ENCYCLOPEDIA OF BEST FILMS

ENCYCLOPEDIA OF
BEST FILMS

A CENTURY OF ALL THE FINEST MOVIES

Volume 2, K–R

JAY ROBERT NASH

ROWMAN & LITTLEFIELD
Lanham • Boulder • New York • London

Published by Rowman & Littlefield
An imprint of The Rowman & Littlefield Publishing Group, Inc.
4501 Forbes Boulevard, Suite 200, Lanham, Maryland 20706
www.rowman.com

6 Tinworth Street, London SE11 5AL, United Kingdom

British Library Cataloguing in Publication Information Available

Library of Congress Cataloging-in-Publication Data

Library of Congress Control Number: 2019939590
ISBN 978-1-5381-3414-6 (cloth : alk. paper)
ISBN 978-1-5381-3415-3 (electronic)

♾™ The paper used in this publication meets the minimum requirements of
American National Standard for Information Sciences—Permanence of Paper
for Printed Library Materials, ANSI/NISO Z39.48-1992.

This work is for my wife, Judy, my son Jay and daughter-in-law Nicole, my daughter Andrea, and all other lovers of good films.

BOOKS BY JAY ROBERT NASH

FICTION

On All Fronts
A Crime Story
The Dark Fountain
The Mafia Diaries

NON-FICTION

Dillinger: Dead or Alive?
Citizen Hoover: A Critical Study of J. Edgar Hoover and His FBI
Bloodletters and Badmen: A Narrative Encyclopedia of American Criminals from the Pilgrims to the Present
Hustlers and Conmen: An Anecdotal History of the Confidence Man and His Games
Darkest Hours: A Narrative Encyclopedia of the World's Greatest Disasters
Among the Missing: An Anecdotal History of Missing Persons from 1800 to the Present
Murder, America: Homicide in the United States from the Revolution to the Present
Almanac of World Crime
Look for the Woman: A Narrative Encyclopedia of Female Criminals from Elizabethan Times to the Present
People to See: An Anecdotal History of Chicago's Makers and Breakers
The True Crime Quiz Book
The Innovators: 16 Portraits of the Famous and the Infamous
Zanies: The World's Greatest Eccentrics
The Crime Movie Quiz Book
Murder among the Mighty: Celebrity Slayings That Shocked America
Open Files: The World's Greatest Unsolved Crimes
The Toughest Movie Quiz Book Ever
The Dillinger Dossier
Jay Robert Nash's Crime Chronology
Encyclopedia of Organized Crime
Encyclopedia of 20th-Century Murder
Encyclopedia of Western Lawmen and Outlaws
Crime Dictionary
Spies: A Narrative Encyclopedia of Dirty Deeds and Double Dealing from Biblical Times to Today
Terrorism in the 20th Century: A Narrative Encyclopedia from the Anarchists through the Weathermen to the Unabomber
"I Am Innocent!": A Comprehensive Encyclopedic History of the World's Wrongly Convicted Persons

POETRY

Lost Natives & Expatriates

THEATER

The Way Back
Outside the Gates
1947 (Last Rites for the Boys)

MULTI-VOLUME REFERENCE WORKS

The Motion Picture Guide (17 volumes)
The Encyclopedia of World Crime (8 volumes)
The Great Pictorial History of World Crime (2 volumes)

INTRODUCTION

Undertaking this work was not a new chore, but an extension of lifelong research. My deep interest in motion pictures began as child in the 1940s when my mother, a singer who seemed to know everyone living in show business, introduced me to films and many of those who made and appeared in them. From childhood, I created and maintained a card system on which I made notes on every film, supplementing in my travels about the world information from movie people—directors, actors, producers, editors, writers, composers, set and art directors, and others—filling cabinets and cabinets of data, images, as well as films. I added to this a collection of books in the film field that easily occupies 20 percent of my personal library of more than 500,000 books.

Further, in my travels as a publisher and editor of various publications (*Literary Times, ChicagoLand Magazine*, etc.), from the early 1960s, as well as through my good friends Ben Hecht (1894-1964; the highest-paid screenwriter of his day), Stanley Ralph Ross (1935-2000; film and TV producer and my co-author of *The Motion Picture Guide*, 17 volumes), Gene Ruggiero (1910-2002; Oscarwinning film editor), along with many others, I met hundreds of Hollywood personalities (actors, actresses, producers, directors) and those related to the film industry in many capacities.

In those meetings, either formal interviews or at social events or chance encounters, I took notes on all the remarks these stellar celebrities made about their own films and the films of others, collecting over a period of more than forty years index cards upon which those remarks were recorded and filed under the title of the film those remarks best represented. Because of space, I was not able to employ these exclusive and revealing quotations in *The Motion Picture Guide*, but they have proven most applicable in this work, which concentrates on the finest films made throughout a century of moviemaking. An index shown in the back matter of this work indicates each person's remarks about specific films under an A-Z name list and where, following each name, there appears an A-Z listing of the films about which each person commented. (The acknowledgments following this introduction provide a list of those personalities.)

My first reference work on films was not published until the early 1980s, after I met and befriended Hollywood producer Stanley Ralph Ross. We met some time before he attended one of my plays then running in Hollywood and we both shared a passion for the history and quality of motion pictures. Learning that Stanley also possessed impressive personal historical archives on films, I proposed that we pool our resources and produce what later became *The Motion Picture Guide* (published from 1984 to 1999), consisting of seventeen volumes of text only and profiling in depth (complete cast, credits, synopsis, etc.) more than 65,000 theatrically released feature films, a work consisting of more than 25 million words, presently residing in every major library and is considered the definitive reference work in print on the subject (and from which, not incidentally, IMDb, the Internet Movie Database, culled the bulk of its credit information).

Of all of those films, as well as the approximately 10,000 worldwide new theatrically released feature films (dealing with no documentaries or made-for-TV or video films) to 2015, I came to realize that less than ten percent of all such films could be reasonably rated as good to masterpiece films (three, four and five-star films by my ratings). Since I had waded through all of the potboilers and programmers in the history of filmmaking, and, knowing what films were worth watching, I determined to produce the present comprehensive work of only the best films.

In the selection of the entries in this work, my criteria demands quality production as well as quality content contained in any film and, of course, a high quality of acting. Production values are based upon how well a film is constructed, from its direction to its story line and script, from its cinematography to its musical score, from its film editing to its art design and set decoration. It is the obligation of any good director to control and carefully supervise all aspects of these separate responsibilities, while visually narrating and smoothly guiding any story on film to its conclusion with consistent continuity and cohesive and effective development of characters and story line at the understandable level of the most unsophisticated viewer. Presuming knowledge or perception by that viewer is always a mistake, and such mistakes are most often made by today's directors.

"No director is a good one when he goes out of his way to make shots that visually remind the audience that he is behind the camera," director John Ford (1894-1973) told this author. Another pantheon director, Howard Hawks (1896-1977), supported that statement when telling me that "the director must be invisible and unsuspected. The story enacted on the screen by the players must make sense without the director leaving any detectable footprints." Hawks' own criteria for a good film was that it had to have at least one great scene in it, and his films invariably had more than one such scene. "Tricky shots with oddball angles are okay now and then if it helps a scene," Hawks added, "but if you overdo that, you're just posturing and strutting." Orson Welles pointed out to me that "we used a lot of unusual shots that had not been fully developed when we did *Citizen Kane*, such as deep focus, but that was to get more visual values into our scenes—and by defining those in the distance with those in the foreground at the same time, all of the characters came naturally alive."

Story and plotline are essential ingredients in any good film. The so-called Golden Age of film (1930s-1940s) was dominated by superlative writers, mostly intelligent novelists and playwrights with deep and inventive talents. These gifted writers had the ability to communicate even the most complicated story with prosaic and understandable scenes, where complex emotions and motives were translated through terse but revealing dialog. Little such "filmic literature" is present in today's films where writers chiefly rely upon the overuse of shock and sensation to produce provocative stories. Characters thusly are less believable, becoming stereotyped and, without being fully developed, preventing any talented actor from reflecting definable character traits with discernible personalities, particularly those that may be otherwise redeemable and inspiring, which is the mainstay of any good film.

Cinematography must visually translate scene for scene the story line without distracting from the actions of the players while logically unraveling all important aspects of that story line in the process. Working in tandem with cinematography, a good musical score should commensurately enhance each type of scene, whether mellifluously or discordantly, to achieve the most effective emotional impression best suited to that scene and its characters. Good editing is simply cleaning up or eliminating excessive footage or lack of continuity that either encumbers or slows down any given scene (and is not and never has been a responsibility to preempt the work of the director). Production design, art direction and set decoration, all essential elements in making a good film, must accurately reflect the period and location of the film, as well as effectively establish its ambience and atmosphere.

This is the criteria I established when producing my seventeen-volume reference work, *The Motion Picture Guide*, and is the same criteria I apply for this work. At the time I was producing that work, this author was visited by film critic Roger Ebert (1942-2013). I had known Ebert since he was a college student at the University of Illinois (he had, in the early 1960s, attended some poetry readings I was producing at Marina City in Chicago). Ebert always contended that *Citizen Kane* is the one and only best film. When he asked me what I thought was the best film ever made, I jocularly told him: "Why that's no problem at all, Roger—the greatest film ever made is *Bela Lugosi Meets a Brooklyn Gorilla* [1952]." Roger's mouth gaped and he finally said: "Are you kidding?"

I replied: "Of course, I am kidding. There is no such thing as the best film ever made." I went on to ask him if *Citizen Kane* was the best western ever produced. Was it the best comedy ever made? Was it the best musical ever made? Was it the best science fiction movie ever made? Was it the best espionage film ever made? Was it the best war film ever made? I pointed out to him that there are many great films separately addressing different themes, genres and subjects. *Citizen Kane* is a drama and, even in that instance, dramas must be subdivided by types of drama in order to determine the best films in that genre—and there are dozens of such films. *Citizen Kane* deals with one man and his corruption through wealth and power. It is senseless to make it compete against other great dramas with widely divergent themes and characters, such as *The Best Years of Our Lives* (1946), which deals with a readjusting generation of wounded persons displaced by war, or *Casablanca* (1942), a drama dealing with star-crossed lovers and the plaintive call to a noble cause. They have wholly separate and individualistic techniques, story lines, motivations, characters and literatures. It is too convenient and simplistic, as would a child filling slots with block figures, to single out only one film and place it at the top of an imaginary filmic totem pole.

I think this was somewhat lost on Ebert, fine film critic that he was, as it is by those who impulsively make up those useless pecking order lists of best films where an uninformed majority decides the jockeying position from one generation to another of such arbitrarily selected films based upon au courant popularity. This is blatantly evident in such ambiguous online sites as Wikipedia and IMDb, which present no recognized authority for any of its statements and thus no worthwhile or acceptable evaluations). This work, however, profiles approximately 7,000 best films, of which several hundred are rated by me as masterpiece (five-star) films in their respective genres. All entries offer something redeemable or worthwhile to qualify for inclusion in this work in accordance with the criteria aforementioned.

Only feature-length, theatrically released films are addressed in this work, covering films from 1913 through 2015. Such features were first produced by Hollywood and a few foreign companies in the early 1910s when shorts were expanded to tell a more complete story with some character development. The standard running time for a feature was then about forty minutes. The average feature film today runs between seventy and two hundred minutes. Between 400 and 600 feature films are made each year by Hollywood and, approximately, another 2,000 worldwide, including documentaries.

Given the enormous budgets for films today, some running into the hundreds of millions, one might believe that such funding is so plentiful as to provide unlimited funding to produce more films than what are actually made. The star system, however, has isolated most Hollywood funds, where the bulk of money goes to a few film celebrities. This system came into existence with the collapse of the studio system in the early 1960s, so that, by the 1980s, a handful of film stars dictated the overall available funds for their own productions.

I am reminded of a film production in which I was involved (where I wrote the script) at that time; the producer, a wealthy Canadian, offered Jack Nicholson's agent, Sandy Bresler, $1 million up front for Nicholson to appear in the film. Bresler had asked for an up front payment of $3 million, and when offered the lesser amount, he flatly turned down the offer. Of course, it is the job of any agent to get whatever he or she can for their clients, but the extravagant payments to such stars might preclude the availability of funds that otherwise might be allocated to smaller-budgeted films where new talent might be exposed and nurtured to maturity. Just the opposite existed under the old studio system where inexpensive programmers or "B" films were produced that showcased thousands of such newcomers.

Further and sadly, Hollywood too seldom tells a good story anymore, let alone constructs and conveys a reasonable plotline and presents admirable characters. It relies upon the most unattractive canned themes and clichéd characters—endlessly predictable rites of passage and coming-of-age tales, or mindless fright films too often peopled by stereotyped serial killers, blood-sucking vampires, soul-clutching devils, perverted parents, and anyone afflicted with drug addiction or any exotic phobia and incurable disease or malady, all of it as ambiguously presented as possible. People struggling with commonplace problems and who constitute most of the walking world, seems to hold little interest for Hollywood.

A generation of writers blossomed and grew rich writing such vacuous screenplays, and equally less talented producers and directors advanced such empty product to the forefront where even the best of actors were compelled to extraneously create their performances if they wanted to work. To be sure, there are still great creative talents such as Steven Spielberg, George Lucas, Ron Howard, Clint Eastwood, George Clooney, Tom Hanks, Meryl Streep, Mel Gibson, Cate Blanchett, Russell Crowe and others who continue to provide and appear in wonderful and entertaining films with good stories (with a beginning, a middle and an end) and have done so in the last three decades, but they are in the diminishing minority.

Most theatrically released feature films today exalt violence and mayhem, assaulting audiences with explicit sex that obliterates true affection and cheapens healthy love. It attacks viewers with visual slaughter and gore at every turn, even in digitalized animation (the chief technical god of Hollywood), eliminating human sensitivity and decency. It has largely abandoned good adult taste. Language in film has turned into that of uneducated savages or gutter rats, the more crude and offensive, the better. The reason for this social sabotage is simply that such language and explicit violence and sex is not permitted on public TV, Hollywood's original chief competitor against its theatrically released feature films.

Some films heralded as superior by others have not been included in this work as the violence employed in these films is overwhelmingly gratuitous. Thus, I do not include certain films extolling violence, vengeance and vigilantism insidiously disguised as heroism, although I do include films where violence is reasonably endemic to character development.

Then again, one must remember that Hollywood is a business that is aimed first, last and always to make money, with art as a remote afterthought. That dollar is nevertheless dwindling as are the better made and worthwhile watching new films. Hollywood stopped thinking about what the public wanted several decades ago. An executive at a major Hollywood studio told me in 1980: "We give the public the kind of films we want to make, the films that return the top dollars. If all they get is what we make then that is what they have to buy."

However, as Abraham Lincoln once said: "You can fool some of the people most of the time, and most of the people some of the time, but you can't fool all the people all the time." By the late 1990s, the attraction to Hollywood's brutal product began to wane, as did box office receipts. Theaters began closing, and ten years later, top video distributors, which had flourished in the suburbs, went out of business. The reason was clear—the suburban upscale viewer, better educated and more sophisticated, was no longer interested in paying to see bad films. Hollywood still peddles such inferior product, but thrives less handsomely from diminishing revenues that stem now from inner-city theaters and foreign distribution.

Hollywood attempted to address the concerns of parents, teachers and librarians regarding its most offensive product by establishing the Motion Picture Association of America, which created its own children's ratings (MPAA; all of which can be found in my reviews) for films released since the late 1960s. However, since this organization is industry sponsored, its ratings are not reliable and have been manipulated in the past to the advantage of production companies and studios and to the disadvantage of parents looking for guidance. I have established my own rating for children (under the age of thirteen), which appears in each and every review, including those going back to the first feature films. This work offers reviews of only theatrically released feature films from 1913 to 2015 and does not address documentaries, feature films exclusively made-for-TV, or video productions.

Hollywood, since the 1970s, has deluded itself into believing that by making certain family-oriented films those films will be acceptable for children because of their basic characters or creatures, for instance, loveable dogs, and have then proceeded to impose upon the story lines of such productions stressful adult situations. They subsequently use the unreliable MPAA rating system as a misleading smokescreen to present such films as acceptable family fare, which they are not. Today's film producers would do well to consult child behavior specialists before undertaking such productions if their films are to be truly aimed at the children's market.

In all fairness, this author wants to emphasize the superlative work of the better angels of Hollywood and the finest product it has produced over the last century and it is that product upon which this work focuses. There is much to be admired, so many thousands of films that it would take the lifetime (as it has this author) of any reader to view them, and I hope the readers of this work will attempt to do exactly that, particularly those four-and five-star films I have extensively profiled. Within the framework of these reviews, the reader will find, following my "Author's Notes," additional production information, "inside" perspectives of participants through exclusive quotes, and a wealth of other information regarding the background and genesis of these films as to their historic and biographical accuracy. All of the text for this work has been freshly written and, to my understanding, its entries far surpass in comprehensiveness any other film work to date.

Jay Robert Nash, Chicago, 2017

ACKNOWLEDGMENTS

My deep appreciation goes to Cathy Edens, page designer for this work, and her production assistant, Diane Anetsberger, as well as to Walter Oleksy for his excellent research in providing updated information on credits and video information for this work. All images employed for this work come from the Jay Robert Nash Collection and are specifically acknowledged by production company and studio in the backmatter. I am also grateful for the comments—exclusively quoted in this work—from hundreds of worldwide personalities used in this work, including, but not limited to Robert Aldrich; Don Ameche; Jean Arthur; Fred Astaire; Mary Astor; Lew Ayres; Richard Basehart; Ralph Bellamy; Jack Benny; Ingrid Bergman; Busby Berkeley; Richard Boone; Charles Boyer; Peter Boyle; Marlon Brando; Charles Bronson; Louise Brooks; Clarence Brown; Charles Bukowski; Henry Bumstead; W. R. Burnett; James Cagney; Frank Capra; Art Carney; Lon Chaney Jr.; Eduardo Ciannelli; Claudette Colbert; Marc Connelly; Elisha Cook Jr.; Gary Cooper; Joseph Cotten; James Craig; Joan Crawford; Donald Crisp; Hume Cronyn; Bing Crosby; George Cukor; Rodney Dangerfield; Bette Davis; Laraine Day; Frances Dee; Marlene Dietrich; Brian Donlevy; Irene Dunne; Douglas Fairbanks, Jr.; Peter Falk; Alice Faye; Henry Fonda; Glenn Ford; John Ford; Samuel Fuller; Greta Garbo; Greer Garson; William Taylor "Tay" Garnett; Samuel Goldwyn; Betty Grable; Cary Grant; Andy Griffith; Alec Guinness; Henry Hathaway; Howard Hawks; Susan Hayward; Rita Hayworth; Ben Hecht; Ernest Hemingway; Katharine Hepburn; Charlton Heston; Alfred Hitchcock; William Holden; Earl Holliman; Bob Hope; Dennis Hopper; Rock Hudson; Ruth Hussey; John Huston; Betty Hutton; Sam Jaffe; Nunnally Johnson; Van Johnson; Boris Karloff; Danny Kaye; Buster Keaton; William Keighley; Brian Keith; Gene Kelly; Deborah Kerr; Henry King; Don Knotts; Stanley Kramer; Stanley Kubrick; Veronica Lake; Hedy Lamarr; Burt Lancaster; Priscilla Lane; Jack Lemmon; Mervyn LeRoy; Harold Lloyd; Ida Lupino; Fred MacMurray; Rouben Mamoulian; Joseph Mankiewicz; Fredric March; George Marshall; Lee Marvin; Groucho Marx; James Mason; Raymond Massey; Walter Matthau; Victor Mature; Leo McCarey; Joel McCrea; Norman Z. McLeod; Steve McQueen; Melina Mercouri; Lewis Milestone; Ray Milland; Vincent Minnelli; Robert Mitchum; Zero Mostel; Paul Muni; Patricia Neal; Tom Neal; Jean Negulesco; Paul Newman; David Niven; Lloyd Nolan; George O'Brien; Pat O'Brien; Laurence Olivier; Dorothy Parker; John Payne; Gregory Peck; Tony Perkins; Christopher Plummer; Otto Preminger; Vincent Price; Anthony Quinn; George Raft; Claude Rains; Basil Rathbone; Nicholas Ray; Michael Rennie; Marjorie Reynolds; Jason Robards Jr.; Edward G. Robinson; Stanley Ralph Ross; Robert Rosson; Gene Ruggiero; Jane Russell; Rosalind Russell; Robert Ryan; George Sanders; William Saroyan; Roy Scheider; Budd Schulberg; George C. Scott; Randolph Scott; Sylvia Sidney; Don Siegel; Jean Simmons; Frank Sinatra; Curt Siodmak; Douglas Sirk; Red Skelton; Ann Sothern; Robert Stack; Barbara Stanwyck; Rod Steiger; John Steinbeck; George Stevens; James Stewart; Paul Stewart; John Sturges; Jessica Tandy; Elizabeth Taylor; Robert Taylor; Spencer Tracy; Claire Trevor; Dalton Trumbo; Lana Turner; King Vidor; Raoul Walsh; Harry Warren; Ruth Warrick; John Wayne; Orson Welles; William A. Wellman; Billy Wilder; Henry Wilcoxon; William Wyler; Jane Wyman; Frank Garvin Yerby; Loretta Young; Robert Young; Darryl F. Zanuck; Fred Zinnemann.

HOW TO USE INFORMATION IN THIS WORK:

The following fields of information apply to all reviews in this work:

Title (in boldface) is the most current title used in the U.S. (alternate titles appear in a separate index).

Star Ratings: ★★★ (good); ★★★★ (excellent); ★★★★★ (masterpiece).

Year of release is the year a film was released in the U.S.

The country in which the film was produced is stated.

The running time is shown in minutes (i.e., 60m; sometimes reels for silent films) at time of release.

Names of producing companies and studios are stated.

Major studios are abbreviated: AA: Allied Artists; COL: Columbia; FOX: 20th Century Fox and 21st Century Fox; MGM: Metro-Goldwyn-Mayer; PAR: Paramount; REP: Republic; RKO: RKO Radio Pictures; UA: United Artists; UNIV: Universal; WB: Warner Brothers.

Color or Black-and-White (B/W) is stated.

Genres specified: Adventure; Animated Feature; Biographical Drama; Children's and Family Film; Comedy, Crime Drama; Drama; Fantasy; Horror; Musical; Mystery; Sports Drama; Spy Drama; Science Fiction; Romance; War; Western.

Author's Children Ratings (the reasons for cautionary and unacceptable film ratings are often explained in text): Recommended; Acceptable; Cautionary; Unacceptable.

MPAA ratings (from the late 1960s; not always available) are stated.

Video Availability: BD: Blu-ray Disc; DVD: Digital Versatile System; VHS: Video Home System (video cassette); 3-D: three-dimensional movies; IV: Internet Viewing (streaming). (All of these video applications can be purchased or rented from local or national video outlets.)

In-depth review and background information (following "Author's Note") appears in each entry.

Cast and credits: p: producer; d: director; cast: cast of six to twelve leading players appearing in a film; w: screenwriter and/or adaptation (with credit for original story, book or play); c: cinematographer (often with additional technical information—i.e., Panavision; Technicolor); m: composer of musical score (for musicals, songs are listed with composers and lyricists); ed: film editor; prod d: production designer; art d: art designer; set d: set decorator or designer; spec eff: special effects or visual effects director.

Indices: Alternate Titles (3438-3449); Events (3450-3464); Fictional Persons (3465-3525); Great Last Lines (3526-3532); Historical Persons (3533-3703); Institutions and Organizations (3704-3723); Lines That Live Forever (3724-3736); Personalities Quoted (3737-3751); Photos: Name Index (3752-3762); Photos: Studio Index (3763-3765); Photos: Title Index (3766-3777); Subject Index (3778-3877).

John Payne, Lee Van Cleef, Neville Brand and Preston Foster in *Kansas City Confidential,* **1952.**

Kadosh ★★★ 1999; Israel/France; 110m; Agay Hafakot/Kino International; Color; Drama; Children: Unacceptable; **DVD; VHS.** This revealing Israeli film is set in Jerusalem's ancient and Orthodox Mea Shearim quarter where men rule the roost and can study the Torah and the Talmud while their wives work, keep house, and have as many children as they can. Abecassis is married to Hattab and are happily and passionately married, but, after ten years, have no children. Hattab's father, the yeshiva's rabbi, wants him to divorce his wife because she is barren and "a barren woman is no woman." But that is not really the case. Hattab is sterile. Meanwhile, Abecassis' sister, Barda, is in love with a Jewish man, Huri, who is unacceptable to the yeshiva as being too secular, and besides, he's a rock singer, so the rabbi arranges the marriage of Barda to a Mea Shearim zealot, Abu-Warda. In a world run by men, the sisters try to satisfy their heart's desires. The word "kadosh" in Hebrew means "to set apart, elevate, or be made special." Subjugation of women themes prohibit viewing by children. (In Hebrew; English subtitles.) **p,** Amos Gitai, Michel Propper; **d,** Gitai; **cast,** Yaël Abecassis, Yoram Hattab, Meital Barda, Uri Ran-Klausner, Yussuf Abu-Warda, Lea Koenig, Sami Huri, Rivka Michaeli, Samuel Calderon, Noa Dori; **w,** Gitai, Eliette Abecassis; **c,** Renato Berta; **m,** Philippe Eidel, Louis Sclavis; **ed,** Monica Coleman, Kobi Netanel; **prod d,** Miguel Markin; **spec eff,** Yaron Yashinski.

Kagemusha ★★★★ 1980; Japan; 162m; Toho-Kurosawa/FOX; Color; Drama; Children: Unacceptable (MPAA: PG); **DVD; VHS.** A samurai warlord, who employs doubles during his battles in killed is one conflict, leaving his lookalike, Nakadai, a petty thief, to take over the fiefdom. In a dual role, Nakadai continue the impersonation with the help of aides, in order to maintain the confidence of his followers. A concubine, however, discovers his charade and exposes him and he is banished from the realm. A decisive battle then ensues, and Nakadai, unable to restrain his desire to seek vindication, takes up a battle flag and rushes into the fray where he is momentarily successful in leading his men until he is fatally killed. He collapses into a lake and floats away, finding the same resting place of the real warlord. This samurai theme is often employed by Kurosawa, and he uses it effectively here with grim irony, incisively exploring role models and loyalties while portraying a powerful pageantry of ancient politics and war. His battle scenes are awash with endless extras, and he deploys his warriors with great military understanding and tactical skill, using color footage, shadow and light for emphasis in these titanic struggles. This film was the co-winner of the

Golden Palm award at the Cannes Film Festival and was introduced in its 1980 premiere in New York by Francis Ford Coppola and George Lucas, at which time the master Japanese director declared that his favorite film was **Star Wars,** 1977. (In Japanese; English subtitles.) **p,** Akira Kurosawa, Masato Ide; **d,** Kurosawa; **cast,** Tatsuya Nakadai, Tsutomu Yamazaki, Ken'ichi Hagiwara, Jinpachi Nezu, Kaori Momoi, Hideji Ôtaki, Daisuke Ryû, Mitsuko Baishô, Masayuki Yui, Hideo Murota; **c,** Takao Saitô, Shôji Ueda (Panavision; Eastmancolor); **m,** Shinichirô Ikebe; **art d,** Yoshirô Muraki.

Kanal ★★★★ 1961; Poland; 91m; Zespól Filmowy/Kingsley International Pictures; B/W; War Drama; Children: Unacceptable; **DVD; VHS.** Intense and unrelentingly oppressive, this film nevertheless will mesmerize viewers seeing this reenactment of the Warsaw Uprising in 1944. The uprising against Nazi occupiers began on August 1, 1944, and the film opens on the fifty-sixth day of fighting where the Polish resistance fighters are on their last legs. They began their open conflict with German troops after hearing that Soviet forces were approaching the city, but the Soviets were not saviors. Stalin ordered those troops to stop short of Warsaw, cruelly calculating that the resistance forces would be wiped out by the more powerful German army and eliminate a segment of dissidents that might later stage a widespread revolution against the Soviets after they replaced the Germans as occupiers. Forty-three members of a decimated platoon of resistance fighters, knowing this, are running out of ammunition and are seemingly trapped in the ruins of a hotel while Nazi soldiers close in on them. Realizing that their cause is lost, the heroic resistance fighters seek to save themselves by retreating into the city's sewers (ergo the title of this film), going in separate groups through its labyrinthine tunnels and avenues that reek with sewage and disease-ridden water, and one by one or in small groups, are killed in the agonizing process. There is a stark feeling of savage claustrophobia in almost all of the uncompromising scenes of this chilling production and a deep sense of hopelessness, which nevertheless accurately profiles the true reality of that tragic and abortive uprising. (In Polish; English subtitles.) **p,** Stanislaw Adler; **d,** Andrzej Wajda; **cast,** Teresa Izewska, Tadeusz Janczar, Wienczyslaw Glinski, Tadeusz Gwiazdowski, Stanislaw Mikulski, Emil Karewicz, Vladek Sheybal (Wladyslaw Sheybal), Teresa Berezowska, Zofia Lindorf, Janina Jablonowska; **w,** Jerzy Stefan Stawinski (based on his short story); **c,** Jerzy Lipman; **m,** Jan Krenz; **ed,** Halina Nawrocka; **prod d,** Roman Mann; **set d,** Leonard Mokicz.

Kansas City Confidential ★★★ 1952; U.S.; 98m; UA; B/W; Crime; Children: Unacceptable; **DVD; VHS.** Former Kansas City policeman Foster turns to crime and plans a million dollar armored car robbery. He

Ralph Macchio and Noriyuki "Pat" Morita in *The Karate Kid*, 1984.

enlists the help of three men, Brand, Van Cleef and Elam, by blackmailing them for supposed criminal evidence he has against them. For safety's sake, he has them wear masks so they can't be identified, even by each other. The heist goes off as planned and the thieves get away with the loot, but police pick up Payne, an innocent man and an ex-con, who was near the scene of the robbery while driving a van similar to the one used in the heist. To clear his name, Payne manages to get away from the police and learns that the thieves fled to Mexico. He trails one of them and beats him for information, but then leaves him to be killed by Mexican police. Payne then assumes the dead man's identity, which gets him in with the thieves and also leads him to fall in love with Foster's daughter, Gray. Payne worms his way into the robbery gang and gets information to use against Foster, while also learning that Foster plans to rat on his partners and collect reward money for turning them in. The finale sees a wild shootout in which Foster and the two surviving gang members are killed. To win Gray's heart, Payne tells police that Foster was a hero for helping him find the two gang members, and Gray swoons in Payne's arms. Excessive violence prohibits viewing by children. (The modus operandi Foster employs in recruiting his fellow thieves was later used by Steve McQueen in the **Thomas Crown Affair**, 1968 and its 1999 remake.) **p**, Edward Small; **d**, Phil Karlson; **cast**, John Payne, Coleen Gray, Preston Foster, Neville Brand, Lee Van Cleef, Jack Elam, Dona Drake, Mario Siletti, Carleton Young, Ted Ryan, Jeff York; **w**, George Bruce, Harry Essex (based on a story by Rowland Brown, Harold R. Greene); **m**, Paul Sawtell; **ed**, George E. Diskant; **set d**, Buddy Small; **art d**, Edward L. Ilou; **spec eff**, Edward R. Robinson (Ray Robinson).

The Karate Kid ★★★ 1984; U.S.; 126m; COL; Color; Sports Drama; Children: Unacceptable (MPAA: PG); **DVD**; **VHS**. Macchio, a teenage dark-haired Italian-American boy, and his mother move from New Jersey to Southern California where she is happy with a new job, but he finds himself to be a virtual outcast among his high school classmates and the blond surfer crowd because of his New Jersey accent and never having ridden a surf board. About a dozen boys who attend a karate school, dominated by Zabka, an especially mean Asian-American rich boy who has a chip on his shoulder, practice karate on him. They beat him badly until Morita, an elderly Japanese-American janitor, uses his karate skills to rescue him and drive the attackers away. Morita promises Macchio he will teach him how to defend himself, using karate in exchange for doing some gardening and other work around his house. Macchio agrees, but is not a fast learner, and soon feels he's being used as a slave. He doesn't understand when Morita tries to teach him the psychology and life skills behind the physical karate moves. It all finally sinks into Macchio's head and he fights Zabka in a regional tournament

and wins, also winning the heart of Shue, a girl he has met along the way to local karate fame. This action-packed entry became a very popular film. Physical violence and profanity prohibit viewing by children. **p**, Jerry Weintraub; **d**, John G. Avildsen; **cast**, Ralph Macchio, Noriyuki "Pat" Morita, Elisabeth Shue, Martin Kove, William Zabka, Ron Thomas, Rob Garrison, Chad McQueen, Tony O'Dell, Andrew Shue; **w**, Robert Mark Kamen; **c**, James Crabe; **m**, Bill Conti; **ed**, Avildsen, Walt Mulconery, Bud S. Smith; **prod d**, William J. Cassidy; **set d**, John H. Anderson; **spec eff**, Frank Toro.

Kate & Leopold ★★★ 2001; U.S.; 118m; Konrad Pictures; Miramax Films; Color; Fantasy/Romance; Children: Cautionary (MPAA: PG-13); **DVD**; **VHS**. Ryan is a beautiful young high-powered marketing maven living in a Manhattan apartment one story below from her former boyfriend, Schreiber, an eccentric scientist. He stumbles upon a portal that can transport persons into another time period if they jump off the Brooklyn Bridge at specific times. He zaps himself back to late-1800s Manhattan with a camera where he takes photos of people attending a party at which a handsome young Victorian duke, Jackman, is about to announce his engagement to a wealthy American heiress. He doesn't love her, but might marry her for her money which his aristocratic family badly needs. Jackman sees party-crasher Schreiber and chases him through Old Manhattan and up the as-yet unfinished Brooklyn Bridge. They both are zapped into the time portal and arrive in 2001, where Ryan and Schreiber had been living. Jackman winds up at Ryan's apartment where he immediately falls in love with her and where she is more than charmed by his looks, accent and his strange-looking apparel. She sees money in the handsome duke and stars him in a television commercial for a low-fat butter substitute. He hates the product and walks off the set for the commercial, criticizing Ryan for having no integrity. She says she can live without that. Their time-travel romance has some problems, but also provides some laughs such as when Ryan's purse is snatched and Jackman borrows a carriage horse and pursues the villain into Central Park to reclaim it. As in all fairy tales, the lovers are finally united, but it takes some doing, which includes Ryan leaping off the Brooklyn Bridge just at the right moment. This well-made film offers a charming new take on old-fashioned romantic comedies, mixed in with the always popular time-travel theme, and with winning performances, especially from Australian actor Jackman. Gutter language prohibits viewing by children. **p**, Cathy Konrad, Christopher Goode; **d**, James Mangold; **cast**, Meg Ryan, Hugh Jackman, Liev Schreiber, Breckin Meyer, Natasha Lyonne, Bradley Whitford, Paxton Whitehead, Spalding Gray, Josh Stamberg, Matthew Sussman, Philip Bosco, Andrew Jack; **w**, Mangold, Steven Rogers (based on a story by Rogers); **c**, Stuart Dryburgh; **m**, Rolfe Kent; **ed**, David Brenner; **prod d**, Mark Friedberg; **art d**, Jess Gonchor; **set d**, Stephanie Carroll; **spec eff**, Connie Brink, Sr. and Jr.

Katyn ★★★ 2008; Germany; 122m; Akson Studio/Koch Lorber Films; Color; Historical/War; Children: Unacceptable; **BD**; **DVD**. Director Wajda offers a strong docudrama about the 1940 massacre of more than 12,000 Polish military officers in the Katyn Forest by Soviet soldiers on orders from Soviet dictator Josef Stalin. Among the victims was Wajda's father. About 10,000 other Polish soldiers were also executed in other locations. The film depicts Poland during WWII and afterward, and adds the fictional story of a Polish officer, Zmijewski, who writes a diary in a Soviet prison on the border of Poland, and of his wife, Ostaszewska, and daughter and the political dangers they face. The Soviet government later blamed the Katyn massacre on Germany. Excessive violence and exposing dead bodies prohibit viewing by children. (In German; English subtitles.) **p**, Michal Kwiecinski, Dominique Lesage, Dariusz Wieromiejczyk; **d**, Andrzej Wajda; **cast**, Andrzej Chyra, Maja Ostaszewska, Artur Zmijewski, Danuta Stenka, Jan Englert, Magdalena Cielecka, Agnieszka Glinska, Pawel Malaszynski, Maja Komorowska, Wladyslaw Kowalski; **w**, Wajda, Przemyslaw Nowakowski, Wladyslaw

Pasikowski (based on a story by Andrzej Mularczyk); **c**, Pawel Edelman; **m**, Krzysztof Penderecki; **ed**, Milenia Fiedler, Rafal Listopad; **prod d**, Magdalena Dipont; **art d**, Marek Kukawski; Ryszard Melliwa; **set d**, Wieslawa Chojkowska; **spec eff**, Jarek Sawko.

Keeper of the Flame ★★★ 1942; U.S.; 100m; MGM; B/W; Drama; Children: Cautionary; **DVD**; **VHS**. Tracy and Hepburn appear in their second film together (their first being **Woman of the Year**, 1942) with this dark and brooding gothic mystery and their charismatic magic is again present in every frame they share together. After American icon Robert V. Forrest drives through an open bridge and is killed, reporter Tracy is assigned to write a profile about this ostensibly great American patriot. He contacts Hepburn, who has become a reclusive widow in long mourning for her deceased husband, living on a vast estate and moving about a great mansion. After some reluctance, Hepburn offers to help Tracy with his profile on her late spouse, but he soon becomes suspicious that not all is right with the comfortable legend Hepburn and others offer about this enigmatic man. When, unseen, and trailing Hepburn to her husband's retreat on their estate, a stone building called "the arsenal," he finds in that house the true identity of the dead man, learning that he was a fanatical fascist and a decided enemy of democracy and the republic and who had established neo-fascist organizations. Tracy believes that Hepburn has had a hand in killing her husband, which she denies, but she finally admits, after Tracy tells her he has fallen in love with her, that she knew that the bridge was out and did not warn her husband, preferring to see him die an American martyr rather than eventually being exposed as an enemy of American ideals. Further, Hepburn shows Tracy her husband's plan to seize power in America with a group of power-mad and wealthy persons, using anti-union, anti-Semitism and racism to divide the country and how she learned of this plot only one day before he was killed. She admits that, after making that discovery, she went horse-riding on the day of his death and saw the washed out bridge, deciding not to tell her husband about it, and believing that a 'clean death in the rain is the best thing that could happen to Robert Forrest." At this point, Whorf, a fanatical supporter and aide of the deceased man, locks Tracy and Hepburn in the stone house and sets fire to it, after fatally shooting Hepburn. He flees, but is struck by a car and killed. Tracy manages to break through the door of the retreat, carrying Hepburn outside where she dies in his arms. Tracy then goes on to write his expose. ***Author's Note***: Although this film did well at the box office, it did not receive widespread critical acclaim, and director Cukor, who was one of Hepburn's favorite helmsmen (considered to be a "woman's director"), told this author: "The film was heavy with propaganda, and although we worked hard to maintain a dramatic story line, the tale had a 'wax-works' feel about it." Cukor invariably allowed Hepburn to interpret her scenes as she saw fit, but, in this production, she was so dominating that the otherwise gentle and reserved director became frustrated at her bold assertions concerning each scene. At one point, Hepburn told Cukor how to set the stone house afire and he sighed, stating to her: "It must be wonderful to know all about acting and all about fires." Tracy was impatient in this film with the endless takes Hepburn insisted upon making and which Cukor invariably accorded her, especially those involving Tracy, but he was, at that time, already emotionally involved with her, and she with him, and their life-long affair permanently cemented. Tracy, at his dogged insistence, nevertheless got top billing and the single-minded Hepburn accepted that billing, objecting less and less with each film in which they appeared together. Writer Garson Kanin, who was a close friend of both Tracy and Hepburn, once asked Tracy why he insisted on being billed above Hepburn. "Why not?" Tracy stated. Kanin replied: "Well, she's the lady, you're the man. Ladies first?" Tracy retorted: "This is a movie, chowderhead, not a lifeboat." Tracy told this author that "the writer for that picture, Donald Ogden Stewart, was also heavily committed to liberal politics so he wrote a script that sometimes sounded more like a political speech, and I objected to that, telling the front office that they were making a propaganda

Bruno Lastra and Rade Serbedzija in *The Keeper: The Legend of Omar Khayyam*, 2005.

film." Hepburn echoed those remarks when she told this author years later that "Spence and I knew that Don Stewart was gilding the political lily with his script for **Keeper of the Flame**. We both complained to Louis B. Mayer, who ran MGM, and reminded him about his old statement of 'if you want to send a message, use Western Union, not my studio.' He turned to an aide and said to him: 'Tell George [Cukor] to have Stewart tone down that political palaver.' Then he looked at me and said: 'Does that make you happy, Miss Hepburn?'" **p**, Victor Saville; **d**, George Cukor; **cast**, Spencer Tracy, Katharine Hepburn, Richard Whorf, Margaret Wycherly, Forrest Tucker, Frank Craven, Stephen McNally, Percy Kilbride, Audrey Christie, Darryl Hickman, Donald Meek, Howard da Silva, Blanche Yurka; **w**, Donald Ogden Stewart (based on the novel by I.A.R. Wylie); **c**, William Daniels; **m**, Bronislau Kaper; **ed**, James E. Newcom; **art d**, Cedric Gibbons; **set d**, Edwin B. Willis; **spec eff**, Warren Newcombe.

The Keeper: The Legend of Omar Khayyam ★★★ 2005; U.S.; 95m; Guide Company Films/Arrival Pictures; Color; Adventure/Fantasy; Children: Unacceptable (MPAA: PG); **BD**; **DVD**. In present-day Houston, Texas, Echahly, a twelve-year-old boy, discovers he is an ancestor of Omar Khayyam, the 11th-Century Persian mathematician, astronomer, and author of the collection of poems *The Rubaiyat of Omar Khayyam*. Filmed on locations in Samarkand, Bukhara, and Uzbekistan, this exciting tale tells how the family connection was passed down through the centuries. The story focuses on the relationship between Khayyam (Lastra) and Hassan Sabbah (Simpson), and their mutual love for a beautiful slave girl, who gets in the way of their bond of eternal friendship. The "Keeper" of the film's title refers to the bearer of the oral history of the Khayyam family over the centuries. Excessive violence and sensuality prohibit viewing by children. **p**, Kayvan Mashayekh, Belle Avery, Sep Riahi; **d**, Kayvan Mashayekh; **cast**, Adam Echahly, Bruno Lastra, Moritz Bleibtreu, Rade Sherbedgia, Vanessa Redgrave, Diane Baker, C. Thomas Howell, Christopher Simpson, Marie Espinosa, Kevin Anding; **w**, Mashayekh, Avery; **c**, Matt Cantrell, Dusan Joksimovic; **m**, Elton Ahi; **ed**, Duncan Burns; **prod d**, Michelle Milosh; **art d**, Giovanni Natalucci; **set d**, Lou A. Trabbie III; **spec eff**, Andre Bustanoby, Christopher Cundey.

Keeping Mum ★★★ 2006; U.S.; 103m; Summit Entertainment; THINK Film; Color; Comedy; Children: Unacceptable (MPAA: R); **BD**; **DVD**. Atkinson is the vicar of the small English country parish of Little Wallop and is so preoccupied with writing sermons that keep parishioners awake that he neglects his wife, Kristin Scott Thomas, seventeen-year-old daughter, Egerton, and younger son, Parkes. He doesn't notice that his wife is being wooed by Swayze, a sexy golf instructor,

Clint Eastwood and Don Rickles in *Kelly's Heroes,* 1970.

his daughter is having relationships with various unsuitable boyfriends, and his son fears going to school where he is bullied. Things begin to change when the family gets a new housekeeper, Smith, who has her own ideas on how to make everything run smoothly for everyone by eliminating the causes of the problems, one by one. Gutter language, nudity and sexual content prohibit viewing by children. **p**, Julia Palau, Matthew Payne, Nigel Wooll; **d**, Niall Johnson; **cast**, Rowan Atkinson, Kristin Scott Thomas, Maggie Smith, Patrick Swayze, Tamsin Egerton, Toby Parkes, Liz Smith, Emilia Fox, James Booth, Patrick Monckton, **w**, Richard Russo, Johnson (based on a story by Russo); **c**, Gavin Finney; **m**, Dickon Hinchliffe; **ed**, Robin Sales; **prod d**, Crispian Sallis; **art d**, Simon Lamont; **spec eff**, Stephen Paton, Gary Cohen.

Kelly's Heroes ★★★ 1970; Yugoslavia/U.S.; 144m; Avala Film/MGM; Color; War Drama; Children: Unacceptable; **BD**; **DVD**; **VHS**. In this rollicking WWII tale, Eastwood is his usual tough and taciturn character, but one with his eyes focused upon a Nazi treasure of gold. While interrogating a captured German officer, Eastwood learns that more than $16 million in gold bars are being held in a small bank in a town behind German lines and he obtains one of those gold bars to prove his point to a motley group of GIs, who join him in raiding that bank, although they must fight their way through German lines to get to it. He enlists men serving under Savalas, a sergeant, as well as Rickles, a greedy supply sergeant, and Sutherland, an off-the-wall eccentric who is in charge of three Sherman tanks. As these men fight their way through the German lines, they recruit more and more GIs to aid them in their quest for the gold. During their battling odyssey, O'Connor, the commanding general in the area, hears that his men are seemingly taking the initiative to attack the enemy on their own and orders his army to attack on all fronts. Meanwhile, after many harrowing exploits, Eastwood and his men reach the Nazi-occupied town, and where they destroy the local garrison and eliminate some German tiger tanks, except for one guarding the bank. Eastwood, Savalas and Sutherland approach the German tank commander and cut a deal with him, offering him and his men a split of the spoils if he throws in with them. He does and blows away the doors of the bank and where Eastwood et al find a towering stack of gold bars, loading this loot onto trucks and departing the town just as O'Connor arrives with victorious American troops. All of the cast members give memorable performances, particularly the conniving Rickles who wisecracks his way through this offbeat but greatly entertaining film, which is more a film about a bank robbery than a war drama. Savalas is also a standout as the frustrated sergeant trying to fight a war, but going along with his men when they decide to get what they can before they may meet death on the battlefield. The strangest of the lot is Sutherland, who is rightly called "Oddball" and who ap-

pears to be either a dangerous mental defective or a latter-day pothead or both. Most of the story line is played for laughs and it gets plenty of them in this often hilarious war spoof, which is sprinkled with some grim life-and-death scenes to keep the film within the framework of the period. *Author's Note*: This film was produced and shot in Yugoslavia, employing landscapes and towns that were similar to the French locations profiled in the script and in keeping with the U.S. Army thrust toward the Rhine in WWII. Savalas told this author that "if you think that this picture is a war movie, you're off the beam. It's a bank heist with World War Two used as a background. All the GIs, who follow Clint to hell and gone are not heroes—they are bank robbers. Got it?" **p**, Gabriel Katzka, Sidney Beckerman; **d**, Brian G. Hutton; **cast**, Clint Eastwood, Telly Savalas, Don Rickles, Carroll O'Connor, Donald Sutherland, Gavin MacLeod, Hal Buckley, Richard Davalos, Harry Dean Stanton, Perry Lopez, Yves Montand; **w**, Troy Kennedy-Martin; **c**, Gabriel Figueroa (Metrocolor); **m**, Lalo Schifrin; **ed**, John Jympson; **prod d&art d**, Jonathan Barry; **set d**, Mike Ford; **spec eff**, Karl Baumgartner.

The Kennel Murder Case ★★★ 1933; U.S.; 73m; WB; B/W; Crime Drama; Children: Cautionary; **DVD**; **VHS**. The urbane and suave Powell stars for the fourth time in what is most likely the best of the Philo Vance murder mysteries, a fast-paced outing with a tricky script. The debonair detective encounters a double murder at a kennel at Long Island, New York. With the aid of his loyal Scottish terrier, Powell is able to sniff out clues after Barrat, a much-disliked collector, is found dead in his locked bedroom following a celebrated dog show. His death is thought to be a suicide by police, but Powell thinks otherwise and his suspicions are confirmed when a coroner examines the corpse and announces that the victim has been stabbed, shot and struck with a blunt instrument. Evidence points to Barrat's brother, Conroy, as the culprit, but that suspect is quickly cleared when Conroy is found dead in a closet, stabbed to death. A number of suspects come under the scrutiny of Powell, all of whom were enemies of these arrogant and wealthy brothers. The bumbling Pallette, the police detective in charge of the investigation, gropes for clues and suspects, but it is the polished Powell who sorts it all out and nails the villain. A good deal of witty humor is displayed in this superior whodunit, those delightful scenes featuring Pallette and Girardot, the coroner, who is constantly complaining that he is always called to examine stiffs when he is either sleeping or at one of his meals. For this man, death is not a somber event, but a pesky annoyance. **p**, Robert Presnell; **d**, Michael Curtiz; **cast**, William Powell, Mary Astor, Eugene Pallette, Ralph Morgan, Jack LaRue, Robert McWade, Robert Barrat, Frank Conroy, Etienne Girardot, Paul Cavanagh, Helen Vinson, James Lee; **w**, Robert N. Lee, Peter Milne, Presnell (based on the novel *The Return of Philo Vance* by S.S. Van Dine); **c**, William Reese; **ed**, Harold McLernon; **art d**, Jack Okey.

The Kentuckian ★★★ 1955; U.S.; 103m; Hecht-Lancaster/UA; Color; Adventure; Children: Cautionary; **DVD**; **VHS**. Lancaster and his young son, MacDonald, plan to leave Kentucky in the 1820s, because the state has become too crowded and "civilized," and look forward to resettling in Texas. Lancaster, however, is sidetracked after visiting a village where McIntire, his relative, is a successful merchant. After encountering beautiful Foster, who is an indentured servant abused by cruel saloon owner Matthau, Lancaster spends most of his traveling money by buying her and setting her free. This incurs the wrath of Matthau, who encourages his bullying son to attack and beat up meek-mannered MacDonald. When Lancaster, who has taken a job with McIntire to earn back enough money to continue his trip to Texas, sees this attack, he intervenes, and so does the brutal Matthau. Using a bullwhip, Matthau savagely lashes Lancaster until he grabs the whip and knocks Matthau cold. He later meets Litel, who arrives on a riverboat and who tries to recruit Lancaster and his son into becoming members of the settlement he plans to establish in Texas. To obtain funds for that trip, Lancaster plays poker with some sharpers on the riverboat and wins their money, but escapes their clutches by leaping from the riverboat and swimming to the shore. He thinks to use his winnings to stay in the area and perhaps marry sophisticated Lynn, but he is then tracked down by two fierce brothers, who want to settle an old family feud by killing him. Matthau aids these killers in trapping Lancaster, but is killed by them when he tries to flee. Lancaster encounters the brothers at a shallow river and they fire at him, shooting his companion, Litel, and Lancaster shoots one of the brothers. As the other brother attempts to reload his musket, Lancaster, clutching a knife, dashes across the river and, just before his assailant can reload and fire at him, sails into the air and crashes the man to earth, killing him. He then tells MacDonald and Foster that they are all going to Texas to "live it bold." A good script, fine score from Hermann, and top action from the athletic Lancaster make for a worthwhile adventure tale. *Author's Note*: Lancaster told this author that he had a "fondness for this picture, as it was the only production where I directed. I didn't achieve everything I want to in **The Kentuckian**, mostly because I was doing two jobs, acting in the film as well as directing, and that taught me a hard lesson. You can't do both well at the same time, and anyone who thinks you can is making a mistake." **p**, Harold Hecht; **d**, Burt Lancaster; **cast**, Lancaster, Dianne Foster, Diana Lynn, John McIntire, Una Merkel, Walter Matthau, Donald MacDonald, John Carradine, John Litel, Rhys Williams, Edward Norris, Clem Bevans, Glenn Strange, Whip Wilson; **w**, A.B. Guthrie, Jr. (based on the novel *The Gabriel Horn* by Felix Holt); **c**, Ernest Laszlo (CinemaScope; Technicolor); **m**, Bernard Herrmann; **ed**, George E. Luckenbacher; **prod d**, Edward S. Haworth; **set d**, Robert Priestley; **spec eff**, Russell Shearman.

Kentucky ★★★ 1938; U.S.; 95m; FOX; Color; Drama/Romance; Children: Acceptable; **VHS**. The State of Kentucky never looked lovelier and inviting than in this lushly photographed film. The story centers on a feud where two families have been at odds since the Civil War when, in 1861, Greene's family took over the stables owned by Brennan's ancestors. Brennan is Young's uncle and is still clinging to that feud while trying to make a comeback by raising a racehorse that might win the Kentucky Derby. Greene works in his family bank, but when his father refuses to give Brennan a loan because of the old feud, Greene, using an alias, goes to work as a horse trainer (which has been his lifelong hobby) for Brennan and meets and falls in love with fetching Young. Just before the horse he is training is to be entered in the Derby, Greene's true identity is discovered by Young and she, siding with her feuding uncle, tells Greene that she no longer wants to see him. Young and Brennan have everything riding on their horse, which is pitted against a horse entered by Greene's family. In what is chiefly a two-horse race, Young's horse wins the Derby. Brennan does not long enjoy his victory, dying of a heart attack. His death, however, brings Young and Greene back together again and they make plans to marry as the old feud is forever buried. Top performances from the entire cast and a lot of exciting horseracing scenes are presented by director Butler. Brennan's bravura performance won him his second Oscar for Best Supporting Actor (his first being **Come and Get It**, 1936; and he would glean a third such Oscar for his performance of Judge Roy Bean in **The Westerner**, 1940). *Author's Note*: Brennan told this author that "I took away three Oscars by playing old, cantankerous men, and I received all three of those awards when I was under the age of fifty. Back then I thought, what will I get when I am really an old man? I'll tell you what I got— the heave-ho. I'm not complaining, mind you. That's just the way life is." **p**, Darryl F. Zanuck, Gene Markey; **d**, David Butler; **cast**, Loretta Young, Richard Greene, Walter Brennan, Douglass Dumbrille, Karen Morley, Moroni Olsen, Russell Hicks, Eddie Arcaro, Bobs Watson, Robert Lowery; **w**, Lamar Trotti, John Taintor Foote (based on the book *The Look of Eagles* by Foote); **c**, Ernest Palmer, Ray Rennahan (Technicolor); **m**, Louis Silvers; **ed**, Irene Morra; **art d**, Lewis Creber, Bernard Herzbrun; **set d**, Thomas Little.

Richard Greene and Loretta Young in *Kentucky,* 1938.

The Key ★★★ 1934; U.S.; 71m; WB; B/W; Adventure; Children: Cautionary; **VHS**. The urbane Powell is an intelligence officer working for the British Black and Tans (a mercenary paramilitary unit so-called because of its black-and-tan uniforms), who arrives in Dublin in 1920 when Irish revolutionaries are fighting to overthrow the British yoke. Powell meets his old girlfriend, Best, who is married to his best friend, Clive, another British officer, and their old flame is rekindled. After Clive is captured by the IRA, the revolutionaries hold him as ransom, demanding the release of one of their leaders, Crisp, who is scheduled to hang. For Best and his love for his friend, Powell arranges for the exchange, but it costs him his own career, as well as a prison sentence. Curtiz does a fine job in presenting in moody and contrasting scenes (thanks to Haller's stark photography) the street fighting and sniper warfare conducted by the IRA, as well as honestly depicting the highhanded tactics employed by the more brutal elements of the Black and Tans. (John Ford's classic production of **The Informer**, 1935, appeared one year after this film, and its visual impact was not lost on that director when he profiled the same tragic struggle in Ireland.) Some of Curtiz's scenes are utterly poetic, such as the mother and child praying before the gates of the prison that holds IRA leader Crisp. Song: "There's A Cottage In Killarney" (Mort Dixon, Allie Wrubel). *Author's Note*: This was Best's debut in American films. Hardy, one of the writers of the play upon which this film is based, served as an intelligence officer for the British Auxiliary Division of the Irish Royal Constabulary during the Irish War of Independence (1919-1921), and who ruthlessly interrogated IRA prisoners, for which he became universally hated in Ireland. **p**, Robert Presnell Sr.; **d**, Michael Curtiz; **cast**, William Powell, Edna Best, Colin Clive, Halliwell Hobbes, Hobart Cavanaugh, Henry O'Neill, J. M. Kerrigan, Donald Crisp, Arthur Treacher, Maxine Doyle, Arthur Aylesworth, Lew Kelly, Dixie Loftin; **w**, Laird Doyle (based on a play by R. Gore Browne and J. L. Hardy); **c**, Ernest Haller; **ed**, William Clemens, Thomas Richards; **art d**, Robert Haas.

The Key ★★★ 1958; U.K.; 134m; Open Road Films/COL; B/W; Drama; Children: Unacceptable; **DVD**; **VHS**. Offbeat but engrossing film sees Loren living in a small apartment in Plymouth, England, during WWII. She is a Swiss-Italian immigrant and the mistress of tugboat captain Howard, who spends his time rescuing sailors from downed convoy ships. He meets and befriends Holden, a Canadian tugboat captain, taking him to that apartment where Holden is immediately taken with the sultry Loren. When Howard feels that his number is up, he gives the key to that apartment to Holden, telling him that that key is traditionally passed from one tugboat captain to another before they meet their deaths in a war that seems to be without end. Howard is killed on his next voyage, and Holden uses the key to enter the apartment, his appearance

Humphrey Bogart, Claire Trevor and Lauren Bacall in *Key Largo*, 1948.

telling Loren that Howard is no more. As a stateless refugee, she blandly accepts Holden as her new lover. Holden truly comes to love her and, unlike her previous relationships, she with him. She tells him that he is the last man to whom she will give herself. Inhibited with his new obligations to Loren, Holden is no longer a risk-taking tugboat captain, becoming overly cautious and even losing his nerve when his ship is trailed by a German U-boat. He comes to believe that, like Howard, his number is up and, in a moment of panic, gives the key to the apartment to Moore, a brutish tugboat captain who has been lusting after the voluptuous Loren. Once at sea, Holden throws caution to the wind and takes on the German U-boat in a surface fight, managing to sink the enemy boat by ramming it with his tugboat. (This scene almost duplicates other WWII films where Allied vessels ram and sink German submarines that have surfaced after believing that their prey is badly damaged, planning to finish off those ships with surface guns, such as **Action in the North Atlantic**, 1943, and **The Enemy Below**, 1957.) Holden, surviving the battle, returns to Plymouth, rushing to the apartment to fined Moore present, handing the key back to him and telling him that Loren rejected him and has left for London. Holden goes to the train station, but Loren has already departed. He vows to go to London and find her and that is where this melodrama ends. The acting is low key, the action substantial and pantheon director Reed does a good job in keeping this somber story from sinking beneath the waves. *Author's Note*: Holden told this author that he felt his role in **The Key** "was all about a man who felt obligated to take care of a woman widowed by war, and does not look upon her as the spoils of war. Poor Sophia is really playing a woman who trades her body to survive in that war and that was not uncommon in those tragic days." **p**, Aubrey Baring; **d**, Carol Reed; **cast**, William Holden, Sophia Loren, Trevor Howard, Kieron Moore, Oscar Homolka, Bernard Lee, Beatrix Lehmann, Noel Purcell, Bryan Forbes, Russell Waters, James Hayter, Irene Handl; **w**, Carl Foreman (based on the novel *Stella* by Jan De Hartog); **c**, Oswald Morris (CinemaScope); **m**, Malcolm Arnold; **ed**, Bert Bates; **prod d**, Wilfrid Shingleton; **art d**, Geoffrey Drake; **spec eff**, Willis Cook.

Key Largo ★★★★★ 1948; U.S.; 101m; WB; B/W; Crime Drama; Children: Unacceptable; **DVD**; **VHS**. Huston presents one of the finest film noir dramas on screen with this dynamic tale where Bogart, Bacall, Robinson, Barrymore and Trevor are marvelous in their divergent and riveting roles. The setting is an old hotel at Key Largo during the off season and where a strange group of men take rooms. Bogart arrives to deliver a medal won by Barrymore's son, killed in WWII, and, as his commander, to tell the wheelchair-bound Barrymore, and the widow of the dead soldier, Bacall, that that son and husband was a hero when dying bravely in Italy. When he steps into the hotel's bar, Bogart meets

Trevor, a hard-drinking lady who is rooting for a horse while listening to a race being described on the radio. He later hears her screaming as Gomez, one of the men accompanying her, locks her in her room. The gum-chewing Gomez explains to Bogart that Trevor "is a lush...after she bends the elbow a few times, she begins to see things—rats, roaches, snakes, bats, you know—a sock in the kisser is the only thing that will bring her out of it." Bacall then tells Bogart that Gomez is a member of a large group that has been allowed to rent rooms only because her father-in-law needs the money and that these men have arrived in a large ocean-going boat that is anchored offshore. He helps her anchor the hotel boat when a storm appears to be brewing and exhibits a fair knowledge of seamanship, which is observed by Gomez and Haade, two of the members of that large visiting party. A number of Seminole Indians then arrive in canoes, seeking the safety of the hotel from the impending storm and these include Silverheels and Redwing, two Indian brothers who are wanted by the law for brawling and who tell Bacall that they intend to give themselves up to the local sheriff, Blue. As the rain begins to fall and the wind increases, Bogart helps Bacall close the shutters to the windows of the hotel while the male visitors become nervous, pacing about as they fan themselves with their hats and while the ancient overhead fans grind slowly around. There is now a clammy, claustrophobic feeling to the interior as the men begin to talk about hurricanes and Haade, an oafish fellow, shows his anxiety by stating: "I hear that a hurricane blows off roofs, uproots trees, puts the snatch on people and they all go flying around in the sky together. That right?" No one answers him. When the phone rings, Bacall moves to answer it, but Gomez blocks her path and answers the phone himself and tells the caller that the party being called (Barrymore) is not available and abruptly hangs up. Upstairs, soaking in a bathtub, smoking a cigar and drinking booze is the corpulent Robinson, who emerges from the tub to be told by Gomez that he and others in the gang had to show their guns to Barrymore, Bacall and Bogart to keep them under control. As Robinson dresses, Barrymore is puzzled, asking the men if they are thieves. Gang member Lewis replies: "That's right, Pop. We're going to steal all your towels." Barrymore calls Lewis and the rest "scum," but Robinson cuts him off and tells Barrymore, Bacall and Bogart that they are *his* guests for a while. A groan is heard, and Rodney, a sheriff's deputy, staggers from a room, his head bloody. He has been attacked and held prisoner by these men, all gangsters, who are waiting to meet with another group of underworld figures to sell off a large amount of counterfeit money. Then Bogart recognizes Robinson as the infamous Johnny Rocco, a onetime big-time gangster (apparently from Chicago with Robinson enacting a prototype of crime boss Al Capone), who has been deported from the U.S. as an undesirable alien. Robinson struts and gloats about his former status as a gangland boss, telling everyone that he will sometime be "back on top." When Bogart defies Robinson, the gang leader hands Bogart a gun and tells him to shoot him while holding another gun on Bogart, but Bogart throws the pistol away. The injured Rodney grabs the gun and tries to escape, but when he attempts to use the weapon he finds it empty of bullets and Robinson kills him. Meanwhile, the Indians seeking shelter from the storm are huddled outside the hotel, begging to come inside, but Robinson keeps them from entering. When all retire to the bar, Trevor begs Robinson for a drink, but he refuses. He then demands that she sings one of her old songs. Trevor, who has not sung in years, agrees when Robinson says he will give her a drink if she sings a song. Trevor, without accompaniment, then struggles to sing an old torch song, "Moaning Low." When she finishes, she asks for that drink, but Robinson refuses, saying with a sneer, "But you were rotten!" Trevor breaks down, weeping. Bogart then stands up, walks behind the bar, pours a drink and takes it to Trevor, who gratefully drinks it. Robinson, retaliating against Bogart's defiance, slaps Bogart's face and he takes it, sitting down next to Bacall, who admires him for his courage. By now the storm outside is howling and whistling. The overhead chandeliers sway with the force of the hurricane now engulfing the area, and Robinson, fearful, paces back and forth, asking how much damage the storm might cause. Barrymore explains how a previous hurricane killed hundreds of people, sweeping them off a neighboring key and blowing a relief train off its tracks and into the sea. Sweating and full of anxiety, Robinson is completely unnerved by the hurricane, which is now sweeping the sea over the land and close to the old hotel, bending back palm trees in its path. Bogart tells Robinson: "What don't you show it your gun? If it doesn't stop, shoot it." The fierce wind then crashes a tree branch through the boarded up window of the saloon and the group flees to another room. With the storm subsided, Blue, the local sheriff, arrives, grilling the gangsters, who tell him they are all tourists from Milwaukee on a fishing trip. When Blue, who has been looking for his deputy, finds the body of Rodney outside, he believes that he has been murdered by the wanted Osceola brothers and he tracks them down and shoots and kills both of them. After Blue leaves, gangster Lawrence, an old associate of Robinson's, arrives with his goons and they eye each other as Lawrence and his money expert examine the counterfeit money Robinson offers him. After confirming that the phony money is good quality, Lawrence pays Robinson a sizeable sum and, feigning friendship, leaves with his gang members. Robinson then learns that the captain of the boat that brought them to the key has fled before the storm and now the gang members plan to escape back to Cuba with the hotel boat, insisting that Bogart, an experienced seaman, captain that boat. Bogart at first refuses, but after Robinson threatens him, he agrees. Before leaving, Trevor, who has stolen a pistol from Robinson, slips the gun to Bogart. The gang and Bogart then depart, going to sea and heading for Cuba. On board the boat, Bogart asks Haade to look over the stern to see if they have picked up any kelp and when he does, Bogart guns the engine and Haade is pitched into the sea. Lewis, who is seasick, shoots and wounds Bogart, but is himself shot by Bogart and killed. Robinson, Gomez and Seymour, the remaining gangsters, are below in a cabin and when Gomez tries to get at Bogart, he is fatally shot. When Seymour refuses to go topside to get at Bogart, Robinson shoots and kills him, and then Robinson calls out to Bogart, saying that he can have his gun and the money he is carrying. He tosses the bag full of money and a gun onto the deck and then starts to emerge, but holding another gun in his hand. Bogart, perched on top of the hood of the boat, sees this ruse and shoots Robinson. He falls, but rises again, trying to shoot Bogart, and is shot again, and yet again, until the gangster is finally dead. Bogart then turns the boat around and heads for Key Largo, calling the Coast Guard and then putting in a call to tell Bacall that he is alive and coming home. The final scene shows Bogart at the wheel of the boat, sailing toward the woman he has come to love. Taut, grim and chilling throughout, this great crime movie from Huston has it all and presents some of the finest performances on film with Trevor winning an Oscar for her unforgettable rendition of a faded, alcoholic nightclub singer clinging to a long-ago past. Robinson is merciless and Bogart quietly heroic where Barrymore, as the crusty old hotel owner, is a wonderful patriarch and Bacall a sensitive and caring woman, who has lost one man but gained another. The stark photography from Freund perfectly matches each scene as does Steiner's stirring score, exuding alternately a deep sense of dread, poignancy and triumph. The script is brilliantly written by Brooks, who updated the original time setting of 1939 to the post-WWII era. *Author's Note*: The play by Anderson upon which this film is based ran for 105 performances on Broadway and starred Paul Muni, who plays a disillusioned Loyalist veteran of the Spanish Civil War where Bogart plays a rather jaded veteran of WWII. There is no doubt that the role played by Robinson is based upon crime czar Al Capone, who died a year before this film was made and who lived like a raja at his large estate on Palm Island, Florida, dying there of paresis of the brain as a result of syphilis. The Robinson character also represents some elements dealing with NYC crime boss Charles "Lucky" Luciano, who was deported from the U.S. shortly after WWII, going to Cuba, before returning to his native Italy. Robinson complains in this film about being deported as if he were "a dirty Red or something." Robinson had recently been threatened by the Hollywood blacklist during the Mc-

Harry Lewis, Dan Seymour, Edward G. Robinson, William Haade and Thomas Gomez in *Key Largo,* 1948.

Carthy era of political witch hunts for his liberal views. "Those lines I speak in **Key Largo** were coincidental," Robinson told this author, "as no one ever accused me of being sympathetic to communism, which I never was. People read a lot of meaning into what an actor says, more so on the screen than on the stage, because the screen has more authority." Though Robinson was second billed to Bogart, he complimented Bogart in the way he deferred to him, stating: "On the set, Bogey gave me every scene and treated me as if I were the star of the picture. Of course, we both went out of our way for Lionel Barrymore. He was seventy then, but he never missed a cue. After some takes, he would sing Irish songs to us in a Yiddish accent and he was hilarious." Huston was particularly fond of Barrymore, telling this author that "he told me on the set of **Key Largo** that his brother John brought on his own bad luck in life when he stole a sacred Eskimo totem pole on an Alaskan fishing trip and then planted that totem pole in his yard at home, and after he did that, John's fortunes immediately went into decline. Lionel insisted that brother John had offended an Eskimo god and that drove him to drink." Trevor told this author that "my own part is based on a showgirl named Gay Orlova, who was Lucky Luciano's mistress and a former showgirl. My name in **Key Largo** is Gaey Dawn, or that is my singing name. Being forced to sing in that picture was embarrassing because I cannot sing a note. It sure shows in my scene when I sing. When I complained about having to do that to John [Huston] he said, 'Oh, don't worry about that—you're supposed to be terrible and it will probably get you an Academy Award. And lo and behold, it did." Gomez, who plays Robinson's right-hand man, told this author that "that picture was one of the best I ever appeared in. The story was great and the cast was astounding. Huston was a master of that kind of picture where everyone and everything is on the dark side. He understood people who lived inside of shadows. Of course, Eddie Robinson walked away with the film. In one scene, Bogey asks him what he wants in life and Eddie says 'More, yeah, that's it, more of everything.' That summed up his character. One of my favorite scenes in that picture, and there are so many good scenes in that film, is where Marc [Lawrence] meets with Eddie after many years and they pretend to be old friends, but you know they are suspicious of one another and would shoot each other at the drop of a hat, but business comes first, the transaction for the counterfeit money. Their goons—and I am one of those characters—stand next to each other, eyeing each other to see if anyone will make a wrong move and go for their gun while the money is being counted. Only John Huston could bring such great tension to a scene like that as he cuts from one pair of goons to another. We're all savage people wearing suits and pretending to be decent folks and none of us are trustworthy." For more details on the characters serving as role models for Robinson in this film, Al Capone and Charles Luciano, see my books, *The Great Pictorial His-*

Thomas Mitchell and Gregory Peck in *The Keys of the Kingdom,* 1944.

tory of World Crime, Volume I (History, Inc., 2004; Capone: pages 503-541; Luciano: pages 544-551) and *World Encyclopedia of Organized Crime* (Paragon House, 1992; Capone: pages 78-98; Luciano: pages 251-256). **p**, Jerry Wald; **d**, John Huston; **cast**, Humphrey Bogart, Edward G. Robinson, Lauren Bacall, Lionel Barrymore, Claire Trevor, Thomas Gomez, Harry Lewis, John Rodney, Dan Seymour, Monte Blue, Marc Lawrence, William Haade, Jay Silverheels, Rodd Redwing, Pat Flaherty, Felipa Gómez; **w**, Richard Brooks, Huston (based on the play by Maxwell Anderson); **c**, Karl Freund; **m**, Max Steiner; **ed**, Rudi Fehr; **art d**, Leo K. Kuter; **set d**, Fred M. MacLean; **spec eff**, William C. McGann, Robert Burks.

The Keys of the Kingdom ★★★★ 1944; U.S.; 137m; FOX; B/W; Drama; Children: Cautionary; **DVD**; **VHS**. A moving and revealing tale that profiles the struggles of a missionary in China, the film begins when Hardwicke, a bishop, arrives to review the work of aging Catholic priest Peck. He must decide whether or not to send Peck to a retirement home in Scotland or keep him at his parish. In looking into this man's past, Hardwicke discovers a startling biography of a self-effacing man who has overcome all external and internal odds to accomplish the spiritual and corporal goals of the Church. In flashback we see Peck as a young boy, McDowall, who witnesses his father's murder by religious bigots—he is killed simply because he is Catholic—and how he matures as Peck, who goes to China to head a parish that is in shambles. He slowly earns the respect of the inhabitants of the village of Tai Pan while contending with Stradner, a severe mother superior, who is a former German aristocrat, and the arrogant Price, a boyhood friend and utter snob, who is his immediate superior and who compels villages to regally carry him about on a litter. He meets and befriends other missionaries in the area—Gleason, a Methodist clergyman who also struggles to maintain his flock, and Gwenn, a fellow Scotsman, who becomes his mentor, while visited on and off by his closest friend, Mitchell, a colorful physician. Through Peck's acts of kindness and affection for his parishioners (in one stunning scene he saves the life of the local Mandarin's son, who is stricken with blood poison), as well as protecting them at the risk of his own life when Japanese invaders attack the area in WWII, the haughty Stradner and others learn the meaning of humility. Peck is marvelous in his second film, one that made him an overnight star, as the resolute, compassionate priest dedicated to enriching the spiritual and corporal life in his region, and director Stahl does not moralize or propagandize Christianity in profiling this touching tale. Newman provides an inspiring score and Miller great lensing. *Author's Note*: Studio boss Zanuck told this author: "We had a great hit with a religious picture when we produced and released **The Song of Bernadette** [1943] so it was reasonable to believe that, in the next year, we would do well with **The**

Keys of the Kingdom and we did." Peck stated to this author that "that role was a gift from Above, and I knew it when I first read the fine script. Zanuck took a chance on me and I gave it my all." Scriptwriter Johnson admitted to this author that "I could not miss with that story, written by a master novelist, Cronin. My problem was that there were so many great scenes in the book that I had a hard time in not using them all." This was evident in that Johnson, always an economical writer who seldom wrote scripts more than 110 pages (the rule of thumb being that one written script page equaled one minute on the screen), brought the script in at 130 pages with producer Mankiewicz adding a few of those pages. **p**, Joseph L. Mankiewicz; **d**, John M. Stahl; **cast**, Gregory Peck, Thomas Mitchell, Vincent Price, Rose Stradner, Roddy McDowall, Edmund Gwenn, Sir Cedric Hardwicke, Peggy Ann Garner, Jane Ball, James Gleason, Anne Revere, Ruth Nelson, Benson Fong, Philip Ahn, Arthur Shields, Edith Barrett, Sara Allgood, Richard Loo, Ruth Ford; **w**, Mankiewicz, Nunnally Johnson (based on the novel by A.J. Cronin); **c**, Arthur Miller; **m**, Alfred Newman; **ed**, James B. Clark; **art d**, James Basevi, William Darling; **set d**, Thomas Little.

Keys to the House ★★★ 2004; Italy/Germany/France; 106m; Color; Drama; Children: Cautionary (MPAA: PG); **DVD**. In this gripping drama, Rossi is a disabled boy left in the care of Favino, an uncle, and Faerovich, his aunt, since he was born after his mother died in childbirth. His father, Rossi Stuart, left him in the hospital and never saw him again. Favino telephones Rossi Stuart and says he should take his son to Berlin where he might get better care at a specialized hospital. Rossi Stuart reluctantly agrees and has his first contact with his son. He gradually feels closer to the boy, but his better instincts are challenged when he arrives in Berlin and befriends Rampling, a woman who is the mother of a disabled young woman. Rampling cautions him that he will suffer if he remains close to his son. Rossi Stuart, however, comes to love his son, and is determined to live with any problems while keeping him. This heartfelt film is well crafted and beautifully acted by the entire cast. (In Italian; English subtitles.) **p**, Enzo Porcelli, Karl Baumgartner, Bruno Pésery; **d**, Gianni Amelio; **cast**, Kim Rossi Stuart, Andrea Rossi, Charlotte Rampling, Alla Faerovich, Pierfrancesco Favino, Manuel Katzy, Michael Weiss, Ingrid Appenroth, Dimitri Süsin, Thorsten Schwarz; **w**, Amelio, Sandro Petraglia, Stefano Rulli (based on their story and the novel *Nati due volte* by Giuseppe Pontiggia); **c**, Luca Bigazzi; **m**, Franco Piersanti; **ed**, Simona Paggi; **prod d**, Giancarlo Basili; **art d**, Didi Richter; **spec eff**, Claudio Napoli.

Khartoum ★★★★ 1966; U.K.; 134m; Julian Blaustein Productions; UA; Color; Adventure/War Drama; Children: Unacceptable; **DVD**; **VHS**. This exceptional adventure tale is also a biopic of two great 19th-Century leaders, British General Charles George Gordon (Gordon of Khartoum, Chinese Gordon, Gordon Pasha; 1833-1885), and the Muslim leader and self-proclaimed Mahdi, Muhammad Ahmad (1845-1885), who match wits and forces in the battle for the fortress city of Khartoum in the Sudan. Heston does a fine job essaying the enigmatic Gordon and Olivier, his skin darkened to deep hues, plays the equally enigmatic Mahdi, who launches his holy war against the infidels by defeating a rag-tag Egyptian army of 8,000 men under the command of Colonel William Hicks, played by Underdown, who is cleverly lured from the El Dueim River and into the desert about 100 miles from Khartoum where Olivier's forces pounce upon those thirst-quenched troops, slaughtering them. When Prime Minister William Gladstone (1809-1898), played by Richardson, learns of the massacre and Olivier's plan to conquer all of Sudan in a holy war (jihad), especially seizing the city of Khartoum with its huge Egyptian population, he summons Heston, asking him to try to make peace with Olivier and avert further massacres as well as evacuate the Egyptians from Khartoum. Heston travels to the Middle East, sailing down the Nile toward Khartoum with Johnson at his side, more as an observer to report Heston's moves to Richardson than the military aide his assignment designates. En route,

Heston learns that the natives no longer respect him and have, for the most part, sided with Olivier in his holy war. When he arrives at Khartoum, however, Heston is greeted as a heroic savior. He takes one guide and goes into the desert, finding Olivier's camp, meeting with him and where Olivier tells him to address him as the Mahdi (anointed one by the Prophet Mohammed), and that "I do not often meet with a Christian, Gordon Pasha. Is it because you are a Christian that I feel myself in the presence of evil?" Heston is unperturbed, retorting: "I think not for I smell the same evil on your own person, and you are not a Christian. So it cannot be that, can it?" Angered by this remark, Olivier tells Heston to leave Sudan, that he does not wish to take his life, and then goes on to say that it is his divine mission to pray in all the great mosques of Cairo, Mecca, Baghdad and Constantinople, meaning that he intends to conquer and rule the entire Arab world. He then menacingly states that the Egyptians must remain in Khartoum and be slain to the last woman and child as a symbol of his divine mission: "I shall take it [Khartoum] in blood and the streets must flow with blood. The Nile must taste of blood for a thousand miles downstream so that the whole of Islam will learn that my miracle is a great and terrible thing, and no man will stand against me." Heston returns to Khartoum, and realizing that Olivier will slaughter all the Egyptians even if they attempt to evacuate the city, he resolves to stay with them, and defend the town against Olivier's hordes. Meanwhile, Heston sends Johnson up the Nile on a heavily armed ship to contact British authorities and to ask that they send an army to the relief of Khartoum. En route, Johnson's boat, packed with fleeing refugees from Khartoum, is attacked by Olivier's men and their fate is in doubt. To better defend Khartoum, Heston orders a huge ditch dug around the city and floods it from the waters of the Nile, creating a moat. Further, Heston plants explosives in underground caches around the city to be set off when and if Olivier's forces attack the city. When the Nile recedes and the moat starts to go dry, Heston receives a message that a British relief army is approaching the city. (Such an army is, indeed, being assembled and its Camel Corps is slowly sent toward Khartoum.) Olivier then summons Heston to his camp and there they meet for the last time. Olivier shows him the severed heads of some of the refugees traveling on the escape boat captured by his men, along with the severed hand of Heston's aide, Johnson. He further tells him that there is no British relief army on the horizon and that he sent that false message to create a hollow hope. He then asks Heston to leave Khartoum, guaranteeing that he will not be harmed. Heston realizes that by remaining in Khartoum, he will most likely be killed, but he will become a martyr around which the British and its Arab allies will rally and bring a new army that will defeat Olivier. Mindful of Olivier's statement that he is the "miracle" that will fulfill the prophecy of Mohammed, Heston states: "I will not leave Khartoum, for I, too, perform miracles. And you shall witness one. While I may die for your miracle, you will certainly die of mine." Heston returns to the city, and at dawn, Olivier's powerful forces attack Khartoum on all sides, many destroyed by the Egyptian defenders with cannons and rifle fire; they nevertheless swarm over the walls, enter the city and slaughter the residents, and when they find Heston, he is killed by a spear. His head is severed and placed on a pole and taken to Olivier's camp where the Arab leader explodes in anger, shouting: "I forbade it! I forbade it!" He knows that Heston's death will hasten the retaliation of the British and its allies. In an epilogue narrated by Genn, it is stated how the plague develops and spreads from eating the corpses left in the sacked city, which destroys Olivier's army and claims his own life within five months, fulfilling Heston's own prophecy and ending Olivier's jihad. This eerie and sumptuous epic is majestically mounted, and every frame of this fine film boasts marvelous and authentic costumes and sets while Dearden's direction is superb in carefully unfolding this strange and compelling story and where Heston and Olivier are riveting in their dueling roles. Scaife's photography is stunning in capturing the exotic landscapes and interiors, as well as the many exciting action scenes, and Cordell's score is well constructed, fusing inspiring martial passages with lyrical and haunting pas-

Laurence Olivier and Charlton Heston in *Khartoum*, 1966.

sages that bespeak the mysteries and mystique of the region and its strange Arab leader. Gordon and the Mahdi are briefly profiled at the beginning of **The Four Feathers**, 1939, and Gordon in **Sixty Glorious Years**, 1938 (by Laidman Browne). *Author's Note*: Producer Blaustein, who had a nagging penchant for authenticity, sent the brilliant and provocative screenplay by Ardrey to the grandson of the Mahdi, and he replied, after reading it: "It is an extremely fine script." That relative stated, however, that his dreaded grandfather and Gordon never met. When Blaustein expressed apologies for taking that liberty, the grandson diplomatically replied: "Ah, but they should have met." Heston told this author that "I think I understood my character. Gordon was as much of a mystic as was the Mahdi. He was a martinet and would not yield on his principles, which is why he lost his life and he knew he would, I believe, when he went to Khartoum. He was a complicated and unpredictable man and I think fatalistic to the core." Olivier, on the other hand, told this author that "the Mahdi was a zealot, a fanatic, but he is not without clever reasoning. He was a master of deception and I play him that way." Some critics complained that Olivier so darkened his skin for the part that he had the appearance of a minstrel performer. In truth, Olivier, a master at mimicking other actors and real-life persons he enacted, borrowed the dark makeup hues employed by Rex Harrison when he plays another great Arab leader, Saladin, in **King Richard and the Crusaders**, 1954. He also employs a rather lisping voice delivery to emphasize the fact that he has a space between his two top teeth, the mark of the anointed one, which he points out to Heston. Olivier admitted to this author that he "used everything in the past that was effective to improve any role I ever played. That is the obligation of any actor—to use every good tool ever invented in making his role believable." Olivier was also a master of mimicking the voices of other actors in the past if he thought those voices might better enhance a part he was playing, such as his role of the Nazi-hunter in **The Boys from Brazil**, 1978, where he mimics the speech patterns of Albert Basserman, a kidnapped diplomat, in **Foreign Correspondent**, 1940, and which he also admitted to me. The great Hollywood stuntman, Yakima Canutt, directed many of the eye-popping action scenes and supervised the amazing stunts performed in this awesome epic. A four-minute prologue narrated by Eliot Ellisofon lushly depicting the region of the Nile, a visual treasure, was unfortunately deleted from the film after its initial release. **p**, Julian Blaustein; **d**, Basil Dearden (Yakima Canutt, action scenes, not credited); **cast**, Charlton Heston, Laurence Olivier, Richard Johnson, Ralph Richardson, Alexander Knox, Michael Hordern, Nigel Green, Hugh Williams, Edward Underdown, Peter Arne, Leo Genn (narrator); **w**, Robert Ardrey; **c**, Edward Scaife (Ultra-Panavision; Technicolor); **m**, Frank Cordell; **ed**, Fergus McDonell; **art d**, John Howell; **set d**, John Bodimeade; **spec eff**, Richard Parker, Cliff Culley.

Charles Chaplin and Jackie Coogan in *The Kid*, 1921.

The Kid ★★★★★ 1921 (silent); U.S.; 68m/6 reels; Charles Chaplin Productions/First National; B/W; Comedy; Children: Acceptable; **DVD**; **VHS**. Though fiercely sentimental, this tale of a lost-and-found child and its unkempt and compassionate savior has endured through the decades as a classic film, the first feature-length production the brilliant Chaplin directed and wrote. The film opens with Purviance, an unwed mother, leaving a hospital with her newborn child. She walks by a church where a young bride appears, clearly unhappy in marrying an older but wealthy man and she sees a flower fall from the bride's bouquet, unknowingly crushed by the groom's foot, one of the many symbolic images Chaplin infuses into this startling film. Realizing she cannot care for her child, Purviance leaves the baby in the back seat of an expensive car with a note pinned to its swaddling clothes and sadly departs. Two thieves steal the car, but, when realizing the child is inside of it and fearing they will be charged with kidnapping, quickly discard the baby by leaving the child in the alleyway of a slum. (The car used for this scene was loaned to Chaplin by its owner, film director D. W. Griffith.) Down the alley strolls Chaplin as the Little Tramp. Finding the child, Chaplin tries to place it in a baby carriage, but its parent, Wilson, drives him away; after reading the note Purviance has left behind, he decides to raise the child himself, while raising suspicions from a passing policeman as he carries the child toward his humble hovel. Purviance, however, has a sudden change of heart and rushes back to the place where the car was parked, but finds it gone and her child with it. Meanwhile, Chaplin converts his meager dwelling into a nursery, using a coffee pot as a baby bottle and its nozzle as a nipple while cutting up a sheet to make diapers. Five years pass and Chaplin is now the father to a small boy, Coogan, who works as his assistant in Chaplin's work as a window repairman. The boy's job is to throw a rock through someone's window and Chaplin then shortly arrives to offer to repair the broken glass pane. Purviance has by now improved her lot, becoming a prominent singer, and who does charity work in the slums. On one such outing to a poverty-stricken area, she encounters Coogan, not realizing that he is her son. After the boy gets into a fight, Purviance goes to Chaplin, believing him to be the boy's father, and encourages him to have a doctor look at Coogan. The physician is not only incompetent, but makes Chaplin's life miserable when, after learning that the boy is not his own, informs the authorities, who then attempt to take the boy from the Little Tramp. Officers seize the boy and, after a struggle with Chaplin, place Coogan in a truck, taking Coogan away. Chaplin pursues over the rooftops of the slum and manages to rescue his adopted son and both of them go into hiding. Meanwhile, the physician shows Purviance the note she left with her child years earlier and now she realizes that Coogan is her child. She places an ad in a newspaper offering a reward for the return of Coogan. Chaplin takes the boy to a flophouse where the owner reads the ad and recognizes the boy, taking him to Purviance while Chaplin is sleeping. When Chaplin awakes he is heartsick to see the boy gone and wanders about. Exhausted, he falls asleep in a doorway and dreams of life in Heaven where the slums are transformed into a clean and happy place and cops wear wings. He is awakened by a beat cop and is surprised that, instead of being arrested for vagrancy, he is taken by the cop to Purviance's residence where Coogan sees him and rushes into Chaplin's arms. Together, they enter Purviance's home for the finale. Chaplin brilliantly fuses pathos and humor in this poignant film, utilizing the same combination he employed in such 1917 silent shorts **Easy Street** and **The Immigrant**. In so doing, he combines serious moments with witty bits of humor, such as his struggle with a pickpocket in the flophouse or when he tries to get rid of the unwanted infant. The touching story stemmed from a deep personal experience by Chaplin, whose own son died of birth defects in 1919. Shortly before making this film, Chaplin went to a vaudeville theater and watched Jack Coogan and his small son Jackie perform on the stage. He was so taken by the boy's antics that he resolved to use him in this film. Coogan is marvelous in his role and would remain Chaplin's lifelong friend. *Author's Note*: Just when it came to Chaplin editing this film, First National locked up the negative as it was named by Chaplin's ex-wife as part of a potential settlement. Chaplin sneaked into the studio with some friends and packed up the many reels containing twelve crates of more than 400,000 feet of negative film. He drove the negative to a hotel in Salt Lake City where he spent endless hours editing the film and then sent the final film to a deserted New Jersey studio, releasing the film under the disguised name of "Blue Moon Film Company." The film was an immediate success, reaping a fortune for Chaplin and establishing him as foremost filmmaker of feature films. **p,d&w**, Charles Chaplin; **cast**, Chaplin, Edna Purviance, Jackie Coogan, Baby Hathaway, Carl Miller, Granville Redmond, May White, Tom Wilson, Henry Bergman, Charles Reisner, Raymond Lee, Lilita McMurray (Lita Grey); **c**, Roland Totheroh; **ed**, Chaplin; **art d**, Charles D. Hall.

Kid Blue ★★★ 1973; U.S.; 100m; FOX; Color; Comedy/Western; Children: Unacceptable (MPAA: PG); **DVD**. Hopper is delightful as an inept young outlaw, who, after botching an attempted train robbery, decides that crime does not pay and that he will go straight. He moves to a small town, Dime Box, Texas, where he takes several menial jobs, but proves that he has no aptitude or inclination for legitimate work and resents those who work for a living, finding them hypocrites. Further, Hopper's every move is scrutinized by Johnson, a suspicious sheriff, who is forever reminding Hopper that he believes that he is up to no good. He is right. Unable to bear his miserable "honest life," Hopper steals a factory payroll at Christmas time and escapes through a weird contraption, with the help of some Indian friends while Johnson conducts a wild goose chase after him. The film is really a parody of the Old West, honest working people and Hopper himself, who acts more like a 1960s hippie than a disgruntled youth living in the 1890s. It is nevertheless well acted and there are more laughs than one might expect in this "sleeper." *Author's Note*: Hopper told this author that "**Kid Blue** was a landmark film, man, a breakthrough film. My character is too cool for all the squares in the town where he lives, and he gets fed up with all their hypocritical ways, so he takes off with their payroll, and he gets away with it, man, all the way. Now, that's a cool film, man." **p**, Marvin Schwartz; **d**, James Frawley; **cast**, Dennis Hopper, Warren Oates, Peter Boyle, Ben Johnson, Lee Purcell, Janice Rule, Ralph Waite, Clifton James, José Torvay, Mary Jackson, Jay Varela; **w**, Edwin "Bud" Shrake; **c**, Billy Williams (Panavision; DeLuxe Color); **m**, Tim McIntire, John Rubinstein; **ed**, Stefan Arnsten; **prod d**, Joel Schiller.

A Kid for Two Farthings ★★★★ 1956; U.K.; 96m; London Film Productions/Lopert Pictures; Color; Comedy/Fantasy; Children: Acceptable; **DVD**; **VHS**. This warm-hearted fantasy, packed with humor, sees Ashmore, a small boy, living with his hard-working mother, Johnson, in a poor Jewish area of London. Johnson works in a small tailor shop for Kossoff, the owner, living in rooms above the shop with Ashmore and where Kossoff tells the boy marvelous tales about a unicorn that can grant anyone their fondest wishes. Ashmore spends two farthings to buy a kid (goat) that has only one horn and believes it is a unicorn, asking it to grant wishes that will help the poverty-stricken people in his neighborhood and some magical things begin to happen that, indeed, aids these penniless people. Dors, a well-endowed blonde, gets her wish when her long-standing beau, wrestler Robinson, wins a bout with towering Carnera, earning enough money to pop the question to Dors. Kossoff is granted his most desired possession when he gets a steam press for his shop. Ashmore is wonderful in his role as a naïve and loving boy as is the rest of the cast, and the film exudes the kind of charm seldom seen in such prosaic stories, due to the care and carefully constructed scenes from pantheon director Reed. **p&d**, Carol Reed; **cast**, Celia Johnson, Diana Dors, David Kossoff, Jonathan Ashmore, Brenda de Banzie, Joe Robinson, Primo Carnera, Lou Jacobi, Irene Handl, Danny Green; **w**, Wolf Mankowitz (based on his novel); **c**, Edward Scaife; **m**, Benjamin Frankel; **ed**, A.S. Bates; **art d**, Wilfrid Shingleton.

The Kid from Brooklyn ★★★ 1946; U.S.; 113m; Goldwyn/RKO; Color; Comedy; Children: Acceptable; **DVD**; **VHS**. Kaye is exceptional in this nonsensical comedy where he is a goofy milkman loving the horse that hauls his milk wagon along its route in Brooklyn as much as he loves his girlfriend, Mayo, an attractive nightclub singer. Kaye visits his sister, Vera-Ellen, and Mayo, who work at the same club, and becomes involved in a brawl with two pie-eyed men, Stander and Cochran. In the fracas, Stander knocks out Cochran, but credit for that blow is given to Kaye, who couldn't punch his way out of a paper bag. The milkman is hailed a hero in that the man he has ostensibly knocked out, Cochran, is the middleweight champion and fight promoter Abel now sees Kaye as a great contender for the title. Kaye wants no part of the ring until Abel tells him that he is setting up a "grudge" match between him and Cochran that will make Kay so rich that he can finally marry Mayo. Kaye agrees and goes into training. Arden, who is Abel's girlfriend, gives Kaye some pointers, having him move about the ring to a Viennese waltz, and after Abel arranges a few fights where Kaye's opponents take dives (in the most ludicrous feigning of knockouts), the milkman comes to believe he is a ferocious boxer. He gets a swelled head and loses Mayo's affection and his sister's respect while Vera-Ellen becomes Cochran's girlfriend. Then Kolb, who is Kaye's boss at the dairy, buys his contract from Abel, planning to give all his winnings to Bainter, who heads a charity for underprivileged children, so all is now riding on the big fight between Kaye and Cochran. Stander, who has switched sides and is now Kaye's ring trainer and handler, plans to fix the fight for Cochran by giving Kaye knockout drops, but he bungles the job and gives the knockout drops to Cochran, who wobbles about the ring during the big match and collapses from the slightest tap from Kaye. (The uproarious choreography for the fight scenes was undoubtedly inspired by Chaplin's classic prizefighting sequence with Hank Mann in **City Lights**, 1931.) The victorious Kaye not only wins enough money to marry Mayo, who is now in his corner, but has enriched the lives of Bainter's poor children. Kaye becomes Kolb's partner at the dairy. Vera-Ellen marries Cochran, who, with Stander, become milkmen working for Kaye. McLeod, known for comedy films, excels with this outlandish and delightful romp. Songs (all from Julie Styne and Sammy Cahn) include: "Pavlova" (a ballet satire performed by Kaye), "Hey, What's Your Name," "Sunflower Song," "Welcome Burleigh," "Josie," "I Love An Old-Fashioned Song," and "You're The Cause Of It All." *Author's Note*: This was the third film where Kaye stars in a Goldwyn production after the producer "discovered" the comedian at a Catskill resort and put him on the big screen, the first two being **Up in Arms**, 1944, and **Wonder Man**, 1945. This film was based upon a Harold Lloyd comedy, **The Milky Way**, 1936, which was based upon a Broadway play, which saw only fifty performances, but it was much more

Busby Berkeley ensemble with the Goldwyn Girls in *The Kid from Spain*, **1932.**

successful than its predecessors, gleaning $5 million from the box office the first time around, easily recouping its budget of $2 million. Kaye told this author that "**The Kid from Brooklyn** was old home week for me. I was born and raised in Brooklyn and the milkmen, like the one I play in that picture, were still driving around in horse-drawn wagons when I was a kid. The milkman on our beat had a horse that would eat anything—carrots, candy, cabbage, including your fingers if you got your hands too close to its choppers. The sound of their hooves clopping along on the streets is one you seldom hear anymore. I always found that sound comforting somehow, something warm and loving out of the past. The milk came in bottles with cream floating at the top and it was delicious." Some of Kaye's early-day friends said that, because he never graduated from high school and ran off to do his own zany comedy skits in small clubs, he would never amount to anything. With Samuel Goldwyn's considerable help, he proved them very wrong. **p**, Samuel Goldwyn; **d**, Norman Z. McLeod; **cast**, Danny Kaye, Virginia Mayo, Vera-Ellen, Steve Cochran, Eve Arden, Walter Abel, Lionel Stander, Fay Bainter, Clarence Kolb, Jerome Cowan, Kay Thompson, Johnny Downs, Betty Blythe, Don Wilson, Joyce Mackenzie, Jack Norton, "Snub" Pollard; **w**, Don Hartman, Melville Shavelson (based on the screenplay by Grover Jones, Frank Butler, Richard Connell; from the play "The Milky Way" by Lynn Root, Harry Clork); **c**, Gregg Toland (Technicolor); **m**, Carmen Dragon; **ed**, Daniel Mandell; **art d**, Stewart Chaney, Perry Ferguson; **set d**, Howard Bristol, Clifford Porter; **spec eff**, John P. Fulton.

The Kid from Spain ★★★ 1932; U.S.; 118m (later cut to 96m); Goldwyn/UA; Musical Comedy; Children: Acceptable; **VHS**. Delightful musical comedy has "Banjo Eyes" Cantor romping through a zany story, avoiding crooks, cops and menacing bulls. Cantor and Young, who plays the scion of a wealthy Mexican family, are college chums caught in a girls' dormitory and are expelled from their college (following a sensational opening number featuring Grable and where the famed Busby Berkeley stages one of his spectacular ensembles). Cantor and Young then go to Young's bank so that the wealthy young man can withdraw his funds to travel back to his native Mexico. Cantor waits outside the bank and suddenly sees robbers emerging with some loot. He then flees, rightly believing that they will be hunting for him as he is an eyewitness who can send them to the clink, and so, too, does O'-Connor, a police detective who wants Cantor to identify the crooks. Arriving at the Mexican border, Cantor is prevented from entering the country until he convinces customs officials that he is a Mexican. When he enters Mexico, he is mistaken for the grandson of the country's great matador, Don Sebastian, and Cantor assumes that false identity. When he arrives at Young's home, he finds his pal romantically involved with

William Haade, Humphrey Bogart and Ben Welden in *Kid Galahad,* 1937.

Hall and Cantor then meets fetching Roberti, and both fall in love. Young, however, is in trouble with Hall's father, who wants his daughter to marry bullfighter Miljan, and Cantor has problems with Miljan's tough friend, Naish, who has eyes for Cantor's new girlfriend, Roberti. Naish then shames Cantor into performing as a matador in the bullring, but Young assures his friend that he will make sure that he confronts a tame bull. Naish, however, switches the docile beast for a fierce bull, and when Cantor enters the ring, he exhibits his ability to outdistance and exhaust the beast by running him around in circles, one of the many hilarious scenes in this mirthful entry. The discombobulating Cantor overcomes the bull with chloroform, wins Roberti's hand, and brings about the same results for pal Young and his girlfriend Hall. Cantor is at the top of his comedic form in this outing and Roberti gives a top flight performance (she being the daughter or the celebrated clown Roberti but whose promising career was cut short when she prematurely died of a heart attack at age thirty-two). McCarey, who does a great job unfolding this zany tale, became known as a pantheon comedy director, making his mark with this film and was soon assigned to helm **Duck Soup**, 1933, where he directed (if that was possible) the Marx brothers. Songs (from Bert Kalmar and Harry Ruby) include: "The College Song," "What A Perfect Combination," "In The Moonlight" and "Look What You've Done." *Author's Note*: Goldwyn believed that he could become the film version of Broadway impresario Flo Ziegfeld, and did exactly that, even to charging and getting more money for his films than what any other producer was then realizing. "My films cost a lot more to make than other musical comedy pictures," Goldwyn told this author, "so it was reasonable that I charge more for people to see them. I got a little nervous when I insisted way back in 1932 that people pay $2 each to see **The Kid from Spain**. They were paying twenty-five to seventy-five cents to see pictures then, but they came to the theaters in droves and were happy to pay that amount to see a great picture. It just goes to show you that quality can pay off." Director McCarey told this author that "Eddie [Cantor] was wonderful to work with, very cooperative and always took direction well as did the entire good cast in **The Kid from Spain**. They all made me look so good that I landed my next job with the Marx brothers in **Duck Soup**, and I went from a dream to a nightmare. Working with the Marx brothers was like entering an asylum where the lunatics were in charge." (See my *Author's Note* for my entry on **Duck Soup**.) p, Samuel Goldwyn; d, Leo McCarey; cast, Eddie Cantor, Lyda Roberti, Robert Young, Ruth Hall, John Miljan, Noah Beery, J. Carrol Naish, Stanley Fields, Paulette Goddard, Betty Grable, Robert Emmet O'Connor, Paul Porcassi, Sidney Franklin, Jane Wyman, Toby Wing; w, William Anthony McGuire, Bert Kalmar, Harry Ruby; c, Gregg Toland; m, Alfred Newman; ed, Stuart Heisler; art d, Richard Day.

Kid Galahad ★★★ 1937; U.S.; 102m; WB; B/W; Sports Drama; Children: Acceptable; **DVD**; **VHS**. Top-notch prizefight film has Robinson as an honest manager, who loses a fight after it is fixed by his crooked rival, Bogart. To dump their gloom, Robinson and his loyal girlfriend Davis host a party at their hotel suite, which is invaded by the gloating Bogart and his thug prizefighter, Haade. When Haade makes a move on Davis, bellhop Morris, who has been delivering drinks for the party, leaps to Davis' defense and promptly knocks out Haade. Davis dubs him "Kid Galahad," and Robinson sees the brawny bellhop as a potential champion in the ring. He and Davis take Morris to their upstate training camp, an old farm, where trainer Carey gets Morris into fighting condition. Bryan, who is Davis' sister, falls for Morris, but Robinson believes that Davis is also romantically inclined toward the young boxer. He matches Morris with a string of fighters, all of whom Morris knocks out. When he finally arranges for Morris to fight Haade, Robinson puts his money on Bogart's fighter, believing that Haade will win, but he does not tell Morris, as he knows the straight-laced boxer would never throw a fight. Robinson also tells Bogart that his man will win and Bogart, thinking the fix is in, tells Robinson that he will put all of his money on his own fighter but, if Haade does not win, Robinson will pay with his life. Throughout the fight, Morris is fighting a losing match as Haade slugs him senseless, but, in the eleventh round, Robinson has a change of heart and urges Morris to box, not slug it out with Haade, and this technique proves successful when Morris catches Haade off guard and knocks him out. Bogart goes crazy and confronts Robinson in Morris' dressing room where both shoot it out, Bogart killed and Robinson mortally wounded. With his dying words, Robinson tells Morris, Carey and Davis that he is dying a happy man as he has brought a great champion to the ring. Morris declares that he is retiring as champion and will never fight again, going off with Bryan with Davis' blessing. All of the acting is solid and believable and the action in the ring is outstanding. This film was remade as **The Wagons Roll at Night**, 1941, starring Bogart, but with a circus setting instead of the boxing ring. It was made again later as a prizefighting vehicle for Elvis Presley, but this was a much inferior production. *Author's Note*: Davis told this author that: "In that picture I am just window dressing for Eddie Robinson. I don't get the hero [Morris] and when Eddie is shot at the end by Bogey, I don't even have a boyfriend anymore, but at least, my sister, who is played by a very good actress—Jane Bryan—gets some happiness before the fade-out." Robinson told this author that "Bogey and I are at it again in **Kid Galahad**, and we wind up shooting each other to pieces once more. We did that in one picture after another and you would think that the public would get a little weary of that routine, but they kept coming back for that same blue plate special. It must have been the way we went out, the bad guy cringing and the good guy sacrificing his life for the good of mankind." Robinson and Bogart also shoot it in **Bullets or Ballots**, 1936; **The Amazing Dr. Clitterhouse**, 1938, **Brother Orchid**, 1940; and **Key Largo**, 1948. p, Hal B. Wallis; d, Michael Curtiz; cast, Edward G. Robinson, Bette Davis, Humphrey Bogart, Wayne Morris, Jane Bryan, Harry Carey, Veda Ann Borg, Frank Faylen, Joyce Compton, Don DeFore, Buddy Roosevelt, Robert Ryan, John Shelton; w, Seton I. Miller (based on the novel by Francis Wallace); c, Tony Gaudio; m, Heinz Roemheld, Max Steiner; ed, George Amy; art d, Carl Jules Weyl; spec eff, Edwin B. DuPar, James Gibbons.

Kidnapped ★★★ 1938; U.S.; 93m; FOX; B/W; Adventure; Children: Acceptable; **DVD**. Baxter, Bartholomew and a fine cast render top flight performances in this exceptional adventure tale, set in the 18th Century when Scotland is warring with England during a Jacobite uprising. Bartholomew is the young heir to a great fortune, but Mander, his greedy uncle, plots to steal that fortune by arranging to have the boy shanghaied and sent to sea. Bartholomew's fortunes improve when he meets the valiant Baxter, a Scottish rebel with a price on his head. Baxter takes Bartholomew under his wing while he evades British authorities, battling adversaries with wit and sword through many escapades, including the undoing of Owen, a calculating and ruthless sea captain. The heroic Baxter overcomes all odds, however, and is able to restore Bartholomew to his rightful position and where Baxter winds up with Whelan in his arms. Director Werker does a credible job in presenting this action-packed yarn, and the costuming sets are commendable in that they appear authentic to the era. The script takes great liberties with the Stevenson tale, but the film is so well done that it improves the basic story line through its exciting visuals. *Author's Note*: This film was shot entirely in California, but its exteriors and sets have the look and feel of fog-bound, mountainous Scotland in every frame. Studio boss Zanuck, who foremost thought of himself as a writer, was the hands-on producer for this film, and like so many other productions, he personally supervised, and was not apologetic for revamping Stevenson's story. "We used the basic plot," he told this author, "but then let our own story take us where we needed to go to get in all the action and sort out the good guys from the bad guys. It's a movie, not a book, and it had to move along quickly to tell its tale. I did my best with that picture and I used every British actor I could lay my hands on, all wonderful players—Smith, Owen, Bruce, Mander, Clive, Hobbes, Love—they all brought reality to that film." **p**, Darryl F. Zanuck (Kenneth Mcgowan); **d**, Alfred L. Werker; **cast**, Warner Baxter, Freddie Bartholomew, Arleen Whelan, C. Aubrey Smith, Reginald Owen, John Carradine, Nigel Bruce, Miles Mander, Ralph Forbes, H.B. Warner, Montagu Love, Halliwell Hobbes, E. E. Clive, John Sutton, Mary Gordon, Zeffie Tilbury; **w**, Sonya Levien, Eleanor Harris, Ernest Pascal, Edwin Blum (based on the novel by Robert Louis Stevenson); **c**, Gregg Toland; **m**, Arthur Lange; **ed**, Allen McNeil; **art d**, Bernard Herzbrun, Mark-Lee Kirk; **set d**, Thomas Little.

Kidnapped ★★★★ 1971; U.K.; 100m; Omnibus Productions/American International; Color; Adventure; Children: Acceptable (MPAA: G); **DVD**. In this, the best of all versions of the Stevenson adventure tale, Douglas is the heir to a great Scottish fortune in the 17th Century. He is cheated out of his inheritance by conniving uncle Pleasence, who has the boy kidnapped and sent to work on a ship at sea under the command of ruthless captain Hawkins. The ship sails for the Carolinas where Hawkins is to sell Douglas into slavery, but the ship rams a small boat, drowning all of its occupants except Caine, a Scottish rebel, who has been fighting for the Jacobites and is a wanted fugitive. Caine and Douglas become close friends after Caine shields the boy from Hawkins' abuse and both wind up battling the captain and his cutthroats, both saved when a storm destroys the ship and Caine and Douglas make their way to the shore where they take refuge in the home of Watson, a distant relative, who implores Caine to make peace with the British. Caine then meets Watson's beautiful daughter, Heilbron, and they form a relationship. Richards, a Scottish turncoat, betrays Watson and Caine by bringing British soldiers to the home and, during the raid, Richards is killed and Watson wounded and captured, but Caine, Douglas and Heilbron escape, going to Edinburgh where they find shelter with Jackson, another Caine relative. Caine asks Jackson to finance his trip to France where he will seek funds to support the Jacobite cause, but Jackson, when realizing that Douglas is the heir to a fortune, goes to Pleasence and gets him to admit that Douglas is the rightful heir and that he has cheated the boy. Pleasence advances the money to Caine, who goes into hiding. When Douglas hears that Watson is about to go on trial for killing Richards and will most probably be condemned, he begs Howard, the British prosecutor, to drop the charges. Howard agrees but only if Douglas testifies as the trial. Heilbron, who has fallen in love with Douglas, realizes that if he testifies, he might himself be charged and condemned, so she finds Caine at his hiding place just before he plans to leave for France and asks for his help. Caine by then has come to realize that the Jacobite cause is lost and, touched by Heilbron's love for Douglas, bravely goes to Howard, admitting that he killed Richards. This sets Watson free, and allows Douglas and Heilbron to have a happy life together. Caine, Douglas, Heilbron and the rest of the cast are stand-

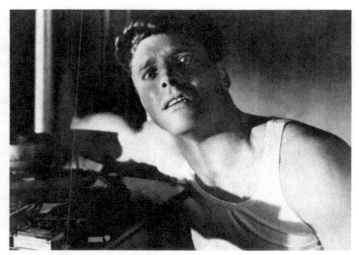

Burt Lancaster in *The Killers*, 1946.

outs in this faithful adaptation of actually two Stevenson tales, with all of its convoluted subplots enmeshed, which might make it somewhat difficult for youngsters to decipher. Accuracy and authenticity in the sets, costuming and on-location shootings are delightful hallmarks of this fine film. **p**, Frederick H. Brogger; **d**, Delbert Mann; **cast**, Michael Caine, Lawrence Douglas, Vivien Heilbron, Trevor Howard, Jack Hawkins, Donald Pleaseance, Gordon Jackson, Freddie Jones, Jack Watson, Peter Jeffrey, Terry Richards, Jack Lambert; **w**, Jack Pulman (based on the novels *Kidnapped* and *David Balfour* by Robert Louis Stevenson); **c**, Paul Beeson (Panavision; Movielab Color); **m**, Roy Budd; **ed**, Peter Boita; **art d**, Alex Vetchinsky; **set d**, Arthur Taksen; **spec eff**, Cliff Culley.

Kiki's Delivery Service ★★★ 2011; Japan; 103m; Nibariki/ G kids; Color; Animated Feature/Adventure; Children: Cautionary (MPAA: PG); **DVD**; **VHS**. A young Japanese girl (Takayama voiceover), in training to become a witch, turns thirteen and must live away from home for a year. She flies off on her broom and later takes a ride on a train and falls asleep. When she awakes she finds herself near a seashore town. There are no witches in the town, so Kiki decides to fill that void. She comes to learn that not everyone welcomes a witch, but the disbelievers do not burn her at the stake. Instead, they merely turn their backs on her. Kiki finds a foster home, and sets up an air delivery service, a perfect business for a witch, and where many exciting escapades unfold. This well-crafted animated tale was produced many years earlier, but not released theatrically in the U.S. until 2011. (In Japanese and English.) **p**, Hayao Miyazaki, Jane Schonberger; **d&w**, Miyazaki (based on the novel by Eiko Kadono); **cast** (voiceovers, English version), Kirsten Dunst, Phil Hartman, Matthew Lawrence, Tress MacNeille, Debbie Reynolds, (Japanese version), Minami Takayama, Rei Sakuma, Keiko Toda, Mieko Nobusawa; **c**, Shigeo Sugimura; **m**, Sydney Forest, Joe Hisaishi; **ed**, Takeshi Seyama; **prod d&art d**, Hinoshi Ono; **spec eff**, Kaoru Tanifuji.

The Killers ★★★★ 1946; U.S.; 103m; UNIV; B/W; Crime Drama; Children: Unacceptable; **DVD**; **VHS**. Lancaster makes his powerful film debut in this fascinating film noir entry based on the tough Hemingway story, and where, at the opening, he is a marked man with two ruthless killers, Conrad and McGraw, looking for him in the small town of Brentwood. These two killers enter a diner where they ask for Lancaster's whereabouts while ordering food. When they get no answers, they round up the three men in the diner, a lone customer, Phil Brown (playing Nick Adams, who is the main character in the Hemingway story, but relegated to a minor role in this film), the owner and the cook, tying them up before they go in search of Lancaster. Brown gets loose and unties the others and then races to Lancaster's rooming house where

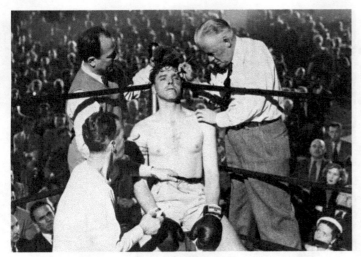

Burt Lancaster, center, in *The Killers*, 1946.

he finds Lancaster lying on a bed. Brown tells him that two killers are on their way to shoot him, but Lancaster, who has been evading these hoodlums for a long time, does not care, saying: "I'm tired of all that running around." Brown then leaves, going to the police, but McGraw and Conrad arrive, kick open the door to Lancaster's room and empty their pistols at him, killing him. This is where the Hemingway tale ends and this film continues, showing O'Brien, as an insurance investigator looking into the case as Lancaster has taken out a life insurance policy, with a hotel maid as the recipient of its benefits. O'Brien's search leads him to Philadelphia police lieutenant Levene, who has been a longtime friend of Lancaster's and who relates his past, shown in flashback when Lancaster was a prizefighter, dating Christine, taking her to a party hosted by Miljan, an underworld fence, and where Lancaster becomes enthralled with Gardner, a sensuous woman singing at the party (he ignores Chirstine, who leaves and later marries Lancaster's pal, Levene). Through Gardner, Lancaster meets many other underworld characters, and after he breaks his hand in a fight and can no longer box, he decides to turn to crime. When Gardner is about to be arrested by Levene for wearing an expensive stolen bracelet, Lancaster takes the rap, saying that he gave her the bracelet and he is sent to prison for robbery. In prison, Lancaster can only think of Gardner while his cellmate, Barnett, an old-time gangster, tells him that, when he gets out of prison, he should go straight. Both men are later paroled and asked to join crime boss Dekker, who is planning a spectacular payroll robbery, but Barnett bows out and urges Lancaster to do the same. Lancaster, however, remains with the gang that also includes Lambert and Corey. Gardner is present when the gang gathers to study Dekker's robbery plans as she is now Dekker's girlfriend, and the only reason why Lancaster has thrown in with this gang is to be close to her. At the last minute before the payroll robbery of a large company is to be committed, Gardner goes to Lancaster, telling him that boss Dekker has changed the meeting place after the robbery, but purposely did not inform Lancaster. The robbery takes place with four men pretending to be employees of that large company. They enter the company offices and steal a huge amount of payroll money at gunpoint, leaving the company and driving off in separate cars while shooting and wounding a security guard. Dekker, Lambert and Corey meet at a remote hideout where they begin splitting up the loot, but Lancaster arrives and, holding them at gunpoint, takes the loot and escapes with it, puncturing the tires of other cars so that he can be pursued. He meets with Gardner at a rendezvous and they plan a life together, but she disappears with the stolen cash, leaving Lancaster flat. Depressed and suicidal, Lancaster tries to take his own life by jumping from the window of the hotel, but Smith, a hotel maid, stops him (and for which Lancaster later names her in his life insurance policy). Lancaster then quits the rackets, going to work in Brentwood as a garage

attendant where Dekker stops for gas and identifies him, later sending his two goons, Conrad and McGraw, to kill him. Following Lancaster's death, a flash forward shows O'Brien's continued investigation, where he takes a room in Lancaster's rooming house next to the room Lancaster had occupied and later finds Lambert rummaging the room, looking for the loot from the robbery. O'Brien and Lambert struggle, but Lambert escapes. Then, with Levene's help, O'Brien meets with Gardner, who suggests they go to a saloon, and once there, she goes to the washroom while Conrad and McGraw enter the place and then move toward O'Brien to kill him. Levene and O'Brien, however, shoot them both dead. O'Brien, Levene and several cops next go to Dekker's palatial home and find Lambert dead and Dekker fatally wounded and dying on a staircase after he and Corey have shot each other. Gardner arrives with no concern for Dekker, who is her husband. Dekker tells O'Brien and the police that he and Gardner deceived the others by setting up Lancaster to take the robbery money so that Gardner could later take it from Lancaster. Gardner begs Dekker to clear her name, but he dies and she knows now that she will be going to prison for her deceitful and criminal actions. O'Brien returns to his insurance boss, MacBride, who tells him that he has performed a good investigation and then tells him to be on the job on Monday. Everything about this chilling crime yarn works well, even though most of it was tacked onto the brief Hemingway story by writers Veiller and Huston. Director Siodmak, an old hand with great dark tales, having directed **The Suspect**, 1944, and **The Spiral Staircase**, 1945, moves this film along with a fast pace while doing a marvelous job of cross-cutting the cleverly constructed scenes in a rather complex story line. Lancaster is riveting in his first role, one that made him a star overnight, and Gardner is stunning as the manipulative and traitorous vixen, having no loyalties to anyone except herself. This role also established Gardner as a leading sex symbol. Rozsa's lower register and dynamic score is foreboding and tension creating, so memorable that it was used as the theme music for the TV series "Dragnet." ***Author's Note***: The robbery depicted in this film is based on the payroll robbery of the Rubel Ice Company in Brooklyn, on August 21, 1934, where four thieves, one disguised as a pushcart peddler, took $427,950. The thieves were caught, but the cash was never recovered. Huston, who worked on the script (not credited as was Richard Brooks, who also worked on the screenplay), told this author that "although the Rubel robbery, one of the largest back in the 1930s, involved robbing an armored car delivery of a payroll to that company, we simply had the thieves enter the front offices of the company and rob that payroll, but we patterned the robbery and the escape after the Rubel heist." Lancaster almost missed getting the role of "the Swede" in this film since producer Hellinger (who paid Hemingway $36,750 for the film rights to the story) thought to use Wayne Morris in that role, but, when Warner Brothers demanded $75,000 for Morris on a loan-out, the producer felt that fee was exorbitant, and had Sonny Tufts test for the role, but did not like the results; a test with Jon Hall also left Helliger dissatisfied. He thought about Van Heflin and even using O'Brien in the role, but changed O'Brien's part to that of the insurance investigator and where O'Brien delivered an excellent and riveting performance. Hellinger was then contacted by Harold Hecht, a down-and-out talent agent, who had Lancaster for a client. "He pitched me to Hellinger, and after I was tested, I got the part," Lancaster told this author. "I was a big fan of Hemingway's, and when I read the script, I told Hellinger that the first sixteen pages stuck to the Hemingway story, but it was a whodunit after that. Hellinger smiled and said: 'You are not a dumb Swede, after all.'" Lancaster never forgot Hecht's efforts in landing him his first feature role and later made Hecht his co-producer on his many independently produced films. Hellinger also thought to have Don Siegel direct this film, but then opted for Siodmak, although Siegel would go on to direct the good 1964 remake of this film. Hemingway was briefly involved in this production, according to Huston, who told this author: "I showed Papa the script and he did a little editing and gave me some pointers that I worked into the screenplay. We got along, as they say, famously, and remained friends as long as he lived." Gardner was forever grateful to Hellinger for casting her in this film, which was her breakthrough movie: "He gave me the big break with a major role in a first-rate feature, and he treated me right from the beginning like a movie star. Mark was a brilliant man and trusted me to give him what he wanted and it was my trust for him that gave me the confidence to give my best in that role in **The Killers**. I am a terrible woman in that film who betrays everyone, but I did not betray Mark Hellinger." Hemingway liked Gardner so much in **The Killers** that he urged (if not insisted) film producers to use her in several other films based on his books, including **The Snows of Kilimanjaro**, 1952, and **The Sun Also Rises**, 1957. She became a Hemingway groupie of sorts and made a point of joining the author and his entourages on his several sojourns. This author first met Gardner in Pamplona, Spain, in 1959, where Hemingway was enjoying the local bullfighting festival and Gardner (not feeling any pain from the flowing Spanish wines) told me as we sat with a dozen other Hemingway admirers in an outside café that "I hope you appreciate the fact that you are sitting in the presence of one of the world's greatest writers." "Yes," I replied, "and one of the world's most beautiful actresses." She smiled and said: "You will go very far, young man." **p**, Mark Hellinger; **d**, Robert Siodmak; **cast**, Edmund O'Brien, Ava Gardner, Albert Dekker, Sam Levene, Virginia Christine, John Miljan, Vince Barnett, Burt Lancaster, Jack Lambert, Charles D. Brown, Donald MacBride, Jeff Corey, Charles McGraw, William Conrad, Queenie Smith, Phil Brown; **w**, Anthony Veiller and (not credited) Richard Brooks and John Huston (based on the story by Ernest Hemingway); **c**, Woody Bredell; **m**, Miklos Rozsa; **ed**, Arthur Hilton; **art d**, Jack Otterson, Martin Obzina; **set d**, Russell A. Gausman, E.R. Robinson; **spec eff**, David S. Horsley.

The Killers ★★★ 1964; U.S.; 93m; UNIV; Color; Crime Drama; Children: Unacceptable; **DVD**; **VHS**. A riveting crime yarn loosely based on the Hemingway short story has Marvin and Gulager arriving at a school for the blind where they shoot and kill a teacher at that school, Cassavetes. The killers are dumbfounded to discover that the victim showed no resistance and inexplicably accepted his fate, and they do not know the person who assigned them to kill Cassavetes. Digging further, they discover that Cassavetes was a former racetrack driver inveigled into driving the getaway car in an armored car robbery and that an enormous amount of stolen cash was never recovered. They further unearth Dickinson, who is the mistress of crime boss Reagan and that Dickinson enticed Cassavetes into driving the getaway car in the robbery, convincing him that they will then betray Reagan and keep the money for themselves. She then betrays Cassavetes, returns the loot to Reagan and marries him. Marvin and Gulager find Reagan and confront him, demanding part of the stolen money, but he shoots and kills Gulager and wounds Marvin, who, in turn, fatally shoots Reagan. Dickinson then arrives and pleads with Marvin, saying that she was merely a pawn in Reagan's hands, but Marvin sees her as a worthless human being (much like himself and everyone else in this film) and kills her. He then tries to flee with the money, but dies from his wounds. Cold-blooded and intensely violent, this film does not equal the original 1946 version, but nevertheless gives a revealing and non-compromising profile of the calculating criminal mind and where Marvin is a standout under Siegel's careful and deliberate direction. This movie was originally produced as a made-for-TV film by NBC, but its excessive violence prohibited its showing on television, so it was distributed as a theatrical release. **Author's Note**: This was Reagan's last film and he later stated that he regretted making it as it was the only film in which he played an utter villain without any redeeming values. He initially refused to play the role until a former agent talked him into performing the part. Two years after this film was released, Reagan was elected governor of California and was on his political path to the White House. Marvin told this author that **"The Killers** was a strange picture where I play a hit man, who turns detective, but only to track down a lot of hidden cash. Ronnie [Reagan] plays a crime boss, and I knock him off. We all thought Ronnie was a washed up actor

Jay C. Flippen, Joe Sawyer, Ted DeCorsia, Elisha Cook Jr. and Sterling Hayden in *The Killing*, 1956.

and he later became the President of the United States. How's that for strange?" **p&d**, Don Siegel; **cast**, Lee Marvin, Angie Dickinson, John Cassavetes, Ronald Reagan, Clu Gulager, Claude Akins, Norman Fell, Virginia Christine, Don Haggerty, Robert Phillips, Kathleen O'Malley, Nancy Wilson; **w**, Gene L. Coon (based on the story by Ernest Hemingway); **c**, Richard L. Rawlings (Eastmancolor); **m**, Johnny Williams; **ed**, Richard Belding; **art d**, Frank Arrigo, George Chan; **set d**, John McCarthy, James S. Redd.

The Killing ★★★★ 1956; U.S.; 85m; UA; B/W; Crime Drama; Children: Unacceptable; **DVD**; **VHS**. The always inventive Kubrick took a leaf from John Huston's classic film noir entry, **The Asphalt Jungle**, 1950, with this startling crime yarn where several men plan the robbery of a racetrack. Hayden, an ex-con, promises girlfriend Gray that he will quit crime after making one last big score, and gathers a group of shady but otherwise legitimate working men to plan and execute that robbery. The members of this motley group are separately profiled by Kubrick. Beyond Hayden, they include Cook, a cashier at the racetrack with a hen-pecking and unfaithful wife (Windsor); Sawyer, who is a bartender at the track in need of cash; DeCorsia, a policeman, who is heavily in debt to bookies; and Flippen, an old friend of Hayden's. The plan involves Hayden waiting at the racetrack's bar and where he and Sawyer will start a fight with a behemoth wrestler, Kwariani, a friend of Hayden's, who is in on the plot, drawing local guards to subdue the berserk wrestler, and while the guards are distracted, Cook will let Hayden into the entrance leading to the cashier's office where, disguised, he will rob the place. Carey, a hulking killer (who is always menacing with heavy eyelids and slurring speech), will park his car on the far side of the track and shoot one of the leading horses in the seventh race, creating another diversion. While all of this is going on, Hayden will drop the loot in a bag from a second-floor window of an office at the track and cop DeCorsia will pick up the bag and, using his patrol car, leave the track and deliver the bag of loot to a previously rented and empty room at a motor court. Hayden will later pick up the loot and take it to Flippen's residence where it will be divided up by the participants. Everything goes as planned, except that Carey, after shooting the horse, has difficulties with parking attendant Edwards and, while attempting to flee, shoots it out with the cops and is killed. Following the robbery, Edwards, who is Windsor's lover, shows up with fellow goon Turkel, at Flippen's house to steal the loot, but Hayden has not yet arrived with it. Cook and his fellow thieves put up a fight and all are killed in the firefight. Hayden arrives to see the carnage and then takes the loot and Gray and goes to an airport, planning to fly away with her. The suitcase carrying the money, however, is overweight and Hayden must pay extra to have it put on a plane. A careless porter, however, packs the case on a carrier

Sam Waterston in *The Killing Fields*, 1984.

so that it bursts open and the money scatters all over the runway. Stunned and seeing all hopeless, Hayden and Gray wait without resistance as police close in on them. This taut little film, the third made by Kubrick, proved to be an overnight hit and brought the director to the attention of major studios. His first two films, each made with budgets with no more than $40,000 each, were miserable failures, and this production was made for a paltry $320,000, but **The Killing** was extremely well crafted by Kubrick and offered a tight and tension-filled script from Kubrick and Thompson and where the stoic Hayden and the entire cast are standouts in their devious and designing roles. *Author's Note*: Kubrick uses actual street scenes and the interiors of shabby apartments and even the racetrack areas are appropriately seedy, littered with debris and dirt and peopled with average-looking characters. He uses a lot of dolly, truck and panning shots, employing the camera as the "fourth wall" to keep the action moving along at a fast pace. "I must admit," Kubrick told this author, "that **The Killing**, and many other pictures I made, was influenced by the work of the great filmmaker Max Ophuls, who was a master of presenting fluid camera work." Further, the settings in which his scenes are shown have a purposeful claustrophobic feeling where his apprehensive characters appear to be cramped and furtive. The film is a visual treat and one that came under considerable study by future filmmakers. **p**, James B. Harris; **d**, Stanley Kubrick; **cast**, Sterling Hayden, Coleen Gray, Vince Edwards, Jay C. Flippen, Ted DeCorsia, Marie Windsor, Elisha Cook Jr., Joe Sawyer, James Edwards, Timothy Carey, Kola Kwariani, Dorothy Adams; **w**, Kubrick, Jim Thompson (based on the novel *Clean Break* by Lionel White); **c**, Lucien Ballard; **m**, Gerald Fried; **ed**, Betty Steinberg; **art d**, Ruth Sobotka; **set d**, Harry Reif; **spec eff**, Dave Koehler, Jack Rabin, Louis DeWitt.

The Killing Fields ★★★ 1984; U.K.; 141m; Enigma/WB; Color; War Drama; Children: Unacceptable (MPAA: R); **DVD**; **VHS**. In what is a riveting film about journalists covering the war in Vietnam and Cambodia in the 1970s, Waterston is a New York *Times* correspondent reporting on that confused politically motivated conflict, but gets most of his news through an energetic and savvy guide, Ngor (won an Oscar for Best Supporting Actor). Director Joffé does not flinch in graphically depicting all the horrors of that war, including slaughterhouse battles and atrocities that will sicken the most sensitive viewer (and is certainly not for children). When American forces begin to withdraw from the area, Ngor, who is the centerpiece of this engrossing film, arranges for his family to leave with those forces, but decides to stay behind and continue to ferret out stories for Waterston and others, but this decision brings great peril and eventual tragedy to him. Waterston is rather feckless in this well-made production, but that matters little for it is Ngor's masterful performance that holds attention throughout. **p**, David Put-

tnam; **d**, Roland Joffé; **cast**, Sam Waterston, Haing S. Ngor, John Malkovich, Julian Sands, Craig T. Nelson, Spalding Gray, Bill Paterson, Athol Fugard, Graham Kennedy, Katherine Krapum Chey, Edward Entero Chey, **w**, Bruce Robinson (based on the magazine article "The Death and Life of Dith Pran" by Sidney Schanberg); **c**, Chris Menges; **m**, Mike Oldfield; **ed**, Jim Clark; **prod d**, Roy Walker; **art d**, Roger Murray-Leach, Steve Spence; **spec eff**, Fred Cramer, Neil Sharp.

Kim ★★★ 1950; U.S.; 113m; MGM; Color; Adventure/ Spy Drama; Children: Acceptable; **DVD**; **VHS**. In this well-told Kipling tale, Stockwell is an adventure-seeking son of a British diplomat living in India in the 1880s. He shuns school and runs away, dressed as an Indian street urchin, wearing a turban and native apparel. He meets kindly lama Lukas, who takes him under his wing, becoming a surrogate father, a holy man who imparts his kindly philosophy and wisdom to the boy, who also comes under the protection of Flynn, a dashing horse thief, who is really an undercover espionage agent for the British. Flynn teaches Stockwell the techniques and tricks of spying and uses him to ferret out information from opposing spies in what Flynn calls "The Great Game." This leads Stockwell into dangerous waters where he encounters devious and evil men, trying to pry information from him through hypnosis, which he resists through Flynn's coaching; he is later almost killed in the high mountains when he and Flynn discover that Russian agents are preparing an invasion by Russian forces at the Khyber Pass and where Lukas dies of old age. Flynn and Stockwell defeat the villains and Flynn returns the boy to his father at the conclusion of this action-packed tale, which director Saville offers with great style. Though some on-location shots were made in India, most of the film was made in California and the Sierra Nevada mountains. **p**, Leon Gordon; **d**, Victor Saville; **cast**, Errol Flynn, Dean Stockwell, Paul Lukas, Robert Douglas, Thomas Gomez, Cecil Kellaway, Arnold Moss, Reginald Owen, Laurette Luez, Michael Ansara, Hamilton Camp; **w**, Gordon, Helen Deutsch, Richard Schayer (based on the novel by Rudyard Kipling); **c**, William Skall (Technicolor); **m**, André Previn; **ed**, George Boemler; **art d**, Cedric Gibbons, Hans Peters; **set d**, Edwin B. Willis; **spec eff**, A. Arnold Gillespie, Warren Newcombe.

Kind Hearts and Coronets ★★★★★ 1950; U.K.; 106m; Ealing Studios/Eagle-Lion Films; B/W; Comedy; Children: Unacceptable; **DVD**; **VHS**. In this superb comedy—one of the funniest films ever to come out of England—Price is a penniless member of the British 19th-Century aristocracy. An utter cad and ne'er-do-well, Price has the ambition to secure the top title and fortune of his family, and to that end, he blithely sets about to eliminate eight of the family members, who precede him in that title pecking order. All of Price's victims are brilliantly played by one person, the amazing Guinness. Price arranges to blow up one uncle before he sends an aunt into space in a failing balloon. Others, one by one, meet similar dire ends, until Price inherits the dukedom he so avidly covets. Further, Price can now pick from two lovely ladies to be his wife, Hobson or Greenwood. But, irony takes a grim hand when Price is then arrested for a crime he has not committed. The husband of Greenwood, his mistress, suddenly dies and Price is convicted of murdering him. He faces execution, but is miraculously reprieved and released from prison after the husband's "suicide note" is too conveniently found. Waiting with loving arms are Hobson and Greenwood, but the rake and serial killer is now impaled upon his own spear—in this case his writing pen, in that he has, while awaiting execution, written his memoirs, telling nothing but the truth, including information that precisely details the murders he has committed; he has negligently left those condemning memoirs in his prison cell, which are later found by astonished officials. Well directed and wonderfully acted by all cast members, this dark and witty satire remains one of the great gems of comedy. *Author's Note*: This was Guinness' third major feature film (after **Great Expectations**, 1946, and **Oliver Twist**, 1948, although he had appeared as an extra in a 1934 British programmer), and he takes every scene and keeps it as his own in his variously fascinating and humorous roles. "Every day I went to the studio in making that film, "Guinness told this author, "I had to ask the producers 'who am I playing today?' I do not have many lines, but that is compensated by the many characters I portray and it was really a matter of makeup and costuming that separates those personalities. They are all rather pompous and aloof persons, haughty and self-contained, so when they meet their Maker it appears that no one will really miss these boring and posturing people." No one, however, missed the great multi-personality roles Guinness delivers in this masterpiece film. **p**, Michael Balcon; **d**, Robert Hamer; **cast**, Dennis Price, Valerie Hobson, Joan Greenwood, Alec Guinness, Audrey Fildes, Miles Malleson, Clive Morton, John Penrose, Cecil Ramage, Hugh Griffith; **w**, Hamer, John Dighton (based on a novel by Roy Horniman); **c**, Douglas Slocombe; **m**, Ernest Irving; **ed**, Peter Tanner; **art d**, William Kellner; **spec eff**, Geoffrey Dickinson, Sydney Pearson.

Kind Lady ★★★ 1951; U.S; 78m; MGM; B/W; Crime Drama; Children: Unacceptable; **VHS**. Ethel Barrymore, that grand lady of stage and screen, is the centerpiece in this suspenseful thriller. She is an elderly, wealthy art collector, who is gulled by confidence man Evans into taking him and his wife, Blair, into her home, along with two devious servants, Lansbury and Wynn. All are in cahoots in that they systematically begin to loot Barrymore's art collection while holding Barrymore a prisoner. No one from the "outside world" comes to her rescue, so she uses her own considerable wits and wisdom to undo the villains. Barrymore is captivating as the victimized woman with a heart of gold and her captors also give superb performances as greedy and heartless creatures in this above average crime yarn. **p**, Armand Deutsch; **d**, John Sturges; **cast**, Ethel Barrymore, Maurice Evans, Angela Lansbury, Keenan Wynn, Betsy Blair, John Williams, Doris Lloyd, John O'Malley, Henri Letondal, Queenie Leonard; **w**, Jerry Davis, Edward Chodorov, Charles Bennett (based on the play by Chodorov and the story "The Silver Casket" by Hugh Walpole); **c**, Joseph Ruttenberg; **m**, David Raksin; **ed**, Ferris Webster; **art d**, Cedric Gibbons, William Ferrari; **set d**, Edwin B. Willis, Jacque Mapes.

A Kind of Loving ★★★ 1962; U.K.; 112m; Vic Films Productions/Governor Films; B/W; Drama; Children: Unacceptable; **VHS**. In this solid and engrossing domestic drama, Bates is a draftsman in a factory in Lancashire, England, who becomes attracted to Ritchie, a secretary working there. She falls in love with him, but he loses interest and begins dating other girls. However, Ritchie has become pregnant. When she tells Bates this, he reluctantly marries her. They honeymoon at a seaside resort and then move in with her domineering mother, Hird, who believes her daughter married beneath her station in life. Ritchie has a miscarriage and loses the baby, and Bates regrets marrying her, so he takes to drinking. The couple decides that the only way they might make a go of their marriage is to escape Ritchie's mother, so they look for a place of their own and that "breaking away" presents another great challenge in their lives. Sexuality and nudity prohibit viewing by children. **p**, Joseph Janni; **d**, John Schlesinger; **cast**, Alan Bates, June Ritchie, Thora Hird, Bert Palmer, Pat Keen, James Bolam, Jack Smethurst, Gwen Nelson, John Ronane, David Mahlowe; **w**, Willis Hall, Keith Waterhouse (based on the novel by Stan Barstow); **c**, Denys Coop; **m**, Ron Grainer; **ed**, Roger Cherrill; **art d**, Ray Simm.

King & Country ★★★ 1964; U.K.; 88m; BHF Films/AA; Drama; Children: Unacceptable; **DVD**; **VHS**. In this grim but compelling drama, Bogarde is a British officer, a legal counsel who is a strict disciplinarian and who goes by the book. He is assigned to defend Courtenay, and who has been charged with desertion during WWI. Bogarde tries to avoid this assignment, which he finds distasteful, but is ordered to proceed to trial, expecting a prompt conviction. When talking with his client, however, Bogarde's attitude begins to change as the sincere

Alec Guinness in *Kind Hearts and Coronets,* 1950.

Courtenay appears to be a legitimate shell-shock victim. He tells Bogarde how he enlisted years earlier only on a dare from friends and how, while he was serving at the front, he learned that his wife has been unfaithful. Then, one by one, all of those in his military unit are killed so that he is left as the lone survivor. Alone in the trenches, Courtenay states that he got fed up and decided to "go for a walk," and left his post, and was later found wandering about aimlessly, his senses jangled by the incessant gunfire at the front. Now full of feeling for his client, Bogarde makes an impassioned speech on Courtenay's behalf, but he fails to move the cold-hearted officers at the tribunal and Courtenay is found guilty of desertion and ordered to be executed by a firing squad. On the night before the scheduled execution, those making up that firing squad filch the best food and liquor from the officers' mess and take it to Courtenay's cell where they party with the condemned man, all getting drunk. In the morning, suffering from terrible hangovers, the members of the firing squad fire at Courtenay, but their drunken aims fail to kill Courtenay and only inflict painful wounds. Bogarde, who presides at the execution, is now compelled to administer the coup de grace by firing a bullet from his revolver into Courtenay's head, ending his life. This uncompromising production indicts the military as having no mercy or compassion and undoubtedly was inspired by the making of the classic war film, **Paths of Glory**, 1957, which treats three soldiers facing a military tribunal, but under different circumstances that nevertheless produce the same horrendous results. **p**, Joseph Losey, Norman Priggen; **d**, Losey; **cast**, Dirk Bogarde, Tom Courtenay, Leo McKern, Barry Foster, Peter Copley, James Villiers, Jeremy Spencer, Barry Justice, Vivian Matalon, Keith Buckley; **w**, Evan Jones (based on the play "Hamp" by John Wilson from the novel *Return to the Wood* by J.L. Hodson); **c**, Denys Coop; **m**, Larry Adler; **ed**, Reginald Mills; **prod d**, Richard Macdonald; **art d**, Peter Mullins.

The King and I ★★★★★ 1956; U.S.; 133m; FOX; Color; Musical; Children: Acceptable; **DVD**; **VHS**. Based on the film **Anna and the King of Siam**, 1946, this remaded version is a musical masterpiece with dazzling performances by Brynner and Kerr. Brynner, in a role he was born to play (he won an Oscar for Best Actor), is the king of Siam and Kerr is hired to teach his many children and wives. Kerr travels in 1862 with her son, Thompson, to Siam and is, after she insists on living apart from the main palace, given a small home of her own. Not only does Kerr bring enlightenment to the children and wives, but inspires Brynner, a chauvinistic monarch with old-fashioned ideas of how to govern, to change his ways and policies and move his country into the modern era. In one of the many subplots, Kerr, after some reasoning and argument, convinces Brynner to release one of his wives, Moreno, who loves another, Rivas, and he slowly evolves from a blustering and arrogant

Yul Brynner and Deborah Kerr in *The King and I*, 1956.

ruler to a compassionate and forward-thinking leader. He and Kerr mentally duel and they banter and bicker about social issues, but a strong bond between them develops and blossoms into a love that is never consummated. The love these two divergent humans have for one another is expressed when Brynner lies on his deathbed for a memorably poignant finale. Lehman's script is brilliant, incisive and true to the original play upon which the original film and this one were based, providing many humorous and tearful moments, but the magnificent score from Rodgers and Hammerstein makes this production one without equal. One of the many highlights of this superb film is a set-piece arranged by master choreographer Jerome Robbins, entitled "The Little House of Uncle Thomas," where the royal children are delightful in presenting the Siamese version of "Uncle Tom's Cabin." This sequence, both hilarious and heart-touching, is presented to visitors to prove that the Siamese are not barbarians. Songs include: "Song of the King," "Something Wonderful," "A Puzzlement," "I Have Dreamed," "March of the Siamese Children," "I Whistle A Happy Tune," "We Kiss In A Shadow," "Hello, Young Lovers," "Getting To Know You" and "Shall We Dance?" Songs originally intended for the film, but deleted, are: "Shall I Tell You What I Think Of You?" "Western People Funny," "My Lord And Master." Kerr's singing voice was looped by dubbing singer Maxi Nixon, who was the wife of film composer Ernest Gold. Alfred Newman and Ken Darby received Oscars for the musical score. The film was an enormous success, gleaning more than $8.5 million at the box office, easily earning back its $4.5 million budget. *Author's Note*: The character wonderfully played by Kerr is based upon Anna Leonowens (1831-1915), who went to Siam and taught (1862-1868) the children and wives of King Mongkut (1804-1868), a Siamese king, who will be forever remembered through the unforgettable performance of Brynner. Some actors are forever linked to the roles they played, such as Clark Gable, who is the one and only Rhett Butler of **Gone with the Wind**, 1939, or Marlon Brando, who is the one and only Stanley Kowalski in **A Street Car Named Desire**, 1951, just as Yul Brynner is the one and only king of Siam. Kerr, too, with the exception of the war drama, **From Here to Eternity**, 1953, the romance film, **An Affair to Remember**, 1957, and some others, is mostly remembered from her performance in **The King and I**. The actress told this author that "It was one of the few films I made where the very hard work was a delight to perform. Every minute of that picture is precious to me and whenever I hear one of its songs, I can see the scene that song represents as vividly as the day when I appeared in that picture." **p**, Charles Brackett; **d**, Walter Lang; **cast**, Deborah Kerr, Yul Brynner, Rita Moreno, Martin Benson, Terry Saunders, Rex Thompson, Carlos Rivas, Patrick Adiarte, Alan Mowbray, Geoffrey Toone; **w**, Ernest Lehman (based on the musical play by Oscar Hammerstein II, Richard Rodgers, from the book *Anna*

and King of Siam by Margaret Landon); **c**, Leon Shamroy (CinemaScope; DeLuxe Color); **m**, Rodgers; **ed**, Robert Simpson; **art d**, Lyle Wheeler, John De Cuir; **set d**, Walter M. Scott, Paul S. Fox.

King Arthur ★★★ 2004; U.S./U.K./Ireland; 126m; Touchstone Pictures/Buena Vista; Color; Children: Unacceptable (MPAA: PG-13); **BD**; **DVD**. In this engrossing and action-packed adventure tale, the legendary King Arthur of England is less enigmatic and his tale is no longer set in the 14th Century, but in 457 A.D. where Arthur, played by Owen, is a valiant Roman officer commanding a small cavalry force during the Roman occupation of Britain and when the Roman Empire was deserting the island as it was thought to be no longer defensible or profitable. Owen leads his men, all of whom are named after those legendary knights—Lancelot, Galahad, Gawain and Tristan—in several rescue missions to deliver Roman dignitaries to the safety of Hadrian's Wall, but he opposes his superiors when they viciously oppress the Woad natives, including one young woman, Guinevere (Knightley), who is later to become Owen's wife, and then leads this tribe in victorious battles against the fierce Saxons. Well acted and with a good script, director Fuqua brings a stirring, action-packed tale to the screen and where Idziak's cinematography is exceptional, particularly the battle scenes in the mountains and on the frozen lake. **p**, Jerry Bruckheimer; **d**, Antoine Fuqua; **cast**, Clive Owen, Ioan Gruffudd, Keira Knightley, Hugh Dancy, Ray Winstone, Ray Stevenson, Stellan Skarsgård, Stephen Dillane, Mads Mikkelsen, Joel Edgerton; **w**, David Franzoni; **c**, Slawomir Idziak; **m**, Hans Zimmer; **ed**, Conrad Buff, Jamie Pearson; **prod d**, Dan Weil; **art d**, Anna Rackard, Yann Biquand; **set d**, Olivia Bloch-Laine; **spec eff**, Steve Cullane, David Brighton.

King Creole ★★★ 1958; U.S.; 116m; Hal Wallis Productions/PAR; B/W; Musical; Children: Acceptable (MPAA: PG); **DVD**; **VHS**. Presley is outstanding as a singing busboy with an attitude and an overactive hip at a cheap Bourbon Street night club in New Orleans. He rescues Jones, a patroness who is being pawed by a drunk during a drinking party. Jones is the girlfriend of a local hoodlum, Matthau, whom she would like to leave, but fears for her life if she did. Presley is still in high school, unable to jump that hurdle after several tries. Jones gives him a kiss and his schoolmates see and razz him about it, so he starts punching. That gets Presley kicked out of school again and he joins a gang of toughs led by Morrow. Presley's father, Jagger, gets him a job at a drug store and tries to talk him into going back to school, but Presley clings to his gang associates, and they rob the drug store while he works and sings there and where Presley falls for Hart, a girl who works at the drug store. Matthau hears Presley sing and introduces him to Stewart, who owns the King Creole nightclub. Presley starts singing there and packs the place. Hart wants Presley to marry her, but he gets arrested for being involved in a hold-up where he is really the victim of a set-up. He learns that Matthau was behind the set-up so he beats him up. Now every hood in town is after him. Presley also beats up Morrow, but is hurt and hospitalized, so Hart takes him to a secluded country place and nurses him back to health. Matthau blames Jones for all his troubles and kills her. He is then killed by one of his own thugs. Deciding to live the straight-and-narrow life, Presley and Hart now plan to get married. This is one of Presley's best and most popular films. Songs include: "Crawfish" (Fred Wise, Ben Wiseman, sung by Presley, Kitty White); "Don't Ask Me Why" (Wise, Weisman, sung by Presley);"As Long as I Have You" (Weis, Wiseman, sung by Presley); "King Creole," "Steadfast, Loyal and True," "Trouble (Jerry Leiber, Mike Stoller, sung by Presley); "Lover Boy" (Sid Wayne, Abner Silver, sung by Presley); "Dixieland Rock" (Aaron Schroder, Rachel Frank, sung by Presley); "Young Dreams" (Schroder, Martin Kalmanoff, sung by Presley); "New Orleans" (Sid Tepper, Roy C. Bennett, sung by Presley); "Hard Headed Women" (Claude Demetri, sung by Presley) Excessive violence prohibits viewing by children. **p**, Hal B. Wallis; **d**, Michael Curtiz; **cast**, Elvis Presley, Carolyn Jones, Walter Matthau, Dolores

Hart, Dean Jagger, Liliane Montevecchi, Vic Morrow, Paul Stewart, Jan Shepard, Candy Candido, Brian Hutton; **w**, Herbert Baker, Michael V. Gazzo (based on the novel *A Stone for Danny Fisher* by Harold Robbins); **c**, Russell Harlan; **m**, Walter Scharf; **ed**, Warren Low; **art d**, Hal Pereira, Joseph MacMillan Johnson; **set d**, Sam Comer, Frank McKelvy.

King Kong ★★★★★ 1933; U.S.; 100m (104m restored version); RKO; B/W; Adventure/Fantasy/Horror; Children: Unacceptable; **DVD**; **VHS**. This film classic offers one heart-pounding scene after another as it unfolds an eerie tale of a strange island forgotten by time and inhabited by Jurassic dinosaurs, dominated by the greatest beast of them all—Kong. The granddaddy of all adventure films, which mixes in its pulsing veins unique fantasy and horror, begins one night in 1932 on a dock in New York Harbor where a looming ship, *Venture*, is anchored. Show business agent Hardy approaches the ship and calls out to a night watchman: "Is this the moving picture ship?" Cabot, the first mate, shouts down to Hardy that it is and the agent boards the ship and is taken to a cabin to meet Reicher, the captain, and Armstrong, a legendary documentary filmmaker known for his exciting nature films profiling exotic lands. He has brought along for his new adventure a good deal of ammunition and a case of gas grenades, but will not tell anyone why he might need such supplies or why he has tripled the number of burly crew members. He asks Hardy if he has found an actress to play the lead in his next film. Hardy tells him, no, that no self-respecting actress or woman would agree to go on a long sea voyage without knowing its destination or its purpose, information that Armstrong has refused to provide. The frustrated Armstrong then conducts his own search for the "right face" among the women lining the Manhattan breadlines in this Depression era as well as rooming houses, but to no avail until he sees a young, blonde woman at an open grocery where she is about to be arrested for stealing an apple. Armstrong pays off the owner and takes the blonde, Wray, to a restaurant where he buys her a good dinner. He then offers her the job in his new movie. At first, she thinks he is handing her a line, but Armstrong tells her that he is not pulling any "funny stuff," and convinces her that he is, indeed, a famous filmmaker and she agrees to take the job. The next day, the *Venture* sails from New York, but Reicher has only vague instructions from Armstrong as to their route and destination. Meanwhile, first mate Cabot meets Wray, annoyed at her presence on deck and thinking that women are bad luck on such voyages. However, he begins to soften toward the beautiful young woman, and she responds in kind. Once the ship is in the Indian Ocean, Armstrong meets with Reicher and Cabot and shows them a map he has purchased from a Norwegian ship captain, one that depicts his mysterious destination, Skull Island. Reicher, an Old Salt who has sailed these waters, tells Armstrong that there is no island in the area. Armstrong then tells him that the island cannot be found on any chart, but it does exist; and, further, the natives on that island have built a huge wall on a peninsula where they dwell to keep out something terrible they both fear and worship and call "Kong," and if this creature exists, he intends to capture it on film. He then asks Wray to do a screen test on the upper deck where she wears a white flowing gown, telling her before he starts his camera that she is to pretend she sees something fierce and terrible and must scream: "It's horrible, but you can't look away...You're helpless...If only you could scream. Cover your eyes and scream, Ann. Scream for your life!" Wray stares into the camera with a look of fright flooding her face and then releases a terrible, piercing scream, one that causes Cabot to wince as he looks down on her from the deck above, saying to Reicher: "What does he think she's really going to see?" The normally confident Cabot is now wary and apprehensive. The following day, as the ship sails through fog-bound waters, Skull Island is suddenly sighted and, in the distance, the native camp and beyond it a towering wall sealing off the rest of that island. From that camp comes the sound of beating drums. The ship anchors and Armstrong takes a small party, including Reicher, Cabot and Wray ashore, as well as his camera. Ap-

Kong and attacking airplanes in *King Kong,* 1933.

proaching the native village, the visitors hear the word "Kong" being repeatedly shouted and they then, while hiding behind some brush, see a native ceremony in progress, one where a young girl is being adorned with flowers and is at the center of a ring of ceremonial dancers dressed in the hairy skins and heads of gorillas as they frenetically pound their chests to the beat of the drums. It is obvious that the girl is about to be sacrificed to "Kong," but the towering, fierce-looking chief, Johnson, sees the interlopers and halts the ceremony. He, along with his witch doctor, Clemento, and some guards, approach the strange-looking visitors, Clemento urging the chief to have the unwanted visitors killed. Johnson sees the fair-haired, white-skinned Wray, and where Reicher serves as an interpreter, offers to buy her. Reicher refuses and Johnson makes a few menacing moves, but Armstrong waves him away, saying they are friends and will return later. The visitors then slowly walk away from the natives, going to their boats and rowing back to their ship. That night, while all are on board the *Venture*, Cabot and Wray express their love for each other. When Cabot is called to a meeting, Wray, left alone on deck, is grabbed by the native witch doctor and others, who have slipped on board the ship, taking her back to the island. One of the kidnapping natives loses his bracelet and this is found by the ship's cook, Wong, who gives the alarm. A frantic search for Wray is conducted, but she is nowhere to be found on the ship. Armstrong orders most of the crew members to man the boats, arming them and taking along the case of gas grenades. By the time they reach shore, Wray has already been prepared as a sacrifice to "Kong," dressed as a native girl, bedecked with garlands, and taken through the huge gates of the wall and tied to a stone altar beyond that wall. The natives then close the gates and slide in place its huge wooden bolt while lining the top of the wall, a large gong then is struck several times to summon from the dense jungle the beast they worship. A loud roar is heard and trees begin to snap beneath the weight of the approaching beast. Wray struggles against the ropes that bind her, but she cannot break free as, suddenly, smashing through the jungle, there appears a colossal prehistoric gorilla, walking upright and standing forty feet tall (appears sixty feet tall in some scenes). It is Kong. Its huge mouth gapes with fierce-looking teeth and its wide-set eyes focuses upon the squirming Wray beneath him. Just at that moment, Armstrong, Cabot, Reicher and crew members arrive, rushing to the gate and peering through a slot to see Kong releasing Wray from her ropes, and while he lifts her in the palm of one gigantic hand, she squirms and struggles while Kong curiously inspects her, until she faints, and Kong turns about and carries her back into the jungle. Driving away the natives, Armstrong and Cabot, along with other crew members, open the gate and, while Reicher and some others remain behind to keep it open for their return, race into the jungle, pursuing Kong in an effort to rescue Wray, who has become the horrific creature's new "bride." Following

Fay Wray and Kong in *King Kong*, 1933.

Kong's footsteps, the men struggle through the jungle, cutting away underbrush until they come to a clearing. They are jolted to a stop at the sight of a foraging dinosaur, a stegosaurus. The beast suddenly sees them and charges at them. They fire their weapons repeatedly at the on-rushing dinosaur, finally felling it. Approaching the beast, it lifts once more to menace them, lashing out with its spiked tail, but more bullets finally kill it. The rescue party continues until it comes to the edge of a vast swamp. Kong has easily waded through these murky waters, but the rescuers are compelled to hastily build rafts and shove off into its foggy midst. As they pole their way to the other side of the swamp, a huge prehistoric water creature emerges, lifting one of the rafts and toppling its occupants into the waters, where it swallows one and then another victim. The survivors reach the far shore and the dinosaur lumbers from the swamp after them. Now, the rescuers are the prey and they run madly through the jungle before the oncoming and thundering beast. One man falls behind and, to save his life, climbs a tree, but when the beast arrives at the tree, it plucks him from his perch, eating him alive. The survivors are now hot on the heels of Kong, who reaches a deep chasm over which stretches a huge log. He walks across this log and then places the now conscious and terrified Wray in the branch of a tall tree before returning to the gorge. The rescuers reach the log, and Cabot makes his way safely across just as Kong returns to the spot and where Cabot hides from him in a cave just inside the cliff, but others are trapped on the log, which Kong lifts with ease and begins shaking them loose so that they fall screaming to their deaths. Several cling desperately to the log, but Kong manages to send them all, including the log, to the bottom of the ravine. He notices movement beneath the cliff where he stands and it is Cabot, pressing against the wall of a shallow cave. Kong reaches down with his hand and probes the area with his fingers, but Cabot stabs him. A creature then begins to climb along a vine toward the top of the cliff and Kong pulls it toward him and kills it, believing that the creature was the prey he was seeking. Kong then hears Wray screaming and he rushes back to the tree where he has placed her to see the king of the dinosaurs, Tyrannosaurus Rex, approaching her. Kong rushes the gigantic beast, which is even larger than he, attacking it. The two behemoths struggle in a fierce fight, biting and clawing at each other until Kong leaps upon the T-Rex's back and brings it to earth, snapping its neck and killing it. He plays with its slack jaw to make sure the beast is dead and then retrieves Wray, heading for his lair. Armstrong, stranded on the other side of the ravine, calls to Cabot, who tells him he will push on to find Wray. Armstrong will return to the village and get reinforcements. Cabot, alone, works his way through the jungles and then enters a huge cave into which Kong has carried Wray. Kong encounters a giant snake-like creature and, putting Wray aside, battles this beast while Cabot arrives in the cavern to witness this struggle, climbing upward to reach Wray.

Killing the snake, Kong takes Wray to his mountaintop retreat where he examines her. When hearing a noise, he puts her down, and at that moment, a giant Pterodactyl swoops down and grabs Wray, who screams; Kong grabs the winged lizard, and while Kong struggles with this beast, Cabot rushes forward, grabs Wray, and begins lowering both of them off the cliff and toward the waiting river below on a long vine. Kong kills the Pterodactyl and then notices that Wray is gone and sees her with Cabot descending toward the river. He yanks the vine toward him, and both Cabot and Wray fall into the river, surviving and swimming away. Kong, enraged, leaves his lair and begins pursuing them in order to reclaim his "bride." Reaching land, Cabot and Wray run wildly through the jungle with Kong in hot pursuit, his thundering steps moving the earth behind them. They reach the native wall and get through the gate, which is bolted behind them just as Kong reaches the wall and where natives and seamen form a sea of humanity behind the gates to support them. Kong begins to bang and bash at the gates while natives on the wall throw spears into him, but his unleashed rage exhibits powerful blows to the gates and the weight of his body against the gates begins to crack the huge wooden bolt, which finally gives way, sending the natives and seamen racing for their lives as Kong invades the village. He stomps on terrified natives, grabbing one and biting off his head (this is only one of several such savage scenes that were later cut for a more sanitized version of this film) and also battles and kills several natives throwing spears at him. By then, Cabot and Wray have joined Armstrong, Reicher, and the remaining seamen on the beach. When Kong arrives to attack them, Armstrong and his men throw several gas grenades that cause the great beast to collapse unconscious. At this point, Armstrong declares that they will not leave the island without their "prize," and that they will build an enormous raft and take Kong to sea with them and back to civilization. "He's always been a king in his world," Armstrong states, "but we will teach him fear...Why, the whole world will pay to see this! In a few months, it will be up in lights— 'Kong, the Eighth Wonder of the World!'" In the next scene we see a marquee on a Manhattan theater emblazoning the very words spoken by Armstrong and where theatergoers in the thousands pay admission to see Kong. The theater fills with spectators, and Armstrong then walks before the curtain to center stage to announce his greatest attraction; when the curtains part, the audience gasps to see Kong standing on a platform, held by a pillory of steel bracelets that pin his arms and legs and where he roars at the startled audience. Armstrong introduces Cabot and Wray as the principals who helped him subdue the great beast, but when a bevy of newspaper reporters arrive on the stage to take photos of Wray and Cabot, their incessant flashbulbs exploding leads Kong to think that they are attacking the one human Kong loves, Wray, and he becomes enraged, breaking one arm loose and then the other as those in the audience flee in screaming panic as does everyone on stage. Kong breaks the bracelets holding his feet and then smashes through the back wall of the theater and begins to create havoc on the street as he searches for Wray, who has been taken to a high rise hotel by Cabot. Kong encounters the elevated tracks of a city train and smashes it, then lifts his head through the broken tracks, which is seen by the motorman of an oncoming train. As the train approaches, Kong stops the train and tears the first car from the tracks, bashing it to pieces and crushing its occupants. Kong then goes in search of Wray, climbing a building and clutches from a room a woman he thinks might be Wray, but, when examining her, realizes she is not and lets her fall to her screaming death. Kong then climbs another building, peering through windows, until he sees Wray in a room with Cabot and thrusts his huge arm through the window, knocking Cabot senseless and grabbing Wray. Armstrong and Cabot are next seen with Cabot recovering from his injury from Kong and talking to city officials, who are told that Kong is now heading for the Empire State Building and has begun to climb the highest (then) building in New York. It is then decided to send armed fighter planes to shoot Kong from the structure, and Cabot goes to the building, hoping to somehow save Wray. Reaching the top of the Empire State Building;

Kong sees the fighter planes approaching and places Wray on a ledge for safety before turning to swing with one mighty arm at the planes that dive and shoot at him while he clings with the other arm to the dome of the building. The fighter planes dive and swoop at the frustrated Kong, shooting him repeatedly. He manages to swipe one plane flying too close to him, sending it crashing in flames toward the streets below. The remaining planes, machine guns blazing, riddle his huge body, striking him in the throat, and after a longing look toward the little human he loves, Wray, Kong falls from his perch, striking the side of the building several times before he falls dead in the street below. Armstrong stands next to the inert corpse of Kong and a policeman says: "Well, the planes got him." Armstrong shakes his head, saying: "Oh, no, it wasn't the airplanes. It was Beauty killed the Beast." Thus ends this utterly chilling and savage retelling of the Beauty and the Beast where the fierce Kong, seen by the world as a dreadful monster, dies in an alien land for his protective love of a human being not much larger than his index finger. Cooper's direction is masterful as he carefully builds anticipation into suspense and then horror until he reveals the terrifying image of the world's most powerful monster. Armstrong, Cabot, Wray and the rest of the cast, including the brief appearances of native chief Johnson, are all standouts in their colorful roles, and, of course, the special effects, even in this early era where such techniques were in embryonic development, are superlative. The film was produced on a budget of $670,000 and was an overnight success, producing more than $1,850,000, much-needed funds for RKO as the studio was close to bankruptcy. It gleaned more than $1 million in its two re-releases in 1938 and 1941. It remains to this day the unequalled horror film in the history of the medium. *Author's Note*: The idea for **King Kong** remained in the fertile mind of its producer-director Cooper for many years. He and his erstwhile co-producer, Schoedsack, had made some astounding and financially successful nature documentaries, **Grass: A Nation's Battle for Life**, 1925, and **Chang: A Drama of the Wilderness**, 1927, shot on location in Africa and Southeast Asia. While producing his first feature-length film, **The Four Feathers**, 1929, Cooper took his cast and crew to Africa and "that is where I saw wild gorillas in the jungle," he told this author in 1967. "I had a brainstorm, and thought I could later make a picture with a giant gorilla with above-average intelligence—and these creatures have considerable intelligence to begin with—and where he would fight to the death with a huge Komodo Dragon. When I mentioned that to Ernie [Ernest Schoedsack], he said: 'Where in the hell are we going to find something like that in this jungle?' After a few days, I told Ernie that I could see this massive gorilla defeating every imaginable creature— they were first giant lizards in my mind and then developed into prehistoric dinosaurs—and even battling them in New York City. Of course, gorillas are tree climbers and the highest perch my imaginary gorilla could climb was the Empire State Building, which had been finished only two years after I got the idea for Kong and it was then the tallest building in the world and I saw him climbing it only to be shot down by a squadron of airplanes. 'Who dangles the banana that gets the gorilla to climb that high?' Ernie laughed. 'And good luck in getting the owners of that building to go along with you!' 'They'll love the publicity,' I told Ernie, 'and besides, we'll do it all with trick photography.' 'That will be *some* trick,' Ernie said, and indeed it was!" At the same time that Kong was stewing in Cooper's fertile mind, special effects genius Willis O'Brien was creating a film that would excel his silent horror class, **The Lost World**, 1925, for which he had created special effects that brought to life (albeit somewhat crudely) prehistoric dinosaurs from the Jurassic period. O'Brien had tinkered with creating dinosaurs on film as early as 1915, when he provided the images for such creatures in a short entitled **The Dinosaur and the Missing Link: A Prehistoric Tragedy**. O'Brien had entitled his next production "Creation" and RKO picked up an option on the story, which, ironically, shared Cooper's separate vision of a group of modern-day explorers stumbling upon a lost world, but in the Amazon jungle of South America where they encounter prehistoric beasts. O'Brien did some preliminary tests for his

Kong in *King Kong*, 1933.

project, but when he showed RKO the budget for all the additional elaborate tests to be made for "Creation," the money-pressed studio turned down the idea and Willis' concept remained in RKO's limbo. In 1931, boy-wonder producer David O. Selznick moved from Paramount to become vice president in charge of production at RKO and invited Cooper, a longtime friend, to share those production responsibilities. Cooper told this author that "I went to New York and went over with David everything that RKO had on the boards. When I looked at the short test Willis had made for something he called 'Creation,' I knew on the spot that he and his visual effects people could make my giant gorilla and all the rest of the prehistoric beasts I had envisioned. David agreed that I should make a test of my own with the giant gorilla and we did, calling that test 'Production 601.'" O'Brien went to work with his top monster-maker, Marcel Delgado, who started by constructing a fully articulate eighteen-inch skeleton or armature of the gorilla, made from aluminum alloy. Employing a combination of sponge and rubber, Delgado added muscles to the gorilla, skillfully covering the entire frame with specially fitted rabbit fur and Kong came to life. "I took one look at what O'Brien and Delgado had made and knew we had captured the beast," Cooper told this author. "I then contacted Edgar Wallace, who had just arrived in Hollywood, and had been signed to a contract by RKO. He was a master mystery writer, and I asked him to write the script for a picture we were then calling 'The Beast.'" Wallace visited O'Brien's shop and, after looking upon the role model, went to work on the script, but, unfortunately, he died on February 10, 1932. "He had not written a word," Cooper said to this author, "but we gave him credit for the picture as one of its writers anyway since he had given me several ideas about how the story should go and little tidbits about the nature of the giant gorilla." Cooper assigned the script to Creelman and Rose, the latter being Schoedsack's wife, and she patterned the character played by Armstrong after her husband, and his partner, Cooper, a man making spectacular nature films. By then, the film was tentatively entitled "The Eighth Wonder" and O'Brien soon had tests for RKO executives to view. He had brought to life the giant gorilla and several prehistoric beasts through stop-motion animation (although his dinosaurs dragged their tails rather than carried them aloft as was later determined by scientists and as depicted in such modern-day epics as **Jurassic Park**, 1993). Simply stated, stop-motion animation involves moving the armature slightly in one exposed frame of film and then continuing its motion by moving the armature in the next exposed frame of film, a tedious, exhaustive job requiring endless patience in that sound film is projected at twenty-four frames per second. Thus, a day's work of such complicated labor where several animated figures move at the same time could provide one second of magical images on the screen for that day. By combining live-action actors into each frame at

Kong battling men in *King Kong*, 1933.

the proper scale, the eighteen-inch models of the prehistoric beasts were made to appear gigantic. In some cases, the animation was filmed ahead of the time where the live-action actors appear and then rear-projected onto a highly reflective screen in front of which the actors later stood, as is the case where Armstrong and his men walk in front of the dying stegosaurus. Without losing too much image quality, the animation was then re-photographed so that the actors could react to what they see on their side of the screen, which was opposite the projector. Once these elements were combined to the proper scale, the scene was then photographed by a camera on the actor's side of the rear-projection screen. Cooper, with O'Brien's considerable aid, successfully employed this process for full and medium shots in sequences requiring little interaction between the beasts and the live-action actors. More complicated scenes required stationary and traveling mattes to be used. In these scenes, O'Brien shot his animated creatures with an area of the frame matted off, meaning that a portion of the frame is covered to keep it from being exposed on film. Cooper then directed the live-action actors in such scenes with the animated portion matted off. The two pieces of separate film are then fitted exactly together through an optical printer and photographed as one. Skull Mountain and other stationary objects were created as miniatures or painted on glass and then matted into larger frames. To enhance the effect, small armatures of humans made to scale replace the live-action actors and these tiny humans become animated when the creatures attack these hapless victims. After the scene showing Kong shaking the actors from the log in the scene at the ravine and Kong's battle with the T-Rex to RKO executives, Cooper received a very enthusiastic response and given the green light to complete the film. At that time, Cooper's partner, Schoedsack, had begun production for an RKO adventure film **The Most Dangerous Game**, 1932, starring Fay Wray and with a cast that included Armstrong and Johnson. When Cooper viewed some early rushes of this film, he decided he wanted Wray, Armstrong and Johnson in the film. "Fay had no idea what the new film was all about," Cooper told this author. "I simply told her that you will be playing opposite a tall, dark leading man. When she later saw Kong, or the portions of the gorilla that would manhandle her, she said: 'Well, he's no matinee idol.' Fay was a brunette so we put a blonde wig on her and she wore that so well, everyone thought it was her actual hair, even Kong." Further, the now fully named **King Kong** and **The Most Dangerous Game** were produced almost simultaneously (although the latter film was released first, opening a full year before **King Kong**) and Cooper took advantage of the huge sets in **The Most Dangerous Game**, using its jungles, mountainous area and even the log over which Kong walks and later destroys along with the hapless sailors clinging to it. With both productions in progress, the actors involved in the two separate films were more than distracted when they would finish

one scene in one film and then be ordered to change their costumes and appear in another scene in the other film. Cooper did not at this time have a finished script, only some scenes he had created in which he could have Wray, Armstrong and Johnson make appearances. He had no leading man up to this time until he considered Cabot, but he forced Cabot to prove his physical prowess by having him climb up and down ropes dangling over a cliff. It was Cabot's first role as a romantic lead. After the scriptwriters filled in the holes, those scenes were shot and principal photography was completed. Everything else rested with O'Brien, who convinced Cooper that more of Kong was needed than the eighteen-inch model and the stop-motion animation of his image, and he and his crew then built life-size portions of the giant gorilla, including an enormous bust of Kong's head and shoulders to be seen in close-ups where Kong snarls and even chomps on beasts and even a few unfortunate humans. Kong's nose, eyes, lips, brows and mouth were mechanically manipulated by three technicians who were positioned inside Kong's head (an idea O'Brien got when he remembered how he once visited the Statue of Liberty in New York Harbor and, along with other visitors, climbed up to stand in the statue's head and peer from little windows to see the harbor and horizon). One of Kong's massive hands is shown many times in the film as it holds Wray in its gentle grasp. One huge foot was made and appears only in one scene where it crushes a native into the dirt. Once O'Brien completed his end of the production, the film was given to sound man Murray Spivack, who proceeded to implant on the sound track in the appropriate scenes the sounds of the jungle creatures, especially the prehistoric beasts, which includes bone-chilling screeches, roars, chirps, and growls, getting exaggerated sounds by recording actual animal sounds and then playing them backward. Spivack also inserted additional sounds such as waterfalls, gunshots and crashing sounds when the prehistoric beasts break through the jungle foliage. Then master screen composer Max Steiner created a full musical score for this film—the first feature to have such a complete score, and it was brilliantly memorable with lower register chords reverberating throughout, along with the frantic beating of drums and hurried "chase" music to heighten the tension in the many harrowing scenes on the island and in Manhattan. Steiner actually composed the music and played it as he viewed scene for scene, establishing the precedent of such important musical scoring. To accentuate the movements of both Kong and the imperiled humans, Steiner created small, eerie-sounding passages. When Johnson, the native chief, takes one deliberate step after another toward Wray, Steiner inserted one menacing sounding note for each step. The film's original budget of $372,000 almost doubled in production to $672,000, and knowing that RKO was in financial trouble, MGM offered to buy the film at $400,000 above its budget, but RKO executives refused and wisely so, as box office returns from its initial release returned three times the cost of the film. **King Kong** was the only film ever simultaneously premiered at two New York theaters—Radio City Music Hall and the RKO Roxy. It met with widespread critical and public approval and stunned audiences with its amazing visual and special effects. Some challenged O'Brien's wizardry, claiming that Kong and the prehistoric beasts were enacted by stunt men in animal suits, but no such tawdry trickery was ever employed in this masterpiece. No reviewer knew that Cooper and Schoedsack appeared in the film as two of the fliers in one of the fighter planes, and, in fact, it was a burst from their plane that finally proves fatal to Kong and sends him crashing dead to earth. "I had every right to kill off Kong," Cooper told this author, "since I created him. He was my Frankenstein, and I felt that it was my responsibility to end his last moments on earth." Wray's appearance in this film made her an overnight star, but her career declined by the end of the 1930s, although she is forever remembered for this wonderful film and was known thereafter as the "the great screamer." Wray told this author in 1976 that "I did not like one scene at all, where Kong's hand is holding me and, with the other hand, begins to strip away my dress so that I am wearing next to nothing, and on top of all that, he smells the shreds of my dress. I thought that was just too crude, even for a gorilla. I also thought that I did too much screaming." She called Kong "my little man" and saw the film only three or four times in her lifetime. "My screaming in pictures, especially in **King Kong**, was my hallmark, I guess. I sailed to England in 1934 on a vacation, and when I got off the boat, a reporter rushed up to me and said: 'Will you please come to the BBC studios with me so you can scream over our airways?' I politely refused to be an idiot. It's a crazy world, isn't it?" The lights of the Empire State Building were dimmed for fifteen minutes in Fay Wray's honor on the night of her death at the age of ninety-six on August 8, 2004. The great sci-fi writer Ray Bradbury told this author that **King Kong** "had more influence on me than any other film from my childhood. After seeing what Willis O'Brien could do with that tragic gorilla, I got it into my head that I could make any fantasy come alive and the world would accept those ideas as they did Kong. He paved the way for me just as he made a path in the jungle with his massive body and giant steps, so I am indebted to that poor lovesick guy, who lost his head and heart and, eventually, his life over a little blonde squirming and screaming in the palm of his hand." **p&d**, Merian C. Cooper, Ernest B. Schoedsack (neither credited); **cast**, Fay Wray, Robert Armstrong, Bruce Cabot, Frank Reicher, Sam Hardy, Noble Johnson, Steve Clemento, Victor Wong, Paul Porcasi, James Flavin, Gil Perkins, Ethan Laidlaw, Blackie Whiteford, Dick Curtis, Walter Ackerman, James Adamson, Bill Williams, Harry Tenbrook, Russ Powell, Lynton Brent, Frank Mills, Jim Thorpe (native dancer), Cooper (airplane flight commander), Schoedsack (observer behind Cooper in same plane); **w**, James Creelman, Ruth Rose (based on a story by Cooper and Edgar Wallace); **c**, Eddie Linden, J.O. Taylor, Vernon L. Walker; **m**, Max Steiner; **ed**, Ted Cheesman; **prod d**, Carroll Clark; **set d**, Clark, Al Herman, Thomas Little, Ray Moyer; **spec eff**, Willis O'Brien, E.B. Gibson, Marcel Delgado, Fred Reese, Orville Goldner, Carroll Shepphird, Marlo Larrinaga, Byron L. Crabbe.

King Kong ★★★ 2005; New Zealand/U.S./Germany; 187m; UNIV; Color; Fantasy/Horror; Children: Unacceptable (MPAA: PG-13); **BD**; **DVD**. Good second remake of the classic 1933 horror film, but one that does not come close to the original. Documentary filmmaker Black assembles a large crew for a huge chartered ship and then recruits Watts as his leading lady for his next opus, but tells no one where they are going. The ship sails to Skull Island, and the visitors encounter natives who have built a giant wall to seal off a ferocious and towering gorilla they call Kong, worshipping the beast as a god and offering human sacrifices to appease his ravenous appetite. When Black, Brody, the first mate of the chartered ship, crew members and Watts visit the native village, they see a human sacrifice being prepared for Kong, and quickly retreat when the natives try to buy Watts so she can also be offered to their flesh-eating idol. Natives later kidnap Watts and she is offered to Kong, who, instead of devouring her, falls in love with the squirming little creature and carries her off, battling prehistoric beasts in the jungle as he makes his way to his lair. Black, Brody and others chase after him to rescue Watts, but many are killed in the pursuit with only Brody finding his way to Kong's mountainous home and where, overcoming incredible hazards, he rescues her and returns her to the village and his associates. Kong, however, chases after them to retrieve Watts, but he is rendered unconscious and placed in the hold of the huge ship. He is taken to New York where he is put on exhibit, but breaks loose to create havoc, finding Watts once more and taking her to the Empire State Building, which Kong climbs to its dome and where he places Watts on a ledge to battle a flight of fighter planes that fatally shoot him, causing him to topple from the building dead. Though this version of the story of the Beauty and the Beast fails to provide the charisma and eerie mystique so perfectly conveyed in the 1933 film, its production values are high and its special effects outstanding. **p**, Peter Jackson, Jan Blenkin, Carolynne Cunningham, Fran Walsh; **d**, Jackson; **cast**, Naomi Watts, Jack Black, Adrien Brody, Thomas Kretschmann, Colin Hanks, Andy Serkis, Evan Parke, Jamie Bell, Lobo Chan, John Sumner; **w**, Jackson, Walsh, Philippa Boyens (based on a

Kong in *King Kong*, 2005.

story by Edgar Wallace and Merian C. Cooper); **c**, Andrew Lesnie; **m**, James Newton Howard; **ed**, Jamie Selkirk; **prod d**, Grant Major; **art d**, Joe Bleakley, Simon Bright, Dan Hennah; **set d**, Bright, Hennah; **spec eff**, Stephen Ingram, Karl Chisholm.

King Lear ★★★ 1971; U.S.; 94m; Edward Small Productions/UA; Color; Fantasy; Children: Unacceptable (MPAA: PG); **DVD**. Peter Brook's film differs from William Shakespeare's play partly because its origins were influenced by *Shakespeare Our Contemporary*, a book by Jan Kott, a Polish critic, whose take on the king was the futility of everything. Lear, brilliantly played by Scofield, faces death by offering his kingdom to his three daughters, Worth, Engel, and Gabold. Worth and Engel connive together to win their father's favor, while Gabold is sincere, but the king is taken in by the two charmers, and Gabold finds herself left out. Lear eventually sees through Worth and Engel and looks for Gabold, but it is too late. A violent family feud ensues and everyone dies. Worth murders Engel by smashing her head on a rock and Gabold is executed. Scofield dies of a heart attack, all of his hopes and plans gone to dust. All's bad that ends bad in this controversial but fascinating film of a play that may be impossible to film as Shakespeare wrote it. Excessive violence prohibits viewing by children. **p**, Michael Birkett; **d&w**, Peter Brook (based on the play by William Shakespeare); **cast**, Paul Scofield, Irene Worth, Cyril Cusack, Susan Engel, Tom Fleming, Anne-Lise Gabold, Ian Hogg, Robert Lloyd, Patrick Magee, Alan Webb; **c**, Henning Kristiansen; **ed**, Kasper Schyberg; **prod d**, Georges Wakhévitch.

King of Alcatraz ★★★ 1938; U.S.; 68m; PAR; B/W; Adventure; Children: Cautionary. Preston, in his film debut, is a radio operator working on board a passenger ship, and his friend Nolan is also an operator on a similar vessel. Both are forever using their communications to outdo each other in outlandish reports, which angers shipping magnate Hall, who assigns them to the same luxury liner and orders them to behave. Both Nolan and Preston then pursue Patrick, the resident nurse on board;as they have both earlier dated her, she wants no more part of them and their shenanigans. The film then segues in story line from comedy to drama when Nolan, Preston and Patrick discover that several gangsters are on board and that their leader is Naish, who is a passenger disguising himself as a "kindly old lady," and who has recently escaped from the federal prison of Alcatraz in San Francisco Bay (ergo the film's title). When the gangsters seize control of the ship and order its captain, Carey, to sail to South America, Nolan and Preston lead an attack on the mobsters and Nolan is shot. Patrick is permitted to receive radio instructions from a physician on how to perform the operation that will remove the bullet. She does this successfully, saving Nolan's life while Preston leads

Robert De Niro and Jerry Lewis in *The King of Comedy,* 1983.

another attack on the gangsters, overwhelming them, but Preston is killed. Patrick and Nolan then face the future together as a deeply bonded couple. Director Florey does a fine job in transitioning this film from a lighthearted comedy to a serious and tension-filled, drama and the cast members are standouts. **p,** William C. Thomas; **d,** Robert Florey; **cast,** Gail Patrick, Lloyd Nolan, Harry Carey, J. Carrol Naish, Robert Preston, Anthony Quinn, Dennis Morgan, Richard Denning, Konstantin Shayne, Paul Fix, Jack Norton; **w,** Irving Reis; **c,** Harry Fischbeck; **m,** Boris Morros; **ed,** Eda Warren; **art d,** Hans Dreier, Earl Hedrick.

King of Burlesque ★★★ 1936; U.S.; 90m; FOX; B/W; Musical Comedy; Children: Cautionary; **DVD**. In this lively musical that offers a bevy of good tunes, Baxter operates a burlesque theater and has ambitions to step up in class by turning his shows into legitimate musicals. Faye is his musical director, who loves him from afar, and Oakie his pal. Baxter then meets Barrie, a down-and-out society lady, and after a whirlwind romance of about a day, they marry, which causes Faye to leave the company. Traveling to London, she becomes a singing hit. After Baxter's new tony musical fails, Barrie divorces him and Baxter takes to drink. Faye, now rich, returns from Europe and, when finding out from Oakie that Baxter is on the skids and knowing that Baxter will never take money from her, convinces Ratoff to pretend to be a millionaire show-backer, giving Ratoff money to invest in Baxter's next show. Baxter returns to the kind of burlesque presentations that originally made him a success, and his new show, starring Faye, is a hit. When Baxter learns that Faye financed the show that restored his career, Baxter falls in love with her and they are now a couple, as is Oakie and Judge, who have been sparking throughout this film. Songs include: "Whose Big Baby Are You?" "I'm Shooting High," "Lovely Lady," "I've Got My Fingers Crossed," "Spreading Rhythm Around" (Jimmy McHugh, Ted Kohler), and "I Love To Ride The Horses" (Jack Yellen, Lew Pollack). *Author's Note*: The colorful and talented Fats Waller makes an appearance in this film but, unfortunately, does not sing any of his own songs. This film was remade as **Hello, Frisco, Hello**, 1943, with John Payne playing Baxter's role and with Faye and Oakie reprising their parts, and that remake also proved to be equally worthwhile watching. **p,** Darryl F. Zanuck; **d,** Sidney Lanfield; **cast,** Warner Baxter, Alice Faye, Jack Oakie, Mona Barrie, Arline Judge, Dixie Dunbar, Gregory Ratoff, Herbert Mundin, Fats Waller, Kenny Baker, Keye Luke, Lynn Bari, Eddie Foy, Jr., Marjorie Weaver, Jane Wyman; **w,** Gene Markey, Harry Tugend, James Seymour (based on a story by Vina Delmar); **c,** Peverell Marley; **m,** Cyril J. Mockridge; **ed,** Ralph Dietrich; **art d,** Hans Peters; **set d,** Thomas Little.

King of California ★★★ 2007; U.S.; 93m; Millennium Films/First

Look International; Color; Comedy; Children: Unacceptable (MPAA: PG-13); **BD**; **DVD**. Douglas, a mental patient with a beard and looking like the Wild Man of Borneo, escapes from an institution and looks for a treasure in gold that he believes the Spanish conquistadors buried years ago near Santa Clarita, California. His wife left him two years ago, and his teenage daughter, Wood, works nights at a McDonald's restaurant and spends days lonely and bored at home in a rundown house in Santa Clarita. When Douglas asks her to go with him on late-night scavenger hunts with a metal detector and shovel, she agrees. Douglas believes he has found the treasure, beneath an aisle in a Costco store. He talks Wood into getting a job in the store so she can steal a key and they can sneak in at night and find the gold. It's a nutcase comedy of sorts or a drama about nutcase people, but has enough quirky moments to consistently entertain. Gutter language, brief drug references, and mature themes prohibit viewing by children. **p,** Randall Emmett, Avi Lerner, Michael London, Alexander Payne, George Parra; **d&w,** Mike Cahill; **cast,** Michael Douglas, Evan Rachel Wood, Willis Burks II, Laura Kachergus, Paul Lieber, Kathleen Wilhoite, Anne Nathan, Arthur Santiago, Ashley Greene, Anna Khaja; **c,** James Whitaker; **m,** David Robbins; **ed,** Glenn Garland; **prod d,** Dan Bishop; **art d,** David Morong; **set d,** Dianna Freas; **spec eff,** Ron Trost, J.C. Machit, Doyle Smiley.

The King of Comedy ★★★★ 1983; U.S.; 109m; Embassy International Pictures/FOX; Color; Drama; Children: Unacceptable (MPAA: PG); **DVD**; **VHS**. De Niro is utterly captivating as a New York groupie admiring comedy TV show host Lewis and ruthlessly goes about emulating him and then planning through a lunatic scheme to replace him on the airways. De Niro hangs around Times Square, chasing after celebrities to get their autographs, but, vain and egotistical for no good reason, he considers himself the greatest comedian in the world (ergo the title of this bizarre but compelling film). He patterns his routines, such as they are, after Lewis, a top comedy star, who hosts a nightly nationally broadcast TV show (it is obvious that Lewis is using Johnny Carson as his role model). De Niro has only one objective in life and that is to appear on Lewis' show where he believes he will become an overnight international star. To that end, he drives away a bevy of autograph seekers surrounding Lewis and then jumps into Lewis' car with him to tell him that he has a wonderful comedy routine to perform on his show. The grateful Lewis tells De Niro to bring his material to his office, but, when De Niro arrives, he is told by a haughty receptionist to first get some club dates and build up his act before returning to Lewis' office. De Niro will not take this no and remains sitting in the reception room. He leaves and then returns, attempting to invade Lewis' inner office and is thrown out by security guards. Believing that he and Lewis have bonded, De Niro, accompanied by his black girlfriend, Abbott, goes to Lewis' country estate and barges in on the comedian. Lewis, by now, is enraged at this invasion of his closely guarded privacy and insults De Niro and then kicks him out. De Niro is now determined to succeed on Lewis' show no matter what comes. He contacts oddball Bernhard, an obnoxious groupie, who has money. They abduct Lewis and hold him hostage, demanding a weird ransom—he must allow De Niro to go on his show before he is released. De Niro appears on the show, does his routine, then goes with Abbott to a bar to watch the prerecorded show before police take him to jail for abduction. Oddly, when he is released from jail, De Niro is acclaimed as the international comedian he has always sought to be, and his autobiography is published and becomes a best-seller. At the end, he has his own network talk show where he is hailed as the king of comedy. Implausible, even idiotic, this is really a savage spoof of TV talk show hosts as well as their audiences and the status-seeking fans of such people. De Niro and Lewis are mesmerizing in their roles and Scorsese does a great job in briskly telling this weirdo tale. **p,** Arnon Milchan; **d,** Martin Scorsese; **cast,** Robert De Niro, Jerry Lewis, Diahnne Abbott, Sandra Bernhard, Shelley Hack, E. Herlihy, Lou Brown, Catherine Scorsese, Joyce Brothers, Victor Borge, Martin Scorsese, Tony Randall; **w,** Paul D. Zimmerman; **c,** Fred Schuler

(DeLuxe Color); **m**, Robbie Robertson; **ed**, Thelma Schoonmaker; **prod d**, Boris Leven; **art d**, Lawrence Miller, Edward Pisoni; **set d**, George DeTitta, Sr., Daniel Robert.

The King of Kings ★★★★ 1927 (silent); U.S.; 155m/14 reels (premiere version); 112m (later edited version); DeMille Productions/Pathé Exchange; B/W/Color; Biographical Drama; Children: Cautionary; **DVD**; **VHS**. Pantheon director DeMille presents a powerful portrait of Jesus of Nazareth in this epic film, one reportedly viewed over the decades by more than eight billion people. As usual, DeMille's penchant for accenting sensuality with deep history is evident in his opening scenes where Logan, playing Mary Magdalene, is seen entertaining a number of men. Learning that Joseph Schildkraut, playing Judas, one of her patrons, is traveling nearby with a carpenter, she mounts her chariot, drawn by zebras, and races to see him. We first see Warner as Jesus when he heals a small girl and are introduced to Peter, his foremost apostle, played by Torrence, and other disciples, who are the adopted sons of Jesus' mother, Mary, played by Cumming, shown as a beautiful and saintly person. Logan arrives to be told by the self-serving Joseph Schildkraut that he is only staying with Warner so that he will become a king after Warner becomes the King of Kings. A series of more miracles are performed by Warner, the raising of Lazarus (Thomson), and the healing of many persons. DeMille interjects a bit of humor when a child asks Warner if he can fix broken legs and after she offers him a legless doll, he fixes the toy. While aiding a poor family, Warner enters a carpenter's shop and, as the son of a carpenter, carves a piece of wood that is then revealed to be a cross that is shown looming over Warner, foreshadowing his own crucifixion. When Warner and his disciples enter Jerusalem, Joseph Schildkraut rouses the inhabitants by urging them to proclaim Warner as king of the Jews, but Warner stops him, stating that he wants no earthly crown. Rudolph Schildkraut, playing high priest Caiaphas, becomes enraged when Joseph Schildkraut makes such proclamations, branding Warner a false prophet. Satan (Brooks) then offers Warner a vast worldly kingdom if he will serve him, but Warner rejects this temptation and later protects Logan and other women accused of adultery, writing in sand the sins of their accusers. When Rudolph Schildkraut threatens to condemn Joseph Schildkraut for advocating Warner as a king, Joseph Schildkraut puts in motion a plan to betray Warner, who then holds The Last Supper with his disciples, asking them to partake of bread and wine that represent his body and blood. Joseph Schildkraut pretends to drink from the cup, but does not and, instead of eating a piece of the bread, drops it to the floor. Cumming, full of foreboding, urges her son to flee for his life, but Warner comforts her and tells her that his life must be sacrificed for the sake of humanity. When all leave the dining area, a dove flutters over the abandoned table. Warner goes to the Garden of Gethsemane where Roman soldiers, summoned by Joseph Schildkraut, arrest him and take him away. Joseph Schildkraut takes the rope that was briefly used to bind Warner and runs off. When seeing that Warner will be condemned, Joseph Schildkraut, horrified, runs off and later uses the rope to hang himself. Warner is then brought before a huge crowd where Pontius Pilate (Varconi) presents him, asking the crowd to decide upon Warner's fate. Cumming and Logan beg for his life, as do many others, but Rudolph Schildkraut spreads money through the crowd to have them shout for Warner's condemnation. Warner is then condemned and carries his own cross to the place of execution, but stops briefly in an alleyway to heal some crippled persons. He is then crucified next to two thieves, and upon his death, the sky blackens and an earthquake shakes the area, great chasms of earth opening and swallowing many of those who have urged Warner's death. The tree from which Joseph Schildkraut has hanged himself is swallowed by the opening and closing earth while the veil covering the Holy of Holies that shrouds the great temple is torn asunder. After Cumming prays and asks God to forgive those who have taken her son's life, the storm abates and the sun shines again. Warner's body is taken from the cross and buried, but, three days later, he emerges from his tomb (to

H. B. Warner as Jesus, center, in *The King of Kings*, 1927.

accent the resurrection, DeMille shot these scenes in color—an early day two-strip Technicolor process—as he did for the opening sequence) and goes to his disciples, asking them to spread his beliefs to the world, telling them that "I am with you always." The film ends when modern cities are shown and where the image of Warner hovers protectively over them. DeMille's direction carefully unfolds this eternal story, and the cast members render fine performances, particularly Warner, who was known forever after for this role. The many action scenes are packed with thousands of extras, and the sets of Jerusalem and the Crucifixion are amazing to behold, as is the cataclysmic earthquake following Warner's death. The film was re-released in 1931 with a synchronized score. *Author's Note*: This film generated widespread controversy and brought down on the director's head angry criticism from Jewish leaders, who stated that DeMille had wrongly profiled the Jews in being responsible for the crucifixion of Jesus. He was accused of maligning Jews everywhere and pandering to the basest emotions of viewers (particularly in the bacchanalian scenes with Mary Magdalene and where the Jews in the crowd condemn Jesus and where many relish in his execution—one female spectator urging the Romans to crucify Warner appears to be ravenously eating popcorn as she sadistically revels in the execution). DeMille was pilloried as a propagandist for the Christian religion, exhibiting enormous bad taste and flagrantly displaying a "warped sense of religion." The film, however, was heralded universally by Christian leaders as a classic and true tale of the Christ. DeMille defended himself by stating that members of the Federal Council of Churches were on hand throughout the production to give advice and who sanctioned the story scene for scene. He emphasized that many members of that Council representing the Catholic, Protestant, Jewish, Muslim and Buddhist faiths were present at the first day's shooting and all joined in prayer. Warner was kept apart from the rest of the cast and most of the crew, as well as the public, where DeMille demanded that no one speak to him, except himself. The director kept the actor aloof from all, to ostensibly promote the mystique and sanctity of his character, but also to keep Warner on the wagon as the actor had a chronic drinking problem (and that problem continued through the remainder of his life), which DeMille religiously kept a secret for many years. He ordered Warner not to appear in public. Warner lived a reclusive life throughout the production and for some time thereafter. The actor ate alone in his tent on location and when driving to and from the set, he wore a black veil over his face as DeMille wanted to preserve Warner's countenance until he presented him as Jesus in his precedent-setting film. DeMille was draconian in his dictates as to the conduct of Warner and all others playing featured parts in this film, requiring them to sign separate agreements with him that they would not do anything "Unbiblical" for five years after appearing in this film, these agreements having

Jacqueline Logan as Mary Magdalene in *The King of Kings,* **1927.**

stiff penalties and prohibiting all involved from participating in swimming in public, going to nightclubs, riding in convertible cars, playing cards in public or attending sports events. None were permitted any interviews with reporters and were ordered not to talk about Warner. "No one saw Warner, except those who acted in scenes with him," Joseph Schildkraut told this author in 1962, two years before his death. "In my scenes with Warner, I was struck by his austerity and reserve and felt that there was really something spiritual about him. We mouthed our words as the script was scant on dialog and when I was close to Warner, I could hear him whispering prayers. His performance as Jesus was magnificent, and I thought it was inspired. After one of our last scenes together, Warner whispered to me: 'I hope and pray that God will forgive me for being so arrogant as to play His Son.' I replied: 'I am playing His betrayer, so pray for me, too, and also add more prayers for my father.'" Schildkraut's father, Rudolph Schildkraut, plays the Jewish high priest, who condemns Jesus. The giant gate that serves as the entrance to Jerusalem was later used in Mirien C. Cooper's classic **King Kong**, 1933, as part of the wall that keeps the giant gorilla from invading the native village. That huge set was torched, along with many other old sets, when producer David O. Selznick created the burning of Atlanta in **Gone with the Wind**, 1939. **p&d**, Cecil B. DeMille; **cast**, H.B. Warner, Dorothy Cumming, Ernest Torrence, Joseph Schildkraut, James Neill, Joseph Striker, Robert Edeson, Sidney D'Albrook, David Imboden, Robert Ellsworth, Jacqueline Logan, Victor Varconi, Montague Love, William (Stage) Boyd, Rudolph Schildkraut, Alan Brooks, George Siegmann, May Robson, Sidney Franklin, Rex Ingram, George F. Marion, Kenneth Thomson; **w**, Jeanie Macpherson; **c**, J. Peverell Marley (two-strip Technicolor in some scenes); **m**, Hugo Riesenfeld (1931 sound version); **ed**, Anne Bauchens, Harold McLernon; **prod d**, Dan Sayre Groesback, Anton Grot, Julian Harrison, Edward C. Jewell; **art d**, Mitchell Leisen; **set d**, Ted Dickson; **spec eff**, Howard A. Anderson.

King of Kings ★★★★ 1961; U.S.; 168m; MGM; Color; Biographical Drama; Children: Cautionary (MPAA: PG-13); **BD**; **DVD**; **VHS**. Director Ray meticulously presents this story with loving care and where Hunter is superlative as Jesus of Nazareth. We see the birth of Jesus in Bethlehem, McKenna (Mary) and Tichy (Joseph) fleeing after hearing that Aslan (King Herod), heeding a prophecy that a child born at the time of Jesus will become the true Messiah, orders all children born at this time murdered. Aslan, however, gripped by fear of his act, suffers a heart attack, and his merciless, power-greedy son, Thring (Herod Antipas) assumes the throne (literally stepping over the prone body of his father in his death throes to sit in that throne). The child grows to be an adult, Hunter, and leaves his father's carpentry work in Nazareth and goes forth to preach his beliefs of love, kindness and living lives free of

sin. He is baptized by Ryan (John the Baptist), who "finds no sin in him." Hunter then calls to his side his disciples, including Dano (Peter) and Torn (Judas) and travels through Judea to preach and even heal the lame and the halt. These miracles do not go unnoticed by the apprehensive and insecure Thring, as well as the Roman governor of Judea, Hatfield (Pontius Pilate). Thring believes that Ryan may be behind these supernatural events and, urged by his wife, Gam, and daughter, Bazlen (Salome), has Ryan arrested and imprisoned for his accusations that Gam is living in adultery. While in prison, Ryan is visited by Hunter, giving him inspiration and courage to face his grim fate, which is beheading after Bazlen performs a sensuous dance for Thring and demands that Ryan be executed for defaming her mother. Hunter goes on to deliver his Sermon on the Mount where Lindfors, the wife of Hatfield, and accompanied by Randell, the head of the Roman troops, who is empathetic toward Hunter, listen and are moved by Hunter's preaching and where he asks his followers to love one another, and obey the Commandments. Meanwhile, thief and brigand, Guardino (Barabbas), plans a revolt, but Torn goes to him, asking him to support Hunter's nonviolent crusade for peace on earth. Guardino agrees when he hears that Hunter will soon arrive in Jerusalem and where Guardino and his warring followers will use that even to attack the Roman troops occupying the city. Hunter enters the city and is greeted by enormous crowds; many of these people are "borrowed" by Guardino and his men, leading them in futile attacks against the Roman fortress where they are slaughtered and where Guardino is captured and imprisoned. Hunter then conducts a Passover Seder, which is Jesus' Last Supper and where Torn has already betrayed him to the Romans, who later arrest and imprison Hunter. He is shown tortured with whippings and a crown of thorns to mock the claim that he is a king. When Hatfield judges him, he finds him innocent of any crime, but pressure from Thring forces him to condemn Hunter to crucifixion. His wife, Lindfors, pressures him to release Hunter and he uses as an excuse a yearly event where clemency is showed to a prisoner. Hatfield offers the crowd Hunter and Guardino to the mob, asking them which of the prisoners should be released and which executed. Guardino's supporters shout down Hunter's supporters and Guardino is released by Randell, who tells him that the wrong man has been given his freedom. Hunter is then forced to carry his cross to Golgotha, the place of execution, and as McKenna and other supporters are present, Hunter is crucified. Following his death, he is entombed, but is resurrected from his tomb and briefly joins his startled disciples, telling them to go throughout the world to preach his message of love and peace, and they are shown on a shoreline before all going their separate ways to do the Lord's bidding. Ray's direction provides thousands of extras in crowd and battle scenes the sweep and great scope of the story, but he also provides many intimate moments where all the players become real human beings and those portraits are exceptional from Hunter, Lindfors, McKenna, Ryan, Dano, Guardino and Randell, and where the haunting voice of Welles cohesively tells the overview of the story in a riveting narration with the kind of authority that only Welles' distinctive baritone voice could render. Rozaa's score is evocative and memorable as well, providing passages that perfectly fit scenes reflecting joy, enlightenment, anguish and sacrifice. *Author's Note*: Director Ray told this author that "**King of Kings** was a film I made with great reservations. I knew the trouble DeMille got into with his own production by putting almost all the responsibility for the crucifixion of Jesus on the Jewish high priest. We carefully avoided that by putting it on the followers of Barabbas, but, of course, they were all Jews, too. I think that Jeff [Hunter] gave the performance of his life and I think he was much more natural and down-to-earth than anyone else playing that next-to-impossible part. His blue eyes are so piercing that I used them in close-ups to mesmerize viewers as he spoke in his gentle voice and I never had him raise that voice in anger. We also gave more play to the role of John the Baptist than anyone else had done and Bob [Ryan] gave me a terrific performance, using all that athleticism he has. His scene in the dungeon where he must struggle to climb to the end of the chains that bind him to touch

Hunter's hand is one of the best scenes I ever put on film, but Jeff and Bob really put it there." **p**, Samuel Bronston; **d**, Nicholas Ray; **cast**, Jeffrey Hunter, Siobhan McKenna, Hurd Hatfield, Ron Randell, Viveca Lindfors, Rita Gam, Carmen Sevilla, Brigid Bazlen, Harry Guardino, Rip Torn, Frank Thring, Guy Rolfe, Royal Dano, Robert Ryan, Michael Wager, Gerard Tichy, Gregoire Aslan, Orson Welles (narrator); **w**, Philip Yordan (narration), Ray Bradbury (not credited); **c**, Milton Krasner, Franz Planer, Manuel Berenguer (Technirama 70; Technicolor); **m**, Miklos Rozsa; **ed**, Harold F. Kress, Renée Lichtig; **set d**, Enrique Alarcon; **spec eff**, Alex C. Weldon, Lee LeBlanc.

The King of Marvin Gardens ★★★ 1972; U.S.; 103m; BBS Productions/COL; Color; Drama; Children: Unacceptable (MPAA: R); **DVD**; **VHS**. Nicholson captivates (and irritates) as a bloviating FM disc jockey working for a Philadelphia radio station who, instead of playing the records all expect, spends endless time telling tales about his brother, Dern, whom he calls "the king of Marvin Gardens." (Anyone who has ever played the game "Monopoly" will remember the yellow square on the board, which is also a real place in Atlantic City.) To further rekindle his fond childhood memories, Nicholson returns to Atlantic City to see brother Dern, finding the city in shambles, its former glories faded (this before the town was reconstructed and became a booming casino center). Nicholson finds Dern working for crime boss Crothers and bails him out of jail where he has been locked up on charges of grand auto theft. Through Dern, Nicholson meets Burstyn, a faded beauty queen, and her daughter, Robinson. Dern confides in his kid brother that he has great ambitions, that he intends to buy an island called Tiki, located in the Hawaiian Islands. He will build a resort there, Dern says, and he and Nicholson will live in comfort and warmth for the remainder of their days. Nicholson, a realist, tells Dern that this is nothing but a fantasy. He becomes alarmed after Dern tells him that he intends to front for Crothers in getting funding for his fantastic island project, which alarms Nicholson, causing him to go to Crothers. The crime boss tells him that he framed Dern on the car theft charge because he has been running around telling people that they are partners and he knows about Dern's plans for the island. Crothers tells Nicholson that if his older brother does not stop his feigned association with him, he will have him killed. Nicholson goes to Dern's home and finds that he is preparing to leave for Hawaii to use Crothers' name in cutting a deal. By this time, Burstyn, who has long been neglected by Dern and who thinks he is really planning to run off with her daughter, Robinson, goes to pieces, grabs a gun and fatally shoots Dern. Nicholson takes his brother's body to Philadelphia for burial and then returns to his DJ job where he continues to wax about his endless memories with Dern. He later visits LaVine, his grandfather, finding him watching old family movies of Nicholson and Dern when they were boys frolicking on the beach at Atlantic City, a powerful and poignant scene that lingers long in memory. Superb performances from the entire cast present an evocative and compelling film that twists warm-hearted nostalgia into deadly reality and where Dern, through direct and foolish action, and Nicholson, through contemplative recollection, are led to rather grim ends, one a premature death, the other a disenfranchising retreat into the past. *Author's Note*: Nicholson's role is undoubtedly based upon Jean Shepherd (1921-1999), who was the unforgettable DJ at WOR in New York City and where he spent five hours of the day talking about his boyhood memories of Indiana. He did not take phone calls on the air and seldom played records, but his mellifluous voice and colorful speech nevertheless enraptured listeners. His memories of his Indiana youth at Yuletide later translated into the classic seasonal film, **A Christmas Story**, 1983. **p&d**, Bob Rafelson; **cast**, Jack Nicholson, Bruce Dern, Ellen Burstyn, Julia Anne Robinson, Benjamin "Scatman" Crothers, Charles LaVine, Arnold Williams, John Ryan, Sully Boyar, Josh Mostel, William Pabst, Gary Goodrow, Imogene Bliss, Ann Thomas, Tom Overton; **w**, Jacob Brackman (based on a story by Brackman and Rafelson); **c**, Laszlo Kovacs (Eastmancolor); **ed**, John F. Link II; **art d**, Toby Carr Rafelson.

Jack Nicholson, Bruce Dern and Julia Anne Robinson in *The King of Marvin Gardens,* **1972.**

King of the Cowboys ★★★ 1943; U.S.; 67m; REP; B/W; Western; Children: Acceptable; **DVD**. The countless fans of Roy Rogers got it all in this film, one of his best. Kids at Saturday matinees at the movies during this World War II year got wholesome entertainment in this film. A handsome singing cowboy captures Nazi saboteurs as a government agent in between riding and roping in rodeo shows. Roy's rodeo riding is a cover for being a U.S. government agent assigned to learn who is blasting military warehouses filled with weapons and other supplies to win the war. He believes the sabotage is connected to a traveling tent show. Joining the show and while singing a few songs, he discovers that the saboteurs get their instructions on where to strike next in coded messages from the show's spiritualist during performances. Rogers unmasks culprit Mohr, the state governor's chief aide, as the brains behind the scheme. The film's title comes from a *Life* magazine article that named Rogers "King of the Cowboys," since Gene Autry, Republic's former top singing cowboy, was off the range and in the army. Songs include "I'm an Old Cowhand" (Johnny Mercer), "Gay Ranchero" (Abe Tuvim, Francia Luban, J. Espinosa), "Roll Along Prairie Moon" (Ted FioRita, Harry McPherson, Al Von Tilzer, Roy Rogers), "Red River Valley" (anonymous, traditional folk song) sung by Rogers with the Sons of the Pioneers. **p**, Harry Grey; **d**, Joseph Kane; **cast**, Roy Rogers, Smiley Burnette, Peggy Moran, Gerald Mohr, Dorothea Kent, Lloyd Corrigan, James Bush, Russell Hicks, Irving Bacon, Bob Nolan and the Sons of the Pioneers; **w**, J. Benton Cheney, Olive Cooper (based on a story by Hal Long); **c**, Reggie Lanning; **m**, Mort Glickman; **ed**, Harry Keller; **art d**, Russell Kimball; **set d**, Charles Thompson.

King of the Gypsies ★★★ 1978; U.S.; 112m; Dino De Laurentiis Co./PAR; Color; Drama; Children: Unacceptable (MPAA: R); **DVD**; **VHS**. Roberts is a handsome young man born into a gypsy family in New York City in the 1930s, but it is a life he did not choose or want. In fact, he hates it. During the 1950s, not wanting to live among gypsies, he runs away and becomes a scam artist dealing in insurance while moonlighting as a singing waiter. He has an otherwise normal life with an apartment and girlfriend and plans to move to California. His grandfather, Hayden, dies and names him the successor and "The King" of all the gypsies, naming him instead of his father, Hirsch. This causes a potentially fatal gypsy family feud among Hirsch, Roberts, and Roberts' mother, Sarandon, and grandmother, Winters, and sister, Shields, and a dispute among gypsy tribal elders about the validity of the purchase of a girl years earlier, who is forced into a future marriage. This incisive, inside look into the lives of modern-day gypsy "tribes" sees an outstanding performance from Roberts, as well as impressive performances from the rest of the cast in a well-directed film. Excessive violence and strong subject matter prohibit viewing by children. **p**, Federico De Laurentiis;

Tyrone Power in *King of the Khyber Rifles*, 1953.

d&w, Frank Pierson (based on the book by Peter Maas); **cast**, Sterling Hayden, Shelley Winters, Susan Sarandon, Eric Roberts, Brooke Shields, Judd Hirsch, Annette O'Toole, Annie Potts, Patti LuPone, Linda Manz; **c**, Sven Nykvist (Technicolor); **m**, David Grisman; **ed**, Paul Hirsch; **prod d**, Gene Callahan; **art d**, Jay Moore; **set d**, Robert Drumheller, John Godfrey; **spec eff**, Edward Drohan.

King of the Hill ★★★ 1993; U.S.; 103m; Wildwood/Gramercy Pictures; Color; Drama; Children: Unacceptable (MPAA: PG); **DVD**; **VHS**. During the 1930s Great Depression, a down and almost out man, Krabbé, takes a desperation job as a traveling salesman of wickless candles in another state. His wife, Eichhorn, is in a sanitarium with consumption, and he has two young sons. He tells his twelve-year-old son Bradford to look after his younger brother, Boyd, and both are to wait for his return in their rooms in a seedy hotel in a city in the Midwest. Bradford is on his own to survive, becoming streetwise and a teller of tall tales. He tells people his father has a secret position in the federal government, and falls under the influence of Brody, a neighborhood shyster. Unable to continue keeping his brother, Bradford sends him to live with a relative. Bradford has to find money for rent, to eat, and somehow keep going to school and not let his teacher, Allen, know how destitute he has become. He meets others living in the hotel, including a friendly alcoholic, Gray, and finds some solace in his fantasies, coming to believe that his great friend is the legendary airplane pilot, Charles Lindbergh, and he uses his imagination to fill his hungry stomach by eating magazine pictures of hamburgers and steaks. Waiting for his father to return and his mother to recover her health, Bradford is unsteadily growing up. The down side of his life is occasionally relieved with some humor, and he and his brother are finally reunited with their father while hope remains that their mother will get well again. Those who were Bradford's age during the Great Depression will associate with this poignant and somewhat painful production and how those hard times shaped and altered a stronger America. The film wonderfully re-creates the 1930s, is well acted, especially by Bradford, and is recommended for older teenagers, but its thematic materials of poverty may be too depressing for children. **p**, Albert Berger, Barbara Maltby, Ron Yerxa; **d&w&ed**, Steven Soderbergh (based on the memoirs of A.E. Hotchner); **cast**, Jesse Bradford, Jeroen Krabbé, Lisa Eichhorn, Karen Allen, Spalding Gray, Elizabeth McGovern, Cameron Boyd, Adrien Brody, Joseph Chrest, John McConnell; **c**, Elliot Davis; **m**, Cliff Martinez; **prod d**, Gary Frutkoff; **art d**, Bill Rea; **set d**, Claire Jenora Bowin; **spec eff**, J.D. Streett IV.

King of the Khyber Rifles ★★★ 1953; U.S.; 100m; FOX; Color; Adventure; Children: Acceptable; **DVD**. Power is a standout as a valiant half-caste British captain in this rousing adventure tale. He is shown leading a supply column to Peshawar, India, when he and his men are attacked by rebellious tribesmen led by Rolfe. After beating off the attack, Power and his men arrive at Peshawar, greeted by their commander, Rennie, and whose beautiful daughter, Moore, becomes romantically involved with Power and he with her. This budding romance angers Justin, who is Power's roommate and who also loves Moore. The jealous Justin then attempts to sully Power's reputation by spreading the news that he is a half-caste, but this does not disturb Rennie, who places Power in charge of a company of native troops and he quickly turns these recruits into a crack company of riflemen, now called the Khyber Rifles. Rennie does become upset when learning that his daughter has fallen deeply in love with Power. Moore is then kidnapped by Rolfe and his men, but Power rescues her, and after being stranded in the desert, they are, in turn, rescued by a search party. Power then learns that Rolfe has captured a group of his men and intends to slaughter them unless the British turn over a shipment of new high-powered rifles to him. Power volunteers to infiltrate Rolfe's camp and where he will kill Rolfe, but Rennie will not permit it. Power disobeys those orders and goes to Rolfe's camp. Rolfe, who is a childhood friend, is convinced by Power that he is tired of being treated as a second-class officer by the British because he is a half-caste, and has deserted his post and is joining the rebels. Power, however, misses an opportunity to kill Rolfe, but his life is spared while Rolfe executes some of his captives instead. Rolfe frees Power, but warns him that he will not be so magnanimous in future. When returning to his British post, Power is arrested for disobeying orders. Rolfe, meanwhile, has inflamed the country and rebellion is everywhere. Power is released and leads his rifle company into battle. When his men accept the rumor that the new rifles issued to them are smeared with lard from pigs, which violates their religious belief, they refuse to use them. Power then orders them to use their swords in an attack on Rolfe's men and they vigorously attack and defeat Rolfe's forces, with Power wounded and Rolfe killed in the assault. The victorious Power is now widely respected by his British counterparts and he wins Moore's hand with Rennie's approval. King directs this action-packed adventure tale with great energy and his battle scenes are exceptional. Power and the cast members give outstanding performances and the cinematography is awe inspiring. ***Author's Note***: Director King told this author that "Ty [Power] performed most of his own stunts in that actioner. I worried that the front office might hear about this as Ty was a great studio asset and Zanuck [head of Fox] would have lopped off my head if Ty had gotten hurt. I also knew that Ty was a great horse rider and swordsman and could handle himself in any physical scenes. I had directed him in **Jesse James** [1939], **The Black Swan** [1942] and **Captain from Castile** [1947] where he rode horses and used swords well, so I did not argue with him when he insisted on doing the stunts for **King of the Khyber Rifles**, but that didn't mean that I didn't sweat a little blood." This film, which was a loose remake of John Ford's **The Black Watch**, 1929, was shot in California, but a second unit captured lush landscapes and mountainous scenes when traveling to northern India for such shots that were integrated into this production. **p**, Frank P. Rosenberg; **d**, Henry King; **cast**, Tyrone Power, Terry Moore, Michael Rennie, John Justin, Guy Rolfe, Richard Stapley, Murray Matheson, Frank de Kova, Argentina Brunetti, Sujata; **w**, Ivan Goff, Ben Roberts (based on the novel by Talbot Mundy and a story by Harry Kleiner); **c**, Leon Shamroy (CinemaScope; Technicolor); **m**, Bernard Herrmann; **ed**, Barbara McLean; **art d**, Lyle Wheeler, Maurice Ransford; **set d**, Walter M. Scott, Paul S. Fox, Fred J. Rode; **spec eff**, Ray Kellogg.

King Richard and the Crusaders ★★★ 1954; U.S.; 113m; WB; Color; Adventure/Biographical Drama; Children: Cautionary; **DVD**; **VHS**. Good actioner where the aloof Sanders plays Richard I (Richard the Lionheart; 1157-1199), who, while conducting the Third Crusade (1189-1192), is wounded by assassins. Harvey, Sanders' only trusted knight, who loves Sanders' ward and cousin, Mayo, attempts to find evidence that will identify the persons behind the attempted murder. Meanwhile, Harrison, in a riveting performance, appears at Sanders' camp, stating that he has been sent by Sanders' avowed Arab enemy, to help him recover. He pretends to be a physician, but he is really that Arab leader (a role based upon Saladin, 1137-1193) and who is also attracted to Mayo. Meanwhile, the villains, Douglas and Pate, arrange to have Harvey disgraced and he falls out of favor with Sanders until he redeems himself, identifies the assassins and jousts with them to the death. Reinstated, Harvey wins the hand of Mayo and where Harrison subtly helps him in his cause. Although Sanders asks Harvey to remain with him in the Middle East to continue his holy war, Harvey and Mayo depart for a more peaceful and happy life in Scotland. Though somewhat overlong, Harvey and Harrison develop their characters to where they hold attention throughout and the production values are high in this costumed epic. **p**, Henry Blanke; **d**, David Butler; **cast**, Rex Harrison, Virginia Mayo, George Sanders, Laurence Harvey, Robert Douglas, Michael Pate, Paula Raymond, Lester Matthews, Anthony Eustrel, Henry Corden, Wilton Graff, Nick Cravat, Leslie Bradley; **w**, John Twist (based on the novel *The Talisman* by Sir Walter Scott); **c**, J. Peverell Marley (CinemaScope; Warner Color); **m**, Max Steiner; **ed**, Irene Morra; **art d**, Bertram Tuttle.

King Solomon's Mines ★★★ 1937; U.K.; 80m; Gaumont; B/W; Adventure; Children: Cautionary; **DVD**; **VHS**. Robeson is a standout in this exciting version of the H. Rider Haggard adventure tale. He is first seen as guide to a group of white explorers led by the attractive Lee, a strong-headed Irish girl wanting to find her father, who was lost years earlier in the wilds of Africa while searching for the legendary treasure known as King Solomon's Mines. Accompanying Lee are explorers Loder, Hardwicke and Young, all of them led through the dense jungles by the enigmatic and closed-lipped Robeson, a towering black native, who seems to be able to overcome all hardships and odds. Robeson leads the party across vast expanses of desert and through deep jungles until they arrive at a village where the natives view the white visitors as gods. The chief, Adams, along with his evil witch doctor, Fairbrother, look upon the interlopers as threats to their authority, and after Robeson declares that he is the rightful heir to the throne (his father had been killed by Adams years earlier and where Adams usurped the throne), they plot to kill the visitors. Young, however, discovers from his notebook that there will soon be a solar eclipse and he and his friends use this natural phenomenon to convince the natives in predicting that event that their magic is more powerful than that of Fairbrother's. Winning over the natives, Robeson is reinstated as king and Adams and Fairbrother are deposed and driven off. Adams refuses to give up, however, and leads a rival tribe in attacking the village, but Adams is killed in the battle and his supporters quit the fight and depart. The white explorers by this time discover the location of the great treasure, but, before they can scoop up the riches, a volcanic eruption collapses the entrance to the mines. Robeson saves the lives of the whites and they leave for England, enriched by the stories of their great adventure if not by King Solomon's treasure. *Author's Note*: The scene where the solar eclipse is employed as magic to gull the natives also appears in **A Connecticut Yankee in King Arthur's Court**, 1949, where Bing Crosby pretends to use magic to blot out the sun during a solar eclipse, thus saving his life and others from execution. **d**, Robert Stevenson; **cast**, Paul Robeson, Cedric Hardwicke, Roland Young, Anna Lee, John Loder, Arthur Sinclair, Robert Adams, Sydney Fairbrother, Arthur Goullett, Ecce Homo Toto, Makubalo Hlubi; **w**, Michael Hogan, Charles Bennett, Ralph Spence (based on the novel by H. Rider Haggard); **c**, Glen MacWilliams; **m**, Mischa Spoliansky; **ed**, Michael Gordon; **art d**, Alfred Junge.

King Solomon's Mines ★★★★★ 1950; U.S.; 103m; MGM; Color; Adventure; Children: Cautionary; **DVD**; **VHS**. One of the classic adventure films, this superb production offers everything—action, suspense, mystery and some of the most eye-popping cinematography ever to capture the lush landscapes of Africa, as well as its exotic beasts,

Stewart Granger and Deborah Kerr in *King Solomon's Mines*, 1950.

fierce tribes and myriad hazards. In this version of the H. Rider Haggard story, Granger is shown as the great white hunter (Allan Quartermain), who is now fully disgusted with his fifteen years in Africa where he has endured endless bloodthirsty clients abusing the ethics of hunting in their desire to wantonly destroy the creatures of the jungle. He has already made plans to retire, leaving for England and looking forward to peace and quiet in its green countryside when he meets beautiful Kerr and her impulsive but sincere brother, Carlson. They both ask Granger to guide them into uncharted territory in search of Kerr's missing husband, who went in search of the legendary King Solomon's Mines, which Granger immediately dismisses as a myth. Kerr, however, is insistent, offering Granger £5,000 if he will serve as their guide to that far-off area, and he accepts, thinking to retire on these funds and that this strange safari will be his last. Accompanied by bearers, the trio embarks, traveling across a vast desert, enduring a fierce sandstorm. A brush fire causes a wild stampede of animals that the adventurers barely survive. They proceed to the jungles where Kerr is compelled to change her cumbersome attire to more suitable traveling clothes and where they encounter one hazard after another, from snakes, scorpions, giant spiders, crocodiles and where they are threatened by drowning in wild rapids. Arriving at a village where the fierce-looking natives appear hostile, they meet Haas, a white renegade, who admits after Granger pressures him that Kerr's husband had been at the village a year earlier, but traveled on looking for King Solomon's treasure. When the natives menacingly close in on Granger's bearers, the hunter rightly concludes that Haas plans to have them all killed and seize their possessions. Granger holds a gun to Haas and orders him to safely accompany them all from the village, which Haas reluctantly does, but, once they are beyond the village, he attacks and kills Granger's chief bearer; Granger, in turn, kills Haas, the gunfire alerting the warriors in the village, who then hunt Granger's party. They escape and are aided by Siriaque, a lone, towering black man, who had earlier joined their party as a bearer. Siriaque serves as their guide as he takes them to a mountainous area, after they scale this region and begin to descend into a valley of green meadows, they encounter other natives similar to their tall-statured guide, all members of the Watusi tribe. Siriaque reveals his abdomen to show ornate carvings on his flesh that indicate that he is the true king of the tribe, and is acknowledged by these tribesmen as such. While Siriaque goes off with his new followers, Granger, Kerr and Carlson travel to the main Watusi village where they meet Baziga, who has usurped the throne, along with his conniving witch doctor, Sekaryongo. When one of the false king's followers makes a move to attack the whites, Granger shoots and kills him and this causes others to treat them with caution, until Sekaryongo indicates that he will take them to the treasure tomb they seek. Sekaryongo leads them into a huge cavern where they find the remains of

Orlando Bloom and Liam Neeson in *Kingdom of Heaven*, 2005.

Kerr's former husband as well as incredible wealth, enormous chests brimming with jewels and gold, one of the world's great treasures. Sekaryongo, however, slips through a crevice and seals the entrance with a large stone, leaving the whites to die of suffocation. They find a narrow shaft, however, providing air and they follow this to an underground river, swimming underwater until they emerge safely into the open countryside. They then see their former guide, Siriaque, and his disciples, and follow them back to the village where the rightful king, Siriaque, challenges imposter Baziga. Both fight to the death, the imposter being killed and Siriaque restored to his throne, and who provides his white friends bearers so that they can return to their civilized world. Superbly directed and acted, this film was produced at a cost of $3.5 million, then an enormous budget, but every penny shows in this thrilling classic. It was an immediate smash hit, returning more than $10 million from its original release. *Author's Note*: The film was shot in Uganda, the Belgian Congo, Tanganyika, Kenya and elsewhere in Africa. The film won Oscars for Best Cinematography, Best Editing and Best Color. Granger, who had been in films for some time, became an international star because of this film and he knew that would be the case, as he told this author, while it was in production: "The care they took in making that film was everywhere, from the costuming to the interiors and exteriors. Everything was authentic-looking down to the last spear. I knew it would be a winner right from the beginning and, oh, my Lord, what it did for my career! I must tell you that I owe much to Errol Flynn, who was offered the part I played before they approached me for the role. Flynn turned it down to do another picture, **Kim** [1950], so he did me a great favor." Carlson told this author that "everyone got ill or sick on that incredible picture. We had to put up with swarms of insects, snakes and every kind of strange disease, but the only one who got through it without getting sick and without a single complaint was Deborah [Kerr]. She was so wonderful and showed so much stamina and courage that she shamed the lot of us into giving everything we had whether we were ill or not." Kerr sloughed off these compliments, saying to this author: "I didn't want anyone fussing over me just because I was a woman. I accepted the hardships just like everyone else and we all did our jobs together. But, make no mistake—that film was very difficult. In one of my love scenes with Stewart [Granger], I felt a little woozy and he joked: 'I can't kiss that well!' I told him that I was feeling the heat, and after someone told me it was 140 degrees, I said that that was impossible, that no one could live in such heat, but they showed me a thermometer and it was true. Well, I said to myself, perspiration or not, if the others can do their scenes in this terrible heat, so can I. We looked exhausted and worn out in some scenes and that was what we were supposed to look like, but I can guarantee you that we *really were exhausted* in those scenes." In one scene dealing with the dancing Masai tribe, more than 500 dancers frenetically whirled, screamed and danced to wildly beaten drums, doing a war dance that went on for two days and culminated when these warriors began throwing spears in all directions that caused the cast and crew members to run for cover and some, like Kerr, even climbed trees. **p**, Sam Zimbalist; **d**, Compton Bennett, Andrew Marton; **cast**, Deborah Kerr, Stewart Granger, Richard Carlson, Hugo Haas, Lowell Gilmore, Kimursi, Siriaque, Sekaryongo, Baziga, Munto Anampio; **w**, Helen Deutsch (based on the novel by H. Rider Haggard); **c**, Robert Surtees; **m**, Mischa Spoliansky; **ed**, Conrad A. Nervig, Ralph E. Winters; **art d**, Cedric Gibbons, Paul Groesse; **set d**, Edwin B. Willis, Keogh Gleason.

Kingdom of Heaven ★★★★ 2005; U.S./U.K./Spain/Germany; 144m; FOX; Color; Adventure; Children: Unacceptable (MPAA: R); **BD**; **DVD**. In this superlative and sweeping historical epic from pantheon director Scott, viewers are uniquely treated to the most realistic visions of ancient crusaders than ever before presented, an utterly absorbing tale that captures the exotic if not bizarre mystiques and mysteries of that long-ago era when religious fever and fanatically clutched dreams of empire ruled the human mind. Set in 1184, five years before the onset of the Third Crusade (1189-1192), Bloom is a blacksmith working in a French village and where he suffers pangs of remorse over his wife's recent suicide. Arriving at the village is Neeson, a baron en route to the Holy Land, accompanied by a group of crusaders, and who introduces himself to Bloom as his father, who asks him to join him in his journey to the Middle East. Bloom refuses and Neeson and his knights ride off. Later, Bloom meets his half-brother, Sheen, who is the village priest and who announces that he has ordered the head of Bloom's wife severed since she committed the religious crime of suicide. When seeing that Sheen is now wearing a cross he has taken from the corpse of Bloom's wife, the blacksmith becomes enraged, killing Sheen, and after retrieving the crucifix, he flees, catching up with and joining Neeson and his followers, Bloom seeking forgiveness by doing service in Palestine. Their party is attacked by soldiers led by Neeson's nephew, ostensibly to capture Bloom, but really to kill Neeson in an effort to seize Neeson's barony. The nephew is killed and the attackers are driven off, but Neeson is wounded with an arrow that is broken off, part of the shaft remaining in his body. The party travels to Messina where Neeson knights Bloom, urging him to serve the King of Jerusalem and aid the helpless, before he dies of his wound. Bloom sails for Jerusalem, but his ship founders in a storm and he and a horse are the only survivors. Releasing the animal from some wreckage, the horse runs off with Bloom in pursuit. He encounters a mounted Muslim and his walking servant. The Muslim, appearing to have some significant rank, demands possession of the horse Bloom has been pursuing, but Bloom refuses to give up the animal and both men fight to the death with Bloom reluctantly killing his opponent. He then orders the servant, Siddig, to guide him to Jerusalem and, upon arrival, frees the servant and gives him the horse. The servant tells Bloom that he has slain a high-ranking Saracen knight and that Bloom will be regarded by Muslims with great respect as a noble cavalier. Bloom is introduced to Norton, King of Jerusalem (Baldwin IV; 1161-1185), who is a young but enlightened leader afflicted by leprosy, which causes him to shield his hideously disfigured countenance from the world by wearing a gold-plated face mask. Bloom swears his loyalty to Norton and then meets Norton's marshal of the city, Irons (Tiberias; Raymond III; Count of Tripoli; 1140-1187), who assumes the role of Bloom's sponsor and adviser as he was a former close friend of his father, Neeson. Further, he meets and is attracted to Norton's beautiful sister, Green, who is married to the conniving and ruthlessly ambitious Csokas (Guy of Lusignan; 1150-1194), a high-ranking knight coveting Norton's throne. To that end, he plans with conspirator Gleeson (Reynold of Chatillon; 1125-1187), a rogue knight, brigand, pirate and mass murderer in league with anti-Muslim forces such as the Knights Templar, to provoke a war with the Muslims, defeat them and, after assuming Norton's crown, become the king of all the Christians in the Holy Land.

Csokas and Gleeson, with the aid of the Templars, attack and destroy a large Muslim caravan, provoking the rage of the great Muslim leader Massoud (Saladin; 1137-1193), who then attacks Gleeson's castle. Bloom, ignoring orders from Csokas and Gleeson, leads his knights in a savage cavalry attack on the approaching Muslim forces to protect the villagers outside of the castle, but his small force is defeated. Captured, Bloom is taken to Massoud's tent where he is greeted warmly by Siddig, the man he thought to be a servant in the desert and whose life he spared. Siddig is, in reality, Massoud's chancellor (Iman ad-Din; 1125-1201), and who, in exchange for saving his life, releases Bloom, who goes to the city of Kerak, which Saladin places under siege. Norton then raises an army and rides with Irons to confront Massoud, negotiating a peace with his promise to punish the culprit, Gleeson, for his wanton attacks on Muslims. Massoud withdraws his army, assuring his generals that he will attack again when better opportunities assure victory. Meanwhile, Norton forces Gleeson to show penance by groveling before him and where Norton slaps him and then compels Gleeson to slavishly kiss his leprosy-infected hand before having him imprisoned. Knowing he is surrounded by enemies, the dying Norton asks Bloom to marry his sister, Green, but the noble Bloom refuses, knowing that her present husband, Csokas, must be killed for that marriage to take place. When Norton dies, Green becomes queen and is pressured by her husband into making him king of Jerusalem. Once assuming the throne, Csokas releases Gleeson, asking him to start a war with the Muslims and this he quickly does by murdering Massoud's sister and where Massoud launches an all-out war against the crusaders. Since Bloom is an outspoken critic of Csokas and his manufactured war with Massoud, Csokas orders some of his knights to murder Bloom, but he avoids assassination. Csokas then convenes a council where he declares war against Massoud "because God wills it." Csokas and Gleeson then lead almost all available fighting men in a powerful army into the desert to seek out the Muslim forces and destroy them. After Irons states that the defense of Jerusalem against Massoud's powerful forces is hopeless, he leaves with his forces for Cyprus. Only Bloom and a few other knights remain in Jerusalem to defend the city. Meanwhile, out of water and weakened by thirst, the army of crusaders are attacked and massacred by Massoud's forces and Csokas and Gleeson are captured. Massoud offers ice water to Csokas only, and when Gleeson takes and drinks this ice water, his throat is cut and he is then beheaded. Massoud then attacks the almost defenseless city of Jerusalem, but Bloom rallies the populace and, using his skills to destroy siege equipment, he repels repeated attacks for three days; during the siege, Csokas is slain before his own followers at the orders of Massoud. Bloom, however, preserves the city until Massoud offers him terms. The defenders are then set free and without threat of harm to return to their lands in Europe while Massoud and his forces occupy Jerusalem. Bloom finds Green among the refugees streaming from the city, and they travel to France together where they marry and settle down outside Bloom's native village. Crusaders then appear looking for the great "defender of Jerusalem," but Bloom denies he is that man, saying he is only a blacksmith. Leading these crusaders is Glen (Richard I; Richard the Lionheart; 1157-1199), king of England, who again asks Bloom if he is the defender of Jerusalem, Bloom insists that he is only a blacksmith and Glen and his men ride off, intent on freeing the Holy Land in what will become the Third Crusade, a warring expedition that Bloom wants no part of as he has renounced war and will now leave peacefully with Green. In keeping with all of his epic films, Scott offers a highly stylized movie with extraordinarily high production values and where huge sets by Max and Klaus and Mathieson's lush cinematography of countless exotic scenes reign supreme. His battle scenes dominate as usual, and his siege of Jerusalem is a superlative set-piece with massive assaults by countless extras highlighted by movable siege towers that are toppled by catapulting defensive ropes and grapples. The exceptional musical score by Gregson-Williams offers a wonderful mix of evocative medieval and Middle Eastern passages befitting each sequence, and the acting from Bloom, Neeson, Massoud, Green, and es-

Frank Sinatra and Tony Curtis in *Kings Go Forth*, 1958.

pecially the repulsive villains, Csokas and Gleeson, is outstanding. This is admittedly a film that does not eschew considerable violence and bloodletting and, as such, prohibits viewing by children and any adult with a sensitive stomach, but Scott's bloodletting is aptly choreographed to fit the actual events he depicts in his capturing of the image of an age when human life had little or no value—a truly mesmerizing and memorable film. **p**, Ridley Scott, Mark Albela, Bruce Devan, Henning Molfenter, Denise O'Dell, Thierry Potok; **d**, Scott; **cast**, Orlando Bloom, Liam Neeson, Jeremy Irons, Edward Norton, Nikolaj Coster-Waldau, Eva Green, Brendan Gleeson, Alexander Siddig, Iain Glen, David Thewlis, Kevin McKidd, Steven Robertson, Marton Csokas, Ghassan Massoud, Jon Finch; **w**, William Monahan; **c**, John Mathieson; **m**, Harry Gregson-Williams; **ed**, Dody Dorn; **prod d**, Arthur Max; **art d**, Maria-Teresa Barbasso, Gianni Giovagnoni, Robert Cowper, Ivo Husnjak, John King, Marco Trentini; **set d**, Sonja Klaus; **spec eff**, Neil Corbould.

Kings Go Forth ★★★ 1958; U.S.; 109m; Frank Ross-Eton Productions/UA; B/W; War Drama; Children: Unacceptable; **DVD**; **VHS**. Stark but engrossing WWII tale set in 1944 sees Sinatra and Curtis serving in the Seventh Army and fighting in France against the Nazis. Sinatra goes on leave in southern France, visiting Nice where he meets fetching Wood, who is living with Dana, her mother. Falling in love with her, Sinatra asks to marry Wood, but she refuses, hesitantly stating as her reason to turn him down is that she is a child from a mixed marriage and her father was black. Her real reason is that she is in love with Curtis. When Sinatra tells Curtis about Wood's background, he tells his friend that her having mixed blood is not important, but, being an utter no-good, Curtis later tells Sinatra that he has never had any notion of marrying the girl, when Wood hears this, she is devastated. Sinatra is so enraged that he seriously considers killing Curtis "by accident" when they next go into battle, but that evil inclination is dismissed when the Germans perform the deed first. In that battle scene, one where Sinatra and Curtis accept a dangerous assignment to scout a German ammunition dump and direct artillery fire to destroy it, Sinatra is also seriously wounded and loses an arm. Following the war, he returns to Nice to find that Dana has died and that Wood has turned her family mansion into a school for war orphans, but it is uncertain whether or not Sinatra and Wood will make a go of it together. Good performances from all the leading players and a taut script make this outing worth the watching. This film concentrates on a love triangle more than offering a broad panorama of the war itself and confines itself to one battle sequence where Curtis is killed and Sinatra is wounded. *Author's Note*: This film was close to Sinatra's heart as he was throughout his spectacular life an activist fighting bigotry; in fact, he received a special Oscar in 1946 for his appearance in a short directed by Meryvn LeRoy, **The House I Live**

Ann Sheridan and Ronald Reagan in *Kings Row,* 1942.

In, 1945, which attacked intolerance and promoted racial equality. Sinatra told this author that "I thought that film with Tony was a little too talky and should have had more action on the battlefield, but it is not really a war film. It deals with racial discrimination and how one man truly loves a woman despite the fact that she has Negro blood and how another man is only using her, with the woman being victimized by her past and her own love for a jerk. Nobody could play jerks better than Tony [Curtis], absolutely nobody." Sinatra gave many memorable performances in roles where he played servicemen—**Anchors Aweigh**, 1945 (a sailor), **On the Town**, 1949 (a sailor), **From Here to Eternity**, 1953 (a soldier), **Some Came Running**, 1958 (a mustered-out soldier), **Never So Few**, 1959 (a U.S. Army captain), **The Manchurian Candidate**, 1962 (a U.S. Army major), **None but the Brave**, 1965 (a sailor), and **Von Ryan's Express**, 1965 (a U.S. Army Air Force colonel)—but, unlike most of the film actors of his generation, he never served in the U.S. armed forces in WWII. Although he was summoned for the draft in WWII, he was, after military doctors inspected him, classified 4-F (not acceptable for military service) because he had a perforated eardrum. An FBI report later revealed that the physicians examining Sinatra at that time of possible induction noted in their records that Sinatra was "neurotic" and "not acceptable material from a psychiatric standpoint." **p**, Frank Ross, Richard Ross; **d**, Delmer Daves; **cast**, Frank Sinatra, Tony Curtis, Natalie Wood, Leora Dana, Karl Swenson, Ann Codee, Edward Ryder, Jacques Berthe, Pete Candoli, Cyril Delevanti; **w**, Merle Miller (based on the novel by Joe David Brown); **c**, Daniel L. Fapp; **m**, Elmer Bernstein; **ed**, William B. Murphy; **art d**, Fernando Carrere; **set d**, Darrell Silvera.

The King's Jester ★★★ 1947; Italy; 92m; Scalera Film/Superfilm Distributing Corp.; B/W; Drama; Children: Unacceptable. Giuseppe Verdi's opera "Rigoletto" is excellently adapted for the screen in this film, which uses the music as background to the drama. Rigoletto (Simon), a hunchbacked clown, is court jester to Brazzi, a lecherous king. Among Simon's duties is to bring the monarch more beautiful young women to be seduced. The problem is that Simon has a beautiful daughter, Mercader. How to keep Brazzi from knowing about her? Simon tries, but Brazzi learns about Mercader, and adds her to his long list of romantic conquests. Simon vows to get revenge. He hires Duranti, a beautiful gypsy dancing girl, to bedazzle Brazzi and then kill him. But Duranti falls for Brazzi and can't bring herself to end the monarch's life. Unaware of this turn of events, Simon returns to collect Brazzi's body and is given a sack with a dead body inside. As he is about to toss it into the river, he hears Brazzi singing and, to his horror, realizes that the body in the sack is his daughter. (In Italian; English subtitles.) **d**, Mario Bonnard; **cast**, Michel Simon, Maria Mercader, Rossano Brazzi, Doris Du-

ranti, Paola Barbara, Elli Parvo, Carlo Ninchi, Juan de Landa, Franco Coop, Corrado Racca; **w**, Bonnard, Carlo Salsa, Simon, Tomaso Smith (based on Giuseppi Verdi's opera "Rigoletto") and Victor Hugo's play "Le Roi s'amuse"); **c**, Ubaldo Arata; **m**, Giulio Bonnard; **ed**, Dolores Tamburini; **prod d**, Florestano Di Fausto; **art d**, Vittorio Nino Novarese; **set d**, Amleto Bonetti.

Kings Row ★★★★ 1942; U.S.; 127m; WB; Drama; Children: Unacceptable; **DVD**; **VHS**. An astounding film for its era and one that still packs an emotional knock-out wallop to this day, this gripping drama incisively depicts with great tension and a brilliant script the kind of tragedy and deep-seated problems invariably associated with big city living, but is centered in small-town America. Unlike the even-keeled domesticity found in Thornton Wilder's **Our Town**, 1940, **Kings Row** unflinchingly but subtly profiles lurking incest, suicide, homosexuality, sadism, insanity and murder that invades the lives of otherwise normal and outgoing people. This film also presents the finest performances of Ann Sheridan, and Ronald Reagan, long before Reagan became the president of the United States. Beginning at the turn of the 20th Century, the town of Kings Row is viewed by five children, who later become the protagonist adults. Beckett (later Cummings as an adult) befriends Thomas (later Field as an adult), who is the strange little daughter of psychiatrist Rains. Beckett's other friends include Croft (later Reagan as an adult), tomboy Todd (later Sheridan as an adult), and the rather snobbish Duvalle (later Coleman as an adult). Beckett learns from a tearful Thomas that she will not be seeing him much more in that her father is taking her out of school and that she will be tutored at home. The five children grow to adults and we now see Cummings as a gifted medical student studying with Rains and where he occasionally meets with Field, but she is mostly distant and seems to live in a dream world. Sheridan is still the outgoing person she was as a child and where she loves both Cummings and Reagan and where Reagan flaunts customs and makes fun of social restrictions. Their former childhood friend, Coleman, is kept from them by her intolerant parents, Coburn, a local-wealthy doctor, and his snooty wife, Anderson, who shield their daughter from her former friends, believing Cummings, Reagan and Sheridan are not suitable company for their daughter. Sheridan then falls deeply in love with the fun-craving Reagan, a playboy with a substantial inheritance; after they become a dating couple, Coleman becomes hysterically jealous, convinced that Sheridan has stolen Reagan's affection from her. Cummings then makes plans to go to Vienna to study, but Field implores him to take her with him. He instinctively does not respond and later learns that his wise grandmother, Ouspenskaya has died of cancer. Further tragedy strikes when Cummings discovers that Field is dead, murdered by her father, Rains, who has then taken his own life. Cummings learns that Rains believed his daughter insane and that is why he ended his life, but it appears that she was pregnant with Rains' own child and Rains could not bear the disgrace of being accused of incest and therefore killed Field and himself. Cummings goes to Vienna to complete his medical education, Sheridan and Reagan continue to see each other, but Reagan's inheritance is suddenly gone, unwisely invested by a money manager; he is compelled to go to work for the railroad for which Sheridan's father, Cossart, and brother, Moriarity, also work. Reagan is then seriously injured, his legs badly damaged in a train accident. Physician Coburn is called to attend to him, although he secretly hates Reagan for forsaking his daughter (even though Coburn and his wife never wanted Coleman to be with Reagan) and because his daughter detests them both for their repressive ways. Instead of performing a normal operation where Reagan's legs are savable, the sadistic Coburn amputates both of his legs. When Reagan comes to after the operation, he looks down upon himself in horror and shock, shouting for Sheridan, who runs to his bedside and holds him as Reagan delivers one of the most memorable lines in film history: "Where's the rest of me?" Cummings then returns from Vienna and finds Kalser, a physician, and her lovely daughter, Verne, living in his old home. Cummings and Verne fall in love and they plan a future together. Cummings then goes to the legless Reagan and, to release him from the depression that consumes him, tells him the truth, that Coburn, a warped and degenerate old man, now dead, needlessly cut off his legs to destroy his life and that he must be courageous enough to face the future and rise above this terrible injustice. Reagan seizes upon this brave notion and vows to live a confident life with Sheridan, his spirits and hopes high, despite the handicap so viciously foisted upon him, ending this emotionally draining film. Director Wood does a fine job of keeping this melodrama from sinking into bathos, and the cast members all render top drawer performances, their scenes dynamically enforced by Korngold's stirring score. *Author's Note*: All the sets for this outstanding film, interiors and exteriors, were shot on the Warner Brothers sound stages. The studio wanted Fox to loan them Tyrone Power to play the role that ultimately went to Cummings, but Fox chief Zanuck refused, telling Jack Warner that Power was his top star and he did not want to loan him out to anyone. Several contract players at Warner Brothers were considered for the role Reagan finally played, including Eddie Albert, Dennis Morgan, Jack Carson and Jeffrey Lynn, but Wood finally selected Reagan, a wise choice, as Reagan worked harder at that part than any before or after, which he later admitted, before enacting the traumatic scene where he discovers his legs are gone, the actor stated later that he went without sleep for many nights in anticipating that scene and his anxiety was such that it is vividly expressed when it came to doing that scene. He did it so well, that it was captured in one take. "Perhaps I never did quite as well again in a single shot," said Reagan. **p**, Hal B. Wallis; **d**, Sam Wood; **cast**, Ann Sheridan, Robert Cummings, Ronald Reagan, Betty Field, Charles Coburn, Claude Rains, Judith Anderson, Nancy Coleman, Kaaren Verne, Maria Ouspenskaya, Harry Davenport, Ernest Cossart, Ilka Gruning, Pat Moriarity, Minor Watson, Ludwig Stossel, Erwin Kalser, Ann E. Todd, Scotty Beckett, Douglas Croft, Joan Duvalle, Mary Thomas; **w**, Casey Robinson (based on the novel by Henry Bellamann); **c**, James Wong Howe; **m**, Erich Wolfgang Korngold; **ed**, Ralph Dawson; **prod d**, William Cameron Menzies; **art d**, Carl Jules Weyl; **spec eff**, Robert Burks.

The King's Speech ★★★★ 2010; U.K./U.S.; 118m; Weinstein Company; Color; Biographical Drama; Children: Unacceptable (MPAA: R); **BD**; **DVD**. This powerful and emotional biopic profiles the reserved and withdrawn Firth as George VI (1895-1952), who, in 1936, was seemingly reluctant to assume the throne of England after his elder brother, Pearce as Edward VIII (1894-1972) abdicated so that he could marry the woman he loved, Best as Wallis Simpson (1896-1986), an American commoner, who was a divorced socialite (both becoming the Duke and Duchess of Windsor). Firth feels that his chronic stammering will impede his ability to properly communicate with the heads of his government as well as the British public. He has given a disastrous public speech in 1925 where his stammering embarrassed him and the royal family and he concludes that there is no cure for his affliction. His wife, Carter, however, persuades him to seek aid from Rush (Lionel Logue, 1880-1953), a London-based Australian speech therapist, but in their first meeting, Rush breaches royal etiquette and protocol by addressing Firth as "Bertie," a pet name used only by members of the royal family, and Firth decides that Rush is unsuitable and thinks to dismiss him. Rush, however, makes a small bet with him that he can deliver without any trouble the "To be or not to be..." monologue from Shakespeare's "Hamlet.' Firth takes up the challenge and records the monologue, but wears headphones while listening to loud music as per Rush's instructions. Believing that he has stammered throughout the recording, Firth dismisses Rush, who gives him a copy of the recording as a keepsake and, to his surprise, later discovers that has delivered the speech without stammering. After his father, Gambon (George V, 1865-1936) makes a Christmas speech to the nation in 1934, he confers with his Firth, his second son, telling him that when his oldest son, Pearce, ascends the throne upon his death, he will be a poor monarch, his womanizing ways

Geoffrey Rush, Colin Firth and Helena Bonham Carter in *The King's Speech*, 2010.

and cavalier deportment bringing ruination upon the royal family as well as the country and that dictators like Hitler and Stalin will appear the only strong leaders in a troubled Europe. Gambon insists that Firth prepare himself to possibly replace his brother by reading Gambon's Christmas speech, and Firth agonizingly attempts to comply. He summons Rush and asks him to resume his speech therapy, but cautions him not to probe into his personal life. Rush agrees and begins to teach Firth how to control his throat muscles and breathing, but nevertheless subtly probes into the psychological reasons for Firth's stammering, slowly learning from Firth how he was a shy child, psychologically affected by the tragic death of his young brother John, and how he suffered injuries as a boy when he was mistreated by an oppressive nanny. Following these revelations, Firth's ability to speak longer sentences without stammering improves and he and Rush become friends. When Gambon dies in 1936, older brother Pearce ascends to the throne, but his ambition to wed a commoner, Best, threatens the monarchy. Pearce believes that Firth has secret ambitions to replace him on the throne by having taken speech lessons and mocks him with his childhood taunt of mimicking his stammering by calling him "B-B-B-Bertie." After Firth confides in Rush his frustration with Pearce, Rush tells him that he, Firth, would be a good king, and Firth tells Rush that such talk is seditious and traitorous, angrily dismissing him once more and telling him that Rush is nothing more than a failed actor and comes from humble origins. After Pearce abdicates, Firth ascends the throne as George VI, and he and his wife, Carter, visit Rush's home, apologizing to him, asking Rush to continue working with Firth. Rush agrees, but purposely angers Firth by demeaning a royal symbol and Firth's angered reply proves to him that he can speak without stammering. It is now 1939, and Firth must make a public address to his country and the world in response to Hitler's invasion of Poland, which has begun WWII, involving Great Britain and almost all other nations. Rush is summoned to Buckingham Palace where Firth makes that speech over the airways through a single microphone in a room with only Rush present, and Firth makes an eloquent, moving speech without any impediments or mistakes. Firth and Carter then step onto a balcony where thousands of citizens cheer the monarchs. A title card at the finale states how Rush was at Firth's side throughout the war when he made subsequent national broadcasts and how they remained close friends for the remainder of their lives. This wonderful biopic is shown with great taste and restraint, but passionately and tellingly reveals how a king can overcome the same seemingly daunting physical obstacles plaguing any average person in the world and where masterful performances from Firth and Rush (and even though briefly, Pearce) are presented in superlative character studies. **p**, Iain Canning, Emile Sherman, Gareth Unwin, Simon Egan, Peter Heslop, Bob and Harvey Weinstein; **d**, Tom Hooper; **cast**, Colin Firth, Ge-

Robert Wagner and Virginia Leith in *A Kiss Before Dying*, 1956.

offrey Rush, Helena Bonham Carter, Jennifer Ehle, Derek Jacobi, Michael Gambon, Claire Bloom, Guy Pearce, Anthony Andrews, Timothy Spall, Richard Dixon, Eve Best, David Bamber; **w**, David Seidler; **c**, Danny Cohen; **m**, Alexandre Desplat; **ed**, Yariq Anwar; **prod d**, Eve Stewart; **art d**, David Hindle, Netty Chapman, Leon McCarthy; **set d**, Judy Farr; **spec eff**, Mark Holt, James Davis III.

Kinyarwanda ★★★ 2011; U.S./France; 100m; Blok Box IMG; African-American Film Festival Releasing Movement; Color; Fantasy; Children: Unacceptable; **BD**, **DVD**. This tense and gripping Romeo and Juliet story set in Africa depicts a young Tutsi female soldier, Freeman, and a Hutu man, Bamporiki, who fall in love during the 1994 Rwandan genocide for ethnic cleansing that killed 800,000 people from the Tutsi minority. Besides their forbidden love are the strict religious and moral codes of the two factions including a Hutu militia tracking down a Tutsi priest, Kennedy, and the Koran's command to give shelter to those in need and the prejudice against a hated faction. Meanwhile, public radio broadcasts inflame the bloodshed by calling for any Hutu to not only kill any Tutsi, but use machetes to dismember them. A Tutsi father sends his young son to a store and encounters Hutu militiamen looking for Tutsi, so the boy leads them back to his own family. In the Bantu language of Rwanda, "Kinyarwanda" means "God spends the day elsewhere, but sleeps in Rwanda." Excessive violence including scenes of the genocide prohibits viewing by children. *Author's Note*: For more details on the Rwandan genocides of 1994, see my *Encyclopedia of World Crime*, Volume VII, A-Q, 1989-1999 (History, Inc., 1999; pages 9, 289-290). **p**, Alrick Brown, Darren Dean, Tommy Oliver, Deatra L. Harris, Joshua Rasplica Rodd; **d**, Brown; **cast**, Cassandra Freeman, Edouard Bamporiki, Cleophas Kabasita, Mazimpaka Kennedy, Hadidja Zaninka, Hassan Kabera, Abdallah Uwimana, Marc Gwamaka, Mutsari Jean, Kena Onyenjekwe, Assumpta Micho; **w**, Brown, Patricia Janvier, Charles Plath (based on a story by Ishmael Ntihabose); **c**, Daniel Vecchione; **m**, John Jennings Boyd; **ed**, Tovah Leibowitz; **prod d**, Sibomana Omar Mukhetar; **art d**, Melissa Slaker.

Kismet ★★★ 1944; U.S.; 100m; MGM; Color; Fantasy; Children: Acceptable; **DVD**; **VHS**. In mythical Baghdad, a beggar-thief-magician, Colman, aspires to have his beautiful daughter, Page, marry the ruler of Baghdad and be its queen. To be accepted among royalty at the palace, Colman masquerades as a prince of a distant land. He befriends the Grand Vizier, Arnold, who, he believes, plans to assassinate the all-powerful Caliph of Baghdad and take his place. Page now lives in the palace, sees a handsome young man, Craig, in the palace garden, and they fall in love. Craig is in disguise as the son of the royal gardener, but in fact he is the Caliph. Colman, meanwhile, has been wooing Arnold's sultry

wife, Dietrich. He plans to have his daughter marry Arnold so he can have Dietrich for his wife. Colman's fine garments are stolen and he is revealed as a beggar, so Arnold orders that Colman's hands be cut off so he can steal no more. Colman suggests that, instead, he kill the Caliph so Arnold can take his place as ruler of Baghdad, and on condition that Arnold abandons Dietrich and marries Page. Arnold agrees, and Colman does some magic tricks in front of Craig, before attempting to stab him. He misses his mark and flees. Arnold and his guards go after Colman, who kills several guards and then kills Arnold. Colman is captured and brought before Craig. When Craig, as the Caliph, learns that Colman is Page's father, he pardons him and makes him a true prince, but banishes him from Baghdad. Colman and Dietrich go off together to a happy future and his wish comes true...his daughter is to marry the ruler of Baghdad, who she happens to love, and she will become queen of the realm. Sumptuously filmed and wellacted, this entertaining fantasy is a keeper. Songs include: "Willow in the Wind," "Tell Me, Tell Me, Evening Star" (Harold Arlen, E.Y. Harburg). *Author's Note*: MGM spent lavishly on this film, more than $3 million and its impressive sets and production values mirror that expense. This story began as a play that was invariably identified with the colorful actor Otis Skinner, who starred in the first Broadway production in 1911 and also appeared in two earlier film versions, a 1920 silent that also featured his daughter, Cornelia Otis Skinner, and in a weakly produced early talkie in 1930. The tale would be produced as a lavish musical in 1955 that somehow appeared lackluster in comparison to this production. The Hays Office, censors of that day, objected to the dance scene in which Dietrich appears (one of only five scenes where she is seen), stating that her costume was too skimpy and that undergarments had to be discernible and that more bangles covering her arms and breasts had to be added. Moreover, Dietrich is made to appear Amazonian in this scene after the makeup department adorned her head with a four-inch topknot hairpiece and had her prancing around with shoes having three-inch heels, so that she stood well over six feet. They painted her fingernails carmine and sprayed her famous legs with gold paint. Her dance was actually no dance at all. Like the slinky "novelty" dance performed by Greta Garbo in **Mata Hari**, 1931, Dietrich provides seductive poses more than dances, bending forward, backward, then prone, all cutaway shots to give the impression of movement than what was literally performed, all of this achieved through clever editing. The censors prohibited the use of the word "harem" in the promotion of this film, but that did not prevent MGM from plastering Dietrich's sensuous poses on divans and next to pillars in its widespread publicity campaign for this production, especially on a huge billboard in New York City's Time Square where the image of this alluring siren beckoned customers to the theater showing this film. **p**, Everett Riskin; **d**, William Dieterle; **cast**, Ronald Colman, Marlene Dietrich, James Craig, Edward Arnold, Hugh Herbert, Joy Ann Page, Florence Bates, Harry Davenport, Hobart Cavanaugh, Robert Warwick, Yvonne De Carlo, Frank Morgan (narrator); **w**, John Meehan (based on the play by Edward Knoblock); **c**, Charles Rosher; **m**, Herbert Stothart; **ed**, Ben Lewis; **art d**, Cedric Gibbons, Daniel B. Cathcart, E. Preston Ames; **set d**, Edwin B. Willis; **spec eff**, Warren Newcombe.

A Kiss Before Dying ★★★ 1956; U.S.; 94m; UA; Color; Crime Drama; Children: Unacceptable; **DVD**; **VHS**. In this taut little thriller, Wagner is a standout as a conniving and murderous youth (unlike his mostly otherwise portraits of the clean-cut boy next door), who kills his girlfriend, Woodward, after learning she is pregnant and that her condition would jeopardize his ambitions to gain her family's wealth. Leith, who is Woodward's sister, does not accept the police report that describes her sibling's death as a suicide and conducts her own investigation. She encounters Wagner, not knowing of his relationship to her sister, and falls in love with him, but, after she discovers that secret relationship, her own life becomes imperiled. Wagner now plans to murder Leith, but, in that attempt, irony and justice take revenge and he falls to his own death. **p**, Robert Jacks; **d**, Gerd Oswald; **cast**, Robert Wagner,

Jeffrey Hunter, Virginia Leith, Joanne Woodward, Mary Astor, George Macready, Robert Quarry, Howard Petrie, Bill Walker, Molly McCart, Marlene Felton; **w**, Lawrence Roman (based on the novel by Ira Levin); **c**, Lucien Ballard (CinemaScope; DeLuxe Color); **m**, Lionel Newman; **ed**, George A. Gittens; **art d**, Addison Hehr; **set d**, James Roach.

Kiss Me Deadly ★★★ 1955; U.S.; 106m; Parklane/UA; B/W; Crime Drama; Children: Unacceptable; **DVD**; **VHS**. Meeker is outstanding as the tough-as-nails private eye Mike Hammer in this hard-hitting whodunit. He is driving his classic convertible on a lonely road when he almost runs over Leachman, who is running wildly away from something or someone. He gives her a lift, but his car is then forced off the road. He is knocked unconscious, and a vicious attacker then tortures Leachman to death with a pair of pliers. Her body is dumped into Meeker's car, and both she and Meeker are sent sailing when the car is pushed off a cliff. Meeker miraculously survives. He begins to investigate, despite a warning from the FBI not to probe further and be thankful that he is alive. Going to Leachman's residence, Meeker finds a book of poetry that provides him a clue, learning also that Leachman's roommate, Rodgers, has fled and is hiding. Meeker's next step is to visit gang leader Stewart where Stewart's bully boys, Elam and Lambert try to roust him, but get the worst of it. Meeker gets little information, but knows now that Stewart is not really the boss behind all the evil events. After Meeker asks his mechanic friend Dennis to help him, he learns that Dennis has been killed, a car dropped on top of him. Worse, Cooper, who is Meeker's secretary, has been kidnapped. Meeker is also kidnapped, but he attacks his abductors and escapes. By then he has learned that there is a key that will explain everything, except that that key had been swallowed by Leachman. Going to the morgue and knowing that an autopsy had been performed on the dead Leachman, Meeker demands that an attendant give him that key. When he refuses, Meeker slams a draw over his fingers and is given that key. Going to a health club, Meeker forces the attendant to identify the locker to which the key belongs. Taking a strange-looking box from that locker, Meeker opens it slightly and a searing bright light shoots from it, burning his hand so that he quickly reseals the leather box. He quickly learns that the box is extremely dangerous as it contains nuclear material. Meeker takes it to his apartment where Rodgers manages to steal the box and takes it to a beach house owned by Dekker, the real brains behind all of the murders and mayhem, and who is holding Cooper hostage. Rodgers' curiosity gets the better of her even after warned by Dekker not to open that box. Thinking that the box contains untold riches, Rodgers, who is a certified nutcase, shoots Dekker to death, and just as Meeker arrives to retrieve Cooper, she also shoots the detective. Rodgers then throws back the lid of the box, which engulfs her in blinding white light, the nuclear material killing her on the spot. Meeker, though wounded, searches the rooms of the beach house, finds Cooper and leads her out of the house and down the beach, throwing her to the sandy beach and shielding her with his body when the house blows up with a terrific roar, which ends this intriguing but ultra-violent Mickey Spillane story. Aldrich's direction keeps this film going at a fast clip, and the acting by Meeker and the cast is well performed and in keeping with the feisty script where just about every character is larcenous, sinister and out for something at the expense of someone else. Aldrich dwells a bit too savagely on some violent scenes, particularly in a scene where he shows Dennis murdered when an assailant releases the hydraulic jacks holding up the car and where the director zooms in for a close-up of Dennis' face to express agony and pain. *Author's Note*: Meeker told this author that "I take a real pounding in that picture. I get knocked out six times, but proved to everyone in Hollywood that I had the hardest head in the business, especially when I kept bouncing back for more. I am normal compared to how Bob [Aldrich] had Gaby [Rodgers] play her part. She walks around like a pop-eyed zombie looking for a fix and she delivers her lines in a monotone—I mean, the character she plays is about the weirdest woman anywhere in or outside of an insane asylum." Stewart was somewhat

Kathryn Grayson and Howard Keel in *Kiss Me Kate*, **1953.**

perplexed by the script, telling this author: "I am playing a gangster in that strange picture, but, you know, I could never figure out my character's end of things. When I asked Bob [Aldrich] about that and suggested that maybe something more might be added to the script, he said: 'The author [Spillane] has no idea either, I am sure—he writes about a lot of violent events and oddball characters and where most everything is left unanswered and that is what we are doing in this picture.'" Aldrich, after reviewing the film before its release, got apprehensive, believing the film would be widely criticized for its excessive violence. "I believe that **Kiss Me Deadly** is an important film noir contribution," he told this author, "but I made a mistake when I wrote an article defending the film's violence, which was necessary to all of its characters and plot, and that was like waving a red cape at a charging bull, because it whipped up a firestorm of protest. But the ruckus I started only caused more people to see the film." Indeed. This film remains a cult classic among most film noir aficionados. **p&d**, Robert Aldrich; **cast**, Ralph Meeker, Albert Dekker, Paul Stewart, Cloris Leachman, Juano Hernandez, Wesley Addy, Marion Carr, Maxine Cooper, Jack Lambert, Jack Elam; **w**, A.I. Bezzerides (based on the novel by Mickey Spillane); **c**, Ernest Laszlo; **m**, Frank DeVol; **ed**, Michael Luciano; **art d**, William Glasgow; **set d**, Howard Bristol.

Kiss Me Kate ★★★ 1953; U.S.; 109m; MGM; Color; Musical; Children: Acceptable; **DVD**; **VHS**. A divorced and still feuding Broadway musical comedy team, Keel and Grayson, star in a new musical adaptation of William Shakespeare's play, "The Taming of the Shrew," created by Cole Porter, Randell. Keel is vain and smug, while Grayson is an abrasive prima donna. They make an unlikely couple off-stage, but are magic together while on the boards together. Two dancers in the production are Miller and Rall. Rall, a gambler, signs Keel's name to an I.O.U. involving several thousand dollars, and two gangsters, Wynn and Whitmore, show up backstage to collect. A series of backstage and on-stage reversals threaten to sink the show, including Keel for having eyes for Miller, which causes Grayson to threaten to leave the show and marry a Texas rancher, Parker. Keel and Grayson finally work out their marital differences, agree to marry again, and the show opens and becomes a hit. Filmed in 3-D, this well-mounted production offers a delightful musical comedy with some great songs and dancing (and with great choreography from Hermes Pan). Songs (all by Cole Porter) include: "From This Moment On," "Wunderbar," "So in Love" (sung by Grayson, Keel); "I Hate Men," (sung by Grayson); "Were Thine That Special Face?," "I've Come to Wive It Wealthily in Padua," "Where Is the Life That Late I Led?" (sung by Keel); "Always True to You in My Fashion," "Why Can't You Behave?" (sung by Miller, Rall); "Kiss Me Kate" (sung by Grayson, Keel, chorus); "Tom, Dick, or Harry," "We

Victor Mature and Coleen Gray in *Kiss of Death*, 1947.

Open in Venice" (sung by Grayson, Keel, Miller, Rall); "Too Darn Hot" (tap dance, Miller). **p**, Jack Cummings; **d**, George Sidney; **cast**, Kathryn Grayson, Howard Keel, Ann Miller, Keenan Wynn, Bobby Van, Tommy Rall, James Whitmore, Kurt Kaszner, Bob Fosse, Ron Randell, Willard Parker, Dave O'Brien, Carol Haney, Hermes Pan; **w**, Dorothy Kingsley (based on the play by Cole Porter, Bella and Sam Spewack from the play "The Taming of the Shrew" by William Shakespeare); **c**, Charles Rosher; **m**, Porter, Andre Previn, Conrad Salinger, Saul Chaplin; **ed**, Ralph E. Winters; **art d**, Cedric Gibbons, Urie McCleary; **set d**, Edwin B. Willis, Richard Pefferle; **spec eff**, Warren Newcombe.

Kiss of Death ★★★★ 1947; U.S.; 98m; FOX; B/W; Crime Drama; Children: Unacceptable; **DVD**; **VHS**. Veteran screenwriters Hecht and Lederer deliver a gripping film noir entry in this tale of a career criminal, Mature, starkly photographed on location in New York by pantheon director Hathaway and where dynamic actor Widmark makes his film debut. Narrating this film is Gray, Mature's girlfriend and future wife, who has loved him from adolescence, and who describes his underworld life, beginning at Yuletide, when Mature and others commit a jewel robbery in a NYC skyscraper. The heist is conducted with efficiency and according to plan with employees being tied up and the gems filched, but one of the office workers touches off an alarm button just as the thieves are leaving. Riding downward in one of the office building's elevators, the thieves are inclined to bolt at the next stop, but Mature keeps them in place as they nervously wait for the elevator to arrive at the lobby floor. The thieves scatter when reaching the lobby, mixing with the crowds exiting the building, but police arrive to seal the entrance. Mature slips into the side entrance of an adjoining shop and then to the street, but a policeman sees him fleeing and orders him to stop. He draws his gun and is shot and wounded while his confederates make their escape. Mature is jailed and, while awaiting trial, Donlevy, a district attorney, asks him to cooperate in identifying his associates in the robbery, but Mature maintains the underworld code of silence by refusing, a defiant act that wins the admiration from another career criminal, Widmark. While Widmark, who is also charged with a crime, is set free, Mature is convicted and sent to prison with the promise from his crooked attorney, Holmes, that his wife and two small girls will be provided for while he is serving time, a promise never kept. While serving his time, Mature is shocked to learn that his wife, depressed for lack of funds, has committed suicide by sticking her head into a gas stove and that his two small daughters have been placed in an orphanage. Enraged at the mistreatment of his family, Mature contacts Donlevy, offering to inform on his former associates. Donlevy cuts a deal with Mature, where Mature agrees to work undercover for the D.A. in getting information on criminal operations and deeds committed by corrupt attorney Holmes

and, especially, gang boss Widmark. When Holmes hears from Mature that he might be indicted for a long-ago unsolved crime, he contacts Widmark to kill a former member of Mature's old gang to silence him regarding that unsolved crime. Widmark goes to the man's apartment but finds only his elderly and crippled mother, Dunnock. Discovering that his quarry has fled, he seeks to send a message to that fleeing criminal by throwing to her death his invalid mother down a flight of stairs while Dunnock is sitting confined in a wheelchair (one of the most brutal murder scenes in filmdom). A parole for Mature, solicited by Holmes, is suddenly granted, but only through the secret arrangements of Donlevy, and Mature is released. He meets again with Gray, falling in love with her, and marrying her and where his two small daughters come to live with them while he works under an assumed name at a blue-collar job provided by Donlevy. Meanwhile, Mature renews his association with Widmark, a ruthless killer, befriending this psychopathic murderer, who brags about killings and robberies before entertaining Mature at a nightclub and then taking him to a bordello. Mature then provides Donlevy with information about Widmark's underworld operations, and the gangster is brought to trial where Mature testifies against him. Surprisingly, however, Widmark wins his case and is set free and now Mature is a marked man. He apprehensively stays up at night, peering from the windows of his house to the street, expecting Widmark and his killers to appear any moment to take their revenge. He then resolves to get solid evidence that will put Widmark behind bars for life. When Donlevy arrives at his home to caution him about taking any action against Widmark, Mature knocks him out and takes Donlevy's weapon. Mature then goes to a NYC restaurant he knows Widmark frequents and, while there, calls Donlevy at his office and tells him to come to that address within a short time and he will catch Widmark red-handed while committing a crime. Mature confronts Widmark and his goons at the restaurant, telling Widmark that he plans to provide more information that will send him to prison, insulting him by calling Widmark a "squirt." The enraged Widmark responds by making threats to Mature, which also includes his wife and children. He then leaves and waits outside with his gunmen in a car parked in front of the restaurant. Mature waits for some minutes, handing the weapon he has taken from Donlevy to a girl at the cash register counter and then bravely steps outside where the car is parked, and where Widmark sits with his gang members. One of the gangsters aims an automatic at Mature and Mature taunts Widmark, challenging him to do his "own dirty work." Widmark grabs the automatic and shoots Mature several times, but the police arrive in several squad cars, and block the street. Widmark races from his car and fires at one of the policemen closing in on him and is, in turn, shot and wounded before he is captured. Donlevy assures the wounded Mature that he has, indeed, provided the evidence that will now imprison Widmark for life. The wounded Mature is carried to an ambulance with Gray's narration stating that he will survive and live out a peaceful life with her and his children. Mature renders a great performance of a man trapped by his own kind and wants nothing more than to live a peaceful life with his family until realizing that he cannot achieve that goal without risking his life. Donlevy is assuring as the resolute D.A., and Holmes is perfectly calculating as the insidious and crooked attorney who runs rackets behind his legitimate and respected lawyer's shingle. Widmark, however, steals every scene as the unbalanced killer, rolling his eyes, snarling threats and providing the most sinister hyena-like laugh ever recorded on film, a truly frightening performance. Hathaway's direction is crisp and well-paced, where he brings gritty realism to this grim crime yarn by his on-location shots of New York's dark and unwelcoming streets and where Brodine's exceptional lensing heightens the taut tale. The 1995 remake of this film was a much inferior production, accenting the violence and without fully developing its characters. ***Author's Note***: Hecht told this author that in writing the script for this film he and close friend Lederer wanted to make their protagonist (Mature) "a lot more human than other gangsters by giving him a deeper loyalty to his own family than his allegiance to those criminal associates that dominate his world. Unlike most underworld types, he has a lot less vanity and puts his loved ones first. That is why he turns informant. His so-called friends desert his wife, causing her to kill herself and his two children wind up in an orphanage. So much for the help he was promised before taking the rap for those friends and going to prison. We had to show how the Tommy Udo character [Widmark] was infinitely worse than the man Vic [Mature] is playing to have Vic appear to be a rather decent fellow—and what could be worse than having that berserk killer [Widmark] shove a helpless woman [Dunnock] in a wheelchair down a flight of stairs to her death?" Director Hathaway was a little disturbed about that scene, telling this author that "I asked Ben [Hecht] if that scene with the woman in the wheelchair wasn't a little too grim and he said: 'She's the victim of a sadistic killer. What would you expect from such a savage murderer like that, dispatching her with a little arsenic in a cup of tea?' Well, Ben was right, so we kept the scene in and it took a lot of guts by Widmark to do that." Widmark said to this author that "I thought when reading about the scene where I shove the old lady down those stairs that I would be typecast for the rest of my life as a psychopath, but it was my first big break in pictures, so I decided that if I am going to show the world I am an insane murderer, who loves bumping off people, I will make them remember just how crazy this guy is and I cluck and cackle at every rotten thing I do in that picture. I knew I would not get any sympathy for that part from moviegoers, but I also knew that hisses get you a lot more attention. And sure enough, in my next picture, I am cast as a kill-crazy crime boss in **The Street with No Name** [1948], and it took me some time to convince producers that I had a reasonable mind and could play sane people." Mature liked his role in this film and thought the production, according to what he told this author, "was more realistic than a lot of the gangster films that had been made in the past. I am trying to support my family and work as a thief just like a man working in an office or delivering the mail. He is not spectacular, just a guy doing a job on the wrong side of the law and where he puts too much trust in the people he works with. The only thing that I thought was not realistic is when, at the end of the picture, I step to the street and ask to be shot. No man, especially a streetwise character like the one I am playing—and I told this to Hathaway—would do such a thing. 'Yes, he would,' Hathaway answered, 'if he knew he was going to be killed anyway and to protect his wife and children by having the police trap his own killer. Besides, you're playing an Italian, and Italians put their families first, last and always.' Well, that made sense, so after I did that scene, I was convinced that my character's sacrifice was really part of my character." **p**, Fred Kohlmar; **d**, Henry Hathaway; **cast**, Victor Mature, Brian Donlevy, Coleen Gray, Richard Widmark, Taylor Holmes, Howard Smith, Karl Malden, Susan Cabot, Mildred Dunnock, John Marley, Millard Mitchell, Jesse White; **w**, Ben Hecht, Charles Lederer (based on a story by Eleazar Lipsky); **c**, Norbert Brodine; **m**, David Buttolph; **ed**, J. Watson Webb, Jr.; **art d**, Lyle Wheeler, Leland Fuller; **set d**, Thomas Little; **spec eff**, Fred Sersen.

Kiss the Blood Off My Hands ★★★ 1948; U.S.; 79m; UNIV; Crime Drama; Children: Unacceptable; **DVD**. In another engrossing film noir entry, Lancaster is in top form as an emotionally scarred WWII veteran who gets into an argument in a London pub where the owner is killed and he flees, hiding in Fontaine's small apartment. A good-hearted nurse, Fontaine believes Lancaster's tale that the killing was an accident and she shields him. Newton, a conniving crook, identifies Lancaster and tries to convince him to join him in a caper, but Lancaster wants no part of it and avoids him. Newton then threatens Lancaster with blackmail, saying that, unless he uses the truck he drives for his work to hijack a load of drugs, Newton will inform the police about the pub killing. Newton's avid aim is to sell the drugs on the black market and make a fortune. Lancaster seems to agree and, on the day of the hijacking, Fontaine gets into Lancaster's truck and Lancaster has a change of heart, taking a different route and not meeting up with Newton. The persistent Newton then goes to Fontaine, telling her that he will betray her boyfriend

Robert Newton and Burt Lancaster in *Kiss the Blood Off My Hands,* **1948.**

to the police over the pub killing unless she persuades him to go through with the hijacking. When she refuses, the short-tempered Newton explodes and makes a menacing move toward her and she shoots and kills him. After Lancaster discovers Newton's demise, he decides to go to the police and admit everything—the pub killing, Newton's diabolical robbery plan and how Fontaine committed justifiable homicide in killing Newton. He knows he faces a prison sentence, but he also knows that the woman he loves will remain free. This convoluted tale is well directed at a clipped pace by Foster, who helmed the superlative spy drama, **Journey into Fear**, 1943, and in addition to the captivating performance by Lancaster, Fontaine and Newton are standouts in their roles. Shot on location in London, the entire production oozes a murky and pervasive atmosphere strikingly similar to another film noir entry, **Night and the City**, 1950, starring Richard Widmark and where all is brutal, uncompromising and seemingly hopeless. *Author's Note*: Lancaster told this author that "I played opposite a terrific actress in that picture—Joan Fontaine, who could convey any emotion with the slight lifting of an eyebrow or a sideways glance. I also had to fight for every scene with that master of evil characters, Bob Newton. All he had to do was clear his throat to take a scene away from anybody. He was gentle as a kitten off the screen, but on-screen he was Jack the Ripper and the French Reign of Terror all in one." **p**, Richard Vernon; **d**, Norman Foster; **cast**, Joan Fontaine, Burt Lancaster, Robert Newton, Lewis L. Russell, Aminta Dyne, Grizelda Hervey, Jay Novello, Colin Keith-Johnston, Reginald Sheffield, Peter Forbes; **w**, Leonardo Bercovici, Ben Maddow, Walter Bernstein, Hugh Gray (based on the novel by Gerald Butler); **c**, Russell Metty; **m**, Miklos Rozsa; **ed**, Milton Carruth; **art d**, Bernard Herzbrun, Nathan Juran; **set d**, Russell A. Gausman, Ruby R. Levitt; **spec eff**, David S. Horsley.

Kiss Tomorrow Goodbye ★★★ 1950; U.S.; 102m; WB; B/W; Crime Drama; Children: Unacceptable; **DVD**; **VHS**. Cagney is at his most ruthless in this stark crime drama. He and Brodie escape from a prison farm and go to Brodie's small hometown, living with Brodie's sister, Payton. Cagney quickly learns that the local officials and most of the police force are corrupt to the bone and he selects two cops, MacLane and Bond, to help him and Brodie in a market robbery Cagney is planning, promising them a portion of the take if they make sure they do not respond to the heist, which is on their beat. Meanwhile, coveting the trampy Payton, Cagney kills her husband, Brand, and mercilessly beats Payton after she tells him that she hates him. He then sets up the daughter of a high-ranking official in a compromising situation to blackmail that powerful politician. He then meets with cops Bond and MacLane, secretly recording their statements to him where they attempt to extort money from him to protect his upcoming robbery and he then uses the

Ward Bond, Harold Huber, Jon Hall, and Raymond Hatton in *Kit Carson*, 1940.

recording to blackmail them into submissive cooperation. After collecting payoff money from the politician, Cagney makes plans to leave town, but with a woman other than Payton. The deserted Payton, however, takes her revenge by shooting and killing Cagney, and, obliquely, justice is further served when the cops and politicians are exposed and arrested. *Author's Note*: Cagney told this author: "**Kiss Tomorrow Goodbye** made big money for Warner Brothers and I am a terrible monster in that picture. There is not a single thing I do that is good, which is why I deserve to get shot down like—what did they call it [smiling broadly]—a dirty rat!" Supporting actor Adler was one of Cagney's favorites, and he admitted to me that Adler taught him some little acting tricks in this film that he had never before experienced and for which he was grateful. "In one scene he is sitting at a desk and when I confront him he raises his head, but he kept his eyes lidded and waited a few seconds before he opened his eyes to look up and glare at me and that was really a chilling moment, one I later taught to the beautiful Dana Wynter when we were doing **Shake Hands with the Devil** [1959]. Boy, could Luther Adler act!" **p**, William Cagney; **d**, Gordon Douglas; **cast**, James Cagney, Barbara Payton, Helena Carter, Ward Bond, Luther Adler, Barton MacLane, Steve Brodie, Rhys Williams, John Litel, William Frawley, Neville Brand, William Cagney; **w**, Harry Brown (based on the novel by Horace McCoy); **c**, Peverell Marley; **m**, Carmen Dragon; **ed**, Walter Hannemann, Truman K. Wood; **prod d**, Wiard Ihnen; **set d**, Joe Kish; **spec eff**, Paul Eagler.

Kit Carson ★★★★ 1940; U.S.; 97m; UA/B/W; Adventure; Children: Cautionary; **DVD**; **VHS**. A rousing adventure tale that presents the stirring story of one of the greatest scouts of the Old West, Kit Carson (Christopher Houston "Kit" Carson; 1809-1868), wonderfully played by Hall, as well as his friend and empire builder, John C. Fremont (John Charles Fremont, 1813-1890), essayed resolutely by Andrews, who escort a wagon train of settlers across the plains against all odds to reach California. Hall and his two frontier pals, Bond and Huber, are first seen scouting a Mexican officer, Stevens, who is stirring up the Indians, urging them to make an attack on a new wagon train of prairie schooners about to leave Fort Bridger in Wyoming sometime in the 1840s. When Hall and his friends arrive at the fort, they are welcomed by pioneer Bridger (Hatton), and all they seek are baths and rest. The three men are taking baths in a communal bathhouse where water runs through the place like a small river and where wooden partitions allow others to bathe in relative privacy, one of those other bathers being the lovely Bari, who loses a bar of soap that floats beneath the partition and is retrieved by Hall, who is embarrassed when he attempts to return it to Bari as he briefly swims beneath the partition. When the wagon train is about to depart for California, Hall is asked to guide the settlers and a unit of

the U.S. Cavalry commanded by Andrews. Hall at first refuses, but he changes his mind after seeing that the attractive Bari is among the pioneers traveling westward and realizing that the settlers are in great danger. As the wagon train proceeds west, it crosses plains and deserts and then enters the western mountains where the Indians trail them, waiting for an opportunity to attack and while their mentor, Stevens, continues to plot against the settlers. At one point, Andrews, who is also attracted to Bari, disagrees with Hall as to which route to take, and he leads his troop into a gorge, leaving the wagon train undefended. Before departing the wagon train, Andrews shouts encouragement and best hopes to the settlers with a traditional Old West farewell: "Green grass and running water!" Once the cavalry has entered dead-end canyon, Stevens and some of his men cascade a series of huge rocks to fall and seal the entrance to the canyon, cutting off the troops from the settlers. The Indians then attack the wagon train where Hall has ordered the wagons to make a circle, and from this defensive position the settlers attempt to fend off the Indians. Realizing that there is no hope of survival without the aid of Andrews and his troops, Hall packs one of the wagons with explosives and races this toward the sealed entrance of the canyon. Meanwhile, Andrews and his men are fighting against Indians and their Mexican advisers, who fire down upon the troopers from hidden positions inside the box canyon. (This scene was all but duplicated by John Ford in his classic cavalry film, **Fort Apache**, 1948, when U.S. Cavalry troops are led into a box canyon by commander Henry Fonda and are slaughtered.) Outside the canyon, Hall drives the explosive-packed wagon toward the sealed entrance and, at the last minute, detaches the horses and rides to safety as the wagon sails against the barrier of rocks, its kegs of dynamite ignited by lighted fuses that explode in a terrific eruption that blows away the rocky barrier and frees Andrews and his men. They then race from the canyon and onto the open prairie where they attack the Indians surrounding the ring of wagons, defeating them and driving off the survivors. Hall, Bond and Huber then capture Stevens and his Mexican soldiers, and torture them to find out that they represent Gordon, a Mexican general, stationed in California and who has sent Stevens to use the Indians in preventing any more Americans from entering the State, which he intends to seize and over which he will preside as a dictator. Bari comes upon Hall's tough interrogation of Stevens and is incensed, believing that Hall is a savage as many have earlier described him. Andrews then learns of Stevens' seditious mission and summarily condemns him to death as a traitor and foreign spy, ordering him and his men shot by a firing squad, which alarms Bari even more. The wagon train then proceeds to California, where the settlers are welcomed by Mexican and American settlers led by Farnum and Maxwell. A fiesta is held to honor Hall and Andrews where Hall learns that Bari loves him and where Andrews gallantly bows out. The trailblazing Hall is embarrassed and tells Bari that he is a pioneer and that life with him would be impossible and that she would be better off with a chivalrous and considerate man like Andrews. Rebuffed, Bari is distraught. Meanwhile, Gordon makes his move, assembling his troops that begin to attack American and Mexican communities, capturing these haciendas one after another. Hall and his friends, however, ride to other communities, asking settlers to join them at Farnum's large hacienda. Andrews then assembles his troops and these collected settlers and positions them in the hills beyond the hacienda, which Gordon and his troops then begin to attack with artillery and rifle fire. The only defenders of the hacienda are Hall, Bond and Huber, who have positioned a number of dummy soldiers at the walls of the hacienda, along with loaded muskets at its loopholes. (The ruse of using dummy soldiers to delude the enemy can be seen in such films as **Beau Geste**, 1939, and DeMille's **Unconquered**, 1947.) These expert marksmen race along the walls firing the muskets with deadly accuracy, felling many of Gordon's men, infuriating him and prompting him to shout: "Don't the fools ever miss?" As Hall and his friends drive back the Mexican troops, Andrews and his men wait in ambush until Hall explodes a prearranged cache of explosives at the hacienda's entrance. Hall, however, is wounded and the fuse to the explosives fizzles. Bari has remained at the hacienda and who tends to Hall's wound just as Gordon's troops swarm forward to seize the hacienda, which will fall unless Andrews and his men are warned by the planned explosion. Bond, when seeing that Hall is about to explode the explosives himself by firing a pistol into kegs of gun powder and where he will be certainly killed, rushes to him, knocks him out, and races to the entrance, leaping atop the explosives and firing that pistol, which creates the explosion and sends the signal to Andrews at the cost of his life. Hearing the signal, Andrews leads his troops and the armed settlers from ambush to envelop and defeat Gordon's forces, causing the would-be dictator to flee for his life. (The tactic of having forces wait in ambush before attacking a seemingly overwhelming enemy force is seen in such films as **The Fighting Kentuckian**, 1949, and John Ford's classic cavalry film, **Rio Grande**, 1950.) The hacienda is saved as is California, which will later join the U.S., and Hall winds up with Bari for the happy finale. Action director Seitz does a great job in presenting this western epic with well-choreographed and breath-taking battle scenes and where cinematographers Mescall and Pittack capture with stunning lensing the grand vistas of the West. Hall, Andrews, Bari, Bond and Huber are standouts, and the script bristles with considerable wit and humor. This superlative production about American pioneers is an often overlooked gem, but nevertheless remains a great adventure film that thoroughly entertains and inspires. **p**, Edward Small; **d**, George B. Seitz; **cast**, Jon Hall, Lynn Bari, Dana Andrews, Harold Huber, Ward Bond, Renie Riano, Clayton Moore, Rowena Cook, Raymond Hatton, C. Henry Gordon, Iron Eyes Cody, Chief Many Treaties, William Farnum, Edwin Maxwell, Harry Strang, Peter Lynn, Charles Stevens; **w**, George Bruce (based on a story by Evelyn Wells); **c**, John Mescall, Robert Pittack; **m**, Edward Ward; **ed**, William Claxton, Fred R. Feitshans, Jr.; **art d**, John DuCasse Schulze; **set d**, Edward Boyle; **spec eff**, Howard A. Anderson, Jack Cosgrove.

Kit Kittredge: An American Girl ★★★ 2008; U.S./Canada; 101m; Picturehouse Entertainment/New Line Cinema; Color; Comedy/Drama; Children: Acceptable (MPAA: G); **BD**; **DVD**. In Cincinnati, Ohio, during the 1930s Great Depression, a teenage girl, Breslin, aspires to become a newspaper reporter. Her father, O'Donnell, owns a car dealership that goes bust, so he goes off to Chicago to look for work, and she is left at home with her mother, Ormond. The mortgage is near being foreclosed, so Ormond takes in some boarders including a magician, Tucci, a nurse, Krakowski, and Cusack, the driver of a mobile library truck. Breslin meets two hobos, Thieriot, who is about her age, and his pal, Smith, who is a little younger, and who call a hobo camp by a river their home. Ormond's few treasures, kept in a box at home, are stolen as neighbors report a rash of robberies and muggings. A footprint beneath a window in Breslin's house is traced to boots found in Thieriot's tent, and he becomes the prime suspect in the treasure box theft. But is he or any of the other hobos stealing things? If Breslin can discover who is guilty, she may finally have a story to sell and become a newspaper reporter. She uses her instincts and reasoning to cleverly solve the mystery and becomes a fledgling reporter. This is a good and entertaining comedy where director Rozema effectively interjects some pensive but absorbing dramatic scenes. **p**, Julia Roberts, Marisa Yeres, Ellen L. Brothers, Lisa Gillan, Elaine Goldsmith-Thomas, Julie Goldstein, Jodi Goldberg, Terry Gould; **d**, Patricia Rozema; **cast**, Abigail Breslin, Julia Ormond, Chris O'Donnell, Stanley Tucci, Joan Cusack, Jane Krakowski, Wallace Shawn, Max Thieriot, Willow Smith, Dylan Smith; **w**, Ann Peacock (based on the Kit Kittredge stories by Valerie Tripp); **c**, David Boyd; **m**, Joseph Vitarelli; **ed**, Julie Rogers; **prod d**, Peter Cosco; **art d**, Michele Brady; **set d**, Odetta Stoddard; **spec eff**, Victoria Holt, Karen Kriss, Aaron Weintraub.

The Kite Runner ★★★ 2007; U.S./China; 128m; DreamWorks SKG/PAR; Color; Drama; Children: Unacceptable (MPAA: PG-13); **BD**; **DVD**. In San Francisco in 2000, a successful author, Amir (Ab-

Abigail Breslin, Julia Ormond and Chris O'Donnell in *Kit Kittredge: An American Girl*, 2008.

dalla) returns to Kabul, Afghanistan, now controlled by the Taliban. In Afghanistan in the 1970s, when he was twelve, Amir (Ebrahimi), a Pushtan, and his wealthy businessman father's Hazara servant, a boy his age named Hassan (Mahmoodzada), bond as close friends and, in fact, treat each other like brothers. They play together and fly kites, such play forbidden by the Taliban. Ebrahimi wants to please his widowed father (Ershadi) whom he believes holds him responsible for his mother's death when giving him birth, and feels that his father favors his friend. The boys enter a kite-flying competition, and afterward, Mahmoodzada is attacked by a Pushtan bully (Assef) and raped. Ebrahimi sees this vicious act, but does not try to help his friend. On the day after Ebrahimi's birthday party, he hides his new watch in Hassan's bed, thus framing him as a thief. Cowardice, jealousy, and betrayal of friendship haunt the boy Amir into adulthood. Grim and often depressing, this film nevertheless presents an incisive and thought-provoking character study. Excessive violence, rape, and gutter talk prohibit viewing by children. **p**, William Horberg, Walter Parkes, E. Bennett Walsh, Rebecca Yeldham; **d**, Marc Forster; **cast**, Khalid Abdalla, Ahmad Khan Mahmoodzada, Atossa Leoni, Shaun Toub, Sayed Jafar Masihullah Gharibzada, Zekeria Ebrahimi, Mir Mahmood Shah Hashimi, Homayoun Ershadi, Nabi Tanha, Elham Ehsas; **w**, David Benioff (based on the novel by Khaled Hosseini); **c**, Roberto Schaefer; **m**, Alberto Iglesias; **ed**, Matt Chesse; **prod d**, Carlos Conti; **art d**, Karen Murphy; **set d**, Maria Nay, Caroline Smith; **spec eff**, Ken Durey, Thomas F. Sindicich, Jason Durey.

Kitty ★★★ 1946; U.S.; 103m; PAR; B/W; Drama; Children: Cautionary; **DVD**; **VHS**. In this sumptuous historical drama, Goddard is the heroine who, like the tale of **Pygmalion**, 1938, rises from poverty to riches through the training and scheming of nobleman Milland. Set in 18th-Century England, Goddard is noticed by Kellaway, playing the famous portrait artist, Thomas Gainsborough (1727-1788). After Kellaway paints her portrait, Goddard comes under the protective and controlling wing of Milland, an impoverished aristocrat, who, along with his alcoholic dowager aunt, Collier, thinks to transform the uneducated Cockney into a grand lady. Milland teaches Goddard the proper speech of the gentry so that she is able to discard her thick Cockney accent, and she is also taught the etiquette and manners employed by the nobility until she becomes a refined and gracious young woman. Her beauty attracts many wealthy suitors, all enticed to her charming side by Milland, who selects rich ironmonger Hoey as her husband. Goddard marries Hoey, a man she does not love as her heart has long ago gone to Milland, but that union quickly ends when Hoey dies. Owen, a dithering duke, who has coveted Goddard for some time, proposes to Goddard and she accepts. Goddard by that time has been expecting a baby from her mar-

Ernest Cossart and Ginger Rogers in *Kitty Foyle*, 1940.

riage with Hoey, but she convinces her new husband, the gullible and adoring Owen (who gives one of his best performances as he trots up and down the grand staircase and through the cavernous halls of his palace) that the child is really his. When the baby is born, Owen's ecstatic delight is so overwhelming that it causes him to collapse from a heart attack. Now the fetching Goddard is not only a duchess, but is free to marry the only man she loves, Milland, and does for a happy fadeout. Director Leisen, who was known as a "woman's director," presents a carefully crafted tale, offering authentic-looking and lavish sets and costumes in what is an opulent film; all the principals give exceptional performances, especially Goddard, who was at the peak of her radiant career, her performance equaled by the always commanding Milland. The film, which won an Oscar for Best Art Direction, was a box office success for Paramount. *Author's Note*: Milland told this author that "I did not particularly like my role in Kitty. I am a bit too much of a fop, using snuff and wearing lace, all that sort of nonsense, and God knows why cultured men of that era pranced around like so many peacocks. It was really Paulette's picture all the way. Leisen doted on her and she gave him a great performance. He was a director, like George Cukor, who always paid more attention to actresses, but that did not bother me since the industry was always male dominated and the gals needed to get a piece of that pie. What did bother me in one scene is where I put on a costume that smelled of perfume. I complained to Leisen about that and he said, 'I had the wardrobe people spray a little cologne on that costume, Ray, so that you would feel the character of the gentleman you are playing.' I said, 'Look, Mitch, I don't smell my way through my roles. Whatever the blazes they sprayed on this outfit is causing me to sneeze.' 'That's great, Ray, great,' he said. "That will go perfectly when you inhale a little snuff and give out a little sneeze. Coincidence is working for you, Ray.' He wasn't smiling and I did not know if he was joking or not, but I played the scene anyway in that smelly outfit in a scene with Paulette and after the take, she said: 'Ray, I think your aftershave is a bit too strong.' When I told her it was the costume, she laughed so hard that she fell off her chair." **p**, Karl Tunberg; **d**, Mitchell Leisen; **cast**, Paulette Goddard, Ray Milland, Patric Knowles, Reginald Owen, Cecil Kellaway, Constance Collier, Dennis Hoey, Sara Allgood, Eric Blore, Gordon Richards, Mary Gordon; **w**, Tunberg, Darrell Ware (based on the novel by Rosamond Marshall); **c**, Daniel L. Fapp; **m**, Victor Young; **ed**, Alma Macrorie; **prod d**, Raoul Pene Du Bois; **art d**, Hans Dreier, Walter Tyler; **set d**, Sam Comer, Ray Moyer; **spec eff**, Farciot Edouart, Gordon Jennings.

Kitty Foyle ★★★ 1940; U.S.; 108m; RKO; B/W; Drama; Children: Acceptable; **DVD**; **VHS**. A grand tearjerker and unarguably a film decidedly for women, this superior production offers a fine performance from the multi-talented Rogers, who abandoned her extraordinary dancing talents to emote her way to an Oscar as Best Actress as a woman seeking what all women seek, true love. Rogers is a young, hard-working woman from the wrong side of the tracks, who lives with her kind-hearted father, Cossart, a slaving blue-collar worker, but she has great aspirations of marrying into High Society. She becomes engaged to Craig, an ethical young physician, but, when the charming Morgan, an old flame who comes from a wealthy Philadelphia main line family, reappears, Rogers abandons Craig and marries Morgan. She has made the mistake of her life as Morgan is a shallow and rather worthless fellow (echoing the words of Ma Joad in **The Grapes of Wrath**, 1940: "Rich men's sons come along and they ain't much good."). After Rogers leaves Morgan, she learns that she is pregnant and then gives birth to a stillborn child, a tragedy Rogers never reveals to Morgan. Craig then re-enters her sad life, and Rogers now realizes that this fine and upstanding man is the person she should have married in the first place, and before the fadeout, she finds true happiness with him. Thickly sentimental and where fine scriptwriters Trumbo and Stewart do not spare the suds, the film is nevertheless immensely absorbing, chiefly through Wood's fine direction and Rogers' superlative acting, handled with considerable restraint. Wood employs a very intimate and effective technique in having Rogers talking to herself in a mirror and then her reflection talking back, a form of stream-of-consciousness that reveals her innermost thoughts and emotions, allowing every viewer to more personally experience her sufferings and joys. *Author's Note*: Rogers told this author that she, more than anyone in the Hollywood community, was shocked when she was given the Academy Award for her role in this film, saying, "I could not believe it, even after I was nominated since almost every great actress of the day were nominated in that year—Katharine Hepburn [**The Philadelphia Story**, 1940], Joan Fontaine [**Rebecca**, 1940] and Martha Scott [**Our Town**, 1940]. I had performed in some films where I did only straight acting before I did **Kitty Foyle**, but they were not exceptional pictures, where **Kitty Foyle** told a very strong story dealing with a woman learning about genuine love and her own motherhood. After I got the Oscar for that picture, I said to myself, well, now you have proven to the world that you can do something other than dancing." So impressed was Hollywood with Rogers' performance that she was considered a top-ranked serious actress—she was the highest paid actress in the U.S. film industry in the year 1943—and she was offered many great dramatic roles for years thereafter, including **To Each His Own**, 1946, and **The Snake Pit**, 1948, roles she turned down and that went to that consummate actress, Olivia de Havilland. Craig, one of her two leading men in this film, told this author: "We all thought the world of Ginger, but up to the time of **Kitty Foyle**, as a dancer and singer. But after my first scene with her in that picture, I left the set and told a friend how I was bowled over by her ability to play her part and I said 'Inside that lively body that has danced through a half dozen pictures with Fred Astaire is a terrific actress!'" **p**, David Hempstead; **d**, Sam Wood; **cast**, Ginger Rogers, Dennis Morgan, James Craig, Gladys Cooper, Eduardo Ciannelli, Ernest Cossart, Odette Myrtil, Mary Treen, K.T. Stevens, Walter Kingsford, Cecil Cunningham, Nella Walker; **w**, Dalton Trumbo, Donald Ogden Stewart (based on the novel by Christopher Morley); **c**, Robert de Grasse; **m**, Roy Webb; **ed**, Henry Berman; **art d**, Van Nest Polglase; **set d**, Darrell Silvera.

Knife in the Water ★★★ 1963; Poland; 94m; Zespol Filmowy; Kanawha; B/W; Drama; Children: Unacceptable; **DVD**; **VHS**. In this engrossing story, the first feature film directed by Polanski, we see a strange love triangle where violence (Polanski's lifelong film penchant) looms and lurks in every frame. Niemczyk is a well-known sportswriter enjoying a fat salary and who has a sensuous, sultry wife, Umecka. The two are riding in their sports car when they pick up Malanowicz, a handsome, young student, giving him a lift, and then offering to take him along on their boating excursion. Once they shove off, Niemczyk realizes that his wife is attracted to Malanowicz, and he becomes jealous. Niemczyk begins taunting the student as they sail through peaceful waters. Niemczyk then brags of his own physical capabilities, ridiculing Malanowicz's inabilities to swim and manage a boat. In frustration, the youth now displays a surly attitude when he withdraws and flourishes a huge hunting knife, which becomes an instrument of menace when he begins displaying his dexterity with it by rapidly jabbing its blade between the fingers of his other hand without cutting any of his fingers. (This harrowing exercise, shudderingly called "Finger Filet," was later shown in great detail by Lance Henriksen, who plays an android in the movie **Aliens**, 1986, and where he performs this trick with lightning speed, jabbing a knife between the outstretched fingers of another crew member in the mess of the spacecraft without injuring the apprehensive participant.) The knife becomes the ever-present symbol of violence and prompts Niemczyk to eventually confront the student, struggling with Malanowicz and causing him to fall overboard. Knowing that the student cannot swim, Niemczyk panics and dives into the water in search of him, but he is nowhere to be found. Malanowicz, however, surfaces and hides behind and clings to a buoy while Niemczyk swims to the shore. Malanowicz then manages to get to the small yacht and, after boarding it, is seductively welcomed by Umecka, and they make love. Umecka later takes the student to shore and still later reunites with husband Niemczyk, confessing her infidelity to him as if it were just punishment for the vicious tyrannies Niemczyk inflicted upon the youth. This well-acted thriller brought Polanski to international attention, and won for him a Venice Film Festival award as well as an Oscar nomination for Best Foreign Film. (In Polish; English subtitles.) **p**, Stanislaw Zylewicz; **d**, Roman Polanski; **cast**, Leon Niemczyk, Jolanta Umecka, Zygmunt Malanowicz; **w**, Polanski, Jerzy Skolimowski, Jakub Goldberg; **c**, Jerzy Lipman; **m**, Krzysztof Komeda; **ed**, Halina Prugar; **prod d**, Boleslaw Kamykowski.

Knight Without Armur ★★★★ 1937; U.K.; 107m; London Film Productions/UA; B/W; Adventure; Children: Cautionary; **DVD**; **VHS**. This stunning adventure tale set before and during the Russian Revolution and its subsequent civil war, magnificently provides a thrilling adventure tale where many leading players offer superlative performances, including the always mesmerizing Dietrich, the gentle and empathetic Donat and the intense Clements, who starred two years later in the classic adventure tale, **The Four Feathers**, 1939. Dietrich is first seen before WWI as an alluring Russian countess attending the Derby in England, accompanied by her father, Lomas, a nobleman who is in the Czar's cabinet. She is adorned in exquisite finery and her radiant personality draws the attention of the crowd. She later marries Trevor, a wealthy nobleman and a colonel in the Russian army, who is a staunch supporter of the Czar. We next see the quiet Donat applying for a passport to travel to Russia. He is a British interpreter, who speaks and writes fluent Russian and aims to translate Russian books once he arrives in that country. Living in St. Petersburg, Donat writes an article and, after its publication, is summoned by authorities, who tell him that the article has been found offensive to the regime in that it is critical of the way of life as decreed by the Czar, and he is ordered to leave Russia within forty-eight hours. Donat visits an old British friend, Culley, dining with him and is then shocked to learn that Culley is an undercover agent for the British government and where Culley makes a strange proposal to Donat. If Donat volunteers to conduct espionage for England, he will arrange for him to remain in Russia. The idea excites Donat's natural desire for adventure and arouses his British patriotism and he agrees. British spymaster Hanray establishes a new identity and passport for Donat, assigning him to monitor the many left-wing organizations that plot to overthrow the oppressive regime of the Czar. Donat then leads the life of a studious radical, frequenting a bookstore operated by Gill and where many radicals gather, all of whom now look upon Donat as one who shares their political aims. One of those youthful revolutionaries is part of a group that attempts to kill Lomas, Dietrich's father, for

Marlene Dietrich and Robert Donat in *Knight Without Armor,* 1937.

his firm policies against all those who might seek to overthrow the Romanov dynasty. The attempt fails, and the assassin, who is wounded and a friend of Donat's, goes to Donat's room for aid and is later found dead there by hunting police, who arrest Donat. He and his close friend Gill are sentenced to hard labor in Siberia and spend endless, freezing nights in the Russian limbo. He and Gill learn that WWI is now raging in Europe and, in 1917, they hear that a revolution has swept Russia. Revolutionaries overthrow the Czar and Dietrich's husband is killed. She flees to her vast estate at Khalinsk, living inside its resplendent white palace, but one morning she finds all the servants gone and, wearing a flowing morning gown, searches the empty rooms for them, and then runs onto the manicured lawns that slope down to a placid lagoon. She sees one servant on the other side of the lagoon, calling to her, but the servant, seemingly terrified, runs off. When Dietrich turns about, she sees hordes of revolutionaries swarming over the crest of a hill and approaching her. Dietrich defies the hundreds of invaders, who seem thunderstruck at the sight of such a beautiful woman and who represents the aristocracy that has ruled the country for so many decades. (This hesitancy to challenge authority in Russia by simple peasants during the Revolution would later be shown in several scenes in **Doctor Zhivago**, 1965, particularly when a Russian officer leaps upon a barrel of water to address deserting Russian soldiers and implores them to turn about and face the German enemy, almost swaying them back to their duty until a revolutionary in their midst shoots him and he ingloriously collapses into the barrel of water and sinks beyond sight.) When all are reluctant to lay hands upon the defiant Dietrich, a woman steps forward from the crowd to shout: "What's the matter with you? She's only a woman!" Dietrich is seized and dragged back to the palace, locked inside her suite of rooms while the rebels destroy priceless paintings and sculptures in their systematic ransacking of the palace, demonstrating their rage at centuries of oppression. Dietrich spends her time in those rooms listening to the incessant shooting of firing squads who execute servants who have loyally served Dietrich and she starts to become unhinged as she awaits what she believes to be her own impending execution. Meanwhile, Gill has been released in Siberia and has named Donat as a commissar and both arrive in Khalinsk where they attempt to establish order among the arguing revolutionaries. Donat is sent by Gill to Dietrich's estate to retrieve her and take her to Petrograd (the city's name changed from St. Petersburg) so that she can face a tribunal. When Donat arrives at the estate, he finds guards outside Dietrich's rooms and enters her suite to find her sitting in a daze and staring into a mirror at her own disheveled image. Donat tells her to "stand up," and she does, turning to shout insults at him and demanding that she be shot along with her servants. Donat quietly tells her that he is taking her to Petrograd where she will have to face trial. To protect her, he has her dress in peasant attire and

Marlene Dietrich bathing in *Knight Without Armor*, 1937.

he protectively guides her through the shouting and arguing revolutionaries who roam the palace. As he is about to leave with Dietrich in a carriage, the two guards who accompanied him to the estate insist on going along. They then ride the carriage to the local train station. The place is empty. Donat takes Dietrich to a waiting room, loading wood into a stove and lighting this to keep the place warm while he makes Dietrich comfortable. While they wait for a train, Donat tells Dietrich that he is British and he recites an English poem for her. She replies by reciting a Russian poem. His poem is full of hope, and her poem is one of foreboding and gloom. When Donat tells the two guards that they are no longer needed, one of them tries to kill Donat, but Donat shoots the guard, and the other guard, after struggling with Donat, races off on horseback. Then Donat and Dietrich hear Petrie, the station master, calling outside. Petrie walks solemnly outside the station shouting: "Your seats, please! Kazan...Moscow...Petrograd!" Donat goes to Petrie, saying: "I don't see the train." Petrie, who has apparently become deranged with the events of the violent revolution, eerily replies: "Sshhh! Trains that are seen are being blown up." Returning to the waiting room, Donat is puzzled, not knowing what to do until he sees through a window many peasants passing the station. When Donat asks one of the peasants where they are going, he is told that they are fleeing before the White Army, which supports the Czar, is counterattacking the area and has already retaken a nearby town from the revolutionaries. Donat and Dietrich then make their way to the town, and Donat releases Dietrich, encouraging her to rejoin members of her own class, the aristocracy. Dietrich is recognized by the commander of the White troops and she is given a room and new fine clothes. After taking a hot bath and adorning herself in a resplendent gown, Dietrich joins the general and presides over a dinner where the White Army officers celebrate her escape from the revolutionaries. Donat, however, makes his way back to the lines held by the revolutionaries and falls in with a massive Red Army that is marching toward the town to attack the Whites. The city is assailed and captured and Dietrich is again captured. Donat, however, has encountered Malleson, a drunken Russian soldier, who is carrying signed commissions to be handed out to commissars, and Donat obtains one of those commissions that makes him a commissar in charge of prisons and prisoners. Donat uses this to obtain Dietrich's release, and while disguising themselves as Cossacks, they escape. Search parties are then shown hunting them through dense woods and Donat covers Dietrich with leaves, telling her that he will return for her. He joins in with the searchers, leading them away from the spot where Dietrich hides, and then later returns to find Dietrich. When she sees him, she runs into his arms and Donat says: 'What were you thinking? That I wouldn't come back?" He kisses her and she responds in kind, both now knowing they love each other. They spend some peaceful days in the forest and where Dietrich takes

a bath in a small brook. Donat then provides her with peasant clothes he has stolen from a nearby village, along with food and wine. They then leave the forest and join a crowd of peasants who block some railroad tracks with their bodies, stopping an oncoming train. Dietrich and Donat clamber into a boxcar and ride the train to Kazan where they are forced into lines of waiting persons being inspected by several commissars. When Dietrich's hands are inspected, it is realized that she is not a peasant and worker. Donat tells one of the commissars, Clements, that he has not been in the army since he has been taking care of his sister, Dietrich, who has been ill. Clements suspects that Dietrich is an aristocrat, but he is immediately taken by her and when another commissar thinks to condemn Dietrich out of hand, believing her to be the countess they have been looking for, Clements brings forth an elderly man, who had been a gardener at Dietrich's estate. The old man looks at Dietrich and then tells the other commissar that he does not know this woman, and that he is willing to swear to his statements "in front of the altar, comrade." When the commissar expresses his doubts, Clements tells him that he will personally escort Donat and Dietrich to Samara where he will make a report about them. The trio boards a train and rides in a compartment together where Donat and Dietrich share their food with Clements, who is obviously now in love with Dietrich. Clements then confesses that he compelled the gardener to lie in order to save Dietrich. While he is sleeping in an upper berth, Clements sees Donat and Dietrich, who have lower berths, kissing and realizes that they are lovers, not sister and brother and that Dietrich is undoubtedly that much sought-after countess. When the train arrives at Samara, Clements, instead of taking Donat and Dietrich to a revolutionary council, shows them the way to the border. He then walks away from them and shoots himself rather than turning them over to the revolutionaries. Donat and Dietrich then find a barge on the Volga River and sail to safety at a border town controlled by the Whites. Dietrich is hospitalized for exhaustion and later put on board a Red Cross train leaving the country, but Donat, thought to be a Red spy, is placed among a group of other revolutionaries and is about to be executed. He escapes, however, and, when learning that Dietrich is on board that train, leaps aboard the train just as it moves out of the station, shouting Dietrich's name. She hears him and opens the window of her compartment to wave frantically at him as he moves toward the compartment and her opening arms for the fadeout. Feyder directs this sweeping epic with meticulous care and with great vitality in keeping with the traumatic events of the titanic revolution that engulfed Russia. Everything about the film is lavish, from its authentic-looking and majestic sets to its appropriately costumed thousands of extras befitting the period (by Georges Benda). Rozsa's wonderful score thunders, entices and enchants and the acting from Dietrich, Donat and the entire cast is outstanding. Dietrich was never lovelier or more charming and gives a riveting essay of a believable Russian countess, who alternately, as one upheaval after another envelopes her, is haughty and demanding, then frantic and vulnerable. Donat is the perfect British agent, a gentleman playing a deadly game with great restraint and stiff-upper-lip resolve. Although he appears toward the end of the film, Clements renders an unforgettable portrait of a sensitive young revolutionary anguishing over the decision to either betray the cause he serves or the woman he has come to love from afar. ***Author's Note***: Dietrich told this author that she believed this film "to be one of my finest roles. Early in my career, I met a beautiful Russian countess, who had survived the Revolution and lived in exile in Paris. Her family had been slaughtered in front of her eyes by the Bolsheviks, but a high-ranking commissar helped her escape from the country while she carried her jewels, more than a half million pounds, in her undergarments. Every man in Paris was in love with her, but she loved only the past and a dashing Russian colonel, who fought with the Whites and was killed during the Russian Civil War. That woman was in my mind in every scene I played in **Knight Without Armour**, and I looked upon that darling Mr. Donat as that colonel. Mr. Donat had a terrible asthmatic condition that caused several delays of the production and when someone told me that Mr. Korda was thinking of replacing him, I went to Mr. Korda and asked him about that, and he said: 'My dear Miss Dietrich, I would no more replace that great actor than I would you. You are both irreplaceable.'" Dietrich was protective of Donat to the point where she assumed the role of his nurse, doting upon him, and even directing a few scenes with him, one of which she carried about, showing this strip of film to her confidantes and even to Korda. After the great filmmaker saw the scene, he said to Dietrich: "You can direct here any time you want." **p**, Alexander Korda; **d**, Jacques Feyder; **cast**, Marlene Dietrich, Robert Donat, Irene Vanbrugh, John Clements, Herbert Lomas, Austin Trevor, Basil Gill, David Tree, Frederick Culley, Laurence Hanray, Evelyn Ankers, Miles Malleson, Hay Petrie, Peter Bull, Torin Thatcher; **w**, Lajos Biró, Arthur Wimperis, Frances Marion (based on the novel *Without Armour* by James Hilton); **c**, Harry Stradling; **m**, Miklos Rozsa; **ed**, Francis Lyon; **set d**, Lazare Meerson; **spec eff**, Ned Mann, W. Percy Day.

Knights of the Round Table ★★★ 1953; U.S; 115m; MGM; Color; Adventure; Children: Acceptable; **DVD**; **VHS**. Taylor is a standout as the chivalrous Lancelot in this good retelling of the story of England's legendary King Arthur and his valiant knights. Ferrer essays Arthur with nobility and Gardner is the fetching Guinevere. Taylor meets Ferrer in a wooded area and neither will give passage to the other so they joust, but neither can best each other and Taylor, when realizing that Ferrer is the king, swears his undying allegiance to him. He later encounters a rogue knight, who has imprisoned Gardner in his castle, and Taylor jousts with him, defeating him and causing Gardner to be released so that Taylor can escort this bride-to-be to her intended, Ferrer. Taylor loses his heart to Gardner and she loves him, but she also loves Ferrer. Meanwhile, warnings from wizard Merlin (Aylmer) predict evil times to come, and they present themselves in the form of the scheming Crawford and her errant and equally diabolical son, Baker, who do all they can to bring down the idyllic realm of Camelot while the valiant Taylor attempts to stem the rising tide of evil. Thorpe, who, a year earlier, directed Taylor in the sumptuous and stirring **Ivanhoe**, 1952, presents an action-packed medieval drama with stunning period sets and costuming backed up by a memorable score from the gifted composer Rozsa. *Author's Note*: Taylor told this author that "MGM had such a great success with **Ivanhoe** that they immediately planned **Knights of the Round Table** as a follow-up, and it was almost as successful, but I think that the beautiful Ava Gardner had more to do with that than I did. A lot of the sets and costumes from **Ivanhoe** were used for that new picture, but no one noticed that. Their eyes were on Ava." **p**, Pandro S. Berman; **d**, Richard Thorpe; **cast**, Robert Taylor, Ava Gardner, Mel Ferrer, Anne Crawford, Stanley Baker, Felix Aylmer, Maureen Swanson, Laurence Harvey, Patricia Owens, Dana Wynter; **w**, Talbot Jennings, Jan Lustig, Noel Langley (based on *Le morte d'Arthur* by Sir Thomas Malory); **c**, Stephen Dade, Freddie Young (CinemaScope; Technicolor); **m**, Miklos Rozsa; **ed**, Frank Clarke; **art d**, Alfred Junge, Hans Peters; **spec eff**, Tom Howard.

Knock on Any Door ★★★ 1949; U.S.; 100m; Santana Pictures/COL; B/W; Crime Drama; Children: Unacceptable; **DVD**; **VHS**. Bogart does his usual exceptional job in this gritty film noir entry from the gifted director Ray and where Derek is also a standout as a conniving slum youth seemingly without any redeeming qualities. Bogart is an attorney attempting to save Derek's life as he is on trial for killing a policeman, and through Bogart's narration we see in flashback the life of the troubled Derek. We see Derek befriended by Bogart while he is an adolescent and how Bogart and his wife, Perry, at her insistence, take the boy on a fishing outing and where he promptly steals items from them. A petty thief living in a slum, Derek's life is altered when he meets and weds Roberts, whose love rehabilitates him so that he takes a legitimate job. He has a hard time adjusting and moves from one job to another, spending most of his income on gambling in an effort to buy Roberts some expensive jewelry. When she tells him that she is pregnant and

Humphrey Bogart, Barry Kelley and Vince Barnett in *Knock on Any Door*, 1949.

they will have a baby, the emotionally unstable Derek cracks up, obsessed with this new financial obligation. He returns to his old life of thievery, now resolved to living a life of crime and adopting his own credo: "Live fast, die young, and have a good looking corpse." Roberts cannot go on living with a career criminal and commits suicide, ending her life and that of her unborn child. Unhinged by this traumatic event, Derek commits another robbery and, when confronted by cop Sully, empties his gun into the policeman. Bogart is then seen in flash forward when Derek cleverly lies to Bogart, claiming innocence, and Bogart believes him and takes his case. At trial, Derek doggedly maintains his pose of youthful innocence, assuming the role of a victim of society, not an offender, a disguise through which shrewd prosecuting attorney Macready sees. Macready relentlessly hammers Derek on the witness stand, but is unable to wring a confession from him until he asks Derek how his wife has died and the memory of her suicide reaches Derek's conscience. He cracks and then blurts out a confession, which stuns Bogart and seals his client's fate. Bogart delivers an impassioned summation—the longest speech on film the actor ever made—where Bogart points out that Derek, like so many other hapless youths, has been a victim of his terrible environment. "Knock on any door," Bogart intones to the jury, and they will find a youth like Derek, who lives in poverty without a father, who sees his boyhood friends brutalized in a reform schools, who lives in miserable poverty and where the slums in which such youths are raised, more than anything else, have created hardened criminals such as Derek". Eloquent though Bogart is, he cannot save Derek from the electric chair. Bogart is with Derek in his cell, comforting him, before Derek walks to his execution. *Author's Note*: This was Derek's first role as a leading player (he had appeared in a few previous films in minor roles) and his stoic presence and monotone delivery shows his novice inabilities but also enhances the artful character he essays. Old pro Bogart helped the young actor throughout the production by giving him acting tips on timing and line delivery, according to what director Ray told this author. "Bogey took one look at his summation written in the script," Ray told this author, "and then came to me and said: 'I have never delivered a speech that long in my life. Impossible!' I told Bogey: 'Look, we'll try it in rehearsal once or twice, and if you feel that you can't do it, we'll try another approach.' Well, he did it in a full rehearsal and he was perfect. 'I don't know if I can do it again when the camera is rolling,' he said. 'You already did,' I told him. I had a camera running when he did the rehearsal and never told him about it and we had it all in that one great take." Ray would go on to helm in the following year another outstanding film noir production, **In a Lonely Place**, 1950, also starring Bogart. **p**, Robert Lord; **d**, Nicholas Ray; **cast**, Humphrey Bogart, John Derek, George Macready, Allene Roberts, Susan Perry (Candy Toxton), Mickey Knox, Barry Kelley, Dooley Wilson, Cara Willliams,

Danny Kaye and Patricia Denise in *Knock on Wood*, 1954.

Chester Conklin; **w**, Daniel Taradash, John Monks, Jr. (based on the novel by Willard Motley); **c**, Burnett Guffey; **m**, George Antheil; **ed**, Viola Lawrence; **art d**, Robert Peterson; **set d**, William Kiernan.

Knock on Wood ★★★ 1954; U.S.; 103m; PAR; Color; Comedy; Children: Acceptable; **DVD**; **VHS**. Kaye is very funny as a ventriloquist whose wooden dummy develops his own personality, talking when Kaye wants him to be silent, and who randomly insults customers (a humorous twist on the more sinister dummies appearing in such films as **Dead of Night**, 1945, and **Magic**, 1978). Burns, who is Kaye's manager, urges Kay to see psychiatrist Zetterling, and the two begin a romance while two opposing groups try to steal the plans for a new super weapon. The blueprints for this weapon wind up being stuffed inside Kaye's uncontrollable dummy, and Kaye then becomes the prey for these ardent spies, who are chasing him hither and yon. The chase sequences are hilarious, including a scene where Kaye, in an effort to escape the secret agents, joins a Russian ballet troupe performing on stage (not dissimilar to Robert Donat escaping agents pursuing him by impersonating a public speaker at a political rally in Alfred Hitchcock's classic, **The 39 Steps**, 1935). Kaye not only outwits the spies before the finale, but he cures Zetterling of *her* mental maladies before they go to the altar together. This is a fine comedic romp that only the zany and child-like Kaye could make successful, one worth the watching. Songs include (all by Sylvia Fine, who was Kaye's wife): "The Drastic Livid History of Monahan O'Han," "Knock On Wood," and "All About You." *Author's Note*: Kaye told this author that he once talked with mystery director Alfred Hitchcock and mentioned that **Knock on Wood** had all the elements of a Hitchcock thriller, except that it substituted comedy for everything sinister, and that he was playing the same kind of hero seen in Hitchcock's films, an innocent man victimized by circumstances. "Hitch gave me that dour look and lifted an eyebrow and then said: 'Danny, if we had done pictures together, you would have been an enormous success and my career would have been utterly destroyed.'" **p,d&w**, Norman Panama, Melvin Frank; **cast**, Danny Kaye, Mai Zetterling, Torin Thatcher, David Burns, Leon Askin, Abner Biberman, Gavin Gordon, Steven Geray, Diana Adams, Virginia Huston, Henry Brandon; **c**, Daniel Fapp (Technicolor); **m**, Victor Young; **ed**, Alma Macrorie; **art d**, Hal Pereira, Henry Bumstead; **set d**, Sam Comer, Ray Moyer; **spec eff**, Farciot Edouart, John P. Fulton.

Knute Rockne—All American ★★★★ 1940; U.S.; 98m; WB; B/W; Biographical Drama; Children: Acceptable; **DVD**; **VHS**. O'Brien is inspiring as the legendary Knute Rockne (1888-1931), who is considered to be one of the greatest college football coaches of all time. O'Brien is shown in several stages of his youth (as Sheffield, Dawson, Wade and,

as an adult, O'Brien), first coming to the U.S. with his immigrating Norwegian parents Qualen and Tree. O'Brien is shown working for the Chicago *Post*, saving enough money to finish his education before embarking for South Bend, Indiana, to attend Notre Dame University (1910-1913) where he also plays an exceptional end for the football team, and we see the precedent-setting forward pass by Gus Dorais (Davis Jr.) to O'Brien that wins the classic game between Army and Notre Dame. Following graduation, O'Brien finds it hard to choose between a career in chemistry or in football when he is offered the job of assistant coach at Notre Dame. Disappointing professor Basserman, who envisions a great career in chemistry for his star pupil, O'Brien is supported by Crisp, a priest who supervises the university, in O'Brien's decision to go into coaching (while teaching chemistry part-time). After a brief courtship, O'Brien marries Page. Emotionally, O'Brien is also married to Notre Dame and the game of football. We see O'Brien instituting many new tactics to the game, his radical backfield shift (which Rockne got the idea for when watching a line of chorus girls at a musical show), refining the forward pass, and the four great running backs for Notre Dame who were known as the "Four Horseman" (Marshall as Don Miller, Lukats as Harry Stuhldreher, Byrne as James Crowley, and Richmond as Elmer Layden), as well as the school's most legendary player, George Gipp (1895-1920), who became Notre Dame's first All-American football player, and is wonderfully played by Reagan. O'Brien sees Reagan as a reluctant recruit to his team, but his outstanding skills soon make him invaluable to the team's success and his tragic premature death from pneumonia is shown with sensitivity and without soapy sentimentality. Moreover, Reagan delivers one of the most memorable lines of his film career when, before dying, he asks O'Brien to tell the team, when it is facing overwhelming odds in a game to "win one for the Gipper." O'Brien is shown asking his team to win on behalf of Reagan's memory at a half-time meeting when the team is losing to Army (in 1929) and how the team roars back to the field and wins the game in the second half. In one of the many moving scenes in the film, four other legendary real-life football coaches appear with O'Brien in defending football when it is accused of a sport too dangerous to play—Pop Warner (Glen Scobey Warner; 1871-1954), Amos Alonzo Stagg (1862-1965), Howard Jones (1885-1941) and William Spaulding (1880-1966). The finale is a sad one where O'Brien flies off for a business meeting and his plane crashes (Rockne and seven others died when their small passenger plane crashed near Bazaar, Kansas, on March 31, 1931) and where his family members and countless friends assemble at his funeral. Bacon does a great job profiling and developing Rockne's colorful character and life, as well as integrating fascinating and exciting football footage of games involving Notre Dame in the Rockne era. *Author's Note*: O'Brien believed that (according to his statements to this author) "this was one of my best performances if not my very best. I had great material to work with, the life of one of America's greatest human beings, whose name will be remembered as long as the sport of football exists. The finest compliments I received for that role came from those four great coaches who appeared in a sequence with me. All of them told me that my mannerisms and the way I delivered my lines could have come straight out of Rockne's mouth. That was praise, indeed, my boy." Reagan aggressively went after the part of George Gipp, and got the part, even though many other actors were being considered for the role. He showed producers pictures of himself in football attire and insisted that the main reason why he entered college was to play football. He was given a test to show his abilities on the gridiron, and he expected some extras to appear for that test with him. He was amazed when O'Brien appeared in full gear and, after encouraging Reagan for the test, did that test with him, a gesture Reagan never forgot, even when he became President of the U.S. **p**, Jack Warner, Hal B. Wallis; **d**, Lloyd Bacon; **cast**, Pat O'Brien, Gale Page, Ronald Reagan, Donald Crisp, Albert Basserman, John Litel, Henry O'Neill, John Qualen, Johnny Sheffield, Kane Richmond, William Marshall, David Bruce, Owen Davis Jr., Nick Lukats, William Hopper, Dickie Jones, Brian Keith,

George Reeves; **w**, Robert Buckner (based on the private papers of Mrs. Knute Rockne); **c**, Tony Gaudio; **m**, Leo F. Forbstein; **ed**, Robert Haas; **spec eff**, Byron Haskin, Rex Wimpy.

Kolya ★★★ 1997; Czech Republic/U.K./France; 105m; Biograf Jan Sverak/Miramax Films; Color; Comedy; Children: Unacceptable (MPAA: PG-13); **DVD**; **VHS**. This 1996 Academy Award winner for Best Foreign Language Film takes place in 1988 Prague shortly before the end of Soviet rule in Czechoslovakia. It is the story of a middle-aged cellist, Sverák, a bachelor who has a nice apartment in a tower and an eye for the ladies. He dates several women, although most of them are married. He was a member of the Prague Philharmonic until they dropped him, so now he plays funerals to pay his debts. A friend's Russian niece offers him money to marry her so she can obtain Czech papers, and he agrees. After their marriage, the bride flies off to Berlin to be with her lover. Her five-year-old son, Kolya (Chalimon), who only speaks Russian, a language which Sverák refuses to learn, had been in the care of an aunt. When the aunt dies, his mother sends him to live with Sverák. At first, Sverák resents the situation, but gradually begins to love the boy, who loves him in return. They have found places in each other's almost empty hearts while Chalimon emotionally takes care of Sverák as Sverák looks after the boy's physical well-being. The story is touching, beautifully acted and photographed. Some sensual scenes prohibit viewing by children. (In Czech; English subtitles.) **p**, Eric Abraham, Jan Sverák, Ernst Goldschmidt; **d**, Jan Sverák; **cast**, Zdenek Sverák, Andrej Chalimon, Libuse Safránková, Ondrej Vetchý, Stella Zázvorková, Ladislav Smoljak, Irina Bezrukova, Silvia Suvadová, Liliyan Malkina, Karel Hermánek; **w**, Sverák (based on a story by Pavel Taussig); **c**, Vladimír Smutný; **m**, Ondrej Soukup; **ed**, Alois Fisárek; **art d**, Milos Kohout; **spec eff**, Pavel Kryml, Boris Masník, Jirí Simunek, Miroslav Snabl.

Kongo ★★★ 1932; U.S.; 86m; MGM; B/W; Horror; Children: Unacceptable; **DVD**; **VHS**. Huston discards his matinee idol image for a savage brute in this shocking horror film. He lives in a ramshackle house in the Congo where he controls the local tribe through his magical instruments—guns. He further abuses through humiliation and physical violence any white person unlucky enough to make his acquaintance. Huston takes out his seething resentment for having become a cripple on the rest of the world, reserving his most intensive hatred for Gordon, who earlier caused him to lose the use of his legs. Huston hideously drags himself about with powerful arms and spends most of his time trying to ruin the lives of everyone else. He hooks young physician Nagel on drugs, and when Bruce arrives, Huston makes a living hell for her, believing her to be the daughter of his nemesis, Gordon, until, through constant and sadistic insult, accusation and threat, he reduces her to a hysterical woman on the brink of losing her mind. Velez is Huston's slavish companion, masochistically accepting his abuse in order to garner any scrap of emotion from him, grateful even for his hatred and wrath. Gordon then arrives and both men struggle to the death, and where Huston kills his old adversary, but not before Gordon informs him that Bruce is not his daughter, but Huston's. Stunned by this revelation, Huston's bestial nature softens and he attempts to make things right by arranging for Nagel and Bruce to safely leave the area. This will be Huston's last act, one of uncommon kindness, as the natives, who are now enlightened about Huston's vulnerability, close in to bring about a gruesome end for this human monster. This remake of the silent horror film, **West of Zanzibar**, 1928, starring Lon Chaney, holds back nothing evil and sinister and where Huston is the living representative of hell on earth, a truly frightening film not suitable for children or any adult with sensitive feelings. It is further amazing that this one got past MGM boss Louis B. Mayer, who prided himself on producing "family films." **d**, William Cowen; **cast**, Walter Huston, Lupe Velez, Conrad Nagel, Virginia Bruce, C. Henry Gordon, Mitchell Lewis, Forrester Harvey, Curtis Nero, Charles Irwin, Sarah Padden; **w**, Leon Gordon (based

Pat O'Brien, right, in *Knute Rockne—All American*, 1940.

on the play by Chester DeVonde, Kilbourn Gordon); **c**, Harold Rosson; **ed**, Conrad A. Nervig; **art d**, Cedric Gibbons.

Kotch ★★★ 1971; U.S.; 113m; ABC/Cinerama Releasing Corp; Color; Comedy; Children: Unacceptable (MPAA: PG); **DVD**; **VHS**. Solid comedy sees Matthau as a grumpy seventy-two-year-old living in the home of his son, Aidman, and with Farr, his daughter-in-law, and their precocious little boy, played alternately by Donald and Dean Kowalski. Matthau takes care of the baby and does a good job of it, but Farr resents his presence and hires Winters as a babysitter to replace Matthau. When Matthau finds Winters making love with her boyfriend, he tells Farr, who fires Winters. Farr nevertheless believes that Matthau is preempting her authority and wants him out of the house and Aidman takes Matthau to inspect a retirement home, which Matthau rejects as his final living space. Instead, he plans to take a long vacation by bus, believing that by the time he returns, Farr will have a change of mind or heart, or both. Before he leaves, however, Matthau, feeling guilty about having had Winters fired, goes to her and finds her pregnant. He gives her some cash and his apology. She later sends him a postcard, saying goodbye and Matthau searches for her, finding her in Palm Springs. He rents a small house for her and him and she stays there while expecting to give birth. They develop a close bond, but Winters then runs off and Matthau later finds her in a mountain cabin. When she is about to give birth, Matthau tries to get her to a hospital, but Winters begins to give birth and they stop at a gas station where Matthau helps Winters give birth in a rest room. Winters has earlier said that she plans to give the baby to a barren couple, but, after the child is born, Winters again departs with the baby, leaving a note for Matthau to tell him that she intends to keep the child, a decision that pleases Matthau, and the film ends. Matthau does a good job as an old man who thinks to do the right thing beyond his own retirement comforts; the cast members are convincing in their respective roles while Lemmon, directing his only film, does a credible job with a complex and quickly shifting story line. **p**, Richard Carter; **d**, Jack Lemmon; **cast**, Walter Matthau, Deborah Winters, Felicia Farr, Charles Aidman, Ellen Geer, Donald Kowalski, Dean Kowalski, Arlen Stuart, Jane Connell, James E. Brodhead, Jessica Rains, Darrel Larson, Biff Elliot; **w**, John Paxton (based on the novel by Katharine Topkins); **c**, Richard H. Kline (Metrocolor); **m**, Marvin Hamlisch; **ed**, Ralph E. Winters; **art d**, Jack Poplin; **set d**, William Kiernan.

Krakatoa: East of Java ★★★ 1969; U.S.; 131m; Cinerama Productions; Color; Adventure; Children: Cautionary (MPAA: PG); **DVD**; **VHS**. In this exciting disaster film involving the titanic volcanic explosion of Krakatoa in 1883, Schell is seen sailing a ship with diverse passengers in search of a vessel containing a fortune in jewels sunken near

Dustin Hoffman and Justin Henry in *Kramer vs. Kramer,* 1979.

that doomed island. On board is Baker, who is the widow of the captain of the lost ship, and Keith, a diver looking for adventure and wealth, as well as balloonists Brazzi and Mineo, diving bell captain Leyton, and Chan, who has brought along a group of female Japanese divers. Moreover, a gang of convicted criminals is on board and en route to prison, and, led by Cannon, these felons take over the ship, but Schell and his crew subdue them and set them adrift in lifeboats. Meanwhile the divers recover the safe from the sunken ship, but find it empty except for a log that tells Baker what she really wants to know, the whereabouts of her son, who was placed by her errant husband in the care of those operating a Catholic orphanage on the island of Krakatoa. Just then the long dormant volcano begins to erupt and the inhabitants, including all those from the orphanage flee, finding safety when Schell picks them up. Baker's son is among these fugitives and he gives Baker the long-sought pearls her husband gave to the boy, and Baker then generously divides the jewels with the passengers just as the volcano erupts, blowing the island to pieces and sending a huge seismic sea wave after the retreating ship. The passengers lash themselves down on the ship, which is eventually engulfed by the wave, but the vessel survives the cascading waters and the fortune seekers live to see another dawn. The story line is a bit crowded, but director Kowalski does a good job in giving a bevy of separate actors some decent character development, and the special effects of the exploding island and the resulting tremendous seismic sea wave are eye-popping and are the highlights of this action-packed adventure tale. The formula employed here is not dissimilar to **Grand Hotel**, 1932, and **Ship of Fools**, 1965, but nevertheless works well. **p**, William R. Forman; **d**, Bernard L. Kowalski; **cast**, Maximilian Schell, Diane Baker, Brian Keith, Sal Mineo, Rossano Brazzi, Barbara Werle, John Leyton, J.D. Cannon, Geoffrey Holder, Peter Graves; **w**, Clifford Newton Gould, Bernard Gordon; **c**, Manuel Berenguer (Cinerama; Technicolor); **m**, Frank De Vol; **ed**, Walter Hannemann, Warren Low, Maurice Rootes; **prod d**, Eugene Lourie; **art d**, Julio Molina, Luis Peréz Espinosa; **set d**, Antonio Mateos; **spec eff**, Lourie, Alex Weldon.

Kramer vs. Kramer ★★★★ 1979; U.S.; 105m; COL; Color; Drama; Children: Cautionary (MPAA: PG); **DVD**; **VHS**. Hoffman (Oscar for Best Actor) is superb in this captivating domestic drama as an art director working for an ad agency in New York City, who is married to Streep (Oscar, Best Supporting Actress), and who suddenly announces that she is leaving him so that she can "find herself." In that search for her identity, the self-serving Streep leaves her small son, Henry, in Hoffman's care, and the stress of taking care of his son causes him to lose a major account and, eventually, his job. Worse, Streep resurfaces and is now suing Hoffman for the custody of the child she abandoned. Streep can afford the lawsuit and expects to win the case, and where her high pay-

ing job will easily allow her to keep Henry at an expensive daycare center. Esteemed attorney Duff is hired by Hoffman and his first advice to Hoffman is to get a job if he expects to win the case and keep Henry. Hoffman manages to get that job, but at a small agency and where he is not making the kind of salary he earlier enjoyed, but it is, nevertheless, a job. When he goes to court, however, and despite the facts in the case, Streep is awarded custody of Henry (as is mostly the result in such cases where the courts invariably favor the mother). In a tearful farewell, Hoffman patiently and lovingly tells Henry that he will not be living with him anymore. Streep's cold heart melts at this scene, and she changes her mind, saying that she will allow Henry to live with Hoffman for a happy fadeout. The superlative performances in an otherwise pedestrian story line, as well as many priceless scenes, such as where Hoffman puts his foot down while trying to get Henry to eat the proper food, makes this film immensely worth the watching, and the interaction between all the principals is marvelously directed by writer Benton. **p**, Stanley R. Jaffe; **d&w**, Robert Benton (based on the novel by Avery Corman); **cast**, Dustin Hoffman, Meryl Streep, Jane Alexander, Justin Henry, Howard Duff, George Coe, JoBeth Williams, Bill Moor, Howland Chamberlain, Jack Ramage; **c**, Nestor Almendros (Panavision; Technicolor); **m**, Henry Purcell, Antonio Vivaldi; **ed**, Jerry Greenberg; **prod d**, Paul Sylbert; **set d**, Alan Hicks.

The Krays ★★★ 1990; U.K.; 119m; Fugitive Features/Miramax; Color; Crime Drama; Children: Unacceptable (MPAA: R); **VHS**. In this absorbing and brutal crime yarn, Gary and Martin Kemp play two of England's real-life arch criminals, twins known as The Krays. Ronald "Ronnie" Kray (1933-1995), played by Gary Kemp, and Reginald "Reggie" Kray (1933-2000), played by Martin Kemp, are the leaders of British organized crime in the 1950s and 1960s, practicing arson, armed robbery, murder and operating assorted rackets in London's East End while operating nightclubs in the tony districts of London's West End. The film depicts their being raised by a dominating mother, Whitelaw, and how they easily involve themselves in crime until they are heading the worst and most dangerous criminal gang in London. While profiling their vicious crimes, neither shows remorse or regret and where Gary Kemp is the more lethal of the two and who dominates Martin Kemp, who more or less follows his brother's orders, finding some relief by marrying, but even that union cannot save him from the eventual long arm of the law. They are shown arrested and convicted on many charges of racketeering and sentenced to life in prison. The Kemp brothers do a good job in essaying these thugs as does Whitelaw as the overly protective and dominating mother who undoubtedly contributed largely in developing the twisted personalities of these criminally bent twins. **p**, Dominic Anciano, Ray Burdis, Stuart St. Paul; **d**, Peter Medak; **cast**, Gary Kemp, Martin Kemp, Billie Whitelaw, Tom Bell, Susan Fleetwood, Charlotte Cornwell, Kate Hardie, Avis Bunnage, Alfred Lynch, Gary Love; **w**, Philip Ridley; **c**, Alex Thomson (Technicolor); **m**, Michael Kamen; **ed**, Martin Walsh; **prod d**, Michael Pickwoad; **art d**, Michael Buchanan; **spec eff**, Ken Lailey.

The Kremlin Letter ★★★ 1970; U.S.; 120m; FOX; Color; Spy Drama; Children: Unacceptable; **DVD**. An unauthorized letter by a U.S. government official saying that America will support the Soviet Union if China acquires the atomic bomb falls into the hands of a Russian agent, and U.S. intelligence agents try to retrieve it. The agent, who has a history of selling Soviet secrets to America, is captured by a colonel, von Sydow, of the Soviet counterintelligence agency, and commits suicide. O'Neal, a U.S. Naval intelligence officer who has a photographic memory and speaks eight different languages with the correct accents, is assigned to a team to recover the letter. His superior, Boone, tells him to contact three other members of the group, who will help him, one of them being a woman, Parkins. O'Neal, however, first undergoes spy training, before going into the field, employing various dirty and dangerous tricks. In one such incident, the family of the head of Soviet counterintelligence, Radd, is taken hostage by U.S. agents, and he is blackmailed for their safe return. A Soviet politician, Welles, then informs a Soviet agent, Andersson, about the inhumane nature of her husband, von Sydow, describing how he slaughtered an entire village of innocent people in order to obtain information. The U.S. spy team sets up surveillance in a Moscow apartment to watch von Sydow's movements. While working in such close quarters, O' Neal and Parkins fall in love. She is captured by Welles, an enemy of von Sydow's, and then O'Neal learns that Welles is a traitor to the Soviets. Meanwhile, the sensitive letter has already been delivered to officials in China. It is revealed that Boone is a double agent working for Welles. Boone then murders both Andersson and von Sydow before he gets his comeuppance. The acting from the entire cast is exceptional, and the convoluted tale with its seemingly myriad subplots nevertheless holds attention throughout. *Author's Note*: Welles told this author that "**The Kremlin Letter** is a very complex story, but anyone who knows anything about espionage knows that that 'Great Game,' as they call it, is one where you fall through one false box into another and then another. Some spies spend their entire lives never knowing all the elements of a case they have worked on, only their end of things. That would leave them terribly frustrated if they had the time to think about it, but they have no time, as people just like them, who know as little as they do, are trying to kill them." **p**, Carter DeHaven, Sam Wiesenthal; **d**, John Huston; **cast**, Bibi Andersson, Richard Boone, Nigel Green, Dean Jagger, Lila Kedrova, Micheál MacLiammóir, Patrick O'Neal, Barbara Parkins, George Sanders, Raf Vallone, Max von Sydow, Orson Welles; **w**, Huston, Gladys Hill (based on the novel by Noel Behn); **c**, Ted Scaife; **m**, Robert Drasnin; **ed**, Russell Lloyd; **prod d**, Ted Haworth; **art d**, Elven Webb; **set d**, Dario Simoni.

Kronos ★★★ 1957; U.S.; 78m; Regal Films/FOX; B/W; Science Fiction; Children: Cautionary; **DVD**; **VHS**. A metal space alien, Kronos, arrives on a California beach. Traveling eastward, it soaks up energy along the way, augmented by taking over the mind of scientist Emery, a personality change that troubles his colleague, Morrow. Kronos gets larger as it absorbs more energy and grows to become 100 feet tall. Morrow, who is clever with electricity, finds a way to short-circuit the monster. That makes it suck up its own energy and it vanishes. Typical of alien invasion films of the 1950s, this film is nevertheless clever enough to entertain. **p**, Kurt Neumann, Irving Block, Jack Rabin, Louis DeWitt; **d**, Neumann; **cast**, Jeff Morrow, Barbara Lawrence, John Emery, George O'Hanlon, Morris Ankrum, Kenneth Alton, John Parish, Jose Gonzales-Gonzales; Richard Harrison, Robert Shayne; **w**, Lawrence Louis Goldman (based on a story by Block); **c**, Karl Struss; **m**, Paul Sawtell, Bert Shefter; **ed**, Jodie Copelan; **prod d**, Theobold Holsopple; **set d**, Walter M. Scott; Chester Bayhi; **spec eff**, Rabin, Block, DeWitt, William Reinhold, Menrad von Mulldorfer, Gene Warren, Wah Chang.

Kundun ★★★ 1997; U.S.; 128m; De Fina-Cappa/Buena Vista; Color; Biography/Drama; Children: Unacceptable (MPAA: PG-13); **DVD**; **VHS**. This biopic of the 14th Dalai Lama of Tibet, who is referred to in Tibetan language as "Kindun" or "The Presence" provides an absorbing character study of this legendary religious leader. His life story begins in 1937 when he was discovered at the age of two (Paichang) in a Tibetan village near the Chinese border. Two years later, he is taken from his parents to the capital city of Lhasa where he begins his schooling and Buddhist spiritual training. When he learns of the Chinese communist threat to take over his country, he writes to U.S. President Harry Truman for help, but gets no reply. As a teenager, Kundun (Tethong) travels to Beijing and meets with Mao Zedong (Lin), who attempts to browbeat him, shouting that "religion is the opiate of the people." Kundun returns to Lhasa, but, in 1969, China crushes a Tibetan revolt and takes over the mountainous country, forcing its Buddhist spiritual leader (Tsarong) to flee to India for sanctuary. Beautifully photographed and well acted, the film's violence prohibits viewing by children. **p**, Barbara

Tulku Jamyang Kunga Tenzin and Lobsang Samten in *Kundun*, 1997.

De Fina, Melissa Mathison, Jeanne Stack; **d**, Martin Scorsese; **cast**, Tenzin Thuthob Tsarong, Gyurme Tethong, Tulku Jamyang Kunga Tenzin, Tenzin Yeshi Paichang, Tencho Gyalpo, Tenzin Topjar, Tsewang Migyur Khangsar, Tenzin Lodoe, Geshi Yeshi Gyatso, Gyatso Lukhang; **w**, Mathison; **c**, Roger Deakins; **m**, Philip Glass; **ed**, Thelma Schoonmaker; **prod d**, Dante Ferretti; **art d**, Alan Tomkins, Franco Ceraolo, Massimo Razzi; **set d**, Francesca Lo Schiavo; **spec eff**, Kevin Hannigan.

Kung Fu Panda ★★★ 2008; U.S.; 90m; DreamWorks Animation; PAR; Color; Animated Feature; Children: Cautionary (MPAA: PG); **BD**; **DVD**. Lovable and cuddly, the animal protagonist of this entertaining entry is lazy panda Po Ping (Black voiceover), who works haphazardly in his parents' noodle restaurant and is a big fan of Kung Fu, and who would rather spend his time at the nearby stadium for the Dragon Warrior Kung Fu competition. By accident, he finds himself in the center of the arena at the stadium. He joins the world of the martial arts and studies with his idols including the legendary Furious Five including aggressive Tigress (Angelina Jolie voiceover), wise-cracking Mantis (Rogen voiceover), Viper (Liu voiceover), Monkey (Chan voiceover), who are all led by Master Shifu (Hoffman). Enter the evil snow leopard Tai Lung (McShane), and where the courageous Po Ping defends everyone from this dangerous creature. Po Ping puts his King Fu skills to the test and defeats the leopard in a spectacular martial arts display. Song: "Kung Fu Fighting" (Carl Douglas; sung by Black, Cee-Lo Green). **p**, Melissa Cobb, Jonathan Aibel, Glenn Berger; **d**, John Stevenson, Mark Osborne; **cast** (voiceovers), Jack Black, Dustin Hoffman, Angelina Jolie, Ian McShane, Jackie Chan, Seth Rogen, Lucy Liu, David Cross, Randall Duk Kim, James Hong; **w**, Aibel, Berger (based on a story by Ethan Reiff, Cyrus Voris); **c**, Yong Duk Jhun; **m**, Hans Zimmer, John Powell; **ed**, Clare De Chenu (Clare Knight); **prod d**, Raymond Zibach; **art d**, Tang Kheng Heng; **spec eff**, April Lawrence (April Struebing), Jonathan R. Cummings, James Cockerham.

Kung Fu Panda 2 ★★★ 2011; U.S.; 91m; DreamWorks Animation; PAR; Color; Animated Feature; Children: Cautionary (MPAA: PG); **BD**, **DVD**. The chubby and lovable panda Po Ping (Black voiceover) is back and is now a protective guard called the Dragon Warrior whose job is to protect his fellow Kung Fu friends in the Valley of Peace. The evil Lord Shen of Gongman City (Oldman voiceover) threatens to destroy the valley with a new weapon of mass destruction. It takes place back in the age of the discovery of gunpowder and fireworks as well as the building of cannon in China. Po and his pals have their King Fu work cut out for them. Returning characters are the Furious Five including aggressive Tigress (Jolie voiceover), wise-cracking Mantis (Rogen voiceover), Viper (Liu voiceover), Monkey (Chan voiceover), and Mas-

Po, the martial arts panda in *Kung Fu Panda*, 2008.

ter Shifu (Hoffman). Plenty of entertaining action can be seen in this above-average animation outing. **p**, Melissa Cobb, Jonathan Aibel, Glenn Berger, Suzanne Buirgy; **d**, Jennifer Yuh Nelson; **cast** (voiceovers), Jack Black, Angelina Jolie, Dustin Hoffman, Gary Oldham, Jackie Chan, Seth Rogan, Jean-Claude Van Damme, Victor Garber, Lucy Liu, David Cross, James Hong, Michelle Yeoh, Denis Haysbert; **w**, Aibel, Berger; **m**, Jon Powell, Hans Zimmer; **ed**, Maryann Brandon, Clare Knight; **prod d**, Raymond Zibach; **art d**, Tang Kheng Heng; **spec eff**, Alex Parkinson.

Kwaidan ★★★★ 1965; Japan; 125m (U.S. release; 161m for Japanese release); Bungei/Continental Distributing; Color; Fantasy/Horror; Children: Unacceptable; **DVD**; **VHS**. Fantasy-horror fans will enjoy this entry that presents four intriguing episodes (three for U.S. viewers) from the gifted Kobayashi, all of these haunting tales written by the brilliant Hearn, an American writer, who made Japan his home in 1890. Mikuni stars in the first episode, entitled "Black Hair," and where he is a samurai, abandoning his wife Aratama to marry Watanabe. Enduring many years of emotional abuse from Watanabe's selfish conduct, Mikuni decides to preserve his peace of mind by returning to the docile and loving Aratama. He finds her at night and sleeps next to her, only to discover to his shock and horror when awakening the next morning that she is dead and the revelation unhinges his mind. Katsuo Nakamura is featured in the second episode, "Hoichi the Earless," and where he is a blind musician performing in a temple and where he is known for his ballads, especially one that exalts the Heike clan, despite the fact that that clan suffered a disastrous defeat in a sea battle in 1185. One night, the ghost of a samurai warrior asks Nakamura to sing for a deceased child of the royal class. After Nakamura renders the song, the temple priests conclude that the singer is spiritually possessed, and they paint Nakamura's body with holy scenes, but they overlook his ears. Those unprotected ears are then lopped off by the returning samurai ghost. This spiritual mutilation, however, strangely enriches Nakamura's miserable life. When he recovers from his bloodied experience, he makes a fortune by recounting his ghostly experiences to wealthy, enthralled listeners. In the third episode, "A Cup of Tea," Ganemon Nakamura sits quietly sipping a cup of tea when he sees the face of another samurai glaring back at him from inside the cup, but he pretends the apparition does not exist. When the face reappears in a second cup of tea, Nakamura quickly drinks down the tea. The samurai again appears that night and attacks him, but Nakamura wounds the assailant and drives him away. The next night, three samurai appear, seeking revenge for their wounded comrade and they, too, attack Nakamura, who manages to drive them off and he is left to wonder, as is the viewer, if these warriors will continue to multiply in seeking relentless revenge until he is over-

come. In the fourth and final episode, "The Woman of the Snow" (edited out of the American release) two woodcutters are trapped by a blizzard and confined to a crude cabin. A female ghost appears as the Snow Witch, and kills one of the woodcutters. She allows the other woodcutter to survive, but only on the provision that he never tell anyone what has occurred. The woodcutter later marries and settles down, telling his wife in detail about the death of his fellow woodcutter in the cabin. The wife then tells him that she knows the story well as she is the Snow Witch! Eerie and compelling, these ghost tales are shown in careful detail, and subtly challenge, as was Hearn's wont in expressing his Western values, the male chauvinism that has dominated Japanese culture for centuries. (In Japanese; English subtitles.) **p**, Shigeru Wakatsuki; **d**, Masaki Kobayashi; **cast**, Rentarô Mikuni, Michiyo Aratama, Misako Watanabe, Katsuo Nakamura, Ganjirô Nakamura, Takashi Shimura, Joichi Hayashi, Kan'emon Nakamura, Noboru Nakaya, Tetsuro Tanba; **w**, Yôko Mizuki (based on stories by Lafcadio Hearn); **c**, Yoshio Miyajima (Tohoscope; Eastmancolor); **m**, Tôru Takemitsu; **ed**, Hisashi Sagara; **art d**, Shigemasa Toda.

L. A. Confidential ★★★★★ 1997; U.S.; 138m; Regency Enterprises/Wolper/WB; Color; Crime Drama; Children: Unacceptable; **DVD**; **VHS**. Superb latter-day film noir tale profiles members of a corrupt LAPD working in collusion with a columnist for a Hollywood gossip magazine to control organized crime in the city in 1953. The film opens with LAPD detectives Crowe and Beckel answering a call about domestic violence at Yuletide. Crowe leaves an unmarked car and stands outside a bungalow listening to a brutish man verbally abusing his wife. Crowe yanks the Christmas adornments from the top of the porch of the house, which draws the man outside where Crowe roughhouses and cuffs him while telling the wife to seek shelter elsewhere until her husband is jailed, early on establishing Crowe's devout hatred for woman-beaters. Beckel, who is more interested in having a good time, tells his partner that they have to pick up some Christmas booze for the seasonal party at police headquarters. Crowe is next seen buying liquor at a small store where he sees beautiful Basinger picking up an order and is instantly attracted to her. When he follows her outside, he sees Smith, a woman sitting in the back of a car with bandages over her nose and whose eyes have been blackened. The man sitting next to the woman, Strathairn, her wealthy sponsor, tells Crowe that everything is all right as does Basinger when getting into the car. The driver, Sandeen, jumps from the car and tries to roust Crowe, but Crowe strong-arms him, pinning Sandeen to the back of the car, examining his identification and taking a gun from him. Sandeen tells him he has a permit to carry the weapon and that he is an ex-cop; Crowe lets him go, returns to his car and drives off with Beckel. Meanwhile, at police headquarters, several Mexican Americans arrive under arrest with detectives shouting that they are responsible for attacking a policeman. Pearce, a sergeant in charge of the desk and the son of a legendary LAPD detective, is approached by detective Spacey, slipping him some payoff money, which Pearce refuses to accept, Spacey being one of many detectives taking payoffs, in this case money he receives from DeVito, a writer for *Hush-Hush Magazine* (based upon *Confidential Magazine*, a celebrity gossip periodical of that day) and who exposes Hollywood scandals in his column. When Crowe and Beckel arrive at headquarters and are told about the arrest of the men who attacked a police officer, the hot-headed Beckel leads other detectives into the lockup area and they are followed by two newspaper men where they witness a wild attack on the prisoners by Beckel, Crowe, Spacey and others and where Pearce vainly tries to stop the mayhem. The police melee is caught on camera when the newsmen photograph the brawl, which results in another LAPD scandal and where LAPD hierarchy is compelled to take punitive action against several of the detectives. Pearce agrees to testify against the offenders, after appearing before a tribunal made up of Police Chief Mahon, LAPD Captain and Chief of Detectives Cromwell, and L.A. District Attorney Rifkin. Crowe refuses to identify those in the brawl and he is suspended, and where he turns over his badge and gun. Spacey, threatened with suspension and where he will no longer be the LAPD adviser to a popular TV show, "Badge of Honor," about the LAPD (based upon the TV series "Dragnet"), a moonlighting job that has made him a minor film industry celebrity, shows his conniving nature by agreeing to identify his fellow detectives. Beckel and others are forced to resign their posts, and Pearce is rewarded for his honesty by being promoted to the rank of lieutenant and, at his request, is posted to the detective bureau, even though Cromwell tries to talk Pearce into going into another LAPD division. Pearce is not welcomed in that post as many of the veteran detectives consider him an informant and turncoat. While Pearce is on duty late at night and alone in the detective squad room, he receives a call telling him that there has been a violent robbery at a small downtown restaurant, the Night Owl. Pearce reports to the dispatcher that he will personally take the case and arrives at the seedy restaurant, telling the beat cop on duty to seal off the area while he investigates. Pearce enters the place to find the counterman dead from gunshots and blood stains everywhere. He follows a running bloodstain to a rest room in back of the place and there discovers several bodies, all shot to death, including Smith and detective Beckel. Cromwell then arrives and Pearce tells him that he is in charge of the case, but Cromwell, his superior, insists that he take over the case, making Pearce his second-in-command. While an investigation into this mass murder and robbery ensues, Cromwell summons the suspended Crowe to a meeting at a restaurant where he returns his gun and badge to him after Crowe agrees to take on a "special assignment," which consists of beating confessions out of out-of-town gangsters, who are attempting to take over rackets from deposed L.A. gangster Mickey Cohen (Guilfoyle). Meanwhile, Pearce is present when Smith's mother, Deacon, identifies her daughter at the morgue after seeing a birthmark on her body, having had difficulty in first making an identification since the young woman's facial features have been altered. Crowe also sees Deacon make the identification after he sees the body of his partner, Beckel, on a gurney at the morgue. Spacey, meanwhile, has been reassigned to the narcotics division, although he keeps his hand in with DeVito, feeding him tips about impending arrests of minor Hollywood figures dealing with illicit affairs and drug use. He tips DeVito to his arrest of Baker, a young actor, and who later introduces Baker to D.A. Rifkin, a practicing homosexual. After Spacey finds Baker brutally murdered, his throat slit in a cheap motel, Spacey sets out to identify Baker's killer. Meanwhile, three young black men are arrested and brought in for questioning as they are thought to be the killers involved in the Night Owl slayings after they are arrested by Pearce and Spacey. Pearce questions them relentlessly and learns that a young girl is being held as a sex slave by another black criminal, and police close in on the culprit's residence with Crowe entering the upstairs apartment where he finds the girl tied to a bed. He then finds her captor, a huge black man, sitting half naked while watching a cartoon show on TV in the front room, and Crowe, who finds any abuse to women intolerable, shoots and kills the man, planting a "throwaway" gun in the man's hand before other officers arrive. Pearce challenges the way in which the culprit died and he and Crowe must be separated by Cromwell to avoid a violent confrontation, Cromwell telling Pearce that he should not disturb Crowe when "his blood is up," and Pearce replies that "his blood is always up." Meanwhile, the three blacks held for the Night Owl killings escape, and Pearce, accompanied by one other detective, tracks them down to a hideout where Pearce uses a shotgun to shoot several of the fugitives and becomes a police hero, given a medal for his valor. Still, Pearce is unconvinced that the men he has killed were not necessarily involved in the Night Owl murders and probes further, getting Spacey's help. At one point, Spacey asks Pearce why he became a policeman and he explains how his father had been murdered by a felon never apprehended.

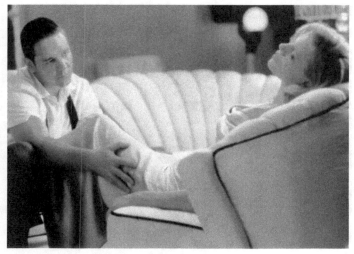

Russell Crowe and Kim Basinger in *L.A. Confidential*, 1997.

Pearce, as a boy, called the killer "Rollo Tomassi," a name he gives to those who "get away with it," and it is felons like that person, who prompted Pearce to become a cop. Meanwhile, Crowe is obsessively drawn to Basinger, establishing a relationship with her after he learns that she is a high-class call girl working for Strathairn, who operates a prostitution ring where his girls have been selected so that they look like Hollywood movie stars, and that included Smith, whose facial injuries had been made by plastic surgery that altered her appearance so that she would look like Hollywood actress Rita Hayworth. Pearce and Spacey investigate Strathairn, but with little result and Crowe and Pearce, in unrelated visits to the home of Smith's mother, Deacon, find the body of Sandeen, who had been Smith's boyfriend, rotting in the basement of her house, another inexplicable murder. While further investigating Strathairn, Pearce visits Basinger, and she makes love to him, even though she is emotionally committed to Crowe. Meanwhile, Spacey has learned that Sandeen and Beckel have been killed after they have been taking over the drug trafficking from the departed Guilfoyle and his lieutenant, Johnny Stompanato (Seganti), and when he goes to Cromwell's residence to tell him that he has learned that both of these errant detectives have had close dealings with him, Cromwell shoots and kills Spacey out of hand. When Cromwell sadistically asks if Spacey has any dying words to leave to the world, Spacey grimly smiles and says before dying: "Rollo Tomassi." It is now evident that Cromwell has betrayed his police office by secretly taking over Cohen's rackets with the aid of a number of venal LAPD detectives and with the support of wealthy Strathairn and columnist DeVito. Cromwell has DeVito brought in for a third-degree interrogation at the deserted motel where Crowe manhandles him, and where DeVito makes sure that Crowe knows that Basinger has had sex with Pearce. Crowe explodes and leaves to search for Pearce and, as Cromwell hopes, to kill him, thus eliminating another detective probing into his underworld affairs. Cromwell then kills DeVito. Crowe then confronts Basinger and she admits having had sex with Pearce and Crowe violates his own credo by viciously hitting her and causing her beautiful face (which has not been altered by plastic surgery to make her look like film star Veronica Lake) to be marked by bruises. He then, still enraged, seeks out Pearce. Pearce by then has, as Spacey before him, discovered Cromwell's underworld operations, becoming suspicious when Cromwell mentions the name "Rollo Tomassi," a name Pearce has uttered only to Spacey, whose body has been found and whose murder is being personally investigated by Cromwell, the very man who murdered him. Crowe then finds Pearce in the archives office of the LAPD offices and attacks him. Pearce stops him by telling him that Cromwell has turned Crowe against him to stop him from identifying the real Night Owl killers, whom, he believes, is Cromwell and a group of de-

Kim Basinger with an Oscar for her role in *L.A. Confidential,* **1997.**

tectives who have helped Cromwell take over the L.A. rackets. They agree to work together and they then find Strathairn dead in his lavish residence. They go to Rifkin and the D.A. orders them from his office and where he is confronted by the death of actor Baker. When Rifkin sloughs off the murder of that young man, Crowe shoves Rifkin's head into a toilet before dangling him from the window of his high-rise office. (This is an illegal interrogation technique first practiced by agents in the Chicago office of the FBI in the early 1930s, as depicted in this author's book, *Citizen Hoover: A Critical Study of J. Edgar Hoover and His FBI,* published by Nelson-Hall, 1972.) Fearing he may fall to his death, Rifkin screams out a confession that he has been blackmailed by Cromwell into helping him take over all the rackets in the city. Then both Crowe and Pearce are separately summoned to the deserted motel, which has been Cromwell's secret headquarters, and they both realize that they have been set up as a bevy of corrupt police detectives led by Cromwell close in on them. They barricade themselves in one of the small motel bungalows and a wild firefight ensues where Pearce and Crowe shoot and kill several of the detectives turned assassins. Both are wounded before Cromwell arrives to point a gun at the injured Pearce, who repeats the name "Rollo Tomassi" to him, and when Cromwell asks who that person is, Pearce tells Cromwell that he is that man, the person "who gets away with it." Before Cromwell can kill Pearce, Crowe revives and drives a knife into Cromwell's leg. Cromwell shoots the already wounded Crowe, but Pearce grabs a weapon and trains it on Cromwell, who then surrenders. When they hear police sirens indicating the approach of patrol cars, Cromwell and Pearce step from the bungalow and Cromwell tells Pearce to hold up his badge so that the approaching cops "will know you are a policeman." Pearce shoots and kills the utterly corrupt Cromwell and then holds up his badge as police squad cars drive toward him. Pearce is then shown being questioned by Police Chief Mahon and D.A. Rifkin, where Pearce reveals the motives and persons behind all the killings and tells them that, for the LAPD to recover its good name, it needs more than one hero (one more than himself) to regain its reputation and he is later shown receiving another award for heroism while newspapers blare a false story that Cromwell died a hero in suppression of police corruption. At the finale, Pearce says farewell to Basinger, who tells him that she is going off on a vacation with Crowe, who sits recovering from his wounds in the back seat of a car and who shakes hands with Pearce before Basinger drives that car away and Pearce looks after it. Hanson's stunning direction marvelously reveals three divergent stories—that of Crowe, Pearce and Spacey—into a cohesive tale where all the missing pieces of this intriguing puzzle come cleverly and effectively into place. The acting from the principals, all relatively unknowns when the film was made, is superb and where the fetching

Basinger as the hooker with a heart captivates with great empathy, poignantly conveying her small world that postures a synthetic lifestyle as grand and glamorous. This is symbolized by her well-appointed bungalow where she conducts her assignations, and where her boudoir is luxurious with an inviting king-sized bed, but when she takes Crowe as her true lover, she leads him to a single bed in a small room littered with the faded childhood keepsakes of yesteryear, her true identity beyond the Hollywood impersonation of her tawdry profession. She deservedly won an Oscar as Best Supporting Actress. The sets, props and costumes are superbly matched to the era of the early 1950s, and the Oscar-nominated score from Goldsmith, one of his best, also nostalgically captures those melodic times when Hollywood's golden era was already slipping into a conveniently remembered past. The script (Oscar for Best Screenplay) bristles with streetwise wit, particularly from the artful Spacey, and the conniving Cromwell (in his finest character portrayal). **L. A. Confidential** is a great salute to the film noir classics of the 1940s and early 1950s, but stands on its own in telling its unique story where the city of Los Angeles is the star. The underbelly of that city is shown through the ostensibly respectable but seamy Strathairn, who, on one hand, is running a lucrative string of prostitutes, and, on the other hand, publicly advocating the launching of the city's freeways for the betterment of his fellow human beings, but for self-serving purposes. By combining Hollywood and prostitution via hookers made to look like Hollywood female stars, as well as showing the relationship between real-life actress Lana Turner (Bakke) and Johnny Stompanato (Seganti)—and a bit of offbeat humor is shown when Pearce cannot tell the difference between a hooker as an ersatz star and the real actress—the hovering and sinister influence of the underworld is cemented to that film industry, evoking the memory of **The Godfather**, 1972, where the Mafia intrudes into Hollywood hierarchy and, obliquely, through Strathairn's posturing as a wealthy L.A. civic leader, mirrors the corrupt civic leader portrayed by John Huston in **Chinatown**, 1974, as well as the L.A. rackets being taken over in the 1930s-1940s by New York City gangster Benjamin "Bugsy" Siegel (1906-1947) as shown in the film, **Bugsy**, 1991. The film's $34 million budget was recouped within a year with worldwide returns exceeding $600 million. ***Author's Note***: The basis for the L.A. police corruption profiled in this riveting film is rooted to the notorious administration of L.A. mayor Frank Shaw (1887-1958) and where corrupt elements of the LAPD worked hand and glove with underworld figures in running the city's rackets until some leading citizens, including former LAPD detective Harry Raymond (his car was blown up by members of the LAPD Intelligence Squad and he was almost killed) led a massive reform movement that saw Shaw recalled and the department wholly revamped with civic-minded officers at the helm. Organized crime had, by that time in the 1930s, reached into the deep pockets of movie moguls through gangster Willie Bioff (William Morris Bioff, 1900-1955), who controlled the International Alliance of Theatrical Stage Employees and Motion Picture Operators, and who extorted millions of dollars each year from studio chiefs on the threat of closing down movie theaters or, chiefly, the projectionists running films in those theaters. Bioff was murdered when his car was rigged with explosives and blew up after he started that car on November 4, 1955, in revenge for Bioff's court testimony against mob bosses in that massive Hollywood extortion racket. For more details on Mickey Cohen, Siegel, Bioff and the L.A. rackets and elements of the corrupt LAPD of the period, as well as the Lana Turner-Johnny Stompanato affair, see my book, *World Encyclopedia of Organized Crime* (Paragon House, 1992; Bioff: page 50; Cohen: pages 106-107; Shaw: pages 361-362; Benjamin "Bugsy" Siegel: pages 363-368) and my two-volume work, *The Great Pictorial History of World Crime*, Volume I (History, Inc., 2004; Siegel: pages 575-583), and Volume II (History, Inc., 2004; Cohen-Turner-Stompanato: pages 877-882). **p**, Curtis Hanson, Arnon Milchan, Michael Nathanson, Brian Helgeland; **d**, Hanson; **cast**, Kevin Spacey, Russell Crowe, Guy Pearce, Kim Basinger, James Cromwell,

Danny DeVito, David Strathairn, Ron Rifkin, Graham Beckel, John Mahon, Simon Baker, Paolo Seganti, Amber Smith, Gwenda Deacon, Darrell Sandeen, Brenda Bakke, Matt McCoy, Paul Guilfoyle; **w**, Hanson, Helgeland (based on the novel by James Ellroy); **c**, Dante Spinotti (Technicolor); **m**, Jerry Goldsmith; **ed**, Peter Honess; **prod d**, Jeannine Claudia Oppewall; **art d**, William Arnold; **set d**, Jay R. Hart; **spec eff**, Eric Rylander, Richard Stutsman, Peter Donen.

The L-Shaped Room ★★★★ 1963; U.K.; 126m; British Lion Film Corp/COL; Drama/Romance; Children; Unacceptable; **VHS**. Caron is exceptional as a sensitive young woman leaving her parents' home in a province of France and moving to London where she has a brief affair and gets pregnant. Rather than have an abortion, she meets with a famous gynecologist, Williams, who drains her of her money while she decides to have the child. Her funds depleted, Caron moves into a seedy boarding house at Notting Hill Gate, a building inhabited by an assortment of eccentrics and misfits, and where she occupies an L-shaped room (ergo the title for this film). She meets struggling writer Bell and they fall in love, a romance that thrills the boarders, including unemployed actresses and hard-working hookers, and the affair becomes the main topic of conversation, although one roomer, Peters, a jazz musician with a conservative streak, is angered at the relationship. Peters, who has learned that Caron is pregnant via another affair, tells his roommate Bell about it, and Bell, incensed at Caron's promiscuity, breaks off the relationship. Desperate to win Bell back, Caron takes some abortion pills provided to her by fading actress Courtneidge, but her motherly instincts surface when she is relieved instead of alarmed when the pills do not work. Bell returns to Caron's side but has difficulty in accepting the fact that Caron now intends to have that baby out of wedlock; after she gives birth at a hospital, Bell visits her, bringing her a story he has written about their original deep relationship, which has become fragile, and one he has entitled "The L-Shaped Room." After Caron leaves the hospital with the baby, she leaves for France and Bell finds his story left by her in his room with a note reading: "It's a lovely story, but it has no end." This is where the film also ends and the viewer is left to wonder if Caron and Bell will ever again unite. Forbes presents a provocative film that incisively provides great character development and where the cast members, including Bunnage, who plays the empathizing landlady at the boarding house, excel in their intriguing roles. Peter Katin performs Piano Concerto No. 1 by Johannes Brahms. **p**, Richard Attenborough, James Woolf, John Woolf; **d**, Bryan Forbes; **cast**, Leslie Caron, Anthony Booth, Avis Bunnage, Tom Bell, Cicely Courtneige, Emlyn Williams, Brock Peters; **w**, Forbes (based on a novel by Lynn Reid); **c**, Douglas Slocombe; **ed**, Anthony Harvey; **art d**, Ray Simm; **set d**, Peter James.

L'Armee des Ombres ★★★ 1969/2006; France/Italy/Germany; 145m; Les Films Corona/Rialto Pictures; Color; War Drama; Children: Unacceptable: **DVD**; **VHS**. Civil engineer Ventura is a French resistance leader in Nazi-occupied France during World War II in 1942. A traitor exposes him for having killed a guard at Gestapo Headquarters in Marseilles, and he is interned in a concentration camp. He escapes and joins his comrades in Marseilles where he strangles the informer. Ventura, aided by Signoret, another member of the resistance group, attempts to rescue a comrade, Cassel, in Lyons, but Ventura is captured and Cassel is killed. On his way to being shot by a firing squad, Ventura escapes. He learns that Signoret has been arrested and, to save herself from being forced into becoming a prostitute, she gives the Gestapo the names of some of those in the resistance movement. She is freed, but, while walking down a street, a resistance group member sees her and kills her. Both the author of the novel on which the film was based (Kessel) and its screenplay writer and director (Melville) had belonged to this resistance movement during WWII. Excessive violence prohibits viewing by children. (In French and Italian; English subtitles.) Released in Europe in 1969, this engrossing film was not shown in the

Nathalie Baye and Philippe Léotard in *La balance*, 1983.

U.S. until 2006. **p**, Jacques Dorfmann; **d&w**, Jean-Pierre Melville (based on the novel by Joseph Kessel); **cast**, Simone Signoret, Jean-Pierre Cassel, Lino Ventura, Paul Meurisse, Claude Mann, Paul Crauchet, Christian Barbier, Serge Reggiani, André Dewavrin, Nathalie Delon; **c**, Pierre Lhomme, Walter Wottitz; **m**, Eric Demarsan; **ed**, Françoise Bonnot; **prod d&set d**, Théobald Meurisse; **spec eff**, Wottitz, Georges Tornero.

La balance ★★★ 1983; France; 103m; Les Films Ariane/International Spectrafilm; Color; Crime Drama; Children: Unacceptable; **DVD**; **VHS**. Léotard is a small-time criminal persecuted by Paris narcotics detective Berry, who threatens to expose the gangster's romance with a prostitute, Baye, while that occupation is illegal in France. Berry tells Léotard he won't expose him if he gives him the names of those in a major drug ring, but Léotard stays silent and faces arrest. A semi-humorous scene evolves in which there is a shootout during a traffic jam and someone gets a bullet in their Sony Walkman. This U.S.-style gangster film transported to Paris was very popular on both sides of the Atlantic, but unacceptable for children because of excessive violence and sexual themes. (In French; English subtitles.) **p**, Georges Dancigers, Alexandre Mnouchkine; **d**, Bob Swaim; **cast**, Nathalie Baye, Philippe Léotard, Richard Berry, Maurice Ronet, Bernard Freyd, Christophe Malavoy, Jean-Paul Connart, Albert Dray, Florent Pagny, Tcheky Karyo; **w**, Swaim, Mathieu Fabiani; **c**, Bernard Zitzermann (Eastmancolor); **m**, Roland Bocquet; **ed**, Françoise Javet; **prod d**, Eric Moulard; **spec eff**, Jean-François Cousson.

La Bamba ★★★ 1987; U.S.; 108m; COL; Color; Biographical Drama; Children: Unacceptable (MPAA: PG-13); **DVD**; **VHS**. Phillips is outstanding in his lively essaying of the exuberant early-day rock singing star Ritchie Valens (Richard Steven Valenzuela; 1941-1959), who was really the forefather of the Chicano rock movement, and who was tragically killed in an accident on February 3, 1959, an airplane crash that also claimed the lives of singing stars Buddy Holly (1936-1959), and J. P. "The Big Bopper" Richardson (1930-1959). The film begins with Phillips living with his hard-working mother, DeSoto, who slaves away at menial jobs and where they live in near poverty. Phillips has a natural singing voice and is talented with the guitar. He begins writing songs and gets a few breaks in recording some of those songs while falling in love with Zerneck, but her bigoted father does not want her associating with any Hispanic Americans. He writes a song for her, "Donna," which becomes a big hit, and their romance survives above and beyond her parents' objections. Meanwhile, Phillips' older brother, Morales, who is struggling with a drinking problem as he is also struggling to become a successful cartoonist, becomes resentful of Phillips'

Lou Diamond Phillips as Ritchie Valens in *La Bamba*, 1987.

successes and believes that mother DeSoto does not care about his own talents and that she loves Phillips much more. When a party is held for Phillips to celebrate one of his musical successes, Morales spoils the party by insulting the startled Phillips in front of relatives and friends. Morales eventually comes around to appreciating his brother's enormous talent, especially when he draws enormous crowds and performs his classic hit, "La Bamba" (which became one of the popular worldwide songs in the world). When everything seems to be going Phillips' way, tragedy strikes when he is killed when flying to an engagement and his plane crashes in 1959, ending a great career. Morales' anguish is eased by the fond memory of his always optimistic and forward-looking brother, recalling scenes between them when they played together as youths. This touching and wonderfully acted film captures the boundless spirit and talents of the memorable Valens. Songs include: "La Bamba," "Come On, Let's Go," "Ooh My Head," "We Belong Together," "Framed," "Lonely Teardrops," "Donna," "Summertime Blues," "Crying, Waiting, Hoping," "Goodnight My Love," and "Who Do You Love?" *Author's Note*: Valens is also portrayed by Gilbert Meigar in **The Buddy Holly Story**, 1978. **La Bamba** was a solid box office success, gleaning more than $52 million in initial release. **p**, Bill Borden, Taylor Hackford; **d&w**, Luis Valdez; **cast**, Lou Diamond Phillips, Esai Morales, Rosanna DeSoto, Elizabeth Peña, Danielle von Zerneck, Joe Pantoliano, Rick Dees, Marshall Crenshaw, Howard Huntsberry, Brian Setzer; **c**, Adam Greenberg; **m**, Miles Goodman, Carlos Santana; **ed**, Don Brochu, Sheldon Kahn; **prod d**, Vincent M. Cresciman; **set d**, Rosemary Brandenburg; **spec eff**, Kevin Pike.

La Belle Noiseuse ★★★ 1991; France/Switzerland; 238m; Pierre Grise Productions/MK2 Diffusion; Color; Drama; Children: Unacceptable; **DVD**; **VHS**. A once-famous painter, Piccoli, has lost the inspiration or courage to continue his art and has put down his brushes, living in a French country mansion in Provence with his wife, Birkin. A young artist, Bursztein, visits with his beautiful girlfriend, Béart. The sight of Béart rekindles the artistic flame in Piccoli and he wants her to be his model for a new attempt at a painting of his nude wife that he abandoned ten years ago. To please Bursztein, Beart agrees to model nude and in the process of painting again, it becomes for Piccoli a war between art and sex. The title of this film is also the title of the painting which means "the beautiful nut," a woman who drives men to distraction. Piccoli paints Beart over the painting he earlier made of his wife, as a form of revenge, he feels, against the power that women have had over him in his life, his dependence on them, and how they have destroyed his talent. This intriguing film probes the nature of artistic talent while incisively examining the power some women have over sensitive men. Nudity and sexual themes prohibit viewing by children. (In French; English subtitles.) **p**, Martine Marignac; **d**, Jacques Rivette; **cast**, Michel Piccolle, Jane Birkin, Emmanuelle Béart, Marianne Denicourt, David Bursztein, Gilles Arbona, Marie Belluc, Marie-Claude Roger, Leïla Remili, Daphne Goodfellow, Susan Robertson, Bernard Dufour; **w**, Rivette, Pascal Bonitzer, Christine Laurent (based on the novella *Le chef-d'oeuvre inconnu* by Honoré Balzac); **c**, William Lubtchansky; **ed**, Nicole Lubtchansky; **prod d**, Emmanuel de Chauvigny.

La Bete Humaine ★★★★ 1940; France; 100m; Paris Film/Century Park Pictures; B/W; Drama; Children: Unacceptable; **DVD**; **VHS**. Gabin, one of France's most powerful and enduring actors (embodying the dynamics of a Spencer Tracy), gives a bravura performance in this dark drama where he is a train engineer and makes the mistake of falling in love with vixen Simon, the wife of fellow worker Ledoux. Fearful that he is about to lose his job, Ledoux persuades Simon to go to his boss to plead for that job, and when she does, she achieves that end, but only by sleeping with the lecherous boss. After Ledoux learns of this assignation, he explodes with rage and jealousy and kills his superior, a murder witnessed by Gabin. To ensure Gabin's silence, Ledoux again uses his wife's wiles, sending her to the engineer where she and Gabin tryst, but the promiscuous Simon falls in love with Gabin and then asks him to kill her husband so that they can be together. Gabin, by this time, is emotionally and mentally torn over his silence about the murder committed by Ledoux and his own lusty inclinations to kill Ledoux in possessing the alluring Simon. Half-crazed, he turns on the female siren, strangling Simon to death. Unable to reconcile his lethal act, Gabin then leaps from a speeding train to his end his own life and this film. Grim and gritty, this production unsparingly depicts love and hate as almost one emotion and which is startlingly conveyed by pantheon director Renoir through the stunning performances of Gabin, Simon and Ledoux. Many believe that this film, indeed, offers Gabin's finest performance. Director Fritz Lang remade this film as **Human Desire**, 1954, but it was a decidedly inferior production. *Author's Note*: Renoir secured permission to use an engine and some attendant cars for this film, capturing the speeding train as it races across farmlands and through tunnels by affixing cameras atop the engine and its cars and, in fact, used one of those cars as a dressing room for his actors. Renoir wrote the script for this chilling film, adding more dimensions to Gabin's character than envisioned by author Zola when he wrote the original novel. The stark lensing from Courant (who lost more than one camera by affixing them to the side of the running train, which were demolished when striking the walls of tunnels through which the train passed) is stunningly realistic, its black-and-white contrasts and shadows greatly impacting another gifted film director, John Frankenheimer, who admitted to this author that **La Bete Humaine** had a great influence in his making of **The Train**, 1964, which deals with French railway workers and their resistance to Nazi occupiers during WWII and where Frankenheimer stated to this author: "That Renoir film implanted so many great scenes in my memory where Gabin and Ledoux are as much the slaves to their emotions as they are to the trains they operate. Burt [Lancaster] and I watched that film together before we made **The Train** and it gave us a lot more than a dozen ideas on the production we began." **p**, Raymond and Robert Hakim; **d&w**, Jean Renoir (based on the novel by Emile Zola); **cast**, Jean Gabin, Simone Simon, Fernand Ledoux, Julien Carette, Blanchette Brunoy, Gerard Landry, Jenny Helia, Colette Regis, Claire Gerard, Germaine Clasis, Renoir; **c**, Curt Courant; **m**, Joseph Kosma; **ed**, Suzanne de Troeye; **prod d**, Eugéne Lourie.

La Buche ★★★ 2000; France; 106m; Canal+/Empire Pictures; Color; Comedy/Drama; Children: Unacceptable; **DVD**; **VHS**. In this amusing comedy, three French sisters whose Jewish parents divorced twenty-five years earlier meet for a dysfunctional family reunion on a Christmas weekend in Paris. The youngest, Gainsbourg, is a computer programmer in love with her career and also with a handsome young man, Thompson. The middle sister, Béart, is married to a rich man, who is about to leave her for a younger woman. The oldest, Azéma, is a gypsy singer in a Russian restaurant and is pregnant by a lover, who has been promising her for twelve years that he will leave his wife when his two daughters are grown, but she doesn't know the couple has four children and a fifth is on the way. Their father, Rich, was a musician and their mother, Fabian, an actress. The film begins with the sisters attending a funeral. The body making cell phone noises inside the coffin belongs to their mother, who has not been told of her husband's death. This starts a series of odd, sometimes funny events involving lovers and lost loves. The film's title refers to the traditional French Christmas dessert, La bûche de Noel, a butter cream cake shaped like a Yule log. (In French; English subtitles.) **p**, Alain Sarde; **d**, Danièle Thompson; **cast**, Sabine Azéma, Emmanuelle Béart, Charlotte Gainsbourg, Claude Rich, Françoise Fabian, Christopher Thompson, Jean-Pierre Darroussin, Isabelle Carré, Samuel Labarthe, Françoise Brion; **w**, Danièle Thompson, Christopher Thompson; **c**, Robert Fraisse; **m**, Michel Legrand; **ed**, Emmanuelle Castro; **prod d**, Michèle Abbé-Vannier; **set d**, Marie-Hélène Sulmoni; **spec eff**, François Dumoulin, Bruno Maillard.

Emmanuelle Béart in *La büche*, 2000.

La Cage au Folles ★★★ 1979; France/Italy; 87m; Da Ma Produzione/UA; Color; Comedy; Children: Unacceptable (MPAA: R); **DVD**; **VHS**. Tognazzi and Serrault have been gay lovers for twenty years. Tognazzi owns a nightclub in St. Tropez, France, where Serrault is the leading "Drag queen." Tognazzi has a "son," Laurent, a boy he adopted and raised as his son, and Serrault as his "uncle." Laurent returns from college to say he's going to marry… a woman. Further complicating matters is that the bride-to-be is the daughter of the secretary of the Union of Moral Order of France (Galabru), and he and his wife (Scarpitta) are planning to be present at the wedding. The son wonders how his in-laws will react to his limp-wristed "father" and "uncle." Serrault, in drag, introduces himself as Laurent's mother, but his actual birth mother, Maurier, shows up at the church wedding to create confusion if not outright mayhem. Based on a long-running play in Paris and throughout Europe, this outing presents a gay comedy of errors and manners that delighted audiences and, as a film, escalates from comedy to farce. Homosexuality, violence, and gutter language prohibit viewing by children. (In French; English subtitles.) **p**, Marcello Danon; **d**, Edouard Molinaro; **cast**, Ugo Tognazzi, Michel Serrault, Michel Galabru, Claire Maurier, Rémi Laurent, Carmen Scarpitta, Benny Luke, Luisa Maneri, Venantino Venantini, Carlo Reali; **w**, Danon, Molinaro, Francis Veber, Jean Poiret (based on the play by Poiret); **c**, Armando Nannuzzi (Technicolor); **m**, Ennio Morricone; **ed**, Monique and Robert Isnardon; **prod d**, Mario Garbuglia; **set d**, Carlo Gervasi.

The Lacemaker ★★★ 1977; France/Switzerland/West Germany; 107m; Action Films/New Yorker Films; Color; Drama/Romance; Children: Unacceptable; **VHS**. Huppert is an innocent and passive apprentice hairdresser living at home with her widowed mother, Dürringer, in Paris, and aspires to become a hair stylist. Meanwhile, she sweeps up and runs errands. She travels to the coast of Normandy with a girlfriend, Giorgetti, and falls in love with a handsome young university student, Beneyton, and they take an apartment together. They are lovers, but he is troubled by her lack of ambition and believes he should be with a woman who shares his interests, including journalism. He finally asks her to leave and she falls ill and is admitted to a mental hospital. Dürringer persuades Beneyton to visit her, and he does, but leaves with their romance still suspended. An engrossing but very sad French take on an ill-fated romance. (In French; English subtitles.) **p**, Daniel Toscan du Plantier; **d**, Claude Goretta; **cast**, Isabelle Huppert, Yves Beneyton, Florence Giorgetti, Anne Marie Dürringer, Christian Baltauss, Renata Schroeter, Michel de Ré, Monique Chaumette, Jean Obé, Chirstian Peythieu, Heribert Sasse; **w**, Goretta, Pascal Lainé (based on the novel *La Dentelliere* by Lainé); **c**, Jean Boffety (Eastmancolor); **m**, Pierre Jansen; **ed**, Joële Van Effenterre; **prod d**, Claude Chevant, Serge Etter.

La Chienne ★★★ 1976; France; 91m; Les Establissements Braunberger-Richebe/Ajay Film Co.; B/W; Drama; Children: Unacceptable; **VHS**. In this strange but compelling tale, Simon is a bank cashier in Paris and is married to a terror of a woman, Bérubet. He meets Maréze, who becomes his mistress, but he doesn't know she is a prostitute in love with her pimp, Flamant. Simon is an amateur painter and Flamant sells some of his paintings under the guise of an American painter. Simon then finds Mareze and Flament in bed together, and when Flamant tells Simon that she loves Flamant, Simon explodes, striking her so hard that she dies from the blow. Police arrest Flamant for the killing and he is sentenced to death while Simon goes free in what was Renoir's perception of ironic justice for a man henpecked by one woman and betrayed by another. Song: "Sois bonne, o ma belle inconnue" (Eugenie Buffet [Toselli]). This film was originally released in France in 1931, but it was not released in the U.S. until 1976. Sexual scenes and violence prohibit viewing by children. (In French; English subtitles.) **p**, Pierre Braunberger, Roger Richebé; **d**, Jean Renoir; **cast**, Michel Simon, Georges Flamant, Janie Maréze, Magdeleine Bérubet, Roger Gaillard, Jean Gehret, Alexandre Rignault, Lucien Mancini, Marcel Courmes, Max Dalban, Viviane Romance; **w**, Renoir, André Girard (based on the novel by Georges de La Fouchardière); **c**, Théodore Sparkuhl; **ed**, Denise Tual, Paul Fejos, Marguerite Renoir; **prod d**, Gabriel Scognamillo; **art d**, Marcel Courmes.

La Dolce Vita ★★★ 1961; Italy/France; 180m; Riama Film/Astor Pictures; B/W; Drama; Children: Unacceptable; **DVD**; **VHS**. Viewers either love or hate this Fellini film, which the director claimed was based upon events and persons he personally experienced or witnessed and/or knew. The comings and goings of his characters are seemingly without meaning or purpose, but this only reinforces the director's profiles of rather useless or exasperating people. His meandering protagonist is Mastroianni, who writes a gossip column for a local scandal sheet, although he has aspirations of writing something serious, which he never gets around to doing. We first see Mastroianni in a helicopter that follows another helicopter that is dragging aloft a giant image of Jesus, as it flies above Rome and where crowds gather to wonder what it's all about (and like most of what is seen in this erratic and disjointed film, it is "much ado about nothing"). That evening Mastroianni visits a nightclub and meets Aimee, a wealthy heiress, who is bored with everyone and everything. They pick up a prostitute, Moneta, and the trio spends the night together. When Mastroianni returns home, he finds his own mistress, Furneaux, has taken sleeping pills to end it all. Rushing her to a hospital to have her stomach pumped, he is told by doctors that she will be all right and he then races off to the airport, joining a bevy of other paparazzo to greet arriving Hollywood starlet Ekberg, an Amazonian

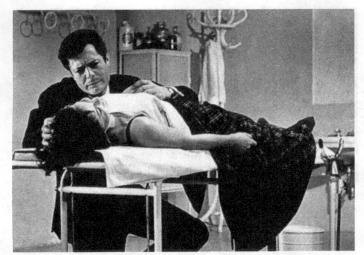

Marcello Mastroianni in *La dolce vita*, 1961.

blonde with an enormous bosom, who enthralls Mastroianni. He takes her on a tour of his Rome, including the Caracalla Baths, St. Peter's Square and the Trevi Fountain. Their idyllic sojourn is violently interrupted when Mastroianni is attacked by Ekberg's insanely jealous boyfriend, bodybuilder Barker. (Barker was Ekberg's husband in real life, and the Ekberg-Barker characters are acutely similar to the voluptuous blonde actress Jayne Mansfield and her bodybuilding husband, Mickey Hargitay.) Extricating himself from this embarrassing situation, Mastroianni then drives from Rome to check out a report that two children have just had a vision of the Virgin Mary. He arrives at a small village where hundreds of people are present to be healed by the holy visitation, but they are enraged when the children admit that they were lying and made up the story for fun. A rainstorm then scatters the crowd. Mastroianni then meets with his gentle father, Ninchi, who is so upset with his son's lifestyle and his smut-seeking journalism that he decides to leave Rome forever and live in a rural district. Mastroianni goes to a restaurant and becomes enamored of waitress Ciangottini, and begins an affair with her, but his peace of mind with his new mistress is undone when he learns that one of his closest friends and a brilliant intellectual, Cuny, has inexplicably killed his two beautiful young children and has then taken his own life. This event so disturbs Mastroianni that he gives up all hope of becoming a serious writer and decides that he will live out his life by simply seeking pleasure at every opportunity, which is what he has been doing all along anyway. He goes to the seaside home of wealthy and dissolute divorcee, Gray, and participates in an orgy. At dawn, he and some of the participants wander onto the beach to see a strange and large dead fish rotting under the hot sun. Mastroianni sees Ciangottini across the canal and she waves at him and shouts words he cannot hear. He then walks away with his friends for the fadeout. No one ever really figured out the meaning of this ambiguous film, and Fellini never bothered to explain its motives, purpose or themes. Its characters have little or no values and seem to be the flotsam and jetsam of Fellini's personal filmmaking world, but, as such, they nevertheless present penetrating and convincing profiles of wastrels and wannabes. While watching this film, one might conclude that Fellini is whimsically (if not perversely) summarizing and stereotyping (typecasting) the overall Italian character to universally represent slaphappy, utterly hedonistic or mindless human beings deliriously overjoyed at being blown willy-nilly to wherever the wild winds take them. *Author's Note*: Actor David Niven was a great admirer of Mastroianni, stating to this author on one occasion: "He is one of the world's greatest actors whose entire career is based upon his playing the indecisive twit who assumes sophisticated airs and he never twitted better than in **La dolce vita**." (In Italian; English subtitles.) **p**, Giuseppe Amato, Angelo Rizzoli; **d**, Federico Fellini; **cast**, Marcello Mastroianni, Anita Ekberg, Anouk Aimee, Yvonne

Furneaux, Magali Noel, Alain Cuny, Annibale Ninchi, Walter Santesso, Lex Barker, Valeria Ciangottini, Jacques Sernas, Nadia Gray; **w**, Fellini, Ennio Flaiano, Tullio Pinelli, Brunello Rondi, Pier Paolo Pasolini (based on a story by Fellini, Flaiano, Pinelli); **c**, Otello Martelli; **m**, Nino Rota; **ed**, Leo Catozzo; **prod d**, Piero Gherardi.

La Marie du Port ★★★ 1951; France; 100m; Films Sacha Gordine/Bellon-Foulke; Drama; Children: Unacceptable. Gabin offers another powerful performance, this time as a well-to-do restaurant owner. His comfortable life is disturbed when the father of his mistress dies and he travels with Brunoy to a small fishing village to attend the funeral. While there Gabin meets and is attracted to Brunoy's younger sister, Courcel, a friendship that quickly develops into a May-December affair. While Gabin finds himself rejuvenated and has more vitality than ever because of this new relationship, Brunoy seems to be unconcerned about his infidelity until Gabin learns that his longtime mistress is having her own affair with the small town's leading Romeo. This intriguing character study closely examines the emotional motivations of its leading players through Carné's deft direction and telling scenes where self-revelation comes dramatically into play. (In French; English subtitles.) **p**, Sacha Gordine; **d**, Marcel Carné; **cast**, Jean Gabin, Blanchetté Brunoy, Nicole Courcel, Claude Romain, Louis Seigner, René Blancard, Robert Vattier, Louise Fouquet, Olivier Hussenot, Jeanne Véniat; **w**, Carné, Louis Chavance, Jacques Prévert, Georges Ribemont-Dessaigne (based on the novel by Georges Simenon); **c**, Henri Alekan; **m**, Joseph Kosma; **ed**, Leonide Azar; **prod d**, Alexandre Trauner; **art d**, Auguste Capelier; **set d**, Maurice Barnathan.

La Marseillaise ★★★ 1939; France; 130m; Compagnie Jean Renoir/World Pictures Corp; B/W; Drama; Children: Unacceptable; **DVD**; **VHS**. Renoir presents a stirring film set during the French Revolution where a battalion of 500 men march from Marseilles to Paris just in time to capture the Tuileries, their march leading to the publication of the Brunswick Manifesto and the eventual overthrow of Louis XVI's monarchy. The film concentrates on the march of the commoners, and where pantheon director Renoir sharply contrasts those peasants from the aristocrats that have been oppressing them for decades. The great "La Marseillaise" is evident throughout the grand march toward Paris, beginning as a little song and enlarging into the country's stirring national anthem. Like his counterpart in Russia, Sergei Eisenstein, Renoir focuses chiefly on the myriad extras in that march, providing close-ups of their haggard and craggy faces, eschewing any extensive dialog and taking a documentary approach to his subject. As such, Renoir provides a moving documentary that captures both the era and overall character of the citizens who became revolutionaries, inflamed by patriotism and their desperate search for "equality, fraternity and liberty." (In French; English subtitles.) **p&d**, Jean Renoir; **cast**, Pierre Renoir, Lise Delamare, Léon Larive, William Aguet, Elisa Ruis, Marie-Pierre Sordet-Dantès, Yveline Auriol, Pamela Stirling, Génia Vaury, Louis Jouvet, Jean Aquistapace; **w**, Jean Renoir, Carl Koch, N. Martel-Dreyfus); **c**, Jean-Paul Alphen, Jean Bourgoin, Alain Douarinou, Jean Louis, Jean-Marie Maillols; **m**, Joseph Kosma, Henry Sauveplane; **ed**, Marguerite Renoir; **prod d**, Léon Barsacq, Georges Wakhevitch; **set d**, Jean Perrier.

La Parisienne ★★★ 1958; France; 86m; Les Films Ariane/UA; Color; Comedy; Children: Unacceptable; **DVD**; **VHS**. Bardot is exceptional in this fine comedy, most likely her best role, where she is the capricious daughter of the French Premier. A prisoner of protocol and politics, Bardot's marriage is arranged for her, but she does not see that as an imposition as she loves her intended, Vidal. The man she is slated to wed, however, and although he loves Bardot, is an incurable flirt, and when Bardot discovers that Vidal is making eyes at another fetching female, she decides to teach Vidal a lesson. She bats her long eyelashes and converts her pouting lips into a come-hither smile at Boyer, an aging prince, who is an older version of Vidal, a notorious flirt. Both fly to a ritzy resort on the Riviera, but Boyer and Bardot both come down with colds that hampers any lovemaking. Desperate to recoup Bardot, Vidal rushes to Bardot's side and, in a series of funny incidents, manages to win back her heart, leaving a rather confused Boyer to continue his womanizing ways. Bardot gets strong support from Vidal and Boyer and director Boisrond presents a clever and inventive comedy with a sure hand. (Dubbed and also in French; English subtitles.) **p**, Francis Cosne; **d**, Michel Boisrond; **cast**, Charles Boyer, Henri Vidal, Brigitte Bardot, Noël Roquevert, Madeleine Lebeau, Fernand Sardou, Claire Maurier, Robert Pizani, Guy Tréjan, Judith Magre; **w**, Annette Wademant, Jean Aurel, Boisrond, Jacques Emmanuel, Michel Boisrond; **c**, Marcel Grignon (Technicolor); **m**, Henri Crolla, André Hodeir, Hubert Rostaing; **ed**, Claudine Bouché; **prod d**, Jean André.

La Passante du Sans-Souci ★★★ 1983; France/West Germany; 110m; Elephant Production/Libra Cinema 5; Color; Drama; Children: Unacceptable; **DVD**; **VHS**. Director Rouffio presents an engrossing portrait of a dedicated peace activist, well essayed by Piccoli. His life is shown in flashbacks and flash forward sequences where we see him as a young boy, being cared for by the maternal-minded Schneider, who, when he becomes an adult, marries him, acting as his wife and mother. Piccoli's life and that of Schneider's changes from a tranquil lifestyle to a horrible nightmare when Piccoli assassinates a Paraguayan ambassador when he learns that his victim is a former Nazi, who has committed many atrocities and has been hiding under an alias. Piccoli's revenge results in tragedy for him and the woman who loves him above all others. Schneider is outstanding in her role in this last film she would make, dying six weeks after this film was released in France. *Author's Note*: Schneider, who became an international star in the 1950s, had a chronic dependency upon alcohol and drugs. She was found dead at age forty-three on May 29, 1982, from an overdose of sleeping pills, and though her death was thought to be a suicide, it was attributed to cardiac arrest. Her fourteen-year-old son, David Haubenstock (his father being stage director Harry Meyen, Schneider's first husband, and who committed suicide in 1979) was found dead on July 5, 1981, impaled on a spiked fence at his grandfather's home, apparently after he fell when trying to climb that fence. Schneider never emotionally recovered from the death of her son, which may have been the reason why she may have taken her own life. Her death mirrored almost the same kind of tragedy that is profiled in her final film. (In French; English subtitles.) **p**, Artur Brauner, Raymond Danon, Jean Kerchner; **d**, Jacques Rouffio; **cast**, Romy Schneider, Michel Piccoli, Helmut Griem, Dominque Labourier, Gérard Klein, Matthiu Carriére, Jacques Martin; **w**, Rouffio, Jacques Kirsner; **c**, Jean Penzer (Eastmancolor); **m**, Georges Delerue; **ed**, Anna Ruiz; **prod d**, Jean-Jacques Caziot, HansJürgen Kiebach; **art d**, Georges Glon; **set d**, Caziot.

La Ronde ★★★★ 1954; France; 97m (110m in 1989 restored version); Films Sacha Gordine/Commercial Pictures; B/W; Drama; Children: Unacceptable; **DVD**; **VHS**. Hailed as one of Ophüls' finest films, this intriguing episodic production offers a bevy of faithless lovers moving like hovering moths to interchangeable flames as they start and then dismiss one affair after another. Signoret is a streetwalker who meets soldier Reggiani, and who uses her and then moves on to have an affair with Simon. The lonely prostitute has long been conditioned to such abandonments and she routinely begins a relationship with Gélin. He, in turn, seduces Darrieux, a married woman whose husband is having an affair with Joyeux. But Joyeux only has eyes for Barrault, a poet who ignores her as he is madly in love with an actress, Miranda. The actress, however, lavishes her love on Philipe. These dizzying and brief love unions come back to the first episode when Philipe encounters and falls in love with Signoret, the tired but indefatigable love symbol in this Ophüls opus. The director keeps these myriad characters and their varied assignations in good order by using the great actor Walbrook as a sort

Anthony Quinn and Giulietta Masina in *La Strada*, 1956.

of master of ceremonies (not dissimilar to the stage manager of **Our Town**, 1940) to stunningly connect and make effective sense of these otherwise disjoined tales. *Author's Note*: Ophüls originally thought to make a film with Greta Garbo (who toyed with the idea of coming out of retirement, which she never did, to appear in an Ophüls production based on a Balzac novel), but when the elusive and reclusive Garbo bowed out, Ophüls opted to make this film, based on the Schnitzler play. The film was released in France in 1950, but its U.S. release was prevented by the New York State censor board that ruled the film "immoral," and it was released four years later in the U.S., after some of its more sensual scenes were deleted. (In French; English subtitles.) **p**, Ralph Baum, Sacha Gordine; **d**, Max Ophüls; **cast**, Anton Wallbrook, Simone Signoret, Gérard Philipe, Danielle Darrieux, Jean-Louis Barrault, Simone Simon, Odette Joyeux, Isa Miranda, Fernand Gravey, Daniel Gélin, Serge Reggiani; **w**, Ophuls, Jacques Natanson (based on the play "Der Reigen" by Arthur Schnitzler); **c**, Christian Matras; **m**, Oscar Straus; **ed**, Léonide Azar; **prod d**, Jean d'Eaubonne.

La Strada ★★★★★ 1956; Italy; 108m; Ponti-De Laurentiis/Trans Lux; B/W; Drama; Children: Unacceptable; **DVD**; **VHS**. In one of his greatest films, Fellini achieves a masterpiece by coupling two wonderful players, Quinn, and Masina (Fellini's wife) to form an unlikely romantic pair. Quinn is a one-man circus, traveling about the countryside on a motorcycle that hauls his tiny house. When arriving in a village, he demonstrates his strong-man abilities by breaking chains when expanding his chest and gathering whatever donations he can inveigle from the unsophisticated peasantry. Knowing that his act is extremely limited, he concludes that he needs an added attraction to keep spectators interested and the lire flowing. When arriving at a seaside town, he sees and "buys" Masina, a slow-witted woman, from her penniless mother. The two begin traveling together, but Masina is treated like a slave by the crude Quinn, who teaches her how to beat a drum and play a few rudimentary notes on a horn and where he uses her to merely attract attention to his strong-man act. Masina, for her part, is somewhat content to be Quinn's assistant, gopher and even occasional love interest, but Quinn's sexual appetite is ravenous and he is forever chasing after other women, crudely seducing them while generally ignoring and sometimes mistreating Masina. Although Masina longs for true love from Quinn, she realizes that he is a hopeless womanizer and loves no one but himself and that he will most likely never change his somewhat savage and unsophisticated ways and she is sadly resigned to her fate as a second fiddle in his life. At one point, Quinn blatantly flirts and runs off with another woman, which breaks Masina's heart and reduces her to tears. She nevertheless continues her shabby life with this brutish man. They later join a small circus that is performing at the outskirts of Rome, where they

Giulietta Masina and Anthony Quinn in *La Strada*, 1956.

meet Basehart, a clown who performs a high-wire act. Quinn and Basehart quickly develop an intense dislike for one another and their traded insults finally prompt Quinn to attack Basehart with a knife, an assault that lands Quinn in jail. Basehart then asks Masina to join him, but she is inexplicably loyal to the abusive Quinn and tells Basehart that she will remain outside the jail until her man is released. When Quinn is finally set free, Masina is waiting for him, but he takes her devotion to him as if it is a debt owed to him, and continues to treat her as his chattel. The two then meet Basehart on a lonely road where Basehart is changing a tire on his worn-out car. Quinn, seething with hatred for the man who caused him to be jailed, then goads Basehart into a fight and where Quinn kills him, although it is evident that taking Basehart's life was not Quinn's real intention. Masina is now so sorrowful over this killing that she is consumed by uncontrollable sobbing, as if she has taken on the remorse for Basehart's death that rightly belongs to Quinn. No longer able to stand Masina's sorrow, the brutal Quinn leaves the poor woman stranded in a mountainous area and with a single keepsake to remind her of her strange relationship with this seemingly uncaring man, the trumpet. Quinn then learns that Masina has died, and the pent-up emotions he has felt for this fine human being that he so mistreated erupts to his surface. He gets drunk and then walks to the sea and bathes himself, as if to wash away the awful abuse he has heaped upon the loving Masina. Quinn then sits down on the beach and weeps, his sobbing causing tears to flood his face, and that is where this powerful drama ends, with a man coming to realize too late that he has lost the one person in his life he truly loved and who loved him. Fellini carefully unfolds this tragedy with a firm hand and where Quinn and Masina give bravura performances in a must-see film, strikingly lensed against a grim background of day-to-day survival, highlighted by the childlike hope the extraordinarily sensitive Masina exudes in every frame. *Author's Note*: Quinn told this author that "I think I surprised a lot of Hollywood people who thought of me as a guy who played nothing but heavies and had no heart or soul. Well, I play that very kind of man in **La Strada**, but, in the end, the world saw that I could also play a person with human emotions and who needs love just like everyone else in this old world of ours. Fellini told me that he saw that in me in a lot of my old pictures, but that no one ever got that kind of performance from me because no one ever asked for it. He was right, but, mind you, I am forever grateful to him for giving me that role and I owe a debt I can never repay to that unforgettable woman, Giulietta Masina, truly one of the world's greatest actresses. Her performance in **La Strada** is one of eternal trust and love. Without her wonderful performance, I would have been nothing more than an ugly toad baking on a flat rock." Quinn also told me that he was not surprised when the Academy failed to nominate him for an Oscar as Best Actor for this great film as the Academy had already nominated

him for an Oscar for Best Supporting Actor in the same year, an award he won for his stunning portrayal of painter Paul Gauguin in **Lust for Life**, 1956. (In Italian; English subtitles.) **p**, Carlo Ponti, Dino De Laurentiis; **d**, Federico Fellini; **cast**, Anthony Quinn, Giulietta Masina, Richard Basehart, Aldo Silvani, Marcella Rovere, Livia Venturini, Gustavo Giorgi, Yami Kamadeva, Mario Passante, Anna Primula; **w**, Fellini, Tullio Pinelli, Ennio Flaiano (based on a story by Fellini, Pinelli); **c**, Otello Martelli, Carlo Carlini; **m**, Nino Rota; **ed**, Leo Cattozzo; **prod d**, Mario Ravasco; **art d**, Enrico Cervelli, Brunello Rondi.

La Terra Trema ★★★ 1965; Italy; 154m; Universalia Film/Mario de Vecchi; B/W; Drama; Children: Unacceptable: **DVD**; **VHS**. Commercial fishermen in a small village in coastal Sicily are victimized by greedy northern businessmen, who control the fishing market. Most of the money goes to them and boat owners. One young man from a poor fishing family returns to the village after serving in World War II and convinces his family to mortgage their house and buy their own boat and fish as independents. The risky effort fails, and they are forced again to depend on the businessmen for their meager living. The cast was made up entirely of village non-actors who speak Sicilian. The film's title refers to the villagers' revolution against the fishing system which sadly does not come about. A lyrical and brilliant film from the gifted Visconti, it was originally shown in Italy in 1947, but not shown in the U.S. until 1965. (In Sicilian; English subtitles.) **p**, Salvo D'Angelo; **d&w**, Luchino Visconti; **cast**, Antonio Arcidiacono, Giuseppe Arcidiacono, Venera Bonaccorso, Nicola Castorino, Rosa Catalano, Rosa Costanzo, Alfio Fichera, Carmela Fichera, Rosario Galvagno, Visconti (narrator); **w**, Visconti, Antonio Pietrangeli (based on the novel *I Malavoglia* by Giovanni Verga); **c**, G.R. Aldo; **m**, Willy Ferrero; **ed**, Mario Serandrei.

La Traviata ★★★ 1983; Italy; 105m; Accent Film/UNIV; Color; Opera; Children: Unacceptable; **DVD**; **VHS**. Giuseppe Verdi's opera is beautifully filmed and sung, set in 1850 Paris, telling the tragic love story of Violetta (Stratas), a beautiful courtesan, and wealthy young Alfredo (Domingo). His father (MacNeil) disapproves of their love affair and convinces Stratas to give up Domingo. She falls ill of tuberculosis and dies in her lover's arms. "Traviata" in Italian means "woman gone astray." Based on the 1852 play "The Lady of the Camellias" or "Camille," by Alexandre Dumas, that haunting tale was also filmed in 1937 as **Camille** and starring Greta Garbo and Robert Taylor. (In Italian; English subtitles). **p**, Tarak Ben Ammar; **d&w**, Franco Zeffirelli (based on the libretto by Francesco Maria Piave from the novel *The Lady of the Camelias* by Alexandre Dumas and the opera "La Traviata" by Giuseppi Verdi); **cast**, Teresa Stratas, Plácido Domingo, Cornell MacNeil, Allan Monk, Axelle Gall, Pina Cei, Maurizio Barbacini, Robert Sommer, Richard Oneto, Renato Cestié; **c**, Ennio Guarnieri; **m**, Verdi, James Levine; **ed**, Franca Silvi, Peter Taylor; **prod d**, Zeffirelli; **art d**, Gianni Quaranta; **set d**, Bruno Carlino.

La vie en Rose ★★★ 2007; France/U.K./Czech Republic; 140m; Legende Films/Picturehouse Entertainment; Color; Biographical Drama; Children: Unacceptable (MPAA: PG-13); **BD**; **DVD**. The life of French cabaret singer Edith Piaf (1915-1963) is memorably essayed by Cotillard. Piaf was called "The Little Sparrow" because she was diminutive and fragile. In her childhood Cotillard lives alternatively with her mother, Courau, an alcoholic street singer, and her father, Rouve, a circus performer, and her paternal grandmother, a madam. When she is twenty, Cotillard becomes a Paris street singer like her mother, and is discovered by nightclub owner Depardieu, who is later murdered. A voice teacher, Barbé, improves Cotillard's singing by coaching her, and advances her career by getting her jobs in concert halls where she soon becomes famous. Her sad love songs are sung from the heart, rooted to her own experiences where her only child dies, and she survives a tragic love affair with championship boxer Marcel Cerdan (Martins).

After Martins-Cerdan dies in a plane crash, Cotillard sinks into depression, alcoholism, and drugs, and tragically dies in 1963 at the age of forty-seven. "La vie en Rose" means "Life through rose-colored glasses," and is the title of one of the great Piaf's most celebrated songs. Cotillard is brilliant in the title role and deservedly won an Oscar as Best Actress. Songs include "La vie en Rose" (Louiguy, Piaf), "Non, je ne regrette rien" (Charles Dumont, Michel Vaucaire), "Milord" (Marguerite Monnot, Georges Moustaki), "L'Hymne á lamour" (Monnot, Piaf), "Les momes de la cloche" (Vincent Scotto, Andre Decaye), "Mon Dieu," "Mon Legionnaire," and "La Foule" all sung by Piaf in recordings; "Frou Frou" (sung by Cotillard); "Il m'a vu toute nue" (performed by Mistinguett, Emmanuelle Seigner); "Padam," "L'Acordeoniste" (performed by accordianist Jil Aigrot); "La Marseillaise" (Claude Joseph Rouget de Lisle). The showing of drug abuse, sexual content, nudity, gutter language and prostitution prohibit viewing by children. (In French; English subtitles.) **p**, Alain Goldman, Timothy Burrill, Marc Jenny, Oldrich Mach; **d**, Olivier Dahan; **cast**, Marion Cotillard, Sylvie Testud, Pascal Greggory, Emmanuelle Seigner, Jean-Paul Rouve, Gérard Depardieu, Clotilde Courau, Jean-Pierre Martins, Catherine Allégret, Marc Barbé; **w**, Dahan, Isabelle Sobelman; **c**, Tetsuo Nagata; **m**, Christopher Gunning; **ed**, Richard Marizy; **prod d**, Olivier Raoux; **art d**, Beata Brendtnerovà, Mick Lanaro, Laure Lepelley-Monbillard, Stanislas Reydellet; **set d**, Stéphane Cressend, Petra Kobedova, Cecile Vatelot, Christine Gilbert; **spec eff**, Kamil Jaffar.

Labyrinth ★★★ 1986; U.K./U.S.; 101m; Henson Associates/TriStar Pictures; Color; Fantasy/Adventure; Children: Unacceptable (MPAA: PG-13); **DVD**; **VHS**. A part-Muppet, part live-action film in which a fifteen-year-old girl, Connelly, who lives in a world of fairy tales, tries to solve the mystery of a labyrinth (a maze). She doesn't like babysitting for her baby brother, Froud, and wishes goblins would take him away. She gets her wish when the Goblin King (Bowie) steals the baby and she is transported to the Goblin King's world. She can get her brother back if she finds her way through a seemingly endless labyrinth to a castle in its center. Songs include "Into the Labyrinth," "Sarah," "Hallucination," "The Goblin Battle," "Thirteen O'Clock," "Home at Last" (Jones; sung by Bowie). Many truly frightening scenes prohibit viewing by young children. **p**, Eric Rattray; **d**, Jim Henson; **cast**, David Bowie, Jennifer Connelly, Toby Froud, Shelley Thompson, Christopher Malcolm, Natalie Finland, Shari Weiser, Frank Oz, and (voiceovers), Brian Henson, Ron Mueck; **w**, Terry Jones (based on a story by Henson, Dennis Lee); **c**, Alex Thomson; **m**, Trevor Jones; **ed**, John Grover; **prod d**, Elliott Scott; **art d**, Terry Ackland-Snow, Roger Cain, Peter Howitt, Frank Walsh, Michael White; **spec eff**, Tony Dunsterville, George Gibbs.

Ladder 49 ★★★ 2004; U.S.; 125m; Touchstone/Buena Vista; Color; Action/Drama; Children: Unacceptable (MPAA: PG-13); **BD**; **DVD**. Phoenix is a rookie Baltimore firefighter, who matures into a seasoned veteran under the guidance of a patient captain, Travolta, in this tribute to firefighters everywhere. Phoenix makes sacrifices to his wife and children during his ten-year rise as a firefighter and in the worst fire of his career he is trapped inside a twenty-story building. There he reflects back on his career and the impact it has made on his life and his wife and children. Firefighting violence and gutter language prohibit viewing by children. *Author's Note*: Many films deal with firefighters and firefighting, most notably **In Old Chicago**, 1937; **Boom Town**, 1940; **Tulsa**, 1949; **Red Skies of Montana**, 1952; **The Towering Inferno**, 1974; and **Backdraft**, 1991. **p**, Casey Silver, Chris Salvaterra; **d**, Jay Russell; **cast**, Joaquin Phoenix, John Travolta, Jacinda Barrett, Robert Patrick, Morris Chestnut, Billy Burke, Balthazar Getty, Tim Guinee, Kevin Chapman, Jay Hernandez, Kevin Daniels; **w**, Lewis Colick; **c**, James L. Carter; **m**, William Ross; **ed**, Bud S. Smith, M. Scott Smith; **prod d**, Tony Burrough; **art d**, Gregory Bolton, Kevin Constant; **set d**, Maggie Martin; **spec eff**, Larry Fioritto.

David Bowie and Jennifer Connelly in *Labyrinth*, 1986.

Ladies in Retirement ★★★ 1941; U.S.; 91m; COL; B/W; Drama; Children: Unacceptable; **DVD**. In this strange and even eerie production, Lupino renders an outstanding performance as a housekeeper and companion to Elsom, a retired British actress who possesses great wealth. She convinces Elsom to allow her two mentally deranged sisters, Lanchester and Barrett, to stay in her mansion, but these weird women so disturb the fragile and ailing Elsom that she asks Lupino to send her oddball sisters away. Lupino cannot bring herself to do this as she knows her sisters will then be sent to an insane asylum, so, in order to protect her siblings, she murders Elsom by strangling her with the collusion of her sisters. The unholy trio continues to live inside Elsom's comfortable home, successfully avoiding queries made by those curious about Elsom's absence. Then Hayward, a relative of Elsom's, arrives and begins to probe. He eventually comes to rightly believe that his aunt has been slain by Lupino or one of her sisters, or all of them, and he stays on to subtly launch his own investigation, playing cat-and-mouse with Lupino until the horrible facts come to the surface. A disturbing, even nerve-wracking film, this thriller holds attention throughout, thanks to Vidor's firm direction of many tension-filled scenes and the performances of Lupino and the rest of the very talented cast. *Author's Note*: Lupino told this author that "I was used to playing hard-bitten women in films before I did **Ladies in Retirement**, but I am an out-and-out killer in that picture and I thought that the only way I can ever get any kind of sympathy from viewers is to play a plain-looking woman. I had to portray her as being driven as mad as her pathetic sisters over her terrible fears of their being locked up in a lunatic asylum. I had to discard my youth and any kind of glamour by appearing with a lot of makeup to be a lot older than what I was then so I could make my character believable. The acting had to do the rest." This compelling and chilling story is based upon a real-life murder case, that of Euphrasie Mercier (b. 1823), who went to work as a housekeeper for a wealthy Frenchwoman, Elodie Menetret, and who murdered her employer, so that she could allow her deranged sisters to live with her in Menetret's sumptuous house. Mercier may have taken other lives, but was, after a relative conducted a private investigation, arrested, charged and convicted in 1886 of only one murder, that of Menetret, and sent to prison for twenty years. For extensive details about the Mercier-Menetret murder, see my book, *Look for the Woman: A Narrative Encyclopedia of Female Poisoners, Kidnappers, Thieves, Extortionists, Terrorists, Swindlers and Spies from Elizabethan Times to the Present* (M. Evans, 1981; pages 292-295). **p**, Lester Cowan, Gilbert Miller; **d**, Charles Vidor; **cast**, Ida Lupino, Louis Hayward, Evelyn Keyes, Elsa Lanchester, Edith Barrett, Isobel Elsom, Emma Dunn, Clyde Cook, Queenie Leonard; **w**, Garrett Fort, Reginald Denham (based on a play by Denham and Edward Percy); **c**,

Lady shares spaghetti with the Tramp in *Lady and the Tramp*, 1955.

George Barnes; **m**, Ernst Toch, **ed**, Al Clark; **prod d**, David S. Hall; **art d**, Lionel Banks.

The Lady and the Duke ★★★ 2001; France; 110m; Pathe Image Production/Sony; Color; Biographical Drama; Children: Unacceptable (MPAA: PG-13); **DVD**; **VHS**. This absorbing biopic is based on the life of Grace Elliott (1758-1823) who is brilliantly played by Russell. She is an English lady living in Paris during the French Revolution of 1792 and who is in love with the French Duke of Orleans (Dreyfus), cousin of King Louis XVI and father of the future French King Louis Philippe. Dreyfus is a sensual man, but a moderate revolutionary. Russell is loyal to the French monarchy and sickened by the growing terror of the revolutionaries. The duke excuses the executions of French aristocracy as a necessary transformation of society in his country. Russell, however, rises to the occasion of such intrusive and violent revolutionaries, such as when a crowd fills Russell's bedroom while she is in a nightgown hiding an aristocrat between her mattresses. She just happens to like excitement, proving it again by smuggling another member of the aristocracy out of Paris to her country house. Though shocked by the horrors brought about by the Revolution, and many of these are effectively depicted by director Rohmer, Russell, like the viewer, is compelled to witness these historical upheavals with obsessive fixations as shown when she watches through a spyglass from a hillside as the king and his family are executed by guillotine. *Author's Note*: The French Revolution has been depicted in many films, but most notably in **Orphans of the Storm**, 1921; **Napoleon**, 1927; **The Scarlet Pimpernel**, 1934; **A Tale of Two Cities**, 1935; **Marie Antoinette**, 1938; and **La Marseillaise**, 1939; Excessive violence prohibits viewing by children. (In French; English subtitles.) **p**, Françoise Etchegaray; **d&w**, Eric Rohmer (based on Grace Elliott's memoir "Ma vie sous la revolution"); **cast**, Lucy Russell, Jean-Claude Dreyfus, Alain Libolt, Charlotte Véry; Rosette, Léonard Cobiant, François Marthouret, Caroline Morin, Héléna Dubiel, Laurent Le Doyen; **c**, Diane Baratier; **ed**, Mary Stephen; **prod d**, Antoine Fontaine; **set d**, Lucien Eymard; **spec eff**, Dominique Corbin, Eric Faivre.

Lady and the Tramp ★★★★ 1955; U.S.; 76m; Disney/Buena Vista; Color; Animated Adventure; Children: Recommended; **DVD**; **VHS**. Adorable tale wonderfully animated has Lady (Luddy voiceover), a very proper Cocker Spaniel, falling in love with Tramp (Roberts voiceover), a streetwise, caring mutt. Lady's life is turned upside down after two Siamese cats arrive at her home and create havoc in trying to eat the family bird and goldfish and, in their insidious process, leave widespread destruction, which is blamed on poor Lady, who has done her utmost to save the bird and fish. Her master believes that the only

way to prevent such mayhem from again occurring is by putting a muzzle on Lady, who then runs away and winds up in a rough area of the town where she is menaced by all sorts of hazards, including a bunch of tough dogs. When cornered by some of these bad bozos, Tramp rescues her and then has his pal, a beaver (Freberg voiceover), use his razor sharp teeth to cut away the confining muzzle. Lady and Tramp then spend the night doing the town and dine a la carte over a shared plate of discarded spaghetti and, in one of so many endearing scenes, also share the same noodle as they each suck their end of that noodle to culminate in a kiss. At Tramp's instigation, they embark on several adventures together, including an ill-advised raid on a chicken coops where they are captured by a dog catcher, winding up at the dog pound, a fate Lady finds embarrassing and causes her to be angry at Tramp. Their love for one another, however, soars beyond all perils and problems and they are shown happily together raising their own family of pups at the joyful finale. All of the voiceovers are perfectly suited to their characters, including the mellifluous voice of singer Peggy Lee, who provides voiceover for several characters, and the charming story is inventive and heartwarming from the first frame to the last, a great film for the entire family. Songs include: "He's A Tramp," "La La Lu," "Bella Notte," "Siamese Cat Song," and "Peace on Earth." *Author's Note*: This was an expensive film for Disney, costing $4 million to make over a three-year period, but it was an instant success and its return staggered even Uncle Walt, filling his coffers with more than $25 million and becoming the third largest grossing film of the 1950s after **The Ten Commandments**, 1956, and **Ben-Hur**, 1959. **p**, Walt Disney; **d**, Hamilton Luske, Clyde Geronimi, Wilfred Jackson; **cast**, (voiceovers), Peggy Lee, Barbara Luddy, Larry Roberts, Bill Thompson, Bill Baucom, Stan Freberg, Verna Felton, Alan Reed, George Givot, Dal McKennon, Lee Millar, The Mellow Men; **w**, Erdman Penner, Joe Rinaldi, Ralph Wright, Don DaGradi (based on the novel by Ward Greene); (Technicolor); **m**, Oliver Wallace; **ed**, Don Halliday; **spec eff**, Ub Iwerks, Bill Fadness, Bruce Tauscher.

Lady Be Good ★★★ 1941; U.S.; 112m; MGM; B/W; Musical; Children: Acceptable; **DVD**; **VHS**. The story is thin in this entertaining musical, one where Young and Sothern are songwriters who were once married but are still song-plugging together and where their love for one another still burns bright. Their close friend, Powell, tries to convince them to make a go of it once more, and her machinations in reuniting them have to overcome their own stubborn natures as well as a lot of funny happenstances. It's all an excuse for the songs and Powell's marvelous dancing, of course, which is the centerpiece of this good romp. Songs include: "The Last Time I Saw Paris" (Jerome Kern, Oscar Hammerstein II), "Fascinating Rhythm," "Hang On To Me," "Oh Lady Be Good," "So Am I," (George Gershwin, Ira Gershwin), "You'll Never Know," "Saudades" (Roger Edens), "You're Words, My Music" (Roger Edens, Arthur Freed) and "Alone" (Nacio Herb Brown, Arthur Freed). *Author's Note*: This film, or its music, without the Kern-Hammerstein number (which was inserted into this production to extend its length), first appeared in a 1924 Broadway hit, and was made as a silent film in 1928, but the story line was scrapped by the writers for this production, substituting the running domestic feud between Young and Sothern as its plot in order to showcase the marvelous tunes. **p**, Arthur Freed; **d**, Norman Z. McLeod; **cast**, Eleanor Powell, Ann Sothern, Robert Young, Lionel Barrymore, John Carroll, Red Skelton, Virginia O'Brien, Tom Conway, Dan Dailey, Jr., Reginald Owen, Rose Hobart, Phil Silvers, Connie Russell, Doris Day; **w**, Jack McGowan, Kay Van Riper. John McClain; **c**, George Folsey, Oliver T. Marsh; **m**, George Stoll; **ed**, Fredrick Y. Smith; **art d**, Cedric Gibbons; **set d**, Edwin B. Willis.

Lady by Choice ★★★ 1934; U.S.; 85m (original release; later version at 76m); COL; B/W; Comedy; Children: Acceptable; **VHS**. Lombard shines in this fun-filled comedy, but Robson, as a raucous and drunken bag lady turned upstanding and moralizing "mother" steals the film.

The story begins with Robson being hauled into court after a bout with booze has caused her to wreck a saloon. The judge, Connolly, would rather not send Robson to the clink. Attorney Pryor, the son of one of Robson's old lovers, convinces Connolly to send Robson to a retirement home for old ladies. At the same time and in the same court, Lombard, a fan-dancer, appears after having been arrested for performing a lewd dance routine, and Connolly lets her off with a warning to mend her morals. To improve her image, Lombard's press agent, Walburn, urges Lombard to "adopt" a mother on "Mother's Day," and she goes to a home for retired old ladies where she identifies Robson, who pretends that she is a grand dame from an old Southern family, although Lombard knows her to be the harridan she had earlier seen at night court. Once she begins living with Lombard, Robson takes her new role to heart, her motherly instincts verbalized when she urges Lombard to quit fan-dancing and become a legitimate performer. Convinced that she can improve her lot, Lombard takes acting, singing and dancing lessons, hoping to break into big time show business. Further, Robson encourages a romance between attorney Pryor and Lombard and they soon fall in love. When Pryor plans to marry Lombard, however, his upper crust family threatens to cut him off without a penny. Lombard refuses to jeopardize Pryor's future and be the instrument of his being ostracized from his family, so she quits her lofty ambitions and returns to the burlesque stage and her floating fans. Robson comes to the rescue and conspires with judge Connolly, who has Lombard hauled back into court; he gives her two choices—she can either go to jail for a year or marry Pryor, who is eagerly on hand to take her as his bride. As one might easily believe, Lombard makes that decision with her heart. *Author's Note*: This tale is so strongly reminiscent of Damon Runyon tales that Swerling, the writer of this pleasant comedy was selected twenty years later to adapt for the screen the Runyon stories that made up the smash Broadway hit that became **Guys and Dolls**, 1955. Robson had performed a similar role a year earlier in **Lady for a Day**, 1933. **d**, David Burton; **cast**, Carole Lombard, May Robson, Roger Pryor, Walter Connolly, Arthur Hohl, Raymond Walburn, James Burke, Henry Kolker, Dennis O'Keefe, Akim Tamiroff; **w**, Jo Swerling (based on a story by Dwight Taylor); **c**, Ted Tetzlaff; **ed**, Viola Lawrence.

The Lady Eve ★★★★★ 1941; U.S.; 94m; PAR; B/W; Comedy; Children: Acceptable; **DVD**; **VHS**. Few would argue that this masterpiece comedy is the best ever produced by pantheon writer-director Preston Sturges and where Stanwyck and Fonda are superlative in this battle of wits and sexes. Fonda is the heir to a vast fortune accrued by father Pallette, a rotund and boisterous brewer who advertises his foremost product with the slogan: "Pike's Pale, the Ale That Won for Yale!" Shy and retiring, Fonda is convinced that every woman on the planet is after his money and has no real concern for him as a human being. To his mind, all women are gold diggers who see him as nothing more than a walking cash register. Fonda's obsessive occupation is traveling about the globe to visit exotic lands where, on these scientific excursions, he can capture strange species of snakes for his studies and, in summarizing this pursuit and oddball lifestyle, is fond of saying: "You know me, nothing but reptiles." Fonda, after finishing a trip up the Amazon, is seen boarding a luxury liner returning to the U.S., but, as he moves up the gangplank, the attractive Stanwyck, who stands on an upper deck, drops an apple that lands on Fonda's head (and thus the film's title). When they meet, Fonda and Stanwyck are taken with each other, and Coburn, Stanwyck's urbane father, a cardsharp and confidence man, agrees with his artful daughter to swindle Fonda out of his fortune, but cautioning her as would any gentleman thief: "Let us be crooked, but never common." The daughter and father are familiar travelers on board luxury liners as they sail the world while bilking suckers in rigged card games. Stanwyck first gets Fonda's attention while he is eating in the ship's luxurious dining room and where several single women blatantly try to get his attention by batting their eyes at him from adjoining tables, or slowly strolling past his table and accidentally dropping handkerchiefs he does

Barbara Stanwyck and Henry Fonda in *The Lady Eve*, 1941.

not retrieve for them. Stanwyck, however, easily snares Fonda as he leaves his table and trips over her outstretched leg. He falls and then picks himself up, and before he can complain, Stanwyck is holding up one of her shoes with a broken heel, so that it appears that it is all Fonda's fault. He makes apologies and then accompanies her to her stateroom where Fonda almost swoons from the smell of Stanwyck's seductive perfume. Fonda is falling fast for her and makes some naïve advances, telling Stanwyck: "You have a definitive nose." She responds: "Do you like the rest of me?" She, too, is genuinely falling in love with the innocent Fonda, and irks her father by telling him that she "is going to be exactly the way he thinks I am." Coburn is also distressed when Stanwyck stalls after he asks her to steer Fonda into a card game where Coburn can easily fleece the naïve, young man. Stanwyck then tells Fonda that her father does "card tricks," and later, Coburn manages to inveigle Fonda into an "innocent" card game. Fonda readily sits down with cardsharp Coburn and Stanwyck, despite protestations from Fonda's thick-headed bodyguard, Demarest. Stanwyck, however, is no longer a willing accomplice to Coburn's crooked card-playing, making sure that Fonda only loses a small amount of money, which vexes Coburn no end. The old sharper, however, turns the tables on his daughter and causes Fonda to lose a substantial sum to him, telling the gulled Fonda to write out a check and "just make it out to cash—$32,000 and no cents." Stanwyck explodes at her father's scamming of the man she now loves, and Coburn, to calm her down, tears up Fonda's check, but he has really torn up another check and has kept Fonda's draft intact. Fonda then arrives to tell Coburn that he loves his daughter and asks Coburn's permission to marry Stanwyck. Coburn pretends shock and Stanwyck is delighted at this romantic turn of events. All that changes drastically when Demarest, the ever loyal family bloodhound, unearths evidence that exposes Stanwyck's crooked past and that of her notorious father. Fonda goes to Stanwyck and confronts her with her past and she candidly admits that she did intend to swindle him, but that she attempted to stop her father from doing that since she is now deeply in love with him. Fonda is too injured to care and tells her they are quits. Hurt at being summarily rejected, Stanwyck vows revenge and contacts Blore, a conniving and fake British aristocrat, who has been a longtime friend of Fonda's family and who remembers Fonda as a "tall, backward boy always toying with toads." Stanwyck convinces Blore to take her to Fonda's family estate and pass her off as his niece. They arrive with Stanwyck wearing a new hairdo and affecting a slight British accent. Fonda accepts her in her new identity because she so closely resembles the Stanwyck he earlier met to be anything other than a different person, or that is his fuzzy reasoning. After some fine comedic moments where Fonda fumbles awkwardly about and where Demarest accidentally spills a serving at dinner on his tuxedo, compelling Fonda to change his

Guy Kibbee and May Robson in *Lady for a Day*, 1933.

clothes, the young heir becomes utterly fascinated with Stanwyck, falling as much in love with her as he did with the previous Stanwyck. He soon proposes and she accepts and they are married. While going on their honeymoon, Stanwyck then takes her revenge just as the couple is about to consummate their union in their stateroom on a speeding train. She begins to recount in tantalizing detail each and every lover she has had in the past, causing Fonda so much pain that he calls off the marriage, demanding an annulment. When Coburn later hears of this disruptive event, he sees a fortune at hand, and urges Stanwyck to demand a staggering settlement in the millions. She wants no part of it, however, since all the anger and revenge has gone out of her and she is left with a burning and persistent love for the straight-laced and naïve Fonda. Stanwyck and Coburn then resume their bilking lifestyle, traveling on board luxury liners, and on one trip heading for South America, Stanwyck again sees Fonda and stops him in his tracks by again tripping him. He is now confused, not knowing which Stanwyck she is, but he knows for sure that he loves her, whoever she is. "I'm married," she tells him. "So am I," he replies. They are, of course, married to one another as no annulment or divorce has ever taken place. When Stanwyck attempts to explain or make any admissions, Fonda stops her and says: "I don't want to understand. I don't want to know. Whatever it is, keep it to yourself. All I know is I adore you. I'll never leave you again. We'll work it out somehow." And they do for a happy ending. This mirthful masterpiece is achieved through the entrancing performances of Stanwyck and Fonda, but that achievement also rests squarely with the brilliant Sturges, who mixes slapstick with satire and whose many cleverly inventive comedic lines pepper the lively script. His direction is a great example of carefully crafted scenes where he slows the pace to achieve the most effective exchanges of dialog and action and speeds up that pace to hurry along to the next unexpected move by the manipulative and love-struck Stanwyck. The entire supporting cast, particularly Coburn, Blore and Demarest, are superb in their roles in this impossible story that is flippant and sparkling at the same time. This film was remade as **The Birds and the Bees**, 1956, a decidedly inferior production. *Author's Note*: Paramount looked upon Sturges as their new "golden boy," especially after the enormous success this film enjoyed. They believed the producer-director-writer to be their foremost provider of comedies, and they gave him as big a budget as he wanted for this production. When Paramount executives suggested strongly that either Madeleine Carroll or Paulette Goddard play the leading lady in this film, Sturges bristled, saying that he had already decided on Stanwyck and had promised the role to her, and if the studio would not let him sign Stanwyck to the part, they could not have him or **The Lady Eve**. Stanwyck told this author that "Sturges went to bat for me and I looked forward to working with him. He was a genius when it came to comedy

and he did not have to argue with writers since he wrote the script himself. He was very decisive, however, about each and every scene, and he would make a lot of quick changes, taking some of our [hers and Fonda's] advice as we went through the production. He made that film under its budget and only two days over its schedule. I think his teaming me with Hank [Fonda] was also a stroke of genius because Hank was the perfect actor for the role of the innocent, young millionaire." Fonda told this author that "Sturges borrowed me from Fox for that film, after I read the script, I told Sturges that the man I am playing 'is either the dumbest cluck that ever walked the face of the earth or thinks that women are some kind of alien species that live on Mars.' Sturges slapped my back and shouted: 'You've got him perfectly, Hank, perfectly!'" **p**, Paul Jones; **d&w**, Preston Sturges (based on the story "The Faithful Heart" by Monckton Hoffe); **cast**, Barbara Stanwyck, Henry Fonda, Charles Coburn, Eugene Pallette, William Demarest, Eric Blore, Melville Cooper, Martha O'Driscoll, Janet Beecher, Robert Greig, Barbara Pepper; **c**, Victor Milner; **m**, Sigmund Krumgold; **ed**, Stuart Gilmore; **art d**, Hans Dreier, Ernst Fegté.

Lady for a Day ★★★★ 1933; U.S.; 96m; COL; B/W; Comedy; Children: Acceptable; **DVD**; **VHS**. Robson is captivating in this warm-hearted comedy about the legendary "Apple Annie," who sells apples at NYC's Times Square and is considered by the area's denizens—from gamblers to panhandlers—as the "queen" of their world, and, in fact, she gently "extorts" small amounts of money from these streetwise natives so that she can continue paying for her daughter's education in Spain. No one knows about that daughter, Parker, and that's the way Robson wants it. Robson has not seen Parker since her birth and pretends in her letters to Parker that she is a wealthy dowager living at a swanky New York City hotel under the name of "Mrs. E. Worthington Manville." Robson has persuaded a bellhop at that ritzy hotel to forward her letters to Parker, which she has written on that hotel's stationery. Then a huge crisis looms when Robson receives a letter from her daughter where Parker informs her that she will be arriving in New York City shortly and will be accompanied by her fiancé, Norton, and his father, Connolly, both members of royalty and who both anxiously look forward to meeting her. William, a high-rolling superstitious gambler, is one of Robson's customers, who believes that her apples have brought him great luck in his many substantial wagers, and when he hears about her current problem, he comes to her rescue. As a personal challenge, William thinks to put on a colossal charade where Robson will appear to be the grand dame she has been impersonating to her daughter. He arranges for her to occupy a suite in the hotel, has dressmakers hurriedly make for her designer gowns and provides her with servants and attendants so that when Parker, Norton and Connolly arrive, they are overawed by this resplendent and distinguished old lady. Though several circumstances threaten to expose Robson's disguise, she manages to see Parker and Norton wed and bids them a loving farewell as they return to Spain and she, now content in life, returns to selling apples at Times Square. Director Capra skillfully brings in a winner with this capricious comedy that gave the venerable Robson, who had been on stage for decades, her most memorable film role. William and the rest of the supporting cast are standouts in this warm-hearted entry, one that was widely welcomed by audiences and critics alike. *Author's Note*: Capra told this author that "little Columbia did not have a lot of cash to buy good properties, but I was lucky enough to buy the story from Damon Runyon for $1,500. But I ran into the usual stone wall when I tried to get Marie Dressler. She wasn't available and then I got lucky again by getting May, a wonderful actress, who could play everybody's mother or grandmother and with a smile that could melt any cold heart. We received four Oscar nominations for **Lady for a Day**, and I was sure that we would win most of them. I was shocked when we went away with none. In fact, I was on my way to the podium to get an Oscar for Best Director after Will Rogers opened the envelope and said 'Come on and get it, Frank.' Then I saw Frank Lloyd walking toward the podium, too, and realized that he was the winner for

Cavalcade [1933], and I was so embarrassed that I wanted to crawl under a rug, but there was no rug to hide under. It was a different story the next year when Columbia won five Oscars for **It Happened One Night** [1934], and I went home with an Oscar for Best Director of that picture. It just goes to show you that if you keep your nose to that grindstone, something good will come your way." **p**, Harry Cohn; **d**, Frank Capra; **cast**, Warren William, May Robson, Guy Kibbee, Glenda Farrell, Ned Sparks, Walter Connolly, Jean Parker, Nat Pendleton, Halliwell Hobbes, Hobart Bosworth, Ward Bond; **w**, Robert Riskin (based on the story "Madame la Gimp" by Damon Runyon); **c**, Joseph Walker; **m**, Howard Jackson; **ed**, Gene Havlick; **art d**, Stephen Goosson.

The Lady from Shanghai ★★★★★ 1948; U.S.; 87m; COL; B/W; Crime Drama; Children: Unacceptable; **DVD**; **VHS**. The genius of Orson Welles is clearly evident in this riveting but complex film noir classic involving the beautiful Hayworth (then Welles' estranged wife), who is a vixen to her alluring core. Welles provides the narration, beginning the film with an opening line in a rather thick Irish brogue that fairly predicts the events to come: "When I start out to make a fool of myself, there's very little to stop me." While taking a stroll in a park, Welles sees Hayworth, who is suddenly molested, but Welles rushes to her rescue, driving off the assailant. Hayworth gives Welles a flirtatious look and then disappears. Sloane, a wealthy, crippled criminal attorney, then hires the unemployed Welles, a sailor, as a member of his crew to serve on Sloane's yacht, which is sailing for Mexican waters. Lo and behold, the sensuous Hayward is on board, but she is, to Welles' startled discovery, Sloane's wife. While Hayworth and Sloane behave oddly toward Welles, he quickly discovers that there are a lot of other strange people on this excursion, and none is stranger than Anders, who is Sloane's law partner, a sweating, obnoxious and sarcastic character who plays a bizarre game with Welles where Welles is to pretend killing him. Then Anders is actually killed, and after Welles has a secret tryst with siren Hayworth and the ship anchors at Acapulco, Welles is accused of murdering Anders. It now becomes apparent to the rather naïve Welles that he has been set up by Sloane and his scheming wife to take the fall for killing Anders, a partner Sloane has long wanted to discard. Welles later meets with Hayworth at an aquarium, and as they stand next to huge glass tanks containing giant swimming sea creatures,Hayworth tries to explain some of the mysteries involving Anders' death, but she gives Welles only piecemeal information that explains little. Welles is still later charged with Anders' murder and brought to trial in San Francisco where, of all people, criminal attorney Sloane takes his case. Sloane, who has never lost a case, however, appears lackluster and even a little unhinged as he displays unorthodox behavior at Welles' trial, even taking the witness stand and having himself cross-examined. It is now apparent that Sloane intends to purposely lose the case to make sure that Welles is convicted, and Welles envisions himself being executed at San Quentin. While being detained in the judge's chamber, Welles attacks a guard and they struggle, reducing the chamber to a shambles until Welles knocks out the guard and escapes, slipping out of the office, down a hall and then mixing in with a jury leaving the building. Welles hides out in a Chinese theater, nervously watching live Chinese entertainers and he is found by Hayworth, who has her Chinese friends spirit Welles from the theater to another location where he is drugged. He comes to his senses inside the fun house of an entertainment center, standing before a maze of mirrors. Hayworth arrives to give Wells some information about her husband's bizarre courtroom performance, but then Sloane arrives, hobbling on canes and holding an outstretched gun, aiming it at Hayworth and/or Welles and the viewer is not sure who he is about to kill, perhaps both, as he now believes that Hayworth has betrayed him for Welles. Hayworth, too, holds a gun, apparently aiming it at Sloane. The maze of mirrors, however, confuses Sloane and Hayworth as they cannot determine which images of their prey are real or which are merely reflections in the many mirrors that surround them. Both begin firing, smashing one mirror after another,

Orson Welles and Rita Hayworth in *The Lady from Shanghai,* **1948.**

until each find their marks, Hayworth mortally shooting Sloane and Sloane then firing a fatal shot into Hayworth. Sloane collapses dead and then Hayworth drops to the floor, writhing in agony. Welles by then clears his head and gropes his way to the exit, turning to see the prone Hayworth begging for his help and crying out: "I don't want to die." Welles gives her an empathetic look, but knows that nothing can be done for her and he staggers outside and into fresh air. Welles is then seen in a long shot as he walks beneath a sullen sky and with the San Francisco skyline in the distance and while he renders his epilogue: "I went to call the cops, but I knew she'd be dead before they got there. I'd be free… Well, everybody is somebody's fool. The only way to stay out of trouble is to grow old, so I'll concentrate on that. Maybe I'll live so long that I'll forget her. Maybe I'll die trying." Thus ends this mysterious tale, one where the mystery remains, in portion, a mystery, which is what Welles has intended all along. He, Sloane, Anders, and all the rest of the cast that make up the engrossing characters, give startling performances, even sex symbol Hayworth. In fact, this may be one of her best dramatic performances, if not her best, but such an appraisal is given while under the influence of Welles' overwhelming and pervasive aura. Everything, such as the last and memorable Hall of Mirror sequence, is fragmentary, unfinished, annoyingly inexplicable, and that structuring of this mesmerizing film is also intentional on the part of the inventive and always unpredictable Welles. *Author's Note*: Welles told this author: "It's a giant frame up, don't you see? Everyone is framing everyone else in **The Lady from Shanghai**, except for the sailor, my character, who is too dumb or trusting to catch on in time. He's the only real victim in the picture. All the rest spend their time betraying each other." The use of jump-cuts and interjected optical oddities created by Welles display a consistent tendency to break up the continuity of the many complex subplots and this may or may not have been intentional in enforcing Welles' penchant to distort throughout this production as primarily exampled in his Hall of Mirrors sequence. I pointed out to Welles that he seemed to have an idea fixe on mirrors, such as his sequence in **Citizen Kane**, 1941, where the tycoon's image is seen many times in telescoping mirrors, and I mentioned that magicians, knowing he was an amateur magician himself (see my Author's Notes for **Black Magic**, 1949, and **Journey into Fear**, 1943, concerning Welles' preoccupation with magic and magicians), routinely employed mirrors in their acts to alter or change their presentations. He laughed, saying: "Mirrors do not always reflect true images, only what the beholder wishes to see. You know what they say about some colossal swindles—that they have been achieved by the use of mirrors, not to say that I intended to swindle anyone in making **The Lady from Shanghai**." Of the many strange shots in this film, I was intrigued by one showing Welles in a close-up that features his profile, chiefly his nose, knowing that Welles never thought

Everett Sloane in *The Lady from Shanghai*, 1948.

his nose was photogenic and was forever, from picture to picture, altering its shape through inventive makeup and acacia gum. While showing that extreme close-up, he also shows in the same frame and at a great distance, Hayworth sunbathing on a rock so that she looks like a tiny speck of a human creature. "She is made to appear insignificant," Welles said, "but nevertheless totally controlling the sailor like some psychic Svengali using his mental powers to possess the mind of a person a block away. My character, indeed, is being led around by his undistinguished nose and he mostly does not care. He understands nothing in his life. He is merely living it. He does not want to understand because he is just smart enough to know that what he might learn is far more dangerous than his ignorance. When he escapes the courthouse, he does not go to a movie theater where he can watch a film and listen to actors speaking in his own language, which he could understand. He takes shelter in a Chinese theater where he does not understand a single word the Oriental actors on the stage are uttering. For him, ignorance is truly bliss. He wants to disappear and to never be found, but, like that victimized rabbit in the magician's hat, he is always being pulled by his ears into the grim light of day." The story of how this film came into being is almost as intriguing as the film itself. Before the making of this film, Welles had worn out his welcome in Hollywood by making many significant films, even a few masterpieces, but most had failed to produce good box office returns. Further, his marriage to Hayworth (they had married in 1943) was on the rocks and the actress was estranged to him, living apart. Welles had relocated in New York where he worked with his good friend, producer Mike Todd, then struggling to produce a Broadway production of "Around the World in 80 Days," but running out of money and telling Welles that he required $50,000 to get the show on the boards. Welles went to the only man he knew had that kind of cash available, the crude and rude boss of Columbia Studio, Harry Cohn. He called Cohn from the backstage of the theater and when he got the mogul on the line, he asked Cohn to cut a deal with him, saying: "If you advance me the $50,000 I will…write and direct a picture. I've got a suspense story that can be made inexpensively." Welles had no suspense story, in fact, no story at all. Cohn seemed willing, but insisted that Welles give him the title of his new film. According to the filmmaker, he frantically looked about and saw a wardrobe mistress sitting in the hallway and where she was reading a pulp novel entitled "The Lady from Shanghai." Welles blurted that mystique-packed title to Cohn, who loved it and agreed to send the cash. The money did not alter the course of Todd's production, which closed after a short run. Meanwhile, Welles was committed to Cohn to do a film and concocted a story that had nothing to do with the original novel, but the rights for it were purchased by Welles for a pittance. He then acquired the rights through William Castle, who served as an assistant director on the film, the rights to another

novel by Sherwood King, but Welles used very little of that story when he banged out his original script, reportedly within seventy-two hours. Cohn insisted that his top star, Hayworth, appear in the leading role as the conniving vixen. Hayworth agreed to do the film, even though she was then battling in court with Welles in trying to conclude a settlement for their daughter, Rebecca Welles, before she was granted a final divorce decree. She felt that Welles would provide for their child from his percentage from the film that Cohn had granted him, so she went into the production, but her relationship with Welles was tenuous throughout the making of the film, it was later claimed that Welles vindictively ordered Hayworth to crop her luxurious long hair and bleach it blonde. When Cohn saw stills of Hayworth's shorn head, he exploded, but he knew that by interfering with Welles, who was then with crew and cast in Mexico making the film, he would invariably slow production and that would cost him even more money. As it turned out, Welles was extravagant with the budget, going over its slated amounts by constantly reshooting scenes and moving his locations between Acapulco and San Francisco, until the production soared beyond $2 million. Moreover, Welles spent a lot of Cohn's cash on his friend, actor Errol Flynn, who was then strapped for money. Welles chartered Flynn's yacht for the film, and it is this vessel that is seen as Sloane's ship throughout the film and where Flynn himself sailed the yacht in and about Mexican waters throughout the production (Flynn can be briefly seen in the film outside of a cantina in Acapulco). The dazzling sequence of the Hall of Mirrors at the amusement park was staged and lighted by special effects master Lawrence Butler, who had provided all the startling special effects for Alexander Korda's stunning fantasy, **The Thief of Bagdad**, 1940, where Butler brought to life a giant genie, captured and emerging from a bottle, flying horses and carpets, a sinister-looking statue that becomes lethally alive and many other magnificent wonders in that magical film. When Welles delivered **The Lady from Shanghai** to Columbia in February 1947, he admitted to Cohn that it needed work and the studio had several writers and editors go labor on the film, deleting a lengthy montage and an airplane sequence, more than fifteen or more minutes sliced away and destroyed, never to be seen again. While this dedicated surgery was being performed on **The Lady from Shanghai**, Welles was off to Europe, seeking other film projects. Hayworth, too, flew to the Continent, but only after she obtained her final divorce decree. At that time, she stated in court that "Mr. Welles showed no interest in establishing a home. Mr. Welles told me he never should have married in the first place, as it interfered with his freedom in his way of life." She was granted that decree on November 10, 1947, five months after **The Lady from Shanghai** was released. Hayworth had only a few terse remarks about this film in our meeting together, telling this author: "I did not care for that picture that much. I was not getting along too well with its director." Louella Parsons, who was the leading Hollywood gossip-monger and whose powerful column was syndicated in the then many Hearst newspapers and aired over Hearst radio stations, savagely attacked Welles at this time. She had long held a grudge against him for his making of **Citizen Kane**, which she and most others knew, critically profiled and revealed the private lifestyle of her employer, media magnate William Randolph Hearst. Further, Parsons was a close friend and booster of Hayworth and strongly sided with the actress in her divorce proceedings against Welles. Parsons railed against the *enfant terrible* of films by calling Welles in print "awesome Orson, the self-styled genius," and concluding that he was "washed up." That, of course, was very far from reality. **p,d&w**, Orson Welles (based on the novel *If I Die before I Wake* by [Raymond] Sherwood King); **cast**, Rita Hayworth, Welles, Everett Sloane, Glenn Anders, Ted de Corsia, Erskine Sanford, Gus Schilling, Carl Frank, Louis Merrill, Evelyn Ellis, Harry Shannon; **c**, Charles Lawton, Jr.; **m**, Heinz Roemheld; **ed**, Viola Lawrence; **art d**, Sturges Carne, Stephen Goosson; **set d**, Wilbur Menefee, Herman Schoenbrun; **spec eff**, Lawrence W. Butler.

Lady in a Cage ★★★ 1964; U.S.; 94m; American Entertainment/PAR;

B/W; Crime Drama/Horror; Children: Unacceptable; **DVD**; **VHS**. De Havilland renders a bravura performance in this chilling and often frightening film, one where her cultured and peaceful world is invaded by street thugs, who make a living hell on earth for her. A successful author, de Havilland lives comfortably in an upscale multi-storied townhouse in New York City. She is somewhat immobilized by an ailing hip and finds it difficult to move about, so she travels between the floors of her townhouse via an elevator. She enters that elevator just when there is a power outage and it becomes stuck between floors. The lift, however, has an alarm bell that de Havilland uses, but to no immediate avail since the Fourth of July is taking place and the noise of the national holiday drowns out the ringing of that alarm bell. De Havilland's twenty-nine-year-old son, Swan, is not there to help her as he has left the house, no longer able to tolerate his mother's dominating and overly protective habits. The constant ringing, however, is finally heard by Corey, a hopeless drunk, who breaks into the townhouse and leisurely loots it, ignoring de Havilland's pleas in his pillaging. He leaves and then returns with Sothern, a bosomy prostitute, as well as three street thugs, who are led by the savage Caan (in his film debut). The punks taunt and tease de Havilland mercilessly as they further rob the place and then begin to destroy the well-appointed rooms. De Havilland, while these cretins carry on their mindless vandalism, manages to pry open a section of the elevator (the cage of the film's title) and drops painfully to a lower floor. By that time, Caan has had an argument with Corey and has killed him and has locked Sothern in the basement. When he comes upon the now freed but injured de Havilland, who can no longer walk, Caan makes a menacing move toward her. De Havilland holds two metal strips that she has pried loose from the elevator in making her escape, and as Caan lunges forward, she drives these strips of metal into his eyes, blinding him. At the sight of this bloody attack Caan's two companions in crime, Billingsley and Campos, flee in horror. De Havilland then painfully crawls toward the entrance of the townhouse as Caan, bleeding and sightless, staggers about, trying to find her. She manages to crawl into the street, and Caan follows her but stumbles forward blindly and is struck and killed by a speeding car. De Havilland's screams are finally heard by the noisy revelers and citizens then rush to her aid, ending this bizarre but compelling tale of horror. This production may or may not have inspired a very similar film, **Wait Until Dark**, 1967, where another disabled woman is sadistically terrorized and threatened with injury and death, until she can outwit her tormentors and bring about savage revenge. *Author's Note*: Davis, who produced and wrote the screenplay for this film, was no stranger to violent crime dramas, having written the script for the chilling **Black Hand**, 1950, which profiles the early-day murderous extortionists, who preyed upon the Italian communities in New York City. Davis stated in writing **Lady in a Cage** that he wrote it as a protest against the increasing widespread violence invading otherwise peaceful communities in America, not unlike the motivations of British author Anthony Burgess, who wrote the violence-packed **A Clockwork Orange**, 1972, in a responsive rage to his own wife being savagely raped by a gang of London street thugs. **p&w**, Luther Davis; **d**, Walter Grauman; **cast**, Olivia de Havilland, Ann Sothern, Jeff Corey, James Caan, Jennifer Billingsley, Rafael Campos, William Swan, Scatman Crothers, Ron Nyman, Charles Seel; **c**, Lee Garmes; **m**, Paul Glass; **ed**, Leon Barsha; **prod d**, Rudolph Sternad; **art d**, Hal Pereira; **set d**, Sam Comer, Joseph Kish; **spec eff**, Paul K. Lerpae.

The Lady in Red ★★★ 1979; U.S.; 93m; New World; Color; Crime Drama; Children: Unacceptable (MPAA: R); **DVD**; **VHS**. Polly Hamilton (Martin), a small-town Midwestern girl, who is abused by her father, leaves home for Hollywood but gets only as far as Chicago where she becomes a seamstress in a sweatshop. She then becomes a dance hall girl for a dime a dance. She is arrested on a prostitution charge and jailed. She is released into the custody of Rumanian Anna Sage (Fletcher), who runs a whorehouse frequented by men of the underworld, from crooked cops to gangsters. Fletcher's bordello is later shut

Ginger Rogers in *Lady in the Dark*, 1944.

down and she and her girls, including Martin, operate a coffee shop. There Martin meets a dapper young man (Conrad) and falls in love with him, without knowing he is the notorious bank robber John Dillinger (1903-1934?), the FBI's Public Enemy #1. Fletcher realizes who Conrad is, so she works a deal with the FBI to help agents capture him in return for not being deported back to her native Rumania. On a hot July night, Fletcher, Martin and Conrad go to the Biograph, an air-conditioned movie theater on Chicago's north side. Fletcher has tipped off the FBI that Conrad will be there, and when they leave the theater after seeing the movie, Conrad is gunned down. Only then does Martin realize Conrad is Dillinger. Reporters label her "The Lady in Red" because she wore a red dress at the theater, and tab her as the woman who set up Dillinger for his death. Martin turns to a life of crime and winds up where she wanted to go in the first place, Hollywood. Although this action-loaded crime yarn is well produced and acted, it has little or nothing to do with the true facts in the Dillinger case and with Polly Hamilton Keele, who was also known as Rita Hamilton. For reliable facts dealing with Dillinger and Hamilton, see my books: *The Dillinger Dossier* (December Press, 1983); and *The Great Pictorial History of World Crime*, Volume II (History, Inc., 2004; pages 1374-1422). It was not Polly Hamilton who was dubbed "the lady in red" by Chicago newsmen following the shooting at the Biograph, but it was Anna Sage, who never wore a red dress that night. She wore an orange skirt. **p**, Julie Corman, Steven Kovacs, Roger Corman (not credited); **d**, Lewis Teague; **cast**, Pamela Sue Martin, Robert Conrad, Louise Fletcher, Robert Hogan, Laurie Heineman, Glenn Withrow, Rod Gist, Christopher Lloyd, Terri Taylor, Robert Forster; **w**, John Sayles; **c**, Daniel Lacambre; **m**, James Horner; **ed**, Teague, Larry Bock, Ron Medico, **prod d**, Jac McAnelly; **art d**, Philip Thomas; **set d**, Keith Hein; **spec eff**, Bill Balles.

Lady in the Dark ★★★ 1944; U.S.; 100m; PAR; Color; Musical; Children: Acceptable; **DVD**. In this entertaining but somewhat offbeat musical, the gifted director Leisen mixes psychiatry with show biz music, a curious blend that somehow works well, but only through the radiant Rogers, who is the alluring centerpiece of this melodious romp into the subconscious. Rogers is the high-powered editor of a top fashion magazine where the pressures of publication are bringing her close to a nervous breakdown. She has three men in her busy life—Milland, Hall and Baxter. She talks about these challenging men to Sullivan, the psychiatrist she visits in getting peace of mind. As Rogers bares her subconscious thoughts, she talks about each man, and these sessions produce in dream sequences the musical numbers. Milland is the contentious advertising manager for the magazine at whom she seems always at odds while Baxter is divorced and who romances Rogers, but she can't handle his amorous advances and so turns to Hall, a he-man type, but he's not

Audrey Totter and Leon Ames in *Lady in the Lake,* 1947.

for her. In the end, Rogers dances straight into Milland's arms for the finale where Auer announces to the viewer: "This is the end, the absolute end!" Songs include: "Artist's Waltz" (Robert Emmett Dolan), "Dream Lover" (Clifford Grey, Victor Schertzinger), "Suddenly It's Spring" (Johnny Burke, Jimmy Van Heusen), "It Looks Like Liza," "Girl Of The Moment," "One Life To Live," "This Is New," and "The Saga Of Jenny" (George Gershwin, Kurt Weil). ***Author's Note***: This was Roger's first color film and the rich old Technicolor process was never lovelier, so much so that this film was nominated for Best Color Cinematography, as well as Best Art Direction. Rogers told this author that "I thought then and still do that that picture was very strange. It was very different than all the musicals I ever made. I am a nutcase needing a psychiatrist and, you may know, in those days, most people did not seek that kind of help. If it got out that you were seeing a shrink, everybody thought you were a raving lunatic that should be locked up in an asylum. But the writers only used that mental mess to give the picture an unusual angle so they could introduce the songs and dancing. I don't do much dancing after all in that picture, only a sort of bump and grind where I had to show a lot of leg in a circus takeoff number done by Gershwin and Kurt Weill, and this is one of the dreams or nightmares I tell my psychiatrist, can you imagine? I don't think the writers knew too much about psychiatry when they wrote that script. If they did, they were making fun of psychiatry, but then, that's what everybody did in those days. Everybody thought that psychiatrists were all crazy themselves! Look at the psychiatrist in that picture, **Bringing Up Baby** [1938; the psychiatrist is played by comedian Fritz Feld]. He's as nutty as a bowl of almonds." **p**, Richard Blumenthal; **d**, Mitchell Leisen; **cast**, Ginger Rogers, Ray Milland, Warner Baxter, Jon Hall, Bary Sullivan, Mischa Auer, Phyllis Brooks, Mary Philips, Fay Helm, Gail Russell, Rand Brooks, Hiliary Brooke, Jack Mulhall, Dennis Moore, Audrey Young; **w**, Frances Goodrich, Albert Hackett (based on the play by Moss Hart, Kurt Weill, Ira Gershwin); **c**, Ray Rennahan (Technicolor); **m**, Robert Emmett Dolan; **ed**, Alma Macrorie; **art d**, Hans Dreier; **set d**, Ray Moyer, Raoul Pène du Bois; **spec eff**, Farciot Edouart, Gordon Jennings, Paul Lerpae.

Lady in the Lake ★★★★ 1947; U.S.; 105m; MGM; B/W; Crime Drama; Children: Unacceptable; **DVD; VHS**. Montgomery is Raymond Chandler's legendary private eye Phillip Marlowe in this gripping film noir tale, one which Montgomery also inventively directs while narrating and introducing the novel "Camera I" as his own protagonist. We do not get to see Montgomery but a few times in this arresting crime drama and, when we do, he is shown in the reflections of windows or in mirrors while looking at himself or the fetching Totter, the red herring femme fatale of the story. All the characters and action is addressed

straight at the camera, which represents Montgomery's character, and though this is somewhat distracting or confusing at times, its uniqueness makes for a very different kind of film. We do see and meet Montgomery in Marlowe's office where he addresses the camera and viewer as if he is talking to a visitor and then begins to explain a caper called "The Lady of the Lake." The camera then replaces Montgomery as he appears in Totter's office. She is an editor of a crime magazine to which he has sent several crime yarns, thinking to quit the private detective business and cash in big as a crime writer. He has come at her request, thinking he is about to cut a publishing deal, but he is mistaken. Totter is not interested in the story he submitted, only his private eye services, asking him to undertake the search of a missing woman, the wife of her publisher, Ames. She explains that Ames wants to locate his wife so that he can divorce her and marry Totter. Sounds reasonable to Montgomery, so he takes the case and begins snooping, his first call made on Simmons, a young, muscle-bound character. It is at first a friendly meeting, but Montgomery asks a question that riles Simmons, causing him to land several blows on Montgomery's face and knocking him out. Montgomery comes to inside a jail cell in Bay City (the location outside L.A. where everything rotten happens in Chandler's always fascinating novels and stories). Hard-as-nails police detective Nolan tells Montgomery that he was found driving around drunk and when he put up a fight, he, Nolan, had to knock him out to subdue him. Nolan hands him back his possessions, including all of his money, the grand total of $18. Nolan then hands Montgomery the copy of the story he had originally submitted to Totter, who then sarcastically reads its title "If I Should Die before I Live," adding: "So you're a story writer, too, huh? The detective business must be on the skids. What are you trying to do—elevate yourself?" Nolan then escorts Montgomery into the office of his boss, police captain Tully, who angrily delivers a sermon to Montgomery about the dangers of drunk driving. Montgomery replies that he has been framed, that he was knocked senseless, booze poured all over him and then thrown into his car, which someone managed to put in motion until the car sailed crazily down the street and over a curb. (This kind of frame-up was shown in **Each Dawn I Die**, 1939, where James Cagney is placed in a car that crashes, killing a man so that Cagney is sent to prison on a manslaughter charge, and this frame-up is also duplicated by Alfred Hitchcock in his classic espionage tale, **North by Northwest**, 1959, spies doing the same thing to an unsuspecting Cary Grant). Tully releases Montgomery, but not before he warns him to stay out of Bay City and Nolan further threatens to beat up Montgomery if he again sees him. Properly chastised, Montgomery returns to Totter, standing with her in front of a mirror to display an ugly closed and blackened eye. He tells Totter that the retainer of $300 she gave him is not enough to cover the kind of beating he took. Further, they learn that the body of a female has been found floating in Little Fawn Lake, and that that body is the wife of Ames' caretaker of his retreat located on that lake. Totter tells Montgomery that she believes that the woman found dead in the lake was murdered by Ames' missing wife and she asks him to go the lake and prove her theory so that Ames can then have his long-vanished wife prosecuted for murder. Montgomery agrees and tells Totter: "You're so full of persuasion. What else would you say you're full of?" Montgomery investigates, but finds that the dead woman is not that of the caretaker. He also finds a pin engraved to Ames' wife from Simmons and decides to risk going back to that dangerous suspect. He does not immediately find Simmons, but the beautiful Meadows, Simmons' landlady, who is looking for Simmons with a gun in her hand. Montgomery lies to her, saying that he is from a finance company and that Simmons is behind in his car payments. Meadows hands the gun to Montgomery, saying she found it on the stairs. The gumshoe ushers her outside and then goes into the house, walking upstairs and, once in the bathroom, finds Simmons dead in the shower, shot to pieces by someone who apparently sent several bullets through the glass shower door while the victim was showering. He also finds a handkerchief bearing Totter's initials. Going to a Christmas party held by Ames, Montgomery takes Totter into another room away from the revelers and he gives her the gun that has been used to kill Simmons wrapped in Totter's handkerchief. Totter denies having anything to do with the Simmons murder and then Ames appears to angrily tell Totter that he has learned that she has hired Montgomery to find his wife against his wishes and that he wants his missing wife left alone. Totter fires Montgomery, telling him that he has cost her the loss of a million dollars, meaning that Ames will not marry her after what she has done. Montgomery is then hired by Ames, asking him to find his wife so he can protect her against what might be a murder charge in the Simmons killing. Montgomery then returns to Simmons' house once more to find police chief Tully and brutal Nolan present. He gives Tully the gun used to kill Simmons, and Tully accuses him of withholding evidence. Nolan becomes abrasive, but this time, before he can throw a punch, Montgomery knocks him down and Tully arrests him for assaulting a police officer. He is again held at the police station, but Tully releases him. Before leaving, Montgomery tells Tully that he believes that Nolan murdered the woman found dead in the lake, but Tully tells him that he is not interested in that slaying as it did not occur in his district and dismisses the idea that Nolan killed anyone. Totter then goes to Montgomery's hotel room to tell him that she is now in love with him, not Ames, but Montgomery ignores her and he is later seen driving down a road with Nolan following him in another car. Nolan forces Montgomery's car off the road, and Montgomery is left semi-conscious from the crash. Nolan runs over to Montgomery's car and pours liquor all over him, setting him up the same way he had been earlier framed for drunk driving. A drunk, however, staggers up to the wrecked car and peers inside. Montgomery grabs the derelict and exchanges identity cards with him and then flees. Police arrive and arrest the drunk and drive off with him. The injured Montgomery manages to get to a phone, calling Totter and asking her to pick him up. Totter arrives and takes Montgomery home with her and he later winds up in her bed where she hands him a mirror and we see in that mirror an ugly laceration on his forehead. She again declares her love for the gumshoe, and Montgomery seems to warm to the idea until Ames appears and offers him $5,000 to go to the Peacock Room and meet with his wife, who has just called him, needing money. He himself cannot go to her, Ames says, because two detectives are trailing him. Montgomery accepts the assignment, but he smells another set-up, so he asks Totter to follow him and bring along some policemen, saying he will leave a trail of rice from the rendezvous to wherever Ames' wife might take him. This plan in place, Montgomery meets Meadows at the Peacock Room, realizing that she is not Simmons' landlady or Ames' wife, but a conniving woman, who had once been Nolan's girlfriend until she jilted him. She tells Montgomery as she holds a gun on him in her apartment that she has impersonated the caretaker's wife and that the lady found floating dead in the lake was, indeed, Ames' wife. Montgomery takes the gun away from Meadows, who is now a nervous wreck; when there is a knock on the door, Montgomery does not find Totter or the police, but the corrupt and brutal Nolan, who grabs the gun and then tells him and Meadows that he intends to kill them both and then report that they have killed each other. The sadistic Nolan shoots Meadows four times, killing her, and then states to Montgomery: "How does it feel dying in the middle of somebody else's dirty love affair?" He tells Montgomery that he has followed his trail of rice and that he destroyed that trail as he followed it. Just before he shoots Montgomery, however, Tully and other cops appear on the fire escape outside the apartment window and they exchange fire with Nolan, killing the berserk cop. The viewer sees Montgomery at the finale where he is in his office, summing up the conclusion to this maze-like case and tying up all the loose ends while Totter arrives to tell him that they have two tickets on the next train leaving for New York. This is where this arresting film ends, one brilliantly and cleverly directed by Montgomery, and where he, Totter, Ames and Nolan render standout performances. The film was well received by critics and the public, which found its inventive style of the "Camera I" approach to be much more than a novelty but a whole new approach to filmmaking.

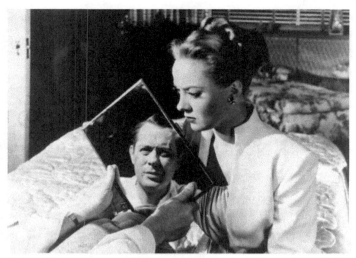

Robert Montgomery and Audrey Totter in *Lady in the Lake,* 1947.

Author's Note: Montgomery told this author that "I wanted to do a film like **Lady of the Lake** for many years, one where the camera had the starring role. I pitched that idea to MGM as early as 1938, but they told me that I was crazy and should stick to acting." Montgomery's break in that regard came when the great director John Ford literally broke a leg while making his classic war drama, **They Were Expendable**, 1945, and Montgomery, who stars in that film, took over the direction for several weeks, finishing the film, and receiving plaudits from MGM and Ford as well for his directorial skills. Now that he had established his ability to direct, Montgomery again pressured the front office to direct a complete film and got the green light, given the Raymond Chandler story, the studio having recently purchased the rights to that hardboiled detective tale. MGM told Montgomery that he could direct the film, but they also wanted to use his star status and he had to appear in it as an actor, which he did, even though he is seen only briefly in several scenes. Studio bosses then became alarmed when they learned how Montgomery intended to use the camera as the star of the film, Louis B. Mayer complaining that he did not want his studio turned into "an experimental laboratory." Montgomery nevertheless had his way, but, as he explained to this author, "I had to train the actors all over again so that they would act directly at the camera, which represented my character. To do that, I sat in a specially made basket just beneath the camera and they emoted directly to me while looking right into the lens." All complied cooperatively, except for Nolan, who had some difficulty in doing the action scenes with Montgomery and where he was literally struggling with the small cameras Montgomery had had technicians strap to his back and arms and where the camera "floats" with his actual movements. "It drove me nuts," Nolan told this author. "I told Bob [Montgomery] that acting directly at a camera was like acting at a blank wall and you don't get the physical response you would from a human being. 'Pretend the camera is that human being,' he told me, 'and you'll be able to do it.' Well, I am a vicious killer in that film and everything I do is mean and angry, so I pretended that the camera was Louis B. Mayer, the boss of MGM, a guy I disliked a good deal, and that somehow worked. At least Bob thought I did the job." For the more difficult shots, Montgomery had technicians build break-away sets, including the cars he drives, one of which was actually cut in two to make the scene of the accident work well. This was Montgomery's last film for MGM as he wanted to make independent films, and his very next film was another classic film noir production, **Ride the Pink Horse**, 1947, where he again is a private eye, but this time is seen throughout the film and where he is a lot tougher than the more pensive Marlowe he portrays in **Lady in the Lake. p**, George Haight; **d**, Robert Montgomery; **cast**, Montgomery, Audrey Totter, Lloyd Nolan, Tom Tully, Leon Ames, Jayne Meadows, Dick Simmons, Morris Ankrum, Kathleen Lockhart,

Arline Judge, Fred MacMurray, David James (baby) and Marlene Dietrich in *The Lady is Willing*, 1942.

Lila Leeds; **w**, Steve Fisher, Raymond Chandler (uncredited, based on the novel by Chandler); **c**, Paul C. Vogel; **m**, David Snell; **ed**, Gene Ruggiero; **art d**, Cedric Gibbons, Preston Ames; **set d**, Edwin B. Willis; **spec eff**, A. Arnold Gillespie.

The Lady Is Willing ★★★ 1942; U.S.; 92m; COL; B/W; Comedy; Children: Acceptable; **VHS**. The ravishing Dietrich is a Broadway musical star, who finds an abandoned baby in the street, takes it home, and wants to adopt it. But she is not married and must have a husband in order to legally adopt the tyke. She offers her new obstetrician, MacMurray, financial help with his research on rabbits, but on the condition that he will marry her so that the baby can be adopted by man-and-wife parents. MacMurray accepts and their marriage becomes one of convenience that nevertheless soon becomes one of genuine love. MacMurray had been previously married and his former wife, Judge, comes to him asking for money. Dietrich thinks MacMurray still loves his ex-wife and leaves him. The baby falls dangerously ill, but MacMurray saves the child's life, and this brings Dietrich and MacMurray back together again for a happy ending. Song: "Strange Thing and I Find You" (Jack King, Gordon Clifford). *Author's Note*: This film takes a large leaf from **Bachelor Mother**, 1939, where shop girl Ginger Rogers finds a baby and decides to adopt the child. **p**, Mitchell Leisen, Charles K. Feldman; **d**, Leisen; **cast**, Marlene Dietrich, Fred MacMurray, Aline MacMahon, Stanley Ridges, Arline Judge, Roger Clark, Ruth Ford, Harry Shannon, Elisabeth Risdon, Charles Lane, Neil Hamilton, Sterling Holloway; **w**, James Edward Grant, Albert McCleery (based on a story by Grant); **c**, Ted Tetzlaff; **m**, W. Franke Harling; **ed**, Eda Warren; **prod d&set d**, Lionel Banks; **art d**, Banks, Rudolph Sternad.

Lady Jane ★★★ 1986; U.K.; 142m; Capital Equipment Leasing/PAR; Color; Biographical Drama; Children: Unacceptable; (MPAA: PG-13); **DVD**; **VHS**. This film grippingly depicts the tragic story of the nine-day rule of Lady Jane Grey (Lady Jane Dudley; 1537-1554) as Queen of England during court intrigue and conflict between the Catholic and Protestant churches in the summer of 1553. Oft-married King Henry VIII dies and Protestant nobles led by John Dudley, the Duke of Northumberland (Wood) conspire to keep England true to the Reformation by having the sickly heir, King Edward VI (Saire) pass over the next in line to succeed him, Princess Mary (Lapotaire), and, instead, leave the crown to his Protestant cousin, Lady Jane Grey (Bonham Carter). Wood and his associates have already gotten Saire to agree to abolish the Catholic churches in England and loot their valuables. Wood arranges for Bonham Carter to marry his handsome teenage son (Elwes). Both of the young people are only sixteen and expected to be easily dominated. Following their wedding the teenagers quickly fall in love

with each other while conspiring to become Queen and King, and while planning to do good deeds for their country. Lapotaire leads a rebel army of Catholics to take back her crown. Political and religious factions win the day and Bonham Carter, Elwes, and Wood are all beheaded. This film takes considerable liberties with the facts, but the acting is superior in this convincing biopic, which is a remake of **Lady Jane Grey**, 1936, a production that more accurately portrays the true historical characters in this tragedy. Nudity and violence prohibit viewing by children. **p**, Peter Snell; **d**, Trevor Nunn; **cast**, Helena Bonham Carter, Cary Elwes, John Wood, Michael Hordern, Jill Bennett, Jane Lapotaire, Sara Kestelman, Patrick Stewart, Warren Saire, Joss Ackland, Ian Hogg, Lee Montague, Richard Johnson; **w**, David Edgar (based on a story by Chris Bryant); **c**, Derek V. Browne, Douglas Slocombe; **m**, Stephen Oliver; **ed**, Anne V. Coates; **prod d**, Allan Cameron; **art d**, Fred Carter, Martyn Hebert; **set d**, Harry Cordwell; **spec eff**, Dave Crownshaw, Dave Eltham.

Lady Jane Grey ★★★ 1936; U.K.; 80m; Gainsborough Pictures/Gaumont; B/W; Biographical Drama; Children: Cautionary. Pilbeam gives a marvelous performance as the teenage Queen of England, her reign lasting only nine days. She plays Lady Jane Grey (1537-1554), who is manipulated into marrying the teenaged Mills so that England can be purged of the Roman Catholic Church, only to be executed after the ends of those controlling her achieve their diabolical goals. The film accurately portrays these royal victims and where the production values are high and where sets and costumes also adhere to historical accuracy. The cast members, particularly the scheming Hardwicke, are standouts in their roles. Many of those appearing in this film were members of London's West End theater community and were somewhat unknown to films at that time, but most later became staples in British filmmaking. **p**, Michael Balcon; **d**, Robert Stevenson; **cast**, Cedric Hardwicke, John Mills, Felix Aylmer, Leslie Perrins, Frank Cellier, Desmond Tester, Gwen Ffrangcon-Davies, Martita Hunt, Miles Malleson, Sybil Thorndike, Nova Pilbeam; **w**, Stevenson, Malleson; **c**, Mutz Greenbaum; **m**, Hubert Bath; **ed**, Terence Fisher; **art d**, Alex Vetchinsky.

Lady Killer ★★★ 1933; U.S.; 76m; WB; B/W; Comedy; Children: Unacceptable; **DVD**; **VHS**. The inimitable Cagney is brusque, clever and very funny in this wild spoof on Hollywood, beginning when he is fired as an usher working at a New York movie theater. He falls into bad company when meeting Dumbrille, Fenton, Hopton and Hatton, along with their trampy girlfriend, Clarke. Cagney helps this unsavory crowd pull off a scam where a version of the old badger game is employed, Clarke inveigling a wealthy married sucker into a compromising position and who is then extorted to keep her silent about his adultery. Cagney's better instincts surface when he expresses his dislike for this kind of unethical work, and after one of the gang members is killed, he quits the underhanded crowd and flees, taking the Super Chief westward until he lands in Hollywood, hiding from the New York police as a down-and-outer. Living like a hobo, unshaven and shabbily dressed, Cagney is spotted at an amusement center by movie director Davidson and his assistants, who are looking for tough-looking characters for their next crime film. Thinking Davidson is a cop, Cagney bolts, but Davidson catches up with him, offering him a job as an actor, and Cagney jumps at the opportunity. Cagney takes the part and is seen pounding rocks in a prison quarry where he is told to hit an abusive guard "and make it look real." He coldcocks the guard and begins getting more substantial roles, mostly as a roughhouse stuntman-actor. He is seen riding a mechanical horse in a western with action shown all about him via rear-screen projection. Meanwhile, throughout this scene, Cagney is driven to distraction by a hysterical if not certifiable director, the screaming Bing. Taking a break, he is given a box lunch and walks about the sound stage until finding an unoccupied dressing room, and where he sits down to munch on a sandwich. The occupant of that dressing room is film star Lindsay, who immediately takes a liking to Cagney, asking him to remain with her and finish his lunch. She then goes out of her way to get Cagney feature roles, and he soon becomes popular with viewers, or so his studio believes while not knowing that Cagney has been writing hundreds of fan letters to himself and having out-of-town friends mail these raving missives to his studio. The studio decides to make a star of this rowdy character and teams him with Lindsay while they begin a love affair. They appear in a historical film that is successful, but one viciously damned by a critic who personally dislikes Cagney. The actor waylays the newspaper columnist in the washroom of the Coconut Grove nightclub and makes him eat his lambasting review and then shoves him into a toilet stall and where, off-screen, we hear the sound of that toilet loudly flushing. Dumbrille and his minions then arrive in Hollywood and try to compel their former confederate into helping them rob the homes of wealthy film personalities, but Cagney cleverly entraps the gang. They are sent to prison, and Cagney, in addition to his valiant screen image, is now hailed a real-life hero, ending up in the arms of the lovely Lindsay. Director Del Ruth delivers an entertaining portrait of Hollywood in the early talkie era, keeping the story line moving along with the whirlwind pace set by the dynamic Cagney, who dominates each and every scene. *Author's Note*: In one scene in this lively romp Cagney again abuses poor Mae Clarke, who had played his gun moll in the film that established Cagney's career as a tough guy, **The Public Enemy**, 1931, and in which he delivered the legendary grapefruit into her face. In this film, Cagney finds Clarke's extortion racket so repulsive that he yanks her out of her bed by her hair, drags her across the floor by that hair and outside where he dropkicks the trollop down the hallway, the most savage treatment he or any other actor ever administered to a woman on screen to that time, but it was all played for laughs and got them. Cagney told this author: "A lot of viewers wrote to me, telling me not to treat women like that, especially by pulling their hair, which was very painful. I wrote back to all those concerned folks that I really wasn't pulling Mae by her hair as she was actually holding on to my wrists when I drag her across the floor and I never yanked a single hair from her beautiful head." **p**, Henry Blanke; **d**, Roy Del Ruth; **cast**, James Cagney, Mae Clarke, Margaret Lindsay, Leslie Fenton, Douglass Dumbrille, Russell Hopton, Raymond Hatton, Henry O'Neill, Marjorie Gateson, Herman Bing, Dennis O'Keefe; **w**, Ben Markson, Lillie Hayward (based on the story "The Finger Man" by Rosalind Keating Shaffer); **c**, Tony Gaudio; **m**, Bernhard Kaun; **ed**, George Amy; **art d**, Robert M. Haas.

The Lady Lies ★★★ 1929; U.S.; 75m; PAR; B/W; Comedy; Children: Acceptable. An entertaining and often very funny film, Huston and Colbert are charming as they find love together, overcoming snobbery and the wild machinations of family members who oppose their union. Huston is a rich widower from the upper class, who meets and falls for the good-hearted and attractive Colbert. He thinks to marry this wonderful woman, but his children, Deering and Brown, along with some other meddling relatives, strenuously object to their marriage based on the fact that Colbert comes from the wrong side of the tracks. Their ridiculous schemes and back-firing sabotage intended to derail the Huston-Colbert romance produces many humorous scenes, but love overcomes all of their wild antics, and Huston and Colbert head for the altar. **p**, Walter Wanger; **d**, Hobart Henley; **cast**, Walter Huston, Claudette Colbert, Charles Ruggles, Tom Brown, Patricia Deering, Betty Garde, Jean Dixon, Duncan Penwarden, Virginia True Boardman, Verna Deane; **w**, Garrett Fort, John Meehan (based on the play by Meehan); **c**, William O. Steiner; **ed**, Helene Turner.

Lady on a Train ★★★ 1945; U.S.; 94m; UNIV; B/W; Crime Drama; Children: Unacceptable; **DVD**; **VHS**. In this quick-paced and engrossing crime thriller Durbin discards her usual singing role for that of a serious actress and does a fine job at it. We first see Durbin traveling on a train en route to New York City where she is scheduled to meet with her attorney, Horton, but, as the train slows down and approaches Grand

Diana Ross and Billy Dee Williams in *Lady Sings the Blues*, 1972.

Central Station, Durbin sees from her compartment window and through a window opposite of hers in an office building a man being murdered. She sees only the killer's back, but recalls the location of the building. When arriving at the station, Durbin goes to the police, but they dismiss her murder report as the product of her imagination, particularly after she admits that she is an avid reader of mystery novels. Getting no response from the police, Durbin then goes to one of her favorite mystery scribes, Bruce, asking him to help her solve the murder. Though Bruce has always created his crime tales out of his imagination and has never probed a real crime in his life, he finds Durbin's proposal challenging and accepts her invitation to aid her in identifying the killer. Durbin then identifies the murder victim when seeing him in a newsreel and she visits the man's family, but she is mistaken for the dead man's mistress, a manipulative nightclub singer. Durbin now becomes a suspect by those family members, including Duryea and Bellamy. When Durbin later finds the nightclub singer murdered (and impersonates her to briefly sing a song), she is now believed to be the killer. Durbin thinks that Duryea is the killer, and she and Bruce try to get him to confess, which leads to a battle royal in the club. Durbin flees with Duryea after her, but she runs into the comforting arms of Bellamy, who takes her to the very room where she originally witnessed the murder from the train. Duryea then arrives, brandishing a gun, but Bruce, who has been hot on Duryea's heels, catches up with him and wrestles the gun from him, handing it to Bellamy, who turns out to be the killer. Before Bellamy can take any more lives, however, police arrive and take him prisoner. Durbin is fetching and very effective in this above average crime tale, which is often played for laughs, until Bellamy realistically reminds everyone that he is truly a deranged killer. *Author's Note*: Alfred La Rue, a bit player who appears in this film and who had appeared in another film with Durbin, **Christmas Holiday**, 1944, also a superior film noir entry, later became a popular western cowboy star, using the sobriquet Lash La Rue. He was always the first to say that he got considerable help from the generous-hearted Durbin in his early Hollywood career. **p**, Felix Jackson; **d**, Charles David; **cast**, Deanna Durbin, David Bruce, Ralph Bellamy, George Coulouris, Allen Jenkins, Edward Everett Horton, Dan Duryea, Jacqueline deWit, Patricia Morison, Elizabeth Patterson, Maria Palmer, Barbara Bates; **w**, Edmund Beloin, Robert O'Brien (based on a story by Leslie Charteris); **c**, Woody Bredell; **m**, Miklos Rozsa; **ed**, Ted J. Kent; **art d**, Robert Clatworthy, John B. Goodman; **set d**, Russell A. Gausman; **spec eff**, John P. Fulton.

Lady Sings the Blues ★★★ 1972; U.S.; 144m; Jobete Productions; PAR; Color; Biographical Drama/Musical; Children: Unacceptable (MPAA: R); **DVD**; **VHS**. Ross, who began her singing career with the Supremes, does a fine job reprising in tone and presentation the unfor-

Margaret Lockwood and Michael Redgrave in *The Lady Vanishes*, 1938.

gettable singing of the legendary Billie Holiday (Eleanora Harris, 1915-1959), who brought so much joy to the world and so much misery to herself. The production values are high and the musical numbers outstanding, but, otherwise, no viewer should view this film with the belief that it represents the true historical facts surrounding this stellar performer's professional career. The film begins in the early 1930s when Ross, a young teenager, is brutally raped in a ramshackle house in Baltimore by a drunk, Caesar. To put her beyond harm's reach, the traumatized teen is sent by her mother, Capers, to live with her mother's friend, Sanford, who, unknown to Capers, runs a whorehouse in Harlem. She goes to work for Sanford as a maid, spending most of her time listening to jazz records and then becomes a member of Sanford's flesh-peddling retinue, becoming the star boarder at the brothel. Ross, however, has loftier ambitions and breaks free to go into show business, getting a job at a nightclub as a dancer, but she cannot put one foot before another and is soon dismissed. She meets Williams, a gambler and smooth operator, and becomes his mistress. He promotes her as a singer, but one much different than the black female singers of that era, who raucously deliver their songs in a caterwauling manner. Ross takes a more gentle approach, singing softly as she manipulates phrasing and tempo in the style of the jazz tunes that has earlier so impressed her, developing her own inimitable style. Her lady-like approach earns her the sobriquet of "Lady Day," and she sees success in nightclubs and later as a top recording star. Ross, however, remains emotionally insecure, despite the love Williams shows her, and takes to drugs to rid the depression that routinely seizes her, particularly after Capers dies, losing the only person in the world she thinks truly cares for her. After a band Ross is singing with in New York is booked on a radio show, she is told that she will not be allowed to perform on the airways, the unstated reason being that she is black; this racist insult causes Ross to rely heavily on drugs. Williams attempts to help her, but her addiction now controls her way of life. Realizing that she is slowly destroying herself, Ross decides to kick the habit and checks into a sanitarium where she struggles toward rehabilitation. More misery is heaped upon her, however, when she is charged and convicted of felonious drug abuse and is sent to prison. Ross then learns that, because of this conviction, her cabaret license to perform in New York has been revoked. Williams comes to her rescue again, guiding her through a tour of the U.S. where she proves that she is clean and is again allowed to perform in New York. She is slated for a concert at Carnegie Hall, and, while Williams is gone, Ross becomes so depressed that she goes back to drugs with the help of Pryor, who is then murdered when thugs invade his apartment. Williams arrives and makes sure that Ross performs at Carnegie Hall, a great success, but she is again denied performances in New York and later jailed for her drug violations, these last offenses causing Ross to be engulfed by drugs until

she tragically and prematurely dies at the age of forty-four. Ross is well supported by Williams and the rest of the cast, and the wonderful songs overcome the otherwise depressing scenes where Ross sinks into drug addiction (which prohibits viewing by children). Songs include: "What A Little Moonlight Can Do" (Harry Woods), "Them There Eyes" (Maceo Pinkard, William Tracy, Doris Tauber), "Mean To Me" (Roy Turk, Fred Ahlert), "I Cried For You" (Abe Lyman, Gus Arnheim, Arthur Freed), "Our Love Is Here To Stay," "The Man I Love" (George Gershwin, Ira Gershwin), "All Of Me" (Seymour Simons, Gerald Marks), "Lady Sings The Blues" (Billie Holiday, H. Nichols), "T'aint Nobody's Busines If I Do" (Porter Grainger, Graham Prince, Clarence Williams), "Don't Explain," "God Bless the Child" (Billie Holiday, Arthur Herzog Jr.), "Strange Fruit" (Lewis Allan), "My Man" (Channing Pollock, Maurice Yvain), "Gimme A Pigfoot And A Bottle Of Beer" ("Kid" Wesley, "Sox" Wilson), "You've Changed" (Bill Carey, Carl Fisher), "Lover Man [Oh Where Can You Be?]" (Jimmy Davis, Jimmy Sherman, Roger "Ram" Ramirez), and "Good Morning Heartache" (Irene Higginbotham, Ervin Drake, Dan Fisher). ***Author's Note***: The great singer's career is not documented accurately in that the producers of this bittersweet film took a wholly fictional approach to all the outstanding persons who helped Holiday in building that career. For instance, Holiday was the lover of the great saxophonist Lester Young from 1939, later married trombonist Jimmy Monroe (in 1941), and simultaneously carried on a long-standing affair with trumpeter Joe Guy, who was her main source of drugs. She divorced Monroe in 1947 when she also broke off her relationship with Guy. Not mentioned at all in this film is the fact that she was discovered by John Hammond in 1933 when she was singing at a small New York nightclub and how Hammond arranged for her to cut her first two records with Benny Goodman and his band. Hammond later stated that Holiday was "the first girl singer I'd come across who actually sang like an improvising jazz genius." Also not mentioned are the popular hits Holiday made when recording with the great Teddy Wilson in 1935-1938, or her work with Count Basie (Basie's name is briefly seen in the film on a theater marquee) or with Artie Shaw in 1937-1938. This author, as a child, met the great Billy Holiday when she was appearing at a nightclub in Milwaukee, Wisconsin, in the late 1940s when I was introduced to her by my mother (who called her "Lady Day") and who was also singing at that club. Not versed in the specialties of the myriad entertainers my mother knew, I asked Holiday what kind of act she performed. "I sing, young sir, I sing," she said. "And, in the next set, my first song will be for you." She sang "God Bless the Child," a moving ballad she had written with Arthur Herzog Jr. in 1939 and recorded on the Okeh label two years later. "She's great," I told my mother, "but she doesn't sound like any other singer I have ever heard before." My mother replied: "No, and you never will—she's one of a kind." She truly was. **p**, Brad Dexter, Jay Weston, James S. White; **d**, Sidney J. Furie; **cast**, Diana Ross, Billy Dee Williams, Richard Pryor, James Callahan, Paul Hampton, Sid Melton, Virginia Capers, Yvonne Fair, Isabel Sanford, Scatman Crothers, Harry Caesar; **w**, Terence McCloy, Chris Clark, Suzanne de Passe (based on the book by Billie Holiday, William Dufty); **c**, John Alonzo (Panavision; Eastmancolor); **m**, Michel Legrand; **ed**, Argyle Nelson; **prod d**, Carl Anderson; **set d**, Reg Allen.

The Lady Vanishes ★★★★★ 1938; U.K.; 96m; Gainsborough/Gaumont; B/W; Spy Drama; Children: Cautionary; **DVD**; **VHS**. Hitchcock's passion for trains (he would travel no other way) is manifested in this classic espionage entry where a marvelous cast superbly enacts exciting roles, all centered on the brutal kidnapping of an elderly woman traveling on a European train. Lockwood, a beautiful young woman, is seen at an inn at a remote Balkan resort. Her vacation over, she is about to return to her home in England to be married to a fellow office worker, but that trip is delayed when an avalanche blocks the railway. Passengers from the snow-locked train stream into the inn looking for rooms and these include an oily attorney, Parker, accompanied by his mistress, Travers; Wayne and Radford, two well-to-do English gentlemen obsessed with the game of cricket and who are desperate to return to England in order to see an important match; Redgrave, a music researcher studying Alpine ballads, and a kindly old woman, Whitty. While dining with Wayne and Radford, Whitty tells them that she is a governess and when she hears a singer warbling outside the inn, she immediately goes to her room and listens carefully to the singer, counting each bar sung. She is then interrupted by a loud banging above her room and, when she steps into the hallway to investigate, she meets Lockwood, who occupies the room next to Whitty's, and who tells her that she, too, is annoyed at the banging. Lockwood complains to Boreo, the manager, who goes to Redgrave's room to find him encouraging several clog dancers to loudly clomp about his room as he records their ritual dance. Redgrave refuses to stop his research and Lockwood offers Boreo money to have the annoying Redgrave evicted, but, when she meets the charming Redgrave, she changes her mind. Meanwhile, Whitty continues listening to the street singer, counting the notes of his song, and when he finishes, she throws him a coin. The next day, the snow has been removed from the tracks and the train is ready to move. The passengers assemble outside the inn, and Lockwood, seeing Whitty struggling with her luggage, leans forward to help her and is struck by a flower pot that has been apparently dropped by some unseen person on a balcony above and intended for Whitty. When Lockwood waves goodbye to her friends from the train, she briefly experiences blurry vision, ostensibly from the slight concussion she received when struck. Lockwood and Whitty occupy a compartment with others and then go to the dining car to have tea. Whitty asks the waiter to make her a cup of tea by using her own brand and she gives him a container with her own tea. While she and Lockwood talk, Whitty tells Lockwood her name, but, at that moment, her words are drowned out as the train rattles over a bridge and she writes her name, "Froy" on the window pane in the condensation gathered there. Lockwood and Whitty return to their compartment and Lockwood falls asleep. When she awakes, Whitty is nowhere to be seen. When she asks the other passengers in the compartment about "the English lady," all these Europeans tell her that "there has been no English lady here." Lockwood sees that Whitty's suitcase is gone and she becomes alarmed. She begins searching the train, but none of the stewards, porters, waiters and conductors can give her any information about Whitty, all saying that no such woman exists on that train. In her now frantic quest to find Whitty, Lockwood again meets Redgrave, who is traveling in third class and where he is watching the performance of some native dancers. Redgrave is, at first, surprised to see that Lockwood is even talking to him and states: "If I thought you were going to be on this train, I'd have stayed another week in the hotel." She explains that she cannot find Whitty and asks his help in finding her. Lukas, a suave and assuring physician, offers to help, but tells Lockwood that he has seen no such person as Whitty, as does Clare, a titled woman. Parker is then asked about Whitty and he denies seeing her. "But you must have," Lockwood states. "She almost fell into your compartment." Parker again says he knows nothing of such a woman and closes the door of his compartment where Travers is reading a magazine. These two are furtive lovers, who have pulled the blinds on the window of their compartment and wish to see no one, particularly the married Parker, who wants no one to know that he is traveling with his mistress. Both have seen Whitty, but Parker tells Travers that they must say nothing about it, as they may later be called as witnesses in a missing person case and that would dangerously bring their adulterous affair into the limelight. Lukas then suggests that Lockwood is most likely hallucinating as a result of having been hit on the head with a pot, but she insists otherwise. When the train comes to a halt at a small town, she and Redgrave look from both sides of the train to see if Whitty gets off, but all they witness is a new passenger being taken aboard on a stretcher, a patient whose face is covered and who is in the care of Lukas. The patient is carried into Lukas' apartment and Lockwood and Redgrave continue their search, meeting Lukas again, who introduces a foreign woman, who is wearing Whitty's clothes

Michael Redgrave, Margaret Lockwood and Dame May Whitty in *The Lady Vanishes,* **1938.**

and tells Lockwood that this is the woman she has mistaken for Whitty while hallucinating. She and Redgrave then go to the dining car, and while the train goes through a tunnel, Lockwood sees the name "Froy" still written on the window pane, and becomes hysterical, screaming that Whitty has been abducted. Conductors try to restrain her and she pulls the emergency handle that stops the train. She faints and wakes up in Lukas' adjoining compartment, and where Lukas tells her that she is ill and he will look after her. She wants none of his attention and leaves with Redgrave, who tells her that he now believes her story about Whitty as he has seen the brand of tea that Whitty gave to the waiter. Lockwood and Redgrave then systematically begin to search the train. Once in the baggage car, they find the equipment of a magician, "The Great Doppo," belonging to Leaver, one of those sitting in Lockwood's compartment. They find a magician's box with a false back used in disappearing acts, and Lockwood then finds Whitty's spectacles. Leaver then arrives and demands that Lockwood give him those glasses, saying that they belong to him. When she refuses, he and Redgrave struggle with Lockwood knocking out Leaver, who is then locked inside his own disappearing box. Lockwood and Redgrave next go to Lukas' compartment to find Lacy, a nun sitting next to the patient whose face is covered in bandages. Redgrave asks the nun if she speaks English, French or any other language, but she remains mute. As Redgrave is about to remove the bandage from the patient, an irate Lukas arrives, stating that Redgrave and Lockwood are endangering the life of his patient. He takes them to his adjoining compartment and gives them some wine, which they appear to drink, and, when both become drowsy from the knockout drops Lukas has slipped into the wine glasses, the insidious doctor tells him that, yes, the patient is, indeed, Whitty, and that she will be removed at the next stop where he will then operate on her, meaning that he will kill her. Lukas admits that the abduction of Whitty is part of a "conspiracy as you term it," adding that he has been kind enough not to overdose their drinks as that would leave them insane. Redgrave and Lockwood appear to become drowsy and fall asleep while Lukas leaves them alone. They have been pretending at being drugged, however, and open a window, breathing in fresh air. Redgrave climbs outside the train and works his way to the adjoining compartment, climbing through its window where he begins to remove the bandages from the face of the patient and where Lacy tells him: "Go on, it is Miss Froy. You needn't worry. You haven't been drugged. He [Lukas] told me to put something in your drinks, but I didn't do it." The foreign woman Lukas has earlier passed off as Whitty is substituted for Whitty, and Whitty is set free and hidden in a closet, and, while Redgrave and Lockwood go back to the adjoining compartment and pretend to be asleep, that substitute is carried on the stretcher from the train when arriving at the next station. Lukas accompanies the woman on the stretcher, who is placed inside an ambulance, but, when

Linden Travers, Naunton Wayne and Basil Radford in *The Lady Vanishes,* **1938.**

he removes the bandages, he realizes that he has the wrong woman. He again boards the train and tells other conspirators, Leaver and Clare, that they must try to kill not only Whitty but Redgrave and Lockwood, too. He then leaves the train. The train proceeds with only a few detached cars in tow, diverted so that it now travels on a branch line, and while Whitty, Redgrave and Lockwood go to the dining car where it is tea time and where all the English travelers are gathered. Once there, Redgrave introduces Whitty and tells Parker, Travers, Wayne and Radford that Whitty has been abducted and that they are now traveling into danger and all must help Whitty to escape. Whitty, by this time, has admitted that she is an agent and, in case she does not make good her escape, gives Lockwood and Redgrave a coded message that relates a secret pact between two European countries and consisting of a song that must be delivered to the British Foreign Office as soon as possible. "Then you are a spy," Lockwood says. Whitty smiles and states: "I have always thought that was such a grim word." When the train comes to a stop in a wooded area, Whitty is lowered from a window and makes her way into a forest. Meanwhile, Lukas and a number of his minions have arrived in cars that park outside the train. An officer boards the train and asks the English travelers to step off the train and get into the waiting cars, but Redgrave knocks out the officer and takes his gun. Radford and Wayne also have weapons and, when Lukas and his men begin firing at the train, the English travelers fire back. Parker, an utter coward, calls his traveling companions insane and tries to surrender, leaving the train and waving a white flag, but he is ruthlessly shot and killed by Lukas' men. While Wayne and Radford hold off Lukas and his minions, Redgrave goes to the deserted engine and gets it started. As the train moves toward the border, Lukas and his men chase it in cars, firing at it, but the train crosses the border, leaving the foreign agents behind. Lockwood and Redgrave then arrive in London and where they plan a life together, having fallen in love. They first go to the Foreign Office to deliver the vital message, but, while waiting outside an office, hear the very song they are to relate being played. They go into that office and see Whitty at a piano, playing that tune and, when Whitty sees them, she reaches out to these two benefactors for a happy reunion. Hitchcock masterfully presents this engrossing espionage tale (where the enemy is not specified but assumed at that time to be Nazi agents of Germany), keeping a fast pace and cleverly unfolding Whitty's identity and mission to build great suspense in one well-crafted scene after another and where Redgrave, Lockwood and Whitty, along with the rest of the cast, render wonderful performances. Lukas is exceptional as the calculating spymaster, and Parker is a standout as the covetous, weak-willed adulterer. *Author's Note*: This was the film that brought Hitchcock to the attention of Hollywood, and he soon left England to make films in America. Hitchcock personally selected Whitty for the pivotal role of the British

spy, but found that in her initial scenes she lacked vitality. The director jarred her from her reserved attitude when, after a few takes, he leaped from his chair, running onto the set, and shouting at the reserved Whitty: "Stop! That was terrible! Aren't you ashamed of yourself?" Whitty thereafter breathed life and animation into her every scene. Hitchcock had little patience with truculent or reticent actors, telling this author that "the best way to deal with actors is to break them down right from the start so that they do it the way the director intends." He had a hard time "breaking down" Redgrave, who was reluctant to do this film as he had been, up to the time of this film, chiefly a stage actor. "Redgrave was difficult from the beginning of that picture," Hitchcock told this author. "He told me right off that he was accustomed to extensive rehearsals and then insisted that we all rehearse his scenes, which might take days. We did a brief rehearsal for his first scene—and I should say that I was humoring him—and then I told him that I was ready to shoot. Well, Redgrave was unnerved by that and he visibly trembled and said: 'In the theater we would have three weeks to rehearse this scene.' I replied: 'I'm sorry. In this medium we have three minutes!' That man complained throughout the production and I became so exasperated with his constant demands for endless rehearsals that I said to him: 'You know that Robert Donat wanted to play your role in the worst way.' That put him in his place, I believe, but I have always felt that Redgrave has given many fine performances as long as he has had a firm director. I had no problems with anyone else in that picture. Paul Lukas, another fine actor, took my direction without comment and did so with such grace that I think he shamed Redgrave into behaving. A cooperative actor can achieve much more than what he or she thinks they can achieve if they will listen to the director. A case in point is Wayne and Radford. Both were rather straight actors not given to comedy. Yet, the roles they play in **The Lady Vanishes** are two very self-concerned British club fellows. They are more concerned about a cricket match than Europe going up in flames. Not until their national honor is challenged do these two persons decide to become involved and then fight like tigers against Lukas and his agents. I needed to have them be very funny in the picture, which needed some humor, and they delivered many humorous moments, even when they both thought that they could never be comedians. Their appearance in that picture was so effective that both went on to do similar humorous roles in other films. I should like to also tell you that I never said that 'actors are cattle.' What I said was that '*some* actors act like cattle.' And they do." **p**, Edward Black; **d**, Alfred Hitchcock; **cast**, Margaret Lockwood, Michael Redgrave, Paul Lukas, Dame May Whitty, Cecil Parker, Linden Travers, Naunton Wayne, Basil Radford, Mary Clare, Catherine Lacy, Googie Withers, Emile Boreo, Philip Leaver, Hitchcock; **w**, Sidney Gilliatt, Frank Launder (based on the story "The Wheel Spins" by Ethel Lina White); **c**, Jack Cox; **m**, Louis Levy, Charles Williams; **ed**, R.E. Dearing; **set d**, Alex Vetchinsky, Maurice Carter, Albert Jullion.

The Lady with the Lamp ★★★ 1951; U.K.; 110m; Herbert Wilcox Productions/Continental Distributing; B/W; Biographical Drama; Children: Unacceptable; **DVD**; **VHS**. Neagle is outstanding in her role as Florence Nightingale (1820-1910), a British nurse who crusades for sanitary medical treatment of soldiers in the Crimean War (1853-1856). The British, French, and Ottoman Empires and the Kingdom of Sardinia fought the Russian Empire over territories of the declining Ottoman Empire, most of the fighting taking place on the Crimean Peninsula. This excellent film focuses on Neagle's political skirmishes to improve the squalor in military hospitals, but impressive war scenes are also shown. Some in Parliament think that her efforts on behalf of wounded soldiers are merely meddling measures that coddle those troops, but Neagle's indefatigable energy and dedication in preserving the lives of these almost forgotten men is an inspiration to those troops and also to the viewer. The title comes from Nightingale going with a lighted oil lamp in the dimly lit hospital wards as she looks after wounded soldiers, who thought of this woman as a saint. The London *Times* reported her efforts to improve hospital conditions in the war, one of the first examples of investigative reporting. Director Wilcox does a great job of showing incisively contrasting scenes between the horrid conditions of the war and the comfortable middle-class homes of British citizens. **p&d**, Herbert Wilcox; **cast**, Anna Neagle, Michael Wilding, Gladys Young, Felix Aylmer, Julian D'Albie, Arthur Young, Edwin Styles, Rosalie Crutchley, Maureen Pryor, Sybil Thorndike, Michael Craig; **w**, Warren Chetham Strode (based on the play by Reginald Berkeley); **c**, Max Greene; **m**, Anthony Collins; **ed**, Bill Lewthwaite; **art d**, William C. Andrews; **spec eff**, Wally Veevers, George Samuels.

Ladybird, Ladybird ★★★ 1995; U.K.; 101m; Channel Four Films/Evergreen Entertainment; Color; Drama; Children: Unacceptable (MPAA: R); VHS. This engrossing tale is based on a true story, depicting a British woman, Maggie Conlan (Rock), who fights with Social Services officials over the care of her four young children from four different fathers, and who have been abusive to her. The children come to the officials' attention when they were injured in a home fire and where Rock is found to be an "unfit mother" and her children are taken from her. She meets a good man, Vega, a Paraguayan immigrant, and they start a family together, but their child is also taken by Social Services. The title comes from the nursery rhyme dating back to 1744: "Ladybird, ladybird, fly away home, your house is on fire, your children shall burn!" Violence prohibits viewing by children. **p**, Sally Hibbin; **d**, Ken Loach; **cast**, Crissy Rock, Vladimir Vega, Sandie Lavelle, Mauricio Venegas, Ray Winstone, Claire Perkins, Jason Stracey, Luke Brown, Lily Farrell, Scottie Moore; **w**, Rona Munro; **c**, Barry Ackroyd; **m**, George Fenton; **ed**, Jonathan Morris; **prod d**, Martin Johnson; **art d**, Fergus Clegg.

Ladyhaw- Century Italy sees Broderick as a clever thief, who awaits execution in the dungeons of Aquila, but he manages to escape via the city sewers. Wood, the Bishop of Aquila, who rules supreme in the area, orders Hutchison, his captain of the guards, to take his men and hunt down Broderick. Hutchison and his soldiers trap Broderick at a marketplace, but he is saved when Hauer, a mysterious knight dressed all in black, attacks and drives back the soldiers, identifying himself as the former captain of these troops. He and Broderick then flee on Hauer's fast horse. When Hutchison reports these events to Wood, the Bishop summons Molina, who is called the wolf hunter, and sends him forth to find both Hauer and Broderick and kill them. As they travel into the wilds, Hauer explains to Broderick that he saved him because he needs his aid to kill the evil Wood, but does not explain his reasons for wanting Wood dead. Traveling with Hauer is a beautiful female hawk, and when they make camp at night, Broderick sees strange events occur. Hauer disappears and a large black wolf is seen running beyond the camp. The hawk is no longer to be seen, but, instead, Broderick meets a beautiful woman, Pfeiffer, who has no fear of the wolf. Following another skirmish with soldiers, Hauer and the hawk are both wounded, and Hauer sends Broderick to take the seriously wounded hawk to the mountain retreat of McKern, a monk who is an enemy of Wood. McKern nurses the hawk; and then Broderick learns the mystery surrounding Hauer and the hawk when the hawk, during the night, turns into Pfeiffer. McKern explains how Hauer and Pfeiffer were betrothed, but Wood, who coveted Pfeiffer, made a pact with the Devil, who placed a curse upon both, so that each would change into another form. Hauer changes into a wolf at night, Pfeiffer into a hawk during the day and only for a fleeting moment at dusk and at dawn, can they have fleeting glimpses of each other, having no memory of their time in animal form, a curse that keeps them "always together, eternally apart." McKern, however, has discovered how the curse can be lifted and that is when, three days hence, a solar eclipse that will produce "a day without a night and a night without a day." On that day, Hauer and Pfeiffer must stand in human form before Wood and the curse will end. To achieve that outcome, the trio travels back to Aquila and, in a bloody encounter, con-

Rutger Hauer holding a curse-bound hawk in *Ladyhawke*, 1985.

fronts the sinister Wood and where these lovers strive to be together. **p**, Richard Donner, Lauren Shuler (Lauren Shuler Donner); **d**, Donner; **cast**, Matthew Broderick, Rutger Hauer, Michelle Pfeiffer, Leo McKern, John Wood, Ken Hutchison, Alfred Molina, Giancarlo Prete, Loris Loddi, Alessandro Serra; **w**, Edward Khmara, Michael Thomas, Tom Mankiewicz, David Peoples (based on a story by Khmara); **c**, Vittorio Storaro (Technicolor); **m**, Andrew Powell; **ed**, Stuart Baird; **prod d**, Wolf Kroeger; **art d**, Ken Court, Giovanni Natalucci; **spec eff**, John Richardson, Joel Hynek, Peter Donen.

The Ladykillers ★★★★ 1956; U.K.; 91m; Ealing/Rank/Continental Distributing; Color; Comedy; Children: Unacceptable; DVD; VHS. This witty, dark crime spoof is highlighted by Guinness' brilliant performance where he is an eccentric professor planning an elaborate robbery. Guinness first appears at the home of Johnson, an elderly lady with her own set of oddities. He rents lodgings from Johnson, saying that he is a musician and will gather his group to practice in his rooms. This pleases Johnson, who looks forward to hearing Brahms and Bach. Guinness' motley gang consists of Parker, Sellers, Lom and Green and they busy themselves in preparing the robbery, one that will allow them all to retire for life. They play recordings at their meetings to convince Johnson they are, indeed, practicing the classics, but they are vexed by her constant interruptions when she unexpectedly appears routinely to bring them tea and cakes. The bumblers somehow manage to pull off the robbery, which nets them £60,000, but, to assure that they are not traced to the stolen money the thieves hide the loot in a locker at a train station and then send the unsuspecting Johnson to retrieve the spoils. Johnson takes a cab to the station, and when returning home, a traffic accident brings her and the trunk she is taking home to the attention of the police, and several officers escort her to her residence. When the crooks see that Johnson is now linked to the police, they fear she may accidentally blab information about her strange boarders to the cops. They grimly resolve that she must be done in, but none are willing to take the life of this sweet old lady. Even after they draw lots, each candidate finds an excuse not to kill Johnson. Panic grips the gang and they all attempt to flee, but, in a series of hilarious misadventures, each culprit is killed, leaving Guinness as the sole survivor, but, he, too, meets his end while trying to hide one of the cadavers. (None of these deaths are presented in grisly presentations but are positioned in ludicrous scenes in the manner of the many deaths appearing in another Guinness classic, **Kind Hearts and Coronets**, 1950.) Johnson now has a trunk full of money and when she goes to the police to tell them about the cache, her tale is dismissed as she has for years been spinning wild tales for the local constabulary, who think of her as merely an eccentric old lady. Resigned to keeping the money, Johnson is last seen

Aamir Khan and Gracy Singh in *Lagaan: Once Upon a Time in India,* **2002.**

handing a large note to a startled hobo passing her in the street and this is where the cleverly spun tale ends. All of the players are exceptional in their roles, although Sellers, then youthfully pudgy, had not by then perfected the skills that would later make him a foremost comedian. The tiny Johnson, however, steals the film with her persnickety performance, one that won for her the British Academy Award. Rose's script is a pure delight, packed with crackling dialog and inventive scenes where the unexpected becomes routine and the ridiculous a normal way of life. He would go on to write many superlative comedy screenplays, including **It's a Mad, Mad, Mad, Mad World**, 1963; **The Russians Are Coming the Russians Are Coming**, 1966; and **The Flim-Flam Man**, 1967. *Author's Note*: Guinness told this author that "in the British mentality, crime is a supercilious pursuit and a waste of good time, which is why such comedies as **The Ladykillers** become successes, at least in Great Britain. To be sure, many criminals are not laughing matters, but we English prefer to profile them as abnormal and odd to the extreme in order to set them apart from rational human beings. That makes sense, don't you think?" **p**, Michael Balcon, Seth Holt; **d**, Alexander Mackendrick; **cast**, Alec Guinness, Cecil Parker, Herbert Lom, Peter Sellers, Danny Green, Jack Warner, Katie Johnson, Philip Stainton, Frankie Howerd, Madge Brindley; **w**, William Rose (based on his story); **c**, Otto Heller (Technicolor); **m**, Tristram Cary; **ed**, Jack Harris; **art d**, Jim Morahan; **spec eff**, Sydney Pearson.

A Lady's Morals ★★★ 1930; U.S.; 87m; Cosmopolitan/MGM; B/W; Biographical Drama/Musical; Children: Acceptable. The wonderful voice of singer Grace Moore highlights this musical biopic of the legendary Jenny Lind (1820-1887), who was called "The Swedish Nightingale," and known as one of the foremost sopranos of the 19th Century. In this highly fictionalized version of the famous singer, Moore is pursued by ardent swain Denny from city to city as she makes her world tour and where the enterprising Denny makes some spectacular efforts to win Moore's affection. Denny finally earns Moore's love when he is struck on the head, causing him to go blind and when she also temporarily loses her voice, their injuries causing them to find solace and affection with each other. Meanwhile, the brawny Beery provides an expansive and boisterous rendition of the colorful showman P. T. Barnum (1810-1891), a character he would reprise in a starring role in **The Mighty Barnum**, 1934. Though the facts are slim in this film, Moore's singing virtuosity (she was a member of the Metropolitan Opera) is superlative and makes the film worth the watching. Songs include: "Lovely Hour" (Carrie Jacobs Bond), "Swedish Pastoral" (Howard Johnson Stothart), "Casta Diva" (from Bellini's "Norma"), "Rataplan" (from Donizetti's "The Daughter of the Regiment"), "The Student's Song," "Is It Destiny," "I Hear Your Voice" (Clifford Grey, Oscar

Straus), and "Oh Why" (Arthur Freed, Herbert Stothart, Henry M. Woods). **p**, Irving Thalberg (not credited); **d**, Sidney Franklin; **cast**, Grace Moore, Reginald Denny, Wallace Beery, Jobyna Howland, Gus Shy, Gilbert Emery, George F. Marion, Paul Porcasi, Bodil Rosing, Joan Standing, Cecilia Parker; **w**, Hans Kraly, Claudine West, John Meehan, Arthur Richman (based on a story by Dorothy Farnum); **c**, George Barnes; **m**, William Axt; **ed**, Margaret Booth; **art d**, Cedric Gibbons.

Lagaan: Once Upon a Time in India ★★★ 2002; India; 224m; Aamir Khan Productions/Sony; Color; Musical/Sports Drama; Children: Unacceptable (MPAA: PG-13); **DVD**; **VHS**. During British rule in India, 1893, Blackthorne, the commander of a local British regiment in central India, announces he will double the Lagaan (land tax) on all villagers. Already feeling over-taxed, the villagers oppose the increase. One of them, Khan, a handsome young man, challenges the British to a game of cricket. If the Indians win, the tax will be canceled for two years, but, if the British win, the villagers will pay three times the tax. The British will field a veteran team of cricket players, but Khan and his fellow teammates have never played the game. Both sides agree and Indians and British from all over the country come to see the game which is symbolic of Indians' determination not to cave in to British authority. Among the few British cheering for the Indians is Blackthorne's beautiful sister, Shelley, who has fallen in love with Khan. In a tension-filled game, the Indians win and, at least, for the moment, they are happy. This exciting film offers fine acting and good direction, made in Bollywood, India's film capital in Bombay. Violence and strong language prohibit viewing by children. (In Hindi, English, Awadhi and Urdu.); **p**, Aamir Khan; **d**, Ashutosh Gowariker; **cast**, Khan, Gracy Singh, Rachel Shelley, Paul Blackthorne, Suhasini Mulay, Kulbhushan Kharbanda, Raghuveer Yadav, Rajendra Gupta, Rajesh Vivek, Sri Vallabh Vyas; **w**, Gowariker, Kumar Dave, Sanjay Dayma, K.P. Saxena (based on a story by Gowariker); **c**, Anil Mehta; **m**, A.R. Rahman; **ed**, Ballu Saluja; **prod d**, Nitin Chandrakant Desai; **spec eff**, Vishal Anand, Sherry Bharda, Shakti Banerjee.

L'Age d'Or ★★★ 1979; France; 60m; Vicomte de Noailles/Corinth Films; B/W; Comedy; Children: Unacceptable; **DVD**; **VHS**. A man (Modot) and woman (Lys) in France are passionately in love with one another, but they are unable to consummate their love because of their families, their own sensibilities, the Catholic Church, and modern society. Lys is strongly drawn to the music of her conductor father, which ties her to longtime bonds. The film, originally released in 1930 and not shown in the U.S. until 1979, was banned in some countries and has remained controversial, partly because of its surrealist scenes and Salvador Dali images. Excessive violence, gutter language and sexual material prohibit viewing by children. (In French; English subtitles.) **p**, Le Vicomte de Noailles; **d**, Luis Buñuel; **cast**, Lya Lys, Gaston Modot, Pierre Prévert, Caridad de Laberdesque, Max Ernst, Josep Llorens Artigas, Lionel Salem, Germaine Noizet, Duchange, Bonaventura Ibáñez, Buñuel; **w**, Buñuel, Salvador Dali (based on the novel by Marquis de Sade [not credited]); **c**, Albert Duverger; **m**, Buñuel, Georges Van Parys (both not credited), and Richard Wagner, Felix Mendelssohn, Ludwig von Beethoven, Claude Debussy; **ed**, Buñuel; **prod d**, Alexandre Trauner; **set d**, Pierre Schildknecht.

Lancer Spy ★★★ 1937; U.S.; 78m; FOX; B/W; Spy Drama; Children: Unacceptable; **VHS**. This exciting WWI espionage tale sees Sanders as a British agent, who impersonates a high-ranking German aristocrat and officer earlier captured in England. Sanders, who is an officer in the British Navy, bears a striking resemblance to the German agent (also played by Sanders) and is recruited in order to masquerade as his doppelgaänger, going to Germany to obtain some vital secrets that must be quickly returned to England. The film opens with Sanders telling his incredible tale to British intelligence officer Atwill, his story then shown in flashback, beginning when, in that disguise as the captured German agent, Sanders makes a daring and spectacular escape from a British jail (a scene that provides one of the greatest action sequences ever put on film). He makes his way to Germany where he is hailed a hero and accepted by everyone, except Lorre, who heads the German secret police. Since Lorre cannot challenge such a distinguished man like Sanders with only his suspicions, he recruits lovely del Rio, an alluring nightclub singer, to get close to Sanders and determine whether or not he is a secret agent. Del Rio establishes a friendship with Sanders, one blossoming into love. When she discovers his true identity, however, del Rio is too much in love with Sanders to betray him, even after Lorre receives from a German agent in England photos of the real Sanders as a British officer. del Rio helps Sanders escape the clutches of the pursuing Lorre and his henchmen as he flees to the safe borders of Switzerland and with the vital German secrets in tow, but she pays the forfeit with her life when Lorre orders her execution by firing squad for betraying Germany. In his first directorial chore, Ratoff, who had been producing, writing and acting in films for many years, offers a thrilling and tense production that unfolds at a quick pace and is brilliantly written by Dunne, his script packed with many offbeat comedic bits enacted by Schildkraut and Ruman as German martinets. Where Lorre renders a chilling performance of the vicious German spymaster, Sanders and del Rio shine in their roles, she being one of the most beautiful women ever to grace the screen. *Author's Note*: Character actor Schildkraut made this film while he was also appearing in **The Life of Emile Zola**, 1937, and for which he won an Oscar as Best Supporting Actor in his role as the persecuted Captain Alfred Dreyfus (1859-1935). Ruman was a Hollywood staple as a blustering German character, and who would almost make a career of such oafish but pricelessly memorable roles, as in **To Be or Not to Be**, 1942; **Berlin Correspondent**, 1942; **Desperate Journey**, 1942; **They Came to Blow Up America**, 1943; **The Hitler Gang**, 1944; and **Stalag 17**, 1953, to name a few. Ruman, along with Schildkraut, Atwill, and even Sanders, would appear as heavies in some of the eight Mr. Moto films (1937-1939) that starred the inimitable Lorre as the uncanny Japanese sleuth. Lorre so hated his role as Mr. Moto that he later claimed it compelled him to take to drugs—he was a morphine addict for many years—albeit Lorre's dependency on that drug began many years earlier; see my *Author's Note* for **Secret Agent**, 1936, and where Lorre caused pantheon director Alfred Hitchcock no end of problems during that production because of his drug addiction. **Lancer Spy** was Sanders' first significant leading role and it made him an overnight star, but in his dual performance, his enactment of the ruthless Prussian officer he impersonates was so riveting that Sanders was subsequently typecast as a heavy, and, for the most part throughout his film career, played insidious, conniving and reprehensible characters. "I did too good of a job playing that Prussian agent if only briefly in my dual roles in **Lancer Spy**," Sanders told this author. "Because of that role everyone wanted me to play such despicable persons thereafter. How do they say it? Falling on your own petard?" The German officer played by Sanders is based upon the captured German agent and naval officer Karl Hans Lody (1879-1914), who was snared in England by British intelligence at the outbreak of WWI, and who was executed at the Tower of London on November 6, 1914. Del Rio's role is certainly based on the WWI German spy, Mara Hari (1876-1917). Instead of betraying an Allied country, del Rio betrays Germany, when it was the other way around for the tragic dancer, Mata Hari, who was shot by a French firing squad on October 15, 1917. For extensive details on Lody and Mata Hari, see my book, *Spies: A Narrative Encyclopedia of Dirty Deeds and Double Dealing from Biblical Times to Today* (M. Evans, 1997; Lody: pages 322-323; Mata Hari: pages 337-342). **p**, Samuel G. Engel; **d**, Gregory Ratoff; **cast**, Dolores del Rio, George Sanders, Peter Lorre, Virginia Field, Sig Ruman, Joseph Schildkraut, Maurice Moscovitch, Lionel Atwill, Luther Adler, Fritz Feld, Lynn Bari; **w**, Philip Dunne (based on a story by Martha McKenna); **c**, Barney McGill; **m**, Arthur Lange, Charles Maxwell; **ed**, Louis R. Loeffler; **art d**, Albert Hogsett; **set d**, Thomas Little.

Littlefoot and family in *The Land Before Time*, 1988.

The Land Before Time ★★★ 1988; U.S.; 69m; UNIV; Color; Animated Adventure; Children: Acceptable (MPAA: G); **DVD**; **VHS**. Delightful animated tale shows the story of an orphaned brontosaurus named Littlefoot (Damon voiceover) born during a great drought between the Jurassic and Cretaceous periods and who attempts to reach the legendary safe haven of the Great Valley where vegetation is lush and plentiful and all dinosaurs live peaceably. Littlefoot befriends Cera (Hutson voiceover), a three-horned dinosaur, along with Ducky (Barsi voiceover), a duckbill lizard; Petrie (Ryan voiceover), a flying lizard that is afraid of flying and heights; and Spike, a stegosaurus. These five baby dinosaurs travel along a path described earlier by Littlefoot's dying mother, going along "the great circle that looks like a longneck [dinosaur]…and the mountains that burn." They encounter many hazards and adventures en route to their promised land, including lava flows and tar pits that threaten to engulf them, while they are all being stalked by a Tyrannosaurus Rex. The five dinosaurs decide to trap their pursuer and drown the flesh-eater, luring him to a watery death, but not before some of them are almost drowned. They all survive, however, and then find the home sweet home they are seeking, the Great Valley. The animation is exceptional, the action well crafted and the story is both homey and poignant, with lively and humorous narration from Hingle. **p**, Don Bluth, Gary Goldman, John Pomeroy; **d**, Bluth; **cast** (voiceovers), Gabriel Damon, Judith Barsi, Helen Shaver, Bill Erwin, Burke Byrnes, Candace Hutson, Will Ryan, Diana Ross, Pat Hingle (narrator); **w**, Stu Krieger (based on a story by Judy Freudberg, Tony Geiss), (Technicolor); **m**, James Horner; **ed**, John K. Carr, Dan Molina; **prod d**, Bluth; **spec eff**, Jim Mann, Dorse A. Lanpher.

The Land Before Time II: The Great Valley Adventure ★★★ 1994; U.S.; 73m; UNIV; Color; Animated Adventure; Children: Acceptable (MPAA: G); **DVD**; **VHS**. The capricious gang of five baby dinosaurs, who have earlier made their way to the Great Valley (now called Peaceful Valley) in the 1988 film, create havoc when Littlefoot (McAfee voiceover), Cera (Hutson voiceover), Ducky (Hogan voiceover), Petrie (Bennett voiceover), and Spike (Paulsen voiceover) prove they are independent by running away and get caught in quicksand, before being rescued by their parents (they were orphans in the 1988 film). They then defy their parents and wander into the Mysterious Beyond where they find two large lizards called eggnappers, trying to steal an egg. The group preserves the egg, which hatches, producing a baby dinosaur, nurturing it and discovering the creature to be a baby Tyrannosaurus Rex. They nevertheless befriended this sharp-toothed creature, naming him "Chompers." After he bites Cera by instinct, Chompers is chastised by the others and runs off. They follow, finding Chompers close to falling into the crater of a live volcano called the Smoking Mountain.

John Payne and Shelley Winters in *Larceny,* 1948.

The eggnappers attack the children, but Chompers comes to their rescue, driving off the attackers. Meanwhile, two adult T-Rex dinosaurs appear to menace everyone, but they have come to retrieve their son, Chompers, and, after they depart the valley, the adult dinosaurs block the entrance to make their home safe again. **p**, Roy Allen Smith, Zahra Dowlatabadi, Nelson Shin; **d**, Roy Allen Smith; **cast** (voiceovers), Scott McAfee, Candace Hutson, Heather Hogan, Jeff Bennett, Rob Paulsen, Linda Gary, Kenneth Mars, Tress MacNeille, John Ingle (narrator); **w**, Dev Ross, John Loy, John Ludin (from characters created by Judy Freudberg, Tony Geiss); **c&m**, Michael Tavera; **ed**, Jay Bixsen; **spec eff**, Kim Jung, Jeff Howard.

The Land That Time Forgot ★★★ 1975; U.S.; 90m; Amicus Productions/American International; Color; Adventure/Fantasy; Children: Cautionary (MPAA: PG); **DVD**; **VHS**. Exciting and well crafted, this adventure fantasy begins after a German U-boat sinks a British ship during WWI, but McEnery, the ethically minded German commander, saves some of the survivors, including McClure and a lone, young female, Penhaligon. When the submarine runs low on fuel, a strange and uncharted Antarctic island is seen, and McEnery finds an underwater entrance to a safe harbor where the climate is tropical and the surrounding terrain consists of dense jungle. When exploring the island, the British survivors and German sailors make a pact to work together in their search for fuel, but they encounter two separate savage tribes of prehistoric humans. They befriend one caveman, who leads them to an area where oil bubbles to the surface and they establish a crude refinery to produce enough fuel for the submarine while fending off attacks from one of the more savage tribes. They also discover that the island is inhabited by flesh-eating dinosaurs from the Jurassic period that consistently endanger them. When they prepare to depart the island, an all-out attack is made on them by the warring tribe and several British and German sailors are killed. McEnery manages to get to his submarine and attempts to sail it through the underwater channel while the live volcano dominating the island explodes. McClure and Penhaligon fail to board the submarine, but survive the tribal attacks and the volcanic eruption, moving northward on the island to seek an uncertain future at film's end. Though this film takes a large leaf from **The Lost World**, 1925, and **Mysterious Island**, 1961, it nevertheless provides a lot of action and no little amount of thrills. **p**, John Dark; **d**, Kevin Connor; **cast**, Doug McClure, John McEnery, Susan Penhaligon, Keith Barron, Anthony Ainley, Godfrey James, Bobby Parr, Declan Muholland, Colin Farrell, Ben Howard, Roy Holder; **w**, James Cawthorn, Michael Moorcock (based on the novel by Edgar Rice Burroughs); **c**, Alan Hume (Technicolor); **m**, Douglas Gamley; **ed**, John Ireland; **art d**, Bert Davey, **set d**, Maurice Carter; **spec eff**, Derek Meddings.

The Landlord ★★★ 1970; U.S.; 110m; Mirisch Corp./UA; Color; Comedy/Drama; Children: Cautionary (MPAA: PG); **DVD**; **VHS**. Bridges is a rich and naive young man, who turns twenty-nine and leaves his sheltered home life to buy a building in a black ghetto in the Park Slope section of Brooklyn. He intends to evict the black tenants and have the building remodeled into an upscale home as his own home. His plans change when he grows fond of the black tenants, especially Sands, the wife of a black radical. He believes he also may have fallen in love with Bey, a mulatto art student, and thinks he might marry her, but that all changes when he makes Sands pregnant. Meanwhile, his mother, Grant, wants him to keep to his original plan for the building and gives her credit card to Bailey, a black tenant, and appoints her as an interior decorator. It's a comic, often satiric take on the racial situation in New York City in the 1960s, one that provides a provocative story and is well acted by the entire cast. Sexual content prohibits viewing by children. **p**, Norman Jewison; **d**, Hal Ashby; **cast**, Beau Bridges, Lee Grant, Diana Sands, Pearl Bailey, Walter Brooke, Lou Gossett, Marki Bey, Melvin Stewart, Susan Anspach, Robert Klein, Trish Van Devere, Hector Elizondo; **w**, Bill Gunn (based on the novel by Kristin Hunter); **c**, Gordon Willis; **m**, Al Kooper; **ed**, William A. Sawyer, Edward Warschilka; **prod d**, Robert Boyle; **set d**, John Godfrey.

Larceny ★★★ 1948; U.S.; 89m; UNIV; B/W; Crime Drama; Children: Unacceptable; **DVD**. Taut crime yarn has Duryea leading a team of swindlers to Florida where they convince Caulfield, who is the widow of a WWII hero, to use up her life savings to construct a monument to commemorate her dead husband's service. The project is a colossal scam, however, and Payne, who fronts for the confidence gang, finds that he is falling in love with the beautiful Caulfield and is now reluctant to bilk her out of her money. Meanwhile, Payne's problems compound when Winters, who is Duryea's promiscuous girlfriend, develops a yen for Payne and begins to make moves on him, which endangers Payne's life as Duryea has a mercurial temper and a psychopathic streak. Payne solves his dilemma by turning himself and the rest of the gang into the police, earning the respect of Caulfield, who ostensibly will be waiting for him when he is released from prison. Tautly directed by veteran helmsman Sherman, Payne, Caulfield, Winters, and, especially, Duryea, give standout performances. *Author's Note*: This film was not initially popular with Winters, who complained to this author that "while I was under contract to Universal for seven years, that studio worked me like a dog, and where I was compelled to appear in twenty films, a lot of them programmers that offered me little opportunity to play anything other than sluts and slatterns. I got fan mail complaining about those roles and one fan asked me why I always wanted 'to play whores in pictures.' And here I was in **Larceny** playing another role like that. I got so mad that during production, I went home and cut my hair and the next day when I showed up for my next scenes, the makeup people almost fainted. Well, since the director [Sherman] was shooting the film in sequence and we were still in the early stages of the production, they made a few changes in the script to say that I had had my hair done over to explain my new look in the picture. Then Universal took advantage of my angry action by promoting my new hairdo and a lot of national magazines ran articles about that. I looked into the mirror and, you know, I actually liked that new look with the close-cropped hairdo and I permanently kept that hairdo. So **Larceny** did me a big favor after all and I remember the picture fondly because of that. Life is almost as strange as a woman's changeable mind." **p**, Leonard Goldstein; **d**, George Sherman; **cast**, John Payne, Joan Caulfield, Dan Duryea, Shelley Winters, Dorothy Hart, Richard Rober, Dan O'Herlihy, Nicholas Joy, Percy Helton, Walter Greaza, Gene Evans; **w**, Herbert H. Margolis, Louis Morheim, William Bowers (based on the novel *The Velvet Fleece* by Lois Eby); **c**, Irving Glassberg; **m**, Leith Stevens; **ed**, Frank Gross; **art d**, Bernard Herzbrun, Richard H. Riedel; **set d**, Russell A. Gausman, Ted Offenbecker, **spec eff**, David S. Horsley.

Larceny, Inc. ★★★ 1942; U.S.; 95m; WB; B/W; Comedy; Children: Acceptable; **DVD**. Robinson is very funny as is the rest of a sterling cast in this humorous gangster spoof where circumstance and coincidence compel Robinson to continue a criminal career after he has resolved to go straight. Shortly before being released from New York's Sing Sing Prison, Robinson tells fellow inmate Crawford, who is also about to be sprung, that he plans to open a dog track. Quinn, another prisoner, overhears these plans and proposes that Robinson instead opens a luggage shop next to a bank and from its basement tunnel into the bank and loot its vault. Robinson courteously declines the idea and, upon his and Crawford's release, they learn that their inept partner, Brophy, has lost the investment for the dog track and, now strapped for cash, Robinson reluctantly goes ahead with Quinn's scheme, leasing the luggage shop. While Crawford and Brophy begin digging in the basement of the shop, Robinson attempts to run the operation as a legitimate business, but has no patience with customers, who do not buy, selling off his inventory at ridiculously low prices and where fellow shopkeepers routinely visit him to wish him luck. Robinson then hires his niece, Wyman, to run things, and she buys an enormous amount of luggage from wholesale salesman Carson, who has eyes for her. When Quinn, still behind bars, learns that Robinson has followed his plan without his knowledge, he feels Robinson is using his scheme without his participation. To make sure he gets his cut from the bank robbery, Quinn breaks out of prison and goes to the shop, and brandishing a gun, forces the fellow thieves to step up their efforts to break into the bank. Realizing that dynamite is required to get through the sturdy walls of the bank, Quinn sets off a massive charge that blows up the shop and is killed and where everyone else survives. Quinn is the only member of the gang held responsible for the robbery attempt as Robinson has already been hailed as a pillar of the community. Having earned respectability, Robinson now decides to buy another luggage shop and follow the straight and narrow path. There are a lot of laughs in this film, especially the endless and futile digging performed by the oafish Crawford and Brophy, and the many transactions made by Robinson. He startles and baffles customers when he repeatedly foists his inventory on them in such a brusque and irrational manner and charges them next to nothing in order for them to take away his expensive luggage. *Author's Note*: Robinson told this author that "**Larceny, Inc.** was another satire on gangsters, only it was even more absurd than two other pictures I made like that—**A Slight Case of Murder** [1938], and **Brother Orchid** [1940]. I spend most of my time trying to get rid of customers while a couple of my men are in the basement trying to break into the bank next door. Instead of getting customers into my shop as would any normal businessman, I shove valises and trunks into their arms, charge them a pittance, and then give them the bum's rush. The shopkeepers in the area think I am nuts, but my actions are later thought to be part of a shrewd promotion campaign that draws a lot more customers into the shop. I am a success in spite of myself. **Larceny, Inc.** is about the wackiest picture I ever made, but it was a personal relief because I did not have to shoot anybody and where I could get my hands on comedy, which I love to perform. Warner Brothers had worn out their welcome with the machine-gunning gangsters of the 1930s, so they softened the images for people like me, Jimmy Cagney and Humphrey Bogart by putting us into a lot of good films where the tough guy appears sympathetic by doing the right thing. Bogey made a film called **All through the Night** [1942] at about the same time I did **Larceny, Inc.**, and where he plays a tough gambler, who rounds up all his cronies to take on and defeat a bunch of Nazis in New York. That picture was also another very good spoof on the kind of characters we all had been playing for years. When I mentioned that to Bogey at the time, he said with that old snarl: 'Eddie, it looks like we're going straight whether we like it or not.'" **p**, Hal B. Wallis, Jack Saper, Jerry Wald; **d**, Lloyd Bacon; **cast**, Edward G. Robinson, Jane Wyman, Broderick Crawford, Jack Carson, Anthony Quinn, Edward Brophy, Harry Davenport, John Qualen, Barbara Jo Allen, Jackie Gleason, William Hopper,

Lassie and Thomas Guiry in *Lassie*, **1994.**

Charles Drake, Ray Montgomery; **w**, Everett Freeman, Edwin Gilbert (based on the play "The Night before Christmas" by Laura and S.J. Perelman); **c**, Tony Gaudio; **m**, Adolph Deutsch; **ed**, Ralph Dawson; **art d**, John Hughes.

L'argent ★★★ 1984; France/Switzerland; 85m; Eos Films/Cinecom Pictures; Color; Crime Drama; Children: Unacceptable; **DVD**; **VHS**. Loosely based on a short story by Leo Tolstoy, this intriguing film relates a tale about a forged 300-franc note passed from one person to another and from shop to shop until it reaches the hands of an innocent heating oil deliveryman and husband, Patey, causing him to turn to a life of crime and become an axe murderer. The title simply means "money," and the film focuses on how the love of money can corrupt even the most innocent of human hearts. Excessive violence prohibits viewing by children. (In French; English subtitles.) *Author's Note*: The story of following an item that changes hands from one diverse character to another is seen in many films, such as **Tales of Manhattan**, 1942, an enthralling Ben Hecht story where a tuxedo changes hands and alters lives, or where an expensive car changes owners in **The Yellow Rolls Royce**, 1964. **p**, Jean-Marc Henchoz, Daniel Toscan du Plantier; **d&w**, Robert Bresson (based on the short story "Faux billet" by Leo Tolstoy); **cast**, Christian Patey, Sylvie Van den Elsen, Michel Briguet, Vincent Risterucci, Caroline Lang, Béatrice Tabourin, Didier Baussy, Marc Ernest Fourneau, François-Marie Banier, Alain Aptekman; **c**, Pasqualino De Santis, Emmanuel Machuel; **ed**, Jean-François Naudon; **prod d**, Pierre Guffroy.

Lassie ★★★ 1994; U.S.; 94m; Broadway Pictures/PAR; Color; Adventure; Children: Cautionary (MPAA: PG); **DVD**; **VHS**. This is a well-done animal film that updates the adventures of the beloved collie that first appeared in **Lassie, Come Home**, 1943, and then in several sequels. In the 1990s, a family leaves the city for the countryside of Virginia. The boy of the family, Guiry, feels lost and alone until a homeless collie joins the family. The dog saves Guiry from a snarling wolf, rescues him from a roaring waterfall, and, perhaps best of all, comforts him by curling up to him with love. It's an excellent entry in the Lassie film pantheon, but cautionary for children because of some pre-teen mischief, mild language, and suspenseful action. **p**, Lorne Michaels, Dinah Minot, Barnaby Thompson; **d**, Daniel Petrie, **cast**, Thomas Guiry, Helen Slater, Jon Tenney, Brittany Boyd, Frederic Forrest, Richard Farnsworth, Michelle Williams, Joe Inscoe, Yvonne Brisendine, Clayton Barclay Jones; **w**, Matthew Jacobs, Gary Ross, Elizabeth Anderson (based on the character of Lassie by Eric Knight); **c**, Kenneth MacMillan; **m**, Basil Poledouris; **ed**, Steve Mirkovich; **prod d**, Paul Peters; **art d**, David Crank; **set d**, Amy Wells; **spec eff**, Joe Digaetano, Robert Vazquez.

Roddy McDowall, Lassie and Donald Crisp in *Lassie, Come Home,* **1943.**

Lassie ★★★ 2006; U.S./France/Ireland/U.K.; 100m; Odyssey Entertainment/Samuel Goldwyn Co.; Color; Adventure; Children: Unacceptable (MPAA: PG-13); **DVD**. The beloved collie returns to 1939 England in this film, where she first appeared in **Lassie, Come Home**, 1943, and then in several sequels. The dog also returns to the original story line of the novel by Eric Knight, in which Lassie is the beloved pet dog and member of a Yorkshire mining family. When the father loses his job as the mine in which he works closes, the dog must be sold to a visiting neighbor, a wealthy duke, O'Toole. When the duke returns to his estate in Scotland, he takes Lassie along. Lassie is well treated but misses her master, so she breaks free from her kennel and undertakes a perilous 500-mile journey to be reunited with her young master, Mason. Beautifully filmed, this production is faithful to both the Knight novel and the original film, but the senseless inclusion of violence and gutter language prohibit viewing by young children. Again, we have the case of producers attempting to make a family film without considering the sensibilities of the children to whom the film is ostensibly addressed. **p**, Charles Sturridge, Ed Guiney, Francesca Barra, Samuel and Victor Hadida, **d&w**, Sturridge (based on the character of Lassie by Eric Knight); **cast**, Peter O'Toole, Samantha Morton, John Lynch, Peter Dinklage, Gerry O'Brien, Steve Pemberton, Eamonn Hunt, Edward Fox, Jim Roche, John Standing, Gregor Fisher; **c**, Howard Atherton; **m**, Adrian Johnston; **ed**, Peter Coulson, Adam Green; **prod d**, John Paul Kelly; **art d**, Colman Corish, Irene O'Brien; **set d**, Johnny Byrne; **spec eff**, Kevin Byrne, Kevin Nolan.

Lassie, Come Home ★★★★★ 1943; U.S.; 89m; MGM; Color; Adventure; Children: Recommended; **DVD**; **VHS**. This classic family film has everything—exciting action, a literate and sensitive script, careful direction, superlative acting, and a wonderful family whose pet, a handsome and a most endearing canine, is at the core of their deepest affections. The perils and setbacks that deprive them of their pet, and the devotion of that pet to those who love him that restores that pet to that family is the stuff of legendary love between animal and man. This prosaic tale begins during the economic depression following WWI and where Crisp and Lanchester live in a small cottage in Yorkshire, England, along with their son, McDowall, and their pet collie, Lassie. In dire need of money, the family barely survives, sharing its meager food with Lassie. To sustain his family, Crisp reluctantly sells Lassie to Bruce, a wealthy duke with a vast estate, and the dog goes to live in Bruce's well-kept kennels and where Taylor, Bruce's granddaughter, gives her love to Lassie. The collie, however, wants no other home than the one he has always known and the companionship of the boy to whom she is devoted, McDowall. She repeatedly breaks free and returns to the small cottage and into McDowall's arms, but he is sadly returned to Bruce's

care. Bruce decides to go on a hunting trip in Scotland and takes Lassie and Taylor along with him, a distance of hundreds of miles. Taylor, who loves the dog as much as McDowall, however, cannot bear to see Lassie pining for her true master, McDowall, and she purposely allows her to escape, knowing she will somehow find her way home to McDowall, Crisp and Lanchester. Lassie then embarks upon her long journey, instinctively going southward toward Yorkshire. She endures all hazards and fierce weather, staying briefly with an elderly farm couple, Webster and Whitty, and, later, with handyman Gwenn, all of these fine people eager to give their care and love to the indefatigable collie. Finally, weak from hunger and exhausted with fatigue, Lassie comes home, found by Crisp, who shares his last meal with the dog and tells wife Lanchester that he will not again break his son's heart and return Lassie to Bruce. Bruce then arrives with Taylor, knowing Lassie has returned to the cottage. Even after he hears the dog whining in another room where Crisp has hidden him, Bruce pretends he does not hear the animal. A generous and considerate person, Bruce has no intention of any longer separating Lassie from McDowall. He offers Crisp, a man he knows to be an animal lover, the job of supervising his dog kennels with the understanding that the great collie will reside with Crisp, Lanchester and McDowall. The happy ending thrillingly concludes when McDowall, returning from school, sees Lassie emerge from the cottage, and where the overjoyed boy takes the collie into his arms, saying: "Lassie, you've come home!" This final scene is indisputably one of the most poignant and touching moments in film history. McDowall, Taylor, Crisp, Lanchester and Bruce, along with the rest of the cast, render stellar performances, but they are overshadowed by the brilliant performance of Lassie. Wilcox's masterful direction patiently tells this story with definitive care addressed to each moving scene, all beautifully lensed by Smith and where the script is sensible without any overdosing of sentimentality. The heart always knows its reasons, and, in this magnificent film, all of its reasons are right. An enormous success, this film had two equally successful sequels, **The Courage of Lassie**, 1946, starring Taylor, and **Hills of Home**, 1948, as well as long-running radio and TV series, and remakes in 1994 and 2006. *Author's Note*: Director Wilcox began as a studio publicist and then as a script clerk for pantheon director King Vidor, and then worked his way up through the MGM ladder to directing screen tests of potential actors, later becoming an assistant director and then a second-unit director, until he was given his first shot at directing a feature film, this one. The front office initially thought this film to be just another programmer. (The film was really spawned in Dore Schary's "B" unit at the studio and MGM executives were amazed to see this film become an overnight classic, reaping more money than what they ever dreamed it would produce.) Wilcox's sister, Pansy Wilcox, married movie mogul Nicholas Schenck, who really held the purse strings for MGM and was actually Louis B. Mayer's boss, albeit the world wrongly believed that Mayer was the supreme boss at that studio. Though he was given his initial jobs at MGM through his nepotistic relationship with brother-in-law Schenck, Wilcox worked hard to finally earn the right to direct this film and its two fine sequels, **The Courage of Lassie**, 1946, and **Hills of Home**, 1948. The venerable character actor Crisp told this author that "that marvelous collie and the two kids [Taylor and Mc-Dowall] should get all the honors for that picture. I think those in the audience had a difficult time deciding on which one of them to love most. I think the collie won out, but only by a nose." McDowall had already become a foremost child film star with the making of Fox's earlier released **My Friend Flicka**, 1943, although he had appeared in many other films as early as 1938, and he was loaned to MGM by Fox for the making of **Lassie, Come Home**. Taylor, on the other hand, had only appeared in one film previous to **Lassie, Come Home**, a programmer called **There's One Born Every Minute**, 1942, produced by Universal, and that studio had no ambitions for the eleven-year-old girl, dropping her brief contract (so much for the keen visions of some film producers). She might never have gotten back into films if it had not been for two men taking nocturnal strolls in Hollywood. Taylor told this author that "my father [a British immigrant who had moved his family to California following the onset of WWII] was taking a walk when he ran into Samuel Marx [who worked for MGM for more than forty years], who was wearing a white helmet and who told my father not to light up any pipes or cigarettes as there was then a blackout. Mr. Marx was the local civilian defense warden making his rounds—this was during the early stages of the war when everyone obeyed these wardens and where blackouts were routine since we thought we might be bombed by the enemy at any moment. My father knew that Mr. Marx was a producer at MGM and that he was making a dog movie [**Lassie, Come Home**] and he begged Mr. Marx to give me a screen test for that film. Mr. Marx looked at the only other film I had appeared in [**There's One Born Every Minute**], and then tested me, and then cast me in **Lassie, Come Home**. The rest is history." The history of Lassie is a much different one. In the first place, the dog playing the female collie is not a female at all, but a male named Pal, a collie purchased for $10 by animal trainer Rudd Weatherwax. He originally used a female collie for the early shooting of the film, but when that dog began shedding, Weatherwax replaced the female with Pal, who was a very smart double doing all the stunts for the original collie. The gifted Pal would, at Weatherwax's command, instantly limp, whine, leap, run, crouch, snarl, or lap the face of any human being. All of the dogs playing Lassie in future would be played by male collies. **p**, Samuel Marx and (not credited) Dore Schary; **d**, Fred M. Wilcox; **cast**, Roddy McDowall, Donald Crisp, Dame May Whitty, Edmund Gwenn, Nigel Bruce, Elsa Lanchester, Elizabeth Taylor, Alan Napier, Arthur Shields, Ben Webster, J. Patrick O'Malley, Pal (Lassie); **w**, Hugo Butler (based on the novel by Eric Knight); **c**, Leonard Smith (Technicolor); **m**, Daniele Amfitheatrof; **ed**, Ben Lewis; **art d**, Cedric Gibbons; **set d**, Edwin B. Willis; Lassie's (Pal's) trainer: Rudd Weatherwax.

Lassie's Great Adventure ★★★ 1963; U.S.; 73m; Wrather Productions/FOX; Color; Adventure; Children: Acceptable; **DVD**; **VHS**. Exciting family fare has Provost, the small son of Lockhart and Reilly, along with their family pet, Lassie, get into a gondola that is suddenly carried skyward during a promotion event at a county fair. While the frantic Lockhart and Reilly organize a search for boy and dog, the balloon sails northward into Canada and lands in the wilds where Lassie saves Provost from many pitfalls and hazards and while they encounter and befriend Kiel, a mute, giant Indian, who further protects them until they are rescued by the Mounties, who have conducted a widespread helicopter search. All's well that ends well in this pleasant outing that offers a lot of good action without traumatizing children. **p**, Robert Golden; **d**, William Beaudine; **cast**, June Lockhart, Hugh Reilly, Jon Provost, Robert Howard, Will J. White, Richard Kiel, Walter Stocker, Walter Kelley, Patrick Waltz; Dick Simmons; **w**, Monroe Manning, Charles O'Neal, Maria Little (based on a story by Sumner Arthur Long and the character of Lassie created by Eric Knight); **c**, Eddie Fitzgerald (Eastmancolor); **ed**, Monica Collingwood; **art d**, George Troast; **set d**, Frank Rafferty; **spec eff**, Harold Murphy.

The Last Angry Man ★★★ 1959; U.S.; 100m; COL; B/W; Drama; Children: Acceptable; **VHS**. Muni gives a powerful performance as an idealistic, uncompromising physician, who has been running a small clinic in Brooklyn for four decades. Baker, his nephew, is an ambitious writer, who pens an article about his hardworking uncle, and when TV producer Wayne reads the piece, he decides he wants to produce a network TV show based upon the dedicated Muni. Baker is delighted as he sees an opportunity to become a writer for TV, but, when Wayne approaches Muni at Baker's urging, the doctor says he wants no part of such a show. Now determined to produce that show, the stubborn Wayne goes to Adler, Muni's oldest and dearest friend (they have gone to school together), asking him to persuade Muni to do the show. Adler agrees, but only on the proviso that Wayne purchases a nice home in a good neighborhood for Muni and his equally hardworking and loyal wife, Pol-

Roddy McDowall and Lassie in *Lassie, Come Home*, 1943.

lock, as they presently live in a crime-infested slum. Adler then goes to Muni and persuades him to appear on the show so that he can emphasize his principles and expose the widespread hypocrisy in the medical profession. While preparing for the show, Muni has become deeply concerned in the welfare of Williams, a street thug who lives in Muni's neighborhood and who has a brain tumor. Muni spends a great deal of his time monitoring Williams' movements and running him down to administer treatment. Just before going on the TV show, Muni is informed that Williams is under arrest for stealing a car and the physician abruptly leaves to give his patient care, but he suffers a heart attack and succumbs while at the police station. Muni was an actor like no other and his forceful personality dominates every scene in this moving film. He gets strong support from Adler, Wayne, Baker and Williams. ***Author's Note***: This was Williams' film debut, and he later admitted that he learned much of his craft from the gifted Muni, who even arm-wrestled with him, showing some tricks in that, too. This was the first film Muni made in seven years and it proved to be his last. He was reluctant to make the film and agreed to go into the production only on the condition that director Mann would allow the actor to have his way with every scene. With that in mind, Muni assumed the role of a film professor, lecturing Mann for hours on end. In one instance, Muni told Mann that one of his scenes had to be "filtered, sifted, refined and distilled," before walking off the set. Mann reportedly turned to Adler and remarked: "What does he think we're making—matzo balls?" **p**, Fred Kohlmar; **d**, Daniel Mann; **cast**, Paul Muni, David Wayne, Betsy Palmer, Luther Adler, Claudia McNeil, Joby Baker, Joanna Moore, Billy Dee Williams, Cicely Tyson, Godfrey Cambridge, Paul Langton; **w**, Gerald Green, Richard Murphy (based on the novel by Green); **c**, James Wong Howe; **m**, George Duning; **ed**, Charles Nelson; **art d**, Carl Anderson; **set d**, William Kiernan.

The Last Bridge ★★★ 1957; Yugoslavia/Austria; 90m; Cosmopol Film/Union Film Distributors; B/W; War Drama; Children: Unacceptable; **DVD**; **VHS**. Schell is a German nurse, who is kidnapped by Yugoslavian partisans during World War II because their doctor died and they need a replacement, at least someone with some medical training. She goes with them unwillingly, but as she gets to know them, she sees them not as bandits and wounded enemies but as human beings who need her help. Traveling with the partisans over mountains and crossing rivers, they are attacked by German troops. Her captivity evolves into an emotional state in which she wonders about her national loyalties, doubts that also question her patriotism. Wicki, the partisan commander, shows her a cemetery and tells her that German soldiers are buried in it, and then gestures with a hand to show the mountains and says, "and there are buried our people, my people, our land." This moving anti-war film offers an extraordinary performance by Schell. War violence pro-

Emil Jannings, left, in *The Last Command*, 1928.

hibits viewing by children. (In German; English subtitles.) **p**, Carl Szokoll; **d**, Helmut Käutner; **cast**, Maria Schell, Bernhard Wicki, Barbara Rütting, Carl Möhner, Pavle Mincic, Horst Hächler, Robert Meyn, Zvonko Zungul, Tilla Durieux, Fritz Eckhardt; **w**, Käutner, Norbert Kunze; **c**, Elio Carniel; **m**, Karl de Groof; **ed**, Herma Diethelm, Paula Dworak; **prod d**, Kosta Krivokapic, Otto Pischinger, Wolf Witzemann.

The Last Chance ★★★ 1945; Switzerland; 104m; Praesens-Film/MGM; B/W; War Drama; Children: Unacceptable; **DVD**. Shot in a documentary style by director Lindtberg, this emotion-packed film realistically portrays three Allied pilots in WWII, who organize and lead a group of refugees fleeing Nazi-occupied Italy over the Alps and to the sanctuary of Switzerland. There are no professional actors performing roles, which are represented by three actual pilots, who had been shot down by the Germans and the refugees are also non-actors and who represent many nations. One of many powerful scenes in this unusual film has the refugees all singing the same song together but in many separate languages. These amateur actors, however, provide exceptional performances in this compelling film. **p**, Lazar Wechsler; **d**, Leopold Lindtberg; **cast**, Ewart G. Morrison, John Hoy, Ray Reagan, Luisa Rossi, Giuseppe Galeati, Romano Calò, Leopold Biberti, Sigfrit Steiner, Emil Gerber, Therese Giehse; **w**, Alberto Barberis, Elizabeth Montagu, Richard Schweizer, David Wechsler; **c**, Emil Berna; **m**, Robert Blum; **ed**, Hermann Haller, René Martinet.

Last Chance Harvey ★★★ 2008; U.S.; 93m; Overture Films; Color; Romance; Children: Unacceptable (MPAA: PG-13); **BD**; **DVD**. Hoffman is a seventy-one-year-old longtime divorced American, a failed jazz pianist who writes jingles for commercials, and who is in London for a weekend to attend the wedding of his beautiful daughter, Balaban, to a handsome young man, Brolin. Hoffman's former wife, Baker, has remarried and his daughter is closer to her stepfather than to him. He thinks he will never meet another woman he would want to marry or who would want to marry him, until he meets Thompson, an attractive unmarried woman, who is 49-years-old and has a boring job where she asks flight passengers to fill out surveys at Heathrow Airport. She also feels that love will pass her by, and she goes on blind dates that friends and her mother Atkins arrange for her, dates that lead nowhere. Hoffman and Thompson get together, but they are a very odd couple and where Thompson represents what Hoffman believes will be his last chance at love and marriage. Thompson, on the other hand, is uncertain as to whether or not Hoffman is the man of her dreams, but they nevertheless wind up together in this entertaining romance film that also provides some incisive character development. Gutter language and adult themes prohibit viewing by children. **p**, Tim Perell, Nicola Usborne; **d&w**, Joel

Hopkins; **cast**, Dustin Hoffman, Emma Thompson, Eileen Atkins, Kathy Baker, Liane Balaban, James Brolin, Richard Schiff, Timothy Howar, Wendy Mae Brown, Bronagh Gallagher; **c**, John de Borman; **m**, Dickon Hinchliffe; **ed**, Robin Sales; **prod d**, Jon Henson; **art d**, Patrick Rolfe, Suzanne Austin; **set d**, Robert Wischhusen-Hayes; **spec eff**, Neal Champion, Charlotte Gray.

The Last Command ★★★★ 1928 (silent); U.S.; 88m/9 reels; PAR; B/W; Drama; Children: Acceptable; **DVD**; **VHS**. The great German actor Jannings gives an unforgettable performance in this stirring drama, and for which he won the first Oscar as Best Actor (which was also given to him for another film produced in the same year, **The Way of All Flesh**, 1927). The film opens with Powell as a Russian émigré transplanted to Hollywood where he has become an important film director. He is looking over many photos of extras for his forthcoming film, based upon WWI and the Russian Revolution when he spots a photo of Jannings and quickly orders an assistant, Raymond, to hire Jannings. When Jannings arrives with a small army of extras pouring into Eureka Studio for Powell's big-budget production, he is given a general's uniform and Jannings begins to prepare for his role. He dresses as the Russian general and places a medal on it, a genuine medal that Jannings personally received from the czar as he was one of Russia's foremost generals before his life as a Hollywood extra. Jannings' hands shake with palsy and his head twitches as he beholds himself in his costume, and this so distracts another actor that he complains. Jannings apologizes, saying that his nervous condition is the result of his having had a traumatic experience years earlier. With that, the story goes to flashback where, ten years earlier, Jannings is, in real life, that powerful Russian general during the communist revolution. He is informed that two actors who have been entertaining his troops are secret revolutionaries and he has one of them, Powell, brought before him. When Powell defies Jannings, the general uses a whip to strike him across his face and orders him jailed. The other actor is the beautiful Brent, an alluring woman to whom Jannings is emotionally drawn. Although Jannings knows that Brent's revolutionary beliefs pose a danger to him, he nevertheless establishes a relationship with her, and, within a week, gives her an exquisite pearl necklace. Brent realizes that Jannings is no oppressive brute, but a man devoted to the czar and who has a noble heart, loving Russia as much as she does. When they are alone together in her room, Jannings sees a partly hidden pistol, but he pretends not to see the weapon; when he turns his back on her, Brent finds that she cannot shoot the man she now loves. As they ride in a military train, the Bolsheviks attack it, and capture Jannings and his men. Brent pretends to hate Jannings and suggests to the revolutionaries that he not be shot along with the rest of his officers, but made to shove coal into the engine's boiler all the way to Petrograd where he will be shot. This done, the train proceeds with Jannings slaving as a stoker, but Brent comes to him while his guards are drunk and not watching, gives Jannings the necklace, telling him to use it to fund his way to freedom in escaping Russia. He leaps from the train, but then watches in agony as the train crashes from a disabled bridge and plunges into the river, killing all on board, including Brent, the woman he loved. In flash forward we now see Jannings in Hollywood and beginning a scene in the film Powell is directing. Seeking revenge for the insult he received at the hands of Jannings ten years earlier, Powell orders Jannings, playing the general he once was, to give an impassioned speech to his dispirited men on the battlefield. Losing his grip on reality, Jannings believes himself to be back in Russia and gives that speech before seizing the czarist banner and then leading his troops in a wild charge against the enemy, one so physically demanding that Jannings suffers a heart attack and, after the scene, asks Powell if he and his troops have won the battle. Powell's hatred for Jannings disappears and he tells Jannings just before he dies that, indeed, he has won the battle. At the finale, the title cards display an ironic exchange of dialog. Raymond states to Powell: "That man was a great actor." Powell replies: "He was more than a great actor. He was a great man." Jannings is riveting as the czarist general living in the past and present at the same time while Powell, Brent and the rest of the cast give fine support. The marvelous styling of pantheon director von Sternberg is evident in every compelling scene in this stylish historical epic where his eye-attracting set-ups and close-ups display deep shadows and contrasting bursts of light that enhance the brooding story and accent the bedeviled mind of Jannings and where the action is often spectacular. **p**, Jesse L. Lasky, Adolph Zukor, B.P. Schulberg; **d**, Josef von Sternberg; **cast**, Emil Jannings, Evelyn Brent, William Powell, Jack Raymond, Nicholas Soussanin, Michael Visaroff, Fritz Feld, Harry Cording, Shep Houghton, Alexander Ikonnikov; **w**, John F. Goodrich, Herman J. Mankiewicz (based on a story by Lajos Biró, von Sternberg); **c**, Bert Glennon; **m**, Robert Israel (2010 composer, new score); **ed**, William Shea; **art d**, Hans Dreier.

The Last Command ★★★ 1955; U.S.; 110m; REP; Color; Adventure/War Drama; Children: Cautionary; **VHS**. Hayden does a fine job playing the inimitable Jim Bowie (James "Jim" Bowie; 1796-1836), knife-fighter and Texas hero. He is seen living comfortably in Texas where he enjoys the friendship of the powerful Mexican ruler of Texas, Santa Anna (Antonio López de Santa Anna; 1794-1876), played by Naish, but Hayden's easy lifestyle is disrupted when fellow Texans Carlson, playing William Barret Travis (1809-1836), and Borgnine, along with others, begin agitating for Texas independence. Hayden takes a conciliatory approach, trying to persuade the Texans to use diplomacy instead of force while he courts Alberghetti, the beautiful daughter of a wealthy Mexican landowner sympathetic to the cause of the Texans. Many oppose a peaceful settlement with Santa Anna, and the hot-headed Borgnine challenges Hayden to a knife fight, a struggle Borgnine loses. Naish's repressive actions, however, soon has Hayden siding with Carlson and others and he becomes one of the leaders of the Texas revolution, going into the Alamo and fighting Naish and his thousands of troops and where he is one of the last heroic defenders to die in that legendary battle (February 23-March 6, 1836). The acting is superior as is the script, and director Lloyd does a good job with the exciting battle scenes. *Author's Note*: Though well made, this film does not compare with John Wayne's epic **Alamo**, 1960, produced and directed by Wayne, who also co-stars in that film with Richard Widmark and Laurence Harvey. This film was originally slated for Wayne, but when he and Republic chief Herbert J. Yates could not get together on the budget (and where Yates insisted that his mistress and reigning Republic star Vera Hruba Ralston, a former Czechoslovakian refugee and figure skater, co-star with Wayne), the independent-minded Wayne abandoned the project and began making plans for his own version of the fight at the Alamo, releasing that film five years later. Yates, however, still wanted to produce a film about this evergreen subject and, perhaps to spite Wayne, went ahead with this production. The struggle for Texas independence is the subject of many other films, notably **Man of Conquest**, 1939; **The Man from the Alamo**, 1953; **Davy Crockett: King of the Wild Frontier**, 1955; the excellent made-for-TV film, **Gone to Texas**, 1986; and **The Alamo**, 2004. **p,&d**, Frank Lloyd; **cast**, Sterling Hayden, Anna Maria Alberghetti, Richard Carlson, Arthur Hunnicutt, Ernest Borgnine, J. Carrol Naish, Ben Cooper, John Russell, Virginia Grey, Jim Davis, Otto Kruger, Russell Simpson, Walter Reed; **w**, Warren Duff (based on the story by Sy Bartlett); **c**, Jack Marta; **m**, Max Steiner; **ed**, Tony Martinelli; **art d**, Frank Arrigo; **set d**, John McCarthy, Jr., George Milo; **spec eff**, Howard and Theodore Lydecker.

The Last Days of Disco ★★★ 1998; U.S.; 113m; Castle Rock Entertainment/Gramercy Pictures; Color; Comedy/Drama; Children: Unacceptable (MPAA: R); **DVD**; **VHS**. Sevigny and Beckinsale are two recent Ivy League college graduate girlfriends working as book editors. They take their customary last stand at a Manhattan disco bar in the early 1980s looking for a night of swinging music and a few drinks while hoping to run into Mr. Right. Those eagerly expected swains appear as Astin, a junior advertising executive, and Leonard, an environ-

Chloë Sevigny and Chris Eigeman in *The Last Days of Disco*, 1998.

mental lawyer, but they're not as Right as the girls hope for. The disco scene presents a lot of fun, but when it ends, the good days of youth and dating after college ends with it. Nudity, drugs, and gutter talk prohibit viewing by children. **p**, Whit Stillman, Edmon Roch, Cecilia Kate Roque; **d&w**, Stillman; **cast**, Chloë Sevigny, Kate Beckinsale, Chris Eigeman, Robert Sean Leonard, Mackenzie Astin, Matt Keeslar, Jennifer Beals, Matthew Ross, Tara Subkoff, George Plimpton; **c**, John Thomas; **m**, Mark Suozzo; **ed**, Andrew Hafitz, Jay Pires; **prod d**, Ginger Tougas; **art d**, Molly Mikula; **set d**, Lisa Nilsson; **spec eff**, Todd Wolfeil, Michael Ventresco.

Last Days of Mussolini ★★★ 1974; Italy; 91m; Aquila/Group 1; Color/B/W; Biographical Drama; Children: Unacceptable (MPAA: PG); **DVD**; **VHS**. Steiger renders a bravura performance in playing Italian dictator Benito Mussolini (1883-1945) during the last few days of the fascist leader. He spends his last days on earth in delusion and apprehension as his supporters desert and his dictatorship crumbles by the hour while his only emotional support is his fiercely loyal mistress, Clara Petacci (1912-1945), well played by Gastoni. Meanwhile, four separate factions are desperately searching for Steiger, who is hiding out in a small mountain retreat with Gastoni and a few others from his collapsed regime. Those seeking the dictator are elements of the Allied forces that want to try him as a war criminal, German troops working to smuggle him out of the country, the provincial Italian government that has sought peace with the Allies, and Italian freedom fighters, mostly communists, who seek revenge on Steiger for his former oppressions against them, and these forces are led by Nero. While Steiger rants and raves and then becomes pensively introspective, Nero learns of Steiger's hideout and subsequently takes him and Gastoni prisoner, but, rather than turn Steiger over to the Allies alive, decides to shoot him. Gastoni frantically tries to save her lover, rushing to his side just as Nero fires and is killed and then Nero shoots and kills Steiger. Their bodies are later strung upside down from the girders of a Milan gas station (these scenes in black and white from the grim newsreel footage of the horrendous event). Lizzani's direction is top notch, as he inexorably brings the hunting factions searching for Steiger closer and closer to their prey and cross-cutting with considerable expertise those scenes and the scenes where Steiger closely reviews his bombastic life and deeds while awaiting inevitable capture and death. *Author's Note*: Mussolini believed almost to the last moment that he would be able to escape his awful past by flying from Italy to Spain where he believed fellow fascist dictator Francisco Franco would welcome him with open arms, but he was captured and shot to death on April 27, 1945, by communist partisans led by a "Colonel Valerio," a ruthless killer and well played by Nero. Mussolini was profiled in many films and TV shows, but most

Basil Rathbone and Preston Foster in *The Last Days of Pompeii*, 1935.

notably by Jack Oakie, who satirizes the Italian dictator in Charles Chaplin's classic, **The Great Dictator**, 1941; Joe Devlin in the 1942 film **The Devil with Hitler**; by Paul Porcasi in the 1942 film **Star Spangled Rhythm**; by Joe Devlin again in the 1943 film **Nazty Nuisance**; exceptionally by Rod Steiger once more in the 1981 film **Lion of the Desert**; by Fernando Briamo in the 1984 film **Claretta**; by Bob Hoskins in the 1985 made-for-TV film **Mussolini and I**; by George C. Scott in the 1985 TV series **Mussolini: The Untold Story**; and by Claudio Spadaro in the 1999 film **Tea with Mussolini**. Steiger told this author: "I suppose they were willing to cast me as Mussolini because of my shaved head and because I bore some resemblance to that bastard. I played that monster in two different films, but with wholly different attitudes. In the first film, **Last Days of Mussolini**, I withdrew into myself as I believe that man did when fear gripped his miserable heart at last and he knew he was being hunted like a dog, the same way he had hunted down tens of thousands of others. In the second film, **Lion of the Desert**, I am playing him at the zenith of his power when he felt he could really conquer the world, with that nut Hitler's help, of course. The problem with playing such deeply hated people is that you have a hell of a time trying to get any sympathy for them from the audience. All you can really do is show them as best you can as they really were." **p**, Enzo Peri; **d**, Carlo Lizzani; **cast**, Rod Steiger, Franco Nero, Lisa Gastoni, Henry Fonda, Lino Capolicchio, Giuseppe Addobbati, Andrea Aureli, Bruno Corazzari, Rodolfo Dal Pra, Francesco Di Federico, Manfred Freyberger; **w**, Lizzani, Fabio Pittorru; **c**, Roberto Gerardi (Eastmancolor); **m**, Ennio Morricone; **ed**, Franco Fraticelli, Jim Bryan; **prod d**, Amedeo Fago; **set d**, Carlo Gervasi; **spec eff**, Massimo Anzellotti, Basilio Patrizi.

The Last Days of Pompeii ★★★★ 1935; U.S.; 96m; RKO; B/W; Biblical Drama; Children: Unacceptable; **DVD**; **VHS**. The brawny Foster, in one of his most dynamic roles in this fine epic, is first seen as a hardworking blacksmith in Pompeii. He is devastated when his beautiful wife, Shea, and their six-month-old son, are run over by a speeding chariot raced by a Roman nobleman. Foster uses up all of his money to pay a doctor and for medicine, but runs out of funds and, to continue paying for the care of his wife and child, enters the arena as a gladiator. He fights desperately and slays his opponent, winning the money needed for the physician and medicine. His incredible effort comes too late as Shea and the child die. Embittered, Foster, who had formerly clung to decent ethics, now believes that the only thing worthwhile in life is money. He goes back to the arena, besting all opponents and ruthlessly slaying them, growing richer and richer with each victory. He then kills one gladiator and, after leaving the arena, sees his dead opponent's son, Holt, waiting vainly for his father. Full of remorse and guilt, Foster adopts the boy and then hires Birch to tutor the boy. Foster's affection

for the boy causes him to be overly cautious in the arena and he is seriously wounded after losing one fight. No longer able to fight as a gladiator, Foster is offered a job by slave trader Mong, but he shows contempt for such a disreputable livelihood, although he later changes his mind and agrees. He raids African villages and takes many prisoners and then goes into the slave-trading business, becoming even richer. After rescuing fortune-teller Tilbury, she foretells that his son will be "saved by the greatest man in Judea," and Foster thinks she is referring to Rathbone, who plays the Roman administrator of the district, Pontius Pilate (and where Rathbone gives a wonderful performance). Foster meets with Rathbone, who urges him to raid a wealthy tribe, stealing their gold and horses. During this raid, Holt is thrown from a horse and seriously injured. Foster hears of "a great prophet," named Jesus, and, frantic to save his son's life, Foster takes Holt to see Jesus, who makes Holt well. Foster then goes to Rathbone, giving him his share of the loot from the raid and where Rathbone appears forlorn, expressing his regret for recently condemning to death an innocent man, Jesus. Foster then prepares to leave Jerusalem with Holt and his faithful servant Hale when he is stopped by one of Jesus' followers, begging the powerful Foster to save Jesus as He labors through the streets carrying his cross. Foster refuses, saying he must take care of his own son and departs with Holt. As they leave Jerusalem, they look back to see three crosses atop a distant hill. Years pass and Foster is now the head of the arena in Pompeii. Having become incredibly wealthy, he lives on a mountainside palace with his son, Wood (as an adult), and servants. Rathbone then pays a visit to Foster and Wood and they recall memories of their times in Judea. Wood talks about his memory of a man who talked of love and peace. Foster interrupts to say that no such man ever existed—an often stated remark by Foster about that man, but Rathbone says: "Don't lie to him. There was such a man." Wood asks about the man's fate and Rathbone says in a deep voice: "I crucified Him." Wood then sees in brief flashback the three crosses on the hill he saw with Foster before departing Jerusalem those long years ago. Unknown to Foster, Wood has by then fallen in love with a beautiful Christian slave girl, Wilson, and, with the help of his tutor, Birch, has been aiding runaway Christian slaves to find safe havens after they have fled his father's arena to avoid being slaughtered in blood sports. Foster is stunned when Wood is arrested and sentenced to die in the arena. Foster vainly begs for his son's life, but the ruthless Roman Prefect, Calhern, refuses to grant Wood mercy. Foster then races to the dungeon at the arena where Wood is being held along with many others and begs the warder, Kolker, to release Wood, offering Kolker a fortune in gold, but the warder refuses. Wood and his beloved Wilson are then herded into the arena along with many other Christian slaves and are about to be slain when the long-smoldering volcanic mountain Vesuvius suddenly erupts. A tremendous explosion rocks Pompeii as the volcano spews fireballs, lava and burning ash down upon the city, which also shakes from a gigantic earthquake. Great buildings, palaces and small dwellings alike crumble in the earthquake and firestorm while the stricken populace flees toward the docks of the sea, clambering into the few available vessels. Foster by then is dazed and sick of heart, believing his son is now dead and with him his palace and great fortune. As he stumbles through the destroyed streets, Foster comes upon the warder, whose son is buried alive beneath some rubble. The warder begs Foster to help him in rescuing his son, but Foster angrily refuses, telling the warder that he would not help him to save his son. Foster then recalls how Jesus saved his own son and Foster helps the warder remove his son from the rubble. He next sees his loyal servant Hale, who tells Foster that he has saved his great fortune, chests filled with gold and priceless gems that slaves carry on litters. Foster orders the chests thrown away and that the litters used to pick up the injured and for Hale to take them to the docks where they can be put aboard vessels departing the flaming city. When they arrive at the docks, Foster sees his son, Wood, along with Wilson, on board the last ship about to sail to sea and the old gladiator gives thanks to Jesus. Just then, Calhern, the cruel Roman Prefect, arrives with his men, intending to seize that last vessel and toss the Christian slaves into the sea. The powerful Foster, however, seals the gate entrance to the docks, holding it closed, even though mortally speared by the Romans, until that last ship sails safely away. As Calhern and his men die within the crashing buildings about them, so, too, does Foster, but, at the fade-out, we see Foster's vision of Jesus, reaching out toward him with open arms. Foster, Rathbone and the rest of the cast do fine work in their roles; Schoedsack, who co-produced three years earlier the classic **King Kong**, 1933 (directed by Cooper, who is producer and co-director of this film), expertly unfolds this epic tale and where the special effects also provide memorable, stunning scenes of the volcanic eruption and earthquake that were not equaled until the making of **San Francisco**, 1936 and its stupendous earthquake scenes. The film did not initially recoup its investment of $237,000 (reportedly three times that amount) until its re-release in 1949, but it remains a minor classic. *Author's Note*: Rathbone told this author that "**The Last Days of Pompeii** offered me a small but significant role as Pontius Pilate. I received considerable praise for my effort in that part, but that was chiefly due to the excellent script and where my character was magnificently written that showed a great economy of words. The sets in that picture were wonderful—spacious and towering and very accurate to the period." Cooper, as he told this author, was disappointed by viewer response to **The Last Days of Pompeii**, saying: "We thought it would do very big box office, but it missed the mark somehow, although we put everything we could into it." **p**, Merian C. Cooper; **d**, Ernest B. Schoedsack, and (not credited) Cooper; **cast**, Preston Foster, Alan Hale, Basil Rathbone, John Wood, Louis Calhern, David Holt, Dorothy Wilson, Zeffie Tilbury, Ward Bond, Henry Kolker, Jim Thorpe; **w**, Ruth Rose, Boris Ingster (based on a story by James Ashmore Creelman, Melville Baker); **c**, J. Roy Hunt and (uncredited) Jack Cardiff; **m**, Roy Webb; **ed**, Archie F. Marshek; **art d**, Van Nest Polglase; **spec eff**, Harry Redmond, Sr. and Jr., Vernon Walker, Marcel Delgado.

The Last Detail ★★★ 1973; U.S.; 104m; COL; Color; Drama; Children: Unacceptable (MPAA: R); **DVD**; **VHS**. A grim but compelling drama has Quaid, a sailor who has been convicted of stealing $40 from the polio charity box, being escorted from his U.S. Navy base at Norfolk, Virginia, to a federal prison in Portsmouth, New Hampshire, where he is to serve an eight-year prison sentence. Quaid's draconian sentence for such petty thievery (one year in prison for each $5 stolen) has resulted because his theft offended the wife of the admiral supporting that charity. Accompanying the affable Quaid are two veteran sailors, Nicholson and Young, who are making a career in the Navy and whose streetwise experience they attempt to impart to the irresponsible and capricious Quaid. En route, the two guards treat the youthful Quaid as avuncular shepherds, trying to show him a good time before he begins his long stretch behind bars. Traveling by train, they stop at one town where they meet Anders, who takes them to a Nicheren Shoshu gathering and where Radner performs an oddball and hilarious dance. Anders then takes Quaid to her room where, instead of seducing him as he hopefully expects, delivers Eastern chants to him that he does not comprehend. Having had similar luck with Anders' friends, Nicholson and Young take Quaid to a brothel, paying Kane to service the bumbling sailor. The three sailors conclude their odyssey when they arrive in snow-bound Portsmouth and where, just before he is to enter the prison, Quaid makes a last request, that the three have a picnic. Nicholson and Young buy hotdogs and they munch this food while stomping around on frozen ground in a park. Quaid tells his companions that the time he has spent with them is the best experience he has had in his miserable life. As they walk along, Quaid suddenly bolts, running wildly away in an attempt to escape imprisonment. Nicholson chases him and, using his automatic, pistol whips the towering Quaid into child-like submission. He and Young then deliver Quaid to the prison and begin their journey back to Norfolk. The film is stark and the on-location sequences are seedy and where the low life reigns, but the amazing performances

John Lone as Henry Pu Yi in *The Last Emperor*, 1987.

from Nicholson, Young and Quaid are so riveting in their sad and dutiful journey that this little film mesmerizes throughout, all enabled through Ashby's excellent direction. The use of four-letter words is so prolific in this film that if they had been omitted, half the dialog would have gone missing, but this kind of gutter talk is nevertheless in keeping with the unsophisticated and poorly educated characters depicted. **p**, Gerald Ayres, Joel Chernoff; **d**, Hal Ashby; **cast**, Jack Nicholson, Otis Young, Randy Quaid, Clifton James, Carol Kane, Michael Moriarty, Luana Anders, Kathleen Miller, Nancy Allen, Gilda Radner; **w**, Robert Towne (based on the novel by Darryl Ponicsan); **c**, Michael Chapman (Metrocolor); **m**, Johnny Mandel; **ed**, Robert C. Jones, Ken Zemke; **prod d**, Michael Haller.

The Last Emperor ★★★★ 1987; China/Italy/U.K./France; 163m (215m director's cut); Recorded Picture Company/COL; Color; Biographical Drama; Children: Unacceptable (MPAA: PG-13); **BD**; **DVD**; **VHS**. Beautifully photographed and well acted, this sweeping biopic portrays the strange life of Puyi (1906-1967), the last emperor of China and the twelfth and final ruler of the Qing Dynasty. The film begins with Lone, playing Puyi, as a captive of Chinese communists, who have taken over the country, and where he attempts suicide, but only brings about unconsciousness, producing the flashback of his life. He is seen in several stages as a child, being reared and pampered as a child in the Imperial Palace of the Forbidden City in Beijing, patiently tutored by Englishman O'Toole, until growing to manhood as Lone. While China undergoes revolution that sees many warlords seize various provinces during the 1920s, Lone remains above it all, living the life of a dissolute playboy and where he comes under the influence of Han, a conniving spy, Eastern Jewel (Yoshiko Kawashima; 1907-1948), a Manchu princess raised in Japan and who has become a Japanese secret agent working for Japanese military intelligence, Kempei Tai. Han uses her heterosexual and lesbian wiles to inveigle Lone into accepting Japanese military protection after the Kempei Tai fakes an attack on the royal residence. Once under that protection, Lone is easily persuaded to become the puppet ruler of Manchukuo (Manchuria), a Japanese-created province in northeast China and southern Mongolia. There Lone and his royal family, including a wife, who hates the Japanese, live in a mansion but under the strict supervision of Japanese military officers, who actually rule the area. Following the collapse of the Japanese military regime in China in 1945, Lone's small world collapses when communists eventually take control. He is imprisoned by communists and endlessly interrogated until he abdicates his throne and renounces all affiliations to the Japanese, his former masters. He is released to work at menial jobs as a peasant. Lone is last seen talking to a small boy when they, along with other spectators, visit the Forbidden City, Lone's birthplace and

Alan Baxter, Moroni Olsen, Edward G. Robinson and Lionel Stander in *The Last Gangster*, 1937.

where his young life showed so much promise, a life that great social upheavals subsequently altered and reduced to obscurity. Director Bertolucci presents a dynamic biopic that is also a riveting epic of the turmoil that engulfed China during the first half of the 20th Century and where all the cast members, particularly Lone, Han, and O'Toole give exceptional performances. *Author's Note*: For more details on Puyi, Eastern Jewel and the Japanese spymasters that manipulated the last emperor of China, see my book *Spies: A Narrative Encyclopedia of Dirty Deeds and Double Dealing from Biblical Times to Today* (M. Evans, 1997; Kenji Doihara: pages 177-182; Eastern Jewel: pages 203-205; Kempei Tai: pages 289-290). **p**, Jeremy Thomas; **d**, Bernardo Bertolucci; **cast**, John Lone, Joan Chen, Peter O'Toole, Richard Vuu, Tijger Tsou, Wu Tao, Ying Ruocheng, Victor Wong, Dennis Dun, Ryûichi Sakamoto, Maggie Han, Ric Young, Vivian Wu, Cary Hiroyuki Tagawa; **w**, Bertolucci, Mark Peploe, Enzo Ungari (based on the autobiography *From Emperor to Citizen, The Autobiography of Aisin-Gioro Pu Yi* by Henry Pu-yi); **c**, Vittorio Storaro (Technicolor); **m**, David Byrne, Ryûichi Sakamoto, Cong Su; **ed**, Gabriella Cristiani, Anthony Sloman; **prod d**, Ferdinando Scarfiotti; **art d**, Maria Teresa Barbasso, Gianni Giovagnoni, Gianni Silvestri; **set d**, Wang Chunpu; **spec eff**, Gino De Rossi, Fabrizio Martinelli, Yang Jingguo, Mario Cassar, Claudio Quaglietti.

The Last Gangster ★★★ 1937; U.S.; 81m; MGM; B/W; Crime Drama; Children: Unacceptable; **DVD**. Robinson's exceptional and expansive performance as a strutting, old-fashioned gangster raises this crime tale above the average. He is shown returning from Europe after having married Stradner, but he finds that his underworld rackets in San Francisco have been mostly taken over by a rival gang. Robinson collects his most loyal goons, especially Stander, and launches an all-out war on the rival gangsters, but is arrested by police after he is fingered by an adversary. Convicted of racketeering and sent to prison for ten years, Robinson is unconcerned about Stradner's future and that of their newly born child. Stradner promises to be a loyal wife, but she is lambasted and hounded by the local press, until Stewart, a young reporter, sees that the woman is decent and honest and writes a story that attempts to correct her sullied reputation. After Stradner visits Robinson in prison, she is stunned by his ruthless nature and barbaric attitude and realizes that she can no longer love this vicious man. Stewart, by then, is in love with Stradner, and, after he convinces Stradner to divorce Robinson, they are married and move to Massachusetts where Stewart becomes the successful editor of a small newspaper. It is ten years later, and Robinson, released from prison, is obsessed with finding his wife and son. He is first contacted by old gang member Stander, who convinces him to put together his old gang and once more take over his old rackets. When Robinson goes to a meeting with those old underworld

associates, however, he is seized by them and tortured as they demand the whereabouts of the money he hid before going behind bars. After getting nowhere with the tight-lipped Robinson, Stander and others kidnap Robinson's ten-year-old son, Scott, and threaten to harm him unless Robinson talks. The old gangster tells them where the money is buried, and, while the gang searches for the hidden cache, Robinson escapes with Scott. After Robinson tries to bond with Scott and to have him call him his father, the boy rebels. He says that his only father is Stewart. Robinson is now enraged and, believing that Stradner has betrayed him and that Stewart has stolen his son's affection, the gangster resolves to kill them both. He takes Scott to his home, but when he sees how loving and caring Stradner and Stewart are, he does the only noble thing in his life by leaving them alone and in peace. Robinson is later found by old rival Baxter, who mortally shoots Robinson. The "last gangster" dies while clutching his son's merit badge, the only keepsake left of a better life he abandoned for a career of crime. *Author's Note*: Robinson told this author that "I had put my foot down with my home studio, Warner Brothers and told them that I was sick and tired of playing snarling gangsters and wanted to do no more parts like that and they promised they would not cast me in such films. They also gave me script approval for my future films with the studio, so they were surprised when I did **The Last Gangster** for MGM. But that picture is not really a film that shows the old-fashioned gangsters I played in earlier films. The character I play is a man, who puts himself before his family and loses that family and all hope of happiness. The fact that he *happens* to be a gangster is almost incidental. Well, Jack Warner didn't see it that way and we had a few strong words together about that picture. As it turned out, that picture was far from being the last film about gangsters as the medium has turned out one such film after another since then, including two I later made, **Key Largo** [1948] and **Hell on Frisco Bay** [1955]." **p**, Lou L. Ostrow; **d**, Edward Ludwig; **cast**, Edward G. Robinson, James Stewart, Rose Stradner, Lionel Stander, Douglas Scott, John Carradine, Sidney Blackmer, Grant Mitchell, Edward Brophy, Don "Red" Barry, Horace McMahon, Alan Baxter, Douglas McPhail, Phillip Terry; **w**, John Lee Mahin (based on a story by William A. Wellman, Robert Carson); **c**, William Daniels; **m**, Edward Ward; **ed**, Ben Lewis; **art d**, Cedric Gibbons.

Last Holiday ★★★ 1950; U.K.; 88m; Associated British Picture Corp./Stratford Pictures; B/W; Comedy; Children: Acceptable; **DVD**; **VHS**. The gifted Guinness is a farm machinery salesman, who learns that he has a rare, incurable disease and will die in a few weeks. A bachelor, he has no close relatives or friends to bequeath his meager savings, so he withdraws it, tells his boss he is going, and drives to a fashionable seaside hotel for a final vacation. The hotel manager, Aslan, welcomes him and he meets Walsh, a woman who calls him a "mystery man." New opportunities arise for him on holiday. He takes time to help people and offers advice to inventor Hyde-White, and is befriended by Cotts, a cabinet minister, who offers him a position, but he respectfully declines it since he believes he has only a short time to live. The hotel staff goes on strike and Guinness leads the residents in doing things for themselves. He then learns he does not have the potentially fatal disease after all, but is then fatally injured in an automobile accident. Before dying, he sends his love to those he knew at the hotel. A delightful dark comedy that wonderfully displays Guinness' measured comedic skills. **p**, J.B. Priestley, Stephen Mitchell, A.D. Peters; **d**, Henry Cass; **cast**, Alec Guinness, Beatrice Campbell, Kay Walsh, Coco (Grégoire) Aslan, Bernard Lee, Wilfrid Hyde-White, Jean Colin, Muriel George, Brian Worth, Esma Cannon; **w**, Priestley; **c**, Ray Elton; **m**, Francis Chagrin; **ed**, Monica Kimick; **art d**, Duncan Sutherland.

The Last Hunt ★★★ 1956; U.S.; 88m; MGM; Color; Western; Children: Unacceptable; **VHS**. In 1883 South Dakota, a longtime buffalo hunter, Granger, has grown tired of the work and quits, while another buffalo hunter, Taylor, is sadistic and loves killing the animals strictly for enjoyment. Taylor coaxes Granger into partnering with him on a final buffalo hunt by offering him enough money that he can't refuse. Some Indians steal their horses, and Taylor hunts them down and kills them in their camp, then takes a beautiful Indian girl as his own. Granger and the girl become attracted to each other, but both fear the emotionally unstable Taylor. As tension mounts between the two men, Taylor kills a white buffalo that is sacred to the Indians and then decides he must kill Granger. While waiting in ambush for Granger, Taylor dies of exposure. This is an unusual role for matinee idol Taylor, who invariably played the hero, but here he is a psychotic killer and he does a very good job convincing the viewer that he certainly is that maniacal predator, and where his death by freezing stiff inside a buffalo hide is lamented by no one. *Author's Note*: Taylor told this author that "I enjoyed playing a rotten human being for a change, the kind of role that offers a lot more meat to chew on. My character not only thrills to killing animals, but he takes pleasure in doing the same thing to human beings and that is someone to be frightened about. Conflict, fright and suspense—those are the main ingredients of any god picture and that one had more than its share of those elements." This film touches upon the lore of Indians holding white buffalos as godlike, but that Native American belief receives a deeper examination in **The White Buffalo**, 1977. **p**, Dore Schary; **d&w**, Richard Brooks (based on the novel by Milton Lott); **cast**, Robert Taylor, Stewart Granger, Lloyd Nolan, Debra Paget, Russ Tamblyn, Constance Ford, Joe De Santis, Ainslie Pryor, Ralph Moody, Ed Lonehill; **c**, Russell Harlan; **m**, Daniele Amfitheatrof; **ed**, Ben Lewis; **art d**, Cedric Gibbons, Merrill Pye; **set d**, Edwin B. Willis, Fred M. MacLean; **spec eff**, Warren Newcombe.

The Last Hurrah ★★★ 1958; U.S.; 121m; COL; B/W; Drama; Children: Acceptable; **DVD**; **VHS**. Tracy gives a lively, colorful performance as an old-fashioned politician and mayor of an Eastern American city with a large Irish-American constituency, presumably Boston, and where his character is certainly based on the multi-termed mayor of that city, James Michael Curley (1874-1958). Tracy is running for reelection and he and his political cronies expect an easy win, until a reform candidate seriously challenges him by exposing Tracy's past shady dealings and where that challenger now has the backing of most of the powerful leaders in the city. Those patrician leaders include Carradine, who runs a conservative newspaper for which Hunter works as a reporter and who is also Tracy's nephew. Hunter, who believes that Tracy is basically a great man, who has always tried to do good for the underprivileged, writes a series of articles that record his uncle's "last hurrah," a campaign packed with old-fashioned street marches, banners and slogans and where Tracy's aides—O'Brien, Brophy, Gleason and Cortez—beat the bushes for votes. In one of his last acts as mayor, Tracy establishes an inexpensive housing project for poor families, but needs a loan from banker Rathbone, who is an ardent member of Carradine's opposition party. When Rathbone refuses to make the needed loan, Tracy makes Rathbone's wealthy, childlike son, Whitehead, an honorary fire department chief, photographing him wearing a helmet, fire horn and other regalia and, rather see his son further ridiculed, Rathbone makes the loan. Tracy's own son, Walsh, is an irresponsible playboy, who spends his time listening to jazz music and womanizing. Tracy is actually friendless and mostly missing his deceased wife, placing a single rose each morning beneath the portrait of his spouse before going about his business. In the end, his most powerful supporters, including Crisp, the Catholic Archbishop, fail to come to Tracy's political aid and he loses the election. He suffers a heart attack and dies, but not before all his affectionate cronies bid him their farewell. Tracy and a wonderful cast bring to life the kind of political atmosphere that is no more in America and are well directed by Ford. *Author's Note*: Tracy told this author that "**The Last Hurrah** was old home week for me. I made a picture with John Ford in 1930 when we made **Up the River**. So three decades later, here I am again with the old master and doing a picture with him again with a title that is prophetic." For some strange reason, O'Brien had a

Spencer Tracy in *The Last Hurrah*, 1958.

hard time being cast for this film, but, as he told this author: "John Ford went to bat for me and insisted that I have a role in **The Last Hurrah**. Mr. Ford never forgot a friend. We did **Air Mail** [1932] together and anyone who ever did a film with him was always good for another role in another picture he was directing. Unlike a lot of people in Hollywood John Ford always remembered those who had worked for him." **p&d**, John Ford; **cast**, Spencer Tracy, Jeffrey Hunter, Dianne Foster, Pat O'Brien, Basil Rathbone, Donald Crisp, James Gleason, Edward Brophy, John Carradine, Ricardo Cortez, Wallace Ford, Frank McHugh, Anna Lee, Ken Curtis, Frank Albertson, Jane Darwell, William Henry, O.Z. Whitehead, Rand Brooks, Edmund Lowe, Mae Marsh, Tom Neal, Helen Westcott; **w**, Frank Nugent (based on the novel by Edwin O'Connor); **c**, Charles Lawton, Jr.; **ed**, Jack Murray; **prod d&art d**, Robert Peterson; **set d**, William Kiernan.

The Last Laugh ★★★★ 1925 (silent); Germany; 90m; UFA/UNIV; B/W; Drama; Children: Cautionary; **DVD**; **VHS**. Jannings, the greatest actor in Germany during the 1920s, offers another bravura performance of a hardworking man who loves his job as the doorman of a leading Berlin hotel. He is dressed in a resplendent uniform and acts with the mannerisms of a major-general. All employees at the hotel defer to Jannings, but, in his advancing years, he begins to falter, making mistakes and, when he can no longer lift heavy luggage, he is demoted to the lowly station of a men's room attendant. Though savagely ridiculed by others, Jannings endures this lowly job in order to survive and does that job conscientiously. In the end, however, he triumphs over all of his persecutors when he inherits a great fortune bequeathed to him by a man who left his belongings with Jannings, as Jannings was the last person to see him alive. Murnau's direction is impeccable, completely telling this prosaic story in startling scenes where Freund's superlative cinematography is stark, crisp and wonderfully lit. Murnau presents this intriguing tale without using the usual title cards invariably attending silent films, a work of pure cinema. **p**, Erich Pommer; **d**, F.W. Murnau; **cast**, Emil Jannings, Maly Delschaft, Max Hiller, Emilie Kurz, Hans Unterkircher, Olaf Storm, Hermann Vallentin, Georg John, Emmy Wyda, O.E. Hasse, Neumann-Schüler; **w**, Carl Mayer; **c**, Karl Freund; **m**, Giuseppe Becce, Florian C. Reithner, Werner Schmidt-Boelcke, Karl-Ernst Sasse; **ed**, Elfi Böttrich; **prod d**, Edgar G. Ulmer; **art d**, Robert Herlth, Walter Röhrig; **spec eff**, Ernst Kunstmann.

The Last Legion ★★★ 2007; U.K./Italy/France; 102m; Dino de Laurentiis/Weinstein Company; Color; Adventure; Children: Unacceptable (MPAA: PG-13); **DVD**; **VHS**. Good action coupled with superior acting aids a well-crafted historical epic to come alive during the last stages of the Roman Empire in 460 A.D. The film begins with the coro-

Aishwarya Rai and Colin Firth in *The Last Legion*, 2007.

nation of Sangster, as Romulus Augustus (460-500?), the heir to the Roman throne, which brings about an attack by Goths, who sack the city and destroy the Roman guard, except for its commander, Firth. Sangster's life is spared, but he is sent to Capri with his tutor, Kingsley, where both are held prisoner at an ancient villa. Exploring the old underground areas of the villa, Sangster comes upon the crypt of Julius Caesar, finding his legendary sword. Kingsley, a philosopher and magician (Merlin), believes that that sword holds magical powers and has been hidden from powerful men, who might otherwise use it for evil ends. Firth, along with martial arts specialist Rai and some loyal legionaries, goes to the island of Capri where the twelve-year-old Sangster is being held captive. When arriving at Capri, Firth and his group battle the boy's captors and escape with Sangster (and the historic sword) taking him and Kingsley to Britannica where they seek the support of what Firth believes to be the only military force that will be loyal to Sangster, the Ninth Legion (or the Dragon Legion). Meanwhile Goths, led by McKidd, hunt Firth's group, seeking to possess the magical sword. Once in Britannica, Firth finds what is left of the Ninth Legion, these once famed warriors having married and settled down, living under the yoke of a ruthless tyrant, Van Gorkum, who controls a large section of the island. When McKidd arrives with his Goths, he allies himself with Van Gorkum, telling him about the sword being carried by Sangster, and the tyrant conducts a savage search for that sword. Meanwhile, Firth cannot get the support of the old legionaries, and he and his small band of warriors retreat to Hadrian's Wall and where they are attacked by Van Gorkum and his men. Just when they are about to be overwhelmed, the members of the old Ninth Legion appear in battle gear and attack the tyrant and his men, leaving the battlefield littered with the dead and dying. Kingsley has killed Van Gorkum by burning him to death, and Sangster has killed McKidd with the legendary sword. Sangster, however, is repulsed by the carnage of battle and hurls the sword so that it pierces a large rock, becoming wedged. Years later, Kingsley appears with James, a young boy named Arthur, taking him to the old battlefield and explaining that Firth and Rai later married as did Sangster, who is James' father, and who took the name "Pendragon," becoming a wise ruler. The camera then closes upon the moss-covered sword lodged in the stone and, just before the fadeout, reveals its name—Excalibur, which suggests the Arthurian legend to come. **p**, Dino de Laurentiis; **d**, Doug Lefler; **cast**, Colin Firth, Thomas Sangster, Ben Kingsley, Aishwarya Rai, Peter Mullan, Kevin McKidd, Harry Van Gorkum, Rory James; **w**, Jez and Tom Butterworth (based on the book by Valerio Manfredi); **c**, Marco Pontecorvo; **m**, Patrick Doyle; **ed**, Simon Cozens; **prod d**, Carmelo Agate; **art d**, Giorgio Postiglione; **set d**, Francesco Postiglione, Alberto Tosto; **spec eff**, Raymond Ferguson, Stefano Pepin.

The Last Metro ★★★ 1981; France; 131m; Les Films du Carrosse/UA; Color; Drama; Children: Unacceptable: **DVD**; **VHS**. In Nazi-occupied Paris during World War II in 1942, an actress, Deneuve, hides her Jewish stage director husband, Bennent, in the basement of a theater. He secretly listens to and watches as she rehearses his new play on-stage with her leading man, Depardieu. Deneuve and Depardieu fall in love and she has to face her personal and political dilemmas. Truffaut, the film's director and writer, drew upon his own experiences in occupied France in creating a very moving political-romantic drama that was well received by both critics and audiences. Sexual themes prohibit viewing by children. Songs include Bei Mir Bist Du Schon" (Sholom Secunda, Chan-Chaplin, Jacob Jacobs, Jacques Larue), "Pierre A Zumba" (A. Lara, Larue), "Mon Amant de Saint-Jean" (E. Carrara, L. Agel), "Sombreros Et Mantilles" (J. Vaissade-Chanty), "Cantique: Pitie Mon Dieu" (A. Kunk). (In French; English subtitles.) **p&d**, François Truffaut; **cast**, Catherine Deneuve, Gérard Depardieu, Jean Poiret, Andréa Ferréol, Paulette Dubost, Jean-Louis Richard, Maurice Risch, Sabine Haudepin, Heinz Bennent, Christian Baltauss; **w**, Truffaut, Suzanne Schiffman (based on a story by Truffaut, Schiffman, Jean-Claude Grumberg); **c**, Nestor Almendros; **m**, Georges Delerue; **ed**, Martine Barraqué; **prod d**, Jean-Pierre Kohut-Svelko.

The Last Mile ★★★ 1932; U.S.; 75m; KBS/Sono Art-World Wide Pictures; B/W; Crime Drama; Children: Unacceptable; **VHS**. Gritty and uncompromising, this prison yarn sees Phillips convicted of murdering his partner and sent to prison where he is placed on Death Row with other condemned prisoners. He arrives just in time to see Stone walk his "last mile" from his cell in the prison block where the condemned prisoners are held to the electric chair and his death, a shuddering experience that further jangles his nerves as he awaits his own execution. Phillips learns about the other inmates and befriends the most surly of the lot, Foster, a career criminal, who has long accepted his fate for the crimes he has committed. The lives of these men are further antagonized by sadistic guards, the most cruel of these being Smith, who taunts and terrorizes the prisoners. Smith commits a serious error, however, when leaning too close to Foster's cell and where Foster strangles him to death, taking his keys and gun. Foster unlocks the cells of the other prisoners, all joining him in a doomed breakout attempt, except for Fix, who refuses to leave his cell and whose mind has long earlier been unhinged by the dreaded anticipation of his own death. Foster captures more guards and locks them into cells before calling Sheridan, the warden' to demand a fast getaway car and a few hours' start. Sheridan refuses to cooperate and orders his guards to besiege the cellblock controlled by Foster. Realizing that he cannot win, Foster steps out into the open to be shot to death. The grim ending, however, has a ray of hope in that Phillips, at the last minute before his scheduled execution, is found to be innocent and is released. Bischoff does a good job in helming the only film he ever directed, thereafter becoming a producer, and Foster, Phillips and the rest give solid performances as the forlorn prisoners. *Author's Note*: The original Broadway production on which this film is based did not have a happy ending and where the character played by Phillips is not reprieved at the end and glumly goes to the electric chair. The play itself was based upon the published memoirs of Robert Blake, *The Law Takes Its Toll*, while he was awaiting his own execution at the Texas State Penitentiary at Huntsville, and where Blake recorded the lives and executions of several of his fellow inmates, until he walked that "last mile" to the electric chair on April 19, 1929. Blake's memoirs were serialized in *The American Mercury*, inspiring twenty-two-year-old playwright Ely John Wexley to write the play about these condemned men. The play was produced on Broadway in 1930 and starred a youthful Spencer Tracy in the role played by Foster in the 1932 film, the character of the unrelenting "Killer Mears." That role brought Tracy to the attention of film producers, who began casting him in tough guy roles. The play was then produced in Los Angeles, and that version saw Clark Gable in the role of "Killer Mears," which, like Tracy before him, brought Gable to the attention of film producers, who began casting Gable in gangster roles. Tracy told this author that "that role had a lot of legs. It got me into pictures and, after Gable did the same part, it landed him in pictures, too. Then we wind up together at MGM and do some of our best films together. Fate is strange, indeed. For years, when we passed each other on the MGM lot, we would wave at each other and say to each other 'Hello, Killer!'" **p&d**, Samuel Bischoff; **cast**, Preston Foster, Howard Phillips, George E. Stone, Noel Madison, Alan Roscoe, Paul Fix, Al Hill, Daniel L. Haynes, Frank Sheridan, Alec B. Francis; **w**, Seton I. Miller (based on the play by John Wexley); **c**, Arthur Edeson; **ed**, Rose Loewinger; **set d**, Ralph M. DeLacy.

The Last Mile ★★★ 1959; U.S.; 81m; UA; B/W; Crime Drama; Children: Unacceptable; **DVD**; **VHS**. Rooney is stupendous in the role of "Killer Mears," a condemned prisoner awaiting execution on Death Row in this solid remake of the 1932 production. Rooney and others are tormented as they await their deaths by a sadistic guard, Barry. Many are driven to half-crazed states, and Rooney, in one unforgettable scene, when seized by hysteria, dances in his cell, cries and laughs in alternating bursts of raw emotion. Barry gets his comeuppance when getting too close to Rooney's cell and where Rooney strangles him and takes his keys and gun. He releases the other inmates and attempts a futile breakout, locking up other guards as well as a fearless and compassionate priest, Overton, who has earlier tried to bring comfort to Rooney and his fellow inmates. The convicts battle the guards besieging the cellblock, but it is a hopeless fight and, after Rooney realizes that his demands will never be granted, steps into the open to be gunned to death. A grim and claustrophobic feeling permeates this prison tale, but one that nevertheless rivets the viewer, chiefly through the intense performance of the inimitable Rooney, a great actor comfortable with any kind of role. Barry, a former B-western star, is exceptional as the cruel guard, and Overton gives a standout performance as the priest trying to bring comfort to those who cannot be comforted. *Author's Note*: This was Michael Constantine's debut in feature films. **p**, Max Rosenberg, Milton Subotsky; **d**, Howard W. Koch; **cast**, Mickey Rooney, Alan Bunce, Frank Conroy, Leon Janney, Frank Overton, Clifford David, Harry Millard, John McCurry, Ford Rainey, Michael Constantine, Don "Red" Barry; **w**, Subotsky, Seton I. Miller (based on the play by John Wexley); **c**, Joseph C. Brun, Saul Midwall; **m**, Van Alexander; **ed**, Robert Broekman, Patricia Lewis Jaffe; **art d**, Paul Barnes; **set d**, Jack Wright, Jr.; **spec eff**, Vincent Brady, Louis DeWitt, Milton Olsen, Jack Rabin.

The Last of the Mohicans ★★★★ 1920 (silent); U.S.; 73m/6 reels; Tourneur Productions/Associated Producers; B/W; Adventure; Children: Unacceptable; **DVD**. Superb telling of the classic Cooper adventure set in 1757 during the French and Indian War. The film opens with Hall and Bedford traveling with a small party through the wilderness to join their father Gordon, a colonel who commands the British bastion of Fort William Henry near Lake Champlain, New York, which is now besieged by the French and their Huron allies. En route, the women and their protector, Woodward, a British major, are attacked by fierce Huron warrior Beery, but Lorraine (Hawkeye), and the only surviving members of the Mohican tribe, Roscoe (Uncas), and Lerch (Chingachgook), come to their rescue, guiding them to the fort and into the arms of Gordon. The fort, however, cannot hold out against the French forces, and Gordon is eventually forced to surrender. The French, however, fail to hold their Indian allies in check and, after Gordon and his troops leave the fort, they are attacked and massacred by the Huron warriors, led by the vicious and bloodthirsty Beery. (This sequence is spectacular and utterly savage as the Indians slaughter the helpless British, man, woman and child, one of the most gruesome scenes ever put on film.) While Hall is rescued by Lorraine and Lerch, Bedford is captured by Beery, but the valiant Roscoe tracks down the bestial Beery and they battle, Beery killing Roscoe and then, when he advances upon Bedford, she leaps from a high cliff to her death, falling close to the Indian youth who

Henry Wilcoxon, center, in *The Last of the Mohicans*, 1936.

sought to save her life. Beery is then confronted by Lerch, who is Roscoe's father, and the two Indians battle to the death with Beery losing his life and leaving Lerch the "last of the Mohicans." The film is beautifully photographed (where the battle scenes were tinted in red), and the direction by Tourneur and Brown (who shot most of the spectacular exterior shots) is poetry on film. All the players give superlative performances, especially Beery, who enacts the most savage role in his long career in films and where he becomes the epitome of evil. *Author's Note*: French director Tourneur, who arrived in the U.S. in 1914 to make films, was noted for his careful narrative development coupled with his aesthetic sense of cinematography, which was more painterly than documentary. This film is considered one of his best, although he did not complete all of the production. Tourneur contracted ptomaine poisoning and then suffered an attack of pleurisy, as well as being injured while exercising on a parallel bar, causing him to be bedridden for almost three months. In his absence, Brown took over all direction and completed all the exteriors, the most effective and stunning sequences of the film, although Tourneur did view all the rushes and made final decisions on all editing for the finished film as well as shooting almost all the interior scenes and had the final decisions on all retakes. **p**, Maurice Tourneur; **d**, Clarence Brown, Tourneur; **cast**, Wallace Beery, Barbara Bedford, Albert Roscoe (Alan Roscoe), Lillian Hall, Henry Woodward, James Gordon, George Hackathorne, Nelson McDowell, Harry Lorraine, Theodore Lerch, Boris Karloff; **w**, Robert A. Dillon (based on the novel by James Fenimore Cooper); **c**, Philip R. Dubois, Charles Van Enger; **m**, Arthur Kay, R.J. Miller; **art d**, Ben Carré, Floyd Mueller.

The Last of the Mohicans ★★★★ 1936; U.S.; 91m; Edward Small Productions/UA; B/W; Adventure; Children: Unacceptable; **DVD**; **VHS**. Outstanding version of the classic Cooper adventure yarn of the French and Indian War sees Scott in one of his greatest roles as the indefatigable Hawkeye, the sharpshooting hero of the wilderness. Scott is accompanied by his two loyal companions, Barrat (Chingachgook) and his son, Reed (Uncas), the only two survivors of the Mohican Indian tribe. Scott is first seen at Albany, New York, arguing with British General James Abercrombie (1706-1781), played by Hare, who is recruiting colonials to fight alongside British troops in New York against the French and their Huron allies. Scott argues that if the colonials leave their homes and farms, they may also leave their families to the mercies of the invading Huron, a risk too great to take. Meanwhile, Wilcoxon, a haughty British major, along with a few soldiers, sets out from Albany for old Fort William Henry on Lake George, which is being besieged by French General Louis-Joseph de Montcalm (1712-1759), played by Stack, along with his Huron allies. Wilcoxon escorts Barnes and Angel, the two beautiful daughters of Buckler, who plays Colonel Munro, a

Madeleine Stowe and Daniel Day-Lewis in *The Last of the Mohicans*, 1992.

character based on George Monro (1700-1757) and who commands Fort William Henry. A friendly Huron, Cabot, is assigned to the group as their guide, but he is a spy working for the French and a ruthless killer. Cabot, in one of his most sinister roles as Magua, leads the trusting British party into an ambush, but Wilcoxon, Barnes and Angel are rescued by Scott, Barrat and Reed, who then take them to Fort William Henry in a circuitous route through the French and Huron lines. Although Buckler extends his gratitude to Scott for saving his daughters, he later orders Scott and the two Mohicans locked up after Scott urges the colonials serving in the militia to secretly abandon the fort in order to go back to their homes and defend their families from the raiding Indians. Meanwhile, the fort is hammered into submission by Montcalm's superior forces, forcing Buckler to surrender with honors. Honor is stained with blood, however, when Cabot and his Huron followers ignore Stack's order to allow the British to retreat peacefully. The Indians invade the now undefended fort and murder the British, and where Cabot takes Barnes and Angel captive, departing with them toward the Huron camp. Scott, Barrat and Reed break out of the stockade and follow. Scott arrives at the Huron camp and asks Chief Sacham (Mong) to set the two British captives free, offering to exchange himself as their captive. Wilcoxon, who has survived the massacre at the fort, then arrives at the Huron camp dressed in the buckskins Scott has usually worn, claiming that he is the celebrated Hawkeye, but Scott tells the chief that Wilcoxon is an impersonator and that he is the one and only Hawkeye. Mong knows of Hawkeye only as the most accurate marksman in the wilderness and compels the two men to fire their muskets at distant targets to see which is telling the truth. Scott wins the match and is accepted as a captive in exchange for Barnes, who leaves with Wilcoxon. Cabot by this time has gone off with Angel and with Reed in pursuit of the fierce Huron. Wilcoxon later musters some British troops and returns to the Huron village just as the Indians are about to burn Scott to death, rescuing him and scattering the Indians. Meanwhile, Reed catches up with Cabot and both men fight with hatchets atop a cliff, Reed losing the battle and falling to his death. When Cabot attempts to claim Angel as his prize the young woman leaps from the cliff to join the Indian who loved her in death. Barrat then arrives, and seeing that Cabot has killed his son, fights with Cabot, and where Barrat hatchets Cabot to death before tossing his body over the cliff. Barrat then builds a ceremonial altar that holds the bodiy of his son, Reed, saying that he is now "the last of the Mohicans." Even though he has loved Barnes, Wilcoxon now bows out and allows Scott and Barnes to be together. The finale sees Scott leading the colonial militia as they go forward with British troops to again take up the battle with the French. Director Seitz does an outstanding job directing this action-packed film, while skillfully coordinating his battle scenes and the various skirmishes, and well balancing the one-

on-one fights and the more tranquil romantic scenes between Scott and Barnes. The cast members are standouts in their roles and the cinematography is superlative, while Webb's heart-thumping score enhances every exciting scene. ***Author's Note***: Scott told this author that "**The Last of the Mohicans** was a big picture for me and it gave me the kind of leading role most actors dream about. I had appeared in a number of western films before doing that picture, which is why I believe I got the part of Hawkeye. Although that picture is more of a pioneering and historical epic than a western, it was truly my big breakthrough. United Artists did not stint on the budget for that picture and went all out to make it a success and it did very well at the box office year after year in many rereleases. The director [Seitz] was an old hand with the story. He had directed a ten-chapter serial version of the tale in the silent era [**Leatherstocking**, 1924], so he knew precisely what to do with all the characters in that great story from James Fenimore Cooper. I thought Bruce Cabot as the treacherous Magua stole every scene and I told him so. He only shrugged and said: 'It's a job.' He had been playing leading men in the early thirties, but he somehow got typecast as a heavy, and he told me that "if I have to play these awful characters, I will play them to the hilt." He certainly did that." **p**, Edward Small; **d**, George B. Seitz; **cast**, Randolph Scott, Binnie Barnes, Henry Wilcoxon, Bruce Cabot, Heather Angel, Phillip Reed, Robert Barrat, Hugh Buckler, Willard Robertson, William Stack, Lumsden Hare, William V. Mong, John Sutton; **w**, Philip Dunne, John L. Balderston, Paul Perez, Daniel Moore (based on the novel by James Fenimore Cooper); **c**, Robert Planck; **m**, Roy Webb; **ed**, Jack Dennis, Harry Marker; **art d**, John Ducasse Schulze.

The Last of the Mohicans ★★★ 1992; U.S.; 112m; Morgan Creek Productions/FOX; Color; Adventure; Children: Unacceptable (MPAA: R); **BD**; **DVD**; **VHS**. Seldom does a remake match up to the original, but this one does, and with great acting, action and authenticity, resplendently and excitingly depicting the Cooper adventure tale, equaling the dynamic two previous productions of 1920 and 1936. Day-Lewis (Hawkeye) and his two lifelong companions, his adopted father, Means (Chingachgook) and brother, Schweig (Uncas), the latter two being the last of the long-ago destroyed Mohican tribe, are seen in 1757 during the French and Indian War. They visit the homestead of Blatchford on the New York frontier where Blatchford tells them that he is assembling local militia to fight with the British troops against the French and their Huron allies as reinforcements going to British-held Fort William Henry, but only with the British promise that the militia can return to their homes and defend their families if the Indians raid those settlements. Meanwhile, Waddington, a British major with a few soldiers, along with guide Studi (Magua, a Huron and spy for the French), embark for Fort William Henry with Stowe and May, the daughters of that fort's commander, Roëves. The party is betrayed by Studi, who, with Huron supporters waiting in ambush, attack the British, but they are driven off when Day-Lewis, Means and Schweig appear on the scene. Day-Lewis and the Mohicans then agree to guide Waddington, Stowe and May to Fort William Henry. En route, they come upon the Blatchford homestead, which has been burned down and all of the family members murdered by raiding Huron. They then slip through the French and Indian lines to reach the fort, where Roëves is amazed to see his daughters. The fort, however, is barely holding on and surrender is inevitable. While Day-Lewis and Stowe develop a close relationship, Day-Lewis works against the wishes of her father by helping the militia volunteers at the fort to secretly leave the fort to aid their families. Day-Lewis, Means and Schweig are summarily condemned and locked up on orders of Roëves. The fort is decimated by enemy attacks and Roëves finally agrees to surrender to Chéreau, playing French General Montcalm (1712-1759) on the promise that he, his troops and their families can retreat peacefully to Albany without further harm. Studi takes issue with Chéreau's terms, saying that his wife and children had been earlier killed by Roëves and his men when his village was destroyed and that he and the Huron allies want bloody revenge. Chéreau orders Studi not to take action, but, after Roëves and his men and their families leave the fort and travel through the wilderness, they are attacked from ambush by Studi and the Huron, the Indians committing a widespread massacre. Studi kills Roëves, removing his heart from his body while he is still alive and telling his victim that he will also kill his daughters to extinguish his bloodline. (This is an exceedingly gruesome and horrific scene.) Day-Lewis, Means and Schweig have by then escaped from the stockade and save Stowe and May, along with Waddington and they take canoes, paddling across Lake George and down a river to find shelter in a cave behind a waterfall. When Studi arrives with a large force of Indian braves, Day-Lewis tells Stowe, May and Waddington to submit to them without resistance and that he will later find and rescue them before he, Means and Schweig leap into the waterfall and are carried downstream. Studi captures Waddington and the sisters and takes them to the Huron village where Studi is chastised by Phillips, the Huron chief, for bringing the wrath of the British down upon his tribe. Studi demands that May remain his captive and squaw and where Waddington and Stowe should be killed as vengeance for British offenses against the Huron. Then Day-Lewis arrives unarmed and offers himself in exchange for the sisters and Waddington, but Phillips decrees that Studi take May with him, and that Waddington die in the flames while Day-Lewis, the long-respected foe of the Huron, take Stowe back to safety to placate the British. Day-Lewis leaves with Stowe while Studi, cursing Phillips for his decision, departs with May and several braves. Once Day-Lewis is outside the camp, he sees Waddington agonizing in pain as he is being burned alive and fires a single shot that hits its mark, killing Waddington and ending his torment. He, Means and Schweib then pursue Studi, with Schweib catching up with the Huron warriors, killing several of them before he faces Studi and where Studi kills Schweib, who falls from top of a cliff. Studi then motions May to follow him, but she turns away and leaps from the cliff to her death. Day-Lewis and Means then arrive, killing many of Studi's warriors, until Means revenges the death of his son, Schweib, in a fierce hand-to-hand fight with Studi, killing Studi and sending his limp corpse over the cliff. Means later holds a burial service for Schweib, stating that he is now the "last of the Mohicans." Day-Lewis and Stowe then depart toward safety and a life together. Mann does a great job in presenting this exciting film, detailing realistic action in many riveting scenes and well-coordinating his battle sequences. The cinematography is exceptional (shot on location in the Blue Ridge Mountains of North Carolina) and the acting superlative and where the costuming is accurate and authentic. This film grossed $75 million during the year of its release. **p**, Michael Mann, Hunt Lowry; **d**, Mann; **cast**, Daniel Day-Lewis, Madeleine Stowe, Russell Means, Eric Schweig, Jodhi May, Steven Waddington, Wes Studi, Maurice Roëves, Patrice Chéreau, Edward Blatchford, Mike Phillips; **w**, Mann, Christopher Crowe (based on the 1936 screenplay by Philip Dunne from an adaptation by John L. Balderston, Paul Perez, and Daniel Moore of the novel by James Fenimore Cooper); **c**, Dante Spinotti; **m**, Randy Edelman, Trevor Jones; **ed**, Dov Hoenig, Arthur Schmidt; **prod d**, Wolf Kroeger; **art d**, Robert Guerra, Richard Holland; **set d**, Jim Erickson, James V. Kent; **spec eff**, Tom Fisher, Henry Millar, Jim Rygiel, Stephen Stanton.

The Last Outlaw ★★★ 1936; U.S.; 62; RKO; B/W; Western; Children: Acceptable; **VHS**. Outlaw Carey is released from prison after twenty-five years, only to find that his old stomping ground, the quiet town of Broken Knee, has grown up into modern Center City. His baby daughter has also changed, becoming Callahan, a beautiful young woman. But outlaws still plague the community, and Carey and his old saddle pals, Gibson and Walthall, have little regard for the younger breed of gunmen. When these younger gunslingers rob the local bank and take Callahan hostage, the old-timers go back into action, this time on the side of the law. This above-average B-western sees great action and exceptional performances from Carey, Gibson and Walthall. The story was originally written by legendary director John Ford, which he first filmed as a silent

Ronald Reagan, Bruce Bennett, and Lloyd Corrigan in *The Last Outpost,* **1951.**

western in 1919. **p**, Robert Sisk; **d**, Christy Cabanne; **cast**, Harry Carey, Hoot Gibson, Tom Tyler, Henry B. Walthall, Margaret Callahan, Frank M. Thomas, Dennis O'Keefe, Alan Curtis, Ralph Byrd, Jack Mulhall; **w**, John Twist, Jack Townley (based on a story by John Ford, E. Murray Campbell); **c**, Jack MacKenzie; **m**, Alberto Colombo; **ed**, George Hively; **art d**, Van Nest Polglase.

The Last Outpost ★★★ 1951; U.S.; 89m; Par; Color; Western; Children: Acceptable; **DVD**; **VHS**. In this rousing and action-loaded oater Reagan and his brother Bennett find themselves as cavalry officers on opposite sides of the American Civil War, with Reagan joining the Confederacy and Bennett serving with the Union. Bennett is sent to command a post in Arizona that is sending gold shipments northward to fund the Union cause and to prevent further raids on those shipments that Reagan and his Rebels are making. Northern spies encourage Apache chiefs Evans (Chief Grey Cloud), Chief Yowlachie (Cochise), and John War Eagle (Geronimo) to take to the warpath and attack the Confederates, but Reagan convinces the Apache leaders to remain peaceful, chiefly because he knows that if they take to the warpath, both Union and Rebel white settlers like Fleming, his ex-fiancée, and her husband, Ridgley, may be killed. All this comes undone when a white man murders an Apache leader and the Indians attack the fort commanded by Bennett and where the fetching Fleming and husband Ridgely have taken refuge. The defenders are slowly reduced in numbers by the savage attacks and it appears that the fort will fall, but the principled Reagan will not allow a massacre of women and children and orders his men to ride to the rescue of the Yankees and their dependents. Northerners and southerners then fight side by side to throw back the Apaches and, after saving the fort and his avowed enemies, Reagan and his Rebels ride off to continue the fight for the Confederacy. Foster's direction is sure and swift, and Reagan, Bennett and cast members are standouts in their colorful roles, especially the veteran western character actor Beery, whose father was celebrated in the silent era for enacting the same kind of roles. ***Author's Note***: This film emanated from Paramount's "B" movie unit headed by Thomas and Pine, but the studio gave them a budget much larger than usual for this production and it shows in its high production values. Reagan, who was three decades away from occupying the White House as the nation's fortieth U.S. President (1981-1989), had his thoroughbred horse, Tarbaby, shipped at Paramount's expense to Arizona where the film was shot on location, which drew some scoffing criticism from the studio wranglers, who predicted that the hot weather and demanding scenes would quickly wear out Reagan's favorite horse. Just the opposite occurred when most of the studio's animals were down with heatstroke and other ailments caused by the demanding climate and environment, but Tarbaby was

Cybill Shepherd and Ellen Burstyn in *The Last Picture Show*, 1971.

running strong and healthy. Bennett (1906-2007), an Olympic champion (Silver Medal for the shot put, 1928), was a reclusive actor, who avoided publicity and had once played the role of Tarzan in a 1935 film (under his given name of Herman Brix). He remained athletic throughout his life, and was parasailing and skydiving into his advanced years, leaping from a plane at 10,000 feet over Lake Tahoe at age ninety-six. He lived to be more than one hundred, but felt that age was only a state of mind, saying that: "We know many young people of ninety and old people of twenty. By my mind, I'm still young." **p**, William H. Pine, William C. Thomas; **d**, Lewis R. Foster; **cast**, Ronald Reagan, Rhonda Fleming, Bruce Bennett, Bill Williams, Noah Beery, Jr., Peter Hansen, Hugh Beaumont, Lloyd Corrigan, John Ridgely, Iron Eyes Cody, Charles Evans, Richard Crane, John War Eagle, Chief Yowlachie; **w**, Geoffrey Homes, Winston Miller, George Worthing Yates (based on a story by David Lang); **c**, Loyal Griggs (Technicolor); **m**, Lucien Cailliet; **ed**, Howard Smith; **art d**, Lewis H. Creber; **set d**, Alfred Kegerris.

The Last Picture Show ★★★★★ 1971; U.S.; 118m; COL; B/W; Drama; Children: Unacceptable (MPAA: R); **DVD**; **VHS**. Sad and poignant, this most memorable film is undoubtedly one of Bogdanovich's finest works, another period production (at the time of the Korean War) that excruciatingly captures the death throes of a small Texas town that has not kept up with the modern era. Bottoms and Bridges are the town heroes as they are the stars of the local football team, although the team has not had a sterling record. Bridges is outspoken and aggressive while Bottoms is withdrawn and sensitive, but who is strongly defensive of a retarded boy (played by Sam Bottoms, Timothy's real life brother), who is the subject of cruel jokes and remarks from loafers and louts hanging out at the local pool hall, which is part of the theater operation run by former cowboy Johnson. The grizzled Johnson is the idol of every boy in town, and who serves as their surrogate father, giving sage advice while forlornly pining for an Old West that is no more. After Bottoms goes to the defense of the retarded youth, Leachman, who is the promiscuous wife of basketball coach Thurman, takes Bottoms under her wing as a lover, an affair that sees its ups and downs throughout the film and where Bottoms throws over his old girlfriend, Taggart, in order to stay with the older woman. Meanwhile, Bridges continues to romance his longtime girlfriend, Shepherd, a self-centered girl, who, like her manipulative mother, Burstyn, wants to marry a rich man. To that end, she attends a nude swimming party held by worthless rich boy Brockette, who really wants nothing to do with Shepherd because she is a virgin. Bottoms and Bridges then take a trip together, going to a Mexican border town, but they are jolted when they return to find that their hero, Johnson, has died. He has left the pool hall to Bottoms, his café to Brennan and the dilapidated movie theater

to Fulton, the elderly woman who has run the concession stand for more years than anyone can recall. The scheming Shepherd then seduces Bridges so that she can lose her virginity and, with that accomplished, runs to Brockette with the news, and he, in turn, rejects her as being repulsive before marrying another girl of his own class. Bridges then takes a job in the oil fields, and Shepherd, now desperate to be married to anyone with a good income, seduces Gulager, the foreman of the firm where her father works, and who has also been a sometimes lover of her mother, Burstyn. Moreover, Shepherd then seduces Bottoms to lure him away from Leachman, and when Bridges learns of this, he flies into a rage and strikes Bottoms with a bottle that causes him to be hospitalized. Bridges then gives up on his home town and joins the army. While Bottoms convalesces, he makes plans to marry Shepherd, but those plans are disrupted when Shepherd's father, Glenn, arrives and takes her away. Burstyn remains briefly with Bottoms to tell him that she and the deceased town idol, Johnson, were once lovers. Bridges returns from basic training and, before being shipped off to fight in the Korean War, he makes amends with old friend Bottoms and the two reminisce about their hometown, watching their "last picture show" together and knowing that the theater is about to close because of the onslaught of television. Before leaving, Bridges asks Bottoms to take care of his car. When Bottoms walks back to the pool hall, he sees Sam Bottoms, the retarded boy he earlier befriended, rush toward him, but who is killed when struck by a speeding car. Dazed and incensed at this senseless death, Bottoms drives Bridges' car at high speeds, but really has no place to go and finally stops outside Leachman's home where Leachman screams at him for humiliating her. Bottoms calms her, reaching out and holding her hand, indicating that their affair is not yet over. This film bathes the viewer with a thick, warm blanket of nostalgia, and every evocative scene produces a strange longing for the past, one that may ache the heart if not certainly stimulate memories of that more gentle time between WWII and the Korean conflict. Few other than Bogdanovich, who employs in this film the techniques of his directorial idols, Howard Hawks and John Ford, could have made such an impactful film and with such care as he skillfully unfolds several stories thorough meticulous cross-cutting and while effectively developing his characters to their fullest. Bottoms, Bridges, Shepherd, Leachman, Burstyn, and particularly Johnson, render unforgettable performances as the lonely denizens of a Texas town doomed by time and change, a moving document that begins with a superb script from McMurtry, and greatly enhanced by the gritty, black-and-white cinematography of master cameraman Surtees. **p**, Stephen J. Friedman; **d**, Peter Bogdanovich; **cast**, Timothy Bottoms, Jeff Bridges, Cybill Shepherd, Ben Johnson, Cloris Leachman, Ellen Burstyn, Eileen Brennan, Clu Gulager, Sam Bottoms, Randy Quaid, Sharon Taggart, Joe Heathcock, Bill Thurman, Gary Brockette, Robert Glenn, Barc Doyle, Jessie Lee Fulton; **w**, Bogdanovich, Larry McMurtry (based on the novel by McMurtry); **c**, Robert Surtees; **m**, (various recordings) Hank Williams, Bob Wills and His Texas Playboys, Phil Harris, Eddie Arnold, Eddie Fisher, Pee Wee King, Hank Snow, Tony Bennett, Frankie Laine, Johnny Ray, Kay Starr, Johnny Sandley, Hank Thompson; **ed**, Donn Cambern; **prod d**, Polly Platt; **art d**, Walter Scott Herndon.

The Last Round-Up ★★★ 1947; U.S.; 77m; COL; B/W; Western; Children: Acceptable; **DVD**; **VHS**. This is the first film produced by Gene Autry Productions and one of the cowboy star's best, which he said was his favorite. He is in charge of rounding up a tribe of Indians encamped on some barren land. The Indians must be relocated because an aqueduct is scheduled to be built at the location. Autry overcomes considerable odds and villains to accomplish his task in this action-packed oater and where considerable stock footage from the Jean Arthur-William Holden film **Arizona, 1940**, from the same studio, was used in this production. Songs sung by Autry include "You Can't See the Sun When You're Crying," "160 Acres in the Valley," "An Apple for the Teacher," "Comin' Round the Mountain," and "The Last Round-

Up." **p**, Armand Schaefer; **d**, John English; **cast**, Gene Autry, Jean Heather, Ralph Morgan, Carol Thurston, Mark Daniels, Robert (Bobby) Blake, Russ Vincent, Ernie Adams, Ted Adams, Jose Alvarado, Trevor Bardette, Iron Eyes Cody; **w**, Jack Townley, Earle Snell (based on a story by Townley); **c**, William Bradford; **m**, Mischa Bakaleinikoff; **ed**, Aaron Stell; **prod d**, Harold MacArthur; **set d**, Frank Tuttle.

The Last Samurai ★★★ 2003; U.S.; 154m; WB; Color; Historical/Action; Children: Unacceptable (MPAA: R); **BD**; **DVD**; **VHS**. A great deal of well-executed action can be seen in this above-average historical epic where Cruise is a veteran of the American Civil War needing work in the 1870s. He takes a job from some American businessmen, who want lucrative contracts with the Emperor of Japan and where Cruise's task is to train Japanese peasant conscripts for the first modern Imperial Army using modern weapons, including firearms. Once trained, their first assignment is to put down a rebellion by Samurai warriors, who remain devoted to their traditional heritage and reject modern warfare including the use of firearms. In their first skirmish, the Samurai defeat Cruise and his army. Cruise is seriously injured in the battle, but the Samurai leader (Watanabe) admires his courage and spares his life. Cruise recovers with a new respect for the Samurai and aids Watanabe in an attempt to save the Bushido traditions. Excessive violence and gutter language prohibit viewing by children. **p**, Edward Zwick, Tom Cruise, Tom Engelman, Marshall Herskovitz, Scott Kroopf, Paula Wagner; **d**, Zwick; **cast**, Cruise, Ken Watanabe, Billy Connolly, Tony Goldwyn, William Atherton, Chad Lindberg, Masato Harada, Masashi Odate, John Koyama, Timothy Spall, Scott Wilson, Shichinosuke Nakamura, Togo Igawa, Satoshi Nikaido; **w**, Zwick, John Logan, Herskovitz (based on a story by Logan); **c**, John Toll; **m**, Hans Zimmer; **ed**, Victor Dubois, Steven Rosenblum; **prod d**, Lilly Kilvert; **art d**, Chris Burian-Mohr, Jess Gonchor, Kim Sinlair; **set d**, Gretchen Rau; **spec eff**, Dick Wood, Stan Blackwell, Romulo Adriano Jr.

The Last Seduction ★★★ 1994; U.K./U.S.; 110m; Incorporated Television Co./October Films; Color; Crime Drama; Children: Unacceptable (MPAA: R); **DVD**; **VHS**. Fiorentino is beautiful, intelligent, and married to Pullman, a doctor who loves her and is as corrupt as she in their greed for money. She persuades him to sell medicinal cocaine to some drug dealers, but, after he does that, she flees with the profits, close to a million dollars, and hides out in a small Midwestern town. Pullman owes some money to a loan shark, so he sends private detectives to find Fiorentino in order to recoup the money. The wily wife seduces Berg, a naive man in town, who is smitten by her beauty, into accepting Fiorentino's plan to get rid of Pullman. No good can come of any of this bad behavior, as Fiorentino learns the hard way. This modern *film noir* entry provides considerable entertainment and offers standout performances from the cast. Violence, gutter language, and sexuality prohibit viewing by children. **p**, Jonathan Shestack, Nancy Rae Stone; **d**, John Dahl; **cast**, Linda Fiorentino, Bill Pullman, Peter Berg, Brien Varady, Dean Norris, Donna Wilson, Mik Scriba, J.T. Walsh, Bill Nunn, Herb Mitchell, Erik-Anders Nilsson; **w**, Steve Barancik; **c**, Jeffrey Jur; **m**, Joseph Vitarelli; **ed**, Eric L. Beason; **prod d**, Linda Pearl; **art d**, Dina Lipton; **set d**, Kathy Lucas; **spec eff**, John Hartigan.

The Last September ★★★ 2000; France/U.K./Ireland; 103m; Matrix Films/Trimark Pictures; Color; Drama; Children: Unacceptable (MPAA: R); **DVD**; **VHS**. Smith and Gambon are a middle-aged British couple living on an old country estate in Ireland in 1920, the time of "The Troubles," and shortly before the British ended their rule in that country. As the Irish war for independence builds to a longtime-coming climax favorable to the Irish, British aristocrats such as Smith and Gambon will lose their privileges. Living with them is their coquettish niece, Hawes, who may or may not be in love with British army captain Tennant, who is unacceptable because his parents were "in trade," and, at the same time, she is attracted to an Irish freedom fighter, Lydon, who has killed

Maggie Smith, Jane Birkin, Lambert Wilson and Michael Gambon in *The Last September*, 2000.

some British soldiers and is hiding in an old mill on the estate. Also living with the aristocrats is a nephew, Slinger, who has been studying at Oxford, and house guests Birkin and Wilson, who are married but homeless, as well as Shaw, a woman from London, who once loved Wilson. Social and political problems are resolved in ways that are not ideal but acceptable to all in this good character study. Nudity and violence prohibit viewing by children. **p**, Yvonne Thunder, Marina Gefter; **d**, Deborah Warner; **cast**, Michael Gambon, Maggie Smith, Keeley Hawes, David Tennant, Lambert Wilson, Jane Birkin, Fiona Shaw, Jonathan Slinger, Gary Lydon, Richard Roxburgh, Tom Hickey; **w**, John Banville (based on the novel by Elizabeth Bowen); **c**, Slawomir Idziak; **m**, Zbigniew Preisner; **ed**, Kate Evans; **prod d**, Caroline Amies; **art d**, Paul Kirby; **spec eff**, Kevin Byrne, Oliver Byrne, Kevin Kearns.

The Last Stop ★★★ 1949; Poland; 110m; P. P. Film Polski/Times Film Corporation; B/W; War Drama; Children: Unacceptable. In this disturbing but powerful docudrama-like film, Drapinska gives a riveting performance as a Jewish woman who, along with her family, is taken by Nazis to the dreaded concentration camp of Auschwitz. Once she arrives at this death camp, Drapinska is separated from her family, selected to be an interpreter. While her family members are murdered, she survives one day at a time at the whims and impulses of sadistic German guards as well as the "capos," or those chosen from the prison population to become administrative workers, who viciously do the bidding of the bestial Nazis. Anxiety mounts as news filters through the camp that the Red Army is approaching to soon liberate the prisoners, and the struggle to survive becomes all the more desperate for Drapinska and her friends. Standout performances from Drapinska and the rest of the cast highlights this grim portrait that indicts the mass murders of Hitler's regime, which is well directed by Jakubowska. (In Polish; English subtitles.) **p&d**, Wanda Jakubowska; **cast**, Tatjana Gorecka, Antonina Gordon-Górecka, Barbara Drapinska, Aleksandra Slaska, Barbara Rachwalska, Wladyslaw Brochwicz, Edward Dziewonski, Kazimierz Pawlowski, Alina Janowska, Mariya Vinogradova; **w**, Jakubowska, Gerda Schneider; **c**, Bentsion Monastyrsky; **m**, Roman Palester; **art d**, Roman Mann, Czeslaw Piaskowski.

The Last Ten Days ★★★ 1956; West Germany/Austria; 113m; Cosmopol-Film/COL; B/W; Biographical Drama; Children: Unacceptable; **DVD**; **VHS**. The legendary German director Pabst offers a fascinating portrait of Nazi dictator Adolf Hitler (1889-1945), well essayed by Skoda, as he cowers in an underground bunker in Berlin during the final days of WWII. The frantic comings and goings of what is left of the German High Command shows slavish generals bowing and scraping to Skoda as he is given false reports about how his troops are throw-

Elizabeth Taylor and Van Johnson in *The Last Time I Saw Paris*, 1954.

ing back the Russian forces while the enemy relentlessly advances toward the center of Berlin. Werner, a soldier doing his duty, arrives at the bunker to deliver a request from a front-line commander seeking Skoda's signature on an order that will send reinforcements to that commander, but there are no reinforcements to send, although the deluded Skoda believes he is still commanding a powerful German army. While waiting for Skoda to make up his mind, Werner quickly realizes that he is the only normal person in this unreal world, and that the bunker is inhabited by lunatics, who still believe that Germany can win the war (and where Werner provides the realistic contrast to these self-aggrandizing and fiercely posturing people). Meanwhile, Tobisch, playing Hitler's mistress, Eva Braun (1912-1945), goes about the bunker chatting with nervous female secretaries as if nothing is amiss and while the place shakes under incessant bombardments, and who becomes ecstatic when hearing that Hitler has decided to finally marry her before they both commit suicide. Pabst provides a shuddering and spine-chilling portrait of Hitler's madness and how that madness infected his mesmerized followers to the last moments of their lives. *Author's Note*: The gifted Pabst had a strange and unpredictable relationship with the Nazi regime. He denounced the Nazis when they rose to power and fled to France, but he then returned to Germany and made films under the Nazi aegis of Paul Joseph Goebbels (1897-1945), who was Hitler's Minister of Propaganda and head of the German film industry. Goebbels also died in the bunker with Hitler, committing suicide with his wife after they killed their six children by having a Nazi physician inject them with morphine. Following the war, Pabst appeared to be an ardent anti-Nazi, stating that he was compelled to make films during Hitler's regime, and he made this film as a way to exonerate himself. The script that depicts the persons and events in **The Last Ten Days** was based upon a novel by Musmanno, who obtained detailed information on those deluded persons and bizarre events in that bunker from Trudl Junge (Gertrude Humps, 1920-2002), and who was one of the female secretaries working in the bunker during Hitler's last days. Junge became a close friend of the rather mindless Eva Braun whose devotion to Hitler was as fanatical as any of his storm troopers. Junge escaped the bunker just before the Russians captured the area and, through Musmanno, took shelter in Austria for several weeks while he paid her 1500 marks for her story. For more details on Adolf Hitler, Eva Braun and the Nazi regime, see my book, *The Great Pictorial History of World Crime*, Volume I (History, Inc., 2004; pages 138-148). (In German; English subtitles.) **p**, Carl Szokoll; **d**, Georg Wilhelm Pabst; **cast**, Albin Skoda, Oskar Werner, Lotte Tobisch, Willy Krause, Erich Stuckmann, Erland Erlandsen, Curt Eilers, Leopold Hainisch, Otto Schmöle, Herbert Herbe; **w**, Erich Maria Remarque (based on the novel *Ten Days to Die* by Michael A. Musmanno); **c**, Günther Anders;

m, Erwin Halletz; **ed**, Herbert Taschner; **prod d**, Otto Pischinger, Werner Schlichting.

The Last Time I Saw Paris ★★★ 1954; U.S.; 116m; MGM; Color; Drama; Children: Cautionary; **DVD**; **VHS**. Director Brooks does a fine job in presenting the tragic love tale from F. Scott Fitzgerald and where Taylor, Johnson and the rest of the cast give sterling performances. Although Fitzgerald set his story after WWI, this version has Johnson arriving in Paris in an attempt to regain the custody of a child he lost through his own mistake. He then recalls his earlier life, which is shown in flashback and where he is going to Paris after the end of WWII to work for an English-language newspaper but with ambitions to become a novelist. After meeting the ravishing Taylor, a wealthy young woman, they wed and settle down in the City of Light and where Johnson goes to work on his first book. The couple seems happy, but when Johnson fails to sell his novel, he becomes depressed and begins drinking heavily and with the loyal but emotionally unstable Taylor joining him. Johnson overdrinks at a party and passes out, and when Taylor tries to enter her home in Paris during a rainstorm, she finds herself locked outside and catches pneumonia that soon claims her young life. Their child is raised by Reed, Taylor's sister, who never approved of Johnson, while he returns to the U.S. He finally becomes a successful writer and then returns to Paris to reclaim that child and this is where the story is shown in flash forward. Johnson begs Reed for the custody of his little girl, but is rebuffed with Reed recalling the bitter memory of his sister's untimely death and for which she holds Johnson responsible. She finally relents, however, when seeing that Johnson loves his daughter more than anything else in his life, and the child is returned to her father. This sad but compelling film is lavishly produced, winning high marks for acting, directing and superlative color lensing by Ruttenberg, who captures the beauty and grandeur of Paris. *Author's Note*: Taylor told this author that this film "really inspired me to be a better actress because I had a part that challenged me—the young woman I am playing has an unpredictable personality. She is mercurial, even a little unbalanced, so I was able to show unusual character traits I did not find in the too normal women I had been playing." Johnson stated to this author that "Elizabeth was so beautiful in that picture that she takes your breath away. We all knew then that she was probably the most beautiful actress on the screen, but she never thought about that. She was too busy being a fine actress. Talent on top of beauty—you can't beat it." **p**, Jack Cummings; **d**, Richard Brooks; **cast**, Elizabeth Taylor, Van Johnson, Walter Pidgeon, Donna Reed, Eva Gabor, Kurt Kasznar, George Dolenz, Roger Moore, Sandy Descher, Celia Lovsky, Odette Myrtil; **w**, Brooks, Julius J. and Philip G. Epstein (based on the story "Babylon Revisited" by F. Scott Fitzgerald); **c**, Joseph Ruttenberg (Technicolor); **m**, Conrad Salinger, Jerome Kern; **ed**, John Dunning; **art d**, Cedric Gibbons, Randall Duell; **set d**, Edwin B. Willis, Jack D. Moore; **spec eff**, A. Arnold Gillespie.

Last Train from Gun Hill ★★★ 1959; Israel/France; 95m; Bryna Productions/PAR; Color; Western; Children: Unacceptable; **DVD**; **VHS**. The Indian wife of a U.S. marshal, Douglas, is raped and murdered. The killer leaves behind a saddle that Douglas recognizes as belonging to his old friend, Quinn, who is now a cattle baron outside the town of Gun Hill. Further complicating matters, Douglas learns that the person who raped and killed his wife is Quinn's son, Holliman. Douglas arrives in Gun Hill and arrests Holliman. He then plans to take Holliman away by the night train to his own town where he can be tried for the rape and murder, but Douglas is trapped in town by Quinn and his henchmen, who are now out to kill him. In the final shootout at the train station, only Douglas is left alive. Solid acting and well-orchestrated action sees this oater as an above-average entry. Excessive violence prohibits viewing by children. *Author's Note*: This film owes a debt to the fine western, **3:10 to Yuma**, 1957, and almost follows the story line of that tense western to the letter. Holliman, who attended a Los Angeles production of one of my plays, "Last Rites for the Boys," told this author that "I appeared with Kirk Douglas in a film a few years earlier, **Gunfight at the O.K. Corral** [1957]. He was one of the most confident actors I ever met, and his intensity charged every scene with electricity." **p**, Hal B. Wallis; **d**, John Sturges; **cast**, Kirk Douglas, Anthony Quinn, Carolyn Jones, Earl Holliman, Brad Dexter, Brian Hutton, Ziva Rodann, Bing Russell, Walter Sande, Ty Hardin; **w**, James Poe (based on the story "Showdown" by Les Crutchfield); **c**, Charles Lang Jr. (Technicolor); **m**, Dimitri Tiomkin; **ed**, Hal Pereira, Walter Tyler; **set d**, Sam Comer, Ray Moyer; **spec eff**, Farciot Edouart, John P. Fulton.

The Last Train from Madrid ★★★ 1937; U.S.; 85m; PAR; B/W; War Drama; Children: Cautionary. In this exciting and tension-filled war tale, we see a number of widely divergent characters fleeing as refugees from Madrid, Spain, then being bombed and attacked by fascist forces. Atwill, a Loyalist general, orders one of his officers, Quinn, to make sure that the last train leaving Madrid makes it safely to Valencia, and Quinn then begins assembling the passengers for that harrowing trip. One of those passengers is Lamour, who has become friendly with Quinn, although she still has feelings for former boyfriend, Roland, who is an ex-officer and a political refugee. Others slated to take the train include Ayres, a cynical newsman who has "adopted" Bradna, an orphan; army deserter Cummings; wealthy baroness Morley; and Mack, a lowly prostitute. Much of the film deals with the struggles of these people, all frantic to seek safety beyond doomed Madrid, as well as the plight of Roland, who is sought by Loyalists as a turncoat. He is a close friend of Quinn's, who allows Roland to board the train and be with Lamour, even though the noble Quinn knows that he will now lose Lamour's affections. Just before the train departs, Atwill arrives at the station, learning that Roland is a passenger on the train. He orders Quinn to remove Roland from the train and summarily shoot him, but Quinn, for the sake of Lamour, holds a gun on Atwill until the train departs. After Lamour and Roland are safely away with the other joyous passengers, Atwill has Quinn arrested and condemned for insubordination. Quinn then forfeits his life to a firing squad out of his love for Lamour. *Author's Note*: This production was controversial in that it was the first feature film focusing upon the Spanish Civil War (1936-1939), a conflict raging at the time and one that was a proving ground between the forces of democracy and that of fascism, although this film makes no political statements and takes not sides, albeit Atwill's performance as the autocratic Loyalist general is more in keeping with the actions of the fascist generals fighting under the banner of Francisco Franco (1892-1975), whose side won the war and established a long-standing fascist state in Spain until his death. Future superstar Alan Ladd appears in this film in a bit part as a soldier, and pantheon director Cecil B. DeMille also appears briefly while stepping from a small house. DeMille made this appearance as a good luck gesture to his new son-in-law, Anthony Quinn, who had married his daughter, actress Katherine DeMille, on October 3, 1937. Quinn told this author that "**The Last Train from Madrid** is about a lot of frightened people trying to get out of a city they know is going to fall into fascist hands. I never understood why they did not have anyone denouncing the fascists in that picture, but Hollywood was just as frightened as those people trying to get onto that train. Paramount did not want to make waves and condemn the fascists outright, probably because they would lose their distribution in Italy and Germany as those countries were supporting Franco in his takeover of Spain. It was a tragic time. The only one in Hollywood who stood up for the Spanish loyalists was Errol Flynn that I can remember. He was fearless and staunchly against the fascists. I think he even went to Spain and fought there secretly for a short time and got into trouble with his studio, Warner Brothers. There was nobody like that man, on or off the screen—a real hero." During the production of this film, the hairdressing and makeup personnel went on strike and, according to statements made to this author by Lamour, "we had to fend for ourselves. We took those hardworking people for granted, but suddenly we had to do our own makeup and fix our hair and we learned just how good those people were and how bad we

Gilbert Roland, Dorothy Lamour, Karen Morley and Anthony Quinn in *The Last Train from Madrid*, 1937.

were at doing their jobs. I always remembered **The Last Train from Madrid** every time I put cold cream on my face." Roland, always a temperamental and vainglorious actor, insisted that none of the featured male actors in the film could wear a mustache and that he be the only one to so adorn his upper lip. Other notable films that portray or touch upon the Spanish Civil War include **Blockade**, 1938; **Arise My Love**, 1940; **The Fallen Sparrow**, 1943; **For Whom the Bell Tolls**, 1943; **Confidential Agent**, 1945; **Arch of Triumph**, 1948; **The Snows of Kilimanjaro**, 1952, and its 2011 remake; **Ship of Fools**, 1965; **Ay; Carmela!**, 1990; **Belle epoque**, 1992; and **Death in Granada**, 1996. **p**, George M. Arthur; **d**, James P. Hogan; **cast**, Dorothy Lamour, Lew Ayres, Gilbert Roland, Karen Morley, Lionel Atwill, Helen Mack, Robert Cummings, Olympe Bradna, Anthony Quinn, Lee Bowman, Evelyn Brent, Alan Ladd (bit part), Francis Ford, Cecil B. DeMille (walk-on); **w**, Louis Stevens, Robert Wyler (based on a story by Elsie and Paul Hervey Fox); **c**, Harry Fischbeck; **m**, Boris Morros; **ed**, Everett Douglas; **art d**, Hans Dreier, Earl Hedrick; **set d**, A.E. Freudeman.

The Last Tycoon ★★★ 1976; U.S.; 123m; PAR; Color; Drama; Children: Unacceptable (MPAA: PG); **DVD**; **VHS**. F. Scott Fitzgerald's unfinished novel comes surprisingly to life through a powerful performance from the always amazing De Niro, playing that last tycoon (which is based upon MGM's chief of production, Irving Thalberg, 1899-1936). The film opens with Mitchum as the actual boss of a major studio (presumably playing Louis B. Mayer, 1884-1957, head of MGM), who is shown nurturing temperamental stars like matinee idol Curtis while bedding down innumerable starlets. Meanwhile, De Niro, who is Mitchum's chief of production, works slowly to take over the studio with or without Mitchum's approval, while fending off threats from union leader Nicholson—both play ping pong together, a wild match that symbolizes the tenacity of their negotiating positions. De Niro, at one point, spots Boulting, a beautiful, young girl on a movie set and later sees her gliding on a float in the studio tank at night and becomes enthralled with her as she reminds him of his dead wife. When he attempts to make love with her, however, he is inhibited by the memory of that deceased spouse. Meanwhile, Russell, Mitchum's daughter, accidentally barges into his office and embarrasses him and her when finding him making love to a woman. Russell is by then head over heels in love with De Niro, but he is too elusive for her to capture his heart. Although Kazan's direction is inventive, and the production values are high and the script witty and provocative, there is no real conclusion to this story as Fitzgerald died before finishing the novel, and Pinter, who based his play on that novel and from which this film stems, is left with an ambiguous finale. It is nevertheless worth the watching to see a good look at Hollywood as it was in its so-called "Golden Age." *Author's*

Richard Widmark in *The Last Wagon*, 1956.

Note: Mitchum told this author that "sadly, the picture does not have a conclusive ending because Fitzgerald died before he finished the book, but we all know the ending anyway. He based his main character on Irving Thalberg, who died prematurely in 1936. Fitzgerald died four years later with only about seventeen chapters, or about half the book finished, and they published that a year after Fitzgerald died. Thalberg was a great man and Fitzgerald was a great author, who also died prematurely. In one respect they are very similar. Both had enormous talent and their brilliant minds made them very special people." **p**, Sam Spiegel; **d**, Elia Kazan; **cast**, Robert De Niro, Tony Curtis, Robert Mitchum, Jeanne Moreau, Jack Nicholson, Donald Pleasence, Ingrid Boulting, Ray Milland, Dana Andrews, Theresa Russell, Peter Strauss, Tige Andrews, Morgan Farley, John Carradine; **w**, Harold Pinter (based on the novel by F. Scott Fitzgerald); **c**, Victor J. Kemper (Panavision; Technicolor); **m**, Maurice Jarre; **ed**, Richard Marks; **prod d**, Gene Callahan; **art d**, Jack T. Collis; **set d**, Bill Smith, Jerry Wunderlich; **spec eff**, Henry Millar.

The Last Voyage ★★★ 1960; U.S.; 91m; MGM; Color; Drama; Children: Cautionary; **DVD**; **VHS**. In this solid disaster drama, the passengers on a luxury liner are suddenly confronted with a sinking ship after an on-board explosion fatally damages the vessel. While many passengers are able to abandon ship, others are trapped in cabins, especially Malone, who is pinned inside of her stateroom while her husband, Stack, frantically tries to free her. When unable to release his wife, he seeks aid from the crew members, most of whom have already abandoned the sinking liner. He finds Strode and a few others, who use their equipment to pry Malone free just as the water is about to close over her head, and she and Stack are rescued as the ship goes down for the Deep Six. The direction and acting is above average, and the well-written story keeps this one afloat. *Author's Note*: Producers Andrew and Virginia Stone were fortunate enough to purchase the old French luxury liner *Isle de France*, which was already designated for destruction, and used this great luxury liner to realistically bring about its watery end. **The Poseidon Adventure**, 1972, takes a large leaf from the story line of this film. Other notable films dealing with the sinking of luxury liners include **Arise, My Love**, 1940 (sinking of the *Athenia* in 1939); **Lifeboat**, 1944; **The Story of Dr. Wassell**, 1944; **Titanic**, 1953; **Abandon Ship!**, 1957; **A Night to Remember**, 1958 (also *Titanic*); and **Titanic**, 1997. **p**, Andrew L. Stone, Virginia L. Stone; **d**, Andrew L. Stone; **cast**, Robert Stack, Dorothy Malone, George Sanders, Edmond O'Brien, Woody Strode, Jack Kruschen, Joel Marston, George Furness, Richard Norris, Marshall Kent; **w**, Andrew L. Stone; **c**, Hal Mohr (Metrocolor); **m**, Rudy Schrager; **ed**, Virginia L. Stone; **spec eff**, A.J. (Augie) Lohman.

The Last Wagon ★★★ 1956; U.S.; 98m; FOX; Color; Western; Children: Unacceptable; **DVD**. In this gritty and uncompromising western Widmark is a trapper who seeks vengeance for the murder of his wife and children. When he kills the man responsible for those slayings, he is arrested and chained to a wagon that is part of a wagon train. Apaches attack the train and kill everyone, except Widmark, who is left for dead, and some children who have been hiding in a wagon. The children revive Widmark and, acting as their surrogate father, assumes the responsibility of getting the children to safety. A hard-hitting and often violent film, this production nevertheless offers a riveting performance by Widmark and the children he shepherds to a safe haven. **p**, William B. Hawks; **d**, Delmer Daves; **cast**, Richard Widmark, Felicia Farr, Susan Kohner, Tommy Rettig, Stephanie Griffin, Ray Stricklyn, Nick Adams, Carl Benton Reid, Douglas Kennedy, James Drury; **w**, James Edward Grant, Daves, Gwen Bagni Gieglud (based on a story by Bagni Gielgud); **c**, Wilfrid Cline (CinemaScope; DeLuxe Color); **m**, Lionel Newman; **ed**, Hugh S. Fowler; **art d**, Lyle R. Wheeler, Lewis H. Creber; **set d**, Walter M. Scott, Chester Bayhi; **spec eff**, Ray Kellogg.

The Last Wave ★★★ 1979; Australia; 106m; Australian Film Commission/World Northal; Color; Drama; Children: Unacceptable (MPAA: PG); **DVD**; **VHS**. Chamberlain is a corporate attorney working in Sydney, Australia, who finds himself in the unusual situation of defending five Aborigines accused of a murder which may have been a ritualized tribal execution where a small group of city Aborigines killed another Aborigine outside a bar one night. One member of the group, Gulpilil, tries to piece together what happened that evening. Western civilization collides with Aborigine culture in this unusual murder mystery complicated by the supernatural with nightmare imagining and strange happenings such as water from nowhere running down a carpeted stairwell, and when school children playing cricket are interrupted by a sudden heavy rain storm when the sky is cloudless. The Aborigines are clearly in touch with some cosmic force that is beyond what white Australians can fathom. This strange but fascinating mystery offers high production values and standout performances from the entire cast. Excessive violence prohibits viewing by children. **p**, Hal McElroy, Jim McElroy; **d**, Peter Weir; **cast**, Richard Chamberlain, Olivia Hamnett, David Gulpilil, Frederick Parslow, Vivean Gray, Nandjiwarra Amagula, Walter Amagula, Roy Bara, Cedrick Lalara, Morris Lalara; **w**, Weir, Tony Morphett, Petru Popescu; **c**, Russell Boyd; **m**, Charles Wain; **ed**, Max Lemon; **prod d**, Goran Warff; **art d**, Neil Angwin; **set d**, Bill Malcolm; **spec eff**, Monty Fieguth, Bob Hilditch, Dennis Smith.

Last Year at Marienbad ★★★ 1962; France/Italy; 94m; Cocinor/Terra Film/Astor Pictures; B/W; Drama; Children: Unacceptable; **DVD**; **VHS**. If not a novelty, this film is certainly an inventive production that challenges as well as exasperates. The film opens at a cavernous chateau where Albertazzi meets Seyrig, a woman he thinks he has met a year earlier at a different resort. Seyrig denies that they have had an affair and insists that she has never before met him. Most of the film occupies Albertazzi's attempt to convince Seyrig that the affair did take place, or is going to imminently take place, or will take place sometime in the future. Pitoëff is a peripheral character, who may or may not be Seyrig's male companion or husband as he seems to be accompanying her at the chateau. The viewer is uncertain that Albertazzi is not imagining these characters, or that he is losing his faculties. Albertazzi narrates this odd story as the camera often takes his POV as he wanders aimlessly about the rather gloomy if not foreboding chateau as if searching for someone or something he cannot or will not specifically identify. Scenes and sequences interpose and these photographic juxtapositions only add further visual confusion to his fragmentary monolog and nothing is resolved, even the eventual confrontation between Albertazzi and Pitoëff. Director Resnais eschews the narrative form of filmmaking here, presenting each scene as one might present a still life painting, but without a cohesive story line or even a loosely organized script as the tale utterly abandons character development and opts for stream-of-consciousness. This unique visual experiment will fascinate some and frustrate others, and still others may dismiss the production as an inside joke parroting some arcane and forgotten Dadaistic prankster á la Tristan Tzara. Certainly, Resnais invites any viewer to create whatever meaning he or she might wish to apply to his filmic puzzle. (In French; English subtitles.) **p**, Pierre Courau, Raymond Froment; **d**, Alain Resnais; **cast**, Delphine Seyrig, Giorgio Albertazzi, Sacha Pitoëff, Françoise Bertin, Luce Garcia-Ville, Héléna Kornel, Françoise Spira, Karin Toche-Mittler, Pierre Barbaud, Wilhelm von Deek; **w**, Alain Robbe-Grillet; **c**, Sacha Vierny; **m**, Francis Seyrig; **ed**, Jasmine Chasney, Henri Colpi; **prod d**, Jacques Saulnier; **set d**, Jean-Jacques Fabre, Georges Glon, André Piltant.

L'Atalante ★★★ 1947; France; 89m; Jean-Louis Nounez/Cine Classics; B/W; Romance; Children: Unacceptable; **DVD**; **VHS**. Writer-director Vigo offers a poetic romance in which a barge captain, Dasté, marries a country girl, Parlo, and they live aboard his boat, *L'Atalante*, with a cabin boy and an old second mate, Simon. Parlo soon grows bored with life on the River Seine, and when the boat arrives in Paris, Dasté gives in to her pleas to take her to a cabaret where she meets a flirtatious peddler. Dasté is jealous and the next morning sails the boat away without his wife. But he soon misses her and falls into a deep depression, so Simon sets off to find her. The story is prosaic but the acting is superior as is the direction and cinematography. Originally made in 1934, this film was not released in the U.S. until 1947. (In French; English subtitles.) **p**, Jacques-Louis Nounez; **d**, Jean Vigo; **cast**, Michel Simon, Jean Dasté, Dita Parlo, Gilles Margaritis, Louis Lefebvre, Maurice Gilles, Raphaël Diligent, Claude Aveline, René Blech, Lou Bonin; **w**, Vigo, Albert Riéra (based on a screenplay by Jean Guinée); **c**, Jean-Paul Alphen, Louis Berger, Boris Kaufman; **m**, Maurice Jaubert; **ed**, Louis Chavance; **art d**, Francis Jourdain.

Late Autumn ★★★ 1973; Japan; 127m; Shochiku Eiga/New Yorker Films; Color; Drama; Children: Unacceptable; **DVD**. Hara is a recently widowed woman who tries to marry off her daughter, Tsukasa, with the help of her late husband's three friends. Tsukasa is not in any hurry to have a husband, which goes against the male tradition that holds that there is little or no place for an unmarried woman in Japanese life. Tsukasa finally gives in and agrees to get married, but her idea of a suitable husband is far from what the three men have in mind for her. Tsukasa is more of a modern Japanese young woman and has trouble giving in to the old traditions, a theme that often recurs in the films of Ozu, one of the great masters of Japanese cinema. Originally produced in 1960, this film was not shown in the U.S. until 1973. Adult themes prohibit viewing by children. (In Japanese; English subtitles.) **p**, Shizuo Yamanouchi; **d**, Yasujirô Ozu; **cast**, Setsuko Hara, Yôko Tsukasa, Chishû Ryû, Mariko Okada, Keiji Sada, Miyuki Kuwano, Shin'ichirô Mikami, Shin Saburi, Nobuo Nakamura, Kuniko Miyake; **w**, Kôgo Noda, Ozu (based on the novel by Ton Satomi); **c**, Yûharu Atsuta; **m**, Kojun Saitô; **ed**, Yoshiyasu Hamamura; **art d**, Tatsuo Hamada.

The Late George Apley ★★★★ 1947; U.S.; 93m; FOX; B/W; Comedy; Children: Acceptable; **DVD**; **VHS**. Colman is a delight in essaying a Boston Brahmin, who thinks that the world ends about ten miles beyond Beacon Hill and, if one is not a Harvard graduate, one is not educated. Wealthy and comfortable in his well-appointed mansion, Colman spends his time bird-watching and avoiding any contact with those not of his upper-upper class. Colman has already decreed that his son, Ney, attend Harvard and that his daughter, Cummins, marry one of her own class, but these edicts are shattered and so is Colman's well-tailored world when Ney falls in love with Brown, who comes from the hinterlands of Worcester, and Cummins begins to date Russell, a young man who is attending (God forbid) Yale. Colman's composure is somewhat restored when Russell begins reciting passages from Emerson, Colman's favorite poet. After Ney is forbidden to marry Brown at the risk of being

Vanessa Brown and Ronald Colman in *The Late George Apley*, 1947.

disinherited, the viewer is left with the notion that Ney will wind up being the same kind of stuffed shirt embodied by father Colman. The film is replete with barbed wit that subtly makes fun of Colman's crusty traditions, and Colman does a wonderful job lampooning his Back Bay character and where his supporting cast members also give superb performances. Director Mankiewicz skillfully shapes this extremely humorous film where pomposity is punctured and lofty airs obliterated. *Author's Note*: This film was hand-picked by Colman, who had the right to select any script he desired, and when he read the screenplay, based on the Pulitzer Prize winning novel by Marquand, he readily agreed to play its memorable character. **p**, Fred Kohlmar; **d**, Joseph L. Mankiewicz; **cast**, Ronald Colman, Peggy Cummins, Vanessa Brown, Edna Best, Richard Haydn, Charles Russell, Richard Ney, Mildred Natwick, Nydia Westman, Percy Waram, Diana Douglas; **w**, Philip Dunne (based on the novel by John P. Marquand and the play by Marquand and George S. Kaufman); **c**, Joseph LaShelle; **m**, Cyril J. Mockridge; **ed**, James B. Clark; **art d**, James Basevi, J. Russell Spencer; **set d**, Thomas Little; **spec eff**, Fred Sersen.

The Late Show ★★★ 1977; U.S.; 93m; Lion's Gate/WB; Color; Comedy; Children: Unacceptable (MPAA: PG): **DVD**; **VHS**. The teaming of Carney and Tomlin in this hilarious spoof on private eyes and film noir in general was a stroke of genius. Carney is an aging private detective who no longer yearns to snoop, even for money, because every time he turns around, something in his body rebels with pain. He gets a visit at his comfortable home from his partner in gumshoeing, Duff, who, unfortunately arrives with a bullet in him that proves fatal. To avenge his partner's demise, Carney takes up the strange trail Duff had been following, that of a missing cat belonging to Tomlin, who has hired Duff to track down and retrieve her beloved feline. Carney is urged to pursue the case by Macy, a pal of Duff's, but he soon learns that Tomlin is a fence, who held out some of her loot from peddling stolen goods to a partner, who then stole her cat in revenge. Carney, Tomlin and Macy then track down the cat abductor only to find him shot to death and carrying valuable stamps stolen from a rich collector in a robbery where the wife of the stamp owner was murdered. They reason that Duff was killed for trying to get his share of the loot from the robbery. When they recover the cat, they also uncover Cassidy, the seductive wife of a fence, Roche. Cassidy admits that she and the collector had been having a secret affair and that she had arrived at the apartment of an associate of Tomlin's now dead associate, who had been blackmailing her over that affair. They then find the body of the partner of Tomlin's deceased associate stuffed into a refrigerator. (If you think this is complicated, you haven't seen anything yet.) Cassidy flees and Carney and Tomlin chase her about the city, a pursuit that excites Tomlin who now thinks she and

Eduard Franz and Lana Turner in *Latin Lovers*, 1953.

Carney are another Nick and Nora Charles, and when she begins to make moves on Carney, the old gumshoe leaves her flat. Carney then visits Roche, telling him that his wife, Cassidy, was being blackmailed for having an affair and Roche, in turn, hires Macy to find the gun that killed the collector's wife. Cassidy also wants to find that gun and she contacts Carney and both go to the collector's home to find that the collector is also a murder victim. The ever snooping Tomlin then discovers the missing gun in her cat's carrying case and she calls Carney to tell him about it, but she gets Macy on the line instead. Macy arrives at Tomlin's residence with Considine, a goon working for Roche, and they demand the gun. Carney and Cassidy then arrive, and Carney, realizing that Tomlin is in real danger, fakes an ulcer attack to disarm the lethal Considine. By this time, Carney has figured it all out and explains á la Sherlock Holmes how Cassidy arranged for the death of the wife of her boyfriend, the collector, and then established the robbery to excuse the murder, but when the collector objected and threatened to call the police, Cassidy killed him, too, and then tried to put the blame on her husband, Roche. That ruse was easily identified by Roche, who killed Duff, who was working with Cassidy, and then went looking for the gun so that he could hold that as evidence against his wife, Cassidy, to keep her in line for the rest of her miserable life. By this time, Roche has arrived and gunfire erupts where Carney fatally shoots Roche, Considine and Macy. With this case neatly and grimly concluded, Carney now feels that he has been living alone too long and he rents a room next to that of the quirky Tomlin and where the pair appear to be heading for a permanent but wildly unpredictable relationship. Director Benton demonstrates superior abilities to spin this intricate tale with subtly humorous scenes that cockle the head and heart. Tomlin's suppressed her usual oddball mannerisms for her role and is outstanding as is the always wonderful Carney, a pillar of sly wisdom and street survival. Macy, too, is a standout as a weaseling character, who would double-cross his mother for a nickel. Although Robert Altman produced this film, the viewer can be thankful that he did not choose to direct, leaving that chore to the talented Benton, who produced a real gem, this being the second film he helmed. **p**, Robert Altman; **d&w**, Robert Benton; **cast**, Art Carney, Lily Tomlin, Bill Macy, Eugene Roche, Joanna Cassidy, John Considine, Ruth Nelson, John Davey, Howard Duff, Lothar Lambert; **c**, Chuck Rosher. (Metrocolor); **m**, Ken Wannberg; **ed**, Peter Appleton, Lou Lombardo; **set d**, Robert Gould, Dennis J. Parrish.

Latin Lovers ★★★ 1953; U.S.; 104m; MGM; Color; Musical/Comedy; Children: Acceptable; **VHS**. In this entertaining musical Turner is a very wealthy and beautiful young heiress, who is not sure men are after her for her money or for herself. But one of the men who loves her, Lund, is even richer than she is, and handsome besides. What is a

filthy rich girl to do? She seeks advice from her analyst, Franz, and his wife, Neumann, but that doesn't help much. Lund, who is more interested in business and making even more millions, flies off on a business trip to Brazil, and Turner follows. There she meets a tango-dancing Brazilian, Montalban, who is also rich, but not as rich as she or Lund, and he's handsome, too. What is a filthy rich girl to do now? Since Lund's feelings for her are nowhere near those of her new Latin lover, Turner gives all her money to Montalban because it hasn't brought her much happiness. Lund marries Turner's secretary, Hagen, and Turner and Montalban tango off together to the altar. Songs include: "Night and You," "Carlotta, You Gotta Be Mine," "A Little More of Your Amour," "Come to My Arms," "I Had to Kiss You" (Nicholas Brodszky, Leo Robin). **p**, Joe Pasternak; **d**, Mervyn Leroy; **cast**, Lana Turner, Ricardo Montalban, John Lund, Louis Calhern, Jean Hagen, Eduard Franz, Beulah Bondi, Joaquin Garay, Rita Moreno, Robert Burton; **w**, Isobel Lennart; **c**, Joseph Ruttenberg; **m**, George Stoll; **ed**, John McSweeney, Jr.; **art d**, Cedric Gibbons, Gabriel Scognamillo; **set d**, Edwin B. Willis, Jacques Mapes; **spec. eff**, A. Arnold Gillespie, Warren Newcombe.

Laugh, Clown, Laugh ★★★ 1928 (silent); U.S.; 73m/6 reels; MGM; B/W; Drama; Children: Cautionary; **DVD**; **VHS**. Chaney again gives a riveting performance, this time as a circus clown. While traveling with his circus, he finds an abandoned child and raises the little girl as his own. She grows up to be a beautiful young woman, Young, who joins the circus as a performer. While gathering flowers one day, Young enters the garden of wealthy count Asther, who falls in love with her at first sight. Young, however, disappears. Asther is seeking help from a physician, asking him to cure him of his uncontrollable laughter and he meets another patient at that time, Chaney, who seeks help from the same doctor while looking for a cure for his melancholia that produces uncontrollable weeping. Asther and Chaney befriend each other and through the clown Asther rediscovers Young. Chaney by this time has grown to love Young as more than a child, now wanting to marry her, but he realizes that the younger Asther also loves Young and would be a more suitable husband. Chaney also knows that Young is devoted to him and to free her and himself from the love that emotionally chains them together, performs a dangerous stunt—"the slide of death"—and is mortally injured. Young is now free to live a happy life with Asther, thanks to the sacrifice of Chaney. Although this film somewhat reprises the theme of an earlier Chaney film, **He Who Gets Slapped**, 1924, this production nevertheless offers a fascinating bittersweet tale and where Chaney performs magically in pantomime to realistically convey a man drowning in sorrow, and where the plot is so well crafted that title cards with dialog are less needed and sparsely employed. *Author's Note*: Young told this author that "I was only fourteen when I did that film with the great Lon Chaney and it was my first leading role in pictures. Mr. Chaney was very kind to me, teaching me all kinds of acting techniques I would use throughout my career. Unlike many actors in the silent period, he never overacted, and he said to me during the making of that picture: 'You do not need to flail your arms about when acting or make broad faces. The camera will pick up any kind of slight movement or subtle gesture and that will work much better for you.' He was so right." **d**, Herbert Brenon; **cast**, Lon Chaney, Bernard Siegel, Loretta Young, Nils Asther, Cissy Fitzgerald, Gwen Lee, Leo Feodoroff; **w**, Elizabeth Meehan (based on the play by David Belasco and Tom Cushing); **c**, James Wong Howe; **ed**, Marie Halvey; **set d**, Cedric Gibbons.

Laughter ★★★★★ 1930; U.S.; 85m; PAR; B/W; Drama; Children: Unacceptable; **DVD**; **VHS**. This much overlooked masterpiece sparkles with the kind of sophisticated wit so woefully absent from today's films and where performances from March, Carroll and Morgan are superlative under d'Arrast's careful and skillful direction. The film opens with Carroll as a top Broadway star of the Follies and where she is inundated with admirers, rejecting all these stage-door Johnnies until she meets kind and caring Morgan, a utilities tycoon, who spends most of his time watching the stock market and counting his endless millions. March, a composer who has always loved Carroll, is shocked with the news of Carroll's marriage to Morgan, a man twice her age, and he leaves NYC for Paris to forget her. When Morgan promptly neglects Carroll, she becomes bored and seeks lively companionship so she has her chauffeur drive her long limousine to Greenwich Village where she visits another old flame, Anders, a sculptor, who is so depressed at his failure to gain recognition and success that he is contemplating suicide. In fact, shortly before Carroll arrives, Anders has smashed a recent work of art and has already written a suicide note, but her presence suddenly brings him back to his senses and he embraces life in the hope that he can renew his old romance with Carroll, although she is seeking only a platonic relationship with him for now. Meanwhile, Ellis, who is Morgan's daughter from a previous marriage, returns from a European jaunt and is met at dockside by Carroll when her luxury liner arrives at NYC. Carroll and Ellis are the same age and have much in common and they soon become close friends. March then returns from Paris and meets Carroll, believing that all the joy of life has gone out of her, mostly due to Morgan's inattention and obsessive preoccupation with his vast business operations. He decides to reenter her life, although Carroll tries to keep him at arm's distance. She cannot resist March's charm, however, and they are soon seeing each other on the sly. Ellis, by this time, has met Anders and they become a couple. Carroll and March are now seeing each other regularly. While they are driving through a rainstorm in the country and running out of gas, they make their way to a deserted house and, once inside, remove their wet clothes and try to dry off, but they are seen in this compromising condition by some local inhabitants and police arrest them for breaking and entering. Jailed, Carroll embarrassingly calls Morgan to bail her and March out of the clink. The ever-forgiving Morgan has them released and his powerful influence causes the charges to be quashed. Morgan then gives a huge ball at his sumptuous mansion, but when Ellis receives a phone call during the fete, she slips away. Her going is closely watched by Carroll, who follows Ellis back to Anders' Greenwich Village loft and there she discovers that Ellis and Anders plan to marry. Carroll, however, believes that Anders is only marrying Ellis because he cannot have her and Carroll confronts the sculptor, demanding that he declare that Ellis is his one and only true love. When Anders will not or cannot make that statement, Ellis, enraged at Carroll's bold action, slaps her and departs. Anders is beside himself and brandishes a gun, threatening to shoot Carroll, but he cannot bring himself to take the life of the woman he really loves and Carroll leaves. As she is departing, however, she hears a shot. Anders has killed himself, a suicide he had been contemplating long before he met Ellis and lost Carroll to another man. Police are called and Carroll is again involved in the spotlight and scandal, but she is exonerated when officials rightly conclude that Anders took his own life. By the time Carroll returns home, the Anders suicide is big news, the story being broadcast over the radio airways and a bevy of newshounds waiting to interview her the moment she arrives at the front door of her mansion. Morgan has by this time (and finally) become upset at this sensational news and demands an explanation from Carroll. Protective of Ellis, Carroll refuses to talk about it and when Morgan pressures her for answers, she tells him that she is leaving him and will seek a divorce. She wants happiness, not riches, and finds that in the arms of March. They are seen sailing away on a luxury liner and, at the finale, they are sipping champagne at a sidewalk café in Paris and where Carroll is again laughing. Beautifully photographed by Folsey and painstakingly directed by d'Arrast, this film is highlighted by incomparable performances from March, Carroll and Morgan and where the supporting cast is also exceptional. What makes this film stand above many others is the script that so well captures the characters of that day and where all are witty, acerbic and incisively observing of the world about them. Not until the rise of such directors as Cukor and Lubitsch did such sophisticated films come further into existence. In many ways, **Laughter** symbolizes the end of the carefree and even reckless 1920s, shortly before the arrival of the grim

Nancy Carroll and Fredric March in *Laughter,* 1930.

and pervasive Great Depression, and its attendant dire poverty that gave no one a reason to laugh. ***Author's Note***: March told this author that "**Laughter** is a very urbane picture, the kind they don't make anymore, one that dwells on the tragedies and triumphs of the upper class that audiences used to look upon with admiration. It is a haunting film with some very unusual characters, especially the artist played by Anders, and one of the most memorable pictures I ever made." d'Arrast directed only a few films, but **Laughter** is certainly his great masterpiece, a time-locked portrait of the so-called Lost Generation that remains a classic to this day. D'Arrast's background is as interesting as this film. He was recuperating at a French field hospital after being wounded on the Western Front in WWI when serving in the French Army and where he met another wounded soldier, George Fitzmaurice, who became a film director in Hollywood and who later asked d'Arrast to come to the U.S. and work with him. D'Arrast (1897-1968) worked as an assistant director in such classics as Charles Chaplin's **The Gold Rush**, 1925, until he was assigned his own productions. He was always at odds with producers as he refused to rush his carefully crafted films and left Hollywood in the 1930s, returning to his family estate in France where his own wealth allowed him to spend most of the rest of his life gambling in Monte Carlo. In making **Laughter**, D'Arrast had the advantage of working with one of Hollywood's most gifted writers, Donald Ogden Stewart, who specialized in subtly lampooning American High Society, as he does here in **Laughter**, and would even more incisively profile the Super Rich in **The Philadelphia Story**, 1940, and for which he would win an Oscar for Best Adapted Screenplay (at his acceptance, Stewart stated that he had no one to thank for receiving that Oscar except himself). Another writer working on the script for **Laughter** was the gifted Herman Mankiewicz, who would work with Orson Welles in producing the script for **Citizen Kane**, 1941. (Anders, who plays the suicidal artist in **Laughter**, also plays a suicidal attorney in **Citizen Kane**.) Both Stewart and Mankiewicz were favored members of the Algonquin Round Table in NYC during the 1920s when they worked for newspapers in the Big Apple at that time, and both knew well the strange man upon whom they based the character of Anders in **Laughter**, Henry "Harry Crosby" (1898-1929), who was the nephew and godson of billionaire J.P. Morgan. Crosby was a dilettante of the arts, who published small literary magazines in Paris and New York, gave lavish parties, was addicted to morphine, worshipped the sun, and, though married, had countless affairs. He hobnobbed with F. Scott Fitzgerald and Ernest Hemingway, and, on December 10, 1929, Crosby murdered his married mistress, socialite Josephine Rotch Bigelow, and then committed suicide in a Greenwich Village loft he had borrowed from an artist friend. Crosby's death, as does Anders' in **Laughter**, symbolizes the end of the Roaring Twenties, a grim finale to a reckless and wild era. For extensive

Vincent Price, Judith Anderson, Gene Tierney and Clifton Webb in *Laura*, 1944.

details on Harry Crosby see my book, *The Great Pictorial History of World Crime*, Volume II (History, Inc., 2004; pages 859-867). **p**, Monta Bell; **d**, Harry d'Abbadie d'Arrast; **cast**, Nancy Carroll, Fredric March, Frank Morgan, Glenn Anders, Diane Ellis, Leonard Carey, Ollie Burgoyne, Eric Blore, Charles Halton, Duncan Penwarden; **w**, Donald Ogden Stewart, Herman J. Mankiewicz, d'Abbadie d'Arrast, Douglas Z. Doty (based on a story by d'Abbadie d'Arrast, Doty); **c**, George J. Folsey; **m**, Vernon Duke; **ed**, Helene Turner.

Laura ★★★★★ 1944; U.S.; 88m; FOX; B/W; Crime Drama; Children: Unacceptable; **DVD**; **VHS**. Stylish and polished, this gem of a film noir entry from the accomplished director Preminger presents an utterly captivating whodunit with outstanding performances from Tierney, Andrews, Price, Anderson and, especially, Webb. This thriller begins when Adams, Tierney's maid, finds the body of her employer, Tierney, the face shot away with a shotgun blast. Enter tough police detective Andrews, who begins interviewing all of Tierney's friends and associates, beginning with the rich, self-centered Webb, a smug, acerbic and powerful columnist and radio commentator. Andrews finds Webb in his richly appointed apartment and where the austere Webb allows Andrews to question him while Webb sponges his body in a marble bathtub. He relates his first experience with Tierney, and we see in flashback her meeting Webb at the Algonquin Hotel where she asks him to endorse a pen her advertising agency is promoting. He refuses, but is attracted to her stunning beauty and poised personality and attempts to establish a relationship with her by later appearing at her agency and where he apologizes and then becomes her self-styled mentor, guiding and shaping her career to considerable success. Webb brags to Andrews how he was responsible for everything good that happened in Tierney's life and how he protected her against invasive suitors, including the devious playboy Price. There is much bad blood between Webb and Price as Andrews learns when he next interviews Anderson, a wealthy socialite, who is Tierney's spinster aunt and who tells Andrews that Webb was jealous of Price because he was engaged to Tierney, the now legendary Laura, but Anderson goes on to state that, despite that engagement, Price is in love with her, not her niece. Andrews then pays one of many visits to Tierney's expensively appointed apartment and gazes longingly at her portrait, one showing a ravishingly beautiful woman. When learning that Price, a womanizing cad, was seeing an attractive model named Diane Redfern while still being engaged to Tierney, Andrews confronts Price. The mealy mouthed Price admits under pressure from Andrews that he had, indeed, been cheating on Tierney and was also seeing her aunt, Anderson, but sloughs off this unseemly behavior as part of his romantic nature. Returning to Tierney's apartment, Andrews dozes off and is then startled to hear a female voice asking him

what he is doing there. He looks up, shocked to see the murder victim, Tierney, standing before him. She threatens to call police unless he leaves her apartment and Andrews explains that he is a police detective investigating her own murder, which apparently has not happened and that someone else has been killed in her apartment and mistaken for Tierney. Andrews then discovers that the murder victim was Redfern, the model Price had been secretly dating. When braced with this information, Price admits that he had taken Redfern to Tierney's apartment while Tierney was vacationing at her country retreat and where she could not be reached since the place had no phone and she had no radio so she could not learn about her own murder. While Price and Redfern were at Tierney's apartment, someone rang the doorbell, and Price states to Andrews that he hid in a closet while Redfern answered the door, and with no lights on inside the apartment so that she was apparently mistaken for Tierney by the killer, who immediately killed Redfern with a double blast from a shotgun that destroyed her face and instantly took her life. Price confesses to Andrews that he found Redfern's body after the killer departed and he also fled because he believed he would be accused of killing Redfern and kept quiet about what he knew, waiting for Tierney to return home and that the police would hopefully by then identify the murderer. Tierney is uncooperative with Andrews, but his patient manner and the affection he demonstrates toward her soon softens her heart and she eventually falls in love with him. Tierney's return from the grave startles and unnerves all who know her, and when Webb first sees Tierney alive, he collapses in a dead faint. Andrews then encourages Webb to have a "reunion" party for Tierney and where all her socialite friends attend, including Webb, Price and Anderson. During that party, Andrews goads Price to the point where Price swings on him and Andrews lands a solid blow to Price's stomach while Anderson plays mother to the playboy, comforting him. Andrews then shocks everyone by arresting Tierney and taking her to headquarters where he grills her under a single lamp, but he has no intention of charging her with Redfern's murder, explaining that he is trying to draw out the real killer. He then takes Tierney home and finds Webb there. When Webb realizes that Tierney has now given her heart to the no-nonsense detective, he derides and degrades Andrews, telling Tierney he is nothing but a lowlife cop and shudders at the idea of Andrews later "pawing" Tierney. He leaves in a huff. Andrews, however, has concluded that Webb is the killer. While earlier visiting Webb's antique-laden apartment, Andrews has noticed a grandfather clock that also has a twin in Tierney's apartment, a gift Webb made to Tierney, and Andrews finds that, in its base of that clock is a secret compartment and there finds in Tierney's copy of that grandfather clock the shotgun used to kill Redfern. He does not remove the weapon, expecting that Webb will later return and try to use it and he will catch the arrogant killer red-handed. Andrews tells Tierney that Webb killed Redfern when he arrived at her apartment while she was away on a vacation she did not announce to anyone, and when Redfern opened the door to Tierney's apartment, Webb mistook her for Tierney while she stood in the darkened apartment, shooting her in a jealous rage over her engagement to ne'er-do-well Price. Andrews now uses Tierney as bait, believing that Webb will try to kill her once more because she has now given her love to Andrews, and his deductive reasoning is rewarded when Webb, indeed, returns to Tierney's apartment just before she is about to retire. Tierney is in her bedroom, brushing her hair and listening to Webb talking on his radio program, while Webb slips into her apartment, retrieves the shotgun from the secret compartment of the grandfather clock, and inserts two shells into the two barrels of the shotgun. Andrews, meanwhile, checks fellow detectives staked outside the apartment building and realizes that Webb has somehow gotten into the building and he races upstairs, unable to get into Tierney's locked apartment. Webb by this time slowly walks into Tierney's bedroom just while an announcer states that his radio address has been a recording and Tierney is shocked to see Webb standing before her, aiming the shotgun at her and telling her that Andrews and no one else will ever have her. Andrews, at that moment, breaks into the apartment through another door and races toward the bedroom as Tierney runs toward him and Webb aims and fires the shotgun at the same time Andrews fires a fatal bullet that strikes and downs Webb. With his dying words, the deranged Webb calls out for Tierney, saying farewell to her with his dying breath, and this is where this intensely suspenseful film ends. Webb steals every scene in this riveting film, and where Preminger gave the actor his freedom of character development, and it is a character (named Waldo Lydecker) never to be forgotten. His scathing wit is comparable to that of a legendary NYC columnist and radio commentator of that day, Alexander Woollcott (1887-1943), who was undoubtedly the role model for Webb's character. Woollcott established the legendary "Round Table" group of NYC's foremost authors and columnists during the 1920s at the Algonquin Hotel, the very hotel where Tierney first meets Webb. Like Woollcott, Webb claims to be a gifted but amateur criminologist and who gives Andrews sideways admiration for solving previous crimes about which he has written in his column. Like many real-life criminals who have not only taunted detectives attempting to solve their murders but actually aided them in their sleuthing tasks (as Richard Loeb helped detectives in searching for clues to the killing of a boy that he had himself murdered in 1924 in Chicago), Webb feeds clues to Andrews during his search for the killer. At one point, while talking to Andrews and meticulously attiring himself after his bath, Webb states, while admiring himself in a mirror: "How singularly innocent I look this morning. Have you ever seen such candid eyes?" He then tells Andrews that, because of Tierney's influence, he had become "the kindest, the gentlest, the most sympathetic man in the world... I should be sincerely sorry to see my neighbors' children devoured by wolves." Although he admires Andrews' dedication to his profession of law enforcement, he also condemns him for his pedestrian way of life and, at one point, to demean Andrews in front of Tierney, repeating a statement Andrews earlier made to him, that "a dame in Washington Heights once got a fox fur out of him!" The incisive and always observant Webb early on realizes that Andrews, before Tierney surfaces in the film, is obsessing with her portrait and an image of a woman he is creating in his own mind without ever having met this young woman. Seeing this, Webb, at one point, suggests that the detective has become the victim of necrophilia, telling Andrews: "Ever strike you that you're acting strangely? You'll end up in a psychiatric ward. I don't think they've ever had a patient who fell in love with a corpse."

Author's Note: Fox chief Zanuck had little regard for the autocratic Preminger and had had some run-ins with him on some previous productions. When Zanuck learned that Preminger had put together preliminary plans to make **Laura**, Zanuck told him that he could produce but not direct the film. Zanuck tried to get Lewis Milestone and Walter Lang to direct the film, which Zanuck said he would personally produce, but both directors, knowing that their friend Preminger wanted to helm the film, refused the assignment. Zanuck then assigned the directorial chore to Rouben Mamoulian, but Preminger continued to lobby for the job. "Otto was a hardhead," Zanuck told this author, "the kind of man you could not reason with and a man who knew everything about everything. The only reason I let him direct **Laura** was because he brought in Samuel Hoffenstein to spruce up the dialog and he did a brilliant job of it. [Hoffenstein had been a friend of Woollcott's and chiefly filled in the character played by Webb, which is based on Woollcott.] Otto then did some tests with Webb and they were so good that I finally decided to let Otto direct the film." The selection of Webb was also not to Zanuck's liking, according to Preminger, who told this author that "Zanuck did not like homosexuals and Webb was of that class of people, although very discreet about that part of his private life. Zanuck wanted Laird Cregar to play the role of the sophisticated killer, but when Webb gave such a great performance in early takes for that part, Zanuck gave up on Cregar, although he ordered me not to give Webb too many close-ups. Zanuck was a man's man—a hunter, a fisherman, someone who went to boxing matches all the time and, at one time said to me: 'I can't stand these fruits and pansies. They make my flesh crawl when I

Clifton Webb and Dana Andrews in *Laura*, 1944.

see them prancing around, these limp-wristed creeps.' When he viewed the finished film, he said: 'I must admit that Webb did a wonderful job, even though all of his mannerisms and his precise schoolmarm deliveries are as fruity as they can be, which is what his strange character is all about.' The beautiful Tierney was not Zanuck's first choice for the leading female role. "Mr. Zanuck wanted Jennifer Jones to play that role in **Laura**," Tierney told this author, "and when she turned down the part, he asked Hedy Lamarr to play that role, but she, too, turned it down. He then took a risk with me and that was the film that really launched my film career." Zanuck had hired Tierney as a contract player after seeing her posing as a model in several fashion magazines. Oddly, Tierney would marry Texas oil tycoon Howard Lee after Lamarr divorced him in 1960. Price told this author that "all of the actors in that great film were told by Mamoulian before he left the production that Otto Preminger was taking over and that he disliked the lot of us and felt that none of us could act worth a lick. Well, when Preminger first came onto the set, Judith Anderson, a great stage actress and a very outspoken person, stepped right up and said: 'I hear that you don't like the way I am playing my part,' and lo and behold, Preminger admitted that he did say that and then proceeded to play out her part word for word and gesture for gesture before the entire cast. And what he did was very good. He is an amazing and very talented man, who always knows what he wants and he gets it." For his part, Mamoulian felt that he had been wrongly replaced as the director of this film, saying to this author: "Preminger was very sneaky, making secret screen tests with Clifton Webb to win over Zanuck so that he could take over the direction of **Laura**. He told Zanuck a lot of garbage about me while I was already directing the early scenes of that picture and that is the kind of sabotage that Otto practiced throughout his career. He wasn't acting when he played that role of the German commander of the POW camp in **Stalag 17** [1953]. That is exactly what Otto is, a ruthless character, who will say or do anything to get his way. He always treated actors and everyone else just the way he treated those unfortunate prisoners of war in **Stalag 17**." For more information on the legendary and brilliant Woollcott, who was the role model for the colorful character played by Webb (as well as the outlandish character Sheridan Whiteside in **The Man Who Came to Dinner**, 1942), see my book, *Zanies: The World's Greatest Eccentrics* (New Century, 1982; pages 418-420). **p&d**, Otto Preminger; **cast**, Gene Tierney, Dana Andrews, Clifton Webb, Vincent Price, Judith Anderson, Grant Mitchell, Dorothy Adams, Lane Chandler, John Dexter, Ralph Dunn, Lee Tung Foo, Jane Nigh, Cara Williams; **w**, Jay Dratler, Samuel Hoffenstein, Elizabeth (Betty) Reinhardt, Ring Lardner, Jr., Jerome Cady (based on the novel by Vera Caspary); **c**, Joseph LaShelle; **m**, David Raksin; **ed**, Louis Loeffler; **art d**, Lyle Wheeler, Leland Fuller; **set d**, Thomas Little.

Alec Guinness and Sidney James in *The Lavender Hill Mob*, 1951.

The Lavender Hill Mob ★★★★ 1951; U.K.; 81m; Rank; Ealing/UNIV; B/W; Comedy; Children: Acceptable; **DVD**; **VHS**. Guinness is again hilarious in another crime spoof not dissimilar in theme and characters to **The Ladykillers**, 1956, but one that offers its own unique comedic story line. Guinness is not a criminal at the film's onset, simply an unnoticed and unspectacular messenger, who, for years, has been delivering gold bullion from smelters to banks, a job of monotonous routine and predictable regimen. Fermenting in his brain, however, is the taunting idea that he can easily abscond with a huge shipment, perhaps as much as £1 million in gold, but is challenged by the idea that he would have no way to smuggle the gold out of the country. To that end, Guinness contacts old friend Holloway, who manufactures paperweights and miniature replicas of famous structures. Needing more help, they enlist the services of two Cockney crooks, Bass and James. The foursome then conducts a hilarious raid on an armored car, taking the gold bars to Holloway's small plant where they melt down the bars and Holloway molds them into miniature copies of the Eiffel Tower and these items are then shipped from England to Paris. A serious problem arises when six of those miniature Eiffel Towers are bought by some school girls and the thieves run crazily about in their attempt to buy them back. One girl, Boyce, holds out, showing it to a policeman at a convention hall where the police are exhibiting curios from their archives of famous crimes they have solved. Guinness and Holloway grab the last Eiffel Tower from Boyce and the police give pursuit, even when the thieves abscond in a police car and begin giving confusing orders over the car's police radio. They manage to get to a subway and it appears that they have finally made good their escape. The epilogue of this zany film concludes with a scene showing Guinness telling his tale of his great gold robbery in a posh café in Rio de Janeiro, his narration actually beginning this offbeat tale. It appears that he has gotten off scot-free until he finishes his drink and then lifts his other hand that shows that he is handcuffed to a detective, the man to whom he has told this tale, and is then walked off into custody. *Author's Note*: Guinness, who appeared in several films that lampooned inept or bumbling criminals (**Kind Hearts and Coronets**, 1950, **The Ladykillers**, 1956), told this author that crime is "an anti-social act basically committed by buffoons, who are invariably trapped by their own outlandish schemes." **p**, Michael Balcon; **d**, Charles Crichton; **cast**, Alec Guinness, Stanley Holloway, Sidney James, Alfie Bass, Marjorie Fielding, Edie Martin, John Gregson, Audrey Hepburn, Peter Bull, Robert Shaw; **w**, T.E.B. Clarke; **c**, Douglas Slocombe; **m**, Georges Auric; **ed**, Seth Holt; **art d**, William Kellner.

L'Avventura ★★★ 1961; Italy/France; 143m; Cino del Duca/Janus Films; B/W; Drama; Children: Unacceptable; **DVD**; **VHS**. Italian filmmaker Antonioni presents a meandering but haunting story that begins with a group of upscale Italian vacationers enjoying an excursion on board a luxurious yacht. The boat anchors off a small rocky island and the passengers disembark to explore the place. While they are walking about, they discover that Massari is missing. Her lover, Ferzetti, is joined by her best friend, Vitti, in a search for her. They and others inspect every crag and outcropping on the small rocky island, but Massari is nowhere to be found. The searchers conclude that Massari somehow left the island and, after their thorough search, return to the yacht and sail back to the mainland. Vitti and Ferzetti continue looking for Massari, but when they cannot locate her, they seem to lose interest in finding her and become more interested in developing a love affair of their own. Vitti then becomes Ferzetti's lover, staying in a luxury hotel. When Vitti falls asleep, Ferzetti goes off on his own and, upon wakening, Vitti cannot find Ferzetti. She leaves the hotel and when Ferzetti returns to their room and finds her gone, begins searching for her. He finds Vitti sitting on a bench in a park, staring at nothing and the camera closes to show Ferzetti also staring at nothing and that is where this strange film ends. Much meaning has been infused into this film, one that offers an ambiguous story line and vacuous characters, and that, of course, is its intent, a subtle indictment of the rich that have so much idle time that they can lose their most cherished loved ones and resume life quickly and establish the same kind of emotional ties without encumbering themselves with the past. There is as little character development here as there is a lack of a cohesive story line, but that, too, is intentional, as Antonioni opts for a stream-of-consciousness approach where the characters are cold-hearted in their ability to accept the loss of others as a day-to-day cost of living. **p**, Amato Pennasilico; **d**, Michelangelo Antonioni; **cast**, Monica Vitti, Gabriele Ferzetti, Lea Massari, Dominique Blanchar, Renzo Ricci, James Addams, Dorothy De Poliolo, Lelio Luttazzi, Giovanni Petrucci, Esmeralda Ruspoli; **w**, Antonioni, Elio Bartolini, Tonino Guerra (based on a story by Antonioni); **c**, Aldo Scavarda; **m**, Giovanni Fusco; **ed**, Eraldo Da Roma; **prod d**, Piero Poletto.

Law and Disorder ★★★ 1958; U.K.; 76m; Paul Soskin Productions/Continental Distributing; B/W; Comedy; Children: Acceptable; **VHS**. Redgrave is a likeable crook and con man, who is successful at his occupation in between jail sentences from the same judge, Morley. Redgrave keeps his son, Burnham, from knowing how he makes his living by telling him he is away a lot because he's a missionary. This works and Burnham worships his father for being a do-gooder. Things start to unravel for Redgrave when Burnham grows up, gets a law degree, and becomes a court aide to Morley. Redgrave senses problems and decides to retire to a seaside fishing village. Old habits are hard to break, however, and he falls in with some local brandy smugglers. They all get caught and Redgrave devises a scheme to discredit Morley, so he will be disbarred. It doesn't work, and Redgrave goes to jail again. His only consolation is that his son never does learn how he has made his living. This delightful comedy is highlighted by outstanding performances from Redgrave and Morley. **p**, Paul Soskin, George Pitcher; **d**, Charles Crichton; **cast**, Michael Redgrave, Robert Morley, Ronald Squire, Elizabeth Sellars, Joan Hickson, Lionel Jeffries, Jeremy Burnham, Brenda Bruce, Harold Goodwin, George Coulouris; **w**, T.E.B. Clarke, Patrick Campbell, Vivienne Knight (based on the novel *Smugglers' Circuit* by Denys Roberts); **c**, Edward (Ted) Scaife; **m**, Humphrey Searle; **ed**, Oswald Hafenrichter; **art d**, Allan Harris.

Law and Disorder ★★★ 1974; U.S.; 103m; Fasdin Cinema Associates/COL; Color; Comedy/Drama; Children: Unacceptable; **DVD**; **VHS**. Two blue collar citizens, O'Connor and Borgnine, become so tired of the unsolved crime in their city that they become self-appointed volunteer policemen. O'Connor, a taxi driver, and Borgnine, a hairdresser, don policemen uniforms and ride with weapons in vehicles with sirens to patrol the streets looking for law-breakers, but they create more problems than they solve. There are some very funny moments in this spoof of inept vigilantes, but the excessive violence prohibits viewing by children. **p**, William Richert; **d**, Ivan Passer; **cast**, Carroll O'Connor, Ernest Borgnine, Ann Wedgeworth, Anita Dangler, Leslie Ackerman, Karen Black, Jack Kehoe, David Spielberg, Joseph Ragno, Rita Gam; **w**, Passer, Richert, Kenneth Harris Fishman; **c**, Arthur J. Ornitz; **m**, Angelo Badalamenti (Andy Badale), Al Elias; **ed**, Anthony Potenza; **art d**, Gene Rudolf; **set d**, Paul Vogt.

Law and Order ★★★ 1932; U.S.; 75m; UNIV; B/W; Western; Children: Unacceptable; **VHS**. Huston gives a dynamic performance as a fierce lawman (his role based on the legendary Wyatt Earp) in one of the first talkies that profiles lawless Tombstone. After incessant gunfights and widespread bloodletting takes place, Huston has had enough, and goes after the gang of killer cowboys, all brothers (based on the Clantons), that includes Woods, Alexander and Ince. Joining Huston in his vigilante crusade against the ruthless gang is his brother, Hopton, and friends Hatton and Carey (who plays a character based on gunman and gambler John H. "Doc" Holliday). Huston and his men shoot it out several times until their final showdown at the O.K. Corral where all of the outlaws die in a wild and blazing firefight. Tombstone is finally cleaned up, but not without considerable bloodletting. The gunfights shown in this film are realistically crude and savage, accurately portraying the actual street battles that occurred in the Old West and where the lawmen are as uncompromising as the murderous outlaws they face down again and again in this vigorous and action-packed oater. *Author's Note*: John Huston, son of Walter Huston, who wrote the screenplay for this film, told this author that "in my research for that picture, I learned that the lawmen [the Earp Brothers] in Tombstone used the same kind of brutal tactics used by the outlaws and there was little difference between them, except that the lawmen knew that the only way to bring law and order to that town was to kill every outlaw in the place. And nobody in pictures could dispatch outlaws better than my father." **p**, Carl Laemmle Jr.; **d**, Edward L. Cahn; **cast**, Walter Huston, Harry Carey, Russell Hopton, Raymond Hatton, Ralph Ince, Harry Woods, Russell Simpson, Richard Alexander, Andy Devine, Walter Brennan, Lois Wilson, Dewey Robinson; **w**, John Huston, Tom Reed, Richard Schayer (based on the novel *Saint Johnson* by W.R. Burnett); **c**, Jackson Rose; **ed**, Phil Cahn; **art d**, John J. Hughes.

The Lawless ★★★ 1950; U.S.; 89m; PAR; B/W; Drama; Children: Unacceptable; **VHS**. Carey is a cautious newspaper editor in a small California town, which is dominated by large farm owners who hire cheap Mexican labor to pick their fruit and vegetables. The film opens during the picking season and where the Mexican migrant farm workers flood the area. They are treated by local inhabitants as sub-humans not worthy of respect or consideration; this attitude is accentuated and acerbated when, at a local dance, migrant worker Rios gets into a fight with a white youth, injuring him before he runs off. The local whites form a lynch mob and go hunting for Rios, and Carey decides that it is his obligation to stand up to mob violence by denouncing the vigilantes. This brings down the wrath of local bigwigs on Carey's newspaper, but the stalwart newsman sticks to his principles and quells the lawlessness while championing the economically oppressed migrant workers. Losey does a good job of presenting character development in this well-told tale of racial bigotry and mob violence. *Author's Note*: Martha Hyer appears in a small role and future teenage idol Tab Hunter also appears in a small role, his film debut. **p**, William H. Pine, William C. Thomas; **d**, Joseph Losey; **cast**, Macdonald Carey, Gail Russell, John (Johnny) Sands, Lee Patrick, John Hoyt, Lalo Rios, Maurice Jara, Walter Reed, Herbert Anderson, Martha Hyer, Tab Hunter; **w**, Geoffrey Homes [Daniel Mainwaring] (based on his novel *The Voice of Stephen Wilder*); **c**, Roy Hunt; **m**, Mahlon Merrick; **ed**, Howard Smith; **art d**, Lewis H. Creber; **set d**, Alfred Kegerris.

The Lawless Breed ★★★ 1953; U.S.; 83m; UNIV; Color; Biographical

Rock Hudson and Julia Adams in *The Lawless Breed*, 1953.

Drama/Western; Children: Cautionary; **DVD**; **VHS**. Hudson gives a standout performance in essaying western gunman John Wesley Hardin (1853-1895). Hudson's gunslinger career is told in flashback as he leaves prison, turning over a copy of his memoirs to a publisher, who begins reading it, Hudson's violent life then unfolding to show his break with his sermonizing father (McIntire), and his allegiance with his uncle (also played by McIntire). He becomes a cowboy, and then a gambler and, after he loses a rigged horserace, takes vengeance on the culprits. When gambling in a saloon, he meets fetching Adams, who later becomes his wife, begging him to settle down, but Hudson's penchant for gambling keeps them on the move from one western town after another and where he invariably gets into gunfights. Being a fast draw, he wins all of these lethal contests, so that he becomes the most notorious gunman in the Southwest and the target of every apprentice gunfighter wanting to make a reputation by killing him. Many episodes show Hudson having encounters with Indians, Union soldiers (he was from Texas, a Confederate state long occupied by the Yankees following the Civil War), and various gunmen, surviving these lethal conflicts but causing Hudson to be a wanted man. He tires of his nomadic lifestyle and finally relents to Adams' pleas, buying a small ranch and living under an alias. He and Adams have a son and while Hudson leaves on a trip to buy some livestock, he is identified as the notorious Hardin and arrested by Texas rangers. He is sent to prison while his son grows to manhood, and when released, he finds that son to be an adult, Gentry, practicing with Hudson's old pistol. He slaps the youth, briefly alienating him, and later saves Gentry from participating in a gunfight, while being wounded in the process. Adams finds both of them and takes them both back to the ranch to nurse Hudson back to health so that he can live out the rest of his life a man of peace. Pantheon director Walsh directs this film with a lot of vitality and moves the story along at a brisk pace. Hudson gives one of his best performances and he is backed up with a sterling supporting cast. *Author's Note*: Walsh admitted to this author that "**The Lawless Breed** was a picture that told a romanticized version of John Wesley Hardin whose life did not end on a happy note. The early part of his life with his father, who was a preacher and a severe man, and his family relationships are all based on fact, but the rest of the story we told was all Hollywood." Walsh's admirable candor reflects the truth in that Hardin, once he took to gambling and roaming, became a much-feared hellion, and though he claimed in his memoirs that he killed forty-two men, the records show that he gunned down at least twenty-seven of that number, which makes him more lethal than the legendary Billy the Kid (1859-1881), many of those shootings occurring during family feuds. Most historians agree that Hardin was probably the fastest gun in the Old West, having two holsters sewn into his vest so that the butts of his six-guns pointed inward, and he drew these guns cross-armed,

Peter O'Toole in *Lawrence of Arabia*, 1962.

saying that that single movement in producing two guns was a faster draw than the conventional drawing from the holster carried on the hip. None of his expertise availed him anything when he was murdered on August 19, 1895, after John Selman Sr., who was involved in a family feud with Hardin, walked into a saloon in El Paso, Texas. Hardin was at the bar, shooting dice with local businessman, H. S. Brown. Hardin rolled the dice and when they stopped on the bar, he said: "Four sixes to beat!" These were the gunman's last words. He looked into the mirror behind the bar to see Selman standing behind him, raise his gun, and, before Hardin could turn about and defend himself, Selman shot Hardin in the back of his head, the shot tearing away half of his head and killing him instantly. Selman, still terrified of this most lethal man in Texas, then stood over the dead Hardin and fired two more bullets into his corpse, one entering his right arm, the other into his chest. Selman was charged with murder, but his defense attorney, Albert Bacon Fall (1861-1944), convinced a jury that Selman acted out of self-defense, despite eye witnesses stating that Selman had committed cold-blooded murder, and he was acquitted. Fall later became U.S. Secretary of the Interior (1921-1923) under the corrupt Harding administration and was sent to prison for illegally leasing government lands to oil tycoons and taking enormous bribes for these underhanded arrangements. For more details on John Wesley Hardin, see my book, *Encyclopedia of Western Lawmen and Outlaws* (Paragon House, 1992; John Wesley Hardin: pages 143-150; John Selman: page 279). **p**, William Alland; **d**, Raoul Walsh; **cast**, Rock Hudson, Julia Adams, John McIntire, Mary Castle, Hugh O'Brian, Dennis Weaver, Lee Van Cleef, Tom Fadden, Race Gentry, Glenn Strange, Richard Garland, Michael Ansara, Francis Ford; **w**, Bernard Gordon (based on a story by William Alland and the autobiography of John Wesley Hardin); **c**, Irving Glassberg (Technicolor); **m**, Herman Stein; **ed**, Frank Gross; **art d**, Bernard Herzbrun, Richard Riedel; **set d**, Russell A. Gausman, Oliver Emert.

A Lawless Street ★★★ 1955; U.S.; 78m; COL; Color; Western; Children: Cautionary; **DVD**; **VHS**. Scott gives a measured and moving performance of a dedicated lawman moving from town to town in Colorado, arresting or shooting down the most dangerous gunmen and outlaws. The strain of establishing law and order takes its toll on Scott, especially in his personal life when his wife Lansbury tells him that unless he hangs up his guns, she will leave him. Scott will not shirk his duty and Lansbury, indeed, departs, while Scott rides on to Medicine Bend, a town controlled by Anderson and Emery, the local powerhouses, who are fighting statehood and who head all the illegal activities, from cattle rustling to robberies. When Scott cracks down on their operations, they hire fast gun Pate to kill Scott, but, in the final showdown, it is Scott's gun that is quicker. After rounding up the culprits and bringing

peace to the town, Scott finally decides that his obligation as a lawman has been met and it is time to retire. He hangs up his guns and Lansbury comes back into his life for a happy ending. Lewis does a fine job directing this above-average oater, where Scott presents a lawman with a complex personality and where he deals with nagging doubts as to the harrowing job he performs, a much different kind of lawman than usually seen in such westerns, which makes this one all the more compelling and worthwhile. **p**, Harry Joe Brown; **d**, Joseph H. Lewis; **cast**, Randolph Scott, Angela Lansbury, Warner Anderson, Jean Parker, Wallace Ford, John Emery, James Bell, Ruth Donnelly, Michael Pate, Jeanette Nolan; **w**, Kenneth Gamet (based on a story by Brad Ward); **c**, Ray Rennahan (Technicolor); **m**, Paul Sawtell; **ed**, Gene Havlick; **art d**, George Brooks; **set d**, Frank Tuttle.

Lawman ★★★ 1971; U.S.; 99m; Scimitar Films/MGM; Color; Western; Children: Unacceptable (MPAA: R); **DVD**; **VHS**. In one of the most severe and unrelenting westerns ever made, Lancaster is a by-the-book lawman, who sets out to bring justice to a crowd of cowboys who have hurrahed his town and, while wildly firing off their six-guns, have killed an elderly man. The cowboys visiting his town are employees of cattle baron Cobb, an otherwise reasonable and considerate man, who orders his straw boss, Salmi, to stop his men and take them out of the town. Lancaster later rides into Sabbath, the town controlled by Cobb, looking for the culprits and meets Ryan, the local sheriff, a once valiant and courageous lawman like Lancaster, but who, after years of gunfights and bloody violence, is now gun-shy and over cautious in his job. Lancaster tells him that he will arrest all of those responsible for the killing of the old man. Ryan rides to Cobb's ranch and asks Cobb to return to Lancaster's town with the guilty parties and face trial, a suggestion that is ignored. Salmi becomes enraged, and later confronts Lancaster and is shot dead by the lawman. Ryan helps Lancaster trap one of the ranch hands, Waite, putting him under arrest. Meanwhile, Lancaster tracks down Duvall, wounding him and putting him behind bars in Ryan's jail. He plans to leave town, but Cobb and his top gunmen gather in the street for a showdown with Lancaster. These include Watson, and Cobb's son, Beck, along with allied rancher Cannon, the common-law husband of North, who is a former flame of Lancaster's and who has tried to convince Lancaster to quit his one-man crusade against the cowboys. Lancaster tells Cobb and his men that he is leaving town, but Watson goes for his gun and Lancaster shoots and kills him. Beck challenges Lancaster and he tells him to put up his gun, but Beck, too, draws on Lancaster and is killed. Cobb, seeing his son dead, then kills himself and, when Cannon loses his nerve and begins to run away, Lancaster shoots him, dead too. Lancaster then mounts his horse and rides out of town and away from the carnage as this grim oater ends. Lancaster, Ryan and Cobb give outstanding performances as does the rest of the fine cast and where Winner, directing his first western, does a good job in applying this Greek tragedy to the Old West. **p&d**, Michael Winner; **cast**, Burt Lancaster, Robert Ryan, Lee J. Cobb, Robert Duvall, Sheree North, Albert Salmi, Richard Jordan, John McGiver, Ralph Waite, John Beck, Joseph Wiseman, Wilford Brimley; **w**, Gerald Wilson; **c**, Robert Paynter (Technicolor); **m**, Jerry Fielding; **ed**, Frederick (Freddie) Wilson; **prod d**, Stan Jolley; **art d**, Roberto Silva, Herbert Westbrook; **set d**, Ray Moyer; **spec eff**, Leon Ortega.

Lawrence of Arabia ★★★★ 1962; U.K./U.S.; 216m; Horizon; COL; Color; Adventure/Biographical Drama; Children: Unacceptable; **DVD**; **VHS**. O'Toole is perfect in essaying the legendary T. E. Lawrence (1888-1935) in this masterpiece adventure biopic from pantheon director Lean. This startling film opens when O'Toole is driving at high speeds in his Brough Superior SS100 motorcycle along a British countryside in May 1935 (while using the alias of Ross) until, to avoid two boys on bicycles, swerves off the road, hits an obstruction, and sails over the handlebars, fatally injuring himself (Lawrence died of his injuries six days later on May 19, 1935, at age forty-six). We next see O'-

Toole as a twenty-nine-year-old officer assigned to the General Staff in Cairo in WWI and where he finds his desk work uninteresting. He is obsessed with the Bedouin way of life (Lawrence was an amateur archeologist who had studied and traveled through Arab countries before the war) and, after a confrontation with his commanding officer, is assigned to work with guerrilla Arab forces fighting the Turks, who are allied with Germany. Forging a close friendship with Guinness (who plays Emir Faisal, 1885-1933), he works with Arab tribe leaders Sharif and Quinn, urging them to attack the Turkish-held port of Aqaba, which, in a sweeping assault while riding camels and horses, and led by O'Toole, the Arabs overrun and capture on July 6, 1917. He then conducts savage raids on the Turkish railroads, blowing up tracks to stop Turkish trains and where the occupants are slaughtered while the Arab attackers loot the trains as spoils of war. O'Toole conducts his own intelligence, going to a Turkish-held town where he is held as a suspect and sexually molested by the homosexual Turkish commander (Ferrer), which alters his perspective so that, after returning to his troops, he shows no mercy to captured Turkish troops. He is interviewed by Kennedy, an American newspaperman (playing a character based on Lowell Thomas, 1892-1981), who writes about him and makes O'Toole an international and legendary hero of WWI. Following the fall of Damascus in 1918, O'-Toole helps to shape his long-envisioned dream of a united Arab state under the leadership of Guinness (that dream was crushed with French forces overwhelmed the city in 1920), before returning to his native England. This stunning and captivating biopic deservedly swept the Oscars for 1963, winning for Best Picture, Best Director (Lean), Best Original Score (Jarre), Best Sound Recording (John Cox), Best Art Direction (Box, Stoll, Simoni), Best Color Cinematography (Young) and Best Film Editing (Coates). The acting is exceptional on all levels, and O'-Toole, although he is lanky and tall where Lawrence was small of stature, totally embodies the great hero in that desert war. Guinness is perfect as the sly and reserved Faisal, and Sharif and Quinn are outstanding as the two divergent tribal chiefs at as much as at odds with themselves as they are with the Turks; Ferrer, as the perverted Turkish commander and Quayle and Hawkins (who plays General Edmund Allenby, 1861-1936) are standouts in their roles as manipulative British officers attempting to control the Arabs for their future domination by the British Empire. Rains, who is the chief of the Arab Bureau who influences O'Toole's appointment as liaison officer to Guinness, also gives a forceful performance as an oily and cunning bureaucrat. Lean's direction is impeccable in each and every scene, capturing the flavor and attitudes of the era and especially the exotic Bedouin lifestyle and O'Toole's enigmatic attraction to the desert, which is pointed out early on by Guinness when he tells O'Toole that he cannot understand the British love of the desert when there is "nothing" in the desert. That unforgiving desert is grimly depicted by Lean in one scene when Sharif finds O'Toole with an Arab guide drinking at a well reserved for Sharif's tribe and shoots and kills the guide for taking water from that well. Water is again the source of lethal confrontation when Quinn and his son alone charge into Sharif's camp of fifty men and challenge them with pistols for drinking at a well reserved for Quinn's tribe. Where Sharif (nominated for an Oscar as Best Supporting Actor) plays a reserved intellectual, Quinn enacts his ideal counterpart—a roaring, raucous, spoils-greedy tribal chief whose magnanimousness is capsulated when he states to O'Toole that he takes nothing for himself and gives everything to his tribe, shouting "I am a river to my people!" Where Lean presents brilliantly organized and executed battle scenes in the desert—the massive attack on Aqaba and attacks against trains in the desert—he subtly profiles the emerging character of O'Toole, from detached British officer to a man later donning resplendent Arab attire as if becoming a tribal chief in flowing white garments. He just as subtly portrays Lawrence's latent homosexuality through O'Toole's odd sponsorship of two orphaned teenage boys whose deaths more grieve him than any number of those he leads into battle, as well as his submissiveness to the caresses of the repulsive homosexual Turkish officer so well

Anthony Quinn in *Lawrence of Arabia,* 1962.

depicted by the accomplished Ferrer, a repugnant role that only a fine actor like Ferrer could masterfully convey. The personal side of Lawrence's life is confined to such scenes as Lean chiefly opted to show Lawrence as the legendary hero the world knew him to be, and, as such, the film remains a classic portrait of one of the world's most heroic but mysterious and decidedly eccentric human beings. *Author's Note*: Lean almost did not make this film, thinking to do an in-depth profile of Mahatma Gandhi (1869-1948), who would be masterfully portrayed in Richard Attenborough's **Gandhi**, 1982. He, instead, chose Lawrence as the subject of his next film and shocked the film world by selecting O'-Toole, a relatively unknown actor, to play Lawrence, albeit O'Toole had just scored high ratings for his London appearance in "Hamlet." Where the real Lawrence was shy and avoided the limelight, O'Toole was dashing and expansive, but O'Toole nevertheless wholly captured Lawrence's enigmatic persona. As was his usual practice, Lean took great pains in preparing the film, spending more than a year studying and filming the terrain in Saudi Arabia before commencing production. He then painstakingly put together the astonishing cast for his great epic. Lean shot many scenes in Saudi Arabia, but the heat was so intense that many of the cast and crew suffered heat strokes, the temperature rising on some days beyond the point of thermometers. The scenes depicting the attack on the city of Aqaba were shot at the seaside of Seville, Spain, where Lean had the town of Aqaba built, duplicating the town since the city had grown to be much larger and was unsuitable for the needed sequence. Structures for the scenes representing Cairo, Damascus and Jerusalem were also lavishly constructed at great expense (the budget soared beyond $15 million), and the desert scene where O'Toole leads his forces to slaughter the retreating Turkish troops was shot in Morocco. The investment into this film was rewarded by an instant critical and public success, the production earning back $70 million in its first release. Guinness told this author that "David Lean is one of the greatest directors of film, a man who knows exactly what he wishes to see in every scene and gets those scenes precisely as he envisions them. I know that well in that I really began my film career with him in **Great Expectations** [1946], and went on to make with him **The Bridge on the River Kwai** [1957]. His attention to accurate detail is beyond reproach, from the inflection of a single word delivered by an actor to the type of ring worn on the little finger of an extra. Nothing misses his eyes which are as reliable as any camera ever made." Quinn told this author that Lean "told me to play my part as the tribal chief very big, so I gave him a man as broad as the desert. I put a lot of putty on my nose to make it bigger and broader and when I speak in that film, I gave every word a lot of volume—you could hear me coming a block away. I had to appear in sharp contrast to Omar Sharif, who plays a more thoughtful Arab leader. I know I sometimes played the buffoon in that picture, but also

Alain Delon in *le Samourai*, **1972.**

a wise leader. That is what David Lean wanted and got." For more details on the intriguing T. E. (Thomas Edward) Lawrence, see my book, *Zanies: The World's Greatest Eccentrics* (New Century, 1982; pages 216-219), **p**, Sam Spiegel, David Lean; **d**, Lean; **cast**, Peter O'Toole, Alec Guinness, Anthony Quinn, Jack Hawkins, Jose Ferrer, Anthony Quayle, Claude Rains, Omar Sharif, Arthur Kennedy, Donald Wolfit; **w**, Robert Bolt, Michael Wilson (based on *The Seven Pillars of Wisdom* by T.E. Lawrence); **c**, F.A. (Freddie) Young (Technicolor); **m**, Maurice Jarre; **ed**, Anne V. Coates; **prod d**, John Box; **art d**, John Stoll, Anthony Masters; **set d**, Dario Simoni; **spec eff**, Cliff Richardson, Wally Veevers.

Le Beau Marriage ★★★ 1982; France; 97m; Les Films du Losange/UA; Color; Comedy/Drama; Children: Unacceptable (MPAA: PG); **DVD**; **VHS**. In this good character study of youthful romance, Romand is a young woman, who moves from Le Mans to Paris to study art history and falls in love with a painter, Atkine. She learns he is married when he gets a phone call from his son. She is now tired of having relations with married men and returns to Le Mans where her friend, Dombasle, introduces her to a handsome cousin, Dussollier, a lawyer from Paris. She tells friends she will marry him, but he does not seem interested in her. She pursues him until he admits to her that he does not love her, which leaves her still looking for the right man and a good marriage. Sexual matter and gutter language prohibit viewing by children. (In French; English subtitles.) **p**, Margaret Ménégoz; **d&w**, Éric Rohmer; **cast**, Béatrice Romand, André Dussollier, Féodor Atkine, Arielle Dombasle, Huguette Faget, Thamila Mezbah, Sophie Renoir, Hervé Duhamel, Pascal Greggory, Virginie Thévenet; **c**, Bernard Lutic; **m**, Ronan Girre, Simon des Innocents; **ed**, Cécile Decugis.

Le Beau Serge ★★★ 1959; France; 98m; Ajym Films/United Motion Pictures Organization; B/W; Drama; Children: Unacceptable; **DVD**; **VHS**. An incisive domestic drama sees Brialy as a theology student, who has lived in a big city for ten years and returns to his home village in France. He does not think it has changed much, but his old friend, Blain, a formerly successful architect, has become a drunk. Brialy learns that his friend's descent into guilt and depression happened after getting married and his son was born malformed. Brialy suggests Blain leave his wife, Méritz. Blain takes this advice, taking up with another woman, Lafont, who is his wife's half-sister. They have a healthy child and this relieves Brialy of his guilt and depression. The title refers to Brialy's name in the film. Sexuality prohibits viewing by children. (In French; English subtitles.) **p,d&w**, Claude Chabrol; **cast**, Gérard Blain, Jean-Claude Brialy, Michèle Méritz, Bernadette Lafont, Claude Cerval, Jeanne Pérez, Edmond Beauchamp, André Dino, Michel Creuze, Chabrol; **c**, Henri Decaë; **m**, Émile Delpierre; **ed**, Jacques Gaillard.

Le Ciel est a Vous ★★★ 1949; France; 105m; Les Films Raoul Ploquin/Siritzky International Pictures Corp.; B/W; Drama; Children: Acceptable. This solid biopic is based on a true story where a French garage owner, Vanel, and his wife, Renaud, are fascinated with flying. They make great sacrifices that pay off when Renaud sets the women's world distance record. The story is based on the 1938 flight of Andree Dupeyron. The director made the film as a flying allegory representing the goals and achievements of those fighting for the French Resistance in World War II. (In French; English subtitles.) **p**, Raoul Ploquin; **d**, Jean Grémillon; **cast**, Madeleine Renaud, Charles Vanel, Jean Debucourt, Raymonde Vernay, Léonce Corne, Raoul Marco, Albert Rémy, Robert Le Fort, Anne-Marie Labaye, Michel François; **w**, Charles Spaak (based on the story by Albert Valentin); **c**, Roger Arrignon, Louis Page; **m**, Roland Manuel; **ed**, Louisette Hautecoeur; **prod d**, Max Douy.

Le Gai Savoir ★★★ 1970; France/West Germany; 95m; Anouchka Films/EYR; Color; Drama; Children: Unacceptable; **VHS**. Director and writer Jean-Luc Godard presents an unusual but fascinating film in which he attempts to dissolve narrative structure to its most basic elements – sound and images. There is no plot. The film shows two young adults, Berto and Léaud, meeting on a movie soundstage to discuss learning and the road to revolution. They speak as footage is shown of a student revolt in Paris, the Vietnam War, and other headline events in the late 1960s. Providing background to their discourse are posters, photographs, cartoons, and music and noise. Though the film was commissioned by the French government, it refused to show it in theaters or on television, so Godard bought back the rights and it was released in 1968, but not shown in the U.S. until two years later, a film that chiefly profiles Godard's radical thoughts on filmmaking. Song: "Cuban Revolutionary Hymn." Mature content prohibits viewing by children. (In French; English subtitles.) **d&w**, Jean-Luc Godard (based on *Emile* by Jean Jacques Rousseau); **cast**, Juliet Berto, Jean-Pierre Léaud; **c**, Georges Leclerc; **ed**, Germaine Cohen.

Le Mans ★★★ 1971; U.S.; 106m; Cinema Center Films/National General Pictures; Color; Drama; Children: Unacceptable (MPAA: G); **DVD**; **VHS**. This exciting film, which takes a docudrama approach, focuses upon the annual twenty-four-hour Grand Prix race car event in France. The focus is on the competition between a German, Rauch, driving a Ferrari 512LM, and an American, McQueen, at the wheel of a Porsche 917. The pressure is on McQueen, partly because in the previous year's Le Mans he caused an accident in which another driver was killed. (The necessity to vindicate oneself appears in many other films, such as Richard Barhelmess attempting to reestablish himself as a professional pilot in **Only Angels Have Wings**, 1939, after having earlier caused the death of another pilot, or Edmund MacDonald trying to earn back the respect of fellow pilots in **Flying Tigers**, 1942, after having caused the death of another pilot in an air race.) During the race, McQueen falls in love with the widow, Andersen, of the man who had been killed because of McQueen's reckless driving. An experienced sports car driver, McQueen did his own driving in the film. Racetrack enthusiasts will find this entry appealing. Sexual scenes, violence, and gutter language prohibit viewing by children. **p**, Jack N. Reddish; **d**, Lee H. Katzin; **cast**, Steve McQueen, Siegfried Rauch, Elga Andersen, Ronald Leigh-Hunt, Fred Haltiner, Luc Merenda, Christopher Waite, Louise Edlind; Angelo Infanti, Jean-Claude Bercq, Michele Scalera; **w**, Harry Kleiner; **c**, René Guissart Jr., Robert B. Hauser (Panavision; DeLuxe Color); **m**, Michel Legrand; **ed**, Ghislaine Desjonquères, Donald W. Ernst, John M. Woodcock; **prod d**, Phil Abramson; **spec eff**, Sass Bedig.

Le Samourai ★★★ 1972; France/Italy; 105m; CICC/Artists International; Color; Crime Drama; Children: Unacceptable (MPAA: PG); **VHS**. Delon is riveting (if not utterly repulsive) as a brutal, calculating professional killer, who plans his murders with cold-blooded precision. He is first seen smoking and lying on a bed in his Spartan room where bottles of mineral water are neatly arranged in a bookcase and a small bird chirps in a gray cage in the middle of the room. Text imposed upon the scene reads: "There is no greater solitude than that of the samurai unless it is that of the tiger in the jungle." Delon has no criminal history as he has carefully planned each of his assassinations with infinite care, providing alibis through his girlfriend (played by Nathalie Delon, the actor's wife). His plans, however, begin to crumble after he fulfills a hit on a nightclub owner, and, while leaving is seen by witnesses, including the nightclub's attractive singer, Rosier. Delon is arrested and placed in a police lineup but no one identifies him as the killer. When released, police tail him, but he loses the tracking cops and meets with one of his employers on a railway overpass where, instead of paying him for his contracted killing, the employer shoots Delon in the arm and flees. Delon returns to his room and treats his arm. He then returns to the nightclub where the bartender, Favart, asks him if he wasn't the man the police suspected of killing his employer, sarcastically adding that "the murderer always returns to the scene of the crime." Delon then meets with the singer, developing a flirtatious relationship with her. Périer, the police superintendent, believes Delon is the killer, but knows he needs more evidence to charge him, so while Delon is away from his apartment, Périer orders police to plant a wiretapping bug in his room, but, while doing so, they disturb the bird in the cage. When returning to his room, Delon notices feathers from the bird on the floor, realizing that his pet has been alarmed by some intruder, and the suspicious Delon searches the room and finds the wiretapping device and disarms it. Périer and other officers then go to Nathalie Delon's apartment and search the place while Périer attempts to cut a deal with her, saying that if she admits that she lied in providing an alibi for Delon, she will not be bothered by the police again. She refuses and orders the cops from her place. Meanwhile, Delon is again confronted by the man who earlier shot him, but this time the man offers him money to perform another murder. Delon refuses, believing this to be a trap. He ties up the man and then goes to the home of that man's boss, Posier, discovering that nightclub singer Rosier also lives there. After shooting Posier to death, Delon returns to the nightclub and, in front of all of the guests, aims a gun at Rosier. She asks why he is about to kill her. Delon states: "I was paid to." A shot rings out, but Delon, not Rosier, falls to the floor dead. A police officer has shot and killed the assassin. Superintendent Périer opens the barrel of Delon's revolver to show that it contains no bullets. This is an unrelenting crime yarn about a man who has no redeeming virtues except his own strange code of the samurai (upon which the title is based), including a suicidal urge to end his life the way he has lived it, through violence. (Dubbed.) **p**, Raymond Borderie, Eugéne Lépicier; **d**, Jean-Pierre Melville; **cast**, Alain Delon, François Périer, Nathalie Delon, Caty Rosier, Robert Favart, Jean-Pierre Posier, Jacques Leroy, Michel Boisrond, Catherine Jourdan; **w**, Melville, Georges Pellegrin (based on the novel *The Ronin* by Joan McLeod); **c**, Henri Decae (Eastmancolor); **m**, François de Roubaix; **ed**, Monique Bonnot, Yo Maurette; **prod d &** **set d**, François De Lamothe.

Le Plaisir ★★★ 1954; France; 97m; Arthur Mayer-Edward Kingsley; B/W; Drama; Children: Unacceptable; **DVD**; **VHS**. This intriguing film is based on three episodic short stories by Guy de Maupassant about pleasure, youth, and death. In the first story, "The Mask," an aging doctor, Dauphin, wears a mask to a ball in order to hide his aging face. In the second story, "The House of Madame Tellier," the keeper of a brothel, Renaud, closes her house for a day so that the ladies working for her can attend the first Communion of Renaud's young niece. This sequence also features Renaud's brother, Gabin, who is having an affair with another madam, Darrieux. In the final story, "The Model," a beautiful model, Simon, throws herself from a window to express her love for a painter, Gelin. She becomes crippled, but Gelin nevertheless marries her and devotes his life to caring for her. Sexuality prohibits viewing by children. (In French; English subtitles.) **p**, Édouard Harispuru, M. Kieffer; **d**, Max Ophüls; **cast**, "The Mask," Claude Dauphin, Jean Gal-

Bryan Forbes in *The League of Gentlemen*, 1961.

land, Gaby Morlay; "The Model," Daniel Gelin, Simone Simon, Jean Servais; "The House of Madame Tellier," Jean Gabin, Danielle Darrieux, Pierre Brasseur, Madeleine Renaud; narrators: Anton Walbrook, Peter Ustinov; **w**, Ophüls, Jacques Natanson (based on three stories by Guy de Maupassant); **c**, Philippe Agostini, Christian Matras; **m**, Joe Hayos, Maurice Yvain; **ed**, Léonide Azar; **prod d**, Jean D'Eaubonne; **set d**, Robert Christidès.

Le Viol ★★★ 1968; France/Sweden; 90m; Sandrews/Freena Films; Color; Drama; Children: Unacceptable. Andersson is a bored Parisian housewife of the upper middle class, who spends another lonely Sunday in her small but nicely decorated apartment. A stranger, Cremer, enters, ties her up, beats her and, with her willingness, takes her to bed and rapes her. That evening, a family friend (also Cremer) is among the guests at a dinner party given by Andersson and her husband, de Pasquale. The romantic liaison may have happened, but the rape has been Andersson's wishful daydream. This strange but compelling film examines female fantasies with some clever introspection. Sexuality prohibits viewing by children. (In French; English subtitles.) **p**, Mag Bodard, Göran Lindgren; **d&w**, Jacques Doniol-Valcroze; **cast**, Bibi Andersson, Bruno Cremer, Frédéric de Pasquale, Katerina Larsson, Claude Becault, Henry Bengtsson, Anne Betzholtz-Murray; **c**, Rune Ericson; **m**, Michel Portal; **ed**, Sophie Bhaud; **art d**, Jan Boleslaw.

Leadbelly ★★★ 1976; U.S.; 126m; Brownstone Productions/PAR; Color; Biographical Drama; Children: Unacceptable (MPAA: PG); **DVD**. Mosley is a standout in this exceptional biopic of blues singer Huddie William "Leadbelly" Ledbetter (1888-1948). A man of considerable talent and possessed of a mercurial temper, Mosley is shown going to a Texas chain gang for murdering a man and later serving a term in prison for stabbing another person. A towering and powerful man, Mosley portrays the singer as he was, uneducated, unfortunate and gifted. Mosley's life is shown in episodic flashbacks, where he deals with three principal persons in his life, his uneducated sharecropper father, Benjamin a Louisiana madam, Sinclair and Manson, the chief prison guard captain. Interspersed in these many scenes are delightful blues sequences offered by HiTide Harris, accompanied by David Cohen, Sonny Terry, Brownie McGhee and Dick Rosmini. **p**, Marc Merson; **d**, Gordon Parks; **cast**, Roger E. Mosley, Paul Benjamin, Madge Sinclair, Alan Manson, Albert Hall, Art Evans, James Brodhead, John Henry Faulk, Vivian Bonnell, Dana Manno; **w**, Ernest Kinoy; **c**, Bruce Surtees (Eastmancolor); **m**, Fred Karlin, **ed**, Moe Howard, Thomas Penick; **prod d**, Robert F. Boyle; **set d**, John A. Kuri.

The League of Gentlemen ★★★ 1961; U.K.; 116m; Allied Film Mak-

Tom Hanks, Rosie O'Donnell and Madonna in *A League of Their Own*, 1992.

ers/Kingsley International Pictures; B/W; Comedy; Children: Cautionary; **VHS**. Hawkins is wonderful as a disgruntled British military officer who is forced into retirement. He takes his revenge by concocting a spectacular robbery where he enlists a number of his old military comrades. This "league of gentlemen" proceed in their plans with military precision, where their every move is detailed to the last minute and in seeing their elaborate machinations the viewer gets a good slice of each man's character and all of it is amusing and even hilarious in some moments. In their well-timed robbery, Hawkins et al employ gas masks, smoke bombs and radio jamming, and get away with £1 million, but all of their well-organized and executed machinations are destroyed by Coote, another military pal, who gets drunk and leads the authorities to the culprits. Director Dearden does a fine job in presenting this subtle crime comedy and where Hawkins and all cast members render memorable performances. This film, although it stands on its own as a very entertaining vehicle, is reminiscent of similar caper films such as **The Lavender Hill Mob**, 1951, **The Ladykillers**, 1956, **Rififi**, 1956, and **Topkapi**, 1964. **p**, Michael Relph; **d**, Basil Dearden; **cast**, Jack Hawkins, Nigel Patrick, Roger Livesey, Richard Attenborough, Bryan Forbes, Kieron Moore, Robert Coote, Terence Alexander, Norman Bird, Patrick Wymark, Nigel Green, Oliver Reed; **w**, Forbes (based on the novel by John Boland); **c**, Arthur Ibbetson; **m**, Philip Green; **ed**, John D. Guthridge; **art d**, Peter Proud.

A League of Their Own ★★★ 1992; U.S.; 128m; COL; Color; Sports Drama; Children: Cautionary (MPAA: PG); **DVD**; **VHS**. Davis takes a trip to the past in 1988 when, as a member of the All-American Girls Professional Baseball League, she travels to Cooperstown, N.Y., to be inducted into the hall of fame. She reflects upon the past and we see in flashback as she and her sister, Petty, are recruited by talent scout Lovitz to play in the newly established women's baseball league in 1943. This league is the brainstorm of Marshall, owner of the Chicago Cubs, who seeks to bolster baseball, which is threatened with a closedown for lack of male players, who are now serving in the armed forces. Davis is already working on a farm and at a dairy while her husband, Pullman, is away fighting in WWII, and she refuses, even though she is a great catcher and hitter. Her younger sister Petty, however, is desperate to leave her small town, and Davis joins up with Petty and both become members after they go through tryouts in Chicago, meeting teammates O'Donnell, Madonna and others. Hanks, a former professional baseball player, who is a drunk and on the skids, is their coach, a job he detests. The girls go through many trials and tribulations, some fighting with each other over petty jealousies and envy, as Hanks sobers up and puts the team into shape. Davis and Petty then fall out when Davis causes her sister to be traded from the Chicago team to a

women's team in Racine, Wisconsin, but they meet again at the women's world series and where Davis and Petty exhaust themselves in competing with opposing teams and each other, but, following the final game, they reconcile, with Davis returning home to be with her husband and to raise a family. Davis and Petty, as well as the rest of the fine cast, render good performances (and surprisingly outstanding athleticism) in this entertaining and often amusing sports entry. **p**, Robert Greenhut, Elliot Abbott, Ronnie Clemmer, Joseph Hartwick, Bill Pace; **d**, Penny Marshall; **cast**, Tom Hanks, Geena Davis, Madonna, Lori Petty, Jon Lovitz, David Strathairn, Garry Marshall, Bill Pullman, Rosie O'Donnell, Ann Cusack, Tea Leoni; **w**, Lowell Ganz, Babaloo Mandel (based on a story by Kim Wilson, Kelly Candaele); **c**, Miroslav Ondricek (Technicolor); **m**, Hans Zimmer; **ed**, Adam Bernardi, George Bowers; **prod d**, Bill Groom; **art d**, Tim Galvin; **set d**, George DeTitta, Jr.; **spec eff**, Christopher Duddy.

Lean on Me ★★★ 1989; U.S.; 108m; Norman Twain Productions/WB; Color; Drama; Children: Unacceptable (MPAA: PG-13); **DVD**; **VHS**. An unorthodox but successful teacher, Freeman, works at a model Paterson, N.J. high school, but he leaves his job in a union dispute in 1967. He returns twenty years later to the school as principal and finds it to be out of control with drug abuse, and where students are terrorized, and teachers are assaulted. Shouting orders for control over a bullhorn and carrying a baseball bat, Freeman tries to get the school under control, but his methods clash with the mayor, North, and superintendent of schools, Guillaume. Freeman tries to frighten a boy on crack by urging him to jump off a roof because he's killing himself anyway, and his draconian actions and policies almost end his career, but he eventually brings order out of chaos. Based on a true story, this hard-hitting film deals realistically with problems that have universally plagued big city America and where Freeman is a standout in his heroic role. Violence, gutter language, and references to drugs prohibit viewing by children. **p**, Norman Twain; **d**, John G. Avildsen; **cast**, Morgan Freeman, Beverly Todd, Robert Guillaume, Alan North, Lynne Thigpen, Robin Bartlett, Michael Beach, Ethan Phillips, Sandra Reaves-Phillips, Sloane Shelton; **w**, Michael Schiffer; **c**, Victor Hammer; **m**, Bill Conti; **ed**, Avildsen, John Carter; **prod d**, Doug Kraner; **art d**, Tim Galvin; **set d**, Caryl Heller.

Leatherheads ★★★ 2008; U.S./Germany; 114m; UNIV; Color; Sports Drama; Children: Unacceptable (MPAA: PG-13); **BD**; **DVD**. Colorful and entertaining period sports drama sees Clooney at the head of an early-day football team. When he loses his sponsor, he convinces WWI hero and Princeton football star Krasinski to join the team. The team, with the dashing and handsome Krasinski leading the way through his blinding speed in running the football, soon begins to see wins and earn an ever-increasing crowd following. Zellweger, a writer for the Chicago *Tribune*, writes articles that boost the fame of the team and its leaders, Clooney and Krasinski, and where both of these brawny players compete for her attentions. Zellweger then learns that Krasinski's claims about his heroic actions during WWI have been grossly inflated and she publishes a story that discredits Kraskinski, who comes to blows with Clooney, but chiefly over the affection Zellweger now shows to Clooney. After a lot of accusations, plots and petty conspiracies by all parties to discredit each other, Krasinski leaves Clooney's team and joins a rival team, both of these teams now meeting in a final showdown match. The teams play tenaciously on a muddy field and it appears that Clooney's team will lose, but Clooney, through a clever ruse, scores the final touchdown that wins the game as well as Zellweger's hand. The acting is good, the action is superb and the production values high in this spirited entry. **p**, Grant Heslov, Casey Silver; **d**, George Clooney; **cast**, Clooney, Renée Zellweger, John Krasinski, Malcolm Goodwin, Matt Bushell, Tommy Hinkley, Tim Griffin, Robert Baker, Nick Paonessa, Lance Barber; **w**, Duncan Brantley, Rick Reilly; **c**, Newton Thomas Sigel; **m**, Randy Newman; **ed**, Stephen Mirrione; **prod d**,

James D. Bissell; **art d**, Christa Munro, Scott Ritenour; **set d**, Jan Pascale; **spec eff**, Kevin Hannigan.

Leave Her to Heaven ★★★ 1945; U.S.; 110m; FOX; Color; Crime Drama; Children: Unacceptable; **DVD**; **VHS**. The stunningly beautiful Tierney gives a mesmerizing performance in this thriller as a selfish, pampered woman so possessed of jealousy that she cold-bloodedly murders anyone who draws the attentions of her husband, Wilde. After meeting Wilde on a train, Tierney learns that he is a successful author and is emotionally drawn to him since he resembles her father. They marry and move to a remote lakeside retreat called "Back of the Moon." All seems peaceful. Tierney fires the handyman and then finds that Wilde pays too much attention to his crippled bother, Hickman. She takes Hickman to the lake and encourages him to swim and when he begins to drown, Tierney ignores him and cruelly watches him sink to his death. Tierney then becomes pregnant, but cannot tolerate the thought of her child later taking attention from Wilde so she walks to the head of a staircase and throws herself down in order to have a miscarriage. When Crain, Tierney's foster sister, comes to live with them, Tierney again is consumed by jealousy, but, instead of plotting Crain's murder, she confesses to Wilde that she allowed Hickman to die in the lake and caused her own miscarriage. Wilde, who has been blind to all of his wife's machinations, now realizes that he is living with a monster. Before he can shed himself of this insane woman, Tierney kills herself, but takes her life in such a way as to leave police enough clues that convince them that Wilde and Crain murdered her so that they could be together. Wilde and Crain are charged with Tierney's murder and prosecuted by attorney Price, who vindictively seeks to have them both executed as he was a former lover of Tierney's. Price's theatrics and vicious treatment of the defendants become obvious to the jury, which finds Wilde and Crain innocent, but Wilde is convicted of being an accessory to murder in that he did not immediately inform authorities about Tierney's confession concerning Hickman's death and that of her own unborn child. Wilde is sent to prison, but Crain is waiting for him at the finale of this shuddering and very grim tale. The acting is exceptional, and Stahl directs this thriller with a sure hand while Shamroy's lensing superbly presents lush color photography. The film was shot on location at Maine, Georgia and Arizona. *Author's Note*: Tierney told this author that "the woman I play in that picture is the most hideous creature I would ever play in any film, and, I believe, worse than any other woman in any picture. A year earlier, I played a sweet and innocent woman in **Laura** [1944] and the next year I am playing an absolute monster." Fox mogul Zanuck had apprehensions about this film, or, at least, Tierney's part, telling this author that "I worried about how the public would take to one of the most beautiful women in the world playing the most despicable person anyone had ever seen, but the audiences were spellbound by her performance and realized that she was, beyond the terrible person she was playing, a fine actress." **p**, William A. Bacher; **d**, John M. Stahl; **cast**, Gene Tierney, Cornel Wilde, Jeanne Crain, Vincent Price, Mary Philips, Ray Collins, Gene Lockhart, Reed Hadley, Darryl Hickman, Chill Wills; **w**, Jo Swerling (based on the novel by Ben Ames Williams); **c**, Leon Shamroy (Technicolor); **m**, Alfred Newman; **ed**, James B. Clark; **art d**, Lyle Wheeler, Maurice Ransford; **set d**, Thomas Little, Ernest Lansing; **spec eff**, Fred Sersen.

Let Him Have It ★★★ 1991; U.K.; 115m; British Screen Productions/COL; Color; Crime Drama; Children: Unacceptable (MPAA: R); **DVD**; **VHS**. Based on true events, this absorbing crime story profiles two teenage boys, nineteen-year-old Derek Bentley (Eccleston), a not-very-bright epileptic, and sixteen-year-old Chris Craig (Reynolds), who are involved in a fatal shooting during a burglary they are committing. A policeman traps them on a warehouse rooftop, and Bentley tells Craig, "Let him have it, Chris." Craig fires the gun and kills the cop. At their trial in 1952, Bentley testified that he was telling Craig to give up the gun, but the younger boy thought Bentley was telling him to shoot the

Gene Tierney and Cornel Wilde in *Leave Her to Heaven*, 1945.

cop. Bentley was hanged for the murder, while Craig, the actual killer, served only ten years in prison. Bentley's parents have since died, but his sister, Iris Bentley, fought a legal battle for a posthumous acquittal for her brother, and the case was reopened after this movie was released. Violence and gutter language prohibit viewing by children. *Author's Note*: For more details on the burglars Craig and Bentley, see my two-volume work, *The Great Pictorial History of World Crime*, Volume I (History, Inc., 2004; pages 268-269). **p**, Luc Roeg, Robert Warr; **d**, Peter Medak; **cast**, Tom Courtenay, Christopher Eccleston, Eileen Atkins, Rebecca Eccleston, Peter Eccleston, Craig Turner, Edward Hardwicke, Ronald Fraser, Tom Bell, Michael Gough, Clive Revill; **w**, Neal Purvis, Robert Wade; **c**, Oliver Stapleton; **m**, Michael Kamen; **ed**, Ray Lovejoy; **prod d**, Michael Pickwoad; **art d**, Henry Harris; **spec eff**, Garth Inns.

Leave It to Beaver ★★★ 1997; U.S.; 88m; Robert Simonds Productions/UNIV; Color; Comedy; Children: Unacceptable (MPAA: PG); **DVD**; **VHS**. This amusing comedy is based on characters in the television series (1957-1963) about a small town Ohio family that starred Jerry Mathers as eight-year-old "the Beaver" and Hugh Beaumont and Barbara Billingsley as his parents, and a follow-up series "The New Leave It to Beaver" (1985-1989). In the 1997 film, teenage Beaver Cleaver (Finley) dreams of getting a bicycle for his eighth birthday so he butters up to his father (McDonald) by joining the town's Mighty Mites football team. Even though Beaver knows nothing about football and runs the wrong way with the ball, he gets his bike, but it's soon stolen by another teenager and it is found later covered in fudge and whipped cream. Meanwhile, Finley's older teenage brother Wally (von Detten) falls in love with a girl named Karen (Christensen) and has other problems with his obnoxious pal Eddie Haskell (Zolotin). Billingsley plays an aunt in the film and Osmond, who played Eddie Haskell on TV, appears as Haskell's father in the film. Gutter language prohibits viewing by children. **p**, Robert Simonds, Kelly Van Horn; **d**, Andy Cadiff; **cast**, Christopher McDonald, Janine Turner, Cameron Finley, Erik von Detten, Adam Zolotin, Alan Rachins, Grace Phillips, Geoff Pierson, Barbara Billingsley, Ken Osmond; **w**, Brian Levant, Lon Diamond (based on the television series by Bob Mosher, Joe Connelly); **c**, Thomas Del Ruth; **m**, Randy Edelman; **ed**, Alan Heim; **prod d**, Perry Andelin Blake; **art d**, Alan Au, Peg McClellan; **set d**, Lisa Robyn Deutsch; **spec eff**, Josh Hakian, James W. Kristoff, Bruno Vilela, Dobbie Schiff.

Leaving Las Vegas ★★★ 1995; U.S.; 111m; Lumiere Pictures; MGM/UA; Color; Drama; Children: Unacceptable (MPAA: R); **DVD**; **VHS**. Cage, an alcoholic Hollywood screenwriter, goes to Las Vegas to drink himself to death, and attracts Shue, a prostitute, who has just rid herself of her sadistic pimp, Sands. She takes Cage under her wing.

Elisabeth Shue and Nicolas Cage in *Leaving Las Vegas*, 1995.

While attempting to make crude sex with her, the drunken Cage falls and breaks a glass table that leaves him bleeding. Their strange romance is depressing and haunting, one where two losers find each other and try to make the best of it. Novelist O'Brien committed suicide two weeks after signing a contract to turn his novel into a film that ironically made millions. Gutter language and sexuality prohibit viewing by children. **p**, Lila Cazés, Annie Stewart; **d&w**, Mike Figgis (based on the novel by John O'Brien); **cast**, Nicolas Cage, Elisabeth Shue, Julian Sands, Richard Lewis, Steven Weber, Kim Adams, Emily Procter, Stuart Regen, Valeria Golino, Graham Beckel; **c**, Declan Quinn; **m**, Figgis; **ed**, John Smith; **prod d**, Waldemar Kalinowski; **art d**, Barry M. Kingston; **set d**, Florence Fellman; **spec eff**, William D. Harrison, Aviv Yaron.

The Left Hand of God ★★★ 1955; U.S.; 87m; FOX; Color; Adventure; Children: Cautionary; **DVD**; **VHS**. Bogart gives another strong performance, this time as an American pilot in China, who has joined warlord Cobb and his ragtag army after his plane crashes. He serves as an adviser to Cobb, and supervisor of Cobb's undisciplined forces, living comfortably at Cobb's mountain retreat with a concubine, Porter. Bogart, however, bristles under Cobb's dictates and knows that if he attempts to escape, he will be shot as Cobb has ordered all deserters executed. After one of Cobb's men shoots and kills a priest, Bogart decides he has had enough. He takes the priest's garments and escapes, going to a small Chinese village to which the dead priest had been posted. Bogart is welcomed by missionaries Marshall and Moorehead as well as a lovely nurse, Tierney. He attempts to comfort the villagers while avoiding religious services while he finds himself attracted to Tierney and she feels uncomfortable since, she, too, is emotionally attracted to him. Bogart finds his position impossible and finally writes the bishop, Reid, confessing his disguise. Then Cobb arrives with his troops and demands that Bogart rejoin him, but Bogart refuses. Cobb tells him that if he does not return to his banner he will destroy the village and everyone in it. Bogart then appeals to Cobb's sporting nature and offers him a deal. They will roll dice and if Cobb wins, Bogart will serve him for five more years. If Cobb loses, he will leave the village unharmed and Bogart will go free. They roll the dice and Cobb loses. He keeps his word and rides off with his men and Bogart later meets Reid, who upbraids him for his irreligious impersonation, ordering him to travel to the coast to face authorities in the matter. Bogart departs, but not before he meets with Tierney, who tells him that she loves him and it is clear that she will follow him and they will later be together. Dmytryk helms this adventure tale with a strong hand, moving the story alone at a brisk pace and where Bogart, Tierney, Cobb, and a fine cast give standout performances. *Author's Note*: Tierney had recently left a sanitarium where she had been treated for a mental breakdown, and Fox chief Zanuck, who had made Tierney a star, had some reservations about her ability to play her part. He asked Dmytryk and Bogart if they had any objections to her playing the female lead and both said they did not, and eagerly looked forward to working with her. The composure and restraint Tierney displays in this film did not indicate for a moment that she was not in control of her part, which she plays to perfection. **p**, Buddy Adler; **d**, Edward Dmytryk; **cast**, Humphrey Bogart, Gene Tierney, Lee J. Cobb, Agnes Moorehead, E.G. Marshall, Jean Porter, Carl Benton Reid, Victor Sen Yung, Philip Ahn, Benson Fong; **w**, Alfred Hayes (based on the novel by William E. Barrett); **c**, Franz Planer (CinemaScope; DeLuxe Color); **m**, Victor Young; **ed**, Dorothy Spencer; **art d**, Lyle Wheeler, Maurice Ransford; **set d**, Walter M. Scott, Frank Wade; **spec eff**, Ray Kellogg.

The Left-Handed Gun ★★★ 1958; U.S.; 102m; WB; B/W; Western; Children: Unacceptable; **DVD**; **VHS**. Newman plays the legendary Billy the Kid (William H. Bonney; William Henry McCarty Jr.; 1859-1881) as no other actor ever played this gunman of the Old West. He arrives at a New Mexico ranch owned by Keith-Johnston (playing John Tunstall, 1853-1878), and is hired as a ranch hand and where the rancher treats Newman with kindness. The homeless, loveless Newman becomes obsessively devoted to Keith-Johnston and, after he is murdered in the Lincoln County range war (1878), Newman, along with pals Best and Congdon, who are as uneducated and unsophisticated as is Newman, conduct a revenge war against the killers, shooting down the rancher's enemies. Storeowner Dierkes, playing Alexander McSween (1843-1878), a Keith-Johnston ally, is also killed, which prompts Newman to continue his lethal crusade against his enemies. Meanwhile, Newman's conduct is tolerated by landowner and one-time friend, Dehner, who plays Pat Garrett (1850-1908), and Newman attends Dehner's wedding, but ruins the festivities when shooting down another faction member. Branded an outlaw, Newman is tracked down by Dehner, who has become a marshal with the expressed orders of capturing the now notorious outlaw. He captures Newman, who is jailed and who awaits trial for several murders, but Newman escapes, killing two guards in the process. Newman takes refuge with a Mexican family whose daughter, Milan, is in love with Newman. His life, however, is ended when Dehner tracks him down to his lair and fatally shoots him. Newman's portrait of the Kid is chilling, where he plays the gunfighter as a mentally unbalanced youth, and where most others emulate the same kind of neurotic posture, particularly Hatfield, who follows Newman about like a gunfighter groupie, collecting memorabilia on Newman as his murders mount and where Hatfield finally realizes that Newman is no western hero, but a young man with feet of clay and a head full of hatred. Billy the Kid has been profiled in many films, most notably by Robert Taylor in **Billy the Kid**, 1941; by Jack Buetel in **The Outlaw**, 1943; Dean White in **Return of the Bad Men**, 1948; by Geoffrey Deuel in **Chisum**, 1970; by Kris Kristofferson in **Pat Garrett and Billy the Kid**, 1973; and by Emilio Estevez in **Young Guns**, 1988 and **Young Guns II**, 1990 (and where Estevez plays a cackling, near-cuckoo Billy, who tells his victims before shooting them: "I'll make you famous"). *Author's Note*: Newman made this film early in his career, having made several appearances in dramatic TV productions and a few feature films. "I was impressed with the script that Vidal wrote about the Kid. He took an altogether different approach with him, one that peered into the gunfighter's psyche. The story examined the reasons why he was the way he was—a lonely, lovesick person, who had been orphaned early in life and whose only friends were people like himself, young cowboys who knew nothing about life except how to shoot guns and ride horses. He was orphaned at an early age and he killed out of revenge for his miserable life and when those few persons who loved him were taken away, he had nothing left but his gun." It is claimed that Billy the Kid killed twenty-one men and was the fastest draw in the Old West, but this is a myth. He most likely killed less than half that number and he never shot it out in the open with an adversary, but killed from ambush. He was a sneaky, back-shooting murderer, vicious, stupid and without any redeeming qualities. For extensive details on Billy the Kid and Pat Garrett, see my book, *Encyclopedia of Western Lawmen and Outlaws* (Paragon House, 1992; Billy the Kid: pages 38-45; Pat Garrett: 133-137). **p**, Fred Coe; **d**, Arthur Penn; **cast**, Paul Newman, Lita Milan, John Dehner, Hurd Hatfield, James Congdon, James Best, Colin Keith-Johnston, John Dierkes, Wally Brown, Ainslie Pryor; **w**, Leslie Stevens (based on the teleplay "The Death of Billy the Kid" by Gore Vidal); **c**, Peverell Marley; **m**, Alexander Courage; **ed**, Folmar Blangsted; **art d**, Art Loel; **set d**, William L. Kuehl.

The Left-Handed Woman ★★★ 1980; West Germany; 119m; Filmverlag der Autoren/New Yorker Films; Color; Drama; Children: Unacceptable; **DVD**. Clever feels that her married life is empty and boring so she decides to leave her husband, Ganz. During the couple's trial separation she attempts to develop other relationships, but is so depressed that she gives it up and returns to her work as a translator. Not much happens but the film does a very good job of dramatizing the effects of a lost relationship while developing penetrating character profiles of people living without love. We are left wondering whether the couple will reconcile or go on to relationships with others. Adult material prohibits viewing by children. (In German; English subtitles.) **p**, Wim Wenders, Joachim von Mengershausen; **d&w**, Peter Handke (based on his novel); **cast**, Edith Clever, Markus Mühleisen, Bruno Ganz, Michael Lonsdale, Angela Winkler, Bernhard Wicki, Nicholas Novikoff, Bernhard Minetti, Rüdiger Vogler, Gérard Depardieu; **c**, Robby Müller (Eastmancolor); **m**, Uli Winkler; **ed**, Peter Przygodda.

The Legend of Tom Dooley ★★★ 1959; U.S.; 79m; COL; B/W; Western; Children: Unacceptable; **VHS**. Grim but well-executed western sees Landon as the hapless Tom Dooley, the story emanating from the folk tale made popular by the Kingston Trio in the late 1950s, which they sing over title credits. Landon is a Confederate soldier, who, along with Pollock and Rust, holds up a Union stage, killing two soldiers in the brutal process. They then learn that the war is over and that their act is branded as criminal and they are now hunted as murderers. They flee southward, but Landon first picks up his girlfriend, Morrow, who comes from a Union family, and they elope. Morrow, however, is accidentally killed, and Landon is eventually hunted down, tried and convicted for murder and is hanged. *Author's Note*: This film takes a few leafs from **Love Me Tender**, 1956, particularly where Richard Egan and others commit a robbery while not knowing that the war has ended. **p&w**, Stanley Shpetner; **d**, Ted Post; **cast**, Michael Landon, Jo Morrow, Jack Hogan, Richard Rust, Dee Pollock, Ken Lynch, Howard Wright, Ralph Moody, John Cliff, Cheerio Meredith, Gary Hunley; **c**, Gilbert Warrenton; **m**, Ronald Stein; **ed**, Robert S. Eisen; **art d**, Don Ament; **set d**, Louis Diage.

The Legend of Bagger Vance ★★★ 2000; U.S.; 126m; DreamWorks/FOX; Color; Sports Drama; Children: Unacceptable (MPAA: PG-13); **DVD**; **VHS**. Intriguing drama that uses the game of golf to rehabilitate Damon, a man haunted by nightmares and who has become an alcoholic following his traumatic experiences in WWI when the company he commanded as a captain is annihilated and where he nevertheless emerged as a recipient of the Congressional Medal of Honor. Damon lives in Savannah, Georgia, and his existence is meager. He has long been estranged from his friends and chiefly the woman he loves and who loves him, Theron, who comes from a wealthy family. Damon had, before the war, been a fine golfer whose promising career was halted by the war and he has not gone back to the clubs since that time. It is now 1930, and Theron now needs Damon's help in that she has organized a championship golfing match to rise needed family funds, one where the two greatest golfers of that era, Bobby Jones (Gretsch) and Walter Hagen (McGill) have agreed to play, but she needs one more player, a native resident, to promote local interest and attendance. Damon at first declines, but then reluctantly agrees to be the third

Will Smith and Matt Damon in *The Legend of Bagger Vance,* **2000.**

player in this much-heralded match and he begins practicing at night, hitting golf balls into a murky distance he cannot see. At that moment, Smith, a black caddy, appears, telling him that he is Bagger Vance (a mythical golfing legend) and that he will caddy for Damon. Smith then begins coaching Damon or emotionally and psychologically encouraging him to use his native skills while overcoming the haunting demons that plague his memory. Damon enters the match and battles to maintain score with Gretsch and McGill while Smith gives him advice on each and every hole. He ignores that advice on several occasions only to lose the hole and must then work hard to catch up, and, throughout the struggle, Damon comes to grips with his nagging memories, overcoming them by the 18th hole where Smith tells him that he no longer needs him and disappears, his caddy duties taken over by his youthful assistant, Moncrief. At that final hole, Damon sinks an impossible putt, and ends with a score the evens that of Gretsch and McGill in a three-way tie. The match is a huge success and Damon has not only regained his self-confidence and new hope for a good life, but also wins back the heart of Theron. The narration begun at the film's beginning by an old man, Lemmon, who is now the aged Moncrief, ends with his final remarks and where he sees the celestial-like Smith once more on the greens beckoning to him and where he follows the legendary Bagger Vance into the hereafter. Well directed by Redford and finely acted by the entire cast, this is a well-written sports drama that will edify all golfing enthusiasts as well as those seeking an entertaining film that also inspires and uplifts. Other notable feature films that profile the sport of golfing include **Trouble in Paradise**, 1932; **Bringing Up Baby**, 1938; **I Love You Again**, 1940; **Going My Way**, 1944; **Follow the Sun**, 1951 (where Glenn Ford plays the great Ben Hogan); **Pat and Mike**, 1952; **Caddyshack**, 1980; **Bobby Jones: Stroke of Genius**, 2004; and **The Greatest Game Ever Played**, 2005 (the incredible victory of 20-year-old Francis Ouimet in the 1913 U.S. Open). *Author's Note*: This was Lemmon's last film, that fine actor dying a year after its release. This film was expensive, costing more than a reported $80 million (much of that going to the exorbitantly paid stars) and it only recouped about half of its investment. Some reviewers thought that Smith's role employed the old stereotype of slavish blacks, but Smith defies that label with a reserved and subtle performance and where his inspiring urgings pour from a human spirit that can never die. **p**, Robert Redford, Jake Eberts, Michael Nozik, Chris Brigham, Joseph Reidy, Karen Tenkhoff; **d**, Redford; **cast**, Will Smith, Matt Damon, Charlize Theron, Bruce McGill, Joel Gretsch, J. Michael Moncrief, Peter Gerety, Lane Smith, Michael O'Neill, Harve Presnell, Jack Lemmon (narrator); **w**, Jeremy Leven (based on the novel by Steven Pressfield); **c**, Michael Ballhaus (Technicolor); **m**, Rachel Portman; **ed**, Hank Corwin; **prod d**, Stuart Craig; **art d**, Angelo P. Graham, W. Steven Graham; **set d**, Jim Erickson,

Karel Fiala (as a cowboy) tossing unknown actor in *Lemonade Joe*, 1967.

Michael Seirton; **spec eff**, Burt Dalton, Rodney M. Byrd, Richard Chuang, Michael A. Chang.

The Lemon Drop Kid ★★★ 1934; U.S.; 71m; PAR; B/W; Comedy; Children: Cautionary; **VHS**. Tracy is terrific as a racetrack tout, a glib talker who cons an ailing old man out of $100 and then skips to a small town where he meets and marries fetching Mack. She convinces Tracy to return to the big city, and they move there and settle down, having a child. All seems promising until Mack learns she has an ailment that threatens her life. Desperate to pay for her medical treatment, Tracy robs a bank and is caught. His wife dies and he is sent to prison. He then learns that his old pals at the racetrack are taking care of his son until he is released from prison and, moreover, he ultimately sees a windfall in that the old man he swindled never pressed charges and, in fact, has left a sizeable amount of money for him and his son, all because Tracy gave him lemon drops that the old man claimed cured his arthritis. Colorful and as fast clipped as a speeding train, this film offers a lot of laughs mixed with just the right amount of pathos to make the fine Damon Runyon story work, cleverly directed by Neilan and with a lively script from Green and McEvoy. **p**, William LeBaron; **d**, Marshall Neilan; **cast**, Lee Tracy, Helen Mack, William Frawley, Minna Gombell, Baby LeRoy, Kitty Kelly, Henry B. Walthall, Robert McWade, Clarence Wilson, Ann Sheridan; **w**, Howard J. Green, J.P. McEvoy (based on the story by Damon Runyon); **c**, Henry Sharp; **m**, John Leipold, Heinz Roemheld; **art d**, Hans Dreier, John B. Goodman.

The Lemon Drop Kid ★★★ 1951; U.S.; 91m; PAR; B/W; Comedy; Children: Acceptable; **DVD**; **VHS**. Though this is a remake of the 1934 film, its story line wanders far afield, but nevertheless offers an outstanding comedy headed by the inimitable Hope, who is a racetrack bookie and handicapper, who, most of the time, handicaps himself. Hope makes a serious mistake when, at a Florida racetrack, he steers King, the girlfriend of gangster Clark, away from a sure thing, and she loses her boyfriend's loot on a nag touted by Hope that comes in last. Now Hope is in big trouble with Clark, who demands the $10,000 King lost or Hope can book a reservation in the hereafter. Hope blows town and arrives in New York City in the middle of winter and close to Christmas. He tries to raise the needed cash from old flame Maxwell, but when she mentions marriage, Hope flies the coop and tries to touch Nolan, a local crime boss, for the money, but Nolan tells him that he is in trouble with the IRS (there is really no love lost between them anyway). There seems little hope for Hope until he notices a Santa Claus standing on a corner and ringing a bell to attract passersby in donating to charity. Hope watches as pedestrians dump coins and bills into the Santa Claus' kettle and then hatches a scheme. He dresses up as Santa and takes a position on a busy street, collecting donations, but he is recognized by a cop who had arrested him years back and he is taken to court where he is convicted and sent to jail for ten days for soliciting charitable funds without a license. Maxwell arrives and bails him out, but Hope now realizes that he can use the same scheme if he operates legitimately. He remembers Darwell, an elderly woman who was denied access to a retirement home because her deceased husband had a criminal record, so he takes over an abandoned casino (owned by Clark) and brings Darwell and many other displaced little old ladies to live there, while using the Santa Claus operation with all proceeds ostensibly going to the support of the elderly women. Hope nevertheless plans to pocket most of the cash. Maxwell and others are all for the plan, thinking Hope has reformed and is now on the path to do-gooder days. After securing a license to operate a charity, it seems like smooth sailing with Hope enlisting an army of confidence men and swindlers to act as street corner Santa Clauses—the most unlikely Khris Kringles ever seen. Trouble rears when Nolan sees Hope's operation as a lucrative racket and tries to muscle in by kidnapping the old ladies as well as Maxwell and ensconcing them in his own mansion in Nyack, which will be the front for Nolan's own version of the charity racket. Hope and his loyal friends, however, literally turn the tables on Nolan as well as Clark, who has returned from Florida, when they arrive at the old casino and where Hope hits a switch that electronically propels gambling tables into view and, at the same time, as arranged by Hope, the cops swarm into the place to put Nolan and Clark under arrest. Hope then resolves to run the charity as a legitimate operation and ends up in the comforting arms of Maxwell. Hope provides many hilarious scenes in this crime spoof, and the cast does a good job in supporting him. One such scene has Hope arriving from Florida in a bone-chilling blizzard that engulfs New York City. He is wearing only his thin, white summer suit and, to keep warm, he filches the coat of a small dog, using this as a vest to keep out the wintry blasts, but all it gets him is the dog's fleas and a lot of Saint Vitas dancing and scratching. Songs include: "They Obviously Want Me To Sing," "It Doesn't Cost A Dime To Dream," and "Silver Bells" (Ray Evans, Jay Livingston). *Author's Note*: Hope told this author that "I was up to no good again in **The Lemon Drop Kid**, but I'm a daisy compared to tough guys like Nolan and Clark. You know the funniest thing about that film is the great cast of characters playing those Santa Clauses—Frawley, Flippen, Melton, Dugan. They were all brawny little guys with faces like leather and they all looked like fireplugs with legs. All Bill Frawley had to do to get a laugh was to give you one of his pop-eyed looks and curl a lip. Those fellows made me look very good." **p**, Robert L. Welch; **d**, Sidney Lanfield; **cast**, Bob Hope, Marilyn Maxwell, Lloyd Nolan, Jane Darwell, Andrea King, Fred Clark, Jay C. Flippen, William Frawley, Harry Bellaver, Sid Melton, Ben Welden, Tom Dugan, Tor Johnson; **w**, Edmund L. Hartmann, Robert O'Brien, Frank Tashlin (based on a story by Edmund Beloin and Damon Runyon); **c**, Daniel L. Fapp; **m**, Victor Young; **ed**, Archie Marshek; **art d**, Hal Pereira, Franz Bachelin; **set d**, Sam Comer, Ross Dowd; **spec eff**, Paul Lerpae, Farciot Edouart.

Lemonade Joe ★★★ 1967; Czechoslovakia; 84m; Filmove studio Barrandov; AA; B/W; Comedy/Western; Children: Acceptable; **DVD**; **VHS**. Fiala is a handsome, straight-shooting cowboy, who sings and plays the piano and who cleans up wild Stetson City, Arizona, in this often hilarious spoof of silent-era American westerns. The Trigger Whiskey Saloon is the gathering place of the good and bad in the dusty cow town, and this is where heroic Fiala, in white hat and white western attire, arrives to rescue beautiful Winnifred Goodman (Schoberová) from the clutches of dastardly Doug Badman (Deyl), the saloon's proprietor, by shooting his pants off. Fiala, known far and wide as "Lemonade Joe," gets everyone in the saloon to do what he does, abstain from alcohol and instead drink Kolaloka, "Crazy Cola" lemonade, for which he is a salesman and who has a deadly aim with a pistol. Deyl's brother, devious gunman Hogofogo (Kopecký) enters to try to save the saloon from Fiala's allies, Schoberová and her father, who are temperance revivalists. Kopecký and his outlaw cronies get the upper hand on Fiala, roping him to a tree and pouring melted chocolate over him from hat to boots, but Schoberová and her father come to his rescue and he learns his true identity. An off-beat, off-the-wall satire based on a 1963 Czech stage production, there is nothing quite like it and the laughs are aplenty. (In Czech; English subtitles.) **p**, Jaroslav Jilovec; **d**, Oldrich Lipský; **cast**, Karel Fiala, Rudolf Deyl, Milos Kopecký, Kveta Fialová, Olga Schoberová, Bohus Záhorský, Josef Hlinomaz, Karel Effa, Waldemar Matuska, Eman Fiala; **w**, Lipský, Jirí Brdecka (based on the novel and play by Brdecka); **c**, Vladimír Novotný; **m**, Vlastimil Hála, Jan Rychlík; **ed**, Miroslav Hájek, Jitka Sulcová; **art d**, Karel Skvor; **set d**, Ladislav Krbec, Milos Osvald, Jiri Rulik; **spec eff**, Vladimír Dvorák.

Lenny ★★★ 1974; U.S.; 111m; Marvin Worth Productions/UA; B/W; Biographical Drama; Children: Unacceptable; **DVD**; **VHS**. Based on a play, this impactful biopic about social comedian Lenny Bruce (Leonard Alfred Schneider; 1925-1966) sees Hoffman deliver a powerful performance in the title role. We see Hoffman becoming popular as a comedian in standard fashion when he meets and falls in love with stripper Perrine, marrying her and obsessing about her. After they have an accident and where Perrine almost loses her life, this traumatic experience causes Hoffman to become even more obsessive about her and it seems to alter his modus operandi on stage. He then opts to mix social commentary with his comedic routines, lacing his monologs with obscenities and profanities (almost every other word), which brings him into conflict with local authorities. Seized by abrupt mood swings, Hoffman becomes hooked on drugs and then, when arrested and charged with obscene public performances (for his foul language), he decides to take on City Hall, battling police departments and officials, which causes him to become a minor cause célèbre, and much of the film is centered on these seemingly endless confrontations where Hoffman fights for his free speech, irrespective of its gutter-glutted content. Permeating the film through Hoffman's mesmerizing performance is his decided death wish or obsession with his own self-destruction, which he brought about on August 3, 1966, when he overdosed on drugs in Los Angeles. This experimental film is far ahead of anything in its day and where Hoffman's life is related through a series of interviews and flashbacks as he pours out his story to an off-camera third party (á la **Citizen Kane**, 1941). The tale is more of a pensive and revealing character study than an ordinary chronicle of a man's life, suitably as erratic, jumbled and confused as Bruce's own existence. Hoffman is superlative in conveying the image and character of this acerbic, insulting and abrasive person, who would have been written off as a social crank had it not been for his sharp wit and incisive social perspectives that pilloried the bigotry and prejudices of his era. *Author's Note*: This author had a personal run-in with the mercurial Bruce when I attended one of his performances with my wife in Chicago in the early 1960s (at Mister Kelly's, a popular nightclub on Rush Street). It was our unfortunate fate to be seated at the first small table directly in front the stage where Bruce was performing and, just after he opened his act and began his stream-of-consciousness monolog, a waitress came to our table, handing me a note from a phone message called in by our babysitter that told us that our oldest child (Lee Travis Nash, age three) was hemorrhaging from the nose. We leaped from our chairs and started to make our way to the exit and our obvious departure incensed Bruce, who thought we were walking out on his act. He screamed obscenities at us as we frantically tried to get to that exit through a packed crowd. My own blood boiled and I turned about, before going through the entrance door of the nightclub to shout back at Bruce: "Shut up, you jerk—our little boy might be bleeding to death!" Bruce stopped his ranting and raving, and, mouth gaping, jumped from the stage and tore through the crowd, grabbing me by the arm before I could leave and saying: "Oh my, God! I am so sorry! Please forgive me!! Please forgive me!" I had to pry his arm loose from my own before we could escape and drive home (going so fast that we were stopped on Lake Shore Drive by police who, after learning of our problem, gave us

Jean Brooks, Dennis O'Keefe and Abner Biberman in *The Leopard Man*, 1943.

an escort home). When arriving home, we found that the babysitter had temporarily stopped the bleeding (from the nose) and had called our pediatrician, who instructed us to take our son to Weiss Memorial Hospital and we rushed him there where that pediatrician cauterized the membranes of our boy's nose. We learned that if our son had continued hemorrhaging, he may have bled to death. Ironically, that life-saving physician was one of the most wonderful men I have ever met in my life, Dr. Benjamin Emanuel, who raised three gifted sons of his own— one became a brilliant medical researcher, another the leading talent agent in Hollywood (Ari Emanuel, co-CEO of the William Morris Endeavor talent agency) and the third, Rahm Emanuel, who is presently the mayor of the city of Chicago. The following day, I got a phone call from none other than Lenny Bruce, and God only knows how he got my phone number at the magazine I was working for in Chicago at that time. He stated: "I wanted to tell you that I am truly sorry for shouting at you and your wife last night. I was up all night thinking about doing that. Is your boy okay?" I told him that all was well and to forget about it, but I knew he wouldn't because I also knew even then that Lenny Bruce carried the world's problems on his back as well as his own like some bizarre and ostracized flagellant whipping himself through life for real and imagined offenses or even for being born, such was his haunted and paranoid nature. Many years later I almost stayed in the house where Bruce died, but declined at the eerie urgings of an oddball Hollywood medium, and that anecdote can be found in my *Author's Note* in my entry for **Ed Wood**, 1994 (Volume I of this work). Life, indeed, is stranger than fiction, and even stranger than Lenny Bruce. **p**, Marvin Worth; **d**, Bob Fosse; **cast**, Dustin Hoffman, Valerie Perrine, Jan Miner, Stanley Beck, Frankie Man, Rashel Novikoff, Gary Morton, Guy Rennie, Michele Yonge, Kathryn Witt; **w**, Julian Barry (based on his play); **c**, Bruce Surtees; **m**, Ralph Burns; **ed**, Alan Heim; **prod d**, Joel Schiller; **set d**, Nicholas Romanak.

The Leopard Man ★★★ 1943; U.S.; 66m; RKO; B/W; Horror; Children: Unacceptable; **DVD**; **VHS**. Great atmospheric chiller sees O'-Keefe as a hustling public relations agent representing a nightclub in New Mexico and where, to achieve a publicity stunt, he rents a leopard, but the creature escapes and reportedly kills a little girl and then stalks the inhabitants of a small town, or, at least, that is what everyone believes. The scene where the little girl is killed is not directly shown, but her death is gruesomely signified after her mother locks her out of her house after she is late in returning home from doing an errand and a pool of blood slowly appears from beneath the front door of that house. Two more brutal deaths are attributed to the missing leopard, but O'-Keefe and his girlfriend, Margo, finally expose the real killer, a human being. This film is typical of the many Val Lewton productions that pro-

Taina Elg, Mitzi Gaynor, Kay Kendall and Gene Kelly in *Les Girls*, 1957.

vide spine-chilling tales, and where director Tourneur does a fine job in maintaining suspense and apprehension by obliquely profiling the violent murders through sound and shadow. **p**, Val Lewton; **d**, Jacques Tourneur; **cast**, Dennis O'Keefe, Margo, Jean Brooks, Isabel Jewell, James Bell, Margaret Landry, Abner Biberman, Ben Bard, Richard Martin, Russell Wade; **w**, Ardel Wray, Edward Dein (based on the novel *Black Alibi* by Cornell Woolrich); **c**, Robert de Grasse; **m**, Roy Webb; **ed**, Mark Robson; **art d**, Albert S. D'Agostino, Walter E. Keller; **set d**, Darrell Silvera, Al Fields.

Les Comperes ★★★ 1984; France; 89m; DD Productions/European International; Color; Comedy; Children: Unacceptable (MPAA: PG); **DVD**; **VHS**. A madcap comedy with a heart has Bierry, a mother, searching for her runaway son, deceiving two lovers from her younger days, a mild-mannered teacher, Richard, and a tough journalist, Depardieu, into thinking each is the boy's father so they will help her find him. Adult themes prohibit viewing by children. (In French; English subtitles.) **p**, Jean-Claude Bourlat; **d&w**, Francis Veber (based on his story); **cast**, Pierre Richard, Gérard Depardieu, Stéphane Bierry, Florence Moreau, Anny Duperey, Michel Aumont, Jean-Jacques Scheffer, Philippe Khorsand, Roland Blanche, Jacques Frantz; **c**, Claude Agostini; **m**, Vladimir Cosma; **ed**, Marie-Sophie Dubus; **prod d**, Gérard Daoudal.

Les Destinees ★★★ 2000; France/Switzerland; 180m; Arcade/Wellspring Media; Color; Drama; Children: Unacceptable; **DVD**; **VHS**. The thirty-year saga of a French family begins in 1900 in Barbazac, France, where a young Protestant minister, Berling, divorces his obsessive wife, Huppert, whom he suspects of having an affair with another man. Out of guilt, he gives his share in the family's porcelain business making fine china in Limoges to her and their daughter, Hansen-Løve. He then marries Béart, a parishioner and the niece of a Cognac distiller, and they live happily in Switzerland until his father dies and the family asks him to return to Limoges to run the porcelain business. His new wife tries to persuade him not to go, but he does. New responsibilities that include running the factory and army service in World War I dramatically change him as well as his marriage. Sexuality prohibits viewing by children. (In French; English subtitles.) **p**, Bruno Pésery, Jean-Louis Porchet, Gérard Ruey; **d**, Olivier Assayas; **cast**, Emmanuelle Béart, Charles Berling, Isabelle Huppert, Olivier Perrier, Dominique Reymond, André Marcon, Alexandra London, Julie Depardieu, Mia Hansen-Løve, Louis-Do de Lencquesaing, Valérie Bonneton; **w**, Assayas, Jacques Fieschi (based on the novel by Jacques Chardonne); **c**, Eric Gautier; **ed**, Luc Barnier; **prod d**, Frédéric Bénard, Gérard Marcireau, Jacques Mollon, Ivan Niclass, Katia Wyszkop; **spec eff**, Hans Frei.

Les Girls ★★★ 1957; U.S.; 114m; MGM; Color; Musical; Children: Acceptable; **DVD**; **VHS**. A somewhat rather involved story line is saved by a bevy of lively song and dance numbers in this spritely musical. The film opens with a successful act in Europe that involves Kelly and three fetching ladies, Elg, Kendall and Gaynor. After the act breaks up, Kendall, who is now married to an English lord, writes her autobiography, but when it is published, along with its scandalous accusations, Elg, who is now married to a French industrialist, files a libel suit that now involves Kelly and Gaynor, who are now married, as well as the contentious Kendall and Elg. Everyone appears in court before judge Daniell and all tell divergent tales about the group, very much in the fashion of **Rashomon**, 1950. None are lying, only telling the same story in different way and throughout these court proceedings we see flashbacks of acts based upon claims and counterclaims, along with some very good musical numbers. Kendall claimed in her book that she was engaged to Kelly and Elg destroyed that relationship in order to land Kelly for herself, and Kelly testifies that he never had interest in either of these ladies, but was always smitten with Gaynor. Further claims involve suicide attempts, but Kelly explains that the girls never tried to take their lives and were almost overcome when staying at one hotel where their room had a faulty gas heater and poor ventilation. All of the bickering and legal challenges come to nothing as everyone resolves their differences for a relatively happy ending. Songs include (all from the gifted Cole Porter) a witty satire on Marlon Brando and his appearance in **The Wild One**, 1954: "Why Am I So Gone (About That Gal)?" as well as "La Habanera," "Ca C'est L'Amour," "Ladies in Waiting," "Flower Song," "You're Just Too, Too," and "Les Girls." *Author's Note*: Director Cukor did not helm too many musicals, but he does a good job on this one, which was shot at the MGM studio, although stock shots and cleverly arranged sets made it appear that the film was shot on location in Europe. Kelly admitted to this author that "**Les Girls** was my last shot at MGM and the studio's last attempt to keep the standard musicals going that had been successful since the mid-1930s. The coming of Rock 'n' Roll ended that wonderful era." Cukor told this author that "I must admit that **Les Girls** gets a bit bogged down with all the courtroom action, but we made up for that with some great musical numbers, which is what it was all about. I also admit that those numbers were really supervised by the very talented Gene Kelly. He breathed more musicals to life at MGM than anyone else at that studio." Kelly did not initially handle the choreography for this film, that task undertaken by Jack Cole, but, when Cole fell ill, Kelly took over the chore. The ravishing and talented Kendall gleaned top marks for her role, but her promising career was prematurely ended when she suddenly died at age thirty-three of leukemia on September 6, 1959, two years after the release of this film. **p**, Sol C. Siegel; **d**, George Cukor; **cast**, Gene Kelly, Mitzi Gaynor, Kay Kendall, Taina Elg, Jacques Bergerac, Leslie Phillips, Henry Daniell, Patrick Macnee, Stephen Vercoe, Barrie Chase; **w**, John Patrick (based on a story by Vera Caspary); **c**, Robert Surtees (Metrocolor); **m**, Cole Porter; **art d**, Gene Allen, William A. Horning; **ed**, Ferris Webster; **set d**, Edwin B. Willis, Richard Pefferle; **spec eff**, Lee LeBlanc.

Les Misérables ★★★★★ 1935; U.S.; 108m; 20th Century Pictures/UA; B/W; Drama; Children: Unacceptable; **DVD**; **VHS**. March, one of filmdom's greatest actors, is at the top of his talent in his mesmerizing essay of Jean Valjean, the persecuted protagonist of Victor Hugo's memorable novel. He steals a loaf of bread to survive and is caught, convicted and unreasonably sent to prison for ten years. March achieves the impossible by escaping from an escape-proof prison and is no longer the compassionate and caring man he was before going behind bars. He is now mean-minded and hating his fellow man until he is taken in by kindly Hardwicke, a bishop in a rural French area. March promptly steals two priceless candlesticks from Hardwicke's residence, but when he is later picked up by local police and brought before Hardwicke, the clergyman tells officers that he has given the candlesticks to March. So taken by this act of mercy, March stays with Hardwicke and, through Hardwick's spiritual guidance, March regains his human sensibilities, returning to his original good nature. March moves on to another town, taking the candlesticks with him with Hardwicke's blessing (as good luck pieces March never intends to sell) and he becomes a successful businessman, and where he adopts a small girl after her mother dies. Using an alias, March's charitable and magnanimous actions earn him the respect of everyone and he is popularly elected the town mayor. Into his life comes Laughton, a police magistrate newly assigned to the area. He is a rigid martinet, who lives by the code of the law and has no compassion for his fellow man. March and Laughton clash over Laughton's severe policies, and Laughton becomes an avowed enemy of March when March intervenes to save Eldridge (March's real-life wife) from imprisonment. When March sees a man trapped beneath a heavy wagon, he rushes to save the man by using his brawny back to momentarily lift the wagon while the man is freed. Laughton sees this great act of heroism, but it only serves to jog his memory of a prison inmate he encountered many years earlier, one having the same kind of almost superhuman strength and he begins to probe into March's past. Laughton then identifies March as the fugitive Jean Valjean, but, before he makes an arrest, he is stunned when learning that another man has been arrested as that very same escaped convict and who is put on trial. March, however, cannot bear to see this man, who has no memory and is obviously mentally retarded, be convicted in his place and goes to the trial where he admits that he is, indeed, the wanted Jean Valjean. (In these scenes, March plays both the accused man and the real Jean Valjean.) He tells officials that he will await their decision and returns home, but, to protect his child, he again flees with his small daughter, taking his money and candlesticks to Paris, where he finds work as a gardener in a convent and where his daughter is raised and educated by the nuns, both of them living in a small cottage on the convent grounds. Years pass and the daughter becomes Drake, a beautiful, young woman, who falls in love with idealistic student Beal. Meanwhile, the dogged Laughton is assigned to a police post in Paris where he is now a powerful inspector and whose job it is to closely monitor young revolutionaries such as Beal. The revolutionaries finally revolt against oppressive conditions, establishing barricades and battling government troops. Drake then begs March to help Beal, who has been wounded during the fighting. March goes to the barricades and carries the wounded Beal through the sewers of Paris with Laughton trailing him. He manages to get Beal to the safety of his home, but Laughton is there to arrest him. Wanting Drake's happiness foremost, March agrees to surrender to Laughton and return to prison, but Laughton, who has been a fist for law enforcement all of his life, relaxes his uncompromising code, realizing the sacrifice March has made out of love, an emotion that he, Laughton, has never allowed to enter his cold heart. The policeman, instead of arresting March, goes to the River Seine, and, unable to enact his duties as an unimpassioned policeman, drops into the river, taking his own life, rather than ruining what is left in the life of his lifelong prey, March, Laughton's only and very grim act of compassion. Boleslawski, an almost forgotten director, helms this film with infinite loyalty to the Hugo story, meticulously following scene for scene the literate and taut script from Lipscomb and getting superb performances from the entire cast. (The film was nominated for an Oscar as Best Picture.) March is utterly captivating in one of his finest roles, which is accentuated and goaded by the despicable character so expertly enacted by the gifted Laughton. Every production detail in this masterpiece perfectly applies to that grim era in French history and where the lensing from genius cinematographer Toland (nominated for an Oscar as Best Cinematography) shows the photographic inventiveness he was to manifest in such films as **Wuthering Heights**, 1939, **The Grapes of Wrath**, 1940 and **Citizen Kane**, 1941. This story was filmed many times, including several crude silent productions, including a 1918 production by Fox, a French version in 1936, and remakes in 1952, 1978 (made-for-TV), 1982, 1995, 1998 and 2012 (with Hugh Jackman as Jan Valjean and Russell Crowe as the dogged police-

John Beal and Rochelle Hudson in *Les Misérables*, 1935.

man Javert; see this entry in the separate index for all 2012 reviews in this volume). *Author's Note*: March told this author that his role in **Les Miserables** "was one of the most demanding parts I ever played, both physically and emotionally. What was foremost in my mind then was that my character was really two persons, a normal and loving man and a hunted fugitive. That wanted criminal of his own past invades his life again and again like a thief in the night to steal his happiness. Fear, like a malignant disease, is always present, threatening his life, and the embodiment of that threat is, of course, the great Charles Laughton. When acting opposite of him, I had a keen sense of danger for no one can intimidate and menace like him and he made me a better actor in every scene with him because of his stunning performance." Zanuck, who personally supervised this film, told this author that he believed that the film was a great success due to March's outstanding enactment of the persecuted Jean Valjean, but added that "Laughton was the perfect counterpoint to March and, although I did not have the habit of going onto the set, I did for one scene and said to Laughton before the cameras rolled: 'You will most likely become the most hated man in the world with the part you are playing.' He replied: 'That bothers me not a bit. I know how to hate back!'" **p**, Darryl F. Zanuck; **d**, Richard Boleslawski; **cast**, Frederic March, Charles Laughton, Cedric Hardwicke, Rochelle Hudson, Florence Eldridge, John Beal, Frances Drake, Ferdinand Gottschalk, Jane Kerr, Marilyn Knowlden, Jessie Ralph, Mary Forbes, John Carradine; **w**, W.P. Lipscomb (based on the novel by Victor Hugo); **c**, Gregg Toland; **m**, Alfred Newman; **ed**, Barbara McLean; **art d**, Richard Day; **spec eff**, Ray Binger.

Les Misérables ★★★ 1952; U.S.; 105m; FOX; B/W; Drama; Children: Unacceptable; **DVD**. Rennie does a good job portraying the persecuted Jean Valjean in this remake of the Hugo classic. The film depicts this saga in three episodes, the first beginning when Rennie is imprisoned for a minor theft and his escape to find a haven with a kindly priest and where he regains his faith in mankind. The second episode is where Rennie establishes himself as a business and social leader in a small town and where he adopts a young girl (Paget), before he is hounded from his home by dogged police inspector Newton. The third episode shows Rennie living peacefully with Paget, who becomes emotionally involved with Mitchell, a young student who is wounded during a Paris uprising and is saved by Rennie, who carries him through the sewers of Paris to safety. Rennie is again confronted by the relentless Newton, but is spared when Newton forsakes his rigid principles and lets him go, taking his own life by drowning in the River Seine. Pantheon director Milestone helms this film with a sure hand and delivers this fine tale with many moving scenes. **p**, Fred Kohlmar; **d**, Lewis Milestone; **cast**, Michael Rennie, Debra Paget, Robert Newton,

Fredric March in *Les Miserables*, 1935.

Edmund Gwenn, Sylvia Sidney, Cameron Mitchell, Elsa Lanchester, James Robertson Justice, Joseph Wiseman, Rhys Williams, Florence Bates; **w**, Richard Murphy (based on the novel by Victor Hugo); **c**, Joseph LaShelle; **m**, Alex North; **ed**, Hugh S. Fowler; **art d**, Lyle Wheeler, J. Russell Spencer; **set d**, Thomas Little, Walter M. Scott; **spec eff**, Ray Kellogg.

Les Misérables ★★★ 1995; France; 175m; Canal+/Les Films 13/WB; Color; Drama; Children: Unacceptable (MPAA: R); **VHS**. Belmondo presents a powerful performance as a modern-day Jean Valjean after his father is imprisoned and killed in a break and his mother commits suicide. He joins the resistance fighters battling the Nazis occupying France during WWII and partakes in a robbery of a Vichy-controlled train. He witnesses the invasion at Normandy in 1944 and later manages a seaside resort in that area, taking in victims of Nazi oppression he has earlier known. A former Vichy police official, however, accuses Belmondo of robbing the Vichy train during the war and Belmondo is imprisoned, but a former resistance fighter battles for Belmondo in court and gets him acquitted. Belmondo returns to the seaside town and is elected mayor and where he presides over the wedding of a girl he shielded from the Nazis years earlier. (In French; English subtitles.) **p,d&w**, Claude Lelouch (based on the novel by Victor Hugo); **cast**, Jean-Paul Belmondo, Michel Boujenah, Jean Marais, Micheline Presle, Philippe Khorsand, Alessandra Martines, Clémentine Célarié, Salomé Lelouch, William Leymergie, Daniel Toscan du Plantier, **c**, Lelouch, Philippe Pavans de Ceccatty; **m**, Michel Legrand, Francis Lai, Didier Barbelivien, Erik Berchot, Philippe Servain; **ed**, Hélène de Luze; **prod d**, Jacques Bufnoir, Laurent Tesseyre; **art d**, Bufnoir; **set d**, Tesseyre; **spec eff**, Dominique Colladant, Georges Demétrau, Guy Monbillard.

Les Misérables ★★★ 1998; U.K./Germany/U.S.; 134m; Mandalay Entertainment/TriStar/COL/Sony Pictures; Color; Drama; Children: Unacceptable (MPAA: PG-13); **DVD**; **VHS**. The brawny Neeson captivates as the persecuted Jean Valjean in the Victor Hugo tale. He is shown being paroled after serving many years behind bars for stealing a loaf of bread. He seeks housing, but no one will rent a room to a former convict until a kindly bishop, Vaughan, takes him in and where Neeson promises him that he will begin a new and better life the next day. Neeson, however, yields to temptation and steals the bishop's silverware before fleeing. He is caught and returned by police to face Vaughan, who tells the officers that Neeson has stolen nothing and, in fact, that he has given the silverware to Neeson, and he further gives the former convict a pair of priceless silver candlesticks. The police depart, and Neeson is overwhelmed by Vaughan's forgiveness and compassion. When Vaughan reminds Neeson of his promise to turn over a

new leaf, Neeson vows that he will keep that promise. Using an alias, Neeson moves to a different town where he becomes a successful industrialist, and where he operates a large factory and treats his employees with kindness and consideration. He befriends Thurman, a single mother, who has turned to prostitution to support herself and when Rush, a police inspector, comes to arrest her, Neeson defends the woman, dismissing him. Rush becomes suspicious, rightly believing that Neeson is a former prison inmate he knew when he was a prison guard, and believes that Neeson is wanted for violating his parole. At that time, another man, McGlynn, a dim-witted person, is charged with being the wanted Jean Valjean. Neeson's conscience cannot allow McGlynn to be sent to prison in his stead and goes before the court to state that he is the man being sought. He awaits the verdict of the court by returning home, but, when he finds Thurman dying and promises to take care of her small daughter, he flees with the little girl, going to Paris and settling there, raising the girl until she grows to young adulthood as Danes. The beautiful young girl falls in love with Matheson, a student and an ardent social reformer, who joins revolutionaries. In the fight at the barricades, Rush is captured, but freed by Neeson, who carries the wounded Matheson through the sewers of Paris to the safety of his own home, but he is trailed by the indefatigable Rush, who finally arrests him. Neeson agrees to go back to prison, but Rush can no longer hound this good man and removes his shackles, placing them on himself as he goes to the Seine and where he commits suicide by drowning as punishment to himself for betraying his strict code of conduct. Neeson is finally a man free to seek happiness. **p**, James Gorman, Sarah Radclyffe, Caroline Hewitt; **d**, Bille August; **cast**, Liam Neeson, Geoffrey Rush, Uma Thurman, Claire Danes, Peter Vaughan, Hans Matheson, Kathleen Byron, Christopher Adamson, Tim Barlow, Timothy Bateson, John McGlynn, Veronika Bendová, David Birkin; **w**, Rafael Yglesias (based on the novel by Victor Hugo); **c**, Jörgen Persson; **m**, Basil Poledouris; **ed**, Janus Billeskov-Jansen; **prod d**, Anna Asp; **art d**, Peter Grant; **spec eff**, Richard Bain, Alex Hope, Jesper Kjölsrud.

Les Parents Terribles ★★★ 1950; France; 86m; Les Films Ariane/DisCina International; B/W; Drama; Children: Unacceptable; **VHS**. De Bray is a strong woman married to a weak and defeated man, André. She is an overly possessive mother and objects to the pending marriage of their handsome young son, Marais, to a beautiful young woman, Day. She has good reason to object because Day is her husband's mistress and he is desired by Marais' aunt, Dorziat. When the tangled web of romances comes to light, de Bray is unable to cope with losing the hold she has over her son and commits suicide. This somber but well-acted domestic drama shows how secret assignations dominate and destroy otherwise rational people. An inferior British remake, **Intimate Relations**, was made in 1953. (In French; English subtitles.) **p**, Francis Cosne, Alexandre Mnouchkine; **d&w**, Jean Cocteau (based on his play); **cast**, Jean Marais, Josette Day, Yvonne de Bray, Marcel André, Gabrielle Dorziat, Cocteau (narrator); **c**, Michel Kelber; **m**, Georges Auric; **ed**, Jacqueline Sadoul; **prod d**, Guy de Gastyne; **art d**, Christian Bérard; **set d**, Pierre Charron.

Let Freedom Ring ★★★ 1939; U.S.; 87m; MGM; B/W (Sepia Tones); Musical; Children: Acceptable; **VHS**. In this rousing musical Eddy is a recently graduated Harvard attorney, who returns to his small town in the West where he finds railroad tycoon Arnold taking over everything. Eddy sides with the settlers, but all of his legal battles are defeated by presiding judge Kibbee, who has been bought by Arnold. To combat the thugs employed by Arnold, Eddy disguises himself as "The Hornet," and abducts the local publisher and a printing press that he uses to produce leaflets that incite action against the oppressive Arnold. When Arnold's goons confront the masked crusader, Eddy is wounded, but he recovers and later convinces McLaglen, Arnold's right-hand man, to switch sides so that he now fights for the settlers and townsfolk, and this overturns Arnold's operation and sends the greedy railroad magnate to the hinterlands. The story line by the gifted Hecht infuses a lot of patriotism and a sense of the spirit of American individualism in an otherwise pedestrian tale, but it is a good excuse for the many good tunes that pepper the tale. Songs include: "I've Been Working on the Railroad" (traditional); "Funiculi, Funicula" (Luigi Denza); "Ten Thousand Cattle Straying" (Owen Wister); "Dusty Road" (Leon and Otis Rene); "Home Sweet Home" (Sir Henry R. Bishop, John Howard Payne), "Love Serenade" (Riccardo Drigo, Bob Wright, Chet Forrest); "When Irish Eyes Are Smiling" (Ernest R. Ball, Chauncey Olcott, George Graf Jr.); "Pat Sez He" (Foster Carling, Phil Ohman); "America" (Henry Carey, Rev. Samuel Francis Smith); and "Where Else But Here" (Sigmund Romberg, Edward Heyman). *Author's Note*: Hecht told this author that "musicals were really not my meat, but MGM wanted a patriotic songfest for their top tenor, Eddy, and I complied with what is basically a western soup stirred with a lot of musical morsels." **p**, Harry Rapf; **d**, Jack Conway; **cast**, Nelson Eddy, Virginia Bruce, Victor McLaglen, Lionel Barrymore, Edward Arnold, Guy Kibbee, Charles Butterworth, H.B. Warner, Raymond Walburn, George "Gabby" Hayes; **w**, Ben Hecht (based on his story); **c**, Sidney Wagner; **m**, Arthur Lange; **ed**, Fredrick Y. Smith; **art d**, Cedric Gibbons; **set d**, Edwin B. Willis; **spec eff**, Jack Hoffman.

Let 'Em Have It ★★★ 1935; U.S.; 97m; Reliance/Astor/UA; B/W; Crime Drama; Children: Unacceptable; **DVD**; **VHS**. Veteran director Wood provides an action-packed gangster film that captures the crime wave that swept the U.S. during the Great Depression. Arlen, Jones and Stephens train to be FBI agents and are then assigned to track down a vicious gang of kidnappers and bank robbers led by cold-blooded Cabot. Bruce, who is Stephens' girlfriend, and who comes from a rich family, is one of the kidnap victims and the agents eventually track down the culprits, dispatching them one by one as well as saving Bruce. Cabot, meanwhile, methodically commits his crimes without conscience or compassion and is utterly ruthless. When his gun moll, Compton, is captured by the police, he shrugs off the loss and immediately takes up with another lowlife lady, Pepper. Now on the run, Cabot goes to a plastic surgeon to have his appearance altered, but the threatened physician takes revenge when, after Cabot removes his bandages, he sees to his horror that the surgeon has branded his face with his initials. The drastic plastic surgery ploy avails Cabot of nothing and he is eventually tracked down and killed in a savage gunfight with agents. Unlike the roaring **G-Men**, 1935, starring James Cagney as an intrepid FBI agent, and was released about the same time (**G-Men** was released on May 4, 1935; **Let, Em Have It** was released on May 17, 1935), this is a more stylish tale about the Bureau and their efforts to quell the notorious Public Enemies of the early 1930s; its more expensive sets and production values boosted it from "B" programmer status to an "A" feature film. Cabot is the riveting character here and he is chilling as a cold-blooded killer. Although the flavor and conditions of the crime spree during this era is well captured, the facts involving the modus operandi of these notorious malefactors are fairy tales concocted by Hoover to improve FBI public relations. *Author's Note*: Cabot's role is an amalgamation of several notorious kidnappers and bank robbers of the 1930s, a portrait that was provided by the Bureau and, chiefly, its director, J. Edgar Hoover, including the many embellishments Hoover manufactured to aggrandize the FBI and his own reputation. The Cabot character presents elements of independent bank robbers and kidnappers John Dillinger (1903-1934?), Charles Arthur "Pretty Boy" Floyd (1904-1934) and the Barker Brothers. The plastic surgery sequence was concocted by Hoover and inserted into this film—he was at the time much feared by Hollywood and his word was law in any scripts dealing with the FBI—and this was based upon the Bureau's claim that Dillinger had had plastic surgery to alter his appearance in order to support its claim that the man who was shot and killed on the night of July 22, 1934, outside Chicago's Biograph Theater, was, indeed, Dillinger, although the dead man did not have Dillinger's appear-

Michael Rennie and Robert Newton in *Les Miserables*, 1952.

ance, a claim this author has always contended in that I obtained the autopsy of the dead man, which utterly refuted Bureau claims in that case. The autopsy revealed that the man killed that night had brown eyes and reliable records showed that Dillinger had blue eyes, as well as the absence of known scars and gun wounds on the corpse that Dillinger possessed, and the fact that the dead man had a terminal heart disease, which Dillinger did not. Following that shooting, the Bureau picked up an underworld physician (charging him with parole violation) and compelled him to give testimony about the so-called plastic surgery he performed on Dillinger, a testimony that ridiculed the Bureau's contention in this matter in that the doctor stated he inserted kangaroo tendons into Dillinger's cheeks to alter his appearance, an impossible medical application that was not challenged in that naive era when plastic surgery was in its formative stages. For more and reliable details on this case, as well as that dealing with Floyd and the Barker brothers (and their erstwhile ally Alvin Karpis, 1907-1979), see my books: *Citizen Hoover: A Critical Study of J. Edgar Hoover and His FBI* (Nelson-Hall, 1972); *Dillinger: Dead or Alive?* (Regnery, 1970); *The Dillinger Dossier* (December Press, 1983); *Bloodletters and Badmen: A Narrative Encyclopedia of American Criminals from the Pilgrims to the Present* (M. Evans, 1973; Barker Brothers: pages 43-51; Dillinger: pages 200-219; Charles Arthur Floyd: pages 242-246; Alvin Karpis: pages 350-355); and *The Great Pictorial History of World Crime*, Volume II (History, Inc., 2004; Dillinger: pages 1374-1422). **p**, Edward Small; **d**, Sam Wood; **cast**, Richard Arlen, Virginia Bruce, Alice Brady, Bruce Cabot, Harvey Stephens, Eric Linden, Joyce Compton, Gordon Jones, J. Farrell MacDonald, Wesley Barry, Barbara Pepper, Dennis O'Keefe; **w**, Joseph Moncure March, Elmer Harris; **c**, J. Peverell Marley, Robert Planck; **ed**, Grant Whytock; **art d**, John DuCasse Schulze.

Let Us Live ★★★ 1939; U.S.; 68m; COL; B/W; Crime Drama; Children: Unacceptable; **VHS**. Taut crime yarn has Fonda and Baxter, both cabdrivers, arrested and charged with robbery and murder. Though they are innocent (and this is clear from the beginning), they are nevertheless convicted and sentenced to death. As they await execution, O'Sullivan, who is engaged to Fonda, believes her boyfriend to be innocent and she prevails upon Bellamy, a pensive police lieutenant, to unofficially reopen the case and probe further. Through misadventures and some harrowing sequences, they finally pinpoint the real culprits, but only an hour before Fonda and Baxter are scheduled to walk the last mile to the electric chair. Brahm, who specialized in film noir productions, does a fine job in maintaining tension and anxiety in this fast-clipped entry, and Ballard's lensing provides effective moody and murky scenes to give a brooding atmosphere of doom. Fonda enacted similar roles in more sumptuously mounted films, **You Only Live Once**, 1937, **The**

Danny Glover and Mel Gibson in *Lethal Weapon*, 1987.

Long Night, 1947, and Hitchcock's semi-documentary production of **The Wrong Man**, 1957. **p**, William Perlberg; **d**, John Brahm; **cast**, Maureen O'Sullivan, Henry Fonda, Ralph Bellamy, Alan Baxter, Stanley Ridges, Henry Kolker, Peter Lynn, Harry Bernard, James Blaine, Ann Doran; **w**, Anthony Veiller, Allen Rivkin (based on a story by Joseph F. Dinneen); **c**, Lucien Ballard; **m**, Karol Rathaus; **ed**, Al Clark; **art d**, Lionel Banks.

Lethal Weapon ★★★ 1987; U.S.; 110m; WB; Color; Crime Drama; Children: Unacceptable (MPAA: R); **BD**; **DVD**; **VHS**. Plenty of action and countless firefights pepper this grim but compelling crime tale where L.A. cop Gibson is a bit touched and suicidal after years of being exposed to the worst underworld elements in the city, and, especially, after the death of his wife in a traffic accident. He is teamed with Glover, a reserved family man, and their new partnership presents many daunting challenges, especially Glover's unwillingness to follow his new partner into Gibson's personal Armageddon. (Gibson's character is really a version of the death-defying role he played in **Mad Max**, 1980, transplanted from futuristic Australia to present-day Los Angeles.) Glover is assigned to investigate a suicide of the daughter of an old friend and learns that the young woman overdosed on tainted drugs that led her to take her own life. While they probe the girl's past, they encounter a pimp she had known, and this leads them to a drug operation where a firefight ensues and Gibson saves Glover's life, which bonds the two. Gibson then learns that the girl's drugs had been dosed with drain cleaner, and he believes that the only person testifying in that death, Naff, a prostitute, may have given that dose to the girl to cause her death. When he and Glover go to interview Naff, they find her dead, her house blown up and Gibson, who has served in Vietnam and knows demolition, identifying a mercury switch at the site and concluding that the explosion was set by professionals. They brace Atkins, the father of the girl who committed suicide and he admits that he had been involved for two years in a widespread operation where drugs have been smuggled from Vietnam by a special operations team that served in that war. Gibson and Glover then learn that the operation is led by a former U.S. general, Ryan, and that his enforcer, Busey, is most likely behind the killings in an effort to silence those even remotely involved in the drug smuggling operations. Before Atkins can convey more information, he is killed by Busey and, after Gibson and Glover relentlessly pursue these culprits, Glover's daughter, Wolfe, is kidnapped and an attempt on Gibson's life is made, but he survives through wearing a bullet-proof vest. After several harrowing exploits, Glover and Gibson save Wolfe, and, in a final firefight, kill Busey, as well as smashing the drug operation. At the finale, Gibson spends Christmas with Glover and his family and he then gives Glover a bullet he intended to use in killing himself, signifying

that he intends to go on living through the friendship he has established with Glover (and to see the inevitable sequels to this strange but dynamic tale). **p**, Richard Donner, Joel Silver; **d**, Donner; **cast**, Mel Gibson, Danny Glover, Gary Busey, Mitchell Ryan, Tom Atkins, Darlene Love, Traci Wolfe, Jackie Swanson, Damon Hines, Ebonie Smith; **w**, Shane Black; **c**, Stephen Goldblatt (Technicolor); **m**, Eric Clapton, Michael Kamen; **ed**, Stuart Baird; **prod d**, J. Michael Riva; **set d**, Marvin March; **spec eff**, Chuck Gaspar, Joe Day.

Lethal Weapon 2 ★★★ 1989; U.S.; 114m; WB; Color; Crime Drama; Children: Unacceptable (MPAA: R); **BD**; **DVD**; **VHS**. Another action-loaded crime yarn has LAPD detectives Gibson and Glover protecting whistle-blower Pesci, a loudmouth accountant, who has exposed a criminal cartel smuggling gold into the U.S. from South Africa (not dissimilar to the character played by Charles Grodin in **Midnight Run**, 1988). Gibson believes Ackland, the Minister of Affairs for South Africa, is somehow involved in the smuggling operation and he begins harassing him while beginning a romance with Ackland's secretary, Kensit. Ackland finally has had enough from the probing cops and orders his top henchman, O'Connor, to kill them both and kidnap and murder squealer Pesci. Gibson and Glover narrowly avoid death and dispatch the killers while, at the same time, they rescue the bumbling Pesci. Ackland, however, manages to shoot and wound Gibson and then holds up his credentials, claiming diplomatic immunity. Glover ignores this protective protocol and fatally shoots Ackland before tending to Gibson just as a horde of LAPD officers arrive for the fadeout. The tale is told with good acting from Gibson and Glover, although Pesci is more annoying than humorous. **p**, Richard Donner, Joel Silver, Jennie Lew Tugend, Steve Perry; **d**, Donner; **cast**, Mel Gibson, Danny Glover, Joe Pesci, Joss Ackland, Derrick O'Connor, Patsy Kensit, Darlene Love, Traci Wolfe, Steve Kahan, Mark Rolston; **w**, Jeffrey Boam (based on a story by Shane Black, Warren Murphy, and characters created by Black); **c**, Stephen Goldblatt (Technicolor); **m**, Eric Clapton, Michael Kamen, David Sanborn; **ed**, Stuart Baird; **prod d**, J. Michael Riva; **art d**, Richard Berger, Virginia Randolph; **set d**, Marvin March; **spec eff**, Matt Sweeney.

Lethal Weapon 4 ★★★ 1998; U.S.; 127m; WB; Color; Crime Drama; Children: Unacceptable (MPAA: R); **BD**; **DVD**; **VHS**. This time Gibson and Glover are battling a Triad smuggling illegal Chinese into the U.S., and they also get involved with a power-mad Chinese general, who is holding several Triad members hostage until receiving a huge ransom. In their search for the culprits, Gibson and Glover are impeded rather than aided by Pesci, who is now an inept private detective, who has unearthed the alien smuggling ring. Numerous firefights ensue and bodies crash and crumple everywhere until the cops defeat the villains during a final battle at a seaside pier and where Gibson almost drowns but is saved at the last moment by Glover. Good action, but Pesci slows down the pace with a lot of cornball routines that don't work. **p**, Richard Donner, Joel Silver, Dan Cracchiolo, J. Mills Goodloe; **d**, Donner; **cast**, Mel Gibson, Danny Glover, Joe Pesci, Rene Russo, Chris Rock. Jet Li, Steve Kahan, Kim Chan, Darlene Love, Traci Wolfe; **w**, Channing Gibson (based on a story by Jonathan Lemkin, Alfred Gough, Miles Millar and characters created by Shane Black); **c**, Andrzej Bartkowiak (Technicolor); **m**, Eric Clapton, Michael Kamen, David Sanborn; **ed**, Dallas Puett, Kevin Stitt, Eric Strand, Frank J. Urioste; **prod d**, J. Michael Riva; **art d**, David Klassen, Richard Mays; **set d**, Lauri Gaffin; **spec eff**, Matt Sweeney, Jon Belyeu, Michael Fink, Bill Maher, Jerry Pooler.

Let's Dance ★★★ 1950; U.S.; 112m; PAR; Color; Musical; Children: Acceptable; **VHS**. Pleasant musical has Astaire and Hutton performing for the GIs during WWII, but Hutton breaks up the act when she tells Astaire that she has just married a soldier. It is suddenly four years later and Hutton is living in a Boston mansion wither her son, Moffett, and her stuffy mother-in-law, Watson. She is bored with the prim and proper

Brahmins and yearns for the old show business life, so she takes her son and gets a job at a nightclub where Astaire is working. Watson, enraged that her grandson is cavorting with such lowlife people, files a custody suit to have Moffett returned to her, but she is foiled when Hutton and Astaire resume their old romance and decide to marry. Not much of a plot, but the music is lively and Astaire's dancing is, as usual, a wonder to behold, all choreographed by Astaire's long-standing associate, Hermes Pan. Songs include (all from Frank Loesser): "Why Fight the Feeling," "Can't Stop Talking," "Oh, Them Dues," "Tunnel of Love," "Jack and the Beanstalk," "The Hyacinth," and "Piano Dance." **p**, Robert Fellows; **d**, Norman McLeod; **cast**, Betty Hutton, Fred Astaire, Roland Young, Ruth Warrick, Lucile Watson, Gregory Moffett, Barton MacLane, Shepperd Strudwick, Melville Cooper, Harold Huber, George Zucco; **w**, Allan Scott, Dane Lussier (based on the story "Little Boy Blue" by Maurice Zolotow); **c**, George Barnes (Technicolor); **m**, Robert Emmett Dolan; **ed**, Ellsworth Hoagland; **art d**, Hans Dreier, Roland Anderson; **set d**, Sam Comer, Ross Dowd; **spec eff**, Farciot Edouart, Gordon Jennings.

Let's Do It Again ★★★ 1975; U.S.; 110m; First Artists/WB; Color; Comedy; Children: Cautionary (MPAA: PG); **DVD**; **VHS**. This entertaining and lively sequel to **Uptown Saturday Night**, 1974, with the same two stars, sees Poitier as a quiet and often bewildered straight man, and Cosby, a fast-talking con artist. They're in Atlanta, Georgia, where Poitier delivers milk and Cosby is a factory worker. Both are members of "The Sons and Daughters of Shaka," a fraternal lodge, assigned to raise money for its old people's home. Cosby has a scheme for making big bucks for the home. He and Poitier will fix an upcoming middleweight title boxing match and bet the lodge's $18,000 building fund on the result and make out like bandits at 5 to 1 odds. They take their wives to New Orleans on vacation, waylay the scrawny contender, Walker, and Poitier hypnotizes him, assuring him he'll feel no pain in defeating the champion. Walker wins, the pals make a pile of money for their lodge, and plan next to fix a heavyweight fight between Muhammad Ali and Sammy Davis Jr.! **p**, Melville Tucker; **d**, Sidney Poitier; **cast**, Poitier, Bill Cosby, Calvin Lockhart, John Amos, Jimmie Walker, Denise Nicholas, Lee Chamberlin, Ossie Davis, Billy Eckstine, George Foreman; **w**, Richard Wesley (based on a story by Timothy March); **c**, Donald M. Morgan (Technicolor); **m**, Curtis Mayfield; **ed**, Pembroke J. Herring; **prod d**, Alfred Sweeney; **set d**, Ruby R. Levitt; **spec eff**, Charles Spurgeon.

Let's Kill Uncle ★★★ 1966; U.S.; 67m; PAR; Color; Horror; Children: Unacceptable (MPAA: PG); **DVD**; **VHS**. In this chilling entry, Cardi is a twelve-year-old boy whose father died and left him a fortune. He is summoned to a remote island by his uncle, Green, who intends to kill him and collect the inheritance. Green, a former British intelligence commander, has authored a book on how to kill. He employs sharks, poisoned mushrooms, tarantulas, fire, and hypnosis to try to do in the boy, but Cardi escapes it all with the help of a girl, Badham, who befriends him. The children go on the offense and it becomes a cat-and-mouse game between them and the lethal uncle, who finally tires, calls it a draw, and leaves the island. Violent subject matter prohibits viewing by children. **p&d**, William Castle; **cast**, Nigel Green, Mary Badham, Pat Cardi, Robert Pickering, Linda Lawson, Reff Sanchez, Nestor Paiva; **w**, Mark Rodgers (based on the novel by Rohan O'Grady); **c**, Harold Lipstein; **m**, Herman Stein; **ed**, Edwin H. Bryant; **art d**, Alexander Golitzen, William D. DeCinces; **set d**, Julia Heron, John McCarthy, Jr.

Let's Talk about Women ★★★ 1964; France/Italy; 108m; Concordia Compagnia Cinematografica/Embassy Pictures Corp.; B/W; Comedy; Children: Unacceptable; **DVD**. Nine intriguing episodes are presented in this film that profiles a handsome young Italian philanderer, Gassman, and his women, who include prostitutes and married women.

Bette Davis killing her lover in *The Letter*, 1940.

In one comic episode, Gassman visits a prostitute at her home and recognizes her husband as an old friend, who won't think of charging Gassman for his wife's services. In another, he is a rag dealer visiting a wealthy and promiscuous woman for her rag collection, but she offers herself instead and he declines, saying he prefers material goods. Sexual themes prohibit viewing by children. (In Italian; English subtitles.) Song: "Ogni Volta" (C.A. Ross, sung by Paul Anka). **p**, Mario Cecchi Gori; **d**, Ettore Scola; **cast**, Vittorio Gassman, Sylva Koscina, Eleonora Rossi Drago; Maria Fiore, Donatella Mauro, Mario Lucidi, Giovanna Ralli, Umberto D'Orsi, Mario Brega, Walter Chiari, **w**, Ruggero Maccari, Scola; **c**, Alessandro D'Eva; **m**, Armando Trovajoli; **ed**, Marcello Malvestito; **set d**, Arrigo Breschi.

The Letter ★★★★★ 1940; U.S.; 95m; WB; B/W; Crime Drama; Children: Unacceptable; **DVD**; **VHS**. Davis, under the careful direction of pantheon director Wyler, gives one of her most captivating performances in this stylish crime drama of deception, betrayal and murder. Set in exotic Malaya before WWII, Davis lives comfortably on a rubber plantation owned and operated by her devoted husband, Marshall. She, however, is not a faithful wife. While Marshall is away, Davis invites her lover, Newell, to visit her, but when she learns that he is breaking off the affair and begins to leave, the tempestuous Davis grabs a revolver and follows Newell to the porch of her home, and then fires every bullet from that revolver into Newell, killing him. The story she tells is in keeping with her sheltered and pampered life where all protect Davis, especially herself when she states to one and all that Newell, a family friend, stopped by to see her on a passing social visit, but then inexplicably tried to take advantage of a woman at home alone by sexually attacking her. She merely defended herself, Davis states, by killing the brute. When learning all of this, Marshall accepts her tale and immediately asks family friend Stephenson, an attorney, to defend Davis. While awaiting trial, Stephenson' assistant, Sen Yung, delivers a letter to the lawyer from Sondergaard, the Eurasian wife of Newell, stating that she is in the possession of a letter Davis sent to her husband, asking him to come and visit her, a damning letter that will prove that Davis was having an affair with Newell. Stephenson is told that he can buy back the letter for $10,000 and this he agrees to do, as does Marshall, who uses up all his cash to buy back the implicating missive, one which Marshall dismisses out of hand. Davis is acquitted and returns home to Marshall, but learns that Sondergaard will not release the letter unless Davis comes to pick it up. Marshall now demands to know the contents of that letter, and Davis confesses the whole story of her relationship with Newell and how she killed him when he rejected her. The astoundingly forgiving Marshall, however, tells Davis that he still loves her and will stay by her side no matter what comes. Financially ruined and emo-

Joan Fontaine and Louis Jourdan in *Letter from an Unknown Woman*, 1948.

tionally destroyed, Marshall cannot really be of any further use to Davis, and she resigns herself to the fate that awaits her at the hands of the vengeance-seeking Sondergaard by stepping into her garden and then walking beyond its walls where Sondergaard and a Malayan enforcer wait for her and where they stab Davis to death. Police arrive to arrest the killers as they try to flee and this is where this strange tale ends. Davis, in a reserved and measured enactment of her calculating and manipulative character, presents a performance of a cold-hearted and utterly selfish woman, who will destroy the lives of anyone challenging her pleasures and lifestyle. Only toward the end does she feel compassion for her long-suffering husband and accept the horrible retribution awaiting her. That performance was exacted from Davis through the patience and incisive helming of Wyler, who always took infinite care with his films, layering his scenes before the viewer as one might unfold the pages of a fine novel. Marshall, too, is superb as the betrayed spouse and Stephenson mesmerizes as the intelligent attorney, who risks his career to aid a friend, this, perhaps, being his finest role. *Author's Note*: Davis had nothing but admiration and respect for Wyler, but she often fought with him over scenes. In one scene, Wyler insisted that Davis deliver a telling line directly to Marshall when she says about her deceased love: "I still love the man I killed." Davis told this author that "Wyler wanted me to look right into his [Marshall's] eyes and deliver that line, but I told him that I should look away when I say that. He insisted I do it his way and I did, and I must admit that, when seeing the film, the scene worked well, but I still think my way would have been more effective. No one could ever change William Wyler's mind. When he saw a scene, well, that is the way it would be, through his eyes and no one else's." Wyler took a different approach, telling this author that "Bette Davis is a great actress, but she is not a director. The reason why she is so good in **The Letter** is that the role she is playing perfectly suited her own dynamic personality—a woman who must always be in control at all costs, and, in this story, even the lives of the men she loves most must be controlled by her or life is not worth living. Bette knew that I knew that about her and so she always went along with me. You see, I also knew that Bette was under the spell of a tragic actress, Jeanne Eagels, who had played the same role in **The Letter** [1929], and that Bette had modeled her acting style on Eagels, including the use of lot of Eagels' strange mannerisms and physical quirks—the abrupt turning of her head, the slow rolling of her eyes, jerking her hands as if to shed water from them, but much of those theatrics, I believe, were caused by the drugs that Eagels had been taking through most of her adult life. To tell you the truth, Eagels was a narcotic to Bette throughout her career." Eagels had had great success in playing Sadie Thompson in the Broadway production of W. Somerset Maugham's "Rain," and went on to appear in the 1929 film version of **The Letter** where Marshall also appears, but as the murdered lover.

She was by then addicted to heroin and her erratic performance in the 1929 film indicates the effects the drug had taken on her. In fact, she was often uncontrollable during the production, and, when she saw the final film, she exploded, ranting and raving as she ran to the screen in the screening room and clawed at it, telling Paramount executives that she hated the man playing her husband and demanded that he be replaced and that the film be shot all over again, and it was, with Reginald Owen playing her spouse. In the remake of the film, Eagels gave an even more expansive rendition of her lethal character, creating an utterly macabre presence on the screen that stunned Davis when she viewed that version before embarking on the Wyler production. It is obvious that Eagels is hallucinating in many of her scenes in that 1929 version, but, instead of creating abhorrence in Davis, that performance inspired Davis somehow and where Davis made Eagels her secret idol. Seven months after making the 1929 version of **The Letter**, Eagels was dead (on October 3, 1929) of an overdose of alcohol, prescription pills, and heroin, ending her life prematurely at the age of thirty-nine. **p&d**, William Wyler; **cast**, Bette Davis, Herbert Marshall, James Stephenson, Gale Sondergaard, Frieda Inescort, Bruce Lester, Cecil Kellaway, Sen Yung, Doris Lloyd, Willie Fung, David Bruce; **w**, Howard Koch (based on the story by W. Somerset Maugham); **c**, Tony Gaudio; **m**, Max Steiner; **ed**, George Amy, Warren Low; **art d**, Carl Jules Weyl.

Letter from an Unknown Woman ★★★ 1948; U.S.; 86m; UNIV; B/W; Drama; Children: Unacceptable; **DVD**; **VHS**. Jourdan is a successful concert pianist, who receives a letter from a woman dying of typhus, a woman he cannot recall, but does with great sorrow as the story unfolds in flashback. He meets Fontaine when he is working hard to become a classic pianist and where they are neighbors. They develop a deep friendship and then love blossoms, but Jourdan leaves to go on his first concert tour, promising Fontaine that he will return to be with her. He goes on to enjoy a great success, but forgets about Fontaine, who, now pregnant with his child, marries another man. Fontaine meets Jourdan again, but he has no recollection of her and he again moves out of her life, until he receives that last, poignant and haunting missive. Fontaine is exceptional in her role as the discarded woman, and the handsome Jourdan, who invariably played blackguards and ne'er-do-wells to perfection, reprises with some compassion and remorse that unsavory character in this memorable entry. **p**, John Houseman, William Dozier; **d**, Max Ophuls; **cast**, Joan Fontaine, Louis Jourdan, Mady Christians, Marcel Journet, Art Smith, Howard Freeman, Betty Blythe, Ilka Grüning, Rex Lease, Celia Lovsky; **w**, Howard Koch (based on the novel *Brief Einer Unbekannten* by Stefan Zweig); **c**, Franz Planer; **m**, Daniele Amfitheatrof; **ed**, Ted J. Kent; **art d**, Alexander Golitzen; **set d**, Russell A. Gausman, Ruby R. Levitt.

Letter to Brezhnev ★★★ 1986; U.K.; 94m; Channel Four Films/Circle Films; Color; Drama; Children: Unacceptable (MPAA: R); **VHS**. In this engrossing tale, two Soviet sailors, Molina and Firth, go ashore in Liverpool to spend a night on the town. Firth speaks enough English to hook them up with two young women, Pigg and Clarke, after they meet at a dockside pub. Clarke is a frozen chicken packer, but Pigg is out of work. Molina and Clarke enjoy an evening in bed together and nothing more than sex is expected. Firth and Pigg, however, fall in love, but the night ends and the boys must leave with their ship. Pigg can't forget Firth so she writes a letter to Soviet leader Leonid Brezhnev, asking him to reunite her with her lover. He surprisingly replies by sending to her a ticket to Moscow and she is uncertain about going there, but she takes the plunge after realizing that, unless she goes to Firth it is unlikely he can come to her. Sexual scenes prohibit viewing by children. **p**, Janet Goddard; **d**, Chris Bernard; **cast**, Alfred Molina, Peter Firth, Tracy Marshak-Nash, Alexandra Pigg, Margi Clarke, Susan Dempsey, Ted Wood, Carl Chase, Sharon Power, Robbie Dee; **w**, Frank Clarke; **c**, Bruce McGowan; **m**, Alan Gill; **ed**, Lesley Walker; **prod d**, Lez Brotherston, Nick Englefield, Jonathan Swain; **spec eff**, John Swinnerton.

A Letter to Three Wives ★★★★ 1949; U.S.; 103m; FOX; B/W; Drama; Children: Acceptable; **DVD**; **VHS**. Well-crafted domestic drama sees the marital lives of three women—Darnell, Sothern and Crain—emotionally disrupted when these ladies are about to embark upon a boat excursion with children along the Hudson River and each receives a letter from another woman that threatens all their marriages. The sender of that letter is a woman, Addie Ross, never shown on the screen, but heard through the voice of Holm, the home-wrecker. All three women recall their marriages and how Ross affected them, each of them believing that their husband has run off with the husband-stealer, and we see in episodic flashbacks those marriages as they blossom and develop. The first is Crain, who marries Lynn, a member of High Society and where she believes she will never fit into his Brahmin class, appearing at a country club affair with him and wearing an out-of-date dress that embarrasses her and causes her to overdrink and appear to be foolish. She hears the name of Addie Ross that night and Lynn states that he has known her and will never forget her. Adding to Crain's fears is that Lynn has left that night on a business trip and will be away for some time. Sothern is the next wife to be profiled in flashback, her story beginning with her marriage to schoolteacher Kirk Douglas and where Sothern writes a radio show that produces for them more income than the lowly pay Douglas receives. He is cynical of such commercial ventures and when the sponsor of the show and his wife appears at a dinner party, the idealistic Douglas sneeringly demeans the show as basically worthless literary content that offers no enhancing knowledge for listeners. He further jeopardizes Sothern's job by stating that his intelligent wife has been corrupted by rampant radio commercialism to produce "drooling pap" to prove to the unwashed millions of listeners that "a deodorant can bring happiness, a mouthwash guarantee success, and a laxative attract romance...Use our product or you will lose your husband, your job and die! Use our product and we'll make you rich, we'll make you famous!" (Douglas' incisive indictment would never be profiled in today's mainstream movies, but films at the time of this production were above and directly combated such commercialism that permeated the competitive radio and infant TV airways at that time, and still do to this day.) Sothern's job now threatens her marriage and she comes to believe that Ross, the "other woman" has definitely stolen her husband. The third wife, Darnell, a beautiful brunette with a materialistic streak, has come from the wrong side of the tracks to marry her boss, Paul Douglas. She has kept herself aloof from him until he agrees to slip the ring on her finger and she then proceeds to demand all the luxuries of life, which establishes an acrimonious relationship between them, until they are constantly bickering and telling each other that they have no love for one another. In the final showdown, Crain and Sothern find, to their great relief, that their husbands are loyal to them and it is Darnell who discovers that her husband, Paul Douglas, has run off with Addie Ross. The kind and gentle Paul Douglas, however, cannot leave Darnell and returns to her side to admit that he had thought to leave her, but that he loves her in spite of her greedy ways, which sobers Darnell and sets her on a loving course with her husband. The acting from the six principals is outstanding, and Mankiewicz's direction is exceptional in carefully unfolding this episodic drama. *Author's Note*: Fox chief Zanuck did not want Mankiewicz to direct this film as he had had many run-ins with him, telling this author that "Joe was always a hardhead. You couldn't tell him anything. I originally wanted Ernst Lubitsch to direct that picture, but he died and I was stuck with Joe." The story was first published in *Cosmopolitan Magazine* in August 1945 under the title of "One of Our Hearts," and its author, Klempner, expanded the tale in an overblown novel, *A Letter to Five Wives* and where Zanuck bought the film rights in 1946. Zanuck conferred with the gifted Lubitsch, but the director died in 1947, two years before the film was finally produced. Zanuck, who by then had reluctantly assigned the truculent Mankiewicz to the production, added in our conversation that "the original story had four wives, but I called Joe and told him that he had one wife too many, so we cut down the story to show three wives

Linda Darnell, Ann Sothern and Jeanne Crain in *A Letter to Three Wives*, 1949.

all thinking they are about to lose their husbands." Zanuck had such apprehensions about Mankiewicz that he told the film's producer, Siegel, that "if he gets a hit with this he'll be unlivable!" Mankiewicz did get a hit with **A Letter to Three Wives** and he did become "unlivable." Holm was not initially slated for her off-screen role in this film as the insidious husband-stealer, and it was, according to her statements to this author "a brilliant bit of business by Mankiewicz to add narration by the actual home-wrecker. When he first called me about doing that part, he said: 'How would you like to be a character never seen on-screen in a movie?' I had no idea what he was talking about and flippantly replied: 'Oh, that's a wonderful idea, because that way I will not have to show my wooden leg.'" Holm's inclusion, and her sweet voice, laced in the acids of jealousy, envy and hate, presented just the right amount of titillating and taunting conflict to heighten the anxieties and fears of the three wives. "Joe went right to the top after making that picture," Zanuck told this author, "as I knew he would, and sure enough, he was hell on wheels every time we talked about another production. He had his way with **Cleopatra** [1963] while I was away and he almost wrecked a studio that had taken me years and years to carefully build. Was he a great director and writer? Sure, but so were dozens of others. Did he think that Fox had more money than the U.S. Mint when he made **Cleopatra**? Yes, and he just about gutted the studio on that money-draining epic. Why? Because he just didn't give a damn about finance and had no business sense whatsoever. Added to that, he was an obnoxious jerk. Just about everyone in Hollywood would rather punch him in the nose than shake his hand." **p**, Sol C. Siegel; **d**, Joseph L. Mankiewicz; **cast**, Jeanne Crain, Linda Darnell, Ann Sothern, Kirk Douglas, Barbara Lawrence, Jeffrey Lynn, Connie Gilchrist, Florence Bates, Hobart Cavanaugh, Celeste Holm, Mae Marsh, Thelma Ritter; **w**, Mankiewicz (based on an adaptation by Vera Caspary of the novel by John Klempner); **c**, Arthur Miller; **m**, Alfred Newman; **ed**, J. Watson Webb, Jr.; **art d**, Lyle Wheeler, J. Russell Spencer; **set d**, Thomas Little, Walter M. Scott; **spec eff**, Fred Sersen.

Letters from Iwo Jima ★★★★ 2006; U.S.; 141m; DreamWorks; Malpaso/WB; Color; War Drama; Children: Unacceptable (MPAA: R); **BD**; **DVD**. Intriguing war epic that shows the Japanese POV about the battle of Iwo Jima (February 19-March 26, 1945) during WWII. Eastwood, who directed and produced this film at the same time he helmed and produced **Flags of Our Fathers**, 2006, which presents the same battle from the American POV (made simultaneously to save money and capture the Japanese audience as well as American viewers). The film begins when the Japanese garrison starts to dig intricate underground defense positions, a labyrinth of interconnecting tunnels that extend from the island's highest point, Mount Suribachi, to the other

James J. Murakami; **set d**, Gary Fettis; **spec eff**, Mike Edmonson, Steven Riley.

Christopher Egan in *Letters to Juliet*, 2010.

Letters from My Windmill ★★★ 1955; France; 160m; Eminente Films/Tohan Pictures Co.; B/W; Drama; Children: Unacceptable; **DVD**; **VHS**. This entertaining episodic film presents three stories by the 19th-century Gallic writer Daudet. Crouzet plays the writer, who goes to an abandoned windmill in Provence to write his tales. The first story, "The Three Low Masses," is about a Catholic priest, Vilbert, who conducts a Mass that is stolen by the Devil. The second story, "The Elixir of Father Gaucher," involves a monk, Rellys, who does the Lord's work with money produced from distilling liquor. The final story, "The Secret of Master Comille," is about a poor miller, Delmont, who almost kills himself while trying to prove that a mythical client he concocted is actually real. (In French; English subtitles.) **p,d&w**, Marcel Pagnol (based on stories by Alphonse Daudet); **cast**, Roger Crouzet, Henri Vilbert, Antonin Fabre, Rellys, Delmont, Fernand Sardou, Robert Vattier, Pierrette Bruno, Serge Davin, Christian Lude, Henri Arius; **c**, Willy Faktorovitch; **m**, Henri Tomasi; **ed**, Monique Lacombe; **prod d**, Robert Giordani, Jean Mandaroux.

Letters to Juliet ★★★ 2010; U.S.; 105m; Summit Entertainment; Color; Drama/Romance; Children: Unacceptable (MPAA: PG); **BD**; **DVD**. An American girl, Seyfried, a *New Yorker* magazine researcher on vacation in Verona, Italy, sees a wall beneath a balcony in a courtyard with thousands of letters written to Shakespeare's Juliet, asking for advice on love, which are answered by the "secretaries of Juliet." One letter particularly interests her and she goes on a quest to find the lovers concerned in it. The letter was written and left there in 1957 by a British woman, Redgrave, who now, fifty years later, asks help in finding a young man she loved, but left behind when she was a teenager. Traveling with Seyfried, but usually away looking for wine and truffles for his New York restaurant, is her fiancé, Bernal. Traveling with Redgrave is her handsome young grandson, Egan, who joins Seyfried and Redgrave on a search for the long-lost lover, Nero. Seyfried and Redgrave become great friends, and Seyfried begins to think Egan might be the love of her life and not Bernal. Redgrave and Nero are, of course, reunited at the end of the film and we can expect Seyfried and Egan to marry. The story is based on an actual wall with such love letters in Verona, and it is beautifully filmed to show the lush Italian countryside, and with attractive actors who bring warmth and charm to their roles. Casting luminous Redgrave and agelessly handsome Nero as her lost love was inspired, since they co-starred as Guinevere and Lancelot in **Camelot**, the 1967 film version of the stage musical, and after having a child together, some years later married. Gutter language prohibits viewing by children. **p**, Ellen Barkin, Mark Canton, Eric Feig, Caroline Kaplan, Patrick Wachsberger; **d**, Gary Winick; **cast**, Amanda Seyfried, Vanessa Redgrave, Christopher Egan, Gael García Bernal, Franco Nero, Marcia DeBonis, Giordano Formenti, Lydia Biondi, Luisa Ranieri, Marina Massironi; **w**, Jose Rivera, Tim Sullivan; **c**, Marco Pontecorvo; **m**, Andrea Guerra; **ed**, Bill Pankow; **prod d**, Stuart Wurtzel; **art d**, Stefano Maria Ortolani, Saverio Sammali; **set d**, Alessandra Querzola; **spec eff**, Andrea Papaleo, Justin Ball, Sarah Barber.

Libel ★★★ 1959; U.K.; 100m; De Grunwald Productions/MGM; B/W; Drama; Children: Cautionary; **VHS**. Compelling tale has Bogarde as a British wealthy peer of the realm. Massie, a Canadian airline pilot, sees Bogarde on TV and identifies him as a fellow POW inmate at a German concentration camp during WWII. Massie publicly accuses Bogarde of being an imposter, claiming that Bogarde is an actor, who has taken over the real life of the British lord. Bogarde, at the insistence of his loyal wife, de Havilland, hires powerful attorney Morley to file a libel suit against Massie and a trial ensues where Hyde-White defends Massie and his damaging claims. Bogarde appears in court as a confused, often dazed witness where he sometimes stutters and demonstrates a failing

lower lying areas of the isle. The Japanese High Command has decreed that the island must be held at all costs to prevent U.S. forces from using Iwo Jima's two airfields to launch air attacks against the main islands of Japan. Ninomiya, a private, is one of a few soldiers who grudgingly begin digging the underground tunnels while the various commanders on the island have divergent military perspectives on how to resist the expected U.S. invasion and where horseman Ihara recalls his pleasant experiences in the U.S., where he established friendly relationships with U.S. military officers, now believing that he will have to fight these very former friends. When the attack finally comes, all of the Japanese ground installations are destroyed and the defenders take to their underground shelters and hidden gun positions like gophers. They unleash a devastating counterattack after U.S. Marines land on the beaches, momentarily halting them, but the Japanese defenders are systematically killed in small groups as the Marines slowly advance to take one position after another. Ihara is wounded and orders his men to retreat to another, safer area and when they depart, he commits suicide. Ninomiya is a member of forces defending Mount Suribachi (a dormant volcano), and when American forces overwhelm the defenders in this area, he and others move through tunnels to other Japanese defensive positions, but these areas, too, are slowly destroyed by the invaders. The fanatical Japanese commanders then demand of their troops that they either blindly attack the Americans in doomed Banzai assaults, or commit Hari-kari (Seppuku), rather than surrender, and most of the soldiers blindly obey, grimly charging into blazing machine-gun fire or painfully killing themselves by exploding grenades against their bodies. Ninomiya, however, has a desire to live, and finds ways to escape the mindless mass suicides, surviving the last firefights of the battle to secretly bury the Japanese commander before surrendering to the Americans. The film is grim and brutal and where the military mentality of that era is shown in all of its savage fury. In an epilogue, Japanese excavators on the island many years following the war unearth buried bags that contain thousands of poignant farewell letters written by the garrison troops to their families before they met their violent and horrible deaths. Out of the 22,000 Japanese troops defending the island, less than 200 survived the Battle of Iwo Jima and where more than 7,000 U.S. troops were killed and many thousands more wounded. (In Japanese; English subtitles.) **p**, Steven Spielberg, Clint Eastwood, Robert Lorenz, Tim Moore, Paul Haggis; **d**, Eastwood; **cast**, Ken Watanabe, Kazunari Ninomiya, Tsuyoshi Ihara, Ryo Kase, Shidou Nakamura, Hiroshi Watanabe, Takumi Bando, Yuki Matsuzaki, Takashi Yamaguchi; **w**, Iris Yamashita, Haggis (based on the book *Picture Letters from Commander in Chief* by Tadamichi Kuribayashi, Tsuyoko Yoshido); **c**, Tom Stern; **m**, Kyle Eastwood, Michael Stevens; **ed**, Joel Cox, Gary D. Roach; **prod d**, Henry Bumstead, memory that cannot recall all of the events occurring during his time at the concentration camp. The jury is almost as confused as Bogarde when one witness after another either reaffirms his true identity or challenges that identity. Finally, one witness appears who is Bogarde's exact double (also played by Bogarde) and where this witness has been a resident at a lunatic asylum. His appearance jogs Bogarde's memory into recalling how this doppelgänger tried to take his identity in that camp and subsequently assume his life when returning to England, and, to achieve that end, attacked him and how Bogarde defended himself by beating the man so badly that he lost his senses. The film ends with Bogarde, the real Lord, vindicated and Massie convicted of libel. This film is loosely based upon a real-life case occurring in France several centuries earlier, and which was profiled in **The Return of Martin Guerre**, 1983. The film **Sommersby**, 1993, takes a leaf from the story line of this film. **p**, Anatole de Grunwald; **d**, Anthony Asquith; **cast**, Dirk Bogarde, Olivia de Havilland, Paul Massie, Robert Morley, Wilfrid Hyde-White, Anthony Dawson, Richard Wattis, Richard Dimbleby, Martin Miller, Millicent Martin, Bill Shine, Ivan Samson, Sebastian Saville, Gordon Stern, Josephine Middleton; **w**, De Grunwald, Karl Tunberg (based on a play by Edward Wooll); **c**, Robert Krasker; **m**, Benjamin Frankel; **ed**, Frank Clarke; **art d**, Paul Sheriff.

Libeled Lady ★★★★ 1936; U.S.; 98m; MGM; B/W; Comedy; Children: Acceptable; **DVD**; **VHS**. A delightful farce with a lot of twists and turns has Tracy as a forceful managing editor of a newspaper, who will do just about anything to get a scoop and where he serves a daily dish of sensationalism to his readers. He gets into big trouble when he prints a false story about Loy that claims she has stolen the affections of a British lord from that peer's wife. Loy promptly sues Tracy and his paper for every penny in their coffers. Tracy thinks to turn the tables on Loy through an elaborate scheme where he hires Powell, a former employee, to marry his girlfriend Harlow whom Tracy has left at the altar so many times that she cannot count the jilts. Powell will then woo Loy and, in the process, and, after Tracy and his newshounds find Powell with Loy, Harlow will then sue Loy for alienation of affections and force Loy to drop her $5 million suit while she drops her own suit. Powell, a clever attorney, however, goes about enacting this ridiculous scheme with his own ambitions in mind. He boards a luxury liner on which Loy and her tycoon father Connolly are traveling and he attempts to ingratiate himself with Loy, who thinks he is nothing much more than a pest and fortune-hunter. Powell, however, develops a friendship with her father, Connolly, after he bones up on fishing techniques and passes himself off as a fellow angler. After they return from their excursion, Powell goes on a fishing outing with Loy and Connolly and gets lost on the river, bumbling about while attempting to catch any kind of fish and falls into the waters only to land a huge fish and where he becomes Connolly's idol as a great fisherman as Connolly has been attempting to land that very fish for years. (This is one of the many hilarious scenes in this mirthful romp.) Powell and Loy then fall in love and when Loy learns that he is married to Harlow, she tests his love for her by proposing that they wed. Powell doesn't hesitate for a moment and they go to the altar, but Harlow is now incensed that she has been charmed by the engaging Powell and storms into his life, charging him with bigamy, even though Loy has by this time, to Tracy's relief, dropped her suit. Powell, however, has the right answer ready, telling Harlow that their so-called marriage was illegal in that the person who married them did not have the legal right to do so as Harlow had not gotten a divorce from a long-ago spouse. Harlow, however, proves that she, indeed, did get that divorce and now Powell exposes Tracy's scheme and where Tracy, to save face with Harlow, finally promises to marry her. Harlow agrees to divorce Powell so his marriage to Loy will remain legal. All's well that ends well, at least, for the moment when this wild film ends. *Author's Note*: Powell and Harlow were carrying on a torrid romance during the production of this film and they were engaged to be married, but Harlow died prematurely eight months after this film was released on June 7,

Myrna Loy, William Powell, Spencer Tracy and Jean Harlow in *Libeled Lady,* **1936.**

1937 (from uremic poisoning brought on by nephritis). **p**, Lawrence Weingarten; **d**, Jack Conway; **cast**, William Powell, Myrna Loy, Jean Harlow, Spencer Tracy, Walter Connolly, Charley Grapewin, Cora Witherspoon, E.E. Clive, Bobs Watson, Hattie McDaniel, Jack Mulhall, Dennis O'Keefe; **w**, Maurine Watkins, Howard Emmett Rogers, George Oppenheimer (based on a story by Wallace Sullivan); **c**, Norbert Brodine; **m**, William Axt; **ed**, Fredrick Y. Smith; **art d**, Cedric Gibbons.

Licence to Kill ★★★ 1989; U.K./U.S.; 133m; Danjag/MGM-UA; Color; Spy Drama; Children: Unacceptable (MPAA: R); **BD**; **DVD**; **VHS**. In the sixteenth entry in the James Bond franchise, Her Majesty's Secret Service Agent 007, Dalton, in his second and final appearance as Bond, is into his most violent adventure, focusing less on humor and sex and more on action. His mission is to stop an evil cocaine drug lord, Davi, and his lieutenant, Zerbe. The film opens with Dalton parachuting into an outdoor wedding. It switches then to Key West, Florida, where Dalton begins a very serious pursuit of Davi and his drug dealing. In one violent scene, Bond's friend, Hedison, loses a leg to a shark, and, in another, a rival for Davi's love has his heart cut out. Bond gets help from two beautiful women, Lowell and Soto. Action follows in the air, on the land, and on and under the sea until Bond finally gets his man in a wild chase. The action is almost non-stop in this thriller, but its excessive violence, sexuality, and drug content prohibit viewing by children. **p**, Albert R. Broccoli, Michael G. Wilson; **d**, John Glen; **cast**, Timothy Dalton, Carey Lowell, Robert Davi, Talisa Soto, Anthony Zerbe, Frank McRae, David Hedison, Wayne Newton, Benicio Del Toro, Pedro Armendariz, Priscilla Barnes; **w**, Wilson, Richard Maibaum (based on characters created by Ian Fleming); **c**, Alec Mills; **m**, Michael Kamen; **ed**, John Grover; **prod d**, Peter Lamont; **art d**, Michael Lamont, Dennis Bosher; **set d**, Michael Ford; **spec eff**, Chris and Neil Corbould, Laurencio Cordero, Sergio Jara, John Richardson.

Lies My Father Told Me ★★★ 1975; Canada; 102m; Drama; Children: Cautionary (MPAA: PG); **VHS**. This poignant and emotionally moving film is set in Montreal in the 1920s, where Lynas is an open-hearted seven-year-old boy living in a small apartment with his father, Birman, mother, Lightstone, and Lightstones' father, Yadin. The boy is neglected by his parents, his father too preoccupied by his pursuit of modern living and involving himself in get-rich-quick schemes. Lynas finds love and comfort only from his grandfather, Yadin, accompanying the old man on Sundays when Yadin travels about the city with an old wagon drawn by an ailing horse, and collects rags and scrap iron. Along his melancholy route, Yadin tells Lynas colorful stories that are drawn upon Jewish folk tales that enthrall and inspire the boy, and through his relationship with his grandfather, he forms a deep and lasting love he does not share

Paul Newman in *The Life and Times of Judge Roy Bean*, 1972.

with his parents. His father, Birman, denigrates Yadin and tells his son that his father-in-law's tales are nothing but hogwash and he should not listen to them, since they are not based upon orthodox Jewish beliefs. Birman's statements are those that constitute the "lies" told to his son, who continues to believe in the old man and his tales, carrying these comforting memories with him into his adulthood. **p**, Anthony Bedrich, Harry Gulkin; **d**, Ján Kadár; **cast**, Yossi Yadin, Len Birman, Marilyn Lightstone, Jeffrey Lynas, Ted Allan, Henry Gamer, Barbara Chilcott, Carol Lazare, Mignon Elkins, Cleo Paskal; **w**, Ted Allan (based on his story); **c**, Paul Van der Linden; **m**, Sol Kaplan; **ed**, Edward Beyer, Richard Marks; **prod d**, Michel Proulx; **art d**, François Barbeau.

The Lieutenant Wore Skirts ★★★ 1956; U.S.; 98m; FOX; Color; Comedy; Children: Acceptable. A lot of laughs are provided by Ewell, who is a former war hero, and now a U.S. Air Force reservist. He is called back to service, but rejected because of a bad knee. His beautiful young wife, North, however, is a former WAC (Women's Army Corps), who is called back into the service and ordered to serve in Hawaii. Ewell follows her there and becomes an army husband, cooking, washing dishes, cleaning the house, and playing bridge with army wives. He tires of his submissive role and comes up with a scheme to convince the base psychiatrist, Platt, that North is having a nervous breakdown, so she can be cashiered and return to him as his day-to-day wife. The plan fails, but nature solves his problem when his wife becomes pregnant. Moreno is also very funny as a dumb brunette Ewell tries not to become attracted to, but who nevertheless creates considerable mayhem for his marriage. Song: "Rock Around the Island" (Ken Darby). **p**, Buddy Adler; **d**, Frank Tashlin; **cast**, Tom Ewell, Sheree North, Rita Moreno, Rick Jason, Les Tremayne, Alice Reinheart, Gregory Walcott, Jean Willes, Edward Platt, Jacqueline Fontaine; **w**, Tashlin, Albert Beich (based on a story by Beich); **c**, Leo Tover; **m**, Cyril J. Mockridge; **ed**, James B. Clark; **art d**, Lyle R. Wheeler, Leland Fuller.

Life, Above All ★★★ 2011; South Africa/Germany; 100m; Dreamer Joint Venture Filmproduction/Sony; Color; Drama; Children: Unacceptable (MPAA: PG-13); **BD, DVD**. A grim but very moving drama about fear and superstition involves AIDS in South Africa. Manyaka, a thirteen-year-old girl living in a village near Johannesburg, tries to cope with the disease's effects on her family including her baby sister's death, her stepfather's alcoholism, her mother's declining health, and her orphaned best friend's prostitution. Not named as AIDS but called "influenza," "this other thing," or "the bug," it is treated by witchcraft or a quack, who gives out herbal supplements, but nothing helps stem the spread of the deadly plague. Sexual content and morose and some violent scenes prohibit viewing by children. (In Sotho/Sepedi; English

subtitles.) **p**, Oliver Stoltz, Greig Buckle, Thomas Reisser; **d**, Oliver Schmitz; **cast**, Khomotso Manyaka, Keaobaka Makanyane, Lerato Mvelase, Harriet Lenabe (Harriet Manamela), Aubrey Poolo, Tinah Mnumzana, Mapaseka Mathebe, Thato Kgaladi, Kgomotso Ditshweni, Rami Chuene; **w**, Dennis Foon (based on the novel *Chanda's Secrets* by Allan Stratton); **c**, Bernhard Jasper; **m**, Ali N. Askin, Ian Osrin; **ed**, Dirk Grau; **art d**, Tracy Perkins, Christiane Rothe; **set d**, Jean-Jacques Chaboissier, Nazo Maloy (Nazo Maloyi), Aime Motomola; **spec eff**, Gerhard van der Heever, Janek Zabielski.

The Life and Loves of Beethoven ★★★ 1937; France; 116m; General Productions/World Pictures Corporation; B/W; Biographical Drama; Children: Cautionary; **DVD**; **VHS**. This sensitive and loving portrait of Ludwig van Beethoven (1770-1827) is wonderfully directed by Gance and where Baur gives a powerful performance of the great composer. The story begins with a child dying and a mother weeping and where Baur sits down at a piano and plays in memory of that lost child. Two sisters, Ducaux and Holt, are in love with Baur. He is engaged to Ducaux, but he has truly loved Holt for many years, his affection remaining unrequited when Holt marries Rozenberg, a count, even though Holt later regrets marrying the aristocrat as her love for Baur never abates. Baur is crushed when Ducaux dies and, slowly becoming deaf, thinks about suicide, but he clings to life through his musical inspirations and moves into an old mill where he composes most of his greatest masterworks. As he ages, Baur, despite his devotion to a selfish and thieving nephew, sinks into poverty and loneliness, although his wealthy aristocratic friends attempt to make his life a bit easier. In one of the many stirring scenes crafted by the gifted Gance, we see Baur engulfed in deafness, dependent upon his acute memory of sound to continue his musical compositions (Beethoven began to go deaf at the age of twenty-six in 1796), while the world about him is permeated with sound—birds chirping, villagers chattering, a street musician playing, the ringing of metal on metal as a blacksmith strikes his anvil—all unheard by Baur as he labors on another masterwork. Gance portrays Beethoven as an idol on a pedestal (he was the director's favorite historical character), and he takes great liberties (as he did when profiling Napoleon Bonaparte in his classic **Napoleon**, 1929) with the actual facts of the composer's life, but his cherished portrait remains a memorable one. (Gance shows, for instance, how Beethoven's landlords coddled and loved him, respecting his great talents, but, in truth, the composer's landlords were forever evicting him, in response to the complaints of tenants and neighbors, who could not tolerate his playing his compositions at all hours of the day and night.) **Immortal Beloved**, 1994, is another good full-blown biopic on Beethoven. (In French; English subtitles.) **p&d**, Abel Gance; **cast**, Harry Baur, Annie Ducaux, Jany Holt, Andre Nox, Jane Marken, Lucas Gridoux, Paul Pauley, Lucien Rozenberg, Yolande Laffon, Jean-Louis Barrault; **w**, Gance, Steve Passeur; **c**, Marc Fossard, Robert Lefebvre; **m**, Ludwig van Beethoven (arranged by Louis Masson); **ed**, Marguerite Beaugé, André Galitzine; **art d**, Jacques Colombier.

The Life and Loves of Mozart ★★★ 1959; Austria; 87m; Cosmopol-Film/Bakros International; Children: Cautionary; **DVD**; **VHS**. Werner, one of Europe's finest actors, does a great job in essaying the mercurial and unpredictable Wolfgang Amadeus Mozart (1756-1791), under the able direction of Hartl. The film concentrates on the last miserable year of Werner as he struggles to pay his debts and is tormented by doubt that challenges his musical genius. He is inspired by Matz, who appears in the premiere of his "Die Zauberflote" ("The Magic Flute") and where she sings the lead role of Pamina (voice by Hilda Güdin). Werner is daffy over this enticing lady, running about with her in fields and even climbing a tree together, ignoring his wife, Kückelmann, while the rather sinister Skoda (playing composer Antonio Salieri, 1750-1825) lurks about menacingly, waiting to create incidents that will disgrace and demean his competitor. The deep animosity between these two is only suggested in a few scenes where Werner's face sours when Skoda's name is uttered. Matz continues to be Werner's obsessive inspiration as he completes his final melodic masterworks before inexplicably dying, and it is she, not Kückelmann, who displays great mourning at his death as she follows his hearse (a death wagon) during a howling windstorm that symbolizes the passing of this musical genius. The final year on earth spent by Mozart was a living hell as he was then growing desperately ill and while creditors hounded him night and day. The film rivets viewer attention through the charismatic performance of the gifted Werner, who is strongly supported by a talented cast. *Author's Note*: "The Magic Flute" is widely recognized as Mozart's paean of praise to Freemasonry as Mozart was an ardent Free Mason, but it was his librettist, Emanuel Schikaneder (1751-1812), who was also a devout Free Mason, and who, more importantly, should be blamed (or credited) for emphasizing the philosophy of Freemasonry in that magical composition. Freemasonry was then outlawed as heresy in Austria and throughout most of Europe at that time, and some claimed that the espousal of Freemasonry by Mozart caused orthodox leaders to plot his demise. The possibility that Mozart was murdered, perhaps at the behest of the manipulative Salieri, as more forcefully depicted in **Amadeus**, 1984 (where Mozart is masterfully played by Tom Hulce as an *idiot savant*, and Salieri is profiled as utterly sinister by F. Murray Abraham), is profiled in detail in my work, *The Great Pictorial History of World Crime*, Volume II (History, Inc., 2004; pages: 793-800). (In German; English subtitles.) **p**, Josef W. Beyer, Julius Jonak, A.I. Paulini; **d&w**, Karl Hartl (based on a story by Hartl, Egon Komorzynski, Franz Tassié); **cast**, Oskar Werner, Johanna Matz, Erich Kunz, Gertrud Kückelmann, Nadja Tiller, Annie Rosar, Hugo Gottschlich, Angelika Hauff, Albin Skoda, Chariklia Baxevanos; **c**, Oskar Schnirch (Eastmancolor); **m**, Wolfgang Amadeus Mozart; **ed**, Henny Brünsch, Leopold Kuhnert, Rudolf Ohlschmidt; **prod d**, Wolf Witzemann; **art d**, Hermann Merotti.

The Life and Times of Judge Roy Bean ★★★ 1972; U.S.; 120m; First Artists/National General Pictures; Color; Western; Children: Unacceptable (MPAA: PG): **DVD**; **VHS**. Newman plays the rapacious and conniving Judge Roy Bean (1825-1903) tongue-and-cheek in this farcical western biopic. He rides into the dusty Texas town of Vinegaroon (in Val Verde County, Texas, near the Rio Grande, in Southwestern Texas) where he sees a wanted poster showing his own image and draws a mustache on it. He is seized by some locals, who bind him to the back of a horse that drags him to the middle of nowhere, but he is rescued by a child, Principal, and makes his way back to that town, which is no more than a group of shanties. Entering the saloon, Newman shoots and kills everyone in the place. Newman then announces that he is the presiding justice of the peace, who now governs the "Law West of the Pecos [River]." He renames the town "Langtry," after his stage idol, Lillie Langtree (1853-1929), a British stage singer, who is the rage in the East at the time. Newman's brand of law is levied not out of the law book he carries, but out of his muddled head and impulses. The town prospers and so does Newman since he virtually robs anyone so foolish as to ride into Langtry with money in their pockets. Moreover, his justice is severe, and he orders random hangings for the slightest infractions (Bean was known as the "hanging judge," but, in fact, he ordered only two executions and one of those condemned men escaped and was never recaptured). There is a lot of traffic in this film, with characters having no relevance to the story drifting in and out of the town and scenes, many of them killed at random by the rowdy denizens. Newman's fortunes decline with the death of Principal and he loses his saloon and is more or less driven out of town. He returns to the place to kill those who took away his saloon, only to die in obscurity and disgrace, except in the eyes of Gardner, who plays Lillie Langtry and makes a visit to the town named after her. Newman gives a powerful performance in his oddball film while playing an oddball historical character. Roy Bean was profiled in several TV productions and, most notably, in two other feature films, **The Westerner**, 1940 (where Walter Brennan gives the most re-

Ava Gardner in *The Life and Times of Judge Roy Bean*, 1972.

liable performance of the artful Bean), and **A Time for Dying**, 1969 (where Victor Jory essays Bean). *Author's Note*: Huston directs this intriguing but somewhat disorganized film with loose reins, allowing many characters to come and go without identification or any development and some of them speak directly into the camera to make comments about Newman as if lapsing into a documentary. "I did that to give a feeling for the complete disorganization of Bean's life and the unruly town he ruled," Huston told this author. "You try ideas and sometimes they work and sometimes they do not." Newman was circumspect about this film, telling this author that "little was known about Bean, so we had to rely on our own notions about how he lived and how he ran that crazy little town on the edge of nowhere." Gardner said to this author that "I really have a very small part in that picture—I get off a train to see this dusty little place, which a strange little man named after me. Everybody in that town is so forlorn and threadbare that I looked quite out of place when I arrive dressed in my finery." For more details on Roy Bean, see my book, *Encyclopedia of Western Lawmen and Outlaws* (Paragon House, 1992; pages 30-32). **p**, John Foreman; **d**, John Huston; **cast**, Paul Newman, Jacqueline Bisset, Ava Gardner, Tab Hunter, John Huston, Stacy Keach, Roddy McDowall, Anthony Perkins, Michael Sarrazin, Victoria Principal, Ned Beatty, Anthony Zerbe; **w**, John Milius (based on a book by C.L. Sonnichsen); **c**, Richard Moore (Technicolor); **m**, Maurice Jarre; **ed**, Hugh S. Fowler; **art d**, Tambi Larsen; **set d**, Robert Benton; **spec eff**, Butler-Glouner.

Life at the Top ★★★ 1965; U.K.; 116m; Romulus Films/Royal Films International; B/W; Drama; Children: Unacceptable; **VHS**. In this sequel to **Room at the Top**, 1959, Harvey is an ambitious young man who gives up the love of his life to marry the boss's daughter, Simmons, only to find that he is being sidelined at work at a mill business and his life is being run by his father-in-law, Wolfit. He is offered a new job in London, but ignores it and tries to keep from falling in love with television celebrity Blackman. When he learns that Simmons is cheating on him with his best friend, Craig, he reconsiders the new job, but wonders if he can make it on ability or just his charm. Simmons persuades him to return to her and he learns that her father actually likes him and plans to leave the business to him when he retires. But Harvey is still unsure if he can run a large company because, after all, he slept his way to the top. Sexuality prohibits viewing by children. **p**, James Woolf, John Woolf, William Kirby; **d**, Ted Kotcheff; **cast**, Laurence Harvey, Jean Simmons, Honor Blackman, Michael Craig, Donald Wolfit, Robert Morley, Margaret Johnston, Ambrosine Phillpotts, Allan Cuthbertson, Nigel Davenport, Edward Fox; **w**, Mordecai Richler (based on the novel by John Braine); **c**, Oswald Morris; **m**, Richard Addinsell; **ed**, Derek York; **art d**, Edward Marshall; **set d**, David Ffolkes.

Mickey Rooney and Judy Garland in *Life Begins for Andy Hardy,* 1941.

Life Begins ★★★ 1932; U.S.; 71m; First National/WB; B/W; Drama; Children: Unacceptable; **VHS**. This taut little drama takes place in a hospital maternity ward where several women are waiting to give birth, chiefly Young, a convicted murderer. Farrell, a cynical and worldly nightclub singer, is about to give birth to twins and does not look forward to that event. Meanwhile, Peterson haunts the ward, unnerving everyone as she is a psychopath, sneaking down corridors and into small rooms while utterly convinced that she, too, is about to give birth, but she is not pregnant and all of these great expectations on her part are wholly imagined. When the "Blessed Event" occurs for Farrell, she changes her mind and is overjoyed when giving birth to twins and belts out the song "Frankie and Johnnie," since she knows no lyrics to any lullaby. It is a much more tragic turn of events for Young, who also gives birth, but dies in the process, stating remorse for her crimes and her prayers for her newly born child. Directors Flood and Nugent do a fine job in balancing the separate stories of the pregnant women and they move the film along at a brisk pace without creating sudsy moments. This film saw a remake as **A Child Is Born**, 1939, a much inferior production. *Author's Note*: This story began as a student play by Mary Axelson, a student at Columbia University in New York City. The play was produced at the university theater before moving on to a Broadway production where it ran for only a week. Executives at Warner Brothers, however, were impressed with the story and bought the film rights, paying only $6,000. Young told this author: "I had a hard time working up a lot of sympathy for my character in **Life Begins** as she is a killer and is not sure she wants to bring a child into a world that has been very cruel to her. Her only joy in life is knowing that though she is dying, her child will live." **p**, Darryl F. Zanuck, Ray Griffith; **d**, James Flood, Elliott Nugent; **cast**, Loretta Young, Eric Linden, Aline MacMahon, Glenda Farrell, Clara Blandick, Preston Foster, Frank McHugh, Vivienne Osborne, Dorothy Peterson, Mary Philips, Gilbert Roland, Bobs Watson; **w**, Earl Baldwin (based on the play by Mary M. Axelson); **c**, James Van Trees; **ed**, George Marks; **art d**, Esdras Hartley.

Life Begins at Forty ★★★ 1935; U.S.; 85m; FOX; B/W; Comedy; Children: Acceptable; **DVD**. In this folksy comedy, which is highlighted by the sly wit of the brilliant Rogers, Cromwell, an innocent youth planning to marry fetching Hudson, a schoolteacher, is accused of a bank robbery. He tells his tale to Rogers, the local newspaper editor, and Rogers champions Cromwell's cause, which alienates totemic social leader and banker Barbier. The banker forecloses on Rogers' newspaper operation after Rogers prints an article attempting to exonerate Cromwell. While Barbier runs for mayor, Rogers and Cromwell begin printing a single sheet newspaper, opposing the banker's election and promoting his new opponent, Summerville, who is the town's drunk and

has been recruited as a candidate by the capricious and avuncular Rogers. Meanwhile, investigators prove that Cromwell is innocent and the bank theft was committed by Beck, Barbier's worthless son. Rogers recoups his newspaper and Cromwell is off to the altar with Hudson. Veteran director Marshall infuses many very funny sequences into this delightful film, including a wild hog-calling contest that leads to mirthful mayhem. Like all of Rogers' films, this one is worth the watching. **p**, Sol M. Wurtzel; **d**, George Marshall; **cast**, Will Rogers, Richard Cromwell, Rochelle Hudson, George Barbier, Jane Darwell, Slim Summerville, Sterling Holloway, Thomas Beck, Jed Prouty, Bobs Watson; **w**, Lamar Trotti, Robert Quillen, Dudley Nichols, William M. Conselman (based on the novel by Walter B. Pitkin); **c**, Harry Jackson; **ed**, Alex Troffey; **art d**, Duncan Cramer, Albert Hogsett.

Life Begins for Andy Hardy ★★★ 1941; U.S.; 110m; MGM; B/W; Comedy/Drama; Children: Acceptable; **VHS**. A more serious entry in the series has teenage Andy (Rooney) refusing to follow his father, Judge Hardy (Stone), into the legal profession after graduating high school. He wants time to think about his future. He decides to leave the small town he grew up in and go to New York City to do that thinking. His parents reluctantly let him go. He meets his sometime girlfriend, Garland, and gets a job as an office boy for $10 a week. His meager salary is just enough for him to get a small apartment, and he makes friends with a struggling young dancer, McDonald, and shares it with him. Soon after, Rooney finds McDonald dead of a heart attack. He gets a loan on his old car to buy a tombstone for his friend. A divorcee, Dane, the receptionist at the office where Rooney works, has eyes for him, and invites him to her apartment for an evening, but he declines. His experiences in the Big Apple convince Rooney that he belongs back in his home town and college is in his future, but he'll decide later about becoming a lawyer or judge. It was Garland's third and final appearance in the Hardy films, but she and Rooney went on to become a very popular movie team. **p&d**, George B. Seitz; **cast**, Mickey Rooney, Lewis Stone, Judy Garland, Fay Holden, Ann Rutherford, Sara Haden, Patricia Dane, Ray McDonald, Ralph Byrd, John Eldredge, Tommy Kelly, Charlotte Wynters; **w**, Agnes Christine Johnston (based on characters created by Aurania Rouverol); **c**, Lester White; **ed**, Elmo Veron; **art d**, Cedric Gibbons; **set d**, Edwin B. Willis.

Life in Emergency Ward 10 ★★★ 1959; U.K.; 86m; Artistes Alliance Ltd.; B/W; Drama; Children: Unacceptable; **VHS**. Craig is a new surgeon in a British hospital, bringing with him an experimental heart lung machine after a trip to America. His colleagues are uncertain about the machine, especially after it is used on an elderly patient who dies. When it is used on a boy with a hole in his heart, it saves his life, and Craig and his machine are then welcomed by the other doctors. Not for children because of strong medical themes. **p**, Ted Lloyd; **d**, Robert Day; **cast**, Michael Craig, Wilfrid Hyde-White, Dorothy Alison, Glyn Owen, Rosemary Miller, Charles Tingwell, Christopher Witty, Rupert Davies, Joan Sims, Douglas Ives; **w**, Tessa Diamond, Hazel Adair (based on their story); **c**, Frank Drake, Geoffrey Faithfull; **m**, Philip Green; **ed**, Lito Carruthers; **art d**, George Beech.

Life Is a Bed of Roses ★★★ 1983; France; 110m; Fideline Films/International Spectrafilm; Color; Comedy/Drama; Children: Unacceptable (MPAA: PG); **DVD**. Three intertwined stories make up this engrossing production. As World War I is about to break out, a French count, Raimondi, has work started on a castle in the Ardennes forest. Work stops during the war, but afterward he uses it to set up a utopian society by brainwashing his friends and his former fiancée, Ardant, and her ex-soldier husband, Dussollier. Flash forward to the 1980s and the castle is used as a place for an educational conference for professors seeking ways to educate children through imagination. Chaplin, an American anthropologist, bets that Azéma, one of the teachers, will be seduced into going to bed with a man at the conference, Arditi, even though the main speaker, Gassman, an Italian skirt-chaser, is attracted to her. While the adults are playing their mature games, children staying at the castle invent a medieval tale about freeing prisoners from the dungeons. We are left to wonder whether the children with their imaginations have more productive educational tools than those produced by the adults. Sexual themes prohibit viewing by children. (In French; English subtitles.) **p**, Philippe Dussart; **d**, Alain Resnais; **cast**, Vittorio Gassman, Ruggero Raimondi, Geraldine Chaplin, Fanny Ardant, Pierre Arditi, Sabine Azçma, Robert Manuel, Martine Kelly, Véronique Silver, André Drussollier; **w**, Jean Gruault; **c**, Bruno Nuytten; **m**, M. Philippe-Gérard; **ed**, Jean-Pierre Besnard, Albert Jurgenson; **prod d**, Enki Bilal, Jacques Saulnier.

Life Is Beautiful ★★★★★ 1999; Italy; 118m; Cecchi Gori Group/Miramax; Color; Drama; Children: Unacceptable (MPAA: PG-13); **DVD**; **VHS**. The colorful and charismatic Benigni (won Oscar for Best Actor) is shown in 1930s Italy looking for work when he meets and immediately falls in love with attractive schoolteacher Braschi (Benigni's wife in real life), and begins awkwardly courting her, despite the fact that she is engaged to a wealthy and stuffy bureaucrat. Benigni cleverly arranges to see Braschi several times, endearing himself to her, but it appears that she will nevertheless go ahead with her marriage, until Benigni dramatically invades her engagement party and takes her away on horseback to embarrass her intended and humiliate her mother, Paredes. She, however, has truly come to love Benigni and they marry, having a son, Cantarini. As the tide of fascism rises in Italy, Benigni mocks and imitates the fascists, at one point leaping upon a table to display his "Aryan belly-button," but this only dangerously marks him as an enemy of the fascist state, and the horse he used to take Braschi away with him is later painted green and marked with anti-Semitic slurs. In 1945, Benigni is seized, along with an uncle, and his son, Cantarini, and ordered onto a train to be taken to a concentration camp. Braschi, who is not Jewish, insists that she accompany her family and, she, too, is taken to that camp. At the camp, Benigni teaches Cantarini a game where he must not cry, call out for his mother, and must hide from camp guards to win points in eventually winning a tank, and, as American forces approach the camp, Nazi guards begin killing the inmates. Benigni convinces his son to hide in a sweatbox as the last test to win a tank and the boy complies as his father is caught by a guard. Knowing he is facing his last moments on earth, Benigni defiantly mocks his guard by goose-stepping to the place of his execution. The next morning, Cantarini climbs from the sweatbox to see American forces enter the camp and he is given his prize when the Americans allow him to ride on a tank. He then sees his mother in the crowds of prisoners streaming from the camp and is reunited with her, only learning later as an adult how his father heroically saved his life by maintaining an inventive ruse to excite his boyhood imagination. This tragicomedy is wonderfully directed by Benigni, and his acting is superb, a memorably poignant performance showing a courageous man with an undying love for life, a truly magical film. (In Italian; English subtitles; English dubbed version.) **p**, Gianluigi Braschi, Elda Ferri, John M. Davis; **d**, Roberto Benigni; **cast**, Benigni, Nicoletta Braschi, Giorgio Cantarini, Giustino Durano, Sergio Bustric, Marisa Paredes, Horst Buchholz, Lidia Alfonsi, Giuliana Lojodice, Amerigo Fontani, Omero Antonutti (narrator); **w**, Benigni, Vincenzo Cerami (based on their story); **c**, Tonino Delli Colli; **m**, Nicola Piovani; **ed**, Simona Paggi; **prod d**, Danilo Donati; **set d**, Luigi Urbani; **spec eff**, Kenneth Cassar, Giovanni Corridori.

The Life of Emile Zola ★★★★★ 1937; U.S.; 116m; WB; B/W; Biographical Drama; Children: Cautionary: **DVD**; **VHS**. Few actors possessed the powerful and dynamic personality of Paul Muni and here he displays all the talents that made him one of the greatest of thespians in his portrayal of French writer Emile Zola (1840-1902). He is first shown as a struggling writer in Paris, sharing an unheated loft with painter Sokoloff, who plays Paul Cézanne (1839-1906). While sitting with

Paul Muni in *The Life of Emile Zola*, 1937.

Sokoloff in a small café, O'Brien Moore appears, hiding from police who have just raided a bordello where she works. Muni invites her to sit at his table and, when officers enter the place to arrest her, Muni tells them to go away and not bother his "friend." Saved from arrest, O'Brien Moore pours out her tragic story to Muni, who writes a novel about her and her tawdry life, titled *Nana*, and it becomes an enormous success. Not knowing that his book has become a best-seller, Muni arrives at his publisher's store and asks for a small advance and the publisher is delighted to pay him considerable royalties. In gratitude, Muni sends O'Brien Moore cash and gifts and then goes on to write many more successful books, becoming rich and famous and moving into a mansion with his wife, Roberts. He is visited in his advancing years by Sokoloff, who has become equally famous, but who chides Muni for not following his youthful ambitions to attack social injustices in his books, as he did in his novel *Nana*. Muni, however, is too old and comfortable to deal with the idealism of his youth, until an event takes place within the hierarchy of the French High Command of the Army. Army intelligence discovers in 1894 that some of its military secrets are being stolen when a French spy working in the German embassy retrieves a memorandum detailing information about a secret French ordnance. Several top French officers immediately conclude that Schildkraut, playing Alfred Dreyfus (1859-1935), a brilliant artillery captain, is the culprit, even though the evidence points to another French officer, Barrat, playing Ferdinand Walsin Esterhazy (1847-1923). The reason why Schildkraut is arbitrarily suspected as being a secret German agent is because he is Jewish and lives far beyond the means of his captain's pay, albeit it is also known that he comes from a wealthy manufacturing family. Schildkraut is summarily found guilty of espionage by a secret tribunal and sentenced to life imprisonment. He is paraded through the ranks and stripped of his insignias and his sword broken. He is then sent to the horrendous French penal colony at Devil's Island in French Guyana (Guiana), where he is confined in a miserable hut, chained to a bed, and where he writes letters to his wife, Sondergaard, imploring her to find a way to prove his innocence. She goes to Muni, known to be the champion of social rights and freedoms, and he agrees to conduct his own investigation. He learns through O'Neill, chief of French intelligence and one of the few honorable French officers in the High Command (playing the noble Colonel Georges Picquart, 1854-1914), that Barrat is the real traitor and that fraudulent documents and testimony by members of the High Command has brought about the wrongful conviction and imprisonment of Schildkraut. Muni then writes his famous "I Accuse," a lengthy indictment of the High Command for its corrupt and criminal treatment of Schildkraut. The article is published, one which accuses the High Command of complicity in railroading Schildkraut and covering up the actions of the traitor, Barrat. The High Command responds by filing charges of libel

William Bendix in *The Life of Riley,* 1949.

against Muni, but, knowing that his forthcoming trial will be rigged before a kangaroo court, he flees to England. Muni's selfless and heroic crusade, however, sees fruit when a new premier takes office and fires the corrupt members of the High Command, and all of the culprits, except Barrat, who also flees to England to live in poverty and disgrace, are either cashiered, jailed or commit suicide. Schildkraut is then vindicated and restored to his position in the French Army. Muni, however, never meets the man he has rescued and dies before Schildkraut can thank him for his intrepid efforts. Carnovsky, playing French writer Anatole France (1844-1924), who is a friend of Muni's and urged the publication of "I Accuse," presides at a memorial in honor of Muni, stating at the end of the film: "He was a moment in the conscience of man." In addition to the superlative performance rendered by Muni (he received an Oscar nomination as Best Actor), the splendid cast members give wonderful and realistic performances, and where Schildkraut is unforgettable as the victimized Dreyfus (he received an Oscar as Best Supporting Actor), and the film won an Oscar as Best Picture, as well as an Oscar for Best Adapted Screenplay. Muni was nominated for Best Actor, as was composer Steiner and director Dieterle. Director Dieterle displays a firm hand in helming this great biopic, skillfully integrating the two tales of Zola's career and the scandalous upheaval of the Dreyfus Affair, while effectively developing in dramatic detail great character development of all the principals of the story. The film was an enormous success, despite the fact that it was informative and literate, proving that the intelligence of American moviegoers was much higher than thought by studio executives and it surprised Warner Brothers executives with its tremendous box office receipts. Although Warner Brothers was lauded for producing a film that attacked bigotry and anti-Semitism, the word "Jew" is not uttered once in the film, although the world knew that Dreyfus was of Jewish heritage. *Author's Note*: The story was first presented to pantheon director Ernst Lubitsch at Paramount, but he candidly admitted that no actor at Paramount was gifted enough to play Zola and he turned the story over to his friend, Henry Blanke, a producer at Warner Brothers, who did have an actor who could play the legendary French writer, Muni, and Muni's towering performance certainly proved Blanke right. Actually, Muni had played a character in this drama, Dreyfus, in a 1924 Maurice Schwartz Yiddish Art Theater play at the age of twenty-nine, and was more than familiar with the story. When he agreed to play Zola, Muni immersed himself with research on his character. "I read everything I could find about him," Muni told this author, "and even talked to some of his living relatives, to better understand his nature and personality, so that when I went before the cameras, I was comfortable in my mind that I could portray this great man with realistic honesty." Dietele told this author that Muni "was like a terrier going after that role, knowing every gesture and mannerism Zola possessed and he

used all that in his great performance. He was the top actor at Warner Brothers and every director knew it. I did not have to ask him for retakes. He knew when they should be made and would do anything to make a scene better. He would exhaust himself in a scene that took only a minute or two to get it just as right as he thought it should be. I sometimes asked myself who was directing this film, me or Muni? I found myself deferring to Muni on just about everything because he had a reliable instinct about how to do every scene. There was no one quite like Paul Muni on the face of the earth. He was patient, demanding and all-knowing and he was also the greatest actor I ever directed. I had the honor to direct Muni in **The Story of Louis Pasteur** [1936], a year earlier, and I directed him three years later in **Juarez** [1939], and he gave the same wonderful performances in those biographical pictures as he did in **The Life of Emile Zola**." Dreyfus has been profiled in a number of films, most notably in **The Dreyfus Case**, 1931, and the exceptional made-for-TV production, **Prisoner of Honor**, 1991, which centers upon the courageous Colonel Picquart, brilliantly essayed by a man ironically named Richard Dreyfuss. For more details about the Dreyfus case, see my books, *Spies: A Narrative Encyclopedia of Dirty Deeds and Double Dealing from Biblical Times to the Present* (M. Evans, 1997; pages 189-192) and *"I Am Innocent!": A Comprehensive Encyclopedic History of the World's Wrongly Convicted Persons* (Da Capo Press, 2008; pages 1-8). **p**, Hal B. Wallis, Henry Blanke; **d**, William Dieterle; **cast**, Paul Muni, Gale Sondergaard, Joseph Schildkraut, Gloria Holden, Donald Crisp, Erin O'Brien Moore, John Litel, Henry O'Neill, Morris Carnovsky, Vladimir Sokoloff, Louis Calhern, Robert Barrat, Ralph Morgan, Harry Davenport, Montagu Love, Robert Warick, Dickie Moore, Florence Roberts, Lumsden Hare, Grant Mitchell, Marcia Mae Jones, Walter Kingsford, Moroni Olsen, Frank Mayo; **w**, Norman Reilly Raine, Heinz Herald, Geza Herczeg (based on a story by Herald, Herczeg and source material "Zola and His Time" by Matthew Josephson); **c**, Tony Gaudio; **m**, Max Steiner; **ed**, Warren Low; **art d**, Anton Grot; **set d**, Albert C. Wilson.

Life of Oharu ★★★ 1964; Japan; 148m; Koi Productions/Toho Company; B/W; Drama; Children: Unacceptable; **VHS**. Tanaka is a fifty-year-old prostitute in the 17th century who is no longer able to attract men. She prays before Buddha while reflecting on her life. When she was young and the daughter of a samurai, she was a lady-in-waiting at the imperial court at Kyoto. She fell in love with a man below her station in life and became his mistress. When their love affair was discovered, her lover was decapitated and Tanaka and her family are banished from the court and the city. Her life afterward is filled with sorrow and humiliation. She fails in an attempt at suicide, later becomes the mistress of a prince, and bears his child, but then he sends her away. Her father sells her and she becomes a prostitute. A wealthy man buys her, but he is discovered to be a criminal and she is sold again. She then marries a merchant and they live together until he dies, and she is then again forced into prostitution. As she is finished recalling the past, her son from the prince asks her to live in his house, which she does, but soon is guilt-ridden by her life and leaves to become a beggar. Not a very happy story, but one so well told that it fascinates throughout. (In Japanese; English subtitles.) **p**, Kenji Mizoguchi, Hideo Koi; **d**, Mizoguchi; **cast**, Kinuyo Tanaka, Tsukie Matsuura, Ichirô Sugai, Toshirô Mifune, Toshiaki Konoe, Kiyoko Tsuji, Hisako Yamane, Jûkichi Uno, Eitarô Shindô, Akira Ôizumi, Kyôko Kusajima; **w**, Mizoguchi, Yoshikata Yoda (based on the novel *Koshuku Ichidai Onna* by Saikaku Ihara); **c**, Yoshimi Hirano, Yoshimi Kono; **m**, Ichirô Saitô; **ed**, Toshio Gotô; **prod d**, Hiroshi Mizutani.

The Life of Riley ★★★ 1949; U.S.; 90m; UNIV; B/W; Comedy; Children: Acceptable; **DVD**; **VHS**. Bendix is very funny as a brawny riveter working in an airplane factory. He is not too smart, but he has a heart of gold and is a dedicated family man. All he wants is a better job while his fetching daughter, Randall, becomes the belle of the neighborhood.

He is suddenly amazed to see himself promoted to a desk job where he knows little or nothing about that executive position, and these scenes, too, are often hilarious. He learns that Randall is now about to marry the boss's son, Daniels, a man she does not love, and then discovers that his loving daughter has gotten him his cushy job only through her agreement to marry Daniels, instead of Long, the young man to whom she has really given her heart. Bendix fixes the problem by stopping his daughter's wedding in the middle of the ceremony and then makes sure that Randall is reunited with Long for a happy ending. *Author's Note*: This film was adapted from a 1944 radio show. A thirty-minute TV series with the same title starring Jackie Gleason ran from 1949 to 1950 (twenty-six episodes) and another thirty-minuteTV series (1953-1958) starred Bendix (212 episodes). **p&d**, Irving Brecher; **cast**, William Bendix, Rosemary DeCamp. James Gleason, Bill Goodwin, Beulah Bondi, Meg Randall, Richard Long, Lanny Rees, Mark Daniels, Ted de Corsia, Victoria Horne, John Brown, Howard Duff; **w**, Brecher (based on a story by Groucho Marx); **c**, William Daniels; **m**, Frank Skinner; **ed**, Milton Carruth; **art d**, John DeCuir, Bernard Herzbrun; **set d**, Russell A. Gausman.

Life with Father ★★★★ 1947; U.S.; 118m; WB; Color; Comedy; Children: Recommended; **DVD**; **VHS**. Powell is utterly captivating and consistently humorous as a successful New York City businessman, who maintains a rigid regimen in his upscale Victorian household and where he runs his family as a drill sergeant might command a platoon of recruits. His loving wife, Dunne, cherishes Powell, but she rebels on occasion when his chauvinistic dictates make life uncomfortable if not intolerable. In reality, Powell loves his family much more than his persnickety lifestyle, but bristles when anyone suggests that a second in his well-ordered life be changed. Powell urges his three red-headed sons to emulate his lifestyle and follow his male-dominating philosophy, telling his oldest son, Lydon, in one scene: "Women have no capacity for thought. They simply get all stirred up." Lydon attempts to follow in his father's entrepreneurial footsteps by peddling some unreliable and unauthorized cure-all medicine, roping his younger brother, Milner, into the scheme. When Dunne falls ill, the boys think that the medicine will help her, so, without telling her, they give her a dose of this vile stuff and she gets even sicker. Dunne, when appearing to be on death's door, extracts from Powell his promise that he will be baptized (something he has never done out of his parents' inadvertent negligence or lack of time). When Dunne recovers, she holds Powell to his promise. He delays, stalls, and finds every excuse he can conjure to avoid that event, but, at the very end of the film, he relents and the entire family climbs into a large horse-drawn carriage on a sunny Sunday and they are off to the church where the ruffled Powell is asked by a neighbor where he is going and where he grumpily replies: "I'm going to be baptized!" (The original line he delivered in that final scene was "I am going to be baptized, dammit!" but this line was cut and Powell redid it for a more acceptable statement of that day.) This film, wonderfully enacted by the entire cast, was a great box office hit, chiefly due to Powell's charming profile of a rigid father who relaxes his own protocols for the sake and love of his adoring family. (He received an Oscar nomination for Best Actor.) Curtiz directs this great family film with vigor and shows infinite care in presenting the tender moments shared between Dunne and Powell, as well as the antics of Powell's children and, notably, the brief scenes where a young Elizabeth Taylor arrives as a visiting cousin and develops an instant crush on Lydon. *Author's Note*: Powell told this author that "I am a stuffy martinet in **Life with Father**, but all my rigid nonsense means nothing when it comes to my love for my family, and that is the message of that great story, that fathers live to nurture their loved ones. They go about convincing themselves every day that they are really in charge when they know in their hearts that their wives really govern the emotional stability of the family, as the wonderful Irene Dunne does in that picture. I studied everything I could about that Victorian era, even though I was born into it, so that I would better understand my role. I did not emulate my own father, but the fathers of that

William Powell, Martin Milner and Irene Dunne in *Life with Father*, 1947.

prim-and-proper and very urbane world. The character was also definitively drawn by Day, who based his book on his own father, and Lindsay's terrific play, which was faithful to the book that I really couldn't miss." The play had been an enormous hit on Broadway, running 3,224 nights. "I was only fifteen when I appeared in **Life with Father**" Taylor told this author, "and I have a small role where I get sappy over Jimmy Lydon because he is attending an Ivy League school. William Powell was very kind to me in that film, as he was to everyone. He was everyone's father in that picture—what a great actor. We all watched his scenes behind the cameras when we were not in scenes with him just to learn what we could about his acting techniques, but no one could ever duplicate that man. He has a marvelous style all of his own." **p**, Robert Buckner; **d**, Michael Curtiz; **cast**, William Powell, Irene Dunne, Elizabeth Taylor, Edmund Gwenn, Zasu Pitts, Jimmy Lydon, Emma Dunn, Moroni Olsen, Elisabeth Risdon, Martin Milner, Clara Blandick, Russell Arms, Arlene Dahl; **w**, Donald Ogden Stewart (based on the play by Howard Lindsay, Russel Crouse, and the book by Clarence Day); **c**, Peverell Marley, William V. Skall (Technicolor); **m**, Max Steiner; **ed**, George Amy; **art d**, Robert Haas; **set d**, George James Hopkins; **spec eff**, Ray Foster, William McGann.

Lifeboat ★★★★★ 1944; U.S.; 97m; FOX; B/W; Adventure; Children: Unacceptable; **DVD**; **VHS**. Exciting and tension-filled adventure film from pantheon director Hitchcock sees a group of passengers and crew members surviving the sinking of an ocean liner in WWII, sitting adrift in a lifeboat on the open sea after their ship has been sunk by torpedoes from a German U-boat. The German submarine has also been sunk by an Allied ship, but that ship does not pick up the survivors. The captain of the U-boat, Slezak, is the only survivor from his sunken vessel and he swims to the lifeboat where he is taken on board. Since he is the only true sailor of the lot, he is elected to helm the lifeboat. The occupants make up a strange group of people—Bankhead is a sophisticated fashion writer, Hull is a manufacturing magnate, Hodiak is an opinionated sailor, Bendix is a thick-witted stoker, Cronyn is a mild-mannered radio operator, Lee a black steward, Anderson is a nurse, and Angel is a dazed mother, who holds her dead baby in her arms until she falls asleep and the child is buried at sea. The artful and cunning Slezak does not steer the boat toward land, but toward a rendezvous at sea with the German mother ship that supplies a number of U-boats. Meanwhile, the fresh water on board diminishes as does the food. Hodiak attempts to catch a fish by using as bait Bankhead's expensive diamond bracelet and loses the gem-encrusted bracelet in the process, sending Bankhead into paroxysms of anger and anguish. The survivors slowly get weaker and weaker, Bendix dying after his injured leg is amputated, but not before he tells the others that he has seen Slezak, who remains strong and is now row-

Hume Cronyn, Tallulah Bankhead and John Hodiak in *Lifeboat*, 1944.

ing the boat toward the German mother ship, that Slezak has hidden water and energy pills that have allowed him to dominate in the fashion of a Nazi superman. When discovering this, the survivors, men and women alike, savagely attack Slezak, battering him senseless and tossing him overboard to a watery death. They then see a vessel steaming toward them and realize it is the German mother ship, but, as it approaches, an Allied warship appears on the horizon and its guns blast and sink the German vessel and then steams toward the survivors to rescue them. Before the ship arrives, a German sailor swims to the lifeboat and is taken aboard. The young sailor threatens the survivors with a pistol, but he is disarmed. Unlike the gruesome demise meted out to Slezak, the survivors, who have regained their compassion, allow the terrified sailor to live and that is where this taut film ends. Hitchcock does a great job in developing his characters where they begin as strangers and evolve as caring friends. Bankhead discards her glamorous and haughty pose and comes down to earth, admitting her emotional attraction to the common-man credo advocated by Hodiak. Hull, who is the personification of the uncaring capitalist, briefly sheds his autocratic ways to embrace the beliefs of the working man. Cronyn, too, changes in that he becomes more assertive and expresses his affection for cowering nurse Anderson, and Lee steps from his shell as an Uncle Tom black to declare his humanity and individualism. Hitchcock inventively makes an appearance in this film as he always hallmarked his films with his own imprimatur, but, in this instance, the confining lifeboat did not offer him the affordability of his usual passerby appearance. His likeness appears in an old newspaper being read by Bendix where he is shown in a fat-reducing ad for an elixir called "Reduco" in before and after photos. For some time after the release of this film, obese viewers wrote to Hitchcock, asking him where they might be able to purchase the mythical "Reduco." The film received Oscar nominations for Best Director, Best Screenplay and Best Black-and-White Cinematography. *Author's Note*: Hitchcock had stock footage taken off the Florida coast and used this footage of a grey and choppy sea in rear-view projection (one of his favorite techniques in combining spectacular scenes with live action) or as process shots. He herded his cast into a lifeboat floating in a large studio tank for weeks, drenching them with water from water-spraying machines, coupled to huge wind-blowing fans and giant water activators. "I was almost drowned," Cronyn told this author, "when I fell overboard and was trapped beneath one of those damned underwater activators. Hitch had had the presence of mind to hire lifeguards who stood around that tank and one of them dove beneath the water and yanked me out of there. Half the time we were either covered with crude oil or we had our clothes drenched with water. After each scene, we climbed out of the lifeboat and went to our dressing rooms, cleaned up, put on dry clothes and then went back to the lifeboat and got drenched

again." Hitchcock told this author that it was "absolutely necessary that we shoot **Lifeboat** in the studio tank. You couldn't have very well gone to sea to do that. You could never get the mobility of the shots. There would have been no way to get level with the people [actors]. As it was, in order to get at the people in the boat, I had to have three lifeboats— one full length, a half of one, and a half of one split down the middle— and we brought up whichever one was useful for the shot. It wasn't just shot in one boat." After Hitchcock got the idea for the story, he assigned the brilliant Steinbeck to write the screenplay, but the two clashed over the script. "I felt that Hitch had an obsession about confining all his action to that lifeboat," Steinbeck told this author. "By doing that, he restricted a hell of a lot of action. When Hitch gets his visions, he sticks with them and then his writers have to figure out how to get him out of the deep holes he digs. His ideas are fantastic, but a lot of them are impossible to translate into reality for the screen and he knows it." Hitchcock had a different view. "John [Steinbeck] wanted to insert a lot of scenes that did not take place in the lifeboat and after I told him that the picture takes place totally in a lifeboat—and that is the title of the film, after all—he stalled, sputtered and stopped. I had to bring in McKinlay Kantor, but he had the same problems with the story line as had Steinbeck. Then I brought in Jo Swerling and he did a pretty good job, but, in the end, as usual, I turned to my favorite screenwriter, Ben Hecht." Hecht told this author that "Swerling had done most of the work for **Lifeboat**. All I did was sharpen the dialog and a few scenes. Hitch always turned to me on most of his films because he knew that I would work with him and not pursue my own fancies. Some writers make the mistake that when they sit down to write a screenplay, they are writing something for themselves, like a novel. When they are writing a screenplay, they are writing for a gang of people all working on a technical concept—a motion picture that involves a lot of talented people who are not writers." The actual star of the film is Bankhead, and Hitchcock literally saved her career by casting her as his leading lady in this film. Her career had taken a nosedive where she had made six unsuccessful films and her stage career had been equally dismal. When Hitchcock offered her $75,000 to play the lead in **Lifeboat**, Bankhead immediately accepted. Hitchcock paid the actress a great compliment by opening the film with a panning shot that scans the debris from the sunken luxury liner until his camera shows the lifeboat and with only one person initially occupying it—a woman with perfectly coiffured hair, her voluptuous body draped with mink and dripping with diamonds—the inimitable Bankhead. In keeping with Hitchcock's sly visual wit, he offers this incongruous image of a woman totally out of place with the grim setting, and, at the same moment, utterly captures her august persona. She is beautiful and selfish to start, but emerges through a bravura performance as the strongest and most morally courageous member of that seemingly doomed group of passengers, an unforgettable role that forever endeared her to worldwide viewing audiences. Hitchcock had nothing but praise for the actress, telling this author that "she endured every conceivable hardship in that picture. She got doused with more than five thousand gallons of water and she got a round of applause from the stagehands in scene after scene." Bankhead caught pneumonia twice during the production and was weak and wobbly legged toward the end of the production, but she persevered and her magnificent performance deservedly won her the prestigious New York Screen Critics award as Best Actress for 1944. (She was not nominated for an Oscar, but that had much to do with the pressure from gossip columnist Louella Parsons, who hated her, and personally lobbied industry voters not to select her at the risk of being lambasted in her column.) Bankhead spent a lot of time with Hitchcock off the set. They lunched together and she took him to the best upscale art galleries in Los Angeles and, on one occasion, urged him to buy a painting by Milton Avery that the director liked. This was the first of many paintings Hitchcock acquired, becoming quite a collector in years to come. "Only Tallulah would have the fortitude to give Hitch a piece of her mind," Cronyn told this author. "Most of us were terrified of the man, even though I knew he was as harmless as a puppy. It was his contemplative and solemn personality that silenced us. He seldom smiled, you know, but that was all an act. He thought everything was funny, not frightening. And he was pretty funny, too. Mary Anderson, who is my love interest in **Lifeboat**, asked me if she thought she could approach Hitch and ask him a few questions that might help her career and I told her she should do that. Well, when he was sitting next to us, Mary asked him those questions and he courteously gave her a few short responses. She then asked him what he thought was her best profile for the camera to shoot. 'What do you think is my best side?' she asked him. Hitch gave her one of those dour looks of his and replied: 'You're sitting on it, my dear.'" The biggest problem for Fox in this production was Bankhead. According to statements made to this author by Fox chief Darryl Zanuck: "She was literally a pain in the butt. A female editor from a powerful women's magazine stormed into my office one day to scream at me about Bankhead, saying that she went to the set of **Lifeboat** to do a story and saw Bankhead climb into that lifeboat with no panties and her bottom exposed to everyone on the set. Can you imagine? I told the woman I would take care of that and immediately called a producer into my office and told him to go to that sound stage and have Hitchcock take care of the matter." The producer did as he was told and, some minutes later, confronted Hitchcock on the set, saying: "The front office has received a complaint that Miss Bankhead is wearing nothing on beneath her dress and I was told to speak to her." Hitchcock shook his head and replied: "Well, you know she's a firebrand and she'll tear you to pieces...She probably hates your guts anyway. I wouldn't talk to her, if I were you. I don't think it's your department." The producer then asked: "Then whose department is it?" Replied Hitchcock: "Either hair dressing or makeup." The tempestuous Bankhead was, indeed, a firebrand, who spoke her piece whenever her mercurial whims urged. She took it into her mind that Slezak was truly the person he was playing, and she several times kicked him in the shins on the set, shouting: "You damned Nazi!" Slezak begged her stop, saying: "Please, Miss Bankhead. I am only *playing a part*." She nevertheless ignored his pleadings and continued to abuse him and she proved then and throughout her life that *she was always playing a part*. Following the release of the film and her winning the New York Critics award for Best Actress, Bankhead gave a lavish press party at the Louis XIV Room in the St. Regis Hotel in New York City. Bankhead's father had been a U.S. congressman and her uncle a U.S. senator (both Democrats from Alabama). She was a decided liberal, but an avowed enemy of communism. When she spotted a female reporter from *PM* at her press party, Bankhead exploded, saying: "Of all the filthy Communist rags that is, it is the most vicious, dangerous, hating paper that has ever been published! It's a dirty Communist sheet! I loathe it! I loathe it! I wouldn't even touch it with my hands. It's cruel, unfair and rotten...I have the maid bring the paper to me with tongs, but I do love 'Barnaby' [a cartoon strip appearing in *PM*]." When someone tried to calm her down, Bankhead roared: "Don't shush me! This isn't your cocktail party! If you don't like what I am saying, get the hell out!" She did calm down a bit, seeming to be conciliatory toward the *PM* reporter by telling her that "you know, you look just like a dear friend of mine." The reporter said nothing, got up and started walking toward the door. Bankhead then shouted after her: "She committed suicide!" **p**, Kenneth Macgowan; **d**, Alfred Hitchcock; **cast**, Tallulah Bankhead, William Bendix, John Hodiak, Walter Slezak, Mary Anderson, Henry Hull, Heather Angel, Hume Cronyn, Canada Lee, William Yetter, Jr., Hitchcock; **w**, Jo Swerling (based on the story by John Steinbeck); **c**, Glen MacWilliams, Arthur C. Miller; **m**, Hugo W. Friedhofer; **ed**, Dorothy Spencer; **art d**, James Basevi, Maurice Ransford; **set d**, Thomas Little.

Lifeguard ★★★ 1976; U.S.; 76m; PAR; Color; Drama; Children: Unacceptable (MPAA: PG); **DVD**; **VHS**. For most young men, being a lifeguard is a summer job during college. For Elliott it is a career and, perhaps, a calling, even as he turns thirty. He loves the fun and sun and girls ogling him on the beaches of Los Angeles, California. When he

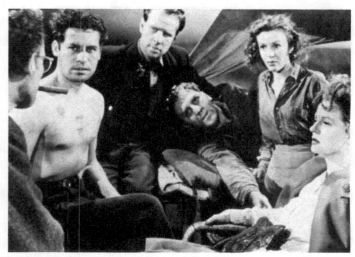

Henry Hull, John Hodiak, Hume Cronyn, William Bendix, Mary Anderson and Tallulah Bankhead in *Lifeboat*, 1944.

meets Archer, his old high school girlfriend at a fifteen-year class reunion with her five-year-old son and learns she is now divorced, his feelings for her rekindle and he begins to wonder if maybe he should get a more "serious" job and marry her. At the same time, Young, an old high school pal, who is a successful Porsche dealer, offers him a better-paying job as a salesman, but he turns it down. Meanwhile, Quinlan, a seventeen-year-old girl, flirts with him and compromises him so his lifesaving job is now in jeopardy. His parents and friends urge him to get out of his Speedos and into a business suit, but he decides to stay a lifeguard for as long as he can. More than a "beach party" film, it is an intelligent look at a man at the crossroads of his life, although it is also a haunting and melancholy film reminiscent of **The Swimmer**, 1968, where Burt Lancaster refuses to accept aging and that life has passed him by. Adult themes prohibit viewing by children. **p**, Ron Silverman; **d**, Daniel Petrie; **cast**, Sam Elliott, Anne Archer, Stephen Young, Parker Stevenson, Kathleen Quinlan, Sharon Clark, Steve Burns, Lenka Peterson, George Wallace, James Van Patten; **w**, Ron Koslow; **c**, Ralph Woolsey (CFI Color); **m**, Dale Menten, Paul Williams; **ed**, Argyle Nelson, Jr.

The Light in the Forest ★★★ 1958; U.S.; 83m; Walt Disney/Buena Vista; Color; Adventure; Children: Acceptable; **DVD**; **VHS**. Exciting and action filled, this Disney entry sees a young white boy kidnapped and reared by members of a Native American Delaware tribe. When he is a teenager (MacArthur), he is traded back to his people in a peace agreement and goes to live with white people in 1760s Philadelphia. He has to learn to fit in with the people his Indian friends taught him to hate. He is befriended by Parker, an army scout, who is assigned to look over his readjustment, and Lynley, an indentured servant girl, who, at first, is hostile to him because her parents have been killed by Indians, but they soon fall in love. His uncle, Corey, is the town bully, a racist and alcoholic, who takes part in raids against Indian villages, and, when he kills an Indian friend of MacArthur's, the boy returns to the tribe that reared him. But the tribal leaders want to use him as a decoy in an ambush against innocent whites. He escapes them and returns to Philadelphia where he confronts his uncle and beats him senseless. MacArthur and Lynley then leave civilization for a new life together in the forest, and Parker marries the minister's daughter, Dru. Songs: "Light in the Forest" (Paul J. Smith, Gil George), "I Asked My Love a Favor" (Smith, Lawrence E. Watkin). **p**, Walt Disney; **d**, Herschel Daugherty; **cast**, James MacArthur, Carol Lynley, Fess Parker, Wendell Corey, Joanne Dru, Jessica Tandy, John McIntire, Joseph Calleia, Iron Eyes Cody, Eddie Little Sky; **w**, Lawrence Edward Watkin (based on the novel by Conrad Richter); **c**, Ellsworth Fredericks (Technicolor); **m**, Paul J. Smith; **ed**, Stanley Johnson; **art d**, Carroll Clark; **set d**, Emile Kuri, Fred

Ronald Colman and Walter Huston in *The Light That Failed*, 1939.

MacLean; **spec eff**, Peter Ellenshaw.

Light in the Piazza ★★★ 1962; U.S.; 102m; MGM; Color; Drama; Children: Cautionary; **DVD**. An upscale American couple, de Havilland and Sullivan, have a beautiful daughter, Mimieux, who is twenty-six-years-old, but, because of a childhood injury to her head, she is mentally disabled with the mind of a ten-year-old. On vacation in Florence, Italy, de Havilland and Mimieux meet Hamilton, a handsome twenty-three-year-old Italian, and the two young people are immediately attracted to each other. At first, de Havilland opposes their mutual affection, but, after getting to know Hamilton better and meeting his friendly and also upscale family, she thinks their marriage might be all right and may actually help her daughter to lead a normal life. De Havilland does not tell Hamilton's parents, Brazzi and Nevinson, about her daughter's mental condition, and Sullivan opposes her marriage and instead wants her placed in an institution, which further strains de Havilland's and Sullivan's own marriage. De Havilland finally tells Brazzi about Mimieux's mental retardation, but the compassionate Brazzi says it does not matter and, over Sullivan's objections, the two are married. A sensitive film with excellent performances and filmed in beautiful Florence where the priceless treasures of the Uffizi Museum are shown for the first time on film. **p**, Arthur Freed; **d**, Guy Green; **cast**, Olivia de Havilland, Rossano Brazzi, Yvette Mimieux, George Hamilton, Isabel Dean, Moultrie Kelsall, Nancy Nevinson, Barry Sullivan, Luciano Barontino, Peppino De Martino; **w**, Julius J. Epstein (based on the novel by Elizabeth Spencer); **c**, Otto Heller (CinemaScope; Metrocolor); **m**, Mario Nascimbene; **ed**, Frank Clarke; **art d**, Frank White; **set d**, Tom Howard.

The Light of Western Stars ★★★ 1930; U.S.; 70m; PAR; B/W; Western; Children: Acceptable; **DVD**; **VHS**. Arlen is an alcoholic cowboy, who sobers up quickly when he sees Brian arrive from the East to claim a ranch once owned by her murdered brother, who was Arlen's best friend. Smitten by Brian, Arlen resolves to help her run the family ranch. Meanwhile, Kohler and his vicious gang of thieves and rustlers do all they can to take over that ranch, but Arlen ingeniously finds ways to outwit and best them and where Brian ends up in the cowboy's arms for a happy trail ending. Considerable humor is shown through some witty scenes and slapstick, but none of this is overdone in producing this above-average oater. This western was twice made in the silent era, 1918 and 1925. It was again remade in 1940, but this version remains the best of the productions based upon the Zane Grey classic. **p**, Harry Sherman; **d**, Otto Brower, Edwin H. Knopf; **cast**, Richard Arlen, Mary Brian, Harry Green, Regis Toomey, Fred Kohler, Guy Oliver, George Chandler, William Gillis, William Le Maire, Lew Meehan, Gus Saville, Syd Saylor; **w**, Grover Jones, William Slavens McNutt (based on the novel by

Zane Grey); **c**, Charles Lang; **m**, Charles Midgely; **ed**, Jane Loring.

The Light That Failed ★★★★ 1939; U.S.; 97m; PAR; B/W; Drama; Children: Cautionary; **DVD**; **VHS**. Colmân gives another riveting performance as an inspired British painter, who, while serving in the Sudan, receives a saber cut on his head during a battle. He returns to England where he recuperates and now has time to fulfill his ambition to become a full-time artist as his wound has disabled him from further military service. While he begins to see old flame Angelus, Colman paints his war experiences in the Sudan, encouraged by his good friend, Huston. His paintings are successful and he goes on to paint portraits, but when his eyesight begins to fail from his old wound, he strives to create a masterpiece, which he titles "Melancholia." Colman hires Lupino, a young Cockney woman from the slums of London and who has eked out a living as a prostitute. She falls in love with Colman, but knows that he will never marry a woman from such a lowly station; while she gives all her affection to him, Colman obsessively demands that she pose for his masterpiece for endless hours, and, to get the right expression and deranged personality from Lupino on canvas, purposely drives her to hysteria. She is driven half mad in the process and, after Colman completes his last work and has by then gone almost blind, Lupino returns to his studio where she savagely attacks the masterpiece, slashing its canvas to shreds and smearing it with paint oils before she runs off. Colman, unaware of what Lupino has done, invites Angelus to view his last great work, and, when she sees it in shambles she does not have the courage to tell Colman that it is in ruins. Lupino then returns, and she drives the final thrust of her rage into Colman's confidence by telling him that she has destroyed his masterpiece, even though she expresses remorse and seeks forgiveness, which the compassionate Colman extends to her. Colman now has nothing to live for, so he travels back to the Sudan where he meets with his old friend Huston and, just as a battle is ensuing, begs Huston to "put me in it." Huston, knowing his dear friend has gone blind and has no desire to go on living, directs Colman toward the battle and he charges with his old troops on a dashing white horse into the heart of the fighting where he is killed. His horse survives and emerges from the smoking melee without its rider. Seeing this Huston turns to another friend, Digges, to say: "God has been merciful, Nilghai. He is dead." Colman's sensitive and often spell-binding performance is nothing less than magnificent as the idealistic painter and pantheon Wellman's meticulous direction fully captures the Kipling tale of advancing male friendship, love of honor and the nobility of the human spirit. ***Author's Note***: Wellman told this author that he loved directing this tale as he was a great admirer of Kipling, but he and Colman clashed many times during the production. Colman was, like only a few others in the film industry, such as Paul Muni, perched on the pedestal of every producer and that he had the uncommon right to select whatever films he wanted to make. "Everyone treated Ronald Colman with kid gloves," Wellman said to this author. "He approached every film in which he appeared as if he were about to conduct Beethoven at the Philharmonic Orchestra. Admittedly, there was no one like him. He never missed a cue or flubbed a line. He was flawless. He was also a perfectionist. In **The Light That Failed**, he wanted every scene precisely his way and as he saw each scene in that picture. He demanded so many retakes that he drove me nuts. I told him repeatedly after he did his scenes that he had done them better than anyone could do them, including himself, but that was not enough for him. 'Let's try it again,' he would say, 'I want to try a slightly different approach on that last line,' or 'perhaps it would be better if I did not turn to her [Lupino] in such a threatening manner, so we should reshoot that scene, I think.' I knew he was living that role as he lived inside the roles of all of the pictures he ever made, but he was making a living hell for me. To tell you the truth, he was one of the greatest actors among great actors and had the most beautiful voice in the history of the motion picture business, but there was only one thing he and I could agree on in that picture and that was that we simply did not like each other." When Colman decided that he would do the film, he also demanded that Vivien Leigh play the role of the slatternly model that ultimately destroys Colman's masterpiece and his life, but to everyone's surprise, Colman did not get his way in this instance. Instead, it went to the determined Lupino. "I wanted that role in the worst way," Lupino told this author. "I tried to see Bill [Wellman], but he kept putting me off. I finally stormed into his office at Paramount and told him that there was no other actress on the face of the earth who could play Bessie [the role of the trollop posing for Colman's painting]. I had gotten a copy of the script and had studied that part and I proceeded to act it out in front of Bill right then and there. When I finished, he stared at me for a moment or two and then said: 'You're Bessie!' That role made my career as I knew it would." Indeed, it did, as Lupino gave a mesmerizing performance of a lonely woman from the gutter whose passion surmounts that of Colman's desire for artistic immortality and one that consumes them both. **p&d**, William A. Wellman; **cast**, Ronald Colman, Walter Huston, Muriel Angelus, Ida Lupino, Dudley Digges, Ernest Cossart, Ferike Boros, Pedro de Cordoba, Ronal Sinclair, Sarita Wooton, Halliwell Hobbes; **w**, Robert Carson (based on the novel by Rudyard Kipling); **c**, Theodor Sparkuhl; **m**, Victor Young; **ed**, Thomas Scott; **art d**, Hans Dreier, Robert Odell.

The Lighthorsemen ★★★ 1988; Australia; 131m; Australian Film Commission/Cinecom Pictures; Color; War Drama; Children: Unacceptable (MPAA: PG); **DVD**; **VHS**. This exciting and often stirring film depicts the exploits of four Australian volunteers serving in the Australian 4th Light Horse Brigade of cavalry fighting in the Palestine and Sinai campaigns of WWI and, chiefly, at the battle of Beersheba on October 31, 1917. Faithfully based on fact and drawing on the lives of four actual participants, the story begins with Sweet, Blake, Walton and McKenzie serving in Palestine. Sweet is wounded in battle and subsequently dies of his wounds, and is replaced by Phelps. When Phelps finds that he cannot for some reason (most probably as a conscientious objector) fire his weapon, he is transferred to a medical unit but where he will nevertheless be exposed to the same gunfire as his compatriots. When Turkish cavalry attacks a British position, British forces hastily retreat, but Andrews, a British major, purposely leaves behind the British plans for an attack on Beersheba, those plans detailing the attack as a diversion. The Australian cavalry then departs for Beersheba, taking with it only limited supplies of water and ammunition and when they confront the German-Turkish forces there, which number about 4,000 defenders, a German military adviser who has obtained the plans left behind by Andrews, tells the Turkish commander that he will not need to call for reinforcements as the attack is only a diversion. Low on supplies and water, time is running out for the Australian forces, and its commander asks British higher-ups for permission to have the Lighthorsemen mount a cavalry charge at Beersheba. The British believe that the attack is suicidal but give reluctant permission, and the 4th and 12th Light Horse Brigades are ordered to form their ranks and prepare to charge. Phelps joins his medical unit, which is to follow in the wake of the incredible charge. The Turkish commander orders his artillery to hold fire until the cavalry dismounts, having his gunners fix the sites of their guns for long range. Then the order to move forward is given and the Australian troopers go forth at a canter, then a trot, until the order is given to make a full-out charge and the troopers go forward at a wild gallop. The Turkish commander then realizes that the Australians are not conducting a diversion, but intend to take the town in a wild cavalry charge and he immediately orders his gunners to adjust the sites of their guns and open fire. As the Australians charge forward, the Turkish shells fall behind their dashing ranks, the Australians riding pell-mell and at great speed to keep "under the guns," and ahead of the stepping barrage that consistently explodes shells behind their ranks. It is a mad flight for life and victory (and one of the most suspenseful and thrilling scenes ever put on film) as the heroic cavalrymen race forward, their charge not dissimilar to those brave British troopers who fought in the Crimean War and who attempted to capture the strongly held Russian positions on the heights at

Jon Blake and Peter Phelps in *The Lighthorsemen*, 1988.

Balaclava on October 5, 1854 (and as were equally and excitingly enacted in **The Charge of the Light Brigade**, 1936, and its 1986 remake). The Australians are now close to reaching the Turkish position, and Walton is killed in that attack. The Australians reach the first line of Turkish defenses, and Blake and others overwhelm the defenders, and take control of the Turkish guns. McKenzie is wounded when the Australians savagely fight with the Turks in the trenches, and Phelps goes to his aid and is also seriously wounded. Blake and others battle their way into the town, capturing Turkish troops. A German officer attempts to blow up the water wells, but Blake and others capture him before he can set off the explosive charge. The incredible battle has been won by the courageous Australians in what is one of the last cavalry charges in modern warfare. The stunning action is masterfully directed by Wincer (where the actual charge is utterly breathtaking), and all the cast members give sterling performances in this fine war film. *Author's Note*: In the actual charge at Beersheba, the Australian cavalry raced across an open area of more than three miles to reach the Turkish line of defense. The 4th Light Horse Brigade lost thirty-one men and thirty-six more were wounded. The British captured more than 4,000 Turkish troops; overall British losses amounted to 171 men. **p**, Jan Bladier, Antony I. Ginnane, Ian Jones, David Lee, Simon Wincer; **d**, Wincer; **cast**, Peter Phelps, John Walton, Tim McKenzie, Jon Blake, Anthony Andrews, Sigrid Thornton, Gary Sweet, Tony Bonner, Bill Kerr, Nick Waters, John Larking; **w**, Jones; **c**, Dean Semler; **m**, Mario Millo; **ed**, Adrian Carr; **prod d**, Bernard Hides; **art d**, Virginia Bieneman; **spec eff**, Steve Courtley, Conrad Rothmann.

Lightnin' ★★★ 1930; U.S.; 96m; FOX; B/W; Comedy; Children: Acceptable; **VHS**. Fans of Will Rogers will love this very funny film where he is a shiftless husband of Dresser, who owns and operates a boarding house that sits squarely between California and Nevada and is conveniently visited by California-based women wanting to get quick divorces in Nevada. Dresser does all the work in the place and her lazy hubby, Rogers, sardonically called "Lightnin'" by Dresser, walks about giving sage advice on everything from the use of patent medicines to how to have a successful marriage. His fetching daughter, Cohan (the actual daughter of entertainer and composer George M. Cohan), meets and falls for McCrea, a young man who has been framed on a charge of embezzlement, and who takes refuge at the boarding house. When a California sheriff arrives with an arrest warrant, McCrea simply walks to another room where he is no longer in California but in Nevada and out of the sheriff's jurisdiction and therefore free from arrest. McCrea and Cohan eventually get together, and Rogers goes on loafing and telling his stories, even though Dresser sues him for divorce; the film concludes with a hilarious courtroom scene where Rogers talks his way back into

Showgirls in *Lights of New York*, 1928.

her good graces. *Author's Note*: This story began as a 1918 play, which became a great success and ran on Broadway for many years. Rogers wanted the role for some time and he made the most of it in this entertaining film, albeit some of his wry remarks would no longer be suitable with today's sensitivities (he makes an offbeat remark about China having the best solution for divorce in that that country girl babies are quickly drowned). **p**, John Golden, Henry King; **d**, King; **cast**, Will Rogers, Louise Dresser, Joel McCrea, Helen Cohan, Jason Robards, Sr., Luke Cosgrave, J.M. Kerrigan, Ruth Warren, Joyce Compton, Rex Bell; **w**, S.N. Berman, Sonya Levien (based on the play by Winchell Smith and Frank Bacon); **c**, Chester A. Lyons; **m**, Arthur Kay; **ed**, Louis R. Loeffler; **art d**, Harry Oliver.

Lights of New York ★★★ 1928; U.S.; 57m; WB; B/W; Crime Drama; Children: Unacceptable; **VHS**. The historic value of this film is that it was the very first all-talking motion picture, one that dwelled upon the contemporary sensationalism of the deadly bootleggers who widely operated in the U.S. during Prohibition. Landis and Pallette migrate to New York to seek their fortunes and buy a barbershop only to find that it is being used as a front for a bootlegging operation run by Oakman, a nightclub owner and the boss of some of the city's rackets. Oakman is a man of few words and his deeds are devastating. He does not hesitate to order the deaths of anyone interfering with his lucrative rackets and, at one point, utters a line that later became a cliché in crime movies, telling a henchman to eliminate a rival gangster and to "take him for a ride." Oakman is murdered, and Landis is framed for the killing after the gun used to kill Oakman is conveniently found on the apprentice barber. Before Landis goes innocently to the electric chair, however, the cops prove that the gun belonged to Costello, a singer at Oakman's nightclub, but she, too, is innocent, until Brockwell, Oakman's mistress, is proven to be the culprit. The story is crude and the dialog terse and packed with street argot and slang, but that makes this tale of assorted and fascinating lowlifes all the more fascinating while director Foy captures all the ersatz allure of the big city's bright lights and nighttime glamour where fast cars, fast women and fast-lived lives are profiled at a dizzying pace. *Author's Note*: Foy, who was the oldest son of famed comedian Eddie Foy, later became head of "B" production at Warner Brothers, cranking out scores of programmers for the studio, but these films, like the similar "B" productions of other studios, proved to be a wonderful training ground for a generation of talented actors, directors, producers, cinematographers and composers. Oakman's ominous line about taking a rival gangster "for a ride" was first enacted in reality in Chicago by Prohibition gangster and bootlegger Earl "Hymie" Weiss (1898-1926), a confederate of North Side boss Charles Dion O'Banion (or O'Bannion; 1892-1924), who, in July 1921, was the first recorded underworld killer

to so dispatch a victim, taking rival bootlegger Steve Wisniewski for a "one-way ride." Weiss kidnapped his victim and drove him to a remote area at the outskirts of Chicago where he killed him, dumping the body in a ditch. Wisniewski, who was an O'Banion truck driver hauling illegal booze, thought to betray his boss and hijack and sell the alcohol. For more details on Weiss and Wisniewski, see my book, *World Encyclopedia of Organized Crime* (Paragon House, 1992, pages 402-403). **d**, Bryan Foy; **cast**, Helene Costello, Cullen Landis, Gladys Brockwell, Mary Carr, Wheeler Oakman, Eugene Pallette, Robert Elliott, Tom Dugan, Tom McGuire; **w**, Hugh Herbert, Murray Roth (based on a story by Charles R. Gaskill); **c**, E. B. Du Par; **ed**, Jack Killifer.

Like Mike ★★★ 2002; U.S.; 99m; FOX; Color; Comedy; Fantasy; Sports; Children: Unacceptable (MPAA: PG); **DVD**; **VHS**. Calvin, a 13-year-old black boy named Bow Wow, and his friends, who live in a Los Angeles orphanage, find an old pair of basketball shoes hanging from a power line. As they go for it on a stormy night, they and the shoes are struck by lightning. The boys are not hurt, but when they take a closer look at the shoes they see the initials "M. J." inside and believe the shoes belonged to basketball great Michael Jordan. Calvin puts on the shoes and finds that he has fantastic basketball powers and may be able to play for the National Basketball Association. Forster, the coach of the local NBA team, gives Calvin tickets to a game and the boy gets in a half-time shooting competition with an NBA star. He sinks so many baskets that he is signed to play in the starting lineup and leads the team to the finals. Gutter language prohibits viewing by children. **p**, Peter Heller, Barry Josephson, Teresa Caldwell, Jeremaine Dupri, Michael Mauldin; **d**, John Schultz; **cast**, Crispin Glover, Anne Meara, Robert Forster, Bow Wow, Morris Chestnut, Jonathan Lipnicki, Brenda Song, Jesse Plemons, Julius Charles Ritter, Eugene Levy, Roger Morrissey, Timon Kyle, Stephen Thompson, Vanessa Williams; **w**, Michael Elliot, Jordan Moffet (based on a story by Elliot); **c**, Shawn Maurer; **m**, Richard Gibbs; **ed**, Peter Berger, John Pace; **prod d**, Arlan Jay Vetter; **art d**, John R. Zachary; **set d**, Suzette Sheets; **spec eff**, Paul J. Lombardi, Ray McIntyre, Jr., Kevin Kipper, Bonnie Kanner.

Lilac Time ★★★ 1928 (silent); U.S.; 80m/11 reels; First National Pictures; B/W; War Drama; Children: Cautionary; **DVD**; **VHS**. Set during WWI in France, a unit of the Royal Flying Corps is stationed on land owned by a French farmer whose daughter is Moore. She is the adopted "daughter of the flying unit," and all of the pilots affectionately treat her as a little sister. Cooper arrives at the unit to replace a pilot, who has been killed in action. When Cooper and Moore meet for the first time, they dislike each other, but they slowly become friendly and then fall in love. Whenever Cooper must take to the air Moore's anxiety increases as she hopes and prays for his safe return. That hazard increases when the entire unit is ordered to fly on what is essentially a suicide mission. Cooper and Moore make their farewells, but Cooper promises that he will return. He does return, but his plane is damaged during the mission and he crash lands into a house at a nearby village. Red Cross workers drag him from the burning wreckage and he is driven to a hospital. Moore, desperate and anxious, rushes to the hospital, but she is crushed when she is told that Cooper is dead. Dazed, Moore begins to wander away, feeling that her life has ended when Cooper calls to her from a hospital window. She rushes to his side and they are united once more for a happy ending. Moore and Cooper are outstanding in this well-crafted film, which features some impressive aerial battle sequences. It also has elements of **Wings**, 1927, in which Cooper also appeared in a supporting role, and offers the same kind of romantic themes to be found in **7th Heaven**, 1927. **p**, George Fitzmaurice, John McCormick; **d**, Fitzmaurice, Frank Lloyd; **cast**, Colleen Moore, Gary Cooper, Burr McIntosh, George Cooper, Cleve Moore, Kathryn McGuire, Eugenie Besserer, Emile Chautard, Jack Stoney, Edward Dillon, Arthur Lake; **w**, Carey Wilson, Willis Goldbeck, George Marion, Jr., Adela Rogers St. Johns (based on the book by Guy Fowler and the play by Jane Cowl,

Jane Murfin); **c**, Sidney Hickox; **m**, Cecil Copping, Nathaniel Shilkret; **ed**, Alexander Hall; **art d**, Horace Jackson.

Lili ★★★ 1953; U.S.; 81m; MGM; Color; Drama; Children: Acceptable; **DVD**; **VHS**. The always charming Caron gives a wonderful performance in this delightful film where she, as a sixteen-year-old, runs away from home to become a waitress in a small carnival. She befriends handsome and kindly Aumont, who is the carnival's magician. His avuncular attitude toward Caron endears him to her, and she translates her affections for him into what she thinks is love, but he is only amused by her and is married to Gabor, who serves as his assistant in his act. Caron pays so much attention to Aumont that she is fired. Emotionally crushed, she finds consolation by watching the puppets in a puppet show at the carnival that is operated by Ferrer, who is a former dancer, but who is embittered for having been crippled in WWII. It is Ferrer who truly loves Caron, and he expresses that love through his heart-warming puppets that Caron comes to identify with; a magical scene takes place when the dancing puppets sing what became a world-famous song, "Hi Lili, Hi Lo" (music by Bronislau Kaper; lyrics by Helen Deutsch). Ferrer, however, cannot express his affection directly to Caron and he finally, seized by overpowering jealousy over her emotional attention to Aumont, slaps her. Caron then packs her bags and is about to leave the carnival, but she now realizes that the love shown to her from the puppets is love being shown to her by Ferrer, and she goes back to him and he take her into his arms for a great happy ending. Caron was nominated for an Oscar as Best Actress and director Walters, who carefully and naturally develops Caron's sensitive character into something beautiful to view, was nominated for an Oscar as Best Director. Kaper did win an Oscar for Best Dramatic or Comedy Score in which he includes another song "Adoration." *Author's Note*: The film was the basis for a 1961 musical titled "Carnival," which was a great hit, starring Anna Maria Alberghetti. The notion of creating Broadway shows from films was then a rare instance, but became commonplace by the 1970s. **p**, Edwin H. Knopf; **d**, Charles Walters; **cast**, Leslie Caron, Mel Ferrer, Jean-Pierre Aumont, Zsa Zsa Gabor, Kurt Kasznar, Amanda Blake, Alex Gerry, Ralph Dumke, Wilton Graff, George Baxter; **w**, Helen Deutsch (based on the story by Paul Gallico); **c**, Robert Planck (Technicolor); **m**, Bronislau Kaper; **ed**, Ferris Webster; **art d**, Cedric Gibbons, Paul Groesse; **set d**, Edwin B. Willis, Arthur Krams; **spec eff**, Warren Newcombe.

Lilies of the Field ★★★ 1930; U.S.; 60m; First National Pictures; B/W; Drama; Children: Unacceptable; **VHS**. Griffith gives a powerfully empathetic performance as a woman who slowly loses everything important in life. She loses her husband in a bitter divorce where she is also deprived of her child. She then drowns her sorrows in nightclubs and jazz joints where she becomes a gold-digging call girl and eventually sinks lower and lower until she is arrested for vagrancy, having no real hope for a better future. The depressing story line is overcome by Griffith's enactment of a "fallen woman," the finest characterization in her career. Spritely directed by Korda, this film offers a bevy of superior songs that include: "I'd Like to Be a Gypsy" (Michael Cleary, Ned Washington), "Sous la fenetre" (Cecile Chaminade), "Song of the Gold Diggers" (Joseph Burke), "I Found You" (Lillian Goodman), "There Was Nothing Else to Do" (Harry Warren, Harry Ruby), "Mechanical Ballet" (Michael Cleary), "Congratulations" (Maceo Pinkard), "Gladly" (Harold Arlen), "Thoughts at Twilight" (Edwin F. Kendall), "La mort de Dea" (Dyck), "Am I Blue" (Harry Akst, Grant Clarke), "Bridal Chorus" (from "Lohengrin" by Richard Wagner). **p**, Walter Morosco; **d**, Alexander Korda; **cast**, Corinne Griffith, Ralph Forbes, John Loder, Eve Southern, Jean Bary, Tyler Brooke, Freeman Wood, Ann Schaeffer, Clarissa Selwynne, Virginia Bruce; **w**, John F. Goodrich (based on the novel by William Hurlbut); **c**, Lee Garmes.

Lilies of the Field ★★★ 1963; U.S.; 94m; Rainbow Productions/UA;

Nuns and Sidney Poitier in *Lilies of the Field*, 1963.

B/W; Drama; Children: Acceptable; **DVD**; **VHS**. This touching and memorable film sees the gifted Poitier, an ex-GI, driving through the Southwest, looking for new opportunities. He stops at a dilapidated farm to get some water for his car's radiator and there meets five German nuns, who have inherited the place and are determined to establish the site as a religious center. Skala, the mother superior, persuades Poitier to remain and do a few chores. He fixes their leaky roof and the nuns send prayer of thanks for the man "sent by God." Poitier stays on to do a few more chores and work the farm, but when they ask him to undertake a major job—building a new chapel, he expresses reservations. He agrees as long as the nuns supply the work materials. When Poitier goes to townspeople to get aid in the project, he is rejected, but he continues nevertheless, and finds one man, Nelson (who is also the director of this film), to help him build the small chapel. Poitier meanwhile patiently teaches the nuns how to speak English—and this is one of the most charming and heartwarming scenes in the film. The materials to build the chapel, however, run out and so does Poitier, but he returns some time later to complete the chapel and, by that time, the townspeople have softened their hearts and pitch in to finish the job. When the nuns gather with the townspeople for the sanctification of the chapel, Poitier leaves as inauspiciously as he arrived to end this thoroughly engrossing film. This little film was a sleeper that saw great success at the box office and it deservedly won for Poitier an Oscar as Best Actor (the first time the award whet to a black man) and it also got nominations for Oscars as Best Picture, Best Supporting Actress (Skala), and Best Cinematography (Haller). **p&d**, Ralph Nelson; **cast**, Sidney Poitier, Lilia Skala, Lisa Mann, Isa Crino, Francesca Jarvis, Pamela Branch, Stanley Adams, Dan Frazer, Nelson; **w**, James Poe (based on the novel by William E. Barrett); **c**, Ernest Haller; **m**, Jerry Goldsmith; **ed**, John W. McCafferty.

Liliom ★★★ 1935; France; 85m; FOX; B/W; Fantasy; Children: Cautionary; **DVD**; **VHS**. Director Lang presents an absorbing fantasy that sees Boyer working as a barker for a merry-go-round at an amusement park in Budapest. He is having an affair with Florelle, who owns the carousel and who is insanely jealous of Boyer. Rignault, a rival barker, tries to get Boyer into trouble by telling Florelle that Boyer is flirting with female customers. Florelle sees Boyer with Ozeray and her girlfriend and insults both female customers. When Boyer defends them, Florelle fires him. He and Ozeray then go on a date and fall in love, and Ozeray moves into Boyer's run-down trailer where he loafs about, takes to drink, and begins arguing with her while she holds onto a job in a photo studio. Florelle then offers Boyer a raise if he will take back his old job with the understanding that their old romance will continue. Boyer, who loves Ozeray, refuses. Ozeray becomes pregnant and now Boyer is desperate to get money to support her and his forthcoming

Jumba and Pleakley in *Lilo & Stitch*, 2002.

child. He teams up with an old friend, Alcover, a professional criminal, to rob a payroll, but the robbery goes awry; hunted by police, Boyer uses a knife to mortally stab himself. When he dies, his spirit leaves his body and he is accompanied by two angels, "God's policemen," who escort him to a celestial court dealing with suicides and where he is told that he must suffer in purgatory for sixteen years. Following that, his spirit will be allowed to return to earth for one day and his behavior on that day will determine where he will spend eternity. Boyer makes that visit and meets with his lovely daughter, giving her a star he has filched on his trip to earth, but when he tells her that he knew her long-ago deceased father and that he was a brute, the girl tosses the star into the gutter. The sobbing girl starts for home, and Boyer catches up with her; when she tells him to go away, he slaps her hand out of frustration and then departs. Upon his return to the Hereafter, Boyer's actions in hurting a child apparently condemns him to Hell, but then the heavenly officials see that, on Earth, the daughter interprets the slap she received as a kiss and asks her mother if such actions can be so translated. Ozeray now believes that Boyer has somehow found a way to spiritually contact their daughter and she tells the girl that a slap can, indeed, be a kiss, remembering her life with Boyer when he was alive and on Earth. With his love thusly conveyed to his daughter, Boyer's spiritual future is now on a course for Heaven and not Hell. Lang does a great job with this sensitive tale from the Molnár play, and his heavenly scenes are beautifully photographed without visual pretensions. Boyer is outstanding in his role of the father willing to sacrifice his eternal fate by expressing in his commonplace way his love for his daughter. This is a superior remake of a 1930 talkie film, which was later adapted for a fine musical, **Carousel**, 1956. *Author's Note*: Lang declared that this film was his favorite production of all the films he helmed during his illustrious career. **p**, Erich Pommer; **d**, Fritz Lang; **cast**, Charles Boyer, Madeleine Ozeray, Florelle, Pierre Alcover, Robert Arnoux, Roland Toutain, Alexandre Rignault, Henri Richard, Marcel Barencey, Raoul Marco, Léon Arvel, Viviane Romance; **w**, Lang, Robert Liebmann, Bernard Zimmer (based on the play by Franz Molnár); **c**, Rudolph Maté, Louis Nee; **m**, Jean Lenoir, Franz Waxman; **art d**, André Daven; **set d**, Paul Colin, Rene Rénoux.

Lilo & Stitch ★★★ 2002; 85m; Walt Disney/Buena Vista; Color; Animated Feature; Children: Cautionary (MPAA: PG); **DVD**; **VHS**. On a distant planet, a scientist (Stiers voiceover) invents a strong, intelligent creature that is nearly indestructible except it cannot swim. The planet's rulers disapprove of his unauthorized genetic experiment, so he is sentenced to jail, but escapes. His creature is to be sent to a prison asteroid, but it also escapes and rides a spaceship to Earth. Arriving in Hawaii, it is pursued by its inventor and his sidekick (McDonald voiceover). It is

adopted by a girl, Lilo (Chase voiceover), who calls it Stitch (Sanders voiceover). She mistakes it for a dog, and tries to civilize it. Lilo's older sister (Carrere voiceover) works in a Hawaiian musical show where her boyfriend (Lee voiceover) is a fire dancer. Stitch is not an easy pet to have around the house, trashing the place and building a model city in Lilo's bedroom, so he can play alien monster. Meanwhile, a social worker is after Lilo and her sister since their parents had been killed in an automobile accident and they are orphans. Lilo's sister is given three days to prove she is a suitable guardian, and Stitch has to escape his alien pursuers. Everyone learns to care for each other as "ohama," the Hawaiian word for family. Songs (include: "Stuck on You" (Jo Leslie McFarland, Aaron Schroeder, sung by Elvis Presley), "Devil in Disguise" (Bill Giant, Bernie Baum, Florence Kaye, sung by Presley), "Hound Dog" (Jerry Leiber, Mike Stoller, sung by Presley), "Heartbreak Hotel" (Presley, sung by Presley), "Burning Love" (Dennis Linde, sung by Wynonna), "Hawaiian Rollercoaster Ride," "He Mele No Lilo" (Mark Keali, sung by the Kamehameha Schools Children's Chorus), "Stitch to the Rescue," "You Can Never Belong" (Alan Silvestri), "Can't Help Falling in Love" (Hugo Petretti, Luigi Creatore, George Davis Weiss, sung by A*Teens). **p**, Clark Spencer; **d&w**, Dean Debois, Chris Sanders; **cast** (voiceovers), Daveigh Chase, Christopher Michael Sanders, Tia Carrere, David Ogden Stiers, Kevin McDonald, Ving Rhames, Zoe Caldwell, Jason Scott Lee, Kevin Michael Richardson; **m**, Alan Silvestri; **ed**, Darren T. Holmes; **prod d**, Paul Felix; **art d**, Ric Sluiter; **spec eff**, Joseph F. Gilland, Rob Nekuhrs, Jason Buske.

Limbo ★★★ 1972; U.S.; 111m; Omaha/UNIV; Color; Drama; Children: Cautionary (MPAA: PG). This engrossing tale offers a film about women whose husbands went missing in action in the Vietnam War (1959-1975). The husband of Nolan, the mother of four children, was listed as missing for several years. Justice, a socialite, refuses to believe her husband was killed. Jackson and her husband had been married only two weeks before he went off to war. She was later notified he was missing in action, and meanwhile has met another man. One of a very few films about the war's effect on the home front and which was made while the war was going on. **p**, Linda Gottlieb; **d**, Mark Robson; **cast**, Kate Jackson, Katherine Justice, Stuart Margolin, Hazel Medina, Kathleen Nolan, Russell Wiggins, Joan Murphy, Mike Bersell, Kim Nicholas, Ken Kornbluh; **w**, Joan Micklin Silver, James Bridges (based on a story by Silver); **c**, Charles F. Wheeler; **m**, Anita Kerr; **ed**, Dorothy Spencer; **art d**, James W. Sullivan; **set d**, Don Ivy.

Limelight ★★★★ 1952; U.S.; 141m; Celebrated Productions/UA; B/W; Drama; Children: Unacceptable; **DVD**; **VHS**. Again the great Chaplin renders a bravura performance in his bittersweet farewell to the musical hall entertainment of yesteryear. Set at the turn of the 20th Century, Chaplin is a famed stage comedian, who discovers Bloom, a dancer so depressed at her career setbacks that she attempts suicide in the boarding house where they both live. Chaplin takes pity on the attractive, young Bloom, taking her in and nursing her back to health. When she recuperates, he encourages her, building her confidence, and aids her in achieving success as a dancer. In one of many endearing scenes, Chaplin teaches Bloom his "laughter therapy," and as her career sees more and more promise, his declines. He finishes in one last show where he uses his old comedic routines with great skill and wonderful humor and where he imagines himself to be a fearless lion tamer, but one who only trains fleas. He stages a comeback that is financed by old friend and theater tycoon Bruce and where he performs with the great Buster Keaton in a side-splitting musical skit where Chaplin's legs appear to miraculously shorten and where he walks lopsided. The skit exhausts him and he collapses into the orchestra pit where he becomes wedged in a large drum. He is carried back onto the stage and says farewell to his adoring audience by stating: "Ladies and gentlemen, I would like to say something, but I am stuck." He is carried backstage and there suffers a heart attack, dying happy in the belief that Bloom has fallen in love with a young composer, Sydney Chaplin, when, in reality, she loves only the indomitable Charles Chaplin. This poignant and memorable salute to the circus and musical hall slapstick comedy of another era is wonderfully reprised by Chaplin, who is really the whole show here, producing and writing the script, starring in and directing the film, as well as composing the haunting score, and winning an Oscar for its main theme song "Eternally." *Author's Note*: Bloom, who was only nineteen when making this film, saw her career soar from her appearance in **Limelight**, although she had debuted on the screen at the age of sixteen. She later praised Chaplin as a great director, but that she "was surprised at how old-fashioned much of what he prescribed seemed—rather theatrical effects that I didn't associate with the modern cinema." **p,d&w**, Charles Chaplin; **cast**, Chaplin, Claire Bloom, Nigel Bruce, Buster Keaton, Sydney Chaplin, Norman Lloyd, Marjorie Bennett, "Snub" Pollard, Charles Chaplin, Jr., Geraldine Chaplin, Josephine Chaplin, Michael Chaplin, Oona Chaplin, Edna Purviance; **c**, Karl Struss; **m**, Charles Chaplin; **ed**, Joe Inge; **art d**, Eugene Lourie.

The Lincoln Lawyer ★★★ 2011; U.S.; 118m; Lionsgate; Color; Crime Drama; Children: Unacceptable (MPAA: R); **BD**, **DVD**. Fascinating crime yarn has McConaughey as a hustling criminal defense attorney, who operates in Los Angeles out of his Lincoln Town Car, picking up random lowlife cases, but he scores big when representing Phillippe, a Beverly Hills playboy whose mother, Fisher, is a real estate tycoon. Phillippe has been accused of assault and battery for savagely beating up prostitute Levieva. When Macy, who is McConaughey's investigator, shows him some police photos depicting the injuries sustained by his client, McConaughey is reminded of similar wounds sustained in a long-ago murder case where his client, Peña, was convicted and sent to prison for life. He now wonders if he should have worked harder on that case, instead of having his client plead guilty in order to avoid a death sentence. McConaughey visits Peña in San Quentin Prison, and his client becomes alarmed when seeing the new photos of the alleged victim of McConaughey's new client, saying that they are the same kind of wounds inflicted on the murdered person for which he went to prison for life. Now McConaughey suspects that Phillippe may have been the real killer in that earlier case, but he hesitates to inform authorities about his suspicion in that it would violate attorney-client confidentiality regulations. McConaughey's suspicions are confirmed that night when Phillippe invades his residence and admits that he, indeed, committed that long-ago murder and subtly threatens McConaughey's family if the attorney talks about his admission. Macy is then found dead, murdered, shot to death with a pistol that Phillippe has apparently taken from McConaughey's residence. In court, McConaughey purposely botches his own case, causing the case against Phillippe to be dismissed, but also has new information about the old murder case involving Peña brought into the trial, which now threatens Phillippe. Seeking revenge on his attorney, Phillippe plans to murder Tomei, McConaughey's ex-wife, and their child, but a tough group of bikers McConaughey has earlier represented appear and trash Phillippe's expensive car and then beat him mercilessly and where McConaughey tells the bikers to send Phillippe "to the hospital, not the morgue." Later, Fisher arrives, gun in hand, admitting that, to protect her pampered and worthless son, Phillippe, she committed the murder for which Peña was wrongly convicted. She shoots and wounds McConaughey, but he fires back and kills her. After recovering from his wound and released from a hospital, McConaughey learns that Peña will now be released from prison. **p**, Sidney Kimmel, Tom Rosenberg, Gary Lucchesi, Richard Wright, Scott Steindorff; **d**, Brad Furman; **cast**, Matthew McConaughey, Marisa Tomei, Ryan Phillippe, William H. Macy, Michael Peña, Frances Fisher, Margarita Levieva, Josh Lucas, John Lequizamo, Bob Gunton, Bryan Cranston, Trace Adkins, Laurence Mason; **w**, John Romano (based on the novel by Michael Connelly); **c**, Lukas Ettlin; **m**, Cliff Martinez; **ed**, Jim McEvoy; **prod d**, Charisse Cardenas; **set d**, Nancy Nye; **spec eff**, Dennis Dion.

Eli Wallach, Mary LaRoche, Robert Keith and Richard Jaeckel in *The Lineup*, 1958.

The Lineup ★★★ 1958; U.S.; 86m; COL; B/W; Crime Drama; Children: Unacceptable; **DVD**. Offbeat but engrossing crime yarn sees Wallach as a professional killer assigned to track down and recover three packets of heroin that have been smuggled into San Francisco and planted on three unsuspecting travelers. Keith, a weird sort of Boswell, accompanies Wallach, eager to write down the last words of each of Wallach's victims. A seaman is Wallach's first victim, killed after he learns what he has been given. The second is the servant of a couple, who also received a packet. The third packet has been planted inside a Chinese doll carried by a little girl. She has discovered the heroin, and, not knowing what it is, has used it to powder the face of her doll. Wallach is disinclined to murder the child and her mother, so he goes to his employer, Taylor, a sadistic criminal boss confined to a wheelchair. They meet on the balcony of a skating rink, and Wallach tries to explain how the third packet was destroyed. Taylor disbelieves him, thinking Wallach had taken the heroin to sell and sneeringly condemns the hit man by saying: "You're dead." Wallach explodes, hurling Taylor from the balcony to his death. He, Keith, and Jaeckel, their getaway driver, then flee, but SFPD detectives Anderson and Meyer, who have been trailing Wallach, give chase. Jaeckel loses his nerve and cracks up the car, killing himself and Keith. Wallach tries to escape, but he is cornered by Anderson and Meyer and shoots it out with the cops and is killed. Siegel, who specialized in such gritty crime films, offers a very violent entry where almost all the characters are ruthless and without human pity or compassion, except when Wallach, who gives a great performance, cannot murder a child, which brings about his downfall. **p**, Jaime del Valle; **d**, Don Siegel; **cast**, Eli Wallach, Robert Keith, Richard Jaeckel, Mary LaRoche, William Leslie, Emile Meyer, Marshall Reed, Raymond Bailey, Robert Bailey, Warner Anderson; **w**, Stirling Silliphant (based on characters created by Lawrence L. Klee in the TV series "The Lineup"); **c**, Hal Mohr; **m**, Mischa Bakaleinikoff; **ed**, Al Clark; **art d**, Ross Bellah; **set d**, Louis Diage; Lawrence W. Butler.

The Lion ★★★ 1962; U.S.; 96m; FOX; Color; Drama; Children: Unacceptable; **DVD**. In this exciting adventure drama, Holden is an American lawyer, called to Africa by his ex-wife, Capucine, who is afraid that their young daughter, Franklin, has grown too attached to the jungle and a pet lion, Zamba. They have raised Zamba since it was born, but it is now a dangerous adult. Capucine has since remarried to Howard, a game warden at a wildlife preserve where they live in Kenya. Holden arrives and soon saves the life of an elderly tribal chief, Zakee, who had been old and ill and left to die, which is the tribe's custom, and who is grateful to Holden. Zakee's son, Oduor, had hoped to become head of the tribe upon his father's death and, furthermore, take Franklin as his wife. But she is only eleven years old, so both Holden and Capucine

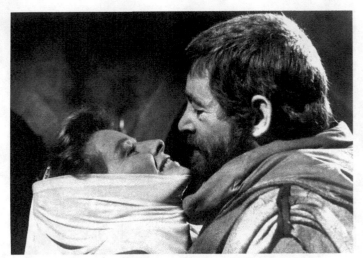

Katharine Hepburn and Peter O'Toole in *The Lion in Winter*, 1968.

object to it. Zakee tells his son that he will never be a man until he has killed a lion, so Oduor plans to kill Franklin's pet. Franklin retaliates by telling Zamba to kill Oduor. By now Howard notices that his wife and Holden are in love again, and wants Holden to return to the U.S. But Zamba saves Franklin from the tribal prince, who is out to kill him, and the former marrieds reunite and Franklin will stay with them in Africa. Well crafted and directed, Holden and the cast members are standouts in their roles, and the cinematography, particularly the exterior shots of the lush, exotic African landscape, is extraordinary. The mature themes and violence prohibit viewing by children. **p**, Samuel G. Engel; **d**, Jack Cardiff; **cast**, William Holden, Trevor Howard, Capucine, Pamela Franklin, Christopher Agunda, Paul Oduor, Makara Kwaiha Ramadhani, Samuel Obiero Romboh, Zakee; **w**, Irene and Louis Kamp (based on the novel by Joseph Kessel); **c**, Ted Scaife (CinemaScope; DeLuxe Color); **m**, Malcolm Arnold; **ed**, Russell Lloyd; **art d**, Alan Withy, John Hoesli.

The Lion in Winter ★★★★ 1968; U.K.; 134m; AVCO Embassy; Color; Biographical Drama; Children: Unacceptable (MPAA: PG); **DVD**; **VHS**. In this strange but captivating historical drama, O'Toole, playing the all-powerful Henry II (1133-1189), ruler of England and most of France, calls a yearly family reunion at a remote French castle where he meets with his estranged wife, Hepburn (Eleanor of Acquitaine; 1122-1204), his three fiercely competitive sons—Castle (Geoffrey; 1152-1212), Terry (John; 1166-1216) and Hopkins (Richard; 1157-1199)—as well as his mistress, Merrow, and her brother, Dalton, who plays Philip II of France (1165-1223). This royal group spends their time under O'Toole's roof bickering and arguing, bringing up the worst old memories while hurling insults at each other. The sons—Castle, Terry and Hopkins are forever quarreling and vying for the affections of O'Toole, each expecting to be named the next king, and Hepburn plays all three of them to her own political advantage (albeit she seems to favor Hopkins, as Eleanor truly did about Richard, who did become Henry's successor). Merrow, who is pregnant with O'Toole's child, wants him to discard his competitive wife and dispatch his three sons so that their child will become the next ruler of England and France, but O'Toole is tossed and turned by his own deep loves for all of these family members while he politically jousts with Dalton to acquire more territory from France and where Dalton plays his sons against him. At one point, when enraged by the acerbic insults from Hepburn, he vows to murder her three sons, having them imprisoned in a dungeon and where they await execution. Hopkins is the only of the three who vows to fight his father if he comes into their prison cell, saying that "when the fall is all you have, you fight," showing the valor that he would later display as Richard the Lion Heart of England. O'-

Toole is all bluster, however, for he cannot bring himself to shed the blood of these sons, even though they have made of themselves his political rivals and are avowedly antagonistic toward him, all wanting his kingdom more than his love. It all comes to nothing, with the rancor and the injuring of deep memories and feelings soothed over when O'Toole leaves, allowing his estranged queen, Hepburn, to retain her regal position and his sons to pursue their individual conquests while they await his eventual demise and their royal inheritance. The performances from Hepburn and O'Toole are superb as they exchange verbal assaults in the high wit of their day while also sharing some memorable tender moments where their love is recalled and rekindled. The rest of the cast, particularly Hopkins, shine in their role,s and Harvey's meticulous direction wonderfully captures that ancient era where the cinematography aptly profiles that long-ago era where hygiene and sanitation is basic and crude and pomp and majesty dwell more in imagination than is shown in any elegant finery and golden crowns. *Author's Note*: Hepburn was particularly fond of this film, telling this author: "I play a woman who has been abandoned by her husband and a mother who must save the lives of her sons when their inheritance of the throne is threatened. I am not unlike any other mother, who will fight for the lives of their children. My only weapon is my wit and my knowledge that my husband—in this case the wonderful O'Toole—still loves me. And what a great weapon I am given in that brilliant script by Goldman. Eleanor was a survivor in her day, more clever, conniving and cunning than her male counterparts. She had to be to go on living and she outlived most of her family after all. I thought that my scenes with the very gifted Hopkins were some of the best in my career." **p**, Martin Poll; **d**, Anthony Harvey; **cast**, Peter O'Toole, Katharine Hepburn, Anthony Hopkins, John Castle, Nigel Terry, Timothy Dalton, Jane Merrow, Nigel Stock, Kenneth Ives, O.Z. Whitehead; **w**, James Goldman (based on his play); **c**, Douglas Slocombe (Panavision; Eastmancolor); **m**, John Barry; **ed**, John Bloom; **art d**, Peter Murton.

A Lion Is in the Streets ★★★ 1953; U.S.; 88m; William Cagney Productions/WB; Color; Drama; Children: Unacceptable; **DVD**; **VHS**. Cagney is again riveting as a crusading southern peddler who takes up the cause of downtrodden sharecroppers and small farmers, who have been for years cheated when selling their cotton crops. Cagney exposes how weights used to scale cotton are rigged by crooked buyers representing Keating, the state's most powerful businessman. With the loving support of wife Hale, Cagney decides to run for office and conducts a wild campaign where he champions the poor farmers and rural people of his state. When one of his supporters, McIntire, is mortally wounded, Cagney drags the dying man into a court to testify on behalf of his cause, but McIntire dies before he can vindicate Cagney, who has been accused of underhanded practices. Cagney, now totally ruthless, nevertheless uses the corpse of his friend to aid his cause. To win election to high office, however, he agrees to work with the very people he has set out to destroy and, in the end, is himself destroyed when one of his own followers, who has learned of his betrayal of the people he has sworn to represent, mortally shoots him and where Cagney dies in his wife's arms. *Author's Note*: The film was an all-Cagney production, with James Cagney starring, his sister, Jeanne Cagney, in a supporting role, and his brothers, William as producer and Edward as story editor. This story was very similar to Robert Penn Warren's novel and the film upon which it was based, **All the King's Men**, 1949, and which, like the Warren story, is based upon the assassinated Louisiana politician and self-styled dictator, Huey Long (1893-1935). "My character in that film is a peddler from the backwaters of a deep southern state," Cagney told this author. "He is an uneducated rabble-rouser just like Long and anyone seeing that film will identify with that character and the character of Long, as they both use the same underhanded political tactics and both are mad for power. I don't think you can mistake the similarities." For more details on Long and, particularly, his assassination, see my book, *The Great Pictorial History of World Crime*, Volume I (History, Inc.,

2004; pages 111-117). **p**, William Cagney; **d**, Raoul Walsh; **cast**, James Cagney, Barbara Hale, Anne Francis, Warner Anderson, John McIntire, Jeanne Cagney, Lon Chaney, Jr., Frank McHugh, Larry Keating, Onslow Stevens, Sara Haden, Ellen Corby, Roland Winters; **w**, Luther Davis (based on the novel by Adria Locke Langley); **c**, Harry Stradling (Technicolor); **m**, Franz Waxman; **ed**, George Any; **prod d**, Wiard Ihnen; **set d**, Fred M. MacLean; **spec eff**, Roscoe Cline.

The Lion King ★★★★★ 1994; U.S.; 89m; Disney/Buena Vista; Color; Animated Adventure/Fantasy; Children: Recommended (MPAA: G); **3-D**; **DVD**; **VHS**. This wonderful African fantasy adventure, presented in the tradition of Disney's earliest and greatest animated feature films, focuses upon a pride of lions. The enchanting film opens with the birth of Simba (Thomas voiceover), who is the son of King Mufasa (Jones voiceover), the present king of the lion pride and the lord of the African Pride Lands. Simba's birth is celebrated as the future king, but Scar (Irons voiceover), the envious brother of Mufasa, who has no heir and wants to become the lord of the Pride Lands upon the death of his brother, plots to kill Simba. Although Mufasa warns his cub son not to go into the shadowy place beyond the plains, the cub, along with his friend, Nala (Calame voiceover), a female lion cub, venture into that dense jungle at the sinister urgings of Scar, who tells Simba that he will see the marvel of the elephant graveyard when entering that area. Once inside the shadowy area, Simba and Nala begin to play, but are attacked by three hyenas, Shenzi (Goldberg voiceover), Banzai (Marin voiceover), and Ed (Cummings voiceover). Mufasa comes to their rescue, driving off the hyenas. He chastises his son for disobeying him, but easily forgives him out of his loving nature. Scar, however, is determined to take over the pride and orders the hyenas to stampede a herd of wildebeest into a gorge where Simba is playing, but, again, Mufasa comes to the rescue, saving his son. When Mufasa attempts to climb to the top of the gorge, however, Scar knocks him back into the gorge and he is killed by the stampeding wildebeests. Scar then convinces Simba that he is responsible for his father's death and tells him to flee and never return. He does, with the hyenas chasing him, but he escapes. Meanwhile, Scar tells the pride of lions that Mufasa and Simba have both been killed and he becomes the king of the Pride Lands and where he allows all of the hyenas to roam freely about. Simba ends his flight in the desert where he collapses from exhaustion, thirst and hunger, but he is found by two sympathetic creatures, Timon (Lane voiceover), a meerkat, and Pumbaa (Sabella voiceover), a warthog, and they nurture him back to health. They take Simba into their community where his childhood is carefree. Growing to an adult (Broderick voiceover), Simba sees his friends being threatened by a hungry lioness, which turns out to be the grown Nala (Kelly voiceover), and he and she soon fall in love. Nala then urges Simba to return to the Pride Lands, saying that Scar has allowed the hyenas to take over their homeland where there is no longer enough to eat or enough water to drink, but Simba, still believing he caused his father's death, refuses. Rafiki (Guillaume voiceover), a sage mandrill, then visits Simba to tell him that his father is still "alive," but only as a reflection in a pond, and Simba returns to the Pride Lands, peering into the water of the pond to see the reflection of his father, Mufasa, who tells him that he has forgotten his responsibilities and must take his rightful place as the king of the Pride Lands. Simba then resolves to gain the crown with the help of his friends Nala, Timon and Pumbaa. He goes to Pride Rock and sees Scar attacking his mother, Sarabi (Sinclair voiceover), and they battle with Scar pushing Simba over a cliff, but he scrambles back and forces Scar to tell the other lions the truth about his father's death. The hyenas attack, but Sarabi, Nala and the other lionesses drive them back while Simba throws Scar from Pride Rock and is killed by the hyenas, who have overheard Scar's remarks about his willingness to betray them. Simba and Nala are later shown where Simba reigns as king of the Pride Lands and he proudly displays a new heir, a lion cub produced by him and Nala, to the other lions. All of the voiceovers are perfectly matched to their characters and

Scene from *The Lion King*, 1994.

the animation is superb, showing lavish landscapes and richly detailed scenes with great dimension and where the score from Zimmer is extraordinarily appropriate to each scene. This is truly a great visual treat for children and the family alike and where the violence is tempered with passion and good-heartedness. **p**, Don Hahn; **d**, Roger Allers, Rob Minkoff; **cast**, Matthew Broderick, Jeremy Irons, Robert Guillaume, Rowan Atkinson, James Earl Jones, Nathan Lane, Moira Kelly, Whoopi Goldberg, Cheech Marin, Niketa Calame, Ernie Sabella, Jim Cummings, Jonathan Taylor Thomas, Madge Sinclair; **w**, Irene Mecchi, Jonathan Roberts, Linda Woolverton, Brenda Chapman; (Technicolor); **m**, Hans Zimmer; **ed**, Ivan Bilancio; **prod d**, Chris Sanders.

Lion of the Desert ★★★ 1981; Libya/U.S.; 173m; Falcon International/United Film Distribution; Color; Biographical Drama; Children: Unacceptable (MPAA: PG); **DVD**; **VHS**. Quinn is exceptional in essaying Libyan tribal leader Omar Mukhtar (1858-1931), who battles Italian forces led by Benito Mussolini (1883-1945), expansively portrayed by Steiger, by using his meager forces in guerrilla warfare for many years. Quinn's forces are woefully lacking modern weapons and suffer one defeat after another at the hands of Italian governor Rodolfo Graziani (1882-1955), played by Reed. Quinn is shown many times displaying mercy and compassion to his enemies, sparing captured Italian soldiers and telling them that Islam forbids the murder of captured soldiers. He is eventually captured and tried as a rebel and condemned, hanged before his followers, but where Italian commanders such as Vallone, salute him in his final moments as a heroic and honorable foe. The score from Jarre is moving and dynamic (he composed the score for **Lawrence of Arabia**, 1962). ***Author's Note***: Steiger told this author that "I played Mussolini very broadly in **Lion of the Desert**. He believed that Italy had a destiny to conquer the weak tribes of Africa, and has no hesitation in slaughtering these helpless people. Fascism never uses reason for its purposes, only the iron fist and I am wielding that fist all the time in that picture." **p&d**, Moustapha Akkad; **cast**, Anthony Quinn, Oliver Reed, Rod Steiger, John Gielgud, Irene Papas, Raf Vallone, Gastone Moschin, Stefano Patrizi, Sky Dumont, Robert Brown; **w**, H. A. L. Craig; **c**, Jack Hildyard (Panavision; Eastmancolor); **m**, Maurice Jarre; **ed**, John Shirley; **prod d**, Mario Garbuglia, Syd Cain; **art d**, Giorgio Desideri, Maurice Cain, Bob Bell; **spec eff**, Kit West.

The List of Adrian Messenger ★★★★ 1963; U.S.; 98m; UNIV; B/W; Crime Drama; Children: Unacceptable; **DVD**; **VHS**. Chilling whodunit presenting many unexpected twists and turns that begins when Merivale gives Scott, a retired British colonel, a list of eleven names, asking Scott to check on the whereabouts of these persons. After Merivale is killed when his plane explodes, Scott begins to investigate the persons on the

Joe E. Marks, Leslie Parrish, Peter Palmer and Billie Hayes in
Li'l Abner, **1959.**

list, finding that each of these individuals has been mysteriously murdered. All of the victims have been former POWs in a Japanese prison camp in Burma during WWII, each betrayed by one in their midst, who informed on them, telling the Japanese about their separate escape attempts. Scott then learns that the killer plots to murder a boy, the last person who is in line to inherit a large estate, that sinister person being a member of the family that owns that estate. Scott figures out the murder plan arranged for the boy, and the killer, instead of his victim, is killed in his stead. Pantheon director Huston takes painstaking care to present this thriller by planting a number of red herrings throughout the clever story line, all superstars playing their roles in disguise, and these include Lancaster, Douglas, Mitchum, Sinatra, Curtis and even the director. The film is peppered with many frightening sequences that are all presented with brooding and moody atmospheric scenes. *Author's Note*: Exteriors for this film were shot on location in Ireland where Huston owned a large estate. Huston told this author: "When it got out that we would be using a number of stars for that picture, even though they were so heavily disguised they could not be easily recognized, I was inundated with requests from half of Hollywood's big names and I had to turn down a ton of them. Though **The List of Adrian Messenger** is a very scary film, it offered a lot of fun for the players where they outdid each other in trying not to be who they really were. I had those big named actors take off their heavy makeup at the end of the film so the viewers could be amazed at not knowing the parts they played and that part of the film was really a guessing game audiences played with that picture." p, Edward Lewis; d, John Huston; cast, George C. Scott, Dana Wynter, Clive Brook, Gladys Cooper, Herbert Marshall, John Merivale, Marcel Dalio, Huston, Kirk Douglas and cameos by Tony Curtis, Burt Lancaster, Robert Mitchum, Frank Sinatra; w, Anthony Veiller (based on the novel by Philip MacDonald); c, Joseph MacDonald; m, Jerry Goldsmith; ed, Terry O. Morse, Hugh S. Fowler; art d, Alexander Golitzen, Stephen Grimes, George Webb; set d, Oliver Emert.

Li'l Abner ★★★ 1959; U.S.; 114m; PAR; Color; Musical Comedy; Children: Acceptable; **DVD**; **VHS**. Al Capp's popular comic strip comes to life with great panache in this very funny musical, which is set in Dogpatch and is peopled by mostly moronic hillbillies. All the leading buffoons are present—the powerful Li'l Abner (Palmer), Daisy Mae (Parrish), Marryin' Sam (Kaye), Stupifyin' Jones (Newmar), Mammy Yokum (Hayes) and Earthquake McGoon (Hoffman)—when they hear that the U.S. government has determined that their mountaintop home is absolutely useless and will be used as an A-bomb testing site. To preserve their oddball heritage, the townsfolk desperately try to impress the government with something important about their community and they come up with Hayes' "Yokumberry Tonic," which produces posi-

tive results for human health and improves everyone's romance, and this elixir seems to turn the trick in convincing the government to look elsewhere to explode its lethal bombs. Palmer offers the elixir to Washington, but General Bullmoose (St. John) also wants it, so he tries to trap Palmer into marrying his secretary (Stevens). Parrish is willing to sacrifice herself to save Palmer from nuclear destruction by agreeing to marry Hoffman, but it turns out that such draconian measures are not necessary and she and Palmer move another step closer to the altar. Meanwhile, the yearly Sadie Hawkins' Day ensues and Daisy Mae is again in pursuit of Li'l Abner, and this time, it appears that she will finally catch up with the evasive young man. The cast, almost all having appeared in the Broadway production, does a wonderful job in this delightful romp and where the costuming from Alvin Colt is exceptional as is the choreography from Michael Kidd and Dee Dee Wood. Songs (all from Gene De Paul and Johnny Mercer) include: "Don't Take That Rag Off in the Bush," "Jubilation T. Cornpone," "If I Had My Druthers," "A Typical Day," "Put 'Em Back The Way They Wuz," "Matrimonial Stomp," "I Wish It Could Be Otherwise," "I'm Past My Time," "Unnecessary Town," "Namely You," "Room Enuff for Us," and "The Country's in the Very Best of Hands." p, Norman Panama; d, Melvin Frank; cast, Peter Palmer, Leslie Parrish, Stubby Kaye, Julie Newmar, Howard St. John, Stella Stevens, Billie Hayes, Joe E. Marks, Bern Hoffman, Al Nesor; w, Panama, Frank (based on their musical and characters from the comic strip created by Al Capp); c, Daniel L. Fapp (VistaVision; Technicolor); m, Nelson Riddle; ed, Arthur P. Schmidt; art d, Hal Pereira, J. McMillan Johnson; set d, Sam Comer, Grace Gregory; spec eff, John P. Fulton.

Little Annie Rooney ★★★ 1925 (silent); U.S.; 94m/9 reels; Mary Pickford Company/UA; Drama; Children: Unacceptable; **VHS**. A more somber outing than what Pickford was known for, this entry presents "America's Sweetheart" in love with Haines, but that romance is violently disrupted when her father, James, a policeman, is killed. Pickford's brother, Griffith, gets it into his head that Haines is the culprit and he shoots and seriously wounds Haines, but his life is saved by Pickford, who offers her blood in a transfusion. She then, with the antic-filled help of the neighborhood children, identifies and captures the real killer and is reunited with Haines for a happy ending. Pickford is her adoring self in this well-crafted whodunit, which is punctuated with a lot of humorous scenes when she is interacting with the kids on her block as they hunt like amateur sleuths for the culprit. p, Mary Pickford (not credited); d, William Beaudine; cast, Pickford, William Haines, Walter James, Gordon Griffith, Carlo Schipa, Spec O'Donnell, Hugh Fay, Vola Vale, Joe Butterworth, Eugene Jackson, Oscar Rudolph; w, Hope Loring, Louis D. Lighton (based on a story by Katherine Hennessey); titles, Tom McNamara; c, Charles Rosher, Hal Mohr; art d, John D. Schulze, Paul Youngblood.

Little Big Horn ★★★ 1951; U.S.; 86m; Bali Productions/Lippert Pictures; B/W; Western; Children: Cautionary; **DVD**. A small cavalry unit led by Bridges learns that the Sioux are planning to ambush and destroy Colonel George Armstrong Custer (1839-1876) and his 7th Cavalry at the Little Big Horn River. They ride after Custer, but one by one of the troopers are killed by arrows shot by Indians from ambush. It is a doomed patrol, all realize, but they feel it their duty to make the attempt to save Custer and his men. The most dangerous assignment for each trooper is when he has to ride point in reconnoitering the whereabouts of the enemy and that is where most of the men are killed. Meanwhile, Bridges comes to suspect that Ireland, his second-in-command, has stolen the affections of his wife, Windsor, and tension between them increases as they make their hazardous trek toward Custer. Good acting and superior direction raises this action-packed, tension-filled oater above the average and where the script is both literate and provocative. *Author's Note*: Warren directs for the first time with this film, which was given a much larger budget by tiny studio Lippert than what it gave to most of its productions. Warren later went on to produce some of the most popular western TV series, including "Rawhide" and "Gunsmoke." **p**, Carl K. Hittleman; **d**, Charles Marquis Warren; **cast**, Lloyd Bridges, John Ireland, Marie Windsor, Reed Hadley, Jim Davis, Wally Cassell, Hugh O'Brian, King Donovan, Richard Emory, John Pickard, Sheb Wooley, Robert Sherwood; **w**, Warren (based on a story by Harold Shumate); **c**, Ernest Miller; **m**, Paul Dunlap; **ed**, Carl Pierson; **art d**, Frank Paul Sylos; **set d**, Ted Offenbecker; **spec eff**, Ray Mercer.

Little Big League ★★★ 1994; U.S.; 119m; Castle Rock/COL; Color; Comedy/Sports Drama; Children: Unacceptable (MPAA: PG); **DVD**; **VHS**. In this humorous if not outlandish film, the owner of the Minnesota Twins professional baseball team, Robards, dies and wills the team to his twelve-year-old grandson, Edwards, who knows the team inside and out and what it needs to make it a winner. The team hates their manager, Farina, so Edwards fires him, but they're not too happy to learn who has been appointed in his place. Edwards has named himself as the new manager. How can they expect to take orders from a boy? But then again, most eventually conclude, what can they lose? They're already down so they have nowhere to go but up. The team does its best, aided by the team's veteran coach, Ashton, and first baseman, Busfield, who is dating Edwards' widowed mother, Crow. Violence and sensuality prohibits viewing by children. **p**, Mike Lobell; **d**, Andrew Scheinman; **cast**, Luke Edwards, Timothy Busfield, John Ashton, Ashley Crow, Kevin Dunn, Billy L. Sullivan, Miles Feulner, Jonathan Silverman, Dennis Farina, Jason Robards; **w**, Scheinman, Gregory K. Pincus (based on a story by Pincus); **c**, Donald E. Thorin; **m**, Stanley Clarke; **ed**, Michael Jablow; **prod d**, Jeffrey Howard; **set d**, Ethel Robins Richards; **spec eff**, Danny Gill, Walter Hart, Mark Galvin.

Little Big Man ★★★ 1970; U.S.; 147m; Cinema Center Films/National General; Color; Western; Children: Unacceptable (MPAA: GP); **DVD**; **VHS**. This oddball, even macabre film begins with Hoffman (who gives an outstanding performance) as a wizened old man telling his life story in the Old West, one where he has known everyone of any note on the frontier (and which Emilio Estevez emulates when recounting his account as an old man when claiming to be Billy the Kid in **Young Guns II**, 1990). Of course the film is really a broad satire from skilled director Penn, which begins when Hoffman (played by Howard as a ten-year-old boy) and his sister, Androsky, are captured by Cheyenne. Androsky escapes, but Howard remains with the Indians and is raised by them, growing to adulthood as Hoffman. He saves the life of a brave, Bellini, and is named Little Big Man and embraced by the chief, George, as a Cheyenne brave. When a segment of the tribe is attacked by white cavalrymen, Hoffman saves his life by cowardly identifying himself as a white man and denouncing his Indian affiliations. He is taken to a settlement where he is "adopted" by pretentious missionary David and his slattern-like wife, Dunaway, who immediately attempts to seduce Hoffman while she is promiscuously sleeping with innumerable others in the town. Hoffman escapes her sexual clutches by leaving and becoming an assistant to Balsam, a traveling drummer selling household goods, notions and patent medicines. Balsam is such a blatant swindler that he is forever being attacked by his victimized clients and, in the process, loses one limb after another until he is reduced to moving about without arms and legs (and where Balsam renders a great but eccentric performance). Hoffman realizes that there is no future with Balsam and departs, later meeting his sister, Androsky, who teaches him how to shoot a six-gun; he becomes a dead shot and is soon known as, after his favorite drink, the "Soda Pop Kid." He befriends gunslinger Wild Bill Hickok (James Butler Hickok; 1837-1876), played by Corey. Hoffman, however, is tired of "civilization" and its endless cruelty and violence, and returns to the Cheyenne, welcomed by George, who considers Hoffman his adopted son. He marries an Indian girl, Eccles, and they have a child, but both are killed when Custer attacks the Indians at their camp at the Wichita River in 1874. Only

Lloyd Bridges, Marie Windsor and John Ireland in *Little Big Horn*, 1951.

Hoffman and George survive the attack, and Hoffman returns to civilization, abandoning his abstinence, following a brief affair with Dunaway, who has become a notorious prostitute, he becomes the town drunk. He again meets Corey, who rescues him from his alcoholism, but watches in horror as the celebrated gunman is fatally shot in the back. Hoffman becomes a mule skinner and scout working for the U.S. Army and commander of the 7th Cavalry, Colonel George Armstrong Custer (1839-1876), who is played by Mulligan (and where Mulligan essays this great hero as a fruity nut, given to screaming temper tantrums while preening himself and obsessively combing his long golden hair, an utter bizarre performance that is more appalling than humorous). Hoffman then serves as Mulligan's scout as they proceed to disaster at the Little Big Horn and where Hoffman tells Mulligan that more Indians than he has ever seen are waiting to destroy him and his command. Mulligan disbelieves him, thinking that Hoffman is trying to deceive him by lying about the number of enemy Indians and so he decides to charge into the Indian hordes where he and his men are massacred (again Mulligan acting like some prissy betrayed woman before he is finally dispatched). Hoffman's life is spared by his old friend, Bellini. He is last seen many years later as an old man telling this improbable tale and bemoaning the fate of the Indians. The story is ridiculous and the characters are acted out as cartooned persons, but the overall effect is a fascinating and utterly absurd distortion of the Old West in the broadest sense of satire. *Author's Note*: Corey, who had long been a character actor in films (and who had been blacklisted in the early 1950s for having once been a communist but made his living by running the Professional Actors Workshop and which had students from James Dean to Jack Nicholson), told this author that his role in this film as Hickok "was not based on any fact. The closest thing I come to being Wild Bill is wearing a big, floppy hat, a flowing mustache and a couple of six-guns. But that was enough since the film is all a pack of great lies. That was what the Old West was really about, I think, a lot of fantastic fabrications everybody believed were true because nobody could check those claims in those days. After I did my scenes in that picture, I would go home, make a pot of coffee and have a good laugh about all the crazy people we were playing. You see, Hollywood doesn't give a damn about facts. It is only concerned about what it can get away with and we got away with everything in **Little Big Man**." **p**, Stuart Millar; **d**, Arthur Penn; **cast**, Dustin Hoffman, Faye Dunaway, Chief Dan George, Martin Balsam, Richard Mulligan, Jeff Corey, Amy Eccles, Kelly Jean Peters, Carol Androsky, Robert Little Star, Annette O'-Toole, Cal Bellini; **w**, Calder Willingham (based on the novel by Thomas Berger); **c**, Harry Stradling, Jr. (Panavision; Technicolor); **m**, John Hammond; **ed**, Dede Allen; **prod d**, Dean Tavoularis; **art d**, Angelo Graham; **set d**, George R. Nelson; **spec eff**, Logan Frazee.

Edward G. Robinson and William Collier Jr. in *Little Caesar,*
1931.

Little Boy Lost ★★★ 1953; U.S.; 95m; PAR; B/W; Drama; Children:
Acceptable; **VHS.** Crosby is a newspaper reporter on a plane to Paris
when he recalls being a war correspondent in France in 1938. We see
him in flashback as he falls in love with a cabaret singer, Maurey. They
marry, and when World War II begins, he joins the French army. The
couple has a baby boy, and when the Germans invade Holland, Crosby
tries to get Maurey out of the country. He is ordered to northern France,
is injured, and sent to a hospital in England where he learns Maurey has
been killed by the Nazi Gestapo. Flash forward and we see Crosby's
plane landing in Paris. He looks for his son, and, with the help of a
friend, Dauphin, and Dorziat, a nun at an orphanage, he is led to a boy,
Fourcade, who may or may not be his son. It turns out the boy is not his
son, but Dorziat urges him to adopt Fourcade. After some soul-searching, Crosby accepts the boy as the child he has lost. A sentimental, warm
story about putting the past behind and going on with the present and
future. Songs sung by Crosby include "The Magic Window," "Cella
M'Est Egal," "A propos de rien" (Johnny Mercer, James Van Heusen),
and a French version of "Oh Susanna" (Stephen Foster). **p**, William Perl-
berg; **d&w**, George Seaton (based on a story by Marghanita Laski); **cast**,
Bing Crosby, Claude Dauphin, Christian Fourcade, Gabrielle Dorziat,
Nicole Maurey, Colette Deréal, Georgette Anys, Henri Letondal,
Michael Moore, Peter Baldwin; **c**, George Barnes; **m**, Victor Young; **ed**,
Alma Macrorie; **art d**, Hal Pereira, Henry Bumstead; **set d**, Sam Comer,
Ross Dowd; **spec eff**, Farciot Edouart, Gordon Jennings, Loyal Griggs.

Little Caesar ★★★★ 1931; U.S.; 79m; First National/WB; Crime
Drama; Children: Unacceptable; **DVD; VHS.** Robinson shot to the top
of stardom with his role as a snarling, unredeemable gangster in this
classic film, the first landmark talkie to profile the seamy side of the
American underworld. He is a man without mercy, killing on his impulse
to gain money and power and that is shown in the open scene of this
horrific film where he drives up to a gas station, enters the office and a
flash of gunfire is seen. He emerges with cash, ostensibly having murdered the attendant and robbed the till, before his driver, Fairbanks, anxiously wheels the coupe onto the road and they make their escape. They
are then shown at a diner where they order spaghetti—both are Italian—
and, while they dine, Robinson reads about a big city crime czar and
proclaims to sidekick Fairbanks that he will someday be a big shot rackets boss and not "just another mug." When arriving at a big city (never
named but apparently Chicago), he goes to the Palermo Club (the name
taken from the Sicilian city that spawned the Mafia) and meets Fields,
a rackets boss, telling him that he is good with a gun and can be of great
service to him. Fields tells Robinson that the use of guns "doesn't go"
with him, but he nevertheless hires him and introduces him to other gang
members that include Hendricks, Stone, Madison and Collier and where

Robinson introduces himself as Cesare Enrico Bandello, and where
Fields gives him the nickname "Little Caesar." Robinson proves to be
fearless and is a born leader, going on capers with the gang and becoming Fields' second-in-command. Meanwhile, Fairbanks, who really
wants no part of crime and has aspirations as a dancer, teams up with
Farrell, a nightclub entertainer and they start a dance act that catches
on. Jackson, a police detective, then visits Fields and tells him he is
going to clamp down on his rackets. Where Fields is timid, Robinson
defies the cop and Jackson tells him that he will soon be arresting him.
"No mug like you will ever put the cuffs on little Rico," Robinson sneeringly snarls. When Fields shows that he is thoroughly intimidated by
the police, Robinson sees this as his chance to take over the mob, telling
Fields that he is getting soft, adding: "You're getting so that you can
dish it out but you can't take it." Robinson meets top crime boss Ince,
who approves of his taking over Fields' operation and where Fields remains as a leader without authority. Robinson then plans to rob the
nightclub where Fairbanks works as a dancer and where Robinson has
pressured him into being a lookout. The club is owned by Black, a rival
gangster, who has had a run-in with Robinson earlier. Ince and Fields
oppose the robbery, but Robinson goes ahead anyway, arriving at the
club with his mob during a New Year's Eve celebration. He holds up
the cashier while Fairbanks nervously watches for the police. Stevens,
the police commissioner, who has been attending the party, emerges in
the foyer where Robinson is committing the robbery and, when he goes
for his gun to stop the thieves, Robinson shoots and kills him. The mob
flees and now Fairbanks is terrified that the police will arrest him. The
bold robbery, however, has established Robinson as a formidable gang
boss and he meets "the Big Boy," Blackmer, a cultured political sachem,
who lives in a resplendent mansion with marbled floors, tapestries and
huge windows offering wide vistas and where Blackmer anoints Robinson as the top boss of the city's underworld. Robinson copies the
lifestyle of Blackmer by moving into a lavish art deco suite of rooms
and is later given a testimonial dinner at the Palermo Club where he is
given a gold watch by his gang members. He later learns that the watch
has been stolen, but the next day he is all smiles when buying some
newspapers on the street and seeing his picture taken at the banquet. As
he strolls down the street, a truck races by and from it a gangster wielding a submachine gun fires at him, riddling a window and wounding
Robinson in the arm. He survives and now believes that he is invulnerable. Stone then arrives to tell Robinson that youthful gang member Collier has the nervous jitters over the killing of the police commissioner
and that he intends to confess his part in the killing to a local priest.
Robinson tracks down Collier, finding him as Collier mounts the steps
of his church en route to the confessional and where Robinson shoots
him to death. (These stairs would be used eight years later as part of the
set where gangster James Cagney would also die in another classic underworld film from Warner Brothers, **The Roaring Twenties**, 1939.)
Robinson now believes that he can run the city and even plans to get rid
of the man who pulls all the strings, Blackmer. He asks Fairbanks to
come back into the mob, but Fairbanks has no stomach for it and, after
Farrell, his dancing partner and love interest backs him up, refuses. Farrell then tells cop Jackson that Fairbanks knows who killed police commissioner Stevens and when Robinson learns that Fairbanks may
inform, he confronts him with a gun, but he cannot bring himself to kill
his former friend and, as the cops close in, he flees with Stone. The cops
pursue and Stone is killed, but Robinson escapes. His fortunes spiral
downward as Robinson goes into hiding, paying almost all his money
to old harridan La Verne, a vicious fence, who hides him in a small, dark
room at the back of her dilapidated store. After La Verne gives Robinson
only a small amount of the money she has been hiding for him, she orders him to leave as police are now searching for him and he is "hot."
Robinson, on the skids, survives in seedy hotels and flophouses, deluding himself into believing that he will somehow "get back on top." Jackson gives an interview to the press, calling Robinson a coward who does
not have the courage to meet him in the open and, after Robinson reads

this in a newspaper, he calls Jackson, threatening him. The police trace the call to a warehouse district and Jackson and other police race to the area. When Robinson sees the police car coming, he runs behind a billboard, gun drawn, but hiding. Jackson stands on the other side of the billboard, ordering Robinson to surrender. Robinson yells, "Come and get me!" Jackson cradles a submachine gun and fires, riddling the billboard, and some of the bullets mortally strike Robinson. He falls, clutching his wounds and, before dying, says, "Mother of Mercy, is this the end of Rico?" Thus the prophetic words shown at the very beginning of the film come to grim fruition where (from St. Matthew) it is stated: "For them that take the sword shall perish by the sword." The film is as grim and ruthless as Robinson's vicious and savage character, each uncompromising scene carefully crafted by pantheon director LeRoy and where Robinson rivets in a mesmerizing performance of a person more beast than man. *Author's Note*: Robinson had been acting in films since 1923, but he had not become a star until appearing in **Little Caesar** as he knew he would and where he told this author that "my part was about a monster of a man, who had no scruples or virtues and would stop at nothing to become rich and powerful. I knew the character would shock the world and leave an unforgettable memory in the minds of viewers. Actually, the producer, Hal Wallis, originally offered me a supporting role [that played by Stone] in the picture, but I insisted that I play the lead or nothing. When I stormed into Wallis' office, I made sure that I was wearing a dark homburg, heavy coat and a cigar clenched in my teeth. I barked at him, while keeping one hand in my coat pocket as if holding on to a hidden gun and he nodded that I would play the leading part." Pantheon director LeRoy, who made many film noir classics (he would direct in the following year the classic **I Am a Fugitive from a Chain Gang**, 1932) decided to make this film when reading the novel in galley proofs. He took those proofs to the studio boss at Fox, Zanuck, who immediately read the story. Zanuck told this author that "I could see right away that the leading player was rotten to the core, completely worthless. Unlike other gangster films up to that time and even afterward, the bad guy always has some good in him, enough to redeem his shabby character. There was nothing like that in this character. He was evil through and through and I knew the film would be a big hit." When making the film, LeRoy stated to this author, LeRoy noticed that Robinson had the habit of blinking rapidly whenever a gun was fired. "No matter how hard Eddie concentrated, he could not prevent himself from blinking every time a gun exploded, so I had the makeup people put little transparent bands of tape to his upper eyelids so that he could not blink when the guns were fired and that did the trick. It even gave him a more menacing look, a blood-thirsty killer staring with large penetrating eyes as he shot his victims to death." LeRoy originally did not have Fairbanks in mind for the role of Robinson's only friend in the film and, after seeing Clark Gable in the L.A. theatrical production of "The Last Mile," had Gable test for the part. When Zanuck saw the test, he exploded, telling LeRoy that he had wasted $500 on testing "a guy with big ears that we would never use in a film." Fairbanks then got the part, but the author, Burnett, thought Fairbanks was too polished and urbane for the role, as did Robinson. In fact, when seeing some of Fairbanks'scenes, he thought the actor, by contrast to the roaring Robinson, appeared to be homosexual, which, of course, was not LeRoy's intent, but the studio later inferred that relationship between Robinson and Fairbanks and is the subliminal reason why Robinson spares Fairbanks' life toward the end of the film. Burnett told this author that "all that homosexual stuff is nonsense as I never wrote any of that into my novel. The Fairbanks character is a heterosexual all along, falling in love with a female dancer. The reason why the Robinson character does not shoot him, even after he knows that he has squealed on him, is that Joe Massara [the character Fairbanks plays] is the only friend Rico has on earth and knows it." LeRoy also supported Burnett's statements, telling this author that Robinson "got upset with me when I began clowning on the set, cracking jokes and pulling a few harmless pranks only to relieve the tension of the grim story. He went to Wallis, the producer, and com-

Edward G. Robinson in *Little Caesar*, 1931.

plained about me and Wallis asked me to cut it out and I did. Eddie Robinson took his job very seriously." Burnett told the story that he got the idea for **Little Caesar** when listening to a local radio broadcast when he lived in Chicago, which was interrupted when gangsters invaded a nightclub celebration and shot up the place, killing a musician who was a friend of Burnett's, and where Burnett swore he could hear the moans of several wounded persons over the airways as the microphone was still open during the raid. He admitted to this author that the character played by Robinson was a combination of two notorious Chicago gangsters and bootleggers Burnett knew about, Al Capone (1899-1947), crime boss of Chicago's South Side, and Charles Dion O'Banion (or O'Bannion, 1892-1924), who was the bootleg boss of Chicago's North Side, and that the Blackmer character, who "pulls the strings" is based on the corrupt Chicago Mayor William Hale "Big Bill" Thompson (1869-1944). For more details on Capone, O'Banion and Thompson, see my books, *World Encyclopedia of Organized Crime* (Paragon House, 1992; Capone: pages 78-98; O'Banion: pages 304-310); *Bloodletters and Badmen* (M. Evans, 1995; Capone: pages 119-130; O'Banion: pages 472-478); and *The Great Pictorial History of World Crime*, Volume I (History, Inc., 2004; Capone and O'Banion: pages 503-541). **p**, Hal B. Wallis, for Darryl F. Zanuck; **d**, Mervyn LeRoy; **cast**, Edward G. Robinson, Douglas Fairbanks Jr., Glenda Farrell, William Collier Jr., Sidney Blackmer, Ralph Ince, Thomas Jackson, Stanley Fields, George E. Stone, Landers Stevens, Noel Madison, Maurice Black, Lucille La Verne, Nick Beta, Ben Hendricks Jr., Armand Kaliz; **w**, Robert N. Lee, Zanuck, Robert Lord, Francis Edwards Faragoh (based on the novel by W.R. Burnett); **c**, Tony Gaudio; **m**, Erno Rapee; **ed**, Ray Curtiss; **art d**, Anton Grot; **set d**, Ray Moyer.

The Little Colonel ★★★ 1935; U.S.; 81m; FOX; Color/B/W; Musical Comedy; Children: Acceptable; **DVD**; **VHS**. Temple is at her charming best in this entertaining musical comedy, which begins with cranky Barrymore, a southern colonel bemoaning the South's loss of the Civil War and complaining that his attractive daughter, Venable, is about to marry a Yankee, Lodge. The couple marries and has a child, Temple. When times become hard and Lodge loses his income, Barrymore takes Venable, Lodge and Temple into his ancestral mansion and where Temple soon bonds with Barrymore's black mammy and housekeeper, McDaniel, and his black butler and jack-of-all-trades, Robinson. Temple uses her considerable charms to win over her grumpy grandfather's heart and, in her delightful way, brings about reconciliation between Barrymore and her parents. The film's finale is a "Pink Party," shot in Technicolor, where Temple sings and dances for a happy finale. The highlight of this film is where the precocious Temple dances with the wonderful Robinson. The cast gives great support to the toddling tot, particularly

Bill "Bojangles" Robinson and Shirley Temple in *The Little Colonel*, 1935.

Barrymore, who is the consummate curmudgeon. Songs include: "Dixie" (aka "I Wish I Was in Dixieland"; Daniel Decatur Emmett), "Oh! Susanna," "My Old Kentucky Home" (Stephen Collins Foster), "Love's Young Dream" (composer not credited; lyrics by Thomas Moore), "Swing Low, Sweet Chariot" (Traditional), "Wade in the Water" (aka "God's Gwinter Trouble De Water"; Traditional Spiritual), "The Sun Shines Brighter (When You Go Singing Along)" (William Kernell, Louis De Francesco). **p**, B.G. DeSylva; **d**, David Butler; **cast**, Shirley Temple, Lionel Barrymore, Evelyn Venable, John Lodge, Sidney Blackmer, Robert Warwick, Hattie McDaniel, Bill "Bojangles" Robinson, Geneva Williams, Dave O'Brien; **w**, William M. Conselman (based on the novel by Anne Fellows Johnston); **c**, Arthur Miller, William Skall (Technicolor); **m**, Arthur Lange, Cyril J. Mockridge, Hugo Friedhofer; **ed**, Irene Morra; **art d**, William Darling.

The Little Foxes ★★★★★ 1941; U.S.; 116m; Samuel Goldwyn; RKO; B/W; Drama; Children: Cautionary; **DVD**; **VHS**. Davis, Marshall and Wyler are teamed again in this powerful drama about a greedy, conniving Southern family, almost each member willing and eager to destroy the others for money. Set at the turn of the 20th Century, this south of the Mason-Dixon line opus begins when family queen bee Davis is approached by her artful brothers, Dingle and Reid, asking that she loan them $75,000 (a very substantial sum in those days) so that they can take advantage of cheap labor by erecting a cotton mill. Davis invites Hicks, a Northern financier, who has proposed the venture, to her richly appointed mansion so that she can give determine his validity. After she is convinced that the family will reap a fortune from the venture, sends her trusting daughter, Wright, to Maryland, to retrieve her ailing husband, Marshall, who has been recovering from a heart attack in a Baltimore institution. Davis immediately goes to work on the still weak and sick Marshall, trying to convince him to put up their share for the investment, $75,000, but Marshall opposes the project, stating that it is morally wrong and will be nothing more than another Southern sweatshop where workers will receive starvation wages. When Dingle and Reid learn that Marshall will not back their new venture, Reid orders his slavish son, Duryea, who works in the local bank Reid controls, to filch some cash-heavy negotiable bonds Marshall has stored in a safe deposit box in that bank. After Davis learns that Duryea has taken the bonds, she exhibits a streak of greediness that outdoes her avaricious brothers by blackmailing them into giving her a share of the new business on the threat that she will tell Marshall about the family arranged theft. Marshall then undoes the plans of his scheming wife by stating that Duryea did not steal his bonds (which he clearly did) but that he, Marshall, gave him those bonds to use as collateral for a loan to fund the project. Davis now viciously nags her husband until his weak heart

gives out. When he has another heart attack, Davis does nothing to help him retrieve his life-saving medicine. Marshall, while on his deathbed, tells daughter Wright not to trust her mother and not to marry her cousin, Duryea, a worthless lout, and seek happiness with Carlson, an upstanding young newspaper editor. After Marshall dies, Davis expresses no remorse for her mistreatment of him, only relief. She successfully blackmails her brothers into giving her two thirds of the new business, but Wright, who has overheard this shady deal, tells her mother that she despises her and holds her responsible for her father's death. She leaves forever, going to Carlson, who has been waiting for her outside the mansion in a rainstorm, and the two go off to be married and see the kind of happy life that never dwelled in Davis' home. Davis is now a wealthy and powerful woman, but at a great cost. With the only two good-hearted persons in her life now gone, Marshall and Wright, she is left alone to ponder her grim and cold-blooded machinations. Davis gives one of her most riveting performances as a woman totally consumed by greed and a lust for power, a performance only achieved under the meticulous guidance of pantheon director Wyler, who unfolds this unsavory tale with great tactical skills in presenting one revealing scene after another to excruciatingly expose the hideous avarice of each character. More sympathetic characters, the sympathetic Marshall, the loving Wright, the noble-minded Carlson, and the warm-hearted Collinge, a wealthy aunt who is a secret alcoholic (and who has been married by Reid only to obtain her family plantation) are shown by Wyler with equally infinite care. Though nominated for eight Oscars in all the top categories (Wright and Collinge were both nominated for Best Supporting Actress), this excellent film won none. It nevertheless remains one of the finest play adaptations ever put on the screen. ***Author's Note***: Davis admitted to this author that "I am an utter bitch in that picture, just awful, not an ounce of decency and compassion in my body. Wyler made sure that viewers would see that about me when he had Greg Toland, the wonderful cinematographer for that picture, shoot a scene where I sit like a stone statue as my husband, poor Herbert Marshall, suffers a heart attack. The close-up is on my face where I show no concern about this dying man, who is trying to get to his heart medicine and where he is seen struggling up some stairs in deep focus—that was Toland's hallmark and which he used to great effect in **Citizen Kane** [1941]—until he collapses and goes out of focus like an old dishrag no longer needed. When I saw the rushes for that scene my blood ran cold as ice. That scene was chilling and nothing could better depict just how cold-hearted a person I am." Wyler told this author that "Bette did not like the film and thought that she did not do a good job with her role, but she is wrong about that. It is one of her greatest roles. She gave me a very hard time in that production and we were arguing back and forth every day and where she fought me on every scene. Bette is one of those persons who can drain you of every emotion and add years to your life in a few minutes. I guess that, too, is a special talent." Producer Goldwyn told this author that "I thought that Hellman had written a great play and I bought the rights after I saw it on Broadway, but, you know, it is a mean and cynical story where the nice people lose out to those who are rotten and corrupt. It works that way in Hollywood, too, young man, believe me." Wright and Duryea make their film debuts in this outstanding entry. **p**, Samuel Goldwyn; **d**, William Wyler; **cast**, Bette Davis, Herbert Marshall, Teresa Wright, Richard Carlson, Dan Duryea, Patricia Collinge, Charles Dingle, Carl Benton Reid, Russell Hicks, Lucien Littlefield; **w**, Lillian Hellman, Arthur Kober, Dorothy Parker, Alan Campbell (based on the play by Hellman); **c**, Gregg Toland; **m**, Meredith Willson; **ed**, Daniel Mandell; **art d**, Stephen Goosson; **set d**, Howard Bristol.

The Little Fugitive ★★★ 1953; U.S.; 80m; Little Fugitive Production Co./Joseph Burstyn; B/W; Drama; Children: Cautionary (MPAA: G); **DVD**; **VHS**. In this engrossing and very touching tale, Andrusco, a ten-year-old Brooklyn boy, runs away from home after his older brother, Brewster, tells him that he, Andrusco, has killed another boy with his cap gun. Brewster has told him the lie because he hates babysitting for his brother and hopes he will run away. Andrusco goes to Coney Island where he collects empty soda bottles for deposit money so he can get on the rides. Williams, the operator of one of the rides, suspects Andrusco is a runaway and notifies the boy's mother, Cushing, who comes for him, takes him back home, and convinces him he has not killed anyone. **p**, Ray Ashley, Morris Engel; **d&w**, Ashley, Engel, Ruth Orkin; **cast**, Richie Andrusco, Richard Brewster, Winifred Cushing, Jay Williams, Will Lee, Charlie Moss, Tommy DeCanio, Ruth Orkin; **c**, Engel; **m**, Eddy Manson; **ed**, Orkin, Lester Troob.

The Little Giant ★★★ 1933; U.S.; 76m; First National/WB; B/W; Comedy/Crime Drama; Children: Cautionary; **DVD**. Robinson does a great job satirizing his previous roles as a tough gangster. He is a bootlegging beer baron in Chicago. When his underworld racket collapses with the return of booze under the Roosevelt administration, Robinson tells his gang members that, instead of starting new rackets, he plans to retire to southern California, take up polo and join High Society. To that end, he takes his ill-gotten bootleg loot and moves to Santa Barbara where he meets Vinson, thinking she is from an upper crust family when, in truth, she is part of a bunch of lowlife swindlers pretending to be the social elite Robinson seeks. Though Robinson is a street savvy crook from Chicago, he is naïve when it comes to sophisticated stock swindles and loses his fortune to Vinson and her associates and is then framed for the vast confidence game. He is about to be convicted by Marston, but Robinson cuts a deal with Marston, asking that he be given enough time to recoup the lost money. He is granted a short period of time to make things right, and Robinson then calls his old Chicago cronies back into action where they strong-arm the crooks into making restitution. In the process, Robinson falls in love with money-strapped Astor in whose heavily mortgaged house he has been living. After Robinson and friends reclaim the stolen money and turn over the culprits to the authorities, Robinson and Astor decide to make a go of it together. There is a lot of fun in this broad spoof of gangsters, and Robinson proves that he has as much talent for comedy as he has for drama. *Author's Note*: "That picture," Robinson told this author, "is as ridiculous as me riding a polo pony. It was, however, a lot of fun, and, for a change, I got to play the good guy, well, a bad-good guy, who strikes a blow for honesty, now that I have turned honest. You know, the fellow who wrote the screenplay for that film, Wilson Mizner, had been some sort of swindler back in the Florida real estate boom in the 1920s, so he used a lot of his tricks when writing about the swindlers shown in **Little Giant**." For more information on the colorful Wilson Mizner, see my book, *Zanies: The World's Greatest Eccentrics* (New Century Publishers, 1982; pages 246-252). **p**, Ray Griffith; **d**, Roy Del Ruth; **cast**, Edward G. Robinson, Mary Astor, Helen Vinson, Russell Hopton, Kenneth Thomson, Shirley Grey, Berton Churchill, Joan Barclay, Guy Usher, Toby Wing; **w**, Robert Lord, Wilson Mizner (based on the story by Lord); **c**, Sid Hickox; **m**, Leo F. Forbstein; **ed**, George Marks, Ray Curtiss; **art d**, Robert M. Haas.

The Little Girl Who Lives Down the Lane ★★★ 1977; Canada; France; 100; Zev Braun Productions/American International Pictures; Color; Horror; Children: Unacceptable (MPAA: PG); **DVD**; **VHS**. In this chilling horror entry, Foster is a thirteen-year-old girl who lives in a secluded house her father rented in a quiet New England seaside community. Anyone visiting around the house only sees her, not her father, and they wonder if the girl lives there alone. Foster makes up stories that her father is away, when, in fact, he is dead. When a curious neighbor comes to the house, Foster pushes her down the basement stairs before she goes about her housework as if nothing has happened. Another neighbor, Sheen, who desires her, asks questions she'd rather not answer. She is meanwhile attracted to a boy her age, Jacoby. Sheen presses her for explanations and she poisons his tea with arsenic. He suspects that and instead drinks her tea, but she outwits him because she had laced her tea figuring he would switch drinks. She murders in order to protect her private world, and we are left to wonder about her

Joseph Dowling, Claude Gillingwater and Mary Pickford in *Little Lord Fauntleroy*, **1921.**

motives and sanity. **p**, Zev Braun, Denis Héroux, Eugéne Lépicier, Leland Nolan; **d**, Nicolas Gessner; **cast**, Jodie Foster, Martin Sheen, Alexis Smith, Mort Shuman, Scott Jacoby, Dorothy Davis, Clesson Goodhue, Hubert Noel, Jacques Famery, Mary Morter, Julie Wildman; **w**, Laird Koenig (based on his novel); **c**, René Verzier; **m**, Christian Gaubert; **ed**, Yves Langlois; **art d**, Robert Prévost; **spec eff**, Christophe Harbonville.

The Little Kidnappers ★★★ 1954; U.K.; 93m; Group Film Productions Ltd./UA; B/W; Drama; Children: Acceptable; **DVD**; **VHS**. Macrae, a Scotsman living on a homestead in Nova Scotia in the early 1900s, is rearing two young grandsons, Whiteley and Winter, whose father died in the Second Boer War (1899-1902). The war was fought between the British and mostly Dutch farmers (Boers) living in the Transvaal of South Africa, who wanted to break away from British rule. Because of the war, Macrae has a strong dislike of all Dutchmen. This leads to Whiteley brawling at school with the son of a Dutchman. Whiteley falls down a cliff and is rescued by the local doctor, Bikel, who is in love with Macrae's daughter, Corri, so the lovers carry on a secret romance. Macrae forbids his grandsons to have a dog, so the boys "kidnap" a baby they find abandoned in a meadow and care for it in a shack. When found, the baby is identified as the child of Macrae's most bitter Dutch enemy. This warm and affectionate story is suitable for the whole family. **p**, Sergei Nolbandov, Leslie Parkyn; **d**, Philip Leacock; **cast**, Duncan Macrae, Jean Anderson, Theodore Bikel, Jon Whiteley, Vincent Winter, Adrienne Corri, Francis De Wolff, James Sutherland, John Rae, Jack Stewart; **w**, Neil Paterson; **c**, Eric Cross; **m**, Bruce Montgomery; **ed**, John Trumper; **art d**, Edward Carrick.

Little Lord Fauntleroy ★★★ 1921 (silent); U.S.; 112m/10 reels; Mary Pickford Company/UA; B/W; Drama; Children: Acceptable; **DVD**. Pickford performs astounding dual roles in this engrossing tale where she is a widowed mother, who also plays her young son, both living in poverty in New York. As the mother she has been married to a British lord, but that marriage was condemned by the family patriarch, Gillingwater, who objected to his son marrying an American commoner, and after Pickford's husband dies, she lives estranged from Gillingwater and the British branch of her husband's family. After Gillingwater's only surviving son dies in a riding mishap, Pickford's son (Pickford herself) becomes the heir to a great British estate. Pickford and the boy are summoned to England and, after they arrive, Pickford (as the boy) becomes Little Lord Fauntleroy. He is separated from his mother, however, as Gillingwater will not allow his mother to stay with him in the ancestral castle since Gillingwater believes her to be nothing more than a gold digger and that she married his oldest son for his money. As the heir,

Douglass Montgomery and Christian Rub in *Little Man, What Now?*, 1934.

Pickford proves to be charming, befriending servants and family friends with ease, and begins to melt Gillingwater's cold heart, which freezes again when a pretender arrives in an attempt to usurp the boy's aristocratic position. A couple of pals from America, however, Marcus and Price, appear and show Gillingwater the proof that Pickford is the rightful heir. Gillingwater then relents, sees how he has wronged the mother, and welcomes her into his home for a happy ending. The many scenes showing Pickford playing the dual roles of mother and son are truly amazing and where, as the mother, she appears to be three or more inches taller than the boy. The scene where they kiss involved elaborate matte processing at that time and took more than fifteen hours to produce, resulting in only a few magical seconds on the screen. **p**, Mary Pickford; **d**, Alfred E. Green, Jack Pickford; **cast**, Mary Pickford, Claude Gillingwater, Joseph Dowling, James Marcus, Kate Price, Fred Malatesta, Rose Dione, Arthur Thalasso, Colin Kenny, Emmett King, Milton Berle; **w**, Bernard McConville (based on the novel by Frances Hodgson Burnett); **c**, Charles Rosher; **m**, Gaylord Carter, Louis F. Gottschalk; **art d**, Stephen Goosson.

Little Lord Fauntleroy ★★★ 1936; U.S.; 102m; Selznick/UA; B/W; Drama; Children; Acceptable; **DVD**; **VHS**. In this third of several versions of the Burnett tale, Bartholomew is the heir to the great British estate, who is summoned to England with his widowed mother, Barrymore, after living in near poverty in New York City. When they arrive, Bartholomew is informed that he is the heir to a great estate and that he is now Little Lord Fauntleroy. Mother and her son, however, are greeted by a stern Smith, who dislikes all Americans and rudely treats Bartholomew and Barrymore with coldness. The boy, however, charms his grandfather with his bright banter and quick mind, showing that he is honorable and deserving of the title he has inherited while also winning the hearts of the many servants and relatives. A pretender arrives to challenge Bartholomew's claim to the estate, but the imposter is proven bogus by Bartholomew and his friends, who provide proof that Bartholomew is the rightful heir. Smith, a wonderful British character actor, is perfect as the unyielding grandfather; Barrymore does a fine job enacting the mother, and Bartholomew is a standout as the little rags-to-riches boy. Fine support is provided by Rooney, as a New York shoeshine boy, and Kibbee, as a colorful Brooklyn grocer. **p**, David O. Selznick; **d**, John Cromwell; **cast**, Freddie Bartholomew, Dolores Costello Barrymore, C. Aubrey Smith, Guy Kibbee, Henry Stephenson, Mickey Rooney, Constance Collier, E.E. Clive, Una O'Connor, Jackie Searl, Jessie Ralph, Dickie Jones, Mary Gordon; **w**, Hugh Walpole (based on the novel by Frances Hodgson Burnett); **c**, Charles Rosher; **m**, Max Steiner; **ed**, Hal C. Kern; **art d**, Sturges Carne; **spec eff**, Virgil Miller, Jack Wagner, Jack Cosgrove.

Little Man Tate ★★★ 1991; U.S.; 99m; Orion Pictures Corp.; Color; Drama; Children: Unacceptable (MPAA: PG); **DVD**; **VHS**. In her debut as a director, actress Foster filmed this absorbing story about a single mother, Foster, whose eight-year-old son, Hann-Byrd, is exceptionally bright, although she doesn't realize it or know what to do about it. Wiest, the operator of a child prodigy institute, does see the genius in the boy and invites him to a summer-long convention for very smart children. Foster is torn between letting Wiest have her son for a summer in which he might develop his intelligence, or keep him at home and to herself. Foster gives in and Wiest takes the boy under her wing, even though she is not a mother and doesn't know how to handle a boy his age, especially one who is a genius. Mature subject matter prohibits viewing by children. **p**, Scott Rudin, Peggy Rajski; **d**, Jodie Foster; **cast**, Foster, Dianne Wiest, Adam Hann-Byrd, Harry Connick, Jr., David Pierce, Debi Mazar, P.J. Ochlan, Alex Lee, Michael Shulman, Nathan Lee, George Plimpton; **w**, Scott Frank; **c**, Mike Southon; **m**, Mark Isham; **ed**, Lynzee Klingman; **prod d**, Jon Hutman; **art d**, Adam Lustig; **set d**, Sam Schaffer; **spec eff**, Phill Norman.

Little Man, What Now? ★★★ 1934; U.S.; 98m; UNIV; B/W; Drama; Children: Unacceptable; **VHS**. Set in Germany during the last stages of the failing Weimar Republic, this intriguing tale has Sullavan and Montgomery as secret newlyweds living in a small town. Montgomery has kept his marriage a secret since his boss does not like to employ married men, but when that secret gets out, the couple is compelled to leave, going to Berlin to live with Montgomery's stepmother, who lives in a lavish home. Montgomery gets a low-paying job in a department store, but he and Sullavan then discover that their home is nothing more than a glorified bordello. Montgomery quits his job and they again depart, finding shelter in a loft owned by an elderly wagon driver where Sullavan gives birth to their son (the "little man" in the title of this film; the allegory of his lowly birth to that of the child in the manger two thousand years earlier is not lost on viewers). The country by then seems to be in political chaos as Hitler's military regime begins to take over the streets, but this small family evades the violence when Montgomery gets a good job in Holland and he, Sullavan and their child leave for a better life. Borzage does a fine job in profiling through symbolic scenes of unrest and the political turmoil of the Great Depression, the rise of European dictatorships in the early 1930s, obliquely heralding the ominous future awaiting everyone in this uncertain and dangerous era and where Sullavan and Douglas render standout performances as a young couple seeking commonplace happiness. **p**, Carl Laemmle, Jr.; **d**, Frank Borzage; **cast**, Margaret Sullavan, Douglass Montgomery, Alan Hale, Catherine Doucet, DeWitt Jennings, Fred Kohler, Mae Marsh, Donald Haines, Christian Rub, Alan Mowbray, Hedda Hopper; **w**, William Anthony McGuire (based on the novel by Hans Fallada); **c**, Norbert Brodine; **m**, Arthur Kay; **ed**, Milton Carruth; **art d**, Charles D. Hall.

The Little Mermaid ★★★★ 1989; U.S.; 83m; Walt Disney/Buena Vista; Color; Fantasy; Children: Recommended (MPAA: G); **DVD**; **VHS**. Loosely based on the fairy tale by Hans Christian Andersen, this version sees Ariel (Benson voiceover) as the mermaid daughter of King Triton (Mars voiceover). She has only one wish and that is that she can be a human living above the sea. She makes a pact with octopus Ursula, the Sea Witch (Carroll voiceover) to give her human legs and meet a handsome young prince (Barnes voiceover) of the world above the waters. Ariel gets her wish, but if the prince does not kiss her within two days, she will have to return to the sea and give her beautiful singing voice to Ursula. This is a wonderful adventure weaving its own special magic and where the distinctive Disney animation is in rich evidence in every frame. One of Disney's best, including the Oscar-winning best song "Under the Sea" (sung by Wright). Other songs include: "Kiss the Girl," "Fathoms Below," "Daughters of Triton," "Part of Your World," "Poor Unfortunate Souls," "Les Poissons" (Alan Menken, Howard Ashman). **p**, Howard Ashman, John Musker; **d&w**, Ron Clements, Musker (based on the fairy tale by Hans Christian Andersen); **cast** (voiceovers), Jodi Benson, Rene Auberjonois, Christopher Daniel Barnes, Pat Carroll, Ben Wright, Paddi Edwards, Buddy Hackett, Kenneth Mars, Hamilton Camp, Mark Hamill, Rod McKuen; **m**, Alan Menken; **ed**, Mark Hester; **art d**, Michael A. Peraza, Jr., Donald A. Towns, Mark Dindal.

The Little Minister ★★★ 1934; U.S.; 104m; RKO; B/W; Drama; Children: Acceptable; **DVD**; **VHS**. A young man, Beal, who is small in stature, arrives with his mother at a rural church in 1840s Scotland and becomes known as the "little minister." The town is run by a few owners of a factory in which the weavers are virtual slaves. They revolt and are aided by a young gypsy, Hepburn, who defies her nobleman guardian, Lord Rintoul (Conroy) by informing the weavers when he dispatches soldiers to break up their gatherings. She and Beal meet and fall in love, but the church's congregation disapproves of their romance. The parishioners change their minds when they learn she is only dressing as a gypsy and is really the ward of Conroy. The lovers may now marry. Despite the heavy plot, the film provides considerable humor and standout performances from Hepburn, Beal and the rest of the cast. (The actors deliver their lines in heavy Scots burrs, requiring viewer concentration, but that makes this well-crafted film all the more worthwhile.) Based on the play by James M. Barrie (author of *Peter Pan*), this story was previously filmed four times during the silent era (1913, 1915, 1921, 1922). **p**, Pandro S. Berman; **d**, Richard Wallace; **cast**, Katharine Hepburn, John Beal, Alan Hale, Donald Crisp, Lumsden Hare, Andy Clyde, Beryl Mercer, Dorothy Stickney, Mary Gordon, Reginald Denny; **w**, Jane Murfin, Sarah Y. Mason, Victor Heerman, Mortimer Offner, Jack Wagner (based on the novel and play by Sir James M. Barrie); **c**, Henry Gerrard; **m**, Max Steiner; **ed**, William Hamilton; **art d**, Van Nest Polglase, Carroll Clark; **spec eff**, Harry Redmond, Sr. and Jr., Vernon L. Walker.

Little Miss Marker ★★★★ 1934; U.S.; 80m; PAR; B/W; Comedy; Children: Acceptable; **DVD**; **VHS**. The first and best in several film versions of the delightful Damon Runyon tale has the adorable Temple in the role that made her an international star. She is left as a $20 marker (or debt) owed to dour-faced and conniving bookie, Menjou, after Temple's father loses everything and takes his life. Menjou bundles the tyke home with him and these opening scenes where he tries to prepare her for bed are hilarious. (This was an extraordinary role for Menjou in that he had established a long career as a suave and urbane matinee idol and here is a shifty gambling tout and, initially, a hard-hearted, wise-cracking money-grubber, rendering one of the finest performances in his distinguished career.) To anyone else, Temple would be the most precocious, sweetest little girl on the face of the earth, but to the hustling Menjou she is a nuisance, if not a pain in the neck. To get the little lady to sleep, Menjou reads her a bedtime story, rattling off a lot of nonsense culled from the local racetrack sheet. Temple becomes fascinated with the story of King Arthur and somehow envisions Menjou (called Sorrowful Jones) as that noble lord of yesteryear. She gives the names of Arthur's most trusted knights and ladies fair to Menjou's male and female cronies, who think the world of her. Menjou then undergoes a personality change as Temple works her charms upon him. Known as the worst tightwad on Broadway, he shocks his pals by letting loose some of his tightly held cash to buy Temple some new clothes and even splurges to purchase a new suit for himself. When it looks like Menjou might lose supervision of Temple as a single guardian, he takes the plunge he has avoided for years and marries his long-standing girlfriend and nightclub singer, Dell, and they adopt the wonderful Temple, who has brought so much joy and love to them and their hustling friends. This standout production, well directed by Hall and with superlative performances from Menjou, Temple and Dell, is enlivened by several songs that include: "Low Down Lullaby" [sung by Dell when she puts Temple to sleep], "Laugh, You Son of a Gun" [played on the piano by Dell and sung by her and Temple], "I'm a Black Sheep Who's Blue"

Adolphe Menjou and Shirley Temple in *Little Miss Marker*, 1934.

[sung by Dell in a nightclub] (all three in 1934; Ralph Rainger, Leo Robin), "The Bowery" [sung a cappella by the knights of the round table] (1892; Percy Gaunt, Charles Hale Hoyt), "Sidewalks of New York" [sung a cappella by the knights of the round table] (1894; Charles Lawlor, James W. Blake), "Bridal Chorus (Here Comes the Bride)" (from "Lohengrin" by Richard Wagner). This film was remade in 1980 with Walter Matthau and Julie Andrews in the starring roles, but it is an inferior production. *Author's Note*: Runyon was not above stealing his own ideas when he later used the Menjou-Dell relationship to effective use in **Guys and Dolls**, 1955, where nightclub singer Adelaide (Vivian Blaine) and gambler Nathan Detroit (Frank Sinatra) finally get hitched after years of enduring a purgatorial engagement. Zanuck, who headed Fox, told this author that "I loaned Shirley [Temple] to Paramount for **Little Miss Marker**. She had made a few films for Fox and I thought she had promise, but lo and behold, after she did that picture, everybody in the world wanted to see her, so Paramount really established her as a Fox star." Dell (1915-1934), who appears in this film at the age of nineteen, had also become an overnight star, after winning a baby beauty contest in her native Hattiesburg, Mississippi and then moving to Louisiana to win the Miss New Orleans Beauty contest in 1930 at age fifteen (beating out seventy-four other contestants, including the ravishing Dorothy Lamour, who would win the contest the following year and go on to become a huge Paramount star). Dell traveled for six months in a vaudeville show until getting a job in 1931 in the Ziegfeld Follies where she wowed audiences by singing "Was I Drunk?" She was signed to a long-term contract by Paramount and appeared in a short, **Passing the Buck**, 1932, and then in three features, all in 1934: **Wharf Angel**, **Little Miss Marker** and **Shoot the Works**. Dell, accompanied by her date, Dr. Carl Wagner, attended an all-night party at a hotel in Altadena, California, leaving that festivity in the early hours of June 8, 1934. En route to Pasadena, the car, driven by Wagner, suddenly left the highway and struck a telephone pole, then a palm tree and finally crashed into a large boulder. Dell was killed instantly and Wagner died a few hours later. When Temple learned of this young woman's death, the little girl, who had emotionally bonded with Dell, was so devastated that she could not continue with the production of **Now and Forever**, 1934, which was delayed until Temple recovered from the shock. Dell continued to receive fan mail for several years after her death and her dressing room at Paramount (No. 101) remained empty and unused for years as many actresses thought it to be "unlucky"; where Irene Dunne and Gladys Swarthout refused to occupy that room. **Little Miss Marker** was released only seven days before Dell's untimely death. **p**, B.P. Schulberg; **d**, Alexander Hall; **cast**, Adolphe Menjou, Dorothy Dell, Charles Bickford, Shirley Temple, Lynne Overman, Warren Hymer, Sam Hardy, John Kelly, Frank McGlynn, Sr., Willie Best; **w**, William R. Lip-

Judy Garland and Douglas McPhail in *Little Nellie Kelly*, 1940.

man, Sam Hellman, Gladys Lehman (based on the story by Damon Runyon); **c**, Alfred Gilks; **m**, Ralph Rainger; **ed**, William Shea; **art d**, Hans Dreier, John B. Goodman.

Little Miss Sunshine ★★★ 2006; U.S.; 101m; Fox Searchlight Pictures; Color; Comedy; Children: Unacceptable (MPAA: R); **BD**; **DVD**. Breslin is a seven-year-old girl who spreads sunshine wherever she goes. She is transfixed when watching a beauty pageant on TV and decides to compete and win this year's crown. Her poor and dysfunctional parents, Kinnear and Collette, support her dream and they take a 700-mile road trip in their Volkswagen bus from Albuquerque, New Mexico, to Redondo Beach, California, so she can enter the finals. Traveling with them is Breslin's grandfather, Arkin, who coaches her in dancing. (He had been ousted from a retirement home for having sex with some of the other residents and for snorting heroin.) Also along for the ride is Collette's gay brother, Carell, who is the leading Proust scholar at a college and who has tried suicide after being dumped by his boyfriend, a graduate student who preferred the college's second leading Proust scholar. Breslin's teenage brother, Dano, hasn't spoken for almost a year, having read Nietzsche and taking a vow of silence while he prepares to apply for flight school. It's a crazy adventure filled with nutty people, and the viewer, thanks to Breslin's sunny personality, will want the youngster to win the beauty contest. Gutter language, sex and drug content prohibit viewing by children. All of the offbeat, if not sometimes unsavory, content also eliminates this otherwise engrossing entry as acceptable family fare. **p**, Albert Berger, David T. Friendly, Peter Saraf, Marc Turtletaub, Ron Yerxa; **d**, Jonathan Dayton, Valerie Faris; **cast**, Abigail Breslin, Steve Carell, Greg Kinnear, Alan Arkin, Toni Collette, Paul Dano, Turtletaub, Jill Talley, Brenda Canela, Julio Oscar Mechoso, Chuck Loring; **w**, Michael Arndt; **c**, Tim Suhrstedt; **m**, Mychael Danna, DeVotchKa; **ed**, Pamela Martin; **prod d**, Kalina Ivanov; **art d**, Alan E. Muraoka; **set d**, Melissa Levander; **spec eff**, Ian Eyre, Adam Avitabile.

Little Nellie Kelly ★★★ 1940; U.S.; 98m; MGM; B/W; Musical; Children: Acceptable; **DVD**; **VHS**. In this fine musical romp that exalts the Irish, Garland falls in love with Murphy, and plans to marry him, even though her father, Winninger, opposes the union. Garland nevertheless goes to the altar with the handsome Murphy and they migrate from Ireland to New York, which also angers old trouper Winninger, who moves there, too. Murphy becomes a cop and Garland has a child, but sadly dies in childbirth. Murphy and Winninger, though battling with each other, raise the little girl, who grows up to be Garland, the spitting image of her mother. And, like her mother, Garland falls in love with McPhail, another Irishman, but who is the son of Winninger's old friend, Shields, a family Murphy has been at odds with for years. It appears that Garland

will not achieve her mother's ambitions, but she finds a way to reconcile the battling family members and goes to the altar with McPhail. Many delightful songs include: "The Irish Washerwoman" (traditional Irish jig), "St. Patrick Was a Gentle Man" (composer unknown), "A Pretty Girl Milking the Cow," "It's a Great Day for the Irish" (1940; Roger Edens), "Columbia, the Gem of the Ocean" (1843; traditional), "The Wearin' of the Green" (traditional), "Believe Me If All Those Endearing Young Charms" (1808; traditional), "Nellie Is a Darling," "Nellie Kelly I Love You" (1922; George M. Cohan), "Happy Birthday to You" (1893; Mildred J. Hill, Patty S. Hill), "Singin' in the Rain" (1929; Nacio Herb Brown, Arthur Freed). **p**, Arthur Freed; **d**, Norman Taurog; **cast**, Judy Garland, George Murphy, Charles Winninger, Douglas McPhail, Arthur Shields, Rita Page, Forrester Harvey, James Burke, George Watts, Ernie Alexander, John Raitt; **w**, Jack McGowan (based on the musical comedy by George M. Cohan); **c**, Ray June; **m**, Roger Edens, George Stoll, George Bassman; **ed**, Fredrick Y. Smith; **art d**, Cedric Gibbons; **set d**, Edwin B. Willis.

The Little Princess ★★★ 1939; U.S.; 91m; FOX; Color; Drama/Musical; Children: Recommended; **DVD**; **VHS**. Hunter is a British army captain, who goes off to South Africa to fight in the First Anglo-Boer War (1880-1881). The war stems from a rebellion of Dutch farmers (Boers) against British rule in the Transvaal that re-establishes their independence. Hunter is widowed and leaves his young daughter, Temple, at an exclusive private school for girls in London run by Nash, a stern woman. Temple is treated like a little princess by Nash until she receives word that Hunter is missing in action and tuition for his daughter has ended. Nash keeps Temple at the school, but now she has to work for her keep, scrubbing floors and cleaning out the fireplace. Temple does the menial work, but refuses to believe her father is dead and visits hospitals in hopes of finding him among the wounded. Meanwhile, she receives a visit from a swami, Romero, who magically redecorates her dismal room into a lavish living area, which gives the girl confidence. Temple eventually finds Hunter in a hospital, but he has amnesia and doesn't know her, until her love reaches him, rekindling his memory of her, and he embraces her for a happy ending. Temple is a little miracle in the movie, perfectly cast in one of the several roles that made her the top child actor in the 1930s. This story was filmed with Mary Pickford as a silent film (1917) and as **A Little Princess**, 1995, with a slightly different plot. **p**, Darryl F. Zanuck; **d**, Walter Lang; **cast**, Shirley Temple, Richard Greene, Anita Louise, Ian Hunter, Cesar Romero, Arthur Treacher, Mary Nash, Sybil Jason, Miles Mander, Marcia Mae Jones, Beryl Mercer; **w**, Ethel Hill, Walter Ferris (based on the novel *The Fantasy* by Frances Hodgson Burnett); **c**, Arthur Miller, William Skall; **m**, Walter Bullock, Samuel Pockrass; **ed**, Louis Loeffler; **art d**, Hans Peters, Bernard Herzbrun; **set d**, Thomas Little.

A Little Princess ★★★ 1995; U.S.; 97m; WB; Color; Family Drama; Children: Recommended (MPAA: G); **DVD**; **VHS**. A slightly changed version of **The Little Princess**, 1939, sees Cunningham as a widowed British army captain, who goes off to fight in World War I, leaving his ten-year-old daughter, Matthews, at a New York boarding school that her late mother had attended. She soon butts heads with Bron, the school's stern headmistress, who tries to stifle the girl's pride and independent streak and belief that every girl is a princess. But her privileged life at the school changes drastically when Bron receives word that Cunningham has been killed in action and his estate taken over by the British government. Instead of being treated as a little princess, Matthews now has to do menial work for her room and board, sharing an attic room with a black servant girl, Chester. Matthews' escape from her new harsh world is in her imagination and magic, remembering her father telling her, "Magic has to be believed – that's the only way it's real." She tells the other girls stories her father told her when they lived in India, about the love between Princess Sita and Prince Rama. She is befriended by a kindly Indian gentleman, Sitahal, and is reunited with her father, who did not die in the war, but was mistaken for a slain soldier and suffered from amnesia. This story was also made as a silent film with Mary Pickford in 1919 and was a very successful Shirley Temple vehicle in 1939. **p**, Mark Johnson, Dalisa Cohen; **d**, Alófonso Cuarón; **cast**, Liesel Matthews, Eleanor Bron, Liam Cunningham, Rusty Schwimmer, Arthur Malet, Vanessa Lee Chester, Errol Sitahal, Heather DeLoach, Taylor Fry, Darcie Bradford; **w**, Richard LaGravenese, Elizabeth Chandler (based on the novel *The Fantasy* by Frances Hodgson Burnett); **c**, Emmanuel Lubezki; **m**, Patrick Doyle; **ed**, Steven Weisberg; **prod d**, Bo Welch; **art d**, Tom Duffield; **set d**, Cheryl Carasik; **spec eff**, Matt Farell, Evelyn Fitzgerald, John Scheele, Jesse Silver.

A Little Romance ★★★ 1979; U.S./French; 108m; Pan Arts/Orion Pictures Corp.; Color; Adventure/Romance; Children: Cautionary (MPAA: PG); **DVD**; **VHS**. Two thirteen-year-olds, a French boy, Bernard, and an American girl, Lane, who goes to school in Paris, meet and begin a little romance. Bernard is the son of a Paris taxi driver, but Lane's parents, Hill and Kellerman, are more upscale. Their parents object to their romance so the kids take a plane to Venice with an adult friend Olivier, who is an engaging pickpocket. In Venice, the young lovers play pranks such as pushing gondoliers into the canals and stealing bikes during a bicycle race. Meanwhile, Lane's parents think she has been kidnapped and police start a search. They find Lane with Olivier and think the worst. Olivier gives himself up, but Lane explains that Olivier was just a chaperone, and the young couple are satisfied that they had a little innocent romance and adventure. **p**, Robert L. Crawford, Yves Rousset-Rouard; **d**, George Roy Hill; **cast**, Laurence Olivier, Diane Lane, Thelonious Bernard, Arthur Hill, Sally Kellerman, Broderick Crawford, Claudette Sutherland, Graham Fletcher-Cook, Ashby Semple, Anna Massey; **w**, Allan Burns (based on the novel *E=MC2 mon amour* by Patrick Cauvin); **c**, Pierre William Glenn; **m**, Georges Delerue; **ed**, William Reynolds; **prod d**, Henry Bumstead; **art d**, François de Lamothe; **set d**, Robert Christides.

The Little Shop of Horrors ★★★ 1960; U.S.; 72m; Santa Clara Productions/The Filmgroup; B/W; Comedy/Horror; Children: Unacceptable; **DVD**; **VHS**. This cult film, shot on a shoestring budget by Corman, a decided filmmaker of the bizarre and macabre, has Haze as a not-too-bright young man working in a slum area florist's shop owned by Welles. To impress girlfriend Joseph, he creates a new floral species which he calls Audrey Jr., after Joseph's name, and all the local lovers of flora and fauna come to admire this new plant. It has a problem, however, and that is it thrives on human flesh and blood and, to keep it alive, Haze starts murdering people and feeding their remains to his ever-enlarging plant, which also talks to him, and incessantly shouts: "Feed me!" Audrey Jr. becomes so large that it takes up almost all the space in the shop and its constant demands for fresh human flesh and blood drives Haze over the brink (he wasn't far from it at the beginning), and he seeks vengeance on his monstrous creation by grabbing a knife and diving into the plant, killing it and himself in the process to end this gruesome black comedy. The film is so absurd, its characters so obtuse and idiotic, that it fascinates while Audrey becomes excruciatingly annoying with its unceasing, shouting demands for human morsels. *Author's Note*: There is no mistaking the notion that Corman got the idea for this weird production after viewing Howard Hawks' classic horror film, **The Thing from Another World**, 1951, which depicts an alien creature of great power that attacks human beings in an Arctic outpost, that creature being a plant form that subsists on human blood. **p&d**, Roger Corman; **cast**, Jonathan Haze, Jackie Joseph, Mel Welles, Jack Nicholson, Dick Miller, Myrtle Vail, Karyn Kupcinet (Tammy Windsor), Toby Michaels, Leola Wendorff, Lynn Storey; **w**, Charles B. Griffith; **c**, Archie Dalzell; **m**, Fred Katz; **ed**, Marshall Neilan, Jr.; **art d**, Daniel Haller.

Little Women ★★★★★ 1933; U.S.; 115m; RKO; B/W; Drama; Children: Acceptable; **DVD**; **VHS**. Though filmed several times as a silent

Frances Dee, Jean Parker, Katharine Hepburn and Joan Bennett in *Little Women*, 1933.

and talkies, this version of the Alcott classic novel remains the very best. The setting is Concord, Massachusetts, during the Civil War, where Byington is raising her four daughters—Hepburn, Bennett, Parker and Dee—while their husband and father, Hinds, is off fighting for the Union. Hepburn has talent as a writer and would like to go off and seek her literary fortune, but she is very close to her sisters and does not want to leave them with insecure feelings at this time of turmoil. The family begins to feel insecure when Dee accepts a proposal of marriage from Lodge, but Hepburn rebuffs the same proposal from Montgomery, and, instead, goes to New York City where she studies with Lukas, a professor who teaches her how to hone her writing skills. The jilted Montgomery finds solace and then love with Bennett and they marry. Meanwhile, Parker grows ill and is dying. Hepburn returns from New York to be at her side. Parker dies as the Civil War ends and Hinds come home to his family. Joining the family is Lukas, who has bonded with Hepburn and that is where this episodic family tale ends. The production is handled with infinite care and sensitivity by pantheon director Cukor, who was, indeed, "a woman's director," and who exacts from all of the female leads stunning performances, particularly from Hepburn, and here her magnificent presence not only sustains deep interest but carries the film to greatness. Everything about this film is flawlessly portrayed, from Cukor's masterful direction to the literate and compelling script from Mason and Heerman (which won the Oscar for Best Adapted Screenplay). Hepburn was not nominated for an Oscar for her superlative performance in this film, but won an Oscar for Best Actress in the same year for **Morning Glory**, 1933. The production values in this film are of the highest quality and it shows in that RKO did not stint on the superb costuming and meticulously constructed historical sets. The sequence showing the party for Montgomery, for instance, is as sumptuous and lavish as can be found six years later in **Gone with the Wind**, 1939. The richness of this masterpiece film bears the indelible stamp of David O. Selznick, who approved of this project, but who left the helm of RKO before this film went into production. His imprimatur, however, is evident in all of the film's enchantingly created scenes; Selznick's penchant for accurate historical detail is loyally enforced by producers Macgowan and Merian C. Cooper, who took over control of the studio when Selznick departed. *Author's Note*: Hepburn told this author: "I had given two very solid performances in that same year and I guess the Academy did not want me to compete with myself by only nominating me for **Morning Glory**, and where I won for that picture, but I must admit that I learned more from George [Cukor] when he was directing **Little Women**." Cukor told this author that "Kate [Hepburn] was always there to give her all in every picture I made with her, but in **Little Women** I told her that she must not give her *all*. I told her that she had to restrain herself so that, in comparison to her co-players, in this instance, the fine

Margaret O'Brien, Janet Leigh, Elizabeth Taylor and June Allyson in *Little Women*, 1949.

actresses playing her sisters, she would appear to be a comforting rock of security and that takes reticence and reserve and I demanded that of Kate and she suppressed her natural urge to be more theatrical. Everything about Kate is wonderfully extravagant, even her distinctive voice with its New England hooks and hinges, but she sacrificed all that to give the world a great performance, one, I think, will never be equaled in that story." So impressed with this film were teachers across the country when it was first released, that tens of thousands of school children were asked to see it in order to view a good representation of American history. Selznick himself studied this film for some time before producing **Gone with the Wind**, and there are strong similarities with both stories, but where the latter is set in the Deep South during the Civil War. **p**, Merian C. Cooper (not credited), Kenneth Macgowan; **d**, George Cukor; **cast**, Katharine Hepburn, Joan Bennett, Paul Lukas, Frances Dee, Jean Parker, Edna May Oliver, Henry Stephenson, Douglass Montgomery, John Davis Lodge, Spring Byington, Samuel S. Hinds, Bonita Granville; **w**, Sarah Y. Mason, Victor Heerman (based on the novel by Louisa May Alcott); **c**, Henry Gerrard; **m**, Max Steiner; **ed**, Jack Kitchin; **art d**, Van Nest Polglase; **set d**, Hobe Erwin; **spec eff**, Harry Redmond Sr. and Jr.

Little Women ★★★ 1949; U.S.; 122m; MGM; Color; Drama; Children: Acceptable; **DVD**; **VHS**. This well-crafted version of the Alcott novel, helmed by pantheon director LeRoy, offers four stellar actresses (Allyson, Taylor, Leigh and O'Brien) as the four New England sisters, who, with their mother, Astor, must take care of themselves during the Civil War while their father, Ames, is away and serving in the Union army. The dashing and handsome Lawford provides the love interest, first as a rejected beau to Allyson and then marrying Leigh and where O'Brien is the tragic sister who grows ill and dies in the comforting arms of Allyson. All give standout performances, as does Brazzi, the wise and avuncular professor, who guides Allyson's aspirations to become a writer and later becomes her paramour, and Astor, the persevering mother living with anxiety as to the fate of her husband and the well-being of her loving daughters. **p&d**, Mervyn LeRoy; **cast**, June Allyson, Peter Lawford, Margaret O'Brien, Elizabeth Taylor, Janet Leigh, Rossano Brazzi, Mary Astor, Lucile Watson, Sir C. Aubrey Smith, Elizabeth Patterson, Leon Ames, Harry Davenport; **w**, Andrew Solt, Sarah Y. Mason, Victor Heerman (based on the novel by Louisa May Alcott); **c**, Robert Planck, Charles Schoenbaum (Technicolor); **m**, Adolph Deutsch; **ed**, Ralph E. Winters; **art d**, Cedric Gibbons, Paul Groesse; **set d**, Edwin B. Willis; **spec eff**, Warren Newcombe.

Little Women ★★★ 1994; U.S.; 115m; COL; Color; Drama; Children: Cautionary (MPAA: PG); **DVD**; **VHS**. Director Armstrong does a fine job in bringing forth this well-told version of the Alcott classic. Ryder (Jo) is exceptional as the guiding spirit of the New England family where she nurtures her three sisters, Alvarado (Meg), Mathis (Amy; as well as Dunst as a younger Amy), and Danes (Beth). Sarandon, too, is a standout in her role as the worried but stalwart mother, waiting for her husband to return from the Civil War as the family faces and overcomes commonplace and traumatic crises. Bale is convincing as the earnest suitor to Ryder and later Alvarado, and Byrne is intensely riveting as the professor, who helps Ryder achieve her literary talents while falling in love with her. *Author's Note*: Veteran character actress Mary Wickes, who resolutely plays the indomitable Aunt, died less than a year after this film's release. **p**, Denise Di Novi, Robin Swicord; **d**, Gillian Armstrong; **cast**, Winona Ryder, Susan Sarandon, Trini Alvarado, Claire Danes, Christian Bale, Eric Stoltz, Kirsten Dunst, Gabriel Byrne, Samantha Mathis, John Neville, Mary Wickes, Florence Paterson; **w**, Robin Swicord (based on the novel by Louisa May Alcott); **c**, Geoffrey Simpson (Technicolor); **m**, Thomas Newman; **ed**, Nicholas Beauman; **prod d**, Jan Roelfs; **art d**, Richard Hudolin; **set d**, Jim Erickson; **spec eff**, William H. Orr, Michael Walls.

The Little World of Don Camillo ★★★ 1953; France/Italy; 107m; Produzione Film/I.F.E. Releasing Corp.; B/W; Comedy; Children: Acceptable; **DVD**; **VHS**. In this delightful and humorous entry, a priest, Fernandel, and a communist mayor, Cervi, squabble over who is the head of a village in the Po valley where life is far from easy. Cervi wants a "People's House" and Fernandel wants a "Garden City" for the poor. Everyone in town is divided on all the issues, the rich vs. the poor, religion vs. atheism. Even lovers are at each other's throats. As much as the priest and mayor feud, they finally cooperate for the good of the villagers. Fernandel, one of France's great comedians, brings his special brand of humor to this very entertaining romp. (In French, Italian; English subtitles.) Orson Welles narrates the English version. **p**, Robert Chabert, Angelo Rizzoli, Marcel Roux; **d**, Julien Duvivier; **cast**, Fernandel, Gino Cervi, Sylvie, Vera Talqui, Franco Interlenghi, Charles Vissiere, Clara Auteri, Italo Clerici, Peppino De Martino, Carlo Duse, Manuel Gary; **w**, Duvivier, René Barjavel (based on the novel by Giovanni Guareschi); **c**, Nicolas Hayer; **m**, Alessandro Cicognini; **ed**, Maria Rosada; **art d**, Virgilio Marchi; **set d**, Ferdinando Ruffo.

The Littlest Hobo ★★★ 1958; U.S.; 77m; AA; B/W; Drama; Children: Recommended; **DVD**; **VHS**. The title refers to a dog, a stray German shepherd, riding from town to town by leaping into cars or on freight trains, like a hobo. On one visit to a town, it rescues a lamb from a slaughterhouse. They become friends and wander off to the lawn of the governor's (Mitchell) mansion. Seeing them, the governor's paralyzed daughter, Stuart, gets the courage to walk again. Charming fun for all ages, especially children, it is a film that also inspires. **p**, Hugh M. Hooker; **d**, Charles R. Rondeau; **cast**, Buddy Hart, Wendy Stuart, Carlyle Mitchell, Howard Hoffman, Robert Kline, Pat Bradley, Bill Coontz, Dorothy Johnson, William E. Marks, Pauline Moore, Larry Thor, Norman Bartold; **w**, Dorrell McGowan; **c**, Perry Finnerman, Walter Strenge; **m**, Ronald Stein; **ed**, Howard Epstein, Arthur H. Nadel; **set d**, Lyle B. Reifsnyder.

The Littlest Horse Thieves ★★★ 1977; U.S.; 104m; Disney/Buena Vista; Color; Drama; Children: Acceptable (MPAA: G); **DVD**; **VHS**. In early 1900s' Yorkshire, England, a coal mine owner, Barkworth, decides to mechanize to increase profits, so he schedules the mine's pit ponies to be destroyed. Two boys, Harrison and Bolgar, with the help of Barkworth's daughter, Franks, rescue the ponies and take them to an abandoned chapel. The ponies are found and the miners vote to go on strike if the animals are harmed. Before any decision can be made, an explosion traps some of the workers in the mine. One of the ponies, a blind animal, leads the others in rescuing the miners. The ponies' lives are spared and the richest man in town, Sim, throws everyone a party. This is a heart-warming film for everyone and will especially appeal to children. **p**, Ron Miller, Hugh Attwooll; **d**, Charles Jarrott; **cast**, Alastair Sim, Peter Barkworth, Maurice Colbourne, Susan Tebbs, Andrew Harrison, Chloe Franks, Benjie Bolgar, Prunella Scales, Leslie Sands, Geraldine McEwan; **w**, Rosemary Anne Sisson (based on a story by Sisson, Burt Kennedy); **c**, Paul Beeson (Technicolor); **m**, Ron Goodwin; **ed**, Richard Marden; **prod d**, Robert W. Laing; **set d**, Hugh Scaife.

The Littlest Outlaw ★★★ 1955; U.S.; 73m; Disney/Buena Vista; Color; Drama; Children: Cautionary; **DVD**; **VHS**. A 10-year-old boy, Velasquez, is the stepson of a cruel horse trainer in Mexico, who abuses a horse while training it to become a champion jumper. The horse is owned by a general, Armendáriz, but when it becomes afraid of jumping and injures his daughter, Maley, while she is riding it, he orders it to be destroyed. Velásquez runs away with the horse, becoming a fugitive. He travels throughout Mexico, meeting various people including other fugitives, and is befriended by a priest, Calleia. The boy and horse are separated later and, after some time, he and the priest see it in a bullring, about to be gored by a charging bull. Velasquez runs into the ring, leaps onto the horse, and rides it away to safety. Armendáriz is impressed by the boy's bravery and spares both him and the horse, the animal now no longer afraid to let his daughter ride on its back. **p**, Larry Lansburgh; **d**, Roberto Gavaldón; **cast**, Pedro Armendáriz, Joseph Calleia, Rodolfo Acosta, Andrés Velázquez, Laila Maley, Gilberto González, Pepe Ortiz, José Torvay, Jorge Treviño, José Ángel Espinosa "Ferrusquilla"; **w**, Bill Walsh (based on a story by Lansburgh); **c**, J. Carlos Carbajal, Alex Phillips (Technicolor); **m**, William Lava; **ed**, Carlos Savage; **set d**, Rafael Suárez.

The Littlest Rebel ★★★ 1935; U.S.; 73m; FOX; B/W; Drama; Children: Recommended; **DVD**; **VHS**. Temple is wonderful as a little Southern girl caught up in the turmoil of the American Civil War. Her father, Boles, is off fighting for the Confederacy when her mother, Morley, becomes ill. Boles sneaks through the Union lines that surround his plantation to see his ailing wife, but he is caught and branded a spy and then condemned to death. Holt, a compassionate Union colonel, who is moved by the pleadings of Temple, arranges for Boles to escape, but he is again captured and this time awaits execution. Temple takes matters into her own careful little hands and travels to Washington, D.C., where she has an audience with President Lincoln (McGlynn). They share an apple and, while crunching away, chat about the war and life in general while Temple pleads for the life of her father. Of course, the Great Emancipator spares her father, and Temple is seen at the finish for a happy reunion with her mother and father, as well as the family's retinue, which includes the unforgettable Robinson. The marvelous dancing sequences with Robinson and Temple are absolutely priceless, especially their endearing performance of "Polly Wolly Doodle" and where the precocious tot keeps amazing pace with the tap dancing Robinson. Songs include: "Polly Wolly Doodle" (traditional; modified music by Sidney Clare; modified lyrics by Buddy G. DeSylva), "Believe Me If All Those Endearing Young Charms" (traditional; lyrics by Thomas Moore), "Turkey in the Straw" (traditional), "(I Wish I Was In) Dixie Land" (Daniel Decatur Emmett), "Sometimes I Feel Like a Motherless Child" (traditional), "Old Folks at Home (Swanee River)" (Stephen Foster), "She and I" (music by Cyril J. Mockridge, Bill Robinson). *Author's Note*: Zanuck told this author that this film "was a box office bonanza for the studio, and the two people who brought in the coins were little Shirley, our biggest star in those days, and the great Bill Robinson. You know, years later, people said that Robinson was playing a stereotyped Uncle Tom in that film, but that is a lot of nonsense. He speaks his own mind with a wise voice in that film and plays nobody's fool. The South had thousands of such fine people working on plantations during and before the Civil War and none of them were stereotypes, just good people living the life that history gave them." **p**, Darryl F. Zanuck, Buddy G. DeSylva; **d**, David Butler; **cast**, Shirley Temple, John Boles, Jack Holt, Karen Morley, Bill "Bojangles" Robinson, Guinn "Big Boy"

Shirley Temple dancing with Bill "Bojangles" Robinson in *The Littlest Rebel*, 1935.

Williams, Willie Best, Frank McGlynn Sr., Bessie Lyle, Hannah Washington, Matthew "Stymie" Beard; **w**, Edwin J. Burke, Harry Tugend (based on the play by Edward Peple); **c**, John F. Seitz; **m**, Cyril J. Mockridge; **ed**, Irene Morra; **art d**, William S. Darling; **set d**, Thomas Little.

Live Free or Die Hard ★★★ 2007; U.S./U.K.; 128m; FOX; Color; Action/Thriller; Children: Unacceptable (MPAA: PG-13); **BD**; **DVD**. A cyber terrorist, Olyphant, hacks into the computers at the FBI's Cyber Crime Division in Washington, D.C. Olyphant achieves his goal through the aid of a sexy kickboxing woman, Maggie Q. The crime happens over the Fourth of July holiday so most of the agents are not available to round up the usual suspects. Local police are called in to help in the emergency, one of them being Willis, a New York cop. He is assigned to go to Camden, New Jersey, locate a suspected hacker, Long, and turn him over to the FBI in Washington for questioning. While on Long's trail, Willis is shot at, but he manages to get to Washington. By then the FBI's computer system has been attacked. More shoot-outs and car chases and explosions follow, but all ends well with Willis nailing Olyphant as the hacker. There's action aplenty in this newest of the three previous films in the series: **Die Hard**, 1988, **Die Hard 2**, 1990, and **Die Hard with a Vengeance**, 1995. Intense violence, gutter language and brief sexual situations prohibit viewing by children. **p**, Michael Fottrell, Stephen James Eads; **d**, Len Wiseman; **cast**, Bruce Willis, Timothy Olyphant, Justin Long, Maggie Q, Cliff Curtis, Jonathan Sadowski, Andrew Friedman, Kevin Smith, Yorgo Constantine, Cyril Raffaelli; **w**, Mark Bomback (based on a story by Bomback and David Marconi and an article "A Farewell to Arms" by John Carlin and characters created by Roderick Thorp); **c**, Simon Duggan; **m**, Marco Beltrami; **ed**, Nicolas De Toth; **prod d**, Patrick Tatopoulos; **art d**, Troy Sizemore, Beat Frutiger, James Hegedus; **set d**, Robert Gould; **spec eff**, Michael Meinardus, Joe D. Ramsey.

The Lives of a Bengal Lancer ★★★★ 1935; U.S.; 109m; PAR; B/W; Adventure; Children: Cautionary; **DVD**; **VHS**. Action director Hathaway superbly presents a rousing adventure tale set in colonial India. Cooper, a seasoned British officer stationed at a remote outpost, is billeted with two new, young officers, Tone and Cromwell, taking them under his protective wing. Tone is brash and challenging, a somewhat annoying know-it-all, and Cromwell is reticent and unsure of himself, particularly after he is received with coldness by Standing, the commanding officer and who is his father. Standing, a by-the-book martinet, when first seeing Cromwell after many years, welcomes him to his new post, but warns his son that he should not seek any favors because of their blood relationship. When Standing later meets all of his officers, he shows no indication that he is Cromwell's father, embarrassing the

Gary Cooper, Richard Cromwell, Franchot Tone and C. Aubrey Smith in *The Lives of a Bengal Lancer*, 1935.

young officer and causing Cooper to label his commander "ramrod." Though Smith, the stalwart second-in-command of the post, urges Standing to "speak to the boy," Standing cannot bring himself to establish a closer relationship with Cromwell, which embitters his son. Tone, meanwhile, taunts Cooper for his protective attitude toward Cromwell, sarcastically calling him "Mother McGregor." Cooper, however, watches as the prankish and cock-sure Tone gets his comeuppance when, while playing a horn used to charm snakes, inadvertently entices a deadly python that weaves only inches away from him, terrifying him and causing him to go on playing and playing lest the snake strike, until Cooper mercifully kills the lethal reptile. Cooper is then given an assignment to find a British spy, Tapley, who is disguised as an Indian and is trying to find out who is organizing the northern tribes to revolt against the British. Taking Tone and Cromwell with him, Cooper finds Tapley and learns from him that Dumbrille, a powerful tribal chief, is the man behind the revolutionary plot. Dumbrille plans to launch an overwhelming attack against the British garrison, but first must steal two million rounds of ammunition that has been shipped to the British. Standing and his officers then make a friendly visit to Tamiroff's resplendent palace, but this is not a social call as Cooper and others are told to scout about to see if they can determine whether or not Tamiroff is siding with Dumbrille. When Tamiroff conducts a "pig-sticking" hunt for the amusement of his British visitors, Sanding is accidentally wounded while protecting his son against a charging boar. Cromwell, who is known to be Standing's son by Dumbrille, is enticed by vixen Burke, who works with Dumbrille, and Cromwell is kidnapped and held as bait where Dumbrille hopes the British lancers will attempt to free him and charge into his well-planned trap. Standing, however, is too smart to be thusly hoodwinked and refuses to send his troops to save his son. Cooper rankles at this and he and Tone then set off on their own to rescue Cromwell, but both are caught and held captive, along with Cromwell. Dumbrille then takes Cooper, Tone and Cromwell to a dungeon where wooden slivers are painfully inserted under the fingernails of Cooper and Tone, but neither will tell Dumbrille anything about the ammunition being sent to the British. Cromwell, however, who no longer believes in serving an army with seemingly uncaring commanders like his father, and whose morale has already been shattered, quickly relents and, before being tortured like his friends, tells Dumbrille what he needs to know about the ammunition. All three are confined in a small jail and they see from its window some days later that very ammunition arrive at Dumbrille's stronghold. Dumbrille then cold-heartedly tells his captives that Standing and his 300 lancers are outside his fortress and are about to attack and be slaughtered, but Cooper and Tone break free and take over a machine gun inside the fortress and begin mowing down Dumbrille's men just as Standing and his lancers charge

forward. Cromwell also escapes the jail and, inspired by the heroic actions of Cooper and Tone, goes after Dumbrille and, after struggling with him in hand-to-hand combat, kills the tribal chief. Standing and his men, however, are still in great peril, and, to save his comrades, Cooper grabs a burning torch and races to the ammunition dump, igniting it and blowing up half the fortress and killing most of Dumbrille's forces, at the sacrifice of his own life. (John Wayne would take a leaf from this exciting scene when making **The Alamo**, 1960, where he, while playing Davy Crockett, blows up an ammunition dump at the cost of his own life.) At a stirring ceremony, Standing posthumously bestows on Cooper the Victoria Cross, pinning the medal to the blanket of his horse while he also honors the heroic actions of the surviving Tone and Cromwell and where he now acknowledges with gratitude the existence of his son. Hathaway directs this action-packed film with vigor, keeping a quick pace and where his military tactics, particularly the cavalry sequences, as well as the harrowing boar hunt, are excitingly staged. The costuming and sets are impressive and the acting from all is superlative. The script is literate and filled with many humorous moments, which largely contributed to the great box office success this fine adventure film enjoyed in its original release and its many re-releases. The film was nominated for many Oscars, including Best Picture, Best Director, Best Screenplay and Best Editing. *Author's Note*: The wonderful sets were so finely created that the always persnickety Cecil B. DeMille used them without little modification when he produced and directed **The Crusades**, 1935. This was the first significant film directed by Hathaway, who admitted to this author that "I wanted to make **The Lives of a Bengal Lancer** for some time. I pushed the front office at Paramount to allow me to make this film when the book came out and the studio bought the rights in 1930 from the author, Major Francis Yeats-Brown, who had served in the lancers. From that point on, I had second unit people go to Northwest India and shoot a great deal of landscape footage and I even went there myself and produced additional footage that I later edited into the story, just enough at the right spots to make that film look authentic in every visual sense. I told Paramount that this picture would make Cooper the world's greatest adventure star in the movies and it did. Coop was wonderful to work with, following every direction without complaint and he always did his scenes better than what I expected. I had the same experience with him when we did another great adventure film together, **The Real Glory** [1939], only the location was in the Philippines." **p**, Louis D. Lighton; **d**, Henry Hathaway; **cast**, Gary Cooper, Franchot Tone, Richard Cromwell, Sir Guy Standing, Sir C. Aubrey Smith, Kathleen Burke, Douglass Dumbrille, Monte Blue, Akim Tamiroff, Mischa Auer, Lya Lys; **w**, Waldemar Young, John L. Balderston, Achmed Abdullah, Grover Jones, William Slavens McNutt (based on the novel by Francis Yeats-Brown); **c**, Charles Lang; **m**, Milan Roder; **ed**, Ellsworth Hoagland; **art d**, Hans Dreier, Roland Anderson.

The Lives of Others ★★★ 2006; Germany; 137m; Arte/Sony; Color; Drama; Children: Unacceptable (MPAA: R); **BD**; **DVD**. In this intriguing Cold War drama, Koch is a successful dramatist in East Germany in 1984. He and his actress-girlfriend, Gedeck, both become stars of the stage and accepted by the communists, even though they do not always follow the party line. The Minister of Culture, Thieme, becomes interested in Gedeck, and has a secret service agent, Mühe, spy on the couple, hoping that evidence will prove Koch disloyal and thus get him out of the way. Meanwhile, Mühe's superior, Turkur, suspects Koch may be leading a double life. Mühe spies on the couple and begins to like them and wants to protect them. But Gedeck is struck by a car and killed and the communists come to realize that the couple is no danger to them. Mühe goes back to routine spy work after having become too involved in the lives of others. Sexuality and nudity prohibit viewing by children. (In German; English subtitles.) **p**, Quirin Berg, Max Wiedemann, Dirk Hamm, Florian Henckel von Donnersmarck; **d&w**, von Donnersmarck; **cast**, Martina Gedeck, Ulrich Mühe, Sebastian Koch, Ulrich Tukur,

Thomas Thieme, Hans-Uwe Bauer, Volkmar Kleinert, Matthias Brenner, Charly Hübner, Herbert Knaup; **c**, Hagen Bogdanski; **m**, Stéphane Moucha, Gabriel Yared; **ed**, Patricia Rommel; **prod d**, Silke Buhr; **art d**, Christiane Rothe; **set d**, Frank Noack; **spec eff**, Hans Seck.

Living Free ★★★ 1972; U.K.; 90m; COL; Color; Adventure; Children: Recommended (MPAA: G); **DVD**; **VHS**. In this fine sequel to **Born Free**, 1966, Hampshire and Davenport replace the original roles of Virginia McKenna and Bill Travers, who essay the real-life Joy and George Adamson. This time, three lion cubs create so much havoc in nearby villages that Hampshire and Davenport, to protect them after Elsa dies, must move the cubs to a game reservation 300 miles distant. Many delightful scenes show the cubs in play and mischief and the nature photography is outstanding in this exciting family fare film. **p**, Paul Radin; **d**, Jack Couffer; **cast**, Nigel Davenport, Susan Hampshire, Geoffrey Keen, Peter Lukoye, Shane De Louvres, Robert Beaumont, Nobby Noble, Aludin Quershi, Charles Hayes, Jean Hayes; **w**, Millard Kaufman (based on the books by Joy Adamson); **c**, Wolfgang Suschitsky (Eastmancolor); **m**, Sol Kaplan; **ed**, Don Deacon; **prod d**, John Stoll.

Living It Up ★★★ 1954; U.S.; 95m; York Pictures/PAR; Color; Musical Comedy; Children: Acceptable; **DVD**. In this good remake of **Nothing Sacred**, 1937, and what is most likely the best in the Martin and Lewis series, Lewis is a station master in the Midwest, who is reportedly exposed to radioactive material and is diagnosed with a terminal illness by local doctor Martin. Lewis is told that he has only a few months to live and, at the urging of Martin, accepts an offer of an expense-free spree on the town in New York City. Reporter Leigh, who writes the tragedy for her newspaper, convinces her boss to pay for this trip while she records Lewis' "last hurrah" on earth. It turns out that Martin has misdiagnosed Lewis' illness and he is not ill at all, but the duo go on that spree and must then pretend that Lewis is slowly dying and dying and dying. The dynamic duo turns this rather lachrymose tale into many fun-filled scenes where the laughs are plenty while Martin romantically pursues the pulchritudinous Leigh. Songs (all from Jule Styne and Bob Hilliard) include: "That's What I Like," "How Do You Speak to an Angel?" "Money Burns a Hole in My Pocket," "You're Gonna Dance with Me Baby," "Champagne and Wedding Cake," and "Every Street's a Boulevard in Old New York." *Author's Note*: Ben Hecht, who wrote the original script for the original 1937 production, wrote the screenplay for this remake, telling this author: "I really did not have to alter much of the story, only making the victim a guy instead of a gal, and that was the Lewis character. I must admit that Lewis was a lot nuttier than the role [Carole] Lombard played in the original film. We traded wit for slapstick, but that's what the public wanted in those days, or, at least, that is what the producers said that the public wanted. Personally, I thought that Lewis was overrated as a comedian. He got his laughs through mugging and pratfalls, the kind of cornball slapstick you see in burlesque, but he is certainly an outstanding clown and there is a real difference between being a clown and a comedian." **p**, Paul Jones; **d**, Norman Taurog; **cast**, Dean Martin, Jerry Lewis, Janet Leigh, Edward Arnold, Fred Clark, Sheree North, Sammy White, Sid Tomack, Sig Ruman, Richard Loo, Grady Sutton; **w**, Jack Rose, Melville Shavelson (based on the musical comedy "Hazel Flagg" by Ben Hecht, Jule Styne, Bob Hilliard, from the story by James H. Street); **c**, Daniel Fapp (Technicolor); **m**, Walter Scharf; **ed**, Archie Marshek; **art d**, Hal Pereira, Albert Nozaki; **set d**, Sam Comer, Emile Kuri; **spec eff**, Farciot Edouart, John P. Fulton.

Lloyd's of London ★★★★ 1936; U.S.; 115m; FOX; B/W; Adventure; Children: Acceptable; **DVD**; **VHS**. Though he is billed fourth in the credits for this sumptuously mounted historical epic, Power is the leading player and his handsome youth and resolute personality captivates throughout. Bartholomew plays Power as a boy and he is shown playing with Scott, who grows up to be Burton, who essays the great British

George Sanders, Madeleine Carroll and Tyrone Power in *Lloyd's of London*, 1936.

naval hero Horatio Nelson (1758-1805). The boys come upon some pirates and overhear their plans to scuttle a commercial ship and abscond with its valuable cargo. They race away to tell officials at Lloyd's of London, the foremost brokers insuring British commercial shipping, but Scott gets lost and only Bartholomew reaches those offices where he is barred from entering. A kindly American visitor, Benjamin Franklin (1706-1790), played by Pogue, hears out the boy and then shepherds him into the hallowed offices where a top executive, Standing, who, when hearing of the piratical plot, orders authorities into action that prevents the theft. Bartholomew is rewarded for his heroic services when Standing gives him a job as an apprentice at the great brokerage house. The boy grows to adulthood as Power, becoming a leading official at Lloyd's, especially after he invents a clever system to relay shipping news from the continent as well as his close relationship with Burton, who is now the adult Nelson, the foremost admiral of the British war fleet. Sanders, however, the arrogant nephew of the first lord of the British admiralty, hates Power for his position of influence and does all he can to discredit Power. When the French Revolution sweeps France, Power travels to that troubled country to aid friends and rescues the beautiful Carroll, making sure she gets to the safety of England, only to learn that she is the wife of his arch foe, Sanders. When the strutting Sanders goes to Lloyd's to secure funds to cover his gambling debts, Power persuades the insurance firm to refuse his request and he becomes Sanders' avowed enemy, who also swears to destroy Lloyd's. The firm begins to decline when it refuses to insure ships after England begins to lose its long war with Napoleon Bonaparte, but the firm is saved when Carroll provides her fortune as collateral to support Lloyd's, and this drives Sanders into a seething rage. When Power brings news that Nelson (Burton) has won a great naval victory over the French at Trafalgar, Sanders vindictively spreads the word that the report is false and that Lloyd's is a colossal fraud. The company is brought to the brink of collapse through Sanders' claims, but confirmation arrives to prove Power correct—it has been a great victory for the British, but at the cost of the life of Powers' dear friend, Nelson (Burton). The company saved, Power goes to Carroll to thank her for her support, and when Sanders finds them together, he challenges Power to a duel. The two men fight to the death and Power is seriously wounded, but Sanders is killed. Carroll remains with Power, nursing him back to health, and it is clear that these formerly star-crossed lovers will now go forward together to seek happiness. The film is richly mounted with impressing sets and costuming and is expertly directed by King. The cast, particularly Power, Sanders and the stunningly beautiful Carroll give standout performances. *Author's Note*: This was Fox's most expensive film to date, costing more than $850,000, but it proved a great box office success and returned that investment many times over in its initial release. The film, though it

Robert Mitchum and Brian Aherne in *The Locket*, 1946.

rigidly conforms in appearance to the period it represents, takes great liberties with the facts concerning Lloyd's and Nelson, as it had with many other epics it produced during the 1930s, these transgressions placed before the feet of studio boss Zanuck. "I did take liberties with the known facts," Zanuck admitted to this author, "in **Lloyd's of London** and other pictures, but you must realize that we were telling dramatic stories where the facts of history had to fit the story line and that audiences wanted a good tale and fine romance and we gave that to them. Only a few complained that a few facts here and there were twisted a bit." Power had been a contract player at Fox for some time until Zanuck decided to put him into this expensive epic and his appearance in **Lloyd's of London** made him a superstar. This was the first of eleven films King would direct with Power as his leading man. It was really King who was responsible for Power's career going into orbit. "I wanted Power for the leading player in **Lloyd's of London** right from the beginning," King told this author. "I went to Zanuck and pleaded with him, but he had Don Ameche signed up for the role. He also had Loretta Young as the leading lady and we were in early production when I went back to Zanuck and told him that Ameche was all wrong for the part and that I needed Power. He relented and Power took over the role, eager to follow my direction, and he was wonderful at that. Young, however, was not. She knew that I was padding Ty's [Power's] part and at the expense of some of her scenes and she blew up. She went to Zanuck and ranted and raved and demanded that Zanuck put Ameche back into the Power role, but the boss stayed with me and told her that her leading man was Tyrone Power. Well, Loretta, who had a temper like a volcano, exploded all over again and then quit the production. Just as well, because then I was able to bring the beautiful Madeleine Carroll in to replace her and she and Ty were perfect together. Loretta didn't talk to me for some time and when she did, I mentioned that I looked forward to doing another picture with her. 'For what?' she said with a sneer, 'so I can be replaced by another blonde floozy?'" **p**, Kenneth MacGowan; **d**, Henry King; **cast**, Freddie Bartholomew, Madeleine Carroll, Sir Guy Sanding, Tyrone Power, Sir C. Aubrey Smith, Virginia Field, Gavin Muir, Douglas Scott, George Sanders, J. M. Kerrigan, Una O'Connor, E. E. Clive, Montagu Love, John Burton, Thomas Pogue, Miles Mander, Lester Matthews, Barlowe Borland, Murray Kinnell, May Beatty; **w**, Ernest Pascal, Walter Ferris (based on the story by Curtis Kenyon); **c**, Bert Glennon; **m**, Louis Silvers; **ed**, Barbara McLean; **art d**, William Darling; **set d**, Thomas Little.

Local Color ★★★ 2006; U.S.; 107m; Alla Prima Productions/Monterey Media; Color; Drama; Children: Unacceptable (MPAA: R); **DVD**. Morgan is a successful artist, who looks back on the summer of 1974 in Port Chester, New York, when he was eighteen and an aspiring artist

whose homophobic father, Liotta, does not appreciate his ambition. Liotta befriends a brilliant older Russian painter, Mueller-Stahl, who lives nearby, but has turned his back on not only art but life after the death of his wife. Liotta begins to reawaken the master's interest in work, which helps him regain his will to live. Meanwhile, Morgan gets his first kiss from the master's neighbor, Mathis. Art master and student learn from each other during a summer they spend together in the Pennsylvania countryside discussing art and life. This well-told story is based on a real-life experience and it provides many engrossing scenes. Gutter language prohibits viewing by children. **p**, George Gallo, Jimmy Evangelatos, Julie Lott, David Peremut, Mark Sennet, Shannon Bae, Dean Blagg, Robert Latham Brown, Bruce Dunn, Alex Kirkwood, Steve Longi, Evan Hoyt Wasserstrom; **d&w**, Gallo; **cast**, Armin Mueller-Stahl, Trevor Morgan, Ray Liotta, Charles Durning, Samantha Mathis, Ron Perlman, Diana Scarwid, Julie Lott, Tom Adams, Nancy Casemore; **c**, Michael Negrin; **m**, Chris Boardman; **ed**, Malcolm Campbell; **prod d**, Bob Ziembicki; **art d**, Bradford Johnson; **set d**, **spec eff**, Nathan Eaans.

Local Hero ★★★ 1983; U.K.; 111m; Enigma Productions/WB; Color; Comedy; Children: Unacceptable (MPAA: PG); **DVD**; **VHS**. Lancaster, in another captivating performance, is a Texas oil tycoon so embarrassed by his riches that he has psychiatrist Chancer regularly visit him and where he encourages Chancer to verbally abuse him for his wealth, even writing obscenities about him on the outside of the windows in Lancaster's skyscraper office suite in Houston. (This self-heaping of humiliation is not dissimilar to the fanatical flagellants, who whipped themselves through public places for their real and imagined sins during the 13th Century and later.) Lancaster, who is not in his right mind (if his character ever has been), often makes statements about astronomy and how its signs mark the fate of human beings, and this seems to be his own credo, religion or standard of living. Lancaster sends Riegert, one of his top young executives, to Scotland where he is to buy out an entire town so that Lancaster's firm can begin drilling offshore, but Riegert becomes inveigled into endless legal maneuvers by shrewd Lawson, who runs the local inn and represents all of the locals. Those locals include Capaldi, who works for the oil firm and who is romancing Seagrove, a diver working for the same company, and Asante, who is the resident vicar. Riegert finds this unusual in that Asante is a black man, who insists he is of Scottish origin. Nothing seems to be what it should be and Riegert finds that he is getting nowhere while Rozycki, the captain of a Soviet trawler, makes routine stops at the village to covertly meet with Lawson. When the plot thickens and Riegert is stalled in completing his deal, Lancaster is summoned in an attempt to sort everything out, which, by then, seems to be impossible. The surprise ending to this charming comedy where the lush Scottish landscape is beautifully photographed, is a wow. The well-directed film provides standout performances from the entire cast' and many entertaining and humorous moments pepper its lively scenes. **p**, David Puttnam; **d&w**, Bill Forsyth; **cast**, Burt Lancaster, Peter Riegert, Fulton Mackay, Denis Lawson, Norman Chancer, Peter Capaldi, Rikki Fulton, Alex Norton, Jenny Seagrove, Jennifer Black; **c**, Chris Menges; **m**, Mark Knopfler; **ed**, Michael Bradsell; **prod d**, Roger Murray-Leach; **art d**, Adrienne Atkinson, Frank Walsh, Ian Watson; **spec eff**, Wally Veevers.

The Locket ★★★ 1946; U.S.; 86m; RKO; B/W; Crime Drama; Children: Unacceptable; **DVD**. Day gives a compelling performance as an inveterate liar and murderess in this chilling film noir entry, well directed by Brahm, and with standout performances from Mitchum, Aherne, Raymond and the rest of the cast. The tale begins when Raymond is visited by psychiatrist Aherne, who warns him not go through with his marriage to Day, that wedding scheduled for only a few hours hence. Aherne tells his story in flashback, how five years earlier he had met with Mitchum, who had been engaged to Day and how Mitchum, shown in another flashback, finds a stolen bracelet in Day's purse. Day, at that time, explains that she was wrongly accused of stealing a locket from a girlhood friend and that terrible accusation caused her to become a compulsive kleptomaniac. Mitchum, an artist, has Day promise him that she will never again steal, but she is later involved in a robbery-murder, but is exonerated when the victim's valet confesses, or so it seems. Mitchum is then seen in flash-forward with Aherne, who is Day's psychiatrist. After the valet is executed and Mitchum comes to believe that Day is still guilty of the murder and kills himself, Aherne blindly believes Day to be innocent and marries her. Aherne later finds a good deal of jewelry that Day has stolen from family friends and they break up. In flash-forward, Raymond hears out Aherne and then confronts his bride-to-be with the psychiatrist's tale, but the beautiful and charming Day convinces the groom that Aherne, not her, is the one suffering from delusions and that he is jealous of Raymond. The groom goes ahead with the wedding, but, as Day walks to the altar, she comes apart and all of her evil actions of the past flood her memory and conscience, causing her to break down and where, instead of becoming another bride is sent to a mental institution. Though convoluted and sometimes a bit confusing, this intriguing crime yarn presents marvelous development of Day's insidious character, subtly portraying an evil woman who will stop at nothing to get what she wants. **p**, Bert Granet; **d**, John Brahm; **cast**, Laraine Day, Brian Aherne, Robert Mitchum, Gene Raymond, Sharyn Moffett, Ricardo Cortez, Henry Stephenson, Reginald Denny, Fay Helm, Myrna Dell, Mari Aldon, Ellen Corby, Martha Hyer; **w**, Sheridan Gibney; **c**, Nicholas Musuraca; **m**, Roy Webb; **ed**, J. R. Whittredge; **set d**, Darrell Silvera, Harley Miller; **spec eff**, Russell A. Cully.

The Lodger ★★★ 1928 (silent); U.K.; 94m/8 reels; Gainsborough Pictures/AmerAnglo/Artlee Pictures; B/W; Crime Drama; Children: Unacceptable; **DVD**. Novello provides a chilling performance in this eerie thriller from Hitchcock. He arrives at night and in a thick fog at a London boarding house owned and operated by Chesney and his wife Ault. They hesitatingly rent a room to him, even though they are, like everyone in the terrified city, suspicious of strangers as a lunatic killer is on the loose, murdering blonde-haired women. The nameless killer is dubbed "The Avenger," but since this film is set in the gaslight era when London was plagued by a maniacal serial killer, "The Avenger" is undoubtedly the ubiquitous Jack the Ripper. Quiet and unassuming, Novello stays much to his room, going out at odd hours and returning, his comings and goings a mystery of Chesney, Ault, and their fetching blonde-haired daughter, Tripp. Novello slowly develops a warm relationship with Tripp and, in one sensitive scene they briefly kiss, almost as an afterthought in their innocent desire to exchange good feelings toward one another. Novello, however, becomes a threat in the mind of Ault as she envisions him pacing in his room above her own, and here the inventive Hitchcock shows the audience what Ault is thinking by depicting Novello nervously pacing as the camera focuses upwardly through a glass floor (although this appears to be a double exposure on the screen). Novello's strange habits soon bring him to the attention of neighbors and many come to believe he is The Avenger. He is trailed and then avidly pursued by a group of people, their ranks swelling until they become a dense and frantic mob that chases Novello through the fog-bound streets of London. When they are about to seize and destroy him, it is learned that he is innocent and that another party is the murderer. Novello explains that his own sister had been killed by the fiend and he was pursuing the actual serial killer. Hitchcock maintains great suspense in this well-crafted film where he plays with light and shadows to heighten viewer anxiety, all adding to Novello's mysterious behavior. *Author's Note*: Hitchcock told this author: "**The Lodger** was the first full-length feature where I emphasized a theme I would later use again and again—that of an innocent man mistaken for a killer and who is wrongly hounded for crimes he did not commit. The picture was very well received and encouraged me to make more such films with similar themes." Though this was a silent film, Hitchcock did not use many title cards to convey his story line as he was able to tell the tale in his clearly

Sara Allgood and Laird Cregar in *The Lodger*, 1944.

defined scenes from one sequence to another. A few of the title cards referring to Novello seemed to carry an "inside message." One card read: "Good thing he doesn't like girls," and other title card reads: "Even if he is a bit queer." I asked Hitchcock if he was not subtly referring in that film to the fact that his leading player, Novello, was homosexual (which Novello was) and replied with subtle humor (in referring to the atmosphere in the film no doubt): "I hadn't the foggiest about that." **p**, Michael Balcon, Carlyle Blackwell; **d**, Alfred Hitchcock; **cast**, Ivor Novello, June (Howard Tripp), Marie Ault, Arthur Chesney, Malcolm Keen, Reginal Gardiner, Eve Gray, Alma Reville, Hitchcock; **w**, Eliot Stannard and (uncredited) Hitchcock (based on the novel by Mrs. [Marie] Belloc Lowndes and her play "Who Is He?"); **c**, Baron Ventimiglia (Gaetano di Ventimiglia), Hal Young; **m**, Ashley Irwin; **ed**, Ivor Montagu; **art d**, C. Wilfrid Arnold, Bertram Evans.

The Lodger ★★★★ 1944; U.S.; 84m; FOX; B/W; Crime Drama; Children: Unacceptable; **DVD**; **VHS**. Hollywood character actor Cregar gives one his greatest performances as a deranged medical researcher in London's gaslight era, who is thought to be Jack the Ripper. A remake of the 1928 Hitchcock film, this production takes a radical departure from that original story in that Cregar is not portrayed as an innocent man wrongly suspected of being that serial killer. His suspicious behavior and ultimate violent outbursts indicate that, if he is not the ubiquitous Jack, he is certainly a dreadful facsimile. Cregar mysteriously appears at a London home owned by Hardwicke and Allgood, asking to rent a room. He is a researcher working at a nearby clinic and, after he rents a room, where he wants all mirrors and pictures removed (shades of the vampire) and asks if he can also use an upstairs attic as a workroom where he can perform his "experiments," which he is allowed to do. Oberon, who is Hardwicke's and Allgood's beautiful daughter and who performs as a theatrical singer in musicals, comes to Cregar's attention, but she seldom sees him since he does not take breakfast, lunch or dinner with the family. He works at night, leaving in the evening to disappear into the fog, carrying a small black bag, and returns in the early morning hours where he keeps to his room and later works in the attic at his "experiments." He is heard walking the floor of his room during the day and when Jack the Ripper begins his murder spree, Hardwicke and Allgood become suspicious of Cregar, thinking he might be the madman serial killer terrifying London. Early before dawn one day, Oberon smells smoke and goes to the basement where she finds Cregar burning what he calls "contaminated" clothing, which he inadvertently brought from his clinic, and the two have a brief conversation. At that time, Oberon retrieves a copy of the newspaper through a basement window that reports another Ripper murder. She, too, now comes to believe that their strange boarder might be the much-wanted killer. She confides her

Martine Carol and Oskar Werner in *Lola Montes*, 1959.

fears to a friend, Sanders, an inspector for Scotland Yard, who has been experimenting with a new forensic science, fingerprinting, and he, along with Hardwicke, take samples of Cregar's prints from his room while he is out, but Sanders fails to match them with the prints he has obtained from the Ripper killings as the prints are from the wrong hand. Meanwhile, Cregar, who is now smitten with the alluring Oberon, decides to attend one of her shows, and when Sanders learns of this, he orders a large contingent of police to accompany Oberon to the theater that night. Officers are everywhere in the theater, but Cregar manages to see Oberon perform in a scantily clad costume that arouses him. When she finishes her performance and returns to her dressing room, she finds Cregar hiding there, waiting for her. He tells her that she has the kind of beauty that drives men insane and that such beauty must be destroyed to preserve the sanity of good men, such as his brother (whom Sanders has earlier discovered died a raving maniac in a lunatic asylum). Cregar begins to strangle Oberon, but she manages to let loose a piercing scream that brings Sanders and police officers on the run to her dressing room. They find her alive and Cregar gone. A mad chase for the berserk Cregar ensues through the back stage area of the theater. Oberon is taken to the stage where she is momentarily guarded, but when left unattended, Cregar, who has climbed into the backstage loft, unleashes a heavy sandbag that crashes toward Oberon and barely misses killing her. Sanders rushes on to the stage and sees Cregar climbing down a metal staircase and fires a shot, wounding Cregar. He nevertheless climbs upward and across a metal ramp with open vents that upwardly send slivers of light rippling across his hulking body and a florid and flushed face distorted with pain and rage, as he moves toward the camera (one of the most chilling scenes on celluloid). Cregar reaches a corner area as Sanders and officers slowly close in on him. He flashes a large, razor-like surgical knife (the kind most certainly employed by the Ripper in his many killings) and his heavy breathing is all that can be heard as he stares wild-eyed like a savage beast at bay at his pursuers. Sanders and a few of the officers make a few steps toward him, and Cregar suddenly whirls about and crashes through a window, his towering, bulky body hurling downward and splashing into the Thames River. (This ending is not in keeping with that of that excellent novel by Marie Belloc Lowndes.) Director Brahm presents a superb early period film noir entry where gaslights flicker and long shadows hold silent, waiting terror and where the fog-bound, glistening wet cobblestone streets of London come alive with lurking and legendary evil. All of the cast members are superlative in their captivating roles, but Cregar dominates every scene with his brooding and threatening persona. *Author's Note*: Cregar and Sanders would be teamed again the following year in an equally mesmerizing film noir entry, **Hangover Square**, 1945, one where Cregar is a deranged composer, who ruthlessly commits murder while suffering peri-

ods of amnesia. The usually unperturbed and urbane Sanders told this author that "that last scene in **The Lodger** where Laird holds us all at bay with that long, shimmering knife and the look of a salivating gargoyle on his face literally sent shivers up my spine, as well as everyone else facing him in that scene. In that terrible moment, he was the personification of that human monster called Jack the Ripper. After that scene, we applauded him, and, being the gentle and humble man that he truly was, he said with a little smile: 'I apologize if I gave anyone fright, except for the filmgoers, of course.'" For extensive details on Jack the Ripper, see my two-volume work, *The Great Pictorial History of World Crime*, Volume II (History, Inc.; pages 1180-1203). **p**, Robert Bassler; **d**, John Brahm; **cast**, Merle Oberon, George Sanders, Laird Cregar, Sir Cedric Hardwicke, Sara Allgood, Aubrey Mather, Queenie Leonard, Doris Lloyd, David Clyde, Helena Pickard, Olaf Hytten, Colin Campbell, Anita Bolster, Billy Bevan, Forrester Harvey, Charlie Hall, Skelton Knaggs; **w**, Barré Lyndon (based on the novel by Marie Belloc Lowndes); **c**, Lucien Ballard; **m**, Hugo W. Friedhofer; **ed**, J. Watson Webb; **art d**, James Basevi, John Ewing; **set d**, Thomas Little.

Lola ★★★ 1961; Italy/France; 90m; Rome Paris Films/Films Around the World; B/W; Drama; Children: Unacceptable; **DVD**; **VHS**. Michel is a bored young man living in Nantes, France. He has no special interest in life until a chance meeting with a woman he knew when he was a teenager. Lola (Aimée) has become a cabaret singer, a single mother devoted to her young son, with hopes that her husband, Harden, who deserted her during pregnancy, will return to her. Michel falls in love with Aimée and it gives his life new meaning. Also in their lives is an American sailor, who is attracted to Lola, and is kind to her son. A young girl about to celebrate her fourteenth birthday, when everything is romantic to her, also enters their lives. The girl's mother is a lonely widow, and an aging woman who misses her son. All romance and illusions crash when Harden returns and takes Aimée and his son away with him. Director Demy does a more than credible job in profiling fragile romance as he carefully develops his characters. Music: Ludwig van Beethoven's *Symphony No. 7*. Sexual themes prohibit viewing by children. (In Italian, French; English subtitles.) **p**, Carlo Ponti, Georges de Beauregard; **d&w**, Jacques Demy; **cast**, Anouk Aimée, Marc Michel, Elina Labourdette, Alan Scott, Annie Dupéroux, Jacques Harden, Margo Lion, Catherine Lutz, Corinne Marchand, Yvette Anziani; **c**, Raoul Coutard; **m**, Michel Legrand; **ed**, Anne-Marie Cotret, Monique Teisseire; **prod d**, Bernard Evein.

Lola ★★★ 1982; West Germany; 113m; Rialto Film/UA; Color; Drama; Children: Unacceptable (MPAA: R); **DVD**; **VHS**. Ten years after the end of World War II, in West Germany in the late 1950s, Lola (Sukowa), a cabaret singer-prostitute works in a brothel that is frequented by the most important men in town including the mayor. The town's new building commissioner, Mueller-Stahl, wants to clean up the town's corruption. This doesn't sit well with one of the town's big shots, Adorf. Sukowa, who is the daughter of the mayor's landlady, flirts with Mueller-Stahl, and he has thoughts of marrying her, but her scarlet reputation, which he only knows through rumor, troubles him. When he learns of her actual tawdry past, he decides it doesn't matter, and plans to go to the altar with Sukowa for a happy ending. (In German; English subtitles.) **p**, Horst Wendlandt, Hanns Eckelkamp, Wolf-Dietrich Brücker; **d**, Rainer Werner Fassbinder; **cast**, Barbara Sukowa, Armin Mueller-Stahl, Mario Adorf, Matthias Fuchs, Helga Feddersen, Karin Baal, Ivan Desny, Elisabeth Volkmann, Hark Bohm, Karl Heinz von Hassel, Christine Kaufmann, Udo Kier; **w**, Fassbinder, Pea Fröhlich, Peter Märthesheimer; **c**, Xaver Schwarzenberger; **m**, Freddy Quinn, Peer Raben; **ed**, Juliane Lorenz, Franz Walsch (Fassbinder), **prod d**, Raúl Gimenez, Rolf Zehetbauer; **art d**, Helmut Gassner.

Lola Montes ★★★★ 1959; France/West Germany; 116m; Gamma Film/Manhattan Films International; Color; Biographical Drama; Children: Unacceptable; **DVD**; **VHS**. In this stunning and superlative film from Ophuls (some call it his masterpiece), the alluring Carol portrays the tempestuous and notorious Lola Montez (1818-1861), Irish-born dancer of Spanish dances, actress, courtesan to several powerful European men, including composer Franz Liszt (1811-1886), and the mistress of mad King Ludwig I of Bavaria (1786-1868), who married her and made her Countess of Landsfeld. The film opens with Carol as an aging Lola Montez and where New Orleans circus master Ustinov introduces her to an admiring audience. In exchange for a quarter from each person, Carol answers a question. Ustinov then begins to relate her life story, which is shown in flashback, her professional career and her various affairs with men in France, Italy, Russia and Poland, as well as her early affair with Liszt (Quadflieg), and finally, her blossoming romance with Ludwig I (Walbrook) and where she becomes a titled lady. (Carol's scenes with Werner, who plays an adoring student, are the most touching in the film.) Carol, who has been performing various circus acts interspersed with the flashbacks narrated by Ustinov, then stands at the top of a high platform, preparing to make a hazardous leap. She appears to be on the verge of fainting, but regains her composure and asks that no net be used. She then makes a successful leap and Ustinov proposes while all the gentlemen in the audience line up to give a dollar each so they can kiss her hand. Visually breathtaking, this film shows the hallmarks of Ophuls' inspired camera choreography, techniques never before or since equaled, but technical methods that were lost on audiences upon its initial release in France where it failed to generate interest. *Author's Note*: Ophuls died in 1957 before the film was released in the U.S., and by then its original 140 minutes had been edited down to 116m (less in some prints), so that its already episodic scenes looked all the more disoriented with the story line and where any sense of Ophuls' original sense of continuity was ignored. The film was released again in 1969 in the U.S. with its restored version. (Dubbed in English.) **p**, Albert Caraco, André Haguet, Anton Schelkopf; **d**, Max Ophuls; **cast**, Martine Carol, Peter Ustinov, Anton Walbrook, Oskar Werner, Henri Guisol, Lise Delamare, Paulette Dubost, Jean Galland, Will Quadflieg, Carl Esmond; **w**, Ophuls, Annette Wademant, Jacques Natanson, Franz Geiger, Claude Heymann, Peter Ustinov (based on the novel *La vie extraordinaire de Lola Montès* by Cécil Saint-Laurent); **c**, Christian Matras (CinemaScope; Eastmancolor); **m**, Georges Auric; **ed**, Madeleine Gug; **prod d**, Jean D'Eaubonne; **set d**, Robert Christidès.

Lolita ★★★ 1962; U.K./U.S.; 152m; Seven Arts/MGM; B/W; Drama; Children: Unacceptable; **DVD**; **VHS**. Mason gives an astounding performance as a college professor in his forties who is enamored of fifteen-year-old Lyon (Lolita). The film opens with Mason walking casually into a room in a filth-ridden mansion where Sellers taunts him and where Mason shoots Sellers to death. Mason then sits down to contemplate how he came to commit this terrible killing. He looks back to see himself (in flashback) as a stuffy, widowed British professor, who relocates to America, getting a job at an Ohio college. He stops off in New Hampshire to deliver a few speeches, but when the home of his host is damaged by fire he is given a room in the sprawling but unkempt home owned by Winters, an overweight, middle-aged woman with intellectual pretensions, whom Mason finds offensive. Mason also finds Winters' romantic advances repulsive, but he tolerates this because he is fascinated by Lyon, who is Winters' teenage, light-headed and lollypop sucking daughter. He reasons that his attraction is based upon a youthful affair with another nubile girl years earlier, an affair never consummated, and that he has emotionally regressed to recapture that failed romance. When Winters proposes marriage, Mason surprisingly accepts, but only to be close to Lyon. Mason writes this all down in a diary where he expresses his loathing for the cloying and possessive Winters, one so intense that he has thoughts of killing her, but that is accomplished after Winters finds and reads his diary and, emotionally unstrung, races outside and is run over and killed by a passing car. Now Lyon's guardian, Mason recovers the girl from a summer camp and they relo-

James Mason and Sue Lyon in *Lolita*, 1962.

cate in Ohio. There Mason enrolls Lyon in an upscale girl's school and they settle down together and are briefly happy until Mason becomes insanely jealous over the attentions Lyon receives from boys her age. Lyon then appears in a school play that is written by Sellers and Lyon is attracted to the playwright, a total degenerate who has Lyon lie to Mason so she can spend some time with him. Mason, who has become a total love slave to Lyon, grows suspicious and takes Lyon on a trip, but, as they drive along, Mason has the sense that they are being followed and his inclinations are correct. Sellers is following them, and, using many disguises (as he so expertly employed in **Dr. Strangelove**, 1964, another film helmed by Kubrick) to secretly meet with Lyon while obliquely taunting Mason. Mason and Lyon then get sick and are hospitalized, but Lyon recovers and slips away from the hospital, going off with the unsavory Sellers. Years go by before Lyon contacts Mason, telling him that she is now married to a blue collar worker, Cockrell, and that she is pregnant and is desperately in need of money. She tells Mason that Sellers took her away from him, and that she stayed with him until he began demanding that they do "weird things" together, and she left him, too. Mason, still in love with Lyon, gives her everything he owns and then sets out to find Sellers and wreak havoc upon him for destroying his boyhood fantasy with Lyon. When finding Sellers, they play a cat-and-mouse game, then play ping pong, and when that game ends, Mason summarily executes the detestable Sellers. To mollify the moral codes of the day an epilogue states that Mason, who is subliminally as degenerate as Sellers is overtly, died in prison of a heart attack, both blackguards thus meeting just ends. The acting by the entire cast is outstanding, and Kubrick directs with an obvious passion for his subject, more clinically approached than graphically, so that he can more easily insert and portray the black humor of this dark drama. *Author's Note*: Kubrick told this author that "I had to approach the subject matter of that story with kid gloves. It really deals with a couple of rotten pedophiles lusting after an underage girl. In the book, she is twelve and we advance that age to about fifteen so we could get past the censors. I thought James [Mason] and Shelley [Winters] deserved Oscars for their great performances, but all we got was an Oscar nomination for the script. That was to be expected in those days where a lot of the older members of the Academy thought I had gone nuts to make a picture like **Lolita** and some even told me that they had doubts about my moral sanity. Well, the picture is tame by comparison to what you see today where nothing is held back and every kind of tasteless, crude thought or exercise about sex is thrown onto the screen like Jackson Pollock would throw paint onto a canvas with his bare hands and all of that is excrement." **p**, James B. Harris; **d**, Stanley Kubrick; **cast**, James Mason, Sue Lyon, Shelley Winters, Gary Cockrell, Jerry Stovin, Diana Decker, Lois Maxwell, Cec Linder, Bill Greene, Shirley Douglas, Peter Sellers; **w**,

Jay Silverheels and Clayton Moore in *The Lone Ranger,* 1956.

Vladimir Nabokov (based on his novel); **c**, Oswald Morris; **m**, Nelson Riddle; **ed**, Anthony Harvey; **art d**, Bill Andrews; **set d**, Andrew Low, Peter James.

The Lone Ranger ★★★ 1956; U.S.; 86m; Wrather Productions/WB; Color; Western; Children: Acceptable; **DVD**; **VHS**. This lively and action-loaded oater sees Moore (The Lone Ranger), who had been playing the masked man for some time on radio and TV, ride onto the screen, full of integrity and valor. He and his erstwhile sidekick, Silverheels (Tonto), learn of a recent rash of Indian uprisings and travel to the area to investigate. They find that this trouble is being caused by greedy Bettger, who wants to mine silver on a mountain held sacred by the tribes and is on Indian land. After overcoming barriers, obstacles and tall odds, Moore and Silverheels round up Bettger and his henchmen and restore peace with the Indians. The Lone Ranger and Tonto, as expected, ride off toward the sunset at the finish with a "Hi ho, Silver!" This solid, above-average western offers a lot of excitement for fans and filmgoers alike. **p**, Jack Wrather, Willis Goldbeck; **d**, Stuart Heisler; **cast**, Clayton Moore, Jay Silverheels, Lyle Bettger, Bonita Granville, Perry Lopez, Robert Wilke, John Pickard, Michael Ansara, Kermit Maynard, Robert Malcolm; **w**, Herb Meadow (based on "The Lone Ranger" legend and characters created by George W. Trendle); **c**, Edwin DuPar (Warnercolor); **m**, David Buttolph; **ed**, Clarence Kolster; **art d**, Stanley Fleischer; **set d**, G.W. Bernsten.

Lone Star ★★★ 1996; U.S.; 135m; Castle Rock/COL; Color; Crime Drama; Children: Unacceptable (MPAA: R); **DVD**; **VHS**. Exciting thriller sees two off-duty soldiers finding a skeleton at an old U.S. Army shooting range, and where Cooper, the sheriff of Rio County, Texas, is called in to investigate. That investigation, which periodically shows in flashback the events of forty years earlier, identifies the remains as that of Kristofferson, who had been the corrupt and violent sheriff at that time. Kristofferson had been succeeded by his deputy, McConaughey, who is Cooper's recently deceased father, and who became a respected and honored leader of the community. The new courthouse is about to be named after McConaughey, but that may not happen in that Cooper now suspects that his father, who was at contentious odds with Kristofferson (almost as he was with his own son Cooper), may have been involved in Kristofferson's death. Friends warn Cooper that his investigation might stir up ancient problems and will create new ones for himself. Cooper nevertheless begins to dig into the case and, in the process, is reunited with an old flame, Peña, a widow with two teenage children and who is now a schoolteacher. Both had a brief romance when they were teenagers, but Cooper's father and mother (Colon) had opposed their relationship and Cooper always believed that it was based on prejudice against his possibly marrying a Hispanic woman. A flashback shows how Colon's husband was shot and killed by Kristofferson and a deputy, James, when he was smuggling illegal aliens into Texas. Cooper's suspicions about his father are confirmed by James, who is now the mayor, and Morton, a local bar owner, who tell him that McConaughey did, indeed, shoot Kristofferson, with the aid of James, to prevent him from killing Morton. McConaughey then purchased a Mexican restaurant for Colon from money he stole from city funds, blaming the theft on the dead Kristofferson, who, McConaughey claimed, had fled following the theft. Thus ends this rather convoluted whodunit (which also explores the past of others in flashbacks in subplots) and one where Cooper also discovers that Kristofferson was also the father of Peña. Despite the fact that he and Pena are half-siblings, Cooper decides to go on having a relationship with her. **p**, R. Paul Miller, Maggie Renzi; **d&w**, John Sayles; **cast**, Kris Kristofferson, Chris Cooper, Matthew McConaughey, Ron Canada, Miriam Colon, Stephen Mendillo, Stephen J. Lang, Elizabeth Peña, Frances McDormand, Joe Morton, Oni Faida Lampley, Eleese Lester, Joe Stevens, Gonzalo Castillo, Richard Coca, Clifton James, Tony Frank, Miriam Colon; **c**, Stuart Dryburgh; **m**, Mason Daring; **ed**, Sayles; **prod d**, Dan Bishop; **art d**, Kyler Black; **set d**, Dianna Freas; **spec eff**, Jack Bennett.

The Lone Wolf Spy Hunt ★★★ 1939; U.S.; 71m; COL; B/W; Spy Drama; Children: Cautionary; **VHS**. In the best of the Lone Wolf series that splendidly mixes comedy and mystery, William (who makes his debut as the legendary jewel thief) gives a fascinating performance. William is abducted by a cabal of crooks, who force him to steal some top secret anti-aircraft plans from the U.S. Army. He foils the plot by filching only half of the plans, and, when released, he goes in pursuit of the espionage agents and where he not only rounds up the culprits, but recoups the stolen secrets, returning them to grateful army officials. Lupino is outstanding in her role as William's wise-cracking girlfriend, as is Weidler, who plays his daughter. *Author's Note*: This film had been filmed twice as silent productions in 1919 and 1929 under the title of **The Lone Wolf's Daughter**. Hayworth received third billing for her role in this film, Columbia already planning to build her into a superstar. Said Lupino to this author: "Rita was a contract player, but Harry Cohn got it into his head that he would make her a star—and this may have come about through their close relationship—so she got queen bee treatment during the production of that Lone Wolf picture where wardrobe gave her specially designed garments and she got her first stand-in, Ellen Duffy. I don't do a lot in that film, but they gave me some good smart-aleck lines to deliver. My big break came that same year after I was cast as the slum girl who becomes a model in **The Light That Failed** [1939], but pictures like **The Lone Wolf Spy Hunt** were a lot of fun to make where the character actors are as interesting as the leading players." **p**, Joseph Sistrom; **d**, Peter Godfrey; **cast**, Warren William, Ida Lupino, Rita Hayworth, Virginia Weidler, Ralph Morgan, Tom Dugan, Don Beddoe, Leonard Carey, Ben Welden, Brandon Tynan, Alec Craig, Marc Lawrence; **w**, Jonathan Latimer (based on a story by Louis Joseph Vance); **c**, Allen G. Siegler; **m**, Joseph Nussbaum; **ed**, Otto Meyer; **art d**, Lionel Banks.

The Loneliness of the Long Distance Runner ★★★★ 1962; U.K.; 104m; Woodfall/Continental Distributing; B/W; Drama; Children: Unacceptable; **DVD**; **VHS**. Courtenay makes an auspicious film debut in this compelling film, one of the first "angry young men" entries made in the early 1960s. He is an uneducated youth living in Nottingham, England, sharing a drab flat with his mother, an uncaring and demanding slattern, who tells him he has to contribute to their support. He is unable to find a job due to his lack of education so he commits a robbery and hides the money in a drainpipe. A storm, however, washes the hidden cash into view and Courtenay is caught and sent to the dreaded reformatory at Borstal where Redgrave is the strict superintendent. Redgrave emphasizes athleticism at Borstal, encouraging the boys to conduct track and field events and where Courtenay, a natural runner (he says he has had a lot of practice by running from the police throughout his childhood), shows outstanding skills. Courtenay has no use for anyone at Borstal and has had only one friend, Bolam. Redgrave sees that Courtenay may be the exceptional runner he needs to compete in a match he has arranged with a local school and tells Courtenay that if he performs well, he will receive special favors at the institution. Courtenay begins rigorous training, and during these trials, he recalls the miserable past that sent him to Borstal, which is shown in a series of flashbacks. He remembers his sweetheart, Jane, and his much-loved father, Madden, who died of a heart attack, and how his mother spent all the insurance money from his father's death on a lowlife gigolo and a TV set. Courtenay trains religiously, and when the big race begins, he starts off with blinding speed, quickly outdistancing all competitors. Just when he is about to cross the finish line, however, Courtenay pulls up short and watches as his competitors go ahead and finish the race. Redgrave is thunderstruck by Courtenay's actions. When Redgrave confronts Courtenay, the young man says nothing, staring at the superintendent with a bland, expressionless face, his actions clearly indicating that he is still an "angry young man" and rebel, who cannot be bought by favors, even in prison, which is where this intriguing tale ends. Courtenay and Redgrave are exceptional in this good character study, which is well directed by Richardson, who carefully employs flashback and present-day scenes in telling a gritty, offbeat tale. **p&d**, Tony Richardson; **cast**, Michael Redgrave, Tom Courtenay, Avis Bunnage, Alec McCowen, James Bolam, Peter Madden, Joe Robinson, Dervis Ward, Topsy Jane, Julia Foster, James Fox; **w**, Alan Sillitoe (based on his short story); **c**, Walter Lassally; **m**, John Addison; **ed**, Antony Gibbs; **prod d**, Ralph Brinton; **art d**, Ted Marshall.

Lonely Are the Brave ★★★★ 1962; U.S.; 107m; UNIV; B/W; Adventure; Children: Unacceptable; **DVD**; **VHS**. Douglas, in a bravura performance, is the consummate outsider, a cowboy who loves his freedom and horse more than modern civilization, which has long ago fenced in the open range he yearns to ride. Riding into Albuquerque on horseback, Douglas goes to see old friends Kane and Rowlands, but learns from close friend Rowlands that Kane is in jail for aiding illegal Mexicans to get into the U.S. To get close to his friend, Douglas purposely gets into a brawl (with Raisch, a disturbed one-armed man who beats him senseless) and is jailed. When sympathetic officers think to release him, he starts a brawl with officers and they then jail him. When he meets with Kane inside the jail, however, his pal wants no part of breaking out of the place, telling him that his rebellious days are over and that he is going to keep himself clean for the sake of his wife, Rowlands. Finding jail intolerable, Douglas breaks out and, finding his horse, sets out for the high mountains with sheriff Matthau and his deputies in pursuit. Matthau soon learns that he is up against a wily opponent as Douglas outguesses him at every twist and turn, moving ever upward through a high mountain range. Matthau secretly respects Douglas, even admires his rugged individualism, but he is dedicated to his task in capturing Douglas with his credo of "either you go by the rules or you lose." Matthau tracks Douglas with a small group of deputies, using a shortwave radio to communicate with his search parties. When Douglas seems to get beyond his reach, Matthau borrows the use of a U.S. Army helicopter to spot the elusive Douglas. The valiant cowboy, however, overcomes all odds and reaches the summit of the mountain range with his loyal horse. He rides over the top, descending to freedom and with Matthau's grudging admiration. When reaching the other side of that mountain in a rainstorm, however, Douglas attempts to cross a busy road and he and his horse are fatally struck by a truck driven by O'Connor, who has been shown in brief scenes before this tragic finale as a symbol of that tragedy to come, as he drives relentlessly toward that terrible rendezvous, one that also symbolizes the end of Douglas' poignantly remembered way of life. The brilliant script from Trumbo and Miller's taut direction, as well as standout performances from Douglas, Matthau

Kirk Douglas and Bill Raisch in *Lonely Are the Brave*, 1962.

and the rest of the cast makes this unusual tale riveting throughout. ***Author's Note***: The gifted Trumbo had been blacklisted for his communist activities in the 1940s and 1950s, but Douglas had courageously hired him, as well as Howard Fast, another such blacklisted writer, to do the script for **Spartacus**, 1960. Trumbo told this author that "Kirk was very impressed with the script as I knew he would be because he is a man who admires individuality and that is what this film is all about. It is the story of a man who lives the life of the Old West, a time of individualism, a man who is eventually destroyed by the automation of the modern age, in this instance a tired driver at the wheel of an unthinking truck." The film was shot on location in and outside of Albuquerque, New Mexico. **p**, Edward Lewis; **d**, David Miller; **cast**, Kirk Douglas, Gena Rowlands, Walter Matthau, Michael Kane, Carroll O'Connor, William Schallert, Bill Raisch, George Kennedy, Karl Swenson, Bill Mims, Bill Bixby; **w**, Dalton Trumbo (based on the novel *Brave Cowboy* by Edward Abbey); **c**, Philip Lathrop; **m**, Jerry Goldsmith; **ed**, Leon Barsha; **art d**, Alexander Golitzen, Robert Emmet Smith; **set d**, George Milo.

Lonely Hearts ★★★ 1983; Australia; 106m; Adam Packer Film Productions/Samuel Goldwyn Co.; Color; Romance; Children: Unacceptable (MPAA: R); **DVD**; **VHS**. Hughes is a thirty-year-old Australian bank clerk. She is dowdy and sexually repressed from living with parents who are both demanding and controlling, especially her father, Gordon, who wants to keep her single. She moves out of the house and into her own apartment. Through a dating service, she meets Kaye, a piano turner and kleptomaniac, who is fifty years old and lives with his mother until she dies. He then registers with the matchmaking service. They have dinner at her apartment, but their first meeting is strained, partly because of Hughes' fear of intimacy. Their families continue to give both of them problems. Kaye's sister, Blake, and her husband, Hardy, intrude on his life, while Hughes' parents keep interfering in her personal activities. Gradually, Hughes and Kaye build a relationship and she joins a play group to which Kaye belongs. The group's director, Finlayson, thinks Hughes is a fine actress. One night, Kaye tries to get more intimate with Hughes, but his advances are more than she can handle and their relationship is endangered. She has to decide whether or not to be more giving to Kaye and to stand up to her domineering father. This is a gentle, charming romantic comedy but not for children because of sexuality. **p**, John B. Murray; **d**, Paul Cox; **cast**, Wendy Hughes, Norman Kaye, Jon Finlayson, Julia Blake, Jonathan Hardy, Irene Inescort, Vic Gordon, Ted Grove-Rogers, Ron Falk, Chris Haywood; **w**, Cox, John Clarke; **c**, Yuri Sokol; **m**, Kaye; **ed**, Tim Lewis; **prod d**, Nigel Angwin.

Lonelyhearts ★★★★ 1958; U.S.; 103m; Dore Schary Productions/UA; B/W; Drama; Children: Unacceptable; **VHS**. This dark

Norman Kaye and Wendy Hughes in *Lonely Hearts*, 1983.

and brooding tale from the brilliant Nathanael West has Clift performing a powerful role of a man entrapped by his own empathy for his fellow human beings. A novice writer, Clift applies for a job with cynical publisher Ryan, who also renders a great performance, and who tries him out as an apprentice reporter and then gives him the unlikely job of writing the newspaper's column to the lovelorn. Clift becomes "Miss Lonelyhearts" and is inundated with letters from lovesick, lonely people. His compassion and empathy is shown in his responses, but he becomes enmeshed with these emotionally disturbed readers, particularly with Stapleton, a neurotic sociopath, who drains Clift of his own emotions and inveigles him into a confrontation that almost proves fatal. One of those love-seeking persons is Loy, who does not write to Clift, but befriends him. She is Ryan's wife, a spouse made lonely and unloved by the savagely sardonic Ryan, a publisher who respects no one and suspects everyone of being self-serving, evil creatures. Ryan encourages his wife's friendship with Clift, but also denigrates both for their emotional dependencies. Ryan perversely goads Clift into bearing his own soul in print and encourages him to develop a relationship with Stapleton, who is married to a crippled husband. After a while, Clift becomes emotionally exhausted, all of his sympathies and compassion sapped. His relationship with his girlfriend, Hart, has almost been wrecked by the debilitating trauma created by his writing chores, but he finally stands up to Ryan and tells him just how jaded and degenerate he is before quitting and going off with Hart to make a better life (in the novel his character becomes a murder victim to the Stapleton character). Grim and unrelenting, this fascinating portrait presents exacting and memorable characters. Clift is the epitome of noble youth, who becomes an emotional sponge willing to take on the psychological ills of the world, saying at one point: "If someone is in trouble, how can you not take them seriously?" Ryan is his deflating counterpart, believing all are corrupt and whose ruthless nature is summed up when he states: "I enjoy seeing youth betray their promises." Ryan's own hatred for humanity is rooted to Loy, never letting her forget that she once betrayed him with another man and where he seeks revenge by making her life as miserable as he can by encouraging her alcoholism. To Ryan, no one is decent, respectable or worthwhile. Clift learns one significant lesson here and that is he cannot arbitrate the emotional fates of nameless humanity and it is enough to keep his own emotional house in order. *Author's Note*: This story had been made as **Advice to the Lovelorn**, 1933, starring Lee Tracy, but it was positioned as a comedy. Ryan told this author that "I don't think I ever played a more savage man than in **Lonelyhearts**. That role as the newspaper publisher is one where I play a person who is really a murderer. He doesn't kill people, but he certainly tries to murder their spirits and their belief in love. You know, Monty [Clift] had a tough time with his role, which would have put most any other actor into a

psycho ward. He was drinking heavily and he had very little stamina. We had to close down each day's shooting at about two in the afternoon, so he could go home and rest. A year earlier, he had been involved in a car crash that almost killed him when he was making **Raintree County** [1957]—and, in fact, I think his co-star in that film and very close friend, Elizabeth Taylor, saved his life by pulling two teeth out of his throat when he almost choked to death. Monty was never a well man and had endless allergies and suffered from colitis all his life—he told me that he had been rejected from the army during World War II because he had chronic diarrhea. He was also homosexual and was very sensitive about that ever getting out to the public. Every wamen he met, I think, wanted to become his mother. I know that Myrna [Loy] was so attracted to him, that she even thought of marrying him—and that is taking your part a little too seriously. Monty generated those feelings in women, that protective motherly instinct, because he seemed so frail and even helpless, like a grown-up handsome child, who was as lost as a toddler in a windstorm. I think he had every phobia known to man. He was a mess, a wreck, and one of the finest actors I ever met." **p**, Dore Schary; **d**, Vincent J. Donehue; **cast**, Montgomery Clift, Robert Ryan, Myrna Loy, Dolores Hart, Maureen Stapleton, Jackie Coogan, Mike Kellin, Onslow Stevens, Frank Maxwell, Frank Overton; **w**, Schary (based on the novel *Miss Lonelyhearts* by Nathanael West and the play by Howard Teichmann); **c**, John Alton; **m**, Conrad Salinger; **ed**, John Faure, Aaron Stell; **art d**, Serge Krizman; **set d**, Darrell Silvera.

The Long Absence ★★★ 1962; Israel/France; 85m; Procinex/Commercial Pictures; B/W; Drama; Children: Cautionary. Valli, the owner of a small bistro in Paris, learns that her husband serving in the French army in World War II is missing in Germany. She waits for sixteen years, hoping for his return, until one day she sees a tramp, Wilson, pass by her café and thinks he may be her missing husband. She follows him to a shack by the Seine River and learns that he has had amnesia since the war. A scar on his head convinces her that he lost his memory in a war injury and he may never regain it, but she is certain he is her husband and determines to spend her life loving and caring for him. Valli and Wilson give strong performances in this telling and poignant production. Song: "Trois petites notes de musique" ("Three Little Music Notes") (George Delerue). (In French; English subtitles.) **d**, Henri Colpi; **cast**, Alida Valli, Georges Wilson, Charles Blavette, Amédée, Paul Faivre, Pierre Parel, Catherine Fonteney, Diana Lepvrier, Nane Germon, Georges Bellec; **w**, Marguerite Duras, Gérard Jarlot (based on the story by Duras); **c**, Marcel Weiss; **m**, Georges Delerue; **ed**, Jasmine Chasney, Jacqueline Meppiel; **art d**, Maurice Colasson.

The Long and the Short and the Tall ★★★ 1962; U.K.; 110m; Michael Balcon Productions/Continental Distributing; B/W; War Drama; Children: Unacceptable; **DVD**. In this engrossing war tale, Todd is a British army sergeant, who leads a troop of soldiers in the Malaysian jungles of Burma in 1942 during World War II. Their mission is to record jungle and troop noises so the recordings can be played back by other troops at base camp to divert the enemy as to their whereabouts. As they proceed farther into the jungle to where they believe the Japanese are, they get farther away from radio range until the only channel they receive is that of a Japanese broadcast. They realize they are only ten to fifteen miles from a Japanese camp. There is friction among the British soldiers. One of the soldiers, Harvey, a troublesome private, is especially at odds with Harris, a corporal. They take a Japanese scout (Takaki) as their prisoner, and this event opens up emotional warfare among those in the British troop as Todd wants to take him to base camp headquarters to be interrogated, but Harvey and some others want the POW killed. Takaki is caught stealing from the troop and is shot and killed by one of the British privates, McCallum. Nearby patrolling Japanese hear the gun shot and attack. Only Harris and McCallum survive the gunfire. Now they are the ones who are POWs and who may be shot. Song: "Bless 'Em All" (Fred Godfrey, Jimmy Hughes, Frank

Lake). **p**, Michael Balcon; **d**, Leslie Norman; **cast**, Richard Todd, Laurence Harvey, Richard Harris, David McCallum, Ronald Fraser, John Meillon, John Rees, Kenji Takaki, Anthony Chinn; **w**, Wolf Mankowitz, Willis Hall (based on the play by Hall); **c**, Erwin Hillier; **m**, Stanley Black; **ed**, Gordon Stone; **prod d**, Terence Verity; **art d**, Jim Morahan; **spec eff**, George Blackwell.

The Long Day Closes ★★★ 1993; U.K.; 85m; British Film Institute/Sony; Color; Biography/Drama; Children: Unacceptable (MPAA: PG-13). Every day is sad and lonely for McCormack, a twelve-year-old boy from a working-class family in Liverpool in 1956. Whenever he can, he escapes home where his father is abusive. He hides from school bullies by going to a local movie theater where he watches classic films. He also listens to music and hears his mother, Yates, sing along with the radio. McCormack finally finds a way to endure his father's abuse and get along with other boys in this intriguing autobiographical tale from prolific British television writer-director Davies, who was from a family of ten and whose father was abusive. **p**, Olivia Stewart, Angela Topping; **d&w**, Terence Davies; **cast**, Leigh McCormack, Marjorie Yates, Anthony Watson, Nicholas Lamont, Ayse Owens, Tina Malone, Jimmy Wilde, Robin Polley, Peter Ivatts, Joy Blakeman; **c**, Michael Coulter; **m**, Bob Last, Robert Lockhart; **ed**, William Diver; **prod d**, Christopher Hobbs; **art d**, Kave Naylor; **set d**, Karen Wakefield; **spec eff**, Martin Body.

Long Day's Journey into Night ★★★★★ 1962; U.S.; 174m; Landau/Embassy Pictures; B/W; Drama; Children: Unacceptable; **DVD**; **VHS**. The powerful Eugene O'Neill play is enacted with great skill by the gifted Hepburn, Richardson and Robards. It is the story of the doomed Tyrone family and where the playwright drew upon his own lifetime experiences as well as that of his closest family members, who come to grips with their terrible afflictions all in one long day in 1912 at their country retreat in Connecticut. Richardson is an esteemed but aging Shakespearean actor, who has, in recent years, been appearing in a widely popular commercial play and has made considerable money, but he has had a lifelong habit of being a skinflint, saving every penny against the threats and hazards of old age. His wife, Hepburn, is regal-like, Catholic born-and-bred, who holds her morals and principles to the highest standard. She has just returned from a sanitarium, but she seems distant, aloof and spiritually apart from her family members. Robards, oldest of Richardson's two sons, has attempted to follow in his father's theatrical footsteps, but he has failed dismally and turned to alcohol, becoming bitter and cynical toward one and all, although he harbors deep affections he cannot bring himself to express. Stockwell is a budding writer, trying to hone his skills, but he is plagued with deep fears about his family. To Richardson, the past is everything and he recalls his theatrical triumphs for his sons, eloquently retelling his exploits on the stage, all of which seem to impress his sons, even though they have heard these tales many times. Hepburn, however, spends little time with the family, staying for long periods in her room, and this makes Richardson nervous. As the day fades and dusk comes, Richardson turns on only a few lights to save money, his penny-pinching manner evident in his every move. Robards is friendly and warm toward his younger brother, Stockwell, but when Hepburn appears in a daze, he and Richardson become moody and morose. Robards then verbally attacks Richardson, accusing him of causing his mother's "condition." Now in his cups and controlled by alcohol, Robards lets loose his darkest emotions, telling Stockwell that their mother is a drug addict and that Stockwell and their father are responsible for this awful affliction. Robards mercilessly relates to young Stockwell how their father, to save money, hired a quack to deliver him at birth in a hotel room and, after their mother could no longer endure the pain inflicted by the quack in his hurried surgery, that quack injected her with morphine, a drug to which she became addicted for life. Hepburn lives with her own guilt in that her father died of tuberculosis and she feels that she has passed this affliction on to her

Katharine Hepburn in *Long Day's Journey into Night*, 1962.

youngest son, Stockwell, who is consumptive. Richardson, however, thinks of Stockwell as an unwanted financial burden and, to save money, has arranged for him to stay at an inexpensive state-operated health clinic and where he will receive only mediocre medical care. Robards then feigns fondness and friendship toward Stockwell, taking him on a pub crawl and where he introduces his youthful brother to his alcoholic friends and prostitutes in sleazy bars. When finally drunk, Robards' hateful feelings burst to the surface and he scathingly attacks Stockwell, telling him that he loves him, but that he also hates him and that he is Stockwell's worst enemy, warning: "Watch out for me, kid!" In his tortured diatribe, Robards tells him that, if he can, he will turn Stockwell into the same kind of boozing, evil-minded person he thinks himself to be. When they return home, they find Hepburn in an utter state of mental confusion, the morphine having taken over her personality, and where she struggles to maintain contact with a family that she, from moment to moment, sees as a group of strangers. Her personality abruptly changes from minute to minute. She is, in one moment, the coquette of decades ago, then a trembling, raving dope fiend, then a loving mother frantically reaching out to her family, then a person who has no identity at all, one without memory or any kind of emotional roots. (These traumatic and highly charged scenes depicted by Hepburn are purgatorial marvels to behold and are achieved as only Hepburn could have managed them, a masterpiece performance never equaled.) And this is where this tragedy ends, without resolution or conclusion, without solace or promise of a better tomorrow as deep and apprehensive night approaches to engulf them all. This past-haunted family becomes enshrouded with the darkness of that night and the darkness of their own tortured souls. Lumet directs with great care, loyally conveying the O'Neill story from the stage version to this superb film. ***Author's Note***: Hepburn wanted the role of the mother for some time and took only a small salary to appear in this excellent production. "I wanted Spence [Spencer Tracy, her lifelong lover] to play the part of the father," Hepburn told this author, "but he said, 'hell, Kate, you're the one for that kind of story, not me. I'm a movie actor.' When I kept pushing him, he asked the producer for $500,000 to play the role, knowing that there was no budget for that kind of salary, and he was turned down, which is exactly what Spence wanted, clever man." Hepburn was nominated for an Oscar for Best Actress for her role in this film, but lost out to Anne Bancroft in **The Miracle Worker**, 1962. All four principals, Hepburn, Richardson, Robards and Stockwell, received the Best Actor/Best Actress award from the Cannes Film Festival. O'Neill was fifty when he began writing this play in 1939, a tale that took its emotional toll on him, and when he finished it, he stated that the story "was of an old sorrow, written in tears and blood." O'Neill's father, James O'Neill (1847-1920), had been a Shakespearean actor, but, in later years, played in the leading role of 'The

Sterling Hayden, Elliott Gould, Nina van Pallandt and Henry Gibson in *The Long Goodbye,* 1973.

Count of Monte Cristo," year after year, growing wealthy. He was a skinflint, who, to save money, had a quack deliver his son, Eugene, in a hotel room (at the Barrett Hotel in Times Square, New York City, on October 16, 1888) and his wife (Mary Ellen Quinlan; Ella O'Neill; 1857-1922), having problems in that childbirth, was given morphine by that quack, addicting her to the drug thereafter. O'Neill's brother, Jamie, tried acting, like their father, but he became a hopeless alcoholic, dying at age forty-five. O'Neill, like the Stockwell character, was consumptive from an early age. This tragic story is autobiographical to its mesmerizing, cathartic core. O'Neill died on November 27, 1953. He lay in a coma for some time in Room 401 of the Sheraton Hotel at Boston, Massachusetts. He came to consciousness briefly, whispering: "I knew it, I knew it. Born in a hotel room and died in a hotel room." With that, his last words, this great American playwright and Nobel Prize winner (1936; four times winner of the Pulitzer Prize, 1920, 1922, 1928, 1957) died at age sixty-five. O'Neill was profiled in several films, chiefly made-for-TV productions, and most notably in **Reds**, 1981, by Jack Nicholson. **p**, Ely Landau, Jack J. Dreyfus, Jr., Joseph E. Levine; **d**, Sidney Lumet; **cast**, Katharine Hepburn, Ralph Richardson, Jason Robards, Jr., Dean Stockwell, Jeanne Barr; **w**, Eugene O'Neill (based on his play); **c**, Boris Kaufman; **m**, André Previn; **ed**, Ralph Rosenblum; **prod d**, Richard Sylbert; **set d**, Gene Callahan.

The Long Good Friday ★★★ 1982; U.K.; 114m; British Lion/Embassy Pictures; Color; Crime Drama; Children: Unacceptable (MPAA: R); **DVD**; **VHS**. Hoskins renders a superlative performance as a sanguine crime boss in England, but whose ruthless streak knows no bounds. He is seemingly at the top of his rackets world when, on Easter weekend, he meets with Constantine, his American counterpart, to conclude a huge land deal in connection with the London Olympics in 1988. Suddenly, Hoskins' well-organized and lucrative world comes crashing down when his buildings are bombed and many of his top enforcers are mysteriously murdered. He thinks that rival bosses are behind these savage attacks and begins a gang war against them, only to discover, too late, that the IRA is his real nemesis, a deadly and unrelenting enemy created by his own doing after some of Hoskins' men robbed a cache of loot used as protection money for the IRA. Hoskins then conducts warfare against the terrorist organization, one he cannot win. Director Mackenzie presents an engrossing crime thriller where its violent scenes are disturbingly taut and its twisting sequences full of inventive surprise. **p**, Barry Hanson; **d**, John Mackenzie; **cast**, Bob Hoskins, Helen Mirren, Eddie Constantine, Dave King, Bryan Marshall, Derek Thompson, Paul Freeman, Leo Dolan, Kevin McNally, Patti Love, P.H. Moriarty, Pierce Brosnan; **w**, Barrie Keeffe; **c**, Phil Meheux; **m**, Francis Monkman; **ed**, Mike Taylor; **art d**, Vic Symonds;

spec eff, Steve Hamilton, David Harris, Ian Wingrove.

The Long Goodbye ★★★ 1973; U.S.; 112m; E-K Corporaton/Lions Gate/UA; Color; Crime Drama; Children: Unacceptable (MPAA: R); **DVD**; **VHS**. Of all the fine Philip Marlowe tales spun by the brilliant crime stylist Raymond Chandler, this one is the strangest and with the most unlikely actor to essay the hardboiled sleuth on film, Gould, who nevertheless gives a captivating performance through the inescapable force of the character he plays. At the opening, Gould is waiting (if not praying) for a case to land on his dirty desk when old friend Bouton arrives and asks him to drive him to Tijuana, Mexico. He does, and when he returns, he is arrested by LAPD detectives, who charge him with aiding and abetting a wanted man. Bouton's wife has been murdered and Bouton is the primary suspect in that case. Gould is released when police receive word that Bouton has committed suicide, and when Gould returns to his abode, he finds voluptuous van Pallandt, who hires him to find her missing husband, Hayden, a famous and wealthy author. Gould tracks down Hayden, finding him an alcoholic and drying out in a seedy sanitarium run by Gibson, a little man with a great greed. The sleuth takes Hayden home, and there Hayden and van Pallandt exchange harsh words and where Hayden demonstrates a streak of violence that causes Gould to suspect that he may have had something to do with the death of Bouton's wife, who was known to Hayden. Gould returns to his unkempt bachelor pad where his neighbors, a bevy of scantily clad young ladies prance about to disco music, and where Gould mourns his recently deceased cat. He then receives an unexpected visit from gangster Rydell and a few of his goons. Rydell demands the return of the money Bouton took from him, revealing to Gould that Bouton was one of his bagmen, running money from Rydell's rackets back to the boss, except that, on his last trip, Bouton absconded to Mexico. All of this is a big surprise to Gould, who is manhandled and knocked about by Rydell's goons before the gangster and his entourage leave, but not without warning Gould to find and return the money or he will be joining his pal Bouton in the Hereafter. To impress Gould with this possible fate, the sadistic Rydell viciously injures his own mistress before they depart. Gould goes to van Pallandt and Hayden, and they give him contradictory statements about Bouton; he then travels back to Mexico where officials verify Bouton's death, but the details are ambiguous, leaving Gould puzzled. Gould goes back to Hayden to find him hosting a beach party with oddball guests and where Gibson shows up and demands his medical fees. When Hayden stalls, the obnoxious pip-squeak doctor savagely slaps Hayden's face and the author pays him his money. (Hayden gives a compelling performance as a drunk, who is stuttering and blubbering most of his lines, dazed and confused in his semi-alcoholic state, a man who is losing what is left of his booze-sodden mind.) That night, Hayden reportedly walks into the ocean and drowns himself. Van Pallandt blames her husband for the death of Bouton's wife, saying that he was having an affair with the woman and his violent nature must have caused him to kill her. Gould does not accept that theory and asks police to reopen the Bouton case, but they refuse. Then the money Rydell has been demanding is surprisingly returned to the rackets boss. Gould tails van Pallandt and, after he sees her meet with Rydell, he is hit by a speeding car and sent to the hospital. Still ailing, Gould leaves the hospital and drives back to Mexico and there he finds Bouton alive. He learns that he has been set up, and, in a rage, Gould winds up killing Bouton so that now he is reliably dead. As he lives at the expensive spa where Bouton has been hiding out, Gould passes van Pallandt, who apparently has murdered her husband as Bouton has his wife so that the two secret lovers can be with each other. That conspiracy has been ruined by Gould, as he knows, and he does a little perverse dance to celebrate his own perverse retribution, which is caught in freeze-frame and where this oddball film noir entry from off-the-wall director Altman ends. Altman takes great liberties with the story and does his own disjointed thing with this tale, presenting a confusing story line where only a few of the loose ends are knotted at the finish, his usual filmic modus operandi.

The whole, absurd tale is unresolved and unsatisfying, but that, too, is its attraction and allure, as it fits the unreal reality of the world of private eyes where, at best, only a piece of the puzzle is ever truly found and the larger mystery remains to nag and haunt. *Author's Note*: Hayden told this author that "I never understood my part in that picture. Altman was not a director who said much about what he wanted. I know that I am playing a drunken author and I am all screwed up, but that was about it. Altman let me do what I thought I should do in every scene, so I gave him a lot of gibberish and he apparently liked that. I didn't think anyone else in that crazy picture knew what they were doing either. When I saw the finished picture I said to myself, for God's sake, you look like you just got a frontal lobotomy!" **p**, Jerry Bick; **d**, Robert Altman; **cast**, Elliott Gould, Nina van Pallandt, Sterling Hayden, Mark Rydell, Henry Gibson, David Arkin, Warren Berlinger, Jo Ann Brody, David Carradine, Arnold Schwarzenegger; **w**, Leigh Brackett (based on the novel by Raymond Chandler); **c**, Vilmos Zsigmond (Technicolor); **m**, John Williams; **ed**, Lou Lombardo.

The Long Gray Line ★★★★ 1955; U.S.; 138m; COL; Color; Biographical Drama; Children: Acceptable; **DVD**; **VHS**. Power gives a wonderful performance of Irish immigrant Martin "Marty" Maher (1876-1961; pronounced "Marr") in this well-directed biopic from pantheon helmsman Ford, and one that also depicts, in nostalgic and memorable scenes, a portrait of the legendary West Point and its dedicated cadets over a period of many illustrious decades. The film begins with Power as an old man, about to be retired from the U.S. Army Military Academy at West Point, New York. He protests this forced retirement to none other than a U.S. President, who is played by Steele. He is then given a grand review where the cadets of "The Long Gray Line" march in review before him and his past comes flooding back in flashback to show him arriving at West Point from Tipperary, Ireland, becoming a waiter in the mess hall at West Point in 1898, and how he then enlists in the U.S. Army, becoming a boxing coach and swimming instructor for the cadets, eventually promoted to the highest noncommissioned position of master sergeant. He is a poor waiter, who breaks so many dishes that the cost of paying for them exceeds his salary. To earn more money to pay for the damages, he enlists (sworn into the army by Stone, who plays major, later five-star general John J. Pershing, 1860-1948), and stays on at West Point, but his mercurial Irish temper gets him into a lot of trouble. Bond, the athletic director at the Point (playing West Point's Herman Koehler, 1859-1927), notices Power and, after Bond roundly beats Power in a boxing match, makes him his assistant. Power then romances O'Hara, an Irish maid at West Point, and they get married. Saving enough money from his army wages, Power then sends for his aged father, Crisp, to travel to America, and he goes to live with Power and O'Hara in a small cottage that has been provided for them on the campus grounds at West Point. O'Hara gives birth to a child, but the baby dies, and she is told that she cannot have any more children. This tragic loss is compensated by the couple when they transfer their maternal and paternal affections to the cadets at the Point, more or less adopting the members of each new class, including Harry Carey Jr., who plays Dwight D. Eisenhower (1890-1969), later a five-star general, commander of Allied Forces in Europe during WWII, and thirty-fourth President of the U.S. Of all the cadets, Francis (in his last film before dying at the age of twenty-five in a plane crash on July 31, 1955, outside Los Angeles) is their favorite, but he violates the strict code of honor and, before graduating, admits to breaking regulations and resigns. Francis later vindicates himself while bravely serving in battle during WWII. O'Hara dies, but Power goes on living, fondly remembered as a strict but compassionate father figure by one generation of cadets to another. When reaching retirement, he begs the President (Steele) to stay on and he is granted that right to remain at West Point. A poignant and stirring film well directed by Ford and with outstanding performances by Power, O'Hara and the rest of the cast. *Author's Note*: The film was expensive to make, costing more than $2 million, but it proved to be a great box

Paul Newman, Anthony Franciosa and Lee Remick in *The Long, Hot Summer*, 1958.

office success, earning back $5 million in its initial release. Ford told this author that "I did not like the use of CinemaScope as I thought it was too gimmicky and that it actually distracted audiences from the story line. I did what I could with that new technique and it worked well when we shot everything on location at West Point. The process allowed us to show the broad plains, the stately buildings, the Hudson River and, especially, the marching ranks of the cadets as they moved beautifully on parade and that is always a sight to make any American's blood run faster. I thought Ty [Power] was perfect in the role of Marty Maher and Maureen [O'Hara] was also ideal in playing his loyal wife, the only person who could cool down that hot Irish temper of his." Maher retired from the U.S. Army in 1928, but stayed on at West Point as a Civil Service employee at the Point's athletic department, not officially retiring until 1946, completing fifty years of service at the Academy. He died at age eighty-four on January 17, 1961, and was buried at West Point. **p**, Robert Arthur; **d**, John Ford; **cast**, Tyrone Power, Maureen O'Hara, Robert Francis, Donald Crisp, Ward Bond, Betsy Palmer, Phil Carey, Harry Carey, Jr., Patrick Wayne, Sean McClory, Peter Graves, Martin Milner, Ken Curtis, Milburn Stone, Erin O'Brien Moore, Mimi Doyle, Willis Bouchey, Jack Pennick, Elbert Steele, Jim Sears; **w**, Edward Hope (based on the book *Bringing Up the Brass* by Marty Maher, Nardi Reeder Campion); **c**, Charles Lawton, Jr. (CinemaScope; Technicolor); **m**, George Duning; **ed**, William A. Lyon; **art d**, Robert Peterson; **set d**, Frank Tuttle.

The Long, Hot Summer ★★★★ 1958; 115m; Jerry Wald Productions/FOX; Color; Drama; Children: Cautionary; **DVD**; **VHS**. Newman is a southern sharecropper with a hot temper and a head for shrewd opportunities. His father was a notorious barn-burner, one who burns down the barns of business adversaries to settle disputes, and Newman seems to be walking in his father's larcenous footsteps as an ambitious arsonist. Newman arrives in a town bossed by wealthy widower Welles, a dominating, obese landowner, who controls vast acres of tillable soil. Newman goes to work as a sharecropper on Welles' land and Welles comes to like the independent-minded young man even more than his own weak-willed son, Franciosa. Welles has another child, Woodward, a feisty daughter who defies him at every turn. A spinster, she has been trying to land rich Anderson, another landowner like her father, but he is under the thumb of his mother, Albertson, who rules her roost as rigidly as Welles dominates his own nest. Welles then tries to feather that nest by matching his daughter with Newman, but Woodward is having none of this. Though she finds Newman attractive in an earthy way, she also thinks him to be vulgar and a lowlife, much inferior to her own station in life. When Franciosa discovers that his father prefers Newman to himself, he takes revenge on Welles by trapping him in a barn and

Harry Langdon in *Long Pants*, 1927.

setting fire to it, believing that Newman will be blamed for this fiery death as he has a reputation of torching such structures, although that reputation is based on rumor, not fact. At the last moment, however, Franciosa cannot bring himself to take his father's life and rescues him from the flames. Meanwhile, after several bristling encounters with the self-confident and often strutting Newman, Woodward comes to realize that she loves this brazen upstart and they decide to marry. The story is complete when Lansbury, who has been Welles' mistress for many years, and Welles decide to go to the altar. Well directed and acted, this Faulkner tale translates well to the screen because the writers took only the most visual elements from the original story and made it a lot less complicated than Faulkner's complex plot and sub-plots. (Other than **Intruder in the Dust**, 1949, **The Tarnished Angels**, 1958, based on Faulkner's novel, *Pylon*, and a few others, including this film, Faulkner's stories do not work well in motion pictures.) ***Author's Note***: Welles told this author that "I do not like my character in **The Long, Hot Summer**, but then that character is not likeable to anyone. He's a tin-pot dictator south of the Mason-Dixon Line and his only desire is to make life miserable for everyone because he is a miserable person. You see, Faulkner's characters are really not that complex—they simply get deeper and deeper into themselves where they sink into their own self-made quicksand. I never cared much for Faulkner's writings. I thought he was overrated, and I was shocked when he got the Nobel Prize for Literature [in 1949]. I met Faulkner when he was trying to write screenplays in Hollywood in the 1940s [Faulkner first went to Hollywood to work with Howard Hawks in 1932]. He was a big boozer and a grumpy sort of guy, who told me that he hated writing for the movies and he hated everyone in Hollywood. I told him, 'the solution is easy, Bill. It's called Union Station [the main train station in Los Angeles]. You go there, get on a train, and leave town.' Well, that's what he eventually did, going back to a little town in Mississippi [Oxford] and I think he drank himself to death there. Something deep and terrible tortured that man and no one ever found out what it was, and I don't think Bill Faulkner found out either." Newman and Woodward met while making **The Long, Hot Summer**. They fell in love and got married shortly thereafter. **p**, Jerry Wald; **d**, Martin Ritt; **cast**, Paul Newman, Joanne Woodward, Anthony Franciosa, Orson Welles, Lee Remick, Angela Lansbury, Richard Anderson, Sarah Marshall, Mabel Albertson, J. Pat O'Malley; **w**, Irving Ravetch, Harriet Frank, Jr. (based on the stories "Barn Burning" and "The Spotted Horses" and the novel *The Hamlet* by William Faulkner); **c**, Joseph La Shelle (CinemaScope; DeLuxe Color); **m**, Alex North; **ed**, Louis R. Loeffler; **art d**, Lyle R. Wheeler, Maurice Ransford; **set d**, Walter M. Scott, Eli Benneche; **spec eff**, L.B. Abbott.

The Long Night ★★★ 1947; U.S.; 101m; Select Productions/RKO;

B/W; Crime Drama; Children: Unacceptable; **DVD; VHS**. Fonda is exceptional as a man barricaded from the police and his past in this fine remake of Marcel Carne's **Daybreak**, 1940. This powerful film noir film opens when Fonda shoots to death a conniving magician, Price, and then takes refuge in his room where he defies the police in a standoff battle and where he reflects upon the events that led to this terrible confrontation. In flashback, we see Fonda getting a job as a sandblaster in a grimy blue collar town on the Ohio-Pennsylvania border. He meets and falls in love with Bel Geddes, a daydreaming young woman whose only ambition is to escape the drab life of this dreary town. Their lives change for the dramatic worse after the cunning and predatory Price arrives to put on his magic act with the assistance of seductive aide Dvorak. Bel Geddes watches the show and meets Price, who immediately begins to make moves on the naïve and trusting young woman while Dvorak tries to entice Fonda, but candidly tells him that her employer is a worthless wolf, a womanizing seducer without morals or scruples. Fonda thinks to defend the woman he loves by confronting Price, telling him to stay away from Bel Geddes, but the artful Price is ready with a quick and surprising answer. He tells Fonda that he is, unknown to Bel Geddes, her actual father and it is he, Price, who tells Fonda that he is not suitable as a future husband for his offspring, and orders Fonda to stay away from his daughter! This is a lie, but so boldly and convincingly conveyed by the glib Price that Fonda believes him. Fonda goes off to contemplate a miserable future without Bel Geddes, which is further aggravated when the insidious Price visits him, threatening him with a gun for inexplicable reasons. Price brags about sexually seducing Bel Geddes and that drives Fonda over the brink. He attacks Price and both men struggle for the gun, which goes off and kills Price and that brings the viewer in flash-forward to the present crisis where Fonda is holding off police in his barricaded room. As Fonda trades shots with police sharpshooters, officers prepare to smoke him out of his room with tear gas, but Bel Geddes arrives and is allowed to talk to Fonda. She pleads with him to surrender and promises that if he is sent to prison, she will be waiting for him and that she loves only him. Fonda relents and a better tomorrow appears in the offing. This gritty and stark film noir entry is in keeping with the brooding Germanic style of pantheon director Litvak and where he exacts from the entire cast superlative performances. ***Author's Note***: Price thought his role in this film was one of the most insidious characters he ever played, telling this author: "I am utterly without human decency in that picture, a cheap magician who extends his tricks to deceive everyone and perversely enjoys wrecking the lives of others. There are such awful creatures in the real world and I play one of them. What a treat it was for me to play opposite the great Henry Fonda. My expansive way of acting in our scenes together simply went to puddles at his feet. His reserve and incredible intensity made my shallow character all the more synthetic and reprehensible." Fonda told this author that "I felt deeply for the character I portrayed in **The Long Night**. He is a trusting soul, like most people, and when his ideals are betrayed, he fights back the only way he knows how—through the same kind of violence that others bring into his life. I was shocked to see that the scene I enacted where I hold off police in a shooting standoff actually took place in New Jersey about a year or so after that picture was released. The man, who barricaded himself against the police, was a decorated World War II hero, just like the character I played in **The Long Night** and who suddenly went berserk and killed a lot of people at random and then holed up in his room and shot it out with police. I have often wondered if he ever saw **The Long Night**. I hope to God the picture did not inspire him to perform those horrible killings." That man was Howard Unruh (1921-2009), who shot and killed thirteen people at random (including three children) in a berserk mass murder spree on September 6, 1949, in Camden, New Jersey. After police broke into his barricaded room and captured him, Unruh, who had been a sharpshooting soldier during WWII, had no explanation for his explosive killing spree where he randomly shot people he saw on the streets of his hometown, stating, before he was taken away: "I would have killed a thousand if I had enough bullets." He was sent to an asylum for the criminally insane and died there on October 19, 2009. For more details about Unruh, see my two-volume work, *The Great Pictorial History of World Crime*, Volume II (History, Inc., 2004; pages 961-965). **p**, Anatole Litvak, Raymond and Robert Hakim; **d**, Litvak; **cast**, Henry Fonda, Barbara Bel Geddes, Vincent Price, Ann Dvorak, Howard Freeman, Moroni Olsen, Elisha Cook Jr., Queenie Smith, David Clarke, Charles McGraw, Ellen Corby, Ida Moore; **w**, John Wexley (based on the 1939 screenplay *To le jour se leve* by Jacques Viot); **c**, Sol Polito; **m**, Dimitri Tiomkin; **ed**, Robert Swink; **prod d**, Eugéne Lourié; **set d**, Darrell Silvera; **spec eff**, Russell A. Cully.

Long Pants ★★★ 1927 (silent); U.S.; 60m; Harry Langdon Corporation/First National; B/W; Comedy; Children: Unacceptable; **DVD**; **VHS**. A lot of good physical comedy is evidenced in this oddball Langdon entry about a young man coming of age (although Langdon was forty-three when making this film). His mother, Brockwell, and father, Roscoe, have kept him childlike for too many years by compelling him to wear knickers or knee pants and when he is given his first pair of long pants, he ventures into the world, drifting away from his childhood sweetheart, Bonner, and going to the big city where he is inveigled into all sorts of risky pursuits by a vamp Bennett. When Bennett winds up behind bars for her underhanded ways, Langdon goes to her rescue and almost undoes himself while Bonner patiently waits for her man to grow up and come back to her welcoming arms, which he does just before the fadeout. There are many great sight gags and slapstick abounds in this appealing entry, but it has some very strange moments, particularly where the cherubic-faced Langdon, under the spell of the vixen Bennett, attempts to do away with the unsuspecting Bonner by luring her into some woods, but botches that feeble attempt in his imagined role as a "lady killer." *Author's Note*: Pantheon director Capra helmed this film, his last one for Langdon. Capra told this author that "Harry got a balloon head when he read that he was as big a star as Harold Lloyd and Buster Keaton. After that, you could not tell him anything. He then started telling me how to direct **Long Pants**. I took him aside and told him that his vanity was wrecking his career and that he had to put his professionalism before his ego. We finished **Long Pants** and then he ordered that I be fired from his production company. That is how I severed my relationship with Harry Langdon. All of Harry's films after that did not do very well and, when the talkies came in, he was pretty much finished. He was a strange little fellow with the kind of forlorn look on his face that made women want to protect him and mothers take him home as you might take home a stray puppy. He wasn't as durable and as inventive as Lloyd or Keaton and could never compare to Chaplin. He kept doing his same comedic routines over and over again until no one wanted to pet him or take him home anymore." **p**, Harry Langdon; **d**, Frank Capra; **cast**, Langdon, Gladys Brockwell, Alan Roscoe, Priscilla Bonner, Frankie Darro, Alma Bennett, Betty Francisco, Billy Aikin, Rosalind Byrne, Ann Christy; **w**, Tay Garnett, Robert Eddy (based on a story by Arthur Ripley); **c**, Glenn Kershner, Elgin Lessley; **ed**, Langdon.

The Long Riders ★★★★ 1980; U.S.; 100m; Huka Productions/UA; Color; Western; Children: Unacceptable; **DVD**; **VHS**. This well-crafted and superbly acted tale of the James-Younger gang accurately depicts the period and the colorful characters of that bygone and violent era when America's middle border was dominated by these most celebrated outlaws. In an inspired piece of casting, several real-life brothers enact the outlaw brothers on the screen. Stacy and James Keach play Frank James (1843-1915) and Jesse James (1847-1882). The Younger brothers are played by David Carradine (Cole Younger, 1844-1916), Keith Carradine (Jim Younger, 1848-1902), and Robert Carradine (Bob Younger, 1853-1889). The Miller brothers, who rode with the James-Younger gang, are played by Dennis Quaid (Ed Miller, 1856-1881) and Randy Quaid (Clell Miller, 1850-1876), and the Ford brothers, who assassi-

James Keach and Stacy Keach as Jesse and Frank James in *The Long Riders*, 1980.

nated Jesse James, are played by Christopher Guest (Charley Ford, 1857-1884) and Nicholas Guest (Bob Ford, 1862-1892). The film opens with the James-Younger gang robbing a bank and where Dennis Quaid needlessly shoots a teller before the gang escapes. He is later kicked out of the gang for his rash gunplay and where James Keach, as Jesse, throws him his share of the loot and tells him to leave or be shot to death. The gang then robs a train before its members split up, most going back to their farms and wives as was the routine of this gang. David Carradine, playing Cole Younger, who was the nominal co-leader of the gang, rides off to Texas where he meets with old flame Reed, who plays prostitute and outlaw Belle Starr (1848-1889). He gets into a knife fight over her affections for her common law husband, Remar (playing Sam Starr, a Cherokee Indian), besting Remar before leaving town and turning his back on Reed. Meanwhile the Pinkertons are avidly hunting the gang members and two of these detectives come upon Keith Carradine (Jim Younger) and his brother, Brophy (John Younger, 1851-1874) as they meet on a narrow trail in the Missouri woodlands. The detectives go for their guns, killing Brophy, but both are killed by the outlaws. The Pinkertons then raid the James farmhouse, believing the outlaw brothers are inside, and throw a smoke bomb through the window that somehow explodes and kills Thrift (the teenage half-brother of Jesse and Frank James) and so badly injures Ryan (playing the mother of Frank and Jesse James) that she loses an arm. The gang gathers with many sympathetic neighbors at a rural burial for Thrift and where many farmers go armed to protect the gang members. This actual incident, more than any other, backfired on the Pinkertons, in that it caused most of the rural people in Missouri to empathize with the gang, these peaceful farmers feeling that the James-Younger boys were being ruthlessly persecuted and they took to protecting and harboring these gang members for years—Jesse James was at large as an outlaw for eighteen years. The gang members then hide out at pig farm operated by Buchanan, but a huge posse attacks the place and Buchanan is killed, along with his hogs while the gang members, some wounded like Stacy Keach, escape. The outlaws recuperate with their families and some visit a local bordello, but all gather again to make a daring raid in Minnesota where they have learned that a bank is holding a great deal of cash. When the gang members arrive and attempt to rob the bank, however, the townsfolk, who have been warned of their coming, barricade the streets and begin shooting at the fleeing outlaws, killing a few and wounding others. The Keach and Carradine brothers, along with Randy Quaid, make their escape, but Quaid is dying from his wounds and the Carradine brothers are so wounded that they cannot continue to ride horses. James Keach insists that he and his brother, Stacy Keach, must leave and ride to freedom and David Carradine (Cole Younger) momentarily trains a six-gun at James Keach, but then puts up the weapon and

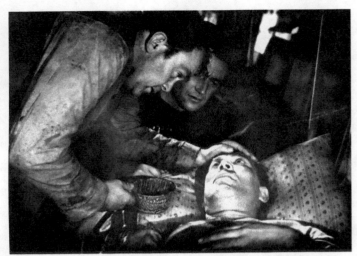

Thomas Mitchell, John Wayne and Ward Bond in *The Long Voyage Home,* **1940.**

says: "I like it better this way, Jesse—I get to see you run." As James and Stacy Keach make good their escape, Quaid dies and the Carradine brothers are captured and taken to a hospital where they refuse to give any information about the departed James boys. James Keach settles with his family and meets with the Guest Brothers (Charley and Bob Ford), planning another robbery, but he is killed by these two, which leaves only Stacy Keach (Frank James) at large. He goes to the top Pinkerton agent, Whitmore, and offers to surrender, but only under the condition that he will be allowed to bury his brother, Jesse, a wish granted. Stacy Keach and Whitmore are last seen riding in an open box-car, accompanying the casket of James Keach and, as they pass a farmer waiting for the train to pass, the farmer recognizes Keach and apparently understands his burial mission and removes his hat in respect. As the train goes off into the distance from the camera POV, banjo music provides an old song about Jesse James to end this exciting and bittersweet tale of the Old West. Hill's taut direction and his attention to detail, the fine and colorful script, the lush lensing and the costuming and sets all accurately portray these legendary outlaws and in more realistic terms than ever before shown. *Author's Note*: For more information on the James-Younger gang, see my books, *Bloodletters and Badmen* (M. Evans, 1995; pages 319-338), *Encyclopedia of Western Lawmen and Outlaws* (Paragon House, 1992; Jesse James: pages 172-189; Younger Brothers: pages 321-323), and *The Great Pictorial History of World Crime*, Volume II (History, Inc., 2004; pages 1342-1360). **p**, Tim Zinneman; **d**, Walter Hill; **cast**, David Carradine, Keith Carradine, Robert Carradine, James Keach, Stacy Keach, Dennis Quaid, Randy Quaid, Kevin Brophy, Pamela Reed, James Remar, Fran Ryan, Savannah Smith, Amy Stryker, Harry Carey, Jr., Christopher Guest, Nicholas Guest, James Whitmore Jr., R. B. Thrift, Shelby Leverington, West Buchanan, Edward Bunker; **w**, Bill Bryden, Steven Phillip Smith, Stacy and James Keach; **c**, Ric Waite (Technicolor); **m**, Ry Cooder; **ed**, Freeman Davies, David Holden; **prod d**, Jack T. Collis; **art d**, Peter Romero; **set d**, Richard Goddard; **spec eff**, Larry Cavanaugh.

The Long Voyage Home ★★★★★ 1940; 105m; Argosy Pictures/UA; B/W; Adventure; Children: Unacceptable; **DVD**; **VHS**. Ford again produces another masterpiece film with this dynamic tale of merchant seamen struggling to survive on a cruel sea during the early period of WWII. Based on four one-act plays by Eugene O'Neill, Ford expertly weaves these tales into a moving profile of lusty seamen attempting to keep their best civilized ideals intact as well as their hopes for a better day as they heroically face life-threatening hardships. There is nothing romantic about this hardscrabble adventure story where the seamen labor long hours. They are seen on their last hours of shore leave on a Caribbean island, cavorting with native dancers, raucously singing and

carousing. Only Hunter, a seaman who keeps to himself, and elderly Shields, remain on board. The men then stagger back to the tramp freighter to take another voyage. When the ship anchors in Baltimore, it takes on a cargo of explosives, which makes the crew members nervous, all knowing that any German U-boat sending a torpedo into the ship might blow them all to pieces. Before the ship sails, Hunter attempts to go AWOL, but is caught by harbor police and taken back on board the freighter. The ship then sails for England, crossing the Atlantic on its perilous journey and where happy-go-lucky Wayne, a young Swedish sailor, has only one ambition, to use his savings to help his family and, when returning home, to settle down on a farm. Many of the veteran seamen—Mitchell, Bond, Fitzgerald and Qualen—are very protective of him, and are dedicated to seeing that Wayne returns home safely to his family. Bond, however, is mortally injured in an accident while his shipmates stand guard next to his bunk and witness his death, despite the attention and care given to him by the empathetic captain, Lawson. Later, while the ship is blacked out at night, one of those on watch on the main deck sees a light flash and an off from a porthole below decks and the alarm is given. Someone on board, the seamen believe, is sending signals, possibly to a U-boat, inviting a German submarine to sink the ship with torpedoes. A frantic search is made below decks and the sailors find Hunter acting suspiciously in their sleeping quarters, which he shares with them. Fitzgerald then tells Mitchell and others that he has been watching Hunter writing notes and hiding them in a tin box and he then accuses Hunter of being a spy for the Germans. Mitchell and others seize the tin box and retrieve the missives stored inside. While Hunter is restrained, Mitchell reads aloud from one of the letters as Hunter agonizes, only to realize with embarrassment that he is reading a letter Hunter has received from his wife, whom he has deserted, along with his children, a loving and plaintive letter begging Hunter to give up his drinking and return to the family that loves him. Mitchell stops reading and places the letter back into the tin box and the sailors sheepishly release Hunter and leave Hunter to recover from the humiliation they have caused him as well as themselves. Hunter had been a naval officer before ruining his professional career with alcohol. (This is one of the most excruciating scenes of personal intimacy put on screen, one which lays bare the meager emotional privacy of sailors, who have no privacy in their cramped quarters and where their individual identities are signified and confined to a bunk and a small locker.) His past now exposed and secret told, Hunter resolutely goes back on deck to keep watch. Wayne calls from his post to him: "All's well, Smitty?" Hunter replies: "All's well, Ole." As the freighter nears England, it is attacked by a German warplane that strafes the vessel with machine-gun bullets. The helpless sailors dive for cover, and Hunter prepares to lower away a lifeboat in the event that the ship is sunk. While uncovering the lifeboat, he is struck and killed, the tarpaulin of the boat flapping over his fallen body as would a shroud and here Ford superimposes for a moment the rippling flag of England to signify the fact that Hunter, despite his personal failings, has given his life for his country. When the freighter finally reaches port in England, the crew members sadly watch Hunter's body removed and placed in a hearse at dockside while his family members arrive to accompany the body to its final burial place. When that party drives away, the crew members go ashore for one last reunion before putting Wayne on a boat bound for his native Sweden. Wayne's wages have been sewn inside his jacket and Mitchell, Qualen, Fitzgerald and others go ashore with him. They go to an inn and begin celebrating and are met by Kerrigan, a tout, who takes them to another pub where trollop Natwick waylays the unsuspecting Wayne, and where she doses his ginger beer with knockout drops. She patiently listens to his simple stories about his home in Sweden until he becomes drowsy. Then, a crew from another freighter, a hated ship because of its captain's underhanded practice of shanghaiing sailors, arrives and carries Wayne away, taking him on board the *Amindra*. When Mitchell and others learn that Wayne has been abducted, he and the others go to the *Amindra* and storm up its gangplank, fighting its crew members and finding Wayne below decks. They remove Wayne safely to shore, but Mitchell is knocked unconscious during the struggle and the *Amindra* weighs anchor, sailing away with the extra crewman its captain has sought, Mitchell. Qualen sees Wayne safely off to his homeward destination and then he and the other sailors straggle back one by one to their own freighter, the *Glencairn*, ready to go to sea and face more hazards once more. As the *Glencairn* weighs anchor and sets back to sea, a newspaper floats by the ship with a headline stating that the *Amindra* has been sunk by a German U-boat, with all on board, including Mitchell, having been lost, this news unknown to Mitchell's friends on board the *Glencairn*. This stark and uncompromising film that so realistically portrays the day-to-day lives of laboring seamen remains one of the great adventure classics and is masterfully directed by Ford. The pantheon director perfectly intertwines four fine O'Neill stories into one great sea saga, carefully developing his distinctively divergent characters and where Ford exacts from his fine cast unforgettable performances from Mitchell, Bond, Fitzgerald, Qualen, Hunter and Wayne. The cinematography from master photographer Toland is outstanding and where Toland uses to marvelous effect his deep focus techniques and where his inventive lighting, from sharp brightness to deepening shadows, accent and emphasize the film's many dynamic scenes. ***Author's Note***: Ford told this author that "Gregg [Toland] should get credit for the whole look of **The Long Voyage Home**. His cameras made the sea and those surviving on it come alive in that picture. No one could light a set like him. He knew just where the shadows should be and where to let in the light along a dim hallway or on a human face. In our setups, I would tell Gregg what I wanted and he always gave me more than I what I envisioned. There was no one like him." Wayne echoed Ford's endorsement when telling this author: "Pappy [Ford] always told the cinematographer what to do in his films, how to set up the lighting and get a composition to the best effect, but, in **The Long Voyage Home**, Pappy relied on Toland to do all that, and Toland gave him one of the most beautifully photographed pictures Pappy ever made. Pappy wanted me to speak with a Swedish accent in that picture and I told him that I could hardly speak English and that if I tried that accent, I would sound like an idiot. But he insisted and so I went to a Swedish actress I knew, Osa Massen, and she coached me on how to pronounce my words with the right accent. When I delivered my first lines with that accent, Pappy grinned and patted me on the back and said, 'you got it down perfectly, Duke.' I later learned that Osa wasn't Swedish at all. She was Danish, but that was close enough." **p**, Walter Wanger; **d**, John Ford; **cast**, John Wayne, Thomas Mitchell, Ian Hunter, Barry Fitzgerald, Wilfrid Lawson, John Qualen, Mildred Natwick, Ward Bond, Arthur Shields, Joseph Sawyer, J. M. Kerrigan, Rafaela Ottiano, David Hughes, Billy Bevan, Jack Pennick, Harry Tenbrook, Constant Frenke, Constantine Romanoff, Carmen Morales, Douglas Walton, Dan Borzage; **w**, Dudley Nichols (based on four one-act plays by Eugene O'Neill, "The Moon of the Caribees," "In the Zone," "Bound East for Cardiff," and "The Long Voyage Home"); **c**, Gregg Toland; **m**, Richard Hageman; **ed**, Sherman Todd; **art d**, James Basevi; **set d**, Julia Heron; **spec eff**, Ray Binger, R.T. Layton.

The Long Wait ★★★ 1954; U.S.; 94m; Parklane Pictures/UA; B/W; Crime Drama; Children: Unacceptable; **VHS**. In this taut film noir entry, Quinn survives a blazing car crash, but he loses his memory and shows up in his hometown with amnesia and no fingerprints. Police have been searching for him as a suspect in a bank robbery, but he has no prints that match the fingerprints left by the culprits. Still under suspicion, Quinn sets out to clear his name and four women, all with widely divergent personalities, help him in his strange quest. While probing, Quinn angers local gangster Evans, who puts out a murder contract for him. He not only manages to evade several attempts on his life, but, with the help of Kay, identifies the real bank robber, Coburn, who heads the bank. Quinn gives a standout performance as an innocent man wrongly accused of committing a crime he cannot even remember. **p**, Lesser Samuels; **d**, Victor Saville; **cast**, Anthony Quinn, Charles

John Wayne in *The Longest Day*, 1962.

Coburn, Gene Evans, Peggie Castle, Mary Ellen Kay, Frank Marlowe, Dolores Donlon, James Millican, Barry Kelley, Jay Adler; **w**, Alan Green, Samuels (based on a novel by Mickey Spillane); **c**, Franz Planer; **m**, Mario Castelnuovo-Tedesco; **ed**, Ronald Sinclair; **art d**, Boris Levin; **set d**, Howard Bristol.

The Long Walk Home ★★★ 1990; U.S.; 97m; Dave Bell Associates; Artisan Home Entertainment; Color; Drama; Children: Unacceptable (MPAA: PG); **DVD**; **VHS**. This engrossing film dramatizes the 1955 racial events in Montgomery, Alabama, when blacks boycotted public transportation because they were forced to sit at the back of a bus. Goldberg is a black maid working for an elite white family headed by Spacek and Schultz, and she feels she is well treated by them, but it is her duty to her race to walk to work in joining the protest against the city's segregation policies, even if it means she will be exhausted and arrive at work late. Goldberg gets up before dawn to walk to her employers' home, and, after a full day's work, arrives home late at night too tired to take care of her own family. Spacek is indignant about it all, not appreciating the significance of the boycott, and has no sympathy for Goldberg or other blacks. Both women gradually learn to understand where each is coming from while maintaining their own dignity. This excellent social film focuses more on the human side of the boycott than the actual event. Song: "Moonglow" from the 1955 film **Picnic** (George Duning, Steve Allen; sung by the McGuire Sisters). **p**, Dave Bell, Howard W. Koch, Jr.; **d**, Richard Pierce; **cast**, Sissy Spacek, Whoopi Goldberg, Dwight Schultz, Ving Rhames, Dylan Baker, Erika Alexander, Lexi Faith Randall, Richard Habersham, Jason Weaver, Mary Steenburgen (narrator); **w**, John Cork; **c**, Roger Deakins; **m**, George Fenton; **ed**, Bill Yahraus; **prod d**, Blake Russell; **art d**, Margery Z. Gabrielson; **set d**, Gretchen Rau; **spec eff**, Mack Chapman.

The Longest Day ★★★★ 1962; U.S.; 178m; FOX; B/W; War Drama; Children: Unacceptable; **BD**; **DVD**; **VHS**. Everything about this great WWII saga is massive, from its brilliant all-star cast (with its several directors) to its army of talented technicians, all wonderfully contributing in the recreation of a single day on earth, the day that the free world launched its attack at Normandy, France, to destroy the evil Nazi empire on June 6, 1944. Opening scenes and the first segment show the preparations of Allied forces as they ready paratroopers to board planes that will take them behind enemy lines in France to support the following amphibious landings and where ground troops board thousands of ships of all kinds for those beach landings. Ryan, who plays Brigadier James M. Gavin (1907-1990), discusses the hazards his men of the 82nd Airborne Division face with his subordinate, Wayne, who plays Lt. Colonel Benjamin H. Vandervoort (1917-1990), who commands the 505th Para-

Robert Mitchum in *The Longest Day*, 1962.

chute Infantry Regiment, which is to lead the attack. Meanwhile, the Allied High Command waits for just the right weather that will make the landings safe enough for the massive assault. Supreme commander, General Dwight D. Eisenhower (1890-1969), played by Grace, confers with British Field Marshal Bernard Montgomery (1887-1976), played by Reid, U.S. Lt. General Walter Bedell Smith (1895-1961), played by Knox, and others before finally making the decision to launch the invasion and, following a good weather report, gives the green light. The second segment depicts the takeoff of hundreds of planes carrying the paratroopers and their drop sites during the night before the landings and where German commanders have intercepted radio communiqués that make them believe that the long-expected invasion is in progress. British planes drop dummy miniature paratroopers that set off firecrackers when landing and this creates diversions and panic among German defenders during the night. Actual British troops land by gliders in other areas and, led by Major John Howard (1912-1999), essayed by Todd, capture and hold a vital bridge at the Orne River, holding off German attackers until they are later relieved by a British column led by Lawford, playing Brigadier General Lord Lovat (Simon Fraser, 1911-1995). Meanwhile, American paratroopers of the 82nd and 101st Airborne Divisions land behind German lines, many of them missing their drop zones. A contingent of these paratroopers land in the middle of the town of Sainte-Mére-Eglise and are slaughtered by German troops. Buttons, who plays Private John Steele (1912-1969), has his chute snagged by the steeple of the town's church and dangles from its roof while Germans fire at him. Defenseless, he goes limp, pretending to be dead. (Steele was later captured by the Germans, but still later escaped and rejoined his unit.) While these nighttime drops are being conducted, the German High Command is in confusion, with only a few of its generals responding with correct appraisals of the invasion, especially General Max Pemsel (1897-1985), chief of German intelligence in the area and who is expertly played by Preiss, and General Erich Marcks (1891-1944), an artillery expert played by Münch, who had predicted in advance and at German war games that the Allies would invade at Normandy, a warning wholly ignored by the German High Command. The third segment shows the great Allied fleet arriving off the coast of Normandy and its heavy warships begin bombarding the coastline to soften up German defensive positions. Steiger, the captain of a U.S. destroyer, tells crew members that they are part of the greatest armada ever assembled and that they will have a story to tell their grandchildren about this day in history, a story that will be told "long after we are dead and gone." Fonda, who plays Brigadier General Theodore Roosevelt Jr. (1887-1944), the eldest son of President Theodore Roosevelt (1858-1919), is shown meeting on board a ship with O'Brien, playing Major General Raymond O. Barton (1889-1963), commander of the 4th In-

fantry Division. Fonda has formally requested that he accompany his men in the first wave to land on Utah Beach, and O'Brien "reluctantly" gives him approval to go ashore with his men. (Barton later stated that he never expected to see Roosevelt alive again, and was amazed to see him after Barton himself went ashore; Roosevelt died a month later in his tent in Normandy of a heart attack and was later awarded the Congressional Medal of Honor.) Fonda later lands with his men at Utah Beach (Roosevelt was the second man to go onto that beach and under heavy fire), finding that the navy has landed them in the wrong area, but Fonda orders his men to go inland, saying: "We are starting the war from right here." As is the case throughout this absorbing film, a number of vignettes are presented to show the average soldier in battle such as MacDowall, a meek-mannered, bespectacled soldier, who wipes out a German machine-gun nest on Utah Beach, while talking to an American sergeant next to him and not knowing that the sergeant is dead. British troops are then shown landing at Sword, Juno and Gold Beaches. At one of those beachheads, More, playing Captain Colin Maud (1903-1980), the beach commander, stalwartly directs traffic on the beach while holding on to his pet bulldog (named "Winston" after Winston Churchill, then the British prime minister). When an armored vehicle stalls, More states that his grandmother always told him that with anything "mechanical, give it a good bash," and with that slams the vehicle with his cudgel and it miraculously starts. He then hurries lingering soldiers like Connery and others ashore, saying "this isn't Piccadilly Circus." American troops then land on the most heavily defended German position at Omaha Beach and where Mitchum, playing Brigadier General Norman Cota (1893-1971), assistant division commander of the U.S. 29th Infantry Division, along with aides such as Albert attempt to organize an attack while under heavy fire. The Germans, by this time, are in shock at seeing this massive invasion. Blech, playing Major Werner Pluskat (d. 1996), who commands a defensive position at Omaha Beach, is amazed to see the Allied armada from his bunker atop a cliff, and when he reports this fleet having thousands of ships to his commander, van Eyck, he is told that the Allies do not have that many ships. As Blech's position is bombarded and his bunker shattered, he shouts over a field phone to van Eyck: "Those five thousand ships you said the Allies don't have—well, they have them!" Blech is ordered to leave his front-line position and to command his troops from a post in the rear. He is later shown driving away from the beachhead and where a column of German troops is strafed and bombed by Allied planes and where Blech's car is wrecked and he is wounded, staggering with wounds toward the rear. As the Allied troops pour ashore at five beaches, Reincke, who plays Josef "Pips" Priller (1915-1961), a German air commander of only two fighter planes (his squadron has been dispersed to many other locations), is ordered to attack the invaders by air. Reincke and his wingman then fly to Normandy and make one pass over the troops coming ashore, strafing them and then heading for safety and where Reincke laughs hysterically, cynically saying: "The Luftwaffe has had its moment of glory!" The German High Command finds the location of the invasion to be a surprise as it has always thought the Allies would attack at Pas-de-Calais, that being the narrowest point of the English Channel between England and France. Hartmann, playing the overall German commander in the area, General Gerd von Runstedt (1875-1953) is thunderstruck with the news, as is Hinz, who plays the brilliant General Erwin Rommel (1891-1944), the famed 'Desert Fox" and the commander of all the German shoreline fortifications. Hinz is shown receiving the news of the invasion at Normandy while on leave with his family in Germany and where he calls himself an idiot for not knowing that the Allies would strike at that location. When Jürgens, playing General Gunther Blumentritt (1892-1967), who is von Runstedt's deputy commander, asks for Hitler's permission to use many German panzer (tank) divisions held in reserve to throw back the invaders, he is refused by General Alfred Jodl (1890-1946), played by Lukschy, who tells Jürgens over the phone that Hitler is sleeping and cannot be disturbed. Jürgens now realizes that at this moment, the war is lost and tells his aide to retrieve some brandy he has been saving for a special occasion. Meanwhile, Free French navy commandoes under the leadership of Marquand, playing Commander Philippe Kiefer (1899-1962), leads his men to the town of Ouistreham, attacking a heavily held German position with a heavy gun installed in a casino that commands the area. His men are being slaughtered (and for harrowing comic relief a bevy of nuns, who are nurses, resolutely led by Renaud, suddenly appear in the middle of the battle to tend to the French wounded) until Marquand, under heavy fire, briefly leaves the area and returns with an Allied tank that blows up the casino and allows the French to take the town. (This battle sequence is one of the most effective in the film, its scenes presented at ground level and with overhead crane shots where a 500-foot crane was used to show the French troops converging down many streets to get to their objective.) Another spectacular sequence (among the many in the awe-inspiring production) shows U.S. Army Rangers attacking the lofty German defensive positions at Pointe du Hoc, and where these heroic troops, including Wagner, Segal, Anka and Sands, scale the cliffs and, in fierce individual combat with German troops, take the place with high casualties, only to find that most of the huge gun bunkers have no heavy guns as the Germans never completed these defenses, causing a shocked Anka to state: "You mean we came all the way up here for nothing?" By this time Wayne, who has broken an ankle and must be carted along with his troops, organizes his men and moves into the town of Sainte-Mére-Eglise and becomes enraged when seeing that some of his men are still swaying dead from trees after having been killed in their drop by defending Germans. He orders a subordinate to "get those boys down!" He is then told that the Germans hold a strong defensive position on high ground outside the town and he orders his men to attack, saying that they will hold this town "until hell freezes over" or when they are relieved by more Allied forces. The worst fears of the Allies are realized, however, and despite all of the gains they have made that day, when Stuart, playing Lt. General Omar N. Bradley (1893-1981), while standing on the deck of an American warship, is informed that the first two waves at Omaha Beach have made no progress and are "floundering." In England, at the Allied High Command nerve center, British commander Genn and American commander Ferrer realize that, unless the troops on Omaha get off that beach, the battle, if not the war, may be lost. Mitchum is then seen commanding his troops at Omaha Beach, telling those cowering beneath a sandbank to obtain weapons from the dead and begin fighting the enemy. He then corrals Hunter, a sergeant commanding a demolition team, and orders him to blow up a huge concrete wall blocking the path of the American troops, and where Mitchum promotes him on the spot to the rank of lieutenant. Hunter gathers his men and places Bangalore torpedoes beneath German barbed wire, blowing this barrier away. While he and his men are under heavy fire, they place all of their explosives beneath the wall. While attempting to get to cover when carrying the wiring to ignite those explosives, Hunter is shot and killed by the enemy, but one of his men retrieves the apparatus and scurries to safety. After Mitchum nods to ignite the explosive, the charge is exploded and a gaping hole in the wall opens. Mitchum's men, cheering, pour through the opening and begin driving back the German defenders and where victory is now inevitable. Beymer, a paratrooper of the 82nd Division, is seen in various sequences—on board a troopship winning thousands of dollars in a crap game run by Buttons and who later becomes lost several times after landing in France, joining other units and then being lost again. He now finds Burton, a downed and seriously wounded RAF pilot at a small French farm where a German officer is draped over a stone wall, having been killed by Burton, who points out that the dead German tried to kill him, but he shot the enemy with his revolver and then further points out that the German is wearing his boots on the wrong feet, caused by his hurried dressing in responding to the invasion. Beymer then states that he has not fired his weapon throughout the whole ordeal, asking "I wonder who won?" That question is answered when Mitchum is shown at Omaha Beach, his men now victorious. He lights a cigar and says to his driver: "Run me up the hill, son."

John Wayne in *The Longest Day*, 1962.

The jeep makes it way up from the beach to join the columns of American soldiers marching inland. The several directors helming the various sequences for this excellent film do wonderful jobs in telling their segments of this great tale, stirringly enhanced by a martial score and where continuity, a foremost problem in welding all of the various sequences together, is marvelously achieved by editor Beetley. The production values are superlative, so effective as to make the viewer think they are reliving that titanic event by witnessing an on-the-scene documentary. The budget for this film, one of the largest ever mounted for a single Fox production, came close to $10 million, but its enormous box office success saw returns exceeding $50 million by the end of 1963, about a year after its initial release in October 1962. *Author's Note*: The film's exteriors were shot at the locations it depicts in England and France, as well as interiors made in Hollywood. Long a pet project of studio boss Zanuck, he had no problem in getting all the international talent he wanted for **The Longest Day**. Zanuck told this author: "After I let it be known that I was looking for the top male stars of the U.S., England, France and Germany, I was swamped with calls and wires from every big name in the business. Everybody wanted to be in that picture and just about everybody who was anybody in those days can be seen in it. That was a big attraction, too, for moviegoers, who sat in audiences and played that guessing game about how many actors they could identify in their various roles. That picture was a lot of fun to make, but it was one of the hardest jobs to do. There were so many separate stories to work into the story line that it became a nightmare to make them all work well together, but we did it by following the timetable of the actual events during that day. The script was already written for us by the real players—the heroic people who fought on that day—and they paid for that story with their blood and lives." One of the greatest stars of that day missed being included in Zanuck's all-star lineup. William Holden had been slated to play the role of the American colonel commanding paratroopers at Sainte-Mére-Eglise, but he had to drop out because of other commitments. "I replaced Bill [Holden] in that picture," Wayne told this author, "but I had to drop the role of the American general [Norman Cota] who was on Omaha Beach, and then Bob Mitchum took over that part. Nobody complained about these changes as we all wanted to be part of a film we knew would be a classic right from the start. All of us wanted to pay homage to those fine young men who fought and died for freedom on that terrible day. God Almighty, could anyone have any idea how it must have been for those boys going in at Omaha Beach? The Germans slaughtered them, but they kept coming and coming. Nothing on earth could stop those boys." [Wayne, a great patriot, was almost in tears when saying these words to me.] Mitchum, who plays the commanding general at Omaha Beach, told this author: "I researched that guy Cota [the commanding general] and he was hard as nails. He

Jean-Pierre Bacri and Virginie Desarnauts in *Look at Me,* 2005.

was in the thick of it all the time on that beach, grabbing GIs and telling them to pick up their weapons and fire back at the Germans, who were shooting down at them from trenches and bunkers on top of a cliff. Hell, it was like shooting fish in a barrel, and Cota knew it. Jeff Hunter plays a fictional GI, a demolition expert, who finally sets up the blast to make a hole in the wall—it was really a huge tank barricade, that was holding up the whole show—so that the troops could get off that damned beach. The reality was that Cota found a bulldozer on the beach that was loaded with explosives and he had a GI drive that damned thing right into that barricade and where he blew it up." Actress Elizabeth Taylor, who married Richard Burton two years after he made this film, told this author that "Richard called his part in **The Longest Day** as 'a plum role.' He said that all he had to do was sit in two scenes, one where he is drinking in an officers' club with another RAF officer [Houston] and another where he is sitting wounded at a French farmhouse talking to a young GI [Beymer]. I saw those two scenes and, to tell you the truth, he was just as good sitting down as if he had been standing up. Richard was always good in any kind of part." The heroism of those fighting that day is depicted in one scene after another, and few were more heroic on that day than General Theodore Roosevelt, who led his men ashore at Utah Beach. "Roosevelt was suffering from arthritis at the time and it was so painful for him to walk that he had to use a cane when he got onto that beach,' Fonda told this author. "He had fought in World War I, and here he was, fighting again in another world war. I only have a few scenes in playing this great man, but they are some of the proudest in my career. Roosevelt fought tooth and nail to lead his men onto that beach that day. He was an old man compared to the boys he commanded, but they didn't come any more courageous. What would we have done without men like that? I will tell you. We would have lost the war." Zanuck had a favorite character in this epic, and that was the real-life Lord Lovat, played by Lawford. "He was the most spectacular man that day," Zanuck told this author. "Lovat was with us in all the scenes where Peter [Lawford] plays him, and on D-Day, he actually went ashore with his bagpiper right next to him and was the first to get onto Sword Beach. We had photos of Lovat landing at that beach and wearing that light-colored sweater and Peter wore the same thing and did everything Lovat did, going at the head of his men to relieve that bridge at the Orne River. Lovat was one of England's greatest heroes. He had been on a half dozen raids, including Dieppe, two years before the Normandy invasion. He got shot in the stomach shortly after the landings at Normandy and had to have half his stomach removed, but six months later he was back with his men, crossing the Rhine to keep after the Germans until they surrendered. That man was the symbol of a fighting England, a country that would not quit, and was the only country standing up to Hitler until we [the U.S.] came into the war. Some critics said that Peter's perform-

ance was too flamboyant, but, hell, he was only doing what Lovat himself actually did. Those critics mistook heroism for flamboyance and I doubt if any of them ever had someone shooting at them." Zanuck personally supervised the shooting of all the exterior shots made for this film, and used as many as eight top cameramen for the Homeric chore. Ever the perfectionist, Zanuck insisted that none of the exteriors be shot until the weather matched that of the original climate existing on D-Day. Of all the stars Zanuck wanted for this film, Wayne was at the top of his list. When the movie mogul initially approached Wayne, however, the superstar turned him down. The two had had an unspecified bitter experience together in the past. "Zanuck kept pestering me about it," Wayne told this author, "until I told him that I would give him the four days of work he wanted, but only if he paid me $250,000. I thought that would shut him up and he would leave me alone. Wow! He turned around and paid me that sum and I did the role. I felt guilty later about doing that to Zanuck. I knew he was paying other top stars about $25,000 each for their cameo appearances. Zanuck gave me top billing. He wanted to use my name and he got it, so, come to think of it, I didn't feel that guilty." (In French and German for some segments; English subtitles.) **p**, Darryl F. Zanuck; **d**, Andrew Marton, Ken Annakin, Bernhard Wicki, Gerd Oswald; **cast**, John Wayne, Robert Mitchum, Henry Fonda, Robert Ryan, Richard Burton, Richard Todd, Sean Connery, Rod Steiger, Jeffrey Hunter, Robert Wagner, Kenneth More, Edmond O'Brien, Arletty, Bourvil, Paul Anka, Jean-Louis Barrault, Hans Christian Blech, Jean Servais, Red Buttons, Fabian, Eddie Albert, Mel Ferrer, Richard Beymer, Gert Fröbe, Leo Genn, Curt Jürgens, Wolfgang Preiss, Dewey Martin [role cut before release], Roddy McDowall, Peter Lawford, George Segal, Tommy Sands, Richard Münch, Stuart Whitman, Sal Mineo, Steve Forrest, Donald Houston, Alexander Knox, Trevor Reid, Peter van Eyck, Paul Hartmann, Werner Hinz, Christian Marquand, Heinz Reincke, Madeline Renaud, Wolfgang Lukschy, Nichols Stuart, Henry Grace, Bob Steele; **w**, Cornelius Ryan, Romain Gary, James Jones, David Pursall, Jack Seddon (based on the book by Ryan); **c**, Jean Bourgoin, Walter Wottitz; **m**, Paul Anka, Mitch Miller, Maurice Jarre; **ed**, Samuel E. Beetley; **art d**, Leon Barsacq, Ted Aworth, Vincent Korda; **spec eff**, Johnny Borgese, Karl Baumgartner, Joseph de Bretagne, Karl Helmer, Augie Lohman, Robert MacDonald, Alex Weldon, Wally Veevers.

The Longest Yard ★★★ 1974; U.S.; 121m; PAR; Color; Comedy/Crime Drama; Children: Unacceptable (MPAA: R); **DVD**; **VHS**. In this entertaining crime comedy, Reynolds is a former superstar quarterback who steals his girlfriend's car and winds up in a Florida prison among thieves and murderers. Reynolds suffers many indignities as an inmate and these incidents provide much of the humor in the film. The warden, Albert, talks him into helming a football match between the inmates and guards, led by Lauter. Albert ups the ante by offering Reynolds an early release if he throws the game so that the guards will win. Reynolds did that once before, but will he do it again? No, he and the convicts win. Lots of fun on the prison gridiron and in a swamp where Reynolds and another inmate play a Laurel and Hardy "tit for tat" scene in which each shovels mud down the other's boots and prison pants. Gutter language and sexuality prohibit viewing by children. *Author's Note*: The theme of a prison warden using his inmates to better his image through competitive sports can be seen in many films, including such productions as **The Loneliness of the Long Distance Runner**, 1962, and **Stir Crazy**, 1980. **p**, Albert S. Ruddy; **d**, Robert Aldrich; **cast**, Burt Reynolds, Eddie Albert, Ed Lauter, Michael Conrad, Jim Hampton, Harry Caesar, John Steadman, Charles Tyner, Mike Henry, Jim Nicholson, Bernadette Peters, Lance Fuller; **w**, Tracy Keenan Wynn (based on a story by Ruddy); **c**, Joseph F. Biroc; **m**, Frank De Vol; **ed**, Michael Luciano; **prod d**, James Dowell Vance; **set d**, Raphael Bretton.

Look at Me ★★★ 2005; France/Italy; 110m; Les Films A4/Sony; Color; Comedy; Children: Unacceptable (MPAA: PG-13); **DVD**. This above-average comedy is set in Paris where Lolita (Berry) is a pretty but plump girl in her twenties, a talented singer, who wants more attention from her father, Bacri, who is a famous but egotistical writer and publisher and who has a beautiful wife, Desarnauts, who is only a few years older than Berry. Berry is in a choir, rehearsing for a concert, and her voice coach, Jaoui, helps her because she hopes she can get Bacri to read her husband's (Grévill) new novel. Berry, meanwhile, falls in love with a struggling journalist, Bouhiza, who may have the same motivation as her voice coach. Everything comes to a conclusion on the night of the concert and Berry is a success, despite some intervening hilarious moments. Gutter language and sexual references prohibit viewing by children. (In French; English subtitles.) **p**, Jean-Philippe Andraca, Christian Bérard; **d**, Agnès Jaoui; **cast**, Marilou Berry, Jean-Pierre Bacri, Jaoui, Laurent Grévill, Virginie Desarnauts, Keine Bouhiza, Grégoire Oestermann, Serge Riaboukine, Michèle Moretti, Jean-Pierre Lazzerini; **w**, Jaoui, Bacri; **c**, Stéphane Fontaine; **m**, Philippe Rombi; **ed**, François Gédigier; **prod d**, Olivier Jacquet; **set d**, Jimena Esteve; **spec eff**, Daniel Lenoir, Frederic Moreau, Sarah Moreau.

Look Back in Anger ★★★ 1959; U.K., 98m; Orion/Woodfall/WB; B/W; Drama; Children: Unacceptable; **DVD**; **VHS**. This film is at the forefront of the "angry young men" tales stemming from a spate of novels and films that depicted the dissatisfaction, disgruntlement and even rage that male youths expressed with economic, social and political issues in the late 1950s and early 1960s. Burton is exceptional in a bravura performance of just such an angry young man. He operates a candy stall in a large open market operated by Pleasence; when he goes home, he routinely abuses his wife, Ure, with verbal insults, his reasons unknown, even to himself, but it seems to have something to do with his day-in and day-out routine of life. Ure's patience endures Burton's barbs and pricks until her close friend, Bloom, convinces her that she should not have to live like this and Ure packs up her bags and moves out. Alone and with no one to abuse, Burton fields about for more companionship and finds it with the unlikely Bloom, a woman he has loathed for most of the film. Their relationship offers little more than give-and-take abuse, with a few tender moments for relief. Ure, meanwhile, who was pregnant before leaving Burton and never told him about it, miscarries. She, too, is now depressed and alone and finds her way back into Burton's arms while Bloom slinks off to her own domicile and lonely existence. Ure and Bloom give standout performances as the females who masochistically seek Burton's love-and-abuse, which is about the same thing, and Richardson faithfully translates the Osborne play to film with a tight hand. Everything about the script is taut and unsparing, but its raw emotional themes may exhaust even the most patient viewer. *Author's Note*: Burton, who had been acting for a decade on film, came to the attention of critics with this film as an actor of immeasurable talent. He had been playing in epics and straightforward dramas, but in his role of an "outsider," he was able to demonstrate a much more far-reaching range of emotions while exploring the psychological makeup of the uncommon common man, who suddenly rebels against the status quo. Writer Osborne was not the first to probe these human depths. George Orwell, one of England's greatest authors, explored those dangerous regions with such works as *Keep the Aspidistra Flying* (1936) and other works where his protagonists defied, ridiculed and rebelled against the middle class way of life in England as Osborne and other writers, such as Colin Wilson (*The Outsider*, 1956), would do a generation later. We each of us yearn to live beyond the walls of the houses we build, believing, naïvely or not, that a better life exists in that unknown beyond. This film, through the magnetic force of Burton's riveting performance, and many others like it, such as **The Loneliness of the Long Distance Runner**, 1962, where Tom Courtenay essays a similar and equally fascinating angry young man, peers with alarming uncertainty into that always alluring beyond. Ure appeared in the original Osborne play and reprises her role here with great skill. She did not appear in too many films and was married to playwright Osborne and later married writer-

Richard Gere and Diane Keaton in *Looking for Mr. Goodbar*, 1977.

actor Robert Shaw, appearing with Shaw in another somewhat angry-young-man film, **The Luck of Ginger Coffey**, 1964. She died prematurely at age forty-three when she accidentally (it was ruled) overdosed on barbiturates on April 3, 1975. Both Burton and Shaw were very much like the angry young men they essayed in films. Both were heavy drinkers and both died at early ages, Shaw at fifty-one from a heart attack in 1978, three years after Ure's death, and Burton from a cerebral hemorrhage in 1984 at age fifty-nine. **p**, Harry Saltzman, Gordon Scott; **d**, Tony Richardson; **cast**, Richard Burton, Claire Bloom, Mary Ure, Edith Evans, Gary Raymond, Glen Byam Shaw, Phyllis Neilson-Terry, Donald Pleasence, S.P. Kapoor, Jane Eccles, Nigel Davenport; **w**, Nigel Kneale, John Osborne (based on the play by Osborne); **c**, Oswald Morris; **m**, Chris Barber; **ed**, Richard Best; **art d**, Peter Glazier.

Look Who's Talking ★★★ 1989; U.S.; 93m; TriStar Pictures; Color; Comedy; Children: Unacceptable (MPAA: PG-13); **DVD**; **VHS**. Alley is an unmarried accountant, who gives birth to a child after an accidental pregnancy to a married businessman, Segal. She needs to find a husband of her own and sets her eyes on a goofy cab driver, Travolta. The action is then told through the eyes and voice of the baby boy (Willis voiceover) in what became a hit comedy and made millions for its producers. This clever comedy provides a lot of good fun including scenes with the baby's cantankerous grandfather, Vigoda, and an eccentric aunt, Dukakis. Gutter language and adult themes including a difficult birth scene prohibit viewing by children. Song: "Cry Baby" (Jerry Ragovoy, Sam Bell; sung by Janis Joplin). **p**, Jonathan D. Krane, Simon R. Lewis; **d&w**, Amy Heckerling; **cast**, John Travolta, Kirstie Alley, Olympia Dukakis, George Segal, Abe Vigoda, Twink Caplan, Jason Schaller, Jaryd Waterhouse, Jabob Haines, Louis Heckerling, and (voiceovers), Bruce Willis, Joan Rivers; **c**, Thomas Del Ruth (Technicolor); **m**, David Kitay; **ed**, Debra Chiate; **prod d**, Reuben Freed; **art d**, Graeme Murray; **set d**, Barry W. Brolly; **spec eff**, William H. Orr (Bill Orr).

Looking for Mr. Goodbar ★★★ 1977; U.S.; 136m; PAR; Color; Drama; Children: Unacceptable (MPAA: R); **DVD**. Keaton gives an exceptional performance as a repressed woman in this disturbing and frightening film, but one well directed by the accomplished Brooks. She is a teacher of deaf and mute children and lives with a dominating father, Kiley, and whose mother, Pointer, is a woman who insists on nice talk only. Keaton seeks a "Mr. Right" in her life, but she looks in all the wrong places, going to singles bars, and sleazy pick-up joints. She meets Atherton, a straightforward young man, who falls in love with her, but he does not satisfy Keaton's obsession for exciting sex, so she turns to Gere, who displays a thick streak of sadism, and his offbeat and abnormal brand of violent sex arouses her, leading her to her last and fatal en-

Peter O'Toole in *Lord Jim*, 1965.

counter with an unhinged bisexual, Berenger, who finally meets Keaton's sadomasochistic demands and winds up killing her in the process. It is an unnerving tale of a woman living in two worlds, one where all is safe and secure and the other where hazards and risks lurk within shadowy bars and cheaply rented dark rooms. This film is not for the squeamish or faint of heart. **p**, Freddie Fields; **d&w**, Richard Brooks (based on the novel by Judith Rossner); **cast**, Diane Keaton, Tuesday Weld, William Atherton, Richard Kiley, Richard Gere, Alan Feinstein, Tom Berenger, Priscilla Pointer, Laurie Prange, Joel Fabiani; **c**, William A. Fraker (Metrocolor); **m**, Artie Kane; **ed**, George Grenville; **art d**, Edward Carfagno; **set d**, Ruby Levitt.

Lord Jim ★★★★ 1965; U.K./U.S.; 154m; COL; Color; Adventure; Children: Cautionary; **DVD**; **VHS**. O'Toole gives a stunning performance as a youthful seaman who, after disgracing himself with an act of cowardice, must prove his courage through incredible feats of bravery, costing the lives of many others as well as taking his own. Based on the great novel by Conrad, O'Toole's search for the redemption of male honor is no more daunting than Percival's indefatigable quest for the Holy Grail. O'Toole is seen serving as an apprentice midshipman in the British merchant marine under the watchful eyes and avuncular guidance of Hawkins, a compassionate skipper of cargo vessels. Quick to learn, O'Toole soon becomes an officer, but is injured and left in Java to recuperate. When he is well, he becomes the executive officer of the *Patna*, a tramp steamer. The ship embarks, carrying an overload of human cargo of religious passengers, Muslem pilgrims en route to the holy city of Mecca. The ship is engulfed by a hurricane and, within moments, it is swamped. O'Toole panics and, forgetting his obligation to his passengers, leaves the ship with the uncaring crew, saving his life. When he reaches port, however, O'Toole sees the rusty *Patna* already in port, having been salvaged by a French vessel. The crew members now scatter, but O'Toole's idealism compels him to go before a naval tribunal and admit his desertion. For abandoning his passengers, O'Toole loses his license and, in utter disgrace, is reduced to surviving on the waterfront as a day laborer. While helping to cart a load of explosives to shore, O'Toole sees one of the natives light a fuse that will blow up the cargo. He fights off the native and saves the cargo, delivering it to Lukas, its owner. Lukas then offers O'Toole a hazardous job where he is to take the explosives, along with rifles and ammunition up river to the remote village of Patusan where the natives are savagely ruled by warlord Wallach. The cargo is being sent by Lukas to his old friend, the chief of the oppressed natives. O'Toole agrees, but finds that he cannot use the motor launch promised to Lukas as its owner, Tamiroff, has been bribed not to lease the craft and O'Toole realizes that Wallach and his cronies have gone to great lengths to deny the arms and explosives to the natives, first by having one of his hirelings blow it up while O'Toole was a member of the cargo crew and second in buying off Tamiroff. Undaunted, O'Toole secures the use of a sailboat and sails up the river with the cargo with two native sailors. When nearing the village, one of the sailors, who is in league with Wallach, kills the other sailor and then dives off the boat, swimming to shore to warn Wallach. O'Toole anchors the boat and takes the cache of explosives and arms ashore, hiding it just before he is captured and brought before Wallach. Though he is tortured, O'Toole refuses to reveal the whereabouts of the hidden arms and this amazes Jurgens, who is Lukas' agent, but who has been bribed by Wallach to work for him. Lavi, a beautiful native girl, helps O'Toole escape that night and he takes the arms and explosives to the native chief. He and Itami, the chief's son, then organize the natives and prepare them to attack Wallach's heavily defended stockade. The natives attack and, after much bloody fighting, and where O'Toole ignites a barrel of gunpowder inside Wallach's inner sanctum, the warlord and his men are all killed, except for Jurgens, who hides in an underground passageway. O'Toole is hailed a hero by the natives and he plans to spend the rest of his life living peacefully with Lavi at Patusan. Jurgens, however, has escaped and teams up with the conniving Tamiroff and they then hire Mason, a river pirate, and his men, to steal the treasure guarded by the natives. They are foiled in their plan by O'Toole and are about to be killed, but the oily-tongued Mason begs for his life and that of his men, promising they will depart and never bother the natives again. He appeals to O'Toole's Christian sense of decency and O'Toole tells the chief that he believes Mason and that he offers his life as a guarantee that Mason and his men will not return to attack the natives. Once Mason and the others leave, however, Mason immediately goes back on his word and returns in one final, savage attempt to gain the native treasure. Their attack is beaten off, but Itami, the chief's son, is mortally wounded. Lukas arrives and pleads with the chief, his old friend, not to hold O'Toole to his promise. The chief gives O'Toole one day to leave the village, but if he remains, he will be killed. O'Toole refuses to leave and, the following morning, he walks to the chief, handing him his loaded gun and then walks away. The chief shoots and kills O'Toole, and his body, along with that of Itami, is then cremated in a ceremony honoring both men as heroes. Brooks does an excellent job combining a great adventure epic with a brooding psychological drama, for which he was inexplicably criticized by some distinguished critics who assumed the roles of protectors of Conrad's 1900 novel, but that was just so much posturing piffle as the integrity and substance of that tale was not violated by Brooks, who did the fine screenplay. The Conrad tale had been filmed as a 1925 silent and none of his psychological works translate well to the screen. Brooks actually enlivens the tale and gives it more flesh and blood than what the author originally provided. O'-Toole's performance is outstanding (and he considers this his finest role, despite the criticism he received in presenting a contemplative and pensive characterization, which was in keeping with the character Conrad profiled). Mason, Lukas, Jurgens, Itami, Lavi, and the rest of the cast are standouts in their roles and the production values are high in this stirring and memorable epic. Kaper also provides an arresting and unique score, played by gamelan musicians, which is all the more appropriate to the exotic settings of the jungle scenes. *Author's Note*: Mason told this author that "I enjoyed doing that picture with Peter [O'-Toole], although I appear only toward the end, and I play the most untrustworthy river rat the world has ever seen. I love playing villains and that character was my most villainous. I must admit, however, I couldn't hold a candle to the bestiality practiced by Eli [Wallach] in that picture. He did a version of Attila the Hun as a savage warlord, and he ate up not only the scenery but half the jungle during that production." Director Brooks admitted to this author that "I let Eli [Wallach] go full tilt in his character, who is a sadist and loves brutality, but it was like letting loose a cyclone. He got some bum raps from the critics for his performance, but if anyone should be blamed, it should be me. However, I still maintain that he and everyone else in that production were perfectly in character with what Conrad wrote." The film was shot on location in Malaysia, Angkor Wat, Malacca, Hong Kong, Lantau Island, and Cambodia, with interiors shot at Shepperton Studios in England. O'Toole complained that the three months of on-location work in Cambodia was "dreadful...sheer hell...a nightmare...all of us knee-deep in lizards and all kinds of horrible insects, and everybody hating us." Dith Pran served as the chief interpreter for the film in Cambodia. He would later be imprisoned as an enemy of the communists taking over the country in 1975 and would even later leave his native country. His exciting life was profiled in **The Killing Fields**, 1984. **p,d&w**, Richard Brooks (based on the novel by Joseph Conrad); **cast**, Peter O'Toole, James Mason, Curt Jurgens, Eli Wallach, Jack Hawkins, Paul Lukas, Daliah Lavi, Akim Tamiroff, Christian Marquand, Ichizo Itami, Tatsuo Saitô, John Richardson; **c**, Frederick A. Young (Super Panavision; Technicolor); **m**, Bronislau Kaper; **ed**, Alan Osbiston; **prod d**, Geoffrey Drake; **art d**, Ernest Archer, Bill Hutchinson; **spec eff**, Cliff Richardson, Wally Veevers.

The Lord of the Rings: The Fellowship of the Ring ★★★ 2001; New Zealand/U.S.; 178m; New Line Cinema; Color; Fantasy; Children: Unacceptable (MPAA: PG-13); **BD**; **DVD**. This exciting screen adaptation of the epic fantasy by J. R. R. Tolkien was a mega hit, making millions for its producers. An ancient ring that was believed to be lost for centuries is found and given to a young hobbit named Frodo (Wood). A wizard, Gandalf (McKellen), believes the ring is the One Ring of the evil Dark Lord Sauron, who wants to use it to destroy the universe, so Frodo must undertake a quest to the Cracks of Doom to destroy it. He goes with hobbit Sam (Astin), Legolas the elf (Bloom), Gimli the dwarf (Rhys-Davies), Aragorn (Mortensen), Boromir (Bean), and three hobbit friends. Their journey as the Fellowship of the Ring takes them over mountains, through blizzards, dense spooky forests, and across roaring rivers as they encounter evil and danger. Their goal is to destroy the one Ring and thereby end the reign of the Dark Lord. An animated version was made in 1978. Battle sequences, scary images, menacing creatures, and excessive violence prohibit viewing by children. **p**, Peter Jackson, Barrie M. Osborne, Tim Sanders, Fran Walsh, Jamie Selkirk, Bob and Harvey Weinstein; **d**, Jackson; **cast**, Elijah Wood, Sean Bean, Orlando Bloom, Cate Blanchett, Ian Holm, Christopher Lee, Ian McKellen, Viggo Mortensen, John Rhys-Davies, Noel Appleby, Sean Astin, and (voiceover) Alan Howard; **w**, Jackson, Walsh, Philippa Boyens (based on the novel *The Fellowship of the Ring* by J.R.R. Tolkien); **c**, Andrew Lesnie; **m**, Howard Shore; **ed**, John Gilbert; **prod d**, Grant Major; **art d**, "Peter" Joe Bleakley, Dan Hennah, Philip Ivey, Rob Outterside, Mark Robins; **set d**, Hennah, Alan Lee; **spec eff**, Steen Bech, Geoff Dixon, Dean Lyon.

The Lord of the Rings: The Two Towers ★★★ 2002; U.S./New Zealand; 110m; New Line Cinema; Color; Fantasy; Children: Unacceptable (MPAA: PG-13); **BD**; **DVD**. The sequel to **The Lord of the Rings: The Fellowship of the Ring**, 2001, begins where the first film left off. The hobbits Frodo (Wood) and Sam (Astin) and their friends continue their quest to destroy the One Ring and stop the Dark Lord from destroying the universe. As the Fellowship of the Ring meets more perils and battles, the enemy, Saruman (Lee) masses his army against the fortress of Theoden (Hill) and the War of the Ring is about to commence. The evil forces of savage gargoyle-like creatures attack the fortress of the good creatures, and where a forest of enlivened trees comes to the rescue. Plenty of action and adventure, but this digitally enhanced production is unacceptable for children because of scary images, violent battle sequences and excessive violence. **p**, Peter Jackson, Fran Walsh, Barrie M. Osborne, Rick Porras, Jamie Selkirt, Bob and Harvey Weinstein; **d**, Jackson; **cast**, Elijah Wood, Orlando Bloom, Cate Blanchett, Sean Bean, Brad Dourif, Christopher Lee, Ian McKellen, Viggo Moretensen, John Rhys-Davies, Sean Astin; **w**, Jackson, Walsh, Philippa Boyens, Stephen Sinclair (based on the novel *The Twin Towers* by J.R.R. Tolkien); **c**, Andrew Lesnie; **m**, Howard Shore; **ed**, Michael

Nicolas Cage and Jared Leto in *Lord of War*, 2005.

Horton; **prod d**, Grant Major; **art d**, "Peter" Joe Bleakley, Dan Hennah, Philip Ivey, Rob Outterside, Mark Robins; **set d**, Hennah, Alan Lee; **spec eff**, Jim Berney, Erina Fon, Joe Letteri, Dean Lyon, Eileen Moran, Jim Rygiel.

Lord of War ★★★ 2005; U.S./France/Germany; 110m; Entertainment Manufacturing Co./Lions Gate; Color; Drama; Children: Unacceptable (MPAA: R); **BD**; **DVD**. Good thriller has Cage as an amoral American immigrant from Ukraine living in Manhattan, who couldn't breathe without a gun. He is a veteran of war zones including Liberia, Sierra Leone, and Afghanistan, and is an international arms dealer in a business suit. When he isn't busy selling weapons, he takes time off to romance a beautiful model, Moynahan, and is pursued by an Interpol agent, Hawke, while one-upping a Cold War arms dealer, Holm, sometimes with help from his handsome cokehead younger brother, Leto. The film is positioned as a dark comedy, but it is hard to laugh at all the violence and there are no laughs involving Cage supplying guns that turn preteens into killers. Though this film makes a weak effort to present satire on the world of war today, the film nevertheless provides plenty of action. Excessive violence, drug use, gutter language and sexuality prohibit viewing by children. **p**, Nicolas Cage, Andrew Niccol, Norman Golightly, Andy Grosch, Chris Roberts, Teri-Lin Robertson, Philippe Rousselet, Douglas E. Hansen; **d&w**, Niccol; **cast**, Cage, Jared Leto, Ethan Hawke, Ian Holm, Donald Sutherland; Bridget Moynahan, Shake Toukhmanian, Jean-Pierre Nshanian, Jasper Lenz, Stephen Gregor, Kobus Marx, **c**, Amir Mokri; **m**, Antonio Pinto; **ed**, Zach Staenberg; **prod d**, Jean Vincent Puzos; **spec eff**, Yann Blondel, Tyrone Stevenson.

The Lords of Flatbush ★★★ 1974; U.S.; 88m; Ebbets Field/COL; Color; Comedy/Drama; Children: Unacceptable (MPAA: PG); **DVD**; **VHS**. A good nostalgic slice-of-life look at some lowlife high school pals with long hair and leather jackets, who organize a gang in 1957 in the Flatbush section of Brooklyn, New York. Filmed on locations in Brooklyn, the story follows the boys' street adventures that include cruising for sex, stealing cars, having a rumble or two with rival gangs, or hanging out in pool rooms or a candy store drinking ice cream sodas. One of the gang, handsome Chico (King) owns a motorcycle, but the girl he wants to take for a ride, Blakely, is the daughter of an army colonel and who is not too fond of his amorous advances, which she considers to be juvenile. Muscular Stanley (Stallone) is conned into marriage by a more willing girl, Smith. Winkler and Mace go along with the other two and are mostly wallpaper. It's an irreverent recollection of high school days in a time when street gangs did not fight to the death and their crimes were misdemeanors, not lethal felonies. Mature themes and sexuality prohibit viewing by children. **p**, Stephen F. Verona; **d**,

Peter Ustinov and Nick Nolte in *Lorenzo's Oil*, 1992.

Verona, Martin Davidson; **cast**, Perry King, Sylvester Stallone, Henry Winkler, Susan Blakely, Paul Mace, Maria Smith, Renee Paris, Paul Jabara, Bruce Reed, Armand Assante, Brooke Adams; **w**, Verona, Davidson, Gayle Gleckler, Stallone; **c**, Edward Lachman, Joseph Mangine; **m**, Joseph Brooks; **ed**, Muffie Meyer, Stan Siegel; **art d**, Glenda Miller.

Lorenzo's Oil ★★★ 1992; U.S.; 129m; UNIV; Color; Drama; Children: Unacceptable (MPAA: PG-13); **DVD**; **VHS**. Though morose and sometimes moribund, this film offers an absorbing character study in profiling the true story of a boy named Lorenzo Odone, who is healthy until the age of seven when he suffers blackouts, memory losses, and other mental problems. He is diagnosed with a rare incurable nerve disease called ALD (Adrenoleukodystrophy) that strikes only young boys and one that doctors say is always fatal. No treatment or cure is known, so his father, Nolte, an economist, and mother, Sarandon, a linguist, learn what little is known about the disease in hopes of discovering something to halt its progress. They get no help from doctors, including Ustinov and a foundation for research and treatment of the disease. Sarandon spends all her time nursing the boy, who becomes bedridden, while Nolte reads every medical book for any information on the disease. Their exhausting efforts lead them to discover a treatment using olive oil. But the film ends without the parents or anyone else finding a way to save Lorenzo, who died sometime after the film was made. Life-threatening scenes prohibit viewing by children. **p**, George Miller, Doug Mitchell; **d**, Miller; **cast**, Nick Nolte, Susan Sarandon, Peter Ustinov, Kathleen Wilhoite, Gerry Bamman, Margo Martindale, James Rebhorn, Ann Hearn, Maduka Steady, Laura Linney; **w**, Miller, Nick Enright; **c**, John Seale; **ed**, Marcus D'Arcy, Richard Francis-Bruce; **prod d**, Kristi Zea; **art d**, Dennis Bradford, Jamie Leonard; **set d**, Karen O'Hara; **spec eff**, John D. Milinac, Craig Barron, Krystyna Demkowicz.

Los Olvidados ★★★ 1952; Mexico; 85m; Ultramar Films/Arthur Mayer-Edward Kingsley; B/W; Drama; Children: Unacceptable; **VHS**. This stark and compelling drama profiles a group of teenage delinquents, who live a life of violence and crime in the slums of 1950s Mexico City. Their leader, Cobo, just released from prison, has become a criminal predator without conscience, leading the others to victimize even the poor not just for money but for the sadistic pleasure it gives them, especially the vindictive Cobo. They push a legless man off his cart and leave him helpless in the street, and throw stones at a blind man playing a guitar, who is begging for a few centavos. A naïve member of the gang, Mejía, hero worships Cobo, and tries to please him, but his conscience won't let him be as cruel. Mejía gets a job to help his mother, Inda, support her three other children, but Cobo interferes, stealing a knife. Police arrest Mejía for the theft and he is sent to a detention center.

A supervisor there sees hope for Mejía and gives him some money to run an errand. While doing this, Mejía runs into Cobo who forces him to give up the money and refuses to let him return to the detention center. They scuffle and Mejía is killed. This is a grim film, but one that realistically portrays the actual conditions in slum-bound Mexico City, a drama from pantheon director Buñuel that is considered to be a masterpiece of its genre, albeit its socially repugnant and brutal scenes places this entry much more into the genre of horror. Excessive violence and criminal exploits prohibit viewing by children. *Author's Note*: Mexico and Mexico City remains to this day a country and city awash with permanent violence, where the wealthy ruling class continue to subjugate the impoverished millions to endless squalor, and which has given birth to uncontrolled crime, particularly the drug-running cartels and their countless annual murders, which have spilled into the southwestern portion of the U.S. If nothing else, Bunuel provides a chilling portrait of those so unfortunate as to be born and raised in this cradle of brutal crime. (In Spanish; English subtitles.) **p**, Óscar Dancigers, Sergio Kogan, Jaime A. Menasce; **d**, Luis Buñuel; **cast**, Estela Inda, Alfonso Mejía, Miguel Inclán, Roberto Cobo, Alma Delia Fuentes, Francisco Jambrina, Jesús García Navarro, Efraín Arauz, Sergio Villarreal, Jorge Perez; **w**, Buñuel, Luis Alcoriza; **c**, Gabriel Figueroa; **m**, Rodolfo Halffter, Gustavo Pittaluga; **ed**, Carlos Savage; **prod d**, Edward Fitzgerald; **art d**, William W. Claridge.

Lost Boundaries ★★★ 1949; U.S.; 99m; Louis De Rochemont/Film Classics; B/W; Drama; Unacceptable; **DVD**; **VHS**. Ferrer makes a standout screen debut in this telling tale of a light-skinned black physician passing for white during the highly segregated 1940s. He and Pearson have been passing for white in a New England town, but decide to move their family to Georgia when a good position is opened to Ferrer. After arriving in Georgia, however, Ferrer is told that the position must be given to a Southern-born physician, although he believes he is suspected of being black after hearing two nurses talk about the reasons why he was not chosen. Ferrer moves his family back to New England and tries to get employment as a black man, but is unsuccessful. He is between two worlds that reject him on both counts. Since his wife is pregnant and he is now desperately in need of money, Ferrer decides to pass for white to more easily get a job and he is given a position where he saves the life of Stevens, a prominent doctor, who then recommends him for an important position in New Hampshire. Although he is encouraged to take a stand, Ferrer opts to remain passing for white in order to provide a better life for his family, which has already been traumatized when its members have been branded blacks and how their social lives have been altered and damaged through prejudice. Ferrer and all the cast members give memorable performances in this strife-torn drama and where Werker directs with great sensitivity. *Author's Note*: Producer De Rochemont had Werker take a docudrama approach to this story, which was in keeping with the producer's long career where he established the significant "March of Time" series. This was not the first film to present the difficulties of blacks passing for white. Of the many films dealing with the subject, the most notable are **Imitation of Life**, 1934, and its 1959 remake and **Pinky**, 1949. **p**, Louis De Rochemont; **d**, Alfred L. Werker; **cast**, Beatrice Pearson, Mel Ferrer, Susan Douglas, Richard Hylton, Rev. Robert A. Dunn, Canada Lee, Grace Coppin, Carleton Carpenter, Morton Stevens, Seth Arnold, Wendell Holmes; **w**, Virginia Shaler, Eugene Ling, Charles Palmer, Furlaud de Kay (based on an article by William L. White); **c**, William J. Miller; **m**, Louis Applebaum; **ed**, David Kummins; **art d**, Herbert Andrews.

Lost Horizon ★★★★★ 1937; U.S.; 125m; COL; B/W; Adventure; Children: Cautionary; **DVD**; **VHS**. In one of director Capra's greatest films and in one of his most magnificent performances, the handsome Colman is a courageous British diplomat, an expert on the Far East, who is seen from the beginning saving dozens of Europeans during a brutal revolution. He gathers these frantic refugees at a remote airport and orders all available planes to fly them out of the area before it is overrun by revolutionaries bent on slaughtering foreigners. He manages to get everyone to safety, remaining behind with a few stranded foreigners until the last available plane taxis onto the runway and then boards that plane with his brother, Howard, along with Mitchell, a conniving crook wanted by the law; Jewell, a prostitute afflicted with tuberculosis; and Horton, an archeologist whose fussiness knows no bounds. The plane roars off and all relax, bundling themselves with heavy coats and blankets as they climb higher and higher into the freezing atmosphere. Colman becomes alarmed when he notices that the plane is not flying to a safe city, but is climbing ever higher and heading toward the Himalayan mountain range and Tibet, known as the "Roof of the World." Colman tries to get into the pilot's compartment, but the door is locked and he discovers that the man flying the plane is Asian, not the European pilot all had expected to be in control. The pilot lands the plane at a remote area where tribesmen, apparently expecting the plane, refuel it, and it then again takes to the air. The plane soars ever upward and northward, until it loses its fuel and crashes in the mountains. The passengers survive, but find that the pilot is dead and his mission remaining a mystery. When the passengers attempt to explore their whereabouts, they find themselves surrounded in deep snow and resign themselves to a freezing death, until a strange-looking party of men arrives at the scene. They are led by a stately and soft-speaking elderly Chinese, Warner, who calmly tells Colman and others that they are being taken to safety and, after adorning heavy parkas, they begin a perilous trek, climbing upward through narrow gorges and craggy passageways, staggering through blizzards of snow and blindly following their unknown guides, until they come to a pass swept by howling winds. They cross a narrow rope bridge and into a small tunnel gouged into the mountainside and emerge into a sun-filled valley surrounded by high mountains. Shedding their heavy winter clothing, the travelers slowly descend into a beautiful world of well-tilled fields and verdant meadows called the Valley of the Blue Moon. The landscapes they behold are magnificent where water and the fruits of the soil are abundant. Amid this wonderful valley is an elegant lamasery of unusual architecture, a many-tiered structure surrounded by terraces and lagoons. The weather is mild in this sun-filled nation unto itself, which the natives call Shangri-La. Everything is plentiful from fish to the fowl of the air. Taken into the vast lamasery where they are greeted by marble-floored, spacious, sun-filled rooms, all elegantly appointed, the Europeans are given their own comfortable quarters and they soon learn that the strange land they have entered is totally absent of greed, hatred, crime and war. Tranquility and peace reigns supreme here, and these weary travelers soon recover their vitality and health. Jewell no longer suffers from tuberculosis, and Horton is excitedly immersed in the exotic flora and fauna of Shangri-La. Mitchell is full of enthusiasm and ideas for new construction methods and the troubled mind of Colman, who has been plagued in dealing with the problems of the world, has found peace of mind. He is further emotionally inspired when seeing a beautiful, young girl Wyatt, who seems pure of heart and untouched by the jaundiced and cynical views of the outside world. Only Howard is unhappy, suspecting that he and his fellow Europeans are somehow being held captive, and his imagination creates thoughts of conspiracy and plots that vex his mind and emotions. Colman, to satisfy his curiosity, goes to Warner, who is the first assistant to the High Lama, to learn more about the mysterious Shangri-La. He is told by Warner that the valley was discovered in 1713 by a missionary, Father Perrault, who established the lamasery as a sanctuary of spiritual contemplation and where the troubles and worries of the outside modern world were banished. Meanwhile, Colman and Wyatt fall in love and he is then asked to visit the High Lama, Jaffe. To his amazement, Colman discovers that the wise and all-knowing Jaffe is the actual Father Perrault, still alive at the age of more than 225 years. Jaffe tells him that he knows he is dying and he has selected the sage and compassionate Colman, a man he has long known about, to replace him as the High Lama of Shangri-La. Jaffe patiently explains that the plane carrying Col-

Ronald Colman and John Howard in *Lost Horizon*, 1937.

man and others was hijacked and flown into the high Himalayas, so that he could be brought to Shangri-La to fulfill his destiny and where he will guide the inhabitants of this sequestered world and preserve the best ideals of civilization while avoiding all of the problems of the outside world, which Jaffe predicts will be eventually destroyed by wars. Shangri-La, however, will survive, says Jaffe, providing a safe haven for those wanting to preserve the best elements, deeds and thoughts of humanity. "For when that day comes," he tells Colman, "the world must begin to look for a new life and it is our hope that they may find it here. For here we shall be with their books and their music and a way of life based on one simple rule—be kind. When that day comes, it is our hope that the brotherly love of Shangri-La will spread throughout the world." All of this is sweet music to Colman, who accepts his role as Jaffe's replacement, planning to marry Wyatt and live out a peaceful life in Shangri-La. His brother, Howard, however, considers this wonderful valley nothing more than a pleasant prison and urges Colman to escape from its alluring confines. Howard has fallen in love with Margo, a beautiful Eurasian woman, who also wants to escape, as she was brought to Shangri-La as a child and wants to return to "the real world." Although Margo appears to be no more than twenty, Warner informs Colman that she is sixty years old and that her youth and beauty has been preserved through the peace and tranquility of Shangri-La. Howard refuses to believe this tale when hearing of it from Colman and demands that Colman accompany him and Margo in returning to the outside world, telling Colman that it is his duty to live up to his obligations to England as well as to aid his own brother. Margo then convinces Colman that Jaffe and his chief aide, Warner, are lying and that these two old men are insane, and that they have made up the tale of near-eternal life existing at Shangri-La to keep the peasants at peace. Margo bribes some porters and they accompany her, Howard and a reluctant Colman as they leave the valley, climbing upward and through the pass. Once they cross the rope bridge, however, they are engulfed by a blinding snow storm and soon the porters fall into a deep ravine to their deaths. Colman, Howard and Margo struggle onward, but that night, Howard and Colman are horrified to see that Jaffe and Warner were telling the truth. Margo, who is now exposed to the outside world, literally ages before their eyes until she is a weak and wizened old woman, her face lined with deep creases and wrinkles, and that night she dies an old woman. The sight of Margo's shriveling, decaying body unhinges Howard's mind, and he ends his life by hurling himself over a cliff. Now Colman, alone, fights his way through blizzards in search of civilization. Wandering through the snowy wilderness, he finally staggers into a village and collapses. Having no memory of his strange experience, he is taken back to England, but when he recovers, he vividly recalls Shangri-La and Wyatt, the woman he loves. Colman immediately departs for Tibet,

Jane Wyatt, Ronald Colman and Margo in *Lost Horizon*, **1937.**

determined to relocate a world that, to all others, remains a fantasy. His friend, Buckler, appears at a London club and tells its members about how he had tried to restrain Colman, but how the adventurer broke away from his keepers time and again until he found a way to get back to the Himalayas. Buckler then lifts his glass in a toast to his ardent friend, saying: "Here is my hope that Robert Conway [Colman] will find his Shangri-La. Here is my hope that we all find our Shangri-La." This is where this tale ends in Hilton's wonderful novel, leaving the reader to wonder if the protagonist will ever return to the Valley of the Blue Moon; but Capra, in a stroke of genius, and knowing that millions of viewers who may have been inspired by Shangri-La would need more than their own envisioned conclusions, provides a dynamic visual ending to this great tale by showing in the last scenes, how Colman desperately and heroically battles wind and snow and impossible odds to reach that distant pass. Colman does find that pass and the rope bridge, crossing it to once more enter Shangri-La, his heaven on earth, and be reunited with the beautiful woman who loves him and has been waiting for him. That heart-pounding finale, as Capra so well knew, is the stuff that movie dreams are made of. His direction is superlative as he meticulously builds this great mystery and adventure tale in scene by careful scene. His character development is a wonder to behold, as he shows his characters altering their personalities under the influence of Shangri-La and where he exacts fine performances from all. It is Colman's film, however, from beginning to end, the story of a world-weary man of wisdom, who comes to believe that the best of mankind's dreams can be attained if one will search for them, even in Utopia. Colman gives one of his finest performances in this masterpiece film, one where he transcends from a cosmopolitan and somewhat skeptical man to one who opens his heart to love and embraces his innocent boyhood belief that all things good and glorious are possible. Walker's soft-focus photography fully captures the dream-like sequences at the lamasery and the astounding sets and special effects are breathtaking, as is Tiomkin's soaring and inspiring score, all greatly enhancing this superlative production. The film was remade as a musical in 1973, with Peter Finch in the Colman role, but it was a much inferior production. *Author's Note*: Capra told this author that "I did not really take any great liberties with the story for **Lost Horizon**, except for that ending where Colman finds his way back to Shangri-La. Those scenes are essential. If I had not provided those scenes, the viewers would never have forgiven me. When he finds Shangri-La again, you see, his triumph is also the triumph of the viewer. He has found happiness and peace away from a world that offers mostly misery and agony and self-destruction." One story, unsubstantiated, held that novelist Hilton based his character (portrayed by Colman) on British mountain climber George Leigh Mallory (1886-1924), who was one of the first to attempt to climb Mount Everest, the

world's highest mountain in 1924 and was seen close to the summit before disappearing (his body was found frozen and intact in 1999). "I asked Hilton about that character," Capra told this author, "and he said that he had a friend, George Leigh Mallory, who disappeared while trying to climb Mount Everest and how he disappeared, but someone in his expedition from below saw him going toward the summit. I think that Hilton was so grieved over the loss of his friend that he found a way to have him survive and wrote about him finding Shangri-La instead of death in his novel [published in 1933]." The name Shangri-La became a household word following the enormous success of this film at the box office. President Franklin D. Roosevelt (1882-1945) called the Presidential retreat in Maryland (then a secret) Shangri-La (and later named Fort David). After American warplanes bombed Tokyo and other Japanese cities during WWII, Roosevelt told the world that the planes had come from "Shangri-La" when, in fact, sixteen B-25 Mitchell medium bombers had been launched from the aircraft carrier USS *Hornet* on April 18, 1942, and was known as the Doolittle Raid, which was led by Lieutenant Colonel James "Jimmy" Doolittle. It had taken author Hilton only six weeks to write the novel, but it took two years for Capra to finish this great film, its budget eventually soared beyond $2,500,000, which was more than half of Columbia's annual budget for all of its films produced that year, an expense that, in Capra's statements to this author "sent Harry Cohn into screaming tirades. He was on the phone to me almost every day when we were in production, shouting and fuming over the costs. At one point, I could no longer hold my temper and shouted back at him: 'For God's sake, Harry, I am giving you one of the best films you will ever release!' He shouted back: 'What good is that to me if I am in bankruptcy and living in the poor house! Finish that goddamn Cloud Cuckoo Land thing now!' That was a literate thing for Cohn to say as I know he never read anything and 'Cloud Cuckoo Land' is something that the writer for **Lost Horizon**, Bob Riskin, had repeatedly said about the story, so Harry was getting that from Bob. It was a line from an old Greek play ["The Birds" by Aristophanes] and Bob was basically a playwright. Bob was a good writer, but I had to make changes in the script for **Lost Horizon**, and I think he secretly resented that because years later he complained that I took credit for a lot of his work, which I never did, but that is Hollywood. Bob, mind you, worked with me on a lot of good films and he always got the credit he deserved, but I did not need someone I worked with back-shooting me when I was struggling to finish **Lost Horizon**. Bob wanted to produce and direct his own films and he was cozying up to Cohn so that Cohn would let him go in that direction on his own. Bob wanted to find Shangri-La, too. I went over schedule with that film. It took about one hundred days to shoot it and I went more than thirty days over the schedule. I must admit that I got swept up in Sam Jaffe's character, that ancient guru living for hundreds of years, and it was like Ponce de Leon looking for eternal youth, you know. I had almost an hour's shooting on that character alone and finally cut it down to about twelve minutes. The film was almost six hours long when I finally got it into the can and we thought we might show it as a two-part film, but we knew that audiences would not really stand for that. My God, **Gone with the Wind** was only half that length when it came out a few years later and some even complained about the length of that terrific film. So I had to work with our editors to cut it down. When we premiered the film, it got a poor response from the audience, some even laughing at the serious scenes with the old priest. I was so embarrassed that I went into hiding, and then went back to it and began cutting all over again." Jaffe told this author that "Capra said that he had made too much of my character, the old priest, so he decided to cut down my role considerably and he reshot all my scenes. In those scenes, he used a soft focus, so that my features were not that definable, even though the makeup people put a lot of aging on my face with deep creases and lines, and Capra put a small light behind me that radiated about my head to give me a saintly look. I spoke almost in a whisper as if my words were coming out of a crypt or a grave and that was Capra's doing, too. I thought at the time, my God, if this man is two hundred and fifty years old, every breath he takes must be torture and I kept that thought when I delivered my lines. Capra told me: 'Everything about this man is ancient. He speaks in the tongue of a man from the past. His manners and his idiom must reflect his own time of hundreds of years ago.' Capra understood that character much more than I did." Jaffe's new scenes were written by Sidney Buchman, who refused to take credit for those sequences, and, when the edited film was finally released, it met with critical praise. It met with mixed responses from audiences, however, and the film did not recoup its initial investment until many years later through re-releases. So miffed was Cohn about the film's expenses that he withheld Capra's annual salary of $100,000 and the director had to sue his boss to receive that payment. The expenses were evident in every frame of this sumptuous film. More than 150 craftsmen worked for two months to build the enormous lamasery (near the Hollywood Way), which was 1,000 feet long and 500 feet wide, surrounded by lily-covered ponds, marbled staircases, lush gardens, sprawling terraces and patios, all done in the modernistic style of Frank Lloyd Wright and with art deco interiors. (The film would win for Goosón an Oscar for Best Art Direction, along with an Oscar going to editors Havlick and Milford.) To capture the high mountain snow scenes, Capra used a huge cold storage warehouse, shooting inside this place for his wintry exteriors (and using black-and-white footage of mountain scenes to supplement these sequences, which is why Capra later stated he could not shoot the film in color, along with the prohibitively expensive three-strip Technicolor process of that day). To show the avalanche that sweeps the porters to their doom, Capra used some stock footage from a 1930 documentary shot by Andrew Marton. On location shoots were made in the Sierra Mountain range, the Mojave Desert, Ojai Valley, Lucerne Valley and Palm Springs. So meticulous was the director that he insisted that all props and animals be in keeping with the exotic setting. He personally tracked down a collection of Tibetan musical instruments, particularly horns, some as long as eight feet, and one that had been retrieved from the high mountain lamasery at Lhasa and used these in the film. Capra converted yearling steers to yaks by covering them with long-haired coverlets and employed the same technique in using Shetland ponies to represent small Tibetan horses. Casting for this film was a challenge for Capra as he wanted Colman in the leading role right from the start, but Harry Cohn did not like Colman, believing him to be too urbane and sophisticated. Capra pointed out to the movie mogul that Colman was the leading box office star. In 1935, twenty-two of Hollywood's top female stars picked him as the most handsome screen actor, even over Clark Gable and Fredric March. Cohn knew Colman was an expensive proposition and, in order to save money, tried to convince Capra to sign up Brian Aherne, instead, but Capra insisted that Colman was "the one and only actor who could do the part," as he stated to this author, adding: "Ronald Colman was not just a great movie star. He was one of the finest actors on the planet with an inner sense for all the characters he played and that always showed on the screen and where viewers never doubted those characters." After signing Colman (who got along famously with the director), Capra went in search for someone to play the ancient missionary. He found A. E. Anson, a ninety-year-old actor, who had been forgotten, and tested him. He liked what he saw and called Anson's home, telling the actor's housekeeper to tell Anson that he had the part. She called back a half hour later, weeping, saying that when she told Anson, he was so overjoyed that he had had a heart attack and died! Next, Capra selected Henry B. Walthal, who had played the Little Colonel in Griffith's Civil War epic, **The Birth of a Nation**, 1915, but Walthal's health failed and he died before Capra could get him into the production. He toyed with the idea of using Charles Laughton for the role of the old guru, but then met and tested Jaffe and, after seeing a few minutes of Jaffe's performance, immediately signed him for the role. Jaffe appears in only a few scenes in this film, his part drastically cut down, but he is forever remembered for this role and for playing another Far Eastern character, an Indian water carrier, in **Gunga Din**, 1939. Howard was on loan from Para-

Julie Hagerty and Albert Brooks in *Lost in America*, 1985.

mount, and he is best remembered for this role, and one other, the arrogant and stuffy fiancé in **The Philadelphia Story**, 1940, directed by George Cukor. Although Howard later stated that he disliked both of these roles, he was grateful to the two directors who had given him these substantial parts, stating: "If it hadn't been for Frank Capra and George Cukor, I would be remembered only as the man who made love to **The Invisible Woman** [1940]." Much of the original footage shot for this majestic film was never recovered, although a latter-day version attempted to restore about seven minutes of recovered soundtrack not originally used. This was incorporated back into the film as it then stood at 125 minutes, with stills added to extend the film to 132 minutes, but this was a crude and ineffective attempt at restoration, a terrible revisionist version that is often and mindlessly foisted upon the public (even from Turner Classic Films, which should know better) and one that demeans Capra's imprimatur and drastically lessens the impact of this classic film in an effort to exalt those rather ghoulish revisionists. **p&d**, Frank Capra; **cast**, Ronald Colman, Jane Wyatt, Edward Everett Horton, John Howard, Thomas Mitchell, Margo, Isabel Jewell, H.B. Warner, Sam Jaffe, Norman Ainsley, Hugh Buckler, John Miltern, Lawrence Grant, John Burton, John T. Murray, Willie Fung, Leonard Mudie, David Clyde, Margaret McWade, Neil Fitzgerald, Ruth Robinson, Val Duran, Wryley Birch, John Tettener, Boyd Irwin, Chief John Big Tree, Noble Johnson, Victor Wong, Milton Owen, Carl Stockdale, Richard Loo, David Torrence, Barry Winton, The Hall Johnson Choir; **w**, Robert Riskin (based on the novel by James Hilton); **c**, Joseph Walker; **m**, Dimitri Tiomkin; **ed**, Gene Havlick, Gene Milford; **art d**, Stephen Goosson; **set d**, Babs Johnstone; **spec eff**, E. Roy Davidson, Ganahl Carson, Harry Redmond, Jr.

Lost in America ★★★ 1985; U.S.; 91m; Geffen Company/Marty Katz Productions/WB; Color; Comedy; Children: Unacceptable (MPAA: R); **DVD; VHS**. In this often hilarious romp, Brooks and Hagerty, a married couple living in Los Angeles, suddenly realize that they do not like their lifestyles. Brooks is an executive at an advertising agency and when he fails to get promoted and is, instead, told that he must relocate to New York City, he tells off his boss and is fired. He convinces Hagerty to quit her job at a department store and see America with him "like **Easy Rider** [1969]" and they liquidate all their assets, buy a recreational vehicle and set off on the road. They do not get very far after they stop in Las Vegas and Hagerty loses all their money when gambling at a casino. They drive to Safford, Arizona, where, out of money, Brooks takes a job as a school crossing guard and where he is ridiculed and taunted by obnoxious students. Hagerty, meanwhile, gets a low-paying job at a restaurant, working for someone half her age. They live in a trailer park and are barely surviving, realizing that they have traded an upscale and

Mercedes Ruehl and Richard Dreyfuss in *Lost in Yonkers*, 1993.

comfortable life for a miserable existence. They pack up again and head for New York City where Brooks pleads with his old employer to get back his old job. Brooks, whose sly comedy is everywhere in this film, directed, wrote the screenplay, and stars in this very entertaining production. **p**, Marty Katz; **d**, Albert Brooks; **cast**, Brooks, Julie Hagerty, Sylvia Farrel, Tina Kincaid, Candy Ann Brown, Maggie Roswell, Hans Wagner, Brandy Rubin, Garry Marshall, and the voices of Rex Reed, Larry King; **w**, Brooks, Monica Johnson; **c**, Eric Saarinen (Technicolor); **m**, Arthur B. Rubinstein; **ed**, David Finfer; **prod d**, Richard Sawyer; **set d**, Richard Goddard; **spec eff**, Dick Albain.

Lost in Translation ★★★ 2003; U.S./Japan; 104m; Focus Features; Color; Comedy/Romance; Children: Unacceptable (MPAA: R); **DVD**; **VHS**. In this amusing comedic romance, Murray is a middle-aged American movie actor whose career and marriage are both in trouble. He goes to Tokyo, Japan, to shoot a whiskey commercial for a quick $2 million. A much younger woman, Johansson, a recent Yale philosophy graduate, also is in Tokyo with her photographer husband, Ribisi, who ignores her and goes off taking pictures of rock stars. Murray and Johansson occupy different suites at the same upscale hotel, meet in the lounge, and become interested in each other. It disturbs her, however, when she discovers that Murray is sleeping with a jazz singer, Lambert. Murray does a funny turn when he needs a translator doing the Japanese commercial. Murray and Johansson, however, do not wind up together. They instead share something they will take away with them and which the audience can only wonder about. Perhaps their brief encounter fails because it is lost in the translation as they try to deal with their inability to understand Japanese. Sexual content prohibits viewing by children. **p**, Sofia Coppola, Ross Katz, Stephen Schible; **d&w**, Coppola; **cast**, Scarlett Johansson, Bill Murray, Akiko Takeshita, Kazuyoshi Minamimagoe, Kazuko Shibata, Take, Ryuichiro Baba, Akira Yamaguchi, Catherine Lambert, Francois du Bois; **c**, Lance Acord; **m**, Kevin Shields; **ed**, Sarah Flack; **prod d**, K.K. Barrett, Anne Ross; **art d**, Mayumi Tomita, Rika Nakanishi; **set d**, Towako Kuwajima, Tomomi Nishio; **spec eff**, Travis Dutch, Robert Rowles.

Lost in Yonkers ★★★ 1993; U.S.; 114m; Rastar Pictures/COL; Color; Comedy; Children: Cautionary (MPAA: PG); **DVD**; **VHS**. In this delightful romp, based upon a Broadway play, two boys, Stoll and Damus, go to live with their stern grandmother, Worth, and their scatterbrained aunt, Ruehl, in a second floor apartment above a candy store Worth owns and operates in Yonkers, New York, in 1942. Their father, Laufer, has deposited his boys in the care of these two unlikely female guardians after his wife has died of a long illness and he is compelled to travel out of town as a salesman. Worth, a strict disciplinarian, did not want to be

bothered in her advancing years with two budding teenagers, but kind-hearted Ruehl has insisted so she puts the boys to work in her store and they don't much like their new lifestyles. All that changes when their mysterious and fascinating uncle, Dreyfuss, appears, a furtive fellow, who is hiding out from a criminal associate, Miranda, after having filched a fortune from Miranda and which is kept in a black bag he carries everywhere. Meanwhile the boys are in search of the $15,000 their grandmother has hidden, believing that this money will help their father and allow them to move back with him. Complicating matters is Ruehl's romance with theater usher Strathairn, who is about as slow witted as Ruehl, and she is seeking $5,000 so they can marry and open up a restaurant she has been dreaming about all her life. Dreyfuss has only one ambition and that is to survive the goons that Miranda has sent after him for the next few days before he can arrange to get out of Yonkers. With a lot of twists and turns from the clever script by Simon, it all comes right in the end, but not without some very subtle and funny moments, including a few harrowing scenes to boot. The cast performs well and Ruehl is exceptional as the slightly unbalanced aunt with a head full of nonsense and a heart of gold. **p**, Ray Stark, Emanuel Azenberg; **d**, Martha Coolidge; **cast**, Richard Dreyfuss, Mercedes Ruehl, Irene Worth, Brad Stoll, Mike Damus, David Strathairn, Robert Guy Miranda, Jack Laufer, Susan Merson, Illya Haase; **w**, Neil Simon (based on his play); **c**, Johnny E. Jensen, A. Troy Thomas; **m**, Elmer Bernstein; **ed**, Steven Cohen; **prod d**, David Chapman; **art d**, Mark Haack; **set d**, Marvin March; **spec eff**, Bill Myatt, Daniel Ottesen.

The Lost One ★★★ 1984; West Germany; 98m; Pressburger Films; B/W; Crime Drama; Children: Unacceptable; **VHS**. Veteran character actor Lorre stars in this chilling and unrelenting crime drama, which opens at a refugee camp in Germany shortly after the end of WWII. He is working as a physician at this camp under an alias, calling himself "Neumeister" ("new man"), but he becomes unnerved when he is given a new assistant, John, who is Lorre's worst nemesis out of the past. They had worked together during the Nazi era when Lorre was a foremost immunologist and John had been his assistant. Lorre invites John to have some drinks with him at the camp's canteen. When they begin to talk, all of Lorre's bad memories come flooding back and are shown in flashback where he and John are working together when Rudolph, a Gestapo officer, informs them that Lorre's fiancée, Mannhardt, has sold the results of Lorre's experiments to the British. Lorre goes to Mannhardt that night, confronting her, and then fondles the pearl necklace encircling her throat before he grabs that throat. In flash-forward, Lorre tells John that he has no memory of killing the woman, but feels that he is responsible for her death and should be punished. Lorre was never named as Mannhardt's murderer as Rudolph and John covered up the slaying; in flashback, we see Lorre in 1943 meeting Hofer, a young woman who has taken Mannhardt's room in the same boarding house where Lorre lives. He begins a romantic relationship with her, but when his murderous instincts drive him to murder, he resists this terrible compulsion and later finds a prostitute, who takes him home with her. When she realizes that Lorre is a homicidal maniac, she screams in terror and he flees, taking a train back to his own boarding house. An air raid siren is heard and the train stops, all the passengers leaving, except for Lorre and Rausch, a lonely woman seeking companionship. When the passengers return to the train, they find the strangled body of Rausch, and Lorre has fled. Lorre blames John for setting him on this course as he has been instrumental in meeting his victims and he begins searching for John, but, instead, discovers a group of anti-Nazi conspirators led by none other than Rudolph. When the Nazis raid the hideout of these anti-Nazis, all are killed or captured except Lorre and Rudolph, who escape. Before Rudolph disappears, he tells Lorre that John is a secret Nazi informer who has brought about the raid and that he, Lorre, should kill him. In flash-forward, we now see Lorre with John, who has become quite drunk and who arrogantly tells Lorre to kill him if he has the nerve, not believing that Lorre will take his life. Lorre, however, has survived the war only to achieve that vengeful act and he shoots and kills John. He then walks to a train yard and stands on the track, turning his back on an oncoming train and covers his face as the train kills him. Thus ends this grim tale, the first and only film Lorre himself directed. *Author's Note*: Well-acted and with a taut script, this grim crime yarn did not do well at the box office nor with critics, who felt that Lorre was merely taking a leaf from Fritz Lang's crime classic, **M**, 1933. Lorre had appeared in that film, one that made him an overnight international star. In this they were wrong, as this film does deal with the same kind of compulsive killer, but he is not a child-killer as was the character in **M**, and the tale explores new psychological territories. If anything, it is a more conclusive tale about a serial killer, seeking vengeance upon his own acts and retribution through his own self-destruction. The stark techniques of this film, with all of its UFA production earmarks of deep shadows and sharply contrasting photography was no longer in public favor. In meeting with Lorre in 1962, the actor told this author that "by the time that picture was released, the public, especially in Germany, did not want to hear about the Nazis anymore. They wanted to see comedies and musicals and anything MGM was peddling. They did not want to be reminded of the terrible events of their past, so my little film did not go anywhere, except to a few theaters and, later, some art houses. I went back into character, playing one nut after another." **p**, Arnold Pressburger; **d**, Peter Lorre; **cast**, Lorre, Karl John, Helmut Rudolph, Johanna Hofer, Renate Mannhardt, Eva-Ingeborg Scholz, Lotte Rausch, Gisela Trowe, Hansi Wendler, Kurt Meister; **w**, Lorre, Axel Eggebrecht, Benno Vigny, Helmut Käutner (based on the novel by Lorre); **c**, Vaclav Vich; **m**, Willi Schmidt-Gentner; **ed**, Carl Otto Bartning; **art d**, Franz Schroedter.

The Lost Patrol ★★★★ 1934; U.S.; 73m; RKO; B/W; Adventure; Children: Unacceptable; **DVD**; **VHS**. Exciting adventure tale from pantheon director Ford has a British patrol scouting the Mesopotamian desert during WWII, their elusive enemy being Arab bandits. As the patrol rides single file over a sand dune, a shot is heard, and Clark, the lieutenant in command, topples dead from his horse. McLagen, a sergeant and next in command, is in a quandary in that Clark has never confided to him the patrol's destination and the map he finds on Clark's body tells him and his men nothing. McLaglen tells the other troopers that Clark kept everything in his head. McLaglen leads the patrol to a small oasis where they replenish water supplies and rest, but unseen Arab snipers begin taking the toll of the soldiers one by one while they fire hidden by the dunes surrounding the oasis. The patrol is trapped by the Arabs and none of the victims see the enemy that takes their lives. Finally, only Ford, Karloff and McLaglen remain alive. They see a British plane flying overhead and it responds to their frantic signals, landing near the oasis. The pilot, Wilson, a British officer, steps from the plane, leisurely tucks a walking stick under his arm and begins to saunter toward the oasis as if on a stroll in Piccadilly Circus while the troopers shout their warnings to take cover. Wilson is shot dead and with him goes their last hope of escape. Seeing this, Karloff, who is a religious fanatic, strips himself of his uniform and, wearing the rags of a mendicant, and holding aloft a makeshift wooden cross, then stoically marches into the desert, his mind snapped and calling to the unseen enemy to embrace Christianity. Ford races after him and, after Karloff is shot, Ford attempts to return to the oasis, but is also shot and killed. Now McLaglen is alone. He buries all of his fellow soldiers placing their swords at each grave, and these sabers gleam ominously as he also digs his own grave and waits heroically with a Lewis machine gun he has taken from the downed plane and at the ready for death at the hands of the ubiquitous Arabs. (This dynamic scene would be recreated in **Bataan**, 1943, where Robert Taylor waits for death after his patrol has been wiped out in a last ditch stand against Japanese invaders in the Philippines in WWII, and the story line for this film would be essentially employed in another WWII drama, **Sahara**, 1943.) The Arabs now attack in the open from all sides of the oasis, streaming down the dunes to fire at McLagen, who mows them down with the machine gun. Deci-

Boris Karloff, Victor McLaglen and Wallace Ford in *The Lost Patrol*, 1934.

mating the enemy, McLaglen shouts at the Arabs to come and get him, but he has apparently killed them all. A British relief column appears and when a British officer asks McLaglen about his men, the exhausted and dazed sergeant, who looks upon these saviors as a mirage, can only point to the graves over which are the upturned sabers, ending this exotic desert saga. Ford does a great job in profiling and developing the characters in this all-male cast and where all render outstanding performances, particularly the colorful Ford, the eccentric Karloff and the indefatigable McLaglen, who was a mainstay actor in many of John Ford's films. McLaglen would win an Oscar the following year for his magnificent performance of an IRA turncoat in Ford's classic **The Informer**, 1935. *Author's Note*: This was a remake of a 1929 film that had Agnew McMaster in the Karloff role and, ironically, Cyril McLaglen, who was Victor McLaglen's brother, playing the part of the sergeant. Ford was given a short schedule to complete this film and outdid himself, completing the film within ten long days of shooting. "I took everyone out to the desert near Yuma, Arizona, to shoot that picture," Ford told this author. "Everyone sweated and panted in the intense heat—I think it was at least 110 degrees every day of those shoots. I heard some of the actors complaining about the heat and I walked over to them and said, 'Look, if the animals can take it and the cameramen and crew members can take it and I can take it, then you can all take it, too.' I didn't hear any complaints after that." Karloff told this author that "my role in that picture is a man who isn't quite right to begin with and he acts peculiar right from the beginning so when he finally exposes his true nature, a religious zealot who believes that Christianity will protect him and he goes into the desert to spread the word of his faith to those who want to kill him for that very reason, well, his fate is sealed. I thought that Mr. Ford was very demanding but, unlike a lot of other directors, he always knew what he wanted and he always got what he wanted. He was not one to inspire actors to their jobs, but always demanded they give their best and it was his force of will that brought about the many fine films he directed." **p**, Cliff Reid; **d**, John Ford; **cast**, Victor McLaglen, Boris Karloff, Wallace Ford, Reginald Denny, J.M. Kerrigan, Billy Bevan, Alan Hale, Brandon Hurst, Douglas Walton, Francis Ford, Howard Wilson, Neville Clark; **w**, Dudley Nichols, Garrett Fort (based on the novel *Patrol* by Philip MacDonald); **c**, Harold Wenstrom; **m**, Max Steiner; **ed**, Paul Weatherwax; **art d**, Van Nest Polglase, Sidney Ullman; **spec eff**, Vernon L. Walker.

The Lost Squadron ★★★ 1932; U.S.; 79m; RKO; B/W; Adventure; Children: Cautionary; **VHS**. In this strange but compelling adventure tale, a group of WWI fighter pilots have found new careers as stunt pilots flying the same kind of fighter planes they have flown during the war but they now fly them in Hollywood films. They are, however,

Mary Astor, Erich von Stroheim and Richard Dix in *The Lost Squadron*, 1932.

under the thumb of dictatorial German director Stroheim, who sadistically demands that they risk their lives in every scene he shoots. A former German fighter pilot, he now punishes his old opponents Dix, McCrea and Armstrong by insisting that they perform impossible and death-risking stunts, seemingly dreaming up any kind of feat that might take their lives. When Stroheim learns that his wife, Astor, is in love with Dix, he plots to murder his romantic rival. He coats corrosive acid on the struts of the biplane flown by Dix, but Armstrong takes off in this plane and is killed in lieu of Dix. After discovering Stroheim's insidious murder scheme, McCrea and Dix take revenge when McCrea shoots and kills Stroheim. Dix then takes him aloft in a fighter plane and dives the plane to the ground, where Dix is killed in a fiery explosion, ending a death feud that had too long lingered after their war was over. Director Archainbaud helms this fascinating story with a fast pace and all of the cast members render standout performances, particularly the pensive Dix and the youthful McCrea. Stroheim does a parody of himself, mimicking his outlandish antics when he was a tyrannical silent film director, particularly his notorious tirades inflicted upon helpless actors in such films as **Foolish Wives**, 1922; **The Merry Widow**, 1925; and **The Wedding March**, 1928. He struts about like some Teutonic peacock, screaming insults at his actors through megaphones. In his every scene, he displays the brutish nature of the Hun. In one scene when Astor displeases him, Stroheim grabs her wrists with such force that he appears on the verge of breaking them. The aerial sequences that simulate WWI dogfights are spectacular and memorable. *Author's Note*: McCrea told this author that "Stroheim took his role to heart all right. He appeared to be a savage. In one scene where he is playing that director and supervising a dogfight, he shouts at an assistant: 'Listen, you, make sure and keep those planes in the cameras and get their action on film—we might get a nice crackup!' He was about as bloodthirsty as they come in that picture and I told him that he was so believable that I thought he really meant what he said. 'Of course, young man,' he replied, 'I mean everything my character says. He is the director and therefore he is supreme among all in Hollywood…including you.' I walked over to Richard Dix and told him what Stroheim said, and I laughed, telling Dix that Stroheim was pulling my leg. Dix did not smile and said in a very serious voice: 'No he wasn't. He is really like that. That man is absolutely crazy. He belongs in a lunatic asylum, not in motion pictures.' As the production went on, Stroheim was as abusive behind the cameras as he was in front of them, insulting everyone and I told Dix that I was growing to hate this man. 'That's exactly what he wants,' Dix said. 'He knows no one loves him, so, for him, hatred is the next best thing.'" d, George Archainbaud; cast, Richard Dix, Mary Astor, Erich von Stroheim, Dorothy Jordan, Joel McCrea, Robert Armstrong, Hugh Herbert, Ralph Ince, Marjorie Peterson, Ralph Lewis; w, Wallace Smith, Herman J.

Mankiewicz, Robert S. Presnell, Humphrey Pearson (based on a story by Dick Grace); c, Edward Cronjager, Leo Tover; m, Max Steiner; ed, William Hamilton.

The Lost Weekend ★★★★★ 1945; U.S.; 101m; PAR; B/W; Drama; Children: Unacceptable; **DVD**; **VHS**. Under the brilliant direction of Wilder, Ray Milland is magnificent in delivering the performance of his life (and for which he won an Oscar as Best Actor) as a writer consumed by an insidious alcoholic condition. His struggle with that addiction is the stuff of true horror, an excruciating experience in human failure and spiritual redemption. This devastating and utterly captivating film opens with the camera zooming in on a New York City apartment window and entering that apartment to show writer Milland at his typewriter about to write his opus while his down-to-earth brother Terry prepares to leave on a weekend business trip. Terry is apprehensive about leaving his brother to his own devices, knowing he is an alcoholic. Milland assures him, however, that all is well and that he is settling down to write some very serious prose. Terry leaves money in a sugar bowl for the cleaning lady and departs while showing considerable apprehension. As soon as he departs, Milland retrieves one of the many bottles of booze he has inventively hidden about the apartment—on a rope dangling from a window ledge, another in a ceiling light fixture, beneath furniture and behind books in a bookcase. He begins to drink as he stares at a blank page rolled into his typewriter. He drinks and writes nothing until he empties the bottle. When the cleaning lady arrives, Milland learns from her that his brother has left her wages in a sugar bowl. He retrieves the cash and then lies to the woman, telling her that Terry forgot to leave her money and asks her to come back another day. Milland, now fortified with money, leaves his apartment and goes to his favorite watering hole, a saloon operated by Da Silva, a compassionate and knowing bartender. Milland buys a drink and then another, becoming eloquent and verbally writing for Da Silva and other patrons in the bar. He points to the street and says: "That's not Third Avenue out there—it's the Nile," and proceeds to describe the grand barge gliding down that legendary river and carrying Cleopatra toward her fatal rendezvous with Marc Antony. Urbane, witty and even inspiring, Milland amuses himself and Da Silva and anyone else who will listen to his literary meanderings where booze unleashes the wellsprings of Milland's fertile imagination. As he entertains himself and others, Milland ruefully counts the number of wet rings left on the bar by the shot glasses of liquor he drinks. Running out of money, Milland begs Da Silva for more booze, but the sympathetic bartender urges him to go home. Meanwhile, his devoted girlfriend, Wyman, a magazine editor, is calling him at his apartment and, when not getting any answer, begins searching for him. In order to obtain more money to buy booze, Milland plays up to Dowling, a call girl who is attracted to his glib conversation and wry wit. He flatters her and she gives him some money and he continues drinking. Running out of cash, Milland goes to an upscale nightclub and sits next to a couple. When the woman goes to a washroom, Milland rummages through her purse, taking some cash, but he is discovered. Rather than press charges, the woman takes pity on Milland, who now looks gaunt and drawn, and he is evicted from the club. Staggering and weak, Milland returns to his apartment where he finds another hidden bottle and begins drowning himself once again, this time hallucinating as liquor has now seized his mind. He suddenly sees a bat flying wildly about the room and he cringes in horror from it in his chair as it dives and sails and shrieks, terrifying him. He then sees a mouse emerge from the crack in a wall and the bat pounces upon it, tearing it to pieces as the prey squeals in agony, its blood gruesomely trickling down the wall. Milland screams in utter terror and he collapses in a faint. Later sobering, he recalls the woman who loves him and whom he loves, Wyman, remembering how they met, and we see a flashback showing both of them claiming their coats following a concert and how embarrassed Milland is when Wyman sees a bottle of liquor tucked into his coat. He also remembers her fur coat, her prized possession and how, after they began their relationship, he pawned that coat to buy liquor, but how she nevertheless forgave him, knowing of his terrible affliction. In flash-forward we now see Milland attempting to recover from his last bout with booze, but still craving alcohol. He attempts to pawn his typewriter to get money to buy liquor but the pawnshops are closed as it is Yom Kippur and the pawnbrokers have locked up their stores. He next goes to Da Silva's saloon and tries to trade in his typewriter, the very symbol of his professional future, for free drinks from Da Silva. The bartender is now disgusted with him, refusing and saying: "You're the writer, Mr. Birnam, not me." Milland staggers from the saloon and wanders down the street, appearing to be a hopeless, meandering vagrant, unshaven, bedraggled and forlorn to the world. Exhausted and weak, he finally collapses in a gutter and is found and taken to Bellevue Hospital, locked up in the alcoholic ward and where he awakes to see Faylen, a male nurse, hovering over him. Faylen sadistically tells him that he is now in the company of raving lunatics who, as night deepens, will have all sorts of hallucinations and will begin screaming so that many of them must be strapped down in their beds. He brutally adds with a satanic smile before leaving the ward and turning off the lights that he was talking to "the doctor the other day and he told me that delirium tremens is a disease of the night. Well... good night." As Faylen predicted, the inmates in the beds next to Milland begin to squirm, toss about, and finally, many of them begin seeing the same kind of terrible visions experienced earlier by Milland. Unable to bear this collective agony, and while some attendants unlock the ward door to rush forward and subdue some of the patients, Milland slips into a hallway, dons the overcoat of a physician, and, using his medical identification card, escapes the hospital. He returns home, utterly fatigued, his lost weekend over. The next day, he opens the door to let Wyman into his apartment. He is clean shaven and assures her everything is all right, but breaks off their relationship, telling her that it is the best for both of them. Wyman is about to leave when she sees a revolver half-hidden from her sight and then realizes that Milland intends to take his own life. They struggle with the weapon and he pleads with her that it is the only way out for both of them. There is a knock at the door. It is Da Silva, who delivers Milland's portable typewriter, telling him that he thought he would need it if he is to write that book he has been talking about, adding that he cleaned the typewriter and that "it works pretty good." Wyman seizes upon this visit to convince Milland that Da Silva's visit was a sign that Milland is to go on living. She tells him that his life is important, and she will stay with him in battling his disease and that together they can overcome it and have a happy life together. Milland and, with Wyman's strong emotional support, resolves to quit drinking, vowing to never drink again. He sits down at his typewriter, rolls a piece of paper into it and types the title of his book, "The Bottle" and we then hear Milland in voiceover as the camera moves through the apartment and out the window, exiting as it has arrived at the beginning of this masterpiece, with Milland ostensibly writing his opening narrative for his book: "And out there in that great big concrete jungle, I wonder how many others that are like me. Poor bedeviled guys on fire with thirst. Such comical figures to the rest of the world as they stagger blindly toward another binge, another bender, another spree..." Wilder's direction is impeccable, carefully building each scene until he crescendos the story with his nightmare visions, all emphasized with his mesmerizing low-key lighting and deep focus photography. Every scene in this riveting and compassionate film belongs to Milland, where he presents an astounding performance transforming from an apparently normal and charming young man to a conniving and wholly untrustworthy human being, as he slowly becomes the slave to the devilish and insidious addiction within him, a modern-day version of Dr. Jekyll and Mr. Hyde, except that the murderer lurking within is out to destroy only one person, himself. This superb film, with its fine supporting cast (Wyman, Terry, Dowling and Da Silva are standouts), though depressing and as debilitating for the viewer as it is for its agonizing protagonist, nevertheless brilliantly inspires at its conclusion where sobriety and reason triumphs over delusion and addiction. It is a film that should be viewed by every

Ray Milland and Jane Wyman in *The Lost Weekend*, 1945.

alcoholic attempting to regain sobriety (whether electing to go to that salvation through the fine organization of Alcoholics Anonymous or to go toward that shining hope alone). This masterpiece gleaned many Academy Awards, winning Best Picture, Best Director (Wilder), Best Actor (Milland), and Best Adapted Screenplay (Brackett and Wilder). Rozsa's dynamic and sometimes eerie score is superlative and he was nominated for an Oscar, but won for his musical score (equally chilling) for another classic film that year, Alfred Hitchcock's **Spellbound**, 1945. *Author's Note*: Once Wilder had the film in the can, however, as he stated to this author, "Paramount had second thoughts about releasing it. They thought it was too depressing, too morose. A lot of powerful organizations wanted that film destroyed and never exhibited. Temperance leaders and their organizations had gotten wind of the picture and were already pressuring the studio to dump it and some liquor organizations, I heard, had offered several million dollars if Paramount would destroy all the prints and the original negative. Also, the front office did not like Milland, who was a matinee idol, playing such a boozy bum-like character. You know, before that picture, Hollywood mostly showed drunks as funny characters and some actors like Leon Errol and Jack Norton [who was a teetotaler] played comic drunks for decades in the movies. That's how the public thought about these stew-bums, just funny little characters with wobbly legs, slipping and collapsing sideways in pratfalls. But that was not the truth or the real case as drunks are pathetic victims of booze, living without purpose or control of their lives. These diseased and miserable creatures were shunned and forgotten when you saw them on the street. God knows, I have seen my share of them in Hollywood, even great actors and actresses, turning into slobbering animals, losing themselves inside the bottle and throwing away great careers. John Barrymore was one of those poor souls and Errol Flynn, who was a buddy of Barrymore's, was on his way to the same destination, until he got control of himself. They thought that by drinking themselves into stupors they somehow got to be more animated and became more interesting people, but they only turned themselves into obnoxious jerks. They thought their slurring insults were witty and memorable when they were simply insults. Well, I argued like hell with the front office for **The Lost Weekend** and they released it and everybody, including myself, was surprised to see the critics falling all over themselves to praise it and the public jamming theaters to see it. That picture did not damage the liquor business, but I think it helped a lot of alcoholics to take stock of their lives and maybe altered their way of life. After that picture, a lot of Hollywood big shots looked at me as a serious director." Wilder was a man who would fight for what he knew would work best in his films. Even though he did not personally like Faylen, the character actor who portrays the vindictive male nurse, the director fought to have Faylen in his film. "Producers wanted me to cast Jack Oakie or Lee

Ray Milland and Howard Da Silva in *The Lost Weekend*, 1945.

Tracy in that role," Wilder told this author, "but I said that I wanted Faylen for that part. He had that kind of repulsive wise-guy attitude for the character where he really doesn't give a damn about the suffering people he is taking care of, and, in fact, resents dealing with these people. He doesn't care whether they live or die." Milland had deep reservations about his role in this film. He was given the brilliant script by Wilder and Brackett by Paramount producer Buddy DeSylva, who wrote a terse note to the actor, stating: "Read it. Study it. You're going to play it." Milland (who was a Paramount contract player, 1934-1948) resisted, thinking he could not do the character justice, but his wife, Muriel, encouraged him to undertake the role. "I did not want any part of that character," Milland told this author. "I thought he was and the story was box office poison, but then everyone kept telling me that I could not lose since Wilder and Brackett, the two smart fellows who wrote the script, had never had a flop. I went ahead with it and that meant going on a severe diet and I even tried over-drinking and that made me sick. By the time we went into production, I had just the right appearance of a gaunt and haggard person. Before that, I did a lot of my own research in New York City, where we did a lot of on-location shooting, but that got me into more trouble than you can imagine." Milland, before the film went into production, contacted a New York City physician, who arranged for Milland to be admitted to Bellevue's alcoholic ward. He was given a plain iron bed, pajamas, slippers and a robe with the hospital's name on it and his clothes were taken away. He planned to spend the night in this ward, but soon became alarmed when the lights were dimmed and the dozens of inmates in neighboring beds began to weep, talk gibberish and some began screaming so that attendants rushed into the ward to strap them down to their beds. An attendant told Milland that most of the patients were former advertising executives and one was the former mayor of a large city. He was given a drink that was given to all inmates at night, paraldehyde, which was designed to settle the stomachs of patients, but it made Milland so sick that he vomited. Milland finally managed to get to sleep, but, in the middle of the night, attendants brought in another patient, who was hysterical and struggling with them and screaming at the top of his lungs. He awoke all the others, and suddenly the place was filled with shouting, screams and "the foulest obscenities I have ever heard," said Milland. "The place had turned into a snake pit and I was staring straight into it. I had to get out of there and right away if I wanted to keep my own senses." Wearing only a bathrobe and forgetting his slippers, Milland raced through the open door and down a back stairway to find an exit on Thirty-Fourth Street. He ran barefooted toward a cab stand, intending to take a taxi back to his hotel, but a cop stopped him. When Milland explained that he was a Hollywood actor doing research for a film, the cop, who did not recognize him, or apparently see his films, saw the robe he was wearing with the Bellevue im-

primatur on it and immediately stepped on Milland's bare feet to corral him. The cop escorted Milland back to Bellevue where the actor had to talk to newly arrived attendants that he was not really a patient, but an actor doing research for a film. After a half hour of such pleadings, he was released. When Milland told Wilder about this odd experience, the inventive director-writer immediately added the Bellevue scene into the script and shot that scene, one of the most frightening in this film, in that ward in Bellevue. The hospital later regretted giving Wilder permission to use its confines as it showed a stark and grim institution, and when director George Seaton later wanted the same permission to shoot scenes at Bellevue for **The Miracle on 34th Street** (where Edmund Gwenn is confined as certifiable for claiming to be the one and only Santa Claus), Seaton was refused as were all other such Hollywood requests. Seaton later stated that when he made his request, the head of Bellevue "practically threw me out because he was still mad at himself for giving Wilder permission to shoot at the hospital. What made him particularly angry was that the picture [The Lost Weekend] showed a male nurse [Faylen] brutalizing an alcoholic [Milland]." Milland further got very bad publicity when he was walking down Third Avenue in New York, his clothes disheveled, looking hollow-eyed and with a thick stubble of a beard, the scene where he is looking for a pawnshop to pawn his typewriter and where Wilder's cameras followed him, but hidden in accompanying vehicles and out of sight to make the scene all the more realistic. Two well-dressed women saw Milland wandering down the street in this terrible condition and, being friends of his wife, Muriel Milland, called her when they returned to California, and they also called the local press, which immediately printed their rumors that Milland was seen in New York on a Homeric bender. Milland said to this author: "My God, it took all that the publicity department at Paramount could do to turn that story around by having those papers run articles to state that I was enacting a scene in the picture." The bar that Da Silva operates is the exact replica of the legendary watering hole, P. J. Clarke's, which is located on Third Avenue. It was built with precise detail as to the original at Stage Five at Paramount Studio. On this set, Milland and Da Silva and others render their memorable scenes, but, while Wilder was shooting these scenes over several days, the director would momentarily stop shooting while a person not connected with the film sauntered onto the set and ordered a drink. Da Silva then produced an actual bottle of whiskey and poured a drink, offering it to the visitor. The visitor would down it, smile and leave the set. This went on for several days and the visitor was always treated with respect, for he was none other than the esteemed writer, critic and humorous wit and actor, Robert Benchley. Where Milland overwhelmed and conquered the great character he essayed, he was overwhelmed when receiving his deserved Oscar for Best Actor. He forgot his acceptance speech and, without a word, accepted the statuette, smiled and walked away. Emcee Bob Hope then quipped: "I'm surprised they just handed it [the Oscar statuette] to him. I thought they'd hide it in the chandelier!" Many in Hollywood were amazed at Milland's performance in this unforgettable film, not the least of whom was his co-star, Jane Wyman. Wyman told this author that "I did not have a lot of scenes with Ray [Milland] in **The Lost Weekend**, and I was not present when he enacted most of his scenes so when I finally saw the picture I was amazed at the great performance he gave. It gave me the willies and, in the scene with the bat and the mouse, I truly believed he was actually hallucinating or was seeing those creatures for real. That's how good he was in that amazing picture. Before he appeared in that picture, everyone thought Ray was a likeable lightweight. Well, he turned out to be a heavyweight champion." Alcoholism and alcoholics have been profiled in many films, most notably in **Broken Blossoms**, 1919; **Anna Christie**, 1930; **The Champ**, 1931; **A Free Soul**, 1931; **State's Attorney**, 1932; **The Wet Parade**, 1932; **What Price Hollywood?**, 1932; **Dinner at Eight**, 1933; **A Tale of Two Cities**, 1935; **A Star Is Born**, 1937; **The Rains Came**, 1939; **The Roaring Twenties**, 1939; **The Great Profile**, 1940; **Across the Pacific**, 1942; **Murder, My Sweet**, 1944; **A Tree Grows in Brooklyn**, 1945;

Key Largo, 1948; **My Dream Is Yours**, 1949; **Under Capricorn**, 1949; **In a Lonely Place**, 1950; **Young Man with a Horn**, 1950; **Come Fill the Cup**, 1951; **Jim Thorpe—All American**, 1951; **Come Back, Little Sheba**, 1952; **The Clown**, 1953; **The Country Girl**, 1954; **The Last Time I Saw Paris**, 1954; **A Star Is Born**, 1954; **Them!**, 1954; **I'll Cry Tomorrow**, 1955; **The Rains of Ranchipur**, 1955; **The Helen Morgan Story**, 1957; **The Sun Also Rises**, 1957; **Too Much, Too Soon**, 1958; **Beloved Infidel**, 1959; **Rio Bravo**, 1959; **The Sound and the Fury**, 1959; **The Entertainer**, 1960; **Days of Wine and Roses**, 1962; **Long Day's Journey into Night**, 1962; **Tender Is the Night**, 1962; **Two Weeks in Another Town**, 1962; **Papa's Delicate Condition**, 1963; **The Carpetbaggers**, 1964; **Cat Ballou**, 1965; **El Dorado**, 1967; **Farewell, My Lovely**, 1975; **The Bad News Bears**, 1976; **The Champ**, 1979; **Arthur**, 1981; **My Favorite Year**, 1982; **The Verdict**, 1982; **Hoosiers**, 1986; **Barfly**, 1987; **A League of Their Own**, 1992; **Leaving Los Vegas**, 1995; **Nixon**, 1995; **Courage under Fire**, 1996; **Flags of Our Fathers**, 2006; **Frost/Nixon**, 2008. **p**, Charles Brackett; **d**, Billy Wilder; **cast**, Ray Milland, Jane Wyman, Phillip Terry, Howard Da Silva, Doris Dowling, Frank Faylen, Mary Young, Anita Bolster, Lilian Fontaine, Audrey Long, Craig Reynolds, the San Francisco Opera Company; **w**, Brackett, Wilder (based on the novel by Charles R. Jackson); **c**, John F. Seitz; **m**, Miklos Rozsa; **ed**, Doane Harrison; **art d**, Hans Dreier, Earl Hedrick; **set d**, Bertram Granger; **spec eff**, Farciot Edouart, Gordon Jennings, Paul K. Lerpae.

The Lost World ★★★ 1925 (silent); U.S.; 106m/10 reels; First National Pictures; B/W; Adventure/Fantasy; Children: Acceptable; **DVD**; **VHS**. This landmark film impressively shows for the first time in a feature-length production the embryonic skills of special effects genius Willis O'Brien and where the Doyle adventure tale is stunningly presented. The film begins in London where newspaper reporter Hughes proposes to Bennett, but she tells him that she cannot become his bride until he makes his mark upon the world. To prove himself, Hughes joins an expedition going to the Amazon and led by eccentric professor Beery and where the explorers plan to locate Love's missing father, a scientist who was lost in the jungle while searching for a plateau that reportedly houses ancient dinosaurs. En route, Hughes and Love fall in love and Hughes forgets his uppity fiancée. The party hacks its way through dense foliage until it comes upon the legendary plateau and its members encounter a pterodactyl, narrowly avoiding this giant flying lizard, a creature thought to be extinct millions of years ago. The explorers fell a giant tree to cross a chasm to reach the plateau and are watched by an ape man hiding in the jungle. As they proceed, the astounded explorers see all kinds of dinosaurs, including flesh-eating monsters and an enormous Brontosaurus, which is attacked by the flesh-eaters and falls from the plateau. The explorers next find a skeleton, learning that it is the remains of Love's father and, just then, a volcanic eruption rocks the area, spewing forth rivers of burning lava from which the prehistoric beasts flee in a wild stampede. The explorers then attempt to escape the plateau by lowering ropes from its cliff, but the ape man appears and tries to foil their efforts. He is killed in the struggle and the explorers lower themselves from the crumbling plateau. The explorers then find the Brontosaurus alive, but mired in a tar pit. Beery determines to save the gigantic beast and bring it back to civilization as a living trophy (shades of King Kong to come) and he manages to crate the beast and transport it back to England. When the ship unloads this enormous cargo, however, the gigantic crate breaks and the beast wanders loose in London. The beast roams the streets of the city, smashing buildings and wrecking thoroughfares. It crosses London Bridge and its sheer weight collapses the span. Splashing into the Thames River, the Brontosaurus swims down the river and to the sea. Hughes, meanwhile, learns that Bennett has married someone else and this now allows him to seek happiness with Love. *Author's Note*: This film was an enormous success as it stunned audiences that had never before seen any prehistoric beasts so well animated. This was achieved by O'Brien through his creation of

Richard Schiff, Julianne Moore, Jeff Goldblum and Vince Vaughn in *The Lost World: Jurassic Park*, 1997.

realistically looking eighteen-inch dinosaurs carefully created by Marcel Delgado, O'Brien's diligent assistant. Placing these miniatures into small jungle sets, they were moved a fraction of an inch per film frame exposure. The overall effect, when these segments were edited into the film with the live action scene with the actors, amazed viewing audiences the world over. O'Brien had, in 1922, created some short film footage showing these miniature creatures and sent them to author Doyle, who was so impressed with his special effects that he publicized O'Brien's achievements and that prompted First National to offer O'Brien a contract to produce this pioneering production. The cost to produce this film exceeded $1 million, a staggering budget for the silent era, but the film earned back its expenses in its original release and, especially, from road show exhibitions where top prices were demanded and paid by curious millions. This film established O'Brien as the foremost special effects artist in Hollywood and he would be instrumental eight years later in creating the memorable **King Kong**, 1933. **p**, Harry O. Hoyt, William Dowling, Earl Hudson; **d**, Hoyt; **cast**, Bessie Love, Lloyd Hughes, Lewis Stone, Wallace Beery, Alma Bennett, Arthur Hoyt, Margaret McWade, Bull Montana, Jules Cowles, George Bunny, Conan Doyle, Gilbert Roland; **w**, Marion Fairfax (based on the novel by Sir Arthur Conan Doyle); **c**, Arthur Edeson; **m**, Cecil Copping; **ed**, George McGuire; **set d**, Milton Menasco; **spec eff**, Willis H. O'Brien, Marcel Delgado, Ralph Hammeras.

The Lost World: Jurassic Park ★★★ 1997; U.S.; 129m; UNIV; Color; Fantasy/Science Fiction; Children: Unacceptable (MPAA: PG-13); **DVD**; **VHS**. In this exciting and well-crafted sequel to **Jurassic Park**, 1993, dinosaurs are discovered to be on an island adjacent to the original isle where Jurassic Park was established. After a girl is attacked by small carnivorous dinosaurs (compsognathus) while her family is picnicking on that island and where she is narrowly saved, Attenborough, whose theme park experiment has proven a failure, attempts to redeem himself by sending Goldblum and others to the island to bring the prehistoric beasts back to the mainland in order to reestablish the park. Meanwhile, Howard, Attenborough's manipulating nephew, who has taken control of the company that controls Jurassic Park, sends his own team to the island for much different and deadly purposes. Goldblum finds that his girlfriend, Moore, is accompanying the other team and when both teams meet on the island, they become the hunted ones instead of the hunters and where many of them are attacked and devoured by these savage beasts. After many harrowing battles and escapes with these creatures, the teams manage to capture and take back to San Diego a huge Tyrannosaurus, but it breaks free and it wreaks havoc in the city, searching for something. Goldblum rightly guesses that this is the mother of the infant that has been taken to the new park earlier, and

Irene Dunne and Charles Boyer in *Love Affair*, 1939.

he and Moore use the baby dinosaur to lure the huge beast back to the cargo ship, but not before the infant dispatches the devious and dangerous Howard. The ship, guarded by U.S. warships, then sails back to the original Jurassic Park, which is now officially declared to be a "nature preserve." Despite a thin story line and static acting from Goldblum and others, the astounding special effects maintain heart-pounding attention throughout. **p**, Gerald R. Molen, Colin Wilson, Kathleen Kennedy; **d**, Steven Spielberg; **cast**, Jeff Goldblum, Julianne Moore, Pete Postlethwaite, Richard Attenborough, Arliss Howard, Vince Vaughn, Vanessa Lee Chester, Peter Stormare, Harvey Jason, Richard Schiff; **w**, David Koepp (based on the novel *The Lost World* by Michael Crichton); **c**, Janusz Kaminski; **m**, John Williams; **ed**, Michael Kahn; **prod d**, Rick Carter; **art d**, Jim Teegarden, Lauren Polizzi, Paul Sonski; **set d**, Gary Fettis; **spec eff**, Mark "Crash" McCreery, Richard Davison, Vicki L. Engel.

Love Actually ★★★ 2003; U.K./U.S./France; 129m; UNIV; Color; Romantic Comedy; Children: Unacceptable (MPAA: R); **BD**; **DVD**. A film to love, and audiences did, big-time, besides earning millions for its producers. Episodic, the story follows eight couples who fall in and out of love in loosely interrelated stories all set during a very busy month before Christmas in London, England. Among the love-struck is a bachelor British prime minister, Grant, who loves the girl who serves him his tea, McCutcheon. The others in this bevy of lovers include Grant's sister, Thompson, her cheating husband, Rickman, his assistant, Linney (who is the only American in the otherwise all-British superstar cast), who loves her co-worker, Santoro, but they are too shy to admit their feelings to each other. Also in this romantic entourage is an aging rock star, Nighy; a British writer, Firth, who has eyes for his Portuguese maid, Moniz; a recently widowed man, Neeson, and his wife's young son by a former marriage, Sangster, and even the President of the United States, Thornton, who flirts with McCutcheon (shades of Bill Clinton!). It's a bit confusing to keep track of the many amorous antics, but it is great fun to watch these lovesick to sappy people frantically mix emotion with desire. Song: "Love Is All Around" (Reg Presley; sung by Nighy). Sexuality, nudity, and gutter language prohibit viewing by children. **p**, Tim Bevan, Eric Fellner, Duncan Kenworthy, Liza Chasin, Debra Hayward; **d&w**, Richard Curtis; **cast**, Colin Firth, Hugh Grant, Liam Neeson, Emma Thompson, Keira Knightley, Bill Nighy, Laura Linney, Billy Campbell, Alan Rickman, Meg Wynn Owen, Rowan Atkinson, Billy Bob Thornton; **c**, Michael Coulter; **m**, Craig Armstrong; **ed**, Nick Moore; **prod d**, Jim Clay; **art d**, Jonathan McKinstry, Rod McLean, Justin Warburton-Brown; **set d**, Caroline Smith; **spec eff**, Richard Conway, Tim Webber.

Love Affair ★★★★ 1939; U.S.; 88m; RKO; B/W; Romance; Children:

Acceptable; **DVD**; **VHS**. In this classic love story Boyer and Dunne, who are both engaged to others, meet aboard a luxury liner and, while sailing the seas, begin to flirt with one another. Boyer, a French painter, and Dunne, a sometimes nightclub singer, soon develop a deep fondness for each other, their emotions blossoming into love. Boyer is engaged to Allwyn and Dunne is the fiancée of Bowman, both wealthy persons they respect and for whom they have warm feelings, but neither loves the persons they are slated to marry. Boyer and Dunne realize that they only love each other and want to be together, but, in fairness to themselves and their intended, they decide to give their romance the test of time. They agree that, if they feel the same way about each other within six months, they will meet at the top of the Empire State Building and begin a new life together. Boyer goes back to Allwyn and his painting and Dunne gets a job as a singer in a nightclub and resumes her relationship with Bowman. The longing that Boyer and Dunne have for one another, however, increases and they both realize that they belong together. Both start out to meet at their rendezvous at the end of the six months, but Dunne is injured in an automobile accident and may be crippled for life. She does not want to burden Boyer as an invalid, so she does not contact him. Meanwhile, Boyer arrives at the rendezvous, but when Dunne fails to appear, he concludes that she has decided to marry Bowman and tries to forget her. He later meets her by chance and comes to realize that she has sacrificed herself for him. He refuses to leave her, however, believing that he can make her well enough so that she can again walk and tells her that he is staying at her side forever, which ends this wonderful and heartwarming production. Boyer and Dunne create many magical moments, and the script from masterful writers Daves, Stewart and others is witty and mirthful, providing many comedic scenes. The cast is superb, particularly the veteran actress Ouspenskaya, who plays Boyer's aging and dying mother, and who instinctively knows that Dunne is the right woman for her compassionate son. McCarey directs with a sure and patient hand, never rushing his scenes and appropriately dwelling on the most significant moments in this captivating romance. Dunne, who has a pleasant singing voice, warbles "Sing My Heart" (Harold Arlen, Ted Koehler) in a nightclub, and when she works briefly at an orphanage, "Wishing" (Buddy De Sylva) is sung by the Robert Mitchell Boy Choir. Other songs include: "Plaisir d'Amour" (Johann Martini, Jean-Pierre Claris de Florian), sung by Dunne and played on a piano by Ouspenskaya, and "Jingle Bells" (1857, James Pierrpont), which is incorporated into the fine score by the accomplished Webb. The film was nominated for Best Picture, Best Screenplay, Best Actress, Best Supporting Actress and Best Song, but this was the year that the colossal **Gone with the Wind**, 1939, swept the Academy Awards. This film was remade as another classic, **An Affair to Remember**, 1957, with Cary Grant and Deborah Kerr as the almost star-crossed lovers, and again in 1994 with the original title with Warren Beatty and Annette Bening, an inferior production. *Author's Note*: McCarey told this author that "Irene Dunne was terrific in that picture because everything about her is genuine. She radiates love and Boyer picked up on that and that is why their scenes in that picture together work so well and seem so normal. Irene was one of the few real 'ladies' I met in Hollywood. My job as a director was to make sure that people felt a lot happier than when they arrived at the theater and **Love Affair** did that. The remake of that picture with Grant and Kerr is a very good one, but I think the 1939 version is the best. I know. I directed both of those pictures. Cary was always duplicating what I did in life and, in fact, a lot of his mannerisms on screen he copied from me and he knows it. He is a very fine actor, but sometimes when I directed pictures in which he appeared I thought I was directing myself." Dunne had nothing but praise for McCarey, telling this author: "He was a master at making little scenes into big ones—a glance or a gesture with a few lines of dialog, well, Leo could turn that into a scene people would remember all the days of their lives. Leo McCarey always knew where the heart was." Boyer echoed these sentiments when telling this author that "McCarey was a genius, who always looked on the bright side. He had a happy heart and a head full of good new ideas every time he showed up on the set. He knew how to show people as very humorous without ridiculing them. He understood how to convey human emotions on the screen with fine sentiment but never becoming sentimental. That was part of his great talent. You may not know this, but he was the man who put Laurel and Hardy together and matching those two wonderful clowns was just another one of Leo's gifts to the world of laughter." **p&d**, Leo McCarey; **cast**, Irene Dunne, Charles Boyer, Maria Ouspenskaya, Lee Bowman, Astrid Allwyn, Maurice Moscovich, Scotty Beckett, Ferike Boros, Mary Bovard, Tom Dugan, Joan Leslie, the Robert Mitchell Boy Choir; **w**, Delmer Daves, Donald Ogden Stewart (based on a story by McCarey, Mildred Cram); **c**, Rudolph Maté; **m**, Roy Webb; **ed**, Edward Dmytryk, George Hively; **art d**, Van Nest Polglase; **set d**, Darrell Silvera; **spec eff**, Vernon L. Walker.

Love and Death ★★★ 1975; U.S./France; 85m; Jack Rollins & Charles H. Joffe Productions/MGM-UA; Color; Comedy; Children: Unacceptable (MPAA: PG); **DVD**; **VHS**. Allen is a cowardly Russian misfit during the Napoleonic wars (what else?), who falls in love with his cousin, Keaton, who loves his deceased brother. Allen is sent to war against his wishes, and makes an inept, shabby soldier, but he manages to become a war hero by being shot out of a cannon. Despite his idiotic heroism, Keaton still does not warm to him, although they have lengthy discussions about sex and other matters, so when a beautiful countess, Georges-Picot, shows interest in Allen, he beds her. Her husband learns of it and challenges Allen to a duel. Keaton feels sorry for Allen, even though he survives the duel, and agrees to marry him. After they wed, they become involved in a plot to assassinate Napoleon, Tolkan. After more lengthy discussions between them, again on sex and other matters, they make various attempts to kill Tolkan, but they are met with one miserable failure after another. Death finally comes, but for Allen in a surrealistic ending. This offbeat take-off on Tolstoy's classic *War and Peace* presents a visual far-out and often entertaining intellectual spoof, but not for children because of its violence and strong sexual themes. *Author's Note*: This film was shot on location in France and Hungary and, other than Allen and Keaton, features many actors from those locales. **p**, Charles H. Joffe; **d&w**, Woody Allen; **cast**, Allen, Diane Keaton, Georges Adet, Frank Adu, Edmond Ardisson, Feodor Atkine, Albert Augier, Yves Barsaco, Harold Gould, Jessica Harper; **c**, Ghislain Cloquet (Panavision; DeLuxe Color); **m**, Sergei Prokofiev; **ed**, Ron Kalish, Ralph Rosenblum, George Hively; **art d**, Willy Holt; **spec eff**, Peter Dawson, Kit West.

The Love Bug ★★★ 1968; U.S.; 108m; Walt Disney/Buena Vista; Color; Comedy/Fantasy; Children: Recommended (MPAA: G); **DVD**; **VHS**. In this delightful romp from Disney, Tomilson is a mean-minded race car driver who owns a Volkswagen Beetle that has a mind all of its own. Tomlinson mistreats the car, but, in losing a race, driver Jones rescues the Beetle, calling it Herbie. This little car (the "Love Bug") takes a liking to Jones and wins race after race for him, but its egotistical owner thinks he's the reason for the wins. Jones' friend Hackett has his doubts about Jones suddenly becoming a racing champion. Then after all of these incredible wins, it becomes confusing as to who really owns Herbie. Tomlinson and Jones make a bet and if Jones wins a final race, he wins Herbie. That last race is a marvelous fight for love and glory. This fine and often hilarious comedy was a huge success and four more **Love Bug** films followed: **Herbie Rides Again**, 1974; **Herbie Goes to Monte Carlo**, 1977; **Herbie Goes Bananas**, 1980; and **Herbie Fully Loaded**, 2005, as well as several television movies and series. **p**, Bill Walsh; **d**, Robert Stevenson; **cast**, Dean Jones, Michele Lee, David Tomlinson, Buddy Hackett, Joe Flynn, Benson Fong, Andy Granatelli, Joe E. Ross, Iris Adrian, Gil Lamb, Pedro Gonzalez-Gonzalez; **w**, Walsh, Don DaGradi (based on the story "Car-Boy-Girl" by Gordon Buford); **c**, Edward Colman (Technicolor); **m**, George Bruns; **ed**, Cotton Warburton; **art d**, Carroll Clark, John B. Mansbridge; **set d**, Hal Gaus-

Woody Allen and Diane Keaton in *Love and Death*, 1975.

man, Emile Kuri; **spec eff**, Howard Jensen, Dan Lee, Robert A. Mattey, Peter Ellenshaw.

Love Crazy ★★★★ 1941; U.S.; 99m; MGM; B/W; Comedy; Children: Acceptable; **DVD**; **VHS**. This superlative laugh riot teams Powell and Loy once again (they appeared six times together as the sleuthing Nick and Nora Charles in the delightful Thin Man series),but here they are a sophisticated married couple where their urbane lifestyle is disrupted and almost destroyed through some innocent folly brought about by the capricious Powell. They are on the verge of celebrating their fourth anniversary when into their tranquil lives comes Bates, Loy's battleax mother, a gossiping, meddling woman, who is, in Powell's opinion (and no doubt that of the world's viewing audience) the most annoying female on the planet. Bates, unexpected visit complicates matters when she falls and sprains her ankle and, unable to move about too well, decides to spend some time with Loy and Powell at their luxurious high rise domicile. While Loy leaves to run an errand, Powell is compelled to entertain Bates by tossing cards into a hat and other folderol. He steps outside to his veranda to view the cityscape and sees on a neighboring terrace a sultry woman, Patrick, an old flame, who is married to wealthy businessman MacBride. Bates overhears a part of the conversation between Patrick and Powell and misconstrues this to mean that her son-in-law is secretly romancing Patrick and imparts this slander to Loy. Loy thinks to turn the tables on Powell by carrying on with Patrick's straight-laced husband, MacBride, but she goes to the wrong apartment and is discovered by thick-witted, brawny Carson, an archery champion, who suddenly makes moves like Tarzan on Loy. Carson, stripped to the waist, then pursues Loy, which unnerves Powell, who tells Loy that his conversation with Patrick was nothing more than innocent chitchat, but Loy believes otherwise and walks out, insisting on a divorce. Powell agrees and then changes his mind. His attorney, Blackmer, tells him that, under the present law, a wife cannot divorce her husband if he is insane. To that end, Powell will pretend to be off his rocker until Loy returns to him. He tells everyone at a party that he is Abraham Lincoln and then runs around freeing the black servants. Loy is wise to his antics and calls his trump by committing him to a lunatic asylum where everyone is certifiable, including the eccentric head doctors, Sokoloff and Rumann. Powell is now trapped inside his own wacky scheme and when he tries to convince authorities at the institution that he is sane, he is told that that is what everyone there claims. He finally escapes and returns home, but in disguise as his own spinster sister. Shaving off his famous mustache, Powell dons a gray wig and dowdy dress and talks in a falsetto voice, arriving on a visit to visit the in-laws, and there is a hilarious bit of business when his dress starts to unravel. He and Loy, however, decide to retire in the same bedroom—by this time Loy is on to Powell

Basil Rathbone in *Love from a Stranger*, 1937.

and they have become reconciled—and the unsuspecting Bates bids the two "ladies" goodnight. Many set pieces provide high-end laughter such as when Powell gets his head stuck between floors when trapped inside a malfunctioning elevator and when, later, the heavyset and henpecking Bates gets shoved into a fountain (causing audiences in that day to thunderously applaud). Although there is considerable slapstick liberally sprinkled throughout this well-mounted production, there is enough sophisticated wit to satisfy any highbrow. Conway directs this lighthearted screwball comedy at a fast clip, providing one riotous laugh after another. **p**, Pandro S. Berman; **d**, Jack Conway; **cast**, William Powell, Myrna Loy, Gail Patrick, Jack Carson, Florence Bates, Sidney Blackmer, Sig Rumann, Vladimir Sokoloff, Donald MacBride, Sara Haden, Kathleen Lockhart; **w**, William Ludwig, Charles Lederer, David Hertz (based on a story by Hertz); **c**, Ray June, William H. Daniels; **m**, David Snell, Lennie Hayton; **ed**, Ben Lewis; **art d**, Cedric Gibbons; **set d**, Edwin B. Willis.

Love Finds Andy Hardy ★★★ 1938; U.S.; 90m; MGM; B/W; Comedy; Children: Acceptable; **DVD**; **VHS**. One of the best of the series, teenage Andy (Rooney) is in trouble with his girlfriend, Rutherford, when he agrees to play escort for his pal's (Reynolds) girlfriend (Turner) to get money to pay off his jalopy. A new girl next door, Garland, comes to visit her aunt and uncle. Rooney doesn't think much of Garland, until she sings at a dance. Rooney takes an interest in Garland until she reminds him that his real girlfriend is Rutherford. It was Garland's first appearance in the series and Turner's first at MGM. Songs: "Meet the Beat of My Heart," "It Never Rains But It Pours" (Mack Gordon, Harry Revel), "In Between" (Roger Edens), all sung by Garland. **p**, Carey Wilson, Lou L. Ostrow; **d**, George B. Seitz; **cast**, Lewis Stone, Mickey Rooney, Judy Garland, Fay Holden, Cecilia Parker, Lana Turner, Ann Rutherford, Mary Howard, Gene Reynolds, Don Castle, Marie Blake, Raymond Hatton, Rand Brooks; **w**, William Ludwig (based on stories by Vivien B. Bretherton and characters created by Aurania Rouverol); **c**, Lester White; **m**, David Snell; **ed**, Ben Lewis; **art d**, Cedric Gibbons.

Love from a Stranger ★★★★ 1937; U.K.; 86m; Trafalgar Productions/UA; B/W; Crime Drama; Children: Unacceptable; **DVD**. A thoroughly chilling drama has Rathbone giving one of his most terrifying performances as a calculating husband out to murder his rich wife, Harding. This brilliantly written thriller begins when the sweet and innocent Harding is on a European vacation and wins a lottery. Her newfound wealth causes strife between her and her fiancé, Seton, so much so that the couple breaks up and Harding goes her own way, straight into the arms of the sophisticated Rathbone. His suavity and charm soon sweeps Harding off her feet. The mysterious Rathbone intrigues Harding and,

despite warnings from friends that Rathbone is a clever fortune-hunter, she falls in love with him and they wed. The marriage, however, is quickly enshrouded with Harding's doubts and eventual suspicions about her husband. Rathbone begins to manifest signs of mental problems and his sudden mood swings convince Harding that not only is he unstable but that her life is in mortal danger. Harding is able to piece together through deduction and the insidious snippets of conversation Rathbone niggardly utters that he is a homicidal maniac, though cleverly covering his compulsion to kill and that he is really a Bluebeard who marries wealthy women in order to murder them and acquire their riches, which is his sinister ambition in the case of the too trusting Harding. Rathbone now knows that Harding knows his true nature, but both toy with each other in a lethal cat-and-mouse game in the final breathtaking scenes together where they are alone in a house and where Rathbone has decided to make his murder move. Rathbone has already tried to kill Harding several times, incidents Harding mistook for mishaps or accidents. It is no accident, however, that Rathbone, on this last night he and Harding will have together, has slipped poison into Harding's coffee. Harding is aware of Rathbone's actions and the two verbally fence with each other, building incredible tension in what is one of the most blood-curdling scenes in film noir. Harding finally and cleverly convinces Rathbone that the coffee he has swallowed contains the poison intended for her. The killer's weak heart finally gives out under the strain and he collapses dead, not knowing that there is no poison in his system. This superlative and often neglected film sees a wonderful script faithfully adapted from the Christie short story by Marion and it is tautly directed by the gifted Lee. Harding, who makes her first appearance in a British film here, shows in a brilliant performance that she is equal to the task of holding her own with the intense and riveting Rathbone, and their mesmerizing scenes together remain a classic of conflict and confrontation. **The Shining**, 1980, takes a great leaf from this classic crime tale. *Author's Note*: Rathbone told this author that his role of the serial lady killer in **Love from a Stranger** "was undoubtedly the most villainous character I ever portrayed and I played quite a number of such villains, but this man is not only evil, he is utterly deranged. He becomes enraged when his true motives are discovered before he can dispatch his victim conveniently and without any strain on his heart. Her [Harding's] only defense, she knows, is if she can bring about his destruction through his own weaknesses, that failing heart and she does and it saves her life. The killer I play in that fascinating picture is really a mentally unbalanced actor, enacting the plots of his own murders, just the same way, I might add, John Wilkes Booth rehearsed and subsequently enacted his assassination of Abraham Lincoln. Booth, too, was a certifiable maniac." In this, Rathbone spoke with considerable knowledge as his distant cousin, Major Henry Reed Rathbone (1837-1911), was a member of the Lincoln party at Ford's Theater and was sitting in the very box with the President when Booth mortally shot Lincoln on the night of April 15, 1865. Rathbone tried to stop Booth from leaping from the presidential box to the stage and was savagely stabbed by Booth before he made good his escape. For more details on Henry Rathbone's involvement in the Lincoln assassination, see my book, *The Great Pictorial History of World Crime*, Volume I (History, Inc., 2004; pages 26-44). **p**, Max Schach; **d**, Rowland V. Lee; **cast**, Ann Harding, Basil Rathbone, Binnie Hale, Bruce Seton, Jean Cadell, Bryan Powley, Joan Hickson, Donald Calthrop, Eugene Leahy; **w**, Frances Marion (based on the short story "Philomel Cottage" by Agatha Christie and the play by Frank Vosper); **c**, Philip Tannura; **m**, Benjamin Britten; **ed**, Howard O'Neill; **art d**, Frederick Pusey.

Love in the Afternoon ★★★ 1957; U.S.; 130m; AA; B/W; Comedy/Romance; Children: Acceptable; **DVD**; **VHS**. This delightful romantic romp, which is filled with a lot of inventive comedic scenes, begins when the impish Chevalier, who is a private eye in Paris, France, snooping on husbands and wives, uses a camera with a telescopic lens to capture wealthy American businessman Cooper dallying with Bourdin, who is married to McGiver. Hepburn, the attractive, fanciful daughter of Chevalier, overhears her father informing McGiver of these boudoir doings and, thinking that McGiver will take mortal revenge upon the interloper, races to Cooper's hotel to warn him. Hepburn arrives in disguise, pretending to be a worldly woman, but Cooper sees through her masquerade and is amused at her posturing but intrigued enough by her sweet pretensions that he wants to see more of her. They have some short meetings where Hepburn relates her many affairs, all of these torrid romances being nothing more than the creation of her fertile imagination. Then Hepburn disappears and Cooper has no idea where to find her. Cooper then meets Chevalier in a steam bath and tells Chevalier of the beautiful young woman he has met and who he now wants to find. Chevalier, not knowing that Cooper is talking about his own daughter, offers his services as a detective to locate this mysterious woman. Chevalier, however, when learning more from Cooper, then realizes that the woman Cooper seeks is Hepburn and Chevalier tells him to put the young woman out of his mind and leave Paris immediately for his own emotional good. (This situation is not dissimilar to another scene in **The Godfather**, 1972, when a father, the owner of a small restaurant in the Sicilian town of Corleone, learns that Al Pacino, an American on the run for murder, shows an interest in his daughter and where the father initially pretends no such young woman exists.) Cooper takes Chevalier's advice and is about to leave for vacation in the provinces when Hepburn arrives at the train station to say goodbye to him. They both are reluctant to say goodbye to each other and come to believe that their May-December romance can bring them both happiness. Cooper then takes Hepburn away with him as they look forward to happiness together. It's a simple story, but so well directed, written and acted that it charms and captivates throughout, especially through the enchanting and memorable performance from Hepburn. Chevalier, too, is a standout, and the always stalwart Cooper is convincing as the aging Romeo, albeit he is a bit long in the tooth for his role. Songs include "Fascination" (F. D. Marchetti, Maurice de Feraudy), "C'est Si Bon" (Henri Betti, Andre Hornez), "I'ame des poétes" (Charles Trenet), "Ariane," "Hot Paprika," "Love in the Afternoon" (Marty Malneck). *Author's Note*: Wilder admitted that Cooper was not his first choice for the male lead in this film, stating to this author that "Cary Grant was at the top of my list, but he turned down the role, as he did for **Sabrina** [1954], a picture that also starred Audrey and I got to thinking that he did not like her for some reason, when all the rest of the world loved her. Next, I tried to get Yul Brynner, but he did not want the part either. Cooper was available at the same time Audrey was ready for the picture, so we cast him. I was surprised to see how he aged in that film. He was not in good health and he seemed to age dramatically each day during the production and, to mask his age, I shot a lot of his scenes in half light or in soft shadows where I showed Audrey in bright sunshine, which accented the differences in their ages and I wanted that to make viewers believe that they would never get together even though they might want them to be a couple. Cooper is really a man reaching back into his past for the love he felt in his youth and he is very lucky at the end to be smart enough to grab on to it and take it with him when he and Audrey go off together. They say that I did this film to honor Ernest Lubitsch. I worked with Lubitsch many years earlier and admired his work and I learned a lot from him. But, I made that picture for its own sake and whatever people say about my motives in making that picture, well, that's just a lot of hooey." **p&d**, Billy Wilder; **cast**, Gary Cooper, Audrey Hepburn, Maurice Chevalier, John McGiver, Van Doude, Lise Bourdin, Olga Valery, Marc Aurian, Vera Boccadoro, Françoise Brion; **w**, Wilder, I.A.L. Diamond (based on the novel *Ariane, jeune fille russe* by Claude Anet; **c**, William Mellor; **m**, Franz Waxman; **ed**, Leonid Azar; **art d**, Alexandre Trauner; **set d**, Oliver Emert.

Love Is a Many Splendored-Thing ★★★ 1955; U.S.; 102m; FOX; Color; Romance; Children: Acceptable; **DVD**; **VHS**. A haunting and well-made romance sees Holden as a married correspondent working

Gary Cooper and Audrey Hepburn in *Love in the Afternoon*, 1957.

in the Far East and falling in love with beautiful Eurasian physician Jones, who works in a British-controlled hospital in Hong Kong. When they first meet, sparks begin to fly, but Jones resists Holden's advances because she fears that no good can come of a sustained relationship with Holden. They nevertheless know that they are made for each other and despite prejudicial advice and arguments from both white and Asian relatives and friends they decide to make a go of it together. Holden, however, is sent to Korea to cover the war and is killed. Jones is devastated, but comforts herself when going to the high and windy hill where she had earlier spent joyous time with lover Holden and now believes that she should be grateful for the brief time God allowed her and Holden to have on this fragile and unpredictable earth. The tall and stately Jones with her chiseled features and high cheekbones does a fine job playing the Eurasian beauty, employing her usual restraint, and Holden is charming and believable as her brash American lover. The direction is handled with sensitivity and the script is literate and provocative. This film features within its memorable score the song "Love Is a Many-Splendored Thing" (Sammy Fain, Paul Francis Webster), which became a super hit. The budget for this film of more than $1.7 million was quickly earned back at the box office where it became a smash, grossing more than $3 million in its initial release. *Author's Note*: Jones received her fifth and final Oscar nomination for Best Actress for her performance in this memorable romance entry and it would be her last significant role as a leading player. In 1981, she purchased the rights to *Terms of Endearment*, a novel by James McMurtry, thinking to produce and star in the film, but its director, James Brooks, candidly told her that she was by then much too old to play the part and it went to Shirley MacLaine, who won an Oscar as Best Actress for that role, an award that Jones had won at the age of twenty-five for **The Song of Bernadette**, 1943. Jones had a special interest in **Love is a Many Splendored Thing** in that she had long been an ardent student of Eastern philosophy, which may have been the reason why she so well understood and conveyed the image of her Eurasian character. Jones had married billionaire Norton Simon in 1971 and controlled his vast estate upon his death in 1993; she lived to the age of ninety, dying in 2009. "I always thought that Jennifer is one of the most beautiful women on the planet," Holden told this author, "and she was no more beautiful than when I worked with her in **Love Is a Many-Splendored Thing**. She was in her thirties then, but she had not really aged. She still had that fascinating Oriental look about her and she was perfect for her part as the Eurasian doctor. We appeared together twenty years later in **The Towering Inferno**, 1974, but we appear only briefly together in that film. And she was still beautiful. She always will be." **p**, Buddy Adler; **d**, Henry King; **cast**, William Holden, Jennifer Jones, Torin Thatcher, Isobel Elsom, Murray Matheson, Virginia Gregg, Richard

William Holden and Jennifer Jones in *Love Is A Many-Splendored Thing*, **1955.**

Loo, Soo Young, Philip Ahn, Jorja Curtright, Donna Martell; **w**, John Patrick (based on the novel *A Many-Splendored Thing* by Han Suyin); **c**, Leon Shamroy (CinemaScope; DeLuxe Color); **m**, Alfred Newman; **ed**, William Reynolds; **art d**, Lyle R. Wheeler, George W. Davis; **set d**, Walter M. Scott, Jack Stubbs; **spec eff**, Ray Kellogg.

Love Is News ★★★★ 1937; U.S.; 77m; FOX; B/W; Comedy/Romance; Children: Acceptable; **DVD**. This terrific screwball comedy has the handsome Power (where he first received top billing) as an energetic reporter working for Ameche's newspaper. Ameche has for some time been trying to get an inside scoop on the lifestyle of Young, a fabulously rich socialite who hates publicity and zealously guards her privacy. After Young becomes enraged with Ameche's newshounds and photographers dogging her, she thinks to turn the tables on the publisher by making an astounding public announcement. She calls a press conference, inviting the representatives of every newspaper in the city, except Ameche's, and states that she is dumping her stuffy fiancé, Sanders, and that her new flame, Power, is not only the love of her life, but that she plans to go to the altar with him, bestowing upon Power as a wedding gift more than $1 million. Ameche explodes and fires Power for not telling him about this great news, but reporter Power is dumbfounded as he knows nothing about it. Now Power is besieged as was Young by every newshound and photographer in the city and he must angrily fend off these pests while trying to discover why his life has been suddenly turned into chaos. He meets with Young and demands an explanation and the two begin feuding, the tough reporter realizing that Young is as feisty as he is. In their love-hate relationship, Power and Young battle through almost every scene. In one hilarious sequence they are locked up in adjoining cells and are shouting at each other. Power, disgusted, lights up his last cigarette and Young then sweetly asks to have a puff. When Power cavalierly offers this to her, she takes the butt and then bites his fingers. He gets his revenge later when dumping her into a mud puddle. These antics are overshadowed by the odious visage of Sanders, a bogus count and fortune-hunter, who arrives to find that he is out in the cold. Undaunted, this consummate cad then pitches frantic woo at Young's equally rich but gullible cousin, Moore. To save Moore from the predatory Sanders, Young now announces that she is dumping Power and that she is returning to the covetous arms of Sanders. This prompts Sanders to promptly discard Moore as his intended victim, believing he has now bagged bigger game with Young, only to discover that she wants nothing to do with the now jilted gigolo and Sanders finds himself permanently out in the cold. None of this makes any sense to Power, who shows up to tell Young an angry piece of his mind. She tries to explain her purposeful sabotaging of her cousin's unworthy romance with blackguard Sanders, but Power is fed up with her shenanigans and departs without hearing her explanations. He returns to his newspaper to find to his amazement that he has been promoted to the powerful position of managing editor, but he is less amazed when discovering that Digges, who is Young's millionaire uncle, has recently bought a large interest in the newspaper. He now accepts his romantic fate, one where he knows that he cannot escape the loving arms of Young (and he does not want to escape in the first place) and both wind up together for a blissful finale. Power is superb as the rugged reporter, and the beautiful Young demonstrates the kind of acting skills that would later win her an Oscar as Best Actress for another great comedy, **The Farmer's Daughter**, 1947. Director Garnett sends this production into high gear, presenting a well-crafted and witty romance with a lot of comedic firecrackers exploding in one scene after another. Sanders, Digges and all the others in the fine cast give standout performances. Songs include: "Love Is News" (Lew Pollock, Sidney D. Mitchell), "The Man on the Flying Trapeze" (Gaston Lyle, George Leybourne), "The Prisoner's Song" (Guy Massey), and "Thanks a Million" (Arthur Johnston). Remade as a musical, **Sweet Rosie O'-Grady**, 1943, and again as a straight romance, **That Wonderful Urge**, 1947, also starring Power in his original reporter's role, and with Gene Tierney as the wealthy socialite who reluctantly falls in love with him. *Author's Note*: "As usual," Sanders told this author, "I do not have a decent bone in my body while playing a phony nobleman in **Love Is News**. I am only out after Loretta's [Young] money, and when she gives me the proverbial bum's rush, I make a play for one of her rich relatives and she upends me again. You know, I am supposed to be a very clever fellow in that picture, who can gull any naïve woman into marrying me, but I am really a dumb cluck, who keeps falling into Loretta's traps. I don't know how viewers could buy all that, but then viewers were a lot more innocent in those days and they suspended their beliefs with any balloon Hollywood would send up." Young had nothing but praise for her co-star, saying that "Ty [Power] was the most handsome man in Hollywood and I had him under my manipulative thumb in that picture, or, at least that's what my character thinks, until she realizes that she has planted him in her heart and will never let him go no matter what schemes and plots she hatches. What woman could not love Ty Power? Every woman in America did in those days and I was no exception." Director Garnett told this author that "we got accused of borrowing too much material for that picture from Frank Capra's **It Happened One Night** [1934], and I think Frank did most of that complaining, but that's not the case. **Love Is News** is a completely different story. Sure, it deals with a wealthy woman, an heiress to a great fortune, but she is not running away from her father. She is running away from the press. The fact that she falls in love with a reporter the way Claudette Colbert fell in love with Clark Gable, who plays a reporter in **It Happened One Night**, is only coincidence." Garnett grinned when adding: "Why, reporters and wealthy socialites fall in love and get married every day, don't they?" **p**, Earl Carroll, Harold Wilson; **d**, Tay Garnett; **cast**, Tyrone Power, Loretta Young, Don Ameche, Slim Summerville, Dudley Digges, Walter Catlett, Pauline Moore, Jane Darwell, Stepin Fetchit, George Sanders, Elisha Cook Jr., Frank Conroy, Eddie "Rochester" Anderson, Lynn Bari, Lon Chaney Jr., Edwin Maxwell, Charles Williams, Julius Tannen, George Humbert, Carol Tevis; **w**, Harry Turgend, Jack Yellen (based on a story by William R. Lipman, Frederick Stephani); **c**, Ernest Palmer; **m**, David Buttolph; **ed**, Irene Morra; **art d**, Rudolph Sternad; **set d**, Thomas Little.

Love Letters ★★★ 1945; U.S.; 101m; PAR; B/W; Drama/Romance; Children: Unacceptable; **VHS**. In this sensitive and often powerful film, Jones gives a superlative performance as a loving but abused woman, who falls in love with the wrong man and must make her way through the fog of amnesia to find true love. The film begins when two soldiers are stationed in Italy during WWII. Sully, a roughneck, asks his friend, Cotten, to write letters to his old girlfriend, Jones, as Sully has no knack for writing love missives, telling Cotten that he "never had any standards, manners or taste." Cotten, who has no girl to write to, writes affectionate love letters to Victoria Remington (Jones), whom he calls his "pinup girl of the spirit." Cotten's letters are full of poetically inspiring prose that causes Jones to fall deeply in love with Sully, thinking that he is writing those letters. When Sully returns home, Jones marries him, but she soon finds out that he is nothing like the man who wrote such wonderful letters to her. He is an unthinking brute, who mistreats her. When returning home one night while drunk, Sully beats Jones so savagely that her stepmother, to protect Jones, stabs Sully to death. Jones, in shock, loses her memory. Sometime later, Cotten arrives to look up old friend Sully, but finds that he is dead and he is told that his wife is also dead. He meets Jones, who calls herself Singleton. As Cotten probes for more details about his friend's murder mystery, he falls in love with Jones, who suffers from amnesia, recalling only snippets of those love letters of long ago that so touched and moved her heart. Through Cotten's tenderness and love, Jones slowly regains her memory and comes to realize that she found "the kind of spirit I found in those letters…a spirit that makes life beautiful…I love that man. I love him more than my own life." When she finds that Cotten is that man, she gives her love to him, the right man, and Cotten gives his love to her, now that he has solved the mystery. Dieterle directs with a patient hand, unfolding his scenes carefully and with great character development. Rand's script is exceptionally literate and knowing, and the performances from Jones (nominated for an Oscar for Best Actress) and Cotten are exceptional in this moving and revealing love story, a modern-day version to some degree of the bittersweet tale of Cyrano De Bergerac, but one having a happy ending. *Author's Note*: Director Dieterle told this author that "**Love Letters** is really a strange mystery after a man is killed and the young woman who thinks she loves him loses her memory of him and can only love the man who sent her the love letters that brought her and that man together. It is another man who wrote those letters, and only when she realizes that is she able to love the right man, who also loves her, does her memory return. It is the story of a troubled mind trying to find its own heart." Cotten felt that Jones "gave a wonderful performance as a traumatized young woman, who has blotted out her memory to protect the image she had for a man who never really existed. I play that man when writing letters for a friend and then have to somehow convince her that the love she got in those letters really came from me. It was a strange tale and I did a similar film with an even stranger love theme when I fall in love with Jennifer [Jones] in **Portrait of Jenny** [1948] where she is a young woman, who has died many years earlier and that is *very strange*, indeed." **p**, Hal B. Wallis; **d**, William Dieterle; **cast**, Jennifer Jones, Joseph Cotten, Ann Richards, Cecil Kellaway, Gladys Cooper, Anita Louise, Robert Sully, Reginald Denny, Ernest Cossart, Byron Barr; **w**, Ayn Rand (based on the novel *Pity My Simplicity* by Chris Massie); **c**, Lee Garmes; **m**, Victor Young; **ed**, Anne Bauchens; **art d**, Hans Dreier, Roland Anderson; **set d**, Ray Moyer; **spec eff**, Farciot Edouart, Gordon Jennings, Loyal Griggs, Paul K. Lerpae.

Love Letters ★★★ 1984; U.S.; 98m; Millenium/New World Pictures; Color; Drama; Children: Unacceptable (MPAA: R); **DVD**; **VHS**. In this intriguing tale, Curtis is a single woman, who is a radio disc jockey and who has a brief, unhappy affair with an older happily married man, Keach, a successful Los Angeles commercial photographer. He doesn't keep his marriage from her, but she insists that he give up his wife, Leverington, and children and marry her. He refuses, and it's like *déjà vu* for Curtis since she comes upon love letters her late mother had written that tell she had a love affair for fifteen years with a married man. Sexual scenes prohibit viewing by children. **p**, Roger Corman; **d&w**, Amy Holden Jones; **cast**, Jamie Lee Curtis, Bonnie Bartlett, Matt Clark, James Keach, Amy Madigan, Brian Wood, Phil Coccioletti, Larry Cedar, Michael Villella, Bud Cort; **c**, Alec Hirschfeld; **m**, Ralph Jones; **ed**, Wendy Greene Bricmont; **prod d**, Jeannine Claudia Oppewall; **art d**, David Brisbin; **spec eff**, Laurel Klick, Bret Mixon.

Love Me or Leave Me ★★★ 1955; U.S.; 122m; MGM; Color; Biog-

James Cagney and Doris Day in *Love Me or Leave Me*, 1955.

raphical Drama/Musical; Children: Cautionary; **DVD**; **VHS**. Day performs one of her finest roles in essaying the biopic of singer Ruth Etting (1897-1978), who, during her heyday of the 1920s and 1930s, was known as "America's Sweetheart of Song." A singer with more than sixty hits in her illustrious career, she was also an actress, appearing on radio and in films. Born in Nebraska, she moved to Chicago to study art and got a job as a lowly costume designer in a nightclub, but had ambitions to become a singer and that is where this dynamic and thoroughly entertaining film begins when Day tries for that first job. She is shown working in a dancehall where customers pay ten cents to dance with girls working there and Day is pushed and shoved about the dance floor while being clutched and pawed by her crude male customers. She refuses to dance with one customer, who takes too many liberties, and she is fired from her job. Leaving the place, Day is spotted by Cagney, who plays gangster Martin "Moe the Gimp" Snyder (who married Etting in 1922 and became her manager as well as her abusive and domineering husband), and he offers to give her a ride. Day thinks he is trying to pick her up, and he gives her his card (he runs a laundry, a legitimate enterprise along illegal rackets) and arranges for her to get a job at a nightclub where Day is put into a bump and grind chorus line. Upon seeing the voluptuous and leggy Day clumsily dancing as a chorus girl, Cagney pressures nightclub owner Tully into giving her a singing job, offering to pay more money than the owner is willing to give to Day as a salary. Further, Cagney encourages pianist Mitchell to give Day strong support in her singing presentations, but this proves to be a mistake in that Mitchell has a romantic eye focused upon the sexy Day. After Day's first solo singing performances, Cagney arranges to have the lead singer suddenly go absent and Day replaces her, becoming a hit, especially after Cagney packs the place with his cronies. (Cagney, when also playing a gangster, had done the same thing in **The Roaring Twenties**, 1939, when making a singing star out of girlfriend Priscilla Lane by getting her a singing job in a nightclub and packing the place with his friends and associates.) Day then becomes a genuine success after delivering one top song after another, and Cagney assumes the role of her manager, getting her jobs on the radio that further promote the sales of her records. Cagney then marries Day and takes her to New York where he gets her into the Ziegfeld Follies. Cagney, however, is a crude thug from Chicago and his bossy ways and interference with Ziegfeld's dance and singing coaches soon make him a pariah, but Day does nothing to defend Cagney. In a rage, he tears up her contract with Ziegfeld and then takes her on a national tour that ends up in Hollywood where Cagney arranges for Day to star in the movies. She again meets accompanist Mitchell and the two resume their friendly relationship that blossoms into love (Day has never loved Cagney) while they work together in developing Day's film career. Cagney, meanwhile, buys an old nightclub and spends

Jeanette MacDonald and Maurice Chevalier in *Love Me Tonight*, 1932.

all his cash refurbishing it, turning it into a posh spa for Hollywood celebrities and where he intends to have Day as his star attraction. He then finds Day kissing Mitchell and explodes, shooting Mitchell (but not fatally) and for which he is jailed. When released, however, Day repays Cagney for shaping and developing her career by appearing as his star attraction at the opening of his nightclub and where Cagney watches her with his old affection and admiration at the finale. Vidor directs this lavish musical biopic with great vitality and Day's singing is as wonderful as her acting. Her scenes with the dynamic Cagney are full of tension and conflict as Day consistently caves into Cagney's demands in order to fulfill her ambitions. Where the magnetic Cagney victimizes Day in providing her with the success she so desperately desires in exchange for her grudging affection (or sex), Day, in turn, victimizes Cagney as a rather ungrateful and contentious spouse, using him to gain fame while belittling and demeaning him for his uncouth ways. The well-written story is candid and uncompromising and as ruthless and aggressive as the Jazz Age it so accurately depicts. The film was a great box office success, returning more than $4 million in its initial release. Songs include: "Shaking the Blues Away" (Irving Berlin), "It All Depends on You" (Ray Henderson; lyrics: Buddy DeSylva, Lew Brown), "I'm Sitting on Top of the World" (Ray Henderson; lyrics: Sam Lewis, Joe Young), "Stay on the Right Side, Sister" (Rube Bloom, Ted Koehler), "You Made Me Love You (I Didn't Want to Do It)" (James V. Monaco, Joseph McCarthy), "Mean to Me" (Fred E. Ahlert, Roy Turk), "Everybody Loves My Baby (but My Baby Don't Love Nobody but Me)" (Spencer Williams, Jack Palmer), "Sam, the Old Accordion Man," "At Sun Down (Love Is Calling Me Home)" (Walter Donaldson), "I'll Never Stop Loving You" (Nicholas Brodszky, Sammy Cahn), "Ten Cents a Dance" (Richard Rodgers, Lorenz Hart), "Never Look Back" (Chilton Price), "Five Foot Two, Eyes of Blue (Has Anybody Seen My Girl?)" (Ray Henderson), "(What Can I Say) After I Say I'm Sorry" (Walter Donaldson, Abe Lyman), "I Miss My Swiss (My Swiss Miss Misses Me)" (Abel Baer, L. Wolfe Gilbert), "My Blue Heaven" (Walter Donaldson, George Whiting), "I Cried for You (Arthur Freed, Gus Arnheim, Abe Lyman) and "Love Me or Leave Me" (Walter Donaldson, Gus Khan). *Author's Note*: Day was not the first choice to play Ruth Etting in this film. It was offered to MGM contract player Ava Gardner, but she turned down the role, believing that producers would dub her voice as they did in **Showboat**, 1951. George Cukor was also slated to direct this film, but he was replaced by veteran helmsman Vidor. Day had, up to the time of this film, been known as the wholesome girl next door, the most prim and proper Hollywood singer, but, in this film, she was asked by producer Pasternak to wear several skimpy costumes, especially when playing a chorus girl where she was required to show a lot of leg, thigh and bosom. She at first resisted, but Pasternak explained

that the role and the era in which the film was set called for such attire and Day finally agreed. Cagney told this author that "I thought Doris [Day] was just terrific in that picture. She was mostly at my studio, Warner Brothers, in her early Hollywood career, and she was mostly in musicals and was not required to do much real acting, but she acted rings around me in **Love Me or Leave Me**. I also thought her style of singing was perfect for the kind of songs she sang. They belted songs out in the twenties and Doris did that so well while playing Ruth Etting. When listening to that great voice of hers, well, she made me long for those days, even though those days were not too kind to me. She's one of the great singers, up there with Jo Stafford, Frances Langford, and Ginny Sims, yes sir." MGM spent more than $50,000 for the rights to the songs used in the film and they also spent considerable money in buying the life stories of Etting, Snyder and Myrl Alderman, who is played by Mitchell in the film and is called "Johnny Alderman.' The script stretched the truth with Etting's real life and Etting said, after seeing the film: "Oh, what a...mess that was...I never at any time was a dancehall girl. It was just a means of working in [the song] 'Ten Cents a Dance.' They took a lot of liberties with my life, but I guess they usually do with that kind of thing." She thought she might sue MGM for those transgressions but then recalled gossip columnist Walter Winchell's warning to those with such inclinations, that legal battles only bring on more bad publicity and Etting dropped the idea. **p**, Joe Pasternak; **d**, Charles Vidor; **cast**, Doris Day, James Cagney, Cameron Mitchell, Robert Keith, Tom Tully, Harry Bellaver, Richard Gaines, Veda Ann Borg, James Drury, Dick Simmons; **w**, Daniel Fuchs, Isobel Lennart (based on the story by Fuchs); **c**, Arthur E. Arling (CinemaScope; Eastmancolor); **m**, George Stoll; **ed**, Ralph E. Winters; **art d**, Cedric Gibbons, Urie McCleary; **set d**, Edwin B. Willis, Jack D. Moore; **spec eff**, Warren Newcombe.

Love Me Tonight ★★★★★ 1932; U.S.; 104m; PAR; B/W; Musical; Children: Acceptable; **DVD**; **VHS**. In one of the greatest musicals ever produced, everything about this wonderful production is orchestrated to seamlessly fit every scene where the music and story line are one without the viewer ever noticing. The film cleverly opens with Chevalier, a Paris tailor, awakening with the sunrise and where the sounds of life greet him. He hears the melody of the early morning workers' tools—the swish of a broom, the scrape of a pick, the whir of a grinding wheel, the clang of a shovel, music to his ears and that of the viewer. The sounds of Paris, by then so expertly in rhythm, are joined by an orchestra when a woman plays a phonograph to present a full melody and where Chevalier stands at the window of his room and sings "That's the Song of Paree." Once in his shop, Roach, a customer, arrives to retrieve his wedding apparel, but Chevalier and Roach are soon distracted when they see a rush of marathon runners streaming past the shop. One of them, Ruggles, a womanizing count, appears in shorts and bearing a makeshift number he has written on a fruit peddler's sign. He is a bogus competitor, having joined the runners after escaping from the home of a woman after her husband unexpectedly appeared. (This inventive and precedent-setting film proved to be a treasure trove for producers, who liberally borrowed from its scenes, such as where Terry-Thomas duplicates the marathon runners sequence in **Make Mine Mink**, 1960.) Ruggles asks Chevalier for some walking apparel and some cash and the tailor obligingly complies. After he leaves, Chevalier and Roach exchange rhyming dialog that evolves into the song "Isn't It Romantic?" When Roach leaves humming this tune, a cabdriver picks up on the song and whistles it while his passenger, a composer, writes down the notes; while later riding a train, he gives the tune lyrics, and this is overheard by some soldiers, who begin singing it as they march across a field. A passing gypsy then plays the song on his violin, which is heard by MacDonald, who lives in a majestic chateau, and she completes the chain, from Chevalier to her (and thus their long-distanced romantic link is established) by singing it. MacDonald is then fending off advances from Butterworth, an ardent suitor, fainting in the process. Her dithering aunts, Patterson, Griffies and Frederici, meanwhile, are busy trying to come up with a cure to remedy MacDonald's all too frequent fainting spells. While this is going on, Loy is plying her wealthy uncle, Smith (the duke) for an advance, and Ruggles then arrives and attempts to borrow money from Loy. He, too, is a nobleman, but so impoverished that he must live on what he can get from Smith. Back in Paris, Chevalier is inundated with complaints about Ruggles, who owes endless creditors considerable money, and Chevalier tells these creditors that he will arrange to have those debts settled. Davis, who is driving a limousine to Biarritz, offers to give Chevalier a ride to the rural chateau where Ruggles lives, but the car breaks down on a narrow road, and while MacDonald is driving her carriage (and singing "Lover") her carriage overturns when she tries to pass the stranded limousine and she lands in the mud. Chevalier, who is standing nearby, retrieves her from the mire, calling her "Mimi" and singing the song about her that would later become Chevalier's trademark song. MacDonald, once her small carriage is righted, goes on her way, but when she returns to the chateau, she again faints. He physician tells her that all of her fainting spells are caused by her lack of having a man in her life. She has been widowed for a few years, having married a man in his seventies when she was sixteen and now she is told that there are only two available males in France who are eligible for her, based on her aristocratic station, a nobleman in his eighties and a boy who has yet to turn thirteen. When Chevalier arrives at the chateau, Ruggles panics and tells everyone that Chevalier is an old friend and a baron while promising Chevalier that he will somehow get the money he owes to all of Chevalier's friends in Paris. Chevalier stays on, impersonating the role of the baron and befriends wealthy Smith, and where a number of hilarious scenes take place, including morning workouts and horseback riding (this scene duplicated in **Auntie Mame**, 1958). Smith, meanwhile, searches through all known sources of French lineage and announces that he cannot find the name Chevalier has been using anywhere to prove that he is of noble birth. Ruggles then says that Chevalier is related to the Austrian Hapsburg princes, but is incognito. Chevalier is ultimately unmasked as an imposter, but, by that time, it doesn't matter as he has charmed everyone, especially the lovesick MacDonald. When he leaves, taking a train back to Paris, MacDonald races after him, has the train stopped, and they embrace for a happy finale, viewers knowing that, irrespective of his lowborn station in life, Chevalier will be with MacDonald forever. The wonderful script sparkles with wit and humor, and Mamoulian's direction is impeccable in every detail while he presents this stunning musical tableau with one spritely tuneful scene after another, a true masterpiece musical in which Chevalier and MacDonald shine and enthrall. Mamoulian's genius for mixing content and style was never more in evidence. They do not come any better than this one. Songs include the abovementioned and (all from Richard Rodgers and Lorenz Hart): "Love Me Tonight," "The Poor Apache," "How Are You?," "Deer Hunt," "A Woman Needs Something Like That" and "The Son of a Gun Is Nothing But a Tailor." *Author's Note*: Mamoulian, who employs the tracking and dolly shots for which he was known, again fuses realism with expressionism, as if painting his scenes as would a Constable. "They were still working on sound techniques to quiet the noises made by the cameras when I made **Love Me Tonight**," Mamoulian told this author. "I let some of that sound in to get the right panning and dolly shots and figured the audiences would take no notice because the scenes were so captivating and this proved to be correct. To have a good sound is important, of course, but, in those days, sound people tried to dominate directors and cameramen, the most important of the crew members, and I was having nothing to do with that. When they told me that the cameras were making too much noise, I told them, 'so what? I won't throw away a good shot just for that.'" Mamoulian, to mollify sound technicians, invented what is called a "blimp" which encased the camera but still allowed it to move so that he could get his dolly, panning and tracking shots, but where it made no noise. **p&d**, Rouben Mamoulian; **cast**, Maurice Chevalier, Jeanette MacDonald, Charlie Ruggles, Charles Butter-

Clark Gable and Joan Crawford in *Love on the Run*, 1936.

worth, Myrna Loy, Sir C. Aubrey Smith, Elizabeth Patterson, Ethel Griffies, Blanche Frederici, Robert Greig, Bert Roach, George Davis, George "Gabby" Hayes; **w**, Samuel Hoffenstein, Waldemar Young, George Marion Jr. (based on the play "Tailor in the Chateau" by Leopold Marchand, Paul Armont); **c**, Victor Milner; **m**, John Leipold; **ed**, William Shea, Mamoulian; **art d**, Hans Dreier; **set d**, A.E. Freudeman.

Love on the Run ★★★ 1936; U.S.; 80m; MGM; B/W; Comedy; Children: Acceptable; **DVD**; **VHS**. In this lively romantic romp, Gable and Tone are rival reporters in Europe where the inventive Gable always seems to scoop Tone, vexing him no end. They both get two assignments, one to cover a celebrated aviator, Owen, who is nothing of the kind, being a vicious spy, and the other is to report on the upcoming nuptials of madcap heiress Crawford, who is about to marry fortune-hunter Lebedeff. (A popular romantic theme in the 1930s, this situation is repeated a year later in **Love Is News**, 1937, where reporter Tyrone Power inadvertently prevents fortune-hunter George Sanders from marrying heiress Loretta Young.) Though Gable is avidly seeking to expose Owen as an insidious espionage agent, Crawford, who hates newspapermen but doesn't know that is Gable's occupation, asks for his help. They, along with Tone, abscond with Owen's plane, flying across Europe and later, in pursuit of the elusive Owen, follow him by car and then in a cart. Owen and his fellow spies then pursue Gable and Crawford, who wind up at Fontainebleau, and, where Meek, the crazy caretaker of the palace, thinks Gable and Crawford are the returning king and queen of France. Gable then wires in his story and, after Crawford learns that he's a newspaperman, leaves him flat, going off with Tone on a train. She is abducted by Owen and his henchmen and Tone is tossed from the moving train. Gable arrives at a farmhouse where he rescues Crawford and prevents Owen from taking off in another plane with the stolen British military secrets. Gable and Tone then capture the lot of spies. Gable, however, leaves the hapless Tone tied to a chair as he and Crawford depart in the plane to seek more adventure, happiness or even a sequel to this whirlwind of a movie. The story line is erratic, but the action is so brisk and the set pieces are so amusing and well acted by Gable, Crawford, Tone and the rest of the cast that the film nevertheless works well and provides consistent entertainment, particularly the scenes at the palace where Gable and Crawford humor the wacky Meek by pretending to be Louis XVI and Marie Antoinette and they perform an awkward minuet that transcends into a hula. *Author's Note*: "That picture did not make much sense," Crawford told this author, "but it was a lot of fun to make. Woody [Van Dyke, the director] was always coming up with some odd ideas to make **Love on the Run** funnier, and he thought that the crazier the idea, the better the picture would be. Audiences liked it, but they were easier to please in those

Jeanette MacDonald and Maurice Chevalier in *The Love Parade*, 1929.

days." **p**, Joseph L. Mankiewicz, W.S. Van Dyke; **d**, Van Dyke; **cast**, Joan Crawford, Clark Gable, Franchot Tone, Reginald Owen, Mona Barrie, Ivan Lebedeff, William Demarest, Donald Meek, George Davis, Billy Gilbert, Leonid Kinskey, Christian Rub, Charles Judels, Charles Trowbridge, Frank Puglia, Richard Alexander; **w**, John Lee Mahin, Manuel Seff, Gladys Hurlbut (based on the story "Beauty and the Beast" by Alan Green, Julian Brodie); **c**, Oliver T. Marsh; **m**, Franz Waxman; **ed**, Frank Sullivan; **art d**, Cedric Gibbons.

Love on the Run ★★★ 1979; France; 94m; Les Films du Carrosse; New World Pictures; Color; Drama; Children: Unacceptable (MPAA: PG); **DVD**; **VHS**. In this absorbing drama from Truffaut, Léaud is a proofreader in love with a record seller, Dorothée, so he divorces his wife, Jade, of five years. The girl he loved when they were teenagers, Pisier, is now a lawyer, who sees him at the divorce proceedings. They do not meet, however, until later when Léaud sees Pisier at a train station. They ride a train together and recall their earlier adolescent love. Léaud, however, loses interest in her and returns to Dorothée. This was the fifth and final entry in the series with the same character that began with **The 400 Blows**, 1959, and starring Léaud and where the protagonist searches his past for the women in his life. He has a desperate need to love, but when meeting up with old flames, he finds that the fires never burned too brightly in the first place. Delerue's score is exceptional and includes the memorable song "L'amour en fuite" (Alain Souchon, Laurent Voulzy). Sexuality prohibits viewing by children. (In French; English subtitles.) **p&d**, François Truffaut; **cast**, Jean-Pierre Léaud, Marie-France Pisier, Claude Jade, Dani, Dorothée, Daniel Mesguich, Julien Bertheau, Jean-Pierre Ducos, Marie Henriau, Rosy Varte, Pierre Dios; **w**, Truffaut, Pisier, Jean Aurel, Suzanne Schiffman; **c**, Néstor Almendros; **m**, Georges Delerue; **ed**, Martine Barraqué; **prod d**, Jean-Pierre Kohut-Svelko.

The Love Parade ★★★ 1929; U.S.; 107m; PAR; B/W; Musical Comedy; Romance; Children: Acceptable; **DVD**. Delightful and entertaining, this songfest offers MacDonald as a love-starved queen of a mythical Balkan country (Sylvania). She receives bad reports about Chevalier, her womanizing emissary to France. His dallying with so many French ladies has gotten him a notorious reputation, and he is recalled to his native country where MacDonald upbraids him for his amorous transgressions. She invites him into her boudoir and demands that he demonstrate the romantic skills that have made him the talk of Paris. Chevalier happily complies and, after sweeping queen MacDonald off her feet, she realizes that he is the man for her and marries him, making him her prince consort (á la Queen Victoria and Prince Albert of England). They get off to a good start until Sylvania becomes

strapped for ready cash and MacDonald seeks to borrow huge sums to stabilize her national economy (shades of America in the 2010s) while Chevalier remains in the shadows, believing he could handle things much better. MacDonald then exercises her queenly authority by making regal demands on Chevalier and he balks, and when she orders him to escort her to the opening of the opera, Chevalier refuses. A saddened MacDonald goes to her royal box alone, but when Chevalier suddenly arrives, her spirits rise, only to be deflated when he tells her that he can no longer be her slavish prince escort and is going to Paris to seek a divorce. Returning from the opera that night, MacDonald concludes that it is wiser to join with Chevalier than separate from him. She goes to his palatial quarters where he takes her into his arms and she makes him king and supreme sovereign of the country for a happy ending. Lubitsch does a wonderful job with this lavishly appointed production, carefully meshing its fine songs with the story line and exacting top-notch performances from MacDonald and Chevalier, Lane, Roth, Pallette and others in a strong cast that round out this insouciant entry. The singing by both MacDonald and Chevalier is stirring and thrilling. Songs (all but one from composer Victor Schertzinger with lyrics from Clifford Grey) include: "Paris, Stay the Same" (sung by Chevalier and Lane), "Ooh, La La" (sung by Lane), "Dream Lover" (sung by MacDonald and chorus), "Anything to Please the Queen" (sung by MacDonald and Chevalier), "Let's Be Common" (sung by Lane and Roth), "My Love Parade" (sung by Chevalier and MacDonald), "Nobody's Using It Now" (sung by Chevalier), "March of the Grenadiers" (sung by MacDonald and chorus), "The Queen Is Always Right" (sung by Lane, Roth and chorus) and "The Wedding March" (composed by Felix Mendelssohn-Bartholdy). The film received six Oscar nominations, including Best Picture, Best Director and Best Actor (Chevalier), but won none. *Author's Note*: This was Lubitsch's first talking film and he makes the most of sound, although there were many passages in the original shooting that had no sound at all, and, to conform to the new medium, Lubitsch inserted sound into those sequences. MacDonald makes her film debut in this production after being discovered by Hollywood while appearing in the Broadway musicals of "Yes, Yes, Yvette," "Angela," and "Boom Boom." She was, however, not to Lubitsch's physical liking. The Germanic director was used to having his leading ladies on the plump side and he thought MacDonald too slender for her role, so he insisted, much to her chagrin, that she stuff herself with hamburgers and milkshakes until she put on more weight. Jean Harlow, who was then an extra before she became a Hollywood star, appears in two scenes, one in the orchestra and another when she is in an opera box. Silent screen film comic Ben Turpin appears briefly doing his cross-eyed routine. **p**, Ernst Lubitsch; **d**, Lubitsch, Perry Ivins; **cast**, Maurice Chevalier, Jeanette MacDonald, Lupino Lane, Lillian Roth, Eugene Pallette, E.H. Calvert, Edgar Norton, Lionel Belmore, Virginia Bruce, Jean Harlow, Ben Turpin; **w**, Ernest Vajda, Guy Bolton (based on the play "The Prince Consort" by Jules Chancel, Leon Xanrof); **c**, Victor Milner; **m**, W. Franke Harling, John Leipold, Oscar Potoker, Max Terr; **ed**, Merrill G. White; **art d**, Hans Dreier.

Love Story ★★★ 1970; U.S.; 99m; PAR; Color; Romance; Children: Cautionary; **DVD**; **VHS**. In the wrong hands, this touching and heart-moving tale would have turned to sentimental slush, but director Hiller made this a memorable film where star-crossed lovers MacGraw and O'Neal give sterling performances, perhaps the best of their careers. O'Neal is in his last year of law school at Harvard when he meets attractive MacGraw, an art student at Radcliffe. They both quickly fall in love and plan to wed, but when O'Neal informs his wealthy father, Milland, about his intentions, the Back Bay patriarch puts down his Brahmin foot after learning that MacGraw is the daughter of a poor Italian baker and comes from the decidedly wrong side of the tracks. Milland tells O'Neal that if he weds MacGraw, he will disown him and he will not receive a dime of his family's carefully hoarded fortune. (This draconian decree is established in many films by such dominating patriarchs, most notably in the comedy, **The Late George Apley**, 1947, where Ronald Colman essays just such a bossy Brahmin.) Undaunted, O'Neal marries the girl of his dreams. Cut off without funds, O'Neal tries to get a scholarship from Harvard, but he is turned down since he is the son of a multimillionaire and he must take various jobs to get that degree, along with help from MacGraw, who works as a vocal coach for a school choir. They take a cheap apartment in a poor neighborhood, but are happy. After O'Neal graduates, he gets a good job in New York and the couple moves into an upscale apartment. Life is bright and full of gladness for them, but, no matter how hard they try, MacGraw cannot become pregnant. Consulting a physician to see if she is barren, O'Neal learns that MacGraw is terminally ill and has only a short while to live. He thinks she is ignorant of this and tries to keep her from knowing this, but she has kept a good face toward this tragedy and, after he knows she knows, O'Neal offers to take her to France, a country she has always wanted to visit. MacGraw refuses, wanting to spend her remaining time on earth at home with O'Neal so they can fully share what is left of their life closer together. She dies in O'Neal's arms and he is devastated, recalling his earlier statement: "What can you say about a twenty-five-year-old girl that died? That she was beautiful and brilliant? That she loved Mozart and Bach, the Beetles and me?" A contrite and regretful Milland appears at the hospital to tell his son that he is sorry for the way he treated him and MacGraw, but it is all too late. O'Neal then delivers a line that is forever associated with this grand but tasteful tearjerker, stating: "Love means never having to say you're sorry." It became the catchword of a generation of young lovers. This sensitive and caring film, although some of its dialog is a bit on the soggy side (but never sappy), is lastingly memorable and takes its place with similar fine bittersweet films dealing with the same theme of star-crossed lovers and where the heroine meets with tragedy. These include **A Farewell to Arms**, 1932, and its 1957 remake; **Love Affair**, 1939, and its great remake, **An Affair to Remember**, 1957; **Dark Victory**, 1939; **Wuthering Heights**, 1939; and **Terms of Endearment**, 1983. The film was nominated for a bevy of Oscars, winning only for Best Original Score (Lai). Shot mostly on location at Harvard, its $2.2 million budget was quickly recouped at the box office where it became an enormous hit, producing a staggering $136 million over the years. *Author's Note*: Most of the top young male movie stars of the day, including Jon Voight, Michael Douglas, Beau Bridges, Michael Sarrazin, and Michael York, turned down the script for this film as did several popular directors of that day until Hiller decided to take on the story. He made the film even better than the best-selling soap opera novel from Segal. **p**, Howard G. Minsky; **d**, Arthur Hiller; **cast**, Ali MacGraw, Ryan O'Neal, John Marley, Ray Milland, Russell Nype, Katherine Balfour, Sydney Walker, Robert Modica, Walker Daniels, Tommy Lee Jones; **w**, Erich Segal (based on his novel); **c**, Dick Kratina (Movielab Color); **m**, Francis Lai; **ed**, Robert C. Jones; **art d**, Robert Gundlach; **set d**, Philip Smith.

Love with the Proper Stranger ★★★ 1963; U.S.; 102m; Boardwalk-Rona/PAR; B/W; Romance; Children: Unacceptable; **DVD**; **VHS**. Wood is superlative as a sweet Italian girl who falls for jazz musician McQueen and then has trouble when getting in the family way. They meet at a summer hotel where McQueen is playing and have a one-night affair. Wood later shows up at McQueen's union hall to tell him that she needs help in finding a doctor. McQueen has no idea where to turn and bluntly tells his regular girlfriend Adams about Wood's pregnancy, seeking her advice. Realizing that McQueen has betrayed her with another woman, Adams has only one bit of advice for the candid (if not naïve) McQueen and that is to get out immediately. Meanwhile, Wood is contending with her family members, mother Santon and her brothers Lembeck and Bernardi, none of whom knows of her delicate condition and who are pressuring her to marry kindly, overweight restaurant owner Bosley. McQueen takes Wood to meet his parents and she is a great hit with them, while he tries to raise the money for an abortionist. Bosley, who learns that Wood is pregnant, then magnanimously tells some peo-

Ryan O'Neal and Ali MacGraw in *Love Story,* 1970.

ple that Wood is pregnant with his child to more easily convince her to marry him. But Wood does not love Bosley, only McQueen, and he loves her, too. Even though he knows he is not the best prospective husband for her, McQueen takes the plunge anyway and he and Wood then plan to go to the altar. This was one of the first films to deal with abortion, which does not take place in any event, and, though the subject is sensitively handled, the producers had apprehensions about audience reception. They needn't have worried as this film proved to be a great success, which was brought about by the top-notch acting from Wood, McQueen and the earthy Italian humor stemming from Lembeck and Bernardi. Ironically, none of the leading players are Italian. The budget for this film was more than $8 million, but it returned more than $415 million at the box office. The film was nominated for five Oscars, including Best Actress (Wood), but won none. McQueen and Wood were also nominated for Golden Globe Awards as Best Actor and Best Actress. **p**, Alan J. Pakula; **d**, Robert Mulligan; **cast**, Natalie Wood, Steve McQueen, Edie Adams, Herschel Bernardi, Anne Hegira, Harvey Lembeck, Tom Bosley, Arlene Golonka, Richard Mulligan, Vic Tayback, Jack Jones (singing); **w**, Arnold Schulman; **c**, Milton Krasner; **m**, Elmer Bernstein, Schulman; **ed**, Aaron Stell; **art d**, Hal Pereira, Roland Anderson; **set d**, Sam Comer, Grace Gregory; **spec eff**, Gerald Endler, Farciot Edouart, Paul K. Lerpae.

The Loved One ★★★ 1965; U.S.; 122m; Filmways/MGM; B/W; Comedy; Children: Unacceptable; **DVD**; **VHS**. This bizarre satire savagely lampoons the funeral business in Hollywood and it would be too grim for any viewer if it had not been for the mesmerizing performances of some of its principal oddball players, chiefly Morse, Comer, Winters and Steiger. Based on the macabre tale from Waugh, the film begins when Morse, a budding British poet, but essentially an awkward cluck, arrives in Hollywood to meet his fussy uncle, Gielgud, an aging art director for films, whose halcyon years are long gone and where he lives in a run-down mansion. After Gielgud hangs himself, Morley, who heads the British community in filmdom, instructs Morse to arrange for his uncle's burial at Hollywood's most resplendent resting grounds, Whispering Glades Memorial Park (which is another name Waugh gives for the illustrious Forest Lawn), which is run by ruthlessly greedy Winters. While contacting unctuous morticians in arranging for his uncle's burial, Morse gets a job at a pet cemetery operated by Winters' brother (also played by Winters), who is as indifferent to the departed animals as his brother is to deceased humans. Morse then becomes associated with Winters' brother, the one running Whispering Glades, and meets sultry mortuary assistant Comer, who, like all of these commercial ghouls, is afflicted by necrophilia, and with a decided fixation on her own future death. The voluptuous Comer is sought after by not only

Doris Day and Rock Hudson in *Lover Come Back*, 1962.

Morse, but Steiger, whose obese and gluttonous mother offends everyone except him, as well as big shot Winters, who is now trying to find a way to "get these stiffs off my property," so he can turn the vast cemetery into a upscale housing area and make more millions. He adopts a plan to dig up all of the corpses at Whispering Glades and send them into space. Steiger, a berserk cosmetologist, who prepares the dead for burial and who adjusts their countenances into comic faces for his own amusement (and God knows what else he does to these hapless cadavers) manhandles Comer while Morse plies her with cornball poetry. She evades the clutches of all, but her quirky ideals are crushed when her idol, Winters, tries to seduce her. Life is no longer worthwhile to Comer and she prefers death, which is what she always preferred in the first place and commits suicide by injecting embalming fluid into her veins. The grieving Morse takes revenge on Winters by exposing Winters' insidious plot to send the corpses on his property into space with the collusion of U.S. Air Force general Andrews. That scheme is to be initiated when a recently deceased astronaut is to be launched into space as his final resting place, a burial hallmark that will ostensibly inspire Winters to send all of the dead at Whispering Glades after him and then sell his vacated land to wealthy retirees. Morse replaces the astronaut's body with that of Comer and she, instead, is sent into space and then Morse publicly exposes Winters' evil scheme, ruining him. He then departs for England to continue his dubious career as a poet. The entire cast provides a lot of entertainment in this wild and raw funeral spoof and where Stander, Hunter and Coburn also add some very funny bits. This one is not for anyone with a squeamish stomach and will appeal to mostly those with a rather jaundiced view of life with an acquired taste for the ghastly and gruesome. ***Author's Note***: Steiger told this author that **"The Loved One** was most likely the strangest picture I ever appeared in. I play a goofy guy named "Joyboy" and if he isn't the weirdest ghoul on the planet, I don't know who is. I mean, this man is only happy when he is preparing the dead "loved ones" to be presented to live people. At one point, I am preparing John Gielgud, that great actor, for his last appearance in his casket and I distort his face to several shocking looks and while I was doing that, Gielgud, who was perfect at playing dead, suddenly bolted upright in a sitting position and scared the hell out of me. Then he said in a soft voice: 'You know they do that, dead people in the morgue, suddenly sit upright for a moment or two—I believe it's the gases in their stomachs or something like that that causes that rather frightening action.' He then loudly passed gas, smiled, closed his eyes and went back to playing dead." **p**, John Calley, Haskell Wexler; **d**, Tony Richardson; **cast**, Robert Morse, Jonathan Winters, Rod Steiger, Anjanette Comer, Dana Andrews, Milton Berle, James Coburn, John Gielgud, Tab Hunter, Margaret Leighton, Liberace, Roddy McDowall, Robert Morley, Lionel Stander, Paul Williams, Jamie Farr; **w**, Terry

Southern, Christopher Isherwood (baesed on the novel by Evelyn Waugh); **c**, Wexler; **m**, John Addison; **ed**, Hal Ashby, Brian Smedley-Aston; **prod d**, Rouben Ter-Arutunian; **art d**, Sydney Z. Litwack; **set d**, James W. Payne; **spec eff**, G.G. Gaspar.

Lovely to Look At ★★★ 1952; U.S.; 103m; MGM; Color; Musical; Romance; Children: Acceptable; **DVD**; **VHS**. In this lively musical, Skelton, Keel, and Gower Champion are three Broadway producers desperately looking for backers for a new musical. Skelton is an heir to a dress salon in Paris, which is in financial trouble. Two other salon heiresses, Grayson and Marge Champion, join them in convincing some of the salon's creditors to back a musical fashion show there. Skelton and Keel both fall in love with Grayson when Miller, Skelton's dancer-girlfriend arrives from New York. After some romantic entanglements, the show is a hit and Grayson and Keel wind up together. This remake of **Roberta**, 1935, presents a breezy romance with some memorable songs (all from Jerome Kern) including "Opening Night," "Smoke Gets in Your Eyes," "Lovely to Look At," "The Touch of Your Hand," "Yesterdays," "I Won't Dance," "You're Devastating," "The Most Exciting Night," and "I'll Be Hard to Handle." **p**, Jack Cummings; **d**, Mervyn LeRoy; **cast**, Kathryn Grayson, Red Skelton, Howard Keel, Marge and Gower Champion, Ann Miller, Zsa Zsa Gabor, Kurt Kasznar, Marcel Dalio, Diane Cassidy; **w**, George Wells, Harry Ruby, Andrew Solt (based on the musical comedy "Roberta" by Jerome Kern, Dorothy Fields, Otto A. Harbach and the novel *Gowns by Roberta* by Alice Duer Miller); **c**, George J. Folsey (Technicolor); **m**, Kern, Carmen Dragon; **ed**, John McSweeney, Jr.; **art d**, Cedric Gibbons, Gabriel Scognamillo; **set d**, Edwin B. Willis, Jack D. Moore; **spec eff**, A. Arnold Gillespie.

Lover Come Back ★★★ 1962; U.S.; 107m; UNIV; Color; Comedy; Children: Acceptable; **DVD**; **VHS**. In what is one of the best Day-Hudson films, the contentious rivals are this time advertising executives battling for clients and with each other. Each works for fiercely competitive agencies on Madison Avenue, and where Day, who has never met Hudson, reports his unethical stealing of clients via his alluring female associates and ample booze parties to the Advertising Council. Hudson circumvents censor and reprimands by sending Adams, his most voluptuous emissary, to the Council and she quickly seduces Council members into giving Hudson a clean bill of advertising health. Hudson rewards Adams by making her the "VIP" girl and puts her into a number of ads for a nonexistent product. Randall, who owns the firm that allegedly produces this new product, becomes confused and mistakenly runs these ads on TV, which proves to be successful, but now forces Randall to invent a product called "VIP." Randall has his top scientist, Kruschen, develop "VIP," but before he finishes the formula, Day is now energetically attempting to steal the product. Believing that Hudson is the company scientist, she has dinner with him and is initially attracted to him, but then becomes enraged when she discovers his true identity and, worse, that he has promoted a nonexistent product (for which she tried to get the advertising account). Day goes back to the Advertising Council and reports this. Hudson is summoned before the tribunal, but, by this time, Kruschen, a decidedly eccentric inventor, has come up with the product, a delicious mint candy with a very distinctive taste. All at the hearing sample the candy, including Day, but none realize the potency of the amazing "VIP," which is similar to drinking several triple martinis. Day is startled to wake up the next morning in bed with Hudson and even more shocked to learn that she and Hudson have gotten married, which is hazily recalled through their titanic hangovers. The enraged Day (she spends much of her time a bit too outraged in this and most of her movies from the 1960s onward) seeks and gets a divorce and then goes to work at the California branch of her firm. She never wants to see Hudson again as long as she lives, but she does, marrying him for real nine months later in the maternity ward of a hospital for a happy and peaceful ending. **p**, Stanley Shapiro, Martin Melcher; **d**, Delbert Mann; **cast**, Rock Hudson, Doris Day, Tony Randall, Edie Adams,

Jack Oakie, Jack Kruschen, Ann B. Davis, Joe Flynn, Howard St. John, Jack Albertson, Donna Douglas; **w**, Shapiro, Paul Henning; **c**, Arthur E. Arling (Eastmancolor); **m**, Frank De Vol; **ed**, Marjorie Fowler; **art d**, Alexander Golitzen, Robert Clatworthy; **set d**, Oliver Emert.

Lovers and Other Strangers ★★★ 1970; U.S.; 104m; American Broadcasting Company/Cinerama Releasing Corp.; Color; Comedy; Children: Unacceptable (MPAA: R); **DVD**; **VHS**. This charming and often hilarious comedy begins on the eve of the marriage between Bedelia and Brandon, a young couple going together for more than a year. Their families are thrilled, but turmoil and endless disruptions ensue among those family members. Castellano is delighted that his son Brandon is finally going to the altar, but he is crestfallen when hearing that his other son, Hindy, is seriously thinking of divorcing his wife, Keaton. Young, the father of fetching Bedelia, has his own big problems when Jackson, his long-standing mistress, tell him that he must now make a final decision to either leave his wife or marry her, or never see her again. Meara, who is Bedelia's sister, then confides that her own marriage is on the rocks because her husband, Guardino, has abandoned sex for the sake of obsessively watching television. Everyone connected to this upcoming marriage has trouble with the opposite sex, even one of the ushers for the wedding, Dishy, who is set up on a blind date with Hailey, Bedelia's cousin, but Dishy gets nowhere with the girl, whose nonstop talking drives him to despair. Despite all of these emotional crises, the participants come to their senses on the day of the wedding and the marriage is smoothly accomplished. Although the film is presented in a series of romantic vignettes, the segments are all seamlessly woven into the clever story line by helmsman Howard and all of the cast members give standout performances. Songs (music: Fred Karlin; lyrics: Robb Rover) include: "Comin' Thru to Me," "For All We Know" and "Keepin' Free." *Author's Note*: So impressive was Castellano (in his first major role) that he was selected to play the part of "Clemenza" in **The Godfather**, 1972, a role that set him on a career of playing gangsters and Mafia types thereafter. This was also Keaton's first major role and, she, too, scored so well that she was also cast as "Kay Adams" who marries Michael Corleone (Al Pacino) in **The Godfather**, 1972, a part that would make her a superstar. **p**, David Susskind, Ronald H. Gilbert; **d**, Cy Howard; **cast**, Diane Keaton, Anne Jackson, Harry Guardino, Gig Young, Bea Arthur, Bonnie Bedelia, Anne Meara, Cloris Leachman, Michael Brandon, Richard Castellano, Sylvester Stallone, Jerry Stiller, Joseph Hindy, Anthony Holland, Robert Dishy, Marian Hailey; **w**, Joseph Bologna, Renee Taylor, David Zelag Goodman (based on the play by Bologna, Taylor); **c**, Andrew Laszlo (Metrocolor); **m**, Fred Karlin; **ed**, David Bretherton, Sidney Katz; **prod d**, Ben Edwards; **set d**, John Allen Hicks.

Loves of a Blonde ★★★ 1966; Czechoslovakia; 90m; CBK/Prominent Films; B/W; Comedy; Children: Cautionary; **DVD**; **VHS**. This pleasant comedy sees Brejchová, a young woman working in a shoe factory in a small town who sleeps with a piano player, Pucholt, while he is playing with a band from Prague. He then leaves her cold, so she follows him to the big city and shocks his very protective parents with whom he lives. Pucholt gets a tongue-lashing from his parents and he tells them that he barely knows the girl. Brejchová leaves and returns to her hometown, telling girls at the factory that she had a wonderful weekend in the city with Pucholt and his parents. Sexual themes prohibit viewing by children. (In Czech; English subtitles.) **p**, Vlado Hreljanovic, Rudolf Hájek; **d**, Milos Forman; **cast**, Hana Brejchová, Vladimír Pucholt, Vladimír Mensík, Ivan Kheil, Jiří Hrubý, Milada Jezková, Josef Sebánek, Josef Kolb, Marie Salacová, Jana Nováková; **w**, Forman, Jaroslav Papousek, Ivan Passer, Václav Sasek (based on the story by Forman, Papousek, Passer); **c**, Miroslav Ondrícek; **m**, Evzen Illín; **ed**, Miroslav Hájek; **prod d**, Karel Cerný; **set d**, Vladimír Mácha.

Loving You ★★★ 1957; U.S.; 110m; Hal Wallis Productions/PAR;

Marian Hailey and Robert Dishy in *Lovers and Other Strangers,* **1970.**

Color; Drama/Musical; Children: Acceptable; **DVD**; **VHS**. Presley is a handsome young hillbilly truck driver who delivers a load of beer to a political rally and attracts the interest of Scott, a publicist, as well as country-western musician Corey, who see him as a possible young singing star. They give him a guitar and he sings and swings from there, becoming a hit. Scott sees him as a hip-swinging goldmine, so she and Corey dress him in a satin western shirt and pants and encourage him to dazzle the girls, becoming a singing guitar-playing sensation in Texas. A fickle fellow, Presley falls in love with Hart, a singer in the band while, at the same time, falls for Scott's more mature charms. A promoter, Gleason, books him into a one-man show at a theater outside Dallas, and Scott buys him a shiny new convertible, telling the press it is the gift of an oil tycoon's rich widow. But Scott offers the car with the condition that the band drop Hart whom she sees as competition for Presley's girl fans and maybe even for her own competition for Presley's personal attentions. Before agreeing to that, Presley drives Hart to her family farm and falls for the simplicity of the country life. Returning to show biz, Presley learns that Scott and Corey were married, but are now divorced. He drives off and crashes his car, but all ends well as Scott and Corey get back together and Presley and Hart sign a television contract and wind up in each other's arms. It was Presley's second film, loosely based on his own career rise, and began a musical series that made him the hottest young male singer in the movies. Songs (all sung by Presley): "Loving You" (Jerry Lieber, Mike Stoller), "Teddy Bear" (Karl Mann, Bernie Lowe), "Lonesome Cowboy" (Sid Tepper, Roy C. Bennett), "Got a Lot of Lovin' to Do" (A. Schroeder, Ben Weisman), "Party" (Jessie Mae Robinson), "Mean Woman Blues" (Claude DeMetrius), "Hot Dog" (Lieber, Stoller). *Author's Note*: "Colonel" Tom Parker, who was Presley's manager, served as a technical adviser on this film and Presley's mother also appears in a bit part. **p**, Hal B. Wallis; **d**, Hal Kanter; **cast**, Elvis Presley, Lizabeth Scott, Wendell Corey, James Gleason, Ralph Dumke, Paul Smith, Ken Becker, Jana Lund, Dolores Hart, Heather Ames; **w**, Kanter, Herbert Baker (based on the story "A Call from Mitch Miller" by Mary Agnes Thompson); **c**, Charles Lang, Jr. (Vistavision; Technicolor); **m**, Walter Scharf; **ed**, Howard Smith; **art d**, Hal Pereira, Albert Nozaki; **set d**, Sam Comer, Ray Moyer; **spec eff**, Farciot Edouart, John P. Fulton.

The Lower Depths ★★★ 1962; Japan; 125m; Toho Company; B/W; Drama/Comedy; Children: Unacceptable; **DVD**; **VHS**. This good adaptation of Maxim Gorky's 1903 stage play is relocated to a flophouse in 19th-century Japan where the married landlady, Yamada, treats everyone harshly except for a thief, Mifune. He is in love with her sister, Kagawa, and, when Yamada realizes this, she kills her husband in a jealous rage. Mifune is arrested and charged with the murder. Yamada loses her mind

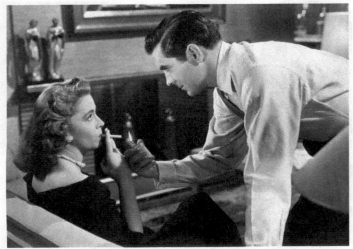

Jayne Meadows and Tyrone Power in *The Luck of the Irish*, 1948.

and the others in the flophouse drink and laugh, glad to be rid of her. Excessive violence and strong subject matter prohibit viewing by children. (In Japanese; English subtitles.) **p,** Sôjiro Motoki, Akira Kurosawa, **d,** Kurosawa; **cast,** Toshirô Mifune, Isuzu Yamada, Ganjirô Nakamura, Kyôko Kagawa, Minoru Chiaki, Kamatari Fujiwara, Akemi Negishi, Nijiko Kiyokawa, Kôji Mitsui, Eijirô Tôno; **w,** Kurosawa, Hideo Oguni (based on the play "Na dne" by Maxim Gorky); **c,** Kazuo Yamasaki; **m,** Masaru Satô; **ed,** Kurosawa; **prod d,** Yoshirô Muraki.

Lucas ★★★ 1986; U.S.; 100m; FOX; Color; Comedy; Children: Unacceptable (MPAA: PG-13); **DVD; VHS.** A sensitive teenage comedy about Haim, a socially shy if not backward thirteen-year-old boy, who feels the first heartbreak of adolescent love when the girl he thinks he loves, Green, and an older teenage friend, Sheen, fall in love. The story takes place in a suburb north of Chicago where, while riding his bicycle, Haim sees a red-haired girl, Green, who is a few years older than he, practicing her tennis swing. He stops and they talk and become friends. That develops into stronger feelings on his part, but she has a crush on the star of the high school football team, Sheen, who returns her romantic feelings. Haim feels jealous of Sheen but Sheen evolves as his friend and becomes his protector from bullies at school, and doesn't want to hurt him by his feelings for Green. More than a typical "teen movie," this well-produced film effectively explores the emotions of teenagers who care about each other. **p,** David Nicksay; **d&w,** David Seltzer; **cast,** Corey Haim, Kerri Green, Charlie Sheen, Courtney Thorne-Smith, Winona Ryder, Thomas E. Hodges, Ciro Poppiti, Guy Boyd, Jeremy Piven, Kevin Gerard Wixted, Emily Seltzer, Sean Hayes; **c,** Reynaldo Villalobos; **m,** Dave Grusin; **ed,** Priscilla Nedd; **art d,** James Murakami; **set d,** Linda Sutton; **spec eff,** Dieter Sturm.

The Luck of Ginger Coffey ★★★ 1964; Canada/U.S.; 100m; Crawley Films/Continental Distributing; B/W; Drama; Children: Cautionary; **DVD; VHS.** Shaw gives a powerful performance as a man always down on his luck. He is nearly forty and living with his family in Dublin where he cannot find any work. To survive and hopefully see a better future, he and his wife, Ure, and their children migrate to Montreal, Canada. Their teenage daughter, McClintock, does not like their new environs, but Shaw tells her that they have no choice and he again finds it difficult to obtain a good job. The family wants to return to Ireland and they have put aside savings for that very purpose, but Shaw has spent all that money and so they are trapped in this new and unwelcoming land. Ure leaves Shaw with the children, but McClintock returns to stay with her father, who finally gets a job as a proofreader for demanding Redmond and also keeps a second job as a delivery man for a laundry. When he thinks that Redmond is about to give him a better paying job as a re-

porter, Shaw quits the laundry, turning down a better offer to work there. He is, however, fired from his job by Redmond, a mean-minded cuss, who gives no reason for dismissing him. Then McClintock begins giving her father no end of headaches and Shaw pleads with Ure to return to keep the teenager in check, which she does. Shaw then desperately tries to get back his job at the laundry, but there are now no openings there. He is beside himself with frustration and succumbs to the "Irish curse," taking to whiskey. He is arrested and jailed, but Légaré, a compassionate judge, does not fine him or sentence him to jail, giving him only a good lecture before releasing him. Shaw steps from the courtroom to see Ure waiting for him and welcoming him into her loving arms. This prosaic tale is well directed and finely acted by Shaw, Ure, McClintock and others, impressively conveying the struggles of working people who want little more in life than to be able to work and have decent lives. *Author's Note*: Shaw and Ure were married at the time of this film. **p,** Leon Roth; **d,** Irvin Kershner; **cast,** Robert Shaw, Mary Ure, Liam Redmond, Tom Harvey, Libby McClintock, Leo Leyden, Powys Thomas, Tom Kneebone, Leslie Yeo, Vernon Chapman; **w,** Brian Moore (based on his novel); **c,** Manny Wynn; **m,** Bernardo Segall; **ed,** Antony Gibbs; **prod d,** Harry Horner; **art d,** Albert Brenner.

The Luck of the Irish ★★★★ 1948; U.S.; 99m; FOX; B/W; Fantasy; Children: Acceptable; **DVD.** In this delightful fantasy, Power is a no-nonsense, ambitious journalist eager to advance his career. While doing a story in Ireland, Power's car breaks down and he walks to a nearby stream. There he meets Kellaway, a weird-looking old man, who is mending old shoes. When asking for directions to the nearest village, Kellaway tells Power to go to a nearby inn. At the inn, Power meets attractive Baxter, who operates the place and tells Power about some Irish legends, including the ancient belief that caches of gold are buried throughout the land by legendary leprechauns, who usually appear to be little, old men. (Leprechauns are mythical fairy-like creatures dwelling in Ireland and who invariably take the forms of old men, who are seen repairing shoes, and who collect gold coins for their services, secreting their caches of gold at the end of rainbows.) While exploring the area later that night, Power again sees Kellaway, following him to a small glen and there wrestles Kellaway to the ground, holding on to him and demanding that he turn over his pot of gold. Power is acting more in jest as he doubts the tales Baxter has told him. He refuses to let go of Kellaway until he turns over his gold. Power, however, refuses to take the gold Kellaway offers and releases the old man. Kellaway, who is, indeed, a leprechaun, is now obligated to grant Power some wishes for releasing him. Power returns to the inn, telling Baxter about his encounter with Kellaway and when he takes her to the glen where he met the little man and tells his story, she thinks he's gone a little crazy. Once he returns to New York, Power quits his news agency, run by his old friend Todd, and is hired by wealthy, right-wing publisher Cobb, who makes him his top speechwriter and pays him an exorbitant salary while introducing him to his beautiful daughter, Meadows. Attracted to each other, it appears that Power and Meadows will eventually marry. He is given an upscale apartment and then tries to hire a manservant to take care of the place. No one applies except for Kellaway (who has prevented all other applicants from seeing Power). Although Power thinks he remembers Kellaway, he cannot exactly recall that encounter and he hires the little man. Through Kellaway's connivance, Power again meets Baxter on the New York City subway. She has arrived in America to collect an inheritance. Power falls in love with her, but when Baxter sees him with Meadows, she thinks he is engaged to another and returns to Ireland. Meanwhile, Kellaway subtly reminds Power of Baxter and points out the fact that he is selling out his ideals to Cobb. Power, however, plans to go on working for Cobb and marry Meadows. When he is about to give a speech on behalf of Cobb, however, Kellaway appears and Power sees Kellaway everywhere in the audience. Instead of endorsing Cobb, Power restates his own idealistic beliefs and then quits Cobb and returns to his old job with Todd. He returns to Ireland with Todd to write another story and marries Baxter, living with her at her inn and where one night, Todd watches Power sneak from his bedroom, go downstairs, and leave outside the door of the inn a bottle of Irish whisky. He then watches as Power looks from a window to see Kellaway scurry up the path to the inn and retrieve the whisky, then hobble happily away. When Todd confronts Power, he smiles and says that Kellaway is "an old friend." Director Koster does a great job in moving this charming fantasy to its happy fruition; Power, Baxter, Cobb and, especially the gnome-like Kellaway, give standout performances, and Sersen's special effects shine as brightly as a leprechaun's gold. *Author's Note*: Veteran actor Barry Fitzgerald had originally been slated for the part of the leprechaun, but commitments elsewhere caused Kellaway to be cast in the role. He had played a similar role as a mythical warlock in **I Married a Witch**, 1942. This was a wise decision as Kellaway steals every scene in this marvelous tale about the mythical characters inhabiting old Ireland. Leprechauns are also extensively and delightfully profiled in **Darby O'Gill and the Little People**, 1959. **p**, Fred Kohlmar; **d**, Henry Koster; **cast**, Tyrone Power, Anne Baxter, Cecil Kellaway, Lee J. Cobb, Jayne Meadows, James Todd, J.M. Kerrigan, Phil Brown, Charles Irwin, Helen Dietrich, Robert Adler; **w**, Philip Dunne (based on the novel by Guy Jones, Constance Jones); **c**, Joseph LaShelle; **m**, Cyril Mockridge; **ed**, J. Watson Webb, Jr.; **art d**, Lyle Wheeler, J. Russell Spencer; **set d**, Thomas Little, Paul S. Fox; **spec eff**, Fred Sersen.

Lucky Devils ★★★ 1933; U.S.; 64m; RKO; B/W; Adventure; Children: Acceptable. This early-day talkie shows a lot of exciting action when profiling Hollywood stuntmen doing every conceivable and inconceivable stunt. The group of daredevils is led by Boyd (who later became the legendary Hopalong Cassidy) and where these dashing figures routinely state that "a stuntman makes a bad husband and a husband makes a bad stuntman." Their harrowing stunts threaten serious injury if not death at almost every turn, and one of them, Bakewell, who has been recently married, is killed while doing a dangerous stunt. A short time later, Boyd and Gargan prevent an attractive young girl, Wilson, from committing suicide. They get her a job at the studio and Boyd falls in love with her, then marries her, but only under the understanding that he will continue to risk his life as a stuntman. When about to perform a stunt, however, Wilson, fearing for his safety, signals him to stop, Boyd hesitates, and his pal Gargan is almost killed. This washes Boyd up with stunts as everyone, including himself, thinks that he has lost his nerve and ability to perform hazardous feats for the movies. Going broke, Boyd takes a job as a crew member, but this does not provide enough money to cover the expenses of Wilson's hospital bill as she is now pregnant and about to deliver a baby. To pay the bill, Boyd undertakes a spectacular stunt and performs it perfectly, regaining his prestige and his job as a leading stuntman. Boyd and Wilson do fine jobs in their roles as does the rest of the cast; Alan Roscoe is a standout as a hysterical film director, who seems to be possessed of more than one devil. *Author's Note*: Some amazing stunts are performed in this film, including stuntmen crashing through plate-glass windows, horrific car crashes and an incredible fight atop a burning roof, to name only a few. The story by Rose, who also appears as one of the stuntmen, is based upon his long career as a Hollywood stuntman. Stuntmen are shown in many films, notably in **The Lost Squadron**, 1932; **Stand-In**, 1937; **Miss Tatlock's Millions**, 1948; **The Bad and the Beautiful**, 1952; **Singin' in the Rain**, 1952; **Westworld**, 1973; **The Great Waldo Pepper**, 1975; **The Stunt Man**, 1980; **F/X**, 1986; **Get Shorty**, 1995; and **The Aviator**, 2004. **p**, David O. Selznick, Marian C. Cooper; **d**, Ralph Ince; **cast**, William Boyd, Dorothy Wilson, William Gargan, Bob Rose, William Bakewell, Julie Haydon, Bruce Cabot, Rochelle Hudson, Alan Roscoe, Lon Chaney Jr., Betty Furness, Roscoe Ates, Sylvia Picker, Julie Haydon, Ward Bond; **w**, Rose, Ben Markson, Agnes Christine Johnston (based on a story by Casey Robinson); **c**, J. Roy Hunt; **m**, Max Steiner; **ed**, Frederic Knudtson, Jack Kitchin; **spec eff**, Vernon Walker, Harry Redmond, Sr.

Helen Walker and Alan Ladd in *Lucky Jordan*, 1942.

Lucky Jordan ★★★ 1942; U.S.; 84m; PAR; B/W; Adventure/Spy Drama; Children: Acceptable; **DVD**; **VHS**. Matinee idol Ladd scores well in this offbeat tale where he is a big shot gangster in New York City, who is having problems with his top lieutenant, Leonard, and who wants to take over his operation. Worse, he is now being besieged by the draft board that wants to take him into the U.S. Army as the period takes place during WWII. Corrigan, who is Ladd's political fixer, tries to get Ladd classified as "4F" by having him labeled "socially undesirable." When that fails, Corrigan arranges to have Ladd "adopted" by an elderly woman, Paige, who is really a lowlife derelict, claiming that Ladd is needed on the home front as he is Paige's only source of support (this ploy is not dissimilar to Carole Lombard "adopting" derelict May Robson in **Lady by Choice**, 1934, to improve her image as a burlesque stripper). Paige warms to Ladd even though he treats her with disdain and we wonder if this hardboiled character ever had a mother. Their son-mother ruse, however, does not wash with the draft board, and Ladd is inducted into the army and shipped off to boot camp where he makes one of the worst soldiers ever to put on a uniform. He sleeps in silk pajamas and refuses to answer reveille. When he does arise from his cot, he manages to avoid training and spends most of his time in the canteen playing pool and where he meets attractive USO worker Walker. Ladd finally goes AWOL, escaping the camp in a car stolen from an army engineer, taking Walker along with him. She begs him to surrender to pursuing MPs, but he will have none of that and, in a fit of anger, she throw a briefcase she thinks belongs to Ladd from the car. Returning to his posh New York City headquarters, Ladd discovers that turncoat Leonard has not only taken over his rackets, but has appropriated his moll, McDonald. Leonard confronts Ladd, admitting that he is selling U.S. military secrets to the Nazis and that the briefcase thrown from the car in which Ladd escaped contains top secrets that are worth a fortune. Ladd battles Leonard and bests him and then goes off with Walker in search of that briefcase. He and Walker become separated, but Ladd locates the briefcase and then hides out with his "adopted" mother, Paige. She mothers him to his annoyance and brags to her lady friends that Ladd is her "son." When he leaves her alone, however, Nazi agents searching for him and the briefcase find Paige and beat her when she refuses to give them any information. When Ladd returns to find Paige injured, he vows vengeance on the Nazis, becoming a patriot who does not "want this country run by guys who beat up old ladies." Ladd corners the Nazis at a remote hideout, and while he waits for U.S. agents to come to the rescue, he and Walker stall the German agents and where Walker, to distract one of their captors, hikes her skirt upward in a seductive leg tease that allows Ladd to disarm the guard and where he subdues the Nazis just as the American agents arrive. Ladd vindicates himself and is now called a hero while earning the respect and love of Walker. A lot of good

Gene Nelson and Doris Day in *Lullaby of Broadway*, 1951.

action and good acting from Ladd, Walker and the cast provides entertainment and considerable tension throughout. *Author's Note*: This film was rushed into production by Paramount to capitalize on Ladd's overnight stardom created by recently released productions of **This Gun for Hire**, 1942, and **The Glass Key**, 1942. This was Walker's film debut and she would prove to be a popular leading lady, dying prematurely of cancer on March 10, 1968, at the age of forty-seven. Her career soared through the early 1940s, but on New Year's Eve, 1946, she picked up three hitchhiking soldiers when she was driving from Palm Springs to Los Angeles. Near Redlands, she struck a dividing island that caused her auto to flip and crash. One of the soldiers was killed and the other two injured. The surviving soldiers sued her, claiming she was drunk while driving at speeds at more than 90 mph, but Walker was later exonerated. The stigma of the soldier's death remained and she found little good work thereafter, appearing in only low-budget films. Ironically, another lady appearing in this film, the voluptuous blonde, Marie "The Body" McDonald, saw similar tragedies visit her own life. She was married six times and, at one time, was reportedly the mistress of West Coast gangster, Benjamin "Bugsy" Siegel (1906-1947), and who, after her own film career went nowhere, reportedly staged her own kidnapping to gain publicity. When she was institutionalized in a psychiatric clinic in Australia, McDonald escaped from that clinic. She later stated that she did not want to take mind-altering drugs prescribed by physicians at that clinic. McDonald died of an overdose of drugs in 1965 at age forty-two. Tuttle, who directed this film, appeared in 1951 before the House of Un-American Activities Committee (HUAC), admitting that he had not only been a communist from 1937 to 1947, but hosted Communist Party get-togethers in New York City where many subversive communists gathered (some going to prison). Tuttle, to preserve his directorial career, named several Hollywood persons such as the gifted director Jules Dassin (who was blacklisted by the industry) as active communists. **p**, Fred Kohlmar; **d**, Frank Tuttle; **cast**, Alan Ladd, Helen Walker, Sheldon Leonard, Mabel Paige, Marie McDonald, Lloyd Corrigan, Dave Willock, Clem Bevans, Anthony Caruso, Yvonne De Carlo, Kirk Alyn, Dorothy Dandridge, Carol Hughes; **w**, Darrell Ware, Karl Tunberg (based on a story by Charles Leonard); **c**, John Seitz; **m**, Adolph Deutsch; **ed**, Archie Marshek; **art d**, Hans Dreier, Ernst Fegté; **set d**, Steve Seymour.

The Lucky Star ★★★ 1982; Canada; 110m; Tele-Metropole International/Pickman; Color; Drama; Children: Unacceptable (MPAA: PG). Jacobi and Hughes, the parents of a teenage Dutch Jew, Marx, are arrested and taken away by the Nazis during the time of the Holocaust in World War II. The boy, who loves and is strongly influenced by American cowboy films, runs off and hides out as a worker on a farm owned by Fletcher. Steiger, a German officer, comes to the farm and Marx takes

him prisoner, the way a cowboy hero would capture a bad man. This bittersweet film is made memorable through the outstanding performances of Steiger and Marx and others, but is not for children because of mature themes and violence. **p**, Claude Léger; **d**, Max Fischer; **cast**, Rod Steiger, Louise Fletcher, Lou Jacobi, Brett Marx, Yvon Dufour, Helen Hughes, Isabelle Mejias, Jean Gascon, Kalman Steinberg, Pierre Gobeil, Guy L'Ecuyer; **w**, Fischer, Jack Rosenthal; **c**, Frank Tidy; **m**, Art Phillips; **ed**, Yves Langlois; **art d**, Michel Proulx.

Lullaby of Broadway ★★★ 1951; U.S.; 92m; WB; Color; WB; Musical; Children: Acceptable; **DVD**; **VHS**. Entertaining musical thin on story line but with many good songs sees Day returning from London after some years, believing that her mother, George, is still a major Broadway star when she is a boozy performer in a sleazy nightclub (taking a large leaf from **Lady for a Day**, 1933). Day is greeted by De Wolfe, the valet for wealthy Sakall, who lives in a huge New Yprk City mansion with battleax wife Bates (when was she anything other?). De Wolfe, a former vaudeville trouper and close friend of George, keeps George's true lifestyle from Day, saying that George owns the mansion and Sakall is only renting it and, meanwhile, arranges for Day to stay in a small room in the vast manor house while trying to sober up George, who is to meet Day at a reunion party. George fails to show up at the party, but Day meets handsome Nelson, an ambitious musical comedy performer, like Day, and romance blossoms. Nelson convinces Stafford, the producer of a new Broadway show, to feature Day with him in an upcoming production while Bates then learns that Day is living in her mansion and suspects hubby Sakall of dallying with the much younger woman. Everything blows up when Day learns the truth about George and plans to return to London. George, however, cleans up her act and meets with Day and they reconcile before Day goes on with the show, and with Nelson dancing and singing at her side in the new Broadway musical, which is a success. Bates learns that Day is no longer a threat and she and Sakall, who is confused throughout by all of these machinations, attend Day's Broadway debut to applaud her performance. Day's singing and the top-flight production numbers keep this songfest sailing along. Songs include: "You're Getting to Be a Habit with Me," "Lullaby of Broadway" (Harry Warren, Al Dubin), "Somebody Loves Me" (George Gershwin, Buddy DeSylva, Ballard MacDonald); "Just One of Those Things" (Cole Porter); "Please Don't Talk About Me When I'm Gone" (Sam H. Slept, Sidney Clare), "I Love the Way You Say Goodnight" (George Wyle, Eddie Pola), "In a Shanty in Old Shanty Town" (music: Jack Little and John Siras; lyrics: Joe Young); "Have You Forgotten" (Nathaniel Shilkret, Dana Suesse), "Zing Went the Strings of My Heart" (James F. Hanley), "We'd Like to Go on a Trip," "You're Dependable" (Sy Miller, Jerry Seelen). *Author's Note*: George sings "It's a Shanty in Old Shanty Town," delivered in her distinctive quavering vibrato, and she is really reprising her role in **The Roaring Twenties**, 1939, where, toward the end of that film, she sings this very song in a low dive. **p**, William Jacobs; **d**, David Butler; **cast**, Doris Day, Gene Nelson, S.Z. Sakall, Billy De Wolfe, Gladys George, Florence Bates, Anne Triola, Hanley Stafford, Murray Alper, Page Cavanaugh Trio; **w**, Earl Baldwin; **c**, Wilfred M. Cline (Technicolor); **m**, Ray Heindorf; **ed**, Irene Morra; **art d**, Douglas Bacon; **set d**, Lyle B. Reifsnider.

Lumumba ★★★ 2000; France, Belgium, Germany, Haiti; 115m; Arte/Zeitgeist Films; Color; Biographical Drama; Children: Unacceptable; **DVD**; **VHS**. This engrossing film profiles the rise to power and assassination of Patrice Emery Lumumba (1925-1961). Lumumba (Ebouaney) was a Congolese independence leader and the first legally elected prime minister of the Republic of the Congo after he helped win its independence from Belgium in June 1960. Just twelve weeks later, he and his government were deposed in a West-supported coup led by his friend but rival for power, Joseph Mobutu (Descas). Mobutu was imprisoned and executed by firing squad, which was sanctioned by the government of Belgium but for which it officially apologized in 2002.

Ebouaney gives an outstanding performance of Lumumba in his rise to power as a black nationalist, his struggle for the Congo's independence and his downfall and murder in this incisive tale about courage and sacrifice in the struggle for freedom. *Author's Note*: Details about Lumumba's career and assassination can be found in my book, *The Great Pictorial History of World Crime*, Volume I (History, Inc., 2004; pages 162-165. Excessive violence prohibits viewing by children. (In French; English subtitles.) **p**, Raoul Peck, Jacques Bidou, Shelby Stone; **d**, Peck; **cast**, Eriq Ebouaney, Alex Descas, Théophile Moussa Sowie, Maka Kotto, Dieudonné Kabongo, Pascal N'Zonzi, André Debaar, Cheik Doukouré, Oumar Diop Makena; **w**, Peck, Pascal Bonitzer, Dan Edelstein; **c**, Bernard Lutic; **m**, Jean-Claude Petit; **ed**, Jacques Comets; **art d**, André Fonsny; **spec eff**, Frederic Moreau.

Lured ★★★ 1947; U.S.; 102m; Hunt Stromberg Productions/UA; B/W; Crime Drama; Children: Unacceptable; **DVD**; **VHS**. Exceptionally well-acted and well-directed thriller sees a lunatic serial killer loose in London and where attractive Ball becomes the bait to catch the murderer. Ball is a taxi dancer in a London nightclub and, after her friend, Chandler, is murdered by a predatory maniac, she is contacted by Scotland Yard inspector Coburn, who asks her to serve as a decoy to help police capture the killer. The madman preys upon lovely, lonely young ladies such as Ball by placing blind ads in the lonely hearts columns, and, once they respond, meets them at secret rendezvous where they are murdered. Having a fondness for Baudelaire, the killer writes his own chilling sonnets to taunt police, these ditties containing cloudy clues about his next intended victim. Suspects quickly surface, including Karloff, an eccentric dress designer, and Calleia, an unsavory white slavery trafficker, who has been importing unsuspecting young women from South America to England to force them into prostitution. Sanders, the glib and suave owner of the nightclub where Ball works, and who is a notorious womanizer, also comes under suspicion as does his docile business partner, Hardwicke. One of these two partners, who is the real killer, tries to pin the murders on his associate while methodically stalking the apprehensive Ball, but, just before the murderer can strike at the last moment, he is identified and captured and Ball's life is saved. Taut direction from Sirk and outstanding performances from Ball and Coburn (unusual in that they were best known for their appearances in light-hearted comedies) maintain and enhance this chilling mystery from beginning to end. *Author's Note*: Though this film is obviously based upon the standout French thriller, **Personal Column**, 1939, directed by film noir specialist Robert Siodmak and starring Maurice Chevalier and Erich von Stroheim, director Sirk told this author that "I never saw that film, so I can only assume that Rosten adapted it from the French production [which he did]. In any event, any good story in any good film made in the past is always worth doing again, as long as you give it new faces and different hats to wear." **p**, James Nasser; **d**, Douglas Sirk; **cast**, George Sanders, Lucille Ball, Charles Coburn, Boris Karloff, Sir Cedric Hardwicke, Joseph Calleia, Alan Mowbray, George Zucco, Robert Coote, Alan Napier, Tanis Chandler, Jimmie Aubrey, Dorothy Vaughan, Sam Harris; **w**, Leo Rosten (based on a story by Jacques Companéez, Simon Gantillon, Ernst Neubach); **c**, William Daniels; **m**, Michel Michelet; **ed**, John M. Foley, James E. Newcom; **prod d**, Nicolai Remisoff.

Lust for Life ★★★★★ 1956; U.S.; 122m; MGM; Color; Biographical Drama; Children: Unacceptable; **DVD**; **VHS**. Douglas and Quinn are both riveting in essaying two of the most gifted painters of their day, Douglas as Vincent van Gogh (1853-1890) and Quinn as Paul Gauguin (1848-1903) in this wonderful and mesmerizing biopic. This magnificent film opens in 1878 with the intense Douglas leaving his home in Holland and going to Le Borinage, a section of the province of Hainaut in Belgium, a grim mining area awash with miserable poverty. He is a religious zealot out to convert the uneducated miners, but when he encounters their impoverished way of life, he takes pity on them and not

George Sanders, Robert Coote and Alan Napier in *Lured*, 1947.

only gives them all his own earthly belongings, but all the worldly goods of his church. Douglas is censured by church officials, who point out that he was to impart spiritual guidance to his flock, not physical generosity. The rebellious Douglas responds by denouncing the church officials as hypocrites and he is summarily dismissed from his position. Donald, Douglas' protective and well-to-do younger brother (Theo van Gogh, successful art dealer; 1857-1891), finds Douglas living in squalor and in such poor health that he takes him home where Douglas slowly recuperates. He reinvigorates his strength through painting, his native talent that begins to demand much of him. When he proposes marriage to a cousin, she rejects him out of hand. So emotionally disturbed at this rebuff is Douglas that he holds his hand over a lighted candle, telling her that he will not remove it from the searing flame until she accepts his proposal. This erratic if not unbalanced behavior compels his sister to order him to leave the family residence, and Douglas goes to The Hague to take up full-time painting. There he meets Brown, a prostitute with a child, who takes up with him. At first, Douglas is happy with his new life. He visits successful painter and distant relative Purcell, who enacts the role of Anton Mauve (1838-1888; he was married to van Gogh's cousin, was a mater colorist and a leader of the painting colony in The Hague). Through Purcell, Douglas learns the use of brilliant colors and follows Purcell's painting style of realism (which invariably featured workers laboring in fields and whose paintings are so realistic that they include horse droppings in his works). Douglas, however, rebels against Purcell's style of art and argues with him, refusing his direction so adamantly that he loses Purcell's friendship and his much-need financial support. Douglas, like van Gogh, is seeking a more vivid and animated style of painting, believing that Purcell and others are presenting static art that merely repeats itself from canvas to canvas. After his funds are gone and Brown leaves him, Douglas moves to Paris to stay with Donald and meets the most famous painters of the day, as well as the leading art critics. He also meets and befriends Quinn, who plays Paul Gauguin, a rebellious and independent-minded painter like himself. Douglas thinks that most of the artists he meets are poseurs but that Quinn is one of the few artists painting with integrity and who, like himself, is truly dedicated to art. Quinn believes that Douglas is also unlike other artists and is wholly committed to art. After Donald sends Douglas to the South of France to paint, he then convinces Quinn to join him, but their friendship soon unravels as each man seems to compete with the other. The passionate Douglas is outspoken in his beliefs about art, gushing his theories and concepts to Quinn while the reserved and pensive Quinn keeps his opinions to himself. Douglas is personally unconcerned about his appearance and keeps a sloppy household where Quinn is meticulous, maintaining neatness and good organization. The conflicting lifestyles and mindsets soon clash in a volatile confrontation.

Kirk Douglas in *Lust for Life,* 1956.

The pipe-smoking Quinn then tells Douglas that he can no longer tolerate his eccentric behavior and his constant demands that his genius be recognized and he departs. Now Douglas is again alone, believing he has lost one of the few true friends of his life. Depressed and agonizing over the loss of once kindred spirit Quinn, Douglas despairs and, losing touch with reality in the middle of the night, seizes a razor and, as if making a bloody act of contrition, slices off his left ear (in reality, van Gogh, in that fit of madness, cut off only a portion of his left ear lobe). He commits himself to an asylum at St. Remy, but his fears and apprehensions continue to cloud his mind even after he is released and he now becomes wholly dependent upon loving brother Donald, who sends him to Sloane, a physician who attempts to stabilize Douglas' troubled mind, but he makes little or no headway. Douglas then departs for Auvers-sur-Oise, where he paints his last landscape, a golden wheat field through which cuts a purple road and above which hover a bevy of crows, these species in the mind of Douglas, being birds of prey or harbingers of death. Upon finishing the canvas, Douglas shoots himself, ending his life on July 29, 1890, thus ending this powerful film. Often depressing and even moribund at times, this film is also inspirational through Douglas' amazing visual achievements as shown in one masterpiece of art after another, which pantheon director Minnelli intermittently presents throughout the production, an awesome array of some of the world's greatest art works. The viewer sees what Douglas sees, the works in the fields, the postman, the baker, the shopkeepers, the peasants and their families, their careworn, lined faces as he paints these landscapes and portraits, and it is as if the viewer is present in a single gallery where the visual marvels of this genius are collected under one majestic roof. **Lust for Life** is one of the most magnificent visual treats ever put on film and the life of its artist is seamlessly interwoven with these spiritually inspiring works, a masterpiece film about one of the world's greatest geniuses of masterpiece art. Douglas was nominated for an Oscar as Best Actor and the film received Oscar nominations for Best Adapted Screenplay and Best Art Direction (color), but only Quinn won an Oscar as Best Supporting Player. *Author's Note*: MGM has expressed interest in making this film as early as 1934 when Stone's novel was first published, but not until 1946 did it begin to actively plan the production, which was initially undertaken by producer Arthur Freed. Since Freed was the mainstay producer for most of MGM's musicals, however, his chores in that regard kept him from the project, which he eventually turned over to the tasteful producer, Houseman, who had had a long association with Orson Welles and his Mercury Players company. Minnelli, one of the studio's most talented and inventive directors was brought in to helm the challenging biopic, but he resisted the use of CinemaScope, later stating that the wider screen "bears little relation to the conventional shape of paintings," but he lost out on that contention and was compelled to employ the new wide screen

process. Minnelli won one significant technical battle, however, arguing that Eastmancolor, then being widely used at MGM, did not offer the kind of soft, subdued tones of color necessary to define van Gogh's art. Eastmancolor sharply defined colors and, in the opinion of the tasteful Minnelli, presented those colors as attackingly garish. He wanted to shoot the film on Ansco film, but the company had long earlier stopped making that kind of color film. He and producer Houseman nevertheless insisted on using this color process and found in the MGM archives about 300,000 feet of Ansco negative film and then compelled that company to produce more negative color film to meet the production needs for **Lust for Life**. Minnelli then led the second unit sent to Europe to shoot all the locations where van Gogh lived and worked. Minnelli recalled a brilliant piece of film from **The Great Waltz**, 1938, which showed a stunning montage of flowers and he used this image when he drew diagrams for the second unit and instructing its filmmakers to capture the budding flowers of blossoming fruit trees at Arles where van Gogh lived and where he (Douglas) opens the shutters of his room to see the splendor of these budding trees. Thus, Minnelli wonderfully captured the breathtaking exteriors for this film, but filming van Gogh's actual paintings (more than 200 such masterpieces were photographed in the homes of collectors and in museums for this film) was another matter. He and Houseman realized that the light employed by motion picture cameras required too much heat and that such heat might distort or misrepresent the true colors of van Gogh's paintings. To have them photographed in their exact likeness, they sent expert portrait photographers around the world to photograph those paintings, using portrait cameras that made time exposures without excessive light. These exposures were subsequently converted into large transparencies, which, in turn, were back-lighted and then re-photographed by motion picture cameras that also employed insert equipment and special lenses to capture every detail from the original transparencies. Douglas, who bore a striking resemblance to the real van Gogh, was approached by Houseman and Minnelli four years before the production of this film when all were making **The Bad and the Beautiful**, 1952, an exceptional portrait on early-day Hollywood, where Douglas was the leading player. Houseman and Minnelli told the star at that time about their concept of doing a film about van Gogh and that he should be the actor to play that gifted but bedeviled artist. Douglas took the part to his heart and made it part of his life, as he did with all of the roles he enacted. He grew a beard (dyed red) and, according to his wife, Anne, "…came home in that red beard of van Gogh's, wearing those big boots and stomping around the house…it was frightening." Douglas was instructed in the rudiments of painting on canvas in the van Gogh style by a French artist and when he paints the canvas of the wheat field, adding the crows onto that memorable canvas, a flock of crows were released off camera, these birds swooping and diving all about him (to get at food carefully placed near the actor in that scene), the fluttering and frantic action that drives him over the brink and to his death. In practice and on screen, Douglas painted more than 900 crows for this production, later stating: "I am not one of the art world's immortals, but at least I can now catch a crow in flight." Quinn told this author that he had "nothing but respect for Kirk, an actor who uses everything in his actor's trick bag in every scene." Quinn added that "I have one line in **Lust for Life**, where Kirk thought I might be talking about his acting style when I am really criticizing van Gogh's insane passion for his art when I say 'If there is one thing I despise, that's emotion in painting.' Kirk knew that that line was in the script, but he thought I delivered that line so decisively that I meant it for him, I think. You know, looking back on that film, I thought we were two very unlikely roommates, and were, without the comedy, not unlike the modern roommates you see in **The Odd Couple** [1968]. That was a very funny film with Jack Lemmon and Walter Matthau, but there was nothing funny about the relationship between Vincent van Gogh and Paul Gauguin. They respected each other but were jealous of each other's talent. They were competing with each other for immortality and they knew it. Gauguin had to get away from this man or wind up being killed by him or maybe killing him and that is not funny." Van Gogh sold only one painting in his lifetime (*Red Vineyard at Aries*, which resides in the Pushkin Museum in Moscow), and his more than 900 other paintings were not sold or made famous until after his death. **p**, John Houseman; **d**, Vincente Minnelli and (not credited) George Cukor; **cast**, Kirk Douglas, Anthony Quinn, James Donald, Pamela Brown, Everett Sloane, Niall MacGinnis, Noel Purcell, Henry Daniell, Madge Kennedy, Eric Pohlmann, Isobel Elsom, Betty Blythe; **w**, Norman Corwin (based on the novel by Irving Stone); **c**, Russell Harlan, F.A. Young (CinemaScope; Metrocolor); **m**, Miklos Rozsa; **ed**, Adrienne Fazan; **art d**, Cedric Gibbons, Preston Ames, Hans Peters; **set d**, Edwin B. Willis, Keogh Gleason.

The Lusty Men ★★★★ 1952; U.S.; 113m; RKO; B/W; Western; Children: Cautionary; **VHS**. In this superlative modern western, wonderfully directed by the gifted Ray, Mitchum, Hayward and Kennedy give outstanding performances while living the exciting and dangerous lifestyles of those following the circuits of western rodeos. Mitchum is a former rodeo star, a champion bronco rider and steer roper, who is so crippled from his many injuries over the years that he can no longer participate in the rodeos that made him famous and momentarily rich. Gored by a Brahma bull, he is now retired and he returns to his old homestead in Oklahoma, to find the treasure he buried as a boy. He finds the owner, a garrulous old man sitting on the front porch of that ancestral home and who allows him to unearth that childhood cache, two nickels and a faded rodeo program. Mitchum then meets a young couple, Kennedy and Hayward, who buy the ranch. Kennedy recognizes Mitchum as a yesteryear rodeo star and hires him, asking him to help him work the ranch. Kennedy later tells him that he has entered some events at an upcoming rodeo and asks Mitchum to give him some pointers. Mitchum agrees and, more or less, trains Kennedy on how best to ride broncos and bulls. Hayward has deep misgivings about her husband's ambitions, but goes along with his plans, which are limited to winning just enough money to pay off their bills and secure their new ranch. She nevertheless is friendly enough toward Mitchum so that he will truly help her husband. Kennedy wins his first few rodeo events and then becomes a rising star, winning more and more events, besting bucking broncos and kicking bulls. His winnings soar and he is soon in the big money bracket. Kennedy loses his down-to-earth attitude as his ego becomes inflated from praise and flattery showered upon him by rodeo star groupies and hangers-on. He becomes a rousing womanizing character, who thinks his rodeo career will go on forever. When Hayward begs Mitchum to straighten out Kennedy, his only response is to tell her to leave Kennedy and take up with him. When she rejects this offer and shows her dogged loyalty to Kennedy, Mitchum has newfound respect for her and agrees to help Kennedy. When Mitchum tries to steer Kennedy away from his swaggering and wasteful ways, where he has abandoned his notion of having a ranch and is now ignoring his wife altogether while paying attention to other women, Kennedy explodes, telling Mitchum he is nothing but a cowardly has-been who has been living off of him and his generosity, wholly forgetting the man who made him a rodeo star. Mitchum responds by going back to rodeos and competes with Kennedy, besting him in every event and proving that he is still a great champion. In the final event, however, Mitchum falls beneath the stomping hooves of a bronco and is fatally injured. Removed from the arena, Mitchum knows he is dying and tells Hayward, who has grown to love him, and Kennedy, not to mourn his passing, that he is dying the way he has lived and that that life made "a thousand bartenders rich." With that, the old rodeo star dies, and his passing so shocks Kennedy back to reason and reality that he quits the rodeos, takes his winnings and leaves with the devoted Hayward to pay off his ranch and live a life with the woman who has remained at his side throughout his travails and transgressions. There is no bathos in these final scenes, so carefully constructed by director Ray, but an unceremonious ending of a man who has died the way he lived in a violent occupation. In addition to Ray's superlative direction, Mitchum gives one of his finest performances as do Hayward and

Susan Hayward and Arthur Kennedy in *The Lusty Men*, 1952.

Kennedy, working with a well-written script from McCoy and Dortort (the latter an experienced cowboy and rodeo rider) and where the grim action is awesomely captured through the stark photography of master cinematographer Garmes. ***Author's Note***: Ray told this author that "I intended to strip away the glamour from the rodeo world and show the actual lifestyle of its participants—a nomadic world that is grim and dirty and very, very dangerous. To my mind, there is little difference between the rodeo riders battling bucking horses and wild, crazed bulls than the matadors who enter the arena to face bulls with red capes. They all risk their lives and the crowds are there to see them injured if not killed. You can call it a sport, but I do not." To this Mitchum added his own criticism, telling this author that "anyone doing most of those stunts at a rodeo has to be a little more than crazy. It is easier to break your neck at a rodeo than it is to drive in the Indianapolis 500. I don't know how they do it and not turn into raving drunks." Hayward stated to this author: "I am not a woman who shuns tough situations, but when we did **The Lusty Men**, I was truly frightened for those cowboys riding at those rodeos. Every time they entered those arenas, they were entering a place of personal destruction if not death." This film was originally titled **Cowpoke**, then retitled **This Man Is Mine** before it was shelved for more than a year, RKO believing it was too violent a film to be released. It was then titled **The Lusty Men** and released. The film was shot on location at rodeos in Tucson, Arizona; Spokane, Washington; Livermore, California; and Pendleton, Oregon, and where actual rodeo stars were filmed, including Les Sanborn, Jerry Ambler and Gerald Roberts, this footage incorporated into the story line. Many films have profiled rodeos and rodeo performers and this one is the very best. Other such films include **Ride 'Em, Cowboy**, 1942; **King of the Cowboys**, 1943; **Bus Stop**, 1956; **The Misfits**, 1961; **The Rounders**, 1965; **Hud**, 1963; **J. W. Coop**, 1971; **The Last Picture Show**, 1971; **Junior Bonner**, 1972; and **Flicka**, 2006. **p**, Jerry Wald, Norman Krasna; **d**, Nicholas Ray; **cast**, Susan Hayward, Robert Mitchum, Arthur Kennedy, Arthur Hunnicutt, Frank Faylen, Jimmie Dodd, John Mitchum, Dennis Moore, Glenn Strange, Chili Williams; **w**, Horace McCoy, David Dortort (based on the novel by Claude Stanush); **c**, Lee Garmes; **m**, Roy Webb; **ed**, Ralph Dawson; **art d**, Albert S. D'Agostino, Alfred Herman; **set d**, Darrell Silvera, Jack Mills.

M ★★★★★ 1933; Germany; 117m; Nero-Film/PAR; B/W; Crime Drama; Children: Unacceptable; **BD**; **DVD**; **VHS**. A masterpiece film from director Lang sees Lorre in his most significant and chilling role, a grim and unrelenting tour de force that incisively profiles a compulsive child killer. Like London before it five decades earlier when it was

Peter Lorre in *M*, 1933.

plagued by the mysterious serial killer Jack the Ripper, Berlin is a city gripped in terror by a serial child molester, who randomly selects little girls on the streets and murders them. Uniformed police and detectives in plainclothes frantically search for the killer while panic ensues among the populace where neighbors turn upon one another, making accusations based upon the flimsiest suspicions. Widespread police raids are conducted in which scores of professional criminals are arrested and brought in for questioning, from pickpockets and burglars to muggers and prostitutes. The city's criminal underworld is in turmoil, its rackets and operations shut down under the intense police pressure. Gang leaders, to protect their lucrative underworld operations, decide to find the killer themselves and bring him or her before their own tribunal and where, if found guilty, he or she will be executed. Meanwhile, the children of the city play innocently in on the streets and in alleyways, mindlessly repeating a gruesome chant, not understanding its true significance: "Just you wait a little while…The evil man in black will come…With his little chopper…He will chop you up." (Lang was ever mindful of London's dreaded Jack the Ripper and here took a leaf from the grim ditty chanted by children in that city when it was beset by that horrendous killer: "Jack the Ripper's dead…And Lying on his bed… He cut his throat…With sunlight soap…Jack the Ripper's dead.") We next see a mother preparing a meal for her little girl. The girl, playing in the street, bounces a ball off a billboard and where the camera momentarily shows a wanted poster for the serial killer and then a shadow slowly crosses the face of the little girl. The girl looks up to see a man, who buys her a balloon and she follows him as he whistles a passage from Grieg's "Peer Gynt" ("Hall of the Mountain King"). As the girl's mother calls frantically for her, the balloon rolls from some shrubbery and sails upward to be snagged on some telephone wires. This latest murder is announced by newspapers with blaring headlines while the killer, Lorre, pens a missive to the press, finishing his letter with "I haven't finished yet." (This is another similarity to the London killings of Jack the Ripper in that that serial killer wrote several taunting letters, one to a news agency, announcing his intent to murder again.) Wernicke, who is chief of Berlin's police detectives, after reviewing the details of the latest murder, comes to believe that the killer is a lunatic and he orders his detectives to search for any underworld figures who have records showing that they are criminally insane. Some detectives interview mental patients and this leads some plainclothesmen to visit Lorre's dingy flat, but they find that he has left. Lorre is lurking on a street, seeing the reflection of a little girl in a store window. He takes a few steps toward her, whistling the eerie bars from "Peer Gynt," but then abruptly stops when he sees the girl's mother appear. Detectives searching Lorre's room find a wrapper for a distinctive brand of cigarettes, the same kind of cigarettes that have been found at the last murder

site and previous killings. Lorre now sees another child and begins following the girl, buying a balloon and whistling a tune that is familiar to the blind balloon seller, who realizes that the same whistling man bought a balloon from him just before the last little girl was killed. The balloon seller tells a beggar that the passing man is the killer and the beggar writes a large "M" in chalk on the palm of his hand and then places this imprint on the back of Lorre's coat. He is now branded as the child killer. When Lorre's next intended victim, the little girl, tries to wipe the telltale "M" from his coat, Lorre sees the mark in the reflection of a store window and now knows that he has been identified with the mark of a murderer. Seized with panic, Lorre races off and hides inside an abandoned office building as news of his identification and where he is hiding is spread throughout the underworld. Gangsters pretending to be police detectives barge into the building and find the cowering Lorre in a storeroom, dragging him away as he screams in protest. Lorre is taken to a huge warehouse basement where the underworld has set up its own tribunal and he is tried under this court as an abhorrent criminal. Staring at Lorre is a number of unsympathetic women, all mothers of the little girls he has slain. Lorre realizes that his life is in jeopardy and he begins to whimper, whine and intermittingly scream in pleading for his life. He states: "I can't help myself…I have no control over this evil thing that's inside me…It's there all the time, driving me out to wander through the streets…It's me, pursuing myself!...I want to escape…to escape from myself!...But, it's impossible!...I must obey!" Lorre's court-appointed attorney mimics his client's plea, saying that Lorre should not be executed because he is a sick man and should be placed in the care of a physician. The prosecutor is relentless, however, condemning Lorre out of hand and he convinces the tribunal to sentence Lorre to death. Just before he can be executed, however, police burst into the basement and the criminals flee in all directions. Officers seize Lorre and drag him away, his screams echoing through the cavernous chamber and this is where this frightening thriller ends. In another version of this mesmerizing story, Lang edited the film from 117m to 99m and tacked on a separate ending, one where Lorre, after being taken from the warehouse basement is shown in a legal court and where he is also sentenced to death while several mothers of his victims express their pity for him, one stating that "We should learn to look after our children more." No child is shown being murdered and where Lang elects to show their deaths through symbols, such as the floating balloon. He employs the early German style of filmmaking, his alternating scenes stark and then murky with deep shadows, all his scenes dominated by low-key lighting. Lorre is consistently shown as a furtive figure, living inside of those shadows, a creature of the night. Lang also uses erratic cross-cutting from the murders to the public response in brief scenes showing reactions from poor and rich to heighten the suspense and permeate a sense of fear. Lorre's performance is one of the most chilling on film, one where he embodies everything repulsive and hideous. ***Author's Note***: Lang believed that **M** was his most significant film and most agree with him. He claimed that he created Lorre's unforgettable character from whole cloth, but it is obvious from Lorre's personality and modus operandi that his character is based upon the notorious German child killer, Peter Kurten (1883-1931), who was called "The Monster of Dusseldorf" and who was condemned and beheaded after being convicted of several murders. "The character I play in that film," Lorre told this author, "was no mystery to me. I read a lot about Peter Kurten and his terrible child slayings and I based my character on that awful man. Lang knew it and I knew it and almost everyone in Germany knew it when they saw the film, but few people in England and in America at the time knew about Kurten, so they thought my character was only a piece of fiction. Unfortunately, I could no more escape from the character I played in that picture than the killer could escape from his compulsion to murder. I was typecast for life as a hateful and insidious murderer and it took years before I got parts where I played a sane or decent person." For more details on Peter Kurten, see my two-volume work, *The Great Pictorial History of World Crime*, Volume II (History, Inc., 2004;

page 1085-1089). (Dubbed in English.) **p**, Seymour Nebenzal; **d**, Fritz Lang; **cast**, Peter Lorre, Otto Wernicke, Gustaf Gründgens, Theodor Loos, Ellen Widmann, Inge Landgut, Fritz Odemar, Paul Kemp, Theo Lingen, Rudolf Blümner, Fritz Gnass; **w**, Lang, Thea von Harbou (based an article by Egon Jacobson); **c**, Fritz Arno Wagner; **m**, Edvard Grieg (from "Peer Gynt"); **ed**, Paul Falkenberg; **prod d**, Emil Hasler; **art d**, Hasler, Karl Vollbrecht.

M ★★★ 1951; U.S.; 88m; COL; B/W; Crime Drama; Children: Unacceptable; **DVD**. Wayne is exceptional in essaying the role of the child killer in this good remake of the Lang masterpiece of 1933. The film follows to the letter the original film, but where the location is not Berlin, Germany, but Los Angeles. Further, Wayne's obsessive sexual perversions are more accented, including his fixation on shoelaces. Director Losey does a good job in maintaining suspense in this frightening entry. **p**, Seymour Nebenzal; **d**, Joseph Losey; **cast**, David Wayne, Howard Da Silva, Luther Adler, Martin Gabel, Steve Brodie, Raymond Burr, Glenn Anders, Norman Lloyd, Walter Burke, John Miljan; **w**, Norman Reilly Raine, Leo Katcher, Waldo Salt (based on the script by Thea von Harbou, Fritz Lang, Paul Falkenberg, Adolf Jansen, Karl Vash and an article by Egon Jacobson); **c**, Ernest Laszlo; **m**, Michel Michelet; **ed**, Edward Mann; **art d**, Martin Obzina; **set d**, Ray Robinson.

Macao ★★★ 1952; U.S.; 81m; RKO; B/W; Crime Drama; Children: Unacceptable; **DVD**; **VHS**. Pantheon director Sternberg employs all of his stylish techniques in presenting this exciting film noir entry where Mitchum is fleeing from police for a crime he did not commit. He meets sultry singer Russell on board a tramp steamer sailing toward Macao, along with detective Bendix, who is posing as a salesman and is after jewel smugglers operating in the Portuguese-held islands off the coast of China, including Macao. Mtichum and Russell, both worldly characters, are attracted to each other, but Russell is wary of the U.S. exserviceman. Once they arrive in Macao, she tries to land a job as a singer in a posh nightclub operated by Dexter, who is the local crime boss and who is running the gem-smuggling operation Bendix seeks to smash. Gomez, the local and very corrupt police official notifies Dexter about the new arrivals, and Dexter, thinking Mitchum is the New York City cop probing his racket, tries to buy him off. He turns Dexter down and stays on while Dexter hires Russell as a singer, but only to learn from her what she knows about Mitchum. Meanwhile, Bendix, knowing Mitchum is low on cash, offers him a sizeable commission if he can sell a stolen diamond necklace, but when Mitchum goes to Dexter, showing him a single diamond from that necklace, Dexter identifies the gem as part of the loot he has earlier fenced and sent to his contacts in Hong Kong. Dexter orders his henchman to seize and hold Mitchum prisoner so he can later question him, but Grahame, Dexter's girlfriend, helps Mitchum escape, mostly because she thinks Dexter is going to abandon her for Russell and believing that Mitchum will take Russell away. Mitchum is now again on the run from Dexter's goons, but Bendix intervenes, saving his life. Bendix, however, is fatally stabbed in the struggle. Before dying, he admits to Mitchum that he is the New York City detective after Dexter and that there is a police patrol boat waiting off Macao to snare the evasive Dexter if he can be lured into the international waters and, if Mitchum helps to capture Dexter, his former criminal charges in the U.S. will be dropped. Dexter, meanwhile, boards his small yacht with Russell, to have a boating party, but Mitchum gets on board and, following a struggle, subdues Dexter and his men, then sails the yacht to the police boat where the smugglers are arrested. Mitchum and Russell then plan to return to the U.S. to make a life together. Sternberg presents a moody and somewhat complicated crime tale where Mitchum, Russell and Grahame are standouts in their roles as desperate people, if not social misfits, trying to survive in a grubbing foreign land and where Dexter and Gomez are appropriately conniving and sleazy. Veteran character actor Sokoloff presents an intriguing coolie, who carries Mitchum and Russell about in his little carriage while mouthing

Jane Russell and Robert Mitchum in *Macao*, 1952.

Oriental platitudes. Songs include (the first three sung by Russell): "One for My Baby" (Harold Arlen, Johnny Mercer); "You Kill Me," "Ocean Breeze" (Jule Styne, Leo Robin) and (as background music) "Come Out Wherever You Are" (Jule Styne, Sammy Cahn). *Author's Note*: Mitchum told this author that "I had made a picture with Jane just a year before [**His Kind of Woman**, 1951] we did **Macao**, and in this one, we compete in disrobing, my beefcake against Jane's cheesecake. The story has a lot of twists and turns and I found it difficult to follow it myself at times. Bill Bendix does a lot of little goofy business in pretending he is a salesman in his role when it's obvious to the world that he's a cop, but Bill always provided a lot of laughs on the set." Russell, too, thought the film was essentially a vehicle to showcase her considerable topside charms. "I did a lot of teasing in that picture," she told this author, "especially in low-cut gowns, but that was the nature of that beast." In one scene, Mitchum accidentally sees her disrobing and Russell quips: "Enjoying the view?" Mitchum replies: "It ain't the Taj Mahal or the Hanging Gardens of Babylon, but it will do." This was the last film Sternberg was to make under his contract with RKO and he felt that too many fingers got into his pie, later complaining that several executives inserted some scenes that disrupted the film's continuity, especially some of the scenes where Mitchum is battling Dexter and his henchman on aboard the yacht. Gomez told this author that "the final fight scene in that picture almost duplicates the ending for another film [**His Kind of Woman**] that starred Bob [Mitchum] and Jane [Russell], and that's where Bob destroys a whole crew of thugs on board another yacht. Sternberg did not like that, but there was little he could do. He was finished at RKO after **Macao**." Ray, who took over some final direction and was not credited for it, told this author that "I directed the fight scene on the yacht with Mitchum, Dexter and others, and did a few little clean-up scenes in the chases along the riverfront. I knew that Sternberg was upset about that, but I needed the work and I tried to keep Sternberg's style in place, but that was really impossible as he was unique in his setups, which were always very detailed. I think he saw his films the way a spider sees the creation of an intricate web. That shows in a lot of his scenes in **Macao**, particularly in his knife fight scene where floats are bobbing along the waterfront, waves sloshing against rotting wharves, a distant foghorn calls out, and Bendix is stabbed repeatedly through an elaborate fishnet. Sternberg had his own style of directing that no one could duplicate." **p**, Alex Gottlieb; **d**, Josef von Sternberg, and Nicholas Ray (uncredited); **cast**, Robert Mitchum, Jane Russell, William Bendix, Thomas Gomez, Gloria Grahame, Brad Dexter, Edward Ashley, Philip Ahn, Vladimir Sokoloff, Trevor Bardette; **w**, Bernard C. Schoenfeld, Stanley Rubin (based on a story by Bob Williams); **c**, Harry J. Wild; **m**, Anthony Collins; **ed**, Samuel E. Beetley, Robert Golden; **art d**, Albert S. D'Agostino, Ralph Berger; **set d**, Darrell Silvera, Harley Miller.

Gregory Peck in *MacArthur*, 1977.

MacArthur ★★★★ 1977; U.S.; 130m; UNIV; Color; Biographical Drama/War Drama; Children: Unacceptable (MPAA: PG); **DVD**; **VHS**. Peck gives a bravura performance, one of the best in his long and sterling career, as the charismatic, dynamic and totemic U.S. General of the Armies, Douglas MacArthur (1880-1964). The film opens with Peck, at the end of his military career, bidding farewell to the cadets of his old alma mater, West Point, after delivering a moving speech that ends with the code of his life: "Duty...Honor...Country." As he speaks, the scene fades to a flashback in early 1942 where Peck is commanding the American and Filipino forces (approximately 70,000 troops) in the Philippines, which has been invaded by a Japanese army of 200,000 men. The battle is a losing one for Peck, who is on the island fortress of Corregidor, which, like neighboring U.S. troops on the Bataan Peninsula opposite Manila Bay, is being bombarded by long-range Japanese guns and bombed from the air by Japanese planes. Knowing that MacArthur and his troops cannot hold out against such overwhelming odds, President Franklin D. Roosevelt (1882-1945), played by O'Herlihy, orders Peck to leave for Australia where he is to organize a relief expedition for the Philippines, this presidential decision made in the belief that such a distinguished commanding officer should not fall into enemy hands. Although Peck initially refuses to obey the order, saying he will stay with his troops and fight with Filipino guerrillas in the hills, he is persuaded to escape with his wife and small boy and he leaves the doomed Corregidor by PT boat (MacArthur elected to evacuate via this surface craft rather than by submarine to prove to the chiefs of staff that the Japanese blockade of the Philippines could be penetrated). He says goodbye to his old friend, Kenyon, playing General Jonathan M. Wainwright (1883-1953), telling him that he "must hold out," promising to return with reinforcements and supplies. He arrives in Australia where Peck states that "I came through and I shall return [to the Philippines]." (This widely quoted statement from MacArthur was later rephrased to state "We Shall Return.") He learns that no plans have been made for a Philippine relief expedition and, in fact, there are very few Allied troops at his disposal in Australia. Peck then organizes an intensive military building up, training raw recruits and telling Australian commanders that he does not intend to defend Australia, but attack Japanese forces that have invaded neighboring New Guinea. Learning that Kenyon has surrendered all the American forces in the Philippines, Peck denounces Kenyon's actions, believing that he has lost his mind. Using American and Australian troops, Peck, who has been named supreme commander of the Southwest Pacific, attacks Japanese positions, but ignores other strongly held enemy positions, adopting a brilliant island-hopping strategy where he starves these Japanese garrisons into submission or surrender by cutting off their supply lines and by bombing their bases from the air. Peck is shown directing his troops as

a front-line commander, often seen in the thick of battle (and this was truly the case with MacArthur, who was dubbed with undeserved acrimony as "Dugout Doug" for supposedly cowering in the deep tunnels on Corregidor, when that was never the case). When his commanders prove ineffective, Peck relieves them, placing new commanders in their place, anyone "who will fight." He begins to win battle after battle, his overall strategy proving successful. He is then asked to visit with President Roosevelt (O'Herlihy) and top U.S. Navy Admiral Chester W. Nimitz (1885-1966), played by Powell, at Pearl Harbor and, at that meeting, Peck convinces O'Herlihy to approve of his plans to retake the Philippines, but only after he shows O'Herlihy a letter he has earlier written wherein he promised to come to the aid of that island nation. With his troops now well trained, Peck is next seen on board a warship of Leyte in the Philippines where he launches his 1944 invasion and is soon seen wading ashore amidt gunfire, stating that many will be surprised to see that "I can't walk on water." While on that beach, Peck delivers over shortwave the precise and moving speech MacArthur delivered that day to the people of the Philippines: "People of the Philippines. I have returned. By the Grace of Almighty God, our forces stand again on Philippine soil—soil consecrated in the blood of our two peoples...Rally to me! Let the indomitable spirit of Bataan and Corregidor lead on! As the lines of battle roll forward to bring you within the zone of operations, rise and strike! Strike at every favorable opportunity! For your homes and hearths, strike! In the name of your sacred dead, strike! Let no heart be faint! Let every arm be steeled! The guidance of Divine God points the way! Follow in His name to the Holy Grail of righteous victory!" As victory is, indeed, achieved, Peck is shown arriving at a Japanese POW camp where he is hailed as a savior by some of the survivors of the Bataan Death March (where the Japanese, following the fall of Bataan, forced tens of thousands of starving and sick prisoners to march without water or food for more than eighty miles to camps on Luzon, viciously slaughtering these helpless troops en route in March 1942 and for which many high-ranking Japanese officers were later condemned as war criminals and executed, including General Masaharu Homma, as well as General Tomoyuki Yamashita, the latter hanged for slaughtering thousands of innocent Filipino citizens in Manila during MacArthur's 1944 invasion of the Philippines). Peck meets with these half-starved men, embracing them in one of the most touching scenes of the film, and telling them that he and his forces are "long overdue." With the Philippines retaken, Peck organizes troops for an invasion of Japan, but is shocked to learn that the U.S. will now employ an atom bomb to force Japan's surrender, and which, in the absence of President Roosevelt, who has died, is ordered dropped by the new President, Harry S. Truman (1884-1972), played by Flanders. Peck then supervises the surrender of Japan on board the American battleship USS *Missouri*, countersigning the surrender document signed by Japanese civilian and military officials. He hands one of the pens he has used for this historic signing to Kenyon, his former commander at Corregidor. Peck is then made governor general of Japan and he institutes widespread reforms, dismantling the industrial and military leaders who led Japan into wars of aggression, and brings about free elections where women are given the right to vote as well as establishing unions for workers. The new Japanese premier is in full agreement with these reforms, stating that Japan will no longer have any military forces and that it renounces war. When a Russian general informs Peck that the Soviets intend to take over some Japanese islands, Peck tells him that such an act will be an act of war and he will meet force with force and that, if such an event occurs, he will throw the Russian general and the entire Soviet diplomatic corps in Japan into prison, his stern warning causing the Soviets to abandon their scheme to appropriate those Japanese islands. Meanwhile, Flanders is irritated by Peck's unwillingness to return to the U.S., but knows that he is governing well in Japan and does not interfere in Peck's operations. All seems tranquil until, in 1950, the North Korean army invades South Korea, setting off the Korean War and where Allied forces are now again under Peck's command. Peck first orders a retreat of Allied forces, but then, in a daring flanking movement by sea, counterattacks through an amphibious assault at Inchon, where the North Korean army is annihilated and driven all the way back to the 38th Parallel, which divides North Korea and South Korea. Meeting with Flanders, Peck tells him that he does not expect that the Chinese communists will join with the North Koreans, but his estimate is wrong and when the Chinese do pour hundreds of thousands of troops into South Korea, the Allied forces are again driven back. Peck wants to attack the Chinese in their homeland, but Flanders forbids it and when the two come to loggerheads, with Peck making public statements that contradict Flanders, the President relieves him of his command. Peck is shown returning to the U.S. to a hero's welcome, awash with tickertape parades and national praise. He is now shown in flash forward at West Point, where he concludes his moving speech to the cadets, the American generals to come, and then ends his military career with a fond farewell. This excellent, well-mounted production captures the substance and flavor of one of the 20th Century's greatest warriors, and Peck superbly essays MacArthur in a stunning performance that incisively shows his vanities, eccentricities, brilliant mind and passionate heart. *Author's Note*: Peck told this author that "to play such a military icon as MacArthur was no little challenge. I had great reservations about my ability to project the many sides of his varied personality. When I accepted the role, I thought the best way to show this man's many faces was to demonstrate those characteristics as if one was opening a door to another room never before entered. Each room held a different man—the warrior, the peace-lover who hated war, the man proud of his achievements, the man fearful of failure—I had to deal with all of those men in that one character." **p**, Frank McCarthy; **d**, Joseph Sargent; **cast**, Gregory Peck, Ed Flanders, Dan O'Herlihy, Ivan Bonar, Sandy Kenyon, Addison Powell, Ward Costello, Nicolas Coster, Marj Dusay, Art Fleming, Russell D. Johnson, Kenneth Tobey, Barry Coe, William Wellman Jr.; **w**, Hal Barwood, Matthew Robbins; **c**, Mario Tosi (Panavision; Technicolor); **m**, Jerry Goldsmith; **ed**, George Jay Nicholson; **prod d**, John J. Lloyd; **set d**, Hal Gausman; **spec eff**, Albert Whitlock.

MacArthur's Children ★★★ 1985; Japan; 125m; Hara/Orion; Color; Comedy/Drama; Children: Unacceptable (MPAA: PG); **VHS**. The title is misleading because the film has nothing to do with General Douglas MacArthur or his children. It is about the impact of Japan's loss in World War II as seen through the eyes of that country's children. The focus is on a small fishing village whose inhabitants try to come to terms with their country's defeat and sudden occupation by MacArthur and American troops. The film is a restrained look into the many postwar transitions in Japan including ethical questions of right and wrong, patriotism and guilt. It opens with a radio broadcast in which Emperor Hirohito announces that Japan has surrendered to the United States and the war is over. Some fifth grade school children stand at respectful attention while listening to the broadcast from a radio on a table. We then follow the children during the next year as the village goes through a love-hate relationship with America. The father of one of the children is tried as a war criminal and executed, and a teacher's fiancé returns from the war, but she is ashamed to see him because she had been raped by another man and tradition makes her feel guilty for having "dishonored herself." On the plus side, some of the children start to play the American game of baseball and their grandmothers sew mitts for them. The town people gradually adjust from a warlike nation to a peace-loving people in this good profile of a whole people in social transition where excellent character development ensues. Violence and sexual matters prohibit viewing by children. (In Japanese; English subtitles.) **p**, Mastao Hara; **d**, Masahiro Shinoda; **cast**, Takaya Yamauchi, Yoshiyuki Omori, Shiori Sakura, Masako Natsume, Hideji Ôtaki, Haruko Kato, Ken Watanabe, Hiromi Gô, Jûzô Itami, Shima Iwashita; **w**, Tsutomu Tamura (based on the novel by Yû Aku); **c**, Kazuo Miyagawa; **m**, Shinichro Ikebe; **ed**, Sachiko Yamaji.

Orson Welles in *Macbeth*, 1948.

Macbeth ★★★ 1948; U.S.; 107m; Mercury Productions/REP; B/W; Drama; Children: Unacceptable; **DVD**; **VHS**. Welles captivates in this moody, murky Shakespearian tale where the apprehensive 11th-Century Scottish nobleman is vexed and nagged by women into murder in order to secure his kingdom, and, in so doing, brings about his own end. This is a highly stylized version of the Immortal Bard's play, one where Welles takes considerable liberties with the original text, peppering the dialog with thick Scottish accents. Supporting players are standouts, but the sets and interiors are often so shrouded in shadow that some of the characters appear to be specters. It is nevertheless a haunting and compelling film worth the watching. *Author's Note*: Welles told this author that "I did not achieve what I wanted in Macbeth. I was given a very limited budget and a crushing schedule—we shot the film in twenty-three days—and my pleas for more funds to improve the sets fell on deaf ears. It is, however, as good a film as I could make with the tools I had on hand." **p**, Orson Welles; **d**, Welles, William Alland (dialog director); **cast**, Welles, Jeanette Nolan, Dan O'Herlihy, Roddy McDowall, Edgar Barrier, Alan Napier, Erskine Sanford, John Dierkes, Keene Curtis, Peggy Webber, Lurene Tuttle, Christopher Welles; **w**, Welles (based on the play by William Shakespeare); **c**, John L. Russell; **m**, Jacques Ibert; **ed**, Louis Lindsay; **art d**, Fred Ritter; **set d**, John McCarthy, Jr., James Redd; **spec eff**, Howard and Theodore Lydecker.

Macbeth ★★★ 1971; U.K./U.S.; 140m; Caliban Films/COL; Color; Children: Unacceptable (MPAA: R); **DVD**; **VHS**. In this unorthodox but interesting version of the Shakespeare tale, Finch ably plays the troubled Scottish lord, who, through treachery and murder, acquires his kingdom, much to the insidious credit of Lady Macbeth, played by Annis. Polanski inventively presents his version of these dark deeds in 11th-Century Scotland by cutting out passages from the original play and converting some of its soliloquies to voiceover monologues, which surprisingly proves effective in telling this sinister tale on film. Further, Polanski considerably inflates the relatively obscure and unimportant character Ross (Stride), making him a leading player when he becomes Finch's insidious and forceful henchman after Finch kills Duncan (Selby). The direction is taut and the acting above par in this lively and innovative tweaking of Shakespeare's diabolic opus. *Author's Note*: Polanski made this film just after his wife and several others were slain by the Manson murder cult in Beverly Hills on August 9, 1969, but he had a hard time getting funds from mainstream Hollywood. He reportedly secured financing from *Playboy* publisher Hugh Hefner, who was persuaded to fund the film by Polanski's good friend, Victor Lownes, Hefner's top executive in England. This may explain why Polanski shocked many critics by inserting an unnecessary scene into Macbeth, one where Annis cavorts nude during a sleepwalking scene, along with

Robert Preston and Joan Bennett in *The Macomber Affair*, 1947.

adding gratuitous graphic violence. Six years after this film was released, the then fourty-three-year-old Polanski was arrested on March 11, 1977, in Los Angeles, on charges of sexually assaulting thirteen-year-old Samantha Geimer. In a plea-bargain arrangement he pled guilty to the charge of "unlawful sexual intercourse with a minor," but when he felt that he might be serving time in prison, he fled the country and has remained a fugitive from U.S. justice since that time, battling against extradition while he continues to live comfortably in Switzerland. Popular opinion in the U.S. and in Europe then and to this day is that he should be extradited and imprisoned, but Polanski has used his powerfully influential connections to remain free, an unsavory latter day Macbeth of sorts. **p**, Andrew Braunsberg; **d**, Roman Polanski; **cast**, Jon Finch, Francesca Annis, Martin Shaw, Terence Bayler, John Stride, Nicholas Selby, Stephan Chase, Paul Shelley, Maisie MacFarquhar, Elsie Taylor, Noelle Rimmington, Noel Davis, Sydney Bromley; **w**, Polanski, Kenneth Tynan (based on the play by William Shakespeare); **c**, Gilbert Taylor (Technicolor); **m**, The Third Ear Band; **ed**, Alastair McIntyre; **prod d**, Wilfrid Shingleton; **art d**, Fred Carter; **set d**, Bryan Graves; **spec eff**, Ted Samuels, Gerald Larn.

The Macomber Affair ★★★ 1947; U.S.; 89m; UA; B/W; Adventure; Children: Unacceptable; **VHS**. Peck is exceptional in his role of the white hunter in Africa shepherding a hunting safari financed by playboy Preston, who is accompanied by his sultry wife, Bennett. Bennett, who has no respect for her husband, rightly believing him to be cowardly and without any sense of manly honor, makes a romantic play for Peck, but the upright Peck will have nothing to do with the cuckolding and deceiving wife. Preston initially displays a thick streak of cowardice during the safari but, through Peck's resolute example, comes to find himself as a man and discovers the courage he requires to go on living. Oddly, this altering change of his personality for the good somehow distresses Bennett, who can no longer pity or condemn Preston. When he later refuses to run from a charging rhino, Bennett fatally shoots him, stating that she was trying to save his life. She is nevertheless tried for murder, but is acquitted. She is now free to be with Peck, who has loved her from afar, but Peck shuns the idea of any future relationship with this dangerous woman and that is where this strange but compelling story ends. Peck, Preston and Bennett are outstanding in their captivating roles, their performances exacted with careful finesse by Korda, a director who had a reputation for developing effective characterizations in almost all of his films. *Author's Note*: Peck stated to this author that "I play a white hunter in that picture, a solid Hemingway story that tests the courage of more than one man and, oddly enough, about five years later, I played a writer in another Hemingway story, **The Snows of Kilimanjaro** [1952] where I am on safari and I am seeking the meaning of

life. Hemingway's characters are searchers, looking for the most elusive things in life and that is what makes them so fascinating." Hemingway stated to this author that "that picture with Peck and Preston stayed with the concept of my story and that was a surprise. Hollywood always wants to tinker with every story it does and usually that makes things worse. They did change things, but I could hear some of my prose in that picture, so they made an effort to keep it honest. I thought Joan Bennett did a very good job as the wife, who is the real hunter of that story." Hemingway had been paid $80,000 for the film rights to the story, but he refused to have anything to do with the script. The producer, Bogeaus, was forever changing the title of the film, arriving on the set unannounced to shout out a new title to director Korda one day after another. When Bogeaus next appeared on the set, interrupting the shooting, he shouted: "I've got it, I've got it! We'll call it 'Congo!'" Incensed with this last of many interruptions, Korda withdrew a penknife, walked up to the producer and flourished the knife. He told Bogeaus that if he ever again came onto the set during the production he would cut out the producer's liver. Other than some stock footage shot in Africa, most of the film was shot on studio sound stages or exteriors at Baja, California. At the time of the shootings in Baja, the actors hired a Mexican marimba band to play at the production campsite. So much did the cast and crew like the band that they later invited the bandleader to bring his musicians to Los Angeles to play at a party celebrating the completion of the film. The bandleader politely refused, saying that most of his musicians had fled to the hills after being accused of committing a recent murder. **p**, Benedict Bogeaus, Casey Robinson; **d**, Zoltan Korda; **cast**, Gregory Peck, Joan Bennett, Robert Preston, Reginald Denny, Jean Gillie, Carl Harbord, Earl Smith, Frederick Worlock, Vernon Downing, Darby Jones; **w**, Robinson, Seymour Bennett, Frank Arnold (based on the short story "The Short Happy Life of Francis Macomber" by Ernest Hemingway); **c**, Karl Struss; **m**, Miklos Rozsa; **ed**, George Feld, Jack Wheeler; **art d**, Erno Metzner; **set d**, Fred Widdowson.

Mad about Music ★★★ 1938; U.S.; 100m; UNIV; B/W; Musical; Children: Acceptable; **DVD**; **VHS**. In her third starring role, Durbin turns in a charming performance as a girl who is left too much alone to live with her vivid imagination. Patrick, a vain, aging Hollywood actress, does not want the world to know that she has a growing daughter that might indicate her own age, so she sends Durbin to a boarding school in Switzerland where she, unlike other students, has no visiting parents. Durbin creates out of her imagination a father who is an adventurer traveling the world. When she is called on to prove the existence of this daring and dashing parent, Durbin becomes desperate. She asks Marshall, a kind-hearted composer, to pretend to be that mythical father. Marshall saves the day and Durbin's face by enacting that role to perfection. Songs include: "Chapel Bells," "A Serenade to the Stars," "I Love to Whistle," (Jimmy McHugh, Harold Adamson); and "Gounod's Ave Maria (music by Charles Gounod, based on the C Major Prelude by Johann Sebastian Bach). **p**, Joe Pasternak; **d**, Norman Taurog; **cast**, Deanna Durbin, Herbert Marshall, Gail Patrick, Arthur Treacher, William Frawley, Marcia Mae Jones, Helen Parrish, Jackie Moran, Christian Rub, Sid Grauman, Rosemary La Planche, Martha O'Driscoll, Franklin Pangborn, John Sutton; **w**, Bruce Manning, Felix Jackson (based on a story by Marcella Burke, Frederick Kohner); **c**, Joseph Valentine; **m**, Charles Previn, Frank Skinner; **ed**, Ted Kent; **art d**, Jack Otterson.

Mad Dog and Glory ★★★ 1993; U.S.; 97m; UNIV; Color; Comedy; Children: Unacceptable (MPAA: R); **DVD**; **VHS**. Wayne "Mad Dog" Dobie (DeNiro) gets his name ironically because he is a shy police crime technician and photographer, who, one day, happens upon a grocery robbery. A street punk shoots the owner and points the gun at Murray, a customer, not knowing he's aiming at a local crime boss. DeNiro persuades the gunman to take the money and run. Murray is so grateful to DeNiro for saving his life that he wants to be friends and offers DeNiro one of his employees, a beautiful girl named "Glory" (Thurman), who tends bar at a comedy club Murray owns and performs there as a stand-up comic. DeNiro has the unusual problem of not being sure about accepting Murray's friendship or romancing Thurman because that would mean he is fraternizing with criminals. Thurman wants to cooperate, telling DeNiro that Murray will take it out on her if she is rejected. DeNiro accepts her and they clinch for a happy ending, but not without several humorous confrontations with the quirky Murray. Scorsese is very good at creating awkward scenes and turning them into natural comedic sequences. Sexuality, language, violence, and drug content prohibit viewing by children. **p**, Martin Scorsese, Barbara De Fina, Steven A. Jones; **d**, John McNaughton; **cast**, Robert De Niro, Uma Thurman, Bill Murray, David Caruso, Mike Starr, Tom Towles, Kathy Baker, Derek Anunciation, Doug Hara, Evan Lionel; **w**, Richard Price; **c**, Robby Müller; **m**, Elmer Bernstein, Terphe Rypdal; **ed**, Elena Maganini, Craig McKay; **prod d**, David Chapman; **art d**, Mark Haack; **set d**, Leslie Pope, Ed Golya; **spec eff**, Edward Drohan.

Mad Dog Morgan ★★★ 1976; Australia; 102m; Mad Dog/Cinema Shares International Distribution; Color; Biographical Drama/Crime Drama; Children: Unacceptable (MPAA: R); **DVD**; **VHS**. Hopper gives a tense performance in this exciting biopic based on the criminal career of outlaw Daniel Morgan (Jack Fuller; c. 1830-1965), who is wanted dead or alive in 1850s Australia. Born in Ireland, Hopper goes to the land down under, hoping to strike it rich in a gold rush. But he has no luck as a gold miner and even less as a highwayman in the Australian outback, getting caught and sentenced to six years at hard labor. When he is released from prison, he has a grudge against everyone, except an aborigine, Gulpilil. Hopper, with Gulpilil as his sidekick, becomes notorious in New South Wales for stealing from the rich, but most others consider them heroes. Hopper's luck runs out when his hideout is surrounded by police and he is shot dead. Extreme violence prohibits viewing by children. **p**, Jeremy Thomas; **d&w**, Philippe Mora (based on the book *Morgan: The Bold Bushranger* by Margaret Carnegie); **cast**, Dennis Hopper, Jack Thompson, David Gulpilil, John Hargreaves, Bill Hunter, Frank Thring, Michael Pate, Wallace Eaton, Martin Harris, Robin Ramsay; **c**, Mike Molloy (Panavision); **m**, Patrick Flynn; **ed**, John Scott, Scott Sousa; **prod d& art d**, Bob Hilditch.

Mad Love ★★★ 1935; U.S.; 68m; MGM; B/W; Horror; Children: Unacceptable; **DVD**; **VHS**. In this bizarre thriller, Lorre, appearing in his first American film, is a brilliant physician so much in love with a woman that his passion drives him into the abyss of insanity. He is smitten by attractive Drake, who is the alluring star of the Parisian Horror Theater, but when he tells her that he loves her, she rejects him out of hand. As a shabby replacement, Lorre buys a life-size replica of Drake used in the theater lobby as an advertisement and takes this home, thinking that he can somehow bring the replication to life. After Clive, who is Drake's husband, a celebrated pianist, loses his hands in a railway accident, a desperate Drake goes to Lorre, pleading that he use his great surgical skills to aid Clive. Lorre, now turned sinister and full of revenge, agrees to help Drake and Clive and he grafts the hands of Brophy, an executed murderer and one-time knife-thrower, onto Clive's stumps. After recovering from surgery, Clive attempts to play the piano, but his hands will not obey. After Lorre kills Clive's stepfather, he employs psychological intimidation to convince Clive that he has done the terrible deed. Clive is further driven to the brink of insanity when Brophy miraculously appears wearing a neck brace and hideous stitches to tell Clive that he has had his head sewn back on by Lorre and he now demands the return of his hands! Only when this gruesome visage returns to Lorre's residence, does the viewer see that it is Lorre impersonating the deceased killer when he removes his mask and awful headgear. To expose Lorre, Drake goes to his home and, seeing the replica of herself, replaces it with her own body and when Lorre appears she pretends to come to life (a la Pygmalion and Galatea of Greek legend). It is Lorre

Uma Thurman and Robert De Niro in *Mad Dog and Glory,* 1993.

who is now totally consumed by insanity (he was not far from it to begin with) and he wraps Drake's long braids about her throat and begins to strangle her. Clive then appears and his hands speak for him, the very hands of a knife-throwing killer that Lorre has grafted to his arms when he expertly throws a knife that instantly kills the maniac, ending this utterly macabre film. Director Freund, who was chiefly a cinematographer, presents unusual camera angles, oblique and distortional shots that emphasize the loss of sanity and here he is greatly aided by two top cinematographers, Toland and Lyons, who freely contribute their own set-up shots to capture the Grand Guignol surrealism that engulfs this fantastic production, a must-see by any horror fan. This was a remake of a 1924 silent film starring Conrad Veidt and it was remade again as **The Hands of Orlac**, 1964, a much inferior film. *Author's Note*: Lorre told this author that "I did not think anyone would believe anything about **Mad Love** and I told Freund that. He shook his head and said, 'they will believe every scene because everyone is crazy in this picture and sane people, and that's everyone in the audience, always accept the insane acts of others for what they seem to be.' I thought he was a little crazy, too, but he was right. Audiences will suspend belief if everything they see is outrageous and we did every outrageous thing we could do in that picture." Oddly, Lorre would appear in another strange and chilling film that dealt with a severed limb, this time a murderous disembodied hand, **The Beast with Five Fingers**, 1946, and which may have been inspired by this production. To provide some sort of comic relief, Freund cast Healy as a wise-cracking newsman, but his brief scenes and attempt at humor seem to fall flat in light of the pervasive gruesomeness of this offbeat but fascinating film. Although the film received high praise when it was released, Charles Chaplin calling Lorre "the greatest living actor," the film was slammed by latter-day revisionist critics. For its time, despite some of its static scenes, it nevertheless remains a minor horror classic. **p**, John W. Considine, Jr.; **d**, Karl Freund; **cast**, Peter Lorre, Colin Clive, Frances Drake, Ted Healy, Sara Haden, Edward Brophy, Henry Kolker, Keye Luke, Harold Huber, Isabel Jewell, Billy Gilbert, Edward Norris; **w**, Guy Endore, Leon Wolfson, John L. Balderston (based on the novel *Les mains d'Orlac* by Maurice Renard); **c**, Gregg Toland, Chester Lyons; **m**, Dimitri Tiomkin; **ed**, Hugh Wynn; **art d**, Cedric Gibbons.

Mad Max ★★★ 1980; Australia; 88m; Kennedy Miller Productions; American International; Color; Adventure/Crime Drama; Children: Unacceptable (MPPA: R); **BD**; **DVD**; **VHS**. The rugged Gibson appears in his first starring role in this futuristic tale, one that established him as matinee heart-throb, as a tough loner cop, who can no longer tolerate the endless battles with vicious and murderous gangs that control the outback roadways and tells his boss that he is retiring. His boss attempts

Mel Gibson in *Mad Max Beyond Thunderdome*, 1985.

to bribe him back into his job by offering him one of the last and fastest cop cars—"the last of the V-8's!" When that does not work, his boss tells him to take a vacation and think about it. Gibson goes to a beach with his wife and child, but both are killed by a group of crazed road gangsters in revenge for the death of one of their members that had been brought about by Gibson. With everything precious in his life gone, Gibson turns into an avenging warrior, donning a black leather ensemble and, after gassing up his V-8, roars off after the culprits, tracking them all down and killing them. Spectacular action takes place during Gibson's violent crusade to destroy the human beasts that have destroyed his family with innumerable car races and crashes and violent explosions and gory executions. **p**, Byron Kennedy; **d**, George Miller; **cast**, Mel Gibson, Joanne Samuel, Hugh Keays-Byrne, Steve Bisley, Tim Burns, Roger Ward, Lisa Aldenhoven, David Bracks, Bertrand Cadart, David Cameron; **w**, Miller, James McCausland (based on a story by Miller, Kennedy); **c**, David Eggby (Eastmancolor); **m**, Brian May; **ed**, Cliff Hayes, Tony Paterson; **art d**, Jon Dowding; **spec eff**, Chris Murray, Richard Wilmot.

Mad Max Beyond Thunderdome ★★★ 1985; Australia; 107m; Kennedy Miller Productions/WB; Color; Adventure; Children: Unacceptable (MPAA: PG-13); **DVD**; **VHS**. In this third entry on the Mad Max action films, Gibson is back as the rugged loner trying to survive in a futuristic world where roving murderous gangs rule the roadways. After his supplies are stolen by aviator Spence, Gibson finds his way to Bardertown, a crudely assembled human outpost in the Australian desert, which attempts to maintain what is left of serviceable technology. The Amazonian Turner is at the time in competition with Rossitto, a conniving engineer, who had assembled the methane extractor that supplies the makeshift town with its electricity and power. Turner sees Gibson as a useful aide who can help her take over the town, and Gibson becomes involved in the power struggle between Turner and Rossitto, which finally sees him again on the desert roads, attempting to rescue children from the murderous clutches of the road gangs. Superlative action dominates this post-apocalypse adventure tale and where Gibson and the cast render solid performances. **p**, George Miller, Terry Hayes, Doug Mitchell; **d**, Miller, George Ogilvie; **cast**, Mel Gibson, Tina Turner, Bruce Spence, Adam Cockburn, Frank Thring, Angelo Rossitto, Paul Larsson, Angry Anderson, Robert Grubb, George Spartels; **w**, Miller, Hayes; **c**, Dean Semler; **m**, Maurice Jarre; **ed**, Richard Francis-Bruce; **prod d**, Graham "Grace" Walker; **art d**, Anni Browning; **set d**, Martin O'Neill; **spec eff**, Steve Courtley, Brian Cox.

The Mad Miss Manton ★★★ 1938; U.S.; 80m; RKO; B/W; Comedy/Crime Drama; Children: Cautionary; **DVD**; **VHS**. Stanwyck and Fonda are standouts in another good "screwball" comedy, using the tried and true story line of an heiress falling in love with a newspaperman. Stanwyck is the "Miss Manton" of the film, but she is not insane, only a madcap wealthy young woman who likes playing pranks and demonstrating strange behavior, like walking her dogs at four in the morning. She romps about with debutante friends (Lester, Bourne and Mercer), but their fun ceases when they discover a body that mysteriously disappears before the police arrive. She is again labeled an irresponsible prankster and a spoiled heiress by newsman Fonda, who insists Stanwyck is having fun at the public's expense by fabricating a murder. Angered at this, Stanwyck and friends turn sleuths and they are now determined to run down the killer. When Fonda writes a story that lambasts Stanwyck for pulling off another hoax, Stanwyck sues his paper for libel. Fonda, who tries to smooth things over, winds up joining Stanwyck and her girlfriends in the amateur detective snooping and together they identify the culprit, Ridges. *Author's Note*: Stanwyck told this author that "Hank [Fonda] and I got along well in that picture and our 'chemistry' if you want to call it that, worked even better when we did **The Lady Eve** [1941] three years later. I don't know what was on the writer's mind [Epstein] when he wrote the script, but I think he felt that turning that comedy into a crime caper would provide more excitement, and I think he was right." Fonda did not want to be in this film, but he was under contract to Walter Wanger. "I was an indentured servant in those days," Fonda told this author, "and my service contract was held by Wanger. He cut a deal with RKO to have me appear in **The Mad Miss Manton**, and I had no choice but to appear in that picture. I have to admit that Babs [Stanwyck] was very good in that film, but she was good in every picture." Similar films with newsmen falling in love with heiresses include **It Happened One Night**, 1934, and **Love Is News**, 1937. **p**, Pandro S. Berman, P. J. Wolfson; **d**, Leigh Jason; **cast**, Barbara Stanwyck, Henry Fonda, Sam Levene, Frances Mercer, Stanley Ridges, Vicki Lester, Whitney Bourne, Ann Evers, Catherine O'Quinn, Linda Terry, Eleanor Hansen, Hattie McDaniel, James Burke, Paul Guilfoyle, Penny Singleton, Kay Sutton, Miles Mander, John Qualen, Leona Maricle, Grady Sutton, Olin Howland, Emory Parnell, Irving Bacon, Leonard Mudie, Walter Sande, Charles Halton; **w**, Philip G. Epstein, Hal Yates (based on a story by Wilson Collison); **c**, Nicholas Musuraca; **m**, Roy Webb; **ed**, George Hively; **art d**, Van Nest Polglase, Carroll Clark; **set d**, Darrell Silvera.

Mad Wednesday ★★★ 1950; U.S.; 79m; California Pictures/RKO; B/W; Comedy; Children: Acceptable; **DVD**; **VHS**. A solid comedy from Sturges sees the silent screen comedian Lloyd twenty years after he appeared in the classic comedy, **The Freshman**, 1925, and, in fact, the film begins with scenes from that film. He has not gone on, as that silent film suggests, to great promise. He is in fact, a lowly bookkeeper working in a drab little office. Unappreciated, he is fired for his years of dogged labor and goes on a wild binge, which brings him into contact with a bevy of Hollywood's best comedic characters: Conlin, a jabbering ex-convict; Pangborn, the master of prissiness; Kennedy, famous for his "slow burn"; Hamilton, the celebrated witch in **The Wizard of Oz**, 1939; and the gravelly voiced Stander. During that madcap spree, Lloyd experiences a spectacular and unlikely series of events that culminates with him waking up to be the owner of a dilapidated and impoverished circus. He must now raise funds to feed the wild animals and allow his seedy performers to go on with the show. His challenges compel him to take extraordinary risks, not the least of which is hanging from a tall building as Lloyd did in his famous **Safety Last!**, 1923, but this time he is menaced by a snarling lion from his own circus. Sturges mixes comedy and thrills in this very funny film, where the viewer will be laughing and nail-biting at the same time. *Author's Note*: Lloyd, though in his fifties, appears only a few years older than his youthful appearance during his Hollywood halcyon days in the silent era, and he, as was the case in all of his previous films, did his own dangerous stunts in this film, which was his last feature production. Sturges, a master of comedy films

(**The Great McGinty**, 1940, **Sullivan's Travels**, 1941, and **The Miracle of Morgan's Creek**, 1944), and Lloyd clashed through most of the film's production. "We had two decidedly different views on how to shoot the story line," Lloyd told this author. "We compromised by shooting each scene his way and then reshooting each scene my way. This was a costly proposition, of course, but Howard Hughes was financing this film and did not object. Well, about halfway through the production, I got tired of fighting with Mr. Sturges, and I let him have it his way, and that turned out just about as good, I think." Hughes and Sturges had put together the production company, California Pictures, for this film, releasing the film through United Artists in 1947 under the title of **The Sin of Harold Diddlebock**, but the film met with tepid audience approval. Hughes withdrew the film, had it edited from 89 minutes to 79 minutes and then released it again under the title of **Mad Wednesday** and it did much better at the box office. **p,d&w**, Preston Sturges; **cast**, Harold Lloyd, Frances Ramsden, Jimmy Conlin, Raymond Walburn, Rudy Vallee, Edgar Kennedy, Arline Judge, Franklin Pangborn, Lionel Stander, Margaret Hamilton, Jack Norton, Robert Greig; **c**, Robert Pattack; **m**, Werner R. Heymann; **ed**, Thomas Neff, Stuart Gilmore; **art d**, Robert Usher; **set d**, Victor A. Gangelin; **spec eff**, John P. Fulton.

Madadayo ★★★ 1998; Japan; 134m; Dentsu Music and Entertainment/Weinstein Co.; Color; Biographical Drama; Children: Acceptable; **DVD**; **VHS**. The great Japanese director Kurosawa's last film tells the gentle, sentimental true story of a retired Japanese university professor in Gotemba, Uchida Haykken-sama (1889-1971), and his devoted former students, especially two of his most ardent pupils, Igawa and Tokoro. After teaching, Haykken-sama (Matsumura) becomes a writer, living in a modest house with his wife, Kagawa, and his books. Allied bombing during World War II force them to live in a hut on a burned-out estate where his adoring former students visit. They ask him each year on his birthday, "Mahda-Kai?" ("Are you ready yet?") He replies, "Madadayo" ("Not yet"), then joins them in drinking an enormous glass of beer. He still wants to live and write and enjoy life. (In Japanese; English subtitles.) **p**, Hisao Kurosawa, Gohei Kogure, Yasuyoshi Tokuma, Yasuyoshi Tokuma; **d**, Akira Kurosawa; **cast**, Tatsuo Matsumura, Kyôko Kagawa, Hisashi Igawa, Jôji Tokoro, Masayuki Yui, Akira Terao, Takeshi Kusaka, Asei Kobayashi, Hidetaka Yoshioka, Yoshitaka Zushi; **w**, Kurosawa, Ishirô Honda (based on essays by Hyakken Uchida); **c**, Takao Saitô, Shôji Ueda; **m**, Shinichirô Ikebe; **ed**, Akira Kurosawa, Ishirô Honda; **art d**, Yoshirô Muraki.

Madame Bovary ★★★ 1949; U.S.; 115m; MGM; B/W; Drama; Children: Unacceptable; **DVD**; **VHS**. French author Gustave Flaubert (Mason) is on trial in Paris for indecency regarding the publication of his sexually controversial novel *Madame Bovary*. He tells a jury why he believes the book is not immoral. The story follows a beautiful young woman, Jones, who leaves a convent to tend to her ailing father. She becomes bored, and when her father's doctor, Heflin, proposes marriage, she accepts. Bored with him because he is not handsome or romantic, she falls in love with a rich wastrel, Jourdan. That love soon dies, too, and she falls in love with Kent, a man who resembles Jourdan. That is not a happy romance, either, and she becomes depressed and commits suicide. MGM pulled out all the stops in producing this film, offering sumptuous sets and costuming and where Jones is outstanding as the sensual, oversexed wife and where Heflin and Jourdan present exceptional performances as her unsatisfying lovers. Pantheon director Minnelli does a fine job in showcasing this sensational story, which was filmed many times in 1933, 1937, 1991 and 2013, but this remains one of the best versions. Minnelli's staging of the lavish "Emma Bovary Waltz" is one of the director's finest sequences where he beautifully handles a huge cast involved in complex choreography. Mature sexual themes prohibit viewing by children. *Author's Note*: Mason, who narrates this film, told this author that "I don't think any other actress brought so much beauty and charm to the character of Emma Bovary

Van Heflin, Jennifer Jones and Eduard Franz in *Madame Bovary,* 1949.

than Jennifer Jones. She is both capricious and sexually attractive and instinctively knew the depths of her character. She was first a devoted wife who will never see riches and then a plaything to get those riches, which leaves her as empty as when she started, a tragic woman from the beginning to the end. I think Jennifer understood this woman so well that she was able to portray her as she was truly written by Flaubert." **p**, Pandro S. Berman; **d**, Vincente Minnelli; **cast**, Jennifer Jones, James Mason, Van Heflin, Louis Jourdan, Christopher Kent (Alf Kjellin), Gene Lockhart, Gladys Cooper, John Abbott, Henry (Harry) Morgan), George Zucco, Ellen Corby, Larry Simms, Paul Cavanagh, Paul Bryar; **w**, Robert Ardrey (based on the novel by Gustave Flaubert); **c**, Robert Planck; **m**, Miklos Rozsa; **ed**, Ferris Webster; **art d**, Cedric Gibbons, Jack Martin Smith; **set d**, Edwin B. Willis; **spec eff**, Warren Newcombe.

Madame Curie ★★★★ 1943; U.S.; 144m; MGM; B/W; Biographical Drama; Children: Acceptable; **DVD**; **VHS**. Garson and Pidgeon, who were teamed in several memorable films, notably **Mrs. Miniver**, 1942, are magical together in this superlative biopic of Marie Curie (1867-1934) and her husband, Pierre Curie (1859-1906), brilliant physicists and chemists, who jointly received the Nobel Prize in Physics in 1903 for their extraordinary research on radioactivity. The film opens with Garson (as Marie Curie) as an impoverished Polish-born student studying in Paris. Basserman, a kindly old professor, gives Garson work as his assistant in researching the magnetism of steel, paying her a few francs to work in his small laboratory. He then tells Pidgeon, a retiring professor, that he can also use his laboratory for his own research and there Pidgeon meets Garson. After learning that she has a brilliant mind with great scientific acumen, he falls in love with her, but is too shy to tell her. When Pidgeon learns that Garson is preparing to return to her native Poland, he finds that he cannot live without her and finds enough courage to ask her to marry him. She has loved him, too, and she does not hesitate to accept his proposal. When they return from their honeymoon, they begin to research some pitchblende that has earlier acted strangely under their applied experiments. Garson persists in discovering the elements contained in pitchblende and Pidgeon joins her in her intensive research, which they conduct in the worst type of environment, working in a deserted small shed without proper heat that they turn into their laboratory. They struggle to continue their experiments, begging for academic funds to continue their research, and are given meager funds. After five years of privation and failure, the couple sees success in isolating and identifying a new element, radium, for which they become the foremost scientists of their day, jointly receiving the Nobel Prize in Physics. The couple buys a comfortable rural home where they raise their two children, living happily until Pidgeon is killed in an accident. Garson continues her scientific experiments and what is only

Lana Turner and Constance Bennett in *Madame X,* **1966.**

suggested but never explicitly profiled in this film is that she most likely has an affair with a young admirer following her husband's death and that is symbolized by the brief appearance of Johnson, who is a student idolizing Garson. Though nominated for Oscars for Best Picture, Best Actor, Best Actress, Best Cinematography and Best Music, this fine production won none. The script is not only well written and literate, but thought-provoking and no more so than in Garson's final speech when she states to her colleagues at a university: "It is by these small candles that we shall see before us, little by little, the dim outlines of the great plan that shapes the universe, and I am among those who think that, for this reason, science has a great beauty, and, with its great spiritual strength, will in time cleanse the world of its evils, its ignorance, its poverty, diseases, wars and heartaches." *Author's Note*: Garson told this author that "playing Madame Curie was, at least to those in France, like playing a scientific saint. This great and dedicated woman is revered around the world and so, in every scene, I walked on eggs, to profile her as the near perfect human being that she truly was." Director LeRoy told this author that "I don't think any other actress in the world could have portrayed Marie Curie as well as Greer Garson did. She possessed the perfect restraint and reserve that completely made up the personality of Marie Curie's dedicated character. While she and Walter [Pidgeon] are trying to identify radium, Greer radiates tremendous confidence that they will somehow make that discovery and in every scene there is something spiritual about her. She was nominated for an Oscar as Best Actress, but she lost out to Jennifer Jones, who also played a very spiritual person in a picture that year, **The Song of Bernadette** [1943]. It was a year of great inspiration in the movies and, God knows, we needed all the inspiration we could get as we did not know if we would win the war in those still dark days [of World War II]." **p**, Sidney Franklin; **d**, Mervyn LeRoy; **cast**, Greer Garson, Walter Pidgeon, Robert Walker, Dame May Whitty, Henry Travers, Albert Bassermann, Sir C. Aubrey Smith, Victor Francen, Elsa Bassermann, Reginald Owen, Van Johnson, Margaret O'Brien, Gene Lockhart, Arthur Shields, James Hilton (narrator); **w**, Paul Osborn, Paul H. Rameau (based on the book by Eve Curie); **c**, Joseph Ruttenberg; **m**, Herbert Stothart; **ed**, Harold F. Kress; **art d**, Cedric Gibbons; **set d**, Edwin B. Willis; **spec eff**, Warren Newcombe.

Madame Rosa ★★★ 1978; France; 105m; Lira Films/Atlantic Releasing Corp.; Color; Drama; Children: Unacceptable; **DVD**; **VHS**. In this engrossing drama, Signoret gives an outstanding performance as a retired prostitute, who is also a Jewish survivor of Auschwitz. She lives in poverty in a six-floor walk-up apartment in the Pigalle section of Paris, and becomes a foster mother to the children of other prostitutes. Her favorite is the oldest, a handsome boy named Momo (Ben-Youb),

an Algerian whom she raises as a Muslim. As she ages and takes in fewer children, Ben-Youb cares for her and earns pennies performing a puppet show on the streets. She makes him promise never to become a male prostitute or pimp, and he is befriended by a male film editor (Bat-Adam). As Signoret ages, she fears the Gestapo is going to find her, so she asks Ben-Youb to hide her if they come for her. She becomes ill, and when a doctor, Dauphin, comes to the apartment, Ben-Youb hides her in a secret room and tells him she has gone to Israel. She dies and Ben Youb continues to keep her in the hidden room until police learn of it and take him away. A strong drama with echoes of the Holocaust that is unacceptable for children because of sexual themes. (In French; English subtitles.) **p**, Jean Bolvary, Raymond Danon; **d&w**, Moshé Mizrahi (based on the novel *Momo* by Emile Ajar [Romain Gary]); **cast**, Simone Signoret, Claude Dauphin, Samy Ben-Youb, Gabriel Jabbour, Michal Bat-Adam, Geneviève Fontanel, Bernard Lajarrige, Mohamed Zinet, Elio Bencoil, Stella Annicette; **c**, Nestor Almendros; **m**, Dabket Loubna, Philippe Sarde; **ed**, Sophie Coussein; **prod d**, Bernard Evein.

Madame Souszatzka ★★★ 1988; U.K.; 122m; Cineplex-Odeon Films/UNIV; Color; Drama; Children: Unacceptable (MPAA: PG-13); **DVD**; **VHS**. Chowdhry is a teenage Indian boy whose parents have moved to London. He lives with his mother, Azmi, after her divorce from his father. Azmi earns small money baking gourmet Indian pastries at home for a department store. When Chowdhry shows skill at playing the piano, and his school teacher refers him to one of the top piano teachers in London, she sells family heirlooms for his lessons. The piano teacher, Madame Souszatzka, MacLaine, is a Russian immigrant, who never achieved the fame she dreamed of as a concert pianist, so she lives that ambition through her students. Gradually, she not only gives the boy piano lessons, but virtually takes over his life. MacLaine's philosophy is "art for art's sake" and she does not want her students to seek financial rewards. Azmi loses her job because of racial discrimination and a suitor shows interest in her. Chowdhry is jealous and decides to support her by playing the piano for money. A booking agent hears him play and wants to start him on a concert career, which MacLaine will fight. But talent and ambition win out and Chowdhry begins a career as a concert pianist with MacLaine applauding him from the audience. This fine drama displays a number of standout performances from MacLaine, Azmi and Chowdhry. Sexual themes prohibit viewing by children. **p**, Robin Dalton; **d**, John Schlesinger; **cast**, Shirley MacLaine, Peggy Ashcroft, Twiggy, Shabana Azmi, Leigh Lawson, Geoffrey Bayldon, Lee Montague, Robert Rietty, Navin Chowdhry, Greg Ellis; **w**, Ruth Prawer Jhabvala, Schlesinger, Peter Morgan, Mark Wadlow (based on the novel by Bernice Rubens); **c**, Nat Crosby; **m**, Gerald Gouriet; **ed**, Peter Honess; **prod d**, Luciana Arrighi; **art d**, Stephen Scott, Ian Whittaker.

Madame X ★★★ 1966; U.S.; 100m; UNIV; Color; Drama/Romance; Children: Unacceptable; **DVD**; **VHS**. Turner is a beautiful young woman from the wrong side of the tracks, who marries rising diplomat Forsythe against the objections of his controlling mother, Bennett. Lonely because Forsythe is frequently away on political business, Turner has an affair with another man, Montalban. When she and Forsythe's son is four years old, her husband's political star rises and he is going to run for governor, Turner breaks off her relationship with Montalban, but he is accidentally killed in a fall down some stairs while in her presence. Bennett threatens Turner that she will disclose her affair with Montalban unless she leaves Forsythe and her son. She agrees and goes off to Mexico where, in need of money, she becomes a prostitute. There she meets con artist Meredith, who plans to blackmail Forsythe by telling him about how Turner has become a fallen woman, so when they return to the United States, Turner kills Meredith. She is brought to trial as Madame X and finds that her son, Dullea, who has become a lawyer, is now her court-appointed defense attorney. He tries hard to defend her although he does not know that she is his mother. Before the jury reaches its verdict, Turner collapses with heart disease and, before she dies, tells

Dullea that he is her son. Turner overcomes what is inherently a maudlin script by effectively enacting a woman of tragedy and woe in this grand tearjerker. This version is the best of previous films of that title made in 1915, 1920, 1929, 1937, 1948 (under the title **The Trial of Madame X**), 1960, and a made-for-TV movie in 1981. *Author's Note*: Turner wisely chose this ten-handkerchief vehicle to revitalize her somewhat dormant production company, telling this author that she chose Hunter "because he had a very good record of successfully producing women's pictures and he and David [Rich] handled **Madame X** with a lot of care, which is why it did well at the box office." **p**, Ross Hunter; **d**, David Lowell Rich; **cast**, Lana Turner, John Forsythe, Ricardo Montalban, Burgess Meredith, Constance Bennett, Virginia Grey, Warren Stevens, Carl Benton Reid, Kaaren Verne, Keir Dullea, Neil Hamilton; **w**, Jean Holloway (based on the play by Alexandre Bisson); **c**, Russell Metty; **m**, Frank Skinner; **ed**, Milton Carruth; **art d**, Alexander Golitzen, George Webb; **set d**, Howard Bristol, John McCarthy, Jr.; **spec eff**, Walter Hammond.

Made for Each Other ★★★ 1939; U.S.; 92m; Selznick International/UA; B/W; Drama/Romance; Children: Acceptable; **DVD**; **VHS**. Though there are some good comedic moments in this above-average romance, it is essentially a drama where brand-new attorney Stewart marries Lombard and both go honeymooning on an ocean liner. Things begin to go wrong right away when Coburn, who is Stewart's boss (and who demonstrates his deafness whenever he does not want to hear someone) orders Stewart to cut his marital romance short and return immediately to try a pressing case. Moreover, Watson, Stewart's mother, is more than irritated that her son so quickly married Lombard, a young woman Watson hardly knew. Coburn is not happy with the Stewart-Lombard union either in that he wanted Stewart to wed his daughter, Weston. Briggs, who is another ambitious attorney working at Coburn's legal firm, then marries Weston, and to celebrate, Stewart invites the newlyweds to dinner, along with Coburn. The dinner party goes awry almost from the beginning with some funny scenes, but all that turns sour when Coburn announces that he has made his new son-in-law, Briggs, a partner at his firm. Stewart is crestfallen as he expected that position. Nothing goes right for Stewart and Lombard thereafter. She has a baby and Stewart is strapped for funds to maintain his burgeoning family, especially after his mother, Watson, moves in with them. The baby becomes ill, needing a special serum, but there is none to be had in New York City. Desperate, Stewart goes to Coburn and passionately pleads for his help. Coburn is moved by Stewart after discovering that Stewart has a knack for delivering heart-moving speeches and he agrees to help. He hires daredevil pilot Quillan to fly his plane from Salt Lake City to New York, carrying the serum, and Quillan pilots his craft through a blinding blizzard, arriving just in time to deliver the serum that save the baby's life. As the baby recovers, Stewart's star rises in Coburn's firm and it appears that it will be smooth sailing for him and Lombard. *Author's Note*: Stewart told this author that "**Made for Each Other** could have drowned in a big tub of bathos if it hadn't been for our director [Cromwell], who knew exactly how to handle sensitive scenes, especially where the child's life is at risk. He did not milk those scenes, but kept them brief enough so that suds didn't spill off the screen. That's always the measure of a good director, knowing where and when to stop. I would like to add that Carole Lombard was terrific in that picture, and whenever she came onto the set she brought with her all the friendly and high-spirited help she could give to the cast and crew. She was wonderful to be with, a real pal, and when she died in an air crash a few years later [January 16, 1942, at Table Rock Mountain, Nevada], we all lost one of the great ladies in the movies." **p**, David O. Selznick; **d**, John Cromwell; **cast**, Carole Lombard, James Stewart, Charles Coburn, Lucile Watson, Eddie Quillan, Alma Kruger, Irving Bacon, Louise Beavers, Ward Bond, Esther Dale, Harry Davenport; **w**, Jo Swerling, Frank Ryan (based on a story by Rose Franken); **c**, Leon Shamroy; **m**, Lou Forbes, Oscar Levant; **ed**, James E. Newcom; **prod**

Lucile Watson, Carole Lombard and James Stewart in *Made for Each Other*, **1939.**

d, William Cameron Menzies; **art d**, Lyle Wheeler; **spec eff**, Jack Cosgrove, Edmund E. Fellegi.

Made in Italy ★★★ 1967; Italy/France; 100m; Documento Film/Royal Films International; Color; Comedy; Children: Unacceptable; **DVD**; **VHS**. This entertaining comedy presents a series of thirty-two short episodes about the fortunes and misfortunes of a group of Italians who take a flight to Sweden. In one scene, a tired mother, Magnani, tries to lead her unemployed husband and three small children across a busy street to buy some ice cream cones. They finally make it to the store, but it is out of ice cream so the owner recommends they buy some at a shop on the other side of the street from which they came. Tourists ask other tourists for directions to historical landmarks, and a young Italian, who learns that his fiancée is involved in robbery, murder, and kidnapping, is relieved because, through it all, she has remained a virgin. Another vignette profiles a young man who goes to great lengths to seduce a married woman and afterward loses interest but can't get rid of her. The varied vignettes add up to an entertaining whole, but not for children because of sexuality. (In Italian; English subtitles.) **p**, Gianni Hecht Lucari; **d**, Nanni Loy; **cast**, Marina Berti, Claudio Gora, Walter Chiari, Nino Castelnuovo, Gina Mucci, Jean Sorel, Virna Lisi, Catherine Spaak, Sylva Koscina, Nino Manfredi, Anna Magnani, Alberto Sordi, **w**, Loy, Ruggero Maccari, Ettore Scola (based on their story); **c**, Ennio Guarnieri; **m**, Gianni Boncompagni, Carlo Rustichelli, Piero Umiliani; **ed**, Ruggero Mastroianni; **prod d&set d**, Luciano Spadoni.

Madeleine ★★★★ 1950; U.K.; 101m; Cineguild/UNIV; B/W; Biographical Drama; Children: Unacceptable; **VHS**. Todd gives a bravura performance in this well-made thriller, based upon a sensational murder case involving wealthy socialite Madeleine Smith (1835-1928). Todd (as Madeleine) lives in comfort with her upscale family in 19th-Century Glasgow, Scotland. She is an attractive young woman, but given to moody spells attributed by others to her lack of male companionship. She meets handsome Desny, an ambitious social climber, and they carry on a secret affair, clandestinely meeting in the maid's quarters of her father's mansion to tryst. Banks, who is Todd's father, a wealthy merchant strictly upholding the Victorian standards of the day, insists that she marry one of her own class, particularly Wooland, a bloodless and boring young man showing little or no virility. Todd continues seeing Desny, but refuses to introduce him to her family, and Desny comes to believe that Todd is merely using him and will eventually discard him and marry someone of her class. Then Todd asks Desny to elope with her, but he refuses, insisting that he be accepted by her parents and that they wed with their approval. Todd attends a fancy ball and, when Desny sees her dancing with Wooland, he is consumed by jealousy and rage.

Ann Todd in *Madeleine,* **1950.**

He threatens Todd with their love letters, saying that unless she formally introduces him to her parents, he will expose the torrid missives to her family. Angered at Desny's threats, Todd becomes engaged to Wooland, but she cannot forget her secret lover and continues to covertly see Desny, but he suddenly dies from arsenic poisoning. Todd is charged with murdering Desny, which causes an international scandal, and her subsequent trial is sensationally covered by the press. Her defense attorney uses every ploy to shield his client and refuses to put her on the witness stand while successfully implanting in the minds of jurors many doubts about her guilt. The jury returns a verdict of "Not Proven" (a peculiar verdict endemic only to Scotland that states that the defendant is not innocent or guilty, a position this clever film also takes in that Todd is never seen overtly bringing about Desny's death but is seen with the inclinations to perform it). Pantheon director Lean, however, gives the viewer an inclination of guilt when he shows Todd, released after the verdict and climbing into her carriage where a small and subtle smile can be seen on her otherwise passive face. Lean directs with great and effective restraint, exacting measured and reserved performances from the enigmatic Todd and desperately maneuvering Desny to heighten tension in each scene he carefully constructs. *Author's Note*: Smith began her secret affair with Pierre Emile L'Angelier in 1855. He did threaten to expose their love letters to her father unless she introduced him as her fiancé. He died of arsenic poisoning on March 23, 1857, and Smith was then brought to trial. It was shown that she had appeared several times at a druggist's office before her lover's death and purchased various amounts of arsenic, signing for this with the name "M. H. Smith" (her full name being Madeleine Hamilton Smith), and claiming that this was to be used for the killing of rats. The prosecution, however, failed to convince a jury of Smith's guilt and she was released, albeit most criminologists and historians, including this one, believe her to be guilty. She married successful artist George Wardle in 1861, had children (Mary and Thomas Wardle), and then, after her husband's death, followed her son to the U.S. in 1909 where she lived in New York City with a man named Sheehy and they lived together until his death. Madeleine Smith died in New York City in 1928 under the name of Lena Wardle Sheehy. Some years earlier, U.S. officials attempted to deport Smith as an "undesirable alien," but these efforts were thwarted through Smith's influence and well-paid attorneys. Years later, an American film company approached her and asked to make a film (silent) about her life. She declined. No one in her immediate social circle at the time of her death knew of her past and they were shocked to learn that she was the notorious Scottish lady who had captured world headlines seven decades earlier. For more details on Smith, see my eight-volume work, *Encyclopedia of World Crime*, Volume IV (CrimeBooks, 1990; pages 2799-2800). **p**, Stanley Haynes; **d**, David Lean; **cast**, Ann Todd, Norman Wooland, Ivan Desny,

Leslie Banks, Elizabeth Sellars, Barry Jones, Barbara Everest, Susan Stranks, Patricia Raine, Edward Chapman, Eva Bartok, John Laurie, Anthony Newley; **w**, Haynes, Nicholas Phipps; **c**, Guy Green; **m**, William Alwyn; **ed**, Clive Donner, Geoffrey Foot; **set d**, John Bryan.

Madeline ★★★ 1998; France/U.S.; 88m; Jaffilms; COL; Color; Comedy; Children: Unacceptable; MPAA: PG; **DVD**. Lovable but mischievous redheaded Madeline (Jones) gets into trouble at a girls' school in Paris, but also solves people's problems. The school mistress, McDormand, has her hands full while coping with her. Madeline's hands are also full trying to find a way to keep Lord Covington (Hawthorne) from selling the school. She does, of course, and she and the school keep going. Consistently entertaining, Jones and McDormand render standout performances. Gutter language prohibits viewing by children. **p**, Saul Cooper, Pancho Kohner, Allyn Stewart; **d**, Daisy Von Scherler Mayer; **cast**, Frances McDormand, Nigel Hawthorne, Hatty Jones, Ben Daniels, Arturo Venegas, Stéphane Audran, Katia Caballero, Chantal Neuwirth, Kristan De La Osa, Clare Thomas; **w**, Malia Scotch Marmo, Mark Levin, Jennifer Flackett (based on books by Ludwig Bemelmans); **c**, Pierre Aim; **m**, Michel Legrand; **ed**, Jeffrey Wolf; **prod d**, Hugo Luczyc-Wyhowski; **art d**, Bertrand Clerq-Roques, Gerard Drolon, Rebecca Holmes; **set d**, Aline Bonetto; **spec eff**, Graham Hills, Graham Longhurst, Daniel Leung.

Madigan ★★★ 1968; U.S.; 101m; UNIV; Color; Crime Drama; Children: Unacceptable; **DVD; VHS**. In this gritty and action-loaded crime yarn, Widmark and Guardino are New York City detectives shown hunting down a wanted killer, Ihnat, a psychopathic gun-happy thief, who has no qualms about taking human life. They find Ihnat in bed with a woman and, while distracted, Ihnat, before he escapes, forces them to turn over their guns, the worst embarrassment any cop can endure. They come before no-nonsense police commissioner Fonda, who scathingly criticizes their irresponsible actions and then orders them to capture Inhat within seventy-two hours or be demoted or even dismissed from the force. Adding to Fonda's woes are accusations from activist black minister St. Jacques, who insists that racists cops have beaten up his son. He then learns that Whitmore, his long-standing friend and his chief inspector, has yielded to pressure to protect a brothel operation. Moreover, Fonda has personal problems in that he is carrying on an extramarital affair with alluring Clark. Meanwhile, Widmark has his own problems with his socialite wife, Stevens, who lives in constant fear that he will sometime be killed in the line of duty, and is also nagged by the thought that Widmark may be secretly seeing an old flame, North. Widmark is constantly bending the rules by taking her to upscale nightclubs and restaurants wherehe eats and drinks "off the cuff" as a police officer. Widmark takes Stevens to a fancy policeman's ball reserved for upper echelon officers, but, after encountering Fonda, feels he must immediately return to his hunt for Inhat, and leaves Stevens in the company of a womanizing police captain (who takes an inebriated Stevens home and beds her). Widmark and Guardino then learn that Ihnat has used their guns to kill two police officers and they intensify their hunt for the berserk murderer. Through an underworld contact, Dunn, a dwarf bookie, they learn about a pimp, Stroud, who has been supplying Ihnat with girls, and they find him at a movie theater, grilling Stroud in the manager's office until he gives them the address where Ihnat is staying. Calling for backup, Widmark and Guardino track down Ihnat to an apartment at 102nd Street in Spanish Harlem, and where Fonda and other high-ranking police officials also arrive. Fonda gives the nod to Widmark and Guardino to go into the apartment and capture the lethal Ihnat, but when they barge into the place, Ihnat uses a woman as a shield while he exchanges gunfire with Widmark and Guardino. Widmark then charges forth, blazing away, killing Ihnat, but is fatally shot by Ihnat. He later dies at a hospital where a grief-stricken Stevens indicts the unresponsive Fonda for being a heartless man, who has no concern for his own men and that her husband was, to him, nothing more than "another lousy cop." Fonda, however, is consoled by the fact that Whitmore, who has resigned, but who has taken back his badge at Fonda's insistence, has raided the brothel operation he was protecting for the sake of his son, a rookie cop being blackmailed by the brothel owner for his gambling debts. Siegel directs this down-to-earth crime tale with a sure hand, effortlessly unfolding several separate characterizations and plots that work well together and where Fonda, Widmark, Whitmore and Stevens are standouts in their roles. *Author's Note*: Widmark told this author that "my character as Madigan is really a dedicated cop, but he wants to do more for his wife [Stevens]. He knows that his duty prevents him from ever improving his lifestyle. He wants too much and knows he can't have it and that is why he goes after the killer at the end. He knows he will be killed, but it is better to die a good cop than an inadequate husband. At least, that's how I saw my character." Fonda was not fond of his role, telling this author that "I was accused of sleepwalking through my role as the police commissioner in **Madigan**, but I am playing a man who is more of a politician than a cop. Everything about that character is circumspect. He is in charge of organized chaos and, to endure all that, he must live above it all, even if he appears to be indifferent to the deaths of the officers he commands. It was a thankless role." **p**, Frank P. Rosenberg; **d**, Donald Siegel; **cast**, Richard Widmark, Henry Fonda, Inger Stevens, Harry Guardino, James Whitmore, Steve Ihnat, Susan Clark, Michael Dunn, Don Stroud, Sheree North, Warren Stevens, Raymond St. Jacques, Bert Freed, Harry Bellaver, Lloyd Gough, Frank Marth, Virginia Gregg; **w**, Henri Simoun (Howard Rodman), Abraham Polonsky (based on the novel *The Commissioner* by Richard Dougherty); **c**, Russell Metty (Technicolor), **m**, Don Costa; **ed**, Milton Shifman; **art d**, Alexander Golitzen, George C. Webb; **set d**, John Austin, John McCarthy; **spec eff**, Albert Whitlock.

The Madness of King George ★★★★ 1994; U.K.; 107m; The Samuel Goldwyn Company; Color; Biographical Drama; Children: Unacceptable (MPAA: PG-13); **DVD**; **VHS**. Hawthorne renders a marvelous performance in essaying England's George III (1738-1820), who, in 1788, began to show signs of mental instability by raving and racing about his palace. Physicians having little or no knowledge of mental disease attempt to cure Hawthorne through physical applications of blistering and purging (bleeding), but to no avail. As the doctors struggle to restore Hawthorne's sanity, his son, Everett, playing the Prince of Wales (George IV; 1762-1830), schemes to take control of the British Empire by having himself named regent and, to that end, sends his own physician, Palmer, to attend to his father, who continues the purging. Distraught over her husband's unstable state of mind, Queen Charlotte (1744-1818), played by Mirren, frantically seeks help and gets it from one of her ladies in waiting, Donohoe, who urges her to have Dr. Francis Willis (1718-1807), played by Holm, who has been treating the insane, to take over Hawthorne's medical supervision. Holm begins by enforcing strict regimens upon Hawthorne, even restraining him in a specially designed waistcoat (an early-day straightjacket) to keep him from harming himself and others. Everett, by then, allies himself with powerful political leaders such as Charles James Fox (1749-1806), played by Carter, who opposes the king's prime minister, William Pitt (1759-1806), played by Wadham, and where Carter urges that Everett be immediately made regent because his father can no longer rule due to his insanity. Holm, by this time, however, had made considerable progress with Hawthorne where the king's faculties have been restored and where he acts in a normal behavior. He is even able to recite passages from Shakespeare, and, at the last minute, he is rushed to Parliament where Hawthorne demonstrates his sanity and thwarts the move to have his ambitious son, Everett, replace him. Hawthorne again assumes the throne and is once more in the arms of his queen, Mirren. Hawthorne's performance is a wonder to behold as he dynamically teeters back and forth from sanity to insanity, a frightening and disturbing characterization that incisively portrays the wanderings and groping of a tortured human mind. *Author's Note*: George III finally did lose his faculties in

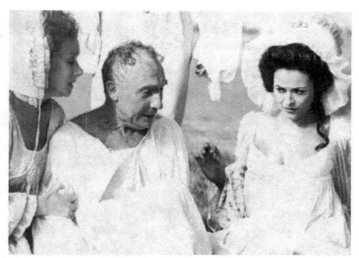

Helen Mirren, Nigel Hawthorne and Amanda Donohoe in *The Madness of King George,* 1994.

1810 after his most cherished daughter, Princess Amelia (1783-1810) died. He wept uncontrollably over her loss, and he began ranting until his ravings and racing about alarmed the court and brought physicians to his bedside to finally announce him insane. The Prince of Wales was appointed regent in 1811 and he became George IV upon the death of his father in 1820. **p**, Stephen Evans, David Parfitt; **d**, Nicholas Hytner; cast, Nigel Hawthorne, Helen Mirren, Ian Holm, Rupert Graves, Julian Wadham, Amanda Donohoe, Rupert Everett, Geoffrey Palmer, Amanda Donohoe, Julian Rhind-Tutt, Anthony Calf, Jim Carter; **w**, Alan Bennett (based on his play "The Madness of George III"); **c**, Andrew Dunn (Technicolor); **ed**, Tariq Anwar; **prod d**, Ken Adam; **art d**, Martin Childs, John Fenner; **set d**, Carolyn Scott; **spec eff**, Alastair Vardy, Stuart Conran, Dave Crownshaw, Kent Houston.

Madonna of the Seven Moons ★★★ 1946; U.K.; 88m; Gainsborough/UNIV; B/W; Drama; Children: Unacceptable; **DVD**. In this intriguing tale, set in the early 1900s, Calvert is a teenage Italian girl, who is raped by a gypsy while walking in the woods and becomes mentally scarred with a split personality. The story flashes forward to the 1940s when, still mentally troubled, she is married to a rich wine merchant. She has the habit of disappearing for long periods of time during which she becomes the moll of a gypsy thief, Granger, living a bizarre life in the House of the Seven Moons in Florence. Songs: "Rosanna," Florentin Carnival" (Hans May, Sonny Miller). **p**, R.J. Minney; **d**, Arthur Crabtree; **cast**, Phyllis Calvert, Stewart Granger, Patricia Roc, Jean Kent, Peter Glenville, Dulcie Gray, John Stuart, Reginald Tate, Peter Murray Hill, Alan Haines, Hilda Bayley, Evelyn Darvell, **w**, Roland Pertwee (based on the novel *The Madonna of Seven Moons* by Margery Lawrence); **c**, Jack Cox; **m**, Hans May; **ed**, Lito Carruthers; **art d**, Andrew Mazzei; **spec eff**, Philippo Guidobaldi.

Maedchen in Uniform ★★★ 1933; Germany; 87m; Deutsche Film-Gemeinschaft/Filmchoice; B/W; Drama; Children: Unacceptable; **VHS**. When her mother dies, Thiele, an independent and spirited teenage girl, is sent to a boarding school run by Unda, a strict Prussian principal. Thiele develops a crush on Wieck, a young female teacher, and they become friends. Thiele impulsively professes her love for Wieck at a party, which sets off a scandal that consumes everyone at the school. A cult classic, it was the first feature film with a pro-lesbian story line. The film was remade in 1958 as an inferior production. *Author's Note*: Lillian Hellman's *The Children's Hour* was produced two years after the release of this film in Germany, and its influence can be seen in the Hellman story, but with a different wrinkle in that Hellman has a female student at an upscale girls' school accusing two young female teachers of being lesbians. **p**, Carl Froelich, Friedrich Pflughaupt; **d**, Froelich, Leon-

An electronic machine shoots magnetic rays in *The Magnetic Monster,* **1953.**

tine Sagan; **cast**, Emilia Unda, Dorothea Wieck, Hedwig Schlichter, Hertha Thiele, Ellen Schwannecke, Gertrud de Lalsky, Marte Hein, Lene Berdolt, Lisi Scheerbach; **w**, Christa Winsloe, Friedrich Dammann (based on the play "Gestern und heute" ["Yesterday and Today"] by Winsloe; **c**, Reimar Kuntze, Franz Weihmayr; **m**, Hanson Milde-Meissner; **ed**, Oswald Hafenrichter; **art d**, Fritz Maurischat, Friedrich Winkler-Tannenberg.

Magic ★★★ 1978; U.S.; 107m; FOX; Color; Horror; Children: Unacceptable (MPAA: R); **DVD**; **VHS**. A great amount of tension and anxiety is generated for this film through the taut and intense performance by the gifted Hopkins. He is an innovative and witty ventriloquist, but his somewhat sinister-looking dummy, "Fats," appears to be even more clever and sharp-witted, stealing all of his master's lines and dominating every stage performance. Hopkins comes to believe that Fats is taking over his personality, controlling his mind and even manipulating his subconscious. He becomes paranoid and decidedly schizophrenic, convinced that Fats is out to destroy him. His agent, Meredith, negotiates a lucrative TV contract, but Hopkins believes that when he is exposed on TV, the world will soon realize that Fats is in control and not him. The deluded Hopkins, believing that Meredith is slyly out to destroy him through such national exposure, kills him, or, he comes to believe that Fats has killed him, such is his irrational thinking. After hiding the body, the panicking Hopkins immediately takes flight, going to a small resort in the Catskill Mountains of Upstate New York to see an old flame, Ann-Margret. Though she is married to Lauter, the aging sexpot is delighted to see Hopkins and wallows in the praise he showers upon her. Her husband, Lauter, however, wants Hopkins to leave. He nevertheless stays and Ann-Margret eagerly trysts with him. Lauter discovers this marital betrayal, but before he can evict the unwelcome Hopkins, the ventriloquist goes berserk once again and kills Lauter, or, it appears that Fats has killed Lauter. Fats then tells Hopkins and Ann-Margret that he will make all future decisions about everything. Later, he gives Hopkins a long knife and orders him to murder Ann-Margret. Fats, however, feels all of his energy draining when he learns that Hopkins, rather than kill more, has taken his own life. At the end of this gruesome and chilling tale, we hear Ann-Margret calling out to Hopkins that she has decided to run away with him, but her voice has become similar to that of Fats, a bizarre and frightening caricature. *Author's Note*: **Magic** owes a great debt to **The Great Gabbo**, 1929, and **Dead of Night**, 1945, where seemingly evil-minded dummies take over the personalities of their ventriloquist masters; other films depicting ventriloquists include **The Unholy Three**, 1925; **The Miracle Woman**, 1931; **Poppy**, 1936; **Mr. Moto's Last Warning**, 1939; **You Can't Cheat an Honest Man**, 1939; **Knock on Wood**, 1954; **Devil Doll**, 1964; **Bugsy Malone**, 1976; **The**

In-Laws, 1979; **Annie**, 1982; **Broadway Danny Rose**, 1984; **Chicago**, 2002; and **The Illusionist**, 2010. **p**, Joseph E. Levine, Richard P. Levine; **d**, Richard Attenborough; **cast**, Anthony Hopkins, Ann-Margret, Burgess Meredith, Ed Lauter, E.J. André, Jerry Houser, David Ogden Stiers, Lillian Randolph, Joe Lowry, Bob Hackman, Mary Munday; **w**, William Goldman (based on his novel); **c**, Victor J. Kemper (Technicolor); **m**, Jerry Goldsmith; **ed**, John Bloom; **prod d**, Terence Marsh; **art d**, Richard Lawrence; **set d**, John Franco, Jr.; **spec eff**, Robert MacDonald, Jr.

The Magic Box ★★★★ 1952; U.K.; 118m; Festival Film Productions/Arthur Mayer-Edward Kingsley; B/W; Biographical Drama; Children: Acceptable; **DVD**; **VHS**. Donat is wonderful in essaying pioneering cinematographer William Friese-Greene (1855-1921), who was the first to patent a motion picture camera (in 1889, three years before Edison's 1892 patent of his Vitascope). The film opens with Donat working as a photographer's assistant in Bristol, England. He branches off to become very successful as a portrait photographer of high society figures, but he spends most of his money on his invention, the motion picture camera. He meets and marries Schell, who is devoted to Donat and his work, but who dies shortly after he achieves success. He marries again to Johnston, who is also supportive of him and endures his many subsequent failures, until the struggling Donat dies at a meeting with film industry leaders. Director Boulting handles this fascinating biopic with great care and enlisted the services of just about every notable British actor in making this fine film. Most of these sterling performers appear in bit parts, and so many flit before the camera that it is hard to keep track of them, such as Olivier, who is a policeman called from his beat to inspect Donat's new invention, and Ustinov, who is a film distributor. *Author's Note*: Friese-Greene began working on his motion picture camera in 1886 and produced his first camera three years later, patenting it, but, within a few years, he used up all available funds to perfect the camera and went bankrupt in 1891, selling the rights to his patented camera for £500. He died, apparently of a stroke, just after he attempted to make a speech at a London convention of filmmakers on May 5, 1921, and was all but forgotten for more than three decades before this film was made. His tombstone at Highgate Cemetery in London reads: "The inventor of Kinematography." **p**, Ronald Neame; **d**, John Boulting; **cast**, Robert Donat, Margaret Johnston, Maria Schell, Renee Asherson, Richard Attenborough, Roland Culver, John Howard Davies, Leo Genn, Marius Goring, Joyce Grenfell, Joan Hickson, Stanley Holloway, Glynis Johns, Mervyn Johns, Barry Jones, Herbert Lomas, Bessie Love, Miles Malleson, Muir Mathieson, Laurence Olivier, Cecil Parker, Eric Portman, Dennis Price, Michael Redgrave, Margaret Rutherford, Basil Sydney, Ernest Thesiger, Sybil Thorndike, David Tomlinson, Peter Ustinov, Kay Walsh, Emlyn Williams, Googie Withers, Joan Young; **w**, Eric Ambler (based on the biography *Friese-Greene, Close-Up of an Inventor* by Ray Allister; **c**, Jack Cardiff; **m**, William Alwyn; **ed**, Richard Best; **prod d**, John Bryan; **art d**, T. Hopewell-Ash; **set d**, **spec eff**, Dario Simoni.

The Magic Christian ★★★ 1970; U.K.; 92m; Commonwealth United/Grand Films; Color; Comedy; Children: Unacceptable; **BD**; **DVD**;**VHS**. Sellers is outstanding in his role as a British nobleman, who is the richest man in the world. He adopts a homeless street boy, Starr, and names him the sole heir to his fortune. He introduces Starr to the family business which is to prey on people's greed by use of the vast holdings of Sellers' financial empire. Together they set out to prove that anyone and anything can be bought if there is enough money involved. Their adventures at sporting events, art galleries, and pheasant hunts turn into lurid displays of bad manners and profiteering. The climax is at the social event of the season, the maiden voyage of Sellers' new pleasure yacht, *The Magic Christian*. British aristocracy is invited aboard and victimized by a vampire, Lee, and others, who insult and demean them. Sellers dumps a fortune into a vat filled with excrement into which the greedy passengers dive while he and Starr leave to go to a park where they meet and laugh at it all. Laced with cameo appearances by stars, it's a wild satire on greed, but, in indicting its subject, some crude and offensive scenes occur. Not for children because of risqué sequences. Songs: "Come and Get It," Rock of All Ages" (Paul McCartney); "Something in the Air" (John Keen); "Carry on Till Tomorrow" (Tom Evans, Pete Ham); "Mad About the Boy" (Noel Coward). **p**, Denis O'Dell; **d**, Joseph McGrath; **cast**, Peter Sellers, Ringo Starr, Isabel Jeans, Wilfrid Hyde White, Richard Attenborough, Laurence Harvey, Christopher Lee, Spike Milligan, Roman Polanski, Raquel Welch, John Cleese, Dennis Price, Yul Brynner, Roland Culver, Peter Graves; **w**, McGrath, Terry Southern, Peter Sellers, Graham Chapman, Cleese (based on the novel by Southern); **c**, Geoffrey Unsworth (Technicolor); **m**, Ken Thorne; **ed**, Kevin Connor; **prod d**, Assheton Gorton; **art d**, George Djurkovic; **spec eff**, Wally Veevers.

The Magic Sword ★★★ 1962; U.S.; 80m; UA; Color; Fantasy; Children: Acceptable; **DVD**; **VHS**. Entertaining fantasy sees Lockwood as a stalwart young knight, the son of a sorceress, Winwood, who dons armor, takes up a magic sword, and goes off on a quest to rescue a princess, Helm, from the clutches of an evil magician, Rathbone. Six knights, magically summoned by Winwood, give him twelve helping hands. Lockwood battles an ogre, some tiny people, Siamese twins, and a two-headed dragon before he accomplishes his task and wins his lady fair. It's a fun adventure with impressive special effects. **p&d**, Bert I. Gordon; **cast**, Basil Rathbone, Estelle Winwood, Gary Lockwood, Anne Helm, Liam Sullivan, Danielle De Metz, Merritt Stone, Jacques Gallo, David Cross, John Mauldin; **w**, Bernard Schoenfeld (based on a story by Gordon); **c**, Paul Vogel (Eastmancolor); **m**, Richard Markowitz; **ed**, Henry Gerstad; **art d**, Frank Bachelin; **set d**, George R. Nelson; **spec eff**, Milt Rice, Gordon.

The Magician ★★★ 1959; Sweden; 100m; Svensk Filmindustri/Janus Films; B/W; Drama; Children: Unacceptable; **BD**; **DVD**; **VHS**. Von Sydow is riveting as a magician who heads a traveling show that presents supernatural illusionist tricks. When the show comes to a town, local police and a medical examiner ask to see a sample of the show before agreeing to a public performance. Disbelievers try to expose them as charlatans, but von Sydow and his troupe are too clever for them by their use of editing, lighting, and special effects. Mature subject matter prohibits viewing by children. This film takes a large leaf from **The Cabinet of Dr. Caligari**, 1921. (In Swedish; English subtitles.) **p**, Allan Ekelund; **d&w**, Ingmar Bergman; **cast**, Max von Sydow, Ingrid Thulin, Gunnar Björnstrand, Naima Wifstrand, Bengt Ekerot, Bibi Andersson, Gertrud Fridh, Lars Ekborg, Tovio Pawlo, Erland Josephson; **c**, Gunnar Fischer; **m**, Erik Nordgren; **prod d**, P.A. Lundgren.

The Magnetic Monster ★★★ 1953; U.S.; 76m; Ivan Tors/UNIV; B/W; Science Fiction; Children: Unacceptable; **DVD**. Agents Carlson and Donovan, working for the U.S. Office of Scientific Investigation, are sent to a hardware store where they find a strong magnetic field has magnetized every metal item there. They trace the source of the magnetism to an airborne flight carrying scientist Mudie, who is dying of radiation poisoning. He has aboard with him a new radioactive element, which grows by creating matter out of energy that it absorbs from metallic objects around it. Carlson estimates that if the substance is not destroyed within twenty-four hours, it will grow large enough to throw Earth out of its orbit. He lures the magnetic monster to an experimental Canadian power station where it is given an energy overdose that destroys it. The exciting yarn is heightened by closing footage from a German film, **Gold, the Magnetic Monster**. Mature subject matter prohibits viewing by children. **p**, Ivan Tors; **d**, Curt Siodmak; **cast**, Richard Carlson, King Donovan, Jean Byron, Harry Ellerbe, Leo Britt, Leonard Mudie, Byron Foulger, John Zarimba, Lee Phelps, Kathleen Freeman; **w**, Tors, Siodmak, **c**, Charles Van Enger; **m**, Blaine Sanford;

Tim Holt in *The Magnificent Ambersons,* 1942.

ed, Herbert L. Strock; **prod d**, George Van Marter; **set d**, Victor A. Gangelin; **spec eff**, Harry Redmond, Jr., Eugen Schüfftan.

The Magnificent Ambersons ★★★★★ 1942; U.S.; 88m; Mercury Productions/RKO; B/W; Drama; Children: Cautionary; **DVD**; **VHS**. In Welles' second great masterpiece (following **Citizen Kane**, 1941), the astoundingly creative director profiles the gentler, kinder and more considerate era of the last decade of the 19th Century, focusing upon a wealthy family living in the American heartland (undoubtedly Indianapolis, Indiana). Holt, the spoiled, egotistical and obnoxious son of the family, is seen whipping his pony in hurrying his buggy along a fashionable street, drawing the attention and disdain of neighbors. Cotten, a soft-spoken and considerate inventor, is in love with Costello, but she marries one of the Ambersons, Dillaway, and he goes through life still loving her. He is shown years later returning to his hometown, having become a successful manufacturer of an automobile, a futuristic invention that some upscale denizens, like Holt, think is nothing more than a crass novelty. By this time Cotten's wife has died and he is a widower. Dillaway has died and Costello is a widow and Cotten renews his romance with her while Holt is attracted to Cotten's fetching daughter, Baxter. She, however, rejects his proposal since Holt refuses to enter a profession or take any kind of job, intending to live out his vainglorious life on his family's wealth. The vindictive Holt then viciously prevents Cotten from further seeing his mother, Costello. Holt and Costello then take a European tour where Costello hopes to forget the memories of the past, but she suffers a heart attack and returns home where Holt continues to prevent Cotten from seeing her, even though she dies asking for him. Holt then receives the shock of his life after Bennett, the family patriarch, dies, and Holt learns that the Amberson fortune is no more and that he must go to work to survive. Moreover, Holt must now close the great mansion where he has lived all his life in comfort and must also find a way to support his most supportive family member, Moorehead, a spinster aunt, who has lived on the leavings of the family. He is crushed when she finally turns on him, telling him that he is essentially a worthless human being who has given no joy to anyone and has lived his life as a lazy, smug and uncaring person not worth anyone's love. Holt is then injured in an accident, but he survives and is visited in the hospital by Moorehead and Cotten, who assures the now emotionally destroyed Holt that Cotten will take care of him, looking upon him as his own son, displaying the kind of generosity and munificence Holt has never shown in life (perhaps proving that kindness is the cruelest cut of all). Welles directs this bittersweet and melancholy story with great skill, providing a visual feast of a lofty element of the American past to show a class of Americans that would not or could not adjust to changing times that brought their old and comfortable world to an end, as they

Cora Sue Collins and Robert Taylor in *Magnificent Obsession*, 1935.

are engulfed by the modern era. He exacts marvelous performances from the entire cast, and Holt was never better in his essay of a young and pompous man shaped and ruined by transient prosperity. Cotten is, as always, touchingly avuncular, and Costello, the one-time silent screen goddess, appears fragile and ghostlike, perfectly enacting the romantic specter Cotten chases but never captures through the years. Moorehead, Sanford, Collins and the rest of the splendid cast are superb in their deeply profiled characterizations, all richly embroidered by Welles, memorable voiceover as he narrates this tragedy of a family frozen in time, dying with its genteel and fleeting landed gentry. Welles moves his fluid camera through the vast halls and grand lounge and dining room, and in and out of spacious bedrooms, of the Amberson mansion to capture its inhabitants, as dated and ornate as the opulent home in which they dwell. The only consistently distinctive voice is that of Welles, where all others coming and going talk in overlapping dialogs, mixed with street sounds and snippet statements from others distant from the story line and main characters. This tale from Booth Tarkington had been filmed as a silent as **Pampered Youth**, 1925, and was remade in 2002, a much inferior production. *Author's Note*: Welles told this author that "in rehearsing the cast members, I asked them to improvise as we went through each scene, allowing them to alter or change their lines as they saw fit, as long as they kept to their characters. I trusted that they knew who they were supposed to be, and no one disappointed me." To that, Cotten stated to this author: "Orson let us be the characters we thought we were playing. We added on our own a line here and there, or maybe just a few words that those characters would say. And this all worked well, as Orson knew it would. He was far ahead of any director of his day, I can tell you." Like Toland before him in **Citizen Kane**, the gifted cinematographer Cortez employs deep focus in many shots to stunningly present the shadowy scenes of the era where all lived under gaslight, and his stark daytime shots are equally arresting and effective. Welles uses every camera technique of the day and many he invented for this film, meshing his setups with dolly, truck and crane shots to keep the tale moving well and to enliven the many long soliloquies, some of these running as long as ten minutes. He marvelously shows an America in transition through his depicted architecture, from filigreed Victorian mansions and office buildings to plain and pedestrian modern structures, one age mournfully overwhelming another, a tintype replaced by a photograph, and he uses the old-fashioned iris up and down to open and close some of his scenes in homage to the passing era he visually and emotionally profiles. "When I was a boy," Welles told this author, "and walking down a street to see some old great house being torn down, I somehow felt pain, as if part of my own past was being destroyed, as if someone was peeling away the layers of my own being. It was hurtful to see them go for I knew they once held laughing and loving families,

and some that never laughed at all. All that came back to me when we did **The Magnificent Ambersons**. I believe that most children in America walked past such grand mansions and said, 'gee, I wished I lived in that house.' I took them into that house in that picture and showed them that it was no paradise at all, that joy was a diminishing thing for those who lived there. The Ambersons and their grand lifestyle and their grand house, well, that's a very deceiving façade. Henry Ford once said that 'wealth is only a means to an end.' Joe [Cotten] is sort of my Henry Ford in **The Magnificent Ambersons**, a man who creates a car and grows rich, but, unlike those who live in the Amberson mansion, he knows that his money cannot buy his happiness. The Ambersons, on the other hand, have money for its own empty sake and no happiness at all. That is part of their tragedy." One of Welles' most delightful scenes is the sleigh ride, one that took him twelve days to get into the can. He shot this scene in a Los Angeles ice factory, setting up an elaborate outdoor set and working with the machinery until he got just the right amount of snow. He also employs mirrors, windows and even glossy furniture to reflect the images of his characters as he did in **Citizen Kane**, these fleeting wraith-like figures suddenly appearing and just as quickly disappearing into deep shadows, as if engulfed by the eternal night of death awaiting us all. This rather somber, if not glum atmosphere permeates the film and audiences responded by angrily talking back to the film in its premiere in Pomona, California, where RKO studio boss George J. Schaefer panicked and later wrote Welles, who was in Brazil preparing for another film (aborted): "It was like getting one sock in the jaw after another for two hours." RKO had invested a then whopping amount of money on **The Magnificent Ambersons**, $1,125,000, and Schaefer immediately ordered film editor (later director) Robert Wise to cut down the film. Welles had earlier edited the film from 148 minutes to 131 minutes (as shown in its Pomona premiere). Wise prudently and carefully edited the film down to 88 minutes, cutting more than 3,000 feet of film, but keeping intact all of its continuity (a spectacular feat unto itself). Then, to give the film a happy ending, Schaefer ordered a final scene added, the hospital sequence where Cotten and Moorehead reassure the injured Holt that he will not be deserted, this sequence directed by Fred Fleck and where composer Roy Webb added music to Hermann's original stirring score. Welles later claimed that by tacking on that final scene, the studio destroyed "the whole heart of the picture." It really did not, as the film remains one of the great cinematic masterpieces. Further demeaning Welles and the film itself, RKO released the film only to second-run theaters as part of a double bill, along with a Mexican Spitfire comedy starring Lupe Velez, a grade-B programmer. The film earned back $625,000 and did not recoup its initial investment until many years later through several re-releases. **p**, Orson Welles; **d**, Welles, Fred Fleck, Robert Wise; **cast**, Joseph Cotten, Dolores Costello, Anne Baxter, Tim Holt, Agnes Moorehead, Ray Collins, Erskine Sanford, Richard Bennett, Edwin August, Georgia Backus, Nancy Gates, Welles (narrator); **c**, Stanley Cortez, Sack Mackenzie, Wells; **w**, Wells (based on the novel by Booth Tarkington); **m**, Bernard Herrmann, Roy Webb; **ed**, Wise, Jack Moss, Mark Robson; **prod d&art d**, Albert S. D'Agostino; **set d**, Darrell Silvera; **spec eff**, Vernon L. Walker, Clifford Stine.

Magnificent Obsession ★★★ 1935; U.S.; 112m; UNIV; B/W; Drama; Children: Acceptable; **DVD**. Taylor and Dunne are superb together in this grand tearjerker. The handsome Taylor is shown as a careless wastrel, killing a gifted surgeon in a car accident, and when he tries to express his regrets to the man's beautiful widow, Dunne, she dismisses him, and, full of emotion and not watching where she is going, is hit by a speeding van and is blinded. Now, Taylor is doubly full of remorse for having caused Dunne this additional and painful injury. He resolves to make amends by doing all he can for Dunne, by befriending her family confidante, the avuncular Morgan. Taylor visits Dunne often and, since she does not know his identity, they become close friends. While on these visits, Taylor learns more about Dunne's deceased husband, a wonderful man who gave of himself to others, doing generous deeds and insisting that he remain as an anonymous donor (this being the "magnificent obsession"). Dunne, with Furness' encouragement, then goes to Paris, to seek a cure for her blindness, and Taylor follows. They begin to fall in love until Dunne then learns of Taylor's true identity and, not being able to forgive him for the death of her husband, she breaks off the relationship. Taylor, however, will not give up the woman of his life. He resolves to make something of himself and begins to study medicine, becoming an accomplished surgeon. Sometime later he learns that Dunne is in a hospital in Virginia and is in need of a life-saving operation, but there is no surgeon with the skills to save her. Taylor, though he has become an accomplished surgeon, doubts whether he can perform the delicate operation, but, with Morgan's encouragement, he does perform that operation and, in the final scene, which made Taylor a superstar, Dunne awakes to find her sight restored and sees the face of the man who gave her that great gift, Taylor. She knows now that she will never leave him again. No one, even those of the hardest of hearts, could resist tearing up after seeing this poignant and emotionally redeeming scene, prevented from being awash in bathos by the sterling performances of Dunne and Taylor and through the careful direction of Stahl. *Author's Note*: Dunne was thirty-five when making this film and Taylor only twenty-four, but his resonant voice and reassuring masculinity seemingly made him appear to be much older than Dunne. Taylor would go on to score another smash a little more than a year later when appearing with the great Greta Garbo in **Camille**, 1937, becoming one of Hollywood's greatest matinee idols. His role was reprised by Rock Hudson in a 1954 remake of this film and it did for Hudson what it did for Taylor, making Hudson an overnight international star. **p&d**, John M. Stahl; **cast**, Irene Dunne, Robert Taylor, Charles Butterworth, Betty Furness, Sara Haden, Ralph Morgan, Henry Armetta, Gilbert Emery, Arthur Treacher, Beryl Mercer, Joyce Compton, Andrea Leeds; **w**, George O'Neil, Sarah Y. Mason, Victor Heerman, Finley Peter Dunne (based on the novel by Lloyd C. Douglas); **c**, John J. Mescall; **m**, Franz Waxman; **ed**, Milton Carruth; **art d**, Charles D. Hall; **spec eff**, John P. Fulton.

Magnificent Obsession ★★★ 1954; U.S.; 108m; UNIV; Color; Drama; Children: Acceptable; **DVD**; **VHS**. In this good remake of the 1935 film, Hudson is the careless young man who accidentally kills Wyman's husband, a man who has practiced doing good deeds for others without seeking recognition for his generosity (the "magnificent obsession"). When Hudson tries to console Wyman over her loss and express his regrets, she angrily dismisses him. But, in trying to avoid him, she is struck by a car and blinded. Hudson then, without her knowing it, befriends the blind Wyman while he begins to study medicine at the encouragement of Kruger, a close friend of Wyman's deceased husband. When Wyman learns that Hudson is the man who brought about her husband's death, she ends their friendship, even though she and Hudson have fallen in love with each other. Hudson continues his studies and becomes a gifted surgeon and, when he hears that Wyman requires a vital operation, he performs that operation, restoring her sight. When Wyman opens her eyes to see Hudson, she can no longer shut him out of her heart, the viewer knowing that these two former star-crossed lovers will now be together. Sudsy and sentimental, this time-tested tearjerker holds up as well as its original and sees two fine performances from Wyman and Hudson, as well as outstanding direction from the talented Sirk. *Author's Note*: "Sentimentality was dripping from every page of the script for that picture when I took it over," Sirk told this author. "There was no way to avoid that. My approach was to have the actors play it terse and straight and not to milk their scenes. That was the only way to make that story at all believable." **p**, Ross Hunter; **d**, Douglas Sirk; **cast**, Jane Wyman, Rock Hudson, Agnes Moorehead, Otto Kruger, Barbara Rush, Gregg Palmer, Paul Cavanagh, Mae Clarke, Lance Fuller, Jack Kelly; **w**, Robert Blees, Wells Root (based on the novel by Lloyd C. Douglas and the 1935 screenplay by George O'Neil, Sarah Y. Mason, Victor Heerman, Finley Peter Dunne); **c**, Russell Metty

Rock Hudson and Jane Wyman in *Magnificent Obsession*, 1954.

(Technicolor); **m**, Frank Skinner; **ed**, Milton Carruth; **art d**, Bernard Herzbrun, Emrich Nicholson; **set d**, Russell A. Gausman, Ruby R. Levitt; **spec eff**, David S. Horsley.

The Magnificent Seven ★★★★ 1960; U.S.; 128m; Mirisch Company/UA; Color; Western; Children: Cautionary; **BD**; **DVD**; **VHS**. This exciting and superbly acted western is an inventive version of Kurosawa's classic film, **The Seven Samurai**, 1956. After Mexican bandit Wallach and his horde of men raid and loot a small Mexican village, the helpless farmers and shopkeepers decide to hire some gunmen to protect their town against these pillaging invaders and cross the border in the U.S. where they approach aging gunslinger Brynner. At first, he is reluctant to take on the job, especially since it pays only a few dollars for several weeks of very dangerous work. His streak of nobleness, however, and his desire to do something worthwhile in a lifetime of dirty deeds, causes him to change his mind. He has already demonstrated that honorable inclination when the townsfolk refuse to bury a local Indian. A traveling salesman has paid for the man's burial, but mortician Bissell cannot find anyone to drive his hearse carrying the body to the local Boot Hill where several armed men are waiting to turn back the hearse, these thugs representing those bigots of the town who do not want an Indian buried among deceased white people. Brynner suddenly decides to drive the hearse and he is joined by McQueen, another gunfighter, who is also down on his luck. The two ride cautiously through the town, watching for those who might shoot them from ambush, while apprentice gunfighter Buchholz, admiring their courage, follows them. Someone fires a shot at them from a second-floor window but is silenced when quick-drawing McQueen fires back. The hearse proceeds to the cemetery, and Brynner warns the armed men waiting there that he intends to see the dead man buried. When one makes a move for his gun, Brynner shoots it from his hand and the vigilantes disperse and the burial ceremony proceeds. Brynner and McQueen decide to aid the Mexican farmers and they proceed to recruit more gunfighters, enlisting the aid of Bronson, Coburn, Vaughn, Dexter and, eventually, the eager Buchholz. Short and fascinating segments show how these men are recruited, all of them down-and-out and near penniless as the day of the gunfighter in the Old West is coming to a close. Bronson is chopping wood at a farm for his board and food, Coburn is working as a cowboy, Vaughn is hiding out in the back room of a store from other gunmen looking to kill him. The seven gunmen arrive in the small Mexican village where they are welcomed by the inhabitants and where they make preparations to resist Wallach and his men when they return, training some of the farmers how to shoot and setting up snares and traps for the bandits. When Wallach arrives, he accuses the villagers of being ungrateful for the mercy he has shown in the past by not taking all of their food. He is

Ann Harding and Louis Calhern in *The Magnificent Yankee*, 1950.

challenged by Brynner and dismisses his threats, but becomes alarmed when he realizes he is facing seven deadly gunmen. A fight ensues when Wallach and his men attempt to flee the village, and where many are shot down or caught in nets and killed at the passes to the village. Wallach survives with a goodly number of his men and regroups. Meanwhile, Buchholz, who is Mexican and knows the mindsets of the farmers, meets attractive Monteros and a romance develops between them. Wallach returns to the village, and with the help of some of the villagers, who now fear that he will vengefully kill them all, he and his cutthroats capture the seven gunfighters. Wallach, magnanimous in victory, gives the gunfighters their freedom, however, telling them never to come back. They are escorted from the village and then given their weapons. Coburn, however, straps on his gun, saying "nobody tells me to run," and the others follow suit. They return to the village where a full-scale battle ensues and where all of the bandits are killed, including Wallach, and where gunmen Bronson, Coburn, Dexter and Vaughn (who has lost his confidence but regains it at the end when shooting down several bandits) are killed, all buried as heroes by the grateful villagers. Buchholz remains with Monteros, and the surviving Brynner and McQueen ride away, having redeemed their tainted careers by saving the village. Sturges directs with great vitality in bringing this action-packed oater to the screen, where his fine ensemble of actors all give standout performances (McQueen, Bronson, Coburn and Vaughn went on to become major stars). The great score (referencing Bartok's "Concerto for Orchestra") from Bernstein became one of the most memorable in film history, and it received an Oscar nomination for Best Dramatic or Comedy Score. Three sequels to this outstanding film were produced, but with less effective results and a TV series (1998-2000) was also produced. *Author's Note*: Although McQueen and Brynner bond on screen, they did not get along too well during the production, McQueen telling this author "Yul treated me like a third banana. He had won an Oscar for **The King and I** [1956] and was a big star. I had been appearing in a lot of TV programmers and he referred to me as a 'TV actor' and that did not set well with me. Either you are an actor or you are not, and it doesn't matter what medium you are appearing in, but Yul was then part of the Hollywood elite and could look down on all of us." Bronson was circumspect about his role in this outstanding western, telling this author that "**The Magnificent Seven** was a big break for me and I knew it. I had appeared in only a few feature films at that time, including **Never So Few** [1959] with Steve McQueen and Brad Dexter, who were both in **The Magnificent Seven**. Brynner was the big name then and we all gave him honors and I was glad to do it since he was such a fine actor. I heard that he and Steve [McQueen] did not get along in that picture, but I got along with Brynner just fine." Sturges told this author that "we shot a lot of that picture in Mexico, but we had problems with the Mex-

ican government that insisted they approve of the script so that Mexico did not look too bad. They were worried about losing tourists from the U.S., so we had to make a lot of revisions and build up the courage of the Mexican villagers and farmers, who fight at the end with the gunfighters to defeat the bandits. Of course, I studied the Kurosawa film until I knew every frame in that classic, but I used a much different approach and different techniques, putting a lot more emphasis on the villagers, who look upon the gunfighters they hire to protect their village as almost as dangerous as the bandits they want to destroy. I also used that wonderful character actor, Sokoloff—he is Russian, you know, not Hispanic—as a sort of Mexican guru, who describes the basic nature of the villagers and who also understands the personalities of the gunfighters. He is the one who sets everything in motion by telling the villagers that they must fight to protect their families and their land." Louis Morheim, who was the associate producer (not credited) for this film, and who was a veteran screenwriter, acquired the English language rights for **The Seven Samurai** for a meager $250. Morheim later stated that he had talked with Kurosawa and asked him why he had made **The Seven Samurai**, and that great director replied: "All I was doing was trying to make a Japanese western." Morheim immediately realized the possibility of making that film into an American western, and instantly bought the English language rights and began lobbying studios for its production. The film was expensive, costing more than $2 million, but it quickly recouped its investment many times over. **p&d**, John Sturges; **cast**, Yul Brynner, Eli Wallach, Steve McQueen, Horst Buchholz, Charles Bronson, Robert Vaughn, Brad Dexter, James Coburn, Jorge Martinez de Hoyas, Vladimir Sokoloff, Whit Bissell, Jim Davis, Rosenda Monteros, Rico Alaniz, Pepe Hern, Natividad Vacio, Mario Navarro; **w**, William Roberts, (not credited writing by Walter Newman, Walter Bernstein; based on the film **The Seven Samurai** and its screenplay by Akira Kurosawa, Shinobu Hashimoto, Hideo Oguni); **c**, Charles Lang Jr. (Panavision; DeLuxe Color); **m**, Elmer Bernstein; **ed**, Ferris Webster; **art d**, Edward Fitzgerald; **set d**, Rafael Suarez; **spec eff**, Milt Rice.

The Magnificent Yankee ★★★★ 1950; U.S.; 89m; MGM; B/W; Biographical Drama; Children: Acceptable; **DVD**; **VHS**. Calhern, in a tour de force performance (which he originally essayed in the long-running Broadway play), is wonderful as the colorful and contentious U.S. Supreme Court Justice Oliver Wendell Holmes Jr. (1841-1935). Calhern is shown when first being appointed to the Court during the administration of President Theodore Roosevelt (1858-1919) and throughout his long judicial career to the time of the administration of Franklin D. Roosevelt (FDR; 1882-1945), who was the fifth cousin of Theodore Roosevelt. Throughout the many court battles depicted, Calhern delivers his wise and pithy opinions while leading American jurisprudence away from formalism and toward legal realism. Several touching sequences show Calhern with his devoted wife, Harding, as well as a bevy of young law clerks, who later become distinguished attorneys and jurists and where he often sides with dissenting jurist Louis Brandeis (1856-1941), ably played by Franz. Ober, who plays western author Owen Wister (1860-1938) and a close friend of Calhern's, narrates the story of this rich life. The script is literate and presents much of Holmes' famous bon mots and epigrams and Sturges directs with great care and skill. *Author's Note*: Holmes, who had been a Civil War hero, retired from the Court at age ninety, then the oldest jurist to serve on that court. Many famous quotes from Holmes appear in this film, but one of his most celebrated lines is missing (no doubt because of its critical nature) and where the illustrious Holmes stated: "The study of law is exquisite, but the practice of it is abominable." Director Sturges told this author that "Dore Schary, who headed production at MGM and was basically a quality writer, wanted to do this picture very much, but he and the rest of us felt that it would get critical acclaim [which it did], but that it would not do much at the box office and was a losing proposition. We were all surprised when the public warmed to the picture, mostly due to the wonderful performance from Louis [Calhern] and it actually made a profit." **p**, Armand Deutsch; **d**, John Sturges; **cast**, Louis Calhern, Ann Harding, Eduard Franz, Philip Ober, Edith Evanson, Richard Anderson, James Lydon, Herbert (Guy) Anderson, John Phillip Law, Ian Wolfe (narrator); **w**, Emmet Lavery (based on his play and the book *Mr. Justice Holmes* by Francis Biddle); **c**, Joseph Ruttenberg; **m**, David Raksin; **ed**, Ferris Webster; **art d**, Cedric Gibbons, Arthur Lonergan; **set d**, Edwin B. Willis; **spec eff**, A. Arnold Gillespie.

Magnolia ★★★ 1999; U.S.; 188m; Ghoulardi Film Co., New Line Cinema; Color; Drama; Children: Unacceptable (MPAA: R); **BD**; **DVD**; **VHS**. Over a rainy night in Los Angeles, two stories about men about to die become intertwined. Both men are estranged from a grown child they seek to find, but neither child wants anything to do with their father. Robards, a television producer, is on his deathbed with cancer. His wife, Moore, is grieving for him, but their estranged son, Cruise, does not want to bury the hatchet, while Robards' male nurse, Hoffman, tries to reunite them. The other father of the story, Hall, host of Robards' most popular television show, also is dying from terminal cancer and his daughter, Walters, is at odds with him. She is having a love-hate relationship with Reilly, a police officer, who must explain to his wife, Dillon, why Walters hates him so much. Meanwhile, a child genius on Hall's kids' quiz show believes the only way to get his father's attention and/or love is to win big, and a former show star, Macy, has grown up and watches as his life peters out. A strong drama about family relationships with a terrific ensemble cast holds attention throughout. Gutter language, drug use, sexuality, and violence prohibit viewing by children. **p**, Paul Thomas Anderson, JoAnne Sellar, Daniel Lupi; **d&w**, Anderson; **cast**, Tom Cruise, Julianne Moore, William H. Macy, John C. Reilly, Philip Seymour Hoffman, Jason Robards, Philip Baker Hall, Alfred Molina, Henry Gibson; **c**, Robert Elswit; **m**, Jon Brion; **ed**, Dylan Tichenor; **prod d**, William Arnold, Mark Bridges; **set d**, Chris Spellman; **spec eff**, Diane, John C., and Lou Carlucci, Dan Rebert.

Magnum Force ★★★ 1973; U.S.; 122m; WB; Color; Crime; Children: Unacceptable (MPAA: R); **BD**; **DVD**; **VHS**. Eastwood again performs with vitality and brings violent justice to San Francisco as Police Inspector "Dirty" Harry Callahan. He and his new partner, Perry, are temporarily reassigned from the homicide department to stakeout duty. They investigate a case in which some of the city's top criminals, who have avoided punishment in the courts through their clever attorneys, are being killed off by unknown assassins. Eastwood discovers that rogue cops and his lieutenant superior, Holbrook, are behind it all as vigilantes taking justice in their own hands. The mayhem ends when Holbrook is killed in a car explosion. Eastwood inadvertently endorses the vigilantism of the four rogue SFPD cops (Soul, Matheson, Urich and Niven) when telling them that "shooting is all right as long as the right people get shot." Well directed and packed with action, Holbrook renders a fascinating performance as the mentor leading the four young cops to their wayward ends, the type of role he also played in **Capricorn One**, 1978, and he is best remembered for his portrayal of "Deep Throat" in **All the President's Men**, 1976, and his one-man show where he gave a great performance as Mark Twain. **Magnum Force** grossed more than $20 million and was one of the most violent and graphically depicted crime films up to that time. The title of this film is drawn from the revolver Eastwood uses to dispatch the bad guys, a .44 Magnum, which he proudly describes as "the most powerful handgun in the world" and where he, like in other such films, challenges a criminal to draw a weapon and fire at him by saying: "Go ahead, and make my day!" This sequel followed **Dirty Harry**, 1971, and produced sequels **The Enforcer**, 1976, **Sudden Impact**, 1983, and **The Dead Pool**, 1988. *Author's Note*: The films **Mulholland Falls**, 1996, and **L.A. Confidential**, 1997, took a leaf from the story line of this film, where cops act as vigilantes to get rid of gangsters, but for different motivations. **p**, Robert Daley; **d**, Ted Post; **cast**, Clint Eastwood, Hal Holbrook, Mitch Ryan,

Catalina Saavedra in *The Maid*, 2009.

David Soul, Tim Matheson, Kip Niven, Robert Urich, Felton Perry, Maurice Argent, Richard Devon, John Mitchum, Will Hutchins, Suzanne Somers; **w**, John Milius, Michael Cimino (based on a story by Milius from original material by Harry Julian Fink, Rita M. Fink); **c**, Frank Stanley (Panavision; Technicolor); **m**, Lalo Schifrin; **ed**, Ferris Webster; **art d**, Jack Collis; **set d**, John Lamphear; **spec eff**, Sass Bedig.

The Maid ★★★ 2009; Chile/Mexico; 95m; Forastero/Elephant Eye Films; Color; Comedy/Drama; Children: Acceptable; **DVD**. In this entertaining comedy, Saavedra is a maid, who has worked for an affluent Chilean family in Santiago for more than twenty years. As she approaches her forty-first birthday she suffers migraine headaches and fainting spells. Her employers suggest they hire a second maid to help with her work. Saavedra will not think of relinquishing any of her duties to anyone else, but it happens and a tough taskmaster, Villanueva, comes to the house. They have a battle of wills and Villaneuva leaves. This happens again with a second maid until a third maid, Loyola, arrives and seems to be immune to Saavedra's combativeness. They eventually bury the hatchet and become close friends, who not only work but live together in harmony. This delightful offbeat comedy stems from a country that seldom sees its films distributed in America. (In Spanish; English subtitles.) **p**, Gregorio González, Issa Guerra, Edgar San Juan, Sebastian Sanchez Amunategui; **d**, Sebastián Silva; **cast**, Catalina Saavedra, Claudia Celedón, Alejandro Goic, Andrea García-Huidobro, Mariana Loyola, Agustín Silva, Darok Orellana, Sebastián La Rivera, Mercedes Villanueva, Anita Reeves, Delfina Guzmán; **w**, Sebastián Silva, Pedro Peirano (based on a story by Silva); **c**, Sergio Armstrong; **ed**, Danielle Fillios; **art d**, Pablo González.

Maid in Manhattan ★★★ 2002; U.S.; 105m; Revolution Studios; COL; Color; Comedy/Romance; Children: Unacceptable (MPAA: PG-13); **BD**; **DVD**. Lopez is a single mother working as a maid in a posh Manhattan hotel, and where she impulsively dons a hotel guest's fur coat and evening dress. Seeing her in such finery, Fiennes, a handsome young hotel guest and heir to an American political dynasty, mistakes her for a socialite and becomes romantically interested in her. When he learns her true identity his thoughts of her as a future wife cool and, although they part friends, they go their separate ways. This modern Cinderella story happens all in one day, producing a lighthearted and entertaining film. Gutter language and sexual references prohibit viewing by children. **p**, Paul Schiff, Deborah Shindler, Elaine Goldsmith-Thomas, Richard Baratta; **d**, Wayne Wang; **cast**, Jennifer Lopez, Ralph Fiennes, Natasha Richardson, Stanley Tucci, Bob Hoskins, Tyler Garcia Posey, Frances Conroy, Chris Eigeman, Amy Sedaris, Marissa Matrone, Priscilla Lopez; **w**, Kevin Wade (based on a story by Edmond Dantés

Robert Newton, Rex Harrison and Wendy Hiller in *Major Barbara*, **1941.**

(John Hughes); **c**, Karl Walter Lindenlaub; **m**, Alan Silvestri; **ed**, Craig McKay; **prod d**, Jane Musky; **art d**, Patricia Woodbridge; **set d**, Susan Tyson; **spec eff**, J.C. Brotherhood, Conny Fauser, Sarah Coatts, Robert Cribbet.

The Major and the Minor ★★★★ 1942; U.S.; PAR; B/W; Comedy; Children: Acceptable; **DVD**; **VHS**. Rogers and Milland are delightful in this very funny Wilder comedy (his American debut as a director). Rogers is an attractive blonde, who can no longer stand the advances of men twice her age and to escape these aging Romeos she decides to return to her hometown in the Midwest. When she goes to buy her train ticket, however, she is shocked to see that prices have soared and she does not have the fare to get to her home in Iowa. She goes to the ladies's room and then disguises herself as a twelve-year-old girl and then buys a ticket at the reduced fare for children, hoping she will not be unmasked until she reaches her destination. She is ogled by a bunch of boys going to a military school and is rescued from their amorous advances by their commander, Milland, a U.S. Army major, who is the head teacher at that school and he takes Rogers under his protective wing, sharing his compartment with her as train space is limited during this wartime period. Rogers, bereft of cash, gets off the train with Milland and the cadets and is billeted at the military academy until Milland can figure out what to do with her. Pretending that she is a homeless waif, Rogers rooms with Lynn, a teenager, who quickly learns of Rogers' masquerade, but keeps silent about it as Rogers starts to fall in love with the gallant Milland. He, however, has a possessive fiancée, Johnson, who is trying to keep him from active service and suspects that Rogers is not all what she appears to be. While at the school, Rogers spends most of her time evading the advances of the cadets, including a ball where all of the boys are chasing after her. She finally manages to get to her home at a nearby town. Milland, who has figured out that she is no little girl at all and is in love with her, tracks her down, but is met by her mother (where Rogers poses as her own mother), who sends Milland on his way. In the end, however, Milland also sees through this additional disguise and returns to find the adult Rogers, taking her into his arms. *Author's Note*: There are some very sexy scenes in this film, particularly involving the adolescent urges of the boys in their eager pursuit of Rogers, but Wilder handles these segments with such lighthearted touches that it all appears to be innocent fun and that, no doubt, caused the censors of the day to turn blind eyes on these segments. Rogers, who is marvelous in her impersonations as a child and her own mother, told this author that "I had a lot of fun with that role where I played a grown woman pretending to be a girl and I remembered all the little nonsense from my own childhood and used some of those gawky manners and goofy sayings to make my impersonation more believable. Without Billy [Wilder] I could never

have gotten away with it. He knew just where to stop the nonsense and where to start it up again." Wilder told this author that "Ginger was a little uncomfortable with some of the scenes where the boys are salivating over her and, at one point, she said to me: 'My God, are these boys trying to get a kiss from me or are they trying to figure out a way to get me into their bunks?' I told her: 'It's probably a little bit of both, but they are only following their natural sexual impulses without knowing that's what it's all about. Play along and try not to be too voluptuous.'" Milland is exceptional in his role as a gentleman who becomes disturbed at romantic feelings toward what he thinks is a child but whose instincts tell him otherwise. He was, particularly in the 1940s, one of Hollywood's great, versatile actors, comfortable in any genre, from comedy (**It Happens Every Spring**, 1949) to crime (**The Big Clock**, 1948), from mystery (**The Uninvited**, 1944) to murder (**Ministry of Fear**, 1944), and from fantasy (**Alias Nick Beal**, 1949) to drama (**The Lost Weekend**, 1945, for which he won an Oscar as Best Actor). "I thought Billy [Wilder] was walking on eggs with that story where a grown man chaperones a girl to a boys' military school and then becomes attracted to her," Milland told this author, "but he handled it like one big hoax. Ginger was so good at impersonating that little girl that we got away with it." **p**, Arthur Hornblow, Jr.; **d**, Billy Wilder; **cast**, Ginger Rogers, Ray Milland, Rita Johnson, Robert Benchley, Diana Lynn, Frankie Thomas, Raymond Roe, Charles Smith, Edward Fielding, Larry Nunn, Lela Rogers; **w**, Wilder, Charles Brackett (based on the play "Connie Goes Home" by Edward Childs Carpenter and the story "Sunny Goes Home" by Fannie Kilbourne); **c**, Leo Tover; **m**, Robert Emmett Dolan; **ed**, Doane Harrison; **art d**, Hans Dreier, Roland Anderson.

Major Barbara ★★★★★ 1941; U.K.; 121m; Gabriel Pascal Productions/UA; B/W; Comedy; Children: Acceptable; **DVD**; **VHS**. Hiller and Harrison are superb in this masterpiece comedy from Shaw, one of his most spritely and satirical comedies, and where pantheon director Pascal presents a broad and brilliant farce that indicts arms manufacturing. The tall and beautiful Hiller is a major in the Salvation Army and whose ideals and stringent socialist beliefs prompt her to indict at every turn the capitalist system and, most importantly, routinely launch blistering attacks against her own father, Morley, who heads an arms manufacturing complex. No one loves Hiller more than Harrison, a youthful professor of literature and Greek history, but all of his amorous advances toward this fetching woman fail to win her heart. Hiller's unrelenting crusade to save the downtrodden from the rich upper class dominates her every waking hour and she can find no time for romance, rebuffing Harrison's every colorful and very funny ploy designed to capture her love. Morley does not make it easy for his dedicated daughter as he is a kindhearted magnate always willing and able to help the poor, but only through the reasonable control of funds. When Hiller challenges her father's stated generosity, Morley offers £50,000 to the Salvation Army to use in its campaign against poverty. To Hiller's amazement, her superior, Thorndike, accepts the donation from Morley and expresses her deep gratitude. So disillusioned is Hiller with Thorndike's action that she quits her post and Harrison then takes her on a tour of her father's factories where she learns that his employees enjoy good salaries and many benefits and are treated with consideration. She becomes a convert to commerce and quickly embraces Morley's philosophy which he sums up with "I am a millionaire. That is my religion" and is soon espousing the credo of capitalism. While now looking forward to a life with Harrison, Hiller tempers her father's beliefs with Shaw's own perspective in the conviction that "the greatest of all evils and the worst of crimes is poverty," and resolves to end poverty by the dissemination of her father's fortune through wise business practices. Though this film was well received in Europe, it did not do widespread business in the U.S. as it was too intellectual for American audiences that also did not respond well to its socialist thinking. Pascal does a masterful job in directing this film, with considerable assistance from French and Lean and where the entire cast is superb, with a delightfully wicked performance from the riveting Newton, who plays a money-hungry character living in a London slum. *Author's Note*: Pascal had scored a success in America with an earlier Shaw vehicle by producing **Pygmalion**, 1938, starring Hiller and Leslie Howard and that was the reason why he was able to convince Shaw to allow him to also put this excellent play on film a few years later. Morley was only thirty-two when playing Hiller's father, while she was twenty-eight at the time. **p**, Gabriel Pascal; **d**, Pascal, Harold French, David Lean; **cast**, Wendy Hiller, Rex Harrison, Robert Morley, Robert Newton, Sybil Thorndike, Emlyn Williams, Marie Lohr, Deborah Kerr, Torin Thatcher, Felix Aylmer, Miles Malleson, Stanley Holloway; **w**, George Bernard Shaw, Anatole de Grunwald (based on the play by Shaw); **c**, Ronald Neame; **m**, William Walton; **ed**, Lean, Charles Frend; **prod d**, Vincent Korda; **art d**, Korda, John Bryan; **spec eff**, W. Percy Day, Peter Ellenshaw.

Major Dundee ★★★ 1965; U.S.; 123m; COL; Color; Western; Children: Unacceptable; **DVD**; **VHS**. Heston is outstanding as is Harris in this off-the-beaten-path western from Peckinpah. Heston is a Union officer commanding a western post where he is holding a number of Confederate prisoners during the last year of the Civil War, including Harris, Heston's boyhood friend, who is scheduled to hang, along with Oates, Johnson, Jones and other rebels for killing a guard in an attempt to escape. After a renegade band of Apaches led by Pate attacks and massacres a Union relief column and a family of ranchers, Heston decides to pursue these killers, but needs additional men for the task. He revokes the execution order for Harris and the rebels he commands on the condition that they will loyally serve under his command and with a motley force of Union troopers, and civilian volunteers, who are also seeking to save some children who have been abducted by the Apaches. They are led by a one-armed scout, Coburn, who is accompanied by an Apache scout, Ruiz, whom almost everyone but Coburn distrusts. The Apaches have fled into Mexico with their captives, but Heston ignores the regulation that prohibits U.S. troops from entering that country and leads his men into Mexico. He enters a poverty-stricken village controlled by French troops (French forces then occupied the country which was under the heel of a puppet emperor, Maximilian von Hapsburg). Heston orders Hutton, a Union lieutenant, to blow a hole in the block house where the French soldiers are holed up. Hutton fires a cannon and, once the door is blown away, the French troops surrender. The Americans find that the townspeople are starving in that the French have taken all their food and summarily hanged many of their leaders. Berger, a beautiful and voluptuous foreign woman, who has been stranded in the country, appears, and both Heston and Harris compete for her attentions. Heston wins out, and he and Berger begin a romance by having a swim together in a nearby river. Heston, however, is wounded by an arrow in a skirmish with the Apaches, and Berger looks after him as he hides in another town occupied by the French. He rejoins his men after recuperating and then finds the elusive Pate and his renegades, destroying them and recouping the abducted children, who are sent under separate escort back to the U.S. Meanwhile, the French have sent a powerful force after Heston, doggedly pursuing the Americans as they attempt to make their way back to the U.S. Just as the Americans reach the river, which is the border between the U.S. and Mexico, the French cavalry arrives in full force and the Americans must battle their way to the river and to freedom. Most escape into the U.S., but Harris, who realizes that the South has lost the war and he believes there is nothing more to live for, wheels his horse about and charges alone into the dense ranks of the French cavalry, and is killed. Heston then leads his men back to his outpost, having achieved his goal. Exciting and action-packed throughout, the film offers a strange story, and where, as usual, Peckinpah liberally peppers his scenes with excessive gore and violence, but this is somehow in keeping with the rugged tale and the crude characters essayed. The story line owes much to **Two Flags West**, 1950, which depicts a Union commander having rebels serve under him at a western outpost and quarreling with the former Confederate officer much the same way Heston

Charlton Heston and Senta Berger in *Major Dundee*, 1965.

and Harris contentiously confront each other in scene after scene in **Major Dundee**. *Author's Note*: Heston did not like doing this film, telling this author that "I expected to receive a complete script, but never really got one. Sam [Peckinpah] is a very creative guy, but he is one of those directors who do their scenes as they go along without a finished script, thinking their own improvisations will cover everything they need, but that does not always work well. It didn't work well with me, I can tell you, and I told that to Sam at the time, too. How we ever finished that picture is a mystery. I did not like the end product. It was disjointed and some scenes appear too abruptly without much connection to the previous scenes. It was sort of 'to hell with the story, just make some intense and memorable scenes' and, to my mind, that is not a complete film. I have many regrets about my appearance in that film and felt even sorrier for [James] Coburn, who is wasted in that picture in a throwaway part. That figures since Sam is a throwaway director." The film was shot on location in Mexico and was an expensive production at that time, costing more than $3.8 million, although it returned over the years more than $15 million. **p**, Jerry Bresler; **d**, Sam Peckinpah; **cast**, Charlton Heston, Richard Harris, Jim Hutton, James Coburn, Michael Anderson, Jr., Senta Berger, Brock Peters, Warren Oates, Ben Johnson, Slim Pickens, Jody McCrea, L. Q. Jones, Michael Pate, Dub Taylor, Jose Carlos Ruiz; **w**, Harry Julian Fink, Oscar Saul, Peckinpah (based on a story by Fink); **c**, Sam Leavitt (Eastmancolor); **m**, Daniele Amfitheatrof, Christopher Caliendo; **ed**, William A. Lyon, Don Starling, Howard Kunin; **art d**, Al Ybarra; **spec eff**, August Lohman.

A Majority of One ★★★ 1961; U.S.; 156m; WB; Color; Comedy; Children: Acceptable; **DVD**; **VHS**. Russell gives an outstanding performance as a Brooklyn widow whose son was killed by the Japanese in World War II. She takes a sea voyage to Japan with her daughter, Rhue, and her diplomat son-in-law, Danton, who has business there. Aboard ship, she meets Guinness (who presents a standout performance), a Japanese businessman who also lost family in the war. Danton learns that Guinness is part of a negotiating team he must deal with on a business-political issue. Guinness and Russell begin to be charmed by each other, and Danton wonders if it is for business-political reasons on Guinness' part. Once in Japan, Danton makes a remark that offends Guinness and a meeting of the negotiating team is called off. Russell will not end her friendship with Guinness and goes to his home. Their cordial reunion results in Guinness going ahead with the business meeting with Danton. A deal is agreed upon, then Guinness makes it known that he loves Russell and wants to marry her. Rhue and Danton object, and Russell, although she loves Guinness, says no to him because of the animosities between their two countries created by the war, which would most likely come between them in the future. A few years later, Guinness

Beulah Bondi and Victor Moore in *Make Way for Tomorrow*, 1937.

is in New York as a Japanese representative to the United Nations. Russell learns of it and is delighted to see her old friend again. A new courtship begins, but we are left to wonder if it will lead to the altar. This is a very charming, gentle story of a cross-cultural romance that was first a long-running play on Broadway and where the gifted Guinness, a master at characterizations, is convincing as the circumspect Oriental. Song: "Oh My Darling Clementine" (Percy Montrose). *Author's Note*: Guinness told this author that "I knew that restraint was necessary when I played a Japanese businessman in that picture. The Japanese do not normally express their emotions and their expressions are subdued. Showing any kind of passion, therefore, becomes a difficulty when one must convey passion, so I had to display little mannerisms to indicate that I was reaching out for Miss Russell, an Occidental woman. To do that, I studied some of Toshiro Mifune's films and even watched **Broken Blossoms** [1919], the great D. W. Griffith film, to see how Richard Barthelmess delicately exhibits his love for an Occidental girl, Lillian Gish, without giving offense, and that is a Japanese credo, not giving offense." Russell saw Guinness, according to her statements to this author, "as an endearing and affectionate man in **A Majority of One**, although all his gestures to indicate he wants more than friendship from me are very subtle. Only a great actor like Alec [Guinness] could have made such a character convincing." **p&d**, Mervyn LeRoy; **cast**, Rosalind Russell, Alec Guinness, Ray Danton, Madlyn Rhue, Mae Questel; Marc Marno, Gary Vinson, Sharon Hugueny, Frank Wilcox, Yuki Shimoda; **w**, Leonard Spigelgass (based on his play); **c**, Harry Stradling Sr. (Technicolor); **m**, Max Steiner; **ed**, Philip W. Anderson; **art d**, John Beckman; **set d**, Ralph S. Hurst.

Make Mine Mink ★★★ 1960; U.K.; 97m; Rank/Continental Distributing; B/W; Comedy/Children: Acceptable; **DVD**; **VHS**. Seyler is a wealthy British Dame, who finds that it is fun to retrieve stolen goods, so she enlists the aid of Terry-Thomas, a retired military officer, to help her and a friend, Duxbury, steal furs for charity. The trio is not too bright about their wacky covert operations and there is lots of slapstick comedy as they perform their shadowy chores as amateur fur thieves. All goes well until Seyler's housekeeper, Whitelaw, who has served time in prison, shows up for work wearing a fur coat and is then suspected of the robberies. To shift the blame from her, Seyler plans a "heist in reverse," to sneak the fur coat back to where they think it was stolen. That exploit only compounds the felony and adds to the laughs. Seyler and her accomplices, nevertheless, will go on to other heists and thoroughly enjoy their nefarious endeavors in this charming comedy. **p**, Hugh Stewart; **d**, Robert Asher; **cast**, Terry-Thomas, Athene Seyler, Hattie Jacques, Elspeth Duxbury, Billie Whitelaw, Jack Hedley, Raymond Huntley, Irene Handl, Ian Fleming, Ron Moody; **w**, Michael Pertwee, Peter

Blackmore (based on the play "Breath of Spring" by Peter Coke); **c**, Reginald Wyer; **m**, Philip Green; **ed**, Roger Cherrill; **art d**, Carmen Dillon.

Make Mine Music ★★★ 1946; U.S.; 75m; Walt Disney/Buena Vista; Color; Animated Musical; Children: Recommended; **DVD**; **VHS**. This wonderful collection of short features has the added attraction of some lively and very entertaining music. "A Rustic Ballad" tells the story of the Martins and Coys, the feuding hillbilly families; "A Tone Poem" is a mood piece set on a blue bayou; "A Jazz Interlude" features a bobbysoxer and her boyfriend jitterbugging at a malt shop; "A Ballad in Blue" visualizes the loss of a lover; "A Musical Recitation" is a reading of the classic baseball story "Casey at the Bat"; "Ballade Ballet" has ballet dancers performing in silhouette; "A Fairy Tale with Music" depicts the Russian story "Peter and the Wolf"; "After You've Gone" has four musical instruments chasing in a surrealistic landscape; "A Love Story" is a charming romance between a fedora and a bonnet; "Opera Pathetique" is the story of "Willie, the Whale Who Wanted to Sing at the Met." Disney brought out a sort-of sequel, **Melody Time**, 1948. Songs include "Shortinin' Bread" (sung by Nelson Eddy), "Largo Al Factotum" from "The Barber of Seville" (Giacomo Donizetti, sung by Eddy), sextet from "Lucia di Lammermoor" (Gaetano Donizetti, sung by Eddy); Clown song from "Punchinello" (sung by Eddy); "Tristan und Isolde" (Richard Wagner, sung by Eddy); "Devil's Song" from "Mephistopheles" (Arrigo Boito, sung by Eddy); Finale to Act III of "Martha" (Baron Friedrich von Flotow, sung by Eddy), "Johnny Fedora and Alice Blue Bonnet" (Allie Wrubel, Ray Gilbert, sung by The Andrews Sisters); "All the Cats Join In" (Alec Wilder, Eddie Sauter, Gilbert, performed by Benny Goodman and His Orchestra, sung by The Pied Pipers); "Without You" (Osvaldo Farres, Gilbert, sung by Andy Russell); "Two Silhouettes" (Charles Wolcott, Gilbert, sung by Dinah Shore); "Casey, the Pride of Them All" (Ken Darby, Elliot Daniel, Gilbert, sung by Jerry Colonna); "The Martins and the Coys" (Al Cameron, Ted Weems, sung by The King's Men); "Blue Bayou" (Bobby Worth, Gilbert, sung by The Ken Darby Chorus); "After You've Gone" (Henry Creamer, Turner Leighton, performed by Benny Goodman, Cozy Cole, Teddy Wilson, and Sid Weiss); "Peter and the Wolf" (Serge Prokofieff). **p**, Joe Grant; **d**, Jack Kinney, Clyde Geronimi, Hamilton Luske, Robert Cormack, Joshua Meador; **cast** (voiceovers), Nelson Eddy, Dinah Shore, Benny Goodman, The Andrews Sisters (Patty, Maxine, Laverne Andrews), Jerry Colonna, Andy Russell, Sterling Holloway, The Pied Pipers, The King's Men, Ken Darby Chorus; **w**, Homer Brightman, Dick Huemer, Dick Kinney, John Walbridge, Tom Oreb, Dick Shaw, Eric Gurney, Sylvia Holland, T. Hee, Ed Penner, Dick Kelsey, James Bodrero, Roy Williams, Cap Palmer, Jesse Marsh, Erwin Graham, Charles Wolcott; **m**, Wolcott, Eliot Daniel, Oliver Wallace, **art d**, Mary Blair, Elmer Plummer, John Hench; **set d**, **spec eff**, Ub Iwerks.

Make Way for Tomorrow ★★★ 1937; U.S.; 91m; PAR; B/W; Drama; Children: Cautionary; **BD**; **DVD**; **VHS**. The home of an elderly couple, Moore and Bondi, is in foreclosure during the latter years of the Great Depression. None of their five children will take both parents to live with them, so Moore goes to live with a daughter, Risdon, and Bondi with her son, Mitchell. The arrangement creates problems for them and the rest of the family until, after some time, Moore tells Bondi he expects to find work in California and will send for her. They say farewell at a train station, reaffirming their lifelong love for each other, yet neither is sure they will ever meet again. This sensitively directed film is touching and revealing, helmsman McCarey believing that it was one of his finest films. When McCarey accepted the Academy Award for Best Director for the comedy **The Awful Truth**, 1937, released the same year, he said: "Thanks, but you gave it to me for the wrong picture," believing **Make Way for Tomorrow** to be his best work. Songs: "When a St. Louis Woman Comes Down to New Orleans" (Arthur Johnston, Sam Coslow, Gene Austin); "Let Me Call You Sweetheart" (Leo Friedman, Harold Rossiter, Beth Slater Whitson); "M-O-T-H-E-R" (Theodore Morse). A few scenes may be too depressing for children. *Author's Note*: McCarey told this author that "**Make Way for Tomorrow** did not get the recognition it should have gotten simply because the Academy did want to deal with aging generations that are woefully abandoned by the younger, on-coming generations. It happens in all ages and in all countries and I depicted that problem with a terrific script and cast, one of my best pictures, if not my very best." **p&d**, Leo McCarey; **cast**, Victor Moore, Beulah Bondi, Fay Bainter, Thomas Mitchell, Porter Hall, Barbara Read, Maurice Moscovitch, Elisabeth Risdon, Minna Gombell, Louise Beavers, Ellen Drew; **w**, Viña Delmar (based on the novel *The Years Are So Long* by Josephine Lawrence and the play by Helen and Nolan Leary); **c**, William C. Mellor; **m**, Victor Young, George Antheil; **ed**, LeRoy Stone; **art d**, Hans Dreier, Bernard Herzbrun; **set d**, A.E. Freudeman; **spec eff**, Gordon Jennings.

Malaya ★★★ 1950; U.S.; 98m; MGM; B/W; War Drama; Children: Cautionary; **DVD**; **VHS**. Tracy and Stewart, two great stars with widely divergent personalities, are teamed in this exciting WWII tale, which is based on an actual covert operation. Stewart is a reporter who knows the Malayan territories, having worked there before the war and also knows where large deposits of much-needed rubber are located. He is recruited to smuggle the rubber out of Japanese-held Malaya, along with super smuggler Tracy, who is released from Alcatraz to perform the deed. Though routinely at odds with each other as to how to achieve their mutual ends, Tracy and Stewart make their way to Malaya and contact a local underworld boss, the aging and venal Greenstreet, to get his cooperation in arranging porters to help them smuggle the rubber through Japanese lines and to U.S. ships waiting off the coast. Tracy and Stewart, whose operations are often stalled by Japanese officer Loo, finally manage to load more than 150,000 tons of rubber onto small river crafts and sail perilously toward the coast and open waters. En route, however, Stewart is killed, but Tracy survives to not only supervise the successful delivery of the rubber to the waiting U.S. ships, but dispatches the insidious Loo in the process. Thorpe directs with a sure hand, presenting many tense moments in the murky Malayan jungles, and the cast does a fine job in essaying their engrossing roles. *Author's Note*: Stewart felt that the story for this film provided a lot of mystery, but "it didn't give Spence and me a lot of conflict, so we had to inject some of that business into our scenes together. Spence carries the film on the sheer force of his personality, but the real scene-stealer in that picture was Greenstreet. That glaring, heavyweight man could steal any scene by simply waddling onto the set. I also thought he was a very funny guy. I caught him throwing water onto his bald head and under the arms of his bulky white suit and when I asked him why he was doing that he said: 'Malaya is a hot country. I know. I've been there. I am not sweating enough in my next scene, so the water is necessary. A sweating man is an interesting man, don't you think?'" The idea for this story came from Manchester Boddy (1891-1967), a newsman and publisher of the old Los Angeles *Illustrated Daily News*. In October 1941, a raging fire destroyed much of the Firestone Rubber Tire Company in Fall River, Massachusetts, and, along with it, most of the U.S. government's stockpile of raw rubber. Knowing that the U.S. would desperately need raw rubber in its impending war with Germany and Japan, Boddy, only a short time before America entered that war, wrote a letter to President Franklin D. Roosevelt (1882-1945) that told Roosevelt the locations of large deposits of raw rubber and how the rubber could be smuggled out of Japanese-held Malaya. Roosevelt wrote back a short time later to tell Boddy that the covert operation had already been launched (reportedly an OSS operation). Boddy subsequently wrote the story for MGM and he is portrayed by Barrymore in the film. **p**, Edwin H. Knopf; **d**, Richard Thorpe; **cast**, Spencer Tracy, James Stewart, Valentina Cortese, Sydney Greenstreet, John Hodiak, Lionel Barrymore, Gilbert Roland, Roland Winters, Richard Loo, Tom Helmore, DeForest Kelley; **w**, Frank Fenton (based on a story by Manchester Boddy); **c**, George Folsey; **m**, Bronislau

John Hodiak, Spencer Tracy and James Stewart in *Malaya*, 1949.

Kaper; **ed**, Ben Lewis; **art d**, Cedric Gibbons, Malcolm Brown; **set d**, Edwin B. Willis; **spec eff**, A. Arnold Gillespie, Warren Newcombe.

Malcolm ★★★ 1986; Australia; 90m; Cascade Films/Vestron Pictures; Color; Comedy/Crime; Children: Unacceptable (MPAA: PG-13); **DVD**; **VHS**. Friels is the Malcolm of the title, a very shy and reclusive young man, who is a gadget-building mechanical genius and is fired for building his own miniature tram and taking it for rides around town. His mother recently died and he needs money to stay in the house they shared. He needs someone to help pay the rent, so he comes upon Hargreaves, a man a few years older, who has just been released from jail, and he moves into the house with him. Hargreaves then introduces Friels to a life of petty crime, encouraged by Hargreaves' girlfriend, Davies. They steal by using some of Friels's gadgets including robots that carry guns and shoot off smoke bombs. Friels and Hargreaves eventually have to pay for their transgressions, which provide some funny moments in their petty crime spree. Gutter language and profanity, along with the sanctioning of a life of crime, even for comedic purposes, prohibit viewing by children. **p**, Nadia Tass, David Parker; **d**, Tass; **cast**, Colin Friels, John Hargreaves, Lindy Davies, Chris Haywood, Charles "Bud" Tingwell, Beverley Phillips, Judith Stratford, Heather Mitchell, Tony Mahood, David Letch; **w&c** Parker; **m**, Paul Coppens, Simon Jeffes; **ed**, Ken Sallows; **spec eff**, Peter Stubbs, Brian Pearce.

Malcolm X ★★★ 1992; U.S.; 202m; WB; Color; Biographical Drama; Children: Unacceptable (MPAA: PG-13); **DVD**; **VHS**. Washington presents another riveting performance in essaying the complex Malcolm X (Malcolm Little; 1925-1965), who comes from a broken family and, after committing burglaries, is sent to prison. While imprisoned, Washington learns and embraces the theories of Elijah Muhammad (1897-1975), played by Freeman, leader of a Black Nationalist movement titled the Nation of Islam. Washington advocates black segregation and isolationism from the predominantly white society of America, as well as urging a "back to Africa" movement. When released, he becomes Freeman's most ardent supporter, and Freeman initially anoints Washington as his heir apparent and appoints him to head his New York City operations. When Washington begins to denounce some of the more violent actions of the movement, he and his family are threatened by radical members of the movement. Washington now lives with fear, and his wife, Bassett, lives in terror that their children may be harmed. Going about with armed guards to protect him, Washington believes that Freeman may be behind the attempt to silence him and, perhaps, kill him. He nevertheless establishes his own black Islamic organization. His home is bombed, but he and his family survive, but later, when appearing at a public rally, Washington is shot to death by a group of radical

Lila Lee, Raymond Hatton, Mildred Reardon and Edmund Burns in *Male and Female*, 1919.

Black Nationalists. *Author's Note*: This film draws much of its content from the excellent documentary, **Malcolm X**, 1972, which was narrated by James Earl Jones and was based upon the same book used in this production. For more details on Malcolm X and, specifically, his assassination, see my two-volume work, *The Great Pictorial History of World Crime*, Volume I (History, Inc., 2004; pages 169-171). **p**, Spike Lee, Marvin Worth, Ahmed Murad, Preston Holmes, Jon Kilik, Monty Ross, **d**, Lee; **cast**, Denzel Washington, Lee, Angela Bassett, Albert Hall, Al Freeman, Jr., Delroy Lindo, Theresa Randle, Kate Vernon, Christopher Plummer, Karen Allen, Peter Boyle, Nelson Mandela, Bill Cosby, Ossie Davis (voice at eulogy); **w**, Lee, Arnold Perl (based on the book *The Autobiography of Malcolm X* by Malcolm X, Alex Haley); **c**, Ernest Dickerson; **m**, Terence Blanchard; **ed**, Barry Alexander Brown; **prod d**, Wynn Thomas; **art d**, Tom Warren; **set d**, Ted Glass; **spec eff**, Steven Kirshoff, Randall Balsmeyer.

Male and Female ★★★ 1919 (Silent); U.S.; 116m/ 9 reels; PAR; B/W; Comedy; Children: Unacceptable; **DVD**; **VHS**. The British class system is satirized in this very funny romp after a shipload of aristocrats is stranded on a remote island. To survive, they have to take orders from their butler, Meighan, the only one with survival skills. Swanson is one of these haughty aristocrats, a lady of high breeding, who falls madly in love with Meighan. However, when they are finally rescued and return to England, her passion for him cools and she marries a man of her own class. DeMille changed the title of the play on which the film was based, "The Admirable Chrichton," because he feared U.S. audiences would think it was a naval story. DeMille's flare for sensuality is evident in this production and for that reason prohibits viewing by children. The story was remade as **The Admirable Chrichton**, 1972. **p&d**, Cecil B. DeMille; **cast**, Thomas Meighan, Gloria Swanson, Theodore Roberts, Raymond Hatton, Robert Cain, Lila Lee, Bebe Daniels, Julia Faye, Rhy Darby, Mildred Reardon, Wesley Barry; **w**, Jeanie Macpherson (based on the play "The Admirable Chrichton" by J.M. Barrie); **c**, Alvin Wyckoff; **m**, Sydney Jill Lehman (1997 release); **ed**, Anne Bauchens; **art d**, Wilfred Buckland.

The Male Animal ★★★ 1942; U.S.; 101m; WB; B/W; Comedy; Children: Acceptable; **DVD**; **VHS**. A charming comedy where Fonda comes to believe that his wife, de Havilland, has renewed her romantic interest in old flame Carson, a former star football player who arrives in their college town to see "the big game." Fonda thinks that Carson is nothing more than a strutting, brawny, boring braggart and dismisses him. He meanwhile has his problems when announcing that he intends to read a letter written by Bartolomeo Vanzetti (1888-1927), an avowed anarchist, who, along with Nicola Sacco (1891-1927), was executed for murder

and robbery on August 23, 1927. He is warned by college dean Simpson and trustees led by Pallette that, if he reads the letter, thought to be inflammatory, to his students, he will most likely be fired from his teaching position. Fonda is championed by school newspaper editor Anderson, who writes an editorial supporting Fonda's intention to read the missive, but he has ulterior motives in that he is in love with Leslie, Fonda's sister-in-law and de Havilland's younger sibling. Leslie, however, is only focused on DefFore, who is the starring halfback on the school's team. After de Havilland urges Fonda to be reasonable and forget about reading the letter to his class, Fonda, a meek and mild-mannered type, explodes, insisting that the First Amendment (Freedom of Speech) is being challenged and threatened and he intends to express his beliefs and read that letter. De Havilland thinks he has become slightly deranged and goes off to a cocktail party with Carson. Fonda then meets with Anderson and they get drunk together. When Fonda goes home in an alcoholic state he encounters wife de Havilland and Carson returning from the cocktail party and, to defend his hearth and home from the interloper, attempts to attack the beefy Carson, but only succeeds in knocking himself cold. Carson carries the unconscious Fonda to his bed but then beats a hasty retreat, having no intention of splitting up a marriage or ever taking de Havilland away (and she has no such inclination either). The next day, a much hung over Fonda reads the controversial Vanzetti letter in the school auditorium, but the trustees and deans relax when they hear that the missive contains no political statements, only a poetic plea for human understanding. Fonda is now a hero to everyone, but he is just as much in love with wife de Havilland, who slipped that all-important letter into his pocket after he forgot to take it with him en route to his reading. Leslie, by this time, changes her mind and forgets about DeFore, now believing that Anderson, a man of deep conviction, is the one for her. Fonda, de Havilland, as well as Carson, who always knew how to profile an annoying oaf, are standouts in this light hearted comedy well directed by Nugent. *Author's Note*: Nugent wrote the screenplay and starred in the original Broadway version of this story. Fonda told this author that "Elliott [Nugent] went out of his way to convince producers that I was the only person to play the lead in the film version of **The Male Animal**, a part I have always liked." Fonda went on to appear in the same role in the Broadway revival of the play, one in which his daughter, Jane Fonda, appeared in as a supporting player. **p**, Hal B. Wallis; **d**, Elliott Nugent; **cast**, Henry Fonda, Olivia de Havilland, Joan Leslie, Jack Carson, Eugene Pallette, Herbert Anderson, Hattie McDaniel, Don DeFore, Tod Andrews (Michael Ames), Ivan Simpson, Charles Drake, William Hopper, Audrey Long, Jane Randolph, Gig Young; **w**, Julius J. Epstein, Philip G. Epstein, Stephen Morehouse Avery (based on the play by James Thurber, Nugent); **c**, Arthur Edeson; **m**, Heinz Roemheld; **ed**, Thomas Richards; **art d**, John Hughes; **spec eff**, Willard Van Enger.

Malta Story ★★★ 1954; U.K.; 97m; Rank/UA; B/W; War Drama; Children: Cautionary; **DVD**; **VHS**. A stirring WWII tale sees Guinness as a British aviator, who is forced to land at Malta when on a reconnaissance mission to Egypt. Through the aerial photos Guinness has taken, British commander Hawkins learns that the Nazis are planning a full-scale attack against the beleaguered island. The Luftwaffe has been bombing the island routinely and keeping much-needed supplies from reaching Malta by British ships. Guinness meets and falls in love with Pavlow, a native Maltese woman working with the British, but his relationship with her is jeopardized when it is learned that her brother, Stock, is covertly working with the Nazis to seize the island. Pavlow, however, is also attracted to her superior, Steel, in what becomes a brief romantic triangle, until Pavlow discovers that Steel is romantically involved with Asherson. Matters are further complicated for Pavlow when her mother, Robson, refuses to take sides between Pavlow's loyalties to the British and the German affiliations established by her son, Stock, especially after he is accused of treason. The highly charged climax comes when Guinness is killed while in the air and about to attack a

German war fleet heading for Malta, and his last words are heard by Pavlow in the British war room on Malta. A great deal of realistic action is provided by extensive British signal corps footage, which is interspersed throughout the film and where deftly created cross-cutting proves very effective to emphasize the wartime perils at Malta and where Guinness and the entire cast give standout performances. *Author's Note*: Guinness told this author that "**Malta Story** did very well in England as it was a prolonged battle close to the British heart, but it was a sideshow of the war to American viewers and that is why it most likely did not do a lot of business in the States." The siege of Malta occurred in the early stages of WWII, where the British-held bastion was most seriously threatened by German forces in 1942, until British relief ships managed to arrive there. Americans, however, were focused at that time on major battles in the Pacific, such as the battles of the Coral Sea and Midway. **p**, Peter De Sarigny; **d**, Brian Desmond Hurst; **cast**, Alec Guinness, Jack Hawkins, Anthony Steel, Muriel Pavlow, Renee Asherson, Nigel Stock, Flora Robson, Peter Bull, Michael Craig, Rosalie Crutchley, Maurice Denham, Gordon Jackson; **w**, William Fairchild, Nigel Balchin, Thorold Dickinson, De Sarigny (based on a story by Fairchild); **c**, Robert Krasker; **m**, Muir Mathieson, William Alwyn; **ed**, Michael Gordon; **art d**, John Howell; **spec eff**, Albert Whitlock, Bill Warrington, Bert Marshall.

The Maltese Falcon ★★★ 1931; U.S.; 80m; WB; B/W; Crime Drama; Children: Unacceptable; **DVD**; **VHS**. In the first version of Hammett's chilling private eye tale, Cortez is the smoothly operating gumshoe, Sam Spade. Daniels is a conniving and beautiful woman who hires Cortez to find her missing sister, a sibling that does not exist, inveigling him into an involved plot where she schemes to obtain a priceless small statuette, the much-sought after Maltese Falcon. After Daniels' accomplice in her dark plot is murdered, Cortez encounters Digges (as Kaspar Gutman) and his evil minions, all seeking that same statuette and where three more persons are murdered in that sinister quest. In the end, Cortez sorts out the puzzle and ensnares the culprits, but has to give up the strange woman, who has captured his heart. Director Del Ruth hurries this fast-paced whodunit along at sometimes breakneck speeds, and Cortez, Daniels and Digges are standouts in their roles, as is Frye, who plays the jittery kill-crazy gunman, Wilmer (Frye had also in this same year appeared as the bedeviled Renfield in **Dracula**, 1931). The brooding San Francisco atmosphere is appropriately set, and where this production presents an opulent world through which these denizens move about in their pursuit of an elusive and dangerous treasure. **d**, Roy Del Ruth; **cast**, Bebe Daniels, Ricardo Cortez, Dudley Digges, Una Merkel, Robert Elliott, Thelma Todd, Otto Matieson, Walter Long, Dwight Frye, J. Farrell MacDonald, **w**, Maude Fulton, Lucien Hubbard, Brown Holmes (based on the novel by Dashiell Hammett); **c**, William Rees; **ed**, George Marks; **art d**, Robert Haas.

The Maltese Falcon ★★★★★ 1941; U.S.; 100m; WB; B/W; Crime Drama; Children: Unacceptable; **BD**; **DVD**; **VHS**. This classic film noir production, which sees the directorial debut of Huston, fascinates from its first frame to its last, a dark and twisting tale of greed, betrayal and murder and where Bogart, as the indomitable private eye, Sam Spade, became a superstar. Bogart is a wise-cracking street-savvy gumshoe, who shares his seedy San Francisco office with partner Cowan (Archer) when into those offices comes Astor, a beautiful but distraught woman, who hires the detectives to find her missing sister. The elusive and errant sister, Astor states, is somewhere in the city with a strange and dangerous man named Thursby. After giving the detectives a substantial retainer, Bogart orders his junior partner, Cowan, to tail Astor, who tells the detectives that she expects to meet Thursby that evening and that her sister might be with him. Cowan dutifully fulfills his assignment, but, when he appears at the end of Bush Street, he is startled to see someone aiming a gun at him and he is then fatally shot, falling backward over a roadway barrier and tumbling down a slope. Bogart then receives

Humphrey Bogart in *The Maltese Falcon*, 1941.

a call while he is in bed at home telling him that Cowan is dead and he rushes to Stockton and Bush streets to inspect the body of his dead partner. Plainclothes detective Bond then shows him the weapon that killed Cowan, not knowing its type and Bogart tells him that it is a "Webley-Forsby .45 automatic, eight shots. They don't make 'em anymore." He then tells Bond that his partner was tailing a man named Thursby, but when Bond probes further, Bogart refuses to give him any more information. When Bogart later calls Astor's hotel, he finds that she has checked out and departed for destinations unknown. Returning to his apartment, Bogart is visited by Bond and his superior, MacLane, a brusque and bullying SFPD lieutenant detective, who demands to know more about Cowan's assignment, and when Bogart gives them only limited information, refusing to name his client (Astor), the policeman more or less suggests that he may have killed his own partner, which enrages Bogart. The cops then inform Bogart that Thursby has been murdered, shot outside his hotel. They suspect that Bogart, too, may have committed this killing, but he provides an air-tight alibi. The cops accept his story, and Bogart pours drinks for all of them, toasting: "Success—to crime!" Returning to his office the next morning, Bogart is greeted by his loyal and underpaid secretary, Patrick, who tells him he has a caller, George, who is Cowan's widow. George embraces Bogart, believing that they might begin a love affair and, like the cops the night before, suggests that Bogart may have dispatched her husband in order to be with her. Bogart brushes her off, then claps his hands when sarcastically mimicking her implications: "Be kind to me, Sam…You killed my husband!" When she begins to weep, Bogart consoles her and then sends her on her way. He then receives a phone call from Astor, who gives him another name and asks that he visit her. When Bogart goes to Astor's new abode, she asks him if he has informed police that she is his client and is relieved to hear that he refused to name her. She then admits that Thursby (who is never seen in this film) was her associate and that he was a very dangerous man, carrying weapons and that he always took the precaution of crumpling up newspapers and scattering them around his room so that he would hear anyone entering his room while he was sleeping. She further tells Bogart that Thursby most likely killed Cowan, but that she has no idea who might have killed Thursby and that unknown parties are threatening her. Bogart tells her that he never believed her story about the missing sister, but agrees to find out about those unknown parties who are stalking her. He takes almost all of her money as a retainer and, by the time he returns to his office, he receives a visit from Lorre, a perfumed little man, who offers him $5,000 for the "black figure of a bird." Bogart tells him he has no idea what he is talking about and then Lorre aims a gun at Bogart, saying, "I intend to search your offices." Bogart quickly disarms the little man, knocking him unconscious and then inspects his wallet to discover that he has

Humphrey Bogart, Peter Lorre, Mary Astor and Sydney Greenstreet in *The Maltese Falcon*, 1941.

several foreign passports under the name of Joel Cairo and a ticket to the Geary Theater. When Lorre comes to, Bogart politely returns his wallet and even his gun. Lorre then aims the gun at him once more and tells him that he intends to search his offices and Bogart, laughing, tells him to go ahead. Later Bogart and Astor meet with Lorre and Bogart demands to know all about "the black bird," but Lorre believes either he or Astor has the item and they begin to quarrel. When Astor mentions that "the fat man" is in San Francisco, Lorre attempts to attack Astor, but Bogart slaps him, saying, "When you're slapped you'll take and like it!" The SFPD cops Bond and MacLane then interrupt the fight between Lorre and Astor and where Lorre complains that Astor attacked him. MacLane tells them that they are all going to the police station, but Bogart tells the cops that it was all a gag. When no one will press charges, the cops, disgusted with the lot of them, leave as does Lorre. Astor remains to tell Bogart that the object everyone is seeking is "a black figure…smooth and shiny…of a hawk or a falcon." She tells Bogart that she and Thursby have been following that bird around the globe as are others, but when he calls her a liar, she admits it, saying, "I've always been a liar." Reclining on a chaise lounge, she holds her head, as if in pain, dramatically adding, "I'm so tired, so tired of lying and making up lies…not knowing what is a lie and what is the truth." Bogart leans forward to kiss her, but looks out the window to see below in the street a man standing in the shadows, the very man Bogart believes has been earlier following him. When later going to Lorre's hotel, Bogart sees the man who has been following him sitting in the lobby and reading a newspaper, or pretending to read that newspaper. When Bogart confronts him, the man, Cook, tells Bogart to "shove off." Bogart calls a friend, Burke, the hotel detective, and points to Cook, saying: "Why do you let these gunsels sit around with guns bulging in their pockets?" Burke tells Cook to leave the hotel, and before he does, Cook snarls, "I won't forget you guys." When Bogart returns to his office, he meets with Astor, asking his secretary, Patrick, to take Astor home with her for safekeeping. George, Cowan's widow, then shows up, but Bogart sends her packing, too. He then gets a call from the fat man, Greenstreet, the very man he has been expecting to hear from, and he goes to Greenstreet's hotel. He meets with him and Cook, Greenstreet's enforcer and Greenstreet begin to tell Bogart about the black statuette everyone is looking for, a Maltese Falcon, but when he is evasive in providing details, Bogart tells Greenstreet to give him more information or not to contact him again and pretends to be enraged when he leaves. He later returns when summoned by Greenstreet, encountering Cook on the street, and when Bogart wise cracks to Cook, the gunman replies: "Keep riding me and you're going to be picking iron out of your liver!" Bogart laughs, replying: "The cheaper the crook, the gaudier the patter." En route to Greenstreet's hotel suite, Bogart disarms Cook, embarrassing him when he turns over

Cook's two automatics to his boss. Greenstreet then pours a drink for Bogart and gives him the astounding details about the much-wanted Maltese Falcon, describing how it is encrusted with jewels from beak to claw, but how it has been disguised with a thick coat of black enamel. He explains how the Falcon was originally intended as a gift to King Charles during the Crusades from the Knights of Malta, but that it was waylaid and, over the centuries, has been sought by those knowing of its existence. He tells Bogart that it might be worth $1 million. Bogart becomes woozy from the drink Greenstreet has given him and then collapses unconscious to the floor. Cook kicks him in the face and he and Greenstreet then depart. Regaining consciousness hours later, Bogart finds in the abandoned hotel suite a newspaper with an encircled announcement of a ship, *La Paloma*, scheduled to arrive in San Francisco that night. Bogart goes to the dock and finds that the ship is on fire and firemen are fighting the blaze. He is told by Parnell, a dock officer, that the passengers and crew members escaped the fire and were all safe. Bogart returns to his office where he and Patrick see a man (Walter Huston, the father of the director, who was not billed) stagger into the office, carrying a package wrapped in newspapers, dropping it to the floor, and uttering: "You know…the Falcon." He collapses on a couch, and Bogart, after seeing that he has been shot several times, tells Patrick that he is dead and that he is the captain of the *La Paloma*. When inspecting the package, Bogart becomes excited, telling Patrick: "We've got it, angel! We've got it!" The phone rings and Patrick answers. It is Astor, giving Patrick an address, then screaming before the line goes dead. Bogart tells Patrick to call the police so that they can attend to the dead man, but not to mention the Falcon. He then takes the enwrapped Falcon and checks it into a baggage room, mailing the claim check to his own post office box. He then takes a taxi to the address Astor gave to Patrick, but it turns out to be an empty lot. After finding Astor at her old address, he takes her to his own apartment, and Greenstreet, Lorre and Cook all meet him there in response to his summons. Greenstreet gives $10,000 in cash to Bogart in exchange for the Falcon, and Bogart tells him that they must wait for it to be delivered. He calls Patrick and tells her to pick up the package and bring it to him. Bogart tells Greenstreet that he expected more than $10,000, but Greenstreet counters by saying that his payment is "genuine coin of the realm. With a dollar of this you can buy ten dollars of talk." Bogart then tells Greenstreet that someone has to be the fall guy for all the murders committed and suggests that Cook, the gunman, be that man. Cook, enraged, makes a move toward Bogart, who knocks him unconscious. While the crooks argue about their shares from the sale of the Falcon, Cook escapes. Patrick then arrives to deliver the package and, after she departs, Astor, Greenstreet and Lorre tear away its wrappings to see the black statuette of the Maltese Falcon. Greenstreet uses a small penknife to slash away at its black enamel coating, expecting to see the encrusted jewels beneath, but, when seeing none, shouts: "It's a fake! It's a phony! It's lead! It's lead! It's a fake!" Bogart confronts Astor, but she says that this is the statuette that was secreted on board the *La Paloma* and she knows of no other. Greenstreet is in a state of near collapse from the defeat, and Lorre explodes, blaming Greenstreet for everything, shouting: "You! It's you who bungled it! You and your stupid attempt to buy it! You, you imbecile! You bloated idiot! You stupid fat-head, you!" Greenstreet, however, is undefeated, resolving to go on searching for the real Falcon. Lorre, who has stopped his whining, agrees to go with him. Greenstreet then trains a gun on Bogart, demanding that he return the $10,000. Bogart gives him the money, but keeps $1,000 "for expenses," and Greenstreet shrugs and leaves with Lorre. Bogart calls the police and tells them to arrest Greenstreet, Lorre and Cook. He is now alone with Astor, the woman he now knows is the actual killer. He tells her that she killed his partner, Cowan, to implicate the murder on her partner, Thursby, but then killed Thursby, too. "Well, if you get a good break," he intones to Astor, "you'll be out of Tahatchapi [woman's state prison in California] in twenty years and you can come back to me then…I hope they don't hang you, precious, by that sweet neck." Astor thinks he is joking. Bogart is not, stating: "I won't play the sap for you! Yes, angel, I'm going to send you over… you're taking the fall!" Astor tries wheedling, telling Bogart that she knows he loves her, but he is resolute in his intentions, telling her that "when a man's partner is killed, he is supposed to do something about it. And it happens that we're in the detective business. Well, when one of your organization gets killed, it's bad business to let the killer get away with it, bad all around, bad for every detective everywhere." He goes on to tell Astor that maybe they love each other, but that does not matter. The doorbell rings, and Astor flashes a wide-eyed look of absolute terror just before cops Bond and MacLane appear. Bogart tells them that Astor killed Cowan and Thursby, gives them the $1,000 bribe Greenstreet has given him and then points to the black statuette of the Falcon. As MacLane takes Astor into custody and walks her from the apartment, Bond briefly holds the statuette and asks Bogart: "What is it?" Bogart takes the statuette into his hands, replying: "The stuff dreams are made of." They walk to the outside landing, and Astor is shown briefly in an elevator with MacLane, stone-faced as the elevator doors close; Bogart and Bond walk down the stairs to end this film noir classic. Huston meticulously directs this film, which loyally conforms to the Hammett novel. Bogart renders a mesmerizing performance, which forever associated the character of Sam Spade to his persona. Every player in this unforgettable film enacts his or her part to perfection, Astor as the lethally conniving vixen, Greenstreet as the evil-minded mastermind, Lorre as Greenstreet's slippery associate, Cook as the dim-witted thug, Patrick as the street-smart secretary, Cowan as Bogart's unsavory partner, George as his deceitful wife, and Bond and MacLane as the uninspired but dogged cops. The film itself is "the stuff of dreams" in that it meets the highest criteria of quality filmmaking. Huston's script is taut, and the dialog crackles with rich characterizations as it unfolds the twisting and turning story as each scene is economically presented, all relative and important to the story's sense and continuity. It is truly an addictive film, one that demands watching again and again to remind the viewer of its richness of content and where the viewer can discover new techniques and nuances from Huston and his players with each new viewing. Edeson's cinematography is a beauty to behold as he captures the visual flavor of San Francisco, its daytime busy streets, its shadowy and murky byways, all the more well accomplished in that most of the film, other than some stock footage of the city, was shot on the Warner Brothers sound stages. Deutsch's score is brilliantly chilling and appropriate to the on-going mystery of the story line. This is actually the third version of the Hammett tale, the first being the 1931 production with Ricardo Cortez and Bebe Daniels, the second being **Satan Met a Lady**, 1936, with Warren William and Bette Davis. *Author's Note*: Huston, who had been for years a contract writer at Warner Brothers, lobbied hard to get his first directorial assignment with this film, but studio chief Jack Warner was leery about his ability to direct a major feature film until producer Blanke went to bat for Huston. Warner approved of the deal, but only if Blanke closely supervised Huston. Knowing that his own job was at risk, the always enterprising Blanke sat down with Huston and gave him his marching orders. Huston told this author that "Henry [Blanke] told me that I had six weeks to make the film and if I went beyond that and a penny more than the $300,000 budget for the film, he would have my neck in a noose and personally tighten that rope until my tongue showed and my eyes popped. Henry was a very smart producer, one who understood everything it took to make a good picture. 'Be careful to make every one of your shots and scenes count,' he told me. 'Shoot every scene as if it is the most important of your career or you will not have a career.' Then the great Hal Wallis, who ran all production at Warner's, got into the act. He, too, personally supervised everything I did and was peering over my shoulder every minute. I hated him, but, to tell you the truth, his presence kept me on my toes and I probably did a better job for his being there." To make sure he wasted no time, Huston drew rough sketches of every scene (a leaf out of Alfred Hitchcock's lifetime filmmaking regimen), positioning all of his truck, dolly, crab, panning and overhead boom shots far ahead of the actual

Lee Patrick and Humphrey Bogart in *The Maltese Falcon,* **1941.**

setups and shootings. He rehearsed the cast for each sequence of scenes, but gave them little direction as they were following his very detailed script that specified most of his directorial requirements. "Not one of our scenes was ever cut because everything was so precise in the script John [Huston] wrote," Astor told this author. "He had laid it all out in so much detail that we had no questions or doubts about what we were supposed to do. I had never seen a director do that before." Lorre, too, was amazed at the economical effort Huston employed in the film, telling this author that "we actually had extra time in the short schedule for **The Maltese Falcon**, even though it was just a matter of weeks. John [Huston] took Bogey, Mary [Astor] and Ward [Bond] and me to his golf club [The Lakeside Golf Club], which was near the Warner Brothers Studio, and we played golf, went swimming or sat around in the lounge drinking and talking about anything and everything, except the picture. It was a smart way for John to get us to relax so that when we went back to work, we were eager to get at our scenes." Cook told this author that "Huston made it all easy for us since he shot the film in the story's sequence and without jumping ahead or behind the story line so that nothing was confusing. He invited me to go on a few of his outings with the rest of the cast, but that wasn't for me. I didn't hang around with anyone, especially other actors. All I wanted to do was to do my work, get my pay, and get the hell out of Hollywood and go back to my home in the Sierra Mountains where I had a cabin and I could fish for trout in peace and could keep my sanity." Huston made a visual treat of the picture by including ceilings to give a confining or ever claustrophobic look to many scenes where his characters are gathered. He allowed the creative Edeson to use low key lighting in many scenes and had him take close-ups of his characters while others bantered in deep focus distance. To emphasize Greenstreet's bulky body, Huston had Edeson shoot from the floor and upward to show Greenstreet's expansive girth, a huge gold watch chain crossing his vest, the image of authority that commanded all the conspirators. A deep friendship between Bogart and Huston was cemented in this film after George Raft turned down the role of Sam Spade because he refused to work with an inexperienced director. When the role was then offered to Bogart, he accepted with enthusiasm (and had he not, there was every likelihood that Huston may have been denied his directorial opportunity). Huston was forever grateful to Bogart for this and showed that gratitude many time over by tailoring some of Bogart's future and greatest roles in **Across the Pacific**, 1942; **The Treasure of the Sierra Madre**, 1948; **Key Largo**, 1948; and **The African Queen**, 1951. Bogart was to state that "I had a lot going for me in that one. First there was Huston. He made the Dashiell Hammett novel into something you don't come across too often. It was practically a masterpiece. I don't have many things I'm proud of…but that's one." **The Maltese Falcon** was also instrumental

Humphrey Bogart and Elisha Cook Jr., in *The Maltese Falcon*, **1941.**

in helping Bogart get his classic role as Rick in **Casablanca**, 1942, in that this was the first film that Ingrid Bergman saw when she was considered for her role as Else in that film and convinced her that she would be acting opposite "a great actor," as Bergman told this author. Hammett personally knew in real life all of the characters in this fascinating story. Sam Spade is really drawn from Hammett's own career as a private detective when he worked for the Pinkerton Agency in San Francisco. His full name is Samuel Dashiell Hammett, but he dropped the first name when becoming a writer in the mid-1920s. He personally pursued and arrested a man in Pasco, Washington, a thief upon whom he based the character of Joel Cairo, who was decidedly effeminate. In the book (published first in *Black Mask* magazine in five installments in 1930 before publisher Alfred A. Knopf put it into book form), Spade's secretary, Effie Perine, before she has Cairo come into Spade's office, tells her boss: "This guy is queer." Huston downplayed the homosexuality of the character, but implied his sexual bent by having him wearing cologne that smells of gardenias. The character Wilmer is also profiled in the book as being homosexual, but his sexual inclination is only obliquely mentioned by Bogart who consistently describes him as a "gunsel." In crime parlance, that word first appears as "gunzel" in *The Gay Cat*, a crime novel published in 1914, which signifies a passive male homosexual, who is also too fast to use his weapon. Even the character Kaspar Gutman is shown in the original novel as having homosexual tendencies; he has no female companions, other than his distant relationship to the conniving Brigid O'Shaughnessy, and all of his close associates are of the ilk of Cairo and Wilmer. Strangely enough, this was Greenstreet's first film. He had long been an established stage actor in England and in New York. The accomplished sixty-two-year-old Greenstreet (then weighing more than 300 pounds), however, was extremely nervous when going into the production for **The Maltese Falcon**. "Sydney [Greenstreet] was very uneasy just before we started production," Astor told this author. "He asked if he could hold my hand before some of those scenes to give him some courage, and I thought, My God, this man is a fine actor. Why would he be so nervous, but he was new to the movies and it was the bright lights of the set that unnerved him, I believe." Lorre told this author that he thought that "Sydney was intimidated by the cameras. I think he thought them threatening, like they were loaded guns pointed right at him. Bogey, Mary and I calmed him down, however, by going to his dressing room and bringing him brandy. After he took a few good shots, he was his old confident self and ready to go on to the set. To see his performance, you would never think he had any anxiety when going before the cameras. His lines were perfect and he was flawless in his part." Lorre would appear in several fine films with Greenstreet thereafter, including **Passage to Marseilles**, 1944; **The Mask of Dimitrios**, 1944; **The Conspirators**, 1944; **Three Strangers**, 1946; and **The**

Verdict, 1946. Actually, the character Gutman is based upon a British rogue, adventurer, theater producer, and sometimes detective, A. Maundy Gregory (1877-1941), a rotund, witty character, who illegally sold titles to would-be British aristocrats. Hammett met the shadowy Gregory in his boozy travels and knew well of his underhanded machinations, and, particularly where Gregory was, at one time, searching for an elusive treasure not unlike the Maltese Falcon. For more details on Hammett and Gregory, see my eight-volume work, *The Encyclopedia of World Crime*, Volume II (D-J) (CrimeBooks, Inc., 1990; Gregory: pages 1379-1380; Hammett: pages 1437-1438). The character of Captain Jacobi, who staggers mortally wounded into Bogart's office carrying the Falcon and with a hat brim pulled low to shroud his face is played by the great actor Walter Huston, the director's father, who insisted on playing this unbilled role as a good luck gesture for his son's first directorial outing, and taking no pay for his brief appearance. His son, an inveterate prankster, however, put his father through the mill, asking him to do his bit part over and over again until he was satisfied. After that day's shooting, Walter Huston went home and soaked in the bathtub, complaining about the many bruises he suffered in stumbling around that day in Bogart's office. He got a call later from what he thought was top Warner Brothers producer Hal Wallis, who said that he had seen the rushes of his scene and stated that his performance was "awful" and then demanded that Huston return the next day and re-do the scene. Walter Huston roared back: "You tell my son to get another actor or go to hell! He made me take twenty falls today and I'm sore all over and I'm not about to take another twenty or even one!" He hung up. It was not Wallis on the phone after all, but John Huston, disguising his voice after Astor, pretending to be Wallis' secretary, got Walter Huston on the phone. Both Huston and Astor laughed uproariously at the prank, but it was no laughing matter to Walter Huston, especially after he learned of his son's impersonation. "Hell, he was mad at me for some time," John Huston told this author, "but he came around with smiles and pats on the back when the film was released." **p**, Hal B. Wallis, Henry Blanke; **d&w**, John Huston (based on the novel by Dashiell Hammett); **cast**, Humphrey Bogart, Mary Astor, Gladys George, Peter Lorre, Barton MacLane, Lee Patrick, Sydney Greenstreet, Ward Bond, Jerome Cowan, Elisha Cook Jr., James Burke, Murray Alper, John Hamilton, Emory Parnell, Charles Drake, William Hopper (not credited), Walter Huston; **c**, Arthur Edeson; **m**, Adolph Deutsch; **ed**, Thomas Richards; **art d**, Robert Haas.

Mamma Roma ★★★ 1995; Italy; 110m; Arco Film; B/W; Drama; Children: Unacceptable. Magnani is a middle-aged prostitute who buys an upper-class apartment in Rome, quits prostitution, and starts a new life as a fruit seller at her own stand. Garofolo, her teenage son, has been reared in the country, but now comes to live with her. He is her pride and joy, but he does not want to study and, after discovering his mother's unsavory background, joins some teenage hooligans. The fruit stand is not bringing in much money, so Magnani drifts back into prostitution. Garofolo becomes a petty thief, is caught after stealing a radio and is sent to prison where he is strapped to a bed and where he later dies. Magnani has to go on living, hard as that will be. When learning that her son, her only joy in life, has died, she thinks to commit suicide by jumping from the balcony of her room, but the sight of the dome of St. Peter's Cathedral in Rome gives her pause and this is where the film ends. A sad, tragic story that is well acted by the accomplished Magnini and Garofolo, its grim scenes, especially Magnini hustling customers at night on Rome's dark streets and Garofolo's prison scenes, and pessimistic attitude may be too depressing for many viewers. There are some airy moments, such as a scene where mother and son dance an awkward tango together and where Garofolo's inept dancing causes Magnini to take a pratfall, but these light hearted scenes are few and far between. *Author's Note*: As was his penchant, Pasolini uses many inexperienced persons to act in brief roles in this production, thinking to bring more realism to his film. This film was released in 1962 but not released in the U.S. until 1995. Strong mature themes including sexuality prohibit viewing by children. (In Italian; English subtitles.) **p**, Alfredo Bini; **d&w**, Pier Paolo Pasolini; **cast**, Anna Magnani, Ettore Garofolo, Franco Citti, Silvana Corsini, Luisa Loiano, Paolo Volponi, Luciano Gonini, Vittorio La Paglia, Piero Morgia, Franco Ceccarelli; **c**, Tonino Delli Colli; **m**, Carlo Rustichelli; **ed**, Nino Baragli; **art d**, Flavio Mogherini; **set d**, Massimo Tavazzi.

A Man Alone ★★★ 1955; U.S.; 95m; Rep; Color; Drama; Children: Unacceptable (MPAA: R); **VHS**. Milland, in his directorial debut, is a gunfighter, who hides out in the home of Bond, a sheriff, while he is pursued by a mob that wants to lynch him for two alleged murders and a stagecoach robbery. Bond is bed ridden with yellow fever, and Murphy, his daughter, helps Milland prove that the town banker, Burr, is the killer and robber. Bond had been in league with Burr, but then comes to Milland's defense. Milland and Murphy have fallen in love and when he is freed, he settles in the town. This superior western takes a different, more psychological approach in profiling the innocent and guilty parties as well as the mindsets of the vigilantes. **p**, Herbert J. Yates; **d**, Ray Milland; **cast**, Milland, Mary Murphy, Ward Bond, Raymond Burr, Arthur Space, Lee Van Cleef, Alan Hale, Jr., Douglas Spencer, Thomas B. Henry, Grandon Rhodes; **w**, John Tucker Battle (based on a story by Mort Briskin); **c**, Lionel Lindon; **m**, Victor Young; **ed**, Richard L. Van Enger; **art d**, Walter Keller; **set d**, Fay Babcock, John McCarthy, Jr.; **spec eff**, Howard Lydecker, Theodore Lydecker.

A Man and a Woman ★★★★ 1966; France; 102m; Les Films 13/AA; Color/B/W; Romance; Children: Unacceptable; **DVD**; **VHS**. Touching and sensitive, director Lelouch presents a simple but intensely visual romance between race car driver and widower Trintignant and Aimée, an actress and widow. They meet when visiting their children, Sire and Amidou, at a boarding house. When Aimée misses her train, Trintignant graciously offers to drive her to her home in nearby Paris and, en route, they share their backgrounds. They again meet the following weekend when visiting their children and they all go sailing and then enjoy a picnic. Trintignant confides to Aimee that his deceased wife lived with too much anxiety, fearing that he would be seriously injured or killed in one of his races and, after he did suffer an accident that injured him and where he nevertheless resolved to go on racing, his wife committed suicide. When Trintignant goes to Monaco to participate in another race, he receives a telegram from Aimée wherein she tells him that she loves him. Trintignant then drives all night to meet Aimee at the town where the boarding house is located, but when they meet and he attempts to make love to her, Aimée distances herself, her feelings for her dead husband preventing her from being with the man she now loves. Trintignant believes that their brief affair is over after Aimée gets on a Paris-bound train and Trintignant begins driving back to Monaco. He thinks about Aimée, not wanting to let her go, and drives to the station to meet her train. When Aimée alights, Trintignant races to her side, lifts her into his arms and swings her about in joy as the film ends. Beautifully crafted and superbly acted by Aimée and Trintignant, and the rest of the cast, this heart-touching love story became enormously popular and most likely produced more budding romances than any other film of the 1960s, its tale greatly aided by Lai's memorable score. *Author's Note*: Lelouch uses many arresting and effective techniques in employing his fluid camera, including the intercutting from scene to scene of color, tinting and black and white, as well as slow-motion, but never excessively, so that his directorial touches do not distract or hinder the story. Lelouch, like John Ford, Howard Hawks and others, is a director's director and his fine and subtle techniques are studied by filmmakers the world over. (In French; English subtitles.) **p&d**, Claude Lelouch; **cast**, Anouk Aimée, Jean-Louis Trintignant, Pierre Barouh, Valérie Lagrange, Antoine Sire, Souad Amidou, Henri Chemin, Yane Barry, Paul Le Person, Simone Paris; **w**, Lelouch, Pierre Uytterhoeven; **c**, Lelouch (Eastmancolor); **m**, Francis Lai, Pierre Barouch; **ed**, Lelouch, Claude Barrois; **prod d**, Robert Luchaire; **spec eff**, Jean Beylieu.

Fred Flintstone in *The Man Called Flintstone*, 1966.

The Man Between ★★★ 1953; U.K.; 100m; London Films/UA; B/W; Spy Drama; Children: Unacceptable; **DVD**. Bloom, a British woman, arrives in West Berlin during the Cold War to visit her doctor brother, Toone, and his wife, Neff, a German citizen. The women take a walk and Neff is followed by Krause, a boy on a bicycle that she seems to know, and, upon their return home, Neff gets a threatening phone call. The next day, Neff takes Bloom into East Berlin where they meet Mason, an attorney, who deals in black market items and also lures people wanted by the communists across the border into the divided city's Eastern sector. Bloom likes Mason without knowing his work, and invites him to dinner at her brother's house. Neff admits to Bloom that she had once been married to Mason, who was a good man until he fell under the influence of the Nazis. Neff thought Mason had died in the war so she remarried, but now that he has turned up alive she realizes she is a bigamist. Mason uses that to get Neff's help in luring Schroeder, a West Berlin man, into communist hands in East Berlin. Neff notifies the police of Mason's plan and a trap is set, but it is foiled when Krause warns Mason. East German police kidnap Bloom, thinking she is Neff. Mason comes to Bloom's rescue and they try to escape over the roofs of the city. Mason sees they are going to be captured and, during a wild chase, he jumps out of a car and is gunned down by East German police as the car with Bloom enters West Berlin and safety. A good espionage film that holds interest throughout, but its excessive violence prohibits viewing by children. **p&d**, Carol Reed; **cast**, James Mason, Claire Bloom, Hildegarde Neff, Geoffrey Toone, Aribert Waescher, Ernst Schroeder, Dieter Krause, Hilde Sessak; Karl John, Ljuba Welitsch; **w**, Harry Kurnitz, Eric Linklater (based on a story by Walter Ebert); **c**, Desmond Dickinson; **m**, John Addison; **ed**, A.S. Bates; **prod d& art d**, Andrej Andrejew.

The Man Called Flintstone ★★★ 1966; U.S.; 89m; COL; Color; Animated Comedy; Children: Acceptable; **DVD**; **VHS**. Based on the television series "The Flintstones" (1960-1966), we see the head of a stone-age family, Fred Flintstone (Reed voiceover), as a dead ringer for a good-guy master spy named Rock Slag (Frees voiceover). When Slag is injured on a case, the Stone Age Secret Service enlists Fred to take his place and keep a bad guy called Green Goose (Frees voiceover) from firing a destructive missile. Fred and his wife (Pyl voiceover) and their neighbor friends Barney (Blanc voiceover) and Betty (Johnson voiceover) go to Rome where Green Goose is operating. Fred and Barney are taken prisoners by Green Goose, but Slag recovers in time to save them. It's a fun time for kids. Other Flintstone movies include **The Jetsons Meet the Flintstones**, 1987, **The Flintstones**, 1994, and **The Flintstones in Viva Rock Vegas**, 2000. Songs: "Pensate Amore" (John McCarthy, Doug Goodwin, sung by Louis Prima); " Team Mates," "Spy

Paul Scofield in *A Man for All Seasons*, 1966.

Type Guy, "The Happy Sounds of Paree," "The Man Called Flintstone," "When I'm Grown Up," "Tickle Toddle" (McCarthy, Goodwin). **p&d,** William Hanna, Joseph Barbera; **cast** (voiceovers), Alan Reed, Mel Blanc, Jean Vander Pyl, Gerry Johnson, Don Messick, Janet Waldo, Paul Frees, Harvey Korman, John Stephenson, June Foray); **w,** Harvey Bulock, Ray Allen (based on their story and story material by Hanna, Barbera, Warren Foster, Alex Lovy); (Eastmancolor); **m,** Ted Nichols, Marty Paich; **ed,** Larry Cowan, Pat Foley, Dave Horton, Milton Krear; **art d,** Bill Perez; **spec eff,** Brooke Linden.

A Man Called Horse ★★★ 1970; U.S.; 114m; Cinema Center Films/National General Pictures; Color; Western; Children: Unacceptable (MPAA: R); **DVD;VHS.** In an intense performance Harris plays an English aristocrat adventuring into the American West in 1825. He is captured by Sioux Indians. As he lives with them he begins to understand and accept their lifestyles and becomes a warrior for the tribe in a harrowing ritual (a brutal test where he is strung up by hooks from the flesh of his chest). Eventually, he becomes the tribe's leader, saving it from destruction. Excessive violence and nudity prohibit viewing by children. Two sequels: **The Return of a Man Called Horse**, 1976, and **Triumphs of a Man Called Horse**, 1983. **p,** Sandy Howard; **d,** Elliot Silverstein; **cast,** Richard Harris, Judith Anderson, Jean Gascon, Manu Tupou, Corinna Tsopei, Dub Taylor, James Gammon, Eddie Little Sky, Michael Baseleon, Lina Marin, Tamara Garina, Iron Eyes Cody, Jackson Tail, Manuel Padilla, Jr.; **w,** Jack DeWitt (based on a story by Dorothy M. Johnson); **c,** Robert Hauser (Panavision; Technicolor); **m,** Leonard Rosenman; **ed,** Philip W. Anderson, Gene Fowler, Jr.; **art d,** Phil Barber; **set d,** Raul Serrano; **spec eff,** Federico Farfan, Jerome Rosenfeld, Tim Smyth.

A Man Called Peter ★★★ 1955; U.S.; 119m; FOX; Color; Biographical Drama; Children: Acceptable; **DVD; VHS.** In this often inspiring film, Todd does an outstanding job essaying Peter Marshall (1902-11949), who was chaplain of the U.S. Senate from 1947 until his untimely death from a heart attack two years later. The Scottish-born Todd is shown early in life when entering the Presbyterian ministry and struggling through his religious posts with loyal wife Peters at his side. His sermons are lively and modern, unlike the stodgy and hortatory lectures usually delivered by other clergy, and, because of this, he develops a loyal and ever increasing following. One of his most devoted parishioners is Tremayne, who is so inspired by Todd's sermons that he leads a crusade to rid his state of political corruption. Todd's reputation reaches the ears of Congress after he takes a post in a Washington, D.C., church and he is then appointed chaplain to the U.S. Senate where he delivers moving and telling sermons, until his premature death at age

forty-six of a heart attack. Peters also gives a remarkable performance as Todd's devoted wife, Catherine Sarah Wood Marshall [LeSourd], who went on to edit many of her husband's sermons that were published in book form; she wrote a popular biography of him that is the basis of this film (and later produce more than 220 religious books). **p,** Samuel G. Engel; **d,** Henry Koster; **cast,** Richard Todd, Jean Peters, Marjorie Rambeau, Jill Esmond, Les Tremayne, Robert Burton, Gladys Hurlbut, Richard Garrick, Gloria Gordon, Billy Chapin; **w,** Eleanore Griffin (based on the book by Catherine Marshall); **c,** Harold Lipstein (CinemaScope; DeLuxe Color); **m,** Alfred Newman; **ed,** Robert Simpson; **art d,** Lyle Wheeler, Maurice Ransford; **set d,** Walter M. Scott, Chester Bayhi.

Man Facing Southeast ★★★ 1987; Argentina; 105m; Cinequanon; FilmDallas Pictures; Color; Drama; Children: Unacceptable (MPAA: R); **DVD; VHS.** In this strange but compelling film, Soto is a gaunt, mysterious man who takes shelter in a psychiatric hospital and claims to be an alien. Quinteros, a doctor assigned to him, is divorced, misses his children (who are in the care of his ex-wife), and plays the saxophone to relax. He becomes fascinated watching Soto, who spends his afternoons in the hospital courtyard facing southeast, which Soto says is the best direction for him to receive alien transmissions. Soto claims to really be an alien, and who has arrived on Earth to learn why humans are so warlike, let people starve, and watch television game shows. Quinteros takes Soto to a concert, and the patient takes the baton away from the conductor and leads the orchestra in Ludwig van Beethoven's Ninth Symphony. Back at the hospital, inmates, who have fallen under Soto's influence, riot and charge the gates like zombies. The hospital director orders massive doses of tranquilizing drugs for Soto, and the alien deteriorates. Excessive violence and the strangeness of this film prohibit viewing by children. (In Spanish; English subtitles.) **p,** Lujan Pflaum; **d&w,** Eliseo Subiela; **cast,** Lorenzo Quinteros, Hugo Soto, Inés Vernengo, Cristina Scaramuzza, Tomas Voth, David Edery, Rúbens Correa, Rodolfo Rodas, Horacio Marassi, Jean Pierre Reguerraz; **c,** Ricardo DeAngelis; **m,** Pedro Aznar; **ed,** Luis César D'Angiolillo; **prod d,** Marta Albertinazzi; **art d,** Abel Facello.

A Man for All Seasons ★★★★★ 1966; U.K.; 120m; Highland Films/COL; Color; Biographical Drama; Children: Cautionary; **DVD; VHS.** Everything about this lavish biopic embodies quality, from the sterling performances of Scofield, Hiller, Shaw, McKern and Hurt, to the lively and incisive direction from pantheon helmsman Zinnemann and the brilliant script from Bolt. Scofield enacts with great restraint and mesmerizing presence the life of Sir Thomas More (1478-1535; Saint Thomas More from his canonization in 1935), who was once a close friend and adviser to England's Henry VIII (1491-1547), and who is portrayed with zest, gusto and no little connivance by the gifted Shaw. These two are the best of friends until Shaw appoints Scofield his Lord Chancellor, replacing the aging Welles, who plays Thomas Wolsey (1473-1530), the truculent Cardinal Archbishop of York, who takes issue with and falls from the favor of Shaw. Scofield, too, becomes a victim of Shaw's tyrannical policies when he refuses to acknowledge Shaw as head of the Anglican Church after Shaw breaks with the Vatican and the Roman Catholic Church when ignoring his marriage vows to Catherine of Aragon (1495-1536) and taking another wife, Anne Boleyn (1501-1536). Scofield, who has resolutely opposed the Lutheran Reformation, also refuses to sign a letter along with other English clergy and aristocrats, asking the Pope to annul Henry's marriage to Catherine, as well as avoiding the taking of an oath that recognizes Shaw as the head of the church in England, thus enraging Shaw, but he keeps his office for the time being. Meanwhile, through Shaw's urgings, McKern, playing Thomas Cromwell (1485-1540), sets traps for Scofield, and uses an ambitious perjurer, Richard Rich (1496-1567), played by Hurt, to have Scofield arrested and imprisoned on charges of treason. He is taken from his lavish estate and his loving wife, Hiller, and daughter, York, and treated like a common felon, surviving in a cramped and dank prison cell until brought to trial. At his trial, where McKern heads the panel of judges, Hurt appears and testifies against Scofield, making outlandish statements and falsely quoting Scofield to prove his treason. Although Scofield masterfully defends himself, the kangaroo court finds him guilty and sentences him to death. Tranquil and firm in his unwavering faith in the Catholic religion, Scofield goes quietly to the block and is beheaded. (The execution of this learned and inspiring man shocked the intellectual and religious world leaders of that day and all the more illustrated the ruthlessness and tyranny of Henry VIII.) Scofield, who had appeared on only four other feature films prior to making his superlative appearance in **A Man for All Seasons**, won the Oscar as Best Actor. The film also won Oscars for Best Picture, Best Director, Best Screenplay (from another medium), Best Color Cinematography and Best Color Costume Design. *Author's Note*: Although the Bolt play was a great hit in London and New York, it struggled for more than six years before it, thankfully, got to the screen. Director Zinnemann told this author that "a lot of studios believed that no one in the small or even big towns of America would want to see this picture about a man who rebels against a British king dead for centuries and gets his head chopped off. Columbia Studio took the plunge and we were all surprised to see that it became a commercial success, but the script and the wonderful performances from Paul [Scofield] and the rest brought that about. I think the story's telling of a man who defied authority fit well with the temper of the 1960s where there was great dissidence and rebellion against that political war in Vietnam and so audiences identified with the story of Thomas More." More's death was a gruesome one. After he was beheaded, his head was displayed on a pole at London Bridge, rotting there for some time until the friend of one of More's daughters climbed that pole and tossed the head to the daughter, who was waiting in a boat on the Thames River. She took it to More's grave where the head was united with the rest of the corpse. For more details on Thomas More, see my book, *"I Am Innocent!": A Comprehensive Encyclopedic History of the World's Wrongly Convicted Persons* (Da Capo Press, 2008; pages 297-299). **p&d**, Fred Zinnemann; **cast**, Paul Scofield, Wendy Hiller, Leo McKern, Robert Shaw, Orson Welles, Susannah York, Nigel Davenport, John Hurt, Corin Redgrave, Colin Blakely, Vanessa Redgrave, Yootha Joyce, Anthony Nichols, John Nettleton; **w**, Robert Bolt (based on his play); **c**, Ted Moore (Technicolor); **m**, Georges Delerue; **ed**, Ralph Kemplen; **prod d**, John Box; **art d**, Terence Marsh.

The Man from Blankley's ★★★ 1930; U.S.; 67m; WB; B/W; Comedy; Children: Unacceptable. Based on the 1903 British play, it was Barrymore's first full-length sound film and a major comedy of the early talkies. The theme involves the difference between British and American social classes in the early 1900s. Barrymore plays a muddle-headed British peer, who wanders drunkenly into the wrong house in which a middle-class couple, Henderson and Fitzroy, are hosting a dinner party in honor of their wealthy uncle, Gran, hoping he will give them financial aid so they can keep up appearances. They need one more guest so they order one from a professional service, Blankley's, and mistake Barrymore for that hired guest. Most of the guests are Americans and the dinner party becomes a bedlam until another guest, Young, recognizes Barrymore as a former lover. Barrymore is outstanding as the capricious interloper, and Young proves fetching in her exceptional performance. *Author's Note*: Young told this author that "I had appeared in twelve other feature films before I made that picture with John Barrymore and I was only eighteen, but full of confidence. Barrymore, who was called The Great Profile, was a handful, I must tell you. And I am talking about his hands as they were everywhere, clutching and grabbing at me when we were off the set. At first I found it amusing and even flattering, but when he kept it up, I told him: 'I want you to stop this boyish nonsense and behave yourself.' He smiled at me and said, 'That's impossible, dear. You're just too beautiful for your own good and mine.'" Mature themes prohibit viewing by children. **p&d**, Alfred E. Green; **cast**, John Barry-

Robert Shaw, Nigel Davenport, Susannah York, Paul Scofield and Wendy Hiller in *A Man for All Seasons*, 1966.

more, Loretta Young, William Austin, Albert Gran, Emily Fitzroy, Dick Henderson, Edgar Norton, Yorke Sherwood, Dale Fuller, Fanny Brice, D'Arcy Corrigan; **w**, Joseph Jackson, Harvey F. Thew (based on the play by F. Anstey); **c**, James Van Trees.

Man from Del Rio ★★★ 1956; U.S.; 82m; UA; B/W; Western; Children: Unacceptable; **DVD**. Quinn impresses as a Mexican gunfighter, who wins in a shootout with a town's sheriff and who was a former outlaw. Townspeople then invite him to replace him as sheriff. Quinn accepts but finds that the town's leading citizens still consider him a gunfighter. His love for a good woman, Jurado, keeps him in town, but Whitney, the owner of the local saloon, wants Quinn to join him in running the town corruptly. Quinn refuses and, after Quinn injures a hand in a brawl, Whitney takes advantage of the situation to challenge him in a shootout. Quinn is determined to go ahead with the shootout, so Whitney backs down and is kicked out of town. Quinn finally wins the respect he wanted and also the girl he loves. Violence prohibits viewing by children. **p**, Robert L. Jacks; **d**, Harry Horner; **cast**, Anthony Quinn, Katy Jurado, Peter Whitney, Douglas Fowley, John Larch, Whit Bissell, Douglas Spencer, Katherine DeMille, Jack Hogan, Guinn "Big Boy" Williams; **w**, Richard Carr; **c**, Stanley Cortez; **m**, Fred Steiner; **ed**, Robert Golden; **art d**, William Glasgow; **set d**, Mowbray Berkeley.

The Man from Laramie ★★★★ 1955; U.S.; 104m; COL; Color; Western: Children: Unacceptable; **DVD**; **VHS**. In this adult western that stands above most oaters, director Mann presents great action, but also provides a deep psychological perspective to the savagery that plagued the American West, where Stewart gives a great performance as a man trying to solve an old massacre. He is the boss of a wagon train delivering goods to a store in Coronado, New Mexico, operated by attractive unwed O'Donnell. He learns that she is engaged to affable Kennedy, the skilled and responsible foreman of a vast ranch owned by stubborn-headed Crisp, who competes with small rancher MacMahon, a lover of many years past. After delivering the goods, Stewart and his men head out with their empty wagons, stopping at some salt flats to take on loads of salt. They are interrupted by cowboys led by Nicol, the sadistic and mercurial son of Crisp, who tells Stewart that he has no right to take the salt from his land and, to prove it, burns his wagons and shoots his mules. When Stewart tries to interfere, he is roped and dragged through a fire, but the punishment is stopped when Kennedy, Crisp's foreman, arrives and orders Nicol and his men to return to the ranch. Kennedy apologizes to Stewart and rides off. Stewart pays off his men, but Ford, one of his drivers, tells him that he would like to work with him, believing Stewart has an ulterior motive for visiting the area. He does, wanting to know who has been selling repeating rifles and ammunition

James Stewart in *The Man from Laramie*, 1955.

to the Apaches, which, he believes, caused the massacre of a U.S. cavalry unit nearby and one which claimed the life of his own brother. Wallace volunteers to investigate by going to Apache territory (he is part Apache, his mother having been a member of the tribe) to see what he can learn. Meanwhile, Stewart goes to Coronado where he again meets Nicol and gets into a fight with him, besting him. Lady rancher MacMahon then prevents Nicol from shooting Stewart by training a rifle on him. Kennedy arrives and he and Stewart get into a battle that is stopped by Crisp, who later pays Stewart for the damages to his wagons and mules. Stewart then tries to get information from O'Donnell and is later attacked by town drifter Elam, who has been earlier tracking him. When Elam is still later found killed, Stewart is arrested and jailed on suspicion, but he is released to the custody of MacMahon on the condition that he go to work for her as her foreman. Stewart is rounding up some strays belonging to MacMahon when he is encountered by Nicol, who begins firing at him. The two take refuge behind some rocks while shooting at each other until Stewart shoots Nicol in the hand, disabling him. Nicol's men then arrive and subdue Stewart and the sadistic Nicol orders them to hold Stewart while he takes his revenge by firing a bullet into Stewart's hand. Again, Kennedy arrives and orders Nicol to leave the area while sending Stewart on his way. Stewart returns to MacMahon's ranch where MacMahon and the visiting O'Donnell treat his painful wound. By now Nicol, enraged at being wounded and seeking revenge against everyone, rides to a mountainous hideout where he has hidden a wagonload of guns (he is the one who has been selling repeating rifles to the Apaches) and he begins to send up smoke signals to summon the Apaches. Kennedy arrives and orders him to stop, telling Nicol that if he fully arms the Apaches widespread massacres will take place. When the berserk Nicol draws on him, Kennedy shoots and kills Nicol and then returns his body to the Crisp ranch where he allows everyone to believe that Stewart has killed Nicol. Following Nicol's burial, the grieving Crisp rides to the MacMahon ranch, intent on killing Stewart, but the old rancher has almost gone blind by now and when he shoots at Stewart he widely misses his mark. Stewart, realizing that Crisp has lost his ability to see, spares his life and returns him to his ranch. Kennedy, meanwhile, who has given his life to Crisp, learns that he will not inherit the vast ranch as Crisp has promised him as long as he has kept errant son Nicol in harness. Now that Nicol is dead and there is no future for him either at Crisp's ranch or in O'Donnell's heart, which she has now given to Stewart, Kennedy goes to the hiding place where the guns are kept and begins sending smoke signals to the Apaches and they respond with smoke signals from a distant mountain range. But before Kennedy can deliver the weapons to the Indians, Stewart, who has been tracking Kennedy, arrives and forces Kennedy to send the wagon load of weapons and ammunition over a cliff where the lethal cache is destroyed. He then orders Kennedy to ride out to meet his Apache friends (Kennedy, along with Nicol, has been selling the Apaches a few rifles at a time in the past), and when the Apaches discover that the weapons have been destroyed, they take their revenge by killing Kennedy. Stewart then returns to MacMahon's ranch to find that she is now nursing Crisp and that, after many years, they will be together while Stewart tells O'Donnell that he will come back for her after he reports to his post at Fort Laramie, Wyoming, where he is a U.S. Cavalry officer, and who has been intent on discovering the facts involving the earlier massacre that claimed the life of his brother, a mystery that he has finally solved. ***Author's Note***: Stewart told this author that Mann "is one of the best western directors in the business. He takes intelligent scripts and translates classic tales, even from Shakespeare, into fascinating stories about the Old West. **The Man from Laramie** is based on Shakespeare's King Lear, as anyone can see. Crisp is that king in the form of a powerful rancher, who is torn between his love for a rotten son [Nicol] and an orphaned boy he has adopted and who had been his loyal foreman [Kennedy], but whose iron fist domination has destroyed them all. You can see such classic tales in many of the films I have done with him [Mann]. I feel most comfortable in westerns and no one I know, except for maybe John Ford, makes westerns better than Anthony Mann." The Stewart-Mann collaboration, indeed, produced many classic westerns other than this production, including **Winchester '73**, 1950; **Bend of the River**, 1952; **The Naked Spur**, 1953; and **The Far Country**, 1955. The brilliant script for **The Man from Laramie** from Yordan also borrows the theme of an errant son rebelling against a dominating rancher father from another fine western, **Vengeance Valley**, 1951, where Robert Walker connives against his father, Ray Collins, who gives more trust to his foreman, Burt Lancaster, than to son Walker as does Crisp to Kennedy than to his spoiled son, Nicol in **The Man from Laramie**. Sons rebelling against dominating fathers in westerns can also be seen in such films as **The Oklahoma Kid**, 1939; **Red River**, 1948; **Winchester '73**, 1950, which also stars James Stewart, where Stephan McNally is a lethal brother who has murdered his own father; **The Lawless Breed**, 1953, where Rock Hudson, playing gunman John Wesley Hardin, rebels against his sermonizing father, John McIntyre; and **Hud**, 1963. **p**, William Goetz; **d**, Anthony Mann; **cast**, James Stewart, Arthur Kennedy, Donald Crisp, Cathy O'Donnell, Alex Nicol, Aline MacMahon, Wallace Ford, Jack Elam, John War Eagle, James Millican; **w**, Philip Yordan, Frank Burt (based on a *Saturday Evening Post* story by Thomas T. Flynn); **c**, Charles Lang (Technicolor); **m**, George Duning; **ed**, William Lyon; **art d**, Cary Odell; **set d**, James Crowe.

The Man from Snowy River ★★★ 1982; Australia; 102m; Cambridge Films/FOX; Color; Western; Children: Cautionary (MPAA: PG); **DVD**; **VHS**. This engrossing western has Burlinson as an eighteen-year-old who has lived all his life on his widowed father's farm in the mountains of Australia. After his father dies in an accident, Burlinson is forced to go down to the lowlands and seek work to earn enough to run the farm. He gets work as a wrangler on the ranch owned by Douglas, one of the wealthiest men in the area, but has to win the respect of the older wranglers. Burlinson falls in love with Douglas' beautiful daughter, Thornton, but knows it's hopeless because he is poor and, at best, he will become a struggling farmer. Douglas has a twin brother, who preferred the life of a wanderer and became Burlinson's father's best friend. A twenty-year-old feud between the brothers comes to a head when Burlinson is accused of letting a prize stallion loose to run with the brumbies (wild horses) in the highlands. Burlinson goes along on a ride with the others to find the stallion. After an exciting horse chase down a mountain, Burlinson finds the stallion and returns it to Douglas' ranch with the wild horses and is hailed a hero. The brothers resolve their feud which had been over a woman who Douglas eventually married. Burlinson continues working for Douglas and has won the respect of the other men, but doesn't quite get his daughter. That looks positive, but viewers must wait until the sequel, **Return to Snowy River**, 1988, which is almost as good and popular as the original and which was a huge hit in America as well as Australia. A terrific family film, but violence may disturb young children. **p**, Geoff Burrowes; **d**, George Miller; **cast**, Tom Burlinson, Kirk Douglas, Sigrid Thornton, Jack Thompson, Terence Donovan, Tommy Dysart, Bruce Kerr, June Jago, Chris Haywood, Kristopher Steele; **w**, John Dixon, Fred Cul Cullen (based on the poem by A.B. "Banjo" Paterson); **c**, Keith Wagstaff (Panavision; Eastmancolor); **m**, Bruce Rowland; **ed**, Adrian Carr; **art d**, Leslie Binns; **spec eff**, Conrad Rothmann.

The Man from the Alamo ★★★ 1953; U.S.; 79m; UNIV; Color; Western; Children: Cautionary; **DVD**; **VHS**. Ford gives another fine performance as a stalwart Texan, who is first seen inside the Alamo, which is under siege by overwhelming Mexican forces during the Texas war for independence in 1836. He and other defenders draw straws to decide which one of them will leave the crumbling fort to warn nearby families of the coming danger from the troops under Santa Ana. Ford escapes the Alamo, but finds that his wife has been killed by Mexican raiders, along with the families of others still fighting at the Alamo. When the Alamo falls, Ford is branded a coward for deserting the fortress and he remains silent, not defending himself or explaining that he purposely left the beleaguered bastion on an assignment. He more or less adopts a wayward Mexican boy who is his only supporter until attractive Adams comforts him over the loss of his wife. He is at odds with army captain O'Brian as he slowly learns that Jory and his band of renegades were responsible for the raids that killed his wife and the others. He is accepted into Jory's unsavory band because of his bad reputation, but eventually brings Jory and his killers to justice, winning Adams' hand at the finale. A gritty and realistic western, Ford represents the anti-hero in many respects, the kind of Old West protagonist director Boetticher was later to enlarge upon in his many films with Randolph Scott (1956-1960). *Author's Note*: Ford told this author that "working with Budd [Boetticher] was a pleasure. He knew what he wanted and wasted no time in his setups and his shots were all well staged and without any loose ends. He did not shoot a lot of close-ups, using them only when they meant something or to make an emphasis. When in production for that picture, I was reminded of a character I had played a few years earlier in **The Big Heat** [1953] where I was doing about the same thing, taking revenge for the murder of my wife, except that that film takes place in a modern big city where in **The Man from the Alamo**, the setting is the Old West." **p**, Aaron Rosenberg; **d**, Budd Boetticher; **cast**, Glenn Ford, Julia Adams, Chill Wills, Hugh O'Brian, Victor Jory, Neville Brand, Jeanne Cooper, Edward Norris, Guy Williams, Brett Halsey, Walter Reed, Dennis Weaver, Stuart Whitman; **w**, Steve Fisher, D.D. Beauchamp (based on a story by Niven Busch, Oliver Crawford); **c**, Russell Metty (Technicolor); **m**, Frank Skinner; **ed**, Virgil Vogel; **art d**, Alexander Golitzen, Emrich Nicholson; **set d**, Russell A. Gausman, Ruby R. Levitt.

Man Hunt ★★★★ 1941; U.S.; 105m; FOX; B/W; Spy Drama; Children: Unacceptable; **DVD**. Thick with menace and murky atmosphere, this exciting espionage tale from pantheon director Lang opens with Pidgeon as a big game hunter vacationing in Bavaria just after the Munich Pact of 1938. While moving through a mountainous area, Pidgeon comes upon Hitler's retreat outside Berchtesgaden and he uses the telescope on his rifle to view the place. When he sees Hitler strolling about on an open patio, he aims his rifle and squeezes the trigger, but fires no shot as there is no bullet in the chamber. He then loads a bullet into the rifle, perhaps thinking to rid the world of the tyrant, but German guards find and seize him, bringing him to Gestapo leader Sanders. When Pidgeon refuses to sign a confession that he was on a mission to assassinate Hitler, Sanders orders that he be tortured. Beaten senseless, he is tossed into a deep ravine and is believed to be dead. Pidgeon, however, survives and escapes, and when Sanders learns of this, he resolves to track down Pidgeon and kill him, much the same way Pidgeon has tracked

Glenn Ford in *The Man from the Alamo*, 1953.

his prey. Pidgeon manages to get to a rowboat and then boards a tramp Danish ship where he hides as a stowaway with the help of cabin boy MacDowall. Though the ship is thoroughly searched by Nazi agent Carradine and others, Pidgeon manages to reach England and leaves the ship. He has, however, lost his passport, which Carradine has found and who now assumes his identity. Pidgeon is trailed by Carradine and others, however, and, after meeting cockney streetwalker Bennett, takes refuge in her room. Pidgeon gratefully buys her an arrow-shaped hatpin, which she clips to her tam-o'-shanter. Pidgeon then attempts to escape Carradine in the London subway system where the two men struggle and a body is later found mangled and unrecognizable after it has been struck by a moving train. The body is identified as Pidgeon after his passport is found on the corpse, but the cadaver is that of Carradine. Pidgeon and Bennett, who have fallen in love, meet again, but only briefly, at London Bridge; he tells her that he is going away but will come back for her, and asks that she keep information about him a secret while he works to identify Sanders and others who are operating in England. When a policeman approaches them, Bennett pretends to be plying her old trade of a prostitute and is hustled away from Pidgeon by the bobby. When Bennett returns to her flat, she finds Sanders and other Nazi goons waiting for her and, when she refuses to give them information about Pidgeon, she is murdered. Pidgeon then goes to a rural area and hides in a cave, but Sanders tracks him down and, while standing outside the cave, produces evidence that he has killed Bennett by pushing the hat ornament Pidgeon has given to Bennett through a crevice in the cave to Pidgeon. Sanders has sealed the cave and tells Pidgeon that he will be released if he finally signs that confession that he intended to assassinate Adolf Hitler. Pidgeon agrees and Sanders removes the stone blocking the entrance to the cave. Pidgeon, however, stalls for time, fashioning a makeshift bow and then shoots the ornamental arrow through the crevice that fatally strikes the arrogant Sanders in the throat, killing him. Pidgeon, now free, joins British forces and is later seen parachuting back into Germany carrying a high-powered rifle with his only assignment being to now complete what he earlier only practiced, the assassination of Hitler. Grim and gritty, Lang does a wonderful job with a limited budget in producing this intriguing spy drama and where Pidgeon and Bennett are standouts. *Author's Note*: The great John Ford was asked to direct this tale, written by stellar scriptwriter Nichols, a longtime Ford associate, but Ford did not like the story and declined. Fox boss Zanuck then assigned the task to Lang, giving him a budget so limited that Lang paid for the set used for the London Bridge out of his own pocket. As was his directorial penchant, Lang shot many scenes with Pidgeon in confining spaces to produce a consistent claustrophobic appearance that greatly adds to the film's tension. Sanders told this author: "Only a few years earlier, I played a Ger-

Johnnie Russell, Joan Bennett and Francis Lederer in *The Man I Married*, 1940.

man agent in **Confessions of a Nazi Spy** [1939], and I am afraid that I played that role so convincingly, that I was typecast. So here I was again shaving my head and being as dishonorably devastating all over again in **Man Hunt** as another Nazi thug. I am desperate to track down and murder poor Walter [Pidgeon] after being embarrassed and ridiculed when he earlier escapes from my evil clutches. The director of that film, Lang, was a brilliant filmmaker, but he was a tough old bird, very demanding, even ruthless in getting what he wanted from the cast and crew. At one point, I thought he should have been playing my part in that picture." **p**, Kenneth Macgowan; **d**, Fritz Lang; **cast**, Walter Pidgeon, Joan Bennett, George Sanders, John Carradine, Roddy McDowall, Ludwig Stossell, Heather Thatcher, Lester Matthews, Bruce Lester, Kurt Kreuger; **w**, Dudley Nichols, Lamar Trotti (based on the novel *Rogue Male* by Geoffrey Household); **c**, Arthur Miller; **m**, Alfred Newman, David Buttolph; **ed**, Allen McNeil; **art d**, Richard Day, Wiard B. Ihnen; **set d**, Thomas Little.

The Man I Love ★★★ 1947; U.S.; 96m; WB-Seven Arts; B/W; Musical/Drama; Children: Cautionary; **DVD**; **VHS**. Lupino captivates in this offbeat musical drama. She gets a job as a torch singer in a night club in Long Beach, California, owned by Alda, who is a tough guy with mob ties. She snubs him in favor of piano player Bennett, who has not quite gotten over an old divorce. He decides to resist Lupino's charms and sign on with a merchant steamer, leaving her to sing more sad songs. Songs: "The Man I Love" (George Gershwin, Ira Gershwin); "Bill," "Why Was I Born?" (Jerome Kern, Oscar Hammerstein II); "If I Could Be with You" (James P. Johnson, Henry Creamer); "Liza" (George Gershwin); "Body and Soul" (Johnny Green); "Silent Night, Holy Night" (Franz Gruber, Joseph Mohr); "Gotta Be This or That" (Sunny Skylar); "Please Don't Talk About Me When I'm Gone" (Sam H. Stept); "How Many Hearts Have You Broken (With Those Great Big Beautiful Eyes" (Al Kaufman); "But I Did" (Joseph Meyer); "Can't We Be Friends" (Kay Swift). **p**, Arnold Albert; **d**, Raoul Walsh; **cast**, Ida Lupino, Robert Alda, Andrea King, Martha Vickers, Bruce Bennett, Alan Hale, Dolores Moran, John Ridgely, Don McGuire, Warren Douglas, Craig Stevens, Jimmie Dodd, Florence Bates, Monte Blue; **w**, Catherine Turney, Jo Pagano (based on the novel *Night Shift* by Maritta M. Wolff); **c**, Sid Hickox; **m**, Max Steiner; **ed**, Owen Marks; **art d**, Stanley Fleischer; **set d**, Eddie Edwards; **spec eff**, Edwin Du Par, Harry Barndollar.

The Man I Married ★★★ 1940; U.S.; 77m; FOX; B/W; Drama; Children: Unacceptable; **DVD**; **VHS**. This well-made anti-Nazi story sees Bennett and her German-American husband, Lederer, visit Germany with their young son in 1938. Lederer becomes brainwashed and joins the Nazi party, then falls in love with Sten, also a Nazi, and demands a divorce from Bennett. When he insists on retaining custody of the boy, she allies herself with Lederer's father, Kruger. Lederer is told that his mother was Jewish and it would be safer for Bennett and the boy if he allow them to return to America, to which Lederer agrees and they escape the clutches of the Nazis at the last minute. **p**, Raymond Griffith; **d**, Irving Pichel; **cast**, Joan Bennett, Francis Lederer, Lloyd Nolan, Anna Sten, Otto Kruger, Maria Ouspenskaya, Ludwig Stössell, Johnny Russell, Lionel Royce, Frederick Vogeding, Ernst Deutsch; **w**, Oliver H.P. Garrett (based on the short story by Oscar Schisgall); **c**, J. Peverell Marley; **m**, David Buttolph; **ed**, Robert L. Simpson; **art d**, Richard Day, Hans Peters; **set d**, Thomas Little.

The Man in Grey ★★★ 1943; U.K.; 93m; Gainsborough; Gaumont; UNIV; B/W; Drama; Children: Unacceptable; **DVD**; **VHS**. Two strangers, Calvert and Granger (she a member of the British women's military service the WRENS, and he an RAF pilot), meet at an estate auction in England during World War II and exchange information about their family histories and possible connections. In a flashback to the 1800s, the story unfolds scenes about their distant relatives. Calvert's ancestor married a cruel womanizing marquis (Mason as the Man in Grey) and she becomes a victim of an actress friend, Lockwood, who hastens her death when she falls ill. Enraged, Granger's ancestor kills Lockwood. This involved but intriguing tale ends in flash forward to 1943 where Calvert and Granger, whose ancestors were unable to find happiness together, fall in love. An engrossing story but too sensual for children. *Author's Note*: This was the first film in which Granger (real name James Stewart) appears in a featured part (he had appeared in several previous films in minor roles), and it was one that quickly identified him to audiences as a dashing leading man. **p**, Edward Black; **d**, Leslie Arliss; **cast**, Margaret Lockwood, Phyllis Calvert, James Mason, Stewart Granger, Harry Scott, Martita Hunt, Helen Haye, Nora Swinburne, Beatrice Varley, Raymond Lovell; **w**, Arliss, Margaret Kennedy (based on an adaptation by Doreen Montgomery of the novel by Lady Eleanor Smith); **c**, Arthur Crabtree; **m**, Cedric Mallabey; **ed**, R.E. Dearing; **art d**, Walter W. Murton.

The Man in Half-Moon Street ★★★ 1945; U.S.; 92m; PAR; B/W; Horror/Romance; Children: Unacceptable; **DVD**. A big notch above most B fright films, this production blends horror and unconditional love. Set in England, Asther, a handsome artist and scientist, falls in love with Walker, his beautiful young model, after painting her portrait, but doesn't tell her that he is eighty years old and staying young looking by unnatural scientific methods, receiving gland implants every decade. He achieves his eternal youth with the help of Schünzel, who accuses him of disregarding their original humanitarian uses of the operations in favor of killing people for their glands. The murder of a medical student prompts Scotland Yard to investigate. Walker learns of Asther's personal fountain of youth, but is so in love with him that she shares his madness. It all ends with Asther suddenly withering to his actual age as an old man and dying. A fascinating tale well told and acted, especially by the underrated Asther. This film was remade as **The Man Who Could Cheat Death**, 1959, an inferior production. Not for children because of mature subject matter. **p**, Walter MacEwen; **d**, Ralph Murphy; **cast**, Nils Asther, Helen Walker, Reinhold Schünzel, Paul Cavanagh, Edmund Breon, Matthew Boulton, Brandon Hurst, Morton Lowry, Forrester Harvey, Ernie Adams; **w**, Charles Kenyon, Garrett Fort (based on the play by Barré Lyndon); **c**, Henry Sharp; **m**, Miklos Rozsa; **ed**, Tom Neff; **art d**, Hans Dreier, Walter Tyler; **set d**, Sam Comer.

A Man in Love ★★★ 1987; France/Italy; 125m; Alexandre Films; Cinecom Pictures; Color; Drama/Romance; Children: Unacceptable (MPAA: R). Coyote is a married American movie star who becomes attracted to his younger leading lady, Scacchi, while filming a new movie in Italy. Scacchi is single, and her American father, Berry, is an alcoholic, and her Italian mother, Cardinale, is dying of cancer. When Berry comes to the set drunk, Scacchi walks off in anger, and Coyote follows her, which develops into more of a sexual relationship than love. Coyote's American wife, Curtis, flies to Italy to be with her husband, and discovers Coyote's passionate affair with Scacchi. Coyote wants it all, his wife, his lover, the devotion of his best friend, Riegert, but ultimately, he mainly loves himself. Nothing much changes for Coyote and Curtis who will keep trying to make a go of their marriage, and his friend Riegert will stand by him, but only Scacchi gains from the romance by maturing and deciding to become a writer, starting a novel about it all entitled "A Man in Love." Nudity and graphic sexual scenes prohibit viewing by children. (In French; English subtitles.) **p**, Diane Kurys, Michel Seydoux; **d**, Kurys; **cast**, Peter Coyote, Greta Scacchi, Jamie Lee Curtis, Claudia Cardinale, Peter Riegert, John Berry, Vincent Lindon, Jean Pigozzi, Elia Katz, Constantin Alexandrov; **w**, Kurys, Olivier Schatzky; **c**, Bernard Zitzermann; **m**, Georges Delerue; **ed**, Joéle Van Effenterre; **art d**, Dean Tavoularis.

Man in the Attic ★★★ 1953; U.S.; 82m; FOX; B/W; Horror; Children: Unacceptable; **DVD**; **VHS**. In this solid remake of the classic **The Lodger**, 1944, Palance gives an intense and captivating performance as an unbalanced pathologist who rents a room in a London boarding house in 1888 when the city is beset by the Jack the Ripper slayings. He becomes obsessed with the beautiful Smith, the daughter of the boarding house owners, but she spurns his advances. As more of the Ripper's victims mount, Smith realizes her life is in danger and seeks the aid of Palmer, a Scotland Yard inspector. When Palance finally decides to end Smith's life, he is foiled by the clever Palmer, and it is Palance's life that is ended. Director Fregonese does a good job in presenting this eerie and frightening tale with a fast-clipped story, atmospheric sets and some inventive shots that sustain suspense. *Author's Note*: For more details on the Jack the Ripper murders, see my two-volume work, *The Great Pictorial History of World Crime*, Volume II (History, Inc., pages 1180-1203). **p**, Robert L. Jacks; **d**, Hugo Fregonese; **cast**, Jack Palance, Constance Smith, Byron Palmer, Frances Bavier, Rhys Williams, Sean McClory, Leslie Bradley, Tita Phillips, Lester Mathews, Harry Cording, Isabel Jewell; **w**, Barre Lyndon, Robert Presnell, Jr. (based on the novel *The Lodger* by Marie Belloc Lowndes); **c**, Leo Tover; **m**, Hugo Friedhofer; **ed**, Marjorie Fowler; **art d**, Lyle Wheeler, Leland Fuller; **set d**, Eli Benneche.

The Man in the Glass Booth ★★★ 1975; U.S.; 117m; The American Film Theater; Color; Biographical Drama; Children: Unacceptable; **DVD**; **VHS**. Schell gives a bravura performance in this *roman á clef* portrait of Adolf Eichmann (Otto Adolf Eichmann; 1906-1962), the Nazi officer who greatly helped to organize the mass extermination of Jews during the Holocaust of WWII. Schell is captured while living in New York and posing as a retired Jewish businessman and then taken to Israel where he is placed on trial, confined in a glass booth (as was Eichmann, who was captured in South America) with Adler as the presiding judge. He is accused of being a German officer during Hitler's regime and how he organized the rounding up and shipping of countless Jews to concentration camps where they were put to death (more than six million such victims were estimated). Schell adroitly and cleverly denies everything, and there is considerable doubt as to his guilt until he is trapped by his own lies by prosecutor Nettleton and receives his deserved death sentence. Director Hiller faithfully follows the successful play upon which the film is based and uses no flashbacks to show the grim concentration camps and mass extermination of the Jews, but holds to a contemporary view where witnesses provide enough shock and sensation in their testimony to hold obsessive interest throughout. *Author's Note*: For more details on Otto Adolf Eichmann, see my eight-volume work, *Encyclopedia of World Crime*, Volume II (CrimeBooks, Inc.; pages 1076-1077). **p**, Ely A. Landau; **d**, Arthur Hiller; **cast**, Maximilian Schell, Lois Nettleton, Lawrence Pressman, Luther Adler, Lloyd Bochner, Robert H.

Peter Coyote and Greta Scacchi in *A Man in Love*, 1987.

Harris, Henry Brown, Norbert Schiller, Berry Kroeger, Leonardo Cimino; **w**, Edward Anhalt (based on the play by Robert Shaw); **c**, Sam Leavitt (Eastmancolor); **ed**, David Bretherton; **prod d**, Joel Schiller; **set d**, Lenny Mazzola.

The Man in the Gray Flannel Suit ★★★★ 1956; U.S.; 153m; FOX; Color; Drama; Children: Cautionary; **DVD**; **VHS**. Peck is superb as a struggling middle-class American businessman in this gripping social drama. He is married to beautiful Jones, has three adorable children, a house with $10,000 mortgage, and uncertain opportunities in facing the future. Moreover, he is haunted by his WWII experiences, one of which involves an extra marital affair that nags his conscience. Peck commutes from his bedroom community in Westport, Connecticut, to NYC by train every day, and while riding toward the Big Apple one morning, he sees a man sitting in front of him and wearing a coat with a fur collar. This stirs a memory of WWII, which is shown in flashback and where Peck and another freezing American officer are evading Germans during a winter battle. Peck sneaks up on a German sentry wearing a warm coat with a fur collar and kills him, stripping him of that coat, but is shocked to see that the sentry he has killed is a youth in his late teens. In other flashbacks, Peck is seen fighting in the Pacific, where he throws a grenade against an enemy position that accidentally kills his best friend and then will not accept the fact that his friend is dead. Still later, in another flashback, Peck is seen with Pavan, a young Italian woman, with whom he has a brief and intense affair, even though he is married to Jones at the time, believing that he will not survive the war (or that is his rationalization that allows him to conduct this illicit affair, a viewpoint shared by many another GI). When returning to the U.S., he resumes his married life with Jones, who is not the most endearing of wives as she is slightly neurotic and demanding, repeatedly urging Peck to better himself for the sake of their three children and improve their lifestyle. To that end, after Peck learns from fellow commuter Lockhart that there is well-paying job for a speech writer at UBC, a large corporation, he applies for that job. He is interviewed by public relations executives O'Connell and Daniell, two rather snooty types with decidedly superior airs. Both of these cynical and rather insidious creatures, who revel in their positions of authority, discourage Peck, offering no promises, but later offer Peck the job of writing speeches for the firm's aggressive and world-beating president, March. Peck and March hit it off well after March impresses Peck as a decent and brilliant corporate leader. March, however, has become a tycoon at the expense of his own family, losing the love of his wife, Harding, and his spoiled daughter, Perreau. Although he has great wealth, March takes pride in the fact that he has kept his nose to the grindstone and now wants to perform humane acts to benefit mankind and that is the gist of what March wants Peck

Gregory Peck and Marisa Pavan in *The Man in the Gray Flannel Suit*, **1956.**

to convey in the speeches he prepares for him. Meanwhile, with his new salary, Peck opts not to buy a new house, but move his family into his ancestral mansion in Westport where he and Jones presently reside, but he is met with opposition by Sweeney, a mean-minded, conniving old caretaker of the mansion, who has taken care of Peck's mother up to the moment of her death and now claims that the feeble-minded woman left the mansion to him. Peck seeks arbitration through a wise and kind-hearted judge, Cobb, who mediates the two claims, and, after Cobb confronts the conniving Sweeney with his obviously forged inheritance documents, the old man threatens to go to court and departs, but Cobb assures Peck and Jones that the family mansion will remain theirs. When Peck later enters an elevator in his office building he is greeted by Wynn, his old sergeant from WWII days, who asks him to meet him after working hours. When they meet, Wynn explains that he and his wife have remained in touch with Pavan in Italy and that, unknown to Peck, Pavan bore his son after he was assigned to another theater of the war and that Wynn, who is a distant relative of Pavan's (Peck was introduced to Pavan by Wynn) has been sending Pavan a little money now and then to support her and the boy. He then asks Peck if he will also donate to the boy's support. This jars Peck and he thinks long and hard about the consequences of his former love affair with Pavan. Meanwhile, Peck works long hours in preparing an important speech for March where he plans to announce the beneficial funding for some needy projects, but that speech is tampered with by the meddling and talentless Daniell and Peck points this out to March, saying that what Daniell has written will make March appear to be insincere and boisterous. This puts Peck's job in peril, but March accepts Peck's wise decisions and keeps what Peck has written. He then asks Peck to accompany him on a business trip to make that speech, but Peck tells him that he is a "nine-to-five" worker, who dutifully goes home to his family when his work is over for the day. March respects him for this, but points out that it takes men like him, who have worked the extra hours of their lives that become the leaders of American businesses and that it is a thankless, lonely way of life, but "someone has to do it." March, who looks upon Peck as the replacement of his own son, who had been killed in the war, nevertheless keeps him on, his own loneliness emphasized when he cannot alter the course of his reckless daughter. Despite Harding's pleadings (she is divorced from March) that March try to talk Perreau out of a marriage with an older man, a fortune-hunter, March fails to convince his daughter to change her mind. She arrogantly walks out on him, leaving March with a sense of failure he has never experienced in his business dealings and he is shown contemplating his losses in life while dining alone in his lavish penthouse. Peck by now has come to grips with his obligation to Pavan and her illegitimate son. He goes to Jones and explains how he met Pavan during the war and had a brief affair with her and that he

has now learned that she has a child by him and he wants to help her, but only if Jones agrees. This news so traumatizes Jones that she explodes and then runs hysterically from their house. Peck later finds her and takes her home. They later appear in the offices of Cobb, the jurist who handled the claim against their house, where Peck explains what happened with Pavan during the war and how he and his wife now want to send monthly payments to Pavan through Cobb and how they will later arrange to make larger payments for the upkeep and education of the boy. Cobb gladly agrees to undertake this chore and tells Jones that it is a great pleasure to meet her, implying that he knows she must be a rare wife in that she has nobly accepted her husband's transgressions and is nevertheless willing to help him support a child that is not her own. When Peck and Jones leave, Cobb watches them from his office window and then states: "This is a day, I am sure, that inspired the poet to say that God is in His Heaven and all is right with the world." Once Peck is inside the family car with Jones and about to drive home, he turns to her and tells her that he adores her and they kiss for the finale. Johnson's sensitive direction shows in every carefully crafted scene from his own brilliant script, and the performances from Peck, Jones, March, Cobb and all the rest of the fine players (particularly the empathetic Wynn and the detestable Sweeney) who give standout support and where Herrmann's dynamic score is appropriately emphatic to each applicable scene. This intelligent and poignant film presents (as did Wilson's fine novel) a memorable microcosm of the generation of Americans who fought in WWII, dubbed by some to be "the greatest generation" of the 20th Century in that it saved the world from tyranny and preserved freedom at great sacrifice (418,000 combat deaths). It incisively profiles through the perspectives of one man the kind of basic decency in post-WWII America by the responsible survivors of that generation that so assiduously built America into the world's foremost super power while resolutely and with considerable personal honor secured a comfortable future for their families. ***Author's Note***: To better grasp the kind of character he was playing, Peck, as he told this author "went to New York City and moved about the advertising and public relations world. I put on a gray flannel suit, then the emblem of such executives, and talked with many of those executives, getting a good feel for the kind of work they did, or did not do, and all of their subtle in-fighting. It is kind of a sneaky world where image is everything and substance really doesn't count for much, but Freddie [March] is a contradiction to that in **The Man in the Gray Flannel Suit** because he is a man who really wants to make a substantial contribution to society in exchange for the riches it has brought him. Freddie is just wonderful in that film and trying to match him word for word in any scene together is next to impossible." Peck recalled his association with director-writer Johnson as a fond one, stating that Johnson "was a director who loved the written word and knew how to convey it to the screen. I worked with him as a writer on many films, and he wrote the screenplay for my first big film, **The Keys to the Kingdom** [1944], and worked on the script for one of my favorite westerns, **The Gunfighter** [1950]. He had directed another film, **Night People** [1954], where I am an army officer outwitting the Russians in Germany after the war, and that was also a pleasant experience, so I really looked forward to doing **The Man in the Gray Flannel Suit** with him. That, too, was a very rewarding experience. Nunnally Johnson was not only a terrific writer and director. He was a great human being." Peck was, however, concerned with acting opposite the raven-haired and exquisitely beautiful Jones. They had played together in **Duel in the Sun**, 1946, but that had been a daunting chore for Peck in that Jones "overwhelmed" him with her torrid portrayal of a tempestuous half-caste and where he vowed never to act with her again. He found, however, in this film, that Jones portrayed the betrayed housewife with much more restraint. Her appearance in this film nevertheless added many woes to director-writer Johnson in that her husband, the powerful Hollywood tycoon, David O. Selznick, according to Johnson's statements to this author "literally bombarded me with memos on how to shoot my scenes with her. He sent memos on how to have her hair styled, how her makeup should be applied, what kind of dresses she should wear. He drove me crazy to the point where I had to go to Zanuck [head of Fox] and complain about it. Well, nobody told Darryl F. Zanuck what to do at his own studio and he sent a message to Selznick that read: 'Listen, you (blankety-blank)! Keep your fingers out of my film!' He got the only response he wanted from Selznick after that. Silence." **p**, Darryl F. Zanuck; **d&w**, Nunnally Johnson (based on the novel by Sloan Wilson); **cast**, Gregory Peck, Jennifer Jones, Fredric March, Marisa Pavan, Lee J. Cobb, Ann Harding, Keenan Wynn, Gene Lockhart, Gigi Perreau, Portland Mason, Arthur O'Connell, Henry Daniell, Mickey Maga, Connie Gilchrist, Joseph Sweeney, Kenneth Tobey, Sandy Descher; **c**, Charles G. Clarke (CinemaScope; DeLuxe Color); **m**, Bernard Herrmann; **ed**, Dorothy Spencer; **art d**, Lyle Wheeler, Jack Martin Smith; **set d**, Walter M. Scott, Stuart A. Reiss; **spec eff**, Ray Kellogg.

The Man in the Iron Mask ★★★ 1939; U.S.; 110m; Edward Small/UA; B/W; Adventure; Children: Cautionary; **DVD**; **VHS**. The swashbuckling Hayward is exceptional in this version of the Dumas classic, where twin brothers (played by Hayward in dual roles) compete for the throne of France. Through the machinations of a powerful cabal, including the insidious Schildkraut, the rightful heir to the throne is imprisoned and forced to wear a hideous iron mask to prevent anyone recognizing him as Louis XIV (1638-1715), the true king of France. His evil-minded, power-mad brother impersonates his twin to keep the royal power while sadistically abusing his queen, Bennett, playing Maria Theresa (1638-1683). William, who plays the heroic D'Artagnan of Three Musketeers fame, reunites with Hale (Porthos), Mander (Aramis), and Roach (Athos), to come to the rescue of the true king, releasing him from his prison cell and switching him with the imposter, who is then compelled to wear the iron mask until his obscure death. Director Whale does a fine job in presenting this exciting fictionalized account of the Sun King, packing it with action, where Hayward and Bennett are standouts as the royal lovers, first estranged when the imposter abuses his beautiful wife, and then as a loving couple when the true and kindhearted king regains his throne. *Author's Note*: James Whale (1889-1957) is best known for his classic horror films, **Frankenstein**, 1931; **The Invisible Man**, 1933; and **The Bride of Frankenstein**, 1935, and was the reigning director at Universal in the early 1930s, but he disliked being exclusively associated with horror films. Following the making of **The Man in the Iron Mask**, Whale's career went into decline, and the wealthy director retreated to his comfortable California home where he held all-male pool parties. He had always been openly gay, an unusual posture in the early years of the film industry since homosexuals invariably hid their sexual habits in that era, but Whale earned a notorious reputation by the late 1920s as a predatory homosexual and was dubbed "The Queen of Hollywood." Although he never swam in his pool as he was deathly afraid of water, he committed suicide by drowning himself in that very pool, leaving a note reading: "The future is just old age, illness and pain..." Hayward was later described as both heterosexual and homosexual; he was described in Noel Coward's diaries as being one of the playwright's lovers. It is not known if there was any sexual relationship between Hayward and Whale. **p**, Edward Small; **d**, James Whale; **cast**, Louis Hayward, Joan Bennett, Warren William, Joseph Schildkraut, Alan Hale, Walter Kingsford, Miles Mander, Bert Roach, Marian Martin, Montagu Love, Doris Kenyon, Albert Dekker, Peter Cushing, Dwight Frye, St. Brenden Choir; **w**, George Bruce (based on the novel by Alexandre Dumas); **c**, Robert Planck; **m**, Lucien Moraweck; **ed**, Grant Whytock; **art d**, John DuCasse Schulze; **spec eff**, Howard Anderson.

The Man in the Iron Mask ★★★ 1998; U.S./France; 132m; UA/MGM; Color; Adventure; Children: Unacceptable (MPAA: R); **BD**; **DVD**. An all-star cast performs a lively remake of the Dumas classic. Paris is starving, but King Louis XIV (DiCaprio) is living a life of luxury while womanizing. The Three Musketeers – Aramis (Irons), Athos

Louis Hayward, Howard Brooks, Joan Bennett, and Montagu Love in *The Man in the Iron Mask*, 1939.

(Malkovich), and Porthos (Depardieu) plan to replace the despot with a twin (DiCaprio), who was hidden away at birth and as an adult was imprisoned behind an iron mask to hide his identity. The musketeers enlist their friend D'Artagnan (Byrne) to accomplish the dangerous mission and free the twin so he can replace the king. They succeed in their perilous mission, but it costs them dearly. Wallace directs this action-filled adventure tale with a firm hand, and DiCaprio shines in his dual roles. The story was filmed in 1939, with Louis Hayward in the leading role, and was presented in two made-for-TV productions in 1977 and 1985, and a second version in 1998. A TV series based on this story was produced in 1968. Violence, some sexuality and nudity prohibit viewing by children. **p**, Randall Wallace, Russell Smith, René Dupont, Paul Hitchcock, Alan Ladd, Jr.; **d&w**, Wallace (based on the novel by Alexandre Dumas); **cast**, Leonardo DiCaprio, Jeremy Irons, John Malkovich, Gérard Depardieu, Gabriel Byrne, Anne Parillaud, Judith Godreche, Edward Atterton, Peter Sarsgaard, Hugh Laurie; **c**, Peter Suschitzky; **m**, Nick Glennie-Smith; **ed**, William Hoy; **prod d**, Anthony Pratt; **art d**, François de Lamothe, Albert Rajau; **set d**, Philippe Turlure; **spec eff**, George Gibbs, Michael J. Morreale, Rob Hodgson, Dario De Gregorio.

The Man in the Middle ★★★ 1964; U.K./U.S.; 94m; Pennebaker Productions/FOX; B/W; Drama; Children: Unacceptable; **DVD**. Wynn is a U.S. Army lieutenant stationed in India during World War II and who walks across a military compound into a barracks where he cold-bloodedly shoots and kills Mitchell, a British staff sergeant. Wynn confesses to the killing, and there are about a dozen witnesses to the strange slaying. Sullivan, an American general, assigns a legal officer, Mitchum, to defend Wynn, and he takes the case when told the defendant is sane and fit for trial. Mitchum then learns from an American army nurse, Nuyen, that Knox, the head of an army Lunacy Commission, discounted psychiatric evidence prepared by a hospital doctor, Wanamaker, who examined Wynn and concluded he was a psychopath unfit for trial. Knox wants a quick guilty verdict so Wynn can be hanged for murder because of ongoing tensions between British and American troops. Mitchum wants Wanamaker to testify at the trial, but Knox squelches this by sending the doctor to a distant posting and Mitchum more or less tells Knox that he is as mentally sick as Wynn. Mitchum then learns the motive for the killing: Wynn was a racial bigot, who shot Mitchell because the sergeant was dating a dark-skinned woman. Now Mitchum hates his client, but has to defend him, so he is a man caught in the middle. Mitchum's legal obligation to Wynn, despite the fact that he detests his client, is aided when Wynn breaks down during the trial and is sent to a hospital instead of being hanged. Intense performances from Mitchum and Wynn sustain attention throughout, although this film is not for children because of its violence. **p**, Walter Seltzer; **d**, Guy Hamilton; **cast**, Robert

Reese Witherspoon and Jason London in *The Man in the Moon*, 1991.

Mitchum, France Nuyen, Barry Sullivan, Trevor Howard, Keenan Wynn, Sam Wanamaker, Alexander Knox, Gary Cookrell, Robert Nichols, Edward Underdown; **w**, Keith Waterhouse, Willis Hall (based on the novel *The Winston Affair* by Howard Fast); **c**, Wilkie Cooper; **m**, John Barry; **ed**, John Bloom; **art d**, John Howell.

Man in the Moon ★★★ 1961; U.K. 98m; Excalibur Films/Trans Lux; B/W; Comedy; Children: Acceptable. More is delightful as a human guinea pig, a professional job he holds with the Common Cold Research Center, but his immunity to such diseases is so formidable that he is unable to catch a cold and is fired. He next gets a job at the National Atomic Research Center, where he is, by virtue of his physical fitness, selected to be the first candidate sent to the moon. More is put through a series of impossible physical tests, including immersion in water tanks, and is deemed the perfect specimen to go to the moon. The prize going to More for his hazardous mission is $280,000, and it looks like it will be some time before he gets to spend that cash as he may be stranded on the moon for some time after landing there. He does not have to deal with that problem, after all, when, after blasting off, his spacecraft simply returns to earth. A very funny outing with a good supporting cast, this film predates by eight years the actual manned moon landings by Neil Armstrong and Buzz Aldrin in Apollo 11 on July 20, 1969. **p**, Michael Relph; **d**, Basil Dearden; **cast**, Kenneth More, Shirley Anne Field, Michael Hordern, Charles Gray, John Glyn-Jones, John Phillips, Norman Bird, Noel Purcell, Bernard Horsfall, Newton Blick; **w**, Dearden, Relph, Bryan Forbes (based on the novel by John Foley); **c**, Harry Waxman; **m**, Philip Green; **ed**, John D. Guthridge; **prod d**, Don Ashton; **art d**, Jack Maxsted.

The Man in the Moon ★★★ 1991; U.S.; 99m; MGM; Color; Drama; Children: Unacceptable (MPAA: PG-13); **DVD**; **VHS**. Witherspoon is a fourteen-year-old girl coming of age in rural Louisiana in 1957. Her father, Waterston, is a loving but strict parent, her mother, Harper, is pregnant with her fourth child, and her older sister, Warfield, is away at Duke University. A new family moves onto the vacant farm next door. The widowed mother has three sons, the eldest, London, is seventeen, a nice guy and handsome. Witherspoon likes to go skinny-dipping in a nearby waterhole and sees London swimming there in boxer shorts. She begins to think he is in love with her, although he sees her more as a friend. Harper is near to delivering her baby, so Warfield comes home to help, and London becomes much more interested in her than in Witherspoon. She becomes jealous of Warfield until tragedy enters and changes everything. London is killed in a farm accident and both sisters grieve his death, but their love as sisters transcends everything as they share the loss of the boy they both loved. A heartfelt drama, but the traumatic introduction of London's untimely death places it far beyond the reach of being a family film and any viewing by children. **p**, Mark Rydell; **d**, Robert Mulligan; **cast**, Sam Waterston, Tess Harper, Gail Strickland, Reese Witherspoon, Jason London, Emily Warfield, Bentley Mitchum, Ernie Lively, Dennis Letts, Earleen Bergeron; **w**, Jenny Wingfield; **c**, Freddie Francis; **m**, James Newton Howard; **ed**, Trudy Ship; **prod d**, Gene Callahan; **art d**, Fredda Slavin; **set d**, Daril Adler; **spec eff**, LaVonne Doane, Neil Stockstill, John Alagna.

The Man in the White Suit ★★★★ 1952; U.K.; 85m; Rank; Ealing/UNIV; B/W; Comedy; Children: Acceptable; **DVD**; **VHS**. Guinness gives another superlative comedic performance in this subtle satire of British industrialism. He is an eccentric chemist working for textile tycoon Parker, and almost all believe him certifiable except for Parker's daughter, Greenwood, who considers Guinness the scientific genius of the age. Guinness takes over Parker's extensive laboratories and prohibits all from entering except one assistant. Parker and his executives, however, cannot restrain their curiosity and, to discover what Guinness is up to, make the mistake of entering that laboratory only to witness another one of his colossal failures, this time an explosion that leaves their clothes smoking and their faces blackened. (This kind of silent-era slapstick is always more appreciated by British audiences in that the onscreen responses by victims in such scenes are not demonstrated by wild antics as evidenced in American comedies, but by quiet and undignified chagrin.) Parker and his fellow magnates continue to tolerate the incessant and annoying noises emanating from that laboratory, constant gurgling, bubbling and belching of roiling chemicals and churlish gases. Greenwood remains staunchly loyal to Guinness, assuring her father that he will someday provide a scientific breakthrough that will vastly reward his investment and, in the process, falls in love with the wacky inventor as she stalls wedding plans with Gough, her insufferably boring fiancé. Finally, Guinness makes his breakthrough, creating a formula that, when added to cloth, allows him to create a pristine white suit that is stain resistant and one that will never wrinkle nor tear, one that appears to be indestructible and will last forever and always appear new. Parker proudly announces this fantastic invention to the world and heralds Guinness as the greatest scientific guru of the modern era. Then the scientific breakthrough is seen for the great danger it poses. Since it cannot be dyed any other color and that it will never be damaged or age, it will inevitably cost countless workers their jobs and stall the worldwide textile industry. Thesiger, the industry's top tycoon, a ruthlessly greedy character, meets with his fellow magnates and they determine that the suit and the formula, if not Guinness, must be destroyed to preserve their industry. Guinness knows now that he and his suit are hunted and he furtively runs hither and yon to escape the pursuing multimillionaires, who avidly chase him about. He is finally cornered by his pursuers on a street during a heavy rainstorm, and when the tycoons begin grabbing and clutching at the white suit he wears, it comes to pieces in their hands until the once resplendent ensemble is in tatters and virtually disintegrates, leaving Guinness ashamedly standing in his underwear. His formula has one terrible flaw. It is destructible by simple rainwater. Dejected, Guinness begins walking away, his embarrassment shielded when a kindly passerby hands him a raincoat. He slowly walks back toward the laboratory and the camera closes upon his somber countenance, which slowly turns to a knowing smile as if to suggest that he now knows what went wrong with his formula and that he knows the remedy to make it right. In the final scene, we hear the gurgling and bubbling noises of the laboratory to indicate that this indefatigable genius will try once more to turn the world of science on its ear. Guinness gives a masterful performance in this mirthful comedy, producing consistently funny scenes that often lead to side-splitting sequences and where this wonderful actor employs all of his subtle techniques to produce the film's uniquely hilarious moments. Greenwood is alluring and captivating and Parker and the rest of the cast are effective in their roles, all guided with expertise by director Mackendrick. ***Author's Note***: Guinness told this author that "I enjoyed appearing in **The Man in the White Suit**, but there was one harrowing scene where I could have been seriously injured. I had to lower myself from a building during the chase scene and I told the director that the wire provided for that stunt was not strong enough to support the weight of my body. He assured me that it was and asked me to go ahead. Sure enough, the wire broke, but I was only about three or four feet from the ground when it did, so my bruises were minor. No one apologized. They seldom or never do when making pictures. In the end, no one wants to be responsible for such untoward events." **p**, Michael Balcon; **d**, Alexander Mackendrick; **cast**, Alec Guinness, Joan Greenwood, Cecil Parker, Michael Gough, Ernest Thesiger, Howard Marion Crawford, Henry Mollison, Vida Hope, Patrick Doonan; **w**, Mackendrick, Roger MacDougall, John Dighton (based on the play by MacDougall); **c**, Douglas Slocombe; **m**, Benjamin Frankel; **ed**, Bernard Gribble; **art d**, Jim Morahan; **spec eff**, Sydney Pearson, Geoffrey Dickinson.

Man Made Monster ★★★ 1941; U.S.; 59m; UNIV; B/W; Science Fiction; Children: Unacceptable; **DVD**; **VHS**. Only one person survives when a bus carrying carnival sideshow performers crashes into hydroelectric lines, electrocuting five others. Hinds, who is a professor of biology, becomes intrigued and invites the survivor, Chaney, to his laboratory where his assistant, Atwill, is conducting experiments to prove his theory that human life can be motivated and controlled by electricity. Atwill persuades Chaney to undergo some tests in which the human guinea pig absorbs increasingly strong electrical charges until he develops considerable immunity and becomes a walking electrical monster. Atwill administers one final mega dose of electricity to Chaney, who becomes superhuman in a body that glows. Chaney also becomes like a robot that Atwill can control. Hinds is fearful that the experiment has gone too far and is dangerous, but, when he tries to stop it, Atwill orders Chaney to kill him, which he does. Chaney is arrested for the murder and sentenced to die in the electric chair. Prison officials are amazed when Chaney's body absorbs the electric charge meant to kill him. Chaney then breaks free and kills the warden. Atwill takes Chaney back to his laboratory and puts him in a rubber suit that preserves his electric energy. Atwill then wants to try his experiment on a young woman, Nagel, with whom Chaney has earlier fallen in love. Chaney, instead, gives Atwill a heavy dose of his own electrical medicine that kills the evil scientist. Chaney then runs off into the night and into a barbed-wire fence that tears his rubber suit and he is drained of his energy and dies. A shocking science fiction thriller (pun intended) that provides lots of science fiction thrills. *Author's Note*: This was Chaney's first significant horror film, which quickly led to his being cast in the leading role for **The Wolf Man**, 1941, and for which he was forever typecast, although he gave some very significant performances in non-horror films, such as his role as Lennie Small, the gentle halfwit giant in **Of Mice and Men**, 1939; his role as an aging, crippled sheriff in **High Noon**, 1952; and the empathetic former chain gang inmate in **The Defiant Ones**, 1958. **p**, Jack Bernhard; **d**, George Waggner; **cast**, Lionel Atwill, Lon Chaney Jr., Anne Nagel, Frank Albertson, Samuel S. Hinds, William B. Davidson, Ben Taggart, Constance Bergen, Byron Foulger, Russell Hicks; **w**, Joseph West (Waggner, based on the story "The Electric Man" by H.J. Essex, Sid Schwartz, Len Golos); **c**, Elwood Bredell; **m**, Hans J. Salter; **ed**, Arthur Hilton; **art d**, Jack Otterson; **set d**, Russell A. Gausman; **spec eff**, John P. Fulton.

Man of a Thousand Faces ★★★★ 1957; U.S.; 122m; UNIV; B/W; Biographical Drama; Children: Cautionary; **DVD**; **VHS**. Cagney captivates in a mesmerizing profile of the great silent screen actor Lon Chaney (1883-1930). No other film actor during the silent era produced so many diversified characters as did Chaney, a master of disguises and perhaps the most accomplished makeup artist in the history of filmdom. He was noted for his hideous, gargoyle-like appearances, fashioned through his own makeup designs. He was an equally accomplished contortionist that could seemingly alter the shape of his body by bending and flexing that body into distorted images in many of his horror films that kept millions

Dorothy Malone and James Cagney in *Man of a Thousand Faces*, 1957.

on the edges of their seats. Cagney is shown born to deaf mute parents, although he is free of these physical afflictions and, knowing what it is to live without sound, becomes a successful mime in vaudeville. He meets beautiful Malone and she becomes his assistant. They fall in love and marry, but when Cagney takes Malone to meet his parents, she becomes hysterical, believing that any child they might have will be congenitally afflicted by the same impairments shared by Cagney's parents. Nothing that Cagney can say or do persuades Malone from this unsubstantiated belief. When they have a child, Malone cannot bring herself to look upon the boy until Cagney brings the baby to her and claps his hands, causing the infant to cry and only then is Malone filled with joy. Cagney becomes a big vaudeville star and Malone, resentful of his fame, competes by cheating on him with a secret lover before she deserts Cagney and her small son (Creighton Chaney, later Lon Chaney Jr., 1906-1973, who also became an actor and noted for his talkie horror films). Cagney then moves with his son to California where he is forced to place his son in a boarding house until he can make enough money to provide a good home for him. To that end, Cagney tries for any character role in the movies, using his own makeup so that he appears to be unique-looking Indians, pirates, cutthroats, renegades, and is soon in much demand and where he begins to get supporting and then leading roles. He meets and marries fetching Greer and by then he is providing a good home for his son. The family often goes to their mountain retreat to fish and where Cagney teaches his son his values. One of the many marvelous scenes in this film has Cagney entertaining his little son by making up to look like a little grandmother who imaginatively stitches his fingers together to pull his hand into a wave from an equally imaginary pull-string. All is tranquil in their lifestyle until Malone reappears. She has lost her voice (ironic in that this was what she most feared for her child) after she tried years earlier to commit suicide by drinking poison. Malone now wants to see her son, but Cagney cannot forgive her for her unfaithfulness and desertion. The loving and caring Greer, however, persuades Cagney to allow their son to visit Malone and the boy, as a teenager and then as a young man, Smith, remains with her, supporting Malone in her old age with his own income as an actor. Cagney disowns his son for showing loyalty to Malone, but, before he dies of throat cancer (the same disease would claim the life of Lon Chaney Jr., as both were heavy smokers), Cagney reconciles with his son and dies in peace. Throughout this somewhat melancholy and bittersweet film, Cagney does some brief but astounding scenes where he duplicates Chaney's incredible disguises and feats from his silent films, notably **The Hunchback of Notre Dame**, 1923; **The Phantom of the Opera**, 1925; and **The Penalty**, 1920. *Author's Note*: Cagney told this author that "it was impossible to perfectly imitate the performances of the great Lon Chaney, but I made a pretty good stab at it. I must admit that I ached for weeks after unwinding my

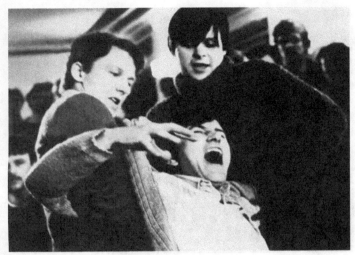

Jerzy Radziwilowicz in *Man of Iron*, 1981.

arms and legs when we did a long scene for **The Penalty**. I really don't know how Chaney was able to distort his body without some of the tricks we used in **Man of a Thousand Faces**. Since he never talked about his techniques, nobody knows." **p**, Robert Arthur; **d**, Joseph Pevney; **cast**, James Cagney, Dorothy Malone, Jane Greer, Marjorie Rambeau, Jim Backus, Robert J. Evans, Celia Lovsky, Jeanne Cagney, Jack Albertson, Roger Smith, Clarence Kolb, "Snub" Pollard, Troy Donahue; **w**, Ivan Goff, R. Wright Campbell, Ben Roberts (based on a story by Ralph Wheelwright); **c**, Russell Metty; **m**, Frank Skinner; **ed**, Ted J. Kent; **art d**, Alexander Golitzen, Eric Orbom; **set d**, Russell A. Gausman, Julia Heron; **spec eff**, Clifford Stine.

Man of Conquest ★★★ 1939; U.S.; 105m; REP; B/W; Biographical Drama; Children: Acceptable; **VHS**. Dix is outstanding in his role of Sam Houston (1793-1863), the man who was foremost in establishing the sovereignty of Texas in its war of independence from Mexico in 1836, and later fought to make it the 28th State of the U.S. in 1845. Dix is shown at his beginnings in Tennessee where he learns the hard-edged rules of American politics from Andrew Jackson (1767-1845; 7th President of the U.S.), wonderfully played by Ellis as a crusty and savvy campaigner, and where Dix becomes governor of the state and marries for the first time. Dix travels to Arkansas where he cements his long-standing relationship with the Cherokee Nation (Houston became an honorary member) and he is married for a second time. Then, at the urging of Ellis (Jackson long lobbied to wrest control of Texas from Mexico and bring it into the Union), Dix goes to Texas where he becomes deeply involved in the revolution against Mexico and its dictator, Santa Ana (1794-1876), ably played as a rather sinister character by Gordon (who again plays a role model of Santa Ana in the fine western, **Kit Carson**, 1940). Dix meets and befriends all of the great Texas heroes who defended and died at the Alamo, Jory, playing William Barret Travis (1809-1836), who commanded the Alamo, Barrat, playing Davy Crockett (1786-1836); and Armstrong, playing Jim Bowie (1796-1836). He also meets Morgan, who plays Stephen Austin (1793-1836), who shaped Texas' constitution. Following the fall of the Alamo (on March 6, 1836, after thirteen days of intense fighting), Dix organizes a rag-tag army of no more than 500 men and, retreating as Gordon pursues him with his own army of several thousand troops. Dix then selects San Jacinto as the decisive battlefield, where he leads his men in a charge against Gordon's encampment (April 21, 1836), overwhelming the Mexican forces, capturing Gordon, and where the wounded Dix dictates peace and Texas independence. Nichols directs this epic with great skill and his battle scenes are well staged. All of the players are exceptional, including Fontaine as Dix's first wife, and Patrick as his second spouse. *Author's Note*: Republic was a small studio that invariably released "B" programmers,

chiefly westerns, but it provided a very large and unusual budget for this film and its high production values show the expense in every frame. **p**, Sol C. Siegel; **d**, George Nichols, Jr.; **cast**, Richard Dix, Gail Patrick, Edward Ellis, Joan Fontaine, Victor Jory, Robert Barrat, George "Gabby" Hayes, Ralph Morgan, Robert Armstrong, C. Henry Gordon, Janet Beecher, Max Terhune, Kathleen Lockhart, Pedro de Cordoba, Leon Ames, Iron Eyes Cody, Chris-Pin Martin, Fay McKenzie, George Montgomery, Jason Robards, Sr., Jim Thorpe, Chief Thundercloud, Chief Yowlachie; **w**, Edward E. Paramore, Jr., Jan Fortune, Wells Root (based on a story by Root, Harold Shumate); **c**, Joseph H. August; **m**, Victor Young; **ed**, Edward Mann; **art d**, John Victor Mackay; **spec eff**, Howard Lydecker.

Man of Iron ★★★ 1981; Poland; 153m; Film Polski/UA; Color; Historical Drama; Children: Unacceptable (MPAA: PG); **DVD**; **VHS**. This fine sequel to **Man of Marble**, 1979, depicts the Gdansk, Poland, student reform movement in 1968 to the Solidarity strikes in 1980 that led to that country's freedom from communist rule and the end of the Cold War. A shipyard strike leader, Radziwilowicz, has become a hardened reform activist despite being harassed by the communist government and a weak, alcoholic television news reporter, Opania, who is assigned to dig up dirt on the strikers. Radziwilowicz, whose father was among those killed in 1970, becomes one of the leading protestors. Opania poses as one sympathetic to the strikers and interviews people who know Radziwilowicz, including the strike leader's wife, Janda, who is being detained by the communists. Opania is not sure where his loyalties lie, either with the strikers or the communists, while Radziwilowicz and Janda survive the perils of political persecution. Actual newsreel footage of the 1968 and 1970 protests are shown and also the later birth of free unions in Poland and success of the Solidarity movement under labor leader Lech Walesa. This powerful social-political film won top honors at the Cannes Film Festival. Violence prohibits viewing by children. (In Polish; English subtitles.) **p&d**, Andrzej Wajda; **cast**, Jerzy Radziwilowicz, Krystyna Janda, Marian Opania, Irena Byrska, Wieslawa Kosmalska, Boguslaw Linda, Franciszek Trzeciak, Janusz Gajos, Andrzej Seweryn, Marek Kondrat; **w**, Aleksander Scibor-Rylski; **c**, Edward Klosinski; **m**, Andrzej Korzynski; **ed**, Halina Prugar-Ketling; **prod d**, Allan Starski; **set d**, Magdalena Dipont.

Man of Marble ★★★ 1981; Poland; 160m; Film Polski Film Agency/New Yorker Films; Color; Drama; Children: Unacceptable; **DVD**; **VHS**. This engrossing production is the first of two films dramatizing Poland's eventual freedom from Soviet domination. Post-World War II Poland is beset by political problems under communist rule that result in a workers' revolt that brings about martial law in 1982. In Krakow, 1976, a university student, Janda, wants to make a documentary about a man, Radziwilowicz, who was well known for his skills as a bricklayer in the 1950s and also has become involved in worker politics. Then he virtually vanishes from the news radar screens when communist leaders disgrace his name and banish him into obscurity. Through her interviews, Janda learns that Radziwilowicz is a crusader for workers' rights and has been crusading for the construction of good housing. Her documentary, which is sympathetic toward the man, is rejected by her superior with the excuse that she has gone over budget on the project. The rise and fall of her subject, a Man of Marble, parallels the history of the Polish workers' movement, which eventually won its country's freedom from communist rule. A sequel, **Man of Iron**, released in 1981, tells the rest of the story leading to Poland's freedom from the Soviets. Violence prohibits viewing by children. (In Polish; English subtitles.) **p&d**, Andrzej Wajda; **cast**, Jerzy Radziwilowicz, Michal Tarkowski, Tadeusz Lomnicki, Krystyna Janda, Jacek Lomnicki, Piotr Cieslak, Wieslaw Wójcik, Krystyna Zachwatowicz, Magda Teresa Wójcik, Boguslaw Sobczuk; **w**, Aleksander Scibor-Rylski; **c**, Edward Klosinski; **m**, Andrzej Korzynski; **ed**, Halina Prugar-Ketling; **prod d**, Wojciech Majda, Allan Starski; **set d**, Maria Osiecka-Kuminek.

Man of the West ★★★★ 1958; U.S.; 100m; Ashton Productions; UA; Color; Western; Children: Unacceptable; **DVD**; **VHS**. In this complex and disturbing production, the last western directed by the skilled Mann, Cooper is entrusted with a sum of money to hire a school teacher for a small town. En route by train to hire that teacher, he is accosted by confidence man O'Connell, who learns of Cooper's mission and tries to bilk him of his funds by convincing him that saloon singer London is a teacher for hire and London reluctantly plays along with the scheme. Before O'Connell can complete his swindle, however, the train is stopped and robbed by the notorious Tobin gang, a ruthless band of psychopathic killers who seem to be all too familiar to Cooper. When the bandits depart, Cooper, O'Connell and London are left behind when the train leaves and they make their way on foot to a nearby cabin Cooper knows about. They find the Tobin gang present, led by their savage and aging leader, Cobb, who suddenly welcomes Cooper with open arms as he is his uncle. O'Connell and London then learn that Cooper is Cobb's favorite nephew and had once been part of this notorious gang with Cobb fondly recalling their robberies and killings. His cousins, Lord, Wilke and Dano (who is a mute), are, however, suspicious of Cooper and distrust his declared reason that he is rejoining the gang. Lord and Wilke, both sadists to the core, salivate over the sensual London and Lord orders her to strip. She slowly removes her clothes (in a scene that may be uncomfortable to many viewers), but before she removes her undergarments, Cobb stops the cruel exhibition and Cooper then, to protect London from further advances by his lusty cousins, tells everyone that London is his woman. Cobb assures Cooper that they will honor that relationship and allows Cooper, London and O'Connell to sleep in a nearby dilapidated barn. Dehner, a fourth cousin, who has replaced Cooper as Cobb's second-in-command, then rides up to the cabin and, when seeing Cooper again, becomes suspicious, thinking he might want to replace him in the pecking order of the gang. Cobb then announces that all of them are going to rob a bank in a nearby Texas town and they begin riding toward their destination. At an encampment, Lord and Cooper get into a fight, again over London, and Cooper beats Lord. He then tears Lord's clothes away in front of London to repeat the humiliation Lord earlier forced upon London. In retaliation, the enraged Lord seizes a gun and fires at Cooper, but kills O'Connell instead. Cobb, upset at his son's dishonorable conduct, then shoots Lord, killing him. (Fathers upholding the code of the Old West at any cost is also demonstrated in another western, **The Big Country**, 1958, where Burl Ives shoots his son, Chuck Connors, for doing the similar underhanded thing.) Cobb then sends Cooper and Dano to scout the bank in the nearby town, but when they arrive they find the place a ghost town with only a Mexican woman living in the deserted bank. Dano is so frustrated that he shoots and kills the woman and Cooper then kills Dano. When Cobb does not hear from Cooper and Dano, he sends Dehner and Wilke to the town where Cooper quickly kills Wilke but has a long gun battle with the cagey Dehner, a mirror image of Cooper's former outlaw self, until finally shooting him to death. Cooper returns to the encampment to find that Cobb has fled to the mountains after having raped London. Cooper stalks his savage uncle to the high country and finds him, telling him that all of his sons are dead, and Cobb challenges him to take his life. Cobb then begins firing wildly at Cooper and Cooper shoots and kills him. He then takes back his money that Cobb has earlier stolen from him, and, with London at his side, rides away, but it is uncertain whether or not they will remain a couple. In this strange but grimly realistic film, Mann shows Cooper as a man who has renounced his outlaw past, but who, when forced back into that terrible lifestyle, is capable of becoming again as savage and lethal as the men with whom he formerly rode. In dispatching his evil family members, he redeems himself for having spent years sharing the crimes of such predatory beasts, these premises based on Shakespearean themes that Mann invariably introduced in almost all of his unique westerns. **p**, Walter Mirisch; **d**, Anthony Mann; **cast**, Gary Cooper, Julie London, Lee J. Cobb, Arthur O'Connell, Jack Lord, John Dehner, Royal Dano, Robert Wilke, Joe Dominguez, Dick

Fredric March in *Man on a Tightrope,* 1953.

Elliott; **w**, Reginald Rose (based on the novel *The Border Jumpers* by Will C. Brown); **c**, Ernest Haller (CinemaScope; DeLuxe Color); **m**, Leigh Harline; **ed**, Richard Heermance; **art d**, Hilyard Brown; **set d**, Edward Boyle; **spec eff**, Jack Erickson.

Man on a Tightrope ★★★★ 1953; U.S.; 105m; FOX; B/W; Drama; Children: Unacceptable; **VHS**. In this brilliantly helmed Cold War drama from pantheon director Kazan, March (one of America's greatest actors) presents an intense and riveting performance where he is the owner of a small Czech circus scheming to find a way to cross the border to freedom and, in the process, take all of his employees and animals with him. He and his family have owned the circus for years, but, after the communists take over Czechoslovakia, they draft all of his young male performers into military service and the new regime denies him any new equipment. The circus is in poor shape, its tent and vehicles all in bad condition, and further, his crew boss, Boone, has become a dedicated communist who watches March's every move. Menjou, a crafty commissar, inspects March's circus and then grills him, telling him that he no longer owns the circus, but that it is the property of the state and he is merely its caretaker. Menjou tells March that he must have his performers do routines that emphasize the communist philosophy, dictates that anger March, but he pretends to obey while he plays for time, even agreeing to fire Wieck, a former duchess, who is one of his performers (a horse rider), but when he later tells Wieck that she is no longer with the circus because of her anti-communist sentiments, he cancels that order and tells her that she will stay on. Grahame, his sultry wife, believes that March's cowering conduct with Menjou indicates a lack of courage and she loses respect for him and, further, March must deal with a rebellious daughter, Moore, who is in love with roustabout Mitchell. After he prevents Moore from running off with Mitchell, March learns that Mitchell is a American soldier who has gone AWOL by crossing the border and both are planning to sneak into Germany, seeking sanctuary and freedom from the Western powers. He tells them that he plans to take the entire traveling circus to freedom as they approach that border in Bavaria, and Mitchell becomes a secret ally in the plot. Almost all the circus performers, except for Boone and his equipment crew members, who are pro-communist, are in on the plot, even D'Arcy, the posturing lion tamer, who, March knows, has been carrying on a mild affair with his wife, Grahame. Before he makes his move, however, March confronts D'Arcy, who tells March that "the curse of my life is that I am a handsome man." March tells him that he knows that he is also a coward and that he should stay with his lions when they make their break for freedom. After wheedling a travel permit from Menjou, March meets with Beatty, the conniving and raucous owner of a rival circus, making secret arrangements with Beatty to keep all of his equip-

Fredric March in *Man on a Tightrope*, 1953.

ment. Knowing that they are being watched by communist commissars, they stage a wild fistfight inside March's office wagon, wrecking the place, with Beatty pretending to be tossed from the wagon and hurling insults at March as he departs. Meanwhile Dehner, who is Menjou's superior, questions Menjou's communist loyalties and good judgment in giving March a travel permit for his circus, but Menjou tells him that he has given March just enough rope by which he will hang him when he believes March will make his move to escape to the West. When Dehner realizes too late that March is attempting to make a break for freedom, he has Menjou arrested and replaced. By that time, the circus is approaching the border, and Mitchell overcomes a communist guard on a roadway and dons his uniform, riding atop one of the circus trucks leading the procession of wagons and dilapidated vehicles as they grind and labor to a military roadblock where they pretend to entertain communist guards. When March gives the signal, Mitchell jumps from the truck and opens fire with a submachine gun, battling the guards as a truck smashes through a barrier and crosses the bridge, the other side of that bridge being the German border (in Bavaria) and where German and U.S. troops welcome the fleeing refugees. The circus wagons and vehicles of all types rumble and ramble across the bridge, the performers running with them to freedom. Mitchell, Moore and the others make it safely to the other side, but March is fatally shot, His wagon, the last vehicle attempting to cross the bridge, is stalled halfway across the bridge and the communist guards begin to close in on it from the Czechoslovakian side of the border. From the German side of the border sits Madame Brumbach, March's elderly mother, glaring at the cowardly D'Arcy, who cannot bring himself to look at her. Then, in the finest moment of his life, D'Arcy, shamed into summoning fortitude he does not know he possesses, races across the bridge, and with his lion-tamer's pistol in hand that now hold real bullets, he courageously fires at the Czech guards, killing some of them as he himself is shot down and while other circus workers free March's wagon and bring it safely across the bridge to freedom. The performers gather outside March's wagon, and a tearful Grahame opens the door of that wagon to tell them that March is dead. She then orders them to give a performance in celebration of their freedom, and the clowns and small band dance and play as the circus proceeds along the roadway, ending this superb drama. Not only does Kazan exact a great performance from March, but draws outstanding portrayals from Grahame, Menjou, Mitchell, Moore and the rest of the cast while he maintains great tension in every cat-and-mouse scene between March and his dogged persecutors and pursuers. The final sequence where the circus performers make their break for freedom is action packed and exciting, as these desperate liberty-loving people frantically try to escape the tyranny that has engulfed their country. This much overlooked classic drama was shot in Bavaria and where Kazan

was compelled to work on a limited budget, but he delivers a powerful and memorable film that depicts in microcosm the political plight that oppressed millions compelled to live behind the Iron Curtain during that bitter Cold War. ***Author's Note***: Kazan offered the role of March's wife to Marlene Dietrich, but she turned down the offer, as did German actress Hildegard Neff (or Knef), until he finally signed Grahame for the part and where she gives an outstanding performance as a dallying but nevertheless loyal wife of a doomed man. "I hired a small German traveling circus [Bimbach Circus] for that picture," Kazan told this author, "and used a lot of its performers, working my own American actors into that troupe. The toughest part of keeping it all organized, especially at the end when the circus makes a break for the border, were the wild animals, especially the big cats, who were dangerous and we had to take care they did not get loose during the wild flight across the bridge. The communist authorities in Czechoslovakia denounced me for making that film and I considered that a compliment. I hate communists and communism as much as I hate fascism and fascists. They are all the same to me, people who want to control and dictate the liberties and freedoms of everyone." Kazan made this film only one year after he had appeared before the House of Un-American Activities Committee in Washington, D.C., that was probing communist activities in Hollywood in 1952. He admitted to this author that, while he was in his "ignorant twenties," between 1934 and 1936, he had been a member of the Communist Party, but had quit the party "along with my friend and playwright Clifford Odets, when communist bosses started telling us that we had to work for the violent overthrow of America. We didn't buy that hogwash and told them to go to hell. Well, here it is, more than twenty years later, and I am before a group of politicians in Washington and they wanted me to name others I knew who belonged to the Communist Party back in the 1930s. I refused, but then I was told that they already had the names of the ones I knew so I gave them what they already knew. I was damned if I was going to wreck my film career for those communists that tried to force me into betraying my country so many years earlier." By that time, Kazan had already established himself as one of the great film directors, having one an Oscar for Best Director for **Gentleman's Agreement**, 1947 (the first to tackle the bigotry of anti-Semitism). He would go on to win another Oscar as Best Director for **On the Waterfront**, 1954 (with Marlon Brando, dealing with criminal corruption among American labor), and direct some of the finest path-breaking social dramas in the history of filmmaking, including this one. His achievements tower above most other Hollywood directors with such classics as **A Tree Grows in Brooklyn**, 1945, dealing with alcoholism; **Boomerang!**, 1947, dealing with a wrongly accused person; **Pinky**, 1949, which was one of the first films to deal with racial bias; **Panic in the Streets**, 1950, which dealt with mass hysteria during the threat of a plague in New Orleans; **A Streetcar Named Desire**, 1951, a powerful drama also set in New Orleans that deals with rape committed against a mentally deluded woman by a cretin-like brother-in-law (Brando); **Viva Zapata!**, 1952 (also Brando), profiling Emiliano Zapata, Mexico's heroic revolutionary leader (ironically a socialist), fighting the corrupt tyrants of his impoverished country; **East of Eden**, 1955, dealing with a modern sibling rivalry and the ancient trauma of the Oedipus complex; and **A Face in the Crowd**, 1957, dealing with a power-mad media-created personality. In 1999, Kazan was given an honorary Oscar for his lifetime achievements in film, presented on that occasion by Martin Scorsese and Robert De Niro, and he won a standing ovation from most of the stellar persons in the audience, except for some who refused to stand up or applaud him, and even some others booed and hissed Kazan for his role in the HUAC hearings almost fifty years earlier. Gregory Peck, who had appeared in Kazan's **Gentleman's Agreement**, had supported the movement to give Kazan that award and, later told this author that "I watched [at those Academy Award ceremonies in 1999] as several distinguished people refused to stand up and applaud the genius of this great man. I don't know if they were communists, socialists or whatever and don't care. I do know that they were ungracious, rude, and brutal people, who, for obvious political reasons, refused to accord a fellow artist his due. There was no excuse for that. None!" **p**, Robert L. Jacks; **d**, Elia Kazan; **cast**, Fredric March, Terry Moore, Gloria Grahame, Cameron Mitchell, Adolphe Menjou, Robert Beatty, Alex D'Arcy, Richard Boone, Pat Henning, Paul Hartman, John Dehner, Dorothea Wieck, Madame Brumbach, Gert Frobe; **w**, Robert E. Sherwood (based on the story "International Incident" by Neil Paterson); **c**, George Krause; **m**, Franz Waxman; **ed**, Dorothy Spencer; **art d**, Hans Kuhnert, Theo Zwirsky.

The Man on the Eiffel Tower ★★★ 1949; U.S./France; 97m; Allen-Tone Film Production/RKO; Color; Crime Drama; Children: Unacceptable; **DVD**; **VHS**. This outstanding film noir tale has Laughton as the sure-handed Inspector Maigret searching for a professional killer. That man is Tone, who gets his thrills by dispatching his victims. Laughton at first is drawn to red herring Meredith, a blind knife-grinder (who also directs this superb film). Laughton identifies Hutton as Tone's employer, who has paid Tone to murder his wife, Roc, in order that Hutton can be with his sensual mistress, Wallace. Laughton, however, does not have enough evidence to prove Tone guilty and he bides for time while Tone taunts him. The strain is finally too much for Tone, who flees with Laughton and his officers pursuing him to the Eiffel Tower. Tone climbs upward with the cops following until the culprit is killed atop the Paris landmark. Tone and Laughton superbly interact to produce a great deal of tension in this well-crafted crime drama by Meredith, who was basically a character actor, this being one of the four films he directed and is his very best. *Author's Note*: Meredith employed the rich Ansco color process for this engrossing film, which was discontinued by the mid-1950s. One of the last major films to employ this process was **Lust for Life**, 1956, to better present the lush colors of hundreds of paintings by master artist Vincent van Gogh. **p**, Irving Allen, Franchot Tone; **d**, Burgess Meredith; **cast**, Charles Laughton, Tone, Meredith, Robert Hutton, Jean Wallace, Patricia Roc, Belita, George Thorpe, William Phipps, William Cottrell, Wilfrid Hyde-White; **w**, Harry Brown (based on the novel *A Battle of Nerves* by Georges Simenon); **c**, Stanley Cortez (Technicolor); **m**, Michel Michelet; **ed**, Louis H. Sackin; **art d**, Rene Renoux.

Man on the Flying Trapeze ★★★★ 1935; U.S.; 66m; PAR; B/W; Comedy; Children: Acceptable; **DVD**; **VHS**. The great W.C. Fields is again hilarious in this domestic romp where he once more must endure the persecutions of an abusing marriage by uncaring and indifferent family members. He is shown gargling several times with the contents of a flask in his bathroom until his wife, Howard, who is in bed in the adjoining room, loudly complains about the noise. Finishing his boozy libations, Fields trundles to bed and is soon snoring peacefully until Howard abruptly awakes him to tell him that she hears "burglars singing in the cellar." Fields asks: "What are they singing?" She insists he confront the interlopers and Fields retrieves a gun. When it accidentally discharges family members come on the run. Lewis, who is Howard's mother, and Sutton, who is Fields' pompous son-in-law, then lambast Fields for his bumbling until Brian, Fields' daughter and his only supporter, appears to tell Lewis and Sutton to stop harassing her father. Fields sets forth to the cellar where he finds two burglars drunk. They have broken into the house, but after finding Fields' barrel of booze-laced apple cider and imbibing some of its contents are now in their cups. Fields joins the party by singing "On the Banks of the Wabash." A cop then arrives and he, too, takes a drink of the cider before joining the group to make a quartet that round out the song. The cop then regretfully tells them all that he must take them to the pokey; the burglars are jailed for breaking and entering, and Fields is locked up for manufacturing alcohol without a license. Howard, Sutton and Lewis refuse to bail him out, but, as usual, Brian comes to his rescue, using all her savings to post bail to have Fields released. Returning home, Fields sits down to a breakfast with Howard, Lewis and Sutton and where Sutton eats most of the food on the table, calling Fields a "jailbird" in the process and where Fields is left with only a burned piece of toast to

Franchot Tone and Charles Laughton in *The Man on the Eiffel Tower*, 1949.

munch on. Sutton then announces that he has found a $15 ticket to a wrestling match, which is a choice seat, vexing Fields no end, who has purchased that very ticket but who cannot admit to having so lavishly spent money for such a luxury. Fields, miserable at having lost that ticket to the filching and conniving Sutton, arrives late at work to warmly greet his secretary, Monti (Fields' real life mistress, who would later write his biography, *W.C. and Me*). Apfel, his superior, is irritated at Fields' tardiness, but endures Fields' irregularities since he is a memory expert who can recall in an instant any vital background on the company's clients. Fields asks Apfel for the day off, stating that his mother-in-law, Lewis, has died. Apfel states that "it must be very hard to lose your mother-in-law." Fields replies: "Yes, it is very hard, almost impossible." Lewis is very much alive, and Fields has fabricated her demise in order to attend the wrestling match. En route, he gets four police tickets for parking his car in the same prohibited spot and then has a flat tire. When changing that tire, it gets loose of his grasp and rolls down a steep hill and Fields chases it. Meanwhile funeral flowers arrive at Fields' home and Howard believes that they represent her husband's death, convinced that he has been killed in an accident. Littlefield, an employee at Fields' company who hates Fields, then calls Howard to ask how Lewis perished and she tells the snooper that her mother is alive and well. Fields, meanwhile, arrives at the wrestling arena as the last customer, desperately offering money to the ticket seller, who tells him that the place has been sold out and promptly slams the ticket window in his face (apparently this wrestling match is the event of the season since everybody who is anyone in town is in attendance). Fields views the match through a knothole in the wooden fence surrounding the arena to see one brawny wrestler throw the other wrestler from the ring with such force that the adversary bounces through the main gate, smashing down the door and out of the arena while knocking down Fields in his tornado-like course. The crowd pours from the arena and among the spectators is Monti, who helps Fields to his feet just as Sutton emerges, who thinks Fields is drunk and is having an affair with his secretary, and he runs home to tattletale this fresh scandal to Howard and Lewis. Fields arrives home to be tongue-lashed by Howard and Sutton for lying about Lewis' non-existent death, a huge fib that has cost Fields his job, thanks to the scheming Littlefield. Fields denies that he is having an affair with Monti, but admits his error in reporting the premature demise of his mother-in-law. When Brian comes to her father's defense, Sutton threatens to hit her and Fields, incensed at his son-in-law's abrasive conduct, finally does something he has wanted to do for a long time; he knocks the obnoxious Sutton cold and then leaves with Brian. They get an apartment and Fields and Brian are searching through newspapers for jobs when Littlefield calls. Brian takes the call, to hear Littlefield apologizing for firing her father and asking that he return to his old job—Apfel has

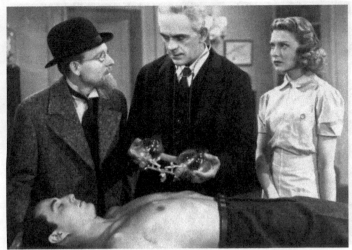

Stanley Brown (on table), Byron Foulger, Boris Karloff and Ann Doran in *The Man They Could Not Hang,* 1939.

demanded the return of his memory expert to deal with another client who is about to arrive. Brian then realizes that her father is in an advantageous position and tells Littlefield that her father must have a new job offer with double his old salary. Littlefield desperately confers with Apfel and matches that offer. Brian insists that Fields receive a long paid vacation, starting immediately, and Littlefield and Apfel agree to that, too. Fields, now in charge of his life, reunites with Howard. He is, at the finale, happily driving a new car while a rainstorm erupts. Fields puts up the top, handing hot coffee to his wife and daughter while the repugnant Lewis and Sutton sit in the rumble seat and are soaked by a downpour that resembles the Great Flood. This wonderful comedy, despite its title, has nothing to do with circuses. The story was written by Fields under one of his ridiculous pseudonyms, Charles Bogle. Although Bruckman received credit as director for this film, it was mostly directed by the gifted and often inspired Fields, who really ran the production. *Author's Note*: Fields based his tale on his own experiences at Paramount where he had been fired but then rehired with a hefty contract following the great success of **It's a Gift**, 1934. Howard was always Fields' favorite on-screen wife. She had been a Metropolitan Opera singer and later a fashion writer. When visiting the set for **Death Takes a Holiday**, 1934, she was asked to take a part in that film and did, remaining in Hollywood to become an established character actress. Brian got her role in **Man on the Flying Trapeze** after Fields noticed the lovely actress as one of his neighbors at Toluca Lake and offered her the job. Fields did not want a lot of regimen imposed during his productions and told the actors that they should "butt in" whenever they thought they should interrupt his bumbling monologs and this Sutton did with alacrity until Fields told Sutton: "I said you could 'butt in,' not take over the leading role!" **p**, William LeBaron; **d**, Clyde Bruckman; **cast**, W.C. Fields, Mary Brian, Kathleen Howard, Grady Sutton, Vera Lewis, Lucien Littlefield, Oscar Apfel, Lew Kelly, Walter Brennan, Edward Gargan, Carlotta Monti, Florence Lawrence; **w**, Ray Harris, Sam Hardy, Jack Cunningham, Bobby Vernon, Frank Griffin, John Sinclair (based on a story by Hardy, Charles Bogle [W.C. Fields]), **c**, Alfred Gilks; **ed**, Richard C. Currier; **art d**, Hans Dreier, A. Earl Hedrick.

Man on the Train ★★★ 2003; France/U.K./Germany/Japan; Cine B/PAR; Color; Drama; Children: Unacceptable (MPAA: R); **DVD**; **VHS**. Intriguing drama sees Rochefort as a retired poetry teacher, who gets off a train in a French provincial town and goes to a pharmacy where he meets bank robber Hallyday. The local hotel is closed for the winter so Rochefort invites Hallyday to stay at his old house. They talk, eat, and drink together and get acquainted. Rochefort says he is about to get a triple heart bypass surgery and Hallyday tells him he plans to rob the local bank. Rochefort offers Hallyday money if he will give up his plan to hold up the bank, but he refuses, saying he has given his word to his associates in crime. Theirs is an odd couple male friendship where, gradually, each man finds something to admire in the other and wishes that in some ways, they could exchange places. By the end of a week they go their separate ways and feel glad for the meeting, but their lives and fates remain unresolved. Gutter language and violence prohibit viewing by children. (In French; English subtitles.) **p**, Philippe Carcassonne, Carl Clifton; **d**, Patrice Leconte; **cast**, Jean Rochefort, Johnny Hallyday, Jean-François Stévenin, Charlie Nelson, Pascal Parmentier, Isabelle Petit-Jacques, Edith Scob, Maurice Chevit, Riton Liebman, Olivier Fauron; **w**, Claude Klotz; **c**, Jean-Marie Dreujou; **m**, Pascal Estève; **ed**, Joëlle Hache; **prod d**, Ivan Maussion; **spec eff**, Eric Martin, Matthias Weber.

The Man They Could Not Hang ★★★ 1939; U.S.; 64m; COL; B/W; Horror; Children: Unacceptable; **DVD**; **VHS**. Karloff fascinates as a scientist, who experiments at bringing the dead back to life with an artificial heart. He is about to open up a student when the intended victim's girlfriend brings the police to the laboratory. Karloff is convicted of murder and hanged, but Foulger, his lab assistant, brings him back to life with an artificial heart. Karloff goes on a rampage, killing the judge and jury that convicted him. Karloff then attempts to release all the inmates in the prison where he was held so he can use them in his evil experiments. When his daughter, Gray, tries to prevent Karloff from releasing these prisoners from their electronically controlled cells she is accidentally electrocuted. Karloff then revives her with an artificial heart before destroying his experiments and himself. *Author's Note*: This grim story was based on the real-life experiments of Robert Cornish (1903-1963), a child prodigy, who graduated with honors from the University of California at Berkeley at age eighteen, and who attempted through similar methods depicted in this film to revive dead dogs in the 1930s. He became convinced in 1932 that he had a method that could restore life to dead creatures and he reportedly revived two dogs in 1934 and 1935, using what he called his teeter-totter board or see-saw application to get blood flowing again in his deceased patients. His request to try his experiments on executed human prisoners was denied, albeit it was reported that he did experiment on some human corpses, seesawing these cadavers up and down to circulate blood while injecting a mixture of adrenaline and anticoagulants, but with no positive results. Experiments with artificial hearts were conducted as early as the late 1940s, but it was not until 1982 when artificial hearts were successfully implanted in two human beings, Barney Clark (survived 112 days beyond surgery) and William Schroeder (survived 620 days beyond surgery). **p**, Wallace MacDonald; **d**, Nick Grinde; **cast**, Boris Karloff, Lorna Gray, Robert Wilcox, Roger Pryor, Don Beddoe, Ann Doran, Joe De Stefani, Byron Foulger, James Craig, Walter Sande, Robert Sterling; **w**, Karl Brown; George Wallace Sayre, Leslie T. White; **c**, Benjamin Kline; **ed**, William Lyon.

A Man to Remember ★★★ 1938; U.S.; 79m; RKO; B/W; Drama; Children: Cautionary; **DVD**. This moving portrait of a passionate physician, superbly essayed by Ellis, depicts his career as a country doctor and is shown in flashbacks where he benefits his fellow man through kindness and consideration. In one scene, Ellis reduces his bill of $100 to $2 for a poor man, who cannot afford to pay him. In another sequence, Ellis convinces a banker to fund muchneeded expenses in supporting a needy hospital. The film is well directed by Kanin in the first film he helmed, and the script from the gifted Trumbo is literate and often inspiring. RKO released this film as a "B" programmer without much promotion, but word of mouth about its fine performances and script saw an unexpected box office success. **p**, Robert Sisk; **d**, Garson Kanin; **cast**, Anne Shirley, Edward Ellis, Lee Bowman, William Henry, John Wray, Granville Bates, Harlan Briggs, Frank M. Thomas, Dickie Jones, Gilbert Emery, Grady Sutton; **w**, Dalton Trumbo (based on the story "Failure" by Katharine Haviland-Taylor); **c**, J. Roy Hunt; **m**, Roy Webb; **ed**, Jack Hively; **art d**, Van Nest Polglase.

The Man Who Came to Dinner ★★★★ 1942; U.S.; 112m; WB; B/W; Comedy; Children: Acceptable; **DVD**; **VHS**. This very funny outing from Kaufman and Hart is based upon the outlandish antics and lifestyle of the eccentric Alexander Woollcott (1887-1943), the New York drama critic and radio personality, who presided over a group of literary lights that regularly gathered at the famed Algonquin Hotel for lunch in the 1920s-1930s. Woolley plays literary guru Sheridan Whiteside (Woollcott), who, while on a nationwide lecture tour with his overindulgent secretary, Davis, agrees to give a talk at a small Ohio town. When visiting this whistle-stop, he slips and falls on some ice outside the resplendent home of his wealthy sponsors, Burke and Mitchell. He is carried into their home where he threatens to sue the socialite couple for every penny they possess. The bumbling family doctor, Barbier, determines that Woolley's injuries are such that he should not be moved and must remain either in bed or in a wheelchair. To placate the irate Woolley, Burke and Mitchell give Woolley the freedom of their mansion, a mistake in that he completely takes charge of the place, ordering its owners to remain in their rooms while he conducts his own business. He uses his considerable charm and persuasion to control the family servants as well as Arms and Fraser, the two youthful but grown children of Burke and Mitchell, urging them to immediately spread their wings and depart the nest. Davis tolerates her boss' high-handed shenanigans, dutifully following his instructions to contact scores of his associates in letting them know that he is ensconced in Ohio, thus dominating the family phone and doorbell. Davis then meets local newspaper editor Travis, who interviews Woolley and who tells the drama critic that he has been writing a play. Travis is taken by Davis and when she responds in kind, Woolley becomes alarmed, believing that he might lose his indefatigable secretary if she marries Travis. To end that relationship, Woolley calls Hollywood siren Sheridan long distance to tell her that he has learned about a new play that is ideal for her talents, believing that she will distract Travis' attentions to Davis. Sheridan arrives and properly vamps Travis into giving her the leading role in his new play, but when Davis learns of Woolley's plan to separate her from Travis, she threatens to quit Woolley's employ. Desperate, and with the help of Durante, another Hollywood personality (playing a role model of zany Harpo Marx), who arrives to cheer up Woolley, they maneuver Sheridan into a life-size mummy coffin that has been sent to Woolley for his perusal with plans to ship it off to Philadelphia with Sheridan still inside. The mansion is inundated with gifts to the famous Woolley from equally famous well-wishers. He receives four live penguins from Admiral Byrd and entrusts these capricious creatures to the care of Woolley's appointed and much-harassed nurse, Wickes (who plays a nurse to Gladys Cooper, Davis's ailing mother, in another film later released that year, **Now Voyager**, 1942). Another admirer sends Woolley a live octopus, and soon the mansion becomes a combination museum and zoo with innumerable celebrities coming and going, such as Gardiner, who plays a role model of playwright-actor Noel Coward. Barbier then again examines Woolley and determines that his original diagnosis is incorrect and that the savant is not suffering from fractured vertebrae and is capable of standing and walking about and leaving the mansion, but Woolley has made too many plans and can't leave the mansion at this time, so he persuades Barbier to reinforce his mandate that he remain right where he is, on the promise the he will arrange to have Barbier's unpublished memoirs put into print and guaranteeing that it will be a bestseller. When Mitchell learns that Woolley has been faking his injuries, he orders him from his house. Before he can be evicted, however, Woolley discovers that Mitchell's sister, Vivian, a sweet but addle-brained spinster, is a notorious lady who had been accused many years earlier of being an axe murderer (based on Lizzie Borden, 1860-1927, who had been accused of murdering her stepmother and father and who Woollcott had written about). Woolley uses this scandalous background

Monty Woolley, Bette Davis and Ann Sheridan in *The Man Who Came to Dinner,* 1942.

to blackmail Mitchell and Burke into staying on until he can complete his Christmas radio broadcast (Woollcott was a celebrated radio personality with a national program called "The Town Crier"). The mansion fills with a bevy of radio technicians and other personnel, along with a full boys' choir, and Woolley does his show. He then patches up Davis' romance with Travis and successfully has Arms and Fraser leave home to seek their fortunes. Now he is ready to depart, but, when he finally leaves the mansion, Woolley falls on some ice and literally breaks a leg and is again carried into the mansion just in time to get a sympathy phone call from First Lady Eleanor Roosevelt, ending this zany comedy. Woolley is wonderful as the totemic, overbearing and unwanted guest, and Davis, Sheridan and the rest of the cast are outstanding in their supporting roles while director Keighley, a workhorse helmsman at Warner Brothers, uses all of his fine techniques to move this terrific comedy along at a break-necking (no pun intended) pace. ***Author's Note***: Director Keighley told this author that "Woolley was perfect in the role. He and Woollcott knew each other. Woollcott actually starred as Sheridan Whiteside, or himself, in a roadshow of this play in 1940. He was too busy with his radio program, however, to appear in the picture, thankfully, and Woolley got the part with Woollcott's approval. When I told Jack Warner that I was first considering Woollcott to play himself in the picture, Jack told me that 'I don't want that nut in that picture. If we take him on, we'll never get rid of the guy. I'll have to build him a house on the back lot!' We had to treat Woollcott with kid gloves because he was then one of the most powerful commentators on radio [a medium Keighley later pursued with great success as a radio host, as he had a memorably mellifluous voice]. Everybody listened to Woollcott's program. He could make or break a novel, a play or a movie in a few lines on the air." Davis was not that happy with her role, telling this author: "I really have a supporting part in that picture, although I got top billing, but Monty [Woolley] is in almost every scene and Jack Warner and Bill [Keighley] gave him special consideration as if they were actually dealing with Alexander Woollcott. I met Woollcott several times and I did not like him. He was pompous, dominating and just like the character Monty was playing; insufferable, I believe is the best description. But he was a big shot with a lot of influence because of his national radio program, so it was like bowing to a rajah when dealing with his alter ego, Monty. Bill [Keighley] actually fawned over Woolley and I told him that that was disgusting, and he only shrugged and said, 'see the boss,' meaning Jack Warner, and nobody wanted to see Jack Warner about anything, so I kept my mouth shut, did my scenes, and took my salary. Bill Keighley was a very good director and could do any kind of film well, from crime to comedy, but he was like Woollcott in many ways. He put on a lot of aristocratic airs that made us all sick to our stomachs, especially Jimmy Cagney, who once said to me, 'if I

Ann Sheridan, Richard Travis, Bette Davis and Monty Woolley in *The Man Who Came to Dinner,* **1942.**

have to do another picture with Keighley I will have to have my stomach pumped!' But he went on doing pictures with him because Keighley was really good at making quality films." The great Dorothy Parker was a friend of Woollcott's, or, at least, a close acquaintance, who had been a member of the celebrated cerebral Algonquin Hotel Round Table group that included such acerbic wits as Robert Benchley, George Kaufman, Moss Hart, Franklin Pierce Adams, Charles MacArthur (writing collaborationist with Ben Hecht), Harpo Marx, Heywood Broun, Marc Connelly, Ruth Hale, Robert E. Sherwood, Harold Ross (publisher of *the New Yorker*) and Parker, to name the most prominent attendees. In one of my several meetings with Parker (some at the famed Algonquin Hotel) in the early 1960s, she told me that "Woollcott used to barge in on friends like Kaufman, who, along with Moss Hart, wrote the play based on him, and continued to be a live-in guest. While staying with Kaufman, Woollcott would charge everything from catered food to gifts to Kaufman until he kicked Woollcott out and told him to stay at his own residence. That's how Kaufman got the idea to write **The Man Who Came to Dinner**. Woollcott tried that routine on me once, but when he saw what a dingy place I was living in and that I insisted he pay half the rent on an hourly basis—I told him that I had to pay a call girl's rate—he beat a fast retreat. He owned an island [Neshobe Island on Lake Bomoseen] in Vermont and built a big house on it and then had us come and visit him. He had us all rowed from the mainland to the place and we would spend the night on that island, but he held us prisoners there and would not call the man rowing the boat to come and pick us up until he finished his endless diatribes. It was **The Man Who Came to Dinner** in reverse. I will tell you that being trapped on an island with Alexander Woollcott was like being trapped in a cage with a polar bear. You either humored him or he would eat you for breakfast! On one such journey to that island, he kept us up all night while reciting passages from some boring new novel he thought was a work of genius. The next morning, when we all sat down to breakfast, he arrived at the head of the table wearing his bathrobe and said: 'I want to tell you all about the most marvelous bowel movement I had this morning,' and proceeded to describe it in detail before encouraging us to eat our scrambled eggs. How's that for a pleasant outing with Alexander Woollcott?" For more details on Woollcott, see my book, *Zanies: The World's Greatest Eccentrics* (New Century, 1982; pages 418-420). **p,** Hal B. Wallis, Jerry Wald, Jack Saper; **d,** William Keighley; **cast,** Bette Davis, Ann Sheridan, Monty Woolley, Richard Travis, Jimmy Durante, Billie Burke, Reginald Gardiner, Elisabeth Fraser, Grant Mitchell, George Barbier, Mary Wickes, Russell Arms, Charles Drake, Ruth Vivian, John Ridgely, Leslie Brooks, Laura Hope Crews, Gig Young; **w,** Julius J. and Philip G. Epstein (based on the play by George S. Kaufman, Moss Hart); **c,** Tony Gaudio; **m,** Frederick Hollander; **ed,** Jack Killifer; **art d,** Robert Haas.

The Man Who Could Work Miracles ★★★ 1937; U.K.; 82m; London Film Productions/UA; B/W; Fantasy; Children: Cautionary; **DVD**; **VHS**. In this whimsical and engrossing fantasy three gods (Sanders, Brandt and Thatcher) discuss in their celestial abode the worthiness of keeping the planet Earth in existence. While debating the questionable values of this tiny but warring and troubled planet, they select a single human being, Young, and bestow upon him miraculous powers to see if his absolute powers will corrupt him absolutely. Young is a meek draper's assistant, who suddenly discovers that he has the ability to move things like turning a lamp around in mid-air. (The ability to employ so-called telekinesis where the mind can move hard objects is demonstrated by John Travolta in **Phenomenon**, 1996, after Travolta is ostensibly exposed to a blast of strange light following an extraterrestrial visit.) When realizing that he has limitless powers, the good-natured Young resolves to stop disease and wars while turning Earth into Utopia. Although his powers seem absolute, Young cannot alter human emotions and finds that no matter what he does, he cannot make Gardner, an attractive shop girl, fall in love with him. Moreover, he incurs the wrath of Richardson, a former army officer, who believes that Young and his powers pose a danger to the world and tries to kill him, but to no avail in that Young has made himself bulletproof. Meanwhile, Young begins to use his powers frivolously to amuse himself. He cures a girl of freckles and then sends an irritating policeman to Hell and then to San Francisco. He becomes so egotistical that he creates a fabulous palace for himself and then summons the world's leaders to that sumptuous residence where he tells them he is now the ruler of the Earth and has the powers to change the destinies of all living things. When these leaders respond with disbelief in his powers (even though they do not question how they all came to be involuntarily within Young's presence), Young angrily demonstrates his omnipotence by ordering the Earth to stop rotating and everything goes flying into space. Young realizes the universal calamity he has caused and he desperately orders that the Earth resume its natural rotation and everything goes back to the time where he was first inside of a pub to learn of his powers and that there is no knowledge of any of the miracles he has earlier brought about. The earth resumes its normal rotation, and Young and all those earlier touched by his miracles go about their lives without remembering any of his spectacular feats. This good Wells fantasy, a sequel to **Things to Come**, 1936, sees a fine performance from Young from pip-squeak to titan and where the special effects are outstanding. **p,** Alexander Korda; **d,** Lothar Mendes; **cast,** Roland Young, Ralph Richardson, Edward Chapman, Ernest Thesiger, Joan Gardner, George Zucco, Joan Hickson, George Sanders, Ivan Brandt, Torin Thatcher, Michael Rennie; **w,** H.G. Wells, Lajos Biró (based on the short story by Wells); **c,** Harold Rosson; **m,** Michael Spoliansky; **ed,** Philip Charlot; **spec eff,** Ned Mann, Lawrence W. Butler, Edward Cohen, Harry Zech, Jack Cardiff, W. Percy Day, Peter Ellenshaw.

The Man Who Fell to Earth ★★★ 1976; U.K.; 139m; British Lion/Cinema 5; Color; Science Fiction; Children: Unacceptable (MPAA: R); **DVD**; **VHS**. In this weird but intriguing science fiction tale Bowie is a humanoid alien who comes to Earth seeking water for his planet, which is very dry and dying. He goes into business with a partner, Henry, who is homosexual, and amasses a fortune by selling gold rings and merchandising some high technology inventions from his home planet. This goes on for three years with the help of a chemistry professor, Torn. Bowie lives comfortably in New Mexico, and a girl, Clark, falls in love with him even though he has a wife and two children on his original planet. Bowie's corporate greed and corruption stand in his way as he tries to build a spaceship so he can return to his desert planet and his family. Torn discovers through X-rays that Bowie is an alien, although by now the extraterrestrial has succumbed to gin and watching television so he is like most other humans. Henry and his lover, Riccardo, fall out of a high hotel window and are killed. The man who pushed them, Casey, has Bowie taken prisoner. More years pass while Bowie is tortured in a deserted hotel. Bowie's company goes bust and Torn goes to work for Casey and marries Clark. Bowie scores something of a financial comeback by recording an album, but reverts to drink and loses hope of ever returning to his home planet. Nudity, violence and gutter language prohibit viewing by children. **p**, Michael Deeley, Barry Spikings; **d**, Nicolas Roeg; **cast**, David Bowie, Rip Torn, Candy Clark, Buck Henry, Bernie Casey, Jackson D. Kane, Rick Riccardo, Tony Mascia, Richard Breeding, Terry Southern; **w**, Paul Mayersberg (based on the novel by Walter Tevis); **c**, Anthony B. Richmond (Panavision); **m**, John Phillips, Stomu Yamashta; **ed**, Graeme Clifford; **prod d**, Brian Eatwell; **set d**, Simon Wakefield; **spec eff**, Harrison Ellenshaw.

The Man Who Knew Too Much ★★★★ 1935; U.K.; 75m; Gaumont; B/W; Crime Drama; Children: Unacceptable; **DVD**; **VHS**. In this early day Hitchcock thriller married couple Banks and Best are vacationing in Switzerland with their daughter Pilbeam when they meet and befriend Fresnay. When Fresnay is mortally wounded, he whispers a secret to Banks, telling him that an important person is about to be assassinated. The plotters behind that assassination scheme to kidnap Pilbeam, telling Banks that, if he remains silent about what he knows, his daughter will be returned to him after they complete their grim assignment. Banks and Best return to London where Banks discovers that the assassination is to be committed there and later learns that the victim is a visiting diplomat, who will be shot and killed at London's Albert Hall. Banks frantically searches for the hideout of the assassins, but when he discovers the lair (and where Pilbeam is being held), he is captured and held hostage on orders of Lorre, who heads the for-hire killers. Meanwhile, Best attends the performance at Albert Hall and, when she spots the assassin, who is about to kill the diplomat, she lets loose a piercing scream that causes the victim to move slightly so that when he is shot, he receives a minor flesh wound. Police then close in on Lorre's hideout and a wild shootout ensues. Here Hitchcock really reenacts the Siege of Sidney Street, where London police shot it out with a group of anarchists (on January 3, 1911), who had committed several earlier murders relative to burglaries they also committed in attempting to fund their international political operations. Lorre and his henchmen are killed in the shootout, except for one assassin, who chases the terrified Pilbeam to the top of the roof of the hideout building, but he is shot dead before he can push the girl to her death. Banks then guides his daughter to safety for a harrowing but happy ending. Banks, Best, Pilbeam and Lorre are standouts in their roles, and pantheon director Hitchcock uses many arresting techniques to sustain suspense throughout for this exceptional thriller. *Author's Note*: Hitchcock really needed this film to be a hit and it was as successful in the U.S. as it was in England and in Europe, buoying the director's career after he had produced a few films that had been poorly received. Hitchcock told this author that "I was, in a way, on probation, and I had a very limited budget for the 1934 version of **The Man Who Knew Too Much**. I could not really shoot live audiences at Albert Hall, so I had Fortunio Matania, a talented artist, paint the audience in detail and then we reflected the painting in a mirror to the camera lens so that it appeared to be a live audience. I was assigned a German cinematographer named Courant and when I gave him specific instructions in English, he pretended to understand me and then began shooting as he wanted on his own. I learned that he understood no English so he thought he was able to pull the wool over my eyes. I then walked up to Courant and gave him his instructions in clear German, which surprised him, and I told him in his own language to follow my instructions to the letter. He was so amazed that he only nodded and did as I wanted after that. Sometime earlier, I had viewed a great crime film, **I Am a Fugitive from a Chain Gang** [1932] by Mervyn LeRoy, and there is a very tense scene in that picture where Paul Muni has just escaped and is sitting in a barber chair with a hot towel over his face when a detective comes into the shop. I admit with all humility that I did something like that in **The Man Who Knew Too Much** when I had Leslie [Banks] turn the tables on a dentist who is part of the conspirators

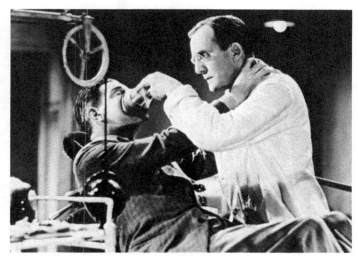

Leslie Banks, in dentist's chair, in *The Man Who Knew Too Much,* **1935.**

and is trying to kill him and he, instead, holds the dentist in his own chair and puts him to sleep with chloroform. Of course, my scene is different from what LeRoy did, but a good idea is still a good idea. Besides, I think a dentist is much more frightening than a barber any day." This was Lorre's first English-speaking film and he told this author that "I was grateful that Hitchcock sent for me to appear in **The Man Who Knew Too Much**. It established my career not only in England, but brought me to the attention of American producers and offers started to come to me from Hollywood. Hitchcock was very kind to me and we became friends and played practical jokes on each other by sending strange gifts to each other in the middle of the night. That stopped after I sent him three hundred singing canaries to his home at three o'clock in the morning." For more information on the Siege of Sidney Street, see my books, *Terrorism in the 20th Century: A Narrative Encyclopedia from the Anarchists through the Weathermen to the Unabomber* (M. Evans, 1998; pages 29-34), and *The Great Pictorial History of World Crime*, Volume II (History, Inc., 2004; pages 1506-1508). **p**, Michael Balcon; **d**, Alfred Hitchcock; **cast**, Leslie Banks, Edna Best, Peter Lorre, Frank Vosper, Hugh Wakefield, Nova Pilbeam, Pierre Fresnay, Cicely Oates, Joan Harrison, Hitchcock; **w**, A.R. Rawlinson, Charles Bennett, D.B. Wyndham Lewis, Edwin Greenwood, Emlyn Williams (based on a story by Bennett, Wyndham Lewis); **c**, Curt Courant; **m**, Arthur Benjamin; **ed**, H. St. C. Stewart; **art d**, Alfred Junge; **spec eff**, Albert Whitlock.

The Man Who Knew Too Much ★★★★ 1956; U.S.; 120m; PAR; Color; Crime Drama; Children: Unacceptable; **DVD**; **VHS**. In this excellent remake of the 1935 production, Hitchcock changes the initial locale from Switzerland to mysterious Marrakesh in French Morocco where Stewart, his wife, Day, and young son, Olsen, are on vacation. They meet Gelin, an affable Frenchman, as they travel by bus toward the city. Once in the city, they take rooms in an upscale hotel, and Stewart and Day are asked by Gelin to join him that evening for dinner. They go to the restaurant, and when Gelin fails to appear, they make new friends of Miles and de Banzie who join them when they have their meal. They then see Gelin at the restaurant, but he ignores them and Stewart is angered at this rebuff. The following day while Stewart, Day and Olsen go to a bazaar, where they also meet Miles and de Banzie, Stewart is shocked to see an Arab staggering toward him with a knife plunged in his back. As Stewart reaches forward to grab the stricken man, his hands come away with black dye from the victim's face, revealing Gelin, who has been in disguise and who, before dying, whispers to Stewart that there is to be an assassination of an important figure. While de Banzie takes Olsen back to the hotel, Miles accompanies Stewart and Day to the local police station where a police inspector grills him and where Miles

Bernard Miles, Brenda De Banzie, Doris Day, James Stewart and Daniel Gelin in *The Man Who Knew Too Much*, 1956.

serves as an interpreter. Miles then assures Stewart that he is going to the hotel to make sure his son, Olsen, is safe. When Stewart and Day return to the hotel, Stewart learns that Olsen has vanished as have Miles and de Banzie and he then learns that the boy is being held hostage to keep Stewart silent about what he has learned from the dead Gelin, an espionage agent, and that Olsen will not be returned until the assassination has been achieved. Stewart and Day return to their hotel in London and, while putting off some visiting friends, Stewart goes in search of his son with only one clue, a man named "Ambrose Chapel." He finds a taxidermist who is operating under that name, but his operation proves to be innocent. Day then discovers that it is a church, not a person, where their son is being held hostage, and both go to the chapel where they see Miles giving a sermon. When Stewart goes to search the place, however, he is thwarted by Miles' henchmen. Knowing that the assassination is to take place at Albert Hall, Day is present during that performance and screams when she sees the assassin about to shoot at a diplomat sitting in a box. The scream causes the diplomat to move so that he is only wounded while the assassin flees. In appreciation for saving his life, the diplomat invites Day and Stewart to his embassy where Day, a former celebrated singer, is asked to play the piano and sing one of her songs. She begins singing "Que Sera Sera" ("Whatever Will Be, Will Be" by Jay Livingston and Ray Evans, winning an Oscar for Best Song), a song she knows is one of her son's favorites, believing that he will hear it and shout out as she and Stewart also believe that Olsen is being held somewhere in the embassy. They are correct and Olsen cries out and Stewart races upstairs and into a room where Miles holds a gun on Olsen, telling Stewart that he will let the boy go only after he is allowed to escape. Miles and Stewart then walk slowly down a grand staircase in the embassy leading to the exit, but Stewart grabs Olsen and topples Miles downward where he is placed under arrest, and Day rushes forward to embrace her son. The traitor who engineered the assassination attempt and his henchmen are then rounded up. Stewart, Day and Olsen return to their hotel room to see their friends still waiting there, and Stewart, who has told them nothing about their harrowing experience, merely tells them "we had to pick up our son," this ironic understatement ending the fine thriller. Although minor locations and plotlines have been altered in this remake of Hitchcock's 1935 production, this version is equally suspenseful and is directed with great economy and skill by Hitchcock, where Stewart, Day and the cast give stellar performances. By this time, however, Hitchcock was one of the foremost film directors in the world and he commanded very substantial budgets. He again uses Albert Hall for one of his settings, and uses the actual premises of that august structure, where, in the original version, he used a set and a painting to represent the audience. In this version, the audience is represented by only some quick shots of spectators in boxes and some orchestra

seats. Highlighting this scene is a full-scale orchestra playing the tension-filled Storm Cloud Cantata, a chorale by Arthur Benjamin. Another song (also from Jay Livingston and Ray Evans) is "We'll Love Again." ***Author's Note***: Stewart had nothing but praise of Day, his co-star in this film, stating to this author that "she was perfect in her role as a deeply concerned mother when her son is abducted. Many thought she would not do well in that part as she had done mostly lighthearted comedies and musicals, but she proved that she could handle dramas, too, along with the best of them. We have a little scene in our hotel room when I must tell her that our son has been kidnapped and I know that, as a husband and physician, she will become hysterical, so I talk her into taking a sedative before I give her that terrible news, and during that scene, Doris brought her great emotional skills to bear as her anxiety mounts and before she learns the truth. Hitch and everybody in that production was very impressed with her." When talking with Hitchcock about this film, I pointed out his penchant for employing sharp instruments to dispatch victims in his many films, and where just such a victim meets his demise in this film when Gelin is dispatched in the bazaar at Marrakesh. (In **Blackmail**, 1929, the heroine defends herself by killing her assailant with a butcher knife; in **The 39 Steps**, 1935, the hero is confronted by a secret agent who falls over him while he is in bed with a knife plunged in her back; in **Dial M for Murder**, 1954, the heroine saves her life by plunging scissors into the back of her assailant; in **North by Northwest**, 1959, a diplomat at the United Nations falls into the arms of the hero with a knife plunged into his back and the hero removes it in front of dozens of witnesses who believe that he is the killer.) "I believe there is nothing more horrific than seeing a person stabbed to death," Hitchcock told me in response to my query. "Most believe that it is much more painful than being shot or blown up, which takes but a few moments, where a stab wound is slow and agonizing and has more visual impact. Also, it allows the victim to retain consciousness long enough to whisper a secret as he does to Stewart in **The Man Who Knew Too Much**, and that whispered secret is the MacGuffin [Hitchcock's term for the plot element that drives the story line] needed in the film." That scene was shot in the actual marketplace in Marrakesh, but there was a serious problem during that shooting as Hitchcock explained. "We used hundreds of natives as extras in that scene," he told this author, "but somehow a rumor spread throughout the crowd that, unless an extra was directly before one of our cameras, they would not be paid. Thus began a slow surge of this large crowd to push and shove in the direction of the cameras. I was sitting some distance away beneath a large umbrella as I watched these extras suddenly begin fighting with each other for positions closer to the cameras until it almost became a full-scale riot. They had to call in more policemen to stop the brawling. After order was restored, I had an interpreter stand on top of a truck and shout through a bullhorn that all would be paid even if they were not shown on camera. He was then promptly pelted with rotten fruit and vegetables for not telling everyone that earlier and then he had the nerve to charge me extra money for making that announcement, claiming that it was 'hazardous duty' pay." **p&d**, Alfred Hitchcock; **cast**, James Stewart, Doris Day, Brenda de Banzie, Bernard Miles, Ralph Truman, Daniel Gelin, Alan Mowbray, Hillary Brooke, Carolyn Jones, Frank Albertson, Hitchcock; **w**, John Michael Hayes, Angus MacPhail (based on a story by Charles Bennett, D.B. Wyndham-Lewis); **c**, Robert Burks (VistaVision; Technicolor); **m**, Bernard Herrmann; **ed**, George Tomasini; **art d**, Hal Pereira, Henry Bumstead; **set d**, Sam Comer, Arthur Krams; **spec eff**, Farciot Edouart, John P, Fulton.

The Man Who Laughs ★★★ 1928 (silent); U.S.; 110m/10 reels; UNIV; B/W; Drama; Children: Unacceptable; **DVD**; **VHS**. Veidt gives a riveting performance as a young man who has his face permanently altered through surgery on orders of James II, to spite Veidt's father, a political rival. His face is changed into a grotesque and permanent wide smile, almost a maniacal-looking toothy grin that makes him appear offensive to everyone. He is given shelter by a traveling showman, who then puts Veidt on public display as a sideshow freak. He later becomes a clown and is celebrated as "the man who laughs." Veidt lives a lonely, loveless life without relatives and friends until he meets and falls in love with Philbin, a beautiful girl, who is blind. She loves Veidt for the good-hearted person he truly is and, despite the ridicule and scorn heaped upon them, they find happiness together. *Author's Note*: Universal first thought to cast the great character actor Lon Chaney Sr., a master of horror films, as the lead in this film, but Veidt proved so effective when testing for the role that he was given the part. **p**, Paul Kohner; **d**, Paul Leni; **cast**, Conrad Veidt, Mary Philbin, Olga Baclanova, Julius Molnar, Jr., Brandon Hurst, Cesare Gravina, Stuart Holmes, Sam De Grasse, George Siegmann, Josephine Crowell; **w**, J. Grubb Alexander, Charles E. Whittaker, Marion Ward, May McLean, Walter Anthony (based on the novel *L'homme qui rit* by Victor Hugo); **c**, Gilbert Warrenton; **m**, William Axt, Erno Rapee, Sam Perry; **ed**, Edward Cahn; **art d**, Charles D. Hall, Thomas O'Neil, Joseph Wright.

The Man Who Lived Again ★★★ 1936; U.K.; 66m; Gainsborough Pictures/Gaumont; B/W; Horror; Children: Unacceptable; **DVD**; **VHS**. This is one of the early British horror films that Karloff appeared in before going to Hollywood, more intriguing and well made than other such productions and where he is again a mad scientist. Karloff has invented a device that can transfer matter where the atoms for one item is scrambled and then reassembled at another location, the transferable item being a brain, which is transferred from one body to another. Karloff presents this theory to a group of scientists, who scoff at his ideas as coming from a deranged mind. Thus rejected, Karloff loses his financial sponsor, Cellier. Incensed, Karloff transfers Cellier's brain to that of Calthrop, his crippled assistant, but this first experiment fails, causing both Cellier and Calthrop to die. Karloff remains dedicated to his science and, suddenly in love with his beautiful female assistant, Lee, attempts to seduce her by saying that they can both enjoy eternal youth and life through his experiments where they can transfer their brains through the ages into always younger bodies. Lee wants no part of this scheme and has earlier given her heart to Loder, Cellier's son, who has become suspicious of Karloff after the disappearance of his father. Karloff tricks Loder into submitting to a brain transfer experiment so that his brain is transferred to Karloff's body and Karloff's brain into Loder's body. Police burst into the laboratory just after the successful completion of this experiment, and Karloff, with Loder's brain, falls from a window and is mortally injured. Lee, who knows that Karloff has performed this last experiment to win her heart (with Loder's brain), is enraged and now demands that the experiment be redone and, while Karloff is still alive, she successfully performs the operation, so that Loder has once more regained his brain and Karloff his own. Before he dies, Karloff, repentant and now wiser for his mad mistakes, admits that it is best that his experiments will cease with his death. Karloff and the cast give standout performances in this well-crafted, well-written horror tale that boasts of superior sets and high production values and where the cinematography is clear and crisp. *Author's Note*: Karloff told this author that "that picture was one of my early ones in England and it had a substantial budget because the producer, Balcon, was a quality filmmaker and could command good financing. You know, the concept that I have as the crackpot scientist in that picture, where he thinks he can transfer matter from here to there, was picked up more than twenty years later and used in **The Fly** [1958], starring my friend, Vincent Price." **p**, Michael Balcon; **d**, Robert Stevenson; **cast**, Boris Karloff, Anna Lee, John Loder, Frank Cellier, Donald Calthrop, Cecil Parker, Lyn Harding, Clive Morton, Bryan Powley, D.J. Williams; **w**, John L. Balderston, Sidney Gilliat, L. Du Garde Peach; **c**, Jack Cox; **ed**, R.E. Dearing, Ben Hipkins, Alfred Roome; **art d**, Alex Vetchinsky.

The Man Who Loved Redheads ★★★ 1955; U.K.; 90m; British Lion/UA; Color; Comedy; Children: Unacceptable. In this delightful comedy, Justin is a youthful British aristocrat severely smitten when he

Conrad Veidt in *The Man Who Laughs*, 1928.

sees a beautiful redhead. His fixation for lassies with reddish tresses continues into his adult years, which includes Shearer, a beautiful red-haired teenager, who reminds him of his first love, making him forget he is married, a father, and has a high position with the foreign office. Justin pretends he is a bachelor and invites Shearer to dinner at the apartment of a friend, Culver. This begins a double life in which he romances more young women who remind him of his first red-hot love. At one of his parties, Elliott, his actor son, arrives, but Justin persuades him not to reveal his marital and paternal identity. Justin and Culver grow old while continuing their girl-chasing ways. One night, while escorting two models to the opening of a show in which Elliott appears, Justin sees his wife, Cooper, and she sees him. He learns that she knew all the time about his chasing redheads, but it hasn't bothered her. Justin is so taken by her loyalty that he vows to give up chasing redheads. When he comes to that adult decision, he doesn't even recognize that a woman standing nearby is the very redhead he first loved. She, like he, has grown older. Shearer, who gives marvelous performances, plays all the redheads in Justin's life. Sexual themes prohibit viewing by children. Music includes excerpts from Pyotr Ilyich Tchaikovsky's "The Sleeping Beauty" ballet. **p**, Josef Somlo; **d**, Harold French; **cast**, Moira Shearer, John Justin, Roland Culver, Gladys Cooper, Denholm Elliott, Harry Andrews, Patricia Cutts, Moyra Fraser, John Hart, Ronald Squire, Kenneth More (narrator); **w**, Terence Rattigan (based on his play "Who Is Sylvia?"); **c**, Georges Perinal (Eastmancolor); **m**, Benjamin Frankel; **ed**, Bert Bates; **art d**, Paul Sheriff.

The Man Who Loved Women ★★★ 1977; France; 120m; Les Films du Carrosse/Almi Pictures; Comedy; Children: Unacceptable; **DVD**; **VHS**. Denner is a standout in this delightful romantic comedy where he is an engineer who has been obsessed with loving women all his life, but once he beds a woman, he loses interest in her. The women, however, hold no grudge and continue to like him after he leaves because he is a charming rogue. He writes his memoirs, which reveal that his mother didn't have time for him because she was too busy having affairs with men. Even when Denner is hospitalized with broken legs from a car accident when he is forty years old, he can't keep his hands off women. When his nurse comes near his bed, he reaches out for her, accidentally unplugging his life support, and dies. Many of his past loves come to his funeral and remember him as a good lover. Sexuality prohibits viewing by children. (In French; English subtitles.) **p**, Marcel Berbert, François Truffaut (not credited); **d**, Truffaut; **cast**, Charles Denner, Brigitte Fossey, Nelly Borgeaud, Genevieve Fontanel, Leslie Caron, Nathalie Baye, Valerie Bonnier, Jean Dasté, Sabine Glaser, Henri Agel; **w**, Truffaut, Michel Fermaud, Suzanne Schiffman; **c**, Nestor Almendros (Eastmancolor) **m**, Maurice Jaubert; **ed**, Martine

Robert Flemyng and Clifton Webb in *The Man Who Never Was*, 1956.

Barraqué; **prod d**, Jean-Pierre Kohut-Svelko.

The Man Who Never Was ★★★★ 1956; U.K.; 103m; FOX; Color; Spy Drama; Children: Unacceptable; **DVD**; **VHS**. Taut and suspenseful throughout, this clever espionage tale (based on a true case) begins when British intelligence officer Webb dreams up a fantastic ruse to deceive and decoy the Nazi High Command during WWII. Webb's scheme is designed to convince the Germans that the much-expected invasion of southern Europe (Operation Husky) in 1943 will take place in Greece and not, as anticipated, somewhere in Sicily or Italy. Cynically labeling his own covert operation as Operation Mincemeat, Webb advises his superiors, including Naismith, that his plan is to have the body of a British officer wash ashore somewhere along the coast of neutral Spain, one that will carry documents that indicate that the forthcoming invasion will take place in Greece. Once the German High Command accepts the information accompanying that planted corpse, Webb believes, it will order most of its reserve forces to Greece and away from the intended landing area, Sicily. Although Webb's plan is thought to be gruesome and ruthless, it is accepted and Webb puts his scheme into motion after he and his assistant, Flemyng locate the body of a British officer and meet with the father of the deceased, asking for his permission to use his son's body and the father, Kelsall, patriotically approves. The dead man's body is preserved while a new identity for that man is created. He is now called "Major Martin," a British intelligence officer. In addition to his military credentials, Webb gives the dead man a financial and social background by establishing a bank account in his name and membership in a club. At the suggestion of Griffin, Webb's assistant, he also gives the man a love life in that he carries a love letter from an imaginary fiancée, a letter written by Griffin. The body, which has been preserved in dry-ice, is then taken by submarine to the coast of Spain, released adrift near Huelva. It is retrieved by Spanish authorities and, as Webb has anticipated, government officials turn over all of the documents found on that body to German intelligence officers in Spain (Germany had earlier been an ally of Spain, which was ruled by fascist dictator Francisco Franco). British intelligence remains uncertain as to whether or not the Germans will accept the ruse as real, but confirmation that the Germans have, indeed, received and copied the information (and then carefully returned it to the corpse for burial) appears in the form of Boyd, a German agent, who comes from Ireland to England to check on the dead man. Boyd goes to "Major Martin's" bank to confirm that he has an account there and then checks his membership in a London club. He boldly goes to Griffin's apartment, to see if she is the girl who has written the love letter to the dead man, but finds Grahame, instead of Griffin, albeit he has found the right girl in that Griffin signed Grahame's name to the love letter. Grahame is distraught at the time, having

recently lost the man she loved in the war, and her grief and emotional state over that man, whom she does not name, ironically convinces Boyd that she is referring to "Major Martin" and he returns to his rented room where he sends a shortwave message to German intelligence confirming that the body and its documents are genuine. The Germans then move army divisions to Greece, which is then an inactive front, and that allows the Allies to make a "soft" landing in Sicily when they begin the invasion of Europe. Webb's successful scheme has saved innumerable Allied lives and, following the war, he visits the dead man's grave, placing a medal at the site in a salute to this unknown warrior, the film ending as it shows the body washing ashore and the viewer hears the haunting words: "Last night, I dreamt a dead man won the fight." Webb is superb in his restrained role of the intelligence officer, and Boyd is outstanding as the cunning German spy while the rest of the cast members all render superlative performances. ***Author's Note***: For extensive details on this great intelligence ruse, see my book, *Spies: A Narrative Encyclopedia of Dirty Deeds & Double Dealing from Biblical Times to the Present* (M. Evans, 1997; pages 332-324). **p**, André Hakim; **d**, Ronald Neame; **cast**, Clifton Webb, Gloria Grahame, Robert Flemyng, Josephine Griffin, Stephen Boyd, Laurence Naismith, Geoffrey Keen, Moultrie Kelsall, Cyril Cusack, André Morell, Michael Hordern, Joan Hickson, Peter Sellers (voice of Winston Churchill); **w**, Nigel Balchin (based on the book by Ewen Montagu); **c**, Oswald Morris (CinemaScope; DeLuxe Color); **m**, Alan Rawsthorne, **ed**, Peter Taylor; **art d**, John Hawkesworth; **spec eff**, Tom Howard.

The Man Who Reclaimed His Head ★★★ 1935; U.S.; 82m; UNIV; B/W; Drama; Children: Unacceptable; **DVD**. Rains is a poor writer, who takes a job writing anti-war editorials for publisher Atwill during World War I. This is fine with him because he's a pacifist. Atwill sends him to some battlefronts where he witnesses the carnage. While he's gone, Atwill courts Rains' wife, Bennett, and upon his return Rains learns of his wife's infidelity. Rains also discovers that Atwill is among those making big money through war profiteering. The combination of it all drives Rains mad and he beheads Atwill. The opening of this film signals the violence and lunacy to come when the viewer hears a scream, a window is broken and then Rains staggers onto a snow-bound Paris street carrying a satchel in one hand and pulling his little daughter by the other. This thriller presents a strong anti-war message and a powerful performance from Rains and where Atwill and Bennett are standouts. ***Author's Note***: Rains told this author that "after appearing in **The Invisible Man** [1933], I was typecast as a man easily provoked into madness and in **The Man Who Reclaimed His Head**, I certainly have enough provocation, but cutting off my rival's head and carrying it about in a satchel, well, that's about as far as you can go with such a character, one would think." **p**, Carl Laemmle, Jr.; **d**, Edward Ludwig; **cast**, Claude Rains, Joan Bennett, Lionel Atwill, Juanita [Baby Jane] Quigley, Henry O'Neill, Valerie Hobson, Henry Armetta, Wallace Ford, Phyllis Brooks, Doris Lloyd; **w**, Jean Bart, Samuel Ornitz, Barry Trivers (based on the play by Bart); **c**, Merritt B. Gerstad; **m**, Heinz Roemheld; **ed**, Murray Seldeen; **art d**, Albert S. D'Agostino; **spec eff**, John P. Fulton.

The Man Who Shot Liberty Valance ★★★★ 1962; U.S.; 123m; PAR; B/W; Western; Children: Unacceptable; **DVD**; **VHS**. Wayne, Stewart, Miles, O'Brien, Strode and, especially, Marvin are outstanding in their roles in this fine Ford western that signifies the taming of America's Old West. The film begins when that violent Old West has gone to boot hill and where an elderly Stewart, accompanied by his aging wife Miles, return to their hometown of Shinbone. Stewart, a U.S. senator, and Miles, are making a melancholy trip to pay homage to a recently deceased rancher, Wayne. They renew their friendships with Devine, the former sheriff of the town, and Strode, Wayne's hired man. While waiting for Wayne to be buried, Stewart gives an interview to the local newspaper, its editor, Young, considering Stewart the great hero of the state, chiefly for dispatching Marvin (Liberty Valance), a notorious killer, many years earlier. As Stewart recalls that violent era, we see in flashback the story of the real hero in that old saga. Stewart is seen traveling by stagecoach as it approaches Shinbone when it is stopped and held up by Marvin and his two equally psychopathic henchmen, Van Cleef and Martin (whose pop-eyed, berserk mannerisms throughout this film are a chilling marvel to behold). Stewart, then a novice lawyer, steps from the stage with other passengers, and when they are robbed, particularly lady passenger Lee, Stewart objects and Marvin beats him so viciously that he believes he has killed him and leaves him for dead as the thieves ride away. Wayne later finds the barely alive Stewart and takes him to Shinbone, depositing him with Miles, who works in the local café with owners Qualen and Nolan. Stewart is given a bed to rest upon as Miles nurses him back to health, feeding him heavy meals while she becomes attracted to him and his ethical beliefs, although she is nominally Wayne's girlfriend. Stewart recovers, but, having lost his money in the robbery committed by Marvin, he is unable to establish a law practice in town. He goes to work as a waiter in the restaurant. When Marvin and his goons visit the café, they ridicule Stewart, and Marvin trips him when he is carrying a steak dinner to serve to Wayne, spilling the steak onto the floor. Marvin orders Stewart to pick up the steak, but Wayne tells Marvin to pick it up himself. Wayne, like Marvin, is handy with his gun and does not fear the brutal thug. Marvin thinks a second time about drawing on Wayne, but before he can retrieve the steak, Stewart picks it up and slams it back onto the plate, shouting: "Now it's picked up!" There are only two persons in Shinbone who stand up to Marvin, Wayne, and O'Brien, a boozy newspaper editor, who is hated by Marvin because O'Brien is forever writing critical articles about Marvin and his brutal conduct, suggesting that he is a thief and murderer. O'Brien then allows Stewart to hang a shingle in front of his small newspaper office where he and O'Brien begin a campaign to bring the territory into statehood, a movement opposed by some of the ranchers, including the cattle-rustling Marvin. When Marvin challenges Stewart, Wayne again comes to the rescue, and, to equip the attorney with some kind of defense, tries to train Stewart in shooting a six-gun, but, in a very amusing scene, he proves to be a bum shot, wholly inexpert in aiming and shooting the weapon. While attempting to train Stewart, Wayne proudly shows him a room that he and Strode have been adding to Wayne's ranch house, a room Wayne says will be a bedroom for him and Miles after the independent-minded Miles finally decides to marry him. A convention is held in Shinbone where delegates are to be chosen to decide on the ratification of statehood, and Marvin storms into the hall, demanding that he be elected as one of those few delegates with his intention to kill the statehood movement. He receives a nomination from Van Cleef, which is seconded by Martin, his two henchmen, but no one votes for Marvin. On the other hand, Wayne, who keeps order with his six-guns ready, nominates both O'Brien and Stewart as delegates and they are almost unanimously elected, with the angry exceptions of Marvin and his two thugs, who leave the hall, promising retribution. That revenge comes when O'Brien prints another attack on Marvin and Marvin arrives with Van Cleef and Martin to wreck O'Brien's offices and press and where they beat O'Brien to death. Marvin then orders Stewart to meet him in the street that night and to bring a gun. Although he has no chance against gunman Marvin, Stewart gets his six-gun and steps into the dark street. Marvin appears and both men shoot at each other with Stewart wounded, but a shot squarely strikes Marvin, killing him. Stewart is hailed a hero and is later elected to several high offices until he becomes U.S. Senator from the state and we see now in flash-forward where Stewart concludes his story to the editor, but adding one significant fact. It was not he who shot Marvin, but it was Wayne, who shot down the killer from across the street. Stewart wants the story corrected, but the editor, Young, refuses, saying: "This is the West. When the legend becomes the fact, print the legend." So Wayne, the true hero, goes unsung to his grave as Stewart, Miles, Strode and Devine accompany the body to its grave to end this bittersweet tale. Ford does a fine job in presenting this exciting story evoking a poignant

Edmond O'Brien and James Stewart in *The Man Who Shot Liberty Valance,* **1962.**

portrayal of the Old West, almost as if making a final salute to the genre, although he would make two more westerns, **How the West Was Won**, 1962 (where he directed only the Civil War scenes), and **Cheyenne Autumn**, 1964. Although well crafted and acted, many elements of the story line in this film can be seen in previous westerns, particularly the character played by O'Brien and his death at the hands of brutal gunmen, as can be seen in the killing of Frank McHugh, who plays a crusading newspaper editor in **Dodge City**, 1939, who is running articles about the town's villain, Bruce Cabot, and his two henchmen, Victor Jory and Douglas Fowley, and who are certainly the role models for Marvin, Van Cleef and Martin. *Author's Note*: When this author asked Ford why he did not shoot **The Man Who Shot Liberty Valance** on location in his usual western exteriors, he replied: "It was the budget. Not enough money to take everybody to Monument Valley or anywhere else. Paramount kept the purse strings tight so I had to use two sound stages at the studio to make that film and I was damned mad about it, I can tell you." Wayne told this author that "I thought it was strange that I had not worked with Jimmy [Stewart] in any pictures until **The Man Who Shot Liberty Valance**. We had talked for years about getting together on a lot of film projects but they never got off the table. He's a hell of an actor and you can't overwhelm him with a lot of bluster or loud talk, no sir. He has all those quiet mannerisms so in our scenes together to compensate for his quiet attitude I kept silent for some time before delivering my lines. I thought to 'out quiet him,' but that didn't work, especially after Pappy [Ford] shouted at me, saying, 'what the hell are you waiting for, Duke? Spit out the line, dammit!' So I started spitting." Stewart, always the gentleman, told this author that "being with Duke in **The Man Who Shot Liberty Valance** was one of my great joys in life. What a fine actor he was. His presence was enormous when he walked on to the set. Everything about him was big, like the West itself. We did one more picture together, **The Shootist** [1976] where Duke is an aging gunfighter who is dying of cancer and I am the doctor who has to tell him that he will soon die. The irony of that picture was that Duke did have cancer at that time and was, indeed, dying. It was his last film, and a great one." Miles told this author [we met at a dinner party in Chicago in 1969 when she was appearing in a play there and when I was the editor-in-chief of *ChicagoLand Magazine*] that "I spent most of my time in that picture frying steaks and making coffee in the kitchen of a restaurant when I am not arguing with Jimmy [Stewart] or Duke." I recall telling Miles that she had dainty feet and that I could tell her what size shoe she wore. When she called me on that, I told her that she wore size 6B and she said: "How in the world would you know that?" I replied: "One of the many part-time jobs I had when going to college was selling women's shoes, my commercial baptism of fire [and the worst job I ever held]." We then spent the next twenty

Michael Caine and Sean Connery in *The Man Who Would Be King,* **1975.**

or so minutes while she had me tell her the sizes of shoes worn by every woman sitting nearby. **p**, John Ford, Willis Goldbeck; **d**, Ford; **cast**, James Stewart, John Wayne, Vera Miles, Lee Marvin, Edmond O'Brien, Andy Devine, John Carradine, Jeanette Nolan, John Qualen, Carleton Young, Woody Strode, Denver Pyle, Strother Martin, Lee Van Cleef, O.Z. Whitehead, William Henry, Anna Lee, Ken Murray, Willis Bouchey, Montie Montana, "Snub" Pollard; **w**, James Warner Bellah, Willis Goldbeck (based on a story by Dorothy M. Johnson); **c**, William H. Clothier; **m**, Cyril Mockridge; **ed**, Otho Lovering; **art d**, Hal Pereira, Eddie Imazu; **set d**, Sam Comer, Darrell Silvera; **spec eff**, Farciot Edouart, Sarah McGrail.

The Man Who Was Sherlock Holmes ★★★ 1937; Germany; 80m; Universum Film/UFA; B/W; Comedy; Children: Acceptable; **DVD**. A delightful comedy sees two confidence tricksters, Albers and Ruhmann, who are mistaken for Sherlock Holmes and Dr. Watson during the 1936 World Exposition in Paris. They go along with the impersonation by tracking down rare but counterfeit stamps. While thus engaged, another man, who looks like Holmes, shows up, but he is really Sir Arthur Conan Doyle (1859-1930), played by Bildt, creator of the fictional Holmes and Watson. Albers and Ruhmann eventually capture a gang of counterfeiters and recover a priceless stamp collection. However, they are arrested as impersonators but are released when Bildt vouches for them, saying he has given them the right to portray his fictional characters. (In German; English subtitles.) **p**, Alfred Greven; **d**, Karl Hartl; **cast**, Hans Albers, Heinz Ruhmann, Marieluise Claudius, Hansi Knoteck, Hilde Weissner, Gunther Ballier, Paul Bildt, Harry Hardt, Lothar Geist, Angelo Ferrari, Erich Dunskus; **w**, Hartl, R.A. Stemmle; **c**, Fritz Arno Wagner; **m**, Hans Sommer; **ed**, Gertrud Hinz-Nischwitz; **prod d**, Otto Hunte, Willy Schiller.

The Man Who Would Be King ★★★★★ 1975; U.K./U.S.; 129m; COL/AA; Color; Adventure; Children: Unacceptable (MPAA: PG); **BD**; **DVD**; **VHS**. The always inventive Huston provides a gloriously entertaining adventure where Connery and Caine are outstanding as two conniving British soldiers in Imperial India. Their tale really begins when their saga has ended as an old and much scarred beggar enters the offices of Plummer (who plays Rudyard Kipling the author of this memorable story) in Lahore, India. At first, the half-mad old man is unrecognizable to Plummer, but, as the rasping beggar begins to tell his tale, he recalls meeting the two men of his story, Caine and Connery, who had visited him many years earlier and asked him to witness a document they provide with his signature, a document that describes their various schemes to make fortunes that have not materialized. We see in flashback as Caine and Connery tell Plummer how they plan to quit the ranks of the British army and seek their own fortunes by going to Kafiristan, a remote mountainous country that has not seen a white man since the days of Alexander the Great. The two men, like Plummer, are Masons, and, in fact, Caine has returned a watch to Plummer he has stolen from him earlier, after Caine sees the Masonic crest on the timepiece. Connery and Caine then embark on a perilous journey, going northward, until they reach the fabled Khyber Pass and then descend into the great valley of Kafiristan, this remote land (Nurestan in present-day northeastern Afghanistan) ruled by warlords living inside ancient walled cities. The inhabitants are uneducated and live crudely without sanitation while worshipping ancient pagan gods. Connery and Caine then meet Jaffrey outside one of these cities; Jaffrey greets them warmly as fellow soldiers as he has been a former corporal in the British army and he becomes their interpreter and guide. The local warlord challenges the two men and Connery bests him in hand-to-hand combat, becoming the leader of the town. He then leads a rag-tag army against a much larger city, and during the battle, an arrow is shot into his chest, but Connery fails to collapse and goes on attacking. When the enemy sees this, they believe that Connery is not only invulnerable but he is the reincarnation of Alexander the Great, who has returned to lead the entire country back to its former days of glory. Connery pulls the arrow from his chest, holding it aloft, but not telling anyone but Caine that he had been saved when the arrow struck the Masonic medal he was wearing beneath his shirt and therefore never penetrated his flesh. Connery is now treated as a god and, even though Caine urges that they both collect the vast amount of jewels and gold they find in the main temple, Connery is too taken by his idolizing followers. While carrying about the arrow that failed to kill him as the symbol of his immortality, Connery decides that he will remain and become king of the country, deluding himself into believing that he might be that reincarnation of Alexander. Caine wants no part of this, but Connery convinces him to remain for a little while to witness his marriage to the most beautiful girl in the country, Shakira Caine (who was Caine's wife in real life). When the trembling girl is brought to him, however, she is too terrified to marry a god and resists Connery, biting and scratching him so that she draws blood. This shocks Connery's followers, who now know that he is only a mortal since gods have no blood in their veins, and both he and Caine are then condemned by the high priests. Both men try to escape, but Connery is killed when falling into a deep gorge and Caine is captured, crucified and then left for dead. In flash-forward we see the beggar finishing his tale to reveal himself to Plummer as Caine, who has somehow survived his incredible adventures and that is where this great saga ends. Huston directs this action-packed adventure with tremendous skill and energy while Connery and Caine provide startling performances that intrigue and charm throughout as two great rascals who dangerously test the gullibility of others and their own luck to the very edge of doom. Plummer, too, is exceptional in his brief but impressive role as Kipling, the great writer who penned this grand story (a novella of 12,000 words, which the author wrote in a few days). This masterpiece adventure film is summed up at the beginning by Caine, who tells Plummer: "We're going away to another place where a man isn't crowded and can come into his own. We are not little men and there's nothing we're afraid of." The film was shot on location in Morocco. *Author's Note*: Director Huston told this author that "I wanted to make **The Man Who Would Be King** ever since I read that story as a boy. What a tale! I tried to convince producers to let me make a film about that story with Clark Gable and Humphrey Bogart in the roles of Danny [Connery] and Peachy [Caine], but everyone thought I was nuts. Later on, I tried the same approach, saying I could make the picture with Richard Burton as Danny and Peter O'Toole as Peachy and again, it was no go with producers. Then my producer, Foreman, somehow convinced Manny Wolf at Allied Artists to cough up the $8 million so we could make the film and, after we signed on two very fine actors, Connery and Caine, we were on our way to Morocco. Going to Afghanistan and the real province where the story was based was impossible since the tribes up there were still warring with each other and we would most certainly have all gotten killed as infidels." (And not much has since changed in that troubled country.) Kipling described Kafiristan with great accuracy, detailing its strange past of idolatry and its ancient links to Alexander the Great in his story, which was published in 1888. Eight years later, in 1896, the Emir of Afghanistan converted Kafiristan to an Islamic state by destroying all of its temples and idols as well as killing its priests, forcing the Islamic religion upon all inhabitants at the threat of death while renaming the province Nurestan. In essaying his fine role as the gifted Kipling (1865-1936), Plummer told this author that "I did quite a bit of research on Kipling. I even listened to an old recording of his voice that we got from BBC and studied photographs of him, and, of course, had read his exciting works, before I played him in **The Man Who Would Be King**." Kipling is also briefly profiled by Reginald Sheffield in another great adventure tale, based on his work, **Gunga Din**, 1939. **p**, John Foreman; **d**, John Huston; **cast**, Sean Connery, Michael Caine, Christopher Plummer, Saeed Jaffrey, Doghmi Larbi, Jack May, Karroom Ben Bouih, Mohammad Shamsi, Albert Moses, Paul Antrim, Graham Acres, Shakira Caine; **w**, Huston, Gladys Hill (based on the story by Rudyard Kipling); **c**, Oswald Morris (Panavision; Technicolor); **m**, Maurice Jarre; **ed**, Russell Lloyd; **prod d**, Alexander Trauner; **art d**, Tony Inglis; **spec eff**, Dick Parker, Wally Veevers, Albert Whitlock, Doug Ferris.

The Man with a Cloak ★★★ 1951; U.S.; 84m; MGM; B/W; Drama; Children: Cautionary; **DVD**; **VHS**. In this suspenseful film, thick with gothic atmosphere (set in 1848), Caron arrives in New York from France seeking to persuade Calhern, a former marshal of France under Napoleon I, into restoring his estranged grandson back into his will. The grandson is Caron's lover, and needs Calhern's wealth to help finance the struggling new Republic. Caron stays in Calhern's sprawling mansion while the dying old man considers her proposal and while Stanwyck, who manages Calhern's affairs, along with his butler, De Santis, and Wycherly, his housekeeper, scheme to kill him and seize Calhern's estate. After Caron gets nowhere with Calhern, she befriends a heavy-drinking, poetry-reciting stranger, Cotten, asking him for her help, and Cotten comes to suspect Stanwyck and De Santis of being up to no good. Caron, along with Cotten's considerable persuasion, change Calhern's mind, and he summons his attorney, Hale, and changes his will, making his grandson his beneficiary. Calhern has earlier placed poison in his brandy, intending to end his life because of the insufferable pain he is enduring. He, however, suffers a stroke and is incapable of speaking and watches in agony as Hale, after completing the changes in the will, drinks the brandy and dies. Calhern's pet raven then swoops up the will and hides it inside a fireplace. Before Calhern succumbs, he tries to indicate to Cotten the location of the hidden will with his eyes, but this last effort fails. Stanwyck realizes that a new will has been written and, following Calhern's funeral, she, De Santis and Wycherly desperately search the mansion in an effort to find the document. Cotten then arrives and, remembering the frantic eye signals from Calhern, deduces the hiding place of the will and finds it. When he attempts to leave the mansion, De Santis attacks him, but Cotten beats him off and manages to escape. The will is then announced with Calhern's fortune going to Caron's lover. Caron then searches for the mysterious Cotten, the man who has always worn a cloak, and goes to his favorite drinking spa. Backus, who is the saloon owner, tells her that the strange Cotten has departed the city, leaving behind his payment for a bar bill, a poem titled "Annabel Lee" and signed "Edgar Allan Poe." This thriller is well directed by Markle and offers a provocative and literate script from Fenton, and where Stanwyck, Cotten, Caron, Calhern and De Santis are outstanding in their respective roles. Song: "Another Yesterday" (music and lyrics by Earl K. Brent; mimed by Stanwyck and sung or dubbed by Harriet Lee). **Author's Note**: Cotten told this author that "playing the great writer Edgar Allan Poe called for restraint. It is widely known that he was a heavy drinker and I show his alcoholism, but not as a drunk who drinks for the sake of drinking. Poe drank from deep psychological prob-

Gregory Peck, Joyce Grenfell and Hugh Wakefield in *Man with a Million*, 1954.

lems and here he steps away from his personal demons to help someone else with their own problems while overcoming his affliction to defeat the villains." Stanwyck thought her role, according to her statements to this author, "was another one of those evil and contemptible women I had been identified with many years earlier, especially after playing that terrible Phyllis in **Double Indemnity** [1944]. I really never escaped that character." **p**, Stephen Ames; **d**, Fletcher Markle; **cast**, Joseph Cotten, Barbara Stanwyck, Louis Calhern, Leslie Caron, Joe De Santis, Jim Backus, Margaret Wycherly, Richard Hale, Nicholas Joy, Roy Roberts, Hank Worden, Mitchell Lewis, Jean Inness; **w**, Frank Fenton (based on a story by John Dickson Carr); **c**, George J. Folsey; **m**, David Raksin; **ed**, Newell P. Kimlin; **art d**, Cedric Gibbons, Arthur Lonergan; **set d**, Edwin B. Willis, Arthur Krams.

Man with a Million ★★★ 1954; U.K.; 90m; Group Film Productions/UA; Color; Comedy; Children: Acceptable; **DVD**; **VHS**. Peck is both charming and very funny in this capricious comedy where, as a penniless American seaman stranded in London, he is arbitrarily selected by two British millionaire brothers, Squire and Hyde-White, to receive a loan of £1 million (in those Victorian days $10 million) to see what might happen to him. The loan, however, is only in the form of a single note in that staggering amount, one that Peck finds impossible to spend. When he offers to pay for a meal with the note, the restaurant owners are shocked into believing he is an eccentric American millionaire, and he is allowed to eat on credit. He is soon being measured for an elegant wardrobe by Saville Row tailors and living in a sumptuous hotel suite. No one presses him for payment, deferring his bills for later settlement. He meanwhile buys some worthless stock that causes the market to respond by buying up more of the stock so that the company's value greatly increases. Peck then meets and falls in love with Griffiths and they plan to marry, but Peck's fate and fortune plummets when he loses the note. When his many creditors learn that he no longer possesses that note, they begin hounding him at every corner. All of his new found friends, except for Griffiths and his faithful butler, Beckwith, turn against him and he is soon facing imprisonment in debtor's prison. Just before Peck is dragged off in disgrace to the pokey, the note is returned to him and he then returns that note to the brothers who made that loan to him. Peck is by then a very wealthy man in that the stock he purchased has earned him a great fortune and he now comfortably faces the future with Griffiths. Neame's direction is top drawer as are all the production values and where the fine sets impressively represent the Victorian era of the story. Peck, who always did well in any genre of film, is outstanding as the lucky (or unlucky) victim of two whimsical millionaires. **Author's Note**: "I look back on that picture with fondness," Peck told this author, "as giving me a very enjoyable role. It's a great story from Mark

Frank Sinatra in *The Man with the Golden Arm*, 1955.

Twain to begin with and it presents a biting satire on the greedy as well as giving a good inside look at British traditions. Money makes most people nervous and a lot of money as is shown in that picture makes everyone a little more than crazy." **p**, John Bryan; **d**, Ronald Neame; **cast**, Gregory Peck, Ronald Squire, Joyce Grenfell, A.E. Matthews, Maurice Denham, Reginald Beckwith, Wilbur Evans, Wilfrid Hyde-White, Hugh Griffith, Joan Hickson, Laurence Naismith, Ernest Thesiger, Mona Washbourne; **w**, Jill Craigie (based on the story "The Million Pound Note" by Mark Twain); **c**, Geoffrey Unsworth (Technicolor); **m**, William Alwyn; **ed**, Clive Donner; **art d**, John Box, Jack Maxsted.

The Man with Bogart's Face ★★★ 1980; U.S.; 106m; Melvin Simon Productions/FOX; Color; Comedy; Children: Cautionary (MPAA: PG); **DVD**; **VHS**. Sacchi, who bears an uncanny resemblance to tough guy movie star Humphrey Bogart, is terrific in this satirical crime yarn (based on **The Maltese Falcon**, 1941, and other Bogart films) where he has his face altered by plastic surgery to look like his movie idol, Bogey, and then opens a cheap office and goes into the detective business, hiring Rowe as his dopey blonde secretary. After Sacchi's picture appears in newspapers following a shooting, he is hired to track down "the eyes of Alexander," two priceless gems stolen from the eye sockets of a statue of Alexander the Great. Several underworld types are also searching for those jewels, including Lom (playing a Peter Lorre character); the bulky Buono, a Greek shipping magnate (parodying actor Sydney Greenstreet); Nero, a secretive Turkish mogul who has alluring Danning for his secretary; and Robinson, a Nazi named Zinderneuf (after the desert fort in **Beau Geste**, 1939), who has recently been released form a Greek jail after serving time as a war criminal. Hussey, too, is looking for the gems as is her father, Kosleck (who played innumerable Nazi characters in the 1940s and whose name is Horst Borsht). After Kosleck is killed by unknown assailants early in the film, bodies begin dropping everywhere. Phillips (playing a parody part of Mary Astor) vies with the others for the gems while the nonstop action takes the viewer through car chases, into lavish mansions, seedy streets, and, at the finale, when Sacchi has obtained the jewels on board a sumptuous yacht anchored at Catalina Island. Buono and Nero, the two millionaires bid for the jewels while stripping to their underwear and Lom is fed to the sharks as assorted mayhem takes place and where Sacchi comes out on top by solving the riddle. All of the cast members are good in this rollicking crime sendup and former stars De Carlo and Raft make brief appearances. *Author's Note*: Fenady wrote the novel based on this movie and produced and wrote the very funny script as well. Sacchi's private eye office was really Fenady's own office at Larchmont and Beverly Boulevard in Los Angeles. The film was financed by Indianapolis

real estate tycoon Mel Simon, who also back **The Stuntman**, 1980. **p**, Andrew J. Fenady; **d**, Robert Day; **cast**, Robert Sacchi, Franco Nero, Michelle Phillips, Olivia Hussey, Victor Buno, Herbert Lom, Gregg Palmer, George Raft, Yvonne De Carlo, Mike Mazurki, Henry Wilcoxon, Sybil Danning, Jay Robinson, Joe Theismann, Martin Kosleck, Larry Pennell, Robert Osborne; **w**, Fenady (based on his novel); **c**, Richard C. Glouner (CFI Color); **m**, George Duning; **ed**, Houseley Stevenson, Jr.; **prod d**, Robert Kinoshita; **set d**, Jerry Adams; **spec eff**, Ira Anderson.

The Man with the Golden Arm ★★★ 1955; U.S.; 119m; Otto Preminger Films/UA; B/W; Drama; Children: Unacceptable; **BD**; **DVD**; **VHS**. Sinatra captivates in an offbeat role as a professional card dealer, who is a heroin addict and who, throughout this grim and often painful film, attempts to beat the habit. Sinatra is shown arriving back in his hometown of Chicago after having taken a lengthy cure in Kentucky and the first person he meets is Stang, a street thief and close friend, as well as conniving drug pusher McGavin, who offers Sinatra a free fix for "old time's sake." Sinatra declines the offer and goes home to his angry wife, Parker, an invalid confined in a wheelchair. To earn good money, Parker urges Sinatra to go back to his old job as a card dealer in Strauss' illegal poker parlor, but Sinatra tells her that he does not want to go back to that old way of life. She pressures him, bitterly reminding him that she is a cripple because of his own carelessness when he crashed a car with her in it while he was driving drunk (Sinatra is a loser in every way). He goes back to work for Strauss and there meets B-girl Novak, an alluring blonde who encourages customers to buy her and themselves drinks, but, after shilling these suckers, she dumps them. Sinatra falls in love with Novak, but he is wracked with guilt over Parker's condition and remains loyal to her. In an effort to begin a new life, Sinatra begins to practice on the drums, believing he can get a job with a small band, but when Parker complains about the noise, Sinatra practices at Novak's apartment. He becomes good enough to have an audition, but before he performs, he must deal one more big poker game and becomes so anxious that he takes a fix of heroin from McGavin. He is then caught cheating and is so severely beaten up that he needs another fix to ease the pain. By the time he goes to the audition, he is a physical and emotional wreck and cannot perform. Meanwhile, McGavin goes to Sinatra's home and finds Parker walking about, and he now plans to tell Sinatra that Parker has been using her "crippled act" to hold on to Sinatra. Before McGavin can relate this grim news to Sinatra, Parker pushes him down a dark, steep flight of stairs and he is killed in the fall. Sinatra is sought by police as McGavin's killer, but he hides out in Novak's apartment, saying that he cannot go to the cops until he rids himself of drugs so he quits "cold turkey," and compels himself to undergo incredible agony in his withdrawal where he rants, whimpers, shouts, cries and pounds on the walls. After three days of this debilitating misery, he believes he has withdrawn from heroin and is ready to talk to the police. He goes to Parker, telling her that he is going to make a clean break with everything and that he is going away with Novak. Parker leaps from her wheelchair and begins to follow him, but when she sees police arriving, she goes to a window and, thinking to end her life, jumps from the window. Sinatra races to Parker's side and holds her in his arms as she dies while Novak stands in the distance waiting to begin that new life with Sinatra. The story is grim and taxing from beginning to end but Sinatra's bravura performance sustains interest, albeit many will find the subject matter too heavy to handle. *Author's Note*: Sinatra told this author that "I worked my butt off on that picture and even studied the way heroin addicts live. There is not much happiness to find in that story, but I think it gives a very good portrait of just how much hell drug addicts go through and what a terrible affliction drugs can be." The truculent Nelson Algren (1909-1981), who wrote the book, conferred with Preminger, and, according to the director's statements to this author "he proved to be a big pain in the neck by telling me how to shoot scenes and how the actors should deliver their lines.

After enough of that nonsense, I told him to stay in Chicago and go back to writing his books and he did. He was an unpleasant, mean little man, who seemed to be angry at everyone." This author's experiences with Algren in Chicago were of a similar nature. Though a brilliant writer, Algren was fiercely competitive with any and all other Chicago writers, who, in his perspective, had no talent. He went out of his way to publicly ridicule other Chicago writers such as Ben Hecht (1894-1964), and, in fact, when Hecht's novel, *Eric Dorn*, was reissued by the University of Chicago in 1963 (Hecht died the following year), Algren pleaded to write an introduction to that work and did, blasting Hecht and the work. I confronted Maurice English (1909-1983), a widely acclaimed poet and the editor at the University of Chicago Press, and asked him why he would reissue Hecht's novel and then paste Algren's acid-dripping introduction in front of it that more or less told people not to read it. English shrugged and said: "We got caught up in Nelson's in-fighting, I guess." When my good friend Tom Fitzpatrick (1927-2002; Pulitzer Prize winning columnist for the Chicago *Sun-Times*) once told Algren to shut up in O'Rourke's Pub, I witnessed Algren's response: He threw a bottle at Fitzpatrick's head that narrowly missed its mark. "You could have killed him," I said to Algren. "Maybe," he replied. Algren most hated Chicago-based writer Saul Bellow (1915-2005), who not only received the Pulitzer Prize but the Nobel Prize for his fine works, and publicly attacked Bellow whenever he could. They both found themselves together in a Chicago Turkish bath one day and spent an hour shouting insults at each other through the billowing steam. You could make Nelson Algren your lifelong enemy by simply getting a byline in an article published in Chicago in those days. He was a dangerous man to know, especially if you were a writer. I think that the only established writer in Chicago who liked Algren in those days was the acerbic Mike Royko (1932-1997), also a Pulitzer Prize winning columnist, who ended his days with the Chicago *Tribune*. Mike was a close friend of mine and I once asked him: "Why do you have any fondness for Algren? You know he's a rattler and has more than one screw loose." Mike replied: "Because he won't take any guff from anybody, and he writes about the mean streets of Chicago better than anyone I know. Besides, it's better to have him as friend than an enemy, if you know what I mean." **p&d**, Otto Preminger; **cast**, Frank Sinatra, Kim Novak, Eleanor Parker, Arnold Stang, Darren McGavin, Robert Strauss, Leonid Kinskey, Shelley Manne, "Snub" Pollard, Shorty Rogers, Will Wright; **w**, Walter Newman, Lewis Meltzer (based on the novel by Nelson Algren); **c**, Sam Leavitt; **m**, Elmer Bernstein; **ed**, Louis R. Loeffler; **prod d**, Joe Wright; **set d**, Darrell Silvera.

The Man with Two Faces ★★★ 1934; U.S.; 72m; First National/WB; B/W; Mystery; Children: Unacceptable; **DVD**. Robinson gives a riveting performance in this tense mystery where he is a Broadway actor. He and his sister, Astor, are among the leading thespians on the New York stage. Astor, however, begins to have mental problems and cannot function, until her husband, Calhern, is gone from her life. Only then does Astor regain her health. She thinks her husband is dead, but he has been in prison and has been released, causing her mental problems to return, and it seems that Calhern is hypnotizing her. Calhern is murdered and Landau, a detective, discovers that Calhern may have murdered several women in the past and was involved in criminal activities. Landau also finds a mustache inside the pages of a Gideon Bible in the room where Calhern died. It turns out that Robinson wore it when he killed his sister's tormentor. But even though Landau knows Robinson is guilty, he simply gives Robinson back his false mustache, telling him to be more careful in the future with such theatrical props and marks the Calhern case "unsolved." Robinson does not stand trial, one of the few instances in films where a man gets away with murder, albeit the finale leaves the impression that Calhern's death has benefited mankind. Violence prohibits viewing by children. *Author's Note*: "Oh, I stagger around in that picture with my mind gone most of the time," Astor told this author. "My memory turns on an off like a wall fan with a bad circuit, because

Mel Gibson in *The Man without a Face*, 1993.

of the evil influence of my husband [Calhern], until Eddie [Robinson] saves my sanity and life." Robinson stated to this author that "my role in **The Man with Two Faces** is rather limited and I appear only when Mary [Astor] gets into trouble with a man [Calhern] who has been manipulating her mind. That was a strange picture and I get away with killing the husband because he has been killing others and I believe that's why it got past the censors." **p**, Robert Lord; **d**, Archie Mayo; **cast**, Edward G. Robinson, Mary Astor, Ricardo Cortez, Mae Clarke, Louis Calhern, Arthur Byron, John Eldredge, David Landau, Henry O'Neill, Dennis O'Keefe; **w**, Tom Reed, Niven Busch (based on the play "The Dark Tower" by George S. Kaufman, Alexander Woollcott); **c**, Tony Gaudio; **ed**, William Holmes; **prod d**, John Hughes.

The Man without a Face ★★★ 1993; U.S.; 115m; Icon Entertainment International/WB; Color; Drama; Children: Unacceptable (MPAA: PG-13); **DVD**; **VHS**. Gibson is a former prep school Latin teacher, half of whose face was disfigured in a fiery automobile accident in which a boy died and where he was convicted of involuntary manslaughter ten years earlier. He lives as a recluse on the outskirts of a Maine coastal town in 1968 and is befriended by Stahl, a fourteen-year-old boy from a dysfunctional family, one of three children from different fathers, and his mother, Whitton, is looking for a fourth husband. The boy hopes to become accepted to a far-off military school his late father had attended, and Gibson tutors him in his second chance to pass an entrance examination. While Stahl deals with his peers and others in town who consider Gibson to be a bad influence, he sleeps over one night at Gibson's house. The next morning the police chief, Lewis, arrives to make some inquiries. When he sees that the boy is wearing only his shorts, Lewis suspects Gibson of being a pedophile. That doesn't prove true, and Stahl improves in his studies so he will pass the exam while Gibson begins to put the tragedy of his past behind him. This impactful film incisively profiles the dangers of judging people without knowing the truth about them. Facial disfigurement, sexual situations and gutter language prohibit viewing by children. **p**, Bruce Davey, Dalisa Cohen; **d**, Mel Gibson; **cast**, Gibson, Nick Stahl, Margaret Whitton, Fay Masterson, Gaby Hoffmann, Geoffrey Lewis, Richard Masur, Michael DeLuise, Ethan Phillips, Jean De Baer; **w**, Malcolm MacRury (based on the novel by Isabelle Holland); **c**, Donald M. McAlpine; **m**, James Horner; **ed**, Tony Gibbs; **prod d**, Barbara Dunphy; **art d**, Marc Fisichella; **set d**, Donald Elmblad; **spec eff**, Brian Ricci, Stephan Ricci.

Man without a Star ★★★ 1955; U.S.; 89m; UNIV; Color; Western; Children: Unacceptable; **VHS**. Douglas is compelling as a drifting cowboy who befriends young man Campbell, teaching him to use a six-gun and defend himself in the Wild West. They both get work as cowhands

Frank Sinatra and Laurence Harvey in *The Manchurian Candidate,* **1962.**

for a female rancher, Crain. She is bent on making a fortune by any means legal or not, and wants Douglas to help her as a range war begins, but, when she hires some gunslingers, he refuses and leaves. He can't forget that his brother was killed in a range war. He goes to a nearby town and renews his friendship with a good-hearted dance hall owner, Trevor. Crain hires a sadistic gunman, Boone, to do what she wants, part of which is to beat up Douglas, which he does in spades. Douglas sees the time has come for action against Crain so he organizes ranchers into standing up to her. Douglas and the ranchers win, but fences are put up to end the era of the open range. Campbell marries another rancher's daughter, while Trevor continues to tend her dance hall, and Douglas rides off, heading farther West to live in what remains of open country, and as far from barbed wire (that has terribly scarred him in the past) as possible. Violence prohibits viewing by children. **p,** Aaron Rosenberg; **d,** King Vidor; **cast,** Kirk Douglas, Jeanne Crain, Claire Trevor, William Campbell, Richard Boone, Jay C. Flippen, Myrna Hansen, Mara Corday, Sheb Wooley, Roy Bancroft, William "Bill" Phillips, Jack Elam; **w,** Bordon Chase, D.D. Beauchamp (based on the novel by Dee Linford); **c,** Russell Metty (Technicolor); **m,** Hans J. Salter, Herman Stein; **ed,** Virgil Vogel; **art d,** Alexander Golitzen, Richard H. Riedel; **set d,** Russell A. Gausman, John Austin.

The Manchurian Candidate ★★★★ 1962; U.S.; 126m; M.C. Productions/UA; B/W; Drama; Children: Unacceptable; **DVD**; **VHS**. In this startling and sometimes shocking drama, having more memorable scenes than most excellent films, Sinatra and Harvey are superb in their roles as Korean War veterans, both of whom having been brainwashed by their communist captors before being returned to the U.S. Harvey is hailed as a great hero and given the Congressional Medal of Honor with the support of all those who have survived in his unit, including Sinatra. Yet, Sinatra, and another member of that unit, Edwards, suffer from recurring nightmares. Both Sinatra and Edwards have come to believe that Harvey is anything but the hero they themselves have proclaimed repeatedly. Sinatra, who remains in the army as a major, is so disturbed that he fails to function well when advising Kelley, the Secretary of Defense, who is repeatedly interrupted at an important hearing by Gregory, a braggadocio U.S. senator, who claims without any proof that there are scores of communists within the federal government (his role undoubtedly based upon Senator Joseph McCarthy, 1908-1957, who conducted widespread hearings into communist subversion of the U.S. during the 1950s, which turned into a reign of witch-hunting terror). The hearings are a shambles and Henderson, who is Sinatra's superior, removes him from his position and orders him to go on an extended vacation to regain control of his emotions and faculties. Sinatra takes a trip to nowhere, and meets voluptuous Leigh on a train, and they fall in love. When they

return to New York City, Sinatra goes to see Harvey, who is now working as an assistant to a liberal news columnist, Corrigan, but Sinatra is shocked to see Silva, who was reportedly a Korean guide to his old unit and who is now working as a houseboy for Harvey. When Sinatra sees Silva, his memory of this man is one where he was present as a communist enforcer when he, Harvey and the rest of his captured unit are being brainwashed by a Chinese commissar, Dhiegh. Sinatra lashes out at Silva, using jujitsu, and Silva likewise counterattacks, both men smashing each other about and wrecking the apartment with savage blows that break furniture until Sinatra pins Silva, viciously twisting his arm and shouting; "What was Raymond [Harvey] doing with his hands [at that brainwashing session]?" Sinatra later recalls that scene and remembers how Harvey, acting like a brainwashed robot, follows the orders of Dhiegh, and indifferently strangles to death one of the American soldiers while the others, all pacified through brainwashing, sit by and do nothing. Police interrupt Sinatra's attack on Silva and he is later bailed out of jail by Leigh, the only person he thought to call. As Sinatra recuperates from his injuries from the fight with Silva, Leigh tells him that she has broken up with her fiancé and will now devote her life to him. All Sinatra can think about, however, is learning why Harvey and the others have been brainwashed. He is then tested by intelligence officers who show him a series of images and Sinatra selects several high-ranking Chinese and Russian commissars who were present at the brainwashing, the very images that Edwards has also pinpointed, now proving that their fears are founded on fact. Sinatra is assigned to investigate Harvey further. By this time, however, the programed Harvey is a dedicated assassin. Dhiegh visits a seedy New York City sanitarium run by Soviet agent Paulsen and where Harvey is being again brainwashed. Paulsen insists that Harvey be tested to make sure that he will carry out his ultimate assignment, the assassination of a frontrunner in the next U.S. presidential race. Dhiegh does not want to disturb "the delicate mechanism" implanted in Harvey, but finally agrees to that test by ordering Harvey to murder his employer Corrigan, to prove he will obey the subliminal orders given to him and also to take over Corrigan's influential newspaper column to further subtly spread the communist doctrine. Harvey dutifully goes to Corrigan's residence, finds him in bed and promptly murders him. Sinatra later follows Harvey to a bar finding him turning cards, and when he sees the queen of diamonds and hears a remark from a customer saying that he told someone to jump in the lake, Harvey, ignoring Sinatra's statements to him, promptly takes a cab, Sinatra following, and goes to Central Park, and resolutely walks to its lagoon and leaps mindlessly into the icy waters (it is wintertime) and a dumbfounded Sinatra pulls him out. Harvey then meets an old flame, Parrish, at a costume party hosted by his mother, Lansbury, and stepfather Gregory, and rekindles his love for her, especially after she appears before him in her costume as the queen of diamonds. They plan to marry and for once Harvey is a happy man, telling Sinatra of his hopeful plans for the future, and how he detests his conniving stepfather. His controller, however, is too strong for him, for that controller is Lansbury herself, the top secret communist agent in the U.S., and she uses a deck of cards to call up the queen of diamonds as the key in controlling Harvey, and then sends Harvey to murder McGiver, a liberal U.S. senator and Gregory's chief political opponent who plans to block Gregory's nomination on the next presidential ticket as vice president. Harvey dutifully walks into McGiver's home and shoots and kills him and, when a startled Parrish appears, he shoots and kills her, too, and then calmly leaves and disappears. Sinatra and his intelligence associates now know that Harvey is nothing more than a killing machine, but they cannot locate him. Harvey indicates to Sinatra that he will be at the convention being held at Madison Square Garden, where the nominees for the next presidential election will be selected, but when Sinatra and others begin to search the packed hall, they have no idea where Harvey may be hiding. Then Sinatra sees a small light flicker in a room at the top of the Garden and he begins racing up ramps and stairs. Meanwhile, Harvey places his Congressional Medal of Honor around his neck and then, with a high-powered rifle with a telescope—

he is a marksman—he aims the rifle at the presidential nominee, but, at the last moment, his mind clearing and now ridden with guilt for the unconscious murders he has committed, shifts the rifle slightly so that he focuses upon Gregory and Lansbury, who sit on the stage, and fires twice, killing them, their bodies spilling on to the stage. Sinatra at that moment bursts through the door of the small room, and Harvey tells him that he is paying for the disgrace and dishonor he has heaped upon himself by ridding the country of two dangerous agents and he then kills himself. In a touching epilogue scene Sinatra recites to Leigh some of the heroic acts performed by other Medal of Honor winners and then mentions Harvey's name, stating he was forced to commit unspeakable acts, but rose above those who had turned him into a murderer and took righteous vengeance. Director Frankenheimer superbly presents a thoroughly thrilling story, carefully building the suspense and revealing its mystery in one layered scene after another and where Sinatra gives a mesmerizing performance that is topped only by the chilling role so intensely enacted by Harvey. Lansbury, it should be noted, who was known for lighthearted comedies up to this time, also gives one of her greatest performances as a power-clutching, sinister person, who has abandoned all love and motherhood for the sake of her political ambitions, a devastatingly memorable portrait of evil and where Gregory is the essence of an oily, shifty and wholly irresponsible politician who is as dominated by Lansbury as is Harvey. This story was remade in 2004, but used the Gulf War where soldiers are brainwashed, a decidedly inferior production. *Author's Note*: Frankenheimer told this author that **The Manchurian Candidate** "is a mixture of fantasy and stark drama. We knew that the Chinese and North Koreans brainwashed some of our men after they were taken captive during the Korean War and compelled them to make public statements that condemned America. We took that idea of brain-scrubbing to its very limit and, perhaps, beyond, and it would not have been believable except for Larry's [Harvey's] amazing performance." Sinatra and Harvey became great friends during the production of this film and Sinatra told this author that "my performance in that picture with Larry [Harvey] may have been the best I ever gave, especially in my crack-up scenes. Larry took the picture, though, and rightfully so. He was magnificent. Here is a guy who kills a lot of people in a picture and comes out at the finale as someone you feel sorry for—now that's a great performance!" **p**, George Axelrod, John Frankenheimer; **d**, Frankenheimer; **cast**, Frank Sinatra, Laurence Harvey, Janet Leigh, Angela Lansbury, Henry Silva, James Gregory, Leslie Parrish, John McGiver, Khigh Dhiegh, James Edwards, Douglas Henderson, Lloyd Corrigan, Albert Paulsen, Barry Kelley, Madame Spivy, Whit Bissell; **w**, Axelrod, Frankenheimer (based on the novel by Richard Condon); **c**, Lionel Lindon; **m**, David Amram; **ed**, Ferris Webster; **prod d**, Richard Sylbert; **art d**, Philip M. Jefferies; **set d**, George R. Nelson; **spec eff**, Paul Pollard.

Manhattan ★★★★ 1979; U.S.; 96m; Jack Rollins-Charles H. Joffe Productions/UA; B/W; Comedy/Romance; Children: Unacceptable (MPAA: R); **DVD**; **VHS**. In this fascinating tale Allen again profiles all of his endless New York City neuroses as well as all of those of the anxiety-driven characters in his life and where Allen mostly discards the kind of one-line adlibbing as seen in his earlier films (such as **Annie Hall**, 1977) to more fully round out his characters. He is a wealthy and successful TV writer, who is now discontent with the medium that has made him rich and famous. Allen lives with charming teenager Hemingway, who is studying drama and is less than half his age (he is forty-two, she is seventeen) and idolizes him. He dreams of becoming an important writer of serious prose and expresses these dreams, as well as his guilt in living with Hemingway, with close friend Murphy. But Murphy has his own domestic problems in that his marriage to Byrne has soured and both he and his wife are drifting apart, mostly due to the fact that Murphy is having an on-and-off affair with Keaton, a phony intellectual woman, who really has no substance. Murphy fobs Keaton off on Allen, who finds her incessant posturing and artsy posing annoying,

Woody Allen and Mariel Hemingway in *Manhattan*, 1979.

until he realizes that Keaton is shamming these ridiculous poses because she thinks that is what expected of anyone claiming to be sophisticated and living in Manhattan, the center of the world for her, Allen and their ilk. (Could any of Allen's films be successful if centered in Keokuk, Iowa?) Beneath all of Keaton's manufactured veneer is a sincere and decent person, one Allen comes to like and they become friends, but not lovers. Allen then visits his ex-wife, Streep, who earlier gained custody of their son in their divorce and is now happily living with lesbian Ludwig. She is busy working on a book about her life with Allen, her divorce and, mostly, her lesbianism. Allen tries to convince Streep not to publish the book, but she goes ahead with it and it proves to be a bestseller that convinces Americans everywhere that Allen is a weirdo. Murphy then dumps Keaton and urges Allen to take up with her and ameliorate his guilt about having a teenage mistress by getting rid of Hemingway. Allen does take up with Keaton and he bluntly urges Hemingway to go to London to study dramatics. The Allen-Keaton affair does not take hold, Allen knowing that Keaton's heart belongs to Murphy and that Murphy feels the same way. He heroically gives up Keaton, urging Murphy to clutch happiness in mid-life by going off with Keaton. Allen then takes the plunge and quits his cushy TV job and sits down to write his great novel, writing the first page of this intended opus over and over again throughout the film. He then thinks of Hemingway and realizes that, despite the age difference, he truly loves her and races off to Hemingway's apartment, catching her just before she is to leave for a six-month stay in London. He tries to persuade her to stay and fears that she will change and even forget him, but she is determined to go. Before getting into a cab going to the airport, Hemingway tells Allen: "You have to have a little faith in people." The look on Allen's face at that telling remark is worth the whole film, which is gem-strewn from scene to scene and where Allen, Keaton, Murphy and Hemingway shine (Streep's role is rather a throwaway caricature). *Author's Note*: Allen elected to shoot this film in black and white to display New York City's grit and grime and it proved effective. Some cities are universally imagined as black and white, particularly the behemoths of New York and Chicago, where towns like Dallas, Phoenix, San Francisco and Los Angeles are somehow imagined in color. It's a matter of sunlight and sanitation. Allen reportedly fought tooth and nail with the MPAA rating people to have the film's rating changed from an "R" (restricted) to a "PG" (parental guidance), but to no avail; the relationship with Allen and the teenage Hemingway is too overtly displayed, albeit this introspective and incisive film is most likely Allen's finest production. **p**, Charles H. Joffe, Jack Rollins; **d**, Woody Allen; **cast**, Allen, Diane Keaton, Michael Murphy, Mariel Hemingway, Meryl Streep, Anne Byrne, Karen Ludwig, Michael O'Donoghue, Bella Abzug, Karen Allen, David Rasche; **w**, Allen, Marshall Brickman; **c**, Gordon Willis (Panavision); **m**, George Gershwin;

Clark Gable and Myrna Loy in *Manhattan Melodrama,* 1934.

ed, Susan E. Morse; **prod d**, Mel Bourne; **set d**, Robert Drumheller.

Manhattan Madness ★★★ 1916 (silent); U.S.; 50m/5 reels; Fine Arts; B/W; Adventure/Comedy; Children: Unacceptable; **DVD**. This well-crafted adventure-comedy provides a delightful blend of laughs and thrills with Fairbanks as a former New Yorker who returns from his ranch in the West. He tells his club cronies he can't wait to return to his cattle and horses, but they bet him $5,000 he will stay in New York for another week. They hire some actors to help them stage a ribbing, including a beautiful actress, Carmen. Fairbanks outwits his pals and wins the heart of the girl. *Author's Note*: Fairbanks was *the* leading matinee idol of that day and was incredibly wealthy. When traveling each day to the Fine Arts Studio in New York City where this film was shot, he commuted with his private yacht via the Hudson and Harlem Rivers. When asked about such extravagance, Fairbanks blithely replied: "Why use an automobile, a taxi or even a streetcar when you have a yacht?" **d**, Allan Dwan; **cast**, Douglas Fairbanks, Jewel Carmen, George Beranger, Ruth Darling, Eugene Ormonde, Macey Harlan, Warner Richmond, John Richmond, Albert MacQuarrie, Norman Kerry, Adolphe Menjou; **w**, Charles T. Dazey (based on a story by E.V. Durling); **c**, Victor Fleming.

Manhattan Melodrama ★★★★ 1934; U.S.; 93m; Cosmopolitan Productions/MGM; B/W; Crime Drama; Children: Unacceptable; **DVD**; **VHS**. This classic, rousing and fast-paced crime yarn from pantheon director Van Dyke sees great performances from Gable, Loy and Powell, demonstrating the dedicated lifelong friendship of two men that leads one of them to a governor's chair and the other to the electric chair. The film opens when the friends are boys traveling with their parents on an excursion boat, the *General Slocum*, in the middle of the East River and where it catches fire on June 15, 1904 (the panic and hysteria that ensued in the real disaster is terrifyingly recaptured by Van Dyke, who was to go on to re-create another horrible disaster, the great earthquake in **San Francisco**, 1936, which occurred two years after the *General Slocum* disaster, on April 18, 1906). The boys, Rooney (who grows up to be Gable), and Butler (who grows up to be Powell) get separated from their families, diving from the sinking ship (one of the worst marine disasters where 1021 persons drowned, mostly immigrants, for the lack of life-saving equipment; the ship's captain, Van Schaick, went to prison for criminal negligence). Carrillo, a family priest, saves their lives, pulling them ashore where the survivors grieve over their loved ones. Sidney, a kindly Jewish businessman who has lost his family, immediately adopts Rooney and Butler. Rooney routinely skips school to shoot craps in alleyways with other boys and pursues a life of petty crime while Butler becomes a good student and stays to the straight and narrow. Tragedy strikes again when Sidney passes a political rally where, of all people

Bolshevik leader Leon Trotsky (1879-1940), played by Lance, rabble-rouses a crowd into a riot and Sidney, who speaks against the communists in defending America, is beaten and then trampled to death in a struggle with stampeding spectators and club-wielding police. (It is a matter of record that Trotsky lived briefly in New York from January to March in 1917 before returning to Europe to participate in the Russian Revolution, but no records exist proving that he made a public speech that caused a riot.) The boys are again orphaned and come under the wing of Carrillo. As they grow up, each takes a different path to success. Gable is now the grown Rooney and he is a big time gambler, operating his own casino, but Powell, who is the grown Butler, puts himself through law school and becomes a celebrated attorney. Gable meets socialite Loy and they fall in love. When one of his gambling patrons loses his yacht to Gable, he makes a present of it to Loy, but it's not riches she wants from him, but reform, asking him to go into some legitimate business and quit the gambling racket. That's not for Gable, who loves living at the edge where danger lurks. Loy pines for a home and children, but Gable stays with his casino and the nightlife. He asks Loy: "What's wrong with you tonight?" "It isn't tonight," Loy replies. "It's every night. Worrying about you, hating what you do, hating who you meet." It is obvious that they are nearing a breakup. Then Gable again meets old pal Powell at the Dempsey-Firpo fight in 1923 and introduces him to Loy, who falls in love with Powell when he is elected district attorney. To celebrate, they go to the famed Cotton Club (profiled in Francis Ford Coppola's crime saga, **The Cotton Club**, 1984) where they use wooden mallets to keep tempo with the band and begin bantering (this was the first of fourteen films in which Powell and Loy appeared and their witty exchanges here would be reprised in those many entertaining films to come, especially when playing private sleuths Nick and Nora Charles in the delightful Thin Man series.) Meanwhile, Gable has trouble with big shot gambler Madison (who plays a character named Manny Arnold and is based upon New York City gambler and crime boss Arnold Rothstein, 1882-1928, reportedly murdered after welching on a huge bet, a killing that remains unsolved to this day) and who has welched on a big wager with Gable. When Gable and his henchman, Pendleton, call on Madison, he pulls a gun and Gable shoots and kills him and then flees with Pendleton. However, Pendleton leaves a coat he has picked up at Gable's apartment, one inadvertently left by Powell when he brought Loy there. After police recover the coat at the murder site, Jackson, who is Powell's ambitious and slippery assistant, brings the coat to Powell, insisting that Gable has worn this coat and is responsible for murdering Madison. Powell examines the coat, believing it to be his and then associates Gable with the Madison killing. Just before Powell is about to indict Gable for the Madison slaying, however, he receives an identical coat by delivery (a new one the clever Gable has ordered made) and one that contains in a pocket a wooden mallet from the Cotton Club where Powell and Loy had earlier celebrated. Powell tries on the coat, finds the mallet and then states: "*This* is my coat!" and dismisses Gable as a suspect in the Madison killing. Loy then leaves Gable for Powell and they marry. She is now a happy woman and encourages Powell to run for the governorship of New York. Jackson, Powell's one-time assistant, however, attempts to blackmail Powell by threatening to expose his wife's former association with Gable and thus prove Powell's collusion in the Madison killing. Loy overhears this threat and, desperate, goes to Gable, asking him to help. Gable, ever Powell's loyal friend and who is still in love with Loy, tracks down Jackson, finding him in the men's room of Madison Square Garden and where he cold-bloodedly shoots Jackson to death. As he leaves the men's room, he sees Russell, a blind beggar sitting in the hallway, waves his hand in front of the man to make sure he is truly blind and then drops some cash into the beggar's hat. Russell is faking. He lifts his dark glasses and looks at the cash and then identifies Gable as he walks way. (This scene duplicates another scene that appears in Fritz Lang's crime classic, **M**, 1933; beggars faking blindness appear in many films, including Lang's thriller, **Ministry of Fear**, 1944.) Gable is brought to

trial, charged with killing Jackson and where the phony blind man identifies him as the last man to leave the murder site. Powell, even though
he still cherishes his friend from their boyhood days, aggressively prosecutes Gable, holding him up as the symbol of the reckless and wild
Prohibition era of widespread violence and corruption. Gable's attorney
tries to defend him, but Gable dismisses his efforts, admiring Powell's
eloquence and fortitude, telling his lawyer: "Class…it's written all over
him." Powell, in his summation to the jury, then demands not only a
conviction, but, and he chokes on the words when saying: "In 1904,
when the *General Slocum* burned, I made a boyish effort to save Blackie
Gallagher's [Gable] life. Today, I demand from you…his death!" Powell
then slips a note to Gable that states: "Sorry, I had to do it." Gable sends
a note back to Powell reading "It's okay, kid. I can take it. Can you?"
Gable is found guilty and sentenced to die in the electric chair. Powell
is then elected governor on the strength of the Gable conviction, but, as
the time of Gable's execution approaches, Loy becomes nervous then
frantic and desperate, begging Powell to commute Gable's sentence. He
refuses, saying he cannot show favoritism even for a boyhood friend he
still loves. As the final hours near for Gable's death, Loy admits to Powell that it was she who went to Gable and begged him to do something
about Jackson and that Gable, out of love for the both of them, killed
Jackson. The shocked Powell goes to the prison and tells Gable that he
cannot allow him to die after knowing what he has done for him, but
the noble Gable tells him that he does not want his sentence to be com-
muted as that would wreck Powell's career. "If I can't live the way I
want then let me die the way I want; says Gable." He then leaves his
cell, and, accompanied by warden Hinds, swaggers from his cell and
bids farewell to the other Death Row prisoners, telling a young prisoner
to "keep your chin up and your nose clean, kid…Die the way you lived,
all of a sudden, that's the way to go. Don't drag it out—living like that
doesn't mean a thing." With that Gable goes to his death and Powell
later resigns from office, admitting publicly what Gable has done on his
behalf. The faithful Loy is waiting for him and asks what he plans to
do. "Try again from the start. Something else." At the finale, Loy walks
with Powell arm in arm, saying: "Let me try with you." Gable and Powell are superb as two friends bonded by love and loyalty and, though totally opposite in lifestyles and perspectives, are similar in their driving
but divergent ambitions, Powell, the lofty and principled crusader,
Gable, the good guy gone wrong but with his own sense of honor. The
theme of close friends wholly opposite each other was portrayed with
almost the identical theme in **Angels with Dirty Faces**, 1938, where
Cagney and O'Brien are lifelong pals, one a gangster who goes to the
electric chair, the other a priest who has failed to reform him. The scene
where Loy asks Gable to help Powell by dealing with the blackmailing
Jackson, is repeated to some degree in **The Roaring Twenties**, 1939,
when old flame Priscilla Lane goes to James Cagney, one-time underworld big shot, and begs him to do something about gangster Humphrey
Bogart, who is planning to kill her husband, Jeffrey Lynn, a crusading
district attorney. The lovely Loy is captivating in the role of a woman
loving two wholly different men. Van Dyke directs in his typical whirlwind pace, packing his scenes with action and hurried lines to effectively
inject more tension and anxiety to the taut script. *Author's Note*: After
playing vamps and vixens for almost a decade, beginning in the silent
era, Loy appears here in her first starring role, albeit she had recently
essayed strong supporting parts in **The Animal Kingdom**, 1932, and
Topaze, 1933. Loy told this author that "Woody [Van Dyke] put us all
through our paces in **Manhattan Melodrama** [the film was shot in
twenty-four days at a budget of $355,000], but I was eager to play my
role where I have two of the best actors in Hollywood interested in me,
Clark Gable and William Powell. Like the characters they play in the
picture, they were complete opposites off screen. Powell was truly a sophisticated gentleman with a natural sense of humor and proved to be a
very good friend. He was a great actor, but so was Gable, even though
Gable always deprecated his abilities. He was always convincing at
playing tough men who are abrupt with women, as he was in **Manhat-**

**Clark Gable, Myrna Loy and William Powell in *Manhattan
Melodrama*, 1934.**

tan Melodrama, but he was really a shy and withdrawn man. He was
a very private person, even though he was easy to like. I could see why
most women in America were in love with him. He had that boyish
charm and no one was more handsome. They called him 'the king' of
Hollywood, but there were many kings in that fantasy land. Gable was
certainly the most desirable prince of any girl's heart, except for, perhaps, Tyrone Power, and that scamp, Errol Flynn." Powell's movie career was literally saved by this film. He had been a matinee idol during
the silent era and was thought to be "washed up" according to some
Hollywood gurus. His teaming with Loy, however, made him a superstar
all over again, and MGM saw the Powell-Loy chemistry working at the
box office (the film recouped its investment and made money almost
immediately when released); they teamed them again in the same year
in **The Thin Man**, 1934, establishing an on-screen love match that
would go on for more than a decade. When this film was shown in
Chicago on July 22, 1934, at the Biograph Theater, FBI agents surrounded the place and, shortly after 10 p.m. that night shot and killed a
man leaving that theater with two women, a man FBI Director J. Edgar
Hoover called Public Enemy Number One, bank robber John Dillinger.
Evidence unearthed by this author over a period of several years that
resulted in the publication of two books, takes serious issue with the
FBI claims in that controversial case. For extensive and exclusive details
on the Dillinger case, see my books, *Dillinger: Dead or Alive?* (Regnery,
1970), *The Dillinger Dossier* (December Press, 1983) and *The Great
Pictorial History of World Crime*, Volume II (History, Inc.; pages 1374-
1422). For details on Arnold Rothstein, see my books *Open Files: A
Narrative Encyclopedia of the World's Greatest Unsolved Crimes* (Mc-
Graw-Hill, 1983; pages 208-210) and *World Encyclopedia of Organized
Crime* (Paragon House, 1992; pages 337-341). For details on the *Gen-
eral Slocum* disaster, see my book *Darkest Hours: A Narrative Ency-
clopedia of Worldwide Disasters from Ancient Times to the Present*
(Nelson-Hall, 1976; pages 212-215). **p**, David O. Selznick; **d**, W.S. Van
Dyke; **cast**, Clark Gable, William Powell, Myrna Loy, Leo Carrillo, Nat
Pendleton, Frank Conroy, Thomas Jackson, John Marston, Edward Van
Sloan, George Sidney, Isabel Jewell, Mickey Rooney, Jimmy Butler,
Shirley Ross, Noel Madison, Donald Haines, Sherry Hall, Samuel S.
Hinds, Bert Russell, Muriel Evans, Claudelle Kaye, Pete Smith, Landers
Stevens, Leo Lance, Leonid Kinskey; **w**, Oliver H.P. Garrett, Joseph L.
Mankiewicz (based on the story "Three Men" by Arthur Caesar); **c**,
James Wong Howe; **m**, William Axt; **ed**, Ben Lewis; **art d**, Cedric Gib-
bons; **spec eff**, Slavko Vorkapich.

Manhattan Murder Mystery ★★★ 1993; U.S.; 104m; TriStar Pictures; Color; Comedy; Children: Unacceptable (MPAA: PG-13); **DVD**;
VHS. New York couple Allen and Keaton send their son off to college

Emmanuelle Beart and Hippolyte Girardot in *Manon of the Spring*, 1987.

and expect their lives will be nice and normal in their apartment building, but nothing of the kind happens. They meet an elderly couple, Adler and Cohen, down the hall and a few days later learn that the wife has suddenly died. Keaton suspects that Adler may have killed her, so he can marry young actress Norris. Allen isn't in any hurry to jump to his wife's conclusions, so she plays sleuth, with the help of friend Alda, who is recently divorced. When Allen's marriage appears to cool if not sour, he becomes jealous and his bumbling gumshoeing gets him into all sorts of trouble. Also at this time, Allen, an editor at a book publishing house, capriciously flirts with Huston, one of his authors, to make Keaton jealous. Bedlam follows as the trio is in pursuit of a maybe killer, getting trapped in an elevator with a dead body, and a shootout in a revival movie theater where clips are shown of film noir classics **Double Indemnity**, 1944, and **The Lady from Shanghai**, 1948, in which men are set up by dangerous women. It turns out there was no murder and the neighbor woman died of heart failure. Song: "I'm In the Mood for Love" (Jimmy McHugh, Dorothy Fields; performed by Erroll Garner). This zany spoof of murder mysteries sustains interest throughout, although the Allen banter is not always up to his usual insightful par. Gutter language and violence prohibit viewing by children. **p**, Robert Greenhut, Joseph Hartwick, Helen Robin; **d**, Woody Allen; **cast**, Allen, Diane Keaton, Alan Alda, Anjelica Huston, Jerry Adler, Lynn Cohen, Ron Rifkin, Joy Behar, William Addy, John Doumanian, Sylvia Kauders, Ira Wheeler; **w**, Allen, Marshall Brickman; **c**, Carlo Di Palma; **ed**, Susan E. Morse; **prod d**, Santo Loquasto; **art d**, Speed Hopkins; **set d**, Susan Bode; **spec eff**, John Andrew Berton, Jr.

Manhunter ★★★ 1986; U.S.; 119m; De Laurentiis Entertainment Group; Color; Crime Drama; Children: Unacceptable (MPAA: R); **DVD**; **VHS**. This absorbing crime yarn has Petersen, a former FBI forensic expert agent, retiring to Florida with his wife, Greist, and their young son, Seaman. Petersen's specialty is studying criminal behavior and putting his mind into that of the criminal at a crime scene to examine the criminal's thoughts and then determine what they might do next. Farina, his former boss, calls Petersen out of retirement to Chicago to help the FBI catch a serial killer known as the "Tooth Fairy" (Noonan), who kills whole families in their homes at random during nights of the full moon, leaving vampire-like bite marks on his victims. Petersen enters the house of the latest victims to try to learn the killer's "mind-set." To learn more about the mind of this deranged killer, Petersen meets with Dr. Hannibal Lecter (Cox), an imprisoned serial killer, who Petersen captured some years earlier, a frightening experience that almost cost Petersen his sanity and life. He learns that the "Tooth Fairy" learns about his victims by studying their home movies, obtaining those movies from a lab in St. Louis. This leads to Petersen discovering Noonan as the killer

and, as he is about to kill Allen, a blind woman, there is a shootout in which Noonan kills several police officers before being shot dead by Petersen. Songs: "Graham's Theme" (Michel Rubini, performed by Michel Rubini); "Seiun" (Masanori "Kitaro" Takahashi, performed by Kitaro); "Freeze" (Klaus Schulze, performed by Schulze); "Evaporation" (David Allen, Barry Andrews, Martyn Barker, Carl Marsh, performed by Schrikeback); "Coelocanth," "This Big Hush," (Schreikback); "Strong as I Am" (Severes Ramsey, Gary Putman, Curt Lichter, Gregory Markel, performed by The Prime Movers); "In-A-Gadda-Da-Vida" (Doug Ingle, performed by Iron Butterfly); "Heartbeat" (Michael Becker, Gene Stashuk, performed by Red 7). This film offers the first screen appearance of the reprehensible character, Lecter, who is later chillingly profiled by Anthony Hopkins in **The Silence of the Lambs**, 1991. **Manhunter** was remade as **Red Dragon**, 2002. Excessive violence and gutter language prohibit viewing by children. **p**, Dino De Laurentiis, Richard Roth; **d**, Michael Mann; **cast**, William Petersen, Kim Greist, Joan Allen, Brian Cox, Dennis Farina, Tom Noonan, Stephen Lang, David Seaman, Benjamin Hendrickson, Michael Talbott; **w**, Mann (based on the novel *Red Dragon* by Thomas Harris); **c**, Dante Spinotti; **m**, Michel Rubini, The Reds; **ed**, Dov Hoenig; **prod d**, Mel Bourne; **art d**, Jack Blackman; **spec eff**, Joseph Digaetano, Wayne Beauchamp, Gusmano Cesaretti.

Manila Calling ★★★ 1942; U.S.; 81m; FOX; B/W; War Drama; Children: Unacceptable. When the Japanese capture the main American radio station in Manila in the Philippines in early 1942 during WWII, station operator Nolan organizes a guerrilla group and finds an advance Japanese unit on a friend's plantation. They seize the site from the Japanese to use their radio transmitter there, and radio operator Wilde transmits information to American forces about conditions in the Philippines. Meanwhile, Landis, a nightclub singer, escapes from the Japanese and gets to the plantation to provide romantic interest. A good early War II propaganda programmer, but some war violence makes it unacceptable for children. *Author's Note*: This film was produced just after the U.S. suffered its most devastating defeat in American military history when more than 70,000 American and Filipino troops surrendered to overwhelming Japanese forces after a grueling four-month battle at Bataan and Corregidor in 1942. American and Filipino resistance fighters continued to fight the Japanese as guerrillas until General Douglas MacArthur reinvaded the Philippines in 1944. "We took a terrible beating over there," Nolan told this author, "and **Manila Calling** was made to reassure the American public that we had not quit altogether in those islands. It was a tough, gritty film that showed how the Japanese butchered prisoners and citizens, but how there were still enough patriots left to fight on and I play one of those guerrillas. Like the Filipinos themselves, I am defiant to the end, with my last line for the closing when I am transmitting to America and say: 'This is Manila Calling…and I ain't no Jap!' **p**, Sol M. Wurtzel; **d**, Herbert I. Leeds; **cast**, Lloyd Nolan, Carole Landis, Cornel Wilde, James Gleason, Martin Kosleck, Ralph Byrd, Ted North, Elisha Cook, Jr., Harold Huber, Lester Matthews, Louis Jean Heydt, Victor Sen Yung, Richard Loo, Leonard Strong; **w**, John Larkin (based on his story); **c**, Lucien A. Andriot; **m**, David Buttolph, Cyril J. Mockridge, David Raksin; **ed**, Alfred Day; **art d**, Lewis Creber, Richard Day; **set d**, Thomas Little.

Manon of the Spring ★★★ 1987; Italy/France/Switzerland; 113m; DD Productions/Orion Classics; Color; Drama; Children: Unacceptable (MPAA: PG); **DVD**; **VHS**. In this good sequel to **Jean de Florette**, 1986, again set in the Provencal countryside of France, it is ten years after the death of a farmer from heartbreak and over-work after two neighbors greedily conspired to deprive his flower farm of water from a spring, which caused his land to dry up and become almost worthless. The two neighbors have acquired it, let the water flow back, and it is rich land again. Cadoret's daughter, Manon (Beart), has grown into a beautiful but poor goat herder. One of the greedy men, Montand, who never married, pressures his nephew, Auteuil, who aided him in the water conspiracy, to marry and have a son so the family name will be carried on. Auteuil is now thirty years old and wealthy, growing and selling carnations on the land Beart's father once owned. Auteuil sees Beart in the fields and falls in love with her, but she loves Girardot, a local schoolteacher. One day she overhears locals talking about what the evil Montand and Auteuil did to her father and she plots revenge. This applies as well to the villagers, who had known what the greedy men were doing and did nothing to prevent them from enacting their sinister scheme. Baert secretly blocks the water supply to the village from another hidden spring, so the village dries up. Beart has her revenge, but too bad for Auteuil, who meanwhile has a moral and ethical conversion. Auteuil regrets his past greed, and truly loves Baert, but he nevertheless loses her to the upstanding teacher, Girardot. Berri's direction carefully unfolds this intriguing social drama and all the cast members render above-average performances. Violence prohibits viewing by children. (In French; English subtitles.) **p**, Pierre Grunstein, Alain Poiré; **d**, Claude Berri; **cast**, Yves Montand, Daniel Auteuil, Emmanuelle Beart, Hippolyte Girardot, Margarita Lozano, Yvonne Gamy, Tiki Olgado; **w**, Berri, Gerard Brach (based on the novel by Marcel Pagnol); **c**, Bruno Nuytten; **m**, Jean-Claude Petit; **ed**, Herve De Luze, Genevieve Louveau; **prod d**, Bernard Vezat; **set d**, Olivier Coutagne, François Dariani, Françoise Doré; **spec eff**, Jean-Marc Mouligne, Paul Trielli.

Manpower ★★★ 1941; U.S.; 104m; WB; B/W; Drama; Children: Cautionary; **DVD**. Robinson and Raft give dynamic performances as two rugged linemen who are close friends, but whose friendship is disrupted by vixen Dietrich. When a fierce storm downs several lines, Robinson climbs to some high wires to make repairs, but, after he touches a live high-voltage wire, one of his legs becomes temporarily paralyzed. While he is recuperating, Raft cheers him up; when he recuperates, Robinson, along with Raft, break the news to Dietrich that her father, Brecher, has been killed during a repair work crisis. She works in a low dive called the Midnight Club as a singer, who, like all the girls working there, shills customers to buy drinks, and seems almost indifferent to her father's death, but Robinson takes a liking to her and, after developing a romance with Dietrich, thinks to marry her. Raft knows all about Dietrich's shady past as he had once been present when Brecher had to bail his daughter out of the pokey for her promiscuous ways. When Raft tries to warn his friend about Dietrich, Robinson dismisses the bad talk about her, saying that she has gotten some bad breaks. Robinson, even though he suspects that Dietrich likes Raft more than she does him, marries the blonde singer and they set up house. After Raft is injured in an accident, Robinson insists that he stay with him and Dietrich to regain his health. While there, Dietrich makes advances on Raft, but he reminds her that she is married to Robinson and does not want any part of her. Depressed at her small-town life, Dietrich decides to abandon Robinson and leave town. Before departing, she stops by her old club to say goodbye to her friends, Arden, Pepper and Compton, but, while there, the police raid the place and she is locked up along with everyone else. Raft hears of this and bails her out. Dietrich tells Raft that he is the only man for her and he hits her and then goes off to work on a repair job, again in a terrible storm. Dietrich then goes to the site where the men are working and tells Robinson that she is in love with Raft and Robinson explodes, climbing high structures holding dislocated and dangerous wires and where Raft is working with others. Robinson then attacks Raft and they battle until Robinson falls to his death. Raft and Dietrich are now left to live a life together, despite the tragedy that has befallen them. Pantheon director Walsh provides an action-packed film with his usual fast tempo, drawing fine performances from his cast, but there were endless problems during the production, chiefly between his leading players. Songs include: "He Lied and I Listened" (1941; music: Friedrich Hollender; lyrics: Frank Loesser; sung by Dietrich), "I'm in No Mood for Music Tonight" (1941; Hollender and Loesser), "Chinatown, My Chinatown" (1906; music: Jean Schwartz; lyrics: William

George Raft, Edward G. Robinson and Marlene Dietrich in *Manpower*, 1941.

Jerome; sung by Beal Wong); "All in Favor Say Aye" (music: Cliff Friend), "Java Jive" (music: Ben Oakland), "The Wedding March" (1843; from "A Midsummer Night's Dream Op 61" by Felix Mendelssohn-Bartholdy), "Bridal Chorus (Here Comes the Bride)" (1850; from "Lohengrin" by Richard Wagner). *Author's Note*: Walsh told this author that "I had my hands full with George [Raft] and Eddie [Robinson] almost right from the start when they both showed too much interest in Marlene [Dietrich] and started competing for her in almost every scene, playing up to her, and I had to take them aside and tell them to quit that out, especially George, who was an amorous guy by nature." Raft did not want to appear to be cowardly in any way, according to Walsh, and complained about one scene where he loses his grip on Robinson and Robinson falls to his death. "Why should I appear to be a weakling in that scene?" Raft rhetorically asked this author in one of our many meetings. "Not a chance. I went straight to Jack Warner and said that I wanted the writer to change that scene where the strap we are both holding onto breaks and Eddie [Robinson] falls and gets killed by accident, so that it doesn't look like I let him go and that I could not hold on to him. Warner shrugged and said okay. You had to fight for your character's honor in every scene in that picture, I can tell you." Robinson had a decided dislike for Raft when they first met on the set, telling this author that "he had been in the movies for a decade and was still flipping that coin and playing the gangster from **Scarface** [1932], but his part in **Manpower** called for a lot more than that and when I gave him a few pointers on how I thought his character could best be portrayed he flared up, shouting at me and saying: 'Who in the hell do you think you are—patronizing me like that?' From that point, our relationship during the production went quickly downhill." Before long, Raft and Robinson were shouting at each other, and, during one scene, they erupted, with both men throwing punches at each other and where Robinson decidedly came out the loser as Raft was a brawler. "I jumped right in to stop that donnybrook," Walsh told this author, "and had a hell of a time doing it as those boys were out for blood. After I got them separated, Robinson walked off the set and later told me that he was quitting the picture, which was a disaster as we were pretty much along in the production and a lot of the budget had been used up. We finally settled the feud between George and Eddie through the Screen Actors Guild, but neither of my stars would talk to each other when off camera after that." Dietrich tried to stay above it all, but found that impossible, saying to this author: "George and Eddie were two tough guys and I was not flattered when Raoul [Walsh] told me that they were quarreling over me off camera. What ridiculous nonsense! I didn't believe they could be so unprofessional until I got a sample of that boyish brawling. One scene called for George to hit me hard and he told me not to worry, and that he would pull his punch. Well, he failed to do that, and accidentally

Frances O'Connor and Harold Pinter in *Mansfield Park*, 1999.

hit me square on the jaw and knocked me down a flight of stairs and I broke an ankle. He came running to me with tears in his eyes, like a little boy, who had just broken a window with a baseball, but I was in no mood to forgive him and I let him stew in his grief until I was well enough to come back on the set and finish the picture. When we completed the picture I turned to Raoul and said: 'You should have shot this picture entirely inside a boxing ring.' He sadly nodded and then gave me a drink of his best brandy from the personal flask he carried." The Raft-Robinson feud continued for many years until the two met on a stage for a benefit. Both men snarled and grimaced at each other. Robinson ordered Raft to "get out of town," and Raft took out his famous coin, flipping it and saying: "Hollywood isn't big enough for the both of us!" They then smiled, embraced, and danced off the stage together. **p,** Mark Hellinger; **d,** Raoul Walsh; **cast,** Edward G. Robinson, Marlene Dietrich, George Raft, Alan Hale, Frank McHugh, Eve Arden, Barton MacLane, Ward Bond, Walter Catlett, Joyce Compton, Barbara Pepper, William Hopper, Lynn Baggett, Diana Barrymore, Faye Emerson, Jane Randolph; **w,** Richard Macaulay, Jerry Wald; **c,** Ernest Haller; **m,** Adolph Deutsch, Friedrich Hollaender; **ed,** Ralph Dawson; **art d,** Max Parker; **spec eff,** Byron Haskin, H.F. Koenekamp.

Mansfield Park ★★★ 1999; U.K.; 101m; Arts Council of England; Miramax; Color; Drama; Children: Unacceptable (MPAA: PG-13); **DVD**; **VHS**. In this engrossing Victorian domestic drama, Fanny, a ten-year-old girl (Taylor Gordon) from a poor family in 1800s England, goes to live with a wealthy uncle, Pinter, and her drug-addicted aunt, Duncan, taking up residence in their resplendent mansion, which is called Mansfield Park. Fanny grows into an attractive young woman (O'Connor). The rich family also includes a drunken elder son, Purefoy; a likable younger son, Miller, who becomes her closest friend; and two daughters, Hamilton and Waddell. Renting a small house on the estate are a conniving brother, Nivola, and sister, Davidtz, from London, who hope to marry into the wealthy family. Nivola initially sets his sights on the daughters, but then focuses on O'Connor, while Davidtz hopes to marry Purefoy, who will inherit the estate because he is the eldest son. Pinter tells O'Connor she is to marry Nivola, but she mistrusts him. Instead, she returns to her original home, but is called back to Mansfield Park when Purefoy falls ill. Nivola presses O'Connor to marry him, but she says no. She is really in love with Miller with whom she shares her writings. While wrestling with her marital future, O'Connor is distressed to learn that Pinter's wealth comes largely from owning slaves in other parts of the world. Pinter then gives O'Connor an ultimatum, either marry Nivola or be returned to the home of her origin in poverty. Honorably, she chooses the latter, but only to marry Miller. Violence, sexual content, and drug use prohibit viewing by children. **p,** Sarah Cur-

tis, Bob and Harvey Weinstein; **d&w,** Patricia Rozema (based on the novel by Jane Austen); **cast,** Frances O'Connor, Jonny Lee Miller, James Purefoy, Lindsay Duncan, Alessandro Nivola, Harold Pinter, Hannah Taylor Gordon, Sheila Gish, Victoria Hamilton, Hugh Bonneville, Justine Waddell; **c,** Michael Coulter; **m,** Lesley Barber; **ed,** Martin Walsh; **prod d,** Christopher Hobbs; **art d,** Andrew Monro; **set d,** Patricia Edwards; **spec eff,** Richard Van Den Bergh, Tim Webber, Drew Jones, Steve Tizzard.

Man's Hope ★★★★ 1947; Spain/France; 88m; Les Productions Andre Malraux/Lopert Pictures; B/W; War Drama; Children: Unacceptable; **DVD**. Author André Malraux (1901-1976) brilliantly directs this stirring and somewhat autobiographical account about the Spanish Civil War (1936-1939), based on his book and experiences during the tragic conflict. Malraux, a flyer, went to Spain in 1936 and enlisted in the services of the Republican Loyalist cause, fighting there until the fascist army of General Francisco Franco (1892-1975) overwhelmed the Spanish Republic, with the considerable aid of fellow fascist dictators Adolf Hitler (1889-1945), of Germany, who provided his bombers and fighters (The Condor Legion) and Benito Mussolini (1883-1945), of Italy, who supplied several divisions of Italian ground troops to supplement Franco's forces. The story shows the efforts of a Loyalist squadron of fliers, who are flying antiquated WWI planes (donated to the Republic by Russia, its only ally in the war) and concentrates on one mission, the destruction of a bridge during the savage battle of Teruel (December 1937-February 1938), and where Malraux and his flying compatriots must locate a new fascist airfield and destroy it, along with the bridge. The airfield is at a secret location and is known by a peasant unable to read a map, so the peasant is taken aloft and leads the squadron by visual identification to the airfield where it is successfully attacked. There is little plot in this tale, which is based on actual operations by the ragtag Republican air force. Malraux intermixes astounding and shocking live footage of the war he and others shot during the conflict, making this fascinating film all the more realistic and revealing, where the sounds and sights of actual gunfire and bombings rivet the viewer. Malraux and other Republican volunteers barely escaped imprisonment before Franco's forces achieved victory, fleeing to France in 1939 and smuggling this film with them. With the fall of France to Germany the following year, this powerful anti-fascist film was secreted and was not released until the war in Europe was achieved by the Allies in 1945. It was not released in the U.S. until two years later. *Author's Note*: Malraux was given the Louis Delluc Award for this film, the highest such honor France could bestow upon him, which really recognized the heroic contributions Malraux and others made in their early fight against fascism. A similar and equally impactful film about the Spanish Civil War, albeit a documentary titled **The Spanish Earth**, 1937, was directed by Joris Ivens and was written by such distinguished anti-fascist writers such as Ernest Hemingway, John Dos Passos, Lillian Hellman, Archibald MacLeish, and others. Hemingway told this author that "Malraux made more than a motion picture with **Man's Hope**. He created an unforgettable image of free men fighting fascism for the first time as a whole people. His film achieved much more than what we had hoped for in **Spanish Earth**, which shows a victimized Spain attempting to defend itself against impossible odds. Malraux showed that the fight could be effectively taken to that enemy." (In Spanish; English subtitles.) **p,** Roland Tual, Edouard Corniglion-Molinier; **d,** André Malraux, Boris Peskine; **cast,** Andrés Mejuto, Nicolás Rodríguez, José Sempere, Julio Peña, Pedro Codina, José María Lado, Serafín Ferro, Miguel del Castillo; **w,** Antonio del Amo, Max Aub, Denis Marion, Peskine (based on the novel *L'espoir* by Malraux); **c,** Louis Page; **m,** Darius Milhaud; **ed,** Malraux, Georges Grace; **set d,** Vicente Petit.

Map of the Human Heart ★★★ 1993; Australia; U.K./Canada; France; 109m; Australian Film Finance Corp./Miramax; Color; Adventure/Drama; Children: Unacceptable (MPAA: R); **DVD**; **VHS**. Bergin, a Canadian cartographer, flies to the Arctic Circle in 1921. On his travels to a remote Inuit village he meets Joamie, an Inuit boy who has tuberculosis, and the compassionate Bergin flies him to Canada for medical treatment. When the boy returns to the village as a young man (as Lee), he has difficulty adjusting between his Eskimo heritage and the Western civilization that has so deeply influenced him. He falls in love with Parillaud, a half-breed girl, but they are separated because of their racial differences. They meet again during World War II when he is a bombardier with the Canadian air force and she is a photo analyzer. But she is now married to Bergin. Besides that burden to deal with, Lee's tribe has fallen on hard times and is starving, his people blaming their misfortunes on the white man (Bergin) who "poisoned" their lives with his visits years earlier. By 1965, Lee is a pathetic drunk, who tells his sad story to a young mapmaker, Cusack, and this is where this somewhat depressing but intriguing tale ends. Gutter language and sexuality prohibit viewing by children. **p**, Vincent Ward, Tim Bevan, Linda Beath, Sylvaine Sainderichin, Paul Saltzman, Timothy White; Bob and Harvey Weinstein; **d**, Ward; **cast**, Jason Scott Lee, Anne Parillaud, Patrick Bergin, John Cusack, Jeanne Moreau, Robert Joamie, Annie Galipeau, Clotilde Courau, Ben Mendelsohn, Jerry Snell; **w**, Louis Nowra (based on a story by Ward); **c**, Eduardo Serra; **m**, Gabriel Yared; **ed**, John Scott, Frans Vandenburg; **prod d**, John Beard; **art d**, Jean-Baptiste Tard; **set d**, Michèle Forest, Diane Gauthier, Joanne Woollard.

Marathon Man ★★★★ 1976; U.S.; 125m; PAR; Color; Spy Drama; Children: Unacceptable (MPAA: R); **DVD**; **VHS**. Full of mystery, fright and oozing evil, this espionage drama from Schlesinger packs a wallop in every frame and where Hoffman, Scheider, and, especially, Olivier, give bravura performances. Hoffman is a dedicated University of Columbia student who is obsessed with running as he trains for an Olympic marathon, jogging along the walkways of the Battery and through Central Park and where he challenges other runners. Sensitive, naïve and even shy, Hoffman must deal with the haunting memory of his father's suicide, a death brought about during the McCarthy witch-hunting era when his father, a liberal educator, was accused of being involved in un-American activities. He has a brother, Scheider, whom Hoffman idolizes, a sophisticated secret American agent involved with many covert activities and much-wanted persons, such as vicious Olivier, a Nazi who has escaped the war criminal dragnets following WWII. Scheider, unlike Hoffman, who lives meagerly in a cold-water flat, lives the high life, traveling about the globe, sporting a tailor-made wardrobe and enjoying the comforts of the best hotels. He is shown in a luxury suite in Paris where he is doing rigorous morning exercises when Woo, a hired Oriental assassin, slips into his room and attempts to strangle him with piano wire, but Scheider is quick enough to place his hand in front of his face and the wire, which painfully cuts into his flesh before he fights the assassin with jujitsu, finally killing him and then calling associates to have the body removed before he seeks medical attention. While being bandaged, Scheider meets with Davane, his controller (the intelligence agency they work for is not specified but is appears to be the CIA). Davane tells Scheider that he believes the attack was made on behalf of those wanting to obtain a priceless horde of gems, chiefly diamonds that have been stolen by Nazi physician and wanted war criminal Olivier from Jewish Holocaust victims in Nazi death camps during WWII, those gems secreted by a brother of Olivier, who recently died in a NYC car accident. The agency for which they work has been shielding Olivier for years in exchange for intelligence information. It is now Scheider's job to contact Olivier in New York, as he has left his deep hiding place in South America and traveled to NYC to obtain those jewels. When Scheider returns to New York, he has a warm reunion with his brother, Hoffman, who has become infatuated with Keller, an attractive young female student at Columbia University. Scheider meets with Olivier, but Olivier believes that he and other agents are after the jewels and he mortally stabs him and then flees with Nazi goons Lawrence and

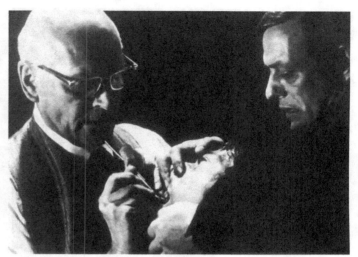

Laurence Olivier, Dustin Hoffman and Richard Bright in *Marathon Man*, **1976.**

Bright. Scheider manages to get to Hoffman's apartment, but dies in his arms unable to utter a single word. Police are called and Hoffman cannot give them any information about his brother's death, stunned as he watches Scheider's body zipped into a body bag and removed. Depressed, he takes a warm bath, but then hears someone moving about in his apartment. He locks the bathroom door, but Olivier's goons break it down and abduct Hoffman, taking him to a warehouse where he is strapped into a dental chair. Olivier then appears, methodically removing dental tools from a bag and meticulously placing them in order as he pries open Hoffman's mouth and begins to painfully probe into a cavity, repeatedly asking "Is it safe?" (These are code words earlier used by Scheider and his associates in response to the question as to whether an agent or a protected person is safe within his covert identity or not.) Hoffman does not know what Olivier is talking about as Olivier sadistically drills into an exposed nerve, and responds by saying, "yes, it's safe," which is not the answer Olivier is seeking. After Hoffman passes out, Olivier concludes that Hoffman has no information and knows nothing about his activities. Hoffman later regains consciousness and escapes, madly running throughout Manhattan streets while Lawrence, Bright, and then Devane pursue him. He obtains his father's gun (the one his father used to commit suicide) and, with the help of Keller and a street gang, he eludes his pursuers. Meanwhile, Olivier goes to a Manhattan bank and finds the thousands of stolen diamonds in his brother's safe deposit box, dumping this fortune into a briefcase. To determine the current value of the gems, he goes to a jewelry store in a predominantly Jewish neighborhood and asks for an appraisal for a few of the gems. One of the jewelers seems to recognize him from the past, and when Olivier sees that the jeweler bears a concentration camp number on his arm, he hurriedly flees the store, but the jeweler follows. He is also recognized by an elderly woman, another concentration camp survivor, who frantically calls out his name "Szell!" When the pawnbroker from the store now realizes that Olivier is the despicable Nazi physician, he follows him down the street, but Olivier suddenly flashes a blade from his coat sleeve and fatally stabs the man before fleeing in a taxi. Hoffman, meanwhile, tracks down Olivier and orders him at gunpoint into a water filtering plant where he takes his revenge by telling Olivier he can have all the diamonds he can swallow and compels Olivier to swallow several gems. Then Hoffman tosses the briefcase full of diamonds into the sewage system, and Olivier, berserk with rage, attempts to slash Hoffman, but falls on his own blade and dies. Hoffman then flees to his remote ancestral home with Keller, whom he suspects of being in on the conspiracy, and Devane, along with Lawrence and Bright, follows him. After Devane shoots and kills Keller, who tries to save Hoffman's life, Hoffman shoots and kills Devane, Lawrence and Bright, and that is where this twisting and mesmerizing tale ends.

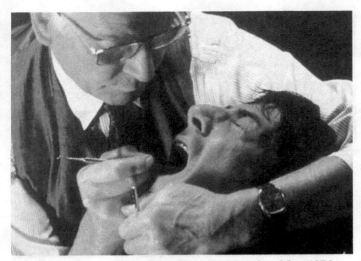

Laurence Olivier and Dustin Hoffman in *Marathon Man,* **1976.**

Schlesinger directs with great style, offering many action-packed (albeit sometimes very disturbing) scenes, and Hoffman is perfect as the naïve victim who suddenly becomes a worldly and canny opponent, somehow vindicating his father's death in that his victimized father found no way to fight back against his political oppressors, but Hoffman, another victim a generation later, certainly does. Olivier gives an astonishing portrait of a vicious Nazi war criminal with no ethics or human compassion. He would play just the opposite character two years later in **The Boys from Brazil**, 1978, as a Nazi hunter (based on Simon Wiesenthal) and where he is tracking wanted Nazi war criminal Gregory Peck (in one of his most extravagant roles). Scheider, too, is marvelous in his role as the secret agent, who, for all his worldly charm, courage and incisive perceptions, is as much a victim as is Hoffman. Devane also captivates as the conniving and wholly untrustworthy intelligence chief, the kind of role his cat-smirking personality personifies. Goldman, who was paid $500,000 for the film rights for his novel and the screenplay, provides a brilliant and witty script, full of surprises and mystery. Shot on location in New York City, this film was an enormous success, returning more than $28 million at the box office. *Author's Note*: Scheider told this author that "there were some comments made to me to have my broken nose fixed before I did **Marathon Man**, but I have always felt that that facial disfiguration gave me some distinction. I earned that broken nose the hard way by getting my brains rattled in my first amateur fight [Golden Gloves Program] in New Jersey in 1947 when a guy named Myron Greenberg gave me the shellacking of my life." Scheider went on to score nine ring victories, all knockouts, from 1948 to 1958. "All of my scenes in **Marathon Man**," he told this author, "take place at the beginning of the story, but John [Schlesinger] gave me a few great scenes, especially the sequence in Paris where I have to overcome a Chinese assassin [Woo], who, I might add, had the most piercing blue eyes I have ever seen in a human head." Some notable films dealing with wanted or escaped Nazis following WWII include **Cornered**, 1945; **The Stranger**, 1946; **Berlin Express**, 1948; **Murderers among Us**, 1948; **The Lost One**, 1951; **The Odessa File**, 1974; **The Man in the Glass Booth**, 1975; and **The Boys from Brazil**, 1978. **p**, Robert Evans, Sidney Beckerman; **d**, John Schlesinger; **cast**, Dustin Hoffman, Laurence Olivier, Roy Scheider, William Devane, Marthe Keller, Fritz Weaver, Richard Bright, Marc Lawrence, James Wing Woo, Madge Kennedy, Treat Williams; **w**, William Goldman (based on his novel); **c**, Conrad Hall (Panavision; Metrocolor); **m**, Michael Small; **ed**, Jim Clark; **prod d**, Richard MacDonald; **art d**, Jack De Shields; **set d**, George Gaines; **spec eff**, Richard E. Johnson, Charles Spurgeon.

March or Die ★★★ 1977; U.K.; 107m; Sir Lew Grade/COL; Color; Adventure: Children: Unacceptable (MPAA: PG); **DVD**; **VHS**. The French Foreign Legion has been romanticized and lampooned in many films, and this one is one of the better profiles of that exceptional military force that accepts the strangest of volunteers with no questions asked. It begins with Hackman (giving an exceptional performance of a Legion commander), who is haunted by the wanton slaughter of his troops on the Western Front in 1918 during WWI. His unit has been decimated and its survivors have been pulled from the trenches, reposted to Morocco and where he must supplement his casualties with new recruits. Among those new recruits sailing with Hackman and his veterans toward Morocco is Hill, a capricious, acrobatic cat burglar; Sherman, an aristocrat craving adventure; Penvern, a musician who wears a top hat; and O'Halloran, a giant former Russian guard for the Imperial Family. The unit's assignment is to guard a scientific expedition led by archeologist Sydow, a curator from the Louvre, who intends to excavate a holy tomb, despite the fact that the natives consider it sacred. Also on board that ship in that voyage into danger is the beautiful Deneuve, who plans to search for her father, also an archeologist, and who was lost during a previous expedition to that tomb. When Hill breaks regulations by leaving steerage on board the ship in an attempt to charm Deneuve, Hackman smugly congratulates him on his inventiveness and then orders him to drink one bottle of wine after another until he collapses drunk. When reaching Morocco, the troops disembark and then travel by train toward their home base in the desert, but the train is stopped in the middle of the drifting dunes by a heavily armed Arab force led by Holm (his role model being Moroccan Arab leader Abd el-Krim, 1882-1963), an old but respected adversary of Hackman's, who warns Hackman not to reenter the sacred ruins or to continue any kind of archeological excavation. Holm then shows Hackman and his men two archeologists captured earlier, one of them being Deneuve's father, both having been blinded, their tongues cut out. They are in rags and are barely alive. Before Holm can execute them in front of Hackman and his men as an abject demonstration of his intentions, Hackman withdraws his pistol and shoots both men dead. The train is then permitted to continue and after the new recruits arrive at the Foreign Legion fort of Bousaada they immediately undergo severe if not savage training. The recruits who do not conform are treated harshly by Bozzuffi, a nononsense officer. He smashes Penvern's top hat as being supercilious and, when Hill gives him a smart remark, he punches Hill in the face, drawing blood and where the defiant Hill merely smiles through his pain. Their final training test consists of marching through the desert with full packs and heavy clothing. They are warned that any stragglers will be left behind in the dunes. It is: "March or die." After the weak Penvern, his feet bleeding, falls from the ranks, he is left to die. Hill, however, goes back for him and carries him to the fort, saving his life and receiving cheers and plaudits from his fellow soldiers. Hackman, though he admires Hill's compassion and valor, brutally punishes him for disobeying orders by having Hill pilloried in the town square where a neckpiece slowly strangles him. Deneuve intervenes, convincing Hackman to release Hill, and promising him that she will not return Hill's attentions, knowing that Hackman, too, is in love with her and is punishing Hill for competing with him for Deneuve's love. The sensitive Penvern then dallies with a prostitute, but after he proves to be impotent, he is ridiculed and then commits suicide. The troops then march to the excavation site, which has been prohibited by Holm, and where Sydow obsessively drives diggers to unearth the sacred relics hidden beneath the desert sands. The archeologist discovers the sarcophagus of "The Angel of the Desert," a legendary Moroccan leader, but just as this discovery is made, Holm arrives with hundreds of armed Arabs. Even after Hackman offers him the coffin of the long-dead leader, Holm is not pacified as he intends to use the violation of the sacred ruins to unite all the tribes in Morocco in an effort to drive the foreigners from his country. He launches a massive attack on all sides of the ruins, and Hackman waits until the last minute before he allows his men to fire. When they do, they mow down with machine guns and rifles the waves of Arabs charging toward them, but most of the defenders are overwhelmed and killed, including Hackman. Hill survives to see Holm approach and salute his dead adversary and then depart with what is left of his men. Hill returns to the Legion post where he says goodbye to Deneuve, who is returning to civilization, and where Hill has decided to remain with the Legion. He is shown at the finale telling new recruits that they must face incredible hardships while serving with the Legion, which is a loyal band of brothers, repeating the words uttered by Hackman: "If the desert doesn't get you, the Arabs will! If the Arabs don't get you, the Legion will, and if the Legion doesn't, I will! I don't know which is worse." Richards directs this film with considerable skill, particularly the battle scenes, unflinchingly showing barbarous conduct, sadism, and much bloodletting, but it is all in keeping with his realistic portrait of the Legion where survival at almost all costs is paramount. Hackman is forceful and compelling in his role as the commander, Deneuve is distantly alluring, and Hill and the others are standouts in their divergent roles. This film did not initially earn back its $9 million budget, gleaning only $1 million at the box office the first time around, but it nevertheless remains a classic through grim portrait of the Legion as it existed during and shortly after WWI. Many films have been based on the exploits of the French Foreign Legion, notably: **Beau Geste**, 1926; **Morocco**, 1930; **Under Two Flags**, 1936; **Beau Geste**, 1939; **The Flying Deuces**, 1939; **The Desert Song**, 1943; **Rogue's Regiment**, 1948; **Ten Tall Men**, 1953; **The Desert Song**, 1953; and **The Mummy**, 1999. **p**, Dick Richards, Jerry Bruckheimer; **d**, Richards; **cast**, Gene Hackman, Terence Hill, Catherine Deneuve, Max von Sydow, Ian Holm, Jack O'Halloran, Rufus, Marcel Bozzuffi, André Penvern, Paul Sherman, Vernon Dobtcheff, Marne Maitland; **w**, David Zelag Goodman (based on a story by Richards and Goodman); **c**, John Alcott (Technicolor); **m**, Maurice Jarre; **ed**, Stanford C. Allen, O. Nicholas Brown, John C. Howard; **prod d**, Gil Parrondo; **art d**, John Graysmark, José Maria Tapiador; **set d**, Julián Mateos, Dennis J. Parrish; **spec eff**, Robert MacDonald.

Marco the Magnificent ★★★ 1965; France/Italy/Yugoslavia; Afghanistan/Egypt; 100 m.; Avala Film/MGM; Color; Adventure; Children: Unacceptable. In this action-loaded adventure tale, Alberti, who plays Pope Gregory X (1210-1276) sends Buchholz, who plays Marco Polo (1254-1324), an adventure-seeking young Venetian sailor, to Asia to introduce Catholic civilization to the Mongol hordes led by Quinn, who plays the all powering ruler of China, Kublai Khan (1215-1294). His journey takes Buchholz through the Holy Land, across the Himalayas and into the Gobi Desert until he finally reaches China. Along the way, Buchholz and his entourage are captured by Tamiroff and his men, who execute one of Buchholz's associates in a bell torture chamber. Sharif, a desert sheik, then helps Buchholz and his men escape to Samarkand where Buchholz is briefly reunited with his father, Girotti. Mongolian bandits chase the travelers and they are aided by whip-wielding Martinelli, who sacrifices her life for Buchholz. Next, Quinn's enemies pursue Buchholz and his party until they escape on a barge belonging to a princess (Moon). Reaching China, Buchholz finds that Quinn is at war with his son, Hossein, in the world's first battle using gunpowder. A narrator then tells that Buchholz remained in China for seventeen years, and when he returned to Italy he was tossed into jail for staying away so long. Marco Polo's travels were made into other movies including **The Adventures of Marco Polo**, 1938; **Marco Polo**, 1962; and a musical movie titled **Marco**, 1973, as well as a 1982 television miniseries, and a 2007 made-for-TV movie. Excessive violence prohibits viewing by children. (In French and Italian; English subtitles.) **p**, Raoul J. Lévy; **d**, Lévy, Denys de La Patellière, Noël Howard; **cast**, Horst Buchholz, Anthony Quinn, Orson Welles, Omar Sharif, Akim Tamiroff, Elsa Martinelli, Robert Hossein, Massimo Girotti, Folco Lulli, Guido Alberti, Lee Sue Moon; **w**, Lévy, de La Patellière, Howard, Jean-Paul Rappeneau, Jacques Rémy; **c**, Claude Renoir, Vladimir Ivanov, Armand Thirard (Franscope; Eastmancolor); **m**, Mario Bua, M.J. Coignard-Helison, Georges Garvarentz; **ed**, Noëlle Balenci, Jacqueline Thiédot, Albert Jurgenson; **prod d**, Jacques Saulnier; **art d**, Veljko

Jeanne Crain and Alan Young in *Margie,* 1946.

Despotovic, Slobodan Mijacevic, Miodrag Miric, Miodrag Nikolic; **spec eff**, Roscoe Cline.

Margie ★★★★ 1946; U.S.; 94m; FOX; Color; Musical Comedy; Children: Acceptable; **VHS**. A terrific high school musical with many comedic scenes is wonderfully evocative of the Roaring Twenties and is told in flashback as the beautiful Crain narrates her "flaming youth" to Todd, her teenage daughter. The tale shows Crain as a teenager at high school where Young and other boys pursue the pretty girl's attention, but her heart throbs only for handsome French teacher Langan. The only feminine competition Crain sees is tall and blonde Lawrence, who attracts a bevy of boys, but their rivalry is a wholesome one where all the snippets and sniping are positioned in a friendly manner. The madcap fancies and fads of the Jazz Age are in evidence in every delightful scene, with girls painting red rouge on their knees and soaking their locks with peroxide while their male counterparts adorn themselves in raccoon coats and spectator shoes. The youngsters rollick through innocent days at school and at home (and where, in a very funny scene, Crain is shown on the debating team), and dreamy nights by kicking up their heels and dancing the frenetic and dynamic "Charleston," but somehow find enough time to complete their studies. Crain manages to win the heart of the evasive Langan, who is shown at the finale as Todd's father. This highly spirited songfest, which, with effective sets and costumes, and a witty script awash with the colorful vernacular of those days, captures that halcyon period and its light-hearted generation as no other musical, with the exception of **Good News**, 1947 (which profiles college students in the 1920s), while providing some of the finest songs of that era. There have been many high school movies (**American Graffiti**, 1973, **Grease**, 1978), but this is one of the best. Songs include: "I'll See You in My Dreams" (Gus Khan, Isham Jones); "Three O'Clock in the Morning" (Dorothy Terriss, Julian Robledo); "A Cup of Coffee, a Sandwich and You" (Billy Rose, Al Dubin and Joseph Meyer); "Ain't She Sweet?" (Jack Yellen, Milton Ager); "Wonderful One" (Dorothy Terriss, Paul Whiteman and Ferde Grofe, from a theme by Marshall Neilan); "Charleston" (Cecil Mack, James P. Johnson); "April Showers" (Buddy De Sylva, Louis Silvers); "Charmaine," "Diane" (Erno Rapee, Lou Pollock); "Collegiate" (Mo Jaffe, Nat Bronx); "Avalon" (Al Jolson, Vincent Rose); "My Time Is Your Time" (Eric Little, Leo Dance); "At Sundown" (Walter Donaldson) and "Margie" (Benny Davis, Con Conrad and J. Russell Robinson). *Author's Note*: Crain told this author that **Margie** was one of her favorite films, although she did have a problem with one comedic device director King kept reintroducing in several scenes and that is "where the elastic on my underwear is always breaking. I told Henry [King] that that gag was wearing just a little too thin and that my embarrassing blush

Tyrone Power and Norma Shearer in *Marie Antoinette*, 1938.

was good for one or may two scenes, but he kept that up, until I told him, 'That's it! The elastic stays in place from now on.'" King laughed when I raised this with him, telling this author: "I think Jeanne was overly concerned what her fans might say. That exquisitely beautiful woman was always a very proper lady. There was nothing risqué about those little personal accidents and it was all done in good fun. I say that a good joke is always worth repeating." **p**, Walter Morosco; **d**, Henry King; **cast**, Jeanne Crain, Glenn Langan, Lynn Bari, Alan Young, Barbara Lawrence, Conrad Janis, Esther Dale, Hobart Cavanaugh, Ann Todd, Hattie McDaniel, Vanessa Brown; **w**, F. Hugh Herbert (based on a story by Ruth McKenney, Richard Bransten); **c**, Charles Clarke (Technicolor); **m**, Alfred Newman; **ed**, Barbara McLean; **art d**, James Basevi, J. Russell Spencer; **set d**, Thomas Little, Frank E. Hughes; **spec eff**, Fred Sersen, Edwin Hammeras.

Marie ★★★ 1985; U.S.; 112m; Dino De Laurentiis/MGM-UA; Color; Biographical Drama; Children: Unacceptable (MPAA: PG-13); **DVD**; **VHS**. Based on a true story, Spacek is excellent as she essays Marie Fajardo Ragghianti (b. 1942), who risks her life as a whistle-blower on political corruption in Tennessee. She leaves a wife-beating husband in 1968 and works as a waitress while putting herself through Vanderbilt University, graduating with degrees in psychology and English while raising her three children including a chronically ill boy. She becomes involved in state politics when Daniels, a legal counsel, Daniels, to Tennessee Governor Ray Blanton (1930-1996), played by Hood, gives her a job, and she works her way up the political ladder to become head of the state parole board. She learns that Hood is influencing the release of some powerful criminals and that he, Daniels, and others are involved in graft. The jailed son of one of Hood's largest re-election campaign contributors demands special care inside the prison. Daniels tries to coax her into ignoring it, but she refuses, so she is railroaded out of her job. Those she tries to expose accuse her of sexual affairs with several men and cheating on her expense accounts. She fights back by hiring an attorney, Thompson, and sues for wrongful dismissal. Her strongest witness, Szarabajka, is killed and Spacek is threatened by hoodlums she believes are on the state payroll. The result is Hood, Daniels, and others are sent to prison and she gets her old job back. This deeply intriguing tale presents a searing indictment of Blanton's corrupt "clemency for cash" scandal of 1977-1979. Mature themes and gutter language prohibit viewing by children. **p**, Frank Capra, Jr.; **d**, Roger Donaldson; **cast**, Sissy Spacek, Jeff Daniels, Keith Szarabajka, Morgan Freeman, Fred Thompson, Lisa Banes, Trey Wilson, John Cullum, Don Hood, Jane Powell; **w**, John Briley (based on the book *Marie: A True Story* by Peter Maas); **c**, Chris Menges (Technicolor); **m**, Francis Lai; **ed**, Neil Travis; **art d**, Ron Foreman; **set d**, Tantar Leviseur.

Marie Antoinette ★★★★ 1938; U.S.; 157m; MGM; B/W; Biographical Drama; Children: Cautionary; **DVD**; **VHS**. MGM pulled out all the stops in making this sumptuous eye-popping epic, based upon the beautiful and controversial Marie Antoinette (1755-1793), Queen of France, played by Shearer, and wife of Louis XVI (1754-1793), played by Morley. The lovely Shearer is the most desired princess in Europe (a Hapsburg) and who is pressured into marrying Morley by her domineering and politically scheming mother, Kruger, who enacts the role of Maria Theresa (1717-1780), Empress of Austria. Shearer gets the shock of her life when first meeting her intended husband, Morley, who is overweight, slow-witted and ungainly, the man of no woman's dreams. She is further repelled by the hostile and sneering Barrymore (Morley's aging but calculating father, Louis XV 1710-1774); and his conniving cousin, Schildkraut (as the Duke of Orleans); and Barrymore's opportunistic mistress, George (Madame Du Barry), who conspire to demean and dismiss the lovely Shearer. On her wedding night, Morley, a sad case, comes to her and admits he is incapable of performing his husbandly duties. Meanwhile adversaries Barrymore, George, and Schildkraut make of her a pariah at the Versailles court. Lonely and emotionally damaged, Shearer immerses herself in lavish balls and fetes where she adorns herself with the most stunning gowns ever seen in any court, extravagantly spending for jewels and fineries from the royal coffers. She meets dashing Power, a handsome count, and they develop a love affair. Meanwhile, Austrian ambassador Stephenson pleads with Shearer to strengthen his country's alliance with France by holding a ball where she is to recognize George as a "woman of royal position." This Shearer does, but she eventually insults George, believing her to be nothing more than Barrymore's sexual plaything. The insult causes Barrymore to explode and where he threatens to annul Shearer's marriage to his son, Morley, and return her to Austria in disgrace. Only Power comforts the now frightened Shearer, but this tenuous position is eased when Barrymore suddenly dies and his weak-willed son, Morley, becomes the new king of France (Louis XVI). Power then tells Shearer that he can love a dauphine of France but not its queen, and leaves her, sailing to America to begin a new life. Shearer vows to be a loyal wife and good queen and thereafter remains faithful to Morley, bearing him two children. However, wealthy Schildkraut, now that Barrymore is dead and George has become an outcast, has himself become the pariah he sought to make of Shearer and, vowing vengeance, begins to finance a revolution to destroy the monarchy. When revolutionaries swarm into Versailles, Schildkraut takes his revenge by having Morley and Shearer put into prison and held there for trial, the outcome of which is known in advance—death by the guillotine. Power, however, has returned from America and arranges for the royal couple and their children to escape. They flee by coach toward the border, hoping to reach safety, but they are stopped at Varennes, are recognized by Calleia, a vicious revolutionary, and are recaptured and again imprisoned. Kept separated with her children from Morley, Shearer later undergoes tremendous agony when ruthless revolutionaries take her children from her. She hears that Morley has been executed and she is then tried and condemned, going to the guillotine. (Marie Antoinette showed incredible courage and disdain for her demise when mounting the scaffold. She accidentally stepped upon the executioner's toes and uttered her last gracious words: "Pardon me, monsieur.") Power is seen standing helpless on a Paris rooftop, witnessing the execution of the woman he loves as he fondles a ring on his finger, one reading: "Everything leads me to thee. Marie Antoinette." Great liberties are taken with the real royal saga, but it is a grand Hollywood re-creation of that tempestuous period, a stunning and memorable historical epic that wholly belongs to the captivating Shearer who gives a marvelous performance and where her supporting players are superlative in their roles. ***Author's Note***: This grandly extravagant production, from its rich sets and amazing costumes had long been prepared for Shearer. Her husband, Irving Thalberg, who had been head of production at MGM for a decade and had been responsible for most of its finest films, began working on this project as early as 1933, but he died in 1936. Nevertheless, scores of MGM craftsmen, wardrobe workers and technicians continued to labor on the production as a smashing comeback to the studio by Shearer (known as the "Queen of MGM"), who had been absent from the screen for two years following her husband's death. However, working behind the scenes to actually sabotage this massive and expensive production was none other than MGM boss Louis B. Mayer. After Thalberg died in 1936, Shearer's attorneys met with Mayer and other MGM executives, demanding that Shearer and her children receive percent of all gross profits produced by MGM through the period of Thalberg's contract with the studio and that extended through 1938, two years after his death (Shearer and her children by Thalberg had already inherited a $4 million estate and many other assets with Thalberg's passing). "Mayer fought tooth and nail against giving Shearer another dime," according to statements made to this author by MGM film editor Gene Ruggiero, who had a strange but inside view of a lot of the executive goings-on at the studio. Ruggiero had been a teenage caddy in New York for Nicholas Schenck (1881-1969), who, along with his brother Joseph Schenck, operated the massive Loew's theater chain through which MGM films were exhibited and held controlling interest in MGM. Schenck took Ruggiero to Hollywood and more or less ordered Mayer to give him a job, and Ruggiero selected the field of film editing where he learned the craft from the ground up. He was at the time of **Marie Antoinette** working under its film editor Kern. Ruggiero told this author that "when Nick Schenck heard that Mayer was trying to chisel money out of the studio's biggest star and the wife of the man who had literally made that studio with some of the world's greatest pictures, he flew to Hollywood. He stopped by my little office where I worked as a film editor—I went on caddying for him for years whenever he came to town from New York—and asked me to accompany him. Well, he marched right into Mayer's big office with no announcement and I am tagging along not knowing what this was all about. Nick, a big bull of a guy, stomped up to Mayer's desk, stuck a fat cigar into his mouth, lit it and began puffing like a steam engine, blowing smoke into Mayer's face. Mayer took all that without a word as he was terrified of only one man, Nick Schenck, who held the purse strings at MGM, and had deep holdings in almost every other studio so that he really owned Hollywood. Nick finally removed the cigar and said: 'Louis, you are a miserable man! I hear you are abusing a widow, Norma Shearer, one of our finest stars, by denying her the proceeds from contracts we signed with Irving [Thalberg]. Without Irving, we would not have this studio and you know it! What the hell is the matter with you? Are you and your associates that greedy that you are going to chisel a widow woman out of what is rightfully due her? You already have more millions than you can ever spend!' He doubled up a fist that was the size of a small frying pan and pounded it so hard on Mayer's desk that it broke a glass figurine that was a prized relic of Mayer's, and said: 'You honor those contracts with Norma, or I will do to you what Salome did to John the Baptist and I will serve your head on a platter to Norma! Do you understand?' Mayer was trembling and speechless. He could only nod. Nick motioned for me to leave with him, but before we got out of Mayer's office, Mayer called out to Nick and said: 'Nick, why, whenever to make one of your visits to me, do you bring Gene along? He works in the film editing department and has no business with these matters.' Nick replied: 'When I brought Gene out here years ago, I promised his mother that I would get him a good job in the picture business and I had you put him to work here, but I want him to know this business from top to bottom. That's why I bring him into your office, Louis. Who knows? He might be running MGM someday.' Then we left Mayer's office and I could not wait to get out of there. Mayer looked at me as Nick's man and I think Mayer always thought I was spying on him on Nick's behalf, but I steered clear of Mayer and the front office all I could. It wasn't until many years later that I learned that I was being paid three times the salary any other film editor was making at the studio and that was Nick's doing. It was like having a guardian angel, I guess." Anyway, Mayer immediately contacted Norma and told her that MGM

Tyrone Power and Norma Shearer in *Marie Antoinette*, 1938.

would honor her husband's contracts and she would receive everything due her. Nick did that, so he was her guardian angel, too." Shearer was further troubled during the production of this film when Mayer removed Sidney Franklin, her favorite director, and replaced him with Van Dyke, a helmsman who put economy first and additional expenses last, never doing more than one or two takes for a scene. In one scene, Shearer demanded another take, even though Van Dyke had done several. The director refused and Shearer walked off the set. She returned the next day to apologize and continued with the production, but it was evident that, with her husband now gone from MGM, she was not to be treated with any special consideration. When leaving the set while wearing one of her ornate costumes, her dress got caught in some cables that yanked her backward so that she landed on her backside, her hooped dress billowing over her head. Crew members broke into loud laughter, something that would never have happened when Thalberg was alive, but Shearer surprised everyone by laughing just as loud. Power's role is mythical and was reduced to that of a character providing romantic relief. He had been loaned out to MGM by Darryl Zanuck, chief of Twentieth Century-Fox. When he saw how his top star was treated, Zanuck vowed to never loan Power out to any other studio and maintained that policy for the next fifteen years. The always manipulating Mayer used this vehicle to also end his expensive relationship with media tycoon William Randolph Hearst, who maintained his own production company on the MGM lot, Cosmopolitan Pictures, which served to produce films for Hearst's actress-mistress Marion Davies. When Davies heard about the **Marie Antoinette** production, she went to Mayer and demanded that she be the star of that film. Of course, Shearer had long been cast in that leading role. Mayer told her that she (Davies) was known by the public as a comedienne and that the role of a tragic woman like Marie Antoinette was not for her. Davies called Hearst, who exploded and decided to move Cosmopolitan Pictures to Warner Brothers and did so, even having Davies' expensively built bungalow at MGM dismantled board by board and then carefully shipped to its new destination in Burbank. This is exactly what Mayer wanted as he had been co-producing Davies' films with Hearst and many of her recent productions had failed at the box office. **Marie Antoinette** was very expensive, its budget topping $1.8 million, but it proved to be an enormous success, mostly due to Shearer's box office popularity. She was nominated for an Oscar but lost out to Bette Davis for **Jezebel**, 1938. Marie Antoinette has been profiled in many films, including **Scaramouche** (Clotilde Delano), 1923; **Captain of the Guard** (Evelyn Hall), 1930; **Mystery of the Wax Museum** (in effigy), 1933; **Madame Du Barry** (Anita Louise), 1934; **Black Magic** (Nancy Guild), 1949; **House of Wax**, 1953 (in effigy); **The Affair of the Necklace** (Joely Richardson), 2001; **Marie Antoinette** (Kirsten Dunst), 2006; and in several TV miniseries; 1963 (a superlative French production with Annie Ducaux),

Spencer Tracy and Ketti Gallian in *Marie Galante*, 1934.

1975 (French; Genevieve Casile), 1979 (animation), and 1999 (U.K.; Elizabeth Berrington), and the made-for-TV movie, **Marie Antoinette** (Karine Vanasse), 2006. **p**, Hunt Stromberg; **d**, W.S. Van Dyke II and (uncredited) Julien Duvivier; **cast**, Norma Shearer, Tyrone Power, John Barrymore, Robert Morley, Anita Louise, Joseph Schildkraut, Gladys George, Henry Stephenson, Reginald Gardiner, Alma Kruger, Henry Daniell, Albert Dekker, Joseph Calleia, Scotty Beckett, Peter Bull, Ruth Hussey, Mae Busch, Howard Da Silva, Harry Davenport, Barry Fitzgerald, George Houston, Mary Howard, Phillip Terry, Zeffie Tilbury; **w**, Claudine West, Donald Ogden Stewart, Ernest Vajda, F. Scott Fitzgerald, Talbot Jennings (based on a book by Stefan Zweig); **c**, William Daniels; **m**, Herbert Stothart; **ed**, Robert J. Kern; **art d**, Cedric Gibbons; **spec eff**, Slavko Vorkapich.

Marie Galante ★★★ 1934; U.S.; 88m; FOX; B/W; Spy Drama; Children: Cautionary; **DVD**; **VHS**. This exciting spy tale, with a clever script and superior acting, sees Gallian in the title role and where she is kidnapped by a drunken sailor, sailing away on a ship, and is later discarded at Yucatan. She makes her way to the Panama Canal Zone and gets a job as a saloon singer. Here she meets and falls in love with the enigmatic Tracy, who is an American agent probing a plot to destroy the Canal, and he enlists Gallian's services in his investigation, falling in love with her, too. Aiding them both are other agents of several foreign countries, but it is Gallian and Tracy who identify and capture the saboteur before any damage can be done. The great torch singer, Helen Morgan, makes some brief appearances while singing in the café where Gallian works and where Morgan warbles "Serves Me Right for Treating You Wrong" (Maurice Sigler, Al Goodhart, Al Hoffman). Other songs include: "Je t'adore," "On a Little Side Street" (Harry Akst, Bernie Grossman); "It's Home" (Jay Gorney, Jack Yellen); "Shim Shammy" (Stepin Fetchit); "Song of the Dreamer" (Jay Gorney, Don Hartman); and "Un peu beaucoup" (Arthur Lange, Marcel Silver). *Author's Note*: Director King, who directs this espionage story with great style, filling it with many shadowy sets and moody atmospheric shots, told this author that "we were ambiguous as to the nationality of the saboteur. We have not only Tracy as the American agent after him, but many other agents of other countries like France and Great Britain involved, too, and we even included an agent from Japan, played by Leslie Fenton, who was Occidental, but who had played many Orientals in many pictures, thanks to good makeup. I had Fenton play his role so that he looks very suspicious, as if he could be that foreign saboteur, and almost at the end of the production, I got a call from a Japanese diplomat in Los Angeles, who politely asked me how that Japanese character was being positioned in **Marie Galante**. The Japanese were very sensitive in those days about how their nationals were being character-ized in the movies. I told this quiet-speaking little man that Fenton was helping Tracy and other agents from preventing the Canal from being destroyed and that was the end of it. Then I read some months after we released the film that American agents had actually caught a bunch of Japanese spies down there in the Panama Canal Zone who were planning to blow up the locks! So I then realized what that inquiry was all about from the Japanese legation in Los Angeles. They wanted to know if we knew what they were up to down there in the Canal Zone." Another very exciting film, **Across the Pacific**, 1942, starring Humphrey Bogart, focuses upon the same tale of sabotage, but this time the saboteurs operating in the Canal Zone are specifically identified as Japanese agents (by that time the U.S. was at war with Japan). **p**, Winfield Sheehan; **d**, Henry King; **cast**, Spencer Tracy, Ketti Gallian, Ned Sparks, Helen Morgan, Sig Ruman, Leslie Fenton, Arthur Byron, Robert Loraine, Frank Darien, Adrienne D'Ambricourt; **w**, Reginald Berkeley (based on the novel by Jacques Deval); **c**, John F. Seitz; **m**, Arthur Lange; **ed**, Harold D. Schuster.

Marigolds in August ★★★ 1984; South Africa; 87m; Serpents/RM Productions; Color; Drama; Children: Unacceptable. This compelling but often disturbing film dynamically profiles the plight of blacks during the apartheid (racial segregation) in South Africa. Segregation was enforced by the National Party government, the ruling party of South Africa, from 1948 to 1994, during which the rights of majority blacks were curtailed and white supremacy was maintained. It tells the fictional story of Ntshona, a black man, during the time of the apartheid. Ntshona makes a passable living working as a gardener and handyman in a white, middle-class, seaside community outside Port Elizabeth. Kani, another black man who is out of work and desperate, comes looking for work and Ntshona, who fears losing his work to him, threatens Kani and chases him away. An older man, Fugard, who is of mixed blood and earns a skimpy living by catching cobras and puff adders in the nearby national park and selling them in Port Elizabeth, helps them by suggesting they work together. The two workers take his advice and their reconciliation is a dramatization of taking the first step toward the goal of racial equity that one day can bring an end to apartheid, which it finally does in 1994. **p**, Mark Forstater; Ross Devenish; **cast**, Winston Ntshona, John Kani, Athol Fugard, Joyce Hesha, Mabel Ntshinga; **w**, Fugard; **c**, Michael J. Davis.

Marine Raiders ★★★ 1944; U.S.; 90m; RKO; B/W; War/Drama; Children: Unacceptable; **DVD**; **VHS**. O'Brien and Ryan are buddies, two Marine Corps officers who take part in the Guadalcanal invasion during World War II. Afterward they are given a short leave in Australia where Ryan falls in love with Hussey. O'Brien breaks it up by having him and Ryan assigned to the States to train recruits. On a return mission to Australia, Ryan and Hussey marry and the pals go off into the war in the Pacific again. This action-packed production is a very good war propaganda film with top flight performances from O'Brien, Ryan and Hussey. **p**, Robert Fellows; **d**, Harold Schuster; **cast**, Pat O'Brien, Robert Ryan, Ruth Hussey, Frank McHugh, Barton MacLane, Richard Martin, Martha Vickers (Martha MacVicar), Russell Wade, Michael St. Angel, Blake Edwards, Greg McClure; **w**, Warren Duff (based on a story by Duff, Martin Rackin); **c**, Nicholas Musuraca; **m**, Roy Webb; **ed**, Philip Martin, Jr.; **art d**, Albert S. D'Agostino, Walter E. Keller; **set d**, Darrell Silvera, Harley Miller; **spec eff**, Vernon L. Walker.

Marius ★★★★ 1933; France; 130m; Les Films Marcel Pagnol/PAR; B/W; Drama; Children: Unacceptable; **DVD**; **VHS**. This is the first of Pagnol's riveting trilogy that includes **Fanny**, 1948, and **Cesar**, 1936. It begins with young man Fresnay working in a Marseilles bar and yearning to go to sea. His father, Raimu, is forever complaining about Fresnay's lack of ambition, but he nevertheless is devoted to his son. Raimu idles away his time with wealthy Charpin, Dullac, a ferry captain, and Vattier, a customs inspector. Meanwhile, Fresnay loves from afar the fetching Demazis, who is the daughter of fishwife Rouffe. Demazis hopes that Fresnay will someday soon ask for her hand in marriage, but he stalls, his longing for the sea postponing any kind of wedding plans. When Charpin asks for Demazis' hand in marriage, however, Fresnay explodes. Demazis is thrilled at Fresnay's passion for her and now believes that he will soon propose to eliminate competitor Charpin, but this does not come to pass after Fresnay learns from Mihalesco that there is a berth open for a sailor on a ship departing that night. Hearing that Fresnay may run away to sea, the desperate Demazis goes to the bar where Fresnay works and tells him that she loves only him and will not marry Charpin. He admits that he loves her and then Milhalesco arrives to tell them that the man who had quit the ship has decided to return to his job and the job for a sailor is no longer available. Fresnay and Demarzis then go to Fresnay's room where they make love. Still they get no closer to the altar as Fresnay's longing for the sea has not abated. After Rouffee finds Fresnay and Demazis making love in the girl's room, she goes to Raimu, demanding that he compel his son to marry her daughter. Raimu tries to do just that, telling Fresnay that he should do the honorable thing and marry Demazis. Mihalesco, however, who serves as a sort of a harbinger of unwelcomed things to come, arrives again and tells Fresnay that there is a job available on another ship about to leave Marseilles and, if Fresnay does not take that job, he probably will never have an opportunity to fulfill his lifelong dreams. The self-sacrificing Demazis now sees how Fresnay is torn between her and his ambitions and tells him that he should take that job as she has decided to accept Charpin's offer of marriage because his wealth will provide comfort for her mother in her old age. Fresnay grabs a suitcase that has long been packed and races toward the docks to sign on board that departing ship while Demazis stalls Raimu. Raimu then tells her that he and her mother are united in that she and his son be married. Realizing her mistake, Demazis becomes ashen-faced as she sees from a window that ship sailing out of the Marseilles harbor and with the love of her life on board and she faints into the arms of the startled Raimu, ending this powerful domestic drama. Korda directs this sensitive story with great skill, fully developing his characters in each scene and where Fresnay, Demazis and Raimu give outstanding performances. *Author's Note*: Though the film is in French, there were no subtitles provided in the 1933 U.S. release, although English subtitles were later provided when this film was re-released in the U.S. in 1948 by Siritzky International Pictures. **p**, Marcel Pagnol, Robert Kane; **d**, Alexander Korda; **cast**, Raimu, Pierre Fresnay, Orane Demazis, Fernand Charpin, Alida Rouffe, Paul Dullac, Alexandre Mihalesco, Robert Vattier, Édouard Delmont, Milly Mathis, Marcel Maupi; **w**, Pagnol (based on his play); **c**, Theodore J. Pahle; **m**, Francis Gromon; **ed**, Roger Mercanton; **art d**, Alfred Junge, Vincent Korda.

The Mark ★★★ 1961; U.K.; 127m; Buckman/Continental Distributing; B/W; Drama; Children: Unacceptable (MPAA: R); **DVD;VHS**. Whitman is compelling in this riveting drama about a young man, who grows into manhood confused about his manliness and where he serves three years in prison for intent to molest a ten-year-old girl. In prison, he is under the care of a psychiatrist, Steiger. Upon Whitman's release from prison, Steiger gets him a job with a company where Whitman falls in love with Schell, a secretary, who is a widow with a ten-year-old daughter. Life looks good for Whitman until Schell's daughter is molested and beaten. A reporter who covered Whitman's previous trial tells police about him and he is picked up for questioning. He has an alibi and is released, but the mark against him as a previously convicted pedophile comes back to haunt him. **p**, Raymond Stross; **d**, Guy Green; **cast**, Maria Schell, Stuart Whitman, Rod Steiger, Brenda de Banzie, Donald Houston, Donald Wolfit, Paul Rogers, Maurice Denham, Amanda Black, Marie Devereux; **w**, Sidney Buchman, Stanley Mann (based on the novel by Charles E. Israel); **c**, Dudley Lovell; **m**, Richard Rodney Bennett; **ed**, Peter Taylor; **art d**, Ray Simm; **set d**, Josie MacAvin.

Bela Lugosi and Elizabeth Allan in *Mark of the Vampire*, 1935.

Mark of the Hawk ★★★ 1958; U.S./U.K.; 83m; Film Productions International/UNIV; Color; Drama; Children: Unacceptable; **DVD**; **VHS**. Poitier gives a strong performance in this engrossing tale about an educated black man struggling with political and racial strife in a colonial African country where the natives want their land and lives back from the British colonists. Poitier returns from schooling abroad to become a legislator. His brother, Macklin, heads a revolt against the ruling whites and Poitier is conflicted as to where his loyalties lie. With the help of his wife, Kitt, and a white missionary, McIntire, he is able to bring about control of the mercurial situation so that it does not escalate into racial warfare. Violence and racial themes prohibit viewing by children. **p**, Lloyd Young; **d**, Michael Audley; **cast**, Sidney Poitier, Clifton Macklin, Eartha Kitt, Juano Hernandez, John McIntire, Helen Horton, Marne Maitland, Gerard Heinz, Patrick Allen, Earl Cameron, Frederick Treves; **w**, H. Kenn Carmichael, Young (based on a story by Young); **c**, Toge Fujihira, Erwin Hillier (SuperScope; Technicolor); **m**, Matyas Seiber; **ed**, Edward B. Jarvis; **art d**, Terence Verity.

Mark of the Vampire ★★★ 1935; U.S.; 60m; MGM; B/W; Horror; Children: Unacceptable; **DVD**; **VHS**. Pantheon horror director Browning returns to his forte genre after a three-year hiatus from the subject since making **Freaks**, 1932. This offbeat but fascinating entry is really a scene-for-scene remake of Browning's silent horror film, **London after Midnight**, 1927, which centers on a bedeviled family headed by Herbert, who, along with his daughter, Allan, and others become the new residents of a sprawling, spooky old castle in Czechoslovakia. The previous resident, Lugosi, reportedly murdered his daughter, Borland, in this creaking and cobwebbed old mansion, and their spirits are rumored to haunt the place in order to drive out anyone thinking to live there. Herbert is then found dead, all of his blood drained away and two curious puncture marks found on his neck. Atwill, the local police inspector, as well as Hersholt, a baron of great wealth, along with physician Meek, decide that they will solve this murder, despite the eerie hazards placed in their probing path. Hersholt, who has taken over the place, magnanimously offers Allan free residence, and she finds solace and love in the form of a handsome young count, Wadsworth. They fall in love and then plan to wed, but things become complicated when Barrymore, a celebrated vampire-hunter, arrives and vows to rid the place of the undead creatures lurking and looming everywhere. To confirm the existence of these creatures, Atwill and Hersholt visit the castle at night, watching from outside a window to see in horror as the murdered Herbert sits at an organ and plays it for Lugosi's pleasure as Borland flies like a fluttering bat about the cavernous living room. Hersholt later that night is confronted by all three vampires, Lugosi, Borland and Herbert, but he manages to flee their clutches. Telling Barrymore of this

Tyrone Power and Basil Rathbone in *The Mark of Zorro,* 1940.

awful experience, the vampire slayer hypnotizes Hersholt and has him recall the events of Herbert's murder. Hersholt seems to be fighting the hypnosis, but finally relents and admits that he killed Herbert in order to prevent Allan's marriage to Wadsworth, as he covets Allan for himself. After murdering Herbert, Hersholt also admits that he drained his blood to make it appear that he had been the victim of a vampire. Barrymore awakens Hersholt and promptly hands him over to police, who are waiting in the wings as per Barrymore's previous arrangements. We then see Lugosi and Borland in a dressing room, changing from their "vampire costumes" as they compliment each other on their performances as actors hired by Barrymore to frighten Hersholt into submitting to hypnosis. Browning presents a moody and frightening film, his massive, gloomy sets and heavily shaded scenes appropriate to the gothic tale, but the twist ending proved to be a letdown with audiences, who craved those that real blood-sucking creatures (as is the case today, particularly with teens, who have made even the most abysmal vampire productions box office successes). *Author's Note*: Browning shot this film as a straight horror film without informing the cast about its trick ending and when he introduced that ending, the cast rebelled, particularly Lugosi, who complained that he would appear to be ridiculous. He and others begged Browning to change the finale back to a realistic vampire conclusion (if one could ever be achieved), but he refused and his rather deflating finish remained. MGM film editor Gene Ruggiero, who had gone to work at the studio as an apprentice assistant film editor while still in his teens in the late 1920s (receiving his first credit in 1939 for **Tarzan Finds a Son!** and was the film editor on a blockbuster, **Ninotchka**, 1939, the same year) told this author that "Browning made everybody mad at MGM with that let-down finish of his **Mark of the Vampire**. He was a big shot director and everybody gave him a wide berth and when he refused to tell anyone about the ending, no one challenged him. Then he tacks on that tricky finish. Eddie Mannix, who was the producer of that film, had a fit when he saw the ending. He went to Browning and told him that the public did not like to be hoodwinked that way and that he was making the actors and the studio look silly and that he should redo the ending. Browning had an iron-bound contract and, after he refused, the studio was stuck with the film the way it was. Browning had directed the granddaddy of all vampire films, **Dracula** [1931], so when it came to horror films, he could get away with anything. He sure got away with one there, leaving Lugosi as a poor red herring." **p**, E.J. Mannix; **d**, Tod Browning; **cast**, Lionel Barrymore, Elizabeth Allan, Bela Lugosi, Lionel Atwill, Jean Hersholt, Henry Wadsworth, Donald Meek, Holmes Herbert, Carol Borland, Jessie Ralph, June Gittelson, Robert Greig, Leila Bennett, Doris Lloyd, Ivan Simpson, Michael Visaroff, Eily Malyon, Guy Bellis; **w**, Guy Endore, Bernard Schubert (based on the story "The Hypnotist" by Browning);

c, James Wong Howe; **ed**, Ben Lewis; **art d**, Cedric Gibbons; **spec eff**, Tom Tutwiler, Warren Newcombe.

The Mark of Zorro ★★★★ 1920 (silent); U.S.; 90m/8 reels; Douglas Fairbanks Pictures/UA; B/W; Adventure; Children: Cautionary; **DVD**; **VHS**. The athletic and dashing Fairbanks is terrific as the wealthy fop turned avenging hero in this first and fine tale of the legendary Zorro. Fairbanks arrives at his ancestral Old California estate in the early 1800s to see that his father, De Gray, who was the governor of the area, has been deposed and replaced by tyrannical Periolat. Under this new and oppressive regime, the peons are taxed into starvation and beaten senseless whenever objecting to such cruel treatment. Fairbanks assumes the disguise of a legendary hero, the masked Zorro, a Robin Hood character, who wears a black ensemble with a flowing cape when he rides to the rescue of the persecuted peons, brilliantly battling with his sword the chief henchmen of the governor, the brutal captain, McKim, and his equally savage sergeant, Beery (Noah Beerry Sr., Wallace Beery's older half-brother). Fairbanks displays in these action-packed fight sequences spectacular acrobatics, leaping from balconies, rooftops and onto speeding horses in battling his foes, and where he scars the faces of his enemies with the telltale mark of "Z" (for "Zorro"). The ravishing De La Motte catches Fairbanks' eye and he tries to woo her while playing a worthless rich idler, doing boring magic tricks to amuse her, but his effete and haughty airs (which Fairbanks exudes with great effectiveness to give the wrong impression of his true nature) so alienates her that she wants nothing to do with him. She then meets his secret counterpart, Zorro (also Fairbanks) and falls in love with the great hero, although she is also courted by the villainous McKim. When McKim cannot win the hand of De La Motte, he arranges for her and her family to be imprisoned, but Fairbanks comes to the rescue once again, this time discarding his disguise as the fop as well as Zorro and, with sword in hand, wins over the governor's soldiers, including Beery (who is bested so many times in swordfights by Fairbanks that he finally throws down his sword and sides with the great hero). McKim is dispatched and Periolat is deposed with the benevolent De Gray restored to the governorship. In the end, thrilled to see that the man she truly loves is Fairbanks, De La Motte willingly gives him her hand as his intended bride. Director Niblo presents nonstop action in this great swashbuckler, infusing into many scenes some clever comedy bits, and Fairbanks shines and thrills in every scene, this being his first great costumer, which led to many of his spectacular adventure tales to come such as **The Three Musketeers**, 1921; **Robin Hood**, 1922; **The Thief of Bagdad**, 1924; **Don Q: Son of Zorro**, 1925; and **The Black Pirate**, 1926. *Author's Note*: Fairbanks had some reservations in doing this role as he had earlier made his mark in films by playing American playboys or range-riders of the Old West and the role of Zorro was a distinct departure from the kind of characters his public then knew. This film, however, was so successful, bringing millions into the UA coffers (Fairbanks, along with his actress-wife Mary Pickford, Charles Chaplin and the great director D. W. Griffith, had founded United Artists only a year earlier in 1919) that it convinced Fairbanks that the adventure genre of swashbuckling swordsmen was the course to chiefly follow and, throughout the silent era, he became the symbol of such onscreen heroes. One of his millions of admirers was a young boy who avidly watched Fairbanks' films over and over, that boy later becoming a Hollywood superstar, Burt Lancaster, who told this author: "No actor on the screen in my childhood more impressed me than the wonderful Douglas Fairbanks Sr. His athletic prowess was unequalled in his time, and most probably was better than anything you see today. I think I was about seven or eight when I first saw **The Mark of Zorro**, and Fairbanks became my all-time hero. He inspired me to emulate his fantastic acrobatics in my own films, such as **The Crimson Pirate** [1952] where I tried to duplicate that unbelievable slide Fairbanks made by slicing downward with his sword into the huge sail of a large ship and sliding downward with it to the deck in **The Black Pirate**. His version was more spectacular and in my version

I almost broke my neck." **p**, Douglas Fairbanks; **d**, Fred Niblo; **cast**, Fairbanks, Noah Beery [Sr.], Marguerite De La Motte, Charles Hill Mailes, Claire McDowell, Robert McKim, George Periolat, Sidney De Gray, Noah Beery Jr., Milton Berle; **w**, Elton Thomas (Fairbanks), Eugene Miller (based on the story "*The Curse of Capistrano:* by Johnston McCulley); **c**, William McGann, Harry Thorpe; **m**, William Axt, William P. Perry (1970 release); **art d**, Edward Langley.

The Mark of Zorro ★★★★ 1940; U.S.; 94m; FOX; B/W; Adventure; Children: Cautionary; **DVD**; **VHS**. Power is magnetic and captivating in one of his greatest swashbuckling roles as the daring Zorro. He returns to his ancestral estate in California during the early 1800s when it was controlled by Spain to find that his fair-minded father, Love, a member of the great landowners (caballeros), has been deposed from his position as governor and replaced by the conniving and greedy Bromberg. Power also witnesses for the first time how Bromberg and his troops oppress the peons by mercilessly taxing them into starvation and poverty, wringing every peso from them at the point of a sword or bayonet. Bromberg's top enforcer is Rathbone, a sadistic captain of the guards who fancies himself a great swordsman. Power resolves to aid his people by pretending to be a fop, his perfumed posturing and prissy manners shocking Love, who believes that his son's education in Spain has taught him little and has turned him into a shallow weakling without honor and courage. This disguise, however, endears him to Sondergaard, the social-climbing wife of Bromberg whose only ambition is to go to Spain and be part of its aristocracy. Power's apparent indifference to the plight of peons pleases Bromberg, who considers Power an ally, but the suspicious Rathbone looks upon Power as a serious rival when Power makes advances toward Bromberg's beautiful niece and ward, Darnell. Power charms Darnell by dancing with her but she is offended by his arrogant and popinjay attitudes when he demeans the peasants and peons, callously ignoring the oppression they endure under Bromberg's savage reign. Thinking their oppressive realm is secure, Bromberg and Rathbone are shocked to learn that a masked rider has suddenly appeared in their midst, posting proclamations that demand the resignation of Bromberg or face his vengeance. The night visitor rides a black horse and is dressed all in black and signs his threatening messages with a "Z" carved into the walls where he posts his proclamations, that "Z" signifying his name, "Zorro." The viewer quickly realizes that Zorro and Love's playboy son is one and the same, Power. Bromberg's troops are attacked many times by the sword-wielding Power, saving the peons from abuse and stealing the tax money extorted from the inhabitants. Pallette, the local friar, is then visited by the masked Power, who asks him to keep the tax money for safekeeping so that it can later be distributed to the poor. This Pallette eagerly agrees to do. The masked Power then daringly visits Bromberg in his guarded residence, entering Bromberg's office through a secret panel where he presses his sword point to Bromberg's throat and orders him to sign his resignation. He then slashes his signature, "Z" with his sword onto the wall of Bromberg's office and then disappears. When the terrified Bromberg thinks to actually resign, Rathbone convinces him to retain his office and promises that he will track down the masked man. Bromberg, meanwhile, encourages Power to make arrangements to marry his niece, Darnell, but she wants no part of the idling Power until he comes to her dressed as Zorro and reveals his true identity. Power continues to raid Bromberg's troops, but Rathbone finds some of the stolen tax money in Pallette's mission and imprisons the friar. When Power makes another social visit to Bromberg, Rathbone confronts him, and Power reverts to his true nature and draws his sword. Power and Rathbone then duel to the death (in one of the most exciting sword duels on film), where Power is wounded, but Rathbone is finally run through by Power. Bromberg calls his guards and has Power arrested, now knowing that Power is the real Zorro. Placed in prison with Pallette, Power tricks the turnkey at the jail into unlocking their cell, but waits inside of that cell until Bromberg arrives with Love and the caballeros to show Power to them

Tyrone Power and J. Edward Bromberg in *The Mark of Zorro,* 1940.

and announce to them that he is the notorious Zorro. Love disbelieves this, but Power then leaps from the unlocked cell and subdues the guards. He then calls on his father and his friends to join him in leading an instant revolt against Bromberg's troops, and a full scale battle ensues inside the walled hacienda. Power works his way through the fighting ranks to scale a wall and race to the gates where the peons are gathered outside with weapons. Power kills the gate guards and opens the gates, allowing the peons to pour into the area and they quickly aid the caballeros in suppressing Bromberg's troops. Bromberg then officially resigns his post and Love replaces him as the governor. Power then hurls his sword into the ceiling of the patio and embraces Darnell, announcing their forthcoming wedding. Mamoulian directs this rousing adventure with great style and where the sets and costuming are lavish and accurate to the period of Old California. Power, Rathbone, Pallette and Darnell are exceptional in their roles, and the script is literate and witty while Newman's score is dynamic and stirring. ***Author's Note***: Although Power does a fine job in his dueling and acrobatic scenes, much of his swordplay was tutored by Fred Cavens, who was one of Hollywood's topnotch experts in dueling and the use of swords, and, in this case, rapiers are employed in the action scenes between Power and Rathbone. "I did not require advice from Fred [Cavens]," Rathbone told this author, "as I had for years schooled myself in the use of swords and had become at an early age an expert at fencing." In fact, Rathbone was a fencing master that had no equal and his expertise with a sword was brilliantly demonstrated in such swashbuckling films as **Captain Blood**, 1935, and **The Adventures of Robin Hood**, 1938, when dueling with the hero of those films, Errol Flynn. Rathbone was twice cut by Power in their harrowing duel, but Rathbone held no grudge about that and, in fact, later stated: "Power was the most agile man with a sword I've ever faced before a camera. Tyrone could have fenced Errol Flynn into a cocked hat." Mamoulian had nothing but praise for his star, stating to this author that "Tyrone Power made his mark as a great cavalier and duelist in **The Mark of Zorro**. Although Douglas Fairbanks did a fine job in that role in the silent days, Power's performance is the most memorable because he presents the full force of his romantic personality in his character even while undermining his true personality with a great impersonation of a worthless idler—you dislike and love the guy all at the same time and that's great acting. I want to add that Rathbone is also one great actor, too. No one can get more hisses from an audience than Rathbone, a man who knows how to play a hateful man. He is a killer in **The Mark of Zorro**, a man who loves to use his sword on easy victims, and I have him accent his obsession with swords in almost every scene where he appears. While sitting at a table and trading insults with Power, I had him constantly use a table knife to jab a piece of fruit to make his veiled threats and to emphasize his lethal nature with edged weapons. In other

Tyrone Power in *The Mark of Zorro*, 1940.

scenes he is invariably flexing his sword or practicing with it as if desperate to find a victim into which he can plunge his blade. I have always believed it to be important to provide characters small but distinctive traits or physical habits that better illustrate their natures." The character of Zorro was created by writer Johnston McCulley, who introduces Zorro in a five-part serial story under the title of "The Curse of Capistrano," which was published in a pulp magazine in 1919. Zorro was most likely based upon the celebrated Mexican bandit of Old California, Joachim Murietta (c.1830-c.1853), who was called "The Robin Hood of El Dorado." For more details on Murietta, see my eight-volume work, *The Encyclopedia of World Crime*, Volume III (CrimeBooks, Inc., 1990; pages 2256-2258). **p**, Raymond Griffith; **d**, Rouben Mamoulian; **cast**, Tyrone Power, Linda Darnell, Basil Rathbone, Gale Sondergaard, Eugene Pallette, J. Edward Bromberg, Montagu Love, Janet Beecher, Chris-Pin Martin, Robert Lowery, Fortunio Bonanova, Ralph Byrd; **w**, John Taintor Foote, Garrett Fort, Bess Meredyth (based on the story *"The Curse of Capistrano"* by Johnston McCulley); **c**, Arthur Miller; **m**, Alfred Newman; **ed**, Robert Bischoff; **art d**, Richard Day, Joseph C. Wright; **set d**, Thomas Little.

Marked Woman ★★★ 1937; U.S.; 96m; WB; B/W; Crime Drama; Children: Unacceptable; **DVD**; **VHS**. This often frightening and realistic crime yarn, based on real facts and characters, begins in NYC where gangster Ciannelli calls his top nightclub hostesses (a euphemism for prostitutes) to a meeting where he announces that they are going to work at his new, lavish bistro. He instructs them to aggressively steer all the customers not only to the club bar and encourage them to liberally buy drinks, but to visit his illegal and crooked gambling tables that are also located in the sprawling club. Davis, the most outspoken of the hostesses, tells him that Ciannelli is establishing only another clip joint designed to bilk customers out of their money. Ciannelli gives her a wicked grin and replies that that is exactly what the new club will be and any hostess who doesn't like it can quit on the spot. Davis and her close friends, Lane, Methot, Marquis, and Jewell, accept their lot and go to work at the new club, but serious trouble for Davis begins after one of her customers, O'Flynn, loses heavily to Ciannelli's gambling tables. He tells Davis that he cannot repay the debt and she warns him to leave town immediately. He is nevertheless murdered before he can flee the city, and Davis swears that she will tell all she knows to crusading district attorney Bogart. When Bogart brings her into court to testify against the racketeer, Davis, who has been threatened by Ciannelli's goons, refuses to give any information in the case. Then Davis' innocent, younger sister, Bryan, goes to the nightclub looking for Davis, and when she refuses the advances of Davidson, one of Ciannelli's associates, Ciannelli murders her. Davis now vows to put Ciannelli behind bars for life and

fully cooperates with Bogart. Ciannelli then sends his goons, led by Welden, to see Davis and they brutally beat her into unconsciousness, scarring her face for life so that she is, in underworld parlance, "a marked woman." Recovering in a hospital, Davis is visited by her friends Lane, Methot, Marquis and Jewell and she begs them to help her take revenge on killer Ciannelli for murdering her sister. Though frightened of Ciannelli and his gangsters, the women collectively unite and agree to all testify against Ciannelli in court. Bogart puts Davis and her friends on the witness stand and this time they tell all. Ciannelli is convicted and sent to prison, along with a number of his goons. Davis and friends then leave the court, but their future is uncertain. Stark and uncompromising, this crime yarn is directed with skill by Bacon, who carefully develops his characters while balancing the action and where Davis gives a stunning performance as a fallen but courageous woman. Bogart is credible in his role as the crusading attorney but has only a few scenes as he was then a contract player at Warner Brothers and not then considered a leading man. Ciannelli, a great character actor, is the embodiment of everything sinister and evil in an outstanding performance. *Author's Note*: Davis had been warring with Jack Warner in a protracted contract dispute and had been on suspension until matters were settled (in her favor), and this film marked her official return to the studio to render one of her greatest performances since her appearances in **Of Human Bondage**, 1934, and **The Petrified Forest**, 1936. Davis told this author: "I thought that when I returned they would take revenge by giving me another stinker of a script, but they surprised me with **Marked Woman**, a great story with a wonderfully sympathetic character and they gave me one of their top flight directors [Lloyd Bacon] to work with. But the old gossip and tongue-wagging about removing me from the top of the heap went on. I heard that Jane Bryan, who was cast as my kid sister, was really being groomed to take my place as a Warner star. Well, I could have cared less about that because Jane was the sweetest young gal I had met in years and we got along like real sisters and I encouraged her to be as aggressive as possible in her scenes with me. Wow! After that, I had to hide her face with a blanket to keep her from stealing my scenes." Davis and Bacon got along well except for one scene where she must return to court after having been disfigured. Davis objected to how the makeup people had covered her face with bandages for that scene and, before shooting that scene, she went to her own physician and had him place the proper surgical bandages on her face and then drove to the studio. When guards at the front gate saw her, they believed she had been in a real accident and called top studio producer Hal Wallis, who ran to the front gate to see if Davis was all right. Before Wallis could say a word, Davis told him: "We film this makeup or we don't film *me* today!" Bacon filmed the scene with Davis wearing the bandages she herself provided. Ciannelli told this author that he thought his role in **Marked Woman** "represented one of the most terrible persons I ever played, but I consoled myself with the thought that I was not playing a character of my own invention. He was based upon a real-life notorious gangster in New York, Charles 'Lucky' Luciano [1897-1962], who had recently been convicted and sent to prison a short time before we made that picture." Luciano, a NYC gangster from the Prohibition era who had helped to form the National Crime Syndicate, was convicted in 1936 on sixty-two counts of compulsory prostitution and sent to prison for between thirty and fifty years, along with several associates. Although Luciano was involved in many divergent rackets, including illegal gambling and drug-selling, his mainstay racket was prostitution; he operated scores of brothels throughout NYC, earning $10,000 a week from the labors of more than 1,000 prostitutes, several of whom testified against him to secure his conviction. For details on Luciano, see my books, *World Encyclopedia of Organized Crime* (Paragon House, 1992; pages 251-256), and *The Great Pictorial History of World Crime*, Volume I (History, Inc., 2004; pages 544-551). **p**, Louis F. Edelman; **d**, Lloyd Bacon; **cast**, Bette Davis, Humphrey Bogart, Lola Lane, Isabel Jewell, Eduardo Ciannelli, Mayo Methot, Jane Bryan, Allen Jenkins, Damian O'Flynn, Rosalind Marquis, John Litel, Raymond Hatton, Ben Welden, William B. Davidson; **w**, Robert Rossen, Abem Finkel, Seton I. Miller; **c**, George Barnes; **m**, Bernhard Kaun, Heinz Roemheld; **ed**, Jack Killifer; **art d**, Max Parker; **spec eff**, Robert Burks, James Gibbons.

Marketa Lazarova ★★★ 1967; Czechoslovakia; 180; Filmove studio Barrandov; B/W; Adventure; Children: Unacceptable; **DVD**. This engrossing drama is based on a 13th-Century Czechoslovakian legend depicting a minor Czech feudal clan that runs afoul of the king when Christianity is replacing Paganism. Velizky and his brother Palch rob travelers for their tyrannical father, Kemr. On one raid they take a young German hostage, but the captive's father escapes to report it to the king. Kemr sends Velicky to ask his neighbor, Kozuch, to join them in war. Kozuch refuses and, in revenge, Kemr abducts Kozuch's daughter, Vásáryová, as she is about to join a convent. The king sends an army against Kemr, and Kozuch joins the fight against him and his clan, which results in slaughterhouse battles. Excessive violence prohibits viewing by children. (In Czech; English subtitles.) **p**, Josef Ouzky; **d**, Frantisek Vlácil; **cast**, Josef Kemr, Magda Vásáryová, Nada Hejna, Jaroslav Moucka, Frantisek Velecký, Karel Vasicek, Ivan Palúch, Michal Kozuch, Martin Mrazek, Václav Sloup, Pavla Polaskova; **w**, Frantisek Pavlícek, Frantisek Vlácil (based on the novel by Vladislav Vancura); **c**, Bedrich Batka; **m**, Zdenek Liska; **ed**, Miroslav Hájek; **art d**, Oldrich Okác; **set d**, Josef Pavlík, Vladislav Rada.

Marley & Me ★★★ 2008; U.S.; 115m; FOX; Color; Comedy; Children: Unacceptable (MPAA: PG-13); **BD**; **DVD**. Based on the book by John Grogan (Wilson), the film opens with Wilson and Aniston, newspaper writers, marrying and moving to Florida. Not eager to be a father, Wilson gives his bride a puppy, Marley. The white Labrador retriever grows up into a 100-pound dog that thinks everything in the house is fair game to eat or tear up. Wilson's newspaper editor boss, Arkin, assigns him to write a column about anything, and so he writes about his crazy life with mischievous Marley. The newspaper column catches on and the paper's readership soars. While Marley continues to age, the couple turns into a family as three children come along. The book and movie were big hits and got lots of laughs. Atrocious animal behavior and the depiction of the death of a dog prohibit viewing by children. **p**, Gil Netter, Karen Rosenfelt; **d**, David Frankel; **cast**, Owen Wilson, Jennifer Aniston, Eric Dane, Kathleen Turner, Alan Arkin, Nathan Gamble, Haley Bennett, Ann Dowd, Clarke Peters, Finley Jacobsen; **w**, Scott Frank, Don Roos (based on the book by John Grogan); **c**, Florian Ballhaus; **m**, Theodore Shapiro; **ed**, Mark Livolsi; **prod d**, Stuart Wurtzel; **art d**, W. Steven Graham; **set d**, Hilton Rosemarin; **spec eff**, J.C. Brotherhood.

Marlowe ★★★ 1969; U.S.; 96m; Cherokee Productions/MGM; Color; Crime Drama; Children: Unacceptable (MPAA: PG); **DVD**; **VHS**. The confident Garner again discards his matinee idol image to enter serious drama (as he did in his powerful performance of Wyatt Earp in **Hour of the Gun**, 1967). This time he is Raymond Chandler's enlightened but hapless sleuth, Philip Marlowe, who is visited in his shabby Los Angeles offices by Farrell, hiring him to find her missing brother, Newman. Garner traces Newman to a cheap hotel, but learns nothing from the hotel manager or from the man now occupying the brother's room. A short time later, both of these men turn up victims, murdered with icepicks, invariably the symbolic murder weapon of underworld gangsters. Probing further, Garner uncovers a cache of photographs showing Hunnicutt, a TV celebrity, in compromising poses with Wynant, a gang boss. Garner is visited by Wynant's enforcer, Lee, a karate king, who orders Garner to drop the case and, to make his point, wrecks Garner's office by smashing his desk in two and breaking up other furniture. Further, abrasive police detective O'Connor suspects that it was Garner who killed the hotel manager. Garner perseveres (as the dogged Marlowe always does) and probes even further until he unearths Newman in the care of

Jane Bryan and Bette Davis in _Marked Woman_, 1937.

physician Stevens, dying, as have the others, from a vicious icepick wound. He then goes to gangster Wynant's posh residence to find him dead, Hunnicutt next to the body, and where she admits killing him. She then tells Marlowe that Farrell is her sister and Newman had been her brother. Garner takes pity on the abused Hunnicutt by arranging evidence to make Wynant's death appear to be a suicide. He then goes in quest of conniving Moreno, a sultry stripper, who is Hunnicutt's friend, but also a former lover of Wynant's. Confronting her, Garner accuses her of killing Wynant, but before she admits her guilt, Stevens, who is Moreno's ex-husband, appears at the strip club and shoots and kills Moreno, before taking his own life. Hunnicutt and Farrell, though disliking each other, are reunited at the end, but little is resolved in this complex whodunit. Garner is very effective as the resolute sleuth, but his character is far from the dynamic personalities of Dick Powell and Humphrey Bogart, who separately essayed the intriguing Marlowe character in **Murder, My Sweet**, 1944, and **The Big Sleep**, 1946. Robert Mitchum, like Garner, played a layback Marlowe in **Farewell, My Lovely**, 1975 (a weak and fractured remake of **Murder, My Sweet**), and Elliott Gould adopts an almost indifferent attitude when playing the character in **The Long Goodbye**, 1973. **p**, Gabriel Katzka, Sidney Beckerman; **d**, Paul Bogart; **cast**, James Garner, Gayle Hunnicutt, Carroll O'Connor, Rita Moreno, Sharon Farrell, William Daniels, H.M. Wynant, Jackie Coogan, Kenneth Tobey, Bruce Lee; **w**, Stirling Silliphant (based on the novel _The Little Sister_ by Raymond Chandler); **c**, William H. Daniels (Metrocolor); **m**, Peter Matz; **ed**, Gene Ruggiero; **art d**, George W. Davis, Addison Hehr, **set d**, Henry Grace, Hugh Hunt; **spec eff**, Virgil Beck, J. McMillan Johnson, Carroll L. Shepphird.

Marnie ★★★ 1964; U.S.; 130m; UNIV; Color; Crime Drama; Children: Unacceptable; **DVD**; **VHS**. Hitchcock leaves his well-worn beaten track in this psychological crime tale that proved to be one of his most introspective but less aggressive productions. The fetching Hedren (Hitchcock's last "cool blonde") takes a job at a large corporation where she is entrusted with the care of the firm's cash flow. This is exactly the position she has sought in that she is a habitual thief, compulsive in stealing to the point of fanatical obsession. Businessman Gabel discovers that his trusted secretary, Hedren, has looted his safe and fled (not unlike the flight of Janet Leigh in **Psycho**, 1960, who is given a large sum of money to bank by her boss but, in a moment of weakness, absconds with the funds, albeit she is not the resolute kleptomaniac Hedren embodies). Investigators soon discover that this same woman has committed many similar robberies by obtaining important jobs at corporations while using aliases and wearing different wigs to alter her appearance. Hedren, meanwhile, leads a comfortable life, albeit she is a mentally tortured woman. She spends much of what she steals for the

Sean Connery and Tippi Hedren in *Marnie*, 1964.

upkeep of an elegant horse, one of the few creatures on earth she loves, the rest to maintain a good lifestyle, while she also sends funds to Latham, her crippled mother living in Baltimore, who seethes with hatred for men and has imparted her loathing for the opposite sex deeply within her troubled daughter. Although she exhibits devotion and love to Latham, Hedren receives nothing in return. Hedreen is crawling with clues, as is later discovered. She is plagued by nightmares and goes into a rage whenever seeing the color red or hearing thunder. She applies for a job with Connery's firm, but Connery, a considerate multimillionaire who takes a deep interest in her, is wise to her ways, knowing she is the woman Gabel has earlier described to him. When Hedren becomes hysterical during a thunderstorm, Connery comforts her, realizing she has deep mental problems and also realizing that he is now emotionally involved with her, and not Baker, the sister of his deceased wife. As Connery expects, Hedren loots his company safe and he catches her in the act, but he tells her will not turn her over to the police if she marries him. Having no choice, Hedren agrees, but on the condition that Connery does not foist sex upon her until she is ready to accept a full marital relationship (whenever that might be). He agrees, but goes back on his word when they are on a shipboard honeymoon, seducing her, and causing her to attempt suicide by drowning herself in the ship's swimming pool, but Connery saves her from that half-hearted attempt. (It is obvious that if Hedren seriously wanted to end her life, she had the entire ocean at her disposal and could have easily accomplished the horrid deed by simply leaping into the sea.) Connery takes Hedren to his ancestral home where she lives in a separate suite of rooms, according to their mutual agreement, and where she presides over a party to which Gabel attends. Gabel believes Hedren looks alarmingly familiar to the woman who robbed his company, but Connery persuades him otherwise. Later, when on a fox hunt, Hedren sees a red jacket worn by one of the riders, and the color triggers her fears into outright hysteria. Connery then takes her to Baltimore where he and Hedren more or less confront her mother, Latham, and the ugly past is unraveled to show that Latham had once been a prostitute and was crippled when fighting with a customer, Dern, during a thunderstorm. After Latham struck Dern with a poker, he fell upon her, causing her to become an invalid. At that moment, Hedren, as a child, thinking Dern was killing her mother, used the poker to crush Dern's skull, killing him. Connery now exposes all of Hedren's fears in one package, her guilt for killing Dern, which causes her fear of men and, ostensibly, her compulsion to steal from them, the color red (being the gore she creates in her childish, mindless murder) and the thunderstorm that engulfed that terrible historical event. Hedren comes to these realizations with the old fear to flee into obscurity, but Connery tells her that she has only one choice—either prison or to remain with him as his wife, leaving the viewer convinced that she will choose the latter course.

Hitchcock (who appears briefly in a hotel lobby as part of his obligatory cameo appearance) employs all of his great technical skills in telling this weird tale and sustains interest throughout, offering a bevy of eye-opening tracking, panning and dolly shots, as well as some rear-view projection shots (the latter being one of his favorite techniques). Hedren and Connery (in his first U.S. film after becoming a superstar in the James Bond films) give standout performances. The film, however, offers a somewhat turgid script that occasionally bogs down the pace and slows tension with two much amateur psychological palaver, nuances and visual red herrings, which is why it did not see the usual broad-based success at the box office that Hitchcock's films otherwise enjoyed. *Author's Note*: Although Hedren had appeared in Hitchcock's **The Birds**, 1963, a year before this picture was made, and one that made her a big star, she was not Hitchcock's first choice to play the troubled Marnie. The director yearned to have his favorite blonde, Grace Kelly, play this role and believed that, even though Kelly had become the Princess of Monaco six years earlier and retired from the screen, he could lure her from her royal perch to play in this film. He sent Kelly the script, convinced that such an introspective role would challenge her always competitive acting skills, although she had already achieved the highest recognition in her profession when winning the Academy Award for Best Actress in **The Country Girl**, 1954. "I tried psychology on her," Hitchcock told this author, "by dangling that script in front of her. She showed signs of interest, and I thought she might do the film, especially since she was only playing one role every day as a princess. The inhabitants of Monaco got upset when they heard about it. They did not want their precious princess demeaning herself by going back into such a commercial medium as motion pictures. So she declined and I went back to Tippi." Psychology plays a large part in many Hitchcock films: **Shadow of a Doubt**, 1943 (a childhood accident that causes the killer to be a woman-hater); **Spellbound**, 1945 (amnesia caused by a guilt complex via the childhood death of a sibling); **Rope**, 1948 (the superman complex driving two killers to commit the "perfect murder"); **Strangers on a Train**, 1951 (father hatred and Oedipus complex); **Rear Window**, 1958 (voyeurism); **Vertigo**, 1958 (fear of heights, voyeurism and necrophilia) **Psycho**; 1960 (mother fixation); and **Frenzy**, 1972 (necrophilia). "I agree with you that it is the foremost obligation of the director to present entertainment," Hitchcock told this author, "but that does not mean that your characters must be robots. All humans contract psychological problems of one sort or another throughout life. Most are not hindered or altered by these mental distractions as they shed them as one would get rid of a virus through a strong immunity system. Others, like Tippi [Hedren] in **Marnie**, are too weak to battle phobias and subliminal fears. Her deep-seated trauma, you must remember, is caused when she is completely vulnerable as a mentally innocent and psychologically defenseless child. That trauma, which continues to live within her, controls her personality and drives her to criminal pursuits." I pointed out to Hitchcock that just such a childhood trauma, the murder of his own father while he is a child, causes Chester Morris to become a lethal gangster in **Blind Alley**, 1939, and where Morris can only recognize that through the aid of one of his hostages, Ralph Bellamy, who is a psychiatrist, so that he is thereafter incapable of taking human life (a film remade with the same excellent results as **The Dark Past**, 1948, with William Holden as the gangster and Lee J. Cobb as the psychiatrist). "I have seen both of those pictures," Hitchcock replied, "and I was impressed by those films and the fine performances they offer. However, the catalyst in those films is a practicing psychiatrist. With the exception of my picture, **Spellbound**, I let some unprofessional person close to the mentally deranged person act as the psychiatrist, and, in that way, the viewer becomes more involved in the revelations and the therapy. The more you involve the audience, the more the picture remains in the viewer's memory." Meeting Hitchcock several times over the years, I came to know his own deep-seated fears and they most likely exceeded in the collective more than any and all demonstrated by the characters in his films. He was, literally, a man who was afraid of everything, although I do not believe those fears and phobias altered a twit of his professional career or impaired his genius in any way, and, in fact, he addressed those fears through portraying others with similar problems in order to deal with his own, but only as incidental self-therapy. To name a few of those fears: Hitchcock was afraid of heights and flying and traveled by train or ship on his transcontinental or intercontinental trips whenever he could. He was afraid of the police (after his father had him locked up in a police cell as a child to show him what would happen to him if he ever broke the law), and that prevented him from ever getting a driver's license (to avoid ever being stopped for a traffic violation), so that he was driven about by his wife, Alma, or a chauffeur in the family limousine. He was afraid of food served in restaurants (preferring to dine at home where his wife, Alma, was a good cook and prepared all his meals), believing that some anonymous chef might poison his food either through whim or sinister intention. He was afraid of burglars lurking outside his home so that he had his servant double lock and bolt every window and door each night. He was even afraid of some of his top performers, like Peter Lorre, Robert Walker and Tallulah Bankhead, whose aggressive and eccentric behaviors unsettled and often unnerved him. **p&d**, Alfred Hitchcock; **cast**, Tippi Hedren, Sean Connery, Diane Baker, Martin Gabel, Louise Latham, Bob Sweeney, Alan Napier, Mariette Hartley, Bruce Dern, John Alvin, Hitchcock; **w**, Jay Presson Allen (based on the novel by Winston Graham); **c**, Robert Burks (Technicolor); **m**, Bernard Herrmann; **ed**, George Tomasini; **prod d**, Robert Boyle; **set d**, George Milo; **spec eff**, Albert Whitlock.

Maroc 7 ★★★ 1968; U.K.; 91m; Cyclone/PAR; Color; Crime Drama; Children: Unacceptable; **DVD**; **VHS**. Taut crime tale has Barry as an undercover agent, who suspects Charisse, a top fashion magazine editor, of doubling as an international jewel thief and smuggler. He sneaks into her home and, using his safecracking skills, finds stolen jewelry in her safe. He then attends a fashion party and persuades Charisse and Phillips, her top photographer, to let him in on their latest heist, smuggling a priceless medallion out of Morocco and replacing it with a fake. But in James Bond–like style, he is distracted by an affair with a beautiful model, Martinelli. She leads him to Barker, a wheelchair-confined rchaeologist, who drowns in his swimming pool a short time after Charisse and Phillips visit him. Elliott, a French police inspector, assigns his own undercover agent, Stewart, to assist Barry in his investigation. After many turns and twists of the clever plot, and with oodles of designer gowns and more dead bodies on display, Barry ends Charisse's adventures into jewel thievery and she becomes the top fashion model in jail. Excessive violence prohibits viewing by children. **p**, John Gale, Leslie Phillips, Martin C. Schute; **d**, Gerry O'Hara; **cast**, Gene Barry, Elsa Martinelli, Cyd Charisse, Leslie Phillips, Denholm Elliott, Alexandra Stewart, Angela Douglas, Eric Baker, Tracy Reed, Maggie London; **w**, David Osborn (based on his story); **c**, Kenneth Talbot (Panavision; Technicolor); **m**, Kenneth V. Jones; **ed**, John Jympson; **art d**, Seamus Flannery, Terry Pritchard.

Marooned ★★★ 1969; U.S.; 134m; COL; Color; Adventure/Science Fiction; Children: Cautionary (MPAA: PG-13); **DVD**; **VHS**. Three American astronauts (Franciscus, Crenna, and Hackman) spend several months in space aboard an orbit lab, then, on preparing to return to Earth, discover that their spacecraft's retro rockets won't fire and they may run out of oxygen and die before (and if) the problem can be fixed. Peck, the NASA base commander on the ground in Houston, suggests that one of the astronauts commit suicide, so the other two will have more oxygen to work on the retro problem. This doe not sit well with anyone, but Crenna decides to sacrifice himself by leaving the spacecraft on the pretext of going out to repair the rockets, and where he detaches himself from the ship and floats off to his death. Franciscus and Hackman despair of being saved, but Soviet cosmonauts come to their rescue with a new supply of oxygen. The two astronauts repair the retro rockets and return safely to Earth. Sturges maintains considerable tension and

Tippi Hedren and Sean Connery in *Marnie*, 1964.

suspense in this well-crafted space adventure, and Franciscus, Crenna and Hackman give standout performances, despite space paraphernalia confining and limiting their physical actions. **p**, M.J. Frankovich, Frank Capra, Jr.; **d**, John Sturges; **cast**, Gregory Peck, Richard Crenna, David Janssen, James Franciscus, Gene Hackman, Lee Grant, Nancy Kovack, Mariette Hartley, Scott Brady, Frank Marth; **w**, Mayo Simon (based on the novel by Martin Caidin); **c**, Daniel Fapp (Panavision; Technicolor); **ed**, Walter Thompson; **prod d**, Lyle R. Wheeler; **set d**, Frank Tuttle; **spec eff**, Chuck Gaspar.

The Marriage Circle ★★★ 1924 (silent); U.S.; 85m/8 reels; WB; B/W; Comedy; Children: Unacceptable; **DVD**; **VHS**. Inspired by Charlie Chaplin's drama, **Woman of Paris**, 1923, this is a sophisticated comedy of manners, if not errors, which is set in Vienna, and where the so-called "Lubitsch touch" is in full evidence. Menjou is a professor, but his life is no bed of roses as he and his wife, Prevost, are always bickering. She tries to seduce Blue, the new husband of her good friend, Vidor. Meanwhile, interloper Hale has a thing for Prevost and sees her dallying as an opportunity to win her, even though he is happily married to Menjou. In a misunderstanding, Prevost thinks Blue is interested in Ralston. Menjou hires a detective to spy on Prevost and all that was muddled ends well as these toying and dabbling couples remain faithful to each other. Lubitsch tweaks the traditions of fidelity and the sanctity of marriage while employing a very clever script, getting top drawer performances from his cast and where his traditionally understated sophisticated comedy scenes are fascinating. **p&d**, Ernst Lubitsch; **cast**, Florence Vidor, Monte Blue, Marie Prevost, Creighton Hale, Adolphe Menjou, Harry Myers, Dale Fuller, Esther Ralston; **w**, Paul Bern (based on the play "Only a Dream" by Lothar Schmidt); **c**, Charles Van Enger; **art d**, Lewis Geib, Esdras Hartley.

Marriage Italian Style ★★★ 1964; France/Italy; 102m; Kayos Productions/WB-Seven Arts; Color; Comedy; Children: Unacceptable; **BD**; **DVD**; **VHS**. Mastroianni is a successful but philandering businessman in Naples, Italy, during WWII, and where he begins an affair with Loren, a seventeen-year-old girl (who looks like a much older voluptuous woman, and is as Loren was thirty years old when this film was released). She becomes his mistress as well as a prostitute. He sets her up in an apartment and she works for him in various businesses. As time passes, she tells him she has three grown sons and one of them is his, but does not tell him which one. He suspects they all might be his and marries her. Both Mastroianni and Loren are standouts in this consistently funny guessing game. (In French and Italian; English subtitles.) **p**, Carlo Ponti; **d**, Vittorio De Sica; **cast**, Sophia Loren, Marcello Mastroianni, Aldo Puglisi, Tecla Scarano, Marilu Tolo, Gianni Ridolfi, Gen-

Hanna Schygulla in *The Marriage of Maria Braun,* 1979.

eroso Cortini, Vito Moricone, Rita Piccione, Lino Mattera, Pia Lindstrom; **w,** Renato Castellani, Tonino Guerra, Leo Benvenuti, Piero De Bernardi (based on the play "Filumena Marturano" by Eduardo De Filippo); **c,** Roberto Gerardi (Eastmancolor); **m,** Armando Trovajoli; **ed,** Adriana Novelli; **prod d,** Carlo Egidi; **set d,** Dario Micheli; **spec eff,** Stefano Ballirano, Stefano Camberini.

The Marriage of Maria Braun ★★★★ 1979; West Germany; 120m; Albatros/New Yorker; Color; Drama; Children: Unacceptable (MPAA: R); **DVD; VHS.** In this, the first of the brilliant Fassbinder's trilogy about women during and after WWII in Germany (followed by **Lola,** 1982, and **Veronica Voss,** 1982), we see Schygulla being married to Lowitsch, a soldier, amid a terrible bombing from Allied planes as the city about them begins to crumble into ruins. The priest presiding over this wedding becomes terrified and races for cover, but Lowitsch runs after him, tackling him, and forces him to complete the ceremoniy. Lowitsch is then immediately sent to the Russian Front, never having consummated his marriage with Schygulla. She returns to her poverty-stricken life with her mother, Uhlen, and sister, Barth. She so pines for Lowitsch that she haunts the railroad stations wearing a sign that asks anyone if they have seen her husband, but to no avail. The war ends and U.S. soldiers occupy her town and Schygulla goes to work as a barmaid and meets Byrd, a black American soldier, who is kind to her, giving her food and supplies for her and her family. After learning that Lowitsch has died during the war, Schygulla becomes Byrd's mistress and, just before one of their trysts, Lowitsch suddenly appears, having been released from a Russian POW camp. Emaciated and starving, Lowitsch nevertheless exerts his rights as a husband and feebly attacks Byrd. When Byrd appears to be gaining the upper hand, Schygulla grabs a bottle and smashes this over Byrd's head, killing him. She is tried for murder, but when Lowitsch learns that she is going to take all the blame for Byrd's death, Lowitsch insists that he and he alone killed Byrd. Lowitsch is sent to prison, again separated from Schygulla, who goes to work for wealthy importer Desny, becoming so indispensable to his business that Desny pays her an exorbitant salary and she then becomes his lover, but Schygulla tortures Desny by telling him that the only man she loves is the imprisoned Lowitsch. Desny's life does not improve when Schygulla becomes wealthy through his business and continues to treat him with a cold heart. Just before Lowitsch is to be released, Desny visits with him and makes a secret deal with him, one where Lowitsch will receive most of Desny's fortune on the condition that, when he is released from prison, he will go to Canada and not return until Desny has died so that Desny can live out his life with the only woman he loves, Schygulla. Though Lowitsch keeps his part of the bargain by going to Canada, he sends a single rose to Schygulla to remind her that he still

loves her. Following Desny's death, and while returning from his funeral, Schygulla sees Lowitsch waiting for her. They go to her lavish home and finally prepare to consummate their marriage of many years earlier. Schygulla strips to black lingerie and becomes for the first time in her life emotionally and sexually aroused, ecstatic in the belief that she is now going to have sex with the only man she has ever loved. Unfortunately (and in what must be one of the most devastating ironies on film), she has, in her excitement, left an unlit gas jet running on the stove, and, when she lights a cigarette as she anxiously approaches Lowitsch, the gas ignites and the house and she and Lowitsch are blown to pieces. This riveting social drama, so carefully presented by Fassbinder, sees outstanding performances from Schygulla, Lowitsch and Desny, and is unarguably Fassbinder's finest film. The film serves as a microcosm of post-WWII Germany when, to survive, it ruthlessly sought to gain freedom through wealth and power, as is demonstrated by the once innocent Schygulla. She learns that her emotions can manipulate events and persons to better her world and to be reunited with the man from whom she had been so cruelly separated, a bittersweet story of starcrossed lovers repeatedly denied happiness through grim fate and merciless happenstance. Fassbinder (1945-1982), the *enfant terrible* and central figure of the New German Cinema, was prodigious, intelligent, inventive, and, in almost all of his films, expresses a consistently cynical and fatalistic viewpoint where happiness is not only elusive but mythical. *Author's Note*: Like so many of the characters seen in his films, Fassbinder was self-destructive, abusing drugs and alcohol. He died on June 10, 1982, in Munich, Germany, of a drug overdose (cocaine and sleeping pills). Found next to him was a film script based on the German communist, Rosa Luxemburg (1871-1919), who, along with Karl Liebknecht (1871-1919), joint leaders of the Spartacus League, were both assassinated by members of the German right-wing Freikorps on January 15, 1919. A very good film on the subject, **Rosa Luxemburg,** was later produced and released in 1987. (In German; English subtitles.) **p,** Michael Fengler, Wolf-Dietrich Brücker, Volker Canaris, Hanns Eckelkamp; **d,** Rainer Werner Fassbinder; **cast,** Hanna Schygulla, Klaus Löwitsch, Ivan Desny, Gisela Uhlen, Elisabeth Trissenaar, Gottfried John, Hark Bohm, George Eagles (George Byrd), Claus Holm; **w,** Peter Marthesheimer, Pea Frohlich, Fassbinder (based on a story by Fassbinder); **c,** Michael Ballhaus (Fujicolor); **m,** Peer Raben; **ed,** Franz Walsch, Juliane Lorenz, Fassbinder; **prod d,** Helga Ballhaus, Norbert Scherer; **set d,** Arno Mathes, Hans Sandmeier, Andreas Willim.

The Marriage Playground ★★★ 1929; U.S.; 101m; PAR; B/W; Comedy; Children: Unacceptable; **DVD; VHS.** This early and funny screwball comedy, set in Italy, involves three sophisticated couples, their divorces, and seven children and stepchildren. The oldest child, Brian, is eighteen and acts as mother to the others because their parents are away a lot. March, a rich American traveling in Italy, befriends Brian and she and the other young people take to him. Brian falls for March but he has a fiancée in Switzerland. Many humorous scenes depict Brian's naïve and innocent pursuit of March, but her determined efforts bear fruit at the finale where he decides he loves Brian more and proposes to her. Sexual subject matter prohibits viewing by children. **d,** Lothar Mendes; **cast,** Fredric March, Mary Brian, Lilyan Tashman, Huntley Gordon, Kay Francis, William Austin, Seena Owen, Philippe De Lacy, Anita Louise, Mitzi Green, Clive Brook (narrator); **w,** J. Walter Ruben, Doris Anderson (based on the novel *The Children* by Edith Wharton); **c,** Victor Milner; **m,** W. Franke Harling.

Married to the Mob ★★★ 1988; U.S.; 104m; Mysterious Arts/Orion; Color; Comedy/Crime Drama; Children: Unacceptable (MPAA: R); **DVD; VHS.** Pfeiffer is unhappily married to high positioned Mafia member Baldwin in Brooklyn. When he is bumped off, she tries to break free of the Mafia world and start a new life. Stockwell, Baldwin's boss, has other plans for her and begins courting her, but she is unresponsive. The FBI begins trailing her, thinking she is Stockwell's new mistress and they might get inside crime information from her. Agent Modine goes undercover as her neighbor and soon falls in love with her. Pfeiffer gets a job as a hairdresser and, even after knowing Modine's been trailing her, she falls for him. They end as an unlikely couple, an FBI agent soon to be married to a mob widow. This offbeat yarn provides some good mixes of comedic moments with some sinister and frightening scenes. Songs: "Mambo Italiano" (Bob Merrill); "Bizarre Love Triangle" (New Order); "Queen of Voudou" (William Borgi); "Ghost in a Bikini," "She's Got Everything" (David Bean); "Burger World Town," "The Same Melody," "Tony the Tiger," "Uncle Ron's Country Cars" (Gary Scetenoir); "Jump in the River" (Sinead O'Connor); "Suspicion of Love" (Chris Isaak); "Welcome to the Real World" (Jane Child); "Happy Birthday to You" (Mildred J. Hill); "Traveling Strangers," "Time Bums" (Ziggy Marley); "Gummy Duppy" (Nina Rawsey). Violence and sexuality prohibit viewing by children. **p**, Edward Saxon, Kenneth Utt, Michael A. Cherubino; **d**, Jonathan Demme; **cast**, Michelle Pfeiffer, Alec Baldwin, Matthew Modine, Dean Stockwell, Oliver Platt, Tara Duckworth, Paul Lazar, Joan Cusack, Mercedes Ruehl, Charles Napier, Frank Aquilino, Anthony J. Nici, Chris Isaak; **w**, Barry Strugatz, Mark R. Burns; **c**, Tak Fujimoto; **m**, David Byrne; **ed**, Craig McKay; **prod d**, Kristi Zea; **art d**, Maher Ahmad; **set d**, Nina Ramsey.

The Marrying Kind ★★★ 1952; U.S.; 92m; COL; B/W; Comedy; Children: Acceptable; **DVD**; **VHS**. Holliday and Ray are in divorce court after seven years of marriage. The judge, Kennedy, asks their reasons for wanting out of the marriage in hopes that they will remember the reasons why they fell in love in the first place. Holliday has always had faith in Ray to succeed and he knows that she brings out the best in him. In flashbacks, we learn they had met in a park, fell in love, married, and had children, one of whom died in a drowning accident. Before the divorce hearing is over, they decide they want their marriage to keep going and they will work out their problems. It's a more realistic portrait of marriage than similar Hollywood films, with some heavy drama mixed in with the humor and where Holliday and Ray shine in their empathetic roles. **p**, Bert Granet; **d**, George Cukor; **cast**, Judy Holliday, Aldo Ray, Madge Kennedy, Sheila Bond, John Alexander, Rex Williams, Phyllis Povah, Mickey Shaughnessy, Griff Barnett, Charles Bronson, Peggy Cass, Harry von Zell; **w**, Ruth Gordon, Garson Kanin; **c**, Joseph Walker; **m**, Hugo Friedhofer; **ed**, Charles Nelson; **art d**, John Meehan; **set d**, William Kiernan.

The Marrying Man ★★★ 1991; U.S.; 115m; Hollywood Pictures; Buena Vista; Color; Comedy; Children: Unacceptable (MPAA: R); **DVD**; **VHS**. Entertaining comedy has Baldwin and Basinger (then a real-life husband and wife) as a millionaire playboy and a torch singer who fall in love, but at the risk of their lives. A multimillionaire heir to a toothpaste fortune, Baldwin has evaded marrying Shue, the daughter of movie mogul Loggia, for some time, but has been pressured to go to the altar by the foul-mouthed, tyrannical Loggia (who does a crude imitation of Harry Cohn, one-time head of Columbia) and he decides to take the plunge. He goes to Las Vegas to have a bachelor party with close friends Reiser, Stevens, Hytner and Dobson, but is emotionally thunderstruck when he and his friends attend a Vegas nightclub and see sexy singer Basinger. Baldwin now has eyes for only one woman, Basinger. When he tries to pick her up after her performance, he is warned that she belongs to a powerful man. Baldwin persists and his charm wins Basinger over, but she is apprehensive about seeing him. She tells him that she will leave a window open at her home and they later secretly meet and make love, their torrid tryst, however, abruptly interrupted by Basinger's other lover, Assante, who plays crime syndicate boss Benjamin "Bugsy" Siegel (1906-1947). Instead of taking violent vengeance on his cheating mistress (the real Siegel had many), the insidious Assante creates what he thinks is a more subtle comeuppance for the betrayal by forcing Baldwin and Basinger to marry (to Assante a fate worse than death). Baldwin drives Basinger to California, offering

Kay Francis, Mary Brian and Fredric March in *The Marriage Playground*, 1929.

her a sum of money for the distress he has caused, but she wants nothing from him and departs. Shortly thereafter, the newspapers run a photo of Baldwin and Basinger being married, and, in a page following an announcement of Baldwin and Shue's impending marriage. Loggia explodes, threatening Baldwin with every kind of torture known to man, and Baldwin states it was all a mistake and says he still wants to marry Shue, who is inconsolable. He then tells Loggia that he will get an annulment from Basinger and, should he fail to marry Shue, will donate a huge amount of money to charity. When Baldwin attempts to get that annulment from Basinger, he finds himself falling in love with her all over again and they marry again. This time, Loggia takes revenge by having thugs beat Baldwin senseless before tossing him into his luxurious swimming pool, Baldwin believing this violent retribution to be fair and just for his former transgressions. Meanwhile, his father dies, and Baldwin is called to Boston to preside over his family's vast holdings. Basinger relocates with Baldwin to that city, but finds the tea parties and quiet social affairs insufferably boring and she yearns to return to California and her singing career. When Baldwin refuses to allow her to pursue her dream, Basinger divorces him and moves back to California. Baldwin follows and remarries her for a third time. He now announces to his friends that he is going to establish a movie studio so he can produce films that will star his beautiful wife, but nothing of the kind happens and Baldwin, neglecting his family business, goes broke. He blames Basinger for his financial woes and they break up again. Baldwin is later seen in a nightclub by his friends, where he tells them that he has established a promising new business, computers, and then shows them a diamond engagement ring and introduces them to his future bride, who turns out to be retread Basinger and who, at the finale of this madcap romp, slides that ring onto her finger. Baldwin and Basinger have appeared in several films together, but this amusing comedy is one of their best (and, ironically mirrors their much troubled real-life marriage). Songs include: "Why Can't You Behave," "Let's Do It" (Cole Porter); "Murder, He Says" (Frank Loesser, Jimmy McHugh); "Satisfy My Soul" (Buddy Johnson); "Honeysuckle Rose" (Andy Razal, Thomas "Fats" Waller); "You're Driving Me Crazy (What Did I Do?)" (Walter Donaldson); "Love Is the Thing" (Ned Washington, Victor Popular Young); "Stompin' at the Savoy" (Benny Goodman, Walter M. Samson, Andy Razal, Chick Webb); "L. D.'s Bounce," "Mama, Look a Boo Boo" (Tim Hauser); "Yardbird Suite" (Charlie Parker); "You Can't Be Mine (and Someone Else's Too)" (J. C. Johnson, Chick Webb). *Author's Note*: Siegel has been profiled in several films, including **The Damned Don't Cry**, 1950 (as a role model for the part played by Steve Cochran); **The Godfather**, 1972 (Alex Rocco); **Bugsy**, 1991 (Warren Beatty), **Mobsters**, 1991 (Richard Grieco); and the made-for-TV movie, **Lansky**, 1999 (Matthew Settle). For more details on Siegel see my

Armand Assante, Alec Baldwin and Kim Basinger in *The Marrying Man*, **1991.**

books, *World Encyclopedia of Organized Crime* (Paragon House, 1992; pages 363-368), and *The Great Pictorial History of World Crime*, Volume I (History, Inc., 2004; pages 575-583). **p**, David Permut, David Streit; **d**, Jerry Rees; **cast**, Alec Baldwin, Kim Basinger, Robert Loggia, Elisabeth Shue, Armand Assante, Paul Reiser, Fisher Stevens, Peter Dobson, Steve Hytner, Jeremy Roberts, Big John Studd; **w**, Neil Simon; **c**, Donald E. Thorin (Technicolor); **m**, David Newman; **ed**, Michael Jablow, Michael R. Miller, Michael Tronick; **prod d**, William F. Matthews; **art d**, Mark Mansbridge; **set d**, Jim Duffy; **spec eff**, Roland Tantin, R.J. Hohman, Robert D. Bailey.

Mars Attacks! ★★★ 1996, U.S.; 106m; Tim Burton Productions/WB; Color; Comedy/Science Fiction: Children: Unacceptable (MPAA: PG-13); **BD**; **DVD**; **VHS**. This offbeat and antic-ridden sci-fi satire has endless ships carrying vindictive and murderous creatures from Mars invading Earth at all points. Ineffectual leaders headed by wishy-washy U.S. President Nicholson, decide to be friends and give the invaders a warm welcome, despite the hysterical pleadings of warmongering general Steiger, urging that the invaders be destroyed. Brosnan, the top scientific adviser to the president, and Short, the White House's press secretary, however, convince Nicholson to extend the olive leaf, which is in response to the Martian message sent worldwide by huge transmitters that repeatedly states "we come in peace." Nicholson announces to the world that a peace conference with the Martians will be held in Nevada, but when his emissary, Winfield, goes to meet the Martian ambassador, Martians swarm from their landed spaceship and, using their blaster guns, begin vaporizing every human in sight, including Winfield, Fox, a TV commentator, and Black, one of the sons of Baker, a gun-toting right-winger, who lives with his large family in a trailer outside of Las Vegas, along with scores of soldiers and spectators. One of those spectators, Bening, who is a recovering alcoholic promoting New Age philosophy, as well as the divorced wife of Las Vegas tycoon Nicholson (in a dual role), manages to escape. Parker, the host of a fashion TV show, is captured and taken on board the Martian ship before it departs. When seeing the wanton devastation and human massacre by the Martians, First Lady Close urges her husband to immediately mount a nuclear attack against the Martians, but he is persuaded by Brosnan that there has been a "cultural misunderstanding" and that earthlings should try once more to make peace before launching any kind of attack, much to the chagrin of the tantrum-consumed Steiger. Lisa Marie, a Martian disguised as a towering, voluptuous woman, then makes her way into the White House, inveigling Short into a tryst, killing him, and then invades the President's bedroom, raking it with machine-gun fire and almost killing Nicholson and Close before she is destroyed. A full-scale world war ensues where Brosnan is captured and joins Parker on board

a Martian spacecraft where their heads are cut off and kept alive in glass containers and where they make verbal love to each other while their truncated bodies are attached to the heads of other creatures in the ongoing and inexplicable experiments being conducted by the wacky Martians. The Martians are victorious everywhere, destroying the Washington Monument, the Eiffel Tower in Paris, London's Big Ben, the Taj Mahal and the facial effigies of American presidents at Mount Rushmore, where they replace those images with the decidedly repulsive-looking faces of Martian leaders. Martians attack the White House, destroying the place, and where Nicholson, Close and their daughter, Portman, barely survive, chiefly through the efforts of self-sacrificing Secret Service agents and two boys who seize blasters from fallen Martians and use them to dispatch many attackers, Ray J. and Brandon Hammond, who are the two mischievous sons of Brown, a professional boxer working as a host at a Las Vegas casino. Nicholson as president makes a final effort to establish peace, but when he meets with the Martian ambassador and holds out his hand in friendship, the Martian's hand turns into a scorpion-like metallic instrument that crawls up his chest, goes over his shoulder and drives a knife into his back, killing him, with the Martian Flag sprouting from Nicholson's back. Then Las Vegas itself is attacked with Martians replacing performers on stage and turning their blasters on employees and guests, destroying tall buildings, including one owned by Nicholson, who is killed with many of his fellow magnates in a business meeting where they hope to commercialize the Martian invasion. Fleeing for their lives is entertainer Jones, Brown, Bening, Rivera (a cocktail waitress and friend of Brown's) and avaricious gambler DeVito, who is vaporized when he tries to buy off a Martian by giving him money and his expensive watch. Jones, Rivera, Bening and Brown make their way to a small airport where all except Brown climb into a small plane, Brown staying behind to hold back a swarm of Martians as they crowd about him and he boxes them one by one to death by smashing their glass helmets, which turns their heads into jelly from his powerful blows. As the small plane flies away to safety, Las Vegas is systematically destroyed, including Baker and his family who are living in a trailer park. His son, Haas, however, survives, and goes in search of the only person he really loves, Sidney, his elderly grandmother, finding her in a retirement home that is being invaded by Martians. He sees two Martians about to kill her with their blasters, but when she removes her headphones, the piercing song she is listening to, "Indian Love Call" (Otto A. Harbach, Oscar Hammerstein II, Rudolf Friml), performed by high tenor Slim Whitman, the vibrations of the song turn the heads of the Martians into jelly, smashing their life-supporting glass helmets. Spiriting Sidney to safety, Haas has discovered the one element that can now destroy the Martians and that song is blared and blasted on loud speakers throughout the world, causing the Martians to die in droves as their spacecraft crash and explode everywhere and where, on once spaceship falling into the sea, the live heads of Brosnan and Parker bid a fond farewell to each other. Epilogue scenes show survivors stepping from the world's rubble everywhere, Brown, Bening and Rivera befriending the birds and animals in the West, and Brown joining his wife Grier and his sons in devastated Washington, D.C. While a Mariachi band plays the "Star Spangled Banner" outside the ruins of the Capitol Building, Portman, the only surviving member of the presidential family, bestows upon Haas, her hero, the Congressional Medal of Honor, and gives accolades to the wheelchair-bound Sidney, for saving the world and where Sidney warns Portman to avoid such disasters in the future. In what is the wackiest, anarchistic sci-fi spoof ever produced, this film offers nonstop zany action and amazing special effects. It is as consistently and absurdly violent as its story line and characters are amusingly impossible and ridiculous, which makes it all the more fascinating and hilarious. Other songs include: "It's Not Unusual" (Gordon Mills, Les Reed; performed by Jones, his theme song), "Humming" (Portishead), "I'm Casting My Lasso Toward the Sky" (Jimmy Wakely, Lee 'Lasses' White), "Headstrong" (E. Antwi, Filo), "Stayin' Alive" (Barry Gibb, Maurice Gibb, Robin Gibb), "Champagne Fanfare"

(George Cates), "Escape (The Pina Colada Song) (Rupert Holmes). *Author's Note*: Steiger told this author that his role in this film "is about as sensible as any other character in that far-out picture. I am screaming at Jack [Nicholson] to nuke the Martians right from the get-go while shouting down my detractors by calling them 'peace mongers.' When I first looked at the script for this picture, I thought that Hollywood had gone nuts, and that Ken Burton had all of his screws loose, but then my curiosity, which has always brought me a lot of good parts, along with my intuition, told me that this picture would do big box office since everyone playing video games would have to see it—the whole film is sort of a crazy video game—and that's about half of the world, at least the young half. Everyone played their roles for laughs and they got them, and these are serious people like Nicholson, Bening, Close, Brosnan, and even that fine singer, Tom Jones, who I thought was the best of all of us, especially when he is performing on stage and is suddenly surrounded by supporting singers that turn out to be these ugly little Martians with the most terrifying, pop-eyed, skull-like faces, and he flips out before running for his life. DeVito, too, has a great little scene, where he tries to con some creepy little Martian from killing him, as if he could buy off this berserk creature before he gets vaporized. Oh, what a lot of fun that picture is!" Films that more seriously depict visits or invasions from Mars to Earth or vise-versa include: **Invaders from Mars**, 1953; **The War of the Worlds**, 1953; the made-for-TV miniseries, **The Martian Chronicles**, 1980; **Mission to Mars**, 2000; and **The War of the Worlds**, 2005. **p**, Tim Burton, Larry Franco, Laurie Parker; **d**, Burton; **cast**, Jack Nicholson, Glenn Close, Annette Bening, Pierce Brosnan, Danny DeVito, Martin Short, Sarah Jessica Parker, Michael J. Fox, Rod Steiger, Tom Jones, Lukas Haas, Natalie Portman, Jim Brown, Pam Grier, Sylvia Sidney, Paul Winfield, Joe Don Baker, Jack Black, Ray J. Brandon Hammond, Janice Rivera, Lisa Marie; **w**, Jonathan Gems, Len Brown, Woody Gelman, Wally Wood, Bob Powell, Norm Saunders (based on a story by Gems); **c**, Peter Suschitzky (Technicolor); **m**, Danny Elfman; **ed**, Chris Lebenzon, Wynn Thomas; **art d**, James Hegedus, John Dexter; **set d**, Nancy Haigh; **spec eff**, Michael Lantieri, Christine Walker, Guy Williams, Daniel Radford.

Marty ★★★★★ 1955; U.S.; 90m; UA; B/W; Drama; Children: Acceptable; **DVD**; **VHS**. There are scores of films profiled in this work that are described as being "heartwarming," but this wonderful masterpiece truly spreads its addictive affection into every corner of the human heart, where Borgnine gives the performance of his life (he won the Oscar for Best Actor). He is a friendly, overweight bachelor who works as a butcher and lives alone with his mother, Minciotti, in their large ancestral home in the Bronx. Borgnine pines for female companionship, but that seems hopeless as he himself admits that he is "no prize," in that he is decidedly homely and ungainly, unattractive in every way to any woman, calling himself a "dog," as he and his friends call unattractive females in their lonely and often humorous pursuit of romance and happiness. Working hard as a butcher, Borgnine is friendly and cheerful to all his customers, and when he gets the opportunity to buy the butcher shop, his ambitions begin to mount, along with the idea that, as a man of property, he might attract some lonely female enough to marry him. Marriage is always foremost in his mother's mind, Minciotti consistently urging Borgnine to go out in the evenings and search for "a nice girl." After work each night, Borgnine meets with his best friend, Mantell, who, like all of their friends, is also an aging bachelor. They meet in their favorite bar, looking over newspapers and sipping beer before beginning a verbal exchange that monotonously captions their lifestyles. "So what do you wanna do tonight, Marty?" Mantell asks. "I dunno, Angie," he replies. "What do you want to do?" They go to a dance hall and, as usual, Borgnine asks a woman to dance, but strikes out, and returns home, his heart and self-respect again injured. His mother urges him to go to a popular dance hall, the Stardust Ballroom, mimicking the words of her son-in-law, Paris, that the place is full of "tomatoes." Borgnine at first refuses, telling Minciotti that he is tired of going to such

Betsy Blair and Ernest Borgnine in *Marty*, 1955.

places and being rejected and coming home with nothing but "heartache," but he then promises her that he will try again. When he does, he sees plain-looking Blair being jilted by a young man who has arrived at the dance hall with her as a blind date. Borgnine asks Blair to dance and they then talk, becoming acquainted, and he winds up escorting her home, promising that he will call her. Blair, like Borgnine, leads a lonely life as a schoolteacher, living with her parents. When, on a date with her, he introduces her to Mantell, and later Minciotti, but she is rejected as a "dog" by Mantell and is considered as a threat by Minciotti, who has come to believe that if Borgnine marries Blair, she will have to go to a retirement home, as has almost been the case with her sister, Ciolli, Paris' mother, who has just been taken in by Minciotti. Knowing he and Blair have much in common and are drawn to each other, Borgnine hesitates, listening to those who tell him that he has made the wrong choice in life and Blair dejectedly waits for his call, one that does not come. Yet, Borgnine knows that his time with Blair has been happy and that he has found the one person who can continue to make him happy. He rebels against family and friends and, while sitting with Mantell and going through the same old regimen about what they might do with their time, Borgnine goes to a phone booth. Mantell and other friends ask him what he is doing and he replies that he is going to call Blair (in one of the most down-to-earth and moving scenes in this masterpiece film): "You don't like her. My mother doesn't like her. She's a dog and I'm a fat, ugly man. Well, all I know is that I had a good time last night. If we have enough good times together, I'm gonna get down on my knees and I'm gonna beg that girl to marry me. If we have a party on New Year's, I've got a date for that party. You don't like her? That's too bad! Hey, Ang, when are you going to get married? You're thirty-three years old and all of your kid brothers and sisters are married. You ought to be ashamed of yourself!" With that, Borgnine closes the phone booth door and calls Blair, and we hear him saying "Hello…hello, Clara?" Mann directs this wonderful film (Oscar for Best Picture) with a sure and deliberate hand (he won an Oscar for Best Director), carefully developing the unforgettable characters in one moving scene after another where the heartstrings play all the captivating music that was present in Chayefsky's original brilliant TV script (Oscar for Best Writing, Adapted Screenplay), and where Borgnine and all of the supporting players are riveting in their superlative performances and where all are pricelessly genuine and memorable. This prosaic but classic tale champions the plain-looking and the lonely while subtly managing to radiate through simple declaration the inward beauty and indefatigable courage of the human spirit. There has never been a film before or after like it. Song: "Marty" (music: Harry Warren; lyrics: Paddy Chayefsky). This film was shot on location in the Bronx and was produced with the meager budget of $343,000, but it surprisingly returned more than $3 million

Katharine Hepburn and John Carradine in *Mary of Scotland*, 1936.

in its initial box office release. *Author's Note*: Minciotti, Ciolli and Mantell reprise their roles from the original 1953 TV production, but Rod Steiger, who played Marty in that original production, either refused to play the part in a feature film or was rejected for the part by producers Harold Hecht and Burt Lancaster. Steiger told this author that "they did not want me in their picture because they had the crazy idea that because I had appeared in the TV version of that great Chayefsky story, people would not line up to pay to see it at the box office. They later said that I turned down the role because their contract would have bound me to them for years. Oh, really? Anyway, Ernie [Borgnine] was simply wonderful in that role and I don't think anyone could have done a better job, including me. Every scene he is in and every little thing he does takes your heart away. For instance, one scene: After he walks Betsy [Blair] home that night and is so happy that he grins with happiness and slams his big fist against a street sign, well, that was a masterstroke as it showed for the first time the pure sign of joy from a man who has lived a joyless life. Yes, Ernie is Marty and Marty is Ernie and that is the way it will always be." The producers were much more concerned about casting Blair as she had, only a few years earlier, become involved with accusations about her pro-communist activities of many years earlier and had been placed on the Hollywood blacklist. Blair's husband at the time was the great director-dancer-actor Gene Kelly, who not only lobbied hard for his wife to get the role in **Marty**, but, when it appeared that she would be dropped from the production after some studio executives began pressuring the producers, Kelly went to the MGM front office where he knew that pressure was being generated and stated that, unless his wife continued in her role for **Marty**, he would fold his participation in the ongoing and costly MGM production of **It's Always Fair Weather**, 1955. Kelly supported this tale when telling this author that "that's about right. I told them I would quit the MGM picture unless they stopped badgering the producers of **Marty** to drop Betsy. It was a terrible time then, everyone caving into those witch-hunting politicians, and some even going out of their way to ruin the careers of others, people they didn't even know, so that they would look good to that bunch of baboons in Washington." Warren, who wrote the theme song for this great film, told this author that "I was delighted to compose that song about a plain-looking guy with no romance and that only includes about half of the males in America all the time. You know, Ernie [Borgnine] calls himself 'ugly' in that picture, but he's just the opposite. As a man, he is inwardly as handsome as Errol Flynn or Ty Power. I get goose bumps every time I see that picture, don't you?" Borgnine felt the same way, saying: "Without **Marty**, I would have had a movie career of playing only mean-minded thugs and heartless guys who didn't give a damn about anyone else. That picture let me show to the world that you might not look so hot to most people, but that you are just as human as anyone

else. What a role, what a story, all from the great mind of Paddy Chayefsky." **p**, Harold Hecht; **d**, Delbert Mann; **cast**, Ernest Borgnine, Betsy Blair, Esther Minciotti, Karen Steele, Jerry Paris, Augusta Ciolli, Joe Mantell, James Bell, Joe Bell, John Beradino, Jerry Orbach; **w**, Paddy Chayefsky (based on his television play); **c**, Joseph LaShelle; **m**, Roy Webb; **ed**, Alan Grosland, Jr.; **art d**, Edward S., Haworth, Walter Simonds; **set d**, Robert Priestley.

Marvin's Room ★★★ 1996; U.S.; 101m; Scott Rudin Productions/Miramax; Color; Drama; Children: Unacceptable (MPAA: PG-13); **DVD**; **VHS**. Streep and Keaton are sisters and estranged since their father, Cronyn, suffered a stroke seventeen years earlier, and live in different states. Keaton doesn't marry and, instead, cares for her father and his sister, Verdon, in her home. Streep has married and her son, DiCaprio, is committed to a mental institution after setting fire to his mother's house. His younger brother, Scardino, seems disinterested in it all. Streep goes to the asylum to take DiCaprio to her home in Florida for a week so he can be tested as a possible bone marrow donor for her sister. DiCaprio tells his mother he didn't know she had a sister. Streep visits Keaton, but doesn't offer to help care for their father. Meanwhile, the sisters' father is bedridden and may finally die after nearly twenty years of hanging on after his stroke. His impending death brings the sisters together again in "Marvin's room," where their father lies dying. This powerful domestic drama sees standout performances from Streep and Keaton. Gutter language and strong adult material prohibit viewing by children. **p**, Robert De Niro, Jane Rosenthal, Scott Rudin, Bonnie Palef, Adam Schroeder, David Wisnievitz; **d**, Jerry Zaks; **cast**, Meryl Streep, Leonardo DiCaprio, Diane Keaton, Robert De Niro, Hume Cronyn, Gwen Verdon, Hal Scardino, Dan Hedaya, Margo Martindale, Cynthia Nixon; **w**, Scott McPherson (based on his play); **c**, Piotr Sobocinski; **m**, Rachel Portman; **ed**, Jim Clark; **prod d**, David Gropman; **art d**, Peter Rogness; **set d**, Tracey Doyle; **spec eff**, Don Canfield.

Mary of Scotland ★★★ 1936; U.S.; 123m; RKO; B/W; Biographical Drama; Children: Cautionary; **DVD**; **VHS**. Ford presents a heroic portrait of the valiant Mary, Queen of Scots (1542-1587), and where Hepburn offers a radiant performance of that ill-starred monarch and March a forceful essay of James Hepburn (1534-1578), 4th Earl of Bothwell, who became Mary's third husband. Hepburn arrives in Scotland from France after having been the wife of Francis II (1544-1560), child king of France and queen consort up to the time of Francis' death. She claims her inheritance to the Scottish throne, but the clan leaders who welcome her are suspicious of her ambitions to rule as they believe the country is better controlled by their collective regency. Most agitated by Hepburn's arrival is Eldridge, who plays Elizabeth I (1533-1603) of England, believing that Hepburn may lay claim to her own throne (Mary and Elizabeth were cousins and she begins conspiring against the new Queen of Scotland). When most of the clan leaders fail to support her, March arrives to give Hepburn his unstinting aid as her most loyal follower, and who falls in love with her at the same time. Adding to Hepburn's woes is Olsen, who plays religious leader and zealot John Knox (1514-1572), who has brought about the Protestant Reformation in Scotland and vigorously opposes Hepburn on the grounds that she is a devoted Catholic. Several of the Protestant clan leaders, headed by Keith, who plays James Stewart (1531-1570), 1st Earl of Moray, Hepburn's illegitimate half-brother, support Olsen and they eventually pressure Hepburn into marrying the foppish Walton, who plays Henry Stuart (1545-1567), Lord Darnley, and who also supports the Protestant movement. Hepburn is now a captive queen in that Walton and Keith control her every move and are suspicious that she is conspiring against them. At their instigation, several clan leaders invade Hepburn's quarters where they seize Carradine, playing David Rizzio (1533-1566), who is Hepburn's private secretary, a poet, and who has strong ties to the Vatican, believing that Carradine has been persuading Hepburn to make Catholicism the official religion of Scotland. Begging for his life and struggling through the queen's chambers with the attackers, Carradine is finally murdered. March arrives at Hepburn's castle and the assassins flee. Meanwhile Walton challenges what authority Hepburn has managed to hold on to, pompously saying that he is the true ruler of Scotland while he is indifferent to their recently born child (it was reported that Darnley believed the child was not his, but an issue between Mary and Rizzio). So menacing does Walton become that he is mysteriously assassinated when his separate palace at Kirk o'Field is blown up on February 10, 1567. Following his death, Hepburn marries the man she truly loves, March. When many clan leaders build an army to overthrow Hepburn, March leaves for the Continent to raise an opposing force, but is imprisoned (and later dies in his cell). Hepburn, meanwhile, is deposed and imprisoned, but manages to escape to England, where Eldridge gives her sanctuary, which turns out to be just another form of imprisonment as Eldridge suspects that her cousin wants to usurp her and keeps her in protective custody for eighteen years. That suspicion becomes a firm belief after forged documents and false accusers make a case against Hepburn and she is tried and condemned for conspiring against Eldridge. The final scene of this well-crafted Elizabethan epic sees Hepburn courageously climbing the scaffold to meet the executioner. Director Ford does a fine job in directing this historical pageant with great vigor and where his richly appointed sets and elaborate costuming befit the era. *Author's Note*: Ford told this author that, to make Hepburn and Eldridge appear as two widely divergent personalities, Hepburn as the vulnerable victim and Eldridge as the cold-blooded and scheming monarch that eventually takes her life, he "shot each of them differently, one having different camera angles and lighting not used for the other. I even had passages in the score for their separate scenes sound differently [heroic and melodious for Hepburn; discordant and harsh for Eldridge]. Kate does a marvelous job as Mary, who was the more beautiful and sensitive of those two competitive queens, and Eldridge was perfect as Elizabeth, who would not hesitate to take anyone's life to preserve her throne." March told this author that "**Mary of Scotland** was Kate's picture from beginning to end and she knew it. Anyone in any a scene with her had to be on their toes. My character is by nature a blustering fellow and that gave me the latitude to bellow and bark, but every time I did, Kate dismissed all that bravado and bellowing with brilliant understatements or even stony silence. She had learned long earlier not to try to out-act other actors, but to use the force of their lines by making them her own through restraint and reservation." Hepburn stated to this author that "I believe the performance I gave in **Mary of Scotland** was one of my best. My God, how could any actress fail with such a great director like John Ford, and such a fine actor as Freddie [March] working with you? There was much more than that—there was the real life drama of the woman herself, more dramatic events and colorful characters, I think, than any queen in history, except for Cleopatra, perhaps, ever experienced. I knew that then and I know it now about Mary, poor, tragic and unloved woman that she was." **p**, Pandro S. Berman; **d**, John Ford; **cast**, Katharine Hepburn, Fredric March, Florence Eldridge, Douglas Walton, John Carradine, Robert Barrat, Gavin Muir, Ian Keith, Moroni Olsen, Ralph Forbes, Alan Mowbray, Frieda Inescort, Donald Crisp, Molly Lamont, Bobs Watson; **w**, Dudley Nichols (based on the play by Maxwell Anderson); **c**, Joseph H. August; **m**, Max Steiner, Nathaniel Shilkret; **ed**, Jane Loring; **art d**, Van Nest Polglase; **set d**, **spec eff**, Vernon L. Walker.

Mary Poppins ★★★★★ 1964; U.S./U.K.; 139m; Disney/Buena Vista; Color; Animated Fantasy/Musical; Children: Recommended. Few films can lay legitimate claim to being a perfect picture, but this one can, being one of the most delightful animated fantasy musicals ever produced and where every frame is a delight to behold. After dour and religiously punctual London banker Tomlinson takes out an advertisement for a nanny to look after his two precocious children, Dotrice and Garber, everything magical begins to happen. It's not that Tomlinson and his flighty wife Johns don't love their offspring. They cherish them, but

Dick Van Dyke and Julie Andrews in *Mary Poppins*, 1964.

they are simply too busy with the outside world, Tomlinson with his endless banking business and Johns with her many crusades for women's rights, to give enough attention to their children, who seek love and affection, and need some handy discipline, more than anything. The children have their own ideas about the ideal nanny and they write down their notions about that mythical person on scraps of paper, but when Tomlinson finds these notes, he dismisses them as childish fantasies, tears them up and throws the pieces into a fireplace. The pieces of paper, however, miraculously come together and then flutter up the flue of the chimney. The following day sees a bevy of nannies arriving to apply for the job, but a fierce wind blows them away and with that wind comes Andrews floating down from on high with her umbrella upraised as if serving as her parachute. Tomlinson is overwhelmed by Andrews and offers her the job and she accepts. She begins by having Dotrice and Garber, two particularly sloppy children, clean up their room, helping them along with one of the many delightful songs that pepper this film. Andrews then takes them for a walk where, in a park, they meet Van Dyke, a chimneysweep, who has a penchant for drawing sidewalk art. They all look down at his drawing and then magically step into that other world where they dance and play with animated penguins that serve them tea before they go to a carousel. The horses they ride then leave the merry-go-round and race across the verdant countryside. The fun ceases when it begins to pour and Van Dyke warns that if they do not leave the picture and return to the reality of their own world, the picture will erode and they will be forever trapped on this magical side of the world. Andrews then takes the children to see her uncle, Wynn, an eccentric old man, who loves to laugh; when he guffaws, he floats to the ceiling and he encourages them to join him by laughing uproariously, and when they do, they also float like balloons to the ceiling. When Dotrice and Garber later tell Tomlinson about these fantastic exploits, their down-to-earth father scoffs, saying it is all nonsense. He thinks to fire Andrews, but her charming ways convince him otherwise, particularly when she suggests that he take his children to his staid and stoic banking institution so they can see what it is that he does for a living. Tomlinson agrees to escort his children to his bank the next day, and that night Andrews sings a song about an elderly woman, Darwell, who sits outside that bank and sells bird seed at two pence a bag, that allows people to feed the birds. The next day, Tomlinson takes his children to the bank and, to give his son, Garber, a sense of financial responsibility, offers him two pence to open a bank account, but Garber would rather spend the money on buying some bird seed and feed the birds. This so disturbs the bank's president that a commotion breaks out and customers believe that there is a financial panic and there is a run on the bank, with customers swamping the tellers' cages demanding the return of their savings. Dotrice and Garber escape the confusion, but, in running away,

Elliott Gould, Tom Skerritt and Donald Sutherland in *M*A*S*H*, **1970.**

they find themselves in a dark and dreary part of London until they are found by Van Dyke, who is, at first, unrecognizable as he is coated in soot and has been at his labors as a chimneysweep. He then takes them on another adventure, leading them to the rooftops of London where he and a bevy of other chimneysweeps dance and sing when showing them how they clean chimneys and keep the homes, fires burning. Meanwhile, Tomlinson is blamed for the panic at the bank for bringing his children to that august institution, but the staid father rebels against such injustice, telling the bank directors what they can do with their bank. When he leaves, to demonstrate his total disgust with his uncaring and aloof profession, he destroys the symbols of that profession by smashing a hole in his bowler hat and turning his elegant umbrella inside-out (and these are but a few of the many wonderful sight gags in this film). Realizing that he has acted like a petty dictator with his family by suppressing his natural love for its members and maintaining a ridiculous regimen of dos and don'ts, Tomlinson becomes a new father and husband, emerging from the basement where he has spent the night to show his amazed children that he has fixed a kite they have earlier broken. The family then goes to a park to fly that kite and enjoy each other's company while Andrews, realizing that she has reunited this loving family, flies away to find another family needing her invaluable services, and that is where this heartwarming fantasy and wonderful family film ends. The direction is superb with technical wizardry abounding in every frame that presents breathtaking animation-live-action sequences. The acting and the songs and beautifully choreographed dancing are superlative. This film was enormously successful, although it had a few carping detractors, who wrongly claimed that it was derivative of **My Fair Lady**, 1964, but without any real foundation as this tale is wholly original and carries the viewer, like its delightful characters, along like a balmy breeze. In addition to Andrews, Van Dyke and the family members, the film offers other notable and memorable faces, including Treacher as the local constable, Baddeley as the Cockney maid, and Owen as a retired admiral, who occupies a neighboring house shaped like a ship and colorfully fires a cannon from its topmast to signal the hour of 6 p.m. each day. The Sherman Brothers, who had long been under contract to Disney, are at the pinnacle of their talents with their magnificent score. Songs (all but the last from Robert B. Sherman and Richard M. Sherman in 1964) include: "Sister Suffragette," "Chim-Chim Cheree," "The Life I Lead," "The Perfect Nanny," "Jolly Holiday," "A Spoonful of Sugar," "Supercalifragilisticexpialidocious," "I Love to Laugh," "Stay Awake," "Feed the Birds (Tuppence a Bag)," "Fidelity Fiduciary Bank," "A Man Has Dreams," "Step in Time," "Let's Go Fly a Kite," "A British Bank," and "Sobre las Olas (Over the Waves)" (1887; Juventino Rosas). *Author's Note*: Irrespective of all of the great films from Disney, this production crowned a career that was

never anything but consistently spectacular. Walt Disney (1901-1966) won more Oscars than any other Hollywood person, gleaning twenty-two competitive Oscars and an additional four honorary Oscars. **Mary Poppins** won four Oscars, one going to Andrews for Best Actress (ironically she had been denied the leading role she created for **My Fair Lady** on the stage, that part going to Audrey Hepburn, but Hepburn was not even nominated that year, although **My Fair Lady** swept most of the awards). The film also won Oscars for Best Original Song ("Chim-Chim Cheree"), Best Original Score (to the Sherman Brothers), Best Film Editing and Best Visual Effects. **p**, Walt Disney, Bill Walsh; **d**, Robert Stevenson; **cast**, Julie Andrews, Dick Van Dyke, David Tomlinson, Glynis Johns, Hermione Baddeley, Reta Shaw, Karen Dotrice, Matthew Garber, Elsa Lanchester, Arthur Treacher, Reginald Owen, Ed Wynn, Jane Darwell; **w**, Walsh, Don Da Gradi (based on the *Mary Poppins* books by P.L. Travers); **c**, Edward Colman (Technicolor); **m**, Robert B. and Richard Sherman, Irwin Kostal; **ed**, Cotton Warburton; **art d**, Carroll Clark, William H. Tuntke; **set d**, Hal Gausman, Emile Kuri; **spec eff**, Peter Ellenshaw, Eustace Lycett, Art Cruickshank, Ub Iwerks.

Masculine Feminine ★★★ 1966; France/Sweden; 103m; Anouchka-Argos/Royal Films International; B/W; Drama; Children: Unacceptable; **DVD**; **VHS**. In this absorbing social drama, Leaud is a naïve young man just out of service with the French Army and disillusioned with civilian life. While searching for romantic love in the 1960s, he meets Goya, a pop singer in a café, and they become roommates. Leaud gets a job interviewing people for a market research firm, while Goya pursues her singing career. They are not a good fit, since he is turned off by the current pop culture of frenetic go-go dancing and noisy jukeboxes. Goya cuts a record that is a hit and becomes pregnant, while Leaud falls out a window in an apparent accident. They spend a lot of time talking about sex and going to the movies [including a sexy Swedish film] and protesting against the Vietnam War while discussing social issues such as birth control. They are microcosms of the rebellious socially aware French youth of the 1960s, who, like most young people the world over in those uncertain times, look perhaps too intensely and apprehensively toward the future. Sexuality prohibits viewing by children. (In French; English subtitles.) **p**, Anatole Dauman; **d&w**, Jean-Luc Godard (based on the stories "The Signal" and "Paul's Mistress" by Guy de Maupassant); **cast**, Jean-Pierre Léaud, Chantal Goya, Marlène Jobert, Michel Debord, Catherine-Isabelle Duport, Eva-Britt Strandberg, Birger Malmsten, Yves Afonso, Henri Attal, Brigitte Bardot; **c**, Willy Kurant; **m**, Jean-Jacques Debout; **ed**, Agnès Guillemot, Marguerite Renoir.

M*A*S*H ★★★ 1970; U.S.; 116m; Aspen Productions/FOX; Color; Comedy/War Drama; Children: Unacceptable (MPAA: PG); **BD**; **DVD**; **VHS**. One of the great cult films, this offbeat and often vicious satire lampoons the medical profession as well as the U.S. Army during the attritional Korean War. It is irreverent, disrespectful, insidiously unpatriotic and incisively telling in depicting the hopelessness and human waste of war. None of the conduct of the these characters in real life would have been tolerated and almost all would have certainly been sent for their thefts, misrepresentations and insubordinate behavior to Leavenworth. This was, however, the time of the 1970s when Hollywood suspended its beliefs far beyond what it expected of any audience. Insulated against any real transparency by its enormous wealth and the power of its medium, Hollywood could afford to indulge in any ersatz dissidence to easily convince a public grown less sophisticated and more gullible that its posture was that of genuine rebellion. In order to get to their new assignment, a field hospital close to the war zone, surgeons Skerritt and Sutherland steal a jeep. When they reach the medical center, all is in chaos, with an anonymous person conducting the loudspeaker announcements, playing offbeat Western and Oriental music that is annoyingly interrupted with announcements of ridiculous sounding films to later be shown to the camp inhabitants, as well as religious announcements and even the secretly recorded sounds of lovemaking between sexy nurse Kellerman and camp commander Duvall. Resident physician Gould, a mental case with a short fuse, befriends the prank-playing Sutherland and Skerritt in their adolescent escapades. At one point, Duvall, who spends most of his off-hours reading the Bible and being sanctimonious, mistakenly shifts the blame for the death of one soldier onto a male nurse and Gould almost strangles him to death. Duvall covets Kellerman, and Burghoff, who befriends the unholy trio of Sutherland, Gould and Skerritt, secrets a microphone under Duvall's bunk where the lovemaking between Duvall and Kellerman is recorded and later played through the ubiquitous loudspeaker system. This causes Kellerman to be called "Hot Lips" and so unsettles Duvall that he becomes a raving moron, who must be taken away in a straitjacket. Schuck, the oversexed resident dentist, then discovers that he is impotent and intends to commit suicide. Sutherland et al. give him a farewell party, providing a suicide pill which is nothing more than a tranquilizer while Sutherland convinces his love interest, Pflug, another sexy nurse, to give her all to save Schuck by sleeping with him after that party, the experience convincing Schuck that he has lost none of his virility and that he should go on living. Gould is then called to perform a delicate surgery in Japan and he takes Sutherland along. Following the surgery, they play an extended game of golf and express their contempt for the war and the military. When they return to the medical center, they are met by Wood, a pompous general, who makes a large wager with Sutherland and friends that his group of soldiers can beat the medical team in a football match. The game ensues with Sutherland et al. winning by employing devious methods, which include rendering their opponents unconscious by injecting sedatives into the adversaries. This story, which is based upon a minor Humphrey Bogart film, **Battle Circus**, 1953 (a serious drama dealing with U.S. Army physicians and nurses in the Korean War), later became a popular 1972 TV series. This film's broad and rather oafish humor sustains interest, but wears more than thin long before all the childish nonsense is used up. Such blatant and unimaginative amusement has long since become passé and old-fashioned, belonging mostly to the easily entertained audiences of the 1970s, even though it cemented the careers of Sutherland and Gould, who each went on playing one weirdo after another with great success. **p**, Ingo Preminger; **d**, Robert Altman; **cast**, Donald Sutherland, Elliott Gould, Tom Skerritt, Sally Kellerman, Robert Duvall, Roger Bowen, John Schuck, G. Wood, Rene Auberjonois, David Arkin, Gary Burghoff, Fred Williamson, Michael Murphy, Bud Cort, Ted Knight, Fran Tarkenton, Johnny Unitas; **w**, Ring Lardner, Jr. (based on the novel by Richard Hooker); **c**, Harold E. Stine; **m**, Johnny Mandel; **ed**, Danford B. Greene; **art d**, Arthur Lonergan, Jack Martin Smith, Michael Friedman; **set d**, Stuart A. Reiss, Walter M. Scott; **spec eff**, Greg C. Jensen, L.B. Abbott, Art Cruickshank.

Mask ★★★ 1985; U.S.; 120m; UNIV; Color; Biographical Drama; Children: Unacceptable (MPAA: R); **DVD**; **VHS**. Based on a true story, this absorbing tale has Stolz as a teenage boy, who is very intelligent and warm to others, but he is suffering from a disease called craniodiaphyseal dyaplasia. The malady causes calcium deposits on the skull that leave his face seriously deformed. He makes light of his condition, telling people he is just another person from the planet Vulcan. His mother, Cher, gives him love but it is no-nonsense "tough love," rearing him as if he might be any normal boy with all the chances for success and happiness other teenagers take for granted. Cher is an atypical mother, riding with a motorcycle gang, going to bed with gang members, and abusing alcohol and drugs. Stoltz's school principal suggests he should be in a special school, but Cher says no way, pointing to the fact that his grades are good and, if the principal persists, she will have her lawyer file suit. Stoltz stays in school and spends a summer as an assistant at a camp for blind children. There he falls in love with a blind teenage girl, Dern, who is not put off by his repulsive-looking face. Theirs is not a sexual relationship but a platonic one where two young people get to like and know each other. As Stoltz continues to accept

Sydney Greenstreet and Peter Lorre in *The Mask of Dimitrios*, 1944.

his face as it is, Cher grows weary of her self-destructive lifestyle and quits the abuse, giving up drinking, drugs, and other men when a man she really loves, Elliott, comes back from a trip and moves into her house. Sexuality, gross deformity, alcohol and drug abuse prohibit viewing by children. Songs include: "Katmandu," "Roll Me Away," "Mainstreet," "Rock 'n' Roll Never Forgets" (Bob Seger, performed by Seger); "Slippin' 'n' Slidin'" (Eddie Bocage, Albert Collins, Richard Penniman, performed by Little Richard [Penniman]. **p**, Martin Starger, Howard Alston; **d**, Peter Bogdanovich; **cast**, Cher, Eric Stoltz, Sam Elliott, Estelle Getty, Richard Dysart, Laura Dern, Harry Carey, Jr., Ben Piazza, Lawrence Monoson, L. Craig King, **w**, Anna Hamilton Phelan; **c**, Laszlo Kovacs (Panavision; DeLuxe Color); **m**, Dennis Ricotta; **ed**, Barbara Ford; **art d**, Norman Newberry; **set d**, Richard J. de Cinces; **spec eff**, Dan Lester.

The Mask of Dimitrios ★★★★★ 1944; U.S.; 95m; WB; B/W; Crime Drama/Spy Drama; Children: Unacceptable; **DVD**; **VHS**. One of the best film noir entries produced in the 1940s, this amazing thriller from Ambler has Lorre in one of his few starring roles (although he is billed fourth), and he is fascinating while serving as a reluctant narrator recording the incredible criminal exploits of Scott, the mysterious and sinister Dimitrios. Lorre, a popular Dutch mystery writer of detective novels, arrives in Istanbul and attends an upscale party where he meets Katch, one of his devoted readers. Katch plays the part of Colonel Haki, head of the Turkish Secret Police (a role also essayed by Orson Welles in another great Ambler thriller, **Journey into Fear**, 1943), who encourages Lorre to write about an arch criminal, Dimitrios Makropoulos (Scott), whose body has just been recently washed ashore from the Bosphorus. Katch, who has never seen Scott alive, so sparks Lorre's imagination with his tales of Scott's "murder, treason, and betrayal," that Lorre asks to see the corpse and is taken to a mortuary to view the deceased arch criminal, and where the observant Lorre notes that the cadaver is wearing a cheap suit, attire unbecoming that of a master criminal. The dead man's past intrigues Lorre, causing him to question Katch: "What is it about a man like that? Why does anyone trust him in the first place?" Katch then relates Scott's earliest recorded crime in Smyrna, where we see Scott in flashback when he is working with Blue as an itinerant fig-packer. Scott convinces the dim-witted Blue to help him commit a robbery, but when they loot a store, Scott shows no pity when strangling the storeowner. Both men go to a low cabaret to celebrate, which is soon invaded by city police, headed by Lackteen. Seeing that the impoverished Blue is spending lavishly for drinks, Lackteen arrests him. Blue calls out for his friend, Scott, who sees his plight, but immediately flees. Blue is later condemned to death for the storeowner's murder even though he insists that Scott is the killer. In flash-forward, after hearing this dark tale, Lorre

Eduardo Ciannelli, Faye Emerson and Peter Lorre in *The Mask of Dimitrios*, 1944.

decides to seek the answers by backtracking Scott's travels and exploits. He books passage on a train going to Sofia. Before the train departs, Greenstreet enters Lorre's compartment to share it with Lorre, who is about to retire, and where the overweight man befriends the writer. (Greenstreet had briefly appeared in an earlier scene when he arrives too late in his strange quest at Lorre's Istanbul hotel to angrily learn from a newspaper that Scott has been killed and his body cremated.) Once he meets Lorre in the train compartment, Greenstreet tells Lorre: "There's not enough kindness in the world. If only men would live as brothers without hatred, seeing only the beautiful things, but, no, there are always people who look on the black side." Before these new friends separate, Greenstreet recommends a hotel in Sofia, and when Lorre arrives in that city, he contacts a journalist friend, Ciannelli, who has written about Scott and who takes Lorre to a low dive owned and operated by mystery woman Emerson. They sit with Emerson and Lorre asks her about Scott, but her memories of this man are too bitter, and she angrily orders them to leave her seedy nightclub. Emerson has second thoughts after Lorre says he saw the body of Dimitrios in Istanbul before it was destroyed and Emerson decides to share her strange memories of Scott and how they met in Sofia in 1923. We then see Scott in flashback while he is living in a room next to Emerson's while starving and unable to pay the rent. She gives him food and loans him money, but expects nothing in return. Surprisingly, Scott shows up later, giving her money, admitting, however, that he has extorted the cash from an elderly suitor of Emerson's. He promises her jewels, money and a fancy apartment as part of their future together. After a diplomat is assassinated in Sofia, police search for Scott, who has become a member of a Bulgarian national party. (The shocking assassination is shown occurring during a rainstorm, a scene where director Negulesco emulates a similar terrifying scene shown in Alfred Hitchcock's classic **Foreign Correspondent**, 1940.) Scott slips into Emerson's now upscale apartment via a rooftop window, drying the rainwater from himself and when police arrive, led by Mercier, Emerson lies by telling the officers that Scott has been with her during the time of the assassination. Though desperately in love with Scott, Emerson is consistently abused by him, and after police leave, he borrows back all the money he has given her, saying he must leave town, but that he will, as in the past, pay her back. She never sees him again, and we see her in flash-forward concluding her tale to Lorre and Ciannelli. With this additional bit of information, Lorre goes back to his hotel room, which he finds in disarray and where Greenstreet is present and training a gun at him. Greenstreet demands to know what Lorre has learned about Scott, but Lorre can give him no helpful information and Greenstreet departs, but not before warning Lorre not to go to his next stop, Belgrade. Lorre does go to that town to find more details about the insidious Scott in the files of the city's criminal records. He then travels

to Geneva where he meets with wealthy arms dealer Francen, who has ostensibly retired he tells Lorre how he once hired Scott as an industrial spy, and we see another prolonged flashback set in Belgrade where Scott befriends government clerk Geray. Scott entertains the mild-mannered Geray and his greedy wife, Hoshelle, taking them to a posh casino where Scott arranges with casino owner Metaxa, who is in league with Francen, for Geray to win considerable sums of money. Scott then takes Geray and his wife to an upscale restaurant where Geray and Hoshelle are entertained by the polished and wealthy Francen, believing they have stepped up into high society. The naïve Geray is then gulled into going back to Metaxa's gaming tables where he now loses an enormous amount of money, which he cannot repay. Scott promises to make his debt good, but only if he steals and gives to him the plans for the Serbian secret minefields in the Otranto Strait. To protect his wife from ruin, Geray agrees and delivers the plans, which Scott, Metaxa and Francen photograph before returning the plans to Geray, who later commits suicide. Scott, however, betrays his employers, Francen and Metaxa, by stealing the photographs at gunpoint with the intent on selling them to the highest bidder. In a flash-forward, Lorre, after learning this twisted tale from Francen, is about to give up on writing about Scott, finding him to be the most despicable criminal and spy he has ever researched. He goes to Paris and meets once more with Greenstreet, who is living in a sumptuous apartment in a deserted building. Greenstreet tells Lorre that he has discovered that the ubiquitous Scott is very much alive and that he wants Lorre to entice Scott to a meeting with a fabulous offer and this Lorre agrees to do. Scott appears at the meeting, gun in hand, but, once he learns that he has been tricked, thinks to kill Lorre and Greenstreet, who now expects to settle an old score where Scott had betrayed Greenstreet and his associates many years earlier. Lorre, however, knocks the gun from Scott's hand, and Greenstreet, who has already been wounded by Scott, picks it up and orders Lorre to go and stay clear of the murder he intends to commit. Lorre ignores Scott's pleas not to leave him with Greenstreet, and, once he has left the apartment, hears shots. The wounded Greenstreet then appears staggering down a flight of stairs with handfuls of big banknotes, but all of this money and the taking of Scott's life amount to nothing in that police arrive to arrest him. Before he is taken away, Greenstreet turns to his friend Lorre and says: "You see, there's not enough kindness in the world," the film ending in a fadeout with this ironic statement. Negulesco directs this film noir masterpiece with great style, utilizing inventive camera angles while keeping the camera mobile as it makes its way through the murky streets, shadowy bistros, elegant casinos and hotels of old Balkan cities and finally on to Paris, all of these fine sets elegantly appointed. Deutsch's eerie score enhances one startling sequence after another, and Lorre, Greenstreet, Scott and the rest of the fine cast give superlative performances of their carefully crafted and distinctive characters. Songs: "Perfidia" (Alberto Dominguez), "Waltz" (from Serenade in Strings in C Major, Op. 48 by Peter Ilyich Tchaikovsky). ***Author's Note***: Lorre told this author that **"The Mask of Dimitrios** has always been one of my favorite pictures. I work against the grain of my typecasting in that picture. I am actually a good guy, or sort of a good guy. I read the Ambler book several times before we went into production and I can tell you that Negulesco—a very conscientious director—hardly changed a word, let alone a scene. They did change my character from being British to Dutch, because of my accent, but that was all that was altered to my knowledge." Negulesco told this author that "Ambler is one of those writers whose work is a blessing to filmmakers. He writes in a very visual style and his scenes translate extremely well on the screen. This was Zachary Scott's first feature film and he is terrific as the elusive Dimitrios. I knew he had great potential and he showed it in that picture. Then he appears in his second film, Renoir's **The Southerner** [1945] the next year, and he gives one of the greatest performances of his life in a film I call a masterpiece, and then he did **Mildred Pierce** [1945] with Joan Crawford, but his career never took off the way it should have and I think it was simply a matter of not getting the right parts that worked with his personality. Do you know who discovered him? It was Jack Warner himself, after he saw Scott in a Broadway show and gave him a contract with Warner Brothers, so all that ridiculous talk about Jack not having any sense about talent is just that, ridiculous talk." The role model for the conniving Dimitrios has always been thought to have been based upon the secretive arms manufacturer Sir Basil Zaharoff (1849-1936), who was accused of secretly creating incidents that started wars, particularly in the Balkans (southeast Europe), especially between Turkey and Greece, and through which he profited enormously, becoming a multimillionaire many times over, but he was so thoroughly hated by national and secret military societies that their assassins sought to kill him throughout most of his adult life, which is why he employed a bevy of doubles. This author once asked Ambler if Zaharoff was, indeed, the role model for Dimitrios. He was reluctant to say, but eventually nodded, stating: "You might say that Dimitrios and several other characters in that book represent some personality traits that were Zaharoff's. He used aliases and lived like a prince in hidden away retreats, little palaces, and had dozens of bank accounts in all of the major cities of Europe. No one ever really knew that strange man." Zaharoff had the habit of conducting his business, where he made deals to sell arms and ammunition, in public parks and at zoos while his armed guards were close by, so he could easily escape if an assassin tried to take his life. He was the first arms dealer to market the deadly machine gun and even sold armed submarines. He funded the secret Black Hand, a Serbian military organization (nothing to do with the Italian "Black Hand" extortionists), which financed the assassination of Archduke Francis Ferdinand in Sarajevo in 1914, which touched off World War I, and through which Zaharoff became even wealthier. For more details on Zaharoff, see my book, *Zanies: The World's Greatest Eccentrics* (New Century Publishers, 1982; pages 421-423). **p**, Henry Blanke; **d**, Jean Negulesco; **cast**, Sydney Greenstreet, Zachary Scott, Faye Emerson, Peter Lorre, Victor Francen, Steven Geray, Florence Bates, Eduardo Ciannelli, Kurt Katch, Marjorie Hoshelle, Georges Metaxa, John Abbott, Louis Mercier, Monte Blue, Frank Lackteen; **w**, Frank Gruber (based on the novel *A Coffin for Dimitrios* by Eric Ambler); **c**, Arthur Edeson; **m**, Adolph Deutsch; **ed**, Frederick Richards; **art d**, Ted Smith; **set d**, Walter Tilford.

The Mask of Fu Manchu ★★★ 1932; U.S.; 72m; MGM; B/W; Horror; Children: Unacceptable; **DVD**; **VHS**. Karloff is the long-nailed evil Oriental doctor seeking a scimitar and golden mask of Genghis Khan so he can become emperor of the world. Englishman Grant is commissioned by the British Secret Service to go to the Gobi Desert and find both objects before Karloff, but is kidnapped by Karloff, who tortures him to reveal where the relics are to be found. Stone, Morley (Grant's daughter), and her fiancé, Starrett, set out to excavate the site where the relics are buried, but are also taken prisoner by Karloff whose beautiful daughter, Loy, has fallen for Starrett. Karloff's sadistic nearly naked torture scene of his prisoners is very sensual as Loy watches lustfully. Stone is being lowered headfirst into a pit of crocodiles, but manages to escape and zaps Karloff with the evil one's own death ray gun. A genuinely spooky horror film that is much too violent for children, this marked yet another vehicle in which the talented Loy was typecast as an Oriental femme fatale. *Author's Note*: "Oh, I can't look at that picture anymore," Loy told this author at one of our meetings [always in NYC where she lived from the early 1960s]. "I am playing another Chinese vixen with only one ambition—to see others in pain. I did that for so many years that I felt like a prop in a Chinese torture chamber." Director Vidor, who presents this well-mounted production with great energy and pace, told this author that "Myrna [Loy] did not like appearing as Boris' vicious Oriental daughter in that picture and told me so, but I told her it was her own fault for being so good in roles like that over the years. She was the epitome of an actress trapped in typecasting, but she broke the mold three years later when she started getting very good roles as sophisticated and witty women and then she got into the Thin Man pictures with

Antonio Banderas in *The Mask of Zorro*, 1998.

William Powell and said goodbye forever to that Oriental lady she hated more than moviegoers did." Karloff, too, told this author that Loy complained about being typecast in this film, "but I told Minnie [Loy's Hollywood nickname, given to her by Victor McLaglen] that 'you shouldn't complain about getting such a gift that keeps your salary going. Why the best friend I have in Hollywood is the Frankenstein monster.' Minnie had talents no one knew about until she appeared in pictures where she was urbane and as smart as her male leading men. Why, four years after we made **The Mask of Fu Manchu** together, everyone forgot about those mean Oriental ladies she had been playing. In 1936, she was called the 'Queen of Hollywood' and was appearing with top stars like Clark Gable and William Powell. Years later, I sent her a set of false long-nails, the kind she had worn in the silent days and the early 1930s when she was playing those slinky Oriental ladies, with a note that read: 'Hold on to these—you never can tell when you might need them again.' Of course, she never did need those nails again." **p**, Irving Thalberg; **d**, Charles Brabin, King Vidor; **cast**, Boris Karloff, Lewis Stone, Karen Morley, Charles Starrett, Myrna Loy, Jean Hersholt, Lawrence Grant, David Torrence, Willie Fung, Allen Jung, Chris-Pin Martin; **w**, Irene Kuhn, Edgar Allan Woolf, John Willard (based on the novel by Sax Rohmer); **c**, Tony Gaudio; **m**, William Axt; **ed**, Ben Lewis; **art d**, Cecil Gibbons; **spec eff**, Warren Newcombe.

The Mask of Zorro ★★★ 1998; U.S./Germany; 136m; TriStar Pictures; Color; Adventure; Children: Unacceptable (MPAA: PG-13); **BD**; **DVD**; **VHS**. In this action-packed adventure tale, Hopkins plays the original Zorro, Don Diego de la Vega, who is a crusader for Mexican peasants (originally portrayed by Tyrone Power in **The Mark of Zorro**, 1940). Hopkins is captured and imprisoned just as Spain concedes California to Mexico's Santa Anna. Twenty years pass and Hopkins' mortal enemy, former governor Montero (Wilson) returns to California from exile in Spain with a plan to become wealthy at the expense of the peasants. Hopkins escapes from prison to find his long-lost daughter, Zeta-Jones, and avenge the death of his wife by one of Wilson's henchmen, and trains Banderas as a new Zorro to take his place. During Hopkins' imprisonment, Wilson raises Zeta-Jones as his own daughter without her knowing her real father is Hopkins. What follows is a lot of exciting swordplay until Banderas and Zeta-Jones win out over Wilson and his army of men. Hopkins is mortally wounded in the final fight, but lives long enough to tell Zeta-Jones that he is her real father and give his blessing for her and Banderas to marry. Song: "I Want to Spend My Lifetime Loving You" (James Horner, Will Jennings). Excessive violence prohibits viewing by children. Other Zorro films include **Behind the Mask of Zorro** (1966) and **The Legend of Zorro** (2005). **p**, Doug Claybourne, David Foster, John Gertz, Steven Spielberg; **d**, Martin

Hazel Court about to be sacrificed in *The Masque of the Red Death,* **1964.**

Campbell; **cast**, Antonio Banderas, Anthony Hopkins, Catherine Zeta-Jones, Stuart Wilson, Matt Letscher, Tony Amendola, Pedro Armendariz, Jr., William Marquez, Jose Perez, L.Q. Jones, Maury Chaykin; **w**, John Eskow, Ted Elliott, Terry Rossio (based on a story by Elliott, Rossio, Randall Jahnson and the character Zorro by Johnston McCulley); **c**, Phil Meheux; **m**, James Horner; **ed**, Thom Noble; **prod d**, Cecilia Montiel; **art d**, Michael Atwell; **set d**, Denise Camargo; **spec eff**, Laurencio Cordero.

The Masque of the Red Death ★★★ 1964; U.S./U.K.; 86m; Alta Vista Productions/American International; Color; Horror; Children: Unacceptable; **DVD**; **VHS**. In another one of his dynamically evil roles, Price plays a Satan-loving 12th-century Italian prince, who invites several dozen of the local nobility to his castle for protection against an oncoming plague, the Red Death. He orders them to attend a masked ball. Court brands herself as the bride of the Devil, but the evil Price shows little interest in her, only a sadistic lust to inflict pain on all of his guests before dispatching them. Court then aids Green and his daughter Asher and her fiancé Weston in their attempt to escape the castle. Green is killed while trying to destroy Price, but Asher and Weston manage to flee from the maniac. During the depravity of the evening, Price sees a hooded stranger dressed in red that he believes to be an ambassador to his master, Satan. But the mystery man reveals he is the Red Death himself and strikes Price down. This offbeat horror tale is typically Corman in that it graphically depicts violence and bloodletting with no attempt to be campy or with any intention to lampoon its gory story line. *Author's Note*: Corman took five weeks to shoot this film, twice as long as his usual shooting schedule. Price told this author that "in that picture, I believe Roger [Corman] was out for blood and the pun is definitely intended." **p&d**, Roger Corman; **cast**, Vincent Price, Hazel Court, Jane Asher, David Weston, Nigel Green, Patrick Magee, Paul Whitsun-Jones, Skip Martin, Robert Brown, Julian Burton; **w**, Charles Beaumont, R. Wright Campbell (based on the stories "The Masque of the Red Death" and "Hop-Frog, or the Eight Chained Orang-outangs" by Edgar Allan Poe); **c**, Nicolas Roeg (Panavision; Pathecolor); **m**, David Lee; **ed**, Ann Chegwidden; **prod d**, Daniel Haller; **art d**, Robert Jones; **set d**, Colin Southcott; **spec eff**, George Blackwell.

Master and Commander: The Far Side of the World ★★★★ 2003; U.S.; 138m; FOX; Color; Adventure; Children: Unacceptable (MPAA: PG-13); **BD**; **DVD**. This superb historical adventure is set in 1805 during the Napoleonic Wars and where Crowe renders a forceful performance as the captain of the British warship, HMS *Surprise*, and who has been assigned to destroy or capture a dreaded French privateer, *Acheron*, a raider that has been preying upon British whaling fleets. The film opens when all on board the *Surprise* hear a bell clanging in the fogbound sea and Crowe sees through his spyglass the very ship he is ordered to destroy bearing down on his small frigate, firing as it sails nearer and nearer, a ship twice as large as the *Surprise*. Crowe orders all hands to battle stations and a running sea fight ensues. In the exchange of cannon fire, the *Surprise* is badly damaged, its rudder blown off and the helm destroyed where its own gunfire seems to do little or no damage and does not penetrate *Acheron's* hull. To escape destruction, Crowe orders crew members to use lifeboats to row the damaged *Surprise* into a fog bank. Making hasty repairs, Crowe, despite the fact that his ship is outgunned and outclassed, turns the *Surprise* about and again attacks the *Acheron*, but is again forced to escape, which he manages through a ruse of floating buoys and lamps. Crowe nevertheless stays to his course, following the *Acheron* around Cape Horn and to the Galapagos Islands. Once reaching the islands, Crowe allows his good friend and ship physician, Bettany, to explore the island to collect its exotic fauna and flora and insect and aviary specimens for Bettany's experiments while they recover the survivors of a whaling ship that has been destroyed by the *Acheron*. Realizing that the French enemy is somewhere close, Crowe orders Bettany and his men to cease their scientific research and return to the *Surprise*, which then sails after the *Acheron*. Bettany, disturbed by having his exploration cut short, accuses Crowe of exceeding his orders, stating that he is now pursuing the enemy out of pride, not duty, an accusation Crowe emphatically denies. Meanwhile, Larkin, who is captain of the ship's marines, sees an albatross flying above the ship, but, when he attempts to shoot the huge bird, he accidentally shoots Bettany, who now suffers a life-threatening wound. Knowing that a delicate operation is needed to save his friend's life and that that operation must be conducted on solid ground, Crowe orders the *Surprise* back to the Galapagos Islands and Bettany is taken ashore where, using a mirror, he operates on himself and saves his own life. Meanwhile, Crowe has Bettany's men continue their scientific research, thus earning back the respect and gratitude of his friend. Crowe has by this time given up his obsessive ambition to find and destroy the *Acheron*, and, when Bettany's explorations and collections are completed, he orders the *Surprise* to prepare to sail for its home British waters. Bettany, however, while finishing his last tour of the island, sees the dreaded *Acheron* anchored on the other side of the island and hurries to warn Crowe. Crowe prepares for battle, but knows that unless the *Surprise* can get very close to the French warship, its cannon will do little or no damage to *Acheron's* hull. Crowe then remembers one of Bettany's insects in his many collections, one that is able to camouflage itself, and this gives Crowe the idea to disguise the *Surprise* as a British whaling ship, which is hastily and cleverly performed, knowing that the French raider will allow a whaling ship to get close enough so that it can be captured as a prize. The ruse works and, after the *Surprise* grapples with the *Acheron*, Crowe leads his crew members and marines onto the enemy ship where fierce hand-to-hand combat ensues and where the British seamen defeat the French defenders and capture the *Acheron*. In search of the *Acheron's* captain, Crowe finds a French doctor below, who has been operating on an officer who has just died, and the surgeon tells Crowe that the deceased is the captain. He then gives Crowe the captain's sword as a symbol of surrender. After both ships are repaired, the *Acheron* is sent to Valparaiso to be turned over to British authorities while Crowe remains with the *Surprise* at the Galapagos. Then Bettany discovers that the French doctor had died, not the much sought-after captain, who impersonated the surgeon in surrendering the ship. Crowe orders his crew to quarters, deciding to accompany the *Acheron* to Valparaiso, although Bettany complains about not having more time to conduct a search for a rare bird at the Galapagos. Crowe tells him that since the bird Bettany is seeking is unable to fly, his specimen will be waiting for him when they return to the islands, and the *Surprise* then sails after the *Acheron* to end this classic adventure. Everything about this film smacks of authenticity, from its life-size vessels that are perfect to the era, to the costuming, weapons, cannons and speech habits of the actors.

Crowe is truly magnetic in his role of the resolute but compassionate captain, and Bettany is excellent in his role as the ship's doctor and as an almost spiritual adviser to Crowe, subtly reminding Crowe as did the savants of ancient Rome caution military conquerors that "all glory is fleeting." Weir's direction is firm and his action and battle scenes are spectacularly executed with knowledgeable precision while he delivers one of the greatest sea sagas ever put on film. Detracting from many scenes is inadequate sound that often fails to allow the brilliant but near-whispering Crowe (a career-long annoying habit) to be distinctly heard, along with many other actors who are permitted to gulp, swallow or muffle their lines. This kind of unprofessional indifference to articulate audibility and poor clarity of sound has been woefully rampant throughout the film industry in the last thirty years where directors are apparently intimidated by the star status of their leading players so that they do not demand that their players clearly enunciate and pronounce their words in delivering their lines by using the diaphragm to understandably project their words as would any professional actor of yore. *Author's Note*: Another such adventure film, **Captain Horatio Hornblower**, 1951, deals with British warships during the Napoleon wars, but that fine film nevertheless presents its sea battles in miniatures (albeit very effectively) while this film has the great advantage of presenting life-size warships of the era. Further, much more attention is given to the lifestyle on board that early 19th-Century man-of-war, where sailors, officers and men alike are shown eating the hardtack food and living the crude and unsanitary lifestyles of that unenlightened era. Everything about this film is gritty and realistic, each scene reminding the viewer of the myriad dangers of the sea and the fragility of life on board such ships. Only ten days of actual shooting took place to depict the *Surprise* at sea (where the ship *Rose*, a life-size reproduction of a British warship, was employed) while the same ship and the *Acheron* were later built as full-scale replicas mounted on gimbals and shot in a large tank. The fierce storm the ship survives was created through digitally enhanced scenes. The scenes at Galapagos were actually shot at those islands, which was unusual in that such footage had been in the past invariably made for documentary films. **p**, Peter Weir, Samuel Goldwyn, Jr., Duncan Henderson, Todd Arnow, Meyer Gottlieb, Bob and Harvey Weinstein; **d**, Weir; **cast**, Russell Crowe, Paul Bettany, James D'Arcy, Edward Woodall, Chris Larkin, Max Pirkis, Jack Randall, Max Benitz, Lee Ingleby, Richard Pates; **w**, Weir, John Collee (based on the novels by Patrick O'Brian); **c**, Russell Boyd; **m**, Iva Davies, Christopher Gordon, Richard Tognetti; **ed**, Lee Smith; **prod d**, William Sandell; **art d**, Bruce Crone, Mark W. Mansbridge, Marco Niro, Héctor Romero; **set d**, Robert Gould; **spec eff**, Robert Alidon, Roy Augenstein, Bret Barrett, Mitchell S. Drain, Stefen Fangmeier, Mark Freund, Pablo Helman.

The Master of Ballantrae ★★★ 1953; U.S./U.K.; 88m; WB; Color; Adventure; Children: Cautionary; **DVD**; **VHS**. This was the dashing Flynn's last film under his longtime Warner Brothers contract that began in 1935 with **Captain Blood**. In this loose adaptation of the novel by Stevenson, Flynn and Steel play two Scottish noblemen brothers, who take no chances on losing the family fortune and estate by intentionally taking opposite sides in a conflict with the king of England. Flynn is part of a rebellion against the king, while Steel remains loyal to the monarch. The king's men are after Flynn, who thinks his brother has betrayed him, so he escapes to the West Indies with a friend, Livesey, who is a soldier of fortune. They both become rich as pirates and return to Scotland so Flynn can marry his longtime sweetheart, Campbell. She meanwhile thought he was dead and became engaged to Steel. After a lot of swordplay, the brothers solve their differences with Steel getting the family fortune and estate, and Flynn riding off to a new life of adventure and romance with Campbell. **d**, William Keighley; **cast**, Errol Flynn, Roger Livesey, Anthony Steel, Beatrice Campbell, Yvonne Furneaux, Felix Aylmer, Mervyn Johns, Charles Goldner, Ralph Truman, Francis de Wolff; **w**, Herb Meadow, Harold Medford (based on the novel by Robert Louis Stevenson); **c**, Jack Cardiff (Technicolor); **m**,

Errol Flynn in *The Master of Ballantrae*, 1953.

William Alwyn; **ed**, Jack Harris; **art d**, Ralph Brinton.

Master of Bankdam ★★★ 1949; U.K.; 105m; Holbein/Eagle-Lion Films; B/W; Drama; Children: Cautionary. This engrossing film presents a well-crafted saga of three generations of an English mill family. Murray and Price are two brothers fighting for the control of their father's (Walls) wool mill in a Yorkshire town. Murray marries a local socialite, uses mill money to finance the building of a new hospital, and is rewarded for that philanthropy by becoming the town mayor. Murray and Price clash over how the mill is operated and the fortune Murray spent on the hospital. Because of Murray's recklessness, Price dies in an accident when a building caves in at the mill. Price's son, Hanley, then tries to prove that his father was killed by his uncle, Murray. Murray assures his father that Price's death was, indeed, an accident, but Walls learns that it was one that Murray could have prevented. Walls dies before he can write a new will, so Murray inherits the mill. Murray marries and has a son, Tomlinson, who is spoiled rotten and grows up to be a coward when workers at the mill go on strike. Murray realizes that his son is not the man to run the mill so he gives that job to Hanley. Song: "The Fire of Your Love" (Paul Wilbur, sung by Maria Var). **p**, Edward Dryhurst, Walter Forde; **d**, Forde; **cast**, Anne Crawford, Dennis Price, Tom Walls, Stephen Murray, Linden Travers, Jimmy Hanley, Nancy Price, David Tomlinson, Patrick Holt, Herbert Lomas, Maria Var; **w**, Dryhurst, Moie Charles (based on the novel *The Crowthers of Bankdam* by Thomas Armstrong); **c**, Basil Emmott; **m**, Arthur Benjamin; **ed**, Terence Fisher; **art d**, George Paterson; **spec eff**, Jack Whitehead.

Masterson of Kansas ★★★ 1954; U.S.; 73m; COL; Color; Western; Children: Cautionary; **DVD**; **VHS**. Montgomery does a good job essaying western lawman Bat Masterson (1853-1921), stalwart sheriff of Dodge City, Kansas, who tries to prove that some cattlemen framed a rancher, Maxwell, for murder. Maxwell had negotiated a treaty with Kiowa Indians led by Silverheels, granting them a reserve in the grass country that the cattlemen want for grazing purposes. Montgomery, fearing the Indians will go on the warpath if Maxwell is executed and they lose their land, begins searching for Bruce, a witness to the murder. Joining Montgomery on the hunt is lawman Wyatt Earp (1848-1929), played by Cowling, and Doc Holliday (1851-1887), played by Griffith. Montgomery and Griffith had been feuding for years, but Griffith is persuaded by Maxwell's daughter, Gates, to help. The bad man leading the cattlemen in all this is Henry, who is brought to justice through the considerable action and gunplay of the probing lawmen. *Author's Note*: Masterson has been profiled in many films, including: **The Woman of the Town**, 1943 (Albert Dekker); **Trail Street**, 1947 (Randolph Scott); **Santa Fe**, 1951 (Frank Ferguson); **The Gunfight at Dodge City**, 1959

Ramon Novarro and Greta Garbo in *Mata Hari,* **1931.**

(Joel McCrea); and **Wyatt Earp**, 1994 (Tom Sizemore). Masterson retired from law enforcement and became a newspaperman in the 1890s, going to work as the chief sports reporter for the New York *Morning Telegraph* in 1901. He was found dead at his desk at the *Morning Telegraph* on October 25, 1921. His last words had been written for his column and read: "There are those who argue that everything breaks even in this old dump of a world of ours. I suppose these ginks who argue that way hold that because the rich man gets ice in the summer and the poor man gets it in the winter things are breaking even for both. Maybe so, but I'll swear that I can't see it that way…" For more details on Masterson, see my book, *Encyclopedia of Western Lawmen and Outlaws* (Paragon House, 1992; pages 227-229). **p**, Sam Katzman; **d**, William Castle; **cast**, George Montgomery, Nancy Gates, James Griffith, Jean Willes, Benny Rubin, William A. Henry, David Bruce, Bruce Cowling, Gregg Barton, Jay Silverheels; **w**, Douglas Heyes; **c**, Henry Freulich (Technicolor); **ed**, Henry Batista; **art d**, Paul Palmentola; **set d**, Sidney Clifford; **spec eff**, Jack Erickson.

Mata Hari ★★★★ 1931; U.S.; 91m; MGM; B/W; Biographical Drama/Spy Drama; Children: Unacceptable; **DVD**; **VHS**. The great Greta Garbo is stunning and utterly captivating as the notorious Dutch dancer, courtesan and WWI spy Mata Hari (Margaret Gertrude Zelle; 1876-1917). She is first seen in this lavish production as the toast of Paris during the war, her exotic dancing drawing the attention of generals and heads of state, trysting with these amorous admirers in order to get secret information for Germany. In one dancing sequence, Garbo displays more of her gorgeous body than ever before or after while wearing a skimpy bikini-like costume as she slides snakelike about the figure of a large Buddha, one having arms that seem to reach out for her and in and around which she enfolds her slinking body, an utterly sensuous if not lascivious dance that censors a few years later would have certainly banned. She is then contacted by her German spymaster, Stone, who directs her to obtain certain secrets regarding an impending Allied troop movement and she goes to Barrymore, an indiscreet Russian general, who has been having an affair with her. At the same time, she meets dashing Novarro, a Russian pilot, and they fall in love. Her loyalty to Germany is tested when she learns that Novarro has the secret information Stone is seeking and she struggles emotionally about betraying the young man whom she loves. Her patriotism wins over and she takes Novarro to bed while her confederates copy the secret plans. When Barrymore learns of Garbo's tryst with Novarro, he explodes and threatens to expose Garbo as a spy and also implicate the unsuspecting Novarro. To protect her secret identity, as well as the man she loves, Garbo shoots Barrymore, killing him. When Novarro thinks to report to Barrymore, Garbo persuades him to fly to Russia. His plane is shot

down and, in the crash, Novarro is blinded. Garbo, hearing of this, abandons her present espionage assignment and rushes to his side in a hospital where she tells Novarro that he is the only man she has ever loved. Stone, in response to Garbo's abandoning her assignment, orders one of his agents to kill her, but the assassin is waylaid by local police. (Stone is about as cold-blooded a spymaster ever seen on the screen, stating when he decides to have his top agent killed: "A spy in love is a tool that has outlived its usefulness.") Garbo is then exposed as a notorious spy and brought to trial by French authorities. Refusing to implicate Novarro in any of her espionage, and so that his memory of her will not be blackened, Garbo pleads guilty and is sentenced to death. Before her execution, she is granted a last request, that the blind Novarro visit her in her cell. He does, believing she is in a hospital dying from an incurable illness, and both swear their love for each other before Garbo, accompanied by nuns, is led to a waiting firing squad and where she is shot to death. Fitzmaurice helms this intriguing melodrama with splendid style, employing many inventive camera shots, and where the sets and costuming are magnificent, complementing in every frame the superb performance from Garbo. The film's literate script takes considerable liberties with the facts involving the infamous spy, but it is Garbo's magnificent performance that most accurately captures the true nature and personality of this ill-starred and tragic woman. *Author's Note*: This was Garbo's eighteenth film, the one and only ever made with Novrro, who was still a great matinee idol. It was her fifth film with Stone and second with Barrymore. She had played a spy in another film, **The Mysterious Lady**, 1928, but this espionage tale had little impact upon audiences. Although the U.S. censor board had not yet been established (until a few years later), the film ran into serious trouble with the British censors, a large market for American films, and they objected to several scenes, particularly one where Novarro is looking down upon Garbo as she reclines on a chaise lounge, while briefly looking at a statue of the Virgin Mary illuminated by candlelight and where Novarro then descends into the enclosing arms of Garbo, as if to suggest that Garbo's seductive allure was far more powerful than any religious symbol. That scene was reshot with the statue of the Virgin Mary replaced with a picture of a soldier's mother over a vigil light. The last scene where Garbo is shot by the firing squad was thought too violent by not only the British censors, but MGM executives. That scene was cut from the initial British release and was later cut from the U.S. re-release (89 minutes), but it remained in the original print initially going to U.S. theaters at 91 minutes. Garbo performed most of the dancing in this film, but, in one sequence of her exotic and strange dance, while undulating and gyrating her hips before the Malaysian Buddha, the camera shows her naked back as she begins to strip away what is left of her skimpy costume, and this sequence may have been performed by one of Garbo's several non-credited doubles, either Elizabeth Taylor-Martin, or most likely, Rae Randall (born Sigrun Salvason; 1897-1934), the latter being her most used double in this film. Randall had appeared in bit parts as a dancer in Cecil B. DeMille's **King of Kings**, 1927, and **The Godless Girl**, 1929, and whose life was as tragic as Mata Hari in that she was found dead on May 4, 1934, in Los Angeles at age thirty-six, and, at first, officials believed she had been murdered, but her death was later attributed to suicide. Garbo told this author that she enjoyed making this film, but then again, Fitzmaurice (one of her favorite director) and Daniels, her most favorite cinematographer (who often showed Garbo in muted close-ups, softening her image to what Garbo called "a warm look") were with her in this production. Garbo never publicly stated her feelings about her appearance in **Mata Hari**, or most of her films, insisting that she never viewed the rushes of any of her films, or watched them when they were released (at least at the premieres), but it is a matter of record that she would, when her films were released to mainstream theaters, drive to small towns outside of Los Angeles, wearing dark sunglasses (her lifelong trademark or disguise tool) and commonplace apparel, and would view her films incognito from beginning to end, being one of the last members of the audience to leave the theater. About this film, or, at least the character she plays, Garbo told this author: "I could identify with Mata Hari, who was thought to be a great interpretive dancer. Her affections for the men who used her brought about her downfall and that is the case with many tragic women. The French shot her out of vengeance, although there was very little proof that she was guilty of causing the deaths of thousands of men as her prosecutors claimed. I believe that in her last conscious moments, Mata Hari was unconvinced that the French would really shoot her, that somehow she would be saved at the last moment. How else could she have appeared to be so brave while standing before that firing squad? Perhaps, I am wrong. She might have accepted her fate and been that brave. We shall never really know, shall we?" Mara Hari was taken from her prison cell and driven to Vincennes early in the morning of October 15, 1917, where she was placed against a stake. She refused a blindfold and waved away a soldier attempting to tie her to the stake. She stood smiling at the twelve men of the firing squad until she was shot. She slumped forward and an officer then fired a bullet into her brain, the *coup de grace*. No one claimed her body. For more details about the spectacular Mata Hari, see my book, *Spies: A Narrative Encyclopedia of Dirty Deeds and Double Dealing from Biblical Times to Today* (M. Evans, 1997; pages 337-342). Like Garbo's double in this film (Rae Randall), Novarro himself would meet a violent end. He was a closet gay and, after his retirement, he was consistently extorted by male hustlers. Two of these predators held him captive in his luxurious Laurel Canyon home before brutally torturing and killing him on October 30, 1968. For details on this case, see my two-volume work, *The Great Pictorial History of World Crime*, Volume II (History, Inc., 2004; pages 890-894). **p**, George Fitzmaurice and (not credited) Irving Thalberg; **d**, George Fitzmaurice; **cast**, Greta Garbo, Ramon Novarro, Lionel Barrymore, Lewis Stone, C. Henry Gordon, Karen Morley, Helen Jerome Eddy, Mischa Auer, Roy Barcroft, Cecil Cunningham; **w**, Benjamin Glazer, Leo Birinski, Doris Anderson, Gilbert Emery; **c**, William Daniels; **m**, William Axt; **ed**, Frank Sullivan; **art d**, Cedric Gibbons.

Mata Hari, Agent H21 ★★★ 1967; France/Italy; 98m; Filmel/Magna; B/W; Spy Drama; Children: Unacceptable; **DVD**; **VHS**. Moreau is the sensuous Mata Hari, exotic dancer and dedicated German spy during World War I. She is ordered to seduce Trintignant, a French captain, and steal needed secret documents. But, instead, Moreau falls in love with him, which leads to her being caught, convicted, and shot as a spy. This is a compelling and straight-forward telling of this well-known espionage tale, but too violent for children. (In French; English subtitles.) Other Mata Hari films were made in 1927, 1931 (the best with Greta Garbo as the notorious spy), 1985, 2003 (made for TV), and 2013. **p**, Eugéne Lépicier; **d**, Jean-Louis Richard; **cast**, Jeanne Moreau, Jean-Louis Trintignant, Claude Rich, Frank Villard, Albert Remy, Georges Riquier, Henri Garcin, Hella Petri, Marie Dubois, Nicole Desailly; **w**, Richard, François Truffaut; **c**, Michel Kelber; **m**, Georges Delerue; **ed**, Kenout Peltier; **prod d**, Claude Pignot.

The Match King ★★★ 1932; U.S.; 79m; First National/WB; B/W; Crime Drama; Children: Unacceptable. William is totally captivating in one of his finest roles, which is based upon one of the world's greatest swindlers, Ivar Kreuger (1880-1932), who was known as the "Swedish Match King." William is shown at the beginning at the pinnacle of his success where he has bilked tens of thousands of persons out of countless millions of dollars through his sophisticated but bogus stock schemes and labyrinthine swindles. He is now faced with exposure and prosecution and contemplates suicide while looking back on his dark and spectacular career, and we see him in flashback in Chicago as a lowly street cleaner. He plans a murder in order to monopolize the most commonplace tool, a simple kitchen match. The suave and polished William easily convinces bankers into backing his valueless firms, transferring (as did Kreuger) the cash from one phony firm to another as he builds a pyramid of companies into a worldwide conglomerate

Warren William in *The Match King*, 1932.

while cornering the market on kitchen matches. He ruthlessly uses women for his financial ends, discarding them when they can be of no more use to him. On his road to riches, William encounters and woos Damita, a wealthy international movie star, who acts and talks like Greta Garbo. (This obvious impersonation is for good reason in that Garbo was one of Kreuger's victims, investing heavily into several of his firms.) When Damita sees that William's house of cards is about to tumble, she leaves him flat. The film acutely imitates reality in many instances, particularly when William negotiates a $40-million-dollar loan from Wall Street to finance his shaky firms (which is identical to what Kreuger actually did). In the end, William, with the law closing in on him, opts to end his life, and this is where this riveting tale ends. Bretherton directs with great skill and hurries this production along at a fast pace as it chillingly recounts the story of a cold-blooded man committing murder, blackmail and forgery to become one of the world's most colossal frauds. The real-life Kreuger shot and killed himself (using an antique pistol once owned by Napoleon I) at his luxurious Paris penthouse on March 12, 1932. As was its wont, Warner Brothers, a studio with the habit of producing films straight from the headlines of the day, seized upon Kreuger's death (as did the author, Thorvaldson, who wrote a quickie novel within a few weeks after Kreuger's demise) and immediately put this film into production. *Author's Note*: When I raised Kreuger's name with Garbo, she shook her head and said: "A fellow Swede and a greater actor than I could ever be. He was the most secretive man I ever knew. He once told me that the secret to his success was 'silence, more silence, and more silence still.' He trained himself never to talk in his sleep to prevent himself from mumbling his secrets. He had nerves of steel and went to the dentist and had serious dental work done, but without ever taking any anesthetic—he was that afraid of revealing how his financial empire worked. Well, the world found out that it did not work and that he had swindled everyone before he shot and killed himself. He taught me one lesson—never to invest in stocks again. After Ivar, I invested in real estate." I asked her how much money she had lost by investing in Kreuger's firms, and she replied: "Oh, I am too embarrassed to tell you the amount. It was a considerable amount. Many others lost a lot more than I did, I am sure. What I lost most was my faith in the man." For more details about Ivar Kreuger, see my books, *Hustlers and Conmen: An Anecdotal History of the Confidence Man and His Games* (M. Evans, 1976; pages 251-255) and *The Great Pictorial History of World Crime*, Volume I (History, Inc., 2004; pages 442-446). **p**, Hal B. Wallis; **d**, Howard Bretherton, William Keighley; **cast**, Warren William, Lili Damita, Glenda Farrell, Juliette Compton, Claire Dodd, Harold Huber, John Wray, Spencer Charters, Murray Kinnell, Hardie Albright, Alan Hale; **w**, Houston Branch, Sidney Sutherland (based on the novel by Einar Thorvaldson); **c**, Robert

Jonathan Rhys Meyers and Rupert Penry-Jones in *Match Point*, 2006.

Kurrle; **m**, Bernhard Kaun; **ed**, Jack Killifer; **art d**, Anton Grot.

The Matchmaker ★★★ 1958; U.S.; 101m; PAR; B/W; Comedy; Children: Acceptable; **DVD**; **VHS**. Booth is delightful as a matchmaker in 1884 Yonkers, New York, who tries to match up a shopkeeper merchant, Ford, with a Manhattan hat maker, MacLaine. Booth really wants Ford for herself, but must appear professional in trying to match him with MacLaine. Booth and Ford go to New York and leave his two male clerks, Perkins and Morse, to run the store in his absence. But these errant and amorous clerks have other things on their mind and go to the big city to kiss any pretty girl they find. By chance, the boys meet MacLaine and her friend, Wilson, and take them to a posh restaurant. The boys, however, are broke and can't pay the bill, until they find Ford's wallet while he is in an adjoining private dining room with Booth. Ford sees his clerks and fires them. It all looks bad for Booth's hopes of matching herself with Ford, but she has another snap up her garter. She helps Perkins open a shop across the road from Ford's in Yonkers. Her scheme works when Ford eliminates Perkins' competition by taking him in as a partner, and Booth winds up with Ford. The plot has a long evolutionary history. It began as a British stage farce, "A Day Well Spent," by John Oxenford, which became a Viennese play by Johann Nestroy. Viennese producer Otto Preminger saw that play in Vienna in the 1920s and filmed it in 1938 as **The Merchant of Yonkers**, which was revised and in 1955 became a Broadway hit. That was made into the musical play and movie **Hello, Dolly**, 1969. No songs in the Booth comedy version. **p**, Don Hartman; **d**, Joseph Anthony; **cast**, Shirley Booth, Anthony Perkins, Shirley MacLaine, Paul Ford, Robert Morse, Perry Wilson, Russell Collins, Rex Evans, Gavin Gordon; **w**, John Michael Hayes (based on the play by Thornton Wilder); **c**, Charles Lang, Jr.; **m**, Adolph Deutsch; **ed**, Howard Smith; **art d**, Hal Pereira, Roland Anderson; **set d**, Sam Comer, Robert Benton; **spec eff**, John P. Fulton.

The Matchmaking of Anna ★★★ 1972; Greece; 87m; Katsourides; Color; Drama; Children: Unacceptable. Vagena, a young woman, has worked as a maid for an older woman, Veaki, for several years. Veaki's daughter, Panou, arranges a marriage between Vagena and a young man, Kalaroglou. While courting Vagena and Kalaroglou gradually begin to know each other and feel the early stages of mutual love. One night, Vagena returns late from a date with Kalaroglou to be told by Veaki and her daughter that they have decided Kalaroglou is not good enough for her. Veaki and her family also begin to think they cannot do without Vagena if she marries, so they try to break up the romance. Vagena's mother also wants to break it up because she needs the money she gets from her daughter. Vagena gives in to the pressures of the others and gives up her brief hopes of marriage. A good but sad domestic story sensitively told, but not for children because of sexual content. (In Greek; English subtitles.) **p**, Dinos Katsouridis; **d**, Pantelis Voulgaris; **cast**, Anna Vagena, Stavros Kalaroglou, Smaro Veaki, Kostas Rigopoulos, Aliki Zografou, Maria Martika, Alekos Oudinotis, Irene Emirza, Mika Flora, Nikos Garofallou; **w**, Menis Koumantareas, Pantelis Voulgaris, Loula Hristara; **c**, Nikos Kavoukidis; **ed**, Dinos Katsouridis; **art d**, Kyriakos Katzourakis.

Match Point ★★★ 2006; U.K./Luxembourg; 124m; BBC Films/DreamWorks; Color; Crime Drama; Children: Unacceptable (MPAA: R); **BD**; **DVD**. A charming and handsome but poor young Irish social climber, Rhys Meyers, is a former tennis pro coaching at a posh London club, who wants to obtain a rich wife. He and a rich young British pupil, Goode, become friends, and Goode's pretty sister, Mortimer, becomes immediately infatuated with Rhys Meyers. Her father, Cox, a corporate tycoon, thinks the match would be fine because Rhys Meyers volleys himself off as a bookish lover of opera, which the father loves. Her mother, Wilton, also approves of Rhys Meyers marrying her daughter. Enter Johansson, a beautiful blonde American actress whose film career is going nowhere and, like Rhys Meyers, is looking for a rich mate. She becomes Goode's fiancée, but she and Rhys Meyers inevitably turn on to each other. Rhys Meyers has to choose between the two lovely women because he can't play both sides of the tennis court at the same time. He marries Mortimer, maybe because her father is making room for him at the top of his conglomerate. Then Goode and Johansson are soon headed for the altar. In the blink of an eye, Goode falls for another beauty and he calls it off with Johansson, and, instead marries the new love of his life. After a year or so, Rhys Meyers and Johansson meet by chance, have a torrid affair, and he now has to choose between her and his wife. He makes Johansson pregnant and that does it for him as the romance turns into a murder mystery. Rhys Meyers lusts after Johansson, but loves his wife and the rich world he entered by marrying her, so he shoots and kills Johansson's landlady, Tyzack, with a shotgun and steals her jewelry to make it look like a burglar had done the crime, then, while making his escape, shoots and kills Johansson with the same shotgun. Police decide the murders are part of a burglary that went wrong, especially after Rhys Meyers convinces the police that he is innocent in the matter. In tennis, "match point" is the final point needed to win a match. Among the jewelry Rhys Meyers makes off with is Tyzack's wedding ring, which he tosses toward the Thames River, but it falls short and lands on the pavement where a drug addict later picks it up and he is, in turn, shot and killed in a robbery. The dead drug addict takes the fall for Rhys Meyers' double murders while he returns to his wife and can continue to rise to the top of the business world. Although this well-crafted tale provides a chilling profile of youthful ambition (it is not a black comedy by any means), it more or less condones murder and deception as part of the modus operandi in achieving those ambitions without any retribution. For this reason, as well as violence and sexuality, viewing by children is prohibited. **p**, Letty Aronson, Lucy Darwin, Gareth Wiley, Nicky Kentish Barnes, Helen Robin; **d&w**, Woody Allen; **cast**, Scarlett Johansson, Jonathan Rhys Meyers, Emily Mortimer, Matthew Goode, Brian Cox, Penelope Wilton, Rupert Penry-Jones, Margaret Tyzack, Alexander Armstrong, Paul Kaye, Janis Kelly, Alan Oke; **c**, Remi Adefarasin; **ed**, Alisa Lepselter; **prod d**, Jim Clay; **art d**, Diane Dancklefsen, Jan Spoczynski; **set d**, Caroline Smith; **spec eff**, Jonathan Bullock, Dean Ford, Matthew Bristowe, Paul Alexiou.

Matchstick Men ★★★ 2003; U.S.; 101m; WB; Color; Drama; Children: Cautionary; MPAA: PG-13; **DVD**. Cage is a seasoned con artist and, along with his protégé, Rockwell, he swindles people into paying ten times what some cheap basement water filters cost in order to win prizes they never collect. Cage is a nervous wreck and an agoraphobic, fearful of travel, which keeps him from expanding his con artistry, so Rockwell sends him to a shrink, Altman. Altman thinks it will help Cage if he gets acquainted with his teenage daughter, Lohman, who is fourteen and whom he's never seen. She visits him for a weekend and she helps steady him while he teaches her the fine art of con artistry. They make an offbeat father and daughter pair of cons and become a family, although a dysfunctional one. The title is another name for con artists because they create temporary identities that are simple and fleeting. Violence, some sexual content, and gutter language prohibit viewing by children. **p**, Ridley Scott, Sean Bailey, Ted Griffin, Jack Rapke, Charles J.D. Schlissel, Steve Starkey, Robert Zemeckis; **d**, Scott; **cast**, Nicolas Cage, Sam Rockwell, Alison Lohman, Bruce Altman, Bruce McGill, Jenny O'Hara, Steve Eastin, Beth Grant, Sheila Kelley, Tim Kelleher; **w**, Nick and Ted Griffin (based on the book by Eric Garcia); **c**, John Mathieson; **m**, Hans Zimmer; **ed**, Dody Dorn; **prod d**, Tom Foden; **art d**, Michael Manson; **set d**, Nancy Nye; **spec eff**, Martin Bresin, Sheena Duggal.

Matewan ★★★★ 1987; U.S.; 135m; Goldcrest/Cinecom; Color; Drama; Children: Unacceptable (MPAA: PG-13); **DVD**; **VHS**. Gritty and uncompromising, this classic tale of unions vs. bosses is set in West Virginia during the 1920s and is based upon a real incident. When a strike is called at a coal mine after bosses cut salaries and bring unskilled black and Italian workers (scabs) to break the strike, these itinerant laborers soon side with the strikers after Union organizer Cooper unifies them in a common cause to improve miserable wages and unsafe working conditions for all. Cooper, who represents the IWW or "Wobblies," strikes up a friendship that promises romance with boarding house owner McDonnell, whose teenage son, Oldham, is a mine worker and apprentice Baptist preacher. Stymied by the unified position of the workers, the bosses hire a small army of private detectives, who are led by Tighe and Clapp, and who have no reservations about murdering workers. They take up residence in McDonnell's boarding house where they try to intimidate Oldham into giving them information about the strikers, but to no avail. Meanwhile, the Italian immigrants and the blacks imported from deep southern states live side-by-side in makeshift tents and bicker and argue with each other until their differences are settled by Jones, a quiet-speaking but commanding African-American worker, and others. Meanwhile, Gunton, a local who appears to be a strong supporter of the strikers, has betrayed his community by becoming a company spy for the detectives, identifying the union ringleaders who are keeping the strike alive and leading the detectives to them where they are summarily tortured for information before being murdered. On one occasion, Oldham witnesses such an execution, identifying Gunton as a traitor. When all fails, the bosses order Tighe and his detectives to wipe out the top strikers, but they are warned by Strathairn, the chief of police for the small town of Matewan (which consists of several buildings sitting alongside a railroad track) that he will oppose such violence and, to prove it, he straps on six-guns as would a sheriff of the Old West, and loads his shotgun. Cooper tries to avert the impending slaughter, but the miners, now armed, will no longer tolerate more abuse and oppression and they are determined to stand up to Tighe and his armed thugs. Mostel, a local businessman and mayor of the small town, joins with Strathairn as they face the heavily armed detectives coming along the railroad tracks and in search of union workers. Mostel warns Tighe, Clapp and others that they have no authority to hunt down the workers and orders them to disarm. The contemptuous detectives go for their guns, and a wild gunfight ensues where Mostel is fatally shot in the stomach. Strathairn fires his two six-guns, killing two of the thugs, and union workers appear from ambush firing on the other detectives while Cooper, who is unarmed and has attempted to prevent the bloodshed, is fatally shot. Tighe flees to McDonnell's boarding house, pleading with McDonnell, but she turns a deaf ear to his lies and shoots and kills him. (A more desired death on film could not be wished in that Tighe represents, in a masterful performance, everything evil and sinister in the world.) In an epilogue, Oldham, who is shown later working in the coal mine, details the fates of the miners and townspeople during the days

Chris Cooper in *Matewan*, 1987.

of "Bloody Mingo." Sayles directs this mesmerizing historical drama with great skill, carefully developing his divergent characters, and where Strathairn, Oldham, McDonnell, Cooper, Tighe and Gunton are standouts in their roles. The gun battle at the finale is one of the most realistic and believable bloody confrontations put on film, one so traumatic, however, that it may disturb sensitive adults (and prohibits viewing by children). *Author's Note*: "Bloody Mingo" references Mingo County, West Virginia, where the actual "Battle of Matewan" occurred on May 19, 1920, between local miners, supported by chief of police Sid Hatfield, and armed members of the Baldwin-Felts Detective Agency. Two miners and the local mayor were killed in the gun battle, and seven detectives, including owner-brothers Albert and Lee Felts, were also killed. **p**, Maggie Renzi, Peggy Rajski; **d&w**, John Sayles; **cast**, Chris Cooper, Mary McDonnell, David Strathairn, Will Oldham, Kevin Tighe, Bob Gunton, Gordon Clapp, Joe Grifasi, Nancy Mette, Jo Henderson, Josh Mostel, Gary McCleery, Renzi, James Earl Jones; **c**, Haskell Wexler; **m**, Mason Daring; **ed**, Sonya Polonsky; **prod d**, Nora Chavooshian; **art d**, Dan Bishop; **set d**, Leslie Pope, Anamarie Michnevich; **spec eff**, Peter Kunz.

Matilda ★★★ 1978; U.S.; 105m; American International Pictures; Color; Comedy; Children: Acceptable; **VHS**. Gould is a talent agent, who is almost out of clients and money when he takes a trip to Australia and discovers a female boxing kangaroo named Matilda. He has a brainstorm and takes Matilda and her trainer, Revill, to America and gets the kangaroo matched to fight a few rounds with professional boxers. This is opposed by an animal rights activist, Carlson, a boxing commissioner, Clark, and other interested parties including a sports writer, Mitchum; a gangster, Guardino; and the current world's boxing champ, Pennell. There are some very funny scenes in this offbeat comedy, a romp that mixes a lot of people familiar in boxing movies with the gimmick of a pugilistic kangaroo, who has her moment in the ring. Song: "When I'm With You I'm Feeling Good" (Carol Connors, Ernie Sheldonh, sung by Pat and Debbie Boone). **p**, Albert S. Ruddy; **d**, Daniel Mann; **cast**, Elliott Gould, Robert Mitchum, Clive Revill, Harry Guardino, Lionel Stander, Roy Clark, Karen Carlson, Art Metrano, Roberta Collins, Larry Pennell; **w**, Ruddy, Timothy Galfas (based on the book by Paul Gallico); **c**, Jack Woolf (Movielab Color); **m**, Jerrold Immel; **ed**, Allan Jacobs; **prod d**, Boris Leven; **set d**, Ruby R. Levitt; **spec eff**, Gerald Endler.

Matinee ★★★ 1993; U.S.; 99m; UNIV; Color; Comedy; Children: Unacceptable (MPAA: PG); **DVD**; **VHS**. Goodman is a showman, who brings a cheap sci-fi horror movie to Key West, Florida, at the time of the Cuban Missile Crisis in 1962. You know it's cheap because of its crude film effects, seedy stage props, and actors adorned in ill-fitting rubber suits. But to Goodman, it's paying homage to old B movies, par-

Kellie Martin and James Villemaire in *Matinee*, **1993.**

ticularly those made by William Castle, so popular at matinees in the 1950s. Goodman does Castle one or two better by wiring theater seats with electrical buzzers, blows ice vapors at the audience, and has an actor dress up like a giant running up and down the aisles and who then throws an ant farm to the ground and yells "You're free! You're free!" Though made on the cheap side, this production presents a lot of zany fun that recalls a kinder, gentler era. Gutter language, violence, and sensuality prohibit viewing by children. **p**, Michael Finnell, Pat Kehoe; **d**, Joe Dante; **cast**, John Goodman, Cathy Moriarty, Simon Fenton, Omri Katz, Lisa Jakub, Kellie Martin, Jesse Lee, Lucinda Jenney, James Villemaire, Robert Picardo, Jesse White, Naomi Watts, Luke Halpin; **w**, Charlie Haas (based on a story by Haas and (no first name) Jerico); **c**, John Hora; **m**, Jerry Goldsmith; **ed**, Marshall Harvey; **prod d**, Steven Legler; **art d**, Nanci B. Roberts; **set d**, Frederick C. Weiler; **spec eff**, Jim Fredburg, Mark Koivu, Dennis Michelson.

The Mating Game ★★★ 1959; U.S.; 96m; MGM; Color; Comedy; Children: Acceptable; **DVD**;**VHS**. This charming, romantic comedy sees Randall, a tax collector, go to a farm to ask why its owners, Douglas and Merkel, have not paid taxes for years. He intends to stay one day to look at their books and estimate their farm income, but stays on as he becomes interested in their wholesome and attractive daughter, Reynolds, and also falls under the spell of the happy family. Randall works out the figures so the government owes the farmers big bucks, and that the farmers do not owe any back taxes. This helps Randall win the farmer's daughter and he leaves his job to become a member of the family. **p**, Philip Barry, Jr.; **d**, George Marshall; **cast**, Debbie Reynolds, Tony Randall, Paul Douglas, Fred Clark, Una Merkel, Philip Ober, Philip Coolidge, Charles Lane, Trevor Bardette, William Smith; **w**, William Roberts (based on the novel *The Darling Buds of May* by H.E. Bates); **c**, Robert J. Bronner (CinemaScope; Metrocolor); **m**, Jeff Alexander; **ed**, John McSweeney, Jr.; **art d**, Malcolm Brown, William A. Horning; **spec eff**, Doug Hubbard.

Max Dugan Returns ★★★ 1983; U.S.; 98m; FOX; Color; Comedy; Children: Cautionary (MPAA: PG); **DVD**; **VHS**. Sentimental but memorable comedy from Simon has errant parent Robards, an old-time gangster, coming back into the life of his estranged daughter, Mason (Simon's wife, for whom he wrote this entertaining vehicle). Mason is a working single mom, struggling to bring up her teenage son, Broderick, when she suddenly begins receiving expensive gifts from an unknown admirer. That admirer presents himself as Robards, her long-vanished father, who seeks to reconcile with her and befriend his grandson Broderick, but Mason wants nothing to do with him. He had run out on her and her mother many years ago, following his shady am-

bitions, which were centered squarely in the underworld, chiefly gambling. Robards truthfully tells Mason that he has a bum ticker and his heart might fail at any time, and that he wants to spend his last days with the only family members he has. The good-hearted Mason (when was she otherwise?) gives in, and allows him to stay with them in their cramped home, but she fears that he might be arrested at any time because of a recent scam Robards has pulled in Las Vegas that netted him a satchel full of money. Mason is particularly concerned because of her recently established friendship with Sutherland, a police detective, fearing that Sutherland might somehow arrest her father and so she plays a cat-and-mouse game with Sutherland while keeping Robards under wraps. Meanwhile, Broderick is awed into admiration for his grandfather's wealth and the many gifts Robards bestows upon him and his mother, but when he presents a new car to them, Mason panics, knowing she cannot easily explain such an expensive gift to Sutherland. Thankfully, the car is stolen, but Sutherland gets on the case, and recovers the auto for her and they begin a tenuous romance while Sutherland's curiosity about her father causes him to probe the old man's background. Robards by this time, seeing Broderick's baseball skills lacking, hires a professional baseball player (Charley Lau) to coach Broderick so that the boy's performance dramatically improves, giving him more self-confidence than he has felt in years. Meanwhile, Sutherland's snooping causes Robards to depart again, but, before vanishing forever, he does one more good deed that dissipates the disillusionment shared by Mason and Broderick. Robards is outstanding as the mysterious Max and Mason, Broderick and Sutherland are also standouts in their roles. *Author's Note*: This was Broderick's film debut, as it was for Sutherland's son, Kiefer Sutherland, who is one of Broderick's pals. Robards told this author that "that Simon story is a nifty and funny one. I enjoyed playing the father stepping out of the past like Santa Claus as he tries to win back the hearts of his daughter and grandson. In the old Greek plays there was a thing called the *Deus ex machina*, sort of an elevator that descends onto the stage to save a hero, who has no way to escape. They called it a 'God Machine. Well, the part I play is like that machine. He miraculously shows up to save his folks from financial and emotional ruin, but complicates their lives and his own through his good intentions. Would that every orphan in the world had such a conscientious and returning father." **p**, Neil Simon, Herbert Ross; **d**, Ross; **cast**, Marsha Mason, Jason Robards, Donald Sutherland, Matthew Broderick, Dody Goodman, Sal Viscuso, Panchito Gomez, Charley Lau, Mari Gorman, Brian Part; **w**, Simon; **c**, David M. Walsh (DeLuxe Color); **m**, David Shire; **ed**, Richard Marks; **prod d**, Albert Brenner; **art d**, David Haber; **set d**, Garrett Lewis; **spec eff**, Alan Lorimer.

Mayerling ★★★★ 1937; France; 96m; Nero Films/Pax Films; B/W; Romance; Children: Unacceptable; **DVD**; **VHS**. Boyer renders one of his greatest performances as Crown Prince Rudolf of Austria (1858-1889) in one of the most poignant love stories ever put on screen. He is the son of Dax, playing the tyrannical Emperor Franz Joseph (1830-1916), the absolute ruler of Austria-Hungary, but in every way is nothing like his father. The film opens with students protesting Dax's iron rule and who are then arrested en masse by police. Among the prisoners is none other than Boyer, who is brought before his father. Dax chastises him for liberal views and then compels him to abandon those radical positions, reminding him that he must preserve the royal bloodline of the Hapsburgs. Boyer's life is made more miserable when Dax imposes upon him a marriage (in 1881) with Laffon, playing Princess Stephanie of Belgium (1864-1945), a royal woman he does not love. Boyer leads a lonely life, estranged from Laffon, finding some joy in hunting and where he establishes his own royal hunting lodge at Mayerling in the Vienna Woods. He is watched night and day by court intriguers and his father's detectives. Knowing this, he evades his trackers one evening and, in disguise, goes to a fair where he meets beautiful Darrieux, who plays Baroness Marie Vetsera (1871-1889); Rudolf and Marie Vetsera met in November 1888 when she was seventeen years old. The two fall in love although Darrieux has no idea that Boyer is the crown prince of Austria. They enjoy themselves by tossing rings around the neck of a swan and by watching a puppet show. The next night, as Darrieux attends the opera, she is startled to see Boyer sitting next to Dax and other members of the emperor's entourage in the royal box. Although she comes from aristocratic parents, Darrieux knows that she cannot ever attain the status of royalty and resigns herself to never seeing Boyer again. Boyer, nevertheless, will not let Darrieux go, and her love for him causes her to secretly meet with him in secret rendezvous, even in rooms of the royal palace. Only through Darrieux's open innocence does Boyer find happiness and is able to forget the endless intrigues of the court. One of Dax's advisers, Debucourt, then discovers the affair, and contacts Darrieux's mother, Regnier, who vows to cure Darrieux "of this madness" by forcing her to accompany her on a trip to Trieste. Thinking that Darrieux has purposely deserted him, Boyer takes to drink, attending parties and imbibing from dusk till dawn. He dallies with other women, but none hold any interest for him. When Darrieux returns, she again meets Boyer, but he is in his cups and seething with anger over her desertion, shouting: "Haven't you ever seen a man drunk before?" She knows about his recent affairs and he lashes out at her, saying: "I'll love all the women in Vienna if I want!" Darrieux shows no anger, only compassion, saying: "Oh, my love, how you suffer!" With this heartfelt statement, Boyer now knows that he has hurt not only himself but the only woman he will ever love and that no matter what might happen, they belong together. Boyer than slips a ring onto Darrieux's finger as a symbol of their eternal union, one ominously inscribed: "United in Love unto Death." Boyer writes a letter to the Pope, asking that his marriage to Laffon be annulled, but the Pope responds by sending his reply to Dax and it is a firm refusal. Dax summons his son and then verbally lashes out at him for his marital transgression, ordering Boyer to somehow remove Darrieux from his memory and giving him an ultimatum: "You have twenty-four hours to end the affair!" That night at a royal ball, the pensive Boyer sits silent with Laffon, but when he sees Darrieux, he shocks one and all by going to her and insists that she dance with him by leading off the grand ball as the first dancers on the floor. While Laffon sits stunned and stone-faced, Boyer and Darrieux defiantly twirl about the huge ballroom, both proclaiming through their actions their love for one another. When Darrieux leaves the ballroom after the ball, Darrieux and Laffon exchange icy stares. Boyer then joins Darrieux and, as snow softly falls, they take a horse-drawn sleigh to Boyer's hunting lodge at Mayerling. The couple knows that their future is hopeless, but they resolve to end their lives together. Darrieux asks that she die before he does, and, after their lovemaking, when she falls asleep, Boyer waits until near dawn (on January 30, 1889) and then shoots and kills her. His faithful servant, Dubosc, comes on the run when hearing the shot, but Boyer tells him it must have been a shot from a hunter in the woods nearby and sends him away. Boyer then lies down next to the lifeless Darrieux, a trickle of blood on her forehead, and then shoots himself. The camera shows Boyer's quivering hand as it reaches out and finally clutches Darrieux's lifeless hand, and this is where this powerful and poetically crafted film ends. Pantheon director Litvak helms this great film with infinite care in unfolding the tale of these star-crossed lovers and where the sensitive Boyer marvelously captures the personality of the tormented Rudolf and where the ravishingly beautiful Darrieux wholly captures the young woman who preferred to die with the man she loved rather than to have a long and loveless life. This exquisite film made international stars of Boyer and Darrieux. Although he had made several films in Hollywood, it was **Mayerling** that elevated Boyer to the status of one of the screen's great lovers and he was much sought by producers the world over to play similar roles and did, such as the equally ill-fated Pepe Le Moko in **Algiers**, 1938. *Author's Note*: Boyer told this author that "Rudolf did not own his own life until he met that beautiful young girl and then decided that life was worthless without her. She felt the same way. Rather than be separated, they chose to end their lives together. A great tragedy, but I do understand their mo-

Charles Boyer and Danielle Darrieux in *Mayerling*, 1937.

tives, all based on their love for one another. For those who do not understand what love can do then they cannot understand this story." Ironically, Boyer chose to end his life in a similar fashion, taking an overdose of barbiturates on August 26, 1978, after the death of his one and only beloved wife, Pat Paterson, who had died four days earlier. The true story of the thirty-one-year-old Rudolf and the seventeen-year-old Marie Vetsera is clouded. When Franz Joseph was informed of his son's death, the royal court first stated that Rudolf had died of an apoplectic attack. They then claimed that he had died of a heart attack when Rudolf had no history of heart ailments. The royal court covered up the death of Vetsera, and, it was reported that she was removed by Austrian soldiers from the hunting lodge so that she appeared to be walking between two burly officers and later riding between them in a carriage, as if she were alive, but her dead body held up by either a broomstick or a sword strapped to her back. She was quickly buried at a graveyard at a small chapel. When the true story of the joint suicides was revealed, the Austrian court insisted that Rudolf had lost his mental faculties when taking his life and that of Vetsera, in order that the Catholic Church (the predominant religion in Austria) allow the Crown Prince to be buried in hallowed ground. No one will ever know the truth of this strange and compelling love story which is best summed up in a memorably haunting line by Keats' "The Eve of St. Agnes": "And they are gone, aye ages long ago, these lovers fled away into the storm." (In French; English subtitles.) **p**, Seymour Nebenzal; **d**, Anatole Litvak; **cast**, Charles Boyer, Danielle Darrieux, Suzy Prim, Jean Dax, Gabrielle Dorziat, Nane Germon, Marthe Regnier, Yolande Laffon, Gina Manés, Jean-Louis Barrault; **w**, Marcel Achard, Joseph Kessel, Irma von Cube (based on the novel *Idyl's End* by Claude Anet); **c**, Armand Thirard; **m**, Arthur Honegger, Hans May; **ed**, Henri Rust; **art d**, Andrej Andrejew.

The Mayor of Hell ★★★ 1933; U.S.; 185m; WB; B/W; Crime Drama; Children: Unacceptable; **DVD**. Cagney is memorable while playing a wisecracking minor gangster with ties to those in high political places and who appoint him deputy inspector of the state reform school. He quickly sees that the warden, Digges, is a sadist, who orders his guards to mistreat the boys, beating them, and serving them bad food. While learning from Darro and other boys of the inhuman treatment they suffer, Cagney falls in love with the school's nurse, Evans. At her urging, he exposes Digges for not only his harsh treatment of the boys, but his pocketing state funds he has withheld from the funds allocated to the food supplied to the boys. Cagney winds up with the girl and makes sure that the institution is properly operated. This role was a turnabout for Cagney in that he is playing a good guy instead of the vicious gangster types he typified in early films of the 1930s. This film was remade as **Crime School**, 1938, with Humphrey Bogart in Cagney's role, which

Nelson Eddy and Jeanette MacDonald in *Maytime*, 1937.

proved to be an inferior production. *Author's Note*: This film was rushed into production, and the cast and crew worked many long hours (before working hour reforms went into place in Hollywood). Cagney complained about this to this author, saying: "That was another programmer where we worked from early in the morning until two or three the next morning. It wasn't unusual to see Archie [Mayo, the director] asleep in his chair. He was exhausted like the rest of us. They kept the pressure on us night and day to bring in those cheap programmers just so the front office could save more money. Everyone felt like an indentured servant." **p**, Lucien Hubbard, Edward Chodorov; **d**, Archie Mayo; **cast**, James Cagney, Madge Evans, Allen Jenkins, Frankie Darro, Dudley Digges, Arthur Byron, Sheila Terry, Robert Barrat, Harold Huber, Dorothy Peterson, Allen "Farina" Hoskins, Hobart Cavanaugh, Fred "Snowflake" Toones; **w**, Chodorov (based on the story "Reform School" by Islin Auster); **c**, Barney McGill; **m**, Leo F. Forbstein; **ed**, Jack Killifer; **art d**, Esdras Hartley.

Maytime ★★★★★ 1937; U.S.; 132m; MGM; B/W; Musical; Children: Acceptable; **DVD**; **VHS**. This wonderful musical is really an operetta that palatably mixes excellent classical music with enormously popular songs and where the MacDonald-Eddy duet (MacDonald's favorite) proves to be magically memorable. This grand tale begins in 1906 when MacDonald is an elderly woman who goes to a May Day celebration where she meets Brown, who tells her that his fiancée, Carver, yearns to have an important singing career. MacDonald then tells her own story which is shown in flashback as she recounts how, forty years earlier when Louis Napoleon ruled France, she, too, had the same ambitions and succeeded in becoming a celebrated opera star. He career is molded by her brilliant singing coach, Barrymore, and, after she sees success, he proposes marriage and MacDonald accepts, but only out of gratitude for what he has done for her. That night, MacDonald goes to the Left Bank and enters a bistro where a group of students is singing and led by Eddy, whose magnificent voice and personality attracts MacDonald. He is taken with her and asks her to dinner and later to a May Day celebration, although MacDonald questions why she is so involved with this young man after she has just accepted Barrymore's proposal. Though both have fallen deeply in love, MacDonald's conscience compels her to tell Eddy that she is about to be married and they go their separate ways, MacDonald becoming the singing toast of Europe and Eddy becoming a famous singer in America. MacDonald then goes to America on tour and is assigned to sing with Eddy in her first American appearance. She and Eddy have never stopped loving each other and they restart their romance, which had begun many years earlier. They agree that they should never again be separated and MacDonald goes to Barrymore, asking him for a divorce so that she can marry the only man she loves. Enraged, Barrymore goes to Eddy's home and shoots and kills him. Flash forward to 1906 where MacDonald concludes her bittersweet tale, telling Carver to abandon her notions of a professional career and devote herself to the only thing that counts in life, the love of a good man such as Brown. Carver, through the tragedy MacDonald has endured, realizes the wisdom of MacDonald's advice and puts aside her singing ambitions and accepts Brown's proposal. MacDonald, left alone in a garden where flower petals flutter gently to the ground, then dies, and her spirit leaves her body to join Eddy's spirit, which has been waiting for her and they reprise one of the wonderful songs in this evergreen and effervescent musical, "Will You Remember (Sweetheart)?" (Rida Johnson Young and Sigmund Romberg). Leonard directs this wonderful musical in a painterly fashion, carefully developing his characters while infusing the musical numbers seamlessly into the superlative story line and where all of its sets and costuming are sumptuous and stunning. MacDonald and Eddy were never in better voices, and Barrymore is riveting as the dominating voice coach who transforms from avuncular friend to possessive and murderous husband. Other songs include: "Now Is the Month of Maying" (traditional with lyrics by Thomas Morley); "Plantons da Vigne" (traditional); "Santa Lucia" (traditional); "Ham and Eggs," "Vivre l'Opera," "Street Singer" (music: Herbert Stothart; lyrics: Robert "Bob" Wright, George "Chet" Forrest); "Student Drinking Song" (Herbert Stothart); "Reverie" (based on Sigmund Romberg airs); "Jump Jim Crow,' "Road to Paradise," "Dancing Will Keep You Young" (Sigmund Romberg, Rida Johnson Young, Cyrus Wood); "Carry Me Back to Old Virginny" (James Allen Bland); "Czaritza" (a bogus opera based on Symphony No. 5 by Peter Ilyich Tchaikovsky with French lyrics by Giles Guilbert); "Les filles de Cadix" (Leo Delibes); "Page's Aria" (from "Les Huguenots" by Giacomo Mayerbeer); "Le Regiment de Sambre et Meuse" (Robert Planquette); "Chi Me Frena" (from "Lucia di Lammermoor" by Gaetano Donizetti); "Nobles seigneur salut," "Une dame, noble et sage" (Gioaechino Mayerbeer, Eugene Scribe); "William Tell," (Gioaechino Antonio Rossini); 'Largo Al Factotum' (from "The Barber of Seville" by Giacchino Antonio Rossini); "Faust" (Charles Gounod); "Tannhauser," "Tristan und Isolde" (Richard Wagner); "Caro Nome," "Anvil Chorus," "Miserere" (from "Il Trovatore" by Giuseppe Verdi); "La Donna E Mobile" (from "Rigoletto" by Giuseppe Verdi); "Sempre Libera" (from "La Traviata" by Giuseppe Verdi); "Sumer Is Icumen In" (traditional since medieval days); "Mazurka" (traditional Polish folk dance); "Napoleonic Waltz" (traditional); "The Last Rose of Summer" (traditional); 'The Sidewalks of New York" (1894; music: Charles B. Lawlor; lyrics: James W. Blake); and 'Columbia; Gem of the Ocean" (1843; Thomas á Becket). *Author's Note*: The original musical stage production of 1917 was so popular that it ran simultaneously in two separate theaters to capacitate the overwhelming crowds. That production was based upon a 1914 German play titled "Wei Einst Im Mai." Movie mogul B. P. Schulberg produced the story as a silent film, **Maytime**, 1923, even though it offered no soundtrack and music. The silent film starred Ethel Shannon and Harrison Ford, who is not related to the present superstar and, in fact, was age ten when the original Harrison Ford retired from the screen. MGM put the talkie version of **Maytime** into production in the early 1930s, with its production chief Irving Thalberg in charge and with Edmund Goulding as the director and where part of the lavish production was shot in Technicolor. Thalberg, however, died and the film was halted. Frank Morgan and Paul Lukas, who were part of the original production, were committed elsewhere when production resumed under Leonard's direction. Barrymore was brought in to replace Lukas and Bing replaced Morgan. The expensive Technicolor footage was destroyed and the film reshot in black and white with MacDonald and Eddy in the leading roles, their third appearance together on screen in a total of eight films they would make together. The film was extremely expensive for those days, its budget going over $1.5 million (but this most likely included the cost of the scrapped Technicolor footage), albeit the film's popularity at the box office returned five times that amount to the MGM coffers in its initial release, making **Maytime** one of the top moneymakers in the 1930s and established MacDonald and Eddy as the foremost singing duets in filmdom. They would reprise their roles from this delightful musical when appearing on the "Lux Radio Theater" in September 1944. Music fans should know that "Czaritza," which was written from Tchaikovsky's music, is really a bogus opera, with special lyrics written by French lyricist Giles Guilbert, much the same way Orson Welles presented a bogus opera, "Salambo," in **Citizen Kane**, 1941, horribly warbled by Dorothy Comingore, a would-be diva. The first time a bogus opera was presented on film occurred when "Carnival" was presented in **Charlie Chan at the Opera**, 1936. **p**, Hunt Stromberg, Robert Z. Leonard; **d**, Leonard; **cast**, Jeanette MacDonald, Nelson Eddy, John Barrymore, Tom Brown, Lynne Carver, Herman Bing, Rafaela Ottiano, Sig Ruman, Walter Kingsford, Harry Davenport, Billy Gilbert, Helen Parrish, Christian Rub, Bobs Watson, Don Cossack Chorus; **w**, Noel Langley, Claudine West (based on the operetta by Rida Johnson Young, Sigmund Romberg); **c**, Oliver T. Marsh; **m**, Romberg, Herbert Stothart; **ed**, Conrad A. Nervig; **art d**, Cedric Gibbons.

McCabe & Mrs. Miller ★★★ 1971; U.S.; 120m; WB; Color; Western; Children: Unacceptable (MPAA: R); **DVD**; **VHS**. In the Pacific Northwest in the early 1900s, a not-too-bright gambler named McCabe (Beatty) teams up with sophisticated Mrs. Miller (Christie), an Englishwoman who makes her living as a prostitute, to become partners running a whorehouse-tavern in a small remote town in a zinc mining territory. Their establishment does good business and they fall in love. All goes well until Auberjonois and Devane, representatives of a large zinc mining corporation, want to buy them out and also all the local mines. Beatty thinks their offer is too low, but Christie says they should take it because they might be shot if they refuse. When the stubborn Beatty stalls on the deal, three hired guns come to settle the deal and Beatty, who has pretended to be a gunfighter, actually shoots two of them dead. Beatty is mortally wounded in a showdown with the remaining gunman, but manages to kill him with a derringer. Beatty dies in the snow and Christie takes up her favorite addiction by going to a Chinese opium den. This far-off-the-beaten track western is awkward in every respect, from its erratic hand-held camera shots to the immature and often offensive dialog, but its crudeness and total unprofessional approach, either through accident or by intention, wholly captures the fumbling inhabitants of a remote, hardscrabble community, exposing in very realistic terms its brutality and savageness. This is a typical Altman film, having a disorganized look and meandering cameras where all is grim and survival brought about only through accident, an Altman hallmark. As usual, his characters invade each other's lines, many speaking all at once so that the viewer is most often confused. Altman purposely injected this consistent annoyance into his productions almost as if he were contemptuous of the viewer (his nature was decidedly dour and cynical). Altman never prepared his cast members or crew members for his shots, going to the set each day to, more or less, "see what would happen." Most of what happened was not productive or pleasant. Altman was expensively tolerated by Hollywood as he enacted the role of the *enfant terrible*, but that image wore so thin that, toward the end of his career, few in Hollywood wanted to work with him. This film was promoted into a cult classic by the druggies of the 1970s, mostly due to Christie's random use of drugs. Altman was a user of marijuana through most of his adult life. Excessive violence and sexuality prohibit viewing by children. **p**, David Foster, Mitchell Brower; **d**, Robert Altman; **cast**, Warren Beatty, Julie Christie, Rene Auberjonois, William Devane, John Schuck, Shelley Duvall, Keith Carradine, Corey Fischer, Bert Remsen, Michael Murphy, Antony Holland; **w**, Altman, Brian McKay (based on the novel *McCabe* by Edmund Naughton); **c**, Vilmos Zsigmond (Panavision; Technicolor); **ed**, Louis Lombardo; **prod d**, Leon Ericksen; **art d**, Al Locatelli, Philip Thomas; **spec eff**, Marcel Vercoutere, Paul Neanover.

Alan Ladd and Frank Faylen in *The McConnell Story*, 1955.

The McConnell Story ★★★ 1955; U.S.; 106m; WB; Color; Biographical Drama; Children: Acceptable; **DVD**; **VHS**. Ladd is outstanding in his resolute essay of American Air Force hero Joseph McConnell Jr. (1922-1954). This fascinating story begins with Ladd as a private in the U.S. Army during the early days of WWII. He is assigned to medical duty, but his real ambition is to be a fighter pilot so he takes private flying lessons on the side in order to qualify. He meets and falls in love with Allyson and they get married and then take up residence at a Texas army base. Ladd is then ordered to Washington for pilot training and Allyson, pregnant, returns to her Massachusetts home to give birth to their daughter. Meanwhile, Ladd becomes a navigator assigned to a bomber and serves in that capacity until the war ends. Ladd stays in the service, and when he learns that old pal Whitmore is now heading a new U.S. Air Force program developing jet fighter planes, he becomes a member of Whitmore's team. He and Allyson have two more children, moving from base to base, until they settle in Apple Valley, California. When the Korean War breaks out, Ladd volunteers for duty as a jet fighter pilot and he sees considerable action, becoming America's top ace by destroying or downing sixteen MiG-15 Soviet-made fighter jets while flying his F-86 Sabre Jet (a record never broken by any other jet fighter pilot). He is given the Silver Star and the Distinguished Service Cross for his aerial combat achievements and then ordered stateside. Although Ladd repeatedly begs his superiors to return him to combat duty, they refuse, saying that he is, as America's top ace, too important to lose in the Korean War. He becomes a test pilot, refusing to ground himself as Allyson begs him to do. None of her tearful pleadings (and no one could plead more tearfully than June Allyson) can change his mind, so she resigns herself to seeing Ladd once more risk his life by testing new warplanes. Finally, he takes to the air to test a plane and it crashes, killing him. Though unabashedly patriotic, this film is well crafted and expertly directed by Douglas (particularly his aerial combat scenes), and Ladd, Allyson, Whitmore and the rest of the cast are standouts in their roles. **p**, Henry Blanke; **d**, Gordon Douglas; **cast**, Alan Ladd, June Allyson, James Whitmore, Frank Faylen, Robert Ellis, Murray Alper, John Alvin, Perry Lopez, Gene Reynolds, Dub Taylor; **w**, Ted Sherdeman, Sam Rolfe (based on a story by Sherdeman); **c**, John F. Seitz (Warnercolor); **m**, Max Steiner; **ed**, Owen Marks; **art d**, John Beckman; **set d**, William L. Kuehl.

The McKenzie Break ★★★ 1970; U.K.; 106m; Levy-Gardner/UA; Color; War Drama; Children: Unacceptable; **DVD**; **VHS**. Tension-filled thriller sees German naval officer Griem, who commands hundreds of German POWs, attempting to outwit an equally savvy prisoner camp commander, Keith, in planning and executing an en masse prison escape in Scotland during WWII. POWs riot and Keith orders his guards

Harvey Keitel in *Mean Streets*, 1973.

to break up their formations with high-pressed water hoses, believing the riot is simply a ruse to disguise a planned escape. One of the prisoners, Janson, a homosexual who has been made a pariah among the POWs, is found unconscious, so severely beaten up that his life hangs in the balance. He mutters something about an escape to Keith, but he is later silenced forever when one of the German POWs gets into the infirmary and strangles Janson to death, this execution ordered by ruthless Griem, a U-boat captain. Keith then bides his time, believing that Griem and others are planning to escape and get to the coast where a German submarine will pick them up. He more or less allows Griem and his most diehard followers to escape at the risk of facing military discipline on charges of negligence. (Keith, an unorthodox Irish captain, has already replaced the regular camp commander, Hendry, a major, and deep conflict exists between them as to how to manage the camp.) Griem and others make good their escape, but Keith and his men doggedly track them down to the coast, capturing or killing one after another. Griem manages to get into a small raft with some of his men and begins rowing toward a German submarine, having arranged a rendezvous with the U-boat. Keith, however, calls in some British warplanes that dive-bomb the submarine, sinking it, leaving Griem with no option but to return to shore and imprisonment. Keith has won their deadly cat-and-mouse game, but at a considerable loss of life on both sides. **p**, Jules Levy, Arthur Gardner; **d**, Lamont Johnson; **cast**, Brian Keith, Helmut Griem, Ian Hendry, Alexander Allerson, John Abineri, Costantin De Goguel, Gregg Palmer, Michael Sheard, Ingo Mogendorf, Barry Cassin; **w**, William Norton (based on the novel *The Bowmanville Break* by Sidney Shelley); **c**, Michael Reed (DeLuxe Color); **m**, Riz Ortolani; **ed**, Tom Rolf; **prod d**, Frank White; **set d**, Keith Liddiard; **spec eff**, Nobby Clark.

Me and Orson Welles ★★★ 2009; U.K./U.S.; 114m; CinemaNX; Freestyle Releasing; Color; Drama; Children: Unacceptable (MPAA: PG-13); **DVD**. An offbeat but compelling drama that uses the famous Orson Welles as a fictionalized character sees Efron, a high school student who thinks to become a professional actor, meeting attractive Kazan in a music store in NYC in 1937. She tells Efron that she is an aspiring playwright and they discuss their mutual ambitions as they become friends. A short time later, Efron finds himself quite by accident at the theater where Orson Welles is rehearsing his Mercury Players for a modern-day version of "Julius Caesar," one with an anti-fascist flavor. Welles, played by McKay, impulsively (or whimsically) asks Efron to test for a part, and then offers him the role of Lucius in the play and Efron accepts. While rehearsing, Efron finds that production assistant Danes is attracted to him and that the entire cast and crew are promiscuous, with McKay sleeping with one of his actresses, although he is

married and his wife at that time is pregnant. As opening night approaches, McKay tells Efron that he fears that the play will fail because he has had nothing but good luck so far and that bad luck is bound to arrive. In a final rehearsal, Efron accidentally sets off the sprinkler system and the entire theater is soaked. McKay accuses Efron of causing this catastrophe, but Efron tells McKay that it was simply the bad luck McKay had been expected, and the mercurial director accepts that reason for the mishap and then suggests that, to break the tension before opening night, all the players take strange partners to bed; McKay beds down with Danes, which angers Efron, who confronts McKay and reminds him that he has betrayed his pregnant wife. McKay explodes and fires him. They later reconcile and the play goes on to see a huge success. McKay then takes Efron aside and fires him again, saying he only wanted him for the premiere and now that Efron's job is done, there is no longer any need for him. The dejected Efron departs, but his spirits soar when he again meets with Kazan, and a romance blossoms between them. It's a little story, but well told and with standout performances from all, but one must ask how alluring this story would be without the use (or misuse) of the magnetic character of the great Orson Welles. A well-made-for-TV film, **RKO 281**, 1999, profiles Welles while he was making **Citizen Kane**, 1941, and offers a riveting portrayal of the genius filmmaker by Liev Schreiber. **p**, Richard Linklater, Ann Carli, Marc Samuelson, Vince Palmo, Holly Gent Palmo, Andrew Fingret, **d**, Linklater; **cast**, Zac Efron, Claire Danes, Christian McKay, Patrick Kennedy, James Tupper, Garrick Hagon, Zoe Kazan, Megan Maczko, Simon Lee Phillips, Thomas Arnold, Simon Nehan, Eddie Marsan; **w**, Vince Palmo, Holly Gent Palmo (based on the novel by Robert Kaplow); **c**, Dick Pope; **ed**, Sandra Adair; **prod d**, Laurence Dorman; **art d**, Bill Crutcher, David Doran, Stuart Rose; **set d**, Richard Roberts; **spec eff**, Neal Champion, Rob Duncan.

Mean Streets ★★★★ 1973; U.S.; 112m; Scorsese Productions/WB; Color; Crime Drama; Children: Unacceptable (MPAA: R); **DVD**; **VHS**. Realistic and often brutal, director Scorsese shows for the first time the lifestyles of young ambitious Italian hoodlums living in NYC's Little Italy, an area north of Canal Street from Chinatown, and up and down the mean streets where they survive. Keitel and De Niro are involved in several petty rackets with Keitel being the dandy, priding himself on his custom-made shirts and well-tailored suits. He lives with his family (this being an Italian tradition in that young men do not leave their family homes until married), and hangs out with other young men also in their twenties in Proval's seedy saloon. Robinson is his girl, but, because she is epileptic, he keeps his relationship with her a secret. De Niro is Robinson's unpredictable cousin, not too bright and a hothead. He easily provokes other hoodlums by his taunting juvenile antics and arrogant behavior, and Keitel is forever getting him out of trouble. De Niro is habitually broke, borrowing money from urbane but lethal loan shark Romanus, and is far behind in the "vigorish" (interest) owed to him; Romanus, when making his rounds to all the night spots in Little Italy, no longer politely reminds De Niro to pay out, but has become outwardly threatening. When Northup returns from Vietnam, Keitel and friends give him a welcome home party, but, disturbed by his wartime experiences, he breaks up the reunion. Meanwhile, Walden, a Jewish girl, enters Proval's bar with her boyfriend, and the boys, all anti-Semitic, insult her and then beat up her boyfriend, but all of this is oblivious to David Carradine, who has gotten drunk and has fallen asleep at the bar. Romanus then arrives and demands money from De Niro, who publicly insults him and now Keitel knows that Romanus has marked De Niro for serious injury if not death and plans to take his friend to a place where no one will look for him—Brooklyn. De Niro wants no part of that, begging Keitel to introduce him to his uncle, Danova, a powerful Mafia leader, so that he can order Romanus to leave him alone and even give him work, but that is the last thing Keitel wants to do, knowing that Danova wants no part of the petty problems of his nephew. He insists that De Niro accompany him to Brooklyn where he will be safe, and they borrow Proval's car. Robinson joins Keitel and De Niro and they drive toward Brooklyn. Unknown to them, Romanus is trailing them in another car with two gunmen. Once Keitel drives into Brooklyn he feels a sense of relief. Romanus and his killers, who are driving behind them, open fire, causing the car to crash. The stunned Keitel looks about him. He is bleeding. Robinson may be dead and so, too, may be De Niro. The viewer never learns their true fates, and that is where this traumatic and disturbing film ends. Scorsese provides a series of scenes rather than a cohesive story line, but, in the process, brilliantly exhibits the characters of these two-bit punks, who are leagues below the lofty Corleones and worlds apart from the hard-working Italians living in the Bronx and profiled in **Marty**, 1955, of a generation earlier. This may be his finest film, although **Raging Bull**, 1980, is most likely Scorsese's most significant contribution. Almost two decades later, he would direct **Goodfellas**, 1990, which deals with the next echelon of Italian criminals, working with the Mafia and where Joe Pesci, a surrogate and maniacally violent replacement for the ambitious Keitel in this story, aspires to become a member of that "family." Keitel, DeNiro, Romanus and Robinson are outstanding in their roles, effectively conveying a communal image of people doomed to live out unpromising lives without ever going beyond the limits of Little Italy. Scorsese focuses upon Keitel and shows all of his many habits and nuances. Keitel acknowledges religious symbols and believes himself to be saintly, far superior to his Little Italy contemporaries, an image he must cling to in order to convince himself that he is not leading a useless life, but he nevertheless, like the compatriots he often sneers at, gets drunk, womanizes, and sadistically enjoys beating up others. *Author's Note*: Scorsese had a free hand with this film, one of the few where he did exactly as he wanted, but he was constrained to work with a small budget, less than $600,000, and much of that was deferred. He had less than two weeks of rehearsal before his six days of actual shooting on location in New York. To save money, he shot the rest of the film in California. Gutter language and excessive violence prohibit viewing by children. **p**, Jonathan T. Taplin; **d**, Martin Scorsese; **cast**, Harvey Keitel, Robert De Niro, Amy Robinson, David Proval, Richard Romanus, Cesare Danova, Vic Argo, George Memmoli, Lenny Scaletta, Jeannie Bell, David Carradine, Robert Carradine, Catherine Scorsese, Martin Scorsese; **w**, Scorsese, Mardik Martin (based on a story by Scorsese); **c**, Kent Wakeford (Technicolor); **ed**, Sid Levin; **spec eff**, Bill Bales.

The Medium ★★★ 1951; Italy/U.S.; 84m.; Transfilm/Lopert Pictures Corp.; B/W; Opera; Children: Unacceptable; **DVD**. Intriguing opera has Powers as a deceptive woman, who conducts séances with the help of a young girl, Alberghetti, and a mute boy, Coleman, who manipulates settings behind curtains. During one séance, Powers feels a hand clutching her throat and thinks a supernatural presence is attacking her, but blames Coleman and throws him out of the house during a rainstorm. Coleman sneaks back into the house to see Alberghetti whom he loves. Powers sees something moving behind a curtain and asks who is there, fearing it is the spirit. When she gets no reply, she fires a gun, killing the boy, who was hiding there. This is a film adaptation of Italian opera composer Gian Carlo Menotti's first international stage success. (Sung in Italian; English subtitles.) Violence prohibits viewing by children. **p**, Walther Lowendahl; **d&w**, Gian Carlo Menotti; **cast**, Marie Powers, Anna Maria Alberghetti, Leo Coleman, Belva Kibler, Beverly Dame, Donald Morgan; **c**, Enzo Serafin; **m**, Menotti; **ed**, Alexander Hammid; **art d**, Georges Wakhévitch.

Medium Cool ★★★ 1969; U.S.; 111m; PAR; Color; Drama; Children: Unacceptable (MPAA: R); **DVD**; **VHS**. Cinematographer turned director Wexler, a native Chicagoan, presents a chilling docudrama of people and events involved with the violent protests and riots occurring in the Windy City during the Democratic Convention from August 26-29, 1968. Almost everybody in this cynical film is uncaring and without human sensitivities, especially Forster, a ruthlessly ambitious news cam-

Robert Forster in *Medium Cool*, 1969.

eraman working for one of the network affiliates in Chicago. He is first seen with his camera assistant Bonerz, both showing their calloused natures when they come upon a car accident and routinely film the wreck and its injured occupants *before* calling an ambulance. Next, Forster encounters McCoy, a black cab driver, who has found several thousand dollars in the back seat of his taxi, apparently left by his last customer. When Forster urges him to turn in the cash so he can make a good story out of the discovery, McCoy refuses and he and his black militant friends then so threaten Forster and Bonerz that the cameramen beat a hasty retreat. (This scene is based upon a real incident where a Chicago cab driver actually did find such a sum and turned in the money; Wexler originally thought to make a separate film out of this incident, but wound up working it into the fragile story line of this film.) Forster then sees a boy, Blankenship, near his car and, believing he is trying to break into his auto, chases him, only to find that the boy has not been attempting to steal anything and has dropped a box containing his pet pigeon. He follows Blankenship to his home, a run-down place in a poor neighborhood where Forster meets his single mother, Bloom, who has moved from West Virginia with her son to seek work, but has found none. Meanwhile, the city is awash with tens of thousands of anti-war protestors pouring into Chicago from many states to disrupt the 1968 Democratic Convention being held at that time and police and protestors are meeting in violent clashes everywhere, these bloody confrontations based upon the then widespread protestations against the Vietnam War. (Wexler inserts considerable documentary footage about that social upheaval that took place a year before this film's release.) Forster begins shooting many of these violent encounters, but when he later learns that his footage has been turned over to the FBI (ostensibly so that Bureau agents can identify the rabble-rousing protestors for later arrest and trial), he gives his boss a piece of his mind and is fired on the spot. Forster, now with time on his hands, begins visiting Bloom and Blankenship as he has become infatuated with Bloom and now ignores his girlfriend, Hill. When the Convention is about to convene, Forster gets a freelance job to shoot the event while he continues to court Bloom. After Blankenship sees Forster in an intimate situation with his mother, Bloom, he becomes disturbed and runs away. Bloom frantically searches for him and Forster later finds her at night at Grant Park where most of the violence is occurring, protestors attacking police formations and the police firing tear gas bombs and cracking heads with their batons. Forster shepherds Bloom from the chaos while they search for Blankenship, who has by this time gone home. While driving about and searching for Blankenship, the street commotion distracts Forster, who runs his car into a tree and Bloom is killed and he is injured. He looks about for some help, and a driver stops his car, sees the accident as a photo op to sell to one of the TV stations, videotapes the accident and,

Frank Sinatra and Shelley Winters in *Meet Danny Wilson*, 1952.

without giving any assistance, drives off, emulating the same callous attitude Forster displayed at the beginning of this film, and that is where this grim film ends. Well crafted and photographed with a lot of tricky shots, including Wexler's trademarked hand-held camera shots (which, when overdone, can be visually annoying), the director takes a side here, depicting the protestors as the victims during that upheaval. The acting is superior but the story line or theme (such as it is) often sinks to blatant anti-government propaganda. *Author's Note*: This author was the editor-in-chief of *ChicagoLand Magazine* at the time of the political clashes at the 1968 Democratic Convention and witnessed what was later termed "a police riot" where police impulsively attacked anyone they thought to be a protestor in the lakeside Lincoln and Grant parks, as well as on the streets of Chicago. At the same time, this author witnessed dozens of out-of-town radicals organizing otherwise innocent high school and college students into contingents or groups that threw rocks and Molotov cocktails at the police. I saw firsthand NYC radical Abby Hoffman (1936-1989) hand out razor blades to teenagers, along with tape, showing them how to affix those razor blades to the tips of their shoes and then how to kick police (and later National Guardsmen) in the shins with these vicious weapons to draw blood. (Hoffman and others, known alternately as the "Chicago Eight" or the "Chicago Seven," were later tried and convicted of inciting to riot, a conviction overturned on appeal.) At one point during the Convention, I stood at the entrance of the Conrad Hilton Hotel on Michigan Avenue and across from Grant Park, the besieged headquarters of the 1968 Democratic Convention. The entrance was protected by dense lines of National Guardsmen holding rifles (no bullets were issued, according to one of those Guardsmen, who worked as one of my assistant editors). Outside those lines of National Guardsmen were thousands of screaming, howling protestors hurling stones and other objects at the troops and at everyone at the guarded entranceway, including author Norman Mailer (1923-2007), Mike Wallace (1918-2012) of "Sixty Minutes" fame, and two Chicago Pulitzer Prize–winning columnists, Mike Royko (1932-1997) and Tom Fitzpatrick (1927-2002). "First it's the cops attacking protestors, now it is armed troops," said Mailer. "We're turning into a fascist state!" At that moment, a beer can sailed over the heads of the National Guardsman and struck Wallace on the forehead, causing a slight gash and a trickle of blood. Wallace coolly withdrew a neatly folded handkerchief and dabbed the blood away. He picked up the empty, crushed can and said: "You would think that if they were going to throw beer at us, they might be considerate enough to make them full cans so that we would have something to drink." Mailer stayed with his propaganda: "Looking at these troops oppressing innocent citizens makes me sick to my stomach." Royko said: "Norman, those punks are no more innocent than the anarchists that bombed Chicago a century ago. You don't know what

you're talking about." In what was a rare occasion, Fitzpatrick agreed with Royko, adding: "You see this bump on my head, Norman? I got this late today when I tried to interview some of those innocent protestors. Before I could open my mouth, one of them hit me in the head with a rock. If you think these birds are so harmless, try and talk to them. They came here for blood and they got it. I don't think you've got the guts to step through the lines of those troops and try to reason with that mob." Mailer glared at Fitzpatrick and then fell silent. We all stood there silent and helpless, all of us the victims of organized anarchy on both sides of that conflict. The title for this film is taken (or altered) from a comment about media analyst Marshall McLuhan, who described television as the "cool medium" and where art imitates life, or Haskell Wexler's version of it. **p**, Jerrold and Haskell Wexler, Tully Friedman; **d&w**, Haskell Wexler (based on the novel *The Concrete Wilderness* by Jack Couffer); **cast**, Robert Forster, Verna Bloom, Peter Bonerz, Marianna Hill, Harold Blankenship, Charles Geary, Sid McCoy, Christine Bergstrom, William Sickingen, Peter Boyle; **c**, Haskell Wexler (Technicolor); **m**, Mike Bloomfield; **ed**, Verna Fields; **art d**, Leon Erickson.

Meet Boston Blackie ★★★ 1941; U.S.; 61m; COL; B/W; Crime Drama; Children: Unacceptable. This is one of the best in the first of a series of fourteen films with Morris as Boston Blackie, an ex-convict who becomes a private investigator. He is aboard a luxury liner returning to the U.S. from a trip to Europe when he finds a dead body in his cabin. Police accuse him of murder and he is compelled to find the real killer and clear himself. Morris discovers that a spy ring is behind the murder, and it operates with the cover of being an ocean-going carnival. Lots of twists, turns and action pepper this superior whodunit. Violence prohibits viewing by children. **p**, Ralph Cohn; **d**, Robert Florey; **cast**, Chester Morris, Rochelle Hudson, Richard Lane, Charles Wagenheim, Constance Worth, Jack O'Malley, George Magrill, Michael Rand, Harry Anderson, Walter Sande; **w**, Jay Dratler (based on his story and characters created by Jack Boyle); **c**, Franz F. Planer; **m**, Michael J. Lewis; **ed**, James Sweeney.

Meet Danny Wilson ★★★ 1952; U.S.; 86m; UNIV; B/W; Drama; Children: Unacceptable; **DVD**; **VHS**. Sinatra plays a hot-tempered singer (when was he not?), who, with pal pianist, Nicol, meets a singer, Winters. Sinatra punches a cop and is thrown in jail, but Winters arranges his bail and gets him a job where she sings at mobster Burr's Chicago nightclub. It doesn't set well with Sinatra that Burr not only demands fifty percent of his earnings, but takes the same cut from Winters, too. Meanwhile, the cops are watching Burr closely because he's a suspect in a murder case. Winters falls for Nicol, and, while Sinatra is drunk, he catches his pal and Winters together. Burr appears and, in a shoving match, Sinatra punches him. Burr pulls a gun aimed at Sinatra but Nicol takes the bullet intended for him. Cops follow Sinatra to Chicago's Wrigley Field baseball park where he shoots and kills Burr. Violence prohibits viewing by children. *Author's Note*: Look for brief appearances from future stars Tony Curtis and Jeff Chandler. The film was made during Sinatra's career slump after being a bobby-sox idol and before scoring big in **From Here to Eternity**, 1953. Not one of Sinatra's best, but the film sustains interest as his wonderful voice is in top form and he sings a lot of great songs: "You're a Sweetheart" (Jimmy McHugh, Harold Adamson); "Lonesome Man Blues" (Sy Oliver); "She's Funny That Way" (Neil Moret, Richard A. Whiting); "A Good Man Is Hard to Find" (Eddie Green); "That Old Black Magic" (Harold Arlen, Johnny Mercer); "When You're Smiling" (Mark Fisher, Joe Goodwin, Larry Shay); "All of Me" (Gerald Marks, Seymour Simons); "I've Got a Crush on You" (George Gershwin, Ira Gershwin); "How Deep Is the Ocean?" (Irving Berlin). **p**, Leonard Goldstein; **d**, Joseph Pevney; **cast**, Frank Sinatra, Shelley Winters, Alex Nicol, Raymond Burr, Vaughn Taylor, Tommy Farrell, Donald MacBride, Barbara Knudson, Carl Sklover, Jeff Chandler, Tony Curtis, Jack Kruschen, Gregg Palmer; **w**, Don McGuire (based on his story); **c**, Maury Gertsman; **m**, Joseph Gershenson; **ed**, Virgil W. Vogel; **art d**,

Bernard Herzbrun, Nathan Juran; **set d**, Russell A. Gausman, Julia Heron; **spec eff**, David S. Horsley.

Meet John Doe ★★★★★ 1941; U.S.; 122m; Frank Capra Productions/WB; B/W; Drama; Children: Cautionary; **DVD**; **VHS**. This is one of Capra's greatest "feel good" films, where optimism, sentiment, and good will triumphs over defeatism and hatred. It's a simple story, one where the heart makes all the moves and they are the right ones. It opens with the feisty Stanwyck working hard as a newspaper writer. She is fired when hard-nosed Gleason becomes the new managing editor of her newspaper and she retaliates by writing her final column, one where she quotes from a letter she has received from an indignant reader about the social conditions of the day. She has, however, invented this idealistic man, naming him "John Doe," and profiling him as a legendary man on a white horse who has appeared out of nowhere to condemn the ruthlessness and corruption heaped upon the honest people of America by greedy tycoons. (Her socialist-like rant is not unlike the FDR "New Deal" of the day that advocated and fought for the common worker while obliquely condemned America's captains of industry.) To drive his point home, the mythical John Doe of Stanwyck's tale states that, as a form of protest against the iniquities of the world, he plans to leap from the top of City Hall on Christmas Eve. Gleason runs the story and the public response is so empathetically enormous that the paper is inundated with countless requests for more information on this mythical person. Gleason demands that Stanwyck turn over the letter she has received from this man. The cornered Stanwyck confesses that she created "John Doe" out of whole cloth, but, to keep her job, she urges Gleason to help her find a man from the great army of American unemployed and present him to the public as the real John Doe in order to sell more newspapers. The hardboiled Gleason is at first reluctant, but, when a rival newspaper calls Stanwyck's story a hoax and that no such man exists, Gleason must now save the paper's reputation by going ahead with the story. He orders Stanwyck to find some hobo and pass him off as the visionary and quixotic John Doe. She finds that very man in Cooper, a broken-down baseball player, who has been riding the rails with fellow hobo Brennan. (These happy-go-lucky drifters first appear in a delightful scene where they play a duet on a harmonica and an ocarina.) Cooper has been a fairly good baseball pitcher until his arm was injured. He agrees to play the role of John Doe on the proviso that money he receives for his impersonation will be used for an operation to fix his arm so that he can return to baseball. Meanwhile, he and Brennan are put up in a fancy hotel suite and these hungry hobos eat just about everything room service can provide while Stanwyck orders a whole new wardrobe for Cooper, including tailored suits. Cooper and Brennan have decided to go along with this charade, but believe that it's nothing more than public relations baloney. Cooper makes a few public appearances while Stanwyck continues to churn out columns on his behalf, ostensibly quoting his platitudes and good will generalities. Even though the public cannot get enough of this man, Gleason feels that the story has been milked enough and wants to end the newspaper stories about John Doe. The ambitious Stanwyck, however, goes to the newspaper's publisher, Arnold, who is the very ruthless magnate she has been condemning, telling Arnold that "If he [John Doe] made a hit around here, he could do it every place else in the country. And you'd be pulling the strings!" Arnold salivates at the idea of using Cooper as a way of molding political opinion to back up his myriad enterprises, and to further enrich his holdings, although he is so wealthy and his estates so far flung that he has his own private police force to protect his fiefdom. Arnold sees Cooper as a national hero who will champion Arnold's causes and espouse Arnold's beliefs, and now intends to use him as a manipulative stooge by which he can attain the White House. Arnold throws all of his influence and media connections—he owns most of the newspapers and radio stations in the state, along with the local politicians being in his hip pocket—into a campaign to establish a national John Doe movement. Cooper, naïve and innocent, is along for a free ride and begins

Barbara Stanwyck, Gary Cooper and James Gleason in *Meet John Doe*, **1941.**

making public speeches written by Stanwyck and to which he adds his own home-spun philosophy and where he pleads for common sense and universal understanding, his prosaically stated generalities aimed at establishing an American Utopia. In one speech, Cooper announces over Arnold's controlled airways: "To most of you, your neighbor is a stranger, a guy with a barking dog and a fence around him. Now, you can't be a stranger to any guy who is on your home team. So tear down the fence that separates you…You'll tear down a lot of hates and prejudices…I know a lot of you are saying to yourself: 'He's asking for a miracle.' Well, you're wrong. It's no miracle. I see it happen once every year…at Christmastime. Why can't that spirit last the whole year round? Gosh, if it ever did, we'd develop such a strength that no human force could stand against us." The public response is almost universally positive and he becomes a great champion for human rights. John Doe Clubs spring up everywhere with the purpose of neighbors helping neighbors and friends assisting friends and where "good will toward man" becomes a grassroots prairie fire. Typical is one John Doe Club, its members going to see Cooper and where Toomey, who works at a soda fountain, and his wife, Doran, tell Cooper that they were so inspired by his speeches that they made an effort to befriend their long-standing neighborhood grouch, MacDonald, whom they have always called "sourpuss" and who has never responded to their greetings, only to discover that his unresponsiveness was based on his poor hearing and how, once they became friends, they established their John Doe Club. Cooper is astounded and so inspired by these fine people that he agrees to Stanwyck's proposal that he stump the country in expanding the John Doe movement, which is exactly what the scheming Arnold desires. As the movement gains tremendous momentum, Arnold plans for a national convention where he will use Cooper and that convention as his political launching pad for the presidency, believing that he will have "ninety percent of the voters" of America in his pocket through the John Doe Clubs. Gleason, though a tough newspaperman, is nevertheless an honest man, and, when he learns of Arnold's scheme, he gets sloppy drunk and then tells Cooper how Arnold plans to use him to wrest control of the John Doe movement for his own political ends. Cooper, enraged, goes to Arnold's estate, barging into his mansion and where he finds Arnold and Stanwyck conferring with other bigwigs. Cooper confronts the tycoon, saying to Arnold: "I'm going down to that convention and I am going to tell those people exactly what you and your fine-feathered friends are cooking up for them." Arnold tells Cooper that if he is so foolish to make such statements, he will brand him a fraud and dismantle the John Doe movement, a movement that he himself has created. "If you can't control it [the movement], you'll kill it!" Cooper says before he knocks one of Arnold's henchmen cold while defying Arnold to try to stop the John Doe movement before departing. Cooper then appears

Cyd Charisse, Vic Damone, and Debbie Reynolds in *Meet Me in Las Vegas,* **1956.**

at a mammoth outdoor convention during a rainstorm, but when he mounts the platform and goes to the podium and speaks through microphones to warn his followers about Arnold, goons seize him and silence him while Arnold tells the crowd that Cooper is not only a phony who never wrote the original letter to his newspaper, but has stolen all the donations gathered from the members of the John Doe movement. This causes the crowd to hurl papers and rotten food at Cooper, who is now a national disgrace. Only a few stand by him, including his old pal Brennan, and Stanwyck, who has seen the errors of her ambitious ways. To revive the movement, Cooper decides that he will prove himself genuine by actually jumping from the top of City Hall on Christmas Eve, as he originally promised to do, or as Stanwyck promised he would do. He is found at the top of that building that night by Arnold and his goons, as well as Stanwyck, who begs Cooper not to commit suicide, telling him that "the first John Doe already died to keep the good will movement alive, and He has kept that idea alive for more than two thousand years…If it's [an idea] worth dying for, then it's an idea worth living for." She faints into Cooper's arms. Then several diehard John Doe Club members, including Toomey and Doran, appear and beg him not to end his life and to go with them to rebuild the movement. Cooper peers over the edge of the building, gives Arnold back his stare, and then agrees to live, carrying Stanwyck as he leaves with his supporters. Gleason, who has all along thought the movement to be a lot of hooey, takes great pride in Cooper's resolve to live and has decided to join the "little people" of the earth. He turns to a chagrined Arnold and says: "There you are, Norton [Arnold], the people! Try and lick that!" He leaves with "the people" while the choral of Beethoven's Ninth Symphony is heard at the fadeout. Capra, as usual, takes great pains to develop the wonderful characters in this stirring film, no less than poetry on film, and where Cooper is the perfect Everyman, Stanwyck the ambitious newswoman, Gleason the seasoned editor, Brennan the dedicated hobo, Arnold the ruthless tycoon, and others are superlative in their fascinating roles. The script, a bit sudsy, but full of great humor, is enhanced by Tiomkin's dynamic and touching score for a film in which the viewer wants to believe as passionately as the members of the John Doe Club want to believe in Cooper, or the fine principles he represents. Cooper had appeared in Capra's earlier tale of a country bumpkin shot to fame in **Mr. Deeds Goes to Town**, 1936, similar in that he is the same kind of unassuming, down-to-earth and gentle man as he is in **Meet John Doe**. *Author's Note*: Capra had long been accused of producing overly sentimental, if not sappy films ("Capracorn"), where his "odor of goodness" was somehow an unpleasant scent, but, as he told this author: "What's wrong with sentiment? Should we be ashamed of feeling good about each other, of loving one another? I think not. Love is the true test of courage. And I am not embarrassed a bit by providing happy endings to my films. The

audience that leaves a film with a happy ending will always go back to a director in hopes of having the same satisfaction with his next picture. I have never disappointed viewers in that regard, never. My beliefs and affections and everything I am is up there on the screen." Cooper told this author that "Frank Capra is one of the great directors because he hides nothing from the viewer. His characters are believable because they believe in simple truths like honesty and decency. They are nobler than all the kings of the earth." Stanwyck told this author that "no one makes pictures like Frank Capra. He cannot make a bad film. It is not in his nature. We all knew that about him and when he asked Coop and me and everyone else to go into his first independent production [**Meet John Doe**], we accepted without even seeing a script. That's how much we trust Frank Capra." This film was Capra's first film through his own production company and where he distributed the film through Warner Brothers, instead of his alma mater, Columbia, which allowed him to work without being hampered by the demands of stringent movie mogul Harry Cohn. He did not have the shooting script in any kind of shape almost up to the first day's shooting. The film was Capra's answer to the then powerful German-American Bund, which was a pro-Nazi organization in the U.S. just prior to America's entering WWII (on December 7, 1941). The film was a great success, and returned a profit of $900,000 in its initial box office release, but, according to Capra, heavy taxes caused him to dissolve his production company a short time later. **p&d**, Frank Capra; **cast**, Gary Cooper, Barbara Stanwyck, Edward Arnold, Walter Brennan, Spring Byington, James Gleason, Gene Lockhart, Rod La Rocque, Regis Toomey, J. Farrell MacDonald, Warren Hymer, Ann Doran, Russell Simpson, Jim Thorpe, Maris Wrixon; **w**, Robert Riskin (based on a story "The Life and Death of John Doe" by Robert Presnell, Richard Connell); **c**, George Barnes; **m**, Dimitri Tiomkin; **ed**, Daniel Mandell; **art d**, Stephen Goosson; **spec eff**, Jack Cosgrove.

Meet Me After the Show ★★★ 1951; U.S.; 86m; FOX; Color; Musical; Children: Acceptable; **DVD**. Broadway musical star Grable learns that her producer-husband, Carey, is cheating on her, so she quits his show. Hoping to get him back, she pretends to have amnesia and returns to Miami where her career as a singer-dancer began. It works and he promises he will never stray again. She admits she faked her amnesia, but that's okay with him and they are reunited. The plot is thin, but Grable is terrific in her dancing and singing numbers, and there are many good songs: "Meet Me After the Show," "Betting on a Man," "Oh, Me, Oh, Mi-ami," "It's a Hot Night in Alaska," "(Ev'ry Day Is Like) A Day in Maytime," "No Talent Joe," "I Feel Like Dancing" (Jule Styne, Leo Robin); "Night Music" (Hal Schaeffer). **p**, George Jessel; **d**, Richard Sale; **cast**, Betty Grable, Macdonald Carey, Rory Calhoun, Eddie Albert, Fred Clark, Lois Andrews, Irene Ryan, Steve Condos, Jerry Brandow, Harry Antrim, "Snub" Pollard, Gwen Verdon; **w**, Mary Loos, Sale (based on a story by Erna Lazarus, W. Scott Darling); **c**, Arthur E. Arling (Techicolor); **m**, Ken Darby; **ed**, J. Watson Webb, Jr.; **art d**, Lyle Wheeler, Joseph C. Wright; **set d**, Thomas Little, Walter M. Scott; **spec eff**, Fred Sersen.

Meet Me in Las Vegas ★★★ 1956; U.S.; 112m; MGM; Color; Drama/Musical; Children: Acceptable; **DVD**; **VHS**. Dailey and Charisse are charming in this entertaining romp through the gambling halls of Las Vegas, chiefly at The Sands. He is a chicken rancher, who cannot stay away from the roulette table where everyone knows that winning against the house is next to impossible. Yet, he wins and wins against the wheel, but only when he holds the hand of the lovely Charisse, who is a ballerina turned leggy nightclub dancer. Realizing that she is his lucky charm, Dailey forms a pact with Charisse. They will go fifty-fifty on all of his wins, as long as she continues to be his hand-holding gambling inspiration. They develop an odd couple romance and fall in and out of love with each other until they can no longer bear to be separated, and decide to go to the altar on the condition that Dailey will allow her to continue her dancing career six months out of the year and she will stay home at the ranch and help Dailey mind the chickens for the rest of the year. Not much of a story line, but the film is salted with many good songs and big name stars (of that day), who make humorous cameo appearances (that may or may not have inspired Stanley Kramer's mega cameo appearances in his comedic epic, **It's a Mad, Mad, Mad, Mad World**, 1963). We see the luck-filled Charisse passing a customer with his back to the camera in one scene as he feeds coins into a slot machine. As he brushes past him, the man suddenly wins the jackpot, money cascading before him and he turns with a perplexed look on his face to be Frank Sinatra. In another scene we see the dour-faced Peter Lorre playing blackjack and telling dealer Oskar Karlweis, to "hit me, you creep!" We see Debbie Reynolds sipping a Coke with Vic Damone and Pier Angeli dining with Tony Martin (Charisse's real-life husband), as well as Jeff Richards, Elaine Stewart, Steve Forrest, Dewey Martin, and, as entertainers playing themselves Jerry Colonna, Lena Horne, Sammy Davis Jr., The Four Aces and Frankie Laine. Songs include (all from Nicholas Brodszky and Sammy Cahn): "If You Can Dream," "The Girl with the Yaller Shoes," "Lucky Charm," "Hell Hath No Fury," "I Refuse to Rock 'n' Roll," "Rehearsal Ballet," "Sleeping Beauty Ballet," and "Frankie and Johnny." **p**, Joe Pasternak; **d**, Roy Rowland; **cast**, Dan Dailey, Cyd Charisse, Agnes Moorehead, Lili Darvas, Jim Backus, Liliane Montevecchi, Cara Williams, George Chakiris, Betty Lynn, Jerry Colonna, Hank Worden, Paul Henreid, Lena Horne, Frankie Laine, Pier Angeli, Vic Damone, Sammy Davis, Jr., Steve Forrest, Robert Fuller, Peter Lorre, Dewey Martin, Tony Martin, Debbie Reynolds, Frank Sinatra, Elaine Stewart; **w**, Isobel Lennart (based on her story); **c**, Robert Bronner (Eastmancolor); **m**, George Stoll, Robert Van Eps, Albert Sendrey; **ed**, Albert Akst; **art d**, Cedric Gibbons, Urie McCleary; **set d**, Edwin B. Willis, Richard Pefferle; **spec eff**, Warren Newcombe.

Meet Me in St. Louis ★★★★ 1944; U.S.; 113m; MGM; Color; Musical; Children: Recommended; **DVD**; **VHS**. In a simple and sweet story that takes place in 1903 in St. Louis, we see a wonderful family headed by parents Ames and Astor, who have four daughters, Bremer, Garland, Carroll, and O'Brien, and a son, Daniels. The older girls, Bremer and Garland, each have boyfriends, Bremer keeping a local boy on the string while carrying on a long-distance romance with a boy away at college, while Garland meets and falls in love with Drake, a young man who moves into the upscale area with his family. Ames is a wealthy businessman, who runs his household as he does his business, with regimen and regulations and no nonsense (not unlike that of William Powell in **Life with Father**, 1947, or David Tomlinson in **Mary Poppins**, 1964, and as Ames would again reprise as the banker-father in **On Moonlight Bay**, 1951, and **By the Light of the Silvery Moon**, 1953). Garland meets Drake, who is a college student, and they soon spark together and eventually plan to marry while O'Brien, in her finest and most memorable role as a child on film, steals almost every scene as the mischievous, precocious and highly imaginative "Tootie." When her big sisters Bremer and Garland host a party in their home, O'Brien sneaks downstairs to crash the party with older sister Carroll, and sing "I Was Drunk Last Night," before O'Brien and Garland perform a marvelous rendition, cakewalk and all, of "Under the Bamboo Tree" (1902; music: Rosamond Johnson; lyrics: Bob Cole). All seems peaceful and promising until Ames comes home one day to proudly announce that he has been promoted and with that promotion is a mandatory move where the entire family must relocate to New York. All in the family, including the colorful and cantankerous cook and maid, Main, and elderly grandfather Davenport, oppose the move, wanting to stay in their comfortable, spacious home and remain with their friends and neighbors in unpretentious St. Louis. So distressed at the news of this move is O'Brien that she buries her dolls in the back yard. (She is a curiosity-seeking child as she naively grapples with worldly issues and she is seen at the beginning of the film telling Wills, who drives a horse-drawn ice wagon and who invariably takes her along on his route through her neighborhood that her

Margaret O'Brien and Judy Garland in *Meet Me in St. Louis*, 1944.

dolls are either dying or dead and for which Wills responds with sympathetic commiseration.) At Christmastime, after Garland sings (undoubtedly the very best rendition) "Have Yourself a Merry Little Christmas" (music: Ralph Blane; lyrics: Hugh Martin), O'Brien, distraught at having to leave the only home she has ever known, runs outside and destroys the large snowman the family has erected on the snow-covered lawn. Earlier, this amazing tyke was wisely given her own sequence where she and older sister Carroll gather with the children in the neighborhood on Halloween Night, throwing broken items into a large street bonfire and where all the children challenge each other to attempt a trick-or-treat with the most dreaded neighbors and the chief local grouch, Newhall, and O'Brien volunteers to face down this scary ogre (he is nothing of the kind). With great trepidation, O'Brien goes to Newhall's porch, rings the doorbell, and, when Newhall opens the door, the terrified little girl finds enough courage to throw some baking soda into his face before racing away. Newhall, smiling, takes it all in good humor. O'Brien breathlessly arrives back at the bonfire to announce to her startled friends that "I killed him!" and she is hailed the heroine of that eerie night. When it comes time to the move scheduled for next spring, the family is desolate and Ames knows it. He cannot bring himself to make his loving family miserable so he declines the promotion and tells everyone that they are staying right where they are, in St. Louis, much to the joy of all. The final scene sees the entire family, Bremer and Garland with their fiancés, Daniels with his intended, Lockhart, and the smaller children present when the magnificent 1904 World's Fair in St. Louis opens, the spectacular lights of its many new illustrious buildings and exhibits lighting up in a dazzling array. All swell with pride in knowing that their hometown is now at the center of the world's attention. Minnelli directs this great musical was his usual meticulous care, carefully framing each scene to seamlessly fit into the next while inserting one great song after another without disrupting the story line and maintaining his character development in his weaving process. Garland, O'Brien, Ames, Astor and the rest of the cast give outstanding performances, and Garland was never more beautiful or in full-throated control of her great voice, the big hit being the unforgettable "Trolley Song" (Ralph Blane, Hugh Martin). Other songs include: "Over the Bannister," "Skip to My Lou," "The Boy Next Door" (Ralph Blane, Hugh Martin); "Meet Me in St. Louis" (1904; music: Kerry Mills; lyrics: Andrew Sterling II); "Yankee Doodle" (traditional); "Goodbye, My Lady Love" (1904; Joseph E. Howard); "You and I" (1944; music: Nacio Herb Brown; lyrics: Arthur Freed); "Down at the Old Bull and Bush" (1903; music: Harry von Tilzer); "Little Brown Jug" (1869; Joseph Winner), "Auld Lang Syne" (traditional Scottish ballad); "Home, Sweet Home" (1823; music: H. R. Bishop); "Kingdom Coming" (1863; music: Henry Clay Work); "The First Noel" (traditional). *Author's Note*: Garland re-

Judy Garland and Tom Drake in *Meet Me in St. Louis*, 1944.

sisted doing this film, believing it had a next-to-nothing story, but Minnelli (they would marry the next year) persuaded her that the wonderful songs and family scenes would handsomely fill in all the gaps and he was right. Garland later stated that this was one of her most favorite films. This was the first time that Minnelli used color in his films and he used it effectively, muting many of his scenes, especially the Christmas scene where Garland sings "Have Yourself a Merry Little Christmas," so that this scene appears warm and gentle and the deep rich hues of the old Technicolor process are in startling evidence. Adding to that imagery, Minnelli recalled the old Currier and Ives prints of yesteryear America and adopted a similar poster style to introduce four seasons of the family's life, summer, fall, winter and spring, using as his pivotal image the family's gothic Edwardian home, with its large front porch and filigreed ornamentations running along its gables, roof edges and columns. He opens each season with a still picture of the lovely Smith home before showing its occupants in action and thus unfolds with such quaint and traditional greeting card introductions the chronology of this fine family over the space of a year. Minnelli prized O'Brien and her appealing innocence in her scenes. She was known as the only child actress who could cry real tears on cue, and, in fact, MGM boss Louis B. Mayer, who never seemed to be able to recall her name, always referred to O'Brien as "the kid who cries on cue." In one scene, however, Minnelli could not get O'Brien to cry those real tears, irrespective of begging, pleading and subtle threats. O'Brien's mother then came to the rescue, telling Minnelli the secret password that always prompted her to weep great tears. "Tell her that her pet dog has been shot and is dead." Minnelli set up his scene and then whispered this terrible line to O'Brien and ordered the cameras to roll. She cried streams of real tears coursing down her cheeks and Minnelli had the scene he needed. When he called cut, O'Brien acted as if nothing had happened and skipped away to attend some tutoring classes (required at all the studios having child actors). "She went home without a thought about what I said to her," Minnelli told this author, "and I went home and felt like such a monster that I could not eat dinner or even breakfast the next morning." Everything about this film was special to Minnelli. He doted on the sets, making sure that all the props specifically applied to the era, and did the same thing in checking everyone's wardrobe. He took his greatest pains with Garland, having master makeup artist Dotty Ponedel (a rather eccentric lady), who enlarged the appearance of Garland's eyes by applying white liner to her lower eyelids, and then tweezed her hairline, raised her eyebrows and gave her a fuller lower lip through careful lipstick application. Although only twenty-one at the time, Garland was beginning to have nervous problems, and she admitted to co-star Astor that she could not sleep at night and that is why she held up production some time by more than an hour or two while the entire cast waited for her to

come onto the set. Astor told this author that "I thought that was just a lot of nonsense and I told Judy that when I stormed into her dressing room one day to complain how she was holding us all up while she primped and primed herself for her next scene. 'Stop drinking coffee at night, or whatever else you are taking [suggesting the drugs that she was taking] and go to sleep early like the rest of us so that when you get up, you will be ready to go to work. Now, get the hell on to that set or I am going home!' She called me 'Mom' throughout the making of **Meet Me in St. Louis**, because I was playing her on-screen mother and so I acted like her mother when I told her to straighten herself out. And she did, appearing promptly on the set after I had that little talk with her. Sadly, I had no idea about the mental and psychological problems Judy was going through at that time. She needed a psychiatrist, not advice from me, and she never got it. I learned later that those quacks at the studio kept giving her sedatives and uppers to keep her going and it was like over-winding an old clock so that the mainspring was so tight that it could snap at any time…and it finally did. Poor Judy, we loved her so much." The story line for this great classic stems from a series of stories titled "The Kensington Stories" by Sally Benson (the home of the Smith family is located at 5135 Kensington Avenue in St. Louis), which appeared in *the New Yorker* in 1941-1942. MGM official Fred Finklehoffe, who read those stories and was enamored of the Smith family profiled in those stories, then bought the film rights of all the stories for MGM for $40,000. Finklehoffe was so enthralled with this tale that he dubbed Ames's voice with his own when Ames sings a memorable duet, "You and I" with Astor. Minnelli gave Lemuel Ayers, who worked under famed art director Cedric Gibbons, complete control of establishing the magnificent exterior sets for this film, all constructed on the MGM back lot where gothic, gabled Edwardian homes with sprawling lawns and broad streets resplendently abounded, at a cost of $200,000, a princely sum at that time. This was Bremer's film debut; she had been a Rockette (dancer) at Radio City Music Hall in New York City and had been discovered when she began a nightclub act. Van Johnson, who was the rising youthful heartthrob of the day, was originally scheduled to play Garland's boyfriend, but, at the last moment, he was inexplicably replaced by Drake. **p**, Arthur Freed; **d**, Vincente Minnelli; **cast**, Judy Garland, Margaret O'Brien, Mary Astor, Lucille Bremer, Leon Ames, Tom Drake, Marjorie Main, Harry Davenport, June Lockhart, Henry H. Daniels Jr., Joan Carroll, Hugh Marlowe, Chill Wills, Robert Sully, Helen Gilbert, Darryl Hickman, Mayo Newhall, Belle Mitchell, Victor Kilian, Robert Sully, Ken Wilson, Robert Emmett O'Connor, Donald Curtis, Mary Jo Ellis, Leonard Walker, John Phipps, Sidney Barnes; **w**, Irving Brecher, Fred F. Finklehoffe (based on the stories by Sally Benson); **c**, George Folsey (Technicolor); **m**, George Stoll, Roger Edens, Conrad Salinger; **ed**, Albert Akst; **art d**, Cedric Gibbons, Lemuel Ayers, Jack Martin Smith; **set d**, Edwin B. Willis; **spec eff**, A. Arnold Gillespie, Warren Newcombe, Mark Davis.

Meet Nero Wolfe ★★★ 1936; U.S.; 73m; COL; B/W; Mystery; Children: Unacceptable; **VHS**. Arnold fascinates as the clever detective Nero Wolfe, who solves mysteries from the comfort of his New York home while growing orchids and drinking gallons of beer, which gives him the proverbial beer belly. A college professor is murdered while playing golf, so Arnold has his assistant, Stander, do the leg work to investigate. Arnold discovers that a young mechanic crated a blow-gun that shoots poisoned darts, but the killer of the professor also kills the mechanic. At the same time, Arnold keeps his personal chef, Qualen, busy whipping up delicious meals. A young woman, Rita Hayworth (credited as Rita Cansino), seeks Wolfe's help in finding her brother, who has gone missing. He, you might suspect, is the inventive mechanic, and killer, played to sinister perfection by Jory. This offbeat mystery is solved through some clever deductions and inventive forensic applications, leaving Arnold to go back to his beer and orchids. Violence prohibits viewing by children. **p**, B. P. Schulberg; **d**, Herbert J. Biberman; **cast**, Edward Arnold, Lionel Stander, Dennie Moore, Victor

Jory, Nana Bryant, Joan Perry, Russell Hardie, Walter Kingsford, Boyd Irwin, John Qualen, Rita Cansino (Rita Hayworth); **w**, Howard J. Green, Bruce Manning, Joseph Anthony (based on the novel *Fer-de-Lance* by Rex Stout); **c**, Henry Freulich; **m**, Howard Jackson; **ed**, Otto Meyer; **art d**, Stephen Goosson.

Melancholia ★★★ 2011; Denmark/Sweden/France/Germany; 136m.; Zentropa Entertainments/Magnolia Pictures; Color; Drama; Children: Unacceptable (MPAA: R); **BD, DVD**. A wedding is about to take place and everyone is apprehensive because a blue planet, Melancholia, is hurtling toward Earth and might destroy it. The bride-to-be, Dunst, has sex with a man on a golf course and the groom-to-be, Alexander Skarsgard, momentarily walks out on her. Dunrst insults her new boss, Sutherland, at a marketing firm and quits. The day of the wedding arrives and those attending include Dunst's estranged parents, Rampling and Hurt, Sutherland, and Kier, the wedding planner. The wedding is small because few family members can stand each other. No scenes of panic or impending disaster are seen as those in the wedding party go on with the ceremony. No cataclysmic event occurs, but Dunst keeps sinking into despair and hopelessness. This offbeat domestic drama presents some engrossing characterizations, but the wedding is far from a typical happy event. Music: Richard Wagner's "Tristan und Isolde." Graphic nudity, sexual content, and gutter language prohibit viewing by children. **p**, Meta Louise Foldager, Louise Vesth, Bettina Brokemper, Remi Burah, Madeleine Ekman, Tomas Eskilsson, Lars Jonsson, Marianne Slot; **d&w**, Lars von Trier; **cast**, Kirsten Dunst, Charlotte Gainsbourg, Kiefer Sutherland, Charlotte Rampling, John Hurt, Udo Kier, James Cagnard, Stellan Skarsgard, Alexander Skarsgard, Brady Corbet, Cameron Spurr, Jesper Christensen, **c**, Manuel Alberto Claro; **ed**, Molly M. Stensgaard, Morten Hojbjerg; **prod d**, Jette Lehmann; **art d**, Simone Grau; **set d**, Louise Drake; **spec eff**, Hummer Hoimark, Christian Kitter, Soren Skov Haraldsted.

Melo ★★★ 1988; France; 112m; Centre National de la Cinematographie/European Classics; Color; Drama; Children: Unacceptable; **DVD**. Two longtime friends from their music conservatory days both become professional violinists in Paris in the 1920s, Dussollier plays on the recital circuit while Arditi plays with a local symphony orchestra. Arditi is married to Azema, but Dussollier remains a single womanizer. The married couple invites Dussollier to their house for dinner and he and Azema play a duet on violins which leads them to begin a torrid affair that ends some time later with Azema throwing herself into the Seine. Arditi then marries Azema's cousin, Ardant, and they have a child. Azema's memory haunts Arditi and affects his work with the orchestra. He decides to move with his wife and child to Tunis and start a new life, when he pays Dussollier a final visit. He wants to learn if his wife did in fact have an affair with his friend. Dussollier denies it and he and Arditi play a final duet together. Based on a 1929 stage play, this film offers an incisive profile of friendship and how one friend goes to painful lengths to protect the emotional memories of the other. Adult situations prohibit viewing by children. (In French; English subtitles.) **p**, Marin Karmitz; **d**, Alain Resnais; **cast**, Sabine Azéma, Fanny Ardant, Pierre Arditi, Andre Dussollier, Jacques Dacqmine, Hubert Gignoux, Catherine Arditi; **w**, Resnais (based on the play by Henri Bernstein); **c**, Charlie Van Damme; **m**, M. Philippe-Gérard; **ed**, Albert Jurgenson; **prod d**, Jacques Saulnier.

Melody ★★★ 1971; U.K.; 103m; Helmdale Productions/Levitt-Pickman; Color; Drama; Children: Unacceptable; **DVD**. Intriguing drama that tests the fantasies and emotions of preteens has Lester as a lonely twelve-year-old boy attending a British school. He falls in love with a girl his age in their music class and she feels the same about him, so they naively decide to get married. They inform their parents, who, of course, are against it. Lester, however, has his school chum, Wild, marry them in a mock ceremony after which the happy couple rides off in an

Lionel Stander and Edward Arnold in *Meet Nero Wolfe*, 1936.

old trolley. Mature themes prohibit viewing by children. Songs: "Teach Your Children" (Crosby, Stills, Nash and Young); "In the Morning of My Life," "Spicks and Specks" (Barry Gibb); "Melody Fair," "Give Your Best to the First of May," "To Love Somebody" (Bee Gees); "Working on It Night and Day" (Richard Hewson, Gordon Gray, sung by the Bee Gees). **p**, David Hemmings, David Puttnam; **d**, Waris Hussein; **cast**, Mark Lester, Tracy Hyde, Jack Wild, Colin Barrie, Billy Franks, Ashley Knight, Craig Marriott, William Vanderpuye, Peter Walton, Camille Davis, Dawn Hope, Kay Skinner; **w**, Alan Parker (based on his story); **c**, Peter Suschitzky (Technicolor); **m**, The Bee-Gees, Richard Hewson; **ed**, John Victor Smith; **art d**, Roy Stannard.

Melody Time ★★★★ 1948; U.S.; 72m; Disney/RKO; Animated Musical Compilation; Children: Recommended; **DVD; VHS**. In this last musical compilation from Disney, the viewer is offered a wonderful selection of delightful tales and scintillating tunes, which truly represents a cross-section of Disney's best shorts, from the inimitable Donald Duck to more classical entries. Clark (voiceover) serves as the linking narrator and host of this visual feast, unfolding each tale with the stroke of a magical paint brush and which begins with a young couple arguing while ice-skating and where the boy saves the girl when she falls through the ice. Witnessing this incident, two rabbits then humorously reenact the scene from their innocent animal perspective until the tale is shown to be a flashback memory of a couple who have had a long and happy marriage. The next piece is titled "an instrumental nightmare" and shows a frenetic bee making honey and buzzing about to avoid musical hazards to the accompaniment of Rimsky-Korsakov's "Flight of the Bumble Bee," but in modern tempo as played by Freddie Martin and his orchestra, a sequence packed with dazzling surrealistic images. Day does all the voices in the third segment that shows the legend of Johnny Appleseed and how this tireless planter finally ages, dies and is escorted to heaven by an angel where he discovers, to his delight, that there are no apple trees, although he can seed heaven with apple blossoms, as a narrator tells us at the finale, that are seen on earth whenever a group of clouds appear in the sky. The fourth delightful treat, which is told in song by the Andrews Sisters, is titled "Little Toot," where a courageous little tugboat gets into trouble and is reprimanded by his father, a large tugboat, and is punished by being sent beyond the twelve-mile limit, but where Little Toot redeems himself in those dangerous waters by saving a large ship in distress during a fierce storm. "Trees," the fifth sequence, is told through music by Fred Waring and his orchestra and beautifully illustrates Joyce Kilmer's wonderful poem, presenting a masterful array of trees as portrayed in color, shadow and light and where everything moves in every frame, showing Disney's best animation. The irrepressible Donald Duck appears in the sixth seg-

Jason Robards and Paul Le Mat in *Melvin and Howard*, 1980.

ment with his old pal, Joe Carioca (from the animated feature **The Three Caballeros**, 1944), where he and Joe are down in the dumps until they take a swig of a cocktail with a special ingredient that causes them to go into a wild Samba (this sequence is titled "Blame It on the Samba") that ends at a café for a wow finish. The seventh and final segment features Roy Rogers (King of the Cowboys) and his Sons of the Pioneers, where Rogers tells tykes Driscoll and Patten the tale of the legendary Pecos Bill when they hear the sounds of coyotes while Roy and ensemble sing as a series of desert night scenes are shown that segues into the animated tale of Pecos Bill. The story relates how Bill is raised by coyotes and how he eventually out-howls them before returning to civilization where he becomes a rootin'-tootin' cowboy and then befriends a great horse named Widowmaker. The close friendship between man and horse is disrupted when Bill meets and falls head over heels in love with attractive Slue Foot Sue. After she and Bill decide to marry, Widowmaker becomes jealous and, when Sue decides to ride the horse, Widowmaker bucks her off so hard that she begins to bounce on her bustle, bouncing ever higher and higher, until she is headed for the moon, never again to see Pecos Bill. So distressed is Bill that he rejoins the coyotes that raised him and howls loudest at the moon for his long lost Sue and that, Rogers explains to Driscoll and Patten, is the reason why coyotes howl at the moon every night. This is a wonderful and finely diversified compendium, full of great fancy and fantasy. Songs include: "Once Upon a Wintertime" (Bobby Worth, Ray Gilbert), "Bumble Boogie" (Nikolai Rimsky-Korsakov, arranged by Jack Fina), "Melody Time" (George Weiss, Bennie Benjamin), "Little Toot" (Allie Wrubel), "Trees" (from the poem by Joyce Kilmer; music: Oscar Rasbach), "Blame It on the Samba" (Ernesto Nazareth, Ray Gilbert), "Blue Shadows on the Trail," and "Pecos Bill" (Eliot Daniel, Johnny Lange). ***Author's Note***: The segments of the bumble bee and "Trees" were later combined for a Disney animated short titled **Contrasts in Rhythm**, 1955, and other segments were incorporated into another Disney release, **Musicland**, 1955. **p**, Walt Disney; **d**, Clyde Geronimi, Wilfred Jackson, Jack Kinney, Hamilton Luske; **cast**, Roy Rogers, Luana Patten, Bobby Driscoll, Ethel Smith, Bob Nolan, Sons of the Pioneers, and the voices of Buddy Clark, Dennis Day, The Andrews Sisters (Patty, Maxene, Laverne Andrews), Fred Waring and His Pennsylvanians, Freddy Martin, Frances Langford, Pat Brady, **w**, Winston Hibler, Erdman Penner, Harry Reeves, Homer Brightman, Ken Anderson, Ted Sears, Joe Rinaldi, Bill Cottrell, Art Scott, Jesse Marsh, Bob Moore, John Walbridge, Hardie Gramatky; **c**, (Technicolor); **m**, Eliot Daniel, Paul J. Smith; **ed**, Thomas Scott, Donald Halliday; **spec eff**, Ub Iwerks, Jack Boyd, Dan Mac Manus, Josh Meador, George Rowley.

Melvin and Howard ★★★ 1980; U.S.; 95m; UNIV; Color; Biograph-

ical Drama; Children: Unacceptable; **DVD**; **VHS**. Often engrossing tale about the so-called meeting between Melvin Dummar (b. 1944) and billionaire eccentric Howard Hughes (1905-1976), and where Dummar claimed to have saved the ailing Hughes after finding him alone in a Nevada desert in 1967 and his later claims that, in gratitude for saving his life, Hughes reportedly left Dummar $156 million in a will that has since been legally determined to be a forgery. Le Mat plays Dummar, who is working as a milkman when he picks up Robards, presumably playing Hughes, on a lonely stretch of a Nevada highway, thinking he is nothing more than an old drifter. He drives Robards to where he wants to go and gives him a quarter to make a phone call. En route, Le Mat gives Robards his advice about how to have a positive attitude and even gets the old, bearded fellow to join him in singing "Blackbird." Le Mat then goes home to wife Steenburgen, who plays a flighty spouse, somewhat of a dingbat who keeps divorcing and remarrying him after he loses one job after another (she won an Oscar as Best Actress). She appears on a TV quiz show, doing an awkward tap dance (as one might see in a toddler training course), and, after answering a few unchallenging questions, wins $10,000. (This sequence is worth the film itself as it presents a biting parody of such goofy quiz shows where intelligence and talent, like batteries, are not included.) Later, after Steenburgen has left him (she becomes a topless stripper without much top in a sleazy nightclub), La Mat is operating a gas station when a well-dressed man leaves a sealed envelope in Le Mat's office. The envelope reportedly contains a will from the now dead Howard Hughes (or so Dummar claimed) that bequeaths $156 million to him for that ride in the desert. Le Mat goes through a lengthy court battle in order to obtain the money, but, in the end, the will is decreed a forgery and Le Mat is again out in the cold. He has had Andy Warhol's promised fifteen minutes of fame. The tale is a pleasant one with LeMat giving an impressive understated performance, and Robards, although he appears only briefly, is mesmerizing in his role of the mysterious stranger. **p**, Art Linson, Don Phillips; **d**, Jonathan Demme; **cast**, Jason Robards, Paul Le Mat, Elizabeth Cheshire, Mary Steenburgen, Chip Taylor, Melvin E. Dummar, Michael J. Pollard, Denise Galik, Gloria Grahame, John Thundercloud, Dabney Coleman; **w**, Bo Goldman; **c**, Tak Fujimoto (Technicolor); **m**, Bruce Langhorne; **ed**, Craig McKay; **prod d**, Toby Rafelson; **art d**, Richard Sawyer; **set d**, Bob Gould; **spec eff**, Karl Miller.

The Member of the Wedding ★★★ 1952; U.S.; 93m; Stanley Kramer Productions/COL; B/W; Drama; Children: Cautionary; **DVD**; **VHS**. Well crafted, this social drama focuses upon a twelve-year-old girl, Harris (who gives an outstanding performance and was twenty-five at the time) and her fantasies as she approaches adolescence and who anxiously awaits the marriage of her older brother, Franz, somehow convincing herself that she will be a member of that wedding party and will even go on the honeymoon with the newlyweds. Awkward and somewhat withdrawn, Harris is rebuffed by other girls her age and spends most of her time idling about the house, talking to the kind-hearted black maid, Waters, or chatting with De Wilde, the younger boy living next door. When she is rejected by the newlyweds, Harris feels utterly rejected and runs away, only to experience a harrowing encounter with a drunken soldier, who attempts to seduce her. She returns to the safety of her home a wiser, more mature child, only to learn that De Wilde has tragically died. Harris weathers this trauma and is later seen a more adjusted teenager as she begins the cycle of dating in this fine rite of passage story. Zinnemann's direction is outstanding as is Mohr's contrasting photography, and the cast members all present standout performances. ***Author's Note***: Producer Kramer told this author that "I was determined to use the cast that appeared in the Broadway play as they were perfect for their roles. I got a lot of pressure from Harry Cohn to use some of his contract players for **The Member of the Wedding**, and that was not an easy fight to win." The original smash play on Broadway ran 492 performances, and Kramer cast Harris, Walter, De Wilde, Hansen and Bolden in the roles they originally enacted. This was the role that established Harris as an international stage and screen star, and De Wilde would achieve the same status after he appeared the next year in the classic western **Shane**, 1953. **p**, Stanley Kramer; **d**, Fred Zinnemann; **cast**, Ethel Waters, Julie Harris, Brandon De Wilde, Arthur Franz, Nancy Gates, James Edwards, Dickie Moore, Hugh Beaumont, Ann Carter, Danny Mummert; **w**, Edna Anhalt, Edward Anhalt (based on the play by Carson McCullers); **c**, Hal Mohr; **m**, Alex North; **ed**, William A. Lyon; **prod d**, Rudolph Sternad; **art d**, Cary Odell; **set d**, Frank Tuttle.

Memories of Me ★★★ 1988; U.S.; 103m; MGM; Color; Comedy; Drama; Children: Unacceptable (MPAA: PG-13); **DVD**; **VHS**. In a moving performance, Crystal, a heart surgeon, suffers a heart attack while operating on a patient. While recovering, he confesses to his girl-friend, Williams, that he lied when earlier telling her that his father, King, was dead. She encourages him to reconcile with his father before it is too late. King, whose hopes of becoming a movie star only took him to the status of being a Hollywood extra, is suffering from a terminal illness. Father and son do bury the hatchet and become friends before either dies. It's a touching father-son drama, where King gives an un-expected and very sensitive performance. Mature subject matter pro-hibits viewing by children. **p**, Billy Crystal, Michael Hertzberg, Alan King; **d**, Henry Winkler; **cast**, Crystal, King, JoBeth Williams, Janet Carroll, David Ackroyd, Phil Fondacaro, Robert Pastorelli, Mark L. Tay-lor, Peter Elbling, Larry Cedar, Sean Connery; **w**, Crystal, Eric Roth; **c**, Andrew Dintenfass; **m**, Georges Delerue; **ed**, Peter E. Berger; **prod d**, William J. Cassidy; **art d**, Russell Smith; **set d**, Sam Gross.

Memphis Belle ★★★★ 1990; U.K./Japan/U.S.; 107m; BSB; Enigma/WB; Color; War Drama; Children: Unacceptable (MPAA: PG-13); **DVD**; **VHS**. This compelling and riveting film profiles the crew of a single U.S. Army Air Force B-17-bomber (of the 324th Heavy Bomb Squadron) during WWII. The bomber is named *Memphis Belle* (after the girlfriend of its no-nonsense captain, Robert Morgan, 1918-2004, played by Modine), and its twenty-fifth mission, this time over Ger-many, the final mission the crew must complete before being safely sent back to the U.S. is the story line for this film. Modine and his crew (as has been the case of the actual crew and bomber upon which this film is based) has been incredibly lucky in that it has managed to survive its previous twenty-four hazardous missions and where other crews and bombers have been routinely destroyed in such missions. The film be-gins on the eve of that final mission where the crew members attend a dance and where one of its members, the tail gunner, who is the talented Connick Jr., plays and sings with the band on the stage while his fellow crew members talk and dance with young British girls. Some, like Gains, a waist gunner with the *Belle*, trusts his lucky charm to see him safely through the mission while navigator Sweeney is utterly convinced that they will all be killed and gets drunk, collapsing in a plane locker. He is found by handsome and happy-go-ucky bombardier Zane the next morning. Zane is able to sober up Sweeney enough so that he is fit to fly, and the *Memphis Belle* then takes off with a flight of other B-17s and is en route from England to Germany (that mission occurred on May 20, 1943, when the *Belle* bombed Wilhelmshaven, Germany). When the *Belle* approaches German air space, it and the other B-17s are attacked by scores of German fighters that are beaten back, with minor damage. The leading plane is shot down and the *Belle* now becomes the point bomber leading the squadron to its destination. Once over the target, the sky is filled with flak from German anti-aircraft guns and more damage is inflicted on the *Belle*, its belly-gunner barely surviving when his turret is destroyed. Zane, the bombardier, tells pilot Modine that he does not have a clear picture of the target because of cloud cover, and Modine decides to make another "run" in hopes of getting a clear target, one that distresses everyone on board since the odds of being destroyed in a sec-ond pass over the target greatly increases. In fact, the desperate Sweeney tries to release the bombs, but Zane fights him off. Modine, as the pilot of the leading plane of the squadron, has made this decision, he tells his

Matthew Modine in *Memphis Belle,* 1990.

crew, so that they can effectively hit the target and not leave the job for another group of bombers. In the second pass over the target, Zane sees an opening in the clouds and drops his bombs and the rest of the squadron follows suit. *Belle* then flies for home, but it is seriously dam-aged and one of its crew members has been wounded. Zane, who has earlier bragged about having attended medical school, is asked to treat the wounded crew member, but he panics, saying he only attended a few medical classes and that "I don't know anything!" Yet, he does treat the wounded gunner, reviving him and cradling him as he and the rest of the crew members pray for their safe return. Meanwhile, at their base, Lithgow, a public relations officer, has arranged a welcome home party for the crew of the *Belle*, but Strathairn, who commands the base, tells him to take down the decorations, saying that he does not want the crew members of the *Belle* to be singled out, which will only emphasize the long odds of all bomber crews in surviving the war. Lithgow protests and Strathairn takes him into his office and compels him to read some of the many letters he has received from parents, wives and other rela-tives of crew members who have been shot down and killed while flying the attritional air war. As Lithgow reads these touching, heart-wringing letters, a montage of black-and-white scenes, grim footage of the actual air war, shows one B-17 after another blown to pieces, or shattered and falling to earth with only a few of their crew members bailing out. Strathairn and Lithgow then hear the roar of the engines of the returning squadron and go to the command tower, counting the surviving planes as they land. They see no *Memphis Belle*. She is still aloft, however, limping toward her base, but one of its wheels has failed to descend and lock into place and its crew members frantically begin to hand-crank the wheel downward as the bomber approaches the landing field. A se-ries of quick cuts shows this desperate work inside the ship while the wheel slowly descends as the plane also descends, coming closer and closer to the ground as all at the field wait anxiously to see if the *Belle* will survive its landing. At the last moment, just before the plane touches down, the wheel locks into place and the *Belle* lands safely. As the plane slowly rolls onto a grassy field, it is still smoking from a fire that has been earlier extinguished, and flak holes are apparent everywhere in its fuselage. It has been shot to pieces, but when it comes to a stop, its crew members (including the injured gunner, who is immediately removed for medical attention) are grateful for their survival. The members of the entire base rush across the field to celebrate the ship's return while Modine breaks open a bottle of champagne from which he and his crew members drink while cheering and laughing and where the camera, in a triumphant boom shot ascends to show the indomitable *Belle* from on high for the fadeout. Director Caton-Jones does a great job in directing this tense war drama, drawing excellent character performances from the cast while integrating stunning aerial combat scenes into the live-

Marlon Brando in *The Men*, 1950.

action sequences, which is supplemented with actual WWII footage. *Author's Note*: This story was earlier told in a 1944 documentary titled **Memphis Belle: The Story of a Flying Fortress**. The actual B-17 of this story was piloted by Captain Robert Morgan (1918-2004), who named the ship after his girlfriend, Margaret Polk, a resident of Memphis, Tennessee. Morgan, as the plane arrived in England before its first mission, wrote to George Petty, who worked with *Esquire Magazine*, and asked that Petty send him a pinup of an attractive girl to put onto his B-17, and Petty sent Morgan a pinup of a curvaceous lady from the magazine's April 1941 edition. Morgan affixed that image and the name of *Memphis Belle* on the front end of his B-17's fuselage. **p**, David Puttnam, Catherine Wyler; **d**, Michael Caton-Jones; **cast**, Matthew Modine, Eric Stoltz, D. B. Sweeney, Billy Zane, Tate Donovan, Harry Connick Jr., David Strathairn, John Lithgow, Jane Horrocks, Sean Astin, Steven Mackintosh, Reed Edward Diamond, Keith Edwards, Courtney Gains, Neil Giuntoli, Jodie Wilson; **w**, Monte Merrick; **c**, David Watkin; **m**, George Fenton; **ed**, Jim Clark; **prod d**, Stuart Craig; **art d**, Norman Dorme, John King, Alan Tomkins; **set d**, Ian Giladjian; **spec eff**, Richard Conway.

The Men ★★★★ 1950; U.S.; 85m; Stanley Kramer Productions/UA; B/W; Drama; Children: Unacceptable; **DVD**; **VHS**. Brando, in a stunning performance, appears here in his first film and in the lead as a WWII soldier struggling to adjust to a debilitating injury that has left his legs paralyzed as a paraplegic and where his anger at his fate consumes his reason and destroys all hope for a decent life. Brando is first shown as a lieutenant leading his men into a German-occupied village and where he is shot in the back by a sniper. He is next shown in a hospital where he resists any notion of rehabilitation, quarreling with his nurses and physicians. Wright, his devoted sweetheart, visits him, but he sends her away, more or less telling her that he is finished as a man and as a human being. Sloane, a physician with great psychological skills, subtly works on Brando, finally convincing him to perform exercises that will strengthen his upper torso. Brando religiously performs these exercises and is soon able to manipulate his movements in a wheelchair and later learns how to drive an automobile specially designed for those with his affliction. Wright, who has never given up on Brando, returns to beg him to seek happiness with her and he agrees to marry her. His wedding, however, is a disaster where he is unable to stand when being wed to Wright. Dejected by his inability to function normally, Brando gets drunk on his wedding night and crashes the car. He is returned to the hospital, which Brando sees as his only sanctuary, but the other paraplegics hold a meeting and decide that he must leave the hospital. Sloane sides with his patients, and Brando is ordered to return home to the woman he has now deserted. Ashamed at his cow-ardice, Brando agrees and goes home to a waiting and loving Wright to begin anew. Zinnemann directs with a clinical style without introducing mawkishness or bathos, addressing this disturbing problem head-on, chiefly through the conduct and characterizations of fellow paraplegics well played by Webb and Erdman, and where Sloane, as the guiding physician also gives a forceful performance. It is Sloane who holds everything together through his firm but compassionate edicts. This memorable film was in keeping with the crusading producer-director Kramer's budding film career. He had produced **Champion**, 1949, a film that indicted the corruption of professional boxing, and **The Home of the Brave**, 1949, a production that exposed racism in the U.S. military. *Author's Note*: Zinnemann has reservations about directing Brando, but, as he told this author, "he proved to be extremely professional and did not impose his method acting upon me, although it was evident that that style was there, just beneath his deliveries in every line he uttered. His style did not infect the other actors, who held their own with him and I think that surprised Marlon." Brando, who had scored big in the Broadway production of "A Streetcar Named Desire," had, at this time, great disdain for Hollywood, stating that producers "never made an honest picture in their lives and probably never will." Kramer wanted Brando for the lead and, according to Kramer's statements to this author "went after him with a lot of ammunition and that was Carl's [Foreman] script. I knew that after Marlon read that sensitive and very witty screenplay, he would change his mind about Hollywood producers, or, at least, this one." Kramer was right. Brando was so impressed with the script that he accepted the lead role and, as was his habit, immediately went into training for his part. "I arranged to stay at a medical center where there was a ward of thirty-two beds," he told this author. "In each one of those beds was a paraplegic, most of them having been injured in the war [WWII]. I watched these bedeviled and brave men deal with their pain and agony and embarrassment at not being able to control their bodies, and where some of them would see false tremors of their paralyzed legs, although they knew that there was no real life there. I studied their mannerisms and their attitudes and took all that with me into the part I played. I was playing all those courageous men in that picture." Brando, an inveterate prankster in those days, also had considerable fun and provided a lot of amusement for the injured men who counseled him at that medical center. He would join them by rolling a wheelchair to a recreation area outside the center and where visitors were suddenly shocked and amazed to see Brando suddenly jump up from his wheelchair (among a sea of such wheelchair-bound paraplegics) and race madly across the lawn. On another occasion, Brando went to a bar with some of these paraplegics, and while they were heavily imbibing, a female religious zealot entered the place and began shrilly lecturing these wheelchair-bound paralyzed men, telling them that if they accepted God's word, they would be cured. Brando fixed a startled look to his face as if he had seen the light, then shakily rose from his wheelchair and staggered with an excruciatingly painful look on his face toward the startled woman, as if miraculously regaining the use of his paralyzed legs through her hectoring sermon. As the mouth-gaping woman beheld Brando's physical transformation, the actor suddenly stood completely erect and then went into a frantic tap-dancing routine, causing the evangelist to collapse in a dead faint. **p**, Stanley Kramer; **d**, Fred Zinnemann; **cast**, Marlon Brando, Teresa Wright, Everett Sloane, Jack Webb, Richard Erdman, Arthur Jurado, Virginia Farmer, Howard St. John, Polly Bergen, Virginia Christine, DeForest Kelley, Forty-five of the Men of Birmingham Veterans Hospital; **w**, Carl Foreman (based on his story); **c**, Robert De Grasse; **m**, Dimitri Tiomkin; **ed**, Harry Gerstad; **prod d**, Rudolph Sternad; **set d**, Edward G. Boyle.

Men in Black ★★★ 1997; U.S.; 98m; COL; Color; Comedy/Science Fiction; Children: Unacceptable (MPAA: PG-13); **BD**; **DVD**; **VHS**. Very funny spoof on sci-fi films opens with Jones and his partner, Hamilton intercepting a load of illegal Mexican aliens on a lonely road and taking one of them, a towering illegal, into the brush where he is shown to be an otherworld creature disguised as a human being and, after he threatens them, Hamilton is incapable of vaporizing him with his blaster. Jones performs the deed while hypnotizing members of a SWAT team that comes to investigate and orders them to blank out what they have seen and go about their business. For his failure to perform, the aging Hamilton is now hypnotized by Jones with an electronic device that blanks out his memory of ever having served in this most secretive of agencies, M.I.B. (Men in Black), which operates as a government agency that covers up all UFO and otherworld alien visitations as well as monitors the otherworld aliens living in the country (there are approximately 1,500 living in disguise in NYC alone). Now Jones must seek a new partner and that prospect is shown as Smith, a NYC detective, who is next shown chasing a felon through the streets of NYC, but he is incapable of corralling this weird and evasive offender as he leaps great bounds and outraces him until Smith corners this weird little man at the top of the Guggenheim Museum. Teetering at the edge of the roof, the desperate felon tells Smith that the world is shortly going to end and then, to his surprise, takes a nose dive off the roof to a splattering death below. Smith is grilled by his superiors about this death, the interrogation taken over by Jones, who is dressed all in black and who uses a device to hypnotize Smith, taking him on a brief tour of shops where similar otherworld creatures reside, until, while they sit in a Chinese restaurant, he convinces Smith to join his secret agency. Smith dutifully goes to a secure bastion-like building where he becomes one of a number of applicants for M.I.B. and is chosen as Jones' ("Agent K") partner. His memory is blanked out and he becomes "Agent J," having no recollection of his former life and going to work with Jones in monitoring extraterrestrials permitted to live on Earth, who are disguised as human beings, including an incident where Smith must assist an alien in giving birth along a roadway. Meanwhile, a spaceship crashes outside a farmhouse, destroying the farmer's truck, and when the farmer, D'Onofrio, goes to investigate, he threatens the visitors with his shotgun and he is killed, the alien being taking over his body. D'Onofrio then goes in search of a prince of another galaxy his species is trying to destroy, and finds and fatally injures that alien (Nussbaum), but who manages to tell Smith that his galaxy can be saved if Smith and Jones find his galaxy which is "on Onion's belt." A search by Jones and Smith, as well as D'Onofrio, for Onion begins, and that turns out to be a cat wearing a necklace with a shimmering small orb that contains that galaxy. Fiorentino, a physician, has taken custody of the cat, at the mortuary where Nussbaum's corpse resides, but D'Onofrio finds her and the cat first and kidnaps both, going to a rendezvous with one its spacecraft at the New York State Pavilion at Flushing Meadows. Jones and Smith are told that unless the galaxy is retrieved, Nussbaum's extraterrestrials will destroy Earth within an hour. They track down the huge bug-like monster and do battle with it, saving Fiorentino, the cat and the galaxy just at the last minute. Jones, however, can no longer function well and so, like his former partner, Hamilton, his memory of his service with M.I.B. is erased and he returns to his former civilian life with Fiorentino becoming Smith's new partner. Director Sonnenfeld does a good job in keeping all of the mayhem in good order, and the cast members render top flight performances while enacting their spectacular roles. The special effects, as the viewer should expect, dominate this wild tale with awesome arrays of blasters and battles while the makeup of the creatures is a marvel to behold. It's all ridiculous great fun, its story line rooted to the undying belief that government officials have for decades been keeping the truth about the existence of extraterrestrials from the public and here that religiously enforced regimen is graphically shown in the astounding antics and operations of M.I.B. This extraordinary film, produced on a $90 million budget, returned an astounding $589 million at the box office. **p**, Laurie MacDonald, Walter F. Parkes, Graham Place, Steven Spielberg; **d**, Barry Sonnenfeld; **cast**, Tommy Lee Jones, Will Smith, Linda Fiorentino, Vincent D'Onofrio, Rip Torn, Tony Shaloub, Siobhan Fallon, Mike Nussbaum, Danny DeVito, Newt Gingrich, George Lucas, Barry and Chloe Sonnenfeld, Steven Spielberg, Sylvester

Will Smith and Tommy Lee Jones in *Men in Black*, 1997.

Stallone, Dionne Warwick; **w**, Ed Solomon (based on a story by Solomon and the comic book characters by Lowell Cunningham) **c**, Don Peterman (Technicolor); **m**, Danny Elfman; **ed**, Jim Miller; **prod d**, Bo Welch; **art d**, Thomas Duffield; **set d**, Cheryl Carasik; **spec eff**, Kyle Ross Collinsworth.

Men in Black II ★★★ 2002; U.S.; 88m; Amblin Entertainment/COL; Color; Comedy/Science Fiction; Children: Unacceptable (MPAA: PG-13); **DVD**; **VHS**. Another great sci-fi spoof sees Smith as the top agent for M.I.B., the ultra-secretive government agency that monitors extraterrestrials living in disguise as humans on Earth. While conducting a routine investigation, Smith learns that Boyle, a destructive queen of an alien planet, has sneaked on to Earth, disguising herself as an alluring lingerie model (her native form shows her to be a hideous hydra-like creature) with the intentions of destroying the planet. Smith now needs the aid of Jones, a former M.I.B. agent, who is the only one knowing how Boyle operates and how to find the Light of Zartha, the only device that will prevent her from demolishing Earth. Smith finds Jones working in a small Massachusetts post office where most of the labors are done by extraterrestrials and Smith zaps his memory, restoring his recollections as a former M.I.B. agent. To find that light, the pair must make several visits to extraterrestrials, including a video shop where they obtain a video with clues to the object they seek while Boyle is seeking the same device. Boyle takes over M.I.B. headquarters, but Jones and Smith, with the help of some strange extraterrestrials called the "Worm Guys," attack the place and battle Boyle and all the worst aliens she has released on earth and while attempting to free Dawson, a pizzeria waitress Boyle has kidnapped, believing that she knows the location of the Light of Zartha, which, the M.I.B. agents know, must be removed from earth before it destroys the planet. A chase ensues where Boyle assumes the form of a giant worm that attacks Jones and Smith, but they manage to destroy the creature and then Dawson, who is really the Light of Zartha, takes off in a spacecraft to return to her home planet and thus saves the world from destruction, all to the emotional dismay of Smith, who has fallen in love with her. Smith and Jones reprise their roles from the 1997 film with good performances, and, again, the special effects are astounding, although the script is not as witty or ironic as the original. But it is nevertheless a thoroughly entertaining parody, where Torn, as the principled director of M.I.B., is again humorously effective. The film was produced on a budget of $140 million and returned $441 million at the box office. **p**, Laurie MacDonald, Walter F. Parkes, Graham Place, Steven Spielberg; **d**, Barry Sonnenfeld; **cast**, Tommy Lee Jones, Will Smith, Rip Torn, Lara Flynn Boyle, Johnny Knoxville, Rosario Dawson, Tony Shalhoub, Patrick Warburton, Michael Jackson, Chloe Sonnenfeld, Peter Graves; **w**, Robert Gordon, Barry Fanaro (based on a

Nehemiah Persoff in *Men in War*, 1957.

story by Gordon and the comic book "Malibu Comics" by Lowell Cunningham); **c**, Greg Gardiner; **m**, Danny Elfman; **ed**, Richard Pearson, Steven Weisberg; **prod d**, Bo Welch; **art d**, Alec Hammond, Sean Haworth, Tom Wilkins; **set d**, Cheryl Carasik; **spec eff**, Jeffrey S. Brink, Bill Sturgeon.

Men in War ★★★ 1957; U.S.; 102m; Security/UA; B/W; War Drama; Children: Unacceptable; **DVD; VHS**. During the Korean War, a tough, battle-worn lieutenant (Ryan) is behind enemy lines and wants to get to a strategic hill where he left his platoon. Ray is a sergeant whose job it is to get Keith, a shell-shocked colonel, to a military hospital. When Ryan's transportation is wrecked, he takes over Ray's jeep with Keith in it and the three get to the hill, but find most of the men in Ryan's platoon are dead and North Koreans have control of the area. Ryan and Ray, with the help of a few others, take the hill back and salute the GIs who fell there. It's a strong anti-war film, shown in gritty scenes of survival by Mann, where Ryan and Ray give standout performances. Bernstein's discordant score is also very effective in enhancing the tension while the combat scenes are realistically presented. Its excessive violence prohibits viewing by children. *Author's Note*: The Korean War has been depicted in many feature films, most notably: **The Steel Helmet**, 1951; **Fixed Bayonets!**, 1951; **Flat Top**, 1952; **One Minute to Zero**, 1952; **Retreat, Hell!**, 1952; **The Glory Brigade**, 1953; **Take the High Ground**, 1953; **The Bridges at Toko-Ri**, 1954; **Men of the Fighting Lady**, 1954; **Prisoner of War**, 1954; **The McConnell Story**, 1955; **The Rack**, 1956; **Time Limit**, 1957; **Pork Chop Hill**, 1959; **The Manchurian Candidate**, 1962; **War Is Hell**, 1963; **M*A*S*H**, 1970; and **MacArthur**, 1977; **p**, Sidney Harmon; **d**, Anthony Mann; **cast**, Robert Ryan, Aldo Ray, Robert Keith, Philip Pine, Nehemiah Persoff, Vic Morrow, James Edwards, L.Q. Jones, Scott Marlowe, Adam Kennedy, Race Gentry, Victor Sen Yung; **w**, Philip Yordan, Ben Maddow (based on the novel *Combat* by Van Van Praag); **c**, Ernest Haller; **m**, Elmer Bernstein; **ed**, Richard C. Meyer; **prod d**, Lewis Jacobs; **art d**, Frank Paul Sylos; **spec eff**, Louis DeWitt, Jack Erickson, Jack Rabin, Lee Zavitz.

Men in White ★★★ 1934; U.S.; 74m; MGM; B/W; Drama; Children: Unacceptable; **DVD**. Gable turns in an impressive performance as a dedicated physician whose medical career is disrupted after he meets alluring vixen Loy, an idling playgirl. He forsakes his impregnated girlfriend, Allan, and abandons his medical research with fellow doctor Hersholt, after Loy convinces him that the only path to success is to practice medicine among the wealthy. The deserted Allan has an abortion, but the operation causes her to contract peritonitis and, while Gable stands helplessly by, she dies. Her death impacts both Gable and Loy, who see the

errors of their selfish ways. Loy, in an uncharacteristic turnabout, then convinces Gable to abandon his lucrative practice and pursue his medical research that will benefit mankind as a much more rewarding way of life. Boleslawski directs this medical melodrama with a firm hand and exacts superior performances from Gable and Loy; in fact, Gable stunned MGM's front office with his powerful performance as he had heretofore been known chiefly as a tough thug in gangster films, and it was this role that convinced MGM to cast him in more heroic roles. The theme of a dedicated doctor abandoning his ethics to become rich by tending to high society appears in many films (most notably in **The Citadel**, 1938, where Robert Donat forsakes dedicated medical research to become rich as a high society doctor), but the idea is fresh and innovative in this early talkie. *Author's Note*: Loy, who appeared in seven films with Gable, said, years later, that "it seems incredible that we were never lovers." Gable, however, during this production, was having a brief affair with Allan, prompting Hollywood guru Anita Loos to later say about him: "Clark had a Babbitt [a chauvinistic character in the novels of Sinclair Lewis] mentality about sex in those days, that old, early American male idea that you must take on any girl that comes your way." Loy told this author that she did not like her role in this film, or most of it, stating: "Here I am once more spoiled rotten to the core—that's poetry, isn't it?—and destroying everyone I meet just for the fun of it. There was no end to those roles, although I did have Clark [Gable] to lead to his destruction. I used to ask myself, 'will I ever get a role where I play a decent person?' I do get to show some compassion at the end of **Men in White**, but that did not drown out the hisses I got through most of that picture. Those roles where I am a reasonable person with some principles finally showed up a few years later, but getting those roles was like pulling teeth from the mouth of the MGM lion." **p**, Monta Bell; **d**, Richard Boleslavski; **cast**, Clark Gable, Myrna Loy, Jean Hersholt, Elizabeth Allan, Otto Kruger, C. Henry Gordon, Russell Hardie, Wallace Ford, Henry B. Walthall, Russell Hopton, Samuel S. Hinds, Frank Puglia, Donald Douglas; **w**, Waldemar Young (based on the play by Sidney Kingsley); **c**, George Folsey; **m**, William Axt; **ed**, Frank Sullivan; **art d**, Cedric Gibbons.

Men of Boys Town ★★★ 1941; U.S.; 106m; MGM; B/W; Drama; Children: Cautionary; **DVD; VHS**. In this sequel to **Boys Town**, 1938, Tracy, playing the legendary Father Edward J. Flanagan (1886-1948) needs money to keep the boys' home open, and has his hands full with the arrival of Nunn, a bitter boy who has been crippled in a beating at a reform school. Rooney and some of the other boys try to help him adjust. Tracy helps with this by giving Nunn a dog. A middle-aged couple, O'Neill and Nash, come looking for a boy to adopt, and choose Rooney. They take him home, but Rooney misses his pals at Boys Town. He drives to a nearby reform school to visit a friend, but isn't allowed inside, so he drives away. He then discovers that a boy from the school, Hickman, is hiding in his car to escape the brutality at the school. Hickman steals $200 in a robbery, and he and Rooney are sent to Hickman's old reform school. Rooney's friend at the reform school commits suicide, and the boy's mother, Revere, appeals to Tracy to expose the harsh treatment there. Tracy convinces authorities to investigate brutality at the reform school and takes Rooney and Hickman to Boys Town. Nunn gets an operation on his legs, but doesn't have the will to try to walk, until his dog is accidentally killed. At the dog's funeral, Nunn stands up at its grave. O'Neill and Nash then give Tracy the money needed to keep Boys Town open. Taurog does a good job keeping this melodrama going at a fast clip, and fine performances come from Tracy, Rooney, Hickman and others. Several traumatic scenes, however, the suicide and accidental death of a dog, may be too disturbing for children. **p**, John W. Considine, Jr.; **d**, Norman Taurog; **cast**, Spencer Tracy, Mickey Rooney, Bobs Watson, Larry Nunn, Darryl Hickman, Henry O'Neill, Mary Nash, Lee J. Cobb, Sidney Miller, Addison Richards, Lloyd Corrigan, Anne Revere, Janet Beecher; **w**, James Kevin McGuinness; **c**, Harold Rosson; **m**, Herbert Stothart; **ed**, Fredrick Y. Smith, Ben Lewis; **art d**, Cedric

Gibbons, Henry McAfee; **set d**, Edwin B. Willis.

Men of Honor ★★★ 2000; U.S.; 129m; FOX; Color; Drama; Children: Unacceptable (MPAA: R); **BD**; **DVD**. Based on the true story of Carl Maxie Brashear (1931-2006), a Kentucky sharecropper's son, this film incisively shows how Brashear slowly broke down the racial barriers inside the U.S. Navy. Gooding plays Brashear, who is armed with only a high school education when he decides, in 1952, to become the first African-American deep sea diver in the U.S. Navy after World War II when racism was still rampant in the country and in the U.S. military. De Niro, a racist and sadist, who is Gooding's trainer, along with Gooding's alcoholic wife, Theron, are just as determined to see Gooding fail. Also strongly opposed to Gooding is his commanding officer, Holbrook. President Harry S. Truman had integrated the U.S. military services, but the navy is slow to change. Blacks in the navy were mainly offered two job choices: cooks or officers' valets. A Harlem librarian, Ellis, tutors Gooding, enabling him to pass a written exam, and he survives a rigged training exercise in which he almost drowns after hours of being submerged. De Niro's prejudicial feelings toward Gooding dissipate when he realizes that Gooding loves deep sea diving just as much as he does. This helps Gooding to complete his training and he finally realizes his ambition as a personal triumph for himself as well as the U.S. Navy. Excellent characterizations are rendered by De Niro and Gooding in this tension-filled drama. Gutter language and blatant expressions of racism prohibit viewing by children. **p**, Bill Badalato, Robert Teitel, Bill Cosby, Stanley Robertson; **d**, George Tillman, Jr.; **cast**, Robert De Niro, Cuba Gooding, Jr., Charlize Theron, Aunjanue Ellis, Hal Holbrook, Michael Rapaport, Powers Boothe, David Keith, Holt McCallany, David Conrad, Joshua Leonard; **w**, Scott Marshall Smith; **c**, Anthony B. Richmond; **m**, Mark Isham; **ed**, John Carter, Dirk Westervelt; **prod d**, Leslie Dilley; **art d**, Lawrence A. Hubbs; **set d**, Kate J. Sullivan; **spec eff**, Boyd Lacosse, Keith Urban, Cosmas Paul Bolger, Jr., Peter W. Moyer, C. Marie Davis, Dan Chuba.

Men of the Fighting Lady ★★★★ 1954; 79m; MGM; Color; War Drama; Children: Unacceptable; **DVD**; **VHS**. Exciting and tension filled, this superlative sea saga tells many tales of jet fighter pilots on board a U.S. carrier (USS *Oriskany*) during the Korean War. The film begins when famed writer James A. Michener, played by Calhern, comes aboard that carrier to hear stories of the heroic and dramatic experiences of some of those aviators that include Johnson, Martin, Wynn, Lovejoy and others. Shown are several combat missions where the aerial dogfights between U.S. and Russian-made fighter jets are spectacular, but the most prolonged and fascinating sequence involves the story of the "blind pilot," one where cocky Martin, a fighter pilot who has never had any use for religion or has never sought God's help, is injured in combat so that he is blinded but still able to fly, although he cannot open his canopy or eject. Johnson, who is flying as Martin's wing man, tells Martin on the radio that he will talk him through this ordeal if Martin closely follows his instructions while they are on their return flight to the carrier. Martin, on several occasions, almost passes out from his wound, but manages to stay on course while doing exactly what Johnson tells him to do, and he slowly comes to realize that he needs more help than that, so he asks for help from God. Both planes (F9F Panther fighter jets) are running out of fuel by the time they spot the carrier, and Johnson talks Martin into a landing (after several passes of the deck) so that he lands safely and survives and where Johnson himself also survives. (This incident was based on a real event.) Marton's direction is top flight, and Johnson, Martin, Wynn and others render good performances, all enhanced by Rozsa's dynamic score. *Author's Note*: Gene Ruggiero, a close friend, edited this film and told this author that "Marton allowed me to insert many scenes from actual newsreel footage into the dramatic combat scenes, and all of the actual combat footage I got myself when I went to Washington and where the U.S. Navy gave me a lot of black-and-white footage and some color footage." Within that footage, Rug-

Robert De Niro and Cuba Gooding Jr. in *Men of Honor,* 2000.

giero found a spectacular crash of a U.S. Navy fighter plane that actually broke in half when striking the main superstructure of a carrier. "Marton took one look at that footage and moaned, saying, "God, I wish we could use it but it's on black-and-white film and we are shooting this picture all in color.' I told him that 'I think I can fix that,' and he gave me a strange look and said, 'if you've got the magic, go to it.' I knew this very talented Hollywood backdrop artist, Warren Newcombe, and I went to him with this thirty-feet of Navy footage and arranged to have the studio pay him $5,000 to paint every frame in that strip of film in color. The results were great and that footage looked like it had really been shot in color. I spliced that strip of colorized film into some live-action shots for the film and it ran in the picture when released." When U.S. Navy experts at the Pentagon saw the film they were amazed and called Ruggiero, asking him where he got that strip of color film, and he replied: "I had it made." They disbelieved him, until he sent them the two cuts of the film he had so expertly doctored with Newcombe's help. This film did exceptionally well at the box office, being released just when the Korean War was ending. **p**, Henry Berman; **d**, Andrew Marton; **cast**, Van Johnson, Walter Pidgeon, Louis Calhern, Dewey Martin, Keenan Wynn, Frank Lovejoy, Robert Horton, Bert Freed, Lewis Martin, George Cooper, Dick Simmons, Jerry Mathers, Dorothy Patrick; **w**, Art Cohn (based on the story "The Forgotten Heroes of Korea" by James Michener and the story "The Case of the Blind Pilot" by Comdr. Harry A. Burns, USN); **c**, George Folsey (Anscocolor); **m**, Miklos Rozsa; **ed**, Gene Ruggiero; **art d**, Cedric Gibbons, Paul Groesse; **set d**, Edwin B. Willis, Keogh Gleason; **spec eff**, A. Arnold Gillespie, Warren Newcombe.

Men of the Sea ★★★ 1951; U.K.; 70m; Associated Talking Pictures/Astor Pictures; B/W; Adventure; Children: Acceptable. Green is a young man in the late 1700s, enlisting in the British navy during the Napoleonic War and who gets into many adventures including rescuing beautiful Lockwood from pirates and finding a lost treasure. It was Reed's first as solo director and it shows the promise of his great films to come. Produced in 1935, this film was not released in the U.S. until 1951. **p**, Basil Dean; **d**, Carol Reed; **cast**, Hughie Green, Margaret Lockwood, Harry Tate, Robert Adams, Roger Livesey, Dennis Wyndham, Lewis Casson, Tom Gill, Frederick Burtwell, Desmond Tester; **w**, Anthony Kimmins, Peggy Thompson (based on the novel *Midshipman Easy* by Frederick Marryat); **c**, John W. Boyle; **m**, Frederic Austin, Ernest Irving, Raoul Kraushaar; **ed**, Sidney Cole; **art d**, Edward Carrick.

Men with Wings ★★★ 1938; U.S.; 105m; PAR; Color; Adventure; Children: Acceptable; **VHS**. Directed by experienced pilot Wellman (who flew in France in the Lafayette Escadrille in WWI), this film shows

Ildiko Bansagi, Klaus Maria Brandauer, directed by Istvan Szabo in *Mephisto*, 1982.

an exciting chronicle of the development of aircraft, beginning with three children flying a kite, O'Connor, Weidler and Cook (much the same way Wellman began a great adventure tale a year later when helming **Beau Geste**, 1939, where children are seen at playing warriors, including O'Connor). They hear about the first successful flight of the Wright brothers at Kitty Hawk, and the viewer then sees Abel, as a reporter eager to test the new flying machine by ascending into the air, only to become one of the first air casualties when he dies in a fiery crash. The children grow up to be MacMurray, Campbell and Milland, where both MacMurray and Milland become early-day pilots with MacMurray marrying childhood sweetheart Campbell. Milland also loves her, but remains close to the two. After several air adventures, MacMurray becomes obsessed with aiding the Chinese, who are being invaded by the Japanese, and he flies off to help China. After he is killed, Milland comforts Campbell and eventually marries her. MacMurray, Campbell and Milland (Milland would also appear in Wellman's **Beau Geste** the following year) are standouts in their roles, and Wellman does a fine job helming this air saga where his aerial sequences are stunning. *Author's Note*: MacMurray told this author that "In **Men with Wings** I am flying those old double-winged planes and I wondered how Bill [Wellman] ever got the nerve to get into any of those broken down crates and actually get them in to the air and ever trust that he could land them in one piece. They were held together by wire and spit, I think. I swore I would never go near any of those old air jalopies again, but, about six years later, I was climbing into those very airplanes when we did **Captain Eddie** [1945, where MacMurray played WWI air ace Captain Eddie Rickenbacker]." **p&d**, William A. Wellman; **cast**, Fred MacMurray, Ray Milland, Louise Campbell, Andy Devine, Lynne Overman, Porter Hall, Walter Abel, Kitty Kelly, Virginia Weidler, Donald O'Connor, Dennis Morgan, John Hubbard, Evelyn Keyes, Joan Leslie, Cheryl Walker; **w**, Robert Carson; **c**, W. Howard Greene (Technicolor); **m**, Gerard Carbonara, W. Franke Harling; **ed**, Thomas Scott; **art d**, Hans Dreier, Robert Odell; **set d**, A.E. Freudeman; **spec eff**, Farciot Edouart, Gordon Jennings, Loyal Griggs.

Mephisto ★★★ 1982; West Germany/Hungary/Austria; 144m; Hessischer Rundfunk/Analysis Film Releasing Corp.; Color; Drama; Children: Unacceptable; **DVD**; **VHS**. A modern version of the "Faust" legend set in Hamburg, Germany, sees stage actor Brandauer become famous for his portrayal of Mephisto, who sells his soul to the devil in exchange for worldly riches. He does this in real life before World War II by supporting the Nazi party so he can move to Berlin and become a stage star in that more important city. He is mainly interested in furthering his career, but also saves some colleagues, who are threatened by the Nazis. The film spans the years from the 1920s to the 1940s during which Bran-

dauer submerses more and more of himself into the actor in him whose primary ambition is to get applause and adulation. The movie won the 1982 Academy Award for Best Foreign Film. Mature subject material prohibits viewing by children. (In German; English subtitles.) **p**, Manfred Durniok; **d**, István Szabó; **cast**, Klaus Maria Brandauer, Krystyna Janda, Ildikó Bánsági, Rolf Hoppe, György Cserhalmi, Péter Andorai, Karin Boyd, Christine Harbort, Tamás Major, Ildikó Kishonti; **w**, Szabo, Péter Dobai (based on the novel by Klaus Mann); **c**, Lajos Koltai (Eastmancolor); **m**, Zdenkó Tamássy; **ed**, Zsuzsa Csákány; **set d**, Nagy János, József Romvári.

The Mephisto Waltz ★★★ 1971; U.S.; 115m; FOX; Color; Horror; Children: Unacceptable (MPAA: PG-13); **DVD**; **VHS**. Jurgens is an aging pianist, who is dying of leukemia and who grants music critic Alda an interview and uses his Satan-like powers to take over Alda's body so he can continue living after he dies. Alda's wife, Bisset, notices changes in him and also becomes possessed after making a bargain with the devil. Jurgens, meanwhile, is having an incestuous affair with his daughter Parkins. Bisset kills Parkins, assumes her body, and winds up with a man who is a combination of Jurgens and Alda. Strange, even bizarre, this one is strictly for horror fans. Music: Franz Liszt's "The Mephisto Waltz." **p**, Quinn Martin; **d**, Paul Wendkos; **cast**, Alan Alda, Jacqueline Bisset, Barbara Parkins, Brad (Bradford) Dillman, William Windom, Kathleen Widdoes, Curt Jurgens, Pamelyn Ferdin, Curt Lowens, Gregory Morton, Berry Kroeger; **w**, Ben Maddow (based on the novel by Fred Mustard Stewart); **c**, William W. Spencer (DeLuxe Color); **m**, Jerry Goldsmith; **ed**, Richard Brockway; **art d**, Richard Y. Haman; **set d**, Walter M. Scott, Raphael Bretton; **spec eff**, Greg C. Jensen.

The Merchant of Venice ★★★ 2004; U.S.; 138m; Sony; Color; Drama/Comedy; Children: Unacceptable (MPAA: R); **DVD**. Based on the play by William Shakespeare, the action takes place in 1596 Venice, a time when Christian enmity toward Jews was a fact of life. Irons, a middle-aged Christian merchant, spits on Pacino, a Jewish moneylender on the Rialto Bridge as a gesture of his contempt for Jews. This starts a tragic chain of events. Irons and a younger man, Fiennes, are friends, so when Fiennes asks for some money, he gives it, not knowing Fiennes is going to use it to marry a young woman, Portia (Collins) by paying her impoverished father for her hand. Irons' remaining money is tied up with merchant shipping at sea, so he grudgingly goes to Pacino, who hates Christians. Pacino offers him a three-month loan at no interest, but if it is not repaid by then, he will exact a pound of flesh from Irons. Pacino's daughter, Robinson, steals his fortune and runs off to marry a young man named Lorenzo (Cox). While Fiennes is wooing Collins, Pacino demands his pound of flesh from Irons. The matter goes to court and a judge must decide if Pacino gets what he wants and which Irons agreed upon, not dreaming Pacino would ever actually expect such a payment. Collins, disguised as a male lawyer, saves Irons from losing his skin. In the end, Pacino is financially ruined and forced to convert to Christianity. Nudity prohibits viewing by children. **p**, Cary Brokaw, Michael Lionello Cowan, Barry Navidi, Jason Piette, Bob Bellion, Jimmy de Brabant, Edwige Fenech, Nigel Goldsack, Luciano Martino, Irene Masiello; **d&w**, Michael Radford (based on the play by William Shakespeare); **cast**, Al Pacino, Jeremy Irons, Joseph Fiennes, Lynn Collins, Zuleikha Robinson, Kris Marshall, Charlie Cox, Heather Goldenhersh, Mackenzie Crook, John Sessions; **c**, Benoît Delhomme; **m**, Jocelyn Pook; **ed**, Lucia Zucchetti; **prod d**, Bruno Rubeo; **art d**, Jon Bunker, Tamara Marini; **set d**, Gillie Delap; **spec eff**, Alain Couty, Sean H. Farrow.

Mermaids ★★★ 1990; U.S.; 110m; Orion Pictures; Color; Comedy; Children: Cautionary (MPAA: PG-13); **DVD**; **VHS**. This offbeat comedy, set in the 1960s, has Cher as an eccentric divorced mother, who has had numerous failed relationships, moving to a new town after each affair ends. She starts a new life in a coastal town in Massachusetts with her two daughters, one fifteen-year-old Ryder and the other, Ricci, a preteen who has a thing for swimming all the time and holding her breath under water. Ryder makes friends with a handsome young handyman, Schoeffling, at a Roman Catholic convent. First, she thinks she might become a nun, even though she's Jewish, because she likes quiet, which she doesn't find at home, but then she feels heart pangs for Schoeffling. A short and husky shoe-store owner, Hoskins, enters their lives when he takes an interest in Cher, but thinks she and her kids are a bit off-kilter and need to come down to earth. Not likely, as Schoeffling gives Ryder a kiss and she is positive that she is pregnant. The title refers to mermaids but the film isn't clear what that means except that Cher wears a mermaid costume to a New Year's Eve party and she and her daughters all may be fish out of water, although Ricci spends most of her time in swimming pools. Mostly, it's a film about a close mother-daughter relationship involving Cher and Ryder. They are total opposites in that Cher wants to live the free life of a modern gypsy and Ryder wants a more stable life. The film ends up in the air with everyone dancing around a table. **p**, Lauren Lloyd, Wallis Nicita, Patrick Palmer; **d**, Richard Benjamin; **cast**, Cher, Bob Hoskins, Winona Ryder, Michael Schoeffling, Christina Ricci, Caroline McWilliams, Jan Miner, Betsy Townsend, Richard McElvain, Paula Plum; **w**, June Roberts (based on the novel by Patty Dann); **c**, Howard Atherton (Technicolor); **m**, Jack Nitzsche; **ed**, Jacqueline Cambas; **prod d**, Stuart Wurtzel; **art d**, Evelyn Sakash, Steve Saklad; **set d**, Hilton Rosemarin; **spec eff**, Brian Ricci.

Merrill's Marauders ★★★ 1962; U.S.; 98m; WB; Color; War Drama; Children: Unacceptable; **DVD**; **VHS**. Exhausting but compelling war film is set in Burma in 1944 in WWII where Chandler commands an American regiment (530th Composite Unit) as General Frank Merrill (1903-1955). After his regiment takes its objective, Chandler is ordered by his commander, Hoyt, playing General Joseph "Vinegar Joe" Stilwell (1883-1946) to march his men farther into Burma behind Japanese lines to attack and capture the vital town of Myitkyina. This seemingly impossible assignment demands that his already weary men must scale a 6,000-foot mountain range where they struggle with pack mules, many falling behind through disease and exhaustion. After taking an objective in en route, the GIs are so debilitated that they initially refuse Chandler's command to go to their main objective and where, in exhorting his men, Chandler suffers a heart attack. Hardin, one of his officers, however, is able to rally the troops and they go on to Myitkyina and, after a hard battle against impossible odds, they take the town from the Japanese defenders. Fuller directs this film with great military expertise, accurately profiling this heroic American force (out of a force of about 3,000 men, only 130 effectives remained after Myitkyina was captured) while developing empathetic and memorable characters within the ranks of the stalwart U.S. troops such as Akins, Hutchins and Brown. Chandler gives on of his best performances, his last one, as he died of blood poisoning before this film was released. **p**, Milton Sperling; **d**, Samuel Fuller; **cast**, Jeff Chandler, Ty Hardin, Peter Brown, Andrew Duggan, Will Hutchins, Claude Akins, Luz Valdez, John Hoyt, Charles Briggs, Chuck Roberson, Chuck Hayward, Pancho Magalona; **w**, Fuller, Sperling (based on the novel by Charlton Ogburn, Jr.); **c**, William Clothier (Technicolor); **m**, Howard Jackson; **ed**, Folmar Blangsted; **art d**, William Magginetti; **spec eff**, Ralph Ayres.

Merry Christmas, Mr. Lawrence ★★★ 1983; Japan/U.K.; 123m; Recorded Picture Co./UNIV; Color; War Drama; Children: Unacceptable (MPAA: R); **BD**; **DVD**; **VHS**. In Java during World War II in 1942, British Col. John Lawrence (Conti), is among those interned in a Japanese prisoner of war camp run by tyrannical and sadistic Takeshi. Conti speaks Japanese and believes he knows how his captors think. The Japanese see the British as dishonorable and weak for having surrendered and for not committing suicide rather than surrendering. Conti, however, considers his Japanese captors to be cruel and not the brave

Winona Ryder and Michael Schoeffling in *Mermaids*, 1990.

or loyal soldiers they think they are. The other prisoners consider Conti a traitor for having any dealings with the enemy. Another British prisoner, Bowie, a major, is put on trial elsewhere for alleged spying. Sakamoto is at the trial and is impressed by Bowie's defiance and courage. Bowie is found guilty and sentenced to death by a firing squad, but it is faked, and Sakamoto has him taken to Takeshi's camp where Bowie is reunited with Conti with whom he served in Libya. Both Conti and Bowie are jailed for alleged camp rules violations but are released on Christmas. Thompson, an Australian prisoner, is going to be executed, but Bowie kisses Sakamoto on both cheeks, causing Sakamoto to collapse. For that, Bowie is buried up to his neck in sand in the hot sun. As the war ends, Takeshi is relieved of command and Bowie dies. Four years later, Conti visits Takeshi and shows him a lock of Bowie's hair when Bowie was buried in the sand pit. Takeshi is moved and tells Conti, "Merry Christmas, Mr. Lawrence." The film is mainly a struggle of wills between the prisoners and their captors and was as equally well profiled in **The Bridge on the River Kwai**, 1957. *Author's Note*: The Japanese High Command knew all about the rules and regulations established by the Geneva Convention regarding prisoners of war, which they did not sign before WWII, and refused to honor its conditions. The brutality and atrocities committed by the Japanese during WWII saw punishment from the West after the war when a goodly number of Japanese commanders were tried and convicted of either ordering or permitting those war crimes, many executed. Excessive violence prohibits viewing by children. **p**, Jeremy Thomas; **d**, Nagisa Ôshima; **cast**, David Bowie, Tom Conti, Ryûichi Sakamoto, Takeshi, Jack Thompson, Johnny Ohkura, Alistair Browning, James Malcolm, Chis Broun, Yûya Uchida, Ryûnosuke Kaneda, Takashi Naitô; **w**, Ôshima, Paul Mayersberg (based on the novel *The Seed and the Sower* by Laurens Van der Post); **c**, Tôichirô Narushima; **m**, Ryûichi Sakamoto; **ed**, Tomoyo Oshima; **prod d**, Shigemasa Toda; **art d**, Andrew Sanders; **spec eff**, Kevin Chisnall, Shulamit Levin.

A Merry War ★★★ 1998; U.K.; 101m; BBC Films/First Look Intl.; Color; Comedy; Children: Unacceptable (MPAA: PG-13); **DVD**; **VHS**. Clever comedy sees Grant as a would-be poet, who quits his job at a London advertising agency where he has been working as a copywriter. He is more of a complainer than he is an angry young man with social grievances. Wanting to see how the lower class lives, he dons old clothes and gets a job at a secondhand book store where he meets and falls for Bonham Carter and then his troubles really begin. This comedy is based on George Orwell's great 1936 satirical novel *Keep the Aspidistra Flying*, referring to an almost indestructible house plant found in many British rooming houses. The war in the title is not so much between the social classes as it is between the sexes, as Grant and Bonham Carter

Mae Murray in *The Merry Widow*, 1925.

try to decide whether to kiss or attack each other. Sexual material prohibits viewing by children. **p**, Peter Shaw; **d**, Robert Bierman; **cast**, Richard E. Grant, Helena Bonham Carter, Julian Wadham, Jim Carter, Harriet Walter, Lesley Vickerage, Barbara Leigh Hunt, Liz Smith, John Clegg, Bill Wallis; **w**, Alan Plater (based on the novel by George Orwell); **c**, Giles Nuttgens (Rankcolor); **m**, Mike Batt; **ed**, Bill Wright; **prod d**, Sarah Greenwood; **art d**, Philip Robinson.

The Merry Widow ★★★★ 1925 (silent); U.S.; 137m; MGM; B/W/Color; Drama/Romance; Children: Unacceptable; **DVD**; **VHS**. In one of his finest films, the imperial Stroheim almost bankrupted the recently established MGM with his excessive takes, sumptuous sets, exorbitant costumes and while ignoring any kind of reasonable schedule. Further, the truculent Stroheim completely ignored the story line of the gushy original stage musical and provides his own melodramatic tale. Despite all this, the film is a silent classic that begins with an army on maneuvers in a Ruritanian kingdom. The officers of a regiment are billeted at a local inn when Murray, the star of the Manhattan Follies, arrives with her entourage. She attracts the attentions of Gilbert and D'Arcy, who are both princes and cousins, the latter the heir to the throne, when Murray lifts her dress to check a run in her stocking. Both young men then compete for her attentions, Gilbert as a gentleman and D'Arcy as a lecherous libertine, a notorious womanizer with no morals, scruples or conscience (exactly like the parts Stroheim himself had earlier played, particularly in **Foolish Wives**, 1922). The princes entertain Murray at dinner and Stroheim presents a humorous scene where both Gilbert and D'Arcy think they are playing footsies beneath the dining room table with Murray when they are toying with their own feet. The romantic competitors then see another rival when Marshall appears; he is a baron and the power behind the throne. All three are next seen in an audience watching Murray perform her act. She presents a rather seductive dance, and Stroheim depicts the innocent love or lust all three men have for the alluring Murray by cross-cutting from parts of her anatomy to close-ups of their faces. Gilbert sees only Murray's beautiful face where the lascivious D'Arcy sees only her moving breasts and undulating hips and where Marshall sees only her nimbly dancing feet (he is a cripple with a foot fetish). Following her performance, Murray rebuffs an invitation from Marshall to dine with him, and, instead, accepts Gilbert's invitation and they retire to an apartment where they sit at a resplendent candlelit table while two blindfolded, scantily clad female musicians entertain them. While Murray and Gilbert have dinner, Stroheim cuts back and forth from that scene to show the dissolute Marshall dining with nubile, skimpily adorned teenagers while D'Arcy hosts a full scale orgy with all of his officers, the kind of bacchanalia for which Stroheim had long earlier become infamous and where voluptuous

women are handled as playthings as D'Arcy proves his incredible marksmanship by shooting the eyes out of a statue. After Gilbert accidentally spills some soup on Murray's gown, she briefly retires to put on a robe, and, as she returns to him, the drunken D'Arcy and his officers invade their apartment. D'Arcy, seeing Murray in the robe, blatantly accuses Gilbert of being a seducer. Gilbert not only denies this accusation, but tells D'Arcy that he and Murray are planning to marry. The enraged D'Arcy storms off and takes out his wrath in a sadistic act of vengeance by beating a helpless, crippled doorman senseless. When Gilbert informs Fawcett and Crowell, the king and queen, of his intentions, they refuse to sanction the marriage between Gilbert and commoner Murray. Thus rejected, the emotionally injured Murray reluctantly accepts Marshall's proposal of marriage after he tells her that his wealth and power will allow her to exact vengeance upon Gilbert and the arrogant royal members that have made her a pariah from their court. Murray's wedding night with Marshall is a disaster where Marshall salaciously indulges his obsessive fetish by playing with Murray's feet, making him so obnoxious and repulsive that the poor woman all but passes out at this disgusting display of perverted love. To Murray's horror (and relief), Marshall's blood pressure boils over while partaking in this sexual perversion and he is instantly immobilized by a stroke. The paralyzed Marshall is bedridden for months, but his sexual fantasies again overwhelm him, driving him to crawl from his bed to a nearby closet and to slavishly embrace Murray's myriad shoes stored there and where Marshall dies. Murray is now free to travel and goes to Paris (and, at this point, the story begins to resemble the original musical story line) where she once again meets Gilbert, but he is drunk and his offhanded remarks lead her to believe that he is only interested in her money (she has inherited Marshall's great wealth and estates) and she lies when telling him that she does not love him but loves the cousin he hates, D'Arcy. Gilbert and D'Arcy then argue and they wind up facing each other in a duel where Gilbert fires his weapon into the air and Murray arrives to see him wounded by D'Arcy, who has no chivalry. Then Fawcett, the king, dies and D'Arcy returns to his kingdom to be present at the funeral and later to claim the crown, but the crippled doorman who has habitually been abused by D'Arcy erupts from the crowd of mourners and assassinates D'Arcy. Gilbert is then shown in his chambers of the palace and where Murray pleads with him to marry her and where he tells her that he cannot wed a woman so wealthy without losing his honor. News is then brought to him that D'Arcy is dead and that Gilbert is now the king. In the final sequence, which appears in color in the original print, a grand coronation is presented with Gilbert and Murray marching in a procession together, presumably toward happiness and marriage and where thousands of extras are present as troops, citizens and members of the court. For all of its excesses and pomp and finery, Stroheim's opus presents a stunning, rich pageantry of a fantasy world, awash with true love, bizarre fetishes and lethal menaces. Gilbert is outstanding as the gentleman officer, and Murray the perfect victim while D'Arcy and Marshall give some of the most bizarre and outlandish performances ever seen on the screen. The film's budget of more than $600,000 was returned with estimated profits of more than $2 million, an astounding success. ***Author's Note***: Stroheim began this production while it was the property of the Samuel Goldwyn Studio, but when that studio was merged into Metro and Goldwyn (becoming Metro-Goldwyn-Mayer or MGM), he was then working at the sound stages and back lot of a new studio in Culver City and he was putting up with a reigning movie queen, Murray (former Ziegfeld Follies star), someone with whom he had never before worked as he preferred his leading players to be unknowns to better manipulate them. Further, Stroheim was again saddled with the supervision of the new studio's production chief, Irving Thalberg, who was the protégé of Louis B. Mayer, head of the newly created MGM. Thalberg and Stroheim had locked heads earlier when they both worked at Universal and Thalberg, knowing Stroheim's penchant for ignoring schedules, immediately began pressuring the director to stay on schedule for **The Merry Widow**. He had Mayer offer

Stroheim, who had not yet been paid for his work on this film, $30,000 in advance, with a $10,000 bonus if he delivered the film on schedule. Stroheim ignored the schedule and went his own way, spending thousands of dollars on specially made shoes for Murray that she never wore and, to emphasize Marshall's foot fetish, shows those shoes in seemingly mile-long closets as he slowly pans over endless boots, slippers, shoes, and shoetrees. After Thalberg saw the rushes of these scenes, he confronted Stroheim, demanding that these scenes be edited down. "The character I am portraying here has a foot fetish!" Stroheim shouted. "He may have a foot fetish," Thalberg replied, "but *you* have a footage fetish!" Moreover, Thalberg found a bill for thousands of dollars for monogrammed underwear that the officers were to wear. He exploded and went to Stroheim again, demanding to know why Stroheim ordered silk, monogrammed underwear for actors that would not be seen on the screen. "Of course the underwear does not show, but the actors *will know* they are wearing such fine garments and that will give them the confidence to properly enact superior beings as officers," Stroheim responded before walking away. Though the cost-conscious Thalberg and the imperialistic director disliked each other immensely, there was pure hatred existing between Stroheim and his leading lady. Just before Murray's big moment in the film, where she is about to begin the waltz (with 350 extras waiting for her to adjust her gown and headdress), and was the closest thing to the original story line Stroheim maintained, the director stepped up to the actress and told her how to perform her initial steps. Murray, a talented and experienced dancer, exploded, screaming: "You dirty Hun! You think you know everything!" She tore her elaborate peacock headdress away and hurled it at Stroheim and began stamping her feet in rage. Stroheim turned on his booted heels and immediately left the studio and remained at home. When hearing that his top star had been insulted, Mayer fired Stroheim and replaced him with Monta Bell. However, Gilbert, D'Arcy, Marshall and the rest of the cast, as well as the crew members, despite Stroheim's arrogant and autocratic ways, remained loyal to him and nothing much happened until Mayer reinstated Stroheim, who then completed the film. His association with MGM, however, was at an end and he was no longer wanted at the studio or any other studio. Stroheim was not only out of work, but would direct (for other studios) only a few more films until the unofficial blacklist imposed upon him by Mayer reduced him to work as an actor. The enmity between Mayer and Stroheim was deep and lifelong, particularly after Stroheim while at a meeting in Mayer's office, told the family-cherishing Mayer, who respected motherhood above all else, that "all women are whores." "Are you saying that my mother and your mother were whores?" Mayer asked. "Of course, they were whores," Stroheim reportedly replied. Mayer then dove at Stroheim, smashing his fists into Stroheim's shaved head until he was blood caked and nearly unconscious and had to be removed to a hospital where his wounds were treated. Stroheim never filed an assault charge against Mayer, although his attorneys urged him to do so. **The Merry Widow** was shown at the Palais des Beaux Arts in Brussels in 1955 and where Stroheim was present. The director ordered that the house lights come up just after the dueling scene, saying: "That is where my story ended, but they insisted on the ending you see now." **p**, Irving Thalberg; **d**, Erich von Stroheim; **cast**, Mae Murray, John Gilbert, Roy D'Arcy, Josephine Crowell, George Fawcett, Tully Marshall, Edward Connelly, Helen Howard Beaumont, Gertrude Bennett, Joan Crawford, Clark Gable, Walter Plunkett; **w**, von Stroheim, Benjamin Glazer, Marian Ainslee (based on the operetta by Leo Stein, Viktor Leon, music by Franz Lehar); **c**, Oliver Marsh, William H. Daniels, Ray Rennahan, Ben F. Reynolds; **m**, Lehar; **ed**, Frank E. Hull, Margaret Booth; **prod d**, Cedric Gibbons.

The Merry Widow ★★★★★ 1934; U.S.; 99m; MGM; B/W; Musical Comedy; Children: Cautionary; **DVD**; **VHS**. In the first talkie version (and the very best) of the great Franz Lehar operetta, pantheon director Lubitsch presents a stunning and captivating masterpiece musical comedy where Chevalier and MacDonald are effervescently unforgettable.

Jeanette MacDonald and Maurice Chevalier in *The Merry Widow*, 1934.

MacDonald is the wealthiest woman living in the mythical kingdom of Marshovia, and the entire country depends upon her spending to keep the national economy afloat. When MacDonald cannot find a suitable suitor, she leaves for Paris to find that man of her dreams and panic ensues in little Marshovia. Barbier, the king, finds Chevalier, a prince, pitching woo in the sacrosanct chambers of his wife, Merkel, and, as punishment, orders him to direct his amour toward MacDonald, telling Chevalier to go to Paris and win MacDonald's heart and return her to her native country before Marshovia goes broke. The worldly Chevalier must either be successful in this assignment or face a court-martial. He leaves for Paris with his slavish valet, Meek, and, when going to the sumptuous bistro Maxim's, meets MacDonald, who is pretending to be a "B" Girl, shilling for the place in order to have male guests buy the most expensive wines and champagne and uses the alias of "Fifi." They are immediately drawn together while they sing and dance, although Chevalier has no idea that MacDonald is his romantic prey. All this changes when the two meet again at the Marshovian Embassy, hosted by ambassador Horton and where MacDonald now knows Chevalier's true assignment. She greets him icily, and nothing he can do convinces her that he has truly fallen in love with her and that his motives are not based strictly on his official assignment. MacDonald and Chevalier then dance in a magnificently choreographed dance number and MacDonald seems to soften toward Chevalier, but then Horton officially announces that she and Chevalier are to be married; MacDonald, enraged, publicly denounces Chevalier, stating that she has been publicly embarrassed and will never again believe a word coming from his mouth. Chevalier is arrested for failing to win MacDonald and shipped back to Marshovia to stand trial. That trial commences with scores of the most beautiful women in the country attending, all having been wooed by the tireless Chevalier. MacDonald arrives to testify against him, stating that he did his best to deceive her, to lie to her and to mislead her, but that he was unsuccessful. Nothing Chevalier says to her has an effect on her vengeance-seeking posture. Chevalier then makes a speech where he says that any man, like himself, who has loved an endless number of women, but who now loves only one with whom he wants to spend the rest of his life should be hanged. The males in the courtroom give him a thunderous applause, but he is nevertheless condemned. He is placed in a cell and is then visited by MacDonald. They begin to argue again, but, standing outside that cell is Horton, Barbier, Merkel and others, who begin sending champagne through the food slot and spray cologne through the bars as a gypsy orchestra plays romantic tunes. Soon the argument softens and we next see the face of a minister as he conducts a wedding ceremony between MacDonald and Chevalier and all ends well. The so-called "Lubitsch Touch" is evident in every frame of this delightful songfest, visually titillating and with a witty and provocative

Leon Ames, Red Skelton, and Douglas Fowley in *Merton of the Movies,* **1947.**

script typified by a humorous line from Horton when he asks Chevalier at one point: "Have you ever had diplomatic relations with a woman?" The huge embassy ball is a marvel to behold, one of the most magnificently choreographed ensembles (by Albertina Rasch) ever put on film. MacDonald and Chevalier are in wonderful voices in singing many great songs that include (all music by Lehar and with new lyrics from Lorenz Hart and Gus Kahn): "Girls, Girls, Girls," "Vilia," "Maxim's," "The Merry Widow Waltz," "Melody of Laughter," "If Widows Are Rich" (music: Franz Lehar; lyrics: Lorenz Hart); "Tonight Will Teach Me to Forget" (music: Franz Lehar; lyrics: Gus Khan); and "Russian Dance" (music: Franz Lehar; lyrics in gibberish to represent the Marshovian language). Remade as an inferior production in 1952, this version did well at the box office although it failed to recoup its huge budget of $1.6 million, falling short by $100,000. *Author's Note*: The accomplished Grace Moore was originally scheduled to play the leading lady in this production, but she refused to be billed after Chevalier, so she was replaced by MacDonald. This was one of thirty operettas composed by the gifted Lehar, produced in Vienna in 1905 and one that became an instant smash hit, perhaps his finest work. Alma Rubens and Wallace Reid appeared in a two-reel silent version of this story in 1912, and Erich von Stroheim directed another and startling silent version in 1925 with Mae Murray and John Gilbert in the leading parts, but that version had very little to do with the original story. A real prince named "Danilo" (Chevalier's character) sued MGM for the misuse of his name and he was paid $4,000 as "nuisance money" to get him to settle out of court. Stroheim also sued when MGM thought to make this film in 1930, saying that the story line for the talkie version plagiarized his script from the 1925 version, and, after some years of litigation, he and his attorneys were paid off and the talkie version began with Chevalier, who was always considered for this version as its leading man and who had by then been a superstar. MacDonald had appeared opposite Chevalier in **One Hour with You**, 1932, and **Love Me Tonight**, 1932. **The Merry Widow** was made simultaneously in English and French with Chevalier and MacDonald appearing in both versions. Chevalier, for some unexplained reason, did not like MacDonald, but their pairing in this film was a stroke of genius that brought together what the public perceived to be the perfect duet. **p**, Irving Thalberg; **d**, Ernst Lubitsch; **cast**, Maurice Chavalier, Jeanette MacDonald, Edward Everett Horton, Una Merkel, George Barbier, Minna Gombell, Sterling Holloway, Donald Meek, Herman Bing, Henry Armetta, Leonid Kinsky. Lane Chandler, Shirley Ross, Akim Tamiroff, Jason Robards, Sr.; **w**, Samson Raphaelson, Ernest Vajda (based on the operetta by Franz Lehar, Victor Leon, Leo Stein); **c**, Oliver T. Marsh; **m**, Lehar, Leon, Stein; **ed**, Frances Marsh; **art d**, Cedric Gibbons, Frederic Hope; **set d**, Edwin B. Willis, Gabriel Scognamillo.

Merton of the Movies ★★★ 1947; U.S.; 83m; MGM; B/W; Comedy; Children: Acceptable; **DVD**; **VHS**. Skelton is a dreamy movie theater usher in the 1920s silent film era. He wins a trip to Hollywood in a publicity stunt to boost the career of Ames. O'Brien, a talent scout, sees star potential in Skelton because of his knack for getting into trouble, and she's right because he becomes a big star with his slapstick antics. Silent film comic Buster Keaton was hired by the producers to teach Skelton slapstick techniques, and they are fun to watch in this entertaining film that gives a nostalgic look at Hollywood's yesteryear. This story was previously made as a silent film in 1924 with Glenn Hunter and also as a sound film, **Make Me a Star**, 1932. **p**, Albert Lewis; **d**, Robert Alton; **cast**, Red Skelton, Virginia O'Brien, Gloria Grahame, Leon Ames, Alan Mowbray, Charles D. Brown, Hugo Haas, Harry Hayden, Douglas Fowley, Dick Wessel, Tom Dugan, Tim Ryan, Mary Treen, John Nesbitt (narrator); **w**, George Wells, Lou Breslow (based on the play by George S. Kaufman, Marc Connelly, and the novel by Harry Leon Wilson); **c**, Paul C. Vogel; **m**, David Snell, Robert Franklyn; **ed**, Frank E. Hull; **art d**, Cedric Gibbons, Howard Campbell; **set d**, Edwin B. Willis.

The Messenger ★★★ 2009; U.S.; 113m; Oscilloscope Laboratories; Color; Drama; Children; Unacceptable; (MPAA: R); **BD**; **DVD**. In this engrossing introspective drama, Foster is a U.S. Army staff sergeant, who is injured when an explosive device detonates near him during the Iraq war. He suffers eye and leg injuries and is sent back to the States to recover. He and his longtime girlfriend, Malone, resume sexual relations even though she is engaged to another man. Foster only has a few months left in his enlistment and is assigned to the Casualty Notification Team in his area. Untrained in the job of a bad news messenger, he is teamed with a career officer, Harrelson, who teaches him about counseling, psychology, and grief management. Foster begins notifying strangers that their loved ones have been injured or killed in the war. Harrelson advises Foster to refrain from showing any personal feelings in the work or it could make things worse for the affected loved ones as well as cause him personal grief and misery. Two of those Foster delivers messages to include a widow, Morton, and an angry father, Buscemi. Foster ignores Harrelson's advice and becomes attracted to Morton while becoming involved in Buscemi's irrational emotions. Gutter language and some sexual content as well as nudity prohibit viewing by children. **p**, Mark Gordon, Lawrence Inglee, Zach Miller, Gwen Bialic; **d**, Oren Moverman; **cast**, Woody Harrelson, Steve Buscemi, Ben Foster, Jena Malone, Eamonn Walker, Yaya Dacosta, Lisa Joyce, Peter Francis James, Samantha Morton, Paul Diomede; **w**, Moverman, Alessandro Camon; **c**, Bobby Bukowski; **m**, Nathan Larson; **ed**, Alex Hall; **prod d**, Stephen Beatrice; **set d**, Cristina Casanas; **spec eff**, John Bair.

The Messenger: The Story of Joan of Arc ★★★★ 1999; France; 148m; Gaumont/COL; Color; Biographical Drama; Children: Unacceptable (MPAA: R); **DVD**; **VHS**. In a startling and riveting performance, Jovovich realistically enacts the legendary role of Joan of Arc (c.1412-1431). We first see Jovovich as Joan at the end of her spectacular life, being burned at the stake. She is next seen as a child (Valentine), playing in the fields beyond her village, but repeatedly going to a small chapel to confess her sins to the local priest, Brooke, who believes she is over-religious. She then leaves to play in a field and there has a supernatural vision of a Christ-like figure. She also later finds an old sword that becomes new and radiates brilliant light. When returning to her village, she sees its buildings set afire by the invading British and is protected by her sister, Greenwood, who hides her behind a wooden wall while she is sexually attacked and then murdered by an invading soldier. Taken away by surviving relatives, she grows up to be teenager Jovovich, who continues to have supernatural visions instructing her to save France from the English. To that end, she rides to Chinon, the court of the Dauphin, played by Malkovich, who later becomes Charles VII (1403-1461). At first, Malkovich will not see her, but his mother, Dunaway, playing Yolande of Aragon (1384-1442) urges him to see Jovovich because, she says, the French public has come to believe that this maid has been sent by God to save France. Malkovich at first attempts to deceive Jovovich when she appears at his court and where another noble pretends to be the Dauphin. Jovovich, however, somehow realizes that she is being duped and searches through the crowd in the hall to find the real Dauphin, kneeling before Malkovich and telling him she has a secret message "from the King of Heaven for you and you only." He takes her into a private room and then emerges with her, telling the court that he is going to allow her to lead his rag-tag army against the powerful English forces that presently besiege Orleans. Jovovich is given armor, a war horse and a banner of her own design and rides away with an escort that includes three of Malkovich's senior knights, Greggory, playing the Jean II, Duke of Alençon (1409-1476); Cassel, playing Gilles de Rais (1404-1440); and Ridings, playing Etienne de Vignolles, known as La Hire (1390-1443), while leading reinforcement to the French army. When she arrives, she tells the senior knight in charge of the army, Karyo, who plays Jean de Dunois (1402-1468), to immediately attack the Tourelles, the strongest bastion held by the English, an order that seems foolish and reckless to all of the cautious knights, who now become skeptical of Jovovich. Karyo admits that he and his commanders are not used to taking orders from a girl. In response, Jovovich cuts her hair and then sends a letter to the English commander that politely requests that he surrender. His response is a shouted insult. While the French commanders prepare a cautious assault, Jovovich rallies the French troops and immediately attacks the Tourelles bastion and, while climbing a ladder, is struck by an enemy arrow in the chest. She is carried to the rear where she pulls the arrow from her chest and then collapses unconscious. When she revives, she again goes to the troops, who thought her dead and are now inspired to see her very much alive and she leads them in another attack in which all the commanders join and where the French gain access to the outer fort when a drawbridge breaks. The French then use an improvised battering ram of logs packed into a huge cart and drive this into the great doors barring the entrance to the inner fort and, when breaking through, the French inflict great slaughter upon the English, its commander fleeing. Jovovich is emotionally disturbed over this human gore and carnage and sees another vision of Jesus bleeding from his face. She orders that none of the prisoners be killed. She saves the life of an English soldier by handing her ring to a French scavenger so that he will not take the man's life. Jovovich again demands that the English give up their siege of Orleans and depart France, but the English regroup and the two armies meet upon an open field. Jovovich rides forward alone to shout at the English that if they do not surrender and depart all will be killed, her words ignored by the English commander. English archers move forward and then English knights on horseback move toward the French troops, but suddenly, inexplicably, the English knights turn around and ride away, followed by the archers and infantry. Jovovich has miraculously won the battle of Orleans and is hailed a national hero. She rides victoriously to Rheims where she stands in the Cathedral to see Malkovich crowned as Charles VII, and then urges him to give her more troops to drive the remaining English from France. Malkovich, however, always the intriguer and engulfed in political conspiracies, puts her off, giving her a token force to recapture Paris, an effort that proves fruitless. Meeting once more with Malkovich, Jovovich is told that he no longer wants to pursue a military course with the English, but will settle their differences with diplomacy and orders Jovovich to go home at the advice of his mother, Dunaway, who tells him that Jovovich has served her purpose and has now become a nuisance. Malkovich then appeases the English by allowing Jovovich to be captured by Burgundians, who are allies to the English, and she is sold to the English. She is then tried for heresy as a witch. In her cell, Jovovich is repeatedly visited by Hoffman, playing "The Conscience" (or perhaps the Devil), who questions her motivations and challenges her claims to having seen supernatural visions. She is tried and condemned and then, in flash=forward to the beginning of this stark and traumatizing film, dies in the flames. This excellent production where

Workers slaving in the underworld in *Metropolis*, 1927.

director Besson helms with great assurance and where his battle scenes are startlingly realistic and gore-smeared offers outstanding performances from Jovovich and Malkovich, as well as all of those playing the captains of the French army. *Author's Note*: Up to the time of this production, the most significant films about Joan of Arc involved a silent film, **The Passion of Joan of Arc**, 1929, where Maria Falconetti plays Joan, chiefly while in confinement and during her trial, and **Joan of Arc**, 1948, where Ingrid Bergman plays a much more sophisticated (and older) Joan. Jovovich's portrayal, however, brings a freshness and vitality to the subject not heretofore seen while she plays Joan as she truly was, as an excitable and inspired teenager. Sadly, the script writers, in an attempt to make their dialog contemporary, insert derogatory appellatives (such as the "F" word) that did not even exist in Joan's day, which annoyingly detracts and demeans this otherwise fine production. **p**, Patrice Ledoux, Luc Besson; **d**, Besson; **cast**, Milla Jovovich, John Malkovich, Faye Dunaway, Dustin Hoffman, Tcheky Karyo, Rab Affleck, David Gant, Joanne Greenwood, Edwin Apps, Vincent Cassel, Bruce Byron, Framboise Gommendy, Richard Ridings, Pascal Greggory, Paul Brooke; **w**, Besson, Andrew Birkin; **c**, Thierry Arbogast; **m**, Eric Serra; **ed**, Sylvie Landra; **prod d**, Hugues Tissandier; **art d**, Alain Paroutaud; **set d**, Robert Le Corre, Ronald Meanti, Alain Pitrel, Jérôme Poirier; **spec eff**, Georges Demétrau, Alain Carsoux.

Metropolis ★★★★ 1927 (silent; revised and enhanced edition: 2010); Germany; 153m; Universum Film/PAR; B/W/Tinted; Fantasy; Children: Unacceptable; (2010 edition: MPAA: PG-13); **DVD; VHS**. This silent film classic from pantheon director Lang is set in the future year of 2000 in a large city ruled by Abel, a heartless capitalist. His only son, Fröhlich, lives a rich, idle life until he meets a young woman, Helm, who cares for the children of the poor workers toiling like slaves in a workers' city below the surface. Following her to the subterranean city, Fröhlich is appalled to see the deplorable working conditions there. He tells his father what he has witnessed and asks him to make positive changes, but his pleas fall on deaf ears. In desperation, Fröhlich gives up his easy life and joins the workers in the lower city, who keep the upper city functioning by providing its energy and fuel. He urges the workers to take peaceful measures for change, but even this angers his father. Abel puts a mad scientist, Klein-Rogge, in his employ to work with any means possible to keep the workers from rebelling, and, to that end, Klein-Rogge kidnaps Helm, who is a Christ-like figure crusading for justice through peaceful protest. Klein-Rogge re-creates Helm into a robot and sends her to appease the workers. He then floods areas of the underworld city to make the workers subservient. Klein-Rogge dies and Fröhlich rescues the real Helm and, together, they save the workers from the flood. Abel finally gets the message that love is the most important

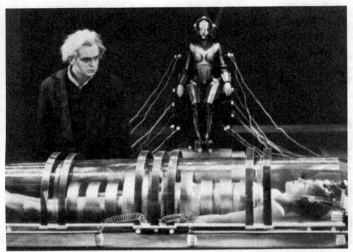

Rudolf Klein-Rogge and Brigitte Helm (encased) in *Metropolis*, 1927.

of human emotions and vows to improve conditions for the workers. Song (in the 1984 re-release), "On Your Own" (Giorgio Moroder, Billy Squier; performed by Squier). Restored versions in 2001 (**DVD**) and 2010 (**BD**; **DVD**). (In German; English subtitles.) *Author's Note*: After Hitler took power in Germany, he had his minster of propaganda, Paul Joseph Goebbels, who supervised all German filmmaking, summon Lang to a meeting where Goebbels, based on Lang's production of **Metropolis**, offered Lang the job as the head of all filmmaking in Germany. Lang told Goebbels that he was flattered and accepted. He then went home, packed his bags, including everything he thought valuable, and fled the country, first going to Paris and later to the U.S. He left his pro-Nazi wife, Harbou, behind. Lang was criticized (by no less a pundit and futuristic writer than H.G. Wells, among many) for making a film that blatantly condemned employers and promoted a tyrannical civilization where machines replaced humans altogether, but the rather stereotyped script for **Metropolis** was not of Lang's own making, but that of his wife, Harbou. Nevertheless, Lang's astounding visuals, camera setups, angles, and the mobile use of his cameras, along with the fantastic sets, established a precedent-setting futuristic hallmark film that became the role model of many such films to come. **p**, Erich Pommer, Giorgio Moroder (1984 restoration); **d**, Fritz Lang; **cast**, Alfred Abel, Gustav Fröhlich, Rudolph Klein-Rogge, Fritz Rasp, Theodor Loos, Erwin Biswanger, Heinrich George, Brigitte Helm, Fritz Alberti; **w**, Lang, Thea von Harbou (based on her novel); **c**, Karl Freund, Gunther Rittau, Walter Ruttmann; **m**, Moroder, Freddie Mercury, Pat Benatar, Adam Ant, Bonnie Tyler; **art d**, Otto Hunte, Erich Kettelhut, Karl Vollbrecht; **spec eff**, Eugen Schüfftan (Eugene Shuftan), Ernst Kunstmann.

Metropolitan ★★★ 1990; U.S.; 98m; Allagash Films/New Line Cinema; Comedy; Children: Cautionary (MPAA: PG-13); **DVD**; **VHS**. It's the season for rich teenage girls in New York City to "come out" in high society as debutantes. A small group of these privileged young ladies of leisure go partying. They are badly in need of male escorts, and a social outsider, Clements, comes to their rescue. He becomes the escort of one of the girls, Farina, but he only has eyes for an old girlfriend, Thompson. His cynical friend, Eigeman, joins him with the girls mainly for the free drinks and meals and more young bachelors come along. The girls go through the debutante season in beautiful gowns with handsome young escorts in rented tuxedos and seem to enjoy themselves but wonder if all this partying and social climbing really prepares them for the future, especially for college and marriage. **p**, Whit Stillman, Peter Wentworth; **d&w**, Stillman; **cast**, Carolyn Farina, Edward Clements, Christopher Eigeman, Taylor Nichols, Allison Parisi, Dylan Hundley, Isabel Gillies, Bryan Leder, Will Kempe, Elizabeth Thompson; **c**, John Thomas; **m**, Tom Judson, Mark Suozzo; **ed**, Christopher Tellefsen.

Mexican Spitfire ★★★ 1940; U.S.; 67m; RKO; B/W; Comedy; **VHS**. Entertaining zany comedy sees Velez in top form, fractured English and mercurial temper and all. The unpredictable Velez elopes with Woods, a promising, young businessman, but Woods' former fiancée, Hayes, won't put up with it and sets out to wreck the marriage. What ensues is a hectic free-for-all pursuit of the newlyweds and nonstop slapstick jammed into almost every scene. Stealing those scenes is the little baldheaded Errol, who plays dual roles as Woods' teetotaler uncle and a wealthy whiskey baron always in his cups; no one in the world could offer a drunk act like the inimitable wobbly legged Errol, and he does so here in one hilarious sequence after another. This was the first of a series of "Spitfire" films produced by RKO and starring Velez and is the best of them. **p**, Cliff Reid; **d**, Leslie Goodwins; **cast**: Lupe Velez, Leon Errol, Donald Woods, Linda Hayes, Cecil Kellaway, Elisabeth Risdon, Charles Coleman; **w**, Joseph A. Fields, Charles E. Roberts (based on a story by Fields); **c**, Jack MacKenzie; **ed**, Desmond Marquette; **art d**, Van Nest Polglase.

Michael ★★★ 1996; U.S.; 105m; Turner Pictures/New Line Cinema; Color; Fantasy/Comedy; Children: Unacceptable (MPAA: PG); **DVD**; **VHS**. Travolta is captivating as a potbellied, womanizing man, who looks like a bum, but wears wings and claims to be the Archangel Michael. He resides at a motel in Iowa owned by Stapleton, and three Chicago tabloid newspaper reporters, Hurt, Pastorelli and MacDowell, are assigned by their boss, Hoskins, to go there and check him out. The reporters talk Travolta into traveling with them back to Chicago for closer examination. While en route by car they begin to have doubts about his celestial authenticity when they see how he chases women, chain-smokes, drinks heavily and swears like a drunken sailor, and then see that his wings begin to lose their feathers. The road trip includes a barroom brawl where Travolta shows his stuff as a battling angel. We learn he has been on Earth before, but this will be his last visit, spreading a little good will here and there. Gutter language and some sensuality prohibit viewing by children. **p**, Nora Ephron, Sean Daniel, James Jacks, G. Mac Brown; **d**, Ephron; **cast**, John Travolta, Andie MacDowell, William Hurt, Bob Hoskins, Robert Pastorelli, Jean Stapleton, Teri Garr, Wallace Langham, Joey Lauren Adams, Carla Gugino, Tom Hodges, Margaret Travolta; **w**, Nora and Delia Ephron, Pete Dexter, Jim Quinlan (based on a story by Dexter, Quinlan); **c**, John Lindley; **m**, Randy Newman; **ed**, Geraldine Peroni; **prod d**, Dan Davis; **art d**, James Tocci; **set d**, Tracey Doyle, Jarrell Jay Knowles; **spec eff**, David Blitstein, Ken Ralston, Stephen Rosenbaum, Louis Cetorelli.

Michael Clayton ★★★ 2007; U.S.; 119m; Castle Rock/WB; Color; Drama; Children: Unacceptable (MPAA: R); **BD**; **DVD**. Clooney is a divorced lawyer, who is a fixer of problems at a high-priced New York law firm. He leaves a poker game and watches his car blow up. Flash back four days earlier when he leaves himself almost broke by paying a loan shark to cover the debts of his brother. The head of the law firm, Pollack, tells Clooney that one of the firm's partners, Wilkinson, has gone crazy by running naked in a parking lot in snowy Milwaukee, and had been the point man representing the firm's defense of a conglomerate client being sued for billions of dollars because of causing poisonous pollution. The client firm is guilty and the law firm knows it's guilty, but it is being paid millions to defend the conglomerate. The smoking gun that could bring the client down is in the hands, or mind, of Wilkinson, and he's gone off some medication and lost it in the parking lot during a hearing on the pollution law suit which involves people dying of cancer. The law firm's chief legal executive on the case, Swinton, wants to stop Wilkinson from testifying about the conglomerate's guilt in the matter. Pollack, on the other hand, orders Clooney to clean up the mess and get the client off or he and the client and the law firm could face financial ruin. Clooney needs money because he is very deep in gambling debt, but his conscience wins in the end and he, his law firm, and the client will all have to pay bit time after the conglomerate is inevitably found guilty. Gutter language prohibits viewing by children. **p**, Sydney Pollack, George Clooney, Steven Soderbergh, Jennifer Fox, Kerry Orent, Steven Samuels, Christopher Goode, James A. Holt; **d&w**, Tony Gilroy; **cast**, Clooney, Tilda Swinton, Tom Wilkinson, Michael O'Keefe, Pollack, Danielle Skraastad, Wai Chan, Alberto Vazquez, Brian Koppelman, Denis O'Hare, Ken Howard; **c**, Robert Elswit; **m**, James Newton Howard; **ed**, John Gilroy; **prod d**, Keven Thompson; **art d**, Clay Brown; **set d**, Paul Cheponis, George DeTitta, Jr., Christine Mayer, Charles M. Potter; **spec eff**, Jeff Brink, Randall Balsmeyer.

Michael Collins ★★★★ 1996; U.K./Ireland/U.S.; 133m; Geffen Pictures/WB; Color; Biographical Drama; Children: Unacceptable (MPAA: R); **DVD**; **VHS**. Neeson renders an energetic and memorable performance of the Irish patriot Michael Collins (1890-1922) in this stirring production that chronicles the Irish fight for independence from Great Britain (1916-1922). The film opens with Hart, a loyal aide to Neeson, attempting to console Roberts, who plays Kitty Kiernan (1892-1945), the fiancée of the slain Irish leader, who has just been killed in an ambush. The film then shows in flashback the last stages of the 1916 Easter Rebellion and where the leaders of that uprising are being rounded up by British troops. Neeson is one of those captured, along with Quinn, who plays Collins' close friend, Harry Boland (1887-1922), as well as the ringleaders, including Rickman, who plays Eamon de Valera (1882-1975). As Neeson and Quinn are led away to be interred in a prison camp, Neeson says to Quinn that the next time "we won't play by their rules. We'll invent our own." All of the ringleaders are summarily shot, except for Rickman, who is also imprisoned (de Valera was an American citizen and for that reason his life was spared). Upon his release, Neeson gives a speech while running for a seat in the Irish Parliament, but the rally is broken up by the Royal Irish Constabulary and he is injured. He is taken by Boland to a remote farm to recover, and there they meet Roberts, who begins a romance with Quinn. When recuperated, Neeson begins organizing IRA guerilla warfare against the Irish Constabulary, which is controlled by the British. He makes little headway until he befriends Rea, who plays Ned Broy (1887-1972), a detective working inside Dublin Castle and a member of the Irish Constabulary, but whose loyalties are rooted to the cause of the IRA. Rea not only provides Neeson with inside information on the enemy's plans and operations, but allows him to sneak into the Castle and where Neeson boldly inspects all of the Constabulary's records about the IRA, discovering that they have but one photo of him that is so poorly made that his likeness is not discernible. He learns that the Constabulary plans to arrest Rickman, who has been released and presides over a shadow IRA cabinet, along with all the members of that cabinet. When warned by Neeson, Rickman forbids any interference, telling Neeson that their arrest will raise a public outcry that will bring about their release. Rickman and others are then arrested, but Neeson and Quinn evade capture. Neeson then leads attacks on remote Constabulary arsenals, collecting weapons, and issues an order that anyone collaborating with the Constabulary or the British will be executed by the IRA. He selects from the IRA's Dublin Brigade the most ardent and lethal members and then orders them to assassinate several members of MI5 (British counterintelligence) that have been working with the Constabulary, particularly its ruthless leader, Dance. (This unit was known as the Cairo Gang, fifteen members of which were assassinated in Dublin on November 21, 1920, earning their sobriquet by holding secret meetings in the back of the Cairo Café at 59 Grafton Street, Dublin.) In retaliation for these mass assassinations, occurring on Bloody Sunday, the Constabulary retaliates by driving an armored car into a Gaelic football match at Croke Park that afternoon where the armored car, supported by armed troops, fire indiscriminately into the crowd, murdering fourteen innocent spectators. (This ill-advised British-sponsored savage atrocity, more than anything else the British did to offend the Irish public at that time, brought more support to the IRA by the Irish public than it could have otherwise hoped to generate and where hundreds of young men volunteered for the secret underground

John Travolta, Robert Pastorelli, Andie MacDowell and William Hurt in *Michael,* 1996.

army and were trained as IRA guerrilla fighters.) By this time, the notorious and dreaded Black-and-Tans had come to Ireland, former British soldiers who had fought in WWI, and where they widely oppressed the Irish public with illegal raids, beatings and outright murders. Then Neeson and Quinn travel to England, where they help Rickman escape Lincoln Prison in Lincolnshire, England, but, instead of joining the fight in Ireland, Rickman tells Neeson that he is going to the U.S. to seek support from President Woodrow Wilson and that he is taking Neeson's right-hand man, Quinn, with him. Before Rickman and Quinn leave, Neeson ruefully tells his friend that Rickman is doing this because he fears leaving them alone in Ireland together. Rickman returns with Quinn from the U.S., failing to get official American support, and states that they must now fight a conventional war against the Constabulary and the British to show that they represent a legitimate government in exile and are not merely terrorists, which Rickman accuses Neeson of being, although Neeson has had no other way in which to combat the enemy. Rickman proposes a frontal attack on the British-controlled Customs House in Dublin and Neeson opposes this, saying the IRA does not have adequate forces to mount such an assault, let alone win an open battle. Rickman and the cabinet overrule him and the attack is made and it is an IRA disaster, most of its members either killed or captured. Neeson and Quinn barely escape themselves as does Rickman and his cabinet members. Neeson later meets with Rickman and tells him that the IRA is so badly damaged that he thinks they cannot hold out for more than a month, but privately tells Quinn that their lifespan is much shorter, perhaps a week. Neeson and Quinn take a brief vacation to a seaside resort with Roberts only to learn in shock that the British have called for a cease-fire, recognizing the IRA as a legitimate entity. Rickman then orders Neeson to go to London and negotiate a peace with the British, his excuse being that the British do not know anything about him and he will therefore be able to negotiate with the British on equal terms. Neeson refuses, saying he is no diplomat, but a guerilla fighter, but he nevertheless takes the assignment and negotiates a peace that only gives Ireland home rule, but not independence. Rickman confronts him by saying that Neeson never had the authority to sign such an agreement and Rickman then withdraws, along with all his supporters from the newly elected Irish Parliament, continuing to wage war against the Irish Free State now commanded by Neeson. (For his part, Collins always insisted that de Valera had him negotiate on behalf of the IRA so that he, de Valera, would not take responsibility for a compromise, the only way in which the British would then accept an agreement.) Ireland ratifies the treaty that Neeson has negotiated, but a civil war breaks out and O'Neill, playing Rory O'Connor (1883-1922), along with other IRA members, occupies the Four Courts in Dublin as a surrogate for Rickman. When Neeson cannot convince O'Neill and others to vacate the

Warren Beatty in *Mickey One*, 1965.

building, he orders a howitzer positioned across the river to blast the place (and this cannonade is startlingly real as shells appear to tear into that resplendent building, blowing pieces of it away). With Four Courts recaptured (O'Connor was executed on December 8, 1922, his death warrant signed by Free State official Kevin O'Higgins, who, a year earlier, had O'Connor serve as his best man at his wedding), Neeson now conducts a civil war against the insurgent IRA led by Rickman and where his dear friend Quinn is fighting against him and is killed in a street battle. By this time, Roberts has fallen in love with Neeson and they plan to get married. Neeson then decides to see if he can negotiate a peace with Rickman and travels to a distant county, but Rickman refuses to meet with him (and it is suggested that Rickman has lured Neeson to this meeting so that he can later be assassinated). In an attempt to return to Dublin, Neeson's small caravan is waylaid by IRA fighters, one of whom fires a fatal bullet into Neeson, ending the life of the celebrated Irish patriot. At the conclusion, Hart is again comforting Roberts in flash-forward and saying: "You've got to think of him the way he was…He was what the times demanded. And life without him seems impossible. He made it possible." A stirring epilogue shows in actual newsreel footage the funeral of Michael Collins, his wreath-wrapped coffin carried on a moving caisson with Free State troops riding with it, as somber and resolute as was that very grim era itself. Jordan directs this film with a firm hand and tells the tale without frills and where standout performances are rendered by Neeson, Rickman, Quinn, Rea, Dance and Roberts. The sets, autos and costumes are accurate to the era, and Goldenthal's dynamic score gives fine support with Irish melodies integrated into the many stirring scenes of this superb film. The plaintive song "Macushla" (Dermot Macmurrow and Josephine V. Rowe) is beautifully sung by tenor Frank Patterson during the film and with the end credits. **p**, Stephen Woolley, Redmond Morris; **d&w**, Neil Jordan; **cast**, Liam Neeson, Julia Roberts, Aidan Quinn, Alan Rickman, Stephen Rea, Charles Dance, Jonathan Rhys Meyers, Sean McGinley, Brendan Gleeson, Owen O'Neill, John Kenny, Ian Hart, Richard Ingram, Ronan McCairbre, Ger O'Leary, Gerard McSorley, Michael Dwyer, **c**, Chris Menges (Technicolor); **m**, Elliot Goldenthal; **ed**, J. Patrick Duffner, Tony Lawson; **prod d**, Anthony Pratt; **art d**, Malcolm Middleton, Arden Gantly, Jonathan McKinstry, Cliff Robinson; **set d**, Josie MacAvin; **spec eff**, Yves De Bono.

Mickey One ★★★ 1965; U.S.; 93m; Florin/Tatira/COL; B/W; Drama; Children: Unacceptable; **DVD**. In another edgy but fascinating film, Beatty is a standup comic, who flees Detroit to escape his gambling debts, believing he is about to be beaten up for not making payments to syndicate mobsters. He goes to Chicago and lives under an alias, hauling garbage for a living. His vanity begins to gnaw at him and he again seeks recognition, so he begins appearing on the stage, but using another name, "Mickey One," although he continues to fear retaliation by the mob. He is booked into an upscale club by his agent, Hart, but before he makes his first appearance he is almost evicted for non-payment of rent. Stewart, who is taking his room, pays his way and the two begin a romance. When he arrives at the club, the owner, Hatfield, tells him that he will perform for only one man, who can book him into all the clubs in the Midwest, but Beatty is so paranoid at this point that he believes that that man is a syndicate enforcer looking for him and when he does his audition, he cuts his rather lame act short and flees. He runs about Chicago, looking for a syndicate crap game so that he can settle with the mob, but is beaten up by a number of doormen all wearing different uniforms. He returns to Hatfield's club where Hatfield tells him that he has paid off his gambling debts and that Beatty is now in bondage to him for life. He resigns himself to this fate after learning that his agent, Hart, has disappeared and Beatty assumes that he has been murdered to help pay for his debt to the mob, and this is where this grim and surrealistic film ends. Beatty is perfect as the apprehensive, paranoid comic with limited talent and with no end of phobias, and Penn paints a frightening portrait of a man trapped by his own errant ways. The jazz played is too loud, the characters are all grotesque (including Tone, who was sixty-one at the time and looks as if he is on death's doorstep) and all seems distorted and as pretentious as the character Beatty embodies, which is exactly what Penn intended. **p&d**, Arthur Penn; **cast**, Warren Beatty, Alexandra Stewart, Hurd Hatfield, Franchot Tone, Teddy Hart, Jeff Corey, Kamatari Fujiwara, Donna Michelle, Ralph Foody, Norman Gottschalk, Dick Lucas, Jack Goodman; **w**, Alan M. Surgal; **c**, Ghislain Cloquet; **m**, Eddie Sauter; **ed**, Aram Avakian; **prod d**, Gordon Jenkins.

Middle of the Night ★★★ 1959; U.S.; 118m; Sudan/COL; B/W; Drama; Children: Unacceptable; **DVD**. In this provocative romantic drama, Novak is a beautiful young divorcée, who is a secretary in Manhattan's tough garment district. Her workaholic boss, March, is a lonely middle-aged widower, who feels his own mortality while he is deeply involved with his stress-creating family, including a grown daughter who can't let go of him. Novak seeks comforting and he provides it while suggesting she find herself a nice young man, but March nevertheless falls in love with her. He asks her to marry him, but she doesn't love him. He wants sex with her, but all she wants is a father figure since her own father left her when she was a child. She meets handsome Philips, a friend from her single years, and March becomes jealous when he learns they are seeing each other. We are left with a lot of questions about the three of them, and the viewer is not sure which man Novak will select in her quest for happiness. **p**, George Justin; **d**, Delbert Mann; **cast**, Fredric March, Kim Novak, Glenda Farrell, Albert Dekker, Martin Balsam, Lee Grant, Lee Philips, Edith Meiser, Joan Copeland, Betty Walker; **w**, Paddy Chayefsky (based on his play); **c**, Joseph C. Brun; **m**, George Bassman; **ed**, Carl Lerner; **prod d**, Leo Kerz; **art d**, Edward S. Haworth; **set d**, Jack Wright, Jr.

Midnight ★★★ 1939; U.S.; 94m; PAR; B/W; Comedy/Romance; Children: Acceptable; **DVD**; **VHS**. Pleasant and humorous romantic comedy has showgirl Colbert struggling to survive in Paris. Cabdriver Ameche takes pity on her and does what he can for her. Colbert's prospects brighten when she is hired by wealthy Barrymore, who assigns her to vamp Lederer, a gigolo paying too much attention to his wife, Astor. Ameche sees Colbert making a play for Lederer, a thoroughly worthless gold digger, and loses respect for her, not knowing that she is performing a job and really has no romantic interest in Lederer. When Barrymore's entourage retires to his lavish chateau, Colbert and Lederer go along. Ameche, who realizes he loves Colbert, despite her flighty flirtations, then shows up at the chateau to save her by indignantly announcing to one and all that he is her husband, which unleashes some hilarious bedlam. Barrymore resolves his differences with Astor, and Ameche gets the girl of his dreams, Colbert, who has been in love with him all along.

Leisen, a woman's director, carefully crafts this romp around Colbert, then one of Hollywood's reigning stars, and her fine performance radiates her special kind of warmth and good-naturedness. *Author's Note*: "He [Leisen] pampered me so much on the set of **Midnight**," Colbert told this author, "that it got to be embarrassing and I told him to 'please pay some special attention to Mary [Astor], but he said, 'I can't do much with her since she is pregnant and we have to cover her up with feathers and frills and keep her seated.' The great John Barrymore was no longer the 'Great Profile,' poor soul. He had so little energy at that time that we all worried if he would get through the production." Astor, who had had a torrid affair with Barrymore many years earlier when he was in his heyday, told this author that "John was on his last legs. Years and years of drinking and whoring and running around had frazzled him down so that he could not remember his cue lines and we all had to help him through every scene. He was once the world's greatest actor of Shakespeare's tragedies and now he had become a tragedy himself." For the energetic and always optimistic Ameche, **Midnight** "was pure pleasure and why not? Claudette is my girl and, like every guy in America, I am in love with her," he told this author. "I am even luckier than all those other guys when she falls for me, a lug driving a hack. That happened all the time in the pictures in those days and audiences always believed it. It was a sweet time to be alive." **p**, Arthur Hornblow, Jr.; **d**, Mitchell Leisen; **cast**, Claudette Colbert, Don Ameche, John Barrymore, Francis Lederer, Mary Astor, Elaine Barrie, Hedda Hopper, Monty Woolley, Armand Kaliz, William Hopper; **w**, Charles Brackett, Billy Wilder (based on a story by Edwin Justus Mayer, Franz Schulz); **c**, Charles Lang, **m**, Frederick Hollander; **ed**, Doane Harrison; **art d**, Hans Dreier, Robert Usher; **set d**, A.E. Freudeman; **spec eff**, Farciot Edouart.

A Midnight Clear ★★★ 1992; U.S.; 108m; A&M Films/Interstar; Color; War/Drama; Children: Unacceptable (MPAA: R); **DVD**; **VHS**. During World War II in 1944 France, a six-man U.S. Army intelligence and reconnaissance squad of young soldiers locates a Nazi platoon that wants to surrender rather than face annihilation in Germany's final war offensive. The GIs and Nazis put their differences on hold at Christmas and spend the holiday together. The GIs include Hawke, Gross, Dillon, and Sinise, who temporarily loses it and runs naked in the snow. At one point, the two combatant groups have a snowball fight instead of tossing hand grenades at each other. But the Nazi surrender plan collapses and both sides are compelled to return to combat. This engrossing war tale offers fascinating and well-developed characters and is directed with a sure hand by Gordon. Gutter language, war violence and sensuality prohibit viewing by children. **p**, Bill Borden, Dale Pollock; **d&w**, Keith Gordon (based on the novel by William Wharton); **cast**, Peter Berg, Kevin Dillon, Ethan Hawke, Gary Sinise, Arye Gross, Frank Whaley, John C. McGinley, Larry Joshua, David Jensen, Curt Lowens, Rachel Griffin; **c**, Tom Richmond; **m**, Mark Isham; **ed**, Don Brochu; **prod d**, David Nichols; **art d**, David Lubin; **set d**, Janis Lubin; **spec eff**, Rick Josephsen.

Midnight Cowboy ★★★★ 1969; U.S.; 113m; Florin Productions/UA; B/W; Drama; Children: Unacceptable (MPPA: R); **DVD**; **VHS**. This offbeat and often unsavory film is not for everyone and most will find it repulsive and repugnant as it centers upon the degenerate activities of a male hustler in the seediest of settings. What saves the film are two magnificent performances from Voight, a tall cherubic-faced young hustler and Hoffman, his carping, conniving pimp. Voight is shown working as a dishwasher in a small hick town in Texas. He naively believes that his youthful, strong body and his handsome face is his ticket to riches and fame, especially once he gets to New York City to wow the beautiful, rich girls waiting to welcome him with loving arms and open checkbooks. Adorned in his best western finery, including Stetson hat and ornate cowboy boots, Voight boards a bus destined for Manhattan. En route, we see in flashback as he recalls his miserable childhood where his father deserts his promiscuous mother and his

Jon Voight in *Midnight Cowboy,* 1969.

grandmother cares for him while she entertains endless "gentlemen callers." After arriving in New York City, Voight rents a room at a tacky boarding house and then cruises the streets, selecting Miles, a loud-mouthed, cheap-looking blonde, as his first customer. She takes him to her richly appointed apartment and they make love. After their tryst, Voight demands his payment, but is startled to hear that Miles has no money and, ironically, Voight loans her some cash to get a taxi. He goes to a bar and meets Hoffman ("Ratso Rizzo"), a cynical little creep of a man, who steals to stay alive and is coughing all the time since he has tuberculosis. After Hoffman learns of Voight's ambitions, he offers to be his "manager" and the gullible Voight agrees to work with Hoffman. Voight's first arranged assignation from Hoffman is to visit McGiver, a religious freak and an aging homosexual. Voight then stays with Hoffman at his residence, a dirty room in an abandoned building. Both are by then suffering from the cold weather and wish they were in the warm clime of Florida. Voight's hustling career spirals downward, until he is servicing a young homosexual in a theater only to learn that this customer is penniless. Hoffman then takes him to an Andy Warhol–type party in Greenwich Village where Voight meets sexy Vaccaro and, after satisfying her, receives a twenty-dollar payment. Life for Voight in the Big Apple is far from what he has envisioned. Meanwhile, Hoffman's physical condition deteriorates and he feels that he will not survive the coming winter, convinced that he will be beaten up and killed by muggers, who constantly roam the streets while searching for easy victims like himself. Believing that Hoffman, the only real friend he has, might survive if he can get to the warm weather of Florida, Voight beats up a male customer, robbing him, and uses the money to buy two bus tickets. He and Hoffman then ride on a bus toward Florida, a destination that is now their hope of salvation. They talk about how good life will be for them once they arrive in Miami (their relationship and expressed wishful dreams not unlike those shared by George and Lenny in **Of Mice and Men**, 1939, and, in a larger sense, Salt's tale unashamedly transplants Steinbeck's great story and its memorable characters from the pristine West to the perverted East). The sick Hoffman, however, will never see the palm trees and white sands of Miami. He dies on the bus, leaving Voight where he began, facing an uncertain future while dearly holding on to a dead man, worthless to the world save for himself. Schlesinger directs with great authority, showing the slime, grime and tawdriness of New York at its worst to win an Oscar as Best Director, and the film deservedly won an Oscar as Best Picture, as well as an Oscar going to Salt for Best Adapted Screenplay. The abruptly changing moods of this film are largely enhanced by the brilliant jazz harmonica playing by Jean "Toots" Theilemans. Songs include: "A Famous Myth," "Tears and Joys" (Jeffrey Comanor); "Everybody's Talkin'" (Fred Neil); "Joe Buck Rides Again," "Fun City," "Midnight

Dustin Hoffman and Jon Voight in *Midnight Cowboy,* **1969.**

Cowboy," "Science Fiction," "Florida Fantasy" (John Barry); "Jungle Jim at the Zoo" (Sam Bronstein, Rick Frank); "He Quit Me" (W. [Warren] Zevon); "Old Man Willow" (Richard Sussman, Michael Shapiro); "Hush, Little Baby" (traditional southern lullaby); "Caisson Song" (1907; Edmund L. Gruber); and "The Last Round-Up (Get Along Little Dogie, Get Along)" (1933; Billy Hill). *Author's Note*: Voight and Hoffman were both nominated for Best Actor, but lost out to John Wayne in **True Grit**, 1969, so, in a less than a metaphysical sense, the clean air and blue skies of the American Old West and its unconquerable hero triumphed after all over the filth, perversion and degeneracy of the modern East and its defeated anti-hero—at least at the Academy Awards. Though utterly fascinating and brilliantly made, **Midnight Cowboy** is also one of the most depressing films ever produced, one that utterly denies the American dream of a better life and a brighter future. This film was originally given an "X" rating by the MPAA, but it later changed the rating to "R" (indicating the willy-nilly unreliability of that industry-sponsored organization). **p**, Jerome Hellman; **d**, John Schlesinger; **cast**, Dustin Hoffman, Jon Voight, Sylvia Miles, John McGiver, Brenda Vaccaro, Barnard Hughes, Ruth White, Jennifer Salt, Linda Davis, J.T. Masters, Sandy Duncan; **w**, Waldo Salt (based on the novel by James Leo Herlihy); **c**, Adam Holender; **m**, John Barry; **ed**, Hugh A. Robertson; **prod d**, John Robert Lloyd; **set d**, Phil Smith; **spec eff**, Joshua Light Show.

Midnight Express ★★★ 1978; U.K./U.S.; Casablanca Filmworks; COL; Color; Drama; Children: Unacceptable (MPAA: R); **DVD**; **VHS**. Tense drama has Americans Davis and Miracle readying their trip back to the U.S. after vacationing in Turkey. Davis, without being seen by Miracle, tapes packages of hashish to his body, but, when they board the plane, he is immediately taken into custody and Miracle is ignored and allowed to leave the country. It is not known how officials knew Davis was smuggling the drugs, the viewer left to wonder if he was singled out from a tip by an informer or that he was simply identified by random selection. Davis is stripped, the drugs founds and he is then taken straightaway to a terrible Turkish prison where guards treat prisoners as animals. Prisoners must fend for themselves as they fight, quarrel and are beaten or even raped without guards interfering. Davis meets others who have been charged with similar drug smuggling and these include Quaid, an American; Hurt, an Englishman; and Weisser, a Scandinavian homosexual with whom Davis later has a brief affair. Kellin, Davis' father, hires attorney Jeffrey to defend his son, but Davis, arrogant in court where he insults the judges, who cannot understand a word of his invective, is found guilty and given a long prison sentence. He vows to take the "midnight express," a euphemism for escape. Davis and Quaid try to dig their way out of the prison but are caught and severely beaten by Smith, a sadistic giant who enforces prison security.

Davis is then placed in a ward for the insane where conditions are even worse. He is later visited by Miracle, who displays her breasts to him so that he can have a last look at a female body and where he masturbates. He then gets into a fierce fight with Diogene, an informer, and bites off the man's tongue. Smith then takes him into a torture room where the 300-pound hulk begins mercilessly beating Davis, but Davis fights back and drives the towering Smith onto a steel spike on the wall used as a clothes rack and upon which the guard is impaled and killed. Davis puts on his guard's uniform and is shown walking from the prison and, in an epilogue, a series of snapshots show him happily reunited with family and friends. Director Parker spares the viewer nothing in this savage but powerful portrait of inhuman conditions in that Turkish prison, a medieval horror chamber where every cruelty and brutality is practiced. Davis, Quaid, Hurt and others give standout performances, but any viewer with a queasy stomach will find this film offensive and unpalatable. *Author's Note*: This film is based on the experiences of Billy Hayes (b. 1947), who was arrested and imprisoned in Turkey in 1970 for drug trafficking, and who was originally sentenced to four years in prison, but when he learned that an additional thirty years was to be applied to his sentence, he escaped in 1975. **p**, David Puttnam, Alan Marshall; **d**, Alan Parker; **cast**, Brad Davis, Randy Quaid, Bo Hopkins, John Hurt, Paul Smith, Mike Kellin, Norbert Weisser, Irene Miracle, Franco Diogene, Michael Ensign, Gigi Ballista; **w**, Oliver Stone (based on the book by Billy Hayes, William Hoffer); **c**, Michael Seresin (Eastmancolor); **m**, Giorgio Moroder; **ed**, Gerry Hambling; **prod d**, Geoffrey Kirkland; **art d**, Evan Hercules.

Midnight in Paris ★★★ 2011; Spain/U.S.; 94m; Gravier Productions/Sony Pictures; Color; Fantasy; Children: Unacceptable (MPAA: PG-13); **BD**, **DVD**. Absorbing fantasy has writer Wilson accompanying his girlfriend, McAdams, and her wealthy, conservative parents, Fuller and Kennedy, on a trip to Paris. Wilson is a successful screenwriter, but is tired of Hollywood and tells McAdams that they should relocate to Paris where he can finish a serious novel and telling her that Paris is unlike any other city in the world and will give him inspiration, particularly when it is raining. The practical McAdams only wants to live in sunny Malibu. While walking through some small streets at midnight, Wilson suddenly sees a 1920s Peugeot carrying partygoers dressed in the clothes of the Jazz Age and they take him along to a party where he is transported back into the past of that era, one that Wilson idolizes. He meets all the famous artists and writers of that era— F. Scott Fitzgerald (Hiddleston), Ernest Hemingway (Stoll), Gertrude Stein (Bates), Alice B. Toklas (Bourou-Rubinsztein), T. S. Eliot (Lowe), along with composer Cole Porter (Heck), as well the famous artists of that era, including Pablo Picasso (Di Fonzo Bo), Salvador Dalí (Brody), and others. Many of them read excerpts from Wilson's unfinished novel, a story about a man operating a nostalgia store. Wilson attempts to bring McAdams into his time travel fantasy, but she believes he is only daydreaming and he alone makes these visits into the past. In one of his time travels, Wilson has an affair with Picasso's mistress, who then takes him deeper into the history of Paris, the 1890s, where he meets the writers and artists of that era. When returning to the present, Wilson discovers that McAdams has been cheating on him and realizes that she is not the girl for him. While walking through the rain, he encounters Seydoux, an antiques art dealer he has earlier met, and they strike up a romance, both not only loving Paris, but each having a deep affection for the Lost Generation of the 1920s. Well crafted and with wonderful recreations of the 1920s settings, this poignant and nostalgic fantasy entertains throughout and is reminiscent of Allen's other nostalgic time traveling production, **The Purple Rose of Cairo**, 1985. p, Letty Aronson, Jaume Roures, Stephen Tenenbaum, Raphaël Benoliel, Helen Robin; **d&w**, Woody Allen; **cast**, Rachel McAdams, Owen Wilson, Kurt Fuller, Mimi Kennedy, Michael Sheen, Nina Arianda, Carla Bruni, Kathy Bates, Marion Cotillard, Tom Hiddleston, Alison Pill, Corey Stoll, Yves Heck, David Lowe, Marcial Di Fonzo Bo, Sonia Rolland, Adrien Brody,

Thérèse Bourou-Rubinsztein; **c**, Darius Khondji, Johanne Debas; **m**, Stephane Wrembel; **ed**, Alisa Lepselter; **prod d**, Anne Seibel; art **d**, Héléne Dubreuil; **spec eff**, Georges Demétrau, Pascal Fauvelle, Jérome Miel, Charles-Axel Vollard.

Midnight Lace ★★★ 1960; U.S.; 110m; Arwin Productions/UNIV; Color; Mystery; Children: Unacceptable; **DVD**; **VHS**. In a consistently tense thriller Day gives a superlative performance as the wife of Harrison, a successful businessman, who lives in London. Her otherwise normal life is disrupted when a strange voice threatens her as she walks through the city's dense fog. Later, while shopping, Day is almost pushed in front of an on coming bus. When she states that she believes someone is attempting to kill her, Loy, her visiting aunt, as well as her protective husband Harrison, do not believe her and think she is hallucinating from stress. Even Scotland Yard inspectors place no credence in Day's claims. She then encounters Gavin, a handsome construction foreman working on a building next door, who seems to be sympathetic, but his odd behavior causes Day to think that he may be the stalker. McDowall, the oddball son of Day's servant, also comes under suspicion by Day. She is then plagued by a series of phone calls from her tormentor, who threatens to kill her at any moment. The stalker, it is revealed, is Harrison, along with his mistress, Parry, who are trying to drive the now unstable Day to suicide, and, failing that, causing her death by misadventure. When Harrison reveals his sinister intentions and attempts to murder Day, she breaks free and makes her way to the dangerous scaffolding next door where Harrison pursues her. Gavin, who has suspected Harrison for some time, appears and rescues Day at the last moment while Harrison falls to his death. Miller maintains suspense throughout by carefully planting the right number of red herrings throughout the plot, and where Harrison, Loy, Gavin and McDowall render good performances. *Author's Note*: Loy told this author that "I don't have much to do in **Midnight Lace** as a wealthy, eccentric woman. I am more concerned about my own creature comforts than the mental well-being of my niece. My God, here is a poor woman threatened by a stalking killer and all I can tell her is that she is imagining everything. I would term my role in that picture as a perfect witch, spelled with a capital 'B.' Rex [Harrison] was having a hard time then. He had lost his wife, Kay Kendall, a year earlier and his career had not gone anywhere. He told me that he really did not want to do this film, but he felt he needed to keep his hand in and he proved to be wonderful as the stalking killer, but Rex was wonderful in all of his roles. Doris tried to boost his spirits by giving him a lot of her Christian Science booklets to read and she was very disappointed when, after the production was over, he did not return them, admitting that he misplaced them." **p**, Ross Hunter, Martin Melcher; **d**, David Miller; **cast**, Doris Day, Rex Harrison, John Gavin, Myrna Loy, Roddy McDowall, Herbert Marshall, Hermione Baddeley, John Williams, Richard Ney, Rhys Williams, Richard Lupino, Hayden Rorke, Doris Lloyd; **w**, Ivan Goff, Ben Roberts (based on the play "Matilda Shouted Fire" by Janet Green); **c**, Russell Metty (Eastmancolor); **m**, Frank Skinner; **ed**, Leon Barsha, Russell F. Schoengarth; art **d**, Alexander Golitzen, Robert Clatworthy; **set d**, Oliver Emert.

Midnight Run ★★★★ 1988; U.S; 126m; UNIV; Color; Comedy; Children: Unacceptable (MPAA: R); **DVD**; **VHS**. Good comedy with many hilarious moments sees De Niro and Grodin deliver memorable performances in this fast-paced crime spoof. De Niro is a former Chicago cop turned bounty hunter working for Los Angeles bail bondsman Pantoliano. He is assigned to capture and return Grodin, who has stolen a fortune from crime syndicate boss Farina and is wanted as a witness against Farina in an upcoming trial. De Niro, through a clever ruse, locates Grodin's hiding place in Manhattan and takes him into custody, but when they are about to fly back to L.A., Grodin, who has an acute fear of flying, throws a fit and both are kicked off the plane. De Niro then books them into a stateroom on board a transcontinental train and they come to know one another, Grodin being an affable and intelligent

Charles Grodin and Robert De Niro in *Midnight Run*, 1988.

thief and De Niro a lonely and frustrated man, who has lost his family and job to another cop. Meanwhile, Farina, knowing that Grodin is being taken back to L.A. to testify against him, sends his goons searching for him with the aid of Kehoe, who is Pantoliano's assistant and who feeds Farina information when hearing periodically from De Niro. Also in search of Grodin is Ashton, De Niro's rival bounty hunter, who thinks to take Grodin away from De Niro and collect a huge payment from Pantoliano, who is playing both bounty hunters against each other in order to regain custody of the elusive Grodin. De Niro and Grodin are forced to leave the train and continue their odyssey westward on foot, and by even stealing vehicles and then riding the rails, but Ashton overtakes them and steals Grodin from De Niro's custody. Ashton then tries to sell Grodin to Farina and his goons but he gets nothing but a beating as the goons quickly locate the hiding place where Ashton has kept Grodin. Meanwhile, De Niro cuts a deal with FBI chief Kotto, saying that he has a tape that will send Farina to prison. De Niro proposes to Kotto that he allow him to meet Farina and offer Farina the tape in exchange for Grodin at a meeting at the L.A. airport, Kotto and his agents can then, when Farina has the evidence that can be used against him in court, arrest and jail him. Kotto accepts this arrangement and the meeting takes place. Farina and his goons are arrested by FBI agents and Grodin is turned over to De Niro's custody. In the end, however, De Niro decides to let Grodin go, and after he does, Grodin gives him $300,000 from the millions he has stolen from Farina and then disappears. De Niro, who has exhausted all of his own money in his Homeric pursuit of Grodin, walks from the airport and asks a cabdriver if he can change a $1,000 bill and the driver tells him that he is nuts and drives off. De Niro then begins walking home. There are many delightful scenes in this very funny film, such as when De Niro and Grodin are completely strapped for cash and arrive in a small town where they go to a bar and where De Niro shows the naïve owner FBI credentials (which he has filched earlier from Kotto), explaining that they are looking for counterfeit bills. They then examine twenty dollar bills from the till, selecting enough cash for their needs by saying that "these are no good" and must be seized before they depart. **p&d**, Martin Brest; **cast**, Robert De Niro, Charles Grodin, Yaphet Kotto, John Ashton, Dennis Farina, Joe Pantoliano, Richard Foronjy, Robert Miranda, Jack Kehoe, Wendy Phillips; **w**, George Gallo; **c**, Donald Thorin; **m**, Danny Elfman; **ed**, Chris Lebenzon, Michael Tronick, Billy Weber; **prod d**, Angelo Graham; art **d**, James J. Murakami; **set d**, George R. Nelson; **spec eff**, Roy Arbogast.

A Midsummer Night's Dream ★★★★ 1935; U.S.; 133m; WB; B/W; Comedy; Children: Acceptable; **DVD**; **VHS**. In this delightful and very best version of the Immortal Bard's great comedy a group of artisans

Anita Louise, center, as Queen of the fairies in *A Midsummer Night's Dream*, 1935.

plan to use creatures of the forest in presenting a play to the royal court. Mitchell (Egeus) insists that de Havilland (Hermia) marry Alexander (Demetrius), and she must forgo the only man she loves, Powell (Lysander). She faces punishment from Hunter (Theseus, Duke of Athens) unless she goes ahead with the wedding while Hunter is also preparing to wed Teasdale (Hippolyta, Queen of the Amazons). De Havilland and Powell cannot tolerate this arrangement and their love for one another forces them to elope and escape to the forest with Alexander pursuing them. Muir, meanwhile, pursues Alexander, since she is daffy in love with him. Meanwhile, the artisans intending to perform the play for Hunter's impending wedding enter the forest, these being Cagney (Bottom), Brown (Flute), Herbert (Snout), McHugh (Quince) and others. The fairies of the forest are ruled by Jory (Oberon), and Louise (Titania), and Jory, who is quarreling with Louise, orders Rooney (Puck) to drop the juice of a passion flower into Louise's eyes so that she will fall in love with the first creature she encounters. Once achieving his assignment, the mischievous Rooney goes on a capricious rampage by turning Cagney's head into that of an ass and this is the creature that Louise first sees when the potion takes affect and she becomes hopelessly in love with him. Using his magic potion, Rooney also changes the feeling the lovers have for one another so that de Havilland and Powell grow to hate one another. All is chaos until the unpredictable fairies, along with Jory, Louise and their minions depart the forest and everything and everyone goes back to normal and where Cagney regains his human head to end this strange dream or nightmare. Reinhardt, who directed the stage version of this vehicle, had as his assistant Dieterle, who was a workhorse for Warner Brothers, and who directed many scenes in this Shakespearean opus with great vitality; the sets and costuming are stunning and sumptuous, and all the players are exceptional. *Author's Note*: Everyone at Warner Brothers and in Hollywood as well were amazed when Jack Warner, who preferred to make modern-day action films based on stories from the daily headlines, surprisingly announced that he intended to make **A Midsummer Night's Dream**, putting aside a huge budget of $1.5 million for the production. Powell, a crooner who had invariably appeared in musicals, said, years later, that he "had no idea about the lines I spoke in that picture." Cagney, too, told this author that "I felt uncomfortable in that picture as I was not that well versed in Shakespeare, but I had a role that allowed me to do a lot of acrobatic business to build up my character. Wearing that damned ass's head, however, was a pain in the neck, literally. The makeup people made it so heavy that it gave me neck and head pains and it was hot as hell beneath that hideous head." Dieterle told this author that "Jack [Warner] wanted to show the world that his studio could produce cultural movies, as toney and classical as anything MGM and Paramount were producing. So he told me to round up every top contract

player at the studio and 'pack them into that artsy picture.' The film was really assigned to the great Max Reinhardt, but he was unfamiliar with movie-making, so Jack [Warner] told me to 'back him up.' Well, I did a lot of backing up after I saw what Ernest Haller had photographed. He had taken Reinhardt's ambiguous directions literally and the rushes showed the forest so blurry with foliage and the actors so muted that you could not tell them for the trees and bushes. I fired Haller and hired Hal Mohr and we reshot all those scenes." [Mohr won an Oscar for this cinematography and another Oscar went to Dawson for Best Editing.] The forest was still too thick and we had to cut half of those bushes and trees from the set, but we could not get rid of a lot of foliage that had been painted to the trees and colored silver so the forest would give that gossamer appearance." The manic, hoarse-voiced Rooney is a wonder to behold in this film in a role that made him one of the leading child actors in Hollywood. He went tobogganing during the production and broke his leg, so that he finished his scenes while sitting on an unseen bicycle being wheeled through the forest by hidden crewmen. **p**, Henry Blanke, Jack L. Warner, Hal B. Wallis; **d**, Max Reinhardt, William Dieterle; **cast**, James Cagney, Dick Powell, Joe E. Brown, Jean Muir, Hugh Herbert, Ian Hunter, Frank McHugh, Victor Jory, Olivia de Havilland, Ross Alexander, Anita Louise, Mickey Rooney, Verree Teasdale, Arthur Treacher, Helen Westcott, Rags Ragland; **w**, Charles Kenyon, Mary McCall, Jr. (based on the play by William Shakespeare); **c**, Hal Mohr; **m**, Leo F. Forbstein, Erich Wolfgang Korngold; **ed**, Ralph Dawson; **art d**, Anton Grot; **set d**, Ben Bone; **spec eff**, Byron Haskin, Fred Jackman, Hans Koenekamp.

A Midsummer Night's Dream ★★★ 1961; Czechoslovakia; 76m; Studio Kresleneho a Loutkoveho Filmu/Showcorporation; Color; Animated Comedy; Children: Recommended; **DVD**; **VHS**. An excellently produced and beautifully photographed puppet version of Shakespeare's comedy presents the classic tale of romantic fantasy nonsense in a forest that won the Cannes Film Festival Grand Prix. This finely crafted animated entry offers a very good introduction of the classic play to younger audiences. Other versions made in 1935, 1969, 1996, 1999. *Author's Note*: This film was originally produced in 1959 and not released in the U.S. until two years later. (In Czech/French; English subtitles.) **p**, Erna Kmínková, Jaroslav Mozis; **d**, Jirí Trnka, Howard Sackler; **cast** (voiceovers), Tom Criddle, Ann Bell, Michael Meacham, John Warner, Barbara Leigh-Hunt, Hugh Manning, Joss Ackland, Alec McCowen, Jean Desailly (narrator, French version); Richard Burton (narrator, English version); **w**, Trnka, Sackler, Jirí Brdecka, Josef Kainar (based on the play by William Shakespeare); **c**, Jirí Vojtá; **m**, Vaclav Trojan; **ed**, Hanna Valachova; **art d**, Trnka.

A Midsummer Night's Dream ★★★ 1967; U.S.; 93m; Oberon/Showcorporation; Color; Fantasy; Children: Acceptable; **DVD**; **VHS**. This fine ballet version of Shakespeare's classic comedy features the New York City Ballet and is wonderfully choreographed by Balanchine, with music by Felix Mendelssohn. **p**, Dick Davis; **d**, George Balanchine, Dan Eriksen; **cast**, Suzanne Farrell, Edward Villella, Arthur Mitchell, Mimi Paul, Nicholas Magallanes, Patricia McBride, Roland Vazquez, Francisco Moncion, Gloria Gorvin, Richard Rapp, Jacques d'Amboise, Allegra Kent; **w**, William Shakespeare; **c**, Arthur J. Ornitz (Eastmancolor); **m**, Felix Mendelssohn; **ed**, Armond Lebowitz; **art d**, Albert Brenner.

Midway ★★★ 1976; U.S.; 132m; Mirisch/UNIV; Color; War Drama; Children: Unacceptable; **DVD**; **VHS**. Where **MacArthur**, 1977, profiled the exploits of General Douglas MacArthur (Peck) in the South Pacific in WWII, this finely directed and well-acted film rightly extolls the great victory achieved by U.S. Admiral Chester W. Nimitz (1885-1966), played by Fonda, who outguesses the attacking maneuvers of Admiral Isoroku Yamamoto (1884-1943), played by Mifune, at the historic naval battle of Midway (June 4-7, 1942). This exciting film opens with the attack by Doolittle's sixteen B-25 Mitchell bombers on Tokyo and other cities on April 18, 1942 (using footage of that bombing run from **Thirty Seconds over Tokyo**, 1944, its original black-and-white footage tinted a rosy red), to herald America's retaliation against Japan for its sneak attack at Pearl Harbor on December 7, 1941. The basic story line opens with Heston, a U.S. Navy officer and experienced fighter pilot, learning that his son, Albert, a young navy fighter pilot, is in love with a Hawaiian girl, Kokubo, and is seeking to marry her, but navy counterintelligence prevents the union because she is of Japanese blood and because she and her parents have been interned because of her parents' demonstrated loyalties to the Emperor and the Japanese war effort. Albert pleads with his father to intervene, and Heston, out of love for his son, breaks the rules and goes to an old friend, U.S. naval counterintelligence chief Nelson, and asks him to suppress the report on Kokubo's parents, pointing out that the allegations therein are outdated and that the Japanese family poses no threat to American security. Nelson is shocked by Heston's request, pointing out that what he proposes is a serious breach of "tampering," but, as a final favor, agrees to reinvestigate the case. Nelson, however, tells Heston that their friendship is at an end. Assured that he can now marry Kukubo, Albert is delighted and grateful to Heston. Then Heston learns from Albert's superior, Robertson, that Robertson has given Albert an assignment that prevents his marriage, Robertson believing that Albert's loyalties are confused. Albert then believes that his father, Heston, has pulled strings to prevent his marriage and has an angry encounter with Heston when he reports for duty on board an aircraft carrier, the same carrier on which Heston is serving and is about to go to sea. Meanwhile, Holbrook, head of U.S. naval intelligence, breaks the Japanese Code (Code Purple, which had been broken earlier by American code analysts) and learns that Mifune is planning to send a powerful task force to attack and capture the American-held island of Midway. After bringing this to the attention of Fonda, plans are immediately made to send the only three American carriers (*Yorktown*, *Hornet* and *Enterprise*) to await the attack. Fonda places Ford (as Admiral Raymond A. Spruance, 1886-1969) in charge of the task force, which also includes carriers commanded by Webber (as Admiral Frank J. Fletcher, 1885-1973). Fonda's top sea commander at that time, Admiral William F. "Bull" Halsey, 1882-1959), played by Mitchum, is then in hospital, suffering from a serious skin disease. Ford goes to Mitchum to get his advice and Mitchum tells him that he must use his own best judgment in dealing with the crafty Mifune, but Ford has already made up his mind in that regard as he has already told Fonda that he intends to "bushwhack" the Japanese task force when it comes within range of Midway. The American carriers sail for Midway and wait off its waters to the northeast until the Japanese task force arrives under the command of Shigeta, playing Admiral Chuichi Nagumo (1887-1944), the Japanese commander who led the attack on Pearl Harbor. After the American commander on Midway sends out PBY scout planes, one of them, at the very end of its scouting range, spots the Japanese task force, but gives few details as to the exact location of the Japanese task force. Shigeta then launches an air attack against Midway, destroying its land-based planes and devastating the island in a savage bombing attack. Ford then orders all of the planes, torpedo planes and dive bombers into the air from all three American carriers, and they begin a desperate search for the Japanese warships. When almost out of fuel, the American planes locate the Japanese task force, the torpedo planes (Torpedo Squadron Eight from the *Hornet*) frantically attacking three of Shigeta's carriers (*Kaga*, *Akagi* and *Soryu*), led by Corbett (playing Lt.-Commander John C. Waldron, 1900-1942), who is killed and whose squadron is destroyed. Only one in that heroic but futile attack (out of the thirty men in that squadron) survives, Dobson (playing Ensign George H. Gay Jr., 1917-1994), whose plane is destroyed, but he manages to stay afloat in the sea and witnesses the destruction of the Japanese fleet. Meanwhile, George (playing Commander C. Wade McClusky Jr., 1902-1976), leading a group of dive bombers (from the *Enterprise*), sees a Japanese destroyer (*Arashi*), sailing at full steam and rightly believes that it is attempting to rejoin the Japanese fleet and or-

Charlton Heston and Cliff Robertson in *Midway*, 1976.

ders his planes to follow it, even though his planes are running out of fuel. His patience is rewarded when he sees the entire Japanese fleet and orders his planes to attack the biggest carrier, *Kaga*, the American dive bombers scoring direct hits on the huge flat top (later sank). (McClusky's decision to follow that destroyer, in the opinion of Admiral Nimitz, "decided the fate of our carrier task force and our forces at Midway.") Shigeta's carriers are caught flatfooted in that he has taken the advice of subordinates to rearm his planes with bombs to make another land attack against Midway, and while his fighter planes are off chasing surviving U.S. torpedo planes, leaving his ships extremely vulnerable in that fueling hoses were snaked across the decks of those carriers while Japanese crew members attempted to refuel planes for that second attack and where bombs for rearming those planes were exposed everywhere on those decks. The result of McClusky's attack leaves the *Kaga* a burning hulk, and the same fate befalls the *Soryu* when Markham (playing Commander Max Leslie, 1902-1985) leads his dive bombers (from the *Yorktown*) in attacking that carrier, and the *Akagi*, too, is bombed and sunk by yet another group of American dive bombers. When told of the great victory by his carriers, Fonda is elated, but tells Holbrook that he "wants that fourth carrier." Meanwhile, Albert is seriously wounded during the attacks but manages to land his plane on its carrier and Heston sees him taken to surgery where he is told that he will survive and where father and son reconcile. That fourth Japanese carrier, *Hiryu*, which has escaped the dive bombers attacking and sinking the other three Japanese carriers, now launches an attack against *Yorktown*, damaging it beyond repair, but Heston and others from that ship and other carriers manage to take to the air and they bomb and sink that last Japanese carrier, *Hiryu*, crippling Japan's ability to thereafter mount any substantial carrier-based attacks against the U.S. in the Pacific for the remainder of the war. Heston, like his son, is wounded in the last attack, and, while attempting to land on board the *Enterprise*, crashes his plane and is killed. Although most of this film is shot as interiors, the live-action newsreel footage is impressive as it shows spectacular aerial combat, and the miniatures used in the battle scenes are also authentic looking. Smight does a good job helming the unwieldy cast, top heavy with star talent, where all the players, many shown briefly in cameo roles, are perfect in their roles. ***Author's Note***: Heston told this author that "I had a tough road to go in **Midway** since I battle my prejudices against the Japanese with my love for a son who loves a Japanese girl. The idea here was to try to bring some closure about the still prevalent anti-Japanese attitude in America for the attack at Pearl Harbor, a revisionist notion that still didn't take when that picture was made. By then the Nazis were mostly a forgotten nightmare, but millions of Americans could not forgive the Japanese for the Pearl Harbor attack." Mitchum, who appears only briefly in the film, told this author that "I had only a two-day shooting

Jimmy McQuaid, Woody Allen and Helena Bonham Carter in
Mighty Aphrodite, **1996.**

schedule. When they told me that I had to get a crew cut to look like Bull Halsey, I told them to go to blazes and that they could give my salary to charity." Ford told this author that "they grabbed a lot of top male talent for that picture and I was just one of the crowd with very little to do, except give the order to attack the Japanese carriers. But that was enough, wouldn't you say?" Fonda told this author that "playing Chester Nimitz was like playing a marble statue. The man was a navy icon and idol, one of its greatest heroes. I was amazed when one of Nimitz's close friends told me that I enacted the man just the way he was, taciturn and measuring his words without a trace of emotion. Don't know to this day as I never met Nimitz if he was correct, but without Nimitz and the men who served under him, we might have lost that war." Paul Frees, a bass-voiced radio announcer, dubbed Mifune's lines, making him sound like a stentorian Japanese relic talking from a deep crypt. **p,** Walter Mirisch; **d,** Jack Smight; **cast,** Charlton Heston, Henry Fonda, James Coburn, Glenn Ford, Hal Holbrook, Toshiro Mifune, Robert Mitchum, Cliff Robertson, Robert Wagner, Robert Webber, Christina Kokubo, Ed Nelson, James Shigeta, Monte Markham, Biff McGuire, Christopher George, Kevin Dobson, Glenn Corbett, Edward Albert, Pat Morita, Erik Estrada, Larry Pennell, Tom Selleck, John Bennett Perry, John Lupton; **w,** Donald S. Sanford; **c,** Harry Stradling Jr. (Technicolor); **m,** John Williams; **ed,** Robert Swink, Frank J. Urioste; **art d,** Walter Tyler; **set d,** John Dwyer; **spec eff,** Jack McMaster.

Mighty Aphrodite ★★★ 1996; U.S.; 95m; Sweetland Films/Miramax; Comedy/Fantasy; Children: Unacceptable (MPAA: R); **DVD; VHS.** Allen and Bonham Carter have an adopted son, who is a genius. Allen becomes obsessed with finding the boy's real parents because he thinks they, too, may be brilliant. He's disappointed when he discovers the boy's mother, Sorvino, is a prostitute and porn star and probably the dumbest person he's ever met. Interwoven is a Greek chorus linking the story of *Oedipus the King,* the Great tragedy by Sophocles about a king whose own faults lead to his downfall. This is one of Allen's most inventive but oddest films where everyone is sleeping with somebody other than their real-life partners. Songs: "Neo Minore" (Vasssilis Tsitanis), "Manhattan" (Richard Rodgers, Lorenz Hart), "Penthouse Serenade/When We're Alone" (Will Jason, Val Burton), "I've Found a New Baby" (Jack Palmer, Spencer Williams), "Take Five" (Paul Desmond), "The 'In' Crowd" (Billy Page), "Li'l Darlin'" (Neal Hefti), "Walkin' My Baby Back Home" (Fred E. Ahlert, Roy Turk), "Horos Tou Sakena" (Stavros Xarhakos), "Whispering" (Richard Coburn, Vincent Rose, John Schonberger), "You Do Something to Me" (Cole Porter), "I Hadn't Anyone Till You" (Ray Noble), "When Your Lover Has Gone" (E. A. Swan), "FAO Schwarz Clock Tower Song" (Bobby Gosh) and "When You're Smiling (The Whole World Smiles with You)" (Mark Fisher, Joe Good-

win, Larry Shaw). Gutter language and sex-related material prohibit viewing by children. **p,** Robert Greenhut, Helen Robin; **d&w,** Woody Allen; **cast,** Allen, F. Murray Abraham, Helena Bonham Carter, Claire Bloom, Olympia Dukakis, Donald Symington, Michael Rapaport, Mira Sorvino, David Ogden Stiers, Jack Warden, Peter Weller, Rosemary Murphy, Paul Giamatti; **c,** Carlo DiPalma; **ed,** Susan E. Morse; **prod d,** Santo Loquasto; **art d,** Tom Warren; **set d,** Susan Bode.

The Mighty Barnum ★★★ 1934; U.S.; 85m; FOX; B/W; Biographical Drama; Children: Acceptable; **VHS.** Beery is perfect as that master of hokum, Phineas T. Barnum (1810-1891). He is dissatisfied with sales at his general notions store in New York City, so he establishes sideshow exhibits of various freaks to attract customers, which brings down upon him the ire of Beecher, his prim and proper wife. The public, however, responds by flocking to his store, but he gets into trouble when his star attraction, La Verne, whom he claims to be the 100-year-old nurse maid to George Washington, is exposed as a fraud, as is Boley, whom Beery has promoted as a genuine bearded woman. The indefatigable Beery remains undaunted and insatiably searches for more and more spectacular attractions and scores big when he signs British singer Jenny Lind (1820-1887), played by Bruce, and where she becomes the toast of New York. (Barnum, under his contract with Lind, paid the singer $1,000 a night for 150 nights.) He then puts under contract his greatest attraction, Brasno, who plays the inimitable midget, General Tom Thumb (1838-1883), who becomes the star of Beery's museum. (Olive Brasno, who was Brasno's real-life wife, plays the female midget married to him in this film.) Beecher, however, can no longer tolerate her husband's wild schemes and his romancing of Bruce and departs for her New England home. Beery then loses Lind after disgracing her at a party through his awkward fumbling, and his dearest friend, Menjou (who plays a character based on James Anthony Bailey, 1847-1906), also vanishes after becoming a hopeless drunk. He loses the museum, but the freaks—giants, midgets, acrobats, and entertainers of all stripes—who have been loyal to him, rally to Beery's support and provide him with enough cash to regain his museum and Beecher then returns to remain at his side. Tragedy then strikes when his museum burns down (the blaze caused by his rivals, according to the film's story line; Barnum's museum burned down on July 13, 1865 and he built another museum, which burned down in 1868, both of mysterious origin and where in both instances, police had to shoot the wild animals escaping from the fires). Beery, however, cannot be defeated. Menjou returns, bringing Beery one of his greatest attractions, Jumbo, reportedly the largest elephant in the world (purchased for Beery by a grateful Bruce), and, as Beery, Menjou and Jumbo head a New York City parade, Beery tells Menjou about their next enterprise— that they will create the finest circus ever seen, one Beery calls "the greatest show on earth!" Lang's direction is skillful in presenting this wonderful panorama of Barnum's exhibits and entertainers. The period is impressively captured in the sprawling sets and rich costuming and the script sparkles with wit and humor, replete with Barnum's many quoted lines, i.e., "There's a sucker born every minute!" Bruce's singing was dubbed by Diana Gaylen. *Author's Note*: Zanuck told this author that "Beery was at first upset when I told him he was going to play a colossal hoaxer, but when he learned that his role was based on P. T. Barnum, he was all smiles and he started dreaming up crazy acts that Barnum never exhibited, creatures from Mars, things like that, until I told him, please, we have more freaks in this film than we can get on camera." **p,** Darryl F. Zanuck; **d,** Walter Lang; **cast,** Wallace Beery, Adolphe Menjou, Virginia Bruce, Rochelle Hudson, Janet Beecher, Tammany Young, Lucille La Verne, George Brasno, Olive Brasno, May Boley, Herman Bing, Donald Meek, Frank Morgan; **w,** Gene Fowler, Bess Meredyth (based on their play); **c,** Peverell Marley; **m,** Alfred Newman; **ed,** Barbara McLean, Allen McNeil; **art d,** Richard Day.

A Mighty Heart ★★★ 2007; U.S./U.K.; 108m; Paramount Vantage; Color; Biography/Drama; Children: Unacceptable (MPAA: R); **BD;**

DVD. This hard-hitting film culls its tale from the headlines of the day. As the U.S. is reacting to the September 11, 2001, terrorist attacks in the nation, a *Wall Street Journal* reporter, Daniel Pearl (Futterman), who is Jewish, and his pregnant reporter wife Mariane (Jolie) are in Karachi, Pakistan, on January 22, 2002, planning to take a flight the next day to Dubai, United Arab Emirates. First, Futterman arranges to interview an Islamic fundamentalist cleric in a Karachi café. When he doesn't return, Jolie begins a search, contacting Pakistani police, American embassy personnel, and the FBI, but gets no information on his whereabouts. We learn that Futterman has been kidnapped by members of a militant group, the National Movement for the Restoration of Pakistani Sovereignty, claiming he was a spy, and was taken to a secret location and, nine days later, was beheaded. Most of the action of the film takes place during Jolie's frantic and courageous week-and-a-half search for her husband, which became worldwide headline news. Excessive violence prohibits viewing by children. **p**, Andrew Eaton, Dede Gardner, Arti Gupta, Brad Pitt, Anita Overland; **d**, Michael Winterbottom; **cast**, Angelina Jolie, Dan Futterman, Irrfan Khan, Archie Panjabi, Mohammed Afzal, Mushtaq Ahmed, Daud Khan, Telal Saeed, Arif Khan, Will Patton; **w**, John Orloff (based on the book by Mariane Pearl); **c**, Marcel Zyskind; **m**, Harry Escott, Molly Nyman; **ed**, Peter Christelis; **prod d**, Mark Digby; **art d**, David Bryan; **set d**, Emma Field-Rayner; **spec eff**, Adam Garner, Marc Knapton, Gus Martinez.

Mighty Joe Young ★★★ 1949; U.S.; 84m; Argosy Pictures/RKO; B/W; Horror; Children: Cautionary; **DVD**; **VHS**. Cooper and Schoedsack, who produced the classic **King Kong**, 1933, reprise their colossal monster here with a smaller but sizeable version, a giant gorilla named Joe Young, who lives on a ranch in Africa and who is the pet of fetching Moore. Armstrong (who starred in **King Kong**, appears with his crew, including cowboy Johnson, looking for another spectacular act to exhibit in New York City, and when he finds Moore and her gigantic gorilla, he convinces her to go with her pet with him to New York and appear in a nightclub act. She agrees and the act begins when she plays "Beautiful Dreamer" on the piano, which slowly rises on a pedestal that is lifted by the powerful Joe Young. The gorilla then plays tug-of-rope with ten of the strongest men on earth, including former heavyweight champion Primo Carnera, where Joe Young easily yanks these men into a tank of water, winning the match. Tragedy strikes when several drunks make their way to Joe Young's cage behind the stage and begin abusing him, hitting him with bottles. He becomes enraged, breaks free of his cage, and goes on a rampage, tearing apart the sprawling nightclub, which has as extra attractions lions kept behind glass cages. Joe Young breaks these glass cages and battles the beasts, tossing them about like toys. When police come to arrest and destroy him, Moore, with the help of Johnson and Armstrong, who now regrets taking Joe Young from his native wilds, flee with the gorilla in a large truck with the police in pursuit. At that moment, a fire breaks out at an orphanage and Moore lets Joe Young free, telling him to climb to the topmost floors of the building to save innocent children trapped there. The valiant gorilla climbs upward, saves the children, and then collapses. He survives, however, and is last seen back at the ranch in Africa with Moore, who has married Johnson, so all's well that ends well. Schoedsack provides a lot of campy excitement in this wild tale, and though it fails to match the awesome impact of **King Kong**, the film does offer great action through the wonderful special effects of Willis O'Brien (who provided the special effects for **King Kong**) and Ray Harryhausen. This film was remade in 1998, but offered a much inferior production. Song: "Beautiful Dreamer" (Stephen Foster). *Author's Note*: The film was produced by Argosy Pictures, which was the production firm owned by pantheon director John Ford. "I had known Cooper and Schoedsack for years when we all worked with RKO," Ford told this author, "so when they pitched me about **Mighty Joe Young**, I thought they might be bringing back the old Kong with a fresh story. It was a good story, but their gorilla just wasn't big enough to match the original." The sequence for the orphanage fire was tinted

Khan Isaque and Dan Futterman in *A Mighty Heart*, 2007.

red in the original release. **p**, John Ford, Merian C. Cooper; **d**, Ernest B. Schoedsack; **cast**, Terry Moore, Ben Johnson, Robert Armstrong, Frank McHugh, Douglas Fowley, Denis Green, Paul Guilfoyle, Nestor Paiva, Regis Toomey, Loura Lee Michel; **w**, Ruth Rose (based on a story by Cooper), **c**, J. Roy Hunt; **ed**, Ted Cheesman; **spec eff**, Willis O'Brien, Ray Harryhausen, Harold Stine, Bert Willis, Linwood Dunn, Peter Peterson, George Lofgren, Marcel Delgado, Fitch Fulton.

Mighty Mouse in the Great Space Chase ★★★ 1982; U.S.; 86m; Filmation/Viacom; Color; Animated Adventure; Children: Acceptable (MPAA: G); **DVD**; **VHS**. Mighty Mouse, the lovable and heroic Superman of rodents, saves the Universe from destruction by the malicious, mischievous, malcontent cat, Harry the Heartless. Sequences were taken from the "space chase" serial of the television show "The New Adventures of Mighty Mouse and Heckle & Jeckle." **p**, Don Christensen, Norm Prescott, Lou Scheimer; **d**, Ed Friedman, Lou Kachivas, Marsh Lamore, Gwen Wetzler, Kay Wright, Lou Zukor; **cast** (voiceovers), Alan Oppenheimer, Diane Pershing; **w**, (based on comic book characters created by Izzy Klein); **c**, R.W. Pope; **m**, Yvette Blais (Ray Ellis), Jeff Michael (Norm Prescott); **ed**, Earl Biddle, James Blodgett, Ann Hagerman; **art d**, Alberto De Mello, James Fletcher.

The Mikado ★★★ 1967; U.K.; 125m; B.H.E./WB; Color; Musical; Children: Acceptable; **DVD**; **VHS**. In ancient Japan, the ruler is called the Mikado (Adams) and anyone disobeying him risks the loss of his head. His handsome young son, Potter, does just that by running away rather than marrying an older, ugly woman, Palmer, whom Adams has chosen for him. Potter becomes a wandering minstrel and enters the town of Titipu where he falls in love with a local beauty, Masterson. But she must marry the local warlord, Reed, who is the town's Lord High Executioner. Now, the Mikado has decreed that there must be at least one execution each month, and Reed cannot find anyone to behead on the month Potter arrives in town. Potter offers his own handsome head on condition that he be allowed to marry Masterson, which will give him one month of happiness. Reed has a problem with that because the law also decrees that the wife of the fellow who loses his head must be buried with him. The great judge, Sandford, tells Reed he will get around that by forging Potter's death certificate. The Mikado now arrives with his intended ugly future daughter-in-law. He is happy to learn that an execution has been performed that month, but then learns the victim was his son. When the fake death certificate is explained, Palmer wants to claim Potter as her husband. But he says he'd rather stay dead than marry her and insists he be allowed to marry Masterson. Adams agrees to let Potter marry the girl of his heart, and Reed, to save his own face and head, agrees to marry Palmer. Such is justice in ancient Japan.

Joan Crawford in *Mildred Pierce*, 1945.

Songs, among the most popular of Gilbert's and Sullivan's, include "The Mikado," "Three Little Maids from School," "I've Got a Little List," "Titwillow, Titwillow," "He's Going to Marry Yum-Yum," "A Wandering Minstrel, I," "The Mighty Troops of Titipu," "The Lord High Executioner," "I Would Kiss You Fondly Thus," "A Short Chop-Chop on a Big Black Block," ""Here's a Howdy-Doo," "The Emperor of Japan and His Daughter-in-Law Elect," "Let the Punishment Fit the Crime (His Object All Sublime)," "The Flowers That Bloom in the Spring" (sung by the cast and members of the D'Oyly Carte Company) (Arthur Sullivan, William S. Gilbert). An earlier production was filmed in 1939 with Kenny Baker as Nanki-Poo and Martyn Green as Ko-Ko. **p**, Anthony Havelock-Allan, John Brabourne; **d**, Stuart Burge; **cast**, Donald Adams, Philip Potter, John Reed, Kenneth Sandford, Thomas Lawlor, George Cook, Valerie Masterson, Peggy Ann Jones, Pauline Wales, Christene Palmer; **w**, William Schwenk Gilbert, Arthur Sullivan; **c**, Gerry Fisher (Technicolor); **m**, Gilbert, Sullivan; **ed**, Alma Godfrey; **art d**, Peter Howitt; **set d**, Disley Jones.

The Milagro Beanfield War ★★★ 1988; U.S.; 117m; Esparza/UNIV; Color; Comedy; Children (Unacceptable; MPAA: R); **DVD**; **VHS**. Bean pickers have bones to pick with a developer, Bradford, in the small town of Milagro, New Mexico. While they toil in the hot bean fields, Bradford plays golf and drinks cool margaritas. Bradford wants to turn the bean fields into a resort development for the rich, which would displace the local Hispanic bean pickers. He has bought out many of the town's inhabitants, but one man, Vennera, stubbornly decides not to sell his bean path. When he illegally taps into Bradford's water supply to irrigate his bean field, he gets local support from those objecting to water use laws that favor the wealthy. Helping Vennera in his Milagro's Last Stand is an activist, Braga, a local newspaper editor, Stern, and a Mexican old-timer, Riquelme, who carries a six-shooter and has a pet pig, along with some senior citizen cronies who carry rifles. The local sheriff, Blades, only wants peace and tries not to take sides, but the governor (state government favors the developer) sends in a tough-as-nails union buster, Walken, and war breaks out between the bean pickers and the developer. The word "Milagra" is Spanish for "miracle," and several minor ones help the Hispanics win their battle. Gutter language prohibits viewing by children. **p**, Robert Redford, Moctesuma Esparza, Charles Mulvehill; **d**, Redford; **cast**, Ruben Blades, Richard Bradford, Sonia Braga, Julie Carmen, James Gammon, Melanie Griffith, John Heard, Carlos Riquelme, Daniel Stern, Chick Vennera, Christopher Walken, Freddy Fender, Tony Genaro; **w**, John Nichols, David Ward (based on the novel by Nichols); **c**, Robbie Greenberg; **m**, Dave Grusin; **ed**, Dede Allen, Jim Miller; **prod d**, Joe Aubel, Tom Roysden; **art d**, Aubel, Brandy Alexander, Pamela Marcotte; **set d**, Thomas L. Roysden; **spec eff**, Mike Reedy,

Paul Russell, Thomas R. Ward, Peter Jamison.

Mildred Pierce ★★★★★ 1945; U.S.; 111m; WB; B/W; Drama; Children: Cautionary; **DVD**; **VHS**. Crawford presents her most stunning performance in this greatest of tearjerkers, a role she was born to play, as they say in Hollywood, a film that won for her the Oscar that had eluded her for so many years. The film opens with a shooting and Crawford (Mildred Pierce) is brought to Los Angeles police headquarters where she is questioned by chief of detectives Olsen. She then tells her story, shown in flashback, beginning when she is a hardworking housewife, married to struggling businessman Bennett while they raise two daughters. The marriage has long earlier gone sour when Bennett fails to provide enough money to keep the family together and he and Crawford repeatedly argue about their older daughter, Blyth (Veda Pierce), who is selfish and spoiled by the doting Crawford. Their younger daughter, Marlowe, becomes ill and dies. Bennett finds solace in the company of another woman and he finally leaves the house. To make ends meet and, to especially keep Blyth in a good school and wearing fine new clothes, Crawford takes a job as a waitress, befriending worldly Arden. Crawford is forever coming up with new ideas to improve customer service and how to provide good, but less expensive food and, when meeting real estate salesman Carson, convinces him to help her establish her own restaurant. Carson goes to playboy Scott, who owns considerable real estate, but is strapped for cash. They cut a deal where Scott turns over some prime property to Crawford so she can build her restaurant on a heavily trafficked corner. The restaurant becomes a huge success, so much so that Crawford expands, until she owns a chain of popular dining operations. Becoming wealthy, Crawford spends all her time either lavishing gifts and providing the good life to Blyth or slavishly working on her restaurants. Blyth, who has been spoiled rotten and is an utter snob, has no regard for her mother, at one point telling Crawford to her face that she is nothing more than "a common frump" and for which Crawford has slapped her so hard that she has knocked her down (and no one could slap harder in a film than Joan Crawford). Blyth later compromises the son of a rich family by telling these bluebloods that she wants a big settlement because she's pregnant and she gets it even though she is lying and is without child. Crawford can no longer tolerate Blyth's deceptive ways and they break up. Blyth becomes a singer in a sleazy nightclub operated by Carson, but Crawford reconciles with her and brings her back under her protective wing. She gives Blyth a new car for her birthday, and Blyth takes a drive with playboy Scott, who holds a percentage in Crawford's operations and now becomes more interested in Blyth than her mother. To give her daughter the social prestige she craves, Crawford marries Scott, making him a partner in her business, but he squanders her fortune and, in a backstabbing move, sells out all of his shares in her restaurant chain, driving it into bankruptcy. Moreover, the rakish Scott begins a secret affair with Blyth, and when Crawford drives to her lavish beach house, she finds Scott with Blyth, and where Blyth scornfully tells her mother that Scott has never loved her and that he is going to leave Crawford and marry her. When Crawford leaves, Scott tells Blyth that she is wrong, that he would never marry such a little tramp like her, and Blyth, enraged, withdraws a gun and empties its bullets into Scott, killing him. Crawford hears the shots and returns to find her daughter pleading to help her, saying that she could not help herself, again pretending to be a victim and depending upon her mother's love for her to protect her. We now see Crawford in flash-forward talking with Olsen at police headquarters, taking the blame for Scott's death, but Olsen tells her that they know who the real killer is and he orders Blyth into his office and books her for the murder, telling Crawford that she cannot this time save her cunning and calculating daughter. Blyth arrogantly tells a tearful Crawford that she will take care of herself before she is led away to be imprisoned. Crawford is now free of a daughter who has inspired her spectacular career and helped to destroy it. She leaves a wiser woman and is met by Bennett, who has always loved her, and they walk together from the portico of the resplendent Town Hall for the fadeout. Pantheon director Curtiz helms this great domestic tale with a firm hand that does not allow sentiment to seep through its many powerful scenes, where he exacts from Crawford the performance of her life as a woman who gives all and takes nothing for the sake of love, while also drawing from Carson, Bennett, Scott and, especially Blyth as the detestable Veda, fine performances. The production values are top notch and the sets and costuming are impressive. The photography from Haller is exceptional as is Steiner's dynamic score. MacDougall's brilliant script (from an equally brilliant novel by Cain) is witty and incisively reveals in its clever dialog the many divergent attitudes, ambitions and machinations of its fascinating characters. In addition to Crawford's Oscar, the film was nominated for Best Picture and Arden and Blyth received Oscar nominations as Best Supporting Actress. The budget for this film was huge at that time, $1,450,000, but it saw an enormous success at the box office and returned $3,500,000 in its initial release (inflation value of about $42 million in 2008). This story was made into a well-crafted TV miniseries in 2011, starring Kate Winslet as Mildred Pierce. Songs include: "You Must Have Been a Beautiful Baby" (Harry Warren, Johnny Mercer), "South American Way" (Jimmy McHugh, Al Dubin), "Please Think of Me" (Murray Mencher, Russ Morgan, Benny Davis), "How Sweet You Are" (Arthur Schwartz), "The Oceana Roll" (Lucien Denni, Roger Lewis), "Sweet Georgia Brown" (Maceo Pinkard), "It Can't Be Wrong" (Max Steiner) and "Waltz in F Flat Major" (Frederic Chopin). *Author's Note*: Oddly, most of the leading ladies in Hollywood at the time wanted nothing to do with this film. Barbara Stanwyck and Bette Davis turned it down and so did Crawford. She had been let go by MGM in 1943 after having been under contract to that studio for eighteen years, but studio boss Louis B. Mayer felt that Crawford's box office draw was fast diminishing and that she was all but finished in Hollywood. Warner Brothers picked up her contract, but she waited months for something to come her way, and when told about the project, she said the story was not for her. Then producer Jerry Wald personally went to Crawford's residence. "He told me that **Mildred Pierce** would be a great hit and it would make me the top female star in the business," Crawford told this author. "Quite frankly, nice man that Jerry was, I did not believe him. He brought the script along and left it with me. Well, after I read that great screenplay, I called Jerry and told him that it was perfect for me, a script I had been waiting for, and that I loved it, I truly loved it." The studio, however, had another serious problem and that was its top director, Curtiz. When Wald told him that he was directing the film and Crawford was the star, Curtiz, who had a mercurial temper, exploded, saying: "Me? Direct that temperamental bitch? Not on your goddamn life! She comes over here [from MGM] with her high-hat airs and her goddamn shoulder pads. I won't work with her! She's through, washed up. Why should I waste my time directing a has-been?" Wald met once more with Crawford, telling her that Curtiz had refused to direct her in **Mildred Pierce** (but without mentioning the director's derogatory remarks about her). Crawford, by then, determined to play the role, did an exceptional thing by bowing to Curtiz' prestige and authority when offering to do a screen test for the part. He agreed, and after he saw that test, he was convinced that Crawford was right for the role and agreed to direct the film, telling Wald: "Okay, I'll work with her, but she better know who's the boss." Curtiz also had the sixteen-year-old Blyth do a screen test before he accepted her in the role of Crawford's daughter, and this practice applied to almost all others in the cast of this film. The first day of production, however, proved to be a disaster. Curtiz exploded when he saw Crawford appear on the set with overly made-up makeup, particularly lipstick that gave her lips a fuller appearance. Accompanying Crawford was her private dress designer, who was carrying a handful of expensive gowns. Curtiz shouted at the designer: "I told you—no shoulder pads!" He then went to Crawford, tearing at her dress, screaming: "You and your damned Adrian shoulder pads!" (Adrian was one of the most successful gown designers in Hollywood at that time.) Crawford was in tears, saying: "Mr. Curtiz. I

Joan Crawford in *Mildred Pierce*, 1945.

bought this dress at Sears, Roebuck and it has no shoulder pads." Curtiz later softened toward the star after he realized the utter devotion she gave to her character and how she went out of her way to be nice to all the cast and crew members (and she particularly went out of her way to help Blyth with her part and for which Blyth was forever grateful). All on the set, including Curtiz, knew that Crawford was presenting a tour de force performance, the greatest of her life. The front office at Warner Brothers was keenly aware of Crawford's ongoing performance in this film and began early on lobbying on her behalf for an Oscar. Powerful Hollywood gossip columnist Hedda Hopper then wrote in her syndicated column, "Insiders say that Joan Crawford is delivering such a terrific performance on **Mildred Pierce** that she is a cinch for an Oscar." Other columnists and radio personalities joined with Hopper and began promoting the award to the actress. When the film was released, millions flocked to see it and everyone agreed that Crawford was back on top as a leading Hollywood lady. Even hardboiled crime writer Cain admired Crawford's performance, sending her a leather-bound edition of his novel and saying: "To Joan Crawford, who brought Mildred to life as I had always hoped she would be and who has my lifelong gratitude." Crawford, however, had second thoughts about attending the Academy Awards, telling Wald and others at Warner Brothers that she felt she would not win and, if she did, she would make "an ass" of herself in any acceptance speech, and so she refused to attend. Further, on the night of the awards, Crawford was at home with a temperature of 104, according to her physician. Her home, however, was filled with news photographers and where Crawford, in her finest nightgown, lay in bed as she listened to the award ceremonies on the radio. When Charles Boyer announced that she had won the Oscar for Best Actress, the photographers filled the bedroom with incessant flashes of light bulbs as they took photos of a smiling Crawford. Wald then appeared with the Oscar, as did many others, including Blyth, along with her most ardent fan, actor Van Johnson, and a contingent of other Hollywood people, to congratulate the star. Crawford then posed reclining with eyes closed while holding onto her Oscar as the photographers continued to take pictures. It was her greatest moment of Hollywood glory (if not revenge for all those who said that she was finished as an actress), and, some of her critics crowed, her second greatest performance. "The Joan Crawford I saw during the making of **Mildred Pierce**," Bennett told this author, "was not the Joan Crawford I had seen in all those slick melodramas from MGM over the years. She was a flesh-and-blood woman, a wife, a mother, and one of the greatest hearts that ever beat before a camera. Being in that picture with her was one of the highlights of my life." (That was a remarkable statement in that Bennett lived to be 100.) It is interesting to note Blyth's name in this film is "Veda," and the fact that many films over the years profiled similar rotten-to-the-

Sean Penn and Victor Garber in *Milk*, 2008.

core women with names commonly beginning with the letter "V," and that includes the selfish "Velma" portrayed by Joan Leslie in **High Sierra**, 1941, where she is an invalid, who plays up to gangster Humphrey Bogart, in order that he pay for an operation that cures her club foot and, when cured, dumps him for another man, or the conniving and murderous "Verna" enacted by Virginia Mayo in **White Heat**, 1949, who is James Cagney's floozy gun moll and who cheats on him with another gangster, Steve Cochran, and even shoots Cagney's mother in the back. What's in a name? To Hollywood such women all had the same moniker and that meant "vixen." In sharp contrast to these horrible harridans is my favorite, the hilarious lady with the double "V," Vera Vague (Barbara Jo Allen, 1906-1974), who played a man-chasing spinster in fifty films and on the radio, chiefly in the 1940s, and regularly appeared with Bob Hope. Barbara got the idea for that zany character when attending a PTA meeting and seeing a woman lecturing the crowd on literature and where that dithering lady could not string one coherent sentence after another, mindlessly changing the subject every five or ten seconds. **p**, Jerry Wald; **d**, Michael Curtiz; **cast**, Joan Crawford, Jack Carson, Zachary Scott, Eve Arden, Ann Blyth, Bruce Bennett, Lee Patrick, Moroni Olsen, Veda Ann Borg, Ramsay Ames, Robert Arthur, Lynn Baggett, Joyce Compton, Robert Evans, Angela Greene, Butterfly McQueen, George Tobias, Jo Ann Marlowe, Barbara Brown, Charles Trowbridge, John Compton; **w**, Ransld MacDougall (based on the novel by James M. Cain); **c**, Ernest Haller; **m**, Max Steiner; **ed**, David Weisbart; **art d**, Anton Grot, Bertram Tuttle; **set d**, George James Hopkins; **spec eff**, Willard Van Enger, Harry Barndollar, Russell Collings.

Milk ★★★ 2008; U.S.; 128m; Focus Features; Color; Biographical Drama; Children: Unacceptable (MPAA: R); **BD**; **DVD**. Harvey Milk (Harvey Bernard Milk, 1930-1978), played by Penn, is a gay camera store owner in San Francisco in 1972, who becomes a gay rights activist and California's first openly gay elected official, winning a seat on the city's Board of Supervisors in 1977. Told in flashback, his camera shop becomes the focal point for the city's growing gay community and he decides to run for political office, with his lover, Franco, as his campaign manager. During almost eleven months as a city supervisor, he is responsible for passing a tough gay rights ordinance for the city. On November 27, 1978, he and Mayor George Moscone (1929-1978) are shot to death by Dan White (Daniel James "Dan" White, 1946-1985), played by Brolin, another city supervisor, who is anti-gay and has resigned but wants his job back. The film also focuses on the gay rights movement in California and the 1978 fight against a statewide effort to bar gays and their supporters from public school jobs. Penn won an Oscar for Best Actor for his performance as Milk. *Author's Note*: For more details on the assassinations of Harvey Milk and George Moscone by Dan

White, see my book: *Murder among the Mighty: Celebrity Slayings That Shocked America* (Delacorte Press, 1983; pages 207-217). Gutter language, sexual content and violence prohibit viewing by children. **p**, Bruce Cohen, Dan Jinks; **d**, Gus Van Sant; **cast**, Sean Penn, Emile Hirsch, Josh Brolin, Diego Luna, James Franco, Alison Pill, Victor Garber, Denis O'Hare, Joseph Cross, Stephen Spinella, Lucas Grabêl, Brandon Boyce; **w**, Dustin Lance Black; **c**, Harris Savides; **m**, Danny Elfman; **ed**, Elliot Graham; **prod d**, Bill Groom; **art d**, Charley Beal; **set d**, Barbara Munch; **spec eff**, Thomas F. Sindicich, Syd Dutton, Bill Taylor.

The Milky Way ★★★ 1936; U.S.; 89m; PAR; B/W; Comedy; Children: Acceptable; **DVD**; **VHS**. Lloyd provides a lot of laughs in this prizefighting romp as a timid milkman, who comes to the aid of his sister, Mack, when she is being harassed by a drunken middleweight championship boxer, Gargan, and his trainer, Stander. When Stander throws a punch at Lloyd, the milkman ducks and the blow knocks out Gargan. Menjou, who is Gargan's manager, learns of it and interviews Lloyd, and the same thing happens again, but this time Menjou envisions big money from promoting Lloyd as a boxing contender and tells photographers and reporters that Lloyd knocked out the champ. Lloyd explains to Menjou that when he was a boy he was bullied and defended himself by learning how to duck. Teasdale, Gargan's girlfriend, teaches Lloyd dancing as fancy footwork skills, which, coupled to his ability to dodge blows, makes Lloyd look good in the ring. Menjou convinces Lloyd that he can be a boxing champ and make a lot of money. Lloyd agrees and, while in training, falls in love with Wilson. Lloyd wins a few fights without knowing Menjou has had them fixed. Lloyd and Gargan are scheduled to fight for the championship, but first they get into an exhibition bout at a party held by philanthropist Gateson, who uses the event to raise milk fund money for underprivileged children. Lloyd learns that he really didn't win the previous fights, so he is terrified about being in the ring with Gargan, but his dancing and dodging saves the day and, becomes the winner. Lloyd winds up a partner in the milk company, but only on the condition that he quit boxing, which he is more than happy to do. This film was remade as an equally delightful comedy with Danny Kaye as **The Kid from Brooklyn**, 1946. Songs: "The Blue Danube Waltz" (Johann Strauss, Jr.), "For He's a Jolly Good Fellow" (anonymous), "Yankee Doodle Dandy" (George M. Cohan), "The Bear Went over the Mountain" (anonymous), "The Skaters' Waltz" (Emile Waldteufel), "A Hot Time in the Old Town Tonight, (Theodore August Metz, Joe Hayden). *Author's Note*: McCarey told this author that "Harold [Lloyd] was a genius before the camera and was hilarious as long as he played his patented character of the innocent boy-next-door victim. You know, he lost his right thumb and forefinger in an accident when he was making **Haunted Spooks** [1920], but he had prosthetic replacements made for those pinkies that he disguised in a paper thin white glove and still managed to do his own stunts with that impairment. He was also a genius at finances and wisely invested his huge salaries when he was on top in the Twenties so that he ended his days with a fortune and lived in a forty-room villa. Nobody could play the fool better than Harold on the screen, but he was nobody's fool away from the camera." **p**, E. Lloyd Sheldon; **d**, Leo McCarey; **cast**, Harold Lloyd, Adolphe Menjou, Verree Teasdale, Helen Mack, William Gargan, George Barbier, Dorothy Wilson, Lionel Stander, Charles Lane, Marjorie Gateson, Anthony Quinn, Milburn Stone; **w**, Grover Jones, Frank Butler, Richard Connell (based on the play by Lynn Root, Harry Clork); **c**, Alfred Gilks; **ed**, LeRoy Stone; **art d**, Hans Dreier, Bernard Herzbrun.

The Milky Way ★★★ 1969; France/West Germany/Italy; 98m; Greenwich-Fraia-U-M; Color; Drama; Children: Unacceptable (MPAA: PG); **DVD**; **VHS**. This fascinating odyssey sees two French drifters, Frankeur and Terzieff, go on a pilgrimage to the shrine at Santiago de Compostela in Spain. The pilgrimage, called the Way of St. James, was one of the most important Christian pilgrimages during medieval times, over which the remains of St. James is carried from Jerusalem to northern Spain and where those remains were buried on the site of what became the city of Santiago de Compostela. En route, the drifters beg for food and hitchhike, meeting various people, who symbolize the main heresies of ages past and the places of Christian beliefs in the world today. Mature subject matter prohibits viewing by children. (In French; English subtitles.) **p**, Serge Silberman; **d**, Luis Buñuel; **cast**, Paul Frankeur, Laurent Terzieff, Alain Cuny, Edith Scob, Bernard Verley, François Maistre, Claude Cerval, Muni, Ellen Bahl, Michel Piccoli, Agnés Capri; **w**, Buñuel, Jean-Claude Carrière; **c**, Christian Matras; **m**, Buñuel; **ed**, Louisette Hautecoeur; **prod d**, Pierre Guffroy.

The Mill and the Cross ★★★ 2011; Poland/Sweden; 92m; Telewizja Polska/Kino Lorber; Color; Drama; Children: Unacceptable; **3-D**; **BD**; **DVD**. This film tells the absorbing story behind the 16th-century painting, "The Way to Calvary" by Dutch artist Pieter Bruegel (1525-1569). Hauer plays the artist of the painting, a large panel about four feet by five and a half feet, full of rich detail, depicting a group of about 500 Flemish people from all walks of life (from peasants and field workers to clerics and noblemen) gathered in a field beneath a mill as Christ is seen carrying His cross. The painting then comes to life as local actors portray those in the masterpiece. Among them are men dressed as soldiers in red tunics escorting Christ to his death, men chopping down a tree in a forest, a horse drawing a cart, a peddler carrying a heavy pack. A young wife with a large number of unruly children can be seen in the painting (and were Bruegel's own family members). This is an innovative, beautifully crafted film that presents a stunning re-creation of a great artist's masterwork, especially exciting in 3-D and Blu-ray. Mature subject matter prohibits viewing by children. (In Polish; English subtitles.) **p**, Lech Majewski, Dorota Roszkowska, Freddy Olsson; **d**, Majewski; **cast**, Rutger Hauer, Charlotte Rampling, Michael York, Oskar Huliczka, Joanna Litwin; **w**, Majewski, Michael Francis Gibson; **c**, Majewski, Adam Sikora; **m**, Majewski, Józef Skrzek; **ed**, Eliot Ems, Norbert Rudzik; **prod d**, Marcel Slawinski, Katarzyna Sobanska; **art d**, Stanislaw Porczyk; **spec eff**, Pawel Tybora.

Miller's Crossing ★★★★ 1990; U.S.; 115m; Circle Films/FOX; Color; Crime Drama; Children: Unacceptable (MPAA: R); **DVD**; **VHS**. Ultraviolent remake of **The Glass Key**, 1935 (and 1942), sees a stunning performance from Byrne as a political fixer working for Finney, the boss of a Midwestern city during the Prohibition era, where the cops and elected officials are as crooked as the crooks they slavishly serve. When Polito, a rival underworld boss, tells Finney that he intends to kill unruly bookie Turturro, Finney refuses to sanction the murder, offering Turturro protection while ridiculing the Italian gangster, enraging Polito and where Polito vows vengeance. Finney has started this war to save Turturro because he is the brother of sultry gun moll Harden, who is having an affair with Finney, even though she has been carrying on a secret romance with Byrne for some time. Byrne opposes his boss, attempting to persuade him not to go against Polito, but Finney, a hot-tempered Irish racketeer, is now dedicated to destroying Polito, but Polito strikes first. He sends two goons to kill Finney in his sprawling house and where they fire machine guns at him, but Finney, also armed with a machine gun, blasts them out of his house and, while dressed in his bathrobe, chases them down a broad street, firing after them until their fleeing car bursts into flames and both are dead. Such bloody open warfare is tolerated since Finney has cowed the public and has the police in his pocket. To get Finney to quit the war, Byrne then tells him that Harden is using him to protect her brother Turturro, and, to prove her disloyalty, tells Finney that he and Harden have been having an affair behind his back. Finney explodes, beats up Byrne and then fires him. Byrne then ostensibly switches sides, going to work for Polito, although Polito's top enforcer, Freeman, a ruthless killer, does not believe Byrne has altered his loyalties. Freeman insists that Byrne prove his loyalty to Polito by murdering Turturro at a remote area outside of town called

Gabriel Byrne and Albert Finney in *Miller's Crossing*, 1990.

Miller's Crossing, and Byrne takes the terrified Turturro to that area as Freeman and other goons wait unseen at a dirt road. Byrne cannot bring himself to kill Turturro, who pleads with tears running down his cheeks for his life; fires several shots, pretending to have killed the errant bookie, Bryne telling Turturro to keep his mouth shut and to disappear. Byrne, however, continues to sow suspicion on Freeman so that Polito will suspect him of being disloyal. Then Turturro resurfaces, and insists that he kill Polito or he will make his existence known to the gangster. Byrne agrees, but, after convincing Polito to murder his top enforcer, Freeman, he tells Polito that Turturro is still alive, thanks to Freeman's doing, and Polito goes gunning for Turturro, who, instead, kills Polito. Byrne then arrives and persuades Torturro to turn over his gun to him. He then tells him that he plans to kill him for betraying him. Turturro then begs for his life once more, but this time his weeping act cannot convince Byrne to spare his life and Byrne shoots him to death. Finney regains his post as top boss of the city and, after forgiving Harden for her emotional betrayal with Byrne, Finney proposes to her and she accepts. Finney then plans to marry Harden and asks Byrne to rejoin him, but Byrne is weary of all the underworld machinations and quits the rackets for the fadeout of this well-made thriller. Finney, Freeman, and Harden give fine support to Byrne's brooding portrayal, and Polito and Turturro give extravagant performances as the two most outlandish characters in this blood-and-thunder production where torn flesh and gory murders are graphically shown by director Coen. Not for the squeamish, this film nevertheless excitingly captures the violent era engulfing its utterly disreputable characters, where the action is well choreographed and the photography is outstanding. Songs: "Danny Boy" (Rory Dall O'Cahan, Frederick Edward Weatherly), "Decatur Street Tutti" (Jabbo Smith), "King Porter Stomp" (Ferdinand "Jelly Roll" Morton, Sonny Burke, Sid Robin), "Come Back to Erin" (Charlotte Allington Barnard), "Runnin' Wild" (A. Harrington Gibbs, Joe Grey, Leo Wood), "Good Night, Sweetheart" (Rudy Valee, Ray Noble, James Campbell, Reginald Connelly). **p**, Ethan and Joel Coen, Mark Silverman; **d**, Joel Coen; **cast**, Gabriel Byrne, Marcia Gay Harden, Albert Finney, John Turturro, Jon Polito, J.E. Freeman, Mike Starr, Al Mancini, Richard Woods, Thomas Toner, Steve Buscemi, Frances McDormand; **w**, Ethan and Joel Coen (based on the novels *Red Harvest* and *The Glass Key* by Dashiell Hammett); **c**, Barry Sonnenfeld; **m**, Carter Burwell; **ed**, Michael R. Miller; **prod d**, Dennis Gassner; **art d**, Leslie McDonald; **set d**, Nancy Haigh; **spec eff**, Peter Chesney, Bob Ahmanson.

The Million ★★★ 1931; France; 83m; Films Sonores Tobis/American Tobis Co.; B/W; Comedy; Children: Acceptable; **DVD**; **VHS**. This rollicking funfest sees a Parisian starving artist, Lefévre, dealing with seemingly endless problems. He is hounded by creditors, and while he

Rene Lefevre and Annabella in *The Million*, 1931.

is embracing the woman whose portrait he is painting, his fiancée, Annabella, walks in on them in his studio. On the plus side, he learns he holds the winning ticket in the Dutch Lottery. On the down side, he has put the ticket in the pocket of a jacket, but Annabella has given the jacket to a criminal, so he can elude the police. The criminal sells the jacket to Ollivier, who sells it to a tenor singing at the Paris Opera House. Meanwhile, some crooks learn of the lottery ticket and they and Lefevre and Annabella go to the opera house to retrieve the jacket, but, during a mad chase, it is thrown out a window and lands on top of a car. Lefevre follows in a taxi, the crooks follow him, and it all ends with Ollivier finding the jacket with the ticket, so Lefevre, rightful owner of the ticket worth a million Dutch florins, wins the lottery and Annabella in the bargain. Pantheon director Clair cleverly employs music to accentuate his most frenetic scenes, heightening tension and increasing the widespread mirth. *Author's Note*: The film's plot was later employed by Ben Hecht in writing the story line for **Tales of Manhattan**, 1942, but where a dress evening coat changes hands many times instead of a jacket. (In French; English subtitles.) **d**, Rene Clair; **cast**, Annabella, Rene Lefevre, Louis Allibert, Paul Ollivier, Constantin Siroesco, Raymond Cordy, Vanda Greville, Odette Talazac, Pedro Elviro, Jane Pierson; **w**, Clair (based on a musical play by Georges Berr, Marcel Guillemaud); **c**, Georges Perinal, Georges Raulet; **m**, Armand Bernard, Philippe Pares, Georges Van Parys; **art d&set d**, Lazare Meerson.

Million Dollar Baby ★★★★ 2004; U.S.; 132m; Lakeshore Entertainment/WB; Color; Sports Drama; Children: Unacceptable (MPAA: PG-13); **BD**; **DVD**. Eastwood (who also directs) and Swank give outstanding performances in this enjoyable sports drama where Eastwood, a gifted boxing trainer, runs a broken-down training gym in Los Angeles. Swank, a waitress from a small Missouri town in the Ozarks, walks into the gym and asks Eastwood to train her to box. He abruptly dismisses her, saying that he doesn't "train girls." Though Eastwood is a no-nonsense guy, he shields a soft heart with a brusque manner and has only one friend, a beaten-up ex-pug, Freeman, who knows that Eastman has been emotionally scarred through a traumatic experience with his estranged daughter and who narrates this tale. Swank determinedly works out at the gym and, with Freeman's help, finally convinces Eastwood to train her to box, but saying that, when she is ready for a match, he will try to get her a manager. His most important advice is that she must protect herself at all costs while fighting in the ring. When ready, Swank gets a manager with Eastwood's assistance, but the manager does a poor job in advising her during her first bout. Eastwood then shows up and brilliantly coaches her so that she wins the match. Swank then exacts a promise from Eastwood that he will not again abandon her, and he manages her professional career thereafter, seeing her win one fight

after another in the women's welterweight boxing division, winning most of her fights by knocking out her opponents in the first round. Eastwood, whose own daughter returns his letters unopened, now adopts a paternal attitude toward Swank, looking upon her as the daughter he has lost. They go to Europe where Swank meets a top flight opponent and wins the match. The good-hearted Swank sends most of her winnings to her ungrateful white trash family, even buying a house for her overweight and selfish mother, Martindale, who tells Swank that such generosity is threatening her welfare and medical payments and adding insult by telling Swank that everybody back home is laughing at her for becoming a professional boxer. Eastwood then arranges a $1 million fight for Swank where she is to meet Rijker, a German ex-prostitute, who holds the women's welterweight championship and is widely known as a dirty boxer, using underhanded methods to win her bouts. At the beginning of the fight, Swank appears to be winning, but Rijker hits her with a sucker punch from behind, knocking her out and where she lands on a stool that causes her to break her neck and leaving her a quadriplegic. Eastwood takes care of Swank, visiting her regularly in a medical center and finally convinces Martindale and the rest of Swank's self-centered relatives to visit her, but they are only concerned with getting her assets through an attorney and have no regard for Swank's dire medical condition. Swank finally sees through their artful ploy and orders them never to see her again, threatening to take away the house she has earlier bought for them. Swank then worsens and must have a leg amputated. She knows she is dying and asks Eastwood to help her end her life, saying that she wants to remember the only great moments of her life, hearing the cheers from the crowds when she won her fights. Eastwood refuses. He then seeks the advice of a priest, O'Byrne, a man he has alienated over the years, who tells him that euthanasia is a terrible sin. Swank, however, attempts several suicides and, no longer able to bear her suffering, Eastwood secretly visits her at night at the medical center and injects adrenaline to end her life before he disappears. Freeman's narration ends this dark finish in a letter being sent to Eastwood's estranged daughter, one that summarizes the fine character of her father. Eastwood directs this tragedy with a sure hand while providing a compelling tale packed with pathos and action, but its dire ending may be too depressing for many and his act of euthanasia (a capital crime under the law) prohibits viewing by children. Euthanasia has been depicted in many films, notably **Ministry of Fear**, 1944; **For Whom the Bell Tolls**, 1943; **Captain from Castile**, 1947; **An Act of Murder**, 1948; **The Greatest Show on Earth**, 1952; **Lawrence of Arabia**, 1962; **It Happened Here**, 1966; **They Shoot Horse, Don't They?**, 1969; **One Flew over the Cuckoo's Nest**, 1975; **Whose Life Is It Anyway?**, 1981; and **The English Patient**, 1996; **p**, Clint Eastwood, Paul Haggis, Bobby Moresco, Tom Rosenberg, Albert S. Ruddy; **d**, Eastwood; **cast**, Eastwood, Hilary Swank, Morgan Freeman, Jay Baruchel, Mike Colter, Lucia Rijker, Brían O'Byrne, Anthony Mackie, Margo Martindale, Riki Lindhome; **w**, Haggis (based on stories from *Rope Burns* by F.X. Toole); **c**, Tom Stern; **m**, Eastwood; **ed**, Joel Cox; **prod d**, Henry Bumstead; **art d**, Jack G. Taylor, Jr.; **set d**, Richard C. Goddard; **spec eff**, Steve Riley.

Million Dollar Legs ★★★ 1932; U.S.; 64m; PAR; B/W; Comedy; Children: Acceptable; **DVD**; **VHS**. A zany, surrealistic comedy not to be confused with a 1939 film of the same name but a different plot starring Betty Grable. In this film, Oakie is a brush salesman in the mythical country of Klopstokia, who falls in love with Fleming, daughter of the country's president, the inimitable and cantankerous Fields. The country is bankrupt and Fields' cabinet conspires to overthrow him. Oakie has a solution. He encourages Fields to enter the 1932 Summer Olympics weightlifting competition in the United States and win a large amount of money offered to medalists by the brush company for which he works. At the Los Angeles Olympics, Fields throws a 1,000-pound weight at Oakie but misses. He does win the competition and a shot put event, saving Klopstokia from insolvency and assuring that Oakie wins Fleming. Songs: "You're in the Army Now" (traditional), "William Tell

Overture" (Gioachino Rossini), "Pomp and Circumstance March No. 1" (Edward Elgar), "It's Terrific (When I Get Hot)" (Ralph Rainger, Leo Robin), "Klopstakian Love Song" based on "One Hour with You" (Richard A. Whiting, Henry Myers), "Sailing, Sailing, over the Bounding Main" (Godfrey Marks). *Author's Note*: This grand farce, which offers a small army of silent slapstick stars doing their priceless bits of funny business, was produced shortly before the 1932 Olympics held in Los Angeles. It savagely lampoons the Olympics and was released at the time the Olympics opened, although sports enthusiasts did not appreciate its stinging parodies as much as expected. The country represented by Oakie, Fields and others is as mythical as the kingdoms where the Marx Brothers dwelled at one time or another (Fredonia, etc.), and where there are spies hiding behind every tree and everyone has superhuman strength, the presidency going to the strongest man in the nation and that is Fields. The very good comedy, **The Mouse That Roared**, 1959, owes much to the plotline (such as it is) of this film. **p**, Herman J. Mankiewicz; **d**, Edward Cline; **cast**, Jack Oakie, W.C. Fields, Andy Clyde, Lyda Roberti, Susan Fleming, Ben Turpin, Hugh Herbert, George Barbier, Dickie Moore, Bruce Bennett, Hobart Bosworth, Billy Gilbert, Charlie Hall, Don Wilson; **w**, Henry Myers, Nicholas T. Barrows (based on a story by Joseph L. Mankiewicz); **c**, Arthur L. Todd; **m**, Rudolph G. Kopp, John Leipold.

Million Dollar Mermaid ★★★ 1952; U.S.; 115m; MGM; Color; Biographical Drama; Children: Acceptable; **DVD**; **VHS**. This well-crafted film is based upon the career of Australian swimmer Annette Kellerman (Annette Marie Sarah Kellerman, 1886-1975), who is played to perfection by the stunning aquatic star Williams. As a girl of ten years (Corcoran), the daughter of a music teacher, Pidgeon, she braves out a leg disorder by becoming a very good swimmer. As a grown woman (Williams), she becomes the best female swimmer in the world. Pidgeon takes a job in London and Williams goes with him. Aboard ship they meet Aussies Mature and White, who own a boxing kangaroo they plan to exhibit in a show in London. Mature suggests to Williams that he manage her swimming career, but she is more interested in studying ballet. The job Pidgeon expected does not materialize and Williams can't find work as a dancer, so she agrees to let Mature manage her as a swimmer. As a publicity stunt dreamed up by Mature, Williams swims thirty miles down the River Thames and her unprecedented swim makes headlines. Mature tries to get her more attention so, taking her to Boston for a long swim, he has her trade in her long, baggy 1920s swimsuit for a daring form-fitting black one-piece number. It shocks a lot of people, and Mature capitalizes on this by notifying the press. She makes more headlines and Mature has her arrested for indecency. The trial goes to court where a judge decides it was all a publicity stunt and releases Williams. Brian, a showman, who books Williams into the famed NYC Hippodrome, later proposes to Williams, but she holds him off. She is then injured, and both Mature and Brian visit her in the hospital. Brian can see that Williams really loves Mature so he walks out of her life and Mature walks permanently to her side. Songs include: "Let Me Call You Sweetheart" (Leo Friedman, Beth Slater Whitson), "The Fountain in the Park" (Ed Haley), "When You Wore a Tulip (and I Wore a Big Red Rose)" (Percy Wenrich), "The Washington Post March," "The Stars and Stripes Forever" (John Philip Sousa), "Sobre las olas (Over the Waves)" (Juventino Rosas), "On the Beautiful Blue Danube," "Emperor Waltz" (Johann Strauss), "Dance of the Reed Flutes" (from The Nutcracker Suite, Op. 71a by Peter Ilyich Tchaikovsky), "Jingle Bells" (James Pierpont), "London Bridge Is Falling Down (traditional), "Gavotte" (François-Joseph Gossec), "Minuet in G" (Ludwig van Beethoven), "Waltz in A Flat Major, Op. 39" (Johannes Brahms). *Author's Note*: Kellerman was the first to present synchronized swimming ensembles when appearing in the huge tank of New York's Hippodrome in 1907, and those aquatic feats are replicated with stunning feats by the beautiful Williams in this film, which was choreographed by the great Busby Berkeley and Audrene Brier. Berkeley employed more than 100 top swimmers to slide

Esther Williams and Walter Pidgeon in *Million Dollar Mermaid,* **1952.**

down fifty-five-foot ramps streaming red and yellow smoke and where the swimmers hold torches to finally form mosaic patterns in the huge tank and where Williams, perched above them on a fifty-foot-high swing, dives into the center of a kaleidoscopic formation while Berkeley's overhead camera captured all the great action. This is one of the finest water ballets ever put on film. Accomplished ballerina Maria Tallchief performs briefly on the stage while enacting the part of the Russian ballerina Anna Pavlova (1881-1931). **p**, Arthur Hornblow, Jr.; **d**, Mervyn LeRoy; **cast**, Esther Williams, Victor Mature, Walter Pidgeon, David Brian, Donna Corcoran, Jesse White, Maria Tallchief, Howard Freeman, James Bell, Queenie Leonard, Betty Lynn; **w**, Everett Freeman; **c**, George J. Folsey (Technicolor); **m**, Adolph Deutsch; **ed**, John McSweeney, Jr.; **art d**, Cedric Gibbons, Jack Martin Smith; **set d**, Edwin B. Willis, Richard Pefferle; **spec eff**, A. Arnold Gillespie, Warren Newcombe.

The Millionaire ★★★ 1931; U.S.; 82m; WB; B/W; Comedy/Drama; Children: Acceptable; **DVD**; **VHS**. A compelling riches-to-rags story has Arliss as the millionaire owner of a major automobile company. He's bored and would like to retire, but Cagney, a life insurance salesman, warns him that retired executives are bad health risks. Arliss answers a newspaper advertisement that offers a garage for sale. Using an alias, he buys half of the garage, and the other half is owned by a decent, hard-working young man, Manners, who becomes his partner and then learns that the girl he loves, Knapp, is Arliss' daughter. Arliss comes to learn that he can be happy as half owner in a garage, although he is still a millionaire, and Manners and Knapp will marry. Florence Arliss, wife of George Arliss, plays his wife in the film which was remade as **That Way with Women**, 1947. The story was by Biggers who created the Charlie Chan detective series. *Author's Note*: This film was made almost at the same time Cagney appeared in the lead role of the classic gangster film. **The Public Enemy**, 1931, and when his star status was net yet secured and where he was briefly playing supporting roles. "I was under contract in those days," Cagney told this author. I got a call and someone at Warner Brothers casting who said to me: 'You're an insurance salesman in a picture called **The Millionaire** starring George Arliss.' Okay, I was an insurance salesman and that was that." **p&d**, John G. Adolfi; **cast**, George Arliss, David Manners, Florence Arliss, Evalyn Knapp, James Cagney, Bramwell Fletcher, Noah Beery, Ivan Simpson, J.C. Nugent, Sam Hardy, J. Farrell MacDonald, Charles Grapewin, Tully Marshall, Ethel Griffies; **w**, Julien Josephson, Maude T. Howell, Booth Tarkington (based on the story "Idle Hands" by Earl Derr Biggers); **c**, James Van Trees; **m**, Leo F. Forbstein; **ed**, Owen Marks; **art d**, Esdras Hartley.

The Millionairess ★★★ 1961; U.K.; 90m; Dimitri de Grunwald Production/FOX; Color; Comedy; Children: Cautionary; **DVD**; **VHS**. The

Marie Dressler and Wallace Beery in *Min and Bill*, 1930.

voluptuous and Amazonian Loren is the lady with all the money, but she is unhappy, having had an earlier marriage gone sour and now wants only to find happiness with the right man. Sim, her avuncular attorney, suggests she see psychiatrist Price to shed her phobias and Price sees nothing but dollar signs in the sultry Loren. They begin to spark until Price makes a derogatory remark about Loren's dominating father and she breaks off the relationship. She next meets Sellers, an Indian doctor whose only interest in life is taking care of the poor and indigent patients at his small clinic. His dedication overwhelms Loren, who asks Sellers to examine her. Before he can turn about, she has shed her clothes and appears only in girdle, nylons, and heels, and displaying as much of her ample charms as propriety allows. Stunned by her beauty, Sellers composes himself and tells Loren to dress immediately and that she appears too healthy to be ill. Loren, however, has made up her mind to have Sellers and, to that end, she buys up all the properties surrounding his clinic and orders the construction of a new and vast medical complex to be added to his clinic. Sellers believes Loren is crazy, telling her that he will go along with her scheme if she takes a job for three months and lives only on the salary she earns. She agrees, but on the condition that Sellers turns a profit with his clinic, tripling his fees for his patients. He agrees, but has no intention of living up to the bargain. Loren works hard and lives up to her end of the agreement, but Sellers fails at his end of the bargain, losing more money than ever. He happily announces his miserable performance to Loren, explaining that his inability to make money proves that he is not the man for her. Crushed, Loren announces that she will give herself to no other man and intends to enter a convent in Tibet. At the last minute, Sellers realizes that he cannot let her go and that he loves her and they come together for a happy fadeout. Asquith does a fine job in presenting this above-average comedy, but he sacrifices much of Shaw's original lines and changes Sellers' character from an idealistic physician to an Indian doctor so that the comedian could enact his favorite caricature and does a hilarious time doing it. Loren is also outstanding in her role as the lovesick rich lady. De Sica, who was Loren's favorite director, makes a brief appearance as a spaghetti salesman. Price is perfect as the conniving money-digging doctor, and Purcell presents a side-splitting imitation of a drunk, one of the best ever essayed on film, while the always clever Sim gives a standout performance as the conniving lawyer expecting to make big bucks if he can maneuver Loren to the altar with Price. **p**, Pierre Rouve; **d**, Anthony Asquith; **cast**, Sophia Loren, Peter Sellers, Alastair Sim, Vittorio De Sica, Dennis Price, Gary Raymond, Alfie Bass, Miriam Karlin, Noel Purcell, Virginia Vernon; **w**, Wolf Mankowitz, Riccardo Aragno (based on the play by George Bernard Shaw); **c**, Jack Hildyard (CinemaScope; Eastmancolor); **m**, Georges Van Parys; **ed**, Anthony Harvey; **prod d**, Paul Sheriff; **art d**, Harry White.

Millions ★★★ 2005; U.K.; 98m; Pathe Pictures/Fox Searchlight; Color; Comedy/Fantasy; Children: Unacceptable (MPAA: PG-13); **DVD**. As the United Kingdom prepares to switch its currency from pounds to euros, a gang robs a train loaded with money on its way to be incinerated. One of the big bags of currency bounces off the train and is found by Etel, a seven-year-old boy, who is walking along the railroad tracks. He talks to saints and thinks the money has come from heaven. His mother died and he and McGibbon, his nine-year-old brother, live with their father, Nesbitt, in a suburb of Liverpool. Etel takes the advice of the saints and decides to be generous with the millions, putting a lot of money in a charity basket and buying pizza for street people. McGibbon figures the money may not be spendable very long, because the currency conversion will take place in a week, so he buys every electronic gadget in the stores, but also urges Etel to invest in real estate, and Etel buys a new house for them. McGibbon also comes up with the idea of turning the pounds into dollars and then using the dollars to buy euros. Meanwhile, the robbers search for the missing loot. The brothers learn that there is a good and bad side to money, especially a lot of it, and what it really means to perform good deeds. The film ends with fantasy overcoming reality as Etel finds himself in Africa where starving villagers consider water from a pump to be worth millions to them and that money is basically useless. Songs: "Hitsville UK" (Joe Strummer, Mick Jones); "Nirvana" (Rojotua and Loxatus); "Hysteria," "Blackout" (Matthew Bellamy, Dominic Howard, Chris Wolstenholme); "La petite fille de la mer" (Vangelis); "Who Wants to Be a Millionaire?" (Keith Strachan, Matthew Strachan); "Tumble and Fall" (Grant Nicholas); "Brazil" (Aro Barrosa); "Deck the Halls" (traditional); "Happy Birthday" (Patty S. Hill, Mildred J. Hill); "Carol of the Bells" (Mykola Dmytrovych Leontovych, Peter Wilhousky); "Little Drummer Boy" (Katherine Davis, Henry Onorati, Harry Simone) and "Silent Night" (Franz Gruber, Joseph Mohr). This would have been a wonderful film for the whole family, but gutter language prohibits viewing by children. **p**, Graham Broadbent, Andrew Hauptman, Damian Jones, Tracey Seaward; **d**, Danny Boyle; **cast**, Aexl Etel, Lewis McGibbon, Daisy Donovan, James Nesbitt, Christopher Fulford, Pearce Quigley, Jane Hogarth, Alun Armstrong, Enzo Cilenti, Nasser Memarzia, Kathryn Pogson; **w**, Frank Cottrell Boyce; **c**, Anthony Dod Mantle; **m**, John Murphy; **ed**, Chris Gill; **prod d**, Mark Tildesley; **art d**, Mark Digby, Denis Schnegg; **set d**, Michelle Day; **spec eff**, Dave Chadwick, Richard Conway, Steve Kane, Melissa Agate, Peter Bach.

Min and Bill ★★★★ 1930; U.S.; 69m; MGM; B/W; Comedy/Drama; Children: Unacceptable; **DVD**; **VHS**. Although this film was initially presented to the public as a drama, it is really a side-splitting comedy where the most unlikely romantic couple, the sixty-two-year-old Dressler, and the fifty-five-year-old Beery (beer belly and saggy, craggy face and all) cavort cantankerously on the screen together in what is one of Hollywood's most memorable duos. Dressler runs a run-down hotel on the waterfront of the California coast and Beery is a fisherman, who is the apple of her eye, but she spends most of her time blackening his for his endless transgressions. Jordan, a pretty, young girl, works very hard for Dressler. She has been left years earlier with Dressler by her mother, Rambeau, an alcoholic streetwalker. Jordan, however, loves Dressler because she knows she has a heart of gold and has been consistently kind to her. Dressler, however, has problems with truant officers, who insist that Jordan be moved to a better home atmosphere and attend school and they compel Jordan to live with strict school principal McGlynn and equally severe wife Gould. Rambeau then shows up, but Dressler, seeing that the drunken harridan has not reformed, begs her to go to San Francisco and stay away from her daughter. Dressler then collects all her savings and spends that on Jordan, sending her to an exclusive boarding school, and there Jordan meets and falls in love with Dillaway (his film debut), a wealthy and decent young man, who does not care about Jordan's poverty-stricken past. They plan to marry, but then Jordan takes a boat back to see Dressler. On that boat is Rambeau, who is caught with a man in her room (Roquemore), although Jordan does not know that shady lady Rambeau is her mother. Rambeau goes to Dressler after learning that her daughter is to marry into wealth and tells Dressler that she intends to blackmail Dillaway's family for a fortune, threatening to expose her own rotten past unless she receives a lot of money. The two women get into a brawl and Rambeau burns Dressler's face with a hot iron, but before this terrible woman can menace Dressler further, Dressler withdraws a gun and shoots Rambeau dead. Bell, a waterfront type who has never liked Dressler, then tells police about the shooting and Dressler, despite the protests and antics of Beery, is arrested and led off to the pokey, but she does not care by this time as Jordan and Dillaway have been married and have sailed away on their honeymoon. Director Hill manages this rough-and-tumble melodrama with great skill, getting from Dressler, Beery and Rambeau outstanding performances and while skillfully unfolding this tearjerker tale. **Tugboat Annie**, 1933, is a fine sequel to this film. *Author's Note*: Dressler had been a superstar in the silent era, but her career had been in a steep decline after talkies arrived. She then appeared with the great Greta Garbo in **Anna Christie**, 1930, and where her status again soared. Dressler's best friend was screenwriter Frances Marion, whose husband was director Hill, and both of them had Dressler in mind for the leading lady when MGM cast her in this film with Beery. The film was an enormous box office success and put Dressler back on top and, until the day of her death in 1934, she was the foremost star at MGM. Dressler was given an Oscar for Best Actress for her appearance in **Min and Bill**, beating out all of the reigning Hollywood stars of that era—Norma Shearer, Marlene Dietrich, Irene Dunne and Ann Harding—to prove that beauty wasn't everything and that the talented ability to move the hearts of millions of moviegoers was. **p&d**, George W. Hill; **cast**, Marie Dressler, Wallace Beery, Dorothy Jordan, Marjorie Rambeau, Donald Dillaway, DeWitt Jennings, Russell Hopton, Frank McGlynn, Gretta Gould, Hank Bell, Jack Pennick, Henry Roquemore; **w**, Frances Marion, Marion Jackson (based on the novel *Dark Star* by Lorna Moon); **c**, Harold Wenstrom; **ed**, Basil Wrangell; **art d**, Cedric Gibbons.

The Mind Benders ★★★ 1963; U.K.; 109m; Novus/American International Pictures; B/W; Science Fiction; Children: Unacceptable; **DVD**; **VHS**. The body of British scientist Goldblatt is found under a moving train and authorities suspect he committed suicide. He has been working as a research professor in the field of sensory perception. A briefcase containing a large sum of money is found nearby, and it is believed he was selling information to the communists and took his life out of guilt and remorse. Bogarde, a friend and colleague, sets out to prove Goldblatt was not a traitor and his death was brought about by the pressure of his work. Bogarde suspects that Goldblatt had been brainwashed by a sensory deprivation method involving isolation experiments, but doesn't know if anyone can really be convinced to do something against their strongest feelings. Bogarde believes brainwashing is possible, but Clements, his superior, disagrees. To test this, Bogarde agrees to be a guinea pig in an experiment in which others will try to make him stop loving his wife, Ure, whom he loves very much. The experiment involves Bogarde submerging himself into a tank of water at a certain temperature, which will strip him of his senses and make him susceptible to any psychological attacks. After emerging from the tank, Bogarde is a different person. When his wife tells him that she is pregnant he begins womanizing with a local young woman, Craig, hardly the actions of a man in love with his wife. Ure goes into early labor and Bogarde rushes to the hospital to help in the baby's delivery, signs that he definitely loves his wife. Bogarde's brainwashing is not a total success since he was able to regain love for his wife, but the experiment is extremely stressful, proving that Goldblatt most probably broke under it. Graphic scene showing childbirth and other trauma-producing scenes prohibit viewing by children. *Author's Note*: Brainwashing has been the subject or an important element of many films, notably **Rain**, 1932; **Miss Sadie Thompson**, 1953; **Prisoner of War**, 1954; **The Rack**, 1956; **The**

Dulcie Gray and Burgess Meredith in *Mine Own Executioner,* 1949.

Manchurian Candidate, 1962; **The Ipcress File**, 1965; **36 Hours**, 1965; **Our Man Flint**, 1966; **On Her Majesty's Secret Service**, 1969; **A Clockwork Orange**, 1971; **Sleeper**, 1973; **The Parallax View**, 1974; **The Stepford Wives**, 1975; **Telefon**, 1977; **Indiana Jones and the Temple of Doom**, 1984; **The Shadow**, 1994; and **The Bourne Legacy**, 2012. **p**, Michael Relph; **d**, Basil Dearden; **cast**, Dirk Bogarde, Mary Ure, John Clements, Michael Bryant, Wendy Craig, Harold Goldblatt, Geoffrey Keen, Terry Palmer, Norman Bird, Edward Fox; **w**, James Kennaway; **c**, Denys Coop; **m**, Georges Auric; **ed**, John D. Guthridge; **art d**, James Morahan.

The Mind of Mr. Soames ★★★ 1970; U.K.; 92m; Amicus/COL; Color; Science Fiction; Children: Unacceptable; **DVD**. Stamp is a young man who has been in a coma since birth and is now thirty years old. Vaughn, an American neurosurgeon, brings him to consciousness. Now he has the body of a grown man but the mind of an infant. Another doctor, Davenport, puts Stamp, who has had no education, through a series of educational programs. Stamp learns so rapidly he becomes a media darling. But the two doctors disagree about the teaching methods used on the patient. Davenport believes in a rigorous in-hospital educational method while Vaughn believes Stamp should experience the outside world and learn more gradually, like a child. Stamp grows restless under the pressure and runs away. He finds the world to be a very hostile place and eventually kills Vaughn while television cameras record the tragedy. Violence prohibits viewing by children. *Author's Note*: Many films deal with persons suffering from comas or coming out of long comas, notably **They Call It Sin**, 1932; **White Zombie**, 1932; **Gabriel over the White-House**, 1933; **Fingers at the Window**, 1942; **I Walked with a Zombie**, 1943; **He Walked by Night**, 1948; **Demetrius and the Gladiators**, 1954; **Belle de jour**, 1968; **Three Women**, 1977; **Rocky II**, 1979; **An American Werewolf in London**, 1981; **The Verdict**, 1982; **Crimes of the Heart**, 1986; **Awakenings**, 1990; **Reversal of Fortune**, 1990; **Forever Young**, 1992; **The Client**, 1994; **Muriel's Wedding**, 1994; **Bean**, 1997; **Open Range**, 2003; and **Insidious**, 2010. **p**, Max Rosenberg, Milton Subotsky; **d**, Alan Cooke; **cast**, Terence Stamp, Robert Vaughn, Nigel Davenport, Christian Roberts, Donal Donnelly, Norman Jones, Dan Jackson, Vickery Turner, Judy Parfitt, Scott Forbes, Christopher Timothy; **w**, John Hale, Edward Simpson (based on the novel by Charles Eric Maine); **c**, Billy Williams (Technicolor); **m**, Michael Dress; **ed**, Bill Blunden; **prod d**, Bill Constable; **art d**, Don Mingaye; **set d**, Andrew Low.

Mine Own Executioner ★★★ 1949; U.K., 108m; London Film Productions/FOX: B/W; Drama; Children: Unacceptable; **DVD**; **VHS**. Offbeat but utterly fascinating psychological drama where Meredith, in a

Hillary Brooke conducting a séance in *Ministry of Fear*, 1944.

bravura performance, is a psychiatrist trying to cure Moore of fierce schizophrenia. Moore has been an RAF pilot in WWII. After being shot down in Burma, he was made a prisoner by the Japanese and suffered unspeakable tortures and privation in a POW camp, these terrors having altered his reason. He has long abused his wife, White, and even threatened to kill her, and Meredith applies intensive treatments to uncover the layers of Moore's fears that have disturbed his mind. When Meredith relaxes his regimen, Moore becomes reckless, impulsively starting an affair with Norden, a sultry married woman. Moore then murders his wife and goes to a tall building, perching on an outside ledge. Meredith thinks to talk him out of suicide by climbing onto that ledge with him, but all of his psychological skills avail him nothing as Moore then jumps to his death. Meredith is brought before a tribunal where he is scathingly criticized in the handling of his patient, Moore, but associate Laurie defends him and helps to save Meredith's professional reputation while Laurie's wife, Gray, gives Meredith stalwart support while he tries to preserve his own sanity during this trial period. Kimmins directs this thriller with a firm hand and, in addition to the outstanding performance from Meredith, exacts top notch portrayals from the rest of the fine cast. *Author's Note*: Dropped from the script is the revealing fact that Meredith is not a practicing physician, but a third-year medical student, who has dropped out of school and has set himself up as a self-styled psychiatrist, who does not have the proper experience, let alone the credentials, to undertake the psychiatric therapy he applies to Moore. Had that been revealed, his failure would have been much more evident to viewers. **p**, Anthony Kimmins, Jack Kitchin; **d**, Kimmins; **cast**, Burgess Meredith, Dulcie Gray, Kieron Moore, Michael Shepley, Christine Norden, Barbara White, Walter Fitzgerald, Edgar Norfolk, Martin Miller, Clive Morton; **w**, Nigel Balchin (based on his novel); **c**, Wilkie Cooper; **m**, Benjamin Frankel; **ed**, Richard Best; **art d**, William C. Andrews; **set d**, Anne Head; **spec eff**, Cliff Richardson, W. Percy Day, Ned Mann.

Ministry of Fear ★★★★ 1944; U.S.; 86m; PAR; B/W; Spy Drama; Children: Unacceptable; **DVD**; **VHS**. One of Lang's most absorbing and frightening films, this espionage tale, set in WWII England, sees Milland (in another riveting performance) as a man being released from a mental institution, only to discover that he is sane and most of the rest of the world is mad. Milland has been the victim of circumstances. To ease the pain of his ailing wife, he had purchased poison and thought to commit euthanasia to ease her terrible agony, but he could not bring himself to administer the lethal dose. His wife, however, when his back was turned, took the poison and died and he was convicted of killing her and sent to the asylum for two years. Upon his release, he goes to a train station to buy a ticket to London, but when he hears the noise from a nearby fair, he strolls to the show to inspect the various stands

where ladies are trying to raise funds for charity under the title of "Mothers of the Free Nations." He guesses the weight of a cake and is guided to a tent where Dyne, a fortune-teller, reads his hand, and, oddly, gives him the weight of the cake he should guess. He leaves and returns to the cake stand, and buys another ticket and guesses another weight for a particular cake. He wins the cake and, just as he is leaving the fair, Duryea hurriedly arrives and goes to the tent to see the fortune-teller and then quickly steps from the tent to see Milland leaving and it is obvious that Milland has been mistaken for Duryea by the fortune-teller and that he now has a cake that is much desired by Duryea and his fellow Nazi spies. Milland goes to the train depot and enters a compartment, placing the cake next to him on the seat. He then hears a tapping noise and sees a blind man, Wyatt, whom Milland helps into the compartment. Milland offers Wyatt a piece of cake, which he accepts, but Milland sees that the blind man is threading the cake, as if feeling for something contained in its doughy substance. (Lang then shows a close-up of Wyatt, whose large unblinking eyes stare vacantly into a void, but, for a few seconds, suddenly and frighteningly focuses upon Milland when Milland is not looking, to clearly indicate that he is impersonating blindness, before resuming that sightless disguise.) While the train rumbles through the darkness, Wyatt continues to knead the piece of cake in his hands until it crumbles everywhere. The train comes to a stop at a remote area during an air raid, the lights in the compartment being turned off. Milland peers from the window to see search lights scanning the sky in the distance and hears the rumble of anti-aircraft guns firing at German bombers. While Milland is thus distracted, Wyatt grabs the cake and brutally strikes Milland over the head with his cane, breaking it, and then fleeing with the cake into the countryside. The dazed Milland follows, trailing Wyatt to the bombed-out ruins of a farmhouse and where Wyatt fires several shots at him until a passing enemy plane drops a bomb that kills Wyatt. When arriving in London, Milland goes to the offices of the "Mothers of the Free Nations" to learn more about that organization that had imperiled his life. He is affably greeted by its supervisors, Reynolds, an attractive, young blonde woman, and her suave and worldly brother, Esmond. Neither can give him any information about the fortune-teller at the fair, saying only that all of the women at that event were volunteers. Esmond, however, offers to take Milland to see Brooke, a medium, who sponsored that fortune-telling sideshow to see if she can shed any light on its operations. Milland and Esmond then go to Brooke's lavishly appointed house where she is about to hold a séance conducted by Dyne, the fortune-teller at the fair who earlier gave Milland the inside information that allowed him to win that ill-fated cake. Milland is asked to participate in the séance and he sits down to a large round table with many visitors joining in and to which Duryea joins at the last minute. When the lights dim and the room darkens, a unknown voice, supposedly from a spirit summoned by Dyne, suddenly accuses Milland of murdering his wife. Before Milland can respond, a shot is heard and, when the lights are turned on, Duryea is lying on the floor, dead, and, when police arrive to investigate, Milland is accused of murdering Duryea. Further, Milland points out that the medium conducting the séance, Dyne, is no longer present and Johnson insists that she was the medium that conducted the séance. Before police can put the cuffs on Milland, he escapes and goes in search of help, finding Sanford, a fussy little private detective, who agrees to aid him. Sanford, however, proves to be of no use and winds up being killed, ostensibly by Nazi spies, who think Milland is in possession of the secret hidden in that cake. Milland then goes to the only person who has shown genuine concern for him, Reynolds, and she takes him to a bookshop where the book dealer hides him in a secret room. In return for hiding Milland, the book dealer asks that Milland deliver a suitcase full of books to Napier, but when he goes to a deserted hotel room with Reynolds and finds no one there, he hears strange noises outside the room. Milland then decides to open the suitcase, but, as he does, his instincts tell him that this is a mistake and he grabs Reynolds and they dive behind a couch just as the suitcase explodes. Milland wakes up in a hospital bed to hear the creaking of a rocking chair, and sitting in it next to his bed is a man dressed all in black and wearing a derby hat, Waram, a Scotland Yard inspector. Waram informs Milland that he is wanted for murder and Milland says that he has no idea how Duryea was shot at the séance, but Waram tells him that he knows nothing about that shooting and that Milland is wanted for killing Sanford, the detective he briefly employed. Waram is convinced that Milland is a lunatic, saying: "They shouldn't have let you out of that asylum." Milland now believes his sanity is in question, but he convinces Waram to accompany him to the ruins of the farmhouse where Wyatt, the blind man, was killed. Waram and several other detectives from Scotland Yard search the ruins but find nothing until Milland sees a bird eating at some of the cake wedged atop a wall of the destroyed farmhouse; the remains of the cake is retrieved and inside of it Waram finds a small strip of microfilm. Waram and Milland go to the British war ministry where Napier works to discover that the microfilm shows a top secret chart of some mine fields, and this is the information that the Nazi spies have been after all along. Waram then traces the Nazis to a men's clothing store where he and Milland find Duryea very much alive as he is a salesman there. Duryea, realizing that he is about to be arrested, makes a phone call (dialing the number with a lethal-looking pair of huge scissors) and tells the person answering that "I think you'll find that when you've worn it once the shoulders will settle." He then goes into a fitting room and uses the scissors to commit suicide. The phone call is traced to Esmond and Duryea's message means that the suit recently delivered to him contains a strip of microfilm hidden in one of its shoulder pads. Before the police can get to Esmond, Milland and Reynolds confront the spymaster. Milland and Esmond struggle over the suit coat, and when Esmond is about to kill Milland, Reynolds shoots and kills Esmond. Both, however, are now in great danger as a group of Nazi spies arrive, led by Napier, and they are chased to the roof of the apartment building where they exchange gunfire with the Nazis. Just when they are out of ammunition, a blaze of gunfire is heard and Waram stoically arrives at the rooftop to indicate that he and other Scotland Yard detectives have dispatched the spies. This relentlessly grim but absorbing film ends with a humorous high note when, just before the fadeout, Milland and Reynolds are shown driving along the British countryside planning their forthcoming wedding and where Reynolds casually mentions their wedding cake. "Cake!" shouts Milland. "No! No cake!" Lang meticulously builds suspense in this superb thriller by carefully unfolding his scenes, filling those scenes with thick atmospheric shots replete with low-key lighting and shadowy sets, Sharp's moody cinematography greatly adds to the brooding tale, where the puzzle of this mystery is solved piece by piece by the inventive Lang. All of the cast members are standouts in their roles and the production values are excellent. *Author's Note*: Milland told this author that "Lang was very demanding. He knew exactly what he wanted in every scene in that spy picture. When I asked him how he saw my character, he said: 'You are innocent. You have been victimized in the past and it is happening again. You do not know what the hell is going on. And when strangers try to kill you for no apparent reason you get pretty damned mad about it.' It was the best advice a director could give to an actor." Reynolds told this author that "Lang was one of those directors who expected you to know everything about your scenes and your character and had very little patience with those who appeared to be unsure. Ray [Milland] was wonderful to work with in that picture. He told me that 'if you show confidence in everything you do in your scenes, you will be fine with the old man' [Lang]. I followed his advice and had no problems with that great director." **p**, Seton I. Miller; **d**, Fritz Lang; **cast**, Ray Milland, Marjorie Reynolds, Carl Esmond, Hillary Brooke, Percy Waram, Dan Duryea, Alan Napier, Eustace Wyatt, Erskine Sanford, Aminta Dyne, Connie Leon, Thomas Louden, Harry Allen, Frank Baker, Byron Foulger, Lester Matthews; **w**, Miller (based on the novel by Graham Greene); **c**, Henry Sharp; **m**, Victor Young; **ed**, Archie Marshek; **art d**, Hans Dreier, Hal Pereira; **set d**, Bertram Granger.

Eileen Heckart and Jane Wyman in *Miracle in the Rain*, 1956.

Miracle in Milan ★★★ 1951; Italy; 100m; Ente Nazionale Industrie Cinematografiche/Joseph Burstyn; B/W; Fantasy; Children: Unacceptable; **DVD**; **VHS**. In this strange but intriguing fantasy, Gramatica, an old, Italian woman, finds a baby boy in her cabbage patch and brings him up as her own. When she dies, the boy, Branduani, is age eleven and enters an orphanage. He stays there until he becomes a young man, Golisano, then leaves to look for work in post–World War II Milan. He finds no employment, so he becomes one of the homeless and helps build crude hovels in a shanty town. Barnabó, a wealthy industrialist, wants to evict the homeless people from the area, in order to dig for oil that he believes is there. Golisano sees the vision of an old woman who gives him a magic dove that will let him grant wishes to the homeless beggars. One of them is greedy and steals the dove. Barnabó now takes over the shanty town area and Golisano and the other homeless people are sent to jail. The dove appears to Golisano in jail and he is able to free himself and the other prisoners. (In Italian; English subtitles.) **p&d**, Vittorio De Sica; **cast**, Gianni Branduani, Francesco Golisano, Paolo Stoppa, Emma Gramatica, Guglielmo Barnabò, Brunella Bovo, Anna Carena, Alba Arnova, Flora Cambi, Virgilio Riento; **w**, Cesare Zavattini, De Sica, Suso Cecchi D'Amico, Mario Chiari, Adolfo Franci (based on the story "Toto il buono" by Zavattini); **c**, G.R. Aldo; **m**, Alessandro Cicognini; **ed**, Eraldo Da Roma; **prod d&art d**, Guido Fiorini; **spec eff**, Ned Mann.

Miracle in the Rain ★★★ 1956; U.S.; 108m; WB; B/W; Drama/Fantasy; Children: Acceptable; **DVD**. Good tearjerker from veteran screenwriter Hecht (who wrote the novel on which the film is based) sees struggling NYC secretary Wyman working for Clark and taking care of her ailing mother, Hutchinson, whose no-good husband, Gargan, has deserted her years ago. Her only companion is Heckart, an aging spinster, but her world changes when she meets a young GI, Johnson, in Central Park during a rainstorm. Although they have little in common, Johnson being a boy from Tennessee and not used to the big city, they fall in love. Their romance is cut short when Johnson's unit is activated and he ships out for overseas duty and where he is killed in action. Johnson's death so debilitates Wyman that she loses her physical strength and force of will to go on living. Withdrawing into herself, Wyman, beset with fever, makes one last effort to regain hope by going to St. Patrick's Cathedral on Fifth Avenue during a rainstorm and there she sees Johnson (or his spirit), who tells her that life is worth living for, no matter what might happen and presses a coin into her hand. Wyman collapses and is later taken home where she begins to regain her health and her hope for a better future, encouraged by the fact that she has that coin Johnson had taken with him to battle and that that coin is evidence that a miracle truly occurred when she last saw the man she loved in that

Betty Hutton and William Demarest in *The Miracle of Morgan's Creek,* **1944.**

rainstorm. The bathos of the story is inescapable, but Mate does a good job in not letting the suds overflow and Wyman and Johnson give top notch performances in this inspiring bit of fancy from Hecht. *Author's Note*: Hecht told this author that "I always admired the stories by O. Henry, and I had stored a few of my own similar tales. **Miracle in the Rain** was one of them, a story I overheard a girl from Brooklyn telling her girlfriend. Girls gave lucky coins to their boyfriends before they went off to war in those days and this coin was more than lucky when it brought some hope to a lovesick girl." Wyman loved her part, telling this author that "my character is like millions of others, working hard and looking only for a little happiness. I meet Van [Johnson] and that happiness comes into my life, but my life almost ends when he is killed in the war. Then a miracle happens, but it only happens through faith and love, when I see Van again, or his spirit comes to me to encourage me to go on living. **Miracle in the Rain** is a great weeper that only Ben [Hecht] could write and make believable." **p**, Frank P. Rosenberg; **d**, Rudolph Maté; **cast**, Jane Wyman, Van Johnson, Peggie Castle, Fred Clark, Eileen Heckart, Josephine Hutchinson, William Gargan, Marcel Dalio, George Givot, Barbara Nichols, Halliwell Hobbes, Alan King, Arte Johnson; **w**, Ben Hecht (based on his novel); **c**, Russell Metty; **m**, Franz Waxman; **ed**, Thomas Reilly; **art d**, Leo K. Kuter; **set d**, William Wallace.

The Miracle of Morgan's Creek ★★★★★ 1944; U.S.; 98m; PAR; B/W; Comedy; Children: Unacceptable; **DVD**; **VHS**. In what is his most outlandish and irreverent comedy, pantheon director Sturges presents a tale so improbable that he managed to get this film past the strict censoring board that ruled the roost of his era. It all begins with scatter-brained, man-chasing Hutton, who lives with her ill-tempered sister, Lynn, and her father, policeman Demarest, in the small town of Morgan's Creek. She goes on a date with a soldier and wakes up the next morning to announce that she has been married and is pregnant, but can't remember the name of the dallying soldier, who has left town. Meek-mannered bank clerk Bracken, who has loved Hutton since childhood, is selected (or ordered) to be Hutton's spouse. He is a man who becomes nervous and sees spots before his eyes at the slightest noise and for that reason he has been rejected for the service (it is war time and almost all young men are members of the armed forces), even though Bracken's most fervent wish is to be a soldier. To save Hutton's reputation, Bracken dresses up in his father's WWI uniform and pretends to be the soldier Hutton has earlier met, using whatever name that vanished swain had, or the best name Hutton can recall, which is nevertheless a ridiculous alias. Everything then goes from the absurd to the disastrous as Bracken is sought for impersonating an officer, corrupting the morals of a minor, forgery, kidnapping and even bank robbery, going in a flash from a complete nonentity to public enemy number one. He

has only one option and that is to flee Morgan's Creek. All looks dire until a miracle occurs when Hutton gives birth to the only sextuplets in the world, making her and Bracken nationwide celebrities and where all is forgiven and forgotten as they ride the promising new crest of willy-nilly fate. Hutton's firecracker personality and Bracken's mousy posture is the perfect mix for this unlikely match, and Sturges wonderfully shows their controversial predicament in one carefully constructed scene after another as he infuses hilarity and no little panic in building toward that maternity miracle. As usual, Sturges employed many of his favorite or stock players for this film, and even had Brian Donlevy and Akim Tamiroff reprise their battling roles and political bosses from **The Great McGinty**, 1940. This film was remade as **Rock-a-Bye Baby**, 1958, an inferior production. *Author's Note*: Sturges, who was in the early 1940s the darling of directors at Paramount, had thought to do this story as early as 1937 and when he heard that the studio was going to destroy its small-town set on its back lot, he begged executives to preserve it so that he could employ the set for this masterpiece comedy. Hutton, who had been a huge fan of Sturges since the early 1940s, admitted to this author that "I drove Preston [Sturges] crazy by always asking him to write a comedy for me and then, one day, he called me up to tell me, 'Okay, Betty, I've got a script for you.' He had written **The Miracle of Morgan's Creek** with me in mind for the young lady who gets into a family way and I was on top of the world with that news. When I read the script I laughed out loud at almost every page. He was a genius when it came to comedy and always knew what would make people laugh." Bracken, on the other hand, was not that receptive to taking another role in a film with Hutton. When Sturges offered him the role of the cringing groom, Bracken told the director that he had appeared with Hutton in a few other films, but that his scenes had been cut down to provide more time for Hutton to sing some songs. Sturges assured Bracken that Hutton would sing no songs in **The Miracle of Morgan's Creek**, and Bracken agreed to play the role. "I'm glad that Preston [Sturges] talked me into doing that picture," Bracken told this author. "It proved to be one of my biggest hits. Actors don't always know what's best for them, but I figured I could not go wrong in a Preston Sturges picture." **p,d&w**, Preston Sturges; **cast**, Eddie Bracken, Betty Hutton, Diana Lynn, Brian Donlevy, Akim Tamiroff, William Demarest, Porter Hall, Emory Parnell, Alan Bridge, Julius Tannen, Chester Conklin, Jack Norton; **c**, John F. Seitz; **m**, Charles Bradshaw, Leo Shuken; **ed**, Stuart Gilmore; **art d**, Hans Dreier, Ernst Fegte; **set d**, Stephen Seymour.

The Miracle of Our Lady of Fatima ★★★ 1952; U.S.; 102m; WB; Color; Biographical Drama; Children: Acceptable; **DVD**; **VHS**. Knowing that tens of thousands of pilgrims crowded into the area of Fatima in Portugal each year to commemorate the miracle reportedly occurring there in 1917, Warner Brothers decided to make this inspiring film. On May 13, 1917, three shepherd children, Lucia dos Santos (1907-2005), played by Whitney, and her cousins, Francisco Marta (1908-1919), played by Ogg, and Jacinta Marta (1910-1920), played by Jackson, while tending their flock outside of Fatima, see the vision of the Virgin Mary (Our Lady of Fatima), the Lady telling them to come to the same spot in the meadow each month on the thirteenth day of the next consecutive six months. The children tell their friend, Roland, an affable town loafer, about their vision, but he cautions them to keep silent about what they have seen, knowing that the present political regime in Portugal is oppressing the Catholic Church and reports of such religious or miraculous visions might bring severe punishment. The Virgin Mary tells the children that she will impart several secrets to them and, on the date of her last appearance, October 13, 1917, she will provide a miracle to convince the world of her visitation. At first the children keep their visions to themselves, but when government officials learn of their experiences, they threaten the parents of the children and then the children with dire punishments. The children are prohibited from further going to the meadow to see the Virgin Mary, but Roland and others come to their aid, even when they are placed in a large prison cell and where the children stun the warders by instantly converting the brutal prisoners into mass prayers and psalm-singing. The children overcome government officials and are allowed to make their visits to the meadow where the Virgin Mary imparts several secrets to the children (later released by the Catholic Church, which eventually endorsed the events at Fatima by stating that they were "worthy of belief"). In their final visit to the meadow on October 13, 1917, Whitney suddenly points to the sun and the sun then does a strange "dance" that is seen by many of the more than 70,000 persons gathered there on that day, one where the sun appeared to change many colors, twirl rapidly and then appeared to be hurling toward earth while radiating intense heat, but then returned to its place. It had rained heavily before this event and all felt their clothes dried. Further, there were many claims of those in the crowd of being cured of varied ailments and impairments. The secrets imparted to the three children were later given by Lucia, the eldest of the children, to the Catholic Church and Church officials released those secrets many years later, including the Virgin Mary's prediction that Soviet Russia would abandon communism, which it did, in 1989-1990. Although the producers took some liberties with this stirring tale, most of the facts are retained and presented in carefully constructed scenes by director Brahm. **p**, Bryan Foy; **d**, John Brahm; **cast**, Gilbert Roland, Susan Whitney, Angela Clarke, Sherry Jackson, Sammy Ogg, Frank Silvera, Jay Novello, Richard Hale, Norman Rice, Frances Morris, Carl Milletaire, Nanette Fabray, Jack Kruschen, J. Carrol Naish, Walter Hampden (narrator); **w**, Crane Wilbur, James O'Hanlon; **c**, Edwin B. DuPar (Warnercolor); **m**, Max Steiner; **ed**, Thomas Reilly; **art d**, Edward Carrere; **set d**, G.W. Berntsen; **spec eff**, Robert Burks.

The Miracle of the Bells ★★★★ 1948; U.S.; 120m; Jesse L. Lasky Productions/RKO; Children: Acceptable; **VHS**. This stirring and memorable film profiles the brief but brilliant acting career of a gifted young actress, wonderfully portrayed by Valli, and as seen through the eyes of MacMurray, the press agent who helps her fulfill her ambitions and falls in love with her, only to lose her to consumption at an early age. The film opens with an impoverished MacMurray arriving by train in Coal Town, Pennsylvania, accompanying Valli's body, which is removed from a baggage car and taken to a local mortuary and is then taken to the small church of St. Michael's, which is the poorest parish in the town and where Sinatra is the local priest. MacMurray tells Sinatra about Valli's past, which is shown in flashback as he narrates, how she left Coal Town at an early age to seek success on the stage and in Hollywood. Valli is shown rehearsing for a play and where she is about to lose her job, but, when press agent MacMurray arrives, he tells the stage manager to "give the kid a break," and he does, so that Valli becomes a successful actress, with MacMurray helping her along the way. At one point, Valli tells MacMurray that it is essential that she becomes a success because the residents of her hometown have little or no hope and that their miserable lives have been spent in the mines and where they live at the level of survival. If, however, she becomes a success and becomes a great film actress, her people can see her on the screen and take shining hope when knowing that one their own has escaped the coal pits and made something of her life. MacMurray is so in love with Valli that he devotes most of his time promoting her into one fine role after another, until he convinces Hollywood movie mogul Cobb to cast her in a major film where she will star as Joan of Arc. Valli works so hard at her role that she becomes ill, but she nevertheless gives a magnificent performance as Joan, and, just after finishing the film, which all consider a masterpiece, she dies. Although Cobb realizes that Valli has made a huge contribution, he refuses to release the film, believing that the public will not want to see a young actress in her first major film appearance and who has recently died, thus depriving the public from its ability to ever see her again in another film. Cobb says that the public will fall in love with Valli and then become angry when realizing that it can never see her in another film. (Cobb's viewpoint is an odd perspective, to say

Porter Hall, Almira Sessions, Betty Hutton, Georgia Caine and Eddie Bracken in *The Miracle of Morgan's Creek*, 1944.

the least, but his logic is rooted to the mind of Hollywood, a mind of which reason does not know.) Although MacMurray tells Cobb that he is crazy, that Valli died to make a great film for him, Cobb is adamant and shelves the picture. MacMurray then spends his last few dollars to take Valli home to Coal Town for burial and where, in keeping with Valli's request, he asks Sinatra to ring the bells of St. Michael's for three days while her body lies in state at his church. Sinatra agrees, but when MacMurray goes to the other, more lucrative churches (Valli requested that all the churches in Coal Town ring their bells for three days to commemorate her passing in her homage to her hometown), he is met with resistance. All of the churches, of all denominations, demand cash to ring their bells, and MacMurray writes checks in the amount of thousands of dollars for this service, all of those checks being worthless as he has no money left in his bank account. He wires Cobb for the money to cover those checks and, at the last minute, Cobb wires the money to him, but as an advance for his promotion of his next film, still refusing to release the Joan of Arc film. Meanwhile, the bells chiming and ringing and tolling hour after hour throughout Coal Town alerts all of its inhabitants and brings the national press to the town to cover the unusual story and where MacMurray works with a bevy of reporters to promote Valli's story. Residents then begin to flock to Sinatra's church, packing it, filling its pews and where there is standing room only. Then, on the last day of the church ringing, churchgoers at St. Michael's, as well as MacMurray and Sinatra, who are present, are all stunned and shocked to suddenly see the giant statues of the Virgin Mary and St. Michael, these huge statuaries flanking Valli's coffin, loudly grind on their pedestals, shaking and rumbling the little church, as they slowly turn to face and look down upon Valli's coffin. Churchgoers sink to their knees, hurriedly making the Sign of the Cross, others murmuring "it's a miracle." The news of this inexplicable event is wired to the press and headlines around the country herald this miracle. When Cobb hears of this, he believes MacMurray has faked this story to promote Valli, an act Cobb believes to be sacrilegious, but he then travels to Coal Town to further investigate. Meanwhile, Sinatra takes MacMurray to the basement of his little church and explains that the two main pillars holding up the church and upon which the huge statues are based were moved by pressures coming from the many mine shafts running beneath the church and that there was no "miracle." MacMurray begs him not to announce this to his parishioners as it will deprive them of the only bright hope that has come into their lives in years, and Sinatra tells him that his religious superiors will later come to the same conclusion and that he cannot perpetuate a hoax. He modifies his statements about this, however, when addressing his congregation, saying that higher authorities will explain the phenomenon. True believers are convinced, however, that the statues moved of their own volition to look lovingly down on the deceased Valli and

Edmund Gwenn, Maureen O'Hara, and John Payne in *Miracle on 34th Street*, 1947.

nothing will move them from this conviction. When Cobb appears, he grudgingly tells MacMurray that he is impressed with his promotional campaign for Valli, and that he will not challenge Providence and has decided to release the film starring Valli after all, particularly now that she has become internationally famous. MacMurray has won after all. Pichel directs this film with great care and elicits fine performances from Valli, MacMurray, Sinatra, Cobb and others. (Valli, a much underrated actress, is absolutely riveting in the scenes where she enacts Joan, and her passion for Coal Town and its downtrodden inhabitants radiates throughout her extraordinary performance.) The script from Hecht, Reynolds and Bodeen is superbly witty and presents one provocative scene after another, as well as giving an incisive view of Hollywood and it promotional campaigns. Harline's score is exceptional and the lensing from De Grasse is outstanding. Sinatra sings one song: "Ever Homeward" (adapted from "Powrot" by Jule Styne; lyrics by Sammy Cahn); other songs: "Miracle of the Bells" (music by Pierre Norman), "Silent Night, Holy Night" (Franz Gruber, Joseph Mohr). *Author's Note*: Hecht told this author that he culled this tale from an actual event where statues moved in a church as if granting a benediction of a deceased person lying in state, an event he insisted had really occurred, saying: "Since all authors believe in the impossible, it was not hard for me to envision this tale and its miracle, which is a miracle if you want it to be." Hecht would again venture into the realm of such phenomenon when writing the script (based on his novel) **Miracle in the Rain**, 1956. "I loved that picture," MacMurray told this author, "and I never saw a better script than the one Ben [Hecht] wrote for **The Miracle of the Bells**. My co-star in that picture was Alida Valli, a great international actress, who was one of the world's most beautiful women as well. Sinatra had not yet hit his stride in the movies, but he showed all of us that he could handle a serious role with great skill when he played that young priest. I thought then and do now that that picture was terrific, one of those pictures that makes you feel good all day long after you see it." **p**, Jesse L. Lasky, Walter MacEwen; **d**, Irving Pichel; **cast**, Fred MacMurray, Alida Valli, Frank Sinatra, Lee J. Cobb, Harold Vermilyea, Charles Meredith, James Nolan, Veronica Pataky, Philip Ahn, Frank Ferguson, Frank Wilcox; **w**, Ben Hecht, Quentin Reynolds, DeWitt Bodeen (based on the novel by Russell Janney); **c**, Robert de Grasse; **m**, Leigh Harline; **ed**, Elmo Williams; **art d**, Ralph Berger, Albert S. D'Agostino; **set d**, Darrell Silvera, Harley Miller; **spec eff**, Russell A. Cully, Clifford Stine.

Miracle on 34th Street ★★★★★ 1947; U.S.; 96m; FOX; B/W; Fantasy; Children: Acceptable; **BD**; **DVD**; **VHS**. In one of Hollywood's most beloved films, particularly at the Yuletide season, veteran character actor Gwenn (Oscar for Best Supporting Actor) tucks this wonderful tale under his arm and walks it into the homes and hearts of every

viewer. The film opens with Macy's Thanksgiving Day Parade and where parade director O'Hara finds the parade's Santa Claus, the wheezing, breath-gasping Helton, intoxicated and unable to even crack a whip from the float that holds his sleigh and reindeer. Gwenn then appears, an elderly man with a rich white beard, who lectures O'Hara for employing such a disgraceful-looking person to impersonate and sully the fine image of Santa. O'Hara looks upon the twinkling-eyed Gwenn as a gift from Heaven, asking his name. "Kris Kringle," he replies. She then asks him if he will replace Helton and he, at first, resists, but O'Hara's desperate pleading win him over and he decides to enact the part for the sake of the thousands of children anxiously waiting his arrival in the parade. Gwenn dons the Santa suit and merrily plays his role with a beaming, smiling face, expertly cracking the whip over the stationary reindeer as he sits within his sleigh atop the moving float and while thousands of children and adults wave and cheer him. So wonderful is Gwenn in his performance that O'Hara offers him the job of Santa at Macy's. He accepts, and to make him welcome, O'Hara invites Gwenn to her home for dinner where he meets Wood, O'Hara's little girl, who has been raised by her widowed mother to see the reality of life and not to believe in fairy tales. When Gwenn tells her he is Santa Claus, Wood disbelieves him, saying that no such person exists, which disturbs Gwenn. He also meets Payne, a young and idealistic attorney who is interested in O'Hara, and who lives in the same apartment building. Payne offers to put Gwenn up during his temporary job with Macy's and Gwenn accepts, becoming his roommate. That night, before Gwenn goes to sleep, Payne asks him whether he tucks his fluffy white beard beneath the covers or not and he draws the covers to his chin so that his beard remains free "to give it air." Wood later goes to Macy's where she sees Gwenn talking to the children and where one little girl, Field, who is a Dutch immigrant unable to speak English, and where Wood is amazed to suddenly hear Gwenn converse with her and then sings a Santa Claus song with her in her native language. Wood now comes to believe that Gwenn just might be the real Santa. Gwenn immediately bonds with all the children sitting on his lap and earnestly telling him their wishes for Christmas, but when some of their parents tell him that they cannot find some of the toys their children want at Macy's, Gwenn, who has kept an exhaustive inventory on such desirable items, tells them where they can get those toys at other stores. Staff members at Macy's panic when hearing this, but then one of the mothers, Ritter, tells a floor walker that Macy's certainly keeps the spirit of Christmas alive by guiding shoppers to other stores to get what they cannot find at Macy's, and that she intends to become a regular Macy's customer thereafter because of the store's Yuletide generosity. When Macy himself, played by Antrim, hears of this, he suddenly realizes that such a good will policy will serve as a promotional bonanza and begins an advertising campaign that Macy's is a store "with a heart." This campaign then inspires all of Macy's competitors to adopt the same magnanimous policy. Meanwhile, O'Hara now has misgivings about Gwenn as he continues to insist that he is the one and only Santa Claus and she thinks he might be delusional and plans to fire him. That notion is overcome when Macy congratulates her for hiring such a benevolent Santa Claus who has spread such wonderful good will for Macy's and gives her a bonus. To put aside O'Hara's misgivings about Gwenn's mental capabilities, store executives order that he be given an examination by autocratic Hall, a deceptive and lying little man who has his own considerable phobias, and even though he is a personnel officer for the store and has no training in psychiatry, he puts Gwenn through a rigorous examination. Gwenn, however, not only passes with flying colors, but disturbs Hall by asking him some pointed questions about himself. Hall then becomes extremely jealous of Gwenn's immense popularity with customers and the Macy's staff and, in an act of vindictiveness, orders Gwenn's slow-witted assistant, Greenman, demoted to a stock boy, branding him "incompetent." Gwenn is enraged at such misconduct and goes to Hall, telling him that he is a small-minded, oppressive man, and when Hall makes a move toward him, Gwenn bops him on the head with his cane, more of a rebuking tap than a serious blow, but Hall, seeing O'Hara and others approaching him, feigns a serious injury and demands that Gwenn undergo a mental examination. Before taking that examination, Payne and O'Hara, who have become deeply attached to Gwenn, appeal to him to not declare his true identity as Santa Claus, but the old man cannot tell a lie and informs those at that hearing that he is the one and only St. Nick. He is then confined until a legal hearing can be held. Payne undertakes to represent Gwenn, but the old man's case looks bleak. He goes before Judge Lockhart, who has been advised by political boss Frawley to give the old man all the consideration he can as the case is a hot political potato. He tells Lockhart that if he judges Gwenn insane, all the children in New York will hate him, and he will further make enemies of every store selling anything for Christmas and all of this means that may not be reelected. Cowan, the district attorney, however, aggressively prosecutes Gwenn, but Payne has Cowan's own son, Hyatt, testify on behalf of Gwenn, the little boy insisting that Gwenn is the true Santa Claus. Then Antrim, as Macy, takes the stand, and he, too, after looking at the smiling Gwenn and remembering all of the wonderful things he did when playing Santa at his store, says that, he, too, believes him to be the genuine Santa, and, before leaving court, sees the conniving Hall sitting at the prosecutor's table and fires him on the spot. Lockhart bends over backward to help Payne, but his evidence in proving Gwenn to be the genuine Santa is so thin that Gwenn's fate seems sealed. Then a strange thing happens. Workers at the main post office in New York City are shown sorting tens of thousands of letters going to Santa Claus, addressed to the North Pole, and one of the workers says that they are stored in the dead letter area, taking up enormous space in the warehouse. Albertson, one of the letter sorters, sees that one letter is addressed to the courthouse where Gwenn is being tried. He then has a bright idea. He tells his supervisor that they can get rid of the letters by having them all delivered to the courthouse where Gwenn is on trial. The following day, Payne is asked by Lockhart if he has any more evidence to prove his case before he renders his judgment, and Payne offers a few letters addressed to Santa that were delivered to the courtroom, stating that this indicates that since these letters were sent to Gwenn, he is the real Santa, and that since the U.S. Post Office has sent Gwenn those letters, that institution recognizes him as the genuine Santa. Cowan then objects, saying that a few token letters do not represent overwhelming evidence that the U.S. Post Office has made such a distinction. Lockhart is compelled to agree, unless Payne can provide more evidence. Payne says he has that evidence, but is reluctant to provide it. Lockhart insists that the evidence be placed on his desk. Payne agrees and then motions to guards to open the courtroom doors; through those doors march a seemingly endless stream of men carrying huge sacks containing letters to Santa Claus, and these letters are dumped onto Lockhart's desk so high that he must push them aside in heaps to be seen. Lockhart then states that since the Post Office, which is an official branch of the U.S. Government, has provided the overwhelming evidence Cowan has demanded in its recognition of Gwenn as the one and only Santa, he agrees with the U.S. Government. Lockhart announces that Gwenn is the true Santa and orders his release. Payne and O'Hara are overjoyed at Gwenn's acquittal and O'Hara asks Gwenn to have dinner with her, Wood and Payne at her home that night, but he smiles while standing outside the courtroom and says that he cannot do that since it is Christmas Eve and he must make his rounds throughout the world to deliver gifts as the real Santa, but will see her the next day at a Christmas party at the home for the aged where he now lives. With that, he is off to bring happiness to millions. Gwenn appears the next day at that party where he distributes gifts, including new and expensive equipment to the resident physician of his retirement home, but when Wood looks through her presents she does not find the gift she has been looking for, believing that there might be some sort of representation of that gift. She concludes that Gwenn is not Santa after all. A short time later, she, O'Hara and Payne are driving through a suburb and Wood suddenly screams for the car to stop. Payne stops the car and Wood alights, running up the steps to a house that has a "for sale" sign. She

Maureen O'Hara, Edmund Gwenn, Natalie Wood and John Payne in *Miracle on 34th Street,* 1947.

races inside with O'Hara and Payne running after her, saying that this is the very house that she wanted for Christmas and that Gwenn has provided that house. As Wood races outside to inspect the backyard, O'Hara and Payne embrace, now planning to wed and seriously consider buying this house where they will begin a new life together with Wood. Payne then congratulates himself for being smart enough to win Gwenn's case until he spots a cane leaning against the wall of the house, a cane that appears to be the very one carried by Gwenn. He then says to O'Hara that, perhaps, he wasn't so smart after all and that more powerful forces were at work in that courtroom. The camera closes on that cane for the fadeout. Gwenn, under director Seaton's careful guidance, renders the most touching and gentle performance on the screen in his unforgettable portrayal of Jolly Old St. Nick, a role so memorable that has been indelibly connected to his persona ever since the release of this enchanting masterpiece. O'Hara, Payne and the endearing Wood, along with the rest of the fine cast, are standouts in their distinctive roles. Songs: "Jingle Bells" (James Pierpont), "National Emblem" (Edwin Eugene Bagley), "Santa Claus Is Coming to Town" (J. Fred Coots), "Sabre and Spurs" (John Philip Sousa), "The First Noel" (traditional), "Twinkle, Twinkle, Little Star" (traditional), "God Rest Ye Merry Gentlemen" (traditional), "To Market, To Market, To Buy A Fat Pig" (traditional), "Sinterklaas Kapoentje" (traditional Dutch song). This story was adapted for several radio and TV programs and was remade as feature films in 1973 and 1994, but these two films paled by comparison to the original. In addition to Gwenn's Oscar for Best Supporting Actor, the film was nominated as Best Picture and it won an Oscar for Best Story (Davies), and Best Adapted Screenplay (Seaton). *Author's Note:* Seaton told this author that "the idea for the picture had been generating with me and Davies [who wrote the original story] for years. We wanted to present a film that really captured the spirit of Christmas, one that punched right through its commercialism, and when we pitched it to Darryl [Zanuck, head of Fox], he seemed lukewarm about it, and gave me a limited budget. Darryl had an instinct for pictures that would really go over, but he was dead wrong about **Miracle on 34th Street**." Zanuck told this author that he did not think the film would do that well, and insisted that "we release it in May [of 1947] when most people start going to the movies—summertime was the biggest box office season in those days. Well, when I looked at the weekly returns, My God, everybody was going to see that picture, week after week, month after month, right up to Christmastime. It was one of the greatest successes we ever had and I didn't mind telling George [Seaton] how wrong I was about it." The film had a budget of $630,000 and returned in its initial box office release more than $3 million. Payne told this author that "George [Seaton] shot most of that picture in New York and I never figured out how he talked Macy's into allowing him to take his cameras into that store and roam

Barbara Stanwyck and David Manners in *The Miracle Woman*, 1931.

around at will, but it proved to give Macy's more great publicity than it could ever buy, and George even went out of his way to include a lot of other major stores in New York, including Gimbel's [Herbert Heyes played Mr. Gimbel], so everyone got a piece of that great pie. I was very fortunate to be teamed with Maureen [O'Hara] as I always thought she was not only one of the most beautiful women on the screen, but a terrific actress. Gwenn, of course, was born for the role of Santa, and I think he knew it. He was as cheerful and merry off camera as he was when the cameras rolled. He told me that he had played some 'very sinister characters in some pictures and now I get to make up for my past sins by playing the happiest and most loved man in the world.' I don't think that anyone who has ever seen that picture can think about Santa Claus without recalling the smiling image of the great Edmund Gwenn." **p**, William Perlberg; **d**, George Seaton; **cast**, Maureen O'Hara, John Payne, Edmund Gwenn, Gene Lockhart, Natalie Wood, Porter Hall, William Frawley, Jerome Cowan, Jack Albertson, Mae Marsh, Thelma Ritter, Percy Helton, Philip Tonge, Harry Antrim, James Seay, Mary Field, Theresa Harris, Alvin Greenman, Anne Staunton, Robert Hyatt, Richard Irving, Jeff Corey, Anne O'Neal, Herbert Heyes, Lela Bliss, Anthony Sydes; **w**, Seaton (based on a story by Valentine Davies); **c**, Lloyd Ahern, Charles Clarke; **m**, Cyril Mockridge; **ed**, Robert Simpson; **art d**, Richard Irvine, Richard Day; **set d**, Thomas Little, Ernest Lansing; **spec eff**, Fred Sersen.

The Miracle Woman ★★★★ 1931; U.S.; 90m; COL; B/W; Drama; Children: Cautionary; **DVD**; **VHS**. Evangelism was and is to this day enormously popular. Two of its early day advocates, Billy Sunday (William Ashley "Billy" Sunday, 1862-1935) and Aimee Semple McPherson (1890-1944), were later profiled in films. Sinclair Lewis' novel, *Elmer Gantry*, which acidly profiled Sunday (as the rip-roaring Gantry) and peripherally included McPherson, was too sensual to film in the early 1930s, but was later produced as a great film in 1960, starring Burt Lancaster. This excellent film from the gifted Capra presents a powerful portrait of a young, attractive female evangelist, which is certainly based on McPherson, who was the leading religious light of the 1920s, until her own secret affair and a questionable faked abduction led to her downfall. This tale opens with Stanwyck as the daughter of a pastor, who has died of a broken heart after he has been released from his parish. Incensed at this mistreatment of a man who has given his life in the service of his religion, Stanwyck goes before parishioners and scathingly indicts their hypocrisy, shocking and angering one and all, except for Hardy, a promoter who sees the fiery young lady as a money-maker. He persuades her to take to the tent-trail of evangelism, traveling the country and spreading the gospel at the grassroots level. Soon the dynamic Stanwyck becomes a widespread success, especially after

Hardy hires an endless stream of supposedly afflicted persons with innumerable infirmities and where Stanwyck ostensibly cures them of all of their ailments, becoming "The Miracle Woman." Stanwyck, despite all the bogus healing, comes to believe that she has a genuine gift as an evangelist and even more energetically spreads her religious beliefs to basically uneducated, naïve and gullible followers. She then takes to the radio to spread her gospel, and Manners, a blind ex-pilot, who is about to leap to his death from a building, hears Stanwyck speaking over the airways and postpones his suicide. He believes that with Stanwyck's help, his faith can be restored as well as his sight. He meets with Stanwyck at her tent before he volunteers to go into a cage with a fierce lion to prove his faith. So moved by this courageous act is Stanwyck that she falls in love with Manners. Meanwhile Hardy is told by Hopton, a greedy press agent, that he wants a larger slice of the pie, and Hardy kills him. When Hardy learns that Stanwyck is growing close to Manners, the shy young man speaking to her through the mouth of his dummy as he has become a ventriloquist, the promoter decides to break up the romance by arranging for Stanwyck to take a trip to the Holy Land. Hardy then tries to bring about his own miracle by striking Manners hard on the head to bring back his sight, a brutal act that achieves nothing. When Stanwyck returns, she is a changed woman, now disgusted with the shamming life she has been leading. She intends to go before her followers and confess that all of her so-called "miracles" have been staged, but before she performs this mea culpa, Hardy sets fire to her tent, burning it down and ending her career. Stanwyck is later shown working for the Salvation Army and getting a wire from Manners, who tells her that he still loves her, and it appears that she will reunite with him for a happy ending. Capra directs this film at a fast clip, and Stanwyck is riveting in her role as the impassioned evangelist and where production values are high and evident throughout every frame. *Author's Note*: Capra told this author that "I felt at the time when that picture was released that the dialog and Babs' [Stanwyck's] speeches were awful corny. But, when looking back, I must admit that everything said was appropriate for the characters and the times, especially when those generalities were addressed to simple folks, who avidly followed evangelists as a way of spiritually uplifting their miserable lives. Will they believe anything? Pretty much, if they think the evangelist is genuine and sincere. It was a matter of showmanship then and it still is." Stanwyck made no bones about the character she was playing when she told this author that "I am enacting Aimee Semple McPherson in **The Miracle Woman**, and everybody knew it then and still do today. A lot of events from her life were used in that picture. I take to the airways to spread the gospel and McPherson was the first evangelist to use the radio to spread her word of God. In fact, she had her own radio station when she was on top of that Bible-belting heap in the Twenties. Also, in the picture, my tent is burned down. McPherson's temple was burned down at one point and mostly finished her career. She was called "Sister Aimee" and I am called "Sister Fallon" in the picture. I think that the only reason why McPherson did not sue the studio is because she did not want a lot of her religious shenanigans exposed in a prolonged legal battle and because she had already been in court for running off with a married man in the 1920s and then faked an abduction to cover her secret affair." For more information on Aimee Semple McPherson and her so-called "abduction" on May 18, 1926 (when she was really having an affair with her radio director, Kenneth G. Ormiston, a married man, at a secret rendezvous), see my work, *The Great Pictorial History of Crime*, Volume I (History, Inc., 2004; pages 636-641). **p**, Harry Cohn; **d**, Frank Capra; **cast**, Barbara Stanwyck, David Manners, Sam Hardy, Beryl Mercer, Russell Hopton, Charles Middleton, Thelma Hill, Harry Todd, June Lang, Dennis O'Keefe; **w**, Jo Swerling, Dorothy Howell (based on the play "Bless You Sister" by John Meehan, Robert Riskin); **c**, Joseph Walker; **ed**, Maurice Wright, **art d**, Mack Parker.

The Miracle Worker ★★★★★ 1962; U.S.; 106m; Playfilm Productions/UA; B/W; Biographical Drama; Children: Unacceptable; **DVD**;

VHS. Bancroft and Duke give powerful portraits of two females struggling to find communication and the light of reason in this mesmerizing classic, based on the lives of Annie Sullivan (Johanna Anne "Annie" Mansfield Sullivan Macy, 1866-1936), played by Bancroft, and Helen Keller (Helen Adams Keller, 1880-1968), played by Duke. Bancroft, whose own sight was impaired and was only partially restored is a graduate of a school for the blind and is asked to become the governess and tutor of a blind and deaf girl, Duke, who lives in the small Alabama town of Tuscumbia. Duke has no way of understanding speech and has no way to communicate with anyone and Bancroft's chore seems impossible, especially when the young girl she is teaching resists with violent fits. Bancroft quickly realizes that she and Duke must live beyond the reaches of Duke's smothering mother, Swenson, and her dominating father, Jory. She insists that the two live apart from the family and her request is accepted and both Bancroft and Duke move to a small house on the Keller property. Bancroft undergoes an almost unceasing traumatic experience with Duke, who acts like a wild animal in a cage, scratching and kicking and biting Bancroft as she resists instruction at every turn, but Bancroft endures the suffering as she understands Duke's own pain, having been brutalized when young by being placed in several institutions where her own blindness was treated and while enduring the loss of the only person ever close to her, a crippled brother who died at a young age. At the end of this traial period, Bancroft sees some progress in that Duke can now dress herself and can now recite the alphabet by touch, although she is unable to put the alphabet together in the sense that they have meaning for items, subjects and human feelings. Bancroft wants to keep Duke in isolation with her for another week or so, but the overly protective Swenson and Jory insist that she be returned to the main house and, when that happens, Duke slips back to a state of erratic, wild behavior. Bancroft, however, remains at the main house, determined to exercise firm but loving discipline. She rebukes and corrects Duke at every turn, particularly when Duke attempts to create emotional outbursts that Bancroft knows is directed at her parents to increase their guilt. At one telling point, Duke tips a pitcher of water at the dinner table and Bancroft drags her outside, compelling her to use the pump to refill the pitcher and then a little miracle occurs. The splashing water drenches Duke, causing her to identify the substance and where she writes the word water in the palm of Bancroft's hand, a wonderful and revealing breakthrough that tells Bancroft that Duke can now associate and employ the alphabet with actual meanings. Duke also realizes that she can intelligently communicate and she excitedly runs about the front yard, frantically touching things, and quickly spelling them out while Bancroft thrills with happiness in having brought this wild child to useful human communication, a magnetic, startling, triumphant scene that ends this stunning and impactful film. Penn, who directed the stage version of this marvelous story, meticulously tells this great biopic, carefully unfolding its emotionally packed scenes as Bancroft and Duke desperately struggle toward enlightenment. Penn deservedly received an Oscar nomination as Best Director, but lost out to David Lean for **Lawrence of Arabia**, 1962. Bancroft, however, won an Oscar as Best Actress, and Duke received an Oscar as Best Supporting Actress, both giving the bravura performances of their lives. Gibson, who authored the brilliant play, received an Oscar nomination for Best Adapted Screenplay. Ruth Morley received an Oscar nomination for Best Black and White Costume Design. The score from Rosenthal impressively works with each obsessive scene where Penn and cinematographer Caparros expertly employ a technique of quick dissolves to heighten the inherently intense drama. *Author's Note*: The play opened on Broadway in October 1959 where Penn directed and Bancroft and Duke enacted the leading parts. When it came time to film this outstanding work, however, studio bosses wanted a big name actress to play Annie Sullivan and proposed Elizabeth Taylor, reportedly offering a $5 million budget to Penn. Studio executives also wanted to replace Duke, pointing out that she was then fifteen years old and was playing a girl of seven. The director, however, was loyal to his stage stars, Penn telling this author that "I was not about

Patty Duke and Anne Bancroft in *The Miracle Worker*, 1962.

to desert them for a big Hollywood payoff. They had worked hard to make those roles their own and they deserved to play those parts on the screen." Penn got a much smaller budget, reportedly about $500,000, and still produced a masterpiece, shooting the film on location at Middletown, New Jersey (to represent Tuscumbia, Alabama), and at Big Sky Ranch at Simi Valley, California. When meeting Bancroft shortly after this film was released, the actress told this author that her role "was just about the toughest job I ever had and I tried night and day to put myself into the person of Annie Sullivan. She must have been one of the world's greatest unsung saints by trying to bring reason, sense and understandability to a child who was nothing more than a wild animal. The fight scene [at the dinner table] I have with Patty [Duke] was so rough that we both had to wear padding beneath our clothes to keep ourselves from getting bruised or worse." That astonishing and painful scene, where Penn used three cameras to record their actions as Bancroft repeatedly tries to teach Duke table manners, takes up nine minutes of the film, but it took five days to get the final cut. Oddly, both Bancroft and Duke were both born with the given name of Anna Marie and were born fifteen years apart in New York. Gibson's play is based upon Keller's own autobiography, which was first adapted in 1953 for an unproduced ballet, before it was produced on TV in 1957 and then went onto the Broadway stage two years later. Keller's journey from ignorance to enlightenment began when Alexander Graham Bell asked the Perkins Institute (established in 1829) to send someone to help Keller and they sent Sullivan, who stayed with Keller as her teacher until her death in 1936. Keller, through Sullivan, overcame her deafness and blindness by learning to read by feeling words on a raised cardboard, her education begun by Sullivan on March 2, 1887, and where Keller then arranged her own sentences on a frame. She learned how to speak at the Horace Mann School for the Deaf in Boston by feeling with her fingers the positions of lips and tongues of others and she later learned how to lip-read when putting her fingers on the lips of others as the words were tapped out by an interpreter on her hand. Her autobiography, *The Story of My Life*, was published in 1902. Keller graduated magna cum laude from Radcliffe College in 1904. In 1913, she began lecturing and, in 1920, she joined with Jane Addams, Felix Frankfurter, Clarence Darrow, Upton Sinclair and others to establish the ACLU. This great woman, shaped by another great woman, Sullivan, spent the remainder of her life aiding the handicapped. **p**, Fred Coe; **d**, Arthur Penn; **cast**, Anne Bancroft, Patty Duke, Victor Jory, Inga Swenson, Andrew Prine, Kathleen Comegys, Maribel Ayuso, Dale Ellen Bethea, John Bliss, Grant Code, Michael Darden, Michele Farr; **w**, William Gibson (based on his play and the book *The Story of My Life* by Helen Keller); **c**, Ernest Caparros; **m**, Don Costa, Laurence Rosenthal, Arthur Siegel; **ed**, Aram Avakian; **art d**, George Jenkins, Mel Bourne.

Glynis Johns as a mermaid in *Miranda*, 1949..

Miracles for Sale ★★★ 1939; U.S.; 71m; MGM; B/W; Mystery; Children: Unacceptable; **DVD**. Young is an illusionist who creates visual tricks that magicians use in their shows while his hobby is exposing fake spiritualists. He tries to protect his fiancée, Rice, after two of her wealthy friends are murdered after they become involved with an occult group. Young learns about the tricks that were made to produce supernatural effects and exposes the criminal, Worlock, a pseudo doctor. This intriguing suspense film was the final directorial effort of Tod Browning (1880-1962), best known for **Dracula**, 1931. Young's character is loosely based on the spectacular life of magician Harry Houdini (1874-1926), who made a lifelong career of exposing phony mediums. **p**, J. J. Cohn; **d**, Tod Browning; **cast**, Robert Young, Florence Rice, Frank Craven, Henry Hull, Lee Bowman, Cliff Clark, Astrid Allwyn, Walter Kingsford, Gloria Holden, William Demarest, Charles Lane, Richard Loo, Phillip Terry; **w**, Harry Ruskin, Marion Parsonnet, James Edward Grant (based on the novel *Death from a Top Hat* by Clayton Rawson); **c**, Charles Lawton, Jr.; **m**, William Axt; **ed**, Fredrick Y. Smith; **art d**, Cedric Gibbons; **set d**, Edwin B. Willis.

Mirage ★★★ 1965; U.S.; 108m; UNIV; B/W; Mystery; Children: Unacceptable; **DVD**; **VHS**. This offbeat but compelling thriller begins when a New York high-rise office building suffers a power failure. The memory of one of those in the building, Peck, a cost accountant for an international conglomerate involved in nuclear manufacturing, goes as blank as the building goes dark. Believing he has amnesia and can't remember the last two years, Peck tries to learn who he was before the blackout. During the power outage, he sees a man, Abel, who was the head of a peace organization, fall to his death from the 27th floor. Offices in the building are now unfamiliar to Peck, as are people he once knew. Also, while in the building, Peck meets a beautiful young woman, Baker, with whom he may have been in love, and she tells him he is alive only because he can't remember the previous two years. Weston, a thug, holds a gun on Peck, and tells him he must go to Barbados and meet a man called "The Major" (Erickson). Peck knocks out Weston and goes to the police, but they don't believe him. He hires a detective, Matthau, to find out what it's all about, but the gumshoe is soon murdered. Peck is followed by gunmen Weston and Kennedy as he seeks the help of a psychiatrist, Harris, who listens to him and concludes that Peck is a chemist, who lost his memory after seeing Abel fall to his death. Peck believes he has discovered a new method of neutralizing radiation. Abel was going to give the formula to a tycoon, Erickson, at his office on the 27th floor, but, during a scuffle, Abel fell from the window. We learn that Peck's discovery was a method of eliminating nuclear fallout, which Abel wanted for peaceful purposes and Peck's conglomerate wanted to sell to the highest bidder. Peck regains his memory, learns that Abel accidentally fell from the window and he then survives the goons chasing him under Erickson's orders. A lot of the plot is as much a mystery as the mirage of the title, but it is so well crafted and enacted that it sustains interest throughout. *Author's Note*: Matthau told this author that "I never figured out how Greg [Peck] lost his memory in that picture and neither did he, or why everybody on the planet was trying to kill him. Since I play a detective who has just put up his shingle, I am no Sherlock Holmes, and I get bumped off for taking him on as one of my first clients. I have played smarter people." Peck was reserved about this film, telling this author that "it's all plot with characterization filled in as you go along, a nifty little puzzle like those you find in the New York *Times*." **p**, Harry Keller; **d**, Edward Dmytryk; **cast**, Gregory Peck, Diane Baker, Walter Matthau, Kevin McCarthy, Jack Weston, Leif Erickson, Walter Abel, George Kennedy, Anne Seymour, House Jameson, Ann Doran, Walter Reed; **w**, Peter Stone (based on the novel *Fallen Angel* by Walter Ericson (Howard Fast); **c**, Joseph MacDonald; **m**, Quincy Jones; **ed**, Ted J. Kent; **art d**, Alexander Golitzen, Frank Arrigo; **set d**, John Austin, John McCarthy; **spec eff**, Albert Whitlock.

Miranda ★★★ 1949; U.K.; 80m; Sydney Box Productions/Eagle-Lion Films; B/W; Fantasy; Children: Acceptable; **DVD**; **VHS**. This delightful, comedy-filled fantasy opens with Jones as a London doctor, who wants to go on a fishing vacation to Cornwall with his wife, Withers, but she suggests he go alone, taking a bachelor holiday. He does just that, falls into the ocean, and is rescued by a beautiful mermaid, Johns, who takes him to an undersea air-filled cave. She converses with him in perfect English, explaining that she learned the language from magazines that people had tossed into the sea. She tells Jones she is lonely and, unless he takes her to London, she will keep him in the cave forever. Jones takes the mermaid home with him, but disguises her as an invalid patient, her tail wrapped in blankets. Withers barely tolerates Johns' presence, while she wonders why this beautiful new woman is living in her house, spending a lot of time in a bathroom when not confined to a wheelchair. On outings in London, Johns casts a romantic spell on every man she sees, including Jones. She beguiles his artist friend, McCallum, and butler-chauffeur Tomlinson, which makes their girlfriends, Holm and Owen, jealous. The only one who discovers that Johns is a mermaid (other than Jones) is her nurse, Rutherford, who is delighted about it. Johns eventually grows homesick for the sea and also becomes pregnant, so Jones takes her back to the ocean where she is swimmingly happy again. Song: "Miranda" (Jack Fishman, Peter Hart). **p**, Betty E. Box; **d**, Ken Annakin; **cast**, Glynis Johns, Googie Withers, Griffith Jones, John McCallum, Margaret Rutherford, David Tomlinson, Yvonne Owen, Sonia Holm, Brian Oulton, Stringer Davis, Maurice Denham, Jean Sablon; **w**, Peter Blackmore, Denis Waldock (based on the play by Blackmore); **c**, Ray Elton, Bryan Langley; **m**, Temple Abady; **ed**, Gordon Hales; **art d**, George Paterson.

The Mirror Crack'd ★★★ 1980; U.K.; 105m; EMI Films/Associated Film Distribution; Color; Mystery; Children: Unacceptable (MPAA: PG); **DVD**; **VHS**. Based on a novel by Agatha Christie, this tale follows her familiar pattern of gathering various people together for one or more murders. This time it's 1953 and a small English village of St. Mary Mead, home of Miss Jane Marple, played by Lansbury, who is an amateur sleuth. She is delighted when an American movie company comes to town to make a movie about the ages-past power struggle between Queen Elizabeth I and Lady Jane Grey, who lost her head in that argument. The actresses playing them are Taylor as Lady Jane and Novak as the queen. Taylor arrives with her husband, Hudson, who is the film's director and who is having an affair with his secretary, Chaplin. The town has bad memories for Taylor since she had earlier suffered a nervous breakdown there. Taylor goes ballistic when she learns that Novak is to play the queen, since the two despise each other. Upon arriving at a manor house where the movie will be filmed, Novak gets death threats. She has come with her husband, Curtis, who is producing the film. Bennett, a woman in town who is at the cast party, dies after drinking a poisoned cocktail. Everyone believes that the drink was meant for Taylor, but the local inspector, Fox, isn't sure, so he asks his aunt, Lansbury, to investigate. She does and, of course, solves the mystery. **p**, John Brabourne, Richard Goodwin; **d**, Guy Hamilton; **cast**, Angela Lansbury, Elizabeth Taylor, Kim Novak, Geraldine Chaplin, Tony Curtis, Edward Fox, Rock Hudson, Anthony Steel, Dinah Sheridan, Wendy Morgan, Margaret Courtenay, Charles Gray, Maureen Bennett, Carolyn Pickles, Pierce Brosnan; **w**, Jonathan Hales, Barry Sandler (based on the novel *The Mirror Crack'd from Side to Side* by Agatha Christie); **c**, Christopher Challis (Technicolor); **m**, John Cameron; **ed**, Richard Marden; **prod d**, Michael Stringer; **art d**, John Roberts; **set d**, Peter Howitt.

The Misfits ★★★★ 1961; U.S.; 124m; Seven Arts/UA; B/W; Drama; Children: Unacceptable; **DVD**; **VHS**. Gable is commanding and compelling in this, his last performance, where he plays a modern-day cowboy, who deludes himself into believing that the West of his youth still retains prosaic ethics and offers a meaningful way of life. Strangely, this was also Monroe's final film, which ended her brief but glamorous reign as the top Hollywood sex symbol. Gable and friends Clift and Wallach are cowboys without horses, driving about in a pickup and working at odd jobs when they encounter the curvy Monroe, in Reno, where she has just separated from her husband, a businessman. A former stripper, Monroe is searching for the meaning of life as well as an understanding life partner and she is attracted to Gable, who talks about a West that is no more, glorifying rodeos and their courageous performers. He invites Monroe to accompany him and his pals on their next adventure, one where they intend to round up wild mustangs and sell them. On her journey, Clift, a former rodeo rider, who harbors a deep hatred for his stepfather and is mentally troubled, makes a play for Monroe, as does Wallach, a one-time bombardier in the U.S. Air Force, but Monroe has given her heart to Gable, a man twice her age, but a man filled with a healthy attitude and with great ambition to live life to the fullest. Then she learns the real reason for their mission. The trio intends to capture the horses and sell them to a firm that will ground them up for dog food. Monroe now thinks that these new friends are horrible monsters having no compassion. When they round up a small herd of mustangs, she begs Gable to let them go. Gable refuses, firm in his belief that no woman should tell a man his business, even though Gable admits that this business is about as low as he has ever gotten. When the leader of the herd resists, Gable shows his supremacy by breaking the horse's spirit in a prolonged battle between man and horse. After subduing the horse, Gable then and only then decides to let the horse and the rest of the herd go, overruling the objections of Wallach and saying that modern developers have turned the West into something "dirty." By releasing the horses, Gable has won back Monroe's love and the two of them drive off to seek their happiness. It's a simple story deftly handled by pantheon director Huston, where Gable demonstrates his ability to render a great performance in one remarkable scene after another. He is boisterous, pensive, amiable and also haunted by his own failures, startlingly demonstrated in one scene where, while he is drunk, he begins to chastise the long absent mischievous small children of his past, children who linger only in his imagination. Miller's sensitive script is often poetic and always meaningful as it mourns the passing of the Old West, if, indeed, it was ever as courageous as Miller envisions it. *Author's Note*: Huston told this author that the 'misfits' the title refers to are the mustangs, but also to the characters in the film. All of the leading players, except for Gable, are really neurotic, and a few of them in real life, Marilyn [Monroe] and Monty [Clift], carried about the same problems. Gable was a stabilizing factor in the production, reliable and always on time for shootings. He not only tolerated poor Marilyn [who was then taking drugs] for being invariably late, but befriended her, and helped her, and gave her a lot of emotional support. Marilyn told me that she thought Gable was 'one of the few real gentlemen I have met in life.' He was not so supportive of Monty, who was an emotional wreck after

Marilyn Monroe and Clark Gable in *The Misfits*, 1961.

having been in that terrible car accident some years earlier and had the physical scars to prove it. Monty habitually showed up late for his scenes and Gable was irked about that. I think the person that upset Gable the most was Wallach, a method actor. At one point, after Eli did one of his scenes, Gable said to him: 'I hear we are having boiled ham for lunch.' Wallach, sort of a wise guy, kept calling Gable 'king,' but that did not disturb him. Gable was almost sixty when he did that picture for me and there were some scenes where he insisted that he do his own stunts, although I was against it. He was still a powerful, broad-shouldered guy and I thought he could handle it, but his battle with that mustang on the desert flats in northern Nevada, probably so weakened him that he had a heart attack two days after we finished the picture and died ten days after that. I carry a lot of guilt about that to this day." Gable's scene called for him to hold on to a rope, which he wrapped around his body, while the wild mustang reared and pulled and stomped, and, at one point, Gable was dragged for more than 400 feet along the dry lakebed in the desert at more than thirty miles per hour during blistering heat that was at 108 degrees. Monroe, who was drinking heavily while taking drugs throughout this production, said, before she died more than a year after the film's release, that she hated her performance in this film, but that undoubtedly had much to do with her crumbling marriage with playwright-screenwriter Miller. Monroe was truly in awe of Gable and stated often that he had been her childhood screen hero and, at one point in one of her more delusionary statements, claimed that she was his child (she had been abandoned at an early age). Clift, who has only one significant scene in this film (where he attempts to have a loving conversation on the phone with his indifferent mother), also drank heavily and used drugs at the time of the production, and he died six years after its release. Huston was criticized for his undisciplined behavior in this film, Wallach later claiming that Huston had been intoxicated while directing some of the scenes in the film. The director did lose so much money at Nevada gambling dens that the production company had to cover his debts. The film was shot on location in Reno and Dayton, Nevada (northeast of Carson City), and Gable's battle with the mustang was shot on a dry lake twenty miles east of Dayton and near a small town called Stagecoach. The area is presently called "Misfits Flat." **p**, Frank E. Taylor; **d**, John Huston; **cast**, Clark Gable, Marilyn Monroe, Montgomery Clift, Thelma Ritter, Eli Wallach, James Barton, Kevin McCarthy, Estelle Winwood, Peggy Barton, Rex Bell; **w**, Arthur Miller; **c**, Russell Metty; **m**, Alex North; **ed**, George Tomasini; **art d**, Stephen Grimes, William Newberry; **set d**, Frank McKelvy; **spec eff**, Cline Jones.

Mishima: A Life in Four Chapters ★★★ 1985; Japan; 121m; Zoetrope Studios/WB; Color/B/W; Biographical Drama; Children: Unacceptable (MPAA: R); **DVD**; **VHS**. This incisive and often powerful

William Holden and Lucille Ball in *Miss Grant Takes Richmond,* **1949.**

film is a dramatized account in four parts of the life of Japan's internationally famous 20th-century author, poet, playwright, actor, and film director Yukio Mishima (1925-1970). His works blended modern and traditional aesthetics, focusing on sexuality, political change, and death. He committed a ritual suicide after a failed political coup. Three of the segments in the film parallel events in his life with his novels *The Temple of the Golden Pavilion* (*Kinkaku-ji*), *Kyoto's House*, and *Runaway Horses*, while the fourth, "The Last Day," takes place on the day of his death, November 25, 1970. Sexuality and ritual suicide prohibits viewing by children. (In Japanese; English subtitles.) **p**, Mataichirô Yamamoto, Tom Luddy, Francis Ford Coppola, George Lucas, **d**, Paul Schrader; **cast**, Ken Ogata, Masayuki Shionoya, Hiroshi Mikami, Junkichi Orimoto, Naoko Ôtani, Gô Rijû, Kyúzô Kobayashi, Yuuki Kitazume, Haruko Kato, Yasosuke Bando, Hisako Manda, Imari Tsujikoichi Sato, Roy Scheider (narrator); **w**, Chieko Schrader, Paul Schrader, Leonard Schrader, Jun Shiragi (based on the novels *The Temple of the Golden Pavilion*, *Kyoko's House*, and *Runaway Horses* by Yukio Mishima); **c**, John Bailey; **m**, Philip Glass; **ed**, Michael Chandler, Tomoyo Oshima; **prod d**, Eiko Ishioka; **art d**, Kazuo Takenaka; **set d**, Kyoji Sasaki; **spec eff**, Catherine Craig.

Miss Fane's Baby Is Stolen ★★★ 1934; U.S.; 70m; PAR; B/W; Drama; Children: Unacceptable; **DVD**; **VHS**. This was the first film about child kidnapping after the baby of aviator Charles Lindbergh was kidnapped and killed in 1932. Baby LeRoy plays the child of Wieck, a famous movie star, who is kidnapped from her luxurious Beverly Hills, California, home. The baby is finally found by Brady, a farmer's wife, and the kidnappers are brought to justice. The film is occasionally lighthearted about the serious subject with Frawley playing his role of police captain for laughs, and some slapstick elements are present, but the story is well crafted and attempts to address the rising number of nationwide kidnappings that became epidemic during the early 1930s. *Author's Note*: Baby LeRoy's real name was Ronald Le Roy Overacker (1932-2001) and he was the persistent headache of curmudgeon actor-comedian W. C. Fields in **It's a Gift** (1934), becoming the youngest movie actor to receive star billing when he was two years old. He retired at the age of four. Fields reportedly once spiked Baby LeRoy's milk with gin. **p**, Bayard Veiller; **d**, Alexander Hall; **cast**, Dorothea Wieck, Alice Brady, Baby LeRoy, William Frawley, George Barbier, Alan Hale, Jack La Rue, Dorothy Burgess, Florence Roberts, George "Spanky" McFarland; **w**, Adela Rogers St. Johns, Jane Storm (based on the novel and story "Kidnapt" by Rupert Hughes); **c**, Alfred Gilks; **ed**, James Smith; **art d**, Hans Dreier, John B. Goodman.

Miss Firecracker ★★★ 1989; U.S.; 102m; Corsair Pictures; Color;

Comedy; Children: Unacceptable (MPAA: PG); **DVD**; **VHS**. This solid comedy has Hunter as a young catfish factory worker who spends her time gutting fish. She is not pleased with her life in the small town of Yazoo, Mississippi, even though she is popular with the young men who nickname her "Hot Tamale." An orphan, Hunter hopes to win more self-respect and that of others by winning the annual local forth of July Miss Firecracker Beauty Pageant. Steenburgen, her self-centered, married cousin, who won the contest years earlier, has come from Atlanta to deliver the keynote address at the pageant. Hunter's closest friends and relatives don't think she has a chance to win, including her eccentric cousin, Robbins, who plans to sell Hunter's rundown family mansion to developers. Hunter's current lover, Glenn, a barker at a carnival that has come to town for the holiday, admires her for trying, even though he also doubts she can win. Hunter thinks she might win if she wears the red "firecracker" dress Steenburgen wore when she won, so she asks a local black seamstress, Woodard, to make her a copy. Woodard does that, even though she mainly makes costumes for bullfrogs. Woodard wins Robbins along the way, and Hunter wins the pageant, and her self-esteem is restored. Sexuality and a senseless scene showing Robbins picking up gory animal road kill prohibit viewing by children. **p**, Fred Berner, Richard Coll; **d**, Thomas Schlamme; **cast**, Holly Hunter, Mary Steenburgen, Tim Robbins, Alfre Woodard, Scott Glenn, Veanne Cox, Ann Wedgeworth, Trey Wilson, Amy Wright, Christine Lahti; **w**, Beth Henley (based on her play "The Miss Firecracker Contest"); **c**, Arthur Albert; **m**, David Mansfield; **ed**, Peter C. Frank; **prod d**, Kristi Zea; **art d**, Maher Ahmad, Debra Schutt.

Miss Grant Takes Richmond ★★★ 1949; U.S.; 87m; COL; B/W; Comedy; Children: Acceptable; **DVD**; **VHS**. In this delightful comedy, Ball (Ellen Grant), is hired by handsome real estate operator Holden (Dick Richmond) as his secretary. Holden has selected her at random when thinking she is too addlebrained and disoriented to interfere with his real money-making operations as a successful bookie. Holden's partners are McHugh, a mental giant with figures, and Gleason, an old-time bookie, who objects to Holden having such an upscale front for their illegal dealings. Ball energetically promotes Holden's real estate holdings to the point where many home-seeking clients appear and where she talks the affable Holden into promoting a new housing project. Holden, however, has serious problems in that he owes considerable money to a gambling syndicate. Holden uses the housing project to raise money that he uses to pay off the syndicate hoodlums and, in the end, the investors and Ball are left holding an empty bag. Holden, however, has fallen for the statuesque Ball and sets out to make amends. He goes to the female boss of the gambling syndicate, Carter, who would like to tear up his markers as she is in love with him, and offers to sell his bookmaking operation to her for $50,000. Carter takes the deal, and Holden then repays the customers Ball has lined up for the housing project. Holden then plans to wed Ball, a secretary, he has learned, who is a lot smarter than what he thought her to be. This comedy moves along at a fast clip under Bacon's firm direction, and Ball and Holden are standouts in their roles and where Ball shows the comedic ability she was to later display in many films and in her long-running television series, "I Love Lucy." In one such scene, she hilariously impersonates a gun moll when invading Carter's lavish home, threatening Carter to give up her claims to Holden. *Author's Note*: Holden told this author that "Lucy [Ball] was not only a knockout redhead, but she was really a gifted comedian. She could take a limp line of dialog and turn it into a firecracker. I learned in that picture that comedy was not all slapstick and a lot of mugging, but was also made up of subtle line deliveries with some restrained gestures." **p**, S. Sylvan Simon; **d**, Lloyd Bacon; **cast**, Lucille Ball, William Holden, Janis Carter, James Gleason, Gloria Henry, Frank McHugh, George Cleveland, Stephen Dunne, Charles Lane, Roy Roberts, Loren Tindall, Will Wright; **w**, Nat Perrin, Devery Freeman, Frank Tashlin (based on a story by Everett Freeman); **c**, Charles Lawton, Jr.; **m**, Heinz Roemheld; **ed**, Jerome Thoms; **art d**, Walter Holscher; **set d**, James Crowe.

Miss Potter ★★★ 2006; U.K./U.S./Isle of Man; 92m; Phoenix Pictures/MGM; Color; Biographical Drama; Children: Cautionary (MPAA: PG); **BD**; **DVD**. Zellweger impressively essays author Beatrix Potter (1866-1943), who lives with her middle-class parents in 1902 London. Her mother, Flynn, who has high society ambitions, has introduced her to several bachelors but Zellweger turns them all down. Since she was a child, she has painted pictures of bunny rabbits and ducklings and made up sweet, sensitive nature stories about them, but her parents do not recognize her as being an artist or author. One day she takes her artwork and stories to a publisher and the junior man in the firm, McGregor, likes and publishes them. Potter's first children's book sells so well that McGregor publishes two more of her works and she steadily becomes a leading artist-author of children's books. Potter and McGregor and his sister, Watson, become her great and only friends. Potter and McGregor fall in love, although her mother disapproves because he is "in trade" and wishes her daughter would marry into society. Her father, Paterson, is more like Beatrix, a gentle man, who, as a young man, aspired to become a painter. Potter's *Tales of Peter Rabbit* and her other books make her famous and rich, but McGregor falls ill and dies before they can marry. Potter buys a country farm where she continues painting and writing her animal stories and, after several years of contentedly living alone in her imaginary world of Peter Rabbit and his friends, marries a kind and gentle realtor, Owen, who has handled the sale of her farm. Songs: "When You Taught Me How to Dance" (Nigel Westlake, Mike Batt, Richard Maltby, Jr.), "Let Me Teach You How to Dance" (Westlake, Maltby, Jr.). This charming, wonderful film sees fine performances from the entire cast. **p**, David Kirschner, Mike Medavoy, Arnold W. Messer, Corey Sienega, David Thwaites, Bob and Harvey Weinstein, Renée Zellweger; **d**, Chris Noonan; **cast**, Zellweger, Ewan McGregor, Emily Watson, Barbara Flynn, Bill Paterson, Matyelok Gibbs, Lloyd Owen, Anton Lesser, David Bamber, Phyllida Law; **w**, Richard Maltby Jr.; **c**, Andrew Dunn; **m**, Nigel Westlake; **ed**, Robin Sales; **prod d**, Martin Childs; **art d**, Mark Raggett, Grant Armstrong; **set d**, Tina Jones; **spec eff**, Victoria Williams, Michael Dawson, Clare Norman, Simon Stanley-Clamp.

Miss Sadie Thompson ★★★ 1953; U.S.; 91m; COL; Color; Drama; Children: Unacceptable; **DVD**; **VHS**. Hayworth tosses her red hair about and shakes her voluptuous body in a steaming and sensual performance as that shady lady of the South Seas, a tempestuous and sizzling character created by austere British author W. Somerset Maugham when writing *Rain* (this being a remake of that tale, **Rain**, 1932). Hayworth shows up on a tropical island that is garrisoned by U.S. Marines shortly after WWII. Brawny Marine sergeant Ray falls in love with Hayworth and proposes marriage, but that romance is snipped in the bud by clergyman Ferrer, a religious fanatic, who knows all about Hayworth's tawdry past and orders her to return to San Francisco to face an old morals charge. She pleads with Ferrer, promising him that she will leave the island and go somewhere else other than back to San Francisco, but he is adamant. Hayworth throws caution to the wind (as usual) and goes to the saloon where the Marines gather and, to flaunt her considerable wares in defiance of Ferrer's edicts, gives a burlesque type performance where she arouses the Marines with a sensuous song and dance, "The Heat Is On," displaying the kind of erotic dancing not usually seen on the screen. Hayworth does a sort of bump and grind in a dress so tight-fitting that her fleshy charms, dripping with sweat, threaten to explode from her revealing attire and she almost causes a riot by the aroused Marines. Ferrer chastises Hayworth for this provocative exhibition, telling her that the only way she can have salvation is to embrace religion and she does, mindlessly submitting to his religious administrations. Ferrer, however, is not after her soul, but her body, and rapes her and then commits suicide. The wiser but worn out temptress then bids farewell to her Marine friends and leaves the island, ostensibly for San Francisco to finally settle her differences with the police in that city. Hayworth gives a dynamic and captivating performance as the tragedy-

Barry Fitzgerald, John Lund, Wanda Hendrix and Robert Stack in *Miss Tatlock's Millions*, 1948.

bound harlot and Ferrer rivets as the religious zealot and where Ray is convincing as the gullible, happy-go-lucky sergeant (although William Gargan played the sergeant as a much more worldly and savvy character in the original **Rain**). Songs (all from composer Lester Lee and lyricist Allan Roberts): "Hear No Evil, See No Evil (Speak No Evil)," "The Blue Pacific Blues," "Marine Song," and "The Heat Is On" (Hayworth's singing voice dubbed by Jo Ann Greer). This film was given a major budget and saw a huge box office success, grossing almost $3 million at the box office in its initial release, even though several state censorship boards banned the film, one of its leaders stating that Hayworth's dance scene was "filthy," and the film "rotten, lewd," and "immoral." It should be noted, however, that the producers of this film sanitized the original story. Exteriors were shot in Hawaii and interiors at the Columbia sound stages. Shot originally in 3-D process and released in that format for two weeks, it was later released in the same year in "flat" process. *Author's Note*: Ferrer, who had won an Oscar for his brilliant performance in **Cyrano de Bergerac**, 1950, only three years earlier, did not like his role, which had been played with much conviction by Walter Huston in **Rain**, stating that he took the part only to offset criticism he had received after being summoned by the House of Un-American Activities (HUAC) to testify in its probing into communist influence in Hollywood (but how this strange role could offset such criticism remains a mystery). Hayworth, who was thirty-four and ten pounds overweight when she did this film, told this author that "I am just another tramp in that picture, but even tramps have hearts and feelings. I tried to show Sadie as a human being, not just a pound of flesh to be bought on the open market." **p**, Jerry Wald; **d**, Curtis Bernhardt; **cast**, Rita Hayworth, Jose Ferrer, Aldo Ray, Russell Collins, Diosa Costello, Harry Bellaver, Wilton Graff, Peggy Converse, Henry Slate, Charles Bronson, Eduardo Cansino, Jr.; **w**, Harry Kleiner (based on the story "Rain" by W. Somerset Maugham); **c**, Charles Lawton Jr. (Technicolor; originally filmed in 3-D); **m**, Morris Stoloff, Lester Lee, Ned Washington, Allan Roberts; **ed**, Viola Lawrence; **art d**, Carl Anderson; **set d**, Louis Diage.

Miss Tatlock's Millions ★★★ 1948; U.S.; 101m; PAR; B/W; Comedy; Children: Acceptable; **VHS**. Hilarious screwball comedy sees a family of lunatics (fetching Hendrix being the only one who is normal), inherit millions from Schuyler Tatlock, an eccentric tycoon, who moved to Hawaii and has not been seen since. Fitzgerald, an employee of the tycoon, contacts stuntman Lund, telling him that his employer has gone missing, but that he does not want that news known to anyone and then asks Lund to impersonate his vanished employer, saying that his masquerade will last only a few days as he presides over the reading of the will, so that other greedy family members will not challenge that will and that the bulk of the funds will go to Hendrix. Lund agrees, dyeing

Sissy Spacek and Jack Lemmon in *Missing*, 1982.

his hair the color of the tycoon and adopting his strange manners. When he meets Hendrix, however, who is supposed to be his younger sister, Lund falls in love with her. After the will is read, Fitzgerald informs Lund that he must continue to protect Hendrix by pretending to be her brother for at least two years, and Lund refuses to carry on the charade for that amount of time. Meanwhile, other family members challenge the will and go after the tycoon's fortune, matters become even more complicated after Lund falls through a roof and is knocked unconscious, only to wake up speaking in his normal voice and acting as his real self. Hendrix thinks the blow to Lund's head has altered her brother's personality and others think Lund is no longer capable of managing his financial affairs, an excuse for the greedy heirs to accelerate their legal moves to seize his fortune. Further, Hendrix is troubled by the fact that she feels affection for Lund that goes beyond sisterly love, but all comes right when the real Schuyler, Neff, shows up with a wife and a passel of children and now Lund and Hendrix, who are not siblings, are able to become man and wife. The dizzying pace and zany antics of the well-acted characters in this film present a whirlwind comedy with many side-splitting scenes. Actor Ray Milland and film director Mitchell Leisen appear as themselves in this delightful romp. Songs: "Sweet Leilani" (Harry Owens), "I Don't Want to Walk Without You" (music: Jule Styne; lyrics: Frank Loesser). **p**, Charles Brackett; **d**, Richard Haydn; **cast**, John Lund, Wanda Hendrix, Barry Fitzgerald, Monty Woolley, Robert Stack, Ilka Chase, Dorothy Stickney, Elizabeth Patterson, Leif Erickson, Bill Neff, Dan Tobin, Hilo Hattie, Haydn, Mitchell Leisen Ray Milland; **w**, Brackett, Richard L. Breen (based on the play "Oh, Brother!" by Jacques Deval); **c**, Charles B. Lang, Jr.; **m**, Victor Young; **ed**, Everett Douglas, Doane Harrison; **art d**, Hans Dreier, Franz Bachelin; **set d**, Sam Comer, Ross Dowd; **spec eff**, Farciot Edouart, Gordon Jennings.

Missing ★★★★ 1982; U.S.; 122m; PolyGram/UNIV; Color; Drama; Children: Unacceptable (MPAA: R); **DVD**; **VHS**. A harrowing and often frightening film from the politically oriented Costa-Gavras has left-wing activist Shea disappearing in a major South American city (the country is not specified, but it is implied to be Chile during the early stages of the Pinochet regime), after his nosy curiosity gets the better of him and he pokes his nose into the political machinations of the current government. Spacek, who is Shea's wife and shares his left-wing views, begins to make frantic inquiries about her missing husband, but everywhere she turns she is met with silence or is stalled by officials, who seem to have no interest in finding Shea. His father, Lemmon, a Christian-Science follower whose political sentiments are right of center and who believes in the American Way, flies to the country and joins with Spacek in searching for Shea. Lemmon does not share his son's political views

or that of Spacek's and the two spend a lot of time bickering about their differing political viewpoints. Both become enraged when the government imposes martial law and citizens are randomly killed when disobeying the slightest infractions. Spacek herself narrowly escapes death when she defies a curfew and is shot at while returning to her hotel. No longer able to tolerate the lame explanations and excuses from American officials, Lemmon explodes, lambasting those officials, especially after he learns that they are conspiring with the present regime to suppress the rights of the natives. Then, Spacek and Lemmon find in a room of executed citizens the body of Regalbuto, a close friend of Shea, and it is glumly assumed that Shea is now dead and that the search for him is futile. Lemmon and Spacek give outstanding performances in this taut drama, playing as much the victims as Shea has become while Costa-Gavras directs with clinical brilliance and unstinting candor and without frills, unfolding one grim scene after another to indict the tyranny of the oppressive regime. *Author's Note*: The story is based upon the disappearance of American journalist Charles Horman (1942-1973), who was swept up in the 1973 coup that brought about the assassination of left-wing Chilean president Salvador Allende (1908-1973) by the Chilean Army's commander-in-chief, Augusto Pinochet (1915-2006), reportedly with considerable collusion from the CIA. Lemmon told this author that "**Missing** is more than a motion picture. It is a powerful visual statement that indicts the corruption of a South American dictatorship with the collusion of powerful American politicians and officials. It is not fiction. It really happened, and the loss I suffer where my own son is a victim of that regime is a small one compared to the people of that country, who are stripped of their freedom and murdered almost by whim." **p**, Edward and Mildred Lewis; **d**, Costa-Gavras; **cast**, Jack Lemmon, Sissy Spacek, Melanie Mayron, John Shea, Charles Cioffi, David Clennon, Richard Venture, Jerry Hardin, Richard Bradford, Joe Regalbuto; **w**, Donald Stewart, Costa-Gavras (based on the book by Thomas Hauser); **c**, Ricardo Aronovich (Technicolor); **m**, Vangelis; **ed**, Françoise Bonnot; **prod d**, Peter Jamison; **art d**, Lucero Isaac, Agustin Ytuarte; **set d**, Linda Spheeris; **spec eff**, Albert Whitlock.

Mission Impossible ★★★ 1996; U.S.; 110m; PAR; Color; Spy Drama; Children: Unacceptable (MPAA: PG-13); **BD**; **DVD**; **VHS**. In the post–Cold War world, American espionage agents Cruise and Voight and Voight's wife, Beart, are sent to Prague on a mission to prevent the theft of a computer file containing the codes and real names of all of America's double agents. Things go wrong and the mission fails, leaving agent Ethan Hunt (Cruise) the lone survivor. He reports the failed mission to the head of the agency, Czerny, who suspects him of being responsible for its failure. Cruise uses the help of an information broker, Redgrave, to find who set him up so he can clear his name. His efforts involve car, train, and helicopter chases. Equally, if not more exciting, is a sensitive computer theft operation in which Cruise hangs upside-down in a harness to avoid anti-theft devices on the floor and infra-red rays guarding the ceiling while delicately inserting a blank compact disc and making a copy of the secret spy identity file. Cruise is successful in accomplishing his mission, the American spies remain unidentified, and he can go on to accept his next mission impossible, or not. Based on the hit television series, 1966-1973 and 1988-1990, created by Bruce Geller, this action-packed thriller will rivet the viewer throughout. Songs: "Theme from Mission Impossible," "The Plot" (Lalo Schifrin), "Dreams" (Dolores O'Riordan, Noel Hogan), "Divertimento in E-Flat Major for String Trio, Third Movement" (Wolfgang Amadeus Mozart). Excessive violence prohibits viewing by children. **p**, Tom Cruise, Paula Wagner, Paul Hitchcock; **d**, Brian De Palma; **cast**, Cruise, Jon Voight, Emmanuelle Beart, Henry Czerny, Kristin Scott Thomas, Vanessa Redgrave, Jean Reno, Ving Rhames, Dale Dye, Marcel Iures, Emilio Estevez; **w**, David Koepp, Robert Towne (based on a story by Koepp, Steven Zaillian, and the television series by Bruce Geller); **c**, Stephen H. Burum; **m**, Danny Elfman; **ed**, Paul Hirsch; **prod d**, Norman Reynolds; **art d**, Frederick Hole, Jonathan McKinstry; **set d**, Peter Howitt; **spec eff**, Eric Allard, David

Beavis, John Knoll, Richard Yuricich.

Mission Impossible II ★★★ 2000; U.S.; 123m; PAR; Color; Spy Drama; Children: Unacceptable (MPAA: PG-13); **BD**; **DVD**. In the post–Cold War period, Ethan Hunt (Cruise), an agent of the IMF, the Impossible Missions Force, an unofficial branch of the CIA, is assigned to find and destroy the supply of a genetically created disease called "Chimera." It is an impossible mission because he is not the only person after samples of the disease. They are also being sought by international terrorists headed by a former IMF agent, Scott, who already stole the cure for the disease and needs Chimera in order to infect the world, out of cussedness or greed or both. Cruise gets help from an international jewel thief, Newton, who happens to be beautiful and with whom he falls in love. She is Scott's former girlfriend and is already infected by the disease, which causes a terrible and quick death. Cruise's mission takes him from Arizona and Utah to Spain and a dizzying car chase along an Australian seaside mountain highway. The impossibly Super Spy manages to get Chimera and its cure in time to save Newton for a possible sequel to this second of the film series based on the television series, 1966-1973 and 1988-1990, created by Bruce Geller. Songs:" Take a Look Around, Theme from M:1-2" (Lalo Schifrin, Fred Durst); "I Disappear" (James Hetfield, Lars Ulrich); "Iko-Iko," "Souca Na Na," "Don Toribio Carambola" (Domingo Gonzalez); "Danza de Ibio," "Viva la Virgin del Carmen," "Aslba y Camino," "Product" (Limp Bizkit); "My Kinda Scene" (Bernard Fanning) and "Scum of the Earth" (Rob Zombie). Excessive violence, brutality, and sexuality prohibit viewing by children. **p**, Tom Cruise, Paula Wang, Terence Chang, Paul Hitchcock; **d**, John Woo; **cast**, Cruise, Dougray Scott, Thandie Newton, Ving Rhames, Richard Roxburgh, John Polson, Brendan Gleeson, Rade Sherbedgia, William Mapother, Dominic Purcell, Anthony Hopkins; **w**, Robert Towne (based on a story by Ronald D. Moore, Brannon Braga, and the television series by Bruce Geller); **c**, Jeffrey L. Kimball; **m**, Hans Zimmer; **ed**, Steven Kemper, Christian Wagner; **prod d**, Thomas E. Sanders; **art d**, Nathan Crowley, Kevin Kavanaugh, Michelle McGahey, Daniel T. Dorrance; **set d**, Kerri Brown, Lauri Gaffin; **spec eff**, David P. Kelsey, Richard Yuricich.

Mission Impossible III ★★★ 2006; U.S.; 126m; PAR; Color; Spy Drama; Children: Unacceptable (MPAA: PG-13); **BD**; **DVD**. Super spy Ethan Hunt (Cruise), who has retired from active duty with the IMF, the Impossible Missions Force, an unofficial branch of the CIA, is called back into action to face his toughest villain yet, Hoffman, an international weapons and information provider. He and three others on his team (Rhames, Meyers, Q) try to rescue one of his trainees, Russell, who has been kidnapped while following Hoffman. This happens during Cruise's main mission, to beat Hoffman for control of a powerful device called the "Rabbit's Foot." The action, and plenty of it, takes Cruise to Berlin, to the Vatican City, to Shanghai for a leap off a skyscraper, and the Chesapeake Bay Bridge, all lifelike thanks to computer-generated imagery. Cruise reprises his trick from a previous film by hanging upside down again in a harness, this time in front of a speeding truck. Of course Cruise accomplishes the impossible mission he accepted and survives to take on another mission, although he is too late to save his wife in this adventure. The third of the film series based on the television series, 1966-1973 and 1998-1990, created by Bruce Geller, this one packs the same action-packed wallop as its two predecessors. Songs: "Mission Impossible Theme," The Plot" (Lalo Schifrin); "We Are Family" (Bernard Edwards, Nile Rodgers); "Come Into My Life" (Jimmy Cliff); "Song 5000" (J.J. Abrams); "Back Door Santa" (Marcus Lewis Daniel, Clarence George Carter); "Best of My Love" (Albert McKay, Maurice White); "A Sunday Kind of Love" (Louis Prima, Anita Nye, Stan Rhodes, Barbara Belle); "Tell Me Something Good" (Stevie Wonder); "Grokspoloitation" (Thomas Dolby, J.J. Abrams); "Impossible" (Kayne West, Carl Mitchell, Armando Manzanero, Sid Wayne); "String Quartet in C Minor" (Ludwig van Beethoven) and "String Quarter in B Major"

Tom Cruise in *Mission Impossible II,* **2000.**

(Joseph Haydn). Excessive violence and sensuality prohibit viewing by children. **p**, Tom Cruise, Paula Wagner, Hai Cheng Zhao, Arthur Anderson, Tao Jiang, Doming Shi, **d**, J.J. Abrams; **cast**, Cruise, Philip Seymour Hoffman, Ving Rhames, Billy Crudup, Michelle Monaghan, Jonathan Rhys Meyers, Keri Russell, Maggie Q, Simon Pegg, Laurence Fishburne, Eddie Marsan; **w**, Abrams, Alex Kurtzman, Roberto Orci (based on the television series by Bruce Geller); **c**, Daniel Mindel; **m**, Michael Giacchino; **ed**, Maryann Brandon, Nick Gibbs, Mary Jo Markey; **prod d**, Scott Chambliss; **art d**, Dennis Bradford, Stephen Bream, Daniel T. Dorrance; **set d**, Karen Manthey; **spec eff**, Renato Agostini, Bruce Law.

Mission Impossible: Ghost Protocol ★★★ 2011; U.S.; 133m; PAR; Color; Spy Drama; Children: Unacceptable (MPAA: PG-13); **BD**; **DVD**. In this fourth entry of the Mission Impossible series, super spy Ethan Hunt (Cruise), an agent of IMF, the Impossible Missions Force, an unofficial branch of the CIA, races against time to find and subdue Nyqvist, a bonkers terrorist, who has gained access to Russian nuclear launch codes and plans a strike on the United States. An explosion causes heavy damage to the Kremlin and the IMF is implicated in the bombing, forcing the U.S. President to invoke "Ghost Protocol" in which the government wants a job done, but offers no help or backup to IMF. Cruise and a new team of agents (Renner and Pegg) go rogue to trace Nyqvist to Dubai, then to Mumbai, to avoid a catastrophic disaster and clear their agency's name. There is lots of excitement along the way, the wildest being Cruise hanging upside-down outside the glass windows of the Burj Khalifa skyscraper in Dubai, at 100 stories, the world's tallest building, which is exciting to see in Blu-ray and even more thrilling in Imax format. Despite a scene in which Cruise dons steel mesh underwear and jumps into a ventilating shaft with spinning fan blades, he manages to survive and accomplish his mission, saving not only himself, but IMF and the United States. Based on the television series, 1966-1973 and 1988-1990, created by Bruce Geller, this is another stunning action-packed entry in the well-crafted series. Songs: "Ain't That a Kick in the Head" (Sammy Cahn, Jimmy Van Heusen) and "The Plot" (Lalo Schifrin). Excessive violence and sensuality prohibit viewing by children. **p**, J.J. Abrams, Bryan Burk, Tom Cruise, Tommy Harper, David Minkowski, Tim Smythe, Matthew Stillman; **d**, Brad Bird; **cast**, Tom Cruise, Jeremy Renner, Simon Pegg, Paula Patton, Michael Nyqvist, Vladimir Mashkov, Samuli Edelmann, Ivan Shvedoff, Anil Kapoor, Ving Rhames, Tom Wilkinson; **w**, Josh Applebaum, André Nemec (based on the television series "Mission Impossible" by Bruce Geller) **c**, Robert Elswit; **m**, Michael Giacchino; **ed**, Paul Hirsch; **prod d**, James D. Bissell; **art d**, Helen Jarvis, Christa Munro, Michael Diner, Michael Turner, Martin Vackár, Grant Van Der Slagt; **set d**, Rosemary

Tim Robbins and Gary Sinise in *Mission to Mars,* 2000.

Brandenburg, Andronico Del Rosario, Elizabeth Wilcox; **spec eff**, Michael Meinardus, Cameron Waldbauer, David Dozoretz, John Knoll, Jason Pomerantz.

Mission to Mars ★★★ 2000; U.S.; 114m; Touchstone Pictures/Buena Vista; Color; Science Fiction; Children: Unacceptable (MPAA: PG); **DVD**; **VHS**. Set in futuristic 2020, the U.S. launches a manned space-craft to Mars. Upon landing, astronauts Cheadle (the commander), Teed, Smith and Outerbridge discover a strange crystal formation within a mountain, but when they further investigate, they are engulfed by a fierce sandstorm that kills all but Cheadle, who transmits an urgent mes-sage to Earth, requesting rescue. A rescue mission is hurriedly assembled and another spacecraft containing astronauts Robbins, Sinise, O'Connell and Nielsen is launched and hurtles in space toward the Red Planet. The ship is caught in a meteorite storm just before landing, which damages the craft and forces the occupants to escape in pressurized suits to get into the module orbiting the planet, but, to save Nielsen, who is drifting away from the module, Robbins sacrifices his life. Sinise, Nielsen and O'Connell use the module to land on Mars and they locate Cheadle, who has survived by building a greenhouse and living on the vegetation he has raised. Cheadle tells them that he believes through his testing of samples on Mars that there is a higher form of life existing there, repre-senting a humanoid structure that was created in the sandstorm that de-stroyed his own ship. Upon investigation and through sending various transmissions, the astronauts see an opening in the structure. Cheadle, Sinise and Nielsen enter the structure while O'Connell waits outside of it in the spacecraft, ordered to take off with or without them if they do not return at a given time. Once inside, the opening of the structure closes, sealing the three astronauts inside and severing communication with O'Connell. They then see a three-dimensional image of the solar system projected before them, one that shows Mars as it appeared ages earlier, covered by water and how a giant asteroid strikes the planet, re-ducing it to ruins. A Martian creature then appears to explain that his species escaped Mars and traveled to a distant star, but sent a spacecraft to Earth, which crashed into one of its oceans and where its DNA even-tually evolved into fish, reptiles and, subsequently human beings, who would, as have these astronauts, eventually land on Mars and recognize themselves as the descendants of the long-ago Martians. The Martian tells the visitors that he will take one of them to his home planet, and Sinise volunteers. He is placed in a cylinder filled with liquid and be-lieves he is going to drown and holds his breath, but the liquid is highly oxygenated and he is able to breathe while encased within the liquid. Nielsen and Cheadle then rejoin O'Connell and they take off for a return trip to Earth, seeing the Martian spacecraft shoot past their own and wishing Sinise a safe journey to a new planet. Though this film was crit-icized by a bevy of film reviewers, who expected more or something other than what they got, the production is extremely well made and its visual design and digital enhancements, particularly the surface of Mars, is so detailed and realistically impressive that the film, along with good acting by the entire cast, is certainly worth the watching. It is reminiscent of some of the stories written by Ray Bradbury in his memorable *The Martian Chronicles* (1950), and Sinise's invitation to accompany the Martian to his own distant planet is a leaf taken from **Close Encounters of the Third Kind**, 1977, but the film nevertheless possesses its own distinctive imprimatur and identity. The Martians are exceptionally shown as benevolent in this film where in most others dealing with these mythical creatures they are decidedly warlike and lethal as can be seen in **The War of the Worlds**, 1953, and its 2005 remake, as well as Tim Burton's wacky send-up, **Mars Attacks!**, 1996. **p**, David S. Goyer, Tom Jacobson, Justis Greene, Jim Wedaa; **d**, Brian De Palma; **cast**, Gary Sinise, Tim Robbins, Don Cheadle, Jerry O'Connell, Connie Nielsen, Peter Outerbridge, Kavan Smith, Jill Teed, Elise Neal, Kim Delaney, Marilyn Norry, Freda Perry, Lynda Boyd, Patricia Harras; **w**, Jim Thomas, John Thomas, Graham Yost (based on a story by Lowell Can-non, Jim Thomas, John Thomas); **c**, Stephen H. Burum (Technicolor); **m**, Ennio Morricone; **ed**, Paul Hirsch; **prod d**, Ed Verreaux; **art d**, An-drew Neskoromny, Thomas Valentine; **set d**, Lin MacDonald; **spec eff**, Garry Elmendorf, Randy Shymkiw, Julie Creighton, Brennan Doyle.

Mission to Moscow ★★★ 1943; U.S.; 124m; WB; B/W; Biographical Drama; Children: Acceptable; **DVD**. Though highly propagandized, this is a well-made biopic of attorney and diplomat Joseph E. Davies (1876-1958), who was the U.S. Ambassador to Soviet Russia, 1936-1938, and who is brilliantly essayed by Huston. The film shows Huston and his family (Harding playing his wife, Marjorie Post Davies) first stopping in Germany before going to Moscow, and where the film depicts the dictatorial regime of Adolf Hitler, with Huston having guarded and ap-prehensive talks with Nazi Foreign Minister Joachim von Ribbentrop (1893-1946), who is played by Daniell. When Huston takes residence in Moscow, however, the film becomes somewhat of a travelogue show-ing contented and well-treated farm and factory workers, although these people were suffering under the same kind of brutal dictatorship of Joseph Stalin (1878-1953), who is played by Kippen. Huston also meets the leading communist leaders, including Maxim Litvinov (1876-1951), played by Homolka, and Vyacheslav Molotov (1890-1986), played by Lockhart. Huston narrates this tale, which was designed to present the Soviet Union as a staunch American ally and holding the same freedom-loving principles as the U.S. and other Western nations. Yet, much of the scenes misrepresent the true history of Stalin's savagely oppressive regime, particularly the segment where Huston describes how Stalin's blood purges of the mid-1930s were designed to ferret out Russian trai-tors in secret league with Nazi Germany and the war-mongering mili-tarists of Japan before WWII began. This, of course, was not the case. Stalin purged almost all of the high command and thousands of junior officers in the Russian army whom he thought might oppose his dicta-torship. The film is not reliable as a visual history, but is a hallmark ex-ample of pure Hollywood propaganda at its best and which is carefully and cleverly presented by pantheon director Curtiz, who was able to ob-tain and insert rare Soviet newsreel footage for this production which, in and of itself, has great value on a documentary basis. Other distin-guished figures shown in this political cavalcade include Winston Churchill (1874-1965), played by Malone; Pierre Laval (1883-1945), played by Chivra; Hjalmar Schacht (1877-1970), played by Basch; Nikolai Bukharin (1888-1938), played by Shayne; Leon Trotsky (1879-1940), played by Goldenberg; General Semen Timoshenko (1895-1970), played by Katch; Anthony Eden (1897-1977), played by Clive Morgan; Ignacy Jan Paderewski (1860-1941), played by Rameau; Mikhail Tukhachevsky (1893-1937), played by Triesault; Cordell Hull (1871-1955), played by Trowbridge; and U.S. President Franklin D. Roosevelt (1882-1945), played by Young. *Author's Note*: Davies, who had a clause in his contract that gave him complete approval of the script, turned down the original script for this film. Veteran screenwriter Koch was then brought in to rewrite the screenplay and, according to Koch's statements to this author: "Davies drove me crazy by picking apart every line of dialog, and wanted the script to be so pro-Soviet Russia that I thought at one point to have my name removed from the credits. I knew that this was a pet project of President Roosevelt and that Davies was conferring with FDR all through the production. The President was desperate to show a good face to Stalin so that Stalin would continue to mount major attacks on the German armies on the Eastern Front, which, Roosevelt felt, would weaken the German armies we would be facing on the Western Front when we later invaded France [D-Day in 1944]. In a way, FDR was really running the show for **Mission to Moscow**, and everybody at Warner Brothers knew it. Who was I to throw a monkey wrench into the American war effort and countermand the desires of the President? I wrote it the way he and Davies wanted it. Curtiz did not like it all and told me so: 'Making that goddamned Stalin look good causes my stomach to turn. He persecuted the Jews just as much as that stinking Hitler, and here I am promoting that murderer. I know we need Stalin in the fight, but every time I go on to the set, I want to puke.'" **p**, Robert Buckner; **d**, Michael Curtiz; **cast**, Walter Huston, Ann Harding, Oskar Homolka, George Tobias, Gene Lockhart, Eleanor Parker, Richard Travis, Helmut Dantine, Victor Francen, Henry Daniell, Roman Bohnen, Manart Kippen, Maria Palmer, Monte Blue, Dudley Field Malone, Charles Trowbridge, Jack Young, Alex Chivra, Felix Basch, Konstantin Shayne, Sam Goldenberg, Kurt Katch, Clive Morgan, Emil Rameau, Ivan Triesault, Cyd Charisse, Warren Douglas, Frieda Inescort, Kathleen Lockhart, Duncan Renaldo; **w**, Howard Koch (based on the book by Joseph E. Davies); **c**, Bert Glennon; **m**, Max Steiner; **ed**, Owen Marks; **art d**, Carl Jules Weyl; **set d**, George James Hopkins.

Mississippi ★★★ 1935; U.S.; 73m; PAR; B/W; Musical Comedy; Children: Acceptable; **VHS**. In this rousing, delightful trip down Old Man River, Crosby is a gentle swain wooing Patrick, a rather haughty Southern belle and whose father, Gillingwater, is the owner of a huge plantation. Miljan, a feisty officer in the Southern Army, also has eyes for Patrick and, to embarrass Crosby in front of her, starts an argument with Crosby and then challenges him to a duel. Crosby thinks Miljan is crazy and refuses to risk his life over an imagined insult. Patrick and Gillingwater, however, look upon Crosby's unwillingness to "defend his honor" as an act of cowardice and he is rejected by Patrick out of hand. Before he leaves, however, he receives the blessing of Bennett, Patrick's younger beautiful sister, who thinks that Crosby's pacifist actions are courageous and not that of a weakling. Disgraced in the eyes of the woman he loves, Crosby joins a showboat operated by the conniving Fields, who sees that the young man has great vocal talents and makes him his star attraction. Crosby warbles his way into the hearts of all the young ladies when the showboat periodically stops to entertain the local inhabitants, but he runs afoul of a roaring braggart and vicious thug, Kohler, who challenges Crosby to a royal battle in a saloon. When it comes time for the showdown, however, the thundering, stomping Kohler is so beside himself with rage over Crosby's taunts that he winds up shooting and killing himself. Crosby is hailed a hero for dispatching the worst scourge on the Mississippi, and Fields makes capital of his victory by renaming Crosby "The Singing Killer." When Bennett arrives to see him singing under his new sobriquet, she becomes disturbed, now believing that the gentle soul she has loved from afar is as violent as most of the men in the South. Crosby tries to explain to Bennett that he is not a bloodthirsty villain and that Kohler did himself in, but Kohler's demise presents yet another problem in that he was a cousin to Patrick and Bennett, another unintentional offense Crosby has made against a family he wants to join. Crosby, by this time, is no longer interested in the aloof Patrick and her airy ways, but has fallen deeply in love with the compassionate and kind Bennett and is now determined to make her his own. To that end, he goes to her plantation, and when encountering

Bing Crosby and W. C. Fields in *Mississippi*, 1935.

bully Miljan, along with his equally offensive friend, Pawley, Crosby thrashes both men to cowering pulps. He then storms upstairs, breaks down the door to Bennett's room, and then takes Bennett into his arms, kissing her. Bennett can no longer resist Crosby and they plan to wed for the fadeout. The tale is a tall one, but in keeping with the tempestuous Old South and its reputation of being chivalrous to the point of idiocy. Crosby is in wonderful voice as he sings some great traditional songs and several Rodgers and Hart tunes, three of which became enormous hits. The cantankerous Fields has several side-splitting scenes, not the least of which is a sequence where he is playing poker with some very mean-looking types and finds that he has dealt himself five aces. While his fellow gamblers leer at him menacingly, Fields discards this overwhelming hand and deals himself some new cards, but these cards are all aces, too! Songs: "Oh! Susanna," "Old Folks at Home (Swanee River)" (Stephen Foster); "Little David" (composer unknown); "Viva La Company" (traditional); "There's No Place Like Home (Home, Sweet, Home)" (Sicilian air, partly composed and arranged by H.R. Bishop); "It's Easy to Remember (And So Hard to Forget)," "Down by the River," "Soon," and "Roll Mississippi" (Richard Rodgers and Lorenz Hart). This was the third and best version of the Tarkington play, the first being a silent production entitled **The Fighting Coward**, 1924. It was remade as an early talkie entitled **River of Romance**, 1929. *Author's Note*: Crosby was not the first selection to play the lead in this film. Producers wanted Lanny Ross in the role, but when they saw some rushes of Crosby trying out for the part, the role went to the great crooner. Crosby told this author that "I never worked with Fields until we made **Mississippi**. He was as much a colorful character off screen as he was before the cameras and anyone trying to take a scene away from him risked body and limb. That man knew every sneaky, slippery and underhanded trick in stealing a scene and he used them all, from fluttering fingers to squinting eyes, in that picture we made together." **p**, Arthur Hornblow Jr.; **d**, A. Edward Sutherland; **cast**, Bing Crosby, W. C. Fields, Joan Bennett, Gail Patrick, Queenie Smith, Claude Gillingwater, John Miljan, Edward Pawley, Fred Kohler, John Larkin, Libby Taylor, Harry Myers, Theresa Maxwell Conover, Paul Hurst; **w**, Francis Martin, Jack Cunningham, Claude Binyon, Herbert Fields (based on the play "Magnolia" by Booth Tarkington), **c**, Charles Lang, Karl Struss; **ed**, Chandler House; **art d**, Hans Dreier, Bernard Herzbrun.

Mississippi Burning ★★★ 1988; U.S.; 128m; Orion Pictures; Color; Crime Drama; Children: Unacceptable; **DVD**; **VHS**. Viewers will be riveted to this hard-hitting crime yarn, based on real events, where FBI agents attempt to identify the killers of three civil rights workers, their investigation leading them to a group of Ku Klux Klan bigots, who rule the roost in a rural Mississippi county. Northern-bred liberal Dafoe is

Piper Laurie, Tyrone Power and Robert Warwick in *The Mississippi Gambler*, 1953.

the young FBI agent in charge of the probe, who is aided by (but is often at odds with) Mississippi native Hackman, a former sheriff, who better understands the backward mentality of the rural people, who shield the culprits, out of pride or fear. Dafoe plays by the rules but gets nowhere until Hackman befriends McDormand, the hard-working wife of deputy sheriff Dourif, and learns the location where the three bodies of the civil rights workers can be located. After they are found in a swamp, Dourif, realizing that McDormand has served as an informant to the FBI, viciously attacks McDormand, her injuries sending her to a hospital. The enraged Hackman seeks violent retaliation, but Dafoe holds him in check.However, Dafoe now agrees to employ Hackman's unorthodox measures. The local mayor, Ermey, is abducted and taken to a shack where he is threatened by a black vigilante, Djola, who forces him to provide the identification of the KKK members involved in the kidnapping-killings. Ermey is then released and we see that Djola is really an FBI agent playing the part of a black terrorist, who has been imported from the North for this special assignment. The information Djola has gotten is not admissible in a court of law, but it now allows Dafoe and Hackman to go after the actual perpetrators and do so, but employ the same kind of subterfuge. Dafoe and Hackman then send notices to all the KKK members involved, ostensibly calling them to a meeting they think comes from their ringleader, local businessman Tobolowsky, and when they meet in a church, all then realize that they have been set up and quickly disperse, but they are now under FBI observation with all of their identities established. Dafoe and Hackman then select the most weak-willed member of the Klan, Vince, and, pretending to be KKK members, attack Vince's home and later, while agents wear hoods, kidnap him, but where he is rescued by other agents, who now appear to Vince as his only means of survival. Vince turns informant and with his information Tobolowsky, Dourif and the others are brought to trial. They are convicted of civil rights violations that send most of the culprits to prison for several years. Meanwhile, Ermey, the mayor of the town, is found by FBI agents in his home, a suicide by hanging. Although Ermey was not a member of the KKK gang that murdered the civil rights activists, he has taken his life, according to Dafoe, because "he was guilty...we are all guilty," This taut and often terrifying film is brilliantly directed by Parker, and Dafoe, Hackman, McDormand and the rest of the cast present electrifying performances. *Author's Note*: The film is based on the June 21, 1964, kidnappings and murders of three civil rights workers (belonging to the Congress of Racial Equality or CORE) in Philadelphia, Mississippi, by members of the Ku Klux Klan, the victims being Michael Henry Schwerner (1939-1964), played by Nauffts; Andrew Goodman (1943-1964), played by Zieff; and James Chaney (1943-1964), played by White. In 1967, seven members of the local KKK, including a deputy sheriff, were convicted in federal court of vi-

olating the civil rights of these three young men, the only federal law that applied to the case at that time, and received prison sentences. This story was also presented as a two-part made-for-TV docudrama titled **Attack on Terror: The FBI vs. the Ku Klux Klan**, 1975. For more information on this case and the long and oppressive history of the Ku Klux Klan in the U.S., see my two-volume work, *The Great Pictorial History of World Crime*, Volume II (History, Inc., 2004, pages 1481-1494). **p**, Robert F. Colesberry, Frederick Zollo; **d**, Alan Parker; **cast**, Gene Hackman, Willem Dafoe, Frances McDormand, Brad Dourif, R. Lee Ermey, Gailard Sartain, Stephen Tobolowsky, Michael Rooker, Pruitt Taylor Vince, Badja Djola, Kevin Dunn, Geoffrey Nauffts, Rick Zieff, Christopher White; **w**, Chris Gerolmo; **c**, Peter Biziou; **m**, Trevor Jones; **ed**, Gerry Hambling; **prod d**, Philip Harrison, Geoffrey Kirkland; **art d**, John Willett; **set d**, Jim Erickson; **spec eff**, Stan Parks.

The Mississippi Gambler ★★★ 1953; U.S.; 99m; UNIV; Color; Adventure; Children: Acceptable; **DVD**. The handsome Power is captivating as a noble gentleman gambler, the son of a New York fencing master, who tries his luck on the Mississippi river boats. He bests Baer in a poker game, and Baer, the arrogant son of a wealthy Southern family, pays off his debt to Power by giving him an expensive necklace that is really owned by his beautiful sister, Laurie. Power will not think of keeping the family heirloom and attempts to return it to Laurie, but the haughty Southern belle rejects his chivalrous gesture, looking upon him as riverboat riffraff and not worthy of her illustrious company. Power then partners with veteran gambler McIntire, both planning to open a posh gambling casino in New Orleans, vowing that their play will be honest and upright. Power makes many new friends through his honest operations, including Cavanagh, the father of Baer and Laurie. He gives Laurie's necklace to Cavanagh, who then returns it to his daughter, but Laurie continues to express contempt for Power. Weak-willed Weaver then loses all his money to Power and takes his life, leaving his attractive sister, Adams, penniless. The compassionate Power then becomes Adams' financial guardian, and when she is seen with him by Laurie, the southern belle becomes jealously enraged—she is secretly in love with Power, but cannot bring herself to admit it. Baer then falls in love with Adams, but she sees only Power, and Baer challenges Power to a duel where Baer fires before the appointed time and Power refuses to fire at him. The disgraced Baer then departs as an outcast from his family, which further incenses the fiery Laurie and, who, out of spite, marries Randell, a banker she does not love. Power later meets Baer on a riverboat, where Baer tries to kill him but dies from his own hand when he accidentally falls on his own knife. Power then learns that Cavanagh is dying after having fought a duel in defending Power's honor and returns to New Orleans to be with his friend in his final hours. Meanwhile, Randell's embezzlement has caused a run on his bank and Power and McIntire lose the fortune when the bank collapses. Undaunted, Power boards another riverboat sailing northward to make another fortune when Laurie arrives to tell him that Randell has abandoned her. She admits that she has always loved Power and he tells her he knows it before taking her into his arms for the happy fadeout. Director Maté unfolds this Southern saga with great vitality, and the production values are high. In addition to Power's forceful performance, Laurie, Baer, Adams and Cavanagh are outstanding in their roles. Songs: "De Lawd's Plan" (Henry Mancini, Frank Skinner), "Haitian Devil Song" (LeRoi Antoine). *Author's Note*: Riverboat gamblers and dueling in the Old South are profiled in such films as **Huckleberry Finn**, 1931; **Mississippi**, 1935; **Steamboat Round the Bend**, 1935; **Showboat**, 1936; **Jezebel**, 1938; **Huckleberry Finn**, 1939; **The Foxes of Harrow**, 1947; **The Secret Life of Walter Mitty**, 1947; **Showboat**, 1951; **The Iron Mistress**, 1952; **The Kentuckian**, 1955; and **The Adventures of Huckleberry Finn**, 1960. **p**, Ted Richmond; **d**, Rudolph Maté; **cast**, Tyrone Power, Piper Laurie, Julie Adams, John McIntire, Paul Cavanagh, John Baer, Ron Randell, Robert Warwick, William Reynolds, Guy Williams, Hugh Beaumont, Anita Ekberg, Gwen Verdon, Dennis Weaver; **w**, Seton I.

Miller; **c**, Irving Glassberg (Technicolor); **m**, Frank Skinner; **ed**, Edward Curtiss; **art d**, Alexander Golitzen, Richard H. Riedel; **set d**, Russell A. Gausman, Julia Heron.

Mississippi Mermaid ★★★ 2009; France/Italy; 123m; Les Films du Carrosse/The Film Desk; Color; Mystery; Children: Unacceptable (MPAA: PG); **DVD**; **VHS**. Belmondo is a millionaire tobacco planter living on the African island of Reunion in the Indian Ocean who has a pen-pal engagement with a beautiful woman, Deneuve. When she arrives on a French ocean liner called the *Mississippi*, he is surprised to find that she doesn't look like the photograph she has mailed to him. She tells him she sent a photo of a less attractive friend, so that he would not marry her for her beauty. He swallows that and marries her, but she soon steals most of his money and runs away. He searches and finds her working as a dance hall hostess on the Riviera. He had planned to kill her, but relents when she explains she was an orphan and was molested as a child. Belmondo believes and forgives her, taking her back to his plantation. He doesn't know that she and her boyfriend, Thénot, murdered the girl in the photo and she assumed her identity and now Belmondo is in more trouble than he knows. This good thriller is highlighted by the chilling performance of the exquisitely beautiful Deneuve, who is the essence of evil, the kind of insidious and artfully lethal character that would be personified by Theresa Russell in **Black Widow**, 1987. Violence and sensuality prohibit viewing by children. Made in 1969, this film was not released in U.S. theaters until 2009. This film was remade in 2001 as **Original Sin** with Antonio Banderas and Angelina Jolie. (In French; English subtitles.) **p**, François Truffaut, Marcel Berbert; **d&w**, Truffaut (based on the novel *Waltz into Darkness* by William Irish (Cornell Woolrich); **cast**, Jean-Paul Belmondo, Catherine Deneuve, Nelly Borgeaud, Martine Ferrière, Berbert, Yves Drouhet, Roland Thénot; **c**, Denys Clerval (Eastmancolor); **m**, Antoine Duhamel; **ed**, Agnès Guillemot; **prod d&set d**, Claude Pignot.

The Missouri Breaks ★★★ 1976; U.S.; 126m; Devon/Persky-Bright/UA; Color; Western; Children: Unacceptable (MPAA: PG); **DVD**; **VHS**. Brando mesmerizes in this oddball oater where he is a berserk gun-for-hire who is employed to track down horse rustlers. His prey consists of a small band of thieves made up of Nicholson, Stanton, Quaid and Ryan. The film opens with Nicholson and company rustling some horses and then setting up a relay station for those horses before they can be sold off, that station being a small farm Nicholson buys and where he pretends to actually work the place. His neighbor, McLiam, who owns a large spread, has a feisty daughter, Lloyd, who attempts to seduce Nicholson, which complicates his life in that he begins to fall in love with her. After several of his horses are rustled and his foreman is murdered in retaliation for the lynching of a rustler, McLiam hires bounty hunter Brando, who immediately suspects Nicholson is no farmer and is part of the rustling gang. Brando visits Nicholson's farm several times, harassing him with an harrowing exhibition of pistol shooting, but Nicholson has finally had enough and goes to McLiam's home where Brando is staying, finding him in a bubble bath. He thinks to shoot him, but forgoes the opportunity. Brando nevertheless tracks down Nicholson's friends. He pretends to be a preacher, befriending Quaid, sharing his dinner with him on the open range and then drowns him the next day. He finds Ryan in an outhouse and shoots him. He sets fire to a hut, driving Stanton out into the open and, while wearing a dress and a bonnet, kills him by hurling a spike-like object into his head. Nicholson is last on his list, but Nicholson has outfoxed him and anticipated his next move. Brando awakes one night on the prairie with a startled look on his face. Nicholson stands over him and laconically remarks: "You've just had your throat slit," and departs, leaving Brando to bleed to death. Nicholson then goes to McLiam's home to wreak vengeance on him, but finds that he has turned idiot. He packs up his belongings and meets one last time with Lloyd. She, too, has packed all she owns and, after they bid farewell, they drive their wagons in oppo-

Marlon Brando and Jack Nicholson in *The Missouri Breaks*, 1976.

site directions. Penn directs this film with skillful care, incisively developing his characters, and Nicholson, Brando and the rest of the cast impressively represent the grim, gaunt and desperate characters they essay. *Author's Note*: "I wanted to show the Old West the way I believe it truly was," Penn told this author. "Even the well-off are shown living crude and unsophisticated lives. Everyone, from the honest ranchers and their wives and children, to the horse thieves, are grubbing along to survive. Their clothes are homespun and threadbare and they have holes in their hats and boots. They live with tired maxims and are haunted by cheap gossip and rumor. When they try to bring some order into their lives by hiring an enforcer with a fierce reputation, they wind up getting a maniac, who further disrupts their lives. Nothing was reliable in those days and that is what I wanted to present." Brando explained his character this way to this author: "I am a certifiable lunatic in **The Missouri Breaks**, a man who enjoys killing people. I am playing the role of a cunning killer, who has an ego that demands that he be much worse than the outlaws he is hired to track down. I suppose that I confused Jack [Nicholson] and other actors in that strange picture with my impromptu gibberish, but that is part of my character. The outlaws I am chasing are reasonable men, but I am crazy as a loon. I use my insanity as a weapon to strike fear in those I am hunting and I always do the unexpected, until Jack [Nicholson] does the same thing to me." **p**, Elliott Kastner, Robert M. Sherman; **d**, Arthur Penn; **cast**: Marlon Brando, Jack Nicholson, Kathleen Lloyd, Randy Quaid, Frederic Forrest, Harry Dean Stanton, John McLiam, John Ryan, Sam Gilman, Steve Franken, Richard Bradford, James Greene, Luana Anders; **w**, Thomas McGuane; **c**, Michael Butler (DeLuxe Color); **m**, John Williams; **ed**, Jerry Greenberg, Stephen A. Rotter, Dede Allen; **prod d**, Albert Brenner; **art d**, Stephen Berger; **set d**, Marvin March; **spec eff**, A. D. Flowers.

The Missouri Traveler ★★★ 1958; U.S.; 103m; C.V. Whitney/Buena Vista; Color; Drama; Children: Acceptable; **DVD**. This well-made drama presents a heartwarming story about De Wilde, a fifteen-year-old orphan who becomes a runaway and tries to make it on his own as a farmer. Merrill, a kindly newspaper editor in a nearby town, takes him under his wing, but he learns some rough lessons while a tough local, Marvin, shows him how to survive in a hard, cruel world. **p**, Patrick Ford, Lowell J. Farrell; **d**, Jerry Hopper; **cast**, Brandon De Wilde, Lee Marvin, Gary Merrill, Paul Ford, Mary Hosford, Ken Curtis, Mary Field, Will Wright, Cal Tinney, Frank Cady, Eddie Little Sky; **w**, Norman Sherman Hall (based on a novel by John Burress); **c**, Winton C. Hoch (Technicolor); **m**, Jack Marshall; **ed**, Tom McAdoo; **art d**, Jack Okey.

Mister 880 ★★★ 1950; U.S.; 90m; FOX; B/W; Drama; Children: Unacceptable; **DVD**; **VHS**. Gwenn gives another memorable performance,

Burt Lancaster, Edmund Gwenn, and Dorothy McGuire in *Mister 880*, **1950.**

this time as a cheerful old man, who is also an amateur counterfeiter in New York City, and who has amazingly managed to elude the police for twenty years. Lancaster, a federal agent assigned to the case, tracks one of the fake bills to McGuire, a translator at the United Nations. She says she got the bill from her neighbor, Gwenn, and Lancaster soon discovers the kindly old gentleman is the counterfeiter. Lancaster and McGuire have fallen in love and it becomes very difficult for Lancaster to turn Gwenn in. He goes to bat for Gwenn, as does McGuire, and where Lancaster points out in court that Gwenn only printed a few bills now and then to survive, and wound up giving most of the money to others in need. A sympathetic judge gives him a reduced sentence. Gwenn takes every scene in which he appears in this fascinating story. Songs: "National Anthem" (Edwin Eugene Bagley), "I'm Looking Over a Four-Leaf Clover" (Harry M. Woods), "Auld Lang Syne" (traditional). **p**, Julian Blaustein; **d**, Edmund Goulding; **cast**, Burt Lancaster, Dorothy McGuire, Edmund Gwenn, Millard Mitchell, Minor Watson, Howard St. John, Hugh Sanders, James Millican, Rico Alaniz, Polly Bailey; **w**, Robert Riskin (based on the *New Yorker* article "Old Eight Eighty" by St. Clair McKelway); **c**, Joseph LaShelle; **m**, Sol Kaplan; **ed**, Robert Fritch; **art d**, Lyle Wheeler, George W. Davis; **set d**, Paul S. Fox, Thomas Little; **spec eff**, Fred Sersen.

Mister Roberts ★★★★ 1955; U.S.; 123m; WB; Color; Drama; Children: Acceptable; **DVD**; **VHS**. In this riveting drama, Fonda, in the title role, is a sensitive cargo officer on board a U.S. Navy supply ship wallowing in the backwaters of the Pacific in WWII. He longs for combat as he thinks he is not contributing to the war effort and is further frustrated by a dictatorial captain, Cagney, who treats his crew members as galley slaves. Fonda finds some solace with Powell, the elderly ship's physician, and is amused by junior officer Lemmon, who is always threatening to vex and harass Cagney by collecting marbles so that he can roll them around above the captain's quarters. Lemmon, in fact, has been avoiding Cagney for months and Cagney is surprised when he discovers that Lemmon is on board and one of his officers, learning that he is in charge of morale and the laundry. Cagney compliments him for his good work, but tells the cowering Lemmon to put less starch in his shirts. At one point, the mercury that Lemmon has been hoarding to make a firecracker to frighten Cagney accidentally explodes and wrecks the laundry, causing the corridors below decks to be filled with suds and providing considerable laughs for Powell and Fonda, but all of Lemmon's goofy ploys do not offset the miserable and oppressive attitude shown by Cagney, who routinely restricts his crew from shore leave. At one point, Lemmon invites some nurses, led by voluptuous Palmer, to inspect the ship, but their visit is short-lived when Palmer discovers that the crew members have been ogling them with binoculars when they

have been showering in their quarters ashore. Meanwhile, Fonda writes another of his many letters to higher command, asking for a transfer to combat duty, but Cagney again routinely refuses to send on the letter, knowing Fonda is the best cargo officer he could have and wants to keep him on board, almost as an indentured servant. Fonda defies him and Cagney takes his revenge by again canceling liberty for the crew. In order to get Cagney's approval to allow the crew liberty, Fonda agrees that he will no longer defy him and will obey his orders without question and that he will not tell anyone on board that he has made this agreement with Cagney. Fonda then seems to be distant and no longer the sympathetic officer the crew members earlier appreciated, but they learn through Powell his sacrifice for them and they smuggle one of his letters from the ship so that it is delivered and Fonda is finally given new orders to transfer to a destroyer where he will see front line action. Before he departs, Fonda is given a makeshift medal from the crew, the Order of the Palm, which mocks the sickly palm tree Cagney nurtures outside his cabin and is the symbol of his tyranny, a medal that Fonda prizes more than if he had received the Congressional Medal of Honor. The news reaches the ship that Fonda has been killed and his last letter to Powell is read to the crew, one that touches them all as he praises their indomitable spirit. The letter is posted, and Lemmon takes Fonda's place, becoming the executive cargo officer. When he hears that Cagney has again given one of his severe commands, he charges up to the captain's quarters, grabs the scrawny palm tree that Cagney keeps outside his cabin and has been nurturing for months, and tosses it overboard, then barges into Cagney's cabin and shouts at him for again restricting the crew, taking up the same defiant role Fonda had maintained and where Cagney realizes that his miserable life has just gotten a lot more miserable. This compassionate and telling story, as did the successful play, focuses largely on Fonda's character. Fonda in his bravura, priceless performance presents a quintessential American male, a humane, optimistic, patriotic and self-sacrificing man, as heroic as any front-line serviceman. Cagney is also superlative as the dominating, petty and cruel captain, a thankless role that he nevertheless presents with consummate vigor and venom. Lemmon is outstanding as the cowering Ensign Pulver (his role later expanded into several offshoot productions) whose empty promises in wreaking vengeance on Cagney are pathetic, but heart-tugging in their boyish intentions and where he transforms into Fonda's strong and resolute character through Fonda's father figure example. Veteran actor Powell, too, provides great emotional stability as the avuncular and sympathetic ship's doctor, and the rest of the cast, including Ford's favorite character actor, Bond, to Adams, Carey, Curtis and others make up a wonderful ensemble of the fun-loving crew longing for peace, home and their loved ones. Song: "If I Could Be With You One Hour Tonight" (James P. Johnson, Henry Creamer). *Author's Note*: This production saw problems long before it got into production. Logan, who wrote the play with Heggen (based on Heggen's novel) as well as the screenplay with Nugent, argued from the beginning with studio bosses, insisting that he direct the film version. He was overruled but mollified by the Warner Brothers front office when they gave Logan more money than what was called for, or essentially paid him *not* to direct the film. As a result, Logan never liked the film and regretted signing over the property for a later produced TV series. Pantheon director Ford was then given the directing job, and he was later replaced by LeRoy, and Logan felt that both of these distinguished directors, in order to present the story in its most common aspects and appeal to the broadest audience, demonstrated Lemmon's comedic pranks and antics as more slapstick than funny mishaps, which Logan never intended. He had, with Heggen as his co-writer when adapting the novel for the stage, certainly wanted to incorporate the farcical elements of the story, but he wanted to underscore and emphasize its serious elements. Lemmon told this author that "I was in the early part of my career then and I did what I was told, playing my part as a youthful buffoon until the end when I mature as a man. I know that Logan did not like my interpretation of Ensign Pulver, but I was following orders from Ford and LeRoy and who was I at that time to tell them what to do? Well, those great directors must have had something on the ball, because the role I played at their very specific instruction got for me an Academy Award as Best Supporting Actor and really sent my career into orbit." Cagney, as he always did, enacts the role of the tyrannical captain, by using all of his eye-catching techniques, from the eye-rolling slow burn to fist-pounding, feet-stomping rage. "I am emotionally adolescent in my role as Captain Morton," Cagney told this author. "Here is a fellow who resents any college-bred officers like Fonda because he has never had much formal education and has come up from the ranks to achieve his position. He takes revenge on poor Fonda for all the abuse and insults he got from college boys when he was waiting tables for them as a young man. This guy lives for revenge, a terrible man, infected with the poison of constant anger. I am more of an easy prop for Fonda's bad situation, a man who has lost his good common sense to a rage that burns in his brain like a wildfire. At least that's how I saw him and that's how I played him. In that same year, I played a similar character, a gangster, who is resentful of entertainment big shots, who give him the air when he promotes a singer [Doris Day], a girl he loves, in **Love Me or Leave Me**, 1955. For that role I received an Oscar nomination, but not for **Mister Roberts**, only because my role was not really that substantial, other than acting as the boogieman." The most serious problem with the production was the disintegrating relationship between Ford and Fonda. Ford had directed Fonda in many films that established Fonda's career as a foremost leading player (**Young Mr. Lincoln**, 1939; **Drums along the Mohawk**, 1939; **The Grapes of Wrath**, 1940), and they had always gotten along with each other. Fonda, however, had distanced himself in later years from Hollywood, preferring to act on the Broadway stage (and also preferring to live in New York City). He had appeared in several hit plays, including "Point of No Return," "The Caine Mutiny Court Martial," and, particularly, "Mister Roberts," and felt that he understood the "Roberts" character better than any director, including his one-time mentor, Ford. For his part, Ford felt that Fonda had "gone high hat with all that toney Broadway methodology," as he told this author. "Like it does with all actors and actresses who become big stage stars, Hank [Fonda] felt that no one could tell him what to do anymore and that he knew everything. Hank's head had gotten as big as the Goodyear blimp because of all that phony praise from Broadway, which feeds an actor's ego with the same kind of poison a junkie shoots into his veins when taking a shot of heroin. He wasn't the Hank Fonda I knew anymore and when I tried to tell him what I wanted, he more or less told me to go to hell, so I popped him hard and sent him to the floor and I don't regret that to this day." Fonda's version of this traumatic encounter that ruptured that relationship forever was recalled much differently. This author met Fonda for the first time in 1956, which was one year after **Mister Roberts** was released, when he was visiting my alma mater, Marquette University, in Milwaukee, Wisconsin, meeting with his old friend, Father Walsh, head of the university's drama department. One of the first questions I put to Fonda was to ask him about John Ford. He sat quietly on a high stool on a small stage, saying nothing for some time and then slowly said with a long hiss: "John Ford is a ssssonofabitch!" He went on to state that "Ford was drinking heavily when the production for **Mister Roberts** began, swilling down two cases of cold beer every day during the production until, on some occasions, he would pass out." After one of the first scenes Fonda had with Powell, Ford called him into his office and Fonda found Ford lying on a couch where, according to Fonda "he was pretty much drunk." Ford had been told by some of the other actors that Fonda had been complaining about Ford's direction in a scene between Fonda and Powell, and where Powell, then getting on in years, fumbled with some of his lines. "Ford didn't bother to get up from the couch and barked at me: 'I understand that you didn't like the work we did today.' I told him that I was not happy with the scene we did with Powell that day. With that, he jumped up and hit me as hard as he could on the jaw and I saw stars and fell backward onto the floor. He stood over me, fists clenched, waiting for me to get up and give him

James Cagney and Henry Fonda in *Mister Roberts*, 1955.

battle, but I was not about to get into a fistfight with an old, drunken man. I shook my head, got to my feet and left without another word to him." It was later reported that Ford and Fonda had several brawls, but these fistfights were the imaginations of gossip-mongers. "Ford later came to me and apologized for attacking me, but I was in no mood to forgive that kind of behavior. He knew we were finished as co-workers and I wanted no more part of him." Ford's deteriorating physical condition ended that relationship when he suffered a gall bladder attack and went to the hospital and where he was replaced by LeRoy. The story was surrounded by dissatisfaction and tragedy from its beginning, particularly when it came to its creator, Heggen (1918-1949), who became so successful when writing the novel and then the play adaptation with Logan that it destroyed his life. The novel is based upon his own life. Heggen, a graduate of the University of Minnesota with a degree in journalism, enlisted in the U.S. Navy immediately after the attack on Pearl Harbor on December 7, 1941. In August 1942, Heggen was commissioned a lieutenant and sent to the Pacific where he served on supply ships in the Atlantic, Mediterranean, and, mostly, in the Pacific. He consistently requested that he be transferred to a destroyer so that he could see front-line duty, but his requests were repeatedly denied by a dictatorial captain. While serving in the backwaters of the war, Heggen wrote vignettes about his fellow crew members and the shenanigans they created to enliven their otherwise dull and eventful service. Heggen described that service where his ship moved from one tranquil port to another as sailing "from Tedium to Apathy and back again, with an occasional side trip to Monotony." Following the war, he wrote the novel, which is largely autobiographical and where he based the "Roberts" character on his own life and experience. The novel proved to be an enormous success, selling more than a million copies and making Heggen rich. His wealth increased when the play adaptation became a Broadway smash with Fonda in the lead role. Pressured to write another bestseller, Heggen complained of "writer's block" and, to stimulate his imagination, took to heavy drinking, supplemented with prescription drugs. He was found dead in a bathtub at age thirty on May 19, 1949. His death ruled a probable suicide through an overdose of alcohol and drugs, although some claimed it was purely an accident. His wealth, including his share of the profits from this film, went to his sister, who lived in the Midwest. **p**, Leland Hayward; **d**, John Ford, Mervyn LeRoy; **cast**, Henry Fonda, James Cagney, William Powell, Jack Lemmon, Betsy Palmer, Ward Bond, Philip Carey, Nick Adams, Perry Lopez, Ken Curtis, Harry Carey, Jr., Patrick Wayne, William Henry, Martin Milner, Duke Kahanamoku; **w**, Joshua Logan, Frank S. Nugent (based on the play by Logan and Thomas Heggen and the novel by Heggen); **c**, Winton C. Hoch (CinemaScope; Warnercolor); **m**, Franz Waxman; **ed**, Jack Murray; **art d**, Art Loel; **set d**, William L. Keuhl.

John Barrymore, right, in _Moby Dick_, 1930.

Misty ★★★ 1961; U.S.; 93m; FOX; Color; Children's Adventure; Children: Recommended; **VHS**. Each year the fire department of Chincoteague, a town on the coast of Virginia, round up the wild ponies of Assateague Island and auction off the colts and yearlings to thin out the herd. Ladd, a twelve-year-old boy, and his younger sister, Smith, are orphans, who live with their grandparents, O'Connell and Seymour. The kids have their hearts set on owning one of the ponies, a three-year-old mare known as Phantom. During the annual Pony Penning Day roundup by locals, the kids capture Phantom and her foal, which they call Misty. They put up $100 at the auction, but a man claims to own the ponies. Phantom goes to live with its owner, but thanks to the help from the locals, Misty can remain with the kids. A beloved story made into a wonderful family-friendly film. **p**, Robert B. Radnitz; **d**, James B. Clark; **cast**, David Ladd, Arthur O'Connell, Pam Smith, Anne Seymour, Duke Farley; **w**, Ted Sherdeman (based on the novel _Misty of Chincoteague_ by Marguerite Henry); **c**, Lee Garmes, Leo Tover; **m**, Paul Sawtell, Bert Shefter; **ed**, Fredrick Y. Smith; **art d**, Duncan Cramer, Maurice Ransford; **set d**, Walter M. Scott, Stuart A. Reiss.

The Mob ★★★ 1951; U.S.; 87m; COL; B/W; Crime Drama; Children: Unacceptable; **DVD**; **VHS**. Crawford, a tough cop, goes undercover to pose as a corrupt New Orleans dock worker to learn which mobsters are running the waterfront. The mob chief, known as "Smoothie" (Crowley), has enforcers Brand and Borgnine find out if Crawford is worthy of trust and they believe he is. Crawford infiltrates the mob, learning to his surprise that Kiley is another cop also masquerading as a crook in order to identify the mob's ringleaders. Using the same brutal tactics as the mobsters they consort with (beating up informants and threatening others with death), both learn that Crowley is the mob leader, and, in a final showdown, Crowley is gunned down by police to bring peace back to the docks. Solid action-packed crime yarn sees good performances all around. _Author's Note_: In one sequence, Crawford and Kiley employ a liquid that glows in the dark in order to follow Crowley's auto, a device used by Basil Rathbone in **Sherlock Holmes and the Secret Weapon**, 1943. **p**, Jerry Bresler; **d**, Robert Parrish; **cast**, Broderick Crawford, Betty Buehler, Richard Kiley, Otto Hulett, Matt Crowley, Neville Brand, Ernest Borgnine, Lynne Baggett, Jean Alexander, John Marley, Diana Barrymore, Charles Bronson, Carleton Young; **w**, William Bowers (based on the novel _Waterfront_ by Ferguson Findley); **c**, Joseph Walker; **m**, George Duning; **ed**, Charles Nelson; **art d**, Cary Odell; **set d**, Frank Tuttle.

Moby Dick ★★★ 1930; U.S.; 80m; WB; B/W; Adventure; Children: Unacceptable; **DVD**; **VHS**. Although this version plays fast and loose with the original Melville tale, it is nevertheless a rousing adventure tale

starring Barrymore, who reprises his role as Ahab from the silent classic, **The Sea Beast**, 1926. Barrymore is an honest seaman, who runs afoul of his evil stepbrother, Hughes, who is a sea predator, both men loving the same woman, Bennett. When both are on a voyage to hunt whales, Hughes knocks Barrymore over the side and his leg is bitten off by the great white whale, Moby Dick. He is plucked from the sea and the stump of his leg is cauterized on deck while several men hold him down as he screams in pain (not a scene for the squeamish). When returning to New Bedford, Barrymore is a hideous sight, stomping about on a peg-leg, and, when Bennett sees him in his painful and debilitating condition, she recoils in horror and runs away from him. This leads Barrymore to conclude that Bennett has fallen out of love with him, a notion that the insidious Hughes has routinely hinted to Barrymore. Alone with his miserable fate, Barrymore is consumed with hatred for the whale that has crippled him and sets sail, now obsessed with killing Moby Dick. He searches the seas for seven years, but finally spots the huge white whale and, in a titanic battle, kills Moby Dick, and, unlike the actual character in the Melville novel, survives and returns to New Bedford where he is reunited with Bennett while the despicable Hughes gets his just desserts. Bacon energetically directs this thriller and Barrymore gives a superlative, restrained performance, albeit he plays his character more as a lighthearted rascal than a man whose soul is darkened through his mad obsession and pursuit of the great whale. Bennett gives a standout performance, as do the rest of the cast members, although the construction of Moby Dick could have been better. _Author's Note_: Barrymore wanted his wife, Delores Costello, to be his leading lady in this film, but when she learned that she was pregnant, she bowed out and Barrymore then selected Bennett for the role, she being the daughter of Richard Bennett, one of Barrymore's old friends from his New York stage days. Joan Bennett had appeared on the stage at the age of four and got her first film role two years later in 1916, becoming a Hollywood child star. She appeared in many silent films before appearing in this film, but she had considerable reservations about dealing with the flamboyant Barrymore. He had a reputation as a rake and heavy drinker, but Bennett quickly learned in her first scenes with the Great Profile that, according to her statements to this author, "he was the perfect gentleman. He was sweet and considerate and treated me with as much respect he gave to actors who had been working with him for years. I needn't have worried about him." **d**, Lloyd Bacon; **cast**, John Barrymore, Joan Bennett, Lloyd Hughes, Noble Johnson, Nigel de Brulier, Walter Long, May Boley, Tom O'Brien, Virginia Sale, John Ince; **w**, J. Grubb Alexander (based on an adaptation by Oliver H.P. Garrett of the novel _Moby-Dick, or The Whale_ by Herman Melville); **c**, Robert Kurrle; **ed**, Desmond O'Brien; **spec eff**, Fred Jackman.

Moby Dick ★★★★★ 1956; U.S.; 116m; Moulin Productions/WB; Color; Adventure; Children: Unacceptable; **DVD**; **VHS**. Pantheon director Huston doggedly keeps faith with the original Melville story (undoubtedly the author's finest work) in this wonderfully crafted masterpiece film that offers a great and distinguished cast and the highest production values, along with the most genuine replication of that dreaded monster of the sea, Moby Dick. This stirring and thrilling tale opens with Basehart entering the seafaring village of New Bedford in 1840, and where he begins his narration with the memorable words: "Call me Ishmael…" He takes a room at the local inn where raucous sailors drink, eat and sleep, only to find that he has a roommate, the fierce-looking Ledebur, a West Indian harpooner whose body is coated with tattoos and flesh carvings, chiefly representing snakes and other creatures. Ledebur consults his collection of bones and strange artifacts and utters strange mystical chants that alarms Basehart, an innocent and somewhat naïve youth craving adventure. That Sunday, Basehart attends the local church where Welles, the pastor, mounts an odd-looking pulpit by climbing up a rope ladder to the dais, which is shaped in the form of a ship's prow that juts over the heads of the silent parishioners. Welles delivers a grim and frightening sermon as he describes in deep-voiced tones (as only he can) the hazards of the sea awaiting any sailor. He illustrates with thundering emphasis the deep perils of the deep and how all of those who go to sea risk not only the loss of their lives, but their immortal souls. Undaunted, Basehart, along with Ledebur, who has become his close friend, think to sign as seaman aboard the *Pequod*. As they approach that anchored sailing ship, they encounter a gaunt man in ragged clothes, Dano, who is named Elijah, after the prophet in the Bible, and who ominously warns them not to go to sea aboard that ship as its destiny is doom. Though Basehart is apprehensive, he nevertheless signs on, becoming a member of the crew, as does Ledebur, who is thought by the ship's owners to be a prize whaler as he is an accomplished harpooner. The ship sails without the crew seeing its legendary captain, Ahab, played by Peck, who emerges from his cabin when the ship is well out to sea, clambering up to the quarterdeck to address the crew. He is a fierce-looking man, his face horribly disfigured with a deep scar that runs the length of his long face to reach a shock of pure white hair on his otherwise dark-haired scalp and who is missing a leg, replaced by a white peg-leg. Peck glaringly tells his crew members that their voyage is not a routine hunt for whales, although they will endeavor to hunt that quarry, but that their primary mission has a deeper, more dangerous purpose, the hunt for the great white whale, Moby Dick, the very sea monster that tore away his leg and scarred his body as well as poisoned his spirit with an all-consuming vengeance, and he asks them to be dedicated to destroying this prey above all else. Peck is a man possessed, mesmerizing the crew as he whips their passions to frenzied compliance, exacting an oath from the entire crew where each man swears allegiance to him and his unswerving purpose to destroy the mythical sea beast. After nailing a gold coin to the main mast, the wild-eyed Peck tells his mesmerized crew that that coin will go to the crew member who first sights Moby Dick. Peck then has his three harpoon men heat the pointed barbs of their harpoons and these are then dipped into the cups of grog from which the crew members drink while they utter crazed chants and death toasts to Moby Dick. All of this bodes ominous fate in the wary mind of first mate Genn, who later goes to Peck in his cabin and begs him to give up his mad quest for the beast that so savagely debilitated him. He asks the sleepless, obsessed Peck to get some rest. Peck glances at the rumpled bedclothes of his bunk and tells Genn that the bunk represents a winding sheath for his burial. He refuses to give up the hunt for Moby Dick, telling Genn that the legendary whale "heaps me." The ship then spots a school of whales and the crew begins hunting them, taking in a rich harvest of catches, lashing the dead whales to the *Pequod* and then carving the blubber, which is lifted in huge slabs to the deck where the blubber is boiled down to make oil. All of the crew members rejoice in knowing that their shares from the catches will be substantial, but then Peck sees another ship approaching and hails its captain, Justice, to come aboard after Justice, calling from his ship, has begged Peck to join him in his search for his son, who has been lost at sea. Justice climbs aboard to show a makeshift hand with a hook that has replaced his own, lost in a battle with Moby Dick, and then tells Peck that his son was in a whaling boat when Moby Dick attacked his ship. Peck is seized with only one thought and that is to abandon all work and sail in pursuit of the whale. He orders Justice from his ship and tells his crew members to quit their killing of the whales. Justice returns to his ship, condemning Peck for refusing to aid him and warning him that he is seeking his own destruction. Peck goes to his cabin and shows Genn his own elaborate sea charts where he has determined the courses of all the whales of the earth and especially the course he believes that Moby Dick takes in his traversing the seas of the world. Sailing on and on, a lookout finally spots the great white whale, and Peck orders all the whaling boats to frantically row after the mammoth whale, which is as scarred as Peck, having innumerable lances, broken harpoons and riggings imbedded and clinging to its white hide. The crew members, led by Peck, who takes to one of the boats, are now as obsessed as their captain in killing the huge whale. Peck's boat comes close enough for him to send a harpoon deep into the whale's side, and the

Gregory Peck, left, with crew members in *Moby Dick,* 1956.

enraged Peck clambers onto the whale, driving the lance again and again into the whale, consumed by his rage and shouting: "To the last I grapple with thee! From hell's heart I stab at thee! For hate's sake I spit my last breath at thee!" He is then lost from view as Moby Dick submerges. The roiling sea is suddenly becalmed until the whale breeches to show Peck seemingly lifeless, entangled in the ship's riggings that coat the beast. As the whale sails, his motion causes one of Peck's arms to move back and forth as if beckoning his crew to follow and, half-mad with this scene, they do, chasing and harpooning the whale, until it turns upon them and, one by one, destroys their boats, sending them to watery deaths. The giant whale then attacks the *Pequod,* the ship that has been hunting him all these years, ramming it and swimming about it to create a giant whirlpool that sucks the ship down and beneath the waves, taking with it its last soul on board, Allenby, the little cabin boy known as "Pip." From its debris floats a coffin with elaborate carvings on it that Ledebur had earlier ordered made for him when he believed he was about to die. The lone survivor, Basehart, swims to the bobbing wooden coffin, clinging to it, and where Basehart, in voiceover, states "only I survived to tell thee…" to end this magnificent film. Director Huston presents this masterpiece in awesome perspectives, providing the most authentic-looking sets and life-size sailing ships, as well as a marvelous replica of the fierce and indefatigable Moby Dick. Peck, Basehart, Ledebur, Genn, Miles, Welles and Andrews (the latter is riveting as the happy-go-lucky second mate) render superb performances in this strange tale, as mesmerizing to the viewer as is Peck's perception of the near mythical whale he seeks to destroy at all costs, even at the sacrifice of his own life. The production values are superlative, and Huston develops the many divergent and colorful characters with infinite care so that each one becomes distinctive and memorable. The film was expensive for its day with a budget of $4.5 million and it returned that plus $700,000 in its box office release. The film was shot on location in Portugal, the Azores, the Canary Islands, Wales and Ireland. Songs (all traditional): "Drummer," "Blood Red Roses" and "Hill an' Gully Rider." *Author's Note*: Huston told this author that "**Moby Dick** was one of the most difficult films I ever made. I wanted perfection and that almost cost the lives of some of the cast and crew members." That penchant for perfection prompted Huston to conduct a search throughout the world for a vessel that conformed to the specifications of the *Pequod* as described by Melville in his novel (where every other chapter dwells on nautical data of his day) and that finally led the director to the port town of Scarborough, England, where he located a 100-year-old three-master with a wooden hull, originally called *Rylands*, which had been used as the *Hispanolo* in Walt Disney's production of **Treasure Island**, 1950, and where it was functioning as a museum. A crew of shipbuilders then refitted the vessel and, after it was made seaworthy, it was christened the *Pequod*

Gregory Peck battling the whale in *Moby Dick*, 1956.

(the ship was later destroyed in a fire in 1972 when anchored in Morecambe, England). Huston then scouted small British and Irish ports and settled on Youghal, Ireland, this little ancient port becoming New Bedford in the film. The director then instructed technicians to make Moby Dick as "the most realistic gigantic whale they could construct," according to Huston's statements to this author. "The recreations of Moby Dick in previous films, like **The Sea Beast** [1926] and the remake of that film [**Moby Dick**, 1930] that starred Jack Barrymore in both of those films was not very realistic-looking, so I resolved to have my Moby Dick look like the real thing or as close to what Melville conceived." To that end, Huston supervised a crew of technicians at Dunlop in Stoke-on-Trent, England, that created a seventy-five-foot-long white whale weighing twelve tons with a steel frame covered by stretched plastic and rubber and with moveable eyes and a mouth and where great spouts of water could be ejected from its blowhole. This mechanical behemoth contained eighty drums of compressed air and a hydraulic system that kept it afloat and was controlled electronically, although it did not swim on its own and had to be towed by a large boat with an underwater cable connected to it. Actually, three such mechanical whales were constructed at a cost of between $25,000 and $30,000 each. "We lost two of the whales at sea," Huston told this author. (They were seen for years bobbing about the Irish Sea and were mistaken for the real thing until officials ordered them destroyed, believing them to be navigational hazards.) "With only one whale left, I was taking no chances for the climax," Huston said. "I drove that whale myself, but we almost lost Greg [Peck] in the process. The towline broke and the tugboat pulling the whale and the tugboat couldn't find the whale as we got lost in a fog bank. Greg was on top of the whale, all tangled up in old nets and ropes the whale was carrying and he believed he was going down for the Deep Six. I could hear him shouting his head off, until the whale was located by the tugboat and another cable was affixed to it. It was all pretty scary." Many of the cast members were injured during the production. Genn was getting into an open boat when its lines gave way and he suddenly fell twenty feet to sea level and Genn fell into it, breaking a leg and spending several weeks in a cast and in hospital, which further delayed production. "I was injured several times, mostly in the arms and once in the head," Basehart told this author, "but my injuries were nothing compared to some others in that picture. We didn't complain to Huston. It would have done no good. He was risking his own life in almost every shot, hanging over the edges of power boats with our cinematographer [Morris] to get every action shot." Peck added to this by telling this author that "Huston was as nutty as my character Ahab in making that picture. He didn't care what happened to himself or anyone else as long as he got that great adventure into the can, but *his* way." It was the way Huston thought Melville would want it, according to his statements

to this author: "I am and always will be a writer, not a director. And my great literary idol was Herman Melville. He had been dead for more than sixty years when I made **Moby Dick** and I owed him a right production. *Moby Dick* was his masterpiece and it deserved to be presented in terms where myth and reality come clashing together and where the beast, which is in all of us, is suddenly actual and alive." Huston had wanted to make this film for many years and originally envisioned his father, Walter Huston, as playing Ahab, but his father died six years before Huston could persuade producers to finance the production and his first choice for Ahab was Peck and he suggested the role to Peck at a party, surprising him. Peck told this author that "I thought that I might do better by playing the role of the reasonable first mate, Starbuck [played by Genn] and suggested to John [Huston] that he play Ahab himself. He kept working on me to take the role and I did, although I have misgivings about my performance to this day." Welles, who really has a cameo role as the thundering preacher, had no misgivings, telling this author that "I did that bit for John [Huston] so that I could get enough money to do my own stage production of *Moby Dick*. So you see we all wanted a version of that incredible story." In writing the script for that story, Huston originally offered the job to James Agee, who considered himself a foremost film expert, but he turned down the offer, saying that he planned to direct a film, but that film was never produced and Agee lost out to Ray Bradbury. That gifted writer diligently worked on the script with Huston, Bradbury telling this author that "John [Huston] went over every word and every comma I put on paper. He told me that 'Melville is looking over our shoulders.' Well, Herman may have been looking over his, but *he* was looking over mine every second and it drove me a little batty. When you think about it, all of it was crazy. Here is a man who is sailing around the world to kill a dumb beast and he doesn't give a damn if it kills him at the same time. It's the story of a lunatic." The film has a singularly memorable visual effect that was achieved by cinematographer Morris when he, under Huston's supervision, created what he called a "desaturation" process that meshed color and monochrome photography and involved three-color inhibitions superimposed on a low contrast black-and-white silver image. The process thus offered muted colors throughout with a consistent golden aquatint tone that duplicated the old whaling prints Huston had located. This was in keeping with the vivid colors Huston had achieved in his rich portrait of French painter Toulouse Lautrec in **Moulin Rouge**, 1952. Not only was Huston a pantheon director, but he was, little known to the world beyond Hollywood, a master of color cinematography. **p**, John Huston, Vaughan N. Dean; **d**, Huston; **cast**, Gregory Peck, Richard Basehart, Leo Genn, James Robertson Justice, Harry Andrews, Bernard Miles, Noel Purcell, Mervyn Johns, Orson Welles, Friedrich Ledebur, Huston, Seamus Kelly, Royal Dano, Edric Connor, Philip Stainton, Joseph Tomelty, Francis De Wolff, Tamba Alleny, Tomm Cleggg; **w**, Huston, Ray Bradbury (based on the novel *Moby-Dick, or The Whale* by Herman Melville); **c**, Oswald Morris (Technicolor); **m**, Philip Sainton; **ed**, Russell Lloyd; **prod d**, Geoffrey Drake, Stephen Drake; **art d**, Ralph Brinton; **spec eff**, Augie Lohman, George Blackwell, Robert Clarke, Charles Parker.

The Model and the Marriage Broker ★★★ 1951; U.S.; 103m; FOX; B/W; Comedy; Children: Acceptable. This charming comedy opens with Ritter, a divorced woman, who runs a dating business and is a matchmaker on the side. When she learns that Crain, a beautiful model, is having an affair with a married man, she can't resist meddling in her life. Ritter gets Crain to go to an unmarried X-ray technician, Brady, whom she knows, on the pretext of finding a missing earring. Ritter hopes they will discover romantic chemistry and Crain will forget the married man. It works like sausage and eggs, and, in thanks, Crain matches Ritter up with a friend, O'Shea. **p**, Charles Brackett; **d**, George Cukor; **cast**, Jeanne Crain, Scott Brady, Thelma Ritter, Zero Mostel, Michael O'Shea, Frank Fontaine, Dennie Moore, John Alexander, Jay C. Flippen, Joyce Makenzie, Mae Marsh, Tommy Noonan; **w**, Brackett, Robert Breen,

Walter Reisch; **c**, Milton Krasner; **m**, Cyril Mockridge, Lionel Newman; **ed**, Robert Simpson; **art d**, Lyle Wheeler, John De Cuir; **set d**, Walter M. Scott, Thomas Little; **spec eff**, Fred Sersen.

Modern Romance ★★★ 1981; U.S.; 93m; COL; Color; Comedy; Children: Unacceptable (MPAA: PG-13); **DVD**; **VHS**. Brooks is a film editor, who is constantly in and out of being engaged to his girlfriend, Harrold, who works at a bank. He is self-centered and very jealous while she has been too willing to let him keep her dangling. He is torn between marriage and the freedom of bachelorhood, so he breaks off their relationship for the umpteenth time. He tries to forget Harrold by every means possible from taking up jogging to absorbing himself in editing a new but cheap science-fiction film. Nothing works and he falls back into his relationship with Harrold by showering her with gifts. He wins her back again, but the old reluctance to marry comes over him again. He finally gets up courage to propose to her during a weekend in the mountains. The couple finally wed, but the end title reports that they divorced only days later, remarried, and divorced again. An often hilarious comedy about a couple that can't live with or without each other. Songs: "You Are So Beautiful," "Love Hurts," "Another One Bites the Dust" (John Deacon); "A Fifth of Beethoven," "God Only Knows," "Along Comes Mary," "She's Out of My Life," "My Own Best Friend," "Sado-Okesa." Sexual content prohibits viewing by children. **p**, Andrew Scheinman, Martin Shafer; **d**, Albert Brooks; **cast**, Brooks, Kathryn Harrold, Tyann Means, Bruno Kirby, Jane Hallaren, Karen Chandler, Dennis Kort, Cliff Einstein, Jerry Belson, George Kennedy; **w**, Brooks, Monica Johnson; **c**, Eric Saarinen; **m**, Lance Rubin; **ed**, David Finfer; **prod d**, Edward Richardson; **set d**, James L. Berkey.

Modern Times ★★★★ 1936; U.S.; 87m; Charles Chaplin Productions/UA; B/W; Comedy; Children: Unacceptable; **BD**; **DVD**; **VHS**. The great comedian Chaplin defied the talking era again (as he had with **City Lights**, 1931), this time nine years after **The Jazz Singer**, 1927, launched the talkie era. This time, Chaplin does include some sound effects and synchronous music. Chaplin plays a lowly factory worker, who slaves on an assembly line, employing two wrenches to tighten bolts as they glide along on a conveyer belt. So engrossed in his methodical, never-changing routine is Chaplin that, when he is diverted for a second and misses a bolt, he dives after it, being carried on the conveyer belt and then run through the huge mechanism, in and around huge spinning gears. Another worker reverses the conveyer belt and Chaplin reemerges, now slaphappy with the experience and turning and tightening imaginary bolts. He takes a break by going to the washroom where he sneaks a cigarette, but the wall suddenly changes into a huge screen where his boss, Garcia, chastises him. Garcia then orders Chaplin to guinea pig a new invention that will speed up the eating habits of workers and thus save time from their lunch breaks. He is strapped into a feeding machine where a turntable with mechanical arms begins to spoon food into his mouth and also provides a rotating cob of corn, another arm wiping his mouth after each mouthful of food with a huge napkin. The machine, however, malfunctions, and its mechanism speeds up the action of the automatic arms so that food is being rapidly stuffed into Chaplin's mouth and the corn cob whirls about so fast that it grinds Chaplin's teeth while another mechanical arm mistakenly dumps a cup of hot soup onto his lap before the elaborate apparatus shatters. Chaplin then returns to the assembly line, but when he resumes his frenetic work, unable to keep up with the nuts and bolts on the conveyer belt, he suddenly goes daffy. He sees a secretary with nuts decorating the back of her dress and he pursues her in order to use his wrenches on those nuts, then races outside the factory and begins tightening the bolts on fire hydrants and after chasing after several passersby, he is subdued by police and sent to an asylum. Ostensibly cured, Chaplin goes in search of another job and when a truck passes him on the street, accidentally dropping its red flag from its tailgate, Chaplin picks up the flag and begins waving it to attract the driver's attention. A group of communists, how-

Charles Chaplin and Paulette Goddard in *Modern Times*, 1936.

ever, see the little fellow as a fellow traveler and they join him in what they think is a political protest march. Police then arrive and arrest the dissident leader, Chaplin, who has no idea why he is being taken to the pokey again. He is placed in a cell with a drug addict and, after imbibing some of the man's drugs, suddenly feels all powerful and then suppresses a wild prison break, and is rewarded for his inadvertent heroism by again being released. He then meets Goddard, who is wanted by the police after she has stolen food to feed her starving family since her father was recently killed in a labor battle. Their friendly meeting is short-lived when officers arrest Goddard and take her to a juvenile home, from which she escapes. Meanwhile, Chaplin, longing for the comforts of his old jail cell, knows exactly how to be placed there. He goes to an upscale restaurant, orders and eats everything in sight and then smilingly tells the waiter that he cannot pay. He is shortly thrown into a paddy wagon en route to jail, but finds Goddard inside the van. The two escape and dream of an idyllic life together in a small and comfortable cottage, but they settle for a dismal little shack. Chaplin then finds work as a night watchman at a luxury department store and he sneaks Goddard into this place of ease and wonderment where she wraps herself in ermine and lies on silk sheets. To speed up his rounds in the store, Chaplin dons roller skates, racing from one time clock to another and then performing for Goddard a startling ballet on skates where he comes dangerously close to flying off a high atrium with a broken railing. When his former assembly line workers appear to tell him that they have been discharged, the generous Chaplin offers them the luxuries and comforts of the sprawling store. For this transgression, Chaplin again winds up in the pokey while Goddard goes to work as a cabaret singer. When released, Chaplin gets a job at the cabaret, and when the lead singer fails to appear one night, Chaplin is pressed into service as his replacement. He appears before the crowd and sings a song in gibberish since he cannot remember its lyrics, but his presentation is so stunning that he brings down the house with thunderous applause. It appears that he is on the verge of finally becoming successful when juvenile authorities again appear to take Goddard away and she and Chaplin then flee. They are last seen walking down a road together, holding hands, and having nothing in life but each other. The film is a marvel to behold as Chaplin performs amazing feats of dexterity fused to his comic routines and some very sensitive and compassionate sequences with gamin Goddard, as well as directing this whirlwind comedy that not so subtly indicts the industrial world and the dehumanization of workers. Songs: "The Prisoner's Song" (Guy Massey), "Hallelujah, I'm a Bum" (Richard Rodgers, Lorenz Hart), "How Dry I Am" (traditional), "In the Evening by the Moonlight" (James Allen Bland), "Je cherche aprés Titine" (Leo Daniderff), "Theme from Modern Times" (Chaplin). *Author's Note*: Although it is easy to identify Fritz Lang's classic **Metropolis**, 1927, and King Vidor's classic,

Charles Chaplin in *Modern Times*, 1936.

The Crowd, 1928, as having great influence on Chaplin when he made **Modern Times**, both of these films placing automation before humanity, he was also influenced by an obscure film, **Oranges and Lemons**, a 1923 comedy short with Stan Laurel (before he teamed with Hardy) where Laurel escapes pursuers by becoming enmeshed in the machinery of a factory. Moreover, as soon as **Modern Times** appeared, Chaplin was sued by the French production company that produced René Clair's classic **A nous la liberté**, 1931, and where those producers claimed that Chaplin had plagiarized scenes from the assembly line sequences in the French production. The suit was dropped when Clair intervened, saying that "God knows I have certainly borrowed enough from him [Chaplin]." For his own defense, Chaplin stated that he got the idea for **Modern Times** as early as 1901 when he worked in London as a printer's apprentice and was amazed to see how the huge printing press he worked on dwarfed him and his fellow workers. **Modern Times** was three years in the making, although it was shot within eleven months, and it proved enormously successful, earning more than $8.5 million in its initial box office release against a budget of $1.5 million. Chaplin had early on planned to have spoken dialog in this film and began writing dialog for the script in 1934, but he later abandoned the notion, believing that all of the millions of fans of his "Little Tramp" character would be disappointed, including those in foreign countries, or so he said. The truth was that Chaplin hated talking films and believed that silent films were much more creative. He was himself an excellent mime and proved it when he and Goddard left on an ocean voyage together following the release of **Modern Times**. They met on board the great Jean Cocteau, poet and filmmaker. Chaplin and Cocteau conversed fluently with each other for several hours although they did not know a single word of each other's language. When asked how this was possible, Cocteau later stated that they conversed in "the living language… The language of mime, the language of poets." Goddard had lived with Chaplin in his Beverly Hills home. Although Chaplin at one point claimed they had been married in China on their Far East voyage following the release of **Modern Times** (and Goddard later claimed they had been legally wed and that she divorced Chaplin in Mexico in 1942), they were never legally married and shared a common-law marriage from 1934 until their breakup in 1938. Chaplin was later criticized by members of the U.S. Congress for being a communist sympathizer and they cited the comedy scene in this film where the communists follow Chaplin down the street. At the time of this film, Chaplin was decidedly critical of U.S. industrialism and from which the only relief workers had, he believed, was from a few laughs he and others could provide, stating: "Machinery should benefit mankind, not throw it out of work… Something is wrong. Things have been badly managed when five million men are out of work in the richest country in the world." He then added: "What kind of filthy world is this, that makes people lead such wretched lives that if anybody makes them laugh they want to kneel down and touch his overcoat, as though he was Jesus Christ raising them from the dead." Chaplin got away with a lot with this production, his persona overwhelming the censors, who would have otherwise insisted upon the deletion of several scenes, including his character living with a young girl, and the drug-taking scene in jail, which had long been forbidden. **p,d&w**, Charles Chaplin; **cast**, Chaplin, Paulette Goddard, Henry Bergman, Stanley Sandford, Chester Conklin, Hank Mann, Stanley Blystone, Allan Garcia, Dick Alexander, Cecil Reynolds, Heinie Conklin, Gloria DeHaven; **c**, Ira Morgan, Roland Totheroh; **m**, Chaplin; **ed**, Chaplin, Willard Nico; **prod d**, Charles D. Hall; **art d**, J. Russell Spencer; **set d**, Hall, Spencer; **spec eff**, Bud Thackery.

Mogambo ★★★ 1953; U.S.; 116m; MGM; Color; Adventure; Children: Cautionary; **DVD**; **VHS**. In an outstanding adventure yarn that provides a subtle love triangle, Gable is a white hunter and safari guide in deepest Africa. He plays reluctant host to Gardner, a sultry showgirl, who says she is the guest of a wealthy maharaja, but that rich potentate never makes an appearance. Gardner and Gable, though drawn together, exchange a lot of combative banter, and it is apparent that Gardner is falling for the self-reliant Gable. All that changes when beautiful, cool blonde Kelly arrives with her husband, Sinden, who is an anthropologist representing various zoos and is studying gorillas. He hires Gable to take him on a safari where he can view gorillas in their natural habitats, and Kelly and Gardner go along on the venture. Gable is soon smitten by Kelly, who encourages his interest, but Gardner warns him that he is getting into dangerous waters. Gable then thinks to tell Sinden of his love for his wife, but he cannot bring himself to injure this kind and considerate man. On another occasion, Gable sees that Sinden might be killed, leaving Kelly to himself, but, at the last minute, his chivalry will not allow Sinden to die and he saves him. The unfaithful Kelly continues to encourage Gable, but his nobility forces him to go to Gardner's tent where he drinks with her and then embraces her and kisses her. When the enraged Kelly finds them in a clinch, she grabs a pistol and shoots Gable in the shoulder. Sinden runs to the tent only to be told by equally noble Gardner that she shot Gable for making advances to her. Thus protected and much the wiser for her transgressions, Kelly then leaves with Sinden. Gardner, too, is about to leave, but Gable asks her to remain with him, realizing that he truly loves her and Gardner stays at his side for the fadeout. Ford does an exceptional job in directing this smoldering tale, drawing fine performances from Gable, Gardner and Kelly while providing some fine jungle action with some amazing wildlife scenes. Shot in Kenya and the French Congo, this was a remake of **Red Dust**, 1932, which starred a much younger and energetic Gable with blonde bombshell Jean Harlow, but the seasoned Gable of **Mogambo** nevertheless projects a powerful presence while Gardner and Kelly spar for his affections. The film did exceptionally well at the box office, gleaning $5.2 million in its first release. Song: "Comin' Through the Rye" (Robert Burns). *Author's Note*: This was the last film Gable did for MGM. The front office thought that his star was fading, but this film put him back on top again and MGM executives wanted him to stay on. He nevertheless took his $400,000 in pension funds and said goodbye. Ford and Gable got along fairly well, although Gable, now advanced in years, had a slight palsy in his hands that caused Ford to do some reshooting of scenes. Gardner thought Ford did not like her as he was a man of few words and seldom complimented his actors. However, Ford told Gardner that she was "damned good, just take it easy" after one scene and she was his friend for life. Ford told this author that "the only reason I did that picture was because I had never been to the French Congo or Kenya and wanted to see those parts of Africa. We had to use some stock footage for the gorillas since they did not exist in the locations where we were shooting." Kelly was infatuated with Gable at the time and they had a brief affair during the production, but it went nowhere as Kelly realized that Gable was twice her age. Gardner at that time was married to singer Frank Sinatra, whose career had taken a nosedive and their marriage was breaking up. Sinatra visited Gardner at one of the African locations, bringing her a mink coat on her birthday, but after he left, Gardner tossed the coat away as if it were an old dishrag. Gable saw her do it and said to Ford: "I'd never let a woman treat me like that." Gardner was pregnant at the time with Sinatra's child, but she miscarried. She told this author that "**Mogambo** was a great adventure for me, but the mosquitoes were the real savages and I found myself bathing three times a day just to get rid of them and all that perspiration." At one point, a local chief told Ford that Gardner was creating problems by bathing in her canvas bathtub in such a way where the young litter bearers could see her in the altogether. Ford went to Gardner and asked her to be more guarded when bathing. Her response was to run through the entire camp stark naked so all the cast and crew could see her ample charms, laughing as she made her mad dash to her tent. Kelly shook her head, mockingly said "tramp!" and then laughed along with the others. **p**, Sam Zimbalist; **d**, John Ford; **cast**, Clark Gable, Ava Gardner, Grace Kelly, Donald Sinden, Philip Staniton, Eric Pohlmann, Laurence Naismith, Denis O'Dea, Samburu, Wagenia, Bahaya, M'Beti; **w**, John Lee Mahin (based on the play "Red Dust" by Wilson Collison); **c**, Robert Surtees, F.A. Young (Technicolor); **ed**, Frank Clarke; **art d**, Alfred Junge; **spec eff**, Tom Howard, Bert Monk.

Moliere ★★★ 2007; France; 120m; Fidelite Productions/Wild Bunch; Color; Comedy; Children: Unacceptable (MPAA: PG-13); **DVD**. Moliere, stage name of the great French actor and playwright (Jean-Baptiste Poquelin [1622-1673]), played by Duris, is given a theater in Paris by the king in 1658 after having toured the country with his company of players. He is undecided whether to write a comedy or a tragedy for his next play even though the king wants him to write a comedy. The film flashes back thirteen years earlier to show Duris being thrown in jail for nonpayment of a debt. A wealthy patron pays his debt and has him freed so he can go to his estate and help him with his wooing of a mistress while keeping their affair from his wife, Morante. Duris does this disguised as a priest and a comedy of romantic errors ensues in this well-crafted production. (In French; English subtitles.) **p**, Olivier Delbosc, Marc Missonnier; **d**, Laurent Tirard; **cast**, Romain Duris, Fabrice Luchini, Laura Morante, Edouard Baer, Ludivine Sagnier, Fanny Valette, Gonzague Montuel, Gilian Petrovski, Sophie-Charlotte Husson, Anne Suarez; **w**, Tirard, Grégoire Vigneron; **c**, Gilles Henry; **m**, Frédéric Talgorn; **ed**, Valérie Deseine, Gilles Granier; **prod d**, Françoise Dupertuis; **set d**, Véronique Melery; **spec eff**, Cédric Fayolle, Chrystèle Barbarat, Loïc Caer.

Molly and Me ★★★ 1945; U.S.; 76m; FOX; B/W; Comedy; Children: Acceptable; **DVD**. British comedienne Fields and Woolley are well-matched in this delightful comedy where she is an out-of-work actress, who takes a job as a housekeeper for stuffy British aristocrat Woolley. He is a retired politician, divorced from his wife, Lloyd, and estranged from his son, McDowall. His life needs shaking up and Fields does just that. Lloyd wants to blackmail Woolley, but Fields enlists her show business friends to create a situation in which Lloyd thinks she has murdered someone and leaves. She also helps Woolley and his son reconcile and Woolley wonders how he can ever do without her. Songs: "Sailor's Hornpipe," "My Bonnie Lies Over the Ocean," "Always Eat When You Are Hungry" (traditional); "The Artfulness, the Sinfulness, the Wickedness of Men," "Good Morning My Dear,); "She Was Poor But She Was Honest" (R.P. Weston, Bert Lee); "Christopher Robin Is Saying His Prayers" (Harold Fraser-Simson, A.A. Milne); "Let's All Sing Like the Birdies Sing" (Tolchard Evans, Stanley Damerell, Robert Hargreaves). **p**, Robert Bassler; **d**, Lewis Seiler; **cast**, Gracie Fields, Monty Woolley, Roddy McDowall, Reginald Gardiner, Natalie Schafer, Edith Barrett, Clifford Brooke, Queenie Leonard, Doris Lloyd, Lillian Bronson, Ethel Griffies; **w**, Leonard Praskins (based on an adaptation by Roger Burford of the novel by Frances Marion); **c**, Charles Clarke; **m**, Cyril J. Mock-

Grace Kelly and Ava Gardner in *Mogambo*, 1953.

ridge; **ed**, John McCafferty; **art d**, Lyle Wheeler, Albert Hogsett; **set d**, Thomas Little; **spec eff**, Fred Sersen.

The Molly Maguires ★★★ 1970; U.S.; 124m; PAR; Color; Biographical Drama; Children: Unacceptable (MPAA: PG); **DVD**; **VHS**. A rousing historical drama, this intriguing film profiles the underground activities of the Irish terrorist group called the Molly Maguires, who killed mine officials and destroyed mines in West Virginia and Pennsylvania in the 1870s in an effort to force mine owners to give better wages and provide better working conditions to the miners. These rampant terrorist activities cause police to seek the aid of the Pinkerton Detective Agency, having one of their bravest operatives, James McParland (1843-1919), played by Harris, to infiltrate the secret organization. In 1876, Harris goes to a small mining town and rents a room from an invalided miner while courting his daughter, Eggar, and, while going to work in the local mine, informs a few miners that he is wanted for murder. While in his cups, Harris pretends to rage against the mine owners and is then approached by several of the secretive Molly Maguires, who introduce them to their resolute and cunning leader, John "Black Jack" Kehoe (1847-1877), played by Connery. Harris is given several tests and is finally inducted into the secret brotherhood and participates in several terrorist attacks and sabotage. When Eggar's father dies, Harris and Connery, now fast friends, break into a company store, steal clothes for the old man's funeral and then set fire to the place. They further bond when Harris helps Connery and others win a brutal football game. Meanwhile, Harris makes secret trips to visit his police contact, providing reports on the Mollies and their operations. Harris learns that Connery and others plan to blow up one of the mines and Harris then turns Connery and others over to the police. Private detectives then make raids against the leaders of the Mollies, shooting them and their wives while they are asleep. Connery is imprisoned and Harris appears in court to testify against him, his testimony sending Connery to the gallows. Eggar then turns her back on Harris, who is branded a Judas turncoat. He, like the real McParland, then leaves the area, promoted to a higher job by the Pinkertons (heading the agency's Denver offices). Ritt, an exceptional action director, offers an uncompromising and passionate tale where the rough-hewn miners are shown in all their grime and ruthless resolution and where the police opposing them are as brutal as the terrorists. Connery and Harris are standouts in their gritty roles as two wholly different Irishmen, one defying the law, the other upholding it at the daily risk of his life. Songs (all traditional): "Eileen Aroon," "Garyowen" and "Cockles and Mussels." *Author's Note*: The film was made for more than $11 million and was shot on location in eastern Pennsylvania, using the very mining areas where the Mollies once operated. It was not a success at the box office, returning only $1.5 million in its initial release. **p**, Martin

Bob Hoskins, Michael Caine and Cathy Tyson in *Mona Lisa*, 1986.

Ritt, Walter Bernstein; **d**, Ritt; **cast**, Sean Connery, Richard Harris, Samantha Eggar, Frank Finlay, Anthony Zerbe, Bethel Leslie, Art Lund, Philip Bourneuf, Anthony Costello, Brendan Dillon, Frances Heflin, John Alderson; **w**, Bernstein (based on the book *Lament for the Molly Maguires* by Arthur H. Lewis); **c**, James Wong Howe (Panavision; Technicolor); **m**, Henry Mancini; **ed**, Frank Bracht; **prod d&art d**, Tambi Larsen; **set d**, Darrell Silvera; **spec eff**, Willis Cook.

Mona Lisa ★★★ 1986; U.K.; 104m; HandMade Films/Island Pictures; Color; Crime Drama; Children: Unacceptable (MPAA: PG-13); **DVD**; **VHS**. Riveting crime yarn sees career criminal Hoskins getting out of prison and looking for work in his trade, but finds that his time behind bars has reduced his stature in the underworld. He goes to Caine, the reigning London crime boss, for work and is assigned to chauffeuring a beautiful, black, and expensive call girl, Tyson, from trick to trick. Hoskins becomes infatuated with Tyson, who, to him, is the embodiment of the beautiful, mysterious, and unattainable woman in the da Vinci painting. Tyson leads him on, but is not the woman he imagines her to be. She needs Hoskins' help because a former pimp wants to cut her face and she also wants him to find a teenage prostitute, Hardie, with whom she is in love and who may or may not be alive. At the finale of this unrelenting tale Tyson kills Caine and his henchman, Peters. There is no happy ending for Tyson because the girl she loved is dead. Hoskins is left without Tyson or his dream of her, but has material for a book. Songs: "Mona Lisa" (Jay Livingston, Ray Evans), "When I Fall in Love" (Victor Young, Edward Heyman), "The Veery Thought of You" (Ray Noble), "In Too Deep" (Genesis), "Bimba Dagli Occhi Pieni di Malia" (Giacomo Puccini). Excessive violence and sexual material prohibit viewing by children. **p**, Patrick Cassavetti, Stephen Woolley, Chris Brown, Ray Cooper, Nik Powell, **d**, Neil Jordan; **cast**, Bob Hoskins, Cathy Tyson, Michael Caine, Robbie Coltrane, Clarke Peters, Kate Hardie, Zoe Nathenson, Sammi Davis, Rod Bedall, Joe Brown; **w**, Jordan, David Leland; **c**, Roger Pratt; **m**, Michael Kamen; **ed**, Lesley Walker; **prod d**, Jamie Leonard; **art d**, Gemma Jackson.

Monkey Business ★★★ 1931; U.S.; 77m; PAR; B/W; Comedy; Children: Acceptable; **DVD**; **VHS**. The Marx Brothers are at their zany best in this wild romp that begins on board an ocean liner where Groucho, Harpo, Chico and Zeppo have stowed away. They spend frantic time moving from one empty cabin to another while evading ship's officers and to avoid being locked up in the brig. Harpo gives up chasing after fetching blonde Todd long enough to get involved with a Punch and Judy show, and where, to evade capture as a stowaway, he pretends to be one of the puppets, his antics delighting all the children on board as well as the adults. The boys then pair up with slick gangster bosses Woods and

Fellowes, and where they pretend to be underworld hoodlums, wildly spewing criminal argot and exhibiting tough-looking mannerisms. Disembarking, the brothers attend a masquerade ball where Hall, the daughter of Fellowes, is abducted by Woods and his goons and the brothers go to the rescue, but are trapped in a barn where they battle the thugs. Groucho leaps from bale of hay to bale of hay as he delivers one-liners and narrates the action for filmgoers (talking directly to "the fourth wall" or the camera, one of his career-long Hollywood ploys, which would be adopted by Bob Hope in many of his comedies) while Harpo and Chico manically chase or are chased by the gangsters until Zeppo decides enough is enough and knocks out the villains to save Hall. Not much of a plot, but the Marx Brothers hold interest throughout with their unpredictable buffooneries and where Harpo strokes his harp and Chico tickles the ivories. Songs: "You Brought a New Kind of Love to Me," "When I Take My Sugar to Tea" (Sammy Fain, Irving Kahal, Pierre Norman), "Pizzicato Polka" (Leo Delibes), "I'm Daffy Over You" (Chico Marx, Sol Violinsky), "Sweet Adeline" (Richard H. Gerard, Harry Armstrong), "O Solo Mio" (Eduardo Di Capua, Giovanni Capurro). The film provides many memorable scenes, not the least of which is where Harpo pretends to be famous singer Maurice Chevalier, miming one of the singer's songs while trying to get through a checkpoint. *Author's Note*: Hecht told this author that "I wrote the story for the Marx Brothers comedy, **Monkey Business**, but when I looked at the film, I saw that it had very little to do with what I wrote. I was not surprised. Those clowns took every story and wrung its neck until the chicken looked like a gooney bird. Years later, I wrote a screenplay for Cary Grant and Ginger Rogers with the same title [**Monkey Business**, 1952] and lo and behold, they actually filmed the story as I wrote it." McLeod told this author that "I directed the Marx Brothers in two films, **Monkey Business**, and **Horse Feathers** [1932], and I can tell you honestly that *they* directed me. They did whatever they wanted and it was useless to complain to the front office about them since old man Zukor [Adolph Zukor, 1873-1976, head of Paramount] thought they were all geniuses. I asked Harpo how he and his brothers ever got into this business and he said: 'We fell into it and we are still suffering from the concussions.'" Groucho told this author that "**Monkey Business** is a subtle version of *The Brothers Karamazov*, and, if you believe that, you'll believe anything." After Groucho's death (in 1977), his children found a gag he had written, asking as a final request that he be buried on top of Marilyn Monroe (he was cremated). Ironically, Monroe made one of her earliest appearances in another film by the same name, **Monkey Business**, 1952. **p**, Herman J. Mankiewicz; **d**, Norman McLeod; **cast**, Groucho Marx, Harpo Marx, Chico Marx, Zeppo Marx, Thelma Todd, Tom Kennedy, Ruth Hall, Rockliffe Fellowes, Harry Woods, Eddie Baker, Cecil Cunningham, Maurice Chevalier (singing voice); **w**, S.J. Perelman, Will B. Johnstone, Arthur Sheekman (based on a story by Ben Hecht, Roland Pertwee [both not credited]); **c**, Arthur L. Todd; **m**, John Leipold, Ralph Rainger.

Monkey Business ★★★★ 1952; U.S.; 97m; FOX; B/W; Comedy; Children: Acceptable; **DVD**; **VHS**. Grant and Rogers are in top form enacting this hilarious comedy from Hecht and Lederer. In an effort to provide a formula that will stop the aging process and restore youth to weary human cells, Grant, an absent-minded chemist, has been experimenting with chimps, but his various formulas have met with no success. His boss, Coburn, the greedy owner of a chemical company, urges Grant to continue his research and not worry about expenses. After Grant leaves his laboratory, one of the chimps gets out of his cage and begins mimicking Grant's experiments, randomly mixing chemicals, then dumps the concoction into the opening of a huge water vat used for the water cooler. A janitor finds the chimp loose and puts him back into his cage and then positions the water vat into the water cooler. Grant returns and mixes another formula and decides to use himself as a guinea pig and drinks it. He then washes away the bitter taste by drinking from the water cooler, but that, too, tastes bitter. Timing his reaction, Grant slowly feels reinvigorated and is then full of energy. Coburn, meanwhile, summons his sexy blonde secretary, Monroe (to prove her to be the dumb blonde she is playing, Coburn, at one point, summarizes her character by handing her a sheet of paper and tells her: "Here, have someone type this") and orders her to find Grant. Monroe locates the now vim and vigorous Grant, who exudes the attitude of a college freshman, out for fun and adventure. He has had his hair cut short in the form of a crew-cut, purchased some loud clothes (checkered jacket, slacks and loafers) and bought an open-air sports car. Grant takes Monroe swimming where he makes high dives (and Monroe attracts all the whistles from the wolves). He takes her roller skating (and where the forty-eight-year-old Grant shows marvelous dexterity and does some fancy moves on the rink) before taking Monroe for a mad drive in his new sports car, which Grant damages slightly after taking a curve too fast. By the time Grant goes home to his wife, Rogers, the formula has mostly worn out. She overlooks his youthful antics as being associated with his research and they then go out to dinner and they later stop by Grant's laboratory where Rogers drinks some water from the cooler. She then begins to feel romantic urges that she has not had for years and talks Grant into taking her to the hotel where they spent their honeymoon, carrying on as a young, excited bride. When Rogers' schoolgirl personality fades, she again visits Grant's laboratory, drinks more of the water from the cooler, and resorts to a prank-playing adolescent. When seeing Monroe, Rogers threatens to pull her "blonde hair out by its black roots." She later calls up an old flame, Marlowe, who thinks he has a chance with her and tries to resume their old relationship. Grant, by this time, has also taken more water from the cooler and has regressed to early childhood where he and a group of neighbor boys play "Indian," capturing Marlowe and tying him to a tree and where Grant snips off Marlowe's hair to give him a Mohican haircut while doing an Indian dance, his frenetic contortions imitated by the laughing boys. Rogers, weary of these games, goes to sleep, awakening as a mature adult, but when she finds a baby lying next to her, she panics, believing that the infant is Grant and that he has somehow returned to puberty. Taking the child to the laboratory, she finds Grant very much a mature adult, but now Coburn and all of his executives and other chemists have drunk water from the cooler and all of them are acting like unruly school children, Coburn chasing Monroe around the room and others hanging from overhead lamps to imitate the chimps in the lab. When the formula finally wears off, everyone is relieved in getting back to normal and the quest for the fountain of youth among these discombobulated people no longer burns bright. They have settled for adulthood and are glad of it. Pantheon director Hawks carefully develops this impossible tale and gets standout performances from Grant, Rogers, Coburn and the rest of the cast, cleverly converting them from adults to human beings aping the antics of chimps to provide a superb comedy. The film did very good business at the box office, taking in more than $2 million in its initial release. Song (sung by Grant): "The Whiffenpoof Song" (music: Tod B. Galloway; lyrics: George S. Pomeroy and Meade Minnigerode). *Author's Note*: Hawks told this author that "Cary [Grant] and I had a long and good relationship where we made a number of fine pictures together, so when it came to doing **Monkey Business**, and we had a lively script from Ben [Hecht], he was ready to do it, even when he hadn't read the script and agreed when I told him the story. We trusted each other. That's what good filmmaking is all about." Grant supported these statements when he told this author that "Howard Hawks never made a bad picture and when he told me about **Monkey Business**, I thought it was going to be **His Girl Friday** [1940] all over again. Even though it was a more modern story, it was still one of those screwball comedies that we did back in the 1930s and 1940s, and it was just as good. I had a lot of fun doing it and when Charles [Coburn], who usually played staid old gents, goes wacky after drinking that fountain of youth formula, well, I cracked up [a rare experience for Grant], and we had to reshoot the scene." Rogers told this author that "I was in the big league with Howard [Hawks] and Cary [Grant] in that picture and where Cary was wonderful to work with. He was never late and never missed a cue and all of his responses were per-

Marilyn Monroe, Cary Grant, and Charles Coburn in *Monkey Business,* **1952.**

fect. The only direction Howard gave me was when I asked him how he saw me when I changed into a little girl, he said, 'if you were a spoiled little brat when you were a kid, then act like one.' That's exactly what I did." **p**, Sol C. Siegel; **d**, Howard Hawks; **cast**, Cary Grant, Ginger Rogers, Charles Coburn, Marilyn Monroe, Hugh Marlowe, Henri Letondal, Larry Keating, Esther Dale, George Winslow, Harry Carey, Jr., Olive Carey; **w**, Ben Hecht, Charles Lederer, I.A.L. Diamond (based on a story by Harry Segall); **c**, Milton Krasner; **m**, Leigh Harline; **ed**, William B. Murphy; **art d**, Lyle Wheeler, George Patrick; **set d**, Thomas Little, Walter M. Scott.

A Monkey in Winter ★★★ 1963; France; 105m; Cite Films/MGM; B/W; Drama; Children: Unacceptable; **VHS**. Gabin renders another fine performance as a reformed alcoholic, who is the owner of a small Normandy inn with his wife, Flon. A younger man, Belmondo, stops there on his way to visiting his estranged young daughter at a Catholic boarding school. Gabin senses Belmondo is troubled about something. They take a liking to each other and Gabin accepts an offer to have a drink. That leads to them getting drunk and telling about their good old days and/or ambitions. Gabin had been a French Marine in China and Belmondo says he dreams of stopping his drifting and drinking and living the good life in Spain. The drinks wear off and Belmondo sees his daughter. He takes her to the inn where Gabin tells them about a Chinese legend involving hordes of monkeys that came down from some mountains and descended on a village. Belmondo recognizes it as an allegory in which he is a wanderer like the monkeys and a villager, Gabin, is the stabilizing force that sends the monkeys back into the mountains. The girl asks Gabin if the story is true and Belmondo, recognizing that Gabin means to help him settle down, tells her yes. A sweet, gentle story but excessive drinking prohibits viewing by children. (In French; English subtitles.) **p**, Jacques Bar; **d**, Henri Verneuil; **cast**, Jean Gabin, Jean-Paul Belmondo, Suzanne Flon, Gabrielle Dorziat, Hella Petri, Marcelle Arnold, Charles Bouillaud, Anne-Marie Coffinet, André Dalibert, Hélène Dieudonné; **w**, François Boyer, Michel Audiard (based on the novel by Antoine Blondin); **c**, Louis Page; **m**, Michel Magne; **ed**, Françoise Bonnot, Monique Bonnot; **prod d**, Robert Clavel.

Monkey Trouble ★★★ 1994; U.S./Japan; 96m; Effe Productions/New Line Cinema; Color; Comedy; Children: Unacceptable (MPAA: PG-13); **DVD**; **VHS**. Birch is a twelve-year-old girl, who is not doing well in grade school and is not happy at home in the Venice Beach area of Los Angeles where she lives with her mother, Rogers, and policeman stepfather, McDonald. She is jealous of the attention her parents give to her new baby brother. She is also upset because Rogers and McDonald won't let her have a dog because they think she is not old or responsible

Martha Raye and Charles Chaplin in *Monsieur Verdoux,* **1947.**

enough to care for and clean up after the animal or any other kind of pet. Keitel, an organ grinder, comes along with his pet monkey. The monkey runs away because Keitel is mean to it, and Birch finds it on her way home from school. They become friends and she takes the monkey home, but keeps her parents from knowing she has made a pet of Dodger (the name she has given the monkey) by hiding it in a knapsack in her room. But Dodger is not housebroken and urinates on the floor and defecates in the bathroom sink. She cleans up the messes and lets her baby brother play with Dodger only because she knows he can't tell on her. She takes Dodger to the Boardwalk to entertain crowds and discovers the monkey has been trained to be a pickpocket. This presents problems when people accuse her of stealing their watches, jewelry, and wallets. Meanwhile, Keitel is frantic to find his kleptomaniac monkey because some crooks want to use it in a big robbery. Keitel finds and takes Dodger, so Birch runs away to find him. It ends with Birch and Dodger being reunited, Keitel going to jail, and Birch getting to keep Dodger because her parents now see how responsible she has become in caring for her pet. Birch is fun to watch, but the capuchin monkey (Finster) steals the show as Dodger. Songs: "Sold for Me," "Posie" (Dylan MacAlinion, Granville Ames); "Who Gets Da Loot" (J.D. Tru, Ross Hogarth); "VB Rap" (Tim Gedemer, Howard Drossin); "Girls" (Darlene Gallegos); "Monkey Shines" (Robert J. Walsh). A fun family film but cautionary for children because of thievery and a moment of menace. **p,** Mimi Polk Gitlin, Heide Rufus Isaacs, John C. Broderick, Ridley Scott; **d,** Franco Amurri; **cast,** Thora Birch, Harvey Keitel, Mimi Rogers, Christopher McDonald, Adrian Johnson, Kevin Scannell, Alison Elliott, Robert Miranda, Victor Argo, Remy Ryan, Finster; **w,** Amurri, Stu Krieger; **c,** Luciano Tovoli; **m,** Mark Mancina; **ed,** Ray Lovejoy, Chris Peppe; **prod d,** Leslie Dilley; **art d,** Nathan Crowley; **set d,** Denise Pizzini; **spec eff,** J.D. Streett.

The Monkey's Uncle ★★★ 1965; U.S.; 87m; Walt Disney/Buena Vista; Color; Comedy; Children: Cautionary; **DVD; VHS.** Kirk is an inventive college boy, who asks his father, Ames, who is a judge, to let him adopt a chimpanzee so he can conduct experiments while raising it as a human being. Ames goes only so far, granting him guardianship but not ownership, so Kirk becomes the monkey's "uncle." Ames is on the college board of regents and is involved in a dispute with a rival, Faylen, who wants to have football banned from the college because he was never chosen to play on the team when he went to school there. Faylen gets the other regents to agree that football players will be summarily flunked if they don't get passing grades. Ames asks his son for help, and Kirk comes up with a scheme of coaching the players in their studies while they are sleeping. This doesn't work as the jocks are all going to be expelled for cheating on exams. Millionaire O'Connell then throws

a monkey wrench (pun intended) into everyone's problems by offering a $10 million grant to the college if it can prove that human-powered flight is possible. Kirk teaches advanced information to the chimp that creates a zany flying machine that solves everybody's problems. The film is a sequel to **The Misadventures of Merlin Jones,** 1963. Song: "The Monkey's Uncle" (Richard M. and Robert B. Sherman). A fun family film that is a bit too flippant in treating the practice of cheating on schoolwork. **p,** Walt Disney, Ron Miller; **d,** Robert Stevenson; **cast,** Tommy Kirk, Annette Funicello, Leon Ames, Arthur O'Connell, Frank Faylen, Connie Gilchrist, Leon Tyler, Norman Grabowski, Cheryl Miller, The Beach Boys; **w,** Tom and Helen August (based on a story by Bill Walsh); **c,** Edward Colman (Technicolor); **m,** Buddy Baker, Richard M. and Robert B. Sherman; **ed,** Cotton Warburton; **art d,** Carroll Clark, William H. Tuntke; **set d,** Hal Gausman, Emile Kuri; **spec eff,** Eustace Lycett, Robert A. Mattey.

Monsieur Hire ★★★ 1990; France; 101m; Henson Associates/TriStar Pictures; Color; Crime Drama; Children: Unacceptable (MPAA: PG-13); **DVD; VHS.** In this absorbing crime tale, Blanc is a middle-aged lonely and reclusive French tailor, who is also antisocial and doesn't like to talk to anyone. But he is not always what he seems to be. He has a police record, keeps pet mice he is kind to, and goes to a bowling alley where he knocks down pins while blindfolded, before visiting prostitutes. He becomes attracted to a blonde young neighbor, Bonnaire, and watches her from his window at night as she meets her boyfriend, Thuillier. Bonnaire visits Blanc and he reveals that he is in love with her. Then Berthon, a young woman in the neighborhood, is murdered, and a police detective, Wilms, suspects Blanc of being the killer because Blanc's neighbors have always thought he was up to no good. Blanc tells Bonnaire that he saw Thuillier murder the girl, but did not tell police for fear she would be considered as an accomplice in the killing. Blanc invites Bonnaire to go with him to Lausanne, Switzerland, and leave Thuillier behind. The film ends with Bonnaire uncertain as to whether Blanc or Thuillier is the real murderer. (In French; English subtitles.) **p,** Philippe Carcassonne, René Cleitman; **d,** Patrice Leconte; **cast,** Michel Blanc, Sandrine Bonnaire, Luc Thuillier, André Wilms, Eric Bérenger, Marielle Berthon, Philippe Dormoy, Marie Gaydu, Michel Morano, Nora Noël; **w,** Leconte, Patrick Dewolf (based on the novel *Les fiançailles de M. Hire* [*Mr. Hire's Engagement*] by Georges Simenon); **c,** Denis Lenoir; **m,** Michael Nyman; **ed,** Joëlle Hache; **prod d,** Ivan Maussion.

Monsieur Verdoux ★★★ 1947; U.S.; 124m; Charles Chaplin Productions/UA; Crime Drama; Children: Unacceptable; **DVD; VHS.** This offbeat crime tale, which is based upon the French bluebeard, Henri Desire Landru (1869-1922), has Chaplin, in an unusual change of character, playing the serial killer of middle-aged women in order to secure their assets. After losing his job as a clerk in a bank, Chaplin, in order to provide for his wife and small son, decides that the easiest course to make money is to murder wealthy women and abscond with their estates. His method is simple. He places enticing advertisements next to the lovelorn columns in French newspapers, describing himself as a man of sophistication, culture and wealth and he is soon inundated with women of like status. Chaplin is very picky about which women he bigamously marries before he murders them and then dissects and burns their bodies in a stove (as was Landru's technique). He methodically dispatches one garrulous woman after another, until he meets the demanding and flamboyant Raye, who proves to be his nemesis in that her suspicions bring the law down upon him. Though Chaplin tries to present this film as a black comedy through his droll and airy characterization, he offers a rather predictable but absorbing story and where he injects grim irony in such scenes where his little boy pulls the tail of a cat and Chaplin wonders how such cruelty has been acquired. To Chaplin, his character is simply a desperate little man attempting to make a living through an unsavory criminal profession. In the end, he puts up little defense for his lethal acts and is resigned to his fate by execution, looking upon that grim fate as simply another way of being fired. Though Chaplin sustains fascinating interest throughout and Raye gives a marvelous performance as a lovesick lady, this is not a tale that will provide any hilarity. It is nevertheless an absorbing curiosity where Chaplin strives mightily for empathy with an unappealing character whose sinister doings minimize the great comedian's attempt at bizarre black humor. Though Landru's murders occurred chiefly from 1914 to 1919, Chaplin sets his story in the early 1930s, during the Great Depression, when uncertainty and apprehension about everything was the norm. The film was not a critical or a commercial success, but has become, over the years, a cult film. *Author's Note*: The script for this film, according to the statements given to this author by Orson Welles, was written by Welles, who then offered it to Chaplin, telling the comedian that he, Welles, wanted to direct the film and where Chaplin would have the starring role as the bigamous wife-killer. "He took the script," Welles said to this author, "but after he read it, he told me that he had never had a director and did not want one. Chaplin then went ahead and made the film and I had to squawk about not getting paid or even getting credit for the script. Well, Chaplin paid me, but, when it came to getting the credit, the only 'credit' he would give me was that I gave him the 'idea' for the story and then took complete credit for writing the screenplay. That was Charlie Chaplin for you. I should have known early on that he was a one-man show and beware to anyone who tried to take the center stage from him." Ironically, the film received only one Academy Award nomination, for Best Original Screenplay, and the award nomination mentioned only one writer, Charles Chaplin. For more details on Henri Desire Landru (who murdered twenty to thirty persons, mostly widows, although French police said that he may have claimed up to 300 victims over many years), see my two-volume work, *The Great Pictorial History of World Crime*, Volume II (History, Inc., 2004; pages 1073-1079). **p,d&w**, Charles Chaplin (based on an idea by Orson Welles); **cast**, Chaplin, Mady Correll, Allison Roddan, Robert Lewis, Audrey Betz, Martha Raye, Ada-May, Isobel Elsom, Marjorie Bennett, Helene Heigh; **c**, Roland Totheroh, Curt Courant; **m**, Chaplin; **ed**, Willard Nico; **art d**, John Beckman.

Monsieur Vincent ★★★ 1948; France; 111m; Edition et Diffusion Cinematographique/Lopert Pictures; B/W; Biographical Drama; Children: Acceptable; **DVD**; **VHS**. St. Vincent de Paul (1581-1660), played by Fresnay, humbly carries on charitable work as he struggles to bring about peace and harmony to peasants and nobles during the Black Plague in Europe. The film follows his birth as a French peasant in 1576 to his days of slavery in Algiers and then his years as a Catholic priest and founder of the St. Vincent de Paul Society ministering to the poor and ill. He was canonized in 1737 for his good works. Spiritually moving, stunningly photographed, this well-mounted production also offers an outstanding performance from Fresnay. *Author's Note*: For more information about the Black Plague (Black Death, 1348-1666), see my book, *Darkest Hours: A Narrative Encyclopedia of Worldwide Disasters from Ancient Times to the Present* (Nelson-Hall, 1976; pages 54-57). (In French; English subtitles). **p**, Viscount George de la Grandiere; **d**, Maurice Cloche; **cast**, Pierre Fresnay, Aimé Clariond, Jean Debucourt, Lise Delamare, Germaine Dermoz, Gabrielle Dorziat, Pierre Dux, Yvonne Gaudeau, Michel Bouquet, Jean Carmet; **w**, Jean Bernard-Luc, Jean Anouilh, Cloche; **c**, Claude Renoir; **m**, Jean-Jacques Grunenwald; **ed**, Jean Feyte; **prod d**, Rene Renoux; **set d**, Robert Turlure.

Monsoon Wedding ★★★ 2002; India/U.S./Italy/Germany/France; 113m; IFC Productions/Focus Features; Color; Comedy/Drama; Children: Unacceptable (MPAA: R); **BD**; **DVD**; **VHS**. Das is a young woman living in modern-day Delhi, India. She is about to marry Dabas, an Indian computer programmer from Texas. Das' parents, Shah and Dubey, arranged the marriage, an ancient tradition in India. Das is a modern Indian woman with a married lover, who is a television host, and agrees to marry Dabas because she doubts her lover will ever divorce his wife and marry her. The engaged couple decide they like each

Lillete Dubey and Naseeruddin Shah in *Monsoon Wedding*, 2002.

other. There are subplots involving the romantic lives of members of both the intended bride's and groom's families, permeated with singing and dancing, typical of films from "Bollywood," the term for India's film industry. The result is a delightful film about the culture class of traditional and modern India, and an arranged marriage that takes place during a monsoon. Songs: "Today My Heart Desires" (Sukhwinder Singh), "Today the Weather Plays Tricks On Me" (Laxmikant Shantaram Kudalkar, Pyarelal Ramprasad Sharma), "Allah Hoo" (traditional), "Chunari Chunari" (Anu Malik, Sameer), "Chura Liya" (Majrooh Sultanpuri, Rahul Dev Burman, Bally Sagoo), "Aaja Nachle" (Bally Sagoo, D. Khanne Wala), "The Lie" (Dahoud Darien, Caezaster), "Nice Guys Finish Last" (Joey Johnson). Rated R for incest, strong language, sex-related dialogue. In English. **p**, Caroline Baron, Mira Nair; **d**, Mira Nair; **cast**, Naseeruddin Shah, Lillete Dubey, Shefali Shetty, Vijay Raaz, Tillotama Shome, Vasundhara Das, Parvin Dabas, Kulbhushan Kharbanda, Kamini Khanna, Rajat Kapoor, **w**, Sabrina Dhawan; **c**, Declan Quinn; **m**, Mychael Danna; **ed**, Allyson C. Johnson; **prod d**, Stephanie Carroll; **art d**, Sunil Chhabra.

The Monster and the Girl ★★★ 1941; U.S.; 65m; PAR; B/W; Horror; Children: Unacceptable; **VHS**. This chilling thriller sees Terry, a church organist, being framed for murder by an organized crime syndicate. In striving to prove his innocence, Terry seeks revenge on gangster Lukas for faking a marriage to Terry's younger sister, Drew, in order to draw her into a life of prostitution. Before Terry is executed, Zucco, a scientist, gets Terry's permission to use his brain after he is dead. Zucco puts Terry's brain into an ape that goes on a rampage and kills Lukas and the crime gang, then is killed by police. Drew then winds up with Cameron, a reporter. Director Heisler does a good job developing his characters in this horror entry, but it is one too violent for viewing by children. *Author's Note*: Moss, the producer, also appeared in some offbeat character roles, the most notable being the methodical assassin in the superlative spy drama, **Journey into Fear**, 1943. **p**, Jack Moss; **d**, Stuart Heisler; **cast**, Ellen Drew, Robert Paige, Paul Lukas, Joseph Calleia, Onslow Stevens, George Zucco, Rod Cameron, Phillip Terry, Marc Lawrence, Gerald Mohr, Tom Dugan, Minor Watson, Cliff Edwards, Abner Biberman, Emma Dunn, John Kellogg; **w**, Stuart Anthony; **c**, Victor Milner; **m**, Gerard Carbonara; **ed**, Everett Douglas; **art d**, Hans Dreier, Haldane Douglas.

Monster's Ball ★★★★ 2001; U.S.; 111m; Lee Daniels Entertainment/Lions Gate; Color; Drama/Romance; Children: Unacceptable (MPAA: R); **BD**; **DVD**; **VHS**. Powerful and moving, this romantic drama sees widower Thornton, and his son, Ledger, working as guards in a Louisiana prison. They live at home with ailing grandfather Boyle,

Paul Lukas and Ellen Drew in *The Monster and the Girl*, 1941.

a man consumed by racism and whose wife committed suicide. Boyle's racist views have infected and influenced his son and grandson. When Thornton and Ledger serve as escorts for Combs, a condemned man going to his execution, Ledger loses his nerve and throws up, an act Thornton interprets as cowardice and for which he takes his son into a washroom and mercilessly beats him. Later, at home, the two confront each other, and, following a fight, Thornton tells his son that he has always hated him (he hates everybody) and Ledger tells Thornton that he has always loved him before committing suicide by shooting himself. Thornton is in shock and buries Ledger in the backyard, locks up his son's room, then quits his job and burns his uniform, acts for which Boyle brands him a "quitter." Meanwhile, Berry, who is Combs' widow, struggles to raise her son, Calhoun, desperately trying to keep him out of trouble but severely criticizing him for any minor infraction and hounding him about his excessive eating and obesity. In need of money, Berry faces eviction from her house and, to meet expenses, takes a job at a diner that Thornton routinely visits. When Berry and Calhoun are walking home one rainy night, Calhoun is struck by a car. Other cars routinely pass Berry as she beckons for help. Thornton drives by, seeing her, but drives on. He then turns around, drives back and picks her and Calhoun up and drives Calhoun to a hospital where the boy dies. The traumatized and distraught Berry turns to Thornton, the only person on earth she knows, and he comforts her, allowing her to cry on his shoulder. He then drives her home. Thornton sees her a few days later when she is leaving the diner and drives her home where she invites him inside. He accepts and the two begin drinking, telling each other about their family losses, Thornton's son and Berry's husband, but Thornton does not tell Berry that he participated in Combs' execution. The two begin to bond and Berry visits Thornton's home where they make love. When Berry later visits Thornton, she finds him gone and where the racist Boyle insults her for being a black woman. When Thornton later learns of this, he realizes that his father's bigotry has led to most of his emotional problems in life and he arranges for Boyle to live in a retirement home. When Berry learns of this and after she is evicted, she agrees to live with Thornton. They develop a deepening love for one another, but then Berry discovers that Thornton was one of the prison guards who executed her husband. She does not abandon him, however. Instead, when Thornton returns home, Berry is waiting for him with ice cream and the two sit on the back porch, as if they were an old married couple, eating the ice cream as the film ends. Forster directs this sensitive and moving story with great care and skill while Thornton and Berry give excellent performances as two persons who overcome their self-destructive emotional histories as well as tremendous racial bias through the indefatigable force of love. (Berry won an Oscar for Best Actress). The film does not pretend to be a social drama analyzing the complex-

ities of the still unresolved racism in the Deep South, but presents the portrait of only a few persons inexorably enmeshed within the all-engulfing web of that bigotry. It nevertheless impressively succeeds in resolving the traumas of the disrupted lives of two lonely human beings seeking and finding life-preserving happiness. The film was produced on a budget of $4 million and returned more than $44 million from the box office in its initial release. Songs: "Broken Up and Blue" (Jill Olson), "(I Never Promised You a) Rose Garden" (Joe South), "Your Love Is My Rest" (John Hiatt), "I Couldn't Love You (More Than I Do Now)" (Jean Wells), "License to Kill" (Bob Dylan) and "I'm Your Man" (The Jayhawks). **p**, Lee Daniels, Milo Addica, Will Rokos, **d**, Marc Forster; **cast**, Billy Bob Thornton, Halle Berry, Taylor Simpson, Gabrielle Witcher, Heath Ledger, Amber Rules, Peter Boyle, Sean Combs, Coronji Calhoun, Charles Cowan, Jr., Taylor LaGrange, Mos Def, Anthony Bean; **w**, Addica, Rokos; **c**, Roberto Schaefer; **m**, Asche & Spencer; **ed**, Matt Chesse; **prod d**, Monroe Kelly; **art d& set d**, Leonard Spears; **spec eff**, David Nami.

Monsters, Inc. ★★★★ 2001; U.S.; 92m; Pixar/Walt Disney Pictures/Buena Vista; Color; Animated Adventure; Children: Acceptable (MPAA: G); **BD**; **DVD**; **VHS**. Superbly crafted animated adventure that hilariously spoofs monsters (taking a leaf from the loveable puppet Cookie Monster of Sesame Street fame), this inventive adventure profiles two worlds, one inhabited by monsters that is empowered by the screams of children in the real world and that real world of children. The goofy-looking monsters sally forth from their world, using closet doors as portals to enter the real world where they collect those screams from children, but these visitations are considered by the monsters as extremely dangerous as they believe human beings are toxic and any monster touching them will be destroyed. The scariest monster is Sulley (short for James P. Sullivan; Goodman voiceover), who is assigned by Randall Boggs (Buscemi voiceover), the head of the monster factory, to solve a serious problem where the manufacturing of monsters is falling off because children are losing their fear of them. Sulley, who lives with fellow monster Mike Wazowski (Crystal voiceover), discovers that Boggs has left a portal open and that a girl (Gibbs), has entered the factory. With Mike's help, Sulley hides the girl in a bag and later escorts her home, discovering that she is not toxic and she makes friends with Sulley and Mike. When they return to the monster factory they find that Boggs has assembled a torture machine to extract more screams from children, a "Scream Extractor," using Gibbs, who has been abducted, as a guinea pig, and when he and Mike attempt to save Gibbs they are banished to the Himalayas. Once they are within those frozen climes, an Abominable Snowman (Ratzenberger voiceover) tells them that they can return to the factory through a portal in the local village. Sulley uses the portal, but Mike, who is fed up with Sulley's misadventures, refuses to return to the factory. Sulley then saves Gibbs from the Scream Extractor, and when Mike suddenly appears, they both defeat Boggs, escaping with Gibbs. Boggs pursues, but when Gibbs laughs, countless stored portals open through which Sulley, Gibbs, and Mike enter and leave while Boggs doggedly chases them. Sulley and Mike then trap Boggs in the human world where he is beaten senseless by some hillbillies when they mistake him for a fierce alligator. Gibbs is returned to the human world, but the portal to Gibbs has been damaged and Mike works hard to restore it, finally reuniting Sulley with his human friend. Moreover, Sulley has solved the problem of empowerment. He has become the head of the factory and now sends the monsters to human children to entertain them and not scare them, their human laughter providing more power than their screams ever did in the past. This entertainingly hair-brained tale presents a wonderful visual treat that is rich with lively and innovative animation and colorful characters that should delight young and old. Song: "If I Didn't Have You" (Randy Newman). **p**, Darla K. Anderson, Karen Dufilho; **d**, Pete Docter, David Silverman, Lee Unkrich; **cast** (voiceovers), John Goodman, Billy Crystal, Mary Gibbs, Steve Buscemi, James Coburn, Jennifer Tilly, Bob

Peterson, John Ratzenberger, Frank Oz, Bonnie Hunt, Laraine Newman; **w**, Docter, Jill Culton, Jeff Pidgeon, Ralph Eggleston, Andrew Stanton, Daniel Gerson, Robert Baird, Rhett Reese, Jonathan Roberts; **m**, Randy Newman; **ed**, Robert Grahamjones, Jim Stewart; **prod d**, Harley Jessup, Bob Pauley; **art d**, Tia W. Kratter, Dominique Louis.

Monte Carlo ★★★ 1930; U.S.; 90m; PAR; B/W; Musical Comedy; Children: Acceptable; **DVD**. This thoroughly entertaining musical sees MacDonald as an impoverished countess, who backs out of a marriage with stuffy duke Allister, taking a train to Monte Carlo where she hopes to win big. A count, Buchanan, falls for her, but MacDonald ignores him. Buchanan then assumes the guise of a hairdresser, who later becomes her servant as butler and chauffeur, and he seems to be more appealing to her in this more slavish role. She falls in love with him, but is tempted to marry the count, not realizing Buchanan is the same man. MacDonald later discovers the two men she loves are one and the same, and finally goes to the altar with the count. The so-called "Lubitsch touch" is in strong evidence in every frame of this charming musical, such as where Buchanan, while impersonating the hairdresser, strokes MacDonald's luxuriant hair as a sign of good luck at the gambling tables. In another unforgettable scene MacDonald sings "Beyond the Blue Horizon," from the open window of her speeding train and she is joined by peasants and farmers working in the fields through which that train travels. The direction is superb (Lubitsch had scored a success with MacDonald and Maurice Chevalier only a year earlier with the smash musical, **The Love Parade**, 1929), and he presents a swift-moving story with high production values boasting extraordinarily lavish sets that, in and of themselves, are sights to behold. Songs: "Beyond the Blue Horizon," "Always in All Ways," "Give Me A Moment Please," "She'll Love Me and Like It," "Day of Days," "Trimmin' the Women," "Whatever It Is, It's Grand" (Richard A. Whiting, W. Franke Harling, Leo Robin). This film was a solid success, furthering the illustrious film career of Mac-Donald, but Buchanan, who was mainly a stage star, generated little interest and did not appear in another major musical film until three decades later when performing with Fred Astaire in **The Band Wagon**, 1953. *Author's Note*: In one of the many meetings this author had with pantheon director Alfred Hitchcock, and where we discussed the films of Ernest Lubitsch, Hitchcock stated that his use of trains in his films held in and of themselves the elements of mystery in that their destinations had not been realized. Hitchcock added: "I didn't see them [trains] like Lubitsch did in **Monte Carlo** when he had Jeannette MacDonald sing 'Beyond the Blue Horizon.' She was having a love affair on the train and he cut to one of the train's pistons going in and out. I guess you could call that 'The Lubitsch Touch.'" **p**, Adolph Zukor; **d**, Ernst Lubitsch; **cast**, Jack Buchanan, Jeanette MacDonald, Claud Allister, Zasu Pitts, Tyler Brooke, John Roche, Lionel Belmore, Albert Conti, John Carroll, Frances Dee; **w**, Ernest Vajda, Vincent Lawrence (based on the play "The Blue Coast" by Hans Müller and the novel *Monsieur Beaucaire* by Booth Tarkington and the play by Evelyn Greenleaf Sutherland based on his novel); **c**, Victor Milner; **m**, W. Franke Harling, Richard Whiting, Karl Hajos, Herman Hand, Sigmund Krumgold, John Leipold; **ed**. Merrill G. White.

Monte Walsh ★★★★ 1970; U.S.; 106m; Cinema Center/National General; Color; Western; Children: Cautionary; **DVD**; **VHS**. This gritty and realistic western offers wonderful characterizations from Marvin and Palance, who are down-at-the-heels cowboys, grateful for any kind of work that will allow them to survive in a fading Old West. Marvin and Palance show up separately at a ranch run by Davis and are hired as hands, meeting an old pal, Ryan. All is well as the cowpokes ride to the nearby town of Harmony for recreation and where Marvin renews his relationship with old flame Moreau, who works in a saloon. Palance meets McLerie, who has inherited a lucrative hardware store after being recently widowed; their romance sees them wed; Palance is now a down-to-earth businessman. These fortunate circumstances come not

Lee Marvin in *Monte Walsh*, 1970.

too soon in that the ranch where he and Marvin have been working closes down. Palance urges the out-of-work Marvin to quit the cowboy lifestyle, saying there is no future there for him and to seek other opportunities. Marvin takes that advice and trails Moreau, who has moved to another saloon in a new town. He asks her to marry him, but she refuses, saying that she has tuberculosis and her time on earth is too short for her to make any wedding plans, although she is flattered by Marvin's offer. Marvin gets drunk and, while staggering about, sees a runaway wild horse crashing about in the town during the middle of the night. His cowboy instincts cause him to rope the bucking horse and, in a wild struggle, he tames the animal, but not until the horse does considerable damage. Its grateful owner is the head of a Wild West show, who offers Marvin a job at a high rate of pay if he will pretend to be "Texas Jack Barrat." Marvin, at first, is tempted, but then rebels against the idea, quitting. He is Monte Walsh, a lowly cowboy, but he has pride in having lived and worked hard and says: "I ain't spitting on my whole life." Meanwhile, saddle mate Ryan, also out of a job, has turned bad and hooked up with some thieves. They rob Palance's store and shoot and kill Palance when he resists turning over the money in the till. Marvin then sets out to bring Ryan to justice, but when he hears that Moreau is dying, he goes to see her, finding her dead and where he arranges for her funeral. Marvin learns that Ryan is hiding out in the same town and he and Ryan finally meet again, stalking each other before shooting it out and where Ryan is killed. Without the love of a woman and with his closest friends dead, Marvin, undaunted and still hopeful, saddles up and rides out to seek another job as a cowboy, the only life he has ever known. Bittersweet and uncompromising, this hard knocks western from Fraker is superbly directed and photographed, and all the grit, grime and hardscrabble elements of the Old West shows in every frame and where Marvin, Palance, Moreau and Ryan (his debut) are outstanding. The demanding and almost unbearable life of the cowboy in the Old West is fully captured here, offering very little optimism for a better way of life, only the hope of survival, one of the more realistic westerns to join the ranks of **Red River**, 1948; **Cowboy**, 1958; **Will Penny**, 1968; **The Culpepper Cattle Company**, 1972; **The Missouri Breaks**, 1976; and **Open Range**, 2003. Song: "The Good Times Are Comin'" (John Barry, Hal David). *Author's Note*: This film marks Fraker's debut as a director. He had been a cinematographer for more than a decade before he was able to convince producers to allow him to direct and he proves tremendous talent in doing so. Marvin told this author that "**Monte Walsh** is about the most sincere picture I ever made. Everything is honest in that film. All the characters are real. No gloss, no glamour, it's so good you can almost smell the horse dung mixing the boiling black coffee. I liked my role, a worn-out saddle tramp with a sense of honor and no matter how miserable life is, my character faces up to it. That's how I think it

Vanessa Redgrave in *A Month By the Lake*, 1995.

truly was in the Old West. There were few choices in those days and the wrong one could get you killed very fast. You take another film I was in, **The Dirty Dozen** [1967], a war picture that became very popular, but that film was not sincere, hokey phony all the way through, all about a bunch of criminal misfits who destroy half the German high command in World War II. I was in that war and, believe me, no such things ever happened. **Monte Walsh**, on the other hand, is a picture you can believe in." **p**, Hal Landers, Bobby Roberts; **d**, William A. Fraker; **cast**, Lee Marvin, Jeanne Moreau, Jack Palance, Mitchell Ryan, Jim Davis, G.D. Spradlin, Bo Hopkins, Allyn Ann McLerie, Richard Farnsworth, Guy Wilkerson, Roy Barcroft; **w**, Lukas Heller, David Zelag Goodman (based on the novel by Jack Schaefer); **c**, David M. Walsh (Technicolor); **m**, John Barry; **ed**, Dick Brockway, Robert L. Wolfe, Ray Daniels, Gene Fowler, Jr.; **prod d**, Albert Brenner; **art d**, Ward Preston; **set d**, Phil Abramson; **spec eff**, Roy Bolton, George Peckham, Daniel Hays.

Montenegro ★★★ 1981; Sweden/U.K.; 96m; Europa Film/Atlantic Releasing Corp.; Color; Drama; Children: Unacceptable (MPAA: R); **DVD**; **VHS**. Anspach is a bored and sexually unhappy American married to Josephson, a straight-laced Swedish businessman in Stockholm whose family members are eccentric (the grandfather thinks he is Buffalo Bill). She gets some relief from her boring married life when Josephson leaves on a business trip and she spends two nights at a ghetto nightclub frequented by some free-living if unkempt Yugoslavian immigrants. Their lives are consumed by sex and violence, and Anspach likes it. She is photographed with a man with a knife in his forehead and sharing the back seat of a car with a sheep. At the club, Anspach becomes attracted to a strong, young peasant, but nothing comes of it. After her husband returns, she goes back to him, but with intentions of loosening up their rigid lives. She has had a taste of life as it can be lived more fully and it has changed her life and marriage, becoming what was then known as a "liberated woman." Songs: "The Ballad of Lucy Jordan" (Shel Silverstein); "The Rhythm" (Neville Cameron); ""I Do, I Do, I Do, I Do," "Why Did It Have to Be Me" (Benny Andersson; Stig Andersson, Bjorn Ulvaeus); "Ramo, Ramo," and "Give Me a Little Kiss" (Roy Turk, Jack Smith, Maceo Pinkard). **p**, Bo Jonsson; **d**, Dusan Makavejev; **cast**, Susan Anspach, Erland Josephson, Svetozar Cvetkovic, Per Oscarsson, Marianna Jacobi, James Marsh, John Zacharias, Marina Lindahl, Bora Todorovic, Lisbeth Zachrisson, **w**, Makavejev, Donald Arthur, Branko Vucicevic; **c**, Tomislav Pinter; **m**, Kornell Kovach; **ed**, Sylvia Ingemarsson; **prod d**, Radu Boruzescu.

A Month By the Lake ★★★ 1995; U.K./U.S.; 92m; Anuline/Miramax Films; Color; Drama/Romance; Children: Unacceptable (MPAA: PG); **DVD**; **VHS**. London spinster Redgrave has spent each April for the last sixteen years on holiday with her artist father at a posh hillside villa on Lake Como in Italy. In 1937, her father dies, and she goes to the villa alone, finding the other guests that April to be brash Americans. Fox, a dapper, middle-aged, but rather formal British army major, checks in as a guest at the spa, and invites Redgrave to cocktails. She forgetfully stands him up when she becomes involved in helping another new arrival, Thurman, a young American woman. Thurman, who recently dropped out of a Swiss finishing school, flirts with Fox. This causes Redgrave to take more of an interest in him. Fox likes Thurman's company, despite being beaten by her in a tennis game. Thurman notices the attraction growing between Redgrave and Fox and decides to quietly help it along. When Fox prepares to leave and return to England, Thurman gives him a rose and a kiss within sight of Redgrave. This backfires by encouraging Fox, although he is years older than Thurman. Cupid enters in the form of a handsome young Italian gigolo, Gasman, who showers attention on Redgrave. True love wins in the end and Fox realizes Thurman is not the woman for him and that he has fallen in love with Redgrave, and the feeling is mutual with her. Thurman can now leave, knowing she has done her job well as a matchmaker. Songs: "A Tripoli" (C. Arona), "Tuli-Tulip Time" (Maria Grevet, Jack Lawrence), "Fascination" (F.D. Marchotti) and "Aida" (Giuseppi Verdi). A gentle, charming film, there is nothing offensive for children, but it is rated PG for moments of sensuality. **p**, Robert Fox, Bob and Harvey Weinstein; **d**, John Irvin; **cast**, Vanessa Redgrave, Edward Fox, Uma Thurman, Alida Valli, Carlo Cartier, Alessandro Gassman, Natalia Bizzi, Frances Nacman, Paolo Lombardi, Riccardo Rossi, Sonia Martinelli, Veronica Wells; **w**, Trevor Bentham (based on a story by H.E. Bates); **c**, Pasqualino De Santis; **m**, Nicola Piovani; **ed**, Peter Tanner; **prod d**, Gianni Giovagnoni; **set d**, Mauro Passi, Joanne Woollard; **spec eff**, Massimo Cristofanelli.

Monty Python and the Holy Grail ★★★ 1975; U.K.; 91m; Python (Monty) Pictures/Cinema 5 Distributing; Color; Comedy; Children: Unacceptable (MPAA: R); **DVD**; **VHS**. One of the better Monty Python films, this satire focuses on the legend of King Arthur, who is in search of the Holy Grail. Arthur (Chapman), King of the Britons, needs knights to sit with him at the roundtable at Camelot. He finds them in the pure Sir Galahad (Palin), brave Sir Lancelot (Cleese), and others. They arrive not on horseback but on foot with their servants, who smack coconuts together to create the sound of horses' hooves (typical of the endless sight gags and ancient slapstick permeating the Python films). Along the way to Camelot they encounter witch trials and survive the Black Plague, but when they get there they decide not to stay. God appears to them from a cloud and tells them (Chapman voiceover) to find the Holy Grail, the chalice from which Jesus drank wine at the Last Supper. Arthur and his knights set off on that quest, but meet many obstacles. The Black Knight (Cleese) refuses to let them pass, so a battle takes place that results in a lot of bloody body parts. Then Lancelot invades a castle to rescue a prince he believes is gay and in distress at a wedding and hacks all the guests to pieces. It all ends in a humongous battle that is broken up by police, who steal the camera that is shooting the film. Songs: "Camelot Song (Knights of the Round Table" (Neil Innes, Graham Chapman, John Cleese); "Monk's Chant," "Sir Robin's Song," "Knights of Ni," "Fanfare," "Sunrise Music," "God Choir," "He's Going to Hell" (Innes); "Big Country" (Keith Papworth); "Homeward Bound" (Jack Trombey); "In the Shadows" (Paul Ferris); "Circle of Danger" (B. Holmes); "Magenta" (Roger Webb); "Love Theme" (Peter Knight); "Starlet in the Starlight" (Kenneth Essex); "The Promised Land" (Stanley Black); "Ice Floe 9" (Pierre Arvay) and "Flying Messenger" (Oliver Armstrong as Graham Whettam). Rated R for extreme violence. **p**, Mark Forstater, Michael White; **d**, Terry Gilliam, Terry Jones; **cast**, Graham Chapman, John Cleese, Gilliam, Eric Idle, Jones, Michael Palin, Connie Booth, Carol Cleveland, Neil Innes, Bee Duffell, John Young; **w**, Chapman, Cleese, Idle, Gilliam, Jones, Palin; **c**, Terry Beadford; **m**, Neil Innes, DeWolfe; **ed**, John Hackney; **prod d**, Roy Smith; **spec eff**, John

Horton, Valerie Charlton, Julian Doyle.

Moon ★★★ 2009; U.K.; 97m; Liberty Films UK/ Sony Pictures; Color; Science Fiction; Children: Unacceptable (MPAA: R); **BD**; **DVD**. This absorbing sci-fi entry is set sometime in the future; space scientist Rockwell has a three-year contract from a mining company as the only person aboard its lunar energy station on the dark side of the moon. His primary job is periodically rocketing back to Earth supplies of helium-3, which is extracted from lunar rocks and is the cleanest and most abundant energy source then used on Earth. His only communication with Earth is through a robot called GERTY (Spacey voiceover). He is weary of being isolated and eager to return to Earth to be reunited with his wife, McElligott, and their infant daughter. With just two weeks left to his mission, he has an accident and falls unconscious. He revives to see a clone of himself, identical in looks and in love with the same wife. Rockwell may be just hallucinating, but we don't know if he becomes one man again and returns to Earth. Songs: "Walking on Sunshine" (Kimberley Rew), "Flute and Harp Concerto K299" (Wolfgang Amadeus Mozart), "Ripples" (Benjamin Wallfisch), and "One and Only" (Nik Kershaw). Sexuality and gutter language prohibit viewing by children. **p**, Stuart Fenegan, Trudie Styler, Nicky Bentham (Nicky Moss), Mark Foligno, Alex Francis, Steve Milne, Deepak Sikka; **d**, Duncan Jones; **cast**, Sam Rockwell, Kevin Spacey (voice only), Dominique McElligott, Rosie Shaw, Adrienne Shaw, Kaya Scodelario, Benedict Wong, Matt Berry, Malcolm Stewart, Robin Chalk, **w**, Jones, Nathan Parker; **c**, Gary Shaw; **m**, Clint Mansell; **ed**, Nicolas Gaster; **prod d**, Tony Noble; **art d**, Hideki Arichi; **spec eff**, Garth Gutteridge, Peter Hutchinson, Stuart Prior, Gavin Rothery, Simon Stanley-Clamp.

The Moon and Sixpence ★★★★ 1942; U.S.; 89m; David L. Loew-Albert Lewin/UA; B/W; Biographical Drama; Children: Cautionary; **DVD**; **VHS**. Sanders is riveting in this superlative biopic, giving one of his finest performances while essaying a role model based upon the gifted and reclusive French painter, Paul Gauguin (1848-1903). Marshall, who plays the author of the story (Maugham, upon whose novel this film is based) narrates this tale, which begins with Sanders as a successful London broker. Having a lifelong and passionate ambition to paint, Sanders befriends Geray, a mediocre but very successful painter, who makes Sanders his protégé and takes him into his home. Geray teaches Sanders all the techniques of mixing paint and the various styles of painting, but the insidious and ungrateful Sanders repays him by seducing his wife, Dudley, and wrecking Geray's life before accepting self-exile to Tahiti. There, as Marshall describes, Sanders comes to grips with himself and his terrible deeds as he begins to earnestly paint one masterpiece after another until he tragically dies. (We do not know if the contemplative Sanders is motivated to produce these outstanding artworks out of guilt or pride of work or by doing penance for the misery he has caused others.) *Author's Note*: Director Lewin inserted tints (sepia tone) in some of his scenes to enhance the artwork and then went to full-fledged color in the final reel to better display the many Gauguin paintings. This was an innovative technique for its day and one not lost on Vincente Minnelli when he went into production for **Lust for Life**, 1956, but where Minnelli used special color film to best exhibit the works of Vincent Van Gogh, played by Douglas. "I did see that film with Sanders, of course, and Lewin was wise to go to color in the last scenes to show Gauguin's works in all their colorful glory. He used the old Technicolor process for that picture and its luxuriant colors is exactly what we needed for **Lust for Life**, but that old process had been abandoned as too expensive by the time we did the Van Gogh picture, so we had to buy up a lot of the old color film stock and even have more manufactured to get the same deep and vivid color quality reproductions." Sanders told this author that "I loved that picture [**The Moon and Sixpence**]. Even though I am playing another cad, I redeem myself through great art. I have another name in the film, but my character is still based on Gauguin. You know, Gauguin was as mean as I ever was

George Sanders in *The Moon and Sixpence,* 1942.

in my worst portrayals. He had a cruel streak that ran right down to his toes." **p**, David L. Loew; **d&w**, Albert Lewin (based on the novel by W. Somerset Maugham); **cast**, George Sanders, Herbert Marshall, Doris Dudley, Eric Blore, Albert Bassermann, Florence Bates, Steven Geray, Elena Verdugo, Robert Greig, Rondo Hatton, Molly Lamont, Mike Mazurki, Irene Tedrow, Heather Thatcher; **c**, John F. Seitz; **m**, Dimitri Tiomkin; **ed**, Richard L. Van Enger; **prod d**, Gordon Wiles; **art d**, F. Paul Sylos.

The Moon is Down ★★★ 1943; U.S.; 90m; FOX; B/W; War Drama; Children: Unacceptable; **DVD**; **VHS**. Grim but effective and moving propaganda film based on Steinbeck's novel and play, the story begins with the Nazi invasion of Norway and where Hardwicke and his German troops occupy a small village. Unlike the German officers portrayed in similar films at this time, Hardwicke is a practical old school officer, who believes that the ruthless Nazi tactics commonly practiced are counterproductive and reduce the amount of coal and products the Germans can otherwise glean for their ongoing war effort. He rules with tolerance if not benevolence without cruelty and punishments, but his wily opponent, soft-spoken Travers, the town mayor, is up to his tricks. Resistance from the villagers is demonstrated again and again as German phone lines are severed, stores destroyed and, after British planes parachute dynamite and arms to the Norwegians, rail lines and German installations are blown up and Nazi soldiers routinely killed. Ballantine, a traitorous villager, turns informant and convinces Hardwicke to take massive reprisals where many of the village leaders, including Travers, are summarily executed. Bowdon takes revenge against the Nazis by inviting van Eyck, a German officer, into her room where she fatally stabs him. The villagers then attack the Germans, defeating them, and then plan an all-out guerrilla war against the invaders. Pichel directs with a firm hand as he delivers a shocking portrait of Nazi oppression and wholesale slaughter, and the cast members, though none are Hollywood stars, give standout performances. *Author's Note*: The original Steinbeck novel for this story was a runaway bestseller with more than a million copies sold in its first run. Steinbeck then wrote a play based on his novel and who stated to this author "that play did not do as well as expected. It ran only nine weeks on Broadway, but when we put it on the road, well, small-town American audiences couldn't get enough of it and it ran for months. It was a defiant message to the Nazis that their brutal tactics would never work in a free society and that's what Americans wanted to hear when we were at war with Germany." Fox, which had produced Steinbeck's classic **The Grapes of Wrath**, 1940, which was a huge success, paid Steinbeck $300,000 for the screen rights to *The Moon Is Down* (a staggering amount for those days). Johnson, who produced and wrote the script (and whose wife Bowdon appears

Richard Dreyfuss in _Moon Over Parador_, 1988.

in the film; she had played the young, pregnant woman in the Joad family in the film production of Steinbeck's **The Grapes of Wrath**, for which Johnson also wrote the screenplay) told this author that "I toned down Steinbeck's hortatory speeches in that story. I felt that he was preaching to his readers and audiences, and even though the message is a good one, no one wants to be lectured." The harsh and uncompromising film did not do well at the box office and, in fact, lost money, which irked Fox studio chief Darryl Zanuck. He blamed the fact that the subject of slave labor, which is depicted throughout the film, was the cause of the film's failure. "**The Moon Is Down** laid an big egg," Zanuck told this author. "The subject of slave labor has no audience appeal and we learned that lesson the hard way when we profiled slave labor in that picture. Sure, the Nazis get killed, but not until everyone has gone through those exhausting and miserable slave labor scenes. It was just too bitter a pill to swallow." **p&w**, Nunnally Johnson (based on the novel by John Steinbeck); **d**, Irving Pichel; **cast**, Sir Cedric Hardwicke, Henry Travers, Lee J. Cobb, Dorris Bowdon, Margaret Wycherly, Peter van Eyck, William Post, Jr., Ludwig Donath, Jeff Corey, Kurt Kreuger, Mae Marsh, Dorothy Peterson, William Prince, Helene Thimig, E. J. Ballantine, Ian Wolfe, Trevor Bardette, Natalie Wood, Pichel; **c**, Arthur Miller; **m**, Alfred Newman; **ed**, Louis Loeffler; **art d**, James Basevi, Maurice Ransford; **set d**, Thomas Little, Walter M. Scott; **spec eff**, Fred Sersen.

Moon Over Miami ★★★ 1941; U.S.; FOX; Color; Musical; Children: Acceptable; **DVD**; **VHS**. This lively musical comedy was one of the entertaining films that gave relief to the American public during the dark days of World War II (its release running well into 1942) and established Grable as the number-one pin-up girl for American GIs. It was the second of three films with the same plot: Three women set out to find rich husbands. Grable and Landis are Texas sisters, who go to Florida with their aunt, Greenwood. They check into a swanky hotel, which serves as their headquarters in their fortune-hunting mission. Grable pretends to be a rich single woman, Landis her secretary, and Greenwood their maid. They soon meet three marital candidates: Ameche, who was once rich but is no longer in the money; Cummings, who is filthy rich; and a waiter, Haley, with no prospects of wealth. After some romantic shenanigans, Grable and Ameche pair off, Landis and Cummings do the same, and Greenwood decides she loves Haley, even though he isn't rich. This film was made earlier as **Three Blind Mice**, 1938, and later remade as **Three Little Girls in Blue**, 1946. Songs: "Moon Over Miami" (Joseph Burke); "What Can I Do for You?," "Miami (Oh Me, Oh Mi-Ami)," "You Started Something," "I've Got You All to Myself," "Is That Good?," "Loveliness and Love," "Kindergarten Conga" and "Solitary Seminole" (Ralph Rainger, Leo Robin). _Author's Note_: Location shots were made at Silver Springs and Cypress Gardens. The well-staged cho-

reography in the several dance numbers was created by the gifted Hermes Pan, who routinely worked on almost all of Fred Astaire's films as they were close associates. Ameche told this author that "**Moon over Miami** was another one of those great little musicals that had plenty of pep. Here I am with two of the most luscious ladies in pictures, Betty [Grable] and Carole [Landis]. How could a guy miss? I got a lot of fan mail on that one from guys asking me questions about those two sensational blondes and I wondered why they weren't writing to them instead of me. Maybe they thought I had some secrets to tell. I didn't." **p**, Harry Joe Brown; **d**, Walter Lang; **cast**, Don Ameche, Betty Grable, Robert Cummings, Carole Landis, Jack Haley, Charlotte Greenwood, Cobina Wright. Jr., Lynne Roberts, Russell Wade, Robert Greig, Minor Watson, Fortunio Bonanova, Hermes Pan; **w**, Vincent Lawrence, Brown Holmes (based on an adaptation by George Seaton, Lynn Starling of the play "Three Blind Mice" by Stephen Powys); **c**, Peverell Marley, Leon Shamroy, Allen M. Davey (Technicolor); **m**, Alfred Newman, David Buttolph, Charles Henderson, Cyril J. Mockridge; **ed**, Walter Thompson; **art d**, Richard Day, Wiard B. Ihnen; **set d**, Thomas Little.

Moon Over Parador ★★★ 1988; U.S.; 103m; UNIV; Color; Comedy; Children: Unacceptable (MPAA: PG-13); **DVD**; **VHS**. Entertaining comedy sees Dreyfuss as a minor actor working on location in the mythical South American country of Parador when its dictator suddenly dies of a heart attack. Julia, the dictator's right-hand man, doesn't want to lose his position of power, so he entices Dreyfuss to impersonate the dictator. Dreyfuss, who is a look-alike for the deceased tyrant, at first declines, but Julia appeals to his thespian ambitions, telling him that his impersonation of the dictator will be his greatest performance, and Dreyfuss accepts, playing the part. This fools the general public but not close friends and employees of the late dictator. There are some hilarious moments and some harrowing sequences as Dreyfuss romps through his charade, especially when romancing the dead president's attractive mistress, Braga. Life at the top, however, is not what Dreyfuss envisioned and, after instituting reforms and aiding the natives, as well as stifling Julia's own ambitions to become the new dictator, Dreyfuss becomes bored in paradise and then decides to resume his humdrum life by returning to New York City. This is a remake (and a better one) of **The Magnificent Fraud**, 1939. Songs: "O Parador" (Will Holt, Leon Capetanos, Paul Mazursky), "Lilli Marlene" (Norbert Schultze, Hans Leip), "Ni Ti Tango, Ni Ti Olvido" (L. Barday), "Begin the Beguine" (Cole Porter), "Besame Mucho" (Consuela Velazquez, Sunny Skylar). Mature content prohibits viewing by children. **p**, Paul Mazursky, Pato Guzman, Geoffrey Taylor; **d**, Mazursky; **cast**, Richard Dreyfuss, Raul Julia, Sonia Braga, Jonathan Winters, Fernando Rey, Marianne Sägebrecht, Dana Delany, Polly Holliday, Michael Greene, Sammy Davis, Jr., Dick Cavett, Edward Asner, Mazursky; **w**, Mazursky, Leon Capetanos (based on a story by Charles G. Booth); **c**, Donald McAlpine; **m**, Maurice Jarre; **ed**, Stuart H. Pappé; **prod d**, Guzman; **art d**, Marcos Flaksman; **set d**, Alexandre Meyer; **spec eff**, Pat Domenico.

Moonlight Sonata ★★★ 1938; U.K.; 86m; Malmar/UA; B/W; Drama; Children: Acceptable; **DVD**. After a plane is forced down in Sweden, two survivors become the guests of a baroness, Tempest, taking residence in her mansion. They are famed Polish pianist Ignacy Jan Paderewski (1860-1941), played by himself, and an American, Farrell. Fortune-hunting Portman flirts with Tempest's sheltered granddaughter, Greene, but Farrell exposes him as a hypnotist and fraud. This leaves the way open for Farrell to romance Greene while Paderewski plays the piano. The thin plot is nevertheless a good excuse for some great music. Songs: "Heroic Polonaise" (Frederic Chopin), "Hungarian Rhapsody" (Franz Liszt), "Moonlight Sonata" (Ludwig van Beethoven), "Minuet in G" (Paderewski). **p&d**, Lothar Mendes; **cast**, Ignacy Jan Paderewski, Charles Farrell, Marie Tempest, Barbara Greene, Eric Portman, W. Graham Brown, Queenie Leonard, Laurence Hanray, Binkie Stuart, Bryan Powley; **w**, E.M. Delafield, Edward Knoblock (based on a story by Hans

Rameau); **c**, Jan Stallich; **m**, Ludwig van Beethoven; **ed**, Philip Charlot; **set d**, Laurence Irving.

Moonlighting ★★★ 1982; U.K.; 97m; Michael White Productions; UNIV; Color; Drama; Children: Unacceptable (MPAA: PG); **DVD**; **VHS**. Solid drama has Irons as a Polish contractor leading a group of workers to London where they will provide cheap labor for a building project, and where they will all earn more money than what they could earn at home. They have one month to renovate a building so their Polish boss can live there. Irons, the only one of the group who speaks English, manages the project. The men experience loneliness and separation from their families as well as temptations. Back in Poland, Soviet soldiers invade Poland and communications are cut off so the workers do not know about events at home or the conditions or safety of their families. A construction accident delays work on a flat for the Polish boss, and Irons scrounges or steals food and supplies to keep going. He knows about the dire events in Poland through reading newspapers, but keeps this news from the workers as long as he can, so they will keep working. When he finally has to tell them about things in Poland they beat him, considering him to be an enemy of Poland. The film is a grim but impressive parody on real events in the early 1980s at the time of the banning of the Solidarity movement in Poland to break free of communist rule. The house the men are remodeling is symbolic of a new Poland and the workmen symbols of the Solidarity movement. **p**, Jerzy Skolimowski, Mark Shivas, Michael White; **d&w**, Skolimowski; **cast**, Jeremy Irons, Eugene Lipinski, Jiří Stanislav, Eugeniusz Haczkiewicz, Edward Arthur, Denis Holmes, Renu Setna, David Calder, Judy Gridley, Claire Toeman, Jenny Seagrove; **c**, Tony Pierce Roberts; **m**, Stanley Myers; **ed**, Barrie Vince; **prod d**, Tony Woollard; **spec eff**, Roy Whybrow.

Moonraker ★★★ 1979; U.K.; 126m; Danjaq/UA; Color; Spy/Adventure; Children: Unacceptable (MPAA: R); **DVD**; **VHS**. This ninth film in the James Bond series was the most expensive to produce, costing almost as much as the first eight put together (budget of $34 million; returned $210 million at the box office). Moore plays Agent 007 in a silver space suit investigating the mid-air theft of a space shuttle and foils a plot by Lonsdale to take over the world. The fetching Chiles serves as Moore's love interest in this action-jammed film which presents many exciting and tense scenes. Songs: "Moonraker" (John Barry, Hal David), "Raindrop Prelude" (Frederic Chopin), "Romeo and Juliet Overture/Fantasy" (Pyotr Ilyich Tchaikovsky), "Tritsch-Tratsch Polka" (Johann Strauss, Jr.), "Theme from **The Magnificent Seven**" (Elmer Bernstein), "Vesti la giubba" from "Pagliacci" (Ruggero Leoncavallo). **p**, Albert R. Broccoli; **d**, Lewis Gilbert; **cast**, Roger Moore, Lois Chiles, Michael Lonsdale, Richard Kiel, Corinne Cléry, Bernard Lee, Geoffrey Keen, Desmond Llewelyn, Lois Maxwell, Toshiro Suga, Brian Keith; **w**, Christopher Wood (based on the novel by Ian Fleming); **c**, Jean Tournier (Panavision; Technicolor); **m**, John Barry; **ed**, John Glen; **prod d**, Ken Adam; **art d**, Charles Bishop, Max Douy; **set d**, Peter Howitt; **spec eff**, John Richardson, Chris Corbould, John Evans, Rene Albouze, Charles Assola, Serge Ponvianne, Anton Furst, Derek Meddings.

Moonrise ★★★ 1948; U.S.; 90m; REP; B/W; Crime Drama; Children: Unacceptable; **VHS**. Offbeat film noir entry set in the South sees Clark as a young man tormented by the memory of his father, who was hanged for murder. The contemplative Clark believes that he has "bad blood" and that he might possess the same kind of killer instincts displayed by his father. A loner, he is taunted by all the other youths of his small town, especially Carey, a vicious thug. The only person who understands and loves Clark is beautiful Russell. Carey again taunts Clark, recalling the terrible deeds of his father, and then attacks him. Clark fights back and kills Carey in an obvious act of self-defense. Feeling that the Mark of Cain is upon him, Clark flees, escaping through some swamps to find his old schoolteacher, Barrymore, a reclusive, wise old woman, who takes him in and begins patiently counseling him until he understands

Ethel Barrymore and Dane Clark in *Moonrise*, 1948.

his motivations. When he no longer feels that he has inherited his father's guilt, he decides to return to town and turn himself into authorities. Director Borzage does a wonderful job in providing a tale thick with tension and moody atmosphere while exacting compelling and empathetic portrayals from Clark and Russell, who are standouts in their roles. Songs: "The Moonrise Song (It Just Dawned on Me)" (William Lava, Harry Tobias), "Lonesome" (William Lava, Theodore Strauss) and "I'll Be Home for Christmas" (Walter Kent, Buck Ram, Kim Gannon). **p&w**, Charles Haas (based on the novel by Theodore Strauss); **d**, Frank Borzage; **cast**, Dane Clark, Gail Russell, Ethel Barrymore, Allyn Joslyn, Rex Ingram, Henry (Harry) Morgan, David Street, Selena Royle, Harry Carey Jr., Irving Bacon, Lloyd Bridges, Houseley Stevenson, Phil Brown, Charles Lane, Clem Bevans; **c**, John L. Russell; **m**, William Lava; **ed**, Harry Keller; **art d**, Lionel Banks; **set d**, John McCarthy, Jr., George Sawley; **spec eff**, Howard and Theodore Lydecker.

The Moon's Our Home ★★★ 1936; U.S.; 80m; Walter Wanger Productions/PAR; B/W; Comedy; Children: Acceptable; **VHS**. This clever and scintillating comedy opens with Fonda as a famous writer of adventure tales and Sullavan as a movie star, but when they meet, they know nothing about each other's fame and use their given names instead of the names by which the world knows them. They fall in love, their romance leading them to the altar, but by then they are aware of their famous alteregos and those egos begin to challenge and bicker, even as they go before Brennan, a justice of the peace who is about to marry them, and who has his hands full when trying to keep peace between them while he joins them in holy matrimony. They take their honeymoon at a New England hotel where they startle discombobulated innkeeper Hamilton (who is hilarious in her role, she being the famed wicked witch in the **Wizard of Oz**, 1939) with their contentious behavior and endless insults. Suddenly the bloom of their romance has turned into an odorous relationship, right down to Fonda's allergy to Sullavan's perfume while their lives are constantly interrupted by those involved in their more famous careers, such as Bondi, who is Sullavan's secretary, religiously reminding her of her obligations as a movie star. Further frustrating these battling lovebirds is Butterworth, an old suitor of Sullavan's who shows up and tries to woo Sullavan away from Fonda. Sullavan, after another confrontation with Fonda, exits, believing that Fonda does not love her and never has. Fonda, however, is devastated at her going and pursues her, finding her and he convinces Sullavan that she is the only woman for him. They will remain together, but it is only a matter of minutes before they are at it again. Seiter directs this romp with a firm hand, and Fonda, Sullavan and the rest of the cast are outstanding in their roles. The script sparkles with wit and biting wisecracks, and that is due to the contribution of Parker and Campbell, who were a mar-

Cher and Nicolas Cage in *Moonstruck*, 1987

ried writing team. ***Author's Note***: Art imitates life, they say, and this was certainly the case in this film. Sullavan had been married to Fonda in real life (from 1931 to 1933), but they were apparently still on talking terms when they did this film together, although, according to what Seiter told this author "after a few scenes, they started arguing off camera and I wound up being a referee throughout the rest of the production. It was strange. Hank [Fonda] and Margaret [Sullavan] were exactly like the characters they were playing in **The Moon's Our Home**. Did they know that? I don't think they cared." Parker told this author that "the characters Hank and Margaret played in that film were based on the adventure writer Richard Haliburton and actress Katharine Hepburn. I told Hank [Fonda] about that when we were making that picture and he said, 'that's news to me. I guess I'm safe since I never read any of Haliburton's books, but I wouldn't tell that to Margaret. She hates Hepburn." Sullavan's own life was riddled with tragedy. After divorcing Fonda, she married the great film director William Wyler (1934-1936), and then married literary agent Leland Hayward (1936-1949), having three children with Hayward, two of whom wound up in mental institutions and eventually committed suicide. Sullavan herself was found dead at the age of fifty in a New Haven, Connecticut, hotel room on January 1, 1960, from an overdose of barbiturates (her death was ruled an accident). **p**, Walter Wanger; **d**, William A. Seiter; **cast**, Margaret Sullavan, Henry Fonda, Charles Butterworth, Beulah Bondi, Henrietta Crosman, Walter Brennan, Dorothy Stickney, Margaret Hamilton, Spencer Charters, Andrea Leeds; **w**, Alan Campbell, Isabel Dawn, Boyce DeGaw, Dorothy Parker (based on the novel by Faith Baldwin); **c**, Joseph A. Valentine; **m**, Boris Morros, Gerard Carbonara.

Moonstruck ★★★★ 1987; U.S.; 102m; MGM; Color; Comedy/Romance; Children: Unacceptable (MPAA: PG); **BD**; **DVD**; **VHS**. Wonderful and heartwarming, this romance sees Cher at the prime of life and still waiting for long-standing beau Aiello to take her to the altar. An Italian American bookkeeper in Brooklyn, Cher is in her late thirties and wonders if she will ever again see a wedding ring on her finger. She has been married and divorced and believes her first union was cursed because she got married at City Hall, instead of at a church. Aiello, a successful businessman and a mama's boy, cannot bring himself to wed the alluring Cher while his mother is still alive. His mother is barely clinging to life, or so it seems, as she has been ailing for years. When it appears that she is on her deathbed, Aiello tells Cher to prepare to be his bride while he flies off to Sicily to bid a final farewell to his mother. Cher then begins making preparations for the nuptials while her father, Gardenia, and mother, Dukakis, express regrets as they do not think Aiello is worthy of their darling daughter. Gardenia, a well-to-do plumber (he installs only the most expensive copper pipes, assuring customers that they will

last forever), meanwhile, is carrying on an affair with a younger woman. Cher, in making her rounds to all of those invited to her impending wedding, meets Cage for the first time, Aiello's truculent and embittered brother. He complains about everything, but chiefly hates Aiello because he claims that he sliced off his hand by accident when Aiello once distracted him. Cage, an earthy, passionate man is just the opposite of brother Aiello, who is fussy and indecisive. Cher, although she does not immediately admit it, is immediately attracted to the explosive and intense Cage. Cher goes to Cage's apartment and, in an effort to befriend him, cooks him a dinner. They drink whiskey and come to know each other. The world-wise Cher tells Cage that he purposely allowed his hand to be cut off because he is essentially a "wolf" that would rather lose a hand than be caught in a trap. Taken by her, Cage impulsively makes love to Cher and they spend the night together while an astoundingly bright and full moon shines down upon them. Cher knows this is going nowhere and tells Cage that she will not have any more relations with her future brother-in-law, but Cage begs her to spend one more evening with him by going with him to the opera. She hesitantly agrees and the next day has a complete makeover at a beauty salon where her hair is colored and styled and her eyebrows plucked before she buys a new gown and shoes to wear to the opera that night. She then goes to her church and to a confessional where she confesses to her priest that she has slept with her fiancé's brother and for which she is given penance. She then meets her mother, Dukakis, who tells her that she knows that her husband, Gardenia, is seeing another woman, but Cher refuses to believe this. Cher has earlier told Dukakis that she intends to marry Aiello even though she does not love him and to which the world-weary Dukakis replies: "Good, when you love them, they drive you crazy because they know they can." That night Cher attends the opera with Cage and, after enjoying a thrilling performance, sees her father Gardenia with a young woman, Gillette, now knowing that her mother was right. While Gardenia and Cher are attending that opera, Dukakis dines alone at her favorite restaurant where she sees Mahoney, a college professor, insulted and doused with water by one of his female students he has been courting. Dukakis strikes up a conversation with Mahoney, advising him to meet his loneliness head-on without such May-December romances, and Mahoney is drawn to her, walking her home and then asking her to spend the night with him. She is flattered, but, after she gives him a maternal kiss, she tells him: "I'm too old for you," and they part. Meanwhile, Cher and Cage have fallen in love and Cher throws caution to the wind and spends another night with Cage. In Sicily, Aiello has told his mother that he is about to marry Cher and the woman has a miraculous recovery and now that she may go on living, Aiello is convinced that he cannot marry Cher. He flies back to the U.S., but before going home, he stops by Cher's residence and finds Dukakis there. She tells him that Cher is out and does not know where she has gone and then asks Aiello why men cheat on women. He says that it might have something to do with men looking for the missing rib that was taken from Adam at the dawn of creation, but Dukakis is more practical, replying that it is because men fear death. Aiello promises to return the next morning. On that morning, Dukakis confronts Gardenia with his affair, which he at first denies. She then tells him: "I just want you to know [that] no matter what you do, you're going to die, just like everyone else." Gardenia says his life is worthless, but Dukakis says it is worthwhile since she loves him and then asks him to stop seeing Gillette. He agrees. Then Cage arrives at Cher's request so that he will sanction the marriage between Cher and Aiello, but when Aiello arrives, he tells Cher that he cannot marry her because his mother is alive and well. Cage seizes this opportunity to immediately propose to Cher in front of the entire family. Cher looks at her mother, Dukakis, who asks her: "Do you love him?" Cher replies, "I love him awful." Cage then asks brother Aiello to give him the ring Cher has returned to him and he does and Cage places it on Cher's finger, saying they are going to be married and the entire family celebrates by having an impromptu party and that is where this love-packed tale ends. Jewison directs this enchanting comedy romance with great skill, its poignant scenes unfolding in practical day-to-day terms to marvelously encapsulate the hopes of common people with uncommon passions. Cher, who was never more beautiful and alluring, is wonderful in her role of a woman in search of true love, her riveting performance deservedly winning for her an Oscar as Best Actress. Dukakis, too, as the forlorn-looking, but very wise mother, won an Oscar as Best Supporting Actress. Cage is terrific as the moody but intense lover, and Gardenia, Aiello and the rest of the cast also render outstanding performances. Shanley's brilliant script that perfectly profiles the tempestuous personalities of these captivating characters also won an Oscar for Best Original Screenplay. This is one of those delightful and memorable films that can be seen again and again to reassure the viewer that the heart has its reasons of which reason does not know and that love, like all the circuitous rivers of the earth, will find its way to a tranquil sea of happiness. **p**, Norman Jewison, Patrick Palmer; **d**, Jewison; **cast**, Cher, Nicolas Cage, Vincent Gardenia, Olympia Dukakis, Danny Aiello, Julie Bovasso, John Mahoney, Louis Guss, Feodor Chaliapin, Anita Gillette, Leonardo Cimino; **w**, John Patrick Shanley; **c**, David Watkin (Technicolor); **m**, Dick Hyman; **ed**, Lou Lombardo; **prod d**, Philip Rosenberg; **art d**, Dan Davis, Barbra Matis; **spec eff**, David Lemmem, Tony Parmelee, Mark Vargo, Ron Moore.

Moran of the *Lady Letty* ★★★ 1922 (silent); U.S.; 68m/7 reels; Famous Players Lasky/PAR; B/W; Adventure; Children: Acceptable; **DVD**. Solid actioner sees the dashing Valentino as a Spanish aristocrat living in San Francisco where he meets attractive Dalton, but their romance is short-lived when he is shanghaied by Long and his gang of smugglers and forced to serve on board their ship, which is sailing to Mexico. En route, they see a vessel, *Lady Letty*, which has caught fire. By the time they reach the ship, they find only one survivor, a sailor. Valentino, however, recognizes the sailor as Dalton, who has disguised herself by wearing men's clothing. Valentino hides and shields Dalton from the other crew members, especially keeping her out of the reach of the lecherous Long, in a series of exciting hide-and-seek adventures, until Long becomes suspicious of the sailor and identifies Dalton. He now intends to possess this lovely creature, but the valiant Valentino confronts him and, in one of the most sensationally staged fights ever put on film, the two men battle the length of the ship and then up into the rigging until they are struggling at the topmost mast and where the evil Long finally falls fatally to the deck. Valentino then takes command and sails away with Dalton in his arms. *Author's Note*: Valentino insisted on doing his own stunts in this film and amazed the cast and crew with his dexterity and athletic prowess. His fight with Long is one of the most spectacular of the silent era and is worth the whole of the film, although the suspense and tension of the story is consistently high throughout this well-crafted production. **p&d**, George Melford; **cast**, Dorothy Dalton, Rudolph Valentino, Charles Brinley, Walter Long, Emil Jorgenson, Maude Wayne, George Kuwa, Cecil Holland, William Boyd, George O'Brien; **w**, Monte M. Katterjohn (based on the novel by Frank Norris); **c**, William Marshall.

The More the Merrier ★★★★ 1943; U.S.; 104m; COL; B/W; Comedy/Romance; Children: Acceptable; **DVD**; **VHS**. This outstandingly cozy if not claustrophobic comedy deals with the housing shortage in Washington, D.C., during WWII, along with a much more serious shortage of available young men, who are off serving in the armed forces. Arthur is a single woman working in Washington who has a small apartment. To do her bit to help the war effort, she agrees to sublet half of her apartment to Coburn, an affable, elderly fellow. He comes to believe that Arthur needs male companionship and begins searching for a suitable beau, finding McCrea, a U.S. Air Force mechanic who has arrived on a special assignment. Coburn, to match-make McCrea to Arthur, then sublets half of his apartment to McCrea. This leads to many complications and a series of very funny sequences, especially over the rights of privacy as the three are in fierce competition for the

Charles Coburn and Jean Arthur in *The More the Merrier*, 1943.

use of the single bathroom. Coburn, however, is unaware that Arthur has been long engaged to Gaines, a stuffy Washington bureaucrat, who dictates her social if not her moral conduct every waking hour of her life. When Coburn does learn of Gaines' existence, he goes out of his way to compromise Arthur so that Gaines comes to believe that she is a loose woman, running around with McCrea, although she and McCrea are by that time falling in love. When Gaines forces a showdown with Arthur, she realizes that the always fault-finding Gaines is not the man for her and she and McCrea tie the knot for a happy ending. This airy farce is skillfully handled by the masterful Stevens, who shot his scenes in the very confining set of the little apartment, using every corner and cranny of that set to eke out a laugh or heartfelt moment. Arthur is her effervescent self, radiating concern for her fellow human beings while trying to understand why she is falling in love with a stranger who has been foisted upon her by another stranger. The upright and sincere McCrea is the perfect but unwitting suitor who has been selected by the designing Coburn, who shines in his role as a clever and very effective Cupid. *Author's Note*: Stevens told this author that "**The More the Merrier** was the last picture I made before I entered the armed forces [he became an officer in the U.S. Signal Corps and shot great documentary footage, including rare color footage that recorded the battles in Europe following the Allied invasion at Normandy in 1944]. I knew little about Jean [Arthur] outside of the films she made, but when I came to work with her, I realized that she was one of the greatest natural comediennes the world had ever seen. She could instinctively pick up on any offbeat action or line and believably twist it into a good laugh, but she did that subtly with her gestures and vocal responses. No one [was] like her and when she got the nomination for Best Actress for her part in the picture, I was very disappointed that she did not get the award, even though that great old gentleman, Coburn, who was also wonderful in that picture, did win [an Oscar as Best Supporting Actor]." Stevens did not mention to me that he himself had been nominated for an Oscar for Best Director and that the film was nominated as Best Film and it also got a nomination for Best Adapted Screenplay. Arthur told this author that "I never expected to get nominated as Best Actress by the Academy for **The More the Merrier**. I thought the picture was a cute little story and that George [Stevens] had made a lot more out of it than what the script showed. I always loved doing comedies because I have always thought that everyone in the world is a character and pretty funny, including myself. You know I have a strange profile. One side of me is okay, but the other makes me look like a horse, don't you think?" (She turned her face left and right to get my appraisal and I told her that both sides were beautiful.) McCrea thought that this film "was above the average, but nothing spectacular. When I saw that it got a lot of Oscar nominations, and

Yul Brynner and Marlon Brando in *Morituri*, 1965.

that Coburn won one, I was somewhat amazed. But, in looking back at that picture, I now realize that it touched the hearts of millions of people, especially the young women during the war, who had no sweethearts, no young beaus knocking on their doors since almost all the young American men were in the service, fighting the war. So they took that little love story back with them into their own small apartments like a precious keepsake." **p&d**, George Stevens; **cast**, Jean Arthur, Joel McCrea, Charles Coburn, Richard Gaines, Bruce Bennett, Frank Sully, Stanley Clements, Ann Doran, Ann Savage, Grady Sutton; **w**, Robert Russell, Frank Ross, Richard Flournoy, Lewis R. Foster (based on a story by Russell, Ross, Garson Kanin); **c**, Ted Tetzlaff; **m**, Leigh Harline; **ed**, Otto Meyer; **art d**, Lionel Banks, Rudolph Sternad; **set d**, Fay Babcock.

Morgan ★★★ 1966; U.K.; 97m; British Lion/Cinema V; B/W; Comedy; Children: Unacceptable; **DVD**; **VHS**. Adapted from a British television play, this captivating film tells the story of a not-very-successful London artist, Morgan (Warner), who takes mental flights of fancy as an escape from reality (not unlike the comedy character portrayed by Danny Kaye in **The Secret Life of Walter Mitty**, 1947). He comes by his quirkiness naturally since his mother, Handl, an old school communist, spends a lot of her time at the grave of Karl Marx. She is at odds with her son because he married a wealthy woman, Redgrave. When she wants a divorce because of his strange ways, such as imagining he is swimming in a jungle, he resists and tries everything to win Redgrave back, especially after Stephens, a man of Redgrave's social class, takes an interest in her. Morgan resorts to kidnapping her, but she is rescued. She decides to marry Stephens, and, at their wedding, Morgan arrives in a gorilla suit to break it up. He goes up in flames and rides a motorcycle to the Thames River. For all this and more he is put into an insane asylum and Redgrave, now pregnant and married to Stephens, visits him and he wonders if the baby is his. She gives him an enigmatic smile and he goes to the garden where he has been tending plants that he has shaped into a giant form of a hammer and sickle, the image of the communist party. Songs: "The Red Flag" "Berceuse pour Danielle" (Pierre Arvay); "Siberian Journey" (Roger-Roger); "The Star Spangled Banner;" (John Stafford Smith, Francis Scott Key); "Parade of the Tin Soldiers" (Leon Jessel); "Lilliburlero" (traditional); "Bash Us Again Bill" (Gus Stephens); "Tangoi Meleva" (Walter Warren); "Desperate Moment" (Kenneth Essex). Explicit scenes of kidnapping and sexuality prohibit viewing by children. **p**, Leon Clore; **d**, Karel Reisz; **cast**, David Warner, Vanessa Redgrave, Robert Stephens, Irene Handl, Bernard Bresslaw, Arthur Mullard, Newton Blick, Nan Munro, Robert Bridges, Bekim Fehmiu; **w**, David Mercer (based on his television play "A Suitable Case for Treatment"); **c**, Larry Pizer; **m**, John Dankworth; **ed**, Tom Priestley, Victor Procter; **art d**, Philip Harrison.

Morituri ★★★ 1965; U.S.; 123m; Arcola-Colony/FOX; B/W; Drama; Children: Unacceptable; **DVD**; **VHS**. A dilapidated German cargo ship departs Tokyo in 1942, headed for Nazi-occupied France under the command of Brynner, a merchant navy officer whose career has been marred by drunkenness. British intelligence learns that the ship is carrying a precious cargo of rubber needed by both sides in World War II. The British devise a daring plan to intercept the ship and capture its cargo. Howard, a British colonel, coerces a German expatriate, Brando, into impersonating an SS officer and board the ship. Brynner is on orders to sink the ship if it is in danger of being intercepted by the British fleet. Brando is to prevent this. Meanwhile, two factions, one consisting of Nazi officers and crew members, the other consisting of anti-Nazi crew members, work against each other along the perilous voyage and where Margolin, a passenger, is discovered to be Jewish, who aids Brando after he confides in her and asks her to persuade some American POWs, who have been taken aboard, to side with him against the Nazis on board. She does so by offering herself to the POWs and is later killed when Brando stages a mutiny. Meanwhile, Brynner, who is an old school German sea captain and who hates the Nazis, eventually sides with Brando, and though the ship is crippled, Brynner sends out a message at the fade-out that is received by the British, giving the ship's location so that the British can seize the precious cargo of rubber. The film presents top acting from Brando and Brynner, along with the rest of the international cast, and offers fascinating and divergent character studies of the divided loyalties of the crew and where the Nazis are profiled with more psychological introspective that went far beyond the stereotypical portraits traditionally found in Hollywood films. Wicki does a fine job directing, and Hall's stark and moody black-and-white lensing adds an eerie and foreboding atmosphere to the film. The word "Morituri" is the plural of a Latin word meaning "about to die," and which underscores the fates of all those traveling upon this doomed ship. *Author's Note*: This production was troubled from the start when its producer Rosenberg, who wanted a three-month production schedule, was told by Fox executives that the film had to be in the can within two months. That did not happen. German director Wicki, new to American filmmaking, was used to taking his time in the films he had earlier made where he was working with smaller casts and crews. "He was very meticulous," Brando told this author, "and I agreed with him that we should take the time we needed to get the scenes right. I believed in necessary retakes, but Wicki went overboard with that, sometimes ordering ten, fifteen, even twenty takes for one scene, until we were all exhausted and all of our inspiration squeezed out of us." This caused the film to go far beyond the production schedule and its budget. A great deal of authenticity can be seen in this film, particularly the ship itself, a 540-foot 1938 Scottish merchant vessel which Rosenberg located in Yokohama Harbor. Further, a marvelously authentic-looking replica of a Japanese submarine was made of plywood at a cost of $80,000 and was also used in the film. The author of the novel upon which this film is based was a German-Jew, who worked in Tokyo as a naval attaché during WWII, until his heritage was discovered and he was recalled to Germany, sailing on a freighter as depicted in this production, and was later "ethnically cleansed" by the Nazis by being sent to the Russian front, where he was expected to be killed, but fortunately survived to write this tale. Margolin's tragic character is somewhat based upon his experiences. **p**, Aaron Rosenberg; **d**, Bernhard Wicki; **cast**, Marlon Brando, Yul Brynner, Janet Margolin, Trevor Howard, Carl Esmond, Martin Benrath, Hans Christian Blech, Wally Cox, Martin Kosleck, Eric Braeden, Gary Crosby, Ivan Triesault, Charles De Vries, Oscar Beregi, William Redfield, Max Haufler, Rainer Penkert, Martin Brandt, Robert J. Wilke, Manfred Lating; **w**, Daniel Taradash (based on the novel by Werner Joerg Luedecke); **c**, Conrad Hall; **m**, Jerry Goldsmith; **ed**, Joseph Silver; **art d**, Herman A. Blumenthal, Jack Martin Smith; **set d**, Walter M. Scott, Jerry Wunderlich; **spec eff**, Emil Kosa, Jr., L.B. Abbott.

Morning Glory ★★★★ 1933; U.S.; 74m; RKO; B/W; Drama; Children: Acceptable; **DVD**; **VHS**. In her third film, Hepburn radiates a magnetic personality and bursts with magical vitality (and for which she won her first of four Oscars as Best Actress, a record) as she leaves her small New England town and goes to New York City to seek fame and fortune on the legitimate stage. Full of expectations, she soon learns that the metropolis is swarming with young, ambitious actresses such as herself and her chances of becoming an overnight theatrical success quickly dim. She meets, however, kindly Smith, a veteran actor, who takes an interest in her, attracted to her bubbling and effervescent personality. After tutoring her with a few acting pointers, Smith takes Hepburn to a cocktail party given by Duncan, a queen bee of the Broadway stage, where Hepburn attracts a lot of raised eyebrows when she spontaneously renders Shakespearean soliloquies on an empty stomach (she hasn't had the money to eat enough) and after having imbibed too much champagne. Most of those at the party dismiss her as a pretentious gatecrasher, but Menjou, an enterprising theatrical promoter, sees promise in the young lady and becomes her manager. The suave Menjou engineers Hepburn to the right people and she meets Fairbanks, a youthful playwright whose new play is about to be produced. Hepburn becomes the understudy of the leading lady, Duncan, the very woman she met at the cocktail party and who branded her an upstart. Duncan is the essence of the stage diva, temperamental, demanding and arrogant, a woman who will not hesitate to tell anyone that they are very fortunate to be within her august presence. Everyone is then faced with a crisis on opening night when Duncan explodes in a fiery tirade and then quits the show. Hepburn is the play's only salvation and she goes onto the boards and gives a magnificent performance that assures the play's success and her own future career in the theater. The story line having the budding actress embroiled in backstage intrigues and then becoming an overnight hit was by then a cliché in films (and almost the same story is presented in the same year with **42nd Street**, 1933). Hepburn's startling performance, however, is so mesmerizing and captivating that she literally lifts this tale far beyond its hackneyed moorings and by which she established herself as a foremost screen actress. *Author's Note*: Hepburn told this author that **Morning Glory** "was, in a way, the story of my own life, as I came from New England and tried to be a success on the stage. The story for the picture was sure fire for audiences then, but it had some unique aspects to it and I think that Lowell [Sherman], who directed, and who was also an actor, understood the mindsets and personalities of actors and that shows in the picture. Lowell said to all of us at the beginning: 'You are all actors and you are not only acting for the world, but for each other—so act till it hurts!' You know, I believe that the picture, **All about Eve** [1950], is taken straight from **Morning Glory**. It has the same characters, the aging, temperamental star that Bette Davis played in that picture, the ambitious young actress that Anne Baxter played in that movie, the manager, the playwright, they are all there. I once asked Bette [Davis] if she was influenced by **Morning Glory** when she did **All about Eve** and she replied: 'Influenced? Hell, I copied it verbatim!' I was twenty-seven years old when I won the Oscar for **Morning Glory**. I had to wait another thirty-five years for my second Oscar [for **Guess Who's Coming to Dinner**, 1968] and then those Oscars kept arriving at my door [**The Lion in Winter**, 1969, shared with Barbra Streisand for **Funny Girl**, 1968; and **On Golden Pond**, 1982]. If you live long enough in this business, you become beloved, like an icon, or a towering statue, and as long as you are working you have a chance to get another brass ring [the Oscar statuette]. They say in Hollywood that the greatest compliment an actress can get is from her own acting community. That's all well and good, but the greatest compliments I ever received were from the moviegoers who kept going to see my pictures. They were the ones who counted and still do." Merian C. Cooper, who made so many superb films (**King Kong**, 1933; **Little Women**, 1933; **The Fugitive**, 1947; **Fort Apache**; 1948, **The Quiet Man**; 1952, and **The Searchers**, 1956; to name a few), served as the executive producer for this film (not credited), and he was the driving

Adolphe Menjou, Katharine Hepburn and Douglas Fairbanks Jr. in *Morning Glory,* 1933.

force that insisted that Hepburn play the role of the aspiring actress. **p**, Pandro S. Berman; **d**, Lowell Sherman; **cast**, Katharine Hepburn, Douglas Fairbanks, Jr., Adolphe Menjou, C. Aubrey Smith, Mary Duncan, Don Alvarado, Fredric Santley, Richard Carle, John Carradine, Robert Adair; **w**, Howard J. Green (based on the play by Zoe Akins); **c**, Bert Glennon; **m**, Max Steiner; **ed**, William Hamilton; **set d**, Van Nest Polglase, Ray Moyer, Chick Kirk; **spec eff**, Harry Redmond, Sr.

Morocco ★★★★ 1930; U.S.; 92m; PAR; B/W; Adventure/Romance; Children: Cautionary; **DVD**; **VHS**. Pantheon director Sternberg presents a classic love story, stylishly mounted and rich in detail, shrouded in the mystique of the Moroccan deserts and where Dietrich (in her American film debut) is captivating and smoldering and Cooper fascinates as her lover. Dietrich is a disillusioned café singer on her way to Morocco by ship when she meets Menjou, a polished and worldly man of wealth, who, like every other male on board, is attracted to the alluring blonde. He offers her his "assistance" in making life easier for her, but she puts him off, tearing up his calling card. When going to work at an upscale nightclub, Dietrich appears before a crowd packed with officers and enlisted men of the French Foreign Legion and must contend with noise from unruly soldiers, but she soon strikes them into silence when performing her first song, "What Am I Bid for My Apples?" She sells an apple to the highest bidder among the crowd while delivering her sultry rendition. Menjou, always her ardent admirer, motions her toward his table, but, at the end of her song, she shocks him and the rest of the audience by turning away from him and going to an attractive woman in the crowd where she strokes her hair and then kisses her on the mouth for the finish. She moves through the crowd to stop at a table where she sees handsome, lanky Cooper sitting with a group of other legionnaires. She offers him an apple, but he is without money and must borrow some francs to buy an apple. She gives him change and also the key to her apartment. Cooper later arrives at Dietrich's abode where they talk, Dietrich expressing in embittered terms her dislike of men and life in general. She is nevertheless taken by the sincere Cooper, who then tells her: "I met you ten years too late." He hands her key back to her and leaves. Dietrich is stunned by Cooper's rejection of her. No man has ever turned her down, and this emotional rebuff causes her all the more to want to know this strange, mysterious legionnaire. As Cooper is returning to his barracks, he sees and meets with Southern, the wife of his commander, Haupt. Southern has followed Cooper to the café and it is apparent that they have had a relationship in the past. Haupt, unobserved by either Cooper or Southern, watches them from a distance in the shadows, seeing Cooper reject his wife and walk away. Meanwhile, Dietrich has become obsessed with Cooper and meets with him, but Southern, now jealous of Dietrich's attentions to Cooper, sends two thugs to attack

Marlene Dietrich and Gary Cooper in *Morocco*, 1930.

them. Cooper soundly beats them up and is later called into Haupt's office to explain why he attacked two innocent citizens. Dietrich, however, comes to Cooper's defense and Haupt reluctantly exonerates Cooper, but lets him know that he is aware of Cooper's past relationship with his wife. Haupt then orders Cooper to accompany him and a detachment on an expedition to a pass where they are to destroy some insurgents, and Cooper now believes that Haupt means to have him killed on that mission. That evening, Cooper learns that Menjou, who is hopelessly in love with Dietrich, plans to propose to her and Cooper, also now in love with Dietrich, accepts that outcome as being a better fate for Dietrich in that she will have a wealthy man to support her, rather than taking chances with a lowly, penniless legionnaire. Suppressing his feelings for her, Cooper visits Dietrich in her dressing room and encourages her to marry Menjou. When her back is turned, Cooper departs, leaving a message on her dressing table mirror that reads: "I changed my mind. Good luck." Believing Cooper does not love her, she accepts Menjou's proposal. When the detachment reaches the pass and encounters the enemy, Haupt orders Cooper to destroy a machine gun nest, and then honorably accompanies Cooper and others to perform the task and Haupt is killed in the process. Dietrich, meanwhile, is given a sumptuous party at Menjou's lavish villa to announce their forthcoming marriage. She and Menjou then learn that Cooper's detachment has returned, but that Cooper is one of the casualties and is in a hospital recovering from his wounds. Dietrich, frantic with love for Cooper, tells Menjou that she must go to him and the understanding Menjou drives her to the outpost. Dietrich finds, however, that Cooper has feigned his wounds to dissuade Dietrich from coming after him and that he is now about to leave with other legionnaires on another mission. The distraught Dietrich bids him farewell and then watches his unit march into the desert. When she sees native women following the men that they love, Dietrich says goodbye to Menjou and, as a wind rises and swirls sand into her face, Dietrich runs after the women, removing her shoes, preferring to be a lowly camp follower than a wealthy woman so that she can be with the man she loves, one of the most impactful romantic scenes ever recorded, to end this enthralling tale. Sternberg's meticulous direction lets no exotic detail escape his searching cameras, from the crowded smoke-filled café to the half-lit, lattice-laced streets of the town and where he visually idolizes Dietrich in every scene. She is mesmerizing as the unpredictable femme fatale, her life rejuvenated when she becomes the victim of love, and who courageously throws everything away for the sake of that love. Hers is an unforgettable performance, stunning American audiences that instantly embraced Dietrich as a foremost screen siren and one that made her an overnight stellar star in Hollywood. Cooper, on the other hand, shocked American viewers in that, unlike his former screen persona, he plays a less than forceful lover, magnanimously giving up the woman

he loves to another man, rather than projecting his well-established image of a rugged, forthright fellow who always seized the day and the woman he wanted. Songs: "What Am I Bid for My Apple?," "Give Me the Man" (Karl Hajos, Leo Robin), "Quand l'amour meurt" (Octave Cremieux, Georges Milandy). ***Author's Note***: Cooper did not like this film and resented the attention Sternberg showered upon Dietrich, who was not only Sternberg's protégé, but his lover. Sternberg had discovered Dietrich in a Berlin nightclub in 1929 and made her an international star with the German production of **The Blue Angel**, 1931, and who took her to Hollywood to make this film, the first of many they would do together (Sternberg had an iron-clad contract to do all of Dietrich's films). Cooper not only resented the doting attention Sternberg gave to Dietrich, but the actor hated the fey gestures and mannerisms Sternberg insisted he employ throughout the production, such as having Cooper put a rose behind his ear, using a fan to disguise a kiss he gives to Dietrich, and smoking cigarettes with a decidedly limp wrist, all these little traits designed by the manipulative Sternberg to present Cooper as not only an indecisive and ineffective lover, but suggesting that he might be homosexual and therefore incapable of having a real sexual relationship with a sensuous woman. Sternberg's attempt to thus minimize Cooper's role as a significant lover (and if not for personal reasons by the director, who was passionately involved with Dietrich) was not lost on the actor, who was contentious with Sternberg throughout the production. Cooper told this author that "Sternberg treated Marlene like a Prussian princess, and to make her feel very special and to make me feel like an unimportant member of the cast, he directed her in German while he talked to me in English." At one point, Cooper let loose a loud yawning noise and the volatile Sternberg glared at him, saying: "If you are sleepy, you can go home." Cooper replied: "Oh, no, it's just that this is America and we don't understand this kraut talk." Sternberg stood up, clenching his fists and stomped his booted feet (he wore jodhpurs and shiny boots as was the traditional director's ensemble for that era), shouting: "Everyone go home! We will not work anymore today! I have been insulted and I want to think this over." Sternberg then stormed into Paramount's front office, demanding that Cooper be replaced, but he was told in no uncertain terms that Cooper was an established star at the studio and would remain in the film and when Sternberg then insisted that Cooper not get top billing with Dietrich, his demand was ignored. He was told to work with Cooper by none other than Paramount chief Adolph Zukor. The next day, Sternberg returned to the set and resumed the production, speaking thereafter only in English, as Zukor ordered him to do. Dietrich, who invariably had romances with her leading men off camera (and this was well known by Sternberg, who tolerated these endless affairs), struck up a relationship with Cooper and the actor reciprocated. Their affair was an on and off relationship that went on for years, even when they were again teamed in **Desire**, 1936. In directing **Morocco**, Sternberg, knowing that the tall Cooper appeared to tower over Dietrich, had Cooper positioned in every scene with her while sitting down, or slouching while standing, and positioning Dietrich in such a way where Cooper was forever looking up at her. This irked the actor no end and who believed this was further designed by Sternberg to impose his own authority over Cooper while making Cooper appear to be another one of Dietrich's love slaves. Actually, Sternberg and Cooper had had a relationship going back several years before making **Morocco** in that Sternberg had begun the direction of a silent film, **Children of Divorce**, 1927, which starred Clara Bow and Cooper, but he was replaced by director Frank Lloyd for reasons that had nothing to do with their working together at that time. Publicly, Sternberg always spoke well of Cooper, at one point stating that he "was one of the nicest human beings I have ever met." Before **Morocco** went into production, Sternberg wholly remade Dietrich's physical personality. He felt that she was too heavy for the tastes of American audiences at the dawn of the 1930s, where new styles demanded that attractive women appear to be thin and sleek, mirroring the craving for Art Deco, where all was plain and simple and without frills and adornments (and where Sternberg was obliquely inspired to this remaking of Dietrich by the futuristic Bauhaus architecture advanced by German architect Walter Gropius, 1883-1969, whom Sternberg greatly admired). Acting as Dietrich's dictatorial Svengali, Sternberg instituted a severe physical regimen for his protégé, having Dietrich's eyebrows shaved and plucked so that her eyebrows presented wide arches over (and to emphasize) her naturally large and expressive eyes. Sternberg brought in dietitians who dictated sparse meals with lean meat and plenty of salads and she underwent constant massages so that her waist was considerably trimmed down. Her famous legs, as displayed in **The Blue Angel**, no longer suited Sternberg, who felt that they were too chubby or beefy, particularly at the thighs, which appealed to European men of that day, but not to American males. He had specialists wrap Dietrich's legs in surgical bandages to reduce and redistribute any fat, particularly about her thighs and ankles and this went on for some time so that, to hide those bandages, Dietrich took to wearing slacks, even at public affairs where she was widely photographed, those slacks exciting the female fashion world and where Dietrich suddenly inspired American women to don similar attire, a fashion trend that swept the country (and where Katharine Hepburn, who was later credited with encouraging that attire through her own constant wearing of slacks, simply emulated Dietrich). The starving diet Dietrich endured for months caused her cheeks to hollow somewhat, which further emphasized her high cheekbones, but some gossips advanced the untruth that she had actually had her back teeth extracted to attain that appearance. To make sure Dietrich was always photographed with her best profile, Sternberg ordered master cinematographer Garmes to shoot only one side of her during the production of **Morocco**. Garmes told this author: "What was I to do after getting such an impossible dictate from Sternberg, keep Marlene in profile throughout the entire picture? That was ridiculous. What I was really doing was shooting her the way Greta Garbo had been photographed back in the Twenties, and Marlene was no Garbo. I went to work setting up lighting that shaded portions of her face and accented those wonderful, large eyes, arching penciled eyebrows, and high cheekbones of hers. When Sternberg saw what I was doing, he asked me about my technique and I told him I had created a "North Light" for Marlene, whatever that meant, but he only nodded and let me go ahead. Sternberg knew I had to photograph Marlene's full face and since he was a master at lighting himself, he knew I was getting what he wanted. We adopted a lot of unusual procedures in the picture, all under Sternberg's direction, like shooting in natural sunlight for the town and desert scenes, and that gave us some rippling shadows, which was not really done then. When it came to shooting close-ups of Marlene, Sternberg had me photograph her against a white wall, and to simulate sunlight, we artificially lit the set, which was shot at the Paramount ranch." Sternberg, for most of his early films, always got what he wanted as he was considered one of the foremost directors of his day, his reputation established by the sumptuous visual banquets his films offered. He was as much a dictator as was the brilliant but insufferable Erich von Stroheim, mercurially explosive when displeased, denouncing anyone who displeased him. (When Sternberg blew up on the set when making the film noir production of **Macao**, 1952, with Jane Russell and Robert Mitchum, Sternberg suddenly threw a fit over a flubbed line and so angered the brawny Mitchum that the actor threatened to throw him off a pier and into deep water where, as Mitchum told this author, he said to Sternberg "I will personally supervise in your drowning, unless you lighten up.") Marlene Dietrich was no exception, telling this author, "Oh, he [Sternberg] was very cruel to me when we made **Morocco**. I spoke very little English then, just having moved to the States to begin making films with him. He told me to speak in a low voice [another distinctive trait that made Dietrich famous] as it made me more appealing, he said. I was learning English when we were making that film and it was difficult for me to utter some words, even full sentences. Sternberg directed me like a schoolteacher [by rote], stating my lines to me in English and then had me repeat them, telling me at one point to count to ten before I delivered a line to Gary [Cooper]. [The line having three words, "Wait for me."] I said the line, but it came

Adolphe Menjou and Marlene Dietrich in *Morocco*, 1930.

out too fast for Sternberg and he went off like a bomb—and he did that all the time—shouting at me: 'If you are so stupid that you can't count to ten slowly and then deliver the line, then count to twenty-five!' I felt like weeping, but I would not give him that satisfaction. I went on to get it correct for him as I always did, but we must have done twenty takes to get it right. Sternberg would do that in almost every scene, retaking the scene over and over and over until he was satisfied. He was a perfectionist and we all tolerated his conduct because we knew he was making great pictures." Sternberg actually went out of his way to make enemies in Hollywood, once declaring that "the only way to succeed is to make people hate you. That way they remember you." Hollywood always remembered Josef Von Sternberg. **p**, Hector Turnbull; **d**, Josef Von Sternberg; **cast**, Gary Cooper, Marlene Dietrich, Adolphe Menjou, Ullrich Haupt, Eve Southern, Francis McDonald, Paul Porcasi, Emile Chautard, Juliette Compton, Albert Conti; **w**, Jules Furthman (based on the play "Amy Jolly" by Benno Vigny); **c**, Lee Garmes, Lucien Ballard; **m**, Karl Hajos; **ed**, Sam Winston.

The Mortal Storm ★★★★ 1940; U.S.; 100m; MGM; B/W; Drama; Children: Cautionary; **DVD**; **VHS**. Although several other Hollywood film studios had earlier denounced through its films the oppressive and hateful regime of Adolf Hitler (the earliest overt attack being Warner Brothers with its **Confessions of a Nazi Spy**, 1939), MGM was one of the last to indict the Nazi tyranny, but did so in this powerful film. Hitler saw this film and immediately banned all MGM films in Germany and the studio's response was to immediately launch more anti-Nazi films, including **Escape**, 1940, where Nazi concentration camps were indicted. **The Mortal Storm** shows the rise of the Nazi Party to power in Germany and where it suppresses the freedoms of that country in the early 1930s, beginning with Morgan, a kindly professor and his family, wife Rich, daughter Sullavan, son Reynolds, and two stepsons, Stack and Orr. Stewart and Young are two boyhood friends as well as suitors seeking Sullavan's hand. After she chooses Young, Stewart returns to his grandmother's alpine farm. He and Young have had a falling out in that Young has joined Hitler's Storm Troopers and Stewart opposes the Nazi philosophy and all of its oppressive measures. At first Morgan is a highly respected teacher at his school, receiving honors for his long-standing service, but when he later ridicules the Nazi propaganda about Germans being superior because of their Aryan heritage, Nazi bigwigs force the faculty to dismiss him. He is later placed in a concentration camp while his stepsons, Stack and Orr, join the Storm Troopers. Rich visits her husband at the camp and sees that he is a dying man, although Morgan puts up a good front and then urges her to leave Germany. She, Reynolds and Sullavan, who has broken off her engagement with Young because of his staunch Nazi beliefs and affiliations, then take a train en route to

Robin Williams in *Moscow on the Hudson*, 1984.

Austria. The train is stopped at the border and their bags are searched. A Nazi inspector finds Morgan's unpublished writings inside of Sullavan's suitcase and, believing she is trying to smuggle out anti-Nazi material, she is detained. Sullavan urges her mother and younger brother to travel on to Austria, promising she will later join them and then she returns to her old home, living there alone. She then goes to Stewart's alpine home where she is reunited with Stewart and welcomed by Stewart's wise old grandmother, Ouspenskaya. Stewart explains that all freedom has been lost in Germany and that they must now flee to Austria, skiing across the border through a mountain pass to get out of the country, and Sullavan agrees. The two begin their perilous journey on skis, but a patrol of Storm Troopers led by Bond and Young arrives at Stewart's home just after they have departed, looking for Stewart, who has been branded an enemy of the state. The Storm Troopers then pursue Stewart and Sullavan, also on skis. The harrowing chase is through steep snow-covered valleys, and just when the Nazis appear to cut off the fleeing pair, Stewart and Sullavan sail through a narrow gorge. The frustrated Storm Troopers fire at them, fatally hitting Sullavan. Though Young feels regret for having shot the woman he loved, he remains steadfast and loyal to his Nazi beliefs. Stewart picks Sullavan up and skis on with her as he holds her in his arms. They cross the border and that is where Sullavan dies, thanking Stewart for taking her to a free country. In an epilogue, the camera tracks the footsteps of Stack and Orr, who are dressed as Storm Troopers as they enter their old, deserted home, a place once filled with happiness and laughter where all of the other occupants are now dead or gone. They hear the joyous conversations of their family in memory and their stepfather's sage words: "I've never prized safety either for myself or my children...I've prized courage." These two young men now have only one family, the Nazi Party. They stand at a window, looking to see the snow falling outside and Orr states his anger over Stewart's escape and survival, saying: "He's free to fight against everything we believe in." Stack, the older of the two, and who has somehow clung to his decency, love of family and freedom, replies: "Yes. Thank God for that!" Orr lashes out by slapping Stack in the face and then runs from the house. Stack looks about forlornly and then leaves and the film ends. The title, of course, represents the wayward stepsons and all of those who flocked to the dark legions of Adolf Hitler that made up the mortal storm of oppression threatening to engulf the civilized world. Borzage directs a moving tale with great skill, his fluid cameras employing quick cuts while presenting clever panning and dolly shots to speed up the action. His camera has the last eerie word as it slowly traces the footsteps of the departed stepsons in the snow as fresh snow begins to cover those tracks as if to say to the world that this evil generation will some time disappear. Sullavan, Stewart, Morgan, Rich, Ouspenskaya, Young and the rest of the cast are

standouts in their roles. Although the element of propaganda is inescapably present, it does not overwhelm the viewer with hortatory sequences, but is shown through the small cruelties inflicted upon good people by the Nazis, such as where Young refuses to tell Sullavan whether her imprisoned father is alive or dead. ***Author's Note***: Young did not like appearing in this film, telling the author that "I hated my part and I found it disgusting that I had to wear a Nazi Storm Trooper uniform. I kept reminding myself that I was playing a part, but I knew that there was no way to redeem my character. He had turned into a savage beast by putting on that uniform. I can't watch that picture and see myself wearing that uniform. I might as well have been wearing a hood and a sheet and playing someone in the Ku Klux Klan...Same thing." Stewart was circumspect about his role when telling this author that "my part is rather small in **The Mortal Storm**. I represent the voice of reason and nobody was listening to that in Germany in those days. I thought that my scenes with Margaret [Sullavan] were some of my best because she was such a sensitive actress, one of those warmhearted souls, who invites your best response. She was one of those persons who made every moment before the cameras something special." Stack told this author that "**The Mortal Storm** was my second film and my role is small, playing one of the stepsons who joins the Nazis. I was well remembered at the end of that film as having the last word when I defiantly condemn the Nazis, and, to quote that line, 'Thank God for that.' It brought me a lot of work and two years later, I was appearing in a Lubitsch picture [**To Be or Not to Be**, 1941] with Carole Lombard as a strong second lead." **p**, Sidney Franklin, Victor Saville (uncredited); **d**, Frank Borzage; **cast**, Margaret Sullavan, James Stewart, Robert Young, Frank Morgan, Robert Stack, William T. Orr, Irene Rich, Bonita Granville, Maria Ouspenskaya, Gene Reynolds, Dan Dailey, Jr., Ward Bond, Tom Drake; **w**, Claudine West, Hans Rameau (Andersen Ellis), George Froeschel (based on the novel by Phyllis Bottome); **c**, William Daniels, Lloyd Knechtel, Leonard Smith; **m**, Bronislau Kaper, Eugene Zador; **ed**, Elmo Veron; **art d**, Cedric Gibbons; **set d**, Edwin B. Willis.

Moscow on the Hudson ★★★ 1984; U.S.; 115m; COL; Color; Comedy; Children: Unacceptable (MPAA: R); **DVD**; **VHS**. Above average comedy sees the frenetic Williams as a saxophonist during the Cold War in the early 1980s. He defects from the Soviet Union while on a visit to the United States and resettles in New York City. After a lot of adjustment problems he gets a job playing saxophone in a band that plays for weddings. America isn't exactly the land of golden opportunity he dreamed of when he defected, but at least he's a free man. Poor, but free, Williams has found love with Alonso. Mature subject matter prohibits viewing by children. Songs: "People Up in Texas" (Waylon Jennings); "Suenos," "Long Day," "Freedom" (David McHugh). **p**, Paul Mazursky, Pato Guzman; **d**, Mazursky; **cast**, Robin Williams, Maria Conchita Alonso, Cleavant Derricks, Alejandro Rey, Savely Kramarov, Elya Baskin, Oleg Rudnik, Alexander Beniaminov, Ludmila Kramarevsky, Ivo Vrzal, Natalie Iwanow, Connie Chung; **w**, Mazursky, Leon Capetanos; **c**, Donald McAlpine (Metrocolor); **m**, David McHugh; **ed**, Richard Halsey; **prod d**, Guzman; **spec eff**, Richard Richtsfeld, Bernie Grill.

Moss Rose ★★★ 1947; U.S.; 82m; FOX; B/W; Mystery; Children: Unacceptable. Cummins is a cockney singer-dancer in London toward the turn of the 20th Century whose female roommate is murdered. She thinks the killer is wealthy Mature who had been dating the girl. She gets an invitation to the large estate where Mature lives with his mother, Barrymore, and learns that he is engaged to Medina. Medina is then killed, and Price (who, for a radical change, is working against evil) is sent by Scotland Yard to investigate. He discovers that the killer of the two young women is not Mature, but Barrymore, who was jealous of them and afraid of losing her beloved son. A good mystery with a standout performance from Barrymore, but violence prohibits viewing by children. This film is reminiscent of the classic thriller, **The Spiral**

Staircase, 1945, which also starred Barrymore, and where a maniacal killer lurks on a large estate. **p**, Gene Markey; **d**, Gregory Ratoff; **cast**, Peggy Cummins, Victor Mature, Ethel Barrymore, Vincent Price, Margo Woode, George Zucco, Patricia Medina, Rhys Williams, Norman Ainsley, Harry Allen; **w**, Jules Furthman, Tom Reed (based on an adaptation by Niven Busch of the novel *The Crime of Laura Saurelle* by Joseph Shearing); **c**, Joseph MacDonald; **m**, David Buttolph; **ed**, James B. Clark; **art d**, Richard Day, Mark-Lee Kirk; **set d**, Paul S. Fox, Thomas Little; **spec eff**, Fred Sersen.

The Most Dangerous Game ★★★★ 1932; U.S.; 63m; RKO; /B/W; Horror; Children: Unacceptable; **DVD**; **VHS**. Grim and taut, this horror entry brings considerable fright to almost every scene. It begins when a fog-bound ship strikes a reef and sinks near a strange island and where a lone survivor, McCrea, a big game hunter and author, swims ashore. He is welcomed by Banks, a Russian count living in a castle-like estate, who tells him that he is also hosting several other guests, who have suffered the same kind of mishap when their ship was wrecked on one of the nearby reefs. McCrea then meets those other four guests, Wray, her brother Armstrong, and two sailors. Banks affords all the luxuries to his guests, but when the survivors talk of leaving the island, Banks puts them off. Banks then tells them of his all consuming passion, and that is hunting the wild and ferocious animals that inhabit the island, and, as he speaks, his fingers a livid scar on his face that resulted with his encounter with a wild buffalo he had been hunting. Wray takes McCrea aside and tells him how Banks has taken the two sailors, one by one, into his trophy room and they have since been mysteriously missing. When Armstrong disappears, McCrea and Wray force their way into Banks' locked trophy room where they are shocked to see upon the room's walls, among the trophies of stuffed animals, a human head. It is soon apparent to the horrified McCrea and Wray that Banks is completely mad, that he lives like a spider on the island, waiting for ships to crash on its dangerous reefs in order that he use the survivors as beasts of prey, for now he hunts not animals but human beings. Banks then appears with two of his men, who are carrying the body of Armstrong. Banks tells McCrea that he respects him as a fellow hunter and asks him to join in his ongoing hunting expeditions for future human beings, but McCrea calls him a lunatic. Banks takes offense, then telling McCrea that if he refuses to be a fellow hunter, he must become the prey; he orders McCrea and Wray to leave his estate and take their chances in the wilds of the island's jungle. The deranged Banks, however, believes in giving his human quarry a sporting chance, so he tells them that he will hunt them with bow and arrow, and, if they survive the hunt, he will allow them to go free. McCrea and Wray are then sent into the wilds and a frantic chase ensues where McCrea and Wray race through the thick jungle, narrowly avoiding its many pitfalls, its steep gorges and clawing wild beasts, while Banks and his men, accompanied by fierce hunting dogs, pursue them. (Directors Schoedsack and Pichel heighten the incredible tension of the chase, one of the most harrowing ever filmed, by quickly cutting from the running McCrea and Wray to telescopic close-ups of the savage dogs on their heels.) Banks, wild-eyed and totally consumed with the excitement of the hunt, frantically blows his hunting horn that all the more accelerates the fear of the running McCrea and Wray while shooting arrows after them that narrowly miss their mark. McCrea and Wray reach a waterfall and one of the dogs attacks McCrea, but he is able to throw it down a steep gorge. Banks arrives and shoots an arrow that apparently strikes McCrea and sends him crashing downward in the cascading waterfall to his death. Banks then captures Wray as his prize and takes her back to his castle. McCrea, however, is very much alive, Banks having killed one of his dogs and not the human being he had been hunting. Reentering the castle, McCrea confronts Banks and his two equally blood-thirsty servants, battling them, killing the henchmen and mortally wounding Banks. He takes Wray to a wharf and they escape in a speedboat. As it goes out to sea, Banks, at a high window of this bastion draws another arrow, but he is

Fay Wray and Joel McCrea in *The Most Dangerous Game,* 1932.

too weak to shoot it and falls from his perch into a courtyard filled with his fierce hunting dogs, meeting a horrible but ironic end. The directors present a true horror classic with this production, one packed with eerie and foreboding atmosphere embodied by the towering castle and the thick jungle, the same producers using the latter set next year in their classic horror epic, **King Kong**, 1933. Banks gives a stunning performance as the mad count and McCrea, Wray and Armstrong are standouts in this must-see film for horror fans. This film would be remade as **A Game of Death**, 1945, an inferior production, and its theme would appear in many other similar films such as **Run for the Sun**, 1956, and **Run of the Arrow**, 1957. Song: "A Moment in the Dark" (Carmen Lombardo). *Author's Note*: Armstrong and Wray, along with Steiner, who composed the chilling score for this film, would all be employed in the making of the producers' next film, **King Kong**, as would Noble Johnson, who plays the tribal chief in that film and where he plays one of Banks' slavish co-killers in **The Most Dangerous Game**. Other than the brief shot of the human head mounted on the wall of Banks' trophy room, the directors also showed a row of severed human heads, but, on second thought, believed that brief scene too grisly and would upset viewers, so the scene was cut before the film was released. McCrea told this author that "the directors of **The Most Dangerous Game** had poor Fay run with me through some of the worst jungle underbrush you could imagine when we were being hunted in that picture by a maniac. We had to do it over and over again until we were exhausted and that's what they wanted on camera. We had so many cuts and bruises that they ran out of iodine. Schoedsack and Pichel were as nutty for realism as that crazy Banks, who was trying to kill us. It is a pretty brutal picture that holds nothing back and there is a strong undercurrent of sadism that made us all feel uncomfortable, but that is part of Banks' strange character. How do writers dream up characters like that? They must have some sort of central casting of their own made up of monsters and maniacs." Wray echoed McCrea's sentiments when telling this author that "the directors gave us a real fright when they told us to start running and that the dogs chasing us might nip at us in that chase through the jungles on the island because they hadn't been fed in several days! Can you imagine? Well, one of those dogs actually bit Joel [McCrea] when he was struggling with it, and since I was standing next to him, I thought, I'm next! That experience, however, was nothing compared to what I faced the following year when I did **King Kong** with the same producers and director. Then it wasn't mad dogs but a gorilla the size of a three-story building." **p**, Merian C. Cooper, Ernest B. Schoedsack; **d**, Schoedsack, Irving Pichel; **cast**, Joel McCrea, Fay Wray, Robert Armstrong, Leslie Banks, Noble Johnson, Steve Clemento, William Davidson, Buster Crabbe, James Flavin, Hale Hamilton; **w**, James Ashmore Creelman (based on a story by Richard Connell); **c**, Henry Gerrard; **m**, Max

Betty Grable and Dan Dailey in *Mother Wore Tights*, 1947.

Steiner; **ed**, Archie E. Marshek; **art d**, Carroll Clark; **set d**, Thomas Little; **spec eff**, Vernon L. Walker, Lloyd Knechtel, Harry Redmond Jr.

Mother ★★★ 1996; U.S.; 104m; PAR; Color; Comedy; Children: Unacceptable (MPAA: PG-13); **DVD**; **VHS**. This delightful domestic comedy sees fine performances from Reynolds and Brooks, who are wonderful together in essaying a renewed mother-son relationship that takes place while Brooks is undergoing a mid-life crisis. A successful science fiction writer, Brooks is undergoing a divorce. He has had women trouble throughout his life and now determines to find out why by moving back in with his mother, Reynolds, who represents his first significant relationship with a female, and where he occupies his old childhood room. Reynolds plays along with Brooks, a bit puzzled but tolerating his endless questions about his childhood and her own past. Many comedic moments take place (particularly how Reynolds demonstrates her penchant for saving leftovers in her freezer, including ancient ice cream) while the fussy Brooks probes Reynolds' past and contends with his successful, overly competitive brother, Morrow. Brooks believes that Morrow has always been Reynolds' favorite child, but in this he is mistaken. He goes on a blind date with air-headed Kudrow, which proves to be a disaster, and then learns Reynolds has a secret talent she has hidden from him and the rest of the family for some time. In the end, Brooks resolves his problems, sort of, and finds that he now has a deeper bond with Reynolds and renewed self-confidence in facing his own future problems. Consistently funny and entertaining, this one is a laugh-filled keeper. Songs: "Mrs. Robinson" (Paul Simon), "Keep on Movin'" (Jazzie B), "Across the Line" (Robert Cray, Richard Cousins, David Olson, Peter Boe, Henry Oden, Joe Louis Walker, D. Amy), "Land of a Thousand Dances" (Chris Kenner), "In My Room" (Brian Wilson, Gary Usher), "Fascination" (F. F. Marchetti), "Humoresque" (Antonin Dvorak), "I Left My Heart in San Francisco" (George C. Cory Jr., Douglass Cross), "Call Me Irresponsible" (Sammy Cahn, Jimmy Van Heusen) and "Downtown" (Tony Hatch). This film proved to be very successful, earning almost $20 million at the box office, proving to be Brooks' highest-grossing production. The film was shot on location in San Francisco and in several small and beautiful communities in Marin County, including Tiburon, Sausalito and Greenbrae. *Author's Note*: Brooks originally offered the role of the mother to Doris Day, but she declined. He next offered the role to Nancy Reagan, who seriously thought about returning to the screen after a forty-year absence, but then decided that she was needed at home to aid her husband, former U.S. President Ronald Reagan, who was then suffering from Alzheimer's disease. Finally, Brooks sent the script to Carrie Fisher, a close friend, asking her to send it on to her mother, Reynolds, who read the script and decided to appear in the film. **p**, Scott Rudin, Herb Nanas, Barry Berg, Adam Schroeder; **d**, Albert Brooks; **cast**, Brooks, Debbie Reynolds, Paul Collins, Laura Weekes, John C. McGinley, Richard Assad, Vanessa Williams, Lisa Kudrow, Rob Morrow, Joey Naber; **w**, Brooks, Monica Johnson; **c**, Lajos Koltai; **m**, Marc Shaiman; **ed**, Harvey Rosenstock; **prod d**, Charles Rosen; **art d**, Chas Butcher; **set d**, Anne D. McCulley.

Mother and Child ★★★ 2010; U.S.; 125m; Everest Entertainment; Sony; Color; Drama; Children: Unacceptable (MPAA: R); **BD**; **DVD**; **VHS**. This absorbing drama tells the story of three women whose lives are linked by their mutual need to be a mother. Bening is a physical therapist, who became pregnant when she was fourteen and gave up her child for adoption thirty-five years earlier. Now she wishes she had that child back. The baby Bening gave up is now a lawyer, Watts, who has a security problem because of having been adopted and uses sex to get ahead in her career. She works for a Los Angeles law firm and has an affair with one of its black partners, Jackson. Another woman, Washington, is happily married, but childless and trying to adopt a child, but its birth mother, Epps, is adamant that her unborn baby will find a good home with caring parents. Next we meet Jones, a nun at a church adoption bureau. Finally, Watts becomes pregnant which complicates her relationship with Jackson and her own feelings about legitimate motherhood. Songs: "Te Quiero" (Juan C. Medina, Martin S. Medina), "Wareika Vibes" (Richard Drury, Keith Finch, Enrico Rodriguez), "Sad Little Song" (Alfred Smith, Jerry Winn), "Latina" (Robert J. Walsh), "Gully Man" (Mike Irwin), "Don't Front on Me" (Owen D. Hunt, Lifford Shillingford), "El Perro" (Alessandro Bertozi, Pedro Llerena), "Being" (Chisty Knowings), "Rapp Star Remixed" (Clint Sands), "Little One" (Lucy Schwart). This is a fascinating American sex stew examining motherhood from many angles. Sexuality, brief nudity, and gutter language prohibit viewing by children. **p**, Lisa Maria Falcone, Julie Lynn, Jonathan McCoy; **d&w**, Rodrigo García; **cast**, Naomi Watts, Annette Bening, Samuel L. Jackson, Cherry Jones, Kerry Washington, David Ramsey, Eileen Ryan, Alexandria Salling, Connor Kramme, Jimmy Smits; **c**, Xavier Pérez Grobet; **m**, Edward Shearmur; **ed**, Steven Weisberg; **prod d**, Christopher Tandon; **set d**, Lisa Fischer; **spec eff**, David Waine, Chris Cline, Mark Dornfeld, Jamie Baxter, Pat Clancey.

Mother Wore Tights ★★★ 1947; U.S.; 107m; FOX; Color; Musical Comedy; Children: Acceptable; **DVD**; **VHS**. Rollicking musical sees Grable as an early 1900s vaudeville song-and-dance girl, who marries her stage partner, Dailey, and they have two daughters. The girls, Freeman and Marshall, grow into their teens and Grable and Dailey go back into show business. Their eldest daughter, Freeman, attends an exclusive finishing school and becomes embarrassed upon learning her parents are singers and dancers, who are going to perform a one-night show near the school. But Freeman changes her mind about her parents' occupation when her stuck-up school chums, who go to the show intending to hoot at the performers, instead cheer them for their wonderful performances. Freeman's graduation is especially warm and fuzzy as she and her parents hug. An innocent, delightful film for the whole family with some wonderful songs: "You Do," "Fare Thee Well Dear Alma Mater," "There's Nothing Like a Song," "Rolling Down to Bowling Green," "Kokomo, Indiana," "This Is My Favorite City" (Mack Gordon, Joseph Myrow); "Burlington Burtie from Bow" (William Hargreaves); "Tra-La-La-La-La" (Harry Warren, Mack Gordon); "Swingin' Down the Lane" (Gus Kahn, Isham Jones); "Lily of the Valley" (L. Wolfe Gilbert, Anatole Friedland); "Stumbling" (Zez Confrey); "Choo'n' Gum" (Mann Curtis, Vic Nizzy); "Daddy, You've Been Like a Mother to Me" (Fred Fisher); "Put Your Arms Around Me Honey" (Junie McCree, Albert von Tilzer); "M-O-T-H-E-R" (Theodore F. Morse, Howard Johnson); "Ta-Ra-Ra-Boom-De-Ay" (Henry J. Sayers) and "Silent Night" (Joseph Mohr, Franz Gruber). *Author's Note*: The story is told through the eyes of the youngest daughter, Marshall, but her voiceover is dubbed by actress Anne Baxter. Renowned ventriloquist Señor Wences (who would become a staple on the Ed Sullivan TV show years later) makes an appearance. Newman and Henderson won Oscars for Best Musical Score. Jackson was nominated for Best Cinematography (color), and Gordon and Myrow received Oscar nominations for the song "You Do." **p&w**, Lamar Trotti (based on the novel by Miriam Young); **d**, Walter Lang; **cast**, Betty Grable, Dan Dailey, Mona Freeman, Connie Marshall, Vanessa Brown, Robert Arthur, Sara Allgood, William Frawley, Ruth Nelson, Stephen Dunne (Michael Dunne), Veda Ann Borg, Sig Ruman, Lee Patrick, Kathleen Lockhart, Mae Marsh, Anne Baxter (narrator); **c**, Harry Jackson (Technicolor); **m**, Alfred Newman, Charles Henderson, David Buttolph; **ed**, J. Watson Webb, Jr.; **art d**, Richard Day, Joseph C. Wright; **set d**, Thomas Little.

Moulin Rouge ★★★★ 1952; U.K.; 119m; Romulus Films/UA; Color; Biographical Drama/Musical; Children; Cautionary; **DVD**; **VHS**. Superb biopic has Ferrer rendering a magnificent portrayal of gifted artist Henri Toulouse-Lautrec (1864-1901), as well as playing his dominating father. The son of wealthy, aristocratic French parents, the artist suffered an accident in childhood that stunted the growth of his legs so that he matured with a normal adult male body, but his legs ceased to grow, so that his deformed body appeared to some as hideous (he was not a dwarf). Ferrer (who painfully enacted the entire film on his knees with a portable dolly to allow him to move about) becomes a painter against the wishes of his draconian father, who wants him to enter business. He further infuriates his father and embarrasses his rich family when he paints the denizens and byways of the colorful district of Montmartre, particularly those performers working at his favorite watering hole, Moulin Rouge, producing marvelously vivid portraits of mimes, comedians, dancers, singers (like Gabor) and even tawdry trollops and ladies of the evening who inhabit the place, along with their gigolos and stage door Johnnies. Ferrer falls in love with Marchand, a manipulating prostitute, who uses him and leaves him. He next falls in love with model Flon, but she, too, leaves him, for another man. Depressed, he drinks to excess and then becomes so ill that he returns to his family estate where his loving and doting mother, Nollier, tends to him. His condition worsens, however, and he dies at the age of thirty-seven, but not before, in the final scenes, he sees all of those wonderful performers he has immortalized through his paintings and who visit him on his deathbed to say their fond and loving farewells. Huston directs this film with great vitality for one of his fondest subjects and begins this wonderful tale with more than twenty minutes of raucous unforgettable cancan dancing and bistro cavorting to set the flavor and times of the painter's era. Huston shows his mastery of color photography through the astounding array of the painter's works, reproducing them in bright and rich hues through the old Technicolor process he was able to employ for this production. *Author's Note*: Toulouse-Lautrec was one of the foremost French painters, along with Van Gogh, Cezanne and Gauguin, of the post-Impressionist period; his original paintings hang in the world's great galleries. One of Toulouse-Lautrec's paintings (of a laundress) sold for more than $22 million in 2005. Huston told this author: "I was always intrigued with the life and work of Toulouse-Lautrec. I knew he lived a miserable and tragic life, but he overcame that through his art and his art stunned the world perhaps later than in his own time. His art is vibrant. It is alive. It talks, sings, walks and dances. I believe that he believed that he died a failure and that is why I added in **Moulin Rouge** that colorful farewell to him from the very people he made famous so that posthumously he would have the tribute he so desperately wanted in life. That sounds conceited, doesn't it? Well, conceit is always necessary if one is to contribute any artistic work to the world. Without it, you lose the nerve, or call it courage, if you like, that is required to do it." **p&d**, John Huston; **cast**, Jose Ferrer, Colette Marchand, Zsa Zsa Gabor, Suzanne Flon, Claude Nollier, Katherine Kath, Jill Bennett, Theodore Bikel, Peter Cushing, Diane Cilento, Christopher Lee; **w**, Huston, Anthony Veiller (based on the novel by Pierre La Mure); **c**, Oswald Morris (Technicolor); **m**, Georges Auric; **ed**, Ralph Kemplen; **prod d&set d**, Marcel Vertes; **art d**, Paul

Jose Ferrer in *Moulin Rouge*, 1952.

Sheriff; **spec eff**, Wally Veevers, Judy Jordan.

Mountains of the Moon ★★★ 1990; U.S.; 136m; Carolco Pictures; TriStar Pictures; Color; Historical Adventure; Children: Unacceptable (MPAA: R); **DVD**; **VHS**. This stirring tale is based on the 1857 expedition of Irish Captain Richard Francis Burton (1821-1890) and British Army Lieutenant John Hanning Speke (1827-1864) to discover the source of the Nile River in darkest, uncharted Africa in the name of Queen Victoria and the British Empire, one of the most important expeditions of the Victorian age of discovery. Bergin (playing Burton), a flamboyant poet, writer, and adventurer, and Glen (playing Speke), a typically reserved English Victorian gentleman and closeted homosexual, become good friends while enduring many hardships of the steamy jungle expedition, but that friendship becomes severely strained by the end of their hazardous and exhausting journey. Separated in the jungle because Bergin falls ill and remains in camp, Glen later reports to the British Royal Geographical Society that he went on to find the source of the Nile in a lake he named Lake Victoria. Bergin disagrees, saying that Glen's findings are inconclusive. Because of these conflicting reports, a second expedition is undertaken by Glen two years later with explorer James Augustus Grant (1827-1892) but without Bergin. Glen returns saying he reached Lake Victoria and then traveled around the lake where on the north side he found the Nile flowing out of it. Bergin insists that since Glen had not followed the Nile from the place it flowed out of Lake Victoria to a location called Gondokoro and a river there, he could not be sure these rivers were the same river. Gondokoro was a trading station now known to be on the east bank of the White Nile in Southern Sudan. The Nile has two tributaries, the White and the Blue Nile. A debate is planned between Glen and Bergin before the Royal Geographical Society on September 18, 1864, but, before either explorer could argue their positions, Glen dies from a rifle shot while hunting (the shooting was accidental, according to reports, but others claimed the fatal wound was self-inflicted; history credits Speke with being the first European to reach Lake Victoria and that he correctly identified it as the source of the Nile). Bernard Hill plays famed missionary Dr. David Livingstone (1813-1873). Well directed, this entry provides good action and plenty of excitement while telling an intriguing story accurately based on facts. Songs: "Kawamba Dance," "Wagogo Soothing Song," "Wagogo Marriage Ritual" (traditional folk songs). *Author's Note*: Sir Richard Burton served for years as a British spymaster in his many exploratory expeditions, chiefly in the Middle East. For more information on this colorful and adventurous man, see my book, *Spies: A Narrative Encyclopedia of Dirty Deeds and Double Dealing from Biblical Times to Today* (M. Evans, 1997; pages 123-124). Nudity prohibits viewing by children. **p**, Daniel Melnick; **d**, Bob Rafelson; **cast**, Patrick

Iin Glen and Patrick Bergin in *Mountains of the Moon*, 1990.

Bergen, Iain Glen, Richard E. Grant, Fiona Shaw, John Savident, James Villiers, Adrian Rawlins, Peter Vaughan, Delroy Lindo, Bernard Hill, Doreen Mantle, Anna Massey, Omar Sharif; **w**, Rafelson, William Harrison (based on the book *Burton and Speke* by Harrison); **c**, Roger Deakins; **m**, Michael Small; **ed**, Thom Noble; **prod d**, Norman Reynolds; **art d**, Maurice Fowler, Fred Hole; **set d**, Harry Cordwell; **spec eff**, David Harris, Ray Lovell, David H. Watkins.

The Mouse That Roared ★★★★ 1959; U.K.; 83m; Highroad Productions/COL; Color; Comedy; Children: Acceptable; **DVD**; **VHS**. Sellers is a scream in this hilarious comedy, a deftly crafted production that mixes farce with satire, and where he plays several roles, all as residents of a mythical tiny nation located somewhere in the Alps and is on the verge of financial collapse. The country, called Grand Fenwick, produces only one product, an excellent wine, but sales for that wine have drastically fallen off because a California firm has produced a similar wine and is selling it at a bargain basement price, undercutting Grand Fenwick's chief export. Prime Minister Sellers has an idea to reverse his nation's miserable fortunes; he tells the Queen (also played by Sellers) that Grand Fenwick has no choice but to take draconian action by declaring war in the United States. Alarmed, the Queen states that such a venture is impossible, but the Prime Minister tells her that he knows that, and that Grand Fenwick will immediately lose the war and then receive the enormous relief funds the U.S. always lavishes upon its vanquished enemies. Grand Fenwick declares war on the U.S. and sends Sellers, in another role as the leader of twenty men armed with bows and arrows and adorned in ancient chain mail, to the U.S. Arriving in New York during an air raid drill, Sellers and his men stumble across inventor Kossoff, who has created for the U.S. an all-powerful Q-bomb, and Sellers captures Kossoff and his daughter, Seberg, making them hostages until the U.S. sues for peace. Having won the war, Grand Fenwick gets an enormous loan from the U.S. while the California firm is compelled to withdraw its competitive wine from the marketplace and the small country is saved. There are many priceless scenes in this mirthful outing, expertly coordinated by director Arnold, that will bring smiles and laughter to viewers, especially from the inventive Sellers and the rest of the cast members, including Landis, who renders a memorable mime, and the blustering McKern, who leads the "loyal opposition" in the tiny country. **The Mouse on the Moon**, 1963, proved to be an ineffective sequel. *Author's Note*: Director Arnold told this author "that we shot the invasion scenes in the deserted streets in New York on a Sunday when everyone was either in church or sleeping it off." He said that he had problems in London where Sellers was appearing in a play "while we were also shooting scenes for **The Mouse That Roared**. In order to get him quickly back and forth from the play ["Brouhaha"]

to the movie set, we had him ride in an ambulance with the siren blaring in order to rush him through the crowded traffic and it was our good fortune that we were not pinched for doing that." In essaying his many roles in this classic comedy, the gifted Sellers took a leaf from his mentor, Alec Guinness, who appeared in one comedy, **Kind Hearts and Coronets**, 1950, where Guinness played eight separate characters. Guinness told this author that he thought Sellers' appearances in his several characters in **The Mouse That Roared** "were extremely convincing. He is like an ever-changing chameleon. He is so good with foreign accents that you would believe him to be one of the foreigners he is playing. The three roles Peter plays in **Dr. Strangelove** [1964] are truly fine impersonations and I particularly liked his role as the American president with not a trace of a British accent. What a clever lad he is!" **p**, Walter Shenson; **d**, Jack Arnold; **cast**, Peter Sellers, Jean Seberg, David Kossoff, William Hartnell, Leo McKern, MacDonald Parke, Austin Willis, Timothy Bateson, Monty Landis, Wally Brown, Bill Nagy; **w**, Roger MacDougall, Stanley Mann (based on the novel *The Wrath of the Grapes* by Leonard Wibberley); **c**, John Wilcox (Eastmancolor); **m**, Edwin Astley; **ed**, Raymond Poulton; **art d**, Geoffrey Drake; **spec eff**, Gerald Endler.

The Mouthpiece ★★★ 1932; U.S.; 86m; WB; B/W; Drama; Children: Cautionary; **VHS**. William captivates as an aggressive district attorney, who takes great pride in his many convictions, until he discovers to his shock and horror that he sent an innocent man to the electric chair, his innocence not established until only a few minutes after his execution. William takes to drink and then becomes cynical about the law. He goes into private practice and begins to represent the very clients he formerly prosecuted, notorious gangster, becoming their slick "mouthpiece." Suave and polished in court, William uses every legal trick he knows to get his infamous clients set free. At one point, he dramatically grabs an exhibit, reportedly a bottle containing poison that his client has used to murder a victim, and, to prove it is not lethal, swallows its contents. William then goes to an underworld doctor, who pumps the slow-acting poison from his stomach. Rolling in underworld money, William lives the high life, womanizing and attending swanky parties. All that changes when he meets upright, clean-living Fox, falling in love with her after she becomes his stenographer. Fox, however, has given her love to an earnest young man, Janney, and rejects William's advances. After Janney is framed for a crime by one of William's clients, William decides to betray the mob and he brilliantly defends Janney, getting him acquitted while implicating his former client. The mob threatens to kill him, but William tells the gang boss that he has enough secret information hidden in a safe deposit box that will send him and all of his gangsters to prison and that that information will be sent to the district attorney if anything happens to him. The gangsters respond by shooting William as he is about to leave for the wedding between Fox and Janney. The grateful Fox is at William's side as he is taken to a hospital and where he tells her that the gangsters will soon be under arrest as his information about them has been sent on to the D.A. The film ends without the viewer knowing if William will survive or not. Flood and Nugent present a hard-hitting crime yarn, packed with action and many tense moments, where William is riveting as the see-sawing attorney who loses sight of this ethics and regains them through his love for an honest, young woman. This film was unsuccessfully remade as **The Man Who Talked Too Much**, 1940, and then again in a successful third version, **Illegal**, 1955, that starred Edward G. Robinson in the role William originally essayed. *Author's Note*: **The Mouthpiece** is obviously based on the celebrated and flamboyant New York City criminal attorney William J. Fallon (1886-1927). A widely read biography, *The Great Mouthpiece: The Life of William J. Fallon* (1931), by Gene Fowler, had been published only a year earlier and the writers of the play upon which this film is based and its screenplay, liberally helped themselves to Fowler's content in creating the colorful character William enacts. The brilliant Fallon (he could read and memorize a good-sized book within two hours) was a graduate of Fordham University and an assistant district attorney for Westchester County in 1915, successfully prosecuting a number of persons until he decided to become rich by switching sides as a criminal defense attorney. He defended such notorious arch criminals as Arnold Rothstein (1882-1928), who fixed the 1919 World Series, and Julius W. "Nicky" Arnstein (1879-1965), who was Fanny Brice's errant husband and who, despite Fallon's considerable efforts, went to prison for stealing bonds. When this film was shown in its first run at a theater in Syracuse, New York, the theater manger blatantly promoted the film as being based on the life of William Fallon, who had died five years earlier (falling dead of a heart attack in a court room while delivering a summation). His daughter, Ruth Fallon, promptly filed a libel suit as well as criminal charges that immediately brought about a $100 fine for the manager. Warner Brothers later settled with her out of court. For more details on Fallon, see my eight-volume work, *The Encyclopedia of World Crime*, Volume II (CrimeBooks, Inc., 1990; pages 1131-1132). **d**, James Flood, Elliott Nugent; **cast**, Warren William, Sidney Fox, Aline MacMahon, John Wray, Guy Kibbee, J. Carrol Naish, William Janney, Stanley Fields, Berton Churchill, Willie Fung, Paulette Goddard, Jack La Rue, Charles Lane; **w**, Joseph Jackson (based on an adaptation by Earl Baldwin of the play by Frank J. Collins); **c**, Barney McGill; **ed**, George Amy; **art d**, Esdras Hartley.

Movie Crazy ★★★★ 1932; U.S.; 84m; Harold Lloyd Corporation; PAR; B/W; Comedy; Children: Acceptable; **DVD**. In what is most likely Lloyd's finest sound comedy, the great silent star lampoons Hollywood and uses considerable content from his own life for this very funny film. A youth living with his parents in rural Kansas, he is obsessed with movies and he impulsively enacts dramatic scenes before his adoring mother and his disapproving father, aping the mugging actors he has seen on the big screen. He sends a letter with his picture to a Hollywood studio, asking for a film test. His letter and photo becomes mixed up at the studio and Lloyd is invited to make a test. When arriving at the studio, he is given the test, but he is not the romantic lead producers expected. Inexperienced and without any acting training, Lloyd awkwardly collides with other actors, misses his cues, stumbles over props and almost destroys the set as he crashes wildly about in an attempt to emote (and here Lloyd presents the old silent era slapstick at its innovative best). He is dismissed from the production and meets attractive Cummings, who is playing the role of a Mexican girl in a film, instantly falling in love with her. When she later removes her costume and heavy makeup, Lloyd meets her again, and not realizing that she is the same girl, falls in love with her, too. Cummings realizes that Lloyd believes her to be two separate women and, to amuse herself, plays along with the idea, but she, too, is falling in love with the innocent and naïve young man. She manages to persuade the head of the studio to give Lloyd another chance, but he again makes such a clown of himself in attempting serious drama that he causes the cast and crew to break into uncontrollable laughter and it is then that the studio boss realizes that Lloyd is a natural comedian and signs him up to a long-term contract to play in comedies, assuring the career he so covetously wanted all along. Lloyd is wonderful in his role, inserting little bits of comedic business in every scene while the film also gives a revealing glimpse of Hollywood production methods during the infant talking era. The film was not inexpensive for its day, its budget going over $675,000, but it was a smash at the box office, gleaning almost $1.5 million in its initial release. **Merton of the Movies**, 1947, takes a large leaf from this film. *Author's Note*: Clyde Bruckman (1894-1955), the director of this film, had long been a successful gag writer and director for silent comedy films that starred Buster Keaton, Stan Laurel, Oliver Hardy and Lloyd. He was considered to be the most inventive creator of sight gags in Hollywood, but, by the early 1930s, he became alcoholic and undependable, being fired from many productions. Keaton and Lloyd tried to help Bruckman by getting him various writing or directorial jobs, but they wound up being either nurses or guards to a hopeless drunk (and Keaton himself

Warren William, second from right, in *The Mouthpiece*, 1932.

had a drinking problem at this time). Lloyd bent over backward to help Bruckman when he made him the director for **Feet First**, 1930, starring Lloyd, and then **Movie Crazy**, but, in both instances, the title of director was titular in that Lloyd really did all the directing. Lloyd told this author that "I had to watch him like a hawk during the production of **Movie Crazy** to make sure he did not wander off the set and hide behind the walls of some sets where he had bottles of booze hidden, and we found them everywhere. He had a lot of problems, but he could not deal with them without drinking. Booze changes some people, like it did Clyde, from a happy, funny person into a sneaky man looking to hide inside of a bottle. All of his friends tried to help him when he could no longer work. We saw that he had a place to live and loaned him money, but it was hopeless. Booze can cost you everything, your loved ones, your home, your career and even your honor. Clyde lost his honor when he did the screenplay for a Joan Davis comedy, **She Gets Her Man** [1945]. When I saw that film, I became very angry. I realized that Clyde had plagiarized my own work from **Movie Crazy**. That was the last straw. I filed a suit against him and the studio [Universal] and won. In the end, Clyde tried to make a comeback with Buster Keaton's help—they were doing some TV shows together in the Fifties, but they flopped. Clyde was at the end of the line, I guess, when he committed suicide, a terrible tragedy and a sad end for a man who had once been so talented." On January 4, 1955, Bruckman reportedly went to a restaurant, ordered a sumptuous meal, and was then physically ejected when he could not pay for that meal. He then went to a phone booth as if to call someone, but, instead, withdrew a pistol he had borrowed from Buster Keaton, and shot himself, ending his troubled life. Many films have profiled Hollywood and movie-making, most notably **Souls for Sale**, 1923; **The Cameraman**, 1928; **The Last Command**, 1928; **Show People**, 1928; **Free and Easy**, 1930; **Paramount on Parade**, 1930; **The Lost Squadron**, 1932; **What Price Hollywood?**, 1932; **Bombshell**, 1933; **Going Hollywood**, 1933; **Lady Killer**, 1933; **Hollywood Hotel**, 1937; **Stand-In**, 1937; **A Star Is Born**, 1937; **Boy Meets Girl**, 1938; **Mad about Music**, 1938; **Hollywood Cavalcade**, 1939; **The Bank Dick**, 1940; **Caught in the Draft**, 1941; **I Wake Up Screaming**, 1941; **Sullivan's Travels**, 1941; **Henry Aldrich Gets Glamour**, 1942; **Holiday Inn**, 1942; **Star Spangled Rhythm**, 1942; **Thank Your Lucky Stars**, 1943; **Follow the Boys**, 1944; **Hollywood Canteen**, 1944; **Anchors Aweigh**, 1945; **Incendiary Blonde**, 1945; **The Jolson Story**, 1946; **Merton of the Movies**, 1947; **The Perils of Pauline**, 1947; **The Miracle of the Bells**, 1948; **Miss Tatlock's Millions**, 1948; **Dancing in the Dark**, 1949; **It's a Great Feeling**, 1949; **Jolson Sings Again**, 1949; **In a Lonely Place**, 1950; **Sunset Boulevard**, 1950; **Callaway Went Thataway**, 1951; **Starlift**, 1951; **The Bad and the Beautiful**, 1952; **Singin' in the Rain**, 1952; **The Country Girl**, 1954; **A Star Is Born**, 1954; **The Barefoot**

Robert Montgomery and Carole Lombard in *Mr. and Mrs. Smith*, 1941.

Contessa, 1955; **The Big Knife**, 1955; **Love Me or Leave Me**, 1955; **Man of a Thousand Faces**, 1957; **Beloved Infidel**, 1959; **La Dolce Vita**, 1961; **Two Weeks in Another Town**, 1962; **Whatever Happened to Baby Jane**, 1962; **8½**, 1963; **The Carpetbaggers**, 1964; **The Loved One**, 1965; **After the Fox**, 1966; **The Godfather**, 1972; **Day for Night**, 1973; **The Way We Were**, 1973; **The Day of the Locust**, 1975; **The Great Waldo Pepper**, 1975; **Hearts of the West**, 1975; **The Last Tycoon**, 1976; **Silent Movie**, 1976; **Annie Hall**, 1977; **All That Jazz**, 1979; **Stardust Memories**, 1980; **The Stuntman**, 1980; **Ragtime**, 1981; **My Favorite Year**, 1982; **The Cotton Club**, 1984; **The Purple Rose of Cairo**, 1985; **Good Morning, Babylon**, 1987; **Cinema Paradiso**, 1988; **Sunset**, 1988; **White Hunter, Black Heart**, 1990; **Barton Fink**, 1991; **Bugsy**, 1991; **The Player**, 1992; **Ed Wood**, 1994; **Get Shorty**, 1995; **Leaving Las Vegas**, 1995; **L.A. Confidential**, 1997; **Wag the Dog**, 1997; **One of the Hollywood Ten**, 2000; **The Anniversary Party**, 2001; **Lost in Translation**, 2003; **The Aviator**, 2004; **Hollywoodland**, 2006; **Bolt**, 2008; **Hugo**, 2011; **Midnight in Paris**, 2011; and **Mulholland Dr.**, 2011. **p**, Harold Lloyd; **d**, Clyde Bruckman, Lloyd (not credited); **cast**, Lloyd, Constance Cummings, Kenneth Thomson, Louise Closser Hale, Spencer Charters, Robert McWade, Eddie Fetherstone, Sydney Jarvis, Harold Goodwin, Mary Doran, Grady Sutton; **w**, Vincent Lawrence (based on a story by Agnes Christine Johnston, John Grey, Felix Adler); **c**, Walter Lundin; **m**, Alfred Newman; **ed**, Bernard Burton; **art d**, William MacDonald, Harry Oliver.

Mr. and Mrs. Smith ★★★ 1941; U.S.; 95m; RKO; B/W; Comedy; Children: Acceptable; **DVD**; **VHS**. In this only full-fledged American comedy from Hitchcock we see married couple Lombard and Montgomery constantly battling over the smallest quibble. They are madly in love with each other and have been since they tied the knot, and promised from that day onward that they would never walk out on each other while having an argument. Some of those arguments go on for days, even weeks, such are their totally opposite, combative natures. The film opens after the couple has been arguing for three days. Lombard ceases her bombardment to lovingly ask Montgomery if he would marry her again. He thinks about it, and, still miffed, says no, even though he still loves her in the deepest way. Lombard is genuinely hurt. When Montgomery goes to his office, he finds Halton, an attorney, waiting for him, telling him that he and Lombard are not legally married because the boundary lines of the state in which they were married were changed just prior to their wedding. When Montgomery returns home that night, Lombard again asks him if he would marry her again and he remains silent, not knowing that Halton has already met with Lombard at their residence and imparted the same information to her about their not being married. She convinces him to take her to a small Italian restaurant

where they spent so much time when they were courting, but the place is under new management and they have a terrible time. The waiter is rude, the service lousy, and the food is so awful that when they try to get the resident cat to eat some of it, the feline adamantly refuses. When they return home, Lombard now believes that Montgomery will not marry or remarry her and she locks him out of the bedroom, telling him that he needn't bother to get a divorce since they are not officially married anyway. Montgomery takes a room at his men's club and spends some time in the steam bath with old pal Carson, but he offers no solution to Montgomery's dilemma. Montgomery is bewildered in how to win back Lombard's affections. Meanwhile, Raymond, who is Montgomery's law partner and has always been in love with Lombard, learns of the breakup and begins pitching woo to Lombard, and she encourages his advances, ostensibly to make Montgomery jealous enough to officially marry her. Lombard seems to go all the way with Raymond when they travel to Lake Placid where they take separate rooms at an inn. Montgomery, however, is not about to give up Lombard and tracks them down and begins interrupting every meeting between Lombard and Raymond, until he enrages Raymond but endears himself to the woman who loves him, Lombard. Realizing that Montgomery truly loves her, Lombard returns to his arms and they plan to finally, officially tie the knot and that is where this charming and entertaining film ends. Hitchcock does a fine job managing this clever comedy, where Lombard and Montgomery shine in their battling roles. *Author's Note*: Hitchcock had established a strong friendship with the earthy Lombard and she had consistently asked him to direct her in a comedic vehicle, a genre that was not normally his bent, but, because of that friendship, he agreed to direct this film, the second to the last made by Lombard (her final film being the classic Lubitsch comedy, **To Be or Not To Be**, 1942) before she died in an air crash. "Carole [Lombard] was a wonderful actress," Hitchcock told this author, "with a natural sense for comedy and I was delighted to direct her in **Mr. and Mrs. Smith**, with that fine gentleman, Robert Montgomery. She had her fun with me on that film. She had heard that I had stated that all actors were cattle, and I do not know where that came from, and when I first walked onto the set, Carole had a little welcoming present for me, three little calves penned inside a wooden fence and with the names of all the leading players written on cards that hung around the necks of those calves. I retaliated by holding up cue cards with her lines written on them in her open scenes. She was a tough cookie and always controlled herself, but the cue cards caused her to muff a few lines. Well, she got back at me once more when I did the cameo part for the picture, one where I am a skid row bum cadging a drink from Bob [Montgomery] outside his office. Carole directed that scene and made me do so many retakes in that little scene that I got a bit dizzy, especially when she ordered the make-up people to add more and more face powder so that I looked like a ghost." Montgomery told this author that "my experience with Hitch was a pleasant one, although we knew that **Mr. and Mrs. Smith** was not his cup of tea, a comedy, and he was more comfortable with his spy thrillers. But we nevertheless had a lot of fun with him and found that this master of suspense had a great sense of humor." The gag about Hitchcock's "cattle" remark would be repeated several times by other actors in his productions. **p**, Harry E. Edington; **d**, Alfred Hitchcock; **cast**, Carole Lombard, Robert Montgomery, Gene Raymond, Jack Carson, Philip Merivale, Lucile Watson, William Tracy, Charles Halton, Esther Dale, Emma Dunn, Betty Compson, Russell Wade, Hitchcock; **w**, Norman Krasna; **c**, Harry Stradling, Sr.; **m**, Edward Ward; **ed**, William Hamilton; **art d**, Van Nest Polglase, Albert S. D'Agostino; **set d**, Darrell Silvera.

Mr. & Mrs. Smith ★★★ 2005; U.S.; 120m; Regency Enterprises; FOX; Color; Comedy; Children: Unacceptable (MPAA: PG-13); **BD**; **DVD**. A married New York couple, Pitt and Jolie, appear to be living a normal life, but are secretly hired assassins. Neither knows that of the other, although they've been married for about five years. Pitt has a suburban business that barely pays the bills, while Jolie owns a Manhattan operation that is lucrative. Pitt keeps his cash and guns in a pit beneath the tool shed, while Jolie stashes her sharp knives and other weapons of human destruction in trays in the kitchen that keep sliding out from under the oven. Each is separately hired to travel to a remote place in the Southwest and kill someone. When the hit is botched, they are instructed to bump off each other. Now they have their work cut out for them, how to keep from earning their fee? They turn their assassin skills on their employers and save themselves for a romp in bed and new assignments. Although this film sends the wrong message, it is well-crafted and offers a clever script and standout performances from Jolie and Pitt. Songs: "Oxidados" (Plastilina Mosh), "Nothin' But a Good Time" (Bret Michaels, C.C. Deville, Rikki Rockett, Bobby Dall), "Mi Dulce Caridad" (Matt Hirt, Francisco Rodriguez), "(Who Discovered) America" (Jason Roberts, William Abers, Raul Pacheco, Justin Poree, Asdru Sierra, Jiro Yamaguchi, Ulises Bella, K.C. Potter, J.B. Eckl), "Express Yourself" (Charles Wright), "Baby Baby" (Amy Grant, Brian Thomas), "Lay Lady Lay" (Bob Dylan), "The Worst Day Since Yesterday" (Flogging Molly), "The William Tell Overture" (Gioachino Rossini), "Making Love out of Nothing at All" (Jim Steinman as James Richard Steiman), "Girl from Ipanema" (Vinicius de Moraes, Norman Gimble, Antonio Carlos Jobim), "Cool Breeze" (William Bergman), "Mongo Bongo" (Pablo Cook as Paul Cook, Tymon Dogg as Timon Stephen, John Murray, Scott Schields, Martin Slattery, Joe Strummer). Violence and sensuality prohibit viewing by children. **p**, Lucas Foster, Akiva Goldsman, Eric McLeod, Arnon Milchan, Patrick Wachsberger, Kim H. Winther; **d**, Doug Liman; **cast**, Brad Pitt, Angelina Jolie, Vince Vaughn, Adam Brody, Kerry Washington, Keith David, Chris Weitz, Rachael Huntley, Michelle Monaghan, Angela Bassett (voice); **w**, Simon Kinberg; **c**, Bojan Bazelli; **m**, John Powell; **ed**, Michael Tronick; **prod d**, Jeff Mann; **art d**, Keith Neely, David Sandefur; **set d**, Victor J. Zolfo; **spec eff**, Michael Meinardus, Greg Curtis.

Mr. Arkadin ★★★ 1962; France/Spain/Switzerland; 93m; Filmorsa; Janus Films; B/W; Drama; Children: Unacceptable; **VHS**. Strange and bizarre, this murky tale fascinates and puzzles at the same time. Welles is a European industrialist so wealthy that he does not know the extent of his riches. After a gun battle ensues on the waterfront of Naples, Italy, Aslan is mortally wounded, but, before he dies, he utters the name of "Arkadin" to Medina and she tells this to her boyfriend, Arden, a cheap confidence man, who identifies that name as the powerful Welles. Arden thinks to make some money from this connection and, through Mori, Welles' daughter, the only person Welles loves on earth, he is introduced to the financial potentate at a lavish party in Spain. Welles immediately identifies Arden as a man attempting to hustle a dollar, but he sees some service in this man, hiring him to look into his own past. Welles states he is suffering from a strange form of amnesia that allows him no memory before the year 1927, except for the recollection of finding a great deal of money in his pockets when wandering along a European street. Welles provides Arden with some contacts, persons who may know something about Welles, asking that Arden report their comments back to him. Arden then undertakes this odd odyssey, locating and interviewing a number of weird persons, who have something to say about Welles, none of their memories of him being good. These include Redgrave, a homosexual antique dealer, who is really a fence of stolen goods; Tamiroff, a tailor; and Auer, who runs a flea circus, to name a few. After Arden talks with these apprehensive and rather furtive people, they begin to meet violent ends. It then occurs to Arden that he has been sent on an errand to identify the locations of those very people and not to collect any information on Welles, and that Welles is using him to track down anyone having any information about him that badly reflects upon his image. Welles has attempted to establish himself among Europe's social elite as a benefactor of mankind and not the murderous white slaver he truly has been. Arden has learned that Welles trafficked in the abduction of attractive young

Orson Welles, Robert Arden and Paola Mori in *Mr. Arkadin,* 1962.

women, abusing them and then selling them to the highest bidder and that this unsavory and reprehensible business has been the foundation of Welles' great fortune. Now having this dangerous information, Arden realizes that his own life is in great danger. Arden contacts Mori and asks her to set up another meeting with Welles by contacting her father, who is en route to his Spanish castle in his private plane, and she does, talking to him on the plane's radio. Now Welles believes that Arden has told his precious daughter all about his terrible white slavery past and he believes that he has lost the love of the only person important to him. Convinced that he has brought disgrace to himself and his family and has sullied Mori's future by inadvertently unraveling his terrible past while trying to eliminate those who helped him create it, Welles, having nothing more to live for, ends his life by leaping from his plane and this is where Welles ends this grim tale. The production values for this film are high, and Welles, who not only stars but extravagantly directs the film, uses many eye-boggling movie-making tricks—scenes shot at strange angles, overlapping dialog (his hallmark from **Citizen Kane**, 1941), and where many stylized scenes so dazzle the viewer with overhead, dolly, and panning shots that focusing on the story becomes, at times, difficult. All of the characters are well played and the story itself is intriguing, but, unlike **Citizen Kane** and Welles' other masterpiece, **The Magnificent Ambersons**, 1942, Welles does not fully develop Arkadin, leaving only one lasting impression of him—a vile and unredeemable character for whom no viewer can find empathy. The film was not the success Welles had hoped for, doing poorly at the box office. Welles later married Mori, his leading young actress in this film. *Author's Note*: Welles labored long and hard at this story, testing it as one of the segments of his radio show several years before shooting the film, and then culling elements of his Harry Lime character from another classic, **The Third Man**, 1950, directed by the brilliant Carol Reed, adding those characteristics to the Arkadin character (where Harry Lime's unsavory past involves drug dealing, Arkadin's past involves white slavery). Welles shot the film from 1954 to 1955 in Italy, Spain, Germany and France. He then spent the next seven years editing **Mr. Arkadin** while trying to find a distributor so that the film was not released in the U.S. until 1962. In one of my meetings with Welles, I asked him if the Arkadin character was based upon the munitions king, Basil Zaharoff, who was called the "Mystery Man of Europe," and who lived in a castle in Spain and in villas about Europe (as does Arkadin), always on the move to avoid assassins (and using doubles to decoy those assassins) while mentioning the fact that I had written about Zaharoff and he was an entry in one of my recent books. Welles nodded and said: "You could say that that character was more Basil Zaharoff than any other person, but I also worked some elements of other people into that character. The character did not work well and that picture did

William H. Lynn and Clifton Webb in *Mr. Belvedere Rings the Bell,* **1951.**

not work well either. It turned out to be a disaster, financially and in many other ways, but only because I lost creative control of that picture." He then asked for a copy of my book and I gave him one (autographed, of course, as I had with a number of my other books over the years). I then asked Welles if he had been inspired to produce **Mr. Arkadin** after seeing **The Mask of Dimitrios**, 1944, a superb tale of an utter rogue that stemmed from an Eric Ambler novel and which had certainly been based on Zaharoff. "Indeed I did see that wonderful film and more than once, and I have a copy of it, which I have studied. Of course that picture is based on Zaharoff, but no one ever fully captured that character on film. Zaharoff was larger than Death, you might say, in one respect. That man started more wars than any other human being so that he could sell his armaments to both sides, and that includes World War One. He was a one-man plague." He then added: "You have considerable knowledge about motion pictures, young man, and I urge you to write a comprehensive work about that subject." I did, having planned for years to undertake such a work, eventually producing the seventeen-volume *Motion Picture Guide* (1986-1990), but, unfortunately, I could not send that work to Welles as this genius died in 1985, one year before I published the first volume of that work, which consists of more than 25 million words on every feature film ever made to that time. For more information on Basil Zaharoff, see my book (a copy of which I gave to Welles), *Zanies: The World's Greatest Eccentrics* (New Century, 1982; pages 421-423). **p**, Louis Dolivet; **d**, Orson Welles; **cast**, Welles, Robert Arden, Paola Mori, Michael Redgrave, Patricia Medina, Akim Tamiroff, Mischa Auer, Katina Paxinou, Jack Watling, Gregoire Aslan, Peter Van Eyck, Suzanne Flon, Frederic O'Brady, Tamara Shane, Gordon Heath; **w**, Welles (based on his novel); **c**, Jean Bourgoin; **m**, Paul Misraki; **ed**, Renzo Lucidi, (not credited), Welles; **art d**, Welles; **set d**, Luis Perez Espinosa, Gil Parrondo, Francisco Prosper.

Mr. Bean's Holiday ★★★ 2007; U.K.; 90m; UNIV; Color; Comedy; Children: Cautionary (MPAA: PG); **DVD**. In this delightful romp, Atkinson is the irrepressible Mr. Bean, who luckily wins a church raffle and a trip to Cannes. But his French holiday is not all fun since he unwittingly separates a boy from his father and then tries to reunite them. He also has an adventure with a hungry vending machine and an egomaniacal director, Dafoe, not to mention being baffled by French public transportation. Along the path of his humorous adventures, Atkinson also discovers bicycle racing and enjoys a brief romance. Songs: "Hawaii 5-0 Theme Tune" (Morton Stevens); "Crash" (Paul Court, Steve Dullaghan, Tracy Tracy as Tracy Spencer); "Love Machine" (Myra Boyle, Miranda Cooper, Nick Coler, Lisa Cowling, Brian Higgins, Shawn Mahan, Timothy Powell); "La Mer" (Albert Lasry, Charles

Trenet); "Too Late, Too Late" (Mr. Hudson); "Boombastic" (Orville Burrell, Floyd King, Jr. Robert Livingston); "Sous le soleil de Bodega," "Gare du nord," "African Market Place" (Michel Estrade, Stefane Mellino, Noel Rota); "Gimme Back My Tie" (Michel Estrade, Stefane Mellino); "Bean Funeral Parlour" (Steven Price); "T'as d'beaux cieux" (Didier Galand, Pierre Yves); "Sonata in a Major-Turkish Rondo" (Wolfgang Amadeus Mozart); "Bucky Wheatcakes" (Imran Hanif); "O Mimo Babbino Caro" (Giacomo Puccini, Giovacchino Forzano); "Celebration" (Robert Bell, Ronald Bell, George Brown, Eumir Deodato, Robert Mickens, Charles Smith, James Taylor, Dennis Thomas, Earl Toon); "Buskers in the Van" (Michel Estrade, Stefane Mellino); "Apres la pluie" (Mellino). **p**, Peter Bennett-Jones, Tim Bevan, Liza Chasin, Eric Fellner, Debra Hayward, Caroline Hewitt; **d**, Steve Bendelack; **cast**, Rowan Atkinson, Willem Dafoe, Steve Pemberton, Lily Atkinson, Preston Nyman, Sharlit Deyzac, Francois Touch, Emma de Caunes, Philippe Spall, Jean Rochefort, Karen Roden; **w**, Hamish McColl, Robin Driscoll (based on a story by Simon McBurney and characters created by Atkinson, Richard Curtis); **c**, Baz Irvine; **m**, Howard Goodall; **ed**, Tony Cranstoun; **prod d**, Michael Carlin; **art d**, Franck Schwarz, Karen Wakefield; **spec eff**, Mark Holt, Philippe Hubin, Jean-Christophe Magnaud, Robert Duncan, Jonathan Fawkner.

Mr. Belvedere Goes to College ★★★ 1949; U.S.; 83m; FOX; B/W; Comedy; Children: Acceptable; **VHS**. Good comedy sees the meticulous and self-reliant Webb as a successful writer, who decides to enter college late in life in order to win a literary prize, believing that his vast intelligence will shorten his time by three years so that he will graduate in one year's time. He at first is thought of as an odd bird by much younger students, but his wit and wiles so amuse and enlighten them that he soon becomes one of the most popular persons on the campus. Temple, a fetching coed, then thinks that she can make a name for herself by writing an article about Webb and she drives him crazy while pestering him for background information. Through a series of very funny mishaps and misadventures, both succeed in reaching their goals, where Webb and Temple, along with the rest of the cast, are standouts in providing a consistently entertaining comedy. *Author's Note*: The Belvedere character was first presented in the hilarious comedy **Sitting Pretty**, 1948, and proved so popular with audiences that Fox launched a series of films about the persnickety Lynn Belvedere, so wonderfully essayed by Webb. **p**, Samuel G. Engel; **d**, Elliott Nugent; **cast**, Clifton Webb, Shirley Temple, Tom Drake, Alan Young, Jessie Royce Landis, Kathleen Hughes, Taylor Holmes, Alvin Greenman, Peggie Castle, Jeff Chandler, Sally Forrest, Kathleen Freeman, Helen Westcott; **w**, Richard Sale, Mary Loos, Mary McCall, Jr. (based on the character "Belvedere" from the film **Sitting Pretty** created by Gwen Davenport); **c**, Lloyd Ahern; **m**, Alfred Newman; **ed**, Harmon Jones; **art d**, Lyle Wheeler, Richard Irvine; **set d**, Thomas Little; **spec eff**, Fred Sersen.

Mr. Belvedere Rings the Bell ★★★ 1951; U.S.; 87m; FOX; B/W; Comedy; Children: Acceptable; **VHS**. Successful lecturer and self-proclaimed expert on everything, Webb is on a tour when he encounters the residents of a retirement home, who are more dead than alive and don't seem to care. He decides to bring youthful new life into these elderly persons by entering the home under an alias and pretending to be a man in his late seventies. Webb soon inspires his fellow retirees to emulate his athletic feats where he sprints through the hallways and recreation areas and does pushups and handstands with ease. Soon the inhabitants are no longer doddering and enfeebled, but are a lively and vibrant bunch, amazing Marlowe, the pastor who supervises the place. Not only does Webb reinvigorate the old folks, but he cements a romantic relationship between Marlowe and the fetching Dru by making Marlowe jealous of Dru's attentions to him. Koster does a fine job directing this fun-filled film where laughs are aplenty and the witty script from MacDougall shines, and where Webb, Marlowe, Dru and the rest of the cast give fine and very humorous performances. **p**, André Hakim; **d**, Henry Koster; **cast**, Clifton Webb, Joanne Dru, Hugh Marlowe, Zero Mostel, William H. Lynn, Doro Merande, Frances Brandt, Kathleen Comegys, Warren Stevens, Hugh Beaumont, Ray Montgomery; **w**, Ranald MacDougall (based on the play "The Silver Whistle" by Robert E. McEnroe and the character "Belvedere" from the film **Sitting Pretty** created by Gwen Davenport); **c**, Joseph LaShelle; **m**, Cyril J. Mockridge; **ed**, William B. Murphy; **art d**, Lyle Wheeler, John DeCuir; **set d**, Paul S. Fox, Thomas Little; **spec eff**, Fred Sersen.

Mr. Blandings Builds His Dream House ★★★ 1948; U.S.; 94m; RKO; B/W; Comedy; Children: Acceptable; **DVD**; **VHS**. Consistently funny, this spritely comedy sees Grant and Loy as a happily married couple with two teenage daughters, but they live in an apartment that has grown much too small for them. A successful advertising executive, Grant, after some persuasion from Loy, decides to buy a home in the country and commute to work. They buy an old country house in ramshackle condition on large acreage, but, against the advice of engineers, who tell them to tear down the building as it is too dilapidated to renovate, they decide to rebuild the basic structure, using architect Denny to design and add more and more rooms to the place. Meanwhile, the construction of the new home is costing a fortune and everything goes wrong with closet doors that will not open and windows that will not shut and endless drilling for a new well to give them fresh water. Loy insists that each family person have their own bathroom, saying to hubby Grant: "I refuse to endanger the lives of my children in a house with less than four bathrooms." Grant testily replies: "For $1,300 [the cost of the additional fourth bathroom] they can live in a house with three bathrooms and rough it!" Among the many hilarious scenes is one where Loy gives Parnell, who is in charge of painting all the rooms, one exotic color after another and where Parnell, when Loy is gone, asks his painter if he understands and he says he will paint various rooms with standard colors. Family attorney Douglas is not much help, as he has been against the move right from the beginning, telling Grant that he has been swindled by a sharp realtor, stating: "You have been taken to the cleaners, and you don't even know your pants are off!" Further, Grant gets stranded in the city when a fierce storm stops the commuter train and when he returns home he finds Douglas wearing his bathrobe and having spent the night at his new and resplendent home, suspicious that he and wife Loy have been up to no good. His fears are groundless, however, as he soon learns, and he and Loy finally have the home of their dreams. Grant overcomes a final crisis as he is about to lose his job, having spent much too much time redoing his dream house, but his family cook, Beavers, comes to the rescue when she gives him a line about one of his top accounts, a brand of ham, when she serves him and the rest of the family breakfast, saying: "If you ain't eating Wham, you ain't eating ham!" The new slogan saves his job, increases his salary and Grant can now begin to pay off the humungous debts he has accrued in building that dream house. Potter directs with a firm hand and Grant, Loy, Denny and Douglas shine in their roles while a bevy of great character actors do their best to add to the mayhem. The clever script from producers Panama and Frank owes much, however, to a similar and uproarious comedy, **George Washington Slept Here**, 1942, starring Ann Sheridan and the inimitable Jack Benny as the husband who gets trapped into buying a run-down house in the country. *Author's Note*: Grant jocularly told this author that "the picture turns that dream every man has about getting a home in the country into a financial nightmare, proving only that money can't buy happiness, but a costly new home can." Loy, equally witty about the film, stated to this author that "Cary and I get involved with that broken-down, old house and each of us sees it as a sort of paradise and we use every dime we have and risk our future just to move into it. Now isn't that reasonable and practical?" **p**, Norman Panama, Melvin Frank; **d**, H.C. Potter; **cast**, Cary Grant, Myrna Loy, Melvyn Douglas, Reginald Denny, Sharyn Moffett, Connie Marshall, Louise Beavers, Ian Wolfe, Harry Shannon, Jason Robards, Sr., Lurene

Melvyn Douglas, Cary Grant, Will Wright, Myrna Loy and Ian Wolfe in *Mr. Blandings Builds His Dream House*, 1948.

Tuttle, Emory Parnell, Lex Barker, Stanley Andrews, Cliff Clark, Frank Darien, Tito Vuolo, Nestor Paiva; **w**, Panama, Frank (based on the novel by Eric Hodgins);, James Wong Howe; **m**, Leigh Harline; **ed**, Harry Marker; **art d**, Albert S. D'Agostino, Carroll Clark; **set d**, Darrell Silvera, Harley Miller; **spec eff**, Russell A. Cully.

Mr. Bug Goes to Town ★★★ 1941; U.S.; 78m; Fleischer Studios; PAR; Color; Animated Feature/Comedy; Children: Recommended; **DVD**; **VHS**. Hoppity, a well-liked young grasshopper (Freed voiceover), who has been away trying to make his fortune, returns broke to Buggsville, a community of insects that live peacefully on a vacant lot in Manhattan. He is eager to marry the girl bug of his heart, Honey (Loth voiceover). He buys her a soda at the Honey Shop owned by her father, lovable old bee Mr. Bumble (Mercer voiceover) who named his gathering place after her. But Hoppity has competition from the richest, not to mention the fattest and meanest bug in town, a sly beetle called C. Bagley Beetle (Pierce voiceover), who has two henchbugs in his employ, Smack the Mosquito (Meyer voiceover) and Swat the Fly (Mercer voiceover). Before Hoppity and Mr. Beetle can fight over Honey, news spreads through Buggsville that a skyscraper is to be built on the lot they call home. Mr. Creeper, the snail (Colvig voiceover) is sure the community faces total destruction when bulldozers start leveling the lot. But ever-optimistic Hoppity is confident things will work out. He is more than sure of this when the skyscraper is built. He scales the building and sees that a young human couple has an apartment on the roof and its beautiful garden would be a paradise for the bugs to move into. But maybe the couple can't afford to keep it. The wife, Mary (Williams voiceover) cares for the garden while her husband Dick (Gardner voiceover), a struggling songwriter, works on music for what he hopes will be a big Broadway hit show. He sends off a song to a publisher and gets a fat check, which assures the couple they will have money to keep their apartment. Hoppity leads Honey and the other bugs to the penthouse garden where they will have a beautiful and safe home. A delight for children, this film had the misfortune of being released in theaters on December 9, 1941, two days after the Japanese attack on Pearl Harbor and that crisis diverted attention from this fine animated feature that would otherwise have done better at the box office. Songs include "We're the Couple in the Castle," "I'll Dance at Your Wedding," "Katy Did, Katy Didn't" (1941; music: Hoagy Carmichael; lyrics: Frank Loesser); "Be My Little Baby Bumble Bee" (1912; music: Henry Marshall; lyrics: Stanley Murphy); "Where Do We Go from Here?" (1917; music: Howard Johnson; lyrics: Percy Wenrich); "Boy Oh Boy" (1941; music: Sammy Timberg; lyrics: Frank Loesser); "Bridal Chorus (Here Comes the Bride)" (1850; from "Lohengrin" by Richard Wagner); "Reveille" (traditional). **p**, Max Fleischer; **d**, Dave Fleischer; **cast**, (voiceovers), Stan Freed, Pauline Loth, Kenny Gardner, Gwen Williams,

Gary Cooper at right holding tuba with Lionel Stander in *Mr. Deeds Goes to Town*, **1936.**

Jack Mercer, Ted Pierce, Carl Meyer, Pinto Colvig, Margie Hines, Guinn "Big Boy" Williams (narrator); **w**, Dave Fleischer, Dan Gordon, Carl Meyer, Pierce, Graham Place, Isidore Sparber, Bob Wickersham, William Turner, Cal Howard (based on a story by Dave Fleischer, Gordon, Pierce, Sparber); **c**, Charles Schettler (Technicolor); **m**, Leigh Harline, Hoagy Carmichael, Frank Loesser, Herman Timberg, Four Marshals and Royal Guards.

Mr. Deeds Goes to Town ★★★★★ 1936; U.S.; 115m; COL; B/W; Comedy; Children: Acceptable; **DVD**; **VHS**. One of Capra's great "common man" films sees Cooper, a modest, kindly young man from a small Vermont town, inherit $20 million from a rich uncle, a vast fortune in these Depression-swept days. The entire town sees him off and Cooper plays along with the local band on his tuba as these good, hardworking people say farewell, while Cooper, Dumbrille, the attorney for Cooper's conglomerate, and Stander, his aide, all say goodbye from the observation car of a departing train. Cooper is national news and when he arrives in New York and enters his uncle's huge mansion, he is dumbfounded by the lavish settings and the slavish servants waiting to serve him. Cynical newspaper editor Bancroft, however, does not buy the "pure and simple" image Cooper projects, calling him a 'cornfed bohunk," and assigns tough female reporter Arthur to cover the story, urging her to ridicule Cooper at every unsophisticated turn he makes. Arthur attempts to get close to Cooper, but, when that fails, she pretends to faint outside his mansion, ostensibly from lack of food, claiming she is unemployed. The chivalrous Cooper picks her up and makes sure she has a good meal and Arthur begins to pump him for information about his life. Cooper's kindness and caring nature soon alters Arthur's opinion of him, and she sees him as he truly is, a decent and honorable man. After he takes her home to her cheap apartment, Cooper reads a poem to Arthur he has written about her, one expressing his love and admiration for her and it melts her heart. She falls in love with him as deeply as he has fallen in love with her. She later takes him to Grant's Tomb where Cooper, in simple terms, tells how he sees Grant from simple Ohio farm boy to becoming President of the U.S. They later go to a celebrated restaurant so that Cooper, a self-styled poet, can meet the city's esteemed writers, critics and poets (undoubtedly based on the famed group of New York City writers who regularly gathered about a round table at the Algonquin Hotel). Cooper is urged to read some of his homespun poetry and, after reciting a few lines, he is widely ridiculed and laughed at, causing Cooper to state: "I know I must look funny to you. Maybe if you came to Mandrake Falls [his home town], you'd look funny to us…But nobody would laugh at you…because that wouldn't be good manners." When one of the writers ridicules Cooper's notion of decency, he knocks the man unconscious and then leaves to undertake

a binge with Arthur under the supervision of writer Catlett, who has admired his rugged defense of his hometown values and thinks of Cooper as a new two-fisted, heroic literary light. En route, Cooper tells Arthur that New Yorkers "work so hard at living, they forget how to live." Arthur struggles with her conscience as she loyally writes lampoons about Cooper for her paper under a pseudonym, but Bancroft suspects that she is softening toward her subject after Arthur tells him that Cooper is "either the dumbest, silliest idiot…or he's the grandest guy alive." She nevertheless continues to depict Cooper's eccentric-appearing antics in print, how he feeds doughnuts to horses hauling delivery wagons, pretends to tickle the feet of statues, slides down the bannister rails of his mansion and wildly chases after fire engines. After Cooper learns that Arthur has betrayed his confidences by writing those ridiculing articles about him, he rejects her. Then an impoverished man, Wray, invades his home, threatening him and demanding money, saying that he has worked all his life and has lost everything and that rich men like Cooper have no concern about him and millions of others suffering during this terrible Depression. Cooper calms the man, offering him help and then decides that he will do what other wealthy men have not done, aid as many families as he can by giving away his fortune. He advertises for farmers to apply to him for loans and he is overwhelmed by thousands of men, mostly farmers who have lost their homesteads. The conniving and manipulative Dumbrille, who has been angling to become the executor of Cooper's estate in order to siphon off its millions, then becomes alarmed and urges two of Cooper's distant relatives to file a suit against Cooper, claiming his estate on the grounds that Cooper is mentally incompetent. A trial then ensues where Cooper remains mute, refusing to testify on his behalf as Dumbrille brings witnesses to describe Cooper's eccentric behavior and mental instability. Even two old maids from his home town testify, stating that Cooper has always been "pixilated" (touched by insanity). Warner, the considerate presiding judge, urges Cooper to speak up on his own behalf, warning that if he makes no defense, he could lose his entire fortune and be institutionalized. He remains silent. Then Arthur stands up in court and publicly apologizes to him for the lambasting articles she has written and declares her love for him, begging him to speak in his own defense, as does her hardboiled editor, Bancroft, who now feels Cooper is an honorable and courageous man. Encouraged by the woman he loves, Cooper then defends himself, telling Warner that he plays the tuba because it relaxes him, just as Warner, Cooper has noticed, "doodles" when listening to stressful testimony to relax himself. He goes on to admit that he did, indeed, feed doughnuts to horses because he was intoxicated, a condition many young men sometimes foolishly create, but that does not make them insane. Further, after he questions the two little old ladies from Mandrake Falls, they admit that they live in their home because Cooper supports them and go on to tell Warner and the court that *everyone* in Mandrake Falls is "pixilated" other than themselves. Dumbrille then insults Cooper and, being the man of action that he is, he hits the scurrilous attorney on the jaw, knocking him out, causing the many penniless farmers and workers who have packed the court to loudly cheer. Cooper apologizes to the court and Warner then concludes: "In my opinion, you are not only sane, but you are the sanest man who ever walked into this courtroom." The case is dismissed and Cooper is carried on the backs of his many supporters, but not before Cooper hugs Arthur to indicate that they are going to have a life together and that is where this stirring film ends. Capra presents a populist classic with this tale by carefully molding his scenes to edge hero Cooper close enough to the abyss, but to save him at the last moment and where Cooper and Arthur are magnificent in their roles as are the rest of the cast members. Capra won an Oscar as Best Director and the film was nominated for Best Picture and nominations also went to Cooper for Best Actor, to Riskin for Best Adapted Screenplay and for Best Sound Recording. *Author's Note*: Capra told this author that Cooper "was my first, last and only selection for the character of Longfellow Deeds. I knew that no other actor could bring the kind of humility and strength to that character and he was just as wonderful in that role as I envisioned he would be." Selecting Cooper's co-star, however, proved to be difficult for the director, although he wanted Arthur in that role after seeing her in a small-budgeted western. He asked Columbia studio chief Harry Cohn to sign her up, but the truculent mogul refused, saying: "she has no name." Capra told Cohn that Arthur "has a great voice." Cohn then said: "Great voice? Did you see her face? Half of it is angel and the other half is horse!" Arthur never forgot hearing this remark and later parroted Cohn's appraisal to this author; see my *Author's Note* for my entry for **The More the Merrier**, 1943. Capra kept after Cohn until he finally agreed to sign Arthur and she proved to be outstanding, although the stubborn Cohn would never admit it. The film also made Arthur a superstar and she would be Capra's leading lady in **You Can't Take It with You**, 1938, and **Mr. Smith Goes to Washington**, 1939. Cooper would appear in one more Capra film, **Meet John Doe**, 1941. Cooper, one of the most popular actors in America for years (he made $500,000 in 1939 and would earn more than $10 million throughout his spectacular career in Hollywood), was circumspect about his role in **Mr. Deeds Goes to Town**, telling this author that "I am just a guy who lives next door to everybody, no one special, so that is why I guess Frank [Capra] picked me for the role of that plain-speaking fellow in **Mr. Deeds Goes to Town**. He plays the tuba, and not too well, and writes cornball poetry and I did things like that as a young man, all young men do those things and, if they're lucky enough, all young men fall in love. I get to fall in love with Jean Arthur, who was just terrific in that picture, and she saves my bacon because she feels the same way about me. A lot of sophisticated people make fun of Frank's [Capra's] films by saying that they are corny and play too much on sentiment. But, what's wrong with that? Americans are sentimental people. We believe in what our hearts tell us. And Frank Capra's films always talk from the heart. That's why his films are great and always will be." Arthur expressed the same sentiments to this author when saying: "The people who don't like Frank Capra's films are people who have never been loved or have never given love to anyone, I think. His films are in step with the world, not only in step, but they skip and hop and dance down every street. Frank [Capra] went to bat for me, fighting to get me that role in **Mr. Deeds Goes to Town**, and I have always been grateful for that and for being part of a film that is considered to be a classic, but we knew just how good it was when we were all putting that wonderful picture together." **p&d**, Frank Capra; **cast**, Gary Cooper, Jean Arthur, George Bancroft, Lionel Stander, Douglass Dumbrille, Raymond Walburn, H. B. Warner, Ruth Donnelly, Walter Catlett, Ann Doran, Emma Dunn, George "Gabby" Hayes, Warren Hymer, Charles Lane, Mayo Methot, Margarete Matzenauer, Spencer Charters, Wyrley Birch, Pierre Watkin, John Wray, Christian Rub, Gustav von Seyffertitz, Irving Bacon; **w**, Robert Riskin (based on the story "Opera Hat" by Clarence Budington Kelland); **c**, Joseph Walker; **m**, Howard Jackson; **ed**, Gene Havlick; **art d**, Stephen Goosson.

Mr. Hobbs Takes a Vacation ★★★ 1962; U.S.; 115m; FOX; Color; Comedy; Children: Acceptable; **DVD**; **VHS**. Consistently funny comedy has Stewart as a St. Louis banker and his wife, O'Hara, and family taking what Stewart hopes will be a nice, quiet vacation for a month on the West Coast. It turns out to be anything but relaxing. The beach house they rent is so run down that the hired cook, Urecal, quits. Their son, Burns, avoids the nearby beach and spends all his time watching television. Their daughter, Peters, refuses to be seen in public because of a mouthful of new braces. Some relatives arrive to give them headaches, and O'Hara finds herself constantly and politely rebuffing wealthy Gardiner, an aging swain and member of a local yacht club, who envisions a summer fling with this attractive married woman. By the end of the month, Stewart has been so worn out he's looking forward to going back to work, but O'Hara has had such a good time she rents the cottage again for the following summer. Song: "Cream Puff" (Johnny Mercer, Henry Mancini). *Author's Note*: Stewart told this author that "I really enjoyed doing **Mr. Hobbs Takes a Vacation**, where, instead of relaxing, I have to be a plumber, carpenter, matchmaker and emotional fixer upper, doing

Gary Cooper and Douglass Dumbrille in *Mr. Deeds Goes to Town*, 1936.

more work than I would do if I were back in my office. I also scare the pants off my son [Burns] when I take him sailing and then we get lost in a fog, but I manage to sail the little boat to safety and get to be the hero all dads want to be. That picture tells the story of millions of fathers, who start out thinking they are going to get some rest on their vacations, but, by the time their vacations are over they are so exhausted from everything rotten that can happen, and it always does, that they are grateful to get back to their jobs where they can get six or eight hours of sleep at night." **p**, Jerry Wald; **d**, Henry Koster; **cast**, James Stewart, Maureen O'Hara, Fabian, John Saxon, Marie Wilson, Reginald Gardiner, Lauri Peters, Valerie Varda, Lili Gentle, John McGiver, Michael Burns, Natalie Trundy, Herb Alpert; **w**, Nunnally Johnson (based on the novel *Hobbs' Vacation* by Edward Streeter); **c**, William C. Mellor (CinemaScope; DeLuxe Color); **m**, Henry Mancini, Johnny Mercer; **ed**, Marjorie Fowler; **art d**, Malcolm Brown, Jack Martin Smith; **set d**, Walter M. Scott, Stuart A. Reiss; **spec eff**, L.B. Abbott.

Mr. Hobo ★★★ 1935; U.K.; 80m; Gaumont British; B/W; Comedy; Children: Acceptable. Arliss plays a lovable vagabond, who, along with his friend Gerrard, is arrested in France for a minor offense. Arliss gives his name as Rothschild and police mistake him for being a member of the British banking firm. They give him some money out of their charity fund and he deposits it in a bank, which is about to go broke, so Arliss' deposit saves the institution from collapse. After Gerrard successfully shields the fortune of a girl from a con artist, he and Arliss begin leading a comfortable life together. This film plays off the success of the smash hit film, **The House of Rothschild**, 1934, which was released a year before this entertaining comedy, and which starred Arliss. **p**, Michael Balcon; **d**, Milton Rosmer; **cast**, George Arliss, Gene Gerrard, Viola Keats, Patric Knowles, Frank Cellier, George Hayes, Mary Clare, Henrietta Watson, Bernard Miles, Mervyn Johns, Cecil Parker; **w**, Guy Bolton, Maude T. Howell, Paul Laffitte (based on the story "Rothschild" by Laffitte); **c**, Mutz Greenbaum; **m**, Arthur Benjamin; **ed**, Charles Saunders; **art d**, Alfred Junge.

Mr. Holland's Opus ★★★★ 1995; U.S.; 143m; Hollywood Pictures/Buena Vista; Color; Drama; Children: Cautionary (MPAA: PG); **DVD**; **VHS**. In a truly memorable role, Dreyfuss, a thirty-year-old composer and musician, married to Headly, takes a teaching position in 1965 at John F. Kennedy High School in Portland, Oregon (a fictional school) to make ends meet and to have enough time to complete the one musical composition that he believes will be a significant contribution to the musical world. Initially, he is aloof with his students, above them all in class and creativity, and he resents the fact that even the football coach, Thomas, outranks him. He believes that he is nothing more than

Richard Dreyfuss and students in *Mr. Holland's Opus*, 1995.

a lowly cog in the educational system, even though he befriends Thomas while assistant principal Macy exhibits a marked dislike for him. Dukakis, the sage but demanding principal, scolds Dreyfuss for his airy ways, telling him that he has an obligation to his students and that teaching is not an avenue by which to merely make a living, but a dedicated mission to bring enlightenment to students above all else. He slowly comes to think of his students as individuals and makes an effort to help them learn about music, innovatively using rock 'n' roll to make them understand the elements of classical music. Headly becomes pregnant, and, instead of hoarding his savings so that he can quit his job and write his opus, Dreyfuss uses the money to buy a home for his family. His son is born during the summer, after he has taught at the school for a year, and, in the fall, he is made head of the marching band. Thomas helps him with that additional chore in exchange for Dreyfuss assigning Thomas' top football player, Howard, to the position of a drummer in the band. Time passes, as shown in a series of newsreel footage that records the events of the Vietnam War and where Howard is among those killed in that attritional conflict, along with the death of John Lennon, a musical icon. Then Dreyfuss and Headly learn that their young son is deaf and Dreyfuss becomes frustrated and depressed at the thought that he will never be able to teach his boy about the joys of music. Headly eagerly learns how to communicate with the boy (Renner at age six), and when Dreyfuss resists learning the same sign language, he and Headly and Renner drift apart. Throughout this period, Dreyfuss becomes so involved with his students that he ignores his family and is tempted to abandon his family when an attractive and talented young female student asks him to leave the school and run off with her, going to New York where they can live together and he can finally write his musical masterpiece. Dreyfuss, however, remains at the school, inspiring many of his students, but he finally reaches an age where he believes it impossible now to find enough finances to have his opus, "The American Symphony," performed, even though, over the years, he has completed that composition. Dukakis then retires and Dreyfuss' old nemesis, Macy, becomes the principal and he immediately calls a board meeting where he gets all the members to agree to eliminate the musical courses, as well as all of the other creative courses that have long been taught at the school, and thus forces Dreyfuss' retirement at age sixty. He thinks of himself a failure, but, on his final day, Dreyfuss is led to the school's auditorium where hundreds of his former students are assembled to pay honor to him, as well as perform his symphony, which Headly and his grown son (Natale, age twenty-eight) have made copies of and distribute to these musical playing students, including Gleason, a former student who has become the governor of the state and plays a clarinet in the orchestra. His students then ask Dreyfuss to conduct his own symphony and he does as Headly and Natale look on with love and admiration

while Dreyfuss' opus is finally heard, that opus not only being his musical composition but the great body of talented and decent adults he has taught from childhood, and who, along with his family, have given him a better understanding and appreciation of their collective personal growths and their real achievements as human beings. Dreyfuss is brilliant in essaying his character, a man who exchanges his most precious ambitions for the self-sacrificing job of teaching others what he knows and loves most, and he is well supported by a superb cast and where Derek's direction is outstanding. This is not only a must-see for music lovers, but will appeal to mainstream viewers wanting a forceful and meaningful drama. Dreyfuss deservedly received an Oscar nomination as Best Actor for his bravura performance (this great and gifted actor has never given a bad performance) while the film did very good box office business, taking in more than $100 million in its initial release. Musical compositions and songs: "Symphony No. 5 in C Minor," "Symphony No. 7 in A Major," "Symphony No. 3 in E-Flat Major" (Ludwig van Beethoven); "Minuet in G Major," "Sleeper's Wake" (Johann Sebastian Bach); "One, Two, Three" (Brian Holland, Lamont Dozier, Edward Holland, John Madara, David White, Leonard Barisoff); "Stranger on the Shore" (Acker Bilk, Robert Mellin); "Stouthearted Men" (Sigmund Romberg, Oscar Hammerstein II); "A Lover's Concerto" (Sandy Linzer, Denny Randell); "Louie, Louie" (Richard Berry); "Keep on Running" (Jackie Edwards);, "The Stars and Stripes Forever" (John Philip Sousa); "I Know an Old Lady" (Alan Mills, Rose Bonne); "Uptight (Everything's All Right)" (Stevie Wonder, Sylvia Moy, Henry Cosby); "Americans We" (Henry Fillmore); "Beautiful Boy," "Imagine" (John Lennon); "Day is Done (Taps)" (Daniel Butterfield); "The Pretender" (Jackson Brown); "I Got Rhythm," "Someone to Watch Over Me," "They Can't Take That Away from Me" (George Gershwin, Ira Gershwin), "I Got a Woman" (Ray Charles); "Ego Trippin' (Part Two)" (Paul Huston, David Jolicouer, Kevin Mercer, Vincent Mason); "Cole's Song" (Michael Kamen, Julian Lennon); 'Visions of a Sunset' (Shawn Stockman); "An American Symphony (Mr. Holland's Opus)" (Michael Kamen). **p**, Robert W. Cort, Ted Field, Michael Nolin, Judith James, William Teitler; **d**, Stephen Herek; **cast**, Richard Dreyfuss, Glenne Headly, Jay Thomas, Olympia Dukakis, William H. Macy, Alicia Witt, Terrence Howard, Damon Whitaker, Nicholas John Renner, Anthony Natale, Jean Louisa Kelly, Joanna Gleason, Balthazar Getty, Forest Whitaker; **w**, Patrick Sheane Duncan; **c**, Oliver Wood (Technicolor); **m**, Michael Kamen, **ed**, Trudy Ship; **prod d**, David Nicols; **art d**, Dina Lipton; **set d**, Jan K. Bergstrom; **spec eff**, Bob Riggs.

Mr. Hulot's Holiday ★★★★ 1954; France; 100m (114m in later releases); Discina Film/Cady Films/Janus Films; B/W; Comedy; Children: Recommended; **DVD**; **VHS**. Tati, that French master of comedic mime (whose talents rank with those of Charles Chaplin and the inimitable Marceau), is absolutely wonderful and hilarious in this uproarious satire of a gentle, discombobulating bachelor, lanky and bone jangling, who takes a vacation to a small seaside resort in Brittany. Oblivious to all about him, he goes along his leisurely way, leaving mayhem and chaos in his unwitting wake. He is attracted to Pascaud, a lovely woman who is staying at his hotel, but he is so shy that the awkward Tati cannot bring himself to make a pass at her. He meets and befriends a bevy of vacationers, people from all walks of life that most people meet when on a holiday, but he touches their lives in unusual ways. Other residents at the hotel include Camax, a forceful, old British maid; Zola, a workaholic, who cannot bring himself to enjoy anything; Carl, an overworked waiter; Dubois, a former military officer, who believes he is still commanding troops; and Lacourt, a constantly henpecked husband, who is forever strolling about at the dictatorial direction of his domineering wife, Gérard. (In one of the many priceless scenes, Gérard is shown collecting seashells, handing them to Lacourt to keep, but, as he walks glumly behind her, he disdainfully tosses them aside without comment as she goes on diligently collecting more seashells.) Everything that can impede, disrupt and otherwise destroy Tati's holiday tales place, but he takes it all in stride as if such events are daily if not hourly normal occurrences. In breakneck, hilarious sequences, he saunters into a grim funeral and a massive American car runs his little sports auto (a well-worn 1924 Amilcar) off the road. Renting a kayak, Tati paddles the craft out to sea only to see it break in half, one end appearing to be a shark and causing boaters and swimmers to panic (this scene may have inspired Spielberg when making **Jaws**, 1975, where he has two boys scuba diving and using a makeshift shark fin to create a panic at a beach). While enmeshed in a wild ping pong game, Tati accidentally pushes against a chair where a card player mistakenly places his card on a nearby table that causes the players to erupt in a fight. He enters a 300-foot long room, crosses it in silence, and, when he closes a door, a priceless Ming vase crashes to the floor. In an anti-climax, Tati wrongly enters a fireworks factory and lights his pipe, which is forever going out, and then casually tosses the still-lit match away before exiting. The factory goes up with spectacular effects, the entire coastline exploding in the most astounding array of pyrotechnics ever seen. The next morning, his vacation over, Tati casually packs his bags and leaves the hotel where only a few adults bid him a fond farewell, but he is cheered by all the local children for whom his appearance has brought endless excitement and delight, as it will to any viewer of this comedy classic. Tati, who directs this masterpiece as well as stars in it, presents a film with very little dialog, but with considerable sound, most of it offbeat and working well with his carefully crafted scenes, although there is little or no plot. Unlike most directors, he does not visually pinpoint the elements to be focused upon, but presents a number of events taking place in the same scene and allows the viewer to visually select the most hilarious element, which is invariably inescapable. In all of his setups he allows the action to take place naturally in the frame, eschewing close-ups, medium or long shots or the lecturing zoom. His directorial perspective is one that does not say "look at this," bur rather "look at what you will," a methodology that Woody Allen elected to employ in his later comedies and to equally good effect. Tati used non-actors in the supporting roles and they were perfect in their parts. He believed that they would be perceived as average tourists, like himself, if they were not professional actors, and in this he was right. The film most deservedly won the Grand Prize at the Cannes Film Festival and it certainly would have won an Oscar for the Best Foreign Language Film, but that category did not then exist at the Academy Awards. *Author's Note*: Tati, born Jacques Tatischeff (1907-1982), directed only six films, but they are all gems, and despite his scant productions, remains one of the pantheon directors of comedies. **The Illusionist**, 2010, an outstanding animated feature, posthumously profiles Tati and is based upon a semi-autobiographical script he wrote in 1956. One of France's greatest comedians, Tati combined the panache of Charles Chaplin, the innocence of Harry Langdon, the deadpan countenance of Buster Keaton and, to some degree, the physicality of Harold Lloyd; all of his films are sheer delights. **p**, Jacques Tati, Fred Orain; **d**, Tati; **cast**, Tati, Nathalie Pascaud, Louis Perrault, Micheline Rolla, André Dubois, Suzy Willy, Raymond Carl, Lucien Fregis, Georges Adlin, Michéle Brabo, Valentine Camax, Jean-Pierre Zola, Marguerite Gérard, René Lacourt; **w**, Tati, Pierre Aubert, Jacques Lagrange, Henri Marquet (based on a story by Tati, Marquet); **c**, Jacques Mercanton, Jean Mousselle; **m**, Alain Romans; **ed**, Suzanne Baron, Charles Bretoneiche, Jacques Grassi; **prod d**, Roger Briaucourt, Henri Schmitt; **spec eff**, Trey Freeman.

Mr. Lucky ★★★ 1943; U.S.; 100m; RKO; B/W; Comedy/Romance; Children: Acceptable; **DVD**; **VHS**. In an intriguing good-guy, bad-guy role, Grant is a gambler in New York City during WWII, who owns a gambling ship that is in much need of repair. He wants to refurbish the vessel and then sail it to Cuba where he can make millions through the wagering of the international set, but he lacks the funds to do the job. While his patient skipper, Bickford, keeps the ship anchored on a New York City dock, Grant contends with another problem. He has received his "greetings" from Uncle Sam and is ordered to report to the draft

Alan Carney, Cary Grant and Laraine Day in *Mr. Lucky,* 1943.

board for induction, but he evades service by assuming the identity of a dead pal, who has been marked "4-F," while his two top confederates, Stewart and Carney, also called up for service, also avoid reporting for duty. While searching for funds, Grant stumbles upon a social organization called the American Relief Society, which is attempting to raise funds in order to send needed medical supplies to the front. He meets one of the society's leaders, Day, an attractive heiress, and, through her trust and the good intentions of her society, he sees an opportunity to turn the big dollar he needs. Grant turns on the charm as only he can and convinces Day, along with Cooper and Johnson, other leaders of the social group, to let him establish a charity where a large gambling event can take place and where all proceeds will then ostensibly go to the society's charitable missions. Grant, of course, plans to run out with the proceeds after the gambling fete is over so that he can refit his gambling ship and live the high life in Cuba with another lucrative gambling operation. A more serious problem arises when Grant learns that the phony I.D. he has appropriated from his dead friend can now send him to prison for life as the dead man is wanted for another crime and that he was a two-time loser. Worse, Cupid intervenes and Grant falls for Day, embracing her noble principles so that when the gambling event is over, he cannot bring himself to steal the proceeds. Stewart, his most hard-hearted henchman, however, has no such generous inclinations, and demands his split at the point of a gun. Grant foils Stewart and turns over the proceeds to the society ladies before vanishing. Day, however, whose heart he has almost broken when she learns of his scheme, is now back in his corner after he has done the right thing, and she chases after him. Through Bickford, the kindly skipper of Grant's old gambling vessel, Day finds Grant and he agrees to not only go straight but serve his country by responding to Uncle Sam's call to arms, all for the love of a good woman. Grant does a fine job leaving the viewer wondering if this great screen hero has turned dastardly through most of the film, and the beautiful Day does a great job in her role of reforming the charming crook. This film was a big winner for RKO, gleaning almost $2 million in profits for the studio from the box office the first time around. It was remade as **Gambling House**, 1950, but that proved to be an inferior production. *Author's Note*: Grant told this author that "I keep everyone guessing about whether or not I am rotten to the core or not in **Mr. Lucky**. I liked that premise of always keeping them guessing, but you had better deliver the good side at the finish if you want to keep viewers happy. They knew that when they made **Casablanca** [1942] with Humphrey Bogart. Is he a good guy or a bad guy? You have to wait until you see the end, ladies and gentlemen, to get that smile on your face and that song in your heart." Day felt that this picture "was one of my best. I stepped into high company when appearing opposite Cary [Grant] in that picture. He made me look good and just being in a scene with him made you feel very

Peter Lorre in *Mr. Moto's Last Warning*, 1939.

confident." The story for this film was hatched by one of Grant's cronies, Milton Holmes, who was the tennis pro at the Beverly Hills Tennis Club where Grant was a member and from whom Grant took lessons. Holmes had written a treatment for this story and after he showed it to Grant, the star thought it had possibilities and he then interested RKO in producing the film. Holmes went on to co-write the screenplay with Scott. **p**, David Hempstead; **d**, H.C. Potter; **cast**, Cary Grant, Laraine Day, Charles Bickford, Gladys Cooper, Alan Carney, Henry Stephenson, Paul Stewart, Kay Johnson, Walter Kingsford, Florence Bates, Rita Corday, Mary Forbes; **w**, Milton Holmes, Adrian Scott (based on the story "Bundles for Freedom" by Holmes); **c**, George Barnes; **m**, Roy Webb; **ed**, Theron Warth; **prod d**, William Cameron Menzies; **art d**, Albert S. D'Agostino, Mark-Lee Kirk; **set d**, Darrell Silvera, Claude Carpenter; **spec eff**, Vernon L. Walker.

Mr. Magoo's Holiday Festival ★★★ 1970; U.S.; 104m; United Productions of America /Maron Films; Color; Animated Film; Children: Recommended; **DVD**. This entertaining feature film is made up of two animated tales with the hilarious near-sighted Mr. Magoo that were originally shown on television. **Mr. Magoo's Christmas Carol** by Charles Dickens, seen on television in 1962, includes the songs "Alone in the World," "It's Great to Be Back on Broadway, "The Lord's Bright Blessing," "Ringle, Ringle," "We're Despicable," and "Winter Is Warm" (Jule Style, Bob Merrill), and **Mr. Magoo's Snow White**, seen on television in 1965. **p**, Lee Orgel; **d**, Abe Levitow; **cast** (voiceovers), Jim Backus, Jack Cassidy, Joan Gardner, Jane Kean, Royal Dano, Morey Amsterdam, Les Tremayne, Pal Frees, John Hart, Marie Matthews, Laura Olsher, **w**, Barbara Chain (based on the book *A Christmas Carol* by Charles Dickens and the fairy tale "Schneewiitchen und die Sieben Zwerge" ["Snow White and the Seven Dwarfs"] by Jackob and Wilhelm Grimm); **m**, Jule Styne; **ed**, Earl Bennett, Sam Horta, Wayne Hughes, George Probert; **prod d**, Corny Cole, Lee Mishkin, Marty Murphy, Tony Rivera, Shirley Silvey, Bob Singer, Richard Ung, Sam Weiss.

Mr. Majestyk ★★★ 1974; U.S.; 104m; Mirisch/UA; Color; Drama; Children: Unacceptable (MPAA: PG); **DVD;VHS**. In this hard-hitting tale about the mistreatment of migratory workers, Bronson is a Vietnam veteran, who becomes a Colorado watermelon farmer and who just wants to live in peace. His workers are threatened by a local organized crime boss, Lettieri, who sends a hit man to kill him after Bronson resists mob control of the workers. Lettieri's goons machine gun Bronson's melon crop into pulp, but he manages to win in a battle with the criminals and it looks like he will finally be able to live in peace. *Author's Note*: Bronson personally felt that migrant workers in the U.S. were widely abused and he used this vehicle to make his social statement, a

good one, telling this author that "local and some state governments in the U.S. talk a lot about defending the rights of these poor migrant workers, but that's mostly lip service. Their lifestyles will never improve unless the public gets involved." **p**, Walter Mirisch; **d**, Richard Fleischer; **cast**, Charles Bronson, Al Lettieri, Linda Cristal, Lee Purcell, Paul Koslo, Taylor Lacher, Frank Maxwell, Alejandro Rey, Jordan Rhodes, Bert Santos; **w**, Elmore Leonard; **c**, Richard H. Kline (DeLuxe Color); **m**, Charles Bernstein; **ed**, Ralph E. Winters; **art d**, Cary Odell; **spec eff**, Robert N. Dawson.

Mr. Moto's Gamble ★★★ 1938; U.S.; 72m; FOX; B/W; Mystery; Children: Unacceptable; **DVD**; **VHS**. Lorre fascinates as the subtle oriental sleuth, Moto, who is shown teaching a criminology course at the University of San Francisco where he has as students Luke, the son of famed Chinese detective Charlie Chan, as well as the bumbling Rosenbloom, who suffers from chronic kleptomania (both providing considerable laughs throughout the film). Huber, a detective for the San Francisco police force, who is a friend of private detective Lorre, invites him to attend an important boxing match between Clark and Baldwin, and where the winner will face the champion, Bond. Fowley, a surly gangster, makes large bets that Clark will not last beyond the fourth round. His wagers and boast prove to be lethally correct in that Clark goes down in the fourth round and dies a short time later. He has been murdered (not unlike the fate of one of the prizefighters profiled in the classic fantasy film **Here Comes Mr. Jordan**, 1941). Huber asks Lorre to help him solve the killing, and the little sleuth goes assiduously to work while the championship fight between Baldwin and Bond is about to take place. While Bari and Baldwin develop a romance, Lorre learns that a huge amount of money has been nationally wagered against Clark (and where bookie Nedell loses a fortune), and goes on to prove that the fight between Clark and Baldwin was rigged by someone involved in the match. He then pinpoints the culprit after his own life has been put in danger. Lorre and the cast do standout jobs in their roles in this above-average mystery and where tension and suspense is sustained throughout. This was the third of eight films in the Moto series, superior to the others in that it has a very good plot and better developed characters. *Author's Note*: Lorre did not like playing Mr. Moto, although the series was very popular, telling this author that "I despised playing that creepy little detective and hated the makeup I had to wear. I have heavy eyelids, but the makeup people so accented them that they made me look hideous and more pop-eyed than I am." Lorre became depressed about his typecast role as Moto that he resumed his abuse of drugs (morphine) to suppress his anger and dislike over having to play the character. The film was not originally intended for the Mr. Moto series, according to studio chief Darryl F. Zanuck, who told this author that "that story was slated for a Charlie Chan picture [**Charlie Chan at Ringside**], but the star of that series, Warner Oland, got sick [died a few months later], so we turned it into a Mr. Moto film. Lorre never like playing Moto and came to me several times, begging me to take him out of the series, but I told him, 'I would, Peter, but you are so good in the role that we could never get another actor to play that part so well.' He walked away, shaking his head, and said: 'I'm sunk! I'm drowning! The whirlpool's got me!'" Bond went on to fame as one of John Ford's most substantial character actors; Stone went on to be "Runt" in the Boston Blackie series and Lon Chaney, Jr., who became the leading star in many low-budget but well-made horror films, appears in a bit part. **p**, Sol M. Wurtzel, John Stone; **d**, James Tinling; **cast**, Peter Lorre, Keye Luke, Dick Baldwin, Lynn Bari, Douglas Fowley, Jayne Regan, Harold Huber, Maxie "Slapsie" Rosenbloom, John Hamilton, George E. Stone, Ward Bond, Paul Fix, Lon Chaney Jr., Pierre Watkin, Charles D. Brown, Russ Clark, Bernard Nedell, Olin Howland; **w**, Charles Belden, Jerry Cady (based on the character created by John P. Marquand), **c**, Lucien Andriot; **ed**, Nick DiMaggio; **art d**, Bernard Herzbrun, Haldane Douglas.

Mr. Moto's Last Warning ★★★ 1939; U.S.; 71m; FOX; B/W; Mystery; Children: Unacceptable; **DVD**; **VHS**. This above-average who-dunit broadens from murder to a widespread sabotage ring and offers so many twists and turns that the viewer might be a bit groggy at the finish. The tale begins when the British fleet at Port Said cancels its joint maneuvers after receiving word that sabotage is afoot. A liner approaching Port Said carries a curious number of passengers, including Irving, the wife, a French admiral, and her daughter, Carroll, who meet the charming Sanders, the garrulous Coote, and Shimada, who is identified as the famed detective, Mr. Moto. After the ship docks at Port Said, Sanders lures Shimada ashore where he is promptly killed by some of Sanders' henchmen. He then takes Irving and Coote to a variety show, the star of which is Cortez, an accomplished ventriloquist, called The Great Fabian. The artful Sanders is in league with Cortez, who heads a group of murderous saboteurs that includes Carradine, Hodgson, and Davidson. Carradine, however, is really a British spy and has infiltrated the organization. The real Mr. Moto, Lorre, then surfaces as the owner of a curio shop in Port Said. The "fake" Mr. Moto (Shimada) had been a Lorre associate and who was posing as the detective while trying to learn the plans being made by Cortez and Sanders. Cortez is operating out of a bar in Port Said that is operated by Field, whom Cortez has smuggled out of England after she was wanted by police. Field, however, has no idea that Cortez is heading a group of saboteurs and thinks him only to be a smuggler. Across the street from the bar is the curio shop operated by Lorre. Coote visits the shop and buys a scarab, but, when leaving, he is attacked and almost killed, but Lorre intervenes and uses his judo skills to save Coote's life. Sanders, who has been trying to find out when the French fleet will arrive in Port Said from Irving, then comes to believe that curio shop owner Lorre is the real Mr. Moto and has Field tail him. Field sees Lorre go the port commander's office where Lorre learns about a strange salvage ship, *Vulcan*, which is commanded by Hodgson. Carradine is then lured to the *Vulcan* by Sanders, who has suspected him of being a double agent, and tells him that he and others plan to start a war between England and France by sinking the French fleet when it arrives at Port Said and enters the Suez Canal. Carradine is then dispatched by Sanders, who traps him in a diving bell. Sanders has by then learned what he needed to know about the arrival of the French fleet and imparts this information to Cortez, but when Field overhears their dreadful plans, she threatens to inform Port Said officials. The suave Cortez talks her out of such rash actions and the culprits proceed with their plans, including the elimination of Lorre. Davidson tries to kill Lorre with a bomb, but Lorre survives the explosion and, with Coote, follows Davidson to a warehouse, but both are captured, tied up and put into sacks and then tossed into the Suez Canal. Lorre, however, uses a sharp object he has grabbed before being trussed up and cuts himself free and then frees Coote, who goes to the police to warn them about the impending sabotage. Sanders then dives into the water, awaiting the signal to detonate a massive underwater cache of explosives that will destroy the French fleet, but Lorre overpowers Sanders and sets off the explosion, killing Sanders and saving the French ships. When he surfaces, however, Cortez is waiting to kill him. Field, however, realizes that she has been viciously used by Cortez, shoots and kills the mastermind. Lorre then unearths the written plans of the saboteurs by finding them inside the dummy used by ventriloquist Cortez, although the viewer is left wondering what country was financing these saboteurs to start a war between England and France. Songs: "Rule Britannia" (1740; music: Thomas Augustine Arne; lyrics: James Thomson), "Over the Waves" (1887; Juventino Rosas), "I Do Like to Be Beside the Seaside" (1907; music and lyrics: John Glover Kind), "My Bonnie Lies Over the Ocean" (1881; music and lyrics: H. J. Fuller), "Moroccan Nights" (1939; music: David Raksin). *Author's Note*: Lorre complained about his role as Mr. Moto in this film as he had earlier about other such appearances, saying: "I don't know why they bothered to give me top billing in that picture as you see Ricardo [Cortez] and George [Sanders] more on camera than me. I suppose it was because I am playing Mr. Moto and that character is the star of the series, and how I hated playing

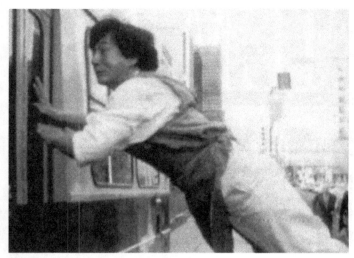

Jackie Chan in *Mr. Nice Guy*, 1998.

that little creep! When **Mr. Moto's Last Warning** came out everybody knew that the Japanese had spies on the West Coast and everywhere in the Pacific and were just itching to get into a war with America and here I am playing this little Japanese detective. I even got some fan letters from people who thought I was one of those spies, passing myself off as an actor in Hollywood! Thank God, Darryl Zanuck decided to end that series that year [1939] and I could get out from beneath that terrible Oriental mask I had to wear—those heavy eyelids and those awful buck teeth." The Mr. Moto series (eight entries in the series, 1937-1939) proved very lucrative for Fox, but studio chief Zanuck felt that the character had reached his peak of popularity by 1939, and became alarmed when he, too, received increasing mail from viewers who had fallen out of love with the Moto character and had become extremely critical of him after reading about Japanese atrocities and Japan's war of aggression in China during that time. Sanders told this author that "Peter carped about his role throughout the picture, saying that he appeared ridiculous when trying to overpower me and other heavies in that film. He only came up to our belly buttons, but nevertheless does away with all the giants towering over him. I agreed with him that it was ludicrous, but we all reminded him that Mr. Moto was, at that time, all knowing and all powerful, or, at least that's what it said on the movie billboards." The director of this film, Foster, had directed a number of Charlie Chan films and went on to helm, with the considerable help of Orson Welles, a masterpiece spy drama, **Journey into Fear**, 1943. **p**, Sol M. Wurtzel; **d**, Norman Foster; **cast**: Peter Lorre, Ricardo Cortez, Virginia Field, John Carradine, George Sanders, Margaret Irving, Joan Carroll, Robert Coote, John Davidson, Leyland Hodgson, Teru Shimada, Holmes Herbert, C. Montague Shaw, Georges Renavent, E. E. Clive; **w**, Philip MacDonald, Foster (based on the character created by John P. Marquand); **c**, Virgil Miller; **ed**, Norman Colbert; **art d**, Lewis Creber, Bernard Herzbrun; **set d**, Thomas Little.

Mr. Nice Guy ★★★ 1998; Hong Kong; 94m; Golden Harvest Co./New Line Cinema; Color; Comedy/Crime Drama; Children: Unacceptable (MPAA: PG-13); **DVD**; **VHS**. The affable and always entertaining Chan is a Chinese television chef, who is sought after by Norton, an Australian drug lord. Norton's goons are looking for Chan because his girlfriend, Fitzpatrick, a news reporter, secretly videotaped a meeting of rival drug gangs fighting over shipments of cocaine and money. The tape incriminates Norton, so he kidnaps Fitzpatrick for the tape, but she has given it to Chan. Now Norton and his henchmen are after Chan and he must rescue his girlfriend and bring the tape to authorities. Chan, an expert kick-boxer, kicks, leaps, and slips his way to rescue Fitzpatrick. Great action includes Chan taking flight on a giant inflatable Godzilla-like monster, landing on a huge wedding cake at a group wedding of bikers,

Ann Blyth and William Powell in *Mr. Peabody and the Mermaid*, 1948.

and nearly getting cut up by a table saw. As is the case with almost all of Chan's films, this crime-related tale is played for laughs and gets a lot of them. Violence, some sensuality, and drug content prohibit viewing by children. **p**, Lam Chua, Leonard Ho; **d**, Sammo Hung Kam-Bo; **cast**, Jackie Chan, Richard Norton, Miki Lee, Karen McLymont, Gabrielle Fitzpatrick, Vince Poletto, Barry Otto, Sammo Hung (Sammo Hung Kam-Bo), Mina Godenzi (Joyce Godenzi); Peter Houghton; **w**, Fibe Ma, Edward Tang; **c**, Raymond Lam (Cineart); **m**, Clarence Hui, Peter Kam, J. Peter Robinson; **ed**, Peter Cheung; **prod d**, Horace Ma; **set d**, Brent Houghton; **spec eff**, Peter Stubbs.

Mr. Peabody and the Mermaid ★★★ 1948; U.S.; 89m; UNIV; B/W; Fantasy; Children: Acceptable; **DVD**; **VHS**. Veteran actor Powell is wonderfully funny in this outlandish fantasy that begins when he visits his avuncular doctor, Smith, complaining about everything as he approaches his fiftieth birthday. Smith tells him that he is suffering from the typical middle-age crisis of too much stress and not enough relaxation and he orders him to take a vacation in the sunny Caribbean. The proper Bostonian businessman and his wife, Hervey, follow Smith's directions and vacation at a resort where Powell goes fishing alone. He hears strange, wordless singing coming from a tiny island that is no more than a rock jutting from the sea and sails close to it, dropping his line into the water. He hooks Blyth, a beautiful mermaid, who does not speak, but is capriciously childlike and affectionate and Powell cannot resist taking this unusual catch home with him, placing her in a soapy bathtub and then later depositing her into a fish pond outside of his beach cottage. Hervey sees Blyth, but only her tail, in the bathtub, and she, along with her friends, again see Blyth in the pond, but again, only her tail, and when Powell insists that what they are seeing is a mermaid, Hervey and company come to think that the tropical sun has baked his brain. Meanwhile, King, a sensuous singer, meets Powell and has designs for him, as Hervey soon realizes even though Powell is oblivious to King's advances. Powell spends so much time doting on Blyth that Hervey thinks he is seeing King and she gets fed up and temporarily departs. Powell's friends think he's gone daffy and abandon him, but Powell does not care as he has not only taught Blyth how to kiss, but has fallen in love with her. In one of the many humorous scenes in the film, Powell goes shopping for a woman's two-piece swim suit, but only wants and buys the top half and then has a tough time explaining to the always mute Blyth that it is necessary that she wear that garment. Meanwhile, Powell gets into more trouble when authorities think that his missing wife, Hervey, has met with foul play and that Powell may be the culprit, but all comes right when Blyth realizes that she is destroying Powell's life and, even though she loves him, decides to return to home in the sea. Powell returns to Boston to be with the very much alive Her-

vey, having only one keepsake of his fantastic experience, Blyth's elaborate and jewel-bedecked comb to preserve his lifelong memory of her. Powell captivates in his role as a man bedazzled by Blyth, who, too, is exceptional, particularly since she mesmerizes without the benefit of any dialog and where Johnson's clever script sparkles and pops. The plaintive song, other then the one sung by King, that is wordlessly hummed by Blyth has haunted viewers for decades and was composed by Dolan. Song (dubbed by Martha Mears for Andrea King): "The Caribees" (music: Robert Emmett Dolan; lyrics: Johnny Mercer). *Author's Note*: Powell told this author: "All men are instinctively fishermen and I think it is every man's desire to catch a mermaid, one of those ethereal creatures man cannot completely possess. The thought of catching and keeping a mermaid is a great male daydream. In **Mr. Peabody and the Mermaid**, my daydream becomes real, at least for enough time to get my blood running a little faster." Johnson told this author that he was amazed to see that another film with almost the identical storyline appeared at the same time as this film: "It was a British picture called **Miranda** [1949] and had a middle-aged man catching a mermaid on a vacation and bringing it home. It was released in England a few months before we released **Mr. Peabody and the Mermaid** in the U.S., but it was not released until the following year in America. To tell you the truth, after I saw that picture, I thought it was pretty good but not as good as ours. Bill Powell made all the difference. Still, it must have been osmosis or something that caused two separate groups of people to make the same story into a film in the same year without knowing each other's intentions. I based my story on a novel and the British picture is based on a wholly separate play. It's almost as much a mystery as the mermaid every man longs to find on the end of his line." **Miranda** presents an almost identical tale with Glynis Johns as a fetching mermaid, and Griffith Jones as the weary middle-aged man who finds and falls in love with her. Other films dealing with mermaids include **Whirlpool**, 1949; **Peter Pan**, 1953; **The Glass Bottom Boat**, 1966; **Local Hero**, 1983; **Splash**, 1984; **The Little Mermaid**, 1989; **Hook**, 1991; **Shrek 2**, 2004; **The Chronicles of Narnia: The Lion; the Witch; and the Wardrobe**, 2005; **Harry Potter and the Goblet of Fire**, 2005; **Hugo**, 2011; and **Pirates of the Caribbean: On Stranger Tides**, 2011. **p**, Nunnally Johnson; **d**, Irving Pichel; **cast**, William Powell, Ann Blyth, Irene Hervey, Andrea King, Clinton Sundberg, Art Smith, Hugh French, Lumsden Hare, Fred Clark, James Logan, Mary Field, Cynthia Corley, Tom Stevenson, Mary Somerville, Bobby Hyatt; **w**, Johnson (based on the novel *Peabody's Mermaid* by Guy Jones, Constance Jones); **c**, Russell Metty; **m**, Robert Emmett Dolan; **ed**, Marjorie Fowler; **art d**, Bernard Herzbrun, Boris Leven; **set d**, Russell A. Gausman, Ruby R. Levitt.

Mr. Rock and Roll ★★★ 1957; U.S.; 101m; PAR; B/W; Drama; Children: Acceptable; **DVD**; **VHS**. O'Brien is a reporter, who writes an article praising a rock star, Randazzo, but her editor rewrites it, attacking the entire rock and roll musical genre. Freed, a disc jockey, goes to the defense of rock and roll, explaining its evolution from Blues, Jazz, and Country and Western music, and urges his young audience to prove they are responsible, caring citizens by raising money for the heart fund. That's all the plot there is, but there is plenty of rock and roll music by some of its greatest performers. **p**, Ralph B. Serpe, Howard B. Kreitsek; **d**, Charles Dubin; **cast**, Alan Freed, Rocky Graziano, Teddy Randazzo, Lois O'Brien, Jay Barney, Al Fisher, Lou Marks, Leo Wirtz, Ralph Stantley, Lionel Hampton, Ferlin Husky; **w**, James Blumgarten; **c**, Maurice Hartzband; **m**, Robert Rolontz; **ed**, Angelo Ross.

Mr. Sardonicus ★★★ 1961; U.S.; 89m; COL; B/W; Horror; Children: Unacceptable (MPAA: PG); **DVD**; **VHS**. This truly frightening film sees Rolfe as Sardonicus, a wealthy British baron searching for a winning lottery ticket in his dead father's grave. The ghoulish experience causes his face to freeze into a horrible grimace (not unlike the hideous grimace permanently affixed to the face of Conrad Veidt in **The Man Who Laughs**, 1928), so he forces a doctor, Lewis, to treat him in order to relax his facial muscles. The result produces an even more grotesque appearance and Rolfe is left with being unable to eat or speak. This chiller is definitely not for children. **p&d**, William Castle; **cast**, Ronald Lewis, Audrey Dalton, Guy Rolfe, Oscar Homolka, Vladimir Sokoloff, Erika Peters, Lorna Hanson, Edith Atwater, Ilse Burkert, Constance Cavendish; **w**, Ray Russell (based on his novella *Sardonicus*); **c**, Burnett Guffey; **m**, Von Dexter; **ed**, Edwin Bryant; **art d**, Cary Odell; **set d**, James M. Crowe.

Mr. Skeffington ★★★ 1944; U.S.; 146m; WB; B/W; Drama; Children: Cautionary; **DVD**; **VHS**. Davis and Rains render memorable performances in this compelling domestic drama that depicts a loveless marriage where neither finds happiness over the years despite their riches and comfortable surroundings. Davis is an attractive socialite with an errant brother, Waring, who has stolen money from Rains' bank to cover his gambling debts. Rains goes to Davis to tell her that he intends to prosecute the young man, but relents when she offers to marry him. After they enter a friendly but distant union, Waring becomes angry, believing that Davis has sacrificed herself to pay for his transgression. He joins the British Air Corps to fight in WWI, the U.S. not having yet entered that war. After he is killed in action, Davis blames Rains for his death, an illogical shifting of guilt, but one that serves to goad their marriage toward its inevitable erosion and collapse. Though pregnant with Rains' child, she separates from him and then divorces him. When her child is born, Rains takes custody and then moves to Europe with the little girl while Davis enjoys the life of a single woman with all the cash she needs as Rains has made a considerable settlement with her. She has many affairs and, after twenty years goes by, she contracts diphtheria while on an outing with her current lover, Drake, a disease that causes her hair to fall out and scars her face so that she is no longer the beautiful woman of yesteryear. The wealthy Rains then returns from Europe with his adult daughter, Riordan, a beautiful girl of eighteen and, after Drake meets and falls in love with her, they marry and move to California, all of which enrages Davis. She then learns from her cousin, Abel, that Rains, who is Jewish, suffered horribly in Europe in a Nazi concentration camp and has returned without a penny to his name and that he has gone blind. Davis, in an act of mercy and compassion, goes to Rains and offers to take care of him for the rest of his life. Not knowing that she is no longer the beautiful woman he once married, Rains accepts, forgiving all of Davis's abuses of the past and they embrace for the finale. Director Sherman does a good job handling the intricate story line woven by the Epstein twins (co-screenwriters of **Casablanca**, 1942, with Howard Koch), and both Davis and Rains are superb in the roles of their tortured characters, one where they really enact a morality tale where they must both lose their core power, Davis her beauty, Rains his riches, in order to exercise the love they have for one another. *Author's Note*: Davis told this author that her role "was more than challenging because I have to age over many years in **Mr. Skeffington**, from a young woman to an old, ugly lady who has been disfigured by disease. Makeup could not achieve what was necessary to be convincing, so in my scenes where I am that young lady, I raised the pitch of my voice, keeping it there and then gradually lowered it as the years passed so that, by the time I am that ugly, old woman, I was talking in my natural lower voice, a baritone I think they call it. Claude [Rains] did not have any such problem. All he had to do was pretend to go blind, stumble about, and fall over furniture." Julius J. Epstein told this author that "we knew **Mr. Skeffington** was a soap opera, but with Bette [Davis] and Claude [Rains] in the leads, we knew that they could lift it beyond all the suds and they did, making it a fine dramatic tragedy. At the end, audiences did not know which one of them they should feel sorrier for and that is the mark of great acting." Rains told this author that "that picture belonged to Bette [Davis] from the beginning to the end and I serve only as the living and impaired excuse that points out the errors of her rather selfish life. In my eagerness to be convincing at having gone blind, I stumbled and fell over some furniture and got a few bruised ribs for my efforts. So much for dedica-

James Stewart and Jean Arthur in *Mr. Smith Goes to Washington,* 1939.

tion." **p&w**, Philip G. Epstein, Julius J. Epstein (based on the novel by "Elizabeth" [Elizabeth von Arnim]); **d**, Vincent Sherman; **cast**, Bette Davis, Claude Rains, Walter Abel, George Coulouris, Richard Waring, Marjorie Riordan, Robert Shayne, John Alexander, Jerome Cowan, Bill Kennedy, Peter Whitney, Ann Doran, Dolores Gray, Andrea King; **c**, Ernest Haller; **m**, Franz Waxman; **ed**, Ralph Dawson; **art d**, Robert Haas; **set d**, Fred M. MacLean.

Mr. Smith Goes to Washington ★★★★★ 1939; U.S.; 129m; COL; B/W; Drama; Children: Acceptable; **DVD**; **VHS**. James Stewart has rendered many great film performances but none ever equaled the one he delivers in this riveting and meaningful masterpiece film (except for perhaps his role in the great fantasy, **It's a Wonderful Life**, 1946, from the same director, Capra). Stewart is a decent and honest young man living in a small town and where he is the head of an organization he has started, the Boy Rangers (a version of the Boy Scouts), whose members do good deeds and have meetings in the woods where they practice bird calls and learn the ways of hiking, hunting and camping. When one of the incumbent U.S. senators of the state dies, Kibbee, the governor, must appoint a replacement, but he has few appealable candidates. While trying to decide who to appoint to this important post, his children urge him to appoint their idol and leader, Stewart. He decides to appoint Stewart, but the state's political boss, Arnold, is not sure that Kibbee has made the right decision until Rains, the senior U.S. senator from the state (who is called the "Silver Knight") tells Arnold that the inexperienced and innocent Stewart will be fine, especially under his guiding control and will vote the way Arnold wants him to vote on all important issues that relate to their state. A banquet is held for Stewart where the Boy Rangers present him with a going away gift, a briefcase, and where the shy and modest Stewart tells everyone that he will never do anything to disgrace his lofty position. He then takes a train to Washington, D.C., accompanied by Rains, and they recall Stewart's father, a crusading editor of a small-town newspaper who was murdered years earlier while attempting to expose a corrupt business group and where Stewart tells Rains that his idealistic father and he, Rains, have inspired him throughout his life. When arriving in Washington, Rains' daughter, Allwyn, and her girlfriends, greet Stewart, soliciting donations for a charity. Rains' political aides, Pallette and others, try to steer Stewart away from newspaper reporters, who nevertheless swarm the new senator and barrage him with endless questions. Stewart is goaded into demonstrating some of the bird calls he has taught to his Boy Rangers, and he is photographed in these ridiculous poses that show his distorted face, those photos later published in the local papers. Stewart then wanders away and, awestruck by the majesty of Washington's elegant historic buildings, he impulsively goes on a rubbernecking bus tour of the city, mar-

James Stewart in *Mr. Smith Goes to Washington*, 1939.

veling at the sights of the Capitol Dome, the Jefferson Memorial, and other landmarks, until he finally goes to the Lincoln Memorial and, full of ebullience, stands before the seated statue of his greatest hero, Abraham Lincoln, and where he watches as a young boy and his grandfather read the words of Lincoln that have been etched upon the wall of the monument (one of so many truly inspiring scenes in this spiritually uplifting film). Stewart then finds his way to his senatorial office and meets his secretary, Arthur, a fetching blonde, who is wise-weary to the ways of Washington's political shenanigans and who is by this time so fed up with political double-dealing and backstabbing that she has long been wanting to quit her job and has told as much to her close friend, Mitchell, a cynical newspaperman, who loves her and wants to marry her. Before Arthur can acclimate Stewart to his job, he sees a number of articles about him, depicting him in pictures and prose as "a clown". He becomes enraged, going after the newspapermen who have lampooned him, tracking them down one by one and knocking them cold until he pursues one of them right into the Washington press club where he is subdued and where Mitchell and others lecture him about the infighting, self-serving realities of American politics and how his own youthful naiveté has brought ridicule to him. He meets later that night with Rains, who soothes his bruised ego, as does Allwyn, who finds him awkwardly attractive (Stewart is forever stumbling over furniture and knocking over lamps when in her presence). Stewart tells Rains that he has disgraced his state and let him down, but Rains calms Stewart and tells him that he can perform a great service if he proposes a bill in the Senate to establish a national boys' camp, a project Stewart has long envisioned, and this gives Stewart new hope. He enlists the aid of Arthur in carefully drafting that bill. Arthur thinks he might be overreaching and too idealistic, but he then inspires her while telling her that the boys' camp represents another American freedom, saying: "Liberty is too precious a thing to be buried in books, Miss Saunders. Men should hold it up in front of them every single day of their lives and say 'I'm free, to think and to speak.' My ancestors couldn't. I can. And my children will." He describes his state as a place of "lazy streams" and "tall grasses," and his visions begin to be part of our own. She falls in love with Stewart and then begins defending him and his lofty principles to the jaded newspapermen in town, such as the acerbic Mitchell. Stewart prepares his bill with Arthur's considerable help and then proposes that bill in the U.S. Senate, where he gets a great round of applause from some boys in the gallery, but when he mentions the site of the proposed boys' camp, Rains and his aides become alarmed as it is the very site where political boss Arnold plans to build a dam and then cash in on a real estate boom. Arthur learns of this and informs Stewart, who cannot believe that Rains (who is really Arnold's political tool) would be a party to such a boondoggle, and Stewart goes to Rains. The avuncular Rains then

talks turkey with Stewart, explaining the grim realities of political life, saying: "You have been living in a boy's world...You have to check your ideals outside the door like you do your rubbers...I've had to compromise. I've had to play ball. That's how states and empires have been built since time began." Stewart is devastated and shocked that his idol has clay feet and he rebels, telling Rains that he will not compromise his idealistic bill that benefits boys to accommodate some "cheap graft" and further tells him that he will expose the corrupt Arnold ring on the floor of the Senate. The next day, before Stewart can get to his feet and make public that scheme, Rains beats him to it, and tells the Senate that the very young man he has sponsored and introduced to that august body is nothing more than a crook, that he planned to establish the boys, camp in order to make great profits from a real estate scam. A hearing is held to consider Stewart's expulsion from the Senate and where several of Arnold's paid stooges give false testimony that supports Rains' false accusations. Stewart, armed with information that will allow him to deliver a filibuster, along with food and water, arrives at the Senate the next day to answer these charges, but only if he can be recognized by the President of the Senate (and Vice President of the U.S.), Carey, a benevolent character, who seems to think Stewart is honest and is being railroaded. Carey surprises the Senate by recognizing Stewart, who then launches his public attack against Arnold, Rains and the powerful political machine that controls his state, depicting how they are attempting to build a phony dam at the location of his proposed camp that will illegally enrich them. As he stalls for time, he reads excerpts from the U.S. Constitution while Arthur contacts his mother, Bondi, asking her to have Stewart's Boy Rangers use their printing press to expose the Arnold ring and Arthur then begins dictating the expose to her and the boys go to work, putting out an extra edition of their newspaper that details Arnold's corruptive methods. Arnold, hearing of this, orders his goons to destroy that edition and they stop the boys from distributing the paper by grabbing copies, manhandling the boys and ruining the printing press. Meanwhile, Arnold mounts a widespread campaign to discredit Stewart through the state's newspapers and radio stations that he mostly controls, and when a citizen's parade is mounted by some of Stewart's supporters, it is disrupted by firemen and police, who turn high-pressured water hoses on them. Stewart, meanwhile, vainly plods on in the Senate, holding the floor against many challenges and only yielding for questions, a procedure he has learned from Arthur, knowing that as long as he can stay awake and continue to talk, he can hold that floor. He is now the center of national attention with newspaper reporters and radio commentators following his every word, all indictments against Arnold and Rains and their powerful ring, so powerful that none of the national news is allowed to be disseminated throughout that state, a fact that Stewart emphasizes in his exhausting filibuster. He is then confronted by countless sacks and baskets of mail, letters and telegrams, from tens of thousands of voters ostensibly from his state, all demanding that he resign from the Senate. Stewart has been at it for almost twenty-four hours, and he is now exhausted, so weak he can hardly stand. He staggers to the assembled bags and baskets filled with mail, examining some of these missives and then holding them up to rightly say that Arnold and his powerful political machine have manufactured "these lies." He appeals to his mentor, Rains, who stands nearby, asking him to remember the lost causes of his own youth, and how he once told him that those causes "were the only things worth fighting for...and he fought for them once for the only reason that any man ever fights for them. Because of just one plain simple rule: 'Love thy neighbor!'" Stewart, having used his last ounce of strength, then falls unconscious to the floor. Some senators and pages go to his aid and a page gives the high sign to Arthur, who has been coaching Stewart from the gallery and indicating to her that Stewart is going to be all right. Witnessing this crucifixion, Rains, consumed by guilt, can no longer stand his betrayal of the young man, and leaves the floor, going to a cloak room where he tries to shoot himself, but he is stopped by other senators. Now consumed with remorse and guilt, Rains stumbles back onto the Senate floor to declare that he and others are the real culprits and that Stewart is not guilty of anything, shouting: "Not that boy!...Not that boy!" The Senate is in pandemonium, and Arthur and her newspaper friends shout with glee to see that goodness has triumphed over evil right there on the floor of the U.S. Senate. Carey, who has been empathetic toward Stewart all along, pops a piece of gum into his mouth, puts his hands behind his head and rocks happily in his chair with a broad smile on his face, and this marvelously moving film ends on a happy if not miraculous note. Capra does a magnificent job of presenting this stirring story, which is seen through the eyes of the patriotic Stewart whose emotions become those of most viewers swept up into the political chaos. This is a draining, spirit sapping tale, but one that also invigorates without being hortatory or hectoring as it roars to its conclusion, leaving its players and viewers still doggedly clinging to their faith in mankind. This masterpiece from Capra, and so brilliantly enacted by Stewart, Arthur, Rains, Arnold and the rest of the cast, presents a grassroots civic lesion told in such impactful visual terms as to assure its place among the greatest of films. We see the political hub of America through the hopeful immigrant eyes of Capra, his implacable beliefs based upon the heroic dreams of every American boy, and through one young man, who will not compromise the ideals of his boyhood for the sake of political expediency and where Capra reiterates with irresistible force his filmmaking standard of "one man, one film." In so doing, he expertly peels back the calluses that have so hardened the consciences of those politicians denying their own good and moral missions through years and years of compromising their principles, particularly in the redeemable Rains, to vindicate and hold dear the most precious values of the naïvely innocent and the pure of heart. Tiomkin mixes many fine Americana tunes in his moving score that emphasize, Capra's common man credo and emotionally supports the film's many stirring scenes. Although this film received eleven Oscar nominations, including Best Film, Best Director for Capra, Best Actor for Stewart, it won only one Oscar, for Best Story, going to Foster, but this was to be expected for the film faced overwhelming competition from **Gone with the Wind**, 1939, which swept the Oscars that year. *Author's Note*: Capra told this author that he had Stewart in mind for the lead in this film "right from the start. I was urged to use Gary Cooper and the film was even originally called 'Mr. Deeds Goes to Washington,' but Gary was too seasoned by then and I needed a boyish-looking actor, but one who had a winning and forceful personality and there was only one like that, Jimmy Stewart. I knew also that I wanted Jean [Arthur] for the female lead as the jaded secretary with motherly instincts and hardened heart she is begging any good man to melt." Arthur told this author that "Frank [Capra] let me go at my role on my own after telling me that 'you have a lot of Washington dirt you can't wash off until this fine young man comes into your life.' That was enough to tell me all I needed to know about my character." Foster's tale about these incongruously matched characters, replete with shifty and corrupt politicians and power-broking bosses like Arnold was originally purchased by director Rouben Mamoulian. When Capra read the story, he asked Columbia mogul Harry Cohn to buy it and he offered Mamoulian $75,000, but, according to what Mamoulian told this author, he was playing a waiting game: "I knew that Frank [Capra] desperately wanted to film that story as much as he knew I wanted to get Cohn to let me film **Golden Boy** [1939]. So when Cohn made that offer, I did not reply. I just sat on the story. I knew Frank was working on him, pressuring him to get that story, so he finally caved in and gave me approval to do **Golden Boy**. I then walked into Harry's office and sold him the Foster story for $1,500 only, the amount I paid for the story, and refused to take his $75,000, doing what I thought was fair. Cohn was not a fair man, ever, and he was so amazed that he almost fell out of his chair, saying, 'Well, I'll be damned!' I got what I wanted and Frank got what he wanted and without having Cohn to pay through the nose for it." Capra diligently went about his usual meticulous preparations for the film by going to Washington, D.C., taking along his trusty assistant director, Art Black, who used a second unit in shooting all the historic landmarks,

James Stewart and Edward Arnold in *Mr. Smith Goes to Washington,* **1939.**

buildings and memorials with specific long shots of stand-ins for Stewart Capra knew he would later employ. He then hired Jim Preston, an expert on the history and functions of the U.S. Senate, and Preston took him to the Senate chamber when it was out of session and where Capra told him to photograph each and every detail of that chamber, right down to the inkwells on the desks of the senators. Capra later used these extensive photo arrays to have his art director, Banks, reproduce that chamber in its every realistic detail. Capra also had Harry Carey, the veteran cowboy star, in mind from the beginning to play the role of the Vice President of the U.S., who presides as President over the Senate. Carey was eager to accept the part, but told Capra that he had reservations, telling him that he had never played such an important person and, in a rare display of ineptitude, Carey muffed his lines repeatedly in his first scenes when he swears Stewart in as a new senator. Seeing that Carey was embarrassed, the always considerate Capra called a lunch break and then took Carey aside and said to him: "Forget Harry Carey the cowboy actor. Swear this new senator in as Harry Carey, the Vice President of the United States." Carey was perfect in the next shot. Capra even knew what kind of score he wanted, going to the gifted but mercurial Tiomkin and telling him to "forget about all those European composers. What we need here is for you to lace your score with American folk tunes." Tiomkin, in his broken English, replied: "In my head is notes like apple pie so American." Stewart told this author that "Frank [Capra] was making a great picture and we all knew it when we were working on it. We gave him everything we had and I even gave him my voice. At the end, when I am supposed to be talking for almost twenty-four hours, he pointed out to me that my voice wasn't hoarse enough, that I would be raspy and almost wheezing after having talked for that period of time. He brought in a doctor who swabbed my throat with a solution that had mercury in it and that caused my vocal chords to swell so that, in my final scene, I sound exactly the way I should sound, like a man who has worn out his voice, along with the rest of his body. I had some concerns about that application the doctor made, but he gave me something to drink later that brought down the swelling and I was fine the next day, thankfully. I knew I was giving one of my best performances in that picture and it remains one of my best performances after all these many years [almost fifty years later when this author had this meeting with Stewart in 1989]. I have Frank Capra to thank for that. Frank believed he had made one of the greatest films of his career and he did, but he was not prepared for the response he got from the big shots in Washington, D.C." That response occurred on October 16, 1939, when Columbia's press department arranged for the premiere showing of **Mr. Smith Goes to Washington** at the DAR's mammoth Constitution Hall in Washington. The place was packed with the Washington press corps, as well as all the leading political figures in Washington—U.S. Senators,

Claude Rains and James Stewart in *Mr. Smith Goes to Washington*, **1939.**

Congressmen, Supreme Court Justices, members of the Executive branch (but not President Franklin D. Roosevelt), more than 4,000 of the most important political leaders and pundits in America. Harry Cohn, the volatile head of Columbia even participated, convinced that his studio was going to pull off the greatest publicity coup in Hollywood history, and he and his top executives attended the premiere, taking a prominent box and where he beamed with pride as a chorus sang patriotic hymns and a band played stirring martial music. Capra was introduced and gave a brief speech that brought a thunderous applause. The film was then run, but, to the horror of Cohn, Capra and others from Columbia, a little more than halfway through the film, guests began to rise from their chairs and leave the auditorium in waves, many of them shouting "Insult!" and "Outrage!" Capra told this author that "I was frozen in my chair, dumbfounded. What had I done so wrong? I looked up to see Harry's [Cohn's] reaction, but he had hurriedly left after hearing the first shout against the picture. I then realized that most of these important Washington figures could not tolerate the idea that I was showing corruption in the U.S. Senate, the highest legislative chamber of the land. I wanted to hide somewhere, but there was nowhere to go, so Lou [his wife] and I sat there, red-faced, taking all of it." That night, Capra had the courage to go to the Washington Press Club for a pre-arranged dinner and he got more lambasting over the film from the press corps members. "One of them was shouting in my face that I had disgraced all Washington journalists by showing Thomas Mitchell in the picture as one of their heavy drinking members. The journalist shouting at me was so drunk that, after he worked himself up into a rage and tried to take a poke at me, he fell flat on his face unconscious. My God, we were almost assaulted, but a few of the more kindred spirits there shielded us as we ran from the place, all those Washington writers shouting and hooting after us. I thought it was the end of my career, and when we went to our hotel room, I was up all night walking back and forth. I was in big time trouble, and for what? Showing a picture that offered reality and truth and I had quickly learned that very little in Washington, D.C., has much to do with such things." Politicians high and low publicly attacked the film for being disrespectful, even flippant, including the venerable U.S. Senator Alben W. Barkley (1877-1956), who later became U.S. Vice President under President Harry Truman. Barkley thundered in the pages of *the Christian Science Monitor* that the film was "a grotesque [distortion of the U.S. Senate]...as grotesque as anything ever seen! Imagine the Vice President of the United States [Carey] winking at a pretty girl [Arthur] in the gallery in order to encourage a filibuster? Can you visualize Jack Garner [John Nance "Texas Jack" Garner, 1868-1967; then the U.S. Vice President] winking up at Hedy Lamarr in order to egg her on? And it [the film] showed the Senate as the biggest aggregation of nincompoops on record!...It showed the Sen-

ate made up by crooks, led by crooks listening to a crook." Capra told this author that the uproar stemmed from "jealousy. I had invaded their private club, their private domain, these press corps people and those politicians, and had showed their inner sanctums the way they might be or even are. They felt that their princely fiefdoms had been exposed for what they were, power pockets where they ruled the roost with no one to question them." Some politicians claimed that the film undermined America's image abroad and that dictators like Adolf Hitler and Benito Mussolini would encourage their followers to see the film to depict the moral corruption of Western democracies (just the opposite was the case as the film was banned in those countries). Some politicians thought the film so dangerous as to be subversive or treasonable, and Hollywood then feared that Washington, D.C., would impose draconian censorships on all films. One unconfirmed Hollywood report stated that Harry Cohn had been offered $2 million to scrap the film by the heads of all other Hollywood studios, so fearful were they of that possible censorship. The film was nevertheless broadly released and, unlike the closeted Washington, D.C., politicians and journalists, the public overwhelmingly endorsed the film by flocking to see it. One can easily believe that the American public, which Lincoln wisely said one could not fool all the time, believed more in the affable, winking image of Harry Carey than they did in all the flustering fulminations from Alben Barkley and his offended ilk. Even Joseph Kennedy, the U.S. Ambassador to England, thought the film damaging, writing to Cohn and asking him not to distribute it, but Cohn, always the wheeler and dealer, stood steadfast with Capra and refused to shelve this masterpiece, showing that this crude, crass, insulting and utterly obnoxious man, possessed the kind of great courage that the film itself displays. "He showed his mettle," Capra told this author. "Harry [Cohn] was raised in New York as a street fighter and no one was ever going to bully him into anything...not in this country!" The film was made on a huge budget (for little Columbia) of $1.5 million, but its enormous popularity at the box office proved Capra (and Cohn) right when more than $9 million came back into the studio's coffers from its initial release. It remains one of the greatest classic films ever made. **p&d**, Frank Capra; **cast**, Jean Arthur, James Stewart, Claude Rains, Edward Arnold, Guy Kibbee, Thomas Mitchell, Eugene Pallette, Beulah Bondi, H.B. Warner, Harry Carey, Astrid Allwyn, Ruth Donnelly, William Demarest, Grant Mitchell, Jack Carson, Pierre Watkin, Porter Hall, Dub Taylor, Fred Hoose, Stanley Andrews, Maurice Costello, Allan Cavan, Dickie Jones, Robert Sterling, Craig Stevens; **w**, Sidney Buchman (based on the novel *The Gentleman from Montana* by Lewis R. Foster); **c**, Joseph Walker; **m**, Dimitri Tiomkin; **ed**, Al Clark, Gene Havlick; **art d**, Lionel Banks; **spec eff**, Fred Jackman, Jr.

Mr. Winkle Goes to War ★★★ 1944; U.S.; 80m; COL; B/W; Drama; Children: Unacceptable; **VHS**. Robinson is captivating as a middle-aged bank clerk who does not like his job and would rather tinker in his repair shop that he has built next to his comfortable home. He finally quits his job and tells wife Warrick that he plans to make a living as a repairman, but she does not think this a good idea and eventually tells him that, unless he returns to his job at the bank, he can live inside his repair shop and not their house. Robinson befriends a troubled neighborhood boy, Donaldson, and helps him through his problems, teaching him the values of honest work. Robinson is then drafted into the U.S. Army, but he does not think he will pass the physical examination. He does and, even though he is forty-four (the U.S. having depleted the available younger men and now needing the older men available to continue the war), is sent to a training camp with Haymes, the son of an old friend. They are trained by veteran soldiers Armstrong and Lane and then ship out to the Pacific. Robinson shows his mettle when he dashes toward a disabled bulldozer under fire, fixes it, and then drives the bulldozer over a Japanese machine gun next, killing the occupants before he is wounded. He survives the battle, but Armstrong and Lane have been killed. Sent home with medals and honors, Robinson arrives at his home town to a hero's welcome and when he returns to his repair shop, his wife Warrick is waiting for him, lovingly taking him back into their house. A well-written script and Robinson's strong performance makes for an entertaining and often inspiring film. *Author's Note*: Robinson told this author that "**Mr. Winkle Goes to War** is one of my favorite 'little' pictures where I play a meek and quiet man and I appeared in another film with a similar character a year later, **Our Vines Have Tender Grapes** [1945]. My character, Winkle, is a tinkerer and has only one ambition and that is to fix things, not destroy them. I did not have to rely on my old personality of menace, until I am drafted and have to go to war and menace the enemy. I was most comfortable in roles like that after I decided to ease into character parts, which I did in the same year when I played the insurance inspector in **Double Indemnity** [1944]. In that picture, I accepted for the first time the third leading part or a supporting role. Ruth Warrick plays my wife in **Mr. Winkle Goes to War**, a very fine actress and I always thought she was one of the most beautiful women in Hollywood." Warrick told this author that "Eddie [Robinson] was a gem to work with in that picture, a great gentleman. He is only about an inch taller than I am [Robinson stood 5'7", Warrick 5'6"], but the director had me wear high heels in our scenes together so that I would be taller than he is to emphasize my role as a domineering wife, but nobody in the movie business could ever dominate Eddie's acting ability." **p**, Jack Moss; **d**, Alfred E. Green; **cast**, Edward G. Robinson, Ruth Warrick, Ted Donaldson, Bob Haymes, Robert Armstrong, Richard Lane, Richard Gaines, Walter Baldwin, William Forrest, Art Smith, Ann Shoemaker; **w**, Waldo Salt, George Corey, Louis Solomon (based on the novel by Theodore Pratt); **c**, Joseph Walker; **m**, Carmen Dragon, Paul Sawtell; **ed**, Richard Fantl; **art d**, Lionel Banks, Rudolph Sternad.

Mrs. Dalloway ★★★ 1998; U.K./U.S.; 97m; First Look International; Color; Drama; Children: Unacceptable (MPAA: PG-13); **DVD**; **VHS**. Redgrave, a wealthy married society matron, hosts an elaborate party in her home in London in 1923. Her thoughts go back to 1890, before she chose a life of comfort and financial security by marrying her stodgy husband, Standing, who is a wealthy cabinet member. Redgrave is bored at her own party, until her long-ago boyfriend, Kitchen, arrives and she remembers how she once loved him, but decided that he wasn't wealthy enough to marry. She also recalls herself as a younger woman (McElhone) and a young woman (Headley) to whom she had been sexually attracted. This woman also comes to the party, now a distinguished member of the nobility. A parallel story unfolds about a young man Redgrave knew, a shell-shocked World War I veteran, Graves, who commits suicide. Redgrave puts up a good front at being the perfect hostess at her party, but her thoughts focus upon the choices she has made in life and what might have been if she had chosen differently. Poignant and with superior performances from Redgrave and the rest of the cast, this nostalgic look back at yesteryear is a haunting and often memorable film. Songs: "Time for Old Time" (Jack Trombey), "Rio Grande" (traditional), "Just a Song at Twilight" (James Molloy, Clifton Bingham), "Addio, del passato" (Giuseppe Verdi). Sensuality and suicide prohibit viewing by children. **p**, Stephen Bayly, Lisa Katselas, Hans De Weers; **d**, Marleen Gorris; **cast**, Vanessa Redgrave, Natascha McElhone, Michael Kitchen, Rupert Graves, Margaret Tyzack; Alan Cox, Sarah Badel, Lena Headly, John Standing, Robert Portal, Oliver Ford Davies, Robert Hardy; **w**, Eileen Atkins (based on the novel by Virginia Woolf); **c**, Sue Gibson; **m**, Ilona Sekacz; **ed**, Michiel Reichwein; **prod d**, David Richens; **art d**, Nik Callan, Alison Wratten; **set d**, Carlotta Barrow, Jeanne Vertigan; **spec eff**, John Horton.

Mrs. Miniver ★★★★★ 1942; U.S.; 134m; MGM; B/W; Drama; Children: Cautionary; **DVD**; **VHS**. A prosaic but poignantly memorable tale, this classic film pays tribute to the fighting spirit of England during its "finest hour" in WWII when it defied and fought Hitler's Nazi juggernaut as seen through the microcosm of an indefatigable British family. Garson, then the foremost actress at MGM is Mrs. Miniver, who is first shown shopping for a hat in downtown London in the summer of 1939.

Greer Garson, Christopher Severn, Walter Pidgeon and Clare Sandars in *Mrs. Miniver*, 1942.

She selects and buys that hat and then returns by train to her home in the small village of Belham, just outside of London, and where she is greeted by station master Travers. This kindly, old gentleman asks her to step inside his small office where he shows her his prized rose, a new hybrid species, and, because he so admires this beautiful and charming lady, he asks her permission to name the rose after her, calling it "Miniver." Flattered, Garson gracefully grants that permission and, touched by Travers' gesture, continues on home. Upon arrival, she learns from her considerate and caring husband, Pidgeon, that he has bought a new car, but he sheepishly admits this purchase with a modicum of guilt. She then admits that she has purchased an expensive new hat and that night she puts it on before they retire and it is shown hanging upon the bedpost in the bed chamber at the end of that tender love scene. The routines of this happy family are then shown in a series of brief scenes culminating when their grown son, Ney, answers the door to see Wright, a beautiful girl who has a special request. She asks that Garson go to Travers and plead with him to withdraw his marvelous hybrid rose in the upcoming flower contest so that Whitty, her grandmother and the aristocratic matriarch of the community, can win the top award for her own rose, a practice that has been going on for years. The meeting spawns a romance between Ney and Wright that ends with them becoming engaged, but just then England is caught up in WWII and the family members make contributions to the war effort while Ney joins the Royal Air Force (RAF). The tide of war turns against the Allies and news comes that the Germans have overrun France and that tens of thousands of British and French troops are trapped at the small port of Dunkirk, across the English Channel. In addition to all of its Royal Navy vessels, the British admiralty calls into service each and every small private vessel in England to help evacuate those troops. Pidgeon and his yachting friends then man their tiny boats and courageously sail to Dunkirk, where, under fire, they retrieve as many stranded soldiers as they can, returning with them to England. In Pidgeon's absence, Dantine, a German pilot, is shot down and becomes a fugitive from British searchers. The wounded Dantine invades Garson's home, holding her hostage at gunpoint and demands food, but while eating, Garson stalls for time until he collapses. The compassionate Garson first checks his wounds before summoning officials to take Dantine away. Pidgeon returns home exhausted, and Garson welcomes him back without telling him about her harrowing experience, putting him to bed and allowing him to sleep, such is the gritty resolve in this stalwart woman and whose courage is equal to that of her loving husband. Garson and Pidgeon then happily learn that their son and Wright will be married, and that joyous event is celebrated by family members and friends. The much-awaited flower show is then held and Whitty, as usual, wins the top prize for her cultivated rose, but she realizes when looking at her entry and the beautiful

Teresa Wright and Greer Garson in *Mrs. Miniver*, 1942.

hybrid rose submitted by kindly, old Travers is far superior to her own, and, instead of announcing herself as the winner, which she has been doing for countless years, she names Travers' entry as the champion, delighting Travers and all present, who are impressed with her magnanimous decision. The Germans then begin to conduct concentrated air attacks on London, bombing the city incessantly almost every night, and those bombs begin to fall in nearby communities such as Belham. In one raid, Garson and Pidgeon gather their two youngest children and go to a makeshift air raid shelter outside their home and sit while they protectively hold on to their children and bombs drop everywhere around them. Throughout this nevre-wracking experience, Garson quietly reads passages from *Alice in Wonderland* to her frightened children, calming them as the bombs continue to explode about them. They survive, but when they emerge from the shelter, they see their lovely home has been badly damaged. Meanwhile, Garson becomes a protective second mother to Wright, her new daughter-in-law, while her son and Wright's husband, Ney, serves in the RAF. While Garson and Wright are driving home, German planes bomb and strafe the area and, after they stop their car, an enemy plane strafes the car and Wright is mortally wounded, dying in Garson's arms. Garson overcomes this terrible tragedy by holding out hope for her son, who is flying with the RAF, and she watches the skies, trying to find her son's plane within the British formations soaring overhead, thinking that all of those pilots are her sons. She goes with Pidgeon and her two small children to church or what is left of it after German bombers have left the once majestic cathedral in ruins and there listens to Wilcoxon, the pastor, who resolutely speaks from the pulpit, saying: "We, in this quiet corner of England, have suffered the loss of friends very dear to us. Some—close to the church. And our hearts go out in sympathy to the two families, who shared the cruel loss of a young girl, who was married at this altar only two weeks ago. The homes of many of us have been destroyed, and the lives of young and old have been taken. There is scarcely a household that hasn't been struck to the heart. And why? Surely, you must have asked yourself this question. Why, in all conscience, should these be the ones to suffer? Children, old people, a young girl at the height of her loveliness. Why these? Are these our soldiers? Are these our fighters? Why should they be sacrificed? I shall tell you why. Because this is not only a war of soldiers in uniform, it is a war of the people—all of the people, and it must be fought not only on the battlefield, but in the cities and the villages, in the factories and on the farms, in the home and in the heart of every man, woman and child who loves freedom. Well, we have buried our dead, but we shall not forget them. Instead, they will inspire us with an unbreakable determination to free ourselves and those who come after us from the tyranny and terror that threatens to strike us down. This is the people's war! It is our war! We are the fighters! Fight it then! Fight

it with all that is in us! And may God defend the right!" And, upon these stirring and patriotic words, this moving and unforgettable film ends. After Prime Minister Winston Churchill saw this film, he declared that it would do more good for the Allied war effort than six full army divisions. He ordered that the speech delivered by Wilcoxon be printed in countless leaflets and these were consistently dropped over enemy positions for the remainder of the war to show the enemy the British resolve to win that war. The Wilcoxon speech is only one of many highlights in this stirring film. Pantheon director Wyler presents an unspectacular tale in a series of spectacular scenes to show the consistent uncommon valor of his characters to lift one's spirit while interspersing little but finely etched poignant scenes that touch one's heart. His patience and diligence, along with the powerful performances from Garson, Pidgeon, Wright and others makes for a masterpiece film that deservedly swept the Academy Awards. The film gleaned Oscars as Best Picture, Best Director (Wyler), Best Actress (Garson), Best Supporting Actress (Wright), Best Adapted Screenplay, and Best Black and White Cinematography (Ruttenberg). Pidgeon was nominated as Best Actor, but lost out to James Cagney in **Yankee Doodle Dandy**, 1942, while Travers was also nominated as Best Supporting Actor. A poor sequel, **The Miniver Story**, 1950, flopped at the box office. ***Author's Note***: Oddly, Garson did not want to play the role of Mrs. Miniver. The role had been turned down by other big MGM stars Norma Shearer and Ann Harding. "None of them wanted to play that part," Wyler told this author, "because none of them wanted to appear on screen with a grown son that would mark their age as an older woman. Such is the female vanity." MGM Studio chief Louis B. Mayer, who was behind this film from the beginning, he being the most enthusiastic Anglophile in Hollywood, called Garson into his office and personally asked that she take on the role. She smiled and politely said no. He then reminded her that MGM had made her rich and one of the great film stars in the world. Garson again smiled and said no. He then used persuasion, even pleaded, but she again refused. He then got tough and threatened to cancel her contract and she again said no. "Mayer then grabbed copies of the script and handed me one," Garson told this author. "He began reading all the parts except mine and ordered me to read my lines back to him and this went on for some time. He delivered his lines passionately and very fast and I had a hard time keeping up with him as he hurried us both through the script. He kept going faster and faster until I felt as if I were a buggy horse being whipped through the streets! He had worked himself into a frenzied state and me along with it and when he stopped he said: 'Well?' I was exhausted and confused and I said, 'all right, I will do it.' I then walked out of his office and when I realized what I had done, I got very weak and fainted. I came to with three secretaries holding me and giving me water and putting a cold compress on my forehead. I saw Henry Wilcoxon a short time later and he congratulated me for taking on the role as Mrs. Miniver. He told me that he thought I would win the Academy Award as Best Actress. I thought he had lost his mind and almost told him so. No one was more surprised than I was when I received the Oscar for that role!" Garson, when accepting the award, gave the longest acceptance speech in the history of the Academy Awards up to that time, almost six minutes. A Hollywood wag attending the ceremonies that night at the Coconut Grove in the Ambassador Hotel in Los Angeles, that night, said that Garson's acceptance speech "was longer than her part in the picture." Mary Pickford, who had helped to establish the Academy Awards, was all but ignored at the ceremonies, having been seated at the very back of the hall with her then husband, Charles "Buddy" Rogers, and who felt that the ceremonies were a colossal flop, saying: "No one could arrange anything so boring." She quit the Academy that night. **Mrs. Miniver** proved to be a colossal success, making more money than even the confident Mayer thought it would produce, taking in almost $9 million in its first box office release, more than recouping its budget of $1.3 million. Many believed that since the film focused on England and its WWII plight, American audiences would not go to see it, but just the opposite occurred. U.S. moviegoers flocked to see the film, chiefly Garson, that stunningly beautiful woman having scored in many recent successes, such as **Goodbye Mr. Chips**, 1939; **Pride and Prejudice**, 1940, and **Blossoms in the Dust**, 1941. Five months after the release of **Mrs. Miniver**, she appeared in another masterpiece, a romance, **Random Harvest**, 1942, with Ronald Colman. The enormous popularity of this film was evidenced quickly when it premiered at the huge Radio City Music Hall in NYC and where 558,000 people rushed to see **Mrs. Miniver** within twenty-five days, packing that theater in almost around-the-clock showings. Mayer became alarmed just before the film was released when he learned that the 38-year-old Garson (born in 1904) was about to marry the 27-year-old Ney, who played her son in the film. Mayer asked Garson not to announce her marriage until long after the film was released, saying that her marriage to a much younger man might be objectionable to some moviegoers, and Garson complied. She did not marry Ney, however, until July 1943, as he was drafted into the U.S. Navy shortly after **Mrs. Miniver** was released. That marriage ended in divorce four years later. Garson married for a third time to multimillionaire E. E. Fogelson (1900-1987), remaining with him until his death (they lived on a large ranch in New Mexico). Years later, many criticized this film as being overly patriotic, and even Garson (who lived to be ninety-one, dying in 1996) half-heartedly apologized for her appearance, saying "...we thought we were doing something important at the time." Wyler, who would win three Oscars (for **Mrs. Mininver**, as well as **The Best Years of Our Lives**, 1946, and **Ben-Hur**, 1959, and an honorary Oscar, the Irving G. Thalberg Award, 1965) said that the film was "synthetic." These anachronistic remarks were made (and pressured from such luminaries as Wyler and Garson), however, in the disillusioned 1970s by mindless and uneducated dilettantes (who passed for film critics without any sense or knowledge of history in those days), and who thought it chic to demean anything patriotic, remarks that ignorantly dismissed the genuine national pride that was prevalent during WWII when the free world was struggling to survive, the overwhelming emotional patriotism of that era being embodied in **Mrs. Miniver** and other such classic films. Mayer, at the time of the production, reminded Wyler that, although England was at war with Germany, the U.S. had not yet entered that war and he warned Wyler to depict the German downed pilot (Dantine) with some sympathy so as not to alienate German-American moviegoers. Wyler disagreed, telling this author that "I told Mayer that if I had a number of Germans in the film, I might give some sympathy *to one of them*, but as I had only one German in the film, I intended to show him as one of Hermann Goering's monsters." (Goering was chief of the German Air Force.) Wyler had Dantine play the downed German pilot like a wild beast at bay and Mayer was glad for it since the U.S. entered the war against Germany before the film was released. Mayer thought that the speech delivered by Wilcoxon was too mild and got permission to have Wilcoxon, then in the service, to briefly return to Hollywood to redo that last scene where his rewritten speech was more impassioned and one that more forcefully indicted the enemy. Wyler himself rewrote that speech, modeling it after the speeches of Winston Churchill, which may or may not have been the reason why Churchill so much liked the film. **p**, Sidney Franklin; **d**, William Wyler; **cast**, Greer Garson, Walter Pidgeon, Teresa Wright, Dame May Whitty, Reginald Owen, Henry Travers, Richard Ney, Henry Wilcoxon, Christopher Severn, Clare Sandars, Brenda Forbes, Helmut Dantine, Rhys Williams, Tom Conway, Peter Lawford, Billy Bevan, Aubrey Mather, Ben Webster, Mary Field, Paul Scardon, Marie De Becker, St. Luke's Episcopal Church Choristers; **w**, Arthur Wimperis, George Froeschel, James Hilton, Claudine West (based on the novel by Jan Struther); **c**, Joseph Ruttenberg; **m**, Herbert Stothart; **ed**, Harold F. Kress; **art d**, Cedric Gibbons; **set d**, Edwin B. Willis; **spec eff**, A. Arnold Gillespie, Warren Newcombe, Max Fabian.

Mrs. Palfrey at the Claremont ★★★ 2005; U.K./U.S.; 108m; Claremont Films/Cineville; Color; Comedy; Children: Unacceptable (MPAA: PG-13); **DVD**. Plowright is a recently widowed woman, who,

Rupert Friend and Joan Plowright in *Mrs. Palfrey at the Claremont*, 2005.

after a long and happy marriage, moves into a London residential hotel, the Claremont, and is virtually forgotten by her family. She falls on the sidewalk and Friend, a penniless young writer, helps her up. She invites him to dine with her at the Claremont hotel, and they both play along when others there assume he is the grandson she hoped would visit her. A friendship develops and she tells him her memories and love for poetry, giving him ideas and encouragement for his writing. Plowright comes to realize that friendship at her senior years can be a very satisfying substitute for romance and Friend, not only enriches his literary knowledge, but gains the maternal affection he has missed in life. Songs: "For All We Know" (Fred J. Coots, Sam Lewis), "The 'Mrs. P' Rap" (Rupert Friend), "It's Never Too Late to Fall in Love" (Sandy Wilson), "Attention Shoppers" (Daniel May). Mature subject matter prohibits viewing by children. **p**, Lee Caplin, Carl Colpaert, Zachary Matz, Matt Devlen, Maxine Nelson-Flitman; **d**, Dan Ireland; **cast**, Joan Plowright, Rupert Friend, Zoe Tapper, Anna Massey, Robert Lang, Marcia Warren, Georgina Hale, Millicent Martin, Michael Culkin, Anna Carteret; **w**, Ruth Sacks (based on the novel by Elizabeth Taylor); **c**, Claudio Rocha; **m**, Stephen Barton; **ed**, Nigel Galt, Virginia Katz; **prod d**, Julian Nagel; **art d**, Fabrice Spelta; **spec eff**, Monette Dubin, Christopher Dusendschon.

Mrs. Wiggs of the Cabbage Patch ★★★ 1934; U.S.; 80m; PAR; B/W; Comedy/Drama; Children: Unacceptable; **DVD**; **VHS**. Lord is impressive as the indomitable Mrs. Wiggs. She and her children plan to celebrate Thanksgiving in their rundown shack with leftover stew, again without Mr. Wiggs, who left them some years earlier. They live in a poor section of town called the Cabbage Patch and the house is due for foreclosure. Venable, a wealthy young lady, who lives in a mansion on the other side of town, brings them a feast. Butler, one of Lord's boys, develops a hacking cough and, Taylor, a newspaper reporter and Venable's boyfriend, takes him to a hospital, but Butler later dies in Lord's arms. The kind-hearted Lord then takes in spinster Pitts and is determined to find the woman a suitable husband. She selects the inimitable Fields, a persnickety man with an appetite that demands haute cuisine. Fields then begins a courtship with Pitts (their romantic scenes together are hilarious) and he thinks to wed the woman, but only if she proves to be a great cook. Pitts, however, cannot cook the simplest meal any more than pigs can fly. Lord makes up for that by preparing a meal that Fields pronounces delicious so that he and Pitts now plan their nuptials. Meanwhile, Middleton, the mean-minded owner of the shack where Lord and family dwell, insists on a $25 mortgage payment or he will evict the brood. All seems hopeless until Meek, the long-lost Mr. Wiggs, reappears. He still wears the threadbare clothes he wore when departing long ago and Lord sees in this confused and discombobulating man little help

Finlay Currie and Irene Dunne (as Queen Victoria) in *The Mudlark*, 1950.

in saving her home, until she rummages through his old coat and discovers the money needed to pay off the mortgage. Then Venable and Taylor settle their long-standing differences and go to the altar and Lord and her family join in the wedding festivities for a very happy ending. Although there are many delightful and uplifting moments in this classic yarn, some of its more tragic scenes (Butler's death) will prove too depressing for children. This story was first filmed as a 1919 silent and was remade in 1942, but neither of those productions can match this superior 1934 version. **p**, Douglas MacLean; **d**, Norman Taurog; **cast**, Pauline Lord, W.C. Fields, ZaSu Pitts, Evelyn Venable, Kent Taylor, Donald Meek, Jimmy Butler, Virginia Weidler, Carmencita Johnson, Edith Fellows, Charles Middleton, Ann Sheridan; **w**, William Slavens McNutt, Jane Storm (based on the play by Anne Crawford Flexner and the book by Alice Hegan Rice); **c**, Charles Lang; **m**, John Leipold; **ed**, Hugh Bennett; **art d**, Hans Dreier, Robert Odell.

Much Ado about Nothing ★★★ 1993; U.K./U.S.; 111m; American Playhouse Theatrical Films/Samuel Goldwyn; Color; Comedy; Children: Unacceptable (MPAA: PG-13); **BD**; **DVD**; **VHS**. A young couple, Claudio (Leonard) and Hero (Beckinsale) have more than their own mutual love on their minds in the week before they marry. They conspire to help Cupid along with their friends, confirmed bachelor Benedick (Branagh), and his match, wit-for-wit Beatrice (Thompson). Don Pedro (Washington), a wealthy and influential friend of everyone at a Tuscan villa, comes to visit with his horse-riding buddies. His half-brother Don John (Reeves), a fellow with a bad attitude who can't stand seeing anyone happy, tries to break up the lovers (Leonard and Beckinsale) by accusing Beckinsale of infidelity. While she is in disgrace, those at the villa get busy convincing Branagh and Thompson that they love each other, which they really do, but are reluctant to admit it, each waiting for the other to melt the ice between them. Reeves' dirty work is found out, Leonard and Beckinsale are reunited, and a double wedding results with them and Branagh and Thompson. This well-crafted joyful romantic comedy sees top flight performances from the entire cast. Song: "Sigh No More, Ladies" (Patrick Doyle). Sensuality prohibits viewing by children. A modern version of the play was made in 2012. **p**, Kenneth Branagh, Stephen Evans, David Parfitt; **d&w**, Branagh (based on the play by William Shakespeare); **cast**, Branagh, Emma Thompson, Keanu Reeves, Kate Beckinsale, Robert Sean Leonard, Michael Keaton, Richard Briers, Imelda Staunton, Brian Blessed, Phyllida Law, Gerard Horan; **c**, Roger Lanser; **m**, Patrick Doyle; **ed**, Andrew Marcus; **prod d**, Tim Harvey; **art d**, Martin Childs; **spec eff**, Nicholas Brooks, Paddy Eason, Pete Hanson.

Muddy River ★★★ 1982; Japan; 105m; Kimura Productions; Unifilms; B/W; Adventure; Fantasy; Children: Unacceptable. Ten years after the end of World War II, the city of Osaka has recovered from devastation and is now enjoying prosperity. Asahara, whose parents, Tamura and Fujita, own a noodle restaurant, becomes friends with Sakurai, a boy who lives with his mother, Kaga, and sister, Shibata, but does not realize their tawdry profession. They live on a *kuruwa-bune* (prostitution boat) on a muddy river. Asahara wonders why Sakurai doesn't invite him to meet his parents. When Asahara loses his pocket money during a festival, Sakurai takes him home to the boat and Asahara learns that Sakurai's mother is a prostitute. Kaga senses that Osaka no longer will tolerate people of her trade, so she takes her son and daughter onto the boat and sails away to another location. Asahara watches as the boat leaves, having lost a friend, but gained some wisdom of his broadening the world. (In Japanese; English subtitles.) **p**, Motoyasu Kimura; **d**, Kôhei Oguri; **cast**, Takahiro Tamura, Mariko Kaga, Nobutaka Asahara, Makiko Shibata, Minoru Sakurai, Yumiko Fujita, Gannosuke Ashiya, Reiko Hatsune, Keizô Kanie, Yoshitaka Nishiyama; **w**, Takako Shigemori (based on the novel by Teru Miyamoto); **c**, Shôhei Andô; **m**, Kurodo Môri; **ed**, Nobuo Ogawa; **prod d**, Akira Naitô.

The Mudlark ★★★ 1950; U.K./U.S.; 99m; FOX; B/W; Drama; Children: Acceptable; **VHS**. A touching and memorable film, set in London in 1875, sees Ray (who gives an outstanding performance) as an innocent London urchin. After he finds a medallion that shows the likeness of Queen Victoria (1819-1901), the naïve orphaned boy decides to meet his monarch and miraculously finds a way to sneak into her residence at Windsor Castle. He evades guards and wanders about its ancient corridors and halls, searching for his queen. After Ray is discovered, the queen's advisers and ministers become alarmed and widespread controversy over this intrusion ensues. The boy explains that all he wants to do is meet the queen and Currie, playing John Brown (1826-1883), the queen's confidante and Scottish manservant, is kindly toward Ray, encouraging Dunne, who plays Victoria, to see him. (Currie's scenes with Ray present many humorous moments, particularly when the boy suggests that Currie has had more than a few stiff drinks and where Currie replies that he has imbibed "only enough to keep off infection, laddie.") Dunne is curious about the boy, but refuses to see him as she has refused to see anyone else since going into her long reclusion of mourning following the death of her beloved husband and consort, Prince Albert (1819-1861). While officials and ministers argue about how the boy was able to penetrate the castle's security, Guinness, who plays Prime Minister Benjamin Disraeli (1804-1881), subtly suggests that Dunne visit with the boy, hoping that her meeting with him will bring her out of seclusion and thus allow him to discuss important matters of state with her. Dunne's curiosity and her maternal instincts finally compel her to meet with Ray and she finds the ebullient boy utterly charming, a historic meeting that ends her seclusion and brings her back into the world of the living. Negulesco draws superb performances from Ray, Dunne, Currie, and Guinness in this warmhearted film, where he manages to convincingly portray the elegance and grandeur of the Victorian era through the many historic sites of London, including Windsor Castle, the Parliament buildings and the Tower of London. *Author's Note*: This was one of Dunne's last feature films and one she found, according to her statements to this author "very trying. The role was not that demanding, but the makeup took hours to prepare every day so that I would look like Victoria. I felt that I was carrying ten pounds of makeup and wig on my head. The boy [Ray] who plays the little orphan and who sneaks into the palace, was wonderful, such wide and expressive eyes and a bubbly way of talking that would charm any woman, let alone a queen." Negulesco told this author that Ray was not the first choice to play the adventurous orphan and that his older brother, Robin Ray, was tested for the part first, but "we thought he was too tall for the role, so we tried his younger brother, Andrew, and he was perfect for the part." Guinness felt that his role in this film "was that of a supporting player. After all, the boy [Ray] is the centerpiece of that marvelous picture. I don't think he ever did much acting before he appeared in that film, but he gives an outstanding performance. It came naturally to him, I think, just being the boy he was and without pretending to be anything else." Ray was ten years old at the time he appeared in **The Mudlark** and would lead a troubled life, particularly in his teens and early twenties. He later attempted suicide, but eventually dealt with his problems and went on to have a successful stage career. **p**, Nunnally Johnson; **d**, Jean Negulesco; **cast**, Irene Dunne, Alec Guinness, Andrew Ray, Beatrice Campbell, Finlay Currie, Anthony Steel, Constance Smith, Ronan O'Casey, Pamela Arliss, Wilfrid Hyde-White, Raymond Lovell, Marjorie Fielding, Constance Smith, Ronan O'Casey, Edward Rigby, Robin Stevens; Michael Brooke, Ernest Clark; **w**, Johnson (based on the novel by Theodore Bonnet); **c**, Georges Perinal; **m**, William Alwyn; **ed**, Thelma Myers; **art d**, C.P. Norman; **spec eff**, W. Percy Day.

Mulan ★★★ 1998; U.S.; 101m; Disney/Buena Vista; Color; Animated Feature/Adventure; Children: Acceptable (MPAA: G); **DVD**; **VHS**. Based on a Chinese folk tale, Hun warriors invade China led by Shan-Yu (Ferrer voiceover), so the emperor (Morita voiceover) calls up all able men to defend the kingdom. A teenage girl (Wen voiceover) learns that her father (Oh voiceover) is to be one of those called up to fight the invading Huns. Since he is old and lame, she disguises herself as a boy and plans to take his place. Stealing his sword, she summons the family ancestors to help her. They order Mushu (Murphy voiceover), a scrawny disgraced dragon, to go with her on her twin quest to defend her family's honor and establish herself as a young woman of strength and character. In the army, she falls in love with a handsome young army captain (Osmond voiceover), serving under his command. While training to be a soldier, she narrowly escapes being exposed at a swimming hole filled with naked fellow soldiers. In the final battle where the Huns attack the Great Wall of China, Mulan devises a defense maneuver that creates a huge avalanche and the Huns are defeated. Mulan's deception is found out, and, according to ancient Chinese law, impersonating a man is treason, but, because of her heroism, instead of being executed, she is hailed a hero. Songs (all by Matthew Wilder, David Zippel) include "Honor to Us All," "Reflection: I'll Make a Man Out of You," "A Girl Worth Fighting For," "True to Your Heart." **p**, Pam Coats; **d**, Tony Bancroft, Barry Cook; **cast** (voiceovers): Ming-NaWen, Eddie Murphy, B D Wong, Miguel Ferrer, Harvey Fierstein, Freda Foh Shen, June Foray, James Hong, Miriam Margolyes, Pat Morita, Marni Nixon, Soon-Tek Oh, Donny Osmond, Lea Salonga, James Shigeta; **w**, Rita Hsiao, Christopher Sanders, Philip LaZebnik, Raymond Singer, Eugenia Bostwick-Singer, Dean DeBlois (based on a story by Robert D. San Souci, John Sanford, Tim Hodge, Burny Mattinson, Barry Johnson, Ed Gombert, Chris Williams, Julius L. Aguimatang, Lorna Cook, Thom Enriquez, Joe Grant, Floyd Norman, Linda Woolverton, Jodi Ann Johnson, Alan Ormsby, David Reynolds, Don Dougherty, Jorgen Klubien, Denis Rich, Joe Ekers, Theodore Newton, Larry Scholl, Daan Jippes, Frank Nissen, Jeff Snow); **m**, Jerry Goldsmith; **ed**, Michael Kelly; **prod d**, Hans Bacher; **art d**, Ric Sluiter; **spec eff**, David Mildenberger, Guner Behich.

Mulholland Dr. ★★★ 2001; France/U.S.; 147m; Les Films Alain Sarde/UNIV; Color; Mystery; Children: Unacceptable (MPAA: R); **BD**; **DVD**. Good whodunit sees Watts as an aspiring actress in Los Angeles. She meets and befriends Harring, who suffers from amnesia after having had an auto accident on Mulholland Drive and who lives in an aunt's apartment. As Watts tries to uncover Harring's identity and past, she is led to a movie director, Theroux, whose new film is taken over by mobsters. The plot thickens with the appearance of Pellegrino, a bungling hit man, and where three people are murdered, all having lesbian affairs with each other. In the end, the puzzle is too overwhelming for Watts, who shoots herself. Even fans of such surrealistic films might have trouble figuring it all out, but it's a well-crafted and well-enacted thriller sustaining interest throughout. Excessive violence, gutter language and sexuality prohibit viewing by children. **p**, Neal Edelstein, Tony Krantz,

Boris Karloff and Bramwell Fletcher in *The Mummy*, 1932.

Michael Polaire, Alain Sarde, Mary Sweeney, Joyce Eliason, John Wentworth; **d&w**, David Lynch; **cast**, Naomi Watts, Laura Elena Harring, Justin Theroux, Dan Hedaya, Brent Briscoe, Ann Miller, Robert Forster, Katharine Towne, Lee Grant, Scott Coffey, Billy Ray Cyrus, Chad Everett; **c**, Peter Deming; **m**, Angelo Badalamenti; **ed**, Sweeney; **prod d**, Jack Fisk; **art d**, Peter Jamison; **set d**, Barbara Haberecht; **spec eff**, Gary D'Amico, Philip Bartko, Chiz Hasegawa.

Mulholland Falls ★★★ 1996; U.S.; 107m; Kayos Productions/WB-Seven Arts; Color; Crime Drama; Children: Unacceptable (MPAA: R); **DVD**; **VHS**. This tough, gritty film noir entry offers a lot of thrills and no little suspense. Set in the early 1950s in Los Angeles, four members of a special anti-gangster police squad known as the infamous "Hat Squad," go after the bad guys, considerably bending the law to achieve their challenging goals. They beat up Petersen, a suspected organized crime figure, and push him off a cliff on Mulholland Drive that is nicknamed "Mulholland Falls," a fatal site in that they routinely throw migrating gangsters from these heights. Nolte, the chief detective heading this squad, and partners Palminteri, Madsen, and Penn, then investigate the murder of Connelly, a woman later identified as an aspiring actress. They learn that she was romantically involved with not only Nolte, but several prominent men, and had secret sex films to prove it, these films used for blackmail. Nolte and his men solve Connelly's murder, but not before Palminteri loses his life. Well directed by Tamahori, Nolte, Palminteri and the rest of the cast give stellar performances in a film not dissimilar to the equally nostalgic **L.A. Confidential**, 1997. Excessive violence and gutter language prohibit viewing by children. Songs: "Harbor Lights" (Jimmy Kennedy, Will Grosz as Hugh Williams), "Mr. Anthony's Boogie" (Ray Anthony, George Williams), "Something Cool" (Billy Barnes), "So Tired" (Russ Morgan, Jack Stewart), "That Certain Party" (Walter Donaldson, Gus Kahn), "Who Me?" (Frank Foster). **p**, Richard D. Zanuck, Lili Fini Zanuck; **d**, Lee Tamahori; **cast**, Nick Nolte, Melanie Griffith, Chazz Palminteri, Michael Madsen, Chris Penn, Treat Williams, Jennifer Connelly, Daniel Baldwin, Andrew McCarthy, John Malkovich, Kyle Chandler, Ed Lauter, Bruce Dern, Louise Fletcher, Rob Lowe, William Petersen; **w**, Peter Dexter (based on a story by Dexter and Floyd Mutrux); **c**, Haskell Wexler; **m**, Dave Grusin; **ed**, Sally Menke; **prod d**, Richard Sylbert; **art d**, Gregory William Bolton; **set d**, Claire Jenora Bowin; **spec eff**, Thomas R. Ward, Samuel E. Price.

The Mummy ★★★★ 1932; U.S.; 73m; UNIV; B/W; Horror; Children: Unacceptable; **DVD**; **VHS**. This chilling horror tale comes hot on the heels of the classic **Frankenstein**, 1931, and where Karloff presents an equally frightening creature in the form of a lethal, mummified priest from ancient Egypt, who is resurrected to wreak havoc on the living.

Boris Karloff in *The Mummy*, 1932.

Set in 1921 in the musty archeological digs of Egypt, scientists Van Sloan, Arthur Byron and their young protégé, Fletcher, are busy examining their latest unearthed discoveries. One of their findings is a strange sarcophagus that they have removed from an unmarked grave and, within it, a mummy, estimated to be 3700 years old. Van Sloan states that the mummified corpse was buried alive and was purposely entombed with the assurance that it would see no afterlife in that the casket has been stripped of all of the usual religious markings accompanying such burials. He further thinks that the corpse was buried in disgrace to indicate that, when alive, the deceased committed some heinous crime. The scientists have also found within that sarcophagus a box upon which is written some words that warn anyone finding this artifact not to open that box and Van Sloan urges his associates to heed that warning. Arthur Byron and Fletcher, however, find that challenge too tempting and, while Arthur Byron takes Van Sloan into the desert to discuss the matter, the curious Fletcher throws caution to the wind and opens the box. He withdraws from the box an ancient scroll and begins transcribing its words and, while he reads those words, the eyes of the mummy flutter open (its eyes and mouth not covered by ancient wrappings) and it begins to slowly move its arms and legs, encased in rags, moving close to Fletcher, who has his back turned away from this horrid creature, until the mummy reaches out an arm to snatch the scroll and where Fletcher screams in horror to see the mummy stagger away into the gloom. Hearing his screams, Van Sloan and Arthur Byron rush back to the tomb to find Fletcher hysterical and consumed by uncontrollable mad laughter. They realize that the young man has gone insane. All Fletcher can say is: "He went for a little walk…You should have seen his face!" The story flashes forward by twelve years to show Manners, who is Arthur Byron's son, on a similar expedition in Egypt and where he meets fellow archeologist Karloff, a man with an ancient-looking face, wrinkled and wax-like in appearance. He is deliberate in taking every step and speaks hesitantly, but he is an invaluable source of information that Manners and others are seeking and Karloff serves as their guide, directing them where to dig for another tomb, that of an ancient Egyptian princess. The scientists find that tomb, just where Karloff has indicated, and they remove the mummy of the princess, along with considerable treasure, taking it to a museum in Cairo. Later, when all have left the museum, Karloff appears with the stolen scroll and reads its incantations, attempting to revive the mummy of the princess, but all his efforts fail. A museum guard appears and Karloff struggles with him, losing the scroll before killing the guard and fleeing. When Karloff later meets Johann, who is Manners' fiancée, he is struck by her resemblance to the long dead Egyptian princess and is convinced that the soul of the princess has been reincarnated in Johann's body. Van Sloan then appears after having been on the trail of Karloff, convinced that he is that living

mummy unearthed in 1921 and has been missing ever since and that he believes that Karloff has designs on Johann. Van Sloan confronts Karloff, but Karloff sneers at Van Sloan, believing his great powers can defeat Van Sloan and any other mortal man. Van Sloan then goes to Arthur Byron, begging him to destroy the scroll that had been recovered at the museum, believing that it will destroy Karloff. The living mummy, however, uses his psychic powers to cause Byron to suffer a heart attack and die before he can destroy the scroll. Karloff then commands Johnson, Byron's black servant, through his psychic powers, to bring him that all-powerful scroll and, once it is in his possession, he psychically summons Johann to his residence. When the mesmerized young woman arrives, Karloff shows her "the pool of remembrance," a swirling body of water that conjures up the ancient images of the Egyptian past that Karloff shared with the princess. We see scenes of Karloff as an all-powerful Egyptian priest and Johann as the princess and how they share their love for one another, but the princess prematurely dies and, desperate, Karloff steals the scroll of life and uses it in an attempt to resurrect her. His incantations are interrupted when he is seized by the Pharaoh's guards and is then condemned on a charge of heresy, ordered to be buried alive in an unmarked grave. Having shown Johann this grim panorama of ancient evil-doings, Karloff announces that she will join him in eternity and he prepares her for a death ceremony. Once he has killed her, he and she will be together in the afterlife, or so Karloff believes. While Johann is under his spell, she dons the gown of the princess and lies down upon the sacrificial altar, but, before Karloff can plunge a dagger into her heart, Johann comes to her senses and implores a nearby statue of the Egyptian goddess of Isis to come to her rescue. Manners and Van Sloan rush into the room and Karloff attempts to kill them with psychic powers, but the statue of Isis comes to life and destroys the sacred scroll of life. All then watch in horror as Karloff disintegrates into dust and bones. Johann is now in the arms of Manners, Van Sloan gratified that his suspicions were correct, and the accursed and stalking mummy that was Karloff is no more. This eerie tale is told in unabashedly bold scenes by Freund, a brilliant cinematographer turned director, and Karloff renders another outstanding performance as the otherworld mummy, another classic horror role that greatly added to Karloff's reputation as the master of frightening film characters. Except for the offbeat **The Mummy's Hand**, 1940, a host of mummy sequels were issued in the next few decades, but all proved to be inferior productions, until a more omnipotent version of the character was impressively resurrected with spectacular visual effects in a spate of new Mummy films in the 1990s and 2000s. *Author's Note*: Where other monster films like **Frankenstein**, 1931, and **Dracula**, 1931, had some historical foundations, at least in folk tales, the story of **The Mummy** was created out of whole cloth by Universal writers. The writers did draw upon the unsubstantiated rumors that some archeologists were cursed for opening the ancient tombs of the pharaohs, but these curses did not emanate from those living in ancient Egypt. Those curses, such as the ones occurring with the discovery of King Tutankhamen's Tomb in 1922, were most likely created by modern-day Egyptians, who wanted to frighten off foreigners from pillaging their chief national treasures, which consisted of their ancient tombs and their contents. Freund does not present the kind of overt terror as seen in other early horror films, other than the opening scenes where Karloff comes alive as the mummy, but sustains suspense and apprehension through his atmospheric shots as his camera floats in dolly and tracking movements through moody, murky sets to give a constant feeling of dread and impending doom. Jack Pierce, the wizard who created the marvelously hideous makeup for **Frankenstein**, does his magic again in this film, creating in the initial scenes a ghastly mummy around Karloff, who was encased with fuller's earth, clay and linen. "It took almost eight hours for Jack to make me up as the mummy for every day we shot those early scenes," Karloff told this author, "and the reason why I moved so slowly and hesitantly is because I was exhausted by the time the cameras rolled and the cloth encasing me was so tight that it restricted my movements. There is one scene where I tell Van Sloan that

'I don't like to be touched.' The reference is easily taken, I think, by the viewer, that my walking corpse is so decomposed and rotting that if anyone brushed up against me, one of my arms or legs would simply fall off." A number of scenes that showed Johann in various reincarnations during various historical periods, such as a martyred Christian in the Roman era, a sacrificial maiden of the Vikings, and a noblewoman during the crusades, were edited out of the film before its release. Oddly, the credits for two actors appearing in those deleted scenes, Henry Victor, who plays a Roman warrior, and Arnold Gray, who enacts a medieval knight, appeared on the screen when the film was originally released. **p**, Carl Laemmle Jr.; **d**, Karl Freund; **cast**, Boris Karloff, Zita Johann, David Manners, Arthur Byron, Edward Van Sloan, Bramwell Fletcher, Noble Johnson, Kathryn Byron, Leonard Mudie, James Crane; **w**, John L. Balderston (based on a story by Nina Wilcox Putnam, Richard Schayer); **c**, Charles Stumar; **m**, James Dietrich; **ed**, Milton Carruth; **art d**, Willy Pogany; **spec eff**, John P. Fulton.

The Mummy ★★★ 1999; U.S.; 125m; UNIV; Color; Horror; Children: Unacceptable (MPAA: PG-13); **BD**; **DVD**. Centuries ago, Egyptian High Priest Imhotep (Vosloo) became intimate with a pharaoh's mistress and paid for the dalliance by being buried alive as a mummy. In the 1920s, Fraser, a soldier of fortune, joins Weisz, a beautiful English librarian-Egyptologist and her entertaining but somewhat scatterbrained brother, Hannah, in a search to find Hamunaptra, the "City of the Dead," beneath which is a reportedly great fortune in treasure. Also, the long-dead mummy is believed to be among those residing in the dead city. Priests who guard the city are afraid that if Imhotep is disturbed, it will release ten plagues on Egypt. Lo and behold, the mummy comes back to life and scares the pants off everyone and unleashes a plague of flesh-eating beetles. Fraser has his hands full, but manages to save the damsel in distress, put the mummy back where it belongs, and they all escape for a sequel. The film shares the same title but a different plot and has some laughs, as well as lots of special effects, unlike the horror classic of 1932. Songs include: "The Tall Palm Tree," "Love Is as Vast as a River" (Metqal Oemawi Metqal, Yunis Al Hilali): "Revive la ilusion" (German Pedro Ibanez). Excessive violence, horrific figures and momentary sensuality prohibit viewing by children. **p**, Sean Daniel, James Jacks, Patricia Carr; **d**, Stephen Sommers; **cast**, Brendan Fraser, Rachel Weisz, John Hannah, Arnold Vosloo, Kevin J. O'Connor, Oded Fehr, Jonathan Hyde, Erick Avari, Bernard Fox, Stephen Dunham; **w**, Sommers (based on a screen story by Sommers, Lloyd Fonvielle, Kevin Jarre, and a 1932 screenplay by John L. Balderston); **c**, Adrian Biddle; **m**, Jerry Goldsmith; **ed**, Bob Ducsay; **prod d**, Allan Cameron; **art d**, Giles Masters, Tony Reading, Clifford Robinson, Peter Russell; **set d**, Peter Howitt; **spec eff**, Chris and Lynne Corbould, Steve Hamilton.

The Mummy Returns ★★★ 2001; U.S.; 130m; UNIV; Color; Horror; Children: Unacceptable (MPAA: PG-13); **BD**; **DVD**. You can't keep a good mummy down, so in this sequel to **The Mummy**, 1999, high priest Imhotep's mummified body wakes up again after his centuries-long sleep and goes back to scaring everyone silly. In this adventure, we learn that Johnson, a Scorpion King, led a killer army in ancient Egypt, but, because he sold his soul to devil-like Anubis, he was erased from history and may now only be a myth. Archeologists Fraser and Weisz from the previous movie are now married and have an eight-year-old son, Boath. Together with Weisz's still entertaining but irresponsible brother, Hannah, they are in search of new artifacts and find the Bracelet of Anubis. Imhotep comes back from the dead again to obtain the bracelet so he can control the Scorpion King's army (still alive after all these years). Boath, who has the bracelet attached to him, is kidnapped. The film has a lot of action including a balloon journey, a magical pyramid with the ominous reputation that no one has ever lived to tell they saw it, and a computer-generated bloody swordplay battle between two armies, one human and the other giant dog-like creatures that run on their hind legs. The humans win the battle, but just barely, while Boath is rescued, and

Jet Li in *The Mummy: Tomb of the Dragon Emperor,* **2008.**

his parents and Imhotep survive to make yet another sequel. Great action and the special effects are impressively spellbinding. Johnson, who plays the Scorpion King, may be recognized by wrestling fans as The Rock, the World Wrestling Entertainment champion. Song: "Forever May Not Be Long Enough" (Glen Ballard, Edward Kowalczyk). Excessive violence prohibits viewing by children. **p**, Sean Daniel, James Jacks; **d&w**, Stephen Sommers; **cast**, Brendan Fraser, Rachel Weisz, John Hannah, Arnold Vosloo, Oded Fehr, Dwayne Johnson, Freddie Boath, Patricia Valasquez, Alun Armstrong, Shaun Parkes, Bruce Byron, Joe Dixon; **c**, Adrian Biddle; **m**, Alan Silvestri; **ed**, Ray Bushey III, Bob Ducsay, Kelly Matsumoto; **prod d**, Allan Cameron; **art d**, Ahmed Abounouom, Giles Masters, Tony Reading; **set d**, Peter Young; **spec eff**, Neil Corbould, David Hunter, Andy Williams.

The Mummy: Tomb of the Dragon Emperor ★★★ 2008; U.S.; 112m; UNIV; Color; Horror; Children: Unacceptable (MPAA: PG-13); **BD**; **DVD**. This third installment of new Mummy series is set not in Egypt but in the Far East in 1946, where the British government hires archeologist-adventurer Fraser and his wife, Bello, to take a relic, the diamond "Eye of Shangri-La" to China. Legend has it that the precious stone can resurrect a long-dead "Dragon Emperor" Han (Jet Li) and point the way to Shangri-La and an eternal pool of life. Arriving in China, the couple finds their adult son, Ford, and Bello's again entertaining irresponsible brother, Hannah. Ford has found the tomb of the emperor and awakened its mummy. Leong, the guardian of the emperor's tomb, tells Fraser and the others that the only way to destroy the emperor is to keep him from reaching Shangri-La or by stabbing him in the heart with a cursed dagger. It's not an easy mission and there is no yellow brick road, but the intrepid Fraser and company manage to end a convoluted plot involving long-dead slaves in the form of skeletons and a battle between armies in which the victors are those who can screw the heads back onto their decapitated comrades. This combination adventure-horror film offers many thrills and laughs that end with the hint that the sequel will take place in Peru. Songs: "My Sweet Eternal Love" (Randy Edelman, Rob Cohen), "Tulsa Oklahoma (Ed Palermo, John Palermo), "Tribeca Bounce" (Bruce Fowler), "Take Me Out to the Ball Game" (Albert von Tilzer, Jack Norworth). Excessive violence prohibits viewing by children. **p**, Sean Daniel, Bob Ducsay, James Jacks, Stephen Sommers, Qin Lei, Josette Perrotta, Doris Tse; **d**, Rob L. Cohen; **cast**, Brendan Fraser, Maria Bello, John Hannah, Jet Li, Michelle Yeoh, Isabella Leong, Anthony Wong Chau-Sang, Russell Wong, Liam Cuningham, David Calder, **w**, Alfred Gough, Miles Millar; **c**, Simon Duggan; **m**, Randy Edelman; **ed**, Kelly Matsumoto, Joel Negron; **prod d**, Nigel Phelps; **art d**, John Dexter, David Gaucher, Isabelle Guay, Nicolas Lepage, Jean-Pierre Pacquet, Scott Zuber; **set d**, Ane Kuljian, Philippe Lord;

The Great Gonzo and Rizzo the Rat in *The Muppet Christmas Carol*, 1992.

spec eff, Mario Dumont, Arthur Wai Kit Lao (Arthur Lao WaiKit), Bruce Law (Bruce Law Wai Yin).

The Mummy's Hand ★★★ 1940; U.S.; 67m; UNIV; B/W; Horror; Children: Unacceptable; **DVD**; **VHS**. An odd mix of horror and humor has Foran and Wallace as comical, out-of-work archeologists in Egypt, who discover the burial place of ancient Princess Anaka. They get funding from Kellaway, an eccentric magician and his beautiful daughter, Moran, and start digging. In their labors they are terrorized by Zucco, an evil high priest, and a living mummy, Tyler, who guards the princess' tomb. After a series of harrowing events, Foran and Ford dispatch Zucco by throwing him down some stairs and then set fire to the stalking mummy. Although this sequel to the classic Boris Karloff film, **The Mummy**, 1932, is nowhere near as frightening, it nevertheless sustains attention throughout with a lot of action and considerable suspense. **p**, Ben Pi; **d**, Christy Cabanne; **cast**, Dick Foran, Peggy Moran, Wallace Ford, Eduardo Ciannelli, George Zucco, Cecil Kellaway, Charles Trowbridge, Tom Tyler, Sig Arno, Eddie Foster; **w**, Griffin Jay, Maxwell Shane (based on a story by Jay); **c**, Elwood Bredell; **m**, Hans J. Salter, Frank Skinner; **ed**, Philip Cahn; **art d**, Jack Otterson; **set d**, Russell A. Gausman.

The Muppet Christmas Carol ★★★ 1992; U.S.; 89m; Jim Henson/Walt Disney/Buena Vista; Color; Comedy/Fantasy; Children: Cautionary (MPAA: G); **DVD**; **VHS**. Charles Dickens' classic story as performed by the Muppets, puppet stars of the popular long-running television series. Set in Victorian London, Caine plays miserly, miserable Ebenezer Scrooge as virtually the only live actor in an otherwise cast of puppets. The Great Gonzo (Goelz voiceover) plays Charles Dickens, Kermit the Frog (Whitmire voiceover) plays Bob Cratchit, Miss Piggy (Oz voiceover) plays Mrs. Cratchit. Caine is visited by the ghost of his deceased former business partner, who tells him three ghosts of Christmas will visit him that night, those of the past, present, and future. These spirits eventually cause Scrooge to become a kind and generous person, reaching out to the needy and where he becomes Santa Claus to his family and friends. Young children may be frightened by the ghosts, but otherwise it is a delightful family film well played by Caine, who considered it one of his best roles and performances. Songs: "Scrooge," "One More Sleep, Til Christmas," "Marley and Marley," "When Love Is Gone," "It Feels Like Christmas," "Christmas Scat," "Bless Us All," "Thankful Heart" (Paul Williams). **p**, Frank Oz, Brian Henson, Martin G. Baker, Jerry Juhl; **d**, Henson; **cast**, Michael Caine, (voiceovers) Dave Goelz, Steve Whitmire, Jerry Nelson, Oz, David Rudman, Don Austen, Jessica Fox, Robert Tygner, Steven Mackintosh, **w**, Jerry Juhl (based on the novel *A Christmas Carol* by Charles Dickens); **c**, John Fenner; **m**,

Miles Goodman; **ed**, Michael Jablow; **prod d**, Val Strazovec; **art d**, Dennis Bosher, Alan Cassie; **set d**, Michael Ford; **spec eff**, David Harris, Simon Clutterbuck.

The Muppet Movie ★★★ 1979; U.K./U.S.; 98m; Henson Associates; ITC Films/Associated Film Distribution; Color; Musical/Fantasy; Children: Acceptable (MPAA: G); **DVD**; **VHS**. The Jim Henson puppets, stars of a long-running television series, appear in their first feature-length movie which was followed by three more Muppets films, **The Muppets Take Manhattan**, 1984, **The Muppets Christmas Carol**, 1992, and **The Muppets**, 2011. Kermit the Frog (Henson voiceover) is persuaded by his agent (DeLuise) to try for a career in Hollywood. This leads him to encourage his friends Fozzie the Bear (Oz voiceover), Miss Piggy (Oz voiceover), The Great Gonzo (Goelz voiceover) and others to do the same. Along the way, Kermit rides a bicycle, rows a boat, and is pursued by a mean fast-food magnate, Durning, who wants him to sign a contract as the trademark of a chain of French-fried frogs' leg restaurants. In their hilarious and haphazard adventures, the puppets become movie stars. Songs include "The Rainbow Connection," "Frog's Legs So Fine," "Movin' Right Along," "Can You Picture That?," "Never Before," "Something Better," "This Looks Familiar," "I'm Going Back There Someday" (Paul Williams, Kenny Ascher). **p**, Jim Henson, David Lazer, Sir Lew Grade; **d**, James Frawley; **cast**, Bob Hope, Milton Berle, Mel Brooks, James Coburn, Dom DeLuise, Charles Durning, Elliott Gould, Madeline Kane, Cloris Leachman, Steve Martin, Richard Pryor, Telly Savalas, Orson Welles, Paul Williams, and (voiceovers) Jim Henson, Frank Oz, Jerry Nelson, Richard Hunt, Dave Goelz, Edgar Bergen; **w**, Jerry Juhl, Jack Burns; **c**, Isidore Mankofsky; **m**, Williams; **ed**, Christopher Greenbury; **prod d**, Joel Schiller; **art d**, Les Gobruegge; **set d**, Richard Goddard; **spec eff**, Robbie Knott, Scott Forbes.

The Muppets ★★★ 2011; U.S.; 103m; Walt Disney; Color; Comedy; Children: Cautionary (MPAA: PG-13); **BD**; **DVD**. A greedy tycoon (Cooper voiceover) wants to drill under The Muppets' old theater, believing oil is there, and three fans (Segel, Adams, and Linz voiceovers) set out to find them since they split up years ago. Kermit the Frog (Whitmire voiceover) lives in Hollywood, Gonzo the Great (Goelz voiceover) is a plumber, Fozzie the Bear (Jacobson voiceover) operates a band, and Miss Piggy (Jacobson voiceover) is a fashion magazine editor in Paris. The fans find them and The Muppets put on one last show that saves their beloved theater. There were three earlier Muppets movies. Crude humor makes this one cautionary for children. **p**, David Hoberman, Todd Lieberman; **d**, James Bobin; **cast** (voiceovers), Jason Segel, Amy Adams, Chris Cooper, Rashida Jones, Steve Whitmire, Eric Jacobson, Dave Goelz, Bill Barretta, David Rudman, Matt Vogel, Peter Linz; **w**, Segel, Nicholas Stoller (based on characters created by Jim Henson); **c**, Don Burgess; **m**, Christophe Beck; **ed**, James Thomas; **prod d**, Steve Saklad; **art d**, Andrew Max Cahn; **set d**, Tracey A. Doyle. Songs include "Life's a Happy Song," "Mahna Mahna" (Christophe Beck), "The Rainbow Connection" (Paul Williams, Kenny Ascher).

The Muppets Take Manhattan ★★★ 1984; U.S.; 94m; Henson Associates/TriStar Pictures; Color; Comedy; Children: Cautionary (MPAA: PG-13); **DVD**; **VHS**. The Muppets graduate from college and take their senior show on the road, hoping to eventually get it on Broadway. They don't find it a piece of cake to sell their show to New York producers, but finally find one. After some problems, the show gets to a theater on Broadway and is a hit for Kermit the Frog (Henson voiceover), Miss Piggy and Fozzie the Bear (Oz voiceovers), Gonzo (Goelz voiceover), and their friends. Crude humor makes this otherwise entertaining vehicle cautionary for children. Songs: "Together Again," "I'm Gonna Always Love You," "He'll Make Me Happy," "You Can't Take No for an Answer," "Sayng Goodbye," "Rat Scat (Something Cookin)," "Right Where I Belong," "Somebody's Getting Married," "Waiting for the Wedding," "He'll Make Me Happy," "The Ceremony" (Jeff Moss); "William Tell

Overture" (Gioachino Rossini). Crude language makes viewing caution- ary for children. **p**, David Lazer, Jim Henson; **d**, Frank Oz; **cast** (voiceovers), Henson, Oz, David Goelz, Steve Whitmire, Richard Hunt, Jerry Nelson, Juliana Donald, Louis Zorich, Art Carney, James Coco, Dabney Coleman, Gregory Hines, Linda Lavin, Joan Rivers, Elliott Gould, Liza Minnelli, Brooke Shields, Edward I. Koch, John Landis; **w**, Oz, Tom Patchett, Jay Tarses (based on a story by Patchett, Tarses); **c**, Robert Paynter; **m**, Ralph Burns; **ed**, Evan Lottman; **prod d**, Stephen Hendrickson; **art d**, Paul Eads, W. Steven Graham; **set d**, Robert Drumheller, Justin Scoppa, Jr.; **spec eff**, Leigh Donaldson, Edward Dro- han, Brian Henson.

Murder! ★★★★ 1930; U.K.; 104m; British International Pictures; B/W; Mystery; Children: Unacceptable; **DVD**; **VHS**. This chilling early day talkie from pantheon director Hitchcock achieves excellence not only through Hitchcock's inventive and masterful scene-to-scene craft- ing, but through a wonderful performance by Marshall, one of the most accomplished actors of his day. He is a member of a jury deliberating the murder trial of beautiful Baring, a young actress, who is found stand- ing over the body of another female player in her traveling theater troupe and who has no recollection of having killed the woman. The jury, other than Marshall, is wholly convinced that Baring is guilty and must be executed by hanging lest she kills again. Marshall is overwhelmed by fellow jurors who pressure him by chanting "guilty!" at him, until that refrain is heard again in the courtroom where Baring is convicted and then sentenced to death. Marshall, who is a knighted, wealthy gentleman and himself a theatrical producer, director and actor, remains uncon- vinced as to Baring's guilt, so much so that he decides to conduct his own investigation into Baring's case in order to expose the flimsy evi- dence that brought about her conviction. He invites Konstam and Chap- man, who are man and wife and two of Marshall's theatrical colleagues, to dine with him at his upscale lodgings. Marshall sees when dining with his friends that Chapman wrongly uses the same spoon from his fruit cup to eat his soup, but, ever the gentleman and not wishing to embarrass his guest over his lack of table etiquette, Marshall himself uses the same spoon to consume the fruit and soup. (Such little but conspicuous bits of business are filmic hallmarks established by the meticulous Hitch- cock.) Marshall is also amused but makes no mention of the fact that Konstam puts on airs to assume the role of a refined woman dining in the company of a knight of the realm, and he protectively overlooks her posturing remarks. Marshall tells his associates that he intends to recre- ate the crime as a play within a play and sets out to reenact the events by first going to the murder scene where he takes lodgings in a shabby rooming house. He is awakened by the solicitous landlady, who brings him his morning tea while he is still in bed, but Marshall's austere de- meanor is quickly shattered when, following the landlady into the room is a bevy of unkempt and dirty children looking to have fun and who unexpectedly leap onto Marshall's bed. One little girl embraces him lov- ingly, but with greasy hands that, for a moment, alarms Marshall. In an instant, however, his humanity forgives the intrusion of this dirt-laden urchin when he gives smiling approval to that little scamp. Marshall's probe leads him to a circus performer, Percy, a half-caste trapeze artist, whom he enlists in the reenactment of the crime. Knowing that a woman was the killer, Marshall also has learned that Percy, a transvestite, has performed on the stage as a female impersonator or drag queen and Mar- shall proves that Percy employed that disguise when killing the victim while he lures Percy into reenacting the murder, trapping and identifying him as the real perpetrator. Baring is set free just before her scheduled execution and winds up in the arms of Marshall, the man who has saved her life. Although some of his scenes are necessarily static because of the restrictions imposed by the crude sound techniques of that day, Hitchcock moves this whodunit along at a brisk pace, using many inno- vative and precedent-setting techniques of his own that greatly enhance the tension and suspense and where Marshall and the cast members are standouts. The director makes his traditional cameo appearance while

Herbert Marshall, left, and Esme Percy, right, in *Murder!*, **1930.**

standing outside the house where the murder occurred at the beginning of the film. Songs: "Symphony No. 5 in C Minor Op.67" (1809; Ludwig van Beethoven), "Prelude" (1865; from Tristan and Isolde; Richard Wagner). ***Author's Note***: The director actually made two versions of this film, one in English with the cast shown herein, and another in Ger- man, with a completely different cast, which went into production after he finished the English version. (This was an early sound day practice, but making two separate productions for the same story was very ex- pensive and this regimen was abandoned as soon as sound technicians found a way to dub films with foreign languages.) Hitchcock spoke Ger- man fairly well, but told this author that he had trouble in making the German version because the actors spoke in unfamiliar dialects, and where, as he said to this author "I didn't understand the cadences of their speech. I got some words here and there, but mostly I did not understand what they were saying and had to work through an interpreter. I had a lot of problems with the leading man of the picture, Alfred Abel, who was playing Herbert's [Marshall's] role. Abel was then a huge film star in Germany. In one scene, I asked him to wear a tweed suit when he vis- its the condemned woman in her prison cell. He appeared in that suit and then wagged his finger at me, shook his head, and said in perfect English: 'I don't visit a girl in these clothes,' and walked off the set. He showed up a short time later dressed in formal wear with striped trousers and insisted that he appear in the scene dressed that way. And that's how it went all along until we finished that German production and where Abel never again spoke anything but German to me." Hitchcock also had many problems with the then difficult early-day sound equipment, telling this author that "sound had just come into the movies and we had to overcome many challenges in working with the cumbersome sound equipment, which confined the movements of the actors as well as the camera." In one scene, Hitchcock had to surmount the difficulty of hav- ing Marshall narrate some of his own thoughts and suspicions while he stands mute before a mirror shaving himself and while listening to clas- sical music coming from a nearby radio. "We could not in those days simply edit in a sound segment for that scene," Hitchcock explained to this author, "so I had Herbert [Marshall] pre-record his thoughts on a wire tape recorder we had in that bygone era, and when I shot the scene where he stands without speaking in front of the mirror and shaving, I ran that tape aloud for the sound equipment to record in that scene, so that viewers could hear what Herbert was actually thinking. Meanwhile, I had a thirty-five piece orchestra playing "Tristan and Isolde" right be- hind the bathroom wall where Marshall is standing to simulate the music that was supposed to be coming from the radio. We had to go to great lengths then to achieve anything out of the ordinary and since anything out of the ordinary is what I have always done, I had to take extraordi- nary measures." Marshall told this author that his role was based on Sir

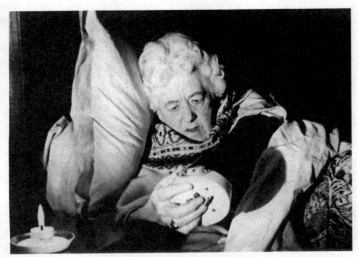

Margaret Rutherford in *Murder at the Gallop*, 1963.

Gerald du Maurier (1873-1934), who was a friend of Hitchcock's, an actor-director who managed a number of theaters. Others claimed that Marshall's character stemmed from Sir Herbert Beerbohm Tree (1852-1917), who managed London's Haymarket Theater and who served as a producer, director and often the star of his productions (and who reportedly fathered a number of illegitimate children, including famed film director Carol Reed), as is the case with Marshall's character. Marshall told this author that he believed "Hitch was making film history with **Murder!** He used so many techniques of his own invention that I marveled at his creativity and I told him how much I admired his courage in taking such an unorthodox approach. He also did something that was unusual for that day and allowed in the scene where I dine with my associates for us to improvise our conversation and we departed considerably from the script's dialog in that scene. I think Hitch had second thoughts about allowing actors such freedom, because, to my knowledge, he never did that again. When we made **Foreign Correspondent** [1940] together, he insisted, by then, that he be in total control of everything in his films. He was having no more of that improvisation from the actors, not a bit. You followed the dialog from the script and to the letter in **Foreign Correspondent** and, I believe, in all the rest of his pictures, or watch out! I am reminded of the scene [in **Murder!**] where I am directing the man I suspect of being the real killer and I compel him to read the very lines that will convict him out of his own mouth and here I am an alter ego of Hitch himself." Hitchcock, never one to let a good scene go unrepeated in his own inventory, would use this same ploy when later making **Stage Fright**, 1950. Hitchcock believed that this film inspired to some degree the classic crime drama, **12 Angry Men**, 1957, stating to this author that "Hank [Fonda] did a picture with me, **The Wrong Man** [1956] and he told me at that time how much of an admirer he was of my pictures and how he had studied them. Well, the next picture he makes is **12 Angry Men**, and what do you think? It's a take-off on my picture, **Murder!** At least, the premise of that picture uses the beginning of my picture and takes it from there. In **12 Angry Men**, Hank is the lone juror in a room full of jurors, who are pressuring him to agree with them in convicting the defendant when he thinks the defendant might be innocent. Like Herbert [Marshall] in my picture, Hank then recreates the murder right there in the jury room to finally turn everybody around so that they find the defendant innocent. I found that picture very appealing and have always thought it was Hank's left-handed way of flattering me." When this author later repeated these remarks to Fonda (who was the chief producer of **12 Angry Men**) in one of my many meetings with the actor, he replied: "That man had a memory like an elephant. He forgot nothing. I think Hitch spent a lot more time watching other people's films than he did his own, not to get ideas, but to see if his own ideas were being used. You might say

he was an unusual film detective, the way he could track down how his own ideas were being used by everybody else. Sure, I watched **Murder!** and more than once before we did **12 Angry Men**. You learn all you can from master directors like Hitchcock if you want to make good films." **p**, John Maxwell; **d**, Alfred Hitchcock; **cast**, Herbert Marshall, Norah Baring, Phyllis Konstam, Edward Chapman, Miles Mander, Esme Percy, Donald Calthrop, Esme V. Chaplin, Amy Brandon-Thomas, Una O'Connor, Joynson Powell, S. J. Warmington, Marie Wright, Hannah Jones, R. E. Jeffrey, Kenneth Kove, Violet Farebrother, Hitchcock; **w**, Alma Reville, Walter C. Mycroft, Hitchcock (based on the novel *Enter Sir John* by Clemence Dane, Helen Simpson); **c**, Jack E. Cox; **m**, John Reynders; **ed**, Rene Marrison; **art d**, J. F. Mead.

Murder Ahoy ★★★ 1964; U.K.; 93m; MGM; B/W; Comedy/Mystery; Children: Unacceptable; **DVD**; **VHS**. That marvelous British character actress Rutherford shines as the dogged amateur detective Miss Marple in this better-than-average Agatha Christie whodunit. Rutherford, one of the trustees of an organization that supervises the use of a boat for wayward youth, witnesses the death of fellow trustee, Longhurst, at one of the organization's meetings. She immediately suspects foul play since Longhurst died shortly before revealing important new information about the boat. She confides her suspicions to police inspector Tingwell, but he sees nothing amiss and dismisses Rutherford's apprehensions. Rutherford, however, embarks upon her own investigation by boarding the yacht, commanded by the stuffy Jeffries, who thinks himself a grand admiral of the seas. Jeffries objects to Rutherford remaining on board, but she overrules him and then begins communicating with lights and other signals from her cabin to her associate, Davis, who has remained on shore. Rutherford discovers that Matthews, an officer on board the ship, has been teaching the delinquent boys how to filch expensive items that are then fenced, but Matthews is suddenly killed, as is his aide, Foster, a matron, before the inventive old lady can bring them to justice. Inspector Tingwell joins Rutherford on the boat to set a trap for the killer, but he himself gets trapped and isolated from Rutherford when the culprit, Mervyn, another trustee, appears. He has been stealing funds from the charity organization and he has been dispatching those who have learned about his underhanded ways. Now he confronts the formidable Rutherford and the two hilariously battle with swords, a fight which Mervyn loses just before Tingwell breaks free and arrests him. The victorious Rutherford is saluted as a hero by Jeffries and the ship's crew just before she departs the boat, ending this delightful crime romp. The story is quick paced and the script witty, and Rutherford captivates in every scene with her unique and endearing gestures and mugging while bird-dogging the perpetrator. Songs: "Rule Britannia" (music: Thomas Augustine Arne; lyrics: James Thomson), "The Sailor's Hornpipe" (traditional). *Author's Note*: Davis was Rutherford's real-life husband and appeared in small roles in many of her films. This marked the final appearance of Rutherford in this entertaining series, her role later taken over by Angela Lansbury. **p**, Lawrence P. Bachmann; **d**, George Pollock; **cast**, Margaret Rutherford, Lionel Jeffries, Charles Tingwell, William Mervyn, Joan Benham, Stringer Davis, Nicholas Parsons, Miles Malleson, Henry Oscar, Henry B. Longhurst, Derek Nimmo, Francis Matthews, Norma Foster; **w**, David Pursall, Jack Seddon (based on the character created by Agatha Christie); **c**, Desmond Dickinson; **m**, Ron Goodwin; **ed**, Ernest Walter; **art d**, Bill Andrews.

Murder at the Gallop ★★★ 1963; U.K.; 81m; MGM; B/W; Comedy/Mystery; Children: Unacceptable; **DVD**; **VHS**. The inimitable lamp-jawed Rutherford is at her funniest in this Agatha Christie whodunit that begins when she and Davis are collecting funds for one of their charities, the Reformed Criminals League. She arrives at a large house to solicit a donation from Currie, an eccentric and wealthy old man, who, after immediately seeing a cat, falls down a flight of stairs to his death. Rutherford's instincts tell her that Currie's death is no accident, but the result of foul play, learning that Currie had a deep-seated fear of cats. After she has found the cat in Currie's residence, along with a muddy footprint of a riding boot, she presents her suspicions to police inspector Tingwell, who, however, tells her that she is barking up the wrong tree and that Currie's death was from natural causes as he died of a heart attack. Undeterred, Rutherford attends the hearing of Currie's will to learn that four of his relatives have been left equal shares of Currie's estate, and when one of them raises the possibility of murder, the elderly woman is later found dead in her cottage by the snooping Rutherford (dispatched with a hatpin and Rutherford again finding a telltale muddy boot print at the crime scene). Robson, the fussy companion to the deceased, then accuses Rutherford of foul play, but inspector Tingwell exonerates her of all guilt and Rutherford keeps on the trail, going to a riding club (owned and operated by Morley, one of the surviving heirs), where Rutherford takes a room at its hotel. She first suspects the always flustering Morley, but then concludes that Robson is the real killer, who is trying to get her hands on a priceless painting left in Currie's will. Rutherford collects the usual suspects, including Robson, and then goes into a frenetic dance, shouting before collapsing to the floor in pretended unconsciousness: "I know who the murderer is!" She is removed to a bedroom to recuperate and Robson appears to administer the coup de grace, but Tingwell, who has been waiting in the wings as per his arrangement with Rutherford, arrests her before she can claim another victim. Her self-assigned mission completed, Rutherford is about to leave the riding club when Morley asks for her hand in marriage, but Rutherford politely declines before going on her merry way. **p**, George H. Brown, Lawrence P. Bachmann (uncredited); **d**, George Pollock; **cast**, Margaret Rutherford, Robert Morley, Flora Robson, Stringer Davis, Charles Tingwell, Gordon Harris, Robert Urquhart, Katya Douglas, James Villiers, Noel Howlett, Finlay Currie; **w**, James P. Cavanagh (based on the novel *After the Funeral* by Agatha Christie); **c**, Arthur Ibbetson; **m**, Ron Goodwin; **ed**, Bert Rule; **art d**, Frank White; **spec eff**, Tom Howard.

Murder by Death ★★★★ 1976; U.S.; 94m; Rastar/COL; Color; Comedy/Mystery; Children: Unacceptable (MPAA: PG); **DVD**; **VHS**. The always clever Simon spoofs the detective films of yesteryear in this hilarious and outlandish film. Capote (named Lionel Twain after the model electric train), an eccentric millionaire, thinks himself to be greater than all the master sleuths on earth. He invites to his eerie mansion those most famous detectives—Sam Diamond/Sam Spade (Falk, accompanied by floozy secretary Brennan), Sidney Wang/Charlie Chan (Sellers, accompanied by son Narita), Jessica Marbles/Miss Marple (Lanchester, accompanied by Winwood), Dick and Dora Charleston/Nick and Nora Charles (Niven and Smith), and Milo Perrier/Hercule Poirot (James Coco, accompanied by Cromwell). As each of these glorious gumshoes arrive, they are greeted by blind butler Guinness, who can't find his way to the washroom, and these apprehensive guests must fend for themselves in going to their rooms while, in the kitchen, a new cook, Walker, arrives, but she is deaf and mute and has no idea of what is expected of her, particularly after Guinness gives her instructions she cannot understand. Meanwhile, the reluctant guests assemble at the dining hall, but without their host present and where Guinness appears and begins to serve them soup he thinks Walker has prepared, but there is nothing that he ladles from the soup dish except air. The host of shrewd detectives soon realize that their collective visit is not a social outing, but that they are being held hostage in Capote's bastion-like fortress, which he electronically controls, sealing the windows and doors with iron bars and grates while challenging them to solve a great murder mystery—his own death, which he elaborately stages before their eyes. Each detective resorts to type in attempting to solve the riddle in order to get out of this madhouse. Sellers uses his inscrutable Oriental counter-logic, but to no end. Niven applies his sophisticated solving methods, but this fails. Falk, who gives the most hilarious performance of the lot as a crass and cunning San Francisco sleuth (which he would reprise with another name and with the same hilarious results in **The Cheap Detective**, 1978,

Eileen Brennan, Peter Falk, Richard Narita, Estelle Winwood, Elsa Lanchester, Peter Sellers, David Niven and Maggie Smith in *Murder by Death*, 1976.

also written by Simon), cannot fill in the puzzle and neither can Lanchester or Coco, who are separately and collectively attacked by mechanical and other devices hatched from Capote's deranged brain. Ceilings begin to descend like giant presses and rooms vanish and reappear like labyrinthine mazes to confuse and discombobulate the exploring detectives, who separately and collectively are as certifiable as Capote, all operating in a crazy mansion, until Capote finally reappears to solve the riddle himself in order to prove that his celebrated guests are nothing more than incompetent nincompoops before he sends them on their idiotic ways. Everyone renders very funny essays in their vaunted roles and even the oily Capote, with his prissy demeanor and annoyingly falsetto voice, is consistently humorous, but only because he is one of the worst actors ever appearing on a screen, which may or may not have been Simon's intention. Simon's script is a scream, packed with witty double entendre and insider quips, especially when the ego-bruised detectives compete with each other's vaunted skills, or the dismal lack of them. Mystery and detective film fans will find this one a sheer delight, but only if they have a sense of humor on the bizarre and madcap side. *Author's Note*: The screams that emit from the door knocker as it is used when guests arrive at Capote's mansion are the actual screams of actress Fay Wray in **King Kong**, 1933. Of all the delightful players in this wild romp, Simon was most impressed by the great Guinness, who told this author that he was "very impressed with the twisting and turning script Simon wrote. He is a master of the unexpected in comedy as **Murder by Death** clearly shows. I had great fun in doing that picture and I believe so did everyone else. A fine parody of those well-remembered detective films of yesteryear." Falk told this author that "Neil Simon? A genius for comedy, no one like him, in a class by himself, yes sir! I loved my character in **Murder by Death**, one where I do a takeoff on Sam Spade and I think I had the juiciest part in the picture. I played the guy as a sleazy, scummy, lowlife, and when Eileen [Brennan] accuses me of pretending to solve crimes by going to gay bars, I become apologetic and full of excuses—please forgive me, Humphrey Bogart! Oh, what a helluva lot of fun that picture was!" Niven was equally enthusiastic about the film, but more reserved when telling this author that "I and Maggie [Smith] choke on our austerity and aloofness in that wonderful satire from Simon. I found myself struggling not to spoil my scenes when reacting to the antics of Sellers and, especially Falk, who is so outlandish that I wanted to go somewhere and laugh for about twenty minutes after each one of his scenes. Peter is not only a fine dramatic actor, but no one performs comedy better than he does. Of course, he made a caricature out of himself, as we all did, but he outdid all of us. After I called him a 'little twit' in one of our scenes together, he took me aside and said, 'Couldn't you call me a big twit instead?' **p**, Ray Stark; **d**, Robert Moore; **cast**, Eileen Brennan, Truman

Peter Whitney, Marjorie Main, Helen Walker and Fred MacMurray in *Murder, He Says*, 1945.

Capote, James Coco, Peter Falk, Alec Guinness, Elsa Lanchester, David Niven, Peter Sellers, Maggie Smith, Nancy Walker, Estelle Winwood, James Cromwell, Richard Narita, Fay Wray (voice); **w**, Neil Simon; **c**, David M. Walsh (Panavision; Metrocolor); **m**, Dave Grusin; **ed**, John F. Burnett; **prod d**, Stephen Grimes; **art d**, Harry Kemm; **set d**, Marvin March; **spec eff**, Augie Lohman.

Murder by Decree ★★★★ 1979; U.K./Canada; 124m; AVCO Embassy Pictures; Color; Horror/Mystery; Children: Unacceptable (MPAA: PG); **DVD**; **VHS**. Plummer superbly plays Sherlock Holmes in this superior thriller and where veteran actor Mason is an equally impressive Dr. Watson. Plummer takes on his most dangerous challenge in tracking down the insidious serial killer, Jack the Ripper, who is randomly murdering lowlife women in London's impoverished Whitechapel district in 1888. (Ironically, the character of Sherlock Holmes first came into creation a year earlier, in 1887, when its author, Arthur Conan Doyle, published his first story about the indomitable detective in *A Study in Scarlet*.) Plummer reluctantly surveys the several slayings committed by the Ripper before he is inspired to dig further after meeting real-life psychic Robert Lees (1849-1931), played by Sutherland, whose mental visions send Plummer on the trail where he discovers a royal cabal of Masons who are covering up the real killer, the lynch pin to his identity being Bujold, the abandoned mistress of a member of the royal household, and who Plummer identifies as the Ripper. He traps the madman at the docks of the Thames, and a terrific battle ensues where Plummer finally bests the serial killer, sending him to a watery death enwrapped in Plummer's weighted scarf (one of the real suspects in that spectacular case reportedly drowned himself and, in the earlier thriller, **The Lodger**, 1944, the Ripper, or the character suspected of being that killer, drowns himself in the Thames). Clark directs with vitality, and the script is intriguing as it unravels the puzzlements of the case. Plummer gets great support from Hemmings, Sutherland, Gielgud and Quayle (the latter playing Sir Charles Warren, 1840-1927, head of the Metropolitan Police) in this outstanding production where the gaslight era of London comes chillingly alive with its enshrouded cobblestone streets and jouncing horse-drawn hansom cabs. Songs: "God Save the Queen" (traditional), "Preludio" (from "Partita fur Violine" by Johann Sebastian Bach), "Abide with Me" (William H. Monk), "Cottage Industry" (Paul Lewis), "A Wanderin' Minstrel" (Arthur Sullivan, Keith Papworth), "Onward Christian Soldiers" (Arthur Sullivan, Edrich Siebert), "Flowers of the Forest" (Traditional). *Author's Note*: Plummer told this author that "anyone playing Sherlock Holmes risks being compared to the great Basil Rathbone, who owned that role for many years. I had to work my character from beneath the shadow of that fine actor to make it my own, not an easy task." **p**, René Dupont, Bob Clark; **d**,

Clark; **cast**, Christopher Plummer, James Mason, David Hemmings, Susan Clark, Anthony Quayle, John Gielgud, Frank Finlay, Donald Sutherland, Geneviéve Bujold, Chris Wiggins; **w**, John Hopkins (based on a story by Clark, the book *The Ripple File* by Elwyn Jones, John Lloyd, and characters created by Sir Arthur Conan Doyle); **c**, Reginald H. Morris (Metrocolor); **m**, Carl Zittrer, Paul Zaza; **ed**, Stan Cole; **prod d**, Harry Pottle; **art d**, Peter Childs; **set d**, Denise Exshaw; **spec eff**, Michael Albrechtsen, Cliff Culley.

Murder, He Says ★★★ 1945; U.S.; 91m; PAR; B/W; Comedy; Children: Cautionary; **DVD**; **VHS**. MacMurray is outstanding in this hilarious comedy where he is a poll taker trying to find a missing co-worker, which leads him to a rural town in the Ozarks where he meets an oddball family living in a dilapidated old house. Main, also absurdly certifiable (and exceptional in her role as she cracks a whip through her menacing scenes) runs the others, who include twin hillbilly brothers, both superbly played by Whitney, who, between them, are at least one teacup short of the Mad Hatter's party. The loony family would just as soon shoot a stranger as let him in the house because they are looking for $70,000, which was hidden somewhere in the place by Pepper, a cousin, after a bank robbery. MacMurray decides that the only sane one around is Walker, daughter of a man supposedly implicated in the bank robbery. MacMurray and Walker team up to decode a deathbed clue left by the family's grandmother, Paige. The old lady gave the clue to MacMurray, a nonsensical song about where the money is stashed, before kicking the bucket, but Main's husband, Hall, tries to poison them as he has poisoned Paige. The bumbling Hall, however, soon accidentally poisons himself. Then Pepper escapes from prison and shows up to retrieve the loot. She has MacMurray sing the song in trying to understand the meaningless lyrics. MacMurray deciphers the clues and it reveals where the loot is hidden. It turns out that Hall has faked his own death, and he and Pepper, along with the nutty twins and Main, chase MacMurray and Walker through secret passageways in the house, but they dispatch their pursuers into a hay baling machine. The nutty family members emerge alive, but snuggly wrapped for police to take them into custody or the funny farm, either destination being suitable for this wacky clan. Walker has vindicated her father and ends in up the arms of MacMurray for a happy fadeout to a frantic frolic. This B comedy is funnier than most A comedies of the decade, with MacMurray, Main, Paige, and Whitney all stealing scenes from each other. *Author's Note*: MacMurray told this author that "**Murder, He Says** is easy to understand since there are only two types of people in that picture, a few sane ones and everyone else is nuts. Marjorie [Main] is wonderful in that picture, sort of a Ma Kettle gone berserk. [Main would first play Ma Kettle two years after this film when appearing with MacMurray in **The Egg and I**, 1947.] The script was something out of *Alice in Wonderland,* and when I told George [Marshall] that most of it did not make any sense, he replied: 'It's not supposed to make any sense—that's what makes it appealing.'" **p**, E.D. Leshin; **d**, George Marshall; **cast**, Fred MacMurray, Helen Walker, Marjorie Main, Jean Heather, Porter Hall, Peter Whitney, Mabel Paige, Barbara Pepper, Harry Allen, Francis Ford, Arthur Hunnicutt, Milton Parsons; **w**, Lou Breslow (based on a story by Jack Moffitt); **c**, Theodor Sparkuhl; **m**, Robert Emmett Dolan; **ed**, LeRoy Stone; **art d**, Hans Dreier, William Flannery; **set d**, George Sawley; **spec eff**, Gordon Jennings, Paul Lerpae.

Murder, Inc. ★★★ 1960; U.S.; 103m; Princess Productions/FOX; B/W; Crime Drama; Children: Unacceptable; **DVD**. Falk is mesmerizing as a conscienceless killer-for-hire in this chilling and shocking film that chronicles the grisly exploits of the lethal gang from a section of Brooklyn, New York, called Brownsville. Called Murder, Inc., the gang operated from the late 1920s until it was exposed and dismantled in the early 1940s. The film opens when an assistant district attorney, Morgan, playing Burton B. Turkus (1902-1982), begins to probe a mob murder that leads him to arrest Falk, playing Abe "Kit Twist" Reles (1906-

1941), one of the worst hit men in the annals of crime. Falk is at first defiant and refuses to cooperate, but Morgan, after finding witnesses to corroborate testimony that will send him to the electric chair, convinces Falk to turn informer and he begins to narrate the gruesome history of Murder, Inc., the enforcement arm of the U.S. crime syndicate, recounting without remorse the many killings he and others performed as murder assignments ("contracts"), where the victims are called "marks" and the killings "hits." (Murder, Inc. killers reportedly committed 400 to 1,000 murders over a fifteen-year period, according to most reliable accounts.) The story not only depicts many gruesome killings where victims are murdered with guns, icepicks and even hatchets, but shows the rise of its most notorious leaders and crime syndicate board members, Albert Anastasia (1902-1957), played by Smith, and Louis "Lepke" Buchalter (1897-1944), played by Stewart. The story then concentrates on Whitman, a hanger-on with the gang, who is inveigled into crime by Falk. Falk forces Whitman and his alluring blonde wife, Britt, to allow Stewart to stay in their home while he is on the run from police, The couple must wait on Stewart as servants while Stewart continues to supervise his underworld operations, sending his closest henchman and enforcer, Bernard, who plays Emanuel "Mendy" Weiss (1906-1944) to commit more murders, especially contracts on those who might testify against Stewart in any future trials. Meanwhile, Falk also commits more murders and then rapes Britt, causing her to turn state's evidence and, after she is murdered by hit men, Whitman begins testifying against Falk. The shabby house of cards that was Murder, Inc. then begins to collapse, and Stewart and Bernard are caught and imprisoned (both Buchalter and Weiss were electrocuted in Sing Sing's electric chair in 1944). Falk does not survive. Kept in hiding in a hotel at Coney Island, he either jumps or is pushed from the window of his room, falling six floors to his death. (Reles' death caused endless controversy in that he was being guarded by six New York City police officers at the time, all of whom were conveniently out of the room when Reles went out of the window at the Half Moon Hotel on November 12, 1941.) This well-crafted film realistically portrays Murder, Inc. through riveting portraits from Falk, Stewart, Bernard, and Smith; Morgan and Oakland, his chief inspector probing the endless murders, are standouts. Another film, **The Enforcer**, 1951, starring Humphrey Bogart as the probing D.A. also dynamically explores the eerie and lethal workings of Murder, Inc. Buchalter was profiled in another film, **Lepke**, 1975, with Tony Curtis playing the gangster, but this proved to be a disappointing and unreliable biopic. *Author's Note*: Falk told this author that "my role as Reles was not one of my favorite characters. The man was a killer robot with no conscience, a savage from the worst jungle in New York. I hated that character but I understood him, his kind of mentality. I have a scene with Stu [Whitman] where I hold out my hands and say: 'What do you think these are for? To take—take! That's all!' Those lines summed up that character, a real monster. I knew guys like that when I was growing up in New York. They'd just as soon kick an old lady in the face for laughs as they would take their next breath. Creeps, the worst scum in the world, better off dead than alive. They had no home life, no decent parents, never went to church or synagogue and a lot of those killers were Jewish, who happily killed people along with their Irish and German and Polish pals. I'm not giving them any excuses. They grew up like wild animals in the streets of New York and they just didn't give a damn about human life, including their own. Abe Reles was probably the worst of the whole damned, stinking lot." For more information on Anastasia, Buchalter, Murder, Inc., and Reles, see my books: *Bloodletters and Badmen* (M. Evans, 1995; Anastasia: pages 28-30; Buchalter: pages 105-110; Murder, Inc.: 450-454); *The World Encyclopedia of Organized Crime* (Paragon House, 1992; Anastasia: pages 27-31; Buchalter: pages 69-73; Murder, Inc.: pages 295-300; Reles: pages 331-332); and *The Great Pictorial History of World Crime* (History, Inc., 2004; Anastasia, Murder, Inc., and Reles: pages 583-590; Buchalter: pages 563-569). **p**, Burt Balaban, Laurence Joachim; **d**, Balaban, Stuart Rosenberg; **cast**, Stuart Whitman, May Britt, Henry Morgan, Peter Falk, David J, Stewart,

Virginia Bruce and Spencer Tracy in *The Murder Man*, 1935.

Simon Oakland, Joseph Bernard, Sarah Vaughan, Morey Amsterdam, Vincent Gardenia, Howard I. Smith, Sylvia Miles, Joseph Campanella, Seymour Cassel, Diane Ladd; **w**, Irve Tunick, Mel Barr (based on the book by Burton Turkus, Sid Feder); **c**, Gayne Rescher; **m**, Frank De Vol; **ed**, Ralph Rosenblum; **art d**, Richard Sylbert.

Murder Is My Beat ★★★ 1955; U.S.; 77m; Allied Artists; B/W; Mystery; Children: Unacceptable; **VHS**. A head is found in a fireplace that is so badly burned that its owner cannot be identified. Policemen Langton and Shayne arrest Payton, a nightclub singer, on suspicion of murder. She insists she is innocent, but is convicted of the crime. While on a train being taken to prison by Langton, she sees a woman in a hotel window that she says is the real killer. Langton believes her and they get off the train to find the woman. They locate Roberts, Payton's former roommate, living in a hotel under an assumed name. Payton disappears and Shayne wants to arrest Langton for letting Payton escape, but agrees to give Langton twenty-four hours to find Payton and solve the murder. In his hurried probe, Langton discovers that Payton has been blackmailed and set up as the killer. Roberts is finally arrested as the culprit and Payton and Langton wind up together for a happy ending to a quirky but fascinating film noir mystery. Excessive violence prohibits viewing by children. *Author's Note*: This was the last feature film in which Payton starred (her last appearance was as an extra in an inferior Frank Sinatra opus, **4 For Texas**, 1963). Following this film, Payton's career collapsed and her personal life became a shambles after she was arrested for passing bad checks, drunkenness and, eventually, prostitution. She died, mostly and sadly forgotten, of a heart attack and liver failure in 1967 at the age of thirty-nine. **p**, Aubrey Wisberg, Ilse Lahn; **d**, Edgar G. Ulmer; **cast**, Paul Langton, Barbara Payton, Robert Shayne, Selena Royle, Roy Gordon, Tracy Roberts, Kate McKenna, Henry W. Harvey, Sr., Jay Adler, Madge Cleveland; **w**, Wisberg (based on a story by Wisberg, Martin Field); **c**, Harold E. Wellman; **m**, Al Glasser; **ed**, Fred H. Feitshans, Jr.; **prod d**, James Sullivan; **set d**, Harry H. Reif.

The Murder Man ★★★ 1935; U.S.; 69m; MGM; B/W; Crime Drama; Children: Unacceptable; **VHS**. This compelling crime yarn sees Tracy as an unpredictable and cunning investigative reporter, who routinely solves murders in order to write about them for his newspaper, scooping all of his competitors. Gossip columnist Bruce has been in love with Tracy for years, subtly attempting to reform his unruly ways, but he is only interested in tracking down culprits, his feats earning him the grudging admiration of his fellow scribes, and the reluctant respect of his editor, who calls him a "crazy, cynical, drunken bum." The unkempt Tracy is all of those things, sleeping in elevators and capriciously riding on a merry-go-round in the middle of the night. Tracy's slaphappy life

Margaret Rutherford and Stringer Davis in *Murder Most Foul*, 1964.

is suddenly disrupted when Stephens, a corrupt financier, ruins Tracy's father, Collier, and brings about the suicide of Tracy's estranged wife. Tracy takes vengeance on Stephens by setting up what he believes to be the perfect crime. He kills Stephens' partner, Eltz, who was equally responsible for Collier's ruination, and pins the murder on Stephens, who is tried for that murder and is convicted and sentenced to death. Cub reporter Stewart, who looks up to Tracy as his journalistic beau ideal, tells Tracy that the editor of their paper wants him to go to Sing Sing's Death House and interview Stephens before he is executed in the prison's electric chair. Tracy visits Stephens, but is unable to keep his own secret of having engineered Stephens' fate, and gloats about how he triumphantly took vengeance upon the crook for ruining his father. Tracy's conscience, however, will not allow the innocent Stephens go to his death and he confesses his guilt to officials, knowing the punishment that awaits him, but not before meeting his last journalistic obligation. Tracy calls his editor and tells him that he has the greatest story he will ever print in his newspaper and that is where this suspenseful and well-delivered film ends. Tracy is outstanding as the outlandish but honest reporter whose sense of decency dictates the course of his rough-and-tumble life while all the fine cast members, including Stewart, who makes his film debut here, give strong support. This film was poorly remade by MGM a year later as a B-programmer entitled **The Perfect Set-Up**, 1936. *Author's Note*: This was Tracy's second film for MGM, his first film for this studio being a programmer, **The Show-Off**, 1934, while Tracy was on loan from Fox, and, after MGM production chief, Irving Thalberg, saw Tracy in that film, he signed him to a seven-year contract, one that would be extended many times until Tracy remained for more than twenty years at that studio. He was first assigned to appear in **Riff-Raff**, 1936, with Jean Harlow, but when Harlow's schedule was disrupted by her personal problems, that film was postponed and Tracy was put into **The Murder Man**. "They bounced me around a lot back then," Tracy told this author, "but I did not complain. I had good, steady work at MGM and I was ready to chew on any bone they threw my way. Jimmy Stewart appeared for the first time in pictures in **The Murder Man**. He was a gangling guy, stood about six-foot-three or more and had the face of a choir boy. He was pretty anxious to make good, but he was nervous about the camera. I took him aside and told him to focus on other players, furniture, his feet, anything but that camera, and that calmed him down and he did fine." Stewart almost did not get the part, as the producer, Rapf, wanted a dwarf to play his character, who is called "Shorty" in the film, but Rapf was persuaded by others to put the tall Stewart in the role with that name as a sight gag and Rapf finally went along with the idea, giving Stewart the part. Stewart told this author that he and Tracy became friends during the production of this film, a friendship that lasted a lifetime, saying: "Spence [Tracy] was just like the char-

acter he was playing, a grinning, jaw-jutting, brawny guy with incredibly quick moves, at least in those days, one of those guys who could charm a snake in and out of a basket. This was my first film and Spence knew I was nervous before I went in front of the cameras. He said to me: 'Look, kid, just pretend the camera isn't there and you'll do fine. Don't worry about stumbling about a little or appearing to be awkward. That's your nature. Just speak your lines clearly and put some guts behind them for the tense scenes.' That's what I did and everything worked okay. It was the best advice I could have gotten and I kept that in mind every time I did another picture. I think that Spence was so convincing in every role he played because he wasn't intimidated by anything or anybody. He was fearless and his strength was that he believed that acting was not as important as living his own private life, which he guarded like a lion. Nobody ever got into his den, except maybe Kate [Hepburn]. When Spence and I did **Malaya** [1950] together almost fifteen years later, I found that he had not changed a bit. He was like the Rock of Gibraltar." Stewart's appearance in **The Murder Man** also impressed Thalberg, who signed him up under a seven-year contract. The character Tracy plays in **The Murder Man**, one of a newspaperman who uses his knowledge about murder to commit one, was based upon Jake Lingle (1891-1930), a crime reporter for the Chicago *Tribune*, who had high contacts with the CPD. In the late 1920s, Lingle, instead of honestly reporting on the crime activities in Chicago, chiefly myriad bootlegging operations during Prohibition, began selling his inside police information (as to when police might raid a speakeasy, gambling den or brothel) to the top crime boss of that day, Al Capone (1899-1947), growing rich from Capone's payoffs. Tracy told this author that "the writers for **The Murder Man** took my character from a newspaperman in Chicago, who fed information to Scarface Capone, and got inside stories on the underworld because of his police contacts and those he had with Scarface. When he switched sides and went with another crime boss, Scarface had him killed, and that was only a few years before we made **The Murder Man**. They bumped off a lot more guys in Chicago in those days than we ever did in Hollywood pictures." Lingle, indeed, after working secretly for Capone for some years, decided to switch allegiances and became secretly employed by North Side Chicago underworld boss George "Bugs" Moran (1891-1957), an avowed enemy of Capone's, while Lingle was still employed by the *Tribune*, feeding Moran the same inside information that he had previously given to Capone. When Capone learned of this treason, he ordered Lingle murdered and the reporter was killed by Leo Vincent Brothers (1899-1950), a St. Louis killer-for-hire, who was imported to Chicago by Capone to perform the murder. Brothers, dressed as a priest, boldly shot and killed Lingle on June 9, 1930, in the underpass of the Illinois Central Railroad terminal in Chicago as Lingle was en route to a racetrack (he was an inveterate gambler who spent most of his money on the horses). Brothers was convicted of this murder and given a fourteen-year prison sentence, but was released in 1940, dying peacefully in bed of heart disease ten years later in St. Louis. Lingle would be the role model for the character portrayed by Martin Balsam in **Al Capone**, 1959. For more information on Capone, Lingle and Brothers see my two-volume work, *The Great Pictorial History of World Crime*, Volume I (History, Inc., 2004; under Capone; pages 503-541). **p**, Harry Rapf; **d**, Tim Whelan; **cast**, Spencer Tracy, Virginia Bruce, Lionel Atwill, Harvey Stephens, Robert Barrat, James Stewart, William Collier Sr., William Demarest, Theodore von Eltz, John Sheehan, Robert Warwick, Lucien Littlefield, Bobby Watson, George Chandler, Fuzzy Knight, Ralph Bushman Jr., Louise Henry, Heinie Conklin, Joe Irving, Ed Coppo; **w**, Whelan, John C. Higgins (based on a story by Whelan, Guy Bolton); **c**, Lester White; **m**, William Axt; **ed**, James E. Newcom; **art d**, Cedric Gibbons; **set d**, Edwin B. Willis.

Murder Most Foul ★★★ 1964; U.K., 90m; MGM; B/W; Mystery; Children: Unacceptable; **DVD**; **VHS**. This breezy and delightful whodunit sees the wonderful Rutherford again as Miss Marple, snooping and sniffing after a killer. She is a member of a jury that must decide the guilt of the defendant charged with murder and, believing much is amiss in the prosecution's case, is the lone hold-out, relentlessly voting "not guilty," which results in a mistrial. She then decides to conduct her own investigation, along with Davis (Rutherford's real-life husband), and the probe begins at the site of the murder. Rutherford fails to enlist the aid of police inspector Tingwell, who is convinced that the accused is guilty. In her probe, Rutherford assumes the role of an actress, joining an acting group headed by Moody, who is more than eager to have her as a member of his troupe, despite her lack of stage experience, after she makes him believe she has considerable funds at her disposal that might be used to fund Moody's theatrical productions. While Rutherford works the boards, two members of the theatrical group are killed and she is now sure that she is on the right track. At considerable personal risk, Rutherford learns that one of the actors in her group has been black-mailed to keep a dark secret from the world, that his mother was executed long ago after murdering her husband. Rutherford confronts the actor, proving that he has committed all the murders, dispatching those who came upon his family's dark past, and neatly wraps up the case for inspector Tingwell, bringing about the exoneration of the imprisoned defendant. Rutherford and the gifted Moody (who so masterfully played Fagin in **Oliver!**, 1968) give exceptionally good and humorous performances while director Pollock, who helmed the four films starring Rutherford as Miss Marple (**Murder She Said**, 1961; **Murder at the Gallop**, 1963; **Murder Ahoy**, 1964; and this entry), moves the film along at a brisk pace, sustaining suspense throughout, and Goodwin's eerie score adds much to its spine-tingling scenes. **p**, Ben Arbeid, Lawrence P. Bachmann (not credited); **d**, George Pollock; **cast**, Margaret Rutherford, Ron Moody, Charles Tingwell, Andrew Cruickshank, Megs Jenkins, Dennis Price, Ralph Michael, James Bolam, Stringer Davis, Francesca Annis, Alison Seebohm, Terry Scott; **w**, David Pursall, Jack Seddon (based on the novel *Mrs. McCinty's Dead* by Agatha Christie); **c**, Desmond Dickinson; **m**, Ron Goodwin; **ed**, Ernest Walter; **art d**, Frank White.

Murder, My Sweet ★★★★★ 1944; U.S.; 95m; RKO; B/W; Mystery; Children: Unacceptable; **DVD**; **VHS**. Powell was pretty much washed up in Hollywood as a crooner no one wanted anymore, but he made a tremendous comeback in this film, proving he was a forceful, serious actor when giving one of the most riveting performances of his life as the tough, principled private eye Philip Marlowe in this film noir masterpiece. Powell is first seen with bandages over his eyes as he sits beneath a single glaring light in a police interrogation room and where detectives grill him about a string of spectacular murders. Powell then tells his story and the tale unfolds in flashback when we first see Powell in his office, located in a shabby part of town (as the dilapidated appearance of his office furniture easily signifies) and where a neon sign flickers outside his second-story window to send grim shadows into his room. Powell suddenly sees as a reflection of that window a towering giant of a man, Mazurki, a brutal thug who has just been released from prison. Mazurki throws some cash onto Powell's desk and then asks him to locate his old girlfriend, a one-time singer named Velma. Powell pockets the advance and goes with Mazurki to a cheap dive in one of the worst areas of Los Angeles, a place where Mazurki's former girlfriend once sang. Powell fails to find out anything about the girl, only that she is long gone, and this provokes Mazurki into a rage. He not only smashes up the place, but hurls its owner, the heavyset Robinson, about like a rag doll before he and Powell depart. When parting from Powell, Mazurki thrusts more cash into the gumshoe's hand and orders him to keep looking for Velma. Powell then locates Howard, who is the widow of the owner of the bar he has visited. Powell, who narrates his sojourn into this labyrinthine crime case, describes Howard as "a charming middle-aged lady with a face like a bucket of mud." The old harridan is a dipsomaniac and, to get information from her, Powell pours her some drinks. He asks her about Velma, the former singer at her husband's

Douglas Walton and Dick Powell in *Murder, My Sweet*, 1944.

dive, and Howard staggers to her feet, saying: "Hold on to your chair and don't step on no snakes," before going into the next room to check her files. He follows her into the room, finding her rummaging through records and finding a photo of a woman and then hiding it. Powell seizes the photo and asks Howard why she tried to hide the photo and she tells him to "beat it," before collapsing in a stupor. When Powell returns to his office building, the elevator operator tells him that a visitor is waiting for him, an effeminate man who "smells nice," and Powell finds well-dressed Walton in his office. (Almost the same scene can be found in another classic film noir entry when the same kind of effeminate visitor, who smells of perfume, is shown into Sam Spade's office in the opening scenes of **The Maltese Falcon**, 1941.) After some jockeying conversation, Powell learns that Walton must meet some men that night on a lonely remote dead-end road and pay them considerable cash in exchange for some stolen gems and he offers Powell $100 to accompany him, a great deal of money for Powell in that he usually gets $25 a day plus expenses for his sleuthing. He accepts and that night he drives with Walton to that murky rendezvous. No one is waiting for them. Powell tells Walton to remain in the car while he carries his gun in one hand and holds a searching flashlight in another as he explores the area. Finding no one, he returns to the car, but is then hit on the head, stating: "I caught the blackjack right behind my ear. A black pool opened up at my feet. I dived in. It had no bottom. I felt pretty good—like an amputated leg." When he regains consciousness, Powell hears a woman's voice asking him if he is all right, but when he looks about, the woman is gone. He then finds Walton dead in the back seat of the car. Powell must now undergo a grilling from Douglas, a police lieutenant, who does not like him and who all but accuses Powell of killing Walton, even though Powell points out to Douglas that it was he who called the police and reported Douglas' slaying. Douglas tells him that "you're not a detective. You're a slot machine. You'd slit your own throat for six bits, plus tax." Douglas then orders Powell to go home and stay out of trouble and to stay away from Walton's associates, including Kruger, Powell hearing this man's name for the first time. Powell returns to his office and this time Shirley is waiting for him, telling him that she is a reporter doing a story on the Walton killing. He does not believe her and, after he rummages through her purse, he quickly discovers that she is not who she says she is. Shirley confesses that she is the daughter of Mander, who owns a priceless jade necklace that was stolen, and it was Walton who tried to buy that rare gem back from the thieves. At Powell's insistence, Shirley drives him to her father's vast estate and they enter a huge mansion where Powell meets Mander and his alluring blonde wife, Trevor. Mander tells Powell that the necklace stolen from him was worth $125,000. When Mander retires, Trevor remains to tell Powell that the necklace was stolen after she attended a social affair, the robbers acting

Anne Shirley and Dick Powell in *Murder, My Sweet*, 1944.

strangely in that they took the necklace she was wearing, but returned one of her rings and that she had given Walton $8,000 to buy back the necklace, but that money, Powell knew, was missing after he discovered Walton dead at the dead-end rendezvous. When Trevor, who is sitting close to Powell on a couch, begins flirting with him, Shirley angrily leaves the room. Trevor then hires Powell to locate the missing jade necklace. Kruger than appears and Powell tells him that he was warned by police not to associate with him, and when Kruger asks what he is doing at Mander's palatial estate, Powell flippantly replies: "I was hired as a bodyguard and I bungled the job and now I am investigating myself." Before going home, Powell tells Kruger that he will later contact him so they can discuss the missing necklace. After arriving home, Powell is shaving in his undershirt when Trevor unexpectedly arrives, telling he has "a nice build for a detective." He replies: "It gets me around." Trevor then pays Powell a retainer of $500 to find her missing necklace and he later takes her to a nightclub. When Trevor goes to the lady's room, Shirley, who has been following the pair, takes Powell aside and offers him $1,000, twice what Trevor has paid him, but on the condition that he has nothing to do with her stepmother, Trevor. Powell says he will consider the offer, and when they part, he is met by the giant Mazurki, who strong-arms him into going with him to see Kruger at Kruger's posh penthouse dwelling. There Kruger grills him about what the police might have said about him, admitting that he is referred to as a "quack," explaining that such a derogatory appellative is unfair in that he is a "psychic physician." Powell then surprises him by telling him what he has learned about Walton, his associate, that Walton was part of a robbery gang, steering wealthy women like Trevor to parties and where, in dark parking lots, Walton's friends could rob them of their jewels. Powell then accuses Kruger of engineering the robbery of the jade necklace. Kruger tells him that he is an avid collector of jade, but does not have the necklace. Believing that Powell has the necklace, he offers to buy it. Powell tells him that he wants nothing to do with Kruger and then Kruger summons goon Mazurki to tell him that Powell knows where his old girlfriend, Velma, is, but will not tell him. Mazurki goes berserk and, during a struggle, Powell is sapped unconscious and then wakes up in a shabby room, groggy, his mind clouded and where he realizes that he has been injected with some sort of mind-bending drug. He tries to clear the fuzzy image of the room, one that appears to be shrouded with smoke, saying: "The window was open but the smoke didn't move. It was a gray web woven by a thousand spiders. I wonder how they got them to work together." After he screams in horror at his situation, a heavyset male guard arrives and then leaves. Later, Powell is able to summon enough strength to sit upright on the bed, saying to himself: "Okay, Marlowe, you're a tough guy. You've been sapped twice, choked, beaten silly by a gun, and shot in the arm [by drugs] until

you're as crazy as a couple of waltzing mice. Now let's see you do something really tough, like putting your pants on!" He forces himself to walk about the room until his head clears and then removes an iron spring from the bed, hides behind the door and screams again. When the guard appears, Powell knocks him unconscious with the iron spring, taking the guard's gun and going downstairs of the ramshackle sanitarium to find Harolde, the physician in charge. He holds the doctor at gunpoint as he tears out the connection of the doctor's phone and then leaves the place, going to a nearby waiting cab. The cabdriver tells him that he is waiting for a fare. He then runs into the dimwitted Mazurki, promising him that he will find his girlfriend, and Mazurki convinces the cabdriver to take Powell home by crushing the cab's meter. Instead, Powell goes to the only friend he has, Shirley, who nurses him. Police lieutenant Douglas then arrives and Powell tells him that Kruger is behind the murders and offers to help Douglas solve the case and Douglas agrees. Powell then meets with Mander, who tells him that he believes his life is in danger. Powell then goes to Mander's lavish beach house with Shirley and they find Trevor there. Shirley leaves and Trevor passionately kisses Powell, telling him that Kruger helped her overcome some psychological problems and then began blackmailing her after discovering some of her affairs in her dark past, threatening to expose her transgressions to her wealthy, elderly husband, Mander. She says that she thought to give Kruger the jade necklace to finally buy him off, but that the necklace was stolen before she could give it to Kruger. She offers Powell a lot of money to kill Kruger, and Powell goes along with the scheme, later going to Kruger's penthouse where he finds Kruger dead. Mazurki, Kruger's killer, then appears, but Powell puts him off, saying he is going to take him to see his old flame, Velma, the next night. On that night, Powell and Mazurki stand outside Mander's beach house and Powell tells Mazurki to come from the beach and into the house when he sees a light in the window. Powell then enters the beach house to find Trevor, who hands him the jade necklace, telling him to use it to entice Kruger before killing him, admitting that the necklace was never stolen and that she held on to it to use if she needed to pay off Kruger later. Powell does not tell Trevor that Kruger is dead. Powell then tells Trevor that he has known all along that she is the missing Velma, and that she has committed many crimes in the past. She holds a gun on him, intending to kill him when Mander appears, also holding a gun, and who shoots Trevor dead for her past indiscretions. Shirley then arrives as does Mazurki. When Mazurki sees Trevor dead and realizing that Mander has killed her, he lunges for Mander. Powell, in an attempt to stop him, leaps forward as Mander fires at Mazurki and the flash from the gun blinds Powell. Mazurki, having been shot three times, falls dead. Powell collapses from the injury to his eyes and is later shown in flash forward as he concludes his tale to the police detectives. Douglas then orders Powell released and taken home by Phillips, a detective who is named Nulty. When Phillips guides the blinded Powell toward a nearby cab on the street, Shirley appears and waves Phillips away, helping Powell into the cab and then sits next to him as the cab drives away. Inside the cab, Powell smells Shirley's perfume, and, after some casual conversation, suddenly says: "Nulty…I haven't kissed anybody in a long time. Would it be all right if I kissed you, Nulty?" With that, Powell and Shirley clinch for the fadeout to this great thriller. Director Dmytryk helms this fascinating whodunit with great skill, exacting a terrific performance from Powell and an equally stunning performance from Trevor as the insidious, scheming and backstabbing siren. Other than the mansion and beach house, all of the sets are suitably seedy and realistic in residing in the tawdry netherworld occupied by Powell, and its supporting players are convincing as the conniving and wholly untrustworthy characters they enact. The production values are high and the visual techniques Dmytryk employs—the dimly lit streets, the seedy interiors of bars and dwellings and the bughouse scene in the sanitarium filled with overlaying images of cobwebs and spider nets—all provide great atmosphere and ambience to this film noir classic. This film was remade with Robert Mitchum playing Philip Marlowe and using the original title employed in Chandler's novel as **Farewell, My Lovely**, 1975. *Author's Note*: This was the first significant film directed by the gifted Dmytryk, who proved with this great crime tale that he was a first-class director (he had been helming B-programmers since 1935). Dmytryk was taken aback when RKO's chief, Charles Koerner, came to him with the script, telling him that he wanted to make a first-class production out of the Raymond Chandler story, even though segments of that tale had been used in **The Falcon Takes Over**, 1942, an RKO B-programmer. "What really amazed me," Dmytryk told this author "was that Koerner wanted to star Dick Powell in the picture as the tough gumshoe, Philip Marlowe. I told him that I could not envision Powell playing such a role since he was known worldwide as a crooner singing songs like "By a Waterfall" and ditties like that. Koerner told me that Powell was washed up as a singer in the movies and was desperately trying to get serious dramatic roles and that he went to Paramount and begged for the part of the insurance man turned killer in **Double Indemnity** [1944], but was turned down and the part went to Fred MacMurray. Koerner pointed out that, if Mac-Murray, who appeared in mostly light comedies, could play such a sinister character, Powell could do the same thing and he really pushed hard for Powell, and since Koerner was allowing me an "A-budget" for the film [more than $400,000] and giving me a shot at a major movie, I agreed to take on Powell." Koerner's motives in this case were spurred by the fact that he originally wanted Powell to sign up to do a series of musicals at RKO, but Powell told him that unless he got the part in **Murder, My Sweet**, there would be no deal. Powell got the part, but he was so impressive in his role that he mostly appeared in films related to the crime genre thereafter in such hard-hitting productions as **Cornered**, 1945, also directed by Dmytryk; **Johnny O'Clock**, 1947; **To the Ends of the Earth**, 1948; and **Pitfall**, 1948. "Dick was great to work with, never complaining about a thing and was ready to do any retake I wanted," Dmytryk told this author. "While we were making **Murder, My Sweet**, I saw this charming, casual singer change into a hard-knuckled character, who would tackle anything. It was an amazing transformation. But maybe that was the real Dick Powell coming out of that lighthearted image they had created for him in the 1930s." The towering Mazurki, who plays Moose Malloy in the film, told the author that "Eddie [Dmytryk] wanted me to appear much taller than Dick in our scenes together, even though Dick was pretty tall himself, only a few inches shorter than me [Powell stood 6'2" and Mazurki a little more than 6'4"]. Eddie had Dick walk in the gutter when we stroll down streets together, and when I try to strangle him, Eddie had Dick standing in only his stocking feet while I was standing on a box choking him. Dick didn't put up a beef about any of that. He was the most cooperative guy in the world to work with." (Such practices were not uncommon in a director's efforts to maximize an actor's height or, conversely, to minimize the height of an otherwise towering actress, such as where Sophia Loren, who stands more than 5'8" had to walk in a trench along a beach or stand in a hole in a floor or on a street when doing scenes with Alan Ladd, who stood 5'6" when they appeared in scenes together in **Boy on a Dolphin**, 1957.) Dmytryk used many innovative devices to emphasize menace in the film, such as using a plate glass instead of normal glass to more clearly reflect and define Mazurki's repulsive and threatening image when Mazurki first comes into Powell's office as a neon light goes on and off outside of Powell's office window. He uses the same plate glass device when Powell lunges for the gun that goes off and blinds him to show that brilliant flash of light from the gunfire. In the drug scenes inside the dilapidated sanitarium, Dmytryk presents a hallucinatory montage of images seen by the drugged Powell, consisting of strange faces, swirling odd objects, hallways that grow smaller in their extensions so that they become confining spaces that restrict Powell's movements and prevent his escape. He then shows Powell in a free fall, Powell going downward into inky blackness. Here Dmytryk shot Powell falling and then reshot the scene with the camera quickly retreating from the action to accelerate Powell's descent (here Dmytryk borrows a technique employed two years earlier by Alfred Hitchcock in his

Claire Trevor and Dick Powell in *Murder, My Sweet*, 1944.

Saboteur, 1942, where secret agent Norman Lloyd falls from the arm of the Statue of Liberty, but Hitchcock may have been influenced by Dmytryk's montage scene when later making **Spellbound**, 1945, where Hitchcock presents a similar nightmare sequence.) Trevor felt that this film, more than any other, as she told this author, "established my reputation as a femme fatale. At least that was an improvement from my being typecast as a tramp in pictures and that started with **Dead End** [1938] where I play an old girlfriend of Humphrey Bogart's—he became a gangster and I became a lowly streetwalker—but in **Murder, My Sweet** I have come up in the world, marrying an old coot with millions and using his money to have anyone killed who knows about my terrible past when I was—guess what—just another fallen woman. I rode the crest of playing crummy gals for years. Any time a producer needed an actress to play the worst kind of woman, he would say, 'oh, get Claire for that role.' Well, it was a living, young man, and a better one than actually being one of those poor and unhappy shady ladies." That typecasting also brought Trevor an Oscar for Best Supporting Actress when she played another fallen woman as a gangster's gun moll in **Key Largo**, 1948. The original title for the novel upon which this superlative film is based was *Farewell, My Lovely*, but the producers thought that title might be misleading, suggesting that the story involved another musical, particularly with Dick Powell starring in it. The title was changed to **Murder, My Sweet**, so that it would be unmistakably identified as a crime tale, and what a crime tale it is. The acerbic and always truculent Chandler, who had a love-hate relationship with Hollywood as a screenwriter and whose novels and stories were adapted for films, thought that **Murder, My Sweet** was the best film adaptation of any of his works because it was so faithfully transcribed from his original text to the screen (and, upon its release, Chandler wrote a thank-you note to its screenwriter, Paxton, praising him for keeping his story so tightly intact). Chandler received no payment for the rights to his novel at the time of production for **Murder, My Sweet**, as he had sold those rights some years earlier. He was nevertheless proud of the fact that the two film noir classics that most established the genre as enormously popular fare with audiences, **Double Indemnity**, 1944, and **Murder, My Sweet**, released in the same year, were "A-budget" productions and that he was associated with both of them, having written the screenplay for the former and that his novel was the source for the latter. (**Murder, My Sweet** was an enormous success at the box office, returning more than four times its budget of $400,000 upon its original release.) In 1948, Chandler wrote to a friend: "**The Maltese Falcon** [1941] did not start the high budget mystery picture trend, although it ought to have. **Double Indemnity** and **Murder, My Sweet** did, and I was associated with both of them. The result is that everybody who used to be accused of writing like [Dashiell] Hammett [author of *The Maltese Falcon*], may now be

A carload of suspects in *Murder on the Orient Express*, 1974.

accused of writing like Chandler." Hammett, of course, was Chandler's chief competitor in the field of crime fiction, their separate detective protagonists, Sam Spade and Philip Marlowe, battling for readers over the decades. Chandler respected Hammett (both were dedicated heavy drinkers and darkly brooding writers), but always felt that Hammett stole most of the literary limelight whenever their unforgettable and highly principled sleuths stepped from their murky shadows to do battle with the evils of the world. Both Hammett and Chandler were great stylists, and where their inventive phraseology stunningly captivates the reader in their haunting dark tales. The uncompromising and principled Sam Spade is a private eye full of wisdom and as enigmatic as a ghost, gaining ground every day. The compromising Philip Marlowe is packed with sarcastic but endearing wit, a flesh and blood shamus losing ground every day, but never his principles. The difference between them is 380 miles, as Sam operates in San Francisco, and Philip in Los Angeles. **p,** Adrian Scott; **d,** Edward Dmytryk; **cast,** Dick Powell, Claire Trevor, Anne Shirley, Otto Kruger, Mike Mazurki, Miles Mander, Douglas Walton, Don Douglas, Ralf Harolde, Esther Howard, Paul Phillips, John Indrisano, Jack Carr, Shimen Ruskin, Dewey Robinson, Ernie Adams, Larry Wheat, Sam Finn; **w,** John Paxton (based on the novel *Farewell, My Lovely* by Raymond Chandler); **c,** Harry J. Wild; **m,** Roy Webb; **ed,** Joseph Noriega; **art d,** Albert S. D'Agostino, Carroll Clark; **set d,** Darrell Silvera, Michael Ohrenbach; **spec eff,** Vernon L. Walker.

Murder on a Honeymoon ★★★ 1935; U.S.; 74m; RKO; B/W; Mystery/Comedy; Children: Unacceptable. Oliver is a school teacher and an amateur sleuth and Gleason a police detective in an amusing mystery, part of a series. While on vacation on Catalina Island, California, Gleason inadvertently becomes involved in a murder investigation. Oliver then pitches in, proving to Gleason that she is as good a sleuth as he is as they banter and battle their way to solving the crime and snaring the culprit. The sharp script was penned by literary wit Benchley, guaranteeing a lot of humorous scenes along the path that leads to the scene of the crime and beyond. This is one of the better entries in a series begun with Oliver and later carried on by Helen Broderick. **p,** Kenneth Macgowan; **d,** Lloyd Corrigan; **cast,** Edna May Oliver, James Gleason, Lola Lane, George Meeker, Dorothy Libaire, Harry Ellerbe, Chick Chandler, Willie Best, Leo G. Carroll, Spencer Charters, Lynne Carver; **w,** Seton I. Miller, Robert Benchley (based on the novel *The Puzzle of the Pepper Tree* by Stuart Palmer); **c,** Nick Musuraca; **m,** Alberto Colombo; **ed,** William Morgan; **art d,** Van Nest Polglase, Perry Ferguson; **spec eff,** Vernon Walker.

Murder on Monday ★★★ 1953; U.K.; 85m; Maurice Cowan-British Lion/Arthur Mayer-Edward Kingsley; B/W; Crime Drama; Children:

Unacceptable; **VHS**. In this taut thriller, Richardson is a British bank official who goes missing for twenty-four hours and when he returns home to his wife, Leighton, he has no memory of where he's been or what he's done. He then learns that money from his sports club has been stolen and the steward who handled the money has been found murdered. To avoid becoming a suspect, Richardson gives police a phony alibi, which makes him a positive suspect. He manages to retrace his steps during the missing hours and proves he is innocent. His recurring amnesia was a result of shellshock Richardson suffered during World War I. Richardson, one of the great actors of the British cinema, is superlative in his role as a man groping for an elusive memory in this highly suspenseful psychological mystery. *Author's Note*: This was the only feature film helmed by Richardson and where his talents as an inventive director are evident as he provides a swift-moving tale that sustains tension and anxiety throughout. **p,** Maurice Cowan; **d,** Ralph Richardson; **cast,** Richardson, Margaret Leighton, Jack Hawkins, Campbell Singer, Michael Shepley, Margaret Withers, Frederick Piper, Meriel Forbes, Gerald Case, Diana Beaumont; **w,** Anatole de Grunwald (based on the play "Home at Seven" by R.C. Sherriff); **c,** Jack Hildyard, Edward Scaife; **m,** Malcolm Arnold; **ed,** Bert Bates; **art d,** Vincent Korda, Frederick Pusey.

Murder on the Campus ★★★ 1933; U.S.; 73m; Chesterfield/First Division; B/W; Mystery; Children: Unacceptable; **DVD**. Starrett is a newspaper reporter working on a story about students who work their way through college. He meets Grey, a college student working as a nightclub singer. One night while driving to her dormitory he accuses her of being in love with the college boy, who rings the chimes in the campus bell tower. After dropping her off at her dorm, he hears a gunshot coming from the tower. Police Captain MacDonald, who comes to the scene, finds him there and suspects him of murdering the college boy, who is the foremost athlete on the campus. Grey also becomes a suspect since she knew the victim. When two more students are murdered, Starrett investigates and learns that a professor, Van Sloan, is the killer. Thorpe, who specialized in mysteries and film noir tales, does a fine job of sustaining suspense throughout this fascinating whodunit. **p,** George R. Batcheller; **d,** Richard Thorpe; **cast,** Charles Starrett, Shirley Grey, J. Farrell MacDonald, Ruth Hall, Dewey Robinson, Maurice Black, Edward Van Sloan, Jane Keckley, Richard Catlett, Harry Bowen; **w,** Whitman Chambers, Andrew Moses (based on the novel *The Campanile Murders* by Chambers); **c,** M.A. Anderson; **m,** Abe Meyer; **art d,** Edward C. Jewell.

Murder on the Orient Express ★★★★ 1974; U.K.; 128m; EMI Film Distributors/PAR; Color; Mystery; Children: Unacceptable (MPAA: PG); **DVD**; **VHS**. A host of great film stars are passengers on the sleek Orient Express that carries them into hazard, mystery and murder in this outstanding whodunit and where Hercule Poirot (Finney), Agatha Christie's indomitable private detective, sorts them all out to find the culprit. The film begins when well-to-do passengers leave Istanbul for Paris in 1934 to board the luxury train, including financial tycoon Widmark, accompanied by his secretary, Perkins, who dislikes him. In fact, Widmark, a ruthless businessman, is hated by a number of persons traveling on that train as it roars its way toward Paris. He has received death threats and when he discovers that the great detective, Finney, is on board the train, he attempts to hire him to investigate, if not serve as his bodyguard, but Finney politely declines, stating that he is on holiday. That night, Widmark is killed in his stateroom and Balsam, one of the executives for the railway, persuades his old friend Finney to investigate. Finney discovers that Widmark has been stabbed repeatedly, in fact a dozen times, pointing to the fact that his killer was so much enraged at the victim that he continued to attack him long after he was dead. After the train is stopped by a huge avalanche of snow and is stalled, Finney conducts a meticulous investigation, diligently interviewing other passengers occupying staterooms in the car in which Widmark was murdered, including Bergman, Connery, Bacall, Redgrave, York, Bisset, Hiller, Gielgud, and Perkins. Finney elaborately recreates the murder, demonstrating for everyone—and all are suspects—exactly how Widmark was killed and then goes on to describe who it was that killed him in a surprise conclusion. Although there is little character development, given the extensive of array of characters profiled, all of the players nevertheless give convincing performances, particularly the exacting Finney, but whose Belgian accent is so thick that it could support an elephant. Of all the stellar stars shining in this extravaganza of rich talent, Bergman's part of a forlorn and abandoned woman won for her a third Oscar as Best Supporting Actress (her first two being Oscars as Best Actress in **Gaslight**, 1944, and **Anastasia**, 1956). Lumet directs with great skill, managing to keep all the players in order and balancing them well with the scenes where Finney is probing their varied, dark backgrounds. The film was shot on location in Turkey, France and England. *Author's Note*: Bergman told this author that "I was amazed when I first saw the number of great talents assembled for that picture. It seemed as if half of Hollywood had joined the cast and what fun we all had in doing that classic mystery." Widmark jocularly told this author that "I am bumped off early in that picture and should be as I am the worst guy in the world. My character is the richest guy in the world, but has spent more time ruining people than making money. Good riddance to bad rubbish as they say." Agatha Christie had long refused to allow this story filmed, but she finally relented. The film, as depicted in the novel, begins with a prologue that shows a montage of a kidnapping that Christie certainly based upon the tragic kidnapping of the Lindbergh baby (son of famed aviator Charles Lindbergh) from his New Jersey home in 1932, two years before Christie published her novel. **p**, John Brabourne, Richard Goodwin; **d**, Sidney Lumet; **cast**, Albert Finney, Lauren Bacall, Martin Balsam, Ingrid Bergman, Jacqueline Bisset, Jean-Pierre Cassel, Sean Connery, John Gielgud, Wendy Hiller, Anthony Perkins, Vanessa Redgrave, Rachel Roberts, Richard Widmark, Michael York; **w**, Paul Dehn (based on the novel by Agatha Christie); **c**, Geoffrey Unsworth (Panavision; Technicolor); **m**, Richard Rodney Bennett; **ed**, Anne V. Coates; **prod d**, Tony Walton; **art d**, Jack Stephens; **spec eff**, Charles Staffell.

Murder She Said ★★★ 1961; U.K.; 87m; MGM; B/W; Mystery: Children: Unacceptable; **DVD**; **VHS**. In this first of the Miss Marple mysteries starring the wonderful Rutherford, the jolly, jowly lady is reading a mystery book while riding on a train, but her enjoyment is suddenly halted when she glances out of the window of that train to see a murder. Rutherford sees the window shade of a passing train suddenly flap upward to momentarily show a man strangling a woman in a compartment on that train. After she informs the railway police and inspector Tingwell (who will be Rutherford's reluctant ally in three more sequels), she is told by these knowing sleuths that no report of any murder has taken place and that they believe Rutherford imagined the gruesome image, particularly since she had been reading a murder mystery when *she thought* she glimpsed the awful killing. Miffed at being so summarily dismissed as an old bitty with rattling faculties, Rutherford is now determined to get to the bottom of that haunting vision. She deduces that the body must have been disposed of somewhere in the neighborhood of a vast estate which her train was passing when she viewed the killing. She goes to that estate, owned by Justice, and offers her services as a maid. Once employed, Rutherford begins searching the place. Her suspicions are confirmed when she finds the body of the woman she saw attacked in a small building on the estate. The corpse is tentatively identified as a French woman, who was once married to a member of the family owning the estate, that family member having been killed in WWII. Rutherford learns that all of the children in the family, who stand to inherit a great fortune, were worried about the French woman as she might have claimed a part of their inheritance. All of the family members come under suspicion, but Rutherford's snooping unearths a more likely suspect, Kennedy, the family physician, and, after two of the sons in the

Margaret Rutherford (as Miss Marple) witnesses a murder on a train in *Murder She Said*, 1961.

family are murdered, Rutherford pinpoints Kennedy as the killer, explaining that he murdered his wife on the train, then passed her body off as that of the long missing French woman to throw suspicion onto family members while then planning to systematically kill off all the family members, except for Pavlow, the remaining daughter, and acquire the family fortune by marrying her. Rutherford is a delight to behold as she goes about her fussy investigations, and Kennedy, Justice and the rest of the cast are standouts in this fascinating whodunit. This film did so well at the box office that it inspired many more sequels featuring Miss Marple, three of them with Rutherford as the indefatigable lady sleuth. **p**, George H. Brown; **d**, George Pollock; **cast**, Margaret Rutherford, Arthur Kennedy, Muriel Pavlow, James Robertson Justice; Thorley Walters, Charles Tingwell, Conrad Phillips, Ronald Howard, Joan Hickson, Stringer Davis; **w**, David Pursall, Jack Seddon, David Osborn (based on the novel *4:50 From Paddington* by Agatha Christie); **c**, Geoffrey Faithfull; **m**, Ron Goodwin; **ed**, Ernest Walter; **art d**, Harry White; **spec eff**, Tom Howard.

The Murderer Lives at Number 21 ★★★ 1947; France; 83m; Liote-Continental Films/Mage Films; B/W; Mystery/Comedy; Children: Unacceptable. This intriguing whodunit begins with Paris police inspector Fresnay investigating the case of a serial killer, who leaves a calling card with the bodies of his victims. Fresnay traces the cards to a boarding house at No. 21 Avenue Junot. Impersonating a Protestant minister, he attempts to gain the confidence of residents, any of whom could be the killer. He learns through a series of humorous situations that there is actually a gang of three men, who kill for a lark, and he brings them all to justice, but not before several darkly humorous misadventures and mishaps occur. (In French; English subtitles.) **p**, Alfred Greven; **d**, Henri-Georges Clouzot; **cast**, Pierre Fresnay, Suzy Delair, Jean Tissier, Pierre Larquey, Noël Roquevert, René Génin, Jean Despeaux, Marc Natol, Huguette Vivier, Odette Talazac; **w**, Clouzot, Stanislas-André Steeman (based on the novel by Steeman); **c**, Armand Thirard; **m**, Maurice Yvain; **ed**, Christian Gaudin; **set d**, Andrej Andrejew.

The Murderers Among Us ★★★ 1948; Germany; 80m; Deutsche Film (DEFA)/Artkino; B/W; Drama; Children: Unacceptable. This was one of the first films from Germany after World War II that focused upon the horrible atrocities and mass genocide (Holocaust) committed by the Nazis and where it attempts to extend the guilt for these heinous crimes against humanity to the German people. Knef is a young woman returning to the ruins of Berlin after being in a concentration camp in 1945. She finds Borchert, a doctor, living in her old apartment and whose psychological depression over the ravages of the war has caused him to become a heavy drinker. They share the apartment and fall in

Charles Gemora (in ape costume) and Sidney Fox in *Murders in the Rue Morgue*, 1932.

love. Borchert fears that Paulsen, a neighbor who was his captain in the German army during the war, might see him with Knef and that Paulsen might jeopardize his relationship with Knef. Paulsen has been part of the Nazi crimes, having given the order to kill more than 100 innocent people, including children and women, in Poland during Christmas in 1942. Borchert had witnessed that massacre and now believes Paulsen, who is retired and a family man, should be punished. He wants Paulsen to be killed, but Knef tells him that justice would best be served if Paulsen stands trial for his Nazi war crimes. Borchert relents and follows her advice, and Paulsen is finally charged with his crimes. (In German; English subtitles.) A hard-hitting tale that exposes the underbelly of post-WWII Berlin and its apprehensive inhabitants sees outstanding performances from Borchert and Knef (who was also known as Neff in the few American films in which she appeared). **d&w**, Wolfgang Staudte; **cast**, W. Borchert, Hildegard Knef (Neff), Arno Paulsen, Elly Burgmer, Erna Sellmer, Hilde Adolphi, Marlise Ludwig, Ursula Krieg, Robert Forsch, Albert Johannes; **c**,. Friedl Behn-Grund, Eugen Klagemann; **m**, Ernst Roters; **ed**, Hans Heinrich; **prod d**, Otto Hunte, Bruno Monden, Alfred Schulz.

Murders in the Rue Morgue ★★★ 1932; U.S.; 61m; UNIV; B/W; Horror; Children: Unacceptable; **DVD**; **VHS**. Lugosi is a mad scientist in this bizarre chiller, one where he has an intelligent gorilla named Erik for a friend and as a business associate. He operates a sideshow in Paris where Erik performs, talking in a garbled language, but this bit of offbeat entertainment is designed only to provide Lugosi money enough to fund his obsession and that is to transform any young woman into a simian form so that Erik will have a female companion (not unlike that of Colin Clive as the mad doctor who thinks to create from dead tissue a mate for his undead monster in **The Bride of Frankenstein**, 1935). To that mad end, Lugosi has been abducting young Parisian women and experimenting on them with his serums, but he fails to transform these victims into apes and their bodies are then thrown into the Seine River. Police find these floating corpses, and Waycoff (who later used the name Leon Ames), a police detective, who is also a medical student, is dumbfounded as to how these hapless females have met their tragic fates. Waycoff and his fiancée, Fox, attend one of Lugosi's shows and Erik immediately takes a liking to Fox, grabbing her bonnet, crushing it. When Waycoff tries to retrieve the hat, the gorilla almost strangles him before Lugosi intervenes. When the couple departs, Lugosi sends his servant, Johnson, to follow them, in order to get Fox's address. Meanwhile, Waycoff asks to examine the blood of a prostitute who has been found dead in the river, but his request is denied. He bribes a coroner's assistant, who provides some samples of the woman's blood, and Waycoff discovers a foreign substance that matches what he has found in the blood of other similar victims. Lugosi then visits Fox and asks her to meet with Erik, but she refuses. Lugosi returns to his lair and then sends Erik to kidnap Fox, and the gorilla abducts the terrified young woman, her screams heard by Waycoff as he is arriving at her residence. He rushes to her room, but the door is locked. Police arrive, break down the door and find nothing, while neighbors claim that, during the scuffle they heard, they also heard an intruder talking in a low voice and in a foreign language, one witness saying it was German, another claiming it was Italian, and yet another Danish. They then find the body of Fox's mother stuffed up a chimney and still clutching a handful of ape fur. Meanwhile, Erik has taken the unconscious Fox to Lugosi's laboratory where Lugosi is about to inject his deadly serum into the girl. When Erik sees this, he becomes enraged and, to protect the girl he loves, he attacks and kills Lugosi. By that time, Waycoff and the police are at Lugosi's door, but Erik grabs Fox and carries her across the rooftops of Paris with Waycoff and the police in pursuit. Waycoff corners the gorilla, who turns upon him, but Waycoff shoots Erik dead, the gorilla falling to the cobblestone street below while Waycoff rescues his fiancée. This film saw several sequels, but they were inferior productions. *Author's Note*: Although Universal initially set aside a budget of about $180,000 for this film and assigned George Melford to direct, producers did not like what they saw in some of its first scenes and fired Melford and brought in the inventive Florey to helm this film. When they cut more than $40,000 from the budget, Florey quit the production. He was lured back to complete the film when given a $10,000 bonus. The film went into the can at 74 minutes, but again the front office meddled with the film, having editors cut it down by about thirteen minutes, which caused a rift between Florey and Universal that lasted for some time. Other than the basic elements, little of the original Poe story was employed in this film. Gemora, who plays Erik the gorilla, performs some great stunts as he clambers and scampers across the rooftops of Paris. **p**, Carl Laemmle, Jr.; **d**, Robert Florey; **cast**, Bela Lugosi, Sidney Fox, Leon Waycoff (Leon Ames), Bert Roach, Betty Ross Clarke, Brandon Hurst, D'Arcy Corrigan, Noble Johnson, Arlene Francis, Herman Bing, Charlotte Henry, Polly Ann Young, Charles Gemora; **w**, Tom Reed, Dale Van Every, John Huston (based on the story by Edgar Allan Poe); **c**, Karl Freund; **ed**, Milton Carruth; **art d**, Charles D. Hall; **spec eff**, John P. Fulton.

Muriel, or The Time of Return ★★★ 2007; France/Italy; 115m; Argos Films; Color; Drama; Children: Unacceptable; **DVD**; **VHS**. Originally made in 1963, this engrossing film was not released in U.S. theaters until 2007. It tells the story of Seyrig, a widow, who sells antique furniture from her apartment in the French seacoast town of Boulonge. She lives with her stepson, Thierree, who has recently returned from military service in the Algerian conflict where he tortured and murdered an Algerian girl named Muriel. Troubled and guilt-ridden, Thierree is haunted by the girl's memory and his deeds. He spends much of his time at home viewing an 8mm film of her. Seyrig's former lover, Kerien, also just back from the conflict in Algiers, comes to visit with his niece, Klein whom Seyrig has never met. Seyrig and Kerien try but are unable to recapture their old love for each other, although Thierree's guilt complex is eased through his relationship with Klein. Songs: "Deja" (Paul Colline, Paul Maye), "Sujux Day" (George Delerue). Violence and sexuality prohibit viewing by children. (In French; English subtitles.) **p**, Anatole Dauman, Pierre Braunberger; **d**, Alain Resnais; **cast**, Delphine Seyrig, Jean-Pierre Kérien, Nita Klein, Jean-Baptiste Thierrée, Claude Sainval, Laurence Badie, Jean Champion, Jean Dasté, Martine Vatel, Julien Verdier; **w**, Jean Cayrol (based on the story by Cayrol); **c**, Sacha Vierny; **m**, Hans Werner Henze; **ed**, Claudine Merlin, Kenout Peltier, Eric Pluet; **prod d**, Jacques Saulnier.

Muriel's Wedding ★★★ 1995; U.K./U.S.; 106m; CiBy 2000/Miramax; Color; Comedy/Drama; Children: Unacceptable (MPAA: R); **DVD**; **VHS**. Collette plays Muriel, a young woman who is bored with her life in a small coastal town in Australia, where she lives with her not-very successful politician father, Hunter, and his subservient wife, Drynan, and her siblings. Not especially attractive or popular, she spends much of her time in her room playing ABBA records and dreaming about getting married. She steals some money and meets a loose-living new friend, Griffiths. They board a plane and take a vacation to an island where Muriel's snobbish friends are on holiday. Changing her name to Mariel, she hopes to also change her life, and it begins to happen. She and her new friend score a hit at a party by doing a mimed dance to the ABBA song "Dancing Queen." They then move to Sydney where Collette has her first sexual experience with a young man, but it comes to nothing. Collette, obsessed with planning her own imagined wedding, haunts shops selling wedding dresses. Eventually she winds up in a marriage of convenience with a South African swimming star needing a wife so he can get an Australian passport. Despite the not-so-perfect marriage, Collette has found herself and is able to enjoy a happier life. Songs: "Dancing Queen," "Waterloo," "Fernando," "Mamma Mia," "I Do, I Do, I Do, I Do," (ABBA: Benny Andersson, Bjorn Ulvaeus, Stig Anderson, Agnetha Faltskog, Anni-Frid Lyngstad); "The Tide Is High" (John Holt); "Sugar Baby Love" (Tony Waddington, Wayne Bickerton); "T Shirts & Jeans" (McLean, Thorp. Dzajovsky); "I Go to Rio" (Peter Allen, Adrienne Anderson); "We've Only Just Begun" (Paul Williams, Roger Nichols); "Hotcha," "Coffee & Tea" (Peter Best). **p**, Lynda House, Jocelyn Moorhouse; **d&w**, P.J. Hogan; **cast**, Toni Collette, Rachel Griffiths, Bill Hunter, Sophie Lee, Rosalind Hammond, Belinda Jarrett, Pippa Grandison, Jeanie Drynan, Daniel Wyllie, Gabby Millgate, Gennie Nevinson, Matt Day; **c**, Martin McGrath; **m**, Peter Best; **ed**, Jill Bilcock; **prod d**, Patrick Reardon; **art d**, Hugh Bateup; **set d**, Glen W. Johnson, Jane Murphy; **spec eff**, Ray Fowler, Paul Gorrie, Roger Cowland.

Murmur of the Heart ★★★ 1971; France/Italy/West Germany; 118m; Nouvelles Editions de Films/Palomar Pictures International; Color; Comedy; Children: Unacceptable (MPAA: R); **DVD**; **VHS**. This light-hearted coming-of-age story about a fourteen-year-old boy has Ferreux growing up in an upper-middle-class family in 1954 in Dijon, France. He feels ignored by his gynecologist father, Gélin, and smothered by his mother, Massari. She takes him to a health spa because he is diagnosed as having scarlet fever, which leaves him with a heart murmur. Massari has an extra-marital affair and Ferreux meets some girls, but nothing comes of those liaisons and they return to a hotel room where they both drink too much and mother and son get a little too close in bed, giving each other mutual comforting, a secret but special incident they agree to keep to themselves. Ferreux then goes off to make love to one of the girls he has met. When Ferreux comes back to the hotel, he finds his mother, father, and brothers there. When they realize through Ferreux's sheepish manner that he has just had his first intimate relations with a girl, they all laugh, including Ferreux. Sexuality and suggested incest prohibits viewing by children. (In French; English subtitles.) **p**, Vincent Malle, Claude Nedjar; **d&w**, Louis Malle; **cast**, Lea Massari, Benoît Ferreux, Daniel Gélin, Marc Winocourt, Fabien Ferreux, Michael Lonsdale, Ave Ninchi, Gila von Weitershausen, Micheline Bona, Henri Poirier, Liliane Sorval, Corinne Kersten, Eric Walter, François Werner; **c**, Ricardo Aronovich; **m**, Charlie Parker, Sidney Bechet, Gaston Fréche, Henri Renaud; **ed**, Suzanne Baron; **prod d**, Jean-Jacques Caziot; **art d**, Caziot, Philippe Turlure.

Murphy's Romance ★★★ 1985; U.S.; 107m; COL; Color; Romance; Children: Unacceptable (MPAA: PG-13); **DVD**; **VHS**. This little story has a big heart, one shared by its appealing leads, Field and Garner. Field, a thirty-three-year-old divorced mother with a twelve-year-old son, Haim, buys a small ranch near an Arizona town with the hopes of starting life afresh. She meets Garner, the local pharmacist, and both are attracted to each other, but Garner, who is much older, keeps his distance. He nevertheless goes out of his way to help Field while befriend-

James Garner in *Murphy's Romance*, 1985.

ing Haim. Then Kerwin, who is Field's no-good ex-husband, arrives with nowhere to stay and the empathetic Field takes him in, allowing him to live on the ranch, but under the condition that their intimate relationship is finished. Field finds that she cannot make ends meet and turns to Garner. He refuses to loan her any money, but, to provide funds to Field, purchases a horse and then boards it with Field, suggesting that she offer to board other horses in order to obtain the necessary funds she needs to keep everything afloat, a plan that works. Kerwin sees that his ex-wife is drawing closer to Garner, and, to disrupt that blossoming relationship, develops a rivalry with Garner, who is not intimidated by this self-enriching lout, but this places stress on Field, who sees her son, Haim, torn between his old allegiance to his father, and to Garner, who has become a much better role model as a male parent. Just when Field thinks to break off any relations with Garner, another woman appears with twin baby boys, who are Kerwin's illegitimate offspring, and Field orders Kerwin to leave. After he departs, Field seeks Garner's counsel, asking his advice on how she should look to the future. They both know that that future involves their own marriage as they have fallen in love with each other. Garner, the inveterate bachelor, tells Field that he has two concerns about their future relationship. The first is that he declares his love for Field and the second that he is much older than she is and is wary of a May-December union. She replies that she loves him, too, and that his age is not important to her. That resolved, Garner and Field now plan to go to the altar. Both Field and Garner are exceptional in their roles as they hesitantly grope for love and happiness while knowing all along that their future lies with each other. Director Ritt helms this tender love tale with skillful patience and where his characters are fully developed so that Field, Garner and Haim become appealing to the viewer and where Ritt allows the course of their lives to naturally unfold. Songs: "Love for the Last Time," "Poetry," "Running Lonely," "Hungry Howling at the Moon," and "I Love You Only" (music and lyrics by Carole King). **p**, Laura Ziskin; **d**, Martin Ritt; **cast**, Sally Field, James Garner, Brian Kerwin, Corey Haim, Dennis Burkley, Georgann Johnson, Dortha Duckworth, Michael Prokopuk, Billy Ray Sharkey, Michael Crabtdree, Anna Levine, Charles Lane; **w**, Harriet Frank, Jr., Irving Ravetch (based on a story by Max Schott); **c**, William A. Fraker (Metrocolor); **ed**, Sidney Levin; **prod d**, Joel Schiller; **set d**, Rick Gentz; **spec eff**, Dennis Dion.

Murphy's War ★★★ 1971; U.K.; 107m; Hemdale/PAR; Color; War Drama; Children: Unacceptable (MPAA: PG-13); **DVD**; **VHS**. Action packed and with a stellar performance from the intense O'Toole, this is the saga of a war waged between two men, even after that war is over. O'Toole is shown at the opening as a happy-go-lucky merchant marine sailor, but his attitude toward life and death changes after his ship is

Peter O'Toole in *Murphy's War*, 1971.

sunk by a German U-boat commanded by Janson, who then orders his men to machinegun all the survivors as they struggle in the high seas. One man escapes this slaughter, O'Toole, who is later rescued by Noiret, who operates a salvage barge on the Orinoco River in Venezuela. Noiret takes the injured O'Toole to a mission where his barge is anchored and O'Toole is nursed back to health by Phillips, a local physician (O'Toole's wife in real life). When recovering, O'Toole meets Hallam, a British fighter pilot who crash-landed his plane after he attacked the U-boat. When Phillips wires a report that the U-boat is hiding up river, her message is intercepted by Janson, and he decides to silence the source of that information by wiping out the small mission. The Germans sail down river and Janson leads some of his men ashore where they find Hallam, shooting and killing him, and then destroy much of the mission, but O'Toole, who has gone into hiding with Phillips and Noiret, escape. After the Germans depart, O'Toole, consumed by vengeance for the attack, decides to wage a one-man war against Janson and his U-boat. He repairs Hallam's plane so that it is in flying condition, but, not having any bombs, uses Molotov cocktails to attack the U-boat. Believing that he has destroyed the submarine, O'Toole returns to the mission, but is shocked to see that the German vessel is intact when it returns to the mission and where Janson conducts another savage attack, destroying the place. O'Toole then takes over Noiret's barge, armor-plating it and tries to use it as a ram to sink the U-boat. He has by then heard that the war is over, news that is also learned by Janson, but, for O'Toole, the war will never be over until he destroys Janson and the U-boat. When Janson realizes that O'Toole will not give up his obsessive attack on his boat, he fires a torpedo at the barge, but it misses and lands harmlessly on the beach. O'Toole retrieves the torpedo, raising it perpendicular with the barge's derrick, then sails the barge so that it floats directly over the U-boat, which, in its frantic maneuvering, has become wedged on an underwater sandbar. O'Toole then positions the hanging torpedo over the U-boat and releases it. The torpedo explodes, destroying the submarine and all on board, but O'Toole, who gets caught up in the barge's fittings, is trapped as the barge also sinks, taking O'Toole to the same watery death he has created for Janson and his crew, and where this private and unrelenting war ends. *Author's Note*: This film is reminiscent of **The African Queen**, 1951, where Humphrey Bogart and Katharine Hepburn use Bogart's tramp steamer to destroy a German gunboat in WWI, and where O'Toole does the same thing in this opus to a German submarine in WWII. **p**, Michael Deeley; **d**, Peter Yates; **cast**, Peter O'Toole, Sian Phillips, Philippe Noiret, Horst Janson, John Hallam, Ingo Mogendort, Harry Fielder, George Roubicek; **w**, Stirling Silliphant (based on the novel by Max Catto); **c**, Douglas Slocombe (Eastmancolor); **m**, John Barry, Ken Thorne; **ed**, John Glen, Frank P. Keller; **prod d**, Disley Jones; **spec eff**, Alan Barnard, Colin Chilvers, Martin Gutteridge.

The Muse ★★★ 1999; U.S.; 97m; October Films; Color; Comedy; Children: Unacceptable (MPAA: PG-13); **DVD**; **VHS**. Brooks is a Hollywood screenwriter who is married to MacDowell and has two children. He has had more than a dozen hits, but is fired by his studio for having lost his "edge." He is used to living high off the hog, but all that has changed and he seeks advice, from Bridges, a friend, who is still writing hit screenplays. En route to Bridges' house Brooks sees a beautiful blonde, Stone, leaving Bridges' residence. Brooks wonders if Bridges is having an affair, but is told that the woman, who Bridges met at a party a few years ago, is one of the daughters of the Greek god Zeus, and is Bridges' "muse." Brooks will give her anything for her help in writing and puts her up in an expensive apartment, catering to her every wish. MacDowell sees them together and suspects her husband is having an affair. It turns out Stone is not a goddess but a placebo, making a good living by giving people confidence to achieve what they want, like a literary hooker. No matter, her influence works and Brooks starts writing his next hit. Lighthearted (if not a little lightheaded), this fanciful tale provides consistent entertainment. Songs: "Super Freak" (Rick James, Alonzo Miller), "Let Your Yeah Be Yeah" (Jimmy Cliff), "The Muse" (Elton John, Bernie Taupin). Nudity prohibits viewing by children. **p**, Herb Nanas; **d**, Albert Brooks; **cast**, Brooks, Sharon Stone, Andie MacDowell, Jeff Bridges, Cybill Shepherd, Monica Mikala, Jamie Alexis, Marnie Shelton, Lorenzo Lamas, Jennifer Tilly, Rob Reiner, Wolfgang Puck, James Cameron, Martin Scorsese; **w**, Brooks, Monica Johnson; **c**, Thomas Ackerman; **m**, Elton John; **ed**, Peter Teschner; **prod d**, Dina Lipton; **art d**, Marc Dabe; **set d**, Anne D. Mc-Culley.

The Mushroom Eater ★★★ 1976; Mexico/Spain; 110m; CCP; Conacite Uno; Color; Drama; Children: Unacceptable; **DVD**; **VHS**. This offbeat but engrossing allegorical drama is set in Mexico in the 1800s, by where a wealthy plantation owner finds Thomas, a black boy, at a waterfall in the jungle and rears him as one of his own children. The man's two legitimate sons dislike the jungle boy, but his daughter accepts him and, as they all mature, she and the boy fall in love with each other. The boy's adoptive mother tries to have an affair with him, but he runs away and his stepmother is killed by a panther that is a family pet. The father is opposed to his daughter and his adoptive son having an interracial romance, so he relegates the boy to the job of mushroom taster. The family throws lavish parties with mushrooms on the menu, but they are never certain if any are poisonous. If Thomas eats a mushroom and dies, the family knows it was poisonous and the other workers on the plantation will know which ones to stay away from and not serve for a party. Rather than become a guinea pig, Thomas runs away and the girl who loves him goes to a waterfall hoping to find him there. He is not there, but the panther is and kills her. Thomas goes back to the waterfall, sees his beloved is dead, and gives up on civilization. Violence and sexuality prohibit viewing by children. (In Spanish; English subtitles.) **d**, Roberto Gavaldón; **cast**, Philip Michael Thomas, Adolfo Marsillach, Isela Vega, Sandra Mozarowsky, Ofelia Medina, Fernando Allende, Quintín Bulnes, Josefina Echánove, Jorge Belanger, Ana Lorena Graham; **w**, Gavaldón, Emilio Carballido, Tito Davison, Fernando Vizcaíno Casas (based on a story by Sergio Galindo); **c**, Miguel Araña, Raúl Pérez Cubero (Eastmancolor); **m**, Raúl Lavista; **ed**, José W. Bustos.

Music of the Heart ★★★ 1999; U.S.; 124m; Craven-Maddalena Films/Miramax Films; Color; Drama; Children: Unacceptable (MPAA: PG); **DVD**; **VHS**. Based on a true story, Roberta Guaspari (Streep), whose husband left her and who has two small children, gets a job as a violin teacher in a Harlem high school for underprivileged children. She wants to introduce them to the beauty of classical music by teaching them to play the violin, explaining to administrators that she bought fifty inexpensive violins while in Greece. The board of education opposes her, but she goes ahead with her idea, and risks losing everything while the system puts every obstacle in her way. One black mother, a racist, idiotically objects to having the children exposed to the music of "dead white men." Streep nevertheless perseveres, and the children have a huge success while performing in a benefit concert at Carnegie Hall with violin virtuosos Isaac Stern, Itzhak Perlman, and Arnold Steinhardt. The educators now realize they were wrong. Songs: "Turn the Page" (Guy Roche, Shelly Peiken); "Con Sandunga" (Julito Collazo); "Descargarana" (Jimmy Bosch); "The Bridge," "Down by Law" (M.S. Shan as Shawn Moltke, Marley Marl as Marlon Williams); "Salsa Pilon" (Orlando Valle); "Make the Music with Your Mouth" (Biz Markie as Marcel Hall, Marley Marl as Marlon Willoiams); "Montuno Allegre" (Aslberto Valladares); "Nothing Else" (Julio Iglesias Jr.); "Go Tell Aunt Rhody," "Revancha de Amor" (Cesar Lemos, Gizelle D'Cole, Fabian Schoffer); "Symphony No. 1" (Marley Marl as Marlon Williams, Craig Curry, Big Daddy Kane as Antonio Hardy); "Now in Marianao" (Yosvany Terry Cabrera); "Roxanne's Revenge" (Roxanne Shante, Marley Marl as Marlon Williams); "One Night with You" (Diane Warren); "Poison" (Kool G. Rap, Marley Marl); "Descarga de Hoy" (Orlando Valle); "Groove Me Tonight" (Abel Talamantez, Alexis Grullon, Tomas Torres); "Orange Blossom Special;" (Ervin T. Rose); "Haydn Trio" (Joseph Haydn); "Baila" (Emilio Estefan, Jr., John Secada, Randall Barlow); "Concerto in D Minor for Two Violins" (Johann Sebastian Bach); "Music of My Heart" (Diane Warren). Sexuality and gutter language prohibit viewing by children. **p**, Susan Kaplan, Marianne Maddalena, Allan Miller, Stuart M. Besser, Walter Scheuer, Sandy Gallin, Meryl Poster, Bob and Harvey Weinstein; **d**, Wes Craven; **cast**, Meryl Streep, Cloris Leachman, Aidan Quinn, Henry Dinhofer, Michael Angarano, Robert Ari, Angela Bassett, Josh Pais, Barbara Gonzalez, Gloria Estefan, Kieran Culkin, Isaac Stern, Itzhak Perlman, Joshua Bell; **w**, Pamela Gray; **c**, Peter Deming; **m**, Mason Daring; **ed**, Gregg Featherman, Patrick Lussier; **prod d**, Bruce Alan Miller; **art d**, Beth Kuhn; **set d**, George DeTitta, Jr.; **spec eff**, Al Griswold, Danny Ferrington, Tyler Foell.

The Music Man ★★★★★ 1962; U.S.; 151m; WB; Color; Musical; Children: Acceptable; **BD**; **DVD**; **VHS**. This wonderful look at yesteryear's American heartland is loaded with humor, memorable characters, and, most of all, great music. It is 1912, and we see in the opening scene a number of traveling salesmen, drummers they were then called, riding on a train and talking in singsong about the most notorious of their clan, the redoubtable Preston, who can sell a pig in a poke to any anyone, especially the naïve suckers in the great state of Iowa, the territory they are traversing. When arriving in River City, Iowa, Preston gets off the train and, after looking over the town, gathers its residents to the town square where he warns them that ancient evil is oozing into their well-ordered and principled lives by pointing out the fact that the local poolroom threatens to destroy the ethics and morals of their youngsters. (This lecturing point is not lost on the discombobulated Ford, the mayor of the town, who owns the poolroom.) To prevent this calamity from taking place, Preston states that the town needs to start a band where their children can learn how to play music that will delight and enrich the entire community. He offers to sell them the instruments and teach the children how to play beautiful music, but the confidence man has no intentions of keeping his promises. He plans to pocket the money from the sale of the instruments and run before those instruments arrive since he knows nothing about music. After listening to Preston's spiel about his superlative credentials as a music master, local librarian and music teacher Jones realizes that he is gulling the townsfolk. The glib Preston, who is falling for the fetching Jones, manages to convince her that he has a shortcut technique in teaching music that he labels a "Think System," one where he is able to teach anyone to play any kind of instrument overnight. He points out that all the children need to do is to "think" the song they are about to play and they will then be able to play it. The glibly persuasive Preston is able to create some small miracles, one involving Howard, a withdrawn little boy who is ashamed of his lisp. Preston gives him some pointers on how to talk and the lad soon overcomes

Shirley Jones and Robert Preston lead the parade in *The Music Man*, 1962.

and abandons that lisp. More important, Preston tackled the always quarreling school board, convincing its bickering four directors to finally embrace his plan for a band and they become so enthusiastic that they all bond in friendship by forming a harmonizing quartet (the players are members of the renowned barbershop quartet, "The Buffalo Bills"). Further, the enterprising entrepreneur collects all the gossips and rumormongers in the town who have been bad-mouthing him, and befriends them and convinces them to form a committee to organize a huge dance to celebrate the arrival of the instruments. Moreover, Jones, has lost her fear of becoming an old maid in that she is now deeply in love with Preston and looks to a future at his side. Her dreams are almost dashed when anvil salesman Hickox arrives to tell Jones that Preston is an utter fraud and that he has wooed a bevy of music teachers in many other small towns, enlisting the support of these trusting and unsuspecting women in order to sell his musical instruments and has then left them in the lurch. Jones implores Hickox not to spread this poisonous talk about town, but the vengeful salesman does just that and soon Preston is the object of distrust if not wrath. The instruments arrive and Preston is brought to City Hall to face the music. His confidence and self-assurance, however, remains intact, and, after the instruments are distributed to the children, he tells them to think the "Minuet in G" and, amazingly they do, while their loving parents, relatives and friends immediately overlook (or under-hear) their squeaking mistakes. The film ends with a massive parade where the band, elegantly attired in colorful uniforms and with rehabilitated confidence man Preston leading the way, marches impressively through the streets, each band member playing his or her instrument to perfection while the townsfolk cheer. Perfection is what this great film truly is, one that so beautifully captures with warmhearted nostalgia a small-town America all treasure in memory. DaCosta, who directed the original 1957 smash play version on Broadway (which ran for 1,375 performances), brings this scintillating, amusing and endearing tale to the screen with infinite care, successfully capturing the image of the American heartland as no other film has ever achieved, its enthralling score remaining in memory over the decades and where Preston is mesmerizing as the brass and audacious salesman, half con man and half visionary. The fresh-faced Jones is also wonderful in her role and where her singing voice is in top form while Gingold, Wickes and Ford give strong support and create many funny moments. Songs include: "Ya Got Trouble," "Piano Lesson," "If You Don't Mind My Saying So," "Goodnight, My Someone," "76 Trombones," "Sincere," "Sadder But Wiser Girl for Me," "Marian the Librarian," "Gary, Indiana," "Being in Love," "Wells Fargo Wagon," "Linda Rose," "Will I Ever Tell You," "Pick a Little, Talk a Little," "Goodnight My Ladies," "Shipoopi," "Till There Was You," "My White Knight" (music and lyrics: Meredith Willson); "Minuet in G" (Ludwig van Beethoven); "Rustle of Spring" (Christian

Clark Gable and Charles Laughton in *Mutiny on the Bounty*, 1935.

Sinding) and "Columbia, the Gem of the Ocean" (David T. Shaw). The film was nominated for an Oscar as Best Picture and won an Oscar for Best Adaptation or Treatment Score (Willson and Heindorf), but strangely the Academy did not nominate Preston for his stellar perform-ance, a gross oversight. ***Author's Note***: Willson based his great musical on his home town of Mason City, Iowa, where, as a young man, he wit-nessed a horrific bank robbery and shootout in 1934 between the bank robbers and local police and where the robbers escaped while using sev-eral citizens as shields, having them stand on the running boards of their fleeing cars. The gang was led by John Dillinger, who, according to Willson, "was never a folk hero to me or anybody in Mason City." Ronny or Ron Howard, who plays a boy in this film, later became a TV star in such offerings as "The Andy Griffith Show" and "Happy Days" and then going on to become a foremost film director. **p&d**, Morton Da-Costa; **cast**, Robert Preston, Shirley Jones, Buddy Hackett, Hermione Gingold, Paul Ford, Pert Kelton, Timmy Everett, Susan Luckey, Ronny (Ron) Howard, Harry Hickox, Charles Lane, Mary Wickes, Barbara Pepper, Hank Worden; **w**, Marion Hargrove (based on the book of the stage musical by Meredith Willson, Franklin Lacey); **c**, Robert Burks (Technicolor); **m**, Willson, Ray Heindorf; **ed**, William Ziegler; **art d**, Paul Groesse; **set d**, George James Hopkins.

The Music Room ★★★ 1963; India; 100m; Aurora/Edward Harrison; B/W; Drama; Children: Unacceptable; **DVD**; **VHS**. Intriguing drama sees Biswas as a man who has inherited almost worthless land that is being eroded by a river, but tries to maintain the lifestyle of his heritage. He keeps one room, the music room, as elegant as possible, hiring the finest musicians and dancers to perform there and invites his most im-portant neighbors to the concerts. His wife, Devi, pleads with him to economize, but he goes ahead to have a puberty party for his son, Sen-gupta, for which he will pay with the last few family jewels that are left in his possession. After his wife and son drown during a thunderstorm while at sea, Biswas goes into a depressed seclusion for four years, until he hears that a neighbor plans a party in his newly built music room. This news inspires Biswas to pull out of his depression as he spends his last money to throw a party in his own beloved music room. However, he loses his sanity in the process and rides off on his son's horse. Thrown by the horse, he dies in the arms of his servants. Adult themes and vio-lence prohibit viewing by children. (In Bengali; English subtitles.) **p,d&w**, Satyajit Ray (based on the novel by Tarashankar Banerjee); **cast**, Chhabi Biswas, Padma Devi, Pinaki Sengupta, Tulsi Lahiri, Kali Sarkar, Gangapada Basu, Waheed Khan, Roshan Kumari, Begum Akhtar; **c**, Subrata Mitra; **m**, Ustad Vilayat Khan, Asish Kumar, Robin Majumdar, Dakshina Mohan Tagore; **ed**, Dulal Dutta; **prod d**, Bansi Chandragupta; **set d**, R.R. Sinde.

Mutiny on the Bounty ★★★★ 1935; U.S.; 132m; MGM; B/W; Ad-venture: Children: Cautionary; **DVD**; **VHS**. Full of excitement and ac-tion, this adventure tale finds few equals in film history, a saga of the sea where one man loses his ship and reputation as a slave-driving cap-tain and the other loses his status and future in the civilized world in order to free himself and his men from a savage tyrant. Based upon the actual mutiny that took place on board the HMS *Bounty* on April 28, 1789, the story begins in December 187 as the merchant vessel is pre-pared to sail from Portsmouth, England, to Tahiti in the West Indies, as-signed to obtain a cargo of breadfruit. Tone (his character based on Peter Heywood, 1772-1831), who is one of the midshipmen assigned to the ship, is shown with his well-to-do family members, eager for the voy-age, and who, as they all have a farewell drink, enthusiastically gives a romantic toast about his visions for that adventure: "Here's to the voyage of the *Bounty*: Still waters and the great golden sea; Flying fish like streaks of silver; Mermaids who sing in the night; The Southern Cross and all the stars on the other side of the world." Boarding the ship, Tone is accompanied by his rich uncle, Stephenson, who wishes him well while Tone is welcomed by other ship officers, including first mate Gable (playing Fletcher Christian, 1864-1793), as well as its captain, Laughton (playing William Bligh, 1754-1817). Laughton, at this junc-ture, gives a strong hint of his sadistic personality when saying to Stephenson: "If you think there is no science in a cat-o'-nine-tails, you should see my bos'n!" (The ship's boatswain's mate is responsible for administering floggings with a whip having nine leather strips, designed to inflict multiple lacerations.)The voyage begins without problems, where the officers and crew work cooperatively together and where Gable, a seasoned sailor, teaches Tone and other midshipmen the rudi-ments of seafaring. Everything begins to go sour when Laughton, a petty, mean-minded tyrant with a penchant for cruelty if not sadism, be-gins to administer excessive punishments toward seamen over the slight-est infractions. Laughton is then told that three large slabs of cheese are missing from the ship's stores and he calls the crew to bear witness to this discrepancy which has been entered into the ship's log. Laughton accuses someone on board of having stolen the cheese, but seaman Craig steps forward to state that he himself removed the three pieces of cheese on Laughton's orders before the ship sailed from Portsmouth and deliv-ered them to Laughton's residence. Laughton, enraged at obliquely being called a manipulating fraud, calls Craig a liar and orders him flogged. Gable protests against Laughton's injustice, but he is silenced by Laughton, who now makes it clear that he will command the ship by terrorizing his crew, stating that his men "respect one law—fear." From that point on, Laughton routinely orders every imaginable punishment meted out to his hapless men. He has his sailors spread-eagled in the riggings of his ship for malingering, whipped for any small act of defi-ance and even has one man keelhauled for taking water without permis-sion, a punishment where the man is dragged by ropes from one side of the ship to the other underwater, and which results in his death. Most of the crew members, who are now fed rancid and tainted food as they sail toward Tahiti, grow to despise and loath, Laughton, viewing him as an inhuman monster, a perspective now held by Gable, who has earlier sailed with Laughton without recriminations (Fletcher Christian had sailed with Bligh on two previous voyages to Jamaica without incident). The tension on board the ship eases when it arrives in the tranquil waters of Tahiti and where it is greeted by thousands of happy natives, rowing their outriggers to the ship to board it and bestow welcoming wreaths of flowers about the necks of the elated sailors. The chief, Bambridge, greets Laughton, who gives him a ceremonial hat and who, in exchange, offers to give Laughton's crew members all the breadfruit they can load on board the *Bounty*. Tone remains ashore, becoming the adopted son of the chief and where he assembles a dictionary of the Tahitian lan-guage. He uses his influence with the chief to get Gable shore leave as Gable has been restricted to the ship on specific orders by the vindictive Laughton after their relationship has become angrily contentious. Both Gable and Tone fall in love with two beautiful Tahitian girls and their life ashore is full of idyllic leisure where they enjoy swimming and lounging on sandy beaches. When the ship is fully loaded with breadfruit, Gable and Tone say farewell to their native girls, but Gable has fallen in love and promises his sweetheart that he will find some way to return to the island and be with her. When the ship embarks for England, Gable attempts to befriend Laughton once more, but Laughton is too consumed with old grudges and makes the return voyage even more miserable and insufferable than before, inflicting terrible punishments upon the crew members. He does not spare the officers in his draconian regimen, taking pains to insult Gable at every turn. At one point, he accuses Gable of lying and theft, but Gable tells him that he will not be goaded into striking his captain, reminded that that would be punishable by hanging. Laughton shows no mercy toward his crew, sending sick men aloft to man the rigging and puts others in irons below deck for sneaking drinks of water (most of the ship's fresh water is used to preserve the breadfruit, which Laughton prizes more than the lives of his men). At one point, Laughton demands that Digges, the kindly but alcoholic ship's doctor, witness a flogging, but the old man is ill in his quarters. Laughton nevertheless orders him topside and, after Digges struggles to the deck, he dies from the strain. Incensed at such brutality, Gable shouts out to the crew to bear witness to what Laughton has done, calling it murder. He later sees Crisp, a rebellious and imprisoned seaman, being abused by Wolfe, a toady to Laughton and an informer. Gable knocks Wolfe down and, in a rage, states he can no longer tolerate such sadistic abuse from Laughton. He gathers the most rebellious crew members and orders them to seize the weapons in the ship's armory and then leads a mutiny. Loyal crew members are beaten and overwhelmed and Laughton is seized in his cabin and brought topside. Tone and other midshipmen try to put down the mutiny, but they are knocked unconscious by brawny mutineers. Gable is now in total control of the ship and he orders Laughton and several others loyal to him to get into a longboat, giving Laughton supplies and his own compass. Laughton shouts at Gable: "But you are taking my ship!" Gable roars back: "The king's ship, you mean, and you're not fit to command it!" Laughton and several others get into the longboat and row away as sailors on board the *Bounty* shout insults at him and where Crisp is prevented from shooting Laughton by Gable. Laughton, consumed by rage at the seizure of his ship, stands up in the longboat, raising a clenched fist at Gable, and shouts: "I'll live to see you, all of you, hang from the highest yardarm of the British fleet!" The crew members then begin contemptuously dumping the breadfruit they had so assiduously collected in Tahiti into the sea, these plants floating ominously in the wake of the *Bounty* as it sails away from Laughton and those in the longboat. Gable sails the ship back to Tahiti, but his friendship with Tone is almost shattered when Tone tells him that he is an unwilling captive in that he had no part in the mutiny, which he condemns. They nevertheless resume their pleasurable lives after returning to Tahiti while Laughton and his men endure terrible hardships at sea. Laughton sails the longboat 3,618 miles to safety, reaching the island of Timor in the Dutch East Indies. (Bligh, who managed to survive with most of his men for forty-nine days in that longboat, was later hailed as a master seaman for achieving this incredible feat of navigation.) Consumed by revenge, Bligh is given command of another ship, the *Pandora*, and sets sail for Tahiti for the purpose of capturing the mutineers and returning them to England for trial. (The real Bligh did not lead that punitive expedition.) When the *Pandora* approaches Tahiti, Gable and most of the mutineers board the *Bounty* with their women, volunteer natives and supplies and sail from the island. Tone and others who have had no part of the mutiny remain on the island, as do a few of the hapless mutineers, and who are all then captured when the *Pandora* arrives at Tahiti, taken back to England to stand trial. Gable sails the *Bounty* on and on through the South Seas until he finds a small island, Pitcairn, whose location has been misplaced on existing sea charts and he selects this stark and lonely rock as the final home for the mutineers, an island he believes no ship searching for him and his men will ever locate. After going ashore, Gable orders

Clark Gable and Charles Laughton in *Mutiny on the Bounty*, 1935.

the *Bounty* set afire and watches it burn from the shore of Pitcairn. One of his men remarks about how well the ship burns and Gable ironically states that it is made of "good English oak." Tone, meanwhile, along with others, is tried in England at a court martial before the British admiralty, presided over by many admirals, including Lord Samuel Hood (1724-1816), played by Torrence, and Lord Horatio Nelson (1758-1805), played by Lister, and where Tone claims his innocence in the mutiny. He describes the awful transgressions of Laughton (who is present and watches with scowling scorn) and how Laughton beat, tortured and killed his men, driving them, and, in particular, Gable, to mutiny. His pleadings are not merely for himself, but for all British seamen, imploring the admirals to alter the terrible procedures of the British navy and that English seamen would serve willingly in their fleets if not shanghaied by press gangs and "not by flogging their backs, but lifting their hearts," and by thus treating their men, the admirals could "sweep the seas for England." Though Tone is condemned, along with others, Stephenson and others plead with the king and Tone is pardoned and then reassigned to another ship. He is greeted on board with his now famous words by another officer, who tells him that they will "sweep the seas for England." Laughton gives a bravura performance as the bestial Bligh, creating an unforgettable character so vicious and lethal that it is hard to imagine that any such person would ever be given the command of a British ship, but Laughton's essay of Bligh is accurate in that Bligh was that very inhuman sea captain, infamous for his brutality and cruelty; in fact, his actions that prompted the historic mutiny also prompted the British navy to institute widespread reforms in its treatment of British sailors, so great good came from the evil acts of this universally despised man. Gable, too, is magnificent, as the upstanding and decent first mate, who finally rebels against the insufferable tyranny of his captain and who shows more compassionate and forceful leadership in leading that mutiny than the detestable tyrant he usurps. Tone is also outstanding in the role of the trusting and loyal midshipman, who has more respect for a mutineer than the captain of his ship, and who exudes great strength in his role as a victim of both sides of the conflict. The reserved Lloyd, an unpretentious and meticulous director, shows his great technical skills in helming this classic sea saga, masterfully meshing the dramatic scenes with the perilous journey of the ship as it sails through storms and becalmed seas and where Lloyd's tropical island settings are lush and inviting. His action scenes are superlative, particularly when showing the actual mutiny, which he depicts in a rapid series of action cuts as mutineers and loyal seamen battle for control of the *Bounty*. The production values are excellent and the stirring score from Kahn and Kaper greatly enhances its many vivid and memorable scenes. The film, which had a great box office success, won an Oscar as Best Picture and Lloyd was nominated as Best Director and, in an unprece-

Charles Laughton, Clark Gable and, extreme right, Alec Craig, in *Mutiny on the Bounty,* **1935.**

dented move, the Academy nominated the film's three leading players, Gable, Laughton and Tone, as Best Actor, which was nevertheless won by Victor McLaglen in **The Informer**, 1935. The film was remade in 1962 with Marlon Brando in the role of Fletcher Christian and Trevor Howard playing Captain Bligh, and again in 1984, under the title **The Bounty**, with Mel Gibson as Christian and Anthony Hopkins as Bligh. *Author's Note*: Lloyd had long wanted to direct this film and had considerable experience in helming other epic sea films, such as the silent classic, **The Sea Hawk**, 1924. Lloyd purchased the film rights to *Mutiny on the Bounty* from authors Nordhoff and Hall for $12,500 (those rights actually entailed the rights to three books assembled as one, *Mutiny on the Bounty*; *Men against the Sea*; and *Pitcairn Island*). Lloyd and his agent, Edward Small, who later became a distinguished film producer, first approached MGM studio chief Louis B. Mayer with the project, where Lloyd offered to turn over the film rights of the story to MGM for free if he was allowed to direct the film. Mayer thought about that proposal and then turned it down, saying that there was not enough love interest in the story and that viewing audiences would not be interested in seeing a film about a mutineer. Mayer pointed out that Australian producer Charles Chauvel had released a film on the subject, **In the Wake of the Bounty**, which had been released in Australia in 1933, albeit a low-budget production starring an unknown Tasmanian actor named Errol Flynn. Lloyd and Small then went to producer Walter Wanger, who was excited about the project, but he wanted Robert Montgomery, an MGM leading man, to star in the role of mutinous Fletcher Christian while Lloyd wanted MGM star Gable to play that role. Lloyd went back to MGM, and this time pitched the project to Irving Thalberg, head of MGM production. Thalberg loved the idea, going to Mayer and convincing him to do the film, saying that the role of Captain Bligh was the lynchpin to the film's success, stating to Mayer: "People are fascinated by cruelty and that's why **Mutiny** will have appeal." Mayer, however, still had reservations and told a confidante that he would wait to see the production of the film consume a great deal of money and then flop at the box office and that his first impression about the film would be confirmed and that his boy genius (Thalberg) would be proven wrong, such were the extravagant and costly games Mayer played as the top movie mogul in Hollywood. Thalberg cut the deal with Lloyd as Lloyd originally proposed to Mayer and Thalberg then bought up the distribution rights of the Australian film, **In the Wake of the Bounty**, from Chauvel, so that the American market would not see that film. Some short segments of that film, however, were excerpted and used as short clips in the promotion of the MGM production. Chauvel had taken the pains to visit Pitcairn Island, filming its unwelcoming landfalls and steep cliffs while also taking underwater shots of the remains of the original *Bounty* that rested inside a reef and in shallow waters of the island. Thalberg,

like Lloyd, believed that only one actor, Gable, should play the part of the rebellious Fletcher Christian, but when he approached the actor to propose the role to him, Gable stubbornly refused to play the part. "Look, Irving," Gable told Thalberg, "I'm a realistic kind of actor. I've never played in a costume picture in my life." Further, Gable refused to shave off his mustache, which he considered his "lucky" charm in the many film successes he had had at MGM and was further troubled by the idea that he would have to wear long hair with a pigtail, knee pants and buckled shoes, the traditional costume of a British naval officer of that day. (The only surviving image of Fletcher Christian, an old woodcut, shows him wearing a beard while serving as first mate on the *Bounty*, which was then contrary to British regulations, but had Gable seen that woodcut, he might have used it to preserve that mustache he so cherished.) Gable was still mindful of his father's warning that acting might turn him into "a painted pretty boy," suggesting the character of a sissy or even that of being homosexual. Gable's father had been a rugged oil rigger in the oil fields of Oklahoma and Texas, and Gable himself had followed that craft as a youth before bumming through the country and becoming, almost as a lark, an actor. Thalberg, however, would not back down, but used a soft approach to the actor, pleading with Gable to do him a favor, and saying: "Do this one for me…I'll never ask you again to play a part you don't want to do." Gable finally agreed, but told Thalberg that he would play Christian the way he truly was, a man's man with no traces of the fop or dandy, and that is exactly what Gable appears to be on the screen, a virile, firm and courageous leader of men. Thalberg then considered Wallace Beery for the role of Captain Bligh, but, on second thought, he and Lloyd believed Beery too American in personality and style to play the role, and they selected Laughton, who had played, with excellent results, cruel and tyrannical characters, in **The Private Life of Henry VIII**, 1933, and **The Barretts of Wimpole Street**, 1934, both smash box office hits and where, in the latter film, Laughton had starred with Thalberg's real-life wife, Norma Shearer, the then reigning queen at MGM, and who thought Laughton would be perfect as Bligh. Laughton, however, when approached with the part by Thalberg, did not agree. He was tired of playing loathsome characters and, when Thalberg attempted to entice him into the role by telling him he would have top billing, Laughton said that that was another reason for him not to do the part since it would immediately cause friction with Gable (who was billed after Laughton). Thalberg used his considerable charm to persuade Laughton to finally take the part, but there was contention between Laughton and Gable right from the beginning. Crisp, who plays one of the rebellious sailors siding with Gable in the mutiny (Thomas Burkitt, who was captured, tried and condemned, hanged at Spithead on October 29, 1792), told this author: "They went at each other like the real Bligh and Christian, hating the sight of each other in every scene. It was not hard for Gable or any of the rest of us to dislike Laughton, great actor that he is, as Laughton took the part of the tyrant, Bligh, very seriously. He treated all of us with disdain on and off the set. He wasn't just playing that role. He was living it." At one point, Laughton, who established forever for himself the image of absolute villainy on the screen, delivered a barking order to Gable, but refused to look at the actor. "Gable exploded," Crisp told this author. "His face went red and he waved to the director [Lloyd] to stop the scene. He then shouted to the director, as only Gable could, while he stood with his fists clenched close to Laughton, telling the director that Laughton was purposely shutting Gable out of the scene. Laughton stood there scowling and said nothing." What Gable shouted was: "Laughton is treating me like an extra! He didn't even look at me when he addressed me! The audience won't see me in the sequence! Laughton hogged it!" Gable walked off the set and refused to appear again with Laughton, who refused to apologize. Lloyd could do nothing to fix the situation, so Thalberg flew from Los Angeles to Catalina Island where the production was on location and implored Gable to return to the production while ordering Laughton to look directly at Gable when addressing any lines to him. Lloyd continued to play referee between Laughton and Gable, and where Laughton proved to be continuously troublesome, repeatedly going to Thalberg to complain about the director, saying that Lloyd knew nothing about handling actors and was only suited to direct extras and props (a gross misstatement in that Lloyd was a superb director, who otherwise got along well with his actors and crew members). Laughton further said that the real star of the film was the ship, *Bounty*, since Lloyd was spending so much time shooting its billowing sails and exterior as it sliced through the seas. Tone, who has the third leading role in the film (he took the part after Robert Montgomery, who was originally considered for the Gable role and was then offered the role of the midshipman and turned it down), told this author in 1962 that "I spent more time trying to keep peace between Gable and Laughton than I did in playing my part in the picture. They were at each other's throats every day, like two male lions trying to take over a pride. It wasn't an easy go for me either in some of my scenes. In one scene, I am ordered topside to the highest mast of the ship during a storm by Laughton as punishment—and I believed Laughton loved doing that since he thought I had truly befriended Gable during the production as I do in the picture. While I was up there, clinging to that mast in that rolling, swaying ship, and in the middle of a storm, I fell and could have been killed, but I grabbed one of the riggings and swung myself back into place and lashed myself to the mast. The camera went overboard and we had to do that scene all over again. There was no stunt man doing that for me. I had to do it myself and all the while I asked myself how in the hell those seamen in those days could endure such a life. By the way, I did befriend Gable in that picture. He was a great actor and a great guy." Lloyd also faced untold hazards and costs that spiraled out of sight when one mishap after another occurred. The ships *Bounty* and *Pandora* were built to life-size structures and made actual voyages to Tahiti and back, voyages of more than 14,000 miles. At Lloyd's insistence (for authenticity), a second unit shot a great amount of footage at Tahiti where almost 3,000 natives were employed, but when that unit returned to the U.S., it was discovered that a technician had forgotten to dehydrate the film that was exposed to the damp tropical climate and that that footage was useless and had to be reshot all over again. The *Bounty* was damaged several times and was repaired at considerable expense. Moreover, when shooting on location off Catalina Island, a storm engulfed the camera barge and more than $50,000 worth of equipment was lost and a technician, trying to save that equipment, drowned in the effort. An eighteen-foot replica of the *Bounty* with two technicians inside of it was swept out to sea by another storm and was lost for two days until it was recovered and where the two technicians were found just barely alive. Though the film proved to be, as Mayer suspected, one of MGM's most costly films to date with a budget of almost $2 million, it was not the failure he predicted. The film had a great success at the box office, returning $4,460,000 to the studio in its initial release. The gifted and insightful Thalberg died a year after this film was released, but he had the satisfaction of knowing before then that he had been right about the film's potential from the first moment he envisioned making it. For more details on the mutiny, see my entry in my eight-volume work, *The Encyclopedia of World Crime*, Volume III (CrimeBooks, Inc., 1990; pages 2269-2270). **p**, Frank Lloyd, Irving Thalberg (not credited); **d**, Lloyd; **cast**, Charles Laughton, Clark Gable, Franchot Tone, Herbert Mundin, Eddie Quillan, Dudley Digges, Donald Crisp, Henry Stephenson, Francis Lister, William Bambridge, Spring Byington, Movita, Mamo Clark, Percy Waram, David Torrence, Ian Wolfe, Ray Corrigan, Dick Haymes, Robert Livingston, Doris Lloyd, Alec Craig, Ivan Simpson, DeWitt Jennings, Stanley Fields, Wallis Clark, Vernon Downing, Dick Winslow, Byron Russell, John Harrington, Douglas Walton, Lionel Belmore, Mary Gordon, Nadine Beresford, Eric Wilton, Marion Clayton; **w**, Talbot Jennings, Jules Furthman, Carey Wilson (based on the novels *Mutiny on the Bounty* and *Men against the Sea* by Charles Nordhoff, James Norman Hall); **c**, Arthur Edeson; **m**, Gus Kahn, Bronislau Kaper, Walter Jurmann, Herbert Stothart; **ed**, Margaret Booth; **art d**, Cedric Gibbons, A. Arnold Gillespie.

At center, **Clark Gable, Charles Laughton and Donald Crisp in** *Mutiny on the Bounty*, 1935.

Mutiny on the Bounty ★★★ 1962; U.S.; 178m; Arcolo Pictures; MGM; Color; Adventure; Children: Unacceptable; **DVD**; **VHS**. High production values and good performances from Howard and Brando enhance this good remake of the 1935 classic. Although the tale follows the same story line as the Lloyd film, it departs dramatically in how Brando essays the character of Fletcher Christian (1864-1793). Unlike the portrayal of Christian by Clark Gable in the 1935 film, Brando plays the rebellious first mate as a posturing, aristocratic fop, mostly concerned about the cleanliness of his knee-high stockings and his frilly laced shirts. While Howard, who enacts the role of the brutal Captain William Bligh (1754-1817), relentlessly ordering his men whipped and beaten for the slightest infractions, Brando takes it all in stride, as if such acts of inhumanity are socially offensive, but nevertheless within the authority of his master. He does little or nothing in the way of softening Howard's savage regimen and confines himself to the comforts of his stateroom as the ship *Bounty* sails for its West Indies destination of Tahiti where it is to load a cargo of breadfruit. Brando wears the uniform of a commissioned officer as first mate, but only Bligh was actually a commissioned officer in the British Royal Merchant Navy (a lieutenant), and where Christian was promoted to an acting lieutenant during the voyage to Tahiti. Harris, who has a strong third lead in the film, plays the role of rebellious seaman John Mills, serving as an Iago to Brando, subtly and insidiously working on Brando's social sensitivities and passion for decorum if not compassion for his fellow sailors to recognize and finally usurp Howard for his transgressions. After the *Bounty* reaches Tahiti, the sailors begin gathering the breadfruit and storing these preciously cultivated plants on board their ship while Brando and other seamen find and fall in love with the beautiful native girls. Howard, who spends most of his time on board the ship, comes ashore to attend a native feast and celebration and is goaded into mimicking a native dance, for which he is scoffed and derided by his crew members, a humiliation Howard does not forget. After the *Bounty* departs Tahiti, Brando is more and more the butt of Howard's criticism and spewing spleen and where Howard degrades Brando as the supercilious, limp-wristed and perfumed person he seems to be. Brando has gone by the book up to this time, but, after he sees an exhausted seaman scrubbing the decks and begging for fresh water, most of that water stingily reserved to keep the breadfruits alive, he goes to a water barrel and ladles some water to the sailor, but Howard intervenes, knocking the water ladle out of his hand and again sneeringly rebuking Brando. Brando fumes like an insulted maiden and then nods approval to Harris and his fellow mutineers to take over the ship. The mutiny is quickly accomplished, and Howard, still defiant, is ordered into a longboat with those loyal to him and told to take his chances with the sea as Brando, Harris and other mutineers sail away in the *Bounty*. Howard manages to sail

John Wildman and Margaret Langrick in *My American Cousin,* **1986.**

that longboat to Timor, surviving to hunt after Brando and his fellow mutineers, but they evade official punishment by locating remote Pitcairn Island, which has been misplaced on the sea charts, and make this isolated and forlorn place their home. Unlike the 1935 film, the story of the mutineers continues to show Brando and his associates settling on the island, but where Brando has second thoughts and considers sailing the *Bounty* back to England to take his chances at a court martial. This alarms Harris and others, who believe that this would spell their doom at the end of hangman's rope. Harris and others set fire to the *Bounty*, and when Brando sees the ship burning, he and a few others row out to it and he attempts to put out the blaze, but is so badly burned that he must be removed from the sinking ship and where he later dies from his terrible wounds. Thus ends this fascinating tale, although the character Brando is playing, Fletcher Christian did not die in the manner portrayed, but was murdered by some of the nine mutineers, who accompanied him to Pitcairn, on September 20, 1793, and where all of the mutineers were killed by each other or by the six Tahitian men and eleven Tahitian women that accompanied them to that island with only John Adams (1767-1829; who used the alias of Alexander Smith) as the surviving mutineer. *Author's Note*: Brando and the film's director, Milestone, an accomplished helmsman, did not get along well during the production. "Marlon was impossible to direct in that picture," Milestone told this author. "He refused to take any of my suggestions and when I insisted that he show more defiance in his confrontations with Howard, he merely shrugged and mumbled words I could not understand. He acted as a petulant child and I later called the picture 'The Mutiny of Marlon Brando.'" Harris publicly stated that the film was "a large, dreadful nightmare for me," blaming Brando's truculence and unresponsiveness as the reason why the film did not work well. For his part, Brando told this author that "I did not want to try to play Fletcher Christian like the he-man Gable portrayed in the early film about the mutiny. That would have been impossible. So I turned the character around a bit, but I think that by adding a lisp to his speech was a mistake and that I made him a little too prissy. We all make mistakes, but my biggest mistake was taking on the role in the first place." The film was excessively expensive, most of its $6 million budget going to the top stars, chiefly Brando, but it nevertheless returned almost $10 million at the box office, mostly because of Brando's appeal with worldwide audiences. For more details on the mutiny, see my entry in my eight-volume work, *The Encyclopedia of World Crime*, Volume III (CrimeBooks, Inc., 1990; pages 2269-2270). **p**, Aaron Rosenberg; **d**, Lewis Milestone; **cast**, Marlon Brando, Trevor Howard, Richard Harris, Hugh Griffith, Richard Haydn, Tarita, Percy Herbert, Gordon Jackson, Chips Rafferty, Noel Purcell, Henry Daniell, Anna Lee, Torin Thatcher, Les Tremayne (narrator); **w**, Charles Lederer, Eric Ambler (uncredited), Borden Chase, William L.

Driscoll, John Gay, Ben Hecht (based on the novel by Charles Nordhoff, James Norman Hall); **c**, Robert L. Surtees (Ultra Panavision; Technicolor); **m**, Bronislau Kaper; **ed**, John McSweeney, Jr.; **art d**, George W. Davis, J. McMillan Johnson; **set d**, Henry Grace, Hugh Hunt; **spec eff**, A. Arnold Gillespie, Robert R. Hoag, Lee LeBlanc.

My American Cousin ★★★ 1986; Canada; 190m; Borderline/International Spectrafilm; Color; Drama; Children: Unacceptable (MPAA: PG); **DVD**; **VHS**. In this absorbing coming-of-age drama, we see Langrick as a twelve-year-old girl living with her parents, Donat and Mortifee, and two younger sisters on a cherry farm in the mountains of British Columbia, Canada, in the 1950s. She is not happy because her parents treat her like a child. One day, her cool cousin, Wildman, arrives by surprise from California in a hot red Cadillac convertible. He's a worldly hunk and she becomes attracted to him, but he also treats her as an adolescent. She later learns that her cousin stole his mother's car and ran away from home. She would like to go off with him, but Wildman is only interested in older girls, the car, and himself, and, after a while, he drives that car and himself off into the sunset. Langrick is a little wiser for the interlude, but not much. Songs: "Some Enchanted Evening" (Richard Rodgers, Oscar Hammerstein II); "Canadian Sunset," "Theme from 'A Summer Place'" (Max Steiner); "Save the Last Dance for Me" (Doc Pomus, Mort Shuman); "I Guess It Doesn't Matter Anymore" (Paul Anka); "Sweet Little Sixteen" (Chuck Berry); "Little Star" (Arthur Venosa, Vito Picone); "Sea Cruise" (Huey P. Smith); "Sh-Boom, Life Could Be a Dream" (Carl Feaster, James Keys, Floyd McRae, Claude Feaster, James Edwards); "There's a Windmill on Your Windowsill" (Will Carter). Sexuality prohibits viewing by children. **p**, Peter O'Brian, Sandy Wilson; **d&w**, Wilson; **cast**, Margaret Langrick, John Wildman, Richard Donat, Jane Mortifee, T.J. Scott, Camille Henderson, Darsi Bailey, Allison Hale, Samantha Jocelyn, Babs Chula, Terence Moore, Brent Severson, Brian Hagel; **c**, Richard Leiterman (Alphacine); **ed**, Haida Paul; **art d**, Phil Schmidt; **set d**, Joey Morgan.

My American Uncle ★★★ 1980; France; 101m; Philippe Dussart/Andrea Films/New World Pictures; Color; Comedy; Children: Unacceptable (MPAA: PG-13); **DVD**, **VHS**. Three stories by Henry Laborit involve the lives of three people discussing behaviorist theories of survival, combat, rewards, punishment, and anxiety. René (Depardieu) is a technical manager at a textile factory who suffers anxiety because of a corporate downsizing. Janine (Garcia) is a self-educated actress, who learns that the wife of her lover is dying and struggles with allowing them to reunite. Le Galle (Pierre) is a controversial career-climbing writer-politician at a crossroads in his life involving a beautiful woman. Their dilemmas are interspersed with comments from the author, Laborit. An American uncle, long expected in the film, like Lefty and Godot, never shows up in this engrossing tale. Sexuality prohibits viewing by children. (In French; English subtitles.) **p**, Philippe Dussart; **d**, Alain Resnais; **cast**, Gérard Depardieu, Nicole Garcia, Roger Pierre, Nelly Borgeaud, Pierre Arditi, Gérard Darrieu, Philippe Laudenbach, Marie Dubois, Henri Laborit, Bernard Malaterre, Laurence Roy; **w**, Jean Gruault (based on the writings of Laborit); **c**, Sacha Vierny (Eastmancolor); **m**, Arié Dzierlatka; **ed**, Albert Jurgenson; **prod d**, Jacques Saulnier.

My Best Friend ★★★ 2007; France; 94m; Fidelite Productions/IFC Films; Color; Comedy; Children: Unacceptable (MPAA: PG-13); **DVD**. This delightful comedy sees Auteuil as a middle-aged bachelor and antique dealer, a handsome, successful man living comfortably, but, at a dinner with a group of his best acquaintances, he comes to realize that none of them really have any fondness for him. They consider him to be arrogant and self-centered, and believe that he does not know the meaning of friendship. He insists to his business partner, Gayet, that he has a great friend, and she challenges him by betting him that if he can produce that friend in ten days, she will let him keep a valuable Greek vase he acquired on the company tab. If he cannot produce a best friend, he must pay for that vase. Auteuil accepts the bet, and then frantically searches though his address book to find someone he can pass off as his best friend. He is unable to find anyone to fit the bill. While taking a taxi ride, he finds the cabbie, Boon, to be annoying because he is a trivia-spouting fellow. But Boon also appears to be warmhearted, and Auteuil, desperate to win the bet, selects Boon to become his best friend. In a series of meetings during the days that follow, Auteuil comes to like Boon and the feeling is mutual, so that before the ten days are up, Auteuil has a real and honest best friend to introduce to Gayet. Auteuil gets to keep the vase, but more important, he has learned from Boon about friendship and how important friends are in life. Songs: "La Paimpolaise" (Theodore Botrel, Eugene Fautrier); "Mercato Bottleneck" (Xavier Demerliac, Alexandre Michel); "Le Canon de la Nation," "Balaton Bolero" (Jean-Stephane Brosse, Xavier Demerliac, Philippe Sirco); "Prelude in A Minor" (Johann Sebastian Bach). Gutter language prohibits viewing by children. (In French; English subtitles.) **p**, Olivier Delbosc, Marc Missonnier; **d**, Patrice Leconte, Jérôme Tonnerre (based on an idea by Olivier Dazat); **cast**, Daniel Auteuil, Dany Boon, Julie Gayet, Julie Durand, Jacques Mathou, Marie Pillet, Élisabeth Bourgine, Henri Garcin, Jacques Spiesser, Philippe du Janerand; **c**, Jean-Marie Dreujou; **m**, Xavier Demerliac; **ed**, Joëlle Hache; **prod d**, Ivan Maussion.

My Big Fat Greek Wedding ★★★ 2002; U.S./Canada; 95m; Gold Circle Films/IFC Films; Color; Comedy/Romance; Children: Unacceptable (MPAA: PG-13); **DVD**; **VHS**. This consistently humorous comedy sees Vardalos, an American girl of Greek ancestry, who is thirty years old and single, working in her family's Chicago restaurant, which is called Dancing Zorba's. Her father, Constantine, dreams of her marrying a nice Greek boy, but she wants to see what the future might bring. She takes some computer classes at college before taking over her aunt's travel agency. She then meets Corbett, a high school English teacher and they date secretly. After Constantine learns about the relationship, he becomes furious because his daughter is dating a young man who is not Greek, but he has to accept him as a future son-in-law and Corbett has to accept Vardalos' big Greek family while the bride happily accepts it all. This sleeper, made for $5 million, proved to be a huge success, taking in more than $368 million at the box office. **My Big Fat Greek Life** was a 2003 sequel. Songs: "Istanbul Coffee Shop," "Ancient Greece" (Daghan Baydur, Richard Keith Thomas); "I'm a Woman" (Jerry Leiber, Mike Stoller); "Wedding March" (Felix Mendelssohn); "Wedding March" (Richard Wagner); "Orea Ee Neefee Mas" (traditional); "Viennese Blood" (Johann Strauss, Jr.); "Tis Nifis Ta Vimata," "Moonkopoulos," "Belly Dance," "Kefi In Katavia," "To Kounoup" (Emanuel Kiriakou); "Stalia Stalia," "All My Only Dreams" (Scott Rogness, Rich Elias); "Secret Garden," "Dear God" (Nick Kutsukos); "Waltz" (from "Coppelia" ballet by Leo Delibes). Sensuality and gutter language prohibit viewing by children. **p**, Gary Goetzman, Tom Hanks, Rita Wilson, David Coatsworth, **d**, Joel Zwick; **cast**, Nia Vardalos, John Corbett, Michael Constantine, Andrea Martin, Louis Mandylor, Gerry Mendicino, Stavroula Logothettis, Constantine Tsapralis, Christina Eleusiniotis, Kaylee Vieira, John Kalangis, Lainie Kazan, Marita Zouravlioff, Sarah Osman, Bess Meisler; **w**, Vardalos; **c**, Jeffrey Jur; **m**, Alexander Janko, Chris Wilson; **ed**, Mia Goldman; **prod d**, Gregory P. Keen; **art d**, Kei Ng; **set d**, Enrico Campana; **spec eff**, Martin Malivoire, Peter Sissakis.

My Blue Heaven ★★★ 1950; U.S.; 96m; FOX; Color; Musical Comedy; Children: Acceptable; **DVD**. In this humorous musical, which is loaded with great songs, Grable and Dailey are a successful radio married couple as they are off the air, their show such a hit that they are asked to move their act to TV. All is well except that Grable wants to have a child. After a medical check, her physicians tell her that she cannot bear children and the couple is desolate, especially when regularly

Dan Dailey, Betty Grable and Mitzi Gaynor in *My Blue Heaven*, 1950.

seeing their close friends, Wayne and Wyatt, who have five adorable children. Grable and Dailey apply at an orphanage to adopt a child, but they have to wade through endless red tape and overcome objections from some sticks-in-the-mud who simply don't like the idea of theater people adopting children, irrespective of how successful they might be. They are finally granted the adoption of a child, but there is a mix-up and they wind up adopting another child and then Grable learns that her doctors were wrong and that she is pregnant and about to have a child, so that they will now have a much larger family than expected and are overjoyed at that fact. Mitzi Gaynor, the pert and pretty singer and dancer, makes her film debut in this above-average songfest where Grable and Dailey are standouts, being reunited after appearing together in the hit **When My Baby Smiles at Me**, 1948. Songs: "My Blue Heaven" (music: Walter Donaldson; lyrics: George Whiting); "What a Man," "It's Deductible," "Cosmo Cosmetics," "Halloween," "I Love a New Yorker," "Live Hard, Work Hard, Love Hard," "Don't Rock the Boat, Dear," and "The Friendly Islands" (music: Harold Arlen; lyrics: Ralph Blane). **p**, Sol C. Siegel; **d**, Henry Koster; **cast**, Betty Grable, Dan Dailey, David Wayne, Jane Wyatt, Mitzi Gaynor, Una Merkel, Don Hicks, Louise Beavers, Laura Pierpont, Bill Baldwin (announcer), Conrad Binyon, Sally Forrest, Mae Marsh, Marion Marshall, Barbara Pepper; **w**, Lamar Trotti, Claude Binyon (based on the story "Storks Don't Bring Babies" by S.K. Lauren); **c**, Arthur E. Arling (Technicolor); **m**, Alfred Newman; **ed**, James B. Clark; **art d**, Lyle Wheeler, Joseph C. Wright; **set d**, Paul S. Fox, Thomas Little, **spec eff**, Gerald Endler.

My Bodyguard ★★★ 1980; U.S.; 96m; FOX; Color; Comedy; Children: Unacceptable (MPAA: PG); **DVD**; **VHS**. Makepeace moves to Chicago with his father, Mull, and grandmother, Gordon (who has an offbeat wisecrack for every occasion). He goes to school where the local bully is Dillon, who terrorizes the boy as he does all the rest of the kids. Dillon operates a protection racket at school, extorting money from all the children with the threat that hulking Baldwin, a huge reclusive boy who talks to no one, will otherwise thrash them to bloody pulps. Schoolyard rumor has it that Baldwin once killed someone, but nobody knows for certain. Makepeace finally tires of shelling out his lunch money to the insidious Dillon and decides that he might as well pay off the source of his anxiety. He goes to Baldwin and offers him his money, but Baldwin is dumbfounded as he knows nothing about the racket Dillon has been operating and that he has no liaison with the extortionist. Makepeace learns that Baldwin has a guilt complex in that he and his brother had once been foolishly playing with their father's gun, which went off accidentally and killed that brother. Baldwin has maintained silence ever since, but he warms to the charming Makepeace and agrees to become his bodyguard. He goes to bully Dillon and forces him to give up all the

Richard Burton and Audrey Dalton in *My Cousin Rachel*, 1952.

money he has taken from the other children and those funds are returned to their owners. Dillon later shows up with a skin-headed thug, a monster of a man, and he battles Baldwin, defeating him. Dillon returns to his racket, but Makepeace has now learned courage from Baldwin, and he confronts and defeats Dillon, who is a coward at heart, and then Dillon's towering thug is also beaten to a pulp by Baldwin in a return rematch. The children are now free of the extortionist and they are shown walking and joking along the shores of Lake Michigan with their newfound buddy, Baldwin, who has become better adjusted through his experience. Well crafted by director Bill and with outstanding performances from Makepeace, Baldwin and Dillon, this film depicts the special problems of schoolchildren too rampant in American schools then and now, which, in this case, is exceptionally solved. *Author's Note*: This film was financed by independent filmmaker Melvin Simon, an Indianapolis real estate tycoon, who moved to Hollywood to make his own unique brand of films like this one, along with several others, such as **The Stunt Man**, 1980, but his films sadly saw limited distribution. Violence prohibits viewing by children. **p**, Don Devlin; **d**, Tony Bill; **cast**, Chris Makepeace, Adam Baldwin, Matt Dillon, Ruth Gordon, Martin Mull, John Houseman, Craig Richard Nelson, Paul Quandt, Hank Salas, Joan Cusack, Dean R. Miller, Jennifer Beals; **w**, Alan Ormsby; **c**, Michael D. Margulies (DeLuxe Color); **m**, Dave Grusin; **ed**, Stu Linder; **prod d**, Jackson De Govia; **set d**, Dave L. Love.

My Brilliant Career ★★★ 1979; Australia; 100m; Greater Union; Analysis Film Releasing Corp.; Color; Drama; Children: Acceptable (MPAA: G); **DVD**; **VHS**. Davis is a headstrong young woman, who grows up in a farming community in Australia's remote outback in the early 1900s where most girls marry early and raise a family. She could marry Neill, a wealthy young man, and, although she loves him, rejects him because she is afraid of losing her independence. Instead, she takes a job as a governess and housekeeper to the family of an illiterate neighbor to whom her father owes money. Turning her back on marriage and having a career alienates her from her family and friends, but she is happy with her choices. This prosaic but moving story sees an outstanding performance from Davis and good support from the cast members. **p**, Margaret Fink; **d**, Gillian Armstrong; **cast**, Judy Davis, Sam Neill, Wendy Hughes, Robert Grubb, Max Cullen, Aileen Britton, Peter Whitford, Patricia Kennedy, Alan Hopgood, Julia Blake, David Franklin; **w**, Eleanor Witcombe (based on the novel by Miles Franklin); **c**, Donald McAlpine (Panavision; Eastmancolor); **m**, Nathan Waks; **ed**, Nicholas Beauman; **prod d**, Luciana Arrighi; **art d**, Neil Angwin.

My Brother Talks to Horses ★★★ 1947; U.S.; 92m; MGM; B/W; Comedy; Children: Acceptable. Set in Baltimore in the early 1900s, this charming comedy sees nine-year-old Jenkins with psychic powers that enable him to talk to race horses. His older brother, Lawford, works in a bank and has a fiancée, Tyler. Their widowed mother, Byington, who takes in boarders, is a bit odd herself as she doesn't think it is strange that Jenkins talks to horses because she routinely sees supernatural beings and events. There's a cute scene in which Byington tickles Jenkins' back and he keeps saying "More, more!" The plot thickens when gangsters discover that Jenkins learns from the horses which nag will win in the next race. When Jenkins is threatened by the thugs, Lawford comes to the rescue, besting the bad guys and saving Jenkins from harm. This is a heartwarming story for everyone including children. *Author's Note*: Of all the many movie stars on the huge MGM lot, Jenkins was the favorite of the studio's chief, Louis B. Mayer, who once said of Jenkins: "That boy is one of the greatest natural actors in the world." Jenkins, with his freckled face and often missing front teeth, was, indeed, one of the most endearing child actors of his day, shining in such films as **The Human Comedy**, 1943; **National Velvet**, 1944; and **Our Vines Have Tender Grapes**, 1945. Director Zinnemann told this author that "Butch was easy to direct [in **My Brother Talks to Horses**]. He had no notions about being a movie star and thought he was having fun. Everything he did came naturally to him. He had a good memory and always delivered his lines on cue and as they were written. The amazing thing was that when he spoke those words it was if they were coming out of his own mind and mouth for the first time. That little guy was a delight." **p**, Samuel Marx; **d**, Fred Zinnemann; **cast**, Jackie "Butch" Jenkins, Peter Lawford, Beverly Tyler, Edward Arnold, Charles Ruggles, Spring Byington, O.Z. Whitehead, Paul Langton, Irving Bacon, Howard Freeman, Lillian Yarbo, Harry Hayden; **w**, Morton Thompson (based on his novel *Joe the Wounded Tennis Player*); **c**, Harold Rosson; **m**, Rudolph G. Kopp; **ed**, George White; **art d**, Cedric Gibbons, Leonid Vasian; **set d**, Edwin B. Willis; **spec eff**, Warren Newcombe.

My Brother's Wedding ★★★ 1985; U.S.; 115m; Charles Burnett Productions/Milestone Film & Video; Color; Drama; Children: Unacceptable (MPAA: PG-13); **DVD**. Silas is an angry young black man living in the Watts neighborhood of Los Angeles, California, who works in the family's dry cleaning business. He has a love-hate relationship with the community, resenting the disadvantages he faces each day. He has a dilemma in having to choose between attending two events on the same day, the funeral of his best friend, who was killed in a car accident, or the wedding of his brother, Kemper, whom he resents for being more successful. Kemper is a lawyer engaged to marry another lawyer, Burnett, who comes from a well-to-do family, and Silas despises her and her family members. Silas would rather skip the wedding, but knows his mother, Holmes, would be furious if he did not live up to his family responsibilities. His choice, like his life, is a muddle and the film ends in a freeze-frame that makes the viewer wonder which event he will eventually attend. This fascinating drama sees standout performances from Silas and the supporting cast members. Gutter language prohibits viewing by children (and this seems to be replete in almost all modern films featuring blacks, as if they were all uneducated lowlife persons, unrefined, uncouth and without a sense of decent conversational skills, which, in the opinion of this author, presents and promotes a subliminal and unfair racist portrait). **p**, Charles Burnett; **d,w&c**, Burnett; **cast**, Everett Silas, Jessie Holmes, Gaye Shannon-Burnett, Ronnie Bell, Dennis Kemper, Sally Easter, Angela Burnett, Monte Easter, Frances Nealy, Sy Richardson; **ed**, Thomas Penick; **prod d, art d, set d**, Penny Barrett.

My Cousin Rachel ★★★ 1952; U.S.; 99m; FOX; B/W; Mystery/Romance; Children: Unacceptable; **DVD**; **VHS**. This gothic tale begins in the early 1800s with a young Richard Burton (in his American film debut) living on a huge estate in Cornwall, England, his mansion close enough to the sea so that its crashing waves can be heard from his living room windows. He has been receiving letters from his cousin, Sutton, who lives in Italy, the last missive alarming Burton in that Sutton states in that letter that he is dying and believes that his beautiful wife, de Havilland, has been systematically poisoning him to death. Sutton dies, and then de Havilland appears and she both attracts Burton as well as alarms him as he cannot rid himself of the suspicion that she may be a murderess, although her charming and winning ways belie such lethal capabilities. Burton nevertheless falls in love with de Havilland, and, after Sutton's will is probated, Burton inherits Sutton's vast riches that are now added to his own considerable assets. All that means little to Burton (whose character is age twenty-five while Burton was then twenty-seven, and he is now involved with an older but alluring woman). He then confronts de Havilland with the letter he received from Sutton, but de Havilland is quick to answer that her husband was suffering from a brain tumor that made him paranoid and where he believed all around him were seeking to kill him. Burton accepts her explanation and he magnanimously gives all he has, his mansion, land, money, the family jewels, to de Havilland, and they are now a happy couple, although they cautiously avoid talking about going to the altar. Then Dolenz, a polished Italian attorney arrives, to conclude de Havilland's affairs, and Burton becomes suspicious that Dolenz is somehow romantically involved with his client and that de Havilland is secretly keeping this affair from Burton. At Dolenz' suggestion, de Havilland prepares her "special tea" for Burton, and, after he drinks it, he becomes violently ill, through its own possible lethal contents or Burton's own imaginary apprehensions, which the viewer is left to determine. Burton becomes hallucinatory, believing in his bedridden deliriums that he has married de Havilland. He slowly recovers through the careful and tender nursing by de Havilland and, once Burton has regained his health, he asks for her hand in marriage. She politely refuses, and this rejection causes Burton to be consumed by rage. He throttles de Havilland, almost choking her to death, but then regains his senses, releases her and humbly apologizes. His rage again mounts when Burton sees de Havilland in what he thinks is a romantic meeting with Dolenz. Then Dalton, a fetching old flame of Burton's, arrives at the estate, and Burton is now happy to hear from de Havilland that she will be leaving the estate. So convinced is Burton that de Havilland has, indeed, murdered Sutton, that he does not tell her that the dilapidated bridge she must cross when leaving is dangerous, and when de Havilland does leave, the bridge collapses and she suffers a fatal fall. Burton races to her side, holding de Havilland in his arms as she dies and where he now has a terrible guilt that he will carry with him for the rest of his life, believing that he has caused de Havilland's death, although the viewer is left with a rather unexplained ending that questions de Havilland's own guilt in Sutton's death. The acting by Burton and de Havilland is superb, and director Koster maintains great tension and anxiety throughout this well-written mystery, where Waxman's eerie and somewhat discordant score adds greatly to this chilling tale. *Author's Note*: Screenwriter Johnson, who was a favorite of Fox boss Darryl Zanuck, was also the producer of this film and really called the shots on its production, and not pantheon director George Cukor, who was originally slated to direct this film. Cukor told Zanuck that he believed he could coax the reclusive Greta Garbo out of her isolated retirement in New York to play the femme fatale role, but when Garbo declined (as she routinely did for so many years when Hollywood attempted to lure her back before the cameras), Cukor then began arguing with Johnson about the script, which Zanuck loved. Unlike most movie moguls of that era, Zanuck, who thought of himself as a writer first and a studio boss second, most often sided with his screenwriters, especially Johnson, and when he took Johnson's side in the debate, Cukor quit the production and Koster was assigned to direct. "George [Cukor] wanted me to rewrite the script to give more scenes and attention to Olivia [de Havilland]," Johnson told this author. "I refused and Zanuck backed me up. George was a "woman's director" and we all knew it, and he did well with many films that focused on women, but my script encompassed much more than that. So it was goodbye to George [Cukor] and hello to Henry [Koster]." The film did not see the

Marisa Tomei, Fred Gwynne and Joe Pesci in *My Cousin Vinny*, 1992.

box office success Fox anticipated, but it did establish the brilliant and mercurial Burton as a Hollywood movie star and secured for him a long-term contract that allowed him to appear in many future and significant feature films. **p&w**, Nunnally Johnson (based on the novel by Daphne du Maurier); **d**, Henry Koster; **cast**, Olivia de Havilland, Richard Burton, Audrey Dalton, Ronald Squire, George Dolenz, John Sutton, Tudor Owen, J.M. Kerrigan, Margaret Brewster, Hamilton Camp; **c**, Joseph LaShelle; **m**, Franz Waxman; **ed**, Louis Loeffler; **art d**, Lyle Wheeler, John De Cuir; **set d**, Walter M. Scott; **spec eff**, Ray Kellogg.

My Cousin Vinny ★★★★ 1992; U.S.; 120m; Palo Vista Productions/FOX; Color; Comedy; Children: Unacceptable (MPAA: R); **DVD**; **VHS**. This hilarious black comedy begins when Macchio and Whitfield, two NCY college students are driving through rural Alabama and stop in a small town to buy food at a convenience store. They neglect to pay for a can of tuna, and their car is shortly pulled over by a policeman and they are arrested and booked. Macchio believes they have been charged for shoplifting the can of tuna and readily admits his error, not knowing that, after he and Whitfield left the store, the clerk had been robbed and shot and killed by two young men fitting his and Whitfield's description. Macchio is charged with murder and Whitfield as an accessory. Macchio makes a frantic phone call to his cousin Vinny (Pesci), who immediately sets out with his fiancée, Tomei, and arrives in the small Alabama town, to tell Gwynne, the presiding judge in the case, that he is representing Macchio and Whitfield. Pesci is a recently graduated lawyer, a mechanic who has worked his way through law school and who is practicing personal injury cases, but he is wholly inexperienced and knows nothing about criminal law. When talking to Gwynne, however, he gives the judge a tall tale about his vast experiences in criminal courts, inferring that he has participated as an attorney in many recent celebrated criminal cases. When asked by Gwynne about his trial successes, Pesci shrugs and says: "Win some, lose some." Gwynne tells him that he goes by the book and hands him a copy of Alabama's criminal jurisprudence that specifies the State's rules and regulations involved in criminal cases, a book Pesci has never read, but takes along with him as he prepares to defend Macchio and Whitfield. He and Tomei take a room at a cheap motel, but they are awakened in the middle of the night by the screeching of hogs being fed in a large feeding pen across the street. Sleepless, Pesci appears in court before Gwynne, who admonishes him for his casual dress and orders him to obtain and wear a suit in accordance with the court's dress codes. After he soils the only suit he has, and is unable to find a cleaners to have it cleaned, Pesci rents the only suit he can find from a costume shop, a garish red formal suit with tails, and when he appears wearing this outlandish garment, Gwynne threatens to cite him for contempt of court, until Pesci explains his circumstances.

Joe Pesci in *My Cousin Vinny*, 1992.

Pesci's inexperience soon becomes evident to his opponent, Smith, the prosecuting attorney, who is amused with Pesci's unorthodox antics in court and where he botches every simple cross-examination with the prosecutor's eyewitnesses, several of whom identify Macchio and Whitfield as the two young men that left the convenience store just after the shooting. Pesci, meanwhile, has continued problems with Gwynne, his defiant behavior bringing several contempt citations while his sweetheart, Tomei, badgers him about getting married. He is further vexed when Tomei loses most of their money to a hulking pool shark and then confronts this towering thug by betting him the lost amount that he can beat him up (Pesci stands only 5'4", a pygmy compared to this giant), and Pesci later collects that bet after the pool shark shows him the prize money, with a few quick punches that doubles up the thug and where Pesci perfunctorily grabs the cash. At one point, Whitfield is so disgusted with Pesci's mishandling of the case that he fires him, and accepts public defender Pendleton, who has a decided stutter and proves even more ineffective so that Whitfield goes back to Pesci. Gwynne, who has always been suspicious of Pesci's boasted credentials, contacts the court in Brooklyn, where Pesci normally practices, discovering that he is not the celebrated attorney he claims to be, but Pesci then tells Gwynne that he practices under different names, causing Gwynne to continue tracking down Pesci's true background. Meanwhile, Smith makes a strong case against the defendants, but Pesci unexpectedly recalls all the eyewitnesses and proves that one could not actually see the robbers leaving the convenience store, another failed to actually see the perpetrators because he was making grits at the time, and yet another witness, an elderly black woman, is so near-sighted that she cannot distinguish anything for any appreciable distances. Smith, however, has an expert FBI witness, Rebhorn, who testifies that the skid marks left by the culprit's car are definitely those coming from the car driven by the defendants, testimony that appears to seal the fate of the defendants. Further, Pesci, who has little sleep because of the nocturnal noises of trains rattling by his hotel (he and Tomei move from one place to another in their desperation to find a tranquil resting place), alienates Tomei by ridiculing some candid photos she has taken of the crime scene, particularly the skid marks of the car used by the robbers, and she walks out on him. He studies those photos and then pleads with Tomei to return to the courtroom to give testimony while asking sheriff McGill to make a phone call for him. Tomei reluctantly takes the stand, stating to Gwynne that she hates her fiancé, and then establishes the fact that she is a master mechanic and describes in unchallenging detail how the skid marks of the car left by the culprits could not have been that of the defendants as they could have been made only by one other car model, destroying Rebhorn's testimony. Rebhorn again takes the stand and agrees that he has been mistaken. Further, McGill takes the stand and testifies that he

has made a phone call to another county where the sheriff there has reported that two youths with the similar appearances to Pesci's clients have been arrested and that their car is the same model that has left the skid marks at the convenience store and that the weapon used to kill the clerk has been found in the possession of those two other young men. Smith now admits he has no case and dismisses all charges against Macchio and Whitfield and they joyously leave the courtroom with Pesci, who also avoids Gwynne's last probe into his background in that Tomei has established yet another alias for Pesci that allows them leave the town. As they drive north toward New York City, Pesci and Tomei resume their bickering about their forthcoming marriage. This delightfully humorous film is well directed by Lynn, and Pesci gives one of his finest performances as a crude, low-born apprentice attorney desperate to save the lives of his clients while Tomei is also superb as the loyal but contentious fiancée (she won the Oscar for Best Actress). Gutter language (unfortunately almost every other word) prohibits viewing by children. Songs: "Way Down South" (Edgar Winter), "It Just Takes One" (Jan Buckingham, David Vidal), "Don't Look at My Shadow" (Stephen Stills), "Secretly" (Dick Manning, Al Hoffman, Mark Markwell), "Stand by Your Man" (Billy Sherrill, Tammy Wynette), "Mind Your Own Business" (David Cole, Robert Clivilles). **p**, Dale Launer, Paul Schiff; **d**, Jonathan Lynn; **cast**, Joe Pesci, Ralph Macchio, Marisa Tomei, Mitchell Whitfield, Fred Gwynne, Lane Smith, Austin Pendleton, Bruce McGill, Maury Chaykin, Pauline Meyers, Raynor Scheine, James Rebhorn, Chris Ellis; **w**, Launer; **c**, Peter Deming; **m**, Randy Edelman; **ed**, Tony Lombardo, Stephen E. Rivkin; **prod d**, Victoria Paul; **art d**, Michael Rizzo, Rando Schmook; **set d**, Michael Seirton; **spec eff**, Dick Cross.

My Darling Clementine ★★★★★ 1946; U.S.; 97m; FOX; B/W; Western; Children: Cautionary; **DVD**; **VHS**. Pantheon director Ford presents a classic western in his depiction of the story of legendary lawman Wyatt Earp (1848-1929), who is superbly played by Fonda. The film opens with Fonda and his brothers Bond (playing Morgan Earp, 1851-1882), Holt (playing Virgil Earp, 1843-1905), and Garner (playing James Earp, 1841-1926) driving a herd of cattle westward. Fonda comes upon Brennan (who plays rancher Newman Hayes Clanton, 1816-1881, the father of several sons, all rustlers), along with his sons Withers (playing Joseph Isaac "Ike" Clanton, 1847-1887), Ireland (playing Billy Clanton, 1862-1881), Libby (playing Phineas Fay "Phin" Clanton, 1843-1906), and Simpson (playing Sam Clanton, a fictitious member of this outlaw clan). Brennan, who has been looking over Fonda's herd, makes Fonda an offer to buy his cattle, but at an inexpensive price. Fonda turns him down and then Brennan suggests that Fonda and his brothers ride into the nearby town of Tombstone and enjoy a night of relaxation. Fonda thinks that a good idea and later rides to Tombstone with brothers Bond and Holt, leaving young Garner behind as he is entrusted with the care of the herd. When Fonda arrives, he immediately goes to a barbershop, but just before barber Hall can shave him, a bullet whistles through the shop, narrowly missing Fonda. Enraged, Fonda steps outside to see people running from the Oriental Saloon. Inside, drunken Stevens, who is called Indian Charlie, is shooting up the place after having driven out its occupants. Fonda demands that the local sheriff, Woods, subdue Stevens, but he refuses to risk his life with the lethal gunman. Disgusted, Fonda goes to the saloon, climbing the outside stairs to the second floor, and enters the place through a window. Several more shots and then the brief sound of a struggle are heard by the townsfolk, who anxiously stand outside awaiting the outcome. Fonda then appears as he drags the unconscious Stevens through the swinging doors of the saloon and deposits him with Roberts, the town mayor, saying to Roberts: "What kind of town is this—serving liquor to Indians?" Stevens stands up to feel a large lump on his head where Fonda has given a blow, and Fonda then orders Stevens out of town, kicking him in the backside to send him on his way. Roberts immediately offers Fonda the post of town marshal, but he refuses and returns to the barbershop to get his shave and haircut. When Fonda and his brothers return to their campsite, they find Garner murdered and their cattle stolen. Fonda, Bond and Holt bury Garner and then ride back to Tombstone where Fonda wakes Roberts up in the middle of the night, accepting the job of town marshal and where he deputizes his two brothers. He then checks into the local hotel where he again meets Brennan, telling him that his herd has been stolen, his brother killed and that he has taken the job of town marshal. Brennan tells him that that might be a dangerous job, but Brennan becomes alarmed when Fonda tells him his name, "Wyatt Earp," who is known as one of the most feared lawmen in the West. Fonda and his brothers then begin to investigate the dark doings of Brennan and his four brutish sons. Fonda is shown gambling at the Oriental and where singer Darnell stands behind him giving signals to a cardsharp. Fonda realizes he is being cheated, but his attention is diverted when Mature, playing the celebrated gambler and quick-draw gunman John H. "Doc" Holliday (1851-1887), sees the cardsharp and then runs him out of town. Fonda then confronts Mature, who draws his gun, but Fonda shows him that he is not wearing a six-gun and invites him to have a drink. Mature does, befriending him and his brothers Bond and Holt, and where Fonda reminds him that he is now the law in Tombstone and that only he has the authority to run anyone out of town. Mowbray, a posturing Shakespearean actor, arrives in town with much pomp and ceremony, and he announces his forthcoming appearance at the local theater, but, on opening night, he is nowhere to be found. A riot almost ensues, but Fonda promises the theater crowd that he will find Mowbray. He and Mature locate Mowbray in a seedy saloon, standing atop a table where he is being forced to perform by the four Clanton brothers. Mowbray struggles to recite some lines from Shakespeare's *Hamlet*, but his memory fails him and Mature recites the lines for him (before seized by one of his many coughing fits; he has consumption as did Holliday). Fonda then tells Mowbray that he is taking him out of the saloon, but, when Withers threatens to stop him, Fonda knocks Withers unconscious with the butt of his gun (a favorite ploy of Earp's when subduing unruly cowboys). Brennan then arrives, seeing that his sons have been cowed, and half-heartedly apologizes for their thug-like behavior, and after Fonda, Mature and Mowbray leave, he savagely turns upon his sons, whipping them and shouting: "When you pull a gun, kill a man!" The next morning, Fonda sees beautiful Downs alight from the newly arrived stagecoach, helping her with her luggage. She is a schoolteacher with the name of Clementine, and Fonda is immediately taken with her, escorting her to the hotel and telling the clerk to provide hot water for her so she can take a bath. Downs has arrived to see her former fiancé, Mature, and finds him that night eating dinner in the kitchen of the saloon with Fonda. Mature tells her that their engagement is over and that he no longer wishes to see her, that they can have no decent life together, his notorious western reputation as a gambler and gunfighter ruining their relationship. Downs, however, stays in town, taking the job of schoolteacher and Fonda becomes her self-appointed protector, dancing with her at a Sunday church meeting that is held outdoors where the local church is under construction. Later that day, Darnell, who is jealous of Downs as she wants Mature for herself, goes to Downs' room and orders her to leave town. Fonda arrives and throws Darnell out of the room. Meanwhile, Mature has left town, but Fonda finds a locket Darnell is wearing that belonged to his slain brother, Garner, and Darnell tells Fonda that she has gotten that locket from Mature. Fonda then thinks that Mature may have been the one who rustled his cattle and killed his brother and he rides after the stagecoach. Catching up with it, Fonda subdues Mature and brings him back to Tombstone where they both confront Darnell that night in her room. She stalls and then hesitantly tells them that she got the locket from Ireland (Billy Clanton), who is waiting outside her window on a porch and who then shoots her and flees. Mature carries the wounded Darnell to the saloon, placing her on a table where he will operate on her. Fonda, by that time, has fired several shots at the fleeing Ireland and, when he sees his brother Holt on horseback in the street, orders Holt to go after Ireland; Holt chases the outlaw as they exchange shots during the wild chase leading toward

Linda Darnell and Henry Fonda in *My Darling Clementine*, 1946.

Brennan's ranch. Meanwhile, Mature operates on Darnell, and she briefly recovers to thank him, but then dies, and Mature feels he has failed himself and Darnell. Then Holt arrives at the Brennan ranch, entering the house to find Ireland in bed, dead, and with Brennan and his other three sons standing over him. As Holt is about to leave, Brennan shoots Holt dead and his body is later dumped on a Tombstone street by Brennan, who tells Fonda that he and his sons "will be waiting for you at the O.K. Corral!" Fonda prepares for that final showdown with Bond and Mature. At dawn, the three men go to the sprawling corral where Brennan and his three sons are waiting. Fonda calls out to Brennan, telling him he has a warrant for Brennan and his sons charging them with the murders of his two brothers, Garner and Holt. Brennan shouts back "Well, you come right in here and serve your warrants, marshal!" His remarks are then followed by gunfire from Brennan and his sons. The battle ensues with Fonda, Bond and Mature shooting and killing all three of Brennan's sons while Brennan takes refuge in a small adobe hut. Fonda tells him to come out, that all his sons are dead. Brennan comes outside, calling for his sons. Fonda says to him: "They're all dead. I'm not going to kill you. I hope you live a hundred years so you can feel just a little what my Pa is going to feel. Now get out of town! Start wandering!" Brennan mounts a horse and slowly begins to ride away, but he turns in the saddle, pulling his six-gun. Bond then rapidly fires his own six-gun, killing Brennan, who topples dead from his horse. Bond then tells Fonda that Mature has been shot and he lies dead in the corral, a handkerchief he has used in his final coughing spell fluttering on the railing of the corral's fence. The final scene of this epic western sees Fonda bidding farewell to the lovely Downs, telling her that, after he visits with his family in California, he plans to return to see her and she welcomes his return. Fonda tips his hat and says: "Ma'am, I sure like that name, Clementine." With that, he rides after his brother Bond on a road that stretches to far vistas of buttes and open country as Downs watches him ride away. Although Ford takes great liberties with the actual facts and characters of this story, it is presented in such vivid and moving scenes that he fully captures the raucous and rowdy nature of Tombstone and, in his carefully organized scenes, presents a gritty image of the Old West very much in keeping with its guzzling gunmen and struggling settlers. Fonda and Mature are standouts in their roles, and the rest of the cast give strong support. Songs: "(Oh My Darlin') Clementine" (1884; music: Percy Montrose; lyrics: H.S. Thompson), "Ten Thousand Cattle" (traditional), "The First Kiss Is Always the Best from Under a Broad Sombrero" (composer unknown), "Oh! Susanna" (1848; Stephen Foster), "Camp Town Races" (1850; Stephen Foster). ***Author's Note***: Ford told this author that "I knew the real Wyatt Earp back in the 1920s when he was a consultant on western films and was living in Los Angeles. He told me all about the gunfight at the O.K. Cor-

Walter Brennan and Henry Fonda in *My Darling Clementine*, 1946.

ral and I recreated that fight just as he described it." Ford, however, for the sake of dramatic license, altered many facts. For instance, Brennan's character of N. E. Clanton was not present at the gunfight at the O.K. Corral, and he may never have met Earp, having been killed two months before the gunfight in Tombstone, on August 13, 1881, by Mexican Federal troops at Guadalupe Canyon in Animas Valley, New Mexico, on the Mexican border, along with five others, who had been rustling Mexican cattle. Virgil Earp was not murdered before the fight, but wounded in it, and only Billy Clanton was killed and in that gunfight, not while attempting to escape after murdering someone, as depicted in the film. Moreover, Mature is shown as a practicing medical doctor when he was a dentist and he did not die at the O.K. Corral, but perished six years later of consumption in a sanitarium. In almost all of the films depicting the celebrated gunfight, including this one, the O.K. Corral is shown as a sprawling area similar to a stockyard where it was, in fact, a rather confining area wedged between two buildings in Tombstone. Moreover, Ford shot the entire film in forty-five days and on location in Monument Valley, his favorite location area, and where he had the town of Tombstone reconstructed. "Pappy [Ford] made a very long film out of **My Darling Clementine**," Zanuck told this author, "and it was just too long for audiences to wait until that final shoot-out, so I told him that we had to cut it down by about thirty minutes, and we did, but very carefully, and with his approval on every cut scene." Zanuck considered Ford to be "the greatest film director of the modern era," or so he stated to this author. Fonda, who by nature, acted with hesitancy in almost all of his films, emphasized those manners in this film at Ford's insistence. Fonda told this author that "Pappy took me aside at the beginning of the production and told me that 'Earp is a very careful man. He never makes a sudden move. He measures every step he takes and slowly moves his hands. He had to if he wanted to survive in those days. I know. Earp told me so. Anyone who made a sudden move in those days was liable to get shot,' and so I followed that good advice and moved about like a snail until I am forced to take action. I slowed down everything I did, even when I am sitting in a chair on a wooden veranda balancing myself on two legs of a chair by switching one leg from another against a wooden post. I did that so slowly that I fell off that chair several times until we got it right." Mature told this author that "Ford wanted me to practice a quick draw with my six-gun, but I did not do that too well, so he had my holster greased and that improved my draw, but then I had to keep wiping away that grease from my fingers. I understand that Holliday carried three or four guns, but I only wear one and that was enough for me. Doc Holliday was a strange bird, an educated man from the South. He developed tuberculosis and moved to the West to get to the dry climate to improve his lungs, but, if he was so interested in preserving his life, why then would he want to risk it by getting into one gun-

fight after another? Like I said, he was a strange bird." Brennan understood his character as soon as he read the script, telling this author: "A total villain, that's what I am in that picture. Old Man Clanton is about the meanest cuss I ever played, but I had played a man pretty much like him about five years earlier when I played the part of Roy Bean [1825-1903] in **The Westerner** [1940], who is a self-appointed judge in a small western town where I use the law to get what I want, fine anyone for anything to get money and hang anyone I don't like. I took all the viciousness from that character and put into my character of Old Man Clanton in **My Darling Clementine**. Everyone takes what they can from the best of others in this business, and I did, too, even from my own roles. After we finished the picture, Ford told me: 'Amazing job, you got that mean old man down perfectly. How did you understand him so well?' I told him that I read up on the subject, a fib. I don't think he saw me act in **The Westerner**, or he would have known how I got that character down pat. I don't think that John Ford watched too many other films, especially westerns. I think he thought he owned the westerns, and I guess he did." The legendary gunfight at the O.K. Corral that occurred in Tombstone, Arizona, on Wednesday, October 26, 1881, at 3 p.m., between lawmen Wyatt Earp and his brothers, along with gunfighter John H. "Doc" Holliday and the outlaw clan of the Clanton and McLaury [or McLowery] brothers and others, resulting in the deaths of Billy Clanton and Tom and Frank McLaury, has been depicted in many other films, including **Doc**, 1971; **Frontier Marshal**, 1939; **Gunfight at the O.K. Corral**, 1957; **Hour of the Gun**, 1967; **Law and Order**, 1932; **Tombstone**, 1993; **Tombstone: The Town Too Tough to Die**, 1942; **Wyatt Earp**, 1994. For all films depicting the Earp brothers, Doc Holliday and the outlaws they faced, see Indices for Historical Events and Historical Personalities. For more factual details on the gunfight, and those involved in that event, see my book, *Encyclopedia of Western Lawmen and Outlaws* (Paragon House, 1992; Wyatt Earp: pages 110-121; Holliday: pages 162-165; Clanton: pages 75-76). **p**, Samuel G. Engel; **d**, John Ford; **cast**, Henry Fonda, Linda Darnell, Victor Mature, Cathy Downs, Walter Brennan, Tim Holt, Ward Bond, Alan Mowbray, John Ireland, Roy Roberts, Jane Darwell, Grant Withers, J. Farrell MacDonald, Russell Simpson, Francis Ford, Mae Marsh, Don Garner, Fred Libby, Charles Stevens, Louis Mercier, Mickey Simpson, Harry Woods, Jack Pennick, Ben Hall; **w**, Engel, Winston Miller (based on a story by Sam Hellman and the book *Wyatt Earp, Frontier Marshal* by Stuart N. Lake); **c**, Joe MacDonald; **m**, Cyril J. Mockridge, David Buttolph; **ed**, Dorothy Spencer; **art d**, Lyle Wheeler, James Basevi; **set d**, Thomas Little; **spec eff**, Fred Sersen.

My Dinner with Andre ★★★ 1981; U.S.; 110m; Saga Produtions; New Yorker; Color; Drama; Children: Cautionary (MPAA: PG); **DVD**; **VHS**. This is one of the strangest films ever made, presenting almost a stream-of-consciousness conversation between two friends, Shawn and Gregory, as they dine together in a restaurant, sharing their lives by discussing every imaginable person and problem on the planet. Gregory, a director, is the more gregarious (if not garrulous) of the two, but Shawn gets in his licks with plenty of provocative palaver. Gregory carries the conversation by relating his experiences, how he dropped out of his practical life and traveled the world to meet one extraordinary person after another, such as a monk who could stand on his fingertips. A good listener, Shawn often counters with challenges to Gregory's wanderlust attitudes and his complete disregard for the social order of things. These are two clever persons, probing each other's minds while asserting their principles of life (or the utter abandonment of them). The passion and force of their conversation holds fascinating attention throughout, as if one is eavesdropping on an important discussion at the next table, and, though their statements are eloquently and creatively delivered, there is much vacuity to it all. The viewer, however, will be addictively sucked into the vortex of their whirlpool verbiage and verbosity, one where Gregory proves to be a great storyteller and Shawn his perfect sounding board. Song: "Gymnopedie 1" (Erik Satie). **p**, George W. George, Beverly Karp; **d**, Louis Malle; **cast**, Wallace Shawn, Andre Gregory, Jean Lenauer, Roy Butler; **w**, Shawn, Gregory; **c**, Jeri Sopanen (Movielab Color); **m**, Allen Shawn; **ed**, Suzanne Baron; **prod d**, David Mitchell; **art d**, Stephen McCabe.

My Dog Skip ★★★ 2000; U.S.; 95m; Alcon Entertainment/WB; Color; Drama; Children: Unacceptable (MPAA: PG-13); **DVD**; **VHS**. This entertaining autobiographical story sees Muniz and his dog in Yazoo, Mississippi, in 1942. His father, Bacon, has lost a leg in the Spanish Civil War and his mother, Lane, tries hard to make her son happy, but the birthday party she throws for him is only attended by senior citizens. His older and only friend, Wilson, is a high school athlete who lives next door, but goes off to World War II before he can teach Muniz his baseball "secrets." Lane thinks what her son needs is a dog, but his father is not in favor of it. Lane nevertheless gives Muniz a dog he names Skip, and they become instant best pals, going everywhere together. Now all the other kids want to be Muniz's friend because he has such a great dog. Skip is also a smart dog in that he befriends everyone in town and makes daily visits to the local butcher, who gives him a slice of bologna sausage (which, in case you didn't know, is pronounced "baloney"). Wilson returns from the war more serious and grown-up, as would be expected, having experienced bloody combat and a similar experience, albeit shown in allegorical microcosm, has Muniz see a deer die before his eyes. This coming-of-age film is based on the boyhood of Willie Morris, who, as an adult, went to Oxford University on a Rhodes scholarship, then to New York for a literary career, including this fond memoir of his beloved dog Skip. Songs: "Tuxedo Junction" (William Johnson, Buddy Feyne, Erskine Hawkins, Julian Dash), "Ration Blues" (Louis Jordan, Collenane Clark, Antonio Cosey), "Old Yazoo" (Fats Waller), "I'm Beginning to See the Light" (Duke Ellington, Don George, Johnny Hodges, Harry James), "There'll Be a Hot Time in the Town of Berlin" (Joe Bushkin, John DeVries), "Lullaby of Broadway" (Al Dubin, Harry Warren), "Chasing Shadows" (Benny Davis, Abner Silver). Violence and gutter language prohibit viewing by children. **p**, John Lee Hancock, Broderick Johnson, Mark Johnson, Andrew A. Kosove; **d**, Jay Russell; **cast**, Frankie Muniz, Diane Lane, Luke Wilson, Kevin Bacon, Bradley Coryell, Daylan Honeycutt, Cody Linley, Caitlin Wachs, Peter Crombie, Clint Howard, Mark Beech, Harry Connick, Jr. (narrator); **w**, Gail Gilchriest (based on the book by Willie Morris); **c**, James L. Carter; **m**, William Ross; **ed**, Harvey Rosenstock, Gary Winter; **prod d**, David J. Bomba; **set d**, Tracey A. Doyle; **spec eff**, Stephen Bourgeois, Matthew Zeringue.

My Dream Is Yours ★★★ 1949; U.S.; 99m; WB; Color; Musical; Children: Acceptable; **DVD**; **VHS**. This girl-next-door-makes-it-big tale offers a number of top songs and begins when Bowman, a conceited singer, refuses to renew his contract for a hit radio show. Talent scout-agent Carson knows what to do about that after he discovers a single mother, Day, and transforms her into a major singing star. Carson and Day fall in love in the process. While Carson helps Day to the top, Bowman's star almost crashes, but he makes a comeback with Day's help. A highlight of the film has Day cavorting with Bugs Bunny and Tweety Bird, this live action and animation sequence owing much to Gene Kelly's dancing with Jerry, the adorable cartoon mouse, in the musical hit **Anchors Aweigh**, 1945. **My Dream Is Yours** is an entertaining remake of the Dick Powell musical **Twenty Million Sweethearts**, 1934, with lots of terrific songs: "Cuttin' Capers" (Harry Warren, Ralph Blane, based on "Canadian Capers" by Guy Chandler, Bert White, Henry Cohen, Earl Burnett); "Freddie, Get Ready" (Harry Warren, Ralph Blane, based on "Hungarian Rhapsody No. 2" by Franz Liszt); "You May Not Be an Angel/But I'll String Along with You" (Warren, Al Dubin); "Love Finds a Way," "My Dream Is Yours," "Someone Like You," "Tic, Tic, Tic," (Harry Warren, Ralph Blane); "You Must Have Been a Beautiful Baby," "Jeepers Creepers" (Harry Warren, Johnny Mercer); "Nagasaki" (Harry Warren, Mort Dixon); "Hooray for Holly-

Frankie Muniz and Enzo/Moose in *My Dog Skip*, 2000.

wood" (Richard A. Whiting); "I'll Sing You a Thousand Love Songs" (Harry Warren); "I Only Have Eyes for You," "With Plenty of Money and You" (Harry Warren, Al Dubin); "Avalon" (Vincent Rose); "Lullaby of Broadway," "I Wanna Go Back to Bali" (Harry Warren); "What's Up, Doc?"(Carl W. Stalling); "Vienna Blood" (Johann Strauss, Jr.); "Five O'Clock Whistle" (Gene Irwin, Josef Myrow); "The Merry-Go-Round Broke Down" (Cliff Friend); "Bull Dog" (Cole Porter). **p&d**, Michael Curtiz; **cast**, Jack Carson, Doris Day, Lee Bowman, Adolphe Menjou, Eve Arden, S.Z. Sakall, Selena Royle, Edgar Kennedy, Sheldon Leonard, Franklin Pangborn, Ada Leonard, Frankie Carle, Mel Blanc (voice), Iris Adrian, Rudolf Friml, Jr., Chili Williams; **w**, Harry Kurnitz, Dane Lussier, Allen Rivkin, Laura Kerr (based on the story "Hot Air" by Jerry Wald, Paul Finder Moss); **c**, Wilfred M. Cline (Technicolor), Ernest Haller; **m**, Harry Warren; **ed**, Folmar Blangsted; **art d**, Robert Haas; **set d**, Howard Winterbottom; **spec eff**, Edwin DuPar.

My Fair Lady ★★★★★ 1964; U.S.; 170m; WB; Color; Musical; Children: Acceptable; **DVD**; **VHS**. This delightful and always enthralling musical, one of the best ever made, is based upon Bernard Shaw's classic play "Pygmalion" and its 1938 non-musical film adaptation starring Wendy Hiller and Rex Harrison, offering a wonderful cast headed by Harrison (reprising his role as the inimitable Henry Higgins), Hepburn, and Hyde-White. It all begins when Harrison is leaving a theater in London and encounters Hyde-White, both being experts in linguistics and having considerable admiration for each other's skills. Harrison believes that he can take the most commonplace guttersnipe and turn that uneducated person into a grand lady by teaching her the proper speech patterns and manners, but Hyde-White has his doubts. To prove his point, when Harrison hears Hepburn, a young cockney girl, bawl out a pitch for her flowers, Harrison selects her as his guinea pig, making a substantial wager with Hyde-White that he can turn Hepburn into that grand lady within a short period of time. Hepburn at first refuses Harrison's offer to make a lady of her, thinking he has ulterior motives and she, being properly raised, will have nothing to do with it, but when she learns that Harrison is a foremost speech instructor, she appears at his upscale residence (where Hyde-White is now staying as a guest) and offers Harrison money for lessons in diction. She feels that if she can improve her manner of speech, she will be able to get a job as a store clerk and stop selling flowers on the street. Harrison, who is wealthy, really has no need of her money, but he agrees to transform her into a lady of high breeding and class, as he is still attempting to win that bet with Hyde-White. Harrison mercilessly puts Hepburn through his exacting regimen, and that also includes a new physical look, where she is scrubbed and perfumed, and her hair perfectly coiffed. Meanwhile, Holloway, who is Hepburn's father, a blue collar worker and a man with

Jeremy Brett, Audrey Hepburn and Rex Harrison in *My Fair Lady*, 1964.

enormous street savvy and considerable wit, appears and demands a few pounds for the "use" of his daughter, believing that her reputation might be sullied if it were to be learned that she is living in the residence of a bachelor, despite the fact that he knows propriety is being strictly observed. Harrison gives him some money and Holloway goes on his merry way, straight to a pub to enjoy his newly found riches with his friends. Hepburn's rigorous education continues, and when Harrison and Hyde-White finally think Hepburn is suitable for public presentation, they adorn her in a resplendent gown, parasol and sun hat and escort her to the races at Ascot. While at this outing, Hepburn turns the eyes of everyone and charms Cooper, Harrison's mother, an austere and demanding dowager who is as discerning as a tax collector and who pronounces Hepburn a perfect lady. Hepburn particularly enamors Brett, a handsome but vacuous young man. Harrison then puts her through one final test, as challenging as the hedgerows of a steeple chase, when he and Hyde-White escort her to a mammoth social ball where everyone who is anyone is present, and where Hepburn is closely scrutinized and becomes the radiant star attraction, even wowing aristocrats and those of royal blood. She passes the supreme test when another linguist, Bikel, meets her and then boasts his knowledge of accents and speech patterns by saying that he will stake his reputation that Hepburn is of royal birth, such is her regal comportment and eloquent speech. When they return home, Harrison and Hyde-White revel in their colossal charade, while complimenting each other on their ability in foisting off a cockney girl on British high society. Ignored and shunned aside, Hepburn departs only to find that her father has improved his financial status after associating with a millionaire earlier recommended by Harrison and has now decided to make an honest woman of his common-law wife, Hepburn's mother, by finally taking the woman to the altar to be officially married. Hepburn, who is in love with Harrison, visits his mother and Cooper gives her advice on how to handle her son. Meanwhile, the love-smitten Brett, who has been wandering outside of Harrison's domicile in hopes of catching a glimpse of the fetching Hepburn, meets with her and proposes marriage. She puts him off and later uses that proposal as a threat to Harrison, who returns home to an empty home, thinking about Hepburn so much that he begins playing recordings of her voice when she first began taking lessons from him. As he sits listening to that cockney accent of old, the record stops but Hepburn's voice continues and now Harrison realizes that Hepburn is in the room with him and that she loves him and he loves her. Without looking at her, he says: "Eliza, get me my slippers," a message that Hepburn perfectly understands, one that means that Harrison loves her and that they are going to have a life together. She dutifully retrieves those slippers and this charming and thoroughly entertaining film ends. Cukor, that inveterate "woman's director," helms this charmer with great expertise, focusing, of course,

on Hepburn, who turns in a marvelous performance, as does the suave and self-assured Harrison and who is strongly supported by the happy and pleasingly avuncular Hyde-White. Production values are superb, from exquisite costuming to richly appointed sets, and every dime of the film's $17 million budget is evident in every frame. Of course, the film contains some of the most unforgettable songs in the history of the medium, an astounding number of these great songs firmly remaining in popular memory. The film, like the original stage production in NYC (1956-1962, having the longest and most successful run of any musical with 2,717 performances; a similar success was achieved in London) was a great box office success, reaping more than $72 million. It won an Oscar as Best Picture and Cukor won an Oscar for Best Director, as well as Harrison winning an Oscar as Best Actor, but glaringly, Hepburn was not even nominated for Best Actress, with Julie Andrews winning that Oscar for Mary Poppins, 1964. The irony (or the revenge of the Academy) was that Andrews starred in the Broadway version of *My Fair Lady* (Harrison, Hyde-White and Holloway also appeared in that record-breaking Broadway production) and was refused the part in the film adaptation in favor of Hepburn, who was thought by Warner Brothers mogul Jack Warner to have more box office appeal. Songs (all in 1956 from Alan Jay Lerner, lyrics; and Frederick Lowe, music): "Why Can't the English," "Wouldn't It Be Loverly," "The Flower Market," "I'm an Ordinary Man," "With a Little Bit of Luck," "Just You Wait," "Servants' Chorus (Poor Professor Higgins)," "The Rain in Spain," "I Could Have Danced All Night," "Ascot Gavotte," "On the Street Where You Live," "The Embassy Waltz," "The Transylvanian March," "You Did It," "Show Me," "Get Me to the Church on Time (I'm Getting Married in the Morning)," "A Hymn to Him (Why Can't a Woman Be More Like a Man)," "Without You," and "I've Grown Accustomed to Her Face." ***Author's Note***: Jack Warner wanted to film the Broadway version for some years and put aside a staggering $20 million budget for its production (it came in under that by $3 million). The always cost-conscious Warner fretted when he went so far as to offer 50 percent of the net of the film to Lerner and Lowe, and to assure its success, he thought to pack the film with stellar talent, thinking to cast either Cary Grant or Rock Hudson in the role played (and owned) by Harrison on the Broadway stage and even thought to have James Cagney play the role Holloway has established in the stage version as the delightfully devious father. He did not want any of the fine talent that had made the Broadway play such a great success. Warner's wild notions, however, were turned around when Grant met with Warner and not only refused to play the part of the know-it-all Henry Higgins, but said to Warner, as Grant told this author: "If you don't put Rex [Harrison] in that role, which he has made famous, I won't even bother to see the picture myself. You have a great built-in cast from the stage production and you would be a fool not to use all of those fine performers in the film." Warner thought the world of Grant and heeded his advice, signing Harrison, Hyde-White and Holloway and others form the stage version, but he balked at Andrews and insisted that Hepburn play Eliza Doolittle, creating considerable debate to this date as to which one would have been better suited to the part. **p**, Jack L. Warner, James C. Katz (1994 restoration); **d**, George Cukor; **cast**, Audrey Hepburn, Rex Harrison, Stanley Holloway, Wilfrid Hyde-White, Gladys Cooper, Jeremy Brett, Theodore Bikel, Mona Washbourne, Isobel Elsom, John Holland, John Alderson, Betty Blythe, Henry Daniell, Queenie Leonard, Alan Napier, Grady Sutton, Marni Nixon (singing voice of Hepburn), Bill Shirley (singing voice of Brett); **w**, Alan Jay Lerner (based on a musical play by Lerner, Frederick Lowe and the play "Pygmalion" by George Bernard Shaw); **c**, Harry Stradling (Technicolor); **m**, Lowe, André Previn; **ed**, William Ziegler; **prod d**, Cecil Beaton, Gene Allen (not credited); **art d**, Allen, Beaton (not credited); **set d**, George James Hopkins.

My Family/Mi Familia ★★★ 1995; U.S.; 128m; American Playhouse; Color; Drama; Children: Unacceptable (MPAA: R); **DVD**; **VHS**. In an engrossing domestic drama that also deals with illegal immigrants from Mexico, Olmos narrates the tale of three generations of an immigrant family in America, he being a writer and a member of the third generation. The saga begins with Vargas, patriarch of the first generation, walking over a year's time from Mexico to Los Angeles in the 1920s. He meets and marries Lopez, who works as a nanny, and they raise a family in a small house in East Los Angeles. During the Great Depression, Lopez is one of thousands of Mexican-Americans rounded up by U.S. Army troops and sent back to Mexico with her babies, even though she and most of the others have become American citizens. She eventually returns to her home, and the children deal with youth culture problems and the police in the 1950s. The film then focuses on one of their sons, Smits, his marriage to Carrillo, a Salvadorian refugee, their son, and his struggle to become a good parent. Over the decades, the family lives in the same house to which one room after another is added to capacitate more and more Mexican immigrants, including a nun, an ex-convict, a lawyer, a restaurant owner, and a boy shot and killed in a gang conflict. This strong saga of a determined Hispanic family's struggles and triumphs is well crafted and enacted. Songs: "Konex Konex," "Guacamaya," "Rosa de Castilla," "Angel Baby" (Rosalie Hamlin); "Sugar Time" (Charlie Phillips, Odis Echols); "Tu Solo Tu" (Fgelipe Valdez Leal); "La Negra" (Ruben Fuentes, Silvestre Vargas), "La Diana" (traditional), "Jesusita en Chihuahua" (Quirino Mendoza), "Flor de Canela" (traditional); "Que Rico el Mambo" (Perez Prado); "One Summer Night" (Danny Webb); "Are You Really Sincere" (Mike Piccirillo); "Celoso" (Jennu Lou Carson); "Guavaberry" (Juan Luis Guerra); "Down on the Riverbed" (David Hidalgo, Louis Perez); "I Love Lucy Theme" (Eliot Daniel, Harold Adamson); "El Rey" (Jose Alfredo Jimenez); "Los Laureles" (Salvador Ringel Gonzalez); "I'm Your Puppet" (Linden Oldham, Dan Penn); "Bachata Rosa," "Senorita" (Juan Luis Guerra); "Zapa Mambo" (Mario Desafinado). Gutter language, graphic violence, and sexuality prohibit viewing by children. **p**, Anna Thomas, Francis Ford Coppola; **d**, Gregory Nava; **cast**, Jimmy Smits, Esai Morales, Edward James Olmos, Scott Bakula, Mary Steenburgen, Jennifer Lopez, Rafael Cortes, Ivette Reina, Amelia Zapata, Jacob Vargas, Alicia del Lago, Constance Marie; **w**, Thomas, Nava; **c**, Edward Lachman; **m**, Mark McKenzie; **ed**, Nancy Richardson; **prod d**, Barry Robison; **art d**, Tony Myers, Adam Lustig; **set d**, Suzette Sheets; **spec eff**, Lou Carlucci, Robert Calvert.

My Father's Glory ★★★ 1991; France; 105m; Gaumont/Orion Classics; Color; Biographical Drama; Children: Acceptable (MPAA: G); **BD**; **DVD**; **VHS**. Based on the boyhood of novelist and filmmaker Marcel Pagnol (1895-1974), who is played by Ciamaca, this filmic memoir portrays an idyllic summer in France during early 1906. When Ciamaca is eleven, he and his schoolteacher father, Caubére, and mother, Roussel, leave the city and spend their summer vacation in a cottage in the hills of Provence. The boy learns about the area from a local girl, Molinas, who becomes his friend. Nothing much happens but the little things like walking in the sun, sitting under a shady tree, listening to birds, and eating local food adds up to warm personal travelogue, packed with charm and family nostalgia. A sequel, **My Mother's Castle**, 1991, depicts more of that summer at the same location. (In French; English subtitles.) **p**, Alain Poiré; **d**, Yves Robert; **cast**, Philippe Caubére, Nathalie Roussel, Didier Pain, Thérèse Liotard, Julien Ciamaca, Victorien Delamare, Joris Molinas, Benoît Martin, Paul Crauchet, Pierre Maguelon; **w**, Robert, Louis Nucéra, Jérôme Tonnerre (based on the novel by Marcel Pagnol); **c**, Robert Alazraki, Christophe Beaucarne, Eric Vallée, Paco Wiser; **m**, Vladimir Cosma; **ed**, Pierre Gillette; **prod d**, Jacques Dugied.

My Favorite Blonde ★★★ 1942; U.S.; 78m; PAR; B/W; Comedy; Children: Acceptable; **DVD**; **VHS**. Cute comedy with plenty of laughs opens when Hope and his partner, a clever penguin, are refining that penguin's act for its film debut after a successful theatrical run. Into their dressing room slips beautiful blonde Carroll, a British spy, who is car-

Philippe Caubére and Nathalie Roussel in *My Father's Glory,* 1991.

rying the secret plans for a shipment of planes to England, which is at war with Germany, and a bevy of Nazi agents are in hot pursuit of her to obtain those plans. Carroll easily convinces Hope to help her make an escape, and he takes her along as part of his act in what turns out to be a cross-country chase between Hope, Carroll, the penguin and pursuing Nazis, until they all reach the Golden State. That chase involves many tricky maneuvers and disguises by Hope, Carroll and even the hilarious penguin as they successfully evade their pursuers and eventually best the beastly bunch. Bing Crosby, Hope's partner in many of Paramount's "Road Show" films, makes a cameo appearance as a travel agent giving Hope and Carroll ridiculous directions (Crosby made a practice of appearing in Hope's solo comedy films). Songs: "Over the Waves" (1887; Juventino Rosas), "Thanks for the Memory" (1937; Ralph Rainger, Leo Robin), "Old Folks at Home (Swanee River)" (Stephen Foster), "When Irish Eyes Are Smiling" (1912; music: Ernest Ball; lyrics: Chauncey Olcot, George Graff), "Wearin' of the Green" (traditional). *Author's Note*: Hope told this author that "Madeleine Carroll, one of the most beautiful women in the movies, is my co-star in that chase picture, and she set the standard of all of those "My Favorite" pictures, so Paramount had to provide me with one beautiful woman after another. Who's complaining? To tell you the truth, the penguin in that picture stole all my best scenes, the little hog!" **p**, Paul Jones; **d**, Sidney Lanfield; **cast**, Bob Hope, Madeleine Carroll, Gale Sondergaard, George Zucco, Lionel Royce, Walter Kingsford, Victor Varconi, Edward Gargan, Dooley Wilson, Milton Parsons, Monte Blue, Isabel Randolph, Carl "Alfalfa" Switzer, Bing Crosby; **w**, Don Hartman, Frank Butler, Barney Dean (based on a story by Norman Panama, Melvin Frank); **c**, William C. Mellor; **m**, David Buttolph; **ed**, William Shea; **art d**, Hans Dreier, Robert Usher; **spec eff**, Farciot Edouart.

My Favorite Brunette ★★★★ 1947; U.S.; 87m; Hope Enterprises; PAR; B/W; Comedy; Children: Acceptable; **DVD**; **VHS**. This is one of Hope's best comedies, replete with one hilarious sequence after another, all based upon Hope doing a pal a favor that threatens his life and limbs. Hope is a mild-mannered baby photographer. His good friend, Ladd, is a tough private detective occupying an adjacent office, and Hope is forever emulating his pal's heroic behavior as a no-nonsense gumshoe á la Sam Spade or Philip Marlowe. Ladd decides to take a vacation from his criminal cases and asks Hope to look after his business and office, and Hope, flattered that his idol so trusts him, agrees. Beautiful Lamour arrives and thinks that Hope is Ladd and hires him to find her missing uncle, a wealthy baron, and gives him a treasure map to guard at all costs, a map that very evil persons are seeking. Dingle, claiming to be one of the baron's friends, accompanies Hope on his search for the missing uncle. Dingle takes Hope to a vast estate where he introduces Hope

Bob Hope and Dorothy Lamour in *My Favorite Brunette*, 1947.

to a wheelchair-bound man, who is supposedly that uncle. Hope then meets Chaney, a physician, who tells him that Lamour is mentally unstable and that her stories about a vanished uncle are nothing more than wild imaginations. Hope is all but convinced that Lamour has sent him on a fool's errand, but when he is about to leave, he sees the invalided uncle suddenly leave his wheelchair, appearing to be in perfect health and Hope takes a photo of the upright man. Dingle sees this and summons his lunatic henchman, Lorre, who knocks out Hope and steals the camera containing the incriminating photo. Hope recovers and later teams with Lamour, both going to the geologist who drew the treasure map, only to find him murdered. Hope is then arrested for the killing and is tried, convicted and condemned. At the last minute before he goes to the electric chair, he is reprieved. Lamour has discovered that Lorre has framed Hope by using the gun that Hope has borrowed from detective Ladd to dispatch the geologist. Her findings have also brought about the arrests of Dingle and his associates, including the psychotic Lorre. Hope is released and winds up in the arms of Lamour for a happy ending. Hope is very funny in this comedic romp, packed with sight gags and wonderful lines and where Lorre is a standout as a weirdo killer. Crosby, Hope's partner in their "Road Show" films, makes another cameo appearance, this time as the hooded executioner, who is about to throw the switch that will fry Hope in the electric chair. When Crosby removes his hood, Hope remarks: "Boy! He'll take any kind of part!" Songs: "Beside You," "My Favorite Brunette" (music: Ray Livingston; lyrics: Ray Evans); "Murder, He Says" (music: Jimmy McHugh; lyrics: Frank Loesser). **p**, Daniel Dare; **d**, Elliott Nugent; **cast**, Bob Hope, Dorothy Lamour, Peter Lorre, Lon Chaney Jr., John Hoyt, Charles Dingle, Reginald Denny, Frank Puglia, Ann Doran, Jack La Rue, Anthony Caruso, Bing Crosby, Betty Hutton, Alan Ladd, John Hoyt, Willard Robertson, Ray Teal; **w**, Edmund Beloin, Jack Rose; **c**, Lionel Lindon; **m**, Robert Emmett Dolan; **ed**, Ellsworth Hoagland; **art d**, Hans Dreier, Earl Hedrick; **set d**, Sam Comer, John MacNeil; **spec eff**, Farciot Edouart, Gordon Jennings.

My Favorite Spy ★★★ 1951; U.S.; 93m; PAR; B/W; Comedy; Children: Acceptable; **DVD**; **VHS**. In this funny outing, Hope is a burlesque comic, who is arrested by NYC police. The cops believe him to be a much-wanted international spy. That spy, who was about to obtain some important microfilm, is arrested by other agents, and now U.S. intelligence agents ask Hope to impersonate that spy because he is a perfect look-alike and they want him to obtain that vital microfilm. Hope overcomes his apprehensions when told that, if he is successful, he will receive a huge cash award. Hope travels to Tangier and there meets alluring Lamarr, the girlfriend of the abducted spy. His impersonation of her sweetheart is so effective that Hope convinces her that he is that

very secret agent she loves. Lamarr is really a double agent, working for the U.S. as well as for Sullivan, who wants to obtain that microfilm. In one humorous mishap after another, Hope manages to avoid detection until the real spy he is impersonating escapes from his captors and arrives in Tangier (he is also played by Hope in a dual role). When that spy is killed, Hope, the comic, has no choice but to confess his charade to the fetching Lamarr, who has fallen in love with the comic. Just when Hope is about to be captured by Sullivan, Lamarr aids him in escaping and she then turns Sullivan and his henchman over to authorities. Lamarr and Hope then retire from the espionage game by establishing a clothing store in New Jersey with the $10,000 award Hope has earned through his hazardous antics. Songs: "Just a Moment More" (music: Jay Livingston; lyrics: Ray Evans), "I Wind Up Taking a Fall" (music: Robert Emmett Dolan; lyrics: Johnny Mercer), "William Tell Overture" (Gioachino Rossini), "Light Cavalry Overture" (Franz von Suppé). **p**, Paul Jones; **d**, Norman Z. McLeod; **cast**, Bob Hope, Hedy Lamarr, Francis L. Sullivan, Arnold Moss, John Archer, Luis Van Rooten, Morris Ankrum, Angela Clarke, Iris Adrian, Frank Faylen, Mike Mazurki, Marc Lawrence, Martha Mears (singing voice for Lamarr); **w**, Edmund Hartmann, Jack Sher, Hal Kanter, Edmund Beloin, Lou Breslow (based on a story by Beloin, Breslow); **c**, Victor Milner; **m**, Victor Young; **ed**, Frank Bracht; **art d**, Hal Pereira, Roland Anderson; **set d**, Sam Comer, Grace Gregory; **spec eff**, Farciot Edouart, Gordon Jennings.

My Favorite Wife ★★★ 1940; U.S.; 88m; RKO; B/W; Comedy; Children: Acceptable; **DVD**; **VHS**. Grant is a successful businessman who remarries after waiting seven years for his missing wife, Dunne, to be declared dead, she having vanished after a shipwreck. Grant marries Patrick, but before they go on their honeymoon, Dunne suddenly resurfaces, having been rescued from a remote island where she and Scott, the only survivors of that shipwreck, have been living together. Grant and Patrick take their honeymoon at Yosemite National Park, but Dunne, still in love with Grant, won't give up on him, and follows him and his new bride to the vacation spot, ruining Grant's nuptials. When he and Patrick return home, they find Dunne in residence and where she has met her two children, who cannot remember her and so he tells them that she is a family friend and this charade continues with many humorous incidents, but Grant becomes alarmed when he learns that Scott was Dunne's only male companion on that island for seven years. The whole mixed-up relationship winds up in court where Patrick wants Grant's former marriage to Dunne annulled so that she will be legally married to Grant, but Grant is not so sure that he wants to be married to her because he still loves Dunne. Bates, the presiding judge in the case, is suddenly faced with sorting out this impossible situation while dealing with the bantering Dunne, the kibitzing Scott, the irate Patrick and the much-confused Grant. The proceedings become a shambles of endless accusations, assertions and assumptions until Bates is thoroughly discombobulated and who cannot tell one wife from another. When Grant fails to strongly support Patrick's angry contentions, Patrick tells one and all she has had enough and Bates winds up annulling her marriage with Grant so that Grant and Dunne can resume their loving marriage. Wonderfully enacted by Grant, Dunne, Scott and Patrick, and with a very witty script, director Kanin, a master of such domestic comedies, does a great job confusing viewers for most of this hilarious film, until bringing this dizzy tale to a reasonable (sort of) and happy conclusion. This film was remade as **Move over Darling**, 1963, with James Garner and Doris Day in the Grant and Dunne roles, but was never as good as the original. Songs: "Jingle Bells" (1857; James Pierpont), "The Skater's Waltz" (1882; Emil Waldteufel). *Author's Note*: Grant told this author that "Irene [Dunne] and I had a hit together in **The Awful Truth** [1937] a few years before we did **My Favorite Wife** together and that screwball comedy worked just as well as the first one. You know Hollywood's principle, when you succeed with one type of story, do it again and again." Comedy director Leo McCarey, who had directed both Grant and Dunne in **The Awful Truth**, was slated to direct this film, but he was injured in a serious car accident shortly before the production was to begin and Kanin was brought in to substitute. **p**, Leo McCarey; **d**, Garson Kanin; **cast**, Irene Dunne, Cary Grant, Randolph Scott, Gail Patrick, Ann Shoemaker, Scotty Beckett, Mary Lou Harrington, Donald MacBride, Granville Bates, Pedro de Cordoba; **w**, Sam and Bella Spewack (based on a story by the Spewacks and McCarey); **c**, Rudolph Maté; **m**, Roy Webb; **ed**, Robert Wise; **art d**, Van Nest Polglase; **set d**, Darrell Silvera.

My Favorite Year ★★★★ 1982; U.S.; 92m; Brooksfilms/MGM/UA; Color; Comedy; Children: Cautionary (MPAA: PG); **DVD**; **VHS**. This is a wonderfully funny film that nostalgically and poignantly recalls the hilarious antics of early day television. The film centers on one episode of a one-hour live show being prepared for uproarious comedy star Bologna. He is tough, sly, crafty, creative, and even has a soft spot in his heart that is larger than he would like to admit. Bologna exhausts and exasperates his staff of brilliant comedy writers that include Macy and others. Ambitious, young writer Linn-Baker is an apprentice scribe working on Bologna's show. He gets an extraordinary assignment to escort and act as guide (and keeper) of a spectacular film star, O'Toole, who has played countless swashbuckling adventurers on the silver screen and who is about to make a guest appearance on Bologna's show. O'-Toole arrives with great fanfare from Hollywood, and Linn-Baker soon finds that the heavy drinking O'Toole is a roaring drunk and a notorious womanizer. They go to the Stork Club where the gallant O'Toole dances with an adoring fan, the middle-aged wife of a businessman, giving her the most exciting moment of her life, but O'Toole also covetously eyes a curvaceous blonde and whose escort jealously guards her against O'-Toole's advances. Linn-Baker, however, impersonates a waiter and clumsily tumbles a tray of food onto the escort that allows O'Toole to escape with the blonde. In the days that follow, Linn-Baker finds himself involved in one wild escapade after another with the irresponsible O'Toole. The actor decides to see an old friend, but when he finds that friend is attending a private party in a high rise apartment building, he lowers himself on a fire hose from its rooftop to the level below where the party is taking place on an open veranda, and where O'Toole almost falls to his death. Linn-Baker next finds himself strolling through Central Park near dawn with O'Toole. The actor relates his colorful Hollywood career and espouses his credos on acting and life, while avoiding any conversation that involves his young daughter, who is at a boarding school as he has been unable to bring himself to see her because he thinks he has failed her as a father. This stroll through the park ends when O'Toole impulsively steals a policeman's horse while the cop is relieving himself in the bushes, and he and Linn-Baker escape while wildly riding that horse through the park. Linn-Baker, while trying to maintain a romance with fetching TV assistant Harper, has taken O'Toole to his home for dinner, where O'Toole charms his mother, Kazan, who endearingly calls O'Toole "Swanee" (his name is Alan Swan), and where Linn-Baker replies: "He's an actor, Mom, not a river." Kazan and other relatives, who idolize the actor, give him sound advice, telling him that the family is everything and this reminds O'Toole of his daughter. When he leaves Kazan's house, the entire population in the neighborhood has gathered to cheeringly see him off. Meanwhile, Bologna plans a skit in his show where he will lampoon union boss Mitchell, a thug with underworld ties and who wears garish ties and pin-striped suits, the very ensemble Bologna, with expanded shoulder pads extending like boards from his shoulders, plans to wear. Mitchell meets with Bologna and warns him not to go through with his parody about him, which only further incites the comedian to go ahead with an even more savage lampooning. Then Bologna learns that his guest star O'Toole is suffering from the DTs, and Linn-Baker is ordered to sober him up and prepare him for his appearance on the upcoming show. Linn-Baker has achieved the impossible in that O'Toole is now ready to make his appearance, but he panics when he discovers that the show is live, saying, "I am a film actor!" He cowers in his dressing room as the show begins with the very skit that Mitchell

Jessica Harper, Mark Linn-Baker and Peter O'Toole in *My Favorite Year,* **1982.**

warned Bologna not to perform. To that end, Mitchell has sent four brawny union thugs to invade the show, and while Bologna and other actors are performing, these goons take part in a staged fight that becomes very real as they pummel and bounce the brawling Bologna about. O'Toole, however, who has been shamed into action by a disgusted Linn-Baker, finally finds his nerve and appears in a balcony above the live audience that thinks the fight on stage where the sets and props are being wrecked are part of the show. Seeing Bologna in real trouble, or just for the daring fun of it, O'Toole grabs a rope and swings from the balcony onto the stage where he battles the goons with Bologna, both spectacularly knocking these toughs senseless for a terrific finish to the show, where the audience thunderously applauds what they think is a staged performance. The film ends with O'Toole taking bows to a standing ovation as he has triumphed on TV as he has in life, since he has earlier gone to see his daughter at her school and has reunited with her. O'Toole gives a marvelously believable performance of an unbelievable character and Bologna is riveting as the rugged TV comedian. Linn-Baker, Kazan, Harper, Macy and the rest of the cast are also standouts in their roles. Director Benjamin directs with superlative skills that move this action-packed and very humorous film along at a dizzying pace. Songs: "Stardust" (1927; music: Hoagy Carmichael; lyrics: Mitchell Parish), "How High the Moon" (1940; music: Morgan Lewis; lyrics: Nancy Hamilton), "Somebody Stole My Gal" (1918; music and lyrics: Leo Wood). The film did brisk box office business in its initial release, returning more than $20 million. *Author's Note*: The film, according to Brooks, is based upon the guest appearance of swashbuckling film star Errol Flynn (who is the role model for O'-Toole), in one of the early episodes of the live TV show "Your Show of Shows," hosted by comedian Sid Caesar (the role model for Bologna). The character of Linn-Baker is based upon Brooks (who was the executive producer for this film) and comedian Woody Allen, both of whom were then working as gag writers for Caesar's show. **My Favorite Year** marked the debut of Benjamin as a director of feature films. Brooks admitted that Flynn's appearance on that show was uneventful and that he and others, who escorted Flynn about during that time, did not befriend or come to know the celebrated actor to any extent and that the character played by O'Toole, though it is based on Flynn's persona or reputation, is otherwise wholly fictional. **p**, Michael Gruskoff, Joel Chernoff, Mel Brooks (not credited); **d**, Richard Benjamin; **cast**, Peter O'Toole, Mark Linn-Baker, Jessica Harper, Joseph Bologna, Bill Macy, Lainie Kazan, Anne DeSalvo, Basil Hoffman, Lou Jacobi, Adolph Green, Cameron Mitchell, Gloria Stuart; **w**, Norman Steinberg, Dennis Palumbo (based on a story by Palumbo); **c**, Gerald Hirschfeld (Metrocolor); **m**, Ralph Burns; **ed**, Richard Chew; **prod d**, Charles Rosen; **set d**, Don Remacle; **spec eff**, Charles R. Schulthies.

Ava Gardner and Robert Mitchum in *My Forbidden Past*, 1951.

My First Mister ★★★ 2001; U.S.; 109m; ApolloMedia/PAR; Color; Comedy; Children: Unacceptable (MPAA: R); **DVD**; **VHS**. High school ends for Sobieski, a misfit seventeen-year-old, who bears tattoos, ear piercings, and dyed hair, and she needs a job. She sees Brooks, a chubby forty-nine-year-old man dressing a men's clothing store window, is intrigued by him, and asks for a job. He owns the store and says she doesn't look like she could sell anything to his customers, but he hires her in spite of his misgivings. They become friends, both being loners, but sex does not come into their friendship. Many humorous incidents occur as these two mismatched co-workers go about selling clothes to customers while they learn much about each other's lifestyles and we learn about two nice people. Songs: "Disconnected Child" (Tim Brecheno, Dave Tomlinson); "I Enjoy Being a Girl" (Richard Rodgers, Oscar Hammerstein II); "Attitude" (Stee Proctor, Lindy Layton); "On Stage" (Antonio Jolly, Donna McConnell); "Beautiful" (Tara Slone, Tony Rabalao, Thomas Payne, Thomas McKay); "Monster" (Gina Birch); "All the Nice Girls Love a Sailor" (Bob Barratt, Colin Frechte); "Soldiers" (Susan Wallace, Tina Root); "I See You Baby" (Andrew Cato; Thomas Findlay, Tod Wooten); "Sandwiches" (Detroit Grand Pubahs); "Beyond the Sea" (Charles Trenet, Jack Lawrence); "Don't Blame the Children" (Horace Hinds. Clive Hunt); "I Think I Love You" (Tony Romeo); "Shakin' All Over" (Racicot Daniel Albert); "Straight to Number One," "Life's Beach" (David Lowe, James Lynch); "Bell, Book and Candle" (Bob Hewerdine); "Don't Look Now" (Michael Sherwood, Julius Robinson); "Retdurn" (Chad Butler, Bun Freeman); "The Girl I Dream About" (Bobby Caldwell); "All the Way" (Sammy Cahn, Jimmy Van Heusen). Gutter language and sexual content prohibits viewing by children. **p**, Carol Baum, Sukee Chew, Jane Goldenring, Anne Kurtzman, Mitchell Solomon, Frank Hübner, Jan Fantl; **d**, Christine Lahti; **cast**, Albert Brooks, Leelee Sobieski, John Goodman, Carol Kane, Mary Kay Place, Michael McKean, Gary Bullock, Henry Brown, Kevin Cooney, Nic Costa, Rutanya Alda, Natasha Braisewell; **w**, Jill Franklyn; **c**, Jeffrey Jur; **m**, Steve Porcaro; **ed**, Wendy Greene Bricmont; **prod d**, Dan Bishop; **art d**, Gary Kosko; **set d**, Kathe Klopp; **spec eff**, Lou Carlucci, Steve Sosner.

My Foolish Heart ★★★ 1949; U.S.; 98m; Samuel Goldwyn/RKO; B/W; Drama; Children: Unacceptable; **VHS**. Hayward gives a bravura performance (nominated for an Oscar) in this grand tearjerker where she is about to lose everything—her husband, her daughter, and her home—because of her excessive drinking and constant depressions. Her marriage has long been an unhappy one and now her husband, Smith, wants a divorce. The cause of it is Hayward's early mistake in getting pregnant by another man and then inveigling Smith into marrying her after she has stolen him from Wheeler, but that old college roommate has remained her only friend. Though she plans to tell Smith that their daughter, Perreau, is not his child, Wheeler convinces her not to reveal that secret. She begins packing her things, but finds an old dress that stirs Hayward's memories and we see her in flashback where it is 1941 and she is attending an upscale New York City party wearing that dress and meets and is swept off her feet by gatecrasher Andrews. They develop an affair, and when she and Andrews are caught necking at her private boarding school, Hayward is expelled. Her mother, Landis, is worried that she has been sexually compromised, and her father, Keith, confronts Andrews, who swears that he and Hayward did not consummate their love affair. Then the Japanese attack Pearl Harbor and America goes to war and so does Andrews, joining the air force. Before he is shipped out to fight overseas, he and Hayward have one last passionate evening together. Hayward later gets a letter from Andrews saying that, when he returns, he will take her to the altar, but he never returns as he is killed in action. Pregnant with Andrews' child, Hayward then comes between Wheeler and Smith so that Smith will marry her and, after that happens, she tells him that the child she bears is his. In flash-forward, we see Hayward deciding that she will do the right thing, and she tells Smith that she will leave and that he can keep Perreau. Smith by then wants a divorce so that he can marry old flame Wheeler, but he compassionately leaves Perreau with Hayward, still believing she is his child, so that Hayward and Perreau can make a life together. In addition to Hayward's fine performance, the entire cast, particularly Keith, offer standout performances in this well-crafted film. Song (which became an enormous hit): "My Foolish Heart" (music: Victor Young; lyrics: Ned Washington). *Author's Note*: Hayward told this author that "**My Foolish Heart** was the first film I did with Goldwyn, who is one of the finest gentlemen in Hollywood. It was full of suds, of course, a woman's film, but the script was so well written [by the Epstein twins, who wrote the screenplay for **Casablanca**, 1942] that its scenes and the dialog overcome all those suds spilling at our feet. I thought Dana [Andrews] was just terrific in the role of my lover and always felt that he was one of the most underrated actors in Hollywood. I was up for an Oscar in that picture, but I lost to Olivia de Havilland and I was not sorry about it. She deserved to win as Best Actress that year for her magnificent performance in **The Heiress** [1949]. My chance would come later, as I knew it would." Hayward would go on to win an Oscar as Best Actress for **I Want to Live!**, 1958. This film was based upon a story by J. D. Salinger that first appeared in *the New Yorker* and later appeared in a collection of nine stories by the author. **p**, Samuel Goldwyn; **d**, Mark Robson; **cast**, Dana Andrews, Susan Hayward, Kent Smith, Lois Wheeler, Jessie Royce Landis, Robert Keith, Gigi Perreau, Karin Booth, Tod Karns, Phillip Pine, Neville Brand; **w**, Julius J. and Philip G. Epstein (based on the story "Uncle Wiggily in Connecticut" by J.D. Salinger); **c**, Lee Garmes; **m**, Victor Young; **ed**, Daniel Mandell; **art d**, Richard Day; **set d**, Julia Heron; **spec eff**, John Fulton.

My Forbidden Past ★★★ 1951; U.S.; 70m; RKO; B/W; Drama; Children: Cautionary; **DVD**; **VHS**. Gardner and Mitchum steam with passion in this above-average tearjerker, where Gardner is the belle of New Orleans in the 1890s, having inherited a great fortune from her grandmother, a woman of wiles and a somewhat notorious past. Gardner has everything in life that a woman would want, except the one thing she cannot have, and that is Mitchum, who is married to Carter. Obsessed with this brawny individualist, Gardner tries to win Mitchum away from his wife, and when that fails (he is a loyal spouse who refuses to dally with her), she uses everything at her considerable disposal to break up Mitchum's marriage. She encourages Douglas, a rake of the first rank, to pursue and woo Carter away from her husband, but that separation comes about through violence when Carter is killed. Mitchum is blamed for her death and is tried and comes close to being convicted until Gardner courageously steps forward to expose all the repulsive skeletons dangling in her closet that bring about Mitchum's exoneration and her own disgrace, such is the unflagging love of a woman for a good man. Mitchum and Gardner are outstanding in their moody roles, and the film boasts high production values with lavish costuming and sumptuous sets. The film bogs down a bit with all of the machinations launched by Gardner, but the viewer's fascination for this beautiful actress and the magnetic personality of the rugged Mitchum is sustained throughout. *Author's Note*: Mitchum told this author that "I felt that my part in that picture was a lot of male window dressing for Ava's [Gardner's] costumes—she wore a new dress for every scene, I think. She's got all the money in the world. She is more beautiful than any other woman. She can have any man in town. So why is she running after me? The reason, if you want to call it that, is because she can't have me. Only women can figure that one out." **p**, Robert Sparks, Polan Banks; **d**, Robert Stevenson; **cast**, Robert Mitchum, Ava Gardner, Melvyn Douglas, Janis Carter, Lucile Watson, Gordon Oliver, Basil Ruysdael, Clarence Muse, Walter Kingsford, Jack Briggs, Will Wright; **w**, Marion Parsonnet, Leopold Atlas (based on the novel *Carriage Entrance* by Banks), **c**, Harry J. Wild; **m**, Frederick Hollander; **ed**, George C. Shrader, **art d**, Albert S. D'Agostino, Alfred Herman; **set d**, Harley Miller, Darrell Silvera.

My Friend Flicka ★★★★ 1943; U.S.; 89m; FOX; Color; Adventure; Children: Recommended; **DVD**; **VHS**. Wonderful family film with stunning western photography sees ten-year-old McDowall returning home from boarding school, miserable at having poorly performed as his bad grades testify and where he is threatened with having to repeat fifth grade. He lives on a ranch where his father, Foster, and mother, Johnson, raise thoroughbred horses. McDowall is a big disappointment to Foster, who demands that he improve his study habits, but Johnson believes that he will improve if Foster grants McDowall his one wish in life, that he gives McDowall a colt to raise on his own. Foster argues that McDowall is just too irresponsible, but finally gives in and is then further dismayed when McDowall chooses a sorrel chestnut filly that is a foal from an unruly mare. Foster, who has a fine knowledge of horse breeding, attempts to persuade his son that the filly is not the right horse for him, but he cannot change McDowall's mind. The filly becomes injured and McDowell, with his parents' considerable help, nurses the horse back to health. Through painstaking work and much love, McDowall raises the horse until it becomes a fine mare and his closest companion. This sensitive and heartwarming film offers a great family story where McDowall, Foster, Johnson and the rest of the cast are superb in their endearing roles and where the photography from Wrigley (of the ranch and its exteriors in Utah) are breathtakingly beautiful and where Newman's stirring score gallops and thunders with the racing horses on that idyllic ranch (where every boy and girl in America will want to live after seeing this truly great film). **p**, Ralph Dietrich; **d**, Harold Schuster; **cast**, Roddy McDowall, Preston Foster, Rita Johnson, James Bell, Diana Hale (Patti Hale), Jeff Corey, Jimmy Aubrey, Arthur Loft; **w**, Lillie Hayward, Francis Edward Faragoh (based on the novel by Mary O'Hara); **c**, Dewey Wrigley (Technicolor); **m**, Alfred Newman; **ed**, Robert Fritch; **art d**, Richard Day, Chester Gore; **set d**, Paul S. Fox, Thomas Little.

My Gal Sal ★★★ 1942; U.S.; 103m; FOX; Color; Biographical Drama/Musical; Children: Acceptable; **DVD**. This colorful and rousing musical is loosely based upon the adventurous life of composer and actor Paul Dresser (Johann Paul Dresser, 1858-1906), zestfully enacted by Mature. After getting into some trouble as a youth in his native Indiana, Mature decides to leave home, telling his stern father, Andrews, that he does not want to be a minister, as his father wants, but wants to compose songs. So as not to sully his family's reputation in pursuits that were then considered unsavory, he changes his name from Dreiser to Dresser (his younger brother is played by Barry Downing, that brother being Theodore Dreiser, who later became a celebrated author and whose book about his older brother is the basis of this film). Seeking adventure and fortune, Mature hooks up with a less than reputable snake oil peddler, playing a banjo and singing his own songs while the peddler

Flicka, Roddy McDowall and James Bell in *My Friend Flicka*, 1943.

pockets cash from suckers. The patent medicine is discovered to be nothing more than sugared water. An angry mob then seizes the peddler and Mature, and they tar and feather them. Mature, injured and embarrassed, is discovered by voluptuous Landis, a member of a traveling vaudeville wagon show, and she shelters him, taking care of him and convincing Catlett, who owns the show, to feature Mature in his acts. Mature performs his songs with Landis as they travel through the country, working in small towns. Hayworth, accompanied by Sutton, watches one of Mature's performances as he plays two pianos, and they ridicule his garish suit. Mature and Landis then attend a theatrical performance where they take vengeance by laughing at Hayworth's singing performance, but Mature realizes that he has wronged Hayworth in that he also knows she is a talented, professional singer. Landis is in love with Mature, but all he can see is the bright lights of New York (and the memory of the ravishing Hayworth), and he leaves her and the show, going to NYC to establish a big time reputation as a composer. He meets Gleason, a promoter of songs in Tin Pan Alley, who has Mature's songs published. Those tunes take hold and he begins to become rich and famous, as does singing star Hayworth. They met again and establish a tempestuous and competitive relationship, battling for the limelight while growing more deeply in love with each other. Hayworth makes Mature even more famous by singing his songs in hit Broadway shows and on the road, including his memorable "On the Banks of the Wabash." They quarrel and break up, and then Mature shows just how much he loves Hayworth by writing his most famous song for her, "My Gal Sal," which Hayworth sings (with Nan Wynn's singing voice) in a terrific ensemble set piece to end this grand musical. Mature is outstanding as the brash and bold Dresser, out to become a world beater, and Hayworth was never lovelier and charming. The production values are high, and Fox did not stint on the costumes, which are as ornate and rich as the 1890s and early 1900s they represent, along with the impressive period sets of that long ago but colorful era. Expensive to produce, Fox nevertheless had a great hit on its hands, the box office returning more than $2 million in the film's initial release. The film won Oscars for Best Art Direction and Set Decoration and Newman was nominated for his lively score. Songs: "I'se Your Honey If You Wants Me, Liza Jane," "Come Tell Me What's Your Answer, Yes or No," "The Convict and the Bird," "Mr. Volunteer," "On the Banks of the Wabash," "My Gal Sal" (Paul Dresser); "On the Gay White Way," "Oh, The Pity of It All," "Here You Are," "Me and My Fella and A Big Umbrella" (Ralph Rainger, Leo Robin); "Daisy Bell" (Harry Dacre). *Author's Note*: Fox chief Darryl Zanuck wanted to originally cast Alice Faye, who had been Fox's top singing star for some years, as the leading lady in this film, but when it came time to produce the film, she was pregnant. He next offered the role to Mae West and Irene Dunne, but both declined the part, as did Betty Grable. "I knew

Victor Mature and Rita Hayworth in *My Gal Sal*, 1942.

that Rita [Hayworth] was at the top of the world at that time," Zanuck told this author. "She had appeared with Ty Power in **Blood and Sand** [1941] for us and made another hit that same year with Fred Astaire in a musical called **You'll Never Get Rich** [1941] for Columbia. I called Harry Cohn at Columbia and cut a deal to get Rita for **My Gal Sal**, and that was that." Mature accepted his part after reading the script but told this author that he was "amazed when I saw a picture of Dresser. The guy must have weighed 300 pounds, an enormous blimp of a guy and he was no romantic leading man by any means, but nobody knew what he looked like then. He had been dead for forty-five years [Dresser died at age forty-nine on January 30, 1906, weighing 250 plus pounds.] Before I first went onto the set, I went to the wardrobe people and got one of those old clown costumes that billowed out to make me look like I weighed 500 pounds and when I showed up in that rig, Rita [Hayworth] and the rest of the cast broke up. I showed them a picture of the real Dresser and said I was merely enacting my part. The director [Irving Cummings] was not amused." Hayworth told this author that "**My Gal Sal** was a lot of fun to do, especially with Vic [Mature] as my leading man. He was always clowning around and never took anything seriously and that's why he is believable and wonderful in that role as that composer from Indiana. And no, young man, I did not use my own voice when singing those songs, but if they had let me, I could have held my own, believe me." **p**, Robert Bassler; **d**, Irving Cummings; **cast**, Rita Hayworth, Victor Mature, John Sutton, Carole Landis, James Gleason, Phil Silvers, Walter Catlett, Mona Maris, Stanley Andrews, Curt Bois, Barry Downing, Hermes Pan, Iron Eyes Cody, Robert Lowery, Terry Moore, Ted North, Chief Thundercloud, Nan Wynn (Hayworth's singing voice); **w**, Seton I. Miller, Karl Tunberg, Darrell Ware (based on the story "My Brother Paul" by Theodore Dreiser from his book *Twelve Men*); **c**, Ernest Palmer (Technicolor); **m**, Paul Dresser, Cyril J. Mockridge, Leigh Harline; **ed**, Robert L. Simpson; **art d**, Richard Day, Joseph C. Wright; **set d**, **spec eff**, Thomas Little.

My Left Foot ★★★ 1989; Ireland/U.K.; 103m; Ferndale Films/Miramax Films; Color; Biographical Drama; Children: Unacceptable; MPAA: R; **DVD**. The inspirational true story of Christy Brown (1932-1981), played superbly by Day-Lewis, who was born with cerebral palsy, but learned to write and paint with his left foot, which was his only controllable limb. Born a quadriplegic into a large, poor Irish family in Dublin, he is ten years old when he is able to maneuver a piece of chalk with the toes of his left foot and writes a word on the floor. His mother, Fricker, recognizes his intelligence when everyone else considers him to be a vegetable. He grows up to become a poet, novelist, and painter with a feisty personality, a drinker who likes women, and an amazing achiever, who overcomes tremendous obstacles. Day-Lewis

won an Oscar for Best Actor and Fricker an Oscar as Best Supporting Actress. Song: "Foggy Dew" (traditional). Gutter language and explicit scenes of deformities prohibit viewing by children. **p**, Noel Pearson; **d**, Jim Sheridan; **cast**, Daniel Day-Lewis, Brenda Fricker, Alison Whelan, Kirsten Sheridan, Declan Croghan, Eanna MacLiam, Marie Conmee, Cyril Cusack, Phelim Drew, Ruth McCabe, Fiona Shaw, Adrian Dunbar; **w**, Sheridan, Shane Connaughton (based on the book by Christy Brown); **c**, Jack Conroy; **m**, Elmer Bernstein; **ed**, J. Patrick Duffner; **prod d**, Austen Spriggs; **set d**, Shirley Lynch; **spec eff**, Gerry Johnston.

My Life as a Dog ★★★ 1987; Sweden; 101m; FilmTeknik/Skouras Pictures; Color; Drama; Children: Unacceptable; **DVD**. This absorbing tale sees Glanzelius as a twelve-year-old boy living with his older brother, Brömssen, and their mother, Liden, in Sweden in 1959. She is dying from tuberculosis which depresses him, so the only happy part of his life is being with his beloved but mischievous dog, a pet that drives his mother to distraction. When she can no longer care for her sons they are sent to live with relatives. Glanzelius lives with an uncle in a small town who works in a glass factory. Glanzelius takes his dog with him and learns about life and death as he meets a variety of people including a tomboy, Kinnaman, who teaches him to box as she worries about her growing breasts; a woman Glanzelius chaperones to pose nude for a sculptor; and a dying old man to whom he reads a lingerie catalog and shows him the pictures. Song: "I've Got a Lovely Bunch of Coconuts" (Fred Heatherton, Povel Romel). Nudity prohibits viewing by children. (In Swedish; English subtitles.) **p**, Waldemar Bergendahl; **d**, Lasse Hallström; **cast**, Anton Glanzelius, Tomas von Brömssen, Anki Liden, Melinda Kinnaman, Kicki Rundgren, Lennart Hjulström, Ing-Marie Carlsson, Leif Ericsson, Christina Carlwind, Ralph Carlsson; **w**, Hallström, Reidar Jönsson, Brasse Brännström, Per Berglund (based on the novel by Jönsson); **c**, Jörgen Persson; **m**, Björn Isfält; **ed**, Christer Furubrand, Susanne Linnman; **prod d**, Lasse Westfelt; **set d**, Tove Hellbom, Pontus Lindblad.

My Life So Far ★★★ 1999; U.K.; 98m; Enigma Productions/Miramax Films; Color; Biographical Drama; Children: Unacceptable (MPAA: PG-13); **DVD**; **VHS**. This often riveting film is based upon the memoirs of Denis Forman (1917-2013), former director of the Royal Opera House at Covent Garden, London, who grew up on a Scottish estate in the late 1920s. As a ten-year-old boy (Norman), he is raised by an eccentric father, Firth, who invents old-fashioned airships and paddlewheel boats, and spends a lot of money on cultivating sphagnum moss, which he believes has high medicinal use. His mother, Mastrantonio, is wearily tolerant of Firth. Her mother, Harris, owns the estate, which Firth hopes she will leave to him some day, although he has competition in that from his tough businessman brother, McDowell, who might instead inherit the property. One day, McDowell arrives with his young French wife, Jacob, who is a professional cellist. Norman develops a crush for her, but Firth falls in love with her. Mastrantonio learns Firth has had an affair with Jacob, but forgives him and Firth and Norman both come to learn that their lives so far have been rewarding. Songs: "On the Sunny Side of the Street," "Dooin' the New Lowdown" (Jimmy McHugh, Dorothy Fields); "Edward Sits Alone" (Colin Matthews); "My Love Is Like a Red, Red Rose" (Robert Burns). Sexual content and nudity prohibit viewing by children. **p**, Steve Norris, David Puttnam, Nigel Goldsack, Bob and Harvey Weinstein; **d**, Hugh Hudson; **cast**, Colin Firth, Rosemary Harris, Irene Jacob, Mary Elizabeth Mastrantonio, Malcolm McDowell, Robert Norman, Tcheky Karyo, Kelly Macdonald, Roddy McDonald, Daniel Baird, Jennifer Fergie, Brendan Gleeson; **w**, Simon Donald (based on the book *Son of Adam* by Sir Denis Forman); **c**, Bernard Lutic; **m**, Howard Blake; **ed**, Scott Thomas; **prod d**, Andy Harris; **art d**, John Frankish; **set d**, Gillie Delap; **spec eff**, David Crownshaw, Terry Schubert, Dominic Tuohy, Jeremy Lovett.

My Life to Live ★★★ 1963; France; 80m; Pathe/Union Film Distributors; Drama; Children: Unacceptable; **DVD**; **VHS**. Godard presents a fascinating visual pastiche that combines the life of one woman, while incorporating his perspectives through twelve sequences of literature, films, prostitution and various other subjects, while also narrating this film. Karina, his wife in real life, plays a Parisian store clerk, who wants something better out of life, and quits her job to become an actress. She is overwhelmed, however, when viewing Carl Dreyer's **The Passion of Joan of Arc**, 1928, starring Maria Falconetti. Never hoping to equal Falconetti's performance, Karina decides the easiest way through life is via prostitution and she sells herself to pimp Rebbot, who, in turn, sells her to another pimp. These human scavengers then quarrel over their "ownership" of Karina, and after they exchange gunfire, they find their "property," Karina, dead. Godard experiments here with this tawdry tale, eschewing his normal "jump-cuts" and allowing his camera to freely roam through his interior and exterior sets for as long as eight minutes per sequence while introducing panning shots where the sounds of machine-gun fire is heard as if to hurry along his visuals. (In French; English subtitles.) **p**, Pierre Braunberger; **d**, Jean-Luc Godard; **cast**, Anna Karina, Sady Rebbot, André S. Labarthe, Guylaine Schlumberger, Gérard Hoffman, Monique Messine, Paul Pavel, Dimitri Dineff, Peter Kassovitz, Eric Schlumberger, **w**, Godard, Marcel Sacotte (based on the book *Où en est la prostitution* by Sacotte and a story by Godard); **c**, Raoul Coutard; **m**, Michel Legrand; **ed**, Godard, Agnès Guillemot; **spec eff**, Jean Fouchet.

My Little Chickadee ★★★ 1940; U.S.; 83m; UNIV; B/W; Comedy; Children: Acceptable; **DVD**; **VHS**. The inimitable Fields and the irrepressible West combine their considerable comedic talents in this oddball satire of the Old West, one offering many hilarious moments and not too little inside jokes (the script was mostly written by West, who specialized in risqué innuendos). West is labeled a rather loose woman after having had an affair with a masked bandit, and the local ladies insist that she leave their fair city lest she continue to sully its otherwise pristine reputation. She is packed on board the next departing train and is now en route to Greasewood City. West meets Fields on that train, believing he is wealthy and carrying a large suitcase stuffed with cash. He is nothing of the kind. Fields is a confidence man carrying a valise packed with phony coupons, but his oozing patter soon convinces West that he is a man of means. The train is then attacked by hordes of Indians, but West dispatches almost all of them with her Annie Oakley type marksmanship, which impresses Fields. West, however, is worried as they approach their destination, believing that her reputation may have preceded her. To appear the essence of propriety, she decides that she should be a married woman when she alights from that train and she selects Fields as her groom. They are married on board the train as man and wife by professional cardsharp Meek, who doesn't have the authority to send himself to the men's room. After they arrive at Greasewood City as man and wife, Fields and West check into the local hotel, but, that night, West has no urge to consummate her marriage and puts a goat in her place in the bed. When Fields turns his bulbous-nosed face toward this creature, he takes a whiff and states: "Darling, have you changed your perfume?" West takes herself to the local saloon where she meets its owner, slippery Calleia, and a romance between them suddenly blossoms. Fields wanders into the saloon and gets involved in a poker game (one of the funniest scenes in the film). Knight, an old cowboy, asks: "Is this a game of chance?" Fields replies: "Not the way I play it!" Fields is later made sheriff of the town, but when he puts on a mask to impress West (knowing she favors masked men lovers), he is arrested and thrown into his own jail, the townsfolk believing he is a notorious bandit. They plan to string him up, but West appeals to the real robber, wherever he may be in the crowd, to step forward and save an innocent man's life. Calleia, it turns out, is the bandit, who nobly returns all he has previously stolen, in order to win West's heart, but he has stiff competition from local editor Foran, who also loves the buxom lady and the two spend much time fighting over her favors. In the end, West tells Fields

Mae West and W. C. Fields in *My Little Chickadee*, 1940.

that their marriage is bogus, which much relieves him of any responsibility as he is planning to go East to sell endless shares of hair-oil wells to eagerly awaiting suckers. Before departing, he says to West (stealing her famous line): "Come up and see me sometime." West retorts (by stealing one of Field's patented lines): "I will...my little chickadee!" Song: "Willie of the Valley" (music: Ben Oakland; lyrics: Milton Drake). ***Author's Note***: Fields and West were teamed for the first time in this film and both were then top stars with West being paid a then whopping $300,000 for writing the script and acting in the film and Fields was paid $125,000 for acting and an additional $25,000 for what writing he added to the script, which consisted mostly of adlibs. West was wary of working with Fields and knew well his reputation of his imbibing antics during film productions so she had a special clause inserted in her contract that prohibited Fields from drinking or smoking on the set or in her presence, which irked the actor a great deal. When the film was completed, West paid Fields a rather offbeat compliment by stating to the press: "There's no one in the world like Bill[Fields]... Thank God!" **p**, Lester Cowan, Jack J. Gross (not credited); **d**, Edward F. Cline; **cast**, Mae West, W.C. Fields, Joseph Calleia, Dick Foran, Ruth Donnelly, Margaret Hamilton, Donald Meek, Fuzzy Knight, Willard Robertson, George Moran, Jackie Searl, Gene Austin, **w**, West, Fields; **c**, Joseph Valentine; **m**, Frank Skinner; **ed**, Edward Curtiss; **art d**, Martin Obzina, Jack Otterson; **set d**, Russell A. Gausman; **spec eff**, John P. Fulton, James V. King.

My Man Godfrey ★★★★★ 1936; U.S.; 94m; UNIV; B/W; Comedy; Children: Acceptable; **DVD**; **VHS**. This masterpiece comedy is brilliantly brought to life through the vibrant and inventive talents of Powell and Lombard and with no little creative effort of the gifted director, La Cava. Set during its own time of the Great Depression, its wonderful humor lies between great wealth and abject poverty and its social conscience discernible through its subtle wit. A scavenger hunt is part of a social affair hosted by Park Avenue rich girls Lombard and Patrick, two spoiled and pampered sisters, who have known poverty only through rumor. Among the items listed in that hunt are goldfish, tennis rackets and "the forgotten man," an anonymous unemployed male to be randomly selected from one of the many hobo jungles blotting Manhattan. Lombard, who is sweet and capricious, and Patrick, sensuously alluring and manipulative, go slumming through a hobo camp on the East River and find among the shacks and shadowy figures of destitute men a tall man of rather regal bearing, Powell. Patrick tells Powell that he is to go along with her as her "trophy" for the evening, but, indignant and angered at her insensitivity, Powell eloquently chastises her for her callousness and menacingly backs her up until she falls onto a pile of rubbish. Incensed, Patrick leaves in a huff, but Lombard remains, in-

William Powell and Alice Brady in *My Man Godfrey*, 1936.

trigued by the decisive and forceful Powell. She tells him that her sister is used to getting her way and she will undoubtedly find some other hobo and take him back to the upscale hotel where they are holding their party and become the winner of the scavenger hunt. To prevent her from doing that, Powell agrees to be Lombard's "forgotten man" and attends the party as Lombard's "trophy." Powell tells the well-dressed partygoers that their hunt is childish and all bristle at his barbs, except Lombard, who is delighted that she has won the hunt and, for the first time, bested Patrick. So thrilled with the urbane and well-mannered Powell is she that she offers him a job as the family butler, a position he accepts. He goes to work at her Park Avenue home, presided over by her millionaire father, Pallette, who is beset by the antics of his daughters as well as that of his charming but addlebrained wife, Brady. Powell quickly adjusts as he puts the household in order, becoming the perfect butler. Lombard, meanwhile, is falling in love with him, but he does his best to avoid her advances while dutifully administering to the needs of everyone. He knows this family well in that he comes from a similar household as he is the offspring of a wealthy Boston family, who fell from their good graces after a ruinous love affair and became one of those millions of "forgotten men." When the family gives a party, one of the guests, Mowbray, sees Powell serving everyone and recognizes him as his old pal from Harvard and a member of the Boston Back Bay elite, but Powell asks Mowbray to keep his background a secret and he does. He tells Mowbray that he had lost all faith in humanity, but regained that faith when living with the men in shantytown where these unemployed unfortunates continued to maintain hope while displaying their indomitable spirit and confidence for the future. Meanwhile, Patrick, who resents Powell, probes his background and then tries to frame him by planting an expensive necklace in Powell's room and then calling the police and inferring that Powell has stolen it. Powell is too clever for Patrick as he has hidden the necklace, and when police detective Gargan cannot locate the necklace, he abandons the investigation. Powell, meanwhile, gets rid of Auer, an arrogant pest and Brady's live-in gigolo, for which the docile Pallette is grateful. When Pallette's company encounters trouble, Powell pawns Patrick's necklace and uses the money to buy stock in Pallette's firm, bolstering it, and when its stock goes up, Powell sees a profit and recoups the necklace, returning it. With Pallette's fortunes now secure, Powell contacts old friend Mowbray and they both invest in building a posh nightclub, which is constructed on the very location where Powell once lived in a shanty. He hires all the bums who have lived there and when the place opens, it becomes an enormous hit. Lombard then makes the picture complete by arriving at the club with a preacher, and insists that Powell marry her and they are wed in his office for a very happy ending. Songs: "Dark Eyes" (1843; composer unknown), "Drink a Highball" (1901; G. B.

Brigham), "Oh Where, Oh Where Has My Little Dog Gone" (1864; traditional). This film was remade in 1957, but was far inferior to the original. **Merrily We Live**, 1938, uses almost the same story, but, it too, does not compare with this film. *Author's Note*: Powell told this author that "**My Man Godfrey** has always been one of my favorite pictures. It's one of those screwball comedies of the 1930s, but it packs a punch and has a lot to say about those caught up in the Great Depression. The boys who wrote the script could have been working in the White House because a lot of what they wrote sounded like FDR's [President Franklin D. Roosevelt] 'New Deal' where the rich are shown to be a lot of silly people and the poor have all the common sense. And isn't that the way of it in all bad times?" Powell and Lombard had been married (1931-1933), but remained good friends and their reunion on screen shows it. Jane Wyman makes her debut in this film as a partygoer. **p**, Charles R. Rogers; **d**, La Cava; **cast**, William Powell, Carole Lombard, Alice Brady, Gail Patrick, Eugene Pallette, Jean Dixon, Alan Mowbray, Mischa Auer, Pat Flaherty, Bess Flowers, Franklin Pangborn, Jean Rogers, Grady Sutton, Jane Wyman; **w**, Morrie Ryskind, Eric Hatch, La Cava (based on the story "1101 Park Avenue" by Hatch); **c**, Ted Tetzlaff; **m**, Charles Previn, Rudy Schrager; **ed**, Ted Kent, Russell Schoengarth; **art d**, Charles D. Hall; **spec eff**, John P. Fulton.

My Mother's Castle ★★★ 1991; France; 98m; Gaumont; Orion Classics; Color; Biographical Drama; Children: Unacceptable (MPAA: PG-13); **BD**; **DVD**; **VHS**. This entertaining sequel to **My Father's Glory**, 1991, is based upon the boyhood of novelist and filmmaker Marcel Pagnol (1895-1974), played by Ciamaca, and depicts the further adventures of his idyllic summer in France during the early 1900s. When Ciamaca is about eleven, he and his schoolteacher father, Caubére, and mother, Roussel, leave the city and spend their summer vacation in a cottage in the hills of Provence. They follow a canal from a train station to the cottage, walking through the backyards of some eccentric people. The summer is romantically eventful for young Ciamaca when he meets a pretty but self-centered girl, Timmerman, but she soon leaves with her family. Most of the film takes place during the walk along the canal and shows the colorful people they meet. Just as charming and wonderful as the first film, but sexuality prohibits viewing by children. (In French; English subtitles.) **p**, Alain Poiré; **d**, Yves Robert; **cast**, Julien Ciamaca, Philippe Caubère, Nathalie Roussel, Didier Pain, Thérèse Liotard, Victorien Delamare, Joris Molinas, Julie Timmerman, Paul Crauchet, Philippe Uchan; **w**, Robert, Jerôme Tonnerre (based on the novel by Marcel Pagnol); **c**, Robert Alazraki; **m**, Vladimir Cosma; **ed**, Pierre Gillette; **prod d**, Jacques Dugied.

My Name s Julia Ross **★★★** 1945; U.S.; 64m; COL; B/W; Mystery; Children: Unacceptable. A young woman named Julia Ross (Foch) gets a job as a live-in personal secretary to a wealthy widow, Whitty, who has a grown son, Macready. The morning after moving into Whitty's mansion in London, Foch awakens to find herself a prisoner at an isolated seaside estate in Cornwall. She is told she is really Macready's wife. The household staff is told she has had a nervous breakdown so they ignore her wild claims and prevent her from escaping. Foch discovers a secret passageway to her room and overhears Macready admit to Whitty that he murdered his real wife in a fit of rage and tossed her body into the sea. Macready tries to kill Foch and when that fails, he tries to escape, but is shot down by police, who have been on his trail for some time. A good mystery yarn, but too violent for children. **p**, Wallace MacDonald; **d**, Joseph H. Lewis; **cast**, Nina Foch, Dame May Whitty, George Macready, Roland Varno, Anita Bolster, Doris Lloyd, Joy Harington, Leyland Hodgson, Olaf Hytten, Queenie Leonard; **w**, Muriel Roy Bolton (based on the novel *The Woman in Red* by Anthony Gilbert); **c**, Burnett Guffey; **m**, Mischa Bakaleinikoff; **ed**, Henry Batista; **art d**, Jerome Pycha, Jr.; **set d**, Milton Stumph.

My Name Is Nobody ★★★ 1974; Italy/France/West Germany; 117m;

Rafran Cinematografica/UNIV; Color; Western; Children: Unacceptable (MPAA: PG); **DVD**; **VHS**. This offbeat, but entertaining spaghetti western is really a satire of the Old West that doesn't take itself seriously. Fonda, once the greatest gunman in the Old West, wants to move to Europe and retire in peace. A young gunslinger, known as "Nobody" (Hill, who grins his way through this film as he does in most others), idolizes him and wants to see him go out in a blaze of shooting glory, so he arranges for Fonda to face a 150-man gang known as The Wild Bunch. Fonda survives a blaze of bullets in a showdown and the film ends with him at a desk, presumably writing his memoirs. (Dubbed in English.) Excessive violence, the hallmark of such Italian westerns, prohibits viewing by children. **p**, Fulvio Morsella, Claudio Mancini, Sergio Leone; **d**, Tonino Valerii; **cast**, Terence Hill, Henry Fonda, Jean Martin, R.G. Armstrong, Karl Braun, Leo Gordon, Steve Kanaly, Geoffrey Lewis, Neil Summers, Piero Lulli, Mario Brega; **w**, Ernesto Gastaldi (based on a story by Gastaldi, Morsella, and an idea by Leone); **c**, Giuseppe Ruzzolini; **m**, Ennio Morricone; **ed**, Nino Baragli; **prod d**, Gianni Polidori; **spec eff**, Eros Bacciucchi, Giovanni Corridori.

My Neighbor Totoro ★★★ 1993; Japan; 80m; Tokuma Japan Communications Co./50th Street Films; Color; Animated Feature; Children: Recommended (MPAA: G); **DVD**; **VHS**. Two girls, Satsuki (Hidaka voiceover, Japanese version; Dakota Fanning voiceover, English version), and her younger sister Mei (Chase voiceover, Japanese version; Elle Fanning voiceover, English version) and their father move into a house in the country so they can be closer to their mother, who is hospitalized. The girls soon discover that the house and nearby forest are inhabited by magical creatures called Totoros. They befriend the Totoros, who take them on some magical adventures. One of these entertaining odysseys involves the girls' encountering a creature called the Cat Bus that runs through the forest on eight paws. There are no villains in this delightful film, merely fascinating creatures that the girls befriend as they discover the wonders of life. Song: "My Neighbor Totoro" (Hayao Miyazaki). This delightful adventure tale provides great family fare and was a huge international hit. (In English and Japanese; English subtitles.) **p**, Toru Hara, Ned Lott; **d&w**, Hayao Miyazaki; **cast** (voiceovers), Noriko Hidaka, Cheryl Chase, Chika Sakamoto, Hitoshi Takagi, Shigesato Itoi, Sumi Shimamoto, Tanie Kitabayashi; (English version voiceovers), Dakota Fanning, Elle Fanning, Pat Carroll, Natalie Core, Paul Butcher, Tim Daly, Kenneth Hartman, Lee Salonga, Frank Welker); **c**, Mark Henley; **m**, Jô Hisaishi; **ed**, Takeshi Seyama; **art d**, Kazuo Oga; **spec eff**, Kaoru Tanifuji.

My Night at Maud's ★★★★ 1970; France; 110m; Les Films de la Pleiade/Pathe; B/W; Drama; Children: Unacceptable (MPAA: PG); **DVD**; **VHS**. In an introspective and moody film, auteur director Rohmer presents another one of his compelling "Moral Tales," this one centered on Trintignant, an upstanding young man adhering to the strictest codes of the Catholic Church. While regularly attending church, Trintignant sees and is enamored of beautiful, blonde student Barrault. He is too shy and withdrawn to approach her. He later meets old friend Vitez at a bookstore, and Vitez suggests that they spend the night at the home of Fabian (Maud), that night happening to be Christmas Eve. They spend time discussing the philosophy of French mathematician and philosopher Blaise Pascal and then Fabian tries to seduce Trintignant, but the chaste and modest young man resists, falling asleep in an armchair. He nevertheless is tempted to violate his code (where he will not sleep with a woman until marrying her) by eventually bedding down with Fabian, but still remains a virgin by refusing to have sex with her. He has saved himself for the beautiful Barrault, and, after he finally meets her, they quickly fall in love and wed. It is then that Trintignant discovers that his wife had not kept the same vows of chastity he so religiously upheld in that she not only had an affair with a married man, but that assignation was with Fabian's ex-husband. Meticulously directed by Rohmer, a stickler for every action by his actors and persnickety about every prop

Roy Rogers, left, in *My Pal Trigger*, 1946.

adorning his sparse sets, the acting from Trintignant and the rest of the cast is outstanding. (In French; English subtitles.) **p**, Pierre Cottrell, Barbet Schroeder; **d&w**, Eric Rohmer; **cast**, Jean-Louis Trintignant, Françoise Fabian, Marie-Christine Barrault, Antoine Vitez, Léonide Kogan, Guy Léger, Anne Dubot, Marie Becker, Marie-Claude Rauzier; **c**, Néstor Almendros; **ed**, Cécile Decugis; **prod d**, Nicole Rachline.

My Pal Trigger ★★★ 1946; U.S.; 79m; REP; B/W; Western; Children: Cautionary; **DVD**; **VHS**. Rogers is a horse trader, who wants to mate a prize mare with a stallion owned by his pal Gabby, but Gabby doesn't want the match to take place. Holt, a gambler, also wants his mare to be mated with Gabby's stallion, but Gabby's horse runs off and mates with Rogers' mare. The stallion is shot dead and Rogers is blamed for it. The mare has a colt that grows up to be Rogers' famous horse, Trigger. A big race is held between Trigger and Holt's horse, and Trigger wins. Holt inadvertently reveals he killed Gabby's stallion and is arrested. This pleasing oater was Rogers' favorite and the most successful of all his movies. Songs: "Livin' Western Style" (Don Swander, June Hershey), "Old Faithful" (Michael Carr, Hamilton Kennedy), "Alla en el Rancho Grande" (Silvano Ramos, Bartley Costello), "Harriet" (Abel Baer, Paul Cunningham). **p**, Armand Schaefer; **d**, Frank McDonald, Yakima Canutt (not credited); **cast**, Roy Rogers, George "Gabby" Hayes, Dale Evans, Jack Holt, LeRoy Mason, Roy Barcroft, Sam Flint, Kenne Duncan, Francis McDonald, Bob Nolan, Sons of the Pioneers, Trigger the Horse; **w**, Jack Townley, John K. Butler (based on a story by Paul Gangelin); **c**, William Bradford; **m**, Morton Scott, R. Dale Butts, Charles Maxwell; **ed**, Harry Keller; **art d**, Gano Chittenden; **set d**, John McCarthy, Jr., Earl Wooden; **spec eff**, Howard and Theodore Lydecker.

My Pal Wolf ★★★ 1944; U.S.; 75m; RKO; B/W; Adventure; Children: Acceptable. This touching, often memorable dog tale sees Edwards and Maricle as a wealthy Virginia couple too busy to spend much time with their young daughter, Moffett, so they hire a British nanny, Esmond, to look after her. Moffett finds a German shepherd that has fallen into a well and brings him home. She calls the dog Wolf and they become great friends, but Esmond sees the dog as a threat to her authority, so she tries to find its owner. It is learned that Wolf was lost while being trained to serve in World War II and, when recovered from Moffett, Wolf is now scheduled to be sent to Europe. Moffett goes to an army training ground nearby and finds Wolf, then asks if she can buy him. She is told that is up to the Secretary of War, Fielding, in Washington, D.C. Moffett travels to Washington, sees Fielding, and he says Wolf has to do his part in the war effort. She reluctantly lets the army have Wolf, but then Fielding tries to make it up to her by giving her a puppy and promises Wolf will come back to her after his war service is concluded. **p**, Adrian Scott;

Rosalind Russell, Brian Aherne and Janet Blair in *My Sister Eileen*, **1942.**

d, Alfred Werker; **cast**, Sharyn Moffett, Jill Esmond, Una O'Connor, George Cleveland, Charles Arnt, Claire Carleton, Leona Maricle, Bruce Edwards, Edward Fielding, Olga Fabian, Grey Shadow the Dog (as Wolf); **w**, Lillie Hayward, John Paxton, Leonard Praskins (based on a story by Frederick Hazlitt Brennan); **c**, Jack MacKenzie; **m**, Werner R. Heymann; **ed**, Harry Marker; **art d**, Carroll Clark, Albert S. D'Agostino; **set d**, Al Fields, Darrell Silvera; **spec eff**, Vernon L. Walker.

My Side of the Mountain ★★★ 1969; U.S.; 100m; PAR; Color; Adventure; Children: Cautionary (MPAA: G); **DVD**; **VHS**. Eccles is a thirteen-year-old boy, who is told by his parents, Perry and Loder, that the family summer vacation trip has been cancelled, so he ventures into the Canadian mountains by himself. He believes that such a trip will be easy, because he's read Henry David Thoreau's *Walden*, and thinks that such a sojourn will be as simple as a walk in the park. He leaves a note telling his parents he'll be back in a year, and departs with some camping gear and his pet raccoon, Gus. He builds a home in a hollow tree and spends some pre-trip time at the library reading about survival in the wilderness. On his trip to the mountains he finds a baby falcon and learns the art of falconry. He meets a wandering folk singer, Bikel, who spends some time teaching him more about living outdoors. The falcon is killed by hunters as winter approaches. Christmas Day comes and Eccles is lonely, until Bikel shows up with Wiggins, the librarian from home. They bring him a Christmas dinner and show him newspaper clippings that tell of his parents' frantic search for him. Eccles decides he's proven that he can survive in the wilds, so he returns home to endless hugs and kisses instead of a scolding. This well-crafted family film provides a lot of exceptional outdoors photography, but nevertheless sends the dangerous message that children can run away to the wilderness and survive. Song: "Baby Elephant Walk" (Henry Mancini). **p**, Robert B. Radnitz; **d**, James B. Clark; **cast**, Ted Eccles, Theodore Bikel, Tudi Wiggins, Paul Hébert, Cosette Lee, Ralph Endersby, George Allan, Dan McIlravey, Frank Perry, Peggi Loder, Max "Slapsie Maxie" Rosenbloom; **w**, Joanna Crawford, Jane Klove, Ted Sherdeman (based on the novel by Jean Craighead George); **c**, Denys N. Coop; **m**, Wilfred Josephs; **ed**, Alastair McIntyre, Peter Thornton; **art d**, George Lack; **set d**, Johnny Allett.

My Sin ★★★ 1931; U.S.; 80m; PAR; B/W; Drama; Children: Unacceptable. The inimitable Bankhead is captivating in this melodramatic tale where she is seen in Panama singing in a low dive. March is one of her admirers, an alcoholic Harvard-trained attorney, who has fallen on hard times. Bankhead also turns tricks as a sometimes prostitute and then quarrels with her pimp and, when he attacks her, she shoots him to death. March comes to her rescue by sobering up and representing her

in court where he masterfully presents a defense that brings about Bankhead's acquittal. The victory causes March to regain his self-confidence and he goes on to resume a successful and lucrative legal career, loaning money to Bankhead so that she can make a new life in NYC, both of them moving to the Big Apple to start life anew. Bankhead, using a new name, establishes a successful interior decorating business and meets handsome, young Kolk, who comes from a wealthy family. When Kolk proposes, Bankhead seeks March's advice as to whether or not she should tell Kolk about her lurid past in Panama. He urges her to make a clean breast of everything so that her marriage to Kolk will have no threatening skeletons in its closet, but Bankhead is hesitant. She finally tells Kolk about her shady past and he tells her that that will not deter his marrying her, but Bankhead sees he is now uncertain and their relationship becomes tenuous. At the last minute, however, Bankhead says goodbye to Kolk and goes to March, the man she truly loves, and, since he has always been in love with her, they decide to make a life together. This was Bankhead's second talkie film (and her third for Paramount) after having appeared in a clunker, **Night Angel**, 1931, and this outing was a great improvement, thanks to a better script and topnotch performances from Bankhead and March, Bankhead's distinctively low-register voice makes her tawdry character all the more memorable. Song (sung by Bankhead): "Crazy Tom" (composer unknown). *Author's Note*: Abbott, the director of this film, was also an accomplished writer, who won an Oscar for Best Screenplay a year earlier for **All Quiet on the Western Front**, 1930. Abbott told this author that "Tallulah was one of those women who could stun you into silence with a single word. She had a dominating character, very forceful, a southern gal with a lot of opinions about everything. When we were making **My Sin**, she came to me with some ideas about how I should direct the film. I told her that since I had very little patience with myself, I had no inclinations to follow her suggestions. Well, she clammed up and we did the picture without further suggestions from her. It was a chilly experience." March recalled little about this film, stating to this author that "all I can recall is that I first see Tallulah in a cantina while I am in a drunken stupor, and when she goes to shake my hand, her own hand is holding a wad of money and she tells me that that money 'is the only thing that matters' in life. We were very crass people in the movies in those days." **p&d**, George Abbott; **cast**, Tallulah Bankhead, Fredric March, Harry Davenport, Scott Kolk, Margaret Adams, Anne Sutherland, Jay Fassett, Lily Cahill; **w**, Owen Davis, Adelaide Heilbron, Abbott (based on a story by Frederick Jackson); **c**, George Folsey; **m**, Johnny Green, Frank Tours; **ed**, Emma Hill.

My Sister Eileen ★★★ 1942; U.S.; 96m; COL; B/W; Comedy; Children: Acceptable; **DVD**. Entertaining comedy sees Russell and her younger sister, Blair (Eileen) arriving from rural Columbus to seek opportunities in New York. They rent a basement apartment in Greenwich Village from Greek building owner Tobias, and encounter a number of colorful if not eccentric persons. That includes Jones, who is always reminding everyone that he once was a football star at Georgia Tech and is forever singing its "Rambling Wreck" fighting song. His wife, Donnell, a worrywart, takes care of her mother, Phillips. Others include MacBride, an irritable cop, who walks the beat in the neighborhood, and two swains, Joslyn, a newspaperman who is daffy over Blair, and Aherne, a magazine editor who becomes romantically involved with Russell after she begins submitting her short stories to him, and which have to pass muster with its obnoxious publisher, Fillmore. The basement flat is constantly being overrun with characters, and their problems and ambitions are translated into mini-plots and tales by Russell, who uses them as the gist of her storytelling. There is no main story line, just a lot of great characters who sustain interest throughout this light-hearted comedy, and with exceptional performances from Russell, Blair, and Aherne. Song: "(I'm a) Ramblin' Wreck from Georgia Tech" (based on the 1895 song of "Son of a Gambolier" by George Ives; lyrics: Frank Roman). *Author's Note*: This film was based on a hit play stemming from a series of stories appearing in *the New Yorker* and written by Ruth McKenney, who moved from Columbus, Ohio, to New York with her sister Eileen, who, in turn, married the celebrated novelist Nathanael West (Nathan Weinstein), author of several books later turned into films, such as **Lonelyhearts**, 1958, and **Day of the Locust**, 1975. The marriage between Eileen McKenney and Nathanael West, sadly, lasted only eight months; they were wed in April 1940 and West died in December 1940. Jeff Donnell, who was often billed as "Miss Jeff Donnell" so that there would be no mistake about her gender, went on to become the TV wife of George Gobel in a 1956 TV comedy series. **p**, Max Gordon; **d**, Alexander Hall; **cast**, Rosalind Russell, Brian Aherne, Janet Blair, George Tobias, Allyn Joslyn, Grant Mitchell, Gordon Jones, Elizabeth Patterson, Richard Quine, June Havoc, Donald MacBride, Frank Sully, Jeff Donnell, Kirk Alyn, Ann Doran, Clyde Fillmore, Minna Phillips, Larry Fine, Curly Howard, Moe Howard, Robert Kellard, Tito Renaldo, Arnold Stang, Forrest Tucker; **w**, Joseph Fields, Jerome Chodorov (based on their play from stories by Ruth McKenney); **c**, Joseph Walker; **m**, Sidney Cutner; **ed**, Viola Lawrence; **art d**, Lionel Banks.

My Sister Eileen ★★★ 1955; U.S.; 108m; COL; Color; Musical Comedy; Children: Acceptable; **DVD**; **VHS**. This remake of the 1942 film is as good or better than the original in that it adds singing and dancing, this time with Garrett as the short story writer arriving with her younger sister, Leigh (Eileen) in New York to look for jobs, fortune, and, perhaps, husbands. They rent a basement apartment in Greenwich Village from Greek building owner Kasznar, and that apartment begins to quickly fill up with assorted characters with colorful backgrounds, all which writer Garrett records. She then submits a story about her beautiful sister (Leigh) to playboy publisher Lemmon, pretending that the story is about herself so she can protect her sister, a pretense that leads to some very funny incidents. Meanwhile, Leigh gets a job performing in a new Broadway show. A lot of mayhem and mishaps dot the story line, culminating when Garrett and Leigh lead a conga line on the street that brings the police on the run. Not having had any success in publishing her stories, Garrett decides that she will pack up her bags and her sister, and return to Ohio. At the last minute, Lemmon arrives to not only tell her that he is going to publish those stories, but asks for Garrett's hand in marriage, while Leigh happily winds up with her most dedicated suitor, York. Thoroughly enjoyable, this film sees a lot inventive dancing (choreographed by the talented Bob Fosse), and songs that include: "As Soon as They See Eileen," "There's Nothing Like Love," "I'm Great," "It's Bigger Than You and Me," "Give Me A Band and My Baby" (music: Jule Styne; lyrics: Leo Robin); "Competition Dance" (composer unknown), "Conga" (composer unknown); "Atmosphere" (composer unknown). *Author's Note*: Lemmon told this author that "**My Sister Eileen** was one of those 'let's have fun' pictures and it was for me. I got to play the piano and sing a little in that one and I enjoy nothing better." This was the first film Lemmon made with director Quine, an actor turned helmsman, and it proved so successful that they would go on together in making **Operation Mad Ball**, 1957; **Bell Book and Candle**, 1958; **It Happened to Jane**, 1959; **The Notorious Landlady**, 1962; and **How to Murder Your Wife**, 1965. **p**, Fred Kohlmar; **d**, Richard Quine; **cast**, Janet Leigh, Betty Garrett, Jack Lemmon, Robert (Bob) Fosse, Kurt Kasznar, Richard (Dick) York, Lucy Marlow, Tommy Rall, Barbara Brown, Horace MacMahon, Henry Slate, Hal March, Queenie Smith; **w**, Blake Edwards, Quine (based on the play by Joseph Fields and Jerome Chodorov from the stories of Ruth McKenney); **c**, Charles Lawton Jr. (CinemaScope; Technicolor); **m**, George Duning; **ed**, Charles Nelson; **art d**, Walter Holscher; **set d**, William Kiernan.

My Six Convicts ★★★ 1952; U.S.; 104m; COL; B/W; Prison Drama; Children: Unacceptable; **VHS**. Based on the autobiographical book by Donald Powell Wilson, this hard-hitting tale profiles a new prison psychologist, Beal, and his six inmate patients. At first, the prisoners are uncooperative, but they gradually warm to him. They and Beal eventu-

Van Heflin, Robert Walker and Helen Hayes in *My Son John*, 1952.

ally learn about themselves through his patient and compassionate treatment and friendship. Beal helps put down a prison break and departs with gifts from the prisoners he has helped to rehabilitate, most importantly earning of all their respect. This film was shot on location at San Quentin State Prison, California. Song: "Columbia the Gem of the Ocean" (David T. Shaw). Excessive violence prohibits viewing by children. *Author's Note*: The always socially conscious Kramer told this author that "I had always wanted to profile on film the backgrounds of prison inmates that motivated them to commit their crimes. Using a psychiatrist [Beal] to shed light on those dark pasts was the can-opener." **p**, Stanley Kramer; **d**, Hugo Fregonese; **cast**, Millard Mitchell, Gilbert Roland, John Beal, Marshall Thompson, Alf Kjellin, Henry (Harry) Morgan, Jay Adler, Regis Toomey, Fay Roope, Carleton Young, John Marley, Byron Foulger, Charles Buchinsky (Charles Bronson); **c**, Guy Roe; **m**, Dimitri Tiomkin; **ed**, Gene Havlick; **art d**, Edward L. Ilou.

My Son John ★★★ 1952; U.S.; 122m; Rainbow Productions/PAR; B/W; Spy Drama; Children: Unacceptable; **VHS**. Hayes, the first lady of the American theater, as she was rightly called, gives a bravura performance as a troubled mother, who sees her favorite offspring, Walker, return from Europe as a person she no longer knows. The enigmatic Walker (in his last film), who is John, also turns in a stunning and thoroughly frightening performance as that strangely altered son. Walker works in Washington, D.C., as a federal employee in a sensitive position, and his absence is sorely noticed when he fails to appear at a farewell party for his two younger brothers, Jaeckel and Young, who have enlisted in the armed forces and are about to go overseas and fight in the Korean War. When Walker finally does appear, he moves back into his old home, but he is not the loving son Hayes has always known. He is cynical and sardonic, mocking his plain-speaking father, Jagger, who often quotes the Bible and is a patriot to the marrow. Walker challenges his father's religious statements at every turn and ridicules Jagger's love of country, smirking and laughing at Jagger's singing a song about "Uncle Sammy" so that his enraged father slaps him. Hayes, distraught and emotionally shaken by her son's callous attitude, becomes confused, now believing that something sinister has entered her otherwise tranquil home. Walker, a college-trained bureaucrat, flaunts his intellectualism (the slow disintegration of her motherly strength and confidence is tellingly conveyed by Hayes in every scene). Walker then begins to get calls from a woman, Winston, who is ostensibly his sweetheart, and who also works in a sensitive position in the federal government. Walker is secretive and guarded about such calls when Hayes makes inquiries about the woman. When Walker is out of the house, Hayes is visited by Heflin, an FBI agent, who patiently asks for her help in providing information about her son, admitting to her that Walker is

Brian Aherne and Louis Hayward in *My Son, My Son!*, 1940.

under FBI investigation as a suspected communist spy. Shocked and stunned by this news, Hayes at first refuses to believe that her adoring son could have turned into a traitorous spy, but, she recalls his mocking attitude; his refusal to see off his younger brothers, who are going to fight in a war against communism; and his refusal to attend church with family members, all support her suspicions that Heflin may have told her the truth. To make sure, Hayes goes to Washington, and confronts Walker, asking him to prove his allegiance to the United States by swearing on a Bible that he is loyal to America. Walker patronizingly smiles and renders that oath to his mother, treating Hayes as if tolerating a naïve and unsophisticated child. She struggles to accept Walker's oath, instinctively believing that he has lied. Her suspicions—Hayes is much more intuitively knowing than the smug Walker can understand—are then supported when Heflin meets again with her to tell her that Walker's girlfriend, Winston, is another KGB-controlled traitor and Soviet agent, working with Walker to steal U.S. top secrets so that this vital information can be funneled to Russian spymasters. Hayes then makes one final appeal to Walker to give up his treasonable activities and remain loyal to America and its great principles and freedoms. Moreover, Heflin calls Walker and urges him to defy the Soviet agents that have turned him into a traitor and spy, telling him to act on behalf of his better nature while he "still has the free will" to do so, and the implication here is that Walker has somehow been brainwashed into becoming an enemy agent. Walker's conscience, which he has not been able to bury or destroy, then compels him to confess his guilt, and, instead of escaping the country by flying to Lisbon to deliver top U.S. secrets that he and Winston have stolen, he returns them to the safekeeping of the FBI. For this betrayal, he is now the target of Soviet assassins, who track him down and fatally shoot him and he dies upon the steps of the Lincoln Memorial, his last words expressing his true love for America. Walker's taped confession is later played before students at his former high school, one that ends with his fervent urging that these young students "hold fast to honor," and this is where the tragic story ends. McCarey directs this film with great patience, using Walker's distorted facial expressions, his furtive movements and shadowy actions to convey the dangerous espionage he practices rather than overtly showing his filching secrets while adroitly interspersing unnerving and emotionally disturbing scenes showing Hayes undergoing the trauma of seeing the son she loves exposed as a traitor. Both Walker and Hayes are superb in presenting their counterpoint characters. The strong element of propaganda is inescapable, however, in that this film was made at the height of the witch-hunting McCarthy era, and it was one of the films that Hollywood made to assure its loyalty to the U.S. At that time, many Hollywood writers had been accused of having communist affiliations, some of them going to prison on contempt after refusing to an-

swer questions at congressional hearings probing secret Soviet activities in the U.S. This much-maligned film is much better than its critics claim it to be. It is truly a chilling and incisive character study of a man struggling to determine his allegiances and a mother attempting to reclaim the lost son so dear to her heart with the threat of Soviet evils serving as a catalyst and those threats were chillingly real. *Author's Note*: McCarey, who was more comfortable with comedies and light-hearted films, was also an ardent patriot and made this film his pet project, basing the tale on a real-life American, who had turned into a communist spy and who worked at the U.S. Department of Justice for several years while blatantly stealing secrets she delivered to her KGB lover. Winston's role is based on that spy, Judith Coplon (Judith Coplon Socolov; 1921-2011), who obtained a job in the U.S. Department of Justice after graduating *cum laude* from Barnard College in 1943, and who, along with KGB spymaster Valentin Gubitchev, a Soviet attaché working at the United Nations in New York, and who was also Coplon's lover, were convicted in 1950 of espionage, albeit those convictions were overturned on technicalities as the FBI had made illegal wire taps of their conversations and, incredibly, arrested both of them while Coplon was flagrantly delivering some secrets to Gubitchev in New York, but without an arrest warrant. Rather than retry the pair, who were obviously guilty of espionage, the Bureau declined to pursue the case as it would then have to reveal much of its jealously guarded files in the case that would lead to the exposure of other counterintelligence operations then being conducted by the FBI. "Coplon was guilty as hell," McCarey told this author, "and everyone knew it. She was convicted and would have gone to prison had it not been for some agents fouling up their procedures. I turned that story around when making **My Son John**, to have Robert Walker in the role of Coplon and Irene Winston act as his Soviet control. Walker was sensational as the deluded American, who spies for Russia and he was as troubled in real life as he was in the film. He was drinking heavily and taking prescription drugs at the same time and running to a psychiatrist every hour on the hour. He was allergic to those drugs and that killed him [on August 28, 1951] just before we finished the production, a great loss. I had to use some stand-ins and backup shots for him in some final scenes to complete the picture. Of course, Helen [Hayes] is marvelous in the picture. I thought she gave such a powerful performance that she truly represented every loving mother in America. A lot of critics kicked me around for making that picture, but they lost sight of just how dangerous the communist spy rings were in those days. American traitors had actually stolen our secrets to the atomic bomb and turned them over to the Soviets and a lot of other important secrets. That's an irrefutable fact. There was a radical left element in Hollywood in those days, a small one to be sure, that supported all of those espionage activities by the Russians, and the rest of us in Hollywood were pretty damned nervous about *their* allegiances, I can tell you!" For more details on Judith Coplon, see my book *Spies: A Narrative Encyclopedia of Dirty Deeds and Double Dealing from Biblical Times to the Present* (M. Evans, 1997; pages 159-163). **p&d**, Leo McCarey; **cast**, Helen Hayes, Van Heflin, Robert Walker, Dean Jagger, Minor Watson, Frank McHugh, Irene Winston, Richard Jaeckel, James Young, Lee Aaker, Erskine Sanford; **w**, Myles Connolly, McCarey, John Lee Mahin (based on a story by McCarey); **c**, Harry Stradling; **m**, Robert Emmett Dolan; **ed**, Marvin Coil; **art d**, Hal Pereira, William Flannery; **set d**, Sam Comer, Emile Kuri; **spec eff**, Farciot Edouart, Gordon Jennings.

My Son, My Son! ★★★★ 1940; U.S.; 116m; Edward Small Productions/UA; B/W; Drama; Children: Cautionary; **DVD**; **VHS**. Aherne is outstanding as a loving but overly tolerant father of an errant and utterly worthless son, also brilliantly played by Hayward. Aherne is shown as an ambitious but impoverished young writer working as a day laborer in the slums of Manchester, England. When a baker loses his delivery man, Aherne offers to help him out and makes the deliveries. He is then offered a full-time job and Aherne takes it, befriending and then reluctantly marrying the baker's single-minded daughter, Hutchinson. When her father dies, Hutchinson manages the bakery, but is always upset with her husband, Aherne, who more busies himself with writing romantic novels than making deliveries. They have a son, who is coddled as a child (played by Beckett) and who is an inveterate cheat and liar, stealing things and then cleverly deceiving his trusting father. When Hutchinson insists that the boy be disciplined, the doting Aherne cannot bring himself to lift a hand to Beckett. In one of the many fascinating scenes in this well-crafted film, Aherne is shown writing his manuscript when a spider lands on one of its pages and he urges it to traverse that page to uphold the old belief that if the insect successfully crosses the page, the work will be a success. When the spider ambles away without crossing the page, Aherne calls after it: "It will be a success in spite of you!" Then one of Aherne's novels is published and it does become a great success. He sojourns to the coal mines to do research for his next novel when he meets and falls in love with the beautiful Carroll, but, being the noble and honest person that he is, Aherne tells her he is married and they sadly part. Aherne's marriage by then has turned into an unhappy one in that Hutchinson considers his occupation as that of an idler. After Hutchinson dies, Aherne goes on to become rich and famous as one of England's foremost authors. He is blessed when he again meets Carroll, who is the love of his life, but, by that time, his son, Hayward, has grown to manhood, and he is also attracted to Carroll. Knowing his father plans to marry Carroll, Hayward purposely makes advances toward her and makes her so uneasy that life becomes intolerable for her and she leaves, breaking Aherne's heart. Hayward then compromises sweet, young Day, wrecking her life as he has so many others; Aherne finally sees the reality of his son's wretched and despicable nature and finally severs his relationship with him. World War I then erupts and Hayward goes to the front as an officer, and Aherne, who has become a war correspondent, meets him while both are at the front lines. In a final meeting, Aherne tries to reconcile with Hayward, whose war experiences has made a much better man of him, and who admits that he has "never been any good" while the self-sacrificing Aherne has always been "too good" to him and everyone else. The strong love father and son have for each other is evident in this touching scene before Hayward goes off on a perilous mission and redeems himself by heroically sacrificing his life for others. Aherne mourns the loss of Hayward in his final telling line, saying "My son, my son!" Director Vidor presents this poignant and moving film with a sure hand, all of its scenes showing superlative production values in costuming and sets, and the script is witty, humorous and intelligent. Carroll, one of the great beauties of that fondly remembered film era is utterly captivating in her every scene. *Author's Note*: The film, as far as the profile of the Aherne role, is largely an autobiographical portrait of Welsh author Howard Spring (1889-1965), who worked himself up from the slums of Cardiff to become a reporter (serving in WWI) and later a hugely popular novelist of romantic fiction. **p**, Edward Small; **d**, Charles Vidor; **cast**, Madeleine Carroll, Brian Aherne, Louis Hayward, Laraine Day, Henry Hull, Josephine Hutchinson, Sophie Stewart, Bruce Lester, Scotty Beckett, Mary Gordon; **w**, Lenore Coffee (based on the novel by Howard Spring); **c**, Harry Stradling; **m**, Edward Ward; **ed**, Fred R. Feitshans, Jr.; **art d**, John DuCasse Schulze; **spec eff**, Howard Anderson.

My Song for You ★★★ 1935; U.K.; 75m; Cine-Alliance/Gaumont; B/W; Musical; Children: Acceptable. In this entertaining musical, Kiepura is an Italian opera singer, who is the idol of women all over Europe and the man every woman is after, except one. Marson keeps running away from him and he has to pursue her. He finally wins her heart, but not before some humorous setbacks. Songs: "My Song for You," "With All My Heart" (Mischa Spoliansky, Frank Eyton); "O Madonna" (Bronislau Kaper, Walter Jurmann, Charles L. Pothier). **p**, Michael Balcon, Arnold Pressburger; **d**, Maurice Elvey; **cast**, Jan Kiepura, Aileen Marson, Sonnie Hale, Emlyn Williams, Reginald Smith, George Merritt, Muriel George, Gina Malo, D.J. Williams, Bruce Winston; **w**, Austin Melford, Robert Edmunds, Richard Benson

Jacques Tati in *My Uncle*, 1958.

(based on the musical "Ein Lied für Dich" ["A Song for You"] by Ernst Marischka); **c**, Charles Van Enger; **m**, Mischa Spoliansky; **ed**, Charles Frend; **art d**, Alfred Junge.

My Uncle ★★★★ 1958; France/Italy; 117m; Gaumont/Continental Distributing; Color; Comedy; Children: Acceptable; **DVD**; **VHS**. Tati, that French master of mime and mirth (as well as one of France's foremost filmmakers), reprises his comedic role of Mr. Hulot, his first appearance as that endearing character made in **Mr. Hulot's Holiday**, 1954. (Tati made only six feature films in his entire career, all of them standouts.) Tati is a man who lives an almost solitary life. He is unkempt, his dwelling a disorderly and disheveled place; he disdains any sense of order as he rebels against modern conveniences that he believes have enslaved most of the so-called civilized world. Zola, his brother-in-law, and sister Servantie, live in an entirely opposite world, their modern house having every known electronic gadget ever invented. Their kitchen is packed with gadgets that open cans, dispose of garbage, and almost cook meals by remote control while their garage door (which later proves truculently temperamental) opens and closes with the click of a finger or a human movement caught by its electronic eye. Their son, Bacourt, is not impressed by the antiseptic atmosphere of his own home, but prefers to visit and remain with his charming and colorful uncle, Tati, and enjoys his uncle's disorganized residence and way of life, both of them deeply bonding as they are truly boys at heart. Although he attempts to avoid, evade and escape modern conveniences, Tati realizes that he must meet modern appliances head on and nevertheless struggles to master the scientific implements that clutter everyone's home and begin to invade Tati's dwelling as well. His life becomes even more complicated when Zola hires him as a representative of his firm and he must now conform to scientific modernization, or so it might seem. Meanwhile, Zola sees the folly of gadgets running his life and turns toward his neglected son to more fully establish a deeper relationship with Becourt. Tati produced and directed this film as well as starring in it and he proves again to be a master of visual comedy, his clever sight gags and subtle slapstick enhancing every scene in this enjoyably delightful film. (In French; English subtitles.) **p**, Jacques Tati, Fred Orain, Louis Dolivet; **d**, Tati; **cast**, Tati, Jean-Pierre Zola, Adrienne Servantie, Alain Becourt, Lucien Fregis, Betty Schneider, J.F. Martial, Dominique Marie, Yvonne Arnaud, Adelaide Danieli; **w**, Tati, Jacques Lagrange, Jean L'Hôte; **c**, Jean Bourgoin (Eastmancolor); **m**, Franck Barcellini, Alain Romans, Norbert Glanzberg; **ed**, Suzanne Baron; **prod d&set d**, Henri Schmitt; **spec eff**, Bertrand Levallois, Ugo Bimar.

My Uncle Antoine ★★★ 1971; Canada; 110m; National Film Board of Canada/Gendon Films; Color; Drama; Children: Unacceptable; **DVD**;

Dennis Morgan and Andrea King in *My Wild Irish Rose*, 1947.

VHS. This absorbing drama opens with Gagnon, a fourteen-year-old orphaned boy living in a small French Canadian mining town in the 1940s with his uncle Antoine (Duceppe) and aunt Cecile (Thibault), who own the general store and undertaking business. Christmas approaches and Gagnon flirts with his foster sister, Champagne, but the elders disapprove of it. Townspeople join them at the store for an annual Christmas party. It is interrupted by news that a boy has died and since his father is away at work at a logging camp, his mother, Loiselle, needs help with the body. Gagnon goes with Duceppe on a dog-sled trip to Loiselle's house. Duceppe has some drinks and, on the return journey with the body, the sled overturns and the body falls out. Duceppe is too drunk to recover it, so Gagnon goes back to town for help. He finds his aunt and a store clerk, Jutra, locked in each other's arms. Gagnon and Jutra go back to find the body, but the casket is missing. They go to Loiselle's house and see that the dead boy's father is there, having found the body and brought it home. It is a Christmas Gagnon will never forget and neither will most viewers. (In French; English subtitles.) **p**, Marc Beaudet; **d&w**, Claude Jutra (based on a story by Clément Perron); **cast**, Jean Duceppe, Olivette Thibault, Jutra, Jacques Gagnon, Lyne Champagne, Lionel Villeneuve, Hélène Loiselle, Mario Dubuc, Lise Brunelle, Alain Legendre, Robin Marcoux; **c**, Michel Brault; **m**, Jean Cousineau; **ed**, Jutra, Claire Boyer; **set d**, Denis Boucher, Lawrence O'Brien.

My Weakness ★★★ 1933; U.S.; 73m; FOX; B/W; Musical; Children: Acceptable. Hotel clerk Harvey falls for more sophisticated Ayres. Her girlfriends take two weeks to transform her into a classy socialite and she wins the man of her dreams. This nifty and charming "Cinderella" fantasy introduced German film star Harvey to American audiences, but she did not succeed as hoped. Songs: "Gather Lip Rouge While You May," "Be Careful," "How Do I Look?" (Buddy G. DeSylva, Leo Robin, Richard A. Whiting). **p**, B.G. DeSylva; **d**, David Butler; **cast**, Lilian Harvey, Lew Ayres, Charles Butterworth, Harry Langdon, Sid Silvers, Irene Bentley, Henry Travers, Adrian Rosley, Mary Howard, Irene Ware, Barbara Weeks; **w**, DeSylva, Butler, Bert Hanlon (based on a story by DeSylva); **c**, Arthur C. Miller; **m**, Arthur Lange, Cyril J. Mockridge; **ed**, Irene Morra; **art d**, Gordon Wiles.

My Week with Marilyn ★★★ 2011; U.K./U.S.; 99m; Weinstein Company/BBC Films; Color; Biographical Comedy; Children: Unacceptable (MPAA: R); **BD**; **DVD**. Humorous biopic sees Redmayne as a young and eager film student, who wants to be involved in the making of a new London-based movie starring Sir Laurence Olivier (1907-1989), played by Branagh. An extra incentive is that film siren Marilyn Monroe (1926-1962), played by Williams, will be Olivier's co-star. Williams arrives and London goes wild over her, but Branagh is less enthusiastic

because he considers her to be decorative but not an actress. She becomes insecure because of his criticism, but finds a friend and supporter in Redmayne, who falls in love with her during their week of shooting the film. Redmayne's tender loving care works wonders on Williams and she becomes even more the actress than Branagh ever dreamed possible. The shoot ends and Branagh and Williams are both happy as they go separate ways, while Redmayne is left to write a book about his weekend with Marilyn. Songs: "When Love Goes Wrong, Nothin' Goes Right" (Harold Adamson, Hoagy Carmichael), "Heat Wave" (Irving Berlin), "Memories Are Made of This" (Frank Miller, Richard Dehr, Terry Gilkyson), "Uno Dos Tres" (Daniel Indart, Jesus Alejandro as Jesus A. Perez-Alvarez), "Aces Wild" (Johnny Ace as John L. Alexander), "Burley Cutie" (Don Robey, David J. Mattis), "You Stepped Out of a Dream" (Gus Kahn, Nacio Herb Brown), "Autumn Leaves" (Joseph Kosma, Jacques Prevert), "That Old Black Magic" (Johnny Mercer, Harold Arlen). This well-made film offers excellent performances from all. Gutter language prohibits viewing by children. **p**, David Parfitt, Bob and Harvey Weinstein, Mark Cooper; **d**, Simon Curtis; **cast**, Michelle Williams, Eddie Redmayne, Julia Ormond, Kenneth Branagh, Judi Dench, Michael Kitchen, Dougray Scott, Derek Jacobi, Emma Watson, Zoë Wanamaker, Geraldine Somerville, Toby Jones, Karl Moffatt; **w**, Adrian Hodges (based on the books *My Week with Marilyn* and *The Prince, the Showgirl and Me* by Colin Clark); **c**, Ben Smithard; **m**, Conrad Pope; **ed**, Adam Recht; **prod d**, Donal Woods; **art d**, Charmian Adams; **set d**, Judy Farr; **spec eff**, Marl Holt, Daniel Baker, Antony Bluff, Alan Church.

My Wild Irish Rose ★★★ 1947; U.S.; 101m; WB; Color; Biographical Musical; Children: Acceptable; **DVD**. A delightful biopic of Irish-American composer Chauncey Olcott (Chancellor "Chauncey" Olcott; 1858-1932), played by Morgan, this rousing and happy musical romp also provides a swarm of lively and lovely songs by Olcott and others. Morgan, whose wonderful tenor voice is everywhere in this song-packed production, spends most of his time writing songs for King, who plays the famed Lillian Russell (1860-1922), as well as pitching woo at her, his amorous advances fended off until he gives up and decides that he truly loves Dahl (in one of her first films), the fetching daughter of an alderman, and takes her to the altar. The writers played fast and loose with Olcott's life. If the composer did all that is shown here, he lived more than ten lifetimes. However, it is the terrific music that counts, and director Butler delivers a staggering number of ballads and song and dance numbers that will enthrall and entertain even the most jaded viewer. Songs: "My Wild Irish Rose," (1899; music and lyrics by Chauncey Olcott); "Mother Machree" (1910; music: Chauncey Olcott, Ernest Ball; lyrics: Rida Johnson Young); "When Irish Eyes Are Smiling" (1912; music: Ernest Ball; lyrics: Chauncey Olcott, George Graff); "One Little, Sweet Little Girl" (1907; music and lyrics: Chauncey Olcott, Daniel J. Sullivan); "I Love the Name of Mary" (1911; music: Chauncey Olcott, Ernest Ball; lyrics: George Graff); "Sweet Inniscara" (1897; music and lyrics: Chauncey Olcott); "Hush-a-Bye, Wee Rose of Killarney," "The Natchez and the Robert E. Lee," "Miss Lindy Lou," "There's Room in My Heart for Them All," "Let Me Dream Some More," "Sing and Irish Song" "Show Me the Way to Kerry Fair" (all in 1947; music: M. K. Jerome; lyrics: Ted Kohler); "The Mirror Song" (music: M. K. Jerome); "Come Down Ma Evenin' Star" (1902; music: John Stromberg; lyrics: Robert B. Smith); "My Nellie's Blue Eyes" (1886; music and lyrics: William J. Scanlan); "You Tell Me Your Dream, I'll Tell You Mine" (1899; music: Neil Moret [Charles N. Daniels]; lyrics: Seymour Rice, Albert H. Brown); "Wait Till the Sun Shines, Nellie' (1905; music and lyrics: Harry von Tilzer); "Will You Love Me in December as You Do in May?" (1905; music: Ernest Ball; lyrics: James J. Walker); "A Little Bit of Heaven" (1914; music: Ernest Ball; lyrics: J. Keirn Brennan); "By the Light of the Silvery Moon" (1905; music: Gus Edwards; lyrics: Edward Madden); 'Twas Only an Irishman's Dream" (1916; music: Rennie Cormack; lyrics: Al Dubin, John J.

O'Brien); "Minstrel Days" (1941; music: M. K. Jerome; lyrics: Jack Scholl); "The Ride of the Valkyries" (1870; from "Die Walkure' by Richard Wagner); "Old Black Joe" (1860; music and lyrics: Stephen Foster); "(I Wish I Was in) Dixie's Land" (1860; music and lyrics: Daniel Decatur Emmett); "In the Evening by the Moonlight" (1878; music and lyrics: James Allen Bland); "Dear Old Donegal" (traditional Irish folksong); "Polly Wolly Doodle" (1880; traditional); "The Irish Washerwoman" (traditional); "Garryowen" (traditional; rewritten with new music and lyrics in 1905 by J. O. Brockenshire); "How Many Miles to Dublin Town?" (traditional Irish folksong). **p**, William Jacobs; **d**, David Butler; **cast**, Dennis Morgan, Arlene Dahl, Andrea King, Alan Hale, George Tobias, George O'Brien, Sara Allgood, Ben Blue, William Frawley, Don McGuire, George Cleveland, Ruby Dandridge, Grady Sutton, Herbert Anderson, Monte Blue, Penny Edwards, Ross Ford, Peggy Knudsen, Florence Lake, William B. Davidson, Oscar O'Shea, Charles Irwin, Clifton Young, Paul Stanton, Douglas Wood, Charles Marsh, Andrew Tombes; **w**, Peter Milne, Sid Fields, Edwin Gilbert (based on a book by Rita Olcott); **c**, Arthur Edeson, William R. Skall (Technicolor); **m**, Chauncey Olcott, Max Steiner; **ed**, Irene Morra; **art d**, Ed Carrere; **set d**, Lyle Riefsnider; **spec eff**, Harry Barndollar, Robert Burks.

The Mysterious Avenger ★★★ 1936; U.S.; 54m; COL; B/W; Western; Children: Acceptable. This above-average action-packed oater sees Starrett as a Texas Ranger, who comes to town to solve a cattle rustling mystery in which two ranchers, McKee and LeSaint, accuse each other of being the culprit. Not an easy job because one of them, McKee, is his father. Starrett discovers that neither is guilty and the real rustler is Oakman, bringing the villain to justice after many chases, shootouts and fights. **p**, Harry L. Decker; **d**, David Selman; **cast**, Charles Starrett, Joan Perry, Wheeler Oakman, Edward LeSaint, Lafe McKee, Hal Price, Charles Locher (Jon Hall), Roy Rogers, Bob Nolan, Sons of the Pioneers; **w**, Ford Beebe (based on a story by Beebe and Peter B. Kyne); **c**, George Meehan; **ed**, Richard Cahoon.

The Mysterious Dr. Fu Manchu ★★★ 1929; U.S.; 80m; Rowland V. Lee Productions/PAR; B/W; Mystery, Children: Unacceptable. Oland (who later starred in the Charlie Chan films) is exceptional as the evil Chinese physician in this first film adaptation of the Rohmer mystery novels. He is consumed by taking revenge against a British officer who served during the Boxer Rebellion (1898-1901) and where he blames that officer for the deaths of his wife and son. Arthur, a white woman who was left in Oland's care as a child when her father was killed in the Rebellion, is used by the evil doctor as his instrument of death. Oland hypnotizes Arthur and, while in a trance and under his control, she dispatches several British officers, but Oland's chief intended victims are King and his son Hamilton. Just when Oland is about to exact his revenge, Scotland Yard, which has been on the trail of the insidious Oland, intervenes, saves King and Hamilton and nabs the bloodthirsty physician and his followers. Director Lee does a good job presenting this chiller where the killers move through murky streets and shadowy sets, creating a gloom and doom atmosphere that heightens the suspense. **d**, Rowland V. Lee; **cast**, Warner Oland, Jean Arthur, Neil Hamilton, O.P. Heggie, William Austin, Claude King, Charles A. Stevenson, Evelyn Selbie, Noble Johnson, Tully Marshall; **w**, Lloyd Corrigan, Joseph L. Mankiewicz, Florence Ryerson (based on the story by Sax Rohmer); **c**, Harry Fischbeck; **m**, Oscar Potoker; **ed**, George Nichols Jr.

Mysterious House of Dr. C ★★★ 1968; Spain/U.S.; Copelia/Childhood Productions; Color; Fantasy; Children: Cautionary (MPAA: G). This curious but absorbing adaptation of Leo Delieb's ballet "Coppelia" is set in a small Spanish village where strange Dr. Coppelius (Slezak) keeps curious townspeople away by setting off explosions as a cover for his workshop filled with life-sized dolls he has created. After a young couple breaks into his house to discover the dolls, the girl then impersonates one of the dolls, which leads to considerable mayhem. **p&d**,

Warner Oland in *The Mysterious Dr. Fu Manchu*, **1929.**

Ted Kneeland; **cast**, Walter Slezak, Claudia Corday, Caj Selling, Eileen Elliott, Marcia Bellak, Kathy Jo Brown, Clara Cravey, Kathleen Garrison, Chris Holter, Sharon Kapner, Terry-Thomas (voice of the Bull); **w**, Ted Kneeland, Jo Anna Kneeland, Victor M. Tarruella (based on the libretto for the ballet "Coppelia" by Charles Nuitter, Arthur Saint-Leon); **c**, Cecilio Paniagua; **m**, Leo Delibes, Adrian Sardo; **ed**, Juan Serra; **prod d**, Florence Lustig; **art d**, Gil Parrondo; **set d**, Roberto Carpio.

Mysterious Intruder ★★★ 1946; U.S.; 61m; COL; B/W; Mystery; Children: Unacceptable. Plenty of suspense will be found in this entry in the series of films based on the CBS radio program "The Whistler." Burns, the owner of a music store, hires private detective Dix to find some rare and very valuable Jenny Lind recordings that went missing. After some kidnappings and arrests, thieves fall out as Mowery is killed by Toomey and Burns gets his records back. Dix is exceptional as a gumshoe compelled to spend as much time fending off clumsy police as he does tracking down the culprits. Excessive violence prohibits viewing by children. **p**, Rudolph C. Flothow; **d**, William Castle; **cast**, Richard Dix, Barton MacLane, Nina Vale, Regis Toomey, Helen Mowery, Mike Mazurki, Pamela Blake, Charles Lane, Paul E. Burns, Stanley Blystone, Harlan Briggs, Jack Carrington, Kathleen Howard; **w**, Eric Taylor (based on a story by Taylor); **c**, Philip Tannura; **m**, George Duning; **ed**, Dwight Caldwell; **art d**, Hans Radon; **set d**, Robert Priestley.

Mysterious Island ★★★ 1961; U.K./U.S.; 101m; American Films; COL; Color; Adventure; Children: Cautionary; **DVD**; **VHS**. Superior adventure tale with a lot of great special effects begins when Union POWs, led by Craig, escape in a Rebel observation balloon that has been positioned at a prisoner compound guarded by Confederate troops during the Civil War. Herbert, one of the Rebel guards, makes the mistake of holding on to one of the balloon's ropes and is taken skyward with the escapees that include journalist Merrill, and Union soldiers Callan and Jackson. Hoping to reach federal lines, Craig and the others, not experienced in handling the balloon, drift helplessly as heavy winds take it out to sea. After some time, the balloon descends, crashing into the sea next to an island lush with tropical foliage. The survivors wade ashore and begin building shelters and searching for food and water. They then add to their company two women, Greenwood and Rogan, who are survivors of a shipwreck. They locate a cave on a high cliff and make that their dwelling, accessing that natural shelter by a makeshift rope ladder. When exploring the island, the group encounters a number of mutant creatures, giant bees, huge crabs and a savage ostrich, which they ride like a horse until killing it for food. (These frightening and behemoth creatures are the inventive creations of special effects wizard Harryhausen.) Also discovered is a cache of weapons, equipment and

Craig Reynolds, Boris Karloff and Ivan Lebedeff in *The Mystery of Mr. Wong*, 1939.

other vital supplies that conveniently washes ashore in a large chest. Those weapons allow the inhabitants to ward off an attack from pirates, who come ashore, but are driven back to their ship, which is then inexplicably sunken by an unseen attacker. The survivors then see a man coming from the sea wearing strange underwater apparel and equipment that permits him to breathe underwater. He introduces himself as the celebrated Captain Nemo (Lom), who has been experimenting with the creatures on the island so that such gigantic mutations might serve to meet the world's shortage of food. The long dormant volcano on the island suddenly begins to erupt, and the inhabitants manage to escape by using the sunken pirate ship, which has been brought to the surface by Lom's apparatus. Lom, however, fails to reach safety as his submarine, which had earlier sunk the pirate ship, is crushed inside a sea cave by volcanic rock and lava. Endfield directs with a sure hand, and the script is witty and provides many humorous scenes, equaled by some very terrifying monsters á la Harryhausen, and where the cast members give topnotch performances. Added to the eerie and menacing atmosphere is a great score from composer Herrmann, who provided the score for **Citizen Kane**, 1941. This classic Jules Verne tale saw several remakes (in 1973, 2010 and 2012), but none compare with this outstanding production. Song: "Toccata and Fugue" (in D Minor BWV by Johann Sebastian Bach). **p**, Charles H. Schneer; **d**, Cy Endfield; **cast**, Michael Craig, Joan Greenwood, Michael Callan, Gary Merrill, Herbert Lom, Beth Rogan, Percy Herbert, Dan Jackson, Harry Monty; **w**, John Prebble, Daniel Ullman, Crane Wilbur (based on the novel *L'lle mystérieuse* by Jules Verne); **c**, Wilkie Cooper (Eastmancolor); **m**, Bernard Herrmann; **ed**, Frederick Wilson; **art d**, Bill Andrews; **set d**, **spec eff**, Ray Harryhausen.

Mysterious Mr. Moto ★★★ 1938; U.S.; 62m; FOX; B/W; Mystery; Children: Cautionary; **DVD**. Lorre again does an outstanding job as the inscrutable Japanese sleuth in this fifth entry of the series. This time Lorre is tracking an insidious group of killers known as the League of Assassins, who dispatch their high-positioned victims as killers-for-hire. To infiltrate this secret cabal, Lorre has himself imprisoned on dreaded Devil's Island as a convicted murderer, so that he can get close to Ames, a member of the League. With the collusion of the prison authorities, Lorre helps Ames escape, and both make their way back to London where Ames rewards Lorre by making him his houseboy. While posing as that servant, Lorre begins to identify other members of the League, sending his information to Scotland Yard. After witnessing some murders by the League, which Lorre is helpless to prevent, he learns that Wilcoxon, a tycoon and prominent member of high society, is scheduled to be the League's next victim. He also learns that the leader of the League employs a street musician to play the song "Madrid" as a signal to other members to commit their assassinations.

Wilcoxon is marked by murder after he refuses to pay off money to the League in a blackmail scheme. Rhodes, who is the leader of the League, then secures a position with Wilcoxon as his assistant and then arranges for Wilcoxon to be murdered while Wilcoxon is visiting an art museum. However, Lorre has learned of the plot and disguises himself as a German vagrant and prematurely sets off the street song that causes Rhodes, not Wilcoxon, to be killed and where the rest of the foul gang is quickly rounded up by police. Well crafted and with an inventive script, this moody whodunit provides great ambience and some very humorous scenes (particularly when Lorre deals with a bunch of ruffians in a London pub) while sustaining suspense. *Author's Note*: Lorre, as he had about other Mr. Moto films reviewed in this work, expressed his hatred of playing Moto, and carped about his appearance in this film, saying to this author: "I get myself thrown into that hellhole of Devil's Island to identify a gang of killers in **Mysterious Mr. Moto**—can you imagine anyone doing such a crazy thing? I don't know who was creepier in that picture, me or the killers I am trying to identify. Ironically, I wound up on Devil's Island or next to it on the mainland prison of French Guiana when I appeared in a picture with Humphrey Bogart, **Passage to Marseilles** [1944], and I escape again in that picture, too. They must have had a lousy prison system there with all of their inmates getting away from them." **p**, Sol M. Wurtzel; **d**, Norman Foster; **cast**, Peter Lorre, Mary Maguire, Henry Wilcoxon, Erick Rhodes, Harold Huber, Leon Ames, Forrester Harvey, Fredrik Vogeding, Lester Matthews, Karen Sorrell (Lotus Long), Mitchell Lewis; **w**, Foster, Philip MacDonald (based on a character created by John P. Marquand); **c**, Virgil Miller; **m**, Charles Maxwell; **ed**, Norman Colbert; **art d**, Lewis Creber, Bernard Herzbrun.

The Mysterious Mr. Wong ★★★ 1935; U.S.; 63m; MON; B/W; Mystery; Children: Unacceptable; **DVD**. Lugosi's extravagant performance as a torturing Chinese nutcase raises this whodunit above the average. He is murdering people in order to obtain the "Twelve Coins of Confucius" and, once these ancient coins are in his possession, he will rule a province in China. Wise-cracking reporter Ford begins snooping into Lugosi's nefarious affairs and unearths a chamber where Lugosi tortures victims in order to get information about the location of the coins. The fetching Judge, who is Ford's fiancée, is abducted by Lugosi, but Ford goes to the rescue and nabs the lunatic before he can do more harm. Well made and with a provocative script (but where ethnic slurs abound, which was not uncommon for that early talkie period), this film was produced by Poverty Row studio Monogram, which, at that time, had no real studio. Monogram produced its films, like this one, at RKO in Culver City and where it rented the lots and sound stages for its inexpensive productions. Monogram was later absorbed, as were almost all the other Poverty Row studios, by Republic Studios. **p**, George Yohalem; **d**, William Nigh; **cast**, Bela Lugosi, Wallace Ford, Arline Judge, Fred Warren, Lotus Long, Robert Emmett O'Connor, Edward Peil, Luke Chan, Lee Shumway, Etta Lee, Richard Loo; **w**, Nina Howatt, Lew Levenson, James Herbuveaux (based on the novel *The Twelve Coins of Confucius* by Harry Stephen Keeler); **c**, Harry Neumann; **m**, Abe Meyer; **ed**, Jack Ogilvie; **art d**, E.R. Hickson.

Mystery Liner ★★★ 1934; U.S.; 62m; MON; B/W; Mystery; Children: Unacceptable; **DVD**; **VHS**. This above-average whodunit sees Beery as the captain of an ocean-going luxury liner. He suffers a nervous breakdown and is relieved of duty. His replacement, Howard, takes over the ship as it is about to be used for an experiment in remote control that inventor Lewis will operate from a laboratory on land. Shortly after the demonstration, Lewis is attacked and nearly killed. Maxwell, a private investigator, learns that the villain is a German passenger, von Seyffertitz, who wants the device for his country. Excessive violence prohibits viewing by children. **p**, Paul Malvern; **d**, William Nigh; **cast**, Noah Beery Sr., Astrid Allwyn, Edwin Maxwell, Gustav von Seyffertitz, Ralph Lewis, Cornelius Keefe, Zeffie Tilbury, Boothe Howard, Howard

Hickman, George "Gabby" Hayes, Slim Whitaker; **w**, Wellyn Totman (based on the novel *The Ghost of John Holling* by Edgar Wallace); **c**, Archie Stout; **m**, Abe Meyer; **ed**, Carl Pierson.

The Mystery of Edwin Drood ★★★ 1935; U.S.; 85m; UNIV; B/W; Horror; Children: Unacceptable; **VHS**. Charles Dickens' unfinished novel is well told in this film adaptation where Rains is a moody choirmaster at a finishing school set in Victorian England. Rains is not the upstanding educator he pretends to be, but leads a secret life as a drug addict (opium). He develops an obsession for a beautiful young student, Angel, who is engaged to his handsome nephew, Edwin Drood (Manners). On Christmas Eve, Rains murders Manners and dumps his body in a quicklime pit. He then tries to pin the murder on Montgomery, a mixed-blood young man, who arrives at the school from India with his twin sister, Hobson. But Rains is found out when the pit is opened and Manners' hand is seen with an engagement ring on it. Dickens died before completing the novel, so it is not known what his ending might have been, but the film's ending works well and Rains is a standout as the drug-crazed choirmaster. This story was made as a silent film in 1914 and remade in 1993 with disappointing results. **p**, Edmund Grainger; **d**, Stuart Walker; **cast**, Claude Rains, David Manners, Valerie Hobson, Heather Angel, Douglass Montgomery, Francis L. Sullivan, Zeffie Tilbury, Ethel Griffies, E.E. Clive, Walter Kingsford. J.M. Kerrigan, Walter Brennan, Will Geer, Helen Parrish; **w**, John L. Balderston, Gladys Unger, Leopold Atlas, Bradley King (based on an unfinished novel by Charles Dickens); **c**, George Robinson; **m**, Edward Ward, Clifford Vaughan; **ed**, Edward Curtiss; **art d**, Albert S. D'Agostino; **spec eff**, John P. Fulton.

The Mystery of Mr. Wong ★★★ 1939; U.S.; 68m; MON; B/W; Mystery; Children: Unacceptable; **DVD**. Karloff is the inscrutable Chinese detective, who is contacted by old friend Wallace, a wealthy gem collector, after Wallace receives a letter threatening his life. Wallace explains that he has come into the possession of the "Eye of the Daughter of the Moon," the largest sapphire in the world, which has been reportedly stolen from a museum in China. Wallace tells Karloff that, in the event that he is killed, the letter should provide clues as to the identity of his murderer. Wallace then discovers that his wife, Tree, is considering divorcing him through the persuasion of her secretary, Reynolds, who has become Tree's lover. Wallace is later shot and killed when the lights go out during a game of charades and Reynolds become the prime suspect, but the young man, through Karloff's diligent snooping, proves to be innocent. Long, who is the family's Oriental maid, then becomes a suspect after Karloff learns that she is dedicated to having the rare sapphire returned to its rightful owner, the museum in China. Long, however, is quickly discarded as a suspect when she, too, is murdered after the anonymous letter Wallace received vanishes. Karloff then deduces that Herbert, Wallace's brother-in-law, is the culprit, handing him over to the police. Karloff has learned that Herbert sought revenge on the gem collector after Wallace abandoned Herbert's sister, who was Wallace's first wife. Director Nigh presents a taut mystery, sustaining suspense throughout, where Karloff is outstanding as the intelligent and articulate sleuth. This was the second in the series on Mr. Wong from Poverty Row studio Monogram, a series that proved to be successful at the box office. *Author's Note*: Karloff told this author that "I particularly liked playing the Wong character. Instead of menacing everyone in sight, I am trying to save lives and bring criminals to justice. The character I play is Oriental, as my makeup describes, but he has a sharp mind and thinks with both Western and Oriental intellectuality, unlike the character Peter Lorre plays in the Mr. Moto series where he is all Oriental in manner and thought." **p**, William Lackey, Scott R. Dunlap; **d**, William Nigh; **cast**, Boris Karloff, Grant Withers, Dorothy Tree, Craig Reynolds, Ivan Lebedeff, Holmes Herbert, Morgan Wallace, Lotus Long, Chester Gan, Bruce Wong; **w**, Scott Darling (based on the short stories by Hugh Wiley); **c**, Harry Neumann; **m**, Ed-

Sinister-looking figures in *The Mystery of the Wax Museum,* **1933.**

ward J. Kay; **ed**, Russell Schoengarth; **art d**, E.R. Hickson.

The Mystery of Mr. X ★★★ 1934; U.S.; 84m; MGM; B/W; Mystery; Children: Unacceptable; **DVD**. Montgomery is outstanding as a suave jewel thief operating in London when he becomes suspected of being a serial killer. One London policeman after another is killed, these murders confounding the best minds at Scotland Yard. To clear himself of suspicion, Montgomery goes after the real killer, who proves to be Mudie, recently released from prison after serving a term of fifteen years and who has been bent on killing a London bobby for each year he has spent in prison. Selwyn directs with considerable style to provide a foggy and mysterious London alive with foreboding characters lurking within the shadowy byways of the great city. *Author's Note*: Montgomery had reservations about playing his character, telling this author that "I never liked playing crooks, even though I am polished and considerate in stealing gems in **The Mystery of Mr. X**. Hollywood somehow felt that heroes could play jewel thieves and no one would think the lesser of them since they were pilfering jewels from wealthy people and not victimizing the poor and that they were nonviolent criminals. Almost everyone in America was poor in the Thirties—that was the time of the Great Depression—so stealing from the rich was somehow acceptable. That was, at least, Hollywood's logic." **p**, Lawrence Weingarten; **d**, Edgar Selwyn; **cast**, Robert Montgomery, Elizabeth Allan, Lewis Stone, Ralph Forbes, Henry Stephenson, Leonard Mudie, Forrester Harvey, Ivan Simpson, Alec B. Francis, Charles Irwin; **w**, Howard Emmett Rogers, Monckton Hoffe, Philip MacDonald (based on the novel *Mystery of the Dead Police* by MacDonald); **c**, Oliver T. Marsh; **m**, William Axt; **ed**, Hugh Wynn; **art d**, Merrill Pye.

The Mystery of the Wax Museum ★★★★ 1933; U.S.; 77m; WB; Color; Mystery; Children: Unacceptable; **DVD**. In one of his most impressive performances, veteran character actor Atwill is a gifted sculptor creating life-size wax figures of beautiful historical characters such as Joan of Arc and Marie Antoinette. These creations are exhibited at his wax museum in London in 1921, but Atwill faces a dilemma in that his museum is about to be closed down for lack of funds. Maxwell, Atwill's conniving partner and financial backer then arrives, stating that the only way he can recoup his investment is to burn down the museum and collect the insurance money. Atwill opposes this arsonist plan, but Maxwell sets fire to the museum and Atwill, horrified that his magnificent wax effigies will be destroyed, struggles with Maxwell. He is knocked unconscious and left to die in the flames as the museum burns to gutted ruins. Atwill, however, survives and is now seen in New York in 1933 forlornly watching from his window the New Year's Eve festivities in the street below. His injuries from the fire have confined him to a wheel-

Nicoletta Braschi and Elizabeth Bracco in *Mystery Train*, 1989.

chair and his hands are crippled so that he can no long sculpt. During those festivities a beautiful and wealthy socialite dies of her dissolute lifestyle by committing suicide through an overdose of drugs. After reporter Farrell goes to investigate the socialite's death, she learns that a man wearing a black cloak and hat and with a repulsively disfigured face invaded the morgue and stole the body of the socialite. The next day, newspaper headlines tell of the bizarre episode, and Farrell's editor orders her to stay with the story. Atwill, meanwhile, has secured funds and is about to open a new museum in New York. Since he can no longer work with his hands, the wax effigies to be exhibited in the museum are created by an odd group of sculptors working under Atwill's close instruction. Within this cadre of workers only youthful art student Vincent seems normal. Betz is a mindless deaf mute, who slavishly obeys Atwill's orders. Carewe, though a drug addict, appears to be gifted in that he finishes a beautiful wax replica of Joan of Arc, almost as exquisite as the effigy Atwill had so proudly displayed in his museum a decade earlier, but the image is strikingly similar to that of the socialite whose body was stolen from the morgue. This resemblance is seen by the sharp-eyed Farrell, who, when visiting the museum with her friend, Wray, comments on its similarity to the dead socialite, but Atwill dismisses her impressions as merely coincidental. Taken with Wray's beauty, Atwill tells her that she resembles his lost wax creation of Marie Antoinette. He asks if she will sometime pose for his sculptors to recreate that effigy and Wray agrees. Meanwhile, the snooping Farrell is also struck by the life-size wax reproduction of Voltaire, which is also on display at the museum, believing it to be almost the exact replica of a famous New York judge, who has recently vanished. (The missing judge is an oblique reference to the notorious disappearance of NYC Judge Joseph Force Crater, 1889-1930, who mysteriously vanished on August 6, 1930, and was never found.) She concludes that these are not merely wax reproductions, but that those of Joan of Arc and Voltaire are merely the preserved corpses of the socialite and the judge that have been coated with wax and then been put on display. She goes to the police and urges them to investigate and they arrest and grill Carewe, who, after being denied the drugs he craves, confesses that the figures of Joan of Arc and Voltaire are, indeed, the stolen bodies of the socialite and the judge. At this time, Wray, who is dating Vincent, goes to the museum, looking for him, but finds Atwill instead, who insists that she immediately pose for his sculptors, obsessed with her beauty, which he says he can preserve forever. His ravings so alarm her that Wray tries to leave, but Atwill shocks her when he stands up and leaves his wheelchair. He is not the invalid he has feigned to be and, further, when he grabs Wray and she struggles with him, Wray strikes Atwill's face, and, to her horror, a piece of it crumbles. Hysterical, she hits him again and again, until his face shatters and, beneath its crusty makeup is revealed a horribly disfigured

countenance, the terrifying image of an ogre that was shaped by the earlier fire. Wray faints and Atwill carries her to his basement laboratory where he removes her clothes and places her in a container over which hovers a vat of boiling wax with which Atwill intends to cover her. Just before he can kill her and spill the boiling wax onto Wray, Farrell arrives with police, who break through the basement door and struggle with Atwill on the catwalk next to the caldron of boiling wax. Atwill fights like a madman, but is finally overcome and knocked off the catwalk and into the boiling hot wax for the gruesome end he had planned for Wray. She is then rescued and reunites with Vincent. Pantheon director Curtiz provides a chilling tale, sustaining suspense throughout as his cameras move throughout the streets of London and New York and in and about the cavernous museum containing its grisly contents, where the sets are stunningly presented. Atwill is captivating and so, too, is Farrell as the wise-cracking newswoman, along with the fetching Wray (who could scream better on film than any leading lady of her era). The film straightforwardly deals with insanity, drug addiction and necrophilia, uncommon ground for its era. This was one of the first all color films where a two-strip Technicolor process was employed. Remade as a very good 3-D version titled **The House of Wax**, 1953, that film starred Vincent Price in Atwill's role and Phyllis Kirk essaying Wray's part. Another loose remake was produced in 2005. *Author's Note*: This film was somehow lost for some years until a print was found in the possession of studio chief Jack Warner and was later restored. Wray told this author that "I had just made **King Kong** [1933] before I was cast in the role of a naïve young woman in **Mystery of the Wax Museum**. The director [Curtiz] was very demanding and hard to understand as he had a thick foreign accent. At one point, he shouted at me, saying: 'You screamed louder for that big gorilla [in **King Kong**] than you are screaming for me. You must scream louder than that picture. We bought your scream!' When we were done, I hardly had any voice left. What a way to make a living." **p**, Henry Blanke; **d**, Michael Curtiz; **cast**, Lionel Atwill, Fay Wray, Glenda Farrell, Frank McHugh, Allen Vincent, Gavin Gordon, Edwin Maxwell, Holmes Herbert, Claude King, Arthur Edmund Carewe; **w**, Don Mullaly, Carl Erickson (based on a play by Charles Belden); **c**, Ray Rennahan (Technicolor); **ed**, George Amy; **art d**, Anton Grot; **spec eff**, Rex Wimpy.

Mystery Science Theater 3000: The Movie ★★★ 1996; U.S.; 73m; Best Brains/Gramercy Pictures; Color; Science Fiction/Comedy; Children: Unacceptable (MPAA: PG-13); **DVD**. Intriguing offbeat sci-fi film has Beaulieu as a mad scientist who creates an evil scheme that will enable him to control the world. First, he plans to torment Nelson and his robots by sending them to what he considers to be a clinker of a film to watch, **This Island Earth**, 1955, about a lobster creature dressed in slacks, expecting it to drive them crazy (this madcap idea was undoubtedly inspired by the technique employed in **A Clockwork Orange**, 1971, that shows habitual felon Malcolm McDowell being compelled to watch Holocaust films to rid himself of his evil inclinations). Nelson watches the film and finds humor that saves his sanity and the Earth. Song: "Love Theme from **Mystery Science Theater 3000: The Movie**" (Charlie Erickson, Joel Hodgson). Fans of the television series spoofing science-fiction films will find this to be a lot of fun. Sexuality prohibits viewing by children. **p&d**, Jim Mallon; **cast**, Trace Beaulieu, Michael J. Nelson, Mallon, Kevin Murphy, John Brady; **w**, Mallon, Nelson, Beaulieu, Murphy, Mary Jo Pehl, Paul Chaplin, Bridget Jones (based on the television series by Joel Hodgson); **c**, Jeff Stonehouse; **m**, Billy Barber; **ed**, Bill Johnson; **prod d**, Jef Maynard; **art d**, Rando Schmook; **set d**, Blakesley Clapp; **spec eff**, Eric D. Howell, Paul Murphy.

Mystery Street ★★★ 1950; U.S.; 93m; MGM; B/W; Mystery; Children: Unacceptable; **DVD**. Engrossing and highly suspenseful, this thriller begins with Sterling, a conniving floozy, having an affair with Ryan, a wealthy married man from a Boston Back Bay family. After Sterling discovers that she is pregnant, she arranges to meet Ryan at a lonely beach area, and, en route to that destination, she encounters Thompson, who befriends her and, feeling him empathetic, tells him her tale. Thompson offers to drive her to her rendezvous with Ryan, but Sterling uses a ruse to steal his car and drives off to meet Ryan. When learning from her that she is pregnant, Ryan realizes that his secure world is about to crumble and panics. He shoots and kills Sterling and then removes her clothing and dumps her body into the ocean. He then drives Thompson's car to a swamp, driving it into a bog, sinking it. Thompson, who has reported his car stolen, then becomes a suspect in Sterling's murder after her body washes ashore. Savvy street detective Montalban, who investigates the case, is not so sure that Thompson is guilty and probes further, bringing Bennett, a Harvard-trained forensic scientist, into the case. When Thompson's car is dredged from the swamp, he is arrested and charged with killing Sterling, but Montalban still has his doubts about the innocent-appearing young man. Lanchester, who is the landlady in the rooming house where Sterling lived, finds Ryan's phone number among Sterling's belongings and soon deduces that he is the girl's murderer. She confronts him, managing to steal the gun used to kill Sterling and then begins blackmailing Ryan. When he later goes to her rooming house to kill Lanchester, Ryan is met by Forrest, Thompson's worried wife, who is accompanied by Montalban. Ryan learns from Lanchester that she has hidden the murder weapon in a locker at a bus station, but before he can do anything about it, Montalban appears and Ryan flees. Montalban, through Bennett's forensic discoveries, has already determined that Ryan is the culprit and, after he obtains the key to that locker, he goes to the bus station the following morning and finds Ryan there, arresting him and charging him with Sterling's murder, which allows Thompson to be reunited with his loving wife, Forrest. Sturges directs this film noir entry with great expertise, taking a semi-documentary approach as was the mode adopted by Hollywood following WWII as seen in similar film noir standouts as **Kiss of Death**, 1947; **The Naked City**, 1948; and **He Walked by Night**, 1948. This entry is as impactful and tension filled as its contemporaries, thanks to fine performances from Montalban, Lanchester, Thompson and Ryan. The film was shot on location in Boston. *Author's Note*: Bennett, who plays the forensic scientist, told this author that "Dore Schary was running things at MGM in those days and, though the studio had not really concentrated on crime films before Schary's takeover from Louis B. Mayer, he wanted to present more of the kind of nitty-gritty crime films others were making. John Huston had just made **The Asphalt Jungle** [1950], one of those documentary type crime films, for MGM, and Schary followed up with **Mystery Street**. I play a forensic expert in that film and we were allowed to use the laboratory at Harvard University to determine the way in which Jan Sterling is killed in that picture by studying her skeletal remains, which I think audiences found pretty fascinating. It was all part of the new kind of realism Hollywood brought to the theaters at that time." **p**, Frank E. Taylor; **d**, John Sturges; **cast**, Ricardo Montalban, Sally Forrest, Bruce Bennett, Elsa Lanchester, Marshall Thompson, Jan Sterling, Edmon Ryan, Betsy Blair, Wally Maher, Ralph Dumke; **w**, Sydney Boehm, Richard Brooks (based on a story by Leonard Spigelgass); **c**, John Alton; **m**, Rudolph G. Kopp; **ed**, Ferris Webster; **art d**, Cedric Gibbons, Gabriel Scognamillo; **set d**, Edwin B. Willis.

Mystery Train ★★★ 1989; U.S./Japan; 110m; JVC Entertainment Networks; Crime/Comedy; Children: Unacceptable (MPAA: R); **BD**; **DVD**. This intriguing offbeat, independently produced film is a mix of comedy and drama, three tales centered on a seedy Memphis hotel where events take place in one night. Weirdo Hawkins is the night clerk and equally strange Lee is the bellboy. The first tale, "Far from Yokohama," deals with Japanese teenage tourists Kudoh and Nagase, both obsessed with Elvis Presley (there is a photo of Presley in every room), and where they try to link Presley to the Statue of Liberty and Madonna. In "Ghost," the second story, Braschi is an Italian widow, who is escorting her husband's body back to Italy for burial, but who is constrained to stay in

Melvyn Douglas and Tala Birell in *Nagana*, 1933.

the cheap hotel because of lack of funds, having lost most of her cash through various scams. She shares a room with garrulous Bracco, who has just broken up with her boyfriend, Strummer, and exhausts Braschi with her nonstop chatter. When she falls asleep, she is visited by the spirit of Presley. In the third tale, "Lost in Space," Strummer, Bracco's estranged boyfriend, gets drunk in a bar and later botches a liquor store robbery where he wounds the owner before he had his two friends, Buscemi and Aviles, escape to hide in the rundown hotel. They spend the night talking about the TV program "Lost in Space," and, when they leave, they run right into a police squad car to be captured. The direction is taut and clever and the characterizations are well enacted to sustain interest throughout. The film was shot on location in Memphis, Tennessee, in 1988 on a budget of $2,800,000, but it did poorly at the box office, returning a little more than half of its expense. Songs: "Mystery Train" (1953; Junior Parker), "Blue Moon" (1934; music: Richard Rodgers; lyrics: Lorenz Hart), "The Memphis Train" (1967; Rufus Thomas), "Pain in My Heart" (Naomi Neville), "Soul Finger" (1967; the Bar-Kays). Nudity and gutter language prohibit viewing by children. **p**, Kunijiro Hirata, Demetra MacBride, Rudd Simmons, Jim Stark; **d**, Jim Jarmusch; **cast**: Youki Kudoh, Masatoshi Nagase, Screamin' Jay Hawkins, Cinqué Lee, Nicoletta Braschi, Elizabeth Bracco, Joe Strummer, Rick Aviles, Steve Buscemi; **w**, Jarmusch; **c**, Robby Müller; **m**, John Lurie; **ed**, Melody London; **prod d**, Dan Bishop; **set d**, Dianna Freas; **spec eff**, Gary L. King.

Nagana ★★★ 1933; U.S.; 62m; UNIV; B/W; Adventure; Children: Acceptable; VHS. Birell is an adventurous countess, who accompanies Douglas, an idealistic doctor, into the African jungle on his search for a cure for Nagana, the native word for sleeping sickness, which is caused by the tsetse fly. On their trek they are plagued by native superstitions and crocodiles, not to mention mosquitoes. Some good exciting scenes and many perils abound in this action-packed tale. *Author's Note*: This film attempted to establish Birell as a clone of Marlene Dietrich or Greta Garbo. A Romanian-born actress, who came to America from German films, Birell never came even close to achieving Dietrich's or Garbo's star status, but continued in B-movies for the next twenty years. Douglas went on to become one of Hollywood's most enduring actors, twice winning Academy Awards as Best Supporting Actor in **Hud**, 1963, and **Being There**, 1979. **p**, Carl Laemmle, Jr.; **d**, Ernst L. Frank; **cast**, Tala Birell, Melvyn Douglas, Miki Morita, Onslow Stevens, Everett Brown, Billy McClain, William R. Dunn, Frank Lackteen, Noble Johnson; **w**, Dale Van Every, Don Ryan (based on a story by Lester Cohen); **c**, George Robinson; **ed**, Robert Carlisle.

Gene Barry, Chuck Connors and Sterling Hayden in *Naked Alibi,* **1954.**

Naked Alibi ★★★ 1954; U.S.; 86m; UNIV; B/W; Crime Drama; Children: Unacceptable. Gritty crime yarn has Hayden as a no-nonsense police detective. Following the murders of three policemen, Hayden points the finger at suave Barry, a prominent leader in local society, an accusation that brings about Hayden's suspension. Tough and taciturn, Hayden will not give up on his belief that Barry is the culprit and he finally flushes his prey from cover. After Barry tells his wife, Henderson, that the pressure created by Hayden has so troubled him that he needs time to work things out, he makes a run for the Mexican border. Barry arrives at Border Town in Mexico, to see his mistress, Grahame, a singer in a sleazy bar. Barry has been leading a double life, one in Mexico as a murderous gangster and one in the United States as a community leader. Hayden then arrives at Border Town and enlists Grahame's aid in tracking down Barry. The hoodlum flees, but Hayden, in a wild chase, scrambles after him over rooftops, where Grahame is shot to death and Barry, in a frantic effort to escape, meets grim justice by falling to his death. Hayden and Barry, as well as Grahame, give standout performances in this well-crafted film noir entry. *Author's Note*: Hayden told this author that he believed his role in this film "was almost as good as my part in John Huston's **Asphalt Jungle** [1950], although I played a hoodlum in that picture and a police gumshoe in **Naked Alibi**. Gloria [Grahame] was exceptional as the floozy singer in that picture and I always believed that she never really got the credit she should have gotten for her fine acting abilities." **p**, Ross Hunter; **d**, Jerry Hopper; **cast**, Sterling Hayden, Gloria Grahame, Gene Barry, Marcia Henderson, Casey Adams (Max Showalter), Billy Chapin, Chuck Connors, Don Haggerty, Stuart Randall, Don Garrett, Richard Beach, Fay Roope, John Alvin; **w**, Lawrence Roman (based on the story "Cry Copper" by J. Robert Bren, Gladys Atwater); **c**, Russell Metty; **m**, Frank Skinner, Hans J. Salter; **ed**, Al Clark; **art d**, Alexander Golitzen, Emrich Nicholson.

The Naked City ★★★★ 1948; U.S.; 96m; Hellinger Productions; UNIV; B/W; Crime Drama; Children: Unacceptable; **DVD**. Grim and uncompromising, this excellent crime tale is helmed by pantheon director Dassin with great skill, employing a documentary approach to the mesmerizing story. Opening with the bathtub murder of a beautiful playgirl, veteran detective Fitzgerald is assigned to the case, along with his eager, young assistant, Taylor. They and others begin a systematic search for the killer by following next-to-nothing clues. Throughout the tedious investigation where plainclothes detectives make seemingly endless inquiries on the streets of New York, producer Hellinger narrates their activities, stating as the camera shows the cops questioning venders, cabdrivers and citizens: "Ask a question, get an answer, ask another." Meanwhile, seasoned investigator Fitzgerald relentlessly drives Taylor and others to their task, repeating his favorite summation of his exhaust-

ing job: "I haven't had a busy day since yesterday." Results of this blanket investigation begin to appear when investigators learn that Hart, a model who worked in the shop where the murder victim bought her dresses, is engaged to Duff, a no account fortune hunter, who once dated the victim. Police further discover prescription drugs in the victim's room that have been provided by a physician, Jameson. Fitzgerald interviews Jameson, who says he knows little about the dead girl, except that she once dated Duff. After Duff is brought in for questioning, he lies about his former association with the dead girl, but, after more grilling, finally admits that he arranged to have the blonde playgirl murdered to protect someone, the actual killer being de Corsia, a murderous and powerful killer-for-hire and former wrestler. While police search for de Corsia, Fitzgerald then learns that the wealthy Jameson was the murdered girl's secret lover and financial sponsor and, after she began blackmailing him, he ordered Duff and de Corsia to get rid of her. Rather than face criminal charges and the destruction of his reputation, Jameson, while being interviewed in his high rise office, quits the world by committing suicide when leaping from one of his office windows. Duff is charged with the murder of the girl and Fitzgerald, Taylor and a host of other officers then begin a frantic city-wide search for de Corsia. Through diligent and dogged police work, Taylor locates de Corsia in his seedy apartment, but de Corsia overwhelms him and escapes. Taylor pursues, along with Fitzgerald and others, chasing de Corsia to the Brooklyn Bridge, where the killer clambers upward on its towering girders, shooting at the police below and shouting defiance. He is finally shot and falls to his death to conclude the case. Taut and suspenseful throughout, Fitzgerald, Taylor, Duff and Jameson are standouts in their roles, and the skilled Dassin maintains a brisk pace in presenting the gritty events as they unfold to reveal the story's grim conclusion, all in his unique semi-documentary approach while shooting on location in the streets, subways and byways of New York, every fascinating scene as grimly realistic as Dassin's other crime films, **Brute Force**, 1947, and **Night and the City**, 1950. *Author's Note*: This film was uniquely photographed by gifted cinematographer Daniels, who shot more than 100 sites in NYC, mostly from the secreted position of a van parked on various streets from posh Fifth Avenue to the debris-strewn streets of Lower Manhattan, thus preventing otherwise normally acting pedestrians from knowing of the camera's presence. A successful ABC TV series emanated from this superlative film, one that showed "slice of life" profiles of New York City's inhabitants, and where Hellinger's cogent closing remarks ending this film were also employed in that series: "There are eight million stories in the naked city. This has been one of them." Hellinger, who had been a successful newspaper columnist in New York in the 1920s, became a Hollywood producer and made many films that realistically profiled his native NYC, not the least of which was the memorable crime yarn, **The Roaring Twenties**, 1939, a bootlegging era saga starring James Cagney and Humphrey Bogart, and where he also serves as the narrator of that film. **p**, Mark Hellinger; **d**, Jules Dassin; **cast**, Barry Fitzgerald, Howard Duff, Dorothy Hart, Don Taylor, Frank Conroy, Ted de Corsia, House Jameson, Jean Adair, Paul Ford, James Gregory, Nicholas Joy, Arthur O'Connell, Nehemiah Persoff, Molly Picon, Hellinger (narrator); **w**, Albert Maltz, Malvin Wald (based on a story by Wald); **c**, William Daniels; **m**, Miklos Rozsa, Frank Skinner; **ed**, Paul Weatherwax; **art d**, John F. DeCuir; **set d**, Russell A. Gausman, Oliver Emert.

The Naked Gun: From the Files of Police Squad ★★★ 1988; U.S.; 85m; PAR; Color; Comedy; Children: Unacceptable (MPAA: PG-13); **VHS**. This satire of police movies spun off from the television series "Police Squad," and follows the antics of Nielsen, an incompetent police lieutenant, who can do nothing right. Queen Elizabeth II of England is paying a visit to New York City, and Montalban, an arch criminal, who is not a fan of hers, plans to assassinate her when she attends a Brooklyn Dodgers baseball game while she accommodatingly passes a hot dog along to a man sitting next to her. Another of the funniest scenes comes at the end of the film when Simpson, a man with a cast on his leg in a wheelchair accidentally goes flying out of the stands at the ball game. Despite all of his ineptitude, Nielsen eventually foils Montalban while putting the queen at considerable disgrace and discomfort. A goofy film full of sight and sound gags that goes its merry way while offering a lot of laughs and good entertainment down a very zany path. Two sequels followed: **The Naked Gun 2 ½: The Smell of Fear**, 1991, and **Naked Gun 33 1/3: The Final Insult**, 1994. Songs: "The Star Spangled Banner" (John Stafford Smith, Francis Scott Key), "I Love L.A." (Randy Newman), "I'm Into Something Good" (Gerry Goffin, Carole King), "Louie, Louie" (Richard Berry), "Trumpet Fanfare" (Stephen Oliver), "God Save the King!" (Henry Carey). Excessive violence prohibits viewing by children. **p**, Robert K. Weiss; **d**, David Zucker; **cast**, Leslie Nielsen, Priscilla Presley, Ricardo Montalban, George Kennedy, O. J. Simpson, Susan Beaubian, Nancy Marchand, Jeannette Charles, Reggie Jackson, Lawrence Tierney, Dick Enberg, Mel Allen, Jim Palmer, Curt Gowdy, Joyce Brothers, John Houseman; **w**, David Zucker, Jerry Zucker, Jim Abrahams, Pat Proft (based on the television series "Police Squad" by Abrahams and the Zuckers); **c**, Robert Stevens (Technicolor); **m**, Ira Newborn; **ed**, Michael Jablow; **prod d**, John J. Lloyd; **art d**, Donald B. Woodruff; **set d**, Rick T. Gentz; **spec eff**, Cliff Wenger, Bruce A. Block.

The Naked Jungle ★★★★ 1954; U.S.; 95m; PAR; Color; Adventure; Children: Cautionary; **DVD**; **VHS**. In this exciting adventure tale, Heston is the wealthy and all-powerful owner of a vast plantation deep in the Amazon jungle. Arriving by boat up the Amazon River—it takes a full day for the vessel to traverse Heston's property—is beautiful Parker, a refined and cultured woman who has married Heston by proxy. When she first meets her new husband, Parker is offended by his cold and even cruel remarks. She makes a little joke and his callous response is: "You have a sense of humor. I don't like humor in a woman." Heston has been too long a reclusive bachelor to realize the wonderful prize he has acquired in Parker. Though she tries to befriend her new spouse, nothing she can do will soften the hard shell he had built where he has insulated himself against the softening embrace of love. Parker makes the mistake of mentioning that she has had a previous marriage. This angers Heston to the point where he tells her to pack her bags and go back to her hometown of New Orleans. Before the emotionally distraught Parker can depart, Conrad, the provincial commissioner, arrives to tell them that strange occurrences are taking place in the jungle where mass migration of all the wild animals is happening. Heston asks Conrad what he thinks is causing this and he replies with one word: "Marabunta," meaning an endless army of legionary ants by the billions that cover the landscape, eating everything in sight, plant and animal (these foraging ants form columns as wide as twenty miles) and that that army is incessantly moving through the jungle and directly at Heston's plantation at six miles a day and devouring all it encounters. Conrad tells Heston that these plagues occur every so often in a century and that nothing can stop the oncoming Marabunta and that the only recourse is to get out of the way of its devastating path. Heston has fought long and hard to establish his plantation and refuses to simply walk away from his property. Parker decides to stay with her man, arguing that if she leaves, the natives will also depart and he will have no one to aid him in his fight with the army of insects. Heston, impressed with Parker's pluck, now sees her in another light, as a companion who will work with him, and he asks her to stay on. Heston scouts the jungle and discovers from a mountaintop the massive army coming his way, a brown and moving coat that covers miles of hills and valleys. Heston prepares for the onslaught by having his native workers build water-filled moats around his plantation, his palatial home surrounded by a high wall. The ants arrive at his plantation and Heston floods their approaches and blows up bridges, but the clever ants, thinking as one entity, use leaves to float across the water and even crawl above the bodies of their dead fellows to reach their destination. Whenever Heston is able to stop the ants at one point, the insects invade

Don Taylor in *The Naked City*, 1948.

another area of his plantation, eating all of his crops and relentlessly crawling toward his walled home. The natives flee in terror, but Heston refuses to give up the fight. He coats himself with grease and fights his way through a swarm of ants until he reaches the dam that holds back waters from which he has originally claimed his lands. Just as the ants reach his walled home where Parker and a few servants are battling the ants by burning timber to halt their path, Heston reaches the dam and manages to blow it up, cascading waters carrying him and the billions of ants away, the waters engulfing and drowning the ants as its crashes against the walls of Heston's home, saving it. When the water subsides and the threat is over, a worried Parker steps from the home to see Heston alive and staggering forward into her welcoming arms to end this harrowing tale. Heston and Parker give exceptional performances in this thriller, and Haskin directs with a firm hand, keeping the story line taut and the anxiety, particularly in the ant attack on the plantation, at high pitch and where the special effects are outstanding. Of all the films based on attacks by insects, including **Them!**, 1954, this is one of the best productions. ***Author's Note***: Heston stated that to this author: "I like working with Eleanor [Parker], a fine actress, who is always prepared and gives her best in every scene. The producer, Pal, knew what he wanted in **The Naked Jungle** as he always did in his many science fiction films [**Destination Moon**, 1950, and **War of the Worlds**, 1953]." **p**, George Pal; **d**, Byron Haskin; **cast**, Eleanor Parker, Charlton Heston, Abraham Sofaer, William Conrad, Romo Vincent, Douglas Fowley, John Dierkes, Leonard Strong, Norma Calderon, Pilar Del Rey; **w**, Philip Yordan, Ranald MacDougall (based on the story "Leiningen Versus the Ants" by Carl Stephenson); **c**, Ernest Laszlo (Technicolor); **m**, Daniele Amfitheatrof; **ed**, Everett Douglas; **art d**, Hal Pereira, Franz Bachelin; **set d**, Sam Comer, Grace Gregory; **spec eff**, Farciot Edouart, John P. Fulton.

The Naked Kiss ★★★ 1964; U.S.; 90m; F&F Productions/AA; B/W; Drama; Children: Unacceptable; **BD**; **DVD**; **VHS**. Absorbing tale has Towers, a prostitute, getting into a violent fight with her pimp, who is trying to cheat her and pull off her wig that would reveal her shaved bald head. She kills him and runs away to a town where she is not known. There she has a brief affair with Eisely, the local police captain. He knows of her past as a prostitute and suggests she work for a town madam, Grey. Instead, she gets a job nursing at a hospital for handicapped children. Dante, a well-respected millionaire philanthropist, who is generous to the children and hospital, falls in love with her. She admits her shady past to him, but he says he will marry her anyway. But the kiss he gives her reawakens something that haunts her, an experience in her past, which a psychiatrist called "The Naked Kiss." Despite that, she buys a wedding dress and goes to Dante's home to show it to him, but finds him in his bedroom with a little girl he is about to molest, so

Cornel Wilde in *The Naked Prey*, 1966.

Towers beats him to death with a telephone. Townspeople brand her a murderer, but, with Eisley's help, the girl is found and, she states that Dante attempted to molest her. The town does an about-face and considers Towers a heroine, but she decides to move on. "The Naked Kiss" reminded her of being molested when she was a little girl. Songs: "Santa Lucia" (Teodoro Cottrau), "Little Child (Mon Enfant) (traditional). This strong and finely made film is not for children because of subject matter and excessive violence. **p,d&w**, Samuel Fuller; **cast**, Constance Towers, Anthony Eisley, Michael Dante, Virginia Grey, Patsy Kelly, Marie Devereux, Karen Conrad, Linda Francis, Bill Sampson, Sheila Mintz; **c**, Stanley Cortez; **m**, Paul Dunlap; **ed**, Jerome Thoms; **art d**, Eugène Lourié; **set d**, Victor Gangelin.

The Naked Prey ★★★★ 1966; South Africa/U.S.; 96m; Sven Persson/PAR; Color; Adventure; Children: Unacceptable; **DVD**; **VHS**. This gritty and consistently terrifying tale begins with Wilde as a safari guide leading an expedition of ivory hunters in the South African jungles in the late 19th Century. The hunters are inconsiderate and self-serving, one of them, van den Bergh, insulting members of a local tribe. They retaliate by attacking the camp and killing all but six of the safari members, taking them prisoner and putting them through various sadistic tortures. One of the white hunters is stripped, coated with mud and two hollow tubes jammed into his nostrils that allows him to breathe as he is then tied to a spit and roasted to death over an open fire as one might roast a pig. Another hunter is hog-tied and feathered and then hacked to death. Van den Bergh is staked out inside a ring of fire which also encloses a deadly cobra that subsequently bites him with death-dealing poison. All of the hunters are thus dispatched in grisly methods except for Wilde, whom the tribe respects as he had earlier objected to the insults they suffered from the hunters. He is offered the "Chance of the Lion," where, after being stripped naked except for a loincloth, he is allowed to run for his life while several of the strongest young braves of the tribe, all of whom have killed several lions, chase and hunt him with spears and knives. Wilde is given a head start of a few hundred yards and, being an excellent runner, sprints off at great speed, surprising his pursuers. One of the braves, eager to achieve the kill, races ahead of the others, despite the shouted warnings of the oldest warrior, who is the leader of the pack. The young warrior closes the distance with Wilde and hurls his spear at him, but Wilde manages to evade the lance and then uses it to kill the young warrior. As his fellow warriors stop to mourn him, Wilde gains more ground in distancing himself from the warriors, now wearing the moccasins and using the knife of the slain warrior as he frantically makes his way toward a distant fort and safety. The death of the young warrior fills the others with vengeance, and they now swear to run Wilde to earth and kill him. Evading deadly snakes,

scorpions and lizards, Wilde plunges ahead with the warriors in hot pursuit. Wilde uses all his skills to set ruses so that he is able to kill two more of the warriors and he then halts the pursuit of the others by setting fire to dry brush that blazes for a great distance. He nevertheless knows that the warriors will not give up their pursuit and he races on. He encounters a village where black slavers have imprisoned the natives, leading them away in halters. Wilde manages to free a few of these hapless victims before the armed slavers fire at him, but he manages to escape into the jungle and later falls into a river and almost drowns. He is saved by a young boy, who has fled the village and the slavers, and Wilde briefly serves as the boy's surrogate father, fishing and eating with him before the boy goes his own way. As Wilde nears the fort and safety, the relentless warriors have gained ground and close in on him. Frantic, Wilde again runs for his life, tearing through the jungles with the warriors closing the distance. Wilde finally breaks through the dense foliage and enters a clearing where he sees on a hill in the distance the fort and where soldiers spot him and move toward him. The warriors also come into the clearing and one is about to hurl a spear at Wilde, but one of the soldiers fires at him, killing him. Wilde, exhausted, then staggers toward the fort and safety. He turns to see the remaining warriors standing at the edge of the jungle, raising their spears to him in respect and admiration for his endurance and physical abilities in surviving the lethal chase (much as the warriors do in saluting the British defenders at the 1879 Battle of Rorke's Drift in Natal, South Africa, in the film **Zulu**, 1964) and then disappear back into the jungle. Wilde not only stars in this exciting film, but is its director, his fourth film as a helmsman, and here he does a marvelous job in profiling the almost non stop action and where he is also exceptional as the pursued victim. There is little dialog in the script, the story line concentrating on the chase, which opens about fifteen minutes from its beginning. The depiction of the pursuit is breathtaking as Wilde brilliantly crosscuts from the pursuers to the pursued, creating tension and anxiety in every harrowing scene. Wilde is believable as the human prey and exhibits a good deal of physical dexterity as he was an athletic performer (and was a member of the U.S. fencing team before it went to the Olympics in 1936). *Author's Note*: Wilde was inspired to make this film after hearing a radio program that told the story of John Colter (c. 1774-c.1813), who is considered to be America's first "mountain man." He was a trapper and member of the celebrated Lewis and Clark Expedition (1804-1806), who left the expedition and remained in the Rocky Mountain area. In 1808, he was captured by Blackfoot Indians, who considered him a fellow brave and he was allowed to save his life by running ahead of several Blackfoot warriors, who chased him for more than five miles through rough terrain until he reached the safety of a trader's fort on the Little Big Horn River (later the site of the Custer massacre) in Montana. In the chase, Colter killed one pursuing Indian and used his blanket and utensils to survive the pursuit. Wilde originally thought to base the film on Colter's experience, but funding provided by South African interests caused him to relocate the story, changing its time frame. The production, all shot in South Africa, was fraught with hazards and problems. Wilde himself suffered many injuries during the chase through the jungles and hills, a lizard attaching itself to his leg at one point and where the creature had to be killed before it could be separated from the actor's leg. He also contracted tick fever, similar to that of malaria, which made him look haggard, but that look of exhaustion gave credibility to his worn out appearance during the chase. Crew members were also plagued during the production, five members going to a hospital after they were repeatedly stung by a swarm of killer bees. The unit manager was bitten by a cobra, and its poison had to be extracted in a minor operation. The chief of the tribe that supplied the warriors in the film generously offered Wilde a fifteen-year-old girl from his tribe as a wife for Wilde, and was surprised when the actor politely refused the gift, telling Wilde that he had six wives and he could not understand why Wilde would be satisfied with only one spouse (Wilde's wife then being beautiful blonde actress Jean Wallace, who accompanied Wilde to South Africa and was present during the production shooting and whose milky white skin caused the chief to think her bloodless). Other films depicting chases where human prey is involved include **The Most Dangerous Game**, 1932 (where Joel McCrea and Fay Wray are hunted on a jungle island by a deranged aristocrat); **Drums along the Mohawk**, 1939 (where Henry Fonda is chased by Mohawk braves for many miles); **Run for the Sun**, 1956 (where Richard Widmark and Jane Greer must outrun Nazi pursuers); and **Run of the Arrow**, 1957 (where Rod Steiger must outrun Sioux braves to survive). **p&d**, Cornel Wilde; **cast**, Wilde, Gert van den Bergh, Ken Gampu, Patrick Mynhardt, Bella Randles, Morrison Gampu, Sandy Nkomo, Eric Mcanyana, John Marcus, Richard Mashiya; **w**, Clint Johnston, Don Peters; **c**, H.A.R. Thomson (Panavision; Technicolor); **m**, Edwin Astley, Andrew Tracey, Wilde; **ed**, Roger Cherrill.

The Naked Spur ★★★★ 1953; U.S.; 91m; MGM; Color; Western; Children: Unacceptable; **DVD; VHS**. Another superlative and "intelligent" western from director Mann sees the always fascinating Stewart as an embittered Civil War veteran. When returning from the war, Stewart finds that he has lost his ranch and, to regain it, must obtain substantial money. To that mercenary end, he becomes a bounty hunter, his first prey being Ryan, a killer with a $5,000 reward for his capture, dead or alive, who has escaped into the wilds of the Colorado Territory. Accompanying Ryan is Leigh, a beautiful but lonely young woman, who wants nothing more than to go to California and live a peaceful life. In his search for the fugitive, Stewart encounters Mitchell, a nomadic, prospecting gold-seeker, who becomes his deputy believing that Stewart is a lawman. They then meet up with Meeker, a cashiered officer from the U.S. Cavalry, a wholly immoral man, who was dishonorably discharged for assaulting a woman. Meeker learns of Stewart's mission and becomes another "deputy," also believing that he is a lawman. The three encounter Ryan and Leigh in a mountainous area and take them prisoner, and Leigh vainly begs Stewart to let her and Ryan go, a plea Stewart ignores. Ryan, an insidious outlaw, realizes that, to escape, he must set his three captors against each other and begins to subtly urge Mitchell and Meeker to kill Stewart, as well as each other, in order for them to get the entire reward, hoping that, through this process of elimination, he will be able to escape. As the group travels for seven days through Indian territory, heading for Abilene, they meet up with hostile Indians and there is a firefight, but Stewart is hampered in his task in that he has injured his leg. He becomes delirious in his sleep and Leigh nurses him. Then Mitchell and Meeker learn that Stewart is a bounty hunter and not a lawman and they both demand a share in the reward Stewart thinks to receive for delivering Ryan to authorities. Stewart reluctantly agrees, but the group travels now with greater insecurity, the three captors all suspecting the others of plotting against them. Ryan, meanwhile, causes Stewart to fall from his horse, further aggravating his injury, but Stewart recovers and continues leading the group toward Abilene. Ryan attempts several escapes, all foiled by Stewart, until Ryan manages to obtain a rifle from Mitchell and retreats to a rocky hilltop where he shoots and kills Mitchell. Stewart and Meeker then battle Ryan in a gunfight until Ryan is killed. His body falls into a raging river, but Meeker lassos the floating corpse, but, when attempting to retrieve it, is drowned. Stewart then hauls Ryan's soaking body to shore and packs it onto a horse. Leigh, who has fallen in love with him, begs him to give up his grim mission, and Stewart, realizing how disgusting and repulsive his goal has become, finally quits the task. He buries Ryan's body and he and Leigh then set out for California to make a life together. Stewart is outstanding as the diehard bounty hunter who altruistically quits his grim quest to salvage his dignity and self-respect, and Ryan is also a standout as an insidious, evil-minded outlaw attempting to escape punishment for his crimes at all cost. Meeker and Mitchell give excellent performances as two men obsessed with greed and bloodlust. Mann's fine direction is taut with suspense and packs a lot of action that he brilliantly choreographs in one telling scene after another. *Author's Note*: Stewart told this author that "**The Naked Spur** is a 'thinking man's' western. It

James Stewart in *The Naked Spur,* 1953.

shows the pursuit and capture of an evil man while also showing a good man struggling with his conscience. It doesn't preach, but shows that struggle in one scene after another as that man tries to hold on to his values. They did not make westerns like that until after World War Two, and I made a lot of them with Anthony Mann, who was simply great in making such films." Ryan told this author that his role in this film "was another one of those sneaky villains who uses basic psychology to divide and conquer the men who have captured him. It was the kind of role I was used to playing, but that one that had some meat to it as my character is as smart as the men who have taken him prisoner. That was due to a very fine script, so good that it got an Oscar nomination, and that is something exceptional for a western." Many films portray bounty hunters mostly in search of wanted felons in the Old West, including **Apache Warrior**, 1957; **The Bounty Hunter**, 1954; **The Bounty Killer**, 1965; **Chisum**, 1970; **Joe Kidd**, 1972; **The Missouri Breaks**, 1976; **The Outlaw Josey Wales**, 1976; **Pat Garrett and Billy the Kid**, 1973; **The Professionals**, 1966; **Ride Lonesome**, 1959; **The Shooting**, 1966; **3:10 to Yuma**, 1957, and its 2007 remake; **The Tin Star**, 1957; **True Grit**, 1969; **Young Guns**, 1988 and **Young Guns II**, 1990; and in the modern era, including **The Bounty Hunter**, 1989; **Five Came Back**, 1939; **The Hunter**, 1980; **L.A. Bounty**, 1989; **The Misfits**, 1961; **No Country for Old Men**, 2007; **Papillon**, 1973; **The Reward**, 1965; and **Wanted: Dead or Alive**, 1987. **p**, William H. Wright; **d**, Anthony Mann; **cast**, James Stewart, Janet Leigh, Robert Ryan, Ralph Meeker, Millard Mitchell; **w**, Sam Rolfe, Harold Jack Bloom; **c**, William Mellor (Technicolor); **m**, Bronislau Kaper; **ed**, George White; **art d**, Cedric Gibbons, Malcolm Brown; **set d**, Edwub B. Willis; **spec eff**, Warren Newcombe.

The Naked Street ★★★ 1955; U.S.; 84m; UA; B/W; Crime Drama; Children: Unacceptable. In this grim but fascinating crime yarn, Bancroft is the nice but naughty sister of mobster Quinn. She gets pregnant by young Granger, a convict on his way to the electric chair, but Quinn gets Granger released so he can marry Bancroft. After she miscarries, the gunshot wedding is unnecessary. Quinn then learns that Granger has been cheating on Bancroft, so he frames him for a murder and Granger is sent back to Death Row. Granger tells Graves, a reporter, about it all and that leads to a police investigation that concludes when officers chase Quinn over rooftops and where he falls to his death. Bancroft then winds up with good guy Graves. Excessive violence prohibits viewing by children. **p**, Edward Small; **d&w**, Maxwell Shane (based on a story by Leo Katcher); **cast**, Farley Granger, Anthony Quinn, Anne Bancroft, Peter Graves, James Flavin, Whit Bissell, Else Neft, Sara Berner, Jeanne Cooper, Mickey Knox, Lee Van Cleef; **c**, Floyd Crosby; **m**, Emil Newman, Ernest Gold; **ed**, Grant Whytock; **art d**, Ted Haworth.

Bette Davis and Wendy Craig in *The Nanny*, 1965.

The Nanny ★★★ 1965; U.S.; 91m; Associated British-Hammer/FOX; B/W; Horror; Children: Unacceptable; **DVD**; **VHS**. Davis is exceptional in playing an English nanny or governess in this grim and taut thriller. She looks after Dix, a ten-year-old boy just released from a home for disturbed children where he spent two years undergoing psychological treatment for drowning his little sister in a bathtub. Soon after he arrives home, his mother is poisoned, but he blames Davis, whom he also has accused in the death of his sister. No one believes him, until an aunt, Bennett, comes to live in the house and sees Davis attempting to kill Dix by smothering his face with a pillow. Bennett has a heart attack and Davis admits to the dying woman she was responsible for the little girl's drowning, but claiming it was an accident. She goes ahead with a plan to drown Dix, but is tormented by memories of the girl's drowning, so she leaves him alive, packs up and departs the house. Violence prohibits viewing by children. **p**, Jimmy Sangster; **d**, Seth Holt; **cast**, Bette Davis, Wendy Craig, Jill Bennett, James Villiers, William Dix, Pamela Franklin, Jack Watling, Maurice Denham, Alfred Burke, Harry Fowler; **w**, Jimmy Sangster (based on the novel by Evelyn Piper); **c**, Harry Waxman; **m**, Richard Rodney Bennett; **ed**, Tom Simpson; **prod d**, Edward Carrick.

Napoleon ★★★★★ 1929 (silent); France; 240m (235m in 1980 restored version); Cine France Films/MGM; B/W; Biographical Drama; Children: Cautionary; **DVD**; **VHS**. Gance produces a masterpiece film in his biopic of French emperor Napoleon I (Napoleon Bonaparte; 1769-1821), an amazing and technically advanced film (for its age) that mesmerized a generation of viewers. Roudenko plays Napoleon as a boy, first shown playing with his classmates in a snowball fight and demonstrating his dexterity and skills as a born leader by engineering that fight as a military exercise. His teachers believe that the inventive and imaginative boy possesses great promise and that he will someday make his mark in the ranks of the French military. However, Roudenko's decisive manner and authoritative bearing makes him no friends and he is ostracized by his fellow students, finding solace and comfort with his pet eagle, the image of that regal bird later becoming the symbol of his military prowess. In revenge for his demanding conduct, his classmates free the bird and Roudenko battles all of them at once until his teachers corral him and toss him into a bank of snow to cool off. Weeping that he has lost his only friend, Roudenko leans against a barrel of a cannon, only to find that the eagle is faithful to him, as it returns to him and perches next to him on that symbolic piece of artillery. In flash-forward we now see Dieudonné as an adult Napoleon, going to his native Corsica where he attempts to bring the island into the cause of the French Revolution. The Corsicans reject Dieudonné's entreaties, and he is threatened with imprisonment, fleeing from the island in a small boat and using as a sail

the Tricolor flag of the Revolution. Upon his return to France, Dieudonné proves his military abilities by defeating a large British force during a storm. Promoted to the rank of captain, he travels to Paris only to discover that the Reign of Terror has ensued where aristocrats are being hunted down and then quickly sent to the guillotine. Dieudonné's own loyalty is then tested by the Committee of Public Safety when it offers him the command of Paris. Not wanting to protect the architects of the Terror against the eventual public outcry he expects, he declines and is then branded a traitor and imprisoned. While incarcerated, Dieudonné meets Manes, who plays the love of his life, Josephine de Beauharnais (1763-1814). They are saved at the last minute from going to the guillotine when one of the prominent leaders of the Revolution, Louis Saint-Just (1767-1794), played by Gance himself, orders the Reign of Terror to be stopped. Dieudonné is then asked to command forces that will oppose Royalists, but he again refuses, stating he will not fight against other Frenchmen, but is willing to fight any invading foreigners. He is disciplined by being sent to serve in a meaningless position at the Office of Topography, but Dieudonné's fertile mind produces a daring strategy to invade Italy. His unenlightened superiors, however, when studying his plan, fail to understand its intricate workings and dismiss it out of hand. The Royalists by then have become more powerful, and their forces threaten to take over Paris. Dieudonné offers his services to defeat them and he leads the Revolutionary forces battling the Royalists in the city's streets, defeating them and becoming a much heralded hero. When attending one of the many parties held to celebrate the survival of the Revolution, Dieudonné again meets Manes and they fall deeply in love and plan their marriage. Wielding her considerable influence with prominent Frenchmen, Manes convinces these leaders to appoint Dieudonné as the commander of the French Army of the Alps. Absorbed by his new position, Dieudonné spends so much time developing his original idea to invade Italy that he forgets to attend his wedding with Manes. He arrives late with Manes fuming, but she becomes even more vexed when Dieudonné orders the priest to rush through the ceremony. He then leaves immediately to take command of the Army of the Alps and his planned invasion of Italy, with Manes having no honeymoon and a husband far from her. Just before going to his post, however, Dieudonné stops at the now deserted convention hall that was the center of the Revolution and there sees the ghosts of the leaders of the Revolution, all asking him to become their new leader. Dieudonné agrees and vows to them that he will end all wars and then sets off to his post in the Alps. After arriving, Dieudonné becomes angry to see the French army he has inherited is in terrible condition, its troops poorly fed, badly clothed and without good morale. He orders his generals to abandon their usual defense strategy and prepare for an attack. The demoralized army is then shown in camp (in the original release the curtains at the theater opened wider to show three screens and where three separate integrated scenes were shown in triptech process) as Dieudonné arrives, his winning character inspiring each man to enthusiastically respond to his call to arms. This part of the film offers a stunning and moving series of scenes over which the initial release presented three tinted colors for each of the three screens, the colors of the French Tricolor flag, one of the most innovative techniques used to that time and causing a breathtaking response from audiences. The film concludes with Dieudonné leading the French army into Italy and presumed victory. This mesmerizing epic was first shown in 1927 at the National Theater and Opera in Paris to great critical acclaim, particularly when the triptech process was revealed to virtually explode its scenes upon three screens and where a full orchestra provided a unique and moving score accompanying this masterpiece. The film was rereleased in 1935 at 140 minutes and with sound effects and dialog dubbed with actors simulating the lip movements of the original actors, not much of which worked very well. Gance presents a Napoleon that is athletic, energetic and all action, eschewing prolonged romantic scenes with Manes. Napoleon's love affairs would be more intensely profiled by Charles Boyer and Marlon Brando in later films. Gance concentrates on Napoleon's early years where other productions, such as the two versions of *War and Peace*, extensively show (through standout performances by Lom and Strzhelcik) his disastrous retreat from Moscow and where Rod Steiger gives a masterful performance at his final military collapse at Waterloo. Napoleon I has been profiled in many films, most notably in **Anthony Adverse**, 1936 (Rollo Lloyd); **Conquest**, 1937 (Charles Boyer); **The Count of Monte Cristo**, 1934 (Paul Irving); **The Count of Monte Cristo**, 2002 (Alex Norton); **Desiree**, 1954 (Marlon Brando); **The House of Rothschild**, 1934 (Louis Shapiro); **The Pearls of the Crown**, 1938 (Jean-Louis Barrault/Emile Drain); **Reign of Terror**, 1949 (Shepperd Strudwick); **War and Peace**, 1956 (Herbert Lom); **War and Peace**, 1968 (Vladislav Strzhelcik); **Waterloo**, 1971 (Rod Steiger); and **The Young Mr. Pitt**, 1943 (Herbert Lom). For the complete listing of forty-seven films profiling Napoleon I, see in this work, the Index for Historical Personalities, Volume II. *Author's Note*: Gance's great opus was subsequently shown in about twenty different versions over the years, all at varying length, including the 1935 sound version, but, over the years, the original silent classic appeared to have been lost. Years later, film historian Kevin Brownlow began assembling segments of the film in a heroic effort to restore the 1927 silent production to its original state and, with substantial funds provided by U.S. and French donors (including Francis Ford Coppola), the film was restored to its almost original state by the early 1980s, where it was shown again with a full orchestra with a new score composed and conducted by Carmine Coppola, the son of donor Francis Ford Coppola. Gance introduced many radical new techniques in this film. At the beginning, to show dimension to the snowball fight, Gance had his cinematographer Kruger place the camera on a sled that was pushed into the snowball fight and then pulled away from it, while camera assistants threw snowballs from behind the camera and snowballs were being thrown directly at the camera to make the audience feel that it was participating in the fight and fun. To increase the drama and chaos of the activities in the convention hall holding the revolutionaries, Gance placed his camera on a pendulum that swayed back and forth into and away from the gesticulating actors to make the hall seem to sway and shudder in accordance with the volatile actions taking place there. These scenes were cross-edited with the storm Dieudonné is battling on his little sailboat as he leaves Corsica and is returning to an unsettled France, similar actions (in mood and character) that Gance titled as the "Double Tempest." Predating CinemaScope by more than two decades, Gance achieved his incredible visual effects (triptechs) by employing a special camera system consisting of three cameras mounted on a tripod, all three cameras operated by a single motor that assured synchronous operation of all three films when they were played together on the wide screens. The amazing result was that Gance was able to uniquely present to audiences a panoramic view of his scenes while, at the same time, presenting separate montages of exciting scenes that could be viewed simultaneously. It is a filmic triumph where the script, acting, direction and production values are unparalleled. **p,d&w**, Abel Gance; **cast**, Albert Dieudonné, Vladimir Roudenko, Gina Manès, Nicolas Koline, Edmond Van Daële, Alexandre Koubitzky, Antonin Artaud, Gance, Suzanne Bianchetti, Marguerite Gance, Annabella; **c**, Jules Kruger, Léonce-Henri Burel, Jean-Paul Mundviller, Nikolai Toporkoff; **m**, Arthur Honegger (1927 release), Carmine Coppola (1980 release); **ed**, Abel Gance; **art d**, Alexandre Benois, Alexandre Lochakoff; **spec eff**, Segundo de Chomón, Paul Minine, Edward Scholl, Eugen Schüfftan, Nicolas Wilcké, W. Percy Day.

The Narrow Corner ★★★ 1933; U.S.; 69m; WB; B/W; Adventure; Children: Unacceptable. Fairbanks is a young Englishman wanted for murder in Australia. Kolker, his rich and influential father, sends him out to sea on a fishing boat, and Fairbanks becomes friends with its captain, Hohl, and the ship's doctor, Toler. Fairbanks meets Ellis on an island, then meets her fiancé, Bellamy, who runs a government plantation. Bellamy becomes depressed over the growing romance between Fairbanks and Ellis and commits suicide. His death makes authorities sus-

Marie Windsor and Charles McGraw in *The Narrow Margin*, 1952.

pect Fairbanks killed him and his future seems bleak until evidence is unearthed that exonerates him. Some fine storms at sea are profiled in this solid adventure yarn, and Fairbanks and the rest of the cast give standout performances in essaying their colorful characters. Based on a novel by W. Somerset Maugham, it was remade as **Isle of Fury**, 1936. *Author's Note*: Bellamy told this author that "from almost the first film I made in Hollywood, I was typecast as a good-natured wealthy guy engaged to the leading lady and who loses out to the leading man. I played those losing fiancés for more years than I can recall until I got the role of my life in playing one of America's greatest presidents, Franklin D. Roosevelt, on the stage and in the picture, **Sunrise at Campobello** [1960]. In **The Narrow Corner**, I not only lose the girl but I take my life over losing her. Now, that's losing big time." Bellamy was a lifelong Democrat and attended the Democratic Convention in 1960, the year that **Sunrise at Campobello** was released and where he was a strong supporter of presidential candidate John F. Kennedy. **p**, Hal B. Wallis; **d**, Alfred E. Green; **cast**, Douglas Fairbanks, Jr., Patricia Ellis, Ralph Bellamy, Dudley Digges, Arthur Hohl, Reginald Owen, Henry Kolker, William V. Mong, Willie Fung, Sidney Toler; **w**, Robert Presnell (based on a novel by W. Somerset Maugham); **c**, Tony Gaudio; **ed**, Herbert Levy; **art d**, Robert M. Haas.

The Narrow Margin ★★★★ 1952; U.S.; 71m; RKO; B/W; Crime Drama; Children: Unacceptable; **DVD**. In one of the best "sleeper" film noir productions in the post-WWII era, L.A. detectives McGraw and Beddoe are assigned to accompany Windsor, the widow of a deceased gangster, from Chicago to Los Angeles on board a westbound train. When they go to her Chicago residence, however, they encounter racketeers bent on killing her before she can give testimony in a L.A. court against her husband's associates. As McGraw and Bedoe are escorting Windsor down the stairs of her rooming house, the mobsters open fire and kill Beddoe. McGraw gives chase, but the killers escape. McGraw must now escort and protect Windsor en route to L.A., and he has her board the westbound train alone, taking a compartment that adjoins his own, believing that the killers are following him as they have identified him as her police escort, but have not identified Windsor as their prey. Once on board the train and moving westward, McGraw finds Windsor uncooperative and demanding, her irritating attitude further aggravating his angry memory that Beddoe, a man with a wife and children, gave his life to protect her, a fact that Windsor barely acknowledges. Meanwhile, while going back and forth to the dining and club cars, McGraw plays cat-and-mouse with several of the killers, who have boarded the train and are searching for Windsor. He encounters Leonard and her young son, Gebert, when entering their compartment to evade one of the trailing killers, and he befriends the boy. He further befriends White,

Charles McGraw and Marie Windsor in *The Narrow Margin*, 1952.

an attractive woman, when visiting the lounge car; later discovers that she is Gebert's mother and that Leonard is the boy's governess. Meanwhile, Clarke, one of the killers, uses the false claim that his briefcase is missing to have a conductor open McGraw's compartment and he searches the washroom and even the closeted beds for Windsor, who is hiding in the adjoining compartment, where she has locked the adjoining door. McGraw arrives and Clarke departs. Maxey, a heavyset train detective, then approaches McGraw, stating that his own sleeping quarters are very confining and, since there is no one occupying the adjoining compartment McGraw has reserved (ostensibly for his dead partner, Beddoe), asks McGraw to make it available for his own use. McGraw arouses suspicion when he adamantly refuses. Virgo, the leader of the killers-for-hire, then confronts McGraw, offering him a substantial amount of money if he turns over Windsor to him and his associates, but McGraw, a by-the-book cop, refuses the bribe. While McGraw is absent from his compartment, one of the killers uses a ruse that persuades Windsor to open the door to her compartment, and when she refuses to turn over documents intended for the upcoming trial, they struggle. Windsor tries to use a revolver she has hidden in her purse but she is killed. When McGraw finds her dead, he realizes that she is not the witness she claimed to be, but an undercover police woman, who has acted as a decoy for the real witness and given her life to protect her, and who, McGraw learns, is White. McGraw later believes that Clarke killed Windsor and picks a fight with him in the men's washroom, beating him to a pulp. He then turns Clarke over to the custody of train detective Maxey, who becomes McGraw's ally (and who remarks about his own obesity by routinely stating that "nobody loves a fat man"). Now McGraw concentrates on protecting White's life, and believes that she will be safe in occupying Windsor's compartment. The killers, however, know that Windsor was a decoy and they are now searching the train for White. Virgo concludes that White is hiding in Windsor's compartment and pretends to be McGraw to gain access. Once inside, he threatens her with a gun, demanding that she turn over the documents the killers have been seeking that will bring about the conviction of a mob boss. McGraw, by this time, is at the other side of the door of the adjoining compartment and he can see Virgo and White through the reflections of the windows of another passing passenger train, knowing exactly where each is standing. He orders White to give Virgo the documents by stepping to a closet and she obeys. As she does, McGraw, aiming his gun at the door where he knows Virgo is standing, fires several times and kills the assassin. As the train speeds toward Los Angeles, McGraw sees a car filled with gunmen racing alongside on a highway and orders Maxey to use the train's phone to call ahead and have police intercept the car. Clarke, by this time, has escaped Maxey, and when the train stops, he leaps from the platform of the observation

car and races down the track to get into the car carrying the gunmen, but just then police cars arrive and capture the mobsters. When the train arrives in L.A., McGraw accompanies White, and he expresses his regrets in wrongly judging the heroic Windsor and even White, whom he has thought to be nothing more than a mobster's gun moll, but now knows that she is a caring mother and decent woman. This taut and highly suspenseful film, directed with great skill by Fleischer, who had earlier made his mark with such standout gritty crime films as **Trapped**, 1949, and **Armored Car Robbery**, 1950, sees great performances from McGraw and Windsor, and exceptional essays from the rest of the cast. Felton's script is terrific (coming from a fine crime novel by Goldsmith, who had earlier provided the gritty tale for another film noir classic, **Detour**, 1945), providing a lot of crackling dialog, particularly the barbed and darkly witty exchanges between the stony-faced and taciturn McGraw and the seemingly coldhearted Windsor, all of it making for a film noir classic. This film was remade with the same title in 1990 with Gene Hackman playing McGraw's role, and Anne Archer playing Windsor's part, but with much less impact. ***Author's Note***: McGraw told this author that "I think that my role in **The Narrow Margin** was one of my best performances, but I have Dick Fleischer to thank for that. He gave me a big break when starring me in **Armored Car Robbery** a few years earlier. He is a very talented and much underrated director." McGraw made his mark as a character actor in many post-WWII film noir classics such as **The Killers**, 1946 (where he and William Conrad established their film personas as the two ruthless killers out to murder Burt Lancaster), **Brute Force**, 1947 (Jules Dassin's riveting prison drama, again starring Lancaster), **The Gangster**, 1947, and **T-Men** (a harrowing classic crime tale where Dennis O'Keefe gives a startling performance as an undercover treasury agent). McGraw, following this film, returned to playing character roles in many films (he is a standout as the sadistic head trainer at a gladiatorial school in **Spartacus**, 1960). He died on July 30, 1980, at the age of sixty-six in a freak accident when he slipped on a bar of soap while taking a shower in his home in Studio City, California, and crashed through the glass shower doors. Fleischer told this author that RKO's front office "skimped on the budget for **The Narrow Margin**, allowing me only $180,000 and considered it a "B" production to be run as part of a double bill with one of their "A" productions. I was determined to do as much as possible with what I had to work with. Other than one stop where Charles [McGraw] and Jacqueline [White] get off at Santa Fe, New Mexico—my only location shooting in the picture—almost all of the film was shot on the set for the Pullman train cars, which I had fixed to the floors of the sound stage [at RKO studio in California]. I simulated movement of the train with rocking movements of the hand-held cameras I used, and I used handheld cameras for most of the movement and action of the actors in the picture as it was the only way to quickly capture the action down the narrow train corridors and in and out of the confining compartments, and I think I was one of the first to use those handheld cameras in making a feature film. When the front office saw what I was doing, they realized that **The Narrow Margin** was very promising, and they gave me more money so that the budget increased to $230,000. The film was a great success at the box office and it saw a lot of rereleases and RKO made a bundle on it." Windsor told this author that "**The Narrow Margin** is one of my favorite pictures, along with another crime film I appeared in, **The Killing**, which was directed by Stanley Kubrick. In **The Narrow Margin**, I play a tough female undercover cop and I give Charles [McGraw], who plays another cop, a very hard time. I was by then seen as an on-screen femme fatale, a cheating wife, a promiscuous gun moll, a conniving vicious woman, who would sell out anyone for a buck. Those were the kind of roles I got and I did the most I could with them. It's the 'bad types' that get all the attention in scenes because viewers want to know why they have such rotten personalities and evil hearts. I got a lot of fan mail that I never wanted when doing those roles, some viewers sending me Bibles and telling me to repent or that I was going to Hell for playing these awful women. Some even threatened me and I turned those letters over to the police. It was scary, but I kept on doing those roles as it was a living and I knew I was good at it. When I got into that typecasting, I said to myself: 'Someone's got to play Medusa, so why not me?'" **p**, Stanley Rubin; **d**, Richard Fleischer; **cast**, Charles Mc-Graw, Marie Windsor, Jacqueline White, Gordon Gebert, Queenie Leonard, David Clarke, Peter Virgo, Don Beddoe, Paul Maxey, Harry Harvey; **w**, Earl Felton (based on a story by Martin Goldsmith, Jack Leonard); **c**, George E. Diskant; **ed**, Robert Swink; **art d**, Albert S. D'Agostino, Jack Okey; **set d**, Darrell Silvera, William Stevens.

Nashville ★★★★ 1975; U.K./U.S./France; 159m; PAR; Color; Drama; Children: Unacceptable (MPAA: R); **DVD**; **VHS**. Complex if not complicated, this is Altman's finest film, one where he pieces together the puzzles of many characters who all attend a weekend music festival in Nashville, the home of country music while, at the same time, a huge political rally is ongoing for a presidential candidate, who is running on the "Replacement Party." Altman deftly cuts back and forth between twenty-four characters, as they participate in both events, offering a dizzying array of charming, oddball and even weird people, who all have their momentary place in the sun, all enhanced and bedazzled by an equally impressive array of musical numbers. Beatty and Murphy, who are promoting the presidential candidate, persuade, cajole and implore the musical personalities to lend their talents in promoting their candidate's political cause. Dominating all the performers is Gibson, a veteran at the country music game, who is idolized by younger performers, but behind whose automatic smile is a thoroughly rotten personality, an insidious, conniving and wholly amoral creature, who will backstab anyone to glean a dollar and more fame than what he already has. Among the contenders to Gibson's throne is Blakley, who has recently recovered from a mental breakdown and is on the verge of suffering another. (Her character appears to be based on country singer Loretta Lynn, who was later profiled in a fine biopic, **The Coal Miner's Daughter**, 1980, with Sissy Spacek as Lynn.) Carradine is one of the many hopefuls eager to make a name for himself as part of a singing trio, and he demonstrates an amazing ability to bed a number of women, including Raines, the wife of Nicholls, one of his singing partners; Tomlin, who is Beatty's wife, and the fetching Chaplin. When Blakley makes her appearance, her angst and mental worries causes her to render a poor performance and her manager and husband, Garfield, promises the disappointed crowd that she will next offer them a free concert to make up for that disappointing outing. Beatty then goes to Garfield and Blakley, asking Blakley to perform at a special rally for his presidential candidate. (The presidential candidate or his described character seems to be based upon third-party presidential candidate George Wallace, 1919-1998, who was invalided following an assassination attempt on him in 1972, three years before this film was released.) Blakley agrees to make that performance, and, meanwhile, Beatty and Murphy hold a stag party for their candidate's financial backers and persuade Welles to sing at this seedy event. Welles is a voluptuous waitress, but she cannot carry a song in a basket. The male spectators note her alluring body and begin chanting for her to "take it off," and the ever enterprising Beatty encourages her to do just that, promising that she will sing at the next political rally. Welles does a crude strip act (which brought about the "R" rating for this film) while the male spectators hoot and holler encouragement (oddly, many of these men were actual members of Nashville's Chamber of Commerce). After Welles completes her awkward stripping performance, she rebuffs Beatty's attempt to take her to bed. Throughout the hectic goings-on, the viewer occasionally sees Hayward slipping in and out of scenes while carrying a violin case. After Gibson and Blakley perform in the final concert, which is a smash success, Hayward vents his inexplicable wrath upon both of them by shooting them. Blakley is carried off the stage by medical assistants, and, seizing the traumatic moment, Harris, an unknown singer, runs to the microphone and begins singing to clutch her desperate moment of fame as Welles waits forlornly in the wings for a big break that will never occur. Brilliant and unsettling, this

Ronee Blakley, Henry Gibson and Barbara Baxley in *Nashville*, 1975.

erratic but mesmerizing film presents a conglomerate of talented and untalented people who are all jockeying and finagling in a collective and frantic effort to grab the brass ring and that also includes Black, who opens a show for country singer Johnny Cash. Songs: "I'm Easy," "It Don't Worry Me," "Honey" (Keith Carradine); "My Idaho Home," "Bluebird," "Dues," "Tapedeck in His Tractor (The Cowboy Song)," "Down to the River" (Ronee Blakley); "Memphis," "Rolling Stone," "I Don't Know if I Found It In You" (Karen Black); "Keep A-Goin,'" "200 Years" (Richard Baskin, Henry Gibson); "For the Sake of the Children" (Richard Baskin, Richard Reicheg); "I Never Get Enough" (Richard Baskin, Ben Raleigh); "Yes, I Do" (Richard Baskin, Lily Tomlin); "The Day I Looked Jesus in the Eye" (Richard Baskin, Robert Altman); "Sing a Song" (Joe Raposo); "The Heart of a Gentle Woman" (Dave Peel); "One, I Love You," "Let Me Be the One" (Richard Baskin); "Rose's Café" (Allan F. Nicholls); "My Baby's Cookin' in Another Man's Pan" (Jonnie Barnett); "Since You've Gone" (Gary Busey); "Trouble in the U.S.A." (Arlene Barnett), "Old Man Mississippi" (Juan Grizzle); "Swing Low, Sweet Chariot" (traditional). *Author's Note*: Altman, as was his wont in all of his films, allowed his players to improvise their monologues and dialogs, some of which proved to be better than the written script and other lines bordering on the moronic, the kind of communal filmmaking that Altman always encouraged. Somehow, Altman, with much cross-cutting of scenes, manages to make his twenty-four characters believable in this lengthy film (more than two and a half hours), all of it worth watching at least once. Most are exceptional in their roles, including the jaded Arkin, a chauffeur who has endured a lifetime of strutting and egotistical performers, and Peel, who is Gibson's much-abused son. Amazingly, Altman shot and completed this film within forty-five days at a meager budget of $2 million, but managed to collect an army of talented people (including Gould and Christie, who play themselves) in promoting this country song opus by effectively employing the "favored nations" clause where all of the players got the same amount of money for their separate performances. Altman was able to collect huge crowds of spectators by offering them free concerts and all the inexpensive food they could eat, especially when showing the final concert that was held at the Parthenon, a replica of the Greek edifice built in 1876, then a part of the State's Centennial Exposition. Susan Anspach was originally slated to play the mentally disturbed singer, but contract disputes caused Altman to abandon her and hire her vocal coach, Blakley. The film received Oscar nominations for Best Film, Best Director and for supporting players, but won only an Oscar for Carradine's popular song "I'm Easy." **p&d**, Robert Altman; **cast**, David Arkin, Barbara Baxley, Ned Beatty, Karen Black, Timothy Brown, Ronee Blakley, Keith Carradine, Geraldine Chaplin, Shelley Duvall, Allen Garfield, Henry Gibson, Scott Glenn, Jeff Goldblum, Bar-

Mickey Rooney and Elizabeth Taylor in *National Velvet*, 1945.

bara Harris, Michael Murphy, Lily Tomlin, Keenan Wynn, Elliott Gould, Julie Christie, David Hayward, Allan F. Nicholls, Gwen Welles, Cristina Raines, Dave Peel; **w**, Joan Tewkesbury; **c**, Paul Lohmann (Panavision; Metrocolor); **m**, Arlene and Jonnie Barnett, Black, Blakley, Gary Busey, Juan Grizzle, Nicholls, Peel, Joe Paposo; **ed**, Dennis Hill, Sidney Levin; **set d**, Robert M. Anderson.

Nasty Habits ★★★ 1977; U.K. /U.S.; 96m; WB; Color; Satire; Children: Unacceptable (MAPP: PG); **DVD**; **VHS**. This clever satire (inspired by the 1972 Watergate scandal) sees Jackson as a nun who schemes and engages in dirty tricks so that she will remain head abbess of a Philadelphia convent. Jackson's character is similar to that of cloistered President Richard Nixon (1913-1994) and Dennis plays a character similar to that of John Dean (1938-). Jackson masterminds a break-in of her competition, invading Dennis' sewing box, which contain love letters from an illicit lover. Wiretappings and bribery raise their ugly heads and even the Vatican (substituting for Congress) becomes involved when Mercouri, a jet-setting missionary, arrives to quell the scandal. Jackson is eventually disgraced by tape recordings and replaced by Meara. Upon leaving, Jackson tells reporters they won't have her to kick around anymore (as Nixon did when he resigned as U.S. President). Jackson and the rest of the cast are darkly delightful in this biting comedy-satire, but one with mature content that prohibits viewing by children. **p&w**, Robert Enders (based on the novel *The Abbess of Crewe* by Muriel Spark); **d**, Michael Lindsay-Hogg; **cast**, Glenda Jackson, Melina Mercouri, Geraldine Page, Sandy Dennis, Anne Meara, Susan Penhaligon, Edith Evans, Jerry Stiller, Rip Torn, Eli Wallach, Mike Douglas, Jessica Savitch, Howard K. Smith; **c**, Douglas Slocombe (Panavision; Technicolor); **m**, John Cameron; **ed**, Peter Tanner; **art d**, Robert Jones; **set d**, Harry Cordwell.

National Lampoon's Animal House ★★★ 1978; U.S.; 109m; UNIV; Color; Comedy; Children: Unacceptable (MPAA: R); **BD**; **DVD**; **VHS**. The fraternity house from heaven or hell, depending on your viewpoint, is the star of this ribald comedy. In 1962, Hulse and Furst, two aspiring college fraternity brothers, are turned down by all of the frat houses on campus except the one with the reputation of throwing drinking parties and having members with the lowest grades and are accepted by the house's main man, Matheson. The college dean, Vernon, wants to shut the house down and plans to do that with the help of the main man of the most conservative frat on campus, Daughton. Furst gets wind of it and takes Daughton's horse to Vernon's office and shoots it, leaving it there over night, where Vernon is shocked to see it the next morning (this is a mimic of the killing of the thoroughbred belonging to the movie mogul intimidated by the Mafia in **The Godfather**, 1972). Meanwhile,

Belushi, the king of gross at the frat house, falls madly in love with Daughton's girlfriend, Weller, and does a Peeping Tom through a window of her sorority house as she undresses. Next day, Belushi starts a food fight at Daughton's frat house that creates a mess of flying vitals. Vernon thinks he can shut down Matheson and Belushi's "Animal House" if everyone in it flunks the mid-term exams. Belushi steals examination answers and gives them to his fellow frat brothers, but they all fail the exams because Belushi unintentionally gave them the wrong answers. Belushi decides it's time for a "toga party," the house's words for a drinking orgy, and it is held with every beautiful girl and sex-starved boy in the house. Vernon closes down the frat house for serving liquor and everyone in it is expelled. These flunked out characters take revenge by wrecking the annual homecoming parade that ends the school year. Fearful of what these unpredictable hellions might do, Vernon reopens Animal House and lets the boys back into school. This film of the absurd was Hollywood's distorted view of collegiate life, parading every type of inanity and sophomoric piece of slapstick it could pack into every frame and, as a result, the film became a huge hit with young male audiences, who spent millions to see it. The film's hallmark was Belushi's outlandish performance where he established his film persona as Hollywood's consummate slob. Crude humor, gutter language and sexuality prohibit viewing by children. Songs: "Animal House," "Dream Girl" (Stephan Bishop); "Shout," "Shama Lama Ding Dong," "Louie, Louie," "Money," "Hey Paula," "Wonderful World," "Twistin' the Night Away," "Let's Dance," "Who's Sorry Now?" (Bert Kalmar, Harry Ruby); "Tosssin' and Turnin'." ***Author's Note***: Belushi told this author that "the director [Landis] pretty much let us do what we wanted in that film and any repulsive thing we could think to do, we did. If anyone in any frat house on any college campus did what we did in that crazy movie, they would have been herded like wild horses and driven into the desert and left there until their bones crumbled to dust, and I mean dust!" **p**, Ivan Reitman, Matty Simmons; **d**, John Landis; **cast**, John Belushi, Tim Matheson, Thomas Hulce, James Daughton, Peter Riegert, Karen Allen, Kevin Bacon, Donald Sutherland, Stephen Furst, Mark Metcalf, Mary Louise Weller, Douglas Kenney, Chris Miller, John Vernon; Landis; **w**, Harold Ramis, Kenney, Miller; **c**, Charles Correll (Panavision; Technicolor); **m**, Elmer Bernstein; **ed**, George Folsey, Jr.; **art d**, John J. Lloyd; **set d**, Hal Gausman; **spec eff**, Henry Millar.

National Velvet ★★★★ 1945; U.S.; 123m; MGM; Color; Drama; Children: Recommended; **DVD**; **VHS**. This beloved tale, one of the finest family films MGM ever produced, opens when ex-jockey Rooney, a nomadic youth with a deep wanderlust, enters a small village in Sussex, England. He befriends Taylor, the beautiful, young daughter of Crisp, a successful butcher, who hires Rooney as an assistant. He is given lodging in the family's barn, a room next to the stable, and is welcomed at the family's dinner table by mother Revere and her other siblings, Quigley, Lansbury and precocious tyke Jenkins, who keeps a pet insect in a bottle. After Taylor wins a raffle and becomes the owner of a horse, she persuades Rooney to train her how to ride that horse in the hopes that she will someday enter professional races. Taylor becomes adept at riding the horse and then pleads with her parents, Crisp and Revere, to allow her to enter the horse in the Grand National race. The entrance fee, however, is prohibitive, until Revere gives Taylor money she has saved, winnings she earned when, years earlier, she swam the English Channel. Rooney and Taylor travel to the Grand National track, but the jockey they have secured backs out and Taylor decides that she will ride her horse. Rooney reluctantly agrees and helps her cut her hair so that she is disguised as a male jockey (no female riders are allowed). Taylor rides her horse in the race (a spectacular and exciting sequence not to be missed) and surmounts all obstacles, her horse leaping every hedgerow, to finish as the winner. Taylor, however, falls from her horse and is rushed to a medical center where a doctor learns that she is a girl and her horse is disqualified. Taylor's incredible feat, however, makes national news (her name is Velvet, thus the title of the film), and she is satisfied that she and her horse have proved themselves and where Crisp, Revere and her siblings welcome her home as a celebrity. Rooney is again consumed by his wanderlust and decides to seek his fortune in the world and departs, but not before a fond farewell occurs between him and Taylor. Brown's direction is superb, and all of the players do exceptional jobs in this wonderfully heartwarming tale. Revere won an Oscar as Best Supporting Actress, but it was Taylor's marvelous performance that riveted international attention and convinced MGM that they had a great star on their hands. She was signed to a long-term contract and would remain with the studio for another two decades, maturing into one of the most beautiful women to ever grace the screen. Kern also won an Oscar for Best Film Editing. The film was later adapted for a 1960 TV series and was remade as **International Velvet**, 1977, a costly ($4 million) failure at the box office. *Author's Note*: Bagnold's novel had been purchased for the screen ten years after its publication, producer Berman, than at RKO, acquiring the film rights with the thought of starring Katharine Hepburn. The property was then purchased by Paramount and later by MGM where movie mogul Louis B. Mayer thought to cast Spencer Tracy in the role of the father and Margaret Sullavan in the role of Velvet, but nothing came of these plans until Berman, then working at MGM, resurrected the story. He was thinking to hire Shirley Temple from Fox, but then considered Taylor. "Mr. Berman had me test for the role of Velvet," Taylor told this author, "but after he saw the test, he told me and my mother that I was too slight and frail for the role. As time passed, I put on some weight and learned how to ride horses and then was tested again when I was a few inches taller. Mr. Berman said that I was all right for the role and that picture made me a star. I had as my co-star the great Mickey Rooney, who really took all of our scenes together—such a great actor—and I found it impossible to take any scenes from little Butch Jenkins, that adorable, freckle-faced little boy, who was everyone's favorite at MGM. **National Velvet** stands out as one of my warmest memories of childhood." Although Taylor proved to be a proficient horse rider during the production, MGM took no chances of her being injured and hired Snowy Baker, an Australian jockey, to double for her in the most harrowing racetrack sequences. **p**, Pandro S. Berman; **d**, Clarence Brown; **cast**, Mickey Rooney, Donald Crisp, Elizabeth Taylor, Anne Revere, Angela Lansbury, Jackie "Butch" Jenkins, Juanita Quigley, Arthur Treacher, Reginald Owen, Terry Kilburn, Arthur Shields, Donald Curtis, Mona Freeman; **w**, Theodore Reeves, Helen Deutsch (based on the novel by Enid Bagnold); **c**, Leonard Smith (Technicolor); **m**, Herbert Stothart; **ed**, Robert J. Kern; **art d**, Cedric Gibbons, Urie McCleary; **set d**, Edwin B. Willis; **spec eff**, Warren Newcombe, A. Arnold Gillespie, Mark Davis.

The Natural ★★★★ 1984; U.S.; 134m; Delphi II/TriStar; Color; Sports Drama; Children: Unacceptable (MPAA: PG); **BD**; **DVD**; **VHS**. Redford is outstanding in one of his finest films, a fantasy sports drama where he possesses incredible talents as a baseball player. The film opens on a farm where Redford's father dies while beneath a tree struck by lightning. The youth makes a baseball bat from the split tree and upon its handle burns the word "Wonderboy." Flash-forward to 1923 and Redford is now a nineteen-year-old draftee for the Chicago Cubs as a miraculous fast-ball hurler. En route to Chicago, his train stops at a carnival where Baker, the most celebrated baseball home-run hitter of the day (called "The Whammer," his brief role based upon the legendary George Herman "Babe" Ruth) challenges Redford to pitch to him while sports writer Duvall witnesses the lightning fast hurler striking him out. When Redford gets back on the train, Hershey, an alluring but disturbed woman, believes he is the greatest baseball player in the world and tries to seduce him. He resists, but when he later arrives in Chicago, Hershey goes to his hotel room, where the mentally unbalanced woman more or less tells Redford that no one will ever possess the greatest baseball player in the world but her and she shoots him. Thinking him dead, Hershey then commits suicide by leaping from a window of Redford's hotel room, plunging to her death. Redford recovers, but his hopeful pitching

Richard Farnsworth and Wilford Brimley in *The Natural*, 1984.

career in baseball is over. (Hershey's character is one of the most bizarre on record in that she has, before ending her life, killed two other promising athletes in order to deny them their riches and fame.) In flash-forward, it is now 1939 and Redford (as Roy Hobbs) is now reporting to the New York Knights, a baseball team with a terrible record and in last place in its league. The middle-aged Redford has been hired by Prosky, who owns half of the team and has given Redford a contract to irk manager Brimley, who owns the other half of the team. Prosky's aim in hiring Redford, Brimley believes, is to saddle him with a dead weight player to further assure his losing streak. Prosky and Brimley, who despise each other, have an agreement, one where Brimley must sell his half of the team to Prosky if he fails to have a winning season and he is on his way to doing just that. Brimley accepts Redford but keeps him on the bench while assistant coach Farnsworth befriends Redford, who then meets alluring blonde bombshell Basinger, and who is the conniving mistress of financial investor McGavin. After Madsen, the slumping star slugger of the team, who is Basinger's boyfriend, is killed by chasing a fly ball and crashing through the wooden fence in the outfield, Brimley reluctantly has Redford replace Madsen. He proves to be an excellent outfielder, and his extraordinary hitting soon inspires his fellow teammates to keep pace with his superior performance. The team begins to win one game after another and is no longer in last place. Prosky and McGavin conspire to undo the team by having Basinger seduce Redford and by wearing him out with endless parties and nightlife, not to mention their ongoing torrid affair. Redford falls into a slump and so does the team, but, while on the road and playing against Chicago, he meets his old flame from his farming youth, Close, who is now widowed and has a small boy. Redford and Close slowly resume their old relationship, but that is almost severed when he returns to New York and the high life offered by the seductive Basinger. Meanwhile, sports writer Duvall recalls Redford as the young pitcher who struck out Baker those many years ago and begins probing his past, learning about the shooting and Hershey's suicide, offering Redford $5,000 for his exclusive life story for his newspaper. Redford declines. He then gets out of his slump and leads the Knights toward the pennant, but he is injured toward the end of the season and his playing days are questionable. He nevertheless rejoins the team to play in the last crucial games and, while throwing over Basinger and resuming his love affair with Close, refuses a huge bribe from Prosky to throw the final game. Toward the end of that final game, Redford comes to bat, representing the wining runner. He sends a powerful drive to right field, but it is a foul and when he returns to home plate finds that his treasured bat, "Wonderboy," with which he has established his fantastic hitting record for the year, is shattered. The bat boy, Wilkosz, who has idolized Redford throughout the season and made his own bat to emulate Redford, offers Redford that

Nelson Eddy and Jeanette MacDonald in *Naughty Marietta*, 1935.

bat. Redford takes it and, though bleeding at his side (blood spots seen seeping through his uniform), hits the next pitch with a powerful home-run blow that sends the ball into the outfield, sailing so high that it strikes one of the huge lights illuminating the field and that sets off one explosion of lights after another, producing a shower of fireworks, while Close stands admiring the man she loves in the stands and his teammates cheer their hero as Redford slowly rounds the bases. Brimley has kept his team and Redford has achieved his goal in life. The final scene in this moving film shows Redford playing catch with his adopted son in a cornfield on a farm while Close watches them. Director Levinson maintains a fast pace and orchestrates some fine and realistic action scenes on the playing field (the baseball scenes were shot at the War Memorial Stadium as the Knights' home grounds and the All-High Stadium, substituting for Wrigley Field in Chicago, both stadiums being in Buffalo, New York), while Redford, Basinger, Brimley, Farnsworth and Close present standout performances. Made for about $28 million, the film saw a box office return of close to $48 million in its initial release. *Author's Note*: More than any other baseball legend, the character Redford essays is most likely based upon Boston Red Sox slugger Ted Williams. Several notable films profile other baseball legends, including **The Babe**, 1992 (Babe Ruth; New York Yankees); **The Babe Ruth Story**, 1948; **Fear Strikes Out**, 1957 (Jim Piersall; Boston Red Sox); **The Jackie Robinson Story**, 1950; **The Pride of St. Louis**, 1952 (Jerome "Dizzy" Dean; St. Louis Browns; Chicago Cubs); **The Pride of the Yankees**, 1942 (Lou Gehrig; New York Yankees); **Safe at Home!**, 1962 (Mickey Mantle, Roger Maris; New York Yankees); **The Stratton Story**, 1949 (Monty Stratton; Chicago White Sox); **The Winning Team**, 1952 (Grover Cleveland Alexander; Philadelphia Phillies; Chicago Cubs; St. Louis Cardinals). **p**, Mark Johnson; **d**, Barry Levinson; **cast**, Robert Redford, Robert Duvall, Glenn Close, Kim Basinger, Wilford Brimley, Barbara Hershey, Robert Prosky, Richard Farnsworth, Joe Don Baker, John Finnegan, Michael Madsen, Mark Atienza, Darren Mc-Gavin, George Wilkosz; **w**, Roger Towne, Phil Dusenberry (based on the novel by Bernard Malamud); **c**, Caleb Deschanel (Technicolor); **m**, Randy Newman; **ed**, Stu Linder, Christopher Holmes; **prod d**, Mel Bourne, Angelo Graham; **set d**, John Sweeney, Bruce Weintraub; **spec eff**, Roger Hansen, Eric Roberts, Roger Dorney.

Naughty Marietta ★★★ 1935; U.S.; 105m; MGM; B/W; Musical/Operetta; Children: Acceptable; **VHS**. Spritely and enchanting, this musical showcases the wonderful singing talents of MacDonald and Eddy (his debut in a major film). A French princess, MacDonald is the unhappy fiancée of Kingsford, a wealthy Spanish nobleman, her imminent marriage delighting her uncle, Dumbrille, a royal prince, who needs Kingsford's wealth. Even though the king sanctions the marriage, MacDonald

is determined to escape a loveless union and flees while substituting herself for her maid and sails to Louisiana in disguise. The maid, Shipman, is glad to momentarily trade places with MacDonald as she has given Shipman the money that will allow her to marry the poor young fellow from Marseilles that Shipman loves. The ship on which Mac-Donald sails carries a number of young women, who are all pledged to marry bachelor colonists in Louisiana, but their voyage is interrupted when pirates stop and raid the ship, taking all the women with them. Coming to the rescue is Eddy, who leads a rescue force that overwhelms the pirates and recoups the terrified women, taking them to the safety of New Orleans. MacDonald immediately falls for hero Eddy, but though he is also taken with her, he keeps his distance as he is dedicated to remaining in the army. The women are quickly paired with their swains, but MacDonald refuses to pick out a spouse and, to make sure she is isolated from any suitor, creates a false past, telling Morgan, the governor, that she has a shady background and is unworthy of marrying any of the local, upright bachelors. She starts a little business where she makes marionettes and pines for Eddy. Dumbrille and Kingsford then arrive at New Orleans and find MacDonald, insisting that she marry Kingsford. Morgan, who learns that MacDonald is a princess, gives a sumptuous ball to honor her and to announce her forthcoming marriage to Kingsford. Eddy, who now realizes he loves MacDonald, shows up at the ball, but MacDonald puts him off, protecting him since Dumbrille has told her that Eddy will be killed if he attempts to steal her away from Kingsford. Eddy nevertheless learns the truth of the matter and proposes that MacDonald elope with him and she happily agrees, both fleeing from the city while protected by Eddy's devoted troops for a very happy ending. The film, well directed by pantheon director Van Dyke, proved to be a great success that cemented the onscreen love team of MacDonald and Eddy with audiences that flocked to see this delightful songfest where the singing voices of MacDonald and Eddy are at their best and the strong cast members (including Huber and Brophy, who contribute considerable mirth) are standouts. This was the first of eight films Mac-Donald and Eddy would make together, their greatest film being **The Merry Widow**, 1934, made later than this film but released earlier. The film was nominated for an Oscar as Best Picture, and won an Oscar for Best Sound Recording (Douglas Shearer). Songs (all in 1910 by Victor Herbert, music; and Rida Johnson Young, lyrics; with additional lyrics by Gus Kahn): "Antoinette and Anatole," "Chansonette," "Tramp, Tramp, Tamp," "Live for Today," "'Neath the Southern Moon," 'The Owl and the Polecat," "Italian Street Song," "I'm Falling in Love with Someone," "Ship Ahoy," "Ah, Sweet Mystery of Life," "Prayer." *Author's Note*: This film was the personal project of the sentimentally bent MGM boss Louis B. Mayer, who had loved the Victor Herbert operetta since seeing it as a young man when it opened on Broadway in 1910. He went to his top producer, Hunt Stromberg, and handed him the old script, telling him to "spruce it up a bit" with some more modern lyrics (provided by the prolific Gus Kahn) and gave him a huge budget to produce the original musical as an extravaganza songfest. Stromberg pulled out all the stops and employed and updated many of the MGM sets that occupied acres on the studio lot and then hired more than 1,000 extras for the crowd scenes, especially for the grand ball held in New Orleans. Mayer had been trying for years to present the perfect singing duo in MGM films. He had starred Lawrence Tibbett and Grace Moore in several films, but they did not click with the public. For **Naughty Marietta**, Mayer first thought to team MacDonald with the brilliant tenor Allan Jones, but he was not available for the production so Mayer, with some guidance from Stromberg, selected a young, handsome, blond-haired man named Nelson Eddy, who had had some small singing parts in MGM films (**Broadway to Hollywood**, 1933; **Dancing Lady**, 1933; and **Student Tour**, 1934) to be MacDonald's singing partner, a decision they would never regret. They first had Robert Z. Leonard at the helm, but when Mayer did not think Leonard was putting enough zip into the film, he had Stromberg bring in W. Van Dyke, who was known for his fast production procedures (he was called "One-take

Woody"), Van Dyke completed the film in his typical whirlwind fashion, ahead of schedule and even under the large budget he had at hand. The film was premiered in Washington, D.C., where thirty-five U.S. senators and several U.S. Supreme Court justices attended. It got a standing ovation. **p**, Hunt Stromberg, W.S. Van Dyke II; **d**, Van Dyke; **cast**, Jeanette MacDonald, Nelson Eddy, Frank Morgan, Douglas Dumbrille, Joseph Cawthorne, Cecilia Parker, Walter Kingsford, Akim Tamiroff, Harold Huber, Edward Brophy, Olive Carey, Walter Long, Edward Norris; **w**, John Lee Mahin, Frances Goodrich, Albert Hackett (based on the book by Rida Johnson Young of the operetta by Victor Herbert); **c**, William Daniels; **m**, Herbert; **ed**, Blanche Sewell; **art d**, Cedric Gibbons.

The Navigator ★★★★ 1924 (silent); U.S.; 59m/6 reels; Buster Keaton Productions/MGM; B/W; Comedy; Children: Acceptable; **DVD**; **VHS**. Keaton is at his best in this hilarious outing, an antic comedy packed with his unique sight gags and slapstick. Inept at everything, Keaton is a millionaire, who suddenly decides to marry McGuire, his long-standing sweetheart, an idle socialite who lives the same kind of pampered life as Keaton. He thinks to sweep her off her feet when offering to wed her and take her on a lavish honeymoon to Hawaii, but when he proposes, she rejects him out of hand for having taken so long in seeking her hand in marriage. Keaton decides to sail to Hawaii alone, but he boards the wrong vessel, *the Navigator*, an ocean-going ship owned by Vroom, McGuire's father, and begins wandering about, puzzled by the fact that no one else is present. McGuire, at the same time, goes on board to look for Vroom, who has sold the ship to a small country then at war. Agents from an enemy country then kidnap Vroom, releasing the mooring ropes of the liner, which then drifts out to sea. As the ship floats along, Keaton and McGuire finally meet and discover they are the only persons on the ship, which has been swept into the Pacific by strong currents, and both encounter one outrageous mishap after another as they try to control the vessel. At one point, they see another vessel and frantically raise pennants to signal for help, but they unwittingly send a signal that informs the captain of that other ship that their own ship is under quarantine and the vessel turns about and sails away. *the Navigator* eventually grounds itself on a reef outside a remote island. To repair a hole in the side of the ship, Keaton dons a diving suit with the help of McGuire. Keaton struggles to get into the diving suit, and when McGuire screws on the helmet, Keaton is smoking a cigarette, and the helmet is soon filled with smoke. His stone face is suddenly changed to an expression of panic as the smoke clouds over the glass plate of the helmet, and he struggles to breathe until McGuire opens the glass plate. Once submerged, Keaton plods about on the ocean floor where he encounters a huge octopus, battling the giant creature by using a swordfish as a blade. While Keaton is underwater and working to repair the ship, natives from the island paddle canoes to the stranded liner and seize McGuire, taking her back to the island for a sumptuous dinner as they are cannibals. Keaton, however, rescues her by coming ashore in the helmeted diving suit. When the natives see him suddenly rise from the deeps they believe he is an all-powerful underwater monster and slavishly worship him, allowing him to wrest McGuire from their control and back to the safety of the grounded ship. The natives, realizing that Keaton is human after all, paddle their canoes to the liner and board it, and where Keaton and McGuire struggle with the hungry cannibals. They manage to escape in a small dingy, but the natives close in on them. Just when all seems lost, a submarine, positioned right beneath the small boat carrying Keaton and McGuire, surfaces to lift them upward and they are saved as the terrified natives paddle back to their island. Keaton provides a mirth-packed film, where he employs every elaborate comedic stunt in his extensive repertoire. The film was a great success, taking in more than $2 million at the box office at its initial release, a return of more than ten times the cost of the film, about $200,000. It established Keaton as a comedian rivaling Harold Lloyd and Charles Chaplin in popularity and inspired him to launch even more

Hamish McFarlane in *The Navigator: A Medieval Odyssey*, 1989.

substantial feature films such as **Seven Chances**, 1925, and his masterpiece, **The General**, 1927. *Author's Note*: Keaton told this author that "I wanted Donald Crisp, a fine dramatic actor and friend, to co-direct **The Navigator** with me. I told him that he should direct the dramatic scenes and I would direct the comedy sequences. When we got into production, Donald told me he wanted to direct the comedy scenes, too, and I told him that would not do and he packed up and went home, so I directed all the scenes in the picture. I got the idea for **The Navigator** when I was reading a newspaper item about how the old ocean liner, *Buford*, was going to be sold for scrap. I immediately bought the old ship, knowing I had the greatest prop I could ever get for a picture. I shot some underwater scenes in a big pool, but that did not work out and we wound up shooting those underwater scenes at Lake Tahoe where the water was very clear. The camera crew had to stay underwater with me, using a camera that was encased in a special box to get the scenes I wanted. It all worked out pretty well, except that the lake water was so cold that we had to keep surfacing every few minutes to warm up and get our blood running again. One of the most interesting things about **The Navigator** was the ship itself. I had a crew of experienced seamen sailing the *Buford*, and several of them told me that they would be glad when the picture was over because they thought the old tub was haunted. They said they heard voices coming from a lot of the cabins and the lower holds, but when they went to investigate they found no one. To tell you the truth, I heard some of those voices, too. Kind of scary, but I don't believe in ghosts much. The old *Buford* used to ferry troops during the Spanish-American War and in World War One and it was used to deport a number of anarchists to Russia after the Red Scare [including anarchist leaders Emma Goldman and Alexander Berkman in 1919]. I guess those folks had a lot to talk about and I suppose that those were the voices in those cabins that the seamen heard—now I sound like I'm going off my rocker, don't I?" **p**, Buster Keaton, Joseph M. Schenck (both not credited); **d**, Donald Crisp, Buster Keaton; **cast**, Keaton, Kathryn McGuire, Frederick Vroom, Clarence Burton, H.N. Clugston, Noble Johnson; **w**, Clyde Bruckman, Joseph Mitchell, Jean Havez; **c**, Byron Houck, Elgin Lessley; **m**, Claude Bolling (1967 version), Robert Israel (1995 version), William Axt (not credited); **ed**, Keaton (not credited).

The Navigator: A Medieval Odyssey ★★★ 1989; Australia/New Zealand; 90m; Arenafilm/Circle Films; B/W/Color; Adventure/Fantasy; Children: Unacceptable (MPAA: PG); **DVD**; **VHS**. This intriguing tale is set in 14th-Century England, beginning in a village that has been spared by the Black Plague, but the villagers, Christian miners, fear that the pestilence will soon engulf them. McFarlane, an eight-year-old boy, has visions that the village will be spared if they dig a path to the other

Conrad Veidt in a dual role with Ann Ayars in *Nazi Agent*, 1942.

side of the world and carry a cross to put on a cathedral in a city of lights before the sun goes down. He further believes that the moon carries the dreaded plague. McFarlane leads four men, including Lyons, his older brother, on a journey that takes them into the 20th Century and they reach Auckland, New Zealand. Now they must find a foundry to cast a spike upon which to hang the cross on a cathedral in McFarlane's dream. The film changes from black and white to color during the transition of the Middle Ages to the modern era. **p**, John Maynard, Gary Hannam; **d**, Vincent Ward; **cast**, Bruce Lyons, Chris Haywood, Hamish McFarlane, Marshall Napier, Noel Appleby, Paul Livingston, Sarah Peirse, Mark Wheatley, Tony Herbert, Jessica Cardiff-Smith; **w**, Ward, Geoff Chapple, Kely Lyons; **c**, Geoffrey Simpson; **m**, Davood A. Tabrizi; **ed**, John Scott; **prod d**, Sally Campbell; **art d**, Mike Becroft; **spec eff**, Paul Nichola.

Nazi Agent ★★★ 1942; U.S.; 105m; MGM; B/W; Spy Drama; Children: Unacceptable; **DVD**; **VHS**. Veidt gives a startling performance as he plays German-born identical twins living in America during the Nazi era in Germany (1932-1945). The Nazi-trained brother uses blackmail to force the good American brother to conduct espionage in America, but, after the Nazis kill one of his close friends, the good brother decides to destroy his evil twin and his henchmen. The good brother kills the Nazi brother and assumes his identity to round up and defeat the enemy agents. Ayars, who loves both brothers, ends up with the good brother in this early and very effective propaganda film where country comes above all else, including the loyalty of brothers. This film is well directed by the accomplished Dassin, and the visual effects where the twins are shown together are startlingly effective. Veidt carries the tale with confidence, introducing small physical nuances that subtly differentiate his dual characters. **p**, Irving Asher, **d**, Jules Dassin; **cast**, Conrad Veidt, Ann Ayars, Frank Reicher, Dorothy Tree, Ivan Simpson, William Tannen, Martin Kosleck, Marc Lawrence, Sidney Blackmer, Moroni Olsen, Mark Daniels, William Post, Jr., Russell Simpson, Joe Yule, Pierre Watkin, Margaret Bert, Barbara Bedford; **w**, Paul Gangelin, John Meehan, Jr. (based on a story by Lothar Mendes); **c**, Harry Stradling Sr.; **m**, Lennie Hayton; **d**, Frank E. Hull; **art d**, Cedric Gibbons, Stan Rogers; **set d**, Edwin B. Willis.

Neapolitan Carousel ★★★ 1961; Italy; 129m; Lux Film; Color; Musical; Children: Acceptable; **DVD**. This entertaining Italian musical effectively combines ballet, opera, popular song, street dancing, and mime patterned after the Commedia dell'Arte, a form of improvised theater begun in Italy in the 16th Century. A group of street musicians has performed from city to city for generations. Stoppa, the group's current patriarch, introduces the various performances. These include "The

Sailor's Lamente;" a ballet called "Naples Incarnate" in which a young Neapolitan girl is courted by several men in costumes from different countries; a tragic romance between a model, Loren, for naughty postcards, and a soldier killed in World War I; a performance of *Michelmamma*, which is the oldest known Italian melody; and a ballet of the invasion of Saracens and the occupation of Naples by French, Spanish, and Germans. There is also a tarantella dance and a massive street dance in Naples. Some outstanding sequences present a sumptuous eye and earful. This film was first released in Europe in 1953, but not shown in U.S. theaters until 1961. (In Italian; English subtitles.) **p**, Carlo Ponti; **d**, Ettore Giannini; **cast**, Paolo Stoppa, Léonide Massine, Achille Millo, Agostino Salvietti, Maria Fiore, Tina Pica, Maria Pia Casilio, Giacomo Rondinella, Sophia Loren, Dolores Palumbo; **w**, Giannini, Remigio Del Grosso, Giuseppe Marotta; **c**, Piero Portalupi (Pathe Color); **m**, Raffaele Gervasio; **ed**, Niccolò Lazzari; **prod d**, Mario Chiari.

Ned Kelly ★★★ 1970; U.K.; 103m; Woodfall/UA; Color; Biographical Drama/Crime Drama; Children: Unacceptable; **DVD**; **VHS**. America's West had its Jesse James and Australia had Ned Kelly (c.1854-1880), an Aussie outlaw who garnered considerable public sympathy in the 1870s. In an offbeat but fascinating performance, Jagger plays the defiant Kelly, who is imprisoned for a crime he did not commit. Upon release, he and his brother, Bickford, and two others, Gilmour and McManus, form a gang and become horse thieves. This leads to a murder, and, cleverly, the governor arrests Jagger's mother, Kaye, in hopes the gang will come out of hiding to rescue her. Kelly offers to give himself up in exchange for his mother's freedom, but the governor declines the deal. Jagger then thinks to rouse the outback folks, mostly of Irish descent, and lead a revolution that will take over Australia, but he and his partners in crime are cornered in a saloon where all but Jagger commit suicide rather than be taken alive. Jagger, as did the real Kelly, takes on a bevy of policemen while wearing his self-fashioned uniform of iron, replete with iron helmet, shooting down several of his opponents before he is wounded and captured. He is tried and condemned to death, telling the judge that he will see him in Hell. A remake was made in 2003; a 1976 film, **Mad Dog Morgan**, told virtually the same story, but Kelly was renamed Morgan. Songs: "Ned Kelly," "She Moved Through the Fair" (Shel Silverstein). Excessive violence prohibits viewing by children. **p**, Neil Hartley; **d**, Tony Richardson; **cast**, Mick Jagger, Allen Bickford, Geoff Gilmour, Mark McManus, Clarissa Kaye, Ken Goodlet, Frank Thring, Bruce Barry, Tony Bazell, Robert Bruning, Bill Hunter; **w**, Richardson, Ian Jones; **c**, Gerry Fisher (Technicolor); **m**, Shel Silverstein; **ed**, Charles Rees; **prod d**, Jocelyn Herbert; **art d**, Andrew Sanders.

Nell Gwyn ★★★ 1935; U.K.; 85m; Herbert Wilcox/UA; B/W; Drama/Romance; Children: Unacceptable; **DVD**; **VHS**. Set in 17th-Century London, Neagle, who plays the beautiful Nell Gwyn (1650-1687), is an uncultured but pretty cockney dance hall girl performing at Drury Lane. She attracts the attention of Charles II (1630-1685), played by Hardwicke, and he becomes more enamored of her than his current concubine, the aristocratic French Duchess of Portsmouth (1649-1734), played by De Casalis. Neagle becomes very devoted and loyal to Hardwicke, but is never accepted by his circle at court. She nevertheless remains his favorite mistress until his death. The American Hays Office, which governed the morality in U.S. films at the time of this production, compelled the producers to shoot a historically inaccurate ending in which Neagle ends up poor and dying in a gutter to show that an adulterous life did not pay. Neagle gives a top flight performance as does Hardwicke. This story was made in 1914 and 1926 as silent films. **p&d**, Herbert Wilcox; **cast**, Anna Neagle, Sir Cedric Hardwicke, Jeanne De Casalis, Muriel George, Helena Pickard, Dorothy Robinson, Esme Percy, Miles Malleson, Moore Marriott, Craighall Sherry, Lawrence Anderson; **w**, Malleson; **c**, F. A. Young; **m**, Philip Braham; **ed**, Merrill G. White; **art d**, Lawrence P. Williams.

Neptune's Daughter ★★★ 1949; U.S.; 92m; MGM; Color; Musical Comedy; Children: Acceptable; **DVD**; **VHS**. Williams and Wynn are partners in a bathing suit company while millionaire playboy Montalban pursues her. Garrett, who is Williams' scatterbrained older sister, is in love with Skelton, a masseur she has mistaken for Montalban, the celebrated captain of the South American polo team. Skelton goes along with a charade as the polo player, but falls in love with Williams. After some songs, jokes, and excellent swimming sequences, Williams and Skelton pair off, as do Garrett and Montalban. Songs: "Baby, It's Cold Outside," "I Love Those Men," "My Heart Beats Faster," "On a Slow Boat to China" (Frank Loesser); "Jungle Rhumba" (Toni Beaulieu). Thoroughly entertaining, the sequences showing the well-choreographed swimming sequences with the beautiful and graceful Williams are imminently watchable while Skelton is exceptional in providing a lot of funny stunts. **p**, Jack Cummings; **d**, Edward Buzzell; **cast**, Esther Williams, Red Skelton, Ricardo Montalban, Betty Garrett, Keenan Wynn, Xavier Cugat, Ted de Corsia, Mike Mazurki, Mel Blanc, George Mann, Frank Mitchell; **w**, Dorothy Kingsley; **c**, Charles Rosher (Technicolor); **m**, George Stoll, Leo Arnaud; **ed**, Irvine Warburton; **art d**, Cedric Gibbons, Edward C. Carfagno; **set d**, Edwin B. Willis.

Network ★★★★ 1976; U.S.; 121m; MGM/UA; Color; Drama; Children: Unacceptable (MPAA: R); **BD**; **DVD**; **VHS**. The brilliant Chayefsky presents an all-out assault on the medium of TV, a fascinating indictment studded with equally brilliant performances from a stellar cast and under the skillful direction of Lumet. Finch, a normally reasonable and reserved TV news anchorman, who has been before the cameras for more than two decades, becomes emotionally and mentally unhinged after he is perfunctorily informed that he is being fired because of his declining ratings. (His fate has befallen many a real TV icon—Johnny Carson quit on top before that happened; Jay Leno lingered too long for the axe—see Author's Note.) Finch has been at the United Broadcasting System (fictional) for most of his adult life and startles his superiors and the world in his very next broadcast. Finch tells his viewers that his life has been for naught, and that he intends to end that life with his final broadcast the following week by committing suicide on live TV. The network's ratings soar with this gruesome news (and Chayefsky here indicts a public as bloodthirsty as Finch's bosses are coldhearted). The fan mail is overwhelming, most imploring Finch to quit his mad plan and, on the night he is scheduled to end it all, he does a volatile turnabout, apologizing to the viewing public and explaining that he was motivated to misspeak his grim intentions because of the vicious treatment he and the rest of the world has endlessly endured from the powers that be. Gesticulating with his waving arms as he stands up from his news desk, Finch shouts at the camera, telling viewers to "go to your nearest window and yell as loud as you can: 'I am mad as hell and I am not going to take it anymore!'" The response in enormous, countless viewers echoing Finch's shout from windows all over the country. Dunaway, a beautiful but scheming junior executive at UBS sees in Finch's outlandish performances the opportunity to become one of the network's leading players by using the nearly deranged Finch to glean the highest Nielsen ratings. Dunaway convinces network bosses that Finch should transform from a reliable newsman to a raving eccentric and proposes that he be signed to a new weekly show where Finch can spew and spout out his now unleashed venom on the world. Holden, an old guard newsman, staunchly opposes this idea even after the artful Dunaway seduces him and where Holden betrays Straight, his loyal wife of twenty-five years. Dunaway then convinces network boss Duvall to do the show where Finch will appear to be the consummate angry man and be promoted as "the mad prophet of the airways." Holden still fights against the idea and is summarily fired, returning later to Straight to beg her forgiveness and realizing that his professional life is at an end (at one point when it is suggested that he write his memoirs, Holden responds by realistically saying that no one will want to read such memoirs from a has-been). Finch goes on the new show to exhibit his

Peter Finch in *Network*, 1976.

rantings and ravings, preaching his own self-styled Gospel and spouting predictions as if he were a gifted psychic or guru who can look into the future. The show is an enormous hit, its Nielsen ratings skyrocketing. Dunaway is now the new executive star at UBS and she concocts one eccentric show after another made up of screaming political activists, paramilitary groups and even dedicated felons, anything to grab the TV ratings for her network. Meanwhile, Finch gets into deep corporate trouble after he learns that the network is going to be secretly sold to a foreign buyer and he denounces the deal on the airways, urging his rabid viewers to contact Washington immediately to oppose the deal. For this worst of transgressions, Finch is brought before conglomerate chief Beatty who gives him a stern short-course in American business ethics (or the total lack of them) and the way the eco-dollar works in the world, chastising him for his ignorance. Finch becomes a reformed man—a madman who is malleable and easily manipulated by authority at this time—and he becomes Beatty's corporate advocate, telling viewers, with Beatty's approval, that they are more or less inconsequential in the world and that they must abide by the higher thoughts of such brilliant business savants as Beatty. Finch's ratings plummet and, in desperation, Dunaway goes to corporate hatchet man Duvall and they both solve the problem by having actual terrorists, who now have their own show, assassinate Finch on live TV! Thus ends this outlandish satire with the gory absurd. Though savagely attacking the TV medium, Chayefsky incisively and tellingly depicts the varied and troubled characters of some of those who control that medium while manipulating public opinion as they extensively line their own pockets. This astounding and richly rewarding film was nominated for Best Picture and Best Director (Lumet), and won Oscars for Finch (Best Actor, the first such award given posthumously as Finch died shortly after the film was completed), for Dunaway (Best Actress) and for Straight (Best Supporting Actress, another precedent in that her performance on screen is the shortest to ever win an Oscar), as well as Oscar nominations for Best Cinematography (Roizman) and Best Editing (Heim). *Author's Note*: When talking with TV host Johnny Carson (after he had retired from his long-running "Tonight Show" in 1992), Carson (1925-2005) told this author that "the character Faye [Dunaway] plays in **Network** is based on a real female network executive—and I won't say her name—who was the most ruthless woman in the business. She would stop making love with her partner to discuss the ratings of her TV shows, to show you what came first on her agenda. She was a real barracuda and Faye played that woman to the frightening hilt." I had appeared on Carson's show on June 17, 1976, when promoting one of my books (*Hustlers and Conmen*), and had come to know him well enough to ask him if he believed that the ruthless goings-on in **Network** were widespread in the real world of television. "More than you will ever know," was his response. "I got out [retired]

Steve McQueen in *Nevada Smith*, 1966.

just before the sharks filled the tank." **p**, Howard Gottfried; **d**, Sidney Lumet; **cast**, Faye Dunaway, William Holden, Peter Finch, Robert Duvall, Wesley Addy, Ned Beatty, Arthur Burghardt, Bill Burrows, John Carpenter, Jordan Charney, Kathy Cronkite, Conchata Ferrell, Darryl Hickman, William Prince, Beatrice Straight; **w**, Paddy Chayefsky; **c**, Owen Roizman (Panavision; Metrocolor); **m**, Elliot Lawrence; **ed**, Alan Heim; **prod d**, Philip Rosenberg; **set d**, Edward Stewart.

Nevada Smith ★★★★ 1966; U.S.; 139m; Embassy/PAR; Color; Western; Children: Unacceptable; **DVD**; **VHS**. McQueen is exceptional as a youthful cowboy in this offbeat but fascinating oater. After his half-breed mother and father are killed by three vicious outlaws—Malden, Kennedy and Landau—McQueen sets out to bring the murderers to justice. Starving and in rags and while armed only with a malfunctioning old six-shooter, McQueen ambushes Keith, a traveling gunsmith and sharpshooter. Keith blithely ignores McQueen's threats, pointing out that the weapon the youth aims at him is useless since its firing pin is damaged. The kindhearted Keith then takes pity on McQueen and invites him to a meal and then more or less adopts him, teaching him his trade and training him how to shoot a gun with accuracy while telling McQueen to abandon any thought of a quick draw since such showy practices usually prove ineffective in dispatching foes. After learning all he can from Keith, McQueen goes his separate way, finding his first prey, Landau, in a small town, where he waylays the outlaw in a cattle pen, battling him and killing him with a knife. He next learns the identity of the second killer, Kennedy, only to find that Kennedy has been captured and sent to a chain gang for another crime. To get close to Kennedy, McQueen commits a purposely bungled crime and is sent to the same chain gang where he befriends Kennedy and then convinces him to escape with him with the help of local girl Pleshette, who has met McQueen while he was working on a road gang and has had an assignation with him (where local women are allowed to enter the prisoner barracks to sexually service the prisoners for money, not unlike the scene in **Spartacus**, 1960, where gladiators are serviced in the same manner). Kennedy and McQueen make their break with Pleshette's help when she provides a skiff for them to use in paddling through the swamps, but she is bitten by a poisonous snake; when Kennedy insists they abandon her, McQueen attacks him. They battle in the water and McQueen kills Kennedy, then takes Pleshette ashore only to see her die from the snakebite. Traveling westward, McQueen, while using the alias of "Nevada Smith," gets into trouble in a small town where he meets Malden, who is leading a band of outlaws and planning the robbery of a gold shipment. Malden takes McQueen into his gang, but is suspicious of him, thinking he might be the youth called "Max Sand," the son of the parents Malden and others have murdered and, having also heard

how that youth has tracked down his two associates (Landau and Kennedy) and killed them. To make sure that McQueen is not "Sand," he brandishes an Indian pouch he has taken from McQueen's mother after assaulting and killing her, bragging about his sexual conquest. McQueen, however, does not respond and Malden now feels assured that McQueen is not the youth looking for him. During the robbery of the gold shipment, Malden becomes separated from the rest of his gang and flees, but McQueen chases him, Malden now knowing that McQueen, indeed, is "Max Sand," the youth out to kill him for the murder of his parents. McQueen chases Malden on horseback to a river where they battle in a savage firefight, where McQueen wounds Malden many times, crippling him for life. Malden screams in agony, begging McQueen to "finish me!" McQueen, however, has exhausted his passion for revenge and leaves Malden a cripple for life as he rides away. Pantheon director Hathaway, a first-rate action helmsman, presents a thoroughly exciting and provocative western with "thinking men" characters that are fully developed—the avuncular Keith, the evasive Kennedy, the conniving Malden and the obsessive McQueen, all of whom render superlative performances. Ballard's photography provides many breathtaking western scenes, and Newman's score is outstanding. ***Author's Note***: This film profiles a character that appeared in the novel and film, **The Carpetbaggers**, 1964, where Alan Ladd plays "Nevada Smith," a rugged cowboy with a violent past, and it is that past that is profiled by McQueen in this film. McQueen told this author that "I play a character that actually lived in the Old West, a cowboy turned gunslinger, who became a close friend of Howard Hughes's father when the old man was wildcatting for oil. Nobody ever really knew what that man was, but some believe it was the silent film cowboy star William S. Hart [1864-1946]. He was born in New York, but went west before the turn of the 20th Century where he got into a lot of scrapes and met gunfighters like Wyatt Earp. The three men I hunt down and kill are played by some fine actors. The most miserable of the lot is Karl [Malden] and I asked him if he enjoyed playing such a rotten S.O.B., and he said, 'I love it—villains are the best characters you can play. Everybody watches their every move, just like you did in our scenes together.' And, boy, did he have the moves, from fingers to toes." **p&d**, Henry Hathaway; **cast**, Steve McQueen, Karl Malden, Brian Keith, Arthur Kennedy, Suzanne Pleshette, Raf Vallone, Janet Margolin, Pat Hingle, Howard Da Silva, Martin Landau, Paul Fix, Gene Evans, Josephine Hutchinson, Lyle Bettger, John Litel, Loni Anderson, Iron Eyes Cody, Strother Martin; **w**, John Michael Hayes (based on a story by Hayes and a character in the novel *The Carpetbaggers* by Harold Robbins); **c**, Lucien Ballard (Panavision; Eastmancolor); **m**, Alfred Newman; **ed**, Frank Bracht; **art d**, Hal Pereira, Tambi Larsen, Al Roelofs; **set d**, Robert Benton; **spec eff**, George C. Thompson, Paul K. Lerpae.

Never a Dull Moment ★★★ 1968; U.S.; 99m; Disney/Buena Vista; Color; Comedy; Children: Acceptable; **DVD**; **VHS**. Good comedy sees Van Dyke as a minor actor, who fears that a mugger is following him, so he hides in a doorway. Hoodlum Bill mistakes him for a hired killer, Elam, who he is supposed to meet. Bill drives Van Dyke to the mansion of a mobster boss, Robinson, who has a love of art and plans to steal a priceless painting at an art museum. Van Dyke tries to convince Provine, who is Robinson's hired art teacher, that he is not the thief (Elam), but she doesn't believe him. Elam then shows up at the mansion and Robinson doesn't know who the real killer is, so he has both occupy a room and figures that the real hit man will survive. Provine now believes Van Dyke is telling the truth and helps him escape from the room. The art heist goes on, with Van Dyke and some of Robinson's goons participating, but Van Dyke foils the theft by leading his fellow thieves on a frantic chase inside the museum during which the thugs are spooked by frightening modern art they cannot understand. Provine alerts police and they arrest the thieves. Robinson later seeks exoneration by saying that he only wanted the painting so he could give it back if the museum was named after him. Van Dyke is hailed as a hero and his future as an actor gets a big boost. This fast-paced comedy is high-lighted by an outstanding performance from Robinson, a real-life art collector, who spoofs his many past films where he essayed a snarling gangster. **p**, Ron Miller; **d**, Jerry Paris; **cast**, Dick Van Dyke, Edward G. Robinson, Dorothy Provine, Henry Silva, Joanna Moore, Tony Bill, Slim Pickens, Jack Elam, Mickey Shaughnessy, Anthony Caruso; **w**, AJ Carothers (based on the novel *A Thrill a Minute with Jack Albany* by John Godey); **c**, William E. Snyder (Technicolor); **m**, Robert F. Brunner; **ed**, Marsh Hendry; **art d**, Carroll Clark, John B. Mansbridge; **set d**, Emile Kuri, Frank R. McKelvy; **spec eff**, Eustace Lycett, Robert A. Mattey.

Never Cry Wolf ★★★ 1983; U.S.; 105m; Walt Disney/Amarok/Buena Vista; Color; Adventure; Children: Unacceptable (MPAA: PG); **DVD**; **VHS**. A film based on the true story of Farley Mowat (Farley McGill Mowat, 1921-), played by Smith, a biologist whom the U.S. govern-ment sends to the northernmost wilds of Alaska to discover if wolves are the reason why caribou herds are diminishing. His research in virtual isolation in the wilderness leads him to conclude that old beliefs about wolves and their threat to caribou are mostly false. He finds that Arctic wolves live mostly on a diet of mice. They only attack weak and sick caribou, which ensures the survival of the fittest caribou, and concludes that wolves play an important beneficial part in the ecosystem of the North. He also comes to believe that humans are a far greater threat to the land, because of hunters, who are responsible for the significant re-duction in caribou herds in recent years. Smith is for a short time not entirely alone, befriended by a wise old Inuit, Ittimangnaq, who teaches him many wolf secrets, and by a younger Inuit, Jorah, who kills wolves only to support his family. At the end of the film, a bush pilot, Dennehy, who has flown Smith into the Arctic, now flies in some land developers that envision having a resort built to bring hunters to the area. The film is an absorbing and sometimes even humorous adventure, particularly after Smith discovers that mice are tasty to eat, so no wonder wolves feast on them. Violence prohibits viewing by children. **p**, Lewis Allen, Jack Couffer, Joseph Strick; **d**, Carroll Ballard; **cast**, Charles Martin Smith, Brian Dennehy, Zachary Ittimangnaq, Samson Jorah, Hugh Web-ster, Martha Ittimangnaq, Tom Dahlgren, Walker Stuart; **w**, Curtis Han-son, Sam Hamm, Richard Kletter, Smith, Eugene Corr, Christina Luescher, Ralph Furmaniak (based on the book by Farley Mowat); **c**, Hiro Narita (Technicolor); **m**, Mark Isham; **ed**, Michael Chandler, Peter Parasheles; **art d**, Graeme Murray; **spec eff**, John Thomas.

Never Give a Sucker an Even Break ★★★ 1941; U.S.; 71m; UNIV; B/W; Comedy; Children: Acceptable; **DVD**; **VHS**. Fields is a filmmaker in this comedic extravaganza (one that embraces the absurd long before such films attempted to position the ridiculous as serious). In one of his most acerbic spoofs of Hollywood, the great curmudgeon concocts the most outlandish plots for his films and he has a brand new one to offer as this film opens and he is en route to his home base, Esoteric Studios. He pauses when approaching the studio, gazing with admiration at an advertisement on a billboard that illustrates his last filmic opus (the **Bank Dick**, 1940), chasing away two young boys who ridicule the film. A fetching lady then catches his eye and his pass at her backfires when her brawny boyfriend appears and promptly sends him over a hedgerow after landing a blow on his bulbous nose. Recovering from this fanciful faux pas, Fields goes to a small restaurant where Gilbert, an obese and obnoxious waitress, verbally abuses him as she tells him that everything he orders is no longer on the menu and all he can order is eggs. She then complains that he is too free with his hands and Fields replies that he "was only trying to guess your weight." Gilbert responds by pouring ice water down the back of his shirt. Fields, soggier for the experience, goes to his studio where he flirts with receptionist Monti (who was the actor's mistress in real life) before being granted an interview with fussy studio producer Pangborn, who dismisses Fields' story for his next film and sends him on his way. Fields next meets with his niece, Gloria Jean, at

Marcia Ralston and W.C. Fields in *Never Give a Sucker an Even Break,* **1941.**

a shooting gallery operated by Errol, and whose two offspring were the boys earlier giving Fields a hard time. Gloria Jean's mother, Nagel, a trapeze artist, is then killed in a fall, and Fields adopts the girl, taking her on a flight to Mexico. Fields is convinced that he will soon be rich by peddling wooden nutmegs to Russian colonists, who have taken up residence south of the border. The plane on which he and Gloria Jean ride has all the comforts of home, including sleeping compartments and even an open-air observation deck. While lounging on that deck, Fields accidentally drops his bottle of booze overboard and desperately dives after it, catching up with the falling bottle in mid-air, and recapping it before he crashes downward, only to land comfortably on an enormous mattress. He meets Miller, an exiled Russian expatriate, and makes awk-ward advances toward the beautiful young woman; he is interrupted when her mother, Dumont, appears and he retreats as she aggressively makes advances toward him. After dallying with these two women, who occupy a luxurious castle-like residence atop a mountain, Fields is re-united with Gloria Jean, but is crestfallen to learn that his nemesis, Errol, has already cornered the wooden nutmeg market in the area. Fields then reconsiders Dumont's attraction to him after he learns that she is fabu-lously wealthy, but when he revisits her, he finds the oily Errol already present and pitching woo to the rich matron. The utterly defeated Fields departs only to be shown back at Pangborn's office where Fields is con-cluding his tale, the entire Mexican adventure being part of the film he has been describing to the producer. Pangborn is so repelled by the ridiculous story that he suffers an apoplectic attack before kicking Fields out of his office. Fields decides to go home to contemplate his disastrous commercial failures; en route, he encounters a heavyset woman, who informs him that it is urgent she get to a maternity hospital immediately and, thinking she is about to have a baby, packs her into his car and drives like a madman through the heavily trafficked streets of Los An-geles. Caroming off other cars and becoming entangled in the ladder of a racing fire engine, Fields nevertheless manages to reach the hospital to deliver the woman, who is only visiting someone and not having a baby after all, and, in the process, Fields utterly destroys his car, stepping from its collapsed ruins with only the steering wheel in his hands. Gloria Jean suddenly appears, smiling and saying: "My uncle Bill…but we still love him!" The film, the most absurd of all of Fields' zany comedies, ends on this oddball note. *Author's Note*: This strangest of all Fields' films was his last feature production. Fields knew that his career was closing and that Universal, his last major studio, would be promoting newer and younger comedians, such as Abbott and Costello, in future productions, so he took his revenge by portraying producer Pangborn as much an idiot as the character Fields himself plays. Fields wrote the script for this film in four months, but producers, along with the Breen Office, the then official Hollywood censoring organization, took excep-

Gina Lollobrigida, Frank Sinatra and Peter Lawford in *Never So Few*, 1959.

tion to a lot of Fields' scenes—where he stares at a young woman's legs, and, especially, his many remarks about drinking. His own drinking was of deep concern yo producers, who hired private detectives to trail Fields at the studio to make sure he was not secretly drinking his favorite rum and pineapple juice on the sly. After Fields received a copy of the script that had been rewritten by a number of studio hacks, he exploded, telling director Cline that his story had been completely destroyed and was even more senseless than the planned senselessness he had created. Fields later stated: "I was going to throw [the script] in their faces when the director [Cline] told me not to. He said: 'We'll shoot your own script. They won't know the difference.' We did—and they didn't." **p**, Jack J. Gross; **d**, Edward Cline; **cast**, W.C. Fields, Gloria Jean, Leon Errol, Charles Lang, Margaret Dumont, Billy Lenhart, Kenneth Brown, Susan Miller, Franklin Pangborn, Mona Barrie, Anne Nagel, Nell O'Day, Jody Gilbert, Jean Porter, Carlotta Monti, Irving Bacon; **w**, John T. Neville, Prescott Chaplin (based on a story by Otis Criblecoblis (W.C. Fields); **c**, Charles Van Enger; **m**, Frank Skinner, Charles Previn; **ed**, Arthur Hilton; **art d**, Jack Otterson; **set d**, Russell A. Gausman.

Never on Sunday ★★★ 1960; Greece/U.S.; 91m; MGM; B/W; Comedy; Children: Unacceptable; **DVD**; **VHS**. Mercouri fascinates in this "hooker with a heart" tale. Dassin, who also produces and directs (he married Mercouri), is shown arriving in Piraeus, Greece. He is an academic-type American enamored with the country, its customs, culture and people. He meets Mercouri, a prostitute, who looks upon her occupation as a legitimate profession and feels no guilt in turning tricks six days a week. She shuns her patrons on Sundays as that day is reserved for her open house where she hosts all manner of visitors with food, wine and song before going to the theater to watch classic Greek plays without understanding their significance. She thinks that "Oedipus" relates a simple family story about a man who loves and respects his mother and that Medea is wholly misunderstood by the hurtful men in her life. Dassin tries to explain the nuances and meanings of these plays to Mercouri, but it is just so much high-blown palaver to her. Falling in love with her, Dassin tries to reform Mercouri and she stops hooking, but only for a brief time, eventually going back to turning tricks. The real transformation takes place with Dassin, who comes to accept Mercouri's way of life (not dissimilar to the influence Anthony Quinn has on the stiff-necked Albert Bates when educating him about the realities of Greek life in **Zorba the Greek**, 1964). The simple tale is highlighted by Mercouri's exceptional performance, one where she charmingly conveys a vibrant humor and love for life, and where Dassin, too, shines in his role as a man whose perspectives of morality gradually alter. This film made an international star out of Mercouri, but when she reprised her role in the same story on Broadway in 1967, she was met with a

lukewarm reception by the public. Dassin was nominated for an Oscar as Best Director, and his script was also nominated while Mercouri received an Oscar nomination as Best Actress. The title song was awarded an Oscar. ***Author's Note***: This film was produced for less than $200,000 and made a fortune worldwide. Dassin had departed Hollywood almost a decade earlier when he became involved in the political witch-hunts for left-wing activists, going to France to direct the classic crime tale **Rififi**, 1956, and then to Greece to make this thoroughly entertaining film. **p,d&w**, Jules Dassin; **cast**, Melina Mercouri, Dassin, Giorgos Foundas, Titos Vandis, Mitsos Lygizos, Despo Diamantidou, Dimos Starenios, Dimitri Papamichael, Alexis Solomos, Thanassis Veggos, Faidon Georgitsis, Nikos Fermas; **c**, Jacques Natteau; **m**, Manos Hatzidakis; **ed**, Roger Dwyre; **art d**, Alekos Tzonis.

Never So Few ★★★ 1959; U.S.; 124m; Canterbury/MGM; Color; War; Children: Unacceptable; **DVD**; **VHS**. Sinatra is a U.S. Army captain in this gritty war tale where he leads a band of American-British skilled OSS (Office of Strategic Services) operatives in Burma during WWII to train Kachin natives in modern warfare. In an ambush mission, they wipe out a Japanese squad and Sinatra then goes to Calcutta to ask for more aid. There he falls for Lollobrigida, girlfriend of a wealthy merchant, Henreid. Sinatra returns to his post in the jungles, seeing many setbacks where his Kachin fighters are waylaid and many are killed. He learns that the Chinese government is outfitting warlord rebels to ambush Allied troops and sell supplies to the Japanese. When one of Sinatra's closest aides, Johnson, is wounded by a Chinese soldier, Sinatra orders all the Chinese prisoners in a village executed. Sinatra is placed on trial for this savage act, but is vindicated after he provides proof that the Chinese government has been sabotaging Allied war efforts and American general Donlevy exonerates him. The result is that the Chinese agree to stop rebels from killing Allied soldiers and promise to defend its borders. Based on true events, the film provides some great action scenes and more than one steamy sequence between Sinatra and the smoldering Lollobrigida. Excessive violence prohibits viewing by children. ***Author's Note***: Sinatra was particularly proud of this film, stating to this author: "We showed a little-known theater of the war in that picture and we were actually portraying a real OSS unit [Office of Strategic Services, Detachment 101 in Burma and others in China] and those heroic people never got the credit they deserved in their part of the war. The picture helped to recognize those heroes." McQueen told this author that "working with Frank [Sinatra] in Never So Few was no picnic. He demanded that everybody give the same one hundred percent he put out in every scene, and even though Sturges was the director, it was Frank who kept us all in line." Sturges echoed McQueen's statements when telling this author: "Frank [Sinatra] was like a terrier on that picture, hounding the cast members to stay on their toes. At one point, I told him that I thought he was my 'enforcer,' but I don't think he took too kindly to that remark." For further information on the OSS, see my work, *Spies: A Narrative Encyclopedia of Dirty Deeds and Double Dealing from Biblical Times to Today* (M. Evans, 1997; William Donovan: pages 183-188; OSS: page 375). **p**, Edmund Grainger; **d**, John Sturges; **cast**, Frank Sinatra, Gina Lollobrigida, Peter Lawford, Steve McQueen, Richard Johnson, Paul Henreid, Brian Donlevy, Dean Jones, Charles Bronson, Philip Ahn, John Hoyt, Whit Bissell, William Smith, Irene Tedrow; **w**, Millard Kaufman (based on the novel by Tom T. Chamales); **c**, William H. Daniels; **m**, Hugo Friedhofer; **ed**, Ferris Webster; **art d**, Hans Peters, Addison Hehr; **set d**, Henry Grace, Richard Pefferle; **spec eff**, Robert R. Hoag, Lee LeBlanc, Cliff Shirpser.

Never Steal Anything Small ★★★ 1959; U.S.; 94m; UNIV; Color; Musical/Crime; Children: Unacceptable; **VHS**. Cagney is an ambitious longshoreman, who aspires to become a union president while singing and dancing throughout this entertaining musical. He falls in love with Jones, wife of an honest lawyer, Smith, and frames him on a charge of corruption to get him out of the way. Cagney also engages in perjury, bribery and grand larceny to get ahead while his girlfriend, Williams, tries unsuccessfully to reform him. It ends with him losing everything including Jones in an offbeat outing that nevertheless sustains interest, all due to the inimitable Cagney and his bravura performance. Songs: "Never Steal Anything Small," "I'm Sorry, I Want a Ferrari," "I Haven't Got a Thing to Wear," "It Takes Love to Make a Home," "Helping Our Friends" (Allie Wrubel, Maxwell Anderson). *Author's Note*: Cagney told this author that "**Never Steal Anything Small** missed its mark a bit. I think the character was just a bit too crooked for his own good and the audience knew it, but I played all of his shenanigans for laughs, never with a thought to inspire anyone to follow his corrupt practices." **p**, Aaron Rosenberg; **d**, Charles Lederer; **cast**, James Cagney, Shirley Jones, Roger Smith, Cara Williams, Nehemiah Persoff, Royal Dano, Anthony Caruso, Horace McMahon, Jack Albertson, Virginia Vincent, Roland Winters; **w**, Lederer (based on the play "The Devil's Hornpipe" by Maxwell Anderson); **c**, Harold Lipstein; **m**, Allie Wrubel; **ed**, Russell F. Schoengarth; **art d**, Alexander Golitzen, Robert Clatworthy; **set d**, Russell A. Gausman, Ollie Emert; **spec eff**, Clifford Stine.

Never Take Candy from a Stranger ★★★ 1961; U.K.; 81m; Hammer Film Productions/Astor Pictures Corp.; B/W; Drama; Children: Unacceptable; **DVD**. A family moves from England to a small town in Canada where Allen, the father, becomes the new high school principal. Accompanying him are his wife, Watford, and their nine-year-old daughter, Faye. Soon after they settle in, Faye loses her purse containing "candy money" while playing in some woods with her eleven-year-old friend, Green. Green tells her she knows where they can get some candy for nothing, and takes her to a secluded mansion. Its owner, an elderly and senile man, Aylmer, had been watching them from a window. They visit Alymer and, that night, Faye tells her parents that Aylmer made her and Green dance before him nude before giving them some candy. Allen files a complaint, but the local police chief, Knapp, is skeptical of Faye's story and says Aylmer is a highly respected and important citizen. The case goes to court where Aylmer's attorney, MacGinnis, gets him acquitted by convincing everyone that Faye made up her story. Allen decides to leave with his wife and daughter and live somewhere else when Faye and Green disappear. A search is made and Aylmer is found in the woods beside the body of Green whom he has murdered. Faye is found nearby, safe and not having witnessed the killing. Well made, this grim film depicts the insidious nature of a child molester, but one not for viewing by children because of its subject matter. **p**, Anthony Hinds, Michael Carreras; **d**, Cyril Frankel; **cast**, Gwen Watford, Patrick Allen, Felix Aylmer, Niall MacGinnis, Alison Leggatt, Bill Nagy, MacDonald Parke, Michael Gwynn, Janina Faye, Frances Green, Estelle Brody; **w**, John Hunter (based on the play "The Pony Cart" by Roger Garis); **c**, Freddie Francis; **m**, Elisabeth Lutyens; **ed**, Alfred Cox, James Needs; **art d**, Don Mingaye, Bernard Robinson.

Never Wave at a WAC ★★★ 1953; U.S.; 87m; Independent Artists/RKO; B/W; Comedy; Children: Acceptable. Enjoyable comedy sees Russell as a divorced Washington, D.C., socialite, who misses her boyfriend, Ching, a lieutenant colonel in the U.S. Army and stationed in Paris, so she asks her father, Dingle, a U.S. Senator, to get her an officer's commission in the WACs (Women's Army Corps), so she can be in Paris with Ching. Dingle thinks it would do her more good if she served as a private and got WAC basic training, so she is sent to Fort Lee, Va. In camp, she meets addlebrained Wilson, a fellow WAC, who is a former striptease burlesque queen (and who is added to this film for laughs as Wilson invariably and effectively played dumb bimbos). Douglas, who is Russell's ex-husband and a consultant with the army, then arrives at the camp and he keeps Russell from going to Paris by having her join a group of WACs assigned to testing new military apparatus. Ching is then sent to the same camp and it's a battle royal over Russell between her boyfriend and ex-husband. Douglas wins and Russell decides she loves him enough to marry him again. General Omar Bradley

Liza Minnelli and Robert De Niro in *New York, New York,* 1977.

(1893-1981) makes a cameo appearance as himself. Song: "WAC Song" (Jane Douglass, Camilla Mays Frank). **p**, Frederick Brisson, Gordon S. Griffith; **d**, Norman Z. McLeod; **cast**, Rosalind Russell, Paul Douglas, Marie Wilson, William Ching, Arleen Whelan, Leif Erickson, Hillary Brooke, Charles Dingle, Lurene Tuttle, Regis Toomey, Frieda Inescort, Jane Seymour, Olan Soule, Truman Bradley (narrator); **w**, Ken Englund (based on a story by Frederick Kohner, Fred Brady); **c**, William H. Daniels; **m**, Elmer Bernstein; **ed**, Stanley Johnson; **art d**, William Flannery; **set d**, Howard Bristol.

The New Land ★★★ 1973; Sweden; 161m; Svensk Filmindustri/WB; Color; Adventure/Drama; Children: Unacceptable; **VHS**. A sequel to **The Emigrants**, 1971, this film is the continuing saga of a Swedish family led by von Sydow that starts a new life on a farm in Minnesota in the mid-1850s. They find the summers and winters to be much harsher than in Sweden, but live a better life, until the American Civil War begins and Sioux Indians engage in a bloody war of their own against the white settlers. Von Sydow's brother, Axberg, leaves the farm to try his luck as a gold miner in California. He never reaches California, but becomes rich from a friend who dies of yellow fever along the way westward, only to lose the fortune by falling victim to a con man. Axberg makes his way back to the family farm where he dies from a disease he contracted along the way. Meanwhile, von Sydow's wife, Ullmann, who has never forgotten Sweden, gives birth to several more children even though it endangers her life. Director Troell depicts a good but hardscrabble story of pioneer Americans in the 1800s and the many perils that challenge their survival. Violence prohibits viewing by children. *Author's Note*: This film depicts the uprising of the Sioux Indians in Minnesota in 1862, where the Sioux conducted what was later dubbed the "Makato Massacre," and where they killed 490 white men, women and children; thirty-eight Indians were hanged in America's largest mass execution (on orders of President Abraham Lincoln); for more information on this uprising, see my work, *The Encyclopedia of World Crime*, Volume III (CrimeBooks, 1990; page 2103). (Dubbed in English.) **p**, Bengt Forslund; **d**, Jan Troell; **cast**, Max von Sydow, Liv Ullmann, Eddie Axberg, Pierre Lindstedt, Allan Edwall, Monica Zetterlund, Hans Alfredson, Agneta Prytz, Halvar Björk, Tom C. Fouts; **w**, Forslund, Troell (based on the novel *The Emigrants* by Vilhelm Moberg); **c&d**, Troell (Technicolor); **m**, Bengt Ernryd, Georg Oddner; **prod d**, P.A. Lundgren.

New York, New York ★★★ 1977; U.S.; 155m; WB; Color; Drama; Children: Unacceptable (MPAA: PG); **BD**; **DVD**; **VHS**. Packed with great songs, this entertaining and well-acted romantic drama opens on the day WWII ends in the Pacific in 1945 De Niro, a selfish, smooth-

Alan Gelfant and Cara Buono in *Next Stop Wonderland*, 1998.

talking New York saxophone player, meets Minnelli, a lounge singer, and they get gigs as a boy-girl act in a nightclub. They fall in love while they struggle with their careers and they aim for the top. They marry and De Niro makes Minnelli pregnant, but he doesn't want to be a father so he walks out on her. She becomes a top singer and movie actress and he a well-known musician and club owner. They meet again and he wants to reunite, but she leaves him cold. ("Hell hath no fury like a woman scorned.") Songs: "Theme from New York, New York," "There Goes the Ball Game," "Happy Endings," "But the World Goes Round" (music: John Kander; lyrics: Fred Ebb); "Night in Tunisia" (Frank Paperelli, Dizzy Gillespie, John Birks); "Opus One" (Sid Garris, Cy Oliver); "Avalon" (Al Jolson, Vincent Rose); "You Brought a New Kind of Love to Me" (Sammy Fain, Irving Kahal; Pierre Norman Connor); "I'm Getting Sentimental Over You" (Ned Washington, George Bassman); "Song of India" (Rimsky-Korsakov); "Don't Blame Me" (Jimmy McHugh, Dorothy Fields); "Blue Moon" (Richard Rodgers, Lorenz Hart); "Don't Get Around Much Anymore," "Do Nothing Till You Hear From Me" (Duke Ellington, Bob Russell); "Once in a While" (Bud Green, Michael Edwards); "You Are My Lucky Star" (Nacio Herb Brown, Bert Freed); "It's a Wonderful World" (Jan Savitt, Jimmy Weston, Harold Adamson); "Hold Tight" (Leonard Kent, Leonard Ware, Edward Robinson, Willie Spottswood, Jerry Blandow); "Bugle Call Rag" (Elmer Schoebel, Billy Meyers, Jack Pettis); "Don't Be That Way" (Benny Goodman, Mitchell Parish, Edgar Sampson); "For All We Know" (S.M. Lewis, J. Fred Coots); Taking a Chance on Love" (Vernon Duke, Ted Fettler, John Latouche); "South America, Take It Away" (Harold Rome); "Just You, Just Me" (Raymond Klages, Jesse Greer); "The Man I Love" (George and Ira Gershwin); "Flip the Dip," "Game Over" (Georgie Auld); "Honeysuckle Rose" (Fats Waller, Andy Razaf); "Hazoy," "V. J. Stomp," "Bobby's Dream," "Once Again, Right Away" (Ralph Burns). **p**, Irwin Winkler, Robert Chartoff; **d**, Martin Scorsese; **cast**, Liza Minnelli, Robert De Niro, Lionel Stander, Barry Primus, Mary Kay Place, Georgie Auld, George Memmoli, Dick Miller, Murray Moston, Lenny Gaines, Jack Haley, Larry Kert; **w**, Earl Mac Rauch, Mardik Martin (based on a story by Rauch); **c**, Laszlo Kovacs (Panavision; DeLuxe Color); **m**, Ralph Burns; **ed**, Bert Lovitt, David Ramirez, Tom Rolf; **prod d**, Boris Leven; **art d**, Harry Kemm; **set d**, Robert DeVestel, Ruby R. Levitt; **spec eff**, Richard Albain.

News Is Made at Night ★★★ 1939; U.S.; 110m; FOX; B/W; Drama; Children: Cautionary. Foster is a newspaper editor who will do almost anything to increase circulation so he prints a campaign to free a man condemned to be executed while accusing a wealthy former criminal of a string of murders. Bari is a reporter who helps him although they're always at war with each other. Of course they love each other and after

the guilty and innocent are sorted out, we know the lovers will get together. Easy-going drama with some good comedy from the supporting cast. Not presently available in any video format. **p**, Edward Kaufman, Sol M. Wurtzel; **d**, Alfred L. Werker; **cast**, Preston Foster, Lynn Bari, Russell Gleason, George Barbier, Eddie Collins, Minor Watson, Charles Halton, Paul Harvey, Charles Lane, Betty Compson, Paul Fix, Paul Guilfoyle; **w**, John Larkin; **c**, Ernest Palmer; **ed**, Nick DeMaggio; **art d**, Richard Day, Chester Gore; **set d**, Thomas Little.

Newsfront ★★★ 1978; Australia; 110m; Australian Film Commission/New Yorker Films; Color/B/W; Drama; Children: Cautionary (MPAA: PG); **DVD**; **VHS**. Solid drama offering a lot of historical newsreel clips sees two brothers, Hunter and Kennedy, as newsreel cameramen for competing companies in Australia between the years 1949 and 1956, a period of social and political changes in the country. They both film breaking news shown in movie theaters, but, while Kennedy prefers to film events close to his home, Hunter is more aggressive and goes wherever events are happening. As competition from television news gets stronger, Hunter leaves for California, hoping to join the movie business in Hollywood. The drama is enhanced by the addition of actual color and black-and-white newsreel clips from events in those years. It's a nostalgic look at an early way of bringing news to the public, later replaced by television. Violence in some of the newsreels prohibits viewing by children. **p**, David Elfick; **d**, Phillip Noyce; **cast**, Bill Hunter, Wendy Hughes, Gerard Kennedy, Chris Haywood, John Ewart, Don Crosby, Angela Punch, John Clayton, John Dease, Bryan Brown, Lorna Lesley, Mark Holden, Bruce Spence; **w**, Noyce, Bob Ellis, Elfick, Philippe Mora; **c**, Vincent Monton; **m**, William Motzing; **ed**, John Scott; **prod d**, Lissa Coote; **art d**, Lawrence Eastwood; **set d**, Sally Campbell.

Next Stop, Greenwich Village ★★★ 1976; U.S.; 111m; FOX; Color; Comedy/Drama; Children: Unacceptable (MPAA: R); **DVD**; **VHS**. Fascinating but often disturbing coming-of-age tale has Baker as a young Jewish youth, who has recently graduated from college and who aspires to be an actor. He leaves his parents, Winters and Kellin, and their Brooklyn apartment and moves to Greenwich Village in 1953 with hopes of living the Bohemian life there, and is relieved to be away from his possessive mother. Baker gets a job in a health food store and takes acting lessons from Egan, who teaches him "Method" acting. He becomes friends with nutsy Brenner, suicide-prone Smith, poet Walken, and black homosexual Fargas. They form a tight-knit group, helping each other when in need, from arranging an abortion for Greene, a girl associated with their crowd, to raising rent money for Baker by throwing a party where guests chip in cash. Baker learns that a movie company is looking for actors to play juvenile delinquents and hopes he will be chosen. His parents arrive and Winters is shocked by how Baker lives and that Greene is his roommate, but Kellin summarily takes Winters back to Brooklyn. The group learns that Smith has killed herself and they comfort each other. Greene tells Baker she is Walken's lover and leaves with Walken and the others to go to Mexico. Baker is left behind, but there is still hope for Baker after he gets a call to go to Hollywood to test as one of the juvenile delinquents. The film is based on the Greenwich Village experiences of producer Mazursky, who played a juvenile delinquent in **The Blackboard Jungle**, 1955. Sexuality and suicide prohibit viewing by children. Songs: "Three to Get Ready," "Blue Rondo á la Turk," (Dave Brubeck); "Perdido" (Juan Tizol); "Yesterdays," "Little Brown Jug" (Joseph Winner). **p**, Paul Mazursky, Tony Ray; **d&w**, Mazursky; **cast**, Lenny Baker, Shelley Winters, Mike Kellin, Ellen Greene, Lois Smith, Christopher Walken, Michael Egan, Dori Brenner, Antonio Fargas, Lou Jacobi, Jeff Goldblum, Bill Murray; **c**, Arthur Ornitz; **m**, Bill Conti; **ed**, Richard Halsey; **prod d**, Phil Rosenberg; **set d**, Ed Stewart.

Next Stop Wonderland ★★★ 1998; U.S.; 104m; Robbins Entertainment/Miramax; Color; Comedy/Romance; Children: Unacceptable

(MPAA: R); **DVD**; **VHS**. Davis, a night nurse, and Gelfant, a former plumber who works at an aquarium and has hopes of becoming a marine biologist, keep crossing paths by accident. One night they see each other while being passengers on a Boston commuter rail line called Wonderland. Davis' matchmaking mother, Taylor, places a personal ad extolling the virtues of her daughter, hoping to find her a boyfriend. Some fellows respond to the ad and they bet on who will be first to get a French kiss from Davis. This leads to Davis and Gelfant discovering each other and falling in love while en route to Wonderland. A gentle and pleasing romantic comedy, Davis and Gelfant are standouts in their roles. Gutter language prohibits viewing by children. **p**, Mitchell Robbins, Laura Bernieri, Rachael Horovitz; **d**, Brad Anderson; **cast**, Hope Davis, Alan Gelfant, Philip Seymour Hoffman, Cara Buono, Callie Thorne, Ken Cheeseman, Pamela Hart, Diane Beckett, Jeremy Geidt, Dave Gilloran, Luz Alexandra, Emma Shaw, Kemp Harris; **w**, Anderson, Lyn Vaus; **c**, Uta Briesewitz; **m**, Claudio Ragazzi; **ed**, Anderson; **prod d**, Chad Detwiller; **art d**, Sophie Carlhian, Humberto Cordero; **set d**, Karen Weber; **spec eff**, Phil Cormier.

The Next Voice You Hear ★★★ 1950; U.S.; 82m; MGM; B/W; Drama; Children: Cautionary; **DVD**; **VHS**. Offbeat but fascinating tale has Whitmore and Davis having an average American family in a Los Angeles suburb with their young son, Gray, and are expecting a baby any day. One night, while listening to the radio, Whitmore hears a voice cut in on a program saying, "This is God. I'll be with you for the next few days." It turns out that everyone in the world listening to any radio heard the same thing. The voice returns over the next six evenings and tells listeners not to fear his pronouncements. Some people react positively, others negatively, but the messages compel all of those countless listeners to reevaluate their moral priorities and spiritual goals in life. Whitmore is exceptional in his role of the average man (if there can ever be such a person). *Author's Note*: Pantheon director Wellman was not that interested in directing this "message" film, but he undertook the job, as he told this author, "because I wanted to prove I could get that film in the can within three weeks and I did." In fact, Wellman completed the film within fourteen days and a cost of $220,000, far less than the $650,000 budget allocated for the production. Whitmore told this author that "Bill [Wellman] ran us ragged when we were doing that picture. Bill did his whirlwind takes, but we did not complain to him. You did not do that with Bill Wellman, a very rugged no-nonsense guy. Nancy [Davis; who would marry future U.S. President Ronald Reagan two years later] went along with Bill, too, as did the rest of the cast and crew members. When we were done, we thought we had been blown through the studio by a cyclone." **p**, Dore Schary; **d**, William A. Wellman; **cast**, James Whitmore, Nancy Davis, Gary Gray, Lillian Bronson, Art Smith, Tom D'Andrea, Jeff Corey, Frankie Darro, Marjorie Hoshelle, Douglas Kennedy, Sherry Jackson; **w**, Charles Schnee (based on a story by George Sumner Albee); **c**, William Mellor; **m**, David Raksin; **ed**, John Dunning; **art d**, Cedric Gibbons, Eddie Imazu; **set d**, Edwin B. Willis.

Niagara ★★★ 1953; U.S.; 92m; FOX; Color; Drama; Children: Unacceptable; **DVD**; **VHS**. Offbeat and riveting, this film noir entry is set at almost everyone's honeymoon nest, Niagara Falls, but for some of the couples visiting this placid place for lovers there will be little or no joy or bliss. Newlyweds Adams and his sultry wife, Peters, arrive to take up residence in a small bungalow. The neighboring bungalow is occupied by Cotten and his voluptuous wife, Monroe, who confides to Peters that her husband is considerably older than she is and she is worried about his mental condition as he has recently been released from an asylum. Peters tells Adams that all is not well with this couple, but the carefree Adams dismisses his wife's concerns. Monroe, meanwhile, cavorts about in tight-fighting dresses that define her curvaceous body and, at one point, does a suggestive dance to sensuous music being played by some admiring young men. When the obsessively jealous Cotten sees

Casey Adams and Jean Peters in *Niagara*, **1953.**

his wife performing this provocative dance, he goes to a record player and smashes the record. Peters later sees the promiscuous Monroe meeting Allan, her young lover, at a secret rendezvous, kissing and embracing the ardent swain. Peters overhears their plans, a scheme to murder Cotten, but when she tells this to Adams, he again thinks she is imagining things. Cotten then disappears and is later reported dead and Monroe is asked to go to the morgue to identify the body. When she does, she recoils in shock to see that the corpse is not Cotten, but that of her lover, Allan. She now knows that Cotten has been on to her cuckolding ways and she is now in fear for her life, rightly believing that hubby Cotten is now stalking her. She collapses at the sight of Allan's body and is taken to a hospital to recuperate. Meanwhile, Peters catches a glimpse of the now furtive Cotten, but when telling Adams, he says that she must be mistaken. (Adams is the classic dumb-cluck husband, who thinks his wife is a bit addlebrained, does not know her own mind, but loves her anyway.) Peters then meets Cotten and, fearful of him, runs away, but almost falls to her death before Cotten saves her. He insists that he is innocent and that his killing of Allan was simply self-defense in that Allan was trying to murder him. Peters is now in a quandary in deciding Cotten's guilt and hesitates about going to the police. Cotten then tracks Monroe, finding her and chasing her to the top of an observation tower where he strangles her to death. Peters is later shown with Adams as they prepare to take a boat ride. She is left alone when Adams and friends go to get gas and Cotten appears, fleeing from the police and commandeering the boat, sailing it out onto the waters that flow toward the lethal falls. Peters implores Cotten to turn the boat around, but he refuses. He takes pity on the hapless woman by steering the boat to a large rock and placing Peters on it before the boat is swept by the rushing current over the falls, where Cotten meets a watery death. Police by then have ordered a helicopter into the air and it hovers above the rock, plucking Peters to safety and returning her to the arms of Adams, who, finally, believes everything Peters has earlier told him. Hathaway directs this nerve-jangling thriller with great skill, and all of the leads provide exceptional performances. Monroe's persona—the jiggling, bouncing walk and the hushed words from her pouting lips—is in full and fleshy evidence throughout. She again gives one of her hallmark neurotic performances and is very convincing. MacDonald's photography, especially of the resplendent Niagara Falls, is outstanding and often breathtaking. **p**, Charles Brackett; **d**, Henry Hathaway; **cast**, Marilyn Monroe, Joseph Cotten, Jean Peters, Casey Adams, Denis O'Dea, Richard Allan, Don Wilson, Lurene Tuttle, Russell Collins, Will Wright, Harry Carey, Jr., Sean McClory, Minerva Urecal; **w**, Brackett, Walter Reisch, Richard Breen; **c**, Joe MacDonald (Technicolor); **m**, Sol Kaplan; **ed**, Barbara McLean; **art d**, Lyle Wheeler, Maurice Ransford; **set d**, Stuart Reiss; **spec eff**, Ray Kellogg.

Joseph Cotten and Marilyn Monroe in *Niagara*, 1953.

Nicholas and Alexandra ★★★★ 1971; U.S.; 183m; COL; Color; Biographical Drama; Children: Unacceptable (MPAA: GP); **DVD**; **VHS**. This carefully crafted and superlatively acted biopic portrays the life and times of Russia's last reigning monarch, Nicholas II (Romanov; 1868-1918), played by Jayston, and his wife Alexandra (Alix of Hesse; 1872-1918), played by Suzman. Their union is plagued by trouble from the beginning when Suzman marries heir apparent Jayston in 1894 after a long courtship, and where the Russian people resent her German origins. To overcome the sentiment against her, Suzman adopts and speaks the Russian language and embraces her husband's religion. Two years later, Jayston is crowned czar of Russia and Suzman becomes his empress. She bears four daughters for Jayston, these female offspring further aggravating the Russian people, who want a male heir to the throne. When Suzman finally gives birth to a son, Alexei (1904-1918), played by Noble, the couple tragically learn that he is afflicted by life-threatening hemophilia. It is learned that this terrible blue-blood disease is inherent in Suzman's lineage (tracing back to Queen Victoria of England). As Noble grows up, he is guarded night and day, the royal family fearful of the dangers of his disease. A slight fall or minor bruise might cause external or internal bleeding, and when this occasionally happens, court physicians are at a loss to treat the boy. The royal couple lives in constant anxiety about their fragile son, withdrawing from public life to family retreats where male bodyguards closely watch the boy's every move. As the family isolates itself, Jayston avoids important matters of state and the increasing unrest of the Russian public, including the many anti-government organizations that evolve, many of a revolutionary nature. When Noble suffers another fall and suffers serious internal bleeding, Suzman turns to a mystic she has recently met, Gregory Rasputin (1869-1916), played by Baker. He is a profligate and womanizing monk, a religious zealot who had a mesmerizing personality. He visits Noble in his bed chamber and there hypnotizes the boy, causing the bleeding to stop. Suzman believes that Baker has great spiritual powers and she appoints him the family's spiritual adviser. She becomes more and more dependent upon Baker as he treats Noble for each succeeding attack. Baker begins to exercise his powers by interfering with government matters to the point where he is the gray eminence behind the throne, and Jayston exercises less and less authority as the ruling monarch. When the royal family leaves the Winter Palace in St. Petersburg to go to a royal retreat on vacation, a massive but peaceful demonstration by workers and peasants approaches the palace (on January 22, 1905), with petitions they wish to give to the czar, asking for better working conditions. The Cossack troops guarding the palace order the demonstrators to disperse, and when they do not, the troops open fire on them, killing and wounding scores before driving the survivors away. This senseless slaughter is labeled "Bloody Sunday" by Bolshevik and communist ag-

itators. Marxist leaders Vladimir Lenin (1870-1924), played by Bryant, and Leon Trotsky (1879-1940), played by Cox, denounce Jayston as the culprit, calling him as "Bloody Nicholas." They begin a concerted campaign to unseat Jayston through revolution. Olivier (playing Count Sergei Witte, 1849-1915), Jayston's top political adviser, urges Jayston to establish democratic reforms in Russia by establishing the Duma (a parliament). The autocratic Jayston reluctantly agrees and Duma leaders like Alexander Kerensky (1881-1970), played by McEnery, demand more and more government concessions and liberties. Meanwhile, Porter, playing the liberal-minded Russian Prime Minister Count Peter Stolypin (1862-1911), is assassinated at the Kiev Opera House, one of many murders committed by the revolutionaries. Then Jayston learns that Baker, while attempting to run the government through blackmail and intimidation, is conducting all sorts of perversions among the aristocracy and he tries to ban the monk from the family household. Suzman, terrified that if Baker is no longer present to stem her son's hemophiliac attacks, Noble will die. She defies her husband and recalls Baker to court to watch over her son. When Germany declares war on Russia and WWI ensues in 1914, Jayston appoints his uncle, Andrews, to lead the ill-equipped and poorly organized Russian army into the field, but the Russians suffer one disastrous defeat after another, until, at the urging of Suzman, Jayston dismisses Andrews and assumes command of his troops even though Jayston is woefully inexperienced in leading what is now a disorganized rabble. Baker adds more strife by secretly attempting to take over the government, but his madman machinations are brought to an end by Potter, who plays Prince Felix Yusupov (1887-1967) after Potter inveigles Baker to a supposed assignation and kills him. Suzman is incensed by this assassination and banishes Potter from Russia. Meanwhile, Jayston's troops lose one battle after another until McEnery, who heads the Duma, demands that Jayston abdicate and that the Duma literally governs Russia. Jayston, despite Suzman's pleas to hold on to the throne for their son's sake, abdicates. The royal family then seeks asylum in England, France and elsewhere, but no country will give Jayston and his family sanctuary because of the oppressive measures his regime has earlier committed. The family and its loyal servants are then sent to Siberia where they are held captive by revolutionary troops until Byrant orders the entire family killed (at Yekaterinburg on July 17, 1918) by an execution squad in the basement of the house where they have been kept. They are shot and bayoneted to death, ending the last monarchy in Russia. Richly mounted, this production superbly and accurately recounts the traumatic last reign of the Romanovs under Shaffner's meticulous direction, presenting an awe-inspiring panorama of Russian history as never before seen on the screen, albeit this tragic story was also well told in **Rasputin and the Empress**, 1932; **Rasputin**, 1938; **Rasputin the Mad Monk**, 1966; and **Rasputin**, 1985. Jayston, Suzman, Noble, and the rest of the cast members are exceptional in their historic roles, and Baker, in particular, enacts the flamboyant and artful Rasputin to the hilt of his insidious character. The script, too, is finely written by Goldman (author of the play and film version of **The Lion in Winter**, 1968) and Bond, well researched and literate, and where all of its characters come to life through brilliant dialog. The action scenes are mesmerizing, and the dynamic score from Bennett enhances the film's many memorable scenes. The film received an Oscar nomination as Best Picture, and Suzman received an Oscar nomination as Best Actress. Yvonne Blake and Antonio Castillo received Oscars for Best Costume Design, and Archer, Box and Maxsted won an Oscar for Best Art Direction, as well as Vernon Dixon for Best Set Decoration. *Author's Note*: George Stevens was first assigned to helm this epic biopic, but he left the production for other chores and several other directors were tasked—Joseph L. Mankiewicz, Charles Jarrott, and Anthony Harvey—but all were dispatched by producer Spiegel, who finally brought Schaffner into the production, after Spiegel was impressed with viewing Schaffner's direction of the blockbuster historic film, **Patton**, 1970. The film was shot on location in Yugoslavia and in Spain. For more information on the last days of the ill-fated Nicholas II and his family, as well as the notorious Rasputin, see my work, *The Great Pictorial History of World Crime*, Volume I (History, Inc., 2004; Nicholas II: pages 79-83; Rasputin: pages 73-79). **p**, Sam Spiegel, Franklin J. Schaffner; **d**, Schaffner; **cast**, Michael Jayston, Janet Suzman, Harry Andrews, Irene Worth, Tom Baker, Jack Hawkins, Timothy West, Laurence Olivier, Eric Porter, Michael Redgrave, Maurice Denham, Vivian Pickles, Ian Holm, Roy Dotrice, Curt Jurgens, Diana Quick, Martin Potter, Alexander Knox, Jeremy Brett, Roderic Noble, Ania Marson, Lynne Frederick, Candace Glendenning, Fiona Fullerton, John McEnery, Michael Bryant, Brian Cox; **w**, James Goldman, Edward Bond (based on the book by Robert K. Massie); **c**, Freddie Young (Panavision; Eastmancolor); **m**, Richard Rodney Bennett; **ed**, Ernest Walter; **prod d**, John Box; **art d**, Ernest Archer, Jack Maxsted, Gil Parrondo; **set d**, Vernon Dixon; **spec eff**, Eddie Fowlie.

Nicholas Nickleby ★★★ 2002; U.K./U.S.; 132m; UA/MGM; Color; Drama; Children: Cautionary (MPAA: PG); **DVD**; **VHS**. This well-made historical drama is drawn from Charles Dickens' classic novel, and sees Hunnam as a British boy living a comfortable upper-class life in the country until his father dies in debt and the family becomes penniless. He moves to London with his mother, Gonet, and sister, Garai, with hopes that his rich but miserly uncle, Plummer, will help them, but, instead, he separates them. Mitchell is sent to work in a boarding school run by a mean headmaster, Broadbent, who beats his charges. When Broadbent beats Hunnam's crippled friend, Bell, they run away, intent on reuniting Hunnam with his mother and sister. Plummer attempts to get revenge on Hunnam by matching Garai with Fox. Some touring actors, Lane and Humphries, enlist the boys in their acting group. Hunnam later finds work in a law firm and all ends well with Hunnam and his family reunited and he falls in love with a beautiful girl, Hathaway, while the cruel and scheming Plummer gets his comeuppance. Well enacted and directed, this production provides a faithful adaptation of the book. Song: "On Ilkla Moor Baht'at" (traditional). This film is a remake of **Nicholas Nickleby**, 1947. **p**, Jeffrey Sharp, Simon Channing Williams, John N. Hart; **d&w**, Douglas McGrath (based on the novel by Charles Dickens); **cast**, Charlie Hunnam, Romola Garai, Tom Courtenay, Anne Hathaway, Jamie Bell, Christopher Plummer, Jim Broadbent, Juliet Stevenson, Stella Gonet, Andrew Havill, Henry McGrath, Hugh Mitchell, Poppy Rogers, Kevin McKidd, Edward Fox, Nathan Lane, Alan Cumming, Timothy Spall; **c**, Dick Pope; **m**, Rachel Portman; **ed**, Lesley Walker; **prod d**, Eve Stewart; **art d**, Tom Read, Andrew Grant; **spec eff**, Chris and Graham Longhurst, Keith Dawson, Andy Jeffery.

Night after Night ★★★ 1932; U.S.; 73m; PAR; B/W; Drama; Children: Unacceptable; **DVD**; **VHS**. Raft makes enough money as a boxer to leave the ring and buy a speakeasy in the 1920s. He falls for Cummings who was a society girl until her father lost a fortune in the stock market crash. At first she thinks he's too much of a mug for her, but she finally falls for him. It was Raft's first starring role and the first talking film for West who stole the picture with her swinging hips and wisecracks. When a hatcheck girl admires her jewelry and exclaims "Goodness!," West retorts: "Goodness had nothing to do with it, dearie." It is suggested throughout most of the film that West's wealth stems from her shady past, possibly a bordello madam until it is revealed that her riches come from the fact that she owns a chain of beauty parlors. *Author's Note*: This was this first time director Mayo worked with West, the voluptuous actress sauntering through his sets and doing exactly what she pleased in every scene. "I couldn't do a thing with her," Mayo told this author. "She was a big star then and Paramount's front office thought she walked on water. When I suggested a few acting points to her, she would only give me that crooked smile and say: "You have a lot to learn, sonny." Raft, a relative newcomer to Hollywood, was equally dumbfounded when West managed to move in front of him in every scene they had together, telling this author that "she stole everything in that picture but the cameras. She was very clever and tricked

Cary Grant and Ginny Simms in *Night and Day*, 1946.

us all up with her moves and jumping cues so that we all looked like a bunch of mannequins or props just standing around so that she could deliver her lines." Raft and West would not appear on screen together until making a comedy forty-four years later, **Sextette**, 1978. They both died two years after that film in 1980 within two days of each other, Raft at age eighty-five and West at eighty-seven. **p**, William LeBaron; **d**, Archie Mayo; **cast**, George Raft, Constance Cummings, Wynne Gibson, Mae West, Alison Skipworth, Roscoe Karns, Louis Calhern, Bradley Page, Al Hill, Harry Wallace, Bill Elliott, Tom Kennedy, Dennis O'Keefe; **w**, Vincent Lawrence, Kathryn Scola, Mae West (based on the novel *Single Night* by Louis Bromfield); **c**, Ernest Haller.

Night and Day ★★★ 1946; U.S.; 128m; WB; Color; Biographical Drama/Musical; Children: Acceptable; **DVD**; **VHS**. Though this film offers a sketchy portrait of the life of the brilliant composer Cole Porter (1891-1964), ably enacted by Grant, its major attractions are the wonderful and memorable songs created by this musical genius. Grant is first shown at Yale where he begins composing his tunes with the encouragement of Woolley (who plays himself as he was a lifelong friend of Porter's in real life), a professor at that august institution. (Porter wrote more than 300 songs while he was a student at Yale.) Grant, upon graduation, struggles to sell his songs while playing and singing with Ginny Simms in a NYC music store (although Porter, in real life, had no such labors in that he came from a very wealthy family in Indiana) until he decides to put on his own musical show, and this he does with Woolley's aid after Woolley persuades many rich Yale alumni to invest in the production. The musical opens, but just as WWI breaks out, dimming its prospects. Grant then enlists in the French army and is seen next in a bombed out village, listening to Senegalese troops chanting as they trudge past him, a haunting chant that causes him to begin a composition, but a German barrage interrupts his concentration and a shell explodes nearby, severely wounding him in the legs. While recovering in a hospital, Grant is attended to by Smith, a nurse, who falls in love with him. During his recuperation, Grant tries to remember what he originally composed in that French village and finally produces the unforgettable "Begin the Beguine." (This element of the film is based on some fact, albeit Porter believed that he never fully recaptured some of the elements of his original composition, and whenever he heard the song, he had some reservations about it.) Smith sees Grant recuperated and sent stateside where he has a string of musical show successes and he later meets Smith again in London and they marry. Grant, however, is not a stay-at-home husband, always on the move to produce more musical shows and, because of his lack of attention to her, Smith departs. Grant's reputation soars as he becomes a stellar figure in the musical world, but only then does his reserved family acknowledge his achieve-

Cary Grant and Monty Woolley in *Night and Day,* 1946.

ments, particularly his grandfather, Stephenson, the family's wealthy patriarch, who wanted Grant to become a lawyer (as did Porter's multimillionaire grandfather in real life). Stephenson finally meets with Grant at the Indiana homestead and they have a drink to toast to Grant's success, where Stephenson finally accords Grant's achievements with personal approval. Stephenson then dies, and while riding a horse in a rainstorm, Grant is thrown when lightning strikes and again injures his legs. He is in and out of the hospital many times where his injured legs are operated upon. While in the hospital, he listens on the radio as his new compositions are played and sung. The finale of this biopic ends when Grant once more recuperates and appears at a Yale alumni gathering, welcomed by Woolley and walking on two canes. Just before the fadeout, Smith reappears to embrace him and it is suggested that they may reunite to seek happiness together. Grant is exceptionally charming in his sensitive role, and Woolley is his entertaining and witty self. Porter's songs are wonderfully showcased with the great Ginny Simms and the unforgettable Mary Martin and others warbling and dancing to his tunes (the dance ensembles are also exceptional, along with the sets, one of which is an outdoor shot at a pool, which is Pickfair, the estate owned by Mary Pickford and Douglas Fairbanks Sr.), albeit many of these memorable songs are presented in truncated form. Curtiz directs with his usual economic skills, rightly accenting the musical aspect of Porter's career and eschewing the nagging nuances of his personal life. Songs (music and lyrics by Cole Porter): "Night and Day" (1932), "Bulldog" (1911), "Blow, Gabriel, Blow" (1934), "In the Still of the Night" (1937), "I'm in Love Again" (1924), "You've Got that Thing" (1929), "An Old Fashioned Garden" (1919), "Let's Do It" (1928), "You Do Something to Me" (1929), "Miss Otis Regrets" (1934), "I'm Unlucky at Gambling" (1929), "What Is This Thing Called Love?" (1929), "I Get a Kick Out of You" (1934), "Rosalie" (1937), "I've Got You Under My Skin" (1936), "Anything Goes" (1934), "Just One of Those Things" (1935), "Love for Sale," (1930), "You're the Top" (1934), "Easy to Love" (1934), "Do I Love You?" (1939), "My Heart Belongs to Daddy" (1938), "Don't Fence Me In" (1934), "Begin the Beguine" (1935); additional songs: "Rock-a-bye Baby" (1886; music: Effie I. Canning), "I Wonder What's Become of Sally" (1924; music: Milton Ager; lyrics: Jack Yellen), "On the Rue de la Paix" (music: Werner R. Heymann), "Bridal Chorus (Here Comes the Bride)" (1850; from Lohengrin by Richard Wagner). Another wholly different slant on the gifted Porter was presented in another and well-done biopic/musical on his life, **De-Lovely**, 2004, that incorporates Porter's gay life, a subject that Hollywood would never touch when producing this film with Grant. *Author's Note*: Porter lived with his wife Linda Lee Thomas in a marriage of convenience as he was homosexual (as was his intimate friend, Woolley). Grant told this author that "playing Cole Porter was like playing a chaperone to his music—that came first

in **Night and Day** and Curtiz [the director] laid down the law on that with all of us right from the beginning. Why not? All everybody wanted to see and hear was his great music. I knew Cole Porter and I was always impressed with him as being a gentleman of great taste. He did not flaunt his gay life. In fact, he guarded that part of his life from the rest of the world like a bulldog. I don't think anyone knew in the days when we made **Night and Day** that he was gay, except insiders in the musical and show business world and they did not talk about it because they all had great respect for Porter, no more than anyone talked about George Gershwin or Lorenz Hart being gay. Nobody cared then and I don't think they do now [in 1984]. These people gave us some of the greatest songs ever written. So did Irving Berlin and Jerome Kern and nobody talks about the fact that they were not gay and were happily married to fine ladies. The way Hollywood is going now, I suppose some day they will make a picture about Porter and show his homosexuality, but they will only be doing that to cash in on some cheap sensationalism and that will be out of place because his music is what should be remembered." **p**, Arthur Schwartz; **d**, Michael Curtiz; **cast**, Cary Grant, Alexis Smith, Monty Woolley, Ginny Simms, Jane Wyman, Eve Arden, Victor Francen, Alan Hale, Dorothy Malone, Tom D'Andrea, Selena Royle, Donald Woods, Mary Martin, Carlos Ramírez, Robert Arthur, Lynn Baggett, John Alvin, Herman Bing, Joyce Compton, Jimmie Dodd, Joe Kirkwood, Jr., Fay McKenzie, Mel Tormé; **w**, Charles Hoffman, Leo Townsend, William Bowers (based on the career of Cole Porter, adapted by Jack Moffitt); **c**, Peverell Marley, William V. Skall, Bert Glennon (Technicolor); **m**, Cole Porter, Max Steiner; **ed**, David Weisbart; **art d**, John Hughes; **set d**, Armor Marlowe; **spec eff**, Robert Burks.

Night and the City ★★★★ 1950; U.K.; 95m; FOX; B/W; Crime Drama; Children: Unacceptable; **DVD**; **VHS**. This riveting and often frightening film noir tale has Widmark as an American in London living the life of a petty hustler and con man. He has ambitious plans to be an underworld kingpin, but his wild schemes never work out. One day he sees Zbyszko, the most famous Greco-Roman wrestler in the world, at a wrestling arena run by the wrestler's son, Lom. Widmark dreams up a get-rich scheme to be Zbyszko's manager, but it backfires on him. He promotes a match between Zbyszko and a mountain called the Strangler (Mazurki). Zbyszko wins the brutal match, but the strain of the wrestling match causes him to die of a stroke soon afterward. Underworld boss Lom now decrees Widmark's murder in revenge for his father's death, and all of the city's gangsters mobilize against him. He is tracked by killers everywhere, seeking the solace of the only woman who still loves him, Tierney, but his furtive actions avail him nothing. He is finally tracked down and killed by hit men. Pantheon director Dassin, who had directed a string of strong film noir classics (**Brute Force**, 1947; **The Naked City**, 1948; **Thieves Highway**, 1949), provides another dark and brooding entry with a terrific performance by Widmark, and where Sullivan, Lom, Withers, and Tierney are standouts. Greene's stark and uncompromising photography captures the seamy side of London as few others have ever done. Songs: "Here's to Champagne" (Noel Gay), "The Right Kind" (Lionel Newman, Charles Henderson), "Don't Fence Me In" (Cole Porter), "I'm Looking Over a Four-Leaf Clover" (Harry M. Woods), "Again" (Lionel Newman), "She Was Poor but She Was Honest" (R. P. Weston), "There's Yes! Yes! In Your Eyes" (Joseph H. Santly), "Yours (Quiereme mucho)" (Gonzalo Roig), "It Happens Every Spring" (Josef Myrow). This film was remade with the same title in 1992, and was almost as good as the original. *Author's Note*: Widmark told this author that "**Night and the City** offered me a great role, one of the best I ever got. In my first film, **Kiss of Death** [1947] I play a mindless killer, but in **Night and the City** I had much more to work with, a character with a lot of dimensions, a desperate 'thinking man's' crook, you could call Harry Fabian, my character. He is too smart for his own good and thinks himself into an early grave." Mazurki told this author that "my role in **Night and the City** was one of the most difficult I ever played. I wrestle a professional wrestler [Zbyszko] in that film and he did not hold back anything in our match together. I was sore for weeks after that, but I kept my mouth shut about it, as I did not want to lose any roles in the future where I might be called upon to again be bounced around like a sack of wheat. Big guys like me had to put up with that all the time. That's how we made our living." Excessive violence prohibits viewing by children. **p**, Samuel G. Engel; **d**, Jules Dassin; **cast**, Richard Widmark, Gene Tierney, Googie Withers, Hugh Marlowe, Francis L. Sullivan, Herbert Lom, Stanislaus Zbyszko, Mike Mazurki, Derek Blomfield, Clifford Buckton, Kay Kendall; **w**, Jo Eisinger, Austin Dempster, William E. Watts (based on the novel by Gerald Kersh); **c**, Max Greene (Mutz Greenbaum); **m**, Franz Waxman, Benjamin Frankel; **ed**, Nick De Maggio, Sidney Stone; **art d**, C.P. Norman.

Night and the City ★★★ 1992; U.S.; 105m; Penta Films/FOX; Color; Crime Drama; Children: Unacceptable (MPAA: R); **DVD**. In this good remake of the 1950 film noir classic, De Niro is a failed New York lawyer having an affair with Lange, a waitress married to Gorman. De Niro has just lost a court case against a famous boxing promoter, King, and wants revenge by catching him in another illegal operation. Without knowing a thing about the boxing racket, he gets help from several people including Warden, King's older brother, who is a retired boxer living in an old age home. They start a partnership where they assemble a number of young boxers and where De Niro thinks he will get rich by promoting professional boxing matches, taking away revenues from King. It all backfires when Warden gets into an argument with one of King's fighters and dies of a heart attack and then King takes his revenge out on De Niro, his goons sending De Niro to the hospital, and where, while on a stretcher being put into an ambulance, De Niro comes to his senses, saying: "Boxing! I must have been out of my mind." Song: "Love Doesn't Matter" (Akon). Violence and gutter language prohibit viewing by children. **p**, Irwin Winkler, Jane Rosenthal, Rob Cowan; **d**, Winkler; **cast**, Robert De Niro, Jessica Lange, Alan King, Jack Warden, Eli Wallach, Barry Primus, Gene Kirkwood, Clem Caserta, Anthony Canarozzi, Regis Philbin, Margo Winkler; **w**, Richard Price (based on the novel by Gerald Kersh) **c**, Tak Fujimoto; **m**, Newton Howard; **ed**, David Brenner; **prod d**, Peter S. Larkin; **art d**, Charley Beale; **set d**, Robert J. Franco.

Night at the Museum ★★★ 2006; U.S./U.K.; 108m; FOX; Color; Adventure/Fantasy; Children: Cautionary (MPAA: PG); **BD**; **DVD**. Humorous and action packed, this adventure has Stiller as an unemployed and divorced not-too-bright man, who gets a job as a night security guard at the New York Museum of Natural History. As the sun sets, everything in the museum comes to life. He learns that these strange events are instigated by an old Egyptian stone that was donated to the museum in 1950 and brings the statues of animals and famous people to life until dawn. Stiller brings his son with him to spend a night as three former night watchmen break into the museum to try to steal the magical stone. Stiller gets help from the historical statues in the museum to stop the thieves and save the museum. Stiller is very funny as the bumbling guard in this innocent adventure, which is especially exciting to see in IMAX format. A sequel followed, **Night at the Museum: Battle of the Smithsonian**, 2009. Songs: "Eye of the Tiger" (James Peterik, Frank M. Sullivan III), "Dem Bones" (traditional), "Tequila" (Chuck Rio), "Mandy" (Richard Kerr, Scott English), "Camptown Races" (Stephen Foster), "She'll Be Comin' Round the Mountain" (traditional), "Weapon of Choice" (Ashley Slater, Sly Stone, Bootsy Collins, Norman Cook, Mista Lawnge, Andres Titus), "September" (Maurice White, Al McKay, Allee Willis), "Tonight" (Dameon Beckett, Ali Dee, Zach Danziger, Julian Davis, Anna Dafonesca, Dave Kelly), "Friday Night" (Tom Fletcher, Danny Jones, Dougie Poynter, Jason Perry, Julian Emery, Daniel Carter). **p**, Chris Columbus, Michael Barnathan, Shawn Levy, Josh McLaglen; **d**, Shawn Levy; **cast**, Ben Stiller, Carla Gugino, Ricky Gervais, Paul Rudd, Dick Van Dyke, Anne Meara, Mickey Rooney, Robin Williams, Bill Cobs, Jake Cherry, Owen

Sig Rumann, Margaret Dumont and Groucho Marx in *A Night at the Opera,* **1935.**

Wilson; **w**, Robert Ben Garant, Thomas Lennon (based on the novel by Milan Trenc); **c**, Guillermo Navarro; **m**, Alan Silvestri; **ed**, Don Zimmerman; **prod d**, Claude Par; **art d**, Michael Diner, Helen Jarvis, Bridget McGuire; **set d**, Lin Macdonald; **spec eff**, Michael Bird, Steven Kirshoff, William H. Orr.

Night at the Museum: Battle of the Smithsonian ★★★ 2009; U.S./Canada; 104m; Color; Adventure/Fantasy; Children: Cautionary (MPAA: PG); **BD**; **DVD**. A sequel to **Night at the Museum**, 2006, this entertaining film, hallmarked by exceptional special effects (as was the original), takes us on more adventures of Stiller, a night watchman in the New York Museum of Natural History. This time he has to rescue two friends, Wilson and Coogan, who have been shipped to the museum by mistake. The museum is being remodeled and the exhibits are going into storage, but by mistake so are the two live men who play exhibits. Songs: "My Heart Will Go On" (James Horner, Will Jennings), "Lovebug" (The Jonas Brothers), "I Only Have Eyes for You" (Harry Warren, Al Dubin), "Ride of the Valkyries" (Richard Wagner), "Blue Moon" (Richard Rodgers, Lorenz Hart), "Life in Technicolor" (Guy Berryman, Jonathan Buckland, William Champion, Christopher Martin, Jon Hopkins), "Fly with Me" (The Jonas Brothers, Greg Garowsky), "Seventh Cavalry Regiment" (traditional), "Bugle Call Rag" (Billy Meyers, Elmer Schoebel, Jack Pettis), "More Than a Woman" (Barry Gibb, Maurice Gibb, Robin Gibb), "That's the Way I Like It" (Harry Wayne Casey, Richard Finch), "Gloriana" (Mark Ford, Stephen Metcalfe), "Let's Groove" (Maurice White, Wayne Vaughn). **p**, Chris Columbus, Michael Barnathan, Shawn Levy; **d**, Levy; **cast**, Ben Stiller, Amy Adams, Owen Wilson, Hank Azaria, Robin Williams, Christopher Guest, Alain Chabat, Steve Coogan, Ricky Gervais, Bill Hader, Jon Bernthal; **w**, Robert Ben Garant, Thomas Lennon; **c**, John Schwartzman; **m**, Alan Silvestri; **ed**, Dean and Don Zimmerman; **prod d**, Claude Par; **art d**, Michael Diner, Anthony Dunne, Helen Jarvis, Grant Van Der Slagt; **set d**, Lin Macdonald; **spec eff**, William H. Orr.

A Night at the Opera ★★★★ 1935; U.S.; 96m; MGM; B/W; Musical Comedy; Children: Acceptable; **DVD**; **VHS**. The manic Marx Brothers are at it again in this music-filled comedy, presenting a dazzling array of on-screen, often side-splitting, comedic scenes while singers Jones and Carlisle deliver many a scintillating song. Groucho is, as usual, the conniving catalyst for the story, a confidence man to the bone. He is seen in Milan with brothers Harpo and Chico, where Groucho is attempting to persuade Dumont, a dowager with an estate of $8 million, to financially back an opera company run by the pompous Rumann and which features singers King and Carlisle, taking the troupe to New York and where they will have a great success, or so Groucho insists. Though

Harpo Marx with trombone in *A Night at the Opera*, 1935.

Carlisle is sweetness personified, King is a strutting stuffed shirt and Carlisle would prefer another singing partner, particularly Jones, after she encounters the street-singing tenor. Dumont finally succumbs to Groucho's incessant blandishments and barrages of operatic victory, especially after he guarantees that he will introduce Dumont to NYC's highest in high society, and she funds the project. All board an ocean liner bound for New York (and before the sailing Carlisle, from the railing of the ship, and Jones, standing on the dock, exquisitely sing the memorable "Alone" to each other). The impoverished Jones has no money to journey with Carlisle to NYC so Groucho inadvertently smuggles him, as well as his brothers Harpo and Chico, on board, all hidden in a large trunk. The stateroom Groucho is given provides one of the most hilarious scenes in any film, so cramped and small that anyone other than Groucho caught occupying that closet-like space would normally be charged with adultery. After the stowaways emerge from the trunk, Groucho orders food, along with every other kind of imaginable service from the ship's workers and soon the cabin is crammed to the gills with waiters spilling food, manicurists trying to hone nails, plumbers trying to fix pipes that are not broken, maids trying to make up a bed that is laden with people. Groucho, struggling to remain on his feet remarks to the audience: "Is it my imagination or is it getting crowded in here?" The pressure of what seems to be more than a dozen or so squirming and struggling bodies erupts when Dumont opens the stateroom door to see the whole bunch spill out into the outside corridor in a colossal crash. (Dumont was padded for the scene so that when the crowd tumbled on top of her, she remained unharmed.) The stowaways play a cat-and-mouse game with stewards and ship's officers until the ship arrives in NYC and the brothers escape detection and disembark while disguised as three foreign dignitaries, after clipping off their beards and pasting them to their own faces and where they are hailed as important visitors, making nonsense speeches, but they flee after Harpo's beard falls off, taking refuge in an upscale hotel with dogged detective O'Connor at their heels. O'Connor locates Groucho in a suite of rooms, and Chico and Harpo move from one room to another, in a bed-hopping chase, confusing O'Connor (as well as viewers). That night the brothers appear at the opera, but the production is in disarray before the curtain goes up after Carlisle tells off King for making advances and is fired. Groucho, too, is fired, but takes his revenge by bollixing up the night's performance. The opera does not open with the scheduled Verdi composition, but with "Take Me Out to the Ball Game," because Harpo and Chico, at Groucho's instigation, have switched the orchestra's sheet music, startling the theatergoers. Marx mayhem then ensues, with Groucho selling peanuts to the audience, Harpo swinging across the stage to cause sets to collapse and Chico arranging to have King kidnapped. Carlisle and lover Jones go on to save the show and become overnight

sensations. The combination of the Marx Brothers' zany comedy and a bevy of memorable songs proved to be a box office bonanza for MGM, returning to the studio coffers more than $3 million in its initial release. Songs: "Il Trovatore" (1853; Giuseppe Verdi), "Alone" (1935; Nacio Herb Brown, Arthur Freed), "All I Do Is Dream of You" (1934; Nacio Herb Brown), "Take Me Out to the Ball Game" (1908; Albert von Tilzer), "Cosi-Cosa" (1935; Bronislau Kaper, Walter Jurman), "I Pagliacci" (1892; Ruggero Leoncavallo), "Sing Ho for the Open Highway! Sing Ho for the Open Road!" (unknown composer), "Santa Lucia" (1849; traditional Neapolitan song), "When the Moon Comes Over the Mountain" (1931; Kate Smith, Howard Johnson, Harry M. Woods), "The Prisoner's Song (If I Had the Wings of an Angel)" (1924; Guy Massey). *Author's Note*: This was the sixth of the thirteen Marx Brothers films and it is one of the funniest. This was their first film for MGM, and where younger brother Zeppo no longer appeared with them, deciding to go into business and stay off the screen. The brothers had been dropped by Paramount, but Irving Thalberg, the production chief at MGM, thought highly of them, and put them into this production. Before the cameras rolled, however, Thalberg wanted to make sure their routines would work and sent the boys on a road tour to four cities where they gave twenty-four performances while writers Kaufman and Ryskind sat in the audience, polishing the gags and subduing the slapstick (if that was humanly possible), until all the routines the brothers had used years earlier on the stage worked for the film. Thalberg was happy with the final script, but studio chief Louis B. Mayer scoffed at the project, telling his boy genius that "those clowns are only going to waste our time with a picture that won't make any money." In this, Mayer was completely wrong and Thalberg was right. Groucho told this author that "Irving [Thalberg] saved our careers. We got thrown out into the cold at Paramount and he took us in at MGM—through the back door, of course. He told us to stay away from Louis B. Mayer, who didn't like us, so I went out of my way to accidentally bump into Mayer whenever I could and where I shook his hand until it almost fell off, telling him what a wise man he was for hiring us. He gave me nothing but a cold stare until after **A Night at the Opera** was released and made a lot of money. Then Mayer went out of his way to shake *my* hand and I told him that I thought he was a wiser man than the wise man I thought him to be when we first met. To tell you the truth, the wisest man in the front office at MGM was Irving Thalberg." **p**, Irving Thalberg; **d**, Sam Wood; **cast**, Groucho Marx, Chico Marx, Harpo Marx, Kitty Carlisle, Allan Jones, Walter Woolf King, Siegfried Rumann, Margaret Dumont, Edward Keane, Robert Emmett O'Connor, **w**, George S. Kaufman, Morrie Ryskind, Al Boasberg, Bert Kalmar, Buster Keaton (not credited), Harry Ruby (based on a story by James Kevin McGuinness); **c**, Merritt B. Gerstad; **m**, Herbert Stothart; **ed**, William LeVanway; **art d**, Cedric Gibbons, Ben Carre; **set d**, Edwin B. Willis.

Night Court ★★★ 1932; U.S.; 92m; MGM; B/W; Crime Drama; Children: Unacceptable; **DVD**; **VHS**. Taut crime tale has Page as the wife of taxi driver Holmes, who accidentally obtains information that could destroy the career of a night court judge, Huston. Corrupt to the bone, Huston learns that Page has this incriminating data and, to shut her up, puts her in jail on a trumped-up charge. Holmes sets out to expose the injustice, and, after risking his life, gets enough evidence to free his wife, clear her name, and send Huston to prison. Huston, Holmes and Page are standouts in this fascinating tale, speedily directed by Van Dyke. **d**, W.S. Van Dyke; **cast**, Phillips Holmes, Walter Huston, Anita Page, Lewis Stone, Mary Carlisle, John Miljan, Jean Hersholt, Tully Marshall, Noel Francis, Reginald Barlow, Frederick Burton; **w**, Bayard Veiller, Lenore J. Coffee (based on the play by Mark Hellinger, Charles Beahan); **c**, Norbert Brodine; **ed**, Ben Lewis; **art d**, Cedric Gibbons.

The Night Fighters ★★★ 1960; U.K./U.S.; 90m; D.R.M. Productions/UA; B/W; Drama; Children: Unacceptable; **VHS**. Well-made tense drama sees Mitchum, an American, joining the Irish Republican Army in 1941 to help drive the British out of Northern Ireland during World War II (1939-1945). He changes his mind when the IRA decides to collaborate with the Nazis, who promise their freedom from Britain. Mitchum thinks the IRA is misguided, so he betrays their cause and then escapes to Liverpool. Garnett directs with skill, and Mitchum presents a riveting performance as he weighs his allegiances and his loyalty to friend Harris, a dedicated IRA fighter. **p**, Raymond Stross; **d**, Tay Garnett; **cast**, Robert Mitchum, Richard Harris, Anne Heywood, Dan O'Herlihy, Cyril Cusack, Eileen Crowe, Niall MacGinnis, Marianne Benet, Christopher Rhodes, Harry Brogan; **w**, Robert Wright Campbell (based on the novel *A Terrible Beauty* by Arthur Roth); **c**, Stephen Dade; **m**, Cedric Thorpe Davie; **ed**, Peter Tanner; **prod d**, John Stoll; **set d**, Josie MacAvin.

Night Flight ★★★ 1933; U.S.; 84m; MGM; B/W; Adventure; Children: Acceptable; **DVD**. An all-star cast well directed by Brown provides many exciting action scenes in this aviation adventure tale, where John Barrymore heads a South American airline that survives by hazardously flying mail over the treacherous Andes Mountain range. Barrymore rigidly insists that his pilots complete their missions at any cost, even at the risk of losing their lives. Gable and Gargan are Barrymore's two most trusted pilots, proving their bravery by following Barrymore's dictates. Lionel Barrymore (John's real-life brother) is the chief foreman for the airlines and, while attempting to protect the lives of the pilots, is in constant confrontations with John, who tells him to stop fraternizing with the aviators, an order Lionel ignores. Gable undertakes one mission while flying through a dangerous storm, communicating with Barrymore via his plane's radio. Then the radio communications cease and Barrymore must break the news to Hayes, Gable's wife, that her husband has been lost. Then Gargan, who is married to Loy, undertakes the same mission, and, he, too, is killed while attempting to deliver the mail. John Barrymore is at the center of this taut drama and dominates its many scenes with his dynamic persona. The theme for this tale would later be adopted for **Only Angels Have Wings**, 1939. *Author's Note*: Director Brown told this author that "MGM was a studio that wanted to pack all of its top stars in one picture after another to assure box office success and **Night Flight** was one of those pictures. [MGM had considerable success in packaging its stars in such films as **Grand Hotel**, 1932, and **Dinner at Eight**, 1933.] Gable was not too happy with the producer, Selznick, thinking that Selznick was typecasting him as a dispensable actor where his character would die or get lost somewhere in the story and Gable was wary of Selznick for years after, even when they did **Gone with the Wind** [1939] together. The Barrymore brothers were terrific in **Night Flight**, but, as usual, fought over every scene together like cats and dogs. In one of their loud arguments, I stepped in and said, 'Why don't you boys stop all this bickering and try to get along with one another?' and John replied with blinking eyes: 'That's like asking us to drop dead.' They liked all that nonsense and I think they thought that all those battles they had with each other got their blood boiling and helped them give better performances. They were gifted people but very strange brothers. In one scene, Lionel has no words and must stand silent as John lectures him, but he nevertheless found a way to steal the scene. When he left the room, he paused at the door and scratched his behind. They were very clever about all that." Brown, who was a flier, provides many exciting aerial sequences with the help of special effects expert Arnold "Buddy" Gillespie, who was also a pilot and was married to the celebrated aviatrix Ruth Elder. Selznick insisted that he be given an on-screen producer's credit, a rarity at MGM at that time, but the front studio acquiesced and thereafter all the producers at that studio insisted that their names be credited to the films they produced. "Selznick promoted himself into a Hollywood big shot that way," Brown said to this author, "and everyone knew he was angling to eventually set himself up as an independent producer. I give him credit, though, and tell you that he was also a very talented guy who instinctively knew what stories would be successful films and he

Jerome Cowan, Edward G. Robinson and Virginia Bruce in *Night Has a Thousand Eyes*, 1948.

was almost always right." **p**, David O. Selznick; **d**, Clarence Brown; **cast**, John Barrymore, Helen Hayes, Clark Gable, Lionel Barrymore, Robert Montgomery, Myrna Loy, William Gargan, C. Henry Gordon, Leslie Fenton, Helen Jerome Eddy; **w**, Oliver H.P. Garrett (based on the novel *Vol de nuit* by Antoine de Saint-Exupéry); **c**, Oliver T. Marsh; **m**, Herbert Stothart; **ed**, Hal C. Kern; **art d**, Cedric Gibbons, Alexander Toluboff; **spec eff**, A. Arnold Gillespie.

Night Has a Thousand Eyes ★★★ 1948; U.S.; 81m; PAR; B/W; Mystery; Children: Unacceptable; **VHS**. Robinson is fascinating as a troubled spiritualist, who predicts dire events for people close to him. He is first seen when Lund and his wife, Russell, come to him after Lund has saved Russell from committing suicide. They explain that Russell was about to take her life after Robinson predicted that Russell would meet that fate. Robinson explains that he has been burdened with a special "gift" to see the future, especially tragic events, saying that "I had become a reverse zombie....The world was dead and I was living." In flashback, we see Robinson as a spiritualist performing on the stage and assisted by fetching Bruce. He is able to pick winners in horse races, giving these tips to his partner, Cowan, who becomes rich through his winning bets, but Robinson places no importance on such futuristic information until he tells a woman in the audience one night to go home quickly after spiritually seeing the woman's young boy threatened by a house fire. The woman rushes home just in time to save her child, an event that rattles Robinson. He next envisions Bruce dying in childbirth and this vision so unnerves him that he quits the stage and lives in isolation for many years. He ends his hermit-like existence after learning that Bruce, who has since married Cowan, has, indeed, died in childbirth, and he has another vision that sees Cowan dying in a plane crash. He moves to Los Angeles to be near Cowan and his daughter, Russell, somehow planning to warn them of his terrible vision. He tells Russell that her father is about to die in that plane crash and begs her to stop Cowan from participating in a coast-to-coast aerial speed race, but Russell's husband, Lund, believes Robinson is deranged. Russell, however, believes Robinson, although she is unable to prevent her father's death and, after Cowan dies and Robinson again predicts that Russell will meet a similar fate, Russell attempts to take her life, but is saved by Lund. In flash-forward, we now see Lund and Russell confronting Robinson, who insists that Russell will soon lose her life. Lund becomes enraged, convinced that Robinson is driving his wife to commit suicide and has him arrested by police. Robinson, however, is soon released after he proves his ability as a soothsayer after telling police that a prisoner will soon commit suicide. When that prisoner takes his life, Robinson is set free. He rushes to Russell's home just in time to see Cowan's partner, the man who had arranged for Cowan's death in the plane crash

Groucho Marx and Lisette Verea in *A Night in Casablanca*, **1946.**

in order to seize Cowan's assets, about to kill Russell. Robinson races forward to stop the killer, but police, who have followed him, think he is about to harm Russell, and, while capturing Russell's assailant, they shoot and kill Robinson. Inside one of Robinson's pockets is found a note the clairvoyant has written, one that has predicted his own death. Tense and eerie throughout, Farrow presents a chilling tale where Robinson mesmerizes and where the supporting players are all standouts in their roles, its many truly frightening scenes enhanced by a bone tingling score from Young. *Author's Note*: This was not the first film in which Robinson had played a character blessed or cursed with the gift to see the dire events of the future, having previously appeared in a similar role in **Flesh and Fantasy**, 1943. Robinson told this author that "the character I play in **Night Has a Thousand Eyes** is completely fictional and I will admit that this man is a walking plague. I have heard about clairvoyants being able to predict the future, but my character sees death and destruction around every corner and I do not believe anyone can be that accurate about such possible coming events. The film presents a lot of hokum, but it was well directed—John Farrow is a top-notch director. As to the story, well, I did that film to make money, not to convince anyone that my character was the all-seeing eye of the future. People will believe what they want about such phenomena." This author was compelled to believe in such phenomena after many firsthand experiences demonstrated the reality of such seemingly unreal occurrences. The first of these was when I was traveling with my mother as a child on a train from Chicago to Green Bay, Wisconsin. We were dining in our compartment when my mother suddenly dropped her fork and knife on her plate and told me to finish dinner as we would be getting off at the next stop. She started to cry and, after I asked her what was wrong, she said: "Your grandfather has just died." I did not know how she could know such a thing. When we got off at the next stop, she called her sister and was told that their father had died only an hour earlier from a heart attack. My mother possessed this "gift" of clairvoyance or ESP, or whatever it is. While sitting with her and my brother Neil at Arlington race track in Illinois one balmy May day—we had gotten to that track early and only a few persons were present in the grandstand and there was nothing posted on the announcement board—she stared out at the track and the green field beyond and said almost offhandedly to my brother: "Neil—there is a horse in the third race today [she then named the horse]. I want you to put $100 on that horse to win." My brother hurriedly rustled through the racetrack paper and found the name of the horse, which, indeed, was to run in the third race, and then told her that she would be wasting her money, that that horse had never won a race. I knew something different and I placed that bet for her as well as one for myself on the same horse and it won, paying off against long odds. That day, I had not only remembered what my mother had said on that

train ride so many years earlier, but another event with her that occurred in June 1963. While visiting with her at her home in Milwaukee, and while she was reading a newspaper in the kitchen, she suddenly began crying, and when I asked her what was the matter, she said: "It's the President…he is going to die in November or December when he goes out West." President John F. Kennedy was assassinated on November 22, 1963, in Dallas, Texas. Before her death, she told me that she knew that I also had this "gift," but I made no note of that then. However, years later, in October 1994, while I was watching a television news report with my wife, Judy, we saw a distraught woman pleading for the return of her two young sons, saying that they had been kidnapped when her car had been stolen. I turned to my wife and said: "That woman killed her sons." Judy was startled, saying: "How do you know such a thing? What a terrible thing to say. The poor woman is begging for the return of her children!" I responded by saying that "she is sobbing, but she is shedding no tears." I knew something else about that woman. I had seen, while watching her, somewhere in my mind, as she sent her car into a body of water with her sons sitting in the back seat and, while they shouted for help, she turned her back and walked away. I later told Judy what I had seen in my mind, and she thought that I was suffering from writer's exhaustion. That woman, Susan Smith, was later convicted and imprisoned for murdering her two young sons. Other such visions have occurred without being summoned, brief illustrations, or sometimes names or street addresses having no connection to my chain of thought, and sometimes in dreams. A few days before his death, I had a deep premonition about Roger Ebert, whom I had known for decades, and, two days later, he died (on April 4, 2013). This I kept to myself as I have on most other such strange occasions. I do not question or probe the reasons for these mental or spiritual impressions or "visitations" with the certain conviction that they are best left unchallenged. Many films have profiled clairvoyants, soothsayers, fortune tellers, psychics or those endowed with ESP; see, in this work, Clairvoyants, Subject Index, in Volume IV. **p**, Endre Bohem; **d**, John Farrow; **cast**, Edward G. Robinson, Gail Russell, John Lund, Virginia Bruce, William Demarest, Richard Webb, Jerome Cowan, Onslow Stevens, John Alexander, Roman Bohnen, Paula Raymond; **w**, Barre Lyndon, Jonathan Latimer (based on the novel by Cornell Woolrich); **c**, John F. Seitz; **m**, Victor Young; **ed**, Eda Warren; **art d**, Hans Dreier, Franz Bachelin; **set d**, Sam Comer, Ray Moyer; **spec eff**, Farciot Edouart.

The Night Holds Terror ★★★ 1955; U.S.; 86m; COL; B/W; Crime; Children: Unacceptable; **VHS**. This thriller is based on a true story of a family held hostage and opens with Kelly driving to his California desert home after a business trip to Los Angeles. He picks up hitchhiker Edwards, who pulls out a gun and orders Kelly to pick up two of his fellow criminal friends, Cassavetes and Cross. All three criminals hold Kelly and his wife, Parks, and their two children hostage in their home. When Edwards learns that Kelly only has ten dollars, he decides to trade in the car for cash. Kelly sells his car and Edwards takes the money. The hoods leave, but take Kelly with them. Parks calls the police against Edwards' orders and, between the phone company and the FBI, the kidnappers are traced to their hideout and are killed in a shootout. Kelly then returns to his family in this tense *film noir*. Song: "Every Now and Then" (Andrew Stone). Excessive violence prohibits viewing by children. **p,d&w**, Andrew Stone; **cast**, Jack Kelly, Hildy Parks, Vince Edwards, John Cassavetes, David Cross, Edward Marr, Jack Kruschen, Joyce McCluskey, Jonathan Hale, Barney Phillips, Roy Neal; **c**, Fred Jackman, Jr.; **m**, Lucien Cailliet; **ed**, Virginia Stone.

A Night in Casablanca ★★★ 1946; U.S.; 85m; UA; B/W; Drama; Children: Acceptable; **DVD**; **VHS**. Set in post-World War II Casablanca, this comedic romp pits the Marx Brothers against a gang of former Nazi thugs. Groucho is hired to run a hotel whose previous managers have all been murdered. French soldier Drake suspects the killers were former Nazis (members of the National Socialist German Workers, Party in

Germany). They especially suspect a German count, Ruman. Drake is falsely accused of collaborating with the Nazis, and he enlists the aid of Harpo and Chico to help clear him. They discover a hoard of war booty, priceless art, cached in the hotel (which is why the hotel managers have been systematically eliminated), and, in addition to clearing Drake's name, they destroy (along with the sets) the nasty culprits. The production also offers some romances and some funny moments including a number of hilarious sight gags, especially when Harpo takes control of a plane and delightfully pushes every button and pulls every knob in the cockpit until the plane crashes into a nightclub, and where Ruman, the chief culprit, is apprehended (the comedic bits for Harpo were written by novice writer Frank Tashlin, who later went on to great success as a screenwriter and director). *Author's Note*: Groucho told this author that "**A Night in Casablanca** was not one of our best pictures, but it was better than a blank screen. Some said that we were winging it and we were on the wane and that was probably all Chico's fault, and, if it wasn't, it was Harpo's fault, or maybe the fault was in our stars, or in our contracts." Actually, Chico talked his brothers into doing this film because of his desperate need of money, chiefly to pay off gambling debts. **p**, David L. Loew; **d**, Archie Mayo; **cast**, Groucho Marx, Harpo Marx, Chico Marx, Charles Drake, Lois Collier, Sig Ruman, Lisette Verea, Harry Semels, Ruth Roman, Arthur Tovey; **w**, Joseph Fields, Roland Kibbee, **c**, James Van Trees; **m**, Werner Janssen, Bert Kalmar, Harry Ruby, Ted Snyder; **ed**, Gregg C. Tallas; **art d**, Duncan Cramer; **set d**, Edward G. Boyle; **spec eff**, Harry Redmond, Jr.

Night Must Fall ★★★★★ 1937; U.S.; 116m; MGM; B/W; Crime Drama/Horror; Children: Unacceptable; **DVD**; **VHS**. One of the most frightening films ever made is made even more frightening through the chilling and unforgettable performance of Montgomery, a subtle, sly and charming serial killer. The film opens in the home of Whitty, a rather demanding elderly woman confined to a wheelchair and living with her doting niece, Russell. They hear that a female guest in a nearby inn has vanished, but dismiss her disappearance as she has been described as "a very flashy woman," suggesting that she is prone to running off with strange men. Then Montgomery comes knocking on their bungalow door, explaining that he had been working as a page at the inn, but is looking for better employment suited to his "special" talents and he charms Witty into hiring him as a handyman. When taking residence in a small room in the large cottage, he places a large, heavy hatbox he has been carrying on a shelf in a closet. Montgomery proves to be a devoted servant, waiting hand and foot on Whitty, amusing her with humorous stories. While constantly flattering Whitty, Montgomery realizes that Russell distrusts him. Though uneducated, he exchanges witty barbs with Russell and she becomes intrigued with his shifty character. Meanwhile, Whitty innocently asks if Montgomery knew the woman who disappeared from the inn and he blithely replies that he did, then describes her as "on the tall side, with thin ankles and one of them bracelets on one of them...Fair hair...thin eyebrows...with white marks where they was pulled out...to be in fashion, you know. Her lips are a bit thin, with red stuff painted around them to make them look more. You can rub it off, I suppose...Her neck—rather thick—she's—very lively." Though Witty takes no note of Montgomery's description, which deals with the woman's physical attributes and says nothing about her personality, Russell shrewdly discerns that Montgomery has a psychopathic nature and becomes alarmed. She fears to leave Whitty in the house with him and finds one excuse after another not to leave the place even when her suitor, Marshal, asks her to go out with him. The cunning Montgomery notices this and bides his time. He locates the hidden family safe and then plans to murder Whitty and even Russell, to complete the theft of the family money. The body of the woman missing from the inn is then located in some nearby woods, officers horrified to find the body decapitated and the head of the victim missing. When Russell learns of this killing, she talks openly about the ordinariness of such heinous acts, stating: "murder is a thing we read about in the papers. It isn't real life.

Robert Montgomery and Beryl Mercer in *Night Must Fall*, 1937.

It can't touch us...but it can...and it's here...all around us...in the forest...in this house. We're living with it." Convinced that Montgomery is the killer, Russell goes to inspect that suspicious-looking hatbox tucked away in Montgomery's closet, but he interrupts her and she finds a way to leave the house, but returns only to find Whitty a corpse and Montgomery about to murder her, too. In a tension-filled scene, Montgomery toys with Russell, but she disarms him by praising his cleverness and wile before she manages to escape. She returns with police, who arrest Montgomery, who insists on taking the hatbox from his closet, which contains the decapitated head of the woman from the inn he has killed, his prized trophy, and we last see him get into a police car and drive away in the darkness of the night until the car's probing headlights can be seen no more for the fadeout. Thorpe provides one of his finest films here, so tense and full of anxiety that there is not a moment when the viewer will not be on edge, thanks to the masterful portrayal rendered by Montgomery in what is undoubtedly his most mesmerizing and insidious role, a startling and shocking portrait of a sinister killer seldom equaled. (Thorpe would later direct another offbeat but fascinating film with Montgomery, **The Earl of Chicago**, 1940, where Montgomery again is out of character as a tough gangster transplanted to England as an aristocrat.) Russell, too, is superb in this masterpiece thriller, as a woman instinctively knowing she has a killer under her roof, but is, at the same time, fascinated by his overwhelming charm and seemingly endearing ways. Whitty, as the trusting old lady, is equally impressive, right up to her final devastating scene when she realizes, at the last moment, that the young man she has trusted is about to murder her. Montgomery was deservedly nominated for an Oscar for his unforgettable performance, and Whitty was nominated as Best Supporting Actress. The film was a huge box office success and was remade in 1964 with Albert Finney in the role of the killer. *Author's Note*: Williams, the gifted writer for this bone-tingling tale, appeared as the youthful killer in the smash stage version in London in 1935, and Whitty played the aged hypochondriac, both reprising their roles when the play moved to Broadway in 1936. Hunt Stromberg, one of MGM's top producers, saw the play in New York and was stunned by its impact, so much so that he could not sleep for nights thinking about it and, when he returned to California, went straight to MGM boss Louis B. Mayer and told him about the story and that he wanted to film it. Mayer, who was dedicated to musicals and family films was shocked and horrified, stating: "Hunt, are you telling me that you want to make a picture in which a man carries a woman's head around in a hatbox?" Stromberg nodded, saying that it would be one of MGM's biggest box office hits. "Mayer could not believe it," Thorpe told this author. "He thought that Stromberg had lost his mind. Hunt later told me that Mayer said to him: 'You get $8,000 a week here at the studio to make great films, but what

Clark Gable, Ben Lyon, Betty Jane Graham and Barbara Stanwyck in *Night Nurse*, 1931.

you are suggesting is as crazy as the man you want to show on the screen.' Then Hunt told Mayer that he not only insisted on making the film, but that he wanted Robert Montgomery to play the psychopathic killer. Mayer really huffed and puffed at that, telling Hunt: 'And you want one of our most charming leading men, Bob Montgomery, a man who plays in comedies and romances, to turn into a lunatic murderer? Now I know you've lost your mind.' Stromberg, however, persisted and fought tooth and nail to get Bob [Montgomery] and he finally won Mayer over with the promise that the film would make more money for the studio than five of its musicals. Montgomery, when he heard about the role, jumped for the part like a hungry dog. He knew that there was more meat in that character than a dozen of the high society characters he had been playing." For his part, Montgomery told this author: "What a role to play! A killer with a mind that must be quicker than all of his intended victims. He is glib and charming and likeable with his every move, and he is also a woman killer without a shred of conscience. That was for me as I knew it was the only way I could get out of MGM's drawing rooms and social teas [on the screen]. Every time I saw Emlyn after that, I thanked him for writing such a memorable character." Mayer, according to some reports, so disliked this film that he ordered all of his people not to vote for any Oscars of any kind for the film, a story to be believed in that Mayer was forever sabotaging his own films to prove that he was always in authority and always right at MGM, a man that, indeed, often bit the hand that fed him, in this case his own. **p**, Hunt Stromberg; **d**, Richard Thorpe; **cast**, Robert Montgomery, Rosalind Russell, Dame May Whitty, Alan Marshal, Merle Tottenham, Kathleen Harrison, Eily Malyon, Matthew Boulton, Beryl Mercer, E.E. Clive; **w**, John Van Druten (based on the play by Emlyn Williams); **c**, Ray June; **m**, Edward Ward; **ed**, Robert J. Kern; **art d**, Cedric Gibbons.

Night Must Fall ★★★ 1964; U.K.; 101m; MGM; B/W; Drama; Children: Unacceptable; **DVD**; **VHS**. This is a good remake of the 1937 film noir classic where Finney is a crazed axe murderer, who charms his way into the home of elderly Washbourne and her daughter, Hamsphire, on the pretense of redecorating it. While romancing Hampshire and playing bizarre games with Washbourne, Finney performs rituals with the heads of victims he keeps in a hatbox in his room. Police track him down and he goes berserk, killing Washbourne. Finney cowers in a bathroom like a frightened little boy, as Hampshire tries to coax him out and he is finally arrested. Finney is scary in an impressive performance, but he cannot match Robert Montgomery's psychopathic performance in the original. Excessive violence prohibits viewing by children. **p**, Albert Finney, Karel Reisz; **d**, Reisz; **cast**, Albert Finney, Susan Hampshire, Mona Washbourne, Sheila Hancock, Michael Medwin, Joe Gladwin, Martin Wyldeck, John Gill; **w**, Clive Exton (based on the play by Emlyn

Williams); **c**, Freddie Francis; **m**, Ron Grainer; **ed**, Philip Barnikel; **prod d**, Timothy O'Brien; **art d**, Lionel Couch.

The Night My Number Came Up ★★★ 1955; U.K.; 94m; Ealing Studios; B/W; Horror; Children: Unacceptable; **VHS**. Exciting thriller has a naval officer appear at a Hong Kong dinner party, where guests goad him into revealing a terrible nightmare. He reluctantly recounts his dark dream, one where he has envisioned a flight in a Dakota from Bangkok to Tokyo with eight persons on board and where the plane crashes into the Japanese mountains, killing everyone on board. Redgrave, an air marshal, listens intently to this grim tale, realizing that he is to shortly take just that flight to Tokyo the following day. Redgrave dismisses the tale since he knows he is flying on a Liberator, but when he and his aide, Elliott, arrive at the airport to take that flight, he is told that equipment failure in the Liberator has caused the flight to be changed and Redgrave must board another plane, a Dakota. He and Elliott board the Dakota and Redgrave sees the very people on board that were described in the dream, including Knox and Sim, but there are only six on board until, at the last minute, two soldiers climb aboard to make the number eight. As the flight continues, Redgrave becomes more and more convinced that the nightmare might very much come true as the plane is tossed about in a terrible storm and the oxygen on board becomes so thin that the passengers find it difficult to breathe, all of this detailed in that awful nightmare. While Redgrave struggles to hold on to his normal cool presence, Elliott battles his increasing anxiety, and Knox, who had been the most skeptical when first hearing the details of that nightmare, comes unhinged by fear in blindly accepting that prediction. The only part of that dark dream that does not come true is when the plane makes a forced landing and where all on board survive. Norman, in his film debut as a director, provides a taut thriller that sustains anxiety and tension throughout, where Redgrave and all cast members provide first-rate performances. This is not a film you will see on board air flights and it is not a film to view before going to an airport to take to the air or you may turn your car around and go home. **p**, Michael Balcon, Tom Morahan; **d**, Leslie Norman; **cast**, Michael Redgrave, Sheila Sim, Alexander Knox, Denholm Elliott, Ursula Jeans, Ralph Truman, Michael Hordern, Nigel Stock, Alfie Bass, Bill Kerr, George Rose, Victor Maddern, David Orr, David Yates, Doreen Aris, Richard Davies, Charles Perry; **w**, R. C. Sherriff (based on a magazine article by Air Marshal Sir Victor Goddard); **c**, Lionel Banes; **m**, Malcolm Arnold; **ed**, Peter Tanner; **art d**, Jim Morahan; **spec eff**, Sydney Pearson, Geoffrey Dickinson.

Night Nurse ★★★ 1931; U.S.; 72m; WB; B/W; Crime Drama; Children: Unacceptable; **DVD**; **VHS**. Stanwyck is outstanding in this provocative tale where she goes to work for Merriam, assigned to care for her two children, Graham and Jones. She learns that Merriam is an utterly worthless and evil person, who is planning to starve her children to death in order to obtain the fortune left to them by her deceased husband and initiates this sinister plan with her lover and family chauffeur, Gable, a ruthless and brutal man. The frightened Stanwyck confides her fears to roommate Blondell, who urges her to go to the police, but Gable stops her from doing this by threatening to kill her if she talks; to make sure he means what he says, he smashes his fist into Stanwyck's face. She does seek help from an unlikely source when meeting and befriending Lyon, a happy-go-lucky bootlegger. When it appears that Merriam and Gable will complete their murderous scheme and take the lives of the children, Lyon appears at the last minute, brandishing a gun, and dispatches the villains while saving the children. He promises to give up his criminal ways and ends up with Stanwyck, who has already given her heart to him. Pantheon director Wellman directs with great skill and provides one tension-filled scene after another; Stanwyck is stunning in her role, one that established her as a foremost dramatic actress. *Author's Note*: The film was released before official censorship had been established and there are many risqué scenes showing the voluptuous Blondell and Stanwyck running about in skimpy lingerie. Wellman told this author that "I was very busy in that year when we made **Night Nurse**. I directed four other films that year [**Other Men's Women**, 1931; **The Public Enemy**, 1931; **The Star Witness**, 1931; and **Safe in Hell**, 1931], and I did not do a lot of retakes in **Night Nurse**, since that was not necessary as all the players, especially Babs [Stanwyck] were right on their toes and missed no cues and did everything I wanted them to do right away. Warner Brothers thought about putting James Cagney into the role of the brutal chauffeur, but I convinced them to put Gable into the part. He was an unknown then and hungry for any kind of role and he was great in that part, one that elevated his status. Warner Brothers refused to give him a contract and hired him as a free agent actor, which was a break, because when he left Warner Brothers after that picture, MGM picked him up and began putting him into pictures as a leading player, not a supporting player, which was the kind of part he had in **Night Nurse**. I did Cagney a favor, too, by keeping him out of **Night Nurse**. He was under contract to Warner Brothers and had he done that role, he might have been stuck in supporting parts where he was typecast as a heavy. I did **The Public Enemy** with Cagney, and, after that picture, he went right to the top of the heap as one of Warner Brothers' most popular leading men." Stanwyck liked her role in **Night Nurse**, but she felt that the great success the film saw at the box office "was all due to Clark [Gable]. He was one of the most darkly handsome men I had ever seen and almost every woman in America shared my view. We could not stop looking at that good-looking guy. Make no mistake. It was Clark who brought the crowds to see **Night Nurse**. In that picture, he had to hit me with his fist and before we shot that scene Clark told me not to worry, that he would pull his punch, but he missed a little bit and I got stung on the kisser and he apologized for that all through the production. Twenty years later, when we did **To Please a Lady** [1950] together, Clark had to do the same thing, but this time he missed my jaw so many times that we had to do many retakes, so fearful was he that he might land that big fist of his on my face. He finally got it right and that swing was about the closest near miss I ever experienced." **p,&d**, William A. Wellman; **cast**, Barbara Stanwyck, Ben Lyon, Joan Blondell, Clark Gable, Blanche Frederici, Charlotte Merriam, Charles Winninger, Edward Nugent, Vera Lewis, Willie Fung, Betty Jane Graham, Marcia Mae Jones, Allan "Rocky" Lane, Jed Prouty; **w**, Oliver H.P. Garrett, Charles Kenyon (based on the novel by Dora Macy (Grace Perkins Ousler); **c**, Barney "Chick" McGill; **ed**, Edward McDermott; **art d**, Max Parker.

Night of June 13th ★★★ 1932; U.S.; 76m; PAR; B/W; Mystery; Children: Unacceptable; **DVD**; **VHS**. Members of several families in a New York suburb become involved in a murder trial. Allen, a neurotic woman, commits suicide and leaves a note blaming her husband, Brook, and his infidelity with a young neighbor, Lee. Brook finds the note and destroys it so as to protect Lee. Police suspect murder and arrest Brook, who is brought to trial. Witnesses at the trial who might clear him nevertheless lie because their testimony might implicate them. Before Brook can be convicted, however, an elderly neighbor, Grapewin, finally comes forward and testifies, exposing the lies of the others, and Brook is freed. This early mystery from Caspary, author of the classic **Laura**, 1944, exhibits a clever script and well-developed characters, which director Roberts skillfully employs in presenting a gripping mystery. **d**, Stephen Roberts; **cast**, Clive Brook, Lila Lee, Charles Ruggles, Gene Raymond, Frances Dee, Mary Boland, Adrianne Allen, Charley Grapewin, Helen Ware, Helen Jerome Eddy, Arthur Hohl, Paul Fix, Kent Taylor; **w**, Agnes Brand Leahy, Brian Marlow, William Slavens McNutt (based on the story "Suburbs" by Vera Caspary); **c**, Harry Fischbeck.

The Night of the Generals ★★★ 1967; U.K./France; 148m; COL; Color; War Drama; Children: Unacceptable; **DVD**; **VHS**. O'Toole gives a chilling performance as a psychopathic German general in WWII, his military status and prestige allowing him to escape punishment for serial

Tom Courtenay and Peter O'Toole in *The Night of the Generals,* 1967.

killings as well as mass murder. This grim but fascinating tale opens in 1942 when a German agent doubling as a prostitute to obtain information is viciously murdered by one of her patrons; her controlling spymaster, Sharif, begins to investigate, and his suspects are three German generals, O'Toole, Gray and Pleasence. His obsessive probe, however, so annoys his superiors that Sharif is transferred to Paris, and where, two years later, the same three generals are stationed. Another prostitute is killed, and Sharif learns that she has been murdered with the same modus operandi employed in the case he dealt with two years earlier; he is now convinced that the culprit is one of those three generals. O'-Toole is shown visiting a museum where he views the works of Vincent Van Gogh, and when he looks upon Van Gogh's self-portrait he recognizes his own madness and becomes weak with the shock. After O'-Toole plants evidence indicating that his orderly, Courtenay, has killed the prostitute, Sharif now rightly believes that O'Toole is the serial killer and enlists the aid of French police detective Noiret to obtain enough evidence to convict O'Toole. So obsessed with bringing O'Toole to justice is Sharif that he ignores Noiret's information concerning a plot to kill Hitler. O'Toole, now knowing that Sharif is hot on his trail, implicates Sharif in the failed attempt to kill Hitler, and Sharif is wrongly arrested and executed for participating in that plot. In flash-forward we now see O'Toole twenty years later about to attend a reunion of the army unit he commanded during the war. He has recently been released from prison after serving time for war crimes (such as the destruction of Warsaw) and in a short time another prostitute is murdered. Noiret, however, who has become a member of Interpol, has never forgotten Sharif and the murder case in Paris, and, with assembled evidence from that case and the new murder committed by O'Toole, confronts O'Toole just before he is to make his appearance before his ardent followers. Rather than face the disgrace of arrest, imprisonment or possible execution for murder, O'Toole calmly steps from the meeting hall and into a room where he ends his life by shooting himself. Director Litvak presents a tense tale where O'Toole rivets in his role of a clever killer, who manages to turn the tables on his accuser, Sharif, who also presents a brilliant and tense performance. All of the cast members are standouts, and the production values are high. **p**, Sam Spiegel, Anatole Litvak; **d**, Litvak; **cast**, Peter O'Toole, Omar Sharif, Tom Courtenay, Christopher Plummer, Juliette Greco, Donald Pleasence, Joanna Pettet, Philippe Noiret, John Gregson, Nigel Stock, Gordon Jackson, Harry Andrews, Coral Browne, Charles Gray, Charles Millot, Yves Brainville, Sacha Pitoeff; **w**, Joseph Kessel, Paul Dehn (based on the books *Die Nacht der Generale* by Hans Hellmut Kirst and *The Wary Transgressor* by James Hadley Chase); **c**, Henri Decae (Panavision; Technicolor); **m**, Maurice Jarre; **ed**, Alan Osbiston; **prod d**, Alexander Trauner; **art d**, Auguste Capelier.

Robert Mitchum in *The Night of the Hunter*, 1955.

The Night of the Hunter ★★★★★ 1955; U.S.; 93m; Paul Gregory Productions/UA; B/W; Crime Drama/Horror; Children: Unacceptable; **BD**; **DVD**; **VHS**. Although the versatile Mitchum was invariably impressive in playing either heroes or villains, he seldom matched his terrifying performance of a maniacal killer in this genuinely frightening film, the only film directed by the gifted actor Charles Laughton, and one that proved to be a masterpiece of classic horror. This haunting film opens during the 1930s when the nation was suffering from the Great Depression and where Graves robs a West Virginia bank, killing two people in the process and then rushes home with $10,000 in stolen cash, hiding the loot inside the doll of his little daughter, Bruce. He has her and her older brother, Chapin, swear that they will never tell where the money is hidden just before police arrive to take him to prison. We next see Mitchum sitting in a seedy burlesque theater where a stripper cavorts on stage and, while other men hoot and holler at her undulating performance, Mitchum squints with hatred at her, instinctively drawing from his pocket and opening a switchblade knife, a weapon he apparently would like to use to end the fleshy performer's act. Before he can follow his murderous inclinations, however, he is arrested for stealing a car and sent to the very prison housing Graves and becomes Graves' cellmate, and where the stoic Graves is awaiting execution. Mitchum stays awake at nights intently listening to Graves muttering in his sleep. Knowing Graves has hidden the cash from the robbery, Mitchum tries to learn the whereabouts from Graves, but when he leans from his bunk above that of Graves to hear Graves talking in his sleep, Graves suddenly awakes and smashes his fist into Mitchum's face. Graves goes to his death without revealing the information that Mitchum so avidly seeks, so when he is released, Mitchum, posing as a back county preacher, travels to Graves' hometown where he charms the locals into believing he is a man of God. In his Gospel-spouting sermons, Mitchum uses his two hands to illustrate his points, the words "love" inked on the fingers of his right hand and "hate" on the fingers of his left hand, using his hands in a dramatic struggle until "Love" triumphs and lays the left hand low. Local leaders Varden and Beddoe think the world of Mitchum and they match him with Graves' naïve and trusting widow, Winters, which is exactly what Mitchum wants, so he can get close to Graves' family and locate the hidden loot. After they are married, Mitchum begins to systematically work on the children to get them to tell where the money is hidden, but Chapin, who has instantly disliked the phony preacher from the beginning, convinces his little sister to keep silent as she carries her doll everywhere with her, the very entity containing that hidden money. After they are wed, Winters expects Mitchum to perform his husbandly duties, but he asks her if she has "procreation" in mind and she says she wants no more children. Mitchum then labels her a lustful woman and demands that she pray for her immortal soul and, as

Winters lies in a trancelike state praying, Mitchum withdraws his switchblade knife and Winters accepts her gruesome fate as he kills her. With their mother gone, the children are now at the mercy of Mitchum, who terrorizes them. The children run from him, hiding in the cellar of their house, and when Mitchum descends in the darkness looking for them, with knife in hand, he stumbles and falls, then, while rising, Chapin releases a board containing heavy jars that slams into Mitchum's head, momentarily knocking him out while the children escape the cellar and race from the house. While Mitchum begins searching for them, Chapin and Bruce run to a houseboat where Chapin tries to rouse old family friend Gleason. The old man, however, is in a drunken stupor after he has earlier seen Winters' body while he was fishing. At that time, he peer down into the water to see Winters's automobile beneath the water and her sitting strapped to the front seat, dead, her throat slit, and her hair waving with the underwater current, a nightmare scene that has caused him to drink himself into a babbling daze. Unable to bring Gleason around, Chapin guides Bruce to a small skiff, placing her inside the boat, and then struggles to push it from the mud and into the river. Just as he manages to free the boat and climb into it, Mitchum arrives wide-eyed and wielding his switchblade, wading into the water after the boat, but the river's current catches the boat at the last second, and it sails beyond his grasp, causing Mitchum to wail like a frustrated madman. The boat sails down the river and the exhausted children gaze about while night birds in trees lining the river look down upon them and a star-filled night sky spreads above them (an exquisitely composed scene). The boat drifts down the river and Chapin manages to bring it ashore where he takes Bruce to a barn and where they fall asleep on the hay. Chapin awakes to hear Mitchum singing in the distance as he tracks the children while riding on a horse (the distant silhouetted figure of a man is shown on a horse plodding along a ridge, this eerie scene achieved by director Laughton by having a midget riding a pony on a confining set shrouded in shadows). Mitchum chants from an old hymn: "Leaning, leaning, safe and secure from all alarms… leaning, leaning…leaning on the everlasting arms." Chapin stares at this distant image, stating, "Doesn't he ever sleep?" After he awakens Bruce, they return to the boat and continue their journey on the river, falling asleep. They are awakened by the voice of a woman and to find that the boat has drifted ashore and next to the property of Gish, who is an elderly, strict-minded but compassionate caretaker of several orphans. She takes Chapin and Bruce into her household, but is unable to get any coherent information from the tight-lipped Chapin, who now distrusts every living adult. The children become part of Gish's family, but the reticent Chapin is slow to respond to Gish's motherly affection until, at Christmas, he receives a gift from her, and then wraps an apple in a doily and presents it to Gish and where she brings a smile to his face by telling him that it is the finest present she has ever received. Later, Castillo, the oldest girl living with Gish, is shopping in the nearby town and innocently informs a stranger who gives her the attention she craves that Chapin and Bruce are staying with Gish. That stranger is Mitchum, who is still doggedly searching for the children. Mitchum then shows up at Gish's house, standing outside its fence, and he tells Gish that he is the father of Chapin and Bruce, saying that they are runaways and he has come to take them back home. He reprises his preacher's "love" and "hate" routine for Gish, but the shrewd old woman sees right through his pretensions and posturing. She then looks at Chapin, who says to her: "He ain't my pa." Gish turns back to stare at Mitchum, saying to him: "No, nor a preacher either!" With that, she herds her brood back into her house and orders Mitchum to depart. He retreats, his face clouding over with an angry look as he calls her "the spawn of the devil." That night Gish moves resolutely from room to room in her house carrying a shotgun, knowing that Mitchum is somewhere lurking outside. As she stands on the screened porch of the house, Gish peers into the darkness to hear Mitchum shout: "I want them kids!" She tells him that he will not get them and Mitchum begins his "leaning" chant, but omitting the important line of "leaning on the Almighty," which Gish fills in for him.

He then makes his move as he tries to break into the house but Gish lets loose a blast from her shotgun, which strikes Mitchum and sends him howling like a wounded animal into Gish's barn. Gish then calls police and, at dawn, Mitchum is shown being dragged from the barn, manacled and under arrest. Chapin, seeing Mitchum being dragged away in the same manner Graves was taken into custody, is overcome by emotion and grabs Bruce's doll, racing to Mitchum and hitting him with it so that it breaks. The hidden money spills out, and Chapin shouts for Mitchum to take the stolen loot. He is thus relieved of the burden imposed upon him by his father, Graves, when he swore that he would keep the whereabouts of the stolen money a secret. Gish and her children are later seen in the town where a lynch mob, led by Varden and Beddoe, who had once been Mitchum's most ardent admirers, are now shouting for Mitchum to be released into their hands so that he can be hanged by the mob. Gish guides her brood clear of the mob as the heavily guarded Mitchum is shown being led from the back of the jail and into a car en route to prison where he will be executed. His executioner later states that he has never liked his job, but that he was pleased to dispatch a monster like Mitchum, and he then returns to his own wife and children. This exceptional film was not well received by critics and was not a success at the box office, but it nevertheless remains a horror classic, with superlative direction by Laughton and astoundingly effective performances by Mitchum, Winters, Chapin, Bruce, Gleason, and the wonderful Gish and where supporting players like Varden and Beddoe are marvelous in their roles. *Author's Note*: Laughton's first and only sojourn into direction saw him employ many of the techniques used by German directors Lang and Sternberg, both of whom he greatly admired, and where he effectively uses shadows and darkness to emphasize the film's most horrific scenes. He also nods to his idol, master filmmaker D. W. Griffith when employing opening and closing iris techniques, particularly in scenes with Gish, who was Griffith's favorite silent film star in his productions. Laughton, from the beginning, when given the script, had only one man in mind for the evil, phony preacher, Robert Mitchum. "He called me one day," Mitchum told this author," and said that he was going to make a Mother Goose story as a nightmare and that, if I played the heavy I would be enacting the role of a 'diabolical crud.' I immediately responded by saying 'Present.' When we got into the production, I was amazed at how skilled Laughton was in directing. He paid attention to every little detail on the sets and his setups were very inventive in capturing that dark fairy tale he was showing. He had a top flight cameraman, Cortez [cinematographer for **The Magnificent Ambersons**, 1942] and Cortez gave him everything he wanted, some really great shots, especially when I am trailing the children as they float down a river in a little boat. Laughton did not like those children and found it difficult to work with them, so he asked me to coach them along and I did as I had become good friends with them—when not trying to slit their throats on camera. I'm not sure that the little girl [Bruce] knew what was really going on, but that was just as good as her wide-eyed stare did the trick. The boy [Chapin] was a very good little actor and he responded well to my suggestions. I told him to keep his emotions inside of him and his mouth shut, like his father told him to do at the beginning of the film and he did that perfectly until he lets out all that steam-pressure emotion when he bursts out crying at the end. I told him to hit me over the head with that doll until it broke and he told me he thought he might hurt me and I told him that my head was as solid as a rock so he did not have any problem in letting me have it." Mitchum thought that Gish dominated every scene he had with her, saying that "she was magnificent. She knew her role and I could not budge her from her character, no matter how many wild moves I made. My God, man, she was there when all the great movies began with Griffith, so she knew every technique there was, but never overused them." For her part, Winters, as she told this author, thought her role "a supporting part. I am again a pretty dumb woman who falls for all of Bob's [Mitchum's] sanctimonious lines, but when he is about to kill me, I put up a little fight with Charles [Laughton], telling him: 'No woman in the

Sally Jane Bruce, Billy Chapin and Robert Mitchum in *The Night of the Hunter,* 1955.

world is just going to lie there and watch some lunatic plunge a knife into her throat.' He gave me that wise uncle smile of his and said, 'Normally not, but you are in a religious trance where you think no harm will come to you—you are as much a religious zealot as your friends and as Bob is a homicidal maniac. Now, will you please let him go ahead and cut your throat so we can get on with the picture?' Well, that cracked me up and I went ahead with the scene and I think it worked fine. Charles was right. I am just as much a nutcase in that picture as as Bob is." The script was written by movie expert Agee (paid $30,000 for the job), but, according to one report, it was overlong when completed. "The script was the size of a telephone book," according to Elsa Lanchester, Laughton's wife, who said she and her husband worked for days to cut down the script so that it was useable. Years later, after the film became a film noir classic, Mitchum was reluctant to talk about the sadistic lunatic he played. "I did not like what I saw in myself in that role," Mitchum told this author. "Maybe I was just a little too good at being that madman, although I did play a similar character, a very bad number who likes killing people, some years later when I did a picture with Gregory Peck called **Cape Fear** [1962], but I was nowhere near the wacko I played in **The Night of the Hunter**. A friend told me about that time that I should stop playing these monsters or I would be typecast for the rest of my career. 'Leave that to Jack Palance,' he said, and I did." The role Mitchum plays is modeled on Harry Powell, the character created by author Grubb in his chilling novel upon which this film is based. Grubb based his character on Harry Powers, a sadistic West Virginia serial killer, who murdered women and children after torturing them in secret chambers he had constructed beneath his garage and who was hanged in 1932; for more information on Powers, see my book, *World Encyclopedia of 20th Century Murder* (Paragon House, 1992; page 456). **p**, Paul Gregory; **d**, Charles Laughton; **cast**, Robert Mitchum, Shelley Winters, Lillian Gish, James Gleason, Evelyn Varden, Peter Graves, Don Beddoe, Billy Chapin, Sally Jane Bruce, Gloria Castillo, Emmett Lynn, **w**, James Agee (based on the novel by Davis Grubb); **c**, Stanley Cortez; **m**, Walter Schumann; **ed**, Robert Golden; **art d**, Hilyard Brown; **set d**, Al Spencer; **spec eff**, Louis De Witt, Jack Rabin.

Night of the Living Dead ★★★ 1968; U.S.; 96m; Image Ten/Continental; B/W; Horror; Children: Unacceptable; **BD; DVD; VHS.** Genuinely frightening, Pennsylvania turns into Transylvania in this horror classic when it is overrun with zombies. O'Dea and Streiner, teenage sister and brother, visit the grave of their father in a remote cemetery. A weird ghoulish old man comes along and grabs O'Dea and Streiner tries to free her, but the man tries to bite him. They struggle, and Streiner hits his head on a tombstone, losing consciousness. O'Dea runs for help and enters an empty farmhouse, then sees the man coming to it. She finds

Buddy Ebsen, Rita Gam and Gregory Peck in *Night People*, 1954.

the decomposed body of a woman in the house, flees from it, and sees Jones, a black man who comes to the house for refuge from some strange men who are pursuing him. Jones kills some of them and boards up O'Dea and himself in the house. The men threatening them are bloodthirsty vampires, one of which is now the dead Streiner. A live family appears in the house and everyone watches television news that reports that recently dead people are coming back to life in funeral parlors, morgues and cemeteries while a mass murderer is being hunted. The reason for the dead returning to life may be because of radiation from another world. After a lot more grisly scenes ensue, such as zombies eating the flesh of everyone in sight and a sheriff's posse arriving to affect O'Dea's rescue, but mistakenly shooting Jones and tossing his body on a burning pile of zombies. Made on a shoestring, the film was a sensational "sleeper" that earned millions and began a zombie industry for director Romero including two updated versions of **Night of the Living Dead** in 1990, a 3-D version in 2006, and sequels **Dawn of the Dead**, 1978, and **Day of the Dead**, 1978 and 2004, as less sophisticated audiences developed an insatiable thirst for zombie films. Excessive violence prohibits viewing by children. **p**, Russell Streiner, Karl Hardman; **d**, George Romero; **cast**, Judith O'Dea, Duane Jones, Hardman, Marilyn Eastman, Keith Wayne, Judith Ridley, Kyra Schon, Charles Craig, Bill Heinzman, George Kosana, Frank Doak; **w**, Romero, John Russo (based on a story by Russo); **c&d**, Romero; **m**, Scott Vladimir Licina; **spec eff**, Tony Pantanello, Regis Survinski.

The Night of the Shooting Stars ★★★ 1983; Italy; 105m; RAI/UA; Color; Drama; Children: Unacceptable (MPAA: R); **DVD**; **VHS**. In Italian folklore, the Night of San Lorenzo is called the Night of the Shooting Stars, when dreams come true. Lozano is a woman, who recalls a night in 1944 when she was six years old and the stars fell. She and her family and neighbors fled their small town in Tuscany when they hear rumors that Nazis plan to blow it up and also the good news that Americans are coming soon to liberate them. The film focuses on a conflict between Italian fascists and peasants at the end of World War II, which is a remembrance of the director's childhood. In a blend of realism and surrealism, the girl, Guidelli, imagines the partisans being Greek warriors and a fascist threatening her life is killed by spears. There is a love affair between senior citizens, but also a scene in which a fascist boy is shot dead by partisans before his father's eyes, causing the father to commit suicide. It ends with some still alive, others dead, and an old man sitting alone in the rain in the town square wondering what it was all about. The night of shooting stars brought nightmares instead of happy wishes coming true. This well-crafted tale offers a fascinating memoir of war mixed with hope and despair. Song: "The Battle Hymn of the Republic" (Julia Ward Howe). (In Italian; English subtitles.) **p**, Giuliani G. De

Negri; **d**, Paolo and Vittorio Taviani; **cast**, Omero Antonutti, Margarita Lozano, Claudio Bigagli, Miriam Guidelli, Massimo Bonetti, Enrica Maria Modugno, Sabina Vannucchi, Giorgio Naddi, Renata Zamengo, Micol Guidelli; **w**, Paolo and Vittorio Taviani, De Negri, Tonino Guerra; **c**, Franco Di Giacomo; **m**, Nicola Piovani; **ed**, Roberto Perpignani; **prod d**, Gianni Sbarra; **spec eff**, Luciano D'Achille.

Night People ★★★★ 1954; U.S.; 93m; FOX; Color; Spy Drama; Children: Unacceptable; **DVD**; **VHS**. Top-notch post-WWII thriller has Peck as a savvy U.S. Army colonel heading an intelligence unit in the American zone of occupied Berlin during the Cold War. The Soviets have spies everywhere and some of them randomly select Avery, an innocent GI, to kidnap and take to East Berlin, holding him captive. It is Peck's job to recoup the young American soldier without creating an international incident or touching off WWIII. He contacts one of his best agents, Bjork, who works for the Soviets while she does undercover work for Peck, and the alluring blonde soon reports that the Soviets are holding the GI until the Americans deliver a wanted elderly couple living in the American sector, Faeber, who was a former German general during the war, and his British-born wife, Esmond, who supports her blinded husband by playing piano in a rundown nightclub. Complicating matters for Peck is Crawford, a wealthy American businessman with influence with top U.S. politicians and who arrives in Berlin and demands that Peck act immediately to bring his son, Avery, to the safety of the American zone. Peck takes Crawford to the nightclub where he shows Crawford the elderly couple, telling him that the Soviets want these people in exchange for his son so that they can then turn Faeber over to former SS men working with the Soviets. Those SS men, still diehard Nazis, want to execute Faeber because he was involved in the plot to kill Hitler in 1944 (and for which he was blinded). The couple, when learning that the Soviets are closing in on them, attempt suicide by taking poison, but they are rushed to a hospital where U.S. Army doctor Abel tries to keep them alive. Meanwhile, Bjork turns up at the hospital at Peck's request and she tells Peck that the Soviets will bring Avery to the hospital in an armed ambulance, but will release him only when Faeber and Esmond are exchanged for Avery and placed in that Soviet ambulance. By this time, Ebsen and Gam, who are Peck's devoted aides, have uncovered the fact that Bjork's loyalties are to the Soviets and that she has been duping Peck all along while pretending to be his double agent. Peck tries to get her drunk, but she is on to him and he forces her to drink some liquor and then knocks her out. Faeber has by this time died, but Esmond is still alive, and the Soviets have agreed that they will accept her alone in exchange for Avery. The Soviet ambulance arrives with heavily armed guards and with a drugged Avery inside the ambulance. Peck bundles Bjork onto a mobile stretcher, covering her face and passes her off as Esmond, stuffing her purse with money so that it will appear that she has betrayed the Soviets by being bought off by the Americans. She is placed inside the Soviet ambulance and Avery is removed to the safety of the hospital and to his grateful father, Crawford, while the Soviets depart, having been outfoxed by Peck. Johnson does a great job in maintaining tension throughout this thriller while Peck is outstanding as the American intelligence officer playing a dangerous game. *Author's Note*: Peck told this author that Johnson was "a fine writer and a brilliant director and I had great confidence in him when we did **Night People** because he did such a fine job on the script when we worked together in making **The Gunfighter** [1950]." Johnson, for his part, said that "Zanuck [chief of Fox] told me that I could direct **Night People**, my first major feature picture, but only if Greg [Peck] approved of me. Greg told Zanuck that he believed I would do a fine job and I got that starting shot thanks to Greg, a great guy and a wonderful actor. You don't go very far in this business without some help, believe me." **p&d**, Nunnally Johnson; **cast**, Gregory Peck, Broderick Crawford, Anita Bjork, Rita Gam, Walter Abel, Buddy Ebsen, Casey Adams, Jill Esmond, Peter van Eyck, Marianne Koch, Ted Avery, Anton Faeber; **w**, Johnson (based on a story by Jed Harris, Thomas Reed); **c**,

Charles G. Clarke (CinemaScope; Technicolor); **m**, Cyril J. Mockridge; **ed**, Dorothy Spencer; **art d**, Hanns Kuhnert, Theo Zwierski.

The Night Runner ★★★ 1957; U.S.; 79m; UNIV; B/W; Drama; Children: Unacceptable; **VHS**. Danton is a standout in this unnerving thriller as a schizophrenic mental patient, who becomes an outpatient because of hospital overcrowding. Before being released, doctors caution him to avoid stressful situations. To avoid the big city and the temptations that landed him in the asylum, he takes a bus to a seaside motel and becomes attracted to Miller, the owner's daughter. Her father, Bouchey, learns of Danton's mental condition and warns him to leave his daughter alone or he will have him recommitted. The stress is too much for Danton and he kills Bouchey. He panics and flees up the beach with Miller and plans to kill her and then himself. He attempts to drown her when the shock brings him back to his senses and he saves her instead and then surrenders to police. **p**, Albert J. Cohen; **d**, Abner Biberman; **cast**, Ray Danton, Colleen Miller, Merry Anders, Eddy Waller, Robert Anderson, George Barrows, Irwin Jay Berniker, Willis Bouchey, Marshall Bradford, Alexander Campbell; **w**, Gene Levitt; **c**, George Robinson; **m**, Joseph Gershenson; **e**, Albrecht Joseph; **art d**, Alexander Golitzen; **set d**, Russell A. Gausman, Ray Jeffers.

Night Shift ★★★ 1982; U.S.; 106m; Ladd Company/WB; Color; Comedy; Children: Unacceptable (MPAA: R); **DVD**; **VHS**. Winkler leaves his high-stress Wall Street job to become a morgue attendant and likes the quiet work until he is assigned to the night shift with partner Keaton, who craves more excitement in his life. Long, a prostitute and neighbor, enters their lives when she complains about losing her pimp. Keaton has a money-making idea to use the morgue at night as a brothel and talks Winkler into going along with it. They hire out Long and her prostitute friends and become what Keaton calls "love brokers." Meanwhile, Winkler falls in love with Long. Kevin Costner has a small and early film role as a young man at a party. This comedy provides consistent amusement despite its unsavory subject, mostly due to Winkler's discombobulating performance. **p**, Brian Grazer; **d**, Ron Howard; **cast**, Henry Winkler, Michael Keaton, Shelley Long, Gina Hecht, Pat Corley, Bobby DiCicco, Nita Talbot, Basil Hoffman, Tim Rossovich, Clint Howard, Kevin Costner, Cheryl Howard, Ron Howard; **w**, Lowell Ganz, Babaloo Mandel; **c**, James Crabe; **m**, Burt Bacharach; **ed**, Daniel P. Hanley, Mike Hill, Robert Kern, Jr.; **prod d**, Jack T. Collis; **art d**, Pete Smith; **set d**, Richard C. Goddard; **spec eff**, Allen Hall.

The Night They Raided Minsky's ★★★ 1968; U.S.; 99m; UA; Color; Comedy; Children: Unacceptable (MPAA: PG-13); **DVD**; **VHS**. Ekland leaves an Amish community in the 1920s and goes to New York City where she hopes to convert lost souls through her wholesome and inspirational biblical scene dancing. Robards, a comedian at the National Winter Garden leased by showman Billy Minsky (1887-1932), played by Gould, wants to embarrass a conservative vice-fighting society attending a show, so he hires Ekland to perform her Bible dancing at a special midnight performance. She believes him about doing a Bible dance and prepares for her performance. Andrews, her furious father, appears at the theater wanting to take her home, and a fight ensues between him and Robards. As Ekland goes on-stage, Andrews accidentally tears her dress. The packed house loves it and encourages her to take off more, so she does, stripping her clothes off in a dance of wild abandon during which the top of her dress falls off. Conservatives in the audience call the police and Minsky's show is raided. Thus, allegedly, the uniquely American art form of burlesque with comedians and striptease dancers is born. Songs: "The Night They Raided Minsky's," "Take Ten Terrific Girls But Only 9 Costumes," "How I Love Her," "Perfect Gentleman," "You Rat, You," "Penny Arcade," "Wait for Me" (Charles Strouse, Lee Adams). Suggestive content and brief nudity prohibit viewing by children. **p**, Norman Lear; **d**, William Friedkin; **cast**, Jason Robards, Britt Ekland, Norman Wisdom, Forrest Tucker, Harry Andrews,

Jason Robards, Britt Ekland and Norman Wisdom in *The Night They Raided Minsky's,* 1968.

Joseph Wiseman, Denholm Elliott, Elliott Gould, Jack Burns, Bert Lahr, Rudy Vallee (narrator); **w**, Arnold Schulman, Sidney Michaels, Lear (based on the novel by Rowland Barber); **c**, Andrew Laszlo; **m**, Charles Strouse; **ed**, Ralph Rosenblum; **pd**, William and Jean Eckart; **art d**, John Robert Lloyd; **set d**, John Godfrey.

A Night to Remember ★★★ 1942; U.S.; 91m; COL; B/W; Mystery; Children: Unacceptable; **VHS**. Entertaining whodunit sees crime writer Aherne and his wife leave their comfortable apartment and move into a basement flat in Greenwich Village so that Aherne will have a better atmosphere to write his tales, but they get more than what they expected when, upon moving in, they find a corpse on their hands. Police detective MacBride (his specialty role, invariably as a dumb flatfoot) is dumbfounded by the murder, and Aherne decides that he will use all he knows to solve the case. A host of strange and spooky suspects then parade through the place, providing an army of red herrings until Aherne pieces the puzzle together, but not before he and Young experience several tense moments. Wallace provides many good harrowing scenes, and Aherne and Young do a good job as amateur sleuths while many of the fine supporting players are convincing as the suspected killer. **p**, Samuel Bischoff; **d**, Richard Wallace; **cast**, Brian Aherne, Loretta Young, Jeff Donnell, William Wright, Sidney Toler, Gale Sondergaard, Donald MacBride, Lee Patrick, Blanche Yurka, Don Costello, Richard Gaines, James Burke; **w**, Richard Flournoy, Jack Henley (based on a story by Kelley Roos); **c**, Joseph Walker; **m**, Werner R. Heymann; **ed**, Charles Nelson; **art d**, Lionel Banks.

A Night to Remember ★★★★ 1958; U.K.; 123m; Rank; Historical Drama; Children: Unacceptable; **DVD**; **VHS**. Superbly directed and acted, this exciting tale accurately and dramatically recounts the ill-fated voyage and sinking of the great luxury liner HMS *Titanic* in 1912. More is the central character in this riveting drama, essaying the part of Charles Herbert Lightoller (1874-1952), who was the second mate (second officer) of the *Titanic*, and is shown with his wife while preparing for the voyage (he would be the senior officer to survive the sinking on April 14, 1912). Other passengers, from those in first class to those traveling steerage, are also shown leaving their homes en route to the ship's departure. Once at sea, we see a cross-section of the passengers, the wealthy settling into their comfortable and expansive suites and enjoying the luxurious lounges and dining hall while the second class passengers stroll decks, envying the upper-class travelers, and while the steerage passengers, mostly immigrants owning very little are happy in their cramped quarters, glad to be traveling to a new land where opportunities await them. More deals with the routines of the ship and all seems tranquil until the vessel strikes an iceberg and where its designer

Rex Harrison in *Night Train to Munich*, 1940.

Thomas Andrews, Jr. (1873-1912), played by Goodliffe, examines the damage, concluding that nothing can save the ship and it will sink within an hour or two. Naismith, who plays the captain (Edward John Smith, 1850-1912), orders that all lifeboats be loaded with women and children and put to sea, knowing that there are not enough such lifeboats to hold all of the 2,224 passengers and crew members on board. More and other officers arm themselves against possible rioting and begin to load women and children into the boats, lowering them into the sea while distress rockets are sent skyward and radio operators Griffith and McCallum send out frantic SOS messages. The captain of the *Californian* receives a report that a large ship nearby is firing rockets, but thinks little of it and does nothing. When Bushell, who plays the captain (Sir Arthur Henry Rostron, 1869-1940) of the *Carpathia*, receives the distress signal, he signals back that he has turned his ship about and is racing toward the sinking *Titanic*. Meanwhile, most of the first class passengers, including many men, are safely lowered in lifeboats while second class and steerage passengers scramble for any available lifeboat, but most are gone and only a few of the female passengers among these passengers find safety in the remaining lifeboats. As the ship begins to sink, the ship's band members heroically remain at their post and play encouraging airs while most stranded on board scramble toward the ship's stern as the water begins to engulf the bow. More attempts to launch a collapsible boat but falls with it into the water. Naismith goes to the bridge and watches as the sea crashes into the area. One of the survivors in a lifeboat is McGuire, who plays Margaret "Molly" Brown, (1867-1932)—the "Unsinkable Molly Brown"—who takes charge of her boat, demanding that swimmers in the water be picked up. Then those in the lifeboats grimly watch as the ship slowly slides downward and soon disappears beneath huge waves from its departing wake. More gathers swimmers in the water and places them atop an overturned lifeboat and keeps them together while waiting for rescue. The *Carpathia* arrives at dawn to rescue 711 survivors. More attends a religious ceremony bereaving the deceased and where the survivors show gratitude to Providence for their rescue. More accompanies Bushell to the deck of the *Carpathia* to be shown the location where the *Titanic* sank, and where he watches the ship's floating debris, beneath which now lie 1,513 victims of this great sea tragedy. Though more than 200 speaking parts are profiled in this moving saga, all of the roles work well under Baker's taut direction and where he provides an unforgettable pageant of poignant and traumatic events involving scores of memorable characters engulfed by the disaster. *Author's Note*: The depiction of the 46,000-ton liner ripped like a tin can by the iceberg (a 300-foot gash through three of the ship's four watertight boiler rooms) is meticulously presented with wonderful special effects; the evacuation scenes are particularly exciting as well as the scenes of the survivors at sea as they

await rescue, these marvelous production values achieved with a budget of $1,680,000 (considerable for its day but meager by today's standards and costs). The story was filmed several times, notably in **Atlantic**, 1930; **Titanic**, 1953; **The Unsinkable Molly Brown**, 1964; **SOS Titanic**, 1979 (made for TV); and **Titanic**, 1997. For more information about the *Titanic*, see my book: *Darkest Hours: The World's Greatest Disasters* (Nelson-Hall, 1976; pages 552-558). **p**, William MacQuitty; **d**, Roy Baker; **cast**, Kenneth More, Ronald Allen, Robert Ayres, Honor Blackman, Frank Lawton, Michael Goodliffe, Anthony Bushell, David McCallum, Alec McCowen, Tucker McGuire, Laurence Naismith, Sean Connery, John Moulder-Brown, Kenneth Griffith, George Rose, John Cairney, Jill Dixon, Jane Downs, Tucker McGuire, James Dyrenforth, Ralph Michael; **w**, Eric Ambler (based on the book by Walter Lord); **c**, Geoffrey Unsworth; **m**, William Alwyn; **ed**, Sidney Hayers; **art d**, Alex Vetchinsky; **spec eff**, Bill Warrington.

Night Train to Munich ★★★★ 1940; U.K.; 95m; FOX; B/W; Spy Drama; Children: Unacceptable; **DVD**; **VHS**. Pantheon director Reed presents a classic espionage tale where Harrison, Lockwood and Henreid give sterling performances in a dangerous cat-and-mouse game. The film opens in an alpine mansion where a man is ranting to his followers, this character undoubtedly based on Adolf Hitler and where he slams a fist down upon a map showing Czechoslovakia. We next see newsreel footage depicting Nazi troops invading that country. German police are then shown arresting Lockwood, the daughter of Harcourt, an armament scientist that the Nazis are seeking, but who has fled to England where he remains in protective custody by British Intelligence. Placed in a concentration camp, Lockwood befriends Henreid, a prisoner in the men's compound, and they talk while divided by a barbed wire fence and where Henreid develops a plan that allows them to later escape. They flee to England and Lockwood is then contacted by British authorities, telling her that she can see her father by contacting Harrison, a British agent, who poses as the operator of a music shop at a seaside resort. Lockwood is attracted to the carefree Harrison, although she is grateful to Henreid for liberating her from the Nazis. Harrison and Henreid, meanwhile, although they do not meet each other at this point, compete for Lockwood's attentions. Harrison then arranges for Harcourt to arrive by sea and to stay in a protected house with Lockwood. Henreid, however, is not the anti-Nazi he seems to be, but a top Nazi agent, who has arranged for Lockwood's escape so that he can locate the much-wanted Harcourt, and, through another clever ruse, he captures Harcourt and Lockwood and smuggles them out of England by a German U-boat. They are returned to Germany where they are held in a Berlin hotel while Harcourt is being grilled about his information concerning armament technologies. Harrison, meanwhile, meets with his intelligence superiors and persuades them to allow him to go to Germany, disguised as a German officer and where he will attempt to liberate Harcourt and Lockwood. Harrison arrives in Berlin, posing as a decorated German army major, who penetrates the German Naval Ministry, befriending an admiral, who allows him to have access to Harcourt and Lockwood. Harrison tells Lockwood to tell everyone that he and she are old lovers and to support his claim that he is a German aristocrat while promising them that he will find a way to get them safely out of Germany. When learning that both are to be sent to Munich by train for further interrogation, Harrison gets himself assigned to that unit accompanying Harcourt and Lockwood and he shares a compartment with them and Henreid, who is suspicious of Harrison, but does not know he is an undercover British agent. While on the train, Harrison enlists the aid of two British gentlemen, Radford and Wayne, who help him subdue and bind and gag Henreid and his guards and where they pose as German guards accompanying Harrison, who escorts Harcourt and Lockwood from the train, commandeering a car and then racing toward the border. They reach an alpine border pass that can only be crossed with cable cars. After overwhelming the German guards there, they prepare to take the cable car to freedom, but Henreid and other German soldiers arrive and lay siege to the cable car building. Harrison holds them off as Lockhart, Harcourt, Radford and Wayne take the cable car to freedom. Harrison, meanwhile, after Henreid's aides have been killed in the ongoing gunfight, is left to battle Henreid. Harrison manages to take the next cable car to freedom while shooting and disabling Henreid, who watches his adversary escape. (This scene is particularly harrowing where Harrison leaps from one moving cable car to another as they pass each other in mid-air, a scene duplicated almost three decades later in **Where Eagles Dare**, 1968.) Reed skillfully provides an action-packed thriller while presenting fully developed characters, and Harrison, Lockwood and Henreid render great performances. Made early in WWII, the Nazis are profiled with some elements of decency and chivalry, although Henreid proves to be completely unscrupulous, and only until later in the war when the Nazis were discovered to be bestial mass murderers did the British perspective of their arch enemy alter and where they showed that enemy in the full light of its actual evils. **p**, Edward Black; **d**, Carol Reed; **cast**, Margaret Lockwood, Rex Harrison, Paul von Hernried (Paul Henreid), Basil Radford, Naunton Wayne, James Harcourt, Felix Aylmer, Wyndham Goldie, Roland Culver, Ian Fleming; **w**, Sydney Gilliat, Frank Launder (based on a story by Gordon Wellesley); **c**, Otto Kanturek; **m**, Louis Levy; **ed**, R.E. Dearing; **art d**, Alex Vetchinsky.

The Night Watch ★★★ 1964; France/Italy; 118m; Filmsonor/Jerand Film; B/W; Crime Drama; Children: Unacceptable; **VHS**. Based on a true prison escape, this gripping tale portrays four cellmates (Constantin, Keraudy, Leroy, and Meunier), who are hardened criminals at the Sante Prison in France and are planning a prison break. Michel, a young inmate awaiting trial for the attempted murder of his wife, Spaak, is transferred to their cell because his own cell is under repair. The four inmates confide their escape plan to Michel, but are unsure if he will join or expose them. Under the cover of the noise of construction by repair crews, the prisoners eventually tunnel down into the sewers beneath the prison. Before they can escape, the warden, Bervil, tells Michel his wife has dropped the charges against him. He tells this to his cellmates but assures them he will go ahead and join them in the escape because he still faces a five-year prison term. His four cellmates are about to go down into the tunnel to make their escape through the sewer when sirens blare and they are caught. They realize that Michel has betrayed them so as to lighten his sentence. Filmed documentary-style, this taut drama sees standout performances from the entire cast. Violence prohibits viewing by children. (In French; English subtitles.) **p**, Serge Silberman; **d**, Jacques Becker; **cast**, Michel Constantin, Jean Keraudy, Philippe Leroy, Raymond Meunier, André Bervil, Marc Michel, Jean-Paul Coquelin, Eddy Rasimi, Jean Becker, Philippe Dumat, Catherine Spaak; **w**, Becker, José Giovanni, Jean Aurel (based on the novel *Le Trou* by Giovanni); **c**, Ghislain Cloquet; **m**, Philippe Arthuys; **ed**, Marguerite Renoir, Geneviève Vaury; **prod d**, Rino Mondellini.

Nightfall ★★★ 1957; U.S.; 78m; Copa/COL; B/W; Drama; Children: Unacceptable; **VHS**. This superior *film noir* entry has Ray as an innocent man on the run from charges of murder and robbery. He meets Bancroft in a restaurant, and is later kidnapped by Keith and Bond, who take him to a deserted oil derrick where he is tortured by his captors while they demand that he tell them where some stolen money is hidden. Ray escapes and goes to Bancroft's apartment, believing that she has set him up. Bancroft insists she has not betrayed him, and agrees to help him find the money. In a flashback we learn that Keith and Bond are bank robbers who killed a doctor and filched his medical bag, thinking it contained their loot. Bond kills Keith in a battle over the loot and uses a snowplow in an effort to run down Bancroft and Gregory, an insurance investigator who is on the trail of the thieves. Ray pulls Bond out of the cab of the snowplow, and after they struggle, Bond is crushed under the plow. Ray is vindicated and winds up with Bancroft for a happy ending. Songs: "Nightfall" (Peter De Rose, Charles H. Cuppett as Charles Harold, Sam Lewis as Sam M. Lewis), "Nocturne Op. 9 No. 2" (Frederic

Anne Bancroft and Aldo Ray in *Nightfall*, 1957.

Chopin), "Red River Valley" (traditional). Excessive violence prohibits viewing by children. **p**, Ted Richmond; **d**, Jacques Tourneur; **cast**, Aldo Ray, Brian Keith, Anne Bancroft, Jocelyn Brando, James Gregory, Frank Albertson, Rudy Bond, Arline Anderson, Monty Ash, María Belmar, Orlando Beltran; **w**, Stirling Silliphant (based on a novel by David Goodis); **c**, Burnett Guffey; **m**, George Duning; **ed**, William A. Lyon; **art d**, Ross Bellah; **set d**, Louis Diage, William Kiernan.

Nighthawks ★★★ 1981; U.S.; 99m; UNIV; Color; Crime Drama; Children: Unacceptable (MPAA: R); **DVD**; **VHS**. Stallone appears in another taut and tension-filled tale where he is a standout as a rugged NYC cop, struggling with a failing marriage with Wagner, and where he and his partner, Williams, are undergoing anti-terrorist training. Ironically, their training is well placed in that international terrorist Hauer arrives in NYC to create havoc and regain his reputation as a leader in his terrible trade. Hauer has recently planted a bomb in a London department store that exploded and killed a number of children (after the real-life London department store bombing committed by IRA terrorists some years earlier), a heinous act that causes him to fall from favor with other leading terrorists (as if to say that there remains in the minds of terrorists some vestiges of selective decency). Along with another rabid terrorist, Khambatta, Hauer kidnaps and holds hostage a number of important persons while killing several people before he apparently escapes. Stallone and Williams, however, are hot on Hauer's trail and they employ a ruse to entice the terrorist and where they kill him in a wild firefight. Hauer's intense portrayal of the fanatical terrorist is truly frightening (equaling his chilling performance the following year as the indefatigable and murderous replicant in **Blade Runner**, 1982) and gives great counterbalance to the fine portraits rendered by Stallone and Williams as they doggedly pursue him in this action-loaded thriller. **p**, Martin Poll; **d**, Bruce Malmuth; **cast**, Sylvester Stallone, Billy Dee Williams, Lindsay Wagner, Rutger Hauer, Persis Khambatta, Nigel Davenport, Hilarie Thompson, Joe Spinell, Walter Mathews, E. Brian Dean, Caesar Cordova, Charles Duval, Tony Munafo, Howard Stein, Tawn Christian, Jamie Gillis; **w**, David Shaber (based on a story by Shaber and Paul Sylbert); **c**, James A. Contner (Technicolor); **m**, Keith Emerson; **ed**, Christopher Holmes; **prod d**, Peter Larkin; **set d**, Fred Weiler; **spec eff**, Nick Allder, Edward Drohan, Walter Tatro.

Nightmare ★★★ 1942; U.S.; 81m; UNIV; B/W; Spy Drama; Children: Unacceptable; **VHS**. Tense espionage tale set in England in WWII sees Donlevy as an impoverished, starving gambler. He breaks into Barrymore's upscale home in search of food, but discovers to his shock the body of a man with a knife plunged into his back. Barrymore arrives and tells Donlevy that either or both of them will be charged with her

Brian Donlevy and Gavin Muir in *Nightmare*, 1942.

husband's death and gives him the option of either being turned over to the police as the guilty party or helping her to hide the body and for a handsome payment. Donlevy chooses the latter course. When police discover the corpse, Donlevy and Barrymore flee, going to her family retreat in Scotland. Barrymore introduces Donlevy to her adopted cousin Muir, a wealthy distillery owner. Strange events take place that lead Donlevy and Barrymore to probe Muir's activities and they discover that he is operating a Nazi spy ring where German agents parachute near his distillery and he shelters and directs them in acts of sabotage. Donlevy and Barrymore place patriotism before protecting themselves on charges of murder, and, working with authorities, they set a trap for Muir and his agents and bag the spies and are later exonerated for the killing of Barrymore's husband, who was in league with the enemy agents and was dispatched by them for allegedly fouling up one of their operations. Though convoluted, this spy drama provides a lot of intriguing twists and turns and many tense scenes where Donlevy and Barrymore give exceptional performances. **p**, Dwight Taylor; **d**, Tim Whelan; **cast**, Diana Barrymore, Brian Donlevy, Henry Daniell, Eustace Wyatt, Arthur Shields, Gavin Muir, Stanley Logan, Ian Wolfe, Hans Conried, John Abbott, David Clyde; **w**, Taylor (based on the story "Escape" by Philip MacDonald); **c**, George Barnes; **m**, Frank Skinner; **ed**, Frank Gross; **art d**, John B. Goodman; **set d**, Russell A. Gausman.

Nightmare ★★★ 1956; U.S.; 89m; Pine-Thomas-Shane/UA; B/W; Crime Drama; Children: Unacceptable; **VHS**. McCarthy is a New Orleans jazz musician who awakens from a dream in which he has fatally stabbed someone in a mirrored room of a mansion. Or was it only a dream, he wonders, when he sees bruises on his body. He tells Robinson, his police detective brother-in-law, about the dream, but Robinson tells him to forget about it. A jazz tune that McCarthy heard in the dream haunts him and he visits Bourbon Street nightclubs hoping to hear it played. While on a picnic with his girlfriend, Russell, and Robinson, McCarthy sees the mansion of his dream and goes there, finding a room of mirrors and a phonograph and record of the song that has been going around in his head. Robinson learns that a murder was recently committed in the mansion and suspects McCarthy so he gives him twenty-four hours to leave the city or he will have him arrested. Robinson later comes to believe that the owner of the mansion murdered his wife and hypnotized McCarthy into believing that he is the culprit. Robinson traps the murderer and McCarthy is freed from his nightmare. Great atmospheric scenes and standout performances from Robinson and McCarthy make this eerie film worth seeing, a superior remake of the original, **Fear in the Night**, 1947. Songs: "What's Your Sad Story" (Richard M. Sherman), "The Last I Ever Saw of My Man" (Herschel Burke Gilbert, Doris Houck). **p**, William H. Pine, William C. Thomas;

d&w, Maxwell Shane (based on the short story by William Irish (Cornell Woolrich); **cast**, Edward G. Robinson, Kevin McCarthy, Connie Russell, Virginia Christine, Rhys Williams, Gage Clarke, Marian Carr, Barry Atwater, Meade Lewis, Ralph Brooks, Billy May and His Orchestra; **c**, Joseph F. Biroc; **m**, Herschel Burke Gilbert; **ed**, George Gittens; **art d**, Frank Sylos; **set d**, Edward Boyle; **spec eff**, Howard A. Anderson.

Nightmare Alley ★★★ 1947; U.S.; 110m; FOX; B/W; Drama; Children: Unacceptable; **DVD**. Power, in one of his most riveting roles, exchanges his matinee idol image for an utterly worthless fellow with ambition so ruthless that he will destroy anything or anyone in his path to success. This offbeat and often eerie film begins when Power gets a job as a roustabout in a seedy carnival. He becomes obsessed by a mind-reading act performed by Keith, an alcoholic, and Blondell. The act, Power learns, is one where Keith uses a code to convey answers to Blondell, culled from questions in the audience and where something personal is discovered about each questioning spectator and then related back to them by Blondell, amazing the audience. Power, a glib and charming man, becomes the barker for this show and gathers those questions, gradually learning the code from Keith and Blondell. He meanwhile becomes disgusted by another act at the carnival that features a geek, a derelict and dipsomaniac, who, in exchange for food, booze and a place to sleep, performs his grisly act in a pit and where he bites off the heads of live chickens (such gruesome and primitive acts were offered by only the seediest of carnivals and were popular in the South and Midwest of the U.S. from the 1880s to the 1930s and where the tragic geeks also bit off the heads of live snakes to "entertain" unsophisticated rural spectators). "How do you get a guy to be a geek?" Power asks the carnival owner. "I can't understand how anybody can get so low." Power becomes successful with the mind-reading act as he gets spectators to write out their questions and then substitutes those small sheets with questions for blank sheets, which he hands to Blondell on stage and where she burns them in a vase while Power hands the actual questions to Keith, who is hidden beneath the stage and who rewrites the questions on a blackboard that is reflected on a mirror that appears in a crystal ball that Blondell reads, and where she gives clever answers that make her appear to be a genuine mind reader. Gray, an attractive artist performing with strongman Mazurki at the carnival, falls for Power and she tells him how Keith and Blondell used to be big-time performers until Keith took to the bottle. She explains that their old act consisted of Keith staying in the audience and simply putting the written questions to his forehead and saying a few words that represented the "code" Keith and Blondell created, that allowed her to give enlightening answers without seeing those written questions. Power tries to pry the code from Keith by giving him bottles of booze, and Keith responds by peering into a crystal ball, and states, as if seeing the past: "Throughout the ages man has sought to look behind the veil that hides him from tomorrow…Wait! The shifting shape begins to clear. I see fields of grass and rolling hills, and a boy. The boy is running barefoot through the hills. A dog is with him." Power, mesmerized by Keith's mental portrait, believes Keith has just peered into his own boyhood and blurts: "His name was Gip—go on." Keith laughs and says: "See how easy it is to hook them? Stock reading…fits everybody…every boy has a dog." In an effort to have Keith reveal how his code works, Power continues to provide the inebriate with booze, but he gives Keith a bottle of rubbing alcohol by mistake and, after Keith drinks this, he dies. Power then pressures Blondell for information on how her code works and, taken with him, she relents after Power begins an affair with her and he is now equipped to begin his own act with Blondell where she performs on stage blindfolded as Power moves through the crowd, feeding her the right answers while using the code. (Blondell delivers a marvelous line to Power before beginning their affair, one which jocularly describes her promiscuousness when she states: "I have a heart like an artichoke—a leaf for everyone.") The unscrupulous Power, however, is without loyalty and soon betrays Blondell by having an affair with Gray, but this backfires when the carnival folk angrily demand that he marry Gray. Power and Gray marry in a shotgun wedding and Power goes off with her to establish his own mind-reading act, becoming a great success where he and Gray perform in high-class nightclubs. Heralded as a great spiritualist, Power astounds sophisticated audiences in Chicago and then meets psychologist Walker, who is as much a scheming person as he is. Cheating on Gray, he begins an affair with Walker so that she will share with him her confidential files about her clients. Power uses such private information to shock those clients when Walker steers them to his act by revealing their secrets, as if Power can peer into their minds and spirits. This sinister association is designed for profit, one where Power and Walker will share in whatever payments or deals Power can manipulate from such gullible people in private séances. In these rigged performances, Power ostensibly puts his rich clients in contact with their deceased loved ones. He begins milking Holmes, a gullible tycoon still in love with a lost love of many years earlier, by having Gray impersonate the returning spirit of that dead woman. Overwhelmed by this vision, Holmes is now convinced that Power has supernatural powers and promises to give him $150,000 to establish a spiritual temple. Power now thinks that he will become a multimillionaire after establishing that temple, but Gray wants no part of his colossal fraud, saying: "You think God is going to stand for that?" At the next séance, Gray betrays Power and admits that she is posing as Holmes' dead girlfriend, which causes Holmes to explode, striking Power and shouting: "You dirty, sacrilegious thief!" Power seeks Walker's help, but she shuns him, warning that if he ever again contacts her, she will reveal how Keith really died (she has learned this secret from the scorned Blondell) and Power gives up everything, leaving town and living as a hobo. He later goes to Roberts, the manager of a cheap carnival, begging for a job, and Roberts offers Power, who appears to be nothing more than a human derelict, a job with the carnival as a geek, the kind of disgusting job Power had condemned at the beginning of the film. He has, however, no illusions about his future, which he has used up in all of his vile machinations, and resigns himself to living out his life as a miserable geek, stating to Roberts: "Mister, I was made for it." This is where this powerful and mesmerizing tale ends, but the Hollywood censorship board insisted that Fox add a final scene where Power is rescued from such a disgusting finale; director Goulding added a scene where Gray finds Power going half mad after performing as a geek and rescues him. Power's amazing performance won for him universal plaudits from the critics and public alike, and the film proved to be a great success. Blondell is superb as the floozy, fake spiritualist, as is Keith, and Walker also provides a chilling performance as a woman as calculating and scheming as Power's repulsive character. Exceptional, too, is Garmes' crisp cinematography that captures both gritty images of the tawdry carnival atmosphere, as well as the glossy and deceiving nightclub and high society world and where Mockridge's haunting score adds greatly to the chilling scenes. *Author's Note*: Fox studio chief Darryl Zanuck prized Tyrone Power above all of his other actors (with the possible exception of Gregory Peck), telling this author that "when I first heard that they wanted to put Ty [Power] into a role where he is an sleazy crook and then, God forbid, a geek, I thought they [Fox producers] had gone nuts. Ty was our leading star and the most handsome actor on the screen. Then Ty comes to me and practically begs me to let him make the picture. I finally said okay, but I thought it was a big mistake. The picture turned out to be a big hit, so that proved something about my own judgment, didn't it?" Goulding had directed Power in another impactful and memorable film, **The Razor's Edge**, 1946, where Power plays just the opposite type of character, a pure-hearted young man seeking truth. His relationship with Power, however, was cemented and Power asked that Goulding direct **Nightmare Alley** and was edified to see how meticulous and effective Goulding was in helming this strange but compelling tale. Mazurki told this author that "**Nightmare Alley** was one of the weirdest films I ever appeared in, very strange picture. I am a dumb strongman at a carnival

Joan Blondell, Ian Keith and Tyrone Power in *Nightmare Alley*, 1947.

and not very nice, but I am a prince compared to the sleazebag Ty Power plays. I thought when we were making that picture that somebody at Fox had lost their marbles by putting Power into such a role, but the picture was a huge hit, so what did I know?" **p**, George Jessel; **d**, Edmund Goulding; **cast**, Tyrone Power, Joan Blondell, Coleen Gray, Taylor Holmes, Mike Mazurki, Ian Keith, Florence Auer, George Beranger, Oliver Blake, Roy Roberts; **w**, Jules Furthman (based on the novel by William Lindsay Gresham); **c**, Lee Garmes; **m**, Cyril Mockridge; **ed**, Barbara McLean; **art d**, Lyle Wheeler, J. Russell Spencer; **set d**, Thomas Little; **spec eff**, Fred Sersen.

The Nightmare Before Christmas ★★★ 1993; U.S.; 76m; Touchstone/Buena Vista; Color; Animated Fantasy; Children: Cautionary (MPAA: PG); **BD**; **DVD**; **VHS**. Tim Burton presents a bizarre film that resembles in no way, except a skewered title, the classic 1822 poem "The Night Before Christmas" by Clement Clarke Moore (1779-1863). This film, however, became a classic of its own. Burton wrote his poem while working as a Walt Disney animator in 1982. It tells the story of Jack Skellington (voice of Sarandon voiceover with the singing voice of Elfman), who celebrates in "Halloween Town" with jazz-playing zombies, a wolf man, and a female Frankenstein scarecrow, played by O'Hara, who is enamored of him. But he becomes bored and ventures into a forest where he discovers the joyous "Christmas Town." He wants to share his wonderful discovery, so he returns to Halloween Town by impersonating Santa Claus and hires three mischief-makers to kidnap the real Santa so he can share his weird idea of Christmas with the world. Mixing Christmas with Halloween proves to be a strange and scary tale, but the film became a huge hit and made many millions. Songs: "Here Comes Santa Claus" (Gene Autry, Oakley Haldeman); "Deck the Halls" (traditional),"Jingle Bells" (James Lord Pierpont); "Jack's Lament," "Jack's Obsession," "Kidnap the Sandy Claws," "Making Christmas," "Oogie Boogie's Song," "Poor Jack," "Sally's Song," "This Is Halloween," "Town Meeting," "What's This?," "Finale" (Danny Elfman). Many of the images may prove to be too frightening for children. **p**, Tim Burton, Denise DiNovi, Kathleen Gavin, **d**, Henry Selick; **cast** (voiceovers), Danny Elfman, Chris Sarandon, Catherine O'Hara, William Hickey, Glenn Shadix, Paul Reubens, Ken Page, Ed Ivory, Susan McBride, Debi Durst; **w**, Caroline Thompson, Michael McDowell (based on a story and characters by Burton); **c**, Pete Kozachik; **m**, Elfman; **ed**, Stan Webb; **art d**, Deane Taylor; **spec eff**, Loretta Weeks, Myles Murphy, Kozachik.

Nights of Cabiria ★★★ 1957; Italy/France; Dino de Laurentiis/Lopert Pictures; B/W; Drama; Children: Unacceptable; **DVD**; **VHS**. Fellini again presents his wife, Masina, in a memorable film where she plays a

Elpidia Carrillo in *Nine Lives*, 2005.

streetwalker with the stereotypical heart of gold, but her persistent optimism raises her character far above its clichéd persona. Masina works the streets in one of the shabbiest areas of Rome where she encounters one setback after another, but none of these depressing experiences daunts or deters her from looking positively on life. She meets a handsome movie star after he becomes involved in a brawl and he cavalierly takes her to his lavish residence where Masina has momentary visions of remaining as the wealthy man's concubine, but just as easily accepts her usual fate when the actor quickly sends her on her way after a brief sexual encounter. Masina then meets shy and withdrawn Perier, a man to whom she is inwardly drawn, more as a mother figure than a lover. She dares to make plans in marrying him, but her hopes are again crushed when Perier steals all her money and deserts her, leaving her only one choice and that is to return to streetwalking. Masina, however, accepts her fate with the strong good will of her heart, and in the closing scene of this absorbing drama she looks directly at the camera and gives a knowing smile that assures the viewer that she will go on living her miserable life but with a strong heart and an indomitable spirit, perfectly translating Fellini's own existential philosophy. (In Italian; English subtitles.) **p**, Dino De Laurentiis; **d**, Federico Fellini; **cast**, Giulietta Masina, François Perier, Franca Marzi, Dorian Gray, Aldo Silvani, Ennio Girolami, Mario Passante, Christian Tassou, Amedeo Nazzari, Gianni Baghino; **w**, Pier Paolo Pasolini (based on a story by Fellini, Ennio Flaiano, Tullio Pinelli, and a novel by Maria Molinari); **c**, Aldo Tonti, Otello Martelli; **m**, Nino Rota; **ed**, Leo Catozzo; **prod d**, Piero Gherardi.

The Nights of Prague ★★★ 1969; 92 min.; Czechoslovakia; Filmove Studio Barrandov; B/W; Drama/Horror; Children: Unacceptable; **DVD**; **VHS**. Three stories were released as one film – two of which, "The Bread Shoes," directed by Schorm, and "The Poisoned Poisoner," directed by Makovec – take place during the Middle Ages. The third and most interesting of the stories is a new version of the Yiddish legend "The Golem" about a Polish rabbi, Klusk, who makes a live clay man that destroys him. Well made and enacted, these allegorical tales entertain and provide some frightening moments at the same time. **d**, Jiri Brdecka, Evalkd Schorm, Milos Makoveck; **cast**, Jan Klusak, Jana Brezkova, Teresa Tuszynska, Milena Dvorska, Milos Kopecky, Josef Blaha, Kveta Fialova, Natasa Gollova, Milan Nedela, Zdenek Dite; **w**, Brdecka; **ph**, Jan Kallis, Frantisek Uldrych.

Nikki, Wild Dog of the North ★★★ 1961; U.S./Canada; 74m; Disney/Buena Vista; Color; Adventure; Children: Cautionary; **DVD**; **VHS**. In this exciting adventure, Nikki, a half-wolf, half-dog raised by trapper Coutu in Alaska's Yukon Territory during the 1890s gold rush, runs into the woods and returns with a new friend, a bear cub. Coutu leashes them

together with rope and takes them down a river in his canoe. The canoe overturns in some rapids and the animals, both still tied together, survive, but find themselves on their own. The rope finally breaks, but they remain together searching for food, water, and Coutu. As winter approaches, the cub goes into hibernation and Nikki is now on his own. He raids the campsite of another trapper, Genest, who captures and trains Nikki to be a pit fighter. A local authority learns of the illegal betting sport and tries to break it up, but Genest tries to sic Nikki on him. Nikki recognizes the man as Coutu and, instead, turns on Genest, who falls on his own knife. Nikki and Coutu are reunited and go off on more adventures. An exciting and wonderful family film but cautionary for children because of some animal violence. **p**, Winston Hibler, Erwin L. Verity (for Walt Disney Productions); **d**, Jack Couffer, Don Haldane; **cast**, Jean Coutu, Émile Genest, Uriel Luft, Robert Rivard, Jacques Fauteux; **w**, Ralph Wright, Hibler, Dwight Hauser (based on the novel *Nomads of the North* by James Oliver Curwood); **c**, William W. Bacon III, Lloyd Beebe, Jack Couffer, Ray Jewell, Donald Wilder; **m**, Oliver Wallace; **ed**, Grant K. Smith; **set d**, Jack McCullagh.

Nim's Island ★★★ 2008; U.S.; 96m; Walden Media/FOX-Walden; Color; Adventure/Fantasy; Children: Unacceptable (MPAA: PG); **BD**; **DVD**. Intriguing tale sees Butler as an oceanographer scientist, who takes his twelve-year-old daughter, Breslin, to live on a deserted tropical island after her mother dies in the ocean. A devoted reader of fantasy adventure novels by her favorite author, Foster, Breslin's imagination is visited by some friendly animals and creatures including a 500-pound sea lion, an iguana, a bearded dragon, and a pelican. Butler leaves her alone for one day to search for a strain of plankton and his boat is damaged in a storm. While she anxiously awaits his return, a cruise ship arrives, but she manages to discourage its passengers from coming ashore to spoil her privacy by pretending it's dangerous. Breslin tries to get a fictional hero in one of Foster's books to find her father (also played by Butler), but, instead, she reaches Foster, who suffers from agoraphobia, a fear of open spaces, and cannot leave her San Francisco home. Foster fights her fear by wanting to help Breslin, so she manages to take a helicopter, swim with a huge whale, and ride a high wire through treetops like Tarzan in a jungle. This enjoyable blend of reality and fantasy provides impressive character development where Breslin learns how to overcome adversity by calling upon her own bravery. Songs: "Stay Up Late" (David Byrne, Christopher Frantz, Jerry Harrison, Martina Weymouth), "Beautiful Day" (Adam Clayton, Dave Evans, Bono (Paul David Hewson, Larry Mullen, Jr.). Violence and gutter language prohibit viewing by children. **p**, Paula Mazur, Murray Pope, Alan Bell; **d**, Jennifer Flackett, Mark Levin; **cast**, Abigail Breslin, Jodie Foster, Gerard Butler, Michael Carman, Mark Brady, Anthony Simcoe, Christopher Baker, Maddison Joyce, Peter Callan, Rhonda Doyle; **w**, Mazur, Flackett, Levin, Joseph Kwong (based on the novel by Wendy Orr); **c**, Stuart Dryburgh; **m**, Patrick Doyle; **ed**, Stuart Levy; **prod d**, Barry Robison; **art d**, Colin Gibson, Jacinta Leong, Deborah Riley; **set d**, Rebecca Cohen; **spec eff**, Bruce Bright, Dan Oliver, Rodney Burke, Scott Gordon.

Nine Hours to Rama ★★★ 1963; U.K./U.S.; 124m; Red Lion/FOX; Color; Biographical Drama; Children: Unacceptable; **DVD**. Intense and provocative, this biopic depicts the murderous actions of religious Hindu zealot Nathuram Godse (1910-1949), excitingly played by Buchholz, who, along with others, plots the assassination of India's foremost leader, Mahatma Gandhi (1859-1948), played by J. S. Casshyap (shown briefly at end). Buchholz is convinced that Casshyap, a nationalist who has always advocated non-violence, is leading the country into chaos because of his partiality toward Musleims, even though Buchholz is a member of Gandhi's political party. He struggles with his convictions as well as his sexual relationship with attractive Gearon, who is married, and who is a strong supporter of Gandhi, and it is over her allegiance to the great leader and their arguments over Gandhi's measures that cause their separation. Buchholz becomes dejected after his application to the British army (England's rule over India was in its last stages) is rejected based upon his Brahmin background, and he seeks solace in the company of Baker, a prostitute, but this shabby relationship brings him nothing but remorse. He returns to Gearon, but she no longer has any love for him and orders him to leave. It is at this moment that Buchholz resolves to murder Gandhi. He begins his journey to Gandhi's retreat, and en route we see in flashback several traumatic moments of his life—the deaths of his father and his child bride in bloody riots; his promise to his mother that he will seek justice, even by violence, for these transgressions; and his associations with radicals, chiefly Borisenko (who plays Godse's co-conspirator, Naryan Apte, 1911-1949), who are bent on killing Gandhi. While Buchholz is on his murderous mission, local police chief Ferrer learns of the plot to kill the Indian leader and he warns Casshyap, who resigns himself to whatever fate awaits him, telling Ferrer that he will not alter his itinerary. Buchholz finally arrives at New Delhi and pushes his way through a crowd greeting Casshyap (who is an amazing Gandhi look-alike) and confronts the great leader. Without a word, Buchholz withdraws a pistol and fires three shots point blank range at his victim (all three shots struck Gandhi squarely in the chest, killing him almost instantly; he reportedly stated "Hai, Rama!"/"Oh, God!"). Buchholz makes no effort to escape and accepts his fate by allowing police to seize him and drag him away into custody. Robson's direction skillfully portrays this tragedy and Buchholz is riveting in his role while Gearon, Baker, Ferrer and Casshyap (who was a 64-year-old teacher) are standouts in their roles. *Author's Note*: Godse and associate Apte were executed by hanging a week after Godse assassinated Gandhi on January 30, 1948; for more information on Godse and Gandhi, see my book, *The Great Pictorial History of World Crime*, Volume I (History, Inc., 2004; pages 156-160). **p&d**, Mark Robson; **cast**, Horst Buccholz, Jose Ferrer, Valerie Gearon, Don Borisenko, Robert Morley, Diane Baker, Harry Andrews, P. Jairaj, David Abraham, Achala Sachdev, Marne Maitland, Harold Goldblatt, J.S. Casshyap; **w**, Nelson Gidding (based on the book by Stanley Wolpert); **c**, Arthur Ibbetson, Ted Moore (CinemaScope; DeLuxe Color); **m**, Malcolm Arnold; **ed**, Ernest Walter; **art d**, Elliot Scott, Ram Yedekar; **set d**, John Jarvis.

Nine Lives ★★★ 2005; U.S.; 115m; Mockingbird Pictures/Magnolia Pictures; Color; Drama; Children: Unacceptable (MPAA: R); **DVD**. Though the title might lead viewers to believe that this film deals with the exploits of a cat, it absorbingly portrays nine women on a hot tin roof, a series of short takes on turning points in the lives of nine southern California women. The episodes include those about a pregnant woman, Penn, who has an encounter in a grocery store with an ex-boyfriend; Baker, a stressed wife, who talks about her upcoming mastectomy with her husband, Mantegna; Spacek, a wife who cares for her dying husband; and Brenneman, a young woman who raises eyebrows by attending the funeral of the wife of her former husband. The stories end with two women, Close and Fanning, visiting a cemetery together. All the women are connected in one way or another in this complex but well-presented drama. Songs: "Memories" (Francois Paterson, Dominic Paterson, Christelle Pechin); "Marjorie," "Riviera Gold," "So Posh" (Richard Friedman); "Tennessee Blossom" (Alain Leroux); "Willow Dream" (Juan Vincente Zambrano); "Tropic Breeze" (Sam Fonteyn); "Garden Song" (David Mallett); "Freedom" (Diego Carlin, Kyme Dang); "Whale Watching" (Jaime Perkins); "Bolero Mi Amor" (Carlos Sarmiento, Marco Siniscalco); "Wetlands" (Paul Lewis). Gutter language, brief sexual content, and some disturbing images prohibit viewing by children. **p**, Julie Lynn; **d&w**, Rodrigo Garcia; **cast**, Sissy Spacek, Kathy Baker, Aidan Quinn, Amy Brenneman, Glenn Close, Joe Mantegna, Robin Wright Penn, Holly Hunter, Ian McShane, Mary Kay Place, Elpidia Carrillo, Lawrence Pressman, Dakota Fanning; **c**, Xavier Pérez Grobet; **m**, Ed Shearmur; **ed**, Andrea Folprecht; **prod d**, Courtney Jackson; **art d**, Amy Lamendola; **spec eff**, Richard Van Den Bergh.

Jane Fonda, Lily Tomlin and Dolly Parton in *Nine to Five*, 1980.

Nine Men ★★★ 1943; U.K.; 68m; EAL/UA; B/W; War Drama; Children: Unacceptable; **DVD**; **VHS**. This exciting and well-enacted war tale profiles nine British soldiers, who were attacked by German planes while on patrol in North Africa during World War II (1939-1945). The captain is killed, leaving the sergeant and seven others to fight off the enemy until help can arrive. The movie was inspired by the Russian film, **The Thirteen**, 1937, which also inspired the American version **Sahara**, 1943. Violence prohibits viewing by children. **p**, Michael Balcon; **d&w**, Harry Watt (based on the story "Umpity Poo" by Gerald Kersh); **cast**, Jack Lambert, Gordon Jackson, Frederick Piper, Grant Sutherland, Bill Blewitt, Eric Micklewood, John Varley, Jack Horsman, Richard Wilkinson, Giulio Finzi; **c**, Roy Kellino; **m**, John Greenwood; **ed**, Charles Crichton, Erik Cripps; **art d**, Duncan Sutherland.

Nine to Five ★★★ 1980; U.S.; 110m; FOX; Color; Comedy; Children: Cautionary (MPAA: PG); **DVD**; **VHS**. This very funny comedy where three women rebel against a chauvinistic boss to create mayhem and mirth begins when Fonda gets a job as a secretary at a large corporation. She makes friends with Tomlin and Parton (in Dolly's great debut where she is terrific). Their boss is Coleman, a conniving, womanizing and thoroughly disreputable character without an ounce of decency in his middle-aged body. Though married, Coleman is forever trying to seduce buxom Parton, offering her gifts and slobbering amour after using the ruse of having her take dictation in his office. He is demanding and overbearing with Fonda and Tomlin, berating them for any minor mistake, a man any woman could instantly learn to despise. Gathering together one evening, the trio of females, while high on pot, pool their collective derision toward Coleman and begin imagining any kind of retaliatory techniques that will produce his comeuppance. (In one hilarious dreamlike sequence Tomlin envisions herself as Snow White and how she perfunctorily dispatches Coleman with poison.) So obsessed are these women in seeking revenge against Coleman that they collectively accept Tomlin's conviction that she has somehow poisoned Coleman and, to cover her tracks, all three go to the morgue to retrieve his body, only to discover that Tomlin's dream is only a dream. Coleman, the next day, is nevertheless very much alive and his old obnoxious self, oppressing these women at every turn until they take drastic measures, kidnapping and taking him to his home while his wife, Mercer, is out of town. Gagged and bound, Coleman is forced to watch endless TV soap operas, entertainment he loathes and which almost unhinges his mind (shades of **A Clockwork Orange**, 1972, where criminal Malcolm McDowell is forced to see Holocaust films to cure him of his evil thoughts). The women, meanwhile, return to work and streamline operations and where everyone works in harmony and with peak efficiency. Coleman, now a wiser and more circumspect man, returns to his position to be greeted

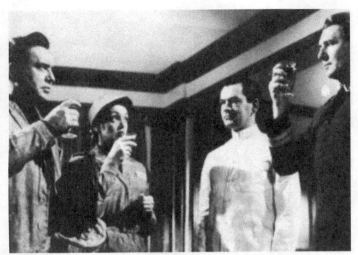

Edmond O'Brien, Jan Sterling, Joseph Bull and Michael Redgrave in *1984*, 1956.

by corporate boss Hayden, who compliments him on the vast improvements in his department and he grudgingly accords recognition to Tomlin, Parton and Fonda, their careers now assured with success. Decidedly a one-way perspective that indicts all men—none of the men in the film are treated with any respect (much the same way Steven Spielberg portrayed men in **The Color Purple**, 1985), this consistently funny film nevertheless provides a thoroughly entertaining female fantasy. **p**, Bruce Gilbert; **d**, Colin Higgins; **cast**, Jane Fonda, Lily Tomlin, Dolly Parton, Dabney Coleman, Sterling Hayden, Elizabeth Wilson, Henry Jones, Lawrence Pressman, Marian Mercer, Ren Woods, Elisabeth Fraser; **w**, Higgins, Patricia Resnick (based on a story by Resnick); **c**, Reynaldo Villalobos; **m**, Charles Fox (DeLuxe Color); **ed**, Pembroke J. Herring; **prod d**, Dean Mitzner; **art d**, Jack Gammon Taylor, Jr.; **set d**, Anne McCulley; **spec eff**, Chuck Gaspar, Matt Sweeney.

1984 ★★★ 1956; U.K.; 90m; Holiday Film Productions/COL; B/W; Science Fiction; Children: Cautionary; **DVD**; **VHS**. Orwell's pervasive and powerful novel comes to life in this well-crafted production where a futuristic world is controlled by "Big Brother" and his faceless followers, and is set in London, which is called Oceana, one of three world organizations that have survived nuclear holocausts. Everything and everyone is controlled and monitored on TV screens and even private lives are strictly surveyed by agents of the Ministry of Love. O'Brien's emotions and instincts have somehow survived incessant indoctrination to remain rebellious against this oppressive lifestyle and its many dictates and dictators. He meets Sterling, who secretly shares his loathing for this society and they begin a clandestine affair. This intimate association is fraught with fear and they risk their lives if detected by agents of the Anti-Sex League or the all-powerful Thought Police. These furtive lovers are walking on eggshells in that two-way microphones have been planted in their homes as they are also present in every other residence and their every word is recorded and evaluated by unknown listeners. They nevertheless resolve to form a secret organization that will overthrow the dictatorship of Big Brother, enlisting Redgrave into their dangerous cause. He proves to be less than reliable, however, as he is a secret agent for Big Brother and he turns both of them over to the Thought Police. O'Brien is tortured into confessing all when confronted by his most innermost fear, the sight of rats after he is exposed to a swarm of these scurrying creatures, he turns in Sterling and screams out love for Big Brother (in the U.S. version of this film; in the British version, he is executed). Sterling suffers the same fate in this somewhat depressing but mesmerizing film, where O'Brien and Sterling are standouts in their roles. **p**, Peter Rathvon; **d**, Michael Anderson; **cast**, Michael Redgrave, Edmond O'Brien, Jan Sterling, David Kossoff, Mervyn Johns, Donald Pleasence, Carol Wolveridge, Ernest Clark,

Patrick Allen, Ronan O'Casey; **w**, William P. Templeton, Ralph Gilbert Bettinson (based on the novel by George Orwell); **c**, C. Pennington-Richards; **m**, Malcolm Arnold; **ed**, Bill Lewthwaite; **prod d**, Terence Verity; **art d**, Len Townsend; **spec eff**, Bryan Langley, George Blackwell, Norman Warwick.

Nineteen Eighty Four ★★★ 1984; U.K.; 113m; Umbrella-Rosenblum Films/Atlantic Releasing Corporation; Color; Science Fiction; Children: Unacceptable (MPAA: R); **DVD**; **VHS**. A good remake of the 1956 film sees Hurt rewriting history in a dictatorial society where everyone's moves are strictly monitored and where he rebels by having a secret affair with Hamilton. He and Hamilton so loathe their oppressive society that dictates their lifestyle that they decide to overthrow its faceless dictator, Big Brother. Burton joins them in their cause, but he turns out to be an undercover agent for the regime and turns them both over to authorities and where Hurt is tortured into denouncing Hamilton and becomes a slavish servant to Big Brother. **p**, Simon Perry, Robert Devereux; **d&w**, Michael Radford (based on the novel by George Orwell); **cast**, John Hurt, Richard Burton, Al Clark, Suzanna Hamilton, Cyril Cusack, Gregor Fisher, James Walker, Andrew Wilde, David Trevena, David Cann, Roger Lloyd Pack, Anthony Benson, Peter Frye; **c**, Roger Deakins (Eastmancolor); **m**, Dominic Muldowney, **ed**, Tom Priestley; **prod d**, Allan Cameron; **art d**, Martin Hebert, Grant Hicks; **spec eff**, Ian Scoones.

1911 ★★★ 2011 China/Hong Kong; 121m.; Beijing Alnair Culture & Media/Well Go; Color/B/W; Adventure; Children: Unacceptable (MPAA: R); **BD**; **DVD**. This well-made historical action film is based on the founding of the Republic of China when nationalist forces led by Sun Yat-sen (1866-1925), played by Chao, and Huang Xing (1874-1916), played by Chan, overthrew the Qing Dynasty in 1911. The film was made to commemorate the 100th anniversary of the Xinhai Revolution, following which Sun Yat-sen was elected provisional president of the new Provisional Republic of China. This was followed by the abdication of the last Qing emperor, Puyi (1906-1967). It was Chan's 100th film and he spent $30 million of his own money to fund it. A film of epic proportions, its excessive violence prohibits viewing by children. Another magnificent film about the 1911 China Revolution is **The Last Emperor**, 1987. **p**, Guoqing Gu, Bin Guo, Peter Lam, Lijuan Liu, Jianhong Qi, Zhonglun Ren, Xiaoyi Shen, Dafang Wang, Lian Yu, Li Zhou, Pxue Zhou; **d**, Li Zhang, Jackie Chan; **cast**, Chan, Winston Chao, Bingbing Li as Bingbing Lee, Chun Sun, Joan Chen, Wu Jiang, Jaycee Chan, Ge Hu, Jing Ning, Shaoqun Yu, Yu-Hang To (as Dennis To), Zhi-zhong Huang; **w**, Xingdong Wang, Baoguang Chen; **c**, Wai Huang; **art d**, Hai Zhao; **spec eff**, Yanming Jiang.

1941 ★★★ 1979; U.S.; 118m; UNIV; Color; Comedy; Children: Unacceptable; **DVD**; **VHS**. Wild and zany, this comedic romp from pantheon director Spielberg presents a host of Saturday Night players in California just after the beginning of WWII and where paranoia reigns over military commanders, who believe that the Japanese have either secretly invaded the United States or are about to do so at any second. Anti-aircraft guns are placed on the rooftops of Los Angeles office buildings and along the coast, one of these 40mm guns left in the care of Beatty, a bumbling but patriotic citizen whose large house is at the edge of a cliff overlooking the Pacific Ocean (and where his wife, Gary, frets over the presence of that gun). While Beatty patrols the coastline, swarms of servicemen flock to a jitterbug contest in a huge dance hall in downtown L.A. where fetching blonde jitterbug Kay is avidly sought by Williams, a thug-like soldier, and dance mad Di Cicco. Meanwhile, Oates commands a jittery army unit to the north of the city, where this gun-happy commander has his men on full alert and firing at anything that moves. He hears a plane overhead and he and his men blast at it, but the P-40 fighter lands safely, and from its cockpit leaps Belushi, who is called "Wild Bill Kelso," a cigar-chomping, beer-gutted pilot seeking Japanese planes that do not exist and is as gun-happy as Oates. After palavering with Oates, Belushi takes off in his fighter, but not before, at Oate's request, he fires several rounds from the guns of his fighter plane so that jingoistic Oates can revel in the mutter of those guns. He then takes off in search of enemy planes. While the top commander of the area, General Joseph "Vinegar Joe" Stilwell (1883-1946), played by Stack, visits a movie theater and grinningly enjoys watching **Dumbo**, 1941, youthful U.S. Army officer Matheson convinces Allen, who is Stack's aide, that he is an experienced pilot and commandeers a transport plane, taking her aloft to have an assignation in the clouds, her most desired form of achieving ecstasy. While they attempt to make love, the plane, on auto-pilot, rolls and dives and soars crazily about. At the dance hall, the competition between Williams and Di Cicco for Kay's attentions erupts into a fight that becomes a widespread brawl between sailors, soldiers and marines, a frantic fight that all but wrecks the place. Above this mayhem flies Matheson and Allen whose plane is spotted by fighter pilot Belushi, and, thinking it to be a Japanese bomber, Belushi states: "Eat lead, squint!" and begins shooting at it. In making one of his attacks, Belushi sees off the coast a Japanese submarine surface, which is captained by Mifune, and accompanied by Nazi naval adviser Lee. Belushi fires at the transport carrying Matheson and Allen, shooting it down so that it crashes in the Le Brea tar pits, but Matheson and Allen survive. Belushi's fighter is then shot down by U.S. anti-aircraft and crash lands on a L.A. street where all is chaos and where Aykroyd commands a tank that shoots out the street lights to create a protective blackout. Stack, hearing all this commotion, steps from the movie theater and Belushi reports to him, saying that he has just been in combat with a Japanese bomber. He then commandeers a motorcycle and races toward an amusement park on the coast, believing the Japanese submarine is located there. That submarine has already been engaged in combat by Beatty, with the aid of friend Stander, when Beatty loads the 40mm gun on his property and fires several shells at the sub that just miss the target, and manages to destroy his own home in the process and where his wife, Gary, just barely survives. Meanwhile, hunter Hamilton and his goofy friend, Deezen, a ventriloquist, accompanied by a wise-cracking dummy, ride high on a Ferris wheel. They fire upon the submarine, which begins shelling the seaside amusement center. Aykroyd arrives with his tank as does Belushi and they, too, fire on the submarine, which returns fire, unleashing the Ferris wheel that rolls along a pier and into the sea, as well as destroying the pier that sinks the tank. Belushi swims to the submarine and climbs into it as it submerges and is taken prisoner, and where Mifune orders the sub to return to Japan. The conclusion sees Stack meeting with Beatty and all of the survivors from the previous night's mayhem and where they resolve to work together to defeat the enemy in the ensuing WWII. Beatty tells Stack that he will not allow the enemy to spoil his Christmas, and he hangs a wreath on the front door of his house, which has been mostly destroyed in his battle with the submarine, and which promptly collapses into the ocean for a crescendo finale. Loaded with low-brow, toilet humor, infantile slapstick and cornball clichés, the action is nevertheless nonstop in a truly madcap film where Spielberg allowed the lunatics to take over the asylum. Made for $32 million, this outrageous comedy returned three times its investment (more than $94 million) in its initial box office release. **p**, Buzz Feitshans; **d**, Steven Spielberg; **cast**, Dan Aykroyd, Ned Beatty, John Belushi, Lorraine Gary, Murray Hamilton, Christopher Lee, Tim Matheson, Toshiro Mifune, Robert Stack, Nancy Allen, John Candy, John Landis, Mickey Rourke, James Caan, Penny Marshall, Joseph P. Flaherty, Frank McRae, Elisha Cook, Jr., Slim Pickens, Lionel Stander, Dub Taylor, Warren Oates, Treat Williams, Bobby Di Cicco, Dianne Kay, Perry Lang, Wendie Jo Sperber, Eddie Deezen, Patti LuPone; **w**, Robert Zemeckis, Bob Gale (based on a story by Zemeckis, Gale, John Milius); **c**, William A. Fraker (Metrocolor); **m**, John Williams; **ed**, Michael Kahn; **prod d**, Dean Edward Mitzner; **art d**, William F. O'Brien; **set d**, John Austin; **spec eff**, Larry Robinson.

Evelyn Keyes and John Payne in *99 River Street*, 1953.

1900 ★★★ 1977; Italy/France/West German; 245m; PEA/PAR; Color; Drama; Children: Unacceptable (MPAA: R); **DVD**; **VHS**. This sweeping epic spans a half century and depicts the characters of a large family in Italy, beginning in 1945 to show the end of WWII and then, in flashback, to Giuseppe Verdi's death in 1901. The story line follows the lives of two young men, De Niro, who is the son of wealthy landowner Lancaster in Parma (where director Bertolucci presents a microcosm of Italy during this chaotic period in which fascism took root in the nation) and Depardieu, who is the son of peasant Hayden. Both boys grow up together, De Niro is a weakling, easily cowed by his dominating father Lancaster, and Depardieu is a strong-willed person who becomes a communist and demands widespread land reforms. They both serve in WWI and return home, De Niro slowly embracing fascism while marrying Sanda, and inheriting his father's vast estates and where Depardieu's wife, Sandrelli, dies after giving birth. Depardieu's communist activities finally cause him to flee when fascists seek to imprison him, but he returns to the area following the war and participates in a trial where De Niro is charged with fascist activities and where he survives the charges and is eventually released. Overlong (the Italian version ran 317 minutes), Bertolucci often dwells too much on the political nuances of the era, but nevertheless elicits powerful performances from De Niro (who has the more difficult role) and Depardieu. **p**, Alberto Grimaldi; **d**, Bernardo Bertolucci; **cast**, Robert De Niro, Gerard Depardieu, Dominique Sanda, Francesca Bertini, Laura Betti, Werner Bruhns, Stefania Sandrelli, Sterling Hayden, Anna Henkel, Alida Valli, Donald Sutherland, Burt Lancaster; **c**, Vittorio Storaro (Technicolor); **m**, Ennio Morricone; **ed**, Franco Arcalli; **prod d**, Maria Paola Maino, Gianni Quaranta; **art d**, Ezio Frigerio; **set d**, Maino; **spec eff**, Andrea Baracca, Ludovico Bettarello.

99 River Street ★★★ 1953; U.S.; 83m; UA; B/W; Crime; Children: Unacceptable; **DVD**. Karlson, a director excelling in film noir productions, presents a suspenseful thriller where Payne is a boxer whose collapsed ring career has compelled him to drive a cab for a living. Castle, his cheating wife, is having an affair with jewel thief Dexter. Payne becomes involved with Keyes, an actress, who is accused of murdering a stage producer, but Payne, who tries to help her out of that homicide, learns that he has been used in a reenactment of that murder so that Keyes can get an acting role in a murder play. Castle is found dead in Payne's cab, and he tries to find a way to clear himself of her death. He learns that Dexter murdered her and clears his own name while Keyes, in trying to right her wrong in using Payne, helps him in his quest for justice and exoneration. Payne, who had earlier played matinee idol roles in comedies and musicals, later turned to tough character parts in many film noirs, and this is one of those better productions. ***Author's***

Greta Garbo and Melvyn Douglas in *Ninotchka*, 1939.

Note: Payne told this author that "I thought that **99 River Street** had a much better script than some of the other crime dramas I appeared in and that my character is more of a victim than my cheating wife, who gets murdered. Every time I turn around in that picture, I get sucker-punched. It's a tough, bare-knuckled film, very realistic, and any working man, who has been blamed for something he did not do, can identify with it." Excessive violence prohibits viewing by children. **p**, Edward Small; **d**, Phil Karlson; **cast**, John Payne, Evelyn Keyes, Brad Dexter, Frank Faylen, Peggie Castle, Jay Adler, Jack Lambert, Glen Langan, Eddy Waller, John Day, Ian Wolfe, Peter Leeds, **w**, Robert Smith (based on a story by George Zuckerman); **c**, Franz Planer; **m**, Arthur Lange, Emil Newman; **ed**, Buddy Small; **art d**, Frank Sylos; **set d**, Al Keggeris; **spec eff**, David Koehler.

Ninotchka ★★★★★ 1939; U.S.; 110m; MGM; Comedy; Children: Acceptable; **DVD**; **VHS**. Garbo is magnificent in this wonderful Lubitsch comedy, the first major U.S. film to profile the dictatorship of Joseph Stalin and the Soviet regime in Russia, albeit its draconian lifestyle was played for laughs rather than presenting a political indictment. The film opens with a Soviet committee of three—Granach, Rumann and Bressart—who arrive in Paris to sell priceless jewels confiscated from the Russian aristocracy during the Revolution in order to buy tractors to cultivate the country and feed its starving masses. Claire, a former grand duchess of Russia, learns that the gems are her very own that were seized during the Revolution and, enraged, hires Douglas, her lover and a nobleman, to recoup the jewels. Douglas gets an injunction against the sale of the jewels pending litigation and then proceeds to corrupt the visiting Soviet committeemen by wining and dining them, so that the pleasures of the Western world are now more attractive to these Soviet visitors than completing their mission. (Lubitsch cleverly demonstrates the corruption of these communist clodhoppers by simply showing waiters arriving outside the door of their hotel room carrying trays laden with haute cuisine and all manner of alcoholic drinks, culminating with three alluring ladies selling cigarettes, and with each arrival of these delicacies we hear a roar of approval from the unseen three committeemen.) Lugosi, the commissar in Moscow in charge of these three clowns, becomes alarmed when he does not receive reports from them, he sends his most dedicated assistant, Garbo, to Paris, to conclude the mission. Garbo is a dedicated communist, and after arriving in Paris, she implants the fear of the Soviet regime once more inside the minds and hearts of Bressart, Rumann and Granach. Douglas finds her a no-nonsense bureaucrat, who never cracks a smile on her beautiful face and Douglas realizes that she may be invulnerable to temptation. Suave and full of charm, Douglas makes many amorous advances to Garbo, and she easily resists his amorous assault and tells him

that love is only "a chemical reaction." He takes her on a tour of the City of Light, showing her its magnificent structures, but such beautiful architecture does not inspire romance; it only reminds Garbo of their structural significance. When returning her to her hotel room, Douglas tries the direct approach, embracing and kissing Garbo. She is somewhat taken aback, as if this is the first time she has ever been kissed, and she responds by saying: "That was restful." Then she admits that she has, indeed, been kissed once before, by a Polish cavalryman, who was killed in a battle. Douglas then works to unleash her sense of humor, taking her to a small café and telling her a joke, but she does not crack a smile. He gives up, telling her that "there's not a laugh in you!" With that, he angrily moves backward in his chair and promptly spills onto the floor. Garbo erupts with a deep-throated, long laugh, one that electrified the world. Her bureaucratic hard shell begins to crumble and soon Garbo is buying Paris gowns and dresses, silk stockings, high-heeled shoes and Paris perfumes, all of which now emphasizes and accents her feminine charms. Douglas takes her on the town where they dance and dine and Garbo drinks a bit too much champagne so that when Douglas deposits her at her hotel suite, she falls asleep in her evening gown. Claire enters the suite and finds the hidden area where her confiscated jewels are stashed and she recoups them and departs. Having regained her jewels, however, is not as important to Claire as keeping Douglas as her lover. She knows that Douglas has fallen for Garbo down to his patent leather shoes and she schemes to get him back into her arms. She tells Garbo that she can have the jewels, but only under the condition that she returns to Moscow on the next plane and has no further communication with Douglas. Knowing that Claire holds the upper hand, Garbo agrees to this plan. She receives the jewels and then returns to Moscow, even though she has fallen deeply in love with Douglas. For his part, Douglas is devastated when Garbo leaves; he tries to travel to Russia, but is denied a visa. He then learns that the three inept Soviet committeemen have returned to Moscow and have been reassigned to a mission in Constantinople, and he rightly guesses that these three incompetent buffoons will again botch their new assignment. They do, and Garbo is again dispatched by Lugosi to straighten out these errant Soviet citizens. When she arrives in Constantinople, she finds that Rumann, Bressart and Granach have opened up a posh Russian restaurant and are in the chips and have no intention of ever returning to the drudgery and dire lifestyle of Soviet Russia. She then learns that their financial backer is none other than Douglas. When Garbo sees Douglas, she rushes into his arms and they make plans to wed. Garbo, too, will not be returning to Russia. Lubitsch superbly directs this film with infinite care, accenting Garbo's exquisite beauty in medium and close-up shots while surrounding her with comedic action from her errant associates and many touching romantic scenes with the amorous Douglas; both render marvelous performances and are greatly aided by a lively, witty script from Brackett, Wilder and Reisch. The film was loosely remade as **Comrade X**, 1940, with Clark Gable and Hedy Lamarr; **The Iron Petticoat**, 1956, with Katharine Hepburn and Bob Hope; and again, as a delightful musical, **Silk Stockings**, 1957, with Fred Astaire and Cyd Charisse. *Author's Note*: Garbo told this author that she came to do this film after Lubitsch called her and told her that he wanted to direct her in a comedy, and she agreed, saying: "He was one of the most gifted directors of that day and I knew I could relax with him. Ernst cared about the pictures he made and the people who worked with him. He took good care of everyone. He took very good care of me in **Ninotchka**." So eager was Garbo to do this film that she took a pay cut, accepting only $125,000 from MGM to make the film (she had received an average of $250,000 per picture from MGM in the past). Garbo and Douglas got along famously during the production, according to Garbo's statements to this author, but her experiences with Claire were unfriendly and even openly hostile in that Claire was the widow of John Gilbert, who was Garbo's on-screen and off-screen lover during her silent film period and whom she jilted at the altar after she agreed to marry him. Ruggiero, who was the film editor of this masterpiece and my lifelong friend, told this author that "Garbo and Claire only talked together when they had to, and that was when they were in some scenes together. Claire had been married to Jack [John] Gilbert, the silent screen star, and he drank himself to death, they say, over losing Garbo, and Claire blamed Garbo for Jack's death, but that was probably unfair. I knew Jack and he drank for a lot of reasons, mostly because his career took a nosedive when talkies came in. I could never understand why Jack would drink himself into a grave over someone like Garbo—a woman who was really too tall for most men, including him [Garbo stood just under 5'8"; Ruggiero stood 5'6"], kind of ungainly, and with large feet—directors went out of their way not to photograph those gunboats—and she has a chest as flat as an ironing board. No explaining a man's tastes in women. Garbo was a great actress, but when it came to real romance in her life, well, she was a flop, I think. She had affairs with women as well as men and she dropped them all as easily as changing the sheets on her bed. That's why she's hiding out in New York under an alias, I suppose, so that none of those old lovers can ever find her. Maybe that's unkind. I know she never liked Hollywood and making films was a pain in the butt for her, except after she finished a picture and got a lot of praise. [An attitude not dissimilar to that of Dorothy Parker, who once wrote: 'I hate writing but I love having written.'] Garbo treated me well enough and even complimented my editing on **Ninotchka**, telling me that 'you took good care of me, Gene.' But I really did not have to do any patchwork on that film. Lubitsch had it all in place. He was like a grandfather doting on every scene and his setups and takes were always on the money. Garbo told me that she could trust Lubitsch to make her scenes shine and protect her, but Lubitsch was like every director in Hollywood. Lubitsch protected Lubitsch." This was Garbo's second-to-last film, and remains one of her finest. She made another comedic romance, **Two-Faced Woman**, 1941, with Douglas again as her romantic leading man, but this effort was a rather clumsy attempt to rekindle their dynamic performances in **Ninotchka**. **p&d**, Ernst Lubitsch; **cast**, Greta Garbo, Melvyn Douglas, Ina Claire, Bela Lugosi, Sig Rumann, Felix Bressart, Alexander Granach, Gregory Gaye, Rolfe Sedan, Edwin Maxwell, Richard Carle, Peggy Moran, George Tobias; **w**, Charles Brackett, Billy Wilder, Walter Reisch (based on a story by Melchior Lengyel); **c**, William Daniels; **m**, Werner R. Heymann; **ed**, Gene Ruggiero; **art d**, Cedric Gibbons; **set d**, Edwin B. Willis.

The Ninth Day ★★★ 2005; Germany/Luxembourg/Czech Republic; 98m; Provobis Films/Kino International; Color; Drama; Children: Unacceptable; **DVD**. This powerful drama is based on the diary of Luxembourgian Roman Catholic priest Jean Bernard (1907-1994), played by Matthes, who was a prisoner in the Dachau concentration camp during World War II (1939-1945). He watches as a fellow clergyman is hanged, then is given a nine-day leave to return home and attend his mother's funeral. But there is a catch to it. During his leave, Diehl, a German Gestapo lieutenant, tries to get him to convince the local bishop to give up resisting the Germans and write a letter to the pope in the name of the Catholic Church of Luxembourg supporting Adolf Hitler (1889-1945). In exchange, Diehl promises that Matthes and his family and other clergymen in his country will be spared persecution. Diehl tells him that if he refuses to persuade the bishop to write that letter to the pope, he will nevertheless be spared if he himself takes a pro-German position. Matthes wrestles with his conscience over being a German collaborator and being safe from torture, imprisonment, and possible death or resisting the Germans. Matthes ultimately chooses not to become a collaborator and face whatever future might come and is sent to Dachau to witness countless crimes and atrocities committed by the Nazis. Tens of thousands of Dutch Catholics were deported for not cooperating with the Germans. Song: "Frauen sind keine Engel" (Mothers are No Angels). Excessive violence prohibits viewing by children. (In German and French; English subtitles.) **p**, Jürgen Haase, Jakob Hausmann, Benigna von Keyserlingk; **d**, Volker Schlöndorff; **cast**, Ulrich

Greta Garbo and Ina Claire in *Ninotchka*, 1939.

Matthes, August Diehl, Hilmar Thate, Bibiana Beglau, Germain Wagner, Jean-Paul Raths, Ivan Jirík, Karel Hromadka, Miroslav Sichmann, Adolf Filip; **w**, Eberhard Görner, Andreas Pflüger (based on the memoir "Pfarrerblock 25487" by Jean Bernard); **c**, Tomas Erhart; **m**, Alfred Schnittke; **ed**, Peter R. Adam; **prod d**, Ari Hantke.

Nixon ★★★★ 1995; U.S.; 192m; Cinergi Pictures Entertainment/Hollywood Pictures/Buena Vista; Color; Biographical Drama; Children: Unacceptable (MPAA: R); **BD**; **DVD**. Director Stone presents a semi-documentary approach in portraying the last days of U.S. President Richard M. Nixon (1913-1994), superbly essayed by Hopkins. He is shown listening to the tape recordings (that he either had destroyed or were accidentally erased) that encompass the events surrounding the Watergate scandal that brought an end to Nixon's presidency and compelled him to resign. While listening to these incriminating tapes, Hopkins reflects on his life and we see in flashback his childhood in Whittier, California, his youthful ambitions as a college student where he is obsessed with football, his political rise and his vice presidency under U.S. President Dwight D. Eisenhower (1890-1969), his defeat for the presidency by John F. Kennedy (1917-1963), his political resurgence and eventual election as president, the film ending with his resignation. Throughout these dark reveries, Hopkins confers with his top aides, Woods (playing H. R. Haldeman, 1926-1993), and Walsh (playing John Erlichman, 1925-1999), in an attempt to fend off his inevitable departure from the White House. Throughout Hopkins' ruminations, we see what appears to be his dependency upon alcohol while he struggles with the scandal that eventually destroys his political career. Hopkins gives a riveting performance, so intense and personalized that he wholly captures Nixon's somewhat paranoid persona, which increases the tension throughout this very good profile, where Stone lends credibility to his subject by interspersing telling newsreel clips between his dramatic scenes. **p**, Oliver Stone, Clayton Townsend, Andrew G. Vajna, Dan Halsted, Eric Hamburg; **d**, Stone; **cast**, Anthony Hopkins, Joan Allen, Powers Boothe, Ed Harris, Bob Hoskins, E.G. Marshall, David Paymer, David Hyde Pierce, Paul Sorvino, Mary Steenburgen, J. T. Walsh, James Woods, Annabeth Gish, Tony Goldwyn, Larry Hagman, Ed Herrmann, Madeline Kahn, Tony Lo Bianco, George Plimpton, Stone (closing narrator); **w**, Stone, Stephen J. Rivele, Christopher Wilkinson; **c**, Robert Richardson (Technicolor); **m**, John Williams; **ed**, Brian Berdan, Hank Corwin; **prod d**, Victor Kempster; **art d**, Richard F. Mays, Donald Woodruff, Margery Zweizig; **set d**, Merideth Boswell; **spec eff**, F. Lee Stone, Robert Calvert.

No Country for Old Men ★★★ 2007; U.S.; 122m; PAR/Miramax; Color; Crime Drama; Children: Unacceptable (MPAA: R); **BD**; **DVD**.

Barbara Rush and Pat Hingle in *No Down Payment*, 1957.

Taut crime yarn begins when Brolin, an impoverished man, is seen in desolate rural Texas in 1980, where he discovers two million dollars, a huge cache left by drug runners who killed each other in a botched transaction. He decides not to report his find to police and keep the money. Bardem, who is a psychopathic killer, knows about it all and is on Brolin's trail as a sheriff, Jones, investigates. Brolin tells his wife, Macdonald, about the money, and she meets him at a motel in El Paso where he is soon found dead. Bardem has followed her to the motel and says he will flip a coin to spare her life if she gives him the money. She says the choice is his, and he leaves with the money, but is injured in a car accident (the viewer is left to wonder about the whereabouts of the money). In a flash-forward we see Jones retired and telling his wife, Harper, that he dreamed he lost some money his sheriff father had given him some years before while rationalizing the bloody drug money murders into twisted fond memories of the good old days. Much of this strange tale is left unresolved and loose ends dangle beyond the fadeout, but the film is well crafted and the cast presents memorable performances. Excessive violence and gutter language prohibit viewing by children. Songs/music: "Puno de tierra" (Michael Elroy Sanchez), "Las mananitas" (traditional), "Blood Trails" (Carter Burwell). **p,** Ethan and Joel Coen, Scott Rudin; **d&w,** Ethan and Joel Coen (based on the novel by Cormac McCarthy); **cast,** Tommy Lee Jones, Javier Bardem, Josh Brolin, Woody Harrelson, Kelly Macdonald, Garret Dillahunt, Tess Harper, Barry Corbin, Stephen Root, Rodger Boyce; **c,** Roger Deakins; **m,** Carter Burwell; **ed,** Roderick Jaynes (Ethan and Joel Coen); **prod d,** Jess Gonchor; **art d,** John P. Goldsmith; **set d,** Nancy Haigh; **spec eff,** Peter Chesney, Peter Chesney, Jr.

No Down Payment ★★★ 1957; U.S.; 105m; FOX; B/W; Drama; Children: Unacceptable; **DVD**; **VHS**. Good "slice of life" tales present the marital problems of some young couples living in a southern California housing development with mortgages requiring no money down. Their day-to-day struggles escalate to lethal events when Hunter, an electrical engineer, kills World War II hero Mitchell for raping his wife, Owens. Mitchell's wife, Woodward, whose only desire is to be a mother, is left a widow. Randall is a used car salesman with big plans that never materialize, prompting his wife, North, to think about divorce. Though this film is more or less a soap opera, it is well crafted and nevertheless offers good performances from some very entertaining young future stars. **p,** Jerry Wald; **d,** Martin Ritt; **cast,** Joanne Woodward, Sheree North, Tony Randall, Jeffrey Hunter, Cameron Mitchell, Patricia Owens, Barbara Rush, Pat Hingle, Robert Harris, Aki Aleong, Jim Hayward; **w,** Philip Yordan (based on the novel by John McPartland); **c,** Joseph LaShelle; **m,** Leigh Harline; **ed,** Louis R. Loeffler; **art d,** Lyle R. Wheeler, Herman A. Blumenthal; **spec eff,** L.B. Abbott.

No Exit ★★★ 1962; U.S./Argentina; 85m; Aries Cinematografica Argentina/Zenith International Films; B/W; Drama; Children: Unacceptable; **VHS**. Based on the existentialist play by philosopher Jean-Paul Sartre (1905-1980), three strangers come together in a brightly lit hotel room. They are Sterne, a famous journalist; Gam, a narcissistic social climbing wife; and Lindfors, a lesbian. At first they take sides, planning to kill each other, but settle for a deep contempt for one another. We learn that these forlorn persons are members of the deceased: Sterne was shot for cowardice; Gam was sex-crazed and married for money, then killed her husband and their baby; and Lindfors committed suicide after seducing a married woman, who then killed herself. A fight ensues, and Gam tries to kill Lindfors with a paper knife. After this trio realizes that they are dead and are to spend eternity together in the room, they are consumed by fits of laughter before falling silent to end Sartre's vision of Hell. **p,** Fernando Ayala, Héctor Olivera; **d,** Tad Danielewski; **cast,** Viveca Lindfors, Rita Gam, Morgan Sterne, Ben Piazza, Mirta Miller, Susana Mayo, Miguel A. Irarte, Carlos Brown, Elsa Dorian, Mario Horna; **w,** George Tabori (based on the play by Jean-Paul Sartre); **c,** Ricardo Younis; **m,** Vladimir Ussachevsky; **ed,** Jacques Bart, Carl Lerner, Atilio Rinaldi; **art d,** Mario Vanarelli.

No Greater Glory ★★★ 1934; U.S.; 74m; COL; B/W; Drama; Children: Unacceptable; **DVD**; **VHS**. This sensitive and well-made film accurately depicts the joys and agonies of childhood and is set during the early 1930s of the Great Depression. Breakston is a lonely and sickly boy, who wants to belong to a military-style street gang led by his idol, Butler. However, Butler despises Breakston because of his physical weakness. He nevertheless allows Breakston to join his gang as a flunky, with the rank of private, while all the others are designated as officers. The boys wear uniforms and carry their own flag, which is later stolen by a rival gang, this theft setting up a gang war. In a heavy rain, Breakston tries to prove himself by invading the enemy gang's camp to recover the flag, but Darro, that gang's leader, holds his head under water repeatedly, causing Breakston to contract pneumonia. A battle is set up between the gangs and Breakston leaves his sick bed to take part, dying in the fight. Butler finally realizes that Breakston was tough and courageous, also realizing the futility and tragedy of street gang activities. Borzage presents a powerful allegorical anti-war story that provides excellent performances from the cast. The events shown herein are based on the autobiographical experiences of Hungarian novelist Molnar. Ironically, both Breakston and Butler were killed a decade later in World War II. **p&d,** Frank Borzage; **cast,** George P. Breakston, Jimmy Butler, Jackie Searl, Frankie Darro, Donald Haines, Rolf Ernest, Julius Molnar, Wesley Giraud, Bruce Line, Samuel S. Hinds, Ralph Morgan, Lois Wilson; **w,** Jo Swerling (based on the novel *The Paul Street Boys* by Ferenc Molnar); **c,** Joseph August; **ed,** Vilola Lawrence.

No Highway in the Sky ★★★★ 1951; U.K.; 98m; FOX; B/W; Drama; Children: Cautionary; **DVD**; **VHS**. In a masterfully restrained performance, Stewart is an aeronautical engineer whose entire life is consumed by his work. He is thought to be eccentric by his superiors at the Royal Aircraft Establishment in England, but they tolerate his odd behavior because of his brilliant display of technical knowledge. Stewart, a widower who lives with his small daughter, Scott, has finished his review on a new and expensive passenger plane, the Reindeer, which has just been put into operation, but, when once more going over his studies, he concludes that the plane has a serious defect. He goes to his boss, Hawkins, telling him that he believes that the plane's tail assembly cannot take too much stress and claims that it will break away from sheer exhaustion from the fuselage after 1,440 hours of in-air flying. Hawkins believes that Stewart's claim is dubious in that he has not yet proven his theory through stress testing of the plane's tail structure, but, to make sure, he sends Stewart on a flight to Labrador where one of the new Reindeer planes has inexplicably crashed. While flying to that destination, Stewart learns that the Reindeer on which he and other passengers are flying has already logged 1,420 hours, and, convinced that his theory is sound, becomes alarmed, believing that this plane, too, will soon crash. He warns the pilot and crew members, alarming them, and is told to remain in his seat until the plane reaches Labrador and talk to no one about his suspicions. He sits next to Dietrich, a famous film star, and, after befriending her, he confides his suspicions about the plane to her, as well as to fetching stewardess Johns. Both women are attracted to this shy and retiring man, but they have doubts about his claims. When the plane lands at Labrador without incident, the plane is scheduled to continue its flight to the U.S., but Stewart, convinced that it will crash before reaching that destination, resolves to save its passengers and destroys the undercarriage of the plane. He is then ordered to return to England to face criminal charges. Dietrich and Johns, however, staunchly believe that Stewart's claims have some validity, and Hawkins, at the risk of his own job, allows Stewart to conduct stress tests on a new Reindeer's tail assembly. For weeks, Stewart labors at that task without sleep while Johns, who has fallen in love with Stewart, moves into his small house to take care of him and his little girl, Scott, although Scott is very self-reliant in that she has been the "little mother" of the house for some time. When Hawkins is about to order testing stopped, the tail assembly on the Reindeer being tested collapses, and Stewart, instead of being labeled an irresponsible crackpot, is hailed a scientific hero. Meanwhile, Dietrich, who is also attracted to him, goes to his home and confronts Johns, telling her that she would be a much better wife for Stewart and departs. Stewart goes home to discover through Johns' diligence that he has saved a great deal of money and he can afford to marry Johns and they plan their future together, along with Scott. Stewart gives an exceptional performance as the gifted aviation expert vexed by a problem he must solve to save countless lives while the beautiful and warm-hearted Johns is vastly appealing, but it is Dietrich who takes every scene in which she appears, her magnetic personality riveting the viewer. *Author's Note*: "There was no way I was going to steal any scenes from Marlene in **No Highway in the Sky**," Stewart told this author. "All she had to do was to bat those heavy eyelids of hers over those penetrating and magnificent eyes and the scene was forever hers. No other actress in the world could match her performances before or since and I can tell you that it was a pleasure just being in a picture with her." Dietrich, for her part, told this author that "falling in love with Jimmy [Stewart] is easy for any woman. He is a man every woman wants to mother and protect, but a man also to be admired, especially in that picture where he is a rather nutty aviation expert, who tells me while we are flying together that the plane might crash at any time. What would you do in such a pickle, I ask you? Well, I did the most practical thing and made the most of it, although I can tell you that that picture gave me some bad thoughts whenever I took an airplane flight. The problem was that Jimmy was not there on those flights to hold my hand and tell me everything was going to be all right." Dietrich dresses to the hilt in this film, wearing Dior designer gowns she charged to Fox, keeping those gowns, along with a mink coat and fur stole. No one complained. Shute provides a sharp and witty script, richly enhanced by fascinating technical information about the plane in question, effectively so in that he had been an aviation engineer before becoming a writer. **p**, Louis D. Lighton; **d**, Henry Koster; **cast**, James Stewart, Marlene Dietrich, Glynis Johns, Jack Hawkins, Janette Scott, Elizabeth Allan, Ronald Squire, Jill Clifford, Felix Aylmer, Maurice Denham, Wilfrid Hyde-White, Bessie Love, Kenneth More; **w**, R.C. Sherriff, Oscar Millard, Alec Coppel (based on the novel *No Highway* by Nevil Shute); **c**, Georges Perinal; **m**, Malcolm Arnold; **ed**, Manuel del Campo; **art d**, C.P. Norman.

No Limit ★★★ 1935; U.K.; 80m; Associated Talking Pictures; B/W; Comedy; Children: Acceptable. Local yokel Formby is confident he has the ability to win the Isle of Man TT race, despite what neighbors in the small town of Wigan think. In preliminary trials, he rides his homemade motorcycle, "The Shuttleworth Snap" (named after himself) to break

Jack Hawkins and James Stewart in *No Highway in the Sky*, 1951.

the current lap record and instantly becomes a dirt bike racing star. As the big race approaches, he expects jealous bikers to stop at nothing to make sure he doesn't even take part in the event. After lots of action and laughs, he does win the race. An early film by the British comic, and one of his funniest, but as yet unavailable for viewing on any video format. **p**, Basil Dean; **d**, Monty Banks, **cast**, George Formby, Florence Desmond, Howard Douglas, Beatrix Fielden-Kaye, Peter Gawthorne, Alf Goddard, Florence Gregson, Jack Hobbs, Eve Lister, Edward Rigby; **w**, Thomas J. Geraghty, Fred Thompson (based on a story by Walter Greenwood); **c**, Robert Martin; **m**, Ord Hamilton; **art d**, J. Elder Wills.

No Longer Alone ★★★ 1978; U.S.; 99m; World Wide Pictures; Worldwide Entertainment Corp.; Color; Drama; Children: Unacceptable (MPAA: PG); **VHS**. This inspirational drama is based upon the life of London stage actress and writer Joan Winmill Brown, who suffered from suicidal tendencies until she had a religious conversion. Told in flashback, as a girl she had an unhappy childhood during which her mother and a cousin died. Her grandfather, also suffering from suicidal tendencies, suffered a nervous breakdown. In the film, Carroll, who plays Brown, has an affair with U.S. Senator Robert F. Kennedy (1925-1968), played by Devol, but, in real life that affair was reportedly not a strong relationship. Her religious conversion comes in 1954 while attending a religious ceremony conducted by evangelist Billy Graham (1918-), who plays himself in this production, and she is moved to respond to an altar call. Brown traveled to America and married William Brown, a Graham executive, and wrote eighteen books, including her autobiography upon which the film is based. Suicidal themes prohibit viewing by children. **p**, Frank R. Jacobson; **d**, Nicholas Webster; **cast**, Belinda Carroll, Roland Culver, James Fox, Wilfrid Hyde-White, Simon Williams, Helen Cherry, Igor Alexander, Joan Alkin, Vivienne Burgess, Joan Winmill Brown (narrator); **w**, Lawrence Holben (based on the autobiography by Joan Winmill Brown); **c**, Michael Reed; **m**, Tedd Smith; **ed**, J. Michael Hooser; **prod d**. John Lageu.

No Love for Johnnie ★★★ 1961; U.K.; 110m; Five Star Films/Embassy Pictures; B/W; Drama; Children: Unacceptable; **VHS**. Finch gives a strong performance as a fictitious member of the British House of Commons. He is a member of the Labour Party and, at age forty-two, he feels frustrated in both his personal and professional life while his desire to win the next election is endangered by his continual quest for love. He has a loveless marriage and is faced with giving up his career or Peach, the woman he loves, a fashion model half his age. Fellow Labour Party members are not happy with him after he skips an important hearing to be with Peach, but she solves his dilemma by deciding against marrying a man twice her age and leaves him. His wife, Crutch-

Clark Gable and Carole Lombard in *No Man of Her Own*, 1932.

ley, decides she wants to save their marriage, but she is a communist, and Labour Party leaders offer him a cabinet seat if he splits with her, which he agrees to do because with Finch, politics come first. Sexuality prohibits viewing by children. **p**, Betty E. Box; **d**, Ralph Thomas; **cast**, Peter Finch, Stanley Holloway, Mary Peach, Donald Pleasence, Billie Whitelaw, Hugh Burden, Rosalie Crutchley, Mervyn Johns, Dennis Price, George Rose, Oliver Reed, Mona Washbourne; **w**, Nicholas Phipps, Mordecai Richler (based on the novel by Wilfred Fienburgh); **c**, Ernest Steward; **m**, Malcolm Arnold; **ed**, Alfred Roome; **art d**, Maurice Carter; **set d**, Arthur Taksen.

No Man Is an Island ★★★ 1962; U.S.; 114m; Gold Coast Productions/UNIV; Color; War Drama; Children: Unacceptable; **DVD**; **VHS**. Hunter is outstanding in essaying U.S. Navy hero George Ray Tweed (1902-1989). Hunter is a radioman stationed at Guam, a seasoned veteran of sixteen years, when the Japanese invade the island on December 10, 1941. The small garrison is quickly overwhelmed, but, instead of surrendering, Hunter and five other U.S. servicemen take to the jungles, resolving to remain at large until U.S. forces attack and take back the island. He takes refuge at a leper colony supervised by a priest, de Cordova, and sends messages of encouragement to the island residents by using the hospital's transmitter. When the Japanese learn of this, they attack the colony, burning the hospital to the ground, but Hunter successfully flees, hiding out in a cave and where he is provided with food by a friendly native family. At large for thirty-four months, Hunter lives hand to mouth, barely surviving as he moves from one hideout to another with Japanese patrols tracking him. The other five U.S. servicemen who escaped with him are hunted down and killed one by one, Hunter remaining the sole survivor. He survives through will power and the aid of island residents, who risk their lives to give him food and shelter, and this instills in him a feeling of confidence in his fellow man, realizing that he nor any other person in such dire circumstances can survive alone (and that no man is therefore an island). Then Hunter spots two U.S. destroyers off the coast of Guam and, after signaling them with a mirror, swims toward one of the warships and he is picked up in a whaleboat and taken on board to learn that the two destroyers are making preparations for the invasion of Guam (which occurred on July 10, 1944). He provides vital information to the U.S. commander that helps U.S. forces to quickly retake the island. Hunter is then joyfully reunited with the many Guam natives who heroically helped him to survive his incredible ordeal. Well directed and tension filled throughout, this film offers an outstanding performance from Hunter, along with high production values, a literate script, and excellent lensing by Kayser. *Author's Note*: Hunter appeared in a similar film two years earlier, **Hell to Eternity**, 1960, where he plays Mexican Ameri-

can Guy Gabaldon (1926-2006), a U.S. Marine hero, who spoke fluent Japanese and who was instrumental in persuading between 800 and 1,500 Japanese troops to surrender during the Battle of Saipan (June 15-July 9, 1944). One of Hollywood's most promising young actors, Hunter (1926-1969) tragically died at age forty-two, following an accidental fall that resulted in a stroke and brain surgery. **p**, John Monks Jr., Richard Goldstone, Rolf Bayer; **d&w**, Monks, Goldstone (based on the World War II experiences of George R. Tweed); **cast**, Jeffrey Hunter, Marshall Thompson, Barbara Perez, Ronald Remy, Paul Edwards, Jr., Bayer, Vicente Liwanag, Fred Harris II, Lamberto V. Avellana, Vic Silayan; **c**, Carl Kayser (Eastmancolor); **m**, Restie Umali; **ed**, Basil Wrangell; **art d**, Benjamin Resella; **spec eff**, Robert R. Joseph.

No Man of Her Own ★★★ 1932; U.S.; 85m; PAR; B/W; Comedy; Drama; Children: Unacceptable; **DVD**. Gable excels as a New York City card sharp who has to go on the lam to avoid a pesky detective, MacDonald. While hiding out in a nearby small town, he meets Lombard, a librarian, and she falls in love with him. On a coin flip with a friend, he marries her, but he is not in love with her. They move to New York where he returns to cheating at card games. After Lombard learns of his errant ways, she begs him to quit, but he feels she's crowding him and tells her he's leaving for South America on a business trip, without her. In fact, he has fallen in love with her and decides to go straight. He turns himself in to MacDonald and gets a three-month jail sentence, with Lombard waiting for him upon his release. Another film with the same title was produced in 1950, but has a much different plot. Gable would later meet and fall in love with another on-screen librarian, Greer Garson, in **Adventure**, 1945, and he would marry her on a whim, leaving her, until her winning ways reforms his carousing lifestyle as a seaman. *Author's Note*: Gable and Lombard met on the set and fell in love, but both were married at that time (Lombard to actor William Powell), and they would not marry until seven years later in 1939. **p**, Albert Lewis; **d**, Wesley Ruggles; **cast**, Clark Gable, Carole Lombard, Dorothy Mackaill, Grant Mitchell, George Barbier, Elizabeth Patterson, J. Farrell MacDonald, Tommy Conlon, Charley Grapewin, Lillian Harmer; **w**, Maurine Watkins, Milton H. Gropper (based on a story by Edmund Goulding, Benjamin Glazer); **c**, Leo Tover; **ed**, Otho Lovering.

No Man of Her Own ★★★ 1950; U.S.; 98m; PAR; B/W; Drama; Children: Unacceptable; **DVD**; **VHS**. In a clever and fascinating impersonation story, Stanwyck becomes pregnant by boyfriend Bettger. Penniless, she takes the identity of pregnant Thaxter when that woman and her husband, Denning, are killed in a train wreck. Thaxter's in-laws, O'Neill and Cowl, and their other grown son, Lund, had never met Thaxter, so they accept Stanwyck and her newborn son into their family. Bettger finds her and blackmails her, threatening that he will expose her, but Lund comes to her rescue and all's well that ends well in this entertaining soap opera. The film was remade as a French film, **I Married a Shadow**, 1983. The 1932 film titled **No Man of Her Own** had a different plot. *Author's Note*: Stanwyck told this author that "I thought that the woman I impersonate, Phyllis [Thaxter] was a lot prettier than I was when we made **No Man of Her Own**. In fact, I never thought that I was pretty and that my leading men were prettier than I was. I had to act around all of that." Bettger, who had considerable stage experience, makes his film debut in this production, proving so effective as a sinister character that he became one of the busiest heavies in Hollywood. **p**, Richard Maibaum; **d**, Mitchell Leisen; **cast**, Barbara Stanwyck, John Lund, Jane Cowl, Phyllis Thaxter, Lyle Bettger, Henry O'Neill, Richard Denning, Carole Mathews, Harry Antrim, Catherine Craig, Dooley Wilson, Esther Dale; **w**, Sally Benson, Catherine Turney (based on the novel *I Married a Dead Man* by William Irish (Cornell Woolrich); **c**, Daniel L. Fapp; **m**, Hugo Friedhofer; **ed**, Alma Macrorie; **art d**, Henry Bumstead, Hans Dreier; **set d**, Sam Comer, Ray Moyer; **spec eff**, Farciot Edouart, Gordon Jennings.

No Man's Land ★★★ 2001; Bosnia; Herzegovina; France; Slovenia; Italy; U.K.; Belgium; 98m; Noe Productions/MGM/UA; Color; War Drama; Children: Unacceptable (MPAA: R); **DVD**. Two wounded soldiers from opposing sides in the Bosnia and Herzegovina fighting in 1993 share a trench in no man's land between the two lines. The Bosnian soldier, Djuric, and the Serbian soldier, Bitorajac, wait for dark, trading insults and learning they both dated the same woman. Meanwhile, also in the trench is another Bosnian soldier, Sovagovic, a Serbian booby-trapped mine underneath him that will explode if he moves. All three will be killed if they aren't very careful. The two soldiers try to help the third by waving white flags, but get no help from Callow, a United Nations field observer. Cartlidge, a British female reporter, comes to help, but Siatidis, a French sergeant, is ordered not to interfere. Cartlidge threatens to expose the situation in a global scandal, so Callow has helicopters sent in to defuse the situation. This tense war tale incisively depicts the fierce partisanship during this conflict and provides top flight acting from the cast. Violence and gutter language prohibit viewing by children. **p**, Marc Baschet, Frédérique Dumas-Zajdela, Cédomir Kolar, Judy Counihan, Marion Hänsel, Dunja Klemenc, Marco Mueller, Igor Pedicek, Cat Villiers; **d&w&m**, Danis Tanovic; **cast**, Branko Djuric, Rene Bitorajac, Filip Sovagovic, Georges Siatidis, Katrin Cartlidge, Serge-Henri Valcke, Sacha Kremer, Alain Eloy, Mustafa Nadarevic, Bogdan Diklic, Simon Callow; **c**, Walther Vanden Ende; **ed**, Francesca Calvelli; **prod d**, Dusan Milavec; **spec eff**, Olivier de Laveleye, Marie Pierre Franck, Blaz Jelnikar.

No Minor Vices ★★★ 1948; U.S.; 96m; Enterprise Productions; MGM; B/W; Comedy; Children: Acceptable; **VHS**. Pleasant comedy with a lot of humorous touches begins when Andrews, an upscale child psychologist, whimsically hires artist Jourdan to capture on canvas "real life" portraits in his office that will depict "the inner selves" of his family and clients. This proves to be a big mistake in that Jourdan's eccentricities border on lunacy and he quickly turns Andrews' office into messy mayhem. Further, he aggressively invades Andrews' home, going after Palmer, Andrews' attractive wife, overwhelming her with his passionate advances. While Andrews tries to undo the domestic turbulence Jourdan has created in his office while putting his medical practice back in order, he must also compete with madman Jourdan for his wife's divided attentions. All of these madcap goings-on are witnessed by Gorcey, who operates a cigar shop opposite Andrews' office, giving sage and funny remarks about the chaos across the street in voiceover. (The leading players also offer voiceover remarks about this odd situation, mimicking the technique of addressing the audience as employed by playwright Eugene O'Neill in his drama, **Strange Interlude**, 1932.) Andrews finally realizes that he has taken his wife and friends and lucrative occupation for granted and works hard to win back their love and respect while ultimately driving cuckoo Jourdan out of his life. Director Milestone does a credible job in delivering an entertaining comedy, but was somewhat out of his element as he was more comfortable with dramas. Andrews, Palmer and Jourdan give good performances, providing many humorous moments in a story that goes from reasonable to the ridiculous. The story was presented as a one-hour radio show produced by Screen Director's Playhouse, and aired on February 22, 1951, with Andrews and Jourdan reprising their roles. *Author's Note*: This was the fourth and final film Andrews would make with Milestone, having had successes with **The North Star**, 1943; **The Purple Heart**, 1944; and **A Walk in the Sun**, 1945. Andrews told this author that "**No Minor Vices** had a lot of potential as a comedy and we all did our best to make it work, but the script needed some boosting so we gave Lewis [Milestone] a lot of our own ideas—some worked and some did not." Andrews actually invested some of his own money into this film, but it did not see the box office success envisioned by its producers. Andrews later stated that the film would have had a better outing if it had been released by United Artists, instead of MGM. Milestone told this author that "I was doing that picture with the people behind Enterprise Productions—

Dana Andrews and Lilli Palmer in *No Minor Vices*, 1948.

David Loew, who came from the Loew family that owned many theaters and distributed films in the old days, and Charles Einfeld—after we had a setback with a very expensive picture they backed, **Arch of Triumph** [1948], and which I directed. To make up for the loss we suffered with that picture, which was a very good one, but did not click with audiences, the producers at Enterprise tried to recoup with **No Minor Vices**, which we did on the wing. Well, they all don't work out. This business is like shooting craps or like waiting for that little ball to land in the right groove on a roulette wheel." **p&d**, Lewis Milestone; **cast**, Dana Andrews, Lilli Palmer, Louis Jourdan, Jane Wyatt, Norman Lloyd, Bernard Gorcey, Roy Roberts, Fay Baker, Sharon McManus, Ann Doran, Beau Bridges; **w**, Arnold Manoff; **c**, George Barnes; **m**, Franz Waxman; **ed**, Robert Parrish; **prod d**, Nicolai Remisoff; **set d**, Edward G. Boyle; **spec eff**, Mario Castegnaro.

No Name on the Bullet ★★★ 1959; U.S.; 77m; UNIV; Color; Western; Children: Unacceptable; **DVD**; **VHS**. In this tense and exceptional oater, Murphy is a cool, cultured professional killer, who rides into Lordsburg, New Mexico. His reputation precedes him, but no one knows who he has come to town to kill. While waiting for him to make his move, the townsmen all become fearful he may be there to kill any one of them and their paranoia becomes universal. He is not really there to kill anyone, but is blamed for the suicide of the wheelchair-bound Stehli, a community leader. Suspenseful and exciting throughout, this is one of Arnold's best outings, and Murphy gives a riveting performance. **p**, Jack Arnold, Howard Christie; **d**, Arnold; **cast**, Audie Murphy, Charles Drake, Joan Evans, Virginia Grey, Warren Stevens, Edgar Stehli, R.G. Armstrong, Karl Swenson, Whit Bissell, Bob Steele, Guy Wilkerson; **w**, Gene L. Coon (based on a story by Howard Amacker); **c**, Harold Lipstein (CinemaScope; Eastmancolor); **m**, Herman Stein; **ed**, Frank Gross; **art d**, Alexander Golitzen, Robert E. Smith; **set d**, Russell A. Gausman, Ted Driscoll.

No, No Nanette ★★★ 1930; U.S.; 98; First National; B/W/Color; Musical; Acceptable; **DVD**; **VHS**. Entertaining musical sees Littlefield, a Bible salesman, innocently helping three women who are in trouble, but he finds himself in trouble when all three arrive at his Atlantic City cottage. There are a number of good songs warbled while Littlefield manages to escape his romantic mess. Most of the film is taken up by musical numbers from the Broadway show and all are well choreographed. The film was remade in 1940 under the same title, and in 1950 under the title **Tea for Two**. Songs: "As Long as I'm with You" (Harry Akst, Grant Clarke); "King of the Air," "Dancing to Heaven," "No, No Nanette" (Edward Ward, Al Bryan); "The Dance of the Wooden Shoes," "Dancing on Mars" (Michael Cleary, Ned Washington, Herb Magidson);

James Stewart, Rosalind Russell, and Charles Ruggles in *No Time for Comedy*, 1940.

"Tea for Two," "I Want to Be Happy" (Vincent Youmans, Irving Caesar); "Were You Just Pretending?" (M. K. Jerome, Herman Ruby). **p**, Ned Marin; **d**, Clarence G. Badger; **cast**, Bernice Claire, Alexander Gray, Lucien Littlefield, Louise Fazenda, Lilyan Tashman, Bert Roach, Zasu Pitts, Mildred Harris, Henry Stockbridge, Jocelyn Lee; **w**, Howard Emmett Rogers, Beatrice Van (based on the Broadway musical by Otto Harbach, Emil Nyitray, Vincent Youmans, Frank Mandel); **c**, Sol Polito (Technicolor); **m**, Vincent Youmans; **ed**, Frank Mandel.

No, No Nanette ★★★ 1940; U.S.; 96; RKO; B/W; Musical; Acceptable; **DVD**; **VHS**. In this good remake of the 1930 film, Neagle is a perky young woman, who tries to save the marriage of her wealthy uncle, Young, on whom some fortune-hunting women have set designs. She enlists the help of Mature, a theatrical producer, who falls in love with her. Carlson, an artist, also comes under her spell when he is asked to help her. Neagle manages to deal with all of this and saves Young's marriage while falling in love with Carlson. This film was made again in 1950 as **Tea for Two**. Songs: "No No Nanette," "I Want to Be Happy," "Tea for Two" (Vincent Youmans, Irving Caesar); "Ochi Chornya" (traditional). **p&d**, Herbert Wilcox; **cast**, Anna Neagle, Richard Carlson, Victor Mature, Roland Young, Helen Broderick, Zasu Pitts, Eve Arden, Billy Gilbert, Tamara, Stuart Robertson, Georgiana Young; **w**, Ken Englund (based on the musical by Frank Mandel, Otto A. Harbach, Emil Nyitray, Vincent Youmans); **c**, Russell Metty; **ed**, Elmo Williams; **art d**, Lawrence P. Williams; **set d**, Darrell Silvera; **spec eff**, Vernon L. Walker.

No Time for Breakfast ★★★ 1978; France; 100m; Action Films/Daniel Bourla; Color; Drama; Children: Unacceptable; **VHS**. Girardot is a French doctor, who is well liked by her patients and co-workers, but her husband, Perier, is a dull fellow. The couple has a pregnant teenage daughter, Huppert, and a neglected son, Coryn. Despite her busy career and home life, Girardot finds time to fall in love with Cassel. She learns she has cancer, but faces an operation bravely and positively. (In French; English subtitles.) **p**, Lise Fayolle, Yves Gasser, Yves Peyrot; **d**, Jean-Louis Bertuccelli; **cast**, Annie Girardot, Jean-Pierre Cassel, François Périer, Isabelle Huppert, William Coryn, Suzanne Flon, Anouk Ferjac, Michel Subor, Josephine Chaplin, Andre Falcon; **w**, Bertuccelli, André G. Brunelin (based on the novel *Un Cri* by Noëlle Loriot); **c**, Claude Renoir (Eastmancolor); **m**, Catherine Lara; **ed**, Catherine Bernard, Francois Ceppi; **prod d**, Yves Demarseille, Gérard Dubois.

No Time for Comedy ★★★ 1940; U.S.; 93m; WB; B/W; Comedy; Children: Acceptable; **VHS**. Stewart is perfect as a budding young playwright living in the hinterlands of Minnesota, who writes a comedy that is accepted for a Broadway production in which successful actress Russell will star. Stewart heads for the Big Apple, a hayseed filled with humor who has written a play about New York without ever having been there. He has been summoned to NYC to be present if any rewrites are required, but he takes his time getting there, visiting the Grand Canyon simply to rubberneck because he has never seen it. He finally arrives as a breath of fresh air for Russell, who is tired of being surrounded by sophisticated cynical types, such as Joslyn, her wise-cracking director. The stammering, withdrawn Stewart soon captures Russell's heart and he falls in love with his charming leading lady, a romance ending when they go to the altar. Stewart then writes several more smash comedies, but success goes to his head and he assumes the veneer of the polished and cynical savant that Russell has always disliked. Wealthy theater matron Tobin then gets his attention when she urges him to stop writing comedies and aim for something higher, like writing great tragedies. Stewart's now inflated ego embraces this lofty ambition at the same time he thinks he is falling in love with Tobin. He writes that tragedy and it is a colossal flop. Russell by this time is deeply worried about losing her husband and, to divert Stewart's fascination from Tobin, establishes a phony romance with Tobin's husband, the dithering Ruggles. Stewart then believes that he is about to lose not only the love of his life, but that he has abandoned his true talent in writing comedy and decides that he will hold on to both by going back to Russell and giving Tobin the heave-ho. In future, he will leave the writing of great tragedies to Eugene O'Neill. Directors Keighley moves this humorous-filled film along at a brisk pace, and Stewart and Russell are outstanding in their roles. The same theme was used a year later in Preston Sturges' marvelous comedy, **Sullivan's Travels**, 1941, where film director Joel McCrea decides to abandon making comedies (like "Ants in Your Pants") and helm heavy dramas. *Author's Note*: This was Tobin's last film; she married director Keighley and lived happily ever after in California, dying at age ninety-five in 1995. Keighley told this author that "**No Time for Comedy** was easy to put in the can because I had top flight people like Jimmy [Stewart] and Roz [Russell] to work with, people who come prepared and know what they are supposed to do. They don't miss cues and their first takes are usually the best ones." Stewart stated to this author that "I liked working with Bill Keighley in **No Time for Comedy**. He is one of those directors who cut right into the meat of each scene, no dallying around or second thoughts. That's why he was one of the great workhorses at Warner Brothers. He did it all—comedies, adventure films, crime and war dramas—and he did them all well, classics like **G-Men** [1935], **The Adventures of Robin Hood** [1938], **The Fighting 69th** [1940], and **George Washington Slept Here** [1942]. He never stepped on any toes and was always on top of his own. He is truly a great director." For her part, Russell stated to this author that "I had to fill some very big shoes in **No Time for Comedy**. The wonderful Katherine Cornell was the leading lady in the original play on Broadway and trying to do what Kit [Cornell] did was impossible, so I did my own version of the actress, and, what do you know, Kit later complimented me on my performance." Julius Epstein, half of the twin writers who wrote the adaptation, stated to this author that "the original play by Behrman was a tightly written piece. We did not have to labor much to get it to work on screen. We added a few lines here and there and some set pieces, but we tried to keep faith with the original play and that was a very good play with a lot of great and funny dialog. There is a scene where Roz [Russell] causes Genevieve [Tobin] to burst into tears and Roz goes to Charlie [Ruggles], who is playing her husband, and he more or less tells her to forget about it, saying: 'I make her cry all the time. It usually ends up with me giving her a check.' I don't remember if that was Behrman's line or ours, but that kind of wisecracking is everywhere in that picture." **p**, Jack L. Warner, Hal B. Wallis; **d**, William Keighley; **cast**, James Stewart, Rosalind Russell, Charles Ruggles, Genevieve Tobin, Louise Beavers, Allyn Joslyn, Clarence Kolb, Robert Greig, J.M. Kerrigan, Frank Faylen, Herbert Anderson, William Hopper, John Ridgely; **w**, Julius J. and Philip G. Epstein (based on the play by S.N.

Behrman); **c**, Ernest Haller; **m**, Heinz Roemheld; **ed**, Owen Marks; **art d**, John Hughes.

No Time for Love ★★★ 1943; U.S.; 83m; PAR; B/W; Comedy/Romance; Children: Acceptable; **DVD**. Colbert, a top New York fashion photographer, reluctantly takes an assignment from her magazine editor to take photos of the tunnel work being done under the city. MacMurray, one of the sandhogs working in the tunnel, gets into a fight with a fellow worker, and Colbert snaps a picture of his punching the other worker. He's shirtless and when the photo is published he is dubbed "Superman." For his pains, MacMurray is fired and Colbert, feeling sorry that she has disrupted his life, hires MacMurray as her assistant, a job he neither likes nor performs well, but he has to live. He meets alluring model Havoc (who, in real life was the sister of burlesque stripper queen Gypsy Rose Lee) and, when Colbert sees that MacMurray is attracted to her, Colbert comes between the pair, realizing that she has fallen for MacMurray. They are opposites, she being sophisticated and he being far from it, or so it seems, but when the tunnel work comes to a halt and all of MacMurray's pals are out of work, Colbert discovers that MacMurray is not merely a burly laborer, but a college-trained engineer, and he develops a machine that will prevent the tunnel from collapsing. He and Colbert end up together, but not before they get into several very funning situations. *Author's Note*: MacMurray told this author that "Claudette [Colbert] is one of the classiest ladies in Hollywood, but she let down her hair in **No Time for Love**, and even gets into a big fight with June [Havoc]. There are some pretty tough cookies in that film playing sandhogs, like Rod Cameron, a big bruiser of a guy but a gentle giant, and there was Tom Neal, who later became Hollywood's bad boy, getting into a lot of trouble and even went to prison for killing his wife." Colbert told this author that "all I can remember from **No Time for Love** is that I got bounced around in brawls in bars and my face was splashed with mud half the time when Fred [MacMurray] and I are always in that awful tunnel. Can you imagine men working in dark, damp places like that all the time? I loved working with Fred and we did more comedies together and he was perfect in those films like **Practically Yours** [1944] and **The Egg and I** [1947]. He had an instinct for comedy and did not like playing sinister characters, although he did them well, too, like the murdering insurance man in **Double Indemnity** [1944], but he tried to steer clear of such roles. I don't think there was a mean bone in his body." **p**, Fred Kohlmar, Mitchell Leisen, **d**, Leisen; **cast**, Claudette Colbert, Fred MacMurray, Ilka Chase, Richard Haydn, June Havoc, Marjorie Gateson, Rod Cameron, Bill Goodwin, Alan Hale, Jr., Tom Neal, Lillian Randolph, Keith Richards, Woody Strode, Rhys Williams; **w**, Claude Binyon, Warren Duff (based on a story by Robert Lees, Fred Rinaldo); **c**, Charles Lang, Jr.; **m**, Victor Young; **ed**, Alma Macrorie; **art d**, Hans Dreier, Robert Usher; **set d**, Sam Comer; **spec eff**, Farciot Edouart, Gordon Jennings.

No Time for Sergeants ★★★★ 1958; U.S.; 119m; WB; B/W; Comedy; Children: Acceptable; **DVD**; **VHS**. Griffith, in his second film (following his riveting appearance as a villain in **A Face in the Crowd**, 1957), displays his great comedic gifts in this hilarious and well-made film. He is a not-too-bright country bumpkin from Georgia, who is drafted into the U.S. Air Force, and is branded by fellow inductees, chiefly the self-serving and conniving Hamilton, as a shirker, which he is not when he is brought in handcuffs to town by the local sheriff to board a bus that will take him and others to their training camp. The gentle and kind-hearted Griffith tolerates a lot of abuse from Hamilton as he undergoes basic training under the direction of McCormick, an aging sergeant and longtime veteran who has been putting up with the goofy and irresponsible antics of trainees for more years than he wants to remember. Troublemaker Hamilton goes too far when he picks on Adams, who is smaller and weaker than Hamilton, and Griffith gives him a lesson in false pride by thrashing him, which, of course, gets him into trouble with McCormick. The naïve Griffith finds a way to disrupt

Andy Griffith and Myron McCormick in *No Time for Sergeants,* **1958.**

and confuse McCormick's training practices, driving McCormick to distraction, if not despair. McCormick believes that serving in the armed forces is a wonderful profession and way of life, as long as no one rocks the boat, and Griffith is forever capsizing that boat with his every turn. Griffith, with a heart of gold that is filled with patriotism and good will (he hears taps for the first time and smiles, saying: "Someone brung their trumpet"), is ordered to clean the latrine as punishment for his foul-ups, and he happily accomplishes that chore so that when McCormick and the company commander inspect the place, they are not only amazed to see it cleaner than ever before but are startled when all the toilet seats snap to attention by uniformly lifting their lids via a crude mechanism Griffith has created and manipulates. Griffith's odd behavior finally causes him to be sent to Air Force psychiatrist Millhollin, but he so confuses the shrink that he is sent back to his barracks without any recommendations. When almost completing his basic training, Griffith and others are sent aloft, but he and Adams fall from the plane and are then listed as "missing, presumed dead." They are far from it. While their fellow servicemen and brass mourn their loss at their funeral, both men suddenly arrive very much alive, which almost causes McCormick to be overcome with an apoplectic seizure. (This scene is taken right out of Mark Twain's *Tom Sawyer*, but nevertheless works well to provide comic relief; the same kind of scene is shown at the end of **Capricorn One**, 1978, when astronaut James Brolin appears at his own funeral, but to expose a corrupt official who has purposely faked his death.) All's well that ends well as Griffith completes his training and plans to make a career of the Air Force, much to the chagrin of the worn-out McCormick. Pantheon director LeRoy directs this delightful romp with great skill, eliciting superb performances from Griffith, McCormick, Adams, Hamilton and others (including the hilarious Don Knotts). Songs: "Gotta Be This or That" (Sunny Skylar), "When My Dreamboat Comes Home" (Cliff Friend, Dave Franklin), "Spirit of Independence" (Abe Holzmann), "My Buddy" (Walter Donaldson), "America, the Beautiful" (Samuel A. Ward), "I Love a Parade" (Harold Arlen), "There's a Long, Long Trail" (Zo Elliott), "The Caisson Song" (Edmund L. Gruber), "The Stars and Stripes Forever" (John Philip Sousa), "The Star Spangled Banner" (composer: John Stafford Smith; lyrics: Francis Scott Key). *Author's Note*: This film is one of several comedies based upon military services, and belongs to the best of those, including **Mr. Roberts**, 1955, and **Stalag 17**, 1953. This comedy undoubtedly inspired the comedy TV series "Gomer Pyle," starring Jim Nabors, a hillbilly recruit, who incessantly vexes and taxes his sergeant. Griffith told this author that "my character in **No Time for Sergeants** offended some hill people, who wrote to me and told me I was making fun of poor folks and that was the last thing in the world that I was doing. I am in that picture a man without education, but one with a rea-

Sidney Poitier and Ruby Dee in *No Way Out*, 1950.

sonable mind and a big heart, who shows up a lot of stuffed shirts. Sophisticated and well-educated persons do stupid things, too, enough of them to create a mess of the world, instead of an Air Force barracks." **p,** Mervyn LeRoy, Alex Segal; **d,** LeRoy; **cast,** Andy Griffith, Myron McCormick, Nick Adams, Murray Hamilton, Howard Smith, Will Hutchins, Don Knotts, Jean Willes, Peter Brown, Dub Taylor, Benny Baker; **w,** John Lee Mahin (based on the play by Ira Levin from the novel by Mac Hyman); **c,** Harold Rosson; **m,** Ray Heindorf; **ed,** William Ziegler; **art d,** Malcolm Brown; **set d,** Robert R. Benton; **spec eff,** Louis Littlefield.

No Trace ★★★ 1950; U.K.; 76m; Tempean Films/Eros; B/W; Mystery; Children: Unacceptable; **DVD**; **VHS.** London crime novelist Sinclair also hosts a weekly radio show with stories listeners think are fiction, but are based on his true-life experiences. He finds himself being blackmailed by Brennan, an American and former criminal associate, and he murders him. Laurie, a Scotland Yard detective friend, asks for Sinclair's help in solving the crime and Sinclair almost manages to escape detection through clouding the case, until Sheridan, his well-meaning secretary, complicates matters by trying to help. Her work leads Laurie to Sinclair's door, causing him to be arrested for the murder. This good mystery provides a lot of clever twists and turns as the much harassed Sinclair essentially searches for himself as the culprit. **p,** Robert S. Baker, Monty Berman; **d,** John Gilling; **cast,** Hugh Sinclir, John Laurie, Dinah Sheridan, Dora Bryan, Barry Morse, Beatrice Varley, Michael Brennan, Michael Ward, Madoline Thomas, Ernest Butcher; **w,** Gilling, Carl Nystrom (based on a story by Baker); **c,** Berman; **m,** John Lanchbery; **ed,** Gerald Landau; **art d,** Walter Scott.

No Way Out ★★★ 1950; U.S.; 106m; FOX; B/W; Crime Drama; Children: Unacceptable; **DVD**; **VHS.** Powerful and shocking, this exceptional crime yarn sees outstanding performances from Widmark, McNally and a newcomer to the screen, Poitier, who are involved with race battles between two warring factions and centered at a county hospital located in a slum area. Poitier is a newly graduated intern, who is given a position at the hospital by McNally, who believes in hiring the most competent physicians no matter the color of their skin, and he assigns Poitier to the hospital's prison ward. The first two patients Poitier treats are Widmark and his brother, Paxton, two slum gangsters, who have been wounded by police while attempting a robbery. Poitier attempts to save Paxton's life, thinking that he is suffering from a brain tumor, but he dies under the operation, and Widmark, a bigot to the bone, accuses him of killing his brother because he was white. Poitier insists that Paxton's death was caused by the tumor and asks to perform an autopsy, but he needs a relative's permission to perform that operation and Widmark adamantly refuses, saying that he does not want his brother's

body butchered by a black doctor. Poitier and McNally then locate Paxton's widow, Darnell, a tough slum lady, who is associated with Widmark's street gang, and she hesitates to give permission. She visits Widmark at the hospital—she has had an adulterous relationship with him in the past—and he tells her that Paxton would be alive if a white doctor had operated on him and persuades her to go with his older brother, Bellaver, a deaf mute, to see Freed, the leader of a white gang, and tell him about what happened. Darnell visits Freed and he tells her that they are going to attack residents living in the city's black ghetto, which the bigoted Freed calls "Niggertown." Black gang leaders, however, have learned about the impending attack and make arrangements to ambush Freed and his gang members. Meanwhile, Poitier learns of this planned attack from Johnson, a black elevator operator at the hospital, and he tries to prevent the battle, but the attack nevertheless ensues, resulting in many injuries, these wounded men brought to the hospital where Poitier and other doctors treat them. An autopsy is then conducted on Paxton and Poitier is vindicated when it is learned that he died from a brain tumor, and Darnell denounces Widmark as a racist. Widmark then escapes, going to McNally's house where he entices Poitier to see him and then threatens to kill him with a pistol he has taken from a guard at the prison ward of the hospital when escaping. Darnell arrives and turns out the lights, which causes Widmark to shoot and wound Poitier in the shoulder. When the lights are turned on, Poitier and Darnell see Widmark writhing in pain from his old gunshot wound and where Poitier has wrested the gun from him. Darnell, who hates Widmark for involving Paxton in a life of crime, as well as his racist attitude, asks Poitier to let Widmark bleed to death, but, ever the conscientious physician, Poitier uses the gun and a strip of cloth to make a tourniquet that stops the bleeding as he tells Widmark that he should stop crying and that he is going to live after all. This film, well directed by Mankiewicz (he received an Oscar nomination for Best Screenplay for co-writing this riveting tale), was extremely controversial in that it profiles the naked racism (on both sides, white and black) in the slums of an unnamed large American city, exposing in ugly detail this sensitive issue as no other film had done up to this time. ***Author's Note***: Studio chief Zanuck, who was forever making superlative socially conscious films, personally supervised the production of this film, telling this author: "It was important to show how widespread and deep racial hatred went in America and we did just that in **No Way Out**. I got a lot of criticism from other studio heads for probing that subject, but, by doing that, we exposed a deep flaw in the country's character, showing the actions of bigots that led to widespread violence. I think that film was very instrumental in supporting the civil rights movement a decade later that brought about a lot of reforms and a better understanding of our racial problems." Widmark told this author that "I play another rotten apple in **No Way Out** and I was getting to think that any time Fox wanted an actor to play a disgusting, repulsive human being, they thought about me in that kind of role. I guess I was good at understanding such jerks and was convincing in playing them. But, mind you, I did not want to be typecast in those roles and told Zanuck about that and he said: 'Don't worry, we'll cast you as a hero in the next three films.' He kept his word. I appeared as a good guy in **Halls of Montezuma** [1950], **The Frogmen** [1951], and **Red Skies of Montana** [1952]." Poitier, one of the most gifted African-American actors on the screen, had only appeared in one other film before appearing in **No Way Out**, and it was this appearance that riveted attention to him by international audiences and catapulted his career into high orbit. His previous film appearance was as an extra in **Sepia Cinderella**, 1947, an inexpensive musical that was made, like many others, for the then 684 theaters in the U.S. that exclusively catered to black audiences, who were discouraged if not outright prohibited from attending other theaters attended by white patrons. Poitier's powerful appearance in this film considerably helped to break down that long-standing color barrier, as Zanuck believed it would. Ossie Davis, another gifted black actor, makes his debut in this film and for the first time appears on screen with his off-screen wife, Ruby Dee. **p,** Darryl F.

Zanuck; **d**, Joseph L. Mankiewicz; **cast**, Richard Widmark, Linda Darnell, Stephen McNally, Sidney Poitier, Mildred Joanne Smith, Harry Bellaver, Stanley Ridges, Dots Johnson, Amanda Randolph, Ken Christy, George Tyne, Bert Freed, Frank Richards, Ray Teal, Maude Simmons, Jim Toney, Robert Adler, Will Wright, Betsy Blair, Ossie Davis, Ruby Dee, Dick Paxton, Jack Kruschen, Barbara Pepper; **w**, Mankiewicz, Lesser Samuels; **c**, Milton Krasner; **m**, Alfred Newman; **ed**, Barbara McLean; **art d**, Lyle Wheeler, George W. Davis; **set d**, Thomas Little, Stuart Reiss; **spec eff**, Fred Sersen.

No Way Out ★★★ 1987; U.S.; 114m; Orion Pictures; Color; Drama/Thriller; Children: Unacceptable (MPAA: R); **DVD**; **VHS**. Costner is a heroic navy officer posted to the Pentagon, reporting to Hackman, the newly appointed Secretary of Defense, and his devoted assistant, Patton. Costner has a brief romantic affair with Young, a beautiful Washington call girl, including a memorable liaison in the back seat of a government limousine, not knowing she is Hackman's mistress. She is shortly afterward found dead, accidentally killed by Hackman in a rage of jealousy. Costner has seen Hackman going into Young's apartment the night of the killing, but can't expose his boss as her killer because of some sensitive reasons. Meanwhile, Costner is assigned to investigate the suspicion that there is a KGB mole in the Pentagon. When a photo of Costner is found in Young's apartment, he becomes a suspect in her killing and has only a few hours to find evidence against Hackman before the photo is enhanced to make him more identifiable and sent out over the Internet. Hackman then puts the blame for Young's death on his loyal aide, Patton, a closet homosexual with strong feelings for him (it was Patton who recommended Costner for his present post). Feeling betrayed every which way, Patton shoots and kills himself. Hackman then tells police that Patton killed Young and also was the KGB mole. But that doesn't end the matter. A final scene shows Costner in a hotel room being interrogated by a man speaking Russian, and we learn that stalwart Costner was the mole, above suspicion because of his naval heroism—he had saved a sailor during a storm at sea. He was an unwilling mole, but nonetheless a Soviet agent, although now KGB officials don't want his services because of his involvement in the Pentagon affair and he becomes a man with no way out and nowhere to go. Superior acting from Costner and Hackman, along with a good script, makes this thriller worthwhile. Songs: "No Way Out" (Paul Anka, Michael McDonald), "Say It" (Anka, Richard Marx), "Wild Thing" (Chip Taylor), "Do Ya Think I'm Sexy?" (Rod Stewart, Carmine Appice), "Twistin' U.S.A." (Kal Mann), "Hail to the Chief" (James Sanderson). This film is a remake of **The Big Clock**, 1948. Violence, nudity and sexuality prohibit viewing by children. **p**, Robert Garland, Laura Ziskin; **d**, Roger Donaldson; **cast**, Kevin Costner, Gene Hackman, Sean Young, Will Patton, Howard Duff, George Dzundza, Jason Bernard, Iman, Fred Dalton Thompson, Leon Russom; **w**, Garland (based on the novel *The Big Clock* by Kenneth Fearing); **c**, John Alcott (Metrocolor); **m**, Maurice Jarre; **ed**, William Hoy, Neil Travis; **prod d**, Dennis Washington; **art d**, Anthony Brockliss; **set d**, Bruce Gibeson; **spec eff**, Terry Frazee, Ken Durey.

No Way to Treat a Lady ★★★ 1968; U.S.; 108m; PAR; Color; Crime Drama/Mystery; Children: Unacceptable; **DVD**; **VHS**. Steiger provides a bravura performance in this thriller, a black comedy where he plays a crafty but psychotic killer, who uses various disguises to trick and strangle his female victims. They are women who remind him of his domineering mother whom he hated. Segal, a harassed New York City police detective, starts getting phone calls from Steiger, who disguises his voice, and they form an odd alliance. Remick is a swinging tour guide who sees Steiger leave her neighbor's apartment and that woman is later found dead there. Remick suspects Steiger of having killed her, while at the same time she falls for Segal. Steiger becomes sure that Remick suspects him, so he intends to murder her. Segal, however, gets to her apartment in time to save her; Steiger escapes only to be shot and killed

Kevin Costner, Gene Hackman, and Will Patton in *No Way Out*, 1987.

by Segal, who has discovered his true identity, the owner of a Broadway theater where he has been a frustrated actor, which enabled him to effectively use his disguises in dispatching his many victims. Violence prohibits viewing by children. *Author's Note*: Steiger told this author that "I had a lot of fun playing all sorts of weirdo characters in that picture. I use a lot of disguises and display a number of impersonations while I am strangling half the female population of New York City. The director pretty much gave me a free hand as to how I interpreted those many offbeat roles. The most difficult part was coming up with different-sounding voices for all the characters I am playing, but I got a lot of help on that from the sound people. I think I did a pretty good job at that, but I am no Paul Muni or Alec Guinness. Both of those great actors played several different characters in some of their films and they were astounding in those multiple roles. I did what any conscientious actor would do and studied those films before I did **No Way to Treat a Lady**." The films Steiger was referring to were **Seven Faces**, 1929, where Muni played seven different characters, and **Kind Hearts and Coronets**, 1949, where Guinness played eight separate characters. **p**, Sol C. Siegel; **d**, Jack Smight; **cast**, Rod Steiger, Lee Remick, George Segal, Eileen Heckart, Murray Hamilton, Michael Dunn, Martine Bartlett, Barbara Baxley, Doris Roberts, Val Avery, Sam Coppola; **w**, John Gay (based on the novel by William Goldman); **c**, Jack Priestley (Technicolor); **m**, Stanley Myers; **ed**, Archie Marshek; **art d**, Hal Pereira, George Jenkins; **set d**, Jenkins.

Noah's Ark ★★★ 1928; U.S.; 135m; WB; B/W; Historical Drama/War Drama; Children: Unacceptable; **DVD**. This fascinating historical epic fuses two story lines, the biblical tale of Noah and his Ark, and WWI, beginning with the building of the Tower of Babel and hordes of worshippers paying homage to the Golden Calf. The scene then flash-forwards to 1914 where O'Brien and Williams are traveling in Europe on the "Oriental Express." O'Brien makes friends with minister McAllister, after O'Brien orders a rude passenger to allow McAllister to take his seat. A flash flood causes a bridge to collapse and the racing train is derailed. O'Brien and Williams rescue several persons from the wreckage with the help of Waite, a prisoner who has managed to free himself from handcuffs that bound him to his now dead police escort. Among those rescued is the beautiful Costello, an actress traveling with a German theatrical group, and she quickly falls in love with the robust and heroic O'Brien. While they seek refuge at a remote inn, Beery, a Russian spymaster, accuses Costello of being a secret German agent and he and O'Brien get into a fight where Beery grabs a bottle, breaking it and attempting to use it as a weapon, but is disabled when his hand is severely slashed in the fight. French troops then arrive to announce that WWI has begun, and O'Brien, Costello and Williams depart for Paris where

George Raft and Joan Bennett in *Nob Hill*, 1945.

O'Brien and Costello marry. After the U.S. enters the war, Williams joins the American army, but O'Brien remains behind, worried that if he leaves to fight with the Allies, Costello will have no support. O'Brien's patriotism, however, soars when he sees American troops marching to the front and he impulsively enlists and goes off to fight on the Western Front, losing touch with Costello. O'Brien meets Williams by chance on the battlefield and accidentally kills him when he throws a hand grenade into a trench Williams and others have captured and Williams dies in O'Brien's arms. Costello, meanwhile, joins a troupe of entertainers giving shows for Allied troops, but Beery resurfaces to again wrongly accuse her of being a German spy and she is arrested, convicted and sentenced to death, based on the false testimony of Beery. While awaiting death, Costello is comforted by McAllister, the minister she and O'Brien befriended years earlier on the train. Irony also presents itself when O'Brien is assigned to the firing squad that is to execute Costello, and he manages to save her at the last minute. A German artillery barrage then reduces to rubble the area where they are staying and, during this devastating bombardment, McAllister likens the storm of war and its oceans of blood to the flood that Noah survived in his ark. In flashback, we see all the players from the modern story playing characters in the biblical scenes, Beery playing the evil king who has forced his subjects to worship idols, and McAllister as Noah, who directs his three sons, O'Brien, Williams and Waite, to build a huge ark on a mountainside in preparing for the impending flood decreed by God to McAllister and to subsequently bring all their relatives and animals of all species to that ark. Beery orders the sacrifice of the most beautiful woman in his realm to propitiate his false gods, and Costello, a McAllister handmaiden, is selected. O'Brien tries to save her, but is captured, blinded and then sent to grind wheat at a stone mill (as was Victor Mature in **Samson and Delilah**, 1949). Before Costello is killed, however, God intervenes and frees O'Brien from his chains and restores his sight, allowing him to rescue Costello and take her to the ark just as the flood engulfs the land and the rest of the world,e Beery tries to board the ark but is refused entrance. The ark's survivors then sail on to a better future. In flash-forward, the final scene shows the German bombardment ceasing and O'Brien, Costello and McAllister then learning that an armistice has been signed and that the war is at an end. Pantheon director Curtiz, an expert at action scenes, provides an exciting and often mesmerizing tale, employing hundreds of extras in his scenes, where O'Brien, Costello and Beery are standouts in their roles. This film, made during the time Hollywood was converting to sound movies, provides sound in the modern sequences of the film but the biblical scenes are silent. *Author's Note*: The film was shot at the Iverson Movie Ranch at Chatsworth, California. Budding actor John Wayne, who was one of the hundreds of extras (as was character actor Andy Devine), and who dou-

bled as a prop and stunt man for this film, told this author that "the site where they shot **Noah's Ark** in Chatsworth was used more than ten years later when I appeared in **Stagecoach** [1939] with Pappy [John Ford]. **Noah's Ark** was a dangerous film where three extras lost their lives in the flood scenes and a lot of others were injured. Dolores [Costello] caught pneumonia and almost died. Curtiz, the director, didn't give a damn about any of that. He was the toughest director in Hollywood and, if an extra lost his life in his films, and many did in some of his films, well, Curtiz figured that was part of the risk they took. A lot of people would not work with him, and that includes me. We thought he was a great director, but that he was a very callous and cynical person. Jack Warner put up with Curtiz because he made more successful big-budget films for him than anyone else. It was all money then as it is now." **d**, Michael Curtiz; **cast**, Dolores Costello, George O'Brien, Noah Beery, Louise Fazenda, Guinn "Big Boy" Williams, Paul McAllister, Myrna Loy, Anders Randolf, Armand Kaliz, William V. Mong, Andy Devine, Joe Bonomo, John Wayne; **w**, De Leon Anthony, Anthony Coldewey (based on a story by Darryl F. Zanuck); **c**, Barney McGill, Hal Mohr; **m**, Alois Reiser; **ed**, Harold McCord; **art d**, Anton Grot.

Nob Hill ★★★ 1945; U.S.; 95m; FOX; Color; Musical; Children: Acceptable; **DVD**; **VHS**. Pleasant period story with many great tunes has Raft owning a San Francisco saloon on the Barbary Coast. He meets Garner, an Irish girl who has traveled from her native Ireland to stay with her uncle, but Raft tells her that her uncle has died and the child, now consumed by grief and loneliness, touches his heart and she becomes her ward. Raft, meanwhile, longs to be accepted by the city's society elite and meets through Garner wealthy socialite Bennett, a beautiful queen bee, who resides in a mansion on Nob Hill. The singing-dancing star of Raft's saloon's shows, Blaine, however, loves him and makes sure he stays where he belongs, on the Barbary Coast and with her. The story is based on two earlier Alice Faye films, **King of Burlesque**, 1934, and **Hello, Frisco, Hello**, 1943. Songs: "I Don't Care Who Knows It," "I Walked Right in with My Eyes Wide Open," "Touring San Francisco" (Harold Adamson, Jimmy McHugh); "On San Francisco Bay" (Gertrude Hoffman, Vincente Bryan); "What Do Want to Make Those Eyes at Me For?" (James V. Monaco, Howard Johnson, Joseph McCarthy); "San Francisco, the Paris of the USA" (Hirshel Hendler); "Holy God, We Praise Thy Name" (Peter Ritter); "San Francisco" (Bronislau Kaper, Walter Jurmann, Gus Kahn); "Hello, Frisco" (Louis A. Hirsch, Gene Buck); "When You Wore a Tulip and I Wore a Big Red Rose" (Percy Wenrich, Jack Mahoney);"When Irish Eyes Are Smiling" (Ernest Ball, Chauncey Olcott, George Graff); "Too-ra-loo-ra-loo-ra, That's an Irish Lullaby" (J.R. Shannon); "Happy Birthday to You" (Mildred J. Hill, Patty S. Hill); "Hello! Ma Baby" (Joseph E. Howard, Ida Emerson); "For He's a Jolly Good Fellow" (traditional). *Author's Note*: "I liked being in those period pictures like **Nob Hill**," Raft told this author, "and where I got to wear a lot of spiffy old outfits and those great derby hats, but, to tell you the truth, I don't have a lot to do in that picture, except to take care of a little girl [Garner] and sit around smiling as I listen to a lot of wonderful tunes. After all, it was a musical and that came first before all my mugging." **p**, André Daven; **d**, Henry Hathaway; **cast**, George Raft, Joan Bennett, Vivian Blaine, Peggy Ann Garner, Alan Reed, B.S. Pully, Emil Coleman, Edgar Barrier, Rory Calhoun, Dorothy Ford; **w**, Norman Reilly Raine, Wanda Tuchock (based on a story by Eleanore Griffin); **c**, Edgar Cronjager (Technicolor); **m**, David Buttolph; **ed**, Harmon Jones; **art d**, Russell Spencer, Lyle Wheeler; **set d**, Thomas Little; **spec eff**, Fred Sersen.

Nobody Lives Forever ★★★ 1946; U.S.; 100m; WB; B/W; Drama; Children: Unacceptable; **DVD**. Garfield gives another dynamic performance in this tough drama where he is a former gambler and confidence man. He returns from the army in World War II to discover that his girlfriend, Emerson, has gone off with another man. Also, his gambling interests have been taken over by a rival faction. To seek more opportunities, Garfield travels to California and gets involved in a scheme to fleece a rich young widow, Fitzgerald, but finds that he is falling in love with her, much to the dismay of his racketeer pals, Brennan and Coulouris. Garfield offers to pay his pals off if they forget about Fitzgerald, but, instead, Coulouris kidnaps her for ransom. Brennan comes to her rescue and he and Coulouris shoot each other dead in a gun fight, leaving Garfield to start a new life with Fitzgerald. *Author's Note*: Negulesco told this author that "Humphrey Bogart was the first choice to pay the lead in **Nobody Lives Forever**, but Bogie was big enough by that time to tell Jack Warner that he would not do the film, so Julie [Garfield, real name Julius Garfinkle] was assigned to the role. He wanted to get out of his contract with Warner Brothers and make independent films, but he did the picture with me and was very cooperative. We felt that the story was a bit hackneyed, so we got together and introduced subtle business that establishes his character as a man who has been displaced by the war and is socially adrift, developing the kind of moody character study that could only work with a gifted actor like Julie. What also made things work well was the fact that Julie greatly admired Geraldine's [Fitzgerald's] talents and that shows in the fine scenes they have together." Violence prohibits viewing by children. **p**, Robert Buckner; **d**, Jean Negulesco; **cast**, John Garfield, Geraldine Fitzgerald, Walter Brennan, Faye Emerson, George Coulouris, George Tobias, Robert Shayne, Richard Gaines, Dick Erdman, James Flavin, Robert Arthur, Rudolf Friml, Jr., Marion Martin, Grady Sutton; **w**, W.R. Burnett (based on his novel *I Wasn't Born Yesterday*); **c**, Arthur Edeson; **m**, Adolph Deutsch; **ed**, Rudi Fehr; **art d**, Hugh Reticker; **set d**, Casey Roberts; **spec eff**, Willard Van Enger, William C. McGann, Paul Detlefsen.

Nobody's Fool ★★★ 1995; U.S.; 110m; Capella International/PAR; Color; Comedy/Drama; Children: Unacceptable (MPAA: R); **DVD**; **VHS**. Newman mesmerizes as an easy-going sixty-year-old beer-guzzler approaching retirement, although he has never really grown up. He lives and works in a small upstate New York town as a sometimes construction worker for Willis, a builder. Newman rents an upstairs room from Tandy, and lives in her house. She was his eighth grade teacher and he is fond of her as they develop a mother-son relationship. His life, when off the job, which is most of the time, mainly involves drinking beer with his buddies at a local bar and flirting with his boss's lovely wife, Griffith. He left his wife, Wilson, and two children thirty years earlier and his now grown son, Walsh, a college teacher whose marriage is on the rocks, comes to town for the Thanksgiving holiday to learn why his father deserted him. Most of the film's action involves a long-running argument with Willis over the theft and recapture of a snow blower and Newman's efforts to win a worker's compensation suit from Willis because of a bad knee. Newman's chief pursuits are focused upon trying to save Tandy's house from her banker son, who wants to destroy the house to make way for a development and where she would be evicted. Newman plays a man who is, ultimately, nobody's fool and finds ways to save Tandy's house and become more of a grandfather, and the final scene shows him fast asleep, taking a well-deserved rest. Slight on action but strong on character development, Newman and Tandy, as well as the rest of the strong cast, provide standout performances that sustain high interest throughout. Songs: "Call Me Irresponsible" (Sammy Cahn, Jimmy Van Heusen), "Ruby, Don't Take Your Love to Town" (Mel Tillis), "The Nearness of You" (Ned Washington, Hoagy Carmichael), "People's Court" (Alan Tew), "Whiskey, Wine and Roses" (Bill Reveles), "Silver Bells" (Ray Evans, Jay Livingston), "Near You" (Francis Craig, Kermit Goell). Gutter language and nudity prohibit viewing by children. *Author's Note*: "Just being in the same picture with a great actress like Jessica [Tandy] was a terrific kick for me," Newman told this author. "There was something so comfortable about being in scenes with her, especially after I rent a room in her home and she more or less adopts me as the son she never had. We lost a very great lady when she passed away." Tandy died in 1994, shortly after completing this film, which was released the following year. **p**, Scott

Jessica Tandy and Paul Newman in *Nobody's Fool*, 1995.

Rudin, Arlene Donovan; **d&w**, Robert Benton (based on the novel by Richard Russo); **cast**, Paul Newman, Jessica Tandy, Bruce Willis, Melanie Griffith, Dylan Walsh, Philip Seymour Hoffman, Philip Bosco, Josef Sommer, Gene Saks, Catherine Dent; **c**, John Bailey; **m**, Howard Shore; **ed**, John Bloom; **prod d**, David Gropman; **art d**, Dan Davis; **set d**, Gretchen Rau; **spec eff**, Tom Ryba, Rod Kiser.

Nocturne ★★★ 1946; U.S.; 87m; RKO; B/W; Crime Drama; Children: Unacceptable; **DVD**; **VHS**. This well-made film noir entry has Raft as a police detective who is assigned to investigate the fatal shooting of a womanizing composer. He suspects that one of the ten women the victim has dumped, but his superiors conclude that the man killed himself. Raft thinks otherwise and tracks down one discarded lover after another, despite being ordered off the case. His main suspect becomes beautiful Bari, to whom he becomes attracted. She leads him to her sister, Huston, a singer who has fallen in love with her pianist, Pevney, and it turns out through Raft's good snooping that he was the killer in a case of jealousy over her. Songs: "Nocturne" (Leigh Harline, Mort Greene); "Why Pretend," "A Little Bit Is Better than None" (Eleanor Rudolph). *Author's Note*: Raft told this author that "**Nocturne** offered a lot of clever twists and as I sifted through almost a dozen suspects, I actually got a bit confused, and I started calling Lynn [Bari] 'Wendy' when we were off the set, until she reminded me that her name was 'Lynn.' The confusion came because Wendy Barrie, another actress in those days, was paling around with my friend Ben Siegel [Benjamin "Bugsy" Siegel, the underworld crime boss of southern California and top lieutenant of the U.S. crime syndicate until his murder in 1947]. I apologized to her, but I was always confusing names in Hollywood. There was a 'Queenie Smith' in **Nocturne**, and I confused her for 'Queenie Leonard,' a British actress. I guess I got those two names mixed up because both of them were singers. Most people don't know that 'Queenie Smith' was once engaged to a guy named Archibald Leach, who was Cary Grant. *His name* I could always remember." Violence prohibits viewing by children. **p**, Joan Harrison; **d**, Edwin L. Marin; **cast**, George Raft, Lynn Bari, Virginia Huston, Joseph Pevney, Myrna Dell, Edward Ashley, Walter Sande, Mabel Paige, Bernard Hoffman, Queenie Smith, Mack Gray, Lilian Bond; **w**, Rowland Brown, Frank Fenton, Jonathan Latimer, Harrison; **c**, Harry J. Wild; **m**, Leigh Harline; **ed**, Elmo Williams; **prod d**, Robert Boyle; **art d**, Albert S. D'Agostino; **set d**, James Altwies, Darrell Silvera; **spec eff**, Russell A. Cully.

None But the Lonely Heart ★★★★★ 1944; U.S.; 113m; RKO; B/W; Children: Cautionary; **DVD**; **VHS**. In one of his finest dramatic roles (nominated for an Oscar), Grant is superb as a carefree British cockney living in the slums of London's Whitechapel just prior to WWII. The

Cary Grant and Jane Wyatt in *None But the Lonely Heart*, 1944.

gloomy area is crowded with shifty denizens, crowded tenements and cheap shops, unchanged from when the sinister and ubiquitous Jack the Ripper roamed its dark streets fifty years earlier. His mother, Barrymore, a shrewd but kind-hearted old lady, runs one of those shops, a second-hand furniture store where petty transactions allow them both to survive. Grant and Barrymore have a love-hate relationship as he comes and goes to and from Barrymore's shop, living in an upstairs room. He thinks of her as an aging miser and she believes him to be incorrigibly shiftless and without purpose in life, and in this she is right. Grant refuses to hold down a regular job, although few are then available in these Depression-era times. He maintains the exterior of a charming rascal with a lot of snappy lines, but he is internally uneasy as he yearns to acquire quick wealth so that he can wed the beautiful and alluring Duprez, the divorced wife of powerful crime boss Coulouris. Wyatt, a pretty cellist who lives nearby, loves Grant, but he looks upon her as an always available companion for an occasional date. Picking up odd jobs, Grant manages to maintain his independence, although he is forever cadging cigarettes from others, such as Shayne, a pawnbroker, who gives him sage advice and who is Barrymore's close friend, as well as drifter Fitzgerald, an avuncular friend always commenting on the dire events of this dark era when war is brewing on the Continent. The insidious Courlouris, knowing that Grant needs cash to continue his romance with Duprez, entices him with offers of riches if he joins his underworld gang and Grant at first resists, but then succumbs and participates in some robberies for which he feels remorse. He quits the gang even though the avaricious Duprez seeks more gifts from him. Grant then learns from Shayne that his mother is suffering from cancer and, without letting her know, he makes a strong effort to bond with her by working in her store and where he spends many hours repairing old furniture and clocks, showing kindness to Barrymore with his every gesture, a new attitude that surprises her as they have never been close. Realizing that her son cannot plan his future—let alone contemplate marriage—without money, Barrymore breaks the law and begins trafficking in stolen items for which she is arrested and imprisoned. Grant visits her in prison, knowing that she is dying of cancer. They at first have little to say to each other, but then Barrymore sobs and tells Grant that she has disgraced him. Grant then breaks down and utters the first words of affection to her, saying: "Didn't disgrace me, Ma. This is your son, Ernie Mott, Ma. This is the boy who needs you and wants you." Barrymore smiles and Grant leaves, promising to return tomorrow. She dies before he returns, and Grant then resolves to stand up against the oppressions of the world, telling Fitzgerald that he is going to enlist in the army and "fight with the men who will fight for a human way of life." Grant then leaves to enlist, becoming what the opening narration of this powerful film implies, the unknown dead soldier of WWII. Odets, who wrote the brilliant script,

directs this memorable film with great skill, his settings appropriately foreboding and ominous as Grant flirts with danger and hazard while seeking something that has evaded him all his life, affection and love, as well as purpose to an otherwise meaningless life. The film was not a box office success, but it remains a classic portrait of that dark era between the two world wars and where the indefatigable Grant represents the spirit of hope. Barrymore's performance is as captivating as Grant's, and their biting exchanges of dialog are exceptional. Barrymore won an Oscar as Best Supporting Actress for her marvelous enactment of a mother, hardened by her sordid surroundings, but desperate for love from her only son. *Author's Note*: Grant told this author that "John and Lionel Barrymore were great actors, but Ethel was the greatest acting talent of the family, a woman who could carry a scene by slowly closing and opening her eyes. I play her son in **None But the Lonely Heart**, and, believe me, I felt like it, only like a little boy in awe of her. The producers got her to play in the picture only after they agreed to pay off all the expense of closing down a huge Broadway hit she was appearing in, *The Corn Is Green*. That cost RKO a lot, but they knew she was worth it and so did I." **p**, David Hempstead; **d&w**, Clifford Odets (based on the novel by Richard Llewellyn); **cast**, Cary Grant, Ethel Barrymore, Barry Fitzgerald, June Duprez, Jane Wyatt, George Coulouris, Dan Duryea, Roman Bohnen, Konstantin Shayne, Rosalind Ivan, John Meredith; **c**, George Barnes; **m**, Hanns Eisler; **ed**, Roland Gross; **prod d**, Mordecai Gorelik; **art d**, Albert S. D'Agostino, Jack Okey; **set d**, Darrell Silvera, Harley Miller; **spec eff**, Vernon L. Walker.

None Shall Escape ★★★ 1944; U.S.; 85m; COL; B/W; Drama; Children: Unacceptable; **DVD**; **VHS**. Knox gives a riveting profile of a diehard Nazi, who is shown at first at his trial where he is charged as a war criminal, flashbacks showing how he came to be branded an unthinking protégé of Hitler's ruthless regime. Crippled during World War I (1914-1918), he returns to his home along the German-Polish border and resumes his career as a teacher. His pro-Nazi (National Socialist German Workers' Party, 1933-1945) leanings cause Hunt, his girlfriend, to leave him. After he sexually assaults a young woman, he is banished from the village. He joins the Nazi party and becomes the local Nazi commandant, waging his own war of terror during World War II (1939-1945). De Toth helms this frightening profile with great care to depict how a good man can become an instrument of evil. **p**, Samuel Bischoff; **d**, Andre De Toth; **cast**, Marsha Hunt, Alexander Knox, Henry Travers, Erik Rolf, Richard Crane, Dorothy Morris, Richard Hale, Ruth Nelson, Kurt Kreuger, Hank Worden; **w**, Lester Cole (based on a story by Alfred Neumann, Joseph Than); **c**, Lee Garmes; **m**, Ernst Toch; **ed**, Charles Nelson; **art d**, Lionel Banks, Perry Smith; **set d**, Frank Tuttle.

The Noose Hangs High ★★★ 1948; U.S.; 77m; Abbott & Costello Productions/Eagle-Lion; B/W; Comedy; Children: Acceptable; **DVD**; **VHS**. Good comedic romp sees those laughable clowns, Abbott and Costello, as window washers, who are mistaken for gamblers and get mixed up with a group of gangsters led by Calleia. The boys do a take-off on their "Who's on First" routine in a skit called "You Can't Be Here," among many other routines and sight gags that fill this outing with mirth and mayhem. **p&d**, Charles Barton; **cast**, Bud Abbott, Lou Costello, Joseph Calleia, Leon Errol, Cathy Downs, Mike Mazurki, Fritz Feld, Ellen Corby, Jimmie Dodd, Pat Flaherty; **w**, John Grant, Howard Harris (based on a story by Daniel Taradash, Julian Blaustein, Bernard Fins); **c**, Charles Van Enger; **m**, Walter Schumann; **ed**, Harry Reynolds; **art d**, Edward L. Ilou; **set d**, Armor Marlowe; **spec eff**, George J. Teague.

Nora Prentiss ★★★ 1947; U.S.; 105m; WB; B/W; Drama; Children: Unacceptable; **DVD**. This intriguing film noir tale opens with Smith as a successful San Francisco doctor, who is unhappily married to De-Camp, and who starts an affair with Sheridan, a nightclub singer. He can't work up the courage to ask his wife for a divorce, so Sheridan moves to New York City to open up at new nightclub. DeCamp dies and Smith fakes his own death before going to New York to see Sheridan again. He learns that his faked death is being investigated as a murder. He takes to drink and becomes jealous of Sheridan's boss, Alda, and they fight. Smith believes he's killed Alda, so he flees and has a car accident that leaves his face disfigured. His face is reshaped with plastic surgery and he thinks all is well with a new countenance that will not be recognized, until he is arrested for his own murder in California. He asks Sheridan and his friends not to reveal his true identity so he is convicted and sentenced to death. He and Sheridan say farewell before his execution. This production plays better than the involved plot suggests, and Smith and Sheridan render top-notch performances. Violence prohibits viewing by children. Songs: "Would You Like a Souvenir?" "Who Cares What People Say?" (M. K. Jerome, Jack, Scholl); "Deep in a Dream" (Jimmy Van Heusen); "Berceuse in D Flat Major, Op. 57" (Frederic Chopin). **p**, William Jacobs; **d**, Vincent Sherman; **cast**, Ann Sheridan, Kent Smith, Bruce Bennett, Robert Alda, Rosemary DeCamp, John Ridgely, Robert Arthur, Wanda Hendrix, Helen Brown, Rory Mallinson, Harry Shannon, Douglas Kennedy, Don McGuire, John Alvin; **w**, N. Richard Nash (based on the story "The Man Who Died Twice" by Paul Webster, Jack Sobell); **c**, James Wong Howe; **m**, Franz Waxman; **ed**, Owen Marks; **art d**, Anton Grot; **set d**, Walter Tilford; **spec eff**, Harry Barndollar, Edwin DuPar.

Norma Rae ★★★★ 1979; U.S.; 110m; FOX; Color; Drama; Children: Unacceptable (MPAA: PG); **DVD**; **VHS**. In one of her finest roles (for which she received her first Oscar, her second for **Places in the Heart**, 1984), Field wholly embodies an uneducated young southern wife, who works in a factory for meager wages and whose life is drastically altered when she decides to join a union. She idolizes her father, Hingle, who dies for lack of the proper medical attention, not to mention a misdiagnosis of his ailments. Her mother, Baxley, is losing her hearing because of the incessant din inside the factory where she works. Divorced, Field has two children from a previous marriage and she meets easy-going but dim-witted Bridges and marries him so that her children will have a father figure, which he proves not to be. Meanwhile, Field, along with everyone in her small town, labor long hours in a cotton mill where they are underpaid and have little or no benefits. Then Liebman, a New York union organizer, arrives in town and attempts to establish a union at the factory, but he meets with universal disdain from the workers, all of whom fear losing their jobs if they even talk to him. Liebman selects the feisty Field as his lynchpin in establishing that union and indoctrinates her against the evils of corporations and company owners who purposely neglect and mistreat their workers to earn more money. She is already well aware of the harsh working regulations and oppressive atmosphere at the factory where strong-armed goons act as supervisors to intimidate the male and female workers. Liebman brings about a dramatic transformation in Field, from a woman without any real ambition to a person now resolved to fight for a better way of life. Her relationship with Liebman annoys and then angers Bridges, who all but demands that the union organizer pack up and leave town. Liebman, however, is as dedicated to his mission as a fierce terrier and continues to prod, goad and stimulate Field until she openly defies factory bosses and is removed from the place under police escort. She is bailed out by Liebman and is then reinstated at her job, but when conditions worsen at the factory, Field again rebels, shutting down her machine and standing atop a table and holding up a sign that reads "UNION" for all of her fellow workers to see. As bosses close in on her, the workers, one by one, shut down their machines, indicating that they are joining Field's strike and are now supporters of the union, and it is clear that the factory will be unionized, despite the severe and insidious methods that bosses have employed to prevent that from happening. With production at a standstill, the management now has no choice but to accept the universal will of its employees. Field has won, but, in essence, all these hardworking and simple people have triumphed after they finally resolve to act as one in

Sally Field in *Norma Rae*, 1979.

helping everyone. In addition to Field's amazing and mesmerizing performance, Liebman, Bridges, and the rest of the cast are perfect in their roles, thanks to Ritt's skillful casting and where his incisive direction elicits fine performances from all while depicting in many telling scenes the drab and unpromising lifestyle of the decaying South where whites and blacks suffer the same dire economic fate. The film was nominated as Best Picture as was the screenplay. In addition to Field's Oscar, Shire and Gimbel won Oscars for Best Original Song, "It Goes Like It Goes." The film enjoyed an enormous box office success, taking in more than $22 million against its original budget of $4.5 million, and it remains one of the best films about unionism, joining the ranks of such fine films as **Hoffa**, 1992, and **On the Waterfront**, 1954. Songs: "It Goes Like It Goes" (music: David Shire; lyrics: Norman Gimbel), "Cindy, I Love You" (Johnny Cash), "It's All Wrong, But It's All Right" (Dolly Parton). **p**, Tamara Asseyev, Alex Rose; **d**, Martin Ritt; **cast**, Sally Field, Beau Bridges, Ron Leibman, Pat Hingle, Barbara Baxley, Gail Strickland, Morgan Paull, John Calvin, Robert Broyles, Booth Colman; **w**, Irving Ravetch, Harriet Frank, Jr.; **c**, John A. Alonzo (Panavision; DeLuxe Color); **m**, David Shire; **ed**, Sidney Levin; **prod d**, Walter Scott Herndon; **art d**, Tracy Bousman; **set d**, Gregory Garrison; **spec eff**, William Van Der Byl.

North by Northwest ★★★★★ 1959; U.S.; 136m; MGM; Color; Spy Drama; Children: Unacceptable; **BD**; **DVD**; **VHS**. No director ever made films about spies better than Alfred Hitchcock and he proves that again in this masterpiece tale of espionage. Again, he relies upon an innocent man arbitrarily selected by fate to be caught up in a maelstrom of intrigue and murder. This time it is the inimitable Grant, who plays a suave, charming and successful New York advertising executive, whose bit of whimsy has led him to parody his own name, "Roger A. Thornhill," by having his personalized matchbooks emblazoned with his initials "R.A.T." He is shown going to the Plaza to have lunch with his wealthy mother, Landis, who thinks her son's lifestyle, if not his profession, is that of an idler and that he has wasted too much of his time with the wrong people, including the two women who have divorced him. He is getting on in life, she points out, and that time is fleeting and so are his opportunities for true love while he continues to indulge himself with the fancies of an aging bachelor. While distracted in conversation with Landis, Grant mistakenly answers the page of a bellhop calling out the name of "George Kaplan." That minor error, however, will lead him down a path fraught with hazard and lurking killers. He is dogged by two hit men, Williams and Ellenstein, but manages to evade them and then he and Landis begin looking for Kaplan, going to Kaplan's room at the Plaza. They find his suits hanging in a closet and his other personal items, Grant even inspecting the man's comb in the bathroom

Cary Grant and Eva Marie Saint in *North by Northwest*, 1959.

to tell Landis that "Kaplan has dandruff." But they find no George Kaplan and discover that a housemaid and a valet at the hotel have never met the mysterious Kaplan. When they leave the room and take an elevator downward, Williams and Ellenstein suddenly slip into that elevator and stand next to Grant, who tells Landis that these are the two men who are trying to murder him. She doesn't believe a word of it, and thinks that their hunt for Kaplan has been nothing but a wild goose chase and, to embarrass Grant for his impossible imaginings, she turns to Williams and Ellenstein and says: "You're not really trying to kill my son, are you?" They grin and then begin laughing as does everybody else in the elevator, including Landis. The only one not laughing is Grant, who, when the elevator arrives at the lobby floor, dashes from it, races through the lobby, goes outside and abruptly dives into a cab others are about to enter. As the cab drives away, Grant sees from its rear window that Williams and Ellenstein have jumped into a cab that is following him. They nevertheless capture him and take him to a rural mansion where he is grilled by Mason, an urbane spymaster of an unknown country. Grant insists that he is not Kaplan, the man Mason and his minions seek, but they disbelieve him, convinced that he is that man, who is an American agent on their trail. Williams and Ellenstein, with the aid of Mason's chief enforcer, Landau, then compel Grant to drink excessive amounts of whiskey until he is drunk. That night they place him behind the wheel of a Mercedes sports car and send him crazily driving along a mountain road, expecting that he will drive off a cliff and be killed. Grant, however, despite being thoroughly inebriated and seeing double, manages to steer the car down the perilous road and into a small town and is followed by a police car until Grant slams the Mercedes into a parked car and he is arrested. Landau and others, who have been following in another car, see that Grant is now in police custody and drive away. Booked and jailed for drunken driving, Grant calls Landis and she arrives with an attorney the next day and where Grant is released after paying a fine. He insists, however, that he was set up by a conspiratorial group headed by Mason with intent to kill him and he leads detectives back to the mansion where Hutchinson, who appears to be the wife of Ober, owner of the estate, tells detectives that Grant had too much to drink at a party she held and borrowed a guest's Mercedes and drove away, all of which Grant denies, but fails to convince detectives that his story is legitimate. All leave and Grant later goes to the United Nations where Ober works, asking to see him. When Ober arrives, Grant tells him that a group of strangers have taken over his country estate and Grant shows Ober a photograph of Mason. He gapes at the photo, his face distorted in shock, but it is not from viewing the photograph as he falls forward into Grant's arms with a knife in his back, thrown by one of Mason's henchmen. Grant impulsively grabs the handle of the knife, holding on to it as Ober falls dead at his feet, and someone photographs

Grant clutching the knife before he flees. Now he is pursued by police for Ober's murder and by Mason's minions, who think him to be a secret American agent, which he is not. In an effort to clear his name, Grant learns that the elusive and ubiquitous Kaplan has left New York for Chicago and Grant goes to Grand Central Station where he sneaks aboard the posh 20th Century, the luxury train en route to Chicago. He goes to the dining car and is seated opposite alluring blonde Saint, who seems to be seducing him as they chat and have dinner. He admits to her with self-effacing irony that his previous two wives divorced him because "I led to dull a life." When the train comes to a stop, Saint sees what appears to be a number of detectives boarding the train and tells Grant about it, suggesting that he go to her stateroom. Saint is then seen sitting in her stateroom reading a book when those detective knock on her door as they have been routinely searching the train car by car. She tells a detective that she has not seen Grant and says, after learning that he is wanted for murder, that she intends to see no one on that train and plans to lock her door, which she does after the detectives departs. Saint then unlocks the panel to the upper berth, releasing the panel to show Grant hiding there. He is perplexed as to her motivations in shielding him, but accepts the fact that she is simply attracted to him and they embrace as the train races westward into the fading dusk. As expected, more detectives are waiting at the station in Chicago when the train arrives, but Grant eludes them by posing as a train porter carrying Saint's luggage. He then goes to the men's room at the station and changes his clothes, shaves and later goes to the upscale Ambassador East Hotel, finding Saint in her room. He learns that she is somehow involved with Mason, but thinks she has his best interests at heart when she tells him that he can locate the ubiquitous Kaplan at a rural destination in Indiana. Grant takes a bus to that remote and lonely place, getting off at a crossroad in the middle of farm fields. He stands waiting for some time, seeing nothing or no one in sight, until a car arrives from a side road and a passenger in that car gets out and stands impassively across the road from Grant. Believing that the man might be Kaplan, Grant crosses the road to briefly talk to the man, only to find out that he is waiting for another bus and is not Kaplan. The man looks to the sky to see a crop-dusting plane and tells Grant that he believes the pilot is acting strangely because he is "dusting crops where there ain't any crops." The bus arrives and the man gets on and the bus drives away and Grant stands alone at the crossroads, utterly dumbfounded. As he stands watching the crop-dusting biplane, he sees it suddenly turn in his direction and fly directly at him. Grant senses danger and begins running along a dirt road with the plane diving and racing after him and firing machine gun bullets at him as it passes over him, that spray of bullets barely missing him. He frantically races from the road and into a cornfield as the occupant or occupants (they are never seen) of the plane continue to fire at him. Once inside the cornfield, Grant cowers as the plane unleashes clouds of anti-pestilent fumes. Holding a handkerchief to his face and coughing, Grant runs from the cornfield and back to the main road where he sees an oncoming oil tank truck approaching. In desperation, he stands before the truck, waving at its driver to stop and the truck halts only inches from him as he falls down. The pilot of the plane, however, aims itself at Grant and dives at him and the truck, crashing into the truck as Grant and the truck drivers run from it just as the oil tank explodes, killing the pilot (or pilots) and where the plane and truck are consumed in a gigantic fireball. Some passersby stop their cars and Grant leaps into a pickup truck, which the driver has left to view the carnage and uses it to drive off. The truck is later seen abandoned on a Chicago street and Grant is then shown reentering the Ambassador East Hotel. Grant now believes that Saint is part of the cabal out to kill him, but he hides his suspicions as Saint allows him to take a shower in her room and sends for a valet to clean his suit. When she leaves, Grant finds an address Saint has written on a notepad, which gives Grant the location of her destination, an upscale auction salon on Michigan Avenue and he goes there. When he sees her with Mason and his men, he confronts her, accusing her of attempting to have him killed. Mason then tells him that he will not leave the place alive as he orders his men to block the exits. Grant takes a seat with the buyers and, as the auctioneer begins to announce the sales of items, Grant begins making ridiculous bids, disrupting the proceedings. When he shouts that one of the priceless items is not genuine, a woman seated nearby states that "one thing is for sure and that is *you* are a *genuine* idiot!" While he creates a fight, police are summoned, which is exactly what Grant wants, and he is hauled off and placed in a police squad car. Officers then get a radio message not to take him to police headquarters, even though they know he is wanted for Ober's murder, but deliver him, instead, to the airport on orders of Carroll, the chief of a U.S. intelligence agency (never specified, but something similar to the CIA or NSA) and he tells Grant that they have known all along that he has been mistaken for one of their agents, Kaplan, a man who has never existed and was a mythical plant to decoy Mason and his group of spies. Carroll explains that Grant has now compromised one of their undercover agents, Saint, who is working to get enough evidence to have Mason and his organization arrested. Carroll asks that Grant continue playing the mythical Kaplan in order to protect Saint. Having fallen in love with her, Grant agrees and he flies with Carroll to Rapid City, South Dakota, where Mason maintains a mountain retreat, which is not far from the historic monument of Mount Rushmore. Once Grant arrives in South Dakota, he enacts a lethal charade as planned by Carroll in order to convince Mason that Saint is, indeed, loyal to him and has no real feelings for Grant. Grant barges in on Mason, Saint and Landau as they lunch in the dining area of the main building at Mount Rushmore, which is crowded with tourists. Grant tells Mason that he is no longer concerned with what he and his friends are up to. He only wants revenge against Saint so that she can "get what's coming to her." Mason, Landau and Saint begin to leave the place, but Grant grabs Saint, who orders him to leave her alone and, when he continues to hold on to her, she withdraws a pistol and shoots Grant several times and he falls to the floor, apparently dead, startling the crowd and creating chaos. Landau then shepherds Mason away from the scene as Saint separately flees the building. Carroll kneels next to Grant, examining his bloody body and signals to spectators that he is dead. Grant's body is then loaded into an ambulance, but before it takes the corpse to the morgue, the ambulance drives to a remote wooded area where a very much alive Grant emerges from the ambulance to meet with Saint, who is in love with him. They have arranged to have her "kill" Grant by shooting blanks at him in order to convince Mason that she is truly a member of his spying cabal. She tells Grant that she is now going to accompany Mason, who is planning to fly out of the country with some top secrets he has obtained in Chicago so that she can recoup those secrets, the evidence that will send Mason and his minions to prison. Grant is then taken at Carroll's orders to a hospital where he is held under guard and under an alias. Carroll tells him that his association with Saint is at an end and he thanks him for his services to his country, but Grant has no intentions of letting the matter drop as he is now desperately in love with Saint and intends to keep her out of harm's way. He escapes from the hospital and makes his way to Mason's remote retreat, seeing from a porch the lavish interior of the living room where Mason and Landau are making preparations to leave the country while Saint is sitting on a couch. Grant climbs to an upper floor and gets into a bedroom that overlooks the living room area, and, to signal Saint that he is present, tosses one of his embossed matchbooks bearing his trademarked initials toward her while Mason and Landau have their backs turned. The matchbook lands on the floor next to Saint but she does not see it. Landau, however, walks close to her and notices the matchbook, picking it up and placing it on a coffee table and Saint then sees that it is a signal from Grant and excuses herself, saying that she has some final packing to do. She meets with Grant in her bedroom, and Grant tells her not to go on that trip, but she is adamant in performing her undercover job. Grant leaves, but lingers on the outside porch to see Mason and Landau alone and where Landau inexplicably insults his boss, starting an argument. The angered Mason then makes a move toward Landau and Lan-

Eva Marie Saint and Cary Grant in *North by Northwest,* 1959.

dau shoots him. Mason stands with a startled look on his face only to discover that he has not been injured. Landau then hands him a pistol, the very one Saint used to shoot Grant earlier, explaining that it is harmless as it holds nothing but blanks, thus exposing Saint's ruse. She is now in mortal danger and Mason tells Landau that, once they are in the airplane and in flight, his deceitful mistress will be pushed out of that airplane to her death. Hearing this, Grant again climbs up to Saint's room to warn her, but she goes ahead with her mission, accompanying Mason to a nearby plane that has landed and is about to take off. Grant slips down the stairs from the bedroom, but is confronted by a heavyset housekeeper, who trains a pistol on him. As Mason and Saint are about to board the plane, they hear gunshots coming from the house, and while Mason is thus distracted, Saint grabs an art object that Mason had purchased at the auction in Chicago, which contains the top secrets, and races off with it. Coming toward her, also on the run, is Grant, who leads her through a wooded area, explaining that he overpowered the housekeeper after discovering that she was using that same pistol containing the blank cartridges. They then try to flee the estate, but all escape routes are blocked by Mason's henchmen. Running through the woods, they come upon the Mount Rushmore monument, standing atop of it and having nowhere to go but downward onto the rocky faces of four U.S. presidents (Washington, Jefferson, Lincoln and Theodore Roosevelt, this scene in keeping with Hitchcock's penchant for including highly recognizable historic landmarks in his films). Mason's thugs pursue them and Williams stops them on a ledge. Grant and Williams struggle and Williams goes over the ledge, screaming as he plunges downward to certain death. As Grant and Saint work themselves downward, Saint falls, but saves herself by clinging to the face of one of the edifices as Grant scrambles to her and clutches her hand while clinging to a ledge with his other hand. Landau then appears, standing at the top of the ledge where he has retrieved the art object containing the vital secrets. Grant asks him for help and Landau cruelly steps on Grant's fingers. Just as Grant is about to slip from the ledge and take Saint with him in a death fall, a shot rings out, a bullet striking Landau, killing him and sending him over the ledge while he drops the art object that breaks to reveal a roll of microfilm, the vital secret sought by Carroll, Saint and other American agents (or the MacGuffin, as Hitchcock puts it, the catalyst for all of the sinister events taking place in this thriller). Mason is then shown in captivity atop the monument, standing with Carroll and other officers, blithely remarking that shooting Landau was "not very sporting of you." The crisis is over and justice has triumphed. Grant is shown reaching for Saint, but he is no longer on the monument. He is sitting on the upper berth of a stateroom in a Pullman train car, pulling Saint upward to him and into his arms, to whimsically reenact their earlier experience on a train, and where Saint tells him that "this is silly," but

Cary Grant and Eva Marie Saint in *North by Northwest*, 1959.

Grant does not care as they are now married and, as they embrace, the final scene shows the train racing into a tunnel (of love, as so overtly implied by the equally whimsical Hitchcock). Grant, Saint, Mason and the rest of the cast give stellar performances under Hitchcock's impeccable direction, where he maintains high anxiety and suspense in every scene, those scenes packed with great action and where the humorous and witty script from Lehman presents one surprising twist after another. This was Landau's first important supporting role and he is superb in radiating an aura of evil, undoubtedly the most insidious and sinister character in the film, a role that accelerated his Hollywood career and established him as a first-rate actor (he had earlier appeared in many TV dramas and had had a small part in Lewis Milestone's Korean War epic, **Pork Chop Hill**, 1959). This superb actor would go on to play many fine roles and win an Oscar for his riveting enactment of the drug-addicted horror film star, Bela Lugosi, in **Ed Wood**, 1994. Songs (as background music or whistled and/or sung by Grant): "It's a Most Unusual Day" (1948; music: Jimmy McHugh; lyrics: Harold Adamson), "Serenade for Strings" (1880; Ilyich Tchaikovsky), "Singin' in the Rain" (1929; music: Nacio Herb Brown; lyrics: Arthur Freed), "Rosalie" (1937; Cole Porter), "I've Grown Accustomed to Her Face" (1956; music: Frederick Loewe; lyrics: Jay Lerner). *Author's Note:* In one of my many meetings with Hitchcock, the director told this author that, although the gifted Lehman wrote the script for **North by Northwest**, he, Hitchcock, had a direct hand in shaping its scenes, as was his wont with almost all of his writers (and as testified by one of his favorite screenwriters, Ben Hecht, who told this author that "Hitch had his fingers on every page I ever wrote for him"). Hitchcock worked closely with Lehman by walking about in a room where Lehman labored at a typewriter (this was Hitchcock's usual routine when working with his writers), verbally telling Lehman his ideas in setting up one scene after another. "**North by Northwest** did not end on Mount Rushmore in one version," Hitchcock told this author. "We got up into Siberia nearly with it, Ernie Lehman and I, and I remember I had a sequence where the girl [Saint] is kidnapped. They [the kidnappers] get her along the straits and they are going along a road in Siberia in an open car and a helicopter [Hitchcock used a helicopter or an early-day auto-gyro in a chase scene in the hills of Scotland in **The 39 Steps**, 1935] from the Alaskan side is chasing the car with a rope hanging from it and they were saying to the girl: 'Grab the rope!' And she's rescued from the car and the heavies try to grab her back...It was the most daring rescue you've ever seen." This scene, however, never made it into the final film, and a number of other spectacular scenes the director envisioned were also not used. "I remember one scene I wanted," Hitchcock went on, "I said: 'Can't we work it in somehow? We ought to have a scene showing a vast plain of ice and two little black figures walking toward each other...enemies or some-

thing...' I don't know what would have happened when they got together. They are going along and there is a hole in the ice, and, suddenly, a hand comes out of the hole. ...You've got to go wild and then tone it down. Where would the hand come from? I don't know. That's what you have to work out afterwards. ...That's the hard work. Get the idea, which is a startling thing, then you've got to say how you came by that. You shock them [the audience] first and explain later. That's the power of technique." I then said to Hitchcock: "You dream up all these outlandish scenes and then see if your writer can make some sense of them and translate them into something real?" Hitchcock nodded and grinned and said: "That's the ticket." The title for this amazing film comes from Shakespeare's "Hamlet" (Act II; scene 2) where Hamlet says to Guildenstern and Rosenkrantz: "I am but mad north-north-west; when the wind is southerly, I know a hawk from a handsaw." The script, according to Hitchcock, took almost a year to write, the director admitting that he got the idea from a NYC reporter he knew, who told him that he ought to make a film about a normal businessman, who is used as a decoy spy. Hitchcock was originally contracted by MGM to direct **The Wreck of the Mary Deare**, 1959, but he and Lehman could not come up with a workable script after a month and gave up on the project (the film was later directed by Michael Anderson and starred Gary Cooper and Charlton Heston). Hitchcock then began developing **North by Northwest**, MGM paying him $250,000 with ten percent of the gross over $8 million; the film made more than $6 million in its initial release and $14 million in rereleases. He had Cary Grant in mind as the victimized businessman turned secret agent right from the start. Grant was long a Hitchcock favorite, the director telling this author that "Cary [Grant] instinctively knew how to play his characters in our pictures together and he seemed to read my mind in how I wanted every scene from him." For his part, Grant told this author that "**North by Northwest** was probably the most physically demanding picture I had made in years and I was no spring chicken when I did that one with Hitch. [He was fifty-five years old at that time, but looked ten years younger since he always worked out; he was then one of the highest paid actors in Hollywood, receiving $450,000 for his role in this film, plus huge overtime payments.] That man could get me to do just about anything except commit suicide, I suppose. Every actor who ever worked with him wanted to please him. His great talents and that wild imagination of his took us everywhere in the world. You just could not let him down or the fantastic stories he wanted to show on the screen. Every picture he did was special and I don't know of any actor who didn't crow to the world when they got a part in one of his pictures—you know, 'I'm doing one with Hitch!' Wow! That was being at the very top." Grant would appear in four of Hitchcock's films, **Suspicion**, 1941; **Notorious**, 1946; **To Catch a Thief**, 1955; and **North by Northwest**. Mason told this author that Hitchcock "cast me as the chief villain in **North by Northwest** because he knew he could rely upon me to give him that aloof and overly confident character, who heads a group of spies. Hitch is very shrewd and takes his time in casting all of his males in his pictures, typecasting for the most part, and expecting them to do exactly what the script calls for and to follow those storyboards he draws—little stick-like figures in small squares for every setup in every scene. He left nothing to chance and when you went before his cameras, he knew you would do exactly what he wanted so he gave little or no direction to the male players. He spent most of his time directing the women in his films, or, specifically, the beautiful leading ladies, but I will not go into detail on that, except to tell you that I think he thought of himself as some sort of Svengali when it came to creating the images for his leading ladies, almost all of them peculiarly blonde, shaping and molding each role as one might make a pretty prop. Since Hitch had Cary [Grant] hopping around from one crisis to the next in **North by Northwest**, I offset all that manic behavior by going into slow motion with my cynical and sinister lines, being as distant and haughty as possible. At one point, I accuse Cary of being a 'peevish lover,' but I can tell you that he was never that by any means. He is competing with me over the attentions of beautiful Eva

Marie Saint, but we both knew that she belonged entirely to Hitch, in front of the cameras, of course." Hitchcock did take great pains with Saint, telling this author that "I decided to transform her into a beautiful, alluring woman, much different from the rather drab young lady she plays in **On the Waterfront** [1954], although I did not have to work too hard to achieve that look for her as she possessed all that glamour to begin with." Hitchcock doted on the actress, selecting all of her apparel for all of her scenes and even coaching the makeup and hairdo specialists on how to have the actress appear in every scene. Again, this master of suspense was taking no chances. **p&d**, Alfred Hitchcock; **cast**, Cary Grant, Eva Marie Saint, James Mason, Jessie Royce Landis, Leo G. Carroll, Josephine Hutchinson, Martin Landau, Les Tremayne, Philip Ober, Adam Williams, Edward Platt, Robert Ellenstein, Philip Coolidge, Patrick McVey, Ken Lynch, Edward Binns, John Beradino, Madge Kennedy, Robert Shayne, Olan Soule, Carleton Young, Nora Marlowe, Doreen Lang, Alexander Lockwood, Stanley Adams, Hitchcock; **w**, Ernest Lehman; **c**, Robert Burks (Technicolor); **m**, Bernard Herrmann; **ed**, George Tomasini; **prod d**, Robert Boyle; **art d**, William A. Horning, Merrill Pye; **set d**, Henry Grace, Frank McKelvey; **spec eff**, A. Arnold Gillespie, Lee LeBlanc, Doug Hubbard.

North Dallas Forty ★★★ 1979; U.S.; 119m; Frank Yablans Presentations/PAR; Color; Sports/Drama; Children: Unacceptable (MPAA: R); **DVD**; **VHS**. Nolte is compelling as a professional football star in this gritty sports tale loosely based on the Dallas Cowboys team of the early 1970s. Nolte is a veteran receiver and he is at odds with management because he questions being doped before a game and for not being part of the club's "family." He shares his fierce independence with his best friend. Davis, and where girlfriends, Haddon and Smith, admire their rebellious natures. Forrest, the team's owner, and coaches Durning and Spradlin want him to cave in to their demands and be more of a team player, which causes constant feuding. The film presents a soft satire on professional football, but also presents a very realistic treatment of the rough, tumble, and often brutal sport now suspected of routinely doping its players. Violence, sexuality, and gutter language prohibit viewing by children. **p**, Frank Yablans; **d**, Ted Kotcheff; **cast**, Nick Nolte, Mac Davis, Charles Durning, Dayle Haddon, Bo Swenson, John Matuszak, Steve Forrest, G.D. Spradlin, Dabney Coleman, Savannah Smith; **w**, Yablans, Kotcheff, Peter Gent (based on the novel by Gent); **c**, Paul Lohmann (Panavision; Metrocolor); **m**, John Scott; **ed**, Jay Kamen; **prod d**, Alfred Sweeney; **set d**, Art Parker; **spec eff**, Joe Mercurio.

The North Star ★★★ 1943; U.S.; 108m; Samuel Goldwyn Productions/RKO; B/W; War Drama; Children: Unacceptable; **DVD**; **VHS**. Good propaganda film that advances the Soviet cause in WWII is focused upon the occupants of a small Russian village called the North Star, chiefly profiling one family where Huston is the patriarch, a kindhearted physician. The film opens with his family members—Baxter, her brother Andrews, her boyfriend Granger, and friends Roberts and Withers—hitching a ride on a wagon driven by Brennan, all on their way to Kiev. As they laugh and sing in the sun, their idyllic day is shattered when German Stuka dive bombers attack the road on which they are traveling, strafing and bombing the area and causing all to flee back to their village. Andrews enlists in the Russian air force as a pilot, and the rest of the family members join the guerrillas, most leaving the village as it is set on fire to prevent its buildings and crops being used by invading German troops. Nazi forces, however, arrive to put out the fires and occupy the place. German interrogators try to find out where the adults have gone and torture Harding, Huston's wife, breaking her arms and legs, but she refuses to give them any information. Stroheim, a German physician who says he hates the Nazis, nevertheless orders that the Russian children be drained of their blood for transfusions applied to wounded German soldiers, one of these children dying from loss of blood. The shocked Huston travels to the hills where he urges the guerrillas to attack the village; an all-out assault is made, and the Germans

Anne Baxter and Farley Granger in *The North Star,* 1943.

are wiped out. Huston finds Stroheim and takes his revenge by shooting him to death. The surviving Russians then burn the village to the ground and move off to join the Russian army in its ongoing war against the Germans. Pantheon action director Milestone presents a horrifying portrait of German atrocities and does not stint on the violence, and where all the cast members playing the villagers are effective in their sympathetic roles. Stroheim and those enacting the Germans are expectedly brutal and unthinking killers. *Author's Note*: This film was made, as were many others during the early days of WWII, at the urging of U.S. President Franklin D. Roosevelt, who wanted to show public support for America's ally, Soviet Russia. His son, James Roosevelt, was then president of Samuel Goldwyn Studios (a rather titular title) and Goldwyn, who really ran things, decided to become the first Hollywood movie mogul to produce a pro-Soviet film as a way of aiding the American war effort. He wanted William Wyler to direct this film, but Wyler, after completing **Mrs. Miniver**, 1942, went into the armed services as did Greg Toland, the gifted cinematographer also originally scheduled to photograph this production. Goldwyn then hired Milestone, who assigned the talented James Wong Howe to the job as cinematographer. Hellman was hired to write the script and Baxter was signed on as the leading lady after Teresa Wright fell ill and could not perform that role. This was the first leading role enacted by Granger, who was eighteen at the time and had been discovered by Goldwyn after he saw his picture in a newspaper advertisement. The film was widely praised when first released, but Hearst newspapers did a turnabout and then attacked the film as blatant Soviet propaganda. It was used in 1947 by members of the House Committee on Un-American Activities (HUAC) as an example of communist influence in Hollywood. The film was later edited down to 82 minutes and renamed **Armored Attack**, eliminating all references to the word "comrade" and deleting the most pro-Soviet scenes. Andrews told this author that "Milestone presented a lot of amazing action in **The North Star**, but that picture was really made to promote U.S.-Soviet relations during the war. Those relations were never very good since Russia was just as much a dictatorship as Germany was in those days. A few years later I appeared in a picture called **The Iron Curtain** [1948], where I played a defecting Russian operative, and that film showed the true political nature of that communist dictatorship." Milestone echoed Andrews' words when telling this author that "I did not like pumping up the Soviet image when making **The North Star**, but I had my marching orders from Goldwyn and he got his from the President. We were at war and the Soviets were our allies." Two years later, Milestone would direct one of the finest WWII films, **A Walk in the Sun**, 1945, which starred Andrews. **p**, William Cameron Menzies; **d**, Lewis Milestone; **cast**, Anne Baxter, Dana Andrews, Walter Huston, Farley Granger, Ann Harding, Walter Brennan, Dean Jagger, Jane With-

Stewart Granger, John Wayne and Fabian in *North to Alaska*, 1960.

ers, Erich von Stroheim, Carl Benton Reid, Ann Carter, Esther Dale, Ruth Nelson, Paul Guilfoyle, Robert Lowery, Martin Kosleck; **w**, Lillian Hellman (based on a story by Hellman); **c**, James Wong Howe; **m**, Aaron Copeland; **ed**, Daniel Mandell; **art d**, Perry Ferguson, McClure Capps; **set d**, Howard Bristol; **spec eff**, Ray Binger, Clarence Slifer.

North to Alaska ★★★ 1960; U.S.; 122m; FOX; Color; Adventure; Children: Acceptable; **DVD**; **VHS**. In this brawling good-natured parody of himself and the Old West, Wayne presents a gentle giant with a heart of gold, who has struck it rich with partners Granger and Granger's kid brother, Fabian, in the Alaskan gold fields. They have a mine that has provided enough wealth for Granger to now marry his unseen mail-order bride, who ostensibly waits for him in Seattle. While Granger prepares a honeymoon cottage for his new bride, Wayne goes off to Seattle to buy more mining equipment and with his promise to Granger that he will return with his new spouse-to-be. While Wayne is gone, the overly trusting Granger befriends sharper Kovacs, who covets the gold mine Granger, Wayne and Fabian have slaved to develop and also cons Granger into buying a fake diamond ring that Granger intends to give to his new bride. Meanwhile, Wayne arrives in Seattle to find that the woman Granger intended to marry has gone off to the altar with another man and, not wanting to disappoint his good friend, selects another woman for him, Capucine, a sultry prostitute working in a bordello, asking her to accompany him to Alaska. She has fallen for Wayne and agrees to go with him, thinking that Wayne intends to wed her. When they arrive in Nome, Alaska, however, Capucine learns that Wayne has taken her there to be Granger's bride. She refuses to wed Granger, and Wayne offers her money for her inconvenience; she throws it back in his face, the take a room in the boarding house run by oily Kovacs, who was a former lover, and tries to rekindle their old romance, but without success. Then Capucine thinks to goad Wayne into marrying her by making him jealous as she plays up to Granger, creating strife between the partners, who are also battling claim jumpers attempting to take over their mine, and fending off legal action by Kovacs, who is also trying to boondoggle them out of their mine. Capucine moves into Granger's cabin, and Fabian develops a wild crush on the older woman. Capucine then comes clean, telling Granger that she is in love with Wayne and, for his friend's sake, he pretends that he is about to marry her, faking a torrid love scene in the cabin that causes Wayne's secreted love for Capucine to boil to the surface and where he rushes into the cabin in a rage, only to fall flat on his face when Granger abruptly opens the door for him. Capucine ends up in Wayne's arms and he and his partners hold on to their mine, but only after a wild fight that involves most of the inhabitants of Nome, one of the zaniest, mud-slinging brawls in the history of the Old West, a colossal donnybrook that ends

this riotous and entertaining film. Packed with great action, Wayne, Granger and the rest of the cast play this tale for laughs, and there are plenty of them to sustain interest throughout. It is hokum at its heartiest. *Author's Note*: "We had a lot of fun with **North to Alaska**," Wayne told this author, "but I worried that we were taking that wild story a little too far…the more broadly we played our parts, the more impossible the story became. It all seemed to work, but we didn't really know that until the public fell in love with that picture." Hathaway supported Wayne's contentions when he told this author that "Duke [Wayne] had some apprehensions about how everybody was going off in all directions in **North to Alaska**, but I told him that the crazier things got, the better the picture would play. I told him: 'The Old West was full of crazy people and that's what audiences love about westerns—anything can happen and the unexpected is expected by filmgoers.' Sure enough, the picture was such a hit, and Duke stayed with that kind of free-and-easy role for the rest of his career." **p&d**, Henry Hathaway; **cast**, John Wayne, Stewart Granger, Ernie Kovacs, Fabian, Capucine, Mickey Shaughnessy, Karl Swenson, Joe Sawyer, Kathleen Freeman, John Qualen, Alan Carney, Douglas Dick; **w**, John Lee Mahin, Martin Rackin, Claude Binyon (based on the play "Birthday Gift" by Laszlo Fodor and an idea by John Kafka); **c**, Leon Shamroy (CinemaScope; DeLuxe Color); **m**, Lionel Newman; **ed**, Dorothy Spencer; **art d**, Duncan Cramer, Jack Martin Smith; **set d**, Stuart A. Reiss, Walter M. Scott; **spec eff**, L.B. Abbott, Emil Kosa, Jr., Barney Wolff.

Northern Pursuit ★★★ 1943; U.S.; 93m; WB; B/W; Adventure/War Drama; Children: Unacceptable; **DVD**; **VHS**. Good action and suspense is offered in this patriotic adventure tale set during World War II in Canada, where Flynn is a stalwart Canadian Mountie whose parents were born in Germany. On routine patrol, he and fellow officer Ridgely come upon Dantine who is unconscious at a campsite. They learn he is a German Luftwaffe officer on a spy mission. To catch the spy ring, Flynn pretends that his loyalties are rooted to Germany and leaves the Mounted Police, infiltrating the German ring, but Dantine, distrusting Flynn, orders him to take along his fiancée, Bishop, as the group makes its way through the snow-covered wilderness to a rendezvous with a German bomber that will destroy strategic Canadian installations. Bishop thinks her sweetheart has turned traitor and wants nothing to do with him, but he vindicates himself with her and the Mounties when he turns the tables on Dantine, turncoat Lockhart and others, foiling their plans and defeating them, thus winning back Bishop's affections and where Flynn is hailed a hero. Song: "The Bonnie Banks O' Loch Lomond" (c.1745; traditional; lyrics: Robert Burns). *Author's Note*: Director Walsh told this author that "**Northern Pursuit** was written for Errol as a vehicle to exploit his athletic heroism, and I had so many action scenes in the picture that it became too much for him and, at one point, he collapsed on the set. When that news got out, we covered up the fact that he was suffering with tuberculosis and said he had a minor respiratory ailment. He also suffered from a weak heart, which is why none of the armed services would take him during the war [WWII], but that never stopped him from doing his own stunts. Errol was just as heroic off screen as he was before the cameras." Much of the plot for this film borrows from the story line used in **Across the Pacific**, 1942, starring Humphrey Bogart and Mary Astor, although that film is set on board a Japanese freighter and ends with Bogart foiling Japanese spies from using a bomber to destroy the locks at the Panama Canal. **p**, Jack Chertok; **d**, Raoul Walsh; **cast**, Errol Flynn, Julie Bishop, Helmut Dantine, John Ridgely, Gene Lockhart, Tom Tully, Warren Douglas, Monte Blue, John Alvin, Tom Drake, John Forsythe, Robert Hutton, Bill Kennedy, Robert Kent; **w**, Frank Gruber, Alvah Bessie (based on the story "Five Thousand Trojan Horses" by Leslie T. White); **c**, Sid Hickox; **m**, Adolph Deutsch; **ed**, Jack Killifer; **art d**, Leo Kuter; **set d**, Casey Roberts; **spec eff**, Roy Davidson.

Northwest Mounted Police ★★★★ 1940; U.S.; 126m; PAR; Color;

Adventure; Children: Acceptable; **DVD**. The indomitable Cooper is outstanding in this exciting DeMille epic that pays homage to the heroic exploits of the red-coated Royal Canadian Mounties. Set in 1885, the story deals with Cooper, a Texas Ranger, who goes to Canada seeking a wanted felon, Bancroft, a renegade who has thrown in his lot with French rebel Louis Riel (1844-1885), played by McDonald, and who is leading another revolution (his first, in 1869, failed) against the British crown (known as the North West Rebellion or the Saskatchewan Rebellion). Bancroft has organized the Indians and half-breeds in the northwest, urging them to attack the British-controlled white settlements and the small fort manned by the Mounties, who were then known as the Northwest Mounted Police, these stalwart redcoats led by Foster, who is in love with beautiful Carroll, a nurse. Carroll's younger brother, Preston, is also a Mountie and is madly in love with Goddard, a half-breed vixen, who loves Preston, but her loyalties are to her villainous father, Bancroft. Cooper meets with Love, the commander of the Mounties, telling him he has a warrant for Bancroft on charges of murder, but Love tells him that the Mounties want Bancroft on a similar charge and Love offers cooperation where Cooper and the Mounties might jointly hunt down and capture the fugitive. Cooper beds down in the barracks of the Mounties and his easy-going ways cause him to make friends with these intrepid men, but he gives Foster pause when Carroll seems to take an interest in the plain-speaking Cooper, who falls in love with her almost at first sight. When he describes the vast rich lands of the Lone Star State to her, Carroll says: "Texas must be Heaven." Cooper replies: "It will be when you get there." Meanwhile, Bancroft has stolen a Gatling gun (an early-day machine gun) and displays its lethal capabilities by firing it and cutting down shrubs and tree branches. McDonald is awed by the weapon, stating: "Blood will run like water." The crass Bancroft snorts: "Blood? You won't notice it much. The Mounted Police wear red coats." Love orders almost all of his men, fifty Mounties, led by Foster, to put down the rebellion, but before they depart on their mission, Goddard, who knows her father and his renegades are waiting in ambush, tricks Preston, who has deserted his post to see her, and ties him up so that he cannot leave with the other Mounties in order to protect his life. He calls her every name he can think of, but Goddard ignores his insults, believing Preston loves her above all else, although his loyalty to the Crown really comes first. Toomey, another Mountie who had been assigned with Preston to act as an advance guard to detect the movements of Bancroft's renegades, is now alone and is killed by the renegades. Cooper, who has remained at the fort, rescues Carroll when the renegades attack the bastion, escorting her by canoe from the carnage. Foster then leads his troops into the ambush where many of his men are killed, but Cooper arrives, lassoing the Gatling gun that is creating much of the slaughter and drags it down a slope, sending it into a lake. He later insists that this heroic feat was accomplished by Preston, who has broken free of his bonds, but has been killed in attempting to rejoin his unit, thus Cooper preserving Preston's good name for the sake of Carroll, the woman of his heart. Foster and a few of the surviving Mounties then boldly march into the camp of the Cree Indian chief, Hampden, where Bancroft insists that the Indians shoot down the Mounties. Hampden, however, believes that the Mounties are gifted with supernatural powers in surviving Bancroft's attack, particularly when Foster boldly steps forth and throws the heavyset Bancroft to the ground, manacling him in the same swift somersaulting movement. Foster then steps forward to place a medal around the neck of Hampden, asking him if he is worthy of receiving such an honor from Queen Victoria. Hampden then kneels before Foster, saying that "the Cree are brothers to the brave." As a gesture of country-to-country good will, Foster turns Bancroft over to Cooper, but Cooper fails to also get the girl in that Carroll remains with the man she truly loves, Foster, and both of them bid farewell to the brave Texan as he rides away with his captive. Packed with action and spectacular exterior scenes, this was DeMille's first color film and he employs the old Technicolor process in every scene by showing rich hues in his costuming and landscapes. The tale is a bit

Robert Preston, Paulette Goddard and Gary Cooper in *Northwest Mounted Police,* **1940.**

hokey, but the acting is superb in this great adventure tale. *Author's Note*: DeMille wanted to shoot this film entirely in the wilds of Canada, but Paramount executives told him that that would be too expensive so he settled for exterior shots outside of Eugene, Oregon, and shot his interiors and some exterior sets at the Paramount sound stages. DeMille originally thought to cast Joel McCrea in the role of the Texas Ranger, but McCrea had commitments elsewhere and DeMille hired Cooper for the role. They had made **The Plainsman**, 1936, together, which had been an amiable relationship. DeMille would make two more films with Cooper, **The Story of Dr. Wassel**, 1942, and **Unconquered**, 1947, the latter production teaming Cooper with Goddard in a revolutionary costume adventure tale. "DeMille was a very demanding director," Cooper told this author, "and very precise when shooting his scenes. He loved historic detail and did a lot of research on costumes and props so that they perfectly fit the era he was filming. He was one of the most conscientious directors I ever knew and that showed when we did **Northwest Mounted Police**. In one scene, he stopped shooting to walk up to an extra wearing an Indian headdress, tearing if off his head and saying: 'This isn't a Cree headdress. This is a Sioux headdress!' The headdress was replaced with the right one before he continued shooting. Some thought he was petty, but his attention to detail always showed in every film and it was impressive." Such was the case when DeMille began shooting close-ups of Hampden, who plays the Cree chief. Hampden's skin, along with the rest of hundreds of extras playing Indians, had been stained to the color of mahogany, but Hampden's eyes were bright blue. DeMille stopped Hampden's scenes until Hampden was fitted with an early-day set of contact lenses (at a cost of $500) that showed the color of his eyes brown. DeMille had more than 300 pine trees planted on Paramount's back lot where he shot some of his exteriors and then hired forest rangers to patrol that area so that the pine trees were not accidentally burned down. The role of the half-breed girl was long in question, DeMille considering a bevy of actresses for that role, including Marlene Dietrich, Simone Simon and Rita Hayworth. Goddard lobbied for the role, sending DeMille several notes, which he ignored. She finally went to Paramount's top makeup artist, Wally Westmore, who stained her skin, redid her hair to inky, stringy black and adorned her in greasy buckskins. Goddard then barged into DeMille's office, cracking a whip and speaking broken English with a thick French accent. She lifted her skirt and put her foot on his desk, knowing DeMille admired small feet on women and hers were petite, and all of this finally convinced DeMille to give her the part. DeMille had some problems with Russian-born Tamiroff, who plays a half-breed and who roared out his lines to the point where DeMille had to repeatedly caution him to deliver his lines in a softer voice. One of the extras, however, a Navajo Indian named Tom Hightree, screamed his warrior chant so loudly and in such a blood-

Spencer Tracy and Robert Young in *Northwest Passage*, 1940.

curdling manner that DeMille stopped the scene and said to him: "Mr. Hightree, please! If you could just moderate your war whoop a little. It's too harrowing. After all, it's only a massacre." Many films have profiled the Royal Canadian Mounted Police; for a comprehensive list of such films (54 entries), see Subject Index under Mounties. **p&d**, Cecil B. DeMille; **cast**, Gary Cooper, Madeleine Carroll, Paulette Goddard, Preston Foster, Robert Preston, George Bancroft, Lynne Overman, Akim Tamiroff, Walter Hampden, Lon Chaney, Jr., Montagu Love, Francis McDonald, Richard Denning, Robert Ryan, Ralph Byrd, Wallace Reid, Jr., Rod Cameron, Chief Thundercloud, Clara Blandick, Phillip Terry, Chief Thunderbird, Chief Yowlachie, DeMille (narrator); **w**, Alan LeMay, Jesse Lasky, Jr., C. Gardner Sullivan (based on the novel *Royal Canadian Mounted Police* by R.C. Fetherstonhaugh); **c**, Victor Milner, W. Howard Greene (Technicolor); **m**, Victor Young; **ed**, Anne Bauchens; **art d**, Hans Dreier, Roland Anderson; **spec eff**, Barney Wolff, Farciot Edouart, Gordon Jennings.

Northwest Passage ★★★★★ 1940; U.S.; 126m; MGM; Color; Adventure; Children: Unacceptable; **DVD**; **VHS**. For sheer excitement and thrills, few adventure films can match this masterpiece saga of the American wilderness superbly brought to the screen by pantheon director Vidor, where the indomitable Tracy fascinates in every scene. Tracy plays the legendary frontiersman Robert Rogers (1731-1795), who organized Rogers' Rangers, a British paramilitary unit that fought guerrilla warfare on behalf of the British during the French and Indian War (1754-1763). The film opens with Young returning to his wealthy family in Portsmouth, New Hampshire, where he, a budding artist, admits that he has been expelled from his school after inserting political comments into his artwork. His criticisms have been aimed at the British, which raises the ire of Hussey's Tory family, she being Young's beautiful fiancée and he has thus jeopardized their impending wedding. He and sidekick and drifter Brennan go to Pendleton's pub and get drunk and, while there, encounter and insult Hussey's father, Hector, a stiff-necked landowner, who summons the police to arrest the pair. Both flee with Pendleton's help and trudge through the wilderness until they come upon a remote inn where they meet Tracy, who is busy sobering his best Indian guide. Tracy's idea of sobering people is strange enough in that he feeds his guide hot buttered rum by the tankard and then gets Young and Brennan to drink so much of the stuff that they, too, become unconscious. They wake up with fierce hangovers outside the fort at Crown Point, which is crowded with Tracy's troops, his rangers, who are all clad in green leather outfits as are they, discovering that, sometime during their drinking binge encouraged by Tracy, they have enlisted in Rogers' Rangers. Young finds himself appointed Tracy's mapmaker and Brennan his aide as the rangers then embark by boat for St. Francis to

conduct a retaliatory raid against the Abenaki tribe (part of the Algonquin Indian Nation) aligned with the French, this tribe having made many vicious and bloody raids against British colonies. The rangers row longboats up the chain of rivers and lakes and while camping the rangers tell Young and Brennan how fierce their enemy is by describing the massacres committed by the Abenakis, how their warriors savagely tortured captured fellow rangers and relatives, prying their limbs from their torsos and tearing out their ribs while still alive before cutting off their heads and using those heads with which to play ball. It is Tracy's assignment to destroy the Abenakis in order to prevent their continuing raids in New England, upstate New York and the Ohio Valley, and then follow a circuitous escape route, knowing that the French and their Indian allies will be pursuing them as they attempt to reach the safety of a British outpost, Old Fort Wentworth. As the rangers work their way through the wilderness, their Indian guides either desert or betray them, and, after a keg of powder accidentally explodes and wounds a number of rangers, Tracy sends the Indians and the wounded men back to Crown Point. He then leads his men by boat through the chain of rivers leading to St. Francis. At one point, the rangers carry and pull their heavy boats over a high and challenging hill (portaging) so they can continue their journey on another river chain until they reach Lake Champlain, which is controlled by the French, and where they hide their boats and continue on foot toward their destination. To avoid enemy forces searching for them, Tracy leads his men through the swamps and some, like Toomey, injure themselves, and are left behind with supplies and extra ammunition, knowing they must now fight to the death when they are found by the French and their Indian allies. When reaching a roaring river, Tracy fords that river by having his men linking arms and forming a human chain that stretches across the river and along which his other men move to reach the far shore and then that chain of men is pulled onto the far bank one by one, Tracy being the last to leave the river. (This is only one scene of many to show the amazing physical feats performed during this great outdoors adventure.) When the rangers finally reach St. Francis, Tracy organizes the raid for the following dawn where his men will be positioned at four points surrounding the Abenaki village and the French fort at its center, instructing his men to slowly close in from all of those points as the enemy is driven by gunfire from one attacking line of men to the next until they are all killed. Before the dawn attack, Tracy and a few others sneak through the Indian village where the enemy sleeps and get into the fort to spike its guns and silently overwhelm a few sentries while others begin setting fire to the Indian tepees. The Indians and French troops then awake and attempt to break out of the closing ring of rangers, but they are shot down or hacked to pieces and where Young is wounded, shot in the stomach. After the enemy forces have been destroyed, Tracy discovers that the main French force stationed there has left, but is expected to return shortly. He collects what food is available, some baskets of corn, and finds several white female prisoners, including Jewell, who has turned savage and curses him. He tells Young that his wound is not mortal and that he can survive, but only if he can keep walking as the rangers retreat, ordering Jewell and a small Indian boy to help him. Weak but resolved to save his life, Young straggles after the retreating rangers. He falls farther and farther behind but somehow regains his strength. The bleeding of his wound stops and Young manages to catch up with the rangers, who are now starving from lack of food. Tracy splits his forces, sending several contingents along different routes so that smaller units can forage for food and all later meet at a rendezvous. When they reach their rendezvous, Tracy finds no British relief force waiting for him as promised, and only two of his units join Tracy's band, a third unit having been ambushed and where two survivors described how their fellows have been massacred and then savagely cut to pieces by the vengeance-seeking Indians. Though exhausted and starving, the rangers, at Tracy's goading and promises of food, stagger forth toward the safety of Old Fort Wentworth. When they reach that fort, however, they find it deserted and in ruins. Tracy attempts to revive his men after they collapse from utter fatigue, ordering them to begin foraging for food, but almost all are too weak to obey his commands. When all seems lost, Tracy and his men hear the faint sounds of drums and fifes and then see a number of boats carrying British troops arriving on the river. Tracy has his men stand to attention as they eagerly watch British troops come ashore, some carrying baskets of food and huge slabs of meat. The British troops then stand to attention and salute the rangers for their incredible heroic feat. Tracy is next shown with his men at Portsmouth where he tells them that they are about to undertake another great adventure, one that will make their trip to St. Francis seem to be nothing more than a "duck hunt," and that they are going to march westward to Fort Detroit and then explore the vast wilderness beyond in order to open up a northwest passage to the Pacific so that the colonies can expand their trade and commerce throughout the Orient. Young, however, is not making this trip, deciding to stay behind with his fiancée, Hussey, and marry her and then go to England to study art. When Brennan is asked if he is going with Tracy, he shakes his head and says: "I've been." Tracy then marches away, but stops to bid farewell to Young, telling him: "I will see you at sundown." Young and Hussey watch the rangers march away and Tracy stands on top of a hill to wave a last goodbye as Young tells Hussey: "That man will never die!" Superlative in every sense, **Northwest Passage** is directed with great skill by Vidor, a masterpiece production where the authenticity of the era and its robust and unforgettable characters are indelibly stamped on every frame. Tracy renders a memorable portrait of an indefatigable frontiersman, undoubtedly one of his greatest roles, and Young, Brennan and the rest of the cast provide outstanding support. The superb lensing by Wagner and Skall captures the great outdoors in vivid colors, presenting one breathtaking action scene after another, all dynamically enhanced by Stothart's stirring score. The film was remade as a TV series in 1958-1959. *Author's Note*: Vidor was endowed with a then enormous budget of more than $2 million and he moved his almost all male cast to Idaho, shooting most of the film around Lake Payette, which resembled the New England locale of Rogers' time. Vidor resolved to make the greatest action-adventure story ever and drove his cast and crew relentlessly for seventy days, overcoming all natural hazards. In the portage scenes where the rangers must use pulleys to take their cumbersome boats over a massive hill, several extras were injured and Young and Brennan narrowly missed being struck by a boat that broke away and crashed down the slope of the hill. "Vidor was obsessed with the story for **Northwest Passage**," Young told this author, "and he drove us in our scenes to the point of exhaustion every day. I told Spence [Tracy] that I thought he was going to kill us all, but Spence just waved off my complaints, saying: 'Hell, it's like going to a boy's camp.'" Brennan, a tough veteran character actor told this author that "that frontier picture was about the toughest one I ever made. I got thorns in my feet every time I took a step and got jabbed in the butt when I sat down on pine cones that were everywhere. The director [Vidor] and I were about the same age, I think, both of us were in our mid-forties, and since he was climbing up every hill and going through all the forests and wading the rivers with us, I said to myself, 'I'm not going to let that guy outdo me,' so I stayed with it—we all did to prove to him that he was not the best man." Vidor had originally thought to have a number of MGM stars appear in the film with Tracy, including Robert Taylor, Wallace Beery and Franchot Tone, but none were available so Young and Brennan were enlisted to support Tracy. The exterior action shots presented challenging ordeals for the actors, particularly Tracy, who was in the center of all the action. The river-crossing scene was particularly exhausting, according to Tracy, who told this author: "I had to anchor myself to a tree on one side of that river, holding onto the next man, who held on to the next man and so on, and the weight of that human chain almost tore off my arm. I wore out two pairs of pants when we made those scenes that took two days to shoot and where we froze in the icy water. I thought I was in good shape going into that production and so did all the rest of the actors, but we found out that, after hiking over hills and wading through swamps day after day, we were a puny lot. God only knows

Ruth Hussey, Robert Young and Spencer Tracy in *Northwest Passage*, 1940.

how Rogers and his men achieved what they did in those tough colonial days. They must have been superhuman." Vidor told this author that "Spence wasn't taking any chances. When we quit for the day, he went straight to his small cabin and got into a warm bed where he read Agatha Christie mysteries. He told the other actors, who usually put away some stiff drinks after the shoots that he was on the wagon for the duration of the production. I think that's what preserved his stamina and, believe me, he needed every ounce of it when I put him through his paces." After several weeks of such back-breaking shooting, however, Tracy told Vidor that he had had enough and threatened to return to Los Angeles, leaving the production, MGM, and his movie career forever. "I had the damnedest time convincing Spence to stay with it," Vidor told this author, "and I used every promise, excuse and outright lie to keep him going until we completed the picture. On the screen Spence was undefeatable, the symbol of courage and physicality, but he was only flesh and blood, like all of us." Vidor had hired more than 300 Indians to play the Abenaki warriors, but they balked at the start of the production, saying that they wanted $10 a day, not the $5-a-day salary Vidor offered them. Tracy solved that problem by telling Vidor to tell the Indians that they were "playing half-breeds, not full-blooded Indians, so that's why they are entitled to only $5 a day." Vidor gave these extras this ridiculous excuse and, surprisingly, the Indians agreed to play their roles at the $5 daily rate. **p**, Hunt Stromberg; **d**, King Vidor, Jack Conway (uncredited); **cast**, Spencer Tracy, Robert Young, Walter Brennan, Ruth Hussey, Nat Pendleton, Robert Barrat, Donald MacBride, Isabel Jewell, Regis Toomey, Montagu Love, Truman Bradley, Louis Hector, Lumsden Hare, Addison Richards, Douglas Walton, Hugh Sothern, Lester Matthews, Andrew Pena, Lloyd Bridges, Rand Brooks, Don Castle, Tom London, Eddie Parker, Ray Teal, Kent Rogers, Verna Felton, Edward Gargan, Gibson Gowland, John Merton, Hank Worden; **w**, Laurence Stallings, Talbot Jennings (based on the novel by Kenneth Roberts); **c**, Sidney Wagner, William V. Skall (Technicolor); **m**, Herbert Stothart; **ed**, Conrad A. Nervig; **art d**, Cedric Gibbons; **set d**, Edwin B. Willis.

Nosferatu ★★★★ 1922 (silent); Germany; 94m; Jofa-Atelier/Film Arts Guild; B/W; Horror; Children: Unacceptable; **BD**; **DVD**; **VHS**. Murnau presents a classic horror tale based upon the Dracula character (who is called Count Orlok to avoid copyright infringement), the first such film based upon this dreaded vampire. The film opens when Wangenheim, a clerk working in a German city, is sent by employer Granach to Transylvania in the Carpathian Mountains to see a strange nobleman, Schreck, who plays Count Orlok. He is an undead vampire, who lives a nocturnal existence, avoiding all rays of the sun while preying upon the living, attacking humans to drain their blood for his unholy survival.

Max Schreck in *Nosferatu*, 1922.

Wangnenheim travels to a small village near Schreck's gloomy castle, where the frightened inhabitants warn him to stay away from the count, telling him that he should not travel at night since a werewolf is prowling in the area. The clerk ignores these warnings and hires a coachman to drive him to the castle, but, as night begins to fall, the coachman refuses to cross the bridge that leads to the castle. Wangenheim then stands at the crossroads until nightfall, until a black coach with black horses and an unidentifiable coachman wearing a shroud arrive, the coach then taking him to the castle. He is welcomed by Schreck, who provides Wangenheim with a plate of food, and they discuss the property Schreck wants to purchase in Germany. When Wangenheim cuts his finger, Schreck seizes the injured finger and sucks away the blood, and Wangenheim quickly withdraws his hand, finding this bizarre action repulsive. Wangenheim then retires to his room. When he awakes in the morning, he discovers two tiny puncture marks on his neck, attributing these bites to either mosquitoes or spiders. He then wanders about the vast castle, but finds no one there. That night, he again sees Schreck, who signs the agreement for the purchase of the house, which is located across the street from Wangenheim's own residence. Wangenheim mentions his wife, Schroeder, to Schreck, showing him a locket that contains her portrait, and Schreck admires the woman, particularly her long, white neck. Wangenheim then writes a letter to his wife, giving it to the castle's coachman to deliver and then retires to his room where he reads a book he has taken from the inn, a book that describes vampires. Wangenheim now comes to believe that his host, Schreck, is among those undead creatures. He becomes frightened and, when he attempts to bolt the door, he finds there is no lock on it. After midnight, Wangeneim sees the door open, seemingly on its own, and also sees Schreck in all his hideous form, a ghastly white skull of a head, fangs protruding from thin lips, and long arms and claws for hands, as he stoically enters the room and Wangenehim collapses unconscious in fear. He awakes to find that he has been again drained of more blood and when he looks from the window of his room he sees below a coach where Schreck is loading coffins before entering the last coffin and the coach then rides away from the castle. Wangenheim attempts to escape, but falls when climbing out of the window and later awakes in a hospital. Meanwhile, a raft carries Schreck's coffins down a river and they are loaded onto a schooner. As the ship sails away, one of the coffins is opened and a swarm of rats scurry from it, quickly spreading pestilence to the crew, causing the seamen to die, one after another. The first mate, believing the source of these uncanny deaths are the coffins, goes to one of them in the hold and opens it to see to his horror Schreck rising from the coffin, and the terrified mate races to the deck and leaps into the sea, drowning himself. Only Nemetz, the captain, remains alive, but he knows his hours are numbered. He straps himself to the wheel of the ship as it sails

through rough seas toward Germany. While the ship sails on, Wangenheim is released from the hospital and hurries home to Germany, where he is reunited with his wife, Schroeder. The ship carrying Schreck then arrives at the docks of the town and, unobserved, Schreck leaves the ship carrying one of his coffins. He moves into the house opposite Wangenheim's home. At dawn, officials inspect the ship, which appears to be a derelict. They find no one on board, except Nemetz, who is dead, still strapped to the wheel of the vessel. Shortly thereafter many citizens begin to strangely die, these deaths attributed to the plague. Granach, Wangenheim's employer, has by this time been confined to an asylum as hopelessly insane. He escapes after killing the superintendent and flees across rooftops using a scarecrow as a decoy. Across the street from Wangenheim's residence, Schreck stands at night at the window of his own house staring at Schroeder while she sleeps. Schroeder is now obsessed with vampires as she has, against Wangenheim's wishes, read the book he brought from Transylvania that describes these undead creatures and learns that a vampire can only be killed if he (or she) is somehow inveigled into attacking a victim and that victim willingly sacrifices himself or herself, delaying the vampire so that it can be engulfed by sunlight and destroyed. Schroeder sees Schreck standing across the way and opens her window, inviting the monster, but she faints. Wangenheim finds her and when she regains consciousness, she begs him to find Gottowt, a professor, who has been battling vampires for some time (a character based on Bram Stoker's Abraham Van Helsing). After Wangenheim departs, Schreck appears in the room and attacks Schroeder. He becomes so obsessed in consuming her blood, however, that he ignores the rising sun and, when the room begins to fill with sunlight, Schreck is petrified and vanishes in a cloud of smoke. Wangenheim returns, but too late to save Schroeder, who dies in his arms. To confirm the end of the monster, the film closes with a final scene depicting Schreck's castle in the Carpathian Mountains as nothing but ruins. Murnau presents a truly frightening film with chilling atmospheric scenes—the ride to the castle, the eerie, shadowy castle itself, the horrific scenes on board the doomed schooner, and the victims in the German town, ending with Schroeder's devastating death. Schreck is masterful in his unnatural and erratic movements and gestures and his makeup is a sight to behold: emaciated face, elongated arms, claw-like hands with talons for fingernails, an unforgettable portrait of stalking evil. ***Author's Note***: Murnau knew that he would be facing legal problems when appropriating the well-established Bram Stoker novel, *Dracula* (he never bothered to contact family members to secure the dramatic rights for the book), so he quickly dissolved the corporation he had established to make this film after completing production to avoid that litigation, which Stoker's wife, Florence Stoker, nevertheless initiated. She won the suit and all prints of the film were ordered destroyed by the courts, but several prints survived and can be seen to this day. Murnau shot the film's exteriors in Wismar, a small port in northern Germany, and he employed a metronome to pace his actors in all of their scenes. Schreck was an experience actor, a married man, but a rather reclusive person, who was jocularly described by a fellow actor as living in "a remote and incorporeal world," and that Schreck took long walks in the woods alone, suggesting that the actor was, perhaps, a real vampire. This contention was, of course, nonsense, but was nevertheless wholly embraced by the producers of **Shadow of the Vampire**, 2000, which depicts Murnau's 1921-1922 production of **Nosferatu** and where John Malkovich plays Murnau and Willem Dafoe appears as Schreck, who is portrayed as a real vampire, a flagrant disservice to Schreck. Following the release of **Nosferatu**, many more vampire films were produced, mostly in the talking era, beginning with the classic **Dracula**, 1931, with Bela Lugosi essaying the vampire. For a complete list of all such horror films centered upon Dracula or vampires, see the Index for Fictional and Historical Characters, Volume II of this work. **p**, Enrico Dieckmann, Albin Grau; **d**, F. W. Murnau; **cast**, Max Schreck, Alexander Granach, Gustav v. Wangenheim, Greta Schroeder, Georg H. Schnell, Ruth Landshoff, John Gottowt, Gustav Botz, Max Nemetz; **w**, Henrik

Galeen (based on the novel *Dracula* by Bram Stoker); **c**, Fritz Arno Wagner, Günther Krampf; **m**, Hans Erdmann, Carlos U. Garza, Richard O'Meara, Bernd Wilden, Peter Schirmann (1969 version), Richard Marriott and Hans Posegga (1989), Timothy Howard (1991), James Bernard (1997), Bernardo Uzeda (2006); **art d & set d**, Albin Grau.

Nosferatu: The Vampyre ★★★ 1979; West Germany/France; 107m; Color; Horror; Children: Unacceptable. Ganz is a real estate salesman in Varna, Germany, in the 1800s whose boss sends him to Transylvania to complete a deal to sell a house in Varna to Kinski, who plays Count Dracula. Ganz leaves his beautiful young wife, Adjani, at home. Unaware that the count is a vampire, Ganz goes to the count's castle. Kinski sees a small portrait of Adjani, lusts for her, and locks Ganz in the castle, then goes to Varna to find his new lady love. Adjani, however, rebuffs him, and then discovers that he is a vampire. She sacrifices herself to him in order to lure him into staying up until dawn and at the first sunlight he dies. The story follows almost the same plotline offered in Murnau's silent 1922 classic. (In German and French; English subtitles.) **p,d&w**, Werner Herzog (based on the novel **Dracula** by Bram Stoker and the film script for **Nosferatu** by Henrik Galeen); **cast**, Klaus Kinski, Isabelle Adjani, Bruno Ganz, Roland Topor, Walter Ladengast, Dan van Husen, Jan Groth, Carsten Bodinus, Martje Grohmann, Rijk de Gooyer; **c**, Jörg Schmidt-Reitwein; **m**, Popol Vuh; **ed**, Beate Mainka-Jellinghaus; **prod d**, Henning von Gierke; **spec eff**, Cornelius Siegel.

Not as a Stranger ★★★ 1955; U.S.; 135m; Stanley Kramer/UA; B/W; Drama; Children: Unacceptable; **DVD**; **VHS**. Mitchum is an intern with strong ambitions of becoming a first-class doctor, not just a successful one. Though he does not love her, he marries de Havilland because she is a highly skilled operating room nurse and has saved money that he decides can help make him a success (by paying for his medical studies). He becomes a doctor in a small town and has an affair with Grahame. De Havilland's patience with him runs thin and she asks for a divorce, even though she is pregnant. Bickford, Mitchum's employer-doctor, has a heart attack and he operates, but Bickford dies in the operation. Mitchum then realizes he's just a man, after all, human like everyone else and he asks de Havilland's forgiveness and she decides to stay with him. Suds of a soap opera invariably bubble to the surface in this one, but the script is intelligent and the acting superior to sustain interest throughout. Song: "Not as a Stranger" (Jimmy Van Heusen, Buddy Kaye). *Author's Note*: "I play a heel again in **Not as a Stranger**, but with some ethics as a doctor," Mitchum told this author, "so I guess I have some redeeming qualities as the critics like to say, but I am a heel nevertheless by always taking advantage of poor Olivia [de Havilland] for my own ends. She puts up with me a lot more than any other woman would tolerate from such an abusive husband, but that's love." Kramer told this author that "I always wanted to probe the ethics of the medical profession and we stepped on a lot of toes when we did **Not as a Stranger**, but we got away with it because the novel was such a great success." When this author talked with Sinatra about his role in the film, he stated: "I don't know what the hell I was doing in that picture, playing an intern, and here I was almost forty years old and with crow's feet around the eyes. Who could believe that? Stanley [Kramer] talked me into doing that picture because it would help at the box office. He always helped me, so I did what any friend would do and pitched in, but do I look like a guy you would trust with a scalpel?" **p&d**, Stanley Kramer; **cast**, Olivia de Havilland, Robert Mitchum, Frank Sinatra, Gloria Grahame, Broderick Crawford, Charles Bickford, Myron McCormick, Lon Chaney Jr., Jesse White, Harry Morgan, Lee Marvin, Mae Clarke; **w**, Edna and Edward Anhalt (based on the novel by Morton Thompson); **c**, Franz Planer; **m**, George Antheil; **ed**, Fred Knudtson; **prod d**, Rudolph Sternad; **art d**, Howard Richmond; **set d**, Victor Gangelin.

Not Without My Daughter ★★★ 1991; U.S.; 116m; Pathe Entertainment/MGM-UA; Color; Drama; Children: Unacceptable (MPAA: PG-

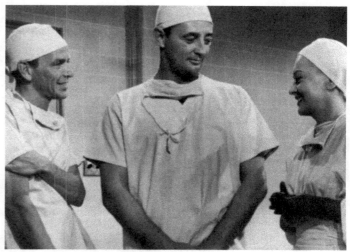

Frank Sinatra, Robert Mitchum and Olivia de Havilland in *Not as a Stranger*, 1955.

13); **DVD**; **VHS**. This often harrowing and fascinating thriller is based on a true story where Molina, an Iranian-born doctor living in Michigan in 1984 with his wife, Field, and daughter, Rosenthal, wants them to meet his family in Iran. He encourages them to take a short vacation there with him, assuring them that they will be safe and free to leave and return to America anytime they wish. Field has her doubts because of unrest in Iran during the regime of its supreme leader Ayatollah Khomeini (1900-1989), but reluctantly agrees. Soon after their arrival in Tehran, Field is distressed about visiting the country, partly because women are treated as second-class citizens or worse. She tells Molina she wants to return to America, but he says he has decided they will remain in Iran and live the rest of their lives there. Field is determined to leave Iran, but not without taking her daughter with her. Field meets Seth, a sympathetic Iranian, who helps her escape with her daughter. Songs: "Happy Birthday to You" (Mildred J. and Patty S. Hill), "Vissi D'Arte from Tosca" (Giacomo Puccini). Spousal abuse prohibits viewing by children. **p**, Harry J. and Mary Jane Ufland; **d**, Brian Gilbert; **cast**, Sally Field, Alfred Molina, Sheila Rosenthal, Roshan Seth, Sarah Badel, Mony Rey, Georges Corraface, Mary Nell Santacroce, Ed Grady, Marc Gowan; **w**, Pat Riddle (David W. Rintels), (based on the book by Betty Mahmoody, William Hoffer); **c**, Peter Hannan; **m**, Jerry Goldsmith; **ed**, Terry Rawlings, Ofer Bedarshi; **prod d**, Anthony Pratt; **art d**, Avishay Avivi, Desmond Crowe; **set d**, Anat Avivi; **spec eff**, Pini Klavir.

The Notebook ★★★ 2004; U.S.; 123m; New Line Cinema; Color; Drama/Romance; Children: Unacceptable (MPAA: PG-13); **BD**; **DVD**. Engrossing drama sees Garner as an elderly man reading a story from a notebook to an elderly woman, Rowlands, both being residents in a nursing home. She is suffering from Alzheimer's and he is ailing from heart trouble. His notebook tells of two teenage lovers, McAdams and Gosling, who meet at a carnival in North Carolina and fall in love. McAdams' wealthy parents, who are on a vacation with her, disapprove of Gosling because he is a lowly mill worker and his family is not rich and so they leave, taking McAdams with them. She waits several years for Gosling to write to her, but letters do not come from him. Actually, he wrote her every day but her mother, Allen, kept his letters from her. During World War II she meets a handsome and rich young soldier, Marsden, and they become engaged. Before she makes up her mind to marry him, she visits Gosling's old home. They meet again and still have strong feelings for each other. Allen gives McAdams the letters Gosling wrote and McAdams reads them for the first time, recalling their young love. Now she has to choose between her first love and her fiancé. Near the end of the movie we learn that the elderly couple and the young couple are the same, but Rowlands only realizes it in fleeting moments as

James Garner and Gena Rowlands in *The Notebook,* **2004.**

she listens to Garner tell the story. Rowlands chose Garner as her husband, and she eventually realizes this when they dance in his hospital room. But here memory fails and she does not know him and they are back to fighting, which they always did when younger, even though they were deeply in love. Then they die in a hospital bed together holding hands. Well scripted and acted, this tale provides a stirring and memorable romance wrapped inside a ten handkerchief tearjerker. Sexual scenes, gutter language and some morose scenes prohibit viewing by children. Songs/Music: "I'll Be Seeing You" (Sammy Fain, Irving Kahal), "Alabamy Home" (Duke Ellington, Dave Ringle), "Where or When" (Richard Rodgers, Lorenz Hart), "Prelude for Piano, Op. 28, No. 4" (Frederic Chopin), "Opus One" (Sy Oliver), "Sonata No. 19 in G Minor for Piano, Op. 49, No.1" (Ludwig van Beethoven). **p**, Lynn Harris, Mark Johnson; **d**, Nick Cassavetes; **cast**, Ryan Gosling, Rachel McAdams, Gena Rowlands, James Garner, Joan Allen, Sam Shepard, James Marsden, Heather Wahlquist, Ed Grady, Andrew Schaff, James Middleton; **w**, Jeremy Leven, Jan Sardi (based on the novel by Nicholas Sparks); **c**, Robert Fraisse; **m**, Aaron Zigman; **ed**, Alan Heim; **prod d**, Sarah Knowles; **art d**, Scott Ritenour; **set d**, Chuck Potter; **spec eff**, Bob Shelley, Lisa Reynolds, Ryal Cosgrove.

Notes from Underground ★★★ 1995; U.S.; 88m; Renegade Films/Northern Lights; Color; Drama; Children: Unacceptable; **DVD**. This provocative modern-day adaptation of the novella by Fyodor Dostoevsky (1821-1881) sees Czerny admitting in notes that he is a sick, dysfunctional, and not very nice man. He is a smalltime bureaucrat whose job it is to approve building plans in the building department at city hall. He considers himself to be an "Underground Man," and his diary notes become a video diary, dramatizing the text. He crashes a party and makes a fool of himself, then takes Lee, a prostitute, to bed while the invited guests go to a whorehouse. He talks Lee into coming to his dingy basement apartment, but when she does, he does what he always does with such tenuous social encounters, destroying their relationship. His life is going nowhere, but that is no surprise to him. A somewhat dark, psychological drama that probes the reasons of life, but perfectly in keeping with Dostoevsky's gloomy and foreboding perspectives. Sexuality prohibits viewing by children. **p**, Alicia Dollard (Alicia Allain), Chris Beckman, Frank J. Gruber, **d&w**, Gary Walkow (based on the novel by Fyodor Dostoevsky); **cast**, Henry Czerny, Sheryl Lee, Jon Favreau, Seth Green, Christine Hanson, Alina Panova, Kristine Pham, Geoffrey Rivas, Eamonn Roche, Charlie Stratton; **c**, Dan Gillham; **m**, Mark Governor; **ed**, Peter B. Ellis; **prod d**, Michael Rizzo; **art d**, Mark Benson.

Notes on a Scandal ★★★ 2006; U.K.; 92m; FOX; Color; Drama; Children: Unacceptable (MPAA: R); **DVD**; **VHS**. Dench is exceptional as a middle-aged spinster and high school teacher befriending a newcomer to her school, a beautiful younger art teacher, Blanchett, who also delivers a stellar performance. Dench becomes sexually attracted to Blanchett, who is married to a former professor, Nighy, and has a teenage daughter, Temple, and son, Lewis, who is afflicted by Down syndrome. Dench keeps her feelings for Blanchett to herself, but writes about them in notebooks. Entries later include those in which she has learned that Blanchett is having an affair with one of her fifteen-year-old male students (Simpson). Dench realizes she has damaging private information about her friend, which gives her a sense of power over her, but is uncertain as to how to use it. Dench thinks to expose Blanchett's dalliance with the underage student, but, instead, uses a fellow teacher, Davis, to reveal the secret. In this treacherous, jealous act, however, Dench's own secret of being a closet lesbian comes to light and both women become victims of their self-destructive deceptions. Cleverly written and inwardly revealing, this drama is well directed by Eyre. Sexual scenes, subject matter, and gutter language prohibit viewing by children. **p**, Scott Rudin, Robert Fox; **d**, Richard Eyre; **cast**, Judi Dench, Cate Blanchett, Bill Nighy, Michael Maloney, Benedict Taylor, Juno Temple, Max Lewis, Joanna Scanlan, Shaun Parkes, Tom Georgeson, Emma Kennedy; **w**, Patrick Marber (based on the novel *What Was She Thinking: Notes on a Scandal* by Zoe Heller); **c**, Chris Menges; **m**, Philip Glass; **ed**, John Bloom, Antonia Van Drimmelen; **prod d**, Tim Hatley; **art d**, Hannah Moseley, Mark Raggett; **set d**, Caroline Smith.

Nothing But a Man ★★★ 1964; U.S.; 95m; Du Art/Cinema V; B/W; Drama; Children: Unacceptable; **DVD**; **VHS**. This well-crafted independent film incisively depicts the hardscrabble life of a black man in the South of the 1960s. Dixon has no desire for anything except to live a simple, peaceful life. While working for a railroad in Alabama, he falls in love with Lincoln, daughter of a minister, Greene, who disapproves of him. They nevertheless marry and relocate to a different town where they buy a house and Dixon gets a job at a saw mill. Dixon endures bigoted insults from his employers, but he won't cower under their threats and prejudices as he tries to start a union. Labeled a troublemaker, he is fired. He is reduced to picking cotton for $2.50 a day or working as a waiter and sometimes at a garage with Lincoln. A customer at the garage belittles him and his threatening response causes him and Lincoln to be fired. Unemployed and unable to support his wife and their infant son, Dixon feels his life has been crushed by racism and he leaves town, perhaps never to return. A very strong and telling story, this film was made at the height of the civil rights movement, and brilliantly lends itself to that good and noble cause. Songs: "Heatwave," "Fingertips," "That's the Way I Feel," "Come On Home," "This Is When I Needed You Most," "I'll Try Something New," "Way Over There," "Mickey's Monkey," "You Beat Me to the Punch," "You've Really Got a Hold on Me," "Bye Bye Baby." **p**, Michael Roemer, Robert Rubin, Robert Young; **d**, Roemer; **cast**, Ivan Dixon, Abbey Lincoln, Julius Harris, Gloria Foster, Martin Priest, Leonard Parker, Yaphet Kotto, Stanley Greene, Helen Lounck, Helene Arrindell, Moses Gunn, Esther Rolle; **w**, Roemer, Young; **c**, Young; **m**, Eddie and Brian Holland, Lamont Dozier; **ed**, Luke Bennett; **art d**, William Rhodes.

Nothing But the Truth ★★★ 1941; U.S.; 90m; PAR; B/W; Comedy; Children: Acceptable; **DVD**; **VHS**. Very funny film has stockbroker Arnold promising his niece, Goddard, that, if she can raise $20,000 for charity he will double it. But he connives so that the donors she solicits refuse to give her more than the $10,000 she's already raised. Goddard secretly gives her new partner, Hope, the $10,000, and asks him to double it. Hope, an inveterate and notorious liar, bets a business partner, Anders, and client, Erickson, that he can tell the truth for twenty-four hours, but, if he loses, they get the money. If he wins, he gets double, or the needed $20,000. Hope is then subjected to twenty-four hours of crazy and impossible attempts to force him to lie about anything. This marathon truth testing provides many hilarious scenes and lots of belly laughs. Hope wins the bet and Goddard achieves her goal. This outing is much funnier than the two earlier films made about this zany tale in 1920 and 1929. *Author's Note*: Hope and Goddard had been paired in two previous and enormously popular comedies, **The Cat and the Canary**, 1939, and **The Ghost Breakers**, 1940, and this entry also proved to be a success at the box office. Hope told this author that "I couldn't miss with Paulette [Goddard] at my side, what a dish! My big challenge in **Nothing But the Truth** was to be honest for a change and tell the truth for twenty-four hours and that was more difficult than all the endless fibs I told in all my pictures. I told Bill [W.C.] Fields that I was doing that picture and that it reminded me of a title of one of his own films, **You Can't Cheat an Honest Man** [1939] and how I was forced to tell the truth for a day and a night. He gave me that squinty-eyed look of his and said: 'Sounds like you are playing the patsy again, or, perhaps, a colossal sap—which do you think it might be?'" **p**, Arthur Hornblow, Jr.; **d**, Elliott Nugent; **cast**, Bob Hope, Paulette Goddard, Edward Arnold, Leif Erickson, Helen Vinson, Willie Best, Glenn Ander, Grant Mitchell, Rod Cameron, Rose Hobart, Mary Forbes, Clarence Kolb; **w**, Don Hartman, Ken Englund (based on the play by James Montgomery, from the novel by Frederic S. Isham); **c**, Charles Lang, Jr.; **m**, Victor Young, Floyd Morgan, Leo Shuken; **ed**, Alma Macrorie; **art d**, Hans Dreier, Robert Usher; **spec eff**, Farciot Edouart.

Nothing But the Truth ★★★ 2008; U.S.; 108m; Battleplan Productions/Yari Film Group; Drama/Thriller; Children: Unacceptable (MPAA: R); **DVD**. This hard-hitting drama sees the fetching Beckinsale as a Washington political columnist, who sees a potential Pulitzer Prize in an article she writes involving the U.S. President. She writes that the President has ignored the findings of a covert CIA operative and went ahead and ordered air strikes against Venezuela. She goes further by naming the agent, Farmiga, whose daughter is in the same school and class as Beckinsale's son, and both women are soccer moms. The government moves to force Beckinsale to name the source of her sensational story, but she refuses and is jailed for contempt and where her case is energetically prosecuted by Dillon. Beckinsale's refusal to cooperate with the government estranges her from her husband, Schwimmer (who plays a rather dimwitted fellow) and strains her relationship with her son. The film draws its story from the true case of Judith Miller (1948-), a *New York Times* reporter who served eighty-five days in prison for refusing to name her source in an article involving President George W. Bush (1946-) and Vice President Richard Cheney (1941-) and their insistence that there were weapons of mass destruction in Iraq, which justified going to war there. Gutter language, sexual material, and violence prohibit viewing by children. **p**, Rod Lurie, Marc Frydman, Bob Yari; **d&w**, Lurie; **cast**, Kate Beckinsale, Matt Dillon, Angela Bassett, Alan Alda, Vera Farmiga, David Schwimmer, Courtney B. Vance, Noah Wyle, Preston Bailey, Floyd Abrams; **c**, Alik Sakharov; **m**, Larry Groupe; **ed**, Sarah Boyd; **prod d**, Eloise Stammerjohn; **set d**, Leslie Morales; **spec eff**, Amanda Nichol Paller, Curt Miller, Chad E. Beck, Eddie Bonin.

Nothing Like the Holidays ★★★ 2008; U.S.; 98m; 2DS Productions/Overture Films/Color; Comedy/Drama; Children: Unacceptable (MPAA: PG-13); **BD**; **DVD**. A good comedy that profiles a Puerto Rican family spending Christmas together in the Humboldt Park neighborhood in west Chicago. Married coupled Molina and Pena own a convenience grocery store and their younger son, Rodriguez, is a veteran who has served in Iraq. Their oldest son, Leguizamo, is a successful New York executive married to a career-driven woman, Messing. Their daughter, Ferlito, is an amateur actress living in Hollywood. This profile of a passionate Latino family and their reunion at Christmas proves that "there is never a dull moment" with this clan. Dinners are laced with heavy drinking, and everyone's worst sides come out, providing some hilarious and provocatively dramatic scenes. Gutter language and drug references prohibit viewing by children. **p**, Robert Teitel, George Tillman, Jr.,

Walter Connolly and Fredric March in *Nothing Sacred*, 1937.

Thomas J. Busch; **d**, Alfredo De Villa; **cast**, Luis Guzman, Alfred Molina, Elizabeth Pena, Freddy Rodriguez, John Leguizamo, Jay Hernandez, Debra Messing, Vanessa Ferlito, Melonie Diaz, Alexander Bautista; **w**, Alison Swan, Rick Najera (based on a story by Teitel, Rene M. Rigal); **c**, Scott Kevan; **m**, Paul Oakenfold; **ed**, John Coniglio, Amy E. Duddleston; **prod d**, Daniel B. Clancy; **art d**, Stephanie Gilliam; **spec eff**, Bob Wiatr, Phillip Palousek, Michael Morreale.

Nothing Sacred ★★★★★ 1937; U.S.; 77m; Selznick International; UA; Color; Comedy; Children: Acceptable; **DVD**; **VHS**. The brilliant Ben Hecht penned a classic when scriptwriting this hilarious film, a clever, black screwball comedy that spoofs the newspaper world of his day as well as a public so gullible as to swallow whole the most fabulous fibs ever to be foisted upon it. March is a cynical newspaperman who will do anything to grab a headline, including creating news out of thin air. He promotes a story where a foreign black potentate, the "Sultan of Marzipan," arrives to donate $500,000 for a new art institution, but this exotic-looking rajah is a fake, a Broadway shoeshine man, Brown, who is impersonating a character March has conjured from his fertile imagination. When the potentate is exposed as a fake (such antics are in keeping with the kind of sensationalism March's tabloid newspaper promotes) Connolly, March's editor, explodes, demoting him to the status of writing obituaries and where he is now compelled to work at a tiny desk amid file cabinets endlessly accessed by researchers, who make it impossible for him to write a word. While March ponders his present self-inflicted humiliation, Lombard, a young woman named Hazel Flagg who lives in distant Warsaw, Vermont, dreams of going to New York City to seek adventure and opportunity, but her hopes are dashed after she has a routine medical checkup with local physician Winninger, and learns from this rather inept doctor that she has contracted radium poisoning and has but a short time to live. March gets wind of this tale and, to get back into the good graces of Connolly by writing one of the great sob stories in history about Lombard, he sets out for rural Vermont. When he reaches the hick town, however, he learns from the discombobulated Winninger that his original diagnosis was incorrect and that there is not a thing wrong with Lombard and she will probably live as long as Methuselah. March will not tolerate such good news as he intends to write that tragic tale about Lombard come hell or high water and he convinces her to fake that illness and travel to New York City where she will live in luxury and see all the sights she has always wanted to see since childhood. Lombard's arrival in New York has been heralded by March's reports and where Connolly, along with Rumann and other financiers wanting to appear generous and sympathetic, provides all the money required to make her final days on earth spectacular. She is welcomed by the mayor and given the key to the city

Carole Lombard is socked by Fredric March in *Nothing Sacred*, 1937.

and then taken to a posh hotel suite where she is showered with gifts, a stunning wardrobe, jewels and endless room service. Treated like a queen, Lombard is swarmed by manicurists and masseurs before March takes her out dining and dancing at an upscale nightclub. She has too much to drink and passes out, but this collapse is immediately interpreted as a relapse due to her so-called terminal illness, and men and women openly weep for her as March carries her out of the place, returning her to her hotel suite. When sobering up, Lombard tours the city where spectators mourn her appearance as a doomed woman. When she appears at a wrestling match at Madison Square Garden with March, the ring announcer points her out to the crowd and demands and gets several minutes of "silent respect" for her and where the crowd stands up as one to render its universal sorrow for her plight. As the days pass, Connolly, who does not know that Lombard is in perfect health and expects to run her obituary any moment, begins to wonder why Lombard has not by this time kicked the bucket. Smelling a rat among his literary legionnaires, Connolly focuses upon the devious March and then orders a team of medical specialists to again examine Lombard. Before these learned doctors arrive, the desperate March decides to wear Lombard out so that she will appear exhausted and emaciated by putting her through impossible physical exercises, but she still looks too healthy, so he begins (in one of the most hilarious scenes) pummeling her so that she will have some bruises and when she puts up a fight, he lands a haymaker on her jaw, knocking her out. The medicos examining her take a look at her terrible condition and conclude that Lombard is at death's door, but she again recovers and Connolly and his financial backers now believe they are being hoodwinked, along with everyone else in New York, and, of course, they are correct. After they discover that Lombard has been feigning her illness, they beg her and March to find a way to end her ebullient life so that their own reputations will survive intact. March and Lombard solve the problem by concocting a memorable fake suicide and, after Hazel Flagg is no more, March and Lombard, who have long earlier fallen in love, marry and sail away to the tropics in disguise, ending this great comedy. Lombard is superlative in her role as she was a natural comedienne and March, who mostly played in dramatic roles, shows great skills in performing his comedic part, while the cast members give strong and believable support in this classic screwball comedy, masterfully directed by Wellman, and the first such zany comedy to be filmed in color. In keeping with Wellman's quick tempo modus operandi, his scenes scurry by so fast that it is difficult to keep pace with one belly laugh after another, a grand and humorous expose of hypocrisy at its zenith. The film was made with a substantial budget of more than $1.2 million. Director Frank Capra liberally borrowed much of the story line of this film for his production of **Meet John Doe**, 1941, and the film was remade as a Broadway musical titled "Hazel Flagg," with

Helen Gallagher in the title role, and then as a poor film remake as **Living It Up**, 1954, with Jerry Lewis playing Homer Flagg and Janet Leigh in the March role of the reporter. Songs: "Give My Regards to Broadway" (1904; George M. Cohan), "Oh du liebur Augustin" (1679; Max Augustin), " Land of Hope and Glory" (1902; Edward Elgar), "Columbia, the Gem of the Ocean" (1843; David T. Shaw), "Three O'Clock in the Morning" (1922; Julian Robledo), "Yankee Doodle" (c.1755; traditional), "Hooray for Hazel Flagg" (music from "Battle Hymn of the Republic"; 1856; music: William Steffe), "Taps" (1862; Daniel Butterfield), "Massa's in De Cold, Cold Ground" (Stephen Foster). *Author's Note*: Hecht admitted to this author that the story line for **Nothing Sacred** was "inspired by some of my antics when I was a reporter in Chicago working for the *Daily News*. No news is not good news in that business and, when things got dull, we 'created' some harmless but exciting events and personalities to spruce up the front page. On one such day, I persuaded my friend and poet, Maxwell Bodenheim (1892-1954), to impersonate a wealthy Indian rajah visiting Chicago, so heavily made up with dark stains to his skin and a fake beard that he passed for the real McCoy. [He used that hokum as the setting in the first scene Hecht wrote for **Nothing Sacred**.] Sometimes we went a little too far. I wrote a news story about how a 'little' earthquake had struck a small part of the South Side of Chicago and quoted my relatives and friends, who insisted that dishes rattled off their shelves and window panes cracked. That set a pack of seismologists on my trail looking for the epicenter of that quake and I had a devil of a time evading their questions. Were my editors in on all those shenanigans? They sure were, but they would never admit it. There must have been a dozen daily newspapers in Chicago in those days and competition for the news was fierce, so everyone tried everything they could think of to beat the other guy with a scoop. There was always a lot of exciting news in Chicago, especially in its humid summertime when you could pluck a great story out of its thick, damp air, and that's just where Hazel Flagg came from, too." Wellman told this author that "Carole [Lombard] was in her element in **Nothing Sacred**, a role perfect for her kind of broad comedy. She was a firecracker off the set as much as before the cameras. When she kept asking me about some of her scenes, I kept my mouth shut since she was doing fine, but she got upset with me, thinking I didn't want to talk to her. One day when I walked onto the set, she and some bozo friends of hers ambushed me. They grabbed me and put me into a straitjacket and then tied me to my director's chair where I was forced to talk to her. It was my own fault. She heard me saying after one take: 'A little fun is the best tonic between scenes.' Well, she had her 'fun' with me all right." Lombard's antics so infected the normally reserved March that, according to his statements to this author, "I went more than along with her, but found myself competing with her to perform the most outlandish things during the production of **Nothing Sacred**. We rented a fire truck one day and drove it around the Selznick lot at breakneck speeds with the siren blaring and while we were clanging its bells, which caused everybody to run out of the soundstages and offices, thinking the whole place was on fire. We brought that truck to an abrupt stop when we saw David O. Selznick standing in our path, hands on hips and a scowl on his face. That put out our fire very quickly." Wellman, too, was infected with Lombard's mirthful manners and even adopted her wisecracking method of talking, stating to her and March at one point before a retake: "Miss Lombard, I know it must be tough for a woman to look into Freddie March's frozen puss and pretend to be in love with him, but close your eyes or something and let's do it just once more." **p**, David O. Selznick; **d**, William A. Wellman; **cast**, Carole Lombard, Fredric March, Charles Winninger, Walter Connolly, Sig Rumann, Maxie Rosenbloom, Margaret Hamilton, Ann Doran, Jinx Falkenburg, Hedda Hopper, Hattie McDaniel, John Qualen, Monty Woolley, Troy Brown, Olin Howland; **w**, Ben Hecht, additional dialogue by Ring Lardner, Jr., Budd Schulberg (based on the story "Letter to the Editor" by James H. Street); **c**, W. Howard Greene (Technicolor); **m**, Oscar Levant; **ed**, James E. Newcom; **art d**, Lyle Wheeler; **set d**, Edward G. Boyle; **spec eff**, Jack Cosgrove.

Notorious ★★★★★ 1946; U.S.; 101m; Vanguard Films/RKO; B/W;
Spy Drama; Children: Unacceptable; **DVD**; **VHS**. Bergman and Grant
were never better than in this masterpiece thriller from Hitchcock, who
brilliantly blends mystery and romance in a sophisticated and clever tale
of dark intrigue. The film opens in an American court where a German-
American businessman is being sentenced for spying for the Nazis and
we then see his daughter, Bergman, throwing a cocktail party at her bungalow where she plans to go on a long voyage aboard a yacht owned by
an elderly millionaire. At that party is Grant, who attracts Bergman's attention so much that she puts off her trip to begin a torrid romance with
him. While driving along a Florida road, Bergman is stopped by a motorcycle cop for speeding, but Grant shows his credentials to the officer,
who salutes him and then rides away without giving Bergman a ticket.
It is then that she learns that he is a federal agent, first resisting him, but
by then she has fallen in love with him. Grant knows that Bergman despises her father's political beliefs and is a loyal American. He persuades
her to travel with him to Rio de Janeiro so that she can renew her acquaintance with Rains, an old beau and friend of her father's, who has
always been attracted to her and who is part of a wealthy chemical cartel
located in Brazil, its members being diehard Nazis. These German expatriates have relocated to Rio shortly after WWII, and are secretly planning to use their wealth and mining properties to revitalize Hitler's
regime. Calhern, an American spymaster and Grant's superior, tells him
to arrange a meeting between Bergman and Rains, ostensibly so that
Bergman can seduce Rains in order to learn more about his operations,
an unsavory chore to which Grant reluctantly agrees and for which
Bergman feels used by him, but she nevertheless agrees to undertake
this repugnant assignment. She and Grant not so coincidentally meet
Rains and others while riding on a bridle path. When Bergman's horse
bolts from Grant's goading and seems to race ahead out of control, Rains
chivalrously charges after her and brings her horse to a halt and they
begin to renew their relationship. The ardent Rains cannot stop himself
from proposing marriage to Bergman, who hesitates, later meeting with
Grant, and telling him about that proposal. He agonizes over his decision, but eventually urges her, for the sake of their country, to marry a
man she does not love. Bergman goes ahead with the marriage, although
she is deeply hurt by Grant's apparent willingness to give her to another
man and now concludes that Grant has never really loved her and has
only pretended affection in order to accomplish his intelligence mission.
Following the marriage, Rains gives a lavish party at his mansion outside of Rio, an estate bordering the ocean, and Grant attends. Bergman
has by then taken a key from Rains' closely guarded key ring that will
open the door to the wine closet in the basement where she believes
Grant may find the evidence he is seeking. The two slip away from the
party and go to the cellar, opening the wine closet where Grant inspects
rows of wine and champagne bottles. Meanwhile, the partygoers are
quickly exhausting the supply of champagne and wine and the steward
tells Rains that they are running low. When Grant is looking at the bottles on a rack in the wine closet, a bottle accidentally falls from a shelf
and breaks, but, instead of wine, he sees black grains of what appears
to be some kind of ore coming from the broken bottle, he takes a sample
of this, and then hides the shards of the broken bottle beneath the rack
before he and Bergman leave. They retreat down the basement hallway
to an outside exit just as Rains appears with his steward to retrieve more
wine, but Rains discovers that the key to the wine closet is missing from
his key ring. He dismisses the steward, saying that the guests will have
to do with what is on hand upstairs and then sees Bergman and Grant
outside the basement door embracing and where Grant kisses her, telling
her to push him away as if he has made unwanted advances, knowing
that Rains is looking at them. Grant leaves and Bergman later explains
that Grant foisted his affections upon her as a former lover, assuring the
suspicious Rains that she has no more feelings for Grant. So much in
love with her is Rains that he is about to accept this explanation until he
discovers later that night that the missing key to the wine closet is now
back on his key ring, which he has placed on a bedroom table and know-

Madam Konstantin, Ingrid Bergman and Claude Rains in
Notorious, **1946.**

ing that only Bergman had access to that key ring. He now realizes his
terrible predicament and, the next morning, he sits anxiously at the bedside of his mother, Konstantin, a firm-minded elderly woman who is his
mentor and a deep-rooted Nazi who never wanted her son to marry
Bergman. "I am married to an American agent," Rains admits to Konstantin, and he fears that, should his associates learn of this, he will, as
has been the case with others, be eliminated by them as a security risk.
"We are protected by the stupidity of your actions," the cool-minded
Konstantin tells him, her long-seated suspicions about Bergman now
confirmed. She has a lethal solution to the problem. They will systematically poison Bergman to death under the pretense that she has gotten
ill, a planned illness that will slowly and eventually take her life and
eliminate her threat to them. Bergman then begins to slowly grow
weaker and weaker. When clandestinely meeting with Grant, he thinks
she is drinking too much and suffering from a hangover, but her condition has been created by the poison Konstantin and Rains are putting
into her coffee. Bergman actually believes she has some unknown ailment, but does not seek medical attention, believing she will soon recover. Then, when meeting with Schunzel, a solicitous member of the
cabal, she sees him mistakenly reach for her cup of coffee and Rains
and Konstantin become alarmed, alerting Bergman to the grim and terrifying fact that her coffee and other beverages being served to her have
been dosed with poison. Meanwhile, Grant, Calhern and other agents
have had the ore taken from Rains' wine cellar analyzed. They learn that
the ore is uranium, an element used in the making of the atomic bomb,
and Bergman has also learned the mountain location where the Nazis
are mining that ore. Bergman is now so ill that she is confined to her
bed, her ailment, unknown to Rains' associates, causing them concern,
but Rains tells them that she will soon recover. Bergman manages to
make a phone call to Grant, whispering that she is dying. Grant drives
to Rains' mansion and arrives while Rains is at a meeting with cabal
members in his study. As he waits in the foyer to see Rains, Grant suddenly decides to take matters into his own hands and climbs the stairs
of the grand staircase leading to the upstairs rooms where he finds
Bergman's bedroom and goes to her, holding her in his arms and telling
her that he loves her above all else. She tells him that she is being systematically poisoned and Grant places a robe around her and helps her
to her feet, then begins to carry her, but Rains and Konstantin arrive.
Grant tells them that he is taking Bergman to a hospital so that the poison
they have given Bergman can be treated. As Grant half-carries Bergman
down the grand staircase, members of the Nazis cabal step from the
study, asking Rains for an explanation. Konstantin urges her panicking
son to say something and Rains informs his associates that he is taking
Bergman to a hospital with Grant's help. He escorts Bergman and Grant
to Grant's car, but Grant, after placing Bergman inside the car and get-

Cary Grant and Ingrid Bergman in *Notorious*, 1946.

ting behind the driver's wheel, locks Rains out of the auto and drives away, leaving Rains alone, and who turns to see his menacing associates summon him inside, undoubtedly to certain death and this is where this riveting and bone-chilling film ends. Hitchcock cleverly presents a subtle spy tale, deftly weaving intrigue through his scenes while also presenting a fascinating and somewhat twisted love story and where Grant and Bergman sizzle in their close-ups, their every embrace engulfing them in deeper hazards. The closer Bergman comes to Rains the closer she flirts with her own death. Her scenes are so suspenseful that they produce excruciating apprehension and fear on the part of the viewer and where Hitchcock took the woman-in-peril plot to the zenith of stressful anxiety. Grant, Bergman and Rains provide stunning performances in this riveting *ménage á trois* that is seen through a glass darkly of Hitchcock's own creation. All that is sinister in the evil machinations of Rains and his cabal is more implied than overtly demonstrated, this approach heightening suspense. The film was produced for $2 million; the investment was quickly recouped at the box office where it became an enormous hit, yielding more than $24 million, staggering gross profits for its day. *Author's Note*: Hitchcock first went to his favorite screenwriter, Ben Hecht, when thinking to make **Notorious**, having had a great success a year earlier with **Spellbound**, 1945, which was written by Hecht. "Hitch called me one day," Hecht told this author, "to tell me that he had a spy story he wanted me to write that would be located somewhere in South America, and that he was working with David O. Selznick in developing the story. Cary Grant and Ingrid Bergman, who were then under contract to Selznick, were part of that package, two of the great stars of that day. I knew I was in for a grind because Hitch liked to work closely with his writers and that meant spending hours and hours with him in a room where he walked about, gazing at the ceiling or his fingernails as he dreamed up one impossible idea after another as we did when I worked with him on **Spellbound**. I think he picked up that work routine from Selznick, who did the same thing with his writers, locking them up in a room with him, sometimes for days on end, to hammer out a script while he rattled off his ideas. David [Selznick] did that with me when I worked for a few weeks with him on **Gone with the Wind**, and he drove me nuts. I would sit at a typewriter banging out his ideas, as I did with Hitch, but most of them wound up in the wastepaper basket. I was all for that because I have always believed that the more concepts you explore, the better are the possibilities of getting a good storyline and a believable script. [When this author first met Hecht and where he more or less became my mentor, his first advice was to say: "Gush out all of your ideas and hold back nothing when you are writing. Blow up the dam and let the water cascade. Then wait a while before you go back to what you have written and clean up the mess, taking out everything that is *precious* to you—

meaning delete everything you have written to impress the world with your writing abilities—and keep everything you have written for the reader that clearly describes your characters and explains your story."] When doing the script with Hitch for **Notorious** we dreamed up every crazy idea we could summon from our imaginations about a group of rich Nazi spies, who have survived the war [WWII; 1939-1945] and are planning to start another one. Hitch kept carping about coming up with what he called a great 'MacGuffin,' the object or reason why all of these secret operations were going on." Hitchcock told a similar story about the development of that lynchpin to the story line of **Notorious** by stating to this author: "Ben Hecht and I were working on **Notorious** and, we had to say, well, what are the Nazis up to down there [in South America]. Ingrid Bergman is sent by the FBI with Cary Grant alongside her, and, until I hit on Uranium 235 in wine bottles, God, we had armed camps down there, the *Graf Spee* crew, the Nazis drilling—you've never seen such a 'MacGuffin.'[The German cruiser *Admiral Graf Spee* was scuttled by its captain in the port of Montevideo on December 17, 1939, to prevent it from falling into British hands in the early stages of WWII.] Actually, it was Hecht who had "hit" upon the subject of Uranium 235, not Hitchcock, after reading about it in a popular science magazine. In 1944, when they were developing **Notorious**, Hecht took Hitchcock to see Dr. Robert Andrews Millikan (1868-1953), a scientist and chairman of California Tech (Nobel Prize-winning physicist known for his research on the electron) and where Millikan spent hours talking with both of them about the "possibility" of splitting the hydrogen atom in order to create a devastating bomb, not telling them that the government-sponsored Manhattan Project had been working on just that for several years (and this was about a year or more before the atomic bombs were dropped on Hiroshima and Nagasaki to end WWII, that war still ongoing). "While we were talking about all this to Millikan," Hecht told this author, "I mentioned using uranium in those experiments since that ingredient had been mentioned in an article I had read about splitting the atom and Millikan got very excited and said, 'no, no, that substance is not involved at all!' Well, okay, we thought, we can go ahead and use uranium then without having any trouble with the government. It turned out that Millikan knew damned well that the government was using uranium to make the atom bomb, but he wasn't about to tell us about it." Hitchcock told this author that "we did not know about it when we left Cal Tech that day that Millikan had alerted the FBI about our visit and I guess he mentioned the fact that we had brought up the word 'uranium' in our conversation with him. Well, what to think? I find out some years later that the minute we left Cal Tech, we were being tailed by FBI agents and that they were monitoring our every move when we were working on **Notorious**. Ben and I worked out a first draft for the picture and then went to Selznick and, after he looked at the script, he said: 'All this stuff you have in here about uranium is just too harebrained. Nobody is going to believe that uranium has anything to do with making some devastating weapon. I will not make a picture like that. We will all look like fools.' Ben and I were shocked by his reaction, but I think now, and I do not have any evidence to support this, that the FBI contacted Selznick and warned him not to make the picture. I have a rather stubborn streak about such things and told Selznick that I was going to make the picture with or without his studio. So what does he do? He gets himself off the hook with the FBI, if he was ever on it, and I think he was, by selling the whole package—yours truly, Ben, Ingrid [Bergman], Cary [Grant] and the script to RKO for $800,000 as well as getting fifty percent of the profits from the picture and that proved to be in the millions. I discovered years later that the FBI sent undercover people to RKO to spy on us while we were in production for **Notorious** and that they were copying the script that Ben was invariably changing under my direction so they could see how we were positioning 'uranium' in the story. They didn't try to stop us, though, until the picture was completed and ready for distribution. By that time [September 1946, the month of this film's U.S. release], the atomic bomb had been used to end the war, but we were nevertheless summoned to the Bureau's L.A. office and agents wanted to know how we found out about uranium being used for the bomb. Ben was ready for them. He simply gave them a copy of a science magazine that had printed an article about the use of uranium in making super bombs years earlier and they were amazed that that article had been printed and that they had never seen it until then. They let us go and when we were outside, I told Ben that it was lucky that he had held on to that magazine. 'I hold on to everything, Hitch,' he said to me, 'as insurance against the whims of the future.' I think Ben held on to that magazine because of the way Millikan overreacted to him when he first mentioned uranium to him. What a very smart fellow was Ben." Everything about **Notorious** bears Hitchcock's brilliant imprimatur, his conceptual techniques in full force, such as a stunning crane shot in the party scene at Rains' mansion where the camera, in one long and breathtaking shot, glides down the grand staircase to hover and then pass over the partygoers in the main foyer and into the ballroom to find Bergman in the crowd, slowly closing in on her, to finally show in a tight close-up the key to the locked wine closet she has stolen and clutches in her hand. Hitchcock was never one to forget his best shots in his previous films, his crane shot in the mansion similar to boom or crane shots he devised for many other films. In **Young and Innocent**, 1938, Hitchcock had his camera on a boom and working its way through a dance hall jammed with dancers as if it were a hunting dog, to find the culprit in the jazz band members, conveniently disguised as all are in blackface, and to then close in on one of the musicians, and closer still to show the telltale clue of the villain's rapidly blinking eyes. In **Foreign Correspondent**, 1940, Hitchcock achieved an amazing crane shot where he shows a huge, rain-swept set in the downtown section of the Hague, his camera looking down upon a square packed with trolley cars, autos and pedestrians, hovering, then almost fluttering like a bird of prey over a crowd, its members shrouded with umbrellas and who are assembled on the steps of an columned office building to greet arriving dignitaries and where, on those steps, a few minutes later, a diplomat is horribly assassinated. In **Saboteur**, 1942, Hitchcock used a similar crane shot to show Robert Cummings and Priscilla Lane evading Nazis by walking down a grand staircase and into a huge ballroom in a New York mansion while a party is going on. **Notorious**, however, boasted many unique shots, the most notable being the longest kissing scene on record to date (more than three minutes), which Hitchcock, like all of his setups and shots, had carefully arranged in advance. The scene takes place in Bergman's flat in Rio, one having a veranda with a spectacular view of the ocean and the city's skyline at night just before she and Grant are to partake in a chicken dinner she has prepared. "We had a problem in those days with the censors," Hitchcock told this author, "who insisted that prolonged kissing on the screen could not be shown as that might arouse or make viewers uncomfortable. Well, I got around that silly notion by having the camera follow Cary and Ingrid about her apartment, sort of closing in on each other as she tells him about the chicken dinner she has prepared for him, and I had them talking about that dinner as they begin to make love. Ben [Hecht] was on the set during that scene and when Cary [Grant] and Ingrid [Bergman] are delivering their ad lib chatter about that, he whispered to me: 'I don't get all this talk about chicken,' which he had not written in the script, and I whispered back, 'you'll see.' I had the camera show them in medium shots as they nibbled on each other's ears, caressed each other's shoulders and kissed each other's cheeks, so that, in the close-ups, they finally worked their way to each other's lips for a very long kiss. The feast they were enjoying, you see, was not the chicken, but each other. That was the main entry, the chicken was dessert. And after the shot, Ben said to me: 'Okay, I get it.'" Bergman thought the world of Hitchcock and she worked well with him, but she had difficulty with one scene, according to her statements to this author: "I could not deliver my line correctly and Hitch kept doing more and more takes, but it simply did not work. He took me aside and asked: 'Ingrid, do you know what this scene is all about?' I told him that I did and, when we started another take, I just

Cary Grant, Ingrid Bergman, Madame Konstantin and Claude Rains in *Notorious*, 1946.

could not get it right, but then, I saw him give me a little smile and I understood how I should deliver that line and we got it right on the next take. Hitch then said to me: 'Good morning, Ingrid.' And I said, 'Good morning, Hitch.'" Grant, who worked with Hitchcock on **Suspicion**, 1941, performed flawlessly in his role, although he told this author that he sometimes "felt uneasy about how I was passing the woman I love to another man so she can learn his secret plans to destroy the Western world. How immoral must you be in the name of patriotism?" Hitchcock, as he remarked to this author, thought Grant "perfect in his part as the agonizing American agent. He never missed a cue and always delivered his lines in keeping with his character, but he is human after all and, as an actor, has his little idiosyncrasies. He was an actor that paid attention to every little detail, and when that detail was out of order, he got annoyed, distracted and even dumbfounded. In one little scene where he is carrying his hat and has to open a door, well, Cary could not do it. He finally turned to me and said: 'Hitch—this is impossible. I have to open this door with my right hand while I am holding on to my hat with the same hand!' I replied: 'Have you considered the possibility of transferring the hat to the other hand?'" **p&d**, Alfred Hitchcock; **cast**, Cary Grant, Ingrid Bergman, Claude Rains, Louis Calhern, Madame Konstantin, Reinhold Schunzel, Moroni Olsen, Ivan Triesault, Alexis Minotis, Wally Brown, Bea Benaderet, Antonio Moreno, Hitchcock; **w**, Ben Hecht; **c**, Ted Tetzlaff; **m**, Roy Webb; **ed**, Theron Warth; **art d**, Carroll Clark, Albert S. D'Agostino; **set d**, Darrell Silvera, Claude Carpenter; **spec eff**, Vernon L. Walker, Paul Eagler.

Notorious Gentleman ★★★ 1946; U.K.; 110m; Independent Producers/UNIV; B/W; Drama; Children: Unacceptable; **VHS**. Harrison gives a fine portrayal as a consummate rake without scruples or values. He is shown as a young English aristocrat, who flunks out of Oxford University and decides to charm his way into a life of leisure and dissipation. He puts into play everything from seduction to betrayals of sweethearts, family and friends, and even marries Palmer for her money. He shows no remorse or desire for redemption and enjoys being a ne'er-do-well. World War II (1939-1945) breaks out and he dies without distinction in the war. Although a wholly disreputable person, Harrison's charming and devious ways sustain interest throughout. **p**, Sidney Gilliat, Frank Launder; **d**, Gilliat; **cast**, Rex Harrison, Lilli Palmer, Godfrey Tearle, Griffith Jones, Margaret Johnston, Guy Middleton, Jean Kent, Marie Lohr, Garry Marsh, David Horne, Alan Wheatley, Joan Hickson, Gilliat (narrator); **w**, Gilliat, Launder (based on a story by Val Valentine); **c**, Wilkie Cooper; **m**, William Alwyn; **ed**, Thelma Myers; **prod d**, David Rawnsley; **art d**, Norman Arnold; **spec eff**, Philippo Guidobaldi.

The Notorious Landlady ★★★ 1962; U.S.; 123m; COL; B/W; Com-

Paul Henreid and Bette Davis in *Now, Voyager*, 1942.

edy/Mystery; Children: Unacceptable; **DVD**; **VHS**. Good comedy begins when Lemmon, a U.S. State Department employee, is transferred from Saudi Arabia to London and rents an apartment in Novak's boarding house, then proceeds to fall in love with his sultry landlady. He's unaware that Scotland Yard detectives suspect her of foul play regarding her missing husband, Reed. Lemmon's boss, Astaire, and inspector Jeffries ask him to snoop around. Reed shows up looking for stolen diamonds in Novak's house, and during a battle, Novak kills him. She is arrested and goes on trial, claiming self-defense. She is exonerated through the testimony of an eye witness, who is only after the reportedly missing gems and a series of hazardous (and funny) situations now threaten Novak, but Lemmon comes to her rescue and they wind up together. Songs: "A Foggy Day in London Town" (George Gershwin, Ira Gershwin); "I Am the Very Model of a Modern Major General," "Come Friends Who Plough the Sea" (William S. Gilbert, Arthur Sullivan). **p**, Richard Quine, Fred Kohlmar; **d**, Quine; **cast**, Kim Novak, Jack Lemmon, Fred Astaire, Lionel Jeffries, Estelle Winwood, Maxwell Reed, Philippa Bevans, Henry Daniell, Ronald Long, Richard Peel, Doris Lloyd; **w**, Blake Edwards, Larry Gelbart (based on the story "The Notorious Tenant" by Margery Sharp); **c**, Arthur E. Arling; **m**, George Duning; **ed**, Charles Nelson; **art d**, Cary Odell; **set d**, Louis Diage; **spec eff**, Dave Koehler.

Notting Hill ★★★ 1999; U.K./U.S.; 124m; Polygram Filmed Entertainment/UNIV; Color; Comedy/Romance; Children: Unacceptable (MPAA: PG-13); **DVD**; **VHS**. Life is simple for Grant, the shy and awkward but handsome young owner of a bookstore in the Notting Hill district of London. His life is disrupted and dramatically altered when Roberts, the Hollywood movie actress he considers to be the most beautiful woman in the world, comes into his store to buy a book. He is so overcome by Roberts' presence that he can hardly bring himself to wait on her. Then he sees her again when he accidentally spills orange juice over her. He suggests she tidy up in his nearby apartment and she thanks him with a kiss. Over the months, they get to know each other much better while they become a news item, engulfing their lives with a frenzied media circus. Grant's friends are amazed that he and Roberts have established a relationship. This unlikely couple, however, end up together and everyone, including strangers, crowd into their wedding for a zany love-fest. The viewer may not learn much about courtship in this offbeat but charming entry, but one will know everything about tai-chi by the ending of this romantic fairy tale. The film owes some of its storyline and characters to **Will Success Spoil Rock Hunter?**, 1957, where advertising executive Tony Randall becomes an "item" after meeting movie star Jayne Mansfield. Songs include "She" (Charles Aznavour, Herbert Kretzmer), "Born to Cry" (Richard Hawley, Jarvis

Cocker, Nick Banks, Candida Doyle, Steve Mackey, Mark Webber),"In Our Lifetime" (John McElhone, Sharleen Spiteri), "Happy Birthday" (Mildred J. and Patty S. Hill), "When You Say Nothing at All" (Paul Overstreet, Don Schlitz), "How Can You Mend a Broken Heart" (Barry and Robin Gibb), "Ain't No Sunshine" (Bill Withers), "Blue Moon" (Richard Rodgers, Lorenz Hart), "You've Got a Way" (Shania Twain, Robert John Lange), "Turn the Lights Down Low" (Bob Marley), "From the Heart" (Diane Warren), "Gimme Some Lovin'" (Spencer Davis, Steve Winwood, Muff Winwood), "No Matter What" (Andrew Lloyd Webber, Jim Steinman). Sexual content and gutter language prohibitviewing by children. **p**, Duncan Kenworthy; **d**, Roger Michell; **cast**, Julia Roberts, Hugh Grant, Samuel West, Richard McCabe, Rhys Ifans, James Dreyfus, Dylan Moran, Hugh Bonneville, Emily Mortimer, Roger Frost, Henry Goodman, Julian Rhind-Tutt, Lorelei King, John Shrapnel, Clarke Peters, Alec Baldwin; **w**, Richard Curtis; **c**, Michael Coulter; **m**, Trevor Jones; **ed**, Nick Moore; **prod d**, Stuart Craig; **art d**, Andrew Ackland-Snow, David Allday, John King; **set d**, Stephenie McMillan; **spec eff**, Dave Crownshaw, Tim Webber.

Now, Voyager ★★★★ 1942; U.S.; 117m; WB; B/W; Romance; Children: Acceptable; **DVD**; **VHS**. This grand tearjerker finds Davis in one of her most popular films, and where her bravura performance as a star-crossed lover assured her status as a great Hollywood legend. She is the dowdy, uncomely daughter of a domineering, wealthy mother, Cooper, living in a Boston mansion where she is treated with less affection than what Cooper shows to her servants. Cooper insists that Davis wear "sensible" apparel, and she is adorned in plain clothes and sturdy but ungainly looking shoes, her overall appearance further made unattractive through her use of thick-lensed glasses that give her the look of an owl. She is overweight, has thick eyebrows, and is easily cowed by Cooper, who seems to bear a deep resentment for her daughter and treats her so harshly and uncaring (if not sadistically) that Davis feels unloved and unwanted, accepting her role in life as an ugly duckling. Her prospects of ever attracting a man, let alone enjoying at least one romance in life, are slim to none and she knows it. Her only real friend is the glamorous Chase (whose mother, in real life, was Edna Woolman Chase, editor-in-chief of *Vogue Magazine* for forty years), who thinks Davis is on the verge of a mental collapse and summons psychiatrist Rains. He realizes that Davis is so emotionally deflated and exhausted by living under her mother's oppressive thumb that the only solution is that she immediately depart the nest. Davis goes to a sanitarium where she gradually builds up her confidence and becomes emotionally stable under Rain's careful guidance and treatment. Within three months, she is transformed into a new woman, losing twenty-five pounds, wearing chic apparel, and can now assert herself as her own person with an individual personality that looks freshly upon the world with hope and courage. When she leaves the sanitarium, Davis, at Rains' urging, takes a South American cruise and, aboard the liner she meets gentle and attractive Henreid, a married man, unhappy with a conniving wife, who sustains her marriage by feigning illness. Davis and Henreid spend a night in Rio, but find that the next day their ship has left without them and they stay on for several more days, falling in love, but Davis believes that this is a dead-end romance since she is convinced that Henreid will never leave his ailing wife. She returns to Boston, resolving to end her relationship with Henreid. When she arrives home, Davis is given an icy reception by her mean-minded mother, Cooper disapproving of Davis' "new" look and attitudes, but her good friend Chase wholeheartedly approves and soon introduces Davis to handsome widower Loder, who soon asks to marry her. When on the verge of accepting, Davis meets Henreid again and realizes that he is the only man in the world she will ever love. She refuses to marry Loder and this rejection causes Cooper to explode, more or less telling Davis that she has missed the only opportunity to marry a man of her "class," Cooper's vitriol and venom spewing forth until she collapses from a coronary attack that takes her life. Davis feels so depressed and guilty over Cooper's demise that she again seeks the solace and support of Rains by going back to his sanitarium. While there, Davis meets Wilson, a young girl, who she discovers to be Henreid's emotionally disturbed daughter. Davis looks upon Wilson as a younger version of herself, suffering from the same emotional stresses she had endured under Cooper's suppressive methods. With Rains' approval, Davis becomes a tender and caring surrogate mother to Wilson, who comes to love her as she, too, regains her self-confidence. Davis now moves back to her Boston mansion and takes Wilson with her, and Henreid visits his daughter to find that she is now a happy, outgoing young girl and agrees with Davis that Wilson's best future is with Davis, allowing Davis to raise her as her own daughter, the child she has never had but wanted in life. Henreid still longs to marry Davis, stating he will find a way for them to be together, but they both know that his situation is hopeless, as he and Davis also know that Henreid cannot leave his wife. As they smoke cigarettes (then thought to be harmless, but a taboo today), Henreid routinely lights both cigarettes, giving one to Davis, a memorable trademark of this film. (That intimate gesture was actually begun by John Gilbert, who lights up two cigarettes and gives one to Greta Garbo in **Flesh and the Devil**, 1927, repeated by Tyrone Power when lighting two cigarettes and giving one to Loretta Young in **Second Honeymoon**, 1937.) They look from the window of Davis' mansion to see a night sky full of twinkling stars; Davis sums up their futures by stating: "Don't ask for the moon when we have the stars." With these poignant words, this moving and superbly crafted film ends. Few actresses could have managed the transformational role achieved by Davis, a one-of-a-kind actress, who instinctively knew how to employ every emotional nuance in her character, transitioning that forlorn and loveless young woman into a self-assured and vibrant human being coming to grips with the challenges and values of life. Rapper's direction is skillfully careful in milking every tear-producing scene in this impactful domestic tale, which is greatly enhanced by one of Steiner's finest scores (and for which he won an Oscar). Cooper is outstanding as the coldhearted mother, who has no love to give to anyone, a chilling performance that got her an Oscar nomination. Rains is also a standout as the empathetic and knowing psychiatrist, while the charismatic Henreid is perfect as the husband hopelessly trapped in a loveless marriage and is the most tragic of the lot in that he will never find fulfilling happiness. *Author's Note*: The great and unique Davis, who had won two Oscars as Best Actress (**Dangerous**, 1935, and **Jezebel**, 1938), received her sixth Oscar nomination for this film and would go on to receive an unprecedented ten Oscar nominations. Davis told this author: "I lost the Oscar that year to Greer [Garson], who played the heroic mother in **Mrs. Miniver** [1942]. How could I compete with her? She was fighting the war for England and all I was doing in **Now, Voyager** was taking off weight and throwing away a lot of ugly dresses. God only knows where the Warner Brothers wardrobe people dug up those terrible-looking rags that only Ma Barker [head of the criminal Barker family] would wear. The makeup people put eyebrows on me that were so thick that I looked ridiculous and I complained about that, telling Wallis [Hal B. Wallis, producer of the film]: 'Look here, it's one thing to make me look like America's Plain Jane; it's another to make me look like Groucho Marx!' Wallis had them trim down the eyebrows a bit, but I still looked absurd. 'Okay,' I said to myself, 'I'll do the ugly duckling thing, but I'll wring its neck until it looks like a swan!' I think I did just that. I guess it was a woman's film all the way because I liberate myself the way women had to liberate themselves during the suffragette days to wear one-piece bathing suits, get the vote, and smoke cigarettes in public. And Paul [Henreid] and I smoke a hell of a lot of cigarettes in **Now, Voyager**. Puffing, puffing, puffing, until the director [Rapper] stopped one scene and shouted: 'Too much smoke. We can't see your faces!' So we blew the smoke away from the camera and finished the scene. I then went to my dressing room and had another coughing fit." Davis was a lifelong heavy smoker, three to four packs a day, and she, in later years, had several bouts with cancer until that disease claimed her fabulous life on October 6, 1989. In a coast-to-coast flight from New York to Los Angeles

Bette Davis and Paul Henreid in *Now, Voyager*, 1942.

and where I was seated next to her on that flight (I was on a book tour and my publisher had inexplicably booked me into first class) and where she talked with me about her many films, Davis, I think, smoked at least two packs of cigarettes before we landed, smoking then allowed on planes. She also had champagne with her breakfast on that flight, telling me that "I need the support [of that bubbly] because I am a bad flier." Any little air disturbance that might cause the plane to bump or jog unnerved her to the point where she asked if she could hold my hand, and I did hold her hand, telling her repeatedly not to worry and that the air disturbances were normal. She asked me if I had ever been a flier to know such things and, to calm her down, I told her that I had logged many hours in the air as an aviator. "If anything happens to the pilots, can you fly this plane?" she asked me. "Of course," I said, "but that will not happen, I guarantee you." I have never flown a plane in my life, but such fibbing seemed to give her the kind of reassurances that she had given to so many millions of viewers in a great lifetime on the screen. It was the least I could do to somehow repay this wonderful and brilliant lady. **p**, Hal B. Wallis; **d**, Irving Rapper; **cast**, Bette Davis, Paul Henreid, Claude Rains, Gladys Cooper, Bonita Granville, John Loder, Ilka Chase, Lee Patrick, Franklin Pangborn, Katherine Alexander, James Rennie, Mary Wickes, Tod Andrews (Michael Ames), Charles Drake, Bill Edwards, Reed Hadley, Bill Kennedy; **w**, Casey Robinson (based on the novel by Olive Higgins Prouty); **c**, Sol Polito; **m**, Max Steiner; **ed**, Warren Low; **art d**, Robert Haas; **set d**, Fred M. MacLean; **spec eff**, Willard Van Enger.

Now You See Him, Now You Don't ★★★ 1972; U.S.; 88m; Disney; Buena Vista; Color or B/W; Juvenile/Comedy; Children: Acceptable (MPAA: G); **DVD**; **VHS**. This good sequel to **The Computer Wore Tennis Shoes**, 1969, offers with the same cast that appeared in the original production. Russell is a college chemistry whiz who finds a serum that can make him invisible. The school is in financial trouble and Russell uses the serum to prevent a planned takeover. During a golf outing, the dean of the college, Flynn, tries to get some money out of wealthy Backus to save the school, and invisible Russell helps Flynn with his game, to secure that financing. Meanwhile, gangster Romero steals some of the serum and uses it so that he becomes invisible in order to rob a bank. On his getaway there is a wild car chase, some of the cars becoming invisible, too. Romero is caught, the school is saved, and Russell materializes again to put the lid firmly on the serum to prevent any future hazards. **p**, Ron Miller; **d**, Robert Butler; **cast**, Kurt Russell, Cesar Romero, Joe Flynn, Jim Backus, William Windom, Michael McGreevey, Richard Bakalyan, George O'Hanlon, Dave Willock, Edward Andrews, Ed Begley, Jr.; **w**, Joseph L. McEveety (based on a story by Robert L. King); **c**, Frank Phillips; **m**, Robert F. Brunner; **ed**, Cotton

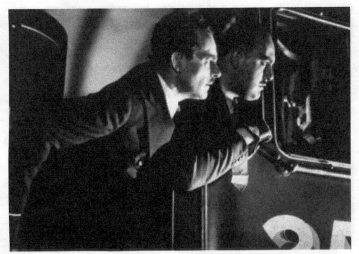

Donald Calthrop and Garry Marsh in *Number Seventeen*, 1932.

Warburton; **art d**, John B. Mansbridge, Walter Tyler; **set d**, Emile Kuri, Frank R. McKelvy; **spec eff**, Danny Lee, Eustace Lycett, Hans Metz.

Nowhere in Africa ★★★ 2003; Germany; 141m; Bavaria Film/Zeitgeist Films; Color; Drama; Children: Unacceptable (MPAA: R); **DVD**; **VHS**. Based on a true story, this gripping domestic drama begins shortly before the start of World War II (1939-1945), where a Jewish family in Frankfurt, Germany, escapes the growing anti-Jewish movement by immigrating to Kenya to begin running a farm. The family consists of a father, Ninidze, who was a lawyer in Frankfurt, a mother, Köhler, and daughter, Kurka, who is five-years-old when the family moves to Africa and who narrates the adventure. She loves Africa from the beginning, but her mother misses the more civilized upscale lifestyle she enjoyed in Germany. As they work a hardscrabble farm in arid country, Kohler longs for a refrigerator, but Ninidze knows there's no going back so the family perseveres without conveniences, working hard to overcome obstacles in order to make a new and freer way of life. Sexual content prohibits viewing by children. (In German; English subtitles.) **p**, Peter Herrmann, Sven Ebeling, Thilo Kleine, Bernd Eichinger, Michael Weber; **d&w**, Caroline Link (based on the novel by Stefanie Zweig); **cast**, Juliane Köhler, Merab Ninidze, Matthias Habich, Sidede Onyulo, Lea Kurka, Karoline Eckertz, Gerd Heinz, Hildegard Schmahl, Maritta Horwarth, Regine Zimmermann; **c**, Gernot Roll; **m**, Niki Reiser; **ed**, Patricia Rommel; **prod d**, Susann Bieling, Uwe Szielasko; **spec eff**, Erwin Gschwind, Pit Rotter.

Number Seventeen ★★★ 1932; U.K.; 63m; British International/Wardour; B/W; Crime Drama/Mystery; Children: Unacceptable; **DVD**; **VHS**. Pantheon director Hitchcock inventively portrays this crime yarn with impressive visuals, his opening shot moving through a dark and eerie London hideout used by gangsters and going up a long staircase. (Hitchcock would duplicate his penchant for staircase shots in his shocking assassination scene in **Foreign Correspondent**, 1940; in **Suspicion**, 1941, when Cary Grant is climbing a long staircase while ostensibly carrying a glass of poison milk to give to wife Joan Fontaine; in **Saboteur**, 1942, where Robert Cummings and Priscilla Lane are trying to avoid spies in a huge mansion; and in **Notorious**, 1946, to float down a grand staircase and into a ballroom to show Ingrid Bergman holding on to a stolen key that will unlock the door to some Nazi secrets, to name a few such scenes.) Lion finds a corpse and becomes involved in the theft of an expensive necklace by a gang of thieves. Lion meets attractive Grey and encounters detective Stuart, who is investigating the death of the murdered man, and, at one point, Stuart and Grey become handcuffed to the bannister of the staircase, but are released. Hitchcock then cuts to Lion taking a wild train ride where the same characters are pas-

sengers and where Stuart is searching for the thieves, the filming ending when the thieves are caught. This early talkie from Hitchcock blends some humor with danger and crime, offering many startling but unresolved scenes more surrealistic than rooted to the realities of the director's later films. Violence prohibits viewing by children. Song: "I Don't Need a Television" (Harry Shalson, John Malvern). **p**, John Maxwell, Leon M. Lion; **d**, Alfred Hitchcock; **cast**, Lion, Anne Grey, John Stuart, Donald Calthrop, Barry Jones, Ann Casson, Henry Caine, Garry Marsh, Herbert Langley; **w**, Hitchcock, Alma Reville, Rodney Ackland (based on the play and novel by Joseph Jefferson Farjeon); **c**, John J. Cox (Jack E. Cox), Bryan Langley; **m**, Adolph Hallis; **ed**, A.C. Hammond; **art d**, Wilfred Arnold; **spec eff**, Bill Warrington.

The Nun ★★★ 1971; France; 135m; Rome Paris Films; Altura Films International; Color; Drama; Children: Unacceptable; **DVD**. This taut tale sees Karina (one of the leading actresses of the French "New Wave" films) as a young woman compelled for financial reasons to enter an 18th-Century convent where she is subjected to all sorts of abusive treatment at the hands of Pulver, a sadistic mother superior. Locked up in a cell and given scant food and water, she is denied simple hygiene conveniences before Pulver attempts to sexually seduce her. She begs for an attorney so that she can have her vows annulled, but this request, like all of her others, is denied. Rabal, a young priest who has also been forced into the clergy, takes pity on her, helping her to escape, but he then tries to rape her and Karina flees from him. She later finds work in a bordello, but her miseries mount with more sadistic treatment so that she commits suicide by throwing herself from the window of the brothel, landing on the street below, arms spread wide, her crumpled figure seen in the form of a cross. Rivette, one of the leading directors of the "New Wave," presents a grim and unrelenting tale, well-enacted by Karina, but one that may offend or repulse sensitive viewers. *Author's Note*: This story was first published in 1796 by French novelist Denis Diderot, although he had written the story in 1760. It was basically a gruesome inside joke. Diderot, to persuade a friend, Marquis de Croismare, to come to Paris, enticed him with letters signed by Suzanne Simonin, a young nun who wanted to annul her vows and reenter the corporal world. When Diderot discovered that his friend was planning to visit the mythical young woman, he wrote to his friend to say that she had committed suicide, his warped joke later transformed into this strange story. The novel and the film upon which it is based was considered an anti-Catholic polemic and was banned in France for some years after it was originally produced in 1966, and it was not released in the U.S. until 1971. (In French; English subtitles.) **p**, Georges de Beauregard; **d**, Jacques Rivette; **cast**, Anna Karina, Liselotte Pulver, Micheline Presle, Francine Bergé, Francisco Rabal, Christiane Lénier, Yori Bertin, Catherine Diamant, Gilette Barbier, Annik Morice; **w**, Rivette, Jean Gruault (based on the novel *Memoirs of a Nun* by Denis Diderot); **c**, Alain Levent (Eastmancolor); **m**, Jean-Claude Eloy; **ed**, Denise de Casabianca; **prod d**, Jean-Jacques Fabre, Guy Littaye.

The Nun's Story ★★★★ 1959; U.S.; 149m; WB; Color; Drama; Children: Cautionary; **DVD**; **VHS**. This fine drama is set in the 1930s and where Hepburn shines in one of her finest roles as the young, headstrong daughter of Jagger, a prominent Belgian surgeon. She becomes convinced that her calling in life is to become a nursing nun in the Congo, then controlled by Belgium, and she enters a convent (the order is not specified) where she undergoes training as a novitiate under the strict tutoring and spiritual guidance of Evans, the mother superior. Evans tells Hepburn that the life she has chosen demands sacrifice and is against nature, but earthly and heavenly rewards await those dedicated to this religious life. Hepburn endures the demands and rigors of the order and is finally accepted as a nun. After taking her vows, she undergoes training at a medical school where she studies how to administer tropical medicine. Though she asks to be assigned to the Congo, she is sent to work in a mental asylum in Belgium where she becomes overly confident and commits the sin of pride by insisting that she can handle a dangerous and deranged patient, even though she has been warned to distance herself from that patient, who comes close to killing her. Jarred back to reality, Hepburn has learned the lesson of false pride, and, now humbled, she is sent to the Congo, but, her wish to treat the black natives there is sidetracked when she is assigned to nurse European whites in a hospital run by no-nonsense physician Finch. Hepburn nevertheless accepts her lot and works hard to bring relief to patients as well as to be one with God's will and purpose. Overworked, she grows ill, suffering a bout of tuberculosis, from which she recovers with Finch's help. For his part, Finch believes that Hepburn brought about her own illness in an effort to avoid being sent back to the convent in Belgium and to avoid its rigid regimen. She is then assigned to accompany an official back to her native land and, after she arrives in Belgium, WWII has just begun and she is sent to work in a hospital in Holland. She witnesses firsthand the brutality of the invading Nazis and, after Jagger is killed by these invaders for aiding some fugitive refugees, Hepburn resolves to become part of the underground fighting the Germans. She struggles with this decision, realizing that she must now renounce her religious vows in order to fight her country's enemies and, after her vow is annulled with Evans' sanction, she is shown leaving the convent all alone and as dedicated to fighting the oppressors as she was earlier dedicated to her religious calling. Pantheon director Zinnemann superbly helms this stirring tale with simple scenes and without visual embellishments, eschewing melodrama and eliciting impactful, reserved performances from Hepburn, Evans, Finch and the rest of the fine cast in what is most likely the best film ever made about this subject. The film was nominated for six Oscars as Best Picture and for the director, screenplay, photography, music and Hepburn as Best Actress, and, incredibly, won none, but this was the year that **Ben-Hur**, 1959, swept the Oscars. The film, however, was a great success, gleaning more than $6 million at the box office in its initial release and remained Hepburn's favorite film. **p**, Henry Blanke; **d**, Fred Zinnemann; **cast**, Audrey Hepburn, Peter Finch, Edith Evans, Peggy Ashcroft, Dean Jagger, Mildred Dunnock, Beatrice Straight, Patricia Collinge, Rosalie Crutchley, Barbara O'Neil, Margaret Phillips, Patricia Bosworth, Colleen Dewhurst, Lionel Jeffries; **w**, Robert Anderson (based on the book by Kathryn C. Hulme); **c**, Franz Planer (Technicolor); **m**, Franz Waxman; **ed**, Walter Thompson; **art d**, Alexander Trauner; **set d**, Maurice Barnathan.

Nurse Betty ★★★ 2000; Germany/U.S.; 110m; Gramercy Pictures/USA Films; Color; Comedy/Crime; Children: Unacceptable (MPAA: R); **DVD**. Zellweger gives a fine performance as a Kansas City waitress with aspirations of becoming a nurse, but she suffers a setback in her life when her husband, a car salesman and loser, is murdered. This sends her into shock and she imagines herself to be the former fiancée of her handsome soap opera idol, Kinnear. She also believes the soap opera is real life, so she goes to Los Angeles to find the hospital where the soap opera character works as a cardiologist. Meanwhile, her husband's murderers, a father and son team, Freeman and Rock, are looking for drugs her husband stole, and Zellweger does not know that those drugs are hidden in the trunk of her car. Freeman is an aging hit man, who planned to retire, but his life becomes complicated when he falls in love with Zellweger. Zellweger and Freeman are both living dreams, but through several strange events, those dreams happily become reality. Songs include "Whatever Will Be, Will Be (Que Sera, Sera)" (Jay Livingston, Ray Evans), "Don't You Know" (Bobby Worth), "Slowly" (Otis Blackwell), "Poor Little Fool" (Sharon Sheeley), "I Won't Be Home No More" (Hank Williams, Sr.), "The Cattle Call" (Tex Owens), "Cold Morning" (Kitty Kat Stew), "Lady Shave" (Sigurdur Kjartansson, Daniel Agust Haraldsson, Birgir Thorarinsson, Magnus Gudmundsson), "If U Don't Want None" (T. Stevens, Kevin Gardner), "That Lonesome Moon" (Wayne Perry, Jerry Marcum), "Just a Touch of Love" (Mark Adams, Dan Webster, Mark Hicks, Raymond Turner, Thomas Locket, Steve Arrington), "Skunk Walk," "Double Cross"

Morgan Freeman and Renee Zellweger in *Nurse Betty,* 2000.

(Neal Sugarman), "Cuando Me Quieres" (Frankie Pine), "Little Lovey Dovey" (Wayne Perry, Tommy Smith). Violence, gutter language, and a scene of sexuality prohibit viewing by children. **p**, Steve Golin, Gail Mutrux; **d**, Neil LaBute; **cast**, Renee Zellweger, Morgan Freeman, Chris Rock, Greg Kinnear, Aaron Eckhart, Tia Texada, Crispin Glover, Pruitt Taylor Vince, Allison Janney, Kathleen Wilhoite; **w**, John C. Richards, James Flamberg (based on a story by Richards); **c**, Jean Yves Escoffier; **m**, Rolfe Kent; **ed**, Joel Plotch, Steven Weisberg; **prod d**, Charles Breen; **art d**, Gary Diamond; **set d**, Jeffrey Kushon; **spec eff**, Larz Anderson.

Nurse Edith Cavell ★★★ 1939; U.S.; 95m; Imperadio/RKO; B/W; Biographical Drama; Children: Unacceptable; **DVD; VHS**. This stirring biopic about English nurse Edith Cavell (1865-1915), wonderfully played by Neagle, shows Naegle working in a small private hospital in German-occupied Brussels during World War I (1914-1918). When the son of a recently deceased patient escapes from a German prisoner-of-war camp, she helps him reach Holland and safety. This leads her to Oliver, a local noblewoman, who is the escaped prisoner's grandmother, and others, who have formed an underground organization to help Belgian, French, British and other solders escape as well. Neagle is warned not to continue her underground activities, knowing that, if caught, she will forfeit her life. She nevertheless continues to smuggle Allied servicemen to freedom and is finally caught by the Germans and executed (in a dramatic firing squad scene). Well made and with standout performances from Neagle and the rest of the cast, this film was not a box office success, but it remains the best account about this legendary British heroine. A silent version was made in 1916. **p&d**, Herbert Wilcox; **cast**, Anna Neagle, Edna May Oliver, George Sanders, May Robson, Zasu Pitts, H.B. Warner, Sophie Stewart, Mary Howard, Robert Coote, Martin Kosleck; **w**, Michael Hogan (based on the novel *Dawn* by Capt. Reginald Berkeley); **c**, Joseph H. August, Freddie Young; **m**, Anthony Collins; **ed**, Elmo Williams; **art d**, Lawrence P. Williams; **spec eff**, Vernon L. Walker.

The Nut ★★★ 1921 (silent); U.S.; 74m; Douglas Fairbanks/UA; B/W; Comedy; Children: Acceptable; **DVD**. Fairbanks, in his last comedy before turning to action films, plays an eccentric inventor in this entertaining comedy. He tries to interest wealthy people in the plan of his society girlfriend, De La Motte, one designed to help needy children relocate from poor neighborhoods to upscale communities. She believes underprivileged children can benefit from living in the homes of the rich. Fairbanks' help involves hosting a party in which he imitates famous historical people and also Charles Chaplin (1889-1977), these impressive impersonations actually performed by Chaplin himself, who

Jada Pinkett and Eddie Murphy in *The Nutty Professor,* 1996.

was a close friend of Fairbanks, and who had formed United Artists Studio with him, Mary Pickford (wife of Fairbanks), and master filmmaker D. W. Griffith, only two years earlier. **p**, Douglas Fairbanks; **d**, Theodore Reed; **cast**, Fairbanks, Marguerite De La Motte, William Lowery, Gerald Pring, Morris Hughes, Barbara La Marr, Frank Campeau, Jeanne Carpenter, Charles Stevens; **w**, William Parker, Elton Thomas (Fairbanks), Lotta Woods (based on a story by Kenneth Davenport); **c**, William McGann, Harry Thorpe, Charles Warrington; **art d**, Edward M. Langley.

Nuts ★★★ 1987; U.S.; 116m; WB; Color; Drama; Children: Unacceptable (MPAA: R); **DVD**; **VHS**. Streisand plays a call girl, who kills a customer in self-defense, but is accused of murder. Her parents try to have her declared mentally incompetent while she stands trial, but she fights for the right to defend herself in court. She doesn't trust anyone, including her court-appointed lawyer, Dreyfuss, and is disruptive during court hearings. We learn she had a miserable childhood, which eventually led to her embracing a life of prostitution. Her father, Malden, sexually abused her when she was younger, and her mother, Stapleton, is a basket case. Dreyfuss gets her off, but she remains what she has always been, an unhappy hooker. Songs: "Here We Are At Last" (Barbra Streisand, Richard Baskin), "Sindhi-Bhairavi" (traditional raga). **p**, Barbra Streisand, Martin Ritt; **d**, Ritt; **cast**, Streisand, Richard Dreyfuss, Maureen Stapleton, Karl Malden, Eli Wallach, Robert Webber, James Whitmore, Leslie Nielsen, William Prince, Dakin Matthews; **w**, Tom Topor, Darryl Ponicsan, Alvin Sargent, Christopher Wilkinson (based on the play by Topor); **c**, Andrzej Bartkowiak; **m**, Streisand; **ed**, Sidney Levin; **prod d**, Joel Schiller; **art d**, Eric Orbom; **set d**, Anne McCulley; **spec eff**, Larry Fuentes.

The Nutty Professor ★★★ 1963; U.S.; 107m; PAR; Color; Comedy; Children: Cautionary; **DVD**; **VHS**. Lewis is very funny in one of his best comedies where he transforms himself from a nerdy, buck-toothed chemistry professor at a small college to a suave, outgoing ladies' man, attracting the most beautiful girls on campus by developing a serum that changes his personality (a comic version of *The Strange Case of Dr. Jekyll and Mr. Hyde*). He falls hard for Stevens, a pretty blonde student attending his class, but it seems that she only has eyes for members of the college football team. Lewis tries to build up his physique by body-building, but he proves to be nothing more than a miserable weakling (when lifting some barbells, his arms become stretched by several feet in an amazing special effects shot). He then resorts to what he knows best, chemistry, and whips up a potent potion that, after swilling down this concoction, alters his physical appearance and personality. He is no longer Professor Julius Ferris Kelp, but is now a man about

town called Buddy Love. He adorns himself in a "hip" wardrobe, slick-backed hair, and then appears at the Purple Pit, the nightclub where all the "in" campus crowd assembles at night. There he wows the girls with his singing and entertaining, including Stevens, but his new personality broadens to the point where he becomes overbearing, obnoxious and repulsively pretentious. His imperfect formula betrays him as it changes his voice back to that of the professor's when it begins to wear off and where Buddy Love makes a hasty retreat only to be replaced by nerdy Professor Kelp, who is left to explain such weird vanishings. When he again appears as Buddy Love at the big dance, his faulty formula again deserts him and he changes back to Professor Kelp in front of the entire student body. He later explains to his students that one cannot change themselves in life and must accept what they are if they are going to be truly loved by anyone. This is a message not needed by Stevens, who has always loved Lewis as Professor Kelp and tells him so as they plan to wed at the finish of this very funny film. *Author's Note*: Lewis supposedly parodied his former partner, Dean Martin, when enacting the part of Buddy Love, but he was really enacting the real Jerry Lewis, who, in later years, became, according to some critics, a pompous, self-aggrandizing and rather unappealing character when appearing on talk shows and telethons. In this film, art truly imitates life. **p**, Jerry Lewis, Ernest D. Glucksman; **d**, Lewis; **cast**, Lewis, Stella Stevens, Del Moore, Kathleen Freeman, Med Flory, Howard Morris, Elvia Allman, Milton Frome, Buddy Lester, David Landfield, Skip Ward, Henry Gibson, Richard Kiel, William Smith, Les Brown and His Band of Renown; **w**, Lewis, Bill Richmond; **c**, W. Wallace Kelley (Technicolor); **m**, Walter Scharf; **ed**, John Woodcock; **art d**, Hal Pereira, Walter Tyler; **set d**, Sam Comer, Robert Benton; **spec eff**, Paul K. Lerpae.

The Nutty Professor ★★★ 1996; U.S.; 95m; UNIV; Color; Comedy; Children: Unacceptable (MPAA: PG-13); **DVD**; **VHS**. Murphy plays an obese, black college science professor, who falls for a new graduate student, Pinkett, but is frustrated by his extra-extra-large suit size. He has been working on a DNA restructuring that he hopes has slimming qualities and drinks the formula. Zap! He slims down immediately, but, in the process, the potion changes him into a lecherous ladies' man called Buddy Love. Now his romantic problems really balloon. After a lot of funny business, he goes back to his old self and size. (Murphy was criticized for racial profiling in that he depicted the professor's family as equally obese black characters, all repulsively shown in scenes where they repeatedly pass gas at dinner while disgustingly gorging themselves.) This is a remake of the 1963 Jerry Lewis movie of the same name. Songs: "Macho Man" (Jacques Morali, Peter Whitehead, Victor Willis, Henri Belolo); "Super Bad," "I Got You (I Feel Good)" (James Brown); "This Is How We Do It" (Montell Jordan, Oji Pierce, Ricky Walters); "Somethin' for Da Honeyz" (Pierce, Doug Rasheed, Claydes Smith, Dennis Thomas, George Brown, Robert Bell, Robert Mickens, Richard Westfield, Alton Taylor, Khalis Bayyan); "Emotionally in Love" (Valerie George, Kyle West); "Bounce 2 This" (Jordan, Schappell); "Close the Door" (Kenneth Gamble, Leon Huff); "I'm So Excited," "Boys Will Be Boys" (Jolyon Skinner, Vit Ren); "Homework" (Danielle LoPresti, Dan Serafini); "Sexyenamutha-Forget It" (LoPresti, Worthy Davis, Andre Berry); "Strokin'" (Clarence Carter); "In the Mood" (Joe Garland, Andy Razsaf); "Little Brown Jug" (Joseph Winner); "Lovin' You" (Dick Rudolph, Minnie Riperton). Crude toilet humor and sexual references prohibit viewing by children. **p**, Brian Grazer, Russell Simmons, James D. Brubaker; **d**, Tom Shadyac; **cast**, Eddie Murphy, Jada Pinkett Smith, James Coburn, Larry Miller, Dave Chappelle, John Ales, Patricia Wilson, Jamal Mixon, Nichole McAuley, Hamilton Von Watts; **w**, Shadyac, David Sheffield, Barry W. Blaustein, Steve Oedekerk (based on the 1963 screen play by Jerry Lewis, Bill Richmond); **c**, Julio Macat; **m**, David Newman; **ed**, Don Zimmerman; **prod d**, William Elliott; **art d**, Greg Papalia; **set d**, Kathryn Peters; **spec eff**, Burt Dalton, Rodney Byrd.

O Brother, Where Art Thou? ★★★★★ 2000; U.K./France/U.S.; 106m; Touchstone/UNIV; Color; Comedy; Children: Unacceptable (MPAA: PG-13); **DVD**; **VHS**. This superb comedy takes its title from a mythical film mentioned in Preston Sturges' classic comedy **Sullivan's Travels**, 1941, a serious, dramatic film about the Great Depression that director Joel McCrea wants to make, instead of the comedies that have made him a success. In truth, the Coen brothers, who produced and directed this film, did make the film, but it was nevertheless a rip-roaring comedy and a masterpiece to boot. The film opens in the year 1937 to show three uneducated crooks, Clooney, Nelson, and Turturro as members of a Mississippi chain gang and where urgent events demand that they immediately escape. Clooney tells his two friends that they must make good their escape as soon as possible since the more than $1.2 million that he stole years earlier from an armored car is hidden in a valley that is undergoing a hydroelectric project and will be flooded in four days to create the Arkabutla Lake. The trio makes good their escape, traveling on foot to the dilapidated farm of Turturro's cousin, Collison, who rids the fugitives of their chains before they bed down in Collison's barn. Collison, however, to obtain needed money, informs on the convicts to receive a reward. Sheriff Von Bargen and his men show up, firing at the barn and setting it afire, but the desperate fugitives escape with the help of Collison's son, Gasaway. Trudging on foot, the three men hear some singing in the distance and discover a group of parishioners gathered at a river where Nelson and Turturro feel the need to be baptized and they submit themselves to a river dousing while Clooney eyes their actions with cynicism, not believing for a minute that such old-fashioned religious rites can save anyone's soul. Continuing their journey, the trio encounters King, a black singer and guitarist, giving him a ride in a vehicle they have stolen. King tells them that he has exchanged his soul for the guitar, the Devil being a white man, who looks very much like Sheriff Von Bargen. They arrive at a rural radio station operated by a blind DJ, Root, and, as King plays his guitar, they record a song titled "I Am a Man of Constant Sorrow," calling their group the Soggy Bottom Boys. After they depart, Durning, along with his slavish son, Pentecost, arrives at the station where Durning plans to do some "politicking" over the airways and where he hears the song recorded by the fugitives. This song, unknown to the so-called Soggy Bottom Boys, becomes an enormous state-wide hit, making them living legends. (The scene in which Clooney, Nelson and Turturro record that song is only one of many sidesplitting sequences in this hilarious film, with close-ups of their florid, pop-eyed expressions as they hammily posture that tune with the amateur exuberance and ebullience of country music fanatics.) After the stolen car in which they are traveling is discovered by police, the fugitives take to walking and then meet up with notorious bank robber George "Baby Face" Nelson (Lester Joseph Gillis, 1908-1934), played by Badalucco, who robs a bank and then takes them for a wild ride, blasting lawmen with his submachine gun as he eludes these pursuers (and acting more of a lunatic than the kill-crazy Nelson ever was in real life, and who had been actually killed by FBI agents three years before the setting of this film, but facts are incidental, if not distracting, in this almost surrealistic production). While they sit chatting with Badalucco by an outdoor fire, the celebrated bank robber appears distracted and bored with his life of crime, giving the fugitives a wad of money and then wandering off into the forest. The trio, when coming upon a river, are enticed by the siren sounds of three ethereal, beautiful women, ostensibly witches, who mesmerize them and seduce them, these three vixens undoubtedly representing the Stygian Witches of ancient Greek mythology (from the *Odyssey*), but where they have disguised their hideous features (the original three witches had but one eye by which to see and one tooth by which to eat among them). Continuing his journey alone, Clooney meets Goodman while he is resting beneath a tree. Goodman is an affable, garrulous, one-eyed Bible salesman, or so he pretends, who tricks Clooney and overpowers him, beating him

John Turturro, Tim Blake Nelson and George Clooney in *O Brother, Where Art Thou?*, 2000.

to a pulp and stealing his money. (Goodman, too, is an allegorical figure in that he represents the one-eyed Cyclopes called Polyphemus as described in the *Odyssey*.) Having been separated from Turturro and Nelson, Clooney and Nelson reunite and later arrive in a small town to meet with Hunter, Clooney's estranged wife, who tells Clooney that she wants no more to do with him and has even told his two small daughters that he has been killed in a train crash. She informs Clooney that she plans to marry McKinnon, who is the political manager of Duvall, the pompous and conniving opposition candidate running for the governorship against longtime incumbent Durning. (Duvall claims to be the reform candidate, using a broom as his political symbol.) Clooney and Nelson then go to a movie theater where they learn that Turturro has been captured and jailed after the river sirens turned him over to the authorities. They break Turturro out of jail and Clooney then admits that there is no great treasure hidden and waiting for them and that he only told that tale to get Nelson and Turturro to help him escape the chain gang so that he could return to Hunter and reconcile with her. Turturro explodes with rage since he had only a few weeks left to serve on the chain gang and that his escape has now added fifty years to that sentence (and this tells the viewer just how dumb Turturro truly is). The trio depart only to stumble on a terrifying vision that night when they come across a secret Ku Klux Klan meeting where a huge crowd wearing white hooded robes are about to lynch King and where they see that the leader (the Grand Wizard) is Duvall. Disguising themselves as KKK members wearing hooded robes, they become the honor guard, but they are identified by Goodman, who is one of the KKK leaders. While chaos ensues, Clooney cuts the wires holding up a towering burning cross that collapses, burning to death several KKK members, including the evil Goodman. The trio, along with King, escape during the melee. Clooney then convinces (as he always does throughout this southern saga) Turturro, Nelson and King to help him win back his wife by sneaking into a large political rally where Duvall and Durning are scheduled to speak. Clooney finds Hunter and tries to persuade her that he has found a new and legitimate calling in life as a singer, but she ignores him. He, along with his friends, then commandeer the stage and sing a country tune and they are recognized as the celebrated Soggy Bottom Boys, the group that everyone has been looking for ever since their hit record took the state by musical storm. Duvall recognizes them from their appearance at the KKK meeting and denounces them, but the crowd turns against him, especially after he is identified as a KKK leader and Duvall is promptly seized, tarred and feathered and run out of town on a rail. Durning, seizing the political turn of events and while all is being aired on the radio, takes the stage to endorse the singing group and, as governor, grants them all full pardons. Hunter tells Clooney that she is taking him back, but only if he finds the original ring he gave to her. He, Nelson

Tim Blake Nelson, John Turturro and George Clooney in *O Brother, Where Art Thou?*, **2000.**

and Turturro then go on a quest for that ring, but, before they depart they see Badalucco in the custody of a mob and being dragged to the local jail. The trio arrives at the valley where Clooney claimed he had hidden the imagined treasure, but they are captured by Sheriff Von Bargen, who ignores their claims that they have been pardoned by the governor and plans to shortcut the courts by promptly hanging them. Their coffins are placed near the place of their hanging, but just before the three are strung up, they hear the rush and crash of cascading water that is now flooding the valley and they are saved while Von Bargen and his men are swept away. The trio survives by floating on top of their own coffins, Turturro and Nelson thanking the Lord for their deliverance. Clooney dismisses Providence as being instrumental in their survival until he sees an old prophecy fulfilled when viewing a cow standing atop a floating house and where the ring he so long ago gave to Hunter is found in the drawer of a floating desk. Clooney is later seen walking freely down a street in his home town with Hunter and his two daughters, but still has troubles as the ring he has given Hunter, she says, is not the one that he originally gave her and that she wants only that one. Clooney knows that he now has an impossible task as that ring is somewhere at the bottom of Arkabutla Lake and this is where this wild fantasy ends. The Coen brothers present a bizarre but utterly captivating tale, employing many eye-popping visual effects and hurrying this wild romp along at a dizzying pace but still offering well-developed characters who are more like cartoon caricatures than real-life persons. The performances from Clooney, Nelson, Turturro and the rest of the fine cast are captivating in every sense of their weird, down home, backcountry portrayals—all humorously uneducated, unsophisticated and unenlightened and headed for doom until Fate or God Almighty takes a hand to set things right. The script is brilliantly appropriate to the locale, period, and the swamp water mentality of its characters, especially that of Clooney, who delivers high-minded and airy speeches in an attempt to present erudition to impress himself as being more important than his dim-witted pals. Produced on a budget of $26 million, the film was a great box office success, yielding more than $71 million in its initial release and was especially popular with folk, bluegrass and country music fans. Songs: "I Am a Man of Constant Sorrow" (traditional); "Po Lazarus," " Tom Devil," "Didn't Leave Nobody But the Baby" (Alan Lomax); "Big Rock Candy Mountain" (1928; Harry McClintock); "You Are My Sunshine" (1940; Jimmie Davis, Charles Mitchell); "Down to the River to Pray" (traditional); "Hard Time Killing Floor Blues" (1931; Skip James); "Keep on the Sunny Side" (1931; A. P. Carter); "I'll Fly Away" (1929; Albert E. Brumley); "Admiration" (1915; William Tyers); "O Death" (traditional); "In the Highways" (Maybelle Carter); "What Is Sweeter" (M. K. Jerome); "In the Jailhouse Now" (1928; Jimmie Rodgers), "Angel Band' (Ralph Stanley); "I Am Weary (Let Me Rest)"

(Pete Roberts); "Lonesome Valley" (traditional); "Indian War Whoop" (Hoyt Ming). *Author's Note*: Clooney reportedly accepted the leading role in this film without reading the script as he was a big fan of the films produced by the Coen brothers. The film employs for the first time the use of digital color correction, which gives the film a somewhat sepia-toned appearance throughout, which was also applied in **Chicken Run**, 2000, a film released shortly after this production. It was shot on location in summer 1999 outside Florence, South Carolina, and Canton, Mississippi. Many films have profiled chain gangs and similar prison systems, notably **Bite the Bullet**, 1975; **The Buccaneer**, 1938; **Carbine Williams**, 1952; **Convicts**, 1991; **Cool Hand Luke**, 1967; **The Defiant Ones**, 1958; **Gone with the Wind**, 1939; **Hallelujah!**, 1929; **I Am a Fugitive from a Chain Gang**, 1932; **Nevada Smith**, 1966; **Papillon**, 1973; **Passage to Marseilles**, 1944; **Strange Cargo**, 1940; **Sullivan's Travels**, 1941; **Take the Money and Run**, 1969; **There Will Be Blood**, 2007; **Tramp, Tramp, Tramp**, 1926; and **Under the Gun**, 1951. For a complete list of fifty-one such films, see Chain Gangs in the Subject Index of this work, Volume II. **p**, Joel and Ethan Coen, John Cameron; **d&w**, Coen brothers (based on the epic poem "The Odyssey" by Homer); **cast**, George Clooney, John Turturro, Tim Blake Nelson, John Goodman, Holly Hunter, Chris Thomas King, Charles Durning, Daniel Von Bargen; Del Pentecost, Michael Badalucco, Ray McKinnon, Wayne Duvall, J. R. Horne, Stephen Root, Brian Reddy, Frank Collison, Quinn Gasaway; **c**, Roger Deakins; **m**, T Bone Burnett; **ed**, Tricia Cooke, Roderick Jaynes (Coen brothers); **prod d**, Dennis Gassner; **art d**, Richard Johnson; **set d**, Nancy Haigh; **spec eff**, Peter Chesney.

O. Henry's Full House ★★★ 1952; U.S.; 117m; FOX; B/W; Adventure/Drama; Children: Cautionary; **DVD**. Few films offering a compendium of separate stories have proven successful, but this lively collection from short story writer O. Henry (William Sydney Porter, 1868-1910) is one of those fine exceptions where all the five separate tales are compactly and expertly shown and enacted by stellar casts, each helmed by superlative directors. Narrated (6 minutes) by the brilliant novelist and Nobel Prize winner John Steinbeck, the first tale, "The Cop and the Anthem" (19 minutes), has the inimitable Laughton as a fussy tramp, who demands his creature comforts, despite his inability to pay for anything. Since winter is approaching and Laughton routinely spends that bone-chilling season within the confines of a warm cell, he begins to plan for that incarceration by purposely committing some offense that will comfortably land him in the pokey. Fate intervenes, however, preventing every abuse Laughton commits from resulting in his arrest. He even attempts a brazen display of mashing by making untoward advances to a pretty blonde, Monroe (in one of her early small parts), but it is Monroe, not Laughton, who is pinched when she is charged with streetwalking. Laughton interprets these strange occurrences as the Hand of God. He goes to a church, and, on bended knees, promises to change the course of his worthless life, to seek employment, and become an upstanding citizen, but when he leaves the church, he is, ironically, arrested for vagrancy, and while vainly protesting, he is bundled off to the hoosegow. In "The Clarion Call" (22 minutes), dedicated lawman Robertson is compelled to arrest old friend Widmark, a charming, conniving crook, and where the two have a battle of wits until the long arm of the law reaches out to bring justice about. "The Last Leaf" (23 minutes) has pretty Baxter dying in a cold-water flat, gazing out the window to see a vine with leaves, and, as she watches each leaf wither, die and be blown away by the wintry winds, she concludes that she will die when the last leaf on that vine is also swept away. She confides this belief to her worried sister, Peters, who imparts her sister's terrible forebodings to elderly artist Ratoff. As the winter deepens, all the leaves, except one, are gone, but that one remaining leaf stubbornly clings to the vine surviving the bitter season, Baxter looking upon it as the symbol of her own struggling life, and its indefatigable presence gives her hope and, eventually, strength enough to fend off death. She recuperates and gets well, only to discover that, upon close inspection, the leaf is not real, but a well-painted replication that Ratoff has rendered, one that he has painted in the bitter cold of night while standing on a ladder against the wall opposite Baxter's window, a courageous hardship that has taken his own life. "The Ransom of Red Chief" (26 minutes) offers a hilarious sequence where two small-time and extremely inept crooks, Allen and Levant, down to their last few dollars and with little prospects, decide to kidnap the child of a well-to-do farmer and hold the boy for ransom. They abduct Aaker, but find to their amazement that his parents have no intention to paying a dime to have their child returned, and, in fact, are relieved that he has been kidnapped. These mystifying actions are soon made clear when Aaker repeatedly turns the tables on them, making Allen and Levant *his* prisoners as Aaker enacts his role of an Indian leader named Red Chief. The would-be kidnappers become so unhappy that they finally pay the parents every dime they have in order that Aaker's indifferent parents take back their monster of a child. In the final sequence, "The Gift of the Magi" (21 minutes), Granger and Crain are a young happily married couple struggling to make ends meet and, at Christmas, they have so little money that it appears that they will not be able to afford to buy each other a present. Crain resolves to make a great sacrifice by selling her luxuriant, long hair, which Granger so much admires, in order that she can buy him an attractive watch chain to go with his only prized possession, his gold-plated watch, which he keeps in the pocket of his vest. She sells her hair and then hides her cropped head in a kerchief. When Granger arrives home, he has a present for Crain, beautiful hair adornments she has long admired in a store window, but he is astounded to see that her long hair is gone. Crain tells him that she needed to sell her hair to buy his gift, and assuring him that her hair will grow back. Crain then gives Granger the watch chain and she then discovers that he has sold his watch to buy her the gift, and both laugh at the irony of their mutual sacrifices. Well made and superbly acted, these poignant and ironic tales will amuse and warm the heart of any viewer. *Author's Note*: Hecht told this author that "I worked on one of the O. Henry stories in that Fox picture, and, to tell you the truth, I did it because I always admired Henry, who was a great reporter. He got into trouble by embezzling funds from a bank where he was working as a teller to pay for his wife's medical expenses [she suffered from tuberculosis, which claimed her life], and then hid out in Honduras where he wrote *Cabbages and Kings* and he was the first to describe a downtrodden South American country as a "banana republic" when writing that amazing work. He finally returned to the U.S. and turned himself in, and got a five-year prison stretch where he met a lot of the colorful crooks he would later write about, including the two bozos who abducted a boy to get some ransom money, and where that boy made their lives a hell on earth until they took the kid back to his parents, who reluctantly accepted him, and that was the story I worked on ["The Ransom of Red Chief"]. Henry had a great influence on my own writing. I read him when I was a kid, and loved the way he profiled his characters, the seats of their pants all worn out, scheming for a buck, and believing that they could all get a piece of the American pie if they used their heads. When he got out of prison, he changed his name from William Sydney Porter to O. Henry, and went where all his best stories were to be found in those days—in hotel lobbies, saloons, baseball parks, and in the streets, especially in New York. He really loved that burg. I told myself that 'someday I am going to meet this man…there is much to learn from him,' but he died [in 1910] a year before I got my first newspaper job in Chicago in 1911. Anyone who wants to learn how to write about real people ought to read his stuff. He knew what was funny. He knew what was sad. And he knew what was true in the human heart. He's right up there with Mark Twain and Jack London." **p**, André Hakim; "The Clarion Call," **d**, Henry Hathaway, **cast**, Dale Robertson, Richard Widmark, **w**, O. Henry, Richard L. Breen; "The Ransom of Red Chief," **d**, Howard Hawks, **cast**, Fred Allen, Oscar Levant, **w**, O. Henry, Ben Hecht, Nunnally Johnson, Charles Lederer; "The Gift of the Magi," **d**, Henry King, **cast**, Jeanne Crain, Farley Granger, **w**, O. Henry, Walter Bullock; "The Cop and the Anthem," **d**, Henry Koster, **cast**, Charles

Anne Baxter in "The Last Leaf" segment of *O. Henry's Full House*, 1952.

Laughton, Marilyn Monroe, David Wayne, **w**, O. Henry, Lamar Trotti; "The Last Leaf," **d**, Jean Negulesco, **cast**, Anne Baxter, Jean Peters, Gregory Ratoff, **w**, O. Henry, Ivan Goff, Ben Roberts; narrator: John Steinbeck; **c**, Lloyd Ahern, Lucien Ballard, Milton R. Krasner, Joseph MacDonald; **m**, Alfred Newman; **ed**, Nick DeMaggio, Barbara McLean, William B. Murphy; **art d**, Chester Gore, Addison Hehr, Richard Irvine, Lyle R. Wheeler, Joseph C. Wright; **set d**, Claude E. Carpenter, Thomas Little, Bruce MacDonald, Fred J. Rode.

O Lucky Man ★★★ 1973; U.K./U.S.; 166m; Memorial **DVD**; **VHS**. Enterprises/WB; Color; Fantasy/Comedy; Children: Unacceptable. McDowell is a young salesman for a coffee company, and this surrealistic film follows his adventures in England and Scotland. He soon learns that, in order to be a successful salesman, he has to abandon his principles, as any good used car salesman would. At the same time, he maintains a detached idealism that distances himself from the greedy and dishonest others in the world. He falls in love with Mirren, daughter of Richardson, who is an evil industrialist, and becomes his personal assistant. After many misadventures he is in a casting call for a film and winds up at a party dancing with all the cast in this film. Songs: "O Lucky Man!," "Poor People," "Sell Sell," "Pastoral," "Arrival," "Look Over Your Shoulder," "Justice," "My Home Town," "Changes" (Alan Price); "Palm Court Theme" (Roy Gubby); "Zingara" (Walter Warren); A bizarre and entertaining film, but too mature and offbeat for viewing by children. **p**, Michael Medwin, Lindsay Anderson; **d**, Anderson; **cast**, Malcolm McDowell, Ralph Richardson, Rachel Roberts, Arthur Lowe, Helen Mirren, Graham Crowden, Peter Jeffrey, Dandy Nichols, Mona Washbourne, Philip Stone; **w**, David Sherwin (based on an idea by McDowell); **c**, Miroslav Ondrícek (Technicolor); **m**, Alan Price; **ed**, David Gladwell; **prod d**, Jocelyn Herbert; **art d**, Alan Withy; **set d**, Harry Cordwell; **spec eff**, John Stears.

O.S.S. ★★★★ 1946; U.S.; 105m; PAR; B/W; Spy Drama; Children: Unacceptable; **DVD**; **VHS**. Exciting and suspenseful, this well-crafted espionage tale shows the operations of the WWII intelligence agency in microcosm as it details the mission of a single unit of O.S.S. (the U.S. Office of Strategic Services) in WWII (1939-1945). The film begins by showing several volunteers being recruited for the service, including Fitzgerald, an attractive, young sculptress specially selected because she has spent time in France studying art; Ladd, a decisive young business executive with public relations experience; Benedict, a rugged young man, who has been a hockey player; and Beddoe, a middle-aged man, who has been a salesman of railroad equipment. They are trained in the spying arts of deception, communication and physical defense, all of them undergoing demanding courses in the use of codes, disguises, mar-

Geraldine Fitzgerald and Alan Ladd in *O.S.S.*, 1946.

tial arts and secreted lethal weapons. They are proficient in speaking and writing French and even taught the European idiosyncrasies of etiquette. For instance, they are taught to always hold a fork with the left hand and to cut food with the right hand when eating. Knowles, a commander in O.S.S., and who recruited Fitzgerald, is most concerned about her safety as he is in love with her. Ladd, too, has fallen for her, and feels that she is not really up to performing a man's job, but Fitzgerald proves in training that she is as clever and effective as any male agent. The unit is then given its mission: to destroy an important railway tunnel in the French railway system. They are dropped at night by parachute into France. Fitzgerald establishes herself as an artist operating a small art supplies shop and she meets Hoyt, an arrogant, suave German staff officer with illusions about art. He is attracted to her and she agrees to sculpt him, creating a bust of him. When she learns that Hoyt will be taking a train that will go through the tunnel her unit is assigned to destroy, she places plastic explosives inside the bust, but when Hoyt picks up this piece of art, he insists that Fitzgerald accompany him on that train trip and she reluctantly agrees. While on the train with Hoyt, Fitzgerald learns that French partisans have stalled the train in the very tunnel that is to be destroyed, but her life is saved when Ladd manages to get her off the train before the plastic explosives ignite and blow up the train and severely damages the tunnel. Instead of showing gratitude, Fitzgerald severely criticizes Ladd for disobeying orders by ignoring his own mission to save her life, telling him: "Never come back for me again! Do you understand? Never come back!" Ladd and Fitzgerald then leave the area while joining a crowd of refugees, but they are later stopped by Gestapo agent Vermilyea. Instead of arresting them, the corrupt Vermilyea takes money from Ladd in exchange for secret information that Ladd then gives to Benedict, the communications agent of the group, and who transmits that information in code via his shortwave radio. Fitzgerald's life then becomes endangered when Hoyt reappears. He has survived the blast in the tunnel and now wears an eye-patch over one eye, which he lost in the explosion, and one side of his face is horribly scarred. He is consumed with vengeance, living for only one purpose, to track down and kill Fitzgerald. He almost traps Fitzgerald and Ladd, but they escape and where Hoyt is left with a consolation prize by identifying Vermilyea as a Nazi turncoat. Ladd and Fitzgerald reunite briefly with Beddoe, but he soon betrays his identity when eating in a restaurant where he makes the telltale mistake of using his fork with his right hand and is promptly arrested. Ladd and Fitzgerald then find a brief safe haven in a farmhouse owned by Dean, who lives with her grandson, Driscoll, and they then play host to a group of drunken German soldiers, one of whom is Webb, another O.S.S. agent working undercover, who gives important information to Ladd regarding the German defenses that may be used against the forthcoming Allied in-

vasion at Normandy. Ladd goes to a distant field and sends a message via a shortwave radio to a circling British plane, relaying the information he has gotten from Webb, but Driscoll arrives to beg Ladd to return to the farmhouse where Gestapo agents and Hoyt have arrested Fitzgerald and Dean. He recalls Fitzgerald's demands that he never go back for her and this time he remains at his post until he has completed sending his message. He then races to the farmhouse to find Fitzgerald and Dean gone and realizes that he has lost Fitzgerald forever. Ladd sits in a chair and weeps over losing the woman he loves. In the final and dynamic scene, Ladd stands at a French crossroad next to a tree with Knowles, his O.S.S. commander, to watch American troops march by, along with their jeeps and tanks, these forces fresh from their successful Normandy landings, a powerful scene that signals the success of that landing based upon the sacrifices made by heroic O.S.S. agents. Director Pichel does a great job in presenting this harrowing tale, maintaining a brisk pace, and Ladd, Fitzgerald, Hoyt and the rest of the cast are all standouts in their memorable roles. The attention to the techniques employed by espionage agents is fascinatingly portrayed in this superlative film, one that also fully develops its courageous characters and incisively depicts their emotional states of mind while under great stress in risking their lives every hour of the day. ***Author's Note***: Ladd, who is exceptional in this film, had been on the outs with Paramount executives after refusing a number of uninspiring scripts, but he immediately accepted his role in this film after reading its script and with the promise from Paramount that he would next be starred in the lead role of **The Great Gatsby**, 1949. When Geraldine Fitzgerald heard about this, she went to Ladd and said: "Oh, do it, do **The Great Gatsby**. You're perfect for it. You're exactly what F. Scott Fitzgerald had in mind." Ladd was reticent in thinking about that challenging role, saying: "I won't be able to do it because I can't act, you know." In this he was wrong. He *was* perfect in that role, playing that character better than anyone before or after him. The O.S.S. (U.S. Office of Strategic Services, 1942-1945) was in charge of U.S. espionage and sabotage, operating in all theaters of WWII, except for the Western Hemisphere, which was the jurisdiction of the FBI (U.S. Federal Bureau of Investigation). The O.S.S. was headed by Major-General William Joseph "Wild Bill" Donovan (1883-1959), who distinguished himself as the leader of this effective intelligence agency that was the precursor to the CIA (U.S. Central Intelligence Agency). Shortly before it closed its offices and was transformed into the CIA, O.S.S. officials offered Hollywood studios the free examination of its myriad files for a three-week period and Paramount jumped at the opportunity, culling from those files many stories that were incorporated into this film. Further, Paramount hired thirty O.S.S. agents to act as advisers and/or bit players in this fine production. This author, who was a member of U.S. Intelligence in the Cold War, has written extensively about the O.S.S.; see my book *Spies: A Narrative Encyclopedia of Dirty Deeds and Double Dealing from Biblical Times to the Present* (1997, M. Evans; CIA: pages: 151-154; Donovan: pages 183-188; O.S.S.: page 375). Other films profiling this secret agency in WWII include **Action in Arabia**, 1944, where George Sanders and Allied agents work to undo the Nazi efforts to unite the Arab tribes to fight for the German cause in WWII; **Background to Danger**, 1943, which has George Raft working with Allied agents in Turkey to undo clandestine operations by a Nazi spy ring run by Sydney Greenstreet; **Cloak and Dagger**, 1946, where physicist Gary Cooper goes behind enemy lines in Italy for the O.S.S., to obtain information about Nazi experiments with the A-bomb; **Decision before Dawn**, 1951, where O.S.S. operatives aid U.S. Army Intelligence in obtaining secret information behind enemy lines in Germany toward the close of WWII; **The Good Shepherd**, 2007, where one man's experiences with this agency in profiled; **Never So Few**, 1959, where O.S.S. agents work with a native guerrilla force under the command of Frank Sinatra in Burma and China in WWII; **Rogue's Regiment**, 1948, which depicts an O.S.S. agent enlisting in the French Foreign Legion to track down a Nazi bigwig, who has escaped and also joined the Legion under an alias;

13 Rue Madeleine, 1947, which has James Cagney leading a team of O.S.S. agents behind the lines in occupied France in WWII; and **Where Eagles Dare**, 1968, where Clint Eastwood, an O.S.S. officer, joins a British team of secret agents on a mission behind the lines in Germany. **p&w**, Richard Maibaum; **d**, Irving Pichel; **cast**, Alan Ladd, Geraldine Fitzgerald, Patric Knowles, John Hoyt, Gloria Saunders, Richard Webb, Richard Benedict, Harold Vermilyea, Don Beddoe, Onslow Stevens, Julia Dean, Gavin Muir, Egon Brecher, Joseph Crehan, Crane Whitley, Bobby Driscoll; **c**, Lionel Lindon; **m**, Daniele Amfitheatrof, Heinz Roemheld; **ed**, William Shea; **art d**, Hans Dreier, Haldane Douglas; **set d**, Sam Comer, Stanley J. Sawley; **spec eff**, Farciot Edouart, Gordon Jennings, Loyal Griggs, Paul K. Lerpae.

Objective, Burma! ★★★★★ 1945; U.S.; 142m; WB; B/W; War Drama; Children: Unacceptable; **DVD**; **VHS**. Flynn gives one of his most powerful and memorable performances in this masterpiece war drama, set in Burma during WWII, and where pantheon director Walsh provides nonstop action as he depicts in realistic detail the harrowing exploits of fifty intrepid American paratroopers. This gripping film opens to show a montage of British, American, Indian and Burmese troops training and preparing to drive back the armies of Japanese that have invaded Burma, narrowing to a single plane that flies over dense jungles, photographing the locale before landing. The film taken is then rushed from the observation plane to a developing laboratory to show the specific location of a Japanese radar installation and surrounding military camp. This information is rushed to General Stilwell (Joseph Warren Stilwell, 1883-1946; commander of American forces in Burma and China, a four-star general), played by Alderson (a startling Stilwell lookalike). Alderson then calls Anderson, who commands a unit of paratroopers, who are then called to a briefing where they are given their assignment to drop behind enemy lines, make their way to the Japanese radar station, destroy it, and then escape by being picked up by planes at a secret landing area. Flynn is given command of this hazardous mission with Prince as his second-in-command. Hull, an elderly newspaper correspondent, is assigned to go on the mission, much to the chagrin of Flynn, who tells him that such physically demanding missions are for younger men, but Hull is determined to go along, despite the waiting perils. He is given a great deal of equipment to carry, plus two parachutes, and then states that something is missing. When Flynn asks what is missing, Hull quips: "The jeep to carry it all." The men then assemble outside two planes while Flynn and Prince check each man's parachute before they board the planes. Once in the air, Hull begins writing down his thoughts, and the wise-cracking Tyne, the paratrooper sitting next to him, goads him with fear by saying that, if his parachute does not open and "we have to pick you up with a blotter, where do you want us to send the blotter?" Hull gives him a sideways look and replies: "To my mother. She collects blotters." The camera closes on many of the paratroopers, showing them in their varied emotional states, some anxious and nervous, some casually reading Bibles, some so oblivious to the dangers they are facing by simply sleeping. One soldier, Caruso, appears so apprehensive that he asks Tobias to push him out of the doorway if he freezes before the jump, but Tobias refuses. Seeing Caruso in a nervous state, Flynn jokes with him, but, when it comes to jumping, Caruso does freeze in the door, and Tobias, who is standing behind him, pushes him into space. The paratroopers land safely in a clearing, gather their opened parachutes and assemble, quickly burying the chutes and then embarking on their journey toward the radar station. They use machetes to hack their way through thick jungle and ford streams and swamps until they reach the outskirts of the Japanese camp. Some of Flynn's men then waylay and kill Japanese guards and then Flynn positions his men on several sides of the camp, fortunate in seeing that the Japanese troops are mostly gathered in their mess hall. The Americans unleash a savage barrage of machine-gun and rifle fire while tossing grenades into the camp, slaughtering the enemy troops as they pour from the mess hall and other buildings. It is all over within a few minutes,

Errol Flynn, center, holding map, in *Objective, Burma!*, 1945.

Flynn and his men cautiously inspecting the camp to find all of its occupants dead. Flynn then orders his demolition teams to destroy the radar installation and all of the camp buildings and, as the paratroopers begin to depart, all of the buildings are destroyed in thundering explosions. It is now imperative that Flynn lead his men quickly to the rendezvous where the planes will meet him and his troops. They make their way to the clearing and communicate with two in-coming planes, Flynn talking with pilot Stevens over a walkie-talkie. The Japanese, however, have been alerted by a spotter, who gives the American position to several commanders, and they assemble hundreds of troops that converge on the small contingent of paratroopers. A scout then reports to Flynn that hundreds of Japanese soldiers are nearby, and Flynn tells Stevens as the planes are descending to land to take to the air and arranges for Stevens to drop supplies to him and his men within two days at another rendezvous deep in the jungle. Moving quickly through the dense jungles with the Japanese hot on their heels, the paratroopers arrive at the rendezvous to see supplies dropped to them. Stevens tells Flynn that there are no other available landing areas and he and his men must now escape by walking out of Burma, a distance of more than 150 miles. Stevens gives Flynn map coordinates to meet him at the next rendezvous where he will again drop supplies. To make sure that at least some of the paratroopers will survive, Flynn splits his forces to take separate routes to the next rendezvous, sending half of his men with his good friend Prince while he leads the others toward that uncertain destination. At the next drop area, supplies are parachuted into a clearing, but when several of Flynn's men go to retrieve the supplies, Japanese troops are waiting in ambush and kill several of them before Flynn and the others beat a hasty retreat. When reaching the rendezvous where Flynn's contingent is to meet up with Prince and his men, they find only two paratroopers from Prince's group, who tell Flynn that Prince and the others were ambushed and slaughtered by the enemy. Flynn pushes on, crossing a river to enter a small Burmese village where his men kill two Japanese guards and then discover that the main Japanese force occupying the village has departed. Flynn and others then find the bodies of Prince's group, all of them brutally mutilated. Prince is found barely alive, and when Flynn kneels next to him, Prince, who has been tortured and is in terrible pain, begs him to kill him. Flynn is saved from that awful deed when Prince then dies. Newsman Hull, witnessing this atrocity, explodes, calling the Japanese troops "immoral, degenerate idiots! Wipe them out, I say! Wipe them off the face of the earth!" (When Bessie, who wrote the story for this film, saw that screenwriter MacDougall had inserted these vitriolic lines in the script, he objected to Jack Warner, saying that *all* Japanese were thus being indicted, but the movie mogul refused to delete the scathing label, pointing out that the public was keenly aware of the notorious atrocities the Japanese had committed dur-

Errol Flynn (holding walkie-talkie) in *Objective, Burma!,* **1945.**

ing WWII and earlier in their invasion of China, such as the Rape of Nanking, where Japanese troops were photographed bayoneting hundreds of Chinese prisoners; the Bataan Death March in the Philippines, where thousands of captured American Filipino troops were routinely murdered by their captors; and the widespread abuse and slaughter of British troops after the fall of Singapore.) The main force of Japanese troops then return to the village and Flynn and his men escape in a fighting retreat, but they are now low on ammunition and food while the exhausted survivors struggle and stagger toward a final rendezvous. Collapsing from fatigue, the paratroopers almost give up hope of survival, but Flynn urges them forward through his resolute leadership (and where Tobias, inspired by Flynn, tells the others to keep moving, saying of Flynn: "I'd follow him down the barrel of a cannon"). They reach the top of a hill, the final destination they have been ordered to find, but there are no reinforcements or supplies waiting for them. The place is as barren as their hopes and all resign themselves to certain death, except for Flynn, who orders them to begin digging foxholes as a last-ditch defense. When none respond, Flynn angrily takes a spade from one of the paratroopers and begins digging, which shames his men into action and all of them dig in, but they later find Hull dead from fatigue and bury him. To their surprise, the paratroopers then hear the roar of a plane overhead and Flynn signals the plane with a mirror, so that the plane drops supplies and food. Refreshed and now with plenty of ammunition, Flynn and his men dig in, knowing that the airdrop has undoubtedly alerted Japanese patrols looking for them and they are right. As night falls, they see from the hill hundreds of Japanese troops in the valley below stealthily moving toward them. After nightfall, the Japanese infiltrate the American positions, some talking in English as they crawl in the dark toward foxholes occupied by the paratroopers, one of them, Hudson, responding to give away his hidden position and being killed. Another paratrooper becomes wary when a Japanese soldier crawling toward him calls out: "Where are you, Joe?" That paratrooper releases a grenade, rolling it toward the Japanese soldier, saying, "I'm right here," then ducks back into his foxhole as the grenade explodes and kills his enemy. He then says: "By the way...my name ain't Joe!" Flynn then sends up a flare that lights up the sky and valley below to show scores of advancing Japanese, and the paratroopers open up on them with intense gunfire and then begin hurling grenades that fell dozens of the enemy and stops the attack as the Japanese race back down the hill in a panicky, running retreat. The surviving paratroopers, including Flynn, rise from their foxholes at dawn only to hear the roar of airplanes. They again take cover in their foxholes, all expecting to see enemy planes bomb their position, but, when they look skyward they see hundreds of U.S. planes, and from them thousands of American paratroopers filling the sky with their chutes as they descend downward, as well as gliders landing nearby and

emerging from these more American troops and equipment. Flynn and his men are ecstatic and jubilantly cheer at this magnificent sight. They leave their position and these ragged, scarecrow-looking soldiers slowly descend the hill, going to their rescuers. When this small group of soldiers arrives at an airfield, Anderson, Flynn's commander, welcomes him and tells him that there is a glider waiting to take him and his men from the area and congratulates him on blowing up the Japanese radar station, which allowed the massive invasion of Burma to occur undetected by the enemy. "This is what it cost," Flynn says, and gives Anderson many dog-tags taken from his fallen men, "not much to send home...a handful of Americans." Flynn and his men then board the glider and it is taken into the air by a transport, flying away to end this exotic saga of war, one of the most impactful and memorable films dealing with World War II. Pantheon action director Walsh maintains a frantic pace throughout this harrowing film, presenting one tension-filled scene after another while showing a clammy-like thick jungle through which the players work their way to and from their mission, and where the battle scenes are superbly choreographed. The powerful and dynamic score from Waxman, filled with exotic-sounding passages, increases the anxiety, the eerie sounds of tropical birds and jungle animals puncturing the soundtrack. Flynn is splendid as the resolute commander, underplaying heroics and relating to his men in very human and compassionate terms, a role he would later claim to be his best. The cast of supporting players are standouts in their roles, all as believable as the actual American soldiers who fought in that theater of war. Much of the story line for this production is taken from a classic adventure film set during the French and Indian wars of the 18th Century, **Northwest Passage**, 1940, but the characters in this film are uniquely appropriate to the 20th Century war that engulfs them. *Author's Note*: Walsh told this author that "Errol had some trouble with that heart murmur of his and got fatigued easily, but he did not complain and kept pace with the rest of the men chopping through the jungles and wading through rivers and swamps. We were fortunate in finding the ideal location to represent the thick Burmese jungle, which was the Lucky Baldwin Santa Anita Ranch [outside of Pasadena]. That place had a lot of tropical trees and plants and dense underbrush and was so realistic-looking that many viewers thought we had actually shot the film in Burma." Although the film was immensely popular and saw a great box office success, the film was unfairly lambasted in England by xenophobic British critics, who thought that the war in Burma was strictly a province of the British army, albeit Stilwell and his American troops fought heroically there as was further depicted in **Merrill's Marauders**, 1962 (which depicted the rigorous and heroic performance of the 5307th Composite Unit of 3,000 U.S. troops in that theater of the war). The film was banned in England and was not distributed there until 1952. "The British handed out a lot of hogwash, claiming that Warner Brothers was trying to convince the world that America had won the war in Burma," Walsh said to this author. "They were either jealous or pretty damned stingy in recognizing the fact that many Americans died fighting in those stinking jungles in Burma. The truth is, they could not have won in Burma without our help and they knew it." **p**, Jerry Wald; **d**, Raoul Walsh; **cast**, Errol Flynn, James Brown, William Prince, George Tobias, Henry Hull, Warner Anderson, John Alvin, Mark Stevens, Hugh Beaumont, Anthony Caruso, Richard Erdman, John Whitney, George Tyne [Buddy Yarus], Erville Alderson, Joel Allen, Rodd Redwing, William Hudson, Asit Koomar, Lester Matthews, John Sheridan, Carlyle Blackwell Jr.; **w**, Ranald MacDougall, Lester Cole (based on a story by Alvah Bessie); **c**, James Wong Howe; **m**, Franz Waxman; **ed**, George Amy; **art d**, Ted Smith; **set d**, Jack McConaghy; **spec eff**, Edwin B. DuPar.

Ocean's Eleven ★★★ 1960; U.S.; 127m; Dorchester/WB; Color; Comedy/Crime Drama; Children: Unacceptable; **DVD; VHS**. Sinatra and his "Rat Pack" are in full force with this lighthearted caper film where he assembles a bunch of his war buddies to commit commando-like robberies of the five top Las Vegas casinos. The idea is to rob the money rooms of the Desert Inn, the Sands, the Riviera, the Flamingo, and the Sahara all at once by separate units of thieves at midnight on New Year's Eve when security will be lax. To achieve this, all of the electronic security systems are shut down by technical expert Conte, who is a member of Sinatra's commando team. As each of Sinatra's units invade the money rooms of each casino (and accessing such closely guarded bastions is much easier in this film than in real life), millions of dollars are stuffed into garbage bags and these are taken to the alley entrances of each casino and placed in garbage disposal containers. Davis, typecast as a black man driving a garbage truck, then arrives in a garbage truck to pick up the loot in those garbage bags, depositing all at a dump to later be retrieved by the thieves. Romero, a smooth operator and gambler, gets on to the scheme and figures that Sinatra is behind the colossal capers and begins negotiating with the casinos and insurance firms for a piece of the pie if he can manage to return the money. Meanwhile, Conte has a heart attack and dies on a Las Vegas street. His mourning friends conveniently use his coffin in which to hide the loot as they prepare to ship the body out of town and with it that loot, which is to later be divided among the thieves. Their plan backfires when Conte's relatives decide to have the body cremated, coffin and all, and the stolen millions ironically go up in smoke. The former commandos break up and go their separate ways, perhaps planning on a reunion that might be more successful in the future. Sinatra does a good job as the freewheeling Danny Ocean, and old pals Martin, Davis, Lawford and others are charming and entertaining in their roles, Milestone directs with a sure hand and with a good wise-cracking script that entertains throughout. This was made again in 2001 under the same title. Songs: "Ain't That a Kick in the Head," "The Tender Trap," "Eee-O-11" (Sammy Cahn, Jimmy Van Heusen); "Learnin' the Blues" (Delores Silvers); "Mother Machree" (1910; Chauncey Olcott, Ernest R. Ball); "Auld Lang Syne" (traditional; lyrics: Robert Burns). *Author's Note*: Sinatra told this author that **"Ocean's Eleven** was no piece of cake to do. We [he, Martin and Davis] were all singing in Vegas at the time, working at night and shooting that picture during the daytime. I can tell you that we were working sixteen hours a day when doing that picture and if that wasn't a backbreaker I don't know what was. But I must all tell you that we all had a hell of a lot of fun doing it. Those were the days when we owned Vegas." **p&d**, Lewis Milestone; **cast**, Frank Sinatra, Dean Martin, Sammy Davis, Jr., Peter Lawford, Angie Dickinson, Richard Conte, Cesar Romero, Patrice Wymore, Joey Bishop, Akim Tamiroff, Henry Silva, Ilka Chase, Buddy Lester, George Raft, Red Skelton, Don "Red" Barry, Richard Boone, Hoot Gibson, Shirley MacLaine; **w**, Harry Brown, Charles Lederer (based on a story by George Clayton Johnson, Jack Golden Russell); **c**, William H. Daniels (Technicolor); **m**, Nelson Riddle; **ed**, Philip W. Anderson; **art d**, Nicolai Remisoff; **set d**, Howard Bristol; **spec eff**, Franklyn Soldo.

Ocean's Eleven ★★★ 2001; U.S.; 116m; WB; Color; Crime Drama; Children: Unacceptable (MPAA: PG-13); **DVD**; **VHS**. Clooney heads a group of eleven dedicated thieves who plan to rob three of Las Vegas' top casinos of more than $150 million in this action-packed thriller and remake of the 1960 production starring Frank Sinatra. Clooney plays Danny Ocean, who gathers his buddies together to make these daring raids against the money vaults in the Vegas casinos, including the snack munching Pitt, who performs some extraordinary acrobatics in penetrating and robbing one of the vaults and where some stunning special effects visually enhance the amazing action. The motivation for the robberies, it seems, is not only the allure of such staggering loot, but the fun all of the robbers enjoy while committing these spectacular heists, with no heed to the old credo of "crime does not pay," albeit their elaborate schemes and modus operandi backfire on all of them. Good direction, high production values and good acting throughout make for a tension-filled thriller. Ironically, this film's budget was almost as much as the thieves are stealing, coming in at a staggering $85 million and producing returns at the box office of more than $450 million. Songs:

Frank Sinatra and Angie Dickinson in *Ocean's Eleven*, 1960.

"Cha, Cha, Cha" (James D'Angelo, Leo Johns, Jimmy Kelleher, Marc Lanjean, Henri Salvador, Marcel Stellman); "Rodney Yates," "Gritty Shaker," "Booby Trappin'," "Lyman Zerga," "Ruben's In," "Planting the Seed," "Stealing the Pinch," "Tess," "Hookers," "Pickpockets," "160 Million Chinese Man," "The Plans" (David Holmes); "Papa Loves Mambo" (Al Hoffman, Dick Manning, Bickley Reichner); "The Projects (P Jays)" (Dan Nakamura, Paul Huston, Tarin Jones, David Jolicoeur); "Spirit in the Sky" (Norman Greenbaum); "Takes My Breath Away" (Giorgio Moroder, Tom Whitlock); "Blues in the Night" (Harold Arlen, Johnny Mercer); "Caravan" (Duke Ellington, Juan Tizol); "A Little Less Conversation" (Billy Strange, Mac Davis); "Spanish Flea" (Julius Wechter); "Clair de lune" (Claude Debussy); "Dream, Dream, Dream" (Jimmy McHugh, Jean Pierre Mottier, Mitchell Parish, Jeannine Melle); "Misty" (Erroll Garner); "Theme from a Summer Place" (Max Steiner); "Moon River" (Henry Mancini, Johnny Mercer); "69 Police" (David Holmes, Phil Mossman, Darren Morris, Italo Salizzatto); "Theme for Young Lovers" (Percy Faith). **p**, Bruce Berman, Susan Ekins, Jerry Weintraub, John Hardy, R. J. Leouis; **d**, Steven Soderbergh; **cast**, George Clooney, Brad Pitt, Matt Damon, Andy Garcia, Julia Roberts, Casey Affleck, Elliott Gould, Bernie Mac, Scott Caan, Eddie Jemison; **w**, Ted Griffin, Harry Brown (1960 version); **c**, Pete Andrews [Steven Soderbergh]; **m**, David Holmes; **ed**, Stephen Mirrione; **prod d**, Philip Messina; **art d**, Keith P. Cunningham; **set d**, Kristen Toscano Messina; **spec eff**, Kevin Hannigan.

October Sky ★★★ 1999; U.S.; 108m; UNIV; Color; Biographical Drama; Children: Unacceptable (MPAA: PG); **DVD**; **VHS**. The true story of Homer Hickam, Jr. (1943-), played by Gyllenhaal, shows him as a seventeen-year-old high school student in Coalwood, West Virginia, who is inspired by the October 1957 launch into orbit of the Soviet Union's artificial satellite Sputnik to learn how to build and launch rockets. His father, Cooper, is a coal mine supervisor who forbids him to work on rocketry and wants him to be a miner. Gyllenhaal can't help himself and goes ahead with the help of school friends, Scott and Lindberg, and the school egghead, Owen. They build a shelter in the woods to undertake a series of trials and lots of errors. Gyllenhaal's high school science teacher, Dern, encourages them to enter the National Science Fair with college scholarships as the prize. The boys learn about rocket fuel and use alcohol from a moonshiner as an ingredient in their formula. They get into trouble when their rocket work is suspected of having started a forest fire, but they prove by use of trigonometry that they are innocent. They take their rocket designs to the 1960 National Science Fair and win both a gold and silver medal in the area of propulsion. Hickam went on to become a NASA engineer designing spacecraft, a Vietnam War medal-winner for heroism, and author of several books.

Jack Lemmon and Walter Matthau in *The Odd Couple*, 1968.

This inspiring story is well played, offering an inventive script. Gutter language and teen sensuality, alcohol use, and some thematic elements prohibit viewing by children. Songs: "Nine Pound Hammer Is Too Heavy" (Charlie Monroe); "My Prayer" (George Boulanger, Jimmy Kennedy); "Jailhouse Rock" (Jerry Leiber, Mike Stoller); "Red & Black," "On Wisconsin" (O'dell Willis, William T. Purdy, Carl D. Beck); "That'll Be the Day" (Norman Petty, Jerry Allison, Buddy Holly); "Yakety Yak," "Searchin'" (Leiber, Stoller); "Smoke Gets in Your Eyes" (Jerome Kern, Otto A. Harbach); "Let the Good Times Roll" (Leonard Lee, Shirley Goodman); "Only You and You Alone" (Andre Rand, Buck Ram); "Ain't That a Shame" (Fats Domino, David Bartholomew); "Speedo" (Esther Navarro); "Why Do Fools Fall in Love" (Frankie Lymon, Morris Levy, Herman Santiago, Jimmy Merchant); "It's All in the Game" (Carl Sigman, Charles Dawes). **p**, Larry Franco, Charles Gordon; **d**, Joe Johnston; **cast**, Jake Gyllenhaal, Chris Cooper, Laura Dern, Chris Owen, William Lee Scott, Chad Lindberg, Natalie Canerday, Scott Miles, Randy Stripling, Donald Thorne; **w**, Lewis Colick (based on the book *Rocket Boys* by Homer H. Hickam, Jr.); **c**, Fred Murphy; **m**, Mark Isham; **ed**, Robert Dalva; **prod d**, Barry Robison; **art d**, Tony Fanning; **set d**, Chris Spellman; **spec eff**, Joe Digaetano, Robert Vazquez.

The Odd Couple ★★★★ 1968; U.S.; 105m; PAR; Color; Comedy; Children: Acceptable; **DVD**; **VHS**. This hilarious comedy sees the perfect matching of Lemmon and Matthau, a delightful duo that would go on to appear in many outstanding comedies together. In this one from stellar comedy writer Simon, they are both bachelors who have lost their wives and decide to room together, a decision that creates more havoc and mayhem in their already dysfunctional lives. Lemmon (playing Felix Ungar) is so much the cleanliness freak, as well as an incurable hypochondriac, that his annoyingly fussy ways and picky nature has caused his wife to throw him out of his domicile. A TV news writer, Lemmon is so depressed that he has attempted suicide, but botched the effort. His mind filled with gloom and doom, he nevertheless arrives at the debris-cluttered apartment occupied by sports writer Matthau (playing Oscar Madison) to attend the regular Friday night poker game where friends Fiedler, Haines, Sheiner and Edelman are present and eagerly looking forward to their usual cutthroat card playing. Lemmon's depression is evident to all, and when he breaks down, the group become deeply concerned about his state of mind. The good-natured Matthau decides to have Lemmon move in with him since he has an extra, unoccupied bedroom. Further, the place is so spacious that there is enough room for both of them, so much so that they should never get in each other's way, or so Matthau wrongly reasons, not knowing that domestic disaster now lurks around every nook and corner of that apartment.

Lemmon immediately takes control of the housekeeping, following his addictive and compulsive obsession to have everything spic and span. He turns the place into a house beautiful showcase where floors shine and not a speck of dust is to be found, but so hounds the unkempt and slovenly Matthau about his cigarette butts, dirty footprints and refusal to eat the specially prepared dishes Lemmon has cooked that they get into classic quarrels. Now Matthau realizes why Lemmon's wife booted him from her premises and schemes a way to do the same thing, but knows in his heart that weirdo Lemmon has no place to go. He thinks to rid himself of this nagging relationship by matching Lemmon with one of the two English sisters, Evans or Shelley, who live in the same building, and arranges a double date. The girls arrive at Matthau's apartment to have a special gourmet dinner that Lemmon has meticulously prepared, and as they chat, one of these addlebrained sisters asks Lemmon what he does for a living and he tells her that he writes the news for a television station. She replies: "Isn't that interesting. Where on earth do you get all your ideas?" Disaster then strikes when Lemmon's meatloaf collapses as does Lemmon, who, in the presence of these empathetic ladies, gushes out his remorse about his failed marriage, sobbing uncontrollably and spoiling Matthau's expectations of a romantic evening with one or both of these fetching women, who are now converted to weeping mother figures as they try to comfort and calm the emotionally distraught Lemmon. They invite Lemmon and Matthau to their apartment, but Lemmon squashes that promising opportunity; when the girls depart, Matthau explodes, and begins to break up the bric-a-brac, soil the doilies and savagely return the apartment back to its original shambles before Lemmon became his excruciatingly annoying roommate. This causes Lemmon to leave, and when the poker-playing buddies reassemble they learn that Lemmon is nowhere to be found and their fears mount by the second. All begin looking for him throughout the city, but they come up empty. They return to Matthau's place and sit glumly at the poker table only to see Lemmon arrive and where he packs his belongings, telling one and all that he is moving in with Evans and Shelley, his compassionate and loving friends, until he can decide on his next move. After he departs, the poker players resume their game, but Matthau, now infected with Lemmon's antiseptic obsessions, begins complaining about how his buddies are messing up the place with their ashes and sloppy eating habits, alerting one and all, including the viewer, that Lemmon's persnickety persona has overwhelmed and altered Matthau's otherwise easy-going personality. Wry, clever, and cunningly humorous, this comedy is a mirth-filled gem brilliantly essayed by Lemmon and Matthau and wonderfully directed by Saks. Simon's script faithfully follows his play, where the acerbic jokes are to the heart of his memorable characters. This film was later made into a very good TV series, "The Odd Couple" (1970-1975), starring Tony Randall as Felix and Jack Klugman as Oscar. A sequel, **The Odd Couple II**, 1998, where Lemmon and Matthau reprise their roles, was far less effective. *Author's Note*: Although the always inventive Simon invariably wrote about his own life, in this instance, he borrowed this unforgettable tale from his older brother Danny, a successful TV writer, who was divorced and was the fussiest man on the face of the earth. He moved in with agent Roy Gerber and Les Colodny, a TV executive and writer, and drove them crazy with his insistence on cleanliness. Danny Simon told Neil many stories about his strained and ridiculous relationships with his roommates, and the brothers originally thought to title this story as "The Odd Trio," but Neil Simon thought that too unwieldy and settled for **The Odd Couple**, writing the play and cutting his brother in for a piece of the pie, since it was based upon Danny's discombobulated life. Lemmon told this author that "I am not the cleaning nut that I play in **The Odd Couple**, although I like to have things somewhat neat. It was easy to go after Walter [Matthau] as he is, quite frankly, a natural slob by nature and lifestyle as he was happy to demonstrate in that very clever comedy." Matthau told this author that "Jack [Lemmon] was perfect as that wacky Felix in **The Odd Couple**. He had that cuckoo's character down pat and was so good at bugging me about my sloppy habits that he really did get on my nerves and actually drove me straight into my character of Oscar so that by close to the end of that picture I wanted to wring his neck. That's acting, my boy!" Matthau had appeared in the original Simon play as Oscar and Art Carney played Felix. When it came to making the film version, however, Paramount insisted that Lemmon, a big name star, take over the role of Felix. The gifted and generous Carney told this author that "Jack [Lemmon] did just as good a job in playing Felix as I would have done in the picture. I have no complaints about him taking over that part. He is a fine actor and was wonderful in that role." **p**, Howard W. Koch; **d**, Gene Saks; **cast**, Jack Lemmon, Walter Matthau, John Fiedler, Herbert Edelman, David Sheiner, Larry Haines, Monica Evans, Carole Shelley, Iris Adrian, Roberto Clemente, Maury Wills; **w**, Neil Simon (based on his play); **c**, Robert B. Hauser (Technicolor); **m**, Neil Hefti; **ed**, Frank Bracht; **art d**, Hal Pereira, Walter Tyler; **set d**, Ray Moyer, Robert Benton, **spec eff**, Paul K. Lerpae.

Odd Man Out ★★★★★ 1947; U.K.; 116m; Two Cities Films/UNIV; B/W; Drama; Children: Unacceptable; **DVD**; **VHS**. Under the brilliant direction of pantheon director Reed, Mason renders one of his most riveting roles as a doomed IRA leader trapped in Belfast, Ireland, following a botched robbery. An inspired Irish rebel, Mason breaks out of prison and then, to fund his revolutionary operations, masterminds a payroll robbery at a mill in Belfast. Mason is unusual as a rebel in that he hates violence, but he nevertheless employs a gun when committing the holdup and, in the process, shoots and kills a man while he himself is critically wounded. An accomplice at the wheel of the escape car panics and drives off, leaving Mason to find his own way to safety. Thus begins a nightmare for the wanted Mason as he is relentlessly pursued by police and the British military. He staggers through the dark streets of Belfast, encountering a number of strange characters, some genuinely attempting to help him, others thinking to sell the fugitive for any reward they might receive. Ryan, his sweetheart, meanwhile, desperately begins searching for him as do a number of his IRA associates that include O'Herlihy and Cusack. The pain from the wound, as well as loss of blood, causes Mason to become sometimes delirious as he makes his torturous way through the byways of Belfast. Two elderly ladies give him a brief respite by taking him into their home where they bandage his wound and give him some tea before he goes on his way. He is found by Mc-Cormick, a drifter, who recognizes him as an IRA leader and hides Mason in a junkyard, placing him in an old bathtub. He is then taken to Newton, a half-mad painter, who has him sit in a chair in his loft and decides to capture Mason's look of death on canvas by painting him. (Newton's lunatic ravings about finally having a living model to paint and the gruesome opportunity of recording the appearance of coming death is one of the most startling sequences in this film or any other.) As his stamina wanes and he drifts in and out of consciousness, Mason hallucinates the image of a friendly priest, as the eccentric Newton furiously slaps paint onto canvas. In a separate scene we see Ryan with that very priest during her frantic effort to find Mason before authorities can apprehend him. With almost superhuman effort Mason leaves Newton and makes his way toward the docks and a ship that might take him from the city and to safety. He plods through the night as snow begins to fall and Ryan finds him, helping him along the riverfront toward that ship, but their escape route is blocked by police, who flood the area with light and train weapons on them, ordering Mason and Ryan to surrender. Mason is too weak to do battle, but Ryan will not go meekly into captivity or let the man she loves be taken alive. She withdraws a gun and, as the police close in, fires at them. The police return fire, a fusillade that mows down Mason and Ryan, leaving their bodies crumpled at the water's edge while snow softly covers them as a white shroud of death to end this sad saga. Reed, who established his reputation as a master filmmaker with this classic film, presents a stunning and mesmerizing odyssey of a man struggling to vainly stay alive in an uncaring world where compassion is fleeting while presenting this grim portrait in re-

James Mason in *Odd Man Out*, 1947.

alistic and often bizarre scenes. The script is literate to the point of poetry, a lyrical flavor lacing the Irish-accented dialog. Krasker's black-and-white photography is starkly gritty, and Alywn's powerful and mellifluous score is hauntingly empathetic to the subject. Mason's bravura performance is wonderfully supported by the rest of the cast members, where Newton, McCormick, O'Herlihy, Cusack and Ryan (her debut) are exceptional in their equally fascinating roles. *Author's Note*: "Reed, brilliant director that he is," Mason told this author, "portrayed me as an almost Christ-like figure in **Odd Man Out**, and that did not sit well with British authorities, I believe, as I am playing a member of the Irish Republican Army, such people generally thought to be outright terrorists. But he took the courageous route to show my character as being human and his purpose hopeless as he becomes the victim to his own altruistic private war. I do believe it was one of my better efforts. I should add that all my scenes with Mr. Newton belonged to him. No one could ever take a scene from that man." The IRA (Irish Republican Army), the underground guerrilla force that has for so long battled British forces in an effort to unite Northern Ireland with the Republic of Ireland to the South, has been portrayed in many other films, notably **Angela's Ashes**, 2000; **Anton**, 2008; **Beloved Enemy**, 1936; **Borstal Boy**, 2001; **The Boxer**, 1997; **Breakfast on Pluto**, 2005; **The Enigma of Frank Ryan**, 2012; **Exiled**, 1999; **Fifty Dead Men Walking**, 2009; **Hunger**, 2008; **I See a Dark Stranger**, 1947; **The Informer**, 1935; **The Jackal**, 1997; **Liam**, 2001; **Midnight Man**, 1997 (made for TV); **Michael Collins**, 1996; **The Night Fighters**, 1960; **Omagh**, 2004 (made for TV); **Ordinary Decent Criminal**, 2000; **Patriot Games**, 1998; **Peacefire**, 2009; **The Quiet Man**, 1952; **The Rising of the Moon**, 1957; **Ronin**, 1998; **Shake Hands with the Devil**, 1959; **Shergar**, 1999; **Ticker**, 2001; **Titanic Town**, 1999; **Veronica Guerin**, 2003; and **The Wind That Shakes the Barley**, 2007. For more information on the IRA, see my book *Terrorism in the 20th Century: A Narrative Encyclopedia from the Anarchists through the Weathermen to the Unabomber* (M. Evans, 1998). **p&d**, Carol Reed; **cast**, James Mason, Robert Newton, Kathleen Ryan, Cyril Cusack, F. J. McCormick, William Hartnell, Fay Compton, Denis O'Dea, W. G. Fay, Maureen Delaney, Dan O'Herlihy; **w**, F. L. Green, R. C. Sherriff (based on the novel by Green); **c**, Robert Krasker; **m**, William Alwyn; **ed**, Fergus McDonell; **art d**, Ralph Brinton; **spec eff**, Stanley Grant, Bill Warrington.

Odds Against Tomorrow ★★★ 1959; U.S.; 96m; HarBel Productions/UA; B/W; Crime; Children: Unacceptable; **DVD**; **VHS**. Begley is an ex-cop who is fired for illegal dealings. He needs two men to help him rob an upstate New York bank, and chooses Ryan, a white ex-convict, and Belafonte, a black man, who is in debt from gambling on the horses. They're both reluctant, so Begley gets Belafonte's creditors to

Robert Ryan and Shelley Winters in *Odds Against Tomorrow*, 1959.

put pressure on him, and Ryan needs money to impress his girlfriend, Grahame, although he is married to Winters. They eventually agree to help Begley rob the bank, but racial tensions arise in the gang because Ryan despises blacks. Begley is shot during the robbery and, unable to make a getaway, takes his own life. Belafonte and Ryan escape to an oil storage building and have a racial fight, shooting at each other. The gunfire turns the building into an inferno and they are both incinerated. When their bodies are found they cannot be told apart, so that in an ironic ending, their deaths are examples that death knows no color. Songs: "My Baby's Not Around," "All Men Are Evil" (Harry Belafonte, Milton Okun). A very interesting *film noir* production with a racial twist that is too violent for children. *Author's Note*: Ryan told this author that "I don't think **Odds Against Tomorrow** got the attention it should have gotten. It deals with the deep-seated racism that is so prevalent today. Again, I am playing a heavy, the kind of bigot I played in **Crossfire** [1947], only this time I hate blacks instead of Jews. What a terrible typecasting to get into." **p&d**, Robert Wise; **cast**, Harry Belafonte, Robert Ryan, Shelley Winters, Ed Begley, Gloria Grahame, Will Kuluva, Kim Hamilton, Mae Barnes, Wayne Rogers, Cicely Tyson; **w**, John O. Killens, Nelson Gidding (based on the novel by William P. McGivern); **c**, Joseph C. Brun; **m**, John Lewis; **ed**, Dede Allen; **prod d**, Leo Kerz; **set d**, Fred Ballmeyer.

Ode to Billy Joe ★★★ 1976; U.S.; 105m; WB; Color; Drama; Children: Unacceptable (MPAA: PG); **DVD**; **VHS**. This grimly offbeat but fascinating drama is set in Tallahatchie, Mississippi, in 1953 where Benson, an eighteen-year-old boy, tells his girlfriend, O'Connor, who is not yet sixteen, that he loves her, despite conflicting feelings that he may be homosexual. He has a few too many drinks at a barn dance and is enticed into a sexual encounter with a man he does not know. Feeling guilty, he hides in the woods, but later admits to O'Connor that he has had sex with a man. O'Connor, whose father refuses to allow her to date before she is sixteen, doesn't want to believe Benson because she likes their lovemaking, mainly at night on the Tallahatchie Bridge over that river. Benson cannot accept his homosexual nature and jumps to his death off of the Tallahatchie Bridge and drowns. Sexual themes and suicide prohibit viewing by children. Songs: "Ode to Billy Joe" (Bobbie Gentry), "There'll Be Time" (Alan and Marilyn Bergman, Michel Legrand). **p**, Max Baer, Roger Camras; **d**, Baer; **cast**, Robby Benson, Glynnis O'Connor, Joan Hotchkis, Sandy McPeak, James Best, Terence Goodman, Becky Bowen, Simpson Hemphill, Ed Shelnut, Eddie Talr; **w**, Herman Raucher (based on the song "Ode to Billy Joe"); **c**, Michel Hugo (Technicolor); **m**, Michel Legrand; **ed**, Frank E. Morriss; **prod d & art d**, Philip M. Jefferies; **set d**, Harry Gordon; **spec eff**, Gene Grigg.

The Odessa File ★★★ 1974; U.K./Germany; 128m; UNIV; Color; Drama; Children: Unacceptable (MPAA: PG); **DVD**; **VHS**. Voight is exceptional in this dark tale of powerful Nazis still operating in Germany in 1963. Voight is a freelance journalist, who reads the diary of an elderly Jewish man after the old man commits suicide. The old man was a survivor of a Nazi concentration camp during World War II (1939-1945). Voight begins an investigation into the reported sighting of Schell, a former German SS captain, who had commanded the camp during the war. Schell had disappeared after the war, but Voight tracks him down and Schell tells him he has no regrets about his command of the concentration camp that killed thousands of Jews. Voight learns about a powerful organization of former SS members called Odessa who seek to advance the philosophy of Nazi Germany. At the same time he is being watched closely by Israeli secret service agents. His own life is soon in danger, and he narrowly escapes death when he is pushed in front of a moving train. He eventually learns there is a link between Schell, Odessa, and his own family. After many harrowing incidents where Voight almost loses his life, he manages to corner Schell and kill him and then exposes the secret SS cabal. Director Neame elicits fine performances from the entire cast and where he maintains tension throughout this riveting drama. Many other films have profiled the Nazi resurgence following WWII, notably **Berlin Express**, 1948; **The Boys from Brazil**, 1978; **Cornered**, 1945; **The Man in the Glass Booth**, 1975; **Marathon Man**, 1976; **Notorious**, 1946; and **The Stranger**, 1946. Song: "Christmas Dream" (Andrew Lloyd Webber, Tim Rice, Andre Heller); **p**, John Woolf, John R. Sloan; **d**, Ronald Neame; **cast**, Jon Voight, Maximilian Schell, Maria Schell, Mary Tamm, Derek Jacobi, Peter Jeffrey, Klaus Lowitsch, Kurt Meisel, Hannes Messemer, Garfield Morgan; **w**, George Markstein, Kenneth Ross (based on the novel by Frederick Forsyth); **c**, Oswald Morris; **m**, Andrew Lloyd Webber; **ed**, Ralph Kemplen; **prod d**, Rolf Zehetbauer; **spec eff**, Richard Richtsfeld.

Odette ★★★ 1951; U.K.; 124m; Herbert Wilcox Productions/Lopert Pictures Corporation; B/W; Spy Drama; Children: Unacceptable; **DVD**; **VHS**. Neagle gives a wonderful and moving performance as the intrepid Odette Sansom Churchill (1912-1995), who served as an undercover agent for England's SOE (Special Operations Executive) during WWII and who proved to be one of Britain's greatest heroines. A native of France, Neagle falls in love with and marries a British soldier, who is killed during the early stages of WWII. When she hears a BBC radio appeal for any photos of the coastal regions of France, she collects her holiday snapshots and mails them, but she sends these photos to the wrong address and they wind up in the British War Office. She is recruited by that office as an agent for SOE, telling her children that she will be working in Scotland for the government, and then undergoes rigorous espionage and sabotage training under Howard, who plays Peter Churchill (1909-1972) an SOE officer who would later marry Odette Sansom. She is then sent secretly to France, working undercover in Marseilles with radio operator Ustinov and where Neagle, via Ustinov's clandestine transmitter, sends vital secret information to England about German operations. She is suspected by cunning Gestapo officer Goring of being a spy and they play a cat-and-mouse game. Goring employs a ruse to trap her and then arrests Neagle, subjugating her to incredible tortures—hot pokers applied to her flesh and her toenails ripped out with pliers by bestial Gestapo interrogators as the sadistic Goring incessantly continues to grill her. The courageous Neagle (as was the case with the real Odette) gives her tormentors no information, and they finally ship her off to a concentration camp at Ravensbruck and there she undergoes further abuses as she awaits her execution. She is saved at the last minute when American troops close in on the camp and Schieske, the camp commander, spares her life, not out of any compassion or mercy, but to use her as a bargaining chip when negotiating his own surrender. (Odette's life was saved when that German camp commander believed that she was married to Peter Churchill, played by Howard, and that he was a relative of then British Prime Minister Winston Churchill, which he was not, and by saving her life, that camp commander thought he would be looked upon favorably by his captors by sparing one of the prime minister's relatives.) After she returns to England, Neagle is hailed a heroine and awarded the George Cross for her courageous service and where she later marries Howard. The film is directed with great skill by Wilcox, who incorporates the fascinating routines of espionage with many dramatic and tension-filled scenes, and the entire cast, particularly Howard and Ustinov, are standouts in their riveting roles. *Author's Note*: Neagle spent more than a year studying for her role, and accompanied Odette, who was hired as a technical adviser for this production, on trips to Marseilles, where Odette operated during the war, and even to the closed-down Ravensbruck concentration camp as well as talking with other SOE agents Odette worked with during the war. Odette praised the actress's dedication to her part, stating: "She [Naegle] was absolutely in toit. In fact, it took one year after the end of the film to get back to normal. She was more upset by doing the film than I was reliving the experience." Maurice Buckmaster (1902-1992), who headed the French Section of SOE during the war and was Odette's superior, plays himself in this film. For more details on this heroic woman, see my book *Spies: A Narrative Encyclopedia of Dirty Deeds and Double Dealing from Biblical Times to the Present* (M. Evans, 1997; Odette Sansom: page 432; SOE: page 452; Peter Churchill: pages 150-151). Other films profiling the activities of SOE include **Against the Wind**, 1949; **Carve Her Name with Pride**, 1958; **Colditz**, 2005 (made for TV); and **Nancy Wake**, 1988 (made for TV). **p&d**, Herbert Wilcox; **cast**, Anna Neagle, Trevor Howard, Marius Goring, Peter Ustinov, Bernard Lee, Maurice Buckmaster, Alfred Schieske, Gilles Queant, Marianne Walla, Fritz Wendhausen; **w**, Warren Chetham-Strode (based on the book by Jerrard Tickell); **c**, Max Green (Mutz Greenbaum); **m**, Anthony Collins; **ed**, Bill Lewthwaite; **art d**, William C. Andrews.

Oedipus the King ★★★ 1968; U.K.; 97m; Crossroads World Film Distributors/UNIV; Color; Drama; Children: Unacceptable; **VHS**. The ancient Greek city of Thebes is cursed by the gods because the king has been murdered. The curse only can be lifted if the present ruler, Plummer, can find and kill the murderer. His investigation leads him to some personal horror in that he learns he killed his own father and slept with his own mother, Palmer, and they had children together. Palmer hangs herself and Plummer tears out his own eyes from guilt and despair. Welles has a brief role as a mountain seer. This is a well-mounted production that faithfully and dynamically presents the classic Greek play by Sophocles. Incest themes and violence prohibit viewing by children. **p**, Michael Luke; **d**, Philip Saville; **cast**, Christopher Plummer, Lilli Palmer, Richard Johnson, Orson Welles, Cyril Cusack, Roger Livesey, Donald Sutherland, Friedrich von Ledebur, Dimos Starenios, Alexis Mann, Oenone Luke; **w**, Michael Luke, Saville (based on a translation by Paul Roche of the play by Sophocles); **c**, Walter Lassally (Technicolor); **m**, Yannis Christou; **ed**, Paul Davies; **art d**, Yannis Migadis.

Of Gods and Men ★★★ 2010; France; 122m; Why Not Productions; Sony; Color; War Drama; Children: Unacceptable (MPAA: R); **BD**; **DVD**. This intriguing tale is set during the 1996 Algerian Civil War where eight French monks of the Trappist Roman Catholic order give spiritual nurturing to an impoverished town. When fundamentalist terrorists engulf the community, the monks must decide whether or not to survive by leaving, or risk their lives by staying and continuing to give spiritual hope to the doomed townspeople. The monks consider their decision, from the aging Lonsdale, to the youngest of them, Wilson, who is scholarly and faith-confident and becomes an example to the others, urging them to remain. They decide to stay, but extremists break into the monastery and abduct the monks. Several months later their bodies are found, but no one claims blame for their murders. Songs: "Seigneur, ouvre mes levres" (Joseph Gelineau), "Puisqu'il est avec nous," "Voici la Nuit" (Dider Rimaud, Philippe Robert), "Nous ne savons pas ton mystere" (Marcel Godard), "Cantique de Mimeon" (Lucien Deiss),

Bette Davis and Leslie Howard in *Of Human Bondage*, 1934.

"Pswaume 142" (Abbaye de Tamie), "O Pere des Lumieres" (Dider Rimaud, Marcel Godard), "Swan Lake" (Pytor Ilyich Tchaikovsky). Violence, disturbing images, and gutter language prohibit viewing by children. (In Arabic, French; English subtitles.) **p**, Etienne Comar, Pascal Caucheteux; **d**, Xavier Beauvois; **cast**, Lambert Wilson, Michael Lonsdale, Olivier Rabourdin, Philippe Laudenbach, Jacques Herlin, Loïc Pichon, Xavier Maly, Jean-Marie Frin, Abdelhafid Metalsi, Sabrina Ouazani; **w**, Beauvois, Comar; **c**, Caroline Champetier; **ed**, Marie-Julie Maille; **prod d**, Michel Barthelemy; **art d**, Yann Megard; **spec eff**, Jacques-Olivier Molon.

Of Human Bondage ★★★★ 1934; U.S.; 83m; Radio Pictures (RKO); B/W; Drama; Children: Unacceptable; **DVD**; **VHS**. Two stunningly great performances by Howard and Davis can be seen in this powerful Somerset Maugham tale. Howard is an idealistic young man, afflicted with a clubfoot, who has aspirations of becoming an artist, but, after studying in Paris, realizes that his artwork will always be second rate, and he decides to enter the medical profession. Howard goes to a restaurant where he meets and is mesmerized by Davis, a blonde vixen named Mildred, who tantalizes him and entices him to the point where he becomes obsessed with her. Withdrawn and insecure due to his disability, Howard finally works up the nerve to ask Davis out on a date and she accepts, which fills Howard's heart with joy. Davis, as is her vicious nature, then cruelly breaks that date by telling Howard that she is going out with salesman Hale, a bully and a braggart. She further injures Howard by sadistically telling him that she could never find any love in her heart for a cripple. It is obvious that Davis is the worst sort of cunning, crafty and scheming lowlife. (And here Davis is magnificent in capturing the complex personality of this most repulsive and deceiving woman.) Howard slowly recovers from this injurious rejection after he meets and is attracted to Johnson, a compassionate young woman, who writes romance novels. Howard, however, is nagged by the image of Davis, who disrupts Howard's relationship with Johnson when she suddenly reappears, telling Howard that the brutish Hale has not only discarded her like an old dishrag, but has left her pregnant and with nowhere to go. The lovesick Howard takes her in, but she again wounds him when she seduces Denny, another medical student and friend of Howard's, and then runs off with Denny. Howard, however, is not rid of this woman. She again returns, this time with her baby, pleading to stay with Howard by saying she has nowhere to go. Howard allows her to stay as he struggles to continue his medical studies, but he distances himself from the dangerous Davis by refusing her offer to make love, and when he leaves, Davis vents her rage by destroying Howard's belongings and even burning some vital bonds necessary in paying for his medical studies. (This vengeful act was duplicated five years later in

Walter Huston and James Stewart in *Of Human Hearts,* **1938.**

The Light That Failed, 1939, where vixen Ida Lupino destroys the masterwork painting created by Ronald Colman, an artist who has gone blind.) Without these funds, Howard cannot continue his studies and takes a job as a salesman, but sees little success as the Depression sets in and few have any money to buy anything. Further, his health fails, but Dee, who has met and has fallen in love with him, along with her compassionate father, Owen, take care of Howard, and he regains his health. He then inherits money that allows him to not only complete his medical studies but have his clubfoot fixed. He marries Dee and begins a happy life when he hears that vixen Davis is in a hospital and is dying. He goes to see her, but she dies before they again meet, and when he leaves he is overwhelmed with a sense of freedom that he is no longer emotionally chained to Davis and is now able to pursue a happy life with Dee. Cromwell directs this traumatic tragedy with a sure hand, fully developing these fascinating characters as novelist Maugham envisioned them. Davis gives one of the greatest performances of her long career, for which she was nominated for an Oscar as Best Actress, but mostly this role established her as a first-rate actress possessing amazing, unique talents. Howard also presents a masterful performance as the sensitive, tortured, tragedy-engulfed Philip Carey. (He and Davis would appear again together in another superb drama, **The Petrified Forest**, 1936, where their romance would again be that of star-crossed lovers.) This film was remade in 1946 and again in 1964, but both were weak efforts to capture the story and characters and could not compare with the original. *Author's Note*: RKO executives were shocked to learn that, after they bought the film rights to the Maugham story, most of their top female stars, including Irene Dunne, Ann Harding and Katharine Hepburn, refused to play the slatternly Mildred. "Not a single leading lady in Hollywood wanted that role," Davis told this author. "I recognized that the character, Mildred, was a vicious person, a flesh-and-blood monster, and I knew that actresses were afraid to be remembered as playing such a terrible person. Not me. I went after that role, something to sink my teeth into after Warner Brothers had been casting me as a forgettable lady in a lot of forgettable films. I went to Jack Warner, who had me under contract, and asked him to loan me out to make that picture. He refused. I kept going back to him until I wore him out and he said, 'okay, go ahead and play that bitch and after you do it, you'll be glad to come back here [to the Warner Brothers studio] and play decent, upright women.' He felt that I would damage my career by playing Mildred. Well, I played her and was nominated for an Oscar and when I went back to Warner Brothers they had to give me better parts, so who won that battle?" Director Cromwell was unhappy by the way Howard, an accomplished actor and international star, was treating Davis. "He thought she was nothing more than a Hollywood starlet," Cromwell told this author, "and he went out of his way to ignore her,

reading a book when he was off camera, and when he fed her lines during rehearsals, he was stone-faced and his voice a monotone. Early during the production I could see that Davis was running away with the picture, and when I told that to Howard, well, he perked up right away and got down to business, using everything he had to hold on to his scenes with her. She was a dynamo and we both knew it. She supervised her own makeup and when she gets sick she looks it, her face more drawn and having the makeup people put more and more white pancake on her face and neck. She is dying toward the end of syphilis after a lifetime of sexual carousing, and, my God, she looked it on her deathbed, the face of a ghost and her eyes blackened, a hideous portrait that Davis herself created. By the end of that picture, Howard and I and everyone else were applauding her. We knew by then that she was a great actress." This film is based upon Maugham's masterpiece novel (published in 1915, selling more than ten million copies), which is largely biographical in that he, like his tormented character, Philip Carey, was a medical student. Like that character, who suffers from a clubfoot, Maugham was afflicted by a lifetime problem of stammering or stuttering, which was most prominent when he was under emotional duress. W. Somerset Maugham (1874-1965) was a closet homosexual, which, because of the times in which he lived where such sexual proclivities were universally condemned, he may have also viewed it as an affliction and which Maugham may have also subliminally attached as an interpreted psychological defect to Carey's character. Maugham's homosexuality developed in him a rather secretive nature that naturally led him into the field of intelligence, where he served as a British spy in Switzerland during WWI and in Russia prior to the 1917 Revolution. Alfred Hitchcock's **Secret Agent**, 1936, is based upon Maugham's novel, *Ashenden*, which depicts the experiences of a gentleman spy. (For more details on Maugham's service and exploits as a British intelligence agent, see my book *Spies: A Narrative Encyclopedia of Dirty Deeds and Double Dealing from Biblical Times to the Present* (M. Evans, 1997; pages 342-345). He was reportedly the highest paid author of the 1930s, growing so rich that he was able to purchase a lavish villa on the Riviera where he lived out his long life. **p**, Pandro S. Berman; **d**, John Cromwell; **cast**, Leslie Howard, Bette Davis, Frances Dee, Kay Johnson, Reginald Denny, Alan Hale, Reginald Sheffield, Reginald Owen, Desmond Roberts, Charles Coleman; **w**, Lester Cohen (based on the novel by W. Somerset Maugham); **c**, Henry W. Gerrard; **m**, Max Steiner; **ed**, William Morgan; **art d**, Van Nest Polglase, Carroll Clark; **spec eff**, Vernon L. Walker, Harry Redmond Sr. and Jr.

Of Human Hearts ★★★★ 1938; U.S.; 103m; MGM; B/W; Drama; Children: Cautionary; **VHS**. The struggling lifestyle in the Ohio Valley before the Civil War is made even more demanding and miserable for Huston's family through his stern credo. Huston is a minister, who zealously embraces poverty as an example to his parishioners, but this results in his wife, Bondi, becoming a household slave as they scrimp and save to survive, and where his son (Reynolds as a boy and Stewart as a young man) grows to hate him because of the hardscrabble life Huston has imposed upon them. When maturing, Stewart's dream is to become a doctor, but his family is so poor that there is little hope that he will ever be able to afford to study medicine. Bondi, however, defies Huston, and sells off some of her belongings and uses up her dowry to send Stewart to an eastern college. Stewart becomes so absorbed with his ambitions to become a physician that he ignores his family. He returns home only when Huston is dying. He then enters the Union Army as a doctor when the Civil War begins. Bondi, now a widow, is left alone and she uses up every penny she has to survive, but is slowly starving, never hearing from Stewart and coming to believe that he may have been killed in battle. Her anxiety about her son's welfare finally compels her to write a letter to President Abraham Lincoln (1809-1865), played by Carradine, begging Lincoln to find out whether her son is alive or dead. Carradine does look into the matter and finds that Stewart is alive and summons him to the White House where he politely reprimands

Stewart for not writing to his mother or contacting her, particularly since she is in great need. A chastised Stewart is given a furlough by Lincoln and he returns home, embracing his neglected mother and promising Bondi that she will never suffer another day and that he will take care of her as a dutiful and loving son. Although inherently melodramatic, pantheon director Brown unfolds this poignant and moving tale with great care, employing impactful scenes that profile his characters so that each projects a separate and strong personality, all of them made memorable through the superlative performances of Huston, Bondi and Stewart (and where Reynolds as a boy is also a standout). Carradine, who appears only briefly as Lincoln, is nevertheless forcefully believable. (See the Index for Historical Personalities in Volume II of this work for a comprehensive list of all films profiling Abraham Lincoln.) Songs: "Bringing in the Sheaves" (1880: music: George A. Minor; 1874: lyrics: Knowles Shaw), "Onward Christian Soldiers" (1871: music: Arthur Sullivan; 1865: lyrics: Sabine Baring-Gould), "The Sweet By-and-By" (1868; music: J. P. Webster; lyrics: S. Fillmore Bennett), "Yankee Doodle" (1755; traditional), "Maryland, My Maryland" (music based on "O, Tannenbaum"; lyrics: James Ryder Randall), "(I Wish I Was in) Dixie's Land" (1860; Daniel Decatur Emmett), "The Battle Cry of Freedom" (1862; George Frederick Root), "There Is a Tavern in the Town" (1891; F. J. Adams), "Battle Hymn of the Republic" (1862; music: William Steffe; lyrics: Julia Ward Howe), "Taps" (1862; Daniel Butterfield). *Author's Note*: "The picture is a heart breaker from the beginning," Brown told this author, "and I had to tone down the suffering of the mother [Bondi] and her son [Reynolds and later Stewart] brought on by Huston. He is a clergyman who takes the Bible too seriously and simply ignores the feelings of the people closest to him and that is the tragedy of this family. It's an old-fashioned story, but it is an honest one that affects every family even today where overbearing fathers kill off any love their family members have for them." Stewart stated to this author that "the syrup gets a little thick in that picture, but the great performances by Huston, who plays my father, and Bondi, who plays my mother, offset a lot of that bathos. I didn't like my character much as I am a deep believer that your mother comes first on this earth and the young man I play ignores his own. A friend of mine went to see the picture when it came out and she then told me that 'I thought you were a nice person—how could you treat your mother like that in that picture, knowing that she was starving to death and not lifting a hand to help her?' Then I knew that **Of Human Hearts** had hit its mark." **p**, John W. Considine, Jr.; **d**, Clarence Brown; **cast**, Walter Huston, James Stewart, Beulah Bondi, Gene Reynolds, Guy Kibbee, Charles Coburn, John Carradine, Ann Rutherford, Leatrice Joy Gilbert, Charley Grapewin, Gene Lockhart, Sterling Holloway, Ward Bond, Phillip Terry; **w**, Bradbury Foote (based on the story "Benefits Forgot" by Honore Morrow); **c**, Clyde De Vinna; **m**, Herbert Stothart; **ed**, Frank E. Hull; **art d**, Cedric Gibbons.

Of Mice and Men ★★★★★ 1939; U.S.; 106m; Hal Roach Studios/UA; B/W; Drama; Children: Unacceptable; **DVD**; **VHS**. Milestone, a pantheon director of action and, particularly, war films, uses all his great skills to present this mesmerizing masterpiece of two lonely ranch workers seeking minor security and a slice of happiness in their world of chronic hardship and poverty. It is the story of two friends, George (Meredith), an intelligent and compassionate man, and Lennie (Chaney), a huge, powerful but dim-witted man with the gentle nature of an eight-year-old child. The two friends are shown at the beginning running from a posse somewhere in the West, narrowly escaping the clutches of the law. They then drift about, picking up odd jobs until they reach the San Joachim Valley in California, where they are hired as full-time hands at a barley ranch, their employer a skinflint with a worthless, self-centered son, Steele, who is married to tramp Field. The two bed down in a bunkhouse with other workers, who discover that Chaney has incredible strength, but is so weak minded that he forgets everything, except his utter dependence upon Meredith, who has inexplicably appointed himself as Chaney's guardian. Chaney loves little animals, but

Lon Chaney Jr. and Betty Field in *Of Mice and Men*, 1939.

when his mind drifts, his petting sometimes changes to crushing caresses that take the lives of these animals. The two friends often amuse themselves with their favorite fantasy, one where they will buy and run a small ranch and where Chaney is promised by Meredith that he can tend to the rabbits so that he can pet the furry creatures, a prospect that delights his childish mind. Bohnen, one of the workers, who is missing a hand and whose only friend is an ancient and foul-smelling dog, overhears the two talking about getting such a place, saying that he will give them his life savings if they take him along to that ranch. At first, Meredith refuses the offer, but then reconsiders when thinking that they might pool their resources, saving their wages and then buying a small ranch he knows about. Meanwhile, the vicious, sadistic Steele begins picking on Chaney, a man much larger than himself, in order to prove his superiority. Bickford, the kind-hearted foreman, however, protects Chaney from Steele's bullying. For his part, Steele believes that Bickford, and perhaps some of the other hands, have dallied with his promiscuous wife, Field, which may be one of the reasons why Steele is so abrasive and anti-social. When Bickford asks Meredith why Chaney is so thick-headed, Meredith tells him that Chaney has been kicked in the head by a horse, but that he is so powerful that he does not know his own strength. Field then finds Chaney a curiosity and begins flirting with the giant, who is dumbfounded by it all. When Steele learns about this, he charges into the barracks and confronts Chaney, who blubbers incoherent responses to Steele's accusations. Steele then explodes and begins punching Chaney in the face, hitting the big man for all he is worth as Chaney cowers under the barrage of savage blows. Meredith can no longer tolerate the punishment his friend is taking and tells Chaney to fight back. Chaney lurches forward and catches Steele's flying fist in mid-air, clutching it in his huge hand and then crushes it, breaking all the bones in Steele's hand until he drops unconscious from the excruciating pain. Bickford then tells Steele that he is to inform his father that he caught his hand in some machinery unless he wants it known that he was injured by a half-witted ranch hand, and Steele agrees that that will be his story. Meanwhile, Field continues flirting with the child-like Chaney. He has been given a puppy to play with, but has killed the little dog by manhandling it with his massive hands. When Field approaches Chaney in a barn, he attempts to caress her hair as he would an animal, and, when she resists, Chaney panics and kills her. Realizing what he has done, he flees to the woods with a posse soon hunting for him (as had been the case at the beginning of the film). Meredith finds Chaney before the posse does and, knowing the fate that awaits the giant, has Chaney look away while he tells them about how they are going to have a ranch together and, as Chaney smiles and thinks about that idyllic haven, Meredith mercifully fires a bullet into his head, ending this trageic-torn tale. The acting by the cast, especially Meredith,

Richard Gere and Debra Winger in *An Officer and a Gentleman,* **1982.**

Chaney (his finest role), Bickford, Field, Steele and Bohnen, is superlative, and the script faithfully follows the powerful Steinbeck novel. Brodine's lensing under Milestone's diligent direction is starkly apt for the story while Copland's exciting score captures the well-choreographed action and the pensive and moody scenes. *Author's Note*: Steinbeck told this author that "I had two stories, **Of Mice and Men**, and **The Grapes of Wrath** [1940] appear on the screen almost within six months of each other. Both were brought to the screen by two great directors, Lewis Milestone [**Of Mice and Men**] and John Ford [**The Grapes of Wrath**]. I felt fortunate that my works were in such good and talented hands. Other writers, I knew, had not been so lucky in Hollywood." Unlike most authors, Steinbeck wrote for Hollywood, producing film adaptations for his own works as well as writing separate and outstanding screenplays. **p&d**, Lewis Milestone; **cast**, Burgess Meredith, Betty Field, Lon Chaney, Jr., Charles Bickford, Roman Bohnen, Bob Steele, Noah Beery, Jr., Oscar O'Shea, Granville Bates, Leigh Whipper, Helen Lynd; **w**, Eugene Solow (based on the novel by John Steinbeck); **c**, Norbert Brodine; **m**, Aaron Copland; **ed**, Bert Jordan; **art d**, Nicolai Remisoff; **spec eff**, Roy Seawright.

Of Mice and Men ★★★ 1992; U.S.; 115m; MGM; Color; Drama; Children: Unacceptable (MPAA: PG-13); **DVD**; **VHS**. A remake of the 1939 film based on Steinbeck's 1937 novel about two drifters who wander California during the 1930s Great Depression dreaming of a better life for themselves. Malkovich is a big, strong, lumbering fellow short on grey matter and Sinise is his compassionate friend and protector, who tells him they will one day have a wonderful ranch together. The dream turns into a nightmare when Malkovich, not realizing his strength, accidentally kills Fenn, a young woman to whom he is attracted. To save him from arrest and execution, Sinise fires a bullet in his friend's head. A fine film with top-flight acting, although not as good as the 1939 production. **p**, Gary Sinise, Russell Smith; **d**, Sinise; **cast**, John Malkovich, Sinise, Ray Walston, Casey Siemaszko, Sherilyn Fenn, John Terry, Richard Riehle, Alexis Arquette, Joe Morton, Noble Willingham, Joe D'Angerio, Moira Harris (Moira Sinise); **w**, Horton Foote (based on the novel by John Steinbeck); **c**, Kenneth MacMillan; **m**, Mark Isham; **ed**, Robert L. Sinise; **prod d**, David Gropman; **art d**, Dan Davis; **set d**, Joyce Anne Gilstrap, Karen Schulz Gropman; **spec eff**, Howard Jensen.

Of Stars and Men ★★★ 1964; U.S.; 53m; Storyboard/Brandon Films; Color; Animated Fantasy; Children: Acceptable; **VHS**. Made in 1961 and released in the U.S. in 1964, this is an animated fantasy based on the book by Harlow Shapley, an American astronomer, one that explores evolution and man's place in the universe, with the possibility of life on other planets. A fascinating film, this film has high production values

and offers a visual delight for audiences of all ages. **p**, John and Faith Hubley (based on the book by Harlow Shapley); **d**, John Hubley; **cast** (voiceovers), Harlow Shapley, Mark and Ray Hubley; **c**, Jack Buehre (Eastmancolor); **m**, Walter Trampler; **ed**, Faith Hubley.

Off the Map ★★★ 2003; U.S.; 108m; Holedigger Films/New Films International; Color; Drama; Children: Unacceptable (MPAA: PG-13); **DVD**. This offbeat but engrossing drama sees a family living in an adobe house with no lights or running water in a remote area of New Mexico. They are poor but live a free life, growing their own vegetables, raiding the nearby city dump. The father, Elliott, gets $320 a month in veterans' benefits and goes fishing with his best friend, Simmons. His wife, Allen, accepts their lifestyle and enjoys gardening in the nude. Their twelve-year-old daughter, Brenneman, is schooled at home. True-Frost, an IRS man, arrives to audit the family's finances because Elliott has reported an annual income of less than $5,000 for several years. However, the agent befriends the family and stays, living in an old school bus on the property. The main focus of the film is Elliott's long-standing depression and how he and the others deal with it, the story line mixing True-Frost's attraction to Allen, which reawakens Elliott's love for and appreciation of her. Nudity and thematic elements prohibit viewing by children. **p**, Campbell Scott, George VanBuskirk; **d**, Scott; **cast**, Amy Brenneman, Joan Allen, Sam Elliott, Valentina de Angelis, J.K. Simmons, Boots Southern, J.D. Garfield, Jim True-Frost, Matthew E. Montoya, Kathy Griego; **w**, Joan Ackermann (based on her play); **c**, Juan Ruiz Anchía; **m**, Gary DeMichele; **ed**, Andy Keir; **prod d**, Chris Shriver; **set d**, David Schlesinger; **spec eff**, James D. Tittle.

The Offence ★★★ 1973; U.K.; 112m; UA; Color; Drama; Children: Unacceptable (MPAA: R); **DVD**; **VHS**. In this gripping crime tale, Connery is a London police sergeant, who is stressed out after twenty years of being involved in cases ranging from murders and rapes to child molestation. He finally cracks when interviewing Bannen, a man suspected of a series of brutal sexual attacks on young girls, and beats him to death. While beating him, Connery reveals to the suspect and to himself that his brutality may be no better than the criminals whose crimes always disgusted him. His aggression, we learn, has stemmed from having been the victim of child molestation when he was a boy. Although somewhat stagey, as is Lumet's style, the film nevertheless provides a compelling story highlighted by Connery's powerful performance. The story line owes much to **On Dangerous Ground**, 1952, a film where Robert Ryan is a detective who brutally vents his pent-up anger and seething inhibitions by savagely beating criminal suspects. Song: "Groupie" (Barry Stoller); Violence and sexual molestation themes prohibit viewing by children. **p**, Denis O'Dell; **d**, Sidney Lumet; **cast**, Sean Connery, Trevor Howard, Vivien Merchant, Ian Bannen, Peter Bowles, Derek Newark, Ronald Radd, John Hallam, Richard Moore, Anthony Sagar, Maxine Gordon; **w**, John Hopkins (based on his play "This Story of Yours"); **c**, Gerry Fisher (DeLuxe Color); **m**, Harrison Birtwistle; **ed**, John Victor-Smith; **art d**, John Clark.

An Officer and a Gentleman ★★★ 1982; U.S.; 124m; Lorimar/PAR; Color; Drama/Romance; Children: Unacceptable (MPAA: R); **DVD**; **VHS**. Solid and heartwarming romantic drama sees slum boy Gere living with a drunken and abusive father, Loggia (not unlike the alcoholic father, Stewart Germain, who haunts and embarrasses Fritz Weaver, a troubled U.S. Air Force officer in **Fail Safe**, 1964). Gere's only prospect in life is that he make good by entering and graduating from a thirteen-week cadet course before being trained as a pilot. He and other plebes have no easy going as their pride is stripped from them as they are put through grueling and challenging training by tough, no-nonsense drill sergeant Gossett (in one of his finest roles, one that won him an Oscar as Supporting Actor). Gossett will tolerate no wisecracks, complaints or backtalk and mostly detests sniveling types. Gossett's only goal in his profession is to either make officers and gentlemen out of these untrained youths or wash them out and send them back to where they came from and he is inclined to do the latter. Gere and Gossett are at loggerheads right from the beginning. Gere believing that Gossett has unfairly singled him out for severe punishment for the slightest infraction, and Gossett believes that Gere has marked him for a patsy and can get around him with his clever banter and charming ways. While on a short furlough, Gere meets and falls for attractive Winger, a mill worker, who is looking for just such a Prince Charming as Gere to rescue her from her drudgery, as does Blount (in her film debut), who meets Gere's friend, Keith. Blount tells Winger that she is fooling herself if she believes that Gere, once he has become an officer and a gentleman, will return for her as she believes that she and Winger are doomed to their class of working people and can never rise above their social station in life. Blount cruelly rejects Keith and this so emotionally destroys him that he commits suicide. Gere, meanwhile, struggles to meet Gossett's near-impossible demands in his rigorous training and is almost washed out (even after challenging Gossett to a fight and where Gossett thoroughly trounces him), but he manages to graduate at the end, thanking Gossett for keeping him on the straight and narrow course. Now that he is an officer and a gentleman and has a rewarding and secure future awaiting him, Gere is about to report to pilot training. Before that happens, he valiantly goes back to the mill where Winger works, and, in one of the most romantic and heart-rewarding scenes in any film romance, he resolutely goes into the mill, walks up to her as she works at her machine, sweeps her off her feet, and passionately kisses her, and then carries her from the place, proving to her and to the rest of the approving filmgoers of the world that he is truly an American knight in shining armor. Gere, Winger, Blount, Keith and Gossett are superb in their roles, with Gossett dominating every one of his scenes through his magnetic and riveting personality. Stewart's script is excellent and true to reality in that he based the story on his own experiences as a U.S. Navy officer. *Author's Note*: Winger received an Oscar nomination as Best Actress for **An Officer and a Gentleman**, and it was her role in this film that established her as a first-rate actress, earning her a berth in **Terms of Endearment**, 1984, where she again was nominated for a Best Actress Oscar, but lost out to Shirley MacLaine, who appeared in that same film. **p**, Martin Elfand; **d**, Taylor Hackford; **cast**, Richard Gere, Debra Winger, David Keith, Robert Loggia, Lisa Blount, Lisa Eilbacher, Louis Gossett, Jr., Tony Plana, Harold Sylvester, David Caruso; **w**, Douglas Day Stewart; **c**, Donald Thorin (Metrocolor); **m**, Jack Nitzsche; **ed**, Peter Zinner; **prod d**, Philip M. Jefferies; **art d**, John Cartwright; **set d**, James I. Berkey; **spec eff**, Joseph P. Mercurio.

The Official Story ★★★ 1985; Argentina; 112m; Historias Cinematografica Cinemania/Almi Pictures; Color; Drama; Children: Unacceptable (MPAA: R); **DVD**; **VHS**. This fascinating drama has Aleandro as a high school history professor living a comfortable life in Buenos Aires, Argentina, in 1983 after the fall of the military dictatorship that took over from the government that had been in power since 1976. Her husband, Alterio, is a successful lawyer and they have a five-year-old adopted daughter, Castro. The film focuses on Aleandro's efforts to learn the identity of the girl's birth mother. Alterio insists the girl was obtained through normal adoption methods in Argentina, but Aleandro wonders if she was stolen from a mother, who was a political prisoner. She loves the girl, but wants to know her story and learn if her birth mother is still alive. Aleandro then meets an old woman, who may be the girl's grandmother, but this meeting leads to no conclusion. Of the 30,000 people who disappeared over the seven years of the military dictatorship (1976-1983), many were children, who were sold to wealthy families. Only the girl knows the official story of her early life, but she was too young to remember any of it. Filming of the movie began in 1983, but was canceled due to threats to the director, actors, and to the family of Analia Castro upon whom the true story is based. Production secretly resumed in 1985 and the film was completed and released. The brave moviemak-

Analia Castro, Héctor Alterio and Norma Aleandro in *The Official Story*, 1985.

ers won the 1986 Academy Award for Best Foreign Language film. Song: "El pais del nome acuerdo" (Maria Elena Walsh). (In Spanish; English subtitles.) Violence prohibits viewing by children. **p**, Marcelo Piñeyro; **d**, Luis Puenzo; **cast**, Norma Aleandro, Héctor Alterio, Analia Castro, Chunchuna Villafañe, Hugo Arana, Guillermo Battaglia, Chela Ruíz, Patricio Contreras, María Luisa Robledo, Aníbal Morixe, Jorge Petraglia; **w**, Puenzo, Aída Bortnik; **c**, Félix Monti; **m**, Atilio Stampone; **ed**, Juan Carlos Macías; **prod d**, Abel Facello; **set d**, Adriana Sforza.

Offside ★★★ 2006; Iran; 93m; Jafar Panahi Film Productions/Sony; Color; Sports Comedy; Children: Cautionary (MPAA: PG); **DVD**. With the establishment of the Islamic Republic in Iran, Iranian women were barred from attending stadiums holding sporting events. This entertaining story is based on a true event occurring in June 2005 when Iran defeated Bahrain to qualify for the World Cup. Some girls want to see the big soccer match so they attempt to enter Tehran's Azadi Stadium dressed as boys. One of them dresses in a soldier's uniform. They are not political activists, only sports fans who want to see a good game. They are told that the reason women cannot attend stadium sporting events is so that men attending can use offensive language as they please. The girls say they simply won't listen, but it does no good and some are arrested, but are not kept in a stadium holding pen for any long period. The girls are ruled "offside," and released, but they have scored their point. Song: "Ey Iran" (Hossein Gol-e-Golab, Ruhollah Khaleghi). Gutter language and thematic elements prohibit viewing by children. Though this tale and the conduct of the Iranian girls are jocularly profiled, Western world critics do not condone the widespread suppression of women's rights in many Islamic countries. (In Persian; English subtitles.) **p&d**, Jafar Panahi; **cast**, Sima Mobarak-Shahi, Shayesteh Irani, Ayda Sadeqi, Golnaz Farmani, Mahnaz Zabihi, Nazanin Sediq-zadeh, Melika Shafahi, Safdar Samandar, Mohammad Kheir-abadi, Masoud Kheymeh-kabood; **w**, Panahi, Shadmehr Rastin; **c**, Rami Agami, Mahmoud Kalari; **m**, Yuval Barazani, Korosh Bozorgpour; **ed**, Panahi; **prod d**, Iraj Raminfar.

Oh, God! ★★★ 1977; U.S.; 98m; WB; Color; Comedy/Fantasy; Children: Acceptable; **DVD**; **VHS**. Delightful comedy sees mild-mannered Denver working as an assistant manager in a supermarket. He is married to Garr and, though he works hard, he doesn't seem to find the next rung up the ladder of success. Then, either by selection or arbitrary whimsy, God selects Denver to be his spokesman on Earth. He visits Denver in the form of an old man, Burns (who is absolutely riveting in his wisecracking savant role), telling Denver that he has been nominated as someone who must now spread His Gospel of love and good will throughout the planet. The withdrawn Denver does not think he is the

Ginger Rogers and Dan Dailey in *Oh, Men! Oh, Women!*, **1957.**

right candidate for this colossal mission, but nevertheless, after several more convincing visits from Burns, he agrees to spread the Good Word. The problem is that no one believes Denver when he begins to disseminate God's messages. His boss at the supermarket fires him and wife Garr thinks he has gone bats. Denver, however, is now inspired as God's messenger and, undaunted, he continues to preach love and understanding and even expose hypocrisy when he appears at a huge evangelical meeting where pretentious and posturing Sorvino presides as a self-appointed evangelist, who is only interested in acquiring wealth and power. Denver is brought to the podium during the meeting to say that he has a message from God for Sorvino, who turns to the audience and blares on his microphone: "He has a message from God for ME!" When Sorvino asks what that message is, Denver bluntly tells him that God thinks that Sorvino should be selling used cars instead of posing as a religious leader. Sorvino explodes and enlists other orthodox religious leaders in joining him in a lawsuit against Denver. He is brought to trial before wise judge Hughes. All the evidence is stacked against Denver, who insists that he had spoken directly to God several times and that God (Burns) asked him to be his representative on Earth. All looks black for Denver until Burns magically (or spiritually) appears in the court and takes the witness stand where He banters with prosecuting attorneys and baffles Hughes by making objects appear and disappear. He states that He is, indeed, God, and that He asked Denver to be His spokesman and while explaining this, Burns also spreads His doctrine of good will toward one and all. To convince everyone in that court that what He has said is de facto, Burns vanishes before everyone's eyes into thin air. The startled Hughes then holds a meeting in his chambers where he tries to evaluate what he and the others have seen, but Burns has left no record of His comments with the stenographer and a tape recording does not yield His voice. In the best interest of the confused court, Hughes dismisses the case and Denver starts looking for another job. As he is driving along, Burns again appears and asks him to continue the Lord's work and Denver agrees. This rollicking comedy proved to be an enormous success, taking in more than $50 million at the box office, making this the seventh highest grossing film for 1977. Gelbart's script was nominated for an Oscar as Best Adapted Screenplay. *Author's Note*: Many films profile heavenly visitors, notably **All Dogs Go to Heaven**, 1989; **All Dogs Go to Heaven 2**, 1996; **Angels in the Outfield**, 1951; **Angels in the Outfield**, 1994; **The Bishop's Wife**, 1947; **Cabin in the Sky**, 1943; **Carousel**, 1956; **A Christmas Carol**, 1938; **A Christmas Carol**, 1951; **The Green Pastures**, 1936; **A Guy Named Joe**, 1943; **Heaven Can Wait**, 1978; **Here Comes Mr. Jordan**, 1941; **The Horn Blows at Midnight**, 1945; **It's a Wonderful Life**, 1947; **Liliom**, 1935; **Michael**, 1996; **The Milagro Beanfield War**, 1988; **The Next Voice You Hear**, 1950; **One Magic Christmas**, 1985; **Scrooge**, 1970; **Stairway to**

Heaven, 1947; and **Strange Cargo**, 1940; for a more complete list of such films, see Heavenly Visitors, Subject Index, Volume II of this work. **p**, Jerry Weintraub; **d**, Carl Reiner; **cast**, George Burns, John Denver, Teri Garr, Donald Pleasence, Ralph Bellamy, William Daniels, Barnard Hughes, Paul Sorvino, Barry Sullivan, Dinah Shore, Jeff Corey, David Ogden Stiers, Moosie Drier; **w**, Larry Gelbart (based on the novel by Avery Corman); **c**, Victor J. Kemper (Technicolor); **m**, Jack Elliott; **ed**, Bud Molin; **art d**, Jack Senter; **set d**, Stuart A. Reiss.

Oh, Men! Oh, Women! ★★★ 1957; U.S.; 90m; FOX; Color; Comedy; Children: Cautionary; **DVD**. Rogers is a bored Los Angeles housewife married to alcoholic movie star Dailey, so she goes to a psychoanalyst, Niven, who is bored with his other patients. He is looking forward to marrying the sultry Rush, but he learns that she is not only dallying about with Dailey, but is seeing Randall, who is as eccentric as Rush. After some very funny incidents, Niven manages to cement the relationship between Rogers and Dailey, but Rush appears to dump him when he criticizes her flirtatious behavior. All is not lost, however, because Rush comes to her senses at the last minute to join Niven on a wedding cruise. Johnson directs with a sure hand and keeps the laughs coming at a fast clip, and his literate and inventive script offers a lot of sharp and witty dialogue. The cast members are standouts. Randall debuts in this, his first feature film, although he had made many appearances in mostly TV sitcoms. *Author's Note*: Niven told this author that "I have plenty to do in that picture as a psychiatrist as Barbara [Rush] and Tony [Randall] play certifiable crackpots. I am chasing after Barbara while Tony is chasing after her and then Ginger [Rogers] starts chasing after me because she is like 'Nora' and wants to escape her 'Doll House.' It was hard to hold on to your sanity and keep track of every oddball at the same time, but we managed it…just." Rogers thought her role in this outlandish comedy "pretty much like a porcelain woman on a pedestal, until I get it into my head that David [Niven], who is a shrink that will tolerate any kind of nonsense, is the man for me and not my boozy husband, Dan [Dailey]. It all works out because I get my head examined and I need it while I am running around after a man, who only wants to organize my goofy mind." Johnson became incensed when he was told by Fox executives that playwright Chodorov's name could not be given credit because he had been blacklisted a decade earlier during the political witch hunts conducted by Congress as having had communist affiliations. "I told them that if they were going to take off Chodorov's name from the credits, they had to remove mine, too, but they refused," Johnson told this author. "It was a double standard in Hollywood all the way in those days." **p,d&w**, Nunnally Johnson (based on the play by Edward Chodorov); **cast**, Ginger Rogers, Dan Dailey, David Niven, Tony Randall, Barbara Rush, Natalie Schafer, Rachel Stephens, John Wengraf, Cheryll Clarke, Clancy Cooper; **c**, Charles G. Clarke (CinemaScope; DeLuxe Color); **m**, Cyril J. Mockridge; **ed**, Marjorie Fowler; **art d**, Lyle R. Wheeler, Maurice Ransford; **set d**, Walter M. Scott, Stuart A. Reiss.

Oh! What a Lovely War ★★★ 1969; U.K.; 144m; Accord Productions/PAR; Color; Musical; Children: Cautionary (MPAA: G); **DVD**. It is hard to believe that anyone could produce and make successful a biting, irreverent satire, let alone a musical, about World War I, but this is exactly what the producers of this amazing film did and they did it with inventive style. The fact that this production did not appear until fifty years after the end of that grim war may have had something to do with the public perception that by then viewed that awful and grim carnage as the foolhardy and insane exploits of kings and emperors, rather than the noble and serious cause its participants originally envisioned. The film begins by showing the royalty and rulers of several European nations gathered together for an affable group photograph and where that portrait explodes with the assassination of Archduke Franz Ferdinand (1863-1914), who is shown being killed at Sarajevo in 1914 and is played by Pithey. As a result, the kings and rulers get into a wild argument, choose sides, and declare war, which is shown as a major attraction in a flashing sign on an amusement pier at Brighton Beach, England. A large family named Smith buys tickets to the attraction and all of its five sons wind up going to the war while a huge sign consistently updates the mounting war casualties. Bogarde and his wife, York, are aristocrats and they do their "bit" by refusing to drink German wines and order their family housekeeper to knit mittens for British soldiers fighting on the Western Front. British Field Marshal Sir Douglas Haig (1861-1928), portrayed by Mills, launches the Somme offensive and then later announces to the public that his forces gained no ground, but that *only* 60,000 troops were killed in this senseless slaughter. All of the Smith sons are killed in the war, the last sibling dying on the very last day of the war and where the scoreboard now announces that nine million have been killed in this war. Only the Smith women survive and are shown in a final shot picnicking next to the graves of their dead, the camera then slowly panning upward to show row on row of white crosses until the hills are dotted with these graves as far as the eye can see. The fine direction, acting and script all contribute to a savage indictment of war, and an astounding number of the Knights of the Realm appear on camera (Sir John Mills, Sir Laurence Olivier, Sir John Clements, Sir Michael Redgrave, Sir Ralph Richardson, Sir John Gielgud). Songs: "Are We Downhearted? No!" (Worton David, Lawrence Wright), "Oh, It's a Lovely War" (John Long, Maurice Scott), "It's a Long Way to Tipperary" (Jack Judge, Harry Williams), "Sing Me to Sleep, Sergeant Major" (G. Clifton Bingham, Edwin Greene), "The Bells of Hell" (traditional), "Belgium Put the Kibosh on the Kaiser" (Alf Ellerton), "I'll Make a Man of You" (music: Herman Finck; lyrics: Arthur Wimperis), "Your King and Country" (Paul Rubens), "Auld Lang Syne" (traditional), "When You Wore a Tulip" (music: Percy Wenrich; lyrics: Jack Mahoney), "Silent Night" (music: Franz Gruber), "Pack Up Your Troubles" (George Asaf, Felix Powell), "Gassed Last Night" (traditional), "Goodbye—ee" (Bert Lee, R. P. Weston), "Roses of Picardy" (music: Haydn Wood; lyrics: Frederick Edward Weatherly), "Comrades" (Felix McGlennon), "Row, Row, Row" (William Jerome, James V. Monaco), "She Was One of the Early Birds" (T. W. Conner), "There's a Long, Long Trail A-Winding" (Zo Elliott, Stoddard King), "Hush, Here Comes the Dream Man" (Fred J. Barnes, R. P. Weston, Maurice Scott), "Mademoiselle from Armentieres" (Harry Carlton, Joseph Tunbridge), "What a Friend We Have in Jesus" (music: Charles Crozat Converse), "Bonsoir Mon Amour" (Rene Lepeltier, Andre Sablon), "Red Wing" (music: Kerry Mills; lyrics: Thurland Chattaway), "Battle Hymn of the Republic" (music: William Steffe; lyrics: Julia Ward Howe), "Onward Christian Soldiers" (music: Arthur Sullivan; lyrics: Sabine Baring-Gould), "Whiter Than the Whitewash" (traditional), "The Church's One Foundation" (music: Samuel Wesley), "Never Mind" (Henry Dent, Tom Goldburn), "I Want to Go Home" (traditional), "Till the Boys Come Home" (Ivor Novello), "The Alley Alley Oh" (traditional), "They Didn't Believe Me" (music: Jerome Kern; lyrics: Herbert Reynolds), "Over There" (George M. Cohan). *Author's Note*: Attenborough, an accomplished actor, was asked to co-direct this film, the first helming of this gifted man, but he soon got into heated arguments with co-director Deighton, who believed that Attenborough was being too soft on the biting material that scathingly criticized the powerful persons who launched that slaughterhouse war of attrition (1914-1918). So heated were their arguments that Deighton finally insisted that his name be removed from the credits. The public was told that the reason for Deighton's departure was over "contractual disagreements," but the truth was that Deighton and Attenborough were at hopeless loggerheads about the treating of the material. There is truly very little that appears in this fascinating film that is funny—it is as sad, poignant and tragic as was that terrible war. That war's plaintive music, which is positioned in ridicule here, nevertheless survives on its own good merits, spiting its detractors as that music is too deeply rooted in the memorable history of that war's human sacrifice to be disturbingly misrepresented by the exceptionally talented revisionists of this production. Although this film

Mark Stevens and June Haver in *Oh, You Beautiful Doll*, 1949.

was broadly acclaimed in Great Britain and did great box office there, this film did only lukewarm business in the U.S. where naked sentiment about that war more hauntingly lingered and where considerable resentment was expressed toward those thinking to denigrate the image (if, indeed, that was the intention) of its hallowed dead or ignore the spiritual significance of the remains occupying the Tomb of the Unknown Soldier. The "Doughboy" is not mocked in America. **p**, Brian Duffy, Richard Attenborough; **d**, Attenborough; **cast**, Dirk Bogarde, Phyllis Calvert, Jean-Pierre Cassel, John Clements, Edward Fox, John Gielgud, Jack Hawkins, Ian Holm, John Mills, Kenneth More, Laurence Olivier, Michael Redgrave, Vanessa Redgrave, Jane Seymour, Maggie Smith, Susannah York; **w**, Len Deighton (based on Joan Littlewood's stage production of Charles Chilton's play "The Long, Long Trail"); **c**, Gerry Turpin (Panavision; Technicolor); **m**, Alfred Ralston; **ed**, Kevin Connor; **prod d**, Donald M. Ashton; **art d**, Harry White; **set d**, Peter James; **spec eff**, Ron Ballanger.

Oh, You Beautiful Doll ★★★ 1949; U.S.; 93m; FOX; Color; Musical/Biography; Children: Acceptable. A rollicking period musical set in the early 1900s portrays New York's Tin Pan Alley of song publishers, where song promoter Stevens meets a struggling composer of operas, Sakall, and suggests his arias could sell as popular songs if he gives them more up-tempo. Needing money, Sakall reluctantly agrees, but changes his name from Albert von Breitenbach to Fred Fisher which preserves his anonymity in case he can later find success composing operas, which he never does. His lovely daughter, Haver, encourages Stevens' idea because she aspires to be a singer and dancer. Sakall becomes a hit composer of popular songs, Haver gets to sing and dance, and she and Stevens fall in love with each other. Songs: "Come Josephine in My Flying Machine" (Fred Fisher, Al Bryan), "Ireland Must Be Heaven, for My Mother Came from There" (Fisher, Howard Johnson, Joseph McCarthy), "Oh, You Beautiful Doll" (Nat Ayer, A. Seymour Brown), "I Want You to Want Me" (Fisher, Bob Schafer, Al Bryan), "When I Get You Alone Tonight' (Fisher, Joseph McCarthy, Joe Goodwin), "Peg O' My Heart" (Fisher, Bryan), "There's a Broken Heart for Every Light on Broadway" (Fisher, Howard Johnson), "Daddy, You've Been a Mother to Me" (Fisher), "Dardanella" (Felix Bernard, Johnny Black), "Chicago/That Toddlin' Town" (Fisher). *Author's Note*: Fisher's real name was Albert von Breitenbach (1875-1942); he founded the Fred Fisher Music Publishing Co. in 1907. Fisher wrote most of the songs in the film, but not the title song. The idea of a composer of operas converting his works to popular songs by changing tempo is also shown in the fine biopic of Sigmund Romberg, **Deep in My Heart**, 1954, where the gifted Jose Ferrer plays Romberg. **p**, George Jessel; **d**, John M. Stahl; **cast**, June Haver, Mark Stevens, S.Z. "Cuddles" Sakall, Char-

Gordon MacRae in *Oklahoma!*, 1955.

lotte Greenwood, Gale Robbins, Bill Shirley, Jay C. Flippen, Andrew Tombes, Eduard Franz; **w**, Albert Lewis, Arthur Lewis; **c**, Harry Jackson (Technicolor); **ed**, Louis Loeffler; **art d**, Lyle Wheeler, Maurice Ransford; **set d**, Paul S. Fox, Thomas Little; **spec eff**, Fred Sersen.

O' Horten ★★★ 2008; Norway/Germany/France/Denmark; 90m; Bulbul Films/Sony; Color; Comedy; Children: Unacceptable (MPAA: PG-13); **DVD**. This gentle farce about a train engineer named Odd Horten, played by Owe, takes place in Oslo. Owe is forced to retire after forty years and wonders what will happen to him. He searches an airport for someone to buy his small boat, chats with a recently widowed owner of a tobacco shop, and rides with an old drunk, who takes pride in driving a car blindfolded. Like the lovable elephant Horton in the Dr. Seuss (Theodore Seuss Geisel) 1950s picture book stories, he is looking for some purpose in life. Adopting a dog helps, but he still hasn't reached a decision on where he goes from here. The story is charming and the production values high and Owe and cast give top flight performances. Nudity prohibits viewing by children. (In Norwegian; English subtitles.) **p**, Bent Hamer, Karl Baumgartner, Christoph Friedel, Alexandre Mallet-Guy; **d**, Hamer; **cast**, Baard Owe, Espen Skjønberg, Ghita Nørby, Henny Moan, Bjørn Floberg, Kai Remlov, Per Jansen, Bjarte Hjelmeland, Gard B. Eidsvold, Bjørn Jenseg; **w**, Hamer, Harold Manning; **c**, John Christian Rosenlund; **m**, John Erik Kaada; **ed**, Pål Gengenbach; **prod d**, Karl Júlíusson; **set d**, Olivier Marcouiller; **spec eff**, Torgeir Busch, Aksel Jermstad, Ivar Rystad, Espen Skjørdal.

Oil for the Lamps of China ★★★ 1935; U.S.; 97m; Cosmopolitan; WB/First National; B/W; Drama; Children: Cautionary; **DVD**. In this gritty drama, O'Brien is the ultimate company man working for an American oil company in a remote part of China. His blind faith in the company nearly destroys his marriage to Hutchinson and his own life. Eldredge, O'Brien's co-worker and best friend, loses money for the company and O'Brien heartlessly fires him. Hutchinson nearly leaves him because of this. He then risks his life to keep $15,000 of company money from falling into the hands of Chinese communists and is shot for his efforts. While recovering in a hospital, he receives notice that his company is rewarding him with a demotion. A company official in New York learns of the injustice and makes things right. O'Brien is exceptional as a man blinded by his slavish sense of obligations to his employers, and the script is sharp and witty. This film was remade in 1941 as **Law of the Tropics**. *Author's Note*: "Pat [O'Brien] is by nature an affable guy," director LeRoy told this author, "and I had to drive him very hard in that picture to get him to mistreat others for the sake of turning a buck for his company until he turned to me one day and said: 'For crying out loud, you're worse than the guy I have to play!'"

O'Brien told this author that "I didn't like my character in **Oil for the Lamps of China**. All I do is kick people around until I get plugged in a battle while trying to save the company's money. Those were the days when the public loved tough guys so we gave them so many of those pictures that they must have felt bruises when leaving the theater." **p**, Robert Lord; **d**, Mervyn LeRoy; **cast**, Pat O'Brien, Josephine Hutchinson, Jean Muir, Lyle Talbot, Arthur Byron, John Eldredge, Donald Crisp, Willie Fung, Tetsu Komai, Henry O'Neil;, Keye Luke; **w**, Laird Doyle (based on the novel by Alice Tisdale Hobart); **c**, Tony Gaudio; **m**, Leo F. Forbstein; **ed**, William Clemens; **art d**, Robert M. Haas.

Oklahoma! ★★★★ 1955; U.S.; 145m; Magna Theater Corporation; RKO; Color; Musical; Children: Acceptable; **DVD**; **VHS**. In this lively and utterly captivating musical (the first Rodgers and Hammerstein Broadway musical adapted for the screen), the viewer is treated to a sumptuous production so filled with wonderful and memorable songs that music lovers will think they have gone to heaven, or Hollywood's best version of that most desired destination. The story profiles the early-day "Sooners" of Oklahoma where the farmers and the ranchers are at traditional odds over range rights and living styles. Cowboys MacRae and Nelson are attracted to fetching farm girls Jones and Grahame. MacRae finds himself competing with farmhand Steiger, a surly and brutish type, for the attentions of Jones, who wants only MacRae, but is intimidated by Steiger, who lives in a small hut on her farm; Nelson finds traveling salesman Albert winning the attention of Grahame. The conniving Albert and Whitmore, who is Grahame's shotgun-toting father, provide most of the laughs, and Steiger does a great job of being an utterly repulsive and crude character no one would want living next to them. The full-throated MacRae and Jones offer many delightful songs, but to provide an extraordinarily choreographed dancing sequence (the Dream Ballet), Jones and MacRae, who had limited dancing abilities, were replaced by substitutes, dancers Linn and Mitchell (this was the first time on screen such replacements were used), which audiences widely accepted, thus establishing a successful precedent for such presentations repeated in many musicals thereafter. The farmers and ranchers come together at an old-fashioned hoe-down where the cowboys and farm hands bid for the picnic lunches prepared by the girls and where MacRae and Steiger get into a fierce bidding match over Jones' finger-licking chicken lunch until MacRae, either out of intense love for Jones or pride in besting the repugnant Steiger, sells off his gun, saddle and horse to win the lunch and the girl. In the end, bully Steiger gets the heave-ho and MacRae ends up with the loveable Jones while Nelson lassos the willy-nilly Grahame and Albert goes merrily on his way to the next county to sell his wares, greatly relieved that he has evaded a wedding knot. Songs (all composed in 1943 by Richard Rodgers, music; and Oscar Hammerstein II, lyrics): "On, What a Beautiful Mornin'," "Kansas City," "The Surrey with the Fringe on Top," "Many a New Day," "I Can't Say No," "People We'll Say We're in Love," "Poor Jud Is Dead," "Out of My Dreams," "Laurey's Dream Ballet," "All'er Nothin'," "The Farmer and the Cowman," "Oklahoma!" *Author's Note*: This smash musical opened on Broadway in March 1943 and had more than 2,200 performances, a staggering success that originally starred Betty Garde, Celeste Holm, Alfred Drake, Howard Da Silva, Lee Dixon, Joseph Buloff, Joan McCracken, Joan Roberts and Bambi Lynn, the latter being the only member of the original cast to appear in the movie version. The film adaptation offered the then newly developed Tod-AO as well as a CinemaScope version, all in rich Technicolor that displayed stunningly beautiful exterior shots. When scouting for the right location, producers concluded that there was no suitable place in Oklahoma to shoot the film so they selected an area outside of Nogales, Arizona, but they waited almost a year before going into production until a large crop of corn could be raised in the area so that it appeared "as high as an elephant's eye." The selection of that location, however, was based on the assumption that the endless sunshine would provide great lensing, but when the film went into production, the cast and crew soon realized that the place was subject to violent squalls and flash flooding. At one point, a limousine carrying an entire week's shooting was washed away in a violent flash flood and the shooting had to be entirely reshot. The cast and crew were more or less held captive at the location for eight months, enough time for MacRae's wife Sheila to arrive, get pregnant, and deliver her baby before the production was over. Zinnemann told this author that "I was not delayed in the way I handled that picture. I am not one to usually do a lot of takes as I envision and plan each scene long before shooting that scene [he was a film editor to begin with, as was Alfred Hitchcock, which is why these two pantheon directors invariably got their films into the can within budget and on time]. It was the weather that stalled the production and it drove us all crazy." Whitmore told this author that "we were in Arizona so long during the making of that picture that I thought we might be stuck there for years." The search for the female lead playing "Laurey" was almost as intense as the search Selznick conducted for years in seeking an actress to play "Scarlett O'Hara" in **Gone with the Wind**, 1939, although Rodgers and Hammerstein had always thought that Jones, who had been in the chorus of their "South Pacific" on Broadway, might be right for the role. She was given a chance to test for that role with MacRae and her singing voice and acting proved to be perfect for the part. At age nineteen, she was signed up to appear in her first film (fifth billing), that appearance launching her career as a superstar. Steiger told this author that "I got to do my own singing in that picture. They say that I have an operatic voice, but someone said that I could not keep in the same key. Well, that is a lot of baloney. I proved when doing a duet with Gordon MacRae ["Poor Jud Is Dead"] in that picture that I could keep in the same key and I got a lot of compliments for doing that song where I sing in harmony with Gordon. So that [exhibiting an uplifted finger] to the naysayers!" Steiger's daughter (with Claire Bloom), Anna Steiger, went on to become an operatic singer. **p**, Arthur Hornblow, Jr.; **d**, Fred Zinnemann; **cast**, Gordon MacRae, Gloria Grahame, Gene Nelson, Charlotte Greenwood, Shirley Jones, Eddie Albert, James Whitmore, Rod Steiger, Barbara Lawrence, Jay C. Flippen, James Mitchell, Bambi Linn, Marc Platt, Ben Johnson; **w**, Sonya Levien, William Ludwig (based on the musical play by Richard Rodgers, Oscar Hammerstein II from the play "Green Grow the Lilacs" by Lynn Riggs); **c**, Robert Surtees (Todd-AO; CinemaScope; Technicolor); **m**, Rodgers; **ed**, George Boemler; **prod d**, Oliver Smith; **art d**, Joseph Wright; **set d**, Keogh Gleason.

Oklahoma Crude ★★★ 1973; U.S.; 108m; Stanley Kramer Productions/COL; Color; Adventure; Children: Cautionary (MPAA: PG); **DVD**; **VHS**. Sterling producer-director Kramer presents a gritty, tough and often humorous tale set during the boom days of Oklahoma wildcatting. Scott is wonderful as an alcoholic drifter with no ethics as he searches about for any opportunity in the oilfields, believing his future is tied to Dunaway, a woman as calloused and mean-minded as Scott. She owns a small piece of land where, atop a steep hill, she erects a derrick, thinking to drill for oil and find it and her fortune. Her only companion and co-worker is Campos, a stoic Indian. Meanwhile, Palance, the enforcer for a land-grabbing oil firm, attempts to pressure Dunaway into selling her property to that firm, but she refuses all offers to buy out her meager piece of land. Mills, who is Dunaway's estranged father and who long earlier deserted her, suddenly shows up, offering to help her bring in the well, but Dunaway so detests him and his errant ways that she sends him packing. (Mills plays a miserable old man looking for sudden riches much the same way Burgess Meredith, a broken down fight manager begs Sylvester Stallone to be his manager after Stallone is given a shot at the heavyweight championship title in **Rocky**, 1976, and who is initially rejected by Stallone just the same way Dunaway rejects Mills.) Mills settles down in a hobo camp and there meets the scruffy Scott, asking him to help his daughter and promising him that he will get a share of the enormous profits awaiting them when Dunaway brings in a gusher. Almost by whim, Scott goes to Dunaway and

George C. Scott, John Mills and Faye Dunaway in *Oklahoma Crude*, 1973.

offers to work on the drilling and she reluctantly accepts him, but makes it clear that she has no romantic interest in him or any other man, bluntly telling him that she hates all men so much that she wishes she had been born with both female and male organs so she could have sex with herself and never have to think about the opposite gender. Palance then arrives with a gang of thugs and they mercilessly beat Dunaway, Scott and Campos, the latter so severely attacked that he dies from his injuries. Driven off the property, Dunaway and Scott go to the local town to seek justice, but local attorney Parfrey tells them that it is useless to go to court since the oil company has bribed all the local judges. Parfrey tells them that the only way they can get back Dunaway's property is to take it back by force. Scott and Dunaway then enlist Mills in their cause and they heavily arm themselves with weapons and ammunition, including hand grenades, and they then attack Palance and his thugs, driving them off the property where the three continue drilling for oil while fending off attacks. Dunaway, Scott and Mills take turns as guards while the others sleep and while Palance has his men surround the hill and where they continuously fire at the occupants of the derrick. A cable breaks and Mills, affixing an iron sheet to his back, heroically climbs the derrick and repairs the cable while bullets ping and twang off the metal sheet. While descending, however, a bullet strikes him and he falls to his death and only then does Dunaway show the deep love she has for her now deceased father. Despite Mills' death, the dogged Dunaway and equally resolved Scott continue drilling, knowing that if the gusher comes in before Palance and his men can take possession of the property their futures are assured with great riches. While they labor under the threat of losing their lives, Dunaway softens toward Scott, now realizing that he has a good heart, and a cautious and strange romance begins. Meanwhile, Palance now believes that the only way to dislodge the stubborn Dunaway and Scott is through a full-fledged attack against the derrick. He and his men then assault the hill from all points, charging upward while firing their weapons. Before they reach the summit of the hill, however, the derrick begins to tremble and then shake and rattle as a tremendous gusher erupts, spewing a rainstorm of crude oil (the Oklahoma crude Dunaway and Scott had slaved to get). Palance and his men cease their attack as they have lost the race and now representatives of many oil companies begin offering Dunaway huge amounts of money to distribute her oil. Scott, thinking his chores are over, begins to walk away, but Dunaway calls out his name to freeze frame him while his eyes widen and his face expresses great expectations. Scott, Dunaway and Mills are superb in their lowlife characterizations, and Kramer directs with superior skill, effectively meshing the action and the contentious love scenes. *Author's Note*: "**Oklahoma Crude** is really a true picture about how it really was in those wildcatting days," Scott told this author. "Everyone in Oklahoma was cutting everyone else's throat

Humphrey Bogart and James Cagney in *The Oklahoma Kid*, 1939.

to jump oil claim. Murdering someone who owned a well that might produce oil was a matter of daily routine. The State was a madhouse in those days and you had to be a certified lunatic to drill for oil and that is exactly the kind of person I play in that picture. Faye [Dunaway] isn't any different and she sacrificed a lot to play that kind of hard-nosed woman. She is a real beauty, but you'd never know that because her face is almost always smeared with oil and dirt. Now, that's what I call a sacrifice." Kramer stated to this author that "**Oklahoma Crude** is not just about the savage conduct of those wildcatters during the oil boom days, but it offers an impossible romance between a man-hating woman, and a man who pretty much hates everyone, proving that love can triumph over everything and anyone." For a list of films on this subject, see Drilling and wildcatting for oil in the Subject Index, Volume IV. **p&d,** Stanley Kramer; **cast,** George C. Scott, Faye Dunaway, John Mills, Jack Palance, William Lucking, Harvey Jason, Ted Gehring, Cliff Osmond, Rafael Campos, Woodrow Parfrey; **w,** Marc Norman; **c,** Robert Surtees (Technicolor); **m,** Henry Mancini; **ed,** Folmar Blangsted; **prod d,** Alfred Sweeney; **set d,** Maury Hoffman; **spec eff,** Chuck Gaspar, Alex Weldon, Albert Whitlock.

The Oklahoma Kid ★★★ 1939; U.S.; 85m; WB; B/W; Western; Children: Acceptable; **DVD; VHS.** Cagney and Bogart exchange their gangster persona for Old West gunslingers in this action-packed oater set in the 1893 Oklahoma land rush when the Cherokee Strip was opened to thousands of settlers. Sothern and his son Stephens are part of those rushing into the Strip to stake claims at the official sound of the gun that starts that race for free land. They find the perfect spot to establish a new town, but find Bogart already at the location with his band of gunmen and where Bogart has already staked a claim. He has, of course, ignored the laws and started for the promising lands ahead of the official land rush, becoming what was called a "Sooner" (getting there sooner than later, the name "Sooner" subsequently becoming the name of anyone from Oklahoma). Bogart is not interested in establishing a town; he only wants the rights to build a lavish saloon on the town's main street and cuts a deal with Sothern and Stephens, who, in exchange for getting Bogart's claim, allow him to have his booze emporium, a decision they will later deeply regret. Bogart soon becomes the local crime boss of the new town, Tulsa, supervising from his saloon headquarters all manner of illegal operations and where the town becomes a hellhole of vice and corruption. Sothern, who has become the leading citizen, decides to run for the office of mayor in order to clean up Tulsa, and Stephens runs for the office of sheriff. Bogart realizes that if Sothern takes office his reign of crime and terror will come to an end so he frames Sothern for a murder. Sothern is jailed and awaits trial when Cagney, his errant son and a notorious outlaw known as the Oklahoma Kid, learns about

Bogart's frame-up. He heads for Tulsa, meeting the attractive Lane en route. She provides the details about Bogart's underhanded ways and Cagney learns that she is his brother's sweetheart. While Cagney rides toward Tulsa, Bogart has Crisp, the upright judge who is to hear Sothern's case, replaced by a judge who is Bogart's paid stooge, and that judge quickly finds Sothern guilty and sentences him to death. Before Cagney arrives in town, Bogart, to assure his hold upon the town, organizes as lynch mob that hangs Sothern. Cagney then arrives in Tulsa and joins with his estranged brother Stephens, now a U.S. marshal, to go after Bogart and his murderous minions. Cagney and Bogart have several run-ins until Cagney and brother Stephens combine forces and invade Bogart's saloon where, in a wild gunfight, Bogart mortally wounds Stephens and Cagney shoots and kills Bogart. Stephens dies in Cagney's arms, but not before Cagney promises that he will abandon his outlaw ways and take care of Lane. Action director Bacon provides a lot of exciting scenes in this above-average western, and Cagney's dynamic personality captures his offbeat character while Bogart is about as sinister as he has ever been in any film, a completely worthless fellow out to destroy mankind. The lensing from veteran cinematographer Howe is exceptional. *Author's Note*: Cagney told this author that "Bogey hated that western picture and told me before we went into production for **The Oklahoma Kid** that 'Jack Warner is punishing me by making me play a western outlaw. Can you imagine me riding around on a horse and pulling a six-gun? What a lot of hooey!' I told him that he shouldn't complain because the wardrobe people gave me a Stetson hat to wear in the picture that was so large that it made me look like a mushroom with legs. Westerns were not really my kind of picture, although, many years later, I made a picture called **Tribune to a Bad Man** [1956], which was a more serious western about a rancher. When I did **The Oklahoma Kid** with Bogey, well, we were under the thumb at Warner Brothers with air-tight contracts and you had to do what the front office wanted. The year after we did that picture, Bogey told me: 'Get this—Jack Warner is putting me into another western [**Virginia City**, 1940] where I not only have to ride a horse and play another outlaw, but I have to use a Mexican accent! He must really hate my guts! I don't know how I'll live this one down.' Well, Bogey survived that picture, which was a pretty good one with Errol Flynn, and, in a few years, he was on top of the heap as a leading man—that was after **Casablanca** [1942]—and he later said to me: 'You won't see me back on that horse, again, Jimmy, never again.' And was he ever right." **p,** Samuel Bischoff; **d,** Lloyd Bacon; **cast,** James Cagney, Humphrey Bogart, Rosemary Lane, Donald Crisp, Harvey Stephens, Hugh Sothern, Charles Middleton, Edward Pawley, Lew Harvey, Ward Bond, Clem Bevans; **w,** Warren Duff, Robert Buckner, Edward E. Paramore (based on a story by Paramore, Wally Kline); **c,** James Wong Howe; **m,** Max Steiner; **ed,** Owen Marks; **art d,** Esdras Hartley.

The Old Dark House ★★★ 1932; U.S.; 70m; UNIV; B/W; Horror/Comedy; Children: Unacceptable; **DVD; IV.** Three travelers, Massey, his wife Stuart, and their friend Douglas, seek shelter from a rainstorm in a remote region of Wales and go to a gloomy old mansion belonging to a strange family presided over by a 102-year-old man, Dudgeon. With him are his obsessive sister, Moore, and atheist son, Thesiger. Two more stranded travelers arrive, Laughton and Bond, and everything in this weird house goes haywire. Moore, who is Thesiger's sister, begins haranguing the guests with her fanatical religious ranting. Then the family's manservant, Karloff, gets drunk, runs amuck, and releases the family's brother, Wills, a psychotic pyromaniac, who has long been locked up in the house, and who now tries to burn it down. The visitors endure a night of madness, but finally manage to escape in the morning. A very funny and spooky film but too weird for children. Song: "Singin' in the Rain" (1929; Nacio Herb Brown, Arthur Freed). *Author's Note*: Massey told this author that "the set for **The Old Dark House** was one of the strangest I have ever seen with its interior angles grotesquely distorted and so dimly lighted that we were tripping over one another, but that was the kind of moody atmosphere the director [Whale] was noted for, and he was on top at Universal since he had made the greatest horror picture in history, **Frankenstein** [1931], a year earlier." Karloff said to this author that "Whale was a genius, but a very strange man—I appeared in his pictures, **Frankenstein** and then **The Old Dark House** and then **The Bride of Frankenstein** [1935] where I again played the monster. Whale had been a prisoner-of-war in a German concentration camp in World War One and I think that terrible experience distorted or altered his mind somewhat. He liked only men and he did not like being known as a director of only horror pictures, but that is how he came to be best known. When the studios would not let him make the films he wanted to make, he gave up on filmmaking. I am told that he spent most of his time holding parties at his big pool at his home where only young men were invited. He later committed suicide by drowning himself in that pool, poor, troubled man." [Two of the leading players in this film, Thesiger and Laughton, were, like Whale, homosexuals.] **p**, Carl Laemmle Jr.; **d**, James Whale; **cast**, Boris Karloff, Melvyn Douglas, Charles Laughton, Raymond Massey, Gloria Stuart, Lillian Bond, Ernest Thesiger, Eva Moore, Elspeth Dudgeon as John Dudgeon, Brember Wills; **w**, Benn W. Levy, R.C. Sheriff (based on the novel *Benighted* by J.B. Priestley); **c**, Arthur Edeson; **ed**, Clarence Kolster; **set d**, Russell A. Gausman; **spec eff**, John P. Fulton.

The Old Fashioned Way ★★★★ 1934; U.S.; 71m; PAR; B/W; Comedy; Children: Acceptable, **DVD**. The inimitable W. C. Fields is again wonderful in this mirthful tale, set in the gaslight era, where he is the Great McGonigle, the manager of a ragged, worn-out troupe of actors touring the country for the umpteenth time while enacting the threadbare play "The Drunkard." The film opens with his bedraggled thespians gathered at a train station where the local sheriff is waiting to serve a summons on Fields for bad debts (which Fields has accumulated all over America). The sheriff holds the summons behind his back, and Fields, seeing this as he approaches from that direction, sets fire to the summons and then stands in front of the sheriff with a twisted grin on his face and where the sheriff says: "I have something for you!" He brings the summons, now aflame, from behind his back, presenting it to Fields, who promptly uses it to light a cigar, thanking the dumbfounded sheriff before he and his actors hastily board the departing train. The travails of these traveling performers see many funny moments as Fields puts up with the antics of daughter Allen, who is in love with Morrison, a singer, and is beset with pesky problems from his eternal nemesis, Baby LeRoy (a child actor who appears in many of Fields' films, always vexing him to the point of apoplexy). While Fields is constantly dodging summons servers, he manages to present a number of hilarious sight gags and routines, including a revised version of his old skit, "Poppy" and later performs one of the most spectacular juggling acts in the history of films. Not known to many is the fact that Fields began on the vaudeville stage as one of the world's greatest jugglers, and he proves that here by juggling four balls, twelve cigar boxes and a stick on one foot and then kicks the entire collection of items to the other foot while pretending to correct a "mistake" in this awesome routine, a feat of dexterity that is worth the entire film. The film ends with Allen and Morrison united and Fields more successful on the boards than ever. *Author's Note*: Fields spent a great deal of time during this production complaining to Paramount's front office about Baby LeRoy, posting his complaints on studio walls where he claimed that the child was stealing his scenes, was a physical menace, and had libeled him in one of his scenes. The precocious child had, during this production, impulsively reached out and tweaked Fields' bulbous nose, but, instead of exploding, the great comedian merely grinned. He later told newsmen in a press conference, who asked if he was sensitive about his large nose, that he took "inordinate pride in my nose. Indeed, I have treatment done on it every day." He then lifted a large glass containing his favorite concoction, rum and pineapple juice, stating with a nod and a wink to the reporters: "My daily treatment." Songs: "A Little Bit of Heaven, Known as Mother"

W. C. Fields and Baby LeRoy in *The Old Fashioned Way*, 1934.

(1934; music: Harry Revel; lyrics: Mack Gordon), "We're Just Poor Folks Rolling in Love" (1934; music: Harry Revel; lyrics: Mack Gordon), "After the Ball" (1893; Charles Harris), "When You and I Were Young, Maggie" (1866; J. A. Butterfield), "Ring de Banjo" (1851; Stephen Foster), "Gathering Shells from the Sea Shore" (1873; music and lyrics: Will L. Thompson), "Old Folks at Home (Swanee River)" (1851; music: Stephen Foster), "Old Black Joe" (1860; music: Stephen Foster), "Die Meistersinger von Nurnberg, WWV96" (1868; music: Richard Wagner), "Home, Sweet Home" (1823; from a Sicilian air, music: H. R. Bishop; lyrics: John Howard Payne), "Comin' thro' the Rye" (traditional), "Yankee Doodle" (c.1755; traditional). **p**, William LeBaron; **d**, William Beaudine; **cast**, W.C. Fields, Joe Morrison, Baby LeRoy (Ronald LeRoy Overacker), Judith Allen, Jan Duggan, Tammany Young, Nora Cecil, Jack Mulhall, Samuel Ethridge, Ruth Marion, Florence Lawrence; **w**, Garnett Weston, Jack Cunningham (based on an original story by Charles Bogle (Fields); **c**, Benjamin Reynolds; **m**, Harry Revel; **art d**, John B. Goodman.

Old Gringo ★★★ 1989; U.S.; 120m; COL; Color; Adventure/Biographical Drama; Children: Unacceptable (MPAA: R); **DVD**; **VHS**. Offbeat but exciting adventure/biopic tale has Fonda going to Mexico as a teacher where she is hired by wealthy landowners to teach their children. She is caught up in the Mexican revolution where rebel Smits is a compassionate general leading revolutionaries and looking to settle old scores with the landowners. He captures Fonda and more or less holds her captive while she meets a strange American, Peck, who has traveled to Mexico on a bizarre mission. Peck's world is in shambles. His wife has recently died and he himself is dying of a disease, but he has sought a quicker and glorious death in Mexico, expecting to be killed in its violent revolution, and thus ending his life on a more spectacular note. Fonda is physically drawn to Peck, who acts as her protector, while she is also attracted to the earthy Smits. Peck, she later learns is none other than the celebrated author, Ambrose Bierce (1842-1913) and whose acerbic writings (he was called "Bitter Bierce") she has always admired, although Peck has taken pains not to reveal his true identity by going under an alias and where he is generally called "Old Gringo." Peck aids Smits and his men when they assault and capture a fortified hacienda, but Peck then begins to insult and goad Smits into killing him in order to fulfill his death wish. The uneducated Smits finds important papers at the hacienda that gives the land rights to the area to the peasants for which Smits has been fighting, but Peck, in a final effort to prompt Smits into killing him, burns those valuable papers. Smits shoots and kills Peck, who dies in Fonda's arms and is oddly grateful for Smits having ended his miserable life and has thus arranged an act of euthanasia that has been concocted for this somewhat bizarre but intriguing tale. Puenzo

Miriam Hopkins and Bette Davis in *The Old Maid,* **1939.**

directs this action-loaded film with a firm hand, and Peck, Smits and Fonda are exceptional in their roles. *Author's Note*: Peck told this author that "a lot of liberties were taken about the unpredictable writer, Bierce. No one ever knew what happened to him after he went to Mexico and got involved with the revolutionaries fighting with Pancho Villa. He was reported missing in 1913 and his body was never found. It is pretty much certain that he took great risks in Mexico, siding with the rebels, but was so insulting to Villa that that revolutionary leader most likely ordered him shot. Villa had a mercurial temper and, like the enemy, had most of the prisoners he captured shot, so one more old and cantankerous American would not make much difference to him." **p**, Lois Bonfiglio; **d**, Luis Puenzo; **cast**, Jane Fonda, Gregory Peck, Jimmy Smits, Patricio Contreras, Jenny Gago, Gabriela Roel, Sergio Calderon, Guillermo Rios, Jim Metzler, Samuel Valadez De La Torre, Pedro Armendariz, Jr., Paul Williams; **w**, Puenzo, Aida Bortnik (based on the novel *Gringo Viejo* by Carlos Fuentes); **c**, Félix Monti; **m**, Lee Holdridge; **ed**, William Anderson, Glenn Farr, Juan Carlos Macías; **prod d**, Bruno Rubeo, Stuart Wurtzel; **art d**, Scott Ritenour, Jorge Sainz; **set d**, Tessa Davies; **spec eff**, Jesus Duran Galvan, Adrian Duran Martinez, Alejandro Duran Vazquez, Fermin Duran Martinez.

The Old Maid ★★★★ 1939; U.S.; 95m; WB; B/W; Drama; Children: Unacceptable; **DVD**; **VHS**. Davis is much different in her role enacting a woman who ages to sixty (she was thirty when doing this film), but she was never better, providing a bravura performance in what is one of the great tearjerkers. She begins as an attractive young woman at the beginning of the American Civil War vying with her fetching cousin Hopkins for the attentions of the handsome Brent, the most desired beau in the county. Brent gets engaged to Hopkins and goes off to fight in the war, but the selfish Hopkins tires of his long absence and refuses to wait for him to return to take her to the altar and marries the wealthy Stephenson, who comes from one of the leading families in Philadelphia. When Brent returns on furlough, he is shocked to see his betrothed married to another man and finds solace in the arms of Davis, who has always loved him. They make love and then Brent goes back to the front and is killed at Vicksburg. Davis, who is pregnant with Brent's child, decides to hide the fact that she is an unmarried mother by pretending to have tuberculosis and therefore needs to cure her ailment by going to Arizona and its dry climate and there she gives birth to a daughter. She moves back to Philadelphia where she establishes an orphanage, placing her child among the children she looks after, but Hopkins knows that the child is that of Davis and her former lover, Brent. When Cowan, who is Hopkins' brother-in-law, thinks to marry Davis, Hopkins tells him that she is too ill to be a good wife and Cowan backs away from the relationship. When he dies, Hopkins, guilt-ridden, invites Davis and her child to live with her in her luxurious mansion and the two reside in that home, Davis' child growing up to be Bryan, who thinks she is an orphan and that Davis is simply an old maid spinster, who has looked after her all her life. For her part, Davis does not reveal to Bryan that she is her mother, believing that she will reveal her true relationship to her after she is happily married to Lundigan. Davis, however, decides to continue to "protect" her daughter Bryan from her closeted scandal by pretending to be her old maid guardian, and Bryan, after she is happily married, continues to think of her that way, saving her last kiss for her favorite old maid protector before going on her honeymoon. Davis is resigned to never tell her daughter the truth and knows she will end her days living with Hopkins, who will forever harbor resentment against Davis for having had an affair with Brent, the man both of them have loved and lost. Davis is superb as the sacrificing mother in this ten-handkerchief film (and where she marvelously ages through some major makeup miracles over a period of several decades); Hopkins is also outstanding as are the rest of the cast members, and director Goulding deftly handles a complex story while carefully developing his characters. *Author's Note*: Much has been said about the combative and confrontational scenes between Davis and Hopkins in this film and where Hopkins struggled to steal many scenes from Davis. "Well, she tried that again and again," Davis told this author, "but she was swimming upstream all the time. I toned down everything I said and did, every gesture, every move and let her run about like a chicken with her throat cut, bleeding all over the scenery, and I knew I took every scene in which we were together. She thought that she could 'out-act' me by being more extravagant and theatrical, but all that did was to make her look hysterical and ridiculous, and, when we finished that picture, Miriam said to me: 'Bette, all I was doing was pouring buckets of water into your ocean.' I took that as a great compliment." **p**, Hal B. Wallis, Henry Blanke; **d**, Edmund Goulding; **cast**, Bette Davis, Miriam Hopkins, George Brent, Donald Crisp, Jane Bryan, Loise Fazenda, James Stephenson, Jerome Cowan, William Lundigan, Cecilia Loftus, Rand Brooks, William Hopper, Doris Lloyd; **w**, Casey Robinson (based on the play by Zoe Akins from the novel by Edith Wharton); **c**, Tony Gaudio; **m**, Max Steiner; **ed**, George Amy; **art d**, Robert Haas.

The Old Man and the Sea ★★★★ 1958; U.S.; 86m; Leland Hayward Productions/WB; Color; Adventure; Children: Cautionary; **DVD**; **VHS**. A moving and powerful allegorical film sees a bravura performance from Tracy, who is an illiterate old Cuban fisherman long on teeth and short on luck. He stoically believes in his lifestyle, living in a small hut near the water's edge in a fishing community where he is held in mocking derision by others as an old, dim-witted fool. He owns a small fishing boat and religiously goes to that boat each dawn with the rest of the fishermen, but not before his only friend, Pazos, a small boy who idolizes him, brings him his morning coffee. Thus warmed for his daily chores, Tracy carries the mast of his boat on his broad shoulders to his boat and then shoves off before dawn, going slowly out to sea while nurturing hopeful thoughts that this day will finally bring him the good catches that have eluded him for so many years. Once he is far out to sea, Tracy drops his lines into the water and waits patiently for a strike and, while waiting, he thinks back upon his life (shown in brief flashbacks), remembering some of the few women he has known, and especially recalls the heroic hand-wrestling battle he had with a powerful opponent when he was a young fisherman endowed with great strength and how, after hours of struggling, he won that exhausting match. While daydreaming, Tracy narrates his thoughts about the decent and honest work of a fisherman, prosaically describing his day's labors and techniques, but, in his wandering reveries, he does not realize that his boat has been carried by the currents far beyond the regular limits of his fishing areas and he has drifted deep into the Gulf Stream, entering another world of the ocean that is utterly foreign to him. A small bird alights on his boat and Tracy welcomes the feathery visitor, but tells the bird that he can have only a momentary rest, and must soon fly off to take his chances with all of the other living creatures as this is the way of the world and nature itself. Then fate arrives to fulfill Tracy's most far-reaching hopes when one of his lines comes alive, running out his line so furiously fast that he becomes alarmed and realizes that he has hooked a gigantic fish. Indeed, he has, as the largest marlin ever to swim in the seas has taken his bait and is now running with his line, surfacing to show its enormous size, as it hurtles into the air and crashes and dives back into the sea again and again and again in a heroic effort to escape the barbed line. Tracy clutches the line to slow its unwinding extensions, the running line slashing and cutting into the flesh of his large and gripping hands; he pours water onto the line to keep it from burning as the marlin, which is much larger than Tracy's boat, drags the fisherman and his small craft further out to sea, plunging into the deep and almost taking the boat downward. The battle continues, seemingly for hours, as Tracy struggles to land the marlin, which he has come to admire as a great adversary. The struggle between man and fish is historic and titanic as it goes on and on, until the old man through dint of physical exertion and sheer will power defeats the mammoth marlin, killing it, and then lashing its huge carcass to the side of his small boat before setting sail for home. The bloody trail of his prey, however, as the old man expected, soon brings his worst fears and enemy—swarms of sharks. They attack the dead marlin, chewing and gnawing away at its once majestic body, mutilating it as the old man savagely fights back with a knife attached to an ore, killing several sharks, and, after the blade is broken off, using the broken oar to hammer at the furiously attacking sharks. The insatiable sharks, however, win this battle, eventually tearing away the flesh of the marlin until only its head, tail and skeleton remain, a grisly and grotesque aquatic artifact that brings the exhausted old man to grief and tears. His magnificent prize, the catch of a lifetime, has been so brutally violated that he is now ashamed of himself for bringing the great fish to such an ignominious end. "You went out too far, old man," he tells himself, a grim and somber soul-searching reminder that he has unnaturally challenged the limits of himself and the nature of the world that makes him human, that compels his mortality and that of the great fish he has conquered and lost to the most dreaded and despised predators of the sea. He agonizes over his empty victory, apologizing to the marlin for bringing it to such a disgraceful and ignominious end, stating: "Fish, I respect you and I love you." He shares the miserable fate of his noble prey for he has been emotionally and spiritually devastated and mutilated by the Homeric and bloody experience. He drifts toward land, seeing the lights of Havana at night and then beaches his boat and its gruesome remains, carrying his mast like the Cross of Christ on his back until its weight and his own fatigue collapses him. He struggles to his shack and, the next morning, tourists gape at the skeletal remains of the fish as the boy visits the old man, only to find him dying. Director Sturges took infinite care with this film, religiously following Hemingway's story line, preserving his prosaic prose through Tracy's simple but powerful narrative and where Tracy is a one-man dynamo, riveting the viewer with one of his most overwhelming performances. Everything about his characterization is as huge and heroic as the giant marlin he catches. Howe's lensing is superb, capturing the azure tranquility of the sea as well as the incredible battles with the landing of the marlin and the desperate and savage struggle with the sharks, and Tiomkin's haunting score is alternatingly and compellingly lyrical and dynamic. *Author's Note*: This film came into existence shortly after Hemingway's novella was published through the concerted efforts of producer Hayward, who was a close friend of the author and his fourth and final wife, Mary (who appears in the film as one of the tourists gaping at the remains of the marlin at the end of the production). Hayward was visiting Hemingway and his wife in Cuba where they were then living when the author gave him the finished copy of his manuscript for *The Old Man and the Sea,* and Hayward hand-carried that story directly to Hemingway's publisher in New York, Scribner's. Prior to its published book form, *Life Magazine* serialized the story in September 1952, the entire issue being sold out the very day it was issued. Almost immediately after

Spencer Tracy in *The Old Man and the Sea,* 1958.

the work became a major selection of the Book-of-the-Month Club, Hayward arranged for Warner Brothers to buy its film rights, paying Hemingway a then substantial sum of $175,000. Hayward and Hemingway put together a partnership for the film production, both quickly agreeing that the only actor who could properly play the old man was the inimitable Tracy. Viertel, who was Hemingway's favorite Hollywood scriptwriter, was chosen to adapt the story for the screen. "There was never a marlin caught the size I described in the book," Hemingway told this author, "so we tried to catch just such a fish and photograph that catch to be used in the movie. We sailed the seas looking for such a marlin and even searched the waters at Capo Blanco off the shores of Peru. We were unsuccessful in finding such a giant marlin to photograph." Such a giant marlin had, indeed existed, and Hemingway knew it. He had seen the remains of just such a marlin captured by an old Cuban fisherman, one that had been reduced to a skeleton by sharks and lashed to the old man's small fishing boat that was anchored near one of Hemingway's drinking spots, and it was the old man's story that Hemingway conveyed in his book. The giant marlin was finally constructed as a huge mechanically operated rubber fish, but when Hemingway viewed this moveable prop, he bluntly stated: "No picture with a f——— rubber fish ever made a dime!" Pantheon director Fred Zinnemann was hired by Hayward to direct the film, but, after four months into production, very little footage had been shot. Tracy, who had become a close friend of Hemingway and his wife, complained that Zinnemann had no work for him. "I was sitting around in an expensive villa packed with a lot of servants giving me greasy food to eat," Tracy told this author, "waiting for some scenes to be sent to me by Zinnemann, but he did not like the script Viertel had written and he and Hayward got into it over that." Zinnemann told Hayward that he wanted to change parts of the story. "I told him [Hayward] that there was too much narration and that made a lot of the scenes static," Zinnemann told this author. "I wanted more action scenes, even taking them from some other stories Hemingway had written and when I mentioned that, well, Hayward blew up. He would not think of it. For him, Hemingway walked on water and he likened every word in that book to the prose of the Holy Bible. Can you believe it?" Hayward then fired Zinnemann, and announced that Zinnemann had left the production due to a "technical" problem, and he hired Sturges to take over the direction. (Sturges had successfully directed Tracy in the powerful drama, **Bad Day at Black Rock**, 1955, which had become a tremendous box office hit.) "I inherited a fairly good script," Sturges told this author, "but we had a hell of a time with the mechanical marlin, so I had to use some considerable second unit footage of a huge marlin being caught, soaring into the air and then crashing into the sea many times, something the mechanical fish could not do, and we showed those scenes at a distance

Ron Moody, Mark Lester (lower foreground) and Oliver Reed in *Oliver!*, **1968.**

so that the fish would look to be proportionately much larger than it really was." The integration of these scenes with the shots of Tracy in his boat was cleverly edited, but the differentiating colors between the second unit shots and the main photography is sometimes discernible. The expenses for the on-location shooting at Cuba began to spiral upward as more and more second unit fishing shots were filmed, and even this did not meet demands so fishing footage from the Disney Studio was acquired, along with private films from several celebrated fishermen, such as Alfred Glassnell of Houston, Texas. More technical equipment was sent from the Warner Brothers studio at a cost of more than $400,000, the overall budget coming in at more than $6 million. For all of their on-location efforts, the crew and cast returned to Hollywood and Sturges shot most of the principal photography at the Warner Brothers tank where its 750,000 gallons of water passed for the Atlantic Ocean. Meanwhile, Tracy, tied to the seemingly endless production, complained in 1957 that "this picture is becoming my life's work [initial photography on the film began in 1955]. By now there is not a chance to make back all the money we will spend, so we are concentrating on making [the film] worthwhile." Tracy had cropped his hair for the production and dyed it white, but, by the end of the production, he did not need any dye as his hair had turned stark white. Tracy grew less and less optimistic about the film, saying "this is for the birds," and that he would sell his interest in the film for "fifteen cents." He and Hemingway had by then fallen out after Hemingway began unfairly blaming Tracy for all the delays involved in the production. When the film was finally released, Tracy received widespread praise for his magnificent performance and received an Oscar nomination for Best Actor, but Hemingway, after seeing the film, acrimoniously carped that Tracy had proved ineffective and called his characterization of the old man as that of a "rich, fat actor," a remark that forever severed the friendship between the author and the actor. Hemingway was later sued by 70-year-old Cuban fisherman Miguel Ramirez, whose skiff carrying the desecrated marlin Hemingway had seen years earlier. Ramirez claimed that he was entitled to the proceeds from Hemingway's book and its subsidiary rights as Hemingway had stolen his story. The suit was later dismissed. **p**, Leland Hayward; **d**, John Sturges; **cast**, Spencer Tracy, Felipe Pazos, Jr., Harry Bellaver, Don Diamond, Don Blackman, Joey Ray, Mary Hemingway, Richard Alameda, Tony Rosa, Carlos Rivero; **w**, Peter Viertel (based on the novel by Ernest Hemingway); **c**, James Wong Howe, Floyd Crosby, Tom Tutwiler, Lamar Boren (Warnercolor); **m**, Dimitri Tiomkin; **ed**, Arthur P. Schmidt; **prod d**, Edward Carrere, Art Loel; **set d**, Ralph Hurst; **spec eff**, Arthur Rhoades.

Old Wives for New ★★★ 1918 (silent); U.S.; 60m; Artcraft/PAR; B/W; Drama; Children: Unacceptable; **DVD**. Callous Dexter marries Ashton

when they're both young, and they give birth to several children. He later neglects her because she's become fat and lazy and he now showers his affections on Vidor. He divorces Ashton and, when Vidor's name is involved in a murder, he leaves her and takes another woman, Manon, to Paris where he marries her. In this early but well-crafted DeMille drama, the perceptive director instinctively seized upon the transition of moral standards in America at that time and translates its national habits in microcosm through the exploits of the womanizing Dexter. Though played for its sensationalism it is nevertheless an excitingly enacted production that did big box office. **p&d**, Cecil B. DeMille; **cast**, Elliott Dexter, Florence Vidor, Sylvia Ashton, Wanda Hawley, Theodore Roberts, Helen Jerome Eddy, Marcia Manon, Julia Faye, Tully Marshall, Alice Terry, Noah Beery, William Boyd; **w**, Jeanie Macpherson (based on the novel by David Graham Phillips); **c**, Alvin Wyckoff; **m**, Louis F. Gottschalk; **ed**, DeMille; **art d**, Wilfred Buckland.

Old Yeller ★★★ 1957; U.S.; 83m; Disney/Buena Vista; Color; Drama; Children: Unacceptable (MPAA: PG); **DVD**; **VHS**. Parker is a Texas farmer, who leaves the homestead to go on a cattle drive in 1869, leaving his wife, McGuire, and two young sons to fend for themselves. A yellow dog comes along and it's mutual love between it and the family, especially the older boy, Kirk, who is fifteen. They have some adventures together involving raccoons, snakes, and bears. One day, Yeller saves Kirk and his younger brother, Corcoran, from some wild hogs, but is injured and it turns out that he has rabies. Heartbroken, when Old Yeller turns on him, Kirk is compelled to shoot and kill the dog. Kirk later gets one of Yeller's puppies and starts a new life with it, having learned some lessons about love and loss. Beautifully produced and superbly enacted, there are many poignant scenes in this moving film, but the tragic and traumatic ending prohibits viewing by children. Song: "Old Yeller" (Oliver Wallace, Hazel George as Gil George). **p**, Walt Disney; **d**, Robert Stevenson; **cast**, Dorothy McGuire, Fess Parker, Tommy Kirk, Jeff York, Chuck Connors, Beverly Washburn, Kevin Corcoran, Spike the Dog; **w**, Fred Gipson, William Tunberg (based on the novel by Gipson); **c**, Charles P. Boyle; **m**, Oliver Wallace; **ed**, Stanley Johnson; **art d**, Carroll Clark; **set d**, Emile Kuri, Fred MacLean; **spec eff**, Peter Ellenshaw.

Oliver! ★★★★★ 1968; U.K.; 153m; Romulus Films/COL; Color; Musical; Children: Cautionary (MPAA: G); **BD**; **DVD**; **VHS**. Pantheon director Reed presents a marvelous musical version of the Dickens classic. Its beginning eliminates the manner in which Oliver goes to the orphanage, showing the precociously endearing Lester (Oliver) eating a meal at that gloomy dungeon-like workhouse. As usual, the boys are suffering from gnawing hunger after receiving their pitiable portions of gruel, and it falls to Lester, who has lost a drawing of straws, to screw up the nerve to ask for a second helping, an unprecedented and daunting request from the draconian Secombe, who is the corpulent and severe headmaster. After Lester timidly makes that request, Secombe roars back: "More? You want more!" He is stunned by this request as it has never been put to him in the history of his awful operation (and one might also ask why anyone would ever want any more of this terrible glutinous glop). Taking the audacious Lester by the ear, Secombe immediately resolves to rid himself of the troublemaking upstart, and leads him through the snow-swept streets of London, offering to sell the boy to anyone who might be so foolish as to buy him. Rossiter, an undertaker living in a small shop with his wife, Baker, and assistant, Cranham, takes Lester and works him to the point of exhaustion. Cranham asks about Lester's background and then makes some insulting remarks about his mother, so disturbing to Lester that the child runs into the crowded streets where he encounters and befriends Wild, a pickpocketing boy wearing a top hat with the name of The Artful Dodger. Lester accompanies Wild to his home, a spacious, shadowy attic where he lives with many other street urchins under the protection and guidance of crafty, old Moody, a master crook named Fagin, who trains these boys in the dark arts of pickpocketing and thievery, selling off the spoils the boys return to him in exchange for his avuncular guardianship. Moody sends Lester to the streets with Wild in his first pickpocketing assignment, but the blonde haired youth is arrested after Wild attempts to filch the pocket of wealthy O'Conor while Moody sees the boy being dragged off to jail. Lester is then brought to court, but insists that he is innocent and his forthright manner touches O'Conor's magnanimous heart, causing him to drop the charges. He decides to take the boy home with him, and suddenly Lester is living in a huge mansion and surrounded by luxury. Meanwhile, Reed, Moody's sinister associate, a killer by nature, plans to kidnap Lester to make sure that he does not inform on Moody's operation and he persuades his sweetheart, Wallis, to abduct the boy and return him to Moody's loft, promising that he will not harm the boy, only make sure that he keeps silent. Wallis performs the deed, but then suspects that Reed intends to kill the boy and, while protecting him, Reed kills her, taking Lester with him as a lynch mob and police pursue him across the rooftops of London. He releases his grasp on Lester to grab a rope in making his escape, but a sharpshooting policeman shoots the villain dead and Lester is returned to O'Conor, who has learned that Lester is his nephew and now intends to make a good home for him. Moody's operation has been broken up because of Reed's evil machinations and he has lost his hoarded ill-gotten gains, but, being the practical thief that he is, resolves to begin again with only Wild at his side to help him "pick a pocket or two." Reed presents a lively and exciting story where Bart's enthralling songs emphasize the twists and turns of the fascinating story line and where Moody steals every scene, although Lester is a standout as are Wild, Reed, Wallis and the rest of the players. Songs (words and music by Lionel Bart): "Oliver!," "Food, Glorious Food," "Boy for Sale," "Where Is Love?," "Consider Yourself," "You've Got to Pick a Pocket or Two," "It's a Fine Life," "I'd Do Anything," "Be Back Soon," "Who Will Buy?," "As Long as He Needs Me," "Reviewing the Situation," "Oom-Pah-Pah," and "My Name," The film won an Oscar as Best Picture and Oscars also went to Reed for Best Director, to Marsh for Best Art Direction and to Bart for Best Musical Score, while nominations went to Moody as Best Actor and Wild as Best Supporting Actor. A special Oscar went to Onna White for choreography. The story was filmed many times as a silent, notably in 1909, 1912, 1916, 1919 and 1922 (starring Lon Chaney Sr., a film banned in England because it was then thought that this production promoted hooliganism), in 1933, and as a classic talkie in 1948 (helmed by another pantheon director, David Lean), an animated version in 1974, twice in 1982 (both made-for-TV productions, one as an animated version), in 1991 (animated version titled **The Adventures of Oliver Twist**), in 1997 (made for TV), and a good Roman Polanski version in 2005, along with several TV series in 1955, 1960, 1962, 1985, 1997, 1999 and 2007. *Author's Note*: This film was lavishly produced with a budget of more than $10 million, and every dime of it shows on the screen via its startling exterior pageants and impressive gaslight era set, where half of old London's inhabitants seem to be prancing and dancing over its cobblestone streets. It doubled its investment at the box office in its initial release. Although Reed does a convincing job of playing the lethal Bill Sikes, his performance was nowhere near as chilling as Robert Newton's essay of that arch criminal in the 1948 version, a terrifying portrayal that influenced Reed's own performance, according to that actor's remarks. **p**, John Woolf; **d**, Carol Reed; **cast**, Ron Moody, Shani Wallis, Oliver Reed, Harry Secombe, Mark Lester, Jack Wild, Hugh Griffith, Joseph O'-Conor, Peggy Mount, Leonard Rossiter, Hylda Baker; **w**, Vernon Harris (based on the musical play by Lionel Bart from the novel *Oliver Twist* by Charles Dickens); **c**, Oswald Morris (Technicolor); **m**, Bart; **ed**, Ralph Kemplen; **prod d**, John Box; **art d**, Terence Marsh; **set d**, Vernon Dixon, Ken Mugglestone; **spec eff**, Allan Bryce.

Olivier, Olivier ★★★ 1993; France; 110m; Oliane Presentations/Sony; Color; Drama; Children: Unacceptable (MPAA: R); **DVD;VHS**. Intriguing tale has Morozof playing Olivier, a nine-year-old boy, who

Mark Lester in *Oliver!*, 1968.

goes missing from his parents' affluent country home outside Paris. His mother, Rouan, always doted on him, so she is frantic when he does not return. His veterinarian father, Cluzet, however, is too preoccupied with his practice to notice him or pay any attention to the couple's preteen daughter, Gatteau, who Rouan also virtually ignores. Gatteau does not hold a grudge against Morozof for being their mother's favorite and loves him, telling him stories about animals and extraterrestrials. One morning, Rouan sends Morozof off on his bicycle to take food to his grandmother. He doe not return and a search is undertaken and an investigation is launched for the boy, conducted by a young police inspector, Stevenin. As months pass and Rouan becomes more distraught, Cluzet accepts a job in Chad. Rouan remains in France, continuing a search for her missing son, and Gatteau remains with her. Six years pass and Stevenin reports to Rouan that he may have found her son. He has unearthed a streetwise fifteen-year-old Parisian youth, Colin, who, among other things, is a hustler of men. Rouan meets with Colin, who is unable to clearly recall his past, but gives hints that he remembers some sort of relationship with her. Cluzet returns from Africa and both he and Gatteau believe Colin is Olivier and are overjoyed at his return. Rouan, however, has doubts and, if Colin really is her long-lost son, what happened to him since his disappearance? These questions and some considerable doubt about Colin's true identity remain to nag Rouan as well as viewers. This film is reminiscent of the thriller, **Changeling**, 2008, where a boy goes missing and is replaced by another impersonating boy, and where the mother of the missing boy, Angelina Jolie, suffers mind-altering anguish over never knowing the fate of her real son. Songs/Music: "Les Anges" (Michel Ferry, William Butler Yeats, Zbigniew Preisner), "Boris Godounov" opera excerpts (Modest Mussorgsky). Sexuality and gutter language prohibit viewing by children. (In French; English subtitles). **p**, Marie-Laure Reyre; **d**, Agnieszka Holland; **cast**, Brigitte Roüan, François Cluzet, Jean-François Stévenin, Emmanuel Morozof, Frédéric Quiring, Faye Gatteau, Carole Lemerle, Jean-Bernard Josko, Lucrèce La Chenardière; **w**, Holland, Régis Debray, Yves Lapointe; **c**, Bernard Zitzermann; **m**, Zbigniew Preisner; **ed**, Isabelle Lorente; **prod d**, Hélène Bourgy; **set d**, Benoît Clémenceau.

Oliver Twist ★★★ 1922 (silent); U.S.; 98m/8 reels; Jackie Coogan Productions/First National; B/W; Drama; Children: Unacceptable; **DVD**; **VHS**. Coogan as Oliver and Chaney as his criminal mentor Fagin are exceptional in this best of the silent films based upon the Dickens classic novel. Coogan is shown as an orphan in a workhouse, then running away to be trained by criminal Svengali Chaney as a pickpocket in 19th-Century London, England, only to be rescued by a wealthy uncle, then abducted and almost killed by a murderous felon,

Lewis Chase, Barney Clark and Harry Eden in *Oliver Twist*, **2005.**

Siegmann, until he is again rescued and restored to the rightful inheritance he has long been denied. Lloyd faithfully tells this enthralling tale with great skill, where production values are high with sumptuous sets, well-orchestrated crowd scenes and superb lensing from MacWilliams and Martin. *Author's Note*: This film was banned in England after British censors determined that Chaney's role too specifically detailed the techniques of pickpocketing and stealing, stating that the film promoted "hooliganism." Coogan was only eight years old when appearing as Oliver whose age is set as ten years old in the novel, but the endearing boy effectively captures and conveys the essence of Dickens' immortal character. **p**, Sol Lesser, Jack Coogan Sr.; **d**, Frank Lloyd; **cast**: Jackie Coogan, Lon Chaney Sr., Gladys Brockwell, George Siegmann, Edouard Trebaol, Lionel Belmore, Carl Stockdale, Eddie Boland, Taylor Graves, Lewis Sargent, James Marcus, Aggie Herring; **w**, Harry Weil, Lloyd (based on the novel by Charles Dickens); **c**, Glen MacWilliams, Robert Martin; **ed**, Irene Mora; **art d**, Stephen Goosson.

Oliver Twist ★★★★★ 1951; U.K.; 116m; Cineguild/Eagle-Lion; B/W; Drama; Children: Unacceptable; **DVD**; **VHS**. This startling and masterfully made film by pantheon director Lean begins as a fierce storm rages and a woman enduring pain and stress makes her way through the dark streets of London to the doors of a workhouse, entering it and collapsing. After giving birth to a boy, she dies, the boy later shown as Davies (Oliver), who is a ward of the workhouse and where life is miserable and the food abominable. Davies is so hungry at a morning meal that he dares to ask taskmaster Sullivan, who runs the workhouse, for more gruel and he is immediately deemed too unruly to remain. Sullivan takes him to undertaker McLaughlin, where Davies is put to work as a slaving apprentice. He is so mistreated by McLaughlin and his wife, Harrison, that Davies runs away, falling in with a gang of boys who are petty thieves and whose ringleader, Newley, playing the top-hatted Artful Dodger, befriends Davies and takes him back to his home, a loft owned by master thief and fence, Guinness, who looks upon all of the boys stealing on his behalf as his sons and where he carefully trains them how to pick the pockets of rich men. After a brief tutoring in this dark art, Davies is sent to the streets with Newley, where he inexpertly attempts to filch the pocketbook of wealthy man Stephenson. Davies is arrested, but the compassionate Stephenson drops the charges and takes the boy to his lavishly appointed mansion where he is delighted to learn that Davies is actually his nephew, the son of Stephenson's niece, who vanished long ago. Vicious killer and robber Newton, who is Guinness' partner in crime, decides to kidnap Davies and hold him for ransom, but, after he abducts the boy, Walsh, Newton's girlfriend, objects and Newton kills her. He then flees with Davies, the police hot on his heels,

and, during the frantic chase, Davies is rescued and Newton is killed. The boy is returned to the protective arms of Stephenson and looks forward to a happy life while Guinness, his pickpocketing ring smashed, is reduced to poverty. He nevertheless resolves to begin his criminal pursuits anew with the always optimistic Newley at his side. Lean presents a grim but utterly riveting film, developing the memorable Dickens characters with great patience and skill in one mesmerizing frame after another; Guinness presents a fascinating performance as the crime-tutoring mentor, and Newton renders (as the murderous Bill Sykes) one of the most terrifying portrayals of a human monster ever recorded on film. *Author's Note*: Davies was an unknown actor when Lean selected him to play Oliver for this production, giving him few lines and relying upon his wonderful facial expressions to establish a convincing Oliver. Guinness, in his marvelous portrayal of master crook Fagin, constructed a long and hooked nose of his own creation that brought considerable criticism from U.S. distributors, who initially refused to release the film in America, stating that Guinness, portrayal could be construed as being anti-Semitic, and, for this reason, the film, produced in 1948 in England, was not distributed in the U.S. until three years later and with some of its scenes with Guinness considerably edited. Guinness told this author: "It is undeniable that Dickens portrayed Fagin as an old Jewish man, who was dedicated to criminal pursuits and that he educated boys in the techniques of stealing. I played him the way Dickens saw him, or, at least the way I saw how Dickens saw him, and I made up my face with an artificial nose to conform to Dickens' description of that man. It was never my intention to present anything anti-Semitic in that characterization." **p**, Ronald Neame, Anthony Havelock-Allan; **d**, David Lean; **cast**, Robert Newton, Alec Guinness, Kay Walsh, John Howard Davies, Francis L. Sullivan, Henry Stephenson, Mary Clare, Anthony Newley, Josephine Stuart, Ralph Truman, Kathleen Harrison, Maurice Denham, Gibb McLaughlin, Peter Bull, Diana Dors; **w**, Lean, Stanley Haynes (based on the novel by Charles Dickens); **c**, Guy Green; **m**, Sir Arnold Bax; **ed**, Jack Harris; **set d**, T. Hopewell Ash, Claude Momsay; **spec eff**, Stanley Grant, Joan Suttie, Les Bowie.

Oliver Twist ★★★ 2005; U.K./Czech Republic/France/Italy; 130m; R.P. Films/Sony; Color; Drama; Children: Unacceptable (MPAA: PG-13); **DVD**. This version of the Dickens classic sees a faithful and well-made adaptation by the controversial Polanski. In the familiar story, ten-year-old orphan Oliver, played by Clark, is ejected from an orphanage in merry old England of the 1800s and into a home not much better. He runs off to London where a pickpocketing urchin, the Artful Dodger, played by Eden, takes him to the den of old crook Fagin, well-enacted by Kingsley, who runs a thieving business that has boys picking the pockets of the rich. Clark meets up with a seasoned robber-killer, Bill Sykes, played by Foreman, and his moll Nancy, enacted by Rowe, who wants out of their relationship but he won't release her. Clark is in deep danger for most of the film during which Foreman is killed and Fagin is arrested for running a gang of boy thieves. Clark visits Fagin in prison where he is condemned to death, and the two almost hug in friendship. Clark has come to think Fagin was not such a bad person and that he was just down and out in London like thousands of others and lived as best he could. Clark is rescued by a kindly bookseller, Hardwicke, who adopts him and sends him to school to become a gentleman. Song: "Newry Town" (traditional). Made also in 1922, 1933, 1948 (the classic drama version by David Lean), 1968 (the classic musical version by Carol Reed) and 1974. Excessive violence, the hallmark of almost all of Polanski's films, prohibits viewing by children. *Author's Note*: Polanski (1933-) remains a fugitive from U.S. justice in that he fled the U.S. following his arrest and conviction (he confessed to the crime) for assaulting a thirteen-year-old girl in 1977. He fled to Europe, was arrested and imprisoned in Switzerland many years later where the U.S. demanded his extradition, but Swiss authorities refused to return him to the U.S. and released him on July 12, 2010. **p**, Roman Polanski, Robert Benmussa, Alain Sarde; **d**, Polanski; **cast**, Ben Kingsley, Jamie Foreman, Leanne Rowe, Barney Clark, Jeremy Swift, Edward Hardwicke, Ian McNeice, Harry Eden, Gillian Hanna, Lewis Chase; **w**, Ronald Harwood (based on the novel by Charles Dickens); **c**, Pawel Edelman; **m**, Rachel Portman; **ed**, Hervé De Luze; **prod d**, Allan Starski; **art d**, Jindra Koci, Jirí Matolín; **set d**, Jille Azis; **spec eff**, Martin Oberlander, Jiff Vater.

The Omen ★★★ 1976; U.S., U.K.; 111m; FOX; Color; Horror; Children: Unacceptable (MPAA: PG-13); **DVD**. Peck is a U.S diplomat stationed in Europe and he and his wife, Remick, are happily married, but want to have children. When Remick's baby is stillborn in a Rome hospital, Peck is approached by a priest, Benson, who suggests they take a healthy newborn infant whose mother has just died in childbirth. Peck and Remick agree and name the child Damien (Stephens). Peck is appointed U.S. Ambassador to Great Britain and the family moves to London where strange events begin happening in their home. At Stephens' fifth birthday party, his nanny sees a vicious-looking dog watching from some trees and publicly hangs herself. Another priest, Troughton, warns Peck that Stephens may be cursed and not human, but the Antichrist. Remick becomes pregnant and Troughton warns Peck that her life may be in danger from Stephens. While trying to enter a locked church during a wind storm, Troughton is struck dead by a lightning rod that falls on his neck. Pregnant Remick loses her baby when she falls off a stepladder after Stephens plays close to it. Warner, a photographer friend, tells Peck that mysterious images are cropping up in his photos. A lot more weird and other-worldly things happen and Peck and Warner go to Israel to meet with McKern, who claims to know how to stop the Antichrist. McKern tells Peck the only way to do that is to plunge seven daggers into Stephens, but Peck refuses to do that to his adopted son. Warner is about to do the killing when he is decapitated by a sheet of glass that slides off a truck. Remick is in the hospital after her baby is stillborn, and Stephens' new nanny, Whitelaw, pushes Remick through a window to her death. Peck then kills Whitelaw and drags Stephens to a church altar where he is about to kill him with one of the daggers. Stephens pleads for his life and police arrive and order Peck to drop the dagger, but he refuses and is shot dead by one of the officers. Stephens attends the funeral of Peck and Remick while smiling innocently at those watching the movie while the song "Ave Satani" ("Hail Satan") is playing on the soundtrack. This thriller is well made and enacted but its excessive violence prohibits viewing by children. Sequels and remakes appeared in 1978, 1981, 2003 and 2006. Songs: "Ave Satani" (Jerry Goldsmith), "The Piper Dreams" (Jerry and Carol Heather Goldsmith). *Author's Note*: Peck told this author that he had "some reservations about doing **The Omen**. I knew it was capitalizing on **The Exorcist** [1973], but when I read the script, I found it literate and well researched on the subject of the Antichrist coming to Earth. I believe that evil does exist for its own sinister ends. You will find that in unrepentant killers, in men who take power and create wars, in those who viciously manipulate and destroy the lives of innocent persons. Much of those horrifying aspects of life can be found in that picture. It is a grim movie that offers little or no hope, but that is the nature of the Satan we portray in that picture." **p**, Harvey Bernhard; **d**, Richard Donner; **cast**, Gregory Peck, Lee Remick, David Warner, Billie Whitelaw, Harvey Stephens, Leo McKern, Patrick Troughton, Martin Benson, Robert Rietty, Tommy Duggan, John Stride; **w**, David Seltzer; **c**, Gilbert Taylor (Panavision; DeLuxe Color); **m**, Jerry Goldsmith; **ed**, Stuart Baird; **art d**, Carmen Dillon; **set d**, Tessa Davies; **spec eff**, John Richardson, George Gibbs.

On an Island with You ★★★ 1948; U.S.; 107m; MGM; Color; Musical; Children: Acceptable; **DVD**. This entertaining songfest sees Williams as a movie star shooting a film on location in Hawaii where she is pursued by Lawford, a handsome young American naval officer assigned as a technical adviser on the set, who is sure she's the girl for him. When Williams shows some hesitancy in going to the altar with Lawford, he kidnaps her and takes her to a nearby island so she can

Gregory Peck, Harvey Stephens and Lee Remick in *The Omen*, 1976.

dance with him to music from his portable radio. He takes her back to the mainland and she doesn't have him arrested and it remains uncertain whether or not they will ever swim off together toward a Hawaiian sunset. Durante provides some laughs and Montalban and Charisse dance together in well-choreographed scenes. Songs: "On an Island with You," "The Dog Song," "Takin' Miss Mary to the Ball," "If I Were You" (Nacio Herb Brown, Edward Heyman); "Anchors Aweigh" (Charles A. Zimmerman); "I Know Darn Well I Can Do without Broadway" (Jimmy Durante); "The Beauty Hula" (Johnny Noble, John Kameaaloha Almeida); "Anapoau" (Johnny Noble); "The Pagan Mask," "All Aboard" (Andre Previn); "The Wedding Samba" (Abe Ellstein, Joseph Liebowitz, Allan Small); "I'll Do the Strut-Away/in My Cutaway" (Harry Donnelly, Jimmy Durante, Irving Caesar); "You Gotta Start Off Each Day with a Song" (Durante); "El Cumbanchero" (Rafael Hernandez); "Nao Tenho Lagrimas" (Max Bulhoes, Milton de Oliveira); "Nightingale" (Xavier Cugat, George Rosner). **p**, Joe Pasternak; **d**, Richard Thorpe; **cast**, Esther Williams, Peter Lawford, Ricardo Montalban, Jimmy Durante, Cyd Charisse, Leon Ames, Kathryn Beaumont, Dick Simmons, Marie Windsor, Xavier Cugat and His Orchestra; **w**, Dorothy Kingsley, Dorothy Cooper, Charles Martin, Hans Wilhelm (based on a story by Martin, Wilhelm); **c**, Charles Rosher (Technicolor); **m**, George Stoll; **ed**, Ferris Webster, Douglass Biggs; **art d**, Cedric Gibbons, Edward Carfagno; **set d**, Edwin B. Willis; **spec eff**, A. Arnold Gillespie.

On Borrowed Time ★★★ 1939; U.S.; 99m; MGM; B/W; Drama; Children: Unacceptable; **DVD**; **VHS**. Watson is orphaned and left in the care of his aged and grumpy grandfather, Barrymore, and the two eventually grow to love each other. Barrymore recognizes Hardwicke as Death when the Grim Reaper comes for him, but Barrymore, employing a ruse, chases Hardwicke up an old apple tree. They have a lengthy discourse on life and death and meanwhile no one in town dies. Barrymore is reluctant to die and leave Watson in the care of aunt Malyon, so he thinks of a way to borrow some time until he can figure out Watson's future. Hardwicke still has powers over life and death in the tree so he coaxes Watson to climb the tree, then makes him fall and break his neck. Barrymore realizes that Watson won't die, but will remain a quadriplegic if he doesn't let Hardwicke down from the tree, so he releases Hardwicke from his promise, but, in recognition of a wily adversary, Hardwicke gives Barrymore more time on earth and the film ends with Barrymore and Watson walking into the future together. Well-acted and directed, this offbeat but fascinating film emphasizes the folly of attempting to cheat Death instead of accepting the inevitable, but few persons alive ever entertain such inevitability. Songs: "The Battle Hymn of the Republic" (William Steffe, Julia Ward Howe), "Jeanie with the Light Brown Hair" (Stephen Foster). **p**, Sidney Franklin; **d**, Harold S. Buc-

Katharine Hepburn and Henry Fonda in *On Golden Pond*, 1981.

quet; **cast**, Lionel Barrymore, Sir Cedric Hardwicke, Beulah Bondi, Una Merkel, Bobs Watson, Nat Pendleton, Henry Travers, Grant Mitchell, Phillip Terry, Truman Bradley, Hans Conried, Dickie Jones; **w**, Alice D.G. Miller, Frank O'Neill, Claudine West (based on a play by Paul Osborn, from a novel by Lawrence Edward Watkin); **c**, Joseph Ruttenberg; **m**, Franz Waxman; **ed**, George Boemler; **art d**, Cedric Gibbons; **set d**, Edwin B. Willis.

On Dangerous Ground ★★★ 1951; U.S.; 82m; RKO; B/W; Crime Drama; Children: Unacceptable; **DVD**; **VHS**. Ryan is riveting in a powerful performance where he plays a tough New York City cop, who has seen so much crime and violence that it has warped his character. He realizes that he is sadistically enjoying beating up suspects and is on the verge of a nervous breakdown. He is sent upstate to cool off and help investigate the murder of a young girl whose body has been found in the winter countryside. There he meets blind Lupino and becomes interested in her, but then learns that her mentally ill brother, Williams, is the chief suspect in the killing. Lupino talks Ryan into finding her brother and taking him into custody before the victim's father, Bond, can kill him. Ryan finds Williams, but the young fugitive thinks Ryan is going to shoot him and instead falls off a cliff to his death. Meanwhile, Lupino has softened Ryan about life and he realizes that there is no future for him in New York. He decides to make a life with Lupino and live the country life. Songs: "Danceland Jive," "Jumpin' Jive" (Roy Webb, Gene Rose); "How Long Did I Dream?" (Jimmy Van Heusen). This well-acted *film noir* production presents considerable violence that prohibits viewing by children. *Author's Note*: Director Ray told this author that "**On Dangerous Ground** lost money at the box office, about $400,000, and RKO blamed me for that, some front office people saying that I should not have split the story line into two separate segments, the first where Ryan is going to pieces in New York, and the second when he moves into a whole new back country world and meets Ida [Lupino], who turns him back into a human being. That was a lot of baloney. The reason why the picture did not make money is because RKO did not promote it." Lupino told this author that "playing a blind person is not a matter of moving about slowly and groping into space. I had to study how such afflicted people think as well as move about without vision. Not looking directly at the other actors was the most difficult thing to do because, for an actor, that is an impulsive and instinctive thing to do." Ryan said to this author that his character in this film "was another tough bird showing his hate with both fists and in the first half of the picture I am not much more than a sadistic cop, but, thank God, the script allowed me to turn into a reasonable person with some compassion, and for me, that was a big break. Most of my previous pictures had typecast me as a bigot or a psychopath." **p**, John Houseman; **d**,

Nicholas Ray; **cast**, Ida Lupino, Robert Ryan, Ward Bond, Charles Kemper, Anthony Ross, Ed Begley, Ian Wolfe, Sumner Williams, Gus Schilling, Cleo Moore; **w**, A.I. Bezzerides, Ray (based on the novel *Mad with Much Heart* by Gerald Butler); **c**, George E. Diskant; **m**, Bernard Herrmann; **ed**, Roland Gross; **art d**, Albert S. D'Agostino, Ralph Berger; **set d**, Darrell Silvera, Harley Miller; **spec eff**, Harold Stine.

On Golden Pond ★★★★ 1981; U.K./U.S.; 109m; IPC Films/UNIV; Color; Drama; Children: Unacceptable (MPAA: PG); **DVD**; **VHS**. Henry Fonda, Hepburn and Jane Fonda are standouts in this prosaic but passionate and telling family drama that takes place at a New England summer cottage, where Henry Fonda is approaching age eighty and realizes that the book is closing for him and he does not like it. He is a retired professor, and his wife, Hepburn, is also about the same age, worried about her husband in that she sees his mind slowly disintegrating after seeing him struggle to recall memories. He is a rather cantankerous old man, who believes that this may be his last summer holiday at a cottage the family has shared for a half of a century and he is not looking forward to seeing his daughter, Jane Fonda, who is about to visit him and Hepburn after some time of being estranged, and Hepburn is also apprehensive about this visit. Jane Fonda then arrives with her husband, Coleman, and his son, MeKeon, from a previous marriage. The boy and Henry Fonda do not get along. The boy is prone to four-letter words and is basically a dedicated smart aleck, and his grandfather would more or less prefer he gets lost somewhere in the woods. When Jane Fonda asks if she and Coleman can leave McKeon in the care of her father and Hepburn, Henry Fonda rebels against the idea, although Hepburn agrees while Coleman, as much a hard head as Henry Fonda, and Jane Fonda depart. The boy and his grandfather are at first at loggerheads, but they slowly warm to each other and finally bond after they spend some time fishing together. Fonda is obsessed with catching an enormous trout in the lake for years, a near mythical fish he calls "Walter," and his dogged resolution in catching that fish almost equals Captain Ahab's obsessive search for the great whale, Moby Dick. While he and McKeon grow closer together, Fonda becomes the boy's mentor, teaching him all the little things that his father, Coleman, has never had time to impart, and McKeon now becomes in Fonda's failing mind the son he never had and always wanted. While fishing for "Walter" Fonda and McKeon suddenly meet mishap when their boat is torn open and both end up in the water. Hepburn becomes alarmed when neither shows up at the cottage for dinner time and she begins searching for them, finding them holding on to a rock in the lake. When they all return to the cottage that night, Fonda and McKeon keep their "adventure" to themselves, which further bonds them in manly confidence. Jane Fonda then returns alone to the cottage, saying that Coleman has returned to California and she and McKeon will join him. When she sees her stepson having such a good time with her father, she becomes resentful in that Henry Fonda never showed much interest in her when she was a child, but Hepburn tells her that such old grudges are foolish to nurture and persuades her daughter to make an effort to understand her father. Jane Fonda does exactly that and her father gives her the warm and gentle responses she has missed all her life and they, too, draw closer so that when she finally leaves with McKeon, she and her father lovingly embrace. After Jane Fonda and McKeon depart, Henry Fonda is suddenly jolted with what he thinks is a heart palpitation. Hepburn gives him a heart pill and he calms down, both thinking that he has again sidestepped the Grim Reaper, and the film closes as both cling to the hope that they will be alive together one more year to return to the cottage the next summer to hear the call of the loons across the lake. Rydell directs this tender tale with great care—a simple but touching story that proved to be an enormous box office hit, mostly due to the outstanding performances of the leading players. Henry Fonda won an Oscar as Best Actor and Hepburn won her fourth Oscar as Best Actress while Thompson took an Oscar for Best Adapted Screenplay. Jane Fonda was nominated for an Oscar as Best Supporting Actress and Grusin received an Oscar nomination for his compelling score, as did Williams for his beautiful cinematography. Made on a budget of $15 million, the film returned almost $120 million at the box office in its initial release. *Author's Note*: This story imitated life in that Henry Fonda and his daughter Jane had not gotten along in many years, and this was the only film in which they appeared together. She had appeared with her father in a 1954 play produced in Nebraska and then became a model and married at an early age to French director Roger Vadim, who thought to remake her into another sex kitten for the screen. Jane's political beliefs were also at odds with her father, but, in a great effort to reunite with him, Jane raised the money to produce this wonderful film, almost as a tribute to her father, who died seven months after **On Golden Pond** was released. The Thompson play upon which this memorable film was based had seen little stage success, having a run off Broadway with 126 performances. Little interest in the film was shown by Hollywood executives until Jane Fonda made a concerted effort to put the film into production. Hepburn told this author that "I think I received a copy of the script about the same time Hank [Fonda] got a copy and we both fell in love with the story right away and wanted to do it. The story is a heart-tugging piece from beginning to end and I was so happy that Hank and I appeared together in it. We had never appeared in any picture together, but we always admired each other's work. **On Golden Pond** was Hank's swansong and we all pretty much knew that, and that made it all the more bittersweet and important. It was our farewell to him and it ended with a kiss." The gratuitous use of four-letter words in this film prohibits viewing by children. **p**, Bruce Gilbert; **d**, Mark Rydell; **cast**, Katharine Hepburn, Henry Fonda, Jane Fonda, Doug McKeon, Dabney Coleman, William Lanteau, Chris Rydell, Troy Garity; **w**, Ernest Thompson (based on his play); **c**, Billy Williams; **m**, Dave Grusin; **ed**, Robert L. Wolfe; **prod d**, Stephen Grimes; **set d**, Jane Bogart; **spec eff**, Matt Sweeney.

On Guard ★★★ 2002; France/ Italy/Germany; 128m; Aliceleo/Empire Pictures; Color; Adventure; Children: Unacceptable; **DVD**. Luchini is a scheming count in France in the early 1700s, and he is to inherit the wealth and estates of his cousin, Perez, a duke, but nonetheless plots against him by keeping it a secret that the duke has a newly born but illegitimate daughter. Perez learns of his daughter's birth and undertakes a journey to a distant castle to marry the girl's mother, who is a baron's daughter. On Perez's wedding night, he and his bride and others in the castle are murdered by Luchini and his henchmen. Before dying, Perez asks one of those attending the wedding, his friend, Auteuil, a sixteen-year-old street urchin, to avenge him, no matter how long it takes. The only ones to survive the massacre are Auteuil and the infant girl, who is the rightful heiress to Perez's fortune. Luchini thinks he has eliminated all who might later jeopardize him, but Auteuil and the girl are taken to safety by a traveling troop of Italian actors. Twenty years pass and Luchini learns that Auteuil and the infant girl survived and he now plots to have them killed. Auteuil, however, gains the confidence of Luchini by working as his bookkeeper under a disguise as a hunchback. Now a skilled swordsman, Auteuil avenges Perez by defeating Luchini in a wild duel with swords. The girl, now a beautiful young woman, Gillain, not only inherits Perez's wealth, but she and Auteuil, who have long loved each other, go to the altar. This new and excitingly produced adaptation of Paul Féval's 1857 novel *Le Bossu* (The Hunchback) was filmed five times earlier as **On Guard** (1924, 1927, 1929, 1942 and 1984), and a 1952 television series was also based on the story. Produced in France in 1997, this top-notch swashbuckler was not seen in America until 2002. Excessive violence prohibits viewing by children. *Author's Note*: This story is reminiscent and takes a leaf from the Alexander Dumas (*père*) novel, *The Corsican Brothers*, which was published in 1844, thirteen years before the Féval work, where twins are denied their rightful inheritance by a tyrant, who seeks to exterminate them and all of their family members, and which was made into several films, most notably **The Corsican Brothers**, 1941, starring the inimitable Douglas Fairbanks, Jr., in the dual role of the twins. **p**, Patrick Godeau, Vittorio and

Vincent Perez in *On Guard*, 2002.

Rita Cecchi Gori, **d**, Philippe de Broca; **cast**, Daniel Auteuil, Fabrice Luchini, Vincent Perez, Philippe Noiret, Marie Gillain, Yann Collette, Jean-François Stévenin, Didier Pain, Charlie Nelson, Claire Nebout, Jacques Sereys; **w**, de Broca, Jean Cosmos, Jérôme Tonnerre (based on the novel by Paul Féval); **c**, Jean-François Robin; **m**, Philippe Sarde; **ed**, Henri Lanoë; **prod d**, Bernard Vézat; **spec eff**, Christian Guillon.

On Her Majesty's Secret Service ★★★ 1969; U.K.; 142m; Eon Productions/UA; Color; Spy Drama; Children: Cautionary; **DVD**; **VHS**. This time, instead of Sean Connery, it is Lazenby, who enacts the role of James Bond in a story that is most likely the best of Ian Fleming's many exciting tales about the celebrated 007 agent of British Intelligence. While searching for criminal mastermind Blofeld (Savalas) in Portugal, Lazenby rescues the attractive Rigg from drowning, only to learn that he has upset her intent to commit suicide. He returns to London only to be told to cease his quest for Savalas, which his superiors consider obsessive, and Lazenby quits the service in disgust. Deciding to pursue Savalas on his own, Lazenby returns to Portugal and again comes to the aid of Rigg by bailing her out of her gambling debts and they are soon lovers. Lazenby is then escorted by toughs to the headquarters of multimillionaire gangster Ferzetti, who offers Lazenby $1 million to preserve the honor of his daughter, Rigg, by marrying her. After Lazenby refuses, he convinces Ferzetti to help him track down Savalas, and Lazenby then pursues the arch criminal to Switzerland where Savalas is attempting to buy the title of count. Lazenby trails the villain to his mountain bastion, a hideout ringed with guards and protective devices, where he learns that Savalas has another fantastic scheme to rule the world, this time by injecting sterility spores into the world's agricultural systems. After one of Savalas' sensual assistants identifies Lazenby as a spy, he is forced to flee, retreating from the place on skis (in one of the most exciting action scenes in any James Bond film). En route to the valley below, Lazenby is saved by Rigg, who arrives by car, and then the two of them use skis to continue their escape while Savalas' minions chase after them. Lazenby realizes that Rigg is the one woman for him and she accepts his proposal of marriage. After they elude pursuers and evade a tremendous avalanche Savalasarranges, Rigg is kidnapped by Savalas' goons and taken to Savalas' mountain fortress. Savalas uses Rigg to demand a strange ransom, that he be given his title of count and that world authorities grant him universal amnesty for all of his past crimes. This outrageous offer is rejected, and Savalas' fortress is bombed by helicopters flown by British agents and Ferzetti's men. Lazenby manages to rescue Rigg and then goes after Savalas in a wild chase down the mountain slope on speeding bobsleds until Savalas takes a wrong turn and meets his end, or so it seems. Lazenby and Rigg are then married, but, on their honeymoon, the insidious and ubiquitous

Doris Day in *On Moonlight Bay*, 1951.

Savalas resurfaces and shoots Rigg, killing her, leaving the shocked Lazenby to mourn the loss of the woman he loved. Hunt directs this action-loaded production with splendid skill, developing Bond's character much more in depth than earlier shown and downplaying the endless gadgets that permeate previous such films in the series. *Author's Note*: After Connery was no longer interested in playing the part of Bond, a worldwide search was made to find his replacement. Lazenby, an Australian model, was more or less signed up in frantic haste to get on with the next Bond production. Lazenby had no experience as an actor and this was his first film. His rather stoic performance, however, was improved through his amazing physical dexterity, which astounded his stunt trainers. "The director of that picture [Hunt] had a lot of problems with George [Lazenby] because he had never acted before," Savalas told this author, "so he concentrated on Diana [Rigg] and me, building up our parts. Well, all that did was make George angry about everything and he was soon growling and barking out his lines on and off the set. It soured the whole production, but Hunt still brought in an exciting picture." **p**, Albert R. Broccoli, Harry Saltzman; **d**, Peter Hunt; **cast**, George Lazenby, Diana Rigg, Telly Savalas, Gabriele Ferzetti, Ilse Steppat, Angela Scoular, Lois Maxwell, Catherina Von Schell, George Baker, Bernard Lee, Joanna Lumley, Bessie Love; **w**, Richard Maibaum, Simon Raven (based on the novel by Ian Fleming); **c**, Michael Reed (Panavision; Technicolor); **m**, John Barry; **ed**, John Glen; **prod d**, Syd Cain; **art d**, Bob Laing; **set d**, Peter Lamont; **spec eff**, John Stears.

On Moonlight Bay ★★★ 1951; U.S.; 95m; WB; Color; Musical Comedy; Children: Acceptable; **DVD**; **VHS**. Pleasant family musical with a lot of great funny moments opens in a small Indiana town around 1917 where banker Ames maintains a large house with his wife DeCamp, daughter Day, his scamp of a son, Gray, and their acerbic housekeeper, Wickes. Ames has his hands full with Gray, who is constantly fibbing his way into trouble, and Day is more of a tomboy, who prefers playing baseball with the neighborhood boys than being a pretty girl attending socials. She abandons her tomboy ways after meeting handsome college student MacRae, who has just moved into the neighborhood, and both begin sparking. MacRae takes her to her first dance at a lake resort where they spoon while canoeing on the peaceful waters and later dance. Ames, however, has reservations about MacRae, who has a lot of radical ideas, and where he is forever spouting socialist concepts that condemn capitalism and banks in general, which is Ames' business. Then Gray creates a town scandal when, after getting into trouble with schoolteacher Corby, spreads the false tale that his father, Ames, is a hopeless drunkard. When this news reaches MacRae's ears, he rushes to Ames' home to protect Day and the other ladies of the house from the alcoholic abuse of an incorrigible inebriate. Of course,

Ames is nothing of the kind and sends MacRae packing and, after discovering Gray's outrageous fabrication, reaches for the spanking strap. Ames and family then attend MacRae's graduation, and Ames, for Day's sake and future, makes peace with the young man when he sees that he and most of the other male graduates have joined the U.S. Army and are about to march off to fight in WWI. It is understood with the hesitant approval of Ames that MacRae will return to marry the fetching Day. Del Ruth directs this lively and entertaining musical with great skill, smoothly integrating the story line with a host of fine songs and where Day and MacRae are at the top of their singing talents. Songs: "Moonlight Bay" (music: Percy Wenrich; lyrics: Edward Madden); "Tell Me" (music: Max Kortlander; lyrics: Will Callahan); "I'm Forever Blowing Bubbles" (music: Nat Vincent, James Kendis, James Brockman; lyrics: John W. Kellette); "Love Ya" (music: Peter De Rose; lyrics: Charles Tobias); "Cuddle Up a Little Closer, Lovey Mine," "Every Little Movement (Has a Meaning All Its Own)" (music: Karl Hoschna; lyrics: Otto A. Harbach); "Ain't We Got Fun" (Richard A. Whiting); "Till We Meet Again" (music: Richard A. Whiting; lyrics: Ray Egan); "Hark! The Herald Angels Sing" (Charles Wesley, George Whitefield, Felix Mendelsohn); "Pack Up Your Troubles in Your Old Kit Bag and Smile, Smile, Smile!" (music: Felix Powell; lyrics: George Asaf); "Oh, You Beautiful Doll" (1911; Nat D. Ayer); "Yoo Hoo" (music: Al Jolson; lyrics: B. G. De Sylva); "Hail to Old I.U" (music: traditional Scottish tune; lyrics [1893]: J. T. Giles); "The Bowery" (music: Percy Gaunt); "Hurry No. 1" (J. S. Zamecnik); "Wintermarchen" (Alphons Czibulka); "It's a Long, Long Way to Tipperary" (Jack Judge). **p**, William Jacobs; **d**, Roy Del Ruth; **cast**, Doris Day, Gordon MacRae, Jack Smith, Leon Ames, Rosemary DeCamp, Mary Wickes, Ellen Corby, Billy Gray, Henry East, Jeffrey Stevens; **w**, Jack Rose, Melville Shavelson (based on the novel *Alice Adams* and the "Penrod" stories by Booth Tarkington); **c**, Ernest Haller (Technicolor); **m**, Max Steiner; **ed**, Thomas Reilly; **art d**, Douglas Bacon; **set d**, William Wallace; **spec eff**, Hans F. Koenekamp, William McGann.

On My Own ★★★ 1992; Italy/Canada/Australia; 97m; Alliance Communications Corp.; Color; Drama; Children: Unacceptable; **DVD**. Absorbing drama sees Ferguson as a teenage boy living at a boarding school in Canada while his father works in Hong Kong and his mother lives in England. When his parents visit for the holidays, he discovers that his mother suffers from schizophrenia, a secret that had been kept from him. He tries to understand her problem and, in the process, comes to terms with his own. Songs: "Piping" (William Blake), "Under His Thumb" (Wendy Morrison), "Take Me to Your Party" (Frank Strangle). Explicit depiction of mental diseases prohibits viewing by children. **p**, Leo Pescarolo, Elisa Resegotti, Will Spencer, Stavros C. Stavrides; **d**, Antonio Tibaldi; **cast**, Matthew Ferguson, Judy Davis, David McIlwraith, Jan Rubes, Michele Melega, Colin Fox, Nicolas Van Burek, Rachel Blanchard, Lanna MacKay, Michael Polley; **w**, Tibaldi, Gill Dennis, John Frizzell (based on a story by Tibaldi, Dennis); **c**, Vic Sarin; **m**, Franco Piersanti; **ed**, Edward McQueen-Mason; **art d**, William Fleming; **set d**, Shelley Nieder; **spec eff**, Brock Jolliffe.

On the Avenue ★★★ 1937; U.S.; 89m; FOX; B/W; Musical Comedy; Children: Acceptable; **DVD**; **VHS**. Several Hollywood stars—Powell, Carroll and Faye—head the cast in this lively and very entertaining musical, which offers by many laugh-filled scenes featuring the zany Ritz Brothers and offers a bevy of fine Irving Berlin tunes. The story line presents a musical inside of a musical in that Powell is directing a Broadway musical starring Faye, and when it premieres, one of the theater-going viewers is the beautiful Carroll, who is shocked to see that her own life is being parodied before the world. Faye is billed as "The Richest Girl in the World" (which is really a profile of the actual life of Doris Duke, 1912-1993, who was given that moniker after inheriting a vast fortune—she died at age eighty leaving an estate of $1.3 billion). Wealthy socialite Carroll will not tolerate such indignities and, following the show, storms backstage to upbraid Powell, insisting that he delete the more outlandish aspects of Faye's character. Powell's showmanship integrity will not be influenced, even though he is dazzled by Carroll's stunning blonde looks and makes a date with her. They are soon an item in the gossip columns, and Powell falls so deeply in love with the heiress that he relaxes his rigid regimen and takes the sharp edges off his show's parody of her. Faye, however, who has been Powell's sweetheart for some time, is livid at Powell's romantic desertion of her and even more furious over his compromising the show's material. She gets even with him and his café society debutante Carroll at the next performance when Carroll returns to see the revised version of the musical, this time bringing with her wealthy father, Barbier, her maiden aunt, Witherspoon, and longtime suitor and fortune-hunter Mowbray (who is, as usual, a consummate cad). Faye's performance is now riddled with even more barbed and biting bits that demean and ridicule Carroll's luxury-bloated lifestyle and that of her opulent family. Her seething satire scandalizing this family so upsets the fulminating Barbier that he files a lawsuit against Powell, charging him with libel. Powell tries to make amends, but Carroll will no longer speak to him and goes even further to settle the score by buying the show from producer Catlett (who gives a delightful portrait of a double-dealing weasel) and alters the musical so that when it is again showcased, Powell is held up to ridicule as Broadway's biggest boob. Carroll tops this turnabout scheme by hiring the entire audience that attends this revised show and where every person in the theater walks out on Powell as he is performing on stage. Powell has had enough. He quits and is then sued by Carroll for breach of contract. The rich girl, to further spite Powell, then agrees to go to the altar with the oily Mowbray, but her aunt, Witherspoon, knows that Carroll's heart belongs to Powell and she stops Carroll from committing grand folly by storming into the wedding and yanking Carroll away from Mowbray, bringing her to her senses and reuniting her with Powell and where they tie the knot at City Hall. The screwball humor in this film is further and delightfully accented by the performance of the oddball Ritz Brothers, where Harry Ritz mockingly mimics Faye in drag and where the humorous and heavyset Billy Gilbert does his discombobulating bit as a restaurant owner. Songs: "Cheek to Cheek," "He Ain't Got Rhythm," "You're Laughing at Me," "The Girl on the Police Gazette," "I've Got My Love to Keep Me Warm," "This Year's Kisses," "Slumming on Park Avenue," (all 1937; Irving Berlin); "There's No Place Like Home (Home, Sweet Home)" (1823; music: H. R. Bishop, from a Sicilian air), "Sailing, Sailing (Over the Bounding Main)" (1880; Godfrey Marks); "A-Hunting We Will Go" (traditional); "Happy Birthday to You" (Mildred J. Hill, Patty S. Hill); "Jingle Bells" (1857; James Pierpont); "Largo al Factotum" (1816; music: Gioachino Rossini; libretto: Cesare Sterbini); "Ochi Chyornye (Dark Eyes)" (Russian folksong); "The Skater's Waltz (Les patineurs)" (1882; music: Emil Waldteufel); "Bridal Chorus (Here Comes the Bride)" (1850; from "Lohengrin"; music: Richard Wagner); *Author's Note*: Zanuck told this author that "we were building up Alice's [Faye] career and put her into **On the Avenue**, but we had no leading singing star at the studio, except for Don Ameche, and he was just not right for the part of the leading man. I wanted Dick Powell, but he was under lock and key at Warner Brothers so I had to go to Jack Warner [for whom Zanuck had once worked as a producer] and beg him to loan me Powell. He did, at a hefty price, of course." Faye told this author that "I got third billing after Madeleine Carroll in **On the Avenue** as she was a big name star then, but I knew the studio was grooming me for the bright lights. They had me sing a very good Irving Berlin number called 'Slumming on Park Avenue' and they had the set look like New York's Hell's Kitchen in that number, I guess because they knew that that was where I came from. I liked working with Dick [Powell], a real professional in every sense and one of the most pleasant and intelligent actors I ever knew. He had a fine tenor voice, but he never wanted to be in musicals and always talked about doing dramas. He did not get that chance until many years later and, when he did, he gave a lot of fine, serious performances, usually as a

Dick Powell and Alice Faye in *On the Avenue*, 1937.

hardboiled detective. Well, I did my thing in **On the Avenue**, and I lose Dick to Madeleine, but that was a foregone conclusion. In the end, I wind up with George [Barbier], which I thought was a bit silly since he was more than twice my age, but it was still the age of the gold-digger and the sugar daddy." **p**, Darryl F. Zanuck; **d**, Roy Del Ruth; **cast**, Dick Powell, Madeleine Carroll, Alice Faye, The Ritz Brothers (Al, Harry, Jimmy Ritz), George Barbier, Alan Mowbray, Cora Witherspoon, Walter Catlett, Douglas Fowley, Joan Davis, Stepin Fetchit, Sig Ruman, Billy Gilbert, Lynn Bari, Marjorie Weaver; **w**, Gene Markey, William Conselman; **c**, Lucien Andriot; **m**, Irving Berlin; **ed**, Allen McNeil; **art d**, William Darling; **set d**, Thomas Little.

On the Double ★★★ 1961; U.S.; 92m; PAR; Color; Comedy; Children: Acceptable; **DVD**. Kaye delights in this military romp. He is an American G.I. in London shortly before the Normandy invasion of Europe during World War II (1939-1945) and looks so much like a British general he's asked to impersonate him, to allow the general to make a secret trip. Kaye is unaware that the general has been a target of assassins. The general dies when his plane crashes, and the plan changes so that Kaye maintains the disguise to confuse the Nazis about where the invasion is to take place. He learns that one of the general's closest friends, Evans, is the chief Nazi spy in England, exposes him, and the Normandy invasion goes off as planned. Songs: "The Mackenzie Hielanders," "Darlin' Meggie," "On the Double Polka" (Sylvia Fine); "Pack Up Your Troubles in Your Old Kit Bag and Smile, Smile, Smile" (Felix Powell, George Asaf); "When the Saints Go Marching In" (traditional); "Battle Hymn of the Republic" (William Steffe, Julia Ward Howe); "Cocktails for Two" (Arthur Johnston, Sam Coslow), "Du, du Liegst Mir in Herzen" (German traditional). A very funny Kaye comedy with a good story line and strong British supporting cast. *Author's Note*: Kaye told this author that "I had been doing impersonations of British upper-crust types in many of my routines [such as his routine in the comedy classic **The Secret Life of Walter Mitty**, 1947, where he imagines himself to be a heroic British flying officer in WWII]. So when I read the script for **On the Double**, I thought, 'perfect for me' and my stiff upper lip character with swagger stick and a tidy uniform. 'Piece of cake, old boy, you know, but then a zillion assassins are out to 'pack me in' and I have to run for my life. Threats, dangers and fear can be turned into something comedic if the victim is preposterous in the first place, and I have always had a knack for being preposterous." **p**, Jack Rose; **d**, Melville Shavelson; **cast**, Danny Kaye, Dana Wynter, Wilfrid Hyde-White, Margaret Rutherford, Diana Dors, Allan Cuthbertson, Jesse White, Gregory Walcott, Terence de Marney, Rex Evans; **w**, Rose, Shavelson; **c**, Harry Stradling Sr. (Panavision; Technicolor); **m**, Leith Stevens; **ed**, Frank Bracht; **art d**, Hal Pereira, Arthur Lonergan;

Gene Tierney and Danny Kaye in *On the Riviera*, **1951.**

set d, Sam Comer, Frank R. McKelvy; **spec eff**, Farciot Edouart, John P. Fulton.

On the Riviera ★★★ 1951; U.S.; 89m; FOX; Color; Comedy; Children: Acceptable; **DVD**; **VHS**. Kaye is perfect in this hilarious comedy where he plays dual roles to the point of confusing everyone, including himself. He is an entertainer performing on the Riviera, who bears an uncanny resemblance to a famous French aviator (who is also played by Kaye). When the famed pilot is delayed from appearing at an important party, Kaye the entertainer is hired to impersonate the flier and he does the doubling with such effectiveness that Tierney, the ravishingly beautiful wife of the pilot, accepts the entertainer as her husband. From that point on, she and just about everyone in the film, as well as viewers, have a tough time separating the two look-alikes, which creates several funny incidents while Kaye manages to sing and dance and even does two good impersonations based on performers in the two earlier films on which this one is a remake, one of Maurice Chevalier in **Follies Bergere**, 1935, and another (in drag) where he sings and dances á la Carmen Miranda, mimicking her appearance in **That Night in Rio**, 1941, top-heavy fruit salad hat and all. Many of the songs Kaye performs were written by his real-life wife, Sylvia Fine. Songs: "Can Can" (1858; Jacques Offenbach); "Chica Chica Boom Chic" (music: Harry Warren; lyrics: Mack Gordon), "Ballin' the Jack" (1913; music: Chris Smith; lyrics: Jim Burris); "On the Riviera," "Popo the Puppet," "Happy Ending" (Sylvia Fine). *Author's Note*: Kaye told this author that "I love doing dual roles in my pictures and in **On the Riviera** I play a stage performer hired to play a celebrated pilot and get to use a French accent and also get to dally with the beautiful Gene Tierney. You know, Darryl Zanuck, head of 20th Century Fox once said that she was 'the most beautiful woman ever to be on the big screen,' and you would not find an argument from me about that." The portrait of Tierney shown in this film is the same portrait of her used in the film noir classic **Laura**, 1944, and in which she stars, with the exception that the earlier film was shot in black and white and this one shows that fine portrait for the first and only time in brilliant color. **p**, Sol C. Siegel; **d**, Walter Lang; **cast**, Danny Kaye, Gene Tierney, Corinne Calvet, Marcel Dalio, Jean Murat, Henri Letondal, Clinton Sundberg, Sig Ruman, Joyce MacKenzie, Marina Koshetz, Gwen Verdon; **w**, Valentine Davies, Phoebe and Henry Ephron (based on a play by Rudolph Lothar, Hans Adler); **c**, Leon Shamroy (Technicolor); **m**, Alfred Newman; **ed**, J. Watson Webb, Jr.; **art d**, Lyle Wheeler, Leland Fuller; **set d**, Thomas Little, Walter M. Scott; **spec eff**, Fred Sersen.

On the Threshold of Space ★★★ 1956; U.S.; 98m; FOX; Color; Drama; Children: Acceptable; **DVD**. This intriguing tale that deals with the early days of space travel sees Madison as a U.S. Air Force physician, who undergoes tests in the mid-1950s to determine the extent of strains and stresses on humans in space travel. Tension is high as Madison risks his life in one test after another while his wife, Leith, lives a life of anxiety and worry and where Hodiak, head of research, also participates in those hazardous tests. The actual techniques and operations of the U.S. Air Force involving such space travel testing were employed in the production, which was shot on location at two U.S. Air Force bases, Elgin in Florida and Holloman in New Mexico. This was Hodiak's last film in that he died of a heart attack at age forty-one just before this film's release. Top flight acting from Madison, Hodiak and the alluring Leith and with firm direction from Webb makes this one worth watching. **p**, William Bloom; **d**, Robert D. Webb; **cast**, Guy Madison, Virginia Leith, John Hodiak, Dean Jagger, Warren Stevens, Martin Milner, King Calder, Walter Coy, Ken Clark, Barry Coe; **w**, Simon Wincelberg, Francis Cockrell); **c**, Joe MacDonald (CinemaScope; DeLuxe Color); **m**, Lyn Murray; **ed**, Hugh S. Fowler; **art d**, Lyle R. Wheeler, Lewis H. Creber; **set d**, Stuart A. Reiss, Walter M. Scott; **spec eff**, Ray Kellogg.

On the Town ★★★★★ 1949; U.S.; 98m; MGM; Color; Musical; Children: Acceptable; **DVD**; **VHS**. No musical until this one was ever largely shot on location in New York, setting not only that precedent but providing one of the most energy-charged songfests to go onto the screen while the story, music and dancing are all beautifully integrated by the gifted Kelly, who directs this film. Three sailors, Kelly, Sinatra and Munshin, are given twenty-four hour passes to see the Big Apple and they leave their ship at the Brooklyn Navy Yard when the sun comes up, having great expectations in meeting the right girls and seeing the city's most spectacular landmarks. They take a subway and see ads promoting the city's monthly "Miss Turnstile," this lovely winner being Vera-Ellen. (New York had for years sponsored a "Miss Subways" contest and many of these fetching girls were later top models, Hollywood starlets and, a few, like Diana Lynn, became movie stars.) Kelly is so taken with Vera-Ellen's picture that he removes it from its frame, intending to take it back with him to his ship to keep him company on many lonely nights at sea. When the three gobs get off at the next stop they are surprised to see Vera-Ellen posing for news photographers. Kelly asks that he be photographed with his dream girl and, after the shot is taken, Vera-Ellen disappears into the massive morning rush-hour crowds. Sinatra and Munshin boost the crestfallen Kelly with promises of meeting any number of other endless beautiful girls, but his heart now belongs only to Vera-Ellen. The boys take a taxi driven by pert and pretty Garrett, who goes gaga over Sinatra (as she did in an equally terrific musical, **Take Me Out to the Ball Game**, 1949, which starred Sinatra, Kelly and Munshin), asking Garrett to race her cab to Columbus Circle where they hope to catch up with Vera-Ellen, thinking she has taken the next train to that destination. They miss connections and Kelly is again deflated when not catching up with his dream girl. Returning to Garrett's cab, Garrett tells the boys that she has finished her night shift and is returning to the garage, but she is so enthralled with Sinatra that she agrees to help the trio find Kelly's elusive heartthrob. Their first stop in this romantic quest is the Museum of Anthropological History, and here Munshin meets Miller, a tall and voluptuous young lady, who is doing a research paper and is looking in admiration at a statue of Prehistoric Man. When Munshin appears as almost an exact duplicate to that long-ago ancestor, Miller suddenly goes crazy for him. In their innocent antics, the group accidentally topples a priceless replica of a dinosaur. The curator is furious and resolves to have them arrested. Miller comes to the defense of the boys, saying: "You ought to be proud that three sailors from the United States Navy got off a ship one day and what did they do? Were they thirsty for hard liquor? No. They were thirsty for culture. Were they running after girls? No. They came running to your museum to see a dinosaur! For months out at sea they were dreaming of your dinosaur." The quest for Vera-Ellen is then resumed, but Garrett believes that the best way they will find this almost mythical girl is that the group members split up, Miller and Munshin going one way, she and Sinatra another, and Kelly on his own. They will meet that night at the observation tower of the Empire State Building (then the world's tallest building) on the corner of 34th Street and Fifth Avenue. (That celebrated romantic rendezvous is the meeting place in many a romance film, including **Love Affair**, 1939; **An Affair to Remember**, 1957, and **Sleepless in Seattle**, 1993, and where the monstrous gorilla meets his doom in the classic horror film, **King Kong**, 1933.) Garrett's plan is more than a little self-serving as she wants Sinatra to herself, but when taking him home to her small apartment she finds to her dismay that her roommate, Pearce, is not at her day job, but is sick in bed with a cold. Meanwhile, Kelly scouts the city, going to Symphonic Hall where he learns that Vera-Ellen is enrolled in a dancing class and he tracks her down. She is taken by Kelly's small-town innocence and agrees to go on a date with him, meeting him and his friends at the Empire State Building. When the six reunite, they decide to go on the town, Kelly naively believing that Vera-Ellen is a great celebrity and not a monthly flash-in-the-pan girl (who is enjoying her fifteen minutes of fame á la Andy Warhol), and Miller and Garrett kindly refrain from bursting Kelly's bubble by telling that all fame is fleeting and that Vera-Ellen's has almost fled. When they arrive at a nightclub, Miller persuades owner Conried to make a fuss over Vera-Ellen so that Kelly will be further impressed, but Vera-Ellen must leave at midnight so Garrett later presses the nose-sniffling Pearce into service to substitute as Kelly's date. First, Kelly takes Vera-Ellen home and she is sorry to say goodbye as she has grown more than fond of the charming sailor, not telling him that she must now go to work to pay for her dancing lessons by performing at a Coney Island sideshow as a cooch dancer. When Kelly returns to the nightclub, Bates tells the group that Vera-Ellen had to leave or lose her job and the group then drives to Brooklyn while police are on their tail for earlier destroying the skeletal remains of the dinosaur. (A cop responding to that complaint and hearing that the dinosaur has collapsed, states: "Collapsed? That's terrible! She's my favorite singing star, that Dinah Shore.") When they finally track down Vera-Ellen, she admits to Kelly that she is not the big star he has envisioned, but only a girl with ambitions to become a dancer and that she is from a small town he has never heard about, Meadowville, Indiana, and, lo and behold, she learns that Kelly comes from that very same town. The cops then arrive to pinch the boys for the collapse of that dinosaur, but the desperate sailors disguise themselves as cooch dancers in the sideshow. Just when they think they have hoodwinked the long arm of the law, they race offstage and run right into the back of a military wagon and are arrested by members of the Navy Shore Patrol. The girls then persuade the MPs to release the boys so that they can enjoy the last few hours of their shore leave and they are later shown reporting for duty where their ship is docked at six a.m., precisely the time their shore leave expires. Vera-Ellen, Garrett and Miller then wave a fond farewell to Kelly, Sinatra and Munshin as they board their ship, and that is where this superb and delightful film ends. The songs are outstanding as is the well-choreographed dancing from Kelly, Miller and Vera-Ellen and where Sinatra was never in better singing voice. Munshin, the clown of the trio, does a fine job with some funny routines, and the direction by Kelly and his longtime partner Donen exceptionally conveys this seamless tale with great vitality and exuberance. Songs: "I Feel Like I'm Not Out of Bed Yet," "New York, New York," "Come Up to My Place" (music: Leonard Bernstein; lyrics: Adolph Green and Betty Comden); "Miss Turnstiles," "A Day in New York" (music: Leonard Bernstein); "Prehistoric Man," "Main Street," "You're Awful," "On the Town," "Count on Me," "That's All There Is, Folks" (music: Roger Edens; lyrics: Adolph Green, Betty Comden). The film won only one Oscar, for Best Musical Score. *Author's Note*: MGM chief Louis B. Mayer was not thrilled about the original Broadway musical, which offered only four songs from Bernstein, calling the film "smutty" because of its sideshow bump-and-grind dancing and "communistic" because, in the

Frank Sinatra, Jules Munshin and Gene Kelly singing at the top of the RCA Building in NYC in *On the Town*, 1949.

play, a black sailor dances with a white girl. Producer Freed, however, the MGM dynamo, who brought so many successful musicals to the screen for that studio, argued with Mayer, telling him that the film would be a great hit and that he would have his associate producer and composer Edens write more songs for the film, with additional support from Green and Comden, who had written the lyrics for the original stage production. Mayer grudgingly agreed, buying the film rights for $250,000 and paying Green and Comden an additional $110,000 for their rewrites. Of the original cast in the 1944 stage version (1944-1946; 462 performances) only Alice Pearce would later appear in the film version. Mayer had emphatically stated that he did not want this film shot on location, but Kelly, who co-directed with choreographer Donen, disagreed. "I went to Mayer," Kelly told this author, "and said that the only way the picture would be a success at the box office was to shoot it on location and show the pride of New York by having the players sing and dance at all of its landmarks [Fifth Avenue, Times Square, at Radio City, Grant's Tomb, Central Park, the Statue of Liberty, the Bronx, the Battery, Coney Island, Brooklyn, Carnegie Hall, Wall Street and the Brooklyn Navy Yard]. 'Look, L.B.,' I said, 'there are eight million people in New York City and they love their town and they will flock to see this picture because it shows their city's greatest attractions inside the story line and surrounds the story with a lot of happy songs and dances. Every guy in New York will take his family to see that film and so will every guy in America.' Well, Mayer was all for that since he bragged that MGM made family films, but he saw the number of people lining up at the box office, too, so he said, 'okay, I'll let you shoot it in New York City, but you have only one week to get the job done.' One week! Can you imagine? But, I took that deal and we did all the shooting inside of that one week [the entire production schedule was completed within forty-seven days, albeit supplemental shots were made at the MGM studio], which almost sent all of us to the hospital from exhaustion." (Ann Miller later claimed, when talking to an uninformed cable TV host, that it was she who convinced Mayer to allow the film to be shot on location in New York, but her claim is easily dismissed in that she was a contract dancer and actress at MGM and held no sway or had any real relationship as to the supervision of productions with Mayer, who would have responded only to that request from the director, Kelly, and his producer, Freed, who also urged Mayer to allow Kelly to make that on-location shooting.) "The shooting in New York for **On the Town** was a backbreaker," Sinatra told this author. "Gene [Kelly] and Stanley [Donen] drove us all nuts for about a week in those shoots. I mean it was night and day because Mayer had given Gene such a tight shooting schedule after Gene talked Mayer into letting him shoot the film on location in New York. But we were all young and full of vinegar so we went into that St. Vitus dance with Gene without complaint. I think that **On the Town** is one of the

Marlon Brando in *On the Waterfront*, 1954.

finest musicals ever made. And it was a shame about Betty [Garrett] when she later got blacklisted by those witch-hunting birds in Washington, but they had her nailed to rights, I guess, after her husband [actor Larry Parks] admitted that he had been a member of the Communist Party, and more or less said Betty had been part of that crowd, too. The witch-hunters may have been doing them a favor because when their film careers folded, they used their money very wisely by building very nice apartment buildings in Los Angeles and grew rich from the rents." Many previous films of all genres used on-location shots of New York dating back to the silent era with master filmmaker D.W. Griffith shooting most of his seventeen-minute crime class short **The Musketeers of Pig Alley**, 1912, in NYC. To name a few others, **The Naked City**, 1948, another crime classic, had been entirely shot on location in New York a year before **On the Town**, and, four years before that, Billy Wilder had many on-location shots taken of his leading player, Ray Milland, staggering through the streets of New York when making the classic drama, **The Lost Weekend**, 1945, which profiled a young, alcoholic writer. In that production, cinematographer John M. Seitz, under Wilder's supervision, took candid footage of New York streets with cameras hidden in a van, the same secretive method employed in **The Naked City** and by cinematographer Rosson when filming **On the Town** in NYC and where Manhattan residents were later shocked to see themselves on camera when the film was released. **On the Town** was made for $2 million and earned that back immediately at the box office, plus adding an initial $1 million to MGM's coffers. Comedienne Judy Holliday made an appearance in this film in one scene in the form of providing voiceover for a character named Daisy, a sailor's date. The following year she catapulted to stardom after appearing as the cuckolded, revenge-seeking housewife in the comedy classic **Adam's Rib**, 1950. **p**, Arthur Freed; **d**, Gene Kelly, Stanley Donen; **cast**, Kelly, Frank Sinatra, Betty Garrett, Ann Miller, Jules Munshin, Vera-Ellen, Florence Bates, Alice Pearce, George Meader, Hans Conried, Bern Hoffman, Lester Dorr, Carol Haney, Judy Holliday; **w**, Adolph Green, Betty Comden (based on the musical play by Comden, Green, Leonard Bernstein from the ballet "Fancy Free" by Jerome Robbins); **c**, Harold Rosson (Technicolor); **m**, Bernstein, Roger Edens, Saul Chaplin, Conrad Salinger, **ed**, Ralph E. Winters; **art d**, Cedric Gibbons, Jack Martin Smith; **set d**, Edwin B. Willis; **spec eff**, Warren Newcombe.

On the Waterfront ★★★★ 1954; U.S.; 108m; COL; B/W; Drama; Children: Unacceptable; **BD**; **DVD**; **VHS**. In what is arguably his finest role, Brando is mesmerizing as a former prizefighter working on the docks of NYC where corruption flourishes in the evil form of crime boss Cobb, who controls a longshoreman union, holding the survival and fate of scores of workers in his money-grubbing hands. Steiger, who also provides a bravura performance (as does Cobb and Malden, who plays a dedicated priest), is a well-educated lawyer on Cobb's payroll and Brando's older brother, a complex man, who loves his younger sibling, but has sold his intelligence, integrity and future to Cobb and is enmeshed within Cobb's felonious and lethal schemes. Brando is kept on Cobb's payroll, occasionally working on the docks and doing Cobb's errands. He spends a lot of time on a rooftop tending to his pigeons and thinking back upon his boxing career, resentful of his status as a has-been fighter. Cobb summons Brando and tells him to make contact with a friend, Wagner, a dock worker who has given Cobb trouble. Brando makes that contact, arranging for his friend to meet him on a rooftop to see his pigeons, but, when Wagner appears, he is suddenly thrown off the roof to his death by some of Cobb's thugs. Brando is shocked to see that he has been used to bring about this murder, saying: "I thought they were only gonna lean on him a little." Galento, one of Cobb's goons, replies sarcastically: "The canary [squealer] could sing, but he couldn't fly!" Brando is further troubled when meeting Saint, the victim's beautiful, blonde sister, who has been away at school and has just returned to find her brother dead. Brando is attracted to Saint and begins to feel that he was responsible for her brother's death and he then suspects that he is on the wrong side of the law in siding with his brother Steiger and Cobb. Saint introduces Brando to Malden, a no-nonsense parish priest, who urges him to cooperate with the crime commission, giving investigators Erickson and Balsam information that will close down the racketeers controlling the waterfront union, but Brando remains "D and D," the motto of the intimidated dockworkers, which means deaf and dumb. Malden persuades some of the dockworkers to attend a meeting in the basement chapel of his church where he urges them to expose Cobb and his henchmen. Henning, one of the most defiant of the workers, asks Malden if he will stand by them if they do what he asks, and Malden promises he will. Brando is at this meeting as a spy for Cobb, but when Cobb's goons attack the chapel, breaking its windows, he grabs Saint and leads her to safety while her father, Hamilton, Henning and others are beaten bloody by Cobb's club-wielding goons when they attempt to escape from the chapel. Hamilton is now frightened for his daughter's life and insists she return to her school, but she is determined to stay and see her brother's murderers brought to justice. Brando continues seeing her, taking her to a saloon, trying to explain how crime bosses like Cobb have always been with them. He later tells Cobb that nothing really happened at the chapel meeting, but Cobb suspects that Brando is being persuaded to turn against him by Saint and Steiger tells Brando to stay away from her, but Brando has no intention of giving up on Saint. He is given a cushy job in the hold of a ship where he loafs on sacks of goods and where Steiger lectures him to "stay in line" and follow Cobb's advice. A freighter then arrives at the port carrying imported liquor and then docks and almost all the dockworkers are allowed to unload the shipment. Henning is working in one of the holds when a heavy load of crated liquor is purposely unleashed, crashing down and killing him. Malden is summoned to give Henning his Last Rites and he then makes an impassioned speech to the workers, telling them that God is down in that hold with them, likening Henning's murder to the crucifixion of Jesus Christ and only they can end such crucifixions by working with authorities to get rid of the hoodlums controlling their union. Goons Galento and Mauriello shout insults at Malden and hurl rotten tomatoes and other debris at him, soiling his clothes. Galento then hurls a can at Malden, which strikes his head and causes a bleeding cut, but the indomitable priest continues his inspired lecture. When Mauriello is about to hurl another object at Malden, Brando, who has earlier warned this thug to stop harassing the priest, steps forth and smashes his fist into Mauriello's ugly face, knocking him down and unconscious. Malden then tells the dockworkers: "Boys, this is my church, and if you don't think Christ is down here on the waterfront, you got another guess coming." Brando by now is in love with Saint and has become so protective of her and so deeply influenced by Malden that Cobb tells Steiger to either get his brother "in line" or be killed. Steiger then meets with Brando (in one of the most moving and intensive self-examinations on film) where he asks Brando to keep silent about Cobb and break off his relationship with Saint, and, when Brando refuses, Steiger points a gun at him. Disgusted with such intimidation, Brando waves the gun away and Steiger, ashamed, tries to rekindle affection between them by recalling Brando's early boxing career, saying that he could have been another "Billy Conn [Light-heavyweight boxing champion]…but that skunk we got you for a manager brought you along too fast." Brando sadly shakes his head and, with tears welling in his eyes, he replies: "It wasn't him, Charley, it was you. Remember that night in the Garden [New York's Madison Square Garden] and you came down to my dressing room and you said, 'Kid, this ain't your night.' My night! I could have taken Wilson [his opponent] apart! So what happens? He gets a title shot outdoors in a ballpark and I get a one-way ticket to Palookaville! You was my brother, Charley. You should have looked out for me a little bit, so I wouldn't have to take them dives for the short-end money." Steiger replies with his usual synthetic older brother pose: "We had some bets down for you…You saw some money." Brando agonizes over the memory, saying: "You don't understand. I could have had class. I could have been a contender! I could have been somebody, instead of a bum, which is what I am. It was you, Charley." Brando has touched his brother's heart and Steiger, who cannot bring himself to take Brando's life, hands him the gun, telling him he is going to need it, and then orders the driver to pull over and lets Brando out, saying that he will tell Cobb that he could not find him. The driver, Persoff, a Cobb goon, then drives the car into a garage owned by Cobb. Brando then goes to Saint's apartment and, after she says she does not want to see him because she thinks he is aligned with her brother's killers, Brando breaks into the place and forcefully kisses her, but, being in love with him, she submits and embraces him. They then hear Cobb's thugs shouting from the street, calling out to Brando: "Your brother's down here—he wants to see you!" Brando and Saint then begin searching for Steiger and are almost run over by a truck that chases them down a narrow alleyway. They then find Steiger dead, hanging from a hook on the exterior wall of a building, a bullet hole and a trickle of blood staining his vicuna overcoat. Brando lowers his brother's body from the hook and holds it, full of rage and swearing to Saint: "I'm gonna take it out on their skulls!" Asking that Saint take care of Steiger's body, Brando, armed with the gun Steiger has given him, goes to a saloon that is often used by Cobb for meetings and holds several of Cobb's goons at bay while waiting to kill Cobb when he arrives. Malden, sent by Saint, shows up, and convinces Brando to take out his revenge by exposing Cobb's racket in providing information to the crime commission probing into Cobb's underworld dealings. He agrees and is soon seen testifying against Cobb and his thugs before the crime commission. Before he leaves, Cobb tells Brando that he will never work again on the docks and he is, more or less, "a dead man." Cobb has ostensibly lost control of the union, but his thugs continue to strong-arm the dockworkers and Westerfield, a Cobb stooge who selects the waiting stevedores each day for work continues to hand out jobs, and this day, he tells everyone that they are working, except Brando, who stands outside the entranceway to the loading docks. Enraged, Brando goes to the gangplank leading to a small shack where Cobb and his goons are holed up, shouting that he is glad that he informed on Cobb. The crime boss steps outside and challenges Brando and Brando races down the gangplank to battle Cobb in a vicious fight where both men mercilessly slug each other and where Cobb's goons interfere to help Cobb beat Brando to a bloody pulp. Malden and Saint locate him behind the floating shack, finding Brando almost unconscious, and Malden tells Brando that he can finally break Cobb's hold on the union if he can stand up, walk back up the gangplank and into the loading area where all the workers are waiting for him. Meanwhile, Cobb, who is also bloodied from the fight, shakily moves up the gangplank, ordering the longshoremen to go back to work, shoving and pushing them, until he comes to Saint's father, Hamilton, who tells Cobb: "You've been pushing me around all my life," and, with that, Hamilton

Marlon Brando and Eva Marie Saint in *On the Waterfront*, 1954.

pushes Cobb so hard that he falls backward and into the water, ultimately humiliating him before a cheering crowd of workers. Brando then regains consciousness and struggles to his feet and, wobbly-legged, staggers up the gangplank. His face a mask of blood, his vision blurred, Brando struggles step by agonizing step toward the open doorway of the loading dock area as his co-workers, as well as Malden and Saint anxiously wait to see if he is able to go to work to finally eliminate the racketeers' hold on the waterfront. In a superhuman effort, Brando does reach the entranceway and enters the area, his co-workers following him, to end the final scene of this impactful and unforgettable masterpiece. Director Kazan, who helmed many superb films, directs this riveting tale with consummate skill, building and expanding his characters in carefully constructed scenes, where Brando and all the cast members brilliantly essay those characters. Each carefully set scene is realistically portrayed in a gray and grim world filled with seedy tenements, debris strewn streets and where the days are overcast and foreboding and nights murky and moving with sinister-looking figures. There is little hope in this unpromising world until Brando's conscience resurfaces and he defiantly risks his life to free his oppressed and downtrodden co-workers from Cobb's underworld bondage. Although he portrays this anti-hero in a more modern world, his role is not dissimilar to that of the reluctant hero he played two years earlier when enacting the part of a peasant leader during Mexico's Revolution of 1910 in **Viva Zapata**, 1952, and where he defies more than one despotic dictator in a valiant effort to establish freedom and the basic rights of his fellow man. **On the Waterfront** deservedly received a staggering twelve Academy Award nominations, winning eight Oscars, to match two other films, **Gone with the Wind**, 1939, and **From Here to Eternity**, 1953. It won for Best Picture, Best Director (Kazan), Best Actor (Brando), Best Supporting Actress (Saint), Best Story and Screenplay (Schulberg), Best Art Direction and Set Decoration (Day), Best Black and White Cinematography (Kaufman) and Best Film Editing (Milford). This film was produced on a meager budget, about $900,000, and proved to be an enormous box office success, returning more than $9.6 million in its initial release. *Author's Note*: Shot entirely on location in Hoboken, New Jersey, the film portrays the widespread corruption on the New York docks as exposed in a twenty-four part newspaper series written by Malcolm Johnson of the New York *Sun*, and published in 1948, focusing upon the racketeers and members of the national crime cartel that controlled the New York docks and extorted millions from shipping lines, as well as taking a large portion of the wages earned by the dockworkers in the form of "dues" to their unions, which the underworld bosses controlled. The series focused upon the murder of a New York longshoreman, who had defied the gangsters. Johnson was awarded the Pulitzer Prize for his shocking expose. Kazan had read this series of articles and had long wanted to

Karl Malden, Marlon Brando and Eva Marie Saint in *On the Waterfront,* **1954.**

do a hard-hitting film about the subject. "He talked Sam Spiegel into doing the film," Schulberg told this author, "and Spiegel wisely went to Columbia's New York office to cut a deal with Jack Cohn [1889-1956], the older brother of Harry Cohn [1891-1958]. Jack ran everything in New York and Harry was head of production in Hollywood, but Gadg [Kazan] and Spiegel knew that Harry had had a tough time with the 'outfit' (national crime syndicate) years earlier when they extorted a ton of money from him and the rest of the Hollywood moguls when they controlled the projectionist's union and he did not want any part of any picture that went after those people. Jack, however, was a crusader, always had been, right from the beginning when he worked for old man Laemmle [Carl Laemmle, 1867-1939, head of Universal Pictures]. The first feature Universal did was inspired by Jack, one that exposed the prostitution rings in New York City [**Traffic in Souls**, 1913], and Jack actually produced and edited that film. They knew that Jack always wanted to make what they call 'socially conscious' films and **On the Waterfront** fit that bill. When Jack told his brother Harry that Columbia had cut a deal to back and distribute the picture, Harry threw a fit, but Jack always got his way. Harry looked up to Jack. Gadg came to me to do the script for **On the Waterfront** and I went at that story like a bearcat." Schulberg would write another riveting expose-type film, **The Harder They Fall**, 1956, starring Humphrey Bogart as a sports writer [like Schulberg], who exposes the gangsters controlling the brutal sport of prizefighting. Kazan and Schulberg would later collaborate on another hard-hitting expose film, **A Face in the Crowd**, 1957. Brando told this author that "there was a lot of talk that Gadg [Kazan] and Budd [Schulberg] made **On the Waterfront** to justify what they did back in the old witch-hunting days when Congress was investigating former Reds and fellow travelers [the House of Un-American Activities Committee or HUAC]. They both became friendly witnesses and named some people, who had also been members of the Communist Party, but they knew that Congress already had those names so they weren't fronting off anyone. I play a guy who turns in a bunch of crumb-bums on the waterfront in the picture so some nuts in Hollywood interpreted that as being similar to what Gadg and Budd did to save their careers from a bunch of political crumb-bums. That's just a lot of hooey. We all did that picture because it told a great story that was based on real facts, on real lives on the New York docks. A lot of those people who went after Gadg and Budd were just jealous of them and the fine pictures they made. Envy does terrible things." Brando was Kazan's first choice for the leading role of the disillusioned prizefighter, but the actor hesitated after reading the script and, after he failed to respond, Kazan went to Frank Sinatra, asking him if he would play the part. Sinatra was about to sign on when Brando finally made up his mind to do the role and quickly signed for the part. Sinatra learned that he was out and exploded.

"I talked with Frank [Sinatra] sometime after that," Steiger told this author. "He was steaming like an old locomotive, swearing and cussing and stomping around whenever anyone mentioned Kazan's name. 'He [Kazan] suckered me into saying I would do the part,' Frank told me, 'so that he could use me to force Brando into taking the role.' Well, I always thought Frank would have done a good job in that role, but no one, not another actor in the world, could have given the performance Brando gave in **On the Waterfront**. I know. I was there with him when he became that tortured human being. He made me look a hell of a lot better in our every scene together. Years and years after we did that picture, people would come up to me and tell me that their most memorable scene about me was when I am sitting in the back seat of that car with Marlon and where he pours out his heart to me and where, after almost destroying him as a human being—my own brother—I decide to sacrifice my life for him." Harry Cohn, who had fought against Kazan's shooting on location in New Jersey, acquiesced to his brother Jack's insistence that Kazan have his way, pointing out that Kazan had proved that on-location shooting brought a powerful visual reality to his films. Kazan had shot his memorable **Boomerang**, 1947, a semi-documentary portrait of a crusading attorney, who saves the life of a drifter wrongly accused of murdering a priest, entirely on location in Stamford, Connecticut. In **Panic in the Streets**, 1950, another hard-hitting film that dealt with the spreading of a lethal disease, Kazan shot the film entirely in New Orleans, fully capturing its seedy waterfront dives and clapboard slum areas. Both of these very successful films had been produced by Fox where Darryl Zanuck was invariably providing American audiences with "socially conscious" productions and all of this was pointed out to Harry Cohn by his mentoring brother Jack, so the usually vociferous Harry Cohn said nothing and allowed Kazan free rein. After the film was completed, Harry Cohn sat with Kazan in Columbia's screening room in Hollywood to preview the film, and where the mogul had no comment about **On the Waterfront**, except when Brando tells Malden, a priest, to "go to hell." Cohn turned to Kazan and said: "Boy, are you going to have trouble with the Breen Office over that 'go to hell' scene. They'll never pass it." The Breen Office was officially the Production Code Administration office, established in 1934 and supervised by Joseph Ignatius Breen (1888-1965), a Catholic layman and former public relations agent. The Breen Office was the official censorship office supported by all of the Hollywood studios, an independent agency with total authority that severely censored any scenes it thought offensive or tasteless. Cohn was amazed when the film was passed without comment by the Breen Office and then began badgering that office with endless written complaints that pointed out that that office had excised many scenes from other Columbia films that were much less offensive than the 'go to hell' scene in **On the Waterfront**, almost as if he were trying to make trouble for his own [or Jack Cohn's] production, such was the inexplicable and vexing mind of Harry Cohn, who had long ago earned the appropriate sobriquet of "White Fang." This was the last film that Brando did with Kazan. He would turn down leading roles in many other Kazan productions, including **Baby Doll**, 1956, **A Face in the Crowd**, 1957, and **The Arrangement**, 1969. Venerable character actor Fred Gwynne (1926-1993) debuted (but was not credited) in his first feature film in **On the Waterfront** as one of Cobb's towering goons. Kazan personally selected and cast a number of others to play those brutal thugs, including two well-known former prizefighters, Tami Mauriello (1923-1999) and Tony Galento (1910-1979). Galento was known in the ring as "Two-Ton" Tony Galento, a colorful character, who got his nickname after explaining that he was late for a fight because he had to "deliver two tons of ice." The heavyweight boxer, who spoke as if he always had a mouthful of marbles, promoted his career by boxing a kangaroo, fighting a 550-pound bear, and wrestling an octopus. He ate fifty-two hot dogs on a bet before going into a fight and trained on beer. He fought heavyweight champion Max Baer, who said Galento "smelled of rotten tuna and a tub of old liquor being sweated out." He fought heavyweight champion Joe Louis on

June 28, 1939, for the title and lost in a TKO in the fourth round. He was notorious as a "dirty" fighter, who used his head to butt his opponents and invariably hit below the belt, just as he does in **On the Waterfront**. **p**, Sam Spiegel; **d**, Elia Kazan; **cast**, Marlon Brando, Karl Malden, Lee J. Cobb, Rod Steiger, Pat Henning, Eva Marie Saint, Leif Erickson, James Westerfield, Martin Balsam, Fred Gwynne, John Hamilton, Tony Galento, Tami Mauriello, John Heldabrand, Rudy Bond, Don Blackman, Arthur Keegan, Abe Simon, Barry Macollum, Anne Hegira, Pat Hingle, Nehemiah Persoff, Ben Wagner, Scottie MacGregor, Tiger Joe Marsh; **w**, Budd Schulberg (based on a story suggested by a series of articles by Malcolm Johnson); **c**, Boris Kaufman; **m**, Leonard Bernstein; **ed**, Gene Milford; **art d**, Richard Day.

On the Yard ★★★ 1978; U.S.; 102m; Midwest Film; Color; Crime Drama; Children: Unacceptable (MPAA: R); **VHS**. An effective portrayal of prison life, this absorbing film focuses upon four inmates. Leader of the group is Waites, and the others are Heard, who is a convicted wife murderer; Kellin, a repeat criminal, who has been in prison more often than he can remember; and Waites' errand boy, Grifasi. A con artist, Kellin has been unable to con the parole board into granting him an early release. Director Silver does a good job in developing his characters, carefully profiling each of the prisoners and how they relate to each other and their incarceration. **p**, Joan Micklin Silver; **d**, Raphael D. Silver; **cast**, John Heard, Thomas G. Waites, Mike Kellin, Richard Bright, Joe Grifasi, Lane Smith, Richard Hayes, Hector Troy, Richard Jamieson, Thomas Toner, Ron Faber; **w**, Malcolm Braly (based on his novel); **c**, Alan Metzger (Technicolor); **m**, Charles Gross; **ed**, Evan A. Lottman; **art d**, Leon Harris.

Once ★★★ 2007; Ireland; 85m; Fox Searchlight; Color; Drama; Children: Unacceptable (MPAA: R); **BD; DVD**. Hansard is a young Dublin band singer and songwriter, making a living by fixing vacuum cleaners in his father's repair shop by day. By night he sings and plays the guitar for money on the streets. Irglova, a young Czech immigrant, who sings and plays the piano like a pro, works at odd jobs by day and cares for her mother and infant daughter by night. She likes Hansard's music and helps him make a demonstration disc, which they hope will land him a recording contract. They get some street musicians to join them in making the record. Through their meetings and songs they fall in love, but their relationship has problems. Irglova is married, but left her husband, Haugh, and took their child to Ireland for a better life, while Hansard still has strong feelings for an Irish girl, who left him to relocate in London. Hansard asks Irglova if she still loves her husband and she replies that she loves him (Hansard), but tells him in Czech, which he doesn't understand. She then tells him that her husband is coming to live with her in Dublin. He asks her to spend a farewell night together and she reluctantly agrees, but later stands him up and he leaves for London to promote his record without being able to say goodbye to her. He calls his ex-girlfriend and she is happy to learn he is going to be in London in a few hours. It's a bittersweet romance about two nice young people and their love for music and each other, but they are ships passing in the night. Made with non-professional actors on an Irish shoestring ($160,000) this "sleeper" nevertheless became a major international money-making success (more than $20 million at the box office), and was later made into a Broadway musical that won a Tony Award as best musical. Songs: "Falling Slowly" (Hansard, Irglova, which won the 2007 Academy Award for best original song); "Once," "And the Healing Has Begun" (Van Morrison); "Say It To Me Now," "All the Way Down," "Lies," "Leave," "Trying to Pull Myself Away," "Fallen from the Sky," "When Your Mind's Made Up" (Glen Hansard); "If You Want Me," "The Hill" (Marketa Irglova); "Whiskey in the Jar" (traditional); "Gold" (Fergus O'Farrell); "Song without Words" (Felix Mendelssohn), "The Fair City Waltz" (Hugh Drumm, Adam Lynch). Gutter language prohibits viewing by children. **p**, Martina Niland; **d&w**, John Carney; **cast**, Glen Hansard, Marketa Irglova, Hugh Walsh, Gerry Hendrick, Alaistair Foley,

Glen Hansard in *Once*, 2007.

Geoff Minogue, Bill Hodnett, Danuse Ktrestova, Darren Healy, Mal Whyte; **c**, Tim Fleming; **m**, Hansard, Irglova; **ed**, Paul Mullen; **prod d**, Tamara Conboy; **art d**, Riad Karim; **spec eff**, Daniel Tomlinson.

Once in Paris . . . ★★★ 1978; U.S.; 100m; Leigh-McLaughlin/Atlantic Releasing Corp.; Color; Drama; Children: Cautionary (MPAA: PG); **VHS**. Rogers is a Hollywood screenwriter, who gets an assignment to go to Paris to try and improve a screenplay for a movie already into production. He and Lenoir, a French actor in the film, who plays a chauffeur, become friends, and at the same time, Rogers begins an affair with British aristocrat, Hunnicutt, who has an adjoining hotel room. The three become friends for the short time Rogers is in Paris to work on the film. Not much happens, but it is a fine example of a superb "little film" where splendid characterizations are achieved. **p**, Frank D. Gilroy, Gérard Croce, Manny Fuchs; **d&w**, Gilroy; **cast**, Wayne Rogers, Gayle Hunnicutt, Jack Lenoir, Philippe March, Marta Andras, Henri Attal, Patrick Aubrée, Jacques Bouanich, Caroline Carliez, Matt Carney, Doris Roberts; **c**, Claude Saunier (TVC Labs Color); **m**, Mitch Leigh; **ed**, Robert Q. Lovett.

Once More, with Feeling ★★★ 1960; U.S.; 92m; COL; Color; Comedy/Romance; Children: Acceptable; **DVD**. In an impressive performance, Brynner plays an eccentric musical genius, who is the conceited conductor of the London Symphony Orchestra. He is kept in check by his wife, Kendall, until she finds him auditioning Field, a sexy young pianist, and she then walks out on him. His career goes into a nosedive and he becomes frantic to find a way to get his wife back. Kendall has meanwhile fallen for Toone, a physicist, and plans to marry him. Brynner reminds her that they never really got married, so, in order to make divorce papers legal, she will have to marry him. She agrees and they marry legally, but then she falls in love with him all over again, and they again become a happily married couple, although she knows Brynner still has a roving eye. Songs: "Old Folks at Home" (Stephen Foster), "The Stars and Stripes Forever" (John Philip Sousa). *Author's Note*: This film owes much to a similar comedy made by Preston Sturges, **Unfaithfully Yours**, 1948, and where, ironically, Rex Harrison, who was Kendall's real-life husband, plays a vain and self-centered orchestra conductor. **p&d**, Stanley Donen; **cast**, Yul Brynner, Kay Kendall, Geoffrey Toone, Shirley Anne Field, Gregory Ratoff, Maxwell Shaw, Mervyn Johns, Martin Benson, Harry Lockart, Colin Drake, Andrew Faulds; **w**, Harry Kurnitz (based on his play); **c**, Georges Périnal (Technicolor); **m**, Muir Mathieson; **ed**, Jack Harris; **prod d**; Alexandre Trauner.

Once Upon a Time in America ★★★ 1984; Italy/U.S.; 229m; Embassy International/Ladd Company; Color; Crime Drama; Children: Un-

Robert De Niro and James Woods in *Once Upon a Time in America*, 1984.

acceptable (MPAA: R); **BD**; **DVD**; **VHS**. Leone presents a riveting episodic crime tale that chronicles Jewish youths growing up in New York City, brilliantly depicting their rise to fame and wealth as successful gangsters in the 1920s and 1930s. Four boys (Tiler, Curran, Moazezi and Bloom) form a gang in the Jewish ghetto of Manhattan's Lower East Side, nominating a boy named "Noodles" (Tiler) as their leader, and they go to work as petty thieves, supervised by a vicious hoodlum, Russo. They then meet another youth named Max (Jacobs), a born organizer with a brilliant mind for criminal pursuits, who persuades them to branch out on their own. Meanwhile, Tiler becomes obsessed with a beautiful, young girl, Connelly, who tells him that she wants to become a dancer and an actress. After Jacobs becomes the co-gang leader with Tiler, the gang rebels against Russo's authority and establishes its own criminal operations, which siphons off Russo's illegal revenues. Russo takes revenge by attacking the youths, and he fatally shoots Moazezi. Tiler retaliates by stabbing Russo to death, and he also stabs a policeman when he is taken into custody. Tiler is sent to prison while Jacobs remains free, continuing to supervise the gang. Twelve years later, in 1932, Noodles (De Niro as an adult) is released from prison and he is welcomed back into the gang, which is still operated by Max (Woods as an adult), and his other two friends, Hayden and Forsythe (now adults). De Niro again meets the girl he had fallen in love with a decade earlier (McGovern as an adult) whose brother runs a speakeasy. The gang has grown powerful and rich through bootlegging and where Woods and De Niro are still co-leaders, but De Niro falls out with Woods after Woods orders the killing of some allied gangsters and De Niro realizes just how ruthless is his old friend. De Niro tries to establish a romance with McGovern, but she puts him off, telling him that she is leaving for California to pursue her acting career in the motion picture field, but, before she departs, De Niro rapes her and later feels remorse for his brutal act. After Prohibition is repealed and bootlegging operations collapse, Woods tells the gang that their next job is to rob the Federal Reserve Bank in New York, which De Niro believes to be suicidal. To prevent his friends from being killed in such a rash robbery, De Niro tips off the police, thinking that they will be arrested instead of being shot down. He later learns that Woods, Hayden and Forsythe have all been killed and he now blames himself for these fatalities, going to an opium den to fend off his overwhelming remorse by drugging himself. He then goes to a train station locker where the gang's substantial loot is stored, only to find that it is all gone. Learning that it was someone else who betrayed his friends and not himself, and that he is now being pursued, De Niro flees the city, going to Buffalo, where he remains for decades, living under an alias. He returns to New York City as an aging, gray-haired man, staying with an old friend, Rapp, saying that he has returned after receiving a letter from a rabbi that tells him that the Jewish cemetery is

about to be converted to a housing development and the bodies of his friends must be interred elsewhere. He then learns that those bodies have already been reburied elsewhere, and Rapp tells him that he got that letter because those hunting for him years earlier knew where he was hiding and that this was simply a message to warn him that he is about to meet the same fate as his gangster friends. When De Niro visits the mausoleum where his friends are now buried, he finds a key hanging on a hook next to their internments, one that is similar to the key to the locker in the train station he visited years ago. He goes to the train station and opens the locker to find a suitcase stuffed with cash and a note saying that this is payment for his next job, which is not specified. He then learns that McGovern, now a successful stage actress, is appearing in a play, and he visits her in her dressing room. She warns him to leave the city at once as his life is in danger and not to go to a party to which he has been invited, one taking place at the home of a powerful politician named Bailey, but he knows who Bailey really is, his old friend Woods. He has also learned that Woods faked his own death and personally killed De Niro's other two friends years earlier and then assumed the name of Bailey, using his gangster fortune to promote his political career. Despite McGovern's warnings, De Niro goes to Woods' party, meeting Woods at his mansion; Woods tells De Niro that he is under federal investigation and, to save his family from disgrace, asks De Niro to murder him, explaining that that is why the suitcase of cash was left for De Niro and that Woods is now paying an old debt to his former friend. De Niro refuses to kill Woods and leaves the mansion. Woods follows and De Niro sees him walk to a slowly moving garbage truck that is grinding up debris and we soon see Woods ending his life by leaping into the bin of the truck to be ground to pieces by its turning screws, and that is where this strange but fascinating film ends. As usual, the gifted Leone presents a lengthy and somewhat disjointed tale, packed with allegorical scenes and where he evokes a bizarre nostalgia for the ultraviolence practiced by American criminals in the 1920s and 1930s, as if to imply that his generational portrait encapsulates the overall lifestyle of America of those periods (and where, in reality, only a very small element of miscreants created such havoc in those eras). De Niro and Woods give exceptionally mesmerizing portrayals of utterly vicious criminals having little or no sense of morals, decency or human compassion—they are essentially worthless persons reveling in their hedonistic lifestyles. Leone unabashedly degrades women in general and presents more than one tasteless, imbecilic and offensive scene in gratuitously, if not perversely, depicting the sub-human sexual nature of his male characters. He blends a mixture of 1930s crime films with a rather superior European perspective that warps his characters into macabre, cartoon-like caricatures, rather than developing realistic and believable human beings. Production values are high and the sets and costuming, along with the period cars, are all richly appointed and appropriate to the eras displayed, albeit, Leone largely ignores any kind of rigid continuity as is his tradition in almost all of his films, and the story line ambivalently (and sometimes annoyingly) drifts about as he leisurely presents his extravagant exegesis on the American underworld. This chauvinistic paean of praise for America's lawless (seemingly based upon hearsay and gossip rather than any true research, as was the case with the novel used for its inspiration) is more of a gruesome but well-made atmospheric curiosity than a visual document reliably conveying the criminal environment it earnestly but naively strives to profile. Although this film influenced many filmmakers to launch similarly violence-dominated films that proliferated in the 1980s and thereafter, it did not do well at the box office, earning back in its initial release only a little more than $5 million, against its whopping $30 million budget. **p**, Arnon Milchan; **d**, Sergio Leone; **cast**, Robert De Niro, James Woods, Elizabeth McGovern, Joe Pesci, Burt Young, Tuesday Weld, Treat Williams, Danny Aiello, Richard Bright, James Hayden, William Forsythe, Tandy Cronyn, Jennifer Connelly, Scott Tiler, Rusty Jacobs, James Russo, Larry Rapp, Brian Bloom, Adrian Curran, Noah Moazezi; **w**, Leonardo Benvenuti, Piero De Bernardi,

Enrico Medioli, Franco Arcalli, Franco Ferrini, Leone, Stuart Kaminsky (based on the novel *The Hoods* by Harry Grey); **c**, Tonino Delli Colli; **m**, Ennino Morricone; **ed**, Nino Baragli; **art d**, Carlo Simi; **spec eff**, Danilo Bollettini, Giovanni Corridori, Jacques Godbout, Gabe Videla.

Once Upon a Time in China ★★★ 1992; Hong Kong; 134m; Golden Harvest/Rim; Color; Action; Children: Unacceptable (MPAA: R); **BD**; **DVD**; **VHS**. This intriguing film is set in late 19th-century Canton and relates the tale of legendary martial arts hero Wong Fei-Hung (1848-1924), who fought against Westerners (British, French, and American) then plundering China. Li's aunt, Kwan, returns to Canton after living in America and becoming totally westernized, and he becomes her protector. This is not an easy task in that his martial arts school and local militia begin to battle with foreign and local government officials over the use of the area's wealth and resources. As violence increases, Kwan begins to question her new Western ideals. There is a lot of political intrigue and martial arts fighting and gunfire, with Kwan being kidnapped but rescued, and where Li kills an American enemy by pressing an unused bullet into the man's forehead with his fingers. The Westerners are beaten, to some extent, and Li becomes a hero and opens his own martial arts school. Action fans will find plenty of excitement in this impressively filmed movie, but excessive violence and bloodshed prohibit viewing by children. Sequels followed in 1992, 1993, 1994. (In Cantonese; English subtitles.) **p&d**, Hark Tsui; **cast**, Jet Li, Biao Yuen, Rosamund Kwan, Jacky Cheung, Steve Tartalia, Kent Cheng, Jonathan Isgar, Yee Kwan Yan, Mark King, Bruce Fontaine, Shun Lau; **w**, Tsui, Yiu Ming Leung, Pik-yin Tang, Kai-Chi Yun; **c**, Tung-Chuen Chan, Wilson Chan, David Chung, Kwok Wah Lam, Arthur Wong, Chung Biu Wong; **m**, James Wong, Romeo Díaz; **ed**, Marco Mak.

Once Upon a Time in the West ★★★ 1969; Italy/U.S.; 175m; PAR; Color; Western; Children: Unacceptable (MPAA: PG-13); **BD**; **DVD**; **VHS**. Offbeat but engrossing western sees some good character development from Italian filmmaker Leone, although these characters are more brutal and savage than anything or anyone riding, walking or crawling through the Old West. It opens with three hired killers in Fonda's employ waiting for a train carrying Bronson (and where Leone flagrantly lifts the same opening from Fred Zinnemann's classic **High Noon**, 1952). Bronson has asked to see Fonda, one of the most feared gunmen in the West, but Fonda is taking no chances with this stranger and has sent a gun-toting reception party to the train station. The train slowly arrives and pulls away to reveal Bronson standing on the other side of the track playing a few mournful chords on a harmonica (it is a brass version of the instrument that was not introduced until 1924, more than fifty years after the setting of this film, but Leone has never bothered about such pesky details). The three gunmen welcome Bronson with their six-guns, but he is not taken by surprise, anticipating this kind of greeting and quickly shoots down all three gunslingers. We next see in flashback a family headed by Wolff, who is awaiting the arrival of his new bride, Cardinale, a prostitute he has met in New Orleans. Cardinale does not arrive, but Fonda and his gunmen do, and they shoot and kill Wolff and his entire family of small children. A land war ensues where Cardinale, who has inherited Wolff's vast real estate, is aided by Bronson and adventurous outlaw Robards in battling crippled railroad magnate Ferzetti, who employs Fonda and his gang of cutthroats as his murderous enforcers, ordering them to "clear the tracks" of the landowners. Ferzetti wants Cardinale's land because he needs the water on her property to operate his trains. Fonda, meanwhile, has ambitions to take over Ferzetti's business, but he rethinks this when the conniving Ferzetti hires a number of Fonda's own gunmen to assassinate their leader. Fonda survives and then thinks twice about becoming a train tycoon. Robards, who is enamored of Cardinale, collects a band of killers and they attack and wipe out Fonda's men and kill Ferzetti in the bloody process. Fonda and Bronson then meet for a final showdown where they

Charles Bronson, Claudia Cardinale and director Sergio Leone on the set in *Once Upon a Time in the West*, 1969.

square off, slowly circling each other, and Fonda now remembers a man he sadistically murdered many years earlier. Leone shows that scene in flashback, depicting Fonda as a much younger gunman, watching with a smile on his face as one of his enemies stands on the shoulders of his younger brother and with a rope around his neck tied to a crossbeam and where, if that younger brother moves or collapses, the other brother will die by hanging. Fonda places a harmonica in the mouth of the younger brother, ordering him to play a tune while the boy slowly begins to lose his strength and sink under the weight of his older brother. The older brother, to end the prolonged and vicious sadism, kicks his younger brother out of the way and hangs himself. Of course, the younger brother is Bronson and he now seeks revenge on Fonda. Now knowing that Bronson is that boy grown to manhood, Fonda goes for his gun, but Bronson pulls his six-gun with lightning speed before Fonda's gun clears its holster and shoots Fonda in the chest. Fonda collapses and Bronson takes the harmonica he has carried for so many years and jams it into Fonda's mouth as a symbolic coup de grace and watches Fonda die. Robards, too, is dying from a wound in the gunfight with Fonda's men, and Bronson, once Robards has breathed his last, drapes his friend's corpse over his horse and rides away, leaving Cardinale with a water monopoly, where she shares her liquid reserves with thirsty railroad workers. Leone's perception of the Old West is unlike any other director in that it is always unrelentingly vicious, brutal and unforgiving as he graphically shows in this weird interpretation of American gunmen, ranchers and railroaders more or less destroying everything in their path. His violent characters are obsessively interesting, and his cinematography is arresting to the point of being breathtaking, but his story line, as is the case in all of his other "spaghetti" westerns, woefully lacks continuity and any kind of reasonable sense of chronological order in his unfolding scenes. Leone paints on film, preferring to provide stirring and memorable single images in one scene after another and he is a master at that, but by insisting that his personal imprimatur be lastingly preserved on film (such vainglorious and egotistical techniques have been religiously eschewed by pantheon directors such as John Ford, Howard Hawks, Billy Wilder, William Wyler and many others, who have all insisted that a director or any member of a cast involved in a film production must always refrain from making his distracting presence known to the viewer in order to preserve the viewer's attention to the story being shown on the screen). *Author's Note*: Fonda told this author that "I have played dopes, dunderheads and a few heroes in pictures, but I never played such a disgusting villain as I did in **Once Upon a Time in the West** and I played that character as a challenge to my abilities, and also to earn my keep." When talking with Bronson about this film, he remarked to this author that "I never thought that **Once Upon a Time in the West** had anything to do with

Julian Arahanga (right) in *Once Were Warriors*, 1995.

the real Old West in America. It was Leone's idea of what went on way back then and I don't think he bothered to do any research about it. When I asked him who impressed him most in American western films, he told me 'Lash La Rue,' who was a small cowboy actor that looked a lot like Humphrey Bogart and appeared in a lot of B westerns. Maybe Leone was kidding me, I don't know. What I do know is that I never learned how to play the harmonica when I did that picture." **p**, Fulvio Morsella; **d**, Sergio Leone; **cast**, Henry Fonda, Claudia Cardinale, Jason Robards, Charles Bronson, Gabriele Ferzetti, Paolo Stoppa, Woody Strode, Jack Elam, Keenan Wynn, Frank Wolff, Lionel Stander; **w**, Leone, Sergio Donati (based on a story by Dario Argento, Bernardo Bertolucci, Leone); **c**, Tonino Delli Colli (Techniscope; Technicolor); **m**, Ennio Morricone; **ed**, Nino Baragli; **art d**, Carlo Simi; **set d**, Rafael Ferri; **spec eff**, Eros Bacciucchi.

Once Were Warriors ★★★ 1995; New Zealand; 102m; Communicado Productions/Fine Line Features; Color; Drama; Children: Unacceptable (MPAA: R); **BD**; **DVD**; **VHS**. Set in 1990s Auckland, New Zealand, a family descended from Maori warriors is plagued by a violent father, Morrison, whose nickname is "Muscles," and being treated by society as outcasts. Although he beats his wife, Owen, when he is drunk, Morrison loves her and his children. After he loses his job, he spends most of his time drinking with friends at a pub. His youngest son, Emile, is in trouble with the police and is finally placed in a foster home, while his elder son, Arahanga, is about to join a tough street gang whose members have their faces tattooed, typical in Maori culture. Morrison's thirteen-year-old daughter, Kerr-Bell, writes stories as an escape from the violent and unhappy home, and then becomes a victim of that violence when she is raped by Curtis, a family friend. When her father wants her to kiss him, she flees the house and hangs herself. Owen finally stands up to Morrison and kicks him out. He takes up residence at the pub and nearly beats Curtis to death with a broken bottle. Owen leaves with the two boys, and returns to the Maori village where she was born. Alone, Morrison has another beer in the pub while sirens wail, police coming for him. A fascinating and well-enacted film, its excessive gutter language, domestic abuse, sexual violence, and substance abuse nevertheless prohibit viewing by children. **p**, Robin Scholes; **d**, Lee Tamahori; **cast**, Rena Owen, Temuera Morrison, Mamaengaroa Kerr-Bell, Julian Arahanga, Taungaroa Emile, Rachael Morris, Jr., Joseph Kairau, Cliff Curtis, Pete Smith, George Henare, Mere Boynton; **w**, Riwia Brown (based on the novel by Alan Duff); **c**, Stuart Dryburgh; **m**, Murray Grindlay, Murray McNabb; **ed**, Michael Horton; **prod d**, Michael Kane; **art d**, Shayne Radford; **spec eff**, Richard Taylor.

Ondine ★★★ 2011; Ireland/U.S.; 111m; Wayfare Entertainment/Mag-

nolia Pictures; Color; Drama/Romance; Children: Unacceptable (MPAA: R); **BD**; **DVD**. Well-made and with superior performances, this romantic drama sees Farrell as a young Irish fisherman, who is divorced and a reformed alcoholic. His ex-wife, Kirwan, lives with their ten-year-old daughter, Barry, who suffers from kidney failure and is confined to a motorized wheelchair. One day while fishing at sea, Farrell pulls up his net and finds in it a young woman, Bachleda, who calls herself Ondine. She pleads with him to take her somewhere secluded, so he takes her to his late mother's house. He tells his daughter a story that is really his own, about a fisherman netting a woman from the sea, and she believes the woman he netted is a *selkie* (a water nymph). Later, we learn that Ondine is really a drug pusher working for a Romanian man, who wants a bag of drugs she lost at sea while trying to escape from the Coast Guard. The bag is ensnared within a lobster trap in the ocean, so the Romanian and an accomplice take Ondine aboard a boat to find the drugs. She trips them so that they fall out of the boat and drown. Farrell marries Ondine so she can stay in Ireland, but they both also love each other. The film is not related to the 1958 ballet "Ondine" about a water nymph by choreographer Sir Frederick Ashton and composer Hans Werner Henze, which was adapted from the novella *Undine* by Friedrich de la Motte Fouque. Songs: "Takk," "All Right" (Sigur Ros); "Travelling" (Michael Nyvang); "One Quiet Night" (Patrick B. Metheny); "Slaibh Na mBan," "The Emigrant's Farewell" (Tony McManus); "Lille" (Lisa Hannigan); "Domes" (Kamran Ince); "Out of the Ocean," "Cape Clear," "Braille" (Lisa Hannigan); "Incrustations" (Lars Gaugaard). Violence, sexuality and gutter language prohibit viewing by children. **p**, Neil Jordan, Ben Browning, James Flynn; **d&w**, Jordan (based on Irish mythology); **cast**, Colin Farrell, Alicja Bachleda, Dervla Kirwan, Alison Barry, Marion O'Dwyer, Tony Curran, Mary O'Shea, Gemma Reeves, Stephen Rea, Norma Sheahan, Emil Hostina; **c**, Christopher Doyle; **m**, Kjartan Sveinsson; **ed**, Tony Lawson; **prod d**, Anna Rackard; **art d**, Mark Lowry; **set d**, Judy Farr; **spec eff**, Kevin Bryne, Kevin Nolan.

The One and Only ★★★ 1978; U.S.; 97m; Balmoral Associates/PAR; Color; Drama; Children: Unacceptable (MPAA: PG); **DVD**; **VHS**. It's 1951 and Winkler, an obnoxious young college senior, marries a fellow student, Darby, despite being disrespectful to her parents. He has aspirations of becoming a hit in show business, but, after the couple moves to New York City, the only job he can get is as a wrestler at a carnival. A promoter, Saks, pushes him, and he becomes a champion professional wrestler. He avoids being beaten up by staging fights that introduce show-wrestling to the sport. Winkler does make a name for himself, but not the way he has envisioned his future. Songs: "The One and Only" (Alan and Marilyn Bergman, Patrick Williams), "My Mammy" (Walter Donaldson, Sam Lewis, Joe Young), "Getting to Know You" (Oscar Hammerstein II, Richard Rodgers). Gutter language prohibits viewing by children. **p**, Steve Gordon, David V. Picker; **d**, Carl Reiner; **cast**, Henry Winkler, Kim Darby, Gene Saks, William Daniels, Harold Gould, Polly Holliday, Herve Villechaize, Bill Baldwin, Anthony Battaglia, Ed Begley, Jr., Charles Frank, Dennis James; **w**, Gordon; **c**, Victor J. Kemper; **m**, Patrick Williams; **ed**, Bud Molin; **prod d**, Edward C. Carfagno; **set d**, Ruby R. Levitt.

One Arabian Night ★★★ 1921 (silent); Germany; 115m/6 reels; Associated First National Pictures; B/W; Drama; Children: Unacceptable; **DVD**. Fascinating tale sees pantheon director Lubitsch at the helm as well as acting the part of a dwarf comedian. He works with a touring troupe of performers that includes a juggler, an elderly woman who charms snakes, and a sensuous dancer, Negri. Lubitsch is in love with Negri, but he cannot bring himself to declare his affection for her. The troupe arrives at an Arab community where Wegener, the local sheik, reigns with an iron fist. Wegener, hearing about Negri's beauty, orders that she be brought to his harem as a replacement for one of his wives, who Wegener believes is unfaithful to him (she has been seeing a local cloth merchant). Negri does not object to joining Wegener's harem, thinking to improve her station in life, but Lubitsch agonizes over losing the woman he has loved from afar. While the ladies of the harem conspire to aid the wife in escaping the clutches of the old sheik, Negri, a designing siren if ever there was one (her traditional vamp role in the silent era), attempts to inveigle the sheik's son into an assignation. When Wegener discovers this infidelity, he becomes enraged and he murders Negri just as Lubitsch comes upon the scene. Lubitsch, horrified and full of revenge, then kills Wegener to end this tragic tale. Though lacking continuity and inter-titles to better clarify the story line, the film is nevertheless packed with Lubitsch's inventive visual techniques (using reverse angles and where the actors stare eerily into the camera), where his images of the desert, the slums of the Arab town and the contrasting majesty of the sheik's palace are breathtaking, enhanced by Richter's elaborate sets. Kupfer proves exceptional as the old lady, especially when she staggers and lurches about while enacting a drunken woman. *Author's Note*: This was the film that got Hollywood's attention and resulted in Lubitsch going to the U.S., where he directed his next film, **Loves of the Pharaoh**, 1922, for Paramount. Negri, too, who had made several films in Europe with Lubitsch, moved to the U.S. and where she became a silent screen star. **p,&d**, Ernst Lubitsch; **cast**, Lubitsch, Pola Negri, Paul Wegener, Jenny Hasselqvist, Aud Egede-Nissen, Harry Liedtke, Carl Clewing, Margarete Kupfer, Jakob Tiedtke; **w**, Hanns Kraly, Lubitsch (based on the stage pantomime "The Arabian Nights" by Friedrich Freska); **c**, Theodor Sparkuhl, Kurt Waschneck; **m**, Friedrich and Victor Hollaender; **art d**, Kurt Richter, Ernö Metzner.

One Day ★★★ 2011; U.S./U.K.; 107m; Focus Features; Color; Drama/Romance; Children: Unacceptable (MPAA: PG-13); **BD**; **DVD**. Well-crafted story sees good performances from Hathaway and Sturgess as a young British couple. They sleep together on the night of their college graduation, July 15, 1988, and then go their separate ways. They are shown each year on the same day and month for the next twenty years, but not always together. Hathaway is smart and aspires to become an author, but it takes time for her to become successful, while success and relationships with women come more easily to Sturgess, especially after he becomes a well-known television host. Hathaway marries Mison while Sturgess marries but divorces. They grow apart from the other people in their lives and grow more closely together, only to find that they belong with each other. Sexual content, partial nudity, gutter language, some violence and substance abuse all prohibit viewing by children. **p**, Nina Jacobson, Jane Frazer; **d**, Lone Scherfig; **cast**, Anne Hathaway, Jim Sturgess, Tom Mison, Patricia Clarkson, Jodie Whittaker, Tim Key, Rafe Spall, Ken Stott, Heida Reed, Gil Alma; **w**, David Nicholls (based on his book); **c**, Benoît Delhomme; **m**, Rachel Portman; **ed**, Barney Pilling; **prod d**, Mark Tildesley; **art d**, Denis Schnegg, Su Whittaker, Katrina Dunn; **set d**, Dominic Capon; **spec eff**, Mark Holt.

One-Eyed Jacks ★★★ 1961; U.S.; 141m; Pennebaker Productions; PAR; Color; Western; Children: Unacceptable; **DVD**; **VHS**. This powerful but offbeat western, full of unusual twists and turns, opens with outlaws Brando and Malden robbing a bank in 1880. They take refuge in a small town where Malden dallies with a local trollop, but is quickly rousted from his revelries when a posse arrives searching for him and Brando. (This scene is duplicated in **Butch Cassidy and the Sundance Kid**, 1969, where Paul Newman as Butch and Robert Redford as the Sundance Kid escape a posse while they are being entertained in a bordello.) The two flee, Malden without his boots, so quickly has he had to make his escape, and ride only one horse together. They reach the summit of a high hill where they fend off the posse, but both realize that they cannot elude their pursuers with only one horse and it is decided that Brando will stay behind and fight off the posse until Malden rides off, obtains another horse and returns with it so that Brando can then flee. Once Malden arrives at a small ranch to obtain a second horse, he rationalizes that, if he returns to Brando, he, too, will be captured, so he abandons his friend and rides away with the sack of gold he and

Marlon Brando directing *One-Eyed Jacks,* **1961.**

Brando looted from the bank, leaving Brando to fend for himself. Running out of ammunition, Brando is surrounded and eventually captured. Sent to a miserable Sonora prison, Brando endures brutal punishment for five years until making his escape with another prisoner, Duran. Traveling northward, Brando and Duran encounter two desperadoes like themselves, Gilman and Johnson, and they team up to form a gang. They plan on robbing the large bank in Monterey, California, but when arriving there, they learn that the town is well guarded by a bevy of heavily armed deputies under Malden, who has gone straight and become the sheriff. He runs the town as his own fiefdom and has a comfortable home, having married Jurado and adopted her grown daughter, Pellicer. Malden is wary of Brando, believing he is seeking revenge for Malden deserting him years earlier, but Brando convinces him that he holds no grudge and lies when he tells Malden that he escaped the posse and has been roaming the West ever since, looking for a place to settle down. He secretly hates Malden and, indeed, seeks revenge, which is demonstrated when he seduces the virginal Pellicer. He and Duran then plot the robbery of the Monterey bank with Gilman and Johnson, who have remained out of sight at a seaside village beyond Monterey. That plan goes awry when Brando returns to Monterey and stops drunken bully Carey, one of Malden's deputies, from abusing a prostitute in a cantina, killing Carey after he attempts to shoot him. Although innocent, the cunning Malden, who believes that Brando still nurtures a deep-seated hatred for him, has him tied to a hitching post and mercilessly whips his bare back before he then smashes Brando's gun hand, breaking all of its bones, to enssure that the quick-draw Brando will not in future pull a gun on him. He then releases him, and Brando goes back to the small village where Gilman and Johnson are waiting, to tend to his wounds. Gilman and Johnson grow impatient waiting for Brando to heal and set out to rob the bank in Monterey on their own, killing Duran when he attempts to stop them. In robbing the bank, they kill an innocent young girl. Malden uses this brutal slaying to arrest the innocent Brando, placing him behind bars in his jail. Brando asks Malden if he will get a fair trial, and Malden replies: "Sure, you'll get a fair trial and then I'm going to hang you!" Brando replies: "You're a real one-eyed Jack in this town, but I've seen the other side of your face." Abused by sadistic deputy Pickens, Brando tricks Pickens into making a wrong move and shoots him before escaping. (This scene duplicates a scene in **The Left-Handed Gun**, 1958, where Paul Newman, playing Billy the Kid, escapes from the Lincoln County Jail after killing two guards, one of them a brutal warder.) Brando returns to fight Malden in the street and shoots and kills him. He then tells Pellicer, whom he has made pregnant, that he will come back for her some time and then rides away. Brando does a more than average job in fully developing his own character and that of Malden and the rest of the players in this,

Jack Nicholson in *One Flew Over the Cuckoo's Nest*, 1975.

the only film he ever directed. The production values are high and the cinematography is impressive, especially when the story moves to the Monterey area and its majestic shorelines. *Author's Note*: Pantheon director Stanley Kubrick was scheduled to direct this film, but Brando, who had complete control of the production, was at odds with Kubrick about how the characters were to be handled; when Kubrick quit, Brando took over the job of helming this strange but compelling western (one not quite as offbeat as **The Missouri Breaks**, 1976, made fifteen years after this film, where Brando plays an absolute nutcase of a bounty hunter). "Stanley is a gifted director," Brando told this author, "but we had big differences over how my character in **One-Eyed Jacks** was to be portrayed, so he went his way and I went mine." When pressed about the basis of the characters and story line, Brando admitted that "yes, there is a lot of similarities to my character in **One-Eyed Jacks** and Billy the Kid and Karl's [Malden's] character to the sheriff that killed the Kid, Pat Garrett. My escape from the jail where I deal with Slim Pickens is also similar to how the Kid escaped, but it ends there since my character lives and Billy the Kid does not survive." Producer Rosenberg was not happy when Brando took over the directorial chores for this film, but he could do little about Brando's decision. The film was scheduled to be shot within sixty days, but Brando, who dwelled on details and was exacting in every shot, took six full months before he completed the production, exposing more than one million feet of film (which Rosenberg described as "a world record") with more than 250,000 feet of film printed (150,000 then being the average). Editor Marshek, under Paramount's instructions, edited the overlong film to 141 minutes. Although much of the self-serving scenes that showed Brando as a Christ-like figure were excised, others remained, particularly the whipping scene, which was likened to the crucifixion of Jesus. Pellicer had been a Rosenberg discovery and she sadly made no other U.S. films; after appearing in a handful of Mexican films, she committed suicide at age thirty. The original budget for this film was $1.8 million, but Brando's extended production period caused the overall budget to soar beyond $6 million and its box office returns on its initial release returned only $4.3 million. **p**, Frank P. Rosenberg; **d**, Marlon Brando; **cast**, Brando, Karl Malden, Katy Jurado, Ben Johnson, Slim Pickens, Larry Duran, Sam Gilman, Timothy Carey, Elisha Cook, Jr., Rudolph (Rodolfo) Acosta, Philip Ahn, Hank Worden; **w**, Guy Trosper, Calder Willingham (based on the novel *The Authentic Death of Hendry Jones* by Charles Neider); **c**, Charles Lang, Jr. (VistaVision; Technicolor); **m**, Hugo Friedhofer; **ed**, Archie Marshek; **art d**, Hal Pereira, J. McMillan Johnson; **set d**, Sam Comer, Robert Benton; **spec eff**, Farciot Edouart, John P. Fulton.

One Fine Day ★★★ 1996; U.S.; 108m; FOX; Color; Comedy; Chil-

dren: Unacceptable (MPAA: PG); **DVD**; **VHS**. This pleasant and well-acted comedy is set in present-day New York City where Pfeiffer is an architect and the divorced mother of a boy, Linz, while Clooney, a newspaper columnist, is also divorced and is the father of a girl, Whitman. Pfeiffer and Clooney meet one morning when Clooney is unexpectedly left with his daughter and forgets that Pfeiffer was to take her to school that day. Both children miss their school field trip and are stuck with the parents. Pfeiffer and Clooney complain to each other about their ex-spouses and fret about not being able to work that day as they planned. Pfeiffer has a presentation to make to clients, and Clooney needs to get to a mayor's press conference to confront him about a scandal. Whitman goes missing and Pfeiffer notifies the police while blaming Clooney for not looking after his daughter properly. Whitman is found and both parents take their kids to a soccer game where Pfeiffer meets her ex-husband, who says he's going on tour as a drummer for Bruce Springsteen, but then admits that that claim is a lie. That night at Pfeiffer's apartment, she and Clooney kiss and soon afterward he falls asleep on her couch, exhausted by the rigors of their fine day. Pfeiffer joins him and they fall asleep together. Songs: "One Fine Day" (Gerry Goffin, Carole King); "The Boy from New York City" (John Taylor, George Davis); "Mama Said" (Luther Dixon, Willie Denson); "Someone Like You" (Van Morrison); "Just like You" (Kevin Moore, John Lewis Parker); "What a Difference a Day Made" (Maria Grever, Stanley Adams); "This Guy's in Love with You" (Burt Bacharach, Hal David); "Love's Funny that Way" (Tina Arena, David Tyson, Dean McTaggart); "Have I Told You Lately?" (Morrison); "Isn't It Romantic" (Richard Rodgers, Lorenz Hart); "For the First Time" (James Newton Howard, Allan Dennis Rich, Jud Friedman); "The Glory of Love" (William Hill); "Heaven's Not Overflowing" (Pepper Keenan, Woody Weatherman); "Quien le Prohibe" (F. "Estefano" Salgado); "Controller" (Victor Thomas, Ted Parsons, Paul Raven, Scott Albert); "Un Bel Di, Vedremo," "One Fine Day" (Giacomo Puccini); "Woman Tangle" (Shabba Ranks, Clifton Dillon); "Optimistic Voices" (E.Y. Harburg, Harold Arlen, Herbert Stothart); "Over the Rainbow" (Harburg, Arlen). **p**, Lynda Obst, Mary McLaglen; **d**, Michael Hoffman; **cast**, Michelle Pfeiffer, George Clooney, Mae Whitman, Alex D. Linz, Charles Durning, Jon Robin Baitz, Ellen Greene, Joe Grifasi, Pete Hamill, Anna Maria Horsford, Gregory Jbara, Robert Klein; **w**, Terrel Seltzer, Ellen Simon; **c**, Oliver Stapleton; **m**, James Newton Howard; **ed**, Garth Craven; **prod d**, David Gropman; **art d**, John Warnke; **set d**, Anne Kuljian; **spec eff**, Jeff Frink, Al Griswold.

One Flew Over the Cuckoo's Nest ★★★★ 1975; U.S.; 133m; Fantasy Films/UA; Color; Drama; Children: Unacceptable (MPAA: R); **DVD**; **VHS**. Disturbingly unnerving and often terrifying, Nicholson and fellow cast members nevertheless provide a powerful and memorable (if not nightmarish) film. He is a crafty and cunning felon—too clever much for his own good this traumatic tale tells—who is serving time on a prison farm and, to escape a work detail, pretends insanity. He is sent to an asylum where conditions are much worse than his previous prison environment in that the ward where he lives is presided over by sadistic nurse Fletcher. He discovers that most of the inmates are no crazier than he is, albeit they have weird traits and quirks. He livens up the place by organizing card games, basketball matches and an outdoor outing and where some of the patients seem to come to life, emerging from their monetized states. The evil-minded Fletcher, however, who hates her job and everyone in the asylum, takes revenge by punishing the inmates for the innocent caprices arranged by Nicholson. Further defying Fletcher, Nicholson goes so far as to smuggle two girls, Moritz and Small, into the ward at night to have sex with some of the inmates. When Fletcher finds Dourif, one of the most troubled patients, in bed with one of the girls, she tells the insecure young man that she is going to inform his mother about this sexual exploit, a threat that so unhinges Dourif that he takes his own life. Nicholson becomes so enraged over Dourif's suicide that he attacks the vicious Fletcher and almost strangles her to death before he is subdued. Fletcher uses this assault to have Nicholson lobotomized so that when he is returned to the ward, he appears before the other patients who have looked upon him as their only relief and comfort in life as a human vegetable, vacant-eyed and totally unresponsive to any remark or motion, which crushes the spirits of all in the ward. Seeing that his only friend has thus been reduced to a living dead man, Sampson, who, like Nicholson, has pretended his lunacy to avoid living in an outside world where persons like the perverse Fletcher have dominated his life, commits euthanasia by smothering Nicholson to death. Following this mercy killing, the giant Sampson stoically goes to the washroom, dislodges a heavy sink and uses it as a battering ram to break through a wall, and he makes his way to freedom, being the only one to fly over this cuckoo's nest. The gifted Forman directs this impactful film with great skill, fully developing his characters and eliciting from his cast outstanding performances, most of these players having had very limited acting experience. Nicholson and Fletcher are riveting in their combative roles, and Nicholson's anti-hero, dedicated to challenging a system he knows he cannot change or defeat, but willing to die in the effort, is reminiscent of Paul Newman's similar doomed lifestyle in **Cool Hand Luke**, 1967, where he plays a defiant, wisecracking prison farm inmate who would rather die at the hands of a dictatorial system than to submit to it. This is not a film for the squeamish or faint of heart and no child should be subjected to its brutal portrayals that nevertheless savagely indict an uncaring and oppressive medical system that imprisons its patients rather than frees them from their mental anxieties. This film swept the Academy Awards, winning for Best Picture and Best Director (Forman). Nicholson deservedly won an Oscar as Best Actor for his mesmerizing performance, and Fletcher won an Oscar as Best Actress in a performance that convinced the world that she was, indeed, one of the most hateful women to walk the earth. Goldman and Hauben won an Oscar for Best Adapted Screenplay, and Oscar nominations went to Dourif as Best Supporting Actor and for Cinematography and Film Editing. Songs: "The Star Spangled Banner" (1814; music: John Stafford Smith; lyrics: Francis Scott Key), "Charmaine" (1926; Lew Pollack, Erno Rapee), "I'm Popeye the Sailor Man" (1933; music and lyrics: Samuel Lerner), "Jingle Bells" (1857, James Pierpont), "Row, Row, Row Your Boat" (traditional), "White Christmas" (Irving Berlin). **p**, Saul Zaentz, Michael Douglas; **d**, Milos Forman; **cast**, Jack Nicholson, Louise Fletcher, William Redfield, Michael Berryman, Brad Dourif, Peter Brocco, Dean R. Brooks, Alonzo Brown, Scatman Crothers, Danny DeVito, Anjelica Huston, Will Sampson, Mwako Cumbuka, Christopher Lloyd; **w**, Lawrence Hauben, Bo Goldman (based on the novel by Ken Kesey and the play by Dale Wasserman); **c**, Haskell Wexler (DeLuxe Color); **m**, Jack Nitzsche; **ed**, Sheldon Kahn, Lynzee Klingman; **prod d**, Paul Sylbert; **art d**, Edwin O'Donovan.

One Foot in Heaven ★★★ 1941; U.S.; 108m; WB; B/W; Drama; Children: Cautionary. March gives a bravura performance as a dedicated Methodist minister, who sacrifices the comforts of life for himself and his family in order to raise impoverished parishes to thriving communities. This episodic tale begins when March is attending a medical school in Canada in 1904 and where he and his devoted wife, Scott, are looking forward to a successful and lucrative life once he becomes a physician. After listening to a moving speech from an evangelist, March quits school and moves to Iowa with Scott to establish a new ministry in a financially pressed community. He and Scott forgo their former lifestyle of fine clothes and better foods and live at the poverty level of most of their parishioners. After establishing this parish as successful, they move on to another town to aid another stricken parish (much the same way Bing Crosby does as a jovial trouble-shooting Catholic priest in **Going My Way**, 1944). They continue this nomadic religious practice for more than twenty years, establishing their own family in the process, but, in one town, their teenage son, Thomas, is wrongly accused of impregnating a young girl. March, however, proves this is not the case and, while redeeming his son's reputation, also shames the community into providing funds to build a new church.

Jeanette MacDonald, Maurice Chevalier and Genevieve Tobin in *One Hour with You*, **1932.**

Moving on to another town, March is exposed to motion pictures by his son, Thomas, who takes him to see a William S. Hart western, which imparts a moralistic message that March later employs in his sermons as he is a man embracing any worthwhile inventions and new ideas that strengthen and inspire the human spirit. At another parish, March is crestfallen when hymns are sung by an off-tuned choir of elderly parishioners and he sparks up the Sunday attendance by replacing that choir with a group of angelic-looking children who sing those hymns on key and in sweet harmony. When March and his sacrificing family finally establish a comfortable lifestyle in a burgeoning parish, he receives word that another community is in desperate need of spiritual guidance, and, true to his dedicated calling, he and his family once more uproot their lives by heading for that needy parish. Before they leave, a hymn is played on the church's new carillon as the entire town turns out to fondly bid them farewell in one of the many touching and memorable scenes in this tender and moving film. Director Rapper does a fine job in telling this inspirational tale, and March and the rest of the cast superbly enact their roles. The sacrifice made by March and his family is reminiscent of the severe sacrifices made by Walter Huston, who plays another dedicated minister in **Of Human Hearts**, 1938, but where Huston's dedication to a life of poverty in proving his faith is much more draconian. Songs: "The Children's Prayer" (from "Hansel and Gretel"; music: Engelbert Humperdinck; lyrics: Adelheid Wette), "Bridal Chorus" (1850; from "Lohengrin" by Richard Wagner), "The Church's One Foundation" (music: Samuel Wesley; lyrics: Samuel Stone), "Yankee Doodle" (traditional), "Put on Your Old Grey Bonnet" (Percy Wenrich), "America (My Country 'Tis of Thee)" (traditional). This film was a great success at the box office and received an Oscar nomination as Best Picture. *Author's Note*: March told this author that "the minister I play in that picture is a religious pioneer, a man who builds for the future and the strong foundations he builds are cemented by the cornerstones of his faith. **One Foot in Heaven** is one of my favorite films. It sends a very positive message without really preaching, that there truly are rewards on earth as there will be in Heaven." **p**, Jack L. Warner, Hal B. Wallis; **d**, Irving Rapper; **cast**, Fredric March, Martha Scott, Beulah Bondi, Gene Lockhart, Elisabeth Fraser, Harry Davenport, Laura Hope Crews, Grant Mitchell, Moroni Olsen, Frankie Thomas, Jerome Cowan, Ernest Cossart, Nana Bryant, Clara Blandick, Charles Drake, Gig Young; **w**, Casey Robinson (based on the biography by Hartzell Spence of his father); **c**, Charles Rosher; **m**, Max Steiner; **ed**, Warren Low; **art d**, Carl Jules Weyl.

One Hour with You ★★★ 1932; U.S.; 80m; PAR; B/W; Musical; Children: Acceptable; **DVD**; **VHS**. A delightful remake of the silent Lubitsch film **The Marriage Circle**, 1924, this musical romp featuring the al-

Adolphe Menjou, Mischa Auer and Deanna Durbin in *100 Men and A Girl,* **1937.**

ways charming Chevalier and the fetching MacDonald begins with a rather risqué opening scene when both are strolling in the main Paris park, the Bois de Boulogne, and where they impulsively begin to kiss each other at a pace that can only be described as furious. Their public necking offends a passing policeman, Judels, who threatens to arrest them for violating proper conduct in public. They happily explain that they are married, but Judels is doubtful about that since he thinks married people have no inclination to display such affection and he tells them that if they are, indeed, married, to go home and conduct their lovemaking in private. They do just that, and after they arrive at their residence, Chevalier turns to the camera and explains to viewers that he was not pulling that policeman's leg, that he and MacDonald are genuinely and legally married. (This is one of Chevalier's many "fourth wall" intrusions in this film as a form of narration and to fill in gaps in the story line; this direct address to the audience technique originated on the stage with Eugene O'Neill's play, *"Strange Interlude,"* written in 1923 and produced in 1928, bringing a Pulitzer Prize to the playwright, and which was later brought to the screen in the same year as this film; Groucho Marx seized upon this technique, as did Bob Hope years later in making direct and humorous aside comments to viewers about the films in which they were appearing.) Chevalier is a successful physician, but he has a roving eye and MacDonald's best friend, Tobin, who is married to Young, knows this, so she visits Chevalier and makes a strong play for him. Suspecting his wife is unfaithful, Young hires private detective Carle to trail Tobin about, and when Carle reports back to Young that Tobin has visited Chevalier, Young goes to Chevalier and tells him that he is planning to divorce his wife and name Chevalier as the reason for his divorce, naming him as co-respondent. When Chevalier tells MacDonald about these troubling circumstances, she is shocked and then thinks to teach Chevalier a lesson by giving him a dose of his own romancing medicine by dallying with Ruggles, who has always been attracted to her. Dismayed by these shenanigans, Chevalier is calmed when MacDonald finally tells him that these dangerously playful ploys must now stop and she promises never again to stray if he will do the same. Chevalier gratefully accepts, promising to do the same. Like most musicals, the story line is paper thin, but this lively outing nevertheless offers captivating songs, snappy dialog and many humorous moments. Songs: "Police Station Number" (music: John Leipold; lyrics: Leo Robin); "One Hour with You," "Three Times a Day," "What Would You Do?" (music: Richard A. Whiting; lyrics: Leo Robin); "We Will Always Be Sweethearts," "What a Little Thing Like a Wedding Can Do," "It Was Only a Dream Kiss," "Oh That Mitzi!" (music: Oscar Straus; lyrics: Leo Robin). *Author's Note*: Lubitsch had long pondered about remaking his silent comedy **The Marriage Circle**, 1924, starring Adolphe Menjou and Florence Vidor. He took great pains to make sure

that the remake was just as good as the original and, through his meticulous efforts, it proved to be just that, but at the cost of director George Cukor, who was originally slated to direct the film. Cukor told this author that "Ernst was in charge of all production at Paramount in those days and his word was law. We got along all right for some time while I was deep into the production of **One Hour with You**, but he then began visiting the set, making more and more suggestions that I change this or eliminate that, until, one day, I said: 'Ernst, you're not going to be satisfied with the final picture unless you do it yourself.' I quit on the spot and he took over the direction. Even though I had done most of the direction for the picture, Ernst thought it was his private property because he had done an original version of the story as a silent picture, so he took exclusive credit as director and I had to go to the Director's Guild for arbitration and he was compelled to give me a co-director credit. Even then, he was niggardly, because on some of the prints I saw later, he listed me only as the 'Dialog Director.' Ernst was a very talented man, but a very possessive one." Before the film went into production, Chevalier was hired as the leading male. He wanted Carole Lombard and Kay Francis as his two leading ladies in the film, but the savvy Lubitsch knew that the womanizing Chevalier wanted those two women in the film because he had romantic inclinations toward both of them. Knowing this would cause trouble on the set, Lubitsch, after considerable argument, persuaded Chevalier to accept MacDonald and Tobin as his leading ladies. Lubitsch had discovered MacDonald and had matched her with Chevalier in **The Love Parade**, 1929. Chevalier never warmed to MacDonald since she was not receptive to his advances, but he accepted MacDonald in this film simply because Lubitsch was then a reigning Hollywood powerhouse. Chevalier also knew that he would also get nowhere off the set with Tobin, who later married film director William Keighley. Chevalier was the heartthrob of just about every woman in the world when this film was made, except for the two women playing his lovers in **One Hour with You**. **p**, Ernst Lubitsch; **d**, Lubitsch, George Cukor; **cast**, Maurice Chevalier, Jeanette MacDonald, Genevieve Tobin, Charles Ruggles, Roland Young, Josephine Dunn, Richard Carle, George Barbier, Kent Taylor; **w**, Samson Raphaelson (based on the play "Only a Dream" by Lothar Schmidt [Goldschmidt]); **c**, Victor Milner; **m**, Oscar Straus, Richard Whiting; **ed**, William Shea; **art d**, Hans Dreier; **set d**, A. E. Freudeman.

One Hundred and One Dalmatians ★★★ 1961; U.S.; 79m; Walt Disney Productions/Buena Vista; Color; Animated Adventure; Children: Recommended; **DVD**; **VHS**. Superb animated tale from Disney presents a delightful film for children and dog-loving viewers of all ages. The story opens when Roger (Wright voiceover) and his dog Pongo (Taylor voiceover) fall in love with Anita (Davis voiceover) and her dog Perdita (Bauer voiceover). Pongo and Perdita mate and produce fifteen adorable Dalmatian puppies, but an evil-minded wealthy woman, Cruella De Vil (Gerson voiceover), intends to have all the puppies for herself. When Roger refuses to sell the adorable offspring to the conniving Cruella, she employs two crafty crooks to steal the puppies and hold them captive in a deserted mansion at the outskirts of London. Roger and Anita try their best to find their lost pups, but are unsuccessful, so Pongo uses his "twilight bark," a system of barking relays that finally identifies the mansion and Pongo, aided by another dog, a cat and a horse, rescues the pups, but he also discovers that the mansion holds ninety-nine Dalmatians that the sinister Cruella has collected in order that they later be sacrificed so that they can be made into a resplendent coat she intends to wear. Pongo leads all of these Dalmatians back to Roger's home and he decides that he will keep them all safe from the evil clutches of Cruella. *Author's Note*: Disney had an army of more than three hundred artists laboring for more than three years to produce this superlative animated delight, where the caricatures are masterfully and sharply defined as individual creatures, all with separate personalities and where Pongo and Perdita not only emulate the traits of their masters, but are similar in appearance (proving the old adage that masters look like their dogs and vice-versa). This film proved to be an enormous success, one of Disney's top moneymakers, taking in $153 million at the box office in its initial release against its original $4 million budget. Songs: "Dalmatian Plantation," "Cruella De Vil" (Mel Leven). **p**, Walt Disney; **d**, Wolfgang Reitherman, Hamilton S. Luske, Clyde Geronimi; **cast** (voiceovers), Rod Taylor, Lisa Davis, Cate Bauer, Ben Wright, Fred Worlock, J. Pat O'Malley, Tom Conway, Queenie Leonard, Marjorie Bennett, Barbara Luddy, Mary Wickes, Basil Ruysdael; **w**, Bill Peet (based on the novel by Dodie Smith); (Technicolor); **m**, George Bruns; **ed**, Donald Halliday, Roy M. Brewer, Jr.; **prod d&art d**, Ken Anderson; **spec eff**, Ub Iwerks, Eustace Lycett.

100 Men and A Girl ★★★ 1937; U.S.; 85m; UNIV; B/W; Musical; Children: Acceptable; **DVD**. Menjou is a classical music trombonist, but, like many other musicians during the Great Depression of the 1930s, is out of work. His energetic daughter, Durbin, forms an orchestra of other out-of-work musicians and persuades Leopold Stokowski to conduct it in a charity event. The concert is a big hit and Menjou and his musician friends find work again. This delightful film with young Durbin again charming audiences was one of the singing actress's most popular films. Songs: "Symphony No. 5, 4th movement (1888; Pyotr Ilyich Tchaikovsky), "It's Raining Sunbeams" (Frederick Hollander, Sam Coslow), "Rakoczy March" (1846; Hector Berlioz), "A Heart That's Free" (1936; Alfred G. Robyn, Thomas Railey), "Zampa Overture" (1831; Ferdinand Herold), "For He's a Jolly Good Fellow" (traditional), "Lohengrin, Prelude to Act III" (1850; Richard Wagner), "Alleluja from the Motet 'Exultate, jubilate," (1773; Wolfgang Amadeus Mozart), "Hungarian Rhapsody No. 2" (1847; Franz Liszt), "Drinking Song" from "La Traviata" (1853; Giuseppe Verdi). **p**, Joe Pasternak; **d**, Henry Koster; **cast**, Deanna Durbin, Adolphe Menjou, Leopold Stokowski, Alice Brady, Eugene Pallette, Mischa Auer, Billy Gilbert, Alma Kruger, Jed Prouty, Christian Rub, Jack Mulhall; **w**, Bruce Manning, Charles Kenyon, James Mulhauser (based on an idea by Hanns Kraly); **c**, Joseph A. Valentine; **m**, Charles Previn, Frank Skinner; **ed**, Bernard W. Burton; **prod d**, John Harkrider; **spec eff**, John P. Fulton.

One Is a Lonely Number ★★★ 1972; U.S.; 97m; MGM; Color; Drama; Children: Unacceptable (MPAA: PG); **VHS**. Jenkins is a college professor who seems to be happily married to attractive, twenty-seven-year-old Van Devere for several years. Then, one day, he leaves with no hint of wanting out of the marriage and files for divorce. She is not an independent and self-supporting person and hopes he will come back to her. She gets work as a lifeguard, despite having a fear of heights that keeps her from diving off the diving board. She and a friend, Elliot, visit Leigh, the president of a club for divorced women. Van Devere and her grocer, Douglas, an older man whose wife of nearly forty years recently died, become friends. Elliot takes Van Devere to the opening of a new art gallery where she meets handsome Markham. He takes her to dinner, then to his apartment, but when he begins to make advances, she flees. Soon afterward, she goes to Markham's apartment and they go to bed together. Van Devere then learns that Markham is married, which ends her affair with him. She also learns that Jenkins is living in Nevada with a teenage girl. At the divorce proceedings, Van Devere states that she does not want any money from Jenkins, only her freedom. Douglas goes missing for some time and she worries about his safety, but he shows up again saying he was away on a business trip. Through all this Van Devere has kept her job as a lifeguard, and now has gained so much confidence that she dives off the diving board, a symbolic act signifying that she has the strength and courage to go on after her divorce. Good acting and a superior script makes this one a cut well above a standard soap opera. Sexuality prohibits viewing by children. **p**, Stan Margulies; **d**, Mel Stuart; **cast**, Trish Van Devere, Monte Markham, Janet Leigh, Melvyn Douglas, Jane Elliot, Jonathan Lippe, Mark Bramhall, Paul Jenkins, Scott Beach, Henry Leff, Dudley Knight, Kathleen Quinlan; **w**, David Seltzer (based on the short story "The Good Humor Man" by

Gary Basaraba, Robbie Magwood and Elizabeth Harnois in *One Magic Christmas,* **1985.**

Rebecca Morris); **c**, Michel Hugo (Metrocolor); **m**, Michel Legrand; **ed**, David Saxon; **art d**, Walter M. Simonds; **set d**, George Gaines.

One Magic Christmas ★★★ 1985; Canada/U.S.; 89m; Disney/Buena Vista; Color; Fantasy/Drama; Children: Unacceptable (MPAA: PG); **DVD**; **VHS**. Christmas is not going to be very merry for the Grainger family because the father, Basaraba, loses his job and he and his wife, Steenburgen, and their two young children, Harnois and Magwood, must vacate their home, which is owned by the company that has just fired Basaraba. The family's holiday will be spent packing for a move while looking for a new place to live. The company can hardly wait to evict them and sends out some prospective new residents to look the house over, and, meanwhile, Basaraba goes to the bank and withdraws $200 to buy Christmas presents, but robber Robson, who is also out of work and desperate, shoots him dead and steals his car for a getaway. Basaraba's children are in the back seat, so they are kidnapped. The car plunges through a bridge railing and the children drown. All this sounds pretty grim for a happy Christmas story, but the mood changes when an angel, Stanton, steps in and the kids miraculously return to life and go to the North Pole and meet Santa Claus, Rubes. In the end, Basaraba also comes back to life and the family has a merry Christmas after all, albeit they are still going to be evicted from their house as jingle bells ring. Offbeat and even weird in spots, this entry nevertheless entertains throughout. Songs: "Sleigh Ride" (Leroy Anderson, Mitchell Parish), "Stop! In the Name of Love" (Eddie Holland, Lamont Dozier, Brian Holland), "Lost in the Stars" (Kurt Weill, Maxwell Anderson), "I'll Be Home for Christmas" (Kim Gannon, Walter Kent). Tragedy and violence prohibit viewing by children. **p**, Peter O'Brian; **d**, Phillip Borsos; **cast**, Mary Steenburgen, Gary Basaraba, Harry Dean Stanton, Arthur Hill, Elizabeth Harnois, Robbie Magwood, Michelle Meyrink, Elias Koteas, Wayne Robson, Graham Jarvis; **w**, Thomas Meehan (based on a story by Boros, Meehan, Barry Healey); **c**, Frank Tidy; **m**, Michael Conway Baker; **ed**, Sidney Wolinsky; **prod d**, Bill Brodie; **art d**, Tony Hall; **set d**, Rondi Johnson; **spec eff**, John Thomas.

One Million B.C. ★★★ 1940; U.S.; 80m; Hal Roach Studios/UA; B/W; Adventure/Horror; Children: Unacceptable; **VHS**. Comedy producer Roach delved into a different genre when offering this fanciful yarn, whimsically mixing the age of dinosaurs with prehistoric yarn, but he nevertheless delivers an exciting tale of two combative human tribes. One consists of the warlike Rock People, who live in the mountains, the other being the peaceful Shell People, who reside at the ocean's edge. Chaney, the fierce chief of the Rock People, argues with his son, Mature, banishing him. Mature roams aimlessly from the mountains, across the plains and eventually finds the Shell People, who take him into their

Lon Chaney Jr. and Victor Mature in *One Million B.C.*, 1940.

tribe, but not before he endures numerous hazards, including attacks from dinosaurs. When hesitantly accepted by the Shell People, Mature meets the fair and buxom Landis, who falls in love with the beefy Mature, instructing him in the ways of table etiquette and civilized behavior. When Chaney leads an attack by the Rock People against the Shell People, Mature acts as a mediator, settling their differences, but before that happens, both tribes are almost wiped out by man-eating dinosaurs and a terrific volcanic eruption. The survivors of the two tribes then realize that their best avenue of survival is to make peace and work together. Other than a few grunts here and there and some scant primitive words unknown to any modern language, communication is largely achieved through sign language; the special effects and the erratic antics of the actors provide the drama. The film was a success, especially with male audiences who flocked to see the scantily clad ladies cavorting about in their bikini-like attire, especially the statuesque and voluptuous Landis, who was one of the leading Hollywood pinups of the day. The film was remade as **One Million Years B.C.**, 1967, with much better effects (stop-action created by Ray Harryhausen), and with Raquel Welch in even skimpier attire, but a production that proved less exciting than the original. For similar films, see Subject Index, Prehistoric Beasts and Man, Volume II. *Author's Note*: Mature told this author that "I thought the picture was one of my weirdest. No lines really in the script, just a lot of running around and battling a bunch of lizards that were shown in rear screen projection, although I got to embrace Carole [Landis] in a few scenes. We worked together the following year in **I Wake Up Screaming** [1941], but she gets bumped off early in that film, and again a year after that in **My Gal Sal** [1942] where I dump her for Rita Hayworth. Poor girl, she never had any real luck. She took her life in 1948 over a broken romance [with actor Rex Harrison]. She was a better actress than most people knew." The lizards to which Mature refers were live ones that substituted for the dinosaurs since Roach decided to approach the special effects inexpensively by simply photographing lizards making menacing moves and then showing them in rear projection (or process shots) in front of which the actors responded. He avoided the more pricy use of creating detailed models of dinosaurs and photographing them for stop-action application as had been employed by special effects wizard Willis O'Brien in **The Lost World**, 1925, **King Kong**, 1933, and other productions. Roach did make a thrust at authenticity by hiring the great pioneering filmmaker D. W. Griffith (1875-1948) to oversee the production as producer and director, announcing on different occasions that Griffith was acting in both capacities. Roach knew that Griffith had produced a rather crude but effective one-reel short about prehistoric life in **Man"s Genesis**, 1912, which he remade the following year under the title of **Brute Force**, and thus believed that Griffith would bring considerable expertise to the subject. However, Griffith was al-

most immediately at loggerheads with Roach about character development. Griffith wanted each leading character to have a distinct personality, but Roach insisted on the traditional stereotypes of cavemen and women grunting and gesticulating communication. This finally led to Griffith telling Roach, after receiving his last paycheck, that he wanted his name removed from the credits of the film; Roach agreed and where Roach took credit for direction and producing. Chaney, who plays the rough-and-tumble leader of the Rock People, had recently made **Of Mice and Men**, 1939, where he appeared in one of his finest roles as a doomed dimwitted ranch hand, attempted to do what Griffith originally envisioned by making his character distinctive. He eagerly went at his role in **One Million B.C.** by doing his own makeup (as his celebrated father, Lon Chaney Sr., was known to do in all of his silent films), and Chaney Jr. created a fascinating image of a grotesque and fierce prehistoric man. "When I appeared on the set in my own makeup," Chaney told this author, "I was told to go back to my dressing room so that makeup people could redo everything it took me hours to create. I ran into trouble right there with the cosmetician's union that insisted that I have all my makeup done by their own people and you could not fight them about that. Well, after they got done with me, I looked just like all the rest of the cavemen, except maybe my beard was a bit longer and dirtier. So much for being creative!" **p**, Hal Roach, Sr., D.W. Griffith (not credited); **d**, Hal Roach Sr., Hal Roach, Jr.; **cast**, Victor Mature, Carole Landis, Lon Chaney Jr., John Hubbard, Jacqueline Dalya, Mary Gale Fisher, Robert Kent, Jean Porter, Dick Simmons, Conrad Nagel (narrator); **w**, Mickell Novack, George Baker, Joseph Frickert, Grover Jones; **c**, Norbert Brodine; **m**, Werner R. Heymann; **ed**, Ray Snyder; **art d**, Charles D. Hall; **set d**, William Stevens; **spec eff**, Roy Seawright.

One Minute to Zero ★★★ 1952; U.S.; 105m; RKO; B/W; War Drama; Children: Unacceptable; **DVD**; **VHS**. Mitchum again provides a powerful performance, this time as a hardened U.S. Army officer trying to maneuver through enemy lines during the Korean War. He meets and falls for fetching Blyth, a naïve and idealistic UN official. She looks upon Mitchum's brusque and taciturn tactics as ruthless and, at first, condemns him, until she realizes that his actions are based on preserving lives, not taking them, as he outwits North Korean troops in evacuating his own men as well as a horde of refugees from the danger zones. Well acted and packed with many exciting action scenes, this war saga sustains interest throughout. Song: "Tell Me, Golden Moon" (music: Nobuyuki Takeoka; lyrics: Norman Bennett). *Author's Note*: Mitchum told this author that "**One Minute to Zero** was made while we were still fighting the Korean War, a war no one wanted to know about, except the relatives and those who loved our boys fighting that so-called 'Police Action' [thus termed by U.S. President Harry S. Truman], but it was no such thing. It was a dirty conflict like all wars and we lost a lot of our people fighting to keep South Korea free and the film we made had a lot to do with that." Garnett, the director of this film, told this author that "I had a limited budget for **One Minute to Zero** so I used a lot of archival footage from the war and wove those scenes into the action and some of that footage was taken by U.S. Army Signal Corps cinematographers, who risked their lives to get those shots, God bless them." Veteran actor McGraw told this author that "I play a sergeant in that film and I play him the way I understand sergeants, who hold all armies together—they take orders and give them and without complaint. I played that character tough, but I could not out-tough Bob [Mitchum], who plays an officer with the mind of a sergeant." **p**, Edmund Grainger; **d**, Tay Garnett; **cast**: Robert Mitchum, Ann Blyth, William Talman, Charles McGraw, Margaret Sheridan, Richard Egan, Eduard Franz, Robert Osterloh, Robert Gist, Roy Roberts, Wally Cassell, Eddie Firestone, Alvin Greenman; **w**, Milton Krims, William Wister Haines; **c**, William E. Snyder; **m**, Victor Young; **ed**, Robert Belcher, Frank McWhorter; **art d**, Albert S. D'Agostino, Jack Okey.

One More River ★★★ 1934; U.S.; 88m; UNIV; B/W; Drama; Children: Unacceptable. Based on British author John Galsworthy's (1867-1933) final novel, this love tale presents a riveting courtroom trial involving Wynyard, who is badly treated by her sadistic husband, Colin Clive, after only eighteen months of marriage. She flees from him in Ceylon, India, and boards a ship back to England. Onboard, she meets charming but penniless Lawton, who falls madly in love with her. They develop a close but platonic relationship, unaware that Clive has hired detectives to watch her. When Clive asks Wynyard to return to him, she refuses and he accuses her of adultery with Lawton. In a highly public and dramatic British divorce trial, Wynyard wants nothing more than to divorce Clive, but to win her case, she has to fight his false accusation to defend her family's honor, and is successful. The movie was Jane Wyatt's film debut. The story is the conclusion of the final trilogy in Galsworthy's *Forsyte Saga*. This superior domestic drama is expertly directed by the accomplished Whale, but it is unfortunately unavailable on any home viewing format. **p**, Carl Laemmle Jr., R. C. Sherriff; **d**, James Whale; **cast**, Diana Wynyard, Colin Clive, Frank Lawton, Mrs. Patrick Campbell, Jane Wyatt, Reginald Denny, C. Aubrey Smith, Henry Stephenson, Lionel Atwill, Alan Mowbray, Kathleen Howard, Gilbert Emery, E. E. Clive, Robert Greig; **w**, Sherriff, William Hurlbut (based on the novel by John Galsworthy); **c**, John J. Mescall; **m**, W. Franke Harling; **ed**, Ted J. Kent; **art d**, Charles D. Hall; **spec eff**, John P. Fulton.

One Night in the Tropics ★★★ 1940; U.S.; 82m; UNIV; B/W; Musical Comedy; Children: Acceptable; **DVD**;n **VHS**. In their rollicking film debut, Abbott and Costello perform some of their most cherished vaudeville skits (reprised on their popular radio show), providing great comedy relief for the budding and turmoil-ridden romance between Jones and Kelly. Jones is an insurance salesman selling a policy to Cummings, who is about to be married, but Jones falls in love with the intended bride, Kelly, complicating matters and doing his utmost to prevent the woman he loves by going to the altar with another man. Jones, a wonderful tenor, is in great voice here, providing many delightful tunes. Songs: "Back in My Shell," "You and Your Kiss," "Remind Me," "Farandola," "Simple Philosophy" (music: Jerome Kern; lyrics: Dorothy Fields); "Your Dream Is the Same as My Dream" (music: Jerome Kern; lyrics: Oscar Hammerstein II and Otto A. Harbach); "Cielito Lindo" (traditional); "Bridal Chorus(Here Comes the Bride)" (from "Lohengrin" by Richard Wagner); "Jonah and the Whale" (traditional). **p**, Leonard Spigelgass; **d**, A. Edward Sutherland; **cast**, Allan Jones, Nancy Kelly, Bud Abbott, Lou Costello, Robert Cummings, Mary Boland, William Frawley, Peggy Moran, Leo Carrillo, Don Alvarado, Russell Wade; **w**, Gertrude Purcell, Charles Grayson, Kathryn Scola, Francis Martin, John Grant (based on the novel *Love Insurance* by Earl Derr Biggers); **c**, Joseph Valentine; **m**, Frank Skinner; **ed**, Milton Carruth; **art d**, Jack Otterson; **set d**, Russell A. Gausman.

One of Our Aircraft Is Missing ★★★ 1942; U.K.; 102m; British National Films/Archers/UA; B/W; War Drama; Children: Cautionary; **DVD**; **VHS**. Tearle is outstanding as the commander of a British Wellington bomber that takes off with its squadron from a British-based airfield to conduct a night raid on Stuttgart, Germany, during WWII. The flight and all of its many perils are recorded in detail as the bomber's crew work their equipment and make navigational and bombing run adjustments as they approach their target, made all the more harrowing when the plane comes under attack from anti-aircraft guns, the flak from these guns causing the plane to leap and jump wildly in the air. After successfully dropping its bombs, the plane is damaged from flak and Tearle orders his crew to bail out. The six crew members parachute downward to land in Nazi-occupied Holland where several Dutch children find them and lead them to a safe haven. They then begin a hazardous journey, moving clandestinely from one secret location to another with the aid of Dutch underground workers such as Withers, a dithering official, Petrie, and a dedicated priest, Ustinov (in one of his first roles). Though the British airmen, who disguise themselves as na-

William Frawley, Bud Abbott, and Lou Costello in *One Night in the Tropics,* **1940.**

tives and thus risk execution as spies, are almost caught by searching Nazis on several occasions, they manage to elude their pursuers, reach the coast and board a small boat that takes them back to England where they again rejoin their squadron and prepare for another raid against the enemy. The exceptional cast and taut direction from master filmmakers Powell and Pressburger (with an important assist by editor Lean, who later became a pantheon British director) present an exciting and moving production, albeit a few windy propaganda speeches slows down some scenes. *Author's Note*: The producers-directors employed an actual Wellington bomber for this film and detailing its technical applications and operations presents additional authenticity to an otherwise stirring film. The same technique was employed by American directors when making **Air Force**, 1943 (Howard Hawks), **Command Decision**, 1948 (Sam Wood), and **Twelve O'Clock High**, 1949 (Henry King) where the American B-17 bomber was shown in detail. **p**, Michael Powell, Emeric Pressburger, John Corfield; **d&w**, Powell, Pressburger (based on a story by Pressburger); **cast**, Godfrey Tearle, Eric Portman, Hugh Williams, Bernard Miles, Pamela Brown, Joyce Redman, Googie Withers, Robert Helpmann, Peter Ustinov, Roland Culver, Robert Beatty, James Donald, Gordon Jackson, Powell; **c**, Ronald Neame; **ed**, David Lean; **art d**, David Rawnsley; **spec eff**, Frederick Ford, Douglas Woolsey.

One of the Hollywood Ten ★★★ 2001; Spain/U.K.; 109m; Bloom Street Productions/Domain Entertainment; Color; Drama; Children: Unacceptable; **DVD**. Goldblum does an exceptional job in essaying Herbert Biberman (1900-1971), a Hollywood writer and director, who was blacklisted as one of the Hollywood Ten by the House Un-American Activities Committee (1938-1975) after he was identified as having had communist affiliations. Goldblum and his actress wife, Gale Sondergaard (1899-1985), played by Scacchi, are fired by Warner Brothers after refusing to testify at the hearings, and Goldblum is imprisoned for six months at the Federal Correctional Institution in Texarkana. Upon his release, he discovers that his Hollywood career is finished, as is his wife's. He manages to direct a screenplay about the 1950-1951 strike of Mexican American miners against the Empire Zinc Company in Bayard, New Mexico. However, the FBI investigates the film's financing and agents try to steal the negatives, telling film processing laboratories not to work on the film, and encouraging the film's crew to set fire to the sets, and then deports one of the film's cast, a Mexican actress, Rosaura Revueltas, played by Molina, on bogus charges. Goldblum stands firm and completes the film, **Salt of the Earth** (1954). The entire cast does a fine job with their roles and the direction from Francis inventively moves the story along at a brisk pace. Songs: "Twinkle in Your Eye" (Richard Rodgers, Lorenz Hart), "When You're Smiling, the Whole World Smiles with You" (Larry Shay, Joe Goodwin, Mark

Gary Cooper and Frances Fuller in *One Sunday Afternoon*, 1933.

Fisher). **p**, Karl Francis, Juan Gordon, Stuart Pollok; **d&w**, Francis; **cast**, Jeff Goldblum, Greta Scacchi, Angela Molina, Christopher Fulford, Antonio Valero, John Sessions, Geraint Wyn Davies, Sean Chapman, Peter Bowles, Jorge de Juan, Teresa J. Berganza, Jorge Bosch; **c**, Nigel Walters; **m**, Victor Reyes; **ed**, John Richards; **prod d**, Hayden Pearce; **art d**, Vincent Mateu-Ferreur as Vicente Mateu; **set d**, Frazer Pearce; **spec eff**, Juan Ramon Molina, Antonio Castillo.

One Sunday Afternoon ★★★ 1933; U.S.; 85m; PAR; B/W; Comedy/Romance; Children: Acceptable; **DVD**. Cooper is wonderful as a mild-mannered young dentist, who goes daffy over the alluring Wray. He nevertheless loses her to the conniving Hamilton and winds up married to gentle and loving Fuller. Cooper still nurtures a secret longing for Wray (as a lovesick boy might pine for an unattainable girl) and tries to think of ways to take revenge on the strutting and arrogant Hamilton, but he is too nice and kind-hearted to give Hamilton his comeuppance. Hamilton gets his just desserts through his own wife, Wray, who, Cooper finally realizes, is nothing more than a selfish, nagging shrew, who is henpecking Hamilton to utter distraction and unhappiness. Cooper also realizes that he has been fortunate, indeed, to have met and married the loving Fuller, the woman who was meant to be his mate for life and begins to appreciate the happiness his marriage has brought to him. This film was remade as a classic comedy starring James Cagney, Olivia de Havilland, Rita Hayworth and Jack Carson as **The Strawberry Blonde**, 1941, and a much lesser effort as a third version in 1948 with the same title as the original. Songs: "One Sunday Afternoon" (1902; music: Harry von Tilzer; lyrics: Andrew Sterling), "In the Good Old Summertime" (1902; music: George Evans; lyrics: Ren Shields), "Goodbye, Little Girl, Goodbye" (1904; music: Gus Edwards; lyrics: Will D. Cobb), "Bill Bailey, Won't You Please Come Home?" (1902; music and lyrics: Hughie Cannon), "Sobre los Olas (Over the Waves)" (1887; music: Juventino Rosas), "Ach Du Lieber Augustine" (German folksong), and "Du, Du Liegst Mir im Herzen" (German folksong). *Author's Note*: Wray told this author that "I never liked my role in **One Sunday Afternoon**. I play a terrible person, very conceited and self-centered and I don't give a hoot for anyone else, especially poor Neil [Hamilton], who plays my unhappy husband. I'd rather be screaming in the hand of that big ape [**King Kong**, 1933, in which Wray appeared as the unwilling love interest to a towering gorilla] than making life miserable for others." **p**, Louis D. Lighton; **d**, Stephen Roberts; **cast**, Gary Cooper, Fay Wray, Frances Fuller, Roscoe Karns, Neil Hamilton, Jane Darwell, Clara Blandick, James Bradbury, Jr., Ed Brady, James P. Burtis; **w**, William Slavens McNutt, Grover Jones (based on the play by James Hagan); **c**, Victor Milner; **m**, John Leipold; **ed**, Ellsworth Hoagland; **art d**, Hans Dreier, Wiard Ihnen; **spec eff**, Farciot Edouart, Gordon Jennings.

1001 Arabian Nights ★★★ 1959; U.S.; 75m; United Productions of America/COL; Color; Animated Comedy; Children: Acceptable; **VHS**. That lovable cartoon character, the near-sighted Mr. Magoo, appears in his first feature-length film, and he is a scream through the discombobulating voiceover of Magoo from the gifted and humorous Backus. The story takes place in long-ago Baghdad where Magoo is a lamp seller and who demands that his lazy nephew, Aladdin (Hickman voiceover), get married. The boy falls in love with the daughter (Grant voiceover) of the sultan (Reed voiceover), but the sultan's right-hand man, a wicked wazir (Conried voiceover), has his evil heart set on her. Magoo comes to the rescue to help Hickman win the princess. A merry romp with lots of magic and some delightful songs: "You Are My Dream," "Three Little Maids from Damascus," "Magoo's Blues" (Ned Washington, George Duning). A live-action film, **Mr. Magoo**, 1997, starred Leslie Nielsen, and there were two Mr. Magoo television shows: "Famous Adventures of Mr. Magoo" (1960) and "Mister Magoo's Christmas Carol" (1962). **p**, Stephen Bosustow; **d**, Jack Kinney; **cast** (voiceovers), Jim Backus, Kathryn Grant, Dwayne Hickman, Hans Conried, Herschel Bernardi, Alan Reed, Daws Butler, Clark Sisters; **w**, Czenzi Ormonde (based on a story by Dick Shaw, Dick Kinney, Leo Salkin, Pete Burness, Lew Keller, Ed Nofziger, Ted Allan, Margaret and Paul Schneider, and the Mr. Magoo character created by John Hubley); (Technicolor); **m**, George Duning; **ed**, Carl Bennett, Skip Craig; **prod d**, Robert Dranko; **art d**, Abe Levitow.

The One That Got Away ★★★ 1958; U.K.; 108m; Rank; B/W; War Drama; Children: Unacceptable; **DVD**; **VHS**. This exciting film is based on the true story of German Luftwaffe Lt. Franz von Werra (1914-1941) whose plane was shot down over England in the early days of World War II (1939-1945), and who was captured and put in a British prison. Werra is expertly played by Kruger, who brags to his captors that he will escape but he fails in two attempts. While on a train to Montreal, and while being transported to a prison camp in Canada, he does escape and makes his way to the United States, which is neutral at the time. Evading extradition to Canada, Kruger then makes his way back to Germany, is decorated as a hero, and returns to the Luftwaffe. Werra, however, died on October 25, 1941, at the age of twenty-seven when his plane suffered engine failure on a practice flight and crashed into the sea north of Vlissingen, the Netherlands. His body was never found. He was the only prisoner of war to escape from a British prison camp. Violence prohibits viewing by children. Songs: "Muss i Denn, Muss i Denn zum Stadtele Hinaus," "Auf, auf zum Frohlichen Tagen," "Horch, was Kommt von Draussen Rein" (German traditional). **p**, Julian Wintle; **d**, Roy Baker; **cast**, Hardy Kruger, Colin Gordon, Michael Goodliffe, Terence Alexander, Jack Gwillim, Andrew Faulds, Julian Somers, Alec McCowen, Robert Crewdson, George Mikell; **w**, Howard Clewes (based on the book by Kendal Burt, James Leasor); **c**, Eric Cross; **m**, Hubert Clifford; **ed**, Sidney Hayers; **art d**, Edward Carrick; **spec eff**, Cliff Culley, Frank George, Bert Marshall, John Stears, Bill Warrington.

The 1,000 Eyes of Dr. Mabuse ★★★ 1966; France/Italy/West Germany; 104m; Central Cinema Co. Film/Ajay Film Co.; B/W; Crime/Horror; Children: Unacceptable; **DVD**; **VHS**. A series of strange murders take place in a hotel in Berlin. An American millionaire, van Eyck, staying at the hotel, saves Addams from killing herself there and they become involved in the investigation of the murders. Police Commissioner Frobe suspects that the killer may be a man who thinks he is in the reincarnation of evil crime genius Dr. Mabuse and Frobe thinks that man is either Preiss, a blind clairvoyant, or Peters, an insurance salesman. We are intentionally misled from here to wonder if Mabuse, presumed to be dead, is back again. This fascinating and puzzling horror mystery is too strange and violent for children. There were two other German Dr. Mabuse films, **Dr. Mabuse Der Spieler**, 1922, and **The Testament of Dr. Mabuse**, 1933. (In German; dubbed in English.) **p&d**, Fritz Lang; **cast**, Dawn Addams, Peter van Eyck, Wolfgang Preiss, Gert

Frobe, Werner Peters, Andrea Checchi, Howard Vernon, Nico Pepe, David Cameron, Jean-Jacques Delbo; **w**, Lang, Heinz Oskar Wuttig (based on an idea by Jan Fethge, from a character created by Norbert Jacques); **c**, Karl Lob; **m**, Bert Grund; **ed**, Walter Wischniewsky, Waltraut Wischniewsky; **prod d**; Erich Kettelhut, Johannes Ott.

One True Thing ★★★ 1998; U.S.; 127m; Monarch Pictures/UNIV; Color; Drama; Children: Unacceptable (MPAA: R); **DVD**; **VHS**. In this revealing and impactful domestic drama, Streep is a mother who dies and the film the deals with how her death affects her family, a story told in flashback. Her husband, Hurt, is a professor of literature, who lives in the past, dwelling on his times when he was a writer for the *New Yorker* magazine twenty years earlier. Her daughter, Zellweger, is an aggressive young journalist whose ambitions are put on hold when Streep falls ill and Hurt asks her to come home and help take care of Streep during the Christmas holiday, which involves cooking, house cleaning, and decorating a tree. Time spent with her mother helps Zellweger to discover what a truly wonderful person her mother truly is, and she also learns more about herself and her needs and ambitions. Songs: "My One True Friend" (Carole King, Carole Bayer Sager, David Foster), "Paraiso de dulzura" (Hector Lavoe), "Do You Want to Dance" (Bobby Freeman), "My Blue Room" (Doug Allen), "If I Only Had a Brain, Heart, and Nerve" (E.Y. Harburg, Harold Arlen), "Body and Soul" (Robert Sour, Johnny Green, Edward Heyman, Frank Eyton), "Friends" (Buzzy Linhart, Mark Klingman), "Season Change" (Lewis A. Martine), "Silent Night" (Franz Gruber, Joseph Mohr). Gutter language prohibits viewing by children. **p**, Jesse Beaton, Harry J. Ufland; **d**, Carl Franklin; **cast**, Meryl Streep, Renee Zellweger, William Hurt, Tom Everett Scott, Lauren Graham, Nicky Katt, James Eckhouse, Patrick Breen, Gerrit Graham, David Byron, Stephen Peabody, Lizbeth MacKay; **w**, Karen Croner (based on the novel by Anna Quindlen); **c**, Declan Quinn; **m**, Cliff Eidelman; **ed**, Carole Kravetz; **prod d**, Paul Peters; **art d**, Jefferson Sage; **set d**, Elaine O'Donnell, Leslie A. Pope; **spec eff**, Steven Kirshoff, J.C. Brotherhood.

One, Two, Three ★★★★ 1961; U.S.; 115m; Bavaria Film; Mirisch; UA; B/W; Comedy; Children: Acceptable; **DVD**; **VHS**. Cagney is dynamically riveting as an all-business U.S. executive of the bottling division of Coca-Cola in Germany, who spends every waking minute pushing and peddling the soda pop. He is struggling to become the top Coca-Cola dog in Europe when airhead Tiffin arrives to see the sights. She is the attractive daughter of Coca-Cola bigwig St. John, who resides in the Georgia headquarters. Cagney assures St. John that his daughter is in safe in his hands, but she is far from that. Although Cagney arranges Tiffin's itinerary and acts like her watchdog during her two-week tour of the Continent, he is unable to prevent her from meeting and falling hard for dingy Buchholz, a wild hippie and a diehard East Berlin communist, a man who represents everything that Cagney is not. Cagney has been banking on getting that top job from St. John (who reprises an offhand version of his blustering "General Bullmoose" character from **Li'l Abner**, 1959), but sees it slipping from his grasp when he learns that Tiffin has married Buchholz. To overcome this disaster, Cagney plants a copy of the *Wall Street Journal* on Buchholz, making him appear to his communist pals that he is a secret capitalist and for which he is tossed into jail and that Buchholz's fall from grace will now allow Cagney to arrange an annulment of Tiffin's marriage to him. Fate further conspires against Cagney when he learns that Tiffin is now expecting Buchholz's baby. He then learns that St. John is soon to arrive in Germany to retrieve his irresponsible daughter so Cagney makes things right for her by using his sexy secretary, Pulver (whose character was later duplicated by Lee Meredith in playing "Ulla" in Mel Brooks' **The Producers**, 1968) to seduce some communist commissioners into releasing Buchholz. Cagney then arranges for Buchholz (who is by now totally disillusioned with communism because of his incarceration) to receive a title as a bona fide aristocrat and puts him through a crash business

James Cagney in *One, Two, Three*, 1961.

course, turning him into an ardent capitalist. After St. John arrives, he is so impressed with his new son-in-law that he gives the big promotion to him and not to Cagney, who then resigns himself to a second fiddle station in life, returning to Atlanta with his wife, Francis, who has proved to be the only dependable person in his life. Pantheon director Wilder presents this wild comedy like a race car, its many side-splitting scenes unfolding with lightning speed. Cagney bursts with energy, so much so that he appears to be manic or, at least, on the verge of a nervous breakdown, especially at the finale when he is ultimately betrayed by someone planting a Pepsi-Cola in a Coca-Cola machine. The crackling script offers many witty and clever lines, and Previn's brilliant score strongly supports the frantic antics of the characters, albeit the jokes are somewhat dated as they were culled from the Cold War headlines of the day. Songs: "Yankee Doodle" (traditional), "Yes! We Have No Bananas" (Frank Silver, Irving Cohn), "Sabre Dance" (Aram Khachaturyan), "Ride of the Valkyries" (from Act III, "Die Walkure" by Richard Wagner), and "Itsy Bitsy Teenie Weenie Yellow Polka Dot Bikini" (Lee Pockriss, Paul Vance). *Author's Note*: Cagney told this author that "Billy [Wilder] drained me of everything I had in **One, Two, Three**, or I wanted to please him so much that I exhausted myself in that picture. I knew it was time to walk away from the cameras when I had to struggle to remember my lines. [He was sixty-two at the time.] Billy's films are always demanding—physically and mentally—and that one about broke my back. So it was goodbye to Hollywood and back to the farm, just the way I retreated when playing George M. Cohan in **Yankee Doodle Dandy** [1942]." Cagney would not appear again in films until twenty years later when playing NYC Police Commissioner Rhinelander Waldo (1877-1927) in Milos Forman's **Ragtime**, 1981. Wilder told this author that "Jimmy [Cagney] was a firecracker in that picture and I had the feeling right from the beginning that he was planning to make it his swansong. He had grown tired of making films and really wanted to stay on his farm and milk his cows or whatever it is they do on farms. [Cagney owned a large dairy farm in upstate New York, as well as a retreat at Martha's Vineyard.] After shooting one scene, he took me aside and said: 'Billy, this isn't for me anymore. The fun has all gone out of it and it's nothing but slavery.' But, he did one hell of a job in **One, Two, Three**." **p&d**, Billy Wilder; **cast**, James Cagney, Horst Buchholz, Pamela Tiffin, Arlene Francis, Howard St. John, Hanns Lothar, Leon Askin, Ralf Wolter, Karl Lieffen, Lilo Pulver, Red Buttons, Sig Ruman; **w**, Wilder, I.A.L. Diamond (based on the play "Egy, kettö, három" by Ferenc Molnar); **c**, Daniel L. Fapp; **m**, Andre Previn; **ed**, Daniel Mandell; **prod d**, Robert Stratil, Heinrich Weidemann; **art d**, Alexander Trauner; **spec eff**, Milt Rice.

One Way Passage ★★★ 1932; U.S.; 67m; WB; B/W; Drama/Ro-

William Powell and Kay Francis in *One Way Passage*, 1932.

mance; Children: Acceptable; **DVD**. Powell and Francis are hauntingly memorable as star-crossed lovers in this melancholy melodrama. Powell is apprehended in Hong Kong by dogged detective Hymer, who is determined to return him to California where, as a convicted murderer, he has an appointment with the executioner at San Quentin. They board an ocean-going liner sailing for that destination, and while on board, Powell meets attractive socialite Francis, falling in love with her. She gives her heart to the suave and polished crook, although she does not know that he is a doomed man. He does not know that she is also doomed in that she is dying from terminal heart disease. The kind-hearted Hymer allows Powell to keep his secret, giving him the freedom of the ship and where Powell appears to Francis to be a successful businessman. Knowing their time together is brief, both agree to meet again later at a Mexican restaurant on New Year's Eve, a romantic rendezvous that, most likely, will never take place. Powell and Francis give startling performances, and Garnett's direction is superb as he was best known for helming heavy dramas and offbeat romance films. Songs: "If I Had My Way" (1914; music: James Kendis; lyrics: Lou Klein), "Where Was I?" (W. Franke Harling), "Till We Meet Again" (1918; music: Richard A. Whiting; lyrics: Ray Egan), "Deep in Your Eyes" (1932; Harry Warren), "On San Francisco Bay" (1906; music: Gertrude Hoffman), "Aloha Oe" (1908; Queen Liliuokalani), "Auld Lang Syne" (traditional Scottish song), "King's Serenade" (music: Charles E. King). ***Author's Note***: Director Garnett wrote the story treatment for this film, working from an idea sketchily presented by Robert Lord. When he thought to take credit for that story treatment, producer Hal Wallis persuaded Garnett against doing so. "The tale is really my own," Garnett told this author, "and I think **One Way Passage** is perhaps my finest work, but that's only because Bill [Powell] and Kay [Francis] were wonderful in their roles as the doomed lovers. They love each other so much that they will not tell each other that there is no hope for either of them, each believing that the other has a good chance in life without them. That, my young friend, is true love." Powell told this author that "**One Way Passage** is one of those pictures that stays in the public's memory as something bittersweet, a story about two people the audience quickly grows to like but knows that they do not have any future together. In fact, they have no future at all. It's more of a tragedy than a romance." **p**, Hal B. Wallis, Robert Lord (both not credited); **d**, Tay Garnett; **cast**, William Powell, Kay Francis, Aline MacMahon, Frank McHugh, Warren Hymer, Stanley Fields, Willie Fung, Roscoe Karns, Allan Lane, Herbert Mundin; **w**, Wilson Mizner, Joseph Jackson (based on a story by Lord); **c**, Robert Kurrle; **ed**, Ralph Dawson; **art d**, Anton Grot.

One Way Pendulum ★★★ 1965; U.K.; 90m; Woodfall Film Productions/Lopert; B/W; Comedy; Children: Acceptable; **VHS**. This delight-ful romp profiles a British family of eccentrics, which includes the father, Sykes, who is building a replica of the Old Bailey courts in the living room; his wife, Leggatt, who hires a maid to eat the leftovers from the family's meals; their daughter, Foster, who hangs out at the zoo watching apes; and their son, Miller, who tries to get his collection of weight scales to play music. Sykes holds a mock trial with his son accused of murder and his wife playing the star witness. Miller is found innocent and that night his scales play the "Hallelujah Chorus" from George Frederic Handel's "The Messiah." It's so noisy, Sykes can't get to sleep. Zany antics provide a lot of fun in the tradition of post–World War II British comedies. Songs: "Rock-a-Bye Baby" (traditional), "Rule, Brittania" (Thomas Augustine Arne), "Lizzie Borden" (Michael Brown). **p**, Michael Deeley; **d**, Peter Yates; **cast**, Eric Sykes, George Cole, Julia Foster, Jonathan Miller, Peggy Mount, Alison Leggatt, Mona Washbourne, Douglas Wilmer, Glyn Houston, Graham Crowden, Kenneth Farrington; **w**, N. (Norman) F. Simpson (based on his play); **c**, Denys Coop; **m**, Richard Rodney Bennett; **ed**, Peter Taylor; **prod d**, Reece Pemberton.

One Woman's Story ★★★ 1949; U.K.; 91m; Cineguild/UNIV; B/W; Drama; Children: Unacceptable; **DVD**; **VHS**. Taut drama sees Todd as a beautiful young woman marrying Rains, an older banker, for his money and achieving a place in society. She comes to find that those things aren't enough. After she goes on holiday to Switzerland and again meets Howard, a lover of nine years earlier, her feelings for him are rekindled. They have a brief affair before going back to their lives. Songs/Music: "Lover's Moon" (Richard Addinsell), "First Love and Last Love" (Addinsell, Joyce Grenfell), "Auld Lang Syne" (traditional). Sensuality prohibits viewing by children. **p**, Ronald Neame; **d**, David Lean; **cast**, Ann Todd, Claude Rains, Trevor Howard, Betty Ann Davies, Isabel Dean, Arthur Howard, Guido Lorraine, Marcel Poncin, Natasha Sokolova, Wilfrid Hyde-White; **w**, Eric Ambler, Lean, Stanley Haynes (based on the novel *The Passionate Friends* by H.G. Wells); **c**, Guy Green; **m**, Richard Addinsell; **ed**, Geoffrey Foot.

Onegin ★★★ 2000; U.K.; 106m; 7 Arts International/Samuel Goldwyn; Color; Drama/Romance; Children: Unacceptable (MPAA: R); **DVD**; **VHS**. Evgeny Onegin (Fiennes, who gives a masterful performance), a handsome, young, but callous aristocrat in 19th-century St. Petersburg, Russia, is restless and melancholy. He has been brought up to be rich and idle, but goes a giant step farther by becoming indifferent to everyone and everything around him. When he inherits a huge estate, he gives it to the serfs, not out of a concern for charity but because owning it might bore him, even though he just lost his own fortune at gambling tables. He can always sponge off friends, he reasons. His best friend, Stephens, who recently married a lovely young woman, Headey, introduces him to her slightly older sister, beautiful and innocent Tatyana (Tyler), who falls hopelessly in love with Fiennes. He returns her adoration by being aloof toward her, feeling he is not made for love and marriage. But he has heart enough to seek the sexual favors of Headey, and when Stephens learns of it, he challenges Fiennes to a duel with pistols. Fiennes kills his best friend and feels remorse, fleeing to Paris. Six years pass and he returns to St. Petersburg and sees Tyler at a ball. He now yearns for her, but she turns her back on him in a "serves you right, you oaf, you missed your chance" denouement. Songs: "Mir ist so wunderbar" (from the opera "Fidelio" by Ludwig van Beethoven), "Le Colporteau" (Sarah Gorby), "Gelder Rose in Bloom" (Isaak Dunayevsky, Julian Hope), "Mandshurian Kummut" (traditional), "Name Day Waltz" (traditional). Sensuality prohibits viewing by children. **p**, Simon Bosanquet, Ileen Maisel; **d**, Martha Fiennes; **cast**, Ralph Fiennes, Liv Tyler, Toby Stephens, Lena Headey, Martin Donovan, Alun Armstrong, Simon McBurney, Harriet Walter, Jason Watkins, Irene Worth, Francesca Annis; **w**, Peter Ettedgui, Michael Ignatieff (based on the poem "Yevgeny Onegin" by Alexander Pushkin); **c**, Remi Adefarasin; **m**, Magnus Fiennes; **ed**, Jim Clark; **prod d**, Jim Clay; **art d**,

Chris Seagers, Vera Zeliskaya; **set d**, Maggie Gray; **spec eff**, Dominic Tuohy, Charles Tait.

The Onion Field ★★★ 1979; U.S.; 122m; Black Marble Productions/AVCO Embassy Pictures; Color; Crime Drama; Children: Unacceptable (MPAA: R); **DVD**; **VHS**. Gritty and graphic in violence and language, this compelling tale, based on a true case, is told from the point of view of two Los Angeles police detectives, Savage and Danson. Where Savage is introspective and quiet, Danson is outgoing and friendly, and whose Scottish heritage surfaces whenever he jovially plays the bagpipes. Both work the Hollywood beat and, after they stop a car with two suspects, recidivist criminals Woods and Seales, the occupants surprisingly confront them with guns. They kidnap both cops and take them to an onion field near Bakersfield, where Danson is summarily and brutally murdered. Savage manages to escape, and both Woods and Seales are hunted down, captured and then put on trial. The police procedures in the capture of the killers is fascinatingly detailed, but the film bogs down somewhat when both are put on trial and seemingly endless court procedures tend to slow the pace. Meanwhile, Savage, who is guilt-ridden over the death of his partner, appears to be on the brink of a nervous breakdown. Further, the insidious and clever Woods, an old hand at the California court systems manipulates its procedures and notoriously lenient attitudes toward criminals to his own advantage. The two killers—each one accuses the other of murdering Danson—receive death sentences, but, through their seemingly endless appeals, both succeed in having their sentences reduced to life imprisonment. *Author's Note*: The actual case took place on March 9, 1963, when LAPD detectives Karl Hettinger (Savage) and Ian James Campbell (Danson) were abducted by armed criminals Greg Powell (Woods) and Jimmy Smith, aka Jimmy Youngblood (Seales), and where Campbell was murdered and Hettinger escaped to later identify the slayers. Smith, to the shock and angry objection of many, was released in 1982. He was returned to prison for parole violations and died behind bars on April 7, 2007, at the age of seventy-six. Powell was never released and, he, too, died in prison on August 12, 2012, at age seventy-nine. Hettinger suffered a nervous breakdown, and was released from the LAPD force in 1966 after being accused of shoplifting. He later worked in law enforcement but died prematurely of liver disease in 1994 at the age of fifty-nine. Wambaugh, who had once been a member of the LAPD, wrote the 1973 novel on which this grim tale is based. **p**, Walter Coblenz; **d**, Harold Becker; **cast**, John Savage, James Woods, Franklyn Seales, David Huffman, Ronny Cox, Christopher Lloyd, Ted Danson, Lillian Randolph, Priscilla Pointer, Diane Hull; **w**, Joseph Wambaugh (based on his book); **c**, Charles Rosher, Jr.; **m**, Eumir Deodato; **ed**, John W. Wheeler; **prod d**, Brian Eatwell; **art d**, Dick Goddard; **spec eff**, Phil Corey.

Only Angels Have Wings ★★★★ 1939; U.S.; 121m; COL; B/W; Adventure; Children: Cautionary; **DVD**; **VHS**. Grant and Arthur romantically clash and click in this excellent adventure tale from Hawks, one where Grant supervises a patchwork air service and where he has to order his pilots to dangerously fly over the Andes Mountains in Peru to deliver mail and freight. Arthur is drifting through South America when she meets affable pilot Beery and chums along with him to his base, but when she meets the tough Grant, she falls head over heels for the no-nonsense boss of the airline, which is owned by hotel and saloonkeeper Rumann and where veteran pilot Mitchell serves as Grant's right-hand man. All of the line's pilots, Carroll, Joslyn, Beery and others, are attracted to the fun-loving Arthur, except for Grant, who considers all women poison, although Arthur's precocious and alluring ways begin to break down his resistance to her feminine charms. Grant seems to melt after sitting down next to Arthur at a piano she is playing and joins with her in lively renditions of "Some of These Days" and "Peanut Vendor." Meanwhile, Grant is plagued by having to order his pilots to fly old planes much in need of repair; his life is further complicated when

Thomas Mitchell, Jean Arthur, Allyn Joslyn and Cary Grant in *Only Angels Have Wings,* **1939.**

Barthelmess, a washed-up pilot, arrives with his seductive wife, Hayworth, and Barthelmess begs Grant for a job flying for his airline. Grant tells Barthelmess that he cannot hire him because he has earlier caused the death of another pilot in an air race, that pilot being Mitchell's brother, and because of that tragic death, none of his pilots will associate with Barthelmess. Hayworth pleads for her husband and Grant relents, giving Barthelmess the dirtiest and most dangerous assignments, which he accepts without complaint. Hayworth, however, is an unfaithful wife and tries her utmost to seduce Grant. He almost succumbs to her alluring enticements, but then realizes that the woman he truly loves is the upright and open-hearted Arthur. Grant is then faced with a dilemma in that he has a hazardous flight to assign but has no available pilot and decides to undertake the mission himself. Realizing that Grant is in great jeopardy, his dear friend Mitchell, who has been grounded by the protective Grant because of his failing eyesight, takes the plane into the air and is killed. Grant has all the while coldly ignored the deaths of previous pilots, but Mitchell's demise shakes him and Arthur sees that Grant is human after all. Grant resumes his duties, but it is evident that Arthur will be at his side throughout the perilous adventures to come. This kind of aviation film was director Hawks' meat in that he was an accomplished pilot and dedicated to the advancement of aviation (he would make a stirring film about of a single U.S. Army Air Force B-17 bomber four years later, **Air Force**, 1943, to promote the use of bombers in WWII). He does an exceptional job of balancing the love scenes between Arthur, Hayworth and Grant and the dangerous action involved in the flights made by the pilots, particularly when flying (in miniature planes) through the snow-capped Andes Mountains, where Barry, occupying a hut atop a mountain peak, guides them through fog-bound areas, which are also occupied by giant flying condors who obstruct and bring about crashes of those flights. Grant and Arthur are splendid together, as they would be four years later when making **The Talk of the Town**, 1943, with Ronald Colman. Songs: "Push 'Em Up" (Howard Jackson), "Gwine to Rune All Night" (Stephen Foster), "The Arkansas Traveler" (Sanford Faulkner), "The Peanut Vendor" (1931; music: Moise Simons; lyrics: L. Wolfe Gilbert, Marion Sunshine), and "Some of These Days" (1910; Shelton Brooks). *Author's Note*: This film liberally takes elements from the plotlines and characterizations of several previous produced aviation films, including **Night Flight**, 1933, **Ceiling Zero**, 1936 (directed by Hawks) and, especially **Flight from Glory**, 1937. Barthelmess' redemption from cowardice and Mitchell's heroic sacrifice although physically disabled is repeated by two other characters appearing in **The Flying Tigers**, 1942. The ménage á troi relationship between Arthur, Hayworth and Grant is almost a duplication of the tangled romance exhibited in **Red Dust**, 1932, where Mary Astor and Jean Harlow vie for the attentions of the brawny Clark Gable. Grant told

Gregory Peck and Barbara Payton in *Only the Valiant*, 1951.

this author that "Hawks was able to convince audiences that they were seeing a lot more than what they got by having all the aerial scenes shot in miniature, but they were done so convincingly that viewers thought they were seeing the real thing in that picture. He shot the entire film with live action players inside a few interiors—a saloon, some shabby rooms in a broken-down hotel and some clapboard offices I use to run that broken-down airline. He was a real genius at making much with very little." This film marked the comeback for silent screen idol Barthelmess, who had not appeared in a film for three years (since **Spy of Napoleon**, 1936), but, according to Hawks' remarks to this author, "he did not have much left in him. Dick [Barthelmess] had come a long way since his days with D. W. Griffith in **Way Down East** [1920] and he had a plum role as the disgraced pilot who has to prove his courage and does. Dick, however, was stoic as stone in his role, the most complex part in the picture, and, no matter how much I pushed him to show some emotion, he remained dispassionate. I think that was his last significant role in a feature film. Thank God, I had Cary [Grant] and Jean [Arthur], who carried that picture in their capable hands. Cary could do any kind of picture and do it well, from comedy to drama. I never had a single problem with him in all of the many pictures we did together. Not one. And that tells you a lot." (Hawks also directed Grant in **Bringing Up Baby**, 1938; **His Girl Friday**, 1940; **I Was a Male War Bride**, 1949; and **Monkey Business**, 1952.) Hawks did include in the original release some segments of actual aerial action performed by legendary stunt pilot Paul Mantz and photographed by Elmer Dyer. Arthur told this author that **Only Angels Have Wings** was "one of my favorite films—I got to play the piano and sing with Cary [Grant]. Now what else could a gal ask for?" **p&d**, Howard Hawks; **cast**, Cary Grant, Jean Arthur, Richard Barthelmess, Rita Hayworth, Thomas Mitchell, Allyn Joslyn, Sig Rumann, Victor Kilian, John Carroll, Donald "Red" Barry, Noah Beery, Jr., Candy Candido, Robert Sterling, Pat Flaherty, Pat West, James Millican; **w**, Jules Furthman and (not credited) Eleanore Griffin, William Rankin (based on the story "Plane from Barranca" by Hawks (not credited); **c**, Joseph Walker; **m**, Dimitri Tiomkin, Manuel Maciste, M. W. Stoloff; **ed**, Viola Lawrence; **art d**, Lionel Banks; **spec eff**, Roy Davidson.

Only the Valiant ★★★ 1951; U.S.; 105m; William Cagney Productions; WB; B/W; Western; Children: Cautionary; **DVD**; **VHS**. Peck's outstanding performance as a rugged and dedicated cavalry officer sustains interest and often fascination throughout this unusual western. He is assigned to take a group of misfit troopers to a pass to block an impending Apache attack against an undermanned fort until a relief force of 400 men can arrive. To accomplish his mission, Peck selects the most rebellious and unruly men, deserters, slackers, cowards and outright psy-

chopaths, all of whom despise him and would like to see him dead, but, after they are put through some rigorous training by Peck, they all realize that none of them will survive without his indefatigable leadership. These include Bond, a ruthless, alcoholic corporal, and troopers Chaney, Brand and Brodie, along with scout Corey and an officer, Young. Further antagonizing the relationship between Peck and Young is the presence of the sensuous blonde, Payton, who is romantically involved with Young, but who gravitates toward Peck to create friction between Young and Peck. After Peck takes this group to defend the pass, he sends Young on a near-suicide mission, one that everyone thinks he should have performed himself, and it is concluded that he has done this to rid himself of a romantic rival. All soon learn that this is not the case and, after the Apaches attack, they see Peck display his true courage, an attack that leaves only three among the defenders alive. Director Douglas does a fine job in handling the action and developing his characters. In addition to Peck, Bond is a standout as the boozy non-commissioned officer, and Young, too, is exceptional as a young officer, who believes he is being victimized by his commander for loving the same woman his commander covets. Song: "Little Brown Jug" (Joseph Winner). *Author's Note*: Peck was reluctant to do this film, stating to this author that "I was under contract to David O. Selznick and when he ran into financial troubles [after recent Selznick releases **The Paradine Case**, 1948, and **Portrait of Jennie**, 1949, failed to see considerable box office returns] he began selling off people like myself who were under contract to him. [Selznick sold Peck to Warner Brothers for $150,000 and Peck received an additional $60,000 for his performance in **Only the Valiant**.] I did not like the script for **Only the Valiant**, but I got my marching orders and did my best with what I had to work with. Fortunately, there were many fine character actors in that picture who did outstanding work and made my job a lot easier. The tragedy of that picture was Barbara Payton, who had been discovered by James Cagney, and she was featured in some of the pictures produced by his producing company that was run by his brother William Cagney and who produced **Only the Valiant**. Barbara was an emotionally high-strung young woman and it proved that she did not manage her private life well. She later got into a lot of notorious situations. When her Hollywood career collapsed, she turned to alcohol and the street life. She was truly a Hollywood casualty of the first order." Payton, later in life, turned to prostitution, living on park benches, mercilessly beaten by pimps, and routinely arrested for solicitation until she moved back to San Diego to live with her parents and where she died prematurely of heart and liver failure on May 8, 1967, at age thirty-nine. **p**, William Cagney; **d**, Gordon Douglas; **cast**, Gregory Peck, Barbara Payton, Ward Bond, Gig Young, Lon Chaney, Jr., Neville Brand, Jeff Corey, Warner Anderson, Steve Brodie, Terry Kilburn, Art Baker, Michael Ansara, Nana Bryant; **w**, Edmund H. North, Harry Brown (based on a novel by Charles Marquis Warren); **c**, Lionel Lindon; **m**, Franz Waxman; **ed**, Walter Hannemann, Robert S. Seiter; **prod d**, Wiard Ihnen; **set d**, Armor E. Marlowe.

Only Two Can Play ★★★ 1962; U.K.; 106m; Vale Film Productions/Kingsley-International; B/W; Comedy; Children: Unacceptable; **DVD**; **VHS**. The brilliant Sellers is a minor staff librarian in this entertaining comedy. He is bored by his job in a small Welsh town and is henpecked by his wife, Maskell. Things heat up when Zetterling, the wife of local councilor Huntley, falls for him. They try to consummate their affair, but keep getting interrupted or side-tracked by many humorous situations. Nothing goes right for them. Sellers writes and publishes a newspaper review that praises a stage production that never takes place in that the theater burns down before the play goes on. Sellers and Zetterling take a car ride and park in a lover's lane where a policeman and her husband find them and think they have had sex together, but they are innocent. Meanwhile, Maskell has an affair with an old flame, Attenborough, a poet who wrote the play that Sellers reviewed. Zetterling tells Sellers she can use her influence to get him promoted to the position of head librarian, but he is afraid of predatory·women like her and declines, becoming instead a mobile librarian. This delightful British comedy has Sellers, one of the British comic greats, exhibiting his many talents and versatility. Sexual situations prohibit viewing by children. **p**, Leslie Gilliat; **d**, Sidney Gilliat; **cast**, Peter Sellers, Mai Zetterling, Virginia Maskell, Kenneth Griffiths, Raymond Huntley, David Davies, Maudie Edwards, Richard Attenborough, Meg Wynn Owen; **w**, Bryan Forbes (based on the novel *That Uncertain Feeling* by Kingsley Amis); **c**, John Wilcox; **m**, Richard Rodney Bennett; **ed**, Thelma Connell; **art d**, Albert Witherick; **set d**, Robert Cartwright.

Only When I Laugh ★★★ 1981; U.S.; 120m; COL; Color; Comedy/Drama; Children: Unacceptable (MPAA: R); **DVD**; **VHS**. Mason, a divorced actress, returns from a ninety-day stay at a hospital for alcoholics, supposedly recovered, as she tries to improve her relationship with her teenage daughter, McNichol, whom she has neglected for years. Her best friends are a gay actor, Coco, and wisecracking Hackett. Mason's former lover, Dukes, writes a new play for her return to Broadway that is based on their troubled relationship. That puts too much pressure on her and she returns to the bottle. Despite this setback, Mason mends her relations with McNichol. Neither the film nor the play upon which it was based constitutes Neil Simon's best efforts, but Mason (Simon's wife in real life) gives an Oscar-nominated best actress performance that vindicates this film, and it is her outstanding performance that sustains interest throughout. Songs: "Heart" (Richard Adler, Jerry Ross), "Machine Gun" (Jimi Hendrix). Sexual themes prohibit viewing by children. **p**, Roger M. Rothstein, Neil Simon; **d**, Glenn Jordan; **cast**, Marsha Mason, Kristy McNichol, James Coco, Joan Hackett, David Dukes, John Bennett Perry, Guy Boyd, Ed Moore, Byron Webster, Peter Coffield, Kevin Bacon; **w**, Simon (based on his play "The Gingerbread Lady"); **c**, David M. Walsh (Metrocolor); **m**, David Shire; **ed**, John Wright; **prod d**, Albert Brenner; **art d**, David Haber; **set d**, Marvin March; **spec eff**, Alan E. Lorimer.

Only You ★★★ 1994; U.S.; 115m; COL; Color; Comedy/Romance; Children: Unacceptable (MPAA: PG); **DVD;VHS**. Zany romantic comedy sees Tomei as a Boston school teacher, who believes soul mates can be united if they can only find each other. This conviction is rooted to her memory that recalls how, when she was eleven years old, she and her brother, Stevens, used a Ouija board and it spelled out the name of the man she believes she is destined to love, D-A-M-O-N B-R-A-D-L-E-Y. A few years later at a carnival, a fortune-teller says she sees that name in her crystal ball and Tomei is now convinced a man with that name will be her future intended. Fourteen years later she is still looking for Damon Bradley while engaged to a dull podiatrist. Ten days before they are to marry, she gets a phone call that her fiancé's high school classmate, Damon Bradley, is going to fly to Venice, Italy. She rushes to the airport, but misses him and the plane, so she and a friend, Hunt, take the next plane to Italy in hopes of finding him. They go to Venice and she meets a young American, Downey Jr., who says his name is Damon Bradley. They spend a night together and fall in love. Then he reveals that his real name is Peter Wright. Tomei is confused and heartbroken, so she leaves him and prepares to return home. Now Tomei learns that the Damon Bradley she has been searching for is at a hotel in Positano. She goes there and meets a good-looking playboy, Zane, who turns out to be a womanizer. It all ends when Stevens admits to Tomei that the whole thing about the Ouija board spelling out the name of her future husband was a prank and he paid the fortune-teller to go along with the deception. Tomei and Stevens are at the airport in Rome when they hear Damon Bradley being paged. Tomei goes to the information desk and finally meets Damon. But he is not especially handsome and Tomei is not attracted to him. She then realizes it is Peter Wright (Downey Jr.) that she loves and they embrace and kiss and board the plane for home, planning to marry. Songs: "Once in a Lifetime" (Michael Bolton, Diane Warren, Walter Afanasieff); "Only You and You Alone" (Buck Ram, Andre Rand); "On the Beautiful Blue Danube" (Jo-

James Coco and Marsha Mason in *Only When I Laugh*, 1981.

hann Strauss, Jr.); "Some Enchanted Evening" (Richard Rodgers, Oscar Hammerstein II); "Swing City," Sloe Gin Fizz" (Richard Iacona); "O Sole Mio" (Eduardo Di Capua, Giovanni Capurro, Alfredo Mazzucchi); "Hallelujah Chorus" from "The Messiah" (George Frederic Handel); "Libiamo Ne' Lieti Calici" from the opera "La Traviata" by Giuseppe Verdi); "Amore Contro" and "Senza Perderci Di Vista" (Eros Ramazzotti, Adelio Cogliati, Piero Cassano); "Overture" from the opera "La Forza Del Destino" by Giuseppe Verdi); "Livin' in the Streets" (Kirk Whalum, Ricky Lawson). Sensuality and gutter language prohibit viewing by children. **p**, Norman Jewison, Robert N. Fried, Charles Mulvehill, Cary Woods; **d**, Jewison; **cast**, Marisa Tomei, Robert Downey, Jr., Bonnie Hunt, Joaquim De Almeida, Fisher Stevens, Billy Zane, Adam LeFevre, John Benjamin Hickey, Siobhan Fallon, Phyllis Newman; **w**, Diane Drake; **c**, Sven Nykvist; **m**, Rachel Portman; **ed**, Stephen Rivkin; **prod d**, Luciana Arrighi; **art d**, Maria Teresa Barbasso, Stephano Ortolani; **set d**, Ian Whittaker; **spec eff**, Dennis Dion.

Open City ★★★★ 1946; Italy; 100m; Excelsa Film/Arthur Mayer & Joseph Burstyn; B/W; War Drama; Children: Unacceptable; **DVD**; **VHS**. Pantheon director Rossellini shocked and impressed the film world when making this extraordinary film that introduced what was termed neorealism in motion pictures, a documentary style where all of his scenes were dramatized but filmed with such realism that viewers believed that they were actually viewing real-life action. That emotionally disturbing action takes place in Rome while that city is occupied by German troops and where, between September 1943 and June 1944 (when American and British troops liberated the city), Italian partisans fight street battles with the Nazis in an effort to rid themselves of their oppressors. Made up of several stories, the first of these features Magnani, one of Italy's great actresses, who is pregnant, her lover belonging to the resistance and who is seized by Germans. She begs the Nazis to release her man, but he is thrown onto a truck heading for prison. Magnani frantically races after that truck and is shot down in the street by German troops. Another character, Fabrizi, is a priest who aids the partisans in escaping the clutches of the Nazis, but his undercover role with the resistance is exposed and he is summarily condemned to death, taken to a field where he is forced to sit in a chair and where an Italian firing squad is ordered to shoot him. Its members do not want to take the priest's life and all of them purposely miss their target. A German officer then goes to Fabrizi and fires a lethal bullet into his head. Feist, who, like almost all of the other actors in this film, was not a leading player until making this film, rivets while playing the German officer in charge of interrogating Italians suspected of being partisans. He employs a number of high-priced Italian prostitutes who entice suspects into his lair and then conducts his examinations, pretending to be sympathetic

Giovanna Galletti and Harry Feist in *Open City*, 1946.

to the Italians but insidiously scheming to eliminate as many suspects as he can. He moves from one luxurious room filled with officers and prostitutes enjoying classical music and sipping expensive liquor to a stark interrogation room where he grills suspects and then sends them into yet another room where they are tortured, their fingernails torn out and their flesh burned until either they confess or pass out or die. Feist presents the consummate portrait of evil, a man with the airs of a civilized human being, who routinely conducts the unconscionable acts of a savage beast. The film is basically grim and offers little hope, but is so naturally and realistically shown that it became a classic after its release. Song: "Mallinata Fiorentina" (1941; music: Giovanni D'Anzi; lyrics: Galdieri). *Author's Note*: Rossellini made the film on a shoe-string budget, hiring music hall actors Magnani and Fabrizi at slave wages and paying next to nothing to all the others going before his cameras. His budget was so limited that he could not afford to view rushes and saw the film only after it was completed. It was only then that Rossellini could afford to edit the raw film and even then he was severely restricted in his ability to make the film cohesive. The final film seems so crudely made that it appears to be a home-made film that shows persons and events in reallife, making it all the more fascinating and revealing. The so-called neorealism attached to this work is the result of abject poverty and not any intentional creativity on the part of its filmmaker as Rossellini himself later admitted. **p&d**, Roberto Rossellini; **cast**, Anna Magnani, Aldo Fabrizi, Marcello Pagliero, Maria Michi, Harry Feist, Vito Annichiarico, Nando Bruno, Giovanna Galletti, Francesco Grandjacquet, Eduardo Passarelli; **w**, Sergio Amidei, Federico Fellini, Rossellini (based on a story by Amidei, Alberto Consiglio); **c**, Ubaldo Arata; **m**, Renzo Rossellini; **ed**, Eraldo Da Roma; **prod d**, Rosario Megna.

Open Range ★★★★ 2003; U.S.; 139m; Touchstone Pictures/Buena Vista; Color; Western; Children: Unacceptable (MPAA: R); **BD**; **DVD**; **VHS**. Gritty and realistic, this fine western sees Duvall driving his herd of cattle across an open range and where his cattle free graze before reaching their destination. Assisting Duvall are three cowboys, Costner, a one-time fast gun who fought in the Civil War and is guilt-ridden over his gunslinger days; Benrubi, a giant but gentle drifter; and Luna, a feisty youth. After Duvall and his men make camp, Benrubi is sent to a local town to get supplies, but he is waylaid by the local sheriff, Russo, and his deputies and is beaten senseless and thrown into jail. This has been done on orders of the local cattle baron, Gambon, an Irish immigrant who rules the area like a tyrant, enforcing his edicts with a large gang of cowboys and gunmen, including gunslinger Coates. When Benrubi fails to return to the camp, Duvall and Costner ride into town where they meet Gambon and Russo at the local jail, where Gambon orders Duvall to

move his herd out of the territory as he will not tolerate free grazers using the open range which he considers private territory for his own cattle. He then allows them to take the badly beaten Benrubi back to camp. When Duvall, who bristles under such orders, takes too much time in moving on, some of his cattle are rustled and he and Costner ride out to investigate. They track down several of Gambon's men and beat them before running them off. Returning to the camp, they find that it has been raided and that Benrubi is dead and Luna critically wounded. They take Luna to the town to be treated by local doctor, McDermott, and they also meet his attractive sister, Bening, to whom Costner is attracted. While the boy is being treated for his wounds, Costner and Bening establish a friendly relationship that later blossoms into romance. In town that night, Costner and Duvall are befriended by livery stable owner Jeter, who tells them that sheriff Russo has several men waiting in hiding to either arrest or shoot them. After encountering Russo in a local restaurant, Costner and Duvall invade Russo's jail, binding him and putting him to sleep with chloroform Duvall has taken from McDermott's office. After Russo's deputies arrive, Costner and Duvall subdue them in the same manner. Duvall and Costner then resolve to face Gambon and his entire gang in a final showdown. Costner meets with Bening once more, telling her, at Duvall's instigation, that he loves her, and she tells him that she will be waiting for him after he confronts Gambon. Both men then purchase cigars and some expensive imported candy, as if these treats are to be their last on earth, and then wait for the cattle baron and his men behind Jeter's barn, where the friendly Jeter acts as a lookout while they enjoy smoking their cigars and eating their candy. Gambon arrives with his men and frees Russo and his deputies, but they are still suffering from the effects of the chloroform so Gambon and his men then go in search of Duvall and Costner. While he sends some of his men searching through the byways of the town for Duvall and Costner, Gambon leads a group of his men, along with Coates, down the main street, and they are soon met by Duvall and Costner. Gambon tells them that they are "dead men" unless they clear out, but Duvall shouts back that they "are not much for running from cowards." Costner then begins to walk toward Coates, asking him: "Are you the one who killed our friend?" Coates grins and says: "That's right. I enjoyed it. And I shot the boy, too." Without another word, Costner draws his gun, aims it at Coates and, before the gunman can respond, shoots him dead by firing a bullet into his head. A gun battle then ensues with Duvall and Costner either killing Gambon's men or driving them off while severely wounding Gambon, who flees. The battle continues through the town (one of the most realistic on-going gunfights ever put on film) where Gambon's men hunt Costner and Duvall as they take refuge in buildings, but these gunmen are shot and killed with the help of Jeter. Gambon, meanwhile, has joined corrupt sheriff Russo and his men and they have captured Luna, who has staggered into town to help Costner and Duvall, threatening to kill Luna unless Costner and Duvall give up their guns, which they are not about to do. They confront Gambon, Russo and his deputies on the street, and, by now, the townspeople are on their side, carrying weapons. Bening, who has arrived to aid Luna, and who has fallen to the ground, tells Russo, who stands over the stricken boy that Russo is "a disgrace." He replies: "I know it. That's just the way it is." Meanwhile, Gambon threatens to kill any of the townspeople who side with Duvall and Costner, saying that he and his men will kill Luna unless they drop their guns, "starting with the gun hand," meaning the deadly Costner. Gunfire then erupts when one of Russo's deputies fires at Costner. Costner kills him, and the townspeople join with Costner and Duvall in unleashing a fusillade of bullets at Gambon, Russo and his men. Russo and all of his deputies are either killed or driven off while the wounded Gambon takes refuge in the jail. Costner is wounded in the leg during the exchange, and Duvall charges into the jail to exchange fire with Gambon, mortally wounding him. The battle over, Duvall and Costner begin to ride away, taking their herd, but Costner by this time has cemented his relationship with Bening and they plan to marry when he returns. Costner, who carefully directs this authentic-looking, action-packed and beautifully photographed film, is superb as the taciturn gunman turned cowboy looking to find roots; Duvall is also outstanding as the good-hearted and wise trail boss. Bening, too, delivers a powerful performance of a woman of the plains who has been waiting for years for the right man to come along, and Gambon, Russo and others in the fine cast are standouts as the evildoers and the townsfolk. Song: "Holding All My Love for You" (Michael Kamen, Julianna Raye). *Author's Note*: This film was shot at Stoney Indian Reservation in Alberta, Canada, and Costner had Duvall in mind for the role of the trail herd boss from the beginning, giving him top billing. Duvall undertook the role with relish as he favored westerns, but he broke six ribs when falling off a horse while training for the part. Costner hand-picked cinematographer Muro as he had worked with Costner on a previous and very successful western, **Dances with Wolves**, 1990. The town cost more than $1 million to build in a remote area with an additional $40,000 in cost to build a road to the shooting site, the overall budget exceeding $22 million. The film was a box office success, returning more than $68 million worldwide in its initial release. **p**, Kevin Costner, Jake Eberts, David Valdes; **d**, Costner; **cast**, Robert Duvall, Kevin Costner, Annette Bening, Michael Gambon, Michael Jeter, Diego Luna, James Russo, Abraham Benrubi, Dean McDermott, Kim Coates, Peter MacNeill; **w**, Craig Storper (based on the novel *The Open Range Men* by Lauran Paine); **c**, James (J. Michael) Muro; **m**, Michael Kamen; **ed**, Michael J. Duthie, Miklos Wright; **prod d**, Gae Buckley; **art d**, Gary Myers; **set d**, Mary-Lou Storey; **spec eff**, Neil Trifunovich, David J. Negron, Jr.

Open Water ★★★ 2004; U.S.; 79m; Plunge Pictures/Lions Gate; Color; Horror; Children: Unacceptable (MPAA: R); **DVD**; **VHS**. This dire horror tale is based on the true story about an American couple, Tom and Eileen Lonergan, played by Travis and Ryan, who accompanied a group of twenty persons on a scuba diving trip to Australia's Great Barrier Reef in 1998. They were accidentally left behind when the crew of the dive boat they are on fails to take an accurate head count before leaving. Alone in the sea and treading water to stay afloat, the couple keep hoping for the boat to come back for them, but meanwhile try to keep themselves safe, especially when they see sharks swimming nearby. Ryan gets a small bite from a shark, but doesn't realize it under his neoprene wet suit. Then Travis gets a larger bite by a shark and Ryan fears he is going into shock. They keep floating in their wetsuits and, as night falls, they must try to keep afloat during a storm, while sharks return and attack Travis, killing him. The next morning, the couple's belongings in a duffle bag still onboard the boat are found by one of the crew and he realizes that the couple has been left behind. Back in the open sea, Ryan had been holding on to her husband overnight until in the morning she realizes he is dead. She releases her hold on him and sharks attack his body in a feeding frenzy. Ryan sees sharks coming for her, so she removes her scuba gear including her diving mask and goes underwater, preferring to drown than be alive when the sharks attack her. The rescuers are too late and find a newly caught shark with a waterproof diving camera inside its stomach. This is a grim tale that offers no hope at its gruesome end, but it is so well produced that it serves as a dramatic warning to those that might undertake the same kind of seagoing outing. Songs: "Isa Lei" (Fijian Farewell Song, traditional), "Hill & Gully Rider" (Jamaican folk song), "Lakonmet Dance" (Rameau Poleon, Henry Sinais, Frances Ashdale), "The Glad Reunion Day" (Adjer M. Pace), "Pump Me Up" (Edwin Yearwood), "Jesus Promised Me a Home Over There" (gospel song, anonymous), "I Ain't Got Long" (Peter Elliot), "Ni Sa Bula" (Fiji folk song), "Yendisare Aimando" (Padaun Suara Mara). Gutter language, nudity and terror prohibit viewing by children. **p**, Laura Lau; **d&w**, Chris Kentis; **cast**, Blanchard Ryan, Daniel Travis, Saul Stein, Michael Williamson, Cristina Zenaro, Jon Charles, Estelle Lau, Steve Lemme; **c**, Laura Lau, Kentis; **m**, Graeme Revell; **ed**, Kentis; **spec eff**, Haven Cousins.

Operation Crossbow ★★★ 1965; U.K.; 115m; MGM; Color; Spy

Blanchard Ryan and Daniel Travis in *Open Water*, 2004.

Drama; Children: Unacceptable; **DVD**; **VHS**. Taut espionage tale sees British agents penetrating the secret German operations that launched the devastating V-1 and V-2 rockets attacking London during the last stages of WWII. After British spy Johnson discovers these operations, Peppard, Kemp and Courtenay are sent on a suicide missions to locate the rocket bases and try to destroy them. All three agents secretly parachute into Germany where they impersonate foreign nationals who have worked on the rockets, with Courtenay and Peppard taking refuge in a small hotel run by Palmer, who is working with British intelligence. Courtenay is exposed and interrogated, but he refuses to reveal any information and is summarily executed. Peppard is then confronted by Loren, the wife of the man he is impersonating, but, after she assures him that she will tell nothing, he allows her to live. Such passionate compunctions are not for Palmer, who realizes that Loren poses a serious threat and kills her. Peppard then manages to gain access to one of the rocket bases where he joins Kemp in contacting Allied bombers that raid the area and destroy the place in a devastating bombardment that takes the lives of Peppard and Kemp. Top-draw action is supplemented with captured Nazi footage on the rockets. The direction from Anderson is superior as is the script, and Peppard, Kemp, Courtenay and Palmer give exceptional performances as the Allied spies. Loren, however, who is provided only for sex appeal and got top billing (her husband, Carlo Ponti, produced) has little to do and appears only briefly in the film. *Author's Note*: The film did not do well at the box office, producers believing that the word "operation" in the title might be misleading, suggesting that the film was a medical story, which was not a popular genre in that decade. The title was changed to **The Great Spy Mission** and the film re-released under that title, but with about the same box office results. A fascinating subplot involves German aviatrix Hanna Reitsch (1912-1979), an ardent Nazi, who tested some of the rockets almost at the cost of her life, and who is effectively enacted by Rueting. Reitsch was a fanatical admirer of Adolf Hitler (1889-1945) and flew a small Storch plane into Berlin just as Soviet troops were about to capture the city, visiting with Hitler in the last few days of his life and promising to fly him to safety. He declined, but since Reitsch was one of his favorites, he offered to share his intended fate with her by giving her a hoarded cyanide tablet with which to take her life. She, instead, flew out of Berlin and was later captured by American troops. Following the war, Reitsch continued her career in aviation, setting many records (particularly in gliders) that stand to this day. **p**, Carlo Ponti; **d**, Michael Anderson; **cast**: Sophia Loren, George Peppard, Trevor Howard, John Mills, Richard Johnson, Tom Courtenay, Jeremy Kemp, Anthony Quayle, Lilli Palmer, Paul Henreid, Helmut Dantine, Richard Todd, Sylvia Syms, Barbara Rueting; **w**, Richard Imrie, Derry Quinn, Ray Rigby (based on a story by Duilio Coletti and Vittoriano Petrilli), **c**, Irwin Hillier (Panavision;

Scott Forbes and Ward Bond in *Operation Pacific*, 1951.

Metrocolor); **m**, Ron Goodwin; **ed**, Ernest Walter; **art d**, Elliot Scott; **spec eff**, Tom Howard.

Operation; Daybreak ★★★ 1975; U.S.; Czechoslovakia; Yugoslavia; 118m; Howard R. Schuster/WB; Color; Spy Drama; Children: Unacceptable (MPAA: PG); **DVD**; **VHS**. Exciting and provocative tale sees a team of Czech resistance fighters successfully assassinate the dreaded Nazi SS leader Reinhard Heydrich (1904-1942), essayed by Diffring, who was known as "the Hangman" after he sent many political enemies to the gallows as well as conducting widespread persecution of the Czech people, which he dominated as a tyrant after the Nazis took over the country. Bottoms, Andrews and Shaw are three Czech resistance fighters who have fled to England and they are trained in the ways of espionage and sabotage with the purpose of killing Heydrich. Following their training, all three parachute into German-occupied Czechoslovakia and they make plans to kill the tyrant. The three track Diffring and narrowly miss killing him until they determine the route his car takes each day to his office and wait for it along its route, one firing at Diffring and his driver, the other finally tossing a bomb into his car, which disables the auto and mortally wounds Diffring, who dies a short time later when doctors fail to save his life. The Nazis capture Shaw, and to protect his wife and family, he identifies Bottoms and Andrews, who are tracked down to the basement of a Prague church where they battle German troops. After running out of ammunition, both men, rather than surrender to the Germans, commit suicide. The film is carefully helmed by director Gilbert, who fully develops his complex characters, and Bottoms, Andrews and Shaw render top-flight performances. *Author's Note*: The film is faithful to the events dealing with Heydrich's assassination in Prague in June 1942, for which the Nazis exacted a terrible revenge by wiping out the town of Lidice and killing all of its male inhabitants, from teenage boys to old men. The three Czech resistance fighters profiled in this film were the actual members of the team that assassinated Heydrich, these being Joseph Gabčík (1912-1942), played by Andrews; Jan Kubis (1913-1942), essayed by Bottoms, both Gabčík and Kubis dying in the Prague church after being betrayed by Karel Curda (1911-1947), played by Shaw, who was rewarded by the Nazis, becoming a member of their secret police and, with a new identity, evaded detection until after WWII when he was arrested, tried for treason and executed. Heydrich has been profiled in many films, notably by Hans Heinrich von Twardowski in Fritz Lang's **Hangmen Also Die!**, 1943, and by John Carradine in **Hitler's Madman**, 1943; for additional films about Heydrich, see the Subject Index, Fictional and Historical Characters in Volume II of this work. For additional information and many images of Heydrich and his assassination, see my two-volume work: *The Great Pictorial History of World Crime*, Volume I (History, Inc., 2004; pages 134-138). **p**, Carter De Haven; **d**, Lewis Gilbert; **cast**: Timothy Bottoms, Martin Shaw, Joss Ackland, Nicola Pagett, Anthony Andrews, Anton Diffring, Diana Coupland, Ronald Radd, Kim Fortune; **w**, Ronald Harwood (based on the novel *Seven Men at Daybreak* by Alan Burgess); **c**, Henri Decae (Technicolor); **m**, David Hentschel; **ed**, Thelma Connell; **art d**, William McCrow, Bob Kulic; **spec eff**, Roy Whybrow.

Operation Mad Ball ★★★ 1957; U.S.; 105m; COL; B/W; Comedy; Children: Acceptable; **DVD**. Lemmon provides a lot of laughs in this outing where he is serving in France after World War II (1939-1945), as a U.S. Army private. He wants to put on a secret "Mad Ball" at an off-limits hotel for the nurses to build up morale at a U.S. surgical hospital that is closing, and also help him win the affections of Grant, a beautiful nurse. She isn't fooled by a fake X-ray he shows her and he goes to the ball alone. At the ball, he sees Grant with his company colonel, O'Connell, but she changes her heart about Lemmon and saves the last dance for him. Kovacs, television comic genius, makes his film debut in this film as a security captain. Songs: "Mad Ball" (Fred Karger, Richard Quine), "Let's Fall in Love" (Harold Arlen), "La Marseillaise" (Claude Joseph Rouget de Lisle), "In the Mood" (Joe Garland), "Pennies from Heaven" (Arthur Johnston). **p**, Jed Harris; **d**, Richard Quine; **cast**, Jack Lemmon, Ernie Kovacs, Kathryn Grant, Arthur O'Connell, Mickey Rooney, Dick York, James Darren, Roger Smith, William Leslie, Sheridan Comerate; **w**, Harris, Blake Edwards, Arthur Carter (based on the play by Carter); **c**, Charles Lawton Jr.; **m**, George Duning; **ed**, Charles Nelson; **art d**, Robert Boyle; **set d**, William Kiernan, Bill Calvert.

Operation Pacific ★★★ 1951; U.S.; 111m; WB; B/W; War Drama; Children: Unacceptable; **DVD**; **VHS**. Solid WWII Navy yarn has Wayne serving on board a U.S. submarine in the Pacific. He is shown emerging from a jungle carrying a baby and later takes it to a hospital where Neal, a fetching nurse, takes care of it. This is not their first meeting in that they have earlier been married, but divorced when she lost a baby in childbirth. Wayne wants to renew his relationship with her, but Neal is hesitant, even though Wayne admits that their breakup was due to his own behavior. She is meanwhile courted by flier Carey, although Wayne is on her mind when he sets sail to sea once more, serving as the executive officer under Bond, who is Carey's father. When the sub sees action, it comes under attack, and Bond, wounded topside, orders the boat to submerge, even though he knows he is sacrificing his life. Wayne follows orders, but is guilt-ridden for losing Bond, who was a father figure to him. He later saves Carey after his plane is shot down and he is wallowing in the sea, an effort that somehow relieves Wayne's conscience over Bond's loss. When both men return to base, they meet Neal again on separate occasions, and Neal, though still in love with Wayne, finds excuses not to see him again until her superior, Brissac, tells her: "You married him for what he is and then tried to make something else out of him, but you couldn't." In the end, Neal realizes that her future is with Wayne and they reunite at the finish. Good action and many fine dramatic moments between Wayne and Neal sustain interest throughout in this well-crafted war tale, where a strong supporting cast provides many talented performances. Songs: "We Watch the Skyways," "It Can't Be Wrong" (Max Steiner), "Eternal Father, Strong to Save (The Navy Hymn)" (music: John B. Dykes; lyrics: William Whiting), "Don't Give Up the Ship" (Harry Warren), "How Many Hearts Have You Broken (With Those Great Big Beautiful Eyes)" (music: Al Kaufman), "What Can You Do with a Drunken Sailor?" (traditional), "Columbia, Gem of the Ocean" (1843; music and lyrics: Thomas a Becket). *Author's Note*: Bond's heroic character in this film is based upon the exploits of U.S. Commander Howard Gilmore, who commanded the U.S. submarine *Growler* that attacked a Japanese convoy on the night of February 6-7, 1943, ramming an enemy warship. Wounded while on deck, Gilmore ordered the submarine to submerge, even though he knew it would cost him his life, an act for which he posthumously received the U.S. Congressional Medal of Honor. Wayne recalled that heroic act when talking with this author about this film, stating: "Most viewers probably thought we made up that scene, but Ward [Bond] plays a real-life Navy hero, who saved his crew by ordering his boat to submerge while he was wounded and unable to get through the hatch. It was great people like that who won that terrible war for us. I thought about that fine man while we were making that picture and he has never been out of my memory." Neal told this author that "appearing with Duke [Wayne] in **Operation Pacific** was a treat for me—what a professional and one of the nicest men I ever met. We are a separated couple in that picture, where I play a nurse. Fifteen years later, I play a nurse taking care of Duke in **In Harm's Way** [1965], which was also about the U.S. Navy in World War Two and some of my fans often confused those two pictures where Duke is a hero in both of them, but he was almost always the hero in all of his pictures and that is the way it should have been." **p**, Louis F. Edelman; **d&w**, George Waggner; **cast**, John Wayne, Patricia Neal, Ward Bond, Scott Forbes, Philip Carey, Martin Milner, Michael St. Angel, William (Bill) Campbell, Paul Picerni, Richard Loo, Milburn Stone, Carleton Young, Virginia Brissac, Jack Pennick; **c**, Bert Glennon; **m**, Max Steiner; **ed**, Alan Crosland, Jr.; **art d**, Leo K. Kuter; **set d**, John Gilbert Kissel; **spec eff**, Hans F. Koenekamp, William McGann.

Operation Petticoat ★★★ 1959; U.S.; 24m; UNIV; Color; Comedy; Children: Acceptable; **DVD**; **VHS**. Delightful comedy sees Grant as a submarine commander in World War II (1939-1945). He narrates the tale by recalling his adventures, especially back in December 1941. The sub is in the Pacific during the evacuation of the Philippines. He has more than the Japanese to deal with as Curtis is a lieutenant aboard and takes on five stranded American nurses, some Filipino families, and a goat. This sets up lots of comedy, and by the time the film ends, Curtis marries one of the nurses, Merrill, and Grant marries another, O'Brien, and the sub is painted pink. The inventive script provides many witty lines and a batch of very funny scenes, particularly when the ladies more or less take over the cramped space in the boat from the tough submariners, who wind up being nursemaids to a number of babies. *Author's Note*: Three separate U.S. submarines were employed in the making of this film, which was shot on location off Key West, Florida, and San Diego. Grant told this author that "the story for that picture was so ridiculous that it proved to be a terrific comedy. Tony [Curtis] had a field day impersonating me in a film made just after we appeared in **Operation Petticoat** together [that film being **Some Like It Hot**, 1959]. During the production of **Operation Petticoat**, I caught him doing imitations of my manners and speech, so he must have been rehearsing for his next picture. I guess you might call that a form of flattery." For his part, Curtis told this author that "there were two great moments in my life—the first when I witnessed the signing of the peace treaty in Tokyo Bay in 1945 when I was stationed in the Navy, the second when I met and went to work with the great Cary Grant in **Operation Petticoat**. Cary had been my movie idol ever since I was a kid and to appear in a picture with him as his co-star made me feel like I had gone to Heaven. There was no greater actor than Cary Grant in Hollywood then or now and anyone who disputes that has not seen his pictures and are just walking around in a fog." **p**, Robert Arthur; **d**, Blake Edwards; **cast**, Cary Grant, Tony Curtis, Joan O'Brien, Dina Merrill, Gene Evans, Richard (Dick) Sargent, Virginia Gregg, Robert F. Simon, Gavin MacLeod, Robert Gist, Marion Ross, Frankie Darro, Arthur O'Connell; **w**, Stanley Shapiro, Maurice Richlin (based on a story by Paul King, Joseph Stone); **c**, Russell Harlan (Eastmancolor); **m**, David Rose; **ed**, Ted J. Kent, Frank Gross.

Operation Secret ★★★ 1952; U.S.; 108m; WB; B/W; Spy Film; Children: Cautionary; **DVD**. Exciting action tale where Wilde is a heroic undercover Free French officer aiding the French underground during WWII. His gallant exploits, however, are tarnished when it is revealed that he may have been a traitor and double agent actually working for the Germans and who brought about the death of underground fighter

Tony Curtis, Cary Grant and Dick Crockett in *Operation Petticoat,* **1959.**

Picerni. The film opens with Wilde, a former member of the French Foreign Legion, who is dropped behind German lines in occupied France to aid the underground, and there he befriends and works with a number of resistance fighters, including Picerni, Malden, Cochran and the attractive Thaxter, a woman who falls in love with him. He is assigned a mission where Wilde must determine the extent of Allied bombing to the ball bearing plant at Schweinfurt. He obtains that information as well as proof of the locations of German V-1 and V-2 rocket sites (in the form of Nazi footage, actual films taken by the German Signal Corps), but while making his way back on a flight, his plane is shot down and he is reported dead. In flash forward, French police investigate the murder of Picerni, one of the French underground fighters, and Wilde is named his killer. His former fellow resistance fighters testify at a court hearing, including the boozy but dedicated freedom fighter Malden (who gives a top-flight performance) and Cochran, who was a communist agent while fighting with the underground. Also testifying is Matthews, who was Wilde's superior in the British Foreign Office during the war, and Novello, who had been a Gestapo agent tracking down resistance fighters before the war ended. Thaxter, too, gives testimony, although her comments are decidedly supportive of Wilde as she still loves him or the memory of him. The most damning statements that paint Wilde as Picerni's killer come from the brash and arrogant Cochran. As each person testifies, we see a flashback showing Wilde in the viewpoints of those witnesses. In the end, it appears that Wilde is a traitor, but the court is then surprised when Wilde appears in its midst to set matters straight and points out the true culprit, Cochran. He then reunites with Thaxter for a happy ending. *Author's Note*: This story is based upon the actual exploits of Colonel Peter Ortiz (1913-1988), a member of the O.S.S. (U.S. Office of Strategic Services that conducted military intelligence and sabotage during WWII, the precursor of the CIA). Ortiz was involved in several clandestine missions behind German lines during the war, where he not only collected vital information, but saved several lives, at one time driving four downed RAF pilots from France to neutral Spain. He was captured by the Germans in August 1944 and spent the rest of the war as a POW in a German concentration camp. Ortiz was one of the most decorated officers in the O.S.S. For more information on the O.S.S., see my book: *Spies A Narrative Encyclopedia of Dirty Deeds and Double Dealing from Biblical Times to the Present* (M. Evans, 1997; William J. Donovan: pages 183-188; OSS: page 375). **p**, Henry Blanke; **d**, Lewis Seiler; **cast**, Cornel Wilde, Steve Cochran, Phyllis Thaxter, Karl Malden, Paul Picerni, Lester Matthews, Dan O'Herlihy, Jay Novello, Philip Carey, Anthony Eisley; **w**, Harold Medford, James R. Webb, Alvin Josephy, John Twist (suggested by *The Life of Peter Ortiz* by Lt. Col. Peter Ortiz, USMCR); **c**, Ted D. McCord; **m**, Roy Webb; **ed**, Clarence Kolster; **art d**, Leo K.

Donald Sutherland and Mary Tyler Moore in *Ordinary People*, 1980.

Kuter; **set d**, William L. Kuehl.

The Optimists ★★★ 1973; U.K./U.S.; 110m; Cheetah/PAR; Color; Drama; Children: Cautionary (MPAA: PG); **DVD**. Sellers fascinates in his role of an old vaudevillian making his living as a busker, performing on the streets of a South London slum with his dog. He befriends two urchins, a preteen girl, Mullane, and her younger brother, Chaffey, who are discouraged because their parents work long hours in blue-collar jobs and they are on their own most of the time. Sellers gives them hope and cheer, taking them along to his street-corner entertaining while they give him companionship. An often heartwarming film, Sellers is a marvel to behold in this serious, dramatic tale. **p**, Adrian Gaye, Victor Lyndon; **d**, Anthony Simmons; **cast**, Peter Sellers, Donna Mullane, John Chaffey, David Daker, Marjorie Yates, Pat Ashton, Pat Beckett, Patricia Brake, Candyce Jane Brandl, Keith Chegwin; **w**, Simmons, Tudor Gates (based on the novel *The Optimists of Nine Elms* by Simmons); **c**, Larry Pizer (Eastmancolor); **m**, George Martin; **ed**, John Jympson; **art d**, Robert Cartwright.

Orchestra Wives ★★★★ 1942; U.S.; 98m; FOX; B/W; Musical; Children: Acceptable; **DVD**; **VHS**. A terrific musical with a lot of great Glenn Miller tunes also provides an inside view of how the big bands in the early 1940s operated and even a deeper view of how their camp following wives coped with their husbands working in those nomadic and enormously popular bands. Montgomery is the handsome lead trumpet player in Miller's band, who meets and falls in love with beautiful Rutherford (who played Scarlett O'Hara's youngest sister in **Gone with the Wind**, 1939) after a whistle stop performance in her small town. They marry and Rutherford travels with the band, along with a number of other wives, who welcome the naïve young wife to their motley mix and where the more jaded of these female spouses believe that her marriage is doomed as the sultry band singer Bari (her vocals looped by singer Pat Friday), a femme fatale of the first rank, has covetous eyes for Montgomery. Bari works her wiles on Montgomery so effectively that he and Rutherford split up and Bari also causes so much trouble that the band is about to break up, its talented members going their separate ways until slick promoter Romero brings them all together again as well as patches up the fractured marriage between Montgomery and Rutherford while Bari gets her comeuppance and all ends well. Songs: "At Last," "(I've Got a Gal in) Kalamazoo," "Serenade in Blue," "People Like You and Me" (music: Harry Warren; lyrics: Mack Gordon); "Chattanooga Choo Choo" (Harry Warren); "Bugle Call Rag" (Jack Pettis, Billy Meyers, Elmer Schoebel); "Moonlight Serenade" (Glenn Miller); and "Boom Shot" (Glenn Miller and Billy May). *Author's Note*: Rutherford was loaned out to Fox for this film by MGM after she

failed to appear in a production by that studio after contracting measles following a War Bond tour in Chicago. MGM boss Louis B. Mayer was miffed because Rutherford had complained about her small role in that upcoming production and absurdly accused her of purposely coming down with the measles to get out of the part, according to Rutherford's statements to this author to which she added: "Mr. Mayer would invent any excuse to allow him to do whatever he wanted to do—he was the most powerful man in Hollywood and everyone was afraid of him, including me." In retaliation, he loaned her out to Fox, but her meaty role and standout performance excited viewing audiences so much that thereafter she was given better roles at MGM. She told this author that "the two persons I remember most and with deep fondness after doing **Orchestra Wives** was that great clown, Jackie Gleason [who plays the role of the band's bass player]. He kept us in stitches when off camera all the time with his clever comedy routines and zany antics. The other person I remember was the great Glenn Miller. He did not have an ounce of conceit in him and was always one of the boys, quiet and gentle, truly a person you could love right away. His premature death during the war was a terrible tragedy." Miller (1904-1944), who is wonderfully essayed by James Stewart in **The Glenn Miller Story**, 1954, disappeared while on a flight from England to France toward the end of WWII on December 15, 1944, when his plane was over the English Channel. News of his death was sketchy, reports saying that the small plane in which he was flying was lost in a fog, but the truth of that event was not revealed until 1985 when WWII pilots and officials admitted that a squadron of Allied bombers had missed its target and, while flying high above Miller's plane, were ordered to jettison their bomb loads; when they did, Miller's plane was struck and blown to pieces. Director Mayo told this author that "Miller was great to work with, always helpful and with a lot of great ideas where we could do some bridging scenes that would naturally introduce the musical numbers in that picture, which was his last where he is on the screen. His band was like no other and that goes for his music, too." Miller appeared in only two films other than this one, **The Big Broadcast of 1936**, 1935, and the memorable **Sun Valley Serenade**, 1941. The charming Rutherford, born in 1917, died at age ninety-four on June 11, 2012, leaving Olivia de Havilland as the only principal player from **Gone with the Wind** still alive (at this writing where she is ninety-five years old). **p**, William LeBaron; **d**, Archie Mayo; **cast**, George Montgomery, Ann Rutherford, Glenn Miller and His Orchestra, Lynn Bari, Carole Landis, Cesar Romero, Virginia Gilmore, Mary Beth Hughes, The Nicholas Brothers (Fayard and Harold Nicholas), Iris Adrian, Tex Beneke, Dorothy Dandridge, Dale Evans, Jackie Gleason, Dick Hogan, Kenneth Howell, Bobby Hackett, Trudy Marshall, Billy May; **w**, Karl Tunberg, Darrell Ware (based on a story by James Prindle); **c**, Lucien Ballard; **m**, Alfred Newman, Leigh Harline (both uncredited); **ed**, Robert Bischoff; **art d**, Richard Day, Joseph C. Wright; **set d**, Thomas Little.

Orders Is Orders ★★★ 1934; U.K.; 62m; Gaumont British; B/W; Comedy; Children: Acceptable; **DVD**;**VHS**. The feisty Gleason is an American movie director who goes to a British army base in England wanting to shoot a movie about the French Foreign Legion and use British soldiers as extras. Maude, the base commander, doesn't want any part of it, but Gleason, with the help of his secretary, is able to go ahead and shoot the film. A good comedy that turns into a broad farce, one that is very funny and offers a clever script, along with a good cast of supporting players. **p**, Michael Balcon; **d**, Walter Forde; **cast**, Charlotte Greenwood, James Gleason, Cyril Maude, Finlay Currie, Percy Parsons, Cedric Hardwicke, Donald Calthrop, Ian Hunter, Jane Carr, Ray Milland, Edwin Lawrence; **w**, Leslie Arliss, Sidney Gilliat, James Gleason (based on plays by Ian Hay, Anthony Armstrong); **c**, Glen MacWilliams; **ed**, Derek Twist; **art d**, Alfred Junge.

Ordinary People ★★★★ 1980; U.S.; 124m; PAR; Color; Drama; Children: Unacceptable (MPAA: R); **BD**; **DVD**; **VHS**. A prosaic domestic tale offers no frills and is almost cruel in its grim portrayals but so realistically presented that it sustains fascination with its characters throughout. The three principal characters are Hutton, the disillusioned and guilt-ridden son of father Sutherland and mother Moore, both self-reliant parents living in Chicago's upscale North Shore. Hutton has been given little attention by Sutherland and hardly any affection from icy Moore, believing that his parents loved Hutton's dead brother much more, that brother and son lost in a boating accident, a death for which Hutton blames himself. Sutherland tries to help the boy by hiring Hirsch, a psychiatrist, who works with Hutton while he struggles with his conscience and also tries to maintain a romance with attractive McGovern. Moore, who has withdrawn into herself, offers him no aid, and her almost indifferent attitude toward Hutton and Sutherland eventually alienates Sutherland. Hutton finally frees himself from a guilt complex through Hirsch's patient and good therapy, as well as establishing a firm romantic relationship with McGovern. The marriage between Sutherland and Moore, however, has been so damaged through Moore's cold-blooded and uncaring posture that Sutherland is preparing to leave her at the film's end. Redford directs with great skill in defining the characters and the script is both intelligent and revealing; Sutherland, Moore and Hutton give outstanding performances. The film deservedly swept the Oscars, winning for Best Picture, Best Director (Redford), Best Screenplay (Sargent) and Best Supporting Actor (Hutton) where Moore, in one of her finest portrayals as a woman everyone could easily despise, was nominated as Best Actress and Hirsch was nominated as Best Supporting Actor. The film was an enormous success, gleaning more than $54 million at the box office at the first time around against a budget of $6 million. Songs: "Canon in D Major" (Johan Pachelbel), "(I Never Promised You a) Rose Garden" (Joe South), "For He's a Jolly Good Fellow" (traditional). *Author's Note*: Moore's startling performance as a self-centered, dispassionate woman was all the more surprising in that she had, until that time, appeared in film and TV comedies, proving herself to be a superlative dramatic actress. Even more amazing was the grim fact that Moore delivered her memorable performance at a time when she lost her only real-life son, Richard, who accidentally killed himself while handling a weapon with a hair-trigger (taken off the market because of his death), and while she was also battling personal problems with diabetes and alcoholism. **p**, Ronald L. Schwary; **d**, Robert Redford; **cast**, Donald Sutherland, Mary Tyler Moore, Judd Hirsch, Timothy Hutton, M. Emmet Walsh, Elizabeth McGovern, Dinah Manoff, Fredric Lehne, James B. Sikking, Basil Hoffman; **w**, Alvin Sargent (based on the novel by Judith Guest); **c**, John Bailey (Technicolor); **ed**, Jeff Kanew; **art d**, Phillip Bennett, J. Michael Riva; **set d**, Jerry Wunderlich, William Fosser.

The Organizer ★★★ 1964; Italy/France/Yugoslavia; 126m; Lux Film/Continental Distributing; B/W; Drama; Children: Unacceptable; **VHS**. This taut futuristic drama is set in 1980 in Turin, Italy, where exploited textile factory workers struggle to achieve better working conditions. They work long hours and, after one of the workers complains, he is suspended without pay for two weeks. Mastroianni, a visiting professor, who has had some experience in workers' rights, helps them organize a strike. Management sends in some strike-breaking goons, and in an ensuing riot, a worker, Lulli, is killed. The incident makes newspaper headlines and Turin's police chief orders the scabs to leave the city. Management tries to get police to go after Mastroianni, but he successfully hides out in the apartment of Girardot, a hooker. Mastroianni gets more disgruntled workers to join the others in marching on the factory, but they are met by more goons and a teenage worker is killed. Police arrest Mastroianni and the workers go back on the job, not having gained anything except having had their grievances heard and the formation of a union that will hopefully bring about reforms in the future. Violence prohibits viewing by children. **p**, Franco Cristaldi; **d**, Mario Monicelli; **cast**, Marcello Mastroianni, Renato Salvatori, Gabriella Giorgelli, Folco Lulli, Bernard Blier, Raffaella Carrá, François Périer,

Lillian Gish and Dorothy Gish in *Orphans of the Storm*, 1921.

Vittorio Sanipoli, Annie Girardot; **w**, Age (Agenore Incrocci), Furio Scarpelli, Monicelli; **c**, Giuseppe Rotunno; **m**, Carlo Rustichelli; **ed**, Ruggero Mastroianni; **prod d** & **set d**, Mario Garbuglia.

Orphans of the Storm ★★★★ 1921 (silent); U.S.; 150m/12 reels; D. W. Griffith Productions/UA; B/W; Drama; Children: Cautionary; **DVD**. Set prior to and during the French Revolution, this stirring tale profiles the fates of two French orphaned sisters caught up in the sweep and chaos of one of France's most turbulent eras, that cataclysmic epoch brilliantly captured on film by master filmmaker Griffith. This opus opens when a commoner is killed by members of an aristocratic family because he dared to marry Emmet, the daughter of a powerful count. The daughter gives birth to a female baby, but the child, sired by that commoner, is taken from her mother and placed on the steps of Notre Dame Cathedral in Paris, along with a purse containing a large amount of money and a brief note stating: "Her name is Louise. Save her." A penniless man bringing his own infant daughter to Notre Dame to leave her there in the hopes that she will be discovered and find a decent home, finds the other child and is so moved by her plight that he decides to raise that child as well as his own daughter, now that he has the funds to provide a decent home. He and his wife move to the provinces and raise both girls as sisters (Lillian and Dorothy Gish), but when the girls are in their teens, a plague devastates the area, killing both parents and leaving Dorothy blind. Lillian, the older sister, becomes Dorothy's surrogate mother and resolves to find a physician who can restore Dorothy's sight. To that end, Lillian takes Dorothy to Paris, meeting en route Wallace, an evil aristocrat, who abducts Lillian. Dorothy is left to wander blind about Paris, almost falling into the Seine River, but is rescued by crippled Puglia. The compassionate Puglia takes Dorothy to his home where he has to protect her against abuse from his cretin-like older brother, Lewis, and his vicious mother, La Verne. (La Verne specialized in playing repulsive characters as she would in **A Tale of Two Cities**, 1935, as the ugly harridan encouraging the beheadings by the guillotine during the Reign of Terror and later enacting in voiceover the wicked queen in **Snow White and the Seven Dwarfs**, 1937.) Meanwhile, Lillian is about to be forced into an orgy by villain Wallace, but young aristocrat Schildkraut saves her after wounding Wallace in a duel, escaping with her, but they are swept up in the street fighting during the Revolution. Lillian meets and befriends revolutionary leader Georges Danton (1759-1794), played by Blue, which angers his fellow revolutionary, Maximilien de Robespierre (1758-1794), played by Herbert. Dorothy, meanwhile, is forced into becoming a street singer by old hag La Verne (the girl terrified into accepting this task after she is thrown into a rat-infested cellar). Schildkraut has become Lillian's protector and exhibits his support for the downtrodden revolutionaries, although he is the

Jean Marais in *Orpheus*, 1950.

nephew of Emmet, Dorothy's real mother, now married to a count, Losee, who is the prefect of police for Paris. When Lillian meets Emmet in her palatial home, she hears the singing voice of her sister, Dorothy, and races toward the door to find her, but she is detained by Losee and his guards. She and Schildkraut are arrested and charged with aiding the revolutionaries and imprisoned in the Bastille. Both are freed when the revolution erupts and the Bastille is stormed and all prisoners released. Schildkraut and Lillian, however, are still thought to be the enemies of the Revolution because of Schildkraut's ties to the aristocracy. They are tried before a tribunal and condemned to death, even though Blue continues to argue for their release even as they are taken to the site of execution. Dorothy, meanwhile, is about to be ravished by the brutish Lewis, but the crippled Puglia finds enough courage to attack his older brother, killing him in a wild knife fight. After saving Dorothy, the heroic Puglia hears that Lillian is about to be executed and goes to the square where she is led to the guillotine. In one of the many harrowing moments of this exciting film, Lillian places her head on the chopping block while the executioner, Wolheim (a great character actor, who, like La Verne, specialized in villains) prepares to send the blade of the guillotine downward to take her life. In a mad race to the scaffold, the crippled Puglia clambers onto the scaffold just before the blade is to descend and stabs Wolheim to death, saving Lillian. The finale to this superlative melodrama sees Emmet confessing her past to husband Losee, who shows compassion by sympathetically accepting her story and where Emmet takes the now homeless Puglia into her household for saving her daughter's life. Dorothy's sight is restored and Lillian marries the dashing Schildkraut. Griffith presents a harrowing and hazardous tale by presenting two alternating story lines where the pace of each increases until the frantic and terrifying conclusion, packing action and great character development throughout, following his successful techniques as displayed in **Intolerance**, 1916, where, like the climactic conclusion to **Orphans of the Storm**, the hero is saved at the last moment from execution. The exceptional acting from the Gish sisters, Schildkraut, La Verne and Puglia memorably preserves their unforgettable characters. *Author's Note*: Griffith had to be talked into making this film by his long-standing star, Lillian Gish, who originally proposed he make this film. He initially told her: "You only want me to make that story because there is a part in it for Dorothy [Gish, her sister]." The great filmmaker dismissed the idea as "an old melodrama," but Gish persisted, pointing out that it was one of the most popular theatrical productions in America, although it had never been brought to the screen, and that it had been successfully produced in more than forty languages and, at the time she proposed filming it, the play had been produced in New York recently in Chinese, Yiddish and German, and was currently running at an Italian theater. She persuaded Griffith to attend one of those productions, and

he was so impressed with Puglia, then appearing in that production, that he hired him on the spot to reprise his role as the cripple in his film version. (In the original release, Puglia is shown being killed after dispatching executioner Wolheim, but this so displeased viewers that Griffith reshot some of his scenes so that he survives at the finish.) Puglia would go on to appear in more than 150 films in various character roles, mostly priests, fathers, politicians, musicians, and restaurant owners and waiters. He is the street vendor in **Casablanca**, 1942, who offers to sell his wares for much less to Ingrid Bergman because she is a friend of his friend, Humphrey Bogart. This production was the last film in which the Gish sisters would appear together and it would be Lillian Gish's last film made with Griffith, the man she respected most in all filmmaking. **p&d**, D.W. Griffith; **cast**, Lillian Gish, Dorothy Gish, Joseph Schildkraut, Frank Losee, Katherine Emmet, Morgan Wallace, Lucille La Verne, Sheldon Lewis, Frank Puglia, Creighton Hale, Monte Blue, Louis Wolheim, Kenny Delmar, Sidney Herbert, Lee Kohlmar; **w**, Gaston de Tolignac [Griffith] (based on the play "The Two Orphans" by Adolphe Philippe Dennery, Eugene Cormon and material inspired by the novel *A Tale of Two Cities* by Charles Dickens and the book *The French Revolution* by Thomas Carlyle); **c**, G.W. Bitzer, Paul H. Allen, Hendrik Sartov; **m**, Lois F. Gottschalk, John Lanchbery, William F. Peters; **ed**, James and Rose Smith; **art d**, Charles M. Kirk; **spec eff**, Edward Scholl.

Orpheus ★★★★ 1950; France; 95m; Andre Paulve Film/DisCina International; B/W; Fantasy; Children: Cautionary; **DVD**; **VHS**. A brilliant fantasy that equals his classic **Beauty and the Beast**, 1947, Cocteau offers a mesmerizing fantasy that begins with Marais as Orpheus, a young poet, who is married to Dea. While they sit at their favorite outdoor café they are horrified to see their friend and fellow poet Dermithe struck and killed by a motorcycle. Marais joins Casares, who is Dermithe's patroness, and they travel in her Rolls Royce, but not to a hospital or the morgue but to an elegant chalet where Dermithe is brought back to life (through clever optical effects where Cocteau runs the motorcycle scene backward so that Dermithe appears to supernaturally rise from the earth). Dermithe and Casares then leave the room by walking through a mirror and into the Underworld. Marais is then returned home in Casares' Rolls Royce by chauffeur Perier, and Marais spends all his time listening to the codes emitted from the car's radio and translates them into poetry. When he sleeps, Casares watches guard over him. Dea, the love-starved wife of Marais, has an affair with Perier, and she, like Dermithe, is then hit and killed by motorcyclists (who represent Death) and Casares sends her to the Underworld. Marais and Perier then use a glove left behind by Casares to walk through a mirror to the Underworld looking for Dea as Perier is now obsessed with her, but Marais' thoughts are now filled with images of the enchantress Casares. Marais then witnesses a trial where Casares pleads with several judges, stating that she has only love for Marais. They agree to free her but on the condition that the wronged Dea is returned from the Underworld. Dea returns to her world but Marais is tasked at never casting his eyes on her again. He attempts to avoid doing this at all costs, which produces some humorous moments, but then sees her when glancing into a mirror and Dea is again sent to the Underworld. A mob then attacks and kills Marais, believing he has murdered Dermithe to steal his poems, and when Marais enters the Underworld Casares kills him so that he will return to his own world and continue to write his poems. Once Marais returns to his world, he is reunited with Dea. Impressionistic and aesthetically created, the film is really a series of thoughts about the creative process, life and death, put to celluloid in Cocteau's innovative style through a series of mesmerizing scenes, where Auric's haunting score enhances the unreality of this strange, even bizarre, tale. (In French; English subtitles.) **p**, Andre Paulve; **d&w**, Jean Cocteau (based on his play); **cast**, Jean Marais, Francois Perier, Maria Casares, Marie Dea. Henri Cremieux, Juliette Greco, Roger Blin, Edouard Dermithe, Rene Worms, Cocteau (narrator); **c**, Nicolas Hayer; **m**, Georges Auric; **ed**, Jacqueline

Sadoul; **prod d**, Jean d'Eaubonne; **set d**, Albert Volper.

Osama ★★★ 2004; Afghanistan/The Netherlands/Japan/Ireland/Iran; 83m; Barmak/MGM; Color; Drama; Children: Unacceptable (MPAA: PG-13); **DVD**; **VHS**. This is the first film made in Afghanistan after the fall of the oppressive Taliban rule (1996-2001) and powerfully indicts the oppressions against women in Afghanistan under Taliban tyrants. Previously, all filming had been banned. The film, based on a true story, is presented in documentary style, opening with Herati, a boy, talking to the camera about the Taliban regime, and how it was especially oppressive to women, not allowing them to work or leave their house without a male escort. These restrictions are then enacted, showing how hard these conditions are imposed on a family solely consisting of three women since their husbands have died in various Afghani wars. They had been nurses until the Taliban closed their hospital. Sahar is a mother who has her twelve-year-old daughter, Golbahari, dress as a boy in order to get a job to support the family. She is renamed Osama, although the film is not about the al-Qaeda terrorist leader Osama bin Laden (March 10, 1957-May 2, 2011). She gets work delivering milk for a family friend, who is only one of two people who know about her masquerade. The other is a boy at school, Herati, who recognizes her and tries to help her keep her secret. Osama's identity is endangered when the Taliban recruit all boys to get schooling, which includes military training and sexual education. After the school's headmaster becomes suspicious of Osama's gender, she is unmasked, arrested, and put on trial, which could mean her death. She is found guilty, but, instead of death, she is given in marriage to a much older man, who already has three wives and who keeps them padlocked in their rooms. He puts the largest padlock on the door to Osama's room. The film ends there, with Osama in a trapped and helpless position so long as the Taliban rules the country. Oppressive treatment of women prohibits viewing by children. **p**, Siddiq Barmak, Julia Fraser, Julie LeBrocquy, Makoto Ueda; **d& w**, Barmak; **cast**, Marina Golbahari, Mohammad Nadir Khwaja, Zubaida Sahar, Mohammad Arif Herati, Gul Rehman Ghorbandi, Khwaja Nader, Hamida Refah; **c**, Ebrahim Ghafori; **m**, Mohammad Reza Darvishi; **ed**, Barmak; **prod d**, Akbar Meshkini.

Oscar and Lucinda ★★★ 1997; U.S./Australia/U.K.; 132m; Australian Film Finance Corp/Fox Searchlight; Color; Drama/Romance; Children: Unacceptable (MPAA: R); **DVD**; **VHS**. Set in the mid-1800s, Fiennes is exceptional as a young priest (of the Church of England). He meets Blanchett, a young Australian heiress, while they are aboard a ship bound for Australia. He is on his way to Australia to become a missionary in the Outback. Blanchett is returning home after buying equipment in London for a glass factory she bought in Sydney because she has a dream of having a church built there entirely of glass and then transported to a remote location in the Outback wilderness where there is no Christian church. They become attracted to each other, not only sexually but because both are addicted to gambling. She uses her winnings to add to her fortune and have the glass church built, and he gives his winnings to the poor. Fiennes bets that he can safely deliver the glass church from Sydney to a churchless ministry in the Outback. He will get her entire fortune if he wins the wager. We're not told his motivation for the bet except, perhaps, he simply loves to gamble, loves her, or can become pastor of the glass church once he gets it to the Outback. Blanchett accepts the bet and the church is built in Sydney. Fiennes' journey with the glass building by river barge is long and treacherous since he must make his way through hostile Aborigine country. When Fiennes finally gets the church to its destination in the Outback, he stands inside of it as it breaks apart and the barge sinks in the river under the church's weight. Unable to get out, Fiennes drowns. Blanchett wins the bet, tragically, because Fiennes was unable to deliver the church safely. This strange but engrossing film is well crafted and enacted by the entire cast. Songs: "Motet—Os Justi" (Anton Buckner), "Haec Dies" (John Sheppard), "Motetten—Lobet die Herrn, alle Heiden, BWV 230"

Marina Golbahari in *Osama*, 2004.

(Johann Sebastian Bach), "Fantasia in C Minor for Piano, Chorus & Orchestra, Op. 80" (Ludwig van Beethoven). Sexuality and violence prohibit viewing by children. **p**, Robin Dalton, Timothy White; **d**, Gillian Armstrong; **cast**, Ralph Fiennes, Cate Blanchett, Ciaran Hinds, Tom Wilkinson, Richard Roxburgh, Clive Russell, Bille Brown, Josephine Byrnes, Barry Otto, Linda Bassett, Geoffrey Rush (narrator); **w**, Laura Jones (based on the novel by Peter Carey); **c**, Geoffrey Simpson; **m**, Thomas Newman; **ed**, Nicholas Beauman; **prod d**, Luciana Arrighi; **art d**, Tom Nursey, John Wingrove; **spec eff**, Steve Courtley.

Oscar Wilde ★★★ 1960; U.K.; 98m; Vantage Films/Four City; B/W; Biography/Drama; Children: Unacceptable; **VHS**. Morley is outstanding in essaying the gifted and controversial Irish writer, Oscar Wilde (1854-1900). He is shown living in London as a successful and famous playwright, who is married to a devoted woman, Calvert, but falls in love with a young nobleman and college student, Neville, who loathes his father, Chapman, the Marquis of Queensbury, who was noted in his own right for devising the rules for professional boxing. Chapman sends Morley a note accusing him of being a sodomite. Neville persuades Morley to bring a lawsuit against his father for libel. The case goes to trial, and Morley, under strong cross-examination by the queen's lawyer, Richardson, breaks down on the witness stand and admits his homosexuality and strong feelings for Neville. He is found guilty of gross indecency and sentenced to two years of hard labor in prison. After serving his sentence, his spirit is broken and he dies in Paris. Morley gives a riveting performance of Wilde, even though he was fifty-two when making this film and Wilde was forty-six when he died, particularly winning empathy when he breaks down in court. Richardson, as the dogged prosecutor, also gives a masterful performance in the courtroom sequences, which are some of the most exciting ever put on film, where acrimony, hate and vengeance is displayed as crackling lightning bolts. This film was remade in 1997 as **Wilde**, with Stephen Fry as Wilde, but with far less effectiveness. Wilde's story was put on film in other productions in **The Trials of Oscar Wilde**, 1960, where Peter Finch played the notorious Irish playwright, but with far less panache and verve than Morley's memorable performance, and in **Oscar Wilde**, a 1972 made-for-TV movie with Klaus Maria Brandauer as Wilde. **p**, William Kirby; **d**, Gregory Ratoff; **cast**, Robert Morley, Phyllis Calvert, John Neville, Ralph Richardson, Dennis Price, Alexander Knox, Edward Chapman, Martin Benson, Robert Harris, Henry Oscar; **w**, Jo Eisinger (based on the play by Leslie and Sewell Stokes); **c**, Georges Perinal; **m**, Kenneth V. Jones; **ed**, Antony Gibbs; **art d**, Scott MacGregor.

Ossessione ★★★ 1976; Italy; 104m; Industrie Cinematografiche Italiane/Ajay Film Co.; B/W; Drama; Children: Unacceptable; **DVD**; **VHS**.

Orson Welles and Suzanne Cloutier in *Othello*, 1955.

Girotti is a young and handsome drifter, who stops at a small roadside restaurant run by de Landa and his wife, Calamai, who is unhappy with her overweight and older husband (she only married him for his money). The two young people fall in love, but Calamai refuses to leave her husband and security and go away with Girotti because he is poor. Girotti leaves but soon returns because he can't forget Calamai. Then Calamai devises a plan to kill her husband and make it look like an accident so she can collect his life insurance as well as keep Girotti as her lover. She gets Girotti to assist her in the murder, but afterwards guilt haunts him and he leaves her again. Girotti takes up with another woman, but returns to Calamai when he learns she is pregnant. Police become suspicious of their close relationship so soon after her husband's death and investigate them. The lovers try to escape, but Calamai is killed in a car crash. Ironically, Girotti is arrested, not for murdering de Landa, but for Calamai's accidental death in the car crash. This film is based on the James M. Cain novel, *The Postman Always Rings Twice*, which was filmed in 1946, and in 1981. **Ossessione** was originally made in 1942, but banned in Italy by Mussolini and finally released in the U.S. in 1976. Songs: "L'amour est un oiseau rebelle" (from the opera "Carmen"; Georges Bizet, Henri Meilhac, Ludovic Halevy), "Je crois entendre encore" (from the opera "The Pearlfishers"; Georges Bizet, Eugene Cormon, Michel Carre), "Di Provensa il Mar, il Suol" (from the opera "La Traviata"; Giuseppe Verdi, Francesco Maria Piave), "E il sol della'anima, la tita e amore" (from the opera "Rigoletto" by Verdi, Piave). Sexuality and violence prohibit viewing by children. (In Italian; English subtitles.) **p**, Libero Solaroli; **d**, Luchino Visconti; **cast**, Clara Calamai, Massimo Girotti, Juan de Landa, Elio Marcuzzo, Dhia Cristiani, Vittorio Duse, Michele Riccardini, Michele Sakara; **w**, Mario Alicata, Antonio Pietrangeli, Gianni Puccini, Giuseppe De Santis, Visconti (based on the novel The Postman Always Rings Twice by James M. Cain); **c**, Aldo Tonti, Domenico Scala; **m**, Giuseppe Rosati; **ed**, Mario Serandrei; **art d & set d**, Gino Franzi.

Otello ★★★ 1986; The Netherlands/Italy/U.S.; 118m; Cannon Films; Color; Opera; Children: Unacceptable (MPAA: PG); **DVD**; **VHS**. This elaborate and rewarding opera production offers a fine version of Giuseppe Verdi's opera based on the play "Othello" by William Shakespeare. The film stars Domingo as the Moor, Otello. In 17th-century Cyprus, ruled by Italy, Otello returns triumphant from a naval battle against the Turkish fleet and is appointed governor of Cyprus. Iago, played by Diaz, an ensign, who is his aide, and resents Domingo's passing him up for the rank of captain in favor of Cassio (Barberini). With the help of Roderigo (Nicolai), a Venetian gentleman who lusts after Domingo's beautiful wife Desdemona (Ricciarelli), Diaz plots to destroy Domingo and Barberini by convincing jealous Domingo that Ricciarelli

is unfaithful and that her lover is Barberini. Diaz gets Barberini drunk and induces him into a brawl with Roderigo, during which Barberini wounds a man. Diaz continues to work on Otello's jealous nature by planting Ricciarelli's handkerchief in Barberini's room and tells Otello he found that incriminating evidence there. Domingo finds Ricciarelli alone in bed and wakes her with a kiss, then accuses her of adultery. She pleads that she is innocent and has been faithful to him, but the enraged Domingo strangles her. Diaz's wife, Malakova, then tells Domingo that Barberini has killed Nicolai, then discovers Ricciarelli is dead and calls for help. Domingo now realizes that Diaz is the villain whose scheming caused him to kill Ricciarelli. Domingo kills him, then stabs himself to death. The play "Othello" was filmed in 1955, 1960, 1965, and 1995. Beautifully photographed, as well as providing outstanding performances, this is a superior filming of the opera, but not for children because of sexuality and violence. (In Italian; English subtitles.) **p**, Menahem and Yoram Globus; **d**, Franco Zeffirelli; **cast**, Placido Domingo, Katia Ricciarelli, Justino Diaz, Petra Malakova, Urbano Barberini, Massimo Foschi, Edwin Francis, Sergio Nicolai, Remo Remotti, Antonio Pierfederici; **w**, Zeffirelli, Masolino D'Amico, Arrigo Boito (based on the play "Othello" by William Shakespeare); **c**, Ennio Guarnieri; **m**, Giuseppi Verdi; **ed**, Franca Silvi, Peter Taylor; **prod d**, Zeffirelli; **art d**, Gianni Quaranta; **spec eff**, Claudio Quaglietti.

Othello ★★★ 1955; U.S./Italy/France/Morocco; 90m; Mercury Productions/UA; Drama; Children: Unacceptable; **DVD**; **VHS**. Although somewhat heavy-handed, Welles's overall production and his own riveting essaying of the doomed Moor Othello sustains interest in this classic Shakespearean tale of jealousy, love and murder. He is a trusting husband until the scheming MacLiammoir implants suspicion in his mind that convinces Welles that his loving wife, Cloutier, is unfaithful, bringing himself to ruin after he murders her in a jealous rage. Welles gives his own broad interpretation to this tale, startling viewers by revealing the story's ending in its opening scenes and where he uses many optical techniques and special effects to achieve arresting shots. *Author's Note*: Welles was hard pressed for money necessary to produce this film, telling this author that "I had to find work elsewhere and appeared in several films in order to put together enough cash to produce **Othello**. That picture was a financing nightmare, I can tell you." Where he took only three weeks to shoot **Macbeth**, 1948, it took more than three years before Welles was about to complete **Othello**. **p,d & w**, Orson Welles (based on the play by William Shakespeare); **cast**, Welles, Michael MacLiammoir, Suzanne Cloutier, Robert Coote, Hilton Edwards, Nicholas Bruce, Michael Laurence, Fay Compton, Doris Dowling, Joseph Cotten, Joan Fontaine, Jean Davis; **c**, Anchise Brizzi, Aldo Graziati (G.R. Aldo), George Fanto, Oberdan Troiani, Alberto Fusi; **m**, Alberto Barberis, Angelo Francesco Lavagnino; **ed**, Jean Sacha, John Shepridge, Renzo Lucidi; **prod d**, Alexandre Trauner, Luigi Scaccianoce.

Othello ★★★★ 1965; U.K.; 165m; BHE Films/WB; Color; Drama; Children: Unacceptable; **DVD**; **VHS**. Olivier gives one of his masterful performances as the troubled Moor, Othello, in what is undoubtedly one of the finest productions on this dire and memorable tale. Olivier plays Othello in blackface, wearing a crucifix and crossing himself, but reverts regularly to his Islamic traditions, mixing Christianity with Islam as much as his own nature marks a double personality, one loving and trusting toward his devoted wife Desdemona, wonderfully played by Smith, the other full of jealousy and rage that has been implanted in Olivier's mind by the scheming Iago, who is essayed outstandingly by Finlay. Olivier's humanizing interpretation of Othello brings more sympathy to that character than in any other production as he articulates his emotional struggle in deciding to take revenge on a loving and kind woman he thinks has betrayed him, and it is the struggle toward that lethal conviction that makes Olivier's performance all the more impactful and lasting. Jacobi as Cassio is also a standout in presenting that character with great restraint, discarding the fulminating and strutting interpretations of that character appearing in other productions. Ever faithful to Shakespeare, this production is more of a play on film than a movie based upon a play. *Author's Note*: Olivier told this author that he felt that his appearance in this production "was essentially faithful to the character, a person of strong convictions, but a man who is corrupted with the paranoia implanted within him by his most trusted aide. He is a man destroyed when he accepts gossip as Gospel. He discards the known for the unknown, like Death itself, and is enveloped by it." **p**, Anthony Havelock-Allan, John Brabourne; **d**, Stuart Burge; **cast**, Laurence Olivier, Maggie Smith, Joyce Redman, Frank Finlay, Derek Jacobi, Robert Lang, Kenneth MacKintosh, Anthony Nicholls, Christopher Timothy, Michael Gambon; **w**, Margaret Unsworth (based on the play by William Shakespeare); **c**, Geoffrey Unsworth (Technicolor); **m**, Richard Hampton; **ed**, Richard Marden; **art d**, William Kellner.

Othello ★★★ 1995; U.S./U.K.; 123m; Castle Rock/COL; Color; Drama/Romance; Children: Unacceptable (MPAA: R); **BD**; **DVD**. Fishburne is convincing in playing Othello, a famous Moorish soldier, who becomes military governor of Cyprus. His courage impresses a young Venetian lady, Desdemona (Jacob), and they secretly marry. One of Fishburne's soldiers, his good friend, Iago (Branagh), is denied a promotion he feels he is entitled to and, to take revenge on Fishburne, spreads lies and makes up incidents that will convince Fishburne that his wife is disloyal to him by sleeping with Cassio (Parker), a lieutenant whom Fishburne promoted instead of Branagh. Fishburne demands that Branagh produce proof of Jacob's infidelity and Branagh produces it by deception, showing Jacob's handkerchief in Cassio's pocket. The false evidence drives Fishburne to kill Jacob by strangling her. He then plunges a dagger into himself to end his agony. The movie follows the play closely, but cuts many lines and adds some scenes not in the play including a sex scene between Fishburne and Jacob, dreams in which Fishburne imagines Jacob having an affair with Parker, and a scene in which the bodies of those killed are buried at sea. *Author's Note*: Fishburne became the first African-American cast as Othello in a major motion picture. The Shakespeare tragedy was previously filmed as a silent movie in 1922 and in talking pictures in 1955 with Orson Welles, 1965 with Laurence Olivier (considered the best version), and in 1980 and 2001. Sexuality and violence prohibit viewing by children. **p**, David Barron, Luc Roeg; **d&w**, Oliver Parker (based on the play by William Shakespeare); **cast**, Laurence Fishburne, Irene Jacob, Kenneth Branagh, Nathaniel Parker, Michael Maloney, Anna Patrick, Nicholas Farrell, Indra Ove, Michael Sheen, Andrew Oumansky, Gabriele Ferzetti; **c**, David Johnson; **m**, Charlie Mole; **ed**, Tony Lawson; **prod d**, Tim Harvey; **art d**, Livia Borgognoni, Desmond Crowe; **spec eff**, Jose Granell, Andy Stevens.

The Other ★★★ 1972; U.S.; 108m; Benchmark/FOX; Color; Horror; Children: Unacceptable (MPAA: PG); **DVD**; **VHS**. Chris and Martin Udvarnocky, nine-year-old twins, live with their family on a farm in Connecticut during the hot summer of 1935. Their loving grandmother, Hagen, has taught them "the game." Murders and morbidity begin happening that worry their widowed mother, Muldaur, and it apprears that Martin is responsible. He is evil and may even be dead. Hagen drags Chris to the family graveyard and demands he face the truth—that Martin has been dead since their birthday when he fell down a well. It's a chilling, spooky tale that ends with Hagen dying in a barn fire and no one learning Chris's terrible secret. Not even the viewer is sure what truly exists in this creepy tale, except that Chris probably killed his brother. Based on the novel by former actor Tom Tryon, this was the Udvarnoky twins' only film. **p&d**, Robert Mulligan; **cast**, Uta Hagen, Diana Muldaur, Chris Udvarnoky, Martin Udvarnocky, Norma Connolly, Victor French, Loretta Leversee, Lou Frizzell, Portia Nelson, Jenny Sullivan, John Ritter; **w**, Thomas (Tom) Tryon (based on his novel); **c**, Robert L. Surtees (DeLuxe Color); **m**, Jerry Goldsmith; **ed**,

Portia Nelson and Martin Udvarnoky in *The Other*, 1972.

Folmar Blangsted, O. Nicholas Brown; **prod d**, Albert Brenner; **set d**, Ruby Levitt.

The Others ★★★ 2001; U.S./Spain/France/Italy; 104m; Cruise-Wagner Productions/ Dimension Films; Color; Horror; Children: Unacceptable (MPAA: PG-13); **DVD**; **VHS**. Kidman retires with her two young children. Mann, and Bentley, to a mansion on the British isle of Jersey in the Channel Islands to wait for her husband, Eccleston, to return from military service in WWII, but fears he is dead. The children have a photosensitivity disease in which they cannot be in direct sunlight without being hurt, so their lives are structured around avoiding sunlight. Three servants arrive, a nanny, Flanagan, an elderly gardener, Sykes, and a young mute girl, Cassidy. Their arrival coincides with some odd happenings in the house such as a piano being played inside a locked room, which convinces Kidman that the house is haunted. Mann draws pictures of four people: a man, a woman, a boy called Victor, and an old woman, and tells Kidman she has seen all four in the house. Kidman finds a "book of the dead" showing pictures of some people who died in the 18th century. She scolds Mann for believing in ghosts, but then hears them herself. She flees the house to get the local priest to bless or exorcize the residence. Meanwhile, the servants seem to be in league against Kidman, siding with the children. While lost in a fog on her way to finding the priest, Kidman sees her husband. She takes Eccleston to the house, but he doesn't seem to know where he is. Then Kidman sees an old woman dressed like her daughter, and attacks her. To her horror, Kidman finds that she attacked her daughter instead. Now Mann is afraid of Kidman. Eccleston tells Kidman he must return to battle at the front and disappears. One morning Kidman awakes to hear the children screaming. She then hears loud noises from the upper story of the house. That night, Mann and Bentley sneak out of the house and find their father as they stumble over some graves, which they see belong to the servants. Kidman then finds photos of the three servants in "the book of the dead." The servants appear, Kidman holds a shotgun on them, and they tell her that they all died of tuberculosis more than fifty years earlier. However, it turns out that Cassidy and Sykes were killed by their mother, Flanagan, who then committed suicide. But there's more… Kidman learns she has gone insane from isolation and, fearing Eccleston was killed in the war, smothered her children before the servants arrived, then shot and killed herself. Flanagan's ghost tells Kidman that they will all learn to live with each other in the house, including Eccleston, who did die in the war. The only benefit from these dire doings is that the children are no longer sensitive to sunlight. Not an easy film to follow, but an effectively chilling ghost story inspired by Henry James' 1898 novella *The Turn of the Screw*. Songs/Music: "I Only Have Eyes for You" (Harry Warren, Al Dubin), "Vals Opus 69 No. 1" (Frederic

Tom Keene and Karen Morley in *Our Daily Bread*, 1934.

Chopin). **p**, Fernando Bovaira, Jose Luis Cuerda, Sunmin Park, Tom Cruise, Bob and Harvey Weinstein; **d&w&m**, Alejandro Amenábar; **cast**, Nicole Kidman, Fionnula Flanagan, Christopher Eccleston, Alakina Mann, James Bentley, Eric Sykes, Elaine Cassidy, Renee Asherson, Gordon Reid, Keith Allen; **c**, Javier Aguirresarobe; **ed**, Nacho Ruiz Capillas; **prod d & art d**, Benjamin Fernandez; **set d**, Emilio Ardura, Elli Griff; **spec eff**, Derek Langley.

Our Betters ★★★ 1933; U.S.; 83m; RKO; B/W; Comedy; Children: Acceptable. High society romp sees Bennett, an American heiress to a hardware fortune, wedded to Mowbray, a stiff-necked British lord. Bored and feeling restricted by the dry and unimaginative decorum of the aristocracy, Bennett breaks free and goes on a rebellious social spree. She defiantly dons black attire for events requiring white apparel and hosts a tea party that turns into a wild and uncontrollable event where everyone is encouraged to discard their manners. Bennett is very funny in turning the heads of her fellow aristocrats as well as turning their traditions upside down, all these enjoyable antics cleverly directed by pantheon director Cukor, who turns this often hilarious tale into a satire lampooning a posturing and pompous aristocracy, one that made the British upper crust uneasy when this film was released. Songs: "The Wedding March" (1843; from "A Midsummer Night's Dream, Op. 61" by Felix Mendelssohn-Bartholdy), "Waltz of the Flowers" (1891-1892; from "The Nutcracker Ballet, Op. 71" by Pyotr Ilyich Tchaikovsky), and "God Save the Queen" (1744; music by Henry Carey). *Author's Note*: Cukor, who was gay, has Davis, a dancing teacher, portray his character as a mincing and effeminate person wearing rouged lips and cheeks, his stereotypical pansy being the closest thing Cukor could then present in capturing a homosexual on film in those days as such characterizations had been strictly forbidden by the American censors (the Hays and later the Breen Office, which was sponsored by all the U.S. studios to protect the morals of the American public). Cukor told this author that "Selznick, who produced **Our Betters** for RKO, allowed me a free hand in putting any accent on the comedic routines in that picture and I worked out a lot of funny business with my actors, especially Constance [Bennett] who was a fine comedienne with a natural and deep sense of humor. That picture so impressed Louis B. Mayer, who was running the show at MGM and was also Selznick's father-in-law that he invited Selznick to set up his own production unit at MGM and Selznick left RKO and took me with him, which was one of the best breaks I ever had in my career." **p**, David O. Selznick; **d**, George Cukor; **cast**, Constance Bennett, Gilbert Roland, Charles Starrett, Anita Louise, Grant Mitchell, Hugh Sinclair, Alan Mowbray, Violet Kemble-Cooper, Phoebe Foster, Minor Watson; **w**, Jane Murfin, Harry Wagstaff Gribble (based on a play by W. Somerset Maugham); **c**, Charles Rosher; **m**, Max

Steiner; **ed**, Jack Kitchin; **art d**, Van Nest Polglase; **spec eff**, Harry Redmond, Sr.

Our Daily Bread ★★★ 1934; U.S.; 80m; King W. Vidor Productions/UA; Drama; Children: Cautionary; **DVD**; **VHS**. The title for this film has been used for many productions, but this one is the standout under that name, a film that powerfully depicts the struggles of the millions of Americans desperately trying to survive during the Great Depression. Morley and Keene, a married couple without jobs and any means of support suddenly inherit a broken-down farm and they move there with the idea of inviting as many similarly jobless persons to be part of a farm collective or a commune where everyone works for the common good of all. The workers slave like worker ants on the farm, sewing corn and wheat and tilling the land, but trouble arrives in the person of sexy Pepper, a vixen who seduces Keene and who, grown restless and depressed at seeing no fruition at the farm, runs away with her. As they make their way to the city, Keene finds a hidden stream of pure water, the very nourishment the crops at his farm need to survive and, in fact, those crops are then withering under a blazing sun that threatens to wipe out everything the commune has been working to create. Thinking on this, Keene's conscience demands that he return to the farm and he does, urging the workers to frantically create an irrigational ditch of some distance that will divert the stream he has found so that it flows to the crops on the farm. In a spectacular sequence of scenes, pantheon director Vidor shows scores of men, women and children frantically using all manner of implements to create a ditch in diverting that stream, shoring the ditch with boulders while desperately chopping down trees and clearing away bushes, a human chain of workers running ahead of each other to create the ditch and keep the water flowing until it courses down into the valley and the waiting, thirsty crops, nourishing these labored plants, reviving them and where all celebrate the fact that they will survive. The irrigation scenes which culminate the struggles of these sincere characters are some of the most dynamic and telling ever put on the screen, capturing mesmerizing images of an anxiety-driven furiousness never equaled. The acting, especially that of Morley, is exceptional, and the script is simple and direct and as plain as calloused on the hands of a hard-working laborer. Though the film saw limited release and did not recoup its investment, it remains a cult classic to this day. Songs: "Just Because You're You" (composer unknown), "Gwine to Rune All Night (De Camptown Races)" (1850; Stephen Foster), "Oh! Susanna" (1848; Stephen Foster) and "You're in the Army Now" (traditional). *Author's Note*: Vidor told this author that "I went to Irving Thalberg at MGM with a proposal for **Our Daily Bread** and, after he looked over the script he gave me a horrified look and told me that he would 'never make a film with a socialist message' and asked me if I was a communist. I told him that I was not, but that had nothing to do with the story. I could not find any studio that would support the picture so I went to private investors. I had so little money to make the picture that I could not afford to hire any established film actors, except for Karen [Morley], who heard about the picture's story and volunteered her services as that story, she said, followed her political convictions. All of the rest of the actors were amateurs, but they proved to be very good in their roles. Even Barbara Pepper, who had limited film experience [she had earlier played a slave girl in Eddie Cantor's comedy, **Roman Scandals**, 1933, and had begun her career in burlesque with Lucille Ball and had appeared in the chorus of a Ziegfeld Follies production] and who plays a scheming tramp, was great in her role. She played that kind of part in many other pictures, until she was sought after as much as Irish Adrian, Marion Martin and Veda Ann Borg, all wonderful actresses who specialized in playing Circe or the kind of brassy blondes oozing seduction and sex to overwhelm any red-blooded male. I thought at the time that **Our Daily Bread** would be the first part of a trilogy based on the downtrodden people in the [Great] Depression, but it did so poorly in distribution that I never got the other two projects off the ground. I guess it was too socialist in nature. After Louis B. Mayer [head of MGM where

Vidor most often worked] saw **Our Daily Bread**, he called me up and said: 'Don't make any more pictures like that, my boy, unless you want to end your career out here [in California] and move to Russia where they make those kind of pictures and where you'll never be able to get a porterhouse steak in Moscow." Morley, who had scored big as Paul Muni's gun moll in **Scarface**, 1932, and whose career was spiraling upward toward success, became deeply involved in left-wing political causes and, by the early 1940s, her film career was almost at an end. It was permanently wrecked in 1947 when she appeared before the U.S. House of Un-American Activities Committee (HUAC) and where she refused to answer questions about her involvement in the Communist Party during the 1930s, her defiance causing her to be put on the Hollywood blacklist. Morley told this author that "McCarthyism destroyed not only my career but dozens of others, all very talented people, because of their political convictions. But I was in deep trouble about my politics many years earlier. Just after making **Scarface**, where I had my best role as Poppy, a woman excited by gangsters and guns, I married Charles Vidor, who was one of the promising directors at MGM. That enraged Louis B. Mayer, who ran that studio and who called me 'a Bolshevik' and that I was out to destroy one of his best young directors and I knew from that point on that Mayer would see to it that I would not get any really good parts at MGM after that and I was right. Mayer was the most powerful of all the old movie moguls and when he branded you for oblivion you were on your way to nowhere. All the other moguls were afraid of him, except Harry Cohn at Columbia, but he was nuts." Morley, who unsuccessfully ran as a candidate for lieutenant governor for New York in 1947 on the American Labor Party ticket, died at age ninety-three on March 8, 2003, at the Motion Picture Country House in Woodland Hills, California. **p&d**, King Vidor; **cast**, Karen Morley, Tom Keene, Barbara Pepper, Addison Richards, John Qualen, Lloyd Ingraham, Sidney Bracey, Henry Hall, Nellie V. Nichols, Frank Minor; **w**, Vidor, Elizabeth Hill, Joseph L. Mankiewicz (based on a story by Vidor); **c**, Robert Planck; **m**, Alfred Newman; **ed**, Lloyd Nosler.

Our Hearts Were Growing Up ★★★ 1946; U.S.; 83m; PAR; B/W; Comedy; Children: Acceptable. Russell and Lynn are college friends roaring through the 1920s who have boyfriend problems with Brown and Edwards. They get them back with the help of a kindly bootlegger, Donlevy. A charming comedy and re-creation of the carefree Jazz Age, based on the adventures of authors Cornelia Otis Skinner (1899-1979), portrayed by Russell, and Emily Kimbrough (1899-1989), essayed by Lynn. This is an entertaining sequel to **Our Hearts Were Young and Gay**, 1944. Unfortunately this worthy film is not presently (at this writing) available in any home-viewing format. **p**, Daniel Dare; **d**, William D. Russell; **cast**, Gail Russell, Diana Lynn, Brian Donlevy, Billy De Wolfe, James Brown, Bill Edwards, William Demarest, Mary Hatcher, Sara Haden, Mikhail Rasumny, Isabel Randolph, Frank Faylen, Byron Barr, Ann Doran, Hobart Cavanaugh, Mona Freeman; **w**, Norman Panama, Melvin Frank (based on the story by Frank Waldman); **c**, Stuart Thompson; **m**, Victor Young; **ed**, Doane Harrison; **art d**, Hans Dreier, Haldane Douglas; **set d**, Sam Comer; **spec eff**, Farciot Edouart, Gordon Jennings, Loyal Griggs, Paul K. Lerpae.

Our Hearts Were Young and Gay ★★★ 1944; U.S.; 81m; PAR; B/W; Comedy; Children: Acceptable. Enjoyable comedy sees Russell enacting the role of author Cornelia Otis Skinner (1899-1979) and Lynn portraying her close friend and fellow author, Emily Kimbrough (1899-1989). After the two girls graduate from college (both Skinner and Kimbrough attended the upscale Bryn Mawr College together), they take a European tour, visiting the hot spots of London and Paris and dallying with a number of eagerly pursuing beaus along the way, including some flirtatious shipboard encounters. Many humorous events present themselves, including a hilarious scene where the girls cavort at an expensive restaurant and are nonplussed in an episode of shedding rabbit capes. After arriving in the City of Light, the girls get themselves locked inside Notre

Gail Russell and Diana Lynn in *Our Hearts Were Young and Gay,* 1944.

Dame Cathedral for a whole night, barely escaping with their reputations intact. Frothy and frilled with the outlandish fancies of the Roaring Twenties, this outing thoroughly amuses and entertains. Its lighthearted scenes capture the flavor of that zany and capricious era so well remembered by the American moneyed class that flitted between the States and the Continent while flaunting flaming youth. An equally entertaining sequel was made two years later, **Our Hearts Were Growing Up**, 1946. Skinner later stated that it was the audacious and adventurous Kimbrough who consistently got them into hot water, saying: "To know Emily is to enhance one's days with gaiety, charm, and occasional terror." *Author's Note*: The generation that succeeded that of Skinner and Kimbrough was enmeshed in the Great Depression and World War II, a hardscrabble era in which such capricious journeys were not affordable. A poignant and telling scene in **Sands of Iwo Jima**, 1949, grimly exhibited the differences between those two generations when a young Marine, portrayed by Martin Milner, races ashore with his unit only to be shot dead by the enemy on the beach. A close-up shows sand upon his opened, lifeless eyes and a book edging from his pocket that displays the title of the popular work by Skinner and Kimbrough, *Our Hearts Were Young and Gay*. Yes those hearts were filled with gaiety, but only for a privileged few, as affirmed by John Wayne, who stars in **Sands of Iwo Jima**, and who stated to this author: "I saw that scene with Marty [Milner] lying dead on the beach with his boy's face frozen by Death and where the camera closes on the title of that book in his breast pocket. I later asked the screenwriter [Harry Brown] why he wrote the scene that way and he said: 'To show that this young American seeks the same joys and happiness the book describes, but will never see either, only the sands of that island in the Pacific.' That book came out shortly before we invaded those Pacific islands, a bestseller, and a lot of our boys were reading it on board transports taking them to battle and many of those great and brave young men would never see London or Paris. That powerful scene of Marty dead on the beach with that book in his pocket has never left my mind. That little scene tells the story of a whole generation with sort of a bittersweet nostalgia for a lifestyle his character, and tens of thousands of others like him, would never enjoy." When recalling all this, tears welled up in Wayne's eyes and, dabbing them away with a dinner napkin—we were eating dinner on board a mine sweeper he had converted into his personal yacht—he said: "I get very emotional about those wonderful boys. The Lost Generation, they say, was made up of those living or visiting in Paris in the Twenties, like Cornelia Skinner and Emily Kimbrough, but America's real Lost Generation was lying dead on that beach where Marty fell to save the world from tyranny." **p**, Sheridan Gibney; **d**, Lewis Allen; **cast**, Gail Russell, Diana Lynn, Charles Ruggles, Dorothy Gish, Beulah Bondi, James Brown, Bill Edwards, Jean Heather, Alma Kruger, Nina Koshetz, Queenie Leonard,

Jo Morrow and Alec Guinness in *Our Man in Havana*, 1960.

Marie McDonald, Noel Neill; **w**, Gibney (based on the book by Cornelia Otis Skinner and Emily Kimbrough); **c**, Theodor Sparkuhl; **m**, Werner Heymann; **ed**, Paul Weatherwax; **art d**, Hans Dreier, Earl Hedrick; **set d**, Ray Moyer, **spec eff**, Farciot Edouart, Gordon Jennings.

Our Hitler, A Film from Germany ★★★ 1980; West Germany; France; U.K.; 407m; TMS Films/Omni Zoetrope; B/W-Color; War/Biography/History; Children: Unacceptable. This experimental film depicts in a combination of dramatic scenes and archival footage the rise and fall of Germany during the years of the dictator Adolf Hitler (1889-1945), who is played by Schubert. Director Syberberg grew up under Hitler's regime, suffering from its tyranny, and recalls the evil of those years, but also found some good in them. Archival footing is in black and white and the film runs with a score by Richard Wagner. Its historical accuracy is up for interpretation. The scenes are presented in Kafkaesque images such as a toga-clad Hitler rising from the grave to Wagnerian strains and much of the imagery stems from the Teutonic slogans and artwork created by the Nazis to vault Hitler to godlike status. *Author's Note*: Originally 442 minutes, the American print was cut to 407 minutes. Violence prohibits viewing by children. (In German; English subtitles.) **p**, Bernd Eichinger; **d&w**, Hans-Jürgen Syberberg; **cast**, Heinz Schubert, Peter Kern, Hellmut Lange, Rainer von Artenfels, Martin Sperr, Peter Moland, Johannes Buzalski, Alfred Edel, Harry Baer, André Heller; **c**, Dietrich Lohmann; **ed**, Jutta Brandstaedter; **prod d**, Hans Gailling.

Our Hospitality ★★★★ 1923 (silent); U.S.; 65m/7 reels (73m 1995 edition); Metro Pictures Corporation; B/W; Comedy; Children: Acceptable; **DVD**. The inimitable Keaton presents a laugh-packed comedy with this delightful tale, set in the Old South of 1831. He is notified that he has inherited an estate in ante-bellum Dixie and he envisions a life of luxury within the halls of a huge pillared mansion. He travels southward on a strange-looking train (the Stephenson Rocket; Keaton was obsessed with anything mechanical and selected this train because it was the oddest-looking ever invented and he had it reconstructed to its finite detail and, following the completion of the production, donated it to the Smithsonian Institute). While on board this rattling train (where the passengers bounce about like rubber balls and pass an odd assortment of creatures and people, including a man who inexplicably hurls rocks at the engineer), Keaton encounters the lovely Talmadge (his wife in real life), having dinner with her. En route he learns that he is staying with her family, a clan that has had a long-standing feud with his now deceased relatives and that he is the last of that kin, which his hosts intend to dispatch. Southern hospitality, however, insists that it would be poor decorum to shoot their guest in their own home, so they plan to eliminate

him once he leaves the premises. Learning this upon his arrival, Keaton employs every device in his trick bag of comedic routines to avoid stepping from the domicile of these dangerous southerners, producing one hilarious sight gag after another. He manages to save himself from execution by escaping the manse dressed as a woman, but his enemies are soon on to his ruse and are in hot pursuit, along with Talmadge, who is now madly in love with him. As Talmadge wildly races after her man, she accidentally falls into water with a fast moving current that quickly takes her perilously close to a lethal waterfall, but Keaton, who also loves the girl, rescues her by using a rope to swing across the churning waters to pluck her at the last minute from doom. (This sequence is one of Keaton's most spectacular and breathtaking stunts, one which he personally performed.) By saving Talmadge, her relatives are so grateful that they decide to quit their feud and embrace Keaton into their family and where he, indeed, not only gets his inheritance, but the girl of his dreams as a bonus for his good deed. This film proved to be one of Keaton's most successful, but it was not put in the can until the Old Stone Face risked his life on several occasions in doing some stunning and dangerous stunts. *Author's Note*: Keaton told this author that "I almost lost my life in **Our Hospitality** twice. In one of the early shots for that picture, I was in a river with a strong current, holding on to a log and the wire controlling that sixteen-foot log broke and sent me downstream in a hurry toward some rapids and I got battered on the head a lot until some crew members fished me out. That gave me a real jar and I thought twice about doing the big stunt at the end of the picture where I have to save Natalie [Talmadge]. Well, when I swung across the river to grab her from rushing water, the wire on that rope also snapped and I pitched straight down into the river head first and I swallowed so much water that I went blank. I almost drowned in that one and they had to take me to a hospital where I was coughing up bilge for hours. Thankfully, the cameras were rolling all the time in both of those takes and they got all the action. We reshot the last scene and got it right, but I made sure that more than one wire was controlling that rope. I had a lot of pain from those stunts and every time an ache talked back to me I was reminded that I was human and mortal and that any more stunts like those might be my last. I loved doing those pictures, but I made up my mind that I was not going to die for them." **p**, Joseph M. Schenck; **d**, Buster Keaton, Jack Blystone; **cast**, Keaton, Natalie Talmadge, Buster Keaton, Jr., Jose Keaton, Joe Roberts, Ralph Bushman, Craig Ward, Monte Collins, Kitty Bradbury, Jack Duffy; **w**, Jean Havez, Joseph Mitchell, Clyde Bruckman; **c**, Gordon Jennings, Elgin Lessley; **art d**, Fred Gabourie.

Our Man Flint ★★★ 1966; U.S.; 108m; ; Color; Spy Drama/Satire; Children: Unacceptable (MPAA: PG); **DVD**; **VHS**. Coburn is an ultra-cool spy in this espionage sendup that mimics the James Bond series, and where the world's weather goes haywire with violent storms and long-dormant volcanoes erupting. Agents working for American intelligence chief Cobb drop like flies, so he recalls former super spy Flint (Coburn) to find out what's going on. Very rich and very much a man after any fetching woman, Coburn takes on the job and discovers that scientists at a secret organization known as Galaxy are bumping off the agents in their ambitions to take over the planet by controlling its weather. Coburn, with the most automatic toothy and insincere smile ever registered on a human face, accomplishes his mission largely with the help of his amazing cigarette lighter which has eighty-three life-saving or annihilating applications. The film was a hit that spawned a 1967 sequel, **In Like Flint**. Violence and sensuality prohibit viewing by children; **p**, Saul David; **d**, Daniel Mann; **cast**, James Coburn, Lee J. Cobb, Gila Golan, Edward Mulhare, Benson Fong, Shelby Grant, Sigrid Valdis, Gianna Serra, Helen Funai, Michael St. Clair, Rhys Williams, James Brolin. Steven Geray; **w**, Hal Fimberg, Ben Starr (based on a story by Fimberg); **c**, Daniel L. Fapp (CinemaScope; DeLuxe Color); **m**, Jerry Goldsmith; **ed**, William Reynolds; **art d**, Jack Martin Smith, Ed Graves; **set d**, Walter M. Scott, Raphael Bretton; **spec eff**, L.B. Abbott, Emil Kosa, Jr., Howard Lydecker.

Our Man in Havana ★★★★ 1960; U.K.; 111m; Kingsmead Productions/COL; B/W; Comedy; Children: Unacceptable; **DVD**; **VHS**. Guinness gives another masterful performance in this droll but hilarious espionage spoof. This time, he is a failed businessman turned British spy in pre-revolutionary Cuba. He runs a shop selling vacuum cleaners in Havana, but has had little success in selling his products to unsophisticated natives who more or less like their floors dirty and their lives unkempt. Urbane Coward, a British spymaster, approaches Guinness, asking him to act as a secret agent in this "weak area" of information. To improve conditions for his teenage daughter, Morrow, Guinness accepts the position, but knows he has no information to pass along to Coward and subsequently British intelligence in London, so, in order to be handsomely paid for any tidbit of secret data, he begins to invent information. Kovacs, the posturing head of the secret police, who has cast a covetous eye on Morrow, grows suspicious of Guinness when seeing him act furtively when sneaking about Havana's streets at night. He begins to spy on Guinness and Guinness, in return, spies on Kovacs, each man creating a vast intrigue where none exists. While O'Hara, an attractive woman who has long been interested in Guinness, becomes alarmed at Guinness' strange behavior, things turn ugly and the macabre enters the story line when someone tries to kill Guinness, and, to save his life, he must dispatch this inexplicable enemy. Pressured by Coward to produce some substantial secrets, Guinness finally gives Coward some bizarre-looking drawings of gigantic war machines supposedly being manufactured by an unknown enemy in the mountains beyond Havana, but these deadly looking machines look very much like the products that Guinness has stocked in his shop, vacuum cleaners. When Coward grows suspicious, Guinness makes a clean breast of things and admits that he has been hoaxing the spymaster. He is ordered back to London and returns there with Morrow, only to see that fickle fortune has another surprise for him. Pantheon director Reed is really presenting a parody of one of his own masterpiece film noir films, **The Third Man**, 1950, mixing subtle comedy with some sinister events while Guinness, Coward and Kovacs are brilliant in their respective roles and with wonderful support from a sterling cast that also includes some standout performances from Ives and Richardson. The mirth oozes from beneath the many layers of the fabricated intrigues, emerging as engaging black humor that will most likely be lost on a less sophisticated viewer, but the film nevertheless remains a classic of its kind. Songs: "La Bella Cubana" (1853; music: Jose White Lafitte), "Domitila, donde vas?" (music: Ricardo Diaz). *Author's Note*: The gloomy atmosphere of Havana had been realistically dictated by recent events in that this film was produced shortly after Fidel Castro (b. 1926) and his communist revolutionaries took over the country and all of its gaiety fled with tens of thousands of political fugitives. "No one was laughing in Havana then," Guinness told this author. "All the old casinos and lavish bistros had been closed down. We [Guinness and his wife Merula] had dinner with Ernest Hemingway and his wife, Mary, but it was a rather glum affair. Hemingway had, I believe, been very supportive of Castro and opposed to the corrupt Batista [Fulgencio Batista, 1901-1973) regime that was overthrown, but then realized that Castro and his bunch were pretty much the same kind of people they had been fighting, and were now oppressing the natives. Hemingway was by then making plans to get out of Cuba. I later ran into Kenneth Tynan [1927-1980; British theater critic and writer] in a bar while we were still in production in Havana, and he asked if I wanted to join him to witness an event for which he had tickets. I asked him what he planned to see and he said: 'They [the communists] are going to shoot a couple of sixteen-year-olds, a boy and a girl. I thought you might like to see that.' I told him that I certainly did not and I have always wondered about what lurked in the mind of Mr. Tynan." **p&d**, Carol Reed; **cast**, Alec Guinness, Burl Ives, Maureen O'Hara, Ernie Kovacs, Noel Coward, Ralph Richardson, Jo Morrow, Raymond Huntley, Maurice Denham, Rachel Roberts; **w**, Graham

Gale Gordon and Eve Arden in *Our Miss Brooks*, 1956.

Greene (based on his novel); **c**, Oswald Morris; **m**, Frank and Laurence Deniz; **ed**, Bert Bates; **art d**, John Box.

Our Miss Brooks ★★★ 1956; U.S.; 85m; Lute Productions/WB; B/W; Comedy; Children: Acceptable. Arden is exceptional as the indefatigable Miss Connie Brooks in this full-length feature that was released right after the popular television series (1952-1956) ended. The film takes us to the start of Arden's adventures, teaching teenagers at Madison High School and pursuing a handsome teacher, Rockwell, who always seems beyond her romantic grasp. A subplot has her trying to make Rockwell jealous by flirting with Porter. Also reprising their roles from the television series are Gale Gordon as the principal Osgood Conklin, Richard Crenna as Walter Denton, and Jane Morgan as Miss Brooks' roommate. Good comedy with many funny moments. Songs: "Brooks Theme" (1952; music: Wilbur J. Hatch), "Whistling Bells" (1955; music: Farian I. Myers). **p**, David Weisbart; **d**, Al Lewis; **cast**, Eve Arden, Gale Gordon, Robert Rockwell, Don Porter, Jane Morgan, Richard Crenna, Nick Adams, Leonard Smith, Gloria McMillan, Joseph Kearns, William Newell, Marjorie Bennett; **w**, Lewis, Joseph Quillan (based on an idea by Robert Mann, from the CBS television series); **c**, Joseph LaShelle; **m**, Roy Webb; **ed**, Fredrick Y. Smith; **art d**, Leo K. Kuter; **set d**, William Wallace.

Our Mother's House ★★★ 1967; U.K.; 104m; Filmways/MGM; Color; Drama; Children: Unacceptable; **DVD**. A touching tale sees seven children living in a large Victorian house with their bedridden mother. She reads to them every night from the Bible and they call it "Mothertime." When she dies, they bury her in the backyard so that no one knows she is dead and to avoid being sent to an orphanage. They continue going to school and each night go to her grave and discuss their low finances. One day, their long-lost father, Bogarde, surfaces. But he is even less responsible than his children, spending their money and bringing women home. He finally tells them they are all illegitimate, which shatters the children's image of their mother as a saint. One of the girls hits Bogarde fatally with a fireplace poker and the children leave the house to face the world a lot more realistically. Violence prohibits viewing by children. **p&d**, Jack Clayton; **cast**, Dirk Bogarde, Maggie Brooks, Pamela Franklin, Mark Lester, Louis Sheldon Williams, John Gugolka, Sarah (Phoebe) Nicholls, Gustav Henry, Parnum Wallace; **w**, Jeremy Brooks, Haya Harareet (based on the novel by Julian Gloag); **c**, Larry Pizer (Metrocolor); **m**, Georges Delerue; **ed**, Tom Priestley; **art d**, Reece Pemberton; **set d**, Ian Whittaker.

Our Relations ★★★ 1936; U.S.; 65m; Stan Laurel-Hal Roach/MGM; B/W; Comedy; Children: Acceptable; **DVD**; **VHS**. Often hilarious romp

Oliver Hardy, Arthur Housman and Stan Laurel in *Our Relations*, 1936.

by classic clowns Laurel and Hardy opens when they are unaware that their long-lost twin brothers are in town, sailors on shore leave in San Francisco, who have a valuable pearl ring entrusted to them by their ship's captain, Toler. A riot of mistaken identities results after a gang of hoodlums tries to steal the ring. The boys are exceptional in their dual roles as they race about San Francisco being chased by thugs and while chasing their look-alikes and while getting mixed up with two bar girls, Adrian and Lona Andre. This film is hilarious and is one of the boys' best feature-length comedies, where Hale and Finlayson help them out in some side-splitting sight gags. Songs: "Ku-Ku" (Laurel and Hardy theme song; music: Marvin Hatley), "The Sailor's Hornpipe" (traditional), "Sailing, Sailing (Over the Bounding Main)" (1880; music: Godfrey Marks), "Happy Birthday to You" (1893; Mildred J. Hill, Patty S. Hill). **p**, Stan Laurel, L.A. French; **d**, Harry Lachman; **cast**, Stan Laurel, Oliver Hardy, Alan Hale, Sidney Toler, Daphne Pollard, Betty Healy, James Finlayson, Iris Adrian, Lona Andre, Noel Madison, Ralf Harolde, Arthur Housman, Virginia Grey, Charlie Hall; **w**, Richard Connell, Felix Adler, Charles Rogers, Jack Jevne (based on the short story "The Money Box" by William Wymark Jacobs); **c**, Rudolph Mate; **m**, Leroy Shield; **ed**, Bert Jordan; **art d**, Arthur I. Royce, William L. Stevens; **spec eff**, Roy Seawright.

Our Town ★★★★ 1940; U.S.; 90m; Sol Lesser Productions/UA; B/W; Drama; Children: Cautionary; **DVD**; **VHS**. Thornton Wilder's superb small-town profile of Grover's Corners, a New England hamlet, comes very much alive with this wonderful production where Craven acts as the town's chronicler and narrator of some of its citizens. Holden is the son of a doctor, who falls in love with Scott, the hardworking daughter of the local editor. Their courtship is strained, but Holden manages to win Scott's hand, and they have a happy but brief marriage that ends when Scott dies in childbirth. This tale is told in three time periods, 1901, 1904 and 1913, showing how Holden and Scott grow up from teenagers to adults as their fates slowly merge and while the adults of the town watch their rites of passage with amusement and concern. The story is simple and direct, showing in detail the joys, triumphs and misfortunes of these carefully developed characters. Director Wood is faithful to the Wilder play (one that was more enacted by small-town productions than any other in the 20th Century) presenting its prosaic tale with dazzling montages, alternating shadowy and brightly lit scenes and focusing on the detail that nostalgically highlights the periods depicted. Scott appears in her first feature film and is outstanding as the ill-starred young and idealistic woman, and Holden is also exceptional as the young man who falls in love with her. Kibbee and Bondi, as Scott's parents, and Mitchell and Bainter as Holden's parents, are wonderful in their compassionate roles as are all of the supporting players.

Copland's moving score enhances every precious scene of this superlative production, and Menzies' sets are impressive, adding to the overall high production value. One somber sequence—where Scott envisions her own death while enduring agony in childbirth and sees herself as a spirit viewing her own relatives and husband Holden while peering upward from her own grave—will be too disturbing for young children. Songs: "Art Thou Weary? Art Thou Languid?" (1868; music: from "Stephanos" by Henry W. Baker; Greek lyrics by the Judean, Stephen of Mar Saba and with the 1862 English translation by John M. Neale), "The Wedding March" (1843; from "A Midsummer Night's Dream, Op. 61" by Felix Mendelssohn-Bartholdy), "Bridal Chorus (Here Comes the Bride)" (1850; from "Lohengrin" by Richard Wagner). ***Author's Note***: Holden thought that his role in this film "was only part of a human community where everyone made up its body and I was an arm. **Our Town** is really a tender story, but it is, in the end, a tragedy where love is lost early to premature death. It's beautifully written and wrenches the heart, but there is something funereal about it. The viewer sees the struggles and joys of these small-town people and, just when you think a happy ending is in sight, wham—the young wife dies in childbirth. A fine picture, but it says a sad goodbye." **p**, Sol Lesser; **d**, Sam Wood; **cast**, William Holden, Martha Scott, Fay Bainter, Beulah Bondi, Thomas Mitchell, Guy Kibbee, Stuart Erwin, Doro Merande, Philip Wood, Spencer Charters, Tom Drake, Frank Craven (narrator); **w**, Thornton Wilder, Frank Craven, Harry Chandlee (based on the play by Wilder); **c**, Bert Glennon; **m**, Aaron Copland; **ed**, Sherman Todd; **prod d**, William Cameron Menzies; **art d**, Lewis J. Rachmil; **set d**, James W. Payne; **spec eff**, Jack Cosgrove.

Our Vines Have Tender Grapes ★★★★ 1945; U.S.; 105m; MGM; B/W; Drama; Children: Acceptable; **DVD**; **VHS**. One of the most heartwarming films ever made profiles a small Norwegian farm family living in Wisconsin. Robinson is the hardworking farmer who strives to make life better for his equally hardworking wife, Moorehead, and, especially, his seven-year-old daughter, O'Brien. Sensitive and caring, O'Brien is shown encountering the joys and tragedies of her child's world. She is devastated after accidentally killing a squirrel, but the always compassionate Robinson comforts her, knowing how tender are her feelings. His kindness extends to making an extra effort to bring simply wonders to O'Brien. When he learns that a circus is going to be passing through his area, Robinson drives to a nearby town with O'Brien and, while the train is briefly stopped at the station, offers one of the circus animal trainers a few dollars to lead an elephant from one of the train's freight cars in order that O'Brien can see the gentle giant, the sight of this creature filling her with wonder and delight. The nearby town of Benson Junction is later awash with excitement when Gifford, a beautiful, young teacher, arrives to teach the local children. Widely spread gossip ensues after local handsome editor Craig begins a hesitant romance with Gifford and where Gifford resists his proposal since she fears being trapped in a small town and its hum-drum lifestyle. When Craig is drafted into the service (it is war time), he asks Gifford to wait for him, but she cannot bring herself to make this commitment. Meanwhile, a disaster occurs when O'Brien and her five-year-old companion, Jenkins, who lives on a nearby farm, vanish into thin air during torrential spring rainstorms. A frantic search ensues, and Robinson and others spot the children floating down a swollen river in a bathtub and manage to rescue them before they are swept from sight. So emotionally upset is Robinson that he is in a quandary as to whether to spank or embrace O'Brien for undertaking this perilous expedition with Jenkins that has almost ended in tragedy. Being a loving father, he can only hug her in gratitude that she has survived her spectacular misadventure. Though fatigued by his daily chores, Robinson always takes enough time to answer O'Brien's many questions, and when she becomes upset when hearing that her friend, Craig, must go away to serve in the armed forces, Robinson patiently explains to her that to preserve "peace on earth" one had to fight to keep that peace. Robinson's simple but humanitarian principles are later demonstrated by O'Brien, who has learned well her father's love for his fellow man after another farmer's farm has been destroyed by a fire and all the livestock killed. The residents of the community gather, and Craig, just before he is to go into service, asks one and all to donate what they can to help the bereft farm family. O'Brien is the first to stand up to state that she is donating her most prized possession on earth, an animal she loves with all her heart, her pet calf. While Robinson beams with pride at his daughter's wonderful sacrifice, O'Brien's gift so moves the community that all of the residents generously pledge livestock, food, supplies, equipment and just about everything it will take to put that destitute farm family back on its feet, one of the most emotionally rewarding scenes ever to appear in any film. Gifford, after seeing this generous and universal outpouring from these simple folk now realizes that there is nothing boring or dull about the people of Benson Junction and that this is one of the finest places on earth to live. She decides to sink her roots in this courageous and compassionate community and tells Craig that she will be waiting for him when he returns after the war is over. Everyone appearing in this stirring and memorable film is outstanding, from Robinson to O'Brien, from Gifford to Craig, from Moorehead to the precocious Jenkins, and every one of its touching and telling scenes is worth watching, a truly great film that will touch every human heart. Songs: "Beautiful Dreamer" (1862; Stephen Foster), "Entry of the Gladiators" (1897; Julius Fucik), "Joy to the World" (1719; music: George Frideric Handel; hymn lyrics: Isaac Watts). *Author's Note*: Louis B. Mayer, head of MGM, proudly pointed to this film as the best example of the kind of family film his studio produced and he personally promoted it, stating that little Butch Jenkins was one of the greatest actors on earth (the freckle-faced boy was his favorite actor at MGM). The film not only advanced Jenkins' career, but was instrumental in getting O'Brien many new good roles. Robinson told this author that "one of the reasons why **Our Vines Have Tender Grapes** was such a success was the fact that it was written by a gifted writer, Dalton Trumbo, whom I had known for years and whose writing I admired. When, some years later, he came under scrutiny by Congress for his left-wing political associations, he was blacklisted. Because I had befriended him and told many persons that I believed he was a talented writer, I, too, came under criticism from some persons in Washington, and that is called 'guilt by association' and that is nonsense." Robinson always felt that his role in this film was "one of my best performances." **p**, Robert Sisk; **d**, Roy Rowland; **cast**, Edward G. Robinson, Margaret O'Brien, James Craig, Frances Gifford, Agnes Moorehead, Morris Carnovsky, Jackie "Butch" Jenkins, Sara Haden, Dorothy Morris, Louis Jean Heydt, Charles Middleton; **w**, Dalton Trumbo (based on the novel *For Our Vines Have Tender Grapes* by George Victor Martin); **c**, Robert Surtees; **m**, Bronislau Kaper; **ed**, Ralph E. Winters; **art d**, Cedric Gibbons; **set d**, Edwin B. Willis; **spec eff**, A. Arnold Gillespie, Danny Hall, Warren Newcombe, Mark Davis.

Our Wife ★★★ 1941; U.S.; 95m; COL; B/W; Comedy; Children: Acceptable. The urbane Douglas is a standout as a talented musician-composer who turns to the bottle after his wife, Drew, divorces him. Hussey enters his life and rescues him from his depression. He finds new inspiration to complete his trumpet concerto, performs it, and it and he are big hits. Douglas and Hussey plan to marry, but now Drew wants him back and will stop at almost nothing to do it. This includes faking a fall down some stairs for sympathy (emulating Vivien Leigh's purposeful fall down a flight of stairs in **Gone with the Wind**, 1939, or the subsequent fall down some stairs made by Gene Tierney in **Leave Her to Heaven**, 1945, but in both of those instances, for different purposes). Hussey sees through this ruse and successfully turns the tables on the devious Drew and keeps Douglas for herself. It's good, light entertainment, suitable for children. Song: "Concerto for Trumpet" (Leo Shuken). **p&d**, John M. Stahl; **cast**, Melvyn Douglas, Ruth Hussey, Ellen Drew, Charles Coburn, John Hubbard, Harvey Stephens, Theresa Harris, Irving Bacon, Hobart Cavanaugh, Betty Blythe, Lloyd Bridges;

Margaret O'Brien, Edward G. Robinson and Agnes Moorehead in *Our Vines Have Tender Grapes,* 1945.

w, P.J. Wolfson (based on the play by Lillian Day, Lyon Mearson); **c**, Franz F. Planer; **m**, Leo Shuken; **ed**, Gene Havlick; **art d**, Lionel Banks.

Out of Africa ★★★★ 1985; U.S.; 161m; Mirage Enterprises; UNIV; Color; Biographical Drama; Children: Unacceptable (MPAA: PG); **BD**; **DVD**; **VHS**. Few films have ever captured the splendor, dangers and excitement of the "Dark Continent" as does this magnificent production, which is based upon the life of author Karen Blixen (who wrote under the pseudonym of Isak Dinesen) and who is superbly enacted by Streep. She is the headstrong and intelligent daughter of a wealthy Danish family who, in 1913, seeks to break free of the social restrictions then imposed upon her gender. She makes a deal with an impoverished aristocrat, Brandauer, offering him financial support in exchange for his marrying her, a union that is to be one of convenience for both of them (as was Karen's true life marriage). They then move to East Africa where they plan to establish a dairy farm, but when they arrive there, Brandauer uses Streep's considerable funds to start a coffee plantation. She meets and forms a deep friendship with big game hunter Redford, although she maintains her marital vows and later has sex with Brandauer, only to learn that he is a womanizing man and from whom she contracts the then life-threatening disease of syphilis. Growing ill, Streep returns to Denmark to undergo painful treatments to cure her condition, taking a new medicine, Salvarsan. In her absence, Brandauer minds the plantation, and after recovering, she returns to the plantation following the end of World War I, but soon discovers that her philandering spouse has continued his errant ways. Streep demands that he leave the house and he does and Streep then slowly develops a romance with the principled Redford. She discovers, however, that Redford cannot be tamed any more than the wild animals of Africa and that his fierce independence, which disdains European customs, wealth and titles, is rooted to the nomadic lifestyle of the Maasai tribe that he so much admires, and that he will never marry her. After he moves into her residence, Redford's staunch lifestyle credo becomes evident. To her dismay, he tells her that no piece of paper, such as a marriage certificate, would cause him to love her any more than what he does. She reluctantly accepts his conditions, further sorrowed when realizing that, because of the effects of syphilis, she can no longer have children. Streep seeks emotional fulfillment by devoting much of her time to teaching tribal children the basics in arithmetic, reading and writing. She meanwhile struggles to maintain the plantation, taking out bank loans to sustain its operations. After her many years of cultivating her land, she finally harvests a financially rewarding crop. A fire, however, devastates the plantation, destroying the harvest and all the equipment needed to continue operations. With the fire goes all of Streep's money, causing her to sell off her land, and she prepares to return to Denmark. The country of East Africa, like

Meryl Streep in *Out of Africa*, 1985.

her own life, is now in transition, as it is about to become a new nation called Kenya. Her long-standing affair with Redford has also vanished, but, after she holds a rummage sale that sees her selling off her last worldly possessions in her comfortable home, Redford returns to have a last dance with her. He tells her that he will fly her to Mombasa in his small biplane within a few days, but he never returns. Streep learns that Redford has been killed after his plane crashed, and the most important person in her life is now gone. After she attends Redford's funeral in the Ngong Hills, her faithful servant, Bowens, takes her to the station where she boards a train taking her to Mombasa and, eventually, her old life in Europe, her great romance with Redford and Africa at a poignant and bittersweet end. She goes on to become a writer spinning memorable tales about the Africa she keeps dear and deep in her heart. Director Pollack does a wonderful job in capturing the African wilds and elicits fine performances from Streep, Redford and Brandauer while sustaining a lively story line, and Watkin's superb cinematography captures the lush landscapes. This film was an enormous success, producing more than $128 million at the box office against an initial budget of $28 million, it swept the Academy Awards, with Oscars for Best Picture, Best Director (Pollack), Best Adapted Screenplay (Luedtke), Best Original Score (Barry), Best Cinematography (Watkin), Best Art Direction and Set Decoration (Grimes and MacAvin), and Best Sound Mixing (Jenkins, Alexander, Stensvold and Handford). Streep also received another nomination as Best Actress, this brilliant actress (some say the most talented film actress in the last thirty years) having received (to this writing) seventeen Oscar nominations and winning three Academy Awards for **Kramer vs. Kramer**, 1979 (Best Supporting Actress), **Sophie's Choice**, 1982 (Best Actress), and **The Iron Lady**, 2011 (Best Actress). Songs: "Sonata in A Major (K.331) 'Rondo alla Turca,'" "Concerto for clarinet and orchestra in A (K.622)," "Sinfonia Concertante in E flat major of Violin and Viola (K.364)," "Three Divertimenti (K.136, K.137, K.138)" (Wolfgang Amadeus Mozart); "For Me and My Gal" (1917; George W. Meyer); "Missouri Waltz" (1914; John Valentine Eppel); "Bridal Chorus (Here Comes the Bride)" (from "Lohengrin" by Richard Wagner); "There Is Beauty in the Bellow of the Beast" (1885; from "The Mikado"; music: Arthur Sullivan; lyrics: William Gilbert); "Auld Lang Syne" (1788; music: traditional; lyrics: Robert Burns); "God Save the King!" (1744; Henry Carey). *Author's Note*: When this author met Ernest Hemingway in 1959 that superlative scribe recommended a number of books to me, one of which was *Out of Africa* (1937), a work he had long admired. Hemingway had gone on his first major hunting safari to East Africa in 1933 and wrote a non-fiction work about his experiences, *The Green Hills of Africa* (1935), published two years before Isak Dinesen's (1885-1962; the author's pen name, using her family's last name) *Out of Africa* was published. She was nominated for the Nobel

Prize, but it was Hemingway, not Dinesen, who won that coveted award. "It was a shame that she never won it," Hemingway told this author, "because she, more than others, deserved that recognition for that fine book, one of the best books about Africa. She made the country come alive, although there was a great and dark tragedy within the walls of her own life." Dinesen took considerable liberties with her own family's heritage in writing that work, which is almost wholly autobiographical in that she did, indeed, marry an impoverished aristocrat and move to East Africa in 1913 on the eve of World War I, but her tale about syphilis plaguing her heroine, as she claimed it destroyed her own personal real life, is in question. It was her father, Wilhelm Dinesen, a Danish army officer, explorer and adventurer from Denmark, who bore that then incurable disease years after he had lived with the Chippewa Indians in Wisconsin in 1872 to 1873 and fathered an illegitimate daughter, who was born after he returned to Denmark. When his legitimate daughter Karen was ten years old, Wilhelm Dinesen was diagnosed with syphilis, reportedly contracted many years earlier from his sexual relations with Indian women, and, upon hearing this, he hanged himself. This traumatic experience emotionally affected Karen throughout her life, albeit she herself was diagnosed with syphilis a year after she married near penniless Swedish Baron Bror von Blixen-Finecke (1886-1946) after she had a failed love affair with his brother. She believed that she had contracted the disease from her husband, but there remains doubt about the true source of the disease. She separated from her husband in 1921 and they were divorced in 1925. By then she had become an accomplished writer, but the sins of the fathers that often plague their offspring certainly visited this tortured woman, harassing her emotions and intellectuality throughout her life. Her affliction of syphilis in one sense served as a cross she needed to bear to lend great empathy to her feminine protagonists, chiefly herself as the victimized role model in *Out of Africa*, this not intended as a criticism but an explanation of the writer's need to create conflict in constructing and rationalizing good drama (and the best of writers use all tools available as would a physician a scalpel or a carpenter a chisel). Further, the part Redford plays in this fine film is also wholly based on a real-life big game hunter, Denys Finch Hatton (1887-1931), who, following Dinesen's divorce, became her lover and moved into her East African residence in 1926 and used it as his home base in organizing his many safaris, chartered by such wealthy sportsmen as Chicago department store magnate Marshall Field and the Prince of Wales. Like Redford in the film, Finch Hatton was killed (on May 14, 1931), when flying his biplane. Unlike the altruistic Redford in the film, Finch Hatton was not always true to Karen in that it is claimed with credibility that he had affairs with other women while living with Dinesen, including a torrid romance with horse trainer and later accomplished Kenyon aviatrix Beryl Markham (1902-1986) in 1930. After Finch Hatton's death, Karen's coffee plantation failed, this during a worldwide economic depression, and, after her family estate sold off her African lands, she returned to Denmark where she lived out her life as an esteemed author. She insisted that she suffered from syphilis throughout her life, but it appears that there was no trace of that disease within her after 1925, some critics stating that she used that affliction as an excuse to permeate and promote her own legend (and one might also wonder if she harbored a deep-seated resentment of her father by genetically inheriting syphilis from him, if, indeed, that was the case, and that she did not otherwise contract the disease as she implies in her writings). She was psychosomatic in her perspective about that affliction, but the truth was that it did not eventually claim her life, a life that was ended due to anorexia nervosa. In Africa, she lived a brave life as an equal in a man's world where danger and death stalked the uninviting sultry savannahs every day and night and where she found a consoling freedom of spirit denied to her in a more socially rigid Europe and where, in that day, no female was considered the equal of any man. In embracing that man's world in Africa, Karen Dinesen also accepted the then widespread belief that its wild animals exclusively existed for the pleasure of big game hunters, of which Ernest Hemingway was a dedicated advocate. Although I was many times offered the opportunity, this author has never sought blood sports or hunted big game, believing that the animals of the wild and those in the so-called domestic world have enough trouble surviving among their own species, let alone contending with the lethal fantasies of some humans, who consider them "fair game." I have, however, long loved fishing, especially after trout and where that prey is most fairly fished when emerging one in the stream with that prey, giving it an equal chance within its own environment and where the adversary is as savvy and cunning as its predator. (While fishing once in Wisconsin, I hooked a Rainbow trout that escaped my net by swimming between my submerged, wader-encased legs, encircling one leg to break the line before swimming free.) Hemingway, a great trout fisherman, once took me on a brief fishing trip in northern Spain, where he instructed me in the techniques of fly-casting. He gave me three of his own hand-made lures, one of which I lost years later on that heroically evasive Rainbow trout. But all of that is a far cry from the widespread slaughter of African game that almost brought these great beasts to extinction and as is often exalted in **Out of Africa**. **p**, Sydney Pollack, Terence Clegg; **d**, Pollack; **cast**, Robert Redford, Meryl Streep, Klaus Maria Brandauer, Michael Kitchen, Malick Bowens, Joseph Thiaka, Stephen Kinyanjui, Michael Gough, Rachel Kempson, Graham Crowden; **w**, Kurt Luedtke (based on the books *Out of Africa* by Karen Blixen, *Isak Dinesen: The Life of a Story Teller* by Judith Thurman, and *Silence Will Speak* by Errol Trzebinski); **c**, David Watkin; **m**, John Barry; **ed**, Pembroke Herring, Sheldon Kahn, Fredric and William Steinkamp; **prod d**, Stephen Grimes; **art d**, Colin Grimes, Cliff Robinson, Herbert Westbrook; **set d**, Josie MacAvin; **spec eff**, David Harris.

Out of the Blue ★★★ 1947; U.S.; 84m; UNIV; Color; Biography; Drama; Children: Cautionary (MPAA: PG); **DVD**; **VHS**. Meek and mild Brent and his domineering wife, Landis, live in a Greenwich Village apartment building in New York City. Other residents are a Bohemian artist, Bey, and his live-in model, Mayo, as well as an invariably inebriated young woman, Dvorak, who believes in free love. While Landis is out, Dvorak calls on Brent and passes out. He thinks she's dead and deposits her on Bey's terrace. Bey takes advantage of the situation by blackmailing Brent, but then Dvorak comes to, and after Landis returns, the mayhem gets into high gear, producing even more hilarious moments in this above-average screwball comedy. Song: "Out of the Blue" (Will Jason, Henry Nemo). This is an inventive comedy of manners and errors but cautionary for children because of mature matter. **p**, Isadore Goldsmith; **d**, Leigh Jason; **cast**, George Brent, Virginia Mayo, Turhan Bey, Ann Dvorak, Carole Landis, Elizabeth Patterson, Julia Dean, Richard Lane, Charles Smith, Paul Harvey; **w**, Vera Caspary, Walter Bullock, Edward Eliscu (based on a story by Caspary); **c**, Jackson Rose; **m**, Carmen Dragon; **ed**, Norman Colbert, Alfred DeGaetano; **art d**, Edward C. Jewell; **set d**, Armor Marlowe; **spec eff**, George J. Teague.

Out of the Fog ★★★ 1941; U.S.; 85m; WB; B/W; Crime Drama; Children: Unacceptable; **DVD**. Garfield renders a powerful performance as a ruthless gangster extorting poor, hardworking fishermen on the Brooklyn waterfront. He meets attractive Lupino, the daughter of fisherman Mitchell, and uses his oily charm to win her attention, even though she knows Garfield is thoroughly corrupt, believing his lie that he will take her away from the struggling poverty she has known all her life. She puts off Albert, a blue-collar worker, who has always loved her and wants to marry Lupino, offering her only a reliable marriage but little financial security. Meanwhile, Garfield discovers that Mitchell and his fishing partner, Qualen, have been for years saving money in order to buy a new boat, and he orders them to turn over their hoarded money while they are in a small boat at sea at night. They reluctantly turn over the money, but Garfield, while standing up in the boat, loses his balance and topples overboard, drowning. He conveniently drops his wallet into the boat before going down for the Deep Six, and Mitchell and Qualen

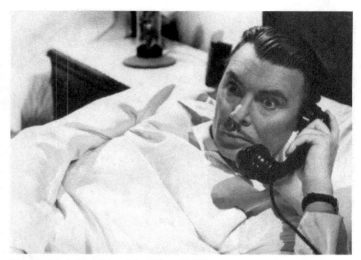

George Brent in *Out of the Blue*, 1947.

recoup their savings. When going ashore, Mitchell and Qualen are met by Homans, a waterfront beat cop, who realizes what has happened, but he turns a blind eye to Garfield's watery demise. Lupino then winds up with Albert for a much happier ending than what the unsavory and brutal Garfield would have provided. Pantheon director Litvak provides an eerie and brooding tale where Garfield's sinister presence looms everywhere like the murky fog rolling in at night. Weyl's waterfront sets of claptrap saloons, stores and cramped living quarters are superb, and master cinematographer Howe presents bone-chilling atmospheric scenes. Lupino, Mitchell, Qualen and the rest of the cast are outstanding in this thriller. Songs: "Concert in the Park," "The Merry-Go-Round Broke Down" (Cliff Friend, Dave Franklin); "Trade Winds" (Cliff Friend); "Whistle While You Work" (Frank Churchill); "South American Way" (Jimmy McHugh); "Anabella" (Eduardo Durant). *Author's Note*: Lupino had appeared with Garfield earlier in the year in the classic **Sea Wolf**, 1941, which was released three months before this film, and when she heard that Humphrey Bogart was cast in the role of the gangster in **Out of the Fog**, she went to studio boss Jack Warner and protested, saying that she did not want to work with Bogart again, having had a difficult time with Bogart when appearing with him in **They Drive by Night**, 1940, and **High Sierra**, 1941. She insisted that Garfield play her evil-minded lover and got her way since Lupino was then a much bigger star at Warner Brothers than Bogart, who had been a character player then slowly emerging into a leading star. After hearing that he had been scratched from **Out of the Fog**, Bogart sent a message to Jack Warner that read: "When did Ida Lupino start casting films at your studio?" Lupino, a strong-willed actress with decided notions about acting and filmmaking and who later became an accomplished director, told this author that "Bogey was just too hard to handle, at least for me. He was getting bigger parts in those days and, to build on his characters, he wanted every actor in scenes with him to play to him, to be submissive to the character he was playing and everyone knew that he was making every effort to become a leading man in pictures. That meant that all the lines you exchanged with Bogart had to favor him in the way they were delivered so that your own lines were more or less toss-away lines and his had more emphasis, making his character more important than any other. I would never go for that as I would not cheat my characters of their importance. To do that would weaken the story line and the picture. I had to battle over every line with Bogey in **They Drive by Night** and **High Sierra**, but, after he was cast in **Out of the Fog**, I put my foot down. I wanted Julie [John Garfield, his given name being Jacob Julius Garfinkle] to play the gangster all along and Jack Warner personally cast him in that part at my request. Julie was terrific in the role—just as tough and menacing as Bogey could ever be—and he thanked me more than once for getting him into that picture, which, I believe, was one of

Jane Greer and Robert Mitchum in *Out of the Past*, 1947.

his favorites. It is a crying shame that that gifted and wonderful man died so young [Garfield died at age thirty-nine of a heart attack]. I believe that, if he had lived longer, he would have won more than one Oscar as Best Actor. He was always a 'Best Actor' in my heart. I don't mean to say that Bogey was not a great actor. He was that, but, to get there, he abruptly cut off lines in scenes with other actors by jumping cues and giving emphasis to his own lines, and he used all the little tricks to step to the forefront of the camera range so that other actors could not be seen or were suddenly in the background. He did that to me, and he did that to a lot of others, like Bill [William] Holden, when Bill was coming up in the pictures and appeared with Bogey in **Invisible Stripes**, 1939, and that is why Bill said: 'I hated that bastard.' Well, that was an unkind remark, but Bogey got to the top by stepping on a lot of toes. Some people like me and Bill Holden never forgot that. You know the old line—you meet the same people going up as you do going down? Well, most of us went up and did not go down, including Bogey, but we are all the same people in this tough business of making pictures and our memories are alive and long." **p**, Hal B. Wallis; **d**, Anatole Litvak; **cast**, Ida Lupino, John Garfield, Thomas Mitchell, Eddie Albert, George Tobias, John Qualen, Aline MacMahon, Jerome Cowan, Odette Myrtil, Leo Gorcey, Robert Homans, Charles Drake, Barbara Pepper; **w**, Robert Rossen, Jerry Wald, Richard Macaulay (based on the play "The Gentle People" by Irwin Shaw); **c**, James Wong Howe; **m**, Heinz Roemheld; **ed**, Warren Low; **art d**, Carl Jules Weyl; **spec eff**, Rex Wimpy.

Out of the Past ★★★★★ 1947; U.S.; 97m; RKO; B/W; Crime Drama; Children: Unacceptable; **DVD**; **VHS**. This film noir classic from pantheon director Tourneur sees Mitchum at his very best in a mesmerizing thriller where he is a hardboiled private detective who knows all the answers, except the one that will save him from his own destruction. His nemesis is the alluring Greer, a cunning femme fatale of the first order, who will deceive and betray anyone to gain wealth and comfort. The film opens when gangster Valentine arrives at a gas station in Bridgeport, California, to get gas and sees the name of the owner, Mitchum. Valentine then finds Mitchum and tells him that Douglas, a wealthy gambler and racketeer, wants to see him. Mitchum has been dreading this visit for some time, but he tells Valentine that he will go to see Douglas at his lavish estate in Tahoe, Nevada. Before making that appointment, Mitchum meets with local lady Huston, who is in love with him, but Mitchum has been reluctant to marry her because of a dark past that has just caught up with him through Valentine's visit. (That meeting is identical to a scene in **The Killers**, 1946, released a year before this film, where gang boss Albert Dekker arrives in a small town to get gas at a station and sees service station attendant Burt Lancaster, a man who has earlier double-crossed him and for whom he has

been vengefully searching.) While taking Huston for a drive, Mitchum explains why their future together is doubtful and tells her about his shady past, which unfolds in flashback as he describes to Huston how he once ran a small detective agency with Brodie, and where he is summoned to Tahoe, Nevada, to see Douglas. The wealthy gambler hires Mitchum, giving him $5,000 to track down his beautiful mistress, Greer, who has stolen $40,000 from him after shooting him, a wound he painfully remembers with vengeful anger. He wants her back, Douglas tells Mitchum, but promises that he will not hurt the woman once she is returned to him. The redoubtable and inventive Mitchum deduces that Greer, although she is clever enough to leave false trails that initially indicated that she has fled to Florida, has really gone to Acapulco, Mexico. Mitchum follows her there, waiting for her to come into a cantina he knows that she often visits. The beautiful Greer does arrive, ordering a drink. Mitchum and Greer are quickly attracted to one another, but Mitchum follows the code of his profession and tells her that must bring her back to Douglas for stealing his money and shooting him. The sweet-faced Greer easily convinces the cynical Mitchum that she is innocent, and that she has stolen nothing from Douglas and never harmed him. In love with her now, Mitchum, instead of returning almond-eyed Greer to Douglas, flees with this lovely creature to make a separate life with her. They find happiness by living under assumed names in a mountain retreat just north of San Francisco, but, one day, Brodie, Mitchum's ex-partner in their gumshoe business, sees Mitchum at a racetrack and follows him to that retreat. The unsavory Brodie tells Mitchum that he is now working for Douglas, who has paid him to find Greer and Mitchum, but that he will forget knowing their whereabouts if he is given a hefty sum of money. Mitchum knows that this is only the beginning of a blackmail scheme that has no end and refuses. The two then get into a battle with fists and, when it appears that Brodie might have the upper hand, Greer shoots and kills Brodie, shocking Mitchum. She then races from the house and drives away. Mitchum later discovers Greer's bankbook, finding that she has, indeed, the $40,000 that Douglas claimed she stole from him, and with this knowledge, realizes that his love for her is entangled in a web spun by a beautiful "black widow." He moves to Bridgeport and opens the gas station and there falls for Huston. His tale concluded, we see Mitchum and Huston in flash forward arriving at Tahoe where Mitchum resolves to set things straight with Douglas. While Huston drives back to Bridgeport, Mitchum confronts Douglas at his modern-styled mansion (which has the architectural motif of having been created by Frank Lloyd Wright). Mitchum is surprised to learn from the scheming and lethal Douglas that he is not seeking to have him killed for betraying him with Greer. Mitchum can make up for failing in his first assignment by undertaking another one on behalf of Douglas. The gambler tells him that he wants Mitchum to go to San Francisco and steal his tax records from a corrupt attorney, Niles, who is holding them as ransom and threatening to turn them over to the IRS unless he receives a huge payoff. Before leaving on this new mission, Mitchum finds Greer at Douglas' mansion, and when they are alone together, she tells him that she has stayed with Douglas only because she fears for her life and that she has always loved only one man, Mitchum. Going to San Francisco, Mitchum contacts Fleming, the seductive secretary working for Niles, who promises him that she will help him obtain Douglas' tax records, but Mitchum, knowing that Fleming is working secretly for Douglas, believes that he is being set up after Fleming arranges a meeting between him and Niles. Mitchum warns Niles that his life is in danger, but the arrogant lawyer ignores the warning and is later murdered by Valentine, this murder attributed to Mitchum, a setup that Mitchum has been anticipating. Mitchum, now wanted for the murders of Brodie and Nile, takes pains to cover his tracks before he returns to Bridgeport to hide out. When Valentine, Douglas' enforcer, arrives in town looking for Mitchum, he is led to a mountainous area by Moore, a mute young man devoted to Mitchum and who kills Valentine. Mitchum then goes back to Douglas, telling him that he plans to turn over what he knows to the IRS, and Douglas offers him $50,000 in an effort to buy him off, stating that he wants Greer turned over to the police for murdering Brodie. Mitchum then breaks off his engagement with Huston, telling her that his dark past has overtaken him and that they have no future together. When he returns to see Douglas, he finds him dead, killed by Greer, who has double-crossed everyone. Mitchum finally accepts the grim fact that he is hopelessly in love with a spider woman. He tells her that they will flee to Mexico, and while she is packing her bags, he calls police to set up a road block that will stop them in their escape to nowhere. When the two are driving to their grim destination, Mitchum then tells Greer all he knows about her treacherous duplicity and murderous ways. In a rage, she fatally shoots him just as they come upon the police roadblock and she then fires at police and is killed when they return a fusillade of bullets. The car crashes and Mitchum spills from it, dead. In Bridgeport, Huston learns from Moore that Mitchum died while going off with Greer, the only woman, lethal or not, in his life, and it appears that she will now give up on him and marry reliable Webb, a local man who has patiently waited for her. Director Tourneur offers a very complex tale, but he displays the story line in such a meticulous manner that all of its complicated elements fall into place in creating this masterpiece of crime and twisted love. The script is both literate and exciting, and all of its fully developed characters come to grim life through the superb performances by Mitchum, Greer, Douglas and the rest of the outstanding cast. Song: "The First Time I Saw You" (from the 1937 film **The Toast of New York**; music: Nathaniel Shilkret). *Author's Note*: Mitchum was not the first candidate for the lead in this film. Tough guys Humphrey Bogart, John Garfield and Dick Powell (who had switched film personas from singer to hardboiled detective in **Murder, My Sweet**, 1944) all turned down the role. The taciturn and brawny Mitchum had only a few leading roles before he was cast as the errant and lovesick gumshoe in **Out of the Past**, but his impact on the public in this fascinating film was enormous and made him an overnight superstar as it did the alluring Greer, as well as furthering the spectacular career of Douglas, this being his second film after appearing in **The Strange Love of Martha Ivers**, 1946. Mitchum appears in close-ups that accent his heavy-lidded eyes, which he claimed were created from his boxing days and because of inherent insomnia, but that made his character all the more appealing in that he had that worried, wearied look so traditional in stereotypical private eyes. That image of fatigue may have also been the result of his heavy pot-smoking, for which he was arrested and jailed in the 1940s, an illegal habit he maintained throughout his life. The always defiant Mitchum obliquely bragged about his drug bust, once stating: "The only difference between me and my fellow actors is that I have spent more time in jail." Mitchum was paid a little more than $10,000 for his role in **Out of the Past**, but, twenty years later, his star status demanded and got $1 million when he appeared in the TV miniseries, "The Winds of War," 1988. Nevertheless, he thought that this film noir classic was, according to his statements to this author, "one of my best pictures ever, but then we had Jacques [Tourneur] running the show and he knew what he was doing. He made RKO shell out a lot of dough by taking us all on location to Mexico and all over California, but those shoots were necessary to give the picture an international look. That doe-eyed Jane [Greer] was a knockout in the picture and we did another one together, **The Big Steal** [1949] a few years later. RKO was then building me up and ran an ad about the picture with a shot showing me with a cigarette dangling from my mouth and Jane holding a smoking gun, the ad saying, 'It's like lightning kissing thunder when Mitchum makes love to a girl with a gun!' Can you imagine the guy who wrote that one? He must have been smoking the same kind of joints [marijuana] I was. Jacques makes a different kind of detective story that shows the guts of its characters, and the RKO ad department promotes it like a Dick Tracy serial. I don't think those promotion guys ever watched the pictures their own studio was making, only looked at a few stills from those pictures before they dashed off whatever trite image came to their very limited

Virginia Huston and Robert Mitchum in *Out of the Past,* **1947.**

minds. I corned one of those goofballs and told him that if he kept promoting me as a nutcase tough guy I would promote him into the nearest garbage can. He grins at me and says: 'Go ahead, hit me. I'd love it!' That's my luck. Instead of a guy willing to put up his dukes, he turns out to be a masochist begging me to beat him up so he can get his sick kicks. Weirdoes like that were thicker than fleas in Hollywood." Greer was always grateful to Tourneur for the way he worked with her in **Out of the Past**, telling this author that "he was one of those very intelligent persons, who could inspire you to do better by working so hard himself. He would talk with me about my character before some scenes as if he were playing the part and I quickly understood how he wanted me to play that character. His wonderful patience helped me give one of my best performances. Of course Bob [Mitchum] and Kirk [Douglas], both terrific actors, made me look very good in every scene when we were together. Let's face it, without those two strong men, I would have had no one to victimize in that picture where I am one of the most evil women ever to walk the earth. What a part!" **p,** Warren Duff; **d,** Jacques Tourneur; **cast,** Robert Mitchum, Jane Greer, Kirk Douglas, Rhonda Fleming, Richard Webb, Steve Brodie, Virginia Huston, Paul Valentine, Dickie Moore, Ken Niles, John Kellogg; **w,** Geoffrey Homes (Daniel Mainwaring), James M. Cain, Frank Fenton (both not credited) (based on Homes's novel *Build My Gallows High*); **c,** Nicholas Musuraca; **m,** Roy Webb; **ed,** Samuel E. Beetley; **art d,** Albert S. D'Agostino, Jack Okey; **set d,** Darrell Silvera; **spec eff,** Russell A. Cully.

Out of This World ★★★ 1945; U.S.; 96m; PAR; B/W; Comedy/Musical; Children: Acceptable. Lively musical with many funny moments sees Bracken becoming a singer with Lynn's all-girl orchestra and they become a success. Problems arise when Lynn tries to find backers to invest in his career and she sells 125 percent interest to investors against the anticipated profits from his earnings. (Overselling stock in an investment is ridiculously demonstrated by an avaricious Zero Mostel in the hilarious Mel Brooks comedy, **The Producers**, 1967, but Lynn, in this film, unwittingly commits this offense with no illegal intentions.) This is all cleared up by the end of this delightfully entertaining film. Bracken's singing is dubbed by Bing Crosby for a standing joke in the movie in which Crosby's sons appear. Songs: "Out of This World," "I'd Rather Be Me," "June Comes Around Every Year" (Harold Arlen, Johnny Mercer). **p,** Sam Coslow; **d,** Hal Walker; **cast,** Eddie Bracken, Veronica Lake, Diana Lynn, Cass Daley, Parkyakarkus (Harry Parke), Donald MacBride, Florence Bates, Gary Crosby, Phillip Crosby, Dennis Crosby, Lindsay Crosby, Don Wilson, Mabel Paige, Ted Fio Rito, Ray Noble, Olga San Juan, Audrey Young; **w,** Coslow, Walter DeLeon, Arthur Phillips (based on stories by Elizabeth Meehan, Coslow); **c,** Stuart Thompson; **m,** Harry Simeone; **ed,** Stuart Gilmore; **art d,** Hans

Sandy Dennis and Jack Lemmon in *The Out of Towners*, 1970.

Dreier, Haldane Douglas; **set d**, Kenneth Swartz.

The Out of Towners ★★★★ 1970; U.S.; 101m; Jalem Productions; PAR; Color; Comedy; Cautionary (MPAA: G); **DVD**; **VHS**. Another hilarious tale from Simon has the exceptionally talented Lemmon, an out-of-town businessman, arriving in the Big Apple with wife Dennis and where he is to have an all-important interview about a new well-paying executive job. While flying toward NYC, the couple refuses food on the plane, planning to have a sumptuous meal at an upscale Manhattan restaurant before checking into their hotel for one night, after which Lemmon will conduct the interview and they will then be returning that day to their home in Dayton, Ohio. What could be simpler? Well, fate proves their lives to be a lot more complex, ensnaring these two visitors into a nightmare experience that changes them overnight from normal, rational humans into desperate, half-crazed creatures. The plane on which they are flying is suddenly denied landing at New York, which is fogged in, so it flies and lands at Boston, and Lemmon and Dennis, after their luggage is misplaced, take a train to NYC, arriving in a fierce rainstorm and where the city has almost come to a stop through strikes by garbage collectors and transit workers. Nothing is moving on the streets and, unable to get a cab (which are invariably hard to acquire even in the best of times in New York), the distressed couple walk to their hotel, the elegant Waldorf, where they are told that, because of their late arrival, their reservations have been canceled and there is no room at the inn for them or anywhere else. They are then befriended by Jarvis, who appears to be a Good Samaritan, telling them that he can get them a room at a comfortable hotel, but, in the process, he filches all their money. They go to a police station to report the theft and, now without funds, the cops tell them that they can find a resting place for the night at an armory, but when en route via police car, the squad car is stolen by hijackers who dump them in Central Park. Trying to sleep in these shadowy wilds, they are again robbed by muggers. At dawn, Lemmon is beaten by two joggers, who mistake him for a rapist. He is then spotted by a mounted police officer in the park, who chases him in the belief that he is a wanted child molester. Desperate to get to his interview, Lemmon is fortunate enough to get a ride from kindly Montalban, a Cuban diplomat, but the car is quickly engulfed with Cuban protestors opposing the Castro regime that Montalban represents and Lemmon narrowly escapes the melee. Haggard, unshaven and filthy, he nevertheless gets to his appointment, and, despite his ungainly appearance, he is offered the job. Lemmon, however, has had enough of New York, and turns down the offer, wanting only to return to Ohio with his wife and live out his life in peace. He and Dennis board another plane that will take him home, but it does not, as it is skyjacked by political nuts, who order the plane to fly to Cuba (this in a day when such real-life skyjack-

ings were commonplace and where the destination was invariably Cuba). Thus ends this hilarious tale where ironic fortune has turned two average travelers into woebegone, butt-sprung, addlebrained persons, who now represent, in delightfully exaggerated portraits, the universal victims of the world. *Author's Note*: Lemmon told this author that "Neil Simon is a genius and can write anything well, for the stage or the screen. He took all the awful things that could happen to a visitor going to New York and crammed them into a twenty-four-hour opus and all of it is funny, only because of the way he wrote his scenes and dialog. Otherwise, **The Out of Towners** would have been a trip to Amityville." **p**, Paul Nathan; **d**, Arthur Hiller; **cast**, Jack Lemmon, Sandy Dennis, Milt Kamen, Sandy Baron, Anne Meara, Robert Nichols, Ann Prentiss, Ron Carey, Phil Bruns, Graham Jarvis, Carlos Montalban, Billy Dee Williams; **w**, Neil Simon; **c**, Andrew Laszlo (Movielab Color); **m**, Quincy Jones; **ed**, Fred Chulack; **art d**, Charles Bailey, Walter Tyler; **set d**, Arthur Jeph Parker.

Out West with the Hardys ★★★ 1938; U.S.; 84m; MGM; B/W; Drama/Comedy; Children: Acceptable. In this fifth and entertaining installment of the popular Hardy Family series, Judge Hardy (Stone) takes the family out West to Arizona to help a friend, who is in a legal dispute and may be run off his ranch. Andy (Rooney) gets in the cowboy spirit by overdressing in western clothes and shows off his nonexistent "cowboy skills" to Jones' young daughter, Weidler. Ride 'em, Andy! Meanwhile, Andy's sister, Parker, falls in love with the ranch foreman, Jones. Stone saves his friend's ranch, Andy learns more lessons about becoming a man, and Parker decides the boy she likes at home is the man for her. One of the most popular films of the series, it was also one of the top-grossing films of the year. **p**, J.J. Cohn; **d**, George B. Seitz; **cast**, Lewis Stone, Mickey Rooney, Fay Holden, Cecilia Parker, Ann Rutherford, Sara Haden, Don Castle, Virginia Weidler, Gordon Jones, Ralph Morgan, Tom Neal, Anthony Allan (John Hubbard); **w**, Kay Van Riper, Agnes Christine Johnston, William Ludwig (based on characters created by Aurania Rouverol); **c**, Lester White; **m**, David Snell; **ed**, Ben Lewis; **art d**, Cedric Gibbons; **set d**, Edwin B. Willis.

Outcast of the Islands ★★★★ 1952; U.K.; 102m; London Film Productions/Lopert Pictures; B/W; Drama; Children: Cautionary; **DVD**; **VHS**. Superlative adaptation of Joseph Conrad's tale sees a riveting performance from Howard as an intelligent and sensitive European adrift in the Far East. He is the operator of a trading post on a remote island, who finds himself without a job when he is suddenly fired. He is aided by an old friend, Richardson, a sea captain, who takes him to another trading post that he and Morley operate and where Howard is reluctantly employed by the demanding Morley. Hiller, who is Richardson's adopted daughter and Morley's wife, however, is attracted to the defiant and single-minded Howard, but she is offended when he disdains her subtle advances and becomes involved with a sultry island girl, Kerima. A devious politician in collusion with one of Morley's competitors uses Howard's association with Kerima to undermine Morley's trading post and Howard then leads an abortive revolt and, after he is exposed as a troublemaker, he and Kerima flee to another island, living in isolation. Richardson finds Howard on that island, urging him to return to "civilization," and Kerima urges Howard to kill Richardson as she believes he is trying to destroy Howard's love for her. Howard not only refuses to murder his friend but tells Kerima that he does not love her or anyone or anything else. Richardson then departs, leaving the embittered and disillusioned Howard to the desolation of his own dark thoughts and to ponder his failures that have caused him to be branded throughout the area as the "outcast of the islands." Pantheon director Reed fully captures the flavor and ill-starred characters of the Conrad story, albeit Howard's character meets an accidental death at the end of the novel and where he survives in the film. The sets, lighting and excellent cinematography from Scaife and Wilcox present a pervasive image of the humid tropics where all is clammy, languid and wallowing in slowly evolving corruption and doom. This visual sense of foreboding is countered by the nobility and decency embodied in Howard's character, which is not dissimilar to that of the protagonist in another well-crafted film about a memorable Conrad character, **Lord Jim**, 1965. Richardson is also outstanding in his role as the compassionate sea captain, and Morley, too, is captivating in his role of a pompous, intolerant and rather loathsome person. The gifted Hiller does as much as she can with her character, Morley's dishrag of a wife, her spirit seeming to shrivel before our eyes as she lives out her loveless life. **p**, Carol Reed, Hugh Perceval; **d**, Reed; **cast**, Ralph Richardson, Trevor Howard, Robert Morley, Wendy Hiller, Kerima, Wilfrid Hyde-White, Frederick Valk, Betty Ann Davies, Dharma Emmanuel, Peter Illing; **w**, William Fairchild (based on the novel by Joseph Conrad); **c**, Edward Scaife, John Wilcox; **m**, Brian Easdale; **ed**, Bert Bates; **prod d**, Vincent Korda; **spec eff**, W. Percy Day.

The Outcasts of Poker Flat ★★★ 1919 (silent); U.S.; 60m; UNIV; B/W; Western; Children: Acceptable. Above-average oater that fuses two Bret Harte stories while employing the same cast for both tales. Carey and Landis are rough-and-tumble westerners who compete for the same girl, Hope, but Carey believes that she will give her heart to Landis, his best pal, because he is much younger and more handsome. Then Carey reads the story of "The Outcasts of Poker Flat" and the film dissolves into that tale where four "immoral" persons are driven from Poker Flat to take refuge in a shanty and wait out a fierce snowstorm and where starvation takes its toll. Great sacrifices are made for others by these otherwise undesirable characters and where Carey gives up the girl he loves to a younger man. In flash forward we see Carey ending the classic tale and concluding that the older cowboy was nothing more than "a durn fool." He promptly proposes to Hope and she accepts and he winds up with the girl of his dreams. Cleverly directed by Ford, who was establishing his mastery in the western genre with just such films as this, and well acted by Carey, Landis and Hope, this version of the Harte story is far better than the two remakes of 1937 and 1952, as well as its several made-for-TV versions. **p**, Pat Powers; **d**, Jack Ford (John Ford); **cast**, Harry Carey, Cullen Landis, Gloria Hope, Joseph Harris, Virginia Chester, Duke R. Lee, Louise Lester, J. Farrell MacDonald, Charles H. Mailes, Vester Pegg; **w**, H. Tipton Steck (based on the stories "The Luck of Roaring Camp" and "Outcasts of Poker Flat" by Bret Harte); **c**, John W. Brown.

The Outfit ★★★ 1973; U.S.; 102m; MGM; Color; Crime Drama; Children: Unacceptable (MPAA: PG); **VHS**. Excellent character study has small-time criminal Duvall being released from prison only to learn that his brother has been shot by hit men in the employ of a crime syndicate boss of a group called The Outfit. Duvall, his brother, and his brother's pal, Baker, had robbed a bank owned by the syndicate. Duvall thinks he's next on the hit list and this is confirmed when his girlfriend, Black, tells him she has been coerced into setting him up as a target by Carey, a gangster who works for The Outfit. Duvall learns that Ryan is the syndicate boss, who is behind all the mayhem and he, with the aid of Baker, begin to systematically disable Ryan's operations until, ironically, the police eventually get him. Songs: "Your Guess Is as Good as Mine" (Steve Gillette, Jeremy Joe Kronsberg), "I Concentrate on You" (Cole Porter), "Rock of Ages" (Augustus M. Toplady, Thomas Hastings). Violence prohibits viewing by children. *Author's Note*: The premise for this film, the robbing of a bank containing crime syndicate funds unknown to the robbers, was also employed in another clever crime film made the same year, **Charley Varrick**, 1973, starring Walter Matthau and also featuring Baker, but where Baker is a hit man out to kill Matthau and his associates for that robbery. A similar theme can be seen in **Payback**, 1999, where robber Mel Gibson commits a heist that contains money belonging to a crime cartel; when he is double-crossed by a partner and loses his share of the loot, he goes after the top members of the cartel to recoup his stolen money. **p**, Carter DeHaven; **d&w**, John

Clint Eastwood in *The Outlaw Josey Wales*, 1976.

Flynn (based on the novel by Richard Stark [Donald E. Westlake]); **cast**, Robert Duvall, Karen Black, Joe Don Baker, Robert Ryan, Timothy Carey, Richard Jaeckel, Sheree North, Marie Windsor, Jane Greer, Joanna Cassidy, Elisha Cook, Jr., Archie Moore, Anita O'Day, Army Archerd; **c**, Bruce Surtees; **m**, Jerry Fielding; **ed**, Ralph E. Winters; **art d**, Tambi Larsen; **set d**, James L. Berkey.

The Outlaw Josey Wales ★★★★★ 1976; U.S.; 135m; Malpaso/WB; Color; Western; Children: Unacceptable (MPAA: PG); **BD**; **DVD**; **VHS**. A consistently fascinating and uncompromising western, this masterpiece from Eastwood (who directs and stars) is set during and after the American Civil War, beginning with Eastwood as a peaceful Missouri farmer living a quiet life with his wife and son. While working in the fields one day, several riders appear wearing Union uniforms and with red boots, these guerrillas thus called "Redlegs." (A similar insignia can be found in the western film **Tombstone**, 1993, where a band of outlaws calling themselves cowboys wear red sashes about their waists to distinguish themselves from ordinary cowhands.) The invaders ride forward with its leader, McKinney, striking Eastwood on the head with his sword, gashing him and knocking him unconscious. He is left for dead as they murder his wife and son and destroy the farm. After recovering and burying his loved ones, the devastated farmer locates a gun and practices shooting until he can hit his targets. He is then visited by another group of guerrillas, southerners led by William "Bloody Bill" Anderson, played by Russell. The Confederate leader asks Eastwood if "Redlegs" have been responsible for killing his family members, and he tacitly nods. "You'll find them up in Kansas," Russell says. "They're with the Union and we're going up there to set things right." Eastwood stares at the ragtag horse riders and replies: "I'll be coming with you." A series of montages then show several Civil War skirmishes and engagements (some of which are taken from scenes in John Huston's **The Red Badge of Courage**, 1951) and which also show Eastwood riding and fighting with Russell and his men. As the war comes to an end, Russell is fatally wounded and Vernon takes command of the Confederate guerrillas, accepting an offer of amnesty. He and his men ride into a Union camp to be disarmed and take the oath of allegiance to the Union, all but Eastwood, who refuses to surrender. While Vernon is restrained, McKinney, who led the raid that killed Eastwood's family, now conducts an ambush where the Rebels are shot down, but Eastwood suddenly appears, shooting several Union soldiers while saving the life of a young Rebel, the severely wounded Bottoms. The two make their escape and are then hunted by Union troopers. The pair evades a group of Union searchers when Eastwood shoots at and severs a rope pulling a ferry loaded with those pursuers, sending them helplessly down river. He and Bottoms continue their flight, but, while camping, two renegades find

Clint Eastwood in *The Outlaw Josey Wales,* **1976.**

them and try to capture Eastwood, his life saved when Bottoms distracts the renegades long enough for Eastwood to shoot them dead. Bottoms then dies of his wounds and Eastwood drapes his body over a horse and sends the animal galloping into a Union camp where he believes the boy will receive a decent burial. Eastwood then rides away and later meets an ancient Cherokee Indian, George, who wears a stove pipe hat and long frock coat, imitating the image of his idol, Abraham Lincoln. He tells Eastwood that he and others of his tribe went to Washington, D.C., in an effort to regain their lands, but achieved nothing except to be met by the Secretary of the Interior, who congratulated them for becoming "civilized." George tells Eastwood that he long regrets the days when he was not civilized. Seeming to be annoyed by the old man, Eastwood nevertheless tolerates his company and they travel westward. At a trading post, Eastwood finds two trappers about to rape Keams, a Cherokee girl who works there, and he shoots and kills them. The girl now believes that Eastwood has taken her for his wife, although he has not, and she follows him and George in their westerly trek, becoming attached to George. They then come upon a covered wagon that has been stopped by a ruthless group of raiders, who are about to kill Trueman and rape her granddaughter, Locke. Eastwood and George shoot down the raiders and rescue the women, taking them with them. After Trueman describes how they were traveling to a beautiful valley and to live in a house her son has built, she invites her rescuers to stay there and they agree. Once arriving at the place, they find it in disrepair, but everyone begins to fix up the place. Eastwood goes to a nearby ghost town, but finds a group of people who have remained, including Jameson, an aging saloon woman; Clarke, a bartender who has no alcoholic drinks to serve; Dano, a one-time gambler; and Verros, an elderly Mexican. Befriending them, they all join him at Trueman's house where they help to make it livable. Meanwhile, Eastwood kills a small group of Comanche warriors and, to prevent a full-scale attack from the tribe, rides to its camp and confronts its chief, Sampson, asking that there be peace between them. Sampson admires Eastwood's courage and makes peace with him, ritualistically cutting their hands to draw blood and mixing that blood in a handclasp that makes them blood brothers. Meanwhile, the homesteaders settle in, only to be attacked by McKinney and his Redlegs, who have tracked them down and are dedicated to killing Eastwood. The homesteaders kill off all the raiders in a pitched battle until only McKinney is left alive. He escapes, riding to the ghost town, but Eastwood, who has been wounded in the battle, finds him and kills the Union guerrilla leader with his own sword. He then goes to the local saloon where Dano and others are telling two Texas Rangers that the notorious Josey Wales is dead, killed in a gunfight, but Vernon, who has accompanied the lawman, recognizes Eastwood and knows different. The Rangers depart, but Vernon remains outside the saloon where he and Eastwood

stare at each other. Vernon tells Eastwood that the war is over, meaning that he will accept the lie that he is dead. Eastwood, instead of killing Vernon, says: "I guess we all died a little in that damn war." He then mounts his horse and rides away, returning to the family he has adopted and where, it is implied, he will finally sink his roots, and this is where this action-packed, well-directed classic western ends. Eastwood is outstanding as the rugged westerner, who comes to realize that he cannot survive alone in a universally hostile West, and all of the supporting players are believable in their hardscrabble roles. There is a deep authentic look to this offbeat but fascinating western (its overall image reportedly copied from the starkly realistic western, **The Great Northfield, Minnesota Raid**, 1972, which Eastwood admired) where the barren landscapes are exceptionally captured through Surtees' superlative cinematography, much of it taken on location in Glen Canyon, Utah. The script provides terse dialog, except for George's elaborate lines that make him all the more humorous and colorful. All is threadbare and nothing glitters in any scene where basic survival comes first and ethereal notions of the grand Old West disappear beneath the clouds of dust kicked up by galloping horses. This masterpiece western is undoubtedly one of Eastwood's finest films, one where he discards the unrealistic type of lone wolf characters he earlier played in the Sergio Leone "spaghetti westerns" and presents a down-to-earth perspective of a rugged individual who comes to believe through the dedication and sacrifice of others that one cannot survive in any hostile environment without the aid of others. His character is not unlike any of those profiled in earlier films that show how chiefly southern guerrillas fighting in the Civil War, as the members of the James-Younger gang, easily transitioned into outlaws following that war. *Author's Note*: Southern guerrillas fighting in the Civil War have been profiled in many films, notably in **Dark Command**, 1940; **Fighting Man of the Plains**, 1949; **Kansas Raiders**, 1950; **The Outriders**, 1950; **Quantrill's Raiders**, 1958; **Red Mountain**, 1951; **Ride with the Devil**, 1999; **Rocky Mountain**, 1950; **Woman They Almost Lynched**, 1953; and **Young Jesse James**, 1960. **p**, Robert Daley; **d**, Clint Eastwood; **cast**, Eastwood, Chief Dan George, Sondra Locke, Bill McKinney, John Vernon, John Russell, Paula Trueman, Sam Bottoms, Joyce Jameson, Royal Dano, Sheb Wooley, Kyle Eastwood, Richard Farnsworth; **w**, Phil Kaufman, Sonia Chernus (based on the novel *Gone to Texas* by Forrest Carter); **c**, Bruce Surtees (Panavision; DeLuxe Color); **m**, Jerry Fielding; **ed**, Ferris Webster; **prod d**, Tambi Larsen; **set d**, Chuck Pierce; **spec eff**, Robert MacDonald, Paul Pollard.

The Outlaws Is Coming! ★★★ 1965; U.S.; 88m; COL; B/W; Comedy; Children: Cautionary; **DVD**; **VHS**. A lot of laughs are provided out West with the Three Stooges in their final full-length film. Larry and Moe are joined by Joe DeRita in getting mixed up in a battle with gunslingers trying to start an Indian uprising by killing off all the buffalo in the territory. The Stooges get help from Annie Oakley (Kovack), Wyatt Earp (Camfield), Bat Masterson (McDonnell), and Wild Bill Hickok (Shannon) in battling outlaws Jesse James (Mack), Billy the Kid (Ginger) and Cole Younger (Sedley). This fun-filled spoof on westerns sees the boys going out in style. **p&d**, Norman Maurer; **cast**, The Three Stooges (Larry Fine, Moe Howard, Joe DeRita), Adam West, Nancy Kovack, Johnny Ginger, Bruce Sedley, Ed T. McDonnell, Paul Shannon, Bill Camfield, Wayne Mack; **w**, Elwood Ullman (based on a story by Maurer); **c**, Irving Lippman; **m**, Paul Dunlap; **ed**, Aaron Nibley; **art d**, Robert Peterson; **set d**, James M. Crowe; **spec eff**, Richard Albain.

The Outriders ★★★ 1950; U.S.; 93m; MGM; Color; Western; Children: Unacceptable; **DVD**. Set at the time of the American Civil War, McCrea leads a fine cast in this above-average oater where he, Sullivan and Whitmore, who are Confederate POWs, escape from a Union prison camp. They are taken in by Corey's Rebel guerrilla band and agree to take part in ambushing a bullion shipment in the southwest, ostensibly to provide the starving South with gold. Once joining that wagon train as scouts and outriders, however, the principled McCrea, along with his friends, decide to protect the passengers and they help them beat off attacks from Corey and his men; McCrea wins the hand of the fetching Dahl, a beautiful widow whose teenage son, Jarman, has come to idolize McCrea. Novarro, who had been a silent screen matinee idol, appears here in one of his infrequent roles and is exceptional as the Mexican owner of the wagon train, as is Sullivan, who is killed for betraying his companions, and Whitmore, a scruffy, broken-down soldier fighting for a cause he knows is lost. *Author's Note*: Novarro would be brutally murdered by two hustlers invading his upscale home in 1968; see my book *The Great Pictorial History of World Crime*, Volume II (History, Inc., pages 890-894). **p**, Richard Goldstone; **d**, Roy Rowland; **cast**, Joel McCrea, Arlene Dahl, Barry Sullivan, Claude Jarman, Jr., James Whitmore, Ramon Novarro, Jeff Corey, Ted de Corsia, Martin Garralaga, Dorothy Adams, Gregg Barton; **w**, Irving Ravetch (based on his story); **c**, Charles Schoenbaum (Technicolor); **m**, Andre Previn; **ed**, Robert J. Kern; **art d**, Cedric Gibbons, Preston Ames; **set d**, Edwin B. Willis; **spec eff**, A. Arnold Gillespie, Warren Newcombe.

The Outside Chance of Maximilian Glick ★★★ 1990; Canada; 107m; National Film Board of Canada/Southgate Entertainment; Color; Comedy/Drama; Children: Acceptable (MPAA: G); **VHS**. Good rite-of-passage film sees Zylberman as a twelve-year-old Jewish boy living with an overbearing Jewish family in a small town in Manitoba, Canada, in the early 1960s. What he wants most in life is a bicycle, but, instead, his family buys him a piano and pushes him to study for his Bar Mitzvah. He takes duo piano playing lessons with Balk, a Christian girl, and falls for her. When his parents learn of this, they forbid him to see her. His rabbi, Rubinek, who would otherwise prefer to be a stand-up comedian, has an unorthodox, fun-loving way of looking at life. Together, they solve their problems with his prejudiced parents and a more traditional Jewish community. This charming and warmly human coming-of-age film later transitioned into a Canadian television series. Songs: "Hoben Mir a Niggundal," "Freilach 42," "Where Were You Before Prohibition?," "Jingle Bell Rock," "Minuet in G" (Johann Sebastian Bach), "Eine Kleine Nachtmusik" (Wolfgang Amadeus Mozart), "Opus 118, No. 2" (Johannes Brahms). **p**, Stephen Foster, Richard Davis; **d**, Allan A. Goldstein; **cast**, Noam Zylberman, Fairuza Balk, Saul Rubinek, Jan Rubes, William Marantz, Aaron Schwartz, Sharon Corder, Ken Zelig, Alec McClure, Howard Jerome, Matthew Ball; **w**, Phil Savath (based on the novel by Morley Torgov); **c**, Ian Elkin; **m**, Graeme Coleman; **ed**, Richard Martin; **prod d**, Kim Steer; **art d**, Phil Schmidt; **spec eff**, Jak Osmond.

The Outsider ★★★★ 1961; U.S.; 108m; UNIV; B/W; Biographical Drama; Children: Unacceptable; **DVD**; **VHS**. Curtis, in one of his most intensive and introspective roles, essays the troubled Ira Hamilton Hayes (1923-1955), a Pima Indian, who was one of the Marines raising the American flag on Mount Suribachi during the Battle of Iwo Jima (February 19-March 26, 1945). Raised in poverty on an Arizona Indian reservation, Curtis decides to enlist during WWII and enters boot camp where he is treated like a unwanted recruit by all except the compassionate and open-minded Franciscus, who befriends him. They finish training and undergo several campaigns together, both of them landing at Iwo Jima and helping to raise the American flag. After Franciscus is killed, however, Curtis goes to pieces, emotionally destroyed at losing the only friend he has ever had. Decorated and hailed a hero, he is flown back to the U.S. to help sell war bonds and inspire more recruitments, but Curtis wants no part of anything that will promote more young men into the service and perhaps bring about the premature death suffered by Franciscus. He takes to drink and becomes unruly, getting into brawls and disobeying his superiors. He is then discharged and finds that he cannot adjust to civilian life when he returns to his reservation. There is he considered a great hero and he reluctantly accepts a mission to travel to Washington, D.C., to be the tribe's representative in a land dispute, but

Arlene Dahl and Claude Jarman Jr. in *The Outriders*, 1950.

he botches the assignment when getting drunk after arriving at the capital and is jailed. He returns in disgrace to the reservation where he is now shunned by all as a man who has brought shame on his tribe. Further, he is told that he will not be considered for a post on the tribal council, a position he has long desired. Feeling his life to be at an end, Curtis packs up some bottles of booze and climbs a mountain where he is later found dead from exposure, an ignominious end for a once great hero. Curtis gives a startling and disturbing performance as Hayes in a somber and often grim film that does not compromise with the truth of his plight. The rampant prejudice against him and others is explicitly depicted by director Mann in all of its damaging ugliness in one unrelenting scene after another. There is a pervasive feel of brutality throughout this superlative film, one where the sensibilities of the human spirit are under a savage assault as furious as that of the Marines storming that hellish island in the Pacific. *Author's Note*: Hayes appeared as himself as a Marine in **Sands of Iwo Jima**, 1949, and was profiled by Lee Marvin in **The American**, 1960 (made for TV), as well as by Adam Beach in Clint Eastwood's **Flags of Our Fathers**, 2006. Curtis told this author that "I believe that my work in **The Outsider** was the best I ever produced, although many critics thought I was miscast as that tragic Indian boy. Ira Hayes fought for his country and was treated by a lot of people like a second-class citizen unworthy of the recognition he won in battle. He was a martyr on the cross of bigotry. I had a good dose of that in my early Hollywood years. I am Jewish, although a lot of people thought I was Italian or something just as good. My friend Sidney Poitier had a hard go of it in Hollywood, and had to fight for any good role and I helped him get into **The Defiant Ones** [1958] with me. That was one of my best films, a Jew and a black guy chained to each other, running from the law, but what we were really running from was prejudice and race hatred. So was Ira Hayes, poor guy, who kept running until he dropped dead. What a fate for an American hero." Curtis considered himself a patriot, having served in the U.S. Navy during WWII, and while serving on board a submarine tender, he watched through binoculars as General Douglas MacArthur and others signed the peace terms that ended WWII on board the USS *Missouri*, which was anchored in Tokyo Bay, on September 2, 1945. "That was the greatest moment of my life," Curtis told this author. **p**, Sy Bartlett; **d**, Delbert Mann; **cast**: Tony Curtis, James Franciscus, Gregory Walcott, Bruce Bennett, Vivian Nathan, Edmund Hashim, Paul Comi, Stanley Adams, Wayne Heffley, Ralph Moody, Jeffrey Silver, James Beck; **w**, Stewart Stern (based on the biography *The Hero of Iwo Jima* by William Bradford Huie); **c**, Joseph LeShelle; **m**, Leonard Rosenman; **ed**, Marjorie Fowler; **art d**, Alexander Golitzen, Ted Haworth; **set d**, Oliver Emert.

The Outsider ★★★ 1980; U.S.; 128m; Cinematic Arts/PAR; Color;

C. Thomas Howell and Diane Lane in *The Outsiders*, 1983.

Drama; Children: Unacceptable (MPAA: R); **DVD; VHS**. Grim and un-relenting profile of the seemingly eternal strife between Protestants and Catholics in Northern Ireland sees naïve Wasson going to Belfast to fight for the IRA. He has been inspired by his grandfather's fiery recollections of fighting the British decades earlier, but he is in for a rude awakening when he finds that the IRA has marked him for death. (Such glorified and IRA tales told to impressionistic youngsters appear in many films, including **I See a Dark Stranger**, 1947, where naïve Deborah Kerr is so inspired to undertake a one-woman war against the British nation that she inadvertently becomes involved in Nazi espionage, almost at the cost of her life.) The IRA, however, is not the noble and purposeful organization so grandly illustrated by Wasson's grandfather. These sinister rebels plan to kill Wasson and blame his murder on the British so that the demise of this young American will show him to be a martyr to their cause. Once he is dead, the rebels believe they can raise huge amounts of money from Irish-Americans to further their operations. The other side shares its portion of brutality in that a British soldier is shown as he mercilessly murders a twelve-year-old boy, and British soldiers in another scene are shown to be sadistically applying torture to a rebel as they conduct an interrogation. Meanwhile, Wasson spends most of his time evading death in one harrowing scene after another. Harsh to the point of being savage, this film, more than most profiling the subject, takes neither side and gives what is most probably the most realistic portrait of the grim conditions in Northern Ireland up to that time. Wasson, Quinn and Hayden, along with the rest of the cast, give outstanding performances under the firm direction of Luraschi, who also wrote the well-crafted script. *Author's Note*: The film was produced for less than $3 million and was shot mostly in Dublin as the filmmakers were not permitted to use the war-torn streets of Belfast; the beginning and end were shot on location in Detroit. **p**, Philippe Modave; **d&w**, Tony Luraschi (based on the novel *The Heritage of Michael Flaherty* by Colin Leinster); **cast**, Craig Wasson, Sterling Hayden, Patricia Quinn, Niall O'Brien, T.P. McKenna, Niall Toibin, Frank Grimes, Elizabeth Begley, Bosco Hogan, Gabriel Byrne; **c**, Ricardo Aronovich; **m**, Ken Thorne; **ed**, Catherine Kelber; **art d**, Franco Fumagalli.

The Outsiders ★★★ 1983; U.S.; 91m; Zoetrope Studio/WB; Color; Drama; Children: Unacceptable (MPAA: PG); **DVD; VHS**. This gruesome but realistic film profiles teenage gangs at war with each other in 1960s Tulsa, Oklahoma. It's the wealthy South Zone gang, "The Socs" (Socials), against the poor North Zone gang, "The Greasers." The Greasers are Ponyboy Curtis (Howell), his two older brothers Soda (Lowe) and Darrel (Swayze), and Johnny (Macchio), Dally (Dillon), Two-Bit Matthews (Estevez), and Steve (Cruise). Five of the Socs attack Howell and his neck is cut with a switchblade in retaliation for Macchio

having been similarly attacked the previous month. Two of the Socs, Garrett and Dalton, confront Greasers Macchio, Howell, and Estevez, who are at a drive-in talking to two Soc girls Cherry (Lane) and Marcia (Meyrink). The girls avoid a gang battle by going home with the Soc boys. Later that night, Macchio and Howell are attacked in a park by Garrett, Dalton and two other Soc boys, who dunk Howell in a fountain. Macchio stabs Garrett fatally with a switchblade. Howell and Macchio hide out in an abandoned church and Howell dyes his hair blond to disguise himself. News comes to them that Lane will take their side in court. The boys go hunting for food but, upon their return, find the church on fire with children trapped inside. They rescue the kids, but Macchio is hospitalized with severe burns and a broken back. Howell and Macchio are praised for their heroism, but Macchio is charged with manslaughter for killing Garrett, while Howell is to be sent to a boys' home. A rumble takes place between the two gangs and the Greasers win. Macchio then dies of his burn wounds. Distressed, Dillon robs a grocery store at gunpoint and is killed by police. Howell is eventually cleared of Garrett's death and is allowed to stay with his brothers. Life, miserable that it is, goes on for the boys in both gangs. This film proved to be an early success for Dillon, Macchio, Swayze, Lowe, and Estevez, all of whom became stars and where Cruise became a superstar. Songs: "Stay Gold" (Carmine Cappola, Stevie Wonder), "Gloria" (Van Morrison), "Loveless Motel" (Buck Barrett), "Jack Daniels If You Please" (David Allan Coe), "Out of Limits" (Michael Z. Gordon), "Mystery Train" (Junior Parker, Sam Philips). Excessive violence, teen drinking, smoking and some sexual scenes prohibit viewing by children. **p**, Fred Roos, Gray Frederickson; **d**, Francis Ford Coppola; **cast**, C. Thomas Howell, Matt Dillon, Ralph Macchio, Patrick Swayze, Rob Lowe, Emilio Estevez, Tom Cruise, Glenn Withrow, Diane Lane, Leif Garrett, Sofia Coppola; **w**, Kathleen Knutsen Rowell (based on the novel by S.E. Hinton); **c**, Stephen H. Burum (Panavision; Technicolor); **m**, Carmine Coppola; **ed**, Anne Goursaud; **prod d**, Dean Tavoularis; **set d**, Gary Fettis; **spec eff**, Dennis Dino.

Outward Bound ★★★ 1930; U.S.; 83m; WB; B/W; Fantasy; Children: Unacceptable; **VHS**. This strange and sometimes chilling drama has a number of passengers on board a ship and not knowing its destination or acknowledging the reasons why they are on board. Francis is the only crew member they encounter, an aging steward who tends to their needs. Howard begins to question their existence until he and the rest finally discover that they are all dead, except for a young married couple, Fairbanks and Chandler. Digges then boards the fog-bound ship in the form of the Examiner, who will judge which destination each passenger will ultimately take (one can assume either Heaven or Hell), and while examining each, we learn their good and bad natures. Howard is sent to live in a small cottage where he will find peace of mind; Mercer, an elderly woman, accepts her role as his housekeeper' and only toward the end do we discover that she is Howard's mother, who gave him up as a child. The fate of Fairbanks and Chandler hangs in the balance since they are suicides, like Francis, and are condemned to forever sail on board this true ghost ship to nowhere, until, on earth, their dog smashes a window and, breathing fresh air, they return to life, leaving the ship and resuming lives with more promise and hope than the dire action that brought them to this eerie voyage. Well enacted by the entire cast, this offbeat fantasy from Sutton Vane provides great atmospheric scenes, thanks to the fine cinematography of Mohr, who employs some inventive lighting and effective use of fog machines. The film was remade as **Between Two Worlds**, 1944, with Paul Henreid and Eleanor Parker as the suicides and John Garfield and Sara Allgood as the son and mother, and Sidney Greenstreet is the Examiner. It was remade again as **The Flight That Disappeared**, 1961. *Author's Note*: This was Howard's first American film, which helped to establish him as a matinee idol and where he reprises his role from the original Broadway play, as do Mercer, Fairbanks, Digges and Watts. **p**, Jack L. Warner; **d**, Robert Milton; **cast**, Leslie Howard, Douglas Fairbanks Jr.,

Beryl Mercer, Dudley Digges, Helen Chandler, Alec B. Francis, Montagu Love, Lyonel Watts, Alison Skipworth, Walter Kingsford, Tempe Pigott; **w**, J. Grubb Alexander (based on the play by Sutton Vane); **c**, Hal Mohr; **ed**, Ralph Dawson.

Over My Dead Body ★★★ 1943; U.S.; 68m; FOX; B/W; Comedy/Mystery; Children: Acceptable. Zany comedy has Berle as a failed mystery writer who can't concoct endings to his plots. He relies on his wife, Hughes, to be the breadwinner in the family. He takes his latest story to the publishing house where she works and where her boss, Denny, doesn't know she is married. Hiding in a closet, Berle overhears Denny and some others talking about their boss having committed suicide over their goofy schemes. Berle thinks this would make a great story, so he has himself arrested as the murderer of the man, who actually committed suicide. He believes he can come up with a plot solution to save himself from the electric chair, but his plan backfires and he is put on trial for murder. After a lot of shenanigans, he barely manages to clear himself and now has a plot with a good ending for his next book. This delightful comedy demonstrated that Berle had the makings of a great comic, which culminated in the late 1940s and early 1950s when he became the number one comedic attraction on TV. **p**, Walter Morosco; **d**, Malcolm St. Clair; **cast**, Milton Berle, Mary Beth Hughes, Reginald Denny, Frank Orth, William Davidson, Wonderful Smith, J. Patrick O'Malley, George M. Carleton, John Hamilton, Milton Parsons, Lon McCallister, Ann E. Todd; **w**, Edward James (based on the novel *As Good as Murdered* by James O'Hanlon); **c**, Lucien N. Andriot; **m**, Emil Newman, Cyril J. Mockridge; **ed**, J. Watson Webb, Jr.

Over the Hedge ★★★ 2006; U.S.; 83m; DreamWorks Animation/PAR; Color; Animated Adventure; Children: Unacceptable (MPAA: PG); **BD**; **DVD**; **VHS**. An exciting computer-animated family action comedy based on characters from the United Media comic strip of that name begins when a starving con artist raccoon (Willis voiceover) in a forest raids a food cache belonging to a hibernating black bear (Nolte voiceover). Nolte wakes up and his food and a red wagon used to carry it are run over by a truck. Nolte gives Willis a week to replace his food or he will eat him, and Willis promises the return of those victuals. Meanwhile, some forest animal friends led by a turtle (Shandling voiceover) awake from hibernation to find their food stores nearly empty. They forage for food, but find a large hedge blocking their way. This leads Shandling to discover a human community on the other side of the hedge, and Willis tells them it's easier to raid the humans' garbage than forage for food. They get enough food to keep them from starving, but they are chased away by one homeowner (Janney voiceover) who hires an exterminator (Church voiceover) to keep them out of her house and garden. There is a falling out among the animals about whether they should return the food or not, and then they see Janney has bought a large supply of food for a party. She tells Church to hide some booby traps in her yard in order to catch any thieving animals, but, working at night, the animals take her party food. Janney calls Church, who briefly traps all the animals except Willis, who escapes with the party food. The animals then take a truck with the food to now-awake Nolte, but it goes out of control and demolishes Janney's house. The animals hide in the hedge, trapped by Willis on one side and Janney on the other. Willis and Shandling give Hammy, a hyperactive squirrel (Carell voiceover) a can of an energy drink that sends him off faster than the speed of light. He sets off an illegal trap Church had installed in Janney's lawn, and all the animals are caught by police. Back in the forest, Shandling tells Willis that if he had explained that he wanted to replace Nolte's food, the others would have helped because "that's what families do," and welcomes him back to the family. Meanwhile, Carell refills their food cache with nuts to last them for a year and the animals escape from the police to enjoy a more peaceful life back in the forest. Songs: "Family of Me," "Heist," "Still," "Rockin' the Suburbs" (Ben Folds); "Lost in the Supermarket" (Joe Strummer, Mick Jones, Paul Simonon, Topper Headon).

Irene Dunne and Charles Coburn in *Over 21*, 1945.

Crude humor and mild comic action of some violence prohibits viewing by children. **p**, Bonnie Arnold, Christian Kubsch; **d**, Tim Johnson, Karey Kirkpatrick; **cast** (voiceovers), Bruce Willis, Garry Shandling, Steve Carell, Wanda Sykes, William Shatner, Nick Nolte, Thomas Haden Church, Allison Janney, Eugene Levy, Catherine O'Hara; **w**, Len Blum, Lorne Cameron, David Hoselton, Chris Poche, Kirkpatrick (based on characters created by Michael Fry, T. Lewis); **m**, Rupert Gregson-Williams; **ed**, John K. Carr; **prod d**, Kathy Altieri; **art d**, Paul Shardlow; **spec eff**, Marty Havran, Heather M. Shepherd.

Over 21 ★★★ 1945; U.S.; 104m; COL; B/W; Comedy; Children: Acceptable. Dunne and Knox are married writers living near a U.S. Army base during World War II (1939-1945). Knox joins up so he can learn more about army life and write about it, but finds the disciplined life of a soldier hard to handle, especially since the other recruits are so much younger than he is and that he shares little in common with them. Meanwhile, Dunne struggles with being an army wife, contending with regulations and restrictions that lead to many humorous scenes. Based on the real-life experiences of Gordon, this tale was adapted for a Broadway stage production (opened on January 3, 1944, with Gordon in the lead, Dunne enacting Gordon's role in the film version), providing a lively comedy that entertains throughout. **p&w**, Sidney Buchman (based on the play by Ruth Gordon); **d**, Charles Vidor; **cast**, Irene Dunne, Alexander Knox, Charles Coburn, Jeff Donnell, Loren Tindall, Lee Patrick, Phil Brown, Cora Witherspoon, Charles Evans, Abigail Adams, Carole Mathews; **c**, Rudolph Mate; **m**, Marlin Skiles; **ed**, Otto Meyer; **art d**, Stephen Goosson, Rudolph Sternad; **set d**, Louis Diage.

The Overlanders ★★★ 1946; Australia/U.K.; 91m; Ealing Studios; UNIV; B/W; War Drama; Children: Unacceptable; **DVD**; **VHS**. Exciting tale is set in Australia at the start of World War II (1939-1945), where Japanese forces threaten the "down under" continent, which causes inhabitants to evacuate and burn everything in a "scorched earth" policy. Rather than kill all of their 500,000 head of cattle, a group led by Rafferty decides to drive them overland halfway across the continent. The arduous journey of 2,000 miles takes fifteen months, and hardships include a cattle stampede that threatens all of the cowboys. Overcoming hazards and hardships, the drovers accomplish their mission, preserving the herd for the much needed troops that will be fighting that war. Song: "Hardships" (composer unknown). This Australian classic provides many harrowing scenes that prohibit viewing by children. **p**, Michael Balcon; **d&w**, Harry Watt; **cast**, Chips Rafferty, John Nugent Hayward, Daphne Campbell, Jean Blue, Helen Grieve, John Fernside, Peter Pagan, Frank Ransome, Stan Tolhurst, Marshall Crosby; **c**, Osmond Borradaile; **m**, John Ireland; **ed**, E.M. Inman Hunter.

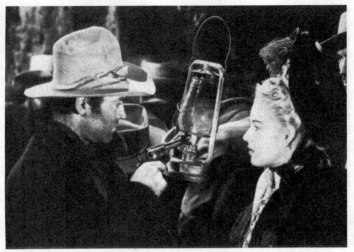

Henry Fonda and Mary Beth Hughes in *The Ox-Bow Incident*, 1943.

Overnight Delivery ★★★ 1998; U.S.; 109m; UNIV; Color; Comedy/Romance; Children: Unacceptable (MPAA: PG-13); **DVD**; **VHS**. Pleasing though adolescent-minded romantic comedy sees Rudd as a Minnesota college student, who suspects that his girlfriend, Taylor, a University of Tennessee college student in Memphis, is unfaithful, and is cheating on him with someone named "Ricker." Heartbroken, he goes to a strip club, gets drunk, and meets one of the club dancers, Witherspoon. She suggests he get back at Taylor by sending her an abusive letter and enclose a photo of himself with her (Witherspoon) while she is posing topless. Rudd does this and also encloses a fake "used" condom in the package, sending it by overnight delivery. After the package is on its way, he learns that Taylor is not cheating on him. "Ricker" is not a man, but a dog belonging to Taylor's girlfriend, and for whom Taylor has been a caretaker. Frantic, Rudd has only twenty-four hours to prevent the package from being delivered. He finds the delivery man, Drake, and asks for the package, but Drake refuses to break the company rules and thinks Rudd is a spy for the company. (This ploy is also shown as the pivotal hazard in **Cause for Alarm!**, 1951, where Loretta Young tries her utmost to prevent the delivery of a letter that will wrongly incriminate her in the death of her husband and where the great character actor Irving Bacon, a by-the-book postman, refuses to turn over that letter to her.) Rudd buys an air ticket to Memphis, but another passenger, Bell, is a serial killer, who takes him hostage. Rudd escapes and gets Witherspoon to drive him to Memphis. En route, they see Drake's truck at a gas station. Rudd breaks into it and finds the package, but, before he can take it, Drake leaves with the truck. On the road again, Rudd and Witherspoon are involved in an accident, and Witherspoon's car falls into a river. Both broke, they have dinner at a diner and are arrested for not paying the bill. They obtain some cash and manage to post bail and are on their way again when they see Drake's truck once more. While Drake has dinner at a diner, Rudd empties the truck's gas tank so as to stall him. A lighted cigarette carelessly sets off a fire and the truck catches fire. The indefatigable Drake, however, is still able to drive the truck, so Rudd and Witherspoon follow by stealing a drunk's car. They finally get to the campus in Memphis, but, by then, Rudd realizes he loves Witherspoon and not Taylor. Rudd also learns that Taylor really was cheating on him with a man called Ricker. He lets Taylor receive his package and letter and confesses his love to Witherspoon, who has also fallen in love with him. Hectic, crude and offensive for some, this film nevertheless holds attention throughout. Songs: "Magnet and Steel" (Walter Egan), "One Way or Another" (Deborah Harry, Nigel Harrison), "Paint Me" (Louise Wener), "Signed, Sealed, Delivered (I'm Yours)" (Syretta Wright, Lee Garrett, Lula Mae Haraway, Stevie Wonder), "Bad Vibes Everyone" (David Lowery, John Hickman, David Faragher), "We Wish You a Lovely Day" (Tom Jennings, Glen Mitchell, Graham

McHugh). Crude sexual content prohibits viewing by children. **p**, Dan Etheridge, Brad Krevoy, Steven Stabler; **d**, Jason Bloom; **cast**, Paul Rudd, Reese Witherspoon, Christine Taylor, Sarah Silverman, Buffy Sedlachek, Richard Cody, Gary Wolf, John Sylvain, William Byrd Wilkins, John Beasley, James Belushi; **w**, Bloom, Marc Sedaka; **c**, Edward J. Pei; **m**, Andrew Gross; **ed**, Luis Colina; **prod d**, Marek Dobrowolski; **art d**, Scott Meehan; **set d**, Diana L. Stoughton; **spec eff**, Ron Trost.

Owning Mahowny ★★★ 2003; Canada/U.K.; 104m; Alliance Atlantis Communications/Sony; Color; Crime Drama; Children: Unacceptable (MPAA: R); **DVD**; **VHS**. Based on the largest one-man bank fraud in Canadian history, this film tells the story of Brian Molony, who, in the film is called Dan Mahowny and played by Hoffman), a twenty-four-year-old rising star at the Canadian Imperial Bank of Commerce, who is a compulsive gambler and deep in debt. As assistant manager of the bank's major branch in Toronto in 1982, he accesses a multi-million-dollar account. To his friends, he is a quiet but humorous person who spends most of his leisure time watching sports on television. He dresses in cheap suits, drives a beat-up old car and lives in a modest apartment with cheap furniture. To his fiancée Driver, and fellow bank employee, he is a shy and withdrawn person, not capable of creating trouble for anyone. No one can guess that he has created phantom accounts and has juggled figures to defraud the bank by skimming $10 million in eighteen months for his own use. The money is used to feed his gambling obsession which involves horse race betting and frequent trips to the casinos in Atlantic City. He actually wants to win a lot, then lose it, just for the excitement of being a high roller, win or lose. A telephone wire tap leads investigators to Mahowny and his eventual arrest. The film presents a fascinating portrait of Mahowny's character rather than how he is caught. Gutter language and sexuality prohibit viewing by children. **p**, Alessandro Camon, Andras Hamori, Seaton McLean, Bradley Adams, Damon Bryant; **d**, Richard Kwietniowski; **cast**, Philip Seymour Hoffman, Minnie Driver, John Hurt, Maury Chaykin, Ian Tracey, Sonja Smits, Chris Collins, Jason Blicker, Vincent Corazza, Roger Dunn, Eric Fink, Sandra Oh; **w**, Maurice Chauvet (based on the novel *No Limit* by Gary Stephen Ross); **c**, Oliver Curtis; **m**, Richard Grassby-Lewis, The Insects (Bob Locke, Tim Norfolk); **ed**, Mike Munn; **prod d**, Taavo Soodor; **art d**, Diana Magnus; **set d**, Erica Milo; **spec eff**, Brock Jolliffe.

The Ox-Bow Incident ★★★★★ 1943; U.S.; 75m; FOX; B/W; Western; Children: Unacceptable; **DVD**; **VHS**. Pantheon director Wellman delivers a masterpiece western with this brooding, bare-knuckle film, one of the first to introspectively examine the root causes and basic character of mob violence so common to that era of the Old West. Based on a real event in 1885 in Nevada, the unsophisticated and rough-hewn characters are embodied by the first two persons to appear on the screen, cowboys Fonda and Morgan, who ride into the tired and declining town of Bridger's Wells, Nevada, after finishing a long and fatiguing cattle drive. They tie up their horses in front of the local saloon, seeking whiskey and relaxation. Within a short time, Fonda locks horns with local cattleman Lawrence, knocking him out in a brief fight, only to hear a man riding into town shouting to one and all that a popular rancher named Larry Kinkaid (Orth) has been killed and his cattle rustled. Lawrence, a hothead, who is the slain rancher's best friend, seethes with anger, shouting to everyone to get mounted so that a posse can immediately pursue, capture and punish the rustlers. Wise and avuncular Davenport, a storekeeper, urges caution, stating: "Don't let's go off half-cocked and do something we'll be sorry for." He believes that the sheriff is most probably at the Kinkaid ranch and that it would be a mistake to capture some strangers and perhaps wrongly accuse them, and to take the law into their own hands. "If we hang these men ourselves," Davenport tells the assembled citizens, "we'll be worse than murderers." Lawrence argues with Davenport and then Davenport, along with Fonda and Morgan, visit Briggs, an indecisive judge, who puts off the matter and where Davenport tells Briggs that it would be a mistake to have the sheriff's deputy, Rich, take charge of the situation as Rich is a decided thug. Lawrence, however, has his way, and Briggs reluctantly sanctions a posse led by Rich and Lawrence, along with Conroy, a former Confederate officer in the Civil War, who appears out of nowhere wearing his old uniform and taking command of the posse. Conroy is an aging but dictatorial person, who orders his mild-mannered son, Eythe, to ride with the posse and all set out in search of the rustlers. Each posse member is riding out of different motivations, all varied and most without principle. Fonda and Morgan join the posse, even though they are opposed to violence, but believe that if they do not join the pursuers they might be considered suspects as they have just newly arrived in town. Rich, a sadist, looks to bring havoc down upon the evildoers purely for the perverted joy it will give him and Lawrence needs to satisfy the vengeance gnawing at him. Whipper, a black man and preacher, joins the posse at the request of some of its members so that this gentle old man can pray for those who might be caught and summarily executed by the rope. The posse, numbering twenty-eight riders, including Darwell, an elderly harridan, roams aimlessly about, overtaking a stagecoach that is under repairs at a mountain pass and where Fonda sees the girl he has always loved, Hughes, only to find that she has just married a wealthy businessman, Meeker, and is on her way to live in style in San Francisco. Meeker proves to be a foppish, arrogant man, lisping his salutations to the posse members, and Fonda considers him a "pompous ass" and that Hughes has made the mistake of her life. The posse rides on and on, finding no rustlers and many want to turn back. Darwell shouts out: "What? We'll be the laughingstock of the country if we turn back now!" Shamed by this fierce old woman, the posse rides into a small valley where they find three men at a campsite, Andrews, Quinn and Ford. Andrews tells the posse members that he and his two helpers are planning to build a ranch in the area, but when fifty head of cattle are found with the Kinkaid brand on them, Andrews, Quinn and Ford quickly become suspects. Andrews says that he paid Kinkaid cash for the cattle and that Kinkaid promised to mail him a receipt. This explanation does not convince the posse members, particularly Rich and Conroy, who have already judged the three men out of hand as rustlers. A gun belonging to Kinkaid is then found on Quinn, and one of the posse members claims that Quinn is wanted for several murders. Quinn says that he found the gun and admits that he is wanted by the law but that he did not kill Kinkaid. Andrews tells the posse members that things look bad for him and his friends, but he insists upon a trial "in this godforsaken country." Conroy replies: "You are getting a trial with twenty-eight of the only kind of judges [that] murderers and rustlers get in what you call this 'godforsaken country.'" Conroy then orders everyone to vote, and seven of them, including Fonda, Morgan, Davenport and Whipper, vote to have the men held for trial. The others, which make up the majority, vote to hang them immediately. Conroy tells the three condemned men that they can write letters to their loved ones before being executed, but only Andrews writes a letter to his young wife and gives it to Davenport. The compassionate Davenport reads the letter and then asks Andrews if he can read the letter aloud to the others, believing that it is so touching and sincere that it will soften their hearts and they will relent and allow the three men to stand trial. Andrews refuses, saying that the letter is personal and that he will not tolerate his last loving thoughts to his wife being exposed to a bunch of sadistic lynch mob members. Then Quinn makes a break for freedom, but is shot while trying to flee. He uses a knife to dig the bullet out in his leg while Ford, a senile old man, stares blankly at his accusers, not really knowing what is going on. The conscientious Fonda, who has objected to Conroy's tyrannical proceedings all along, interferes, saying that the three men should be held for trial, accusing Conroy of railroading the three men. He is brutally silenced by Rich, who clubs him with a gun; the three men are bound with their hands tied behind their backs and placed on horses, three ropes tied around their necks, which are tossed over the limb of a sturdy tree. Two members of the posse, the vicious Lawrence and the

Ted North, Victor Kilian, Henry Fonda, Henry Morgan and Harry Davenport in *The Ox-Bow Incident,* 1943.

equally sadistic Darwell, enthusiastically volunteer to whip two of the horses forward and Conroy selects his son, Eythe, to be the third executioner, although Eythe has already voted with the other six men to put off the execution. Conroy compels Eythe to this gruesome task in order to "make a man" of him. At Conroy's order, Lawrence and Darwell whip two of the horses forward, but, when Eythe refuses to do the same, Conroy slugs him unconscious with his pistol and whips the third horse forward to leave the three men dangling. He then orders Lawrence to "finish it," and Lawrence fires rifle bullets into each of the hanging men. Fonda, Davenport, Morgan and four others, who had objected to the mass execution, watch stunned as the participating posse members mount their horses and begin to ride from the site of the execution. The posse then encounters the local sheriff, Robertson, who states that Kinkaid is alive and was only wounded and that he has captured the rustlers. When he learns from Davenport that "all but seven" of the posse members lynched three innocent men, Robertson barks to the culprits: "The Lord better have mercy on you. You won't get any from me!" Later, when members of the posse assemble at the local saloon in Bridger's Wells, they collect $500, which is to be given to Andrews' widow and his children. Fonda, who has been given Andrews' letter by Davenport and who intends to deliver that letter and the collected funds to Andrews' widow, then compassionately reads that letter as the lynch members grimly consider their own fates. He ends his reading with an emotional plea to the world as stated by Andrews in his last message while alive: "A man just naturally can't take the law into his own hands and hang people without hurting everybody in the world, because he's not just breaking one law, but all laws. Law is a lot more than words you put into a book, or judges or lawyers or sheriffs you hire to carry it out. It's everything people have found out about justice and what's right and wrong. It's the very conscience of humanity. There can't be any such thing as civilization unless people have got a conscience, because if people touch God anywhere, where is it except through their conscience? And what is anybody's conscience except a little piece of the conscience of all men that ever lived?" Fonda, who has read this letter with a hesitant and almost groping manner, folds and pockets the letter, and he and Morgan then set out to deliver it, concluding this powerful film. Wellman takes great pains to develop all of his characters, even down to the smallest character parts where each is shown to either have or not possess that "conscience" about which Andrews so eloquently speaks in his final letter. Great performances are rendered by the conscientious Fonda and Morgan, as well as Darwell enacting the sanctimonious "mother" of the lynch mob, along with Conroy as the tyrannical father who is mad for power (and who, after his son Eythe leaves his home, closes the door to that mansion and we hear a shot, ostensibly where the ruthless Conroy has taken his own life, not over supervising the lynching of three innocent men, but by los-

Henry Fonda and Henry Morgan in *The Ox-Bow Incident*, 1943.

ing control over his son). Andrews gives one of his finest performances as the leader of the victimized trio, intensely desperate to vindicate himself even when he knows there is no help for it. Everything appears rough-hewn and hardscrabble in this grim and gritty anti-lynching tale, the most impactful ever to be put on the screen up to that time. Miller's starkly lit scenes add reality to each sequence in a setting that is atmospherically dark and foreboding, the landscape sets as uninviting and hostile as the shallow-souled posse members. Songs: "Red River Valley" (traditional), "Great Camp Meeting in the Promised Land," (traditional spiritual), "Lonesome Valley" (traditional spiritual). Though this film did not do well at the box office, it remained one of Wellman's favorite films, as it did for Fonda. One of the reasons why this film was criticized (some critics calling it "claustrophobic") was that Wellman opted to shoot most of the film with interior sets, instead of outdoors, so that he could better provide the moody lighting and atmosphere he wanted, and more easily direct his actors on the sets of the foreboding landscapes. The outdoor set for the town of Bridger's Wells was the western set at the Fox lot, which was used many times in other western films produced by the studio, including **River of No Return**, 1954, and **Warlock**, 1959. This film was later remade by Fox in 1955, an abbreviated adaptation (only 55 minutes) that saw limited distribution. Other notable western films profiling lynch mobs include: **Across the Sierras**, 1941; **Along the Great Divide**, 1951; **The Baron of Arizona**, 1950; **Blazing Saddles**, 1974; **Broken Arrow**, 1950; **Dodge City**, 1939; **Fighting Man of the Plains**, 1949; **Fury at Furnace Creek**, 1948; **Gunfight at the O.K. Corral**, 1957; **Hang 'Em High**, 1968; **The Hanging Tree**, 1959; **Johnny Guitar**, 1954; **Journey to Shiloh**, 1968; **A Man Alone**, 1955; **The Man from the Alamo**, 1953; **Masterson of Kansas**, 1954; **My Little Chickadee**, 1940; **No Name on the Bullet**, 1959; **The Oklahoma Kid**, 1939; **Rage at Dawn**, 1955; **Rango**, 2011; **Stars in My Crown**, 1950; **Three Hours to Kill**, 1954; **The Tin Star**, 1957; **Unforgiven**, 1992; **Warlock**, 1959; **Woman They Almost Lynched**, 1953; **Wyatt Earp**, 1994; and **Young Guns II**, 1990; for a more comprehensive list see Ku Klux Klan and Lynch Mobs in the Subject Index, Volume II. *Author's Note*: The socially conscious Wellman had lobbied Fox studio boss Darryl F. Zanuck for several years (beginning in 1940) for permission to make this film, but Zanuck, who was one of the foremost filmmakers of socially conscious films in those days, had deep reservations. "I went to Darryl," Wellman told this author, "and promised him that I would do two pictures he wanted made, **Thunder Birds** [1942], and **Buffalo Bill** [1944] if he let me do **The Ox-Bow Incident**. He shook my hand on it, and I went to work on the first picture, but suddenly Darryl was away from the studio, in the service during the war [WWII]. I went to William Goetz, who was running the studio for Darryl in his absence, although Darryl was still the boss. Goetz hedged and

hawed and got a bunch of other top producers to back up his "no" to me about **The Ox-Box Incident**, telling me that the story was just too grim and would not go over with audiences that wanted either musicals and comedies to take their troubled minds off the war, or war films that showed the Japs and Germans being skewered on bayonets. To hell with it, I said to myself, and went over Goetz's head. I sent a wire to Darryl that stated: 'This is to remind you of our handshake.' After Darryl got that wire, he sent one of his own to Goetz, telling him to let me go ahead with the picture." What Goetz and others feared was that the film might inspire more lynching, but such activity in the U.S. was in decline with only three such events occurring in 1943, the year this film was released (and where fifty years earlier as many as 231 persons had been lynched in 1892; more than 2,000 victims of such mob violence had occurred in the U.S. since records were maintained, beginning in 1880). Actually, Wellman had begun lobbying to do this film at Paramount and where a producer at that studio, Harold Hurley, purchased the rights to the book for $6000. "Hurley then got it into his head," Wellman said to this author, "that he wanted, of all people, Mae West, to play the part of the old woman, who rides with the posse and have Mae play that character as some sort of a wisecracking person to bring some light and humor into that otherwise grim story. Well, I told Hurley that he was nuts and that if Mae got into that picture, she would ruin the whole thing and I would not have anything to do with her because I knew what a prima donna she was. Hurley could not do a thing with the story at Paramount and, after he got low on money, I bought the rights from him for $6,500 and then then I went to work on Darryl for whom I had made a number of successful pictures." Wellman made sure that he lined up Fonda for the leading player of the conscientious cowboy by hiring Trotti as the screenwriter to adapt the story for the screen, knowing that the gifted Trotti had done a number of scripts for films in which Fonda starred. "When Bill told me that he was doing **The Ox-Bow Incident**," Fonda told this author, "and that Lamar [Trotti] was producing and writing the script, I told him that I would do it. It was a great story that sent the kind of message to the world I wanted to be part of, especially since Trotti had written scripts for some pictures of mine, like **Young Mr. Lincoln** [1939] and **Drums along the Mohawk** [1939], and both of those pictures had been directed by Pappy [John Ford], a great director. Bill [Wellman], too, was one of the best directors in the business and took a lot of care in the films he made and we thought pretty much the same way about things. As usual there was a hook. I had to agree to play in a comedy [**The Magnificent Dope**, 1942] for Fox, so I agreed to do that picture just to work with Bill on **The Ox-Bow Incident**." Andrews, who had appeared in only a few films prior to doing this film, told this author that "I had to fight for that role of the young rancher who is lynched, but it was Bill [Wellman] who had seen some of my pictures and got me into **The Ox-Bow Incident**, a role that helped me get a lot more important parts, such as **The Purple Heart** [1944] and my big breakthrough picture, **Laura** [1944]. You know, the actor who plays the old addlebrained cowhand who is lynched with me, Francis Ford, was John Ford's older brother and who was a terrific actor and is magnificent as that old befuddled man, the most pathetic victim of the three of us. He had appeared as an old scout in **Drums along the Mohawk** with Hank [Fonda] and where he goes off his head after the Indians capture and burn him alive in that picture and where his younger brother, John [Ford] was directing. I heard that the two Ford brothers did not get along since Francis was a big name silent screen star and started in pictures before he got John his first jobs at Universal back in the silent era and that John always used his older brother in his films, but went out of his way to abuse him by unnecessarily shouting at him. Hank [Fonda] told me that John mistreated Francis because he could not bear to be indebted to Francis and treated everyone else who had helped him establish his career the same way. Pretty strange doings, don't you think? The other man lynched with me was Tony Quinn, who plays a defiant Mexican cowpuncher. He was very intense in that picture and that picture, too, helped his career." Quinn, like Andrews, had been struggling to get substantial parts in Hollywood for a number of years, and told this author that "I don't have a lot of lines in **The Ox-Bow Incident**, and I am in only a few scenes. Bill [Wellman] told me on the set of that picture: 'You know, Tony, you are doing it just right, with plenty of anger, but where are you getting all that steam?' I told him that I was angry about not getting bigger parts and that gave him a laugh, but it wasn't funny to me. Bill gave me a bigger part the next year when he did **Buffalo Bill** [1944] and I got to play Yellow Hand, the Indian leader who is killed by Joel McCrea in that picture in a big battle. When we finished that picture, I told Bill, 'I want to thank you for getting me a bigger part, even though you hanged me in the last picture and scalped me in this one.' Lawrence, who plays one of the most vicious lynch mob members, told this author that "I jumped for joy when Bill [Wellman] cast me in **The Ox-Bow Incident**. I had a role that was almost as big as Hank Fonda's. What a break that was and I always loved playing villains, you know, the kind of people everyone loves to hate. A lot more years went by before I got roles as good as that one, like the crime boss in **The Black Hand** [1950] and the greedy bookie in **The Asphalt Jungle** [1950]. Bill Wellman, God bless him, helped me get those roles when he put me at the head of that posse out to hang anybody available." **p&w**, Lamar Trotti (based on the novel by Walter Van Tilburg Clark); **d**, William A. Wellman; **cast**, Henry Fonda, Dana Andrews, Mary Beth Hughes, Anthony Quinn, William Eythe, Henry (Harry) Morgan, Jane Darwell, Harry Davenport, Dick Rich, Chris-Pin Martin, Paul Hurst, Victor Kilian, Matt Briggs, Leigh Whipper, Willard Robertson, Ted North, Francis Ford, Margaret Hamilton, Frank Orth, George Meeker, Rondo Hatton; **c**, Arthur Miller; **m**, Cyril J. Mockridge; **ed**, Allen McNeil; **art d**, Richard Day, James Basevi; **set d**, Thomas Little, Frank E. Hughes.

Pack Up Your Troubles ★★★ 1932; U.S.; 68m; MGM; B/W; Comedy; Children: Acceptable. Consistently funny comedy sees Laurel and Hardy in the U.S. Army in World War I (19141-1918) when their buddy, Dillaway, is killed in France. Since they promised to look after his baby girl, Lynn, if he died in the war, they try to find the child after they are mustered out following the Armistice. She is in the care of their pal's rich father, Tucker. The boys are invited to Tucker's mansion and it looks like they are going to live on easy street, but the cook, Marshall, recognizes them as his enemies back in basic training and, after a lot of humorous antics, drives them from the house. More hilarious scenes occur over mistaken identities and a bank robbery in this second feature-length comedy from the boys, their first being **Pardon Us**, 1931, after many short comedies, both talking and silent. Songs: "Dance of the Cuckoos" (1930, Marvin Hatley), "Pack Up Your Troubles in Your Old Kit Bag and Smile, Smile, Smile" (1915, Felix Powell), "Semper Fidelis/Always Faithful" (1888, John Philip Sousa), "You're in the Army Now" (traditional), "My Buddy" (1922, Walter Donaldson), "K-K-K Katy" (1918, Geoffrey O'Hara), "Bridal Chorus/Here Comes the Bride" (1850, Richard Wagner). **p**, Hal Roach; **d**, George Marshall, Raymond McCarey; **cast**, Stan Laurel, Oliver Hardy, Tom Kennedy, Grady Sutton, Donald Dillaway, Jacquie Lynn, James Finlayson, Billy Gilbert, Charles Middleton, Paulette Goddard; **w**, H.M. Walker; **c**, Art Lloyd; **m**, Marvin Hatley; **ed**, Richard Currier.

Pack Up Your Troubles ★★★ 1939; U.S.; 75m; FOX; B/W; Comedy; Children: Acceptable. Zany comedy has the Ritz Brothers working as vaudevillians, who lose their jobs during World War I (1914-1918), so they join the army and are sent to France to become mule skinners. There they meet an American girl, Withers, whose father, Schildkraut, is a French officer. Some French soldiers mistake the Ritz Brothers for German spies, and try to capture them, but they escape in a balloon and land in Germany. They capture a German general and get back to France to become heroes. Typical Ritz Brothers low comedy and slapstick are

Des Cave, Milo O'Shea and Peggy Cass in *Paddy,* 1970.

in force here, but it's so well done in this outing that the laughs keep coming. Song: "Who'll Buy My Flowers?" (Jule Styne, Sidney Clare). **p**, Sol M. Wurtzel; **d**, H. Bruce Humberstone; **cast**, Jane Withers, The Ritz Brothers (Al, Harry, Jimmy Ritz), Lynn Bari, Joseph Schildkraut, Stanley Fields, Fritz Leiber, Lionel Royce, Leon Ames; Georges Renavent; **w**, Lou Breslow; Owen Francis; **c**, Lucien N. Andriot; **m**, Samuel Kaylin; **ed**, Nick DeMaggio; **art d**, Richard Day, Albert Hogsett; **set d**, Thomas Little; **spec eff**, Louis J. Witte.

Paddy ★★★ 1970; Ireland; 97m; Dun Laoghaire/Allied Artists; Color; Comedy; Children: Unacceptable; **VHS**. Good comedic outing has Cave as a butcher's assistant in Dublin, Ireland. He tries to support his family after his father deserts them, but hates the constant nagging he receives from family members to improve their lifestyle. His older drinking buddy, O'Shea, gets him an entry-level job at an insurance company and Cave has some affairs with different women. One of them, Molloy, gets pregnant, but says she'll marry someone else because Cave is too irresponsible. O'Shea consoles him while Cave takes up with an American tourist and things look more promising. A charming comedy but sexual situations prohibit viewing by children. Songs: "Paddy," "Oop Oomp Ee Doo" (John Rubinstein, David Colloff), "Maureen" (Rubinstein, Stephen Michaels). **p**, Tamara Asseyev; **d**, Daniel Haller; **cast**, Milo O'Shea, Des Cave, Dearbhla Molloy, Maureen Toal, Peggy Cass, Judy Cornwell, Donal LeBlanc, Lillian Rapple, Desmond Perry, Marie O'Donnell; **w**, Lee Dunne; **c**, Daniel Lacambre, Néstor Almendros (Eastmancolor); **m**, John Rubinstein; **ed**, Christopher Holmes; **set d**, Tim Booth.

Paid ★★★ 1930; U.S.; 83m; MGM; B/W; Crime Drama; Children: Unacceptable; **DVD**. Crawford is a standout as a victimized woman who serves three years in prison for a crime she did not commit. Once out of prison, she and a former prison friend plan a scam in which old men can be sued for breach of promise in what was called the "heart balm" racket. It's Crawford's way of getting back at the men who set her up for the prison rap, but she eventually softens and settles down. Songs: "Happy Days Are Here Again" (Milton Ager, Jack Yellen), "The Sidewalks of New York" (1894; Charles Lawlor, James W. Blake). This story was filmed as silent pictures in 1917 with Alice Joyce, and 1923 with Norma Shearer, both under the title of the stage play "Within the Law." Mature themes prohibit viewing by children. **p&d**, Sam Wood; **cast**, Joan Crawford, Robert Armstrong, Marie Prevost, Douglass Montgomery, John Miljan, Purnell Pratt, Louise Beavers, Polly Moran, Jed Prouty, Tyrrell Davis, William Bakewell; **w**, Lucien Hubbard, Charles MacArthur (based on the play "Within the Law" by Bayard Veiller); **c**, Charles Rosher; **ed**, Hugh Wynn; **art d**, Cedric Gibbons.

William Boyd and Clark Gable in *The Painted Desert*, 1931.

Paint Your Wagon ★★★ 1969; U.S.; 158m; PAR/Miramax; Color; Musical; Children: Unacceptable (MPAA: PG-13); **DVD**; **VHS**. Marvin and Eastwood are exceptional in this offbeat but colorful and very lively musical about fortune-seekers in the Old West and where a number of memorable songs are offered. Hard drinking and rambunctious Marvin and calm and cool Eastwood become unlikely partners as gold prospectors during the California Gold Rush (1849-1850). They buy and share a wife, Seberg, who is purchased by Marvin for $800, but Marvin is left out in the cold when she falls in love with Eastwood. Lots of action follows, including hijacking a stagecoach, kidnapping six prostitutes, and turning their mining camp into a boomtown. They even find time to do some gold mining. Marvin eventually moves on, leaving Seberg and Eastwood to start a new life together. Mature material prohibits viewing by children. Marvin and Eastwood did their own singing, but Seberg's voice was dubbed by Anita Gordon. Songs: "They Call the Wind Maria," "I'm On My Way," "I Still See Elisa," "Hand Me Down That Can of Beans," "I Talk to the Trees," "Whoop-Ti-Ay!," "There's a Coach Comin' In," "Wand'rin' Star," (Frederick Loewe, Alan Jay Lerner), "The First Thing You Know," "A Million Miles Away Behind the Door," "The Gospel of No Name City," "Best Things," "Gold Fever" (Andre Previn, Lerner); *Author's Note*: A number of scenes show Marvin and Eastwood enacting a plan to pick up the gold dust that has over the years fallen through the cracks of the boarded floors of the shanties in which the miners live. To retrieve this gold dust, they and a few others dig a series of tunnels throughout the area to filch the gold, but this underground labyrinth eventually gives way and with it goes the whole mining town, these scenes alone costing more than $2 million. Costs spiraled upward when the roads around Baker, Oregon, where the film was being shot on location, were washed out. The company paid a roadway firm to repave the road, forty-six miles of it at $10,000 a mile. The area was dense with hippies who had migrated to the area in the druggie drop-out 1960s, and many of these drifters were hired as extras. They promptly formed a union and then demanded more salaries and concessions and got them, further inflating the overly expensive budget. Marvin admitted to this author that "I can't sing for a lick and everyone knew it, but I croaked out my own songs in that picture and even my closest relatives held their noses when I asked them how they liked my singing in **Paint Your Wagon**." Nevertheless, Marvin's performance was so outlandish that he is fascinating and his terrible warbling helped to make this film a cult classic. **p**, Alan Jay Lerner; **d**, Joshua Logan; **cast**, Lee Marvin, Clint Eastwood, Jean Seberg, Harve Presnell, Ray Walston, Tom Ligon, Alan Dexter, William O'Connell, Ben Baker, Alan Baxter, Robert Easton; **w**, Lerner, Paddy Chayefsky (based on the musical play by Lerner, Loewe); **c**, William A. Fraker (Panavision; Technicolor); **m**, Lerner, Loewe; **ed**, Robert C. Jones; **prod**

d, John Truscott; **art d**, Carl Braunger; **set d**, James I. Berkey; **spec eff**, Maurice Ayres, Larry Hampton, Daniel Hays.

The Painted Desert ★★★ 1931; U.S.; 79m; Pathe Exchange/RKO; B/W; Western; Children: Cautionary. Above-average oater sees Farnum and MacDonald finding a deserted covered wagon in which they find a baby and where Farnum adopts the child, raising the boy as his own and sending him off to college. The discovery of the child (not unlike the fleeing outlaws in **3 Godfathers**, 1948, who find a dying woman with a newborn child in a covered wagon) creates a long-standing feud between Farnum and MacDonald. When Boyd, who is Farnum's grown adopted son, returns from college with an engineering degree, he attempts to resolve the differences between old friends Farnum and MacDonald. Meanwhile, Boyd meets and woos MacDonald's attractive daughter, Twelvetrees, who is also drawn to the cultured Boyd, but who has another suitor, Gable, a tough cowboy. Gable resents the interloper and, after Boyd begins tunneling for tungsten, Gable viciously settles matters by blowing up Boyd's mine. This brings the two men together for a knock-down, drag-out battle where Boyd emerges victorious. He not only bests Gable and wins the hand of the fetching Twelvetrees, but manages to patch up the old feud between Farnum and MacDonald. The script is literate and the acting by all is superior and what is most attractive in this action-packed western is Snyder's lensing that captures the breathtaking desert landscapes. This was Gable's first feature-length talkie, and he would go on to make several more films where he would play the heavy, villainous characters his manly good looks and deliberate manners would soon overcome to make him the top matinee idol of the mid-1930s. Boyd appeared in a handful of feature films, such as **The Painted Desert**, before immersing himself in the Hopalong Cassidy westerns that would make him a household name in years to come. The film was shot mostly in location at Dinosaur Canyon, seventy miles northwest of Flagstaff, Arizona. *Author's Note*: At the climatic finale where the mine is blown up on October 11, 1930, technicians setting the dynamite and black powder to create the explosion did not anticipate that the hard rock inside the mine shaft would blow outward after they set more than two tons of explosives in the abandoned mine tunnel located in the face of a 400-foot cliff. They believed that the shaft would simply crumble. The resulting explosion, however, caused a shower of large rocks to strike and knock down more than a dozen technicians, sending most of them to hospitals located in Tuba City and Flagstaff. Gable and Boyd, who were in this final scene, standing about 200 feet from the blast, narrowly escaped injuries as a shower of heavy rocks and boulder rained down upon the area. **p**, E. B. Derr; **d**, Howard Higgin; **cast**, William Boyd, Helen Twelvetrees, William Farnum, J. Farrell MacDonald, Clark Gable, Charles Sellon, Wade Boteler, Will Walling, Edmund Breese, Al St. John; **w**, Higgin, Tom Buckingham; **c**, Edward Snyder; **m**, Francis Gromon; **ed**, Clarence Kolster; **art d**, Carroll Clark.

The Painted Hills ★★★ 1951; U.S.; 68m; MGM; Color; Adventure; Animal Drama; Children: Cautionary; **DVD**; **VHS**. In this seventh and final Lassie movie at MGM, Kelly strikes it rich after years of gold prospecting. Returning to town, he discovers that his partner died and left a son, Gray, fatherless. He decides to leave his dog, Lassie, with Gray to cheer him up. Back at camp Kelly finds that his partner, Cowling, doesn't want to share their gold and lures Kelly to his death. Lassie, with human deduction capabilities, figures out what happened, so Cowling poisons the dog. Lassie survives and pursues Cowling, sending him over a cliff. A good film but too violent for children, although the action is superior and the rich lensing is impressive. This was director Kress' first feature film as a helmsman; he had previously been a film editor at MGM. **p**, Chester M. Franklin; **d**, Howard F. Kress; **cast**, Paul Kelly, Bruce Cowling, Gary Gray, Art Smith, Ann Doran, Chief Yowlachie, Andrea Virginia Lester, Brown Jug Reynolds, Mitchell Lewis, Charles Watts, Lassie ("Shep"); **w**, True Boardman (based on the novel *Shep of the Painted Hills* by Alexander Hull); **c**, Alfred Gilks, Harold Lipstein

(Technicolor); **m**, Daniele Amfitheatrof; **ed**, Newell P. Kimlin; **art d**, Cedric Gibbons, Leonid Vasian; **set d**, Edwin B. Willis; **spec eff**, Warren Newcombe.

The Painted Veil ★★★ 1934; U.S.; 85m; MGM; B/W; Drama; Children: Cautionary; **VHS**. Garbo's almost mythical mystique is ever present in this above-average drama where, in Austria, she lives a lonely life until marrying charming Marshall, a physician and her father's research associate. She travels with him to China where Marshall immerses himself in his practice to the point where he neglect his spousal responsibilities. The neglected and love-craving Garbo turns elsewhere for the affection she needs, finding it with handsome Brent, a political attaché in the British Embassy, who dotes on her. Their love affair, which Garbo hides from her husband, is discovered by Marshall. Instead of rejecting Garbo out of hand, he offers her two options: she can either remain with Brent and end her marriage with him, or accompany him to the interior where he must battle a death-dealing plague of cholera, which is about the most uninviting offer that could be made to any woman. She discusses this with Brent, who tells her that his political career would not survive a scandal if she were to stay with him, using this lame excuse to ease himself out of their romance. Garbo, rather than desert Marshall, goes with him into the interior and there nurses the myriad cholera victims while Marshall tirelessly applies his skills in combating the epidemic. He then apologizes for neglecting her before stating that he must go farther into the regions to treat the spreading cholera, saying that she can either wait for him or return to civilization. After Marshall departs, Garbo remains and continues nursing victims. When he returns they both rekindle their love for one another and reaffirm their wedding vows. After Marshall has a section of the town burned to stamp out the disease, an angered Chinese property owner stabs him. Just then Brent arrives, asking Garbo to go away with him, but she has learned that Marshall is now wounded and, after rejecting Brent, flies to Marshall's side where she tends to his wound until he has recovered, knowing that she will remain at his side no matter what comes in the future. Garbo's performance is nothing short of magnificent in one telling scene after another. In one such scene she sits with a veiled face while having dinner with Marshall, and where her suspicions about what he may or may not know regarding her secret affair with Brent are exhibited in her quiet mannerisms and slowly shifting eyes, conveying subtle terror and creeping apprehension. Garbo used her body as well as her emotions in all of her films and does not stint here. When she learns that Marshall is wounded and may die, her agony over his condition is coupled with her own remorse at betraying him and where she physically exhibits that agony by standing outside his hospital room with her shoulders hunched inward and her back bent forward, her body translating the emotional anxiety and sorrow she feels for him and for her own disservice to his love. MGM spent lavishly on this Somerset Maugham story, more than $1 million, but it did not initially recoup its investment at the box office. Song: "Bridal Chorus (Here Comes the Bride)" (1850; from "Lohengrin" by Richard Wagner). *Author's Note*: Garbo told this author while we sat together in her NYC penthouse apartment that "Mr. Boleslawski was a very considerate director, a gentleman who understood female emotions and was very helpful in guiding my character in **The Painted Veil** so that my character would be believable. If a character does not appear sincere then the audience has no confidence in the story or any other character in that story. We achieved sincerity in that picture." When I raised the point that **The Painted Veil** had many similarities to another Garbo film, **Wild Orchids**, 1929, a silent production that offered a musical score and sound effects, Garbo replied: "Yes, you have a good memory—that picture also deals with a wife's infidelity, but it takes place in Java, not in China, and the wife is seduced by a forceful prince. I suppose the wife gives in because her husband has ignored her so that he can hunt tigers or something like that, so, yes, there are similarities." Garbo reportedly had a torrid romance with one of her co-stars in **The Painted Veil**, George Brent, who fell madly in love with her.

Greta Garbo and George Brent in *The Painted Veil*, 1934.

That affair was abruptly ended by Garbo when Brent insisted that they marry. She was not then or at any other time, inclined to go the altar. **p**, Hunt Stromberg; **d**, Richard Boleslawski; **cast**, Greta Garbo, Herbert Marshall, George Brent, Warner Oland, Jean Hersholt, Katharine Alexander, Cecilia Parker, Soo Yong, Beulah Bondi, Walter Brennan, Richard Loo, Keye Luke; **w**, John Meehan, Salka Viertel, Edith Fitzgerald (based on the novel by W. Somerset Maugham); **c**, William Daniels; **m**, Herbert Stothart; **ed**, Hugh Wynn; **art d**, Cedric Gibbons.

The Painted Veil ★★★ 2007; China/U.S./Canada; 125m; WIP/WB; Color; Drama/Romance; Children: Unacceptable (MPAA: PG-13); **BD**; **DVD**. In this good remake of the 1934 film, Watts is a beautiful young London socialite, who marries a dull young bacteriologist, Norton, mainly to get away from her mother. Soon after they marry, she has an affair with Schreiber, a married British vice consul. Norton threatens to divorce her on the grounds of adultery unless she goes with him to a remote area of China where he has volunteered to treat victims of an unchecked cholera epidemic. Watts doesn't really love Norton and doesn't want to go with him to China, so she begs him to divorce her quietly. He agrees, provided Schreiber will leave his wife and marry her. Schreiber says no to the idea and Watts is forced to accompany Norton to China. When they get to the remote village they will call home, Watts sees that she will be living in near squalor. Their marriage is still not a happy one and Watts is left alone most of the time as Norton works, so she volunteers to work in the music room at an orphanage run by French nuns under the supervision of Rigg, a Mother Superior. Their mutual love of children helps to unite them as nothing had before. Watts then finds she is pregnant but unsure as to the identity of the real father. Norton has always loved her and says it doesn't matter to him. The cholera epidemic spreads and Norton sets up a camp outside of the village. He comes down with the disease and Watts nurses him, both discovering they now love each other deeply. But Norton dies and Watts is heartbroken. Five years pass, and while shopping in London with her son, Watts meets Schreiber by chance on a street. He suggests they get together again and suspects he may be the boy's father. Watts rejects Schreiber's offer and walks away. Her son asks who the man is, and she replies, "No one important." Songs: "Gnossienne No. 1" (Erik Satie), "A la Claire Fontaine" (traditional), "Reste avec moi/Abide with Me" (William H. Monk, Henry F. Lyte), "Su San Qi Jie" (traditional), "Le furet du bois joli" (Pierre De Berville). Sexual situations, partial nudity, disturbing images, and brief drug content prohibit viewing by children. This film and the 1934 version saw a remake under the title of **The Seventh Sin**, 1957. **p**, Naomi Watts, Edward Norton, Bob Yari, Sara Colleton, Antonio Barnard, Yasmine Golchan, **d**, John Curran; **cast**, Watts, Norton, Diana Rigg, Liev Schreiber, Sally Hawkins, Juliet Howland,

Doris Day, John Raitt and Carol Haney in *The Pajama Game*, 1957.

Toby Jones, Catherine An, Marie-Laure Descoureaux, Bin Li, Bin Wu, Alan David; **w**, Ron Nyswaner (based on the novel by W. Somerset Maugham); **c**, Stuart Dryburgh; **m**, Alexandre Desplat; **ed**, Alexandre de Franceschi; **prod d**, Juhua Tu; **art d**, Mei Kunping, Xinran Tu, Yanrong Xing; **set d**, Peta Lawson; **spec eff**, Jinguo Yang, Yimin Yang.

Paisan ★★★★★ 1948; Italy; 134m; OFI/Arthur Mayer and Joseph Burstyn; B/W; War Drama; Children: Unacceptable; **DVD**; **VHS**. Riveting and realist, this superb film from the brilliant Rossellini (who offered a similar documentary-type feature film in the equally stunning **Open City**, 1945) is offered in six separate slices of life or sequences that uniformly fit into the overall story line, where the world "paisan," meaning "countryman" befits each segment. The first segment opens with the Allied invasion of Sicily in 1943 and the last segment ends with the 1944 Italian capitulation. In the first segment, Van Loon, an American soldier from New Jersey, is ordered to guard Sazio, a young Sicilian woman, and he spends a night with her in a gloomy castle that is in ruins (which represents the emotional and psychological conditions of the Italian people at that time). Since Sazio refuses to speak a single word or display any emotion, Van Loon must try to befriend her without verbal communication. In the second sequence we see Johnson, a black U.S. Army MP waking from a nap in Naples to find his shoes stolen. He chases a street waif, Pasca, who has filched his shoes, tracking him down to a cavern only to find him and scores more starving urchins cowering there. He cannot bring himself to arrest the boy and add more misery to him so Johnson simply walks way without his shoes. Rome is the site of the third tale where Michi, a streetwalker, encounters a drunken GI, Moore. He tells her that he is obsessed with a beautiful young Italian girl who gave him a drink of water when he rode into Rome atop his tank, along with other U.S. troops when liberating the city. She understands exactly what he is talking about since she was that girl, but Moore is so inebriated that he never recognizes her. The next story harrowingly deals with Gori, an Italian partisan, and White, a U.S. nurse, both having been thrown together by fate and are desperately trying to work their way through the German lines to reach the safety of the Allied lines in Florence. The fifth tale has a Jew, a Protestant and a Catholic meeting with a group of Franciscan monks at a monastery where they all realize that they are all one under the same God, despite their different religious denominations. The sixth and final sequence shows OSS and British troops fighting alongside Italian partisans against German forces that eventually overwhelm all of the Allied fighters. Though segregated, Rossellini's separate tales all work well together to give an overall image of a country in turmoil while struggling to be free of the oppressive German yoke and, in the process, offers joy and tragedy, humor and sadness, where all of the actors are impressive in their variety type roles. ***Author's Note***: This film, a product of what was termed "neo-realism" as was **Open City**, went a long way in cementing the notion that the people of Italy were never in favor of the fascist regime so rigidly enforced by its dictator, Benito Mussolini, as if disavowing the bad manners of a distant relative, but the grim fact was that most Italians did support fascism as long as it was in their best interests to do so. Mussolini ruled for more than two decades and Rossellini and many of his ilk flourished under that dictatorship— Rossellini was a close friend of Vittorio Mussolini, an ardent and brutal fascist and one of the dictator's two sons, who sponsored Rossellini's early day film career. When Mussolini was deposed, Rossellini and others, who had enjoyed the luxuries of that tyrannical regime, quickly switched political sides, and his films became anti-fascist in nature and attitude. He simply stopped filming fascists haranguing Italians from lofty balconies and began filming the debris-strewn gutters of his country, but, hypocritical or not, he nevertheless brilliantly recorded a whole people in economic and social turmoil and transition. Tyrants like Mussolini come and go, but people like Rossellini endure forever, at least in the Italian cinema. (In Italian; English subtitles.) **p**, Roberto Rossellini, Rod E. Geiger, Mario Conti; **d**, Rossellini; **cast**, Carmela Sazio, Robert Van Loon, Gar Moore, Benjamin Emanuel, Dots Johnson, Maria Michi, Harriet Medin, Renzo Avanzo, Giulietta Masina, Giulio Panicali; **w**, Sergio Amidei, Federico Fellini, Rossellini, Geiger (based on stories by Victor Haines, Marcello Pagliero, Amidei, Fellini, Rossellini, Klaus Mann, Vasco Pratolini); **c**, Otello Martelli; **m**, Renzo Rossellini; **ed**, Eraldo Da Roma.

The Pajama Game ★★★ 1957; U.S.; 101m; WB; Color; Musical; Children: Acceptable; **DVD**; **VHS**. This lively musical should delight any and all lovers of musicals. It begins when employees of the Sleeptite Pajama Factory want a seven-and-a-half-cent hourly raise. After management refuses their demand, the employees form a grievance committee headed by feisty Day, who takes complaints to the shop superintendent, Raitt, a handsome and clever fellow. Day spoils the movement by falling in love with him and vice versa. The simple plot turned into a dandy movie musical based on the Broadway hit. Day is a firecracker in motion and her antics produce a lot of humor while she curvaceously fills the top half of pajamas, the bottom half occupied by Raitt, or so the enticing advertisements for this charming vehicle promote. The well-presented songs are memorable, and the dancing, choreographed by Bob Fosse, is inventive and impressive, with the camera's movements taking part in those exciting dancing ensembles. Panning and tracking shots are integrated within the dance numbers so that the camera appears to be one of the dancing partners, particularly in the stunning comedic tango involving Chaney. Songs: "The Pajama Game," "Racing with the Clock," "I'm Not at All in Love," "I'll Never Be Jealous Again," "Hey There," "Once-a-Year-Day," "Small Talk," "There Once Was a Man," "Herenando's Hideaway," "7 ½ Cents," "A New Town Is a Blue Town," "The New Superintendent" (Richard Adler, Jerry Ross). **p&d**, George Abbott and Stanley Donen; **cast**, Doris Day, John Raitt, Carol Chaney, Eddie Foy, Jr., Reta Shaw, Barbara Nichols, Thelma Pelish, Jack Straw, Ralph Dunn, Owen Martin; **w**, Abbott, Richard Bissell (based on their Broadway musical from Bissell's novel *Seven and a Half Cents*); **c**, Harry Stradling (Warner Color); **m**, Richard Adler, Jerry Ross; **ed**, William Ziegler; **art d**, Malcolm Bert; **set d**, William Kuehl.

Pal Joey ★★★★ 1957; U.S.; 111m; Essex Productions/COL; Color; Musical; Children: Acceptable; **DVD**; **VHS**. In a much overlooked musical with a strong story line and packed with many wonderful Rodgers and Hart songs, Sinatra is outstanding as a self-serving heel and womanizing singer who arrives in San Francisco and gets a job warbling at a nightclub where he goes after every available chorine. He cannot, however, make any headway with Novak, a beautiful blonde dancer. Sinatra and the rest of the entertainers are then summoned to a command performance at the swanky mansion of Hayworth, a wealthy widow who lives atop Nob Hill with the rest of the upper crust. When Sinatra meets her, however, he recognizes her as a one-time stripper, who bared her charms in working her way to a fortune. Hayworth is attracted to Sinatra, but he has eyes only for Novak, who holds him at arm's length. When Hayworth offers Sinatra money to open his own club, Chez Joey, he is all ears and plans to open that bistro with Novak in a featured role. Hayworth then sees Novak as her opposition and holds back the financing, telling Sinatra that he can have his club, but not with Novak involved. Novak, who has fallen in love with Sinatra, goes to Hayworth and begs her to fund Sinatra's club, and the rich widow agrees, but only on the condition that the blonde entertainer is not part of the package, and Novak agrees. After Sinatra hears of this, he now realizes that Novak truly loves him enough to sacrifice her golden opportunity, he turns down Hayworth flat, deciding that being with Novak is more rewarding than being a comfortable and bought man and becoming for the first time in his life an honorable and caring person, who will, like Novak, sacrifice his career for the sake of love. Sinatra is terrific in his transformational role and is at the top of his singing talent while Novak is alluring and sympathetic and Hayworth, too, is outstanding as the rich vamp vainly trying to fill the void of her wealth with what she most craves in life, affection. Hayworth's voice was never very strong and all her vocals are looped by Jo Ann Greer. The same went for Novak, her voice looped by Trudi Erwin. The costuming, sets and choreography are all superb, and stunning cinematography from Lipstein and taut direction from Sidney make this musical shimmy and shine. Sinatra's vocals are excellent, and he aggressively delivers one knockout tune after another, all of them dynamically arranged by the gifted Nelson Riddle. Of the fourteen songs offered, ten were part of the original musical Broadway production upon which this film was based, the other four added from other Rodgers and Hart productions. Songs: "I Could Write a Book," "There's a Small Hotel," "My Funny Valentine," "The Lady Is a Tramp," "Zip," "What Do I Care For a Dame," "I Didn't Know What Time It Was," "A Great Big Town," "Bewitched," "That Terrific Rainbow" (music: Richard Rodgers; lyrics: Lorenz Hart); "Plant You Now, Dig You Later," "Take Him," "Do It the Hard Way," and "Happy Hunting Horn" (music: Richard Rodgers). *Author's Note*: This story line for this lively and thoroughly entertaining musical emanated from short stories written by John O'Hara that appeared in the *New Yorker*, these tales written as letters by a conceited, womanizing dancer, who existed only in O'Hara's imagination and were signed, "Your Pal Joey." Producer George Abbott was so impressed with these tales that he persuaded O'Hara to write the book for the stage production, its music and lyrics provided by the stellar Rodgers and Hart. The Broadway musical opened in 1940 with Gene Kelly in the lead and with supporting players Vivienne Segal, Leila Ernst and June Havoc, along with a charming chorus boy named Van Johnson. It met with considerable critical success but audiences were unsettled by the offbeat content that showed the hero as a self-serving sensualist and where many risqué scenes unnerved some of the more delicate female theatergoers, and where the more sophisticated viewers picked up on the sexual double entendre contained in one tune after another. The musical closed after 198 performances, but Columbia nevertheless bought the film rights and tried to interest James Cagney, Cary Grant and others in playing the lead of the cad, but all turned down the rather repugnant role, even after Columbia screenwriters sanitized the script. Irene Dunne, Ethel Merman, Gloria Swanson and Grace Moore were approached and they, too, turned down the role of the femme fatale leads. By the time the war ensued, the project was shelved, but when the play was revived in the 1950s and Columbia saw the queues of ticket-buyers waiting to purchase tickets to the Broadway production, the studio decided to go ahead with the film adaptation. After Marlon Brando appeared with Sinatra in the smash musical **Guys and Dolls**, 1955, Columbia studio boss Harry Cohn asked him to play the lead in **Pal Joey**, but Brando said no. "Marlon [Brando] told [Harry] Cohn that he should talk to me about doing that part," Sinatra told this

Kim Novak and Frank Sinatra in *Pal Joey,* 1957.

author, "but Harry and I did not get along too well." Cohn had withheld a plum part in **From Here to Eternity**, 1953, from Sinatra, compelling the singer to practically beg for that role; when he played it, Sinatra won an Oscar for his performance, which turned around Sinatra's declining career and the tables on Cohn, and, within a few years, Sinatra was a top box office draw. "I was at that time," Sinatra said to this author, "in a position to tell Cohn that I would do the lead in **Pal Joey**, and I put money where my mouth was, investing in the picture, and where I got a piece of that big pie, one of my smarter moves in life." Hayworth told this author that "Frank [Sinatra] was wonderful to work with in **Pal Joey**. He was the driving force behind that picture, and he treated us all with great respect. I am so much a vamp in that picture that the only thing missing in my scenes is a rose clenched in my mouth. We all had a lot of fun doing **Pal Joey**, and that was due to Frank, one of the great live wires in the business." Ironically, Sinatra appeared in two films that year, both released in October 1957 and where he plays saloon singers, one in **Pal Joey**, the other film being **The Joker Is Wild**, 1957, based on the life of Joe E. Lewis (1902-1971) and whose singing voice was brought to an end when gangsters slit his throat in Chicago for defying Capone goons, causing him to become a classic nightclub comedian. Chicago was also the setting for the original production of **Pal Joey**, but scriptwriters changed the locale to San Francisco and transformed the leading player from a dancer to a singer to keep pace with Sinatra's professional persona. **p**, Fred Kohlmar; **d**, George Sidney; **cast**, Rita Hayworth, Frank Sinatra, Kim Novak, Barbara Nichols, Bobby Sherwood, Hank Henry, Elizabeth Patterson, Leon Alton, Barrie Chase, Pierre Watkin, Hermes Pan, John Hubbard, Robert Reed; **w**, Dorothy Kingsley (based on stories by John O'Hara and the musical play by O'Hara, Richard Rodgers, Lorenz Hart); **c**, Harold Lipstein (Technicolor); **m**, Rodgers and Hart, George Duning (not credited); **ed**, Viola Lawrence, Jerome Thoms; **art d**, Walter Holscher; **set d**, Louis Diage, William Kiernan.

Pale Rider ★★★★ 1985; U.S.; 115m; Malpaso/WB; Color; Western; Children: Unacceptable (MPAA: R); **BD**; **DVD**; **VHS**. Offbeat but fascinating western sees a group of hardworking miners in California in the 1880s being oppressed by Dysart, a large mine owner, who sends his thugs into the mining camp where they destroy the place to the point of savagely shooting and killing the dog of fourteen-year-old Snodgress. She sorrowfully buries her pet, praying for a miracle from on high that will help the miners and her family. The leader of the miners, Moriarty, visits a nearby town to get supplies, but is beaten by Dysart's goons until Snodgress' prayers are answered in the form of a tall, taciturn man, Eastwood, who arrives and takes on the goons, beating them senseless and rescuing Moriarty. In gratitude, Moriarty invites Eastwood to his ram-

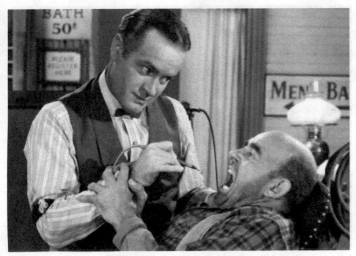

Bob Hope and Nestor Paiva in _The Paleface_, 1948.

shackle home to have a meal, when he sits down to dinner, it is revealed that he is wearing a religious collar, and he is thereafter called "Preacher." Dysart's son, Penn, when hearing about Eastwood's intervention, sends Kiel, a giant thug, to deal with him. Eastwood and Moriarty are next shown as they struggle to remove a huge boulder from Moriarty's claim (here director Eastwood takes a leaf from a classic western showing the titanic struggle by Van Heflin and Alan Ladd in **Shane**, 1953, in removing a huge tree trunk from Heflin's farm). Kiel arrives and smashes the boulder with one sledgehammer blow. He then confronts Eastwood, who summarily dispatches the hulking thug with a hammer blow to the head and another to the groin. Dysart returns from a business trip in Sacramento to find his plans to clear out the miners stymied and he offers to buy them out at $1,000 each on the condition that they leave within twenty-four hours or he will have his stooge marshal, Russell, drive them out. While Eastwood is inexplicably away, Moriarty persuades the miners to refuse Dysart's offer. The frustrated Penn then attempts to kidnap or rape Snodgress to intimidate the miners, but Eastwood appears and shoots Penn in the hand, returning Snodgress to her mother. Russell and his men then gun down McGrath, a miner, and Eastwood and Moriarty retaliate by blowing up Dysart's mine. Eastwood then rides into town and guns down all of Dysart's goons as well as dispatching Russell and his men. Dysart is about to kill Eastwood from ambush when he is shot dead by Moriarty. Having wiped out all the bad guys, Eastwood mounts his horse and begins riding off toward the snow-capped mountains in the distance while Snodgress shouts out her thanks to him for saving the mining community, her scream of gratitude echoing through the hills (almost exactly the way Brandon De Wilde, the son of farmer Van Heflin, shouts after Alan Ladd, the gunfighter who has saved the farming community and who is riding wounded into the sunset at the end of **Shane**, upon which **Pale Rider** heavily depends). Eastwood directs this action-loaded tale with a taut hand; and the performances from all are convincing, Eastwood somewhat reprises his "no name" gunfighter character from earlier Sergio Leone "spaghetti westerns." The film met with popular success at the box office (like most of Eastwood's westerns), earning more than $41 million against a $6.9 million budget, making it one of the highest grossing westerns of the 1980s. The film was shot on location in late 1984 at Columbia State Park, California, and in the Sawtooth National Recreation Area in the Boulder Mountain range, north of Sun Valley, Idaho. **p&d**, Clint Eastwood; **cast**, Eastwood, Michael Moriarty, Carrie Snodgress, Christopher Penn, Richard Dysart, Sydney Penny, Richard Kiel, Doug McGrath, John Russell, Charles Hallahan; **w**, Michael Butler, Dennis Shryack; **c**, Bruce Surtees (Technicolor); **m**, Lennie Niehaus; **ed**, Joel Cox; **prod d**, Edward Carfagno; **set d**, Ernie Bishop; **spec eff**, Chuck Gaspar, Jeffrey A. Wischnack.

The Paleface ★★★ 1948; U.S.; 91m; PAR; Color; Comedy/Western; Children: Acceptable; **DVD**; **VHS**. Hope is hilarious as an inept and cowardly dentist, who has gotten his dental degree through correspondence courses. He goes west to start a practice and meets Calamity Jane (1852-1903), played by Russell, and who is wanted by the law. She is trying to find the villains selling guns to the Indians, hoping that, if she captures them, the law will forgive her past crimes. She marries Hope so they can go undercover as man and wife to look for the gunrunners, but then she falls in love with him. He, of course, thinks he's the luckiest man alive for being hitched to such a voluptuous beauty (which Calamity Jane in real life was not). They join a wagon train, and after it is attacked by Indians, Russell's sharp-shooting drives them off. She gives the credit to Hope, and he becomes a hero and also a target for both the Indians and the gunrunners. This very funny spoof on westerns has many side-splitting scenes, not the least of which are those involving Hope's hopeless attempts to treat dental patients and where he inevitably pulls the wrong teeth while reducing his agonizing patients to laughing hyenas after administering laughing gas to ease their pain. This film was followed by a sequel **The Son of Paleface**, 1952, with the same stars and again remade under the title **The Shakiest Gun in the West**, 1968, with Donn Knotts in the Hope role. Songs: "Buttons and Bows" (Jay Livingston, Ray Evans; sung by Hope, Russell) which won the Academy Award for best song, "Meetcha Round the Corner" (Livingston, Evans; sung by Hope, Iris Adrian [dubbed by Annette Warren]), "Get a Man" (Joseph J. Lilley). **Author's Note**: This film, according to Hope's statements to this author, "made fun of all those other westerns where sultry ladies like Jane [Russell] were steaming up the screen and where I am such an idiot that I deserve to be shot on sight by any drunken cowboy who has nothing better to do than plug me." Russell told this author that "**The Paleface** was sort of a takeoff on **The Outlaw** [1943], which I had appeared in some years earlier, a picture that had some notoriety because of the cleavage shown, chiefly mine. Bob [Hope] was great to work with and had us all in stitches all the time. Such a very funny guy, but he could be a problem because you had to keep from laughing in a scene where you were supposed to keep a straight face. And do you know why he was always funny? Because he made fun of himself and that is always the trait of a great comedian. Whenever I get blue I think about people like Bob and have a good laugh." For a compilation of films about Calamity Jane and the actresses who played her, see Calamity Jane, Index, Fictional and Historical Characters, Volume IV of this work. **p**, Robert L. Welch; **d**, Norman Z. McLeod; **cast**, Bob Hope, Jane Russell, Robert Armstrong, Iris Adrian, Robert (Bobby) Watson, Jack (Jackie) Searl, Joseph Vitale, Charles Trowbridge, Clem Bevans, Jeff York, Iron Eyes Cody, Jody Gilbert, Kermit Maynard, Sharon McManus; **w**, Edmund Hartmann, Frank Tashlin, Jack Rose; **c**, Ray Rennahan (Technicolor); **m**, Victor Young; **ed**, Ellsworth Hoagland; **art d**, Hans Dreier, Earl Hedrick; **set d**, Sam Comer, Bertram Granger); **spec eff**, Farciot Edouart, Gordon Jennings.

The Palm Beach Story ★★★★ 1942; U.S.; 88m; PAR; B/W; Comedy; Children: Acceptable; **DVD**; **VHS**. Though the screwball comedies of the 1930s were on the wane when this uproariously funny film was made, it buoyed the genre back to the surface while presenting a star-packed cast and another improbable but utterly charming tale from pantheon director Sturges. It begins with McCrea and Colbert as a happily married couple who have been struggling to survive financially for five years while McCrea, an inventor, tries to put his creations to work. He obtains no funding, and Colbert then hatches an idea that will aid the man she loves. She will divorce him, find and marry a wealthy man, and then use that new husband's riches to finance McCrea's inventions. What could be any more reasonable (or screwier) than that? After she and McCrea abandon their apartment, the penniless Colbert is rescued by Dudley, a tycoon in the wiener business who walks around with his pockets stuffed with large bills, and he hands Colbert enough cash so that she can take the train bound for Palm Beach, Florida, where all fortune-hunters go to cultivate rich wives or husbands. Colbert's train trip is not uneventful. She runs into a pack of wacky millionaires who all belong to a hunting club, including Demarest, Norton, Ates, Greig, Conklin, Jett and Robinson. These certifiable loons are always arguing about who is the best shot and, while toting their rifles about, begin shooting out the windows of the train for sport (and what could be more reasonable than that except for, perhaps, a lion hunt on board an ocean liner). While on board that train, Colbert meets a more reserved rich man, Vallee, a multimillionaire who believes in spending his money, but who keeps a meticulous record of all of his expenses, irrespective of how frivolous and expensive those purchases might be. He falls hard for Colbert and, after she alights at Palm Beach, he buys her a lavish new wardrobe and the most expensive jewelry her petite body can carry and then asks her to be his guest on board his luxury yacht, an invitation she accepts. There Colbert meets Astor, who is Vallee's sister, a woman who has gone through five husbands and is always on the lookout for another, even though she is currently wedded to Arno, a man who speaks a language no one can understand, including himself (his confusing verbosity presents several side-splitting scenes). McCrea then shows up, trying to dissuade Colbert to give up her crazy marriage scheme, but she is more persuasive in convincing McCrea to pretend that he is her brother, a pretense that causes man-crazy Astor to make moves on him, intending to have him as her next spouse. Then Vallee proposes to Colbert and a wedding takes place, but it is a double nuptial in that those marrying Vallee and Astor are the identical twins to Colbert and McCrea. Sturges (who makes a brief appearance on camera shows up á la Alfred Hitchcock while carrying some luggage to Vallee's yacht) does a wonderful job in sorting out all the crazy characters and maintaining a hectic pace to produce this outlandish and delightful story, where Colbert, McCrea, Astor and Vallee are outstanding in their preposterous roles. Songs: "Goodnight Sweetheart" (1931; Ray Noble, Jimmy Campbell, Reginald Connelly), "Isn't It Romantic?" (1932; music: Richard Rodgers; lyrics: Lorenz Hart), "Sweet Adeline" (1903; music: Harry Armstrong; lyrics: Richard H. Gerard), "Old Folks at Home (Swanee River)" (1851; Stephen Foster), "Old Black Joe" (1860; Stephen Foster); "Frankie and Johnny" (traditional), "A Hunting We Will Go" (traditional), "Merrily We Roll Along" (traditional, but loosely based on "Good Night Ladies," 1847, by Edwin P. Christy), "William Tell Overture" (1829; Gioachino Rossini), "Bridal Chorus (Here Comes the Bride)" (1850; from "Lohengrin" by Richard Wagner), "Wedding March" (1843; from "A Midsummer Night's Dream" by Felix Mendelssohn Bartholdy), 'Romeo and Juliet Overture" (1868; music: Peter Ilyich Tchaikovsky), "Listen to the Mockingbird" (1855; music: Richard-Milburn; lyrics: Septimus Winner). *Author's Note*: McCrea told this author that "working with Preston [Sturges] was like working with a dynamo. The man never stayed put for a second, always full of ideas and acting out characters like some guy doing an Irish jig on St. Paddy's Day. I had done a picture with him, **Sullivan's Travels** [1941], which did pretty good box office and, right after that, he was after me to do **The Palm Beach Story**, and that was fine with me. You couldn't have a better, smarter director than that live wire of a man." Colbert had nothing but praise for Sturges, telling this author: "He was not only a brilliant director, who knew how to handle every scene, but was a gifted writer, who wrote his own scripts, so he lived with those scenes night and day until the picture was completed. He liked everything a bit off center, somewhat strange, but always funny in a heart warming way, because he loved people, all kinds of them, and he had an instinct on how to find everyone's funny bone." Astor enjoyed playing the role of the self-centered sister—she is called "Princess" in the film—telling this author: "Preston told me to play my character like a woman always shopping in a store, only she is always shopping for a new husband. 'There's nothing wrong with your character,' he said to me, 'except that she's spoiled rotten and thinks she is entitled to be that way because she can afford to buy anything she wants. So I want you to shop and keep shopping through every one of your scenes.' Preston wanted to do **The Palm Beach Story** because Hollywood was turning out endless war films at

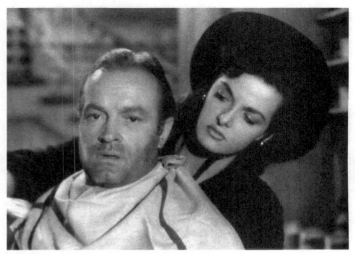

Bob Hope and Jane Russell in *The Paleface*, 1948.

that time because we were at war, but less and less comedies. 'People need to laugh more than ever right now,' he told me, 'and that's why we're making this picture.' And when the picture came out, people laughed and laughed." **p**, Paul Jones; **d&w**, Preston Sturges; **cast**, Claudette Colbert, Joel McCrea, Mary Astor, Rudy Vallee, Sig Arno, Robert Warwick, Jimmy Conlin, William Demarest, Jack Norton, Robert Greig, Roscoe Ates, Chester Conklin, Franklin Pangborn, Robert Dudley, Fred "Snowflake" Toones, Monte Blue, Sturges; **c**, Victor Milner; **m**, Victor Young; **ed**, Stuart Gilmore; **art d**, Hans Dreier, Ernst Fegté.

Palmy Days ★★★ 1931; U.S.; 77m; UA; B/W; Musical Comedy; Children: Acceptable; **VHS**. "Banjo Eyes" appears in one of his best comedies, a zany romp into the spiritual world that is awash with crooks and crazy people. Cantor is an assistant to Middleton, a phony psychic, who owns an art deco bakery. Cantor is mistaken for an efficiency expert and is put in charge. His inefficiency is limitless and that causes endless problems to arise when the psychic and his gang attempt to rob the bakery's payroll. Cantor is blamed, but exonerates himself through a series of delightful songs and dances in a film that served well to show off his considerable comic abilities. Cantor conducts many of his celebrated routines, including a "blackface," a scene where he is in drag, and another hectic chase, all well integrated with the songs and dances. The high-kicking Greenwood gets energetically into the act while frantically attempting to ensnare Cantor into a romance he resists with childlike apprehensions. Additional highlights include the beautiful Goldwyn Girls in numbers spectacularly choreographed by the great Busby Berkeley. Songs: "Bend Down, Sister" (Con Conrad, Ballard MacDonald, David Silverstein), "There's Nothing Too Good for My Baby" (Harry Akst, Eddie Cantor, Benny Davis), "Yes, Yes, My Baby Said Yes, Yes" (Conrad, Cliff Friend), "Dunk Dunk Dunk" (Conrad, MacDonald), "Jingle Bells" (James Pierpont), "Falling in Love Again" (Friedrich Hollaender, Samuel Lerner), "Happy Days Are Here Again" (Milton Ager, Jack Yellen), "The Wedding March" (Felix Mendelssohn-Bartholdy). **p**, Samuel Goldwyn; **d**, A. Edward Sutherland; **cast**, Eddie Cantor, Charlotte Greenwood, Spencer Charters, Barbara Weeks, Paul Page, George Raft, Charles Middleton, Harry Woods, Berkeley, and among the Goldwyn Girls are young Betty Grable, Virginia Grey, and Toby Wing; **w**, Morrie Ryksind, Keene Thompson, David Freedman, Eddie Cantor (based on a story by Ryskind, Freedman, Cantor); **c**, Gregg Toland; **m**, Alfred Newman; **ed**, Sherman Todd, Stuart Heisler; **art d**, Richard Day; **set d**, Willy Pogany.

Palooka ★★★ 1934; U.S.; 86m; Edward Small/UA; B/W; Comedy; Children: Acceptable; **VHS**. Gravel-voiced Durante is at the top of his comedic form as a fight promoter. After he sees championship boxing

Louise Brooks in *Pandora's Box,* 1929.

potential in Erwin, a young pug called Joe Palooka, Durante becomes his fight manager. He puts him up against Cagney (the younger brother of the imitable James Cagney), a drunken champ who is easily beaten by Erwin. Durante and Erwin are well cast in the boxing comedy that spun off into a series of low-budget **Joe Palooka** comedy films made in the 1940s with Leon Errol and Joe Kirkwood, Jr., and has no connection with this fun-filled film except for its two main characters. Durante sings his trademark song, "Inka Dinka Do" (Ben Ryan. Durante); other songs: "The Band Played On" (Charles B. Ward, John F. Palmer), "Like Me a Little Bit Less, Love Me a Little Bit More" (Burton Lane, Harold Adamon), "M-O-T-H-E-R, a Word That Means the World to Me" (Theodore Morse, Howard Johnson), "Count Your Blessings" (Ferde Grofe, Sr.), "Palooka, It's a Grand Old Name" (Joseph Burke). **p,** Edward Small; **d,** Benjamin Stoloff; **cast,** Jimmy Durante, Lupe Valez, Stuart Erwin, Marjorie Rambeau, Robert Armstrong, Mary Carlisle, William Cagney, Thelma Todd, Gus Arnheim and His Orchestra, Tom Dugan, Louise Beavers, Fred "Snowflake" Toones, Guinn "Big Boy" Williams; **w,** Jack Jevne, Arthur Kober, Gertrude Purcell, Murray Roth, Ben Ryan (based on the comic strip by Ham Fisher); **c,** Arthur Edeson; **ed,** Grant Whytock; **art d,** Albert D'Agostino.

Palookaville ★★★ 1996; U.S.; 92m; Playhouse International/Samuel Goldwyn; Color; Comedy; Children: Unacceptable (MPAA: R); **DVD; VHS.** Entertaining comedy sees Trese, Gallo, and Forsythe as friends, who are only looking for some easy money to enliven their going-nowhere lives in a nowhere town. They try robbing a jewelry store, but that botched caper merely demonstrates what bumbling amateurs they are as crooks. After watching an old movie on television, they think they can get away with an armored-car robbery. While plotting the caper, their dysfunctional families give them one headache after another and everything that can go wrong with their heist does. Songs: "Doo Wa Ditty/Blow That Thing" (Roger Troutman, Larry Troutman), "My Man" (Anna Domino), "Armored Car Robbery" (Rob Webb), "Lovin' You" (Rudolph Riperton, Kimiko Kasai), "The Morning After" (Earl Forest, Robert Talle), "Virgen de la Macarenas" (Bernardo Bautista Monterde, Antonio Ortiz Calero), "Me Tienes Sufriendo" (Angel Santiago). Gutter language prohibits viewing by children. **p,** Uberto Pasolini, Scott Ferguson; **d,** Alan Taylor; **cast,** Adam Trese, Vincent Gallo, William Forsythe, Gareth Williams, Frances McDormand, LisaGay Hamilton, Bridgit Ryan, Kim Dickens, Suzanne Shepherd, Robert Lupone; **w,** David Epstein; **c,** John Thomas; **m,** Rachel Portman; **ed,** David Leonard; **prod d,** Anne Stuhler; **art d,** Roswell Hamrick; **spec eff,** Drew Jiritano.

Pandora's Box ★★★★ 1929 (silent); Germany; 109m (133m, restored

version); Nero Film/Moviegraphs; B/W; Crime Drama/Horror; Children: Unacceptable; **DVD; VHS.** Brooks, in one of her most startling and impressive performances, plays an artful and promiscuous femme fatale as no other actress has ever done. She is a sultry vamp named Lulu, who inveigles Kortner, a wealthy banker, into an obsessive affair where she constantly tantalizes him with her considerable sensual charms and eventually inveigles him into marrying her. She is a woman utterly without principles or scruples and knows no sense of fidelity or faithfulness, and has been encouraging a separate affair with Kortner's son, Lederer, who is mesmerized by Brooks. There is no end to her sensuality, even when she dances a tango with Roberts, who plays a lesbian at her wedding party, and where she and Roberts make sterile lesbian love together in that arresting scene. When Kortner exhibits jealousy about her relationship with his son, Brooks murders him on the first day of their marriage. She is charged with Kortner's death, but flees Germany with the infatuated Lederer chasing after her. They settle together in London, but are soon reduced to poverty. Brooks, to support them, becomes a streetwalker, which appeals to her masochistic sensuality. On Christmas Eve, she meets Diesel, a man interested in her, but, after he tells her he has no money to pay for her sexual favors, Brooks says: "Come on, I like you." Taking him to her room, Brooks dances seductively for him, and, just before they embrace, she sees to her horror and perverse fascination, a gleaming knife gripped in his hand, one that Diesel plunges into her stomach, killing her and where she ecstatically dies in that embrace, realizing in her death throes that she has become another victim of Jack the Ripper, the notorious fiend that stalked prostitutes in the West End of London in 1888. Brooks is riveting as the erotic Lulu, a part that she indelibly made her own and one that established her as a foremost international film star, under the sure and careful direction of German master filmmaker Pabst. The lighting and shadows employed by Pabst in his wonderfully atmospheric scenes suggest from sequence to sequence the sinister tragedy to befall the irresponsibly fallen woman Brooks eventually becomes, as if throughout she is daring and inviting that horrible fate from the first moment she appears on the screen. It is a shocking and unforgettable tale of emotional and sexual perversions that results in savage retribution. *Author's Note*: Pabst had long wanted to make this film, but had found no actress that could play Lulu. He sent his agents throughout Germany, interviewing scores of young, attractive women, even interviewing them on subways, at bus stops and in cafés and shops, but to no avail. Then Pabst saw an American film in which Brooks appeared and immediately decided that she was the only one who could play Lulu. He sent a wire to her studio, Paramount, asking to hire her for **Pandora's Box,** but got no response from the studio. At that time, however, Paramount was making the technical transition from silent to talking films and they, like most other studios, told their contract players that they would have to take salary cuts or walk away from any and all agreements. Brooks was one of those players. "I was not about to be treated like that," Brooks told this author. "These studio bosses felt they could abuse anyone and get away with it and I told Zukor [Adolph Zukor, 1873-1976; head of Paramount] that talking films were 'vulgar' and that I wanted no part of them or with Paramount and I walked out of his office. When I quit, however, there was a very considerate producer there, Mr. Schulberg [B. P. Schulberg, 1892-1957], who told me about the offer from Mr. Pabst in Germany and I told him that I would do the picture and immediately booked a voyage to Germany [on board an ocean liner]. My decision was based on my anger at how Paramount treated me, even though I knew nothing about the character I would be playing in Mr. Pabst's picture and I also knew nothing about Mr. Pabst. It was a fortunate decision because, at that very time, Mr. Pabst was talking with Marlene Dietrich about appearing in **Pandora's Box** as Lulu. He got a wire at that very moment from Mr. Schulberg at Paramount telling him that I would do the role and then Mr. Pabst politely told Dietrich that he had another actress for the part." Pabst later stated that he did not really think Dietrich was right for the part of Lulu, saying: "Dietrich was too old [Dietrich was twenty-eight years old and Brooks was twenty-three at that time] and too obvious—one sexy look and the picture would become a burlesque." Jack the Ripper has been profiled by many actors in many other films including **Bridge across Time**, 1985 (Paul Rossilli); **From Hell**, 2001; **Jack the Ripper**, 1960 (Ewon Solon); **Jack the Ripper**, 1973 (TV miniseries); **Jack the Ripper**, 1988 (TV series); **The Lodger**, 1928 (Ivor Novello); **The Lodger**, 1944 (Laird Cregar); **Lulu**, 1980 (Udo Kier); **Man in the Attic**, 1953 (Jack Palance); **Murder by Decree**, 1979 (Peter Jonfield); **The Phantom Fiend**, 1935 (Ivor Novello); **The Ripper**, 1997; **Room to Let**, 1950 (Valentine Dyall); **Seven Murders for Scotland Yard**, 1971; **A Study in Terror**, 1966 (John Fraser); **Time after Time**, 1979 (David Warner); **Waxwork II: Lost in Time**, 1992 (Alex Butler); and **Waxworks**, 1929 (Werner Krauss). For more definitive details on Jack the Ripper, see my two-volume work, *The Great Pictorial History of World Crime*, Volume II (History, Inc., 2004; Jack the Ripper: pages 1180-1203). **p**, Heinz Landsmann, Seymour Nebenzal; **d**, G.W. (George Wilhelm) Pabst; **cast**, Louise Brooks, Fritz Kortner, Franz (Francis) Lederer, Carl Goetz, Krafft-Raschig, Alice Roberts, Daisy d'Ora, Gustav Diesel, Michael von Newlinsky, Siegfried (Sig) Arno; **w**, Ladislaus Vajda (based on the plays "Erdgeist" and "Die Büchse der Pandora" by Frank Wedekind); **c**, Günther Krampf; **m**, Peer Raben (1997 restoration); **ed**, Joseph Fleisler; **art d**, Andrej Andrejew.

Panhandle ★★★ 1948; U.S.; 85m; Monogram/AA; B/W (Sepia tone); Western; Children: Unacceptable; **DVD**; **VHS**. Action-packed realistic western sees Cameron as a former Texas marshal turned gunman is a fugitive in Mexico. He learns from beautiful Downs that her fiancé, Champion, who is his brother, a crusading newspaperman in the Texas Panhandle, has been mysteriously murdered in Sentinel, Texas. Disregarding that he is wanted in Texas, he rides north to the Panhandle to search for his brother's killer. He learns that Hadley, who tries to control the town, is the man he's after and shoots him dead, then stays in town with Downs, keeping her in the family. It's a good story and is well acted, but its violence prohibits viewing by children. **p&w**, Blake Edwards, John C. Champion (based on their story); **d**, Lesley Selander; **cast**, Rod Cameron, Cathy Downs, Reed Hadley, Anne Gwynne, Edwards, Champion, Dick Crockett, Francis McDonald, J. Farrell MacDonald, Rory Mallinson, Jeff York, Trevor Bardette; **c**, Harry Neumann; **m**, Rex Dunn; **ed**, Richard Heermance; **art d**, Dave Milton, Vin Taylor; **set d**, Raymond Boltz, Jr.

Panic ★★★★ 1947; France; 91m; Filmsonor/Film Rights International; B/W; Children: Unacceptable; **DVD**; **VHS**. Chilling crime yarn has Romance getting out of jail for a crime committed by her lover, Bernard, a pathological killer who has earlier murdered an old maid in a Paris suburb at the time of Romance's release. Romance meets Bernard, but the two pretend they do not know each other as Romance makes moves on Simon, who falls in love with her. Simon's love for Romance invites his own destruction in that Bernard throws suspicion on Simon as the serial killer after implanting those suspicions in the minds of angry neighbors who then falsely accuse Simon. A mob gathers seeking justice and Simon is killed, but he has known the identity of the killer all along and leaves behind a photograph that will prove the guilt of the true murderers. Well directed by Duvivier and with exceptional performances from Romance, Bernard and Simon, this film has gone on to become a minor film noir classic, offering many tension-filled moments while incisively employing love for perverse and sinister purposes. (In French; English subtitles.) **d**, Julien Duvivier; **cast**, Viviane Romance, Michel Simon, Paul Bernard, Charles Dorat, Lucas Gridoux, Louis Florence, Marcel Peres, Max Dalban, Emile Drain, Guy Favieres; **w**, Duvivier, Charles Spaak (based on the novel *Les Fiancailles de M. Hire*); **c**, Nicolas Hayer; **m**, Jacques Ibert; **ed**, Marthe Poncin; **prod d**, Serge Pimenoff.

Panic in the Streets ★★★★ 1950; U.S.; 96m; FOX; B/W; Drama;

Paul Douglas, Richard Widmark and Alexis Minotis in *Panic in the Streets*, 1950.

Children: Unacceptable; **DVD**; **VHS**. Widmark does an exceptional job as a conscientious U.S. Navy physician who is called by police to examine the body of a man murdered on the docks of New Orleans. He discovers to his horror that the disease-ridden corpse has Bubonic Plague, or what was commonly referred to as the Black Death, a devastating disease that claimed the lives of millions in Europe from 1348 to 1666. To prevent panic from gripping the city, Widmark insists to Douglas, the police official supervising the criminal investigation, that no news about the disease be released to the press. Douglas is skeptical about Widmark's diagnosis, but agrees to quash the information but only for a short period of time, giving Widmark a deadline to confirm his diagnosis. Meanwhile, Widmark and Douglas conduct a frantic search for the killer so that he and the victim can be identified and all parties associated with them placed in quarantine. Tirelessly working on the case takes its toll on Widmark's marriage to Bel Geddes as he neglects her and his young son. Then Widmark locates an Armenian freighter already at sea and he and Douglas, with the help of the Coast Guard, board the vessel to discover that the murdered man had been a stowaway on the rat-laden ship and had suffered from a strange disease. The ship is quarantined, and Widmark and Douglas then trace the stowaway's movements to an Armenian café located near the New Orleans docks. When the proprietor sees a photo of the dead man, he becomes nervous and goes to his wife. Both know the victim, but the wife orders her husband to keep quiet so that they will not lose their license. The wife, who has been recently suffering from a strange malady, dies the next day, and Widmark diagnoses her death as the result of the Plague. Her husband now talks freely to him and Douglas, and his information leads them to a vicious gangster, Palance, and his right-hand goon, the greasy, fat Mostel, the two men responsible for the death of the murdered victim. With police and Widmark chasing them through the warehouses and docks of New Orleans, both are trapped beneath a wharf and where Widmark captures the whining Mostel. Palance, however, ambushes Widmark from a hiding place and knocks him senseless and then tries to escape by climbing up the anchoring rope of a large freighter. Douglas holds back policemen aiming weapons at him, saying that the Plague-ridden Palance "is going nowhere." Palance, while shinnying up the rope hawser, is stopped by a shield known as a rat-catcher, preventing him from climbing any farther (this scene symbolic in that he, like the disease-laden rats attempting to board a ship is thus prevented from going on board). Losing his grip, Palance falls into the water and is fished out by police and taken into custody. Widmark and Douglas, their ordeal at an end, wind up as good friends. Widmark then returns to his wife and son, exhausted but victorious in his quest to deal with a potential and lethal epidemic. All of the principal players and supporting actors give outstanding performances, from the patient and dedicated Widmark to

Linda Bruhl, Glynis Johns and Jackie Gleason in *Papa's Delicate Condition*, 1963.

the stoic and preserving Douglas, from the manic and psychopathic Palance to the oily and utterly repugnant Mostel. The direction from Kazan is superb, bringing the kind of gritty realism to the story for which he was best known in such moving tales that are similar in location as **A Streetcar Named Desire**, 1951 (located in New Orleans) and **On the Waterfront**, 1954 (located on the New Jersey docks), and where his pace commensurately increases from scene to scene to heighten suspense and anxiety. *Author's Note*: Widmark told this author that "Gadg [Kazan] was in his element when directing **Panic in the Streets** and where we did the picture entirely in New Orleans. He liked to work that way, far from the studio and its controlling front office people. He was a demanding guy, but he never asked any of us to do anything he would not do himself. Nobody could outwork Gadg." For his part, Kazan told this author that "I never liked the title of that picture because it's a little misleading since no panic really takes place in the streets of New Orleans since no news about the Plague is leaked to the press. I used a lot of non-professional actors in that picture and I think I had more fun doing that picture than any other I ever made." **p**, Sol C. Siegel; **d**, Elia Kazan; **cast**, Richard Widmark, Paul Douglas, Barbara Bel Geddes, Jack Palance, Zero Mostel, Dan Riss, Tommy Cook, Wilson Bourg, Jr., Beverly C. Brown, Lewis Charles, Kazan; **w**, Richard Murphy, Daniel Fuchs (based on the stories "Quarantine" and "Some Like 'em Cold" by Edna and Edward Anhalt); **c**, Joe MacDonald; **m**, Alfred Newman; **ed**, Harmon Jones; **art d**, Lyle Wheeler, Maurice Ransford; **set d**, Thomas Little, Fred J. Rode.

Pan's Labyrinth ★★★ 2007; Spain/Mexico; 118m; Estudios Picasso/Picturehouse Entertainment; Color; Drama/Fantasy; Children: Unacceptable (MPAA: R); **BD**; **DVD**. This well-made gothic fairy tale for adults is set in 1944 fascist Spain. Baquero is an eleven-year-old girl who is fascinated with fairy tales. She travels with her pregnant mother, Gil, to live with her new stepfather-to-be, Lopez, who turns out to be a ruthless Spanish army captain. At night, she meets a fairy who whisks her to an old farm in the center of a labyrinth. The fairy tells her she is a princess, but she must prove herself by surviving three perilous tasks. If she fails, she will never see her real father again, and he is the king. The challenges teach her important lessons of life, especially in these hazardous times. A beautifully filmed fantasy, graphic violence and gutter language nevertheless prohibit viewing by children. (In Spanish; English subtitles.) Songs: "Long, Long Time Ago," "The Labyrinth," "Rose, Dragon," "The Fairy," "The Fairy and the Labyrinth," "Three Trials," "The Moribund Tree and the Toad," "Guerilleros," "A Book of Blood," "Mercedes Lullaby," "The Refuge," "Not Human," "The River," "A Tale," "Deep Forest," "Waltz of the Mandrake," "The Funeral," "Mercedes," "Pan and the Full Moon," "Ofelia," "A Princess" (Javier Navarrete); "Soy un pobre presidiario"

(Torres Larrode, Raphael de Leon, C. Cam, Daniel Montorio). **p**, Alvaro Augustin, Alfonso Cuaron, Bertha Navarro, Guillermo del Toro, Frida Torresblanco; **d&w**, del Toro; **cast**, Ivana Baquero, Ariadna Gil, Sergi López, Maribel Verdu, Doug Jones, Alex Angulo, Manolo Solo, Cesar Vea, Roger Casamajor, Ivan Massague, Gonzolo Uriarte; **c**, Guillermo Navarro; **m**, Javier Navarrete; **ed**, Bernat Vilaplana; **prod d**, Eugenio Caballero; **spec eff**, Reyes Abades.

Papa's Delicate Condition ★★★ 1963; U.S.; 98m; Amro Productions/PAR; Color; Comedy; Children: Acceptable; **DVD**; **VHS**. Gleason is endearingly charming as a doting father who has a drinking problem. He is liked by everyone and will do anything to please his wife, Johns, and others or even himself. When his little girl, Bruhl, wants a pony in a circus parade, he buys the entire circus. It's the last straw for Johns and she sends him packing. He goes to Texarkana where Johns' father, Ruggles, is running for his third term as mayor in 1900. Gleason arrives with the circus and helps get Ruggles reelected. This makes Johns so happy, she forgives Gleason and the family is reunited. A warmhearted family comedy based on the biography by silent film star Corinne Griffith (1894-1979), who is played by Bruhl. Songs: "Call Me Irresponsible" (Jimmy Van Heusen, Sammy Cahn), "Bill Bailey, Won't You Please Come Home?" (Hughie Cannon). *Author's Note*: Gleason ironically plays a man with a drinking problem in this film and admitted to this author that "I probably drink to excess in **Papa's Delicate Condition**, but I reform in order to save my marriage and win back the love of my little girl, a role tailor made for a guy like me. There's nothing wrong with drinking as long as it doesn't control your life, but I must admit that it has abruptly interfered with my own more than once." Gleason stated at one time: "Drinking removes warts and pimples. Not from me but from the peopled I look at." **p&w**, Jack Rose (based on the book by Corinne Griffith); **d**, George Marshall; **cast**, Jackie Gleason, Glynis Johns, Charles Ruggles, Laurel Goodwin, Linda Bruhl, Ned Glass, Murray Hamilton, Elisha Cook, Jr., Charles Lane, Juanita Moore, Frank Albertson; **c**, Loyal Griggs (Technicolor); **m**, Joseph J. Lilley: **ed**, Frank P. Keller; **art d**, Hal Pereira, Arthur Lonergan; **set d**, Sam Comer, James W. Payne; **spec eff**, Farciot Edouart, Paul K. Lerpae.

Paper Moon ★★★★★ 1973; U.S.; 102m; Directors Company/Saticoy Productions/PAR; B/W; Comedy; Children: Unacceptable (MPAA: PG); **DVD**; **VHS**. In this poignant, touching and utterly memorable tale, O'Neal and his real-life daughter, Tatum, present bravura performances in Bogdanovich's most significant film, a true masterpiece of Americana. The setting is the Midwest in 1936 during the first term of President Franklin D. Roosevelt (1882-1945), who is the idol of nine-year-old Tatum, and who has recently been orphaned after her mother dies. Attending that woman's funeral is the adult O'Neal, who had been the dead woman's lover. Neighbors implore the young man to take Tatum to live with relatives in St. Joseph, Missouri, and, out of compassion for the child and his memories about her deceased mother, he agrees. He soon comes to regret this decision as little Tatum is more than a handful. She swears, smokes and expresses herself as would a worldly and much-too-sophisticated adult, all of which her former neighbors have described as "adorable" and "cute," but, to O'Neal, she only a demanding pain in the neck, a little girl with an obnoxiously fierce individuality. Before departing the area, O'Neal, a small-time confidence man, scams the brother of the man who caused the accidental death of his former lover, bilking him out of $200. After buying a new car, O'Neal escorts Tatum to the local train station and buys a ticket to St. Joseph, planning to put the child on the train bound for that destination. Before she leaves, he takes her to a restaurant and buys her lunch, but Tatum throws a screaming tantrum, claiming that he has cheated her out of her inheritance, the $200 O'Neal has gleaned, claiming that that money was really a payment in return for her mother's death and belongs to her. Moreover, Tatum all but states that O'Neal is her real father, which he emphatically denies, but she nevertheless continues to yell that "we have the same jaw!" Embarrassed and feeling obligated to the child, O'Neal agrees to take her along with him as he scams his way across Kansas and Missouri, slowly heading for St. Joseph. En route, he successfully sells expensive monogrammed Bibles to the widows or widowers of deceased spouses, using the local obituary columns in small-town newspapers from which to select his victims. He tells these suckers that their recently departed mates had ordered a specially monogrammed Bible (which he has monogrammed with his own embossing equipment) and these gullible and still mourning marks readily pay exorbitant amounts to acquire the last items their loved ones have selected in life. Tatum accompanies O'Neal on his porch to front-door visits, her precocious poses designed to endear O'Neal to his customers. She preempts his pitch in one of his sales by instantly recognizing a wealthy woman as being able to pay much more than what O'Neal intends to ask, and Tatum gets the woman to pay double for the embossed Bible. On another such visit, however, after she sees a poor woman with many scantily clothed children, Tatum kills O'Neal's sale, compelling him to give away the Bible free to the impoverished widow. She further becomes a scamming partner with O'Neal when convincing a naïve department store clerk to give her more change for the actual bill she has used to pay for an item, claiming that the bill she has remitted was a gift to her and had writing on it from a relative. That bill is discovered in the till, one exchanged by O'Neal in an earlier transaction at the store, and she is given the extra and undeserved cash. While the two come closer together through these illegal bonding sessions, that relationship is challenged when O'Neal takes Tatum to a carnival, where O'Neal meets and falls for slatternly Kahn, a buxom and pretentious tart, who claims to be a dancer, but she is a sensual adventuress simply looking for a sugar daddy to support her, along with an impoverished black girl, Johnson, who serves as Kahn's maid. Kahn and Johnson now become part of O'Neal's entourage. While they are picnicking alongside a road, Tatum refuses to get back into the car, angry that she has to sit in the back seat. O'Neal pleads with her, saying that Kahn must soon get to a bathroom. "She's always going to the bathroom," Tatum says. "She must have a bladder the size of a peanut!" After Kahn pleads with Tatum, the little girl takes pity on the woman and returns to the car. Kahn and Johnson then accompany O'Neal and Tatum to a hotel where Tatum and Johnson become friends and where Johnson tells Tatum how she dislikes Kahn, describing her as a cheap gold digger, adding that she is no dancer at all but a conniving prostitute. Tatum then resolves to get rid of this brassy and intruding lady who has gulled O'Neal into a romantic trance. Tatum convinces a randy hotel clerk that Kahn wants him to visit her in her room, and after he enters Kahn's room, Tatum arranges for O'Neal to find the clerk and Kahn in a compromising clinch. O'Neal, as Tatum hoped, immediately dumps Kahn and he and Tatum drive off for greener pastures. O'Neal then makes the mistake of swindling $625 from a bootlegger on the promise of delivering top-notch bootleg booze. He sells the bootlegger his own liquor and then discovers that his victim has a brother, Hillerman, who is a corrupt sheriff, who gets onto O'Neal's trail. Hillerman arrests O'Neal, holding him in his office and demanding the return of the cash O'Neal has taken from his brother, that money hidden in Tatum's cloche hat. Tatum manages to hoodwink a deputy and she and O'Neal escape, but, when they arrive at St. Joseph, Hillerman and his thugs arrive and beat O'Neal senseless. All but broke, the badly shaken O'Neal drives a broken-down truck to deliver Tatum to her relatives, and she is given a warm welcome (only because they have no idea that she is a modern-day version of Calamity Jane packaged into the misleading little body of a young girl). O'Neal bids goodbye to Tatum and drives off down a country road, but she runs after him, insisting that she is his daughter. He shouts at her: "I don't want you riding with me no more!" She screams back: "You still owe me $200!" As they argue while standing in the road, the ancient truck's brakes give way, and the vehicle begins to roll down the hill; they run after it, jumping into its cabin. They, the truck and untold adventures to come continue on down the road and into the far midwestern landscape to end this won-

Tatum O'Neal and Ryan O'Neal in *Paper Moon*, 1973.

derful, bittersweet tale of America's yesterday. The portrait of the Depression-era period that Bogdanovich so expertly presents is irresistible and addictive, as blatantly prosaic as its earthy and very believable characters. There are no frills in each and every hardscrabble scene where faces are careworn and weathered, homes and hotels drab and dilapidated, clothes threadbare and where ancient vehicles labor along dusty roads that seem to lead to nowhere. The performances from the eternally optimistic O'Neal, the tenacious Tatum, the pathetic Kahn, the futureless Johnson and all of the rest of the cast are outstanding while Sargent's script offers dialog that captures just the right flavor, nuance and argot of that long ago age still vividly residing in some living memories. Genuine humor radiates from characters seeming at a glance to be quaint, although they are as realistically blunt as the times and generation they so accurately represent. There is great entertainment here, but also an unforgettable visual document where its nostalgic time period stands comfortably still, unmolested by great events and oblivious to a changing future. Both Kahn and Tatum O'Neal were nominated for Oscars as Best Supporting Actress, and Tatum, who made her film debut in this evocative film, walked away with the statuette, becoming the youngest recipient of such an award in the Academy's illustrious history. Sargent received an Oscar nomination for Best Adapted Screenplay. The public loved this film, chiefly to see O'Neal and his daughter acting together, and showed it at the box office where more than $30 million was returned in the initial run against a $2.5 million budget. Songs: "It's Only a Paper Moon" (1933; music: Harold Arlen; lyrics: E. Y. Harburg, Billy Rose), "I Found a Million Dollar Baby (in a Five and Ten Cent Store)" (1931; music: Harry Warren; lyrics: Mort Dixon, Billy Rose), "Rock of Ages" (1830; music: Thomas Hastings; lyrics [1776]: Augustus Montague Toplady), "About a Quarter to Nine" (1935; music: Harry Warren; lyrics: Al Dubin), "Flirtation Walk" (1934; music: Allie Wrubel; lyrics: Mort Dixon), (It Will Have to Do) Until the Real Thing Comes Along" (1936; Alberta Nichols, Mann Holiner, Sammy Cahn, Saul Chaplin, L. E. Freeman), "Just One More Chance" (1931; music: Arthur Johnston; lyrics: Sam Coslow), "One Hour with You" (1932; music: Richard A. Whiting; lyrics: Leo Robin), "The Object of My Affection" (1934; Pinky Tomlin, Coy Poe, Jimmy Grier), "A Picture of Me Without You" (1935; Cole Porter), "My Mary" (1941; Jimmie Davis, Stuart Hamblen), "The Banks of Ohio" (traditional), "Georgia on My Mind" (1930; music: Hoagy Carmichael; lyrics: Stuart Gorrell), "After You've Gone" (1918; music: Turner Layton; lyrics: Henry Creamer), "Let's Have Another Cup of Coffee" (1932; Irving Berlin), "Sunnyside Up" (1929; music: Ray Henderson; lyrics: Buddy De Sylva, Lew Brown). *Author's Note*: Bogdanovich, a great admirer of pantheon directors John Ford and Howard Hawks, about whom he has made two documentaries, is best known for his well-crafted period films like this one, as well as **The**

Steve McQueen and Dustin Hoffman in *Papillon*, 1973.

Last Picture Show, 1971, and **The Cat's Meow**, 2001. He reportedly had a very difficult time in helming **Paper Moon**, chiefly in handling Tatum O'Neal, stating that this sophisticated little girl gave him "one of the most miserable experiences of my life." The film was shot on location at Hays, Kansas, and many other locations in the state, along with St. Joseph, Missouri. **p&d**, Peter Bogdanovich; **cast**, Ryan O'Neal, Tatum O'Neal, Madeline Kahn, John Hillerman, P.J. Johnson, Jessie Lee Fulton, Jim Harrell, Lila Waters, Noble Willingham, Bob Young, Randy Quaid; **w**, Alvin Sargent (based on the novel *Addie Pray* by Joe David Brown); **c**, Laszlo Kovacs; **m**, various composers of 1930s song classics; **ed**, Verna Fields; **prod d**, Polly Platt; **set d**, John Austin; **spec eff**, Jack Harmon.

Papillon ★★★★ 1973; U.S./France; 151m; Corona General/Solar Productions/AA; Color; Biographical Drama; Children: Unacceptable (MPAA: R); **BD**; **DVD**; **VHS**. McQueen is superlative in this, his finest role, where he enacts the life of French criminal Henri Charriére (1906-1973). Charriére was known as "Papillon," a defiant prisoner serving time at the hellish French penal colony in French Guiana and Devil's Island, and who, after many attempts, finally made good his escape. McQueen is shown being convicted of murdering a French pimp, although he strenuously denies his guilt, and is sentenced to life imprisonment in 1931, two years later being sent to the prison camp maintained in French Guiana. He is shown being herded with other prisoners by French troops to a dock in Marseille in 1933 where he and others take a ship for Cayenne, French Guiana. On board, McQueen befriends Hoffman, another prisoner, a sophisticated, bespectacled stock swindler who has hidden gems on his person. The burly McQueen saves Hoffman from being robbed by other prisoners while they sleep in hammocks in a prison hold on board the ship. Hoffman has swallowed some rare jewels to assure his comfort and security while serving time in prison, but other prisoners learn of this and think to kill him while he sleeps and slice open his stomach and retrieve those gems, a plan aborted by McQueen, who kills one prisoner and knocks the other senseless. McQueen's life-saving act dumbfounds Hoffman as no one has ever done him a favor in life. When they arrive at Cayenne, the prisoners find that it is the most punishing place on earth, suffering from the sultry weather and the constant abuse from savage guards as they work in the dense jungles where they must slave away at clearing swamps and building a road to nowhere. At one point, McQueen and Hoffman are ordered by a guard to capture a huge alligator as it has been attacking workers and they struggle with the beast to the point of exhaustion, a chore whimsically ordered by their captor. After a guard attacks Hoffman, McQueen again saves his friend from punishment by attacking the guard and then making an attempt to escape, which diverts all attention by other guards to focus upon him and

forget all about Hoffman. McQueen is quickly captured and placed in solitary confinement, living on meager rations, where he loses weight and strength, although Hoffman shows his gratitude to McQueen by having nourishing food smuggled to him. To stave off madness, McQueen paces his small cell, but is watched by guards who patrol the cells from a walkway above, peering through ceiling grates to monitor every move made by prisoners. Smithers, the severe warden of the colony, learns that the defiant McQueen has been receiving extra food smuggled to him, and when McQueen refuses to identify his supplier, more time is added to his solitary confinement. He cannot provide such information in any event since he does not know the identity of his benefactor, who has sent him only a few encouraging but cryptic brief notes, which McQueen has eaten along with that secreted food. After serving his complete sentence in solitary, McQueen is released and is welcomed by Hoffman, who lives more comfortably than any other prisoner, having used his hoarded jewels to bribe guards and officials and, as McQueen has all along suspected, been the man smuggling food to him out of gratitude for having earlier saved his life on more than one occasion. Hoffman tries to convince McQueen to give up all thoughts about escape, arguing that Hoffman's attorneys will some time arrange for his parole and also McQueen's release, but McQueen thinks this is wishful thinking, believing that Hoffman's greedy wife is already spending Hoffman's money and has no plans to help him to freedom. McQueen uses some of Hoffman's money to bribe a guard and he and another prisoner then make an escape, but when Hoffman sees McQueen and the other prisoner climbing over a wall and are about to be apprehended by another guard, Hoffman knocks the guard cold and climbs the wall, breaking an ankle when falling to the other side. McQueen helps him into the jungle where they find a boat that has been hidden for them, but find that it is rotten. Then Quade, a man marked with tattoos, finds them and shows the bodies of two bounty hunters he has killed, men that were waiting for McQueen and others. Quade tells them he was once a prisoner and had been hoodwinked the same way. He sends them to a leper colony where McQueen meets its leader, Zerbe, bravely smoking the same cigar the disease-ridden Zerbe offers him to see if he has courage. After McQueen smokes the cigar, Zerbe befriends him, then gives McQueen and fellow prisoners a boat and some supplies and the trio make for the open sea. Exhausted and out of water and food, they finally make landfall, only to be seen by police leading a native, Sierra, under guard. While Hoffman distracts the guards, McQueen and Sierra make a break, fleeing into the jungle. Sierra leads the way through treacherous areas he knows well but is impaled upon a mantrap that native hunters have set, and McQueen continues on the run with those native hunters, working with the police, tracking him through the jungle. They shoot poisoned arrows at him, one striking him in the back just as he reaches a cliff and he topples over it and into a churning pool of water. He is later found downstream by a peaceful tribe. He is taken in and nursed back to health by Assan, the attractive daughter of tribal chief Jory and who so much admires the tattoo McQueen has on his chest (one of a butterfly that has earned him the nickname of "Papillon") that he asks McQueen to apply the same image to his own chest, and this McQueen laboriously does, under the understanding that, if he botches this crude surgery and harms Jory in any way, the natives may take his own life. He works all night on Jory and the surgery proves a success. Jory, in gratitude, gives McQueen a small sack containing a number of priceless pearls. The comfortable conditions in the village suddenly change for McQueen when he awakes one morning to find that the nomadic tribe, including Assan, has suddenly vanished, deserting their village, and McQueen is now all alone. He travels to civilized towns and finds a place to sleep in a nunnery. When Morrison, the mother superior, becomes suspicious of him, McQueen gives her one of the pearls he has gotten from Jory. She promptly summons police, who arrest him, but nevertheless keeps the pearl. McQueen is returned to the penal colony and is again thrown into solitary confinement. Upon his release, he is sent to Devil's Island, a rocky isle lashed by crashing waves and vicious currents and where no natural landfall exists. McQueen occupies a small cottage and discovers his neighbor is Hoffman, who, at first, wants nothing more to do with him, but later rekindles their friendship, explaining that he has resigned himself to life imprisonment and is content to tend to the small garden next to his cottage. He urges McQueen to adopt the same peaceful life, but, even though he has aged and physically deteriorated, as has Hoffman, McQueen doggedly clings to his ideas about how to escape the supposedly "escape-proof" Devil's Island. McQueen studies the tides and then concludes that an escape from the island is possible if he rides a bale of coconuts on the "seventh wave" that will take him out to sea. When he tells this to Hoffman and asks him to join him in that escape attempt, Hoffman agrees that he will make the escape attempt with his old friend. McQueen makes a strong net that contains the coconuts, but, just before he is about to escape, Hoffman arrives and tells him that he will not be going with him. McQueen nods, expecting that decision from Hoffman. Then, while waiting for the "seventh wave to come in," McQueen throws his gerrymandered life raft from a cliff and leaps after it. He clings onto the raft and, indeed, the wave, as McQueen anticipated, sweeps him out to sea and he sails away from Devil's Island, which is the dramatic and triumphant conclusion to this thoroughly exciting and magnificently made film. Director Schaffner does an outstanding job in carefully showing this fascinating tale while detailing in one explicit scene after another the horrors inflicted upon the prisoners at the penal colony in French Guiana (a prison system now defunct). McQueen is astoundingly effective in his stoic but resolute character, and Hoffman, too, presents an utterly captivating performance as a conniving confidence man making for the first time in his life a true friendship. All of the rest of the cast members, particularly Zerbe, Jory, Smithers and Quade, render standout performances, and the production values are top notch as all aspects of the time period are presented with the utmost authenticity. Shot in Spain and in the jungles of Jamaica, this film was a very costly production for its time, its budget exceeding more than $13.5 million (with McQueen receiving $2 million, Hoffman $1,250,000 and Schaffner $750,000 for their excellent services), but it proved to be an enormous box office success, returning more than $55 million in its initial release. Song: "Ballet Music from Faust" (Charles Gounod). Goldsmith, who composed the stirring and memorable score for this masterpiece film, received an Oscar nomination for Best Original Dramatic Score. *Author's Note*: McQueen told this author that "we shot the last scene in the picture on a cliff at Maui, Hawaii, and I actually jumped from that cliff into the sea and what a thrill that was, one of the greatest of my life. But when I later thought about it, well, hell, I could have killed myself. My exhilaration and expectation in making that jump clouded my reason, I think. It was not a matter of courage, but common sense and I did not have much common sense when I insisted on doing that stunt myself. I was trying to impress myself, I guess, but I would think twice before I did something like that again." The French penal colony at French Guiana that includes the offshore Devil's Island has been profiled in a number of films, including: **The Devil Doll**, 1936; **Devil's Island**, 1939; **Escape from Devil's Island**, 1935; **Hell on Devil's Island**, 1957; **I Escaped from Devil's Island**, 1973; **L'affaire Seznec**, 1993 (made for TV); **The Life of Emile Zola**, 1937 (which depicts Alfred Dreyfus' incarceration at Devil's Island); **Passage to Marseille**, 1944; **Strange Cargo**, 1940; **Terror of the Bloodhunters**, 1962; **We're No Angels**, 1955; and **Women of Devil's Island**, 1962. **p**, Franklin J. Schaffner, Robert Dorfmann; **d**, Schaffner; **cast**, Steve McQueen, Dustin Hoffman, Victor Jory, Don Gordon, Anthony Zerbe, Robert Deman, Ratna Assan, William Smithers, Gregory Sierra, John Quade, Barbara Morrison, Ellen Moss, Woodrow Parfrey, Bill Mumy, George Coulouris, Victor Tayback, Ron Soble, Richard Farnsworth, Dalton Trumbo; **w**, Trumbo, Lorenzo Semple, Jr. (based on the autobiographical novel by Henri Charriere); **c**, Fred Koenekamp (Panavision; Technicolor); **m**, Jerry Goldsmith; **ed**, Robert Swink; **prod d**, Anthony Masters; **art d**, Jack Maxsted; **spec eff**, Alex Weldon, Albert Whitlock.

Louis Jourdan in *The Paradine Case*, 1947.

Paprika ★★★ 2006; Japan; 90m; Madhouse/Sony; Color; Animated Fantasy; Children: Unacceptable (MPAA: R); **DVD**. Exciting tale has scientists at a foundation for psychiatric research inventing a device that enables people to record and watch their dreams. This device is stolen and used to enter people's minds when they are awake and distract them with other people's dreams. A sprite named Paprika (Hayashibara) rescues the device from evil hands in a story that warns of Big Brother controlling everyone's minds. Songs: "Parade," "Mediational Field," "The Blind Spot in a Corridor," "Welcome to the Circus," "A Tree in the Dark," "Escapee," "Lounge," "The Shadow," "A Drop Filled with Memories," "Chaser," "Prediction," "The Girl in Byakkoya, White Tiger Field" (Susumu Hirasaw). Violence and sexual images prohibit viewing by children. (In Japanese; English subtitles.) **p**, Jungo Maruta, Masao Takiyama; **d**, Satoshi Kon; **cast** (voiceovers), Megumi Hayashibara, Toru Emori, Katsunosuke Hori, Kôichi Yamadera, Toru Emori, Akio Ohtsuka, Hideyuki Tanaka, Satomi Koorogi, Daisuke Sakaguchi, Mitsuo Iwata; **w**, Seishi Minakami, Kon (based on the novel by Yasutaka Tsutsui); **c**, Michiya Katou; **m**, Susumu Hirasawa; **ed**, Takeshi Seyama; **art d**, Nobutaka Ike.

The Paradine Case ★★★ 1947; U.S.; 125m; Vanguard Films/Selznick Releasing Organization; B/W; Crime Drama; Children: Unacceptable; **DVD**; **VHS**. Pantheon director Hitchcock takes us into the courtroom in this intriguing crime tale where the enigmatic and alluring Valli is accused of killing her rich, blind husband and is defended by barrister Peck. He has a difficult time with his reticent client as Valli gives him little defense evidence to go on; Peck is further hampered when he falls in love with the beautiful Valli, even though he is devoted to his loving wife, Todd. Further, Peck has rough-sledding with Laughton, a draconian judge, who dislikes him, the feeling being mutual with Peck as Laughton has earlier made advances to Todd and was rebuffed by her. (Laughton is an injudicious if not ruthless jurist in that he shocks his wife, Barrymore, who has shown compassion for Valli, by blatantly stating that he intends to send the woman to the gallows irrespective of any kind of defense Peck might make on her behalf.) Peck then learns that Jourdan, a handsome young man who is the stableman at the estate Valli has inherited upon the death of her husband, is Valli's lover. He confronts Valli, thinking it was Jourdan who murdered his employer. Valli is fiercely protective of Jourdan, refusing to discuss her relationship with him and adamantly insisting that Jourdan be kept out of the case. Peck defies her and puts Jourdan on the stand and, even though Peck manages to shift suspicion to him, Jourdan maintains his innocence. When Jourdan later takes his life, Valli blames Peck for scandalizing Jourdan and bringing about his suicide. She further stuns Peck when she admits that she poisoned her husband to death, and he even-

Warren Beatty and Walter McGinn in *The Parallax View*, 1974.

tually loses the woman to the executioner. Hitchcock sustains fine mystery and considerable suspense throughout this dark story, but its script, which had been heavily doctored by the always intrusive Selznick often leads to some blind alleys. This was the American film debut for Valli as it was for Jourdan. *Author's Note*: Hitchcock originally wanted Greta Garbo to play the accused murderess, but she declined, telling this author years later that "it was not the kind of part I ever wanted to play. The character is a cold-blooded murderess, a woman full of hate. I have always played women full of love. I like Mr. Hitchcock's pictures, but I did not want to be victimized by him by playing a woman no one could love. He should have known that about me. Some directors place their actors first in their concerns. Mr. Hitchcock always comes first." To be fair, Hitchcock was hampered and harassed from the beginning with this film in that he was under a rigid contract to movie mogul Selznick, "and he drove me nuts throughout the entire production," Hitchcock told this author. "Selznick was not difficult—he was impossible! He had his hands in every aspect of the picture. When I told him I could not get Garbo and then wanted Ingrid Bergman to play the femme fatale, he stalled me, and then Bergman told me no, she would not do the role and that was because she just did not want to work with Selznick again because of his manipulative ways. Instead of Garbo or Bergman, Selznick gave me Valli. I wanted Ronald Colman or Laurence Olivier to play the attorney, but Selznick insisted that Peck play the part. I wanted Robert Newton to play the lover and Selznick handed me Jourdan. Then he went about changing everything in the script that Ben Hecht had originally written. My God, there was no end to his invasions." Hecht told this author that "David Selznick was obsessed with controlling everything and everybody in all of his productions. Sometimes that worked and sometimes it did not. He grabbed a good script I had done for Hitch for **The Paradine Case** and took it apart and rewrote it and rewrote it. I had worked for a few weeks with him on the script for **Gone with the Wind** [1939] a decade earlier and he put me through hell with that one, so I told Hitch that I would not do anything more on **The Paradine Case** if I had to work with David." Peck, who was one of Fox's top stars and on loan to Selznick for this production, was also unhappy about how the production lagged, stating to this author: "We would do a scene and then Selznick would change it and the script and Hitch would have us do it all over again. Working with Selznick was like crawling into a cement mixer." Hitchcock, who always prided himself in completing his films on schedule and within budget, was completely hamstrung by Selznick, finally completing the film in ninety-two days, a three-hour-long opus that has cost more than $3 million to make, about the initial budget of Selznick's colossal **Gone with the Wind**. "We had the Devil in editing that film down to a presentable time frame and the hardest part was making sense of its continuity after those deep edits. Of course,

David was involved with that, too. I did get my way by casting Ann [Todd] as Greg's [Peck's] wife, but we had to cut some of her scenes and some fine scenes of the great Ethel Barrymore went with those edits and Ethel had done some wonderful scenes as Laughton's wife where Laughton drives her to the brink of madness. You know, Laughton told me that he appeared in two courtroom pictures, **The Paradine Case** and, ten years after that one, **Witness for the Prosecution** [1957], directed by Billy Wilder, telling me: 'Hitch, you had me playing a vicious judge in **The Paradine Case**, but I liked it much better when Billy had me playing a barrister like Gregory Peck played in the first picture, but in Billy's picture I win my case and everybody loves me for it. Very few people love anyone in **The Paradine Case**.'" **p**, David O. Selznick; **d**, Alfred Hitchcock; **cast**, Gregory Peck, Ann Todd, Charles Laughton, Charles Coburn, Ethel Barrymore, Louis Jourdan, (Alida) Valli, Leo G. Carroll, Joan Tetzel, Isobel Elsom, "Snub" Pollard, John Williams, Hitchcock; **w**, Selznick, Alma Reville, James Bridie (based on the novel by Robert Hichens); **c**, Lee Garmes; **m**, Franz Waxman; **ed**, Hal C. Kern, John Faure; **prod d**, J. McMillan Johnson; **art d**, Thomas Morahan; **set d**, Emile Kuri, Joseph B. Platt; **spec eff**, Clarence Slifer.

Paradise Alley ★★★ 1978; U.S.; 107m; PAR; Force Ten Productions/UNIV; Color; Drama; Children: Unacceptable (MPAA: PG); **DVD**; **VHS**. This gritty, well-enacted tale is set in the tough Hell's Kitchen neighborhood of New York City in 1946. Stallone, one of three Italian brothers, hustles and panhandles for money during an economic downturn, but he is an unhappy man because he and his siblings are not living up to his expectations. Older brother Assante is an injured veteran of World War II (1939-1945) working as an undertaker. The youngest brother (Canalito), also the biggest and strongest, delivers ice and shows promise as a wrestler at a nightclub called Paradise Alley. This gives Stallone the idea that Canalito could make big money as a professional wrestler, and he persuades Canalito to enter the ring; Assante becomes Canalito's reluctant manager while Archer, an attractive but tired woman, is trying to establish a relationship with Assante. The brothers have a falling out, but Canalito wins a big wrestling match in a rainstorm and they are reunited, and Assante finally accepts Archer's love. Stallone, Assante, Canlito and Archer all render top-flight performances (as do McRae, who plays a huge black wrestler named Big Glory and who lives in the basement of the wrestling club where he works, and Conway, who plays a petty and zany gangster) in this offbeat but fascinating period drama. The script is sharply witty and funny, and the characters are well developed by director Stallone. Violence and mature themes prohibit viewing by children. Songs: "Too Close to Paradise" (Bill Conti, Carole Bayer Sager, Bruce Roberts); "(Meet Me in) Paradise Alley," "Annie's Back in Town" (Tom Waits), "Angel Voice," "Please Be Someone to Me" (Frank Stallone); "Frere Jacques" (traditional). **p**, John F. Roach, Ronald A. Suppa, Jeff Wald; **d&w**, Sylvester Stallone; **cast**, Stallone, Lee Canalito, Armand Assante, Frank McRae, Anne Archer, Kevin Conway, Terry Funk, Joyce Ingalls, Joe Spinell, Aimee Eccles; **c**, Laszlo Kovacs (Panavision; Technicolor); **m**, Bill Conti; **ed**, Eve Newman; **prod d**, John W. Corso; **art d**, Deborah Beaudet; **set d**, Jerry Adams; **spec eff**, Jeff Frink.

The Parallax View ★★★ 1974; U.S.; 102m; Doubleday Productions; PAR; Color; Crime Drama; Children: Unacceptable (MPAA: R); **DVD**; **VHS**. This riveting thriller begins when a prominent U.S. senator is assassinated by a waiter at the Seattle Space Needle. Three years later, Prentiss, a television reporter who covered the killing, seeks the help of newspaper reporter Beatty because she has noticed that other reporters covering the killing are dying mysteriously and she fears she may be next. During Beatty's investigation, Prentiss supposedly commits suicide, but he suspects she was murdered. He comes to suspect the murders have been part of a conspiracy involving an enigmatic training institute, the Parallax Corporation. He enrolls in the institute and uncovers those responsible for the plot but with no little hazard to himself.

Songs: "Buttons and Bows" (Jay Livingston, Roy Evans), "Blue Hawaii" (Ralph Rainger, Leo Robin), "Moon River" (Henry Mancini, Johnny Mercer), "Wild and Wooly West" (Paul Francis Webster, Sammy Fain). *Author's Note*: It will not be lost on viewers that the setting and victim involved in the killing shown at the beginning of this film is not dissimilar to the assassination of U.S. Senator Robert F. Kennedy in Los Angeles in 1968. Violence prohibits viewing by children. **p&d**, Alan J. Pakula; **cast**, Warren Beatty, Paula Prentiss, William Daniels, Walter McGinn, Hume Cronyn, Kelly Thordsen, Chuck Waters, Bill Joyce, Jim Davis, Kenneth Mars, Ford Rainey, Stacy Keach, Sr., Anthony Zerbe; **w**, David Giler, Lorenzo Semple, Jr. (based on the novel by Loren Singer); **c**, Gordon Willis (Panavision; Technicolor); **m**, Michael Small; **ed**, John W. Wheeler; **prod d**, George Jenkins; **set d**, Reg Allen; **spec eff**, Tim Smyth.

Paranoiac ★★★ 1963; U.K.; 80m; Hammer Film Productions/UNIV; B/W; Horror; Children: Unacceptable; **VHS**. Frightening film has Reed as a wealthy young psychotic living under the thumb of an aunt, Scott, in a palatial mansion outside London. One day, Davion, his long-dead brother arrives to claim the family inheritance, stating that he never committed suicide, only disappeared. It turns out that Davion is an imposter, who has been sent by Bonney, son of the attorney for the family estate and who has been stealing from the family trust fund, or so it is claimed. Davion moves into the mansion and must deal with incessant attacks on his life by a mysterious assailant while Reed annoyingly plays an eerie organ that is about to drive the mentally unstable Scott over the edge. Reed, a genuine lunatic, is the real culprit, having killed his actual brother years earlier and who has kept the corpse in a mummified state. This engrossing horror entry was later successfully dramatized in a British television miniseries, **Brat Farrar**, 1986. **p**, Anthony Hinds; **d**, Freddie Francis; **cast**, Janette Scott, Oliver Reed, Sheila Burrell, Maurice Denham, Alexander Davion, Liliane Brousse, Harold Lang, Arnold Diamond, John Bonney, John Stuart; **w**, Jimmy Sangster (based on the novel *Brat Farrar* by Josephine Tey); **c**, Arthur Grant; **m**, Elisabeth Lutyens; **ed**, James Needs; **prod d**, Bernard Robinson; **art d**, Don Mingaye; **spec eff**, Les Bowie, Kit West.

Paranormal Activity ★★★ 2009; U.S.; 86m; Blumhouse Productions/PAR; Color; Horror; Children: Unacceptable (MPAA: R); **BD**; **DVD**. An unmarried young couple moves into a rented, furnished suburban San Diego home and becomes disturbed by a nightly demonic presence. This chilling tale is enacted by unprofessional actors, but they are convincing as two people who reportedly experienced the terrors, Featherston, a graduate student in English, and Sloat, a day trader. They start filming overnight with a video camera in an upstairs bedroom where they hear strange noises that keep them awake and they soon realize to their shock that they are not alone. Made on a shoestring, this film made a fortune. Nothing is really resolved, but there are a lot of spooky goings-on, in fact enough to fill four sequels, **Paranormal Activity 2**, 2010; **Paranormal Activity 3**, 2011; **Paranormal Activity 4**, 2012; and **Paranormal Activity 5**, 2013. Song: "Numb" (Chester Bennington). Gutter language and violence prohibit viewing by children. **p**, Oren Peli, Jason Blum; **d&w**, Peli; **cast**, Katie Featherston, Micah Sloat, Mark Fredrichs, Amber Armstrong, Ashley Palmer, Crystal Cartwright, Randy McDowell, James Piper; **c&ed**, Peli.

Paratrooper ★★★ 1954; U.K.; 88m; Warwick Film Productions/COL; Color; War Drama; Children: Unacceptable; **VHS**. Ladd is a standout in this well-made WWII drama where he shuns responsibility after having ordered a friend to jump from a plane about to crash. He nevertheless lands the plane safely only to learn that has friend has died when his parachute failed to open. Shocked and dismayed, Ladd resigns his commission in the U.S. Air Force and goes to England, volunteering to serve as a British paratrooper. He is willing to do his duty, but unwilling to assume any leadership even though his commander, Genn, sees that

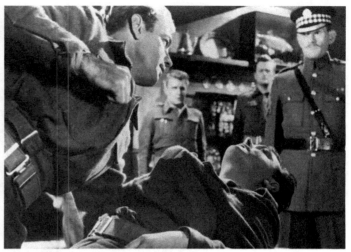

Alan Ladd, left, and Harry Andrews, right, in *Paratrooper,* 1954.

Ladd is a natural leader of men as he quietly probes Ladd's past. While in training, Ladd becomes romantically involved with Stephen, who works as a parachute packer, but their romance is interrupted when Ladd's unit is ordered to fight in North Africa. Once there, the paratroopers are ordered to retake an airfield from German forces. They get trapped in a mine field, however, and it appears that all are doomed, especially when Genn and the rest of the officers are wounded or killed. That leaves it up to Ladd to take command and he does, repeatedly firing a bazooka that explodes the mines and opens a path for the paratroopers to escape. They accomplish their mission, and once they return to their base, Ladd accepts the fact that he will become a leader of these men in future battles. Good action and above-average acting, along with a literate and clever script, makes this war tale come alive. Song: "Red River Valley" (traditional). *Author's Note*: The British press was somewhat critical of this film in that it was very protective about the services rendered by British troops in certain theaters of the war during WWII and felt that Ladd's character, an American, might prove to be the outstanding hero in a contingent of British paratroopers. Ladd held a press conference before the film was in production in England and told London reporters: "Look, I didn't come over [to England] to conquer anything or anybody. All I'm going to do is play the part of a guy who comes to England to learn to fight. Got that? I said learn to fight, not to teach." The film was a success in the U.S., as well as England, and Ladd received praiseworthy reviews and even gleaned a commendation from the venerable Winston Churchill, who stated that he was impressed with Ladd's performance. **p**, Irving Allen, Albert R. Broccoli; **d**, Terence Young; **cast**, Alan Ladd, Leo Genn, Susan Stephen, Harry Andrews, Donald Houston, Anthony Bushell, Patric Doonan, Stanley Baker, Anton Diffring, Lana Morris; **w**, Richard Maibaum, Frank S. Nugent, Sy Bartlett (based on a story from the book *The Red Beret* by Hilary St. George Sanders); **c**, John Wilcox (Technicolor); **m**, John Addison; **ed**, Gordon Pilkington; **art d**, Edward Carrick; **set d**, Freda Pearson; **spec eff**, Cliff Richardson.

Pardon My Past ★★★ 1946; U.S.; 88m; Mutual/COL; B/W; Comedy; Children: Acceptable. Despite a plot involving mistaken identity that is sometimes overused in films, this one provides a very funny comedy. MacMurray stars in dual roles as exact duplicates, but neither man knows the other exists. One of them, Eddie, and his pal Demarest, get mustered out of the service and travel to Wisconsin to start a mink farm, but they don't realize that the life of gambling playboy Francis, the other man who is MacMurray's look-alike, is a mess. Francis has left the country owing a large gambling debt. Tamiroff, the gambler to whom Francis owes $12,000, thinks Eddie is Francis and threatens to kill him unless he gets paid the debt immediately. Eddie locates Francis to get

Lou Costello, chorus girls and William Demarest in *Pardon My Sarong*, 1942.

the money, but everyone thinks he's Francis. After a lot of funny situations, Eddie manages to straighten out the confusion. He winds up with the fetching Chapman and Francis, MacMurray's alter ego, remains with his wife, Johnson, while Dumbrille, the conniving family attorney, is thwarted in his insidious efforts to steal the family estate. *Author's Note*: MacMurray told this author that "**Pardon My Past** is one of those screwball comedies that confuses everyone because I am playing two men who are exact look-alikes, but in this picture, we never use the 'double image' technique—in other words I never appear on the screen with my other self and if that is too confusing, well, you have to see the picture to find out which one I am playing from scene to scene. A year before I did that picture, I did one called **Murder, He Says** [1945] and, in that picture I have to deal with identical twins [played by Peter Whitney] who are out to bump me off and I could never quite tell one twin from the other." Actually, MacMurray does such a fine job in his dual roles in this film and it is fairly easy to identify one look-alike from the other because of the distinct mannerisms he gives to each. **p&d**, Leslie Fenton; **cast**, Fred MacMurray, Marguerite Chapman, Akim Tamiroff, William Demarest, Rita Johnson, Harry Davenport, Douglass Dumbrille, Karolyn Grimes, Dewey Robinson, Hugh Prosser; **w**, Earl Felton, Karl Kamb (based on a story by Patterson McNutt, Harlan Ware); **c**, Russell Metty; **m**, Dimitri Tiomkin; **ed**, Richard Heermance; **prod d**, Bernard Herzbrun; **set d**, Edward G. Boyle.

Pardon My Sarong ★★★ 1942; U.S.; 83m; Mayfair/UNIV; B/W; Comedy; Children: Acceptable; **DVD**; **VHS**. In this delightful romp, Abbott and Costello employ many of their old but clever burlesque routines to good use. They are Chicago bus drivers who accidentally steal their own bus. To escape a company's warrant for their arrest, they tag along with Paige, a playboy, sailing on a boat and winding up on a tropical island where they become mixed up with jewel thief Erickson. It's all fun and nonsense with some spectacular chase scenes through the island's jungle, mixed with a lot of good songs: "Do I Worry" (Stanley Cowan, Bobby Worth); "Shout, Brother, Shout" (Clarence Williams); "Java Jive" (Milton Drake, Ben Oakland); "Lovely Luana," "Vingo Jingo," "Island of the Moon" (1942; Don Raye, Gene de Paul); "Deep in the Heart of Texas" (1942; music: Don Swander; lyrics: June Hershey). *Author's Note*: Universal produced a number of Abbott and Costello films that were designed to compete with the Bing Crosby–Bob Hope films produced by Paramount; the studio's competitive plan worked well, this Bud and Lou outing becoming an enormous box office hit, their biggest to date. **p**, Alex Gottlieb; **d**, Erle C. Kenton; **cast**, Bud Abbott, Lou Costello, Virginia Bruce, Robert Paige, Lionel Atwill, Leif Erickson, Nan Wynn, William Demarest, Samuel S. Hinds, Marie McDonald, Jennifer Holt, Jack La Rue, Charles Lane, Audrey Long, Marjorie Riordan, The Ink Spots (Charles Fuqua, Hoppy Jones, Bill Kenny, Deek Watson), Tip Tap & Toe (Samuel Green, Ted Fraser, Ray Winfield); **w**, True Boardman, Nat Perrin, John Grant; **c**, Milton Krasner; **m**, Frank Skinner; **ed**, Arthur Hilton; **art d**, Jack Otterson; **set d**, Russell A. Gausman.

Pardon Us ★★★ 1931; U.S.; 56m; Hal Roach/MGM; B/W Comedy; Children: Acceptable; **DVD**; **VHS**. This is the first Laurel and Hardy feature film after the boys had made many hilarious shorts, and it is, lulu of a comedy. The boys make home-brew beer during the Prohibition era (1920-1933) when it is illegal to make or sell alcoholic beverages. They try to sell some of their beer to a policeman and wind up in a prison in the South. Laurel has a loose tooth that causes him to make a sound like a raspberry when he speaks, which gets him into trouble with guards, but this earns him the respect of a hardened criminal called "The Tiger" (Long), who thinks Laurel is very brave. Long plans an escape and takes the boys with him, but in a mix-up, Long is caught and the boys escape. They are near cotton plantations so they put on blackface to hide out among cotton-pickers. While there they do a dance as Hardy sings a delightful number. The prison warden, Lucas, happens to be driving in the area when his car breaks down. He encounters Laurel and Hardy, realizing that they are the escaped convicts and returns them to prison. Long then starts a riot, and the boys inadvertently put it down and are rewarded with a pardon. Lucas tells them to return to whatever they were doing before going to prison, and Laurel, complying with the warden's advice, then tries to sign him up for a keg of illegal beer. Song: "Lazy Moon" (1903; music and lyrics, Bob Cole, Rosamond Johnson). **p**, Hal Roach; **d**, James Parrott; **cast**, Stan Laurel, Oliver Hardy, Walter Long, Wilfred Lucas, James Finlayson, June Marlowe, Stanley J. Sanford, Charlie Hall, Frank Austin, Eddie Baker, James Parrott, Etude Ethiopian Chorus; **w**, H.M. Walker (not credited), Laurel; **c**, Jack Stevens; **m**, Leroy Shield; **ed**, Richard Currier.

The Parent Trap ★★★ 1961; U.S.; 124m; Disney/Buena Vista; Color; Comedy; Children: Acceptable; **DVD**; **VHS**. Pleasant comedy has Mills enacting teenage twins who meet for the first time at summer camp. They are daughters of divorced parents, and they switch planes so as to meet the parent they never knew (O'Hara and Keith), then contrive to reunite them. The plot involves a lot of innocent but very funny shenanigans that provides a winning dual performance by Mills, one of the best child stars of the 1960s. This film was remade in 1998 with Lindsay Lohan in the dual role. Songs: "The Parent Trap," "Let's Get Together," "For Now for Always" (Richard M. Sherman, Robert B. Sherman); "Colonel Bogey March" (Kenneth Alford); "Nocturne in E-flat major, Op. 9, No. 2" (Frederic Chopin);"Symphony No. 5" (Ludwig van Beethoven); "Wedding March" (Felix Mendelssohn-Bartholdy); "Bridal Chorus (Here Comes the Bride)" (from "Lohengrin" by Richard Wagner). **p**, George Golitzen; **d&w**, David Swift (based on the novel *Das doppelte Lottchen* by Erich Kastner); **cast**, Hayley Mills, Maureen O'Hara, Brian Keith, Charles Ruggles, Una Merkel, Leo G. Carroll, Joanna Barnes, Cathleen Nesbitt, Ruth McDevitt, John Mills, Frank De Vol, Irene Tedrow; **c**, Lucien Ballard (Technicolor); **m**, Richard M. and Robert B. Sherman, Paul Smith; **ed**, Philip W. Anderson; **art d**, Carroll Clark, Robert Clatworthy; **set d**, Emile Kuri, Hal Gausman; **spec eff**, Ub Iwerks, Bob Broughton.

The Parent Trap ★★★ 1998; U.S.; 127m; Meyers/Shyer Co./Disney/Buena Vista; Color; Comedy; Children: Cautionary (MPAA: PG); **DVD**; **VHS**. This is a good remake of the 1961 film starring Hayley Mills with the same plot, and here the twins are played by Lindsay Lohan in her first screen role. Identical teenage twins are separated at birth and are each raised by one of their biological parents who have separated. The girls discover each other for the first time at summer camp and plan to bring their parents back together which they finally do. There are two sequels to the 1961 film, **Parent Trap 2**, 1986, and

Parent Trap 3, 1989. Songs: "LOVE" (Bert Kaempfert, Milton Gabler), "Happy Club" (Bob Geldof, Karl Wallinger), "Soulful Strut" (Eugene Record, William Sanders), "Top of the World" (Richard Carpenter, John Bettis), "Bad to the Bone" (George Thorogood), "The Great Escape March" (Elmer Bernstein, Albert Stillman), "Do You Believe in Magic" (John B. Sebastian), "There She Goes" (Lee Anthony Mavers), "Here Comes the Sun" (George Harrison), "Never Let You Go" (Gabriel Gilbert, Nick Laird Clowes, Frank Berman, Christian Berman, Jeff Coplan, Matthias Hass), "Life in a Northern Town" (Gilbert, Laird-Clowes), "Parents Just Don't Understand" (Pete Harris, Will Smith, Jeffrey A. Townes), "In the Mood" (Joe Garland), "Let's Get Together" (Richard M. Sherman, Robert B. Sherman), "Everyone Merenge" (Joe Bones Johnson), "I Love You for Sentimental Reasons" (Deek Watson, William Best), "How Bizarre" (Alan Jansson, Paul Fuemana), "Ev'ry Time We Say Goodbye" (Cole Porter), "This Will Be (An Everlasting Love)" (Charles Jackson, Marvin Yancy), "Am I the Same Girl" (Dusty Springfield). **p**, Charles Shyer; **d**, Nancy Meyers; **cast**, Lindsay Lohan, Dennis Quaid, Natasha Richardson, Elaine Hendrix, Lisa Ann Walter, Simon Kunz, Polly Holliday, Joanna Barnes, Maggie Wheeler, Ronnie Stevens, Michael Lohan, Ali Lohan, Dina Lohan; **w**, Meyers, David Swift, Shyer (based on the novel *Das doppelte Lottchen* by Erich Kastner); **c**, Dean Cundey; **m**, Alan Silvestri; **ed**, Stephen A. Rotter; **prod d**, Dean Tavoularis; **art d**, Alex Tavoularis; **set d**, Gary Fettis; **spec eff**, Stuart Brisdon.

Parenthood ★★★ 1989; U.S.; 124m; Image Entertainment/UNIV; Color; Comedy; Children: Unacceptable (MPAA: PG-13); **DVD**; **VHS**. Steve Martin does a good job as the much-harassed head of a household in the Midwest. He has a plateful of problems, dealing with his wife, and she with him while they attempt to raise rebellious children, deal with job pressures, and all the while learning to be good spouses and parents. There are many funny scenes involving eccentric family members, "black sheep" relatives and not too few skeletons in the family closet, all cohesively and delightfully presented by top-notch director Howard. Many of Martin's comedies widely miss the mark (as too adolescently moronic or silly), but this one is on target. Songs: "I Love to See You Smile" (Randy Newman), "Pigs in Zen" (Eric Avery Weiss, Perry Farrell, David Novarro, Stephen Perkins), "Close to You" (Burt Bacharach, Hal David). *Author's Note*: Howard and Grazer and the writers reportedly based the plot on their own experiences, and their remembered domestic predicaments make up an entertaining comedy. Gutter language prohibits viewing by children. **p**, Brian Grazer; **d**, Ron Howard; **cast**, Steve Martin, Mary Steenburgen, Dianne Wiest, Jason Robards, Rick Moranis, Tom Hulce, Keanu Reeves, Martha Plimpton, Harley Jane Kozak, Leaf (Joaquin) Phoenix, Clint Howard, Rance Howard; **w**, Lowell Ganz, Babaloo Mandel (based on a story by Ganz, Mandel, Howard); **c**, Donald McAlpine; **ed**, Daniel Hanley, Michael Hill, **prod d**, Todd Hallowell; **art d**, Christopher Nowak; **set d**, Nina Ramsey; **spec eff**, Bob Cooper, Kevin Harris.

Paris Blues ★★★ 1961; U.S.; 98m; Pennebaker Productions/UA; B/W; Drama/Musical; Children: Acceptable; **DVD**; **VHS**. Handsome white Newman and handsome black Poitier are expatriate jazz musicians living in Paris where racism is not an issue. They both fall in love with American girls on vacation, Newman with Woodward, and Poitier with Carroll, and are faced with a dilemma, whether to move back to America with the girls or stay in Paris and enjoy the freedom it allows them. Carroll convinces Poitier to face the bigotry in the U.S. by returning to his native land to make a life with her, but Newman, who believes he would be deserting his studies in classical music, sends Woodward (his real-life wife and their fourth film together) back to the States alone. The highlight of the film is the wonderful jazz numbers and the appearance of the legendary Louis "Satchmo" Armstrong. *Author's Note*: Newman told this author that he felt that **Paris Blues** "captured the anti-culture feelings for the States some Americans had when they remained in Paris

Nastassja Kinski in *Paris, Texas*, 1984.

after World War Two just the same way F. Scott Fitzgerald and Ernest Hemingway lived in Paris after World War One to write their stories and novels. Paris has always been a haven for the creative and I think we make that point in **Paris Blues**." Newman's trombone playing is dubbed by Murray MacEachern and Poitier's saxophone playing is dubbed by Paul Consalves. Songs: "Take the 'A' Train" (Billy Strayhorn); "Mood Indigo" (Barney Bigard, Duke Ellington); "Autumnal Suite," "Wild Man Moore" (Duke Ellington). **p**, Sam Shaw; **d**, Martin Ritt; **cast**, Paul Newman, Joanne Woodward, Sidney Poitier, Diahann Carroll, Louis Armstrong, Barbara Laege, Andrew Luguet, Marie Versini, Aaron Bridgers, Guy Pedersen; **w**, Jack Sher, Irene Kamp, Walter Bernstein, Lulla Rosenfeld as Lulla Adler (based on the novel by Harold Flender); **c**, Christian Matras; **m**, Duke Ellington; **ed**, Roger Dwyre; **art d**, Alexandre Trauner.

Paris, Texas ★★★ 1984; West German/France/U.K./U.S.; 147m; Argos/Road Movies/FOX; Color; Drama; Children: Unacceptable (MPAA: R); **DVD**; **VHS**. Stanton, an off-the-wall but always fascinating character actor, is mesmerizing in his leading role of a man displaced from family and friends after his mind has failed. He is shown entering a saloon in Texas, where he collapses. A physician revives him, but Stanton will give no answers to the doctor's questions. The doctor finds a Los Angeles phone number on Stanton's person and calls it, getting Stockwell, Stanton's brother, on the line and describing the man he is treating. Stockwell recognizes the man as his brother and goes to Texas, only to find that Stanton has disappeared. Stockwell finds him wandering vacant-eyed and tells him that he will take him to Los Angeles, explaining that he and his wife, Clement, have been taking care of Stanton's son, Carson, after he vanished four years earlier. After Stanton refuses to fly, Stockwell rents a car and the two begin a two-day journey toward L.A., with Stanton still refusing to talk about anything. Finally Stanton speaks, but hesitantly, showing Stockwell an old photo of a vacant lot that represents property Stanton says he has purchased in Paris, Texas, the place where he believes he was born. When they arrive in L.A., Carson is hesitant to accept Stanton as his father, but they slowly grow closer together after Stockwell shows some home movies of Carson and Stanton together years earlier and with Kinski, who is Stanton's estranged wife and Carson's mother. Stockwell then reveals that Kinski regularly deposits money in Carson's name each month at a bank in Houston, Texas, and Stanton then decides that he will go there and attempt to find Kinski. Carson asks to go along, and father and son travel to Texas, bonding even closer during the journey. They arrive at Houston, and Carson recognizes his mother, Kinski, as she leaves the bank. Stanton follows her to a striptease club and finds Kinski performing there and then leaves and takes Carson to

Herbert Heyes and Gene Evans in *Park Row*, 1952.

a hotel, telling him to wait in his room. Stanton returns to the club and tells Kinski that he married her when she was young and how jealousy caused him to take to drink and caused her to leave him. He then tells her where she can find Carson, and Kinski goes to the hotel and finds her son. As they embrace, Stanton drives away from Houston, again alone. Gritty and uncompromising, this is an emotionally debilitating but fascinating story, andStanton gives a magnificent performance as a man who has ruined his life and attempts and achieves redemption through self-sacrifice. **p**, Anatole Dauman; **d**, Wim Wenders; **cast**, Harry Dean Stanton, Hunter Carson, Nastassja Kinski, Dean Stockwell, Aurora Clement, Bernhard Wicki, Edward Fayton, John Lurie; **w**, L. M. Kit Carson, Sam Shepard; **c**, Robby Müller; **m**, Ry Cooder; **ed**, Peter Przygodda; **art d**, Kate Altman.

Park Row ★★★★ 1952; U.S.; 83m; Samuel Fuller Productions/UA; B/W; Drama; Children: Cautionary; **VHS**. The always enterprising Fuller presents a moving story of a crusading early-day journalist, dynamically essayed by Evans, who quits his job at an institutional newspaper and branches off on his own to start a new newspaper in New York's Park Row. His aim is to publish a hard-hitting newspaper that will expose corruption and focus upon plaguing social evils and where truth comes before politics. With the help of some good friends, including experienced and elderly reporter Heyes, and Kovacs, who plays the part of linotype inventor Ottmar Mergenthaler (1854-1899), Evans manages to begin publishing his crusading paper, which alarms his former employer, wealthy Welch, who looks upon newspaper publishing as a business, not a social service, where profits come before ethical criteria. After Evans' paper begins to become popular and competitive with her own newspaper, the ruthless Welch uses every underhanded trick to hamper and eventually destroy Evans' newspaper. The always innovative Evans has Kovacs perfect his linotype machine, which allows Evans to publish his newspaper more quickly than his competitors. Further, he begins a drive to collect pennies from children to pay for the construction of the base upon which the Statue of Liberty will stand, this magnificent gift being then made to the U.S. by France. As his circulation soars, Evans meets with one obstruction after another, barriers placed in his path by competitor Welch. After Evans' paper is wrecked and his employees injured by one of Welch's overzealous associates, Welch comes to realize what great harm she has done to this man, a person she has not only come to respect, but one she now loves. She makes amends by allowing Evans to share her own operation in resuming his crusading publications, now sharing Evans' absolute dedication to the freedom of the press. *Author's Note*: Fuller told this author that **"Park Row** was a picture I wanted to make all my life. When I could not get a dime out of anyone in Hollywood to fund the production, I

withdrew everything I had in the bank [$200,000], except for $1,000 to cover my expenses for vodka and cigars, and put it all into the production, which we shot and put in the can within two weeks. I thought I did one of my best jobs on that picture and I also thought that Gene Evans, Herbert Heyes, Mary Welch and the rest of the cast were wonderful in their roles. The film saw poor distribution and I lost every penny I put into the picture, but I have no regrets. I still consider it to be one of my finest efforts." Ironically, six years later, Heyes and Welch both died on the same day, May 31, 1958. **p,d&w**, Samuel Fuller; **cast**, Gene Evans, Mary Welch, Bela Kovacs, Herbert Heyes, Tina Pine, George O'Hanlon, J. M. Kerrigan, Forrest Taylor, Don Orlando, Neyle Morrow; **c**, Jack Russell; **m**, Paul Dunlap; **ed**, Philip Cahn, **prod d**, Theobold Holsopple; **art d**, Ray Robinson; **spec eff**, Roscoe S. Cline.

Party Girl ★★★ 1958; U.S.; 99m; MGM; Color; Crime Drama; Children: Unacceptable; **DVD**; **VHS**. Taylor is exceptional as a crippled, successful criminal attorney who works exclusively for Chicago crime boss Cobb (giving an energy-charged performance of an Al Capone type underworld czar) in this exciting and well-crafted tale from Ray, one of Hollywood's most gifted and underrated directors. Suave and sophisticated, Taylor effectively employs his affliction in court to win the sympathy of juries by hobbling painfully about on a cane in making his eloquent summaries. After delivering one such impressive address, he wins an acquittal on a charge of murder for Ireland, Cobb's top killer, and Cobb then throws a large party to celebrate the legal victory. He orders a number of his most attractive chorus girls in one of his nightclubs to attend that party, and the sensuous Charisse is one of those girls. Ireland makes a play for her at the celebration, but the statuesque beauty rebuffs him as she becomes fascinated with Taylor, who barely tolerates the crude behavior of the party-carvorting felons he represents. Slightly attracted to Charisse, he escorts the dancer home, and they slowly begin an affair where Charisse tries to convince Taylor to break with Cobb and develop a different kind of legal practice. He informs her that their love affair is really going nowhere since he is already married to an estranged wife, Kelly, who rejected him because of his crippled leg. He then hears about a new type of surgery in Sweden that might correct his affliction and travels there, having a dangerous operation. Meanwhile, Charisse fends off the sexual advances of Ireland and others as she waits for Taylor to return. When Taylor arrives from Sweden, he is walking perfectly, his operation having been a complete success. Kelly, Taylor's selfish, shrewish wife, then learns that he is no longer a cripple, and she goes to Charisse, telling her that she plans to resume her marriage with him. Taylor, however, loves only Charisse, stating he will divorce Kelly, marry her and break with Cobb after handling one more case for the kingpin. The defendant, one of Cobb's killers, is, however, slain in an on-going gang war, and Taylor is wounded in the attack. He is arrested and held as a material witness in the killing; prosecutor Smith tells him that, unless he testifies against Cobb, Taylor will undoubtedly be sent behind bars where he will never see the lovely Charisse again. He agrees to be a witness against Cobb, but only if police give Charisse protection. Cobb learns of this betrayal and has Charisse kidnapped, holding her as a ransom to assure Taylor's silence. Taylor then meets with Cobb where he attempts to persuade Cobb to release Charisse, but the irate mob boss threatens to scar her face for life with acid that he holds in a vial. While police gather outside Cobb's headquarters, Taylor suddenly strikes Cobb causing the acid to splash into his face, blinding him and sending him staggering about in agony toward the windows of the building and he is suddenly shot to pieces by a hail of bullets. Taylor and Charisse then clinch for the fadeout. Though melodramatic in the style of the 1930s gangster films, this entry nevertheless sustains consistent interest through some fine performances and a clever script that well defines its characters. Charisse performs a spectacular jazz-dance number suitable to the sleazy environment of the story, a leggy, hip-slinking routine in a nightclub where goon Ireland salivates over her curvaceous body and Taylor admires her grace and style. Song: "Party Girl" (music:

Nicholas Brodszky; lyrics: Sammy Cahn). *Author's Note*: Director Ray told this author that "I had the benefit of two fine actors going for me in **Party Girl**—Bob [Taylor] and Lee [Cobb], and they both provide enough fireworks to keep the pace of the picture at high speed. I more or less let Cyd [Charisse] handle her steamy dance routine as I am not a Busby Berkeley when it comes to choreography, but I think she did an outstanding job. She is very seductive in **Party Girl**, more sensuous in that picture I think than in any other in which she appeared and she brought more sizzle to her part than I expected." Taylor told this authorthat he took his role very seriously, going to physicians and studying the bone structures of those with crippled legs as well as studying the motion of men in hospitals who had deformed legs in order to perfect his hobbling gait in the film. Taylor said to this author that "I play an underworld mouthpiece that is pretty much like the celebrated criminal lawyer William Fallon, who legally represented a lot of big shots in the Twenties. I read up on his courtroom style and tricks, like using a watch to bring a jury's attention to a point I am making. I achieve some incredible legal victories in that picture, but so too did Fallon. He wasn't called 'The Great Mouthpiece' for nothing." (Fallon represented more than 120 homicide defendants, getting most of them off, during his spectacular legal career in New York.) Cobb saw his character clearly as being based on "that monster Al Capone, who ran everything in Chicago during the bootlegging days. He gave big parties just as I do in **Party Girl**, and while I am grinning and glad-handing guests, I am telling some of my thugs to go out and bump off someone, and that is exactly the kind of person Capone was, too. I had played a few years earlier a similar character in **On the Waterfront** [1954] when I am bossing a dockworker's union and having people killed to protect my rackets. To tell you the truth, I never understood how such people could live with themselves, but I always instinctively understood how to play those terrible creatures." Ireland, who was always a strong supporting player (although he was a leading player in a few feature films such as **All the King's Men**, 1949) was uncomfortable in his role as one of Cobb's killers, telling this author: "Ray had me play that gangster like some sex-crazed nut. He has only one idea and that is to get poor Cyd into bed, having me purring and whispering obscenities into her pretty ear and calling her 'Puss' in the most suggestive ways. I don't think I ever played such a creepy, disgusting character and I knew that I was making Cyd uneasy in those scenes where she probably thought I was about to rape her in front of the entire cast and crew. I apologized to her about the way I came on to her in those scenes, but, being a grand gal, she only smiled and said: 'You're doing your job and a good one.' It comes down to this—you have to have a frightening menace in a picture like that and I was her menace, as well as Lee [Cobb]. Here is Cyd, for crying out loud, with one guy trying to molest her, and another guy [Cobb] who is about to toss acid in her face. Now that's a hell of a lot of menace for any woman!" Capone, the character on which Cobb's role is based, has been profiled in many films, including **Al Capone**, 1959 (Rod Steiger); **Baby Face Nelson**, 1996 (F. Murray Abraham); **Boardwalk Empire**, 2012-2013 (cable TV series; Stephen Graham); **Bonanno: A Godfather's Story**, 1999 (made for TV; Lou Vani); **Capone's Boys**, 2002 (Julian Littman); **Capone**, 1975 (Ben Gazzarra); **Dillinger and Capone**, 1995 (F. Murray Abraham); **Frank Nitti: The Enforcer**, 1988 (made for TV; Vincent Guastaferro); **The George Raft Story**, 1961 (Neville Brand); **Little Caesar**, 1931 (role model for Edward G. Robinson); **The Little Worm**, 1999 (Vincent Riotta); **Mobsters**, 1991 (Titus Welliver); **Night at the Museum: Battle of the Smithsonian**, 2009 (John Bernthal); **Party Girl**, 1958 (role model for Lee J. Cobb); **The Purple Gang**, 1960 (Saverio LoMedico); **Road to Perdition**, 2002 (Anthony LaPaglia; scenes deleted); **The St. Valentine's Day Massacre**, 1967 (Jason Robards Jr.); **Scarface**, 1932 (role model for Paul Muni); **The Scarface Mob**, 1959 (made for TV; Neville Brand); **The Untouchables**, 1959-1963 (TV series; Neville Brand); and **The Untouchables**, 1987 (Robert De Niro). For more details on Al Capone (1899-1947) and William Fallon (1886-1927), see my books

Cyd Charisse and Robert Taylor in *Party Girl*, 1958.

Bloodletters and Badmen (M. Evans, 1995; Capone: pages 119-126; Capone Gang: pages 126-130); *The Great Pictorial History of World Crime*, Volume I (History, Inc., 2004; Capone: pages 503-541); *Encyclopedia of World Crime*, Volume II (CrimeBooks, Inc., 1990; Fallon: pages 1131-1132). **p**, Joe Pasternak; **d**, Nichola Ray; **cast**, Robert Taylor, Cyd Charisse, Lee J. Cobb, John Ireland; **w**, George Wells (based on a story by Leo Katcher); **c**, Robert Bronner (CinemaScope; Metrocolor); **m**, Jeff Alexander; **ed**, John McSweeney, Jr.; **art d**, Randall Duell, William A. Horning; **set d**, Henry Grace, Richard Pefferle; **spec eff**, Lee LeBlanc.

A Passage to India ★★★★ 1984; U.K.; U.S.; 164m; EMI Films/COL; Color; Drama; Children: Unacceptable (MPAA: PG); **BD**; **DVD**; **VHS**. This excellent drama takes place during the 1920s in India when that country was undergoing its early independence movement from the control of British authority. Davis, accompanied by elderly Ashcroft, sail to India from England to visit Ashcroft's son, Havers, who is Davis's fiancé and the magistrate of Chandrapore. Through school superintendent Fox, the two women are introduced to brilliant Guinness, an eccentric Indian professor of the Brahmin caste. Banerjee, a gentle physician, then meets Ashcroft at a mosque overlooking the Ganges River on a moonlit night, and these two sensitive persons establish a friendship. Later, Davis and Ashcroft tell Banerjee that they would like to see the "real India," rather than attend the teas, polo and cricket events held by the British. Banerjee suggests that the two women might like to see the archeological treasures of the Marabar Caves and tells them that he would be willing to hold an excursion for them and other Westerners. The two women readily accept this invitation, and Banerjee then conducts the exploration of the caves with a large number of excursionists, including Davis and Ashcroft. Suffering from claustrophobia, Ashcroft suddenly leaves one of the caves so that she can be in the open air, but she urges Davis and Banerjee to continue exploring the caves, which they do, taking only one guide with them. While Davis and a guide explore one cave, Banerjee briefly leaves the pair to have a cigarette, but when looking for Davis and the guide, he sees Davis suddenly running from the area, her clothes disheveled and covered with blood. Banerjee returns to his village, only to be arrested and charged with sexually attacking Davis, an accusation by Davis that sets off widespread unrest between Indian natives and Westerners. Ashcroft states that she believes that Banerjee is innocent of these charges before she sails for England; she dies of a heart attack during the voyage and her corpse is resigned to the sea. Banerjee is brought to trial and Davis appears to testify against him, but she shocks and disappoints her Western supporters, who believe that she has been raped by the devious Banerjee, when Davis suddenly exonerates Banerjee by telling the court that he is innocent.

Judy Davis in *A Passage to India*, 1984.

Banerjee is carried from the court by jubilant supporters while dejected Westerners now feel that they have been victimized by an overly impressionistic and decidedly confused young woman. Fox shelters and comforts Davis as the only Westerner still willing to support her until she severs her engagement with Havers and leaves India. Banerjee breaks off his long-standing friendship with Fox, believing that Fox has betrayed their trust. He then abandons his Western attire and severs all ties to Westerners, moving to Kashmir in the Himalayas of Northern India where he opens a clinic, exclusively treating Indian natives. Years later, he reconciles his ruptured friendship with Fox and then writes a letter to Davis in which he expresses his thanks for bravely telling the truth in his case. Pantheon director Lean presents an anxiety-filled tale that is handled with the utmost care as he probes the racial suspicions of that less sophisticated day in India, this superb drama being Lean's last film and where he came out of retirement to make this film after a fourteen-year hiatus, having given up on filmmaking after receiving critical reviews for his production of **Ryan's Daughter**, 1970. (It is never made clear just how Davis got into the condition of having her clothes bloodied and disheveled, and the viewer is left to theorize that she either caused these injuries herself or that these injuries were inflicted upon her by the guide or that she accidentally fell down the hill leading from the caves.) The performances from all are magnificent, wholly capturing their troubled characters. The film received eleven Oscar nominations, including for Best Picture, Lean for Best Director and Davis for Best Actress. Ashcroft won an Oscar as Best Supporting Actress, becoming the oldest such female recipient (at age seventy-seven) to that time, while gifted composer Jarre won his third Oscar for Best Original Score, a composition that underscores the subtle apprehensions of the times and enhances the tension of a traumatic event that may or may not have happened, but that nevertheless brought about widespread social upheaval. The film was based on a play that stemmed from an E. M. Forster novel, that Broadway production opening at New York's Ambassador Theater on January 31, 1962, and running for 109 performances. *Author's Note*: Guinness' role in this film was all too brief for the actor, tersely telling this author that "**A Passage to India** was not a rewarding experience for me." The fact remains that Guinness was shocked when most of his scenes in this film wound up on the cutting room floor, the actor blaming Lean for such devastating editing; the long-standing good relationship between Guinness and Lean completely collapsed, neither man ever talking to the other again. Further frustrating Lean were several acrimonious encounters he had with Davis, who reportedly told Lean that, because he had not directed a film in more than a decade, he had "lost his touch" as a gifted director. The racial and sexual themes employed in this outstanding production can be seen in other films depicting the social conflicts in India, including **Gandhi**, 1982;

and, in particular as to the sexual relations between mixed races, in **Bhowani Junction**, 1956; **The Rains Came**, 1939; and **The Rains of Ranchipur**, 1955. **p**, John Brabourne; **d&w**, David Lean (based on the play by Santha Rama Rau and the novel by E.M. Forster); **cast**, Judy Davis, Victor Banerjee, Peggy Ashcroft, James Fox, Alec Guinness, Nigel Havers, Art Malik, Saeed Jaffrey, Clive Swift, Richard Wilson, Antonia Pemberton, H.S. Krishnamurthy; **c**, Ernest Day (Technicolor); **m**, Maurice Jarre; **ed**, Lean; **prod d**, John Box; **art d**, Clifford Robinson, Leslie Tomkins, Herbert Westbrook, Ram Yedekar; **set d**, Hugh Scaife; **spec eff**, Robin Browne.

Passage to Marseille ★★★★ 1944; U.S.; 109m; WB; B/W; Adventure/War Drama; Children: Unacceptable; **DVD**; **VHS**. Hard-hitting and filled with action, this mesmerizing adventure takes place during the early stages of WWII and involves a number of patriotic prisoners suffering the horrors of the penal colony in French Guiana. The film, which employs more multi-dimensional flashbacks than any other in memory (a flashback within a flashback within a flashback), begins when foreign correspondent Loder visits a Free French airfield in England to write about its heroic volunteers, who are repairing, manning and flying bombers that are attacking German installations in Nazi-occupied France. Loder interviews Rains, the French commander of the base, learning about one crew made up of former prisoners at the penal colony of Cayenne, French Guiana, the story chiefly focusing upon one of those prisoners, Bogart, a crusading liberal French journalist. We see in flashback how Bogart and several other prisoners—Dantine, Tobias, Lorre, and Dorn—are found drifting in a small boat at sea and are rescued by a French freighter commanded by Francen. The men claim that they are survivors from another ship that has been torpedoed by a German U-boat and they are given shelter on board and made members of the crew. Francen is a strong anti-fascist, as is Rains, a French army officer on board, but they keep their allegiances to themselves so as not to alert Greenstreet, an outspoken fascist French officer, who is also on board, and who is working, as are others on board, as a secret collaborationist with the Nazis. Rains then talks with the five shipwreck survivors, and they tell him the truth about themselves, admitting that they are escapees from Cayenne; each, in another flashback, is depicted for their separate offenses: Lorre as a pickpocket, Tobias a powerful thug and former farmer, Dantine as a killer, Dorn as an army deserter, and their leader, Bogart, a journalist who was framed for murder by the French fascists he opposed in France. In yet another flashback, Bogart's story is shown in detail, and we then see him working as a journalist in France before the war. He lives in Paris and there meets and marries Morgan. Bogart works for a small liberal newspaper, reporting how France is systematically and secretly working with the Nazis, exposing such collaborationists as Pierre Laval (1883-1945). Fascist thugs invade Bogart's newspaper, wrecking it and killing one of its employees while collaborationist gendarmes stand by and do nothing. Blamed for the murder, Bogart flees with Morgan to the countryside and hides out in a small town, but he is captured and then railroaded into the penal colony at Cayenne where he becomes embittered and disillusioned, even though he is the inspiration of defiance that seethes within his friends. Sokoloff, an elderly man and former prisoner who collects rare butterflies and is a zealous patriot, loves France. He tells Dorn, Lorre, Tobias, Dantine and Bogart that he might be able to provide them with a boat to escape the penal colony, but only if they swear that if they make a successful escape, they will volunteer to fight for France. This they do and the five men make their escape and, in a flash forward are now again with Rains on the freighter, concluding their story. As the freighter sails for the French port of Marseille, news is received that France has gone to war with Germany. Greenstreet tells Francen that the ship must get to Marseille as quickly as possible since the freighter is carrying vital nickel ore, and he wants to turn over this shipment to fascists. Francen refuses, planning to take the ship and its important cargo to England. Greenstreet, Ciannelli and others then attempt to take over the ship, and a full-scale battle ensues where Bogart and his friends join with Francen, Rains and others in killing Greenstreet and his fascist followers and take control of the ship. Conried, another fascist and the ship's radio operator, then sends a message that alerts two German bombers that attack the ship with bombs and machine-gun fire, killing several seamen; Bogart, Lorre and others fire back at the diving planes, shooting both of them down, but at a great cost of life with Lorre and mess boy Roy killed. The ship, however, now sails to England, and in a flash forward we again see Rains concluding his story with Loder, where both go to the airfield to await the return of the Free French squadron that has attacked German installations and is on its way back to its base. The last plane to arrive is one flown by Dorn and where Bogart is a gunner. In former flights, Dorn has flown briefly off course so that Bogart could drop a message in a small metal container on a farm where his wife, Morgan, and small son live. In this last flight, however, the bomber has been damaged during its attack against the Germans and Bogart fatally wounded, so the bomber must head for its home base and Bogart does not have the chance to drop his last message to his wife and son. The bomber lands and its crew carries the wounded Bogart to a stretcher where Rains and Loder see him die. He is buried at a cliff overlooking the English Channel, where Rains reads that last message Bogart has written to his son, a boy he has never seen as he was sent to Cayenne before he was born. The moving message Rains reads encourages Bogart's son to believe in and fight for freedom at all costs. In conclusion, Rains states: "That letter will be delivered!" The final scene in this powerfully presented film depicts the squadron of Free French bombers flying to France to attack German installations and where one breaks formation to fly over the farm where Morgan and her son are waiting to receive that final message. Pantheon director Curtiz, a master of great action scenes, provides one stirring scene after another, particularly the sultry sequences at Cayenne where the prisoners labor and suffer under ann abusive penal system and the violent mutiny on board the freighter and the subsequent attacks against the ship by German bombers. Though a bit unwieldy through Curtiz's use of flashbacks within flashbacks this superlative film sustains deep fascination with its fully developed characters and intriguing story throughout. Bogart is superb as the victimized journalist who strikes a blow for freedom at every turn, and the rest of the cast, many appearing in Bogart's great hit, **Casablanca**, 1942 (Rains, Greenstreet, Lorre, Dantine, Mercier and the wonderful Mexican singer Corinna Mura) render top-flight performances. *Author's Note*: Lorre told this author that "**Passage to Marseille** was the second picture where I was trying to survive in the French penal colony at Cayenne. I was in a picture called **Strange Cargo** [1940] and I played an informer who turns in convicts for payoffs from the warden, a wholly despicable character. In the Bogart picture, however, I vindicate myself by dying heroically after shooting down a German plane. Bogey took his part in that picture very seriously. He told the director [Curtiz] that he was not going to wear his toupee in the scenes where we are on the ship and have escaped from Cayenne so that he would look older and worn out from his terrible prison experiences and I admired him for that. Bogey did not give a hoot for matinee idol images. He told me when we were making that picture: 'I am an ugly guy and the uglier I look in a picture, the more convincing I am in the role.' Well, he was damned convincing in **Passage to Marseille** where he looked like the whole world had been beating him up, but he was still standing at the end, ugly puss, balding head and all." Lauren Bacall, who had been recently hired as a starlet and was being considered for the featured role opposite Bogart in the upcoming film, **To Have and Have Not**, 1944, was brought to the set of **Passage to Marseille** and there met Bogart for the first time, the man she would fall in love with and marry in 1945. Many films have depicted the penal colony at French Guiana (including its adjunct, Devil's Island), including: **The Devil Doll**, 1936; **Devil's Island**, 1939; **Escape from Devil's Island**, 1935; **Hell on Devil's Island**, 1957; **I Escaped from Devil's Island**, 1973; **L'affaire Seznec**, 1993 (made for TV); **The Life of Emile Zola**, 1937 (which depicts Alfred Dreyfus' incarceration at

Helmut Dantine, George Tobias, Humphrey Bogart, Billy Roy and Philip Dorn in *Passage to Marseille*, 1944.

Devil's Island); **Pappillon**, 1973; **Strange Cargo**, 1940; **Terror of the Bloodhunters**, 1962; **We're No Angels**, 1955; and **Women of Devil's Island**, 1962. **p**, Hal B. Wallis; **d**, Michael Curtiz; **cast**, Humphrey Bogart, Claude Rains, Michele Morgan, Philip Dorn, Sydney Greenstreet, Peter Lorre, George Tobias, Helmut Dantine, John Loder, Victor Francen, Vladimir Sokoloff, Eduardo Ciannelli, Mark Stevens, Monte Blue, Hans Conried, Charles La Torre, Louis Mercier, Billy Roy, Frank Puglia, Harry Cording; **w**, Casey Robinson, Jack Moffitt (based on the novel *Men without a Country* by Charles Nordhoff and James Norman Hall); **c**, James Wong Howe; **m**, Max Steiner; **ed**, Owen Marks; **art d**, Carl Jules Weyl; **set d**, George James Hopkins; **spec eff**, Jack Cosgrove, Edwin Du Par, Harry Redmond, Jr., Rex Wimpy.

Passchendaele ★★★ 2010; Canada; 114m; Damberger Film & Cattle Co./Echo Bridge; B/W-Color; War Drama; Children: Unacceptable (MPAA: R); **DVD**; **VHS**. This outstanding war drama is based upon the war heroism of Canadian Army Sgt. Michael Dunne (1880-1917), who fought with the 10th Battalion known as "The Fighting Tenth" in all the major Canadian battles of World War I (1914-1918). Dunne set the record for the highest number of individual bravery awards for a single battle, at Passchendaele in Belgium. Also called the Third Battle of Ypres, it was fought by the British and Canadians against the German empire, taking place on the Western Front between June and November 1917 in an effort to control ridges near the city of Ypres in West Flanders which were major supply lines for the Germans. Dunne is played by Gross, who is wounded in an earlier battle and sent home to Calgary, Canada. While recovering from his injuries, he falls in love with nurse Dhavernas. Gross recovers and returns to the war mainly to look after her headstrong brother, Dinicol. Dunne performs almost superhuman feats to keep Dinicol alive, but dies in the battle and where Dinicol survives and where the Allies win, but at a horrific cost of dead and injured. Australia had its tragic Gallipoli in Turkey in 1915-1916 (profiled in **Gallipoli**, 1981); Canada had Passchendaele. This award-winning Canadian film is excellently acted by Gross, expertly photographed in both battle and pastoral scenes, and offers a fine supporting performance by Harrington as a young colonel. Graphic war violence and some sexuality prohibit viewing by children. Song: "After the War" (Paul Gross, David Keeley). **p**, Paul Gross, Francis Damberger, Niv Fichman, Frank Siracusa; **d&w**, Gross; **cast**, Gross, Caroline Dhavernas, Joe Dinicol, Meredith Bailey, Jim Mezon, Michael Greyeyes, Adam John Harrington, Gil Bellows, James Kot, Jesse Frechette; **c**, Gregory Middleton; **m**, Jan A.P. Kaczmarek; **ed**, David Wharnsby; **prod d**, Carol Spier; **set d**, Janice Blackie-Goodine; **spec eff**, James Paradis.

The Passenger ★★★ 1975; Italy; 126m; Compagnia Cinematografica

Michel Piccoli and Hanna Schygulla in *Passion*, 1982.

Champion/MGM; Color; Drama; Children: Unacceptable (MPAA: PG-13); **DVD**; **VHS**. In this riveting and visually impressive tale, Nicholson is a frustrated war correspondent researching a documentary in the Sahara Desert. He cannot find the war he's been assigned to cover when he is unable to achieve an interview with guerrilla fighters in the desert hills. He meets a gunrunner who dies suddenly and assumes his identity because they look similar and it gives him the opportunity to escape his past and begin a new life. This leads to perils beyond which Nicholson could never imagine. After some action and mystery, including taking money from a terrorist group, his impersonation is exposed when his wife, Runacre, doesn't recognize him, but a lover (Schneider) he finds along the way makes that revealing and hazardous identification. Nicholson, who offers a bravura performance, learns the hard way that being a passenger on a dead man's life can be worse than living your own. Violence, nudity and gutter language prohibit viewing by children. *Author's Note*: This haunting film was the first in which the gifted Antonioni did not wholly work with his own script, although he did rewrite some scenes. **p**, Carlo Ponti; **d**, Michelangelo Antonioni; **cast**, Jack Nicholson, Maria Schneider, Jenny Runacre, Ian Hendry, Steven Berkoff, Ambroise Bia, Jose Maria Caffarel, James Campbell, Manfred Spies, Jan-Baptiste Tiemele, Angel del Pozo; **w**, Mark Peploe, Peter Wollen, Antonioni (based on a story by Peploe); **c**, Luciano Tovoli (Metrocolor); **m**, Ivan Vandor; **ed**, Antonioni, Franco Arcalli; **art d**, Piero Poletto; **set d**, Osvaldo Desideri.

Passion ★★★ 1982; France/Switzerland; 88m; Sara Films/UA; Color; Comedy/Drama; Children: Unacceptable (MPAA: R); **DVD**; **VHS**. This amusing and unusual film offers an insider's view of the nature of work, love, and filmmaking as explored in this film and seen on a movie set, in a factory, and at a hotel. While the independence movement Solidarity takes on the communist government in Poland, a Polish film director, Radziwilowicz, has to remain in France to make a film for television. Schygulla owns a hotel where the film crew stays. She lives with Piccoli, who runs a factory where he has fired Huppert, a floor worker. Both women are attracted to Radziwilowicz, while hotel maids quit and become movie extras and where those extras engage in sexual play off-camera, and where Radziwilowicz, who has no story for the film, wonders why a plot is always necessary in a film. (In French; English subtitles.) Song: "Freres humains, l'amour n'a pas d'age" (Leo Ferre). Sexuality prohibits viewing by children. **p**, Armand Barbault, Catherine Lapoujade, Martine Marignac, Alain Sarde; **d**, Jean-Luc Godard; **cast**, Isabelle Huppert, Hanna Schygulla, Michel Piccoli, Jerzy Radziwilowicz, Laszlo Szabo, Jean-Francois Stevenin, Patrick Bonnel, Barbara Tissier; **w**, Godard, (uncredited) Jean-Claude Carriere; **c**, Raoul Coutard; **ed**, Jean-Luc Godard; **prod d**, Jean Bauer, Serge Marzolff.

Passion Fish ★★★ 1992; U.S.; 135m; Atachafalaya/Miramax; Color; Drama; Children: Unacceptable (MPAA: R); **DVD**; **VHS**. Life electrifyingly imitates art in this solid drama where McDonnell, a New York daytime soap opera actress, is paralyzed after an automobile accident and confined to a wheelchair. She retreats to her family's dilapidated, empty house in Louisiana where she takes to hard drinking and wallows in self-pity and where she offends every caregiver. A new black nurse, Woodard, brings positive change, but not until some initial slam-bang conflicts occur between patient and nurse and where they enrich each other's lives by becoming friends. Songs: "Attack of the Mutant Guitars" (Duke Levine); "Bayou Pon Pon," "Oh, Negresse," Grand Mamou," "La danse de Mardi Gras" (traditional); "Zydeco Queen" (Willis Prudhomme); "Poor Man Two Step" (John Delafose); "Bwanas' Garden" (James MacMitchell, George G. Recile). Gutter language prohibits viewing by children. **p**, Sarah Green, Maggie Renzi; **d&w**, John Sayles; **cast**, Mary McDonnell, Angela Bassett, Alfre Woodard, David Strathairn, Leo Burmester, Elaine West, Linda Castle, Leigh Harris, Michael Mantell, Lenore Banks, Will Mahoney, Nelle Stokes, Brett Ardoin, Daniel Dupont; **c**, Roger Deakins; **m**, Mason Daring; **ed**, Sayles; **prod d**, Dan Bishop, Dianna Freas.

The Passion of Anna ★★★ 1970; Sweden; 101m; Cinematograph AB/UA; Color; Drama; Children: Unacceptable (MPAA: R); **DVD**; **VHS**. Bergman again offers a cryptic and enigmatic film with this strange drama that begins when Ullmann, a crippled woman, visits a lonely farmhouse on an island, asking its only resident, Sydow, if she can use his phone. An ex-convict and dedicated hermit, Sydow allows her the use of his phone, but when she leaves, she forgets her purse. Sydow examines its contents to find her name and address, along with an old letter from Ullmann's husband that details their failing marriage. When returning the purse to Ullmann, Sydow meets her friends Andersson and Josephson. Ullmann and Sydow develop a relationship where she moves into Sydow's old farmhouse, but everything begins to go wrong when they hear reports about a maniacal murderer who is ravaging the countryside. Ullmann momentarily thinks Sydow might be that homicidal lunatic, especially after he explodes in a fit of anger and menaces her with an ax. The real killer, however, sets Sydow's barn on fire and Ullmann saves Sydow from burning to death, escaping the place as she drives wildly down a road and where Sydow now accuses her of trying to kill him as she may have killed her husband and son in an accident years earlier, one that left her a cripple. Ullmann calms down and brings the car to a halt and Sydow gets out, acrimony and ill-will overwhelming whatever good feelings both have had for one another. Ullmann realizes this and severs her life with Sydow by simply driving away, which ends this bizarre story. Although many claim this film to be a Bergman masterpiece, it is far from it, although it is certainly worthy of viewing, given the intense and arresting performances rendered by Ullmann and Sydow. The prosaic storyline allows little character development and where the main characters are rather one dimensional. Beautifully photographed, this film nevertheless is a clinical exercise by Bergman where he wields his director's knife and scalpel to cleverly establish suspicion and apprehension between two persons, who remain strangers to each other and within whom there is no empathy or love. (In Swedish; English subtitles.) **p**, Lars-Owe Carlberg; **d&w**, Ingmar Bergman; **cast**, Liv Ullmann, Max von Sydow, Bibi Andersson, Erland Josephson, Erik Hell, Sigge Furst, Seva Holst, Annika Kronberg, Hjordis Pettersson; **c**, Sven Nykvist (Eastmancolor); **ed**, Siv Lundgren; **prod d**, P. A. Lundgren; **spec eff**, Ulf Nordholm.

The Passion of Joan of Arc ★★★★★ 1929 (silent); France; 110m/10 reels; Société Generale des Films/M. J. Gourland; B/W; Biographical Drama; Children: Unacceptable; **DVD**. This powerful biopic of Joan of Arc (c.1412-1431) concentrates on the nineteen-year-old heroine's trial for heresy after she was turned over to the British and brought before a tribunal of clergymen. Played by Falconetti (in one of the most mesmerizing performances ever put on celluloid), she faces her accusers bravely, and they, in turn, denounce her for wearing men's clothing and for heresy in her claims of having had conversations with several saints, especially St. Michael. Falconetti tells her judges that "a great victory" will eventually free her from prison. In response, she is ordered to renounce her visions and is then shown the many savage instruments of torture that may be used to break her spirit and force a confession. (Director Dreyer visually dwells upon these horrendous-looking devices, each one of these menacing tools providing visual apprehension and anxiety.) Falconetti faints when seeing these horrible torture tools and is removed to her cell where she remains delirious, only to awaken with a fever and weakened after physicians have bled her (as was the archaic medical practice of the day when treating fevers). Begging that she be allowed to make confession with a priest (as Joan repeatedly requested throughout her trial), she is told that if she signs a confession, she will be rewarded by seeing the Eucharist, which represents the body and blood of Jesus Christ. Exhausted and psychologically tormented by her judges, Falconetti defies her accusers once again, refusing to confess and renounce her visions. She is placed upon a litter and carried to a churchyard where she is shown the funeral pyre that awaits her and the image of her impending execution by burning causes her to relent and she is returned to her cell where her head is shaven. Falconetti focuses upon a pile of straw, which she envisions as the Crown of Thorns that was placed upon Jesus' head before His crucifixion, and this vision gives her strength. She reaffirms her belief in her visions and refuses to confess, bravely demanding that she now be taken to the place of execution. Her demand is met with terrible agreement as she is then removed to a stake in a town square and tied to it while wood is piled about her and then set afire. The death scenes enacted by Falconetti under the intense direction of Dreyer, who focuses upon her expressive face in severe close-ups, is both excruciating and almost unbearable to view. As she slowly succumbs within the rising flames, the crowd that earlier and eagerly sought her death now recoils in horror and shocking revelation that a saintly woman is being burned to death and its members widely begin to shout and condemn the executioners. (A British soldier among the guards at Joan's execution at Rouen on May 30, 1431, hurriedly made a cross for her from two wooden sticks and gave this to her to hold shortly before her execution. The chief executioner, Geoffrey Therage, stated that he "greatly feared to be damned" for putting Joan to death.) In death, however, Falconetti's claim that she would be freed from prison by a great victory is symbolized by that death where her spirit is freed and her martyrdom forever established. Dreyer does a magnificent job of profiling Falconetti with astounding close-ups made from astonishing angles, his camera always subjective and invariably focusing upon the actress while enmeshing her and the story line with a series of equally impressive montages that capture the dark mood of the court and its Goya-like faces. Falconetti's performance is thought to be the greatest ever put on film, and anyone seeing this startling masterpiece will most likely agree. What is even more amazing is that this is the only film where she appeared in a featured role, having appeared in only a few early silent productions. Song: "Voices of Light" (from the score in the 1995 version; Richard Einhorn). *Author's Note*: Dreyer, a Danish director, was hired by France's Société Generale des Films to produce a film about a great French historical character and he chose Joan of Arc, who had been canonized a saint in 1920 by the Vatican. "I wanted to interpret a hymn to the triumph of the soul over life," Dreyer later explained when selecting Joan for his subject. He hired Joseph Delteil to write the screenplay as Delteil had written an enormously popular novel about the great French heroine, *Vie de Jeanne d'Arc*. After Dreyer looked over Delteil's script, he immediately abandoned almost all of its scenes and used as a basis for his own script the 1921 book written by Pierre Champion that recorded the actual trial of Joan of Arc. He at first thought to hire American actress Lillian Gish for the lead role, but he saw Falconetti performing as a boulevard comedienne and felt she possessed all the expressive qualities that would embody his vision of Joan

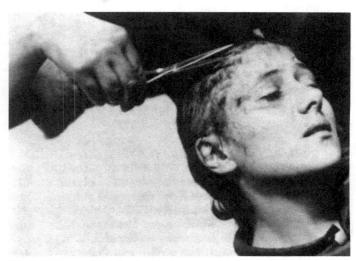

Maria Falconetti having her hair cropped in *The Passion of Joan of Arc*, 1929.

of Arc, even though Falconetti was thirty-six years old when playing the nineteen-year-old Joan. However, no actress since Falconetti has been able to enact Joan to the perfection of Falconetti's truly immortal performance. Ingrid Bergman played the part in **Joan of Arc**, 1948, and she did a wonderful job in that role, but she admitted to this author that "no one on this earth can match Maria Falconetti's performance of Joan. I know that and so does every actress since her day." That performance so unnerved British authorities that they banned this film from distribution in England in its initial release, believing it was adamantly anti-British, but the film became a classic overnight and it was widely shown in England from 1930 onward. Joan of Arc has been enacted by many distinguished actresses in other films, notably **Daughters of Destiny**, 1954 (Michele Morgan); **Joan of Arc**, 1935 (Angela Sollaker); **Joan of Arc**, 1948 (Ingrid Bergman); **Joan of Arc**, 1952 (made for TV; Sarah Churchill); **Joan the Woman**, 1916 (Geraldine Farrar); **The Messenger: The Story of Joan of Arc**, 1999 (Milla Jovovich); **The Miracle of the Bells**, 1948 (Alida Valli, playing an actress essaying Joan of Arc in a film); **Joan of Arc**, 1999 (made for TV; Leelee Sobieski); **Saint Joan**, 1957 (Jean Seberg); **Saint Joan the Maid**, 1929 (Simone Genevois); **The Story of Mankind**, 1957 (Hedy Lamarr); and **The Trial of Joan of Arc**, 1965 (Florence Carrez). **d&w**, Carl Theodor Dreyer (screenplay credit also was given to Joseph Delteil but his material was not used); **cast**, Maria (Melle) Falconetti, Eugene Silvain, André Berley, Maurice Schutz, Antonin Artaud, Michel Simon, Jean d'Yd, Louis Ravet, André Lurville, Jacques Arnna; **c**, Rudolph Maté; **m**, Victor Alix, Leo Pouget; **ed**, Dreyer; **set d**, Jean Hugo, Hermann Warm.

The Passionate Thief ★★★ 1963; U.S.; 106m; Titanus/Embassy Pictures Corp.; B/W; Comedy; Children: Unacceptable **VHS**. Offbeat comedy with a lot of strange twists begins with Magnani as a struggling actress, who is alone in Rome and feeling insecure on New Year's Eve. A friend invites her to a party and she meets an old acting acquaintance, Toto, who joins a professional pickpocket, Gazzara, in stealing from people celebrating in the city. They have some zany adventures at several parties and restaurants until Gazzara is arrested after getting drunk and toppling into the Trevi Fountain. Magnani falls for Gazzara, but she is unaware of his thievery. He steals a necklace from a Madonna statue and she is blamed for it. She serves a short prison sentence and Toto is waiting for her when she is released. Songs: "Una zebra a pois" (Lelio Luttazzi), "Tintarella di Luna" (De Filippi, Franco Migliacci).This comedy will delight most viewers, but excessive drinking and mature subject matter prohibit viewing by children. (In Italian; English subtitles.) **p**, Silvio Clementelli; **d**, Mario Monicelli; **cast**, Anna Magnani, Toto, Ben Gazzara, Fred Clark, Edy Vessel, Gina Rovere, Toni Ucci, Kurt Polter, Mac Ronay, Alberto De Amicis, Gianni Bonagura, Rik Van Nutter; **w**,

Stanley Holloway in *Passport to Pimlico*, 1949.

Suso Cecchi D'Amico, Agenore Incrocci, Furio Scarpelli, Monicelli (based on the stories "Ladri in chiesa" and "Risate di Gioia" by Alberto Moravia); **c**, Leonida Barboni; **m**, Lelio Luttazzi; **ed**, Adriana Novelli; **prod d**, Piero Gherardi, Giuseppe Ranieri.

Passport to Pimlico ★★★★ 1949; U.K.; 84m; J. Arthur Rank/Ealing Studios/Eagle-Lion; B/W; Comedy; Children: Acceptable; **DVD**; **VHS**. Hilarious outing that takes the absurd to the ridiculous and back again with some of the finest comedic talents in England appearing in this thoroughly entertaining romp. After some children roll an old tractor tire down a hill in Miramont Gardens of the Pimlico district of London, it rolls into a hole and sets off a bomb left over from World War II. The explosion opens wide an old cellar that yields a treasure trove of jewels, artwork and coins, as well as an old parchment. Professor Rutherford examines the ancient document and states that it is a genuine edict from King Edward IV, ceding the property and surrounding area to Charles VII, the last duke of Burgundy, meaning that this district no longer belongs to England and all of its present inhabitants are foreigners. Burgundian law demands that the duke or his living heir form a council to negotiate with the British government. A desperate search for that living heir produces Dupuis, who proves that he is the last surviving relative of the duke's, and he, in turn, establishes that council with conniving shopkeeper Holloway as its head. The council decrees that it is not governed or restricted by post-war regulations, including the present rationing and the area is soon inundated with confidence artists, entrepreneurs and outright crooks, as well as mobs of eager shoppers wanting to buy all the goods they had been earlier denied. To stem the tide of these legal law-breakers, the British government sets up barriers around the entire district and shoppers have a difficult time trying to re-enter their own country. When a female shopper complains that she is being restricted from returning to her London home, a bobby replies: "Don't blame me, lady, if you choose to go abroad to do your shopping!" The Burgundians retaliate by stopping all London transit, buses and subway trains that enter the area, demanding that residents declare their possessions and/or pay a tax, and tying up the city's transportation system and causing an irate British government to cease all negotiations. The district is cut off from all other districts and its residents are encouraged to migrate to legitimate areas of London. The "Burgundians" send their children from the area for safety (as Londoners did during the Blitz during WWII), but the adults stay stubbornly in place, even though their electricity, food and water is completely shut off. They state that they have enough gin and chips to keep them going. They raid a hydrant outside their border and pump fresh water into their area, but that causes a flood in their storage area that spoils all of their hoarded food. Sympathetic Londoners, however, continue to aid the beleaguered

Burgundians by tossing food parcels over the barriers much the same way West Berliners threw food supplies to East Berliners over the Berlin Wall during that earlier crisis. Even milk and live pigs are flown into the area and dropped to the Burgundians from helicopters. The British negotiators, Radford and Wayne, are widely censored and criticized for their draconian measures, but a solution is found when local banker Huntley proposes that Burgundy make a generous loan to England in the form of the treasure found with the old regal document and that England annex Burgundy back into its fold, which is done with alacrity just as a torrential rainstorm soaks the entire city, including Pimlico. The acting, direction and script for this outlandish but thoroughly entertaining comedy get top marks, and the production values are high. Songs: "I Don't Want to Set the World on Fire" (Eddie Seiler, Sol Marcus, Eddie Durham, Bennie Benjamin), "Music from the Movies" (Louis Levy), "The Sun Is Shining" (Charles Hawtrey), "Knees Up Mother Brown" (Harris Weston, Bert Lee), "Mulberry" (Kenneth Leslie-Smith), "Explosion," "Chaos" (Charles Williams). *Author's Note*: The story for this film was inspired by an event that took place not in England but in Canada and where the maternity ward of the Ottawa Civic Hospital was officially declared by the Canadian government to be extraterritorial for a certain period in order that Princess Margaret of the Netherlands, who was born there at that time, and whose government was in exile, would not lose her right to the throne. Ironically, the film was not shot on location in Pimlico, but in London's Lambeth district. Some of the story elements for this tale were applied to the story line for **The Mouse That Roared**, 1959, another British comedy providing similar mayhem and mirth. **p**, Michael Balcon; **d**, Henry Cornelius; **cast**, Stanley Holloway, Hermione Baddeley, Margaret Rutherford, Paul Dupuis, Basil Radford, Naunton Wayne, Jane Hylton, Raymond Huntley, Betty Warren, Barbara Murray, Michael Craig; **w**, T.E.B. Clarke; **c**, Lionel Banes; **m**, Georges Auric; **ed**, Michael Truman; **art d**, Roy Oxley.

Pat and Mike ★★★★ 1952; U.S.; 95m; MGM; B/W; Comedy; Children: Acceptable; **DVD**; **VHS**. This delightful and consistently humorous outing sees another classic coupling of Hepburn and Tracy (their seventh and final film together for MGM). Hepburn is a physical education instructor at a small college in California. She is also a whiz at any sport, performing excellently until visited at those events by Ching, a professor who is in love with her, but whose presence of authority somehow inhibits and compels Hepburn to perform poorly. After entering an amateur golf tournament, Hepburn is approached by Tracy, a brusque but clever sports promoter, who thinks Hepburn has great athletic potential, and by managing her sports career he will improve his finances. To assure that he makes money on the tournament, Tracy injudiciously offers Hepburn a bribe to perform badly, but she indignantly refuses. She is nevertheless intrigued with his proposal that he represent her in the fields of golf and tennis after realizing that he is a knowledgeable sports manager—he is already managing heavyweight boxing contender Ray (who gives a terrific performance of a punch-drunk pug). She agrees to turn pro, and Tracy institutes rigorous training where he virtually controls Hepburn's life, his strict regimen causing the independent-minded Hepburn to rebel and where more than one confrontation ensues. Tracy's draconian training, however, pays off when Hepburn begins winning matches, but then Ching arrives to watch her play tennis star Gussie Moran. Hepburn becomes so discombobulated when seeing Ching in the stands that she loses control of her game, envisioning her opponent (in a very funny sequence) as having a tennis racket many times larger than her own and when she returns the ball to that opponent she imagines (and sees) the net purposely rising by itself to block her shots to favor Moran. She loses the match and when she is later seen in an innocent encounter with Tracy by Ching, she loses her fiancé, with Ching walking out on her, but it's all for the best in that Hepburn now realizes that the good-hearted Tracy is the man of her heart (as he was in real life). Hepburn further shows her affection through her physical prowess when she disables a couple of thugs, who are Tracy's silent partners and are trying to put the financial squeeze on him; Hepburn tosses these bozos (including Buchinski, who later became Charles Bronson) about like tennis balls. In the end, Tracy and Hepburn make a life together while planning to make her a star at the courts and links. Cukor's direction is superb, and he elicits outstanding performances from Tracy and Hepburn, the witty script from Kanin-Gordon is brilliantly awash with wit and humor (they received an Oscar nomination for their screenplay). *Author's Note*: The script writers actually based Hepburn's character on the spectacular sports career of the great female athlete Bab Didrikson Zaharias, a point not lost on the shrewd Cukor, who told this author that "the character was so close to Zaharias that the front office thought that she might sue the studio, but we got around that by asking Babe to appear in the movie as one of Kate's competitors on the golf links and she did." Hepburn said to this author that she thought "**Pat and Mike** was one of the best pictures Spence and I ever made together and we had so much fun doing it that it never seemed like work at all. Of course, we had wonderful George Cukor directing everything and he was always very careful to never let any loose strings trip us up." Tracy told this author that "I use a New York accent in that picture, half Brooklyn and half Lower East Side. I had one line where I am looking at Kate walking away from me and I say to a crony: 'Not much meat on her, but what there is is cherce.' I fractured that last word of 'choice' with a Brooklyn accent and George [Cukor] thought I had made a mistake and asked me to do the scene again and I said that word the same way and then he got my meaning and left it in. The only way to direct a director is by performing for them." Chuck Connors, who plays a police caption, was, like so many others in the film, a professional sports player (baseball), but here he plays a police captain in his film debut. **p**, Lawrence Weingarten; **d**, George Cukor; **cast**, Spencer Tracy, Katharine Hepburn, Aldo Ray, William Ching, Charles Buchinski (Charles Bronson), Phyllis Povah, Jim Backus, Chuck Connors, Mae Clarke, Frankie Darro, Carl "Alfalfa" Switzer, Gussie Moran, Babe Didrickson Zaharias, Don Budge, Alice Marble, Frank Parker, Helen Dettweiler, Tom Harmon; **w**, Ruth Gordon, Garson Kanin; **c**, William Daniels; **m**, David Raksin; **ed**, George Boemler; **art d**, Cedric Gibbons, Urie McCleary; **set d**, Hugh Hunt, Edwin B. Willis.

Pat Garrett and Billy the Kid ★★★ 1973; U.S.; 122m; MGM; Color; Biographical Drama/Western; Children: Unacceptable (MPAA: R); **DVD**; **VHS**. Rather than present the traditional story of Billy the Kid (1859-1881), played by Kristofferson, and his friendly nemesis, Pat Garrett (1850-1908), essayed by Coburn, this film takes a more subtle, introspective approach to that toying and dangerous relationship. Coburn is profiled as an outlaw getting on in years and who yearns for a more peaceful life. He accepts the role of lawman after he receives a substantial payment from cattle barons and railroad tycoons, who are represented by Robards, the shrewd governor of the New Mexico Territory, Lew Wallace (1827-1905). Coburn's only assignment is to capture and imprison Kristofferson, who has been plaguing the state by shooting down several persons in the bloody Lincoln County cattle war. This is a chore Coburn dislikes in that he and Kristofferson have been longstanding friends, but he nevertheless performs his duty, locating Kristofferson and telling him that he should leave the territory or that he will be forced to arrest him. Kristofferson exudes the arrogance and bloated confidence of youth and disregards Coburn's warning. Coburn then finds Kristofferson and arrests him, locking him up in the Lincoln County Jail. He is then told that he will most likely be railroaded in a quick trial that will take him to the gallows. Kristofferson, while going to an outhouse, steps from that privy with a gun in his hand (planted there by a friend) and shoots and kills deputies Armstrong and Clark, who have been guarding him, and he makes his escape (that spectacular escape occurred on April 28, 1881, about two weeks after Billy the Kid had been sentenced to death). Coburn, who was out of town when

Spencer Tracy and Katharine Hepburn in *Pat and Mike,* 1952.

Kristofferson escaped (as was Garrett), is now dedicated to recapturing his old friend, dead or alive. He hires Elam to help him hunt down the Kid, and then Robards hires another lawman, Beck, to aid Coburn, but whose job it is to monitor Coburn's hunt for Kristofferson, Robards believing that Coburn likes the Kid too much to bring him to justice. Elam locates Kristofferson at a small ranch and, after having dinner with him and the family, Kristofferson and Elam square off, but Elam is no match for fast gun Kristofferson and knows it, but he goes for his gun anyway and is killed. Coburn then kills Jones, one of Kristofferson's closest friends and, then doggedly pursues Kristofferson to Jones' ranch, arriving there with Beck and another lawman, Jaeckel, late at night. While looking through a bedroom window, Coburn sees Kristofferson making love to Coolidge, but the considerate lawman allows the Kid to finish his tryst. When Kristofferson hears a commotion outside, he steps forth into the moonlight with his gun strapped to his hip. Seeing Coburn, Kristofferson hesitates and Coburn draws first, firing and killing him. Coburn later stands in front of a mirror, not liking what he sees and blasts the mirror to pieces with his six-gun. Coburn rides away the next day as the local residents look sullenly after him. The erratic and unpredictable Peckinpah presents a grim and gritty western, and Coburn and Kristofferson are believably realistic in their roles and the hardscrabble Old West is portrayed at its scruffiest. Robards, Elam and others provide good supporting performances, and the production values are superior throughout this exciting tale. This was the film debut of singer Bob Dylan, but his role is specious and unnecessary as a printer who accompanies Kristofferson on his nomadic journey to an early death. *Author's Note*: The film was shot on location at Durango, Mexico, a favored Hollywood shooting locale. Kristofferson met and fell in love with Coolidge during this production and they were married in August 1973, the same month this film was released (that marriage ending eight years later in 1980). Peckinpah played fast and loose with the facts surrounding Billy the Kid, claiming that this production was "the best film I ever made." He had, however, inserted many self-indulgent if not whimsical scenes that were later cut from the film by a bevy of film editors, fifteen minutes or more slashed from the film, including a prologue and epilogue, the latter showing how Coburn's character, Garrett, was killed many years later, as if to present retribution for Garrett's slaying of his old friend. When Peckinpah saw the deep cuts in his film, he angrily demanded that his name be removed from the credits, but that credit nevertheless stubbornly remained in place. Robards told this author that director Peckinpah "had a lot of ideas that might improve the picture. Some did and others were just crazy notions that had nothing to do with the story line or the characters. He was one of those advocates of improvising as you went along, but this was not really a fictional tale and we all kept reminding him that he was supposed to be showing real-life

Subir Bannerjee in *Pather Panchali*, 1955.

characters from actual history. I think he saw Billy the Kid as his alter ego and Pat Garrett as MGM's front office, the sheriff coming to suppress his creativity and clamp him in a jail cell where his ideas could not be put into practice. I won't argue about his talent, but Sam is not a traditional director like John Sturges, and his disciplines are much different than most other directors I have known." Robards had appeared three years earlier in Peckinpah's offbeat western, **The Ballad of Cable Hogue**, 1970, and had played gunman Doc Holliday in a Wyatt Earp western, **Hour of the Gun**, 1967, which was directed by Sturges. Billy the Kid has been profiled by many actors and in many films, including: **Billy the Kid**, 1925 (Franklyn Farnum); **Billy the Kid**, 1930 (Johnny Mack Brown); **Billy the Kid**, 1941 (Robert Taylor); **Billy the Kid**, 1964 (Jack Taylor); **Billy the Kid**, 1989 (made for TV; Val Kilmer); **Billy the Kid**, 2013 (Christopher Bowman); **Billy the Kid Returns**, 1938 (Roy Rogers); **Billy the Kid vs. Dracula**, 1966 (Chuck Courtney); **The Boy from Oklahoma**, 1954 (Tyler MacDuff); **Chisum**, 1970 (Geoffrey Deuel); **Dirty Little Billy**, 1972 (Michael J. Pollard); **A Girl Is a Gun**, 1971 (Jean-Pierre Leaud); **I Shot Billy the Kid**, 1950 (Don "Red" Barry); **I'll Kill Him and Return Alone**, 1967 (Peter Lee Lawrence); **The Kid from Texas**, 1950 (Audie Murphy); **The Law vs. Billy the Kid**, 1954 (Scott Brady); **The Left Handed Gun**, 1958 (Paul Newman); **The Outlaw**, 1943 (Jack Buetel); **The Outlaws Is Coming!**, 1965 (Johnny Ginger); **The Parson and the Outlaw**, 1957 (Anthony Dexter); **Pat Garrett and Billy the Kid**, 1973 (Kris Kristofferson); **Return of the Bad Men**, 1948 (Dean White); **Son of Billy the Kid**, 1949 (William Perrot); **Strange Lady in Town**, 1955 (Nick Adams); **The Tall Man**, 1960-1962 (TV series; Clu Gulager); Timemaster, 1995 (George Pilgrim); **Young Guns**, 1988 (Emilio Estevez); and **Young Guns II**, 1990 (Emilio Estevez). For more details on Billy the Kid and Pat Garrett, see my book, *Encyclopedia of Western Lawmen and Outlaws* (Paragon House, 1992; Billy the Kid: pages 38-45; Pat Garrett: pages 133-137). Graphic violence prohibits viewing by children. **p**, Gordon Carroll; **d**, Sam Peckinpah; **cast**, James Coburn, Kris Kristofferson, Richard Jaeckel, Katy Jurado, Chill Wills, Barry Sullivan, Jason Robards, Bob Dylan, R.G. Armstrong, Luke Askew, John Beck, Jack Elam, Emilio Fernandez, Paul Fix, Slim Pickens, Harry Dean Stanton, Elisha Cook, Jr., Gene Evans, Bruce Dern, Peckinpah; **w**, Rudy Wurlitzer; **c**, John Coquillon (Panavision; Metrocolor); **m**, Dylan; **ed**, Roger Spottiswoode, Garth Craven, Robert L. Wolfe, Richard Halsey, David Berlatsky, Tony De Zarraga; **art d**, Ted Haworth; **set d**, Ray Moyer; **spec eff**, A.J. Lohman.

A Patch of Blue ★★★ 1965; U.S.; 105m; MGM; B/W; Drama; Children: Unacceptable; **DVD**; **VHS**. This touching and sensitive film has Hartman accidentally blinded at age five by her prostitute mother, Win-

ters. Hartman spends the next thirteen years living with her in a small Los Angeles apartment they share with her grandfather, Ford. She meets and falls in love with a kindly office worker, Poitier, unaware that he is black. They meet in a park every afternoon and he teaches her how to survive in the city. Winters learns of their relationship and forbids Hartman from seeing him again because of his color. Hartman nevertheless continues seeing Poitier and he suggests she attend a school for the blind, which she does. They love each other, but he asks her to meet more men so she is certain about her feelings for him. She insists that she loves him and knows he is black, but it doesn't matter to her. He suggests that they wait a year, but it is evident that they will eventually marry. Winters gives an outstanding performance as the slatternly and bigoted mother, one that won her an Oscar as Best Supporting Actress, and the film catapulted the gifted Poitier into becoming a top star. Sexuality prohibits viewing by children. **p**, Pandro S. Berman; **d&w**, Guy Green (based on the novel *Be Ready with Bells and Drums* by Elizabeth Kata); **cast**, Sidney Poitier, Shelley Winters, Elizabeth Hartman, Wallace Ford, Ivan Dixon, Elisabeth Fraser, John Qualen, Kelly Flynn, Debi Storm, Renata Vanni, Saverio LoMedico; **c**, Robert Burks; **m**, Jerry Goldsmith; **ed**, Rita Roland; **art d**, George W. Davis, Urie McCleary; **set d**, Henry Grace, Charles S. Thompson; **spec eff**, Robert R. Hoag.

Pather Panchali ★★★ 1955; India; 122m; Government of West Bengal/Sony; B/W; Drama; Children: Unacceptable; **DVD**; **VHS**. This fascinating tale is set in rural Bengal, India, in the 1920s, where a boy named Apu (Subir Banerjee) lives with his poor parents in a dilapidated ancestral home in a village. His father, Kanu Banerjee, earns a meager living as a priest and dreams of becoming a successful poet and playwright, so he leaves for the city. Apu is left living with his mother, who also cares for his older sister, Dasgupta, who is a habitual thief, and an elderly aunt, Devi. The film is the first of a trilogy considered to be substantial domestic films that includes **Aparajito**, 1956, and **The World of Apu**, 1959, a saga following the lives of an indefatigable Indian family. Songs: Indian traditional songs played on the sitar by Ravi Shankar; "It's a Long Way to Tipperary" (Jack Judge, Harry Williams). Mature themes prohibit viewing by children. (In Bengali; English subtitles.) **p&d**, Satyajit Ray; **cast**, Kanu Bannerjee, Karuna Bannerjee, Subir Bannerjee, Uma Dasgupta, Chunibala Devi, Runki Banerjee, Reba Devi, Aparna Devi, Haren Banerjee, Tulsi Chakraborty; **w**, Bibhutibhushan Bandyopadhyay, Ray (based on the novel by Bandyopadhyay); **c**, Subrata Mitra; **m**, Ravi Shankar; **ed**, Dulal Dutta; **prod d&art d**, Bansi Chandragupta.

Pathfinder ★★★ 1989; Norway; 86m; Filmkameratene A/S/Carolco; Color; Adventure; Children: Unacceptable; **VHS**. This exciting and well-crafted film begins when a warlike people called the "tjuder" roam Lapland in northern Scandinavia in 1000 A.D. They brutally kill a family in a remote area, including the parents and their little daughter. Their teenage son, Mikkel Gaup, sees the slaughter, but manages to escape and reaches other Lapps, but they worry that he may have been followed, so they flee to the coast. Gaup remains alone to avenge his family's murder. Unfortunately, the barbarians get to him and force him to lead them to the others on the coast. Bravely, he manages to kill them before they can attack the other Lapps. Excessive violence prohibits viewing by children. **p**, John M. Jacobsen; **d&w**, Nils Gaup, **cast**, Mikkel Gaup, Ingvald Guttorm, Nils Utsi, Henrik H. Buljo, Helgi Skulason, Inger Utsi, Svein Scharffenberg, Knut Walle, John Sigurd Kristensen, Sara Marit Gaup; **c**, Erling Thurmann-Andersen; **m**, Kjetil Bjerkestrand, Marius Muller, Nils-Aslak Valkeapaa; **ed**, Nils Pagh Andersen; **prod d**, Harald Egede-Nissen; **art d**, Per Mork; **spec eff**, Per Mork.

Paths of Glory ★★★★★ 1957; U.S.; 88m; Byna Productions/UA; B/W; War Drama; Children: Unacceptable; **DVD**; **VHS**. This masterpiece from pantheon director Kubrick is unarguably one of the greatest anti-war films ever made, ranking with such classics as **All Quiet on**

the Western Front, 1930; it presents in starkly shocking terms and images the senseless slaughter of troops in a near useless war of attrition to edify the egos and vanities of the high command. Douglas (his production company responsible for bringing this unforgettable film to the screen) gives one of his finest performances as the commander of a decimated regiment of the French army positioned along the western front in 1916. Douglas anticipates that his worn-out troops will be relieved and sent to the rear for recuperation, but the almost whimsical notions of the French high command, represented by shrewd general Menjou, have other plans for Douglas and his men. Menjou arrives at the headquarters of Macready, a general who commands the division in which Douglas' regiment serves, telling Macready that his division has been inactive too long and it must make a concerted attack within forty-eight hours against a strong German position called the Ant Hill. Upon taking that position, Menjou implies, Macready can certainly anticipate a promotion. Although Macready knows that the Ant Hill is all but impregnable, he agrees to make the attack, envisioning the attainment of higher rank. Pompous and self-centered, Macready then appears in the trenches occupied by Douglas' troops, his uniform immaculate, his boots polished to a high gloss, moving along the trench system (and the camera tracking him through this snakelike labyrinth, a technique that Kubrick would effectively and dynamically employ throughout this superlative action film). He briefly stops to exchange a few cursory words with the exhausted soldiers, superficially asking them questions about their conditions, but Macready's air of unconcern is evident in his every gesture. He stops before one soldier, Bell, who is shell shocked, and where Bell gives him a rambling, incoherent response. Macready slaps the soldier as if to bring him to his senses, but this only reduces Bell to a sobbing hulk and Macready orders Freed, a sergeant standing nearby, to have Bell immediately transferred from the regiment, calling him mentally incompetent. (The slapping scene would be repeated in the film **Patton**, 1970, based on a real WWII incident, which brought about the censor and dismissal of U.S. General George S. Patton Jr., but in this instance, Macready acts with impunity as did the generals of WWI, fearing no action from high commands that were traditionally and habitually autocratic in their conduct toward their troops on both sides of the conflict.) When Macready arrives at Douglas' dugout command post, he bluntly tells him that his regiment is to lead the attack against the Ant Hill. Knowing that the German bastion is impregnable, Douglas refuses, stating that such an attack will not only fail, but that most of his men will be uselessly slaughtered in such a suicidal assault. Macready states that the attack is the idea of the high command and that they expect reasonable losses but that if the attack is energetically made it will succeed and the Ant Hill will be taken. (The actual attack by the French army in 1916 was made against Fort Douaumont in the Verdun sector, a bloodbath of an attack that took tens of thousands of French casualties.) Knowing how protective Douglas is of his men, Macready tells him that unless he agrees to lead the attack he will be relieved of his command. Rather than allow some replacement commander to impersonally send his troops into battle, Douglas reluctantly agrees, telling Macready that he will "take the Ant Hill." That night, Douglas orders Morris, a cowardly and alcoholic lieutenant, to take a patrol into no man's land to reconnoiter the area the regiment will have to traverse in the impending attack. Morris selects two soldiers to accompany him, Meeker, a man he has disliked from civilian life, and Dibbs. The three men then slip over the top of their trench and into the darkness of the bombed-out area. When they advance a short distance, Morris sends Dibbs ahead to scout the terrain, but when he does not soon return, Morris becomes unduly anxious, telling Meeker that Dibbs has probably been killed and that they should return to their lines before they are killed. Meeker angrily accuses Morris of cowardice. When the Germans send up a flare that illuminates the ghastly looking lunar-like landscape, Morris throws a grenade at a nearby ruins, thinking it occupies Germans, and then flees toward his own lines. Meeker then goes in search of Dibbs and finds him dead in the ruins, his body steaming from the explosion of the

Kirk Douglas in *Paths of Glory*, 1957.

grenade Morris has thrown and which has killed his own man. Morris is then shown sitting in his dugout where he is writing out a false report of his patrol while heavily drinking. Meeker arrives to angrily accuse Morris of desertion and willfully killing one of his own soldiers, Dibbs, calling him a liquor-besotted animal. Morris first tries to placate Meeker, but when Meeker tells him that he will report him, Morris tells him that his word against that of an officer will count for nothing and it will be he, Meeker, not him, Morris, who will stand court martial for falsely accusing an officer of cowardice and desertion. Douglas than appears demanding Morris' report, and Morris tells him that his report about the patrol is not quite finished. Meeker thinks twice about reporting Morris' dereliction of duty and his irresponsible killing of Dibbs and he leaves without reporting Morris's criminally negligent behavior to Douglas. Morris then blatantly lies to Douglas, telling him that Dibbs was killed by German machine-gun fire when he gave away their position by coughing. That night Douglas' men talk about the attack to be made the next day, one private, Turkel, an introspective and intellectual soldier, telling the troubled Meeker that what he fears most is not being shot, but being bayoneted as that would most probably be the most painful way to be wounded or to die. Meeker listens to Turkel with little interest as he is occupied by his own thoughts about the abortive patrol led by Morris. At dawn, Douglas appears walking solemnly through his trench line while reviewing his troops, these soldiers now readying themselves for the attack while clutching rifles with fixed bayonets, fearing doom and knowing that there will be, as Douglas has earlier stated, very little artillery coverage so as not to alert the enemy of the attack. At the appointed time, Douglas climbs to the top of a parapet and blows his whistle and his men clamber over the trench, hundreds of them streaming into the ravaged no-man's-land, working their way forward through craters, barbed wire and ruins from previous bombardments and attacks. The Germans at the Ant Hill open up with scything machine gun fire and mortars that mow down and blow up the French troops. Meanwhile, Macready views the attack from a rear position, witnessing the slaughter through a telescope. When he scans the French front lines, he discovers that one company, commanded by the cowardly Morris, has not left the trenches. Incensed, Macready orders his own artillery to shell the French position and kill his own troops, calling them cowards. Stein, the commander of the artillery, "respectfully" refuses to order the shelling of the French position, and Macready explodes, telling Stein that he is now facing a court martial. Douglas, by this time, has made his way partially into no man's land, but seeing his troops slaughtered and making little or no headway and realizing that some of his troops have not left the French front line, returns to that position to find Morris whining that the attack is a failure and it is "impossible" for his soldiers to even leave the trench. As Douglas' troops fall back into his trench system, he tries

Ralph Meeker and Kirk Douglas in *Paths of Glory,* 1957.

to rally them once more, shouting for them to resume the attack and blowing his whistle, but when he again tries to leave the trench, he is driven back into it by the weight of a falling French soldier. The assault has utterly failed, and Macready seeks vengeance not on the enemy but on his own troops for failing to achieve an objective he and others have known all along was doomed to failure. He shouts at his subordinate, Anderson, a toady-like officer: "If those little sweethearts won't face German bullets, they'll face French ones!" With that, he intends to charge scores of soldiers with cowardice and dereliction of duty and have them court martialed and shot by firing squads. He then meets at his luxurious chateau with Menjou and Douglas where he says that one hundred of Douglas' soldiers should be shot. Douglas points out that his men in the past have proven to be brave. Macready sneers, saying: "They are scum…the whole rotten regiment, a pack of sneaking, whining, tail-dragging curs." Douglas then belittles Macready's demand by mockingly stating: "Why not shoot the entire regiment?" He then offers himself as the culpable party, but Menjou waves away this sacrificial idea, stating that the high command does not want to slaughter its own troops and then asks Macready to state a reasonable number of soldiers to be charged with cowardice and Macready settles for three men, one from each company of Douglas' regiment, who are to be tried before a military tribunal. Douglas, who has been a criminal attorney in civilian life, insists on defending those three soldiers and he is grudgingly allowed to represent the three men selected for trial—Meeker, Turkel and Carey. Meeker has been selected by his company commander, Morris, so that Morris can eliminate a future witness who might testify about his own cowardice. Turkel has been selected because he is thought to be an argumentative radical, and the towering Carey has been chosen because he is dim-witted. Douglas then appears before a tribunal headed by Capell, who summarily refuses Douglas to bring forth witnesses to testify to the good comportment of the three accused men or any other evidence that would prove them simply scapegoats. The three soldiers are then asked to give verbal descriptions of their conduct during the battle. Turkel and Meeker explain that they advanced along with others in their units, but both were wounded and found their way back to the French lines. Carey explains that he advanced with his unit until everyone around him, except another private named Meyer, were killed and he and Meyer then returned to the French line. Douglas then asks Carey why he did not, after all of his fellow soldiers had been killed, continue to attack the Ant Hill. Carey gives him a crooked smile and says: "Just me and Meyer, sir? You've got to be kidding." Carey, who is not really the dimwitted soldier others think he to be, realizes why Douglas has asked such a ridiculous question and adds, directing his comments to the court: "I knew that me and Meyer should have taken the Ant Hill, but we came on back." When Douglas tries to point out

that Turkel had been awarded citations for his earlier heroic conduct in battle, Capell interrupts him, stating that Turkel "is not be tried for his former bravery but for his current cowardice." Anderson, who acts as a prosecutor, simply labels all three soldiers as cowards, saying that they are "a blot on the honor of the French nation" and then demands their conviction and death by firing squad. Douglas protests the fact that no stenographic record of the trial has been kept and that he has been prevented from providing any evidence that might exonerate his clients, adding that the kangaroo court is simply railroading his clients and that its actions constitute a "stain" and "a mockery of human justice." He pleads with the court to show mercy, but it summarily orders all three defendants to death by firing squad. A sumptuous last meal is brought to the three men as they are held in a stable converted into a prison area, but Carey refuses to eat any of the food, believing it might be poisoned. "First they poison you and then they shoot you?" asks the cynical Turkel. Meeker and Turkel discuss the possibility of escape, but Carey tells them that guards are everywhere and it is impossible. Meeker sees a cockroach crawling near him and says that it will be alive after he is dead and will have more contact with his family than he will. Carey leans forward and crushes the cockroach, saying grimly: "Now you have the edge on him." A priest, played by Emile Meyer, then enters the area, asking the three condemned men if they want to make confessions and receive absolution. Meeker asks Meyer to receive his confession, but before Meeker can begin, Turkel, now beside himself, mocks the priest, calling Meyer sanctimonious and then strikes him when Meyer tries to console him. Meeker shoves Turkel away from Meyer, telling him to calm down, but when Turkel attempts to hit Meyer again, Meeker hits him with a powerful blow that sends Turkel toppling and where he strikes his head against a concrete pillar and is unconscious. Freed, the tough sergeant who is in charge of the firing squad then appears with a doctor, who determines that Turkel has received a skull fracture and he gives Turkel an injection, stating that he will most likely remain unconscious throughout his own execution and that Freed is to strap the comatose Turkel to a stretcher and is told to squeeze Turkel's cheeks before he is shot so that he will appear to be alive when killed. Carey then kneels to give his confession to Meyer, but he is now gripped by fear and is racked with uncontrollable sobbing. Douglas has not given up on the three condemned men. On the night before the execution, he goes to Menjou's lavish headquarters, a palatial estate where Menjou is hosting a fete and he interrupts Menjou by asking for a private audience. When the two are alone together, Douglas begs Menjou to interfere with the execution. The coldhearted Menjou replies: "Troops crave discipline and one way to maintain discipline is to shoot a man every now and then." After Menjou refuses to interfere in the execution, Douglas, who has learned that Macready has ordered French artillery to fire on his own troops during the attack on the Ant Hill, presents that information in the form of sworn statements from many French officers to Menjou, along with an affidavit from Stein, the artillery commander, who had refused to obey Macready's order and is himself awaiting court martial. Menjou ignores Douglas' attempt to pressure him into granting a reprieve to the three soldiers and returns to his party, but is sure to take the documents along that incriminate Macready. Douglas now realizes that the situation is hopeless. The following morning, he is present, as is Macready and Menjou where French troops are in formation to witness the executions. Meeker, Turkel and Carey are then marched past the ranks toward three waiting wooden posts, escorted by Freed and his firing squad; Meyer walks with the sob-racked Carey, attempting to console him. The three men are tied to the posts and then Morris, who has been forced to command the firing squad by Douglas and who knows him to be an utter coward, steps forward to offer each man a blindfold. His gesture is useless with the still unconscious Turkel, who is trapped to a stretcher which rests perpendicular to a post and where Freed squeezes his cheeks to bring a bit of color to them as earlier instructed. Carey accepts a blindfold from Morris and sobs as it is affixed over his eyes. Morris then approaches

Meeker, who refuses the blindfold and Morris, knowing how he has deeply wronged this man, says in a low but unconvincing voice: "I am sorry." All three men are then shot to death by the firing squad, and Anderson performs the unpleasant chore of administering the coup de grace by firing single bullets into the men still alive. Later that morning, Menjou and Macready are having breakfast and where Macready states: "The men died wonderfully." Douglas arrives and Macready repeats the same praise for the executed soldiers to Douglas. Menjou then tells Macready that Douglas, who has appeared at Menjou's orders, has brought charges against Macready for ordering French artillery to shell the positions of his own men. Macready explodes, accusing Douglas of being disloyal (he had earlier promised Douglas that he would "break him" of his rank just before the tribunal sat in judgment of the three soldiers). Menjou, however, endorses Douglas' charges, saying that Macready will have to stand up to such charges in a court of inquiry. Macready seethes with anger, telling Menjou: "So that's it! You're making me the goat of the whole affair." He then accuses Menjou of "stabbing" him in the back and storms from the room. The manipulative and always artful Menjou then offers Douglas Macready's job, one where he will be promoted to the rank of general, a promotion, Menjou states, "you have so carefully planned for." Douglas, incensed, replies: "Sir, would you like me to suggest what you can do with that promotion?" The offended Menjou immediately orders Douglas to apologize for such an insult or be placed under arrest. Douglas says: "I apologize for not revealing my true feelings. I apologize for not being entirely honest with you sooner—that you are a degenerate, sadistic old man and you can go to hell before I apologize to you now or ever again!" Ever the politician, Menjou wryly smiles and, in an act of diplomatic conciliation, states: "Colonel Dax, you're a disappointment to me. You've spoiled the keenness of your mind by wallowing in sentimentality. You really did want to save those men and you were not angling for Mireau's [Macready's] command. You're an idealist and I pity you as I would the village idiot. We're fighting a war, Dax, a war we've got to win. Those men didn't fight and they were shot. You brought charges against General Mireau and I insisted that he answer them. Wherein have I done wrong?" Douglas can only reply: "Because you don't know the answer to that question, I pity you." He leaves and returns to his regiment to find his troops in a large hall, solemnly contemplating their next battle. Douglas arrives outside the hall and tells Freed to allow his troops some brief relaxation before ordering them once more into the front line trenches. Inside the hall, Hausner, the proprietor, brings forth a young and innocent German girl, Christian, to sing for the troops. She begins hesitantly as the French soldiers hoot and whistle at her, knowing she represents the nationality of the enemy. As she bravely sings "Soldier Boy" in German, the mood of the soldiers softens and a great wave of emotion sweeps throughout their ranks as they begin to empathetically join with the girl in singing this plaintive song, some smiling appreciatively, some weeping for the common plight of all soldiers in all nations in this terrible war, one of the most heart-rendering and conscience-exorcising scenes ever put on film. Douglas listens to his men humming and singing with Christian, realizing that his men still cling to human decency and genuine love, despite the dehumanizing rigors that have been imposed upon them, and then walks away and into his headquarters to end this startling and uniquely fascinating war drama. Kubrick wastes not a second in this masterpiece film, carefully presenting its story with inventive camera angles and using all of the action techniques available to his lensing—dolly and tracking shots, boom and crane shots and where he exacts from Douglas, Macready, Menjou, Meeker, Morris, Turkel, Carey, Meyer and all of the other cast members outstanding performances in characterizations that are separately and distinctively memorable. Kubrick mixes the heroism and dedication of Douglas and his troops with counterbalancing portraits of utter cowardice and the insidious nature of high command generals, who almost whimsically squander the lives of the men for whom they are militarily and morally responsible (a living document and indictment of the actual commanders in the war

Kirk Douglas, George Macready and Richard Anderson in *Paths of Glory,* **1957.**

on both sides of the conflict). The futility of war and its organizers and managers are incisively and revealingly exposed and more effectively than what had ever been achieved in the history of film. Little music is employed, only the stirring French anthem, "La Marseillaise" at the beginning and "Soldier Boy" at the end, both presented in marital mode. Songs: "La Marseillaise" (1792; Claude Joseph Rouget de Lisle); "Kunstlerleben (Artist's Life) Op. 316 (1867; Johann Strauss), "Der Treue Husar (Soldier Boy)" (German folk song). *Author's Note*: Douglas had long been interested in filming the Humphrey Cobb novel, which had been published in 1934 and had savagely indicted the French high command for its wanton slaughter of its own troops, particularly at the 1916 Battle of Verdun where tens of thousands of French soldiers were killed in an effort to take one dilapidated fort, which had no real military objective and where the author based his story on an actual incident of a military tribunal railroading soldiers to execution. Cobb's novel, because of its attack on the French high command, was all but banned in France, and he was not welcomed as a visitor in that country then or thereafter. Douglas rightly viewed the story as a powerful indictment against war and decided to fund the production himself (at a cost of about $900,000), hiring a then relatively unknown director, Kubrick (both would form a deep friendship and would go on to make the epic **Spartacus**, 1960, together). Kubrick admitted to this author that "yes, of course I used a lot of the techniques that [Lewis] Milestone used in **All Quiet on the Western Front** [1930], and even some of the action shots that [Howard] Hawks got into **Sergeant York** [1941]. I would have been a fool to ignore them since they had captured the images of the war better than any others." When talking with Milestone about this Kubrick film, that director told this author that "Kubrick indirectly flattered me no end. After seeing **Paths of Glory**, I realized that he used most of my techniques such as my tracking shots when he was shooting the battle scenes in no man's land, and where a truck shot passes before the front rank of men as they attack and they are shot down by machine-gun fire as they scramble toward the camera and that duplicates several of my own scenes in **All Quiet on the Western Front**. Kubrick also used my technique of setting off explosive charges to make them appear like mortar explosions in a stepping sequence of explosions that rips through the ranks of the advancing French troops, just as I did, only I showed French and German troops being torn to pieces in that way." Hawks, like Milestone, admired Kubrick's work in **Paths of Glory**, telling this author that "he is a smart and savvy guy. He used all the tricks we all had in our bags. He has Douglas and Macready on separate occasions marching down the trenches to inspect their men just the way I showed the Doughboys in the trenches in **Sergeant York** [1941], in long tracking or truck shots. Why not? We all used whatever we could to make our pictures visually effective, especially in action scenes. I did the same thing in

Kirk Douglas, center, and Wayne Morris, right, in *Paths of Glory,* **1957.**

Sergeant York by using some of my techniques from another World War One picture I made called **The Road to Glory** [1936], and when we made that one, I used some techniques from a French picture about that war called **Wooden Crosses** [1932], as did Bill [William] Keighley when he made **The Fighting 69th** [1940], another World War One picture, and, in fact, I used some of Keighley's great action scenes from that picture by editing them into **Sergeant York**, which was produced by the same studio [Warner Brothers]. All of those panning and tracking or truck shots were invented and used by the old master, D. W. Griffith, when he made his own masterpiece about war, **The Birth of a Nation** [1915]. Griffith had his actors enacting Civil War soldiers attacking trenches and he put his camera on a small railroad track to move along with them as they run forward and also to frontally pan that action as they also run toward the camera so you see the fluid action of them running forward as well as panning them as they race toward the camera with the point of view of the opposing soldiers waiting to repel that attack. That genius translated his mind's eye right through the motion of his cameras. Any director, who does not study and copy the techniques of earlier films when making any picture, is not worthy of being a director. Kubrick did all that when he made **Paths of Glory** and he did it better than most. He deserves a big pat on the back." Kubrick, to better accommodate his bulky camera equipment in his tracking shots within trenches, had the trenches made six feet wide, instead of the four-feet-wide trenches traditionally constructed during WWI. "There were a lot of difficulties in making **Paths of Glory**," Kubrick told this author. "Then, again, most of my pictures are tough nuts to crack. Keeping the continuity and visual sense from one scene to the next in such involved story lines presents a lot of technical and creative problems. Also, I had difficulties with a few of the actors. Menjou, a veteran actor, resented me from the start because I was a new director to him, an upstart, I guess. He argued with me in almost every one of his scenes and I made him do a lot of those scenes over and over again until I got what I wanted. At one point, I asked him to do one scene that was one too many to his liking and he blew up, calling me every name he could think of that might make me explode. But I kept my mouth shut and my fists clenched and said nothing and let him blow off his artistic steam until he was all worn out with it. After he used up all his anger, I quietly and politely asked him to do the scene again and he did it without further complaint and got it the way I wanted it. Another actor in that picture, Timothy Carey, was a headache right from the beginning. I had used him to play a hired assassin in **The Killing** [1956], and, although he was a very effective menace on the screen, he was a bigger menace off the screen. The guy was erratic and played a lot of psychopaths and wackos and I think that all went to his head, and God knows what was always brewing in that weird mind of his. He stood more than six-feet-five-

inches, a hulking giant of a man and he used his size in an attempt to intimidate other actors in his scenes with them, especially actors who were much smaller, like Kirk [Douglas], even though no one could ever intimidate Kirk. That was Carey's way to try to awkwardly hog or steal a scene and it never worked with me. He was doing pretty good then, making about $1,000 a day for his work in **Paths of Glory**, but he wanted more scenes or attention, believing that he was eventually going to become a leading player—good luck with that and that gargoyle face of his—and to bring himself to the attention of the press while we were making the picture in Germany, Carey crudely faked his own kidnapping, a publicity stunt that backfired because our producer [James Harris] fired him when we got on to his self-promotion scheme and that set Carey back a bit in his career. This guy was always looking for a way to get his monster face into the movie magazines. He was once arrested by studio cops at Fox for climbing the studio fence while dressed in armor so that he could be considered for a part in **Prince Valiant** [1954]. To tell you the truth, Carey was terrific as the mentally disturbed soldier in **Paths of Glory**, but off the screen he was a much more disturbed actor." Meeker, who portrays one of the victimized soldiers, told this author that "I only had a few scenes with Tim [Carey] in **Paths of Glory**, but they were memorable. Before each scene, he would be mumbling or cursing under his breath, as if he was about to bash someone's head, and I thought he had a screw loose. I told him as a joke that, after he was shot on camera by the firing squad, and his final scenes were ended, he would be out of his misery in making the picture, but he did not smile. He only glared at me as he did everyone else and that glare was enough for you to never give that guy your home phone number." Shot on location in Bavaria, Germany, and near Munich, some of the palatial estates in that area served as the headquarters for the generals and one was employed for the tribunal judging the three soldiers. This film was all but banned in France, many of its top officials attempting to persuade United Artists, its distributor, to shelve the film. The production was not released in France until two decades later, in 1975. It was proscribed by the fascist-controlled government of Francisco Franco in Spain (for its anti-military stance), and Germany did not allow distribution of this film until two years after its release in order to placate angry high-positioned French militarists. It barely returned its initial investment of $900,000 in its initial box office release in the U.S., but it has since been accepted worldwide as a classic anti-war film. Christian, the attractive young girl who sings at the end of the film, married Kubrick following the completion of the film and remained his wife until his death in 1999. Ironically, Morris, who is superb as the cowardly French lieutenant, served in the U.S. Navy during WWII, flying an F6F Hellcat fighter plane from the USS *Essex* (CV-9) and where he shot down seven Japanese planes, becoming an ace, as well as helping to sink five enemy ships and for which he was awarded four Distinguished Flying Crosses and two Air Medals. **p**, James B. Harris; **d**, Stanley Kubrick; **cast**, Kirk Douglas, Ralph Meeker, Adolphe Menjou, George Macready, Wayne Morris, Richard Anderson, Joseph Turkel, Susanne Christian (Christiane Kubrick), Jerry Hausner, Timothy Carey, Bert Freed, Emile Meyer, Kem Dibbs, Fred Bell, John Stein, Harold Benedict; **w**, Kubrick, Calder Willingham, Jim Thompson (based on the novel by Humphrey Cobb); **c**, George Krause; **m**, Gerald Fried; **ed**, Eva Kroll; **art d**, Ludwig Reiber; **spec eff**, Erwin Lange.

Paths to Paradise ★★★ 1925 (silent); U.S.; 78m; Famous Players-Lasky/PAR; B/W; Comedy; Children: Acceptable; **DVD**. This light-hearted and well-made comedy sees Griffith as a confidence man who takes all the money Compson, a top crook, has fleeced from victims in San Francisco's Chinatown. They meet again at a millionaire's mansion where she is dressed as a maid and he as a detective, both of them there to steal a priceless necklace. They team up and steal it with no difficulty, but then police pursue them as they try to escape to Mexico. After a frantic chase, the thieves elude their pursuers, fall in love and marry, and decide to go straight, returning the necklace. Another version of this story, **Hold That Blonde**, was made in 1945. **d**, Clarence G. Badger; **cast**, Betty Compson, Raymond Griffith, Tom Santschi, Bert Woodruff, Fred Kelsey, Clem Beauchamp, Edgar Kennedy, Ellinor Vanderveer, Leo White; **w**, Keene Thompson (based on the play "Heart of a Thief" by Paul Armstrong); **c**, H. Kinley Martin.

The Patriot ★★★ 1916 (silent); U.S.; 50m; Kay-Bee Pictures/Triangle; B/W; Western; Children: Unacceptable. Hart, a veteran of the Spanish-American War (1898) returns home to find his mine was stolen by government swindlers. He goes to Washington to plead his case but is ignored. Returning home, he finds his little boy dead, killed by the swindlers. Renouncing his country, he joins a Mexican bandit, Laidlaw, who plans a raid on Hart's hometown. During the battle, Hart saves Stone, a boy the same age as his son. In seeing this boy, Hart comes to his senses and he helps the townspeople drive off the bandits. The film ends touchingly with Hart heading home with the boy and having regained his love of country. Unfortunately, the film is not available on any format. **p**, Thomas H. Ince; **d**, William S. Hart; **cast**, Hart, George Stone, Francis Carpenter, Joe Goodboy, Roy Laidlaw, Milton Ross, P. Dempsey Tabler, Charles K. French; **w**, Monte M. Katterjohn (based on his story); **c**, Joseph H. August; **art d**, Robert Brunton.

The Patriot ★★★★ 1928 (silent/part talkie); U.S.; 113m; PAR; B/W; Drama; Children: Unacceptable. The last days in the life of the mad Russian czar Paul I (1754-1801), son of Catherine the Great (1729-1796), are depicted in stunning detail by pantheon director Lubitsch. Jannings, who plays the mentally disturbed Paul, retreats to his palace for fear of assassination because of his lunacy and can only trust Stone, his longtime loyal friend, who plays Paul's most trusted adviser, Count Peter Ludwig von der Pahlen (1745-1826). Jannings displays that insanity in many startling scenes—throwing a puppy from a window, punching his mistress in the face, screaming about mythical enemies and issuing one draconian and impossible edict after another that will further oppress the downtrodden Russian people. Stone, however, thinks first of his country and enlists the aid of a palace guard, Cording, to carry out Jannings' assassination. This is not a difficult recruitment in that, earlier, Jannings has publicly humiliated Cording when inspecting his guards. He stops before Cording and, while examining the guard's uniform, sees that a button is missing. Jannings flies into a rage, poking a finger into Cording's face before he hooks his thumb into Cording's mouth (this personal degradation being what might be called the "Lubitsch Touch") and then proceeds to mercilessly whip the helpless and cowering guard. Jannings' mistress, Voronina, is enlisted in Stone's murderous cabal by the revenge-seeking Cording as she has been Cording's mistress up to this time. She is assigned to lure Jannings to her bed chambers where the murder is to take place, but, instead, she warns Jannings of the plot. Jannings goes to Stone, but Stone assures him that Voronina's warning is nothing more than an unsubstantiated rumor and that Jannings is perfectly safe behind the walls of his palace. That night Stone and Cording conspire again to kill Jannings. Cording fatally shoots Jannings, then, in revenge for having to sacrifice his mistress to the plot, fatally shoots Stone, who, while dying, admits that he has been a bad friend, but a good Russian patriot. Jannings gives a riveting and intense performance as a czar slowly going insane, one consumed by fear and doubt, those apprehensions physically recorded in every frame of this suspenseful film; Stone renders an equally impressive performance of great restraint as he struggles with his conscience in plotting to murder his closest friend. The film received Oscar nominations for Best Film, Best Director, Best Actor (Stone), and Best Art Direction (for Dreier's magnificent marble palace sets) and won an Oscar for Best Writing Achievement. Violence prohibits viewing by children. *Author's Note*: The original complete version of this film was lost and no known copies exist; this author viewed a truncated version of the film that was owned by Oscar winning film editor Gene Ruggiero, who privately screened that version for this author, stating: "To make some space in

Emil Jannings and Florence Vidor in *The Patriot*, 1928.

their storage area, Paramount's vault people made a mistake and tossed out the original prints of that picture, along with a lot of other classic films, thinking that a negative was held somewhere else." Ruggiero's edited copy of this film was one, he stated, that had been used by the studio's publicity department that had excised sequences from the film for publicity purposes. "After talking films came in," Ruggiero told this author, "nobody cared about the old silent films, like **The Patriot**, except maybe people like me, who wanted to study them and use their great techniques for new pictures, and they did not preserve a lot of the classics, which they later came to regret. So the likes of Lubitsch and Jannings and others went into the trash can. Hollywood was a wasteful town back then." **The Patriot** was made as a part talkie and Janning's thick German accent (which later doomed his career in talkies) was thought to be an encumbrance by the front office, so his voice was dubbed, but when Jannings objected to this, his own voice was restored to the partial soundtrack. The post-synchronized dialog that was edited into this film was done without Lubitsch's participation and Jannings utters only a few words, most notably his cries for help ("Pahlen! Pahlen!") before he is assassinated. After Jannings' Hollywood career collapsed, he returned to Germany and appeared in many historical films that endorsed the Nazi credos and were supervised by Adolf Hitler's minister of propaganda, Joseph Goebbels, who, in 1941, hailed Jannings as Germany's number one artist. Following Germany's surrender in 1945, Jannings (1884-1950) surrendered to American troops, showing his Academy Award statuette to GIs to prove his close association with America (or, at least, Hollywood). He was nevertheless detained and underwent a denazification process, never attempting to make a film comeback. He became an Austrian citizen in 1947, dying of liver cancer three years later. Harry Cording (1891-1954), a bulky British actor, specialized in heavies, invariably playing assassins and killers and easily made the transition from silent films to talkies, appearing as an assassin in **The Adventures of Robin Hood**, 1938, and going on to play villains in eight of the fourteen Sherlock Holmes films starring Basil Rathbone and Nigel Bruce. Paul I has also been profiled in two Russian films: **Assa**, 1987 (Dmitry Dolinin) and **Poor, Poor Pavel**, 2003 (Viktor Sukhorukov). Paul I was not, as shown in this film, shot to death. He was strangled to death by one of nine guards who entered his bed chamber on the night of March 11-12, 1801, at Pahlen's instructions. Paul cried out: "Don't kill me! I will abdicate!" His killer reportedly replied: "No sire, you will never abdicate. If we let you free, you will have us all killed and remain in power and Russia will be destroyed." For more details on the assassination of Paul I, see my two-volume work, *The Great Pictorial History of World Crime*, Volume I (History, Inc., 2004; page 12). **p&d**, Ernst Lubitsch; **cast**, Emil Jannings, Florence Vidor, Lewis Stone, Vera Voronina, Neil Hamilton, Harry Cording, Tullio

Logan Lerman, Beatrice Bush, Sky McCole Bartusiak, Mika Boorem, Trevor Morgan and Mel Gibson in *The Patriot*, 2000.

Carminati, Carmencita Johnson; **w**, Hans Kraly, Julian Johnson (based on the play "Der Patriot" by Alfred Neumann, stage adaptation by Ashley Dukes, and the story "Paul I" by Dimitri Merezhkovsky); **c**, Bert Glennon; **m**, Gerard Carbonara, Domenico Savino, Max Bergunker; **ed**, Lubitsch; **art d**, Hans Dreier.

The Patriot ★★★ 2000; Germany/U.S.; 165m; COL; Color; War Drama; Children: Unacceptable (MPAA: R); **BD**; **DVD**; **VHS**. Gibson gives a powerful and magnetic performance in this above-average drama centered on the American Revolutionary War, where he essays a character that is chiefly based upon the enigmatic American hero, Francis Marion (1732-1795), better known as the "Swamp Fox," albeit Gibson is nicknamed "The Ghost." Like Marion, he becomes famous for implementing guerrilla warfare in the South against the British (Marion was known as being one of the fathers of American guerrilla warfare, much the same way the fictional character Robin Hood initiated such military tactics in the days of Richard the Lionheart (1157-1199). Isaacs serves as his evil nemesis, playing a role rooted to the much despised Banastre Tarleton (1754-1833), a British cavalry officer, who reportedly gave no quarter to the enemy and was considered an inhuman butcher. A veteran of the French and Indian War (1754-1763), Gibson is a widower with seven children living comfortably at a successful plantation in South Carolina. When the American Revolution breaks out, Gibson is reluctant to join the rebels, having had enough bloodshed in the previous war. His oldest son, Ledger, however, joins the Continental Army and, some years later, after Charleston falls to the British, Ledger, who has become a dispatch rider, returns home wounded after participating in a nearby battle. Gibson takes in wounded soldiers from both sides of the battle, tending to their wounds when Isaacs appears with his dragoons. Isaacs orders all of the British wounded evacuated and then orders his subordinates to execute all the American wounded and Gibson's house burned to the ground, Gibson protesting against these cruel and murderous acts. Isaacs threatens him with death, along with that of his family, which Gibson cherishes most, and he stands by as the wounded Continentals are summarily shot and his son, Ledger, is placed in captivity. When Smith, Gibson's second-oldest boy, who is barely a teenager, attempts to free his older brother from British guards, Isaacs shoots and kills him, calling him a "stupid boy" before riding away. Before his mansion burns to the ground, Gibson, in a rage at the arrest of one son and the vicious murder of another, tells his oldest daughter to herd the rest of the family to a shelter in the fields and then races inside his burning home to retrieve his old weapons of war, guns and a tomahawk. Arming his next two oldest sons with muskets, he and they then go in pursuit of the British guards who are escorting Ledger, finding them in a wooded area and where they ambush the British soldiers,

killing most of them one by one with musket fire. Gibson then attacks the remaining British guards, killing each one of them with his tomahawk, the last so brutally slaughtered that his savagery shocks Ledger and the younger boys. A lone British soldier survives the ambush and he later tells a startled Isaacs that a single man, who appeared out of nowhere, was responsible for killing the British guards, calling him "a ghost." After leaving his children in the care of his widowed sister-in-law, Richardson, Gibson and Ledger join the troops under the command of Cooper, an old friend of Gibson's who fought with him in the French and Indian War, and who, along with the rest of the Continental army, has just suffered another ignominious defeat at the hands of British General Lord Charles Cornwallis (1738-1805), who is brilliantly played by Wilkinson. Because of his past experience, Gibson is made a colonel and ordered to recruit volunteers for a militia unit designed to harass and pin down British troops under Wilkinson while the regular Continental Army retreats and reorganizes. While Ledger recruits upstanding citizens for the militia from a nearby town when appearing at a church meeting, Gibson recruits a bevy of hardened woodsmen and cutthroats in a pub. Helping to train these recruits in military skills is French officer Karyo, who finds them difficult if not impossible soldiers. Karyo represents France's intention to aid the Americans, but all he can do is say that that aid will arrive sometime in the future. Gibson then leads the militia in many attacks on British convoys, capturing supplies and even the personal effects and two pet dogs belonging to Wilkinson. Gibson, reading some of Wilkinson's captured correspondence, states: "I have just been inside the mind of a genius." After ferries and bridges are burned and Wilkinson's supply routes and communication system is destroyed by Gibson's militia, Wilkinson upbraids Isaacs, telling him that these reprisals by the colonials is a result of his, Isaac's, brutal tactics. When Gibson outwits Wilkinson in getting several of his captured militia released, Wilkinson decides to fight fire with fire and reluctantly allows Isaacs to use whatever means necessary to destroy Gibson and his men, and Isaacs unleashes a storm of savage attacks against the local inhabitants supporting the militia, including burning down a church with all of its parishioners, including Brenner, who has recently married Ledger, along with her family, after the residents refuse to give Isaacs any information about Gibson and his militia. Meanwhile, Gibson has emotionally committed himself to Richardson, who has loved him for a long time. She continues to take care of his young children as he and Ledger and what is left of the militia continue their guerrilla warfare, but the militia is trapped in a ruse set by Isaacs and Isaacs personally kills Ledger, who dies in Gibson's arms. Gibson resolves to fight on and he and his militia join the regrouped Continental Army under the command of General Nathanael Greene (1742-1786), played by Stahl, and where this force meets Wilkinson's army. When it appears that the battle will be lost when the militia flees from its front-line position, the British troops race after them with bayoneted muskets, but when they chase the fleeing militia over a ridge, they find the militia under Gibson reorganized and waiting for them, as well as formations of regular troops of the Continental Army. These troops then unleash savage fusillades that devastate the British units. Wilkinson sees the battle lost and retreats, but Isaacs appears with his dragoons. They, too, are halted by the Continental forces, and Gibson and Isaacs come face to face in mortal combat, battling each other with sword and tomahawk. Gibson is wounded and Isaacs is about to behead him with his sword when Gibson lunges from a crouched position to drive a bayonet into Isaacs, killing his long-standing enemy. Following the battle and the end of the war, Gibson returns to his old burned-out plantation with his children and Richardson at his side, intending to begin a new life and where many of his former militia members arrive to help him rebuild that home. Emmerich directs this action-packed film with great skill, particularly the well-orchestrated battle scenes (full-scale recreations of the battles of Camden, South Carolina, on August 16, 1780, and Guilford Courthouse, North Carolina, on March 15, 1781), and Gibson, Ledger, Wilkinson, Isaacs, Richardaon, and the rest of the cast give standout performances. Songs:

"Boney" (traditional), "Leanin' on the Lawd Side" (traditional), "The British Grenadiers" (traditional). Excessive violence and bloodletting prohibits viewing by children. **p**, Gary Levinsohn, Dean Devlin, Mark Gordon, Peter Winther; **d**, Roland Emmerich; **cast**, Mel Gibson, Heath Ledger, Joely Richardson, Jason Isaacs, Chris Cooper, Tchéky Karyo, Rene Auberjonois, Lisa Brenner, Tom Wilkinson, Donal Logue, Adam Baldwin, Gregory Smith, Andy Stahl; **w**, Robert Rodat; **c**, Caleb Deschanel (Technicolor); **m**, John Williams; **ed**, David Brenner, Julie Monroe, Christopher Holmes; **prod d**, Kirk M. Petruccelli; **art d**, Barry Chusid; **set d**, Victor J. Zolfo; **spec eff**, Terry Chapman, David Hill, Jens Döldissen.

Patriot Games ★★★ 1992; U.S.; 117m; Mace Neufeld/PAR; Color; Crime Drama; Children: Unacceptable (MPAA: R); **BD**; **DVD**; **VHS**. In this above-average sequel to **The Hunt for Red October**, 1990, Jack Ryan (Ford) is on vacation in London when he foils an assassination attempt on Fox, a member of the Royal Family. Ford kills one of the assailants, Miller, while the man's brother, Bean, looks on. Bean then targets Ford and his family, but is killed in a skirmish with Ryan aboard a boat that then explodes. Good action and a taut story that sustains interest throughout. Songs: "Theme from Harry's Game," "The Washington Post March" (John Philip Sousa); "The Pride of Our Land" (The Blended Spirits). Extreme violence prohibits viewing by children. **p**, Mace Neufeld, Robert Rehme; **d**, Phillip Noyce; **cast**, Harrison Ford, Anne Archer, Patrick Bergin, Sean Bean, Thora Birch, James Fox, Samuel L. Jackson, Polly Walker, J.E. Freeman, James Earl Jones, Richard Harris, Alex Norton; **w**, W. Peter Iliff, Donald Stewart (based on the novel by Tom Clancy); **c**, Donald M. McAlpine; **m**, James Horner; **ed**, William Hoy, Neil Travis; **prod d**, Joseph Nemec III; **art d**, Joseph P. Lucky; **set d**, John M. Dwyer; **spec eff**, Paul Clancy, Dale L. Martin, Peter Fern, Michael Dawson.

Patterns ★★★★ 1956; U.S.; 83m; Jed Harris/Michael Meyerberg; UA; B/W; Drama; Children: Unacceptable; **DVD**; **VHS**. Few films have ever depicted such a devastating portrait of ruthlessness in business as does this superlative film, a story written by the brilliant Serling and offering bravura performances from Heflin, Sloane and Begley. Heflin is brought from a field office in Ohio to New York at the request (or orders) of Sloane, who heads a large conglomerate, not really knowing what his new and highly paid new position will be, which causes him to express his anxiety with his supportive wife, Straight. He briefly meets Sloane and is given a luxurious office in the executive suite next to that of Begley, who has been for years the second-highest executive in the firm, an outgoing and friendly man advancing in years and who dotes upon his son, Welsh, who is at college. At their first conference with Sloane, Heflin is startled to see Sloane belittle Begley, demeaning his plans for the firm and dismissing them as business techniques and tactics that are old-fashioned if not archaic and out-of-touch with modern times. Unnerved, Begley, following the meeting, tells Heflin that Sloane's bark is louder than his bite and he continues to find excuses for Sloane's insulting and abusive behavior as he goes out of his way to help Heflin adjust. Heflin busies himself with some new projects and is then shocked to learn that Sloane is grooming him to replace Begley, a man Heflin has come to like and respect as a decent and kind-hearted human being, everything that the cold-hearted Sloane is not. Sloane continues to heap insult after insult on Begley, thinking that such vicious treatment will bring about his resignation, but Begley clings to his job as the only reason for him to go on living even though Heflin compassionately urges him to quit and live out a peaceful life. Sloane's programmed system of abuse, however, finally takes its toll when Begley dies of a heart attack in his office when realizing that Sloane intends to force him to end his business career by making his life intolerable. His son, Welsh, appears to see his father, but Heflin shields the naïve youth and then confronts Sloane, telling him that he intended not to take the job he has offered, and that Sloane has all but caused Begley's death. Now that Begley is

Van Heflin and Elizabeth Wilson in *Patterns*, 1956.

gone, however, Heflin states that he will replace him, but only if Sloane understands that he, Heflin, will fight him tooth and nail on every issue and make of Sloane's life the kind of living hell he has created for Begley. Sloane, who has ruled the roost as a dictator, now realizes he has met his match in the tenacious Heflin and accepts the challenge, apprehensively stating: "Now it begins." Cook's direction is outstanding in moving this startling and tension-filled film along, and everyone in the cast proves to be fascinatingly believable in their roles. Though no one received any awards for this terrific drama, several Oscar nominations should have been made, particularly for Sloane and Begley, who give some of the finest portrayals of their illustrious careers. No score was presented with this production, but it is not missed for a second as the story and its characters command the viewer's focused attention throughout and create all the various moods and nuances through their riveting enactments. ***Author's Note***: This story began when Serling wrote an original script for the Kraft Television Theater, which was produced in 1947, with Sloane and Begley in the roles they play in this film and with Richard Kiley enacting the part Heflin plays in the film version. The TV production won for Serling his first of six Emmy Awards. Serling told this author that "I did not pull any punches in **Patterns**. I knew a corporate leader just like the character Everett [Sloane] so wonderfully and effectively plays. He was utterly ruthless and ran his company like any dictator running a banana republic. Anyone who got in his way he hounded and verbally abused until that executive quit. You can find savage people like that in any kind of business around the world and in **Patterns** he is a consummate composite character of such hideous monsters." Heflin told this author that "I thought that **Patterns** was one of the most demanding roles I ever played, only because I was up against such gifted actors as Everett [Sloane] and Ed [Begley]. They both ran me ragged in my scenes with them, never missing a cue or slowing a scene, two tigers pouncing with every line and movement. It was like being in a ring with two heavyweight champion fighters, both boxing my ears back." Begley was a dynamo actor of great versatility, who had appeared in more than 10,000 radio shows (and whose marvelous and distinctive bass voice demanded the ear's attention). Begley told this author that "there are only a few writers in this country like Rod Serling who can capture the deep and dark personalities of people who are otherwise stereotypes and make them come alive in a way no one ever envisioned. Rod did that with a broken down prizefighter in **Requiem for a Heavyweight** [1962] and where Anthony Quinn is anything but a punch-drunk fighter. He achieved such portraits in **Patterns**, one of the most emotionally draining but revealing portraits of modern-day business you will ever see, thanks to Everett's [Sloane's] unforgettable performance. To tell you the truth, no one can scare the hell out of everyone like Everett can. Did you ever see him in **The Enforcer** [1951] where

George C. Scott as General George Patton in *Patton*, 1970.

he plays a criminal mastermind who turns murder into a business? That performance is not unlike his portrayal of the boss in **Patterns**, who murders the human spirit of his employees, or when he plays an assassin in **Prince of Foxes** [1948] where he gouges out the eyes of helpless Tyrone Power to entertain some party guests. In **Patterns**, Everett is gouging out the eyes of human conscience, his own. Those performances will make your blood run cold, believe me, and only Everett could give such performances." A similar portrait of American corporations and businessmen is presented in the outstanding **Executive Suite**, 1954, starring William Holden and Fredric March and where March is a devious executive out to take over a company, but his tactics are much more circumspect and insidious than the flagrant tyranny Sloane exercises in this excellent film. This was character actor Duggan's first appearance in a film. **p**, Michael Myerberg; **d**, Fielder Cook; **cast**, Van Heflin, Everett Sloane, Ed Begley, Beatrice Straight, Elizabeth Wilson, Joanna Roos, Valerie Cossart, Eleni Kiamos, Ronnie Welsh, Shirley Standlee, Andrew Duggan, Jack Livesy, John Seymour, James Kelly; **w**, Rod Serling (based on his television play); **c**, Boris Kaufman; **ed**, Dave Kummins, Carl Lerner; **art d**, Richard Sylbert.

Patton ★★★★★ 1970; U.S.; 172m; FOX; Color; Biographical Drama/War Drama; Children: Unacceptable (MPAA: GP); **BD**; **DVD**; **VHS**. In a bravura and unforgettable virtuoso performance, Scott wholly captures the enigmatic spirit and magnetic personality in the dynamic character of General George S. Patton (1885-1945) in this masterpiece biopic and war film, a role for which he deservedly won an Oscar as Best Actor. The film opens with a monologue as Scott appears on a stage with a giant American flag in the background and where he declares his principles and ethics in fighting a war as if addressing an audience of new U.S. Army recruits. He is brusque, direct and uncompromising as was Patton himself, one of the greatest fighting generals of America or any other nation and one who largely contributed to the victory of Allied forces in Europe following the 1944 Normandy invasion. The film focuses upon Patton's WWII exploits, beginning with his arrival in North Africa. An American tank unit is shown devastated near Kasserine Pass in Tunisia in February 1943, a resounding American defeat inflicted by units of the Africa Corps, commanded by the brilliant German field marshal Erwin Rommel (1891-1944), played by Vogler. American general Omar Bradley (1893-1981), portrayed by Malden, appears while driving through the ruins of the battle, disgusted at what he sees, heaps of dead GIs upon which vultures are feeding, believing that a new and more resolute commander with better tactical and strategic talents is sorely needed and that man appears to take command of the area in the form of Scott, who makes Malden (as Patton did Bradley) his second-in-command. Scott quickly imposes severe dis-

cipline on his slack troops and makes of them crack fighting units that meet the Africa Corps again at the Battle of El Guettar in 1943 in the Tunisia Campaign, where Scott's tanks soundly defeat Rommel's armored units and where, when the tide of victory turns in his favor, he cries out with jubilance: "Rommel, you magnificent bastard, I read your book!" Scott is later disappointed to learn that Rommel, whom he deeply respects, did not lead his men at that battle and was in Germany at the time with an illness. One of his aides comforts him with the ego-soothing logic that since he has defeated Rommel's forces, he has also defeated Rommel. Scott quickly establishes a reputation as a fighting general, eager to attack at every point of the enemy's positions and, after winning more battles, becomes deeply respected and even feared by his German counterparts and where his competitive other half, British field marshal Bernard Montgomery (1887-1976), played by Bates, evidences some military jealousy if not resentment. When Scott commands American troops in Sicily, he doggedly attacks German positions, gaining more ground than Bates' forces, even though he has been ordered to support his British ally and not spearhead the Allied attack. Where Malden, as his second-in-command, adopts cautious tactics, Scott insists upon audacity, believing that relentlessly pursuing and attacking the enemy is the only way to win the war. He drives his men as one might flog a stubborn mule and, when finding subordinate commanders either too slow to execute his orders or energetically assault German positions, irrespective of the odds and casualties that might be suffered, he fires these commanders in the field and immediately promotes junior officers to their posts, saying that he will do the same thing to them if they do not perform well and with alacrity. He summons one of his best generals, Doucette, who plays General Lucien K. Truscott (1895-1965), not only asking him to launch an amphibious attack against the Germans, but to do it within twenty-four hours. When Doucette complains that he needs more time, Scott refuses to allow him that time, warning him that he should not be overly cautious. Scott's aim in this attack, it is implied by Malden, is not to merely defeat the enemy in a lightning and unexpected assault, but, by doing so, beat the British forces under Bates' command to Messina and capture that city, so that the glory of a successful Sicilian campaign will be credited to the 7th American Army Scott commands, or, chiefly, to himself. Scott sees himself as the reincarnation of many legendary warriors in the past and claims to have visions of battlefields and conquests through the ages, as if he were a mystic or clairvoyant, his visions coupled to his abiding habit of quoting poetry, especially the couplets and stanzas he has written as an amateur poet years earlier. Doucette accomplishes his mission and Scott takes Messina, but at a substantial loss of life, which causes Scott (Patton) to be nicknamed "Old Blood and Guts," one soldier adding as he trudges along a dusty Sicilian road toward Messina in the wake of Scott's jeep: "Yeah, our blood, his guts." When Bates (Montgomery) arrives triumphantly at the head of his troops in Messina, he is crestfallen to see Patton and his forces assembled in the main square and waiting for him. Bates grimly salutes his competitor and then disgustedly leads his men away. Scott is at the zenith of his military career, hailed as one of the most victorious generals among the Allied forces, when he made the blunder of his life after visiting a U.S. Army medical center. He stops to comfort badly wounded men and then sees Considine, an unharmed soldier sitting glumly on a bed. When Scott asks him what is wrong with him, Considine breaks down, sobbing, saying that he can't take the shelling and firing on the front lines. Enraged at what he views to be a shirking coward, Scott slaps Considine and then orders doctors to "get this coward out of here!" The widely publicized slapping incident (as it did in Patton's experience) brings about censor and criticism from the Supreme Allied Commander, General Dwight D. Eisenhower (1890-1969), who orders Scott to make a public apology through the ranks of all of his command for slapping the shell-shocked soldier. Scott dutifully appears before these troops and, despite the humiliation he feels, makes that apology. He is then relieved of his command and is replaced by the even-tempered, by-the-book Malden. Rather than be sent back to the States, Scott is ordered to go to London and he is there placed in command of a non-existent army, inspecting dummy installations that are designed to deceive German intelligence into believing that he will lead that army in an invasion at Calais, an espionage ruse that works in that many German divisions are sent to Calais and not to Normandy where the real invasion takes place on June 6, 1944. Following the invasion, Eisenhower reinstates Scott, placing him under the command of Malden and where Scott leads the U.S. 3rd Army. He drives his troops forward with lightning strikes that cut deep into the German defenses, winning battle after battle. When the Germans launch a massive counterattack near Bastogne that surrounds the 101st U.S. Airborne Division, Scott pulls his tank units and troops from their front lines and, in a legendary drive to Bastogne, breaks through the German lines and rescues the 101st Airborne Division, ending the last German offensive during the war and concluding the Battle of the Bulge (Battle of Ardennes II, 1944-1945). Scott then turns his army about and attacks the Germans in other sectors, but it is, ironically, Bates (Montgomery) who is credited with defeating the last remnants of the German army, and Bates is honored with knighthood. Following the surrender of German forces, Scott gives a press conference where he injudiciously states that the real enemy is now the Soviet Union and that the Allies must inevitably face the Russians in an all-out war, remarks that again bring him criticism and causes him to be relieved. He bids a fond farewell to his staff members and then meets for a last time with Malden before he takes a walk with his pet dog for the fadeout of this great biopic (Patton was fatally injured in an auto accident on December 9, 1945, and died twelve days later on December 21, 1945). Schaffner directs this film with great skill, offering well-orchestrated battle scenes and incisively developing and revealing the myriad nuances of the visionary Patton through the consistently compelling performance by Scott, who won an Oscar for that utterly captivating performance (he refused the award). The many sides of Patton are revealingly shown, such as his utter ruthlessness of command where he sees a cart drawn by two stubborn mules holding up one of his armored columns on a bridge and summarily shoots these dumb animals, having their carcasses tossed into a river (a scene thought by activists against animal cruelty so abusive that they successfully lobbied to have that scene excised from the film when it was shown on mainstream TV). His eagerness to lead is demonstrated when he is shown conducting the most trivial chores such as clearing up a logjam of several armored columns by personally replacing a GI to direct that traffic on a muddy battlefield. His conviviality and esprit de corps is demonstrated as he walks and rides through the ranks of his men, chatting with them and urging them onward to one objective after another. His utter compassion and devotion to his troops (those who would fight) is movingly demonstrated when he visits the wounded, kneeling at their hospital bedsides to pray for them or even when he receives a report from a wounded officer on a battlefield and then kneels at his side and, to express his deep affection and respect for the man's valor, kisses him on the forehead as a loving father would a son. At that same battlefield, strewn with damaged tanks and littered with dead, he also admits to himself his warrior's perverse passion for war, saying, "God help me, I do love it so." He is not a man without humor or wit and, in one scene, when responding to a newsman remarking about his "pearl-handled" revolvers, he corrects the reporter by telling him that only a New Orleans pimp would have such a weapon and proudly points out that his weapons are ivory-handled. He is, above all else and in every scene, a relentless and heroic leader, faithfully representing the true epitome of General George S. Patton Jr. Malden also gives a convincing performance in the role of the more docile and politically correct General Omar Bradley, and the rest of the cast give exceptional supporting performances, but the film is really a one-man show conducted by the mesmerizing Scott. The film also won as Best Picture, Best Director (Schaffner), Best Original Screenplay (Coppola and North), Best Film Editing (Fowler) and Best Art Direction. Songs: "To the Color" (traditional bugle call), "The Washington Post" (John Philip Sousa), "God Save the

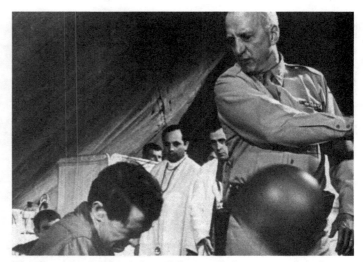

Tim Considine, sitting left, and George C. Scott recreating the slapping incident in *Patton,* 1970.

King!" (traditional), "The Stars and Stripes Forever" (John Philip Sousa). *Author's Note*: The slapping incident shown in the film only exhibits one of two such real life incidents created by Patton. He slapped two American soldiers on two separate occasions for complaining of battle fatigue, a psychological malady Patton would never recognize as a real and debilitating illness. He slapped and verbally abused Private Charles H. Kuhl at a hospital in Nicosia on August 3, 1943, and slapped Private Paul G. Bennett on August 10, 1943, for the same reason. For that, Eisenhower relieved him and held him in reserve in England, but the real decision to keep Patton available for battle following the 1944 Normandy Invasion was actually made by Secretary of War Henry L. Stimson (1867-1950), who insisted that Patton remain available as a battlefield commander due to the need for his "aggressive, winning leadership in the bitter battles to come before final victory." Almost all the top brass, including Eisenhower, and even the retired General John J. Pershing of WWI fame, wanted to send Patton home, but Stimson overruled them. Scott told this author that "everyone wanted to kick Patton out, but the Secretary of War was smarter than that." Scott stated that he studied everything he could find about Patton before playing the role, as well as watching all the newsreels about him to "learn how he walked and talked and all of his peculiar mannerisms and he had a lot of those." Regarding his rejection of the Oscar for his role in **Patton**, Scott told this author: "I turned the Oscar down, but they gave it to me anyway. [His statuette presently resides at the Virginia Military Institute in Lexington, Virginia.] I watched a hockey game instead of that two-hour meat parade they call the Oscars. Don't get me wrong. The Oscar stands for a lot of great talent and it is a wonderful award. It's the ceremony that I can't stand and how careers hang in the balance based on whether or not someone gets that Oscar, and all that hoopla really isn't for a lot of fine talent—it's a boring show designed to make a hell of a lot of money." He said to this author that he did not really think the script was as good as it could have been and that Patton was somewhat "misrepresented" in the film and that it was "next to impossible to accurately show such a great legendary man in his true light," further stating to this author that "Karl [Malden] drove me crazy in that picture. Every response he gave me had that smirk of his glued to it. He was like a lapdog I could not shake. In every scene, there was old smiley giving me a half-ass grin to whatever I said. I know he was playing down his role as Omar Bradley, who was called the 'Soldier's General' I guess because he was not as severe as Patton was, but Karl might have given his character more character. Then again, Bradley was Eisenhower's toady. It was Patton who won all of Bradley's battles for him. But in playing 'Mr. Nice Guy' Karl was just about the most ineffective general ever played on the screen. I told him, 'for crying out loud, Karl, why don't you put some guts into your part?' He gave me that smile again and said: 'That's

Sidney Lumet with Thelma Oliver and Rod Steiger on the set of *The Pawnbroker*, 1965.

your role.' I have a scene with one of the ugliest dogs on God's green earth and that pooch had more dimension and charisma than Karl in that film. In fairness to him, Karl made me look awfully good by assuming that benign and avuncular character that emphasizes my stern father figure image for every GI in the European theater of that war. It was men like that who won that terrible war and saved the free republics of the earth. Thank God we had men like Patton in Europe at that time and MacArthur and Nimitz and Halsey in the Pacific, all of them great leaders who appeared when we most needed them." For his part, the always affable and generous Malden told this author that "George [Scott] gave the performance of his life in **Patton**—no one can ever match it. It was greatness personified. He did not need any help from me or anyone else. He did it all on his own." On a personal note: My stepfather served under Patton in Europe and fought in one of Patton's armored units. His tank was destroyed one day and he sat semi-conscious at the side of the road when a jeep came to a stop in front of him and an officer got out, kneeled, and gave him a drink of water from his canteen. "I wasn't looking at him," my stepfather told me many years later, "as I was gulping down his water when he asked me: 'Can you fight, son?' I replied: 'You're damned right I can, buddy.' Then I looked up to see three stars on his helmet. It was Patton." My stepfather was promoted on the spot and given another tank. "Patton later ate mess with my unit and he ate the same GI food we were eating," my stepfather added. "I had your mother's name, 'Jerrie,' painted on the side of that new tank. A few days later, Patton stopped my tank and told me that that name, 'Jerrie,' meant 'German,' or, at least that's what the Brits called the Germans. 'No, sir,' I told him, 'that's my wife's name.' He pointed his riding crop at the name and said: 'Good for you. Drive that tank and that name right into Berlin!' I would have driven it straight into hell for that guy." **p**, Frank McCarthy; **d**, Franklin J. Schaffner; **cast**, George C. Scott, Karl Malden, Michael Bates, Stephen Young, Michael Strong, Karl Michael Vogler, Edward Binns, John Doucette, Frank Latimore, Morgan Paull, Carey Loftin, Albert Dumortier, Bill Hickman, James Edwards, Lawrence Dobkin; **w**, Francis Ford Coppola, Edmund H. North (based on factual material from the book *Patton: Ordeal and Triumph* by Omar N. Bradley, Ladislas Farago); **c**, Fred Koenekamp (CinemaScope; DeLuxe Color); **m**, Jerry Goldsmith; **ed**, Hugh Fowler; **art d**, Urie McCleary, Gil Parrondo; **set d**, Antonio Mateos, Pierre-Louis Thevenet; **spec eff**, Alex Weldon, L.B. Abbott, Art Cruickshank.

The Pawnbroker ★★★★ 1965; U.S.; 116m; Landau Company/AA; B/W; Drama; Children: Unacceptable; **DVD**; **VHS**. Most likely no actor other than the great Steiger could have played his complex and psychologically troubled character in this singularly unique film of a man whose thoughts and actions are dictated by a horrible past. He is a cold-

hearted and seemingly unfeeling man operating a small pawnshop in the Spanish Harlem section of New York. Those entering his shop bring their pathetic woes and troubles along with the meager items they seek to pawn, all miserable and desperate persons and some are predators with the natures of savage beasts. Steiger is passively noncommittal to everyone and everything, even though his outgoing assistant, Sanchez, a life-loving Puerto Rican, tries to bring Steiger out of his shell by kidding him and making awkward jokes. Fitzgerald, a local social worker, attempts to crack Steiger's hard shell and gets the same results. After she asks him why he is so bitter, Steiger replies: "I am not bitter…that passed me by a million years ago. I am a man of no anger. I have no desire for vengeance for what was done to me. I have escaped from the emotions. I am safe within myself. All I ask and want is peace and quiet." He gets neither as he remains indifferent to everything and everyone in his life. Kimbrell is the only person with whom Steiger finds any human comfort as they share a terrible past together. Both were inmates at a German concentration camp where Steiger's wife was raped and murdered by Nazis and his two young children executed. Kimbrell is a widow, her husband having been killed by the Nazis. Their unsteady affair is further jeopardized by Lumet (father of the director), who is Kimbrell's father and who is critical of their relationship. Peters owns the shop where Steiger works, but Steiger is shocked to learn that Peters funded the pawnshop from his earnings as a pimp, although Peters insists that Steiger has known that that was the source of his money since they first met and perversely compels Steiger to admit he had knowledge of Peters' pimping operation right from the beginning. When Oliver, a young black woman who is Sanchez's girlfriend, appears in the shop to pawn an inexpensive gem, Steiger offers her very little money. To induce him to pay her more, she lowers the top of her dress to display her breast, an act that reviles and disgusts Steiger, causing him to see in a brief flashback, the ugly fate that befell his wife and family (and these flashbacks momentarily appear throughout the film as Steiger's visual memories of his tortured past jar his present with these lightning bolt scenes). When Sanchez persists in trying to humanize Steiger, the pawnbroker begins to cruelly ridicule him and this so angers Sanchez that he arranges for some thieves to rob the store. When the thugs demand all of Steiger's cash, he adamantly refuses to pay them anything. He cares not for their threats and all but challenges them to shoot him to death. Seeing this, Sanchez changes his mind or heart and jumps in front of Steiger just as the thieves fire their guns and he is fatally shot, dying in Steiger's arms. Only when he sees Sanchez dying, a young man who has vainly tried to be his friend, does Steiger become human. Upon the youth's death, his rage against the inhumanity that has been embedded within him is demonstrated with the same kind of brutality that has indelibly marked his life. He forces his hand down upon a paper spike upon which he has impaled receipts until it goes completely through his hand as a form of self-punishment or retribution for the bloodless and insensitive behavior of the world that he himself has displayed. He then walks the dark, debris-strewn streets alone with his thoughts and misery to end this fascinating tragedy. Lumet directs with uncompromising skill in presenting a New York that is grim if not grotesque, everything about it being seedy and uninviting and where its denizens display a creeping moral decay that seems to keep pace with the mounting debris that clogs its gutters and litters its sidewalks and where Steiger presents one of his greatest performances. Sanchez as the friendly Latino and Peters as the calculating black pimp also give powerful performances. Songs: "I Don't Wanna Be a Loser" (B. Raleigh, M. Barkan), "Soul Bossa Nova" (Quincy Jones). *Author's Note*: This film saw widespread criticism from many civic and activist organizations. Black activist groups objected to the merciless portrayal of Peters as one without a redeemable bone in his body, and the Legion of Decency condemned the film for the scene where Oliver bares her breast, one of the first times in a mainstream film such a scene occurred. Jewish organizations also damned the film, stating it was anti-Semitic in that Steiger's Jewish character appears to be nothing more than a money-grubbing person without any compassion or human values. Steiger's towering performance (and for which he was paid $25,000), however, could not be denied by Hollywood and he received a nomination as Best Actor, but lost to Lee Marvin for his comic gunslinger in **Cat Ballou**, 1965. "I hoped to win that Oscar then," Steiger told this author, "because, as they say, hope springs eternal, but in my heart I knew that I would not get the award because **The Pawnbroker** was not broad-based entertainment. It was an introspective and very grim study of a human being who has had his soul savagely torn apart. A friend told me later that the reason why I did not get the Oscar was because Hollywood was fearful that if it gave recognition to such an emotionally exhausting picture, the award would spawn more such films that were too much out of the mainstream of box office fare. That would seriously damage the industry's business. He was right. Filmmaking is a business and sometimes it can be an art, but only if business comes first. I got the Oscar two years later for **In the Heat of the Night** [1967], so that evened things out, I suppose. Then I made the mistake of turning down the lead role in **Patton** [1970] because I did not want to glorify war, and George C. Scott did it and won the Oscar. Take a false step and you can break your leg in this business. In that case, I took that false step and fell straight down into an open manhole. I always felt that if I had accepted the role in **Patton**, I could have been seriously considered for the lead in **The Godfather** [1972], but that role went to Marlon [Brando]. That's why I tell young actors to measure your moves very carefully." p, Roger Lewis, Philip Langner; d, Sidney Lumet; **cast**, Rod Steiger, Geraldine Fitzgerald, Brock Peters, Jaime Sanchez, Thelma Oliver, Marketa Kimbrell, Baruch Lumet, Juano Hernandez, Linda Geiser, Raymond St. Jacques, Morgan Freeman, Reni Santoni; **w**, David Friedkin, Morton Fine (based on the novel by Edward Lewis Wallant); **c**, Boris Kaufman; **m**, Quincy Jones; **ed**, Ralph Rosenblum; **prod d&art d**, Richard Sylbert; **set d**, Jack Flaherty.

Pay or Die ★★★★ 1960; U.S.; 111m; AA; B/W; Crime Drama; Children: Unacceptable; **DVD**. This hard-hitting crime tale is faithfully based upon the career of crusading New York Police Lt. Joseph Petrosino (1860-1909), a pioneer in the fight against organized crime in America and who is powerfully played by Borgnine. Long a stalwart and dedicated NYPD detective, Borgnine has long been battling the Sicilian mobsters that prey upon the residents of New York's Little Italy, a bustling neighborhood beginning at Canal Street. He is promoted to the rank of lieutenant and is placed at the head of an Italian Squad that is dedicated to eliminating the widespread extortion racket run by a group of gangsters, called the Black Hand. Small shopkeepers are forced to pay for protection or be beaten or killed. The most reluctant to pay are blown up along with their shops. After marrying Lampert (her film debut), Borgnine begins tracking down one savage gangster after another. He saves the life of famed opera singer Enrico Caruso (1873-1921), played by Caine, from a Black Hand scheme, and then solves the bombing of a store where several young girls are killed, including the daughter of Ellenstein, one of the wealthy businessmen who are behind the Black Hand operations. Although Borgnine and his dedicated group of detectives prove effective, Borgnine realizes that the only way by which he can identify the masterminds behind the widespread Black Hand operations is to go to Sicily and look through the police records there and to personally identify wanted criminals who have relocated in New York's Little Italy, persons known to him under aliases, many of these being otherwise respected businessmen in Little Italy. He receives funds for that mission and travels to Palermo, Sicily. He identifies the Black Hand ringleaders, and mails copies of their criminal records to New York, but is shot and killed by Mafia assassins before he can return to the U.S. The chief culprit, however, is captured in New York when attending Borgnine's wake. A similar and equally effective story of Petrosino's heroic services is told in **Black Hand**, 1950. Violence prohibits viewing by children. *Author's Note*: Borgnine told this author that "Joseph Petrosino was an unsung hero in New York. Outside of Little Italy, few people later knew about him and I thought that I helped to

Ernest Borgnine, center, in *Pay or Die*, 1960.

honor this great man when appearing in **Pay or Die**. I studied his life and career before I played him in that picture. He was just as fierce and tough as any of the murderous gangsters of his day and was utterly fearless. He went after these killers alone most of the time and fought them on the streets of Little Italy where he used his fists to arrest them and then drag them down the streets so that the Italian residents could see that these mobsters could be defeated. It was a rewarding experience for me. This time I was playing a decent and dedicated man, unlike the kind of thugs and villains I had played in earlier pictures like **Bad Day at Black Rock** [1955] where I am so terrible that I try to pick a fight with one-armed Spencer Tracy, but I get my comeuppance when, even though he has only one working arm, he tosses me around like a sack of potatoes. Actually, I used some of those moves that Tracy made on me when I manhandled gangsters in **Pay or Die**, so even that experience with the great Tracy came in handy." Details of the operations of the Black Hand can be found in my entry for the Mafia in my two-volume work, *The Great Pictorial History of World Crime*, Volume II (History, Inc., pages 1448-1462). **p&d**, Richard Wilson; **cast**, Ernest Borgnine, Zohra Lampert, Alan Austin, Renata Vanni, Bruno Della Santina, Franco Corsaro, Robert F. Simon, Robert Ellenstein, Howard Caine; **w**, Richard Collins, Bertram Millhauser; **c**, Lucien Ballard; **m**, David Raksin; **ed**, Walter Hannemann; **prod d**, Fernando Carrere; **art d**, Darrell Silvera; **spec eff**, Milton Olsen.

Payback ★★★ 1999; U.S.; 100m; Icon Entertainment Intl./PAR; Color; Crime Drama; Children: Unacceptable (MPAA: R); **BD**; **DVD**. Gibson is outstanding in this action-packed crime yarn. He is a street-wise, tough former Marine who is betrayed by a one-time partner, Henry, and shot in the back by his drug-addicted ex-wife, Unger. He survives and begins a campaign of revenge that involves recovering his share, half of the $140,000 robbery of an Asian crime gang. The loot has been passed on to "The Outfit," a gangster organization led by Devane, Coburn and Kristofferson, who run the city. Gibson's campaign of payback takes him into a world of heroin dealers, prostitutes, sadomasochists, gunmen, crooked cops, and a place of torture. His only friend along the way is Bello, a prostitute, but her loyalty is in doubt, since she works for The Outfit. Trouble really begins for Gibson when he falls into the hands of Coburn, a crime boss, and his adventures in the sewer of life have just begun. For one thing, mob thugs smash Gibson's toes with a hammer before he is dumped into a car trunk and taken to an apartment rigged with a plastic explosive to blow up. The savvy Gibson, however, turns the tables on the mob bosses, and when the apartment blows up, it is the mob leaders who are inside to receive the fatal blast. Gibson and Bello then drive off to Canada and a new and less violent life. Songs: "Anniversary Song" (Al Jolson, Saul Chaplin),

Barry Sullivan and Bette Davis in *Payment on Demand*, 1951.

"It's a Man's Man's Man's World" (James Brown, Betty Newsome), "Sway" (Pablo Beltran, Norman Gimbel), "Smoke Gets in Your Eyes" (Jerome Kern, Otto A. Harbach), "Ain't That a Kick in the Head" (Jimmy Van Heusen, Sammy Cahn), "Voodoo Child" (Jimi Hendrix), "The Thrill Is Gone" (Rick Darnell, Roy Hawkins), "Luck Be a Lady" (Frank Loesser), "You're Nobody Till Somebody Loves You" (James Cavanaugh, Russ Morgan, Larry Stock), "If I Had My Life to Live Over" (Moe Jaffe, Harry Tobias, Larry Vincent). Excessive violence, gutter language, drug and sexual content prohibit viewing by children. **p**, Bruce Davey; **d**, Brian Helgeland; **cast**, Mel Gibson, Kris Kristofferson, James Coburn, Gregg Henry, William Devane, Maria Bello, Deborah Kara Unger, David Palmer, Lucy Liu, Jack Conley, John Glover, Bill Duke; **w**, Helgeland, Terry Hayes (based on the novel *The Hunter* by Donald E. Westlake as Richard Stark); **c**, Ericson Core; **m**, Chris Boardman; **ed**, Kevin Stitt; **prod d**, Richard Hoover; **art d**, Troy Sizemore; **set d**, Sandy Struth; **spec eff**, Bob Stoker.

Payday ★★★★ 1973; U.S.; 103m; Fantasy Films/Cinerama; Color; Drama; Children: Unacceptable (MPAA: R); **DVD**; **VHS**. Torn is superlative in his riveting performance as a cynical and unlikable country-western singer. Constantly manipulating those around him to satisfy his selfish needs, he even sets up his limousine driver to take the fall for his fatally stabbing one of his fans. The film incisively and sometimes alarmingly explores the dark side of performing in the struggle for fame and fortune, showing the groupies, the drug users and the miserable day-to-day grind of such a demanding life. Songs: "She's Only a Country Girl," "Slowly Fadin' Circle," "Lovin' You More," "Baby Here's a Dime" (Shel Silverstein); "Road to Nashville" (B. Smith, T. McKinney); "Flatland" (McKinney); "Payday" (Ian & Sylvia Tyson). Violence and drugs prohibit viewing by children. **p**, Martin Fink. Don Carpenter; **d**, Daryl Duke; **cast**, Rip Torn, Ahna Capri, Elayne Heilveil, Michael C. Gwynne, Jeff Morris, Cliff Emmich, Henry O. Arnold, Bobby Smith, Dallas Smith, Richard Hoffman, Walter Bamberg; **w**, Carpenter; **c**, Richard C. Glouner (CFI Color); **m**, Shel Silverstein, Ian and Sylvia Tyson, Ed Bogas, Tommy McKinney; **ed**, Richard Halsey.

Payment on Demand ★★★ 1951; U.S.; 90m; Gwenaud Productions/RKO; B/W; Drama; Children: Unacceptable; **DVD**; **VHS**. Davis renders a riveting performance in this above-average domestic drama. She is married to Sullivan, a lawyer and a top executive at a steelmaking firm. She thinks their marriage is fine after twenty years when he shocks her by asking for a divorce. She tells her teenage daughters, Lynn and Castle, about Sullivan's intentions, and then discovers Sullivan is having an affair with Dee, a beautiful school teacher. Davis threatens to sue him for adultery unless he pays her and their daughters

in the form of a large property settlement. Sullivan agrees and, while waiting for that legal agreement to be completed, she takes a vacation to Haiti where she meets an elderly divorced woman, Cowl, who is a sad case, a rum drinker who pays gigolos for romance, and this gives Davis a grim portrait of what might be her own future. Lynn cables Davis that she is going to be married, so Davis journeys home by ship and has an affair with Sutton, a businessman, who admits he is married and has children. Back home, Davis and Sullivan attend the wedding and both realize that they still love each other and they reconcile for a happy ending. Song: "A Woman's Intuition" (Victor Young, Ned Washington). This soap opera would have sunk into the suds if it were not for the outstanding performance from Davis. This film was made before but released after she scored big in **all About Eve**, 1950. *Author's Note*: Davis told this author that "my role in that picture is about a woman who fights tooth and nail against being divorced until her husband [Sullivan] betrays her. Then she's all for it until she sees what is waiting for her on the other side of the curtain and says to herself, 'to the blazes with that woman scorned nonsense,' and fights to keep her marriage together, and that is the best advice I could give to any woman who thinks to dump her hubby in the nearest garbage can when trouble comes along." **p**, Jack H. Skirball, Bruce Manning; **d**, Curtis Bernhardt; **cast**, Bette Davis, Barry Sullivan, Jane Cowl, Kent Taylor, Frances Dee, Betty Lynn, John Sutton, Peggie Castle, Otto Kruger, Walter Sande, Richard Anderson, Natalie Schafer, Moroni Olsen; **w**, Manning, Bernhardt; **c**, Leo Tover; **m**, Victor Young; **ed**, Harry Marker; **art d**, Carroll Clark, Albert S. D'Agostino; **set d**, Darrell Silvera, Albert Orenbach.

The Pearl ★★★★ 1948; Mexico/U.S.; 85m; Aguila Films/RKO; B/W; Drama; Children: Unacceptable; **VHS**. In this superb allegorical tale we see the fantasy of great riches realized for a poor couple in a small fishing village in western Mexico, only to see their good fortune turn their lives into a nightmare. Armendariz, in another superlative performance, plays a struggling fisherman who finds a huge, perfect pearl in his catch and envisions how his life will vastly improve and that he can now take care of his loving wife, Marques, and their son. Once it is learned that Armendariz possesses this great prize, he and Marques are inundated by greedy, ruthless predators. Rooner, the village physician, who is nothing more than an avaricious doctor, is only one of these persons, who despises the fishermen and sells his services only to the wealthy. Before Armendariz finds the pearl, his son is bitten by a deadly scorpion, but Rooner refuses to treat the boy and Armendariz is compelled to take the boy to a native healer, but he later dies and that death amounts to murder in the eyes of Armendariz. Once Armendariz possesses the pearl, Rooner and his brother, Wagner, a loan shark, set out to swindle the gem from him. Nothing but evil accompanies the pearl and its promised wealth, causing Armendariz in the end to become a killer. He takes the pearl to the sea and throws it back into the Pacific Ocean, hoping somehow that this propitiating gesture will somehow restore his former lifestyle where he was poor but nevertheless happy with a loving family. Fernandez directs this powerful Steinbeck tale with great skill, and Armendariz, Marques and the rest of the cast give stellar performances, all enhanced through Figueroa's beautiful lensing. This outstanding film, however, did not do well at the box office in a day when more straightforward stories were the usual fare. *Author's Note*: Steinbeck, who invariably and effectively wrote about the downtrodden and the impoverished, as he did about the "Okies" in his immortal **The Grapes of Wrath**, 1940, or the blue-collar workers in Central California in **Tortilla Flat**, 1942, and **Cannery Row**, 1982, wrote *The Pearl* with the same kind of poor people in mind, but interjecting the good fortune upon those who had formerly been forgotten by God. "I told a story about how riches do not always bring happiness to even the poorest of us," he told this author, "and the filming of that story was made with great care and with a wonderful cast. I think it did not do well with the public because the public wants to see newly found riches translate into instant security if not comfort and none of that happens in that story. They were disappointed, but riches always disappoint." Fernandez, the director of this film, wanted Hollywood screen star Olivia de Havilland to play the lead in this film, but that never happened either, much to Fernandez's sorrow as he was personally and deeply in love with the actress (from afar). He somehow compensated for her absence by convincing the officials of Mexico City to rename the street where he was raised to "Dulce Olivia" ('Sweet Olivia"). The actress, for years, was ignorant of Fernandez's love for her. **p**, Oscar Dancigers; **d**, Emilio Fernandez; **cast**, Pedro Armendariz, Maria Elena Marques, Fernando Wagner, Gilberto Gonzalez, Charles Rooner, Juan Garcia, Alfonso Bedoya, Raul Lechuga, Max Langler; **w**, John Steinbeck, Fernandez, Jack Wagner (based on the novella by Steinbeck); **c**, Gabriel Figueroa; **m**, Antonio Diaz Conde; **ed**, Gloria Schoemann; **art d**, Javier Torres Torija.

Pearl Harbor ★★★ 2001; U.S.; 183m; Touchstone Pictures/Buena Vista; Color; War Drama; Children: Unacceptable (MPAA: PG-13); **BD**; **DVD**; **VHS**. In this well-made tale, we see two boys in a Tennessee farm field playing inside the wreck of an old biplane in 1923, both having youthful ambitions of becoming fliers. They grow to become Affleck and Hartnett, both now U.S. Army pilots flying P-40 warplanes and stationed at Mitchell Field in New York under the command of Major James Doolittle (1896-1993), convincingly enacted by Baldwin, and where they come under criticism for flying their planes during an exercise in unorthodox air maneuvers that challenge each other's skill. Affleck later meets army nurse Beckinsale and they begin a relationship that is abruptly severed when he announces that he has joined the Eagle Squadron in England and where he intends to be in aerial combat with German planes then attacking that country. Though he asks her not to see him off, Beckinsale nevertheless arrives to bid him farewell, telling him that she loves him and will wait for him. His pal, Hartnett, and the rest of the pilots stationed in New York, along with Beckinsale and the army nurses, are then reassigned to the tropical and enviable post at Pearl Harbor, Hawaii. Then news comes that Affleck has been shot down and presumed dead while in combat over the English Channel, and Beckinsale is devastated when hearing this from Hartnett. She later again meets Hartnett and they begin an affair, but then Affleck, who was only missing in action, returns to find that his girlfriend is now in love with his best friend. He and Hartnett have an argument at the Hula Bar on the night of December 6, 1941, one that erupts into a savage fight. After battering each other, they drive off together, talk reasonably about how events occurred and fall asleep. They wake up to the news that Pearl Harbor is now being attacked by waves of planes from Japanese carriers and they drive to a small airfield that has not yet been destroyed, climbing into the only two available P-40 fighter planes. Meanwhile, Beckinsale and the rest of the nurses in her unit race to the hospital while they are being strafed by diving Japanese planes and there frantically treat the many casualties that arrive there; Beckinsale saves the life of one Army Air Force officer by stopping his main artery from hemorrhaging. The Japanese planes are also diving on all U.S. military installations, strafing and bombing these locations, but they chiefly concentrate on the destruction of the U.S. fleet anchored at Pearl Harbor, bombing and sinking one battleship after another. By this time Affleck and Hartnett are airborne, managing to take off just as Japanese planes arrive and are followed in the air by several fighter planes as they desperately maneuver to escape destruction, managing to outfly the Japanese pilots and destroy their enemies one by one. (These aerial dogfights are stunningly orchestrated through awesome special effects and are highlights of this film as is the actual attack of the U.S. battleships.) Following the attack on Pearl Harbor, Baldwin (Doolittle) organizes a raid against Japan in retaliation for the sneak attack at Pearl Harbor, an attack to be made with sixteen B-25 Mitchell medium bombers, which are placed upon the carrier USS *Hornet*. Affleck and Hartnett, because of their bravery and expertise in aerial combat over Pearl Harbor, are selected by Baldwin to be two of the pilots flying two of those bombers. They both fly their bombers over Tokyo (the Doolittle Raid took place

Ben Affleck, Kate Beckinsale and Josh Hartnett in *Pearl Harbor*, 2001.

on April 18, 1942) and blast the city before flying to China. Running out of fuel, both crash-land their bombers, but Hartnett is killed when saving Affleck's life from Japanese ground troops trying to capture him. Affleck survives and accompanies Hartnett's remains when returning to Pearl Harbor and to the waiting arms of Beckinsale. This well-crafted film is really a romance between three persons, one of whom is tragically killed, and where the traumatic events of the Pearl Harbor and Tokyo attacks overwhelm that romance as it overwhelmed the lives of every American at that time. Affleck, Hartnett, Beckinsale, Baldwin, and the rest of the cast are standouts in their roles, and the production values are high for this very expensive film ($140 million budget against an initial return of $198 million). Songs: "There You'll Be" (Diane Warren); "Bunk Bed Blues," "Tiny Shouderpads" (Bruce L. Fowler); "Little Brown Jug" (William Finnegan Jr.); "Washington in the News" (Jack Shaindlin); "Blues in the Night" (Harold Arlen, Johnny Mercer); "Jeepers Creepers" (Harry Warren, Johnny Mercer); "Jumpin' at the Woodside" (Count Basie); "Hilo March" (traditional); "Lei Ika Mokihana" (Henry W. Walau); "Kaulana Ohilo Hanakahi" (Lena Machado); and "Miss You" (Henry, Harry and Charlie Tobias). *Author's Note*: Cuba Gooding Jr. has a small part in this film, but a significant one in that he plays the heroic Doris "Dorie" Miller (1919-1943), who served as a cook on the USS *West Virginia*, one of the battleships attacked by the Japanese planes at Pearl Harbor. Miller manned a .50-caliber machine gun in the conning tower of the ship, and although he was untrained for the job, his accurate firing reportedly hit several Japanese fighters passing the ship at low altitude. He then helped to carry the mortally wounded skipper of the ship, Captain Mervyn Bennion (1887-1941; posthumous recipient of the Congressional Medal of Honor), from the ship and is credited with saving the lives of many other sailors when the order to abandon ship was issued. For his heroic action, Miller later received the U.S. Navy's then third highest award, the Navy Cross, the first black U.S. sailor ever to receive the award. The roles played by Affleck and Hartnett were loosely based on the heroic exploits of two U.S. Army pilots, who were leaving an all-night poker game when the Japanese attacked. They immediately drove to the remote Haleiwa fighter base and took off in two P-40 planes that were waiting armed and ready for them (they had called the field and ordered the planes fully gassed and armed). One was George Welch (George Lewis Schwartz; 1918-1954), who engaged many Japanese fighters, shooting down two of them, and the other was his friend and wingman, Kenneth M. Taylor, (1919-2006), who is credited with shooting down four Japanese dive bombers during the attack. Both men were awarded the Distinguished Service Cross. Another small but very important role in **Pearl Harbor** is enacted by Voight, who is dynamic and convincing as the wheelchair-bound President Franklin D. Roosevelt (1882-1945), who suffered from

Carmen Filpi and Pee-wee Herman in *Pee-wee's Big Adventure*, 1985.

infantile paralysis and had lost the use of his legs many years before becoming president. Other films profiling the Japanese sneak attack at Pearl Harbor include **Admiral Yamamoto**, 1968; **Air Force**, 1943; **December 7th**, 1943; **Eleanor and Franklin: The White House Years**, 1977 (made-for-TV); **From Here to Eternity**, 1953; **In Harm's Way**, 1965, **Remember Pearl Harbor**, 1942; **Secret Agent of Japan**, 1942; **Tora! Tora! Tora!**, 1970; **War and Remembrance**, 1988 (TV miniseries); **We've Never Been Licked**, 1943. The Doolittle Raid was also depicted in **Destination Tokyo**, 1943; **Midway**, 1976; and **Thirty Seconds over Tokyo**, 1944. President Franklin D. Roosevelt has been profiled by many actors in many other films, including **Annie**, 1982 (Edward Hermann); **Annie**, 1999 (made-for-TV; Dennis Howard); **The Beginning or the End**, 1947 (Godfrey Tearle); **Bertie and Elizabeth**, 2002 (made-for-TV; Robert Hardy); **Churchill: The Hollywood Years**, 2004 (Henry Goodman); **Cradle Will Rock**, 1999 (himself in archive footage); **Edge of Darkness**, 1943 (voiceover of Jack Young); **Eleanor and Franklin**, 1976 (made-for-TV; Edward Hermann); **Eleanor and Franklin: The White House Years**, 1977 (made-for-TV; Edward Hermann); **The First Front**, 1949 (Nikolai Cherkasov); **First to Fight**, 1967 (Stephen Roberts); **The Great Battle**, 1973 (Stanislaw Jaskiewicz); **Hyde Park on Hudson**, 2012 (Bill Murray); **Ike: The War Years**, 1979 (TV miniseries; Stephen Roberts); **J. Edgar**, 2011 (David A. Cooper); **J. Edgar Hoover**, 1987 (made-for-TV; David Ogden Stiers); **MacArthur**, 1977 (Dan O'Herlihy); **The Pigeon That Took Rome**, 1962 (Dick Nelson; scenes deleted); **The Private Files of J. Edgar Hoover**, 1977 (Howard Da Silva); **Sunrise at Campobello**, 1960 (Ralph Bellamy); **This Is the Army**, 1943 (Jack Young); **Truman**, 1995 (made-for-TV; himself, archive footage, funeral procession); **War and Remembrance**, 1988 (TV miniseries; Ralph Bellamy); **World War II: When Lions Roared**, 1994 (made-for-TV; John Lithgow); and **Yankee Doodle Dandy**, 1942 (Jack Young). **p**, Jerry Bruckheimer, Michael Bay; **d**, Bay; **cast**, Ben Affleck, Josh Hartnett, Kate Beckinsale, Alec Baldwin, James King, William Lee Scott, Cary-Hiroyuki Tagawa, Jon Voight, Cuba Gooding, Jr., Dan Aykroyd, Scott Wilson. Peter Firth, Tom Sizemore, Sean Faris, Nicholas Farrell; **w**, Randall Wallace; **c**, John Schwartzman (Technicolor); **m**, Hans Zimmer; **ed**, Roger Barton, Mark Goldblatt, Chris Lebenzon, Steven Rosenblum; **prod d**, Nigel Phelps; **art d**, Martin Laing, Jon Billington, William Ladd Skinner; **set d**, Jennifer Williams; **spec eff**, John Frazier, Eric Brevig, Yves De Bono.

The Pearl of Death ★★★ 1944; U.S.; 69m; UNIV; B/W; Mystery Children: Unacceptable; **DVD**. This is the ninth in the outstanding series of fourteen films that stars Rathbone and Bruce as Sherlock Holmes and Dr. Watson. In this intriguing and well-written whodunit, Rathbone and his bumbling assistant, Bruce (who provides many funny mo-

ments), investigate the theft of a valuable pearl that is linked to a series of brutal murders. The pearl has been stolen from a museum, its theft accidentally brought about by Rathbone himself when he mocks the electronic security system by briefly turning it off (stating: "Electricity, the false prophet of security"). They discover the pearl is hidden in one of six busts of Ludwig van Beethoven (1770-1827) and the owners of those busts are then systematically murdered by a brutal killer, Hatton, who is the Hoxton Creeper and who kills his victims by breaking their backs, always at the third vertebra, a medical fact that does not go unnoticed through the indefatigable sleuthing of Rathbone, this modus operandi allowing Rathbone to identify the killer and where he finally brings the criminal mastermind, Manders and his hulking killer, Hatton, to justice. Violence prohibits viewing by children. *Author's Note*: Rathbone told this author that "Hatton [1894-1946] was cast as the killer in that picture simply because of his grotesque appearance. The poor man had been gassed when fighting in World War One. [Rathbone himself served in British military intelligence, 1915-1919, and was decorated for bravery for his services on the Western Front.] He later developed a strange disease called acromegaly, which brings about horrible disfigurement, usually of the face. Hatton suffered from a severe case of this incurable disease, which made him look like a gargoyle carved in the Medieval Ages." Hatton played villains in many films during the 1930s and early 1940s, but the disease finally took its toll. After he appeared in **The Pearl of Death**, he developed diabetes and went slowly blind until his heart gave out, all brought about by acromegaly. "Universal kept him working right up to the time he died," Rathbone told this author. "He invariably played roles like the Creeper and the studio was later and unjustly criticized for that. They made sure he had a job and a steady income and that is more than what a lot of others got in those days." **p&d**, Roy William Neill; **cast**, Basil Rathbone, Nigel Bruce, Dennis Hoey, Evelyn Ankers, Miles Mander, Rondo Hatton, Ian Wolfe, Charles Francis, Holmes Herbert, Mary Gordon; **w**, Bertram Millhauser (based on the story "The Six Napoleons" by Sir Arthur Conan Doyle); **c**, Virgil Miller; **m**, Paul Sawtell; **ed**, Ray Snyder; **art d**, John B. Goodman, Martin Obzina; **set d**, Russell A. Gausman, E.R. Robinson.

The Pearls of the Crown ★★★ 1938; France; 118m; Cineas/Lenauer International Films; B/W; Historical Drama; Children: Cautionary; **DVD**. Guitry, who wrote and directed this fine and fascinating film (most likely his least theatrical production and one of his most inventively constructed stories), tells the tale of the seven fabulous pearls that once adorned the British Crown. Three of the pearls were forever lost, and the other four are shown in several sequences belonging to celebrated historical characters—England's Henry VIII and Elizabeth I, France's Napoleon III, and his empress, Eugenie. Guitry plays four of the historical roles while Moreno, Pienne and Harding play two roles each. The story unfolds as one pearl after another passes from one hand to another through the ages. The episodic story is somewhat confusing at times as Guitry decided to have his characters speak in three separate languages throughout the film—French, Italian and English—so that only those with trilingual capabilities can most easily enjoy this absorbing drama. (In French, Italian and English; English subtitles.) **p**, Serge Sandberg; **d**, Sacha Guitry; **cast**, Guitry, Jacqueline Dulebac, Lyn Harding, Marguerite Moreno, Yvette Pienne, Marcel Dalio, Ermete Zacconi, Arletty, Renée Saint-Cyr, Enrico Glori, Barbara Shaw, Claude Dauphin, Robert Seller; **w**, Guitry; **c**, J. (Jules) Kruger; **m**, Jean Françaix; **ed**, W. (William) Barache, Myriam (Borsoutsky); **art d**, Jean Perrier.

Pee-wee's Big Adventure ★★★ 1985; U.S.; 90m; WB; Color; Comedy; Children: Cautionary (MPAA: PG); **DVD**; **VHS**. Often hilarious comedy has Reubens as a childlike, eccentric man who goes on a cross-country search for his beloved shiny new bicycle after it is stolen in broad daylight by Holton, a man having a similar lack of maturity. After many humorous and outlandish adventures man-child and bike are finally reunited for a deliriously happy ending. Kids loved this film but caution is advised for younger children because of some unsafe images. Songs: "Burn in Hell" (Dee Snider), "Tequila" (Chuck Rio). **p**, Robert Shapiro, Richard Gilbert Abramson; **d**, Tim Burton; **cast**, Paul Reubens (Pee-wee Herman), Elizabeth Daily, Mark Holton, Diane Salinger, Judd Omen, Irving Hellman, Monte Landis, James Brolin, Morgan Fairchild, Phil Hartman, Tony Bill, Milton Berle, Burton; **w**, Hartman, Michael Varhol, Reubens; **c**, Victor J. Kemper; **m**, Danny Elfman; **ed**, Billy Weber; **prod d**, David L. Snyder; **set d**, Thomas L. Roysden; **spec eff**, Chuck Gaspar, Joe Day.

The Pelican Brief ★★★ 1993; U.S.; 141m; WB; Color; Crime Drama/Mystery; Children: Unacceptable (MPAA: PG-13); **DVD**; **VHS**. This solid mystery opens when two Supreme Court justices with little in common are assassinated and a New Orleans law student, Roberts, who does some sleuthing, believes there is a connection. She writes a brief suggesting who may have killed them and gives it to her professor, Shepard, with whom she is having an affair. Shepard gives the brief to a friend who works for the FBI and when the director reads it, he lets the White House know about it. The president, Culp, is afraid that if the brief becomes public, one of the richest men in America could be implicated and he also could be smeared so he tells the FBI chief not to take any action on it. Shepard is blown up in his car and Roberts narrowly escapes, but becomes a target and turns to an investigative journalist, Washington, for help. This leads to a videotape that leads to a solution and Roberts and Washington wind up together in the Caribbean sunshine. Songs: "Blues for Carol" (Clarence Hollimon); "Nearly," "Just for Now" (Danny Gould); "The Creole Song," "Tippy Ty O" (Lynn August); "Air Conditioner Blues" (Carl Sonny Leyland); "Chain of Fools" (Don Covay); "Dancing in the Rain" (Rik Slave, Marc St. James, Patrick Catania); "Clarinet Marmalade" (Larry Shields, Henry Ragas); "The Lipsetter," "Wiggle" (Rod Piazza); "One Way Street" (Mike Darby, Irene Sage); "My Mammy" (Sam Lewis, Joe Young, Walter Donaldson); "Troisieme Lecon De Tenebres a 2 Voix" (Francois Couperin); "Choral, Komm, O Tod, Du Schlafes Bruder" (Johann Sebastian Bach); "Coach Theme" (John Morris), "The Morning Theme" (Michael Karp); "You Drive Me Crazy" (Greg Ginn). Somewhat weak on motivation, the involved political machinations boost the story line to sustain interest throughout. Violence and gutter language prohibit viewing by children. **p**, Alan J. Pakula, Pieter Jan Brugge; **d&w**, Pakula (based on the novel by John Grisham); **cast**, Julia Roberts, Denzel Washington, Sam Shepard, John Heard, Tony Goldwyn, James B. Sikking, William Atherton, Robert Culp, Stanley Tucci, Hume Cronyn, John Lithgow, Cynthia Nixon; **c**, Stephen Goldblatt; **m**, James Horner; **ed**, Tom Rolf, Trudy Ship; **prod d**, Philip Rosenberg; **art d**, Robert Guerra; **set d**, Lisa Fischer, Rick Simpson; **spec eff**, Conrad Brink, Gerald Scaife, John Nelson.

Pelle the Conqueror ★★★ 1988; Denmark/Sweden; 157m; Per Holst Filmproduktion/FOX; Color; Drama; Children: Unacceptable; **DVD**; **VHS**. At the close of the 19th century, a boat filled with Swedish immigrants arrives at the Danish island of Bornholm. Aboard are a father, Sydow, and young son Pelle (Hvenegaard), who have come to Denmark looking for work. They find it on a large farm, but are treated as inferiors. Hvenegaard starts to learn to speak Danish but continues to be harassed as a foreigner. The two persist and refuse to give up their dream of a better life than the one they abandoned in Sweden. Too mature for children, the film nevertheless provides an absorbing drama with a strong social message. It won the Oscar as Best Foreign Language Film. (In Danish, Norwegian; English subtitles.) **p**, Per Holst; **d**, Bille August; **cast**, Pelle Hvenegaard, Max von Sydow, Erik Paaske, Bjørn Granath, Astrid Villaume, Axel Strøbye, Troels Asmussen, Kristina Törnqvist, Karen Wegener, Sofie Gråbøl; **w**, August, Per Olov Enquist, Bjarne Reuter (based on the novel by Martin Andersen Nexø); **c**, Jørgen Persson; **m**, Stefan Nilsson; **ed**, Janus Billeskov Jansen; **prod**

Madge Evans, Bing Crosby, Donald Meek and Edith Fellows in *Pennies from Heaven*, 1936.

d, Anna Asp; **spec eff**, Claus Bjerre, Michael Kvium, Kristian Lund, Lasse Spang Olsen.

Pennies from Heaven ★★★ 1936; U.S.; 81m; Emanuel Cohen Productions/COL; B/W; Musical; Children: Acceptable; **DVD**; **VHS**. Delightful musical packed with a lot of outstanding tunes (including the Oscar-winning title song) sees a fine performance from the crooning Crosby. He is first shown in prison after having been wrongly convicted of smuggling. Before he is to be released, Crosby is given a note from a convicted murderer, who is about to be executed, begging Crosby to aid his impoverished relatives and move them into his ancestral mansion. Crosby dreams of going to Venice and becoming a singing gondolier, but his compassion compels him to first look up the relatives and he finds ten-year-old Fellows and her ailing, aging grandfather, Meek, barely surviving in squalor. He takes pity on them and escorts them to their family estate, which turns out to be a dilapidated old mansion that, for all of its shabby and dreary appearances, could pass for a first-class haunted house. Crosby nevertheless ensconces Fellows and Meek and himself at this broken-down domicile, and they are soon visited by Evans, a beautiful social worker, who disapproves of the lifestyle of this makeshift family and thinks that Crosby and Meek are poor guardians for Fellows. She sets in motion court proceedings that are aimed at placing the child in an orphanage. To avert this emotional tragedy, Crosby hatches a plan to convert the old house into a restaurant called The Haunted House Café, hoping that he can, through this operation, provide enough funds to maintain Fellows and the feeble Meek. He enlists the aid of a bevy of colorful characters to put the old place in order, and, after it opens, the café becomes a great success and Evans abandons her plans for Fellows as she makes plans of her own that involve a romance with Crosby. Airy and far-fetched as were the usual plotlines for musicals in the 1930s, the film is nevertheless thoroughly entertaining and where the songs and their presentations, particularly through Crosby and his full-throated tenor singing and the rollicking music from Louis "Satchmo" Armstrong and his band, make all the difference. Songs (all written in 1936): "Pennies from Heaven" (AA); "Skeleton in the Closet," "Now I've Got Some Dreaming to Do," "What This Country Needs," "So Do I," "Let's Call a Heart a Heart," "One Two Button Your Shoe" (music: Arthur Johnston; lyrics: Johnny Burke); "Old MacDonald Had a Farm' (traditional). ***Author's Note***: Crosby told this author that "Jo Swerling [who wrote the screenplay for this film] was a very colorful character. He and his family moved from Russia when the czar was running things and lived in New York. He sold newspapers there until he got a job at a newspaper and then became a reporter and later a playwright. He ran around with pals like Ben Hecht and Charles MacArthur, and those fellows got him some jobs in Hollywood turning out scripts.

Irene Dunne and Cary Grant in *Penny Serenade*, 1941.

Jo was always full of jokes and crazy ideas, but somehow his ideas worked well with pictures, especially in the 1930s when audiences would accept almost any kind of far-out story and Jo had a million of those. He got the idea for the haunted house routine in **Pennies from Heaven** from a boyhood experience when he was playing in a deserted mansion in New York City. The hairs on his head stood straight up when he heard a voice saying from another room: 'None of us ghosts like kids playing around here, so we're going to stuff you up a chimney!' He ran like hell out of there and later learned that the voice he heard was the foreman of a wrecking crew that was about to take the old house down. Writers are like mothers. They use every bit of decent food they've got to feed the family, and Jo always had a lot of tasty things cooking on his stove. He died some years back and so did Ben Hecht. Judging by the puny scripts Hollywood is turning out now, we could sure use those fellows." **p**, Emanuel Cohen; **d**, Norman Z. McLeod; **cast**, Bing Crosby, Madge Evans, Edith Fellows, Louis Armstrong, Donald Meek, John Gallaudet, William Stack, Nana Bryant, Tom Dugan, Nydia Westman, Lionel Hampton; **w**, Jo Swerling (based on the story "The Peacock's Feather" by Katherine Leslie Moore); **c**, Robert Pittack; **m**, William Grant Still; **ed**, John Rawlins; **art d**, Stephen Goosson.

Penny Serenade ★★★ 1941; U.S.; 119m; COL; B/W; Drama/Romance; Children: Cautionary; **DVD**; **VHS**. This sentimental tale must have produced the sale of countless handkerchiefs after audiences realized from the first few minutes of this film that it was not the kind of comedy for which Grant had been earlier noted. Although it has some fine comedic moments, this film offers an emotional roller coaster ride with many heart-wrenching scenes. It opens with Dunne about to divorce Grant, but when she plays an old record and while she listens to "Penny Serenade," she thinks back upon her marriage with nostalgic fondness. In flashback, we see Grant working as an enterprising newspaper reporter and Dunne is a clerk in a store. When they meet it is love at first sight and, following their wedding, they move to Japan, a country to which Grant has been assigned. Dunne becomes pregnant and the couple looks forward to the birth of their first child, but a horrific earthquake occurs just as Dunne is about to give birth and causes her to miscarry. They move back to the States, and Grant purchases a struggling newspaper in a small town. Since Dunne can no longer have children, the couple tries to adopt, but their miserable earnings from the all but failing newspaper puts a damper on their chances of getting a child from any adoption agency. Then Bondi, a woman with great compassion who represents an adoption agency, makes it possible for them to adopt a child, and they are given a baby upon whom they dote, love and care for, but tragedy again strikes when the child grows ill and dies. The emotional blow to Grant and Dunne is crushing and in its devastating wake

their marriage begins to crumble. In flash-forward, just as Grant and Dunne are to be divorced, they are offered another child to adopt and they seize this opportunity at happiness, that adoption bringing the couple back together again to end this well-crafted film with a smile and a kiss. The film is peppered with many fine songs that Dunne plays upon her record player. Songs: "You Were Meant for Me" (music: Nacio Herb Brown; lyrics: Arthur Freed), "Just a Memory" (Lew Brown, Ray Henderson, Buddy G. DeSylva), "The Japanese Sandman" (music: Richard A. Whiting; lyrics: Raymond B. Egan), "The Missouri Waltz" (music: John Valentine Eppel; lyrics: J. R. Shannon), "The Moon Was Yellow" (music: Fred E. Ahlert; lyrics: Edgar Leslie), "I'm Tickled Pink with a Blue Eyed Baby" (music: Pete Wendling; lyrics: Charles O'Flynn), "Charleston" (music: James P. Johnson; lyrics, 1923: Cecil Mack), "My Blue Heaven" (music: Walter Donaldson; lyrics: George Whiting), "Auld Lang Syne" (traditional; lyrics: Robert Burns), "Bridal Chorus (Here Comes the Bride)" (from "Lohengrin" by Richard Wagner), "The Wedding March" (Felix Mendelssohn-Bartholdy), "Poor Butterfly" (music: Raymond Hubbell; lyrics: John Golden), "Happy Birthday to You" (Mildred J. Hill and Patty S. Hill), "Silent Night, Holy Night" (music: Franz Gruber; lyrics: Joseph Mohr), "Three O'Clock in the Morning" (music: Julian Robledo; lyrics: Dolly Morse), "These Foolish Things (Remind Me of You)" (music: Harry Link; lyrics: Holt Marvell/Eric Maschwitz, Jack Strachey), "Ain't We Got Fun?" (music: Richard A. Whiting; lyrics: Raymond B. Egan, Gus Khan), "The Prisoner's Song" (1924; Guy Massey), and "To a Wild Rose" (music: Edward MacDowell). ***Author's Note***: Dunne told this author that "I deeply identified with my character in **Penny Serenade** because I adopted a child [Mary Frances, age four, in 1938] and I know what it means to assume the greater responsibility that comes with adoption. I get very emotional in that picture and my tears were as genuine as those women who shed tears when they saw that picture. It is one of my favorites." Grant told this author that "**Penny Serenade** was a weeper, indeed, and it almost washed me away. Only Irene [Dunne] could bring tears to the eyes of everyone on any set and in any picture, and I was no exception. A great actress and a great woman and I think that when we made that picture most Americans looked upon her as a wonderful mother figure, and that helped to make the picture a huge success. Of course, we had the great George Stevens directing and he handled everything so well that the picture never slipped into the bathtub." Stevens stated to this author that "working on that picture with Cary [Grant] and Irene [Dunne] was a breeze, both of them accomplished actors. **Penny Serenade** is really a fragile story and it could have been easily ruined through overacting. The story begged for extravagant theatrics, but Cary and Irene used a great deal of restraint in the most sorrowful scenes, making their characters all the more believable and the story convincing. Their performances are so wonderful that they make the viewer want to see them survive their tragedies and find happiness together. And that's called great acting." **p&d**, George Stevens; **cast**, Irene Dunne, Cary Grant, Beulah Bondi, Edgar Buchanan, Ann Doran, Eva Lee Kuney, Leonard Willey, Grady Sutton, Dorothy Adams, Billy Bevan; **w**, Morrie Ryskind (based on the story by Martha Cheavens); **c**, Joseph Walker; **m**, W. Franke Harling; **ed**, Otto Meyer; **art d**, Lionel Banks.

The People against O'Hara ★★★ 1951; U.S.; 101m; MGM; B/W; Drama; Children: Unacceptable; **DVD**; **VHS**. Tracy is somber and riveting in this grim crime tale as an alcoholic district attorney forced into retirement, but he returns to law practice to defend Arness, the son of family friends, on a murder charge. Under stress, Tracy slips back into his old drinking habit and loses the case to shrewd prosecutor Hodiak. Arness has been found guilty only because he had refused to reveal where he was on the night of the killing. Tracy later learns that he was with a lady friend, Duguay, and did not want her implicated, so he refused to have her be a witness in his case. In desperately trying to exonerate Arness, Tracy has ruined his own career by paying a reluctant witness to testify on his client's behalf, a violation discovered by Hodiak. His life and career in shambles, Tracy redeems himself by learning that the real killer is Campbell, and he traps the murderer at a meeting where he wears a recording device that tapes Campbell's admission of guilt for the police. Tracy, however, is killed, along with Campbell, when police attempt to capture the culprit and they are both shot down in a fierce crossfire. This grim but fascinating *film noir* entry marks the first time that Tracy appeared on screen with his longtime friend, O'Brien. *Author's Note*: O'Brien, following WWII, strangely found that few studios were willing to hire him for substantial roles. "Spence came to my rescue," O'Brien admitted to this author, "leaning on MGM's front office to give me a strong supporting role in **The People against O'Hara**. He was a great guy and he did things like that for a lot of people and never talked about it." Ruggiero, who edited this film, told this author: "That Tracy film where he plays a drunken lawyer was a cinch to work on because Sturges was a very conscientious director and watched continuity and followed the story line. He left no loose ends. I always looked forward to working on films made by people like Sturges, but some other directors at MGM gave me nightmares. They would leave a scene dangling in mid-air or lose a character and never think about it and even sometimes forget to shoot a complete scene that made up all the sense to a story. Those directors were chummy with studio bosses, so they got away with all that and left guys like me to clean up their mess while they went golfing or boozing at the Polo Lounge." **p**, William H. Wright; **d**, John Sturges; **cast**, Spencer Tracy, Pat O'Brien, John Hodiak, Diana Lynn, James Arness, Eduardo Ciannelli, Yvette Duguay, Jay C. Flippen, Mae Clarke, William Campbell, Richard Anderson, Henry O'Neill, Charles Bronson; **w**, John Monks, Jr. (based on the novel by Eleazar Lipsky); **c**, John Alton; **m**, Carmen Dragon; **ed**, Gene Ruggiero; **art d**, Cedric Gibbons, James Basevi; **set d**, Jacque Mapes, Edwin B. Willis; **spec eff**, A. Arnold Gillespie, Warren Newcombe.

People Will Talk ★★★ 1951; U.S.; 110m; FOX; B/W; Comedy; Children: Acceptable; **DVD**; **VHS**. This incisive and intelligent film exposes the hypocrisy practiced by some in the academic world, particularly in the medical profession, although it is most probably too literate (and full of bon mots most will not perceive) for mainstream audiences. Grant, in one of his most sophisticated, reserved and tightly controlled performances, is a physician teaching at a medical college and where his unorthodox medical credo is to treat the patient and not a specific disease, applying common sense psychology in the process. The mind, he believes, can cure as well as any prescribed drug and he is widely loved at the school, even though he has an odd assortment of close friends, including Currie, his manservant, who has twice been convicted of murder, and Slezak, a scientist devoted to toy trains and the eating of knockwurst. The one person who despises Grant is Cronyn, a dry-minded professor of anatomy, who has more interest in cadavers than live human beings. While Grant is giving a lecture, Crain, a pretty young medical student, faints in his class, and he soon discovers that she is pregnant. After she attempts suicide, Grant again comes to her rescue and tells her that his original diagnosis was incorrect and he marries her and inherits another strange friend, her father, Blackmer, a dissolute drunk, who is nevertheless a witty and charming person. Meanwhile, while not lecturing on his offbeat medical theories and adjusting to marital life with Crain, Grant spends time conducting the college orchestra in playing Brahms and Wagner. His life is utterly disrupted when the vicious Cronyn spreads unsubstantiated gossip about Grant and his association with former felon Currie to the college dean, Ruysdael, who then convenes a meeting of the college's board members that act as a tribunal and where Grant must explain his strange relationships. Grant brings forth Currie, who movingly explains his past and convinces all but Cronyn that he is good-willed and benign, and Grant receives the board's endorsement to remain at the college. He nevertheless patiently continues to assure the unsteady Crain that he did not marry her out of pity and truly loves her. Well directed by Mankiewicz, who adapted the screenplay from the Goetz play, the cast and production values are ex-

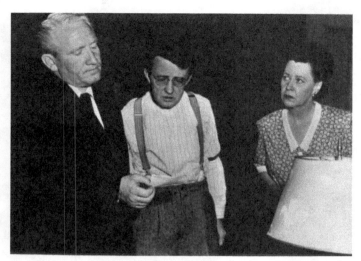

Spencer Tracy, Arthur Shields and Louise Lorimer in *The People against O'Hara*, 1951.

ceptional in this off-center but intriguing comedy. Songs: "Gaudeamus Igitur" (traditional), "Academic Festival Overture" (Johannes Brahms), "Prize Song" (Richard Wagner), "A Hot Time in the Old Town" (Theo. A. Metz), "Happy Birthday to You" (music: Mildred J. Hill; lyrics: Patty S. Hill). *Author's Note*: Grant thought that Mankiewicz's script for this film "was more intellectual than the usual fare produced at Fox, but he had the backing of Darryl Zanuck, who ran the studio and Zanuck was a writer at heart and really liked the kind of introspective comedy the picture represented. Mankiewicz was thumbing his nose at college highbrows in that script and it's really a very clever satire about how college professors think and act, but it was all delivered sotto voce, and that's why the film did not go over as well as expected. The next year I played an experimental researcher developing a youth serum in **Monkey Business** [1952]. Wit went out the door with that one and anything crazy and zany walked in and that picture was a smash hit. You've got to give the lady what she wants, not what you think she should want." Cronyn told this author while we dined together in New York's Oyster Bar that "I never liked that picture much. Like a lot of the professors we play, it is just too damned wordy, but then Mankiewicz was always too wordy. He was always trying to impress everyone that he was a great writer, but the public doesn't give a damn about that. They want to be entertained. I suppose I am biased about that picture because I did not like the character I played, another weasel, and, by that time, I was worn out with playing weasels." **p**, Darryl F. Zanuck; **d&w**, Joseph L. Mankiewicz (based on the play "Dr. Praetorius" by Curt Goetz); **cast**, Cary Grant, Jeanne Crain, Finlay Currie, Hume Cronyn, Walter Slezak, Sidney Blackmer, Basil Ruysdael, Margaret Hamilton, Billy House, Jack Kelly, Billy Mauch, Ray Montgomery, Joyce Mackenzie, Carleton Young; **c**, Milton Krasner; **m**, Johannes Brahms, Richard Wagner; **ed**, Barbara McLean; **art d**, Lyle Wheeler, George W. Davis; **set d**, Thomas Little, Walter M. Scott; **spec eff**, Fred Sersen.

Pepe ★★★ 1960; U.S.; 195m; COL; Color; Comedy/Musical; Children: Acceptable; **VHS**. Cantinflas (Fortino Moreno Reyes) provides a lot of very funny moments as a young Mexican whose beloved horse is sold to Dailey, a Hollywood movie star. Cantinflas journeys to Hollywood to get his horse back and comes in contact with many movie stars. A number of good musical numbers accompany the many comedic scenes, not the least of which is when Cantinflas finally gets to dance with his fantasy woman, voluptuous Janet Leigh, who indulgingly tolerates his awkward advances. This film was designed to capitalize on Cantinflas' debut in **Around the World in 80 Days**, 1956. Songs: "That's How It Went, All Right," "Faraway Part of Town" (Andre Previn, Dory Previn as Dory Langdon); "Pepe" (Hans Wittstatt, Dory Previn); "The Rumble" (Andre Previn); "Lovely Day/Concha Nacar" (Agustin Lara, Marie

Milla Jovovich in *A Perfect Getaway,* 2009.

Teresa Lara, Dory Previn); "Tequila" (Chuck Rio); "Mimi" (Richard Rodgers, Lorenz Hart); "September Song" (Kurt Weill, Maxwell Anderson); "Hooray for Hollywood" (Richard A. Whiting, Johnny Mercer, Sammy Cahn). **p&d**, George Sidney; **cast**, Cantinflas, Dan Dailey, Shirley Jones, Carlos Montalbán, Vicki Trickett, Matt Mattox, Hank Henry, Suzanne Lloyd, and cameo appearances by Maurice Chevalier, Bing Crosby, Bobby Darin, Sammy Davis Jr., Jimmy Durante, Judy Garland, Greer Garson, Jack Lemmon, Dean Martin, Kim Novak, Debbie Reynolds, Edward G. Robinson, Frank Sinatra, Janet Leigh. **w**, Claude Binyon, Dorothy Kingsley (based on a story by Sonya Levien, Leonard Spigelgass, and the play "Broadway Magic" by Leslie Bush-Fekete); **c**, Joseph MacDonald (CinemaScope; Technicolor); **m**, Johnny Green; **ed**, Viola Lawrence; **prod d**, Ted Haworth; **set d**, William Kiernan.

Pepe Le Moko ★★★★★ 1941; France; 94m; Paris Film/Arthur Mayer & Joseph Burstyn; B/W; Drama; Children: Unacceptable; **DVD**; **VHS**. Gabin gives one of his most stunning and memorable performances as an amorous gangster who bosses the criminal underworld of the Casbah, a section of Algiers that no policeman dares enter. He, like the real-life French mobster upon which this story is based, brags that, when and if the police ever capture and kill him, hundreds of mourning women will appear at his wake. Gabin controls his gang members through charm, not violence, while he supervises widespread thieving and other rackets, his dynamic personality cementing dedicated loyalty with his underworld followers. Fabre, who is Gabin's grandfather, approves of everything Gabin does and further acts as a fence for all the stolen goods that Gabin's henchmen bring to him. Gabin is protected by legions of denizens in the Casbah, most fanatically by his mistress, Noro. When she learns that Charpin, one of the few Casbah inhabitants who hates Gabin, has arranged to have Gabin captured when he visits his grandfather's home, she warns her lover just before the cops close in and Gabin escapes slightly wounded following a gunfight. Before he makes his escape, however, Gabin glimpses beautiful Parisian tourist Balin, who is being escorted by Gridoux, a tough police inspector dedicated to capturing Gabin. Just before Gabin departs, Gridoux more or less tells Gabin that he will eventually get him, saying: "It is written, Pepe." Gridoux then escorts Balin back to her hotel outside of the Casbah. Gabin, meanwhile, takes store of his life, admitting to himself that he is weary of his furtive life of crime and yearns for the old carefree days of Paris. He wants to quit the rackets and sever his long-standing relationship with mistress Noro. Then Gil, one of Gabin's top associates, is betrayed by Charpin, who lures Gil from the Casbah with the lie that his mother is ill, but, before Gil dies from wounds he receives in a gunfight with police, he shoots and kills Charpin as he frantically pleads for his life while bumping into a jukebox that suddenly comes alive with blaring

music. Meanwhile, Balin, who has seen Gabin earlier, is intrigued with this handsome and daring rogue and she visits him in the Casbah where they begin a romance that blossoms into a torrid affair. Noro, jealous of the affair, then schemes against her lover with Gridoux, telling the detective about Balin's attraction to Gabin. Gridoux then goes to Granval, the man who escorted Balin to Algiers, a wealthy, older man. When Granval hears from Gridoux that Balin is seeing a notorious brigand, Granval orders Balin never to visit the Casbah again. She refuses, but before she again meets with Gabin, Gridoux informs her that her lover, Gabin, has been killed. Emotionally devastated, Balin decides to sail back to France. Gabin learns of this and, now knowing that he loves Balin above all else, decides that he will give up the rackets once and for all and try to join her. Noro warns Gabin that if he attempts to leave the Casbah, he will certainly be captured, but Gabin ignores her warning. Noro, now convinced that Gabin is throwing her over for Balin, betrays him once again to Gridoux by telling the police inspector that Gabin is going to the docks to board the ship carrying Balin. Gridoux waits for the master thief to arrive and captures him, handcuffing him. Gabin begs one last favor, that he watch the boat sail from the harbor, and Gridoux grants him that favor. The boat begins to sail away and suddenly Gabin sees Balin standing at the stern. He shouts to her, but she cannot see him as she focuses her gaze upon the Casbah, the place where she found love with Gabin. As the boat sails on, the totally disillusioned Gabin withdraws a knife and drives it into his stomach, committing suicide to end this tragedy between two star-crossed lovers. Duvivier directs this masterpiece tale with consummate skill, fully developing his characters and where Gabin, Balin, Noro and others magnificently capture their earthy and compelling characters. This classic story was remade with equal high quality as **Algiers**, 1938, with Charles Boyer as Pepe and Hedy Lamarr as his lover, and remade again as a good musical, **Casbah**, 1948, starring Tony Martin and Yvonne de Carlo. *Author's Note*: This film was shot on location in Algiers, Sete and Marseille, the exteriors shot by the Hakim brothers (who also recruited the talented Ygerbuchen to write the score) and was made one year before its American remake, **Algiers**, but it was not released in the U.S. until several years after **Algiers**. The producers of this film first offered the leading part to Boyer, but he turned it down, then changed his mind and appeared in the American version when Gabin refused to appear in the U.S. remake, Gabin saying that he did not want to go to the U.S. because, like French wine, he did not "travel well." Duvivier admitted that he was greatly influenced by American gangster films of the early 1930s, notably **Scarface**, 1932, when making this film, but he infuses an absorbing romantic element into his crime tale, adding his own poetic touches to each memorable scene and thus produced a singularly distinctive and utterly captivating film that stands on its own as a classic. (In French; English subtitles.) **p**, Raymond Hakim, Robert Hakim; **d**, Julien Duvivier; **cast**, Jean Gabin, Mireille Balin, Line Noro, Lucas Gridoux, Gabriel Gabrio, Fernand Charpin, Saturnin Fabre, Gilbert Gil, Marcel Dalio, Charles Granval; **w**, Duvivier, Henri Jeanson, Detective Roger d'Ashelbe (Henri La Barthe), Jacques Constant (based on the novel by d'Ashelbe); **c**, Jules Kruger, Marc Fossard; **m**, Vincent Scotto, Mohamed Ygerbuchen; **ed**, Marguerite Beauge; **prod d**, Jacques Krauss.

A Perfect Getaway ★★★ 2009; U.S.; 98m; Rogue/UNIV; Color; Mystery; Children: Unacceptable (MPAA: R); **BD**; **DVD**. This suspenseful thriller sees drug-addicted psychopathic killers on the loose in otherwise tranquil tropical Hawaii. Three couples are involved. Newlyweds Jovovich and Zahn are honeymooning in the lush jungles of the island of Kauai when they meet two disgruntled teenagers, Hemsworth and Shelton. Jovovich and Zahn learn of a gruesome murder and fear the killers may be the teenagers. Then they meet tough-talking Olyphant and his sunbathing girlfriend, Sanchez. Amid the beautiful scenery lurks terror and we learn that the killers are the least likely of the couples, Olyphant and Sanchez, but not before the mayhem and mystery is solved. Songs: "Hey, Hey, Hey" (Tracy Adams), "Paradise" (Daniel J.

Black), "Need Your Love" (Michael Rubin Campbell, Brinsley Forde, Angus Gay, Tony Robinson), "Boom Chic Boom Chick," "Red Dress Baby Doll," "Ghetto Chronic" (Tracy Adams). Gutter language, violence, sexual references and drug use prohibit viewing by children. **p**, Robbie Brenner, Ryan Kavanaugh, Tucker Tooley, Camille Brown, Ken Halsband, Geoffrey Taylor; **d&w**, David Twohy; **cast**, Steve Zahn, Timothy Olyphant, Milla Jovovich, Kiele Sanchez, Marley Shelton, Chris Hemsworth, Anthony Ruivivar, Dale Dickey, Peter Navy Tuiasosopo, Wendy Braun, Jim Cruz; **c**, Mark Plummer; **m**, Boris Elkis; **ed**, Tracy Adams; **prod d**, Joseph C. Nemec III; **spec eff**, Charlie Bonilla, Tim Carras, Jonah Loop.

A Perfect Murder ★★★ 1998; U.S.; 107m; WB; Color; Crime Drama; Children: Unacceptable (MPAA: PG); **DVD**; **VHS**. In this good remake of the Alfred Hitchcock classic, **Dial M for Murder**, 1954, millionaire New York industrialist and financial wizard Douglas considers his wife, Paltrow, to be his most treasured acquisition. But he doesn't give her the warmth or romance she craves, so she becomes involved with Mortensen, a struggling artist, who gives her what her husband doesn't. When Douglas learns of her infidelity, he plots to commit the perfect murder, killing her and inheriting her large trust fund in the insidious process. It doesn't work out as planned since he gets caught in a climactic shootout. Songs: "Velvet Night" (Chris "Hambone" Cameron, Richard Davis), Black Alley Rap" (Cameron, Davis, Stevie Butler), "Biala Mi Gente" (Cameron, Ruben Alvarez), "Park Jam" (Davis), "The Sands of Time" (Cameron, Tad Robinson). Davis presents a good mystery but it cannot top the original. Violence, sexuality and gutter language prohibit viewing by children. **p**, Anne and Arnold Kopelson, Peter Macgregor-Scott, Christopher Mankiewicz, Mitchell Dauterive, Nana Greenwald; **d**, Andrew Davis; **cast**, Michael Douglas, Gwyneth Paltrow, Viggo Mortensen, David Suchet, Sarita Choudhury, Michael P. Moran, Novella Nelson, Constance Towers, Will Lyman, Maeve McGuire; **w**, Patrick Smith Kelly (based on the play "Dial M for Murder" by Frederick Knott); **c**, Dariusz Wolski; **m**, James Newton Howard; **ed**, Dov Hoenig, Dennis Virkler; **prod d**, Philip Rosenberg; **art d**, Patricia Woodbridge; **set d**, Debra Schutt; **spec eff**, Jeff Brink, Nathan Lafionatis.

The Perfect Specimen ★★★ 1937; U.S.; 97m; WB; B/W; Comedy; Children: Acceptable. Flynn abandons his swashbuckling image when appearing in this film, his first comedy, and does a good job of amusing himself and his fans by playing a sheltered multimillionaire. He is physically perfect, intellectually brilliant, and socially inept when it comes to the world beyond the gates of his vast estate. His life has been rigidly managed by his grandmother, Robson, the tyrannical family matriarch, who has dictated Flynn's every movement since birth. When learning about this reclusive tycoon, adventurous newspaper reporter Blondell resolves to get a story about him and invades his estate. She finds Flynn falling from a tree as he tests Newton's theory of gravity. The fetching Blondell intrigues Flynn enough for him to accompany her into the world beyond the protected confines of his estate to explore a society he has never known and, perhaps, understand his fellow man. After he leaves, it is believed that he has been kidnapped and held for ransom, and a desperate search is conducted to locate him. This leads to many funny predicaments and a lot of laughs, even when Flynn decides to enter the ring as a prizefighter and there comports himself with unexpected dexterity and prowess (as he would when enacting heavyweight champion James J. Corbett five years later in the exceptional biopic **Gentleman Jim**, 1942). Flynn and Blondell encounter many oddball characters in their exploratory trek as detectives search for Flynn (harried along their way by Robson's dithering secretary, Horton, in a very funny portrait), and a lot of quirky events unfold that add to the merriment and where Flynn makes the greatest discovery of his life by falling in love for the first time and with none other than Blondell, who was never lovelier and adorable than in this delightful outing. Pantheon director Curtiz, always superlative when it came to action films, keeps

Michael Douglas and Gwyneth Paltrow in *A Perfect Murder*, 1998.

this very entertaining story moving at a fast clip and uses a lot of inventive camera shots in the process. Flynn proved that he could handle comedy well and proved it again four years later when he appeared in another delightful comedy, a whodunit spoof called **Footsteps in the Dark**, 1941, where he plays another wealthy young man who thinks himself another Sherlock Holmes and sets out to solve baffling murder mysteries. The story for this film is really a takeoff on **It Happened One Night**, 1934, but in reverse in that the leading character is a wealthy man who goes missing and the reporter is a wisecracking blonde. Song: "As Sure As You're in Love" (M. K. Jerome). *Author's Note*: To promote this film, particularly Flynn's impressive exhibit of pugilism, the publicity department at Warner Brothers released a report that Flynn, a native of Tasmania, had represented Australia as a member of its boxing team in the 1928 Olympics held in Holland. This was a surprise to Flynn, who immediately went to the front office to complain about this fabrication, stating that he had never participated in that distinguished athletic event. Film editor Gene Ruggiero, who owned a small nightclub in Santa Monica at the time (a sideline business to his film editing job at MGM) told this author that "Errol came into my club one night and told me how the publicity people at Warner Brothers had promoted an outright lie about his being in the Olympics as an amateur prizefighter and how Jack Warner told him to dummy up about it after he complained about that phony claim. Errol quoted Warner, saying: 'Don't worry about it. The story will just go away and everyone will forget about it.' Errol belted down a lot of drinks that night and said: 'Sure, it will go away and when the press finds out about it, I will go away with that fake story. What the hell are they doing in that publicity department? Trying to wreck my career?' Well, the phony story haunted Errol so much—he was always a straightforward guy—that he later went to the newspapers and set them straight and, because of his honesty, they did not make any ballyhoo out of it. You know what they say, 'Honesty is the best policy.' Errol was later bum-rapped by two young ladies, who claimed he sexually attacked them at two different times and both were lying just to get money from him and he was innocent of that, too. I think everybody tried to take advantage of Errol because he was such a great hero on the screen and they were jealous of the guy. His biggest enemy in life was a notorious reputation he never earned and didn't deserve." **p**, Hal B. Wallis, Harry Joe Brown; **d**, Michael Curtiz; **cast**, Errol Flynn, Joan Blondell, Hugh Herbert, Edward Everett Horton, Dick Foran, May Robson, Beverly Roberts, Allen Jenkins, Dennie Moore, Hugh O'Connell, James Burke, Harry Davenport, Granville Bates; **w**, Norman Reilly Raine, Lawrence Riley, Brewster Morse, Fritz Falkenstein (based on a story by Samuel Hopkins Adams); **c**, Charles Rosher; **m**, Heinz Roemheld; **ed**, Terry Morse; **art d**, Robert Haas; **spec eff**, Byron Haskin.

Mark Wahlberg and George Clooney in *The Perfect Storm*, 2000.

The Perfect Storm ★★★ 2000; U.S.; 130m; WB; Color; Adventure; Children; Unacceptable (MPAA: PG-13); **DVD**; **VHS**. Tension-filled disaster tale, based upon the actual loss of the fishing vessel *Andrea Gail*, which was engulfed by a massive hurricane (described at the time as "the perfect storm") on October 28, 1991, about 180 miles northeast of Sable Island, and where its crew of six fishermen were lost to the sea. Clooney plays the skipper of this 72-foot-long boat, a scraggly, tough fisherman, and, like the rest of his scruffy, hard drinking crew members, he is always optimistic about the next big catch. His drinking and almost pathological dedication to his job has brought about his divorce and where he seldom sees his two young daughters. His luck at sea has also been running against him. When the vessel sails back to the port of Gloucester, Massachusetts, its holds are almost empty while Clooney's competitors exhibit holds packed with fish. He resolves to change his bad fortune by going far out to sea and fishing where few sail, off the Flemish Cap where endless schools of swordfish swim, or so he believes, the primary catch that is always sought. The vessel sails through choppy seas at the tail of a growing storm, and Clooney's hunch becomes a reality when they begin to harvest a great number of swordfish, he and his laboring crew members joyous at their good fortune. Then their ice-making machine breaks down and they realize that, unless they immediately sail back to port, their catch of fish will spoil. However, they get news that an impending hurricane is gathering between their position and the port. They decide to risk the storm, believing that they might beat the storm to the coast. In the meantime, a sister fishing vessel is damaged and calls for help. A U.S. Coast Guard helicopter arrives, the storm disabling it and the occupants are compelled to ditch into the sea, but are rescued by a nearby Coast Guard cutter. Clooney and his men are now struggling to keep the *Andrea Gail* upright as it is savagely rocked and pummeled by rising seas of forty-to fifty-foot waves. Two of the crew members topple overboard, and then Clooney sees a gigantic "rogue wave" (some of the waves in this actual storm were reportedly as high as 100 feet) and he tells Wahlberg, who is at the controls of the vessel, to steer the boat straight at the wave in an attempt to ride over it. This Wahlberg does, but the enormous wave breaks and the boat flips upside down, trapping all on board inside as it goes down, except for Wahlberg, who is tossed into the sea. He swims frantically as the vessel sinks and his own fate is sealed since he is not wearing a life jacket. All members are later reported lost at sea to end this tragedy and where the relatives of the lost seamen gather at the dock (in a scene reminiscent of **Captains Courageous**, 1937, a classic film about Gloucester fishermen) while Clooney's voice is heard soliloquizing the significance of being a fisherman. Petersen, who directed the powerful WWII sea adventure **Das Boot**, 1982, does a great job of presenting the hardships and perils of deep sea fishermen and his lensing of the growing storm

that turns the sea into a savage cauldron of swirling, crashing waves signaling doom is breathtaking to behold. The acting from Clooney, Wahlberg and the rest of the cast is exceptional, and even the fish (created through computer graphics) are impressive. The cinematography and special effects are outstanding in their candid portrayal of a vicious and uncompromising sea where all is harsh, threatening and, eventually, obliterating. Songs: "Yours Forever (Theme of The Perfect Storm)" (James Horner, John Mellencamp, George Green); "No Woman, No Cry" (Vincent Ford); "Hungry Heart" (Bruce Springsteen); "Rhythm of My Heart" (Marc Jordan, John Capek); "Heart of Saturday Night" (Tom Waits); "Man in the Box" (Jerry Cantrell, Layne Staley); "The Big Rock," "The Last Deputy" (Lennie Niehaus); "Tush" (Billy L. Gibbons, Dusty Hill, Frank Beard); "End of the Line" (Gregg Allman, Warren Haynes, John Jaworowicz, Allen Woody); "Eternal Father, Strong to Save" (William Whiting). *Author's Note*: The actual *Andrea Gail* reportedly had stability problems in that its resistance to capsizing was in doubt. The film was made for a whopping $140 million, but proved highly successful at the box office, returning more than $328 million worldwide. There is a singular similarity to this story and the classic Ernest Hemingway novel and film upon which it is based, **The Old Man and the Sea**, 1958, in that Clooney's character (as was the case with his real-life role model) made the same fateful decision embraced by Hemingway's Mexican fisherman and that is that they both elect to sail far beyond their normal and safe fishing areas and thus invite unpredictable disasters that might engulf them and do. **p**, Gail Katz; **d**, Wolfgang Petersen; **cast**, George Clooney, Mark Wahlberg, Diane Lane, John C. Reily, Mary Elizabeth Mastrantonio, William Fichtner, Bob Gunton, Karen Allen, Cherry Jones, Michael Ironside, Christopher McDonald; **w**, Bill Wittliff (based on the book by Sebastian Junger); **c**, John Seale (Technicolor); **m**, James Horner; **ed**, Richard Francis-Bruce; **prod d**, William Sandell; **art d**, Chas Butcher, Bruce Crone; **set d**, Ernie Bishop; **spec eff**, Walt Conti, John Frazier.

The Perils of Pauline ★★★ 1947; U.S.; 96m; PAR; Color; Biographical Drama/Musical; Children: Acceptable; **DVD**; **VHS**. Fun-loving Pearl White (1889-1938) is played by the energy-packed Hutton, who earns $5 a day working in a garment factory sweatshop in the early 1900s, but that all changes when she does a comic vaudeville performance of a Shakespeare play. It leads to her going to Hollywood and becoming one of the queens of the silent serials in **The Perils of Pauline**, 1914, in which she is always in physical danger. All of the great old silent film stunts and gags are present, where Hutton is always on the verge of being tied to a railroad track and run over by an oncoming locomotive, or dangling in mid-air on a high building or cliff and is about to be let loose to meet her doom. She finds time to have a romance with the handsome Lund while being constantly menaced (on camera) by Panzer, who, like Farnum and others, was brought out of retirement for this very entertaining and nostalgic jaunt down memory lane. Songs: "I Wish I Didn't Love You So," "Poppa, Don't You Preach to Me," "The Sewing Machine," "Rumble, Rumble, Rumble" (1947, Frank Loesser); "Poor Pauline" (Charles McCarron, Raymond Walker). *Author's Note*: Hutton told this author that "meeting and working with some of those great silent stars in **Perils of Pauline** was like stepping back into one of those tiny theaters that they used to have when I was a kid and when I first saw some of these wonderful people on the screen and here I was doing a picture with them. Is that fate? Pearl White was gone by then, but I thought about her every day on the set and I tried to do her routines as she did them in the old days. I watched all of the films about her I could see so that I could do her justice, but there was only one Pearl White." White began her career as a circus performer but, after injuring her spine in a stunt (falling off a galloping horse in a ring), she became a secretary and was noticed by silent film producer Harry Davis. He cast her in a three-reel adventure tale, **The Life of Buffalo Bill**, 1912, which starred William F. "Buffalo Bill" Cody (1846-1917), after the leading lady grew ill. Through this production she met Louis Gasnier, who starred her in her legendary serial. Since White had been physically debilitated by her circus injury, her more acrobatic scenes were enacted by doubles who were actually men of small statures wearing women's wigs and shot at angles so as not to show their faces. Two other films with the same title as this film were made in 1933 and 1967, but have different plotlines. **p**, Sol C. Siegel; **d**, George Marshall; **cast**, Betty Hutton, John Lund, Billy De Wolfe, Constance Collier, William Demarest, Frank Faylen, Paul Panzer, William Farnum, Chester Conklin, "Snub" Pollard, James Finlayson, Heinie Conklin, Bert Roach, George Marshall, Jr., Noreen Nash, Max "Slapsie Maxie" Rosenbloom; **w**, P.J. Wolfson, Frank Butler (based on a story by Wolfson suggested by incidents in the life of Pearl White and Charles W. Goddard's original silent movie serial, **The Perils of Pauline**); **c**, Ray Rennahan (Technicolor); **m**, Robert Emmett Dolan; **ed**, Arthur Schmidt; **art d**, Hans Dreier, Roland Anderson; **set d**, Sam Comer, Ray Moyer; **spec eff**, Farciot Edouart, Gordon Jennings.

Persepolis ★★★ 2007; France/U.S.; 108m; Color; Animated Feature/Biographical Drama; Children: Unacceptable (MPAA: PG-13); **DVD**. Based on the autobiography of Marjane Satrapi (b. 1969), this poignant coming-of-age story of a precocious young Iranian girl, Mastroianni, begins during the Islamic Revolution of the 1979. She watches events as the dream of her idealistic father, Abkarian, mother, Deneuve, and grandmother, Darrieux, is fulfilled with the defeat of the Shah. But then she finds that the new Iran run by Islamic fundamentalists becomes another oppressive regime. Fearing for her safety, her parents send her abroad to Vienna to study and to have a better life. She soon finds herself in an alien and uncomfortable world and, after she returns home, an expatriate at the age of twenty-four, she doesn't know where she really belongs. The title is a reference to the ancient Iranian city. Songs: "Eye of the Tiger" (James Peterik, Franck Sullivan III); "Roses of the South," "Persian March" (Johann Strauss, Jr.). Violent images, sexual references and drug content prohibit viewing by children. (In French; English subtitles.) **p**, Xavier Rigault, Marc-Antoine Robert, Tara Grace; **d&w**, Vincent Paronnaud, Marjane Satrapi; **cast** (voiceovers), Chiara Mastroianni, Catherine Deneuve, Danielle Darrieux, Simon Abkarian, Gabrielle Lopes Benites, François Jerosme, Sophie Arthuys, Jean-François Gallotte, Mathias Mlekuz; (English version voiceovers): Amethyste Frezignac, Gena Rowlands, Sean Penn, Iggy Popp, Aoife Stone; **m**, Olivier Bernet; **ed**, Stephane Roche; **prod d**, Marisa Musy; **spec eff**, Cyril Cosenza.

Persona ★★★★★ 1967; Sweden; 85m; Svensk Filmindustri/Lopert Picture Corporation; B/W; Drama; Children: Unacceptable; **DVD**; **VHS**. This masterpiece from Bergman is one of his most challenging films and where he immerses the viewer within his existential tale. It opens with a bare bulb and a reel of film on a projector, then the countdown leader of the first reel, as if watching a homemade movie or a film out of the early silent period, and the viewer sees a montage of slapstick comedic scenes and cartoons. The story or plotline then unfolds with Ullmann, a celebrated actress, who inexplicably stops speaking her lines while enacting "Electra." Andersson becomes her constant nurse, taking Ullmann to a seaside cottage to recuperate and where she vigilantly cares for her, but soon Bergman begins to focus more on Andersson than Ullmann and where he employs the clever use of light and grades of shadows to show the growing similarities between patient and nurse. In a passionate effort to inspire Ullmann to speak again, Andersson begins talking to her, revealing her innermost thoughts, anxieties and emotions. In so doing, the viewer realizes that Andersson is as mentally and emotionally troubled as Ullmann. While Ullmann can only respond silently with facial and body gestures, Andersson speaks for both of them, slipping deceptively (and deviously as her tortured mind allows) from sanity to insanity and then back again, a chilling and unnerving portrait of a tortured soul that teeters between two distinct but identical personalities in a remarkable display of visual schizophrenia and identity transfer-

Liv Ullmann in *Persona,* 1967.

ence. In an amazing juxtaposition of camera techniques, Bergman shows the viewer the melting and merging of both of their faces into one, producing a visual impact that is singularly stunning and unforgettable. The film ends with the film slipping out of the projector so that the viewer is left to see nothing but the bare bulb, bringing the story (or its brilliant technique) to full circle. The performances from Ullmann and Andersson are nothing short of magnificent, and Bergman is at the peak of his artistry with this superlative film where he perfectly mixes his favorite stew of psychology, art, reality, surrealism, life and death. The cinematography from Nykvist, Bergman's favorite cameraman, is unparalleled in quality and beauty. (In Swedish; English subtitles.) **p,d&w**, Ingmar Bergman; **cast**, Bibi Andersson, Liv Ullmann, Margaretha Krook, Gunnar Bjornstrand, Jorgen Lindstrom; **c**, Sven Nykvist; **m**, Lars Johan Werle; **ed**, Ulla Ryghe; **prod d**, Bibi Lindström.

Personal Column ★★★ 1941; France; 111m; Speva Films/Pax Films, Inc.; B/W; Crime Drama; Children: Unacceptable; **VHS**. Offbeat but chilling crime whodunit sees a number of women being murdered in Paris by a serial killer. After police deduce that all of the victims are young women who answered advertisements published in the personal columns (ergo the title) of newspapers, they go to Dea, who is the roommate of one of the victims, asking her to serve as a decoy to entice the killer into a police trap. She is reluctant to do this, but then agrees and is interviewed by a number of men seeking to hire female employees for various jobs, from maids in hotels to house servants. None of the prospective employers prove to be suspicious. While continuing to be bait for the killer, Dea meets and falls in love with charming Chevalier, a nightclub singer. They plan to marry, but just before they go to the altar, Chevalier is arrested and charged with the serial killings. Dea does not believe Chevalier is guilty and sets out to prove him innocent. She concludes that Chevalier has been framed by one of the men who earlier interviewed her and she confronts this deceptive killer, prompting him to attack her, but police are nearby and rescue her and catch the real killer. Chevalier is set free to live out a happy life with Dea. Siodmak, a director noted for his fine film noir productions (**The Spiral Staircase**, 1945, **The Dark Mirror**, 1946, **Cry of the City**, 1948 and **Criss Cross**, 1949), offers a well-made and very clever film with enough red herrings to fill anyone's plate while providing great suspense and many thrilling moments through his expert use of lighting and shadows. Dea, Chevalier and the rest of the cast are standouts in their roles. The film has a good remake in **Lured**, 1947, starring Lucille Ball in one of her best dramatic roles as the luscious bait to a killer. *Author's Note*: This film was made in 1939, shortly before Germany invaded France, and prints of this film were smuggled out of the country, some making their way to Hollywood where the censors edited out several scenes of Dea with men interview-

Parker Posey and Tim Guinee in *Personal Velocity*, 2002.

ing her, these scenes thought to be then too risqué for American viewing; the film saw limited exhibition in that truncated version. (In French; English subtitles.) **p**, André Paulvé, Michel Safra; **d**, Robert Siodmak; **cast**, Maurice Chevalier, Erich Von Stroheim, Pierre Renoir, Marie Déa, André Brunot, Jean Temerson, Jacques Varennes, Madeleine Geoffroy; **w**, Jacques Companéez, Ernst Neubach, Simon Gantillon; **c**, Marcel Fradetal, Michel Kelber, Jacques Mercanton; **m**, Michel Michelet; **ed**, Yvonne Martin; **art d & set d (prod d)**, Georges Wakhvitch, Maurice Colasson.

Personal Velocity: Three Portraits ★★★ 2002; U.S.; 86m; Blue Magic/UA; Color; Drama/Romance; Children: Unacceptable (MPAA: R); **DVD**; **VHS**. Solid domestic drama sees three women reach critical turning points in their lives. Sedgwick is a working-class young woman from a small town in New York State, who leaves her abusive husband and begins a journey to reclaim her lost power. Posey is an ambition-driven editor, who struggles with her infidelity in an unexciting marriage. Balk ran away from home and got pregnant and finds herself in a relationship she doesn't want. The direction is taut, the script is well written, and the performances are above-average. Violence, strong sexuality and gutter language prohibit viewing by children. **p**, Alexis Alexanian, Lemore Syvan, Gary Winick; **d&w**, Rebecca Miller (based on her book); **cast**, Kyra Sedgwick, Parker Posey, Fairuza Balk, John Ventimiglia, Ron Leibman, Wallace Shawn, David Warshofsky, Leo Fitzpatrick, Tim Guinee, Patti D'Arbanville; **c**, Ellen Kuras; **m**, Michael Rohatyn; **ed**, Sabine Hoffmann; **prod d**, Judy Becker; **set d**, Maus Drechsler, Heather Loeffler.

Persuasion ★★★ 1995; U.K./U.S./France; 107m; BBC Films/Sony; Color; Drama/Romance; Children: Unacceptable (MPAA: PG); **DVD**; **VHS**. Set in 1814 England, Root is the twenty-seven-year-old daughter of a financially troubled aristocratic family, who is persuaded by family members to break off her engagement to Hinds, a young seaman of no position or fortune. He returns after eight years as a rich and successful sea captain from the Napoleonic Wars and is now a highly eligible bachelor. He courts another young woman, but Root succeeds in persuading him that she still loves him and they are reunited. This superior dramatization of the Jane Austen novel sees exceptional performances from Root and Hinds. Songs: "Prelude in B," "Nocturne in B," "Prelude in G" (Frederic Chopin); "Sarabande in B," "Sarabande in D" (Johann Sebastian Bach); "The Minstrel Boy" (Thomas Moore); "The Dusky Night" (traditional). Sensual material prohibits viewing by children. **p**, Fiona Finlay, George Faber, Rebecca Eaton; **d**, Roger Michell; **cast**, Amanda Root, Ciarán Hinds, Susan Fleetwood, Corin Redgrave, Fiona Shaw, John Woodvine, Phoebe Nicholls, Samuel West, Sophie Thompson, Judy Cornwell, Simon Russell Beale, Felicity Dean; **w**, Nick Dear

(based on the novel by Jane Austen); **c**, John Daly; **m**, Jeremy Sams; **ed**, Kate Evans; **prod d**, William Dudley; **art d**, Linda Ward; **spec eff**, Chris Reynolds, Colin Gorry.

Pete 'n' Tillie ★★★ 1972; U.S.; 100m; UNIV; Color; Comedy/Drama; Children: Unacceptable (MPAA: PG); **VHS**. Tillie, played by Burnett, is thirty three years old, single, and fears that if she doesn't marry soon she'll be an old maid. But she's anxious about meeting her newest blind date, Pete, essayed by Matthau. He's a wise-cracking fellow, who flirts with women in order to hide his insecurities. Their relationship results in an agreement to marry, despite their differences. The marriage begins with relative peace and happiness, but, after their son Montgomery dies of leukemia, both begin to drift apart (taking a leaf from a great tearjerker, **Penny Serenade**, 1941). Matthau, an inveterate womanizer, begins seeing other women, and the marriage is almost on the rocks with Matthau living apart from Burnett. Both are miserable without each other, and Matthau returns to Burnett to tell her that the only real happiness he has had is with her and they reconcile, planning to make a go of it once more. Good performances from Burnett and Matthau make this comedic drama superior to the usual domestic bathos found in similar tales. Mature themes prohibit viewing by children. ***Author's Note***: Matthau told this author that "I am a prankster and a punster and a poor spouse for Carol [Burnett] in **Pete 'n' Tillie**. Like a lot of husbands, I think that the grass is always greener on the other side of the fence, but, just like what happens to such wandering clucks, I realize that there's no place like home. I had some dimension to work with in the character I play, thanks to Julie [Epstein], who wrote the script, one of the fellows who turned out the screenplay for **Casablanca** [1942]." Epstein told this author that "Walter [Matthau] and Carol [Burnett], both very talented persons, made my chief characters believable in **Pete 'n' Tillie**. I was amazed at Carol's wonderful restraint in that picture. She dumped all that hammy mugging she did on her TV comedy show and played it straight down the line and did a great job of a woman marrying late in life, losing a son, then her husband, and almost her reason to live until she and Walter find they can't live without each other. That's the stuff their dreams are made of." Burnett's impressive appearance marked her second appearance in a feature film, her first being **Who's Been Sleeping in My Bed?**, 1963, made nine years earlier and where she had a small role in that comedy. **p&w**, Julius J. Epstein (based on the novella *Witch's Milk* by Peter De Vries); **d**, Martin Ritt; **cast**, Walter Matthau, Carol Burnett, Geraldine Page, Barry Nelson, Rene Auberjonois, Lee Montgomery, Henry Jones, Kent Smith, Philip Bourneuf, Whit Bissell; **c**, John Alonzo (Panavision; Technicolor); **m**, John Williams; **ed**, Frank Bracht; **art d**, George C. Webb; **set d**, John P. Austin, Joseph J. Stone.

Pete Kelly's Blues ★★★★ 1955; U.S.; 95m; WB; Color; Drama/Musical; Children: Unacceptable; **DVD**; **VHS**. Few films have captured the jazz era of the 1920s as well as this much underrated but fine musical drama, where Webb gives one of his finest performances as a cornet player leading a jazz band in 1927 Kansas City, Missouri, a town then dominated by ruthless bootleggers and kill-crazy crime bosses like O'Brien. Into Webb's life struts blonde flapper Leigh, a wealthy lady who gives rowdy parties and has a yen for jazz. She falls in love with Webb, overcoming his resistance to any long-standing relationships based upon his fly-by-night lifestyle where he and his band move from city to city. O'Brien forces Webb to take on a singer, Lee, a lady with a sultry voice born for the blues (her role of a lush is not dissimilar to that of Claire Trevor in **Key Largo**, 1948, except that Lee could sing like no other thrush). Webb and his boys are dedicated to jazz and visit a tavern where black entertainers perform and there hear the great Fitzgerald sing two wonderful songs. Things turn for the worse when O'Brien decides to extort dues from the band members as their self-appointed agent, and this causes drummer Milner to angrily explode, attacking the gangster, a rash act that seals his fate as he is later murdered. Such violence so alarms Marvin, who is Webb's closest friend and a wise-cracking clarinetist in the band, that he decides to go elsewhere, having gotten a gig in New York. He asks Webb to join that band, but when Webb learns that Leon Bismark "Bix" Beiderbecke (1903-1931) is the star cornet player in that band, he declines to join up and decides to tough it out in Kansas City. The brutal O'Brien continues to make life miserable for everyone, and when he finds Lee hitting the bottle again, he pistol whips her so viciously that she becomes insane and is sent to an institution, which is where Webb finds her mindlessly murmuring to herself (in a stunning performance that earned her an Oscar nomination). Webb tries to have police detective Devine arrest O'Brien for his transgressions, but, before that happens, he and Leigh are trapped in a deserted dance hall by O'Brien's goons and Webb shoots it out with them, killing one. When another henchman wrongly shoots and mortally wounds O'Brien, he tosses his gun away and flees. O'Brien dies in agony on the dance hall floor as Leigh and Webb depart. They are later seen in a jammed club where Webb and his band are playing to an appreciative audience to end this action-packed film. Webb produced and directed this lively tale, where the sets, props and costuming accurately reflect the flavor and style of the Roaring Twenties, and studded it with a lot of great jazz numbers played by Dick Cathcart (who dubs Webb's cornet playing), Matty Matlock, Moe Schneider and George Van Epps. The outstanding singing from Fitzgerald and Lee are priceless sound gems in this very entertaining film. Produced for $2 million, the film was popular at the box office, returning $5 million in its first release. Songs: "Just a Closer Walk with Thee" (traditional); "I'm Gonna Meet My Sweetie Now" (music: Jesse Greer; lyrics: Benny Davis); "Sugar (That Sugar Baby of Mine)" (Maceo Pinkard, Sidney D. Mitchell, Edna Alexander); "Somebody Loves Me" (music: George Gershwin; lyrics: Buddy G. DeSylva, Ballard McDonald); "Hard Hearted Hannah" (Milton Ager, Jack Yellen, Charles Bates, Bob Bigelow); "Bye Bye Blackbird" (music: Ray Henderson; lyrics: Mort Dixon); "Sing a Rainbow," "He Needs Me" (Arthur Hamilton); "Ella Hums the Blues" (Ella Fitzgerald); "Smiles" (Lee S. Roberts); "Pete Kelly's Blues" (music: Ray Heindorf; lyrics: Sammy Cahn); "Breezing Along with the Breeze" (Haven Gillespie, Seymour Simons, Richard A. Whiting); "I Never Knew" (music: Ted Fio Rito; lyrics: Gus Kahn); "Oh, Didn't He Ramble" (W. C. Handy); "After I Say I'm Sorry" (music: Walter Donaldson; lyrics: Abe Lyman). **p&d,** Jack Webb; **cast,** Webb, Janet Leigh, Edmond O'Brien, Peggy Lee, Andy Devine, Lee Marvin, Ella Fitzgerald, Martin Milner, Than Wyenn, Jayne Mansfield; **w,** Richard L. Breen; **c,** Hal Rosson (Warnercolor); **m,** Ray Heindorf, David Buttolph, Sammy Cahn, Arthur Hamilton; **ed,** Robert M. Leeds; **prod d,** Harper Goff; **art d,** Feild Gray; **set d,** John Sturtevant.

Peter Ibbetson ★★★★★ 1935; U.S.; 88m; PAR; B/W; Fantasy/Romance; Children: Cautionary; **DVD; VHS.** Here is a wonderful story for the always young at heart, a mystical, surrealistic tale insisting that love can transcend and conquer all misery, torment and even death itself. Cooper is a struggling architect, who is assigned to design and build some structures on a large estate in Paris. When inspecting the place, memories of his childhood recall how he once played in one of the gardens at that estate with another youngster, a beautiful girl to whom he lost his heart. The garden is now overgrown with weeds and is in disarray. His employer is a wealthy duke, Halliday, who wants Cooper to design new stables for his horses, but Cooper disagrees with Halliday's attractive wife, Harding, about how the buildings are to be constructed and he is summarily dismissed. Harding thinks twice about her actions and Cooper is rehired, and she permits Cooper to construct the buildings according to his own creative designs. (Cooper's fierce individualism as an architect would be further magnified fourteen years later when he played a Frank Lloyd Wright type architect in **The Fountainhead,** 1949.) In talking with Cooper, Harding notices that he has a peculiar mannerism that she identifies as that of the boy she once played with in her garden and they then both recall their childhood memories together. This rekindles the love they once had for one another, a love

Ida Lupino and Gary Cooper in *Peter Ibbetson*, 1935.

that inexorably bonds them together. The possessive and jealous Halliday sees them together in what he believes is an intimate moment and later confronts Harding, but she assures Halliday that her relationship with Cooper is only based upon the innocence and naiveté of childhood and nothing more. Cooper is allowed to complete his work, but before he departs, he meets again with Harding and embraces her in a friendly gesture. Halliday witnesses this embrace, and, suspicious that Cooper and his wife have been having an adulterous affair all along, confronts Cooper and Harding with a gun. Enraged, he thinks to kill Cooper, but Cooper, in defending himself, hurls a chair at Halliday that causes the gun to go off and where Halliday accidentally and fatally shoots himself. Cooper is arrested, tried and convicted of murder and sentenced to life imprisonment. In his cell, Cooper finds comfort in recalling his childhood memory with Harding, seeing himself with her once again in that lush and beautiful garden (not unlike the magical garden that brings solace to Margaret O'Brien playing a lonely little girl in **The Secret Garden,** 1949); his dreams become so vivid that he talks about them in his sleep, disturbing guards, who conclude that he is an unruly inmate and they angrily beat him so brutally that his spine is injured. As he suffers terrible pain and is in a semi-conscious state, Cooper is visited in his cell by Harding, who tells him that since they are separated in life, they can only be together in his dreams and, if he clings to that belief, it will happen. To bolster his faith in her statements, Harding informs Cooper that she will send him a ring, a token that represents her beliefs, a treasurable item that will signify their eternal love for one another. Cooper receives that ring the next day and now believes that the impossible is possible and that his dreams have somehow become reality when Harding visited him. As the years unfold, Cooper and Harding grow old, but in Cooper's dreams they are always young and happy together. When Harding dies, she tells Cooper that she will be waiting for him in their garden, and when Cooper perishes, they are finally reunited for eternity. Pantheon director Hathaway does a marvelous job in presenting this evocative and powerful tale; he presents the dream sequences in such a convincing manner that one embraces those ethereal images, making of them one's own cherished reality. Cooper's dreams are so effectively exhibited that they are easily shared by the viewer, instilling a desire to see love conquer, a longing deep and abiding within the human spirit that demands the eventual happiness of these starcrossed lovers. The invariably stoic Cooper is unusually sensitive and feeling in this outstanding film as he is drawn into Harding's spiritual embrace. She, too, is mesmerizing in her other world presence of a warm and inviting specter beckoning and bolstering Cooper's faith and trust. Many distinguished filmmakers have rightly termed this film a classic, not the least of whom was Luis Brunel, who stated that it was "one of the ten best films ever made." The film did not do well in the

Peter Pan and Wendy spying on the pirates in *Peter Pan*, 1953.

U.S. when it was released, but it was a smash hit in Europe. ***Author's Note***: Hathaway told this author that "only Coop [Gary Cooper] could have made his character in that picture believable. He was one of the few actors who acted without any phony theatrics in those days. That is because he understood his character and could make him believable." Cooper told this author that "**Peter Ibbetson** is a very special picture for me. I have to live out my life mostly in fantasy scenes and none of those scenes would have meant anything to anyone if Henry [Hathaway] had not used that iron grip of his to make them real instead of fantastic. The scenes are muted and he toned everything down, but those scenes still give you the feeling that you are somewhere else than on this planet. He is one of the great directors." The transference of tangible and meaningful objects from the spiritual to the material world, such as Cooper receiving Harding's ring in this film, has been shown in a number of productions, most dramatically in **Miracle in the Rain**, 1956, where Jane Wyman receives a lucky coin she has given to her lover, Van Johnson, who is killed in WWII, but nevertheless reappears in spirit to return that coin and tell her that their love will last forever. The script for that film was written by my mentor, Ben Hecht, based upon his novel and who admitted to this author that "I was certainly inspired by the novel that presents that haunting love story [*Peter Ibbetson*], but there are many other such tales that go back centuries and you will find stories like that in the folk tales of Europe as far back as the Medieval Ages. There must be something to those stories or they would not have survived the ages, and that something, my boy, is love." The novel by George du Maurier was published in 1891 and it was first filmed under the title of **Forever**, 1921, starring Wallace Reid and Elsie Ferguson. It was later produced as a stage play starring John and Lionel Barrymore and Constance Collier as the female phantasm. Collier later adapted the story for this 1935 version that saw no less than nine writers working on the script. The story was also presented in a one-hour episode of the Ford Theater's TV series in 1951, with Richard Greene and Stella Andrew as the languishing lovers. **p**, Louis D. Lighton; **d**, Henry Hathaway; **cast**, Gary Cooper, Ann Harding, John Halliday, Ida Lupino, Douglass Dumbrille, Virginia Weidler, Dickie Moore, Doris Lloyd, Gilbert Emery, Donald Meek, Christian Rub, Elsa Buchanan, Leonid Kinskey; **w**, Vincent Lawrence, Waldemar Young, Constance Collier, John Meehan, Edwin Justus Mayer (based on the novel by George du Maurier and the play by John Nathaniel Raphael); **c**, Charles Lang; **m**, Ernst Toch; **ed**, Stuart Heisler; **art d**, Hans Dreier, Robert Usher; **spec eff**, Gordon Jennings.

Peter Pan ★★★★★ 1953; U.S.; 77m; Walt Disney Productions/RKO; Animated Adventure; Children: Recommended; **BD**; **DVD**; **VHS**. This delightful Barrie tale of the boy who refused to grow up was never made and presented better than in this animated masterpiece from Disney. The film begins with Conried as the no-nonsense father of a household in London, England, and where he disapproves of his oldest and fanciful daughter Wendy (Beaumont voiceover) telling adventurous stories about a mythical boy named Peter Pan (Driscoll voiceover, who makes a distinctive appearance in that this was the first time Peter was ever played by a boy) to his younger children. Conried insists that no such person as Driscoll exists, and, after he directs Beaumont and the family dog to leave the nursery, he and his wife (Angel voiceover) depart to go out on the town. The moment they leave, Driscoll appears with Tinker Bell (Kerry voiceover), a tiny, glittering fairy, and where Driscoll demands that Beaumont return his shadow back to him, which Beaumont has somehow captured. The other children (Luske and Collins voiceovers) awake and Driscoll tells them that they will have nothing but fun and adventure when he takes them to Never Neverland, and, best of all, when they are there they will never have to grow up and be annoying adults like Conried, who do not know how to have fun anymore. Tinker Bell is not in favor of this idea, especially since she does not like Driscoll giving so much attention to Beaumont, but Driscoll, as he always does, has his way, and Beaumont, Luske and Collins follow him as they all fly from London to Never Neverland. After some mildly harrowing experiences, they are threatened by fierce pirates—their ship is anchored next to Never Neverland, and they are led by Captain Hook (also Conried voiceover), who is desperate to capture Driscoll since it was Driscoll who earlier cut off his hand in a sword fight. Conried and his top henchman, Mr. Smee (Thompson voiceover) plot to capture Driscoll and his friends, along with kidnapping an Indian princess, but Conried grows nervous when he sees a huge crocodile swimming nearby, knowing that it was this creature that ate his severed hand and wants to devour the rest of him. The pirates narrowly miss capturing Driscoll and other children, who then meet a band of lost boys who have made Driscoll their leader. Meanwhile, Driscoll becomes angry at Tinker Bell after he learns that she used a trick that might have gotten Beaumont killed and he orders her banished forever from their company (although Driscoll later forgives her). Driscoll then takes Beaumont to see some mermaids, who think to drown the girl, but they become terrified when seeing Conried and they swim away. Then Driscoll and Beaumont, while spying on Conreid, see that he has captured Tiger Lily (Orr voiceover), the Indian princess, and Conried demands that Orr reveal the whereabouts of Driscoll so that he can capture him. Meanwhile, the lost boys, along with Luske and Collins, have been captured by Orr's father, the Indian Chief (Candido voiceover) and his warriors and Candido tells the boys that if his daughter is not returned by sunset, they will all be burned at the stake. Driscoll solves that problem by rescuing Orr and returning her to Candido and her mother, Candido's squaw (Foray voiceover), a very bossy woman. Driscoll is then honored by the tribe for rescuing Orr. The indefatigable Conried, however, will not give up his pursuit of his nemesis, Driscoll, and after he captures Tinker Bell (Kerry voiceover), locking her inside of a lantern as a makeshift prison cell, he compels her to reveal Driscoll's hideout, but she gets Conried to promise that he will not lay "a finger or a hook" on Driscoll, a promise Conried has no intention of keeping. Beaumont, Luske and Collins are getting weary of their endless adventures with Driscoll and want to return home and they tell the lost boys that they should come along with them and that their parents will adopt them. Before they depart, however, Conried and his henchmen capture the lot of them, leaving a time bomb behind that is about to blow up Driscoll, who has refused to return with the children. At the last second, however, Tinker Bell (Kerry voiceover) appears out of nowhere to snatch the bomb from Driscoll and save his life. Driscoll finds Kerry intact within the rubble and then they both prevent Conried from forcing the children from walking the plank. The children then battle the pirates to a standstill until they all flee with the crocodile hungrily chasing them. The lost boys decide they will stay in Neverland, and Driscoll uses the abandoned pirate ship to sail him and Wendy and Luske and Collins back to London. Once back in London, the boys are found sleeping in their beds in the nursery and Beaumont is sleeping at its open window. Father Conried, who has relaxed his ideas about Beaumont's stories, then arrives and peers from the window with Beaumont to see what seems to be a pirate ship sailing in the sky and the magical image reminds him of his own boyhood dreams, that image then slowly breaking up to become part of the drifting clouds. The animation and production values of this enchanting film are superlative, and the smallest details of every character and the environment of each scene come brilliantly alive with movement and in rich color. The story line is humorous and exciting throughout as each scene inventively unfolds. Truly a masterpiece, this wonderful film joins Disney's illustrious classics of **Alice in Wonderland**, 1951; **Bambi**, 1942; **Dumbo**, 1941; **Fantasia**, 1940; **Pinocchio**, 1940; and **Snow White and the Seven Dwarfs**, 1937. Songs: "The Second Star to the Right," "You Can Fly, You Can Fly, You Can Fly!," "What Makes the Red Man Red?," "Your Mother and Mine," "The Elegant Captain Hook," (music: Sammy Fain; lyrics: Sammy Cahn); "A Pirate's Life" (music: Oliver Wallace; lyrics: Erdman Penner); "Following the Leader" (music: Oliver Wallace; lyrics: Ted Sears, Winston Hibbler); "Never Smile at a Crocodile" (music: Frank Churchill). *Author's Note*: Walt Disney had planned to make this film as early as 1935, two years before he made his first feature-length animated film, **Snow White and the Seven Dwarfs**, 1937, and, in 1939, two years after making **Snow White and the Seven Dwarfs**, he contacted the estate owning the film rights (the Great Ormond Street Hospital in London, which served as the trustee of all of J. M. Barrie's literary properties as per his will) and acquired the rights to film the story. With the advent of WWII, however, Disney put the film project on the back burner while he produced many other feature-length animated films, not reviving the project for a decade, and when he did, he went full tilt at it, spending more than $4 million on the film, then a staggering budget. The cost was so high due to the fact that Disney, in keeping with his penchant for perfection, first made a full-length live-action film of the story, which was exclusively seen and used by his artists, who drew each scene for the animated version from the live-action scenes in the first version and where Conried and many of those appearing in voiceover in the animated version appeared in full costume and on finished sets of the live-action version. Dancer Roland Dupree played Peter in the live-action version. Peter Pan has been played in many other productions, most notably in **The Adventures of Peter Pan**, 1989 (TV series; Noriko Hidaka); **FairyTale: A True Story**, 1997 (Anna Chancellor); **Finding Neverland**, 2004 (Kelly Macdonald); **Happy Birthday, Peter Pan**, 2005 (TV special; Rupert Grint voiceover; Jeremy Sumpter); **Hook**, 1991 (Robin Williams as an adult; and Ryan Francis, Jewell Newlander Hubbard, Max Hoffman and Matthew Van Ginkel as Peter in various stages as a boy); **Neverland**, 2003 (Rick Sparks); **Neverland**, 2011 (TV series; Charlie Rowe); **Peter Pan**, 1924 (Betty Bronson); **Peter Pan**, 1960 (made-for-TV; Mary Martin); **Peter Pan**, 1962 (made-for-TV; Michael Ande); **Peter Pan**, 1976 (made-for-TV; Mia Farrow); **Peter Pan**, 2000 (made-for-TV; Cathy Rigby); **Peter Pan**, 2003 (Jeremy Sumpter); **Shrek**, 2001 (Michael Galasso voiceover); and **Too Many Kisses**, 1925 (Harpo Marx, as the Village Peter Pan). **p**, Walt Disney; **d**, Hamilton Luske, Clyde Geronimi, Wilfred Jackson; **cast** (voiceovers), Bobby Driscoll, Kathryn Beaumont, Hans Conried, Margaret Kerry, Bill Thompson, Heather Angel, Paul Collins, Tommy Luske, Candy Candido, Corinne Orr, June Foray, Tom Conway (narrator); **w**, Ted Sears, Bill Peet, Joe Rinaldi, Erdman Penner, Winston Hibler, Milt Banta, Ralph Wright (based on the play by Sir James M. Barrie); **m**, Oliver Wallace; **ed**, Donald Halliday; **spec eff**, George Rowley, Blaine Gibson, Joshua Meador, Dan MacManus.

Peter Rabbit and Tales of Beatrix Potter ★★★ 1971; U.K.; 90m; GW Films/MGM; Color; Ballet/Fantasy; Children: Recommended (MPAA: G); **DVD**; **VHS**. A delightful live action-film with dances choreographed by Frederick Ashton and performed by the British Royal Ballet in which Peter Rabbit and other characters created by

Kenneth Branagh and Emma Thompson in *Peter's Friends***, 1992.**

Beatrix Potter enact some of her beloved animal tales. Peter steals vegetables from Mr. McGregor's garden, some mice invade a doll house and go bonkers when they discover the food is plastic, and Jemima Puddle-Duck escapes a crafty fox, who wants her for supper. The emphasis is on humor and it's very entertaining for anyone of any age. **p**, Richard Goodwin; **d**, Reginald Mills; **cast**, Frederick Ashton, Alexander Grant, Julie Wood, Ann Howard, Bob Mead, Garry Grant, Sally Ashby, Brenda Last, Michael Coleman, Wayne Sleep; **w**, Goodwin, Christine Edzard (based on stories and characters created by Beatrix Potter); **c**, Austin Dempster (Technicolor); **m**, John Lanchbery; **ed**, John Rushton; **prod d**, Christine Edzard; **spec eff**, Tom Howard.

Peter's Friends ★★★ 1992; U.K.; 101m; British Broadcasting Co.; Samuel Goldwyn; Color; Comedy/Drama; Children: Unacceptable (MPAA: R); **DVD**; **VHS**. Seven friends, who were members of an acting group, graduate from Cambridge University, England, in 1982, and then go their separate ways. Ten years later, one of the group's members, Branagh, now a Hollywood movie writer, inherits a large estate from his father and invites the others to spend New Year's holiday with him there. They soon discover that their lives have all changed a lot since college days. It's a combination of comedy and drama involving friendship, marriage, fidelity, materialism, and coping with death and loss, so closely reminiscent of **The Big Chill**, 1983, that one might think it to be a remake. The film nevertheless presents an absorbing drama peppered with a lot of humorous scenes. Songs: "What's Love Got to Do with It" (Graham Lyle, Terry Britten), "You're My Best Friend" (John Deacon), "Girls Just Want to Have Fun" (Richard Hazard), "Hungry Heart" (Bruce Springsteen), "Give Me Strength" (Eric Clapton), "Don't Get Me Wrong" (Chrissie Hynde), "Everybody Wants to Rule the World" (Roland Orzabal, Ian Stanley, Chris Hughes), "My Baby Just Cares for Me" (Walter Donaldson, Gus Khan), "Rio" (Michael Nesmith), "As the Days Go By" (L. Thomas), "Let's Stay Together (Al Green, Al Jackson Jr., Willie Mitchell), "I Guess That's Why They Call It the Blues," "Un bel Di" (from the opera "Madame Butterfly" by Giacomo Puccini), "If You Let Me Stay" (Terence Trent D'Arby), "King of Rock & Roll" (Prefab Sprout), "The Way You Look Tonight" (Jerome Kern, Dorothy Fields), "Roger's Coffee Commercial Jingle" (Hugh Laurie), "Orpheus in the Underworld" (Jacques Offenbach). Mature subject matter prohibits viewing by children. **p&d**, Kenneth Branagh; **cast**, Branagh, Emma Thompson, Hugh Laurie, Stephen Fry, Imelda Staunton, Phyllida Law, Alphonsia Emmanuel, Richard Briers, Alex Scott, Edward Jewesbury; **w**, Martin Bergman, Rita Rudner; **c**, Roger Lanser; **ed**, Andrew Marcus; **prod d**, Tim Harvey; **art d**, Martin Childs; **spec eff**, Pete Hanson, Mark Nelmes, Janek Sirrs.

Leslie Howard, Dick Foran, Bette Davis and Humphrey Bogart in *The Petrified Forest,* 1936.

Pete's Dragon ★★★ 1977; U.S.; 128m; Disney/Buena Vista; Color; Fantasy/Adventure; Children: Recommended; MPAA: PG; **DVD**; **VHS**. Set in early 1900s New England, this entertaining and well-crafted film sees Marshall, a nine-year-old orphan, running away from mean adoptive parents with his only friend, Elliott (Callas), an imaginary cartoon dragon. They escape to a fishing village in Maine and live with Reddy, a friendly lighthouse keeper, and her father, Rooney. This is a delightful live-action film in which only the dragon is animated and visible only to Marshall, which creates a lot of humorous adventures. While Callas gets Pete into and out of a lot of trouble, Pete saves his friend from a doctor, Dale, who wants Elliott for medical purposes. Songs: "The Happiest Home in These Hills," Boop Bop Bopbop Bop (I Love You, Too)," "I Saw a Dragon," "It's Not Easy," "Passamashloddy," "Candle on the Water," "There's Room for Everyone," "Every Little Piece," "Brazzle Dazzle Day," "Bill of Sale" (Al Kasha, Joel Hirschhorn). **p**, Ron Miller, Jerome Courtland; **d**, Don Chaffey; **cast**, Helen Reddy, Jim Dale, Mickey Rooney, Red Buttons, Shelley Winters, Sean Marshall, Jane Kean, Jim Backus, Charles Tyner, Gary Morgan, Jeff Conaway, Cal Bartlett; **w**, Malcolm Marmorstein (based on a story by Seton I. Miller, S.S. Field); **c**, Frank Phillips (Technicolor); **m**, Irwin Kostal; **ed**, Gordon D. Brenner; **prod d**, John B. Mansbridge; **art d**, Mansbridge, Jack Martin Smith; **set d**, Lucien M. Hafley; **spec eff**, Eustace Lycett, Art Cruickshank, Danny Lee.

The Petrified Forest ★★★★ 1936; U.S.; 82m; WB; B/W; Crime Drama; Children: Unacceptable; **DVD**; **VHS**. Howard is superb as an idealistic but disillusioned drifter in this tension-filled drama adapted from the successful Broadway stage production by the gifted Sherwood (a playwright who was also one of President Franklin D. Roosevelt's top speech writers). Howard finds himself bumming his way through Northern Arizona, and, while hitchhiking, passes a petrified forest of unanimated trees turned to rock, seeing this uninviting image as a symbol of a frozen human society where all is lifeless and hopeless. He comes across a remote way station that is a combination gas station and diner, which is owned by Hall and where Hall's daughter, Davis, serves as a waitress, who also cares for her aging and cantankerous grandfather, Grapewin. Howard, the only customer, orders a meal, and after Davis serves him his food, they begin a conversation. She tells him that she dreams of becoming an artist and going to France to study, but that she has no funds to make the trip. Howard spins some tales about France and how he lived there when he was a young and ambitious writer, who authored one book. He describes how he became the kept husband of a wealthy woman and how he squandered his life and without writing anything more, until she tired of him and they separated. He then migrated to America and has been hoboing his way across the country in search of some meaning to his life. Davis' story is similar in that she has lived without her mother, a French war bride, who married Hall when he was a serviceman in WWI, but how that marriage ended and her mother moved back to France, leaving Davis in the care of her father and grandfather. She is frustrated at living in isolation in the arid Arizona desert, its vistas and rocky landscapes she has captured in some of her murals, paintings she shows to Howard as the first to ever see them and which so impress him that he believes her talent can be fulfilled if she, indeed, goes to France to study. They share their love for poetry, especially the works of François Villon (1431-1463), and Davis passionately reads some of Villon's passages to Howard, one ending with "this is the twain for which we two are met," a line that later comes to have great significance for the both of them. Grapewin is not in touch with Davis' reality; he dwells only in the past of pioneers and the legendary gunmen of the Old West. He prides himself with his memory of once having met the notorious outlaw Billy the Kid (1859-1881), telling Howard, as he does anyone else who will listen to his oft-told tales, that the Kid took a shot at him once, "but he missed me." Meanwhile, Foran, a one-time college football player, who works as the gas attendant, grows jealous of the attentions Davis gives to Howard, but Howard assures the beefy swain that he will soon be moving on and that possibility arrives in the form of wealthy Harvey, his demanding wife, Tobin, and their servile black chauffeur, Alexander. Realizing that Howard has no ride, Davis, who is now infatuated with the genteel writer, persuades Harvey to give Howard a ride to their next destination. She not only forgives Howard for his inability to pay for the meal she has served him, but gives the impoverished Howard "change" in the form of a silver dollar, so that he has some spending money. Her father, Hall, is not present while Davis is running the place as he has gone off to one of his meetings with others who belong to a paramilitary fraternity called the Black Horse Troop. After Howard bids a friendly farewell to Davis, the car in which he is riding is stopped by gangster Bogart and his three henchmen, Morris, Sawyer and Thompson, who order Harvey, Tobin, Alexander and Howard from their car as the gang's car has broken down. Bogart is the notorious Duke Mantee, who is Public Enemy Number One, a robber and killer being sought in several states (his role model in the play and its film version is based upon bank robber John Dillinger (1903-1934?), the celebrated Indiana bandit of the early 1930s). The gang arrives at the diner and takes over the place as Bogart waits for a gun moll to join him. Howard, Harvey, Tobin, and Alexander later arrive on foot at the diner and all of them, along with Davis, Foran and Grapewin are held hostage by Bogart and his thugs. Everyone is fearful of Bogart and his men except Grapewin, who sees Bogart as another Billy the Kid and Howard, who has nothing to fear because he has given up on life. Howard engages Bogart in conversation, cynically calling him "the last great apostle of rugged individualism," but Bogart is indifferent to such mocking praise as he nervously waits for his woman to arrive, telling one and all that they can stay alive if he follows their orders and stay in their seats. Hall then shows up with some of his club members, and they, too, are held hostage. While Davis is out of the main dining area, Howard suddenly gets an idea and produces the only valuable thing he has on earth, his insurance policy. He signs over the policy to Davis as his only beneficiary and then asks Bogart to shoot and kill him before he departs. At first, Bogart thinks Howard is joking, but Howard is in dead earnest, telling the gangster: "It couldn't make any difference to you, Duke. After all, if they catch you, you can hang only once." Bogart still disbelieves Howard's suicidal notion, but tolerates the idea, especially after Howard tells him that he is worth nothing to Davis alive, but, if dead, he can give her the money that will take her out of her dead-end lifestyle and into the world of her dreams in France. After hearing news that the woman Bogart has been waiting for has been arrested by police and that posse members are closing in on the diner, Bogart and his fellow gangsters prepare to flee. Just at the last moment, Howard reminds Bogart of his promise to shoot him and Bogart obliges, saying: "So long pal, I'll be seeing you soon." He fatally shoots Howard and leaves, only to be shot down by police. Meanwhile, the self-sacrificing Howard dies in Davis' arms, and she repeats her favorite line from Villon: "This is the end for which we twain are met." Howard is magnificent in his role of a doomed member of the Lost Generation, a man who has had no purpose in life until discovering that purpose is to give up his life for the young woman he has come to love. Davis, too, gives a bravura performance as a talented young woman searching for a way to find happiness in a world beyond a petrified forest that symbolically represents her hopeless confines. Bogart, in his first major role, is a sinister, brooding menace, rasping and growling life or death orders, a truly frightening figure to behold. The rest of the players are also standouts in this fast-paced crime tale from action director Mayo, and the literate script is packed with entertaining lowbrow humor while offering many tender scenes between Howard and Davis. Song: "I'd Rather Listen to Your Eyes" (Harry Warren). *Author's Note*: Davis told this author that "there was never two such different actors as Leslie [Howard] and Bogey [Bogart]. They were in real life just the way they were in **The Petrified Forest**. Leslie was the ultimate gentleman, always kind and considerate and Bogey barked and snarled like a bulldog, although he never had the murderous streak he shows in that picture, although I think once or twice he wanted to brain Jack Warner, who was head of the studio, but so did I and a lot of others. When Jack bought the film rights of the stage production and was about to sign up Leslie for the picture, Jack said he wanted someone else to play the part of Duke Mantee. Leslie, who had appeared with Bogey in the stage production, told Jack that he would not sign unless Jack hired Bogey, too. Well, you didn't tell Jack Warner anything, but when Leslie threatened to walk away from the picture, Jack caved in and hired Bogey." Mayo echoed Davis' comments about Howard's actions in the matter, reminding this author that Bogart was so grateful to Howard that he named one of his children "Leslie" after the man who got him his first starring role in this film. "But Jack Warner made Bogey pay for that," Mayo told this author. He was the kind of guy who took sly revenge on everybody. He could not do that to Howard, who was too big a star in those days, so he took it out on Bogey by putting him into gangster roles in one film after another until Bogey went nuts at playing goons and gunmen. Bogey was a very unhappy man in those years, stereotyped into all those roles where he had to play killers. I know, I directed him in **Black Legion** [1937] and when we did that picture, he has to play a man who joins a hooded group like the Ku Klux Klan and must kill his best buddy, Dick Foran, who appeared with him in **The Petrified Forest**. Bogey told me at that time: 'Now Jack Warner has me bumping off people while I am hiding under a hood and a black robe. I told him that I'm sick and tired of playing these lunatics, but all he says is 'if you don't like it, quit.' He has been trying to get rid of me since **The Petrified Forest** by giving me every crummy character in the world to play. I'm going to outlast him, that's what I'll do, until I get a role that gets me out of the gangster closet.' Well, Bogey won in the end when he played good guy detective Sam Spade in **The Maltese Falcon** [1941], and then he becomes a romantic hero in **Casablanca** [1942] and everybody wanted him as a leading man, including Jack Warner, who was no fool, because he saw dollar signs every time he saw Bogey." Jack Warner talked with Edward G. Robinson, asking him to play the Duke Mantee role before he attempted to sign up Howard. Then, after Howard forced Warner to give the part to Bogart, Warner, according to Robinson's statements to this author "came back to me and said that he had to give the part to Bogey, which was fine with me. I was playing so many underworld bosses in gangster films at Warner Brothers in those days that losing one such role only meant that I would be doing another such role in another gangster picture. Bogey was terrific in **The Petrified Forest** and after we all saw that performance we knew that he had the makings of being a great actor, everybody, except, perhaps, Jack Warner." Playwright Sherwood admitted that he used bank robber John Dillinger as the role model for his character Duke Mantee, and before Bogart essayed the role on Broadway, he studied newsreel footage of Dillinger in captivity in Crown

Joan Caulfield as a nightclub dancing girl in *The Petty Girl*, 1950.

Point, Indiana (and where Dillinger escaped from that so-called "escape-proof" jail in 1934). Bogart wears the same ensemble Dillinger wears in those newsreel clippings, an open-collared shirt and unbuttoned vest and he moves in the same manner Dillinger exhibited, his arms bent at the elbows, hands limp to the front as if he is about to reach for a pistol. Bogart's facial features were similar to that of Dillinger's, one of the reasons why he was originally typecast in the role of the fierce gangster. For more details on Dillinger, see my books, *Dillinger: Dead or Alive?* (Regnery, 1970); *The Dillinger Dossier* (December Press, 1983); and *The Great Pictorial History of World Crime* (History, Inc., 2004; pages 1374-1422). **p**, Hal B. Wallis; **d**, Archie Mayo; **cast**, Leslie Howard, Bette Davis, Genevieve Tobin, Dick Foran, Humphrey Bogart, Joe Sawyer, Porter Hall, Charley Grapewin, Paul Harvey, Eddie Acuff, Adrian Morris, Slim Thompson, John Alexander; **w**, Delmer Daves, Charles Kenyon (based on the play by Robert E. Sherwood); **c**, Sol Polito; **m**, Bernhard Kaun; **ed**, Owen Marks; **art d**, John Hughes; **spec eff**, Willard Van Enger, Fred Jackman, Warren Lynch.

The Petty Girl ★★★ 1950; U.S.; 88m; COL; Color; Biography/Musical Comedy; Children: Acceptable; **DVD**; **VHS**. Lively musical sees Cummings as a New York City calendar artist, who is famous for his portraits of beautiful women. He becomes fascinated with Caulfield, a prim and proper but beautiful college professor on vacation in the big city and tries to get her to pose for his artwork. She declines the offer, but he's determined to win her over so he follows her back to her college. She gets fired over his shenanigans and goes to New York to settle matters with Cummings but, instead, falls in love with him, poses for him, and they marry. This musical biopic is loosely based on the career of artist George Petty (1894-1976) whose "pin-up girl" art decorated many G.I. lockers, tanks, jeeps and airplanes during World War II (1939-1945). Songs: "Fancy Free," "Calypso Song," "I Loves Ya," "The Petty Girl" (Harold Arlen, Johnny Mercer). **p&w**, Nat Perrin (based on a story by Mary McCarthy); **d**, Henry Levin; **cast**, Robert Cummings, Joan Caulfield, Elsa Lanchester, Melville Cooper, Audrey Long, Mary Wickes, Frank Orth, John Ridgely, Tippi Hedren, Kathleen Howard, Movita, Mabel Paige, Jean Willes; **c**, William Snyder (Technicolor); **m**, Morris Stoloff, George Duning; **ed**, Al Clark; **art d**, Walter Holscher; **set d**, William Kiernan.

Petulia ★★★ 1968; U.S.; 105m; Petersham Pictures/WB-Seven Arts; Color; Drama; Children: Unacceptable; **DVD**; **VHS**. In this solid drama Christie is a beautiful but kooky San Francisco socialite, who has been married to Chamberlain, a handsome naval engineer, for only six months, but she is already unhappy in the marriage because he's abusive. She seeks solace with Scott, a recently divorced doctor. Christie pursues

Hope Lange and Lana Turner in *Peyton Place*, 1957.

Scott relentlessly while he dates other women. But Scott isn't sure he wants to marry anyone as zany as Christie, which leads to complications for both of them. Sexuality prohibits viewing by children. Songs: "Road Back" (Peter Albin, Janis Joplin, Peter Albin), "Down on Me" (Joplin), "Viola Lee Blues" (Noah Lewis). **p**, Raymond Wagner; **d**, Richard Lester; **cast**, Julie Christie, George C. Scott, Richard Chamberlain, Arthur Hill, Shirley Knight, Pippa Scott, Kathleen Widdoes, Roger Bowen, Richard Dysart. Ruth Kobart; **w**, Lawrence B. Marcus (adapted by Barbara Turner from the novel *Me and the Arch Kook Petulia* by John Haase); **c**, Nicolas Roeg (Technicolor); **m**, John Barry; **ed**, Antony Gibbs; **prod d**, Tony Walton; **set d**, Audrey Blasdel.

Peyton Place ★★★ 1957; U.S.; 108m; FOX; Color; Drama/Romance; Children: Unacceptable; **DVD**; **VHS**. This good soap opera begins when Varsi looks back on her teenage years in a New England town in the 1950s. Beneath the town's seeming tranquility and hum-drum lifestyles are many dark secrets involving sexual attraction and repression, rape, gossip, intolerance, and class snobbery. Varsi's sexually suppressed mother, Turner, finds herself aroused by Philips, a new high school principal, who tries to learn why she is cold toward him. Meanwhile, Varsi falls in love with rich young Coe and his parents object to the match. A murder trial straightens things out for happy endings for the main characters, but not without some tension-filled moments. What was a steamy best-selling novel became a more mature movie. Songs: "Serenade in Blue," "You'll Never Know," "Chattanooga Choo Cho," "I Had the Craziest Dream" (Harry Warren); "Blue Moon" (Richard Rodgers); "Auld Lang Syne" (Robert Burns); "Washington Post March" (John Philip Sousa); "Keep Your Sunny Side Up" (Ray Henderson); "You Tell Me Your Dream, I'll Tell You Mine" (Neil Moret. Seymour Rice, Albert H. Brown); "Sweet Genevieve" (Henry Tucker, George Cooper); "Beautiful Dreamer" (Stephen Foster); "Joy to the World" (Lowell Mason); "Adeste Fidelis (O Come All Ye Faithful)" (John Francis Wade). Gutter language and sexual themes prohibit viewing by children. **p**, Jerry Wald; **d**, Mark Robson; **cast**, Lana Turner, Lee Philips, Lloyd Nolan, Arthur Kennedy, Russ Tamblyn, Terry Moore, Hope Lange, Diane Varsi, David Nelson, Barry Coe, Betty Field, Mildred Dunnock, Leon Ames, Lorne Greene, Ray Montgomery; **w**, John Michael Hayes (based on the novel by Grace Metalious); **c**, William Mellor (CinemaScope; DeLuxe Color); **m**, Franz Waxman; **ed**, David Bretherton; **art d**, Lyle Wheeler, Jack Martin Smith; **set d**, Walter M. Scott, Bertram Granger; **spec eff**, L.B. Abbott.

Phantasm ★★★ 1979; U.S.; 88m; New Breed/Avco Embassy; Color; Horror; Children: Unacceptable (MPAA: R); **DVD**; **VHS**. Creepy horror tale has Baldwin, a fifteen-year-old boy whose parents have just died, living with Thornbury, his older brother. Fearful of losing his brother,

Baldwin follows him to a funeral where he sees Scrimm, a tall undertaker, lift a coffin on his own. Baldwin investigates and discovers a nightmarish world where Scrimm and his flying spheres shrink to half their normal size and Scrimm reanimates them as slaves. Baldwin, Thornbury, and a friend, Bannister, discover that Scrimm is using his mortuary as a base for connecting with the dead in order to take over the world. A very strange horror film that spawned three sequels: **Phantasm II**, 1988; **Phantasm III: Lord of the Dead**, 1994; and **Phantasm IV: Oblivion**, 1998. Song: "Sittin' Here at Midnight" (Bill Thornbury). **p**, Don A. Coscarelli, Paul Pepperman; **d&w**, Coscarelli; **cast**, A. Michael Baldwin, Bill Thornbury, Reggie Bannister, Kathy Lester, Terrie Kalbus, Kenneth V. Jones, Susan Harper, Lynn Eastman, David Arntzen, Ralph Richmond; **c**, Coscarelli (Technicolor); **m**, Fred Myrow, Malcolm Seagrave; **ed**, Coscarelli; **prod d**, Kate Coscarelli as S. Tyer; **art d**, David Gavin Brown; **spec eff**, Pepperman, Willard Green.

Phantom Lady ★★★ 1944; U.S.; 87m; UNIV; B/W; Mystery; Children: Unacceptable; **VHS**. This eerie, well-done whodunit has unhappily married Curtis spending the evening with a hat-wearing woman he picked up in a bar. Returning home, he finds his wife strangled and becomes the prime suspect in her murder. All of his alibis about where he was and who he was with fail as no one seems to remember seeing the phantom lady or her hat. Curtis is arrested for the killing and jailed, but has hopes that his erstwhile secretary, Raines, will find the mystery woman. Meanwhile, we learn that Tone, an eccentric artist, killed Curtis' wife because she refused to go away with him after their affair ended. Tone offers to help Raines find the mystery woman and her hat, never really intending to help, and this leads to them finding the hat in the possession of Helm. Raines deduces that Tone is the killer, and Tone realizes she is on to him, but, before he can dispatch her, police inspector Gomez rescues her as Tone leaps from a window to his death. Curtis is freed, and he and Raines will live happily ever after. Song: "Chick-ee-Chick" (1944, Jacques Press, Eddie Cherkose). Violence prohibits viewing by children. **p**, Joan Harrison; **d**, Robert Siodmak; **cast**, Franchot Tone, Ella Raines, Alan Curtis, Aurora Miranda, Thomas Gomez, Fay Helm, Elisha Cook, Jr., Andrew Tombes, Regis Toomey, Joseph Crehan, Doris Lloyd, Virginia Brissac, Milburn Stone; **w**, Bernard C. Schoenfeld (based on the novel by William Irish [Cornell Woolrich]), **c**, Woody Bredell; **m**, Hans J. Salter; **ed**, Arthur Hilton; **art d**, John B. Goodman, Robert Clatworthy; **set d**, Russell A. Gausman, L.R. Smith.

The Phantom of the Opera ★★★★★ 1925 (silent, reissued with sound in 1929); U.S.; 93m/9reels; UNIV; B/W; Horror; Children: Unacceptable; **DVD**. Chaney, in his most famous film, gives a towering and memorable performance as a horribly disfigured composer whose genius is mixed with a madness that drives him to murder in an effort to control a beautiful, young woman he can never possess. Chaney hides his hideous face from the world by wearing a mask and lives in the labyrinthine underground chambers beneath the Paris Opera, which leads to the vast network of the city's underground sewer system. He is in love with Philbin, an understudy to the reigning diva, and he guides Philbin toward stardom by coaching her from behind secret passages and panels until she perfects her singing. Chaney then compels the diva to quit the opera by unleashing a huge chandelier that collapses upon an audience watching the diva's performance of a Richard Wagner opera, killing and maiming many operagoers. After enticing Philbin to his underground lair, Chaney professes his eternal love for her, telling her that he will allow her to return to the stage, but only if she promises that she will break off her relationship with Kerry, her handsome young lover. Philbin gives him that promise, but, after she is released, she meets with Kerry and both plan to immediately go to England after her final performance. The ubiquitous Chaney, nevertheless, overhears their plans, and he abducts Philbin right in the middle of her performance, taking her to his underground lair, with Kerry and a Secret Service agent in hot pursuit. A mob then gathers and these irate, torch-carrying citizens also invade the underground byways of the sewer system, wading through its slimy rivers and scum-coated lakes in a desperate search for Philbin. (Universal would employ such torch-carrying mobs in the many Frankenstein films to come to the point where such crowd scenes became clichéd.) As Kerry and the mob search for the madman, Chaney removes his mask to reveal his ghastly visage to Philbin, his skeletal, hollow-eyed face a mask of death that horrifies and terrifies her (this being one of the most famous horror scenes in film history). With Philbin in tow, Chaney runs from the mob, going to the ground level and racing past Notre Dame Cathedral (the mammoth set used for another classic Chaney film, **The Hunchback of Notre Dame**, 1923) with hundreds of enraged citizens hot on his heels. He seizes a hansom cab and drives its horses wildly through the streets, but when it overturns, Philbin is thrown clear and Chaney continues his flight on foot, running wildly through the streets until he reaches the Seine River. With the river to his back and crowds closing in at the right and left, Chaney halts the mobs by reaching into his cloak, as if to withdraw a terrible weapon, and does the same thing with the other hand. His pursuers freeze in fright until he laughs madly as he exposes an empty palm. Enraged at being hoodwinked, the crowd then rushes forward to overwhelm Chaney, its members furiously beating him to death and then throwing his lifeless body into the Seine to end his reign of terror (Alfred Hitchcock took a leaf from this grim finale by presenting a similar film-ending mob chase in **The Lodger**, 1927, which was based upon another human monster, Jack the Ripper). Chaney is mesmerizing as the Phantom, and the production values are superb in this classic film. *Author's Note*: When this film was initially previewed by a number of film critics in 1923, the year in which it was produced, they told Universal Studio boss Carl Laemmle that the film was just too frightening and would fail at the box office unless considerable comic relief was inserted into the film. The studio then added several more scenes to the film with such Mack Sennett comedians as Chester Conklin, but these scenes required more title writing and these titles were also added to the film, but when it was again previewed in San Francisco, most thought that the plotline was now so distorted and fragmented that little sense could be made of it. The film went back to the editing room where the comedy scenes were all but eliminated and several extraneous subplots were deleted. The film was finally released in 1925 with great ballyhoo and it proved to be an enormous success, one of Universal's biggest financial smashes to date and where Chaney was vaulted into the ranks of Chaplin, Garbo and Fairbanks, this film, more than any other to that date, making him a superstar. **p**, Carl Laemmle; **d**, Rupert Julian; **cast**, Lon Chaney, Mary Philbin, Norman Kerry, Arthur Edmund Carewe, Gibson Gowland, John Sainpolis, Snitz Edwards, Mary Fabian, Virginia Pearson, Olive Ann Alcorn, Chester Conklin, Carla Laemmle; **w**, Raymond L. Schrock, Elliott J. Clawson (based on the novel *Le fantome de l'opera* by Gaston Leroux); **c**, Virgil Miller, Milton Bridenbecker; **m** (1929 sound re-release, Sam Perry); **ed**, Maurice Pivar; **prod d**, Ben Carré; **art d**, Charles D. Hall; **set d**, Russell A. Gausman; **spec eff**, Jerome Ash.

The Phantom of the Opera ★★★ 1943; U.S.; 92m; UNIV; Color; Horror; Children: Unacceptable; **DVD**; **VHS**. In this superior remake of the 1925 classic, Rains is outstanding in playing the deranged and grotesquely disfigured Phantom, dwelling in his dank and shadowy chambers beneath the Paris Opera. The film opens with Rains playing with the Paris Opera as a violinist, but he must struggle with each performance as he suffers from a partly paralyzed hand. Withdrawn and living alone, Rains has but one burning passion that keeps him alive and that is his love for beautiful Foster, a singer in the chorus, who has ambitions of becoming a diva. Knowing this, Rains secretly pays for her expensive singing lessons that she accepts as coming from an unknown benefactor and where she is trained by singing instructor Carrillo. Frustrating Rains is the fact that Foster is courted by opera tenor Eddy, as well as Barrier, who is a police inspector, and that Rains never makes his love for Foster known to her. Rains is emotionally destroyed when

Lon Chaney and Mary Philbin in *The Phantom of the Opera*, 1925.

he is dismissed by Puglia, the head of the opera company, who tells him that his playing has been growing steadily worse, undoubtedly due to his afflicted hand. Now low on funds, Rains goes to Carrillo, begging him to continue to coach Foster in her singing lessons, even though he can no longer pay for them. Carrillo refuses, even though he admits that Foster has the promising talent to become a diva. To get money for those lessons, Rains takes his masterpiece composition, a concerto, to a publisher, but then comes to believe, even though there is a mix-up in the sale of the composition, that Mander, the owner of the opera, has stolen his concerto. He confronts Mander, and, in a state of rage, strangles him, but while he is so assaulting Mander, Carson, who is Mander's mistress, hysterically tries to stop Rains by throwing acid in his face. Screaming in agony, Rains flees and disappears. Police unsuccessfully search for him while he hides in the vast sewers of Paris and then very odd occurrences begin to take place at the opera house. After props, masks and food disappear, stage hands attribute the missing items to ghosts, claiming that the place is haunted. A few nights later, Foster hears a voice seeming to come through a wall in her dressing room that tells her that she is about to become the greatest opera singer in Paris. Then Farrar, the reigning diva, suddenly grows ill, after Rains has drugged her, and Foster, who has been trained as her understudy, takes her place in a performance that rockets Foster's career to overnight stardom. Rains, who wears a mask while dwelling in his underground hideout, listens to that performance, cherishing Foster's success as if it were his own, and in a perverse sense, it is. When Farrar recovers, she accuses Eddy of administering the drug that prevented her from performing, saying that he did it to advance Foster's career because he is in love with the girl. Police inspector Barrier investigates and pronounces Farrar's claims false, but Farrar then takes her revenge on Foster by having her put back into the chorus for the duration of Farrar's extensive contract. When the now deranged Rains learns about this, he sneaks into Farrar's dressing room while wearing an opera costume and mask and strangles her to death. He flees from pursuers, slipping through one of the many secret passageways he has earlier discovered that honeycombs the opera building, but Eddy, who is wearing a costume almost identical to what Rains is wearing, is then detained by Barrier, who closes down the opera while he conducts an investigation. Rains soon identifies himself as the killer when he sends messages that demand that Foster be made the lead singer at the opera now that Farrar is dead. Barrier thinks to set a trap for Rains that he believes will force Rains into the open by reopening the opera and making Andre (who makes her film debut in this production) the leading singer, instead of Foster. Indeed, when Rains learns of this, he does come from his subterranean lair, but not in a way Barrier expects. While Andre is performing on stage, Rains, above the ceiling of the opera house, cuts the ropes holding the huge chandelier, which crashes

A masked Claude Rains unleashing a chandelier in *Phantom of the Opera*, 1943.

into the orchestra area, crushing scores of operagoers and creating widespread pandemonium. During the ensuing mayhem, Rains grabs Foster and takes her to his underground hiding place where he tells her that everything he has done was done because of his deep love for her. In an uncontrollable impulse, Foster snatches away the mask that hides his face to reveal a horrible, pulpy mass of quivering flesh with out-of-place eye sockets, a mask of death that sends her into shock. At that moment, Eddy and Barrier enter the chamber and seize Foster from Rains' clutches, taking her to safety just as the ceiling of the chamber gives way and Rains disappears beneath a huge avalanche of bricks and rocks, leaving behind only his mask and his violin. Once again at the surface, Foster disappoints both swains by telling Eddy and Barrier that she has no thought of marriage now that the path is clear for her to resume a sterling career as the diva of the opera. Lubin does a fine job in presenting this gothic tale, coordinating and balancing the romance between Foster and Eddy and Barier and the evil machinations of Rains, who is outstanding as the demented Phantom, adding the empathetic dimension of pathos to his otherwise wholly menacing character. Unlike the silent version, this one takes full advantage of color by using the old Technicolor process to produce deep and rich hues in every scene, as well as to interject (too much so for the liking of some critics) considerable operatic passages, arranged, adapted or composed by Edward Ward and where Eddy's singing was never better. Songs: "Lullaby of the Bells" (Edward Ward), "Martha" (excerpt; Friedrich von Flotow), "Amore et Gloire" (music: Fredric Chopin; lyrics: George Waggner), "Le Prince Masque du Caucasus" (4th Symphony; music: Peter Ilyich Tchaikovsky). The film received two Oscars for Best Color Cinematography (Greene) and Best (Color) Art Decoration (Goodman and Golitzen). *Author's Note*: Universal did not stint on this production, lavishly spending more than $1.5 million for its production, a staggering budget in those days. Many new and elaborate sets, particularly the underground chambers and byways through which Rains traverses, were especially built, with the exception of the opera house, and where Universal used in this production the original set from the classic 1925 film starring Lon Chaney Sr. Foster, who sings beautifully in this film, nevertheless did not appear in another major film, even though she was kept under contract by Universal for some period of time. Rains told this author that "the script for **The Phantom of the Opera** was very lengthy and it was a great challenge to me." By this he meant that it was one of the most difficult scripts to put to memory as Rains not only memorized his own lines in every film in which he appeared but the entire script. "The makeup people in that picture gave me a much different disfigured face than the one employed by Chaney in the silent version. His was basically the recreation of a skull with eyes behind it. Mine was a mess of quivering chopped liver." **p**, George Waggner; **d**, Arthur Lubin; **cast**,

Nelson Eddy, Susanna Foster, Claude Rains, Edgar Barrier, Leo Carrillo, Jane Farrar, J. Edward Bromberg, Fritz Feld, Frank Puglia, Steven Geray, Hume Cronyn, Fritz Leiber, James Mitchell; **w**, Eric Taylor, Samuel Hoffenstein (based on an adaptation by Hans and John Jacoby of the novel *Le fantome de l'opera* by Gaston Leroux); **c**, Hal Mohr, W. Howard Greene (Technicolor); **m**, operatic score, Edward Ward, Waggner; **ed**, Russell Schoengarth; **art d**, John B. Goodman, Alexander Golitzen; **set d**, Russell A. Gausman, Ira S. Webb; **spec eff**, John P. Fulton, Russell Lawson.

The Phantom of the Opera ★★★ 1962; U.K.; 84m; Hammer/UNIV; Color; Horror; Children: Unacceptable; **DVD**; **VHS**. Lom does a standout job of the Phantom in this remake of the 1943 version, which is set in early 1900s London. Gough is a corrupt aristocrat who steals the life's work of poor composer Lom. In a struggle to stop the printing of his music with Gough's name on it as the composer, Lom breaks into the printing office and accidentally starts a fire that leaves his face disfigured. Years later, Lom returns to terrorize the London Opera House where one of his stolen operas is being performed. A stagehand is murdered, and the audience sees the body hanging from a ballast rope. Aukin, the prima donna performing in the opera, is so terrified that she quits and is replaced by newcomer Sears, in whom both Gough and Lom have taken a romantic interest. Lom later abducts Sears and keeps her prisoner in his secret underground hideaway, but she is eventually rescued by de Souza, her fiancé. During the opera, as Lom attempts to escape, the chandelier falls and crushes him. Music: "Joan of Arc" (Edwin Astley). Violence prohibits viewing by children. This story was also filmed in 1929, 1943, 1989, 1998, and 2004. **p&w**, Anthony Hinds as John Elder (based on the novel by Gaston Leroux); **d**, Terence Fisher; **cast**, Herbert Lom, Michael Gough, Heather Sears, Edward de Souza, Thorley Walters, Harold Goodwin, Martin Miller, Liane Aukin, Sonya Cordeau, Marne Maitland; **c**, Arthur Grant (Technicolor); **m**, Edwin Astley; **ed**, Alfred Cox; **prod d**, Bernard Robinson; **art d**, Don Mingaye.

The Phantom of the Opera ★★★ 2005; U.K./U.S.; 143m; WB; Color; Horror/Musical; Children: Unacceptable (MPAA: PG-13); **BD**; **DVD**. The enormously popular Broadway musical about this classic horror tale was brought to the screen in this exciting production. Butler is a facially disfigured musical genius, who terrorizes the 1870 Paris Opera House because of his unrequited love for Rossum, a beautiful soprano. He would kill for her and proves it by crossing swords with his rival, Wilson, for her affections. True love wins out in the end, but we do feel sympathy for the love-struck phantom. Well made and enacted, the highlight of this superior production is its thoroughly entertaining music. Songs: "Auction at the Opera Populaire," "Think of Me," "Angel of Music," "Little Lotte," "The Mirror," "Music of the Night," "Magical Lasso," "Notes," "Prima Donna," "Poor Fool, He Makes Me Laugh," "Il Muto," "Why Have You Brought Me Here?," "Raoul I've Been There," "All I Ask of You," "Masquerade," "Why So Silent," "Ultimatums," "Journey to the Cemetery," "Wishing You Were Somehow Here Again," "Wandering Child," "We Have All Been Blind," "Twisted Every Way," "Don Juan," "The Point of No Return," "Down Once More," "Track Down This Murderer," "Learn to Be Lonely," "Think of Me," "The Music of the Night" (Andrew Lloyd Webber, Charles Hart, Richard Stilgoe); "The Phantom of the Opera" (Webber, Hart, Stilgoe, Mike Batt); "Hannibal" (Jean-Luc Chalumeau). Violence prohibits viewing by children. **p**, Andrew Lloyd Webber, Eli Richbourg; **d**, Joel Schumacher; **cast**, Gerard Butler, Emmy Rossum, Patrick Wilson, Miranda Richardson, Minnie Driver, Cairan Hinds, Simon Callow, Victor McGuire, Jennifer Ellison, Murray Melvin, Kevin R. McNally, James Fleet; **w**, Schumacher, Webber (based on the stage musical by Webber and the novel *Le fantome de l'opera* by Gaston Leroux); **c**, John Mathieson; **m**, Webber; **ed**, Terry Rawlings; **prod d**, Anthony Pratt; **art d**, John Fenner, Paul Kirby; **set d**, Celia Bobak; **spec eff**, David M.V. Jones, Nathan McGuinness.

Phantom Raiders ★★★ 1940; U.S.; 70m; MGM; B/W; Mystery; Children: Unacceptable; **BD**; **DVD**. Pidgeon is exceptional in the role of detective Nick Carter in this second and final film of the series. Pidgeon and his diminutive assistant, Meek, are assigned by London insurers to investigate the mysterious sinking of British cargo ships in Panama. The ships are sunk after leaving the canal with supplies for the Allies in Europe during World War II (1939-1945). Pidgeon discovers that an American gangster and nightclub owner, Schildkraut, is behind the sinking and brings him to justice. This is a sequel to **Nick Carter, Master Detective**, 1930. A film with the same title, but about the Vietnam War, was made in 1988. **p**, Frederick Stephani; **d**, Jacques Tourneur; **cast**, Walter Pidgeon, Donald Meek, Joseph Schildkraut, Florence Rice, Nat Pendleton, John Carroll, Steffi Duna, Cecil Kellaway, Dwight Frye, Hugh Beaumont, May McAvoy, Joe Yule; **w**, William R. Lipman, Joseph Fields (based on a story by Jonathan Latimer and the Nick Carter radio shows); **c**, Clyde De Vinna; **m**, David Snell, Daniele Amfitheatrof; **ed**, Conrad A. Nervig; **art d**, Cedric Gibbons; **set d**, Edwin B. Willis.

The Phantom Tollbooth ★★★ 1970; U.S.; 90m; MGM; Color; Animated Adventure; Children: Recommended (MPAA: G); **DVD**. This inventive tale sees a boy bored with life, but that all changes one day when he finds a toll booth in his bedroom. He gets behind the wheel of his toy car and drives through the booth, entering a world full of adventure where society is divided into letters and numbers, each letter and digit thinking it is more important than all others. With the help of a dog, he changes considerable chaos into order and returns home. This well-crafted production provides a lot of fun and adventurous nonsense for kids. Songs: "Milo's Song," "Time Is a Gift," World Market," "Numbers Are the Only Thing That Count," "Rhyme and Reason Reign" (Lee Pockriss, Norman Gimbel); "Don't Say There's Nothing to Do in the Doldrums," "Noise, Noise, Beautiful Noise" (Pockriss, Paul Vance). **p**, Chuck Jones, Abe Levitow, Les Goldman; **d**, Jones, Levitow, David Monahan; **cast**, Butch Patrick, and (voiceovers) Mel Blanc, Daws Butler, Candy Candido, Hans Conried, June Foray, Patti Gilbert, Shep Menken, Cliff Norton, Larry Thor, Les Tremayne, Michael Earl; **w**, Jones, Sam Rosen (based on the children's novel by Norton Juster); **c**, Lester Shorr (Metrocolor); **m**, Dean Elliott; **ed**, William Faris; **prod d**, Maurice Noble; **art d**, George W. Davis, Charles Hagedon; **set d**, Henry Grace, Chuck Pierce.

Phar Lap ★★★★ 1984; Australia; 107m; Michael Edgley International/FOX; Color; Sports Drama; Children: Cautionary (MPAA: PG); **DVD**. Engrossing and superlatively directed and acted tale presents the story of the great Australian racehorse, Phar Lap (1926-1932), a thoroughbred affectionately known as "Bobby" that won many Australian major races and became the third highest stakes winner in the world. Phar Lap died mysteriously in April 1932 after winning the Agua Caliente Handicap in Tijuana, Mexico, and it was suspected that underworld figures had poisoned the horse to further prevent it from winning races that were otherwise fixed. That death begins this film and the story is then told in flashback where, five years earlier, the horse arrives by boat from New Zealand, being lowered in a sling, a thoroughbred purchased unseen by horse owner Leibrman. After Leibrman sees the colt, he thinks little of it, telling trainer Vaughan to sell it immediately. Vaughan disagrees, saying that the horse has great pedigree and shows promise. Leibrman agrees to lease the horse to Vaughan for three years and where Leibrman will have only one third of the horse's winnings. Burlinson becomes the horse's handler, and he and Phar Lap establish a deep bond. When Burlinson complains to Vaughan that the horse is being worked too hard, Vaughan fires him, but when the horse stops eating after Burlinson is gone, Vaughan reinstates Burlinson and Phar Lap begins eating again. Phar Lap does not do well in its initial races, and Burlinson realizes that it should be held back at the beginning of each race as the horse likes to come from behind to overtake its com-

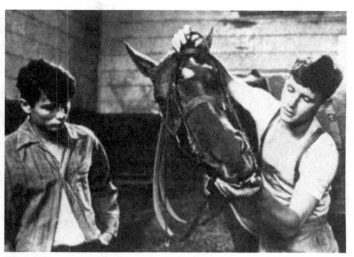

Ross O'Donovan, Phar Lap and Tom Burlinson in *Phar Lap*, 1984.

petitors; when this is practiced, Phar Lap begins to win race after race. Leibrman tries to capitalize on his investment by placing heavy wagers on the outcome of Phar Lap's races, a financial tactic Vaughan opposes. To increase the odds against the horse, Leibrman scratches Phar Lap from running in the Melbourne Cup, and after someone tries to shoot the horse, Burlinson takes Phar Lap into hiding at a stud farm at the outskirts of Melbourne. Leibrman, at the last minute, reenters Phar Lap in the 1930 Melbourne Cup, and the horse, in a spectacular burst of speed, wins the race. It is now believed that the horse, which has earned the nickname of "The Red Terror," will beat any competitor and it is handicapped by having weights added to the jockey and saddle in future races to give competitors a fair edge, but unfairly imposing a great hardship on the horse and it loses its next race. Leibrman then offers to sell his share of ownership in Phar Lap to Vaughan, but he refuses. Vaughan then fakes an injury for the horse and, believing that Phar Lap is now lame, Leibrman sells his share to Vaughan for far less than what he originally asked. Phar Lap then miraculously recovers from an injury it never had and goes on to win his next race with ease and Leibrman realizes that Vaughan has outwitted him. Leibrman then comes to think that Phar Lap can make more money by racing abroad and enters him into the Agua Caliente Handicap in Mexico. Vaughan refuses to accompany the horse to Mexico, Burlinson is promoted to the status of trainer and accompanies the horse to Mexico with Leibrman and where he clashes with Leibrman about how the horse is being treated. Before the big race, Leibrman tells jockey, Elliott, to lead the horse from the start of the race and not hold him back and then come from behind after Leibrman hears that some of the jockeys have been bribed by underworld gamblers to box in Phar Lap during the race so that the horse cannot break into the open. Burlinson, however, convinces Elliott to race the horse in the manner Phar Lap has been running in his successful races and the horse wins, but suffers a bloody split hoof. Following the race, the great horse grows ill and dies, Leibrman and others speculate that he has been poisoned by underworld figures. Exciting throughout, this excellent production sees outstanding performances from Leibrman, Burlinson and Vaughan; the races are well orchestrated by director Wincer; where he also presents impressive period scenes that accurately depict the lifestyles of the early 1930s. Songs: "Phar Lap-Farewell to You" (Jack Lumsdaine), "Baby Face" (music: Harry Akst; lyrics: Benny Davis), "Painting the Clouds with Sunshine" (music: Joseph Burke; lyrics: Al Dubin), "California Here I Come" (music: Joseph Meyer; lyrics: Al Jolson, Buddy G. DeSylva), "Little White Lies" (Walter Donaldson), "Along the Road to Gundagai" (Jack O'Hagan), "There's a Rainbow 'Round My Shoulder" (music: Dave Dreyer; lyrics: Al Jolson, Billy Rose), "Follow the Swallow" (music: Ray Henderson; lyrics: Mort Dixon, Billy Rose). The film was a great

Jean Carson and Edward Andrews in *The Phenix City Story*, 1955.

success in Australia, taking in more than $24 million (in U.S. dollars) at the box office, but fared far less when it was released in the U.S. *Author's Note*: Autopsies later indicated that Phar Lap had not died of poisoning, but from an infection that took the horse's life. Towering Inferno, the thoroughbred gelding that plays Phar Lap in this film, ironically had, like Phar Lap, its life foreshortened when it also met a tragic end, being killed when it was struck by lightning on April 15, 1999. **p**, John Sexton; **d**, Simon Wincer; **cast**, Tom Burlinson, Ron Leibman, Richard Morgan, Robert Grubb, Simon Wells, Kelvyn Worth, Justin Ridley, Martin Vaughan, Brian Granrott, Celia De Burgh, Steven Bannister; **w**, David Williamson (based on the book *The Phar Lap Story* by Michael Wilkinson); **c**, Russell Boyd; **m**, Bruce Rowland; **ed**, Tony Paterson; **prod d**, Lawrence Eastwood; **spec eff**, Conrad Rothmann.

The Phenix City Story ★★★ 1955; U.S.; 100m; PAR/Miramax; B/W; Crime Drama; Children: Unacceptable; **DVD**; **VHS**. Filmed in semi-documentary style and based on true events, this hard-hitting crime yarn tells of Phenix City, Alabama, "the wickedest city in the U.S." It is run by a crime syndicate that has grown rich on prostitution, drugs, and crooked gambling. Kiley returns from military service to a law practice and finds the town preying on soldiers at Fort Benning, Georgia, which is located just across the river from the wide-open town. He helps his father, McIntire, get elected attorney general, but McIntire is brutally murdered. The job goes to Kiley and he enlists the Alabama National Guard to help him clean up the corruption run by crime czar Andrews. The exciting *film noir* opens with a thirteen-minute prologue in which the actual citizens of Phenix City describe the pre-clean-up events. Violence prohibits viewing by children. Song: "Phenix City Blues" (Harold Spina). *Author's Note*: McIntyre portrays Albert Patterson (1894-1954), who was assassinated in June 1954, just after he won the nomination to become the Democratic candidate for Alabama's attorney general. Patterson had been running on a reform platform that promised to destroy the operations of organized crime figures in the state. Director Karlson, who specialized in above-average *film noir* productions, would go on to direct another gritty semi-documentary film based on a similar southern reformer in **Walking Tall**, 1973. **p**, Samuel Bischoff, David Diamond; **d**, Phil Karlson; **cast**, Richard Kiley, John McIntire, Kathryn Grant, Edward Andrews, Lenka Peterson, Biff McGuire, Truman Smith, Jean Carson, Kathy Marlowe, John Larch; **w**, Crane Wilbur, Daniel Mainwaring; **c**, Harry Neumann; **m**, Harry Sukman; **ed**, George White; **art d**, Stanley Fleischer.

Phffft! ★★★ 1954; U.S.; 88m; COL; B/W; Comedy; Children: Acceptable; **DVD**; **VHS**. This very good comedy has Lemmon, a lawyer, and Holliday, a television soap opera writer, divorcing after eight years of marriage. He blames their marital problems on Gear, her interfering mother, and she blames Carson, Lemmon's womanizing pal, for the breakup. Both begin dating others, but whenever they accidentally meet, they remember the good times of their past together. They both take mambo dance lessons and one night they find themselves dancing together in a nightclub at a mambo contest. They realize they miss each other and reconcile. Down to earth and unspectacular, this comedic tale, however, provides top-drawer performances from Lemmon and Holliday, working from Axelrod's fine script. *Author's Note*: Lemmon told this author that this film "has a lot of terrific ingredients to make it appealing to widespread audiences. The picture shows characters like millions of people in real life, who make the mistake of splitting up under angry impulses. They come to realize that they have blown away the real happiness they have in life, and that is being with the person they have always loved and will always love. All marriages have ups and downs. It's all a matter of how you ride that roller coaster to keep a marriage in place." **p**, Fred Kohlmar; **d**, Mark Robson; **cast**, Judy Holliday, Jack Lemmon, Jack Carson, Kim Novak, Luella Gear, Donald Randolph, Donald Curtis, Merry Anders, Shirlee Allard, Frank Arnold; **w**, George Axelrod (based on his story); **c**, Charles Lang; **m**, Friedrich Hollaender; **ed**, Charles Nelson; **art d**, William Flannery; **set d**, William Kiernan.

The Philadelphia Story ★★★★★ 1940; U.S.; 112m; MGM; B/W; Comedy; Children: Acceptable; **DVD**; **VHS**. This utterly entertaining comedy became a classic when it was first released, achieving that stellar status through the superlative direction of Cukor and magnificent portrayals from Hepburn, Grant and Stewart. This stunning film opens with a bang when Grant is shown leaving Hepburn with bags in hand from the front door of their resplendent home. She marches after him, throwing his golf bag and clubs after him, breaking one of his golf clubs over her knee and flinging the broken pieces at him before she starts to walk back into the house. Grant, enraged, storms after her, turns her around, doubles a fist and is about to punch her square in the jaw, but, instead, uses his open hand to push her in a sailing motion to the floor. We next see Hepburn as the vivacious and brilliant daughter of a wealthy family living outside of Philadelphia. She is about to go to the altar with Howard, a rich executive of a huge coal company, who is also a boring stick-in-the-mud. Those impending nuptials, along with Hepburn's well-organized life, however, are about to go into a tailspin at the arrival of her ex-husband, Grant, a rich playboy with more scruples and wisdom than anyone realizes. Grant has learned that Daniell, a media tycoon who publishes a successful scandal magazine, *Spy Magazine*, intends to disgrace Hepburn's family and besmirch her wedding ceremony by publishing an expose about a torrid, secret love affair involving her dallying but endearing father, Halliday. To blunt Daniell's probe into the matter, Grant preemptively arranges for Daniell's top reporter, Stewart, and photographer, Hussey, to interview Hepburn and her family members. She and those family members greet Stewart and Hussey by putting their best feet forward while practicing exaggerated etiquette and elaborately displayed manners. Stewart's down-to-earth nature is annoyed if not angered by what he sees as well-orchestrated and obviously pretentious behavior. Howard, however, is offended by the intrusiveness of the press, resenting the presence of Stewart and Hussey and considers them invaders of his upcoming privately arranged wedding to Hepburn. She, on the other hand, spends much of time not with Howard, but with her ex-hubby Grant, quarreling with him. Hepburn is almost too obsessed with Grant as a discarded husband and, on the night before she is to be married, she drinks too much bubbly and becomes slightly intoxicated. She takes a swim in the family pool, but not before pushing a small toy sailboat in front of her, one that is a replica of the boat she and Grant once sailed when they were still married, a sailboat called *The True Love*. Stewart, who joins her in her drinking merriment, relaxes enough to tell Hepburn how he feels about her, saying: "You're lit from within. You're the golden girl, full of light and warmth and delight." He kisses her just as she passes out and he then carries her to her bedroom. After depositing her in her chamber, Stewart goes to the terrace of her mansion to be confronted by an enraged Howard. The indignant bridegroom is about to beat Stewart to a pulp, but Grant, thinking to deal a more merciful blow, knocks out Stewart in one punch and Howard stomps off to mull things over, but not before telling Grant that he is responsible for causing trouble by sponsoring these interlopers and warns him not to be on the grounds or near his wedding the following day. Stewart regains consciousness and, puzzled, asks Grant why he hit him. Grant explains that he did him a favor because Howard would have hit him much harder. The hangover Hepburn endures the next day is Homeric, one where her only thoughts are of relief through drinking tomato juice and seeking any shady spot on her estate. Howard, still seething with anger over the previous night's travails, lectures Hepburn on her disgraceful conduct with Stewart. To emphasize the extent of his indignation, he calls off their wedding. Family members hearing of this tell Hepburn that the wedding must take place, irrespective of Howard's departure, since the guests are already arriving and calling off that ceremony would constitute an unforgivable faux pas. Hepburn agrees that such a colossal social blunder is unthinkable, although she now has no man to marry. The valiant Stewart then volunteers to replace the stiff-necked Howard, telling Hepburn that he loves her. She is touched by Stewart's sincere act of affection, but gently rejects his gallant offer. She likes Stewart, but she does not love him. With Hepburn anxiously peeking from another room to see the guests filling the hall where her wedding is to take place, Grant comes to her rescue by dictating the words she repeats to the guests, telling them that she will not disappoint their expectations because she is going through with the wedding and the man she is about to wed is Grant. This overjoys Hepburn as Grant is the only man she has ever loved. Her father, Halliday, escorts her down the aisle toward the waiting minister, as well as Grant, and where Stewart acts as best man; Hepburn tells Halliday that she now feels "like a human being," her journey to the altar ending this charming and delightful classic. This tale is packed with wit and humor and many amusing scenes involve other players such as Hepburn's precocious kid sister, Weidler, who does an awkward ballet performance while singing "Lydia, the Tattooed Lady," and Young, a womanizing uncle, who impulsively pinches the behind of every adult female in sight. The film nevertheless belongs to Hepburn; her eccentric mannerisms were never better suited to the character she is playing, and she does a magnificent job playing that character. Grant is the stalwart emotional pillar of her life, although she will not admit it until the very last moment, and, he, too, is captivating in his every scene. Stewart is also brilliant, arriving as a cynical newspaperman and leaving as a sensitive guy who still loves the girl going to the altar with another man. Cukor's direction superbly develops the characters while maintaining a brisk pace and presenting clever turns and twists in the story line to keep the viewer wondering which man's arms will eventually and permanently embrace the ebullient Hepburn. Donald Ogden Stewart won an Oscar for Best Adapted Screenplay, and Stewart surprised just about everyone, including himself, by winning the Oscar for Best Actor. The film was nominated for Best Picture, Best Director (Cukor), Best Actress (Hepburn), and Best Supporting Actress (Hussey). Songs: "Lydia, the Tattooed Lady," "Over the Rainbow" (both in 1939; music: Harold Arlen; lyrics: E. Y. Harburg); "I've Got My Eyes on You" (1940; Cole Porter), "Sobre las olas (Over the Waves)" (1887; Juventino Rosas); "Wedding March" (1843; from "A Midsummer Night's Dream" by Felix Mendelssohn-Bartholdy); "Bridal Chorus" (1850; from "Lohengrin"; music: Richard Wagner). This film was remade as a delightful musical starring Bing Crosby, Frank Sinatra and Grace Kelly, titled **High Society**, 1956. *Author's Note*: Hepburn was absent from the Hollywood scene in 1939, the year when so many great films were produced and released as she was busy playing the leading lady in the stage production of this story where Joseph Cotten plays the role of the former husband and Van Heflin enacts the sardonic newspaperman. "I went to Broadway to do that show," Hepburn told this author,

James Stewart, Cary Grant and Katharine Hepburn in *The Philadelphia Story,* 1940.

"at a time when everyone in Hollywood was saying that I was box office poison, but, when **The Philadelphia Story** opened on Broadway, it was sweet to the taste of the audience and poisoned no one." In making this acting adjustment, Hepburn most likely made one of her wisest career decisions, one that revitalized her career and brought her substantial riches. Playwright Barry had actually written the play with Hepburn in mind, although the actual character she plays was based on Helen Hope Montgomery Scott (1905-1995), who married a close friend of Barry's. Scott was an eccentric socialite, who came from a wealthy Philadelphia family and epitomized the free-spirited elegance that is found in Hepburn's unforgettable character. In accepting the part of the leading lady in the play, Hepburn shrewdly not only took no salary, but covered twenty-five percent of the play's costs. In return, she got 45 percent of the profits, and when the play became a smash hit, those profits were considerable. She further controlled the sale of the play's screen rights and went to the top studio at that time, directly negotiating with its tough boss, Louis B. Mayer. He wanted those rights for MGM as soon as he saw that the play was a success, but he never expected to deal directly with Hepburn, who proved to be a tenacious negotiator. She demanded and got a payment from him of $250,000 for her acting services, and, moreover, his guarantee that she could select her own director and screenwriter to adapt the play, as well as her costars. Cukor, who was Hepburn's favorite helmsman (he had directed her in **Bill of Divorcement**, 1932; **Little Women**, 1933; **Sylvia Scarlett**, 1935; and **Holiday**, 1938), was immediately signed up, and so, too, was Donald Ogden Stewart, who was Hepburn's long-standing friend and who was one of the wittiest writers in Hollywood. She selected Grant as the man to play her ex-husband, having appeared with him in earlier films such as **Sylvia Scarlett** and the classic **Bringing Up Baby**, 1938, and **Holiday**, 1938. Grant demanded and got top billing and a salary of $137,000. (He gave the entire amount to the British War Relief Fund to aid his native country, England, then being at war with Germany.) "I knew Cary was the perfect man to play the ex-husband, although Joe [Cotten] did a wonderful job in that role in the stage production," Hepburn told this author. "Doing **The Philadelphia Story** with Cary was old home week for me. We always worked well together, like ham on rye." Grant told this author that "Kate [Hepburn] had her role in **The Philadelphia Story** under lock and key, and she opened the door to me and invited me to sit down in its parlor with her. Her portrayal in that picture of a strong but very vulnerable woman was truly a tour de force. We all thought that she would get the Oscar for it, but it went to Ginger [Ginger Rogers, for **Kitty Foyle**, 1940], although Ginger did a smashing job in that picture. Well, Kate had already won an Oscar [for **Morning Glory**, 1933, her third film], and we all knew she would be winning more of those statuettes in the future." Hepburn set the record (to date) by twelve Acad-

Shelley Winters in *Phone Call from a Stranger*, 1952.

emy Award nominations and winning four Oscars as Best Actress; in addition to **Morning Glory**, she won for her roles in **Guess Who's Coming to Dinner**, 1967; **The Lion in Winter**, 1968, and **On Golden Pond**, 1981. Stewart had been selected to play the newspaperman by Hepburn after she saw his magnificent performance in **Mr. Smith Goes to Washington**, 1939. Stewart told this author: "No one was more surprised than me when I got a call from Kate [Hepburn], asking me if I would appear in **The Philadelphia Story** with her and Cary [Grant]. Would I? You bet and right away. Working with them and George [Cukor] in the picture was one of the highlights of my life. I got another shock when I won the Oscar for my role in that picture. I never for a moment thought I would win and that my good friend Hank Fonda would take the Oscar that year for his great performance in **The Grapes of Wrath** [1940] and, in fact, I voted for him. Throughout the years, whenever I looked at my Oscar, I would think that it should have been standing somewhere on a shelf in Hank's home, not mine." Cukor told this author that "no matter what anybody says, Jimmy [Stewart] deserved that Oscar for his role in **The Philadelphia Story**. He made a powerful transformation from a cynical, disbelieving newshound to a sensitive and caring guy who falls in love with a girl he sets out to smear with scandal. When Jimmy expressed his love for Kate, it is a revelation to him that he can bring himself to voice such raw emotions, and he did that with such believable sincerity that won every viewer's heart. There has always been something innocent about Jimmy that compels any viewer to believe every word he says. Only Jimmy could have handled that transformation so effectively and convincingly and he did that without any help from me. He won that Oscar fair and square." Cukor edified MGM by bringing this film under schedule, putting the finished film in the can within eight weeks. Although Mayer and other studio executives believed the film would do well, they were shocked to see it break all box office records at the illustrious Radio City Music Hall in New York where it took in $600,000 within six weeks. Although James Stewart was surprised to receive his Oscar at the Academy Awards, Donald Ogden Stewart was not amazed to receive his Oscar. He had told a friend before the Oscars were announced that "I wrote a dog-biting satire on high society in America, but I tweaked its nose with a big smile, so they'll give me the Award." They did, and when he accepted that award, the writer unabashedly and immodestly told everyone gathered at the Awards that night: "I have no one to thank but myself!" **p**, Joseph L. Mankiewicz; **d**, George Cukor; **cast**, Cary Grant, Katharine Hepburn, James Stewart, Ruth Hussey, John Howard, Roland Young, John Halliday, Mary Nash, Virginia Weidler, Henry Daniell, Lionel Pape, Rex Evans, Hillary Brooke; **w**, Donald Ogden Salt and (uncredited) Waldo Stewart (based on the play by Philip Barry); **c**, Joseph Ruttenberg; **m**, Franz Waxman; **ed**, Frank Sullivan; **art d**, Cedric Gibbons; **set d**, Edwin B. Willis.

Phone Call from a Stranger ★★★★ 1952; U.S.; 105m; FOX; B/W; Drama; Children: Cautionary; **DVD**; **VHS**. Several intriguing tales are well presented in this episodic drama that begins when Merrill leaves his wife, Westcott, who is deserting him and their children for a lover. En route to Los Angeles, Merrill meets Winters on board an airplane and she tells him how she has lost an important Broadway tryout, but that she is looking forward to seeing her loving husband, Craig Stevens, who manages an L.A. nightclub owned by her mother-in-law, Varden, who disapproves of Winters and has been wanting her son to get rid of her. After the plane develops some engine problems it lands at a small air station in the Midwest for repairs, and Merrill meets another passenger, Rennie, a physician, who, after learning that Merrill is an attorney, asks his legal advice. Rennie tells him that he is going to California to face charges involving an incident five years earlier when he killed three persons in a car accident while he was intoxicated. Rennie wants to make a clean breast of everything for the sake of his son, Donaldson, whom he dearly loves. Merrill and Rennie then meet Wynn, a noisy traveling salesman, who tells cornball jokes and who brags about his knockout wife, Davis. He asks that they all have a drink sometime after they arrive in Los Angeles, so they can discuss their harrowing adventure (about the plane being forced to land for repairs). Even though Merrill and Rennie do not seek or want Wynn's brassy company, they all exchange phone numbers out of courtesy. They all board the plane again and it takes off, but it is caught in a terrible storm and is forced to crash land. Merrill is knocked unconscious, and when he revives, he sees that the three persons he has been talking to—Winters, Rennie and Wynn—have been killed. As one of the few survivors, Merrill gets airline officials to agree that, instead of the airline informing the relatives about the deaths of the three persons he has come to know, he personally meet with relatives and give them the sad information about their untimely deaths. When visiting Straight, Rennie's widow, Merrill sees that Donaldson is about to run off, but he patiently explains how his father loved him and Donaldson decides to remain with Straight to see her through this crisis. Merrill next visits Craig Stevens and his hard-hearted mother, Varden, and he lies about Winters, saying that she got the part in the new Broadway show and was returning to her husband to celebrate, news that bolsters her husband's faith in her and deflates Varden's bad opinion about Winters. His last visit is to see Davis, who is Wynn's widow, and Merrill is shocked to see that she is paralyzed and confined to her bed and is far from the stunning beauty Wynn boasted about. Davis, in one of her finest cameo roles, confesses to Merrill that she treated Wynn with the same kind of disdain and indifference practiced by everyone else, but, after she cheated on him and ran off with Warren Stevens, she was crippled for life as result of an accident and how Stevens then abandoned her. She then explains that the compassionate Wynn not only forgave her, but took her back and dutifully took care of her thereafter, bragging about her beauty and wonderful personality. Davis, who has learned the lesson of true love through Wynn, now urges Merrill to call his wife and try to keep his marriage together and this Merrill does, making plans to reconcile with Westcott. Superlative acting is seen from the entire cast, and Negulesco's direction is top drawer where he manages to seamlessly merge one tale into another to present a very effective episodic film. The story was aired in a sixty-minute broadcast on the "Lux Radio Theater" on January 5, 1953, with Shelley Winters and Gary Merrill reprising their roles. Songs: "The Daring Young Man on the Flying Trapeze" (music: Gaston Lyle; lyrics: George Leybourne), "Again" (music: Lionel Newman; lyrics: Dorcas Cochran), "The Old Gray Mare" (traditional). ***Author's Note***: Davis told this author that "I only appear in a small scene in **Phone Call from a Stranger**, but that little scene was packed with emotion as I deal with the death of a husband who was a much better person than I have been. He was the saint and I was the sinner. He was a man of no importance to anyone, but to me he was the most loving and caring person on earth and I have to somehow convey that to Gary [Merrill, who was married to Davis at the time]. Small as that part was, it was one of the most difficult to portray in my entire career." Director Negulesco added to Davis' contention by telling this author that "Bette felt that in her scene where she talks about a dead husband who has forgiven her betrayal that she should display no hysterics, no weeping or sobbing, but that she speak matter-of-factly about this man to convince viewers that he was, indeed, larger than life, and she was right. That scene clinched the success for **Phone Call from a Stranger**. Bette was always right when following her instincts." **p&w**, Nunnally Johnson (based on the story by I.A.R. Wylie); **d**, Jean Negulesco; **cast**, Shelley Winters, Gary Merrill, Michael Rennie, Keenan Wynn, Evelyn Varden, Warren Stevens, Beatrice Straight, Ted Donaldson, Craig Stevens, Helen Westcott, Bette Davis, Hugh Beaumont; **c**, Milton Krasner; **m**, Franz Waxman; **ed**, Hugh Fowler; **art d**, Lyle Wheeler, J. Russell Spencer; **set d**, Thomas Little, Bruce Macdonald; **spec eff**, Ray Kellogg.

Piaf—The Early Years ★★★ 1982; France; 104m; Les Films Feuer and Martin/FOX; Color; Biographical Drama; Children: Unacceptable (MPAA: PG); **DVD**; **VHS**. This good biopic centers on France's most celebrated singer of the 20th Century, Edith Piaf (1915-1963), torch singer extraordinaire. Her songs were largely biographical in that they reflected the sorrows and loves of her own life. Ariel does an exceptional job at portraying this passionate woman, her early songs sung by Betty Mars. The tale shows how Piaf recovers from temporary blindness, her street performances with her father, and her tenuous relationship with her sister, played by Christophe. (That sister, Simone Berteaut, wrote the book on which this film is based.) The film also profiles Piaf's first marriage to a Parisian blue-collar worker, and the birth of a child, a union that worsened as her singing career soared to great success as the country's leading chanteuse. This film was originally produced in 1974, but was not released in the U.S. until eight years later. A sequel, **Edith and Marcel**, 1984, details the singer's relationship with French heavyweight prizefighter Marcel Cerdan. Piaf herself appeared in only a few films, notably in **French Can-Can**, 1956, and **Royal Affairs at Versailles**, 1957. (In French; English subtitles.) **p**, Cy Feuer, Leopold Wyler, Ernest H. Martin; **d**, Guy Casaril; **cast**, Brigitte Ariel, Pascale Christophe, Guy Trejan, Pierre Vernier, Jacques Duby, Anouk Ferjac, Sylvie Joly, Yvan Varco, Michel Bedetti, Francois Dyrek, Betty Mars (vocals for Ariel); **w**, Casaril, Francoise Ferley, Marc Behm (based on the book *Piaf* by Simone Berteaut); **c**, Edmond Sechan (Eastmancolor); **m**, Ralph Burns; **ed**, Henri Taverna, Louisette Hautecoeur; **art d**, Francois de Lamothe.

The Pianist ★★★★★ 2002; France/Poland/Germany/U.K.; 150m; R. P. Productions/Heritage Films/Focus Features; Color; Biographical Drama; Children: Unacceptable (MPAA: R); **BD**; **DVD**; **VHS**. This superb biopic of pianist Wladyslaw Szpilman (1911-2000), a Polish Jew, who is brilliantly played by Brody, begins in September 1939 when the Germans invade Poland. Brody is playing on the radio when its station in Warsaw is bombed. As WWII begins, Brody and his Jewish family rejoice when they hear that England and France have declared war on Germany and they believe these allies will soon help defeat the invading Germans. Nothing of the kind happens. Germany conquers Poland with lightning speed, and German troops occupy Warsaw where Nazi officials quickly begin to oppress its Jews, forcing them to wear armbands bearing the "Star of David." Within a year, Brody and his family are forced to live within the barricaded Warsaw ghetto that pens in all of the city's Jews and where its residents are compelled to live in squalor and starvation, and, at one point, he and his family see an entire Jewish family murdered by SS guards during a raid across the street from their home. Brody's family is finally rounded up in 1942 and they are all sent to the Treblinka concentration camp to be exterminated, but Brody escapes through the efforts of a member of the Jewish Ghetto Police. He survives by working as a slave laborer, learning that those Jews remaining in the Ghetto are planning an uprising against the Nazis. He aids the rebels by smuggling weapons to them, but then sees the uprising

Adrien Brody in *The Pianist*, 2002.

crushed. He survives by moving from one hideout to the next with the help of Jews and non-Jews. By 1944, Warsaw lies in ruins and Brody finds shelter in an abandoned house, but he is found by Kretschmann, a German officer, who discovers that Brody is a pianist and, being a music lover, asks him to play something on the grand piano in the house. Brody plays Chopin's Ballad in G Minor, which so moves Kretschmann that he allows Brody to go on hiding in the house, living in the attic and to which Kretschmann regularly brings him food. When the Germans retreat from Warsaw in 1945, Kretschmann says goodbye to Brody, telling him that he hopes to hear him play the piano someday on the radio in Warsaw and then gives him his overcoat to keep warm and departs. A short time later, Brody is almost shot and killed when he is mistaken for a German officer by Polish resistance fighters, who then take him into custody. Kretschmann is later imprisoned by the Soviets, but asks a former prisoner, a musician, if he knows Brody and when he says he does, Kretschmann asks him to contact Brody to help bring about his release. Brody finally hears of Kretschmann's imprisonment, but when he visits the camp, he finds the prisoners gone. It is later learned that Kretschmann (playing William Hosenfeld, 1895-1952) has died while in Soviet captivity. Directory Polanski provides a great story and does not shirk from depicting the bestial brutality of the Nazis while carefully detailing the agonizing lifestyle of the Jewish people, along with Brody's own life as he seeks to constantly survive the seemingly endless hazards of the Holocaust. The production values are outstanding while the lensing realistically conveys the shuddering and unforgettable images of that gruesome period, interspersed with stunning passages of music that transcend and spiritually triumph over the ravages of war and inhumanity to mankind. Songs: "Nocturne in C Minor" (1830), "Ballad No. 1 in G Minor, Op. 23" (1835-1836), "Grande Polonaise Brillante, Op. 23 Allegro Molto" (1830-1831; Fredric Chopin), "Sonata No. 14 in C Minor Op. 27/2" (1801; Ludwig van Beethoven), "Suite No. 1 BWV 1007 for Solo Cello" (1717-1723; Johann Sebastian Bach), "Tantz, Tantz Yidelekh" (traditional), "Umowilem sie z nia na dziewiata" (1937; Henry Vars), "Marsz Strzelcow" (1863; Wladyslaw Anczyc), "Polish National Anthem" (traditional). **p**, Roman Polanski, Robert Benmussa, Gene Gutowski, Alain Sarde; **d**, Polanski; **cast**, Adrien Brody, Thomas Kretschmann, Frank Finlay, Emilia Fox, Michal Zebrowski, Ed Stoppard, Maureen Lipman, Jessica Kate Meyer, Julia Rayner, Wanja Mues; **w**, Ronald Harwood (based on the book by Wladyslaw Szpilman); **c**, Pawel Edelman; **m**, Wojciech Kilar; **ed**, Herve De Luze; **prod d**, Allan Starski; **art d**, Nenad Pecur; **set d**, Wieslawa Chojkowska, Gabriele Wolff; **spec eff**, Alister Mazzotti, Hans Seck, Kazimierz Wróblewski.

Pickpocket ★★★ 1963; France; 75m; Compagnie Cinematographique de France/New Yorker; B/W; Drama/Crime Drama; Children: Unac-

Jean Peters and Vic Perry in *Pickup on South Street*, 1953.

ceptable; **DVD**; **VHS**. Fascinating crime yarn sees La Salle as a lonely young man, who takes to picking pockets as a hobby and is arrested. In jail, he reflects on the morality of crime, but, after he is released, he rejects the help friends offer to put him on the straight and narrow. He returns to pickpocketing, this time taking lessons from an expert thief, Kassagi. La Salle feels that picking pockets is the only way he can express himself and he is now on his way to becoming a professional thief. Look for no redemption here as this profiles a novice in crime who has opted to become a recidivist and for that reason prohibits viewing by children. Song: "Suite de Symphonies d'Amadis" (Jean-Baptiste Lully). **p**, Agnes Delahie; **d&w**, Robert Bresson; **cast**, Martin La Salle, Marika Green, Jean Pelegri, Dolly Scal, Pierre Leymarie, Kassagi, Pierre Etaix, Cesar Gattegno, Sophie Saint-Just, Dominique Zardi; **c**, Leonce-Henri Burel; **ed**, Raymond Lamy; **prod d**, Pierre Charbonnier.

Pickup on South Street ★★★ 1953; U.S.; 80m; FOX; B/W; Crime Drama; Children: Unacceptable; **DVD**; **VHS**. In one of his most riveting roles, Widmark plays a professional pickpocket in NYC, but he picks one too many pockets and winds up being involved with communist spies. He is clever, artful and utterly without scruples, a thief to the marrow. He has one soft spot and that is for Ritter. She is an aging, ailing woman and former pickpocket (who tutored Widmark in the art of stealing in his formative days, and where he looks upon her as a mother figure). Ritter sells cheap neckties to eke out a living, supplementing her income by also selling information on other criminals to the police. Widmark, a "three-time loser," picks the wallet owned by Peters, an attractive brunette, only to discover to his amazement that he has stolen some top secret microfilm Peters has been unwittingly transporting for her lover, Kiley. Although Peters believes Kiley is an attorney, he is a communist spy, and when Kiley learns that she has had her pocket picked and has lost the microfilm, he orders Peters to track down the pickpocket and retrieve that vital microfilm. Meanwhile, federal agents have been trailing Peters in hopes of obtaining information that will allow them to arrest Kiley and his fellow spies. Peters is brought in for questioning by police detective Vye at the request of federal agent Bouchey, who tells Peters that her boyfriend Kiley is a communist spy and that they are after that microfilm. She and the federal agents then locate the whereabouts of Widmark through Ritter, who tells them that they can find Widmark at a shack on the waterfront. Peters visits Widmark and he roughs her up, giving her back her wallet, but not the microfilm, which he knows is valuable and he has hidden. She later returns and offers him several hundred dollars that Kiley has given her to buy back the microfilm. Widmark keeps the money and sends her on her way with only a piece of the microfilm. When federal agents appeal to Widmark to help them, he ignores their pleas. He does not care about communists or any

secrets they might be stealing from the U.S. His only concern is to sell the microfilm for a fortune. Kiley, meanwhile, begins hunting for Widmark and finds Ritter. When she refuses to tell him anything about Widmark, Kiley kills her. Kiley later meets with Peters, who had fallen for Widmark and is working with the federal agents. When she gives him only part of the microfilm, Kiley realizes that Widmark has kept the last vital frame and he explodes, savagely beating Peters into unconsciousness. Federal agents waiting nearby to trap Kiley find Peters beaten senseless, and she is rushed to a hospital. Kiley manages to escape from agents in Peters' apartment building by lowering himself to the basement in a dumb waiter where he overpowers an agent and then flees. Widmark visits Peters in the hospital, learning that she has risked her life to protect him, something no one has ever done for him and he also realizes that he loves her. He now seeks revenge for her beating, as well as the death of Ritter, the only other person he has ever cared about. He waits at his shack for Kiley, who shows up, but he successfully hides from Kiley, and when Kiley leaves, Widmark follows him to a subway station where he finds Kiley passing the incomplete microfilm to another communist spy. Widmark knocks that contact cold and then battles with Kiley, who flees with Widmark in pursuit. They fight through the station and then onto the subway tracks until Widmark knocks Kiley onto the tracks and before an oncoming train. Widmark and Peters are then shown at police headquarters where Vye releases him, but tells him that he will later arrest him for another offense and send him to prison. Widmark, however, has decided to reform and go straight while making a life with Peters. When Vye repeats his prediction that Widmark will again turn to crime, Peters replies: "You wanna bet?" She and Widmark then leave arm in arm. Widmark was never more convincing as a shifty, unreliable, deceitful character until redeeming his errant behavior by falling in love with Peters and embracing her American patriotism. Peters gives a startling and unexpected performance as a sultry mistress risking her life for the sake of her country (a woman more sadistically beaten than in any other film in recent memory), and Kiley is absolutely mesmerizing in one of his most intense roles as the insidious communist agent who will stop at nothing to accomplish his secret mission. So outstanding is Ritter's performance as the worn-out police informant (who tells Kiley before he kills her that he will be doing her a favor by putting her out of her misery) that she deservedly received an Oscar nomination as Best Supporting Actress. Fuller's vigorous direction presents a fast-paced tale packed with action and offering moody and murky scenes that perfectly befit the sinister characters stalking the streets of New York and along its seedy waterfront. Fuller abandons the stereotypical profiles then voguishly offered in anti-communist films and presents a much more complex scenario in his subtle character development of the communist agents, notably Kiley, who is consumed by angst and anger. Songs: "Again" (music: Lionel Newman), "Mam'selle" (music: Edmund Goulding; lyrics: Mack Gordon). Other films profiling espionage and communist spies during the Cold War include **Arctic Flight**, 1952; **Billion Dollar Brain**, 1967; **Counterspy Meets Scotland Yard**, 1950; **Diplomatic Courier**, 1952; **The Double**, 2011; **From Russia with Love**, 1964; **Funeral in Berlin**, 1966; **The Hunter**, 1952 (TV series); **I Was a Communist for the F.B.I.**, 1951; **The Ipcress File**, 1965; **The Iron Curtain**, 1948; **The Manchurian Candidate**, 1962; **My Son John**, 1952; **Night People**, 1954; **North by Northwest**, 1959; **Notorious**, 1992 (made-for-TV); **The Quiller Memorandum**, 1966; **Salt**, 2010; **Security Risk**, 1954; **The Spy Who Came in from the Cold**, 1965; **The Thief**, 1952; **The Third Man**, 1950; **Topaz**, 1969; **Torn Curtain**, 1966; **The Whistle Blower**, 1987; **The Woman on Pier 13**, 1949. *Author's Note*: This film was originally conceived as a straightforward crime tale about drug pushers and written by Dwight Taylor under the title of "Blaze of Glory," but when director Fuller was assigned to helm the film, he had other ideas when meeting with studio head Darryl F. Zanuck. "Fuller wanted to change the story to communist spies instead of drug peddlers," Zanuck told this author. "Since the HUAC hearings [U.S. House of Un-American Activities Committee] were then in the news and everyone was pointing fingers everywhere and calling them hidden communist agents, I thought his idea was a good one and gave him the green light." Fuller told this author that "Zanuck wanted to find a dramatic part for dancer and singer Betty Grable, who was one of the studio's top stars then. I had a battle with him over that, even though I agreed with him that Betty had done a good job in a dramatic role when she appeared with Vic [Victor] Mature in a tough crime story, **I Wake Up Screaming** [1941]. She just wasn't the woman to play the leading lady in **Pickup on South Street**. Betty was too wholesome and the public would have screamed bloody murder if she was seen being beaten to a pulp on the screen, which is what happens to that character several times. 'Okay, Sam,' Zanuck said to me, 'which one of our actresses should have the hell kicked out of her?' I laughed at that, but then saw that he was not kidding and really did not like the idea of any woman being mercilessly beaten. I told him that Shelley Winters would probably be a good candidate. She had been mistreated a lot in several pictures and she had played some alluring loose women—cheating wives and floozy girlfriends. But then I could not get Shelley for the picture. I then thought that Jean [Peters], a very sensuous-looking actress with sultry dark features, would be ideal for the role of the sexy leading lady, but Zanuck told me that 'she will never play a role like that. She turned down some pictures where she said that the roles were 'too sexy.' [Peters had rejected parts in **Yellow Sky**, 1948, and **Sand**, 1949, and for these refusals was briefly dropped from the studio payroll, but reinstated to go on to perform in more prissy performances.] Jean had just appeared in **Niagara** [1953], which had been a big hit, but where Marilyn Monroe got all the attention because she was the sexpot of that picture. When I described to Jean the kind of part she would be playing in **Pickup on South Street**, she told me right away that she would do it and I think Monroe's performance in **Niagara** aroused her competitiveness and that she could sizzle scenes just as good as Monroe. Jean never complained about wearing skimpy dresses, showing a lot of leg and cleavage or even taking a bubble bath in **Pickup on South Street**. She did her own stunts when she had to be beaten up and she got plenty of bruises to show for it. I think she was out to prove that she could be as sexy as Monroe or any other screen siren and she did prove that. I think her performance in that picture is one of the best she ever gave." Widmark told this author that he thought his role in this film "took a lot out of me. I looked upon my character as a guy having a split personality, half crook and half human being and where I have to struggle with myself to either go on being a hateful, sneaking thief, or a good guy who should do the right thing. The guy really has little or no character until he meets a girl who does not play him for a sucker and falls in love with him. He doesn't know how to treat her, so he slaps her around and beats her up because that's the only kind of attention he has ever gotten in life. The guy is a crud all along and I kept asking myself, when am I going to be able to turn this bum into a decent human being? Jean [Peters] was simply great in that film. She gets beaten up by me and Richard [Kiley] so much that I thought she would quit the picture, but she hung in there and took all that punishment and still came up with a smiling face. The person who stole that picture is Richard [Kiley]. Compared to my character, a sneak thief without any principles, Richard is evil personified. He is so dedicated to the communist cause that he becomes a pathological killer, murdering women without batting an eyelash. This is a guy you want to see dead as soon as possible and that's why he took the film. What a great performance!" **p**, Jules Schermer; **d&w**, Samuel Fuller (based on the story by Dwight Taylor); **cast**, Richard Widmark, Jean Peters, Thelma Ritter, Murvyn Vye, Richard Kiley, Willis B. Bouchey, Milburn Stone, Parley Baer, Ray Montgomery; **c**, Joe MacDonald; **m**, Leigh Harline; **ed**, Nick De Maggio; **art d**, Lyle Wheeler, George Patrick; **set d**, Al Orenbach; **spec eff**, Ray Kellogg.

The Pickwick Papers ★★★ 1954; U.K.; 130m; George Minter/Arthur Mayer-Edward Kingsley; B/W; Comedy; Children: Acceptable; **DVD**;

Kim Novak and William Holden in *Picnic,* **1955.**

VHS. This solid and thoroughly entertaining comedy begins when some middle-class and middle-aged Englishmen form the Pickwick Club to study English life. They send the group's namesake, Mr. Pickwick (Hayter) and some other club members traveling across England to report back on interesting things they find along the way. They frequently encounter Mr. Jingle (Patrick), who becomes a source of trouble for all who know him. Hayter also becomes a victim to misunderstandings that bring him problems with the law. It's a very funny, whimsical film with some wonderful British character actors. **p**, Noel Langley, George Minter; **d&w**, Langley (based on the novel by Charles Dickens); **cast**, James Hayter, James Donald, Nigel Patrick, Joyce Grenfell, Hermione Gingold, Hermione Baddeley, Donald Wolfit, Harry Fowler, Kathleen Harrison, Alexander Gauge; **c**, Wilkie Cooper; **m**, Antony Hopkins; **ed**, Anne V. Coates; **art d**, Frederick Pusey.

Picnic ★★★★ 1955; U.S.; 115m; COL; Color; Drama/Romance; Children: Unacceptable; **DVD**; **VHS**. Few leading men could have been as convincing and compelling as Holden is in this powerful study of a young drifter beginning to feel his age and doubting his rootless lifestyle after he falls hopelessly in love with a beautiful small-town girl, Novak. Based upon the Pulitzer Prize–winning play by Inge, the film begins when Holden arrives in a small Kansas town while the residents prepare to celebrate Labor Day. He looks up an old pal, Robertson, who is delighted to see him, introducing him to his fiancé, Novak. Holden and Novak take one look at each other and they are both love-smitten. Robertson's father is the wealthiest man in the county, and Holden thinks to ask Robertson for a job with one of his father's operations but is sidetracked when Robertson asks him to join in the local festivities. The handsome and strapping Holden, who bares his chest and flexes his muscles, soon captivates Strasberg, who is Novak's impressionable younger sister, as well as schoolteacher and spinster Russell (in one of her most endearing and funniest performances). All starts out amiably as Holden befriends O'Connell, a bachelor Russell has been trying to talk, pressure, persuade, cajole, beg and implore to marry her, but the canny middle-aged O'Connell has thus far succeeded in avoiding the altar. Holden attends the community picnic and participates in many of its down-home events, from minor athletic competitions to fast-eating contests. He watches with admiration as Novak sails along a river as the prom queen and suddenly begins to make plans of doing something with his otherwise shiftless life, like getting a good job, settling down, and, mostly, marrying Novak. When the boat docks, Holden and Novak do a slow dance atop the boat deck to the song "Moonglow," a classic love scene that prompted just about every woman in America to want that same dance with Holden, a dance he hated to perform. As the evening wears on, Holden brags about his adventures to anyone who will listen, his

William Holden and Susan Strasberg in *Picnic*, 1955.

most rapt listener being Russell. She begins drinking from the bottle of booze O'Connell has brought along (shielded from sight by newspapers) until she is high as a kite and is flagrantly ogling Holden's bare chest as seen through his unbuttoned shirt. With liquor inflaming her lust, the frustrated Russell can no longer stand the strain and she jumps forward, ripping the shirt from Holden's back in an awkward but obvious attempt at innocent play that is not so innocent, humiliating him in front of everyone. When Robertson later learns that Holden and his best girl Novak are emotionally involved, he gets into a fight with the powerful Holden, who beats him up. After attacking his best friend in a fight he has tried to avoid, Holden is now hunted by the police. He takes Novak home and, for the first time in his life, nobly tells her the truth about himself, that he is nothing more than a self-glorifying hobo with no opportunities and that she would have no future with him and he departs. Meanwhile, Russell has finally coerced O'Connell into marrying her and she is overjoyed, bidding farewell to her spinster friends as she and O'Connell motor down the street to begin their honeymoon, which promises to be too energetic to O'Connell's liking. Novak dreams of the same sweet fate as her mother, Field, urges her to find her happiness and security with Robertson while Holden quickly makes an exit from the town the same way he arrived, by hopping a freight train, riding the rails toward a big city. Novak, however, realizes that love is the only thing that matters to her, not security, and she quickly packs her bags, planning to catch up with Holden and taking a bus that is heading in the same direction as the train on which Holden rides, both vehicles converging in a retreating overhead shot that ends this nostalgic and touching film. Logan does a masterful job in telling this tender love story as well as developing its many colorful characters, and Howe's expert lensing presents a colorful panorama of small-town America. Holden is superb in his role as a man adrift in a world where all seems comfortable, secure and permanent within the uneventful lives of those he comes to meet and befriend, but where his own futureless life is nakedly exposed. To the world he enters, Holden is an amusing if not unsettling outsider to be tolerated and viewed as one might patronize a visiting overnight carnival to excitingly play its petty sideshow games, eagerly munch on its mustard-smeared hotdogs, and leisurely stroll through the wake of trailing sawdust when that carnival departs. Everything about this film is poignantly wistful and evocatively charming as it gently stirs and summons the prosaic memories of every small town in America. Russell and O'Connell are also exceptional in their roles as two middle-aged persons not wanting much more out of life than a little happiness and love. Songs: "Ain't She Sweet" (music: Milton Ager; lyrics: Jack Yellen), "In the Gloaming" (music: Annie Fortescue Harrison; lyrics: Meta Orred), "Moonglow" (Will Hudson, Edgar De Lange, Irving Mills), "Love's Sweet Song" (G. Clifton Bingham, J. L. Molloy), "It's

a Blue World" (Bob Wright, Chet Forrest). ***Author's Note***: Playwright Inge produced a number of successful plays that concentrate on small-town America, earning him the sobriquet of "The Playwright of the Midwest." This author first met William Inge (1913-1973) a year after this film was released and when he visited Father John Joseph Walsh (1914-2005), a Jesuit priest who was the director of the Theater Department (Marquette University Players) at Marquette University from 1951 to 1965, and where this author was then a student. Walsh was regularly visited by celebrated playwrights, actors and actresses. I met Henry Fonda for the first time when he visited Walsh, and, in the same year, 1956, I met Inge. At that time he told me that **Picnic** was autobiographical for the most part and he had "based all of the characters on people I knew well when living in my mother's boarding house in Kansas. A number of spinster school teachers lived there and I came to know what lonely lives they led. They were sweet and kind to me as a child, but I could sense then as I do to this day, how empty and sad their lives truly were. I grouped all of those ladies into one character in 'Picnic' [Russell's character], and made her all the more determined to change the course of her unpromising life by badgering a bachelor into marrying her. There was nothing spectacular about that, except that that is quite an achievement in most small towns where nothing ever changes much." When asking Inge's advice about how to write plays, he told this author: "Become an actor, get on the stage so that you know where everyone needs to be when they are talking to each other on that stage, and then write your play from the point of view of the actors, not the audience. That way you have believable interaction and dimension between your characters, instead of drawing them like characters on a flat mural as if you were sitting in the audience." I followed this sound advice and subsequently wrote four plays that were produced, but never on the scale or with the impact produced by the superlative works of William Inge. Holden told this author that **Picnic** was "not a picture I wanted to make. I was much too old for the character I wound up playing [he was thirty-seven at that time]. It was a great story and beautifully adapted by Dan Taradash and Josh Logan, but I fought against doing it until I was overwhelmed by the great convincer—a lot of money. I wasn't too excited about acting opposite Kim [Novak], who was being groomed for stardom by Harry Cohn at Columbia. She is a beautiful lady, but a wooden Indian to play against. I don't think she could raise her voice much above a whisper even when screaming. I did a dance with her in that picture that was ballyhooed by the studio publicity department—you know the stuff—'steaming, sizzling,' all that stuff, but it was one of the hardest scenes I ever did because I am the world's worst dancer and I hated pretending that I was graceful and quick with my feet." In fact, when Logan was filming this scene, Holden stopped in the middle of the shot and turned to choreographer Miriam Nelson, saying: "I can't do it! I'm a lousy dancer!" Nelson replied: "You don't have to be Gene Kelly. It's only a little ad lib dance…" The patient Logan took Holden and Nelson that night to a small dance club in Hutchinson, Kansas, where the film was being shot on location (some interior scenes were later shot at the Columbia Studio in Burbank) and played some soft music from the jukebox. He then had Holden dance with Nelson until Holden felt comfortable in doing the dance scene with Novak the next day and where Logan was able to finally complete the scene. Holden believed that this dance scene was really hazardous stunt work and told Columbia boss Cohn that he wanted an additional payment of $8,000 for performing such a "dangerous" stunt. Rather than argue with the actor and delay the production, Cohn gave Holden the payment. Holden, however, never warmed to Novak, who refused to attend any of the get-togethers the cast held nightly after each day's shooting. This was Novak's first role as a leading lady in a major film, although she had appeared in a few earlier films as a supporting actress. She was reportedly terrified of flubbing her lines or botching a scene. Instead of attending cast dinners and parties, she allegedly went to church and prayed that she would be successful in **Picnic**. When hearing about these chapel visits, Holden snorted: "She'd be better off if she spent more time learning her lines and less time reciting her rosary." Holden purposely went out of his way to appear incorrigible during the production of **Picnic**. When Harry Cohn made a slight remark about one scene, Holden gave the studio boss all of the pieces of his mind. The actor further frightened director Logan when Holden attended a production party hosted by Logan, and where, after downing a number of stiff martinis, he climbed onto the window ledge of Logan's hotel suite, which was fourteen floors above ground, and told jokes as he teetered on that ledge and everyone held their breath. He later attended a party Rosalind Russell hosted in her hotel suite, which was ten floors above ground, and where Holden did the same thing, standing on the window ledge after belting down several strong drinks. The unflappable Russell, however, only smiled at his antics and said to her guests: "If we don't pay any attention to him, he'll stop this nonsense." The guests ignored Holden's prankish behavior and he soon climbed down from his dizzying perch. Russell nevertheless always liked the actor, later saying of him: "He's strong as an ox, stubborn as a monkey, and luckier than anything." Holden's luck ran out on November 16, 1981, when, after having too many drinks (it is assumed), he stumbled or collapsed or slipped on a rug and struck his head on the edge of a teak bedroom table, a blow that deeply lacerated his forehead and, being alone and unattended, bled to death. **p**, Fred Kohlmar; **d**, Joshua Logan; **cast**, William Holden, Kim Novak, Rosalind Russell, Betty Field, Susan Strasberg, Cliff Robertson, Arthur O'Connell, Verna Felton, Reta Shaw, Nick Adams, Raymond Bailey, Elizabeth Wilson, Shirley Knight, Phyllis Newman; **w**, Daniel Taradash (based on the play by William Inge); **c**, James Wong Howe (Technicolor); **m**, George Duning; **ed**, Charles Nelson, William A. Lyon; **prod d**, Jo Mielziner; **art d**, William Flannery; **set d**, Robert Priestley.

Picnic at Hanging Rock ★★★ 1979; Australia; 115m; UNIV; Color; Horror/Mystery; Children: Unacceptable (MPAA: PG); **DVD**; **VHS**. From a novel supposedly based on a true story, this intriguing tale begins when Lambert, a school teacher, and her teenage girl students go on a picnic to Hanging Rock in a remote area in Victoria, Australia, on St. Valentine's Day in 1900. While their classmates are napping, Lambert and three of the girls, Morse, Roberts, and Gray, decide to climb to the top of the high rock and are never seen again. The film follows those who disappeared and those who stayed behind, asking a lot of questions, but leaving us to guess what might have become of those who disappeared. Songs/Music: "Doina: Sus Pe Culmea Dealului," "Doina Lui Petru Unc" (Gheorghe Zamfir); "Eine Kleine Nachtmusik, 2nd Movement" (Wolfgang Amadeus Mozart); "Piano Concerto No.5 in E Flat Major, 2nd Movement" (Ludwig van Beethoven); "Prelude No. 1 in C Major" (Johann Sebastian Bach); "String Quartet No 1 in D Major, 2nd Movement" (Peter Ilyich Tchaikovsy). Frightening scenes prohibit viewing by children. **p**, Jim McElroy, Hal McElroy; **d**, Peter Weir; **cast**, Rachel Roberts, Anne-Louise Lambert, Vivean Gray, Helen Morse, Kirsty Child, Anthony Llewellyn-Jones, Jacki Weaver, Frank Gunnell, Karen Robson, Jane Vallis; **w**, Cliff Green (based on the novel by Joan Lindsay); **c**, Russell Boyd (Eastmancolor); **m**, Bruce Smeaton; **ed**, Max Lemon; **art d**, David Copping.

Picture Bride ★★★ 1994; Japan; 95m; Cecile Films/Miramax; Color; Drama/Romance; Children: Unacceptable (MPAA: PG-13); **DVD**; **VHS**. This fine story is centered upon Kudô, a 16-year-old Japanese girl who travels to Hawaii in 1918 to marry a man she has never met, she and her intended having only exchanged photos and letters. Upon meeting him, Kudô is surprised to find her future husband is twice her age and, further, he does not own a sugar cane plantation he claimed was his, but works on it. She nevertheless marries him to escape an unhappy life in Japan, and, despite hardship and struggle, she finds unexpected happiness with him. Top-drawer acting and an excellent drama sustain interest throughout. Mature themes prohibit viewing by children. **p**, Lisa Onodera; **d**, Kayo Hatta; **cast**, Yûki Kudô, Cary-Hiroyuki Tagawa, Tamlyn Tomita, Akira Takayama, Yôko Sugi, Christianne

Donna Reed and Hurd Hatfield in *The Picture of Dorian Gray,* 1945.

Mays, Toshirô Mifune, Jason Scott Lee, Michael Ashby, James Grant Benton, Peter Clark; **w**, Kayo Hatta, Mari Hatta (based on a story by them and Diane Mei Lin Mark); **c**, Claudio Rocha; **m**, Mark Adler; **ed**, Mallory Gottlieb, Lynzee Klingman; **prod d**, Paul Guncheon; **spec eff**, Archie Ahuna.

The Picture of Dorian Gray ★★★★ 1945; U.S.; 110m; MGM; B/W/Color; Horror; Children: Unacceptable; **DVD**; **VHS**. Oscar Wilde's eerie novel comes alive in this well-made horror classic that exactingly profiles the sinister nature of the wealthy and forever young Dorian Gray, who is superbly enacted by Hatfield. The angelic-looking Hatfield is a young, rich aristocrat living in 19th-Century London. His character is slowly molded by Sanders, an older, more sophisticated aristocrat, who advocates a hedonistic lifestyle that the impressionable Hatfield embraces. It is soon scandalously rumored that Hatfield is participating in all kinds of evil orgies where masochism and sadism is freely exhibited (but never shown). He begins visiting a dance hall where he sees and meets singer Lansbury, falling in love with her. He brings great joy to her life when he proposes marriage, but, at the last moment, he callously jilts her, emulating the same kind of cruel conduct displayed by his mentor, Sanders. At this time, Gilmore, who is Hatfield's close friend and a gifted artist, paints the young man's portrait, a masterpiece of finite detail that exhibits his penetrating eyes, high cheekbones and full head of hair, a stunning image of masculine handsomeness. When alone and admiring his own image, Hatfield makes a pact with the painting (or the Devil) where he trades his immortal soul in order to remain forever young and handsome as depicted in that portrait, and this results in the portrait taking on the cares and aging that would normally besiege Hatfield's own human flesh. While Hatfield remains youthful and unchanged, the painting slowly turns into a corrosive, hideous image, visually translating the endless transgressions and sins against mankind that Hatfield commits into an image of ghastly looking sores and decaying flesh, the face of a monstrous gargoyle. Gilmore finds the portrait hidden in an attic room of Hatfield's lavishly appointed mansion and recoils in horror at what he sees, discovering Hatfield's secret of always remaining youthful, a secret Hatfield keeps by murdering Gilmore. Years later, Hatfield, who appears just as youthful as decades earlier, meets Reed, who is Gilmore's beautiful niece, and he begins a romance with her. Unaware of Hatfield's lurid and evil past, Reed continues to see Hatfield, despite the warnings of Lawford, a young man who loves her and believes Hatfield has long ago murdered her uncle, as does Fraser, a sailor and who is Lansbury's brother. Both Lawford and Fraser separately investigate Hatfield's past, Fraser meeting his death at the hands of Hatfield. Lawford then breaks into Hatfield's mansion and, finding the hidden portrait in the attic room, he shows this horrific paint-

James Cagney and Alice White in *Picture Snatcher*, 1933.

ing to Reed and Sanders and where Sanders now understands how the secretive Hatfield has maintained over the decades his ageless appearance. Before Hatfield can be brought to justice, however, he confronts that painting and, in an effort to redeem his immortal soul, denounces it and drives a dagger into it, but he has killed himself, and when he collapses dead to the floor, all of the corrosion the painting has born all these years are transmitted to its rightful owner and bearer, the dying remains of Hatfield, who lies upon that floor with a face of decayed and pulpy flesh, the painting resuming its original state to show the youthful and handsome Hatfield at the time of its creation and before its real life model made that terrible bargain with Satan. Director Lewin expertly presents a consistently frightening film, but where the evil doings of Hatfield are more implied than shown, until that grotesque painting is displayed on screen in all of its hideousness. When the viewer finally sees that portrait, the film goes from black and white to Technicolor in showing that portrait (painted by artist Ivan Albright), a sudden, flashing image accompanied by a musical crescendo, more frightening than any lightning bolt displayed in a Frankenstein film or the opening of a casket lid in a Dracula movie. Hatfield's performance is one of subtle brilliance, exuding shuddering dread as, like a vampire, he feeds upon his own image, drawing the lifeblood of that painting to perpetuate an external but false image of perpetual youth within a body that is otherwise rotting from moral decay. Lansbury, who gives one of her finest performances as the naïve and trusting dance hall singer, received an Oscar nomination as Best Supporting Actress, and Gibbons and Peters were nominated as Best Art Direction (for their black-and-white art direction); the gifted cinematographer Stradling received an Oscar for Best Cinematography Black and White. Songs: "Goodbye, Little Yellow Bird" (music: William Hargreaves; lyrics: C. W. Murphy), "Moonlight Sonata" (Ludwig van Beethoven), "Prelude for Piano, Op. 28, No. 24 in D Minor (The Storm)," "Prelude in E, Op. 28, No. 4" (Fredric Chopin), "La Ci Darem La Mano" (from "Don Giovanni" by Wolfgang Amadeus Mozart), "Youth" (Herbert Stothart). *Author's Note*: The abrupt and visually effective transition from black and white to color in showing the altered state of Dorian Gray on canvas in this film was a technique later adopted by director William Dieterle in his outstanding production of **Portrait of Jennie**, 1949, starring Jennifer Jones and Joseph Cotten, but where the portrait of Jones shown in color at the end of that wonderful fantasy film that is otherwise presented in black and white presents a beautiful and benign image. Among the fine cast appearing in **The Picture of Dorian Gray** is Sanders, who specialized (after so being typecast) in playing ultra-sophisticated but unsavory characters and he never better played such a ne'er-do-well than in this film. Sanders told this author that "for the first time in my career in playing a disreputable rake, I appear somewhat appealing and sympathetic,

and even amusing, but that is only because Hurd [Hatfield] plays an inhuman ogre in **The Picture of Dorian Gray**. It was a relief to see someone 'out-cad' me for a change." **p**, Pandro S. Berman; **d&w**, Albert Lewin (based on the novel by Oscar Wilde); **cast**, George Sanders, Hurd Hatfield, Donna Reed, Angela Lansbury, Peter Lawford, Lowell Gilmore, Richard Fraser, Miles Mander, Mary Forbes, Robert Greig, Dorothy Ford, Joe Yule; **c**, Harry Stradling; **m**, Herbert Stothart; **ed**, Ferris Webster; **art d**, Cedric Gibbons, Hans Peters; **set d**, Edwin B. Willis; **spec eff**, A. Arnold Gillespie, Warren Newcombe, Mark Davis.

Picture Snatcher ★★★ 1933; U.S.; 77m; WB; B/W; Drama; Children: Acceptable; **DVD**. This tough and gritty film profiles the excesses of the tabloid newspapers of the 1920s, beginning when ex-convict Cagney goes straight as a newspaper reporter and falls in love with Ellis, the daughter of O'Connor, the policeman who arrested him. Bellamy, the managing editor of a tabloid newspaper in New York City and Cagney's boss, convinces O'Connor that Cagney is an okay guy. Cagney then makes a big mistake, using his relationship with Ellis to take a photo at an execution. O'Connor loses his lieutenant stripes because of this and forbids Cagney to see Ellis again. But when one of Cagney's former friends kills two policemen, Cagney takes his picture and the killer is brought to justice. Cagney wins back O'Connor's respect and Ellis' hand for a happy ending. How Cagney snaps the photo at the execution was based on a true event. Songs: "I'm Forever Blowing Bubbles" (1918, James Kendis, James Brockman, Nat Vincent), "For You" (1930, Joseph Burke), "Young and Healthy" (1933, Harry Warren), "My Old Man" (1933, Bernard Hanighen). *Author's Note*: This film focuses upon one of the most sensational newspaper events of the Roaring Twenties, and that is the scene where Cagney snaps a photo of a convicted murderer being executed in the electric chair while using a hidden camera. That real life event involved convicted murderer Ruth Snyder (1895-1928), who, along with her lover, Henry Judd Gray (1893-1928), a married corset salesman, who beat Snyder's husband, Albert Snyder, to death. Both were convicted and sentenced to death in Sing Sing's electric chair. On the night of Snyder's execution, January 12, 1928, Tom Howard, a photographer for the New York *Daily News*, who was part of the press corps invited to witness that execution, entered the death chamber and took a seat in the first row. He had affixed a small camera secreted beneath a trouser leg, one that had a cord running up that leg to his waist where he held a plunger that would activate the camera and take a picture. Just when the electric current was sent into the chair and coursed through Snyder's body, forcing it to surge against the straps holding her inside the chair, Howard lifted his trouser and took the picture, which was published as the entire front page of the *News* the next day, the kind of photo that had thus far been prohibited. It was this sensational event that was enacted in **Picture Snatcher**. Cagney told this author that "Warner Brothers got a lot of heat from the New York prison people for recreating the *News* photo, but, like the newspaper that sold a lot of copies of that photograph, Warner Brothers sold a lot of movie tickets for doing the same thing. In those days, we were making movies right off the front pages of newspapers and **Picture Snatcher** was one of those movies." For more details on the Ruth Snyder case, see my book, *World Encyclopedia of 20th Century Murder* (Paragon House, 1992; pages 523-529). **p**, Ray Griffith; **d**, Lloyd Bacon; **cast**, James Cagney, Ralph Bellamy, Patricia Ellis, Alice White, Robert Emmett O'Connor, Robert Barrat, Ralf Harolde, Hobart Cavanaugh, George Chandler, Cora Sue Collins, Sterling Holloway; **w**, Allen Rivkin, P.J. Wolfson, Ben Markson (based on a story by Daniel Ahern); **c**, Sol Polito; **ed**, William Holmes; **art d**, Robert M. Haas.

Pie in the Sky ★★★ 1964; U.S.; 86m; Barbroo Productions/Allied Artists;☐ B/W; Drama; Children: Unacceptable. Grim but fascinating rite-of-passage film sees Bray, a young boy, being forced to leave home in rural America because his embittered, widowed father can't afford to feed or house him anymore. Bray hitchhikes to Manhattan where he meets up with another boy, Charlemagne, a con artist his age, who controls the shoeshine and newspaper sellers, forcing them to pay him protection money. Bray wins most of Charlemagne's money in a crap game, but is then beaten by Charlemagne's enforcers. Bray is then befriended by Grant, a prostitute, and lives with her until she is arrested for soliciting. He is later taken in by a black couple, but he decides to return home where he and his father begin a closer relationship. This well-crafted independent film offers an outstanding performance from Bray and the rest of the cast, but it unfortunately saw limited distribution and is (at this writing) unavailable in any video format. Mature themes, violence and prostitution prohibit viewing by children. **p**, Merrill S. Brody, Allen Baron, Dorothy E. Reed; **d&w**, Baron; **cast**, Lee Grant, Richard Bray, Jaime Charlemagne, Michael Higgins, Robert Marsach, Robert Allen, Sylvia Miles, Ruth Attaway, Robert Earl Jones, Roscoe Lee Browne, Charles Jordan; **c**, Brody, Donald Malkames; **m**, Robert Mersey; **ed**, Ralph Rosenblum; **art d**, Charles Rosen.

The Pied Piper ★★★ 1942; U.S.; 86m; FOX; B/W; War Drama; Children: Unacceptable; **DVD**. Woolley gives an exceptional performance as an Englishman who inadvertently turns into the protective shepherd of a flock of displaced children. He is on a fishing vacation in eastern France when the Germans invade in 1940 during World War II (1939-1945). He prepares to return to England and is persuaded to take along two children, McDowall and Garner. Gradually more children are added as Woolley, a modern-day Pied Piper, takes them to German-occupied northern France. Preminger, a German officer, first opposes Woolley and his humanitarian mission, but eventually allows him to continue because he wants his pre-teen niece to escape with him. An effective propaganda film made early in the war, this production displayed more benevolence on the part of a German officer (Preminger) than what would later be shown in films as the war progressed and German atrocities were discovered. *Author's Note*: Woolley had been an English and drama teacher at Yale University before he decided to switch careers and become an actor in the mid-1930s (making his debut in **Ladies in Love**, 1936, as an extra). His luxuriously cultivated beard and his kindly, avuncular nature soon earned him bigger parts until he became a much-sought-after supporting player. Making his film debut at the age of forty-nine, Woolley was one of the oldest thespians to do so, but he was surpassed in that regard by the likes of Sydney Greenstreet, who made his film debut at the age of sixty-one in **The Maltese Falcon**, 1941, and John Houseman, who appeared in his first film in **Seven Days in May**, 1964, at the age of sixty-two, albeit Houseman had appeared in a short three decades earlier (in **Too Much Johnson**, 1938). Violence prohibits viewing by children. **p&w**, Nunnally Johnson (based on the novel by Nevil Shute); **d**, Irving Pichel; **cast**, Monty Woolley, Roddy McDowall, Anne Baxter, Otto Preminger, J. Carrol Naish, Lester Matthews, Jill Esmond, Peggy Ann Garner, Edward Ashley, Marcel Dalio, Helmut Dantine; **c**, Edward Cronjager; **m**, Alfred Newman; **ed**, Allen McNeil; **art d**, Richard Day, Maurice Ransford; **set d**, Thomas Little.

Pierrepoint: The Last Hangman ★★★ 2007; U.K./U.S.; 107m; UK Film Council/IFC First Take; Color; Biographical Drama; Children: Unacceptable (MPAA: R); **DVD**. This taut biopic is loosely based on the life of Britain's most prolific hangman, Albert Pierrepoint (1905-1992), well enacted by Spall. A grocery deliveryman, he moonlighted by following his father's occupation to become known for his efficiency and compassion as the "best hangman in the land." From 1933 to his resignation in 1956, he executed 608 people, many of them being convicted WWII war criminals such as Josef Kramer (1906-1945), the brutal commandant of the Bergen-Belsen Concentration Camp and who was known as the "Beast of Belsen." He also hanged the notorious William Joyce (1906-1946), an Irish-American convicted of treason who made many propaganda broadcasts during WWII on behalf of the Nazis and was called "Lord Haw-Haw." Songs: "Makin, Whoopee" (Walter Donaldson, Gus Kahn); "Curtain Up" (L. Rawle); "You're a Very Good Pal

Roddy McDowall, Anne Baxter, Monty Woolley and Otto Preminger in *The Pied Piper*, 1942.

of Mine," "Jealous Heart" (Jenny Carson); "A Life on the Ocean Wave" (Henry Russell); "Voices of Spring" (Johann Strauss, Jr.); "Moonlight Promenade" (Ib Glindemann). Violence and nudity prohibit viewing by children. **p**, Christine Langan; **d**, Adrian Shergold; **cast**, Timothy Spall, Juliet Stevenson, Eddie Marsan, Simon Armstrong, Ann Bell, Nicholas Blane, Cavan Clerkin, James Corden, Clive Francis, Christopher Fulford; **w**, Bob Mills, Jeff Pope; **c**, Danny Cohen; **m**, Martin Phipps; **ed**, Tania Reddin; **prod d**, Candida Otton; **art d**, Andrea Coathupe; **spec eff**, Hugh Goodbody, James Clarke.

Pierrot le fou ★★★ 1968; France/Italy; 110m; Films Georges de Beauregard/Pathe Contemporary Films; Color; Comedy; Children: Unacceptable; **DVD**; **VHS**. This well-made zany comedy sees Belmondo as an unhappily married man recently fired from his job at a Paris television broadcasting company. He is bored and decides to run away to the Riviera with his children's babysitter, Karina. Belmondo soon learns that Karina is inexplicably being chased by gangsters. She uses Belmondo to get a suitcase full of money and then runs off with a boyfriend. The utterly deflated Belmondo paints his face blue and decides to blow himself up by tying sticks of red and yellow dynamite to his head. At the last minute, he decides against suicide and tries to extinguish the fuse, but that fails and he blows himself up. Songs: "Ma ligne de chance," "Jamais de ne t'ai dit que je t'aimerai toujours" (Antoine Duhamel, Serge Rezvani). Mature themes and violence prohibit viewing by children. (In French; English subtitles.) **p**, Georges de Beauregard; **d&w**, Jean-Luc Godard (based on the novel *Obsession* by Lionel White); **cast**, Jean-Paul Belmondo, Anna Karina, Graziella Galvani, Aicha Abadir, Henri Attal, Pascal Aubier, Raymond Devos, Roger Dutoit, Samuel Fuller, Pierre Hanin, Jimmy Karoubi; **c**, Raoul Coutard; **m**, Antoine Duhamel; **ed**, Françoise Collin; **prod d**, Pierre Guffroy.

Pigskin Parade ★★★ 1936; U.S.; 95m; FOX; B/W; Musical Comedy; Children: Acceptable; **BD**; **DVD**; **VHS**. This enjoyable college film is packed with comedy, romance, good songs, and exciting football action, serving as the film debut of Judy Garland, who was then fifteen years old. Haley is the coach of a Texas college football team whose star player is farm boy Erwin and who is discovered while throwing watermelons great distances as one might hurl footballs. The team does so well it's invited to the Yale Bowl. The football plotline serves as a showcase for a lot of young talent and it delivers great entertainment throughout. Besides Garland, other future superstars include Betty Grable in an early role and Alan Ladd as a student. Songs: "It's Love I'm After," "The Balboa," "The Texas Tornado," "You Do the Darndest Things, Baby," "You're Slightly Terrific," "T.S.U. Alma Mater" (Lew Pollack, Sidney D. Mitchell); "We'd Rather Be in College," "Down

Henrietta Crosman, Hedda Hopper, Marian Nixon and Norman Foster in *Pilgrimage*, 1933.

with Everything," "Woo! Woo!," "We Brought the Texas Sunshine Here with Us," "Football Song" (The Yacht Club Boys: James V. Kern, Charles Adler, George Kelly, Billy Mann); "Fox Chase" (traditional); "Oh Susanna" (Stephen Foster). **p**, Darryl F. Zanuck, Bogart Rogers; **d**, David Butler; **cast**, Stuart Erwin, Patsy Kelly, Jack Haley, Johnny Downs, Betty Grable, Arline Judge, Dixie Dunbar, Judy Garland, Tony Martin as Anthony Martin, Grady Sutton, Elisha Cook Jr., Eddie Nugent, Lynn Bari, Alan Ladd; **w**, Harry Tugend, Jack Yellen, William Conselman (based on a story by Arthur Sheekman, Nat Perrin, Mark Kelly); **c**, Arthur C. Miller; **m**, David Buttolph; **ed**, Irene Morra; **art d**, Hans Peters; **set d**, Thomas Little.

The Pilgrim ★★★★ 1923 (silent); U.S.; 40m; Charles Chaplin/Associated First National; B/W; Comedy; Children: Acceptable; **DVD**. This very funny comedy has Chaplin escaping from prison where he was serving a term for stealing his landlady's mortgage money. On the lam, he puts on a preacher's black suit and white collar. Arriving by train at the town of Devil's Gulch, he is mistaken for the new minister and continues his impersonation. In one of Chaplin's funniest scenes, he pantomimes the story of David and Goliath from the pulpit. Later he is discovered as a convict by Murray, a vigilant sheriff, who takes Chaplin to the Mexican border and gives him the choice of either going back to prison or facing Mexican bandits, who are at war with each other. Murray then kicks Chaplin across the border. The little fellow then runs off with one foot on each side of the border. Song (in a 1971 reissue): "I'm Bound for Texas" (Chaplin). **p,d&w**, Charles Chaplin; **cast**, Chaplin, Edna Purviance, Sydney Chaplin, Mai Wells, Dean "Dinky" Riesner, Tom Murray, Kitty Bradbury, Mack Swain, Loyal Underwood, Henry Bergman, Marion Davies; **c**, Roland Totheroh; **ed**, Chaplin; **art d**, Charles D. Hall.

Pilgrimage ★★★ 1933; U.S.; 96; FOX; B/W; Drama; Children: Unacceptable; **DVD**. Pantheon director Ford offers a solid domestic tale that depicts Crosman as a possessive mother who won't let her grown son, Foster, live his own life. He falls in love with Nixon, but, to keep them apart, Crosman deliberately enlists Foster into the army and he is sent to fight in World War I (1914-1918). Foster leaves for war having made Nixon pregnant, but she does not let him know, and he is soon killed in battle. Ten years pass and, embittered and refusing to acknowledge Foster's son, Crosman goes to France as a "Gold Star Mother." There, she meets La Verne, another mother whose son was killed in the war, but the woman is not bitter and, while under her influence, Crosman's heart softens. She visits her son's grave and meets war veteran Murphy, befriends him, and takes him home with her. Murphy's mother, Hopper, disapproves of his choice for marriage (Angel), but Crosman

tells Hopper she made that very mistake with her own son and Hopper relents. Crosman then goes to Nixon for forgiveness, accepts her grandson, and all ends well. Songs: "Dear Little Boy of Mine" (Ernest Ball, J. Keirn Brennan), "The Sidewalks of New York" (Charles Lawlor, James W. Blake), "How 'Ya Gonna Keep 'Em Down on the Farm" (Walter Donaldson, Sam Lewis, Joe Young). Mature themes prohibit viewing by children. **d**, John Ford; **cast**, Henrietta Crosman, Heather Angel, Norman Foster, Lucille La Verne, Maurice Murphy, Marian Nixon, Jay Ward, Robert Warwick, Betty Blythe, Francis Ford, Charley Grapewin, Hedda Hopper; **w**, Philip Klein, Barry Conners, Dudley Nichols (based on the story "Gold Star Mother" by I.A.R. Wylie); **c**, George Schneiderman; **m**, R.H. Bassett; **ed**, Louis R. Loeffler; William Darling.

Pillow Talk ★★★ 1959; U.S.; 105m; Arwin/UNIV; Color; Comedy; Children: Acceptable; **DVD**; **VHS**. In this good comedic romp Hudson is a playboy songwriter and Day is an interior decorator, both sharing a two-party telephone line. She's frustrated because she can't make or receive calls since he's always on the line talking to his girlfriends. They meet not knowing they are phone sharers, and Hudson decides to add Day to his list of conquests. He learns that she detests the man with whom she shares the phone line, so he pretends to be someone else, a Texas country boy who is girl-shy. Day falls for Hudson's romantic palaver and also for him, but goes ballistic when she finds out that Hudson is the man who has been aggravating her on her phone line. The lovers quarrel, and she takes revenge on Hudson for his deceitful ways by designing his apartment as a gaudy-looking assignation house. He explodes and plucks Day from her domicile, carrying her to that very den of seduction, depositing her there, but she gives in and takes him into her arms for a happy ending. Songs: "Pillow Talk" (Buddy Pepper, Inez James), "Roly Poly" (Elsa Doran, Sol Lake), "Inspiration," "I Need No Atmosphere," "You Lied," "Possess Me" (Joe Lubin, I.J. Roth). Day and Hudson clicked in this, the first of several delightful romantic comedies they would do together, all of these entertaining productions seeing great success at the box office. **p**, Ross Hunter, Martin Melcher; **d**, Michael Gordon; **cast**, Rock Hudson, Doris Day, Tony Randall, Thelma Ritter, Nick Adams, Julia Meade, Allen Jenkins, Marcel Dalio, Lee Patrick, Mary McCarty, Hayden Rorke; **w**, Stanley Shapiro, Maurice Richlin (based on a story by Russell Rouse, Clarence Greene); **c**, Arthur E. Arling (CinemaScope; Eastmancolor); **m**, Frank De Vol; **ed**, Milton Carruth; **art d**, Richard H. Riedel; **set d**, Russell A. Gausman, Ruby R. Levitt; **spec eff**, Clifford Stine, Roswell Hoffmann.

'Pimpernel' Smith ★★★ 1942; U.K.; 120m; British National/UA; B/W; Spy Drama; Children: Unacceptable; **VHS**. This tension-filled espionage tale is set in mid-1939, when England and Germany are preparing for war. Howard, a professor pretending to be a fop, takes his students on an archaeological dig to the Continent. They discover he is really a brave patriot, smuggling persecuted scientists and other enemies of the Germans out of the country. After some close calls in Germany with Gestapo agent Sullivan, Howard escapes across the border to neutral Switzerland, vowing to return. A World War II (1939-1945) spin on the Scarlet Pimpernel spy adventures which were also filmed in 1934 with Howard as the hero, and in 1966, 1982, and 1999. Violence prohibits viewing by children. **p&d**, Leslie Howard; **cast**, Howard, Francis L. Sullivan, Mary Morris, Philip Friend, Hugh McDermott, Raymond Huntley, David Tomlinson, Manning Whiley, Basil Appleby, Sebastian Cabot, Michael Rennie; **w**, Anatole de Grunwald, Roland Pertwee, Ian Dalrymple (based on a story by A.G. Macdonell, Wolfgang Wilhelm and a character from the novel *The Scarlet Pimpernel* by Baroness Emmuska Orczy); **c**, Mutz Greenbaum; **m**, John Greenwood; **ed**, Douglas Myers; **set d**, Duncan Sutherland.

The Pink Panther ★★★★ 1964; U.S.; 115m; Mirisch G-E Productions; UA; Color; Comedy; Children: Acceptable; **BD**; **DVD**; **VHS**. Sellers, one of the world's greatest comedians, is hilarious as the bumbling and wholly inept French detective, Inspector Clouseau, as he searches for a mastermind jewel thief in this first of many films based on the same character. The ultra-sophisticated Niven is the celebrated thief called "The Phantom," a robber with an insatiable appetite for rare gems and he is now on the trail of one of the most fabulous and coveted jewels in the world, a priceless diamond called "The Pink Panther" (which has earned its sobriquet due to a tiny flaw that resembles the shape of a panther), one owned by alluring Cardinale. Niven has checked into a swanky alpine ski resort located near a lavish Roman villa owned by Cardinale, and he intends to filch that jewel, but French Inspector Sellers is also on his trail as he has been for fifteen years, along with Interpol and a half dozen other noted law enforcement agencies. The chief reason why no one, especially Sellers, has ever caught Niven red-handed in his many daring robberies is that Niven is assisted by an equally clever accomplice, who always warns him at the last minute when police are closing in, so that he can make his escape. That accomplice is none other than Capucine, who is Sellers' sultry wife and Niven's long-standing (or long prone) mistress. Meanwhile, Wagner, who is Niven's nephew and who has patterned his life after his celebrated uncle as a masterful jewel thief, arrives at the resort and is equally intent on stealing "The Pink Panther" from Cardinale. Using his boyish charms to entice Cardinale into an affair, Wagner plans to purloin that gem before his avaricious uncle can snatch it. After Cardinale announces that she will be hosting an elaborate costume ball at her villa, Sellers tells her that the jewel thief will most likely attend that fete as that will offer the thief his best opportunity to steal the jewel. Cadinale resolves to put the jewel in the safe in the library instead of wearing it at the ball. The villa is packed with costumed guests that night, including two wearing the same kind of gorilla costume and both separately invade the library to crack the safe. Both discover that the fabulous jewel is gone and, in its place, is a white glove, the calling card of the celebrated "Phantom." After the lights go out, pandemonium reigns and the gorilla-clad thieves flee the villa, driving madly through a nearby village, only to crash their cars at a fountain. Sellers nabs both Niven and Wagner and they are later brought to trial, charged with stealing "The Pink Panther," even though the jewel has not been recovered and only circumstantial evidence confronts them. In defending his clients Niven and Wagner, attorney Le Mesurier calls Sellers to the witness stand and begins to mercilessly grill him, proving that Sellers has been present at every one of the notorious thefts for which Niven has been accused of committing over the last fifteen years, and guilt now shifts from Niven and Wagner to focus upon Sellers. Realizing his predicament, Sellers perspires with anxiety as Le Mesurier hammers home his accusations against him and, to wipe away his apprehensive sweat, Sellers reaches into his pocket to withdraw a handkerchief, at the end of which dangles the much-sought-after jewel. The courtroom is stunned to see this de facto evidence that squarely convicts Sellers out of hand. Niven and Wagner are released and Sellers is packed off to serve a prison sentence, but not before he is swarmed by dozens of attractive women obsessively enamored of him, now that he has been identified as the daring jewel thief. Cardinale regains her jewel and unites with Wagner while Niven and Capucine go on a vacation to South America. Before they begin that idyllic sojourn, Niven states that he will later send a letter to authorities admitting that he arranged for the jewel to be planted on Sellers so that the bumbler will be released from custody and be free to pursue his rambling, incoherent and inconclusive investigations. Niven, Wagner, Capucine and Cardinale all give standout performances in this delightful comedy caper, one directed at a dizzying pace by the accomplished Edwards and where the lensing and sets are also outstanding. Sellers, who appears less on screen than his costars, nevertheless steals this film by enacting the most inept, clumsy and outrageous detective in law enforcement history, his uniquely displayed histrionics producing one hysterical and guffawing scene after another. Song: "It Had Better Be Tonight" (music: Henry Mancini; English lyrics: Johnny Mercer; Italian lyrics: Franco Migliacci). Mancini's song brought him an Oscar nomi-

Peter Sellers in *The Pink Panther*, 1964.

nation and he stayed with the series, going on to do the scores for many of the sequels. This film was a huge box office hit, taking in more than $10 million in its initial release. The enormous popularity of this film prompted a spate of sequels and spinoffs, including **Curse of the Pink Panther**, 1983 (Roger Moore as Inspector Clouseau); **Inspector Clouseau**, 1968 (Alan Arkin as Inspector Clouseau); **The Pink Panther**, 1993-1996 (TV series); **The Pink Panther**, 2006 (Steve Martin as Inspector Clouseau); **The Pink Panther Show**, 1969-1976 (animated TV series); **The Pink Panther 2**, 2009 (Steve Martin as Inspector Clouseau); **The Pink Panther Strikes Again**, 1976 (Peter Sellers as Inspector Clouseau); **The Return of the Pink Panther**, 1975 (Peter Sellers as Inspector Clouseau); **Revenge of the Pink Panther**, 1978 (Peter Sellers as Inspector Clouseau); **A Shot in the Dark**, 1964 (Peter Sellers as Inspector Clouseau); **Son of the Pink Panther**, 1993; and **Trail of the Pink Panther**, 1982 (Peter Sellers as Inspector Clouseau). *Author's Note*: Actor Niven knew director Edwards for some time before making this film, as he told this author, adding that his role was very demanding and required a lot of hard work: "I met Blake [Edwards] when he was directing and writing stories for a producing company in which I had a stake, called Four Star Television. I was immediately impressed with his talent for comedy, which is the hardest type of story to write and direct, I think. When he later contacted me and asked me to appear in **The Pink Panther**, I did not hesitate because I knew this talented man knew what he was doing when it came to comedy. The role that I play in that film is patterned after the character Cary [Grant] plays in Hitchcock's **To Catch a Thief** [1955], who is a retired master jewel thief, although my character has no intention of ever retiring from filching jewels. I knew it would not be a cushy job. Acting out a comedy may appear to be off-handed and casual, but it is the most demanding of work. One false gesture can throw away a scene or the wrongly accented word can cause a funny scene to fall flat. Doing comedy is like performing ballet—you must be on your toes all the time." Sellers took off considerable weight for this film by gulping down diet pills for a year before going into its production. He reportedly modeled his character of Inspector Clouseau after Captain Matthew Webb (1848-1883), who was the first recorded person to successfully swim the English Channel (in 1875), and who later posed for a popular box of matches that was trademarked with his image, one showing him proudly mugging a face with a luxuriant mustache, an image that Sellers saw and then mimicked in doing his unforgettable character of Inspector Clouseau. In delivering his thickly French-accented lines, Sellers invented his own fractured use of the English language, mangling and mauling his words and, in the hilarious process, providing a laugh for each mispronounced syllable. Sellers was not Edwards' first choice for the role of the inept detective. He first offered the role to Peter Ustinov, but trouble between the actor and

Ethel Waters and Jeanne Crain in *Pinky*, 1949.

producers caused Ustinov to be fired from the production, and Edwards then turned to Sellers, who was not then an international star, but his appearance in this film catapulted him into that stellar status. The bathtub scene showing Capucine where she hides Wagner beneath its bubbling suds caused both actors considerable discomfort in that an industrial-strength foaming agent was inadvertently used that caused both actors to suffer skin burns; Wagner, who was totally submerged beneath these harmful suds for some time, reportedly suffered partial blindness for several weeks. Capucine was not Edwards' first selection for the role of Clouseau's cheating wife. He first offered that part to Ava Gardner, but her terms and salary demands were so draconian and high priced that Edwards withdrew his offer. He then went to Janet Leigh, but she also turned down the role as she had recently been married and wanted to spend a long honeymoon with her fourth husband, Robert Brandt (her third husband being actor Tony Curtis). Brandt and Leigh would remain married (1962-2004) until her death. "Capucine was a stroke of luck for Blake [Edwards]," Niven told this author, "because she was perfect for the role, really playing two roles in one, half mother figure to her twit of a husband [Sellers] and playing the other half as a sex-craving vamp torridly making love to me in another room. She is one of the sexiest looking women in the business—on screen, that is." The other leading lady in this film, Cardinale, spoke faltering English, so her lines were dubbed by Gale Garnett, a twenty-year-old voice understudy. **p**, Martin Jurow; **d**, Blake Edwards; **cast**, David Niven, Peter Sellers, Robert Wagner, Capucine, Claudia Cardinale (Gale Garnett voiceover), Brenda De Banzie, Fran Jeffries, Colin Gordon, John Le Mesurier, James Lanphier; **w**, Edwards, Maurice Richlin; **c**, Philip Lathrop (Technicolor); **m**, Henry Mancini; **ed**, Ralph E. Winters; **art d**, Fernando Carrere; **set d**, Reginald Allen, Jack Stevens, Arrigo Breschi; **spec eff**, Lee Zavitz.

The Pink Panther Strikes Again ★★★ 1976; U.K./U.S.; 103m; Amjo/UA; Color; Crime Comedy; Children: Unacceptable (MPAA: PG); **DVD**; **VHS**. In another and very good sequel in the Pink Panther series, Lom, head of the French police, escapes from a mental asylum and sets out to kill his bungling nemesis, Chief Inspector Jacques Clouseau, hilariously played by Sellers, who, through his flagrant incompetence, has ruined Lom's career. Lom comes up with a scheme to build a Doomsday death ray machine and have someone else kill Sellers or he will wipe out entire cities and even countries. He enlists the help of twenty-two assassins from all over the world while Sellers tries to put Lom back in the asylum. After much madness and many sight gags, Sellers, who creates more mayhem than those out to destroy him, gets Lom back into his padded cell. Violence prohibits viewing by children. Songs: "Until You Love Me," "Come to Me" (Henry Mancini, Don

Black); "Tip-Toe thru' the Tulips with Me" (Joseph Burke, Al Dubin); "Thank Heaven for Little Girls" (Frederick Loewe, Alan Jay Lerner); "Over the Rainbow" (Harold Arlen, E.Y. Harburg). **p&d**, Blake Edwards; **cast**, Peter Sellers, Herbert Lom, Lesley-Anne Down, Burt Kwouk, Colin Blakely, Leonard Rossiter, Andre Maranne, Byron Kane, Dick Crockett, Richard Vernon, Dudley Sutton, Omar Sharif; **w**, Edwards, Frank Waldman; **c**, Harry Waxman (Panavision; DeLuxe Color); **m**, Henry Mancini; **ed**, Alan Jones; **prod d**, Peter Mullins; **art d**, John Siddall; **spec eff**, Kit West.

Pinky ★★★★ 1949; U.S.; 102m; FOX; B/W; Drama; Children: Unacceptable; **DVD**; **VHS**. In keeping with studio boss Darryl F. Zanuck's penchant for addressing serious social issues in films produced by Fox, this fine production came into existence at his crusading insistence, a superlative story that exposes racism against black Americans. Crain is a beautiful and intelligent young woman who has been studying to become a nurse in a New England town and where she has passed for white, even though she is of mixed blood, having a black grandmother, Waters. While at school, she meets and falls in love with white physician Lundigan, who knows about the miscegenation in her life, but nevertheless proposes marriage to her. Crain refuses to go the altar, believing that a mixed marriage would never work and saying that she will never abandon her racial heritage (although her rigid attitude tolerates rather than triumphs over this social challenge). She returns to the South to live with her grandmother, who has spent many years working for Barrymore, a stubborn, old white woman with considerable wealth. When Barrymore grows ill, Crain becomes her nurse, administering to her night and day with such devotional care that Barrymore's heart softens and she ultimately looks upon Crain as a daughter. Before she dies, Barrymore alters her will, leaving most of her considerable estate, including her large mansion, to Crain. But, after Barrymore dies, her relatives contest the will, particularly since Crain is part black, employing in their repugnant arguments ancient "Jim Crow" ordinances that disenfranchise blacks. In racially torn courtroom proceedings, Crain prevails and legally inherits Barrymore's estate. The chief reason why Crain wins her case is that she begs Ruysdael, a former judge with strict ethics, to represent her, and he brilliantly argues her case against race-hating relatives, who represent the widespread prejudices of the community. When Crain later thanks Ruysdael for winning her case, he tells her that though justice has been served in her case, the interests of the town were not. He has upheld judicial scruples, but against the white social traditions of the South, indicating through his resentful remarks that he has betrayed his own class in defending her. Though she faces an uphill battle against widespread racial bias, she nevertheless turns the mansion into a school and nursing home for blacks. Crain, in one of her most impressive performances, struggles throughout this tense story in dealing with her white and black allegiances as she is torn between the attitudes and perspectives of two wholly different worlds, belonging to both, and Waters is wonderful as her loving grandmother, who prefers that Crain would not assert her racial heritage and more or less let sleeping dogs lie. Barrymore, that grand old lady of the American stage, offers a riveting performance where she transforms from a suspicious, mean-natured elderly woman into a loving mother figure. Crain received an Oscar nomination for Best Actress, and Waters and Barrymore received Oscar nominations as Best Supporting Actress for their superlative performances. Kazan presents this controversial tale with great sensitivity, and his fully developed characters come alive and are wholly believable. The script from Dunne and Nichols is intelligent and incisive in detailing the very real racial problems existing in the Deep South. Despite apprehensions from distributors, **Pinky** was a success throughout the nation, including in the South, with the exception of a few small towns that banned the film as "prejudicial to the best interests" of their citizens, slyly mirroring the obliquely stated prejudices that the conservative jurist Ruysdael artfully utters to Crain. ***Author's Note***: Zanuck had planned to do this film for some time and was spurred to make the film with the recent appearances of films that addressed racial prejudice against blacks, particularly **Lost Boundaries**, 1949 (from Film Classics), released five months before this film and which also dealt with miscegenation involving a fair-skinned black doctor in the South; **Home of the Brave**, 1949 (from Stanley Kramer and United Artists), which was released three months before this film and which dealt with racial bias in the U.S. military; as well as **Intruder in the Dust**, 1949 (from Clarence Brown and MGM and against the wishes of studio boss Louis B. Mayer), released one month before this film and dealt with race hatred against blacks in the South. Zanuck hired the redoubtable John Ford to direct **Pinky**, but Ford quit after two weeks into the production, telling Zanuck that his heart was not in the project (Ford told this author that the real reason was that he could not work with Waters, saying "the woman refused to take any direction from me as she was conducting her own civil rights crusade"). Zanuck told this author that "I was actually relieved to hear that Pappy [Ford] was leaving the production because, after looking at its dailies, I and others at Fox believed he was stereotyping blacks as 'Uncle Tom' and 'Aunt Jemima.'" Zanuck immediately called Kazan, who took over the production and completed it within eight weeks. One wonders why Zanuck did not initially ask Kazan to direct in the first place since Kazan had been the chief director for most of Fox's formidable social issue films, helming such significant productions as **A Tree Grows in Brooklyn**, 1945 (alcoholism); **Boomerang!**, 1947 (the wrongly accused); and **Gentleman's Agreement**, 1947 (anti-Semitism), albeit it had produced other social issue films helmed by other directors such as William Wellman's **The Ox-Bow Incident**, 1943, which indicted vigilantism. Kazan told this author that "**Pinky** was not difficult and everybody involved in the picture cooperated, although I could never light a fire under Jeanne [Crain], who seemed to daydream through the whole picture. The only scene where she shows some fire is when two white thugs attack her after they hear that she is not white, but has mixed blood. I heard rumors that Ethel Waters gave Ford a hard time, but she and I got along well together. I really don't know why Ford left the production, but I can tell you that replacing him was like stepping into the shoes of a giant. I think that Zanuck hired Ford before me because Ford had directed **Young Mr. Lincoln** [1939] for Fox, and maybe Zanuck thought that because Ford did such a great job with that subject, he understood blacks and racial issues in America. Perhaps Ford understood Lincoln and not so well the black slaves he set free and the racial prejudice against them that lingered like an open sore for decades after that. Ford also directed a great picture called **The Grapes of Wrath** [1940] for Fox, a film Zanuck was going to do at all costs, a startling picture that dealt with another important social issue, the displacement of the 'Okies' during the Great Depression, showing the widespread prejudice against these poor, uneducated people. But the people in that picture were white and maybe Ford could identify with them where he could not with black persons. I am only guessing on that. I admired Ford and his pictures all my life and, to me, there was no greater film director. Sometime after **Pinky** was released, I got a letter that was postmarked from Jackson, Mississippi, that said: 'We invite you to come to our town where we will give you a special party for making that picture, coon lover.' The sender did not sign a name, only the initials 'KKK' ["Ku Klux Klan"]. I kept that letter for some time and would take it out and look at it and wonder what kind of mind that person had until I concluded that that person had no mind at all and I burned the letter." **p**, Darryl F. Zanuck; **d**, Elia Kazan; **cast**, Jeanne Crain, Ethel Barrymore, Ethel Waters, William Lundigan, Basil Ruysdael, Kenny Washington, Nina Mae McKinney, Griff Barnett, Frederick O'Neal, Evelyn Varden, Juanita Moore; **w**, Philip Dunne, Dudley Nichols (based on the novel *Quality* by Cid Ricketts Sumner); **c**, Joe MacDonald; **m**, Alfred Newman; **ed**, Harmon Jones; **art d**, Lyle Wheeler, J. Russell Spencer; **set d**, Thomas Little, Walter M. Scott; **spec eff**, Fred Sersen.

Pinocchio ★★★★ 1940; U.S.; 88m; Walt Disney Productions/RKO; Color; Animated Adventure/Fantasy; Children: Cautionary; **BD**; **DVD**;

Jiminy Cricket and Pinocchio in *Pinocchio*, 1940.

VHS. In his second animated feature-length film, Disney presents the marvelous and totally captivating tale of a wooden puppet that transforms into a boy, but not before he undergoes many harrowing adventures that test his right to become a human being. This classic film begins when the inimitable Jiminy Cricket (Edwards voiceover) sings "When You Wish Upon a Star" while he sits upon a book titled "Pinocchio" and begins to narrate its metamorphic story of how a wooden puppet miraculously became a boy of flesh and blood. Geppetto (Rub voiceover), an elderly and kind woodcarver and owner of a small toyshop, is shown putting the final touches of a painted smile on his newly created marionette, a puppet he names "Pinocchio." The lonely old man then retires and, while in bed, sees through an open window the Wishing Star and makes a wish that the puppet were a real boy, a son of his own. As Geppetto sleeps, along with his pets, a cat named Figaro, and a goldfish called Cleo, the Blue Fairy (Venable voiceover) leaves the Wishing Star to appear in the toyshop, and her magic wand turns the puppet into a live being, although he is still made of wood. The beneficent Blue Fairy promises Pinocchio that, if he learns right from wrong and proves himself to be brave and unselfish, he will turn into a real boy, and then provides him with a moral guide, the wisecracking Jiminy Cricket, who is to serve as Pinocchio's conscience, and, if he, too, performs well, he will receive a gold badge of honor. Upon wakening, Geppetto, Figaro and Cleo are delighted at seeing the puppet very much alive and the old woodcarver provides him with books and then sends him off to school, telling him to mind his teacher and be good. He and Jiminy Cricket then embark for school, but, en route, they encounter two very devious and clever creatures, a sly fox called J. Worthington Foulfellow (Catlett voiceover), who calls himself "Honest John," and his equally cunning friend, Gideon (Blanc voiceover), a conniving cat. The pair realize that such an extraordinary person as a live puppet is worth a great deal of money and they plot to steer Pinocchio from his course, telling him that school is a waste of time and he can have a lot more fun by becoming an actor on the stage and where all adventure and excitement awaits him. Jiminy Cricket warns the marionette not to heed such bad advice and urges him to go to school, but the temptation of the stage as Foulfellow and Gideon describe in such colorful and inviting terms overwhelms the puppet and he decides to follow them to fame and become a thespian, singing "An Actor's Life for Me" with them as they lead him to Stromboli (Judels voiceover), an evil-minded stage manager, who tells Pinocchio that he will make him a great star of the theater. We next see Pinocchio performing on Stromboli's stage, dancing and singing "I've Got No Strings" as he moves about with several other lifeless puppets, all controlled by the huge Stromboli, a puppet master who is up to no good. Jiminy Cricket watches Pinocchio perform and sees that the audience heartily approves of his stage antics, coming

Stromboli and Pinocchio in *Pinocchio*, 1940.

to believe that, perhaps, Pinocchio has made the right decision and that he, indeed, belongs on the stage where he can make a name for himself and that he needs no spiritual guide. When the performance is over, the little cricket goes backstage to bid farewell to Pinocchio only to find to his horror that the mean-minded Stromboli has imprisoned the wooden boy inside a cage and hears the puppet master threaten him, saying that if he does not do exactly what he is told, he will be broken into kindling and burned. "When you grow too old, you will make good firewood," the enormous Stromboli direly warns him. He then hurls a hatchet into another marionette that he has chopped up, another wooden boy bearing a faint smile on its splintered face. After Stromboli departs, Jiminy Cricket tries desperately to unlock the cage and free Pinocchio, but his efforts are in vain. At that moment, the Blue Fairy appears and asks Pinocchio how he came to be imprisoned and be so cruelly treated. Pinocchio begins to spin one excuse tied to another, all lies, and, as he rattles off these fabrications, his wooden nose begins to grow longer and longer (political cartoonists would later seize upon this startlingly memorable illustration to indict public figures caught lying to their constituents by extending the lengths of their noses to outlandish proportions). The more lies Pinocchio tells, the longer his nose grows until branches sprout from it. The Blue Fairy then tells him that "a lie grows and grows until it's as plain as the nose on your face." After this humiliating lesson, the Blue Fairy restores Pinocchio's nose to its normal size and then releases him from the cage after he and Jiminy Cricket give their promises that the wooden boy will behave. Hurrying toward home, Pinocchio is again accosted by the always calculating Foulfellow and where "Honest John" again persuades him to take the wayward path, this time describing all the adventure and fun to be had at the wonderful Pleasure Island, Pinocchio joins a group of eager boys being picked up by a coachman (Judels voiceover), who is in league with Foulfellow in shanghaiing the boys and selling them, the sinister coachman saying that "they never come back...as boys." The coach arrives at Pleasure Island, and the boys race to the many sideshows and games, Pinocchio and Jiminy Cricket partake in the fun, the coachman watching them go and saying with a terrible prediction: "Give a bad boy enough rope and he'll soon make a jackass of himself." Pinocchio makes friends with another boy named Lampwick (Darro voiceover), who leads him to a pool hall shaped like an eight ball and where they shoot pool, drink beer and smoke, even though the little cricket, who is now working overtime as a conscience, warns Pinocchio against these dangerous pastimes. After Lampwick ridicules the cricket and Pinocchio pretends he is not even there, the little fellow has had enough and walks out. "You'd think something is going to happen," Lampwick says in a mocking voice. Lampwick suddenly grows donkey's ears, and, as Pinocchio stares at him in shock, the boy then sprouts a donkey's tail. Pinocchio instinctively

laughs, and when Lampwick responds in laughter his voice is that of a hee-hawing donkey. Lampwick transforms into a donkey and Pinocchio, who has also sprouted donkey ears and a tail, is then about to undergo a complete transformation when Jiminy Cricket arrives to lead him away. As they flee, they see that all of the other boys, having been changed into donkeys, are being herded into a pen by the owners of Pleasure Island, who routinely sell these donkeys as part of their evil operation. After Pinocchio and Jiminy Cricket arrive at the toyshop, they find a note left by the Blue Fairy that tells them that Geppetto has taken Figaro and Cleo and has gone in search of the lost Pinocchio, but, while searching at sea, all three have been swallowed alive by a great whale called Monstro and, though they are still alive and living in the whale's stomach, there is little hope for them. Pinocchio decides he will save his adopted father and his pets and sets out to find Monstro, but Jiminy Cricket is fearful and apprehensive about such a rescue venture. Both leap into the sea and begin walking along its bottom, startled to see all the schools of fish scatter whenever they ask where they can find Monstro. They then see the huge whale swimming toward them as he feeds on the fleeing schools of fish. Monstro then settles at the bottom, slumbering, and Jiminy Cricket boldly taps on its clenched teeth with his cane, and utters a gurgling shout: "Hey, blubbermouth—open up!" The whale comes awake and, as it opens its gaping mouth and swallows a school of fish, it also swallows Pinocchio and Jiminy Cricket. (Seen from the perspective of the inside of the whale, this startling scene depicts the cascading onrush of water avalanching into the whale, mixing the school of fish with Pinocchio and the little cricket as they tumble and toss head over heels into the belly of the beast, one of the most memorable animated sequences ever put onto film.) Pinocchio and Jiminy Cricket find Geppetto alive, along with Figaro and Cleo, dwelling on the remains of his wrecked boat, and, though they are delighted to see the wayward puppet and the erstwhile cricket, Geppetto tells them that their situation is hopeless and that they will all eventually perish inside the whale's belly as he does not cough up any of its content and only takes in whatever he needs to eat. Thinking hard on this, Pinocchio gets an idea, telling Geppetto to build a fire and saying that, after Monstro gets a good snort of the smoke from the fire, he will be forced to sneeze, and that should blow them out of his stomach. They build a fire, along with a raft from the remains of the shattered boat, and, after the smoke begins to curl up Monstro's snout, the whale, indeed, exhales a gigantic sneeze that sends the raft and all of its occupants out of its mouth with a mighty blast and onto the open sea. The whale, angry at being deceived, races after the raft and overtakes it, its gigantic tail slamming down upon the raft to splinter it and hurling its occupants into the water. Pinocchio sees the failing Geppetto going down and he paddles his unconscious father to shore. When Geppetto revives, he finds Figaro, Cleo and Jiminy Cricket alive, but the wooden boy is lifeless, having spent his life to save his father. Taking the puppet home with him, Geppetto's misery and sorrow cannot be consoled by Figaro, Cleo or Jiminy Cricket as he mourns for the loss of the only boy, wooden or not, that he has ever had. The voice of the Blue Fairy is then heard, repeating her words from the beginning of the film where she stated that if Pinocchio proved himself to be unselfish and brave, he could become a real boy. Suddenly, miraculously, the weeping Geppetto hears a voice saying: "Father, what are you crying for?" Without looking in the direction of the voice, Geppetto absentmindedly replies: "Because you're dead, Pinocchio...now lie down." Geppetto then looks up to see (in a hilarious and heartwarming triple take) that Pinocchio is not only very much alive, but that he is now a flesh-and-blood boy, the very much alive son he always wanted and prayed for. Geppetto takes the boy into his arms while Figaro dances and Cleo swims about in joyous delight. Jiminy Cricket then turns to the viewer and says: "This is practically where I came in." Looking skyward to see a twinkling star, he gives his thanks to the Blue Fairy for all her wonderful and miraculous aid. Suddenly appearing on his chest is a glimmering gold badge that reads "Official Conscience/18Kt." He, too, is now full of joy as he goes on his way, reprising that unforgettable tune, "When You Wish Upon a Star." This masterpiece of animation presents one wonderful scene after another, awesomely detailed through multi-plane camera setups that achieve its sharp dimensions and exacting detail in objects and characters. Those vividly animated characters are so finely detailed that everything about them—their ears, eyes, noses, mouths, arms, legs—moves all the time and in all the scenes, a magnificent triumph of artistry that took many years and many artists to create. As was the case in all of Disney's animated feature films, the backgrounds also come vividly alive in rich hues where leaves sway and quiver in breezes and water is rippled by the wind. By contrast to animation that followed where characters and backgrounds appear to be unimaginatively flat, this film comes alive in every precious and memorable frame and where the brilliantly conceived and presented story line is cogent and cohesive, maintaining meticulous continuity throughout. Its production values are impeccable, setting a standard that even latter-day Disney artists seldom equaled. This film was an enormous success at the box office and saw the same results in its many rereleases and sold millions of copies when issued in various video formats over the years. It won an Oscar for Best Musical Score (Harline, Smith and Washington), and another Oscar for Best Song ("When You Wish Upon a Star" by Harline and Washington). Songs (all in 1939): "When You Wish Upon a Star," "Little Wooden Head," "Hi-Diddle-Dee-Dee," "An Actor's Life for Me," "Give A Little Whistle," "I've Got No Strings" (music: Leigh Harline; lyrics: Ned Washington). *Author's Note*: In the original 1883 children's novel by Italian author Carlo Collodi (1826-1890), Pinocchio exhibits an unsavory character, being obnoxious, insulting, and utterly selfish, but Disney softened his personality to a more naïve and innocent creature. Also, in the original story, the mean-minded puppet actually kills the little cricket when it tires of listening to the cricket's lectures, but the cricket returns as a ghost as the puppet's nagging conscience. This, of course, would never do for Walt Disney (1901-1966), who not only has that inimitable cricket survive throughout his masterful production, but has him wear the traditional white gloves that adorned the hands of many other Disney characters such as Mickey Mouse and Goofy. Although some of the animals in his feature films do die, like the mother in **Bambi**, 1942 (not on camera), Disney took great pains not to show the death of animals in his productions. As a boy he vowed to never again kill a living creature after he thoughtlessly killed a small owl, and it was in those boyhood years that he also vowed to later somehow find a way to personalize all animals (or "humanize" them) as he believed they all possessed distinctive personalities. Although **Pinocchio** always had a warm place in Disney's heart, of all of his animated feature films, he most liked **Bambi**, 1942, and **Dumbo**, 1941, and he most disliked **Alice in Wonderland**, 1951, and **Peter Pan**, 1953, because too many of their characters lacked "warmth" and "heart." (Unlike popular belief, Disney's corpse was not frozen at his direction under any dictates from any will, and is not in death residing in a frozen condition to await resurgent life; he was cremated upon death and his ashes were interred at Forest Lawn Memorial Park in Glendale, California.) One of the fine voiceovers for this film is that of Cliff Edwards (Clifton A. Edwards, 1895-1971), who was also called "Ukelele Ike" and who possessed a high tenor singing voice, one that reached "C" above high "C" on the last note of his thrilling and unforgettable rendition of "When You Wish Upon a Star." Edwards sang the first sound rendition of the song "Singin' in the Rain" in 1929. Edwards had been one of the most popular singers in the 1920s and early 1930s, but his career had taken a nose dive until he appeared in **Pinocchio**, and where he again became much in demand, although he was used sparingly by Disney thereafter, appearing in a singing voiceover role as the high tenor of a group of singing crows who warble "When I See an Elephant Fly" in **Dumbo**, and again as Jiminy Cricket in **Fun and Fancy Free**, 1947. Pinocchio has been portrayed by many actors as live-action characters or in voiceovers for animated characters appearing in many other productions, including **The Adventures of Pinocchio**, 1972 (TV miniseries; Andrea Balestri); **The Adventures of Pinocchio**, 1996

Pinocchio and Geppetto in *Pinocchio*, 1940.

(Jonathan Taylor Thomas voiceover); **Disney's House of Mouse**, 2001-2003 (animated TV series; Michael Welch); **Geppetto**, 2000 (made-for-TV; Seth Adkins); **The New Adventures of Pinocchio**, 1999 (Gabriel Thomson); **Once upon a Time**, 2011 (TV series; Eion Bailey); **Pinocchio**, 2002 (Roberto Benigni); **Pinocchio**, 2008 (made-for-TV; Robbie Kay); **Pinocchio and the Emperor of the Night**, 1987 (Scott Grimes voiceover); **Shrek**, 2001 (Cody Cameron voiceover); **Shrek Forever After**, 2010 (Cody Cameron voiceover); **Shrek the Third**, 2007 (Cody Cameron voiceover); **Shrek 2**, 2004 (Cody Cameron voiceover); and **Who Framed Roger Rabbit**, 1988 (Peter Westy voiceover). Cartoon voiceover master Mel Blanc (who provided the unique voices for Bugs Bunny, Daffy Duck, Porky Pig, Sylvester, Tweety Bird and many other cartoon characters in shorts and feature-length films) provided the voice for Pinocchio in a 1953 radio adaptation of the story. **p**, Walt Disney; **d**, Ben Sharpsteen, Hamilton Luske (sequence directors Norman Ferguson, T. Hee, Wilfred Jackson, Jack Kinney, Bill Roberts); **cast** (voiceovers), Dickie Jones, Christian Rub, Cliff Edwards, Evelyn Venable, Walter Catlett, Frankie Darro, Charles Judels, Don Brodie, Marion Darlington, Jack Mercer, Patricia Page, Mel Blanc; **w**, Ted Sears, Otto Englander, Webb Smith, William Cottrell, Joseph Sabo, Erdman Penner, Aurelius Battaglia (based on a story by Collodi [Carlo Collodi]; (Technicolor); **m**, Leigh Harline, Paul J. Smith, Ned Washington; **art d**, Charles Philippi, Hugh Hennesy, Dick Kelsey, Terrell Stapp, John Hubley, Kenneth Anderson, Kendall O'Connor, Thor Putnam, McLaren Stewart, Al Zinnen.

The Piper's Tune ★★★ 1962; U.K.; 62m; ACT (Association of Cinema Technicians)/CFF (Children's Film Foundation); B/W; Children's Adventure; Children: Cautionary; **VHS**. A group of children try to flee France during the Napoleonic Wars (1800-1815) so they journey over the Pyrenees Mountain range hoping to find safety in Spain. A doctor impersonating a spy they trust turns them in to the authorities, but they inventively manage to escape to freedom. The Napoleonic Wars were a series of wars that were sparked by the French Revolution of 1789 and waged by a number of European nations against Emperor Napoleon Bonaparte's (1769-1821) French Empire. An excellent family film, but caution is advised for viewing by younger children due to violent war scenes. **p**, Robert Dunbar; **d**, Muriel Box; **cast**, Mavis Ranson, Roberta Tovey, Angela Whitw, Malcolm Ranson, Brian Wills, Graham Wills, Christopher Rhodes, Frederick Piper, Charles Rolfe, Delene Scott; **w**, Michael Barnes (based on a story by Frank Wells); **c**, Kenneth Reeves; **m**, William Davies; **ed**, Jean Barker.

Pippi in the South Seas ★★★ 1974; Sweden/West Germany; 86m; Beta Film/G.G. Communications; Color; Adventure; Children: Recom-

Gene Kelly in *The Pirate*, 1948.

mended (MPAA: G); **DVD**; **VHS**. Nilsson is wonderful in this exciting tale of the precocious nine-year-old Swedish girl with superhuman strength and who has a lot of fun making life miserable for pompous adults, while, like Peter Pan, insisting on never growing up. The daughter of a buccaneer captain, she has four best friends, neighbor kids, Sundberg and Persson, and a horse and a monkey. In this adventure based on the popular children's novels, they all go to the South Pacific to rescue Nilsson's father from pirates, who are after his buried treasure, sailing there in a balloon. They find her father, Wolgers, just as he is about to be tortured by pirates demanding where he has buried his treasure after his ship was wrecked. Nilsson rescues Wolgers and then causes the pirates to vainly chase about the island after her as she defeats them at every turn. She finally leaves her pursuers stranded on the island after she, Wolgers and her friends use the pirate ship to sail away. Songs: "Here Comes Pippi Longstocking," "Come On, Come On, Pirates" (Jan Johansson, Astrid Lindgren); "Sleep All," "Pirate Fabbe," "Mother Is Sweet," "Merja Mojsi," "Kalle Teodor" (Georg Riedel, Astrid Lindgren). There is a good sequel, **Pippi on the Run**, 1977. (In Swedish; English subtitles.) **p**, Olle Nordemar; **d&w**, Olle Hellbom (based on the Pippi Longstocking books by Astrid Lindgren); **cast**, Inger Nilsson, Maria Persson, Pär Sundberg, Beppe Wolgers, Martin Ljung, Jarl Borssén, Alfred Schieske, Wolfgang Völz, Nikolaus Schilling, Thor Heyerdahl; **c**, Kalle Bergholm (Movielab Color); **m**, Georg Riedel, Jan Johansson; **ed**, Jan Persson, Jutta Schweden; **set d**, Leif Nilsson.

Pippi on the Run ★★★ 1977; Sweden/West Germany; 94m; Iduna Film Produktiongesellschaft/G.G. Communications; Color; Adventure; Children: Recommended (MPAA: G); **DVD**. In this fine sequel to **Pippi in the South Seas**, 1974, Nilsson is again captivating as she plays Sweden's favorite precocious nine-year-old girl who possesses superhuman strength. This time she goes with her sibling neighbors, Sundberg and Persson, when they run away from their strict parents. On their journey they befriend Afredson, an eccentric peddler, going from town to town, riding on top of a train, and zooming high in a flying car, until the runaway brother and sister come to learn they like it much better at home after all. Songs: "Mother's Little Lazybones," "Summer Song," "Lira Lara Loppan" (Georg Riedel, Astrid Lindgren); "In a Deep, Endless Forest" (Carl Olof Rosenius); "Hey, Pippi Longstocking" (Jan Johansson, Konrad Elfers, Lindgren, Wolfgang Franke, Helmut Harun); "Goodbye Pippi Longstocking" (Anders Floija, Christian Bruhn). (In Swedish; English subtitles.) **p**, Olle Nordemar; **d**, Olle Hellbom; **cast**, Inger Nilsson, Pär Sundberg, Maria Persson, Hans Alfredson, Benno Sterzenbach, Öllegård Wellton, Walter Richter, Fredrik Ohlsson, Kurt Zips; **w**, Astrid Lindgren (based on her Pippi Longstocking books); **c**, Kalle Bergholm (Movielab Color); **m**, Georg Riedel, Christian Bruhn;

ed, Jan Persson, Jutta Schweden; **art d**, Stig Limer.

Piranha ★★★ 1978; U.S.; 94m; New World; Color; Horror; Children: Unacceptable (MPAA: R); **DVD**; **VHS**. In a good blend of comedy and horror, this parody of **Jaws**, 1975, sees Menzies as a female detective searching for a couple who went missing in the backwoods. She and Dillman team up to trace the missing couple to a supposedly deserted army base with a deep pool. As they pull a switch to drain the pool, McCarthy, a mad scientist, tells them they have just released some super-bred piranha into a nearby river. He says he bred the man-eating fish at the government's request, to be used against the Viet Cong in the Vietnam War (1961-1975), but the war ended before the fish could be used. Now the killer fish are swimming toward a children's summer camp in which Dillman's daughter is enrolled. Bartel, a camp director, unaware of the approaching piranha, orders the children into the river for an inner-tube race. Many of the children become lunch for the piranha, who then swim on to a new lakeside resort and eat people there at its grand opening. Dillman finally manages to lure the piranha into a smelt fishery and poisons them. An entertaining horror film for fans of that genre, but this film's ultraviolence prohibits viewing by children. A poor remake was issued in 2010. **p**, Jon Davison; **d**, Joe Dante; **cast**, Bradford Dillman, Heather Menzies, Kevin McCarthy, Keenan Wynn, Dick Miller, Barbara Steele, Belinda Balaski, Melody Thomas, Bruce Gordon, Barry Brown, Eric Braeden; **w**, John Sayles (based on a story by Sayles, Richard Robinson); **c**, Jamie Anderson (Metrocolor); **m**, Pino Donaggio; **ed**, Dante, Mark Goldblatt; **art d**, Bill and Kerry Mellin; **set d**, Jeff Ayres; **spec eff**, Jon Berg.

The Pirate ★★★★ 1948; U.S.; 110m; MGM; Color; Musical; Children: Acceptable; **DVD**; **VHS**. Kelly is at his acrobatic dancing best and Garland at her finest singing voice in this lively and entertaining musical, which is set in the Caribbean island of San Sebastian in the 1820s. Garland, a native girl, is obsessed with a legendary pirate named Macoco, who is called "Mack the Black," and she fantasizes about a romantic entanglement with this daring buccaneer. After learning about Garland's fantasy, Kelly, a wandering minstrel, decides to impersonate the pirate to win Garland's love. Slezak, who is a heavyset older man and Garland's intended, angrily denounces Kelly after he appears in the town to state that if Garland is not turned over to him, he will summon his bloodthirsty pirates to devastate and loot the place. Just as Garland is about to sacrifice herself for the good of her community, she learns that Kelly is an imposter and he and she have a wild battle while singing "Love of My Life." Kelly then discovers that the much respected and leading businessman in the town, Slezak, is really the much-feared Macoco, although he has been ostensibly in retirement for some time. Whether or not Slezak is the pirate she once dreamed about no longer interests Garland as she is now hopelessly in love with the amorous Kelly and she decides to spend the rest of her life with this colorful entertainer, going off with him to perform with him and his troupe of players. The film ends with Kelly and Garland performing a rousing song and dance routine with the exceptionally talented Nicholas Brothers while dressed as clowns (with some blackened out teeth and their fake bulbous noses glowing red) and singing the great Porter song "Be a Clown" to end this fine production. Minnelli traditionally handles this film with his usual frenetic pace and exhibits his flair for the spectacular by having Kelly do outstanding stunts, scaling high buildings and swinging on huge drapes from one structure to another in his romantic pursuit of Garland. The sets themselves are majestically breathtaking as are the period costumes and props, and the choreography, particularly in the Pirate Ballet performed by Kelly, is superb. Songs: "Nina," "Mack the Black," "Be a Clown," "You Can Do No Wrong," "Love of My Life" (music and lyrics: Cole Porter); "Sweet Ices, Papayas, Berry Man," "Sea Wall," "Sarafin" (Roger Edens); "The Ring," "Not Again," "The Tight Rope" (Lennie Hayton); "Pirate Ballet" (Cole Porter, Roger Edens, Conrad Salinger). The film did not do as well as expected at the box office, returning $2,290,000 against a then staggering $3,768,000. *Author's Note*: MGM spent lavishly on this production, its wardrobe expenses alone exceeding $140,000. One of the reasons given for the film's box office failure was that Minnelli helmed an old-fashioned musical that offered topdrawer songs from Porter and others, but that the dance routines were pretty much the same kind of ensembles found in most other musicals up to that time with the exception of some of Kelly's acrobatic sequences. Any attempt at dramatic performances was abandoned for tongue-and-cheek mugging and extravagant histrionics, almost as if Minnelli was parodying the period musicals of yesteryear. That approach was defended by Kelly, who told this author that "we hammed it up a lot in **The Pirate** because that is what street entertainers did in those days. They were not performing Shakespeare." MGM had purchased the film rights of the Behrman stage production for $225,000, that play having run for 177 performances in 1942 and with the luminary married couple of Alfred Lunt and Lynn Fontaine in the leading roles. "There was trouble right from the beginning with Judy [Garland] in **The Pirate**," Kelly told this author. "I appeared with her in **For Me and My Gal** [1942] and we had a terrific time in doing that picture together. But when it came to **The Pirate**, well, she went to pieces, poor gal, and began accusing everyone of sabotaging her performance and ruining her career, including me and her husband, Vincente Minnelli, who was directing that picture. It was one of my worst nightmares and I don't know how we ever got that one done." Minnelli said to this author that "Judy had been away from the studio [MGM] for some time and had not done a picture since **Till the Clouds Roll By** [1946]. She was pregnant with our daughter [Liza Minnelli] during that production, and so much of her was showing that in the last few numbers she sang in **Till the Clouds Roll By**, and I directed those numbers although Dick Whorf was the director of the film, she stood behind tables and counters. When we went into production on **The Pirate**, her mood swings increased and she began falling back on the use of pills—and God knows where she got them because I tried to find out and couldn't—and those pills further increased those abrupt mood swings of hers. She would hide out in her dressing room or sometimes not even come to the studio and when she did appear on the set, we got one explosive argument after another from her. We tried very hard to calm her down and make her happy, but nothing could convince her that we were not secretly plotting to destroy her. It was a miserable time for all of us." Garland had a lifetime problem with weight and was forever going on diets and supplemented that regimen with barbiturates, chiefly Seconal, a sedative with hypnotic properties, to combat her dramatic mood swings where she would be either reclusive and noncommunicative or outrageously combative. More than once while on the set of **The Pirate**, Garland began screaming, hysterically accusing both Minnelli and Kelly that they were in league together to demolish her career by Minnelli giving Kelly all the major scenes and reducing her role to that of an inconsequential supporting player and where she was being used as "a moving prop." She smoked incessantly throughout the production, her chain-smoking using up a reported four or more packs of cigarettes a day (80 cigarettes a day), and more than once she collapsed and had to be taken home in a limousine still wearing her costume and camera makeup. Her paranoia mounted to the point that she told everyone she knew that the world had turned against her, and even told gossip columnist Hedda Hopper that one of those who was out to crush her career was her own mother. Because of Garland's no-shows and temper tantrums, Minnelli went beyond schedule, taking 135 days to complete **The Pirate**. "By the time we finished the picture," Kelly told this author, "Judy just about hated everybody connected with it, even though everybody she hated still loved her very much. She had always gotten along with Cole [Porter], who was one of the finest composers in the world and a nicer guy you could never meet. Well, Judy felt that he, too, was somehow scheming to wreck her career and when we finished the film she refused to talk to him anymore. Cole forgave her, though. We all did, and we went on forgiving her when she got worse and worse and maybe that was the wrong thing to do. She needed therapy, but she would not

Gene Kelly and Judy Garland in *The Pirate*, 1948.

go to any therapist and relied on those damned sedatives and that's what killed her. [On June 22, 1969 Garland was found dead in her rented London townhouse by her fifth husband of ninety days, musician Mickey Deans, that death due to 'an incautious self-overdose' of barbiturates, according to a coroner's report.] What a great loss. What a great tragedy." One of the best musical numbers in the film, "Be a Clown," featured the marvelous dancing of the gifted Nicholas Brothers. This scene was not seen in some theaters in the Deep South at the time of its 1948 release because that scene was edited out by local distributors who refused to show black entertainers, such as the Nicholas Brothers, appearing in films then exhibited in Southern theaters catering to only white audiences and where no black citizen could buy a ticket to gain entrance. **p**, Arthur Freed; **d**, Vincente Minnelli; **cast**, Judy Garland, Gene Kelly, Walter Slezak, Gladys Cooper, Reginald Owen, George Zucco, Lola Albright, Dick Simmons, O.Z. Whitehead, Marie Windsor; **w**, Albert Hackett, Frances Goodrich, Joseph Than (not credited), (based on a play by S.N. Berman); **c**, Harry Stradling (Technicolor); **m**, Cole Porter, Lennie Hayton, Conrad Salinger; **ed**, Blanche Sewell; **art d**, Cedric Gibbons, Jack Martin Smith; **set d**, Edwin B. Willis.

The Pirates of Penzance ★★★ 1983; U.K./U.S.; 112m; UNIV; Color; Musical; Children: Cautionary (MPAA: G); **DVD**; **VHS**. Top-flight performances and a bevy of wonderful and witty songs are offered in this very entertaining film based on the Broadway musical and the comic operetta by Gilbert and Sullivan. Smith is meant to be an apprentice to a ship's pilot, but Lansbury, his hard-of-hearing maid, mistakes his wish for that of wanting to become a pirate. He sails with Kline, king of the Pirates of Penzance, and, while ashore, meets the eight daughters of the major general, Rose. Smith falls in love with all of them but only one of them, Ronstadt, agrees to marry him. Smith wants to retire as a pirate when he turns twenty-one, but Kline, who wants to keep him a pirate aboard his ship, tells Smith his birthday falls on a leap year, so it will be some time before he can blow out any cake candles and depart the piratical life. Rose's home is then attacked and cutthroat pirates get away with all of his daughters. Never fear, Smith, Kline and his not-so-fierce Pirates of Penzance rescue them. Songs: "Overture," "Pour, Oh Pour the Pirate Sherry," "When Fredric Was a Little Lad," "On Better Far to Live and Die," "Oh False One, You Have Deceived Me," "Climbing Over Rocky Mountain," "Stop, Ladies, Pray," "Oh Is There Not One Maiden Breast," "Oh Sisters, Deaf to Pity's Name," "Poor Wandering One," "Hold Monsters," "Stay, We Must Not Lose Our Senses," "I Am the Very Model of a Modern Major General," "Act I Finale," "Oh Dry the Glistening Tear," "Now for the Pirate's Lair," "When the Foeman Bares His Steel," "When You Had Left Our Pirate Fold," "Away, Away, My Heart's on Fire," "Stay, Fredric, Stay," "Ah, Leave Me Not to Pine,"

Chow Yun-Fat and Johnny Depp in *Pirates of the Caribbean: At World's End,* 2007.

"Oh Here Is Love and Here Is Truth," "Sergeant, Approach," "No, I Am Brave," "When a Felon's Not Engaged in His Employment," "A Rollicking Band of Pirates, We," "With Cat Like a Tread," "Slightly Softly to the River," "My Eyes are Fully Open (from Ruddigore)," "Act II Finale" (music: Arthur Sullivan; lyrics: W. S. Gilbert). Dangerous swordplay and other pirate action makes this cautionary viewing by children. **p,** Joseph Papp, Timothy Burrill; **d&w,** Wilford Leach (based on the operetta by Sir William Gilbert, Sir Arthur Sullivan); **cast,** Kevin Kline, Angela Lansbury, Linda Ronstadt, George Rose, Rex Smith, Tony Azito, David Hatton, Anthony Arundell, John Asquith, Mohamed Aazzi, Tim Bentinck; **c,** Douglas Slocombe (Panavision; Technicolor); **ed,** Anne V. Coates; **prod d,** Elliot Scott; **art d,** Ernest Archer, Alan Cassie; **set d,** Peter Howitt; **spec eff,** Brian Johnson.

Pirates of the Caribbean: At World's End ★★★ 2007; U.S.; 169m; UNIV; Color; Adventure/Fantasy/Horror; Children: Unacceptable (MPAA: PG-13); **BD; DVD.** In this third action-packed outing of the series, Depp, Bloom, Knightley, and Rush face new foes, Davy Jones (Nighy) and a nobleman, Hollander, who want to get rid of the pirates and rule the seas. Depp and the others summon help from the Pirate Lords from the four corners of the Earth to fight them. After many adventures the heroes defeat their enemies. Again, the spectacular special effects provide the most arresting and memorable scenes, and Depp continues to appear as the most unlikely fey pirate ever to ravage the seas. Songs: "Only Found Out Yesterday" (Keith Richards), "Hoist the Colors" (Ted Elliott, Terry Rossio), "Yo Ho (A Pirate's Life for Me" (Xavier Atenico, George Bruns). There are three other films in the series, **Pirates of the Caribbean: The Curse of the Black Pearl,** 2003; **Pirates of the Caribbean: Dead Man's Chest,** 2006; and **Pirates of the Caribbean: On Stranger Tides,** 2011. Excessive violence and morbidity prohibit viewing by children. **p,** Jerry Bruckheimer; **d,** Gore Verbinski; **cast,** Johnny Depp, Geoffrey Rush, Orlando Bloom, Keira Knightley, Jack Davenport, Bill Nighy, Jonathan Pryce, Lee Arenberg, Stellan Skarsgård, Tom Hollander, Naomie Harris; **w,** Ted Elliott, Terry Rossio; **c,** Dariusz Wolski; **m,** Hans Zimmer; **ed,** Stephen Rivkin, Craig Wood; **prod d,** Rick Heinrichs; **art d,** John Dexter, Bruce Crone, William Hawkins William Ladd Skinner; **set d,** Cheryl A. Carasik; **spec eff,** Allen Hall, Mark Hawker.

Pirates of the Caribbean: The Curse of the Black Pearl ★★★ 2003; U.S.; 143m; Disney/Buena Vista; Color; Adventure/Fantasy/Horror; Children: Unacceptable (MPAA: PG-13); **BD; DVD.** The first of the **Pirates of the Caribbean** series, this action-loaded sea opus follows the adventures of eccentric pirate Captain Jack Sparrow, essayed by Depp, and Bloom, a brave young blacksmith, in rescuing the beautiful Knight-

ley, Bloom's love, who has been kidnapped by the cutthroat pirate Barbossa, well enacted by Rush. Rush and the crew of his pirate ship the *Black Pearl* are under an ancient curse to live among the undead until they make a blood sacrifice. After many adventures, Depp takes a medallion from Rush's treasure chest and becomes immortal in order to kill him in a wild swordfight. Rush survives, however, and Depp and Bloom are to be hanged, but Depp escapes and Bloom is pardoned to marry Knightley. Depp is then rescued and made captain of the *Black Pearl.* Spectacular special effects are seen throughout this offbeat but fascinating film where Depp swashbuckles his way along the piratical sea lanes. The see-sawing transformations of the pirates from flesh-and-blood to horrific skeletal creatures are truly terrifying and are strongly reminiscent of the great special effects achieved by artist Ray Harryhausen. Songs: "Yo Ho (A Pirate's Life for Me)" (Xavier Atencio, George Bruns), "Pirate Music" (Craig Eastman). There are three other films in the series, **Pirates of the Caribbean: Dead Man's Chest,** 2006; **Pirates of the Caribbean: At World's End,** 2007; and **Pirates of the Caribbean: On Stranger Tides,** 2011. Excessive violence and morbidity prohibit viewing by children. **p,** Jerry Bruckheimer; **d,** Gore Verbinski; **cast,** Johnny Depp, Geoffrey Rush, Orlando Bloom, Keira Knightley, Jack Davenport, Jonathan Pryce, Lee Arenberg, Mackenzie Crook, Damian O'Hare, Giles New; **w,** Ted Elliott, Terry Rossio; **c,** Dariusz Wolski; **m,** Klaus Badelt; **ed,** Stephen Rivkin, Craig Wood, Arthur Schmidt; **prod d,** Brian Morris; **art d,** Derek R. Hill, James E. Tocci, Donald B. Woodruff; **set d,** Larry Dias; **spec eff,** Terry Frazee, Donald Frazee, Danny Cangemi.

Pirates of the Caribbean: Dead Man's Chest ★★★ 2006; U.S.; 151m; Disney/Buena Vista; Color; Adventure/Horror; Children: Unacceptable (MPAA: PG-13); **BD; DVD.** In this second of the exciting sea adventure series, Depp owes a debt to Davy Jones, played by Nighy, who is the captain of the pirate ship *Flying Dutchman.* Bloom and Knightley are to be hanged unless then can get Hollander's compass. Bloom takes on another adventure with Depp and they overcome the villains again. The main attraction of this film, along with its companion films, is its outstanding special effects and where Depp becomes again a visual curiosity as he continues to enact the swishiest swashbuckler ever appearing in any pirate film. (Any pirate worth his old salt would have slit Depp's throat at the first flickering of Depp's flying fingers or at the sight of the thick mascara encasing his ogling orbs.) Song: "Two Hornpipes" (Skitch Henderson). There are three other films in the series, **Pirates of the Caribbean: The Curse of the Black Pear,** 2003; **Pirates of the Caribbean: At World's End,** 2007; and **Pirates of the Caribbean: On Stranger Tides,** 2011. Excessive violence and morbidity prohibit viewing by children. **p,** Jerry Bruckheimer; **d,** Gore Verbinski; **cast,** Johnny Depp, Orlando Bloom, Keira Knightley, Jack Davenport, Bill Nighy, Jonathan Pryce, Lee Arenberg, Stellan Skarsgård, Tom Hollander, Geoffrey Rush; **w,** Ted Elliott, Terry Rossio; **c,** Dariusz Wolski; **m,** Hans Zimmer; **ed,** Stephen Rivkin, Craig Wood; **prod d,** Rick Heinrichs; **art d,** Bruce Crone, John Dexter, William Hawkins, William Ladd Skinner; **set d,** Cheryl A. Carasik; **spec eff,** Michael Lantieri, Eric Allard, Joel Harlow.

Pirates of the Caribbean: On Stranger Tides ★★★ 2011; U.S.; 136m; Disney/Buena Vista; Color; Adventure/Horror; Children: Unacceptable (MPAA: PG-13); **BD; DVD.** The fourth in the action-packed pirate series is even more exciting in 3-Dimension. Depp crosses paths with Cruz, a woman from his past, who is the daughter of pirate Blackbeard, essayed by McShane. They and Rush are all searching for the elusive Fountain of Youth, but none of them locate that mythical spring providing eternal life. Breathtaking special effects awesomely sail this actioner to its final destination, despite the weird, offbeat and distracting hip-swaying antics of Depp, who mocks his character and the story line and is as convincing a pirate as Pee-wee Herman (Paul Reubens) might have been if enacting the same role (but who might have provided a lot more laughs). Songs: "Tripping the Stairs" (traditional), "Jolly Sailor Bold" (John Deluca, David Giuli, Matthew Sullivan), "Mermaids" (Hans Zimmer, Eric Whitacre), "Tango" (Eduardo Cruz). There are three other films in the series, **Pirates of the Caribbean: The Curse of the Black Pearl**, 2003; **Pirates of the Caribbean: Dead Man's Chest**, 2006; and **Pirates of the Caribbean: At World's End**, 2007. Excessive violence, gutter language, nudity and sexual content prohibit viewing by children. **p**, Jerry Bruckheimer; **d**, Rob Marshall; **cast**, Johnny Depp, Geoffrey Rush, Penélope Cruz, Ian McShane, Kevin McNally, Sam Claflin, Stephen Graham, Keith Richards, Greg Ellis, Richard Griffiths, Judi Dench; **w**, Ted Elliott, Trery Rossio; **c**, Dariusz Wolski; **m**, Hans Zimmer; **ed**, David Brenner, Wyatt Smith; **prod d**, John Myhre; **art d**, Drew Boughton, John Chichester, Robert Cowper, Zack Grobler, Tomas Voth; **set d**, Gordon Sim; **spec eff**, Neil Corbould, John Frazier, Mark Hawker, Peter Haran.

The Pit and the Pendulum ★★★ 1961; U.S.; 80m; Alta Vista/MGM; Color; Horror; Children: Unacceptable; **DVD**; **VHS**. The classic horror tale from Poe is brought to the screen in a suspenseful and chilling production that sees Kerr going to Spain in the mid 16th Century to learn more about the death of his sister, Steele, who was married to Price, master of a medieval castle on a mountaintop. Price's father had been a torturer in the castle during the Spanish Inquisition (1481-1834), a brutal heritage that eventually invades Price's psyche. Price says Steele died of a blood disease, but Kerr is suspicious. He investigates with the help of Price's sister, Anders, and learns that Steele died from fright and she may have been buried alive in the castle's dungeon. Eventually, Kerr learns that Steele conspired with her lover, Carbone, the family doctor, in an attempt to drive Price mad and subsequently inherit his fortune. Price does go mad, believing he is his executioner father, and fights with Carbone, who falls into a pit in the castle and dies. Price then straps Kerr to a table in the pit and proceeds to bring down a swinging pendulum with a large blade attached to cut him in half, but Anders comes to Kerr's rescue. Price falls to his death in the pit and Kerr and Anders embrace as this grim thriller ends by showing Steele still alive, walled up in the castle dungeon. This story was remade in 1991 and 2009. Excessive violence prohibits viewing by children. *Author's Note*: Price told this author (with no little tongue and cheek) that "I can't recall how many times I have played murderous lunatics, psychopaths, insane scientists and berserk physicians, but my heart always warmed to anything Edgar Allan Poe wrote and that is why I so enjoyed playing the maniac in **The Pit and the Pendulum**. I don't think any of my contemporaries who played similar roles thought the way I do about playing such reprehensible and disgusting characters. I have always felt that, in such roles, I was representing the evil side of mankind and have enjoyed doing it. Perhaps that sounds strange or sick, but it's the truth. However, I do not make jokes at funerals, such as my friend Peter Lorre was wont to do and Peter played his own goodly number of maniacal killers in his career. We both went to the funeral for Bela Lugosi [died August 16, 1956] and I was startled to see that Bela was wearing his cape from his Dracula films while reposing in an open casket. Someone told me that Bela had requested that that cape, his trademark from playing that vampire, go with him to his grave. Peter took one look at Bela wearing his Dracula cape and turned to me, and said without a hint of a smile on his face: 'Do you think we should drive a stake through his heart just to be on the safe side?' As I have said, I do not make jokes at funerals, but Peter Lorre certainly did. I think the difference between Bela and me was that I have played many macabre characters before going home to enjoy life, but Bela's only joy was living and dying within the image of only one such macabre character that he played and who made him famous, that character being the most unsavory citizen of Transylvania." **p&d**, Roger Corman; **cast**, Vincent Price, John Kerr, Barbara Steele, Luana Anders, Antony Carbone, Patrick Westwood, Lynne Bernay, Mary Menzies, Larry Turner, Charles Victor, Randee Lynne Jensen; **w**, Richard Matheson (based on the story by Edgar Allan Poe); **c**, Floyd Crosby (Panav-

Vincent Price and Barbara Steele in *The Pit and the Pendulum*, 1961.

ision; Pathe Color); **m**, Les Baxter; **ed**, Anthony Carras; **prod d & art d**, Daniel Haller; **set d**, Harry Reif; **spec eff**, Pat Dinga, Ray Mercer, Albert Whitlock.

Pitfall ★★★★ 1948; U.S.; 86m; Regal Films/UA; B/W; Crime Drama; Children: Unacceptable; **VHS**. Powell is riveting in this uncompromising film noir tale where he is a happily married man in comfortable suburbia and then becomes involved in a torrid extramarital affair ringed with thieves and killers. Powell is married to devoted wife Wyatt and has an admirable young son, Hunt. He makes his living as an insurance agent, earning enough to afford a good home in the suburbs, a new car every year or so, and has a promising future. All that changes when he is assigned to recover all the goods stolen from a store insured by his firm, or any items the thief has purchased with money received for selling those stolen items. The convicted thief, Barr, is behind bars serving time for the robbery and he is not about to aid Powell in his quest for those stolen items. To locate those items, Powell is given the help of Burr, a conniving private detective, and they both soon locate Scott, an alluring husky-voiced blonde, who has been enjoying pleasure cruises by using Barr's luxury boat, but Powell tells her that that boat will be confiscated to help ameliorate Barr's theft. The dismayed Scott thinks to hold on to the boat by enticing Powell into an affair and, in this she is right. Powell, bored with his ho-hum life, yearns for excitement and falls for the attractive Scott. This angers the calculating Burr as he has made his own plans for Scott. Burr goes to Powell and threatens him, telling him to stay away from Scott and that he has his own designs for her, but, by this time, Powell, who cannot live with the guilt of his philandering, has decided to end his affair with Scott. Burr is not satisfied with Powell's decision, believing that he will go back to the irresistible Scott and, to prevent that from happening, he arranges for Barr to be released from prison. Burr gets Barr drunk and fills him full of lurid stories about Scott and Powell so that Barr, in a drunken rage, sets out to kill Powell. Scott then warns Powell that Barr is gunning for him and he waits for the felon with gun in hand. As expected, Barr barges into Powell's home, but, before Barr can kill his rival, Powell shoots the invader to death. Powell then confesses his betrayal to wife Wyatt, who, though shocked, stands by him, even though she tells him that their marriage will never be the same. Burr then kidnaps Scott, forcing her to leave town with him, but she turns the tables on the overweight detective and kills him. The deaths of Burr and Barr implicate Powell, but he is cleared of both of these killing's and it is the vixen Scott who is arrested. A weary and wiser man, Powell returns to his wife and son, but he now knows that he has permanently damaged his life and marriage and he has little hope that it can ever be repaired. Director de Toth, who specialized in *film noir* productions (**Passport to Suez**, 1943; **Dark Wa-**

Marlene Dietrich and John Wayne in *Pittsburgh*, 1942.

ters, 1944), presents a consistently tense and taut tale with an intelligent script, and Powell is well supported by Wyatt, Scott, and particularly, Burr, who gives a chilling performance that personifies ruthlessness. This story was again presented when it was aired on radio on October 17, 1949, in a broadcast of Screen Director's Playhouse and where Powell, Wyatt and Burr reprise their roles. **p**, Samuel Bischoff; **d**, Andre de Toth; **cast**, Dick Powell, Lizabeth Scott, Jane Wyatt, Raymond Burr, John Litel, Byron Barr, Jimmy Hunt, Ann Doran, Selmer Jackson, Margaret Wells, Dick Wessel; **w**, Karl Kamb (based on the novel by Jay Dratler); **c**, Harry Wild; **m**, Louis Forbes; **ed**, Walter Thompson; **art d**, Arthur Lonergan; **set d**, Robert Priestley.

Pittsburgh ★★★ 1942; U.S.; 91m; Charles K. Feldman Group/UNIV; B/W; Drama; Children: Cautionary; **DVD**; **VHS**. Superior performances from Dietrich, Wayne and Scott mark this coal-besmirched saga as a winning tale about two hardworking miners who fall in love with the same alluring woman. Wayne and Scott are working as coal miners in the deep, dank shafts of Pittsburgh, close friends who do not shirk from the most demanding labors. While attending a boxing match, both see the attractive Dietrich sitting at ringside and they mistake her for a high society woman because of her expensive-looking attire. After the duo befriend her, Dietrich admits that she comes from the same common dirt heritage both men share. She describes herself as a "hunky" having been born and raised in a coal town, just as they have been. Wayne nevertheless calls Dietrich "Countess," after her aristocratic behavior, and quickly falls in love with her while the less aggressive Scott loves her from afar, but she shocks Wayne by telling him that their romance is at a dead end since she has resolved never to marry one of her own kind, a miner. Offended and hurt, Wayne then determines to raise himself from his working-class life and achieve a higher social and financial status by cutting a deal with a steel firm that soon sees him a successful businessman. As he becomes rich and powerful, Wayne no longer focuses on Dietrich but sets his sights on Allbritton, the fetching daughter of a wealthy businessman and a member of high society, with ambitions to join that social peerage. Meanwhile, Scott, who has joined with Craven to establish an independent coal company that is aimed at improving the income and conditions of miners, becomes Dietrich's companion, although she has not yet committed her heart to him. Wayne, who has not been in touch with either Scott or Dietrich, then gets cold feet on the night before he is to marry Allbritton. He goes to Dietrich, telling her that he really wants no part of high society and loves only Dietrich, explaining that "it got a bit chilly uptown and I thought I'd come down here where it's warmer." Feeling as if Wayne has treated her like a second-hand lover and a sop to his disappointments in life, the unpredictable and tempestuous Dietrich slaps his face (which is about as close

to a punch in the nose that any woman has ever landed on a male's human face in a movie). Wayne is humiliated and humbled, and returns to the business of making money and acquiring power, becoming hard-hearted if not mean-minded along the way. He marries Allbritton, but the marriage is not a happy one since Wayne's love is only for Dietrich. He vents his spleen on the very persons he has always magnanimously supported, his workers, breaking his promises to them. When Scott, who is working in alliance with Wayne, asks for more funding to continue research for a new medicine developed from coal tar that might relieve worldwide suffering, Wayne cruelly refuses, saying that there is no profit in the project. Then Gomez, who heads a worker's organization, asks to review the accounting ledgers of Wayne's firm, a right Wayne has earlier granted to the workers. Wayne refuses and the workers, feeling that Wayne has not lived up to his promises in guaranteeing fair wages and has betrayed them, then go on strike. Wayne tries to turn around a bad situation but only makes it worse by going into the mine and where he attempts to force workers to perform their duties at the threat of beating them with his fists. He gets a response from Scott, who defends the workers in a slam-bang, knock-down fistfight, which leaves both men injured. This encounter erodes Wayne's business to the point where it fails, mostly due to his stubborn unwillingness to meet his workers' demands and fairly settle the strike. He is now broke and has lost all his contacts and friends, Allbritton discarding him as she would a soiled handkerchief. Dietrich, who has been seriously injured in a mine accident, then marries Scott, but both will have nothing more to do with Wayne because of his brutal tactics and lack of business ethics. Wayne starts all over again, getting a job in Scott's expanding and successful company, but working under an assumed name so that no one will know his identity. He works hard and regains his healthy work ethics as well as earning the respect of his superior until he is sent to see Scott, who is to consider Wayne for an executive job with the firm. Scott, who is shocked to find out that his new employee, with such a glowing work record, is none other than Wayne. Scott believes that Wayne is up to no good, and is about to confront Wayne with his fists until Dietrich arrives to smooth things over by telling Scott and Wayne that their obligation is not to renew old feuds, but to show "devotion to our country," as America is then at war. All renew their friendships, and Scott makes Wayne a partner in his firm as they plan to work in harmony to increase production in order to support the war effort, a patriotic resolve that ends this rollicking and entertaining drama. The production values of this film are high and the action is exciting and believable as is the likable, down-to-earth script, and, along with the fine performances by the entire cast, these elements contributed to a huge box office success. The film was unfairly criticized as being a propaganda tool for the war effort, but the then normal infusion of such patriotic sentiments in scripts were universal in American moviemaking during WWII, and where such propaganda (if one can call it that) in this production constitutes not much more than a passing but very much needed positive remark. *Author's Note*: This film came hot on the heels of **The Spoilers**, 1942, another rock-'em-sock-'em film also starring Dietrich, Scott and Wayne, one that was so popular that it spawned **Pittsburgh**. Dietrich did not care too much for either Wayne or Scott because she thought that most tall and powerfully built men were neither cultured nor smart (and in this she was wrong about both of them, although both men were tall, Scott standing more than six-foot-two inches and Wayne standing six-foot-four inches). Dietrich had earlier criticized Gary Cooper (standing six-foot-three inches), her costar in **Morocco**, 1930, as not being too intelligent and having no sophistication, but her perspective about him was undoubtedly established after Cooper verbally clashed with the director of that film, Josef von Sternberg, who was then Dietrich's lover and mentor. She held the same opinion about Wayne, who had manhandled her (as the scripts dictated) in some previous films they had done together. She told this author that "I got a little revenge on Duke for his pushing me around in **The Spoilers** and in **Seven Sinners** [1940, in which she also starred with Wayne] in a scene in **Pittsburgh** where I am called upon to slap his face hard. I slapped Duke's face harder than I ever slapped anyone, so hard that one side of his face went bright red. It was lucky that the picture was not filmed in color or it would have shown. He did not indicate that he had any pain after we took that shot, but I did. That slap was like hitting the side of a huge rock and my hand went limp with pain. I went to my dressing room and soaked it in ice water for twenty minutes. The only satisfaction anyone got from that slap was the director." Wayne told this author that he thought Dietrich "was one of the best actresses of her time. She was very independent and very feisty. She hit me so hard in **Pittsburgh** that I saw stars, but I wasn't about to tell her about that. In that story I jilt her for another woman [Louise Allbritton] and I think that she somehow took that personally." Scott vividly recalled that scene when we talked years later, telling me that "Duke could never figure out why Marlene hit him so hard in **Pittsburgh**. He asked me what I thought she might have against him and I said: 'You're bigger than she is. Isn't that enough?'" **p**, Charles K. Feldman; **d**, Lewis Seiler; **cast**, Marlene Dietrich, Randolph Scott, John Wayne, Frank Craven, Louise Allbritton, Shemp Howard, Thomas Gomez, Ludwig Stössel, Samuel S. Hinds, Paul Fix; **w**, Kenneth Gamet, Tom Reed, John Twist (based on a screen story by George Owen, Reed); **c**, Robert De Grasse; **m**, Frank Skinner, Hans J. Salter; **ed**, Paul Landres; **art d**, John B. Goodman; **set d**, Russell A. Gausman, Ira Webb; **spec eff**, John P. Fulton.

A Place in the Sun ★★★★★ 1951; U.S.; 122m; PAR; B/W; Crime Drama/Romance; Children: Unacceptable; **DVD**; **VHS**. Pantheon director Howard Hawks once stated that if a director could manage to have one or even two great scenes in a film, the film was a superior achievement, even a great film. This masterpiece film from the brilliant Stevens, a remake of **An American Tragedy**, 1931, which is based upon the great Dreiser novel, does exactly that. Stevens offers one great scene after another in this moving story, until the tragic finale, and where Taylor was never more beautiful and appealing and Clift never so compelling and empathetic, both giving the performances of their lives. Shot in gritty black and white in the style of a documentary (in keeping with the true and tragic story upon which the film is based), each sequential scene instills a mounting visual sense of foreboding. Clift is first seen working as a bellhop and meeting his wealthy uncle, Heyes, who owns a clothing factory, and he tells the young man to come and see him some time should he be looking for a job. Clift, an ambitious young man, decides to improve his impoverished life. His mother, Revere, a deeply religious caretaker of a shelter for homeless persons, gives him her blessings and a lecture before Clift begins hitchhiking toward a big city in hopes of getting a job from Heyes. While on the road, an expensive convertible passes him as he tries to hitch a ride, but Taylor, the beautiful girl behind the wheel, only smiles at him and beeps the car's horn before speeding away. He is in awe of the girl's stunning beauty as he fixes his eyes upon the convertible as it speeds down the road. Once in the city, Clift meets Heyes, who gives him a low-level job in his factory, telling him that he can expect no favors because he is related to him and must prove himself before seeing any kind of advancement. Clift works hard and is soon promoted after he submits suggestions on how to improve production in his department. At that time, he meets and establishes a relationship with factory worker Winters, who is impressed with Clift because of his relationship to the owner, not realizing that that provides him with no special privileges. After Heyes is told that Clift has been promoted, he decides to invite his poor relation to a party at his mansion, and when Clift attends, he keeps mostly to himself at that gathering, realizing that Heyes and his family consider him a "black sheep" of the family because of his low station in life. He spends some time in a recreation room where he shoots pool and where Taylor (her wealthy family and that of Heyes are leading members of the local high society) finds him. Taylor and Clift are immediately attracted to each other and they begin to see each other on a regular basis, falling deeply in love. Clift by then has aspirations of marrying this ravishingly beautiful society

Elizabeth Taylor and Montgomery Clift in *A Place in the Sun*, 1951.

girl, a marriage that will undoubtedly lift him from the ranks of the working class and catapult him into wealth and social prestige, especially since he has the hesitant approval of Taylor's parents. Meanwhile, Winters shocks Clift by telling him that she is pregnant and begins pressuring him to marry her, but he puts her off, pursuing his romance with Taylor. Winters tries to arrange an abortion, but, after that fails, she insists that Clift marry her. Clift tells her that he will soon have a meeting with some importantly placed persons who will improve his financial situation and allow him to marry her and take care of her and their expected child, but that meeting is really an invitation from Taylor for Clift to spend time with her family and friends at their retreat at Loon Lake. Clift enjoys that holiday, swimming and boating with Taylor, and where he also meets her wealthy, fun-loving friends, believing that he is soon to enter this much coveted world of high society and the leisure class. While vacationing, Clift hears a story about how a couple went boating on the lake and that the man's body was never found. The story takes root in Clift's troubled mind as a sinister plot that will eliminate the existence of Winters, a woman who threatens to destroy his dreams of escaping poverty and marrying Taylor, the girl of his dreams. Winters exhibits that intent after she sees a newspaper article with a picture of Clift with Taylor and her friends enjoying an outing and, realizing that Clift lied to her about that important meeting, takes action. While Clift is enjoying a dinner party at Taylor's home and where he is about to be named to an important business position that will allow him to marry Taylor, he receives a phone call. In answering the call, he hears Winters on the line, and she tells him that she is at a nearby bus station and that if he does not come to get her, she will go to where he is and expose their relationship to his high society friends. Unnerved, Clift makes an excuse to Taylor and her family, saying that he must leave, but will soon return. He then goes to see Winters and, the next morning, glum and desperate, Clift takes Winters to the local City Hall to be married, but, since it is Sunday, the place is closed (as Clift knew it would be), and Clift, desperately stalling for time and a way out of his pinioning relationship with Winters, suggests that they stay at a nearby lake until the City Hall opens the next day. He takes her to a remote, small lake and nervously rents a boat from a man, who appears to be suspicious of his behavior after Clift gives him a false name and especially after Clift asks the man if anyone else is boating on the lake. The man tells him that no one else is on the lake. Clift rows Winters far out onto the lake at dusk and, while the light is fading, Winters bares her heart to Clift, describing in simple but touching terms how she envisions their happiness together, especially after their child is born. Clift appears to have a change of mind, moved by Winters' loving statements, and he seems to abandon his plans to murder her when Winters, awkwardly and suddenly, stands up in the boat. Before Clift can take any action, she falls

Elizabeth Taylor and Montgomery Clift in *A Place in the Sun*, 1951.

and causes the boat to capsize. Clift swims frantically about the boat, but cannot find Winters, who has drowned. He swims to shore and later reappears at Taylor's home where her father, Strudwick, gives his approval for him to marry his daughter. Meanwhile, Winters' body is recovered and police determine that she has been murdered and a search for her companion ensues. When Clift hears of this, he flees through some woods, but runs into a gaunt-looking man who asks: "Are you George Eastman?" Arrested, Clift is put on trial, where Burr, an aggressive state's attorney, obsessively prosecutes him. Although Clift takes the witness stand and denies that he killed Winters, he states that he had had that thought in mind, but that her death was accidental. Burr ridicules his contention and dramatically reenacts what he thinks took place on that lake, having a rowboat brought into the court. Burr stands in the rowboat and describes to the jury how the helpless, pregnant Winters sat in that boat and how Clift then picked up an oar—and here Burr picks up an oar and holds it menacingly over his head—and how Clift brought that oar down with all of his might to crush Winters' head, and with that, Burr smashes the oar onto the boat, breaking it, causing its splinters to violently fly throughout the court. His wild demonstration, correct or not, is stunningly damning. Clift is convicted of murdering Winters and sentenced to death. Taylor, devastated, can barely keep up with her college studies, and before Clift is about to be executed in the electric chair, she visits him against the wishes of her parents and where she bids him a loving farewell. All worthwhile in life has escaped Clift as he ponders his grim fate in his prison cell while accompanied by a priest, Frees, and to whom Clift admits that he did, indeed, think to kill Winters, and is therefore guilty in his mind in bringing about her death and, thus, deserves to die (a scene not dissimilar to the ending of **The Postman Always Rings Twice**, 1946, where John Garfield rationalizes a deserving execution for having murdered one person but not another for which he is about to be put to death). Although Stevens stresses the Taylor-Clift love affair (and provides some of the most smoldering and passionate close-up shots of their embraces and kisses ever put on the screen), he loses none of the impact of the overall powerful story, carefully crafting each scene as he unfolds that tragedy, where Clift, Taylor and Winters, all star-crossed lovers in a fatal triangle, are riveting in their roles, giving magnificent performances. Their actions and reactions are natural, humanly hesitant and sometimes even fumbling as their characters grope for a happy future, first, in a day where they seemingly have found a place in the sun and, last, as the dark night of tragedy slowly engulfs them all. Strudwick is exceptional as Taylor's protective father, who is liberal minded enough to invite a poor young man into his upper-crust world and allow him to marry his daughter, and Burr is utterly mesmerizing as the dogged prosecutor determined at all costs to send a young man to the electric chair. Revere, who appears only briefly

as the sermonizing mother from whom Clift so desperately wants to escape, presents a startling and unforgettable portrait of a religious zealot, a vacuously hypocritical and spiritually barren person, who has fanatically sacrificed her life and that of her son's future through her sanctimonious conduct and where her love for Clift is niggardly given. It is Clift's longing for true love and his desire to live a life beyond the self-imposed poverty his mother has created for him that drives him incessantly toward his grim fate, all of this incisively delineated by the gifted Stevens. Ironically, toward the end of his then declining career through drugs and alcohol, Clift played another drifter with a mother fixation in **The Misfits**, 1961, but one where he is idiotically devoted, unlike his character in **A Place in the Sun**, to an uncaring mother. Mellor's lensing for **A Place in the Sun** is cinematography at its best, capturing in stark, discernible scenes the contrasting worlds of the rich and the poor. At one hand he records the uninspiring and methodical hum-drum daily labors of blue-collar workers and their fatiguing assembly lines and monotonous time clock punch cards. On the other, he displays the dramatically different moneyed social set by detailing the carefree ambience and idyllic lifestyle of a youthful, lounging leisure class, generously and extravagantly spending time at play. We see within the broad vistas of Mellor's photography an inviting tranquil lake through which expensive motorboats slice, and where its lapping waters are ringed by towering and sheltering trees. From somewhere among that darkening forest one hears the plaintive if not ominous call of a lurking loon that eerily beckons at sundown, and where that night the body of a young woman lies at the bottom of that lake. All of what Mellor captures with his cameras, of course, constitutes his translation of the exacting and telling visual perceptions of Stevens, for every scene in this masterpiece film was conceived and dictated by that genius. The film was a great critical and box office success, yielding $7 million to Paramount against a budget of $2,300,000. The film was nominated for an Oscar as Best Picture, and Stevens won an Oscar for Best Direction. Oscars also went to Wilson and Brown for Best Screenplay, to Waxman for Best Dramatic Score, to Mellor for Best Cinematography, and to Edith Head for Best Costume Design (Black and White). Songs: "Out of Nowhere" (1931; Edward Heyman, Johnny Green), "Bear Ye Another's Burdens" (1912; Mabel J. Rosemon), "Rescue the Perishing" (1870; music: Howard Doane; hymn lyrics: Fanny Crosby), "Mona Lisa," (1941; Jay Livingston, Ray Evans), "Alma Mater" (music: Franz Waxman; lyrics: Frank Loesser), "At the Race" (Rudolph G. Kopp), "Pouplet d'Or" (Robert Emmett Dolan), "My Silent Love" (Edward Heyman, Dana Suesse), "Blue Hawaii" (Ralph Rainger, Leo Robin), "Camper's Life" (Frank Skinner), "Oloha Oe" (Queen Liliuokalani). *Author's Note*: Stevens, following his usual meticulous procedures, took a great deal of time making this film, which became Paramount's premier film for 1951. He did endless retakes to perfect each scene and used up more than 400,000 feet of film before he finally put the complete production into the can. Stevens shot the film on location at Lake Tahoe, but was constrained to go into production during wintertime, caused considerable problems in that expensive snow-melting machines had to be used in converting the locale to an summer image. Even though the lake was freezing cold at the time, Taylor bravely water-skied and swam in it while appearing sultry in a skimpy bathing suit. "She was only seventeen when she was hired for that picture," Stevens told this author, "and she was worried about acting opposite Monty [Montgomery Clift] because she knew he was a 'Method Actor' and kept telling me that he was probably too moody and too sensitive to put up with her Hollywood style of acting. I told her that Monty was a very nice young man and she would get along famously with him. Well, she did, and, in fact, they became a number." Paramount's publicity department promoted the onscreen love affair between Taylor and Clift, but, off screen, that romance was very real. Clift fell in love with Taylor just as his character does, although he first met her when she served as his date when she was fifteen when he escorted her to the premiere of **The Heiress**, 1949 (in which he appeared with Olivia de Havilland), a date arranged by studio publicists. Taylor and Clift would remain close friends right up to the time of his death. "Oh, there was never an actor or a man like Monty," Taylor told this author. "He was like a young god when he showed up on the set of **A Place in the Sun**, one of the handsomest men I ever met, although I had known him briefly a few years earlier. There was so much emotion and energy inside of him that he let it out only a little at a time in his scenes and always at the right moment. He hypnotized me and everyone else when we were making that picture, as much as he did the millions of people who saw that picture. You could not take your eyes off of him, not for a second. You wanted to look at that wonderful young man as long as you could stay awake." Stevens told me that "Monty was never any problem when we did **A Place in the Sun**. He understood his character completely and, no matter how many retakes I ordered, he was right there giving me everything he had in every take. Unfortunately, my experience with Shelley [Winters] was not as pleasant. I had a very hard time with that lady, although she gave a marvelous performance of the woman Monty discards for Elizabeth [Taylor]." When Winters was first suggested for the role of the common frump girlfriend, Stevens rejected her out of hand, telling studio bosses that she was not right for the part since she usually played "brassy, loud-mouthed blondes." Winters, however, wanted that role so badly that she pressured all the most important people she knew to have them persuade Stevens to give her the part. Author Norman Mailer told this author that "I did Shelley a favor after she asked me to contact George [Stevens] and I sent him a note saying that she would be great in the part of the scorned woman." Stevens acknowledged to this author that he had received that letter from Mailer, adding: "and a hell of a lot more notes and phone calls. God, that woman had everyone contacting me to tell me to give her that part. She was the biggest schmoozer in Hollywood—went to all the parties, showed up at all of the premieres, and dined in at least ten famous restaurants in Hollywood every night, so that she could meet everybody she knew and did not know so that she could later use them for contacts to get roles. And she did that night and day to get the part in **A Place in the Sun** until I finally agreed to meet with her." That meeting occurred in a restaurant, and when Stevens showed up he could not find Winters anywhere until he looked once again at a very plain-looking dishwater blonde sitting at table wearing no makeup and attired in a cheap, plain-looking dress. "I was amazed," Stevens told this author. "She looked as common as dirt and she knew that is what the character had to look like in **A Place in the Sun**. Savvy woman." Winters was shy and retiring when talking to Stevens that day, and he was impressed enough with her appearance and delivery that he said he would give her the part if she did a screen test that met with his approval. Winters agreed and Stevens waited and waited as Winters found one excuse after another to avoid those scheduled tests. "I could not wait any longer and I had to cast that part so I took a chance and hired her. Then my troubles began." Winters told this author many years after Stevens' death that "George [Stevens] was a brilliant director, but he was also one of the most demanding directors on the face of the earth. He was Zeus and you had to find a way to get to Mount Olympus to talk to him. I admit that I did everything I could to get him to give me that role, but I made the mistake of my life because he turned my life into living hell." Stevens, years earlier, told this author that "Shelley first showed up on the set with a lot of makeup on and dolled up like a Christmas tree and I told her to go back to her dressing room and make herself look just like the way she appeared when we met in that restaurant. But I had to keep sending her back to her dressing room because she insisted on looking like what she called 'a halfway decent looking woman.' I told her: 'You can't afford to look like that! You're a limp dishrag, got it? You can't afford mascara! You can't afford rouge! You can't afford lipstick! You're too damned poor!'" Winters told this author: "That man ran me ragged about my appearance in the picture like the hound of hell, every second, until I was so worn out that all I could do was whimper my lines like some little frightened mouse. I was so exhausted that I was ready for a hospital bed or a padded cell and I did not care which one I got. George told me that I was getting better at

Montgomery Clift and Elizabeth Taylor in *A Place in the Sun*, 1951.

it because now I looked ugly, repulsive, disgusting, vulgar and distasteful, a woman no one would want and that is the character he wanted." Stevens told this author that "by the end of the production, Shelley delivered the character needed for the story, but it was a battle with her all the way to the finish, and, by the time we wrapped it up, she was no longer talking to me. I did not care. She had done her job—finally." The role so magnificently played by Winters was indelibly and permanently linked to her persona, and she would thereafter be invariably cast in such roles by almost every film director for the rest of her career. Unlike the character of George Eastman as written by Theodore Dreiser in his classic novel, *An American Tragedy*, and essayed in the 1931 film with that title, Stevens gave that character more empathy and a less calculating personality. I pointed out to Stevens that the role model for George Eastman, the character played by Clift, Chester Gillette (1883-1908), was a ruthless killer who, indeed, crushed the head of his pregnant girlfriend, Grace "Billie" Brown, with a tennis racket while they were boating on Big Moose Lake, New York (on July 11, 1906), and that there was no possibility that the victim accidentally drowned as Stevens implies in his version of the story. Gillette was so crass and uncaring about his victim that he showed no remorse whatsoever at his trial and was only interested in signing autographs for the scores of young women enamored of the handsome young killer so that he could have enough money to pay for catered meals in his prison cell while subsequently awaiting execution in the electric chair at New York's Auburn Prison on March 30, 1908. "I know all that," Stevens told this author, "but had I showed the character in that light, the romance of the story would have gone to pieces. Don't forget, it is first a romance before any hint of crime destroys that romance and the two lovers. I did not make any excuses for the man. In the end, he admits that he thought about killing that poor girl and convicts himself in his own mind. George Eastman needed to be as human as everybody else in his world, and, by God, he was in **A Place in the Sun**, thanks to Monty's great humanity." For more details on Chester Gillette and Theodore Dreiser, see my entry on Gillette in my *World Encyclopedia of 20th Century Murder* (Paragon House, 1992; pages 233-234). **p&d**, George Stevens; **cast**, Montgomery Clift, Elizabeth Taylor, Shelley Winters, Anne Revere, Keefe Brasselle, Fred Clark, Raymond Burr, Herbert Heyes, Shepperd Strudwick, Frieda Inescort, Walter Sande, John Ridgely, Paul Frees, Ted de Corsia, Kathryn Givney, Robert J. Anderson; **w**, Michael Wilson, Harry Brown (based on the novel *An American Tragedy* by Theodore Dreiser and the stage adaptation by Patrick Kearney); **c**, William C. Mellor; **m**, Franz Waxman; **ed**, William Hornbeck; **art d**, Hans Dreier, Walter H. Tyler; **set d**, Emile Kuri; **spec eff**, Farciot Edouart, Loyal Griggs, Gordon Jennings.

A Place of One's Own ★★★ 1949; U.K.; 92m; Gainsborough Pic-

Danny Glover and Sally Field in *Places in the Heart*, 1984.

tures/Eagle-Lion; B/W; Mystery; Children: Unacceptable. This eerie and well-made mystery begins when Mason, an elderly retired tradesman, buys an old, large house. He gets a very good bargain with his purchase only to learn that no one sought to acquire the place because of persistent rumors that it is haunted. The story claims that the spirit of a young woman who tragically died in the old house continues to haunt the place. The tale annoys Mason as he and his wife, Mullen, take occupancy, and where Mason says: "If there is one thing I cannot stand it is mystery." After the couple takes residence they hire a housekeeper, Lockwood, and, shortly thereafter, weird things begin to take place in the house, but that does not convince Mason that his employee is possessed of the spirit of the long-ago dead woman, particularly when Lockwood seems to go into a trance and these strange events take place. Then Lockwood becomes seriously ill and a doctor is summoned, and Mason learns that the doctor is the same physician who treated the woman who died in the house forty years earlier. The doctor saves Lockwood's life and departs. Police then arrive to make inquiries, telling Mason and Mullen that the doctor's body was found dead in his carriage several hours before Mason has stated that he arrived at his home to treat the ailing Lockwood. Only then does Mason no longer scoff at the tales about the haunted house, now believing that the spirit of the dead woman, along with the spirit of the doctor, had met in his presence to conclude a spiritual rendezvous that had remained unfinished for forty years. Mason is excellent in this impressive spiritual whodunit and where he is made to appear to be a man many years older than his age (he was thirty-four when doing this film), and Mullen, too, is outstanding as his superstitious wife willing to believe that every creaking board of their residence represents the heave footfall of a troubled spirit. Lockwood, an outstanding actress, plays her part stoically, until she appears to be seized by that bedeviled spirit of long ago. Director Knowles employs many clever camera set ups and moves his camera fluidly throughout the old house with arresting panning and tracking shots, maintaining suspense as he hurries this thriller to its conclusion. Thesiger, the beak-nosed, pinch-faced character actor who gave such an outstandingly bizarre and fruity portrayal of the mad physician in the classic horror film, **The Bride of Frankenstein**, 1935, makes his appearance as the strange physician in this film to add his own special brand of fey fright. Songs: "String Quartet No. 2: Nocturne" (Alexander Borodin), "Waltz of the Flowers" (Peter Ilyich Tchaikovsky), "Prelude No. 14" (Fredric Chopin), "Hydropaten Waltz, Op. 149" (Jozsef Gungl). This film was produced in England in 1945, but not released in the U.S. until four years later in 1949. *Author's Note*: Mason told this author that "the script for **A Place of One's Own** offered very interesting characters, normal people who are caught up in ghost story they refuse to believe until they are compelled by circumstances to accept it. Our director

[Knowles] did a very good job of interjecting frightening scenes without resorting to histrionics and blatant bed sheets flowing and flapping about up and down staircases and in corridors. The presence of the ghost is implied through sounds and the movements of the shifting old house and, most effectively, through the reactions of those living in it and that provided considerable tension." **p**, R. J. Minney; **d**, Bernard Knowles; **cast**, James Mason, Margaret Lockwood, Barbara Mullen, Dennis Price, Helen Haye, Michael Shepley, Dulcie Gray, Moore Marriott, Gus Mc-Naughton, Ernest Thesiger; **w**, Brock Williams (based on the novel by Sir Osbert Sitwell), **c**, Stephen Dade; **m**, Hubert Bath; **ed**, Charles Knott; **art d**, John Elphick; **spec eff**, Philippo Guidobaldi.

Places in the Heart ★★★★ 1984; U.S.; 111m; Delphi II Produtions; TriStar Pictures; Color; Drama; Children: Unacceptable (MPAA: PG); **DVD; VHS**. This powerful drama movingly depicts racial tension and economic strife during the Great Depression, where Field gives another masterful performance of a widowed housewife struggling to survive while raising two children, a girl, James, and boy, Hatten. Set in 1935 in Waxahachie, Texas, Field is at home when her husband, Baker, the local sheriff, is shot and killed by White, a drunken black teenager, who is then dragged through the streets of the town before his lifeless body is dragged from the rear of a truck by enraged white vigilantes and taken to Field's home as a grim token of retribution. By that time, Field's sister, Crouse, and her husband, Harris, arrive and Crouse orders the vigilantes to leave the premises and they later hang White's corpse from a tree. Glover, a black drifter, later arrives and asks for any kind of work Field might give him. She has him chop some wood and he is paid a small amount of money. He then begs Field to give him room and board since he is homeless and the prospect of getting any employment in these hard economic times is impossible. In return, he promises that he will not only do all of the needed chores, he will plant cotton on a barren piece of land she owns, knowing that he can raise a good crop from his former experiences as a sharecropper. She refuses and, before he leaves, the desperate Glover steals some of her tableware. Smith, a conniving and unctuous banker, then arrives to tell Field that a payment of $240 will soon be due, and, if it is not promptly paid, she and her family will be evicted and she will most likely have to split up her family with her daughter going to live with some relatives and other relatives caring for her son. Smith suggests that he can solve her problem by selling off her house, but she would nevertheless realize little money and would soon be homeless and lose guardianship of her children. She refuses this deal, and, when Glover is picked up and charged with stealing her silverware, Field does not press charges and has Glover released. She hires him to plant that crop of cotton, telling him he must stay out of trouble and can live in a shed on her property. Field then goes to Smith and tells him that she thinks that she will be able to make payments and keep her house from the proceeds of a cotton crop she plans to cultivate on her property. Smith is doubtful that she will succeed, but Field embarks upon the daunting challenge. Glover accompanies her to a seed store where the owner tries to sell Field some poor cotton seed that Glover identifies as such and where he advises Field to buy another brand with more quality, which she does while the storeowner displays his dislike for Glover for his interfering ways. Glover begins planting the cotton and befriends Field's son, Hatten. When the boy tells Glover that his father was killed by a black man, Glover confides in the boy by giving him his superstitious secrets and displaying charms (horseshoes, chicken bones, peppers and garlic) designed to ward off evil, these "protective" objects enamoring the boy. While Glover, Field and her children struggle to raise the cotton crop, Smith pays a visit to Field's residence, bringing with him his brother-in-law, Malkovich, who is blind, having lost his sight while fighting in World War I. Smith pretends to be a generous and charitable person, but he is just the opposite, a self-serving and rather heartless fellow, who uses the excuse of tolerating Field's late payments to his bank by imposing the care of his brother-in-law on Field and leaves Malkovich with her, thus unburdening himself with a handicapped relative. She accepts Malkovich as her boarder and he proves to be a kind hearted and wise friend. Meanwhile, Field's brother-in-law, Harris, begins cheating on her sister, Crouse, by having an affair with Madigan, which causes Field and her family considerable stress. All of these problems evaporate when the town is struck by a fierce and devastating tornado, Field and Glover barely manage to find and bring Hatten and James to the storm cellar of their house before it is badly damaged by the storm. The town of Waxahachie is destroyed by the tornado, the school house crushed and many children killed and injured. With cotton prices dropping, there seems little chance that Field will meet her bank payment, but she nevertheless resolves to harvest her cotton crop and sell it at a local cotton gin. She, Glover, family members and friends furiously pick cotton on her thirty-acre spread, battling intense heat and insects and suffering blisters, burns and sickness, but they persevere to produce that crop and Field takes her cotton to the gin and, with Glover's help, negotiates a selling price that will allow her to keep her property and her family together. Then members of the Ku Klux Klan raid Field's house and drag Glover from his shed, beating him, until Malkovich steps outside with a gun and begins firing into the air. Although he is blind and cannot see the hooded invaders, he recognizes them by their voices and identifies them and this causes them to depart. Glover then packs up his belongings and says farewell to Field and her children. Before departing, he leaves them some small tokens by which they might remember him. Field thanks him for his great help and tells him that he should be proud that he was instrumental in bringing in the first cotton crop in the area. The film ends at a church gathering where all give thanks for their blessings and where Field states that she has a place in her heart for all of her loved ones. This gritty tale of hardworking people dealing with racial prejudice and economic survival is presented with great and meticulous care by director-writer Benton, who was born in Waxahachie, Texas, in 1932 and where he based his characters on many real-life persons who lived in that small town. Field, Glover, Crouse, Madigan, Harris and Lane all give exceptional performances in this memorable slice of Americana. The film was a solid box office success, earning almost $35 million in its initial release against a budget of $9.5 million. Field won an Oscar as Best Actress, her second such win (following her Oscar win for **Norma Rae**, 1979), and Benton won an Oscar for Best Screenplay. It received Oscar nominations for Best Picture, Best Director, Best Supporting Actress (Crouse), Best Supporting Actor (Malkovich), and Best Costume Design. Song: "In the Garden" (music and lyrics: Austin Miles). *Author's Note*: Many of the elements of this story are closely reminiscent of **To Kill a Mockingbird**, 1962, and, to some degree, **Intruder in the Dust**, 1949, insofar as the profiling of bigotry and racial prejudices and the protective measures Field takes in shielding Glover. See extensive compilations of films depicting the Ku Klux Klan and Lynch Mobs in the Subject Index of this work, Volume IV. **p**, Arlene Donovan; **d&w**, Robert Benton; **cast**, Sally Field, Lindsay Crouse, Ed Harris, Amy Madigan, John Malkovich, Danny Glover, Yankton Hatten, Gennie James, Lane Smith, Terry O'Quinn, De'voreaux White; **c**, Néstor Almendros (Technicolor); **m**, John Kander; **ed**, Carol Littleton; **prod d**, Gene Callahan; **art d**, Sydney Z. Litwack; **set d**, Lee Poll, Derek Hill; **spec eff**, Calvin Joe Acord, Bran Ferren, Mitch Wilson.

The Plainsman ★★★★ 1936; U.S.; 113m; PAR; B/W; Western; Children: Unacceptable; **DVD**; **VHS**. Director DeMille presents wonderful adventure and exciting action in this highly romanticized version of the relationship between western gunslinger Wild Bill Hickok (James Butler Hickok; 1837-1876), who is resolutely essayed by Cooper, and Wild West hellion Calamity Jane (Martha Jane Canary; 1852-1903), energetically played by Arthur. The great showman takes considerable liberties with the facts involving these two colorful Old West characters, as he does in profiling William F. "Buffalo Bill" Cody (1846-1917), General George Armstrong Custer (1839-1876), Cheyenne Indian warrior Yellow Hand (d. 1876), and Jack McCall (1853-1877), who was Hickok's

Victor Varconi, Gary Cooper and Jean Arthur in *The Plainsman*, 1936.

killer and is played by Hall, but, in his flamboyant process he nevertheless presents a rip-snorting and irresistible tale. Cooper is seen just after being mustered out of the Union Army, following his service in the Union Army during the American Civil War and is leaving for the West after arriving on a steamboat, en route to Hays City, Kansas. He notices a large shipment of crates being received by trader Bickford and where one of those crates is dropped by a black stevedore (who is brutally clubbed by Bickford for his error) and is jarred open to reveal a load of repeating rifles that Cooper suspects Bickford of selling to warring Indians. Cooper then encounters an old friend, Arthur, who is the whip-snapping stagecoach driver about to drive the stage to Hays City, and who has always been in love with Cooper (he feels the same way about her, but has no intention of ever telling her his feelings). He then meets an old friend, Ellison, who plays the legendary Buffalo Bill Cody, along with Ellison's new wife, Burgess. Cooper had been earlier asked by Burgess why they must travel on a Sunday, to which he replies: "There's no Sunday west of Junction City, no law west of Hays City, and no God west of Carson City." All of them board the stagecoach and Arthur whips the horses toward their destination as Cooper rides with her atop the stage. Along the way, the coach stops when Indian scout Hayes is seen lying beside the roadway, seriously wounded. He tells Cooper that he was attacked by Cheyenne Indians using repeating rifles and now Cooper is convinced that Bickford is supplying the Indians with those weapons and that a plains war is about to erupt. Once they arrive at Hays City, Cooper gives his information about the Indian attack and the gun-runners to Miljan, who plays General Custer, and who then orders Ellison to guide a cavalry column carrying ammunition to an outpost and orders Cooper to locate his old friend, Yellow Hand, chief of the Cheyenne, and try to persuade him not to go to war. Meanwhile, Arthur provides shelter for Burgess while Ellison is away escorting the ammunition column. When Arthur hears that Cheyenne warriors are approaching the cabin, she hides Burgess and then confronts Varconi and other warriors who invade her cabin. She tries to buy them off by offering them trinkets and hats, but they take her prisoner. Cooper later sees Arthur being led on a rope by the Indians to Yellow Hand's camp, but he, too, is taken prisoner after he fails to negotiate Arthur's release. Held prisoner at the Cheyenne camp, Yellow Hand, played by Harvey, demands to know the whereabouts of the ammunition column led by Ellison, but Cooper refuses to give him that information. Seeing that Arthur is in love with Cooper, he uses her to obtain that information, torturing Cooper by dangling him over a roaring fire. Harvey tells Arthur that Cooper will die in the flames unless she tells him the whereabouts of the ammunition column, but if she gives him that information, Cooper's life will be spared and she and Cooper will be set free. Frantic with fear and concern over Cooper's fate, Arthur breaks down and gives Harvey

Gary Cooper, center, in *The Plainsman*, 1936.

the information and she and Cooper are then released, although Cooper is filled with disgust over Arthur's actions. While traveling back to Hays City, they see the ammunition column, along with Ellison, under siege by Harvey and his warriors as they defend themselves on a small island and where the soldiers are being picked off one by one by Indians surrounding them. Cooper then orders Arthur to make her way back to Miljan so that he can bring his troops to the rescue and he then joins Ellison and the besieged troopers on the island. The siege begins to take a terrible toll until only a handful of the troopers, along with Ellison, who is wounded, survive and where Cooper urges them to hold on to their nerves and continue fighting, even though some want to give up. Just as the Cheyenne make one more savage charge through the shallows of the river surrounding the island (the action during this battle is excitingly breathtaking), the beleaguered defenders hear the sound of a distant bugle blaring the charge and then see Miljan at the head of a cavalry column heroically dashing forward, with pointed sword, he and his troopers riding pell-mell into the Indian columns to break their charge and send them scurrying. Cooper then returns to Hays City and seeks out Bickford, the culprit who has armed Yellow Hand and his warriors, and, to enrich himself, has knowingly sent the Cheyenne on the warpath. Hall, who plays Jack McCall, Bickford's insidious paid informant, learns that Cooper is looking for Bickford and Bickford then offers gold to three army deserters led by Woods to kill Cooper. The three deserters take positions outside of Bickford's store and, when Cooper approaches, Woods blocks his path and insults him. Cooper realizes that the army deserters are substituting for Bickford and orders them to step aside, but Woods goes for his gun and Cooper fast draws his six-guns and kills all three men. (This thrilling gunfight recreates to some degree the actual gunfight Hickok had with two disorderly soldiers of the U.S. 7th Cavalry, who were stationed at Hays when Hickok was then the town marshal; the soldiers attacked him, and Hickok wounded one and fatally shot the other in the struggle on July 17, 1870.) Wounded in the fight, Cooper recovers while Bickford flees with his men, taking another shipment of guns toward Deadwood, South Dakota Territory. Wanted for the shooting of the soldiers, Cooper trails after Bickford, but Ellison is assigned by Miljan to track him down and bring Cooper back to stand trial for the shootings. Ellison finds Cooper in some woods where he has been waiting for him and he invites him to have breakfast. Ellison tells him that, though he is his friend, he is obligated to take Cooper back to Hays to stand trial, although Ellison knows he is no match for Cooper's fast draw. Before they confront each other, they hear some movement in the woods and discover Quinn, a Cheyenne warrior, loudly practicing an Indian rite to his gods. When they disarm and question Quinn, he brags about a great victory achieved by Sioux and Cheyenne warriors where they surrounded and destroyed the cavalry forces of

Custer (Miljan) and, as Quinn describes that fight, Miljan is shown as Custer and where he is making his last stand with his troopers and is killed. Realizing that the Cheyenne are about to also attack troops commanded by General Wesley Merritt (1836-1910), played by MacQuarrie, Cooper and Ellison agree that MacQuarrie must be warned, Ellison riding to warn MacQuarrie and Cooper going to Deadwood to try to stop Bickford from further arming the Indians. Ellison, taking Quinn in tow, departs, but not before telling Cooper that "you are still my prisoner." Cooper replies that he "will see you in Deadwood." When Cooper arrives in Deadwood, he finds that Arthur has opened a saloon and he renews his relationship with her, but when he sees Bickford arrive with his wagons and men, he goes to the street and confronts the gun-runner, telling him to remove the hides covering the freight in his wagon. Bickford climbs to the top of a wagon and, while pretending to remove a hide, goes for his gun. With a lightning-draw, Cooper shoots him dead. He then herds four of Bickford's men into Arthur's saloon, holding them there until Ellison can arrive in Deadwood with troops commanded by MacQuarrie. While waiting, Cooper (like Hickok) makes the mistake of sitting at a table and playing poker with these thugs by exposing his back to the slippery Hall, while Arthur is out of the saloon. One of the thugs, Kohler, tells Cooper that he has no intention of going for his gun because the only way anyone can kill Cooper is by shooting him in the back, a remark intended for Hall as a suggestion to do that very thing. Hall finds a gun in a drawer behind the counter and aims it at Cooper, firing and fatally shooting the legendary gunman, who topples to the floor as the thugs and Hall flee. Arthur, hearing the shot, races inside to cradle Cooper in her arms. Ellison then arrives with MacQuarrie and his troops and they round up Bickford's men and Hall. Ellison and MacQaurrie then stand above the body of Cooper and the mourning Arthur to state that they all owe Cooper a debt of gratitude for stopping another Indian uprising. DeMille directs this western opus with his usual flair for action and presents plenty of it, from gunfights to Indian attacks, all meticulously orchestrated. He dos not restrain the histrionics of some of his actors, such as those playing the besieged troopers in the fight on the island, especially the battle-fatigued Frank Albertson and Irving Bacon, who think, when they first hear the faint sound of a bugle from the on-coming relief column, that the dead are calling them to their graves and become hysterical until Cooper calms them down. Cooper is perfect as the taciturn Hickok and Arthur is ideal as Calamity Jane, feisty and caring with him all in the same breath and where she exhibits some considerable expertise with a whip. Ellison, Miljan, and especially the brutal Bickford, all give outstanding performances in this rousing and memorable western epic. Songs: "When Johnny Comes Marching Home" (Louis Lambert), "Yankee Doodle" (1755; traditional), "Rock-a-bye Baby" (1886; Effie I. Canning), "(I Wish I Was in) Dixie's Land" (1860; Daniel Decatur Emmett), "Oh Susanna" (1846; Stephen Foster), "The Battle Cry of Freedom" (1862; George Frederick Root). *Author's Note*: DeMille always relied upon experienced actors, but he made an exception for the first and only time by "discovering" Burgess in the Paramount's commissary, an eighteen-year-old starlet with no experience. He was so taken with her beauty that he cast her in a leading role in this film as Ellison's wife, but she tragically died of pneumonia shortly before the film was completed, as did, ironically, the leading screenwriter for the film, Young. As was his custom, DeMille dwelled on the costuming, props and sets for this western, insisting on authenticity in that the apparel worn by his actors befitted the era, along with the type of six-guns they used (he provided seventy such weapons from his own private collection for such use by his actors). DeMille hired more than 2,500 Sioux and Cheyenne Indians to perform in the film, shooting most of these extras in remote areas in Montana and using that footage in rear projection with his leading actors playing in front of the action on huge outdoor sets recreating the locales on Paramount's six-acre back lot. DeMille hired Cooper and Arthur after seeing them perform so well together in **Mr. Deeds Goes to Town**, 1936, but Arthur, as she told this author, was "nervous about working with the great DeMille.

Everyone knew that he would not tolerate a flubbed line or a miscue, so I sweated blood when delivering my lines as he watched me like a hawk. He got a little upset with me when I did not crack a whip I must use in corralling Coop toward me with enough force. I told him that I did not want to hurt him. 'You can't hurt him,' DeMille said, 'he's a big strapping man and he can take a stinging whiplash.' DeMille then turned to Coop [Cooper] and said, 'can't you?' Coop nodded and said, 'Yep.' I think that was the first time I ever heard him say 'Yep,' which everyone later said was his favorite trademarked word." Cooper told this author that his appearance in **The Plainsman** went "very smoothly. You could get along with DeMille as long as you followed everything he said to the letter. Wild Bill was my kind of character and I played him as the deliberate man he truly was and that is the character DeMille wanted, so we got along well." DeMille did not get along so well with Bickford, one of the most forceful character actors in Hollywood. In one scene where Bickford is menacing Cooper in a threatening manner, DeMille asked Bickford to take another approach, but Bickford kept delivering the scene with the same intonation in his words and using the same stance when confronting Cooper. DeMille stopped the scene and walked up to the burly Bickford, standing so close to him that their noses almost touched and said: "You are to try to intimidate Mr. Cooper, but don't you *ever* attempt to intimidate *me*!" Bickford nodded and, with the next take, Bickford followed DeMille's instructions. In his obsession for authenticity, DeMille insisted that a genuine Cheyenne Indian play the part of the warrior Cooper and Ellison find in the forest and who narrates the Custer Massacre in his native tongue. Paramount's casting office sent him Quinn, who performed that role just as DeMille envisioned the part being played. "I had appeared in only three pictures before getting that part in **The Plainsman**," Quinn told this author. "I was getting small parts in B-films when I answered a casting call for a Cheyenne brave that could give a war chant in his native language. I lied to the casting director and told him that I was a pure-blooded Cheyenne and spoke the language fluently. Before doing the scene with DeMille, to convince everybody that I was what I said I was, I insisted on putting on my own Indian costume and war paint, telling everyone that that was the way a Cheyenne warrior dressed and looked when he was ready for battle. I then did that scene for DeMille, hopping around with my own type of Indian war dance and I grunted out a lot of words that I thought sounded like what an Indian would say to himself after celebrating the massacre of Custer and his men. Of course, everything I said was a lot of gibberish, but I spat out those made-up words so forcefully and jerked my arms around and stomped the earth like a crazed warrior hopped up on peyote that DeMille bought the whole crazy bit and we did it in one take. DeMille then turned to one of his assistants and said: 'Now *that* is a *real* Indian!'" Quinn later married DeMille's adopted daughter, Katherine DeMille (in 1937, a year after the release of this film), who was also an actress, having five children with her before the marriage ended in 1965. "I trapped myself into a stereotype when I conned my way into that part in **The Plainsman**," Quinn told this author, "because directors thought that I could only play Indians. Years later I found myself playing Chief Crazy Horse in **They Died with Their Boots On** [1942], so being so damned smart in deceiving DeMille and the public, too, because audiences really believed my character as that Cheyenne warrior, well, all that did was to send me on the road to the reservation and a teepee." Many actors have essayed Wild Bill Hickok in many films, notably **Across the Sierras**, 1941 (Bill Elliott); **Calamity Jane**, 1953 (Howard Keel); **Dallas**, 1950 (Reed Hadley); **The Iron Horse**, 1924 (Jack Padjan); **The Lawless Breed**, 1953 (Robert Anderson); **Little Big Man**, 1970 (Jeff Corey); **The Outlaws Is Coming!**, 1965 (Paul Shannon); **Pony Express**, 1953 (Forrest Tucker); **Wild Bill**, 1995 (Jeff Bridges); **The White Buffalo**, 1977 (Charles Bronson); and **Wild Bill Hickok**, 1923 (William S. Hart). For more detailed compilations of films featuring Hickok, as well as Calamity Jane, William F. "Buffalo Bill" Cody, George Armstrong Custer and Yellow Hand see Index: Historical Characters, Volume II. For extensive details on James Butler "Wild Bill"

Astronaut Charlton Heston in *Planet of the Apes*, 1968.

Hickok, see my book, *Encyclopedia of Western Lawmen and Outlaws* (Paragon House, 1992; pages 155-160). **p&d**, Cecil B. DeMille; **cast**, Gary Cooper, Jean Arthur, James Ellison, Charles Bickford, Helen Burgess, Porter Hall, Paul Harvey, Victor Varconi, John Miljan, Frank Albertson, Anthony Quinn, George "Gabby" Hayes, Fuzzy Knight, Harry Woods, Monte Blue, Fred Kohler, George MacQuarrie, Francis Ford, Hank Worden, Chief Thundercloud; **w**, Waldemar Young, Harold Lamb, Lynn Riggs, Jeanie Macpherson (based on the stories "Wild Bill Hickok" by Frank J. Wilstach and "Wild Bill Hickok, the Prince of Pistoleers" by Courtney Ryley Cooper); **c**, Victor Milner, George Robinson; **m**, George Antheil; **ed**, Anne Bauchens; **art d**, Hans Dreier, Roland Anderson; **set d**, A.E. Freudeman; **spec eff**, Barney Wolff, Gordon Jennings, Farciot Edouart, Dewey Wrigley.

Planet of the Apes ★★★★ 1968; U.S.; 112m; APJAC Productions; FOX; Color; Horror/Science Fiction; Children: Cautionary (MPAA: G); **BD**; **DVD**; **VHS**. This superb sci-fi film, loaded with great action and special effects, proved so successful that it spawned many sequels and remakes, most of which also proved to be superior entries in the genre. Heston is outstanding as the commander of a U.S. spacecraft on an extended mission when the ship malfunctions and crashes on a strange planet. Only three of the crew, Heston, Gunner, and Jeff Burton, survive the landing and they soon find themselves among a tribe of humans that are living in the stone age, none of whom having the ability to speak. As they forage for food in a dense jungle with these non communicating creatures, they suddenly hear a strange blasting horn and then gunshots. As the astronauts flee with the other humans, they see, to their horror, apes wearing military uniforms and riding horses, all heavily armed and firing guns while pursuing the humans on horseback through the woods and tall grass. The apes employ nets to ensnare and capture the humans as if corralling wild animals, and then place them into cages. In the savage hunt, Heston is rendered as speechless as the cavemen captured after being shot in the throat. He and other captives are taken to the town of the apes and imprisoned. Meanwhile, his companions have suffered much more than Heston, Jeff Burton having been killed during the hunt. Gunner, too, has been captured and he is quickly silenced after he speaks when taken to a laboratory where top ape scientist Evans immediately performs a lobotomy that renders him mute. While recovering in his cell, Heston is treated kindly by other ape scientists Hunter and McDowall, who look upon him as a pet and come to believe that Heston possesses superior intelligence because of his attempt to communicate through his miming gestures. Evans tries to prevent Hunter and McDowall in further communicating with Heston as he knows that Heston is a human being with superior intelligence. Then Heston escapes, but is chased throughout the ape town and is finally recaptured, regaining

Apes in pursuit of humans in *Planet of the Apes*, 1968.

his ability to speak and shouting: "Take your stinking paws off me, you damned, dirty ape!" When Hunter and McDowall hear Heston speak, they resolve to keep him from the clutches of Evans, who has ordered Heston destroyed. They aid him in making an escape and take him to the "Forbidden Zone," an archeological dig that McDowall has been secretly developing to learn more about the sub-human species Heston represents, showing him curious and disturbing artifacts about Heston's species. At that time, Evans arrives with his soldier apes and attempts to capture McDowall, Hunter and Heston, but Heston turns the tables on Evans and captures him. While holding Evans hostage, Heston compels the ape leader to admit the truth, and Evans tells him how Heston's own species once ruled the planet, but their constant warring between nations brought their civilization to an end, allowing the apes to become the masters of the planet. With that, Heston steals a horse and intends to find some haven of civilization away from the dominating apes, but Evans prophetically tells him that "you will not like what you find." Heston rides from the "Forbidden Zone" and rides along a seashore, his horse galloping through its lapping waves until he has a vision that horrifies him more than anything he has experienced on this unknown planet. He drops limply from his horse and sinks to his knees, pounding his fists in rage into the sand, and saying: "You bastards! You finally did it! You blew it up! Damn you all to hell!" The camera then shows from Heston's point of view an iconic structure, but only the shattered head and arm of the Statue of Liberty, which is buried in the sand, and Heston now realizes that he has, in his long space journey, returned to his own native Earth and, during his time in space, the human race has destroyed its civilization through a nuclear holocaust. The scene that ends this fascinating film remains a classic finale to one of the most enduring science fiction films ever produced. Director Schaffner (who would go on to helm such classics as **Patton**, 1970; **Nicholas and Alexandra**, 1971; and **Papillon**, 1973) presents a totally fascinating portrait of a different world from the odd but acceptable perspectives of its ape masters, one that convincingly supports the image of that drastically altered world with marvelous sets and believable makeup (by John Chambers, who received an Oscar for his impressive ape creations) for the fine actors sweating beneath those ape costumes. The script from the gifted Serling is both witty and sardonic, grimly parodying the foibles and follies of the human race while ominously predicting its dire, self-destructive future, magnificently mixing fantasy with science fiction. Goldsmith's distinctively alarming and inventive score works well with every scene, and Shamroy's lensing is also superlative in capturing the many well-orchestrated action scenes as well as the more rational moments when apes and humans take stock of their violent past, disruptive present and a fearfully uncertain future. *Author's Note*: Heston was leery when he was first approached with an offer to appear in this film, telling this au-

thor that "I thought the idea was something out of an old serial in the late 1930s, a crazy notion for a picture, but when I read the script, I quickly changed my mind. It was written by a very talented writer, Rod Serling, and his writing is so lyrical and brilliantly conceived that it is very close to fine poetry. He and another scriptwriter [Wilson] had put together a thrilling tale that became more and more believable as I turned every page of that script, one that shows in startling detail what could have happened after Armageddon took place on Earth. That's when I decided to do the picture. Doing that picture was no picnic. I always keep in pretty good shape, but the almost non-stop action in that picture wore me out and I was amazed at how exhausting my role had become. I don't think I ever did such a more physically demanding role than in **Planet of the Apes**." **p**, Arthur P. Jacobs; **d**, Franklin J. Schaffner; **cast**, Charlton Heston, Roddy McDowall, Kim Hunter, Maurice Evans, James Whitmore, James Daly, Linda Harrison, Robert Gunner, Lou Wagner, Woodrow Parfrey, Jeff Burton, Army Archerd; **w**, Michael Wilson, Rod Serling (based on the novel *Monkey Planet* by Pierre Boulle); **c**, Leon Shamroy (Panavision; DeLuxe Color); **m**, Jerry Goldsmith; **ed**, Hugh S. Fowler; **art d**, Jack Martin Smith, William Creber; **set d**, Walter M. Scott, Norman Rockett; **spec eff**, L.B. Abbott, Art Cruickshank, Emil Kosa, Jr.

Planet of the Apes ★★★ 2001; U.S.; 119m; FOX; Color; Horror/Science Fiction; Children: Unacceptable (MPAA: PG-13); **BD**; **DVD**. Great action and special effects can be seen in this updated version of **Planet of the Apes,** 1968, which spawned a number of sequels. In this remake, Wahlberg is an Air Force astronaut on a routine reconnaissance mission where his spacecraft accidentally detours through a space time wormhole and crash lands on a mysterious planet where primitive humans are dominated by higher-evolved talking apes. A ape army led by Roth and his most trusted warrior, Duncan, threatens the planet. Wahlberg, with the help of a friendly chimpanzee activist, Bonham Carter, and a small band of human rebels, reaches a sacred temple where they discover the secrets to mankind's past and the key to its future, while defeating the apes. A sequel to this film was **Rise of the Planet of the Apes**, 2011. Other earlier films were **Beneath the Planet of the Apes**, 1970; **Escape from the Planet of the Apes**, 1971; **Conquest of the Planet of the Apes**, 1972; **Battle for the Planet of the Apes**, 1973; and television films and series also based on the same premise and characters. Music: "Rule the Planet Remix" (Paul Oakenfold). Excessive violence prohibits viewing by children. **p**, Richard D. Zanuck; **d**, Tim Burton; **cast**, Mark Wahlberg, Tim Roth, Helena Bonham Carter, Kris Kristofferson, Michael Clarke Duncan, Paul Giamatti, Estella Warren, Cary-Hiroyuki Tagawa, David Warner, Erick Avari; **w**, William Broyles, Jr., Lawrence Konner, Mark Rosenthal (based on the novel by Pierre Boulle); **c**, Philippe Rousselot; **m**, Danny Elfman; **ed**, Chris Lebenzon; **prod d**, Rick Heinrichs; **art d**, John Dexter, Sean Haworth, Philip Toolin; **set d**, Rosemary Brandenburg; **spec eff**, Garth Inns, Mark Freund, Bill George, Nathan and Emma McGuinness, Peter W. Moyer.

Planet of the Vampires ★★★ 1965; Spain/Italy; 86m; AIP (American International Pictures); Color; Horror/Science Fiction; Children: Unacceptable; **DVD**; **VHS**. Consistently frightening sci-fi film begins in the near future when two spaceships from Earth are sent to investigate the mysterious planet Aura. Sullivan, captain of one of the spacecraft, sees the companion spaceship vanish. Landing on Aura, Sullivan and his crew find the wreckage of their companion spaceship and see that its crew all killed each other. A scientist concludes that Aura is inhabited by vampires seeking to inhabit the bodies of humans. Sullivan also learns that the aliens plan to leave Aura and resettle on Earth and suck it dry of human blood. Sullivan plans to escape Aura, but suspects that some of his crew members may have become vampires, and he must determine who is normal and who is a lurking vampire before returning to Earth. A good horror film that provides consistent fright throughout, but its excessive violence prohibits viewing by children. **p**, Fulvio Lucisano; **d**, Mario Bava; **cast**, Barry Sullivan, Norma Bengell, Ángel Aranda, Evi Marandi, Stelio Candelli, Franco Andrei, Fernando Villena, Mario Morales, Ivan Rassimov, Federico Boido, Alberto Cevenini; **w**, Bava, Alberto Bevilacqua, Callisto Cosulich, Louis M. Heyward, Ib Melchior, Antonio Román, Rafael J. Salvia (based on the story "One Night of 21 Hours" by Renato Pestriniero); **c**, Antonio Pérez Olea, Antonio Rinaldi (Colorscope; Pathe Color); **m**, Gino Marinuzzi, Jr.; **ed**, Romana Fortini, Antonio Gimeno; **set d**, Giorgio Giovannini; **spec eff**, Bava, Carlo Rambaldi.

Platinum Blonde ★★★ 1931; U.S.; 89m; COL; B/W; Comedy; Children: Acceptable; **DVD**; **VHS**. Pantheon director Capra presents an incisive look at the divergent class differences between the rich and the poor through the eyes of a hard working newspaper reporter, Williams. At the same time, Capra presents a nifty romantic triangle as two women, Young and Harlow, vie for Williams' attention while he adds a considerable amount of humor in this entertaining comedy. Williams works for a scandal sheet edited by Breese, an editor who demands that his reporters produce a scoop for his front page every day. Williams gets the opportunity to have that scoop when he gets hold of a batch of letters written by wealthy cad Dillaway to a conniving chorus girl, who has sued Dillaway for breach of promise (which was the rage and raw meat content for the tabloids of that era of the 1920s and 1930s). Williams, however, decides not to socially destroy Dillaway because he is enamored of Dillaway's beautiful, younger sister, Harlow (the "platinum blonde" in the film's title). As Williams turns over Dillaway's letter to him, he gratefully introduces the reporter to the vivacious Harlow, a leading lady in the social set, and they begin a relationship that disturbs Young, a female reporter who works with Williams and has loved him from afar. Young is devastated when Williams marries Harlow, but is helpless as she remains in the romantic doldrums and Williams then gets a good dose of the leisure class. Williams soon comes to dislike if not despise Harlow's hypocritical relatives, particularly the obnoxious and biased Hale, who is Harlow's aristocratic mother. With all the money and time to play that he can ever have, Williams soon grows bored with his newfound lifestyle among the social elite and he yearns to return to writing. He decides to write a play lampooning his arrogant in-laws, but, since he has never written one, he calls upon Young's advice and invites her to be his collaborator. She is thrilled to rejoin Williams if only to be at his side as a writing colleague and she goes to work with him in Harlow's mansion. Young also brings along a bevy of colorful newspaper reporters and editors, who turn Harlow's estate into a fun palace, ridiculing its permanent occupants and vexing its major domo, Hobbes, who plays the snootiest head butler ever to disdainfully sniff his way in and out of a scene. Harlow, who has been away enjoying her usual social swirls, returns to her mansion to find this crowd of rowdy, hard-drinking people taking over her domicile and explodes by angrily ordering these lowlife invaders from the premises. Williams takes her offensive remarks to his friends as a personal insult and gives Harlow a piece of his mind, a verbal blast that indicts her and her entire tribe of pretentious relatives and friends. They later dissolve their union and now Williams sees that the woman he most loves and who loves him is the patient Young and they plan a life together. Capra directs with a furious pace in presenting this hectic comedy, drawing good performances from Williams, Harlow, Young and the rest of the cast in the process, and the inventive Swerling (a veteran newspaperman), Robert Riskin and Dorothy Howell provide a witty script peppered with some very good comedic scenes. Song: "A Bird in a Gilded Cage" (1900; music: Harry von Tilzer; lyrics: Arthur J. Lamb). Capra would expand upon the theme of the wealthy and high society five years later when producing his masterpiece, **Mr. Deeds Goes to Town**, 1936, which also deals with the scandal-mongering tabloids, as does his earlier classic comedy-romance, **It Happened One Night**, 1934. Other films profiling scandal sheets or tabloids include **Buried Alive**, 1939; **Cain and Mabel**, 1936; **Dirt**, 2007-2008 (TV series); **Five Star Final**, 1931; **The**

Jean Harlow, Robert Williams and Loretta Young in *Platinum Blonde*, 1931.

Front Page, 1931; **The Front Page**, 1974; Go to Hell, 1999; **His Girl Friday**, 1940; **L.A. Confidential**, 1997; **Lonelyhearts**, 1958; **Love Is News**, 1937; **The Murder Man**, 1935; **The Naked Truth**, 1995-1998 (TV series); **Picture Snatcher**, 1933; **Scandal Sheet**, 1931; **Scandal Sheet**, 1939; **Scandal Sheet**, 1952; **Scandal Sheet**, 1985 (made-for-TV); **Sex and the Single Girl**, 1964; **The Story on Page One**, 1959; **While the City Sleeps**, 1956; and **Winchell**, 1998 (made-for-TV). *Author's Note*: Capra told this author that "I had a hard time with Jo [Swerling] when we first met and he chopped up my script for **Ladies of Leisure** [1930], telling Harry Cohn, head of Columbia, that I wrote terrible scripts that were 'inane, pompous, and unbelievable,' and that my script for **Ladies of Leisure** was 'a putrid piece of gorgonzola.' Jo told Cohn that he hated Hollywood and hated Cohn and did not like me much either, calling me Cohn's 'little tin Jesus.' Well, here I was assigned to do another picture that was written by Jo and Bob Riskin and Dottie Howell, but I must tell you that it was a corker that not only had one terrific comedy scene after another but also allowed me to show the real workings of newspapers in those days, especially the tabloids, which I had always wanted to do. So I felt indebted to Jo and Bob and Dottie and I worked with Jo and Bob in making my next picture with Babs [Barbara] Stanwyck, **The Miracle Woman** [1931], and they gave me another terrific script for that picture, too." Riskin would prove to be one of Capra's most long-lasting script collaborators, writing nine screenplays for Capra and the director basing four more films on Riskin's writings. Young told this author that "Frank Capra was always wonderful to work with, such a charming and gentle man, and always full of ideas. No director ever planned his camera setups as carefully as Frank, except for, perhaps, Alfred Hitchcock, who drew little sketches of his camera setups and then had his crew and camera people religiously follow those drawings. **Platinum Blonde** was a lot of fun to do, especially with Jean [Harlow] who had a great sense of humor and was always making very funny remarks, but never at the expense of anyone, except maybe that bully over at MGM, Wallace Beery, who verbally abused her, even in his sleep. What I remember most about that picture was that its two stars, Jean and Bob [Williams] died tragically early in life. Bob was a natural comedian, a handsome, sleepy-eyed fellow who could make you laugh with a wrinkled brow and a sly grin. He got rave reviews when **Platinum Blonde** was released and critics were all saying that he would soon become Hollywood's next big star, but, only a few days after the film was released, he suddenly died of an appendicitis attack [on November 3, 1931] and he was only thirty seven years old. Jean, too, did not have long to live. She died six years later [on June 7, 1937] and she was only twenty-six. I think of those two early tragic deaths every time I think of **Platinum Blonde**, a very funny film for most everyone, but for me, it represents deep sorrow." **p**, Harry Cohn;

Tom Berenger, Mark Moses and Willem Dafoe in *Platoon*, 1986.

d, Frank Capra; **cast**, Loretta Young, Robert Williams, Jean Harlow, Halliwell Hobbes, Reginald Owen, Edmund Breese, Donald Dillaway, Walter Catlett, Louise Closser Hale, Bill Elliott; **w**, Jo Swerling, Dorothy Howell, Robert Riskin (based on the story by Harry E. Chandlee, Douglas W. Churchill); **c**, Joseph Walker; **m**, David Broekman; **ed**, Gene Milford; **art d**, Stephen Goosson.

Platoon ★★★★ 1986; U.K./U.S.; 120m; Hemdale Film/Cinema 86/Orion Pictures; Color; War Drama; Children: Unacceptable (MPAA: R); **BD**; **DVD**; **VHS**. Gritty and uncompromising, this view of the Vietnam War (1955-1975) from director Stone differs greatly from many other Hollywood productions. His portrait is one of survival in a land where all is hostile, from the oppressive heat, deadly insects and poisonous snakes, and a savage and fanatical enemy lurking beneath the ground and within the dense jungle foliage. College dropout Sheen, who has volunteered for duty in this attritional war, is assigned to a company of soldiers who do not share his ideals and are only concerned with surviving the war. After a brief firefight with troops of the North Vietnamese Army (NVA), Sheen is upbraided by ruthless sergeant Berenger for having recklessly thrown a grenade that has wounded another American soldier, even though this thoughtless act has been performed by another soldier. Sheen nevertheless bonds with a small group of soldiers, especially David, Depp and Whitaker, while another sergeant, Dafoe, a considerate and ethical non-com, becomes his avuncular mentor. During a patrol, Sheen sees some of his fellow soldiers killed by booby traps and finds another tied to a post who has been savagely mutilated. When the patrol enters a village, Sheen discovers an elderly woman and an injured young man cowering in a spider hole, and when they emerge, he loses control, screaming at them and believing they are in league with the enemy. He is shocked to his senses when Dillon steps forth and beats the wounded young man to death. Berenger then begins to grill the local chief, an old man, but when his wife interferes and begins haranguing Berenger, he summarily shoots her to death. He then seizes the chief's daughter, threatening to shoot her, too, if he is not given information about the enemy. Dafoe then arrives and, after he sees the wanton slaughter of these civilians, tongue-lashes Berenger for his criminal behavior. Moses, the indifferent and irresponsible lieutenant who commands the unit, then breaks up the pushing-shoving argument between Dafoe and Berenger and orders his men to burn the village. While departing, Sheen prevents some soldiers from raping two young girls. (A similar, more brutal depiction of such sexual savagery on the part of U.S. soldiers in Vietnam is shown in **Casualties of War**, 1989, where Michael J. Fox vainly tries to stop a group of GIs from raping and eventually murdering a young Vietnamese girl.) When the patrol returns to its base, the company commander, Dye, warns his men

that if he discovers any soldier having committed illegal killings, that soldier will face a court-martial, a caution that alarms Berenger as he now worries that Dafoe might reveal his actions to his commander. On the next patrol, Sheen sees his friends Whitaker and Depp wounded during an ambush by hidden enemy troops and where a mortar strike on the uncertain enemy position explodes among the Americans. Dafoe then takes Sheen and another soldier on a reconnaissance patrol to locate and counter-ambush flanking enemy troops, but races ahead of them and is lost from sight. Berenger meanwhile orders the rest of the platoon to retreat as he goes in search of Dafoe and, when finding him, wounds him. He then finds Sheen and tells him that Dafoe has been killed by enemy fire, a report that Sheen does not believe. The retreating troops are evacuated by helicopter, including the wounded Depp, who dies before reaching base. As the copters begin to lift off and fly away from the area, Sheen sees Dafoe emerge from the jungle wounded, with enemy troops on his trail, and he is finally killed by his dogged pursuers. Now Sheen knows that Berenger was lying and, at the base that night, he tells other soldiers that Berenger is deranged and dangerous, but Berenger arrives and threatens him, scarring his face with a knife. Whitaker is sent home, wishing Sheen luck, which seems to be running out on him, especially when the platoon is now ordered to take up a frontline defensive position to repel an expected attack by overwhelming enemy forces. The GIs occupy deep foxholes masked with brush and logs, and Sheen shares one of these with Glover as night falls and the enemy approaches; the sounds of their footfalls and the breaking of foliage heralds that ominous approach (and here Stone employs the same kind of anxiety-packed tension as can be found in many other war films such as the GIs waiting for Japanese troops to attack their position in **Bataan**, 1943; **The Pride of the Marines**, 1945, and **Sands of Iwo Jima**, 1949). The enemy then makes an all-out assault on the American defense line, and though many are killed by the GIs, they overrun the area, shooting and killing most of the defenders, and the cowardly McGinley uses the body of his foxhole companion to hide from the enemy. Glover and Sheen are wounded while the company command area is also overrun and where commander Dye bravely calls down an air strike on his own area to destroy the enemy, one that will also take the lives of his own men. Sheen finds Berenger leaving the fight, but he turns on Sheen, knowing that he possesses knowledge that can send him to prison. He knocks Sheen to the ground and is about to kill him when the American fighter planes arrive, dropping devastating napalm bombs that obliterate the enemy, the flames scorching and scything jungle and humans alike. The next morning, Sheen regains consciousness and sees Berenger, horribly wounded. Picking up a weapon, he points it at Berenger, who orders him to shoot him and Sheen complies. Sheen then thinks to end his own life, but reinforcements led by his friend Quinn arrive; Glover and the wounded Sheen are taken to the reestablished base where they are put aboard helicopters en route home, and a much safer and saner world. As the copter lifts off, Quinn stands on the ground, bidding farewell to his friend and thumping his chest to indicate that he will stay in the fight to the last. The copter flies away, and Sheen looks back sorrowfully to see innumerable bodies of foes and friends being tossed into bomb craters as their common graves. Stone shows no mercy to the viewer in his bloody portrait of war, one so realistic and horrific that it shocked audiences when it was released, but so expertly presented that it received an Oscar for Best Picture and Stone received an Oscar for Best Director; the film also received Oscars for Best Editing (Simpson) and Best Sound Mixing. Berenger and Dafoe each received Oscar nominations as Best Supporting Actor and Stone also received an Oscar nomination for Best Screenplay. An enormous success at the box office, Platoon earned more than $138 million in its initial release against a $6.5 million budget. Songs: "Adagio for Strings" (Samuel Barber), "White Rabbit" (Grace Slick), "Track of My Tears" (William Robinson, Marvin Tarplin, Warren Moore), "Okie from Muskogee" (Merle Haggard), "Oh! Susanna" (1848; Stephen Foster). Excessive violence, gutter language and sexuality prohibit viewing by children. *Author's Note*: **Platoon** was shot within fifty-four days and on location on the Philippine island of Luzon, where Stone employed several Vietnamese refugees as extras. Stone, who served as an infantryman in the Vietnam War in 1968, claimed that he wanted to present a wholly different view of that war from the version presented in the more stylish production of the war as depicted in John Wayne's **The Green Berets**, 1968. He draws a portrait of American troops that are chiefly the flotsam and jetsam of American society, social misfits, school dropouts, the offspring of essentially uneducated blue-collar families, and where a goodly number of those GIs are blacks, who have come from disenfranchised lifestyles in the U.S. (and in this his portrayal of that social makeup is largely correct, although he takes a leaf from the portrait of the cowardly black soldier, enacted by Woody Strode, in **Pork Chop Hill**, 1959, Strode being one of those disenfranchised African-American citizens who has nothing worthwhile waiting for him if he is fortunate enough to survive that war). Stone's platoon, however, is manned by more repulsive sociopaths, psychopaths and cowards than ever made up a single unit in American military history, far exceeding the collection of misfits profiled in **The Dirty Dozen**, 1967. His savage and revealing indictment of that woefully mismanaged political war is nevertheless accurate in its unrelenting portrait of the day-to-day inhuman brutalities inflicted upon a generation of American youth and the civilians of Vietnam by that war, a war as unpopular and unsanctioned now as it was when it was being waged. The use of drugs by the troops is openly exhibited in **Platoon**, but I was aware of that use when my younger brother, Jack, a U.S. Marine, who fought and was wounded in that war, explained how morphine was freely administered to American troops before any anticipated action to dull their senses, as well as the flagrant indecision displayed by Vietnamese authorities during that conflict. "We were ordered to take a hill one day," that brother said to me, "and we took it and were then ordered to abandon it after some South Vietnamese politician in Saigon demanded we give up the place. We then got orders to retake the hill and did it, after a South Vietnamese general countermanded the politician's order. Going up and down that hill cost the lives of more than twenty of our men, all because two men in Saigon could not make up their minds." Many other films have portrayed the Vietnam War at the front and at home, most notably **Apocalypse Now**, 1979; **The Beautiful Country**, 2005; **Birdy**, 1984; **Born on the Fourth of July**, 1989; **Casualties of War**, 1989; **Coming Home**, 1978; **The Deer Hunter**, 1979; **Full Metal Jacket**, 1987; **Getting Straight**, 1970; **Go Tell the Spartans**, 1978; **Good Morning, Vietnam**, 1987; **The Green Berets**, 1968; **Hamburger Hill**, 1987; **Medium Cool**, 1969; **The Messenger**, 2009; **Rescue Dawn**, 2007; **Running on Empty**, 1988; **The Siege of Firebase Gloria**, 1989; **Some May Live**, 1967; **The Stunt Man**, 1980; **Tigerland**, 2000; **We Were Soldiers**, 2002; and **Who'll Stop the Rain**, 1978, all of which are profiled in this work. For additional films, including made-for-TV productions and TV series, see Index, Historical Events, Vietnam War, in Vol. II of this work. **p**, Arnold Kopelson, A. Kitman Ho; **d&w**, Oliver Stone; **cast**, Tom Berenger, Willem Dafoe, Charlie Sheen, Johnny Depp, Keith David, Francesco Quinn, Forest Whitaker, Kevin Dillon, John C. McGinley, Francesco Quinn, Chris Pedersen, Bob Orwig, Corkey Ford, Mark Moses, Dale Dye, Corey Glover; **c**, Robert Richardson; **m**, Georges Delerue; **ed**, Claire Simpson; **prod d**, Bruno Rubeo; **art d**, Rodell Cruz, Doris Sherman Williams; **spec eff**, Yves De Bono, Rudy Candaza.

Play Dirty ★★★ 1969; U.K.; 118m; Lowndes Productions/UA; Color; War; Children: Unacceptable; **DVD**. Gritty war tale sees Caine as a British oil executive assigned to work with the British army in North Africa during World War II, where he busies himself by handling port duties for incoming fuel and supplies. Green, a British colonel in charge of a tough group of commandos, is ordered to take Caine with them on a dangerous mission 400 miles behind Nazi lines. Caine tries unsuccessfully to stay behind in the safety of the port, but his military expertise works against his ambitions to save his own hide. Davenport, the leader

Michael Caine and Nigel Davenport in *Play Dirty*, 1969.

of the "Dirty Dozen" British group (made up of ex-convicts), does not want Caine along, considering him a liability, but Green insists that Caine be included and he is eventually pressed into service and undergoes the mission. Disguised in German uniforms, the British commandos trek across the German-held desert and engage in some hazardous battles before they manage to accomplish their mission. Caine and only three men surviving the near suicidal mission are then shot and killed by British soldiers after mistaking them as enemy soldiers as they are wearing German uniforms. Caine gives a pensive but compelling performance as a reluctant hero and gets strong support from the dynamic Green and the rest of the cast. Songs: "Lili Marlene" (Norbert Schultze, Hans Leip), "You Are My Sunshine" (Jimmie Davis, Charles Mitchell), "Tornerai" (Dino Olivieri, Nino Rastelli). *Author's Note*: Many films have profiled the desert campaigns in North Africa during WWII, notably **The Desert Fox: The Story of Rommel**, 1951; **The Desert Rats**, 1953; **Five Graves to Cairo**, 1943; **Immortal Sergeant**, 1943; **Patton**, 1970; **Raid on Rommel**, 1971; **Sahara**, 1943; and **Tobruk**, 1967. Excessive violence prohibits viewing by children. **p**, Harry Saltzman; **d**, Andre De Toth; **cast**, Michael Caine, Nigel Davenport, Nigel Green, Harry Andrews, Patrick Jordan, Daniel Pilon, Martin Burland, George McKeenan, Bridget Espeet, Bernard Archard, Aly Ben Ayed; **W**, Lotte Colin, Melvyn Bragg (based on a story by George Marton); **c**, Edward Scaife (Technicolor); **m**, Michel Legrand; **ed**, Jack Slade, Alan Osbiston; **art d**, Tom Morahan, Maurice Pelling, Elven Webb; **spec eff**, Kit West.

Play It Again, Sam ★★★★ 1972; U.S.; 85m; PAR; Color; Comedy; Children: Cautionary (MPAA: PG); **DVD**; **VHS**. Allen is again hilarious in one of his finest comedies, this time as a film reviewer plagued by every neurosis known to mankind. A manic movie maven, his favorite film is **Casablanca** [1942]; this film opens with Allen, mouth agape, watching the closing scenes of that film in a San Francisco revival theater, and he immerses himself inside the persona of that film's leading tough guy character, Humphrey Bogart. However, Allen has none of Bogart's manly attributes of resolution, confidence and courage. He is a trembling, teetering titmouse of a fellow, who has just lost his wife, Anspach, who can no longer tolerate his inert life, telling him: "You're one of life's great watchers [of movies]. I'm not like that. I'm a doer." After Anspach departs, Allen thinks to begin dating again, but the idea of attempting to establish any kind of relationship with another woman gives him so much anxiety that he suffers mental fatigue. Depressed and forlorn, he is visited in an apparition of the great man himself, Bogart (played in wonderful parody by Lacy, who bears an amazing likeness to Bogart as he wears his traditional trench-coat and puffs incessantly on cigarettes). Bogart becomes his avuncular adviser, encouraging him

Woody Allen and Diane Keaton in *Play It Again, Sam*, 1972.

to go out into the world and find the right woman. His advice to Allen is direct, if not severe, saying: "Dames are simple. I never met one that didn't understand a slap in the mouth or a slug from a forty-five." Allen ventures again into the dating world after being encouraged by close friends Keaton and Roberts, a married couple who have known Allen for years and put up with his constant complaints and alleged allergies. They arrange a date with Salt, but she will have nothing to do with him after he acts like some abusive character out of one of Bogart's gangster movies. He next dates sex-craved Viva, but their romance winds up at a dead end. Allen then meets sweet but naïve Bang, but this encounter turns to disaster when bikers beat him up and make off with the confused girl. Keaton decides to cook a dinner for Allen to cheer him up after her husband Roberts leaves on another business trip (he is forever going to business meetings and woefully neglects his wife). Allen, who has always been attracted to her, has a candlelight dinner with Keaton, champagne and all, and thinks to make a move on her, but lacks the courage. Bogart then appears (and only Allen ever sees this tough guy mirage) to inspire Allen to make an advance, but, after Allen kisses Keaton, the surprised woman becomes disoriented and quickly departs. However, she returns a short time later, and she and Allen spend the night together. The next morning, Keaton is consumed by guilt and remorse at having betrayed Roberts, who then unexpectedly returns home. Roberts senses that something is wrong and concludes that she is seeing another man, confiding these suspicions to Allen, telling him that he loves Keaton more than anything and, if he discovers the identity of that other man, he will kill that romantic interloper. Roberts is then compelled to take another business trip, but Keaton resolves to go to the airport to assure him that she still needs and wants him. Allen, too, rushes to the airport, accompanied by his otherworld mentor, Bogart, who continues to give him advice on how to keep the marriage between Keaton and Roberts intact. The three stand on the runway of the San Francisco Airport as fog rolls in and Allen is delirious with joy in that it is the exact setting of the final scenes in his favorite film, **Casablanca**, and he has the opportunity to duplicate Bogart's lines. He admits to Roberts that he loves Keaton, but insists that she and Roberts get on the plane together to keep their marriage together and they do so. Allen, who has now become confident and strong-willed to manage his own affairs, tells Bogart that he no longer needs him and they part as fast friends, with Bogart calling after Allen with his most memorable line from **Casablanca**: "Here's looking at you, kid." Thus ends this sentimental sojourn into the filmic past Allen so admires and loves. The presence of Bogart (Lacy) throughout the film poignantly represents the intellectual and emotional ties Allen has displayed throughout his illustrious comedic career with the Hollywood of yesterday, and he does it with such humorous flair that the viewer is caught up in his imaginary

relationship with tough guy Bogart. Allen, Keaton, Roberts and the rest of the cast are outstanding in their roles, all deftly directed by Ross, and Allen's brilliant script presents a bevy of entertaining bon mots and clever asides (particularly in the dialog exchanges with Bogart and Allen). It is first-class nostalgia sandwiching the nervous and uncertain present with the noble and reliable past, packaged with the kind of off-beat humor that only the brilliant Allen can conjure. What a delight. Songs: "Blues for Alan Felix" (Oscar Peterson), "As Time Goes By" (Herman Hupfeld), "La Marseillaise" (1792; Claude Joseph Rouget de Lisle). *Author's Note*: The production was shot in San Francisco instead of Allen's beloved New York since New York City was then suffering widespread labor strikes. The story is based upon Allen's play, which opened on February 12, 1969, and ran for 453 performances, closing on March 14, 1970, and Allen, Keaton, Roberts and Lacy reprise their roles in this superlative film. This was the first of six film appearances Keaton and Allen would make together. Although Ross directs this film, and brings a firm sense of dramatic organization that is lacking in Allen's previous films that are mostly made up of sight gags and slapstick, such as his earlier outings **Bananas**, 1971, and **Take the Money and Run**, 1969, Allen's imprimatur is everywhere in every scene. Endemic to the great success this film enjoyed is Lacy's impressive role as the inimitable Bogart, reminding the viewer in his every scene that he, more than most, would be the one man anyone would want in a crisis. Allen would extend his clever nostalgic use of old Hollywood by going so far as to have a character step from the screen in an old 1930s melodrama and into the real world of that same era to bring love and joy to an otherwise forlorn and lonely woman in the equally entertaining **The Purple Rose of Cairo**, 1985. **p**, Arthur P. Jacobs; **d**, Herbert Ross; **cast**, Woody Allen, Diane Keaton, Tony Roberts, Jerry Lacy, Susan Anspach, Jennifer Salt, Joy Bang, Viva, Suzanne Zenor, Diana Davila, Mari Fletcher, Michael Greene; **w**, Allen (based on his play); **c**, Owen Roizman (Technicolor); **m**, Billy Goldenberg; **ed**, Marion Rothman; **prod d**, Ed Wittstein; **set d**, Doug Von Koss.

Play Misty for Me ★★★★ 1971; U.S.; 102m; UNIV; Color; Crime Drama; Children: Unacceptable (MPAA: R); **DVD; VHS**. Eastman makes a spectacular debut as a director in this classic tale that turns the life of a free-wheeling bachelor into a murderous nightmare as he is stalked by a woman who refuses to be anything other than a one-night plaything. Eastwood stars in the role of a handsome, young disk jockey living the high life in laid-back Carmel, California. He has a pad by the sea and plays whatever cool songs suit him as they suit most his devoted listeners, who are also cool and laid-back. Although Eastwood is not looking for any strings attached to him, he has a steady girlfriend, Mills, an artist, who is equally independent minded. Mills tells him that she wants a break from their relationship so that she can contemplate her lifestyle, future and art, and leaves the area. Left alone and without his romantic creature comforts, Eastwood goes on the hunt for some companionship, finding more than what he expects when frequenting his favorite drinking spa. He encounters Walter, a sophisticated and attractive woman, who, it turns out, is one of his biggest fans, a listener who has regularly asked him to play Errol Garner's "Misty" for her and which he has routinely done almost on a nightly basis. They retire to Walter's upscale residence, both agreeing that this tryst will be only a one-night affair, and, in the morning, Eastwood goes on his carefree way. The following night, however, he is shocked and disturbed to see Walter unexpectedly appear at his home, more or less implying that she is about to move in and become his life mate. Courteous and kind, Eastwood tolerates her intrusion, but tells her that he has no intention of continuing an affair with her. Walter, however, is not taking no for an answer. Meanwhile, Mills returns and, after having mulled over things, tells Eastwood that she wants to remain with him, news that is welcomed by the DJ. While spending all his free time with Mills, Eastwood distractively puts off Walter, who persistently calls him. When those calls become overwhelming, Eastwood arranges a meeting with Walter where he deliberately and patiently explains that they have no relationship together and that he is seeing another woman and that he wants all contact between them to cease immediately. Walter goes to pieces, babbling that she loves only Eastwood and that they must make a life together. Eastwood firmly tells her that she must leave, and she responds to this order by immediately slashing her wrists; Eastwood frantically binds up her wounds, calling a physician, who tells Eastwood to keep her sedated and in his house until she recuperates and has regained her senses enough to leave for her own domicile. Guilt-ridden, Eastwood complies, but becomes a prisoner to his patient as she begins to whine and plead and beg whenever he attempts to leave his own home. He slips out of the house to go to an important meeting with Hervey, the female owner of the radio station where he works, and all goes well at that restaurant meeting until he and Hervey are interrupted by Walter. She suddenly appears to scream at Eastwood that he is cheating on her with another woman, Hervey. Eastwood angrily hustles her out of the restaurant, but when he returns, Hervey, embarrassed by Walter's accusations, calls the meeting to an end. Eastwood returns to his home to find that the entire place has been torn to pieces, his personal clothing shredded and belongings smashed. He finds his housekeeper on the verge of dying after having been slashed several times with a razor wielded by Walter. Police are summoned, and detective Larch, takes over the case, which is now a criminal matter. Walter is located by Larch and she is then determined to be insane and is institutionalized. After she is placed in a sanitarium, Eastwood breathes a sigh of great relief, now believing this grim episode in his life is only a bitter memory. He goes back to Mills, who later tells him that she has acquired a new roommate and that the three of them should get together. When Eastwood goes to the station that night, he receives a phone call from a listener, asking him to "play 'Misty' for me," recognizing the voice as that of Walter. She explains that she has been cured of her mental maladies and is all right now and is calling to say goodbye. Eastwood says farewell (and good riddance), but, later that night while he sleeps, he awakes to see Walter hovering over him with a knife raised, one she is about to plunge into him. In a quick move, Eastwood manages to avoid the blade Walters slashes toward him and, before he can disarm her, she races out of the house and into the night. Eastwood then concludes that the scheming Walter has escaped the sanitarium and is hiding out in disguise as Mills' new roommate and he contacts Larch to check on Mills. When he later goes to Mills' home, Eastwood finds Larch dead inside Mills' residence, seeing a pair of scissors plunged into his chest. Frantically searching for Mills, Eastwood finds her alive but bound and gagged just as Walter is about to slash her to death with a razor. Eastwood goes after the hysterically screaming woman, who, in her crazed actions, slashes wildly at him, cutting him several times, until Eastwood can send a crashing fist into Walter's face, the powerful blow propelling her onto a terrace and where she tumbles over the railing, plummeting to her death on the rocks below. This shocking psychological thriller is superbly directed by Eastwood, who carefully builds his story and characters to mounting tension without telegraphing the ever-increasing hazards and eventual mayhem to come. Walter gives a stunning performance of an insidious, mentally disturbed person bent on murderous revenge when denied the love she so desperately craves. Eastwood's selection of Carmel, California, as a backdrop for this startling film is a shrewd one, in that this resort area for the leisure class is the perfect setting for its developing and unprecedented violence as its calm and comfortable surroundings lull the viewer into a false sense of security, the bloodletting to come from Eastwood otherwise seldom seen in such a haven of tranquility and peace. This film proved to be such an enormous success that it established Eastwood as a first-rate director, allowing him to helm many a fine film to come. Shot on the meager budget of $750,000, the film returned more than $10,600,000 at the box office in its initial release. Songs: "Misty" (Errol Garner); "The First Time Ever I Saw Your Face" (Ewan McColl); "Preacher's Blues" (Gene Connors), "Willie and the Hand Jive" (Johnny Otis); "Country Preacher" (Joseph Sawinul); "Feelin' Fine," "Dirty

Jessica Walters and Clint Eastwood in *Play Misty for Me*, 1971.

Boogie" (Gator Creek); "It's Not Unusual" (Gordon Mills, Les Reed). *Author's Note*: Eastwood so liked the Monterey, California, area that he took residence there and even became Carmel's mayor (1986-1988). Up to the time of directing this film, Eastwood had appeared as an actor in chiefly successful western films, including the spaghetti westerns he made with Italian director Sergio Leone. He had always wanted to become a film director and asked CBS to allow him to direct some of the episodes of "Rawhide," the TV western series in which he was starring, but the network refused to let him get behind the camera. The story for this eerie tale was written by Jo Heims (1930-1978), a former model and dancer, who was a friend of Eastwood's and who optioned the script from her. After he failed to interest any studio in producing the film, Eastwood turned the script back to Heims, who then sold it to Universal. Two years later, Eastwood went to Universal and convinced executives to allow him to direct the film, promising the studio that he would not only bring it in under budget and ahead of time, but that he would take a percentage of the profits and no salary. He completed the film in record time, using only $750,000 of the production's $1,242,000 budget, which elated studio bosses. With this film, Eastwood became known as a reliable, no-nonsense director, who could complete popular films on schedule and under budget and that assured his success with Hollywood studios in the many years to come. The song "The First Time Ever I Saw Your Face," sung by Roberta Flack during a love scene in the film, went to the top of the charts. **p**, Robert Daley; **d**, Clint Eastwood; **cast**, Eastwood, Jessica Walter, Donna Mills, John Larch, Jack Ging, Irene Hervey, James McEachin, Clarice Taylor, Donald Siegel, Duke Everts, George Fargo, Cannonball Adderley and his Quintet; **w**, Jo Heims, Dean Riesner (based on a story by Heims); **c**, Bruce Surtees (Technicolor); **m**, Dee Burton; **ed**, Carl Pingitore; **art d**, Alexander Golitzen; **set d**, Ralph Hurst.

The Playboy of the Western World ★★★★ 1963; Ireland; 100m; Four Provinces Films/Janus Films; Color; Comedy; Children: Cautionary; **VHS**. This superlative production is set in a quiet village in early 1900s County Mayo, Ireland, and, especially, one young woman, McKenna, falls under the spell of Raymond, a charming but roguish young stranger, who appears among the residents one day. He claims to a crowd of boisterous patrons in a rowdy pub to have killed his father, one of the most disliked men in the area, and, oddly enough, is universally admired for the crime, until his irate father shows up very much alive and in pursuit of his deceitful and cowardly son. The stage masterpiece of satire from Synge, one of Ireland's greatest playwrights, is well transferred to the screen and captures through the wonderful performances of Raymond, McKenna and the rest of the cast the hero-worshipping thinking of a mob made up of unsophisticated and generally

Tim Robbins in *The Player*, 1992.

uneducated persons. Colorful and captivating, this broad farce sustains mesmerizing interest from beginning to tend. **p**, Brendan Smith, Denis O'Dell; **d&w**, Brian Desmond Hurst (based on the play by John Millington Synge); **cast**, Siobhan McKenna, Gary Raymond, Elspeth March, Michael O'Brian, Liam Redmond, Brendan Cauldwell, John Welsh, Niall MacGinnis, Eithne Lydon, Finnuala O'Shannon; **c**, Geoffrey Unsworth (Eastmancolor); **m**, Sean O'Riada.

The Player ★★★ 1992; U.S.; 124m; Avenue Pictures/Fine Line Features; Color; Comedy/Crime Drama; Children: Unacceptable (MPAA: R); **BD**; **DVD**. Intriguing insider's look at Hollywood where Robbins is a movie studio executive who hears story pitches from screenwriters and decides which have the potential to be made into films. He begins receiving death-threatening postcards he believes are from a screenwriter whose pitch he rejected. He has no idea, however, about the identity of the culprit since he only gave a green light to twelve scripts out of 50,000 submissions. He narrows the suspects down to one, D'Onofrio, whose girlfriend is Scacchi. But D'Onofrio is murdered and police suspect Robbins because he was the last person to see the victim alive. A year passes and Robbins gets a phone call from a man who says he wrote the threatening postcards and pitches a story about a studio executive who kills a writer and gets away with murder. Robbins considers the pitch to be blackmail and makes a deal with the caller in which he will approve the script if the caller stops any blackmailing. So we are left to conclude that Robbins killed the wrong man, but gets away with it. The ridiculous premise for this tale is so outlandish as to be consistently amusing, but its rationale and "dirty tricks" mentality nevertheless satirizes a ruthless Hollywood. Songs: "Snake," "Drums of Kyoto" (Kurt Neumann); "Precious" (Les Hooper); "Tema para Jobim" (Jerry Mulligan, Joyce); "Entertainment Tonight" (Michael Park). Gutter language and sexuality prohibit viewing by children. **p**, David Brown, Michael Tolkin, Nick Wechsler, Scott Bushnell; **d**, Robert Altman; **cast**, Tim Robbins, Greta Scacchi, Fred Ward, Whoopi Goldberg, Peter Gallagher, Brion James, Cynthia Stevenson, Vincent D'Onofrio, Dean Stockwell, Richard E. Grant, Sydney Pollack, Lyle Lovett, Dina Merrill, Jeremy Piven, and guest appearances by Steve Allen, Harry Belafonte, Cher, Peter Falk, Louise Fletcher, Jack Lemmon, Nick Nolte, Burt Reynolds, Julia Roberts, Susan Sarandon, Rod Steiger, Patrick Swayze, Robert Wagner, Bruce Willis and others; **w**, Michael Tolkin (based on his novel); **c**, Jean Lepine; **m**, Thomas Newman; **ed**, Maysie Hoy, Geraldine Peroni; **prod d**, Stephen Altman; **art d**, Jerry Fleming; **set d**, Susan Emshwiller.

Playtime ★★★ 1973; France/Italy; 108m; Jolly Films/Continental Distributing; Color; Comedy; Children: Acceptable; **DVD**; **VHS**. Tati again plays the inimitable Monsieur Hulot, who quietly rebels against modernity as he and a group of American tourists get lost in a maze of modern architecture and appliances in a futuristic Paris. As usual, Tati inadvertently and innocently creates mayhem wherever he goes, and, after creating havoc in the corridors of this towering steel and glass structure, he runs into an old friend and goes home with him, only to find to his horror that everyone in the area lives inside of the same unimaginative modern glass homes he so much dislikes. In escaping from this area, Tati finds himself inside a huge edifice still under construction, another crazy-quilt glass and steel structure intended to be a nightclub, but the gangling, pipe-puffing Tati brings the place to ruins as he rambles and bumbles his way through the place before the great comedian exits at the finale. A subtle comedy filled with delightful visual humor that emphasizes Tati's masterful miming routines, this film nevertheless proved to be a dismal financial failure, wrecking Tati's ability to finance future films. *Author's Note*: Tati had not made a film for ten years until producing **Playtime** and he used every dime he had made from his previous films to complete this film. The film presents several adversities, not the least of which was that Tati presents a next-to-nothing story line. Although he never offered strong plots in his previous films, those classic films were rooted to themes having strong characters such as in **My Uncle**, 1958, where Tati visits his in-laws and who live in a home so modern that its electronic gadgets control their lives and all of those around them, a theme Tati again employs but to much less effectiveness in **Playtime**. In **Playtime**, Tati, unlike his previous films, does not condition the viewer to expect a comedic scene through well-established events, but merely has his own central character wander about to create one melee after another, expecting the viewer to know when to laugh without telescoping his sight gags and slapstick. Where, as in his other films, he is an interloping outsider entering undisturbed lifestyles to create his comic mayhem when interacting with normal characters, Tati discards the use of such counterbalancing characters in **Playtime** and wholly depends upon his own erratic and discombobulated character to carry the story line. That character is lovable and fascinating, but his omnipotent presence without the existence of contrasting characters thins the blood of this otherwise entertaining film, and Tati's inventive bits of comedic business are somewhat diminished by becoming just more of the same. In lampooning the glass-and-steel architecture that dominated the 1960s and 1970s, Tati decided to build an enormous and very expensive set that displayed such modern structures, one that Tati envisioned as Paris' look of the future, and he spent all of his money in creating what later came to be known as "Tativille." That set of unattractive modern structures was considered by many important Parisians at that time to be a direct slap in the face at the ultra-modern Pompidou Center, which was then under construction (1971-1977). The Pompidou Center is a massive steel and glass structure, with reinforced concrete, which aptly houses Paris' museum of modern art, the largest such museum in Europe, the very type of architectural design Tati so thoroughly disliked. (In French; English subtitles.) **p**, Bernard Maurice, Rene Silvera; **d**, Jacques Tati; **cast**, Tati, Barbara Dennek, Jacqueline Lecomte, Rita Maiden, France Rumilly, France Delahalle, Valerie Camille, Erika Dentzler, Nicole Ray, Yvette Ducreux, Nathalie Jem; **w**, Tati, Jacques Lagrange, Art Buchwald; **c**, Jean Badal, Andreas Winding; **m**, Francis Lemarque; **ed**, Gerard Pollicand; **prod d**, Eugene Roman.

Plaza Suite ★★★ 1971; U.S.; 122m; PAR; Color; Comedy; Children: Cautionary (MPAA: PG-13); **DVD**; **VHS**. Three stories make up the story line for this very entertaining comedy, all taking place at the Plaza Hotel in New York City, where the gifted Matthau plays three much different characters. In the first episode he is a successful businessman, staying at the Plaza with his wife, Stapleton, in a hotel room she believes is the very room in which they honeymooned twenty-four years earlier. She wants him to pep up what she considers a failing marriage. It turns out that Matthau is cheating on Stapleton with his secretary, Sorel, and thinks such marital disloyalty is his right for having become such a successful businessman, although he holds out a little hope that his marriage will survive. In the second episode, Matthau is a brash film producer, who tries to get his former flame, Harris, interested in him again. Although she is married, Harris is a movie fan and Matthau drops every Hollywood name he can think of to finally get her into his bedroom at the Plaza. In the third tale, Matthau and his wife, Grant, try to get their daughter, Sullivan, out of the bathroom before her approaching wedding. She locks herself in because she is unsure of herself. Matthau climbs out onto a high ledge to try to get into the bathroom, but is plagued by pigeons and a thunderstorm. Carey, who is Sullivan's fiancé, arrives, and orders her to "cool it!" Sullivan obediently unlocks the door. The wedding goes on and the happy couple ride off on a motorcycle. Matthau and Grant can breathe again. Hiller does a fine job in presenting this delightful marital comedy, based on the Neil Simon hit stage play, where Matthau, Stapleton, Harris and Grant shine. Song: "Tangerine" (Johnny Mercer, Victor Schertzinger). *Author's Note*: This was the second of three films scripted by Simon that was directed by Hiller, who also helmed **The Out-of-Towners**, 1970, and **The Lonely Guy**, 1984. Matthau told this author that "**Plaza Suite** is sort of a **Grand Hotel** [1932] but played for laughs. I play three different guys who have all done pretty well in life except in the marriage and parent departments, and the only way those characters produce laughs is through the great lines written by that genius for comedy, Simon." **p**, Howard W. Koch; **d**, Arthur Hiller; **cast**, Walter Matthau, Lee Grant, Barbara Harris, Maureen Stapleton, Louise Sorel, Dan Ferrone, Jose Ocasio, Thomas Carey, Jenny Sullivan, Augusta Dabney, Alan North; **w**, Neil Simon (based on his play); **c**, Jack Marta, Albert Taffet (Technicolor); **m**, Maurice Jarre; **ed**, Frank Bracht; **prod d**, Arthur Lonergan; **set d**, Reg Allen.

Please Don't Eat the Daisies ★★★ 1960; U.S.; 112m; Euterpe/MGM; Color; Comedy; Children: Acceptable; **DVD**; **VHS**. This pleasant comedy sees drama critic Niven and wife Day and their four children and dog move from a crowded Manhattan apartment to an old house in the country. Day settles in to the suburban life but suspects Niven, working in the city, is having an affair with Broadway star Paige. Day must deal with in-laws, new neighbors and four pesky kids all at once while hard-working Niven must overcome his wife's suspicions. It all works out and the family stays in the old country home for a happy ending. Niven and Day are in top comedic form in this fun-filled family film, one that was successful enough to prompt a TV series, 1965-1967, by the same title and with Pat Crowley and Mark Miller in the leading roles. Songs: "Please Don't Eat the Daisies" (Joe Lubin), "Any Way the Wind Blows" (Marilyn Hooven, Joseph Hooven, 'By' Dunham), "Que Sera Sera /Whatever Will Be Will Be" (Jay Livingston, Ray Evans). *Author's Note*: Niven told this author that "it was a lot of fun to play a critic in **Please Don't Eat the Daisies**, especially where I can dish out the dirt instead of being on the receiving end [as an actor]." Paige had been away from the big screen for three years, her last feature film being **Silk Stockings**, 1957. This was the first reappearance on the big screen in a feature film for Kelly in sixteen years. The theme for this entertaining jaunt to the suburbs from the Big Apple takes a leaf from similar comedies, including the hilarious **George Washington Slept Here**, 1942, and the equally laugh-packed **Mr. Blandings Builds His Dream House**, 1948. **p**, Joe Pasternak; **d**, Charles Walters; **cast**, Doris Day, David Niven, Janis Paige, Spring Byington, Richard Haydn, Patsy Kelly, Jack Weston, Margaret Lindsay, John Harding, Carmen Phillips, Guy Stockwell; **w**, Isobel Lennart (based on the book by Jean Kerr); **c**, Robert Bronner (CinemaScope; Metrocolor); **m**, David Rose; **ed**, John McSweeney, Jr.; **art d**, Hans Peters, George W. Davis; **set d**, Henry Grace, Jerry Wunderlich; **spec eff**, Lee LeBlanc, Matthew Yuricich.

Please Give ★★★ 2010; U.S.; 90m; Sony; Color; Comedy/Drama; Children: Unacceptable (MPAA: R); **BD**; **DVD**. Entertaining tale has Platt and Keener as husband and wife who operate a store selling used furniture, and they live in a cramped Manhattan apartment with their

Rebecca Hall and Thomas Ian Nicholas in *Please Give,* 2010.

teenage daughter, Steele. They bought the next-door apartment in which its cranky elderly renter, Guilbert, will live until she dies. Living with her are Hall and Peet, two grown granddaughters, one care-giving and generous and the other cynical and sharp-tongued. The five neighbors try to cope with many issues including marriage, parenting of a teen, boredom, a first date, and care for a terminally ill woman. In the sometimes painful process, they all learn it's a matter of more giving than taking. Songs: "No Shoes" (Paranoid Larry), "Cool Bop" (Pete Thomas), "Sail Away" (Steve Martin), "Tones of Meditation" (Clinton Rusich), "Windcheater" (Apathetic). Gutter language, sexuality and nudity prohibit viewing by children. **p**, Anthony Bregman; **d&w**, Nicole Holofcener; **cast**, Catherine Keener, Amanda Peet, Oliver Platt, Rebecca Hall, Elise Ivy, Josh Pais, Sarah Steele, Ann Guilbert, Griffin Frazen, Reggie Austin, Scott Cohen, Paul Sparks; **c**, Yaron Orbach; **m**, Marcelo Zarvos; **ed**, Robert Frazen; **prod d**, Mark White; **art d**, Lauren Fitzsimmons; **set d**, Kim Chapman, Kris Moran; **spec eff**, David Isyomin, Mark Russell, Chris Gelles.

The Pleasure of His Company ★★★ 1961; U.S.; 115m; Perlsea; PAR; Color; Comedy; Children: Acceptable; **DVD**; **VHS**. Astaire is a standout in this upbeat comedy where he shows up to see his daughter married. That offspring is Reynolds, a San Francisco debutante, who has been hoping that her playboy father, Astaire, will attend her wedding to Hunter, a young cattle rancher. Reynolds has not seen Astaire in fifteen years and, when he arrives, she is taken by his charming ways. Astaire nevertheless disrupts the household of his ex-wife, Palmer, and her husband, Merrill, while befriending and subsequently stealing their male Chinese cook, Fong. He even has hopes of winning Palmer back, but that is not in the cards. Astaire at first tells Reynolds that down home Hunter is not good enough for her, and after Reynolds argues with Hunter, she calls off the wedding, telling everyone that she intends to travel with her worldly father and look after him. Astaire feels that he is far from dotage and needing a caregiver and then turns everything around so that Reynolds eventually decides to go to the altar, providing Astaire with great relief. When he departs, he leaves everyone feeling good for having had him at the wedding. Songs: "The Pleasure of His Company" (Alfred Newman, Sammy Cahn), "Lover" (Richard Rodgers, Lorenz Hart). *Author's Note*: "Sorry, folks, but there is no dancing in **The Pleasure of His Company**," Astaire pointed out to this author, "only a lot of good comedy business. I get to play the role that every man wants in life, a family member who comes and goes as he pleases and with no strings or responsibilities. Not everything goes my way, but I do manage to abscond with the family cook." Celebrated film dress designer Edith Head makes a rare cameo appearance in this film. **p**, William Perlberg; **d**, George Seaton; **cast**, Fred Astaire, Debbie

Barbara Stanwyck in *The Plough and the Stars*, 1936.

Reynolds, Lilli Palmer, Tab Hunter, Gary Merrill, Charles Ruggles, Harold Fong, Elvia Allman, Pat Colby, Eleanor Audley, Edith Head, Jeffrey Sayre, Bert Stevens; **w**, Samuel A. Taylor (based on the play by Taylor, Cornelia Otis Skinner); **c**, Robert Burks (Technicolor); **m**, Alfred Newman; **ed**, Alma Macrorie; **art d**, Ha; Pereira, Tambi Larsen; **set d**, Sam Comer, Frank R. McKelvy; **spec eff**, Farciot Edouart, John P. Fulton.

The Pledge ★★★ 2001; U.S.; 124m; Morgan Creek/WB; Color; Crime Drama; Children: Unacceptable (MPAA: R); **DVD**; **VHS**. Riveting and gritty crime tale sees another outstanding performance from Nicholson. He is a sheriff in Reno, Nevada, who retires and pledges to Clarkson, the mother of a girl murdered in the mountains, that he will find the real killer. He thinks police arrested the wrong man after discovering it is the third killing in the area in the recent past with the victims all being young, blonde, pretty and small for their age. He buys an old gas station in the mountains near the crimes and, with the help of Eckhart, a private detective, searches for a tall man, who drives a black station wagon, gives toy porcupines to girls as gifts, and calls himself the wizard. Nicholson finds clues from a drawing by the dead girl and becomes friends with Wright Penn, a female bartender, and her small, blonde daughter, Roberts, and they move in with him. Nicholson suspects that Noonan, a local minister, is the killer because his black station wagon bears the imprint of a porcupine body. Nicholson uses Roberts as bait, but, when she too becomes a victim of the killer, he descends into madness. Though unfulfilling and somewhat depressing, this film nevertheless offers a chilling portrait of just how helpless and ineffective law enforcement is when dealing with ubiquitous serial killers. Songs: "Nwalhulwana" (Humberto Carlos Benefica), "Da Da Da" (Jerry Hannan), "Slowdown" (Ben Green), "The Other Side of Town" (Steve Earle), "Poor Twisted Me" (James Hetfield, Lars Ulrich), "Through the Years" (Steve Dorff, Marty Panzer), "Why" (David Baerwald). Violence and gutter language prohibit viewing by children. **p**, Sean Penn, Michael Fitzgerald, Elie Samaha; **d**, Penn; **cast**, Jack Nicholson, Aaron Eckhart, Patricia Clarkson, Vanessa Redgrave, Robin Wright, Helen Mirren, Sam Shepard, Benicio Del Toro, Tom Noonan, Mickey Rourke, Pauline Robert; **p**, Harry Dean Stanton; **w**, Jerzy Kromolowski, Mary Olson-Kromolowski (based on the book by Friedrich Dürrenmatt); **c**, Chris Menges; **m**, Hans Zimmer, Klaus Badelt; **ed**, Jay Cassidy; **prod d**, Bill Groom; **art d**, Helen Jarvis; **set d**, Lesley Beale; **spec eff**, David Gauthier, Bill Mills.

The Plot against Harry ★★★ 1989; U.S.; 81m; King Screen Productions/New Yorker Films; B/W; Comedy/Crime Drama; Children: Unacceptable; **DVD**; **VHS**. A middle-aged smalltime Jewish gangster is released after serving a prison term and finds that the Manhattan world he knew has changed so much he no longer knows it. He wants to go into the catering business but is hampered by paranoia in that he thinks everyone is out to get him, especially blacks and Hispanics, who now control the numbers and other rackets in his old neighborhood. At the same time, he tries to get back with family members who want nothing to do with him. The film was not released until twenty years after it was made because of lack of interest, but found its audience later on the independent film circuit. Gutter language prohibits viewing by children. **p**, Michael Roemer, Robert M. Young; **d&w**, Roemer; **cast**, Martin Priest, Ben Lang, Maxine Woods, Henry Nemo, Jacques Taylor, Jean Leslie, Ellen Herbert, Sandra Kazan, Ronald Coralian, Max Ulman, Louis Basile, Margo Solin (Margo Ann Berdeshevsky); **c**, Young; **m**, Frank Lewin; **ed**, Georges Klotz, Terry Lewis.

The Plough and the Stars ★★★ 1936; U.S.; 72m; RKO; B/W; Drama; Children: Unacceptable; **VHS**. Pantheon director Ford presents a powerful panorama of the Easter Rebellion in Ireland in 1916 where insurgents attempt to overthrow British control of that fiercely independent country. Stanwyck manages a boarding house in Dublin, but is troubled when her husband, Foster, talks revolution, fearing the worst for him and Ireland, if rebellion erupts. She uses every type of persuasion to finally convince Foster to quit his association with the Irish Citizen Army (a synonym for the Irish Republican Army). Foster is then informed that he has been made a captain of a unit in that underground army, which bolsters and inflates Foster's Irish patriotism, and he accepts that post. Stanwyck sees nothing but disaster as Foster becomes enmeshed in planning the uprising. She vainly tries to have him quit the rebels and, on Easter Sunday, April 24, 1916, Foster and the rebels seize several important buildings in Dublin, and Foster commands the insurgents that occupy the General Post Office. At first, the rebels see what appears to be victory as they triumphantly defeat pro-British forces, but their attempt to establish an independent Republic of Ireland fails after strong British reinforcements arrive along with heavy artillery that begins to bombard the buildings occupied by the rebels. As she prophesized, Stanwyck's visions of tragedy engulf her and Foster and all those who take place in the Easter Rising. Ford directs this haunting story with vitality and superbly orchestrates its battle scenes while meshing the domestic plot with the politics of that era, although he would later admit that its unwieldy elements caused him much trouble. Stanwyck is outstanding in her role as a woman torn between her deep love for her husband and his passionate patriotism, which she shares with Foster, but is unwilling to lose him to its cause. Foster, who had convincingly played a similar role of an IRA commander in Ford's superlative **The Informer**, 1935, is equally impressive in his role as a dedicated patriot. All of the supporting players were mostly made up of the Dublin-based Abbey Theatre Players, including Fitzgerald, McCormick, O'Dea, Crowe, and Shields (who plays the great Irish patriot, Patdraic Pearse, 1879-1916, and was Fitzgerald's brother, using another name so as not to trade on his sibling's theatrical fame) and all of them, including the wonderful O'Connor, provide memorable performances as troubled citizens during that tragic conflict. *Author's Note*: Ford told this author that "Arthur [Shields] was very helpful during the production as I did not know most of the Abbey Players and he served as an unofficial assistant director in organizing their appearances in their scenes, positioning them and coaching their cue lines." Shields would go on to work in more Ford films and undertake the same behind-the-camera role with the director in such productions as **Drums Along the Mohawk**, 1939; **The Long Voyage Home**, 1940; and **How Green Was My Valley**, 1941. Stanwyck had great regard for Ford, telling this author that "he was a genius with epics and he could show sentiment in a scene by just the way he positioned his cameras skyward as his characters fall to earth. When I first read the script by Dudley [Nichols] I saw that my role was more of a supporting player and complained about that. The front office at RKO then pressured Pappy [Ford] to add more romantic scenes for me, which he did, but he did not like it. He was all business with me after that and I followed his instructions to the letter. He was not a man you wanted to anger, even though I had done just that, so I steered clear of that Irish temper of his, which was just as hot-headed and explosive as the extras running through the streets in that picture during the rebellion scenes. I must admit that those electrifying scenes were so inspiring that the Irish in me or my adrenaline was urging them on. That's how good Pappy was in recreating scenes like that, a true master." When RKO producers insisted that more romance be inserted into the story line, Ford and Nichols protested, arguing that the substance of O'-Casey's political message would be diminished, but the front office had its way. After Ford completed the film, producers, without Ford's knowledge, had George Nichols Jr. reshoot some scenes to further expand the romance between Stanwyck and Foster, and then released the film. Ford went ballistic when he heard about this tampering and demanded that his name be removed from the credits, but he was shown a copy of his contract with the studio, and one clause allowed producers to arbitrarily add or delete scenes in any films he made for RKO. Ford glumly went his way, vowing to never again work with the studio. He would, however, after establishing his own production company, Argosy Pictures, distribute his classic western trilogy through RKO (**Fort Apache**, 1948; **She Wore a Yellow Ribbon**, 1949; and **Rio Grande**, 1950). O'Casey used the image of the flag flown by the Easter Rising rebels for the title of his moving tale, that flag bearing the image of a plough with stars surrounding it. Many films have profiled the IRA (Irish Republican Army; established 1913), depicting its members as both heroes and terrorists, including such productions as **Angela's Ashes**, 2000; **Anton**, 2008; **Beloved Enemy**, 1936; **Borstal Boy**, 2001; **The Boxer**, 1997; **Breakfast on Pluto**, 2005; **The Eagle Has Landed**, 1976; **The Enigma of Frank Ryan**, 2012; **Exiled**, 1999; **Fifty Dead Men Walking**, 2009; **Five Minutes of Heaven**, 2009; **Hunger**, 2008; **I.R.A.: King of Nothing**, 2007; **I See a Dark Stranger**, 1947; **The Informer**, 1935; **The Jackal**, 1997; **Liam**, 2001; **The Man Who Never Was**, 1956; **Midnight Man**, 1997 (made-for-TV); **Michael Collins**, 1996; **The Night Fighters**, 1960; **Odd Man Out**, 1947; **Omagh**, 2004 (made-for-TV); **Ordinary Decent Criminal**, 2000; **Patriot Games**, 1998; **Peacefire**, 2009; **The Quiet Man**, 1952; **The Rising of the Moon**, 1957; **Riot**, 1996; **Ronin**, 1998; **The Secret Invasion**, 1964; **Shake Hands with the Devil**, 1959; **Shergar**, 1999; **Sword in the Desert**, 1949; **Ticker**, 2001; **Titanic Town**, 1999; **Veronica Guerin**, 2003; **The Wind That Shakes the Barley**, 2007; and **The Year London Blew Up: 1974**, 2005 (made-for-TV). **p**, Cliff Reid; **d**, John Ford; **cast**, Barbara Stanwyck, Preston Foster, Barry Fitzgerald, Denis O'Dea, Eileen Crowe, Una O'Connor, Arthur Shields, Moroni Olsen, J. M. Kerrigan, F. J. McCormick, Bonita Granville, Erin O'Brien-Moore, Wesley Barry, Mary Gordon, Doris Lloyd, Francis Ford, Jack Pennick; **w**, Dudley Nichols (based on the play by Sean O'-Casey); **c**, Joseph H. August; **m**, Roy Webb; **ed**, George Hively; **art d**, Van Nest Polglase; **set d**, Darrell Silvera.

The Ploughman's Lunch ★★★ 1984; U.K.; 107m; Goldcrest Films International/Samuel Goldwyn; Color; Drama; Children: Unacceptable (MPAA: R); **VHS**. This well-crafted production is centered on the politics in England during the early 1980s, indicting the Conservative government of Prime Minister Margaret Thatcher (1925-2013). Pryce is a mediocre and politically indifferent radio journalist and historian seeking fame and fortune while bending with the breeze and times. His lackadaisical perspectives sharpen at the time of the British Conservative Party Conference following the end of the short but controversial Falklands War in 1982. The war was between Great Britain and Argentina over sovereignty of the islands east of Argentina. Thatcher flexed her muscles and won praise for decisively deploying British forces. At this time, opportunist cad Pryce has a brief affair with Harris, a Socialist historian so that she will help him with his research. He becomes more successful professionally, but at the price of his integrity. He becomes,

Jonny Lee Miller and Liv Tyler in *Plunkett and Macleane, 1999.*

however, in his assault on the Thatcher administration, just another sniping revisionist attempting to rewrite history to suit the needs of the political present. The film's title comes from a popular British workingman's meal consisting of bread, cheese, a pickled egg, and beer. Songs: "War Front" (Trevor Duncan), "Dramatic Interludes" (Hans May), "Gale Warning" (Ronald Hammer). Sexuality prohibits viewing by children. **p**, Simon Relph, Ann Scott; **d**, Richard Eyre; **cast**, Jonathan Pryce, Tim Curry, Rosemary Harris, Frank Finlay, Charlie Dore, David de Keyser, Nat Jackley, Bill Paterson, William Maxwell, Paul Jesson, Andy Rashleigh, Margaret Thatcher (archive footage); **w**, Ian McEwan; **c**, Clive Tickner; **m**, Dominic Muldowney; **ed**, David Martin; **prod d**, Luciana Arrighi; **art d**, Michael Pickwoad.

Plunkett & Macleane ★★★ 1999; U.K.; 99m; Arts Council of England/USA Films; Color; Adventure; Children: Unacceptable (MPAA: R); **DVD**. Colorful and action-packed, this exciting tale is set in 18th-Century England where William Plunkett (c.1692-c.1791), played by Miller, and Captain James Macleane (James Maclaine, 1724-1750), essayed by Carlyle, form a pact to enter the hazardous profession of highway robbery. They are social opposites since Plunkett has always followed criminal pursuits and Macleane was raised as a gentleman, who, after depleting his family's wealth through his wastrel ways, turns to crime. The pair establishes a gentleman's agreement to relieve aristocrats of their riches. Known as "The Gentlemen Highwaymen" they become notorious. One day, they hold up a coach carrying Lord Chief Justice Gibson (Gambon) and Miller falls in love with his beautiful niece, Tyler. Police Detective Scott also loves Tyler and tries to capture both Plunkett and Macleane, but they're too clever for him, evading his entrapments while they continue robbing the rich to fund their plans to migrate to America. Those plans go terribly awry, however, their eventual destination being the scaffold. Scott directs with great skill in handling this period tale and where production values are high in accurately profiling that long-ago era in sets, costuming and props. Miller and Carlyle are exceptional in their roles as the brigands, and the action scenes that permeate the film are extremely well orchestrated. Songs: "No 9" (Craig Armstrong, Marius De Vries); "Hell," "Whore," Sailors" (Martyn Jacques); "Childhood," "Hypnotic" (Armstrong); "Houses in Motion" (David Byrne, Brian Eno, Christopher Frantz, Tina Weymouth, Jerry Harrison). Excessive violence prohibits viewing by children. *Author's Note*: For more details on these two colorful characters, see my eight-volume work, *Encyclopedia of World Crime*, Volume III (CrimeBooks, 1990; under Maclaine, James, pages 2055-2056). **p**, Tim Bevan, Eric Fellner, Rupert Harvey, Jonathan Finn, Natascha Wharton; **d**, Jake Scott; **cast**, Jonny Lee Miller, Robert Carlyle, Liv Tyler, Michael Gambon, Alan Cumming, Ken Stott, Nicholas Farrell, Iain Robertson, Tommy

Spencer Tracy and Gene Tierney in *Plymouth Adventure*, 1952.

Flanagan, Stephen Walters, James Thornton, Terence Rigby, Christian Camargo; **w**, Robert Wade, Neal Purvis, Charles McKeown, Selwyn Roberts; **c**, John Mathieson; **m**, Craig Armstrong; **ed**, Oral Norrie Ottey; **prod d**, Norris Spencer; **art d**, Jindrich Kocí; **spec eff**, Dave Bonneywell, Jaroslav Stolba, Andy Williams, Joss Williams, Clive Beard.

Plymouth Adventure ★★★ 1952; U.S.; 105m; MGM; Color; Adventure; Children: Acceptable; **DVD**; **VHS**. Pantheon director Brown expertly helms a fascinating and exciting tale of the first American colonists voyaging to the New World in 1620 on board the sturdy ship *Mayflower*, captained by Christopher Jones (c. 1570-1622), who is forcefully played by Tracy. He is a no-nonsense skipper and is skeptical about the survival skills of his 102 passengers, all Pilgrims migrating to America to escape the religious persecutions of their religion. On board is the ethical and brilliant-minded William Bradford (c.1590-c.1657), played by Genn, and who is the leader of this dedicated band of travelers (Bradford would later become the governor of the Plymouth Colony, 1621-1657). Accompanying him is the ravishingly beautiful Tierney, who plays his wife, Dorothy, and who immediately catches Tracy's eye. Also on board are a bevy of other passengers who will become famous in the history of their colony, including carpenter John Alden (1599-1689), played by the upbeat Johnson, originally a crew member, who becomes involved with the attractive Priscilla Mullins (c.1602-c.1685), a colonist. Jones plays Pilgrim preacher and leader William Brewster (c.1566-1644), and Drayton essays the group's military captain, Miles Standish (c.1584-1656), who trains some of his men while on board in the use of flintlocks in any anticipation of conflict with the American Indians they may encounter when arriving in the New World. Cavanagh plays John Carver (1584-1621), who was one of the leaders of the Pilgrims and would become the first governor of the Plymouth Colony. Tracy at first treats his passengers as naïve sheep going to the slaughtering hardships of America and has no regard for their religion or altruistic beliefs. He tells Dehner, a Pilgrim passenger, while looking out to sea that "I put my faith in my ship and she's never failed me. Don't put your faith in men and you'll never be disappointed." The hardships at sea are as daunting as those that await these intrepid voyagers, especially when food and water runs short on the long voyage and Tracy imposes severe rationing. He meanwhile slowly falls in love with the gentle Tierney, even though she does not return his subtle affections, remaining loyal to her caring husband Genn, who inspires all by his resolute leadership and deep religious convictions. As the *Mayflower* sails westward it encounters a savage storm where it is pummeled, rocked and lashed by a roiling and ravaging sea, huge waves engulfing it while near hurricane winds whistle and whine through its creaking and groaning decks and masts (one of the finest

storms at sea ever put on film, thanks to the brilliant action choreography by Brown and captured by master cinematographer Daniels). While fighting the storm and heroically helming his ship through titanic waves, Tracy sees the deep and universal beliefs and trust his passengers have in God and their deliverance and begins to gain new respect for them. When the *Mayflower* makes landfall at Plymouth, Tracy, by this time, no longer shares the disregard and contempt his crew members have for the passengers, especially Bridges, who plays his first mate and gives a riveting performance as a conniving and vicious seaman, who has no regard for human life and would, if allowed, throw all the passengers overboard to rid himself of their burdensome presence. By this time, Tierney has become emotionally involved with Tracy, but, rather than betray her marriage, she either accidentally falls or purposely drops into the sea and drowns (which actually happened while Bradford was away on a brief exploratory expedition), a death that devastates Genn and where the guilt-ridden Tracy does all he can to console the bereaved husband. As the settlers begin to construct their crude homes and forage for food to sustain themselves through the winter, Tracy (as was the case of the actual Captain Jones), tells Genn and his followers that he will not desert them through the hardships that await them in their first winter at Plymouth. Instead of sailing back to England as was originally agreed in his contract with the Pilgrims, he will, despite the angry protests of Bridges and other crew members, keep the *Mayflower* in the harbor as an available haven for the settlers. When spring comes, Tracy also contradicts his original plans and promises Genn that he will return to England, fill his ship with supplies, and return to Plymouth to further aid the settlers with whom he has now deeply bonded; the final scene shows the *Mayflower* embarking on that next voyage. Brown directs with a firm hand, and Tracy, Tierney, Genn and the rest of the cast are standouts in their historic roles in this memorable, action-packed tale that remains faithful to the facts of history. Song: "Confess Jehovah Thankfully" (1612; Henry Ainsworth). ***Author's Note***: The drowning death of Bradford's wife Dorothy is shrouded by time, and the facts in the case only state that she somehow "fell" from the deck of the *Mayflower* and that her death was accidental (but where Brown implies that Tierney takes her own life rather than consummating an illicit relationship with Tracy). Brown does religiously stick to the facts in showing the settlers building frame houses after arriving at Plymouth, rather than log cabins, those log cabins first constructed by Swedish settlers in 1638 when establishing later settlements along the Delaware. Tracy told this author: "I don't know why Clarence [Brown] did not lose his mind when he was directing **Plymouth Adventure** because he was handling dozens of actors at the same time and jumping from one scene to another with a lot of different people. That would have driven me nuts and that's one of the reasons why I never wanted to direct. You have to be a ringmaster, a juggler and a horse rider all at the same time. Directing is not for me, brother!" The film did take its toll on Brown, who told this author that "**Plymouth Adventure** was one of the most exhausting films I ever directed. The script was unwieldy and they kept changing the scenes during the production, taking out this and adding that, and I had to do a lot of retakes until I got dizzy trying to keep the continuity of the film. At one point I thought I was about to direct Leo [Genn] in a scene and I walked to the set to find Van [Johnson] waiting for me. I liked Van, a very good actor and an affable guy, but he was miscast for his role of John Alden, because he had a much too modern personality, and he was still doing that 'young man next door' routine, which I could not shake out of him. That picture was the last one for me. I was all drained out and walked away from the cameras, although I have had some regrets since then in doing that." One of the passengers on board the *Mayflower* was John Billington (c.1580-1630), who is played by Sherman, a rather truculent member of the colony, who later proved to be obstreperous and uncooperative as a settler, and became so lazy that he murdered his neighbor, John Newcomen, in order to acquire that man's cleared lands and for which he earned dark fame as America's first convicted murderer (as a white settler in the Plymouth, Massachusetts, colony) and for which he was hanged. For more details on Billington, see my book, *Bloodletters and Badmen* (M. Evans, 1973, 1983, 1991, 1995; page 73). **p**, Dore Schary; **d**, Clarence Brown; **cast**, Spencer Tracy, Gene Tierney, Van Johnson, Leo Genn, Barry Jones, Dawn Adams, Lloyd Bridges, John Dehner, Lowell Gilmore, Paul Cavanagh, Noreen Corcoran, Dennis Hoey, Kathleen Lockhart, Rhys Williams, John Sherman; **w**, Helen Deutsch (based on a novel by Ernest Gebler); **c**, William Daniels (Technicolor); **m**, Miklos Rozsa; **ed**, Robert J. Kern; **art d**, Cedric Gibbons, Urie McCleary; **set d**, Edwin B. Willis, Hugh Hunt; **spec eff**, A. Arnold Gillespie, Warren Newcombe, Irving G. Ries.

Pocahontas ★★★ 1995; U.S.; 81m; Disney/Buena Vista; Color; Animated Adventure; Children: Acceptable (MPAA: G); **DVD**; **VHS**. Delightful Disney version presents the legendary romance between British Captain John Smith (1580-1631; Gibson voiceover) and the fetching Indian princess Pocahontas (c.1595-1617; Bedard voiceover) in the New England colony of Virginia. Gibson leads a band of sailors and soldiers to the New World to plunder its riches. Native American chief Powhatan (d. 1618; Means voiceover) has pledged his daughter, Bedard, to the village's greatest warrior, but she falls in love with Gibson, which creates problems for Means, who sees the new settlers from across the sea as interlopers into his lands. The British governor (Stiers voiceover), who is the leader of the Virginia Company, levels forests as he and his men search for gold. When settlers open fire on the Indians, who try to prevent the destruction of their sanctuary, the Indians retaliate and they capture Gibson, planning to execute him. Bedard pleads for Gibson's life, and Means, who loves his daughter and can deny her nothing, allows Gibson to live. The film plays fast and loose with the facts, more comfortably relying on myths, but the tale is told with such inviting scenes and with such a tender story line that it nevertheless provides consistent entertainment for young and old. Songs: "If I Never Knew You" (Emilio Estefan, Jr., Buchanan); "Colors of the Wind," "The Virginia Company," "Steady as the Beating Drum," "Just Around the Riverbend," "Listen with Your Heart," "Mine, Mine, Mine," "Savages" (Alan Menken, Stephen Schwartz). *Author's Note*: According to the legend, Smith was captured in 1607 by Indians. When Powhatan was about to personally execute him by crashing his club down upon Smith's head, Pocahontas raced forward and placed her head on top of Smith's own head, which prevented her father from completing his gruesome chore. At the time this colorful canard took place, Pocahontas would have been about eleven or twelve years old. She was later captured by the English in 1617 during an Indian war and held hostage. While in captivity, she converted to Christianity, taking the name Rebecca. She married white planter John Rolfe in 1614, bearing his son, Thomas Rolfe, in 1615. Her union with Rolfe marked the first recorded interracial marriage in the history of America. Where the Disney people took great liberties with the facts of the story (such as they are), their artists painfully and meticulously produced a beautifully animated production, working more than five years to perfect its animation and stunning color hues. The angular shapes and facial expressions of the characters presented great difficulties for those artists, but they overcame problems to present wonderfully fluid animation of characters through rotoscoping. Bedard, who provides the voiceover for Pocahontas, was also the live model for her animated character. The rugged Gibson appears for the first time in a film where his singing voice is heard. To be politically correct, Disney hired mostly Native Americans to play the parts in the film and consulted Indian experts to counsel producers in the way the Indians were presented, but some Indian activists nevertheless openly condemned the film when it was released, claiming that the Indians were shown as stereotypes. **p**, James Pentecost; **d**, Mike Gabriel, Eric Goldberg; **cast** (voiceovers), Mel Gibson, Linda Hunt, Christian Bale, Irene Bedard, Judy Kuhn, David Ogden Stiers, John Kassir, Russell Means, Billy Connolly, Joe Baker; **w**, Carl Binder, Susannah Grant, Philip LaZebnik (based on an idea by Mike Gabriel and a story by Glen Keane, Joe Grant, Ralph Zondag, Burny Mattinson, Ed Gombert, Kaan Kalyon, Francis Glebas,

Meeko, Pocahontas and Flit in *Pocahontas,* 1995.

Robert Gibbs, Bruce Morris, Todd Kurosawa, Duncan Marjoribanks, Chris Buck, Tom Sito); **c**, Ed H. Lee Peterson (Technicolor); **m**, Alan Menken; **art d**, Michael Giaimo.

Pocketful of Miracles ★★★ 1961; U.S.; 136m; Franton Productions; UA; Color; Comedy; Children: Acceptable; **DVD**; **VHS**. Other than a short in 1964, this was the last film helmed by pantheon director Capra, one that was wrongly lambasted by critics and did not do well at the box office, but it is nevertheless a fine comedy with the exceptional talents of Davis, Ford, Lange, Falk, O'Connell and Mitchell heading a wonderful cast. Based on the Damon Runyon play and the script from **Lady for a Day**, 1933 (also directed by Capra), the film tells the tale of a broken-down old woman named Apple Annie, played marvelously by Davis, who sells apples to the denizens along Broadway in New York City, her favorite patron being high-roller gambler Ford, called Dave The Dude. Superstitious, Ford thinks that if he buys an apple a day from Davis that kind-hearted gesture will ward off any evils, particularly from competitive racketeers. Falk, his wise-cracking bodyguard, and Shaughnessy, his chauffeur, think that this daily purchase of apples from Davis is an exercise in futility. Lange, who is Ford's devoted girlfriend, thinks his financial support of Davis (he pays her a lot more for an apple than she asks) is swell, just like everything Ford does, except when he plans to merge his operations with tough Chicago gangster Leonard. Lange smells nothing but trouble from this collaboration between Leonard and Ford, so she urges Ford to give up his racketeering. As a diehard member of the underworld, however, Ford has no intentions of walking away from his lucrative enterprises. (The relationship between Lange and Ford is not dissimilar to that of blonde entertainer Adelaide and her long-standing gambler-lover, Nathan Detroit, in **Guys and Dolls**, 1955, based on another tale from Runyon.) Ford becomes disturbed when he does not find Davis at her usual corner along Broadway and begins to search for her, finding her in a low down dive in the Bowery where she is loaded to the gills, explaining to him in a besotted litany that she has a beautiful, young daughter, Ann-Margret, who has been raised and educated abroad since infancy and where Davis has paid all her bills from her diligent apple-selling. Davis has learned that Ann-Margret is coming to New York with her fiancé, Mann, and his rich father O'Connell, expecting to have Davis present when she is married, that trusting daughter believing that her mother is a wealthy dowager. (Another such mother-daughter charade is presented in **Lullaby of Broadway**, 1951, where Doris Day arrives in the Big Apple, believing that her mother, Gladys George, is a big-time musical star, who has been supporting her upbringing and education abroad while her mother is nothing more than a lush singing in a dive, all of this kept from her by fellow trouper, Billy De Wolfe.) Davis is thinking of suicide and that

Bette Davis and Thomas Mitchell in *Pocketful of Miracles*, 1961.

she would rather end it all than embarrass and disappoint her child. Ford is shocked and, to preserve his good luck charm, comes to Davis' rescue by installing her in an upscale apartment suite, replete with butler Horton. He even hires Mitchell, a drunken disbarred judge, to enact the role of Davis' husband while buying her a new wardrobe and where Lange lends a hand by arranging cosmetic experts to improve Davis' careworn appearance so that she is transformed into a grand lady. When Ann-Margret, Mann and O'Connell arrive from Spain, O'Connell is overwhelmed with Davis' opulent lifestyle and agrees to give his son and bride-to-be a large endowment that will provide comfort and security in their forthcoming union. Davis has acted her part so perfectly that her impersonation runs away from her and she escalates the masquerade by telling O'Connell that she will hold one of the greatest high society bashes in his honor and where he will meet New York's social elite. Ford, meanwhile, is getting pressure from gangster Leonard to conclude their merger and he wants to fold the big front he has established for Davis, but the persuasive old lady convinces him to finish what he started by holding that social party and Ford packs the place with his Broadway chums and their gals, from racetrack touts to striptease artists. When the masquerade becomes known to members of the city's high society, however, they, too, join in the fun, and make their appearances, all impressing O'Connell, Mann and Ann-Margret, who finally sail back to Europe still believing that Davis is the social queen of New York. By this time, Ford has had second thoughts about going into business with the dangerous Leonard and makes Lange joyfully happy by quitting the rackets and where they plan to move to Maryland and live a quiet life. Davis, too, has prospects for a better future when she seriously considers a marriage proposal from Mitchell, who tells her that his love for her is so strong that he will give up booze to make her happy. Though overlong, the film offers fascinating performances from Davis and Ford and the rest of the cast, their energy and panache inspired through Capra's careful construction of each humorous scene. The title song and Falk (as Best Supporting Actor) received Oscar nominations. The title song from Van Heusen and Cahn became a big hit, going to the top of the charts, and the Kodak Corporation later acquired the use of the song to promote its pocket cameras. Songs: "A Pocketful of Miracles" (1961; music: Jimmy Van Heusen; lyrics: Sammy Cahn), "God Rest Ye, Mer-ryGentlemen" (traditional), "Deck the Halls" (Welsh traditional), "Jingle Bells" (1857; James Pierpont), "Good King Wenceslas" (traditional), "A Hot Time in the Old Town" (1896; Theo A. Metz), "Arabian Dance" (1892; from the "Nutcracker Suite, Op. 71a" by Peter Ilyich Tchaikovsky), "Bridal Chorus (Here Comes the Bride)" (1850; from "Lohengrin" by Richard Wagner), "None But the Lonely Heart" (1880; Peter Ilyich Tchaikovsky), "March" (1892; from the "Nutcracker Suite, Op. 71a" by Peter Ilyich Tchaikovsky), "My Bonnie (Lies Over

the Ocean)" (1881; music: H. J. Fuller), "The Man on the Flying Trapeze" (1867; Gaston Lyle), "The Riddle Song (I Gave My Love a Cherry)" (traditional; new lyrics: Frank Capra), "Polly Wolly Doodle" (traditional), "On the Beautiful Blue Danube" (1867; Johann Strauss), "String Quartet in E, Op. 13 No. 5: Minuet" (Luigi Boccherini), "Mexican Hat Dance" (traditional), "Auld Lang Syne" (traditional). *Author's Note*: Davis told this author that "I loved that Damon Runyon story **[Pocket Full of Miracles]** because it's bigger than life and that's what making pictures is all about. Those were the kind of pictures Frank [Capra] always made, and that's why I wanted to play that old battle-axe Apple Annie, who becomes a social prima donna. You know, I almost did not get that part. They were thinking of casting Helen Hayes in that role, but she was out of the country at that time and not available and then they offered the role to me. When the makeup people began to work on me to make me look like death warmed over, I told them, just go ahead and turn me into an old bag, which is what I am playing, lay on the wrinkles and sacks under the eyes and don't stint on the waddles under the chin." Ford told this author that he got the part in **Pocket Full of Miracles** "after Frank [Capra] stopped at my table in a restaurant where we were both having lunch. He asked me: 'What are you doing next, Glenn?' I replied: 'Your next picture, Frank.'" Capra only nodded and then went back to his office, telling this author many years later: "I really did not have Glenn [Ford] in mind for the role of the racketeer in **Pocket Full of Miracles**, but when I met him in that restaurant and he told me that he wanted to be in my next picture, I seriously thought about him and concluded that he was perfect for the leading man. I called his agent and cut the deal." Falk, who is exceptional as Ford's strong-arm man, was seen by Kanter, the writer of the script, in a riveting role as lethal gangster Abe "Kid Twist" Reles in **Murder, Inc.**, 1960, and, according to Falk's statements to this author, "he went to Capra and convinced him to give me the role of Glenn Ford's enforcer in **Pocketful of Miracles**, believing that I had a hidden flair for comedy and that was one of the biggest breaks of my life. It got me out of being typecast as thugs, and, when Frank Sinatra saw me in that Capra picture, he later gave me the choice role of a wacky gangster in **Robin and the 7 Hoods** [1964], and that's when my career took off. It's all in the breaks, kid." The towering character actor Mazurki also appears in this film essaying another of his patented roles, telling this author: "The call went out for every guy who ever played a goon and I was one of the first to show up and got a part—a couple of grunting lines, look menacing, and that's it. A lot of guys complained about being stereotyped, but that was what I did all the time and it put meat and potatoes on the plate." **p&d**, Frank Capra; **cast**, Glenn Ford, Bette Davis, Hope Lange, Peter Mann, Arthur O'Connell, Peter Falk, Thomas Mitchell, Edward Everett Horton, Mickey Shaughnessy, David Brian, Sheldon Leonard, Ann-Margret, Ellen Corby, Barton MacLane, John Litel, Jerome Cowan, Willis Bouchey, Fritz Feld, Jack Elam, Mike Mazurki, Frank Ferguson, Jay Novello, Gavin Gordon; **w**, Hal Kanter, Harry Tugend, Jimmy Cannon (based on the story "Madame La Gimp" by Damon Runyan and the 1933 screenplay "Lady for a Day" by Robert Riskin); **c**, Robert Bronner (Panavision; Eastmancolor); **m**, Walter Scharf; **ed**, Frank P. Keller; **art d**, Hal Pereira, Roland Anderson; **set d**, Sam Comer, Ray Moyer; **spec eff**, Farciot Edouart.

Poil de carotte ★★★★ 1933; France; 108m; Les Films Marcel Vandal et Charles Delac/Harold Auten; B/W; Drama; Children: Unacceptable; **VHS**. Duvivier directs a sensitive and moving film, loosely based upon the Cinderella tale, and centered on Lynen, a pre-adolescent red-haired boy, events taking place during one summer while a family is on vacation. Lynen is abused by his mother, Fonteney, who gave birth to him while having an affair with a man with red hair. She favors his almost adult siblings, while his stepfather, Baur, withdraws to hunting and making friends. Meanwhile Lynen slaves at challenging tasks imposed upon him by Fonteney and his siblings. To relieve his misery and suffering, Lynen and his girlfriend, Segall, rehearse a marriage ceremony in a forest as animals burst into song, and it is with these forest creatures that the boy establishes loving bonds. These idyllic moments are consistently interrupted by Fontenery, who continues to use Lynen as an indentured servant, exhausting him to the point where he thinks about ending his life. Baur, however, who has recently been elected mayor, and who has tried to establish a relationship with Lynen, hears that the boy is about to hang himself and he races to his rescue. He and Lynen have a heart-to-heart talk, and Baur becomes a real father in the boy's eyes, inspiring him to go on living and convincing him that he will enjoy a better way of life. Lynen, Baur, Fortenay and Segall render top flight performances in this consistently touching drama. Duvivier does not anoint Lynen with sainthood, but effectively profiles him as a normal boy, full of mischief and innocent love while being irresponsible and caring at the same time, thus realistically capturing the erratic nature of childhood. The photography from master cinematographer Thirard, who worked film cameras for more than forty years, is superb, and he captures the boy and his story with imaginative camera angles, offering more fluidity than seen in most other films of that period. This popular Renaud story was filmed as a silent in 1925 and again in 1973, but with much less impact than this compelling production. *Author's Note*: Duvivier discovered Lynen while the impoverished boy was walking along a street and, even though Lynen had no acting experience, the director cast him in the lead role of this film. Duvivier rightly believed that Lynen's natural childish flair for theatrics would provide a refreshing image. He instructed Lynen to ignore the camera and act out each scene as if he were playacting with his urchin friends and thereby drew from the boy an outstanding performance. Lynen would go on to appear in more films throughout the 1930s, providing money to his otherwise penniless family that allowed them to survive and eventually see a more financially stabilized lifestyle. Robert Lynen proved to be an exceptionally brave adult, participating in the French underground during WWII, when he was captured by the Nazis in Marseilles in 1943. He was branded as a member of the French resistance and was imprisoned in a German concentration camp in Karlsruhe, Germany, where he was put to death on April 1, 1944, at the age of twenty-two. Sexuality prohibits viewing by children. (In French; English subtitles.) **d&w**, Julien Duvivier (based on the novels *Poil de carotte* and *La bigote* by Jules Renard); **cast**, Harry Baur, Robert Lynen, Catherine Fonteney, Louis Gauthier, Simone Aubry, Maxime Fromiot, Colette Segall, Marthe Marty, Christiane Dor, Jean Borelli; **c**, Armand Thirard, Monniot; **m**, Alexandre Tansman; **ed**, Marthe Poncin; **art d**, Aguettand, Carré.

Point Blank ★★★ 1967; U.S.; 92m; Bernard-Winkler/MGM; Color; Crime Drama; Children: Unacceptable; **DVD**; **VHS**. Director Boorman provides a grim but fascinating crime tale that sees Marvin as a gunman who steals money from the mob with the help of Vernon. They hide out on the island of Alcatraz where Vernon shoots Marvin point-blank to get the loot. As Marvin starts to go under he sees Vernon has his arm around Marvin's untrustworthy wife, Acker. They leave him for dead, but Marvin survives, swims to shore (a feat achieved by only one prisoner at Alcatraz), and the film gets more violent with convoluted criminal activities in flashbacks and flash forwards as Marvin seeks and achieves revenge. He gets that revenge after meeting Wynn in San Francisco, who tells Marvin that he is the poorly paid mob's bookkeeper, and, in exchange for a share of the loot from the robbery Marvin might recover, tells Marvin where he can find the faithless Acker. Marvin goes Los Angeles and to her apartment and blasts it to pieces, but does not kill Acker, who has been abandoned by the ruthless Vernon and who meets her end by subsequently committing suicide. Marvin then finds Acker's sister, Dickinson, and uses her as decoy to invade Vernon's heavily-defended penthouse. While Dickinson beds Vernon, Marvin sneaks into the place, but Vernon falls to his death before Marvin can take his vengeance. Vernon, however, did not have the loot Marvin has sought and he learns that he must now go after mob bosses Strong and Bochner, who is married to Haynes. Strong and Bochner, however,

Lee Marvin and Sharon Acker in *Point Blank*, 1967.

know Marvin is gunning for them and they set a trap for Marvin, but the wily gunman is too smart for them and it backfires, and where Strong and Bochner are killed. In his search for the culprits, Marvin now encounters O'Connor, who is the right-hand sub-boss of the unknown mob leader; Marvin and O'Connor agree to conduct another robbery involving mob money, and O'Connor believes that he will become the top boss of the mob after pulling that heist. When O'Connor and Marvin attempt to commit that robbery in San Francisco, however, O'-Connor is shot dead by Wynn, who, it turns out, is not a bookkeeper but the top mob boss. He compliments Marvin on helping him root out all of the traitorous persons in his mob and then offers him a lucrative position, but Marvin sees this as a ruse by which Wynn will also kill him; Marvin, a now much wiser man, departs for saner, safer pastures. This film was remade as **Payback**, 1999, with Mel Gibson reenacting Marvin's role, which proved to be just as effective and exciting as this original production. Song: "Mighty Good Times" (Stu Gardner). *Author's Note*: This story as originally penned by Westlake, a rather pedestrian crime writer, takes much of its plotline from the betrayals and underworld schemes profiled in **The Killers**, 1946, which, ironically, starred Burt Lancaster, an actor with whom Marvin later had trouble when making **The Professionals**, 1966, where Marvin was drinking to such excess and failing to show up on time for shootings that Lancaster, according to director Richard Brooks "was ready to throw Lee [Marvin] from the top of a cliff to sober him up." Marvin, who also ironically appeared in the 1964 remake of **The Killers**, told this author that "**Point Blank** is a very violent film and violent crime films always seem to go over with audiences because viewers have a sick fascination with violent criminals. There was just too damned much of it in **Point Blank**, though, and I contributed most of that by shooting everyone and anything in sight and that's why it didn't make the kind of money everyone expected." The film was shot on a $3 million budget and initially returned $3.2 million from the box office in its initial release. For more details on the one man bank robber, John Paul Scott, who did escape Alcatraz by swimming to the San Francisco shore on December 16, 1962, see my *Encyclopedia of World Crime*, Volume I (CrimeBooks, Inc., 1990; under "Alacatraz," page 69). Excessive violence prohibits viewing by children. **p**, Judd Bernard, Robert Chartoff, (not credited) Irwin Winkler; **d**, John Boorman; **cast**, Lee Marvin, Angie Dickinson, Keenan Wynn, Carroll O'Connor, Lloyd Bochner, Michael Strong, John Vernon, Sharon Acker, Kathleen Freeman, Roberta Haynes; **w**, Alexander Jacobs, David Newhouse, Rafe Newhouse (based on the novel *The Hunter* by Donald E. Westlake as Richard Stark); **c**, Philip H. Lathrop (Panavision; Metrocolor); **m**, Johnny Mandel; **ed**, Henry Berman; **art d**, Albert Brenner, George W. Davis; **set d**, Keogh Gleason, Henry Grace; **spec eff**, J. McMillan Johnson.

Ed Harris in *Pollock*, 2000.

Poison Pen ★★★ 1941; U.K.; 79m; ABPC (Associated British Picture Corporation)/REP; B/W; Drama; Children: Unacceptable. This intriguing psychological drama has residents in a small British village becoming shocked and frightened after they begin receiving hate-filled "poison pen letters" that make scandalous accusations. This results in a murder and a suicide that prompt police to hire a handwriting analyst, who tracks down and identifies the writer as Robson, the well-respected spinster sister of the village vicar, Tate. Unfortunately, Robson, who initially appears to be a rock of sanity and wisdom, has become mentally unstable. Robson provides a powerful and memorable performance of an aging woman whose mind has been warped through years of repression and unfounded suspicions. Songs: "Dreaded Moments" (J.S. Zamecnik); "Foxtrot" (Sydney Baynes); "Whispering" (John Schonberger, Vincent Rose, Richard Coburn); "Montage," "Playout" (Harry Acres); "Voluntary" (George Griggs). *Author's Note*: The talented McDowall, who plays a choir boy in this film, migrated to America following this production and began a long and successful U.S. film career, beginning with a starring role in John Ford's masterpiece, **How Green Was My Valley**, 1941. Mature themes prohibit viewing by children. **p**, Walter C. Mycroft; **d**, Paul L. Stein; **cast**, Flora Robson, Robert Newton, Ann Todd, Geoffrey Toone, Reginald Tate, Belle Chrystall, Edward Chapman, Edward Rigby, Athole Stewart, Mary Hinton, Wilfrid Hyde-White, Roddy McDowall; **w**, William Freshman, N.C. Hunter, Esther McCracken, Doreen Montgomery (based on the play by Richard Llewellyn); **c**, Philip Tannura; **ed**, Flora Newton.

Pollock ★★★ 2000; U.S.; 122m; Brant-Allen/Sony; Color; Biographical Drama; Children: Unacceptable (MPAA: R); **DVD**; **VHS**. The life and career of American abstract expressionist painter Jackson Pollock (1912-1956), portrayed by Harris, is well presented in this fascinating biopic. The film starts at the end of the 1940s when Harris lives in a small apartment with his brother in New York City, drinking too much and only occasionally exhibiting his paintings in group shows. He meets a fellow artist, Harden, who puts her career aside to be his companion, lover, champion, wife, and caretaker. They move to the Hamptons where he sobers up and achieves a new style that critics praise. But Harris can't fight off the demons driving him to drink and his life ends tragically and prematurely. Songs: "The Mighty Blues" (improvisation by the Port of Harlem Jazzmen); "It's Sad But True" (Harold Green, Michael Stoner, Martin Block); "Sing, Sing, Sing" (Louis Prima); "The Hut-Sut Song" (Leo Killion, Ted McMichael, Jack Owens); "Del Album De Mis Ensuenos" (Bruno Balz, Jim Cowler); "Joseph, Joseph" (traditional); "He's Funny That Way" (Charles Daniels, Richard A. Whiting); "The Honey Song" (Arbie Gibson, Curtis Massey); "Blues in the South" (William Johnstone);, "Dodo's Bounce," Vine Street Breakdown" Jack Laud-

erdale); "Mahogany Hall Stomp" (Spencer Williams); "Old Dan Tucker" (traditional); "Get with the Beat" (Billy Nix, Harry Glenn); " Hot Lips Baby" (Rose Marie McCoy, Fred Mendelsohn, Napoleon Brown); "Central Avenue Drag" (Pete Johnson); "The World Keeps Turning" (Tom Waits, Kathleen Brennan). Gutter language and sexuality prohibit viewing by children. **p**, Ed Harris, Fred Berner, Jon Kilik, James Francis Trezza, Cecilia Kate Roque; **d**, Harris; **cast**, Harris, Marcia Gay Harden, Tom Bower, Jennifer Connelly, Bud Cort, John Heard, Val Kilmer, Amy Madigan, Robert Knott, David Leary, Jeffrey Tambor, Sada Thompson; **w**, Barbara Turner, Susan J. Emshwiller (based on the book *Jackson Pollock: An American Saga* by Steven Naifeh, Gregory White Smith); **c**, Lisa Rinzler; **m**, Jeff Beal; **ed**, Kathryn Himoff; **prod d**, Mark Friedberg; **art d**, Teresa Mastropierro, Peter Rogness; **set d**, Carolyn Cartwright; **spec eff**, Mark Bero, Steve Kirschoff.

Pollyanna ★★★★ 1920 (silent); U.S.; 58m; Mary Pickford Company/UA; B/W; Comedy/Drama; Children: Acceptable; **DVD**. Pickford shines in a memorable film most associated with her illustrious film career. She is the indomitable daughter of James, a missionary who has taught her to always be "glad" in the face of any adversity. After James dies, Pickford is taken to live with her mean-minded aunt, Griffith, a spinster who resents just about every living creature after having been jilted early in life by Prior, who has become a well-to-do physician. While Griffith selfishly withholds her affection from Pickford, the girl makes friends with everyone in the small town, her love and optimism so impressing the man who once loved her mother that he adopts one of Pickford's homeless little friends, Ralston. While saving the life of a child, Pickford is hit by an automobile, and Griffith's heart softens toward the girl, summoning physicians, who tell Griffith that the girl will most likely never walk again and will remain an invalid. Pickford pleads with Griffith to call upon the services of Prior, who has earlier befriended her, and Griffith overcomes her bitter memories of Prior and displays her love for Pickford by asking Prior to examine the girl. Prior not only finds a way to provide Pickford with a complete cure and where she will again regain her ability to walk, but Griffith and Prior reconcile and renew their old romantic relationship. The film ends with one of the most endearing finales when Pickford plays "family" with her friend Ralston, taking their "children" on an imaginary free ride on a trolley car. Pickford's exuberance for life and her gallantry toward her fellow humans is evident in every poignant frame of this delightful production. Song: "Rock-a-Bye Baby" (1884; Effie I. Canning; played on theater organs during the initial release). The film was an enormous success, grossing more than $1 million, a then staggering box office return. In 1928, Pickford stated that this film was one of her favorite films, but she somewhat demeaned the film in the 1950s, bowing to the pressure from critics of any films showing sentimentality. *Author's Note*: Though unabashedly sentimental, this film will warm the hearts of any viewer, despite the irrational derision shown in later decades for sentimentality, which coldheartedly demands that one should feel guilty for having a soft heart. There is nothing shallow or synthetic about sentimentality, which is a decided strength, not a weakness, where one bravely expresses open affection and concern for one's fellow human beings as well as all things living. The marvelous and healthy optimism Pickford shows throughout this wonderful tearjerker inspires the viewer to believe that the world, despite its agonies and trials, is nevertheless a fine place in which to live. (Even the tough and uncompromising Ernest Hemingway once wrote: "The world is a fine place and worth fighting for.") Irrespective of seemingly endless skeptics, cynics and gloom-and-doom naysayers, it is exactly that, the world being the welcoming and inviting place one makes of it. It became fashionable to condemn sentimentality in the 1950s, and that trend was never better illustrated than in a line delivered by Adolphe Menjou, playing a French general in the incisive anti-war classic **Paths of Glory**, 1957, when he accuses Kirk Douglas, commander of some of his troops, of being too compassionate, stating: "You've spoiled the keenness of your mind by wallowing in sentimentality." This is a statement from a cold-blooded, ruthless and utterly merciless general, who has arbitrarily sanctioned the executions of three innocent soldiers as sacrificial compensation for his own military failure. Sentimentality, on the other hand, has been the bulwark of all of Walt Disney's greatest animated classics (**Bambi**, 1942; **Dumbo**, 1941; **Pinocchio**, 1940; and **Snow White and the Seven Dwarfs**, 1937), all of which are impregnably shielded from condemners of sentimentality by the universal approval of a public wanting to instill such warmhearted sentimentality within the developing characters of their innocent children and while doggedly refusing to discard such heartfelt notions from their own childhoods. The destiny of **Pollyanna** and its Victorian ideals (ethics that were as good then as they are now) is dictated, thankfully, by the heart and not the mind, and where the heart has its greater reasons of which the mind can never know (albeit no one ever entirely abandons reason when dealing with their sentiments). In any seemingly insurmountable crisis, the author has always believed in mostly following the heart and not the mind in taking, if not the easiest, the better path, and thereby, irrespective of great pitfalls that chiefly hazard selfish goals, preserve the best element of what some describe as man's immortal soul. **Pollyanna** was remade in 1960 with Hayley Mills and again in 2003. **d**, Paul Powell; **cast**, Mary Pickford, J. Wharton James, Katherine Griffith, Helen Jerome Eddy, George Berrell, Howard Ralston, William Courtleigh, Herbert Prior, Doc Crane, Joan Marsh; **w**, Frances Marion (based on the novel by Eleanor H. Porter and the play by Catherine Chisholm Cushing); **c**, Charles Rosher; **art d**, Max Parker.

Pollyanna ★★★ 1960; U.S.; 134m; Walt Disney/Buena Vista; Color; Comedy; Children: Acceptable; **DVD**; **VHS**. Mills is exceptional as a happy and spunky girl, who comes to a town in 1912 that is embattled by feuds and intimidated by her stern aunt, Wyman. Mills does all she can to get everyone to make peace, but to no avail, and they wish she would simply go away. Many in the town, like Moorehead, are cranky, old people, who find the child annoying, especially when she befriends another orphan, Corcoran, and begins playing games with him, but the children eventually soften Moorehead's heart, along with hermit Menjou, who first chastises the children for playing on his property before inviting them into his home where he shows them his collection of delicate glass prisms that reflect and diffuse brilliant slivers of light throughout his home. Mills also converts Malden, a fire-and-brimstone preacher, into a calmer clergyman after he reads a slogan on an amulet Mills wears around her neck, one that her deceased father, a missionary, had given her, that reads: "If you search for the evil in man expecting to find it, you certainly will." This quote (attributed to Abraham Lincoln but created by scriptwriter Swift) so impresses Malden that his next sermon is one of love and joy instead of threats of eternal damnation. Egan, who is the local doctor and who had been Wyman's childhood sweetheart, then arranges a fair to raise money for a new orphanage and, though Wyman prohibits Mills from attending that gala, the girl escapes from Wyman's home through a window with Corcoran's help and both attend the fair. Mills wins a doll, the first she has ever had, and goes home delighted. She attempts to reenter Wyman's home by climbing an apple tree to get to her bedroom window, but, when the doll falls from her grasp, she reaches for it, and falls, suffering serious injuries that leave her legs paralyzed. Everyone's attitude is altered toward Mills after they learn about her serious medical condition. In a touching, tearful scene, the whole town turns out to bid her good wishes as she leaves for Baltimore to have an operation. Mills' effervescent optimism has altered the lives of many of these people for the better, even curmudgeon Menjou, who now plans to adopt Corcoran as his son. The once embittered Wyman, too, has changed her stubborn ways and even reconciles with Egan. Everyone has captured Mills' indomitable spirit of seeing the good side of even the worst situations. Songs: "America, America"/"America the Beautiful" (1895, Samuel A. Ward, Katharine Lee Bates); "Pollyanna's Song," "Whoop Ta Doodle Day" (Hazel George as Gil George); "Early One Morning" (traditional); "I'll Take You Home

Heather O'Rourke in *Poltergeist*, 1982.

Again Kathleen" (Thomas Payne Westendorf); "When You and I Were Young, Maggie" (J. A. Butterfield, George W. Johnson); "Listen to the Mocking Bird" (Richard Milburn, Septimus Winner as Alice Hawthorne); "Goodnight Ladies" (folk song attributed to Edwin P. Christy). *Author's Note*: The name "Pollyanna" became synonymous with looking on the bright side, if perhaps naively. The film was shot on location in Santa Rosa, California, and throughout the winemaking area of Napa Valley. It was Mills' first film in the United States, after starring with her father John Mills in **Tiger Bay**, 1959, in England. After Mrs. Walt Disney saw that film in England where Walt Disney was looking to cast actors for this film, she urged her husband, Walt, to sign up the girl and he did, starring her in this memorable production. This was the final film in which Menjou appeared. He was a conservative millionaire and very much like the crusty, old man he plays in the film, but the spreading "good will" of everyone involved in the production soon melted Menjou's heart. The antique train and old-fashioned fire engine used in the film were from the private collection of Ward Kimball, who had long been a Disney animator and who had established a toy train museum in San Gabriel Valley where more than 10,000 model trains were on display. **Pollyanna** was first made as a silent film with Mary Pickford in 1920, as a TV series in 1973, and remade in 2003 as a made-for-TV movie. **p**, Walt Disney; **d&w**, David Swift (based on the novel by Eleanor H. Porter); **cast**, Hayley Mills, Jane Wyman, Richard Egan, Karl Malden, Nancy Olson, Adolphe Menjou, Donald Crisp, Agnes Moorehead, Kevin Corcoran, James Drury; **c**, Russell Harlan (Technicolor); **m**, Paul Smith; **ed**, Frank Gross; **art d**, Carroll Clark, Robert Clatworthy; **set d**, Emile Kuri, Fred MacLean; **spec eff**, Ub Iwerks.

Poltergeist ★★★ 1982; U.S.; 114m; MGM/UA; Color; Horror; Children: Unacceptable (MPAA: R); **DVD**; **VHS**. Genuinely scary horror film sees ghosts haunting the recently constructed house of a young family who, at first, seem to entertain everyone, but then terrorize and suck the youngest child, O'Rourke, into limbo. A clairvoyant, Rubinstein, is called in and she says the house stands on a sacred Indian burial ground and their spirits are unhappy. She manages to retrieve O'Rourke from limbo, but not without many harrowing and nerve-wracking moments, before she exorcises the house. Apparently rid of the ghosts, the family is taking no chances and parents Nelson and Williams decide to put it up for sale anyway. Hooper does a great job in managing this fright-filled tale, where special effects wizards Wood and Jarvis provide many astounding scenes. This film became a big hit, producing more than $121 million at the box office in its initial release against a budget of $10.7 million. The film spawned three other films: **Poltergeist II: The Other Side**, 1986; **Poltergeist III**, 1988; and **Poltergeist: The Legacy**, 1996. Song: "The Star-Spangled Banner" (John Stafford Smith, Francis

Tyrone Power and Thomas Gomez in *Pony Soldier*, 1952.

Scott Key). Violence and frightening scenes prohibit viewing by children. **p**, Steven Spielberg, Frank Marshall; **d**, Tobe Hooper; **cast**, Craig T. Nelson, JoBeth Williams, Beatrice Straight, Dominique Dunne, Oliver Robins, Heather O'Rourke, Michael McManus, Virginia Kiser, Martin Casella, Richard Lawson, Zelda Rubinstein; **w**, Spielberg, Michael Grais, Mark Victor (based on a story by Spielberg); **c**, Matthew F. Leonetti (Panavision; Metrocolor); **m**, Jerry Goldsmith; **ed**, Michael Kahn; **prod d**, James H. Spencer; **set d**, Cheryal Kearney; **spec eff**, Michael Wood, Jeff Jarvis.

Pony Express ★★★ 1953; U.S.; 101m; PAR; Color; Western; Children: Unacceptable; **VHS**. Great action appears throughout this lively and exciting western, which is a loose remake of the 1925 silent version directed by James Cruze. Heston is a standout as Buffalo Bill Cody (William F. Cody; 1846-1917) and Tucker is equally impressive playing Wild Bill Hickok (James Butler Hickok; 1837-1876). They join forces to establish the Pony Express mail route from St. Joseph, Missouri, across the Great Plains and over the Rocky Mountains and Sierra Nevada Mountains to Sacramento, California. Heston meets fetching Fleming and her brother, Moore, while riding through the plains of Utah as he charts the route for the intended Pony Express and befriends them, having more than a casual interest in the alluring, titian-haired Fleming. What he does not know is that both have naively joined a cabal to have California secede from the Union, believing that the state is too distant from the U.S. seat of government in Washington, D.C., to mean anything to the present Union. The culprits plotting that secession are Randall, a foreign agent, who expects to get rich once the state secedes and is bought by a foreign country, and stagecoach owner Brandon, who wants to preserve his monopoly of delivering the mail to the exclusion of the Pony Express. To prevent the Pony Express from linking the U.S. to California, Brandon promotes an Indian war by supplying Hogan, who plays Yellow Hand (d. 1876), a leading Cheyenne warrior, with rifles and ammunition. Heston finds it next to impossible to extend the operations of the Pony Express after Hogan and his warriors repeatedly attack its mail riders. He befriends Tucker after they have a friendly sharpshooting competition, enlisting Tucker's aid in combating the Indian problem. They head for Sacramento, California, where they intend to establish the final Pony Express station, but Heston is waylaid by Indians. The captured Heston is then ordered to fight for his survival in a tomahawk battle with Hogan and he undertakes this fierce struggle almost at the cost of his life, barely emerging victorious after killing Hogan. (In reality, Cody, while acting as a U.S. Cavalry scout, killed and scalped Yellow Hand, a Cheyenne sub-chief at the Battle of Warbonnet Creek on July 17, 1876, in northwestern Nebraska; this action was later termed the "First Scalp for Custer" in retaliation for the Custer massacre by the Sioux earlier

that year and for which Cody was awarded the Congressional Medal of Honor.) Heston goes on to successfully establish the Pony Express, despite ambushes from outlaws out to rob the mails, and also, with Tucker's help, brings about the statehood of California while winning Fleming's hand in the epic process. Drama and romance are added to what real facts are provided, but the film does a good job of recreating this true and hazardous adventure saga of the Old West. *Author's Note*: Heston admitted to this author that "**Pony Express** is a dime novel version of that adventurous operation and where a lot of true facts were sacrificed to make an exciting picture. We were not out to educate the public but to entertain it. That's what Hollywood always does. If you want the real facts, you can find them in any good history book." The ten-day horseback journey of the Pony Express between St. Joseph, Missouri, and Sacramento, California, was conducted mostly by courageous teenage boys, who battled harsh weather, hostile Indians, and outlaws seeking to rob the mail, along with California Separatists, who tried to shut down the operation. Historically, the Pony Express operated for only eighteen months, from April 3, 1860, until October 1861 when the operation was shut down as the telegraph and railroads by then delivered mail faster. Many actors have portrayed the celebrated Buffalo Bill and Wild Bill Hickok, notably (Buffalo Bill): **Annie Get Your Gun**, 1950 (Louis Calhern); **Annie Oakley**, 1935 (Moroni Olsen); **Buffalo Bill**, 1944 (Joel McCrea); **Buffalo Bill and the Indians**, 1976 (Paul Newman); **Hidalgo**, 2004 (J. K. Simmons); **The Iron Horse**, 1924 (George Waggner); **The Plainsman**, 1936 (James Ellison); **Wild Bill**, 1995 (Keith Carradine) and (Hickok): **Across the Sierras**, 1941 (Bill Elliott); **Calamity Jane**, 1953 (Howard Keel); **Dallas**, 1950 (Reed Hadley); **The Iron Horse**, 1924 (Jack Padjan); **The Lawless Breed**, 1953 (Robert Anderson); **Little Big Man**, 1970 (Jeff Corey); **The Plainsman**, 1936 (Gary Cooper); **The White Buffalo**, 1977 (Charles Bronson); **Wild Bill**, 1995 (Jeff Bridges); and **Wild Bill Hickok**, 1923 (William S. Hart). For more extensive film listings citing these historical characters and films based upon them, see Historical Characters, Index, Volume II, of this work. For more details on James Butler "Wild Bill" Hickok, see my book *Encyclopedia of Western Lawmen and Outlaws* (Paragon, 1992; pages 155-160). Violence prohibits viewing by children. **p**, Nat Holt; **d**, Jerry Hopper; **cast**, Charlton Heston, Rhonda Fleming, Forrest Tucker, Jan Sterling, Porter Hall, Henry Brandon, Michael Moore, Richard Shannon, Stuart Randall, Lewis Martin, Pat Hogan, Jim Burk; **w**, Charles Marquis Warren (based on a story by Frank Gruber); **c**, Ray Rennahan (Technicolor); **m**, Paul Sawtell; **ed**, Eda Warren; **art d**, Hal Pereira, Albert Nozaki; **set d**, Sam Comer, Bertram Granger; **spec eff**, Farciot Edouart.

Pony Soldier ★★★ 1952; U.S.; 82m; FOX; Color; Adventure/Western; Children: Cautionary; **DVD**; **VHS**. Power gives a compelling performance as a Royal Canadian Mountie in this action-packed western saga. He is on the trail of renegade Indians in 1876 in the Northwest wilds of Canada. Power is assigned to follow Randall, a Cree chief who has led his tribe from its reservation to cross the border into Montana where it has been illegally raiding buffalo herds and where warrior Mitchell has led a band of Cree Indians in a wagon train raid, capturing attractive Edwards and escaped convict Horton. Power's only companion is Gomez, an apprehensive half breed guide, who knows the territory, but fears for his life at the hands of the unpredictable Indians. After several days, Power and Gomez located the Cree tribe and Power forcefully confronts Randall, ordering him and his followers to return to their reservation in Canada. Randall, impressed with Power's commanding presence, meets with his sub chiefs and agrees to return to the reservation if Power provides supplies; Power agrees to do so. While Power closely bonds with an Indian boy, Numkena, he also develops a close relationship with Edwards. Mitchell, along with some of his warriors, however, adamantly refuses to leave the U.S. territory. Then Horton kills Mitchell's brother while making an escape. He is recaptured and is about to be executed, torn apart while tied to two horses about to be whipped into opposite directions when Power intervenes and convinces Randall to prevent Horton's death. In retaliation, Mitchell abducts Edwards, taking her to the high mountains where he intends to sacrifice her to his gods by burning her alive at the stake. Power pursues the renegade and, after a fierce fight, kills Mitchell and saves Edwards. He then leads Randall and his tribe back toward the reservation with Edwards at his side for a romantic ending. *Author's Note*: Beautifully photographed by cinematographer Jackson, the film was shot on location at Sedona, Arizona, and director Newman hired more than 450 Navajo Indians to play members of the errant Cree tribe. The production was hampered by severe snowstorms and, during one shooting episode, Newman called a halt after seeing a strange and alarming flash of light that whited out filming, this being a nuclear test explosion taking place in Nevada three hundred miles distant. Gomez told this author that "Ty [Power] was all man and insisted on doing his own stunts in **Pony Soldier**, even though some of them were very dangerous and over the protests of the director [Newman]. He did not like his image of a handsome matinee idol and was always trying to prove himself as a real man and a fine actor, and he was both. He did the same thing during the war [WWII] when he enlisted in the Marines and became a pilot. He flew a lot of hazardous missions over Iwo Jima and Okinawa and nobody ever heard about that as he was not about to broadcast his heroic exploits. He was truly a brave man and more of a hero in real life than he ever was on the screen in a swordfight or riding a horse. He went on testing himself and that proved to be his undoing, because he insisted on doing some difficult swordfight stunts while they were making **Solomon and Sheba** [1959], and the exertion caused him to have a heart attack that killed him [on November 15, 1958]. No one knew that he always had a weak heart. He died at the age of forty-four. What a great loss of such a great human being." Many films have profiled the heroic exploits of the Royal Canadian Mounted Police, notably: **The Canadians**, 1961; **Death Hunt**, 1981; **The Missouri Breaks**, 1976; **Northern Pursuit**, 1943; **Northwest Mounted Police**, 1940; **Rose Marie**, 1936; **Rose Marie**, 1954; **Saskatchewan**, 1954; and **The Untouchables**, 1987. For a more detailed listing of such films, see Subject Index, Volume II, of this work. **p**, Samuel G. Engel; **d**, Joseph M. Newman; **cast**, Tyrone Power, Cameron Mitchell, Thomas Gomez, Penny Edwards, Robert Horton, Anthony Numkena, Adeline De Walt Reynolds, Howard Petrie, Stuart Randall, Richard Boone, Chief Bright Fire, Michael Rennie (narrator); **w**, John C. Higgins (based on a magazine story by Garnett Weston); **c**, Harry Jackson (Technicolor); **m**, Alex North; **ed**, John W. McCafferty; **art d**, Lyle Wheeler, Chester Gore; **set d**, Thomas Little, Fred J. Rode; **spec eff**, Ray Kellogg.

Ponyo ★★★ 2011; Japan; 101m; Studio Ghibli/GKids; Color; Animated Fantasy; Children: Acceptable (MPAA: G); **DVD**. In this well-crafted animated tale a five-year-old boy in Japan, the son of a sailor, lives a quiet life in a house on a cliff overlooking the ocean with his mother. One day he finds a bottle with a beautiful goldfish inside and calls her Ponyo. She is not an ordinary goldfish but a princess, the daughter of a wizard and a goddess. She uses her father's magic to transform her into a human and falls in love with the boy. This creates an imbalance in the world and her father sends mighty waves to find his daughter. The boy and girl survive many adventures and save the world while Ponyo realizes her dream of remaining a human. Songs: "Ponyo on the Cliff by the Sea" (Joe Hisaishi, Katsuya Kondo, Hayao Miyazaki), "Mother Sea" (Joe Hisaishi, Hayao Miyazaki). (In Japanese; English subtitles.) **p**, Kathleen Kennedy, Frank Marshall, Steve Alpert, Toshio Suzuki; **d&w**, Hayao Miyazaki; **cast** (voiceovers, English version), Noah Cyrus, Cate Blanchett, Matt Damon, Liam Neeson, Tina Fey, Cloris Leachman, Lily Tomlin, Betty White; (voiceovers, Japanese version), Yuria Nara, Tomoko Yamaguchi, Kazushige Nagashima, Yûki Amami, George Tokoro, Kazuko Yoshiyuki, Akiko Yano; **c**, Atsushi Okui; **m**, Jô Hisaishi; **ed**, Hayao Miyazaki, Takeshi Seyama; **art d**, Noboru Yoshida.

The Poor Little Rich Girl ★★★ 1917 (silent); U.S.; 65m; Artcraft Pictures Corporation; B/W; Comedy/Drama; Children: Cautionary; **DVD**.

Mary Pickford in *The Poor Little Rich Girl*, 1917.

Pickford renders an outstanding performance as an ignored eleven-year-old girl in this touching melodrama. She lives in the lap of luxury, but that is of no consequence to her because she is denied the only thing in life she needs and wants, loving concern and care. She is so protected within the confines of her father's vast estate that she has no idea of what transpires in the outside world and where she is virtually held in isolation as one might be held a prisoner behind bars. Her wealthy father, Wellesley, has no time for her as his every hour is consumed with making money and attending to his vast business interests. Her mother, Traverse, equally dismisses Pickford as a bothersome annoyance, giving all her time to her social affairs instead of spending any time with the child. Even the snooty household servants can find no time for Pickford, abusing her feelings while literally pushing her out of their way as they go about their daily chores. Pickford's play is a desperate attempt to get attention, which causes endless chaos within the household, and when she throws a tantrum she is punished for it. At one point, she is humiliated when, as punishment, she is ordered to don boy's clothing, a cruel and symbolic abuse showing not only how she is deprived of love but of her own identity as a girl. When Hicks, another girl from a similarly wealthy family, visits Pickford, this guest proves to be so arrogant and obnoxious that Pickford, after vainly attempting to make friends with her in innocent play, responds to her insults by getting into a fight with her and where the offensive Hicks gets her comeuppance. Although she struggles to find any little bit of happiness, Pickford meets with nothing but meanness, anger and even fear as she becomes terrified by her nightmares (these genuinely frightening sequences show an enormous snake menacing her and, in another well-crafted sequence, where her father contemplates suicide). The miserable and unhappy Pickford then becomes seriously ill through a servant's carelessness, but this changes everything as her parents and their servants now realize the worth of this loving little girl and she finally receives the affection she has so long craved, which is the best tonic she can receive in making a recovery. Pantheon director Tourneur, who directed many of Pickford's films, skillfully helms this production, his camera shots providing inventive angles and fluid scenes, especially the harrowing nightmare sequences. In addition to Pickford's stunningly convincing performance, the supporting players are standouts in their roles, much to the thanks of the meticulous Tourneur. *Author's Note*: Pickford was apprehensive in doing this film, as she was then twenty years old and was unsure as to whether or not she could convince audiences in playing a little girl half her age. The script, which was based upon the 1913 play by Eleanor Gates and starred Viola Dana, a future screen star, was written by Pickford's close friend and adviser, Frances Marion. When beginning production at Paramount's studio in Fort Lee, New Jersey (where most early films were produced as Hollywood was then in its formative stages as

Michael Whalen, Shirley Temple and Claude Gillingwater in *Poor Little Rich Girl,* **1936.**

a film production center), Pickford began introducing many new production ideas that somewhat distracted if not annoyed the by-the-book Tourneur, who was always described as "serious" by Pickford and Marion. While preparing to go on the set one day, Pickford noticed a mirror on the table in her dressing room that was at an angle and where sunlight from a nearby window reflected through it at an upward angle onto her face and where she believed that that intense ray of light made her appear much younger, the very age of the girl she was playing. She went to Tourneur and told him about her discovery and asked that he rig a light that would only flood her face from an upward angle so that its intense rays would bleach out any wrinkles about her eyes or the slightest furrows on her forehead, and this Tourneur did, having a technician make a special light that was later called a "baby spot," an innovative light that would be universally employed thereafter to make actors appear more youthful. Tourneur was less enthusiastic to embrace many of the inventive scenes Pickford and Marion wanted to add to the production. When they urged him to insert a mud fight involving Pickford as comic relief, Tourneur put his foot down, saying, "but that is not in the original play script." He further stated that such antics were unheard of by wealthy offspring of his native France. Both reminded him that Pickford was playing an American girl and in America any kind of play practiced even by the lowborn hoi polloi would be embraced by the richest child seeking universal fun. After some argument, the scene was incorporated and added greatly to the much-needed frolic in the story line. Further, Pickford and Marion insisted that Tourneur make Pickford appear to be smaller than her actual diminutive height (she stood only a half inch more than five feet) so when she descends a staircase, the windows in the backdrop are much taller. When she passes an entranceway, two footmen seem much taller than Pickford, and this illusion Tourneur easily accomplished by having them stand on bricks. Tourneur made sure that all of those actors playing the adults in the film were much taller people than Pickford. When he was asked by Marion to have all the furniture and sets made much larger to further diminish the image of Pickford's size, Tourneur refused, saying: "No, I am certain that Miss Pickford will make herself fit the scene." The film was produced through Pickford's own company and, after she showed it to Paramount studio boss Adolph Zukor and several of his executives, they sat silent and unresponsive. "All of the things Frances [Marion] and I had thought so funny on the set fell absolutely flat in the projection room," Pickford later stated. "I went home to bed without dinner and quietly cried myself to sleep. Frances took it even harder." Zukor and his closest advisers seriously considered not releasing the film, believing that it could damage if not destroy Pickford's career. They then decided to risk the film by releasing it in a few theaters and it met with such tremendous approval that the film was then broadly distributed. It received rave reviews that drove

millions to the theaters to see it, and despite all apprehensions it became the most successful film in Pickford's career to date. The film so entrenched within the public mind Pickford's image of a little girl that she would go on playing that kind of part for many years to come and continue to win public favor—she had become the Peter Pan of the silent film era where viewers insisted that she never grow up and always remain that sweet and darling little girl, and that is exactly how this great actress is best remembered. **p**, Adolph Zukor; **d**, Maurice Tourneur; **cast**, Mary Pickford, Madlaine Traverse, Charles Wellesley, Gladys Fairbanks, Frank McGlynn, Sr., Emile La Croix, Marcia Harris, Charles Craig, Frank Andrews, Herbert Prior; **w**, Frances Marion (based on the play by Eleanor Gates); **c**, Lucien N. Andriot, John van den Broek; **prod d**, Ben Carré.

Poor Little Rich Girl ★★★ 1936; U.S.; 79m; FOX; B/W; Musical; Comedy; Children: Recommended; **DVD; VHS**. Temple is at her most adorable in this musical romp where she is the daughter of Whalen, a wealthy widowed soap manufacturer. He thinks she can benefit from going to school and being around other children, but she'd rather stay home with him. He insists, and her nurse, Haden, takes her on a train to go to the private school, but the train is in an accident, which gives Temple the opportunity to run away and be on her own. She winds up at a boarding house for show business people and claims to be an orphan, so entertainers Faye and Haley take her in and make her part of their song-and-dance act. The trio gets hired to sing on a radio show sponsored by Gillingham, Whalen's rival in the soap business. Whalen hears of the act on the radio and finds his lost daughter, joyful to have her back with him, despite the fact that she has been promoting products produced by his keenest rival. Not only does Whalen recoup his precocious daughter Temple, but falls in love with Gillingham's secretary, Stuart, while searching for the evasive Temple. All the musical numbers are presented with zest, and the production values throughout are excellent. This good vehicle for Temple's talents was a remake of the 1917 silent film starring Mary Pickford, an equally superior film. Songs: "When I'm with You," "Oh My Goodness," "You've Gotta Eat Your Spinach, Baby," "But Definitely," "Buy a Bar of Barry's," "Military Man," "Peck's Theme" (1936, Harry Revel, Mack Gordon), "London Bridge Is Falling Down" (traditional). *Author's Note*: As can be expected, Temple dominates this film and stars Faye and Haley only make their appearances until the film is halfway over. Faye told this author: "I think my appearance in that Shirley Temple picture is about the briefest in my career, except for, maybe, **Now I'll Tell** [1934], but who was I to complain? Shirley was the biggest star of the day and that was only right because no one on God's green earth could top that little tyke." Faye's appearance caused the front office at Fox to believe that her image needed to be softened, so, following this film, she was made over with a new look where her heavy eyebrows were plucked and thinned to pencil line shapes and her hair was completely redone with new coiffeur styles. Also appearing, but only for eighty seconds, is a new singer with a wonderful tenor voice named Dick Webster, who later appeared in starring roles in many films, including non-musicals, under the more recognized name of Tony Martin. He would marry the alluring and talented dancer Cyd Charisse, a marriage that lasted for sixty years until her death in 2008, Martin dying in 2012 at the age of ninety-nine. **p**, Darryl F. Zanuck; **d**, Irving Cummings; **cast**, Shirley Temple, Alice Faye, Gloria Stuart, Jack Haley, Michael Whalen, Sara Haden, Jane Darwell, Claude Gillingwater, Henry Armetta, Lynn Bari, Billy Gilbert, Tony Martin, Fred "Snowflake" Toones; **w**, Sam Hellman, Gladys Lehman, Harry Tugend, Frances Marion (based on stories by Eleanor Gates, Ralph Spence); **c**, John F. Seitz; **m**, Cyril J. Mockridge; **ed**, Jack Murray; **art d**, William S. Darling, Rudolph Sternad; **set d**, Thomas Little.

Popi ★★★ 1969; U.S.; 113m; UA; Color; Comedy; Children: Unacceptable (MPAA: G); **DVD; VHS**. Warmhearted domestic tale sees Arkin as a widowed Puerto Rican father of two young sons, Alejandro and Figueroa, who call him Popi. He is worried about their miserable lifestyle in the run-down neighborhood of Spanish Harlem. Arkin works three jobs to support them, which leaves little time to supervise their activities. He wants to marry his girlfriend, Moreno, and move the family to a better home in Brooklyn, but he can't afford to fulfill that dream. Meanwhile, he and his family are at the mercy of criminal predators and have little recourse, even after street thugs victimize the boys and steal their clothes. One day Arkin notices that Cubans who have escaped to America and arrived in New York City have been given exceptional welfare benefits, so he comes up with an idea to improve family conditions. He takes the boys to Miami Beach and sets them adrift in a rowboat, hoping they will be rescued as Cuban political refugees and offered asylum in America. The boys do become adrift in that stolen rowboat off the coast of Miami, and are rescued. Taken to a hospital, they become heroes as thousands of people shower them with gifts while some wealthy persons state they want to adopt the boys. Arkin visits them in the hospital and tries to convince the boys that they would be better off with rich parents, but they argue about it and are overheard by members of the hospital staff. Their deception is exposed and they return to their impoverished life in Spanish Harlem, a still poor but happily reunited family. Hiller directs this sensitive tale with great care and skill, and Arkin provides a powerful and charismatic performance, as do Alejandro and Figueroa. Song: "Popi" (Dominic Frontiere, Norman Gimble). **p**, Herbert B. Leonard; **d**, Arthur Hiller; **cast**, Alan Arkin, Rita Moreno, Reuben Figueroa, Miguel Alejandro, Arny Freeman, Joan Tompkins, Anthony Holland, Louis Zorich, Antonia Rey, Barbara Dana; **w**, Tina Pine, Lester Pine; **c**, Andrew Laszlo (DeLuxe Color); **m**, Dominic Frontiere; **ed**, Anthony Ciccolini; **art d**, Robert Gundlach; **set d**, Sol Stern.

Poppy ★★★ 1936; U.S.; 73m; PAR; B/W; Comedy; Children: Acceptable; **DVD**; **VHS**. Fields is wonderful as a conniving confidence man and carnival hustler full of his usual blarney and bloviating palaver. He appears with his adopted daughter, Hudson, in the small town of Green Acres. After seeing and catching a wayward pup, Fields takes the canine to a saloon and places the little dog on the bar; he begins talking to it, and the dog appears to talk back to him as Fields employs his deceptive ventriloquism. When he asks the dog what it will have, it replies: "Milk in a saucer." The saloonkeeper is astonished at seeing a talking dog and immediately offers Fields $20 for the pup. Fields accepts the payment and begins to depart, but just before he leaves, the ostensibly irate dog shouts to him: "Just for selling me, I'll never talk again!" The saloonkeeper is crestfallen when Fields returns to state: "He probably means it, too. He's awfully stubborn." With that, he departs, leaving the dog and the saloonkeeper staring at each other. Fields and Hudson then set up a booth at the local fair where they fleece suckers in the old shell game and where Fields is not above bilking his fellow concessionaires out of their money with other confidence tricks. While her father is busy conning the locals, Hudson meets Cromwell, the mayor's son, and they begin a romance and become engaged. Fields by this time has learned that the rich Putnam family is about to be evicted from its vast estate because the legal heir to that estate has been missing since childhood. Fields seizes upon this opportunity by having a crooked attorney friend of his put together a bogus legal document contending that Hudson is the missing heiress to the Putnam estate. Meanwhile, Hudson and Cromwell hold a social event to announce their engagement, where Fields plays a mean game of croquet (a variation of his old vaudeville golfing routine), beating all the social elite through his crooked game playing while he circulates the news that Hudson is the missing heiress to the Putnam fortune. When his scheme is later exposed, Hudson, who was unaware of her stepfather's actions, runs off and is sheltered by Eburne, a kindly old woman, who knew the Putnam family well and sees that Hudson bears a striking resemblance to the mother of the missing heiress. When she finds that Hudson is wearing a locket she has had since childhood, it proves that Hudson is, indeed, that missing girl. This discovery rights all wrongs and Hudson goes ahead with her plans to

W.C. Fields and Rochelle Hudson in *Poppy,* 1936.

marry Cromwell while Fields is no longer attempting to evade pursuing police. Before he departs for greener pastures and the gullible marks that live there, he and Hudson have a touching farewell meeting, where she tells him that she can no longer be his faithful companion as he travels the roads to fortune. Fields smiles and, before departing, tells her: "Let me give you one word of fatherly advice: 'Never give a sucker an even break!'" Sutherland, who directed many of Fields' films, delivers a fun-filled story with many mirthful moments, and Fields' outlandish behavior, snide and funny remarks, and his adept performance in pulling off one scam after another provide consistent and often hilarious entertainment throughout. Songs: "Poppy" (1936; music: Friedrich Hollaender; lyrics: Sam Coslow), "A Rendezvous with a Dream" (1936; music: Ralph Rainger; lyrics: Leo Robin), "Gwine to Rune All Night (De Camptown Races)" (1850; Stephen Foster), "Mary Had a Little Lamb" (traditional children's song), "Pop Goes the Weasel" (c.1853; unknown composer). *Author's Note*: This is a delightful remake of Fields' superb silent comedy, **Sally of the Sawdust**, 1925, which was based upon Fields' smash 1923 Broadway stage hit where he performed his amazing juggling routines, which do not, unfortunately, appear in this film. The great comedian did not display his usual vim and vigor in that he was ill throughout most of this production. That illness was caused when, early on in the production, Fields accidentally fell from his bicycle, a prop he often used when escaping from pursuing police; he broke a vertebra, compelling him to wear a restraining back-brace throughout most of the production and exhibited considerable pain whenever he had to move actively about. Fields suffered such intense pain that he would do a scene perfectly and then pass out. Restricted in his movement, he was doubled in the long shots and the over-the-shoulder shots by Johnny Sinclair. Since some of his scenes were cut to spare the comedian more agony, Sutherland filled in these small gaps with some brief musical numbers and increased the subplot involving Hudson and Cromwell. The film still remains as another Fields gem glittering brightly in his illustrious repertoire, and his off-screen antics are the stuff of legend. For more details on the colorful life of Fields, see my book *Zanies: The World's Greatest Eccentrics* (New Century, 1982; pages 125-134). **p**, William LeBaron; **d**, A. Edward Sutherland; **cast**, W. C. Fields, Rochelle Hudson, Richard Cromwell, Catharine Doucet, Lynne Overman, Granville Bates, Maude Eburne, Bill Wolfe, Adrian Morris, Rosalind Keith, Ralph Remley, Wade Boteler, Tom Herbert, Cyril Ring, Dewey Robinson; **w**, Waldemar Young, Virginia Van Upp (based on the play by Dorothy Donnelly); **c**, William C. Mellor; **m**, Friedrich Hollaender; **ed**, Stuart Heisler; **art d**, Hans Dreier, Bernard Herzbrun; **set d**, A.E. Freudeman.

Porgy and Bess ★★★★ 1959; U.S.; 138m; Samuel Goldwyn Com-

Dorothy Dandridge and Sidney Poitier in *Porgy and Bess*, 1959.

pany/COL; Color; Drama/Musical Operetta; Children: Unacceptable; **DVD**; **VHS**. A moving if not disturbing romantic tale is centered among blacks living on "Catfish Row" in Charleston, South Carolina, and offers magnificent songs from Gershwin (and his two collaborators, lyricists Heyward and his brother Ira). Poitier (Porgy) is an ethical young crippled man who moves about on a goat cart. He has given his heart to alluring tramp Dandridge (Bess), who is a heroin addict and gets her "happy dust" from drug peddler Davis, who is also in love with her and is forever attempting to get her to move with him to New York and live the high life in the Big Apple. The slum area in which they live is full of desperate and unhappy people, such as the beautiful Carroll, who has lost her fisherman husband to a hurricane, and the brutish Peters, a burly stevedore, who covets Dandridge and treats Poitier as dirt. Peters gets into an argument with Fluellen during a crap game and kills him, then flees into hiding while the denizens of "Catfish Row" collect burial money for the deceased gambler by passing a saucer through the ranks of those attending his funeral (and the donations are meager, indeed). Dandridge, now that Peters had gone into hiding, takes up with Poitier. Peters returns and demands that Dandridge stay with him. Overcoming his handicap, Poitier kills Peters in a wild fight and then he goes into hiding. When he later begins searching for Dandridge, he finds that she has finally given in to Davis and has accompanied him to New York. Poitier, however, will not give up on her and vows to follow her to the Big Apple, hoping to find her and the happiness that has evaded him throughout his miserable life. Preminger directs this earthy tale with a strong hand; he draws from Poitier, Dandridge and the rest of the cast superlative performances, and Davis is a standout in his role as the conniving character of Sportin' Life. The memorable musical numbers are handled with great care and the film offers high production values throughout, particularly from Shamroy's outstanding cinematography, which captures the hurricane sequence with breathtaking lensing. Songs: "Summertime," "A Woman Is a Sometime Thing," "Here Comes the Honey Man," "They Pass By Singin'," "The Crap Game," "Gone, Gone, Gone," "My Man's Gone Now," "I Ain't Got No Shame," "What You Want With Bess?," "O Doctor Jesus," "Street Vendors' Cries," "God and Me," "Clara, Clara," "Morning Sounds," "O Lawd, I'm On My Way" (music: George Gershwin; lyrics: DuBose Heyward); "I Got Plenty o' Nuttin'," "Bess, You Is My Woman Now," "Oh, I Can't Sit Down," "It Ain't Necessarily So," "I Loves You Porgy," "A Red Headed Woman," "There's A Boat Dat's Leavin' Soon for New York," "O Bess, Where's My Bess" (music: George Gershwin; lyrics: Ira Gershwin). *Author's Note*: After Heyward authored the novel *Porgy* about this classic story, published in 1925, he and his wife, Dorothy Heyward, converted the tale into a successful Broadway drama that was produced in 1927 and ran for 367 performances. The authors then met with George and Ira

Gershwin and they all collaborated in the Broadway operetta production of 1935, which ran for only 124 performances and with an all-black cast. Both the 1927 drama and the 1935 operetta were directed by the gifted Rouben Mamoulian. The reason why the operetta did not received the attention it deserved in 1935 was due to critics unable to accept its lowlife characters and the unorthodox Gershwin tunes as being a legitimate opera. Some then and later took issue with how blacks were portrayed as stereotypes (especially the character of Porgy, thought to be an Uncle Tom, albeit he slaves for no white master), and where Duke Ellington condemned "Gershwin's lampblack Negroisms," although Ellington praised a 1952 revival production, reversing himself and saying, "Gershwin the greatest." It toured briefly but saw the same unsuccessful results with some of its black members complaining that racial restrictions and segregation played a part in its failure, and, to some degree, their claims were legitimate. The operetta was produced again as a Broadway production in 1942 and proved to be more successful than its predecessors, running for nine months, and it has routinely seen revival productions since that time. On May 8, 1957, Goldwyn purchased the rights to "Porgy and Bess" from Ira Gershwin for $600,000 plus ten percent of the gross profits and under the stipulation that all the principal roles be played by African-American performers. Mamoulian was the logical choice to direct the film version since he had helmed the two Broadway productions in 1927 and 1935, but he was hired only after Elia Kazan, King Vidor and Frank Capra declined the directorial chore, and he was then signed up for the film version, which was the last production personally undertaken by the venerable but unpredictable Goldwyn. Nash was hired to write the script after a host of other writers declined and he delivered a very lengthy screenplay in December 1957. Mamoulian worked closely with Nash for several months to trim the story while supervising the pre-recording of the songs. Meanwhile, Goldwyn tried to sign up Harry Belafonte to play the leading role as he was then the most prominent black actor in Hollywood, but Belafonte turned down the part and the role then went to Poitier, a rising new African-American film star. Poitier orally agreed to do the part for $75,000, but then tried to back out of the production, reportedly based on peer pressures that he would be doing his race a disservice in playing an Uncle Tom, but Goldwyn threatened to sue him and his agent for breach of an oral contract, and, fearing that a resulting lawsuit might jeopardize his career, particularly his upcoming role in Stanley Kramer's superb crime drama, **The Defiant Ones**, 1958, Poitier agreed to do the part. Mamoulian and Goldwyn then assured Poitier that he would later look back upon his contribution with pride. The role for Bess had always been slotted for Dandridge, who had become a star after appearing in **Carmen Jones**, 1959, the contemporary version of Bizet's opera, "Carmen," which had been directed by Preminger, who would later take over the directorial chores from Mamoulian and who was then having an affair with Dandridge, treating her as he did all others as a self-styled Svengali. Although Dandridge had a good singing voice, it was thought to be limited in capturing the range of the songs she had to warble so her voice was looped by Adele Addison. Poitier had no singing ability whatsoever, so Robert McFerrin was brought in to do all of Poitier's songs. Carroll's singing voice, albeit she sang ballads well, was looped by Loulie Jean Norman, and Attaway's voice was looped by Inez Matthews. Peters, who had a powerful voice, sang his own songs, as did the inimitable Bailey, and, of course, Davis sang in his own voice, but was somewhat criticized in that his delivery was more in the style of a 1950s nightclub singer than in the more traditional style of the early 1900s, which is the time setting for this story. Goldwyn first thought to hire Cab Calloway to play the role that eventually went to Davis, but Calloway told the producer that he was just too busy with other projects (but most likely declined because he did not really want to play that rakish rogue character). Davis, however, had early on lobbied hard for the part by arranging his own audition at a private party held in Judy Garland's home, where Lee Gershwin, Ira's wife, attended with Goldwyn. Mrs. Gershwin was shocked at the abusive gutter language Davis used at that "audition" and asked Goldwyn (who referred to Davis at that time as "a monkey") to promise her that he would never hire Davis for any role in **Porgy and Bess**, which he did, telling Davis that night, "you're just not right for the part." Davis, however, would not give up, barraging Goldwyn with requests to play the role of Sportin' Life. He even went so far as to ask his good friend Frank Sinatra to intervene. Sinatra told this author that "I went to bat for Sammy and personally asked Sam [Goldwyn] to cast him in **Porgy and Bess**, and so did a lot of my friends and associates." Goldwyn (in his typical style of malapropism statements) told this author that "Frank [Sinatra] and others in his crowd were all over me and for weeks to take Sammy [Davis] into **Porgy and Bess**. My God, they were ringing my phone every ten minutes. They drove me nutmeg [sic] until I finally signed him on, and then I told Sammy 'now that you have the part, I want you to personally call every one of those people that called me about you and tell them to let me die in peace.'" Ironically, Calloway, who had turned down the role Davis so desperately wanted and got, later essayed that very role on the cast album when Davis was prohibited from participating because of his commitment to another rival record company. "I think the reason why a lot of black actors and performers did not want to be part of the picture," Goldwyn told this author, "is because they knew the story really dealt with a lot of controversial elements, like fornication, the use of drugs, a lot of violence, including murder and whores selling their bodies. We weren't making all of that up—those were the historical conditions in that black slum in Charleston back in those days and that's the way it was shown in the theatrical versions." Serious problems beset the production almost from the start. All the expensive sets for the production were destroyed, along with the expensive costuming, in a studio fire on July 3, 1958, and at an estimated cost of $2 million (the overall budget for the film would soar to $7 million and never recoup its investment, returning less than half of its original budget). Mamoulian then decided, according to his statements to this author, "that the smartest thing to do was to take the whole cast and crew to Charleston and shoot it on location in one of the slum areas that would certainly pass for the old 'Catfish Row' area Heyward first wrote about. I went to Sam [Goldwyn] and told him that that is what we had to do, and he exploded. I guessed he would do that because I knew that he never liked on-location shootings and always wanted to keep his productions inside studio sound stages so that he could get at the director and meddle in the on-going production, and Sam did that all the time. Well, we went back and forth about that until he said: 'You have betrayed me,' and then he fired me and hired Otto [Preminger] to take over **Porgy and Bess**. Otto had done the same thing to me when he took over the direction of **Laura** [1944] and where he took all the credit for all the work I had already done on that picture, too! That man was like a bird of prey, waiting like a vulture to pounce whenever trouble arose." Mamoulian received his full fee for his work, but Preminger took the only credit as director as Mamoulian's efforts were all centered in pre-production. Preminger knew full well that Goldwyn would be visiting the set to make one change after another or, especially, insist on inserting additional scenes. "I circumvented all that," Preminger told this author, "by shooting very long scenes with medium and long shots as continuing shots and very few close-ups, so I allowed no room in the production for Goldwyn to insert any additional scenes, unless at a very high cost, and Goldwyn always tried to avoid such costs. I had thus stymied the man and got my way. It was the only way by which to get that picture completed on schedule." As usual, Preminger brought his own style of dictatorial, if not cruel, attitudes to the production and where he made Dandridge's life more miserable than he had throughout their troubled long affair, which by the time of the production, had mostly ended. (She had become pregnant with his child and, after Preminger had refused to marry her, he urged her to have an abortion.) Dandridge displayed emotional insecurity and a lack of self-assurance throughout the production and Preminger did not help by excessively criticizing her performance, but she nevertheless delivered an outstanding and memorable Bess. Gold-

Dorothy Dandridge and Sidney Poitier in *Porgy and Bess*, 1959.

wyn spent a great deal of money promoting the film, insisting that the distributor advertise it as an "American Folk Opera," but that did not help when it was first released in major cities in the South, like Atlanta, where it was labeled racist and where Goldwyn pulled the film as he did in many other such instances. The film nevertheless won for Best Scoring (André Previn and Ken Darby), and Irene Sharaff was nominated for Best Costume Design (Color). Poitier, years later (as Goldwyn predicted he would do), stated: "Other roles may come and go, but I expect the role of Porgy to stay with me for a lifetime." Also staying with him are the songs from George and Ira Gershwin, which will last forever. **p**, Samuel Goldwyn; **d**, Otto Preminger; **cast**, Sidney Poitier, Dorothy Dandridge, Sammy Davis, Jr., Pearl Bailey, Brock Peters, Leslie Scott, Diahann Carroll, Ruth Attaway, Clarence Muse, Joel Fluellen, Earl Jackson, Moses LaMarr, Margaret Hairston, Ivan Dixon, Antoine Durousseau, Claude Akins, Helen Thigpen, Maya Angelou, Geoffrey Holder; **w**, N. Richard Nash (based on the operetta by George Gershwin (music) and DuBose Heyward (libretto and lyrics) with additional lyrics by Ira Gershwin, from the stage play by DuBose and Dorothy Heyward, and the novel by DuBose Heyward); **c**, Leon Shamroy (Todd-AO; Technicolor); **m**, Gershwin; **ed**, Daniel Mandell; **prod d**, Oliver Smith; **art d**, Joseph C. Wright, Serge Krizman; **set d**, Howard Bristol.

Pork Chop Hill ★★★★ 1959; U.S.; 97m; MGM-Pathe Communications/UA; B/W; War Drama; Children: Unacceptable; **DVD**; **VHS**. Stirring, memorable and historically impactful, this riveting war tale centers upon one action during the Korean War (1950-1953), the first Battle of Pork Chop Hill, which took place in April 1953. Peck, who commands an infantry company, essaying its actual commander, 1st Lieutenant Joseph J. Clemons Jr., K Company, 31st U.S. Infantry, is ordered to retake Pork Chop Hill, which has been overrun by communist Chinese forces. He and his men are aware of the fact that the war is coming to an end and that the assault on Pork Chop may be nothing more than a bloody exercise in futility. While he receives his order to attack Pork Chop, Peck is told by his commander: "Remember this— you've got 135 men, all of them thinking of the peace talks at Panmunjom. It's a cinch that they won't want to die in what may be the last battle." Peck and his men are then driven in trucks to the jump-off point and begin climbing the hill in the middle of the night, stealthily going forward, until they reach a line of barbed wire; At that point, floodlights from an American position mistakenly turn on and bathe the area with searing light that allows Chinese defenders to see the approaching Americans; the Chinese open up with withering firepower while tossing grenades that shoot down and blow up many of Peck's men. After Peck signals the Americans at the other position to turn off

Gregory Peck in *Pork Chop Hill*, 1959.

those lethal lights, he and his men assault the top trenches of the hill. The GIs take some of the enemy positions, but must doggedly fight to take the rest of the hill the following morning, a victory that has cost Peck the lives of half of his men and where another supporting company has been all but wiped out, only ten men in that company led by Landau (in his film debut) surviving. Toward the summit, Peck and his men find other GIs, who have barricaded themselves inside a bunker and have survived the initial Chinese takeover of Pork Chop and they all celebrate, only to be bombarded by mortar shells in a Chinese counterattack. During these actions, Peck sees Strode, a tall and powerful GI, evading action. Peck had earlier found Strode malingering during the initial night attack and had ordered him to "keep up with me" during that assault. When Peck sees that Strode is using a wounded GI to evade action by escorting that wounded man to the rear when he needs no real assistance, he orders another black GI, Edwards, a corporal, to watch Strode closely. When Strode asks why he, a fellow black, is ordering him about, Edwards firmly replies: "Because I have an interest in everything you do." While Peck and his men continue to beat off repeated attacks by the Chinese, he is overjoyed to see that a fresh company of GIs led by Torn have arrived to reinforce the position. Ironically, Torn is Peck's brother-in-law, and their "old home" meeting reduces Peck's anxiety as Torn's men fill in the gaps along the labyrinth trench system atop the hill. Torn, however, is shocked to see that he and his men have not come upon an American victory as is believed by higher command, but that Peck and his men are barely hanging on to their positions. Then another officer from the battalion level arrives to tell Peck that Torn's company is to be withdrawn as it is understood by higher command that they are no longer needed because the enemy has been totally defeated, which enrages Peck and who tells the officer that just the opposite has taken place, that he has very few men left in his own company and, if Torn and his men withdraw, he does not think that he will able to hold the hill if further attacked. Meanwhile, the U.S.-U.N and Chinese negotiators at Panmunjom come to a stalemate when Chinese representatives indicate that their troops will continue their assault on Pork Chop. U.S. Admiral Reid steps from the peace talks to confer with other Allied commanders, all coming to realize that the Chinese really don't care about Pork Chop Hill as it has no tactical or strategic value in the war. Their savage and near suicidal assaults, Reid rightly concludes, are merely to test the Allies in seeing whether or not the Allies are willing to spend lives as freely as the Chinese have been doing. It is a test of brute force. By this time, Peck and a handful of men remain atop Pork Chop as Torn obeys orders and reluctantly takes his company from the hill. In rounding up all of his available men, Peck finds Strode cowering in a bunker and orders him to join the rest of his men in a last-ditch stand at the top of Pork Chop. Strode points a rifle at Peck and refuses,

saying that he will not go to prison on charges of desertion, but Peck tells him that he has a last chance to redeem himself by joining him and the other men, Strode finally agrees and he and Peck take up positions in foxholes at the top of the hill. As they wait for the assault, the GIs hear from loudspeakers positioned everywhere in the area by the Chinese, an enemy propagandist, Amonsin, plead with them to surrender for the sake of their loved ones back in the States while playing plaintive love songs to nostalgically remind them of home. The GIs ignore these messages appealing to their emotions and dig in. The Chinese then launch a massive attack, and when the GIs seem to be overrun, Peck gathers a handful of survivors and he and they take shelter in a dugout, barricading it just as Chinese troops fill the trench outside that dugout they blast the barricaded dugout with flamethrowers. Just when it looks as if Peck and the other defenders are close to being killed, fresh U.S. troops appear, swarming up the hill and into the trenches to wipe out the Chinese attackers. The battle-weary Peck and other survivors are then shown staggering down the hill, too exhausted with fatigue to celebrate the victory, but one that has demonstrated to the Chinese that the U.S. and its allies will, indeed, spend whatever lives are necessary to defeat dictatorships such as communism. Peck is superb as the resolute commander, who shows both stern discipline and compassion toward his men while dealing with what appears to be a hopeless situation. The supporting cast members are also outstanding in their roles, especially Strode, who portrays the black soldier shirking from duty while fearing for his life; or Guardino, a machine gunner, who shouts and weeps at the same time when his buddy, Peppard, is killed; or Blake, a pint-sized soldier who destroys an enemy machine gun nest and is severely wounded but who refuses to go to the rear and continues fighting. The almost nonstop action is masterfully captured by pantheon director Milestone, who brilliantly choreographs the day and night battle scenes, and Leavitt's cameras fluidly capture those grim and tension-filled scenes with eye-catching panning and tracking shots and where his boom shots have the camera racing through the trenches and over the battle-scarred landscapes of that shell-torn hill, closing in on one poignant or ironic scene after another to offer a truly realistic panorama of horrific warfare. This was the imprint that Milestone had established with two earlier classics. ***Author's Note***: Peck established his own company, Melville Productions, with producer Bartlett, to make this film, and both eagerly sought Milestone to be its director. "He [Milestone] had directed several classic war films," Peck told this author, "so he was the logical choice to direct **Pork Chop Hill**. He did a great job with that picture and should have gotten more recognition than he did for doing it. It really makes up a tetralogy of his war films, dealing with the First [1], Second World Wars [2] and the Korean War [1], which a lot of nitwits called a 'police action.' Well, I can tell you that no cops were getting killed in Korea, but a lot of brave Americans did, along with a lot of other heroic men from many other countries, all of them fighting communist aggression there." Those several earlier classic war films directed by Milestone were **All Quiet on the Western Front**, 1930 (World War I), **A Walk in the Sun**, 1945, and **Halls of Montezuma**, 1951 (World War II), the first dealing with the German perspective in WWI, the second from the GI view in WWII during the Salerno Invasion of 1943, and the third dealing with Marines fighting on Okinawa. Milestone told this author that he was unhappy at the fact that about twenty minutes were edited out of the film because "Greg's [Peck's] wife, Veronica, a very strong-willed lady, took a look at the picture and complained that Greg was showing up in the picture too late, so a lot of what I thought was important preamble went by the boards. Greg was great to work with, though, a fine gentleman. I had a lot tougher times working with a lot of others, who were arrogant producers and always thought they knew more than I did about making pictures. Carl Laemmle, the little old man who ran Universal, was like that, always butting in. When I was making **All Quiet on the Western Front** and where Lew [Ayres] gets killed at the very end, well, Uncle Carl, as they called him, came to me and said, 'Oh, this is terrible, that poor young man dying at the end. Can't we have a happy ending to the picture instead?' I told him: 'All right, Uncle Carl, you want a happy ending. Let's show the Germans winning the war.' He gave me his sternest look and said, 'that's not a bit funny.' He went back to his office and left me alone after that." Many films have profiled the Korean War, most notably **The Bridges at Toko-Ri**, 1954; **Fixed Bayonets!**, 1951; **Flat Top**, 1952; **The Glory Brigade**, 1953; **The Great Imposter**, 1961; **Heartbreak Ridge**, 1986; **I Want You**, 1951; **Love Is a Many Splendored Thing**, 1955; **The Manchurian Candidate**, 1962; **M*A*S*H**, 1970; **MacArthur**, 1977; **The McConnell Story**, 1955; **Men in War**, 1957; **Men of the Fighting Lady**, 1954; **One Minute to Zero**, 1952; **Prisoner of War**, 1954; **The Rack**, 1956; **Retreat, Hell!**, 1952; **Sayonara**, 1957; **The Steel Helmet**, 1951; **Take the High Ground!**, 1953; **Time Limit**, 1957; **War Hunt**, 1962; and **War Is Hell**, 1963. For a more extensive listing of films about the Korean War, see Index, Historical Events, Volume II, of this work. **p**, Sy Bartlett; **d**, Lewis Milestone; **cast**, Gregory Peck, Harry Guardino, Rip Torn, George Peppard, Carl Benton Reid, James Edwards, Bob Steele, Woody Strode, George Shibata, Norman Fell, Robert Blake, Biff Elliot, Martin Landau, Carl Benton Reid, Gavin MacLeod, Bill Wellman, Jr., Harry Dean Stanton, Clarence Williams III, Viraj Amonsin; **w**, James R. Webb (based on the book by Brig. Gen. S.L.A. Marshall, USAR); **c**, Sam Leavitt; **m**, Leonard Rosenman; **ed**, George Boemler; **prod d**, Nicolai Remisoff; **set d**, Edward G. Boyle; **spec eff**, David Koehler.

Port of 40 Thieves ★★★ 1944; U.S.; 58m; Rep; B/W; Crime/Drama; Children: Unacceptable. This suspense-packed film sees Bachelor as a homicidal maniac who murders her rich husband for the inheritance so she can marry her lover. She then fears her lover will talk, so she kills him by pushing him down an elevator shaft. Roberts, her daughter by her first marriage, suspects her and is able to bring her to justice. The acting is superior thanks to a good script, taut directing by the accomplished English and good lensing from Marta, a gifted cinematographer. *Author's Note*: Like most inexpensive films made at Republic, English employs chiefly one set, a penthouse, a generic construction in that it could be used, with some minor alterations, again and again in later films without too much additional cost. English was the studio workhorse when it came to producing and directing Republic's many serials and was responsible for more than half of those lucrative serials during their most popular era. **p**, Walter H. Goetz; **d**, John English; **cast**, Stephanie Bachelor, Tom Keene (as Richard Powers), Lynne Roberts, Olive Blakeney, Russell Hicks, George Meeker, Mary Field, Ellen Lowe, Patricia Knox, John Hamilton, Harry Depp; **w**, Dane Lussier; **c**, Jack Marta; **m**, Morton Scott; **ed**, Richard Van Enger; **art d**, Russell Kimball.

Port of Shadows ★★★★ 1938; France; 91m; Cine-Alliance/Film Alliance of the U.S.; B/W; Drama; Children: Unacceptable. Gabin gives a powerful performance as a disillusioned French army deserter, who arrives at night in Le Havre, wanting to leave France. He finds civilian clothes, a little money, a passport, and a dog. He also meets Morgan, who is seventeen and growing up too fast. He gives her courage to resist local shop owner Simon, who traffics in stolen goods and covets Morgan. Simon tells Gabin that he will provide him with a passport if he kills Morgan's boyfriend, but Gabin refuses. Simon later murders that boyfriend and Gabin, in retaliation, smashes Simon's head with a brick. Gabin's plight seems hopeless until he meets Le Vigan, a poet who has also given up on life and who gives him his passport so that Gabin can escape to another country and, perhaps, enjoy a better lifestyle. A ship is leaving for Venezuela, but, in running to board that ship, Gabin is shot and killed by gangster Brasseur. Carne presents a moving but disturbingly grim portrait where death pervasively seems to be preferable to life. Gabin provides a stunning performance as a man without a future, and Morgan (who is alive and well at age ninety-three at this writing) also gives an exceptional performance as the love-craving girl who

Joseph Cotten and Jennifer Jones in *Portrait of Jennie,* 1949.

is denied the affection she so desperately seeks. The lensing, too, is superb, capturing the eerie, fog-shrouded streets and docks of Le Havre as Carne's doomed characters grope their way toward peace and happiness that always seems to elude them. *Author's Note*: Ironically, this production was first envisioned by producers at Germany's UFA studio, but when Nazi Minister of Propaganda Joseph Goebbels read its script, he refused to make the film, stating that its leading character, a deserter, represented "decadence." Then Raoul Ploquin, who headed French productions at UFA, gave a copy of the novel upon which this story is based to Carne and he became intrigued with the tale, deciding to film the story, one that was later described as a film that helped to establish French "Poetic Realism." Carne had production problems right from the start with France's Minister of War, who insisted that the word "deserter" could not be used in the film and that the soldier's uniform Gabin wears be given "respect." The gloom and doom that dominates the film was later interpreted to be the national attitude at that time, one that offered France no hope in escaping WWII, that war erupting one year after this film was released. A top-ranking Vichy Government official later blamed this film for his country's plight by stating: "If we have lost the war, it is…the fault of **Port of Shadows**." Producer Rabinovitch, who had purchased the rights of the novel, argued incessantly with Carne to give the film a happier ending, but to no avail, at least when it came to Gabin's fate. Prevert, the scriptwriter who collaborated with Carne on **Jenny**, 1936, and **Bizarre, Bizarre**, 1937, did, however, soften Morgan's character considerably, making her an innocent victim of events rather than the slattern she was originally portrayed in the novel and where she is a vicious prostitute, who has no compunction about killing her pimp and living to enjoy the riches stemming from his miscreant ways. After Germany defeated France in 1940 and occupied most of the country, this film was banned from viewing and a concerted effort was made to destroy all copies of this film; several prints nevertheless survived. Excessive violence prohibits viewing by children. (In French; English subtitles.) **p**, Gregor Rabinovitch; **d**, Marcel Carne; **cast**, Jean Gabin, Michele Morgan, Pierre Brasseur, Michel Simon, Edouard Delmont, Raymond Aimos, Robert Le Vigan, Rene Genin, Marcel Peres, Jenny Burnay, Roger Legris; **w**, Jacques Prevert (based on a novel by Pierre Dumarchais as Pierre Mac Orlan); **c**, E. Schufftan; **m**, Maurice Jaubert; **ed**, R. Le Henaff; **prod d**, Alexandre Trauner.

Portrait of Jennie ★★★★ 1949; U.S.; 86m; Vanguard Films/Selznick International; B/W/Color; Fantasy/Romance; Children: Acceptable; **DVD**; **VHS**. Cotten is magnificent as a struggling painter in this haunting fantasy where he falls in love with Jones, a girl from another era. Jones was never more captivating and enthralling as that ethereal apparition that only Cotten can see, a stunning performance that is as mem-

Cecil Kellaway and Joseph Cotten in *Portrait of Jennie*, 1949.

orable today as it was when this superlative film was first released. The film opens with Cotten sitting in New York City's Central Park, an unsuccessful artist who is as unsure of his future as is this uncertain year of 1932 of the Great Depression. Suddenly, from nowhere, Jones appears as a young, beautiful girl, who talks to Cotten, but uses words from a long ago lexicon. Wearing old-fashioned clothes from the Edwardian era, she tells him that she is a student in a convent and that her parents are entertainers, high wire artists performing at the Hammerstein Opera House, which, oddly, has been closed decades earlier. Jones sings a strange song for Cotten, one that proves to be prophetic: "Where I come from nobody knows and where I'm going everything goes. The wind blows, the sea flows—and nobody knows." She then disappears and Cotten asks himself if her visit was nothing more than his own daydreaming. While struggling to improve his art, Cotten is encouraged by art dealers Barrymore and Kellaway, who buy some of his artwork, although they believe he needs to improve his techniques. Jones then reappears several times, almost always when Cotten visits Central Park, although each time she seems to be somewhat taller and older and each time she further captivates Cotten's heart, even though she continues to vanish as quickly as she appears. Meanwhile, to support himself, Cotten paints a patriotic mural of Michael Collins (1890-1922) and his men during the Easter Uprising of 1916 for a saloonkeeper, a job arranged by Cotten's friend, Wayne, a regular patron of that Irish bar. A cabdriver, the optimistic Wayne is a bit of a philosopher and who believes in Cotten's artwork and his integrity, encouraging him to continue his paintings. He is more than encouraged when Jones reappears and sits for a portrait that Cotten paints, telling him at that time that she is about to graduate from the convent. She again disappears, and Cotten takes the portrait to Barrymore and Kellaway, both seeing that he has now become a very talented artist with this painting and where he has refined his unique artistic techniques; they believe that he will soon become a widely recognized painter. By this time, Cotten has learned that Jones' parents were killed many years ago in an accident while performing their high wire act, puzzled by the fact that those deaths occurred decades earlier. Cotten locates the convent where Jones is about to graduate and watches her and her fellow students at those proceedings. He later returns to meet with Gish, the mother superior of the convent, who tells him that Jones, indeed, had been one of her long ago students, but, after graduation, she died in a fierce New England hurricane during the 1920s. He goes to Barrymore, who advances him money so that he can travel to Land's End Light, the site where Jones was reportedly lost at sea, and he rents a boat. Sailing toward the lighthouse, his boat is engulfed in a savage storm, and he barely manages to reach the abandoned lighthouse. Jones then appears in a small sailboat that is being tossed about by the storm and meets Cotten one final time, telling him that the

love they have for one another will last throughout time. They embrace, but are then torn apart by the savage storm that drags Jones back into the sea, leaving Cotten unconscious. Barrymore, who has been summoned to his side by local authorities after he has been rescued, hears from the recovering Cotten that he has had a final rendezvous with the young woman he loves, the very woman in the portrait Barrymore has purchased. Cotten vividly describes his last encounter with Jones to Barrymore. He realizes that Barrymore wants to believe him, but finds his story impossible, until he is given a scarf found with when he was rescued. It is Jones' scarf, he tells Barrymore, and she now believes that this young woman did, indeed, step from the past to enter the present where she remains within Cotten's heart. The film ends as Cotten's portrait of Jones, a portrait of Jennie, hangs in the National Museum of Art (and where the film goes to Technicolor to exhibit that beautiful painting). Director Dieterle masterfully presents this fantasy romance with tender loving care, muting Jones' scenes through August's superb cinematography to make her appear spiritual and apart from the rest of the very real and struggling world in which Cotten lives. Tiomkin's lyrical and melodic score haunts and enhances this bittersweet tale of starcrossed lovers reaching toward each other from different ages to emphasize the belief that love can transcend anyone's lifespan and time itself. It is a delicate other world story so deftly managed that it becomes charmingly believable. Songs: "Nuages," "The Girl with the Flaxen Hair," "Arabesque No. 1 in E" (Claude Debussy); "Jennie's Song" (music: Bernard Herrmann; lyrics: Robert Nathan). ***Author's Note***: One of this author's mentors, Ben Hecht, wrote the narrated forward to this film: "Out of the shadows of knowledge, and out of a painting that hung on a museum wall, comes our story, the truth of which lies not on our screen but in your heart." Actually, Hecht wrote scripts for two other outstanding romance films that involve "miracles" compelled by love, **The Miracle of the Bells**, 1948, and, most notably, **Miracle in the Rain**, 1956, where a memento is left behind after the spiritual visit of a lost loved one, just as Cotten is left with Jones' scarf at the end of **Portrait of Jennie**. Hecht told this author that "Selznick wanted something that would telegraph the story in **Portrait of Jennie** with a narrated introduction. He always wanted to set the right perspective just the same way he had narration begin **Duel in the Sun** [1946, which also starred Jones and Cotten], so I wrote that little bit of introduction for that very good picture. It's really a story of a man falling in love with a ghost that becomes real. Another picture was made about that time that did the same thing called **The Ghost and Mrs. Muir** [1947], and that was also a fine story where a live woman and a long-dead sea captain fall in love and finally get together in the hereafter. People believe in love and that's why they want to believe in stories like that. Faith in that is all the proof they ever need." Dieterle told this author that "David [Selznick] was in and out of that production like a ferret, always changing this and that, from the dialog to the way the sets were arranged, but mostly in the scenes where Jennifer [Jones] appears. He married her about the time of that picture and he worshipped the ground she walked on. Mind you, she is a great actress and is wonderful in **Portrait of Jennie**. She has a quality about her that is very spiritual." Cotten, when talking with this author, remembered how "David [Selznick] commissioned John Brackman, a very accomplished painter, to paint Jennifer's portrait, the one I supposedly paint in the picture, and she spent a lot of time going back and forth to Brackman's studio in Connecticut to pose for that portrait. After David married Jennifer, he put that portrait on a wall in their home, and, to him, it was more of a prized possession than most of his films." This was August's last film; he died of a heart attack toward the end of the production, and cinematographer Lee Garmes completed the film (without credit). Bernard Herrmann was originally hired to do the score, but he quarreled with Selznick and finally quit and was replaced by Tiomkin. Albert Sharpe, the fine character actor playing the Irish saloonkeeper who commissions Cotten to paint the heroic mural of Michael Collins, went on to delightfully enact the title role in **Darby O'Gill and the Little People**, 1959, another great fantasy film, one that is peopled by dizzily dancing leprechauns. This production marked the film debuts of Wayne, Nancy Davis (Mrs. Ronald Reagan) and Nancy Olson. It was not successful at the box office and did not recoup its estimated $4 million budget. **p**, David O. Selznick; **d**, William Dieterle; **cast**, Jennifer Jones, Joseph Cotten, Ethel Barrymore, Lillian Gish, Cecil Kellaway, David Wayne, Albert Sharpe, Henry Hull, Florence Bates, Felix Bressart, Clem Bevans, Robert Dudley, Nancy Davis, Anne Francis, Brian Keith, Nancy Olson; **w**, Paul Osborn, Peter Berneis, Leonardo Bercovici (based on the novel by Robert Nathan); **c**, Joseph August, Lee Garmes (not credited); **m**, Dimitri Tiomkin; **ed**, William Morgan; **prod d**, J. McMillan Johnson; **set d**, Claude Carpenter; **spec eff**, Clarence Slifer, Paul Eagler, Johnson.

The Poseidon Adventure ★★★ 1972; U.S.; 117m; Kent Productions; FOX; Color; Adventure; Children: Unacceptable (MPAA: PG); **DVD**; **VHS**. Above-average disaster film sees a top-flight performance from Hackman, who stars in this film as a rebellious and decisive priest. He is aboard a luxury liner that is suddenly engulfed in a tidal wave while everyone is celebrating New Year's Eve, the ship being capsized and where many passengers nevertheless initially survive while the ship is mostly underwater. Some of the survivors want to try to stay at the top of the ship, which is now really at the bottom, while Hackman insists they must work their way to the bottom of the ship, which is really at the top. Only ten passengers agree with him and follow him through a labyrinth of cramped passageways, electrical conduits and, even submerged areas through which they must swim. They finally reach the dangerous boiler rooms, which are belching fire from burning oil, and must make their way by climbing and crawling over pipes and cables and where some perish in the effort, including Hackman, until survivors reach the crankshaft of the ship and emerge to be rescued by helicopters. Some exceptional performances are rendered by Borgnine and Stevens and Albertson and Winters, who play two married couples and where the wives are lost. Neame does a fine job coordinating the many hazardous scenes, and the production values are high through superior lensing from Stine. Songs: "The Song from the Poseidon Adventure" (1972; Al Kasha and Joel Hirschhorn), "Give Me the Simple Life" (1946; Rube Bloom), "For He's a Jolly Good Fellow" (traditional), "Auld Lang Syne" (1788; traditional; lyrics: Robert Burns). The film proved to be an enormous success at the box office, taking in more than $93 million in its initial release against a $5 million budget. Many other films have depicted the sinking of ocean liners, most notably **Abandon Ship!**, 1957; **Arise My Love**, 1940; **History Is Made at Night**, 1937; **The Last Voyage**, 1960; **Lord Jim**, 1965; **Titanic**, 1953; and **Titanic**, 1997. *Author's Note*: This film spawned a rash of disaster films and made producer Allen even wealthier than the riches he had gleaned from producing the popular TV series **Lost in Space** (1965-1968), and **The Time Tunnel** (1966-1967). The novel on which this exciting tale is based was written by sportswriter Paul Gallico, who used his experiences on the *Queen Mary* for the story line. While traveling on that ship during WWII when it had been converted to a troop ship, Gallico and his fellow GIs were tossed about when the ship was struck by an enormous wave during its voyage, one that almost capsized her. When sailing on the same luxury liner years after the war, the ship was again struck by a freak tidal wave that Gallico claimed sent passengers from one side of the ship to the other. The *Queen Mary*, which was anchored at Long Beach as a museum at the time of this production, was used for scenes leading up to its capsizing; a model of the *Queen Mary* was shown in a very impressive special effects sequence where the ship is capsized by a mountainous wave during a storm. Borgnine told this author that "**The Poseidon Adventure** took a lot out of me. It was a very physical film where we had to do a lot of our own stunts because of the medium and close-up shots. At one point, we had to swim underwater and that about did me in, as it did poor Shelley Winters, especially since she had to gain weight for her character. Gene [Hackman] was in great shape and had no problem in pulling himself hand over hand along pipes and ca-

Gene Hackman in *The Poseidon Adventure*, 1972.

bles. After one scene I joked with him, saying: 'Did you ever think of becoming a stunt man?'" Said Winters to this author: "Oh, brother, I wouldn't want to do that picture again! I thought I would drown when I had to swim underwater holding my breath for God knows how long. You know, I have always thought that actors have more than a few screws loose because we are willing to do things like that." **p**, Irwin Allen; **d**, Ronald Neame; **cast**, Gene Hackman, Ernest Borgnine, Red Buttons, Carol Lynley, Roddy McDowall, Stella Stevens, Shelley Winters, Jack Albertson, Pamela Sue Martin, Arthur O'Connell, Leslie Nielsen; **w**, Stirling Silliphant, Wendell Mayes (based on the novel by Paul Gallico); **c**, Harold E. Stine (Panavision; DeLuxe Color); **m**, John Williams; **ed**, Harold F. Kress; **prod d**, William Creber; **set d**, Raphael Bretton; **spec eff**, L.B. Abbott, Matthew Yuricich, A.D. Flowers.

Possessed ★★★ 1947; U.S.; 108m; WB; B/W; Drama; Children: Unacceptable; **DVD**. Crawford is compelling in this powerful psychological drama. She is first seen walking the streets of Los Angeles in a dazed condition looking for a man named David. She collapses in a diner and is taken to the psychiatric ward of a hospital. In flashbacks, she reveals her obsession for David (Heflin) as a result of a borderline personality disorder which leads to murder. In flashback we see Crawford as a nurse tending to Bryant, the mentally unbalanced wife of millionaire Massey. After Massey hires Heflin, an engineer, to construct some business buildings, Crawford becomes obsessed with Heflin. He likes her but is not in love with her and finally leaves because of her possessiveness. The deluded Bryant believes that Crawford and her husband are having an affair and she drowns herself. Crawford sees Massey through this crisis and earns his love and she finally accepts his proposal and marries him. She is, however, still in love with Heflin and, after Heflin falls in love with Brooks, Crawford is consumed by passion and possessiveness and shoots him dead. This sends Crawford into greater mental instability and she is institutionalized but, in the end, is not held accountable for murder because of her mental condition. Songs: "Carnaval, Opus 9" (Robert Schumann), "Emperor Waltz" (Johann Strauss, Jr.). This story has nothing to do with another film with the same name, **Possessed**, 1931, in which Crawford also appeared as the leading lady opposite a young Clark Gable, Crawford having the distinction of being the only female film star to appear in two films with the same title. *Author's Note*: Bette Davis, who was Warner Brothers' top female star at the time, was first offered the lead role in this film, but she turned it down as she was then about to have a baby and it went to Crawford. Producer Wald believed that Crawford was the only other actress at the studio who could believably portray the neurotic personality of the film's leading lady. Crawford told this author that "I was getting Bette's hand-me-downs in those days, but the part was a good one and I did the best I

Cecil Kellaway, John Garfield and Lana Turner in *The Postman Always Rings Twice*, 1946.

could with it. I even visited mental hospitals and observed the conduct and mannerisms of some of the patients. One of them later sued the studio. She claimed I was copying her lunacy! Can you imagine that?" The suit was later dropped. **p**, Jerry Wald; **d**, Curtis Bernhardt; **cast**, Joan Crawford, Van Heflin, Raymond Massey, Geraldine Brooks, Stanley Ridges, John Ridgely, Moroni Olsen, Erskine Sanford, Peter Miles (as Gerald Perreau), Douglas Kennedy, Don McGuire, Monte Blue; **w**, Silvia Richards, Ranald MacDougall (based on a story by Rita Weiman); **c**, Joseph Valentine, Sidney Hickox; **m**, Franz Waxman; **ed**, Rudi Fehr; **art d**, Anton Grot; **set d**, Fred M. MacLean; **spec eff**, Robert Burks, William McGann.

Postcards from the Edge ★★★ 1990; U.S.; 101m; COL; Color; Comedy/Drama; Children: Unacceptable (MPAA: R); **DVD**; **VHS**. This fascinating film is based on the book by actress Carrie Fisher about her drug addiction and problems with her actress-mother, Debbie Reynolds. Streep plays the film actress, who is drug addicted, and her career is on the skids. She spends some time at a detoxification center and afterward her film company insists that, as a condition of continuing to employ her, she must live with her mother, MacLaine. Once a big movie star, MacLaine has become an alcoholic. It's a hard choice for Streep to live with her since she has had a long-standing problem living in her mother's shadow and being treated like a child. They become a very odd couple but finally reach something of a balance in their relationship through understanding each other a little better. Songs: "I'm Checkin' Out" (Shel Silverstein), "I'm Still Here" (Stephen Sondheim), "You Don't Know Me" (Cindy Walker, Eddy Arnold), "From This Moment On" (Cole Porter), "I Love to Be Unhappy" (Gilda Radner, Paul Shaffer). Gutter language prohibits viewing by children. **p**, Mike Nichols, John Calley; **d**, Nichols; **cast**, Meryl Streep, Shirley MacLaine, Dennis Quaid, Gene Hackman, Richard Dreyfuss, Rob Reiner, Mary Wickes, Conrad Bain, Annette Bening, Simon Callow, Gary Morton; **w**, Carrie Fisher (based on her book); **c**, Michael Ballhaus; **m**, Carly Simon; **ed**, Sam O'Steen; **prod d**, Patrizia Von Brandenstein; **art d**, Kandy Stern; **set d**, Chris A. Butler; **spec eff**, Alan E. Lorimer, Bill Hansard.

The Postman ★★★ 1994; Italy/France/Belgium; 108m; Cecchi Gori Group; Tiger Cinematografica/Miramax; Color; Biographical Drama; Children: Unacceptable (MPAA: PG); **DVD**; **VHS**. Absorbing biopic about Pablo Neruda (1904-1973), the celebrated Chilean poet and politician, who is expertly played by Noiret. He is shown exiled to a small island for political reasons. Noiret receives so much mail that Troisi, the unemployed son of a fisherman, is hired as an extra postman who is to hand-deliver the poet's mail to him. Poorly educated, Troisi learns to love poetry, and he and Noiret become friends. Troisi loves

Cucinotta, a local beauty, and gets Noiret's help in poetically wooing and winning her. Although this film takes a large leaf from the tale of **Cyrano de Bergerac**, 1950, and its 1990 remake, this is nevertheless a tender and charming movie that was made on a shoestring but found a large worldwide audience. Troisi and Cucinotta give outstanding performances in this well-crafted romantic drama. Song: "Madreselva" (Francisco Canaro, Luis Cesar Amadori). (In Italian; English subtitles.) **p**, Gaetano Daniele, Mario and Vittorio Cecchi Gori; **d**, Michael Radford; **cast**, Massimo Troisi, Philippe Noiret, Maria Grazia Cucinotta, Renato Scarpa, Linda Moretti, Sergio Solli, Carlo Di Maio, Nando Neri, Vincenzo Di Sauro, Orazio Stracuzzi; **w**, Radford, Anna Pavignano, Furio Scarpelli, Giacomo Scarpelli, Massimo Troisi (based on the novel *Ardiente Paciencia* by Antonio Skármeta and a story by Furio Scarpelli and Giacomo Scarpelli); **c**, Franco Di Giacomo; **m**, Luis Bacalov; **ed**, Roberto Perpignani; **prod d**, Lorenzo Baraldi.

The Postman Always Rings Twice ★★★★★ 1946; U.S.; 113m; MGM; B/W; Crime Drama; Children: Unacceptable; **DVD**; **VHS**. Crime writer James M. Cain had scored big with his tale of **Double Indemnity**, 1944, and this crime yarn matches that grim and sordid romance-and-murder story with equal shock and compelling fascination. In what is arguably their finest performances, Garfield and Turner enact the conspiratorial and lethal lovers who plan and execute the killing of Turner's husband, Kellaway, but not before telegraphing their intentions to a shrewd district attorney. Garfield, a drifter with an "itch" to keep moving, thumbs a ride with Ames along the coast highway in California; Ames drops him off at a roadway gas station and diner where Garfield sees a "man wanted" sign. Ames drives off, wishing Garfield good luck. Garfield is cheerfully greeted by Kellaway, the diner's owner, who tries to persuade him to take the job being offered, that of a handyman, promising him good food, a warm bed and decent wages. The wanderlust-bound Garfield is disinclined, but, when he sees Turner, Kellaway's young, sexy, blonde wife, he changes his mind, taking the job just to be near Turner. The two soon draw closer together as Turner explains that she only married Kellaway, a man twice her age, to escape poverty, but she is now trapped in another kind of cage, one that offers her a loveless union and where she has no control over Kellaway's operations. The two become lovers, furtively meeting for secret trysts until they decide to run off together. Turner changes her mind while they are on the road and forced to hitchhike, and, while covered with dust and dirt, she decides to return to the diner where, at least, she has some financial security and comfort. Garfield, now obsessed with her, goes back to the diner with her. The two then slowly hatch a scheme where Kellaway will appear to accidentally die in his bathtub as Garfield rigs an electrical circuit to turn off the lights just when the old man is getting into his tub. After the lights go off, however, Turner finds Kellaway still alive and, panicking, calls for a doctor. Garfield and Turner are next shown standing in a hospital hallway outside Kellaway's bedroom door, and Ames, the man who had originally driven Garfield to the diner, appears with York, a motorcycle cop, accompanying him. Ames introduces himself as the local district attorney, and he is more than curious about Kellaway's "accident" as he has long been suspicious of the relationship between Turner and Garfield. When Kellaway regains consciousness at the hospital, he recognizes Turner and has no idea what has happened to him. As far as everyone is concerned, he accidentally fell in the bathtub when the lights inexplicably went out. When Garfield and Turner return to the diner, Ames and York follow them, and when they arrive at the diner, they find a cat dead at the foot of a ladder outside the place, Garfield points out that the cat short-circuited a wire that blew out the lights, an explanation that Ames and York accept. The lethal lovers are thus protected through happenstance, but they renew their plans to murder Kellaway after he tells them that he is about to sell the diner and move to his ancestral home where Turner is expected to take care of his ailing sister, and to Turner, this is a fate worse than death. On the night before Kellaway is to conclude the sale of his diner, he gets tipsy with Garfield, singing as he celebrates his impending retirement. He, Garfield and Turner then step outside to get into the family car with Turner driving. Ames, who lives nearby, stops to see them get into the car and watches them as they drive off. Turner suggests that they take the scenic mountain road en route to Santa Barbara, and, once they drive along that road, Garfield, who is sitting in the back seat, crashes a bottle over Kellaway's head, killing him. He and Turner then get out of the car and push it over the cliff to see the car slide downward, caroming off rocks, but it only descends a short distance, so they climb down to the car. Garfield, while reaching inside the car to grab the wheel, pushes the car forward with Turner's help. The car suddenly lurches downward with Garfield inside of it, crashing in its descent. Shocked and now alone, Turner begins to hysterically scream for help as she climbs desperately to the top of the cliff. When she reaches the roadway, she is met by Ames, who has been following her car. Garfield has survived the crash and is bedridden in a hospital where Ames visits him, telling him that he believes that he and Turner killed Kellaway, which Garfield adamantly denies. Ames then tries another approach, saying that he now believes that only Turner killed Kellaway and that she made him the scapegoat and, using all the pressuring persuasion he can, convinces Garfield to sign a complaint against Turner to further prove his own innocence. After Ames leaves, Cronyn, who has been hired as Turner's shrewd defense attorney, visits Garfield, but when he learns that he has signed a complaint against his client, he tells him to remain silent and that he will handle the case from that point onward. When Garfield and Turner appear in at a preliminary hearing, Cronyn, in a clever move, first pleads his client guilty and then later tells Ames that he knows he has no real evidence to convict his client and tells him that he will plea bargain Turner to the lesser charge of manslaughter in exchange for a light sentence. Ames agrees, and Turner hesitantly pleads guilty to manslaughter at Cronyn's insistence and is then given probation. She is free and so is Garfield, both of them returning to the diner which is now owned by Turner. She has nothing but contempt for her fellow conspirator after Garfield signed that complaint against her and she treats him like dirt as she plans to remodel the place and turn it into a lucrative business, even trading off her now notorious reputation to attract customers. Cronyn tells Turner that he will take no fee for getting her released, telling her to keep the $10,000 in insurance money she has received for Kellaway's death, but cautions that she and Garfield, if they are to go on living together, should get married. Both wed, but Turner continues to mistreat Garfield. Reed, a former private detective for Cronyn, then attempts to blackmail Turner and Garfield with a signed confession of murder Turner had earlier given to Cronyn, but one that was never shown to the prosecution and has been locked up in the attorney's safe until Reed has stolen it. Reed makes a call on Turner and Garfield, but Garfield beats him up and forces Reed's associate to deliver the original statement and all of its copies to them before he and Turner send the would-be blackmailers on their way. Turner next takes a trip to the East Coast when her ailing mother dies and, while she is away, Garfield has a brief affair with Totter. When Turner returns, she had softened toward Garfield and the couple make up after they swim far out to sea at Turner's request and where she can no longer swim back to shore. Garfield, however, helps her return to the shore and she now knows through this test that he still loves her. As they drive back toward the diner, she tells Garfield that she loves him and they look forward to a better life together. But, just at that time, an oncoming truck swerves into their car and Turner is killed. Garfield survives only to be charged with Turner's death, Ames getting a conviction and where Garfield is sentenced to be executed. Even though he claims his innocence, Garfield while in his cell and just before going to his execution, admits to Ames that even though he is not guilty of killing Turner, he is guilty of killing Kellaway. He states: "You know, there's something about this, which is like expecting a letter you're just crazy to get, and you hang around the front door for fear you might not hear him [the postman] ring. You never realize that he always rings twice....The truth is, you always hear him

Lana Turner and John Garfield in *The Postman Always Rings Twice*, 1946.

ring the second time, even if you're way out in the back yard." He then turns to Dillon, a priest who is there to administer the Last Rites, and says: "Father, could you send up a prayer for me and Cora [Turner], and, if you can find it in your heart, make it so that we're together...wherever it is." Garnett brilliantly directs this film noir masterpiece with a firm hand, drawing superlative performances from Garfield, Turner, Kellaway, Ames and Cronyn, and Wagner's excellent lensing captures with one arresting and inventive shot after another all the sordid and torrid scenes in this mesmerizing thriller. Songs: "She's Funny That Way" (1928; music: Neil Moret; lyrics: Richard A. Whiting), "There's A Tavern in the Town" (1883; composer/lyricist unknown). *Author's Note*: Garnett employed many subtle techniques for this film, telling this author that "I had Lana [Turner] always wearing white in the film, except twice when she wears black for the deaths of others and the reason for that is that white symbolizes purity and virginity, neither of which her character embodies, so that touch is ironic if not cynical. We also used narration which Julie [Garfield, born Jacob Julius Garfinkle] speaks from beginning to the end from his death house jail cell, and that was a trademark by then because the same technique was used in another picture based on a James M. Cain crime novel, **Double Indemnity**, where an insurance agent [Fred MacMurray] narrates how he and a married woman [Barbara Stanwyck] have murdered her husband. They both do it for the same reason, insurance money, a motive for murder that you will find in a lot of Cain's novels. Julie was never better than in that role of the drifter who falls for a real spider woman and Lana surprised even me by giving the performance of her life as a woman as evil as Medusa." Turner told this author that Garfield was "one of the most magnetic male leading men I ever met. He was like a walking dynamo, so charged with electricity that you could feel the current whenever you got near him. We had so many great lines in that picture and we were firing those lines at each other as if we were firing pistols. He was very quick with his cues and you had to stay on your toes to keep up with him, but you could never overtake him, never. He was just too fast for everyone. His instincts were perfect. He always knew just when to slow down and just when to speed everything up. There was never anyone like Julie on the face of this earth, a truly great actor. He made me look so good in that picture and it is my favorite to this very day." Cronyn thought his role in this film was "the pivotal character...he not only saves those two killers, but condemns them to go on living with each other where they can stay up nights wondering when each will try to kill the other. I think my role as that conniving and utterly amoral attorney is about the most evil person I have ever portrayed, and that it tops the sadistic police captain I play in **Brute Force** [1947]. I really hated that part, which was more one-dimensional than the attorney I play in **The Postman Always Rings Twice**. Now that part had real meat on its

Conrad Veidt and Cedric Hardwicke in *Power*, 1934.

bones." Cain's original novel was published in 1934, proving to be a bestseller, but, after MGM bought the drama rights to the book, it soon realized that its controversial contents would never pass the then Hollywood censors. The story was adapted for the stage, but saw only a limited run in 1936 with Richard Barthelmess and Mary Philips as the murderous lovers and Joseph Greenwald as the victimized husband. A French version was filmed as **Le Dernier Tournant**, 1939. Luchino Visconti wholly appropriated the story in his film **Ossessione**, 1943, but its prints were blocked by MGM from U.S. distribution until 1977 and that film saw only limited distribution. Garfield and Turner reprised their roles in a thirty-minute radio adaptation for the Screen Guild Theater on June 16, 1947. A terrible remake was produced in 1981 with Jack Nicholson and Jessica Lange. This film, and Cain's original novel, is based on two murder cases involving lethal wives who killed their husbands: Eva Rablen, who poisoned her husband to death in 1929 and went to prison for life in California, and Ruth Snyder, who, with her lover, Judd Gray, a diminutive corset salesman, murdered Snyder's husband for his life insurance in 1927, and both went to the electric chair at New York's Sing Sing Prison. For details about these cold-blooded killers, see my book *Look for the Woman* (M. Evans, 1981; Rablen: page 327; Snyder-Gray: pages 346-348). **p**, Carey Wilson; **d**, Tay Garnett; **cast**, Lana Turner, John Garfield, Cecil Kellaway, Hume Cronyn, Leon Ames, Audrey Totter, Alan Reed, Jeff York, Philip Ahlm, Morris Ankrum, Betty Blythe, Tom Dillon; **w**, Harry Ruskin, Niven Busch (based on the novel by James M. Cain); **c**, Sidney Wagner; **m**, George Bassman; **ed**, George White; **art d**, Cedric Gibbons, Randall Duell; **set d**, Edwin B. Willis; **spec eff**, A. Arnold Gillespie, Warren Newcombe, Mark Davis.

Power ★★★ 1934; U.K.; 105m; Gaumont British; B/W; Drama; Children: Unacceptable. This gripping story profiles life in the 18th-century Jewish ghetto of Wurtemburg, Germany. Veidt, in a dynamic performance, is "Jew Süss," who accumulates wealth and power by yielding his lover, Hume, to an evil duke, Vosper. His manipulative machinations come back to haunt him as her father gets revenge by accusing him of being a gentile. Veidt redeems his spirit by clinging to his faith and insisting that he is Jewish and is hanged. Mendes directs this venerable tale with a forceful hand, and Veidt and the rest of the cast are standouts in their roles. Songs: "Gigue," "Passacaglia" (George Frideric Handel); "Pur di Gesti," "Minuet," "Gavotte" (Jean-Baptiste Lully). *Author's Note*: This film, produced in England, mirrors the then on-going persecution of Jews in Germany by the Nazi regime. Veidt, who had been a film star in Germany, fled that regime after openly denouncing it, and became a leading player in British and American films, ironically enacting the very Nazis who had oppressed him in such films as **Escape**,

1940; **All through the Night**, 1941; **Nazi Agent**, 1942; and, in his most memorable role as Major Strasser, **Casablanca**, 1942. Mature themes prohibit viewing by children. This film is also known under the title of **Jew Süss**. **p**, Michael Balcon; **d**, Lothar Mendes; **cast**, Conrad Veidt, Benita Hume, Frank Vosper, Cedric Hardwicke, Gerald du Maurier, Paul Graetz, Pamela Mason, Joan Maude, Percy Parsons, Dennis Hoey, Francis L. Sullivan; **w**, A.R. Rawlinson, Dorothy Farnum (based on the novel by Lion Feuchtwanger); **c**, Roy Kellino; **m**, Jack Beaver, Bretton Byrd, John Greenwood, Charles Williams; **ed**, Otto Ludwig; **art d**, Alfred Junge.

The Power and the Glory ★★★ 1933; U.S.; 76m; FOX; B/W; Drama; Children: Unacceptable; **DVD**. Tracy renders a riveting performance as a man driven by ambition, his life as a businessman retold following his funeral. Most recall the man with dislike, describing him as a ruthless tycoon, but Morgan, his former secretary, then tells his wife about his employer and we see in flashbacks the unfolding of Tracy's mercurial career. Tracy plays a railroad track worker looking for unsafe rails who rises to head the company through hard work and dedication. He marries Moore, his school teacher, who goads and guides him to success, while remaining faithful to him. In climbing the ladder of success, however, Tracy loses touch with his family. While negotiating a merger with another railroad company, Tracy becomes infatuated with Vinson, the daughter of the rival company owner. After Tracy informs Moore that he wants a divorce so that he can marry Vinson, that loyal wife of so many years ends her life by stepping in front of a bus. Tracy marries Vinson, but, when he learns she is having an affair with his grown son, Jones, he commits suicide. This was one of the first films in which Tracy was given a role in which he could display his great talents and in his bravura performance subtly reveals the many-sided aspects of his complex character. Songs: "Nearer My God, to Thee" (1856; music: Lowell Mason; lyrics: Sarah F. Adams), "Ave Maria" (1825; music: Franz Schubert). A 1944 film with the same title has a different story, based on a novel by Grahame Greene. *Author's Note*: Some story elements and the film's innovative artistic production techniques, employing a style called "narratage" (a combination of narration and montage scenes not necessarily connected in chronological sequences) were used eight years later in Orson Welles' **Citizen Kane**, 1941. The gifted and innovative writer for this script, Sturges, set precedent when cutting a deal with producer Lasky where he received a percentage of the profits of the film instead of a salary, this deal unnerving many movie moguls, who then considered writers nothing more than hired hands. Lasky admitted that he did this deal after being so impressed with the script Sturges gave him (rather than telling him the story), one that was an actual scene-for-scene shooting script and where Lasky ordered that the film be made directly from that script. The dire opening of the film, beginning with the subject's death, was later used in **Citizen Kane**, as well as many other films to then recall in flashback the life of the deceased. Tracy told this author that "until I got the part in **The Power and the Glory**, I had been playing lugs and thugs in pictures like **Up the River** [1930] and **20,000 Years in Sing Sing** [1932], but Sturges' script offered me a filet to sink my teeth into, instead of the usual hamburgers they plopped onto my plate." The original negative and many of the prints for this film were destroyed in a fire, but a complete print was reconstructed many years later by the American Film Institute. Mature themes and suicide prohibit viewing by children. **p**, Jesse L. Lasky; **d**, William K. Howard; **cast**, Spencer Tracy, Colleen Moore, Ralph Morgan, Helen Vinson, Phillip Trent (as Clifford Jones), Henry Kolker, Sarah Padden, J. Farrell MacDonald, Frank Beal, Edith Fellows, Mary Gordon, Russell Simpson; **w**, Preston Sturges; **c**, James Wong Howe; **m**, Peter Brunelli, Louis De Francesco, J.S. Zamecnik; **ed**, Paul Weatherwax; **art d&set d**, Max Parker.

A Prairie Home Companion ★★★ 2006; U.S.; 105m; Picture House Entertainment; Color; Musical Comedy; Children: Unacceptable

(MPAA: PG-13); **DVD**; **VHS**. This entertaining film recreates through a hodge-podge of inventive scenes (typical Altman scattershot sequences that deal with large ensembles and disconnected scenes) that occur backstage during the final broadcast of the popular variety radio show hosted by down-home humorist Garrison Keillor as performed live at a theater in St. Paul, Minnesota. Stars of the show are accompanied by famous guest stars. Songs: "Back Country Shuffle" (Pat Donahue); "Atlanta Twilight," "Ladies at the River," "Duct Tape Underscore" (Richard Dworsky); "Smooth Talker" (Donahue, Dworsky); "Guy Noir," "Baby, Baby, Be My Man," "The Day Is Short" (Dworsky, Keillor); "I Used to Work in Chicago," "Go Tell Aunt Rhodie" (traditional); "Pisca-cadaquoddymoggin" (Robin Williams, Keillor); "Yishomingo Blues" (Spencer Williams); "Independence Rag" (Pat Donohue, Andy Stein); "Won't You Come Home Bill Bailey," "Blues at the Fair," "Mudslide," "Guy's Shoes," "Waitin' for You" (Donohue); "Strappin' the Strings" (Stein); "Slow Days of Summer," Goodbye to My Mama," "Bad Jokes" (Keillor); "Softly and Tenderly" (Will Thompson); "Grandfather's Clock" (Henry Clay Work); "Old Plank Road" (Robin and Linda Williams); "My Minnesota Home," "The Old Folks at Home" (Stephen Foster); "Whoop-I-Ti-Yi-Yo," "Frankie and Johnny," "Beboparerop Rhubarb Pie," "Shortnin' Bread" (traditional, Keillor); "You Have Been a Friend to Me," "Gold Watch & Chain" (A.P. Carter); "Coming Down from Red Lodge" (Peter Ostroushko); "When the Bloom Is On the Sage" (Fred Howard Wright, Nathaniel Hawthorne Vincent); "Rollin' in My Sweet Baby's Arms" (Lester Flatt); "She Is More to Be Pitied than Censured" (William B. Gray); "Let Your Light Shine on Me," There is a Tavern in the Town" (traditional); "Coffee Jingle" (Kate MacKenzie, Keillor); "The Prince of Pizza Commercial," "A Bunch of Guys," "Summit Avenue Rag" (Dworsky); "Red River Valley" (traditional), "While Ye May" (Kevin Kline, Robert Herrick); "In the Sweet By and By" (S. Fillmore Bennett, Joseph Phillbrick Webster). *Author's Note*: This was Altman's last film, the director dying of leukemia five months after it was released at the age of eighty-one. Risqué and off-color humor prohibit viewing by children. **p**, Robert Altman, Wren Arthur, Joshua Astrachan, Tony Judge, David Levy; **d**, Altman; **cast**, Garrison Keillor, Meryl Streep, Lily Tomlin, Kevin Kline, Woody Harrelson, Tommy Lee Jones, Lindsay Lohan, Virginia Madsen, John C. Reilly, Maya Rudolph, Robin Williams; **w**, Keillor (based on a story by Keillor, Ken LaZebnik and Keillor's radio program); **c**, Ed Lachman; **ed**, Jacob Craycroft; **prod d**, Dina Goldman; **art d**, Jeffrey Schoen; **set d**, Tora Peterson; **spec eff**, Steve Hintz, Kevin G. Miller.

Prancer ★★★ 1989; U.S./Canada; 103m; Cineplex-Odeon Films; Orion Pictures; Color; Adventure; Children: Acceptable (MPAA: G); **DVD**; **VHS**. Delightful seasonal film sees Tickell, the eight-year-old daughter of Elliott, a poor widowed farmer in Three Oaks, Michigan, where she can hardly wait for Santa Claus at Christmas. One of Santa's reindeers falls from a display in town, and, after Tickell finds a live deer with an injured leg, she assumes it is Prancer from the display, and has come to life. She hides him in her father's barn and feeds him cookies until his leg heals and she can return him to Santa. She is helped by Vigoda, a friendly veterinarian, as well as Leachman, a reclusive woman in town. Elliott discovers the deer and plans to sell him to the local butcher, not for venison, but as an advertising display. But Tickell's love and Vigoda's care heal Prancer and he is set free where she sees him flying into the sky to rejoin Santa's other deer pulling his sleigh on Christmas Eve. Meanwhile, Elliott's heart has now warmed because of Tickell's tenderness and love. This is a charming story where director Hancock does not overly lard his scenes with bathos and where all the cast members are standouts. **p**, Raffaella De Laurentiis, Mike Petzold, Greg Taylor; **d**, John Hancock; **cast**, Sam Elliott, Cloris Leachman, Rutanya Alda, Abe Vigoda, Michael Constantine, Rebecca Harrell Tickell, John Joseph Duda, Ariana Richards, Mark Rolston, Walter Charles; **w**, Taylor; **c**, Misha Suslov; **m**, Maurice Jarre; **ed**, Dennis O'Connor, John Rosenberg; **prod d**, Chester Kaczenski; **art d**, Marc Dabe; **set d**, Judi

Charlton Heston and Susan Hayward in *The President's Lady*, 1953.

Sandin; **spec eff**, Mike Menzel, Craig Barron.

The President's Analyst ★★★ 1967; U.S.; 103m; Panpiper/PAR; Color; Comedy; Children: Unacceptable; **DVD**; **VHS**. Psychiatrist Coburn is appointed to be the President's analyst, which makes him sought after by those who want to know what the nation's leader thinks on all subjects. He soon becomes stressed out by the job and paranoid as spies are everywhere in an attempt to learn the President's thinking. Coburn can no longer tolerate the strain and runs away, teaming with gun-toting, karate-kicking liberals, who create their own kind of mindless mayhem. Secret Service police from many countries search for him in order to enlist his services or to kill him so that no one else can capture him. Coburn learns that the telephone company and computers really rule the country with a group of automation midgets running everything. This clever but bizarre spoof of spy films acidly lampoons American culture and politics, a thinking man's satirical comedy that is, however, too mature for viewing by children. Coburn is exceptional in this hilarious romp, displaying a decided talent for comedy. Songs: "Inner Manipulations" (Barry McGuire, Paul Potash), "She's Ready to Be Free" (The Clear Light: Bob Seal, Robbie Robison, Doug Lubahn, Dallas Taylor, Michael Ney, Cliff De Young, Ralph Schuckett), "Joy to the World" (George Frideric Handel). **p**, Stanley Rubin; **d&w**, Theodore J. Flicker; **cast**, James Coburn, Godfrey Cambridge, Severn Darden, Joan Delaney, Pat Harrington Jr., Barry McGuire, Jill Banner, Eduard Franz, Will Geer, William Daniels, Joan Darling, Arte Johnson; **c**, William A. Fraker; **m**, Paul Potash, Lalo Schifrin; **ed**, Stuart H. Pappé; **prod d**, Pato Guzman; **art d**, Hal Pereira, Al Roelofs; **set d**, Robert Benton, Arthur Krams; **spec eff**, Albert Whitlock.

The President's Lady ★★★ 1953; U.S.; 96m; FOX; B/W; Biographical Drama/Romance; Children: Unacceptable; **DVD**. This adventure-packed biopic profiles the tempestuous romance and controversial marriage between Andrew Jackson (1767-1845), seventh President of the United States, and Rachel Donelson Robards (1767-1828). The film begins in 1791 in Nashville, Tennessee, when Rachel, played by Hayward, is married to Connor, a philandering local businessman. She meets attorney Jackson, played by Heston, and sparks immediately fly between them. Bainter, Hayward's mother, suggests she take a breathing spell away from Connor by going to Natchez, Mississippi. Since the region is dangerous, Heston takes Hayward there by riverboat, but, en route, Indians attack the boat. Heston manages to fight them off and their survival bonds them closer together. Heston wants to marry Hayward and suggests that she have her marriage to Connor voided in Natchez. Heston's law partner, McIntire (playing John Overton, 1766-1833, who later became Jackson's presidential adviser), sends him a

Raul Julia, Bonnie Bedelia and Harrison Ford in *Presumed Innocent,* 1990.

note saying Connor is suing Hayward for divorce on grounds of adultery with Heston. Thinking the divorce has gone through, Heston marries Hayward. They return to Nashville where they learn that Hayward's divorce action was not complete when she and Heston married, which creates a scandal that jeopardizes Heston's plans to run for public office. The divorce becomes final and Hayward and Heston marry again. Political opponent Betz raises the issue, claiming Heston stole another man's wife and that Heston and Hawyard are bigamists. They fight a duel in which Heston is wounded, but Betz is killed. (Betz plays Charles Dickinson, 1780-1806, a longtime foe of Jackson's, both dueling to the death on May 30, 1806, in Adairville, Kentucky, going across the state line since dueling was then outlawed in Tennessee.) Heston vows to Hayward that he will make her a great and important lady someday. Time passes and the Democratic Party chooses Heston to run for President. While Heston is making a campaign speech, Hayward listens while standing in the crowd. When Heston is heckled about Betz's death and his marriage scandal, she faints. She falls ill and, before Heston learns he has been elected President, Hayward dies in his arms, never living to become "First Lady." The film does not cover Jackson's heroism in the War of 1812 when his troops said he was "as tough as old hickory wood," thus earning the sobriquet of "Old Hickory." Heston is exceptional as the young and hotheaded Jackson, and Hayward gives a strong performance of the only woman in Jackson's life. The script faithfully follows the Stone novel, which correctly profiled Jackson. Songs: "Sally Goodin," "Cotton Eyed Joe," "Possum Up a Gum Stump" (music: Urban Thielmann); "Leather Britches" (traditional); "German Dances" (Ludwig van Beethoven); "Yankee Doodle" (traditional). Mature themes prohibit viewing by children. *Author's Note*: Heston told this author that his performance "was as close as I could make it to that colorful and sometimes unpredictable man. Jackson was a capable lawyer and a natural politician but he was a pioneer at heart and he loved the wilderness, and, I think, that is why he loved Rachel Donelson, because she was very much like that wildness, untamed and free-spirited." Hayward laughed when recalling this film for this author, stating: "Jackson's Rachel was as tough as he was, a backwoods person with as much bark on her as you could find on Old Hickory. She smoked a pipe and so do I in that picture. It was a lot of fun doing that picture with Charlton, except when I had to be made up as an old woman of more than sixty and that took hours to achieve, but the makeup people did a fine job. When I saw the picture and myself in old age, I said to myself, 'I hope I look that good when I reach the age of sixty.'" She never did; Hayward, born in 1917, died at the age of fifty-seven on March 14, 1975, of brain cancer. Zanuck told this author that "we had problems on the set of **The President's Lady** because 'Red' [Hayward] was always arguing with Connor, the actor who plays her estranged husband. That was ironic because Con-

nor was once engaged to marry her and had run off with her sister instead of taking 'Red' to the altar and she never forgave him for that." Many other films have profiled the feisty Andrew Jackson, including: **Bridger**, 1976 (made-for-TV; John Anderson) **The Buccaneer**, 1938 (Hugh Sothern); **The Buccaneer**, 1958 (Charlton Heston); **Davy Crockett: King of the Wild Frontier**, 1955 (Basil Ruysdael); **The Eagle and the Sea**, 1926 (George Irving); **The Fighting Kentuckian**, 1949 (Steve Darrell); **The First Texan**, 1956 (Carl Benton Reid); **The Frontiersman**, 1927 (Russell Simpson); **Gone to Texas**, 1986 (made-for-TV; G. D. Spradlin); **The Gorgeous Hussy**, 1936 (Lionel Barrymore); **Lone Star**, 1952 (Lionel Barrymore); **Man of Conquest**, 1939 (Edward Ellis); **My Own United States**, 1918 (F. C. Earle); **Pirates of Treasure Island**, 2006 (Thomas Downey); **Privateer**, 2009 (Corin Nemec); **The Remarkable Andrew**, 1942 (Brian Donlevy); **War of 1812**, 1999 (TV miniseries; Richard Clarkin); and **The Wedding of Lilli Marlene**, 1953 (Robert Ayres); **p**, Sol C. Siegel; **d**, Henry Levin; **cast**, Susan Hayward, Charlton Heston, John McIntire, Fay Bainter, Whitfield Connor, Carl Betz, Charles Dingle, Margaret Wycherly, James Best, Trudy Marshall, Jim Davis; **w**, John Patrick (based on the novel by Irving Stone); **c**, Leo Tover; **m**, Alfred Newman; **ed**, William B. Murphy; **art d**, Leland Fuller, Lyle R. Wheeler; **set d**, Paul S. Fox; **spec eff**, Ray Kellogg.

Pressure Point ★★★ 1962; U.S.; 91m; Larcas/UA; B/W; Drama; Children: Unacceptable; **DVD**; **VHS**. Producer Stanley Kramer invariably tried to provide great social messages with his films, and this one is no exception. This powerful tale dealing with anti-Semitism sees Poitier as an African-American prison psychiatrist, who finds his professionalism tested when he is assigned to counsel Darin (in his fourth film of an all-too-brief career). The case is unraveled in flashback as Poitier is giving counsel to another psychiatrist, Falk, who is having difficulty with his practice. Darin is shown as a disturbed inmate, who has bigoted Nazi tendencies. He admires the Nazis of yesteryear, and we see some of the rallies held by the American Bund before the beginning of WWII and learn much about these hate-filled members of the National Socialist German Workers' political party from 1920 to the end of World War II, 1939-1945. Darin's past is crowed with misery, where he is abused by a mean-minded, drunken father, and a shrewish, bedridden mother. Darin cleverly pretends to be cured of his deep racial hatreds, convincing others at the institution that he is rehabilitated, and he is released from prison, despite Poitier's objection. Darin then murders an old man and is later executed for the crime, thus vindicating Poitier's staunch objections to having this psycho released. This film not only offers a good perspective on the many applications of psychology, but exposes insidious racism and bigotry in a very impactful manner. Poitier, Darin, and the rest of the cast are standouts, including Gordon, who would go on to play the utterly charming and worldly son of Jason Robards Jr. in the hilarious **A Thousand Clowns**, 1965. Songs: "Here Comes the Bride/Bridal Chorus" (Richard Wagner), "The Star-Spangled Banner" (John Stafford Smith, Frances Scott Key). *Author's Note*: Kramer, who had earlier produced **The Defiant Ones**, 1958, which starred Poitier and Tony Curtis, told this author that he felt that "Sidney is one of the most sensitive and thoughtful men in the acting business and only a very few could have matched his introspective performance in **Pressure Point**. He is a vastly underrated actor." Kramer had previously dealt with anti-Semitism promoted by the Nazi regime in **The Juggler**, 1953, and **Judgment at Nuremberg**, 1961. Mature themes, racism and bigotry prohibit viewing by children. **p**, Stanley Kramer; **d**, Hubert Cornfield; **cast**, Sidney Poitier, Bobby Darin, Peter Falk, Carl Benton Reid, Mary Munday, Howard Caine, Gilbert Green, Barry Gordon, Richard Bakalyan, Lynn Loring; **w**, Cornfield, S. Lee Pogostin (based on the story "The Fifty-Minute Hour" by Robert M. Lindner); **c**, Ernest Haller; **m**, Ernest Gold; **ed**, Cornfield, Frederic Knudtson; **prod d**, Rudolph Sternad; **art d**, George C. Webb; **set d**, George Milo.

Presumed Innocent ★★★ 1990; U.S.; 127m; WB; Color; Crime

Drama; Children: Unacceptable (MPAA: R); **BD**; **DVD**; **VHS**. Cleverly crafted and puzzling whodunit has Ford, a prosecutor and right-hand man of prosecuting attorney Dennehy, who assigns him to investigate a killing after Scacchi, Ford's colleague and mistress, is murdered. Ford, who has been unfaithful to his wife, Bedelia, becomes the prime suspect, and, after dangerously probing the case, comes to believe that Scacchi was killed while investigating a bribery case involving Dennehy. That hazardous lead turns out to be a red herring after Ford discovers that Bedelia killed Scacchi out of jealousy. Songs: "MacNamara's Band" (Shamus O'Connor, John J. Stamford), "Country Dreams" (Jim Jacobsen as Peter Morris), "Let the Drummer Loose" (Richard Wolf, Bret Mazur, Y.C. Smith). Excessive violence prohibits viewing by children. **p**, Sidney Pollack, Mark Rosenberg; **d**, Alan J. Pakula; **cast**, Harrison Ford, Brian Dennehy, Raul Julia, Bonnie Bedelia, Greta Scacchi, Paul Winfield, John Spencer, Joe Grifasi, Tom Mardirosian, Anna Maria Horsford; **w**, Pakula, Frank Pierson (based on the novel by Scott Turow); **c**, Gordon Willis; **m**, John Williams; **ed**, Evan Lottman; **prod d**, George Jenkins; **art d**, Bob Guerra; **set d**, Carol Joffe.

Pretty Baby ★★★ 1978; U.S.; 110m; PAR; Color; Historical Drama; Children: Unacceptable (MPAA: R); **BD**; **DVD**, **VHS**. This sordid and often disgusting tale starkly depicts in very realistic terms the wide open prostitution rampant in New Orleans in 1917 where Sarandon is a prostitute living with her twelve-year-old daughter, Shields, in Storyville, the red light district of the city. They live in the fancy brothel of Madame Nell (Faye) where Sarandon works. Ernest J. Bellocq (John Ernest Joseph Bellocq; 1873-1949), a photographer, who is played by Carradine, takes pictures of the women in the whorehouse and is attracted to both Sarandon and Shields. Faye auctions Shields' virginity and the winner pays $400 to spend the night with her. Sarandon marries a wealthy client and moves to St. Louis, Missouri, leaving Shields in the brothel. Carradine proposes to Shields and she accepts him and moves to his house. Sarandon later gives up her past life and goes to Carradine's house to reclaim Shields. Carradine wants Shields to remain with him, but she decides to go with her mother, leaving him a sad, lonely man. Based on some real characters including Bellocq, this is a compelling film and is well enacted by the entire cast. Mature themes and prostitution prohibit viewing by children. Songs: "Pretty Baby" (Egbert Van Alstyne, Tony Jackson, Gus Kahn); "Tiger Rag" (Edwin B. Edwards, Nick LaRocca, Tony Sbarbaro, Henry Ragas, Larry Shields); "Winin' Boy Blues," "Big Lip Blues" (Ferdinand "Jelly Roll" Morton); "Creole Belles" (J. Bodewalt Lampe); "Swipesy" (Scott Joplin, Arthur Marshall); "Moonlight Bay" (Percy Wenrich); "Heliotrope Bouquet" (Scott Joplin, Louis Chauvin); "The Ragtime Dance" (Scott Joplin); "Careless Love" (traditional); "Madamoiselle from Armentieres" (traditional); "Where Is My Wandering Boy Tonight?" (Robert Lowry); "After the Ball" (Charles K. Harris). *Author's Note*: Storyville flourished for twenty years, from 1897, until social reformers pressured politicians to close it down in 1917. Its bordellos featured many of the celebrated African-American jazz bands and singers of that era, these exceptionally talented people going on to legitimate fame and fortune. The name of this Red Light District was originally "Storeyville," named after a local politician, Sidney Storey, a city committeeman who mapped out the area in 1896. For extensive details on this notorious New Orleans district, see my work *Encyclopedia of World Crime*, Volume IV (CrimeBooks, Inc., 1990; pages 2861-2864). **p&d**, Louis Malle; **cast**, Keith Carradine, Susan Sarandon, Brooke Shields, Frances Faye, Antonio Fargas, Matthew Anton, Diana Scarwid, Barbara Steele, Seret Scott, Cheryl Markowitz; **w**, Polly Platt (based on a story by Platt, Malle from the book *Storyville, New Orleans: Being an Authentic Account of the Notorious Redlight District* by Al Rose); **c**, Sven Nykvist (Metrocolor); **ed**, Suzanne Fenn, Juliet Taylor; **prod d**, Trevor Williams; **set d**, Jim Berkey.

Pretty Boy Floyd ★★★ 1960; U.S.; 96m; Le-Sac/Continental; B/W;

Brooke Shields in *Pretty Baby*, 1978.

Crime Drama; Children: Unacceptable; **DVD**. This is a taut and riveting biopic of Oklahoma bandit Charles Arthur "Pretty Boy" Floyd (1904-1934), dynamically portrayed by Ericson. Released from prison after serving a term for a stickup, Ericson tries to start an honest life by becoming a boxer. He does well in the ring, but his good looks get him the name of "Pretty Boy," a moniker he hates. He leaves the ring and gets a job on an oil rig, but he loses that job after he has an affair with a married woman and her husband exposes his prison record. He then learns that his father has been murdered by a farmer, who has had a long-standing feud with the family. Ericson tracks down the farmer and kills him, which leads him into a life of serious crime. He acquires partners Newman, York, and Kenneally, and a new girlfriend, Harvey. Months of bank robberies and killings take Ericson to Kansas City, Missouri, where he takes part in the killing of an FBI agent and three local lawmen. The bloody battle becomes known as the Kansas City Massacre, and Ericson becomes the FBI's Public Enemy Number One. Ericson flees to a farm in Ohio, but FBI agents track him there and he is gunned down on October 22, 1934. Song: "Black Emanuelle" (Del Serino, Bill Sanford). This well-told crime biopic was made on a small budget, and the story is excitingly presented with exceptional performances from the cast, although the story line follows the FBI version of events, some facts of which are still in doubt. Ericson came to the movies after starring on Broadway in the play "Stalag 17," but lost the film role to William Holden, who won the best actor Oscar for the 1953 movie. Ericson's movie career continued for some years but, despite looks and talent, he never became a top star. *Author's Note*: Floyd insisted right up to the time of his death that he never participated in the Kansas City Massacre, telling that to FBI Agent Melvin Purvis after he was wounded while fleeing an Ohio farmhouse. According to reliable reports, rather than take Floyd alive and to preserve J. Edgar Hoover's dogged contention that Floyd was responsible for the Kansas City Massacre, Purvis ordered a local police officer to execute Floyd and the bandit was summarily shot to death. For more details on Floyd, see the entry on Floyd in my *Encyclopedia of World Crime*, Volume II (CrimeBooks, Inc., 1990; pages 1182-1188). For a detailed account of the Kansas City Massacre, see my book *The Great Pictorial History of World Crime*, Volume II (History, Inc., 2004; pages 951-958). Floyd was profiled by many actors in several other films, including: **A Bullet for Pretty Boy**, 1970 (Fabian); **Dillinger**, 1973 (Steve Kanaly); **The FBI Story**, 1959 (Bob Peterson); **Guns Don't Argue**, 1957 (Doug Wilson); **The Kansas City Massacre**, 1975 (made-for-TV; Bo Hopkins); **Public Enemies**, 2009 (Channing Tatum); **The Story of Pretty Boy Floyd**, 1974 (made-for-TV; Martin Sheen); **The Verne Miller Story**, 1988 (Andrew Robinson); and **Young Dillinger**, 1965 (Robert Conrad). **p**, Monroe Sachson; **d&w**, Herbert J. Leder; **cast**, John Ericson, Barry Newman, Roy Fant,

Richard Gere and Julia Roberts in *Pretty Woman*, 1990.

Joan Harvey, Carl York, Philip Kenneally, Jason Evers (as Herb Evers), Effie Afton, Shirley Smith, Casey Peyson, Peter Falk, Al Lewis; **c**, Charles Austin; **m**, William Sanford, Del Sirino; **ed**, Ralph Rosenblum.

Pretty in Pink ★★★ 1986; U.S.; 96m; PAR; Color; Comedy/Drama; Children: Unacceptable (MPAA: PG-13); **DVD**; **VHS**. Ringwald is a high school senior who works in a record shop and has a crush on McCarthy, a rich boy at her school; they date, but friends in their different social circles object. Meanwhile, Cryer, a boy of her own social set, is in love with her but is shy and doesn't show his feelings for her. She goes to her senior prom without a date, but looks adorable in a pink dress of her own making. At the prom, Cryer encourages Ringwald to accept McCarthy despite what others think, and Ringwald and McCarthy kiss in the parking lot, a happy future ahead for them as a couple. A new girl enters Cryer's life, her presence promising a possible future for them. This well-crafted film presents a good example of teenage high school life and romance in the 1980s, and Ringwald and the cast members are charming and convincing. Songs: "Pretty in Pink" (Roger Morris, John Ashton, Duncan Kilburn, Vince Ely, Tim Butler, Richard Butler); "Wouldn't It Be Good" (Nik Kershaw); "What's It Going to Be" (Maggie Lee); "Love" (John Lennon); "Round, Round" (Neville Keighley); "Pursuit" (Winston Sharples); "Rave-Up/Shut-Up," "Positively Lost Me" (Jimmie Podrasky, Doug Leonard); "Copacabana, At the Copa" (Barry Manilow, Bruce Sussman, Jack Feldman); "Thieves Like Us" (Arthur Baker, New Order); "Elegia" (New Order); "If You Leave," "Whisper/Touch" (Dean Chamberlain); "Bring on the Dancing Horses" (Will Sergeant, Ian McCulloch, Les Pattinson, Pete DeFreitas); "Do What You Do" (Michael Hutchence, Andrew Farriss); "Shell-Shock" (New Order, John Robie); "Try a Little Tenderness" (Harry M. Woods, J. Campbell, Reginald Connelly); "Cherish" (Terry Kirkman); "Please Please Please Let Me Get What I Want" (Morrissey, Johnny Marr); "Rudy" (Bruno); "Left of Center" (Suzanne Vega, Steve Addabbo); "Getto Know Ya" (Jesse Johnson). Sexual themes prohibit viewing by children. **p**, Lauren Shuler; **d**, Howard Deutch; **cast**, Molly Ringwald, Andrew McCarthy, James Spader, Jon Cryer, Harry Dean Stanton, Annie Potts, Jim Haynie, Alexa Kenin, Kate Vernon, Andrew "Dice" Clay; **w**, John Hughes; **c**, Tak Fujimoto; **m**, Michael Gore; **ed**, Richard Marks; **prod d**, John W. Corso; **set d**, Bruce Weintraub, Jennifer Polito; **spec eff**, John Frazier.

Pretty Poison ★★★ 1968; U.S.; 89m; FOX; Color; Crime Drama; Children: Unacceptable; **DVD**; **VHS**. Quirky but fascinating crime tale has Perkins as an emotionally disturbed young man, who is released from an institution and where he has been held for burning down his aunt's house with her in it. He meets Weld, a pretty, sexy girl, who blindly believes his story that he is a secret agent. A high school cheerleader, she is as unstable as Perkins, easily persuaded to help him try to destroy a lumber mill he says is poisoning the area's water. She kills a guard at the lumberyard, and Perkins is suspected. They plan to marry and then escape to Mexico, but Weld's mother, Garland, shows up to stop them. Weld shoots her mother and wants Perkins to dump the body in a river. Instead, he drives the corpse to the police. Weld tells the cops Perkins killed the guard and her mother and they believe her, and he is convicted and sent to prison. Weld is free to create more murderous mayhem, but is being closely watched at the film's end. Perkins is exceptional as Weld's mentally unstable pawn, and Weld, who had established an acting career based on playing innocent, sweet, young girl roles, surprises with her shuddering performance of a an utterly ruthless and vicious killer. Song: "The Thunderer" (John Philip Sousa). This film was remade as a television movie in 1996. *Author's Note*: Perkins told this author that "my role in **Pretty Poison** is not much different from the part I played in **Psycho** [1960], which, I guess, typecast me in playing deranged persons ever after. Well, even nutty people have to make a living—right?" Perkins delivered this last remark with a wide grin. Violence and sexuality prohibit viewing by children. **p**, Noel Black, Marshal Backlar; **d**, Black; **cast**, Anthony Perkins, Tuesday Weld, Beverly Garland, John Randolph, Dick O'Neill, Clarice Blackburn, Joseph Bova, Ken Kercheval, Don Fellows, George Ryan; **w**, Lorenzo Semple, Jr. (based on the novel *She Let Him Continue* by Stephen Geller); **c**, David Quaid (DeLuxe Color); **m**, Johnny Mandel; **ed**, William Ziegler; **art d**, Jack Martin Smith, Harold Michelson; **set d**, John Mortensen; **spec eff**, Ralph Winigar, Billy King.

Pretty Village, Pretty Flame ★★★ 1996; Yugoslavia; 115m; Cobra Films/Fox Lorber; Color; War Drama; Children: Unacceptable; **DVD**; **VHS**. Impactful war tale sees friends since boyhood, a Muslim, Pejakovic, and a Serb, Bjelogrlic, becoming enemies twelve years later during the Bosnian civil war in 1992. Both are wounded and in a Belgrade hospital together where they reflect upon their former friendship and how the war has drastically changed them. Songs: "Bacila je sve niz rijeku," "Igra rokenrol cela Jugoslavija." Excessive violence prohibits viewing by children. **p**, Dragan Bjelogrlic, Goran Bjelogrlic, Milko Josifov, Nikola Kojo; **d**, Srdjan Dragojevic; **cast**, Nikola Pejakovic, Dragan Bjelogrlic, Dragan Maksimovic, Zoran Cvijanovic, Milorad Mandic, Dragan Petrovic, Nikola Kojo, Lisa Moncure, Velimir "Bata" Zivojinovic, Petar Bozovic; **w**, Dragojevic, Biljana Maksic, Pejakovic (based on a story by Vanja Bulic); **c**, Dusan Joksimovic; **m**, Aleksander Habic, Lazar Ristovski; **ed**, Petar Markovic; **prod d**, Milenko Jeremic; **spec eff**, Petar Zivkovic.

Pretty Woman ★★★ 1990; U.S.; 119m; Touchstone/Buena Vista; Color; Comedy/Romance; Children: Unacceptable (MPAA: R); **BD**; **DVD**. Handsome, rich, and ruthless businessman Gere specializes in taking over companies and then selling them off piece by piece (not unlike Michael Douglas playing the business barracuda in **Wall Street**, 1987). On a business trip to Los Angeles, he meets attractive Roberts, a high-class prostitute, and offers her considerable money if she will stay with him for a week while he breaks into the "rich and famous" scene of society parties and polo matches. She agrees, accepting $3,000 and the use of his credit cards and then goes on a Rodeo Drive shopping spree, although she is unsophisticated in that she usually buys her clothes at bargain basement stores. Elizondo, manager of the hotel they stay at, helps her pick the right dresses and coaches her on dinner etiquette. Gere is amazed and delighted by her transformation into a more sophisticated beauty and they soon make love on the grand piano in the hotel lounge. They go to a polo match where Alexander, Gere's attorney, tells Roberts he'll hire her after Gere is finished with her, but she's insulted (and this is somewhat incongruous in that Roberts' profession is selling her body). Roberts and Gere fly in his private jet plane to San Francisco and attend the opera. Roberts relates to the plot of Verdi's "La

Traviata" about a rich man falling in love with a courtesan (which examples their modern-day affair). She and Gere spend the next day together and have sex and she admits she's fallen in love with him. Gere is no longer consumed with business and enjoys his time with Roberts, relaxing and having sex with her, but isn't inclined to marry her. Alexander is upset that Gere's mind is no longer focused on business, and he blames Roberts, and he then tries to rape her. Gere arrives in time to stop Alexander and orders him out of his hotel room. Roberts moves into the apartment of a girlfriend, San Giacomo, and plans to leave Gere and get a college education. Gere climbs up the fire escape, despite his fear of heights, and with some roses between his teeth and as "La Traviata" plays in the background, he tries to win her heart. It reminds Roberts of her childhood dream of being a princess and being rescued from a tower by a knight on a white horse, although she sees that Gere has come there in his white limousine. Gere and Roberts kiss on the fire escape and women in audiences all over the world cry with joy, making the film one of the top grossing movies of the decade. It was the final film for Bellamy who plays a businessman in this film. The romance elements of this film are reminiscent of **An Officer and a Gentleman**, 1982, which also starred Gere. This touching fairy tale is full of syrup and soggy handkerchiefs, but it is nevertheless well made and enacted and it is most likely the favorite film of all those shady ladies strolling up and down Sunset Boulevard, hoping and praying to meet a man like Gere. Roberts was, at one time, called "the most beautiful woman in the world" by *Cosmopolitan Magazine*. This megahit produced more than $463 million from the box office in its initial release against a $14 million budget, and sent Gere and Roberts to superstardom. Songs: "Oh, Pretty Woman" (Roy Orbison, William Dees), "Five for Louie" (Karen Hernandez), "King of Wishful Thinking" (Martin Page, Peter Cox, Richard Drummie), "Real Wild Child (Wild One)" (Johnny O'Keefe, Johnny Greenan, Dave Owen), "Show Me Your Soul" (Anthony Kiedis, Flea, Chad Smith, John Frusciante), "Fame 90" (David Bowie, John Lennon, Carlos Alomar), "Life in Detail" (Robert Palmer, Allen Powell), "Tangled" (Scott Cutler, Jane Wiedlin), "Kiss" (Prince), "Wild Women Do" (Matthew Wilder, Gregory Prestopino, Sam Lorber), "The Four Seasons" (Antonio Vivaldi), "Richard Gere Piano Solo" (Richard Gere), "Songbird" (Kenny G), "You Don't Understand" (Clarence Williams, Spencer Williams, James P. "Jimmie" Johnson), "One Sweet Letter from You" (Harry Warren, Sidney Clare, Lew Brown), "Fallen" (Lauren Wood), "La Traviata" selections (Giuseppe Verdi), "It Must Have Been Love" (Per Gessle), "No Explanation" (David Foster, Linda Thompson-Jenner, Bill LaBounty, Beckie Foster), "She Rescues Him Right Back" (Thomas Pasatieri). Sexuality and gutter language prohibit viewing by children. **p**, Arnon Milchan, Steven Reuther, Gary W. Goldstein; **d**, Garry Marshall; **cast**, Richard Gere, Julia Roberts, Ralph Bellamy, Jason Alexander, Laura San Giacomo, Alex Hyde-White, Amy Yasbeck, Elinor Donahue, Hector Elizondo, Judith Baldwin; **w**, J.F. Lawton; **c**, Charles Minsky; **m**, James Newton Howard; **ed**, Raja Gosnell, Priscilla Nedd-Friendly; **prod d**, Albert Brenner; **art d**, David Haber; **set d**, Garrett Lewis; **spec eff**, Gary Zink.

Priceless ★★★ 2008; France; 106m; France 2 Cinema/Samuel Goldwyn; Color; Comedy/Romance; Children: Unacceptable (MPAA: PG-13); **BD**; **DVD**. In this tawdry but tempting comedy Tautou is a gold-digging prostitute who goes after one rich elderly man after another on the French Riviera. One night, she mistakes Elmaleh, a bartender, for a new rich prospect, and takes him to her hotel room where her sugar daddy has passed out. Tautou and Elmaleh have a hot evening together and then go their separate ways. A year later they meet again but this time the sugar daddy finds out and dumps her. Tautou and Elmaleh both need money so he joins her in her love-for-sale business, she going after more rich men and he pursuing rich women. Songs: "Jaleo" (Christian Prommer, Roland W. Appel, Rainer Truby, Concha Buika), "What's the Use" (Jamie Lidell), "Whatever Lola Wants" (Richard Adler, Jerry Ross), "Cheaper to Keep Her" (Mack Rice), "Brother Where Are You?"

Greer Garson, Vernon Downing, Laurence Olivier and E. E. Clive in *Pride and Prejudice*, 1940.

(Matthew Herbert Remix), "Alone" (Don Ellis), "Amour delices et conterebasse" (Guy Pedersen, Raymond Guiot), "Sort Me Out" (Alexis Slioussarenko, Winston McAnuff), "Calling Out" (Lyrics Born, Charles Berman, Alain Gagnon, Francois Lanctot, Yves Legare, Claude Chapleau), "Can't Take My Eyes Off You" (Bob Gaudio, Bob Crewe), "Can't Take My Mind Off of You" (Feat Lennie Hibbert). Sexual scenes and nudity prohibit viewing by children. (In French; English subtitles.) **p**, Philippe Martin; **d**, Pierre Salvadori; **cast**, Audrey Tautou, Gad Elmaleh, Marie-Christine Adam, Vernon Dobtcheff, Jacques Spiesser, Annelise Hesme, Charlotte Vermeil, Claudine Baschet, Laurent Claret, Jean de Coninck; **w**, Salvadori, Benoît Graffin, Franck Bauchard; **c**, Gilles Henry; **m**, Camille Bazbaz, David Hadjadj; **ed**, Isabelle Devinck; **prod d**, Yves Fournier; **art d, set d, spec eff**, Cédric Fayolle.

Pride and Prejudice ★★★★★ 1940; U.S.; 118m; MGM; B/W; Comedy/Drama/Romance; Children: Acceptable; **DVD**; **VHS**. Garson and Olivier are superlative in this masterpiece film from pantheon director Leonard, one that wholly captures the manners, morals and marital pursuits of the early 1800s in England. Other than the set time period (which was advanced by a decade for production reasons), this magnificent production keeps dogged faith with the characters and story line as portrayed in Jane Austen's classic novel. Boland and Gwenn are two happily married persons living comfortably in a large home in a rural area, spending more time than what they would want in worrying about and arranging for the marriages of their five beautiful but very different daughters— Garson, O'Sullivan, Rutherford, Hunt and Angel. Gwenn, an endearing father, is frustrated and hampered in finding suitable spouses for his offspring by his garrulous wife Boland, whom he nevertheless adores. The daughter of a shopkeeper, Boland is forever promoting the charms and graces of her lovely daughters, which embarrasses Gwenn, an old-fashioned gentleman adhering to the strict decorum of the day. Nevertheless, the couple needs to find suitable suitors in order to marry off their children and have further family progeny in order to protect their modest income and estate from being acquired by Cooper, an avaricious cousin with a decided mean streak. The family as well as the town is awash with gossip and rumor when two new handsome, young men arrive, these eligible bachelors being Olivier and Lester. Boland immediately sets her sights on these two swains as good marital prospects for her daughters. Lester is easily attracted to the family, but Olivier, a rather haughty fellow, looks down his nose at these locals as unsophisticated people not worthy of his august company. Garson is attracted to Olivier, but she resents his arrogant ways, and, to teach him a lesson, refuses to dance with him when they attend a local ball. Her standoffish manners intrigue the pensive Olivier, finding Garson all the more alluring as he slowly advances and she slowly retreats, the fox after the hare, or via

Keira Knightley and Matthew Macfadyen in *Pride & Prejudice*, 2005.

versa. He is further intrigued when Garson manages to deftly handle his equally snobbish dowager aunt, Oliver (whose snooty and pretentious performance is another gem in this sterling production). Meanwhile, O'-Sullivan and Lester fall in love, although Inescort, Lester's sister, who is as arrogant as is Olivier, persistently reminds her brother that O'Sullivan's family is several social notches down from their own. When Olivier also points out to Lester that Gwenn's family is not equal to their social class, Lester sadly bows to the pressure from his peers and departs for London, which emotionally devastates O'Sullivan. Olivier, however, is still taken by Garson and when they next meet, he tells her that he loves her and that he wants to marry her, but makes the faux pas of telling her that he is willing to do this, in spite of the low social station of her family. Insulted and hurt, Garson rejects his proposal, which stuns the otherwise overly confident Olivier. Cooper, meanwhile, visits Gwenn and his family, unhappy at the sight of a healthy Gwenn and realizing that, to acquire Gwenn's estate, he must marry into the family, instead of waiting for Gwenn to die and claim his inheritance. To that end, he proposes marriage to Garson, but she looks upon the conniving Cooper as one might observe a curling, twisting snake, and refuses his offer. Trouble arises when the trusting and innocent Rutherford falls in love with Ashley, a soldier, and then runs off with him, ostensibly to elope, although Ashley is hesitant in making their union legal. The impending scandal that is about to engulf Gwenn's otherwise happy family is averted through the noble efforts of Olivier. He locates the furtive couple and provides Ashley with enough money so that he and Rutherford can now marry. Olivier's grand gesture so enthralls Garson that she now realizes that Olivier is a fine and decent human being, and, when she sees him once more, she agrees to marry him. Gwenn is more than satisfied when hearing this news, and the dithering Boland becomes ecstatic with joy, now knowing that some of her daughters are safely leaving the nest. Leonard's direction is impeccable as he carefully molds each loving scene of this wonderful story, adding very human touches to each distinct character. Beyond the soaring performances of Garson and Olivier, all of the cast members are superb in their roles. Huxley's brilliant script offers just the right blend of wit, humor and upbeat perspectives. The production values—from the rich costuming (precisely accurate for the period), to the sumptuous and well-appointed sets, to Freund's brilliantly lighted cinematography and Stothart's lilting and moving score—represent the finest in filmmaking. Songs: "Flow Gently Sweet Afton" (1786; music: Alexander Hume; lyrics: Robert Burns), "Pomp and Circumstance March No. 1 in D Major, Op. 39" (1901; Edward Elgar), "On Wings of Song, Op. 34/2" (1835; Felix Mendelssohn-Bartholdy), "Wedding March" (1842; Felix Mendelssohn-Bartholdy), "Ballet of the Unhatched Chicks" (1886; from "Pictures at an Exhibition" by Modest Mussorgsky), "Now Is the Month of Maying" (1595;

Thomas Morley), "Charlie Is My Darling" (traditional Scottish folk song), "Drink to Me Only With Thine Eyes" (traditional English folk song), "Comin' Thro' the Rye" (traditional Scottish folk song), "Summer Is Icumen In" (traditional English folk song). *Author's Note*: The Austen novel was written over several years, from 1793 to about 1797, but no one wanted to publish the work until 1813 when it was first put into print. The play adaptation of this work by Helen Jerome did not appear until 1935 when it was produced in New York (ran 219 performances at the Plymouth Theater, from November 5, 1935, to May 1936) and where Adrienne Allen (then married to actor Raymond Massey) played Elizabeth Bennet, the role that Garson would call her own in the 1940 film production. The novel was actually in public domain when MGM thought to produce it as a film, but the studio nevertheless purchased the film rights from playwright Jerome at the urging of Irving Thalberg, who was then chief of MGM production and who originally envisioned the story as a vehicle for his wife, actress Norma Shearer, who was then the queen at MGM. Thalberg, however, died and the production was put on hold. After MGM revived the story some years later, Clark Gable, then the reigning star at the studio, was offered the role of Darcy, the part Olivier would later enact. Gable, however, refused to appear in another period costume drama, rightly believing his rough-hewn persona did not fit such characters. Gable had appeared in one costume drama, **Parnell**, 1937, a biopic about Irish politician Charles Stewart Parnell (1846-1891), a dismal failure and where he gave what is universally believed to be his worst on-screen performance. "After Gable turned down the role in **Pride & Prejudice**," Olivier told this author, "they offered it to me and I accepted that assignment under the understanding that MGM would consider Vivien [Leigh, his wife at the time] for the role of Elizabeth Bennett. That was not to be." At that time, some at MGM agreed with Olivier, believing that Leigh would do well in the lead role, but MGM studio boss Louis B. Mayer put his foot down. "I was amazed to hear that Mr. Mayer insisted that I play the part of Elizabeth Bennett in **Pride & Prejudice**," Garson told this author. "Certainly, I wanted that prized role, but I never imagined that I would get that part." Mayer at that time was grooming Garson for superstardom after she appeared in MGM's smash hit, **Goodbye Mr. Chips**, 1939, with Robert Donat (who was also briefly considered for the role of Darcy as was Robert Taylor and Errol Flynn), a role for which she received her first of six Academy Award nominations as Best Actress. Production problems presented themselves in that MGM wanted to film this great film in color, but all available Technicolor film had been exhausted in the making of **Gone With the Wind**, 1939. The time frame for the Austen story was moved from the late 1700s to the early 1800s because the costuming for that latter period presented more opulent and impressive apparel as it was the age of the British dandies. Leonard, a master of lighthearted films was named to helm this film after several other directors were either rejected, including George Cukor, or declined the herculean task of presenting the complex story and its myriad characters. **p**, Hunt Stromberg; **d**, Robert Z. Leonard; **cast**, Greer Garson, Laurence Olivier, Mary Boland, Edna May Oliver, Maureen O'Sullivan, Ann Rutherford, Frieda Inescort, Edmund Gwenn, Marsha Hunt, Heather Angel, Edward Ashley, E.E. Clive, Bruce Lester, Melville Cooper, Karen Morley; **w**, Aldous Huxley, Jane Murfin (based on the play by Helen Jerome and the novel by Jane Austen); **c**, Karl Freund; **m**, Herbert Stothart; **ed**, Robert J. Kern; **art d**, Cedric Gibbons; **set d**, Edwin B. Willis.

Pride & Prejudice ★★★ 2005; France/U.K./US; 129m; Focus Features; Color; Comedy/Drama/Romance; Children: Unacceptable (MPAA: PG); **BD**; **DVD**. Based on Austen's 1813 novel, this entertaining film follows the attempts at marriage by five sisters in an upscale English family as they seek rich husbands while dealing with the rigid social issue of that day that insisted that women be nothing more than decorations in a male-dominated society. Knightley plays Elizabeth Bennet, the beautiful and eldest of the sisters, and Macfadyen is Darcy, a young, handsome, and wealthy man of great social stature. He is nevertheless aloof and prejudiced against girls of lower station in life. Also handsome and wealthy young Woods becomes a neighbor and Mr. and Mrs. Bennet (Sutherland and Blethyn) and their daughters meet him at a ball, along with his haughty sister, Reilly, and his reserved friend, Macfadyen. Woods becomes enchanted with Jane Bennett, who is played by Pike, while Knightley takes an instant dislike to Macfadyen after she overhears him talking about her in what she thinks to be an insulting and demeaning manner. Pike becomes slightly ill on a visit to Woods' mansion, and Knightley goes there to chaperone her, engaging in verbal sparring with Macfadyen and Reilly. A pompous clergyman begins to court Knightley, but she despises him. Friend, a handsome, young, and charming army lieutenant, arrives, and the sisters all fall under his charming spell. He gains Knightley's sympathy by telling her that Macfadyen cheated him out of his inheritance. At another ball, Macfadyen surprises Knightley by asking for a dance, and they spend that dance snapping at each other with witty sarcasm. The next day, the clergyman proposes marriage to Knightley, but she declines, as politely as possible, while he assures her that he will continue to seek her hand. Pike expects Woods to propose to her, but he unexpectedly departs for London, persuaded to break off relations with Pike by his arrogant sister, Reilly, who insists that Pike is too much beneath her sibling's station in life. Knightley takes Pike to London to recover from her broken heart by staying with relatives, the Gardiners (Wilton and Wight). The clergyman then proposes to the most unattractive sister, Blakely, and she accepts, only because that marriage will mean a life of security. Knightley sees Macfadyen again at the mansion of his aunt, Lady Catherine, who is played by Dench, and he is impressed by Knightley's wit and her deft handling of the haughty dowager. Knightley then becomes upset when learning that Macfadyen had joined with Reilly in discouraging the romance between Woods and her sister, Pike. Macfadyen picks this unfortunate time to propose marriage to Knightley, but makes the mistake of saying that he loves her "most ardently," despite her "lower rank." Knightley is insulted and flatly turns him down, and Macfadyen leaves in shock. Soon after, he writes her a letter explaining that Friend is a gambler, who attempted to elope with Macfadyen's fifteen-year-old sister, Merchant, so that he could obtain her inheritance, then abandoned her when learning that he would not receive the money. Next, the youngest Bennet sister, Malone, runs away with Friend and her family fears social ruin. But then it is learned that Malone and Friend have married and that Macfadyen has paid for their wedding. Woods then proposes to Pike and she accepts. Dench then meets with Knightley, demanding that she never see Macfadyen again because of Knightley's lower station in life. Knightley refuses her demand and shortly after meets Macfadyen and where he again proposes marriage. Softened by the discovery of his recent kindnesses to her sister Malone, and admitting to herself that she loves him, Knightley finally accepts. Pride and prejudice no longer keep them apart, and the lovers embrace and kiss for a happy ending. This faithful adaptation of the novel provides a lavishly produced story with exceptional acting, but it simply cannot match the 1940 Greer Garson-Laurence Olivier version or the superlative 1995 British Masterpiece Theatre television miniseries. It is nevertheless far superior to the 1980 TV miniseries and the 2003 feature film production. The film was also produced as a present-day version ntitled **A Modern Pride and Prejudice**, 2011. Songs: "Greensleeves," "The Young Widow," "Wakefield Hunt," "The Bishop," "Dutch Dollars," "Tythe Pig," "Black Bess," "Duke of Glouchester's March" (traditional); "Letter to Henry Purcell," "Meryton Townhall," "Dawn" (Dario Marianelli). **p**, Tim Bevan, Eric Fellner, Paul Webster, Jane Frazer; **d**, Joe Wright; **cast**, Keira Knightley, Matthew Macfadyen, Donald Sutherland, Brenda Blethyn, Rupert Friend, Simon Woods, Judi Dench, Talulah Riley, Rosamund Pike, Jena Malone, Carey Mulligan, Claudie Blakley, Tom Hollander, Penelope Wilton, Peter Wight, Kelly Reilly, Meg Wynn Owen; **w**, Deborah Moggach, Emma Thompson (based on the novel by Jane Austen); **c**, Roman Osin; **m**, Dario Marianelli; **ed**, Paul Tothill; **prod d**, Sarah Greenwood; **art d**, Ian Bailie, Nick Gottschalk, Mark Swain; **set d**, Katie Spencer;

Cary Grant, Sophia Loren, and Frank Sinatra in *The Pride and the Passion*, 1957.

spec eff, Hugh Goodbody, John Moffatt.

The Pride and the Passion ★★★ 1957; U.S.; 132m; Stanley Kramer Productions/UA; Color; Adventure; Children: Unacceptable; **DVD**; **VHS**. Producer Kramer abandoned his usual message themes to make this impressive spectacle, a stirring and exciting adventure tale set during the Napoleonic wars. Grant, a British officer and ordnance expert, is assigned to retrieve one of the largest cannon ever constructed after it has been left behind by a retreating Spanish army. He goes to Spain and enlists the aid of guerrilla leader Sinatra and his followers, including Sinatra's mistress, Loren, to locate and then drag, pull and push this mammoth artillery piece to a safe area where the British can put it to military use. Sinatra and his people laboriously pull the enormous cannon from the bottom of a gorge with pulleys and winches created by Grant, but once it is repaired, Sinatra tells Grant that he will not turn over the cannon to him until it is used to bombard the walled fortress of Avila, which is being held by French forces, and where he and his ragtag army can then penetrate the defenses of that city and free that city from Napoleon's dictatorial control. Grant gives his reluctant approval and thus begins a marathon march across Spain with hundreds of people dragging the cannon across plains, through deserts, over hills and through cities and towns, all with the help of the patriotic civilian population, as the citizens of each village and town help the guerrillas accomplish their exhausting mission. At one point, the cannon is almost discovered by searching French troops, but Sinatra and the citizens of one town hide the cannon inside a towering cathedral where it is again repaired and then it is moved once more toward its military objective. Meanwhile, Grant finds the sultry, earthy Loren so attractive that he falls in love with her and she returns his affection in kind, but their romance is doomed by the near suicide assault on Avila by Sinatra and his followers. Once they arrive at that city, Grant supervises the bombardment of its massive walls, the belching cannon sending huge cannon balls to eventually breach a portion of one wall so that Sinatra and his followers, now numbering in the thousands, can pour through the breach and take the city. In the attack, Sinatra is killed as is Loren, and Grant is devastated, no longer concerned about the massive cannon, which has been ruptured during the cannonade. He finds Sinatra's body and, as a gesture to honor the Spanish patriot, carries it to the town square and deposits it at a large fountain. Kramer does a fine job in orchestrating the crowd and battle scenes, a daunting chore in that he was dealing with many thousands of extras, and this is the real reason to view this historical epic. Planer's lensing is outstanding as his cameras capture the stirring action while displaying the broad Spanish landscapes in rich color, and Antheil's dynamic score appropriately represents the turbulent period. Songs: "The British Grenadiers" (traditional), "Rule, Britannia!" (music:

Frank Sinatra and Sophia Loren in *The Pride and the Passion*, 1957.

Thomas Augustine Arne; lyrics: James Thomson). ***Author's Note***: This was Loren's second American film, after **Boy on a Dolphin**, 1957, having made a reputation in Italy as a sexpot in many risqué Italian films that focused upon her voluptuous and statuesque body, vying with other Italian screen sirens such as Gina Lollobrigida and Silvana Mangano. Her acting, in these days, consisted chiefly of hip-swinging and cleavage exposure (she was paid $200,000 for her role). Even though Italian producer Carlo Ponti, who was then promoting her career into U.S. films, ordered Loren to take a crash course in English for this film, she delivers her lines in such a fractured and wrongly accented manner that it is almost impossible to understand her. "Poor woman," Sinatra told this author, "she could not get with it in English. We got along well because I could talk to her in Italian. She told me that she was worried that her lines were coming out all wrong in English and that she would appear to be ridiculous. I told her to act with her fantastic face, her huge, brown eyes and that great body of hers and she would be fine." Grant did not care much for his role, telling this author that "my part of that British officer was one of the worst miscasting of my career. Because I was born in England did not mean that I could therefore be the epitome of an upper-class Englishman and what I knew about cannons could be comfortably squeezed into an olive bottle. I was leery about ever doing any historical epics after making **The Howards of Virginia** [1940], because that picture was a terrible box office flop, and I did not ever want to repeat that experience, so I refused the role in **The Pride and the Passion** when it was first offered to me, but Stanley [Kramer] talked me into it. He could talk anyone into anything." Grant met Loren for the first time in this production (they would appear together a year later in **Houseboat**, 1958) and, though he was fifty-three at the time and married to actress Betsy Drake, he fell deeply in love with the twenty-two-year-old Italian actress. She was then deeply involved with Ponti, who was forty-five and was also married, but she and Grant reportedly had a torrid affair throughout the production of **The Pride and the Passion**. "Sophia was the only reason why I could keep Cary [Grant] in the picture," Kramer said to this author, "because he hated his role and wanted to quit every ten minutes. Sophia kept his attention going all the time, though, and, after we would end a scene, they would go off together alone. Cary was the most cool-headed actor in Hollywood, but he completely lost his head over Sophia. He was simply nuts about her." Grant proposed to Loren, but she turned him down, preferring to later on marry Ponti, who divorced his wife to marry her. Kramer was beset with logistical problems during the production, particularly when it came to hiring and organizing the swelling armies of his extras, to the point where he felt "overwhelmed and that is something for me. I wound up hiring just about every Spaniard we met as we moved from one location to another with that damned big cannon." The most challenging problem

Kramer had was dealing with the temperamental Sinatra, who, by then, was a superstar. "I knew the man when he was a pleasant singer and just an average Joe, but, after he won that Academy Award for his appearance in **From Here to Eternity** [1953], there was no holding him. He had become a prima donna. He insisted that his private car be flown to Spain at our expense. He did not like Francisco Franco, who was running the country at that time, and he was always making public insults about him that caused us a lot of problems. Like Cary, Frank threatened to quit the picture almost every ten minutes and he finally left me high and dry so that we had to make up some shots with him back in Hollywood." Sinatra told this author that "I hated doing that picture because I could not stand being in Spain at that time, a country that was run by a fascist bastard! That was Francisco Franco [1892-1975], who had taken over the country back in the 1930s with the help of those bums Hitler and Mussolini. I was so steamed up about that jerk that I hung a sign from the balcony of my hotel room that read 'Franco is a fink' or something like that, and, boy, did I get into a lot of trouble over that. Next thing you know, I am visited by some of his fascist stooges ordering me to take the sign down and threatening me with all sorts of strong-arm stuff." I had a similar experience in that same year when I was serving in the U.S. military and stationed in Europe and while I was on a vacation to Madrid. I was sitting at an outside café and saw a row of children, who could not have been older than ten or twelve, all chained together and paraded down a street as if they were dangerous felons by two Guardia Civil officers. A crying mother of one of the children begged to have her child released and was brutally slapped in the face by one of the guards. After being told that these children were being publicly humiliated for violating a nighttime curfew, only one of Franco's many draconian edicts, I loudly cursed the dictator. A man wearing dark glasses rose from a table next to me and showed his secret police credentials and then arrested me, taking me to a local prison where I was, without being charged, summarily thrown into an unlighted dungeon crowded with other prisoners. The place stank of putrid water that had leaked from a sewer and flooded the stone floor. Scores of persons sloshed about in that knee-high foul water, groping like blind men in that dark pit, and calling out to others in many languages while getting little response. Above us were rafters crowded with scurrying, squealing rats that occasionally fell into the water and attempted to survive by clinging onto the water-soaked trouser legs of the prisoners, some of whom shouted in agony after being bitten. This living nightmare could have been envisioned by Franz Kafka, a scene so grotesque that only a Goya could have captured it on canvas. I was fortunate to be an American as our local attachés were prompt in responding to complaints about U.S. citizens. One soon appeared and I was taken from this awful watery pit and brought to an office where a Spanish official asked me why I had verbally maligned Spain's present head of state. I told him that I did not like Franco's oppression of innocent children and women, his suppression of the freedom of the press, and his general disregard for all human rights in this otherwise great nation. He nodded, spoke a few words to the American attaché, and I was released, but not before that Spanish official told me to leave his country and never return. I did not leave until a week later and I did return many times while Franco remained the dictator of that country and after he, thankfully, and for the merciful delivery of the Spanish people, passed from this earth. When I told this story to Sinatra, he said: "Imagine that, the both of us in the same country at the same time and we each squawk about that creep. I get a lecture and you get thrown into the clink. If you had been Spanish, they would have shot you. You know that, don't you?" **p&d**, Stanley Kramer; **cast**, Cary Grant, Frank Sinatra, Sophia Loren, Theodore Bikel, John Wengraf, Jay Novello, Jose Nieto, Carlos Larranaga, Philip Van Zandt, Paco el Laberinto; **w**, Edna and Edward Anhalt (based on the novel *The Gun* by C.S. Forester); **c**, Franz Planer (VistaVision; Technicolor); **m**, George Antheil; **ed**, Ellsworth Hoagland, Frederic Knudtson; **prod d**, Rudolph Sternad; **art d**, Fernando Carrere; **spec eff**, Willis Cook, Maurice Ayres.

The Pride of St. Louis ★★★ 1952; U.S.; 93m; FOX; B/W; Biographical Drama/Sports Drama; Children: Acceptable; **VHS**. Dailey is terrific as the colorful baseball player Jerome Herman "Dizzy" Dean (Jay Hanna Dean; 1910-1974), one of the fastest pitchers in the major leagues. The Ozark-born Dailey is discovered while playing for a semi-pro team, the Houston Buffalos, and is signed to a contract to play for the St. Louis Cardinals. He thinks baseball is nothing more than recreation, but when he goes to work for the Cardinals, he becomes serious about the game and begins pitching in earnest, as does his brother, Crenna, who plays Dizzy's real-life younger brother and also a fast-ball pitcher, Paul Dee "Daffy" Dean (1912-1981). Both become superstars of the game and take the Cardinals to a winning World Series. Throughout their great exploits and wild antics on the mound and outside the ballpark, Dailey manages to win the heart of Dru, marrying her. Many of Dizzy's prankish exploits are displayed in this good-natured and fun-filled film, including his legendary striking out of three dangerous hitters while his teammates sat on the ground at his orders. After establishing many records, Dailey is injured and forced into early retirement, but he takes up a new job as a radio sports announcer (Dean continued in that role for television). His fractured English and homespun way of speaking, however, rises the ire of some grammar teachers, who lobby to have him removed from the airways, but Dru and others come to his defense and, in a moving plea at a hearing, he wins the hearts of the then controllers of the American airways and is given the green light to go on fracturing the English language as he sees fit. Dean actually got an irate letter from an English teacher where she complained that he was constantly using the word "ain't" and, because of the use of that non-word, was corrupting the youth of America. Dean wrote back to her, stating: "A lot of folks who ain't sayin' ain't, ain't eatin'. So, Teach, you learn 'em English and I'll learn 'em baseball." This film is well directed by Jones, who incorporates a lot of real-life sports footage that shows the real Dean in action (from a distance). The script from Mankiewicz, who co-wrote **Citizen Kane**, 1941, with Orson Welles, is wonderfully inventive and loaded with great humor, wholly capturing the lively and unpredictable character of the legendary Dean. In addition to Dailey's fine performance, Dru, Crenna and the rest of the cast are standouts. Songs: "Take Me Out to the Ball Game" (1908; Jack Norworth, Albert von Tilzer), "Hold My Mule While I Dance Josey" (traditional), "Honey" (Richard A. Whiting), "Stompin' at the Savoy" (Edgar M. Sampson), "National Anthem" (Edwin Eugene Bagley). *Author's Note*: Dean achieved 1,163 strikeouts with 150 wins and 83 losses and had an ERA of 3.02. He played for the St. Louis Cardinals, 1930, 1932-1937; the Chicago Cubs, 1938-1941; and the St. Louis Browns, 1947, before retiring and becoming a sports announcer for CBS. He often signed off as that unforgettable announcer by saying: "Don't fail to miss tomorrow's game!" Before the 1934 season, Dean bragged that he and his brother Paul would win forty-five games together for the Cardinals, then called the "Gashouse Gang." He won thirty games and Paul Dean won nineteen, for a total of forty-nine wins. Dizzy was named the National League's MVP for 1934. He was inducted into the Baseball Hall of Fame in 1953. **p**, Jules Schermer; **d**, Harmon Jones; **cast**, Dan Dailey, Joanne Dru, Richard Hylton, Richard Crenna, Hugh Sanders, James Brown, Leo T. Cleary, Robert Board, Harris Brown, John Butler, John Call, Chet Huntley; **w**, Herman J. Mankiewicz (based on a story by Guy Trosper); **c**, Leo Tover; **m**, Arthur Lange; **ed**, Robert Simpson; **art d**, Lyle Wheeler, Addison Hehr; **set d**, Thomas Little, Stuart Reiss; **spec eff**, Fred Sersen.

Pride of the Marines ★★★★ 1945; U.S. 120m; WB; B/W; Biographical Drama/War Drama; Children: Unacceptable; **DVD**. Garfield, in one of his finest roles, essays the U.S. Marine hero Al Schmid (Albert Andrew Schmid; 1920-1982) in this superlative biopic and war tale. Garfield is a carefree blue-collar worker in Philadelphia, who rooms with Ridgely and his wife Doran and their daughter Todd, the teenage Todd idolizing Garfield. The matchmaking Doran thinks that Garfield

Richard Crenna, Joanne Dru and Dan Dailey in *The Pride of St. Louis*, 1952.

should find a girl to marry and sets up a blind date for him with girlfriend Parker, but Garfield has no intention of going to the altar; when they go on that date, he insults her by more or less telling her that all she is after is a wedding ring. He takes her bowling and makes fun of her lack of athletic experience, although he is attracted to her while uselessly trying to teach her how to bowl. All Parker can do is throw gutter balls that never kiss a pin. Garfield continues to heckle her about her designing ways until Parker explodes and tells him off, loudly stating: "I've had a terrible time with an awful drip!" Spectators at the bowling alley give her a round of applause as she leaves Garfield flat and with his mouth gaping. The attractive Parker remains in Garfield's mind and he finds her as she leaves work, pulling his car alongside a curb crowded with people waiting for a bus. He tells her that their sick child is crying for her and wants her to come home. One of the men in the crowd, Haade, tells Parker to do the right thing, be a good mother and go home and take care of her sick child. She gives him a disgusted look and tells Haade that her child has "two heads" and then gets into the car and drives off with Garfield. "Imagine that," says the thick-witted Haade, "a kid with two heads." Parker wants nothing to do with the tough Garfield, but he shows up while she is going out with another man on a date and Garfield pretends that Parker has been two-timing this fellow, who indignantly leaves Parker. She finally softens toward Garfield and they begin dating. Garfield falls in love with her, kissing her for the first time while they are out on a winter hunt. Their plans to marry are interrupted when they hear the news that the Japanese have attacked Pearl Harbor and Garfield soon enlists in the Marine Corps. Parker promises to wait for him, and though he asks her not to come to the train station to see him off, she is nevertheless there and when he sees her in the crowd, he gives her an engagement ring before leaving. Following training, Garfield is sent with his machine gun detachment to fight on Guadalcanal, and he is seen with Clark and Caruso as they relieve others and take over a dugout equipped with a .50-caliber machine gun. They wait until dark, expecting another attack by the Japanese. They have been fighting hard on this front for some time, and their situation is summed up by Caruso, a former prizefighter, who states: "No sleep…no chow… no mail…not enough planes…not enough navy…not enough doctors… we're on the ropes and the referee is up to eight." All along their murky front they can hear the noise of the enemy moving toward them through the swampy creek that faces them and then they hear the enemy call out: "Marine—tonight you die!" The attack ensues with swarms of Japanese soldiers first creeping forward camouflaged as bushes and shrubs and they are shot down and then they rush forward in groups and are shot down. The attack increases as the Japanese add more men, now charging forward in waves, firing blindly at the Marine entrenchments. Some try to flank the dugout, and Clark kills them with his submachine gun.

Eleanor Parker, John Garfield and Ann Todd in *Pride of the Marines*, 1945.

Caruso mans the heavy machine gun, firing short bursts at Clark's command while Garfield feeds the muttering, chattering gun its ammunition belt. Caruso is then shot dead in the head; Clark is wounded, leaving only Garfield to man the machine gun; where Clark tells him to fire only short bursts. The Japanese continue the attack, fanatically charging forward into Garfield's blazing fire, only to be scythed like wheat by its blistering bullets. An enemy bullet pierces the machine gun's water jacket, and Garfield loudly prays for the gun not to jam as he continues firing. On and on come the Japanese and with every renewed attack, Garfield shoots down the enemy. One of the wounded Japanese close to the dugout hurls a grenade that explodes at its opening, and Garfield is hit, blinded by the blast. He gropes for and retrieves his sidearm, raising the .45. Clark pleads with him not to shoot himself, but Garfield has no intention of doing that as he waves the pistol toward the enemy, crying out to Clark: "Tell me where they are…tell me where they are!" We next see Garfield at a military hospital in San Diego, where Clark and others from Guadalcanal are recovering from their wounds. After several examinations, Garfield can only see a blur from one eye and is told that he will most likely be blind for the rest of his life. Now embittered, he decides not to return to his hometown of Philadelphia and asks caretaker DeCamp to write to Parker, saying that he no longer wants to marry her and asking DeCamp not to mention the fact that he is blind. Garfield feels that he can no longer support a wife and will be nothing but a burden to Parker should he marry her. Parker, however, knows Garfield's true condition from DeCamp and also talks with Clark, who accompanies Garfield back to Philadelphia by train and where they arrange for Parker to pretend that she is a U.S. Navy officer who will be driving Garfield to a military hospital when they arrive in Philadelphia. En route, Clark tries to give Garfield hope, telling him that many blind persons adjust to their infirmity and go on to have productive and happy lives, but Garfield is resigned to a gloomy future. When Clark finally says goodbye to Garfield and tells him that he will probably go back in action, he tells him that "when I hit the beach, I'll mark the first Nip for you, Al." Garfield, remembering his terrible wound, bitterly replies: "Get him in the eyes! Right in the eyes!" When arriving at the train station, Clark guides Garfield to Parker's side and, without a word, she takes him to a car, has him take a back seat and then drives away with him, taking him back to Ridgely's home. As he is led up the steps to that home, he realizes that he has been returned home and that Parker is at his side. Angry, he demands that she take him to a hospital but young Todd sees him and embraces him and welcomes him home and Garfield says that, for the girl's sake, will pretend that he has returned to this family. After a family reunion dinner, he is left alone with Parker, telling her that they have no future together because he is blind, but she tells him that that does not matter. He stumbles about and knocks over a

Christmas tree and she holds him in her arms, telling him that if he leaves her she will be left to stumble the same way through life without him. Garfield finally accepts Parker's love and they plan to go ahead with their marriage. Garfield is next shown receiving the Navy Cross and, following the ceremony, he is joined by Parker. As they are about to go home, Garfield, who has regained partial vision of one eye (as did Schmid) tells her, "let's get that yellow cab over there," indicating that he is improving, but cautions her that their life together will not be easy and that is where this superb film ends. In addition to Garfield's bravura performance, Parker is wonderful in enacting her warmhearted and loving character, a woman as feisty and independent as the man she comes to love. Clark, too, as the staunch and very brave buddy, is outstanding and gives one of the finest performances of his long career, and Ridgely, Doran and Todd are endearing as Garfield's good-natured second family. Daves directs this film with a sure hand, all of his fine scenes exhibiting a realism seldom seen in the 1940s, his battle scenes starkly realistic and are some of the most harrowing tension-filled scenes ever portrayed. Daves also employs many inventive techniques, particularly the nightmare visions Garfield has during his rehabilitation and his return home, seeing himself at first returning home with his sight intact and embracing Parker and then as a blind man wearing dark glasses and groping about with a white cane and being rejected by Parker. In presenting these remarkable scenes, Daves achieves an eerie and unnerving effect of total apprehension through the use of double printings, negative images and telescopic shots. **Pride of the Marines** remains one of the greatest war films ever made. Songs: "Auld Lang Syne" (traditional Scottish ballad; lyrics: Robert Burns), "In the Evening by the Moonlight" (1878; James Allen Bland), "U.S. Marine Corps Hymn" (AKA: "Marine's Hymn"; 1868; from "Genevieve de Brabant" by Jacques Offenbach), "It Came Upon a Midnight Clear" (music [1850]: Richard Storrs Willis; lyrics [1849]: Edmund Hamilton Sears), "Semper Fidelis" (1888; John Philip Sousa); "Symphony No. 4 in E Minor, Opus 98: 1st Movement" (1885; Johannes Brahms), "America the Beautiful" (1882; Samuel A. Ward), "Old Black Joe" (1853; Stephen Foster). The film was a smash hit at the box office and was later aired on December 31, 1945 by Lux Radio Theater as a sixty-minute radio adaptation where Garfield, Clark and Parker reprised their roles. It was again aired on June 15, 1946, on the Academy Award Theater in a thirty-minute radio adaptation, again with Garfield reprising his role. ***Author's Note***: This film came into existence after Garfield read an article about Al Schmid in *Life Magazine* and contacted screenwriter Maltz, who wrote the script (based on a book about Schmid by Roger Butterfield); Warner Brothers assigned Daves to direct, the same director of the classic war film, **Destination Tokyo**, 1943, that starred Cary Grant and Garfield. Actually, Garfield had met Schmid while Schmid was on a bond rally tour and knew him during his rehabilitation period. Before going into production, Garfield spent time with Schmid and his wife Ruth, befriending them. (This film would remain one of Garfield's favorites.), Maltz inserted much working-class philosophy into his fine script, content that was later used to demonstrate his communist tendencies by the U.S. House Committee on Un-American Activities (HUAC) that later brought about Maltz's blacklisting, along with that of screenwriter Alvah Bessie, who wrote a twenty-six-page screen treatment for the film. Clark, who speaks much of Maltz's social messages in the film, did not agree with some of the quasi-political views held by his character, telling this author: "Maltz and others were trying to get a lot of their communist beliefs into mainstream pictures like **Pride of the Marines**, and that steamed me up a lot, especially because they were doing it off the backs of true American heroes. Julie [Garfield] believed in all that horse dung and we got into so many arguments about it that we could not get along together. In fact, we did not talk to each other ever again, except for the scenes we had together and where we had to talk as friends. The strange thing was that in one of my speeches to him I tell him that I will have just as hard a time getting through life as he will as a blind man because I am Jewish and a lot of people will not hire me because of that. I could see a few little twinges on Julie's face when I was saying that because he *was* Jewish and he knew all about that kind of cruel bigotry." Garfield and Clark were wholly at odds in their political beliefs. Garfield was an ardent, liberal Democrat where Clark was a conservative Republican. Al Schmid was a member of the 11th Machine Gun Squad of the 2nd Battalion in the 1st Marine Regiment of the 1st Marine Division. The fight in which Schmid was engaged and wounded, blinded by a grenade thrown by a dying Japanese soldier close to his dugout machine gun nest, was called the Battle of Alligator Creek (or the Battle of the Tenaru), occurring on the night of August 21, 1942, where Japanese Colonel Kiyonao Ichiki (who committed suicide after the attack failed) hurled 800 of his crack troops against well-entrenched Marine positions defending Henderson Field on the east side of the Lunga perimeter. The M1917 Browning heavy machine gun fired by Schmid and others was struck several times by bullets, puncturing its water jacket and leaving it "red hot" during the action throughout the night. More than 200 dead Japanese soldiers were found piled up in front of the machinegun nest occupied by Schmid, Corporal LeRoy Diamond and Private John Rivers, all of whom were awarded the Navy Cross. Schmid regained the use of one eye. He is buried at Arlington National Cemetery. Many films have profiled the historic battle at Guadalcanal (August 7, 1942-February 9, 1943), notably **Battle Cry**, 1955; **First to Fight**, 1967; **The Flying Leathernecks**, 1951; **The Gallant Hours**, 1960; **Guadalcanal Diary**, 1943; **The Pacific**, 2010 (cable-TV miniseries); **South Sea Woman**, 1953; **Tarawa Beachhead**, 1958; and **The Thin Red Line**, 1998. **p**, Jerry Wald; **d**, Delmer Daves; **cast**, John Garfield, Eleanor Parker, Dane Clark, John Ridgely, Rosemary DeCamp, Ann Doran, Ann Todd, Warren Douglas, Don McGuire, Tom D'Andrea, Mark Stevens, Anthony Caruso, Moroni Olsen, Harry Shannon, Dave Willock, Truman Bradley, William Haade; **w**, Albert Maltz, Marvin Borowsky (based on the book by Roger Butterfield); **c**, Peverell Marley; **m**, Franz Waxman; **ed**, Owen Marks; **art d**, Leo Kuter, Max Parker; **set d**, Walter F. Tilford; **spec eff**, L. Robert Burks, Edwin Dupar.

The Pride of the Yankees ★★★★★ 1942; U.S.; 128m; Samuel Goldwyn Productions/RKO; B/W; Sports Drama; Children: Acceptable; **DVD**; **VHS**. Everything about this sensitive and warmhearted sports biopic is eloquent, from its brilliant, humor-filled script to its careful direction, and, especially, stellar performances from Cooper, Wright, Brennan and the rest of a sterling cast. It tells the memorable story of the legendary New York Yankee first baseman, Lou Gehrig (Henry Louis "Lou" Gehrig; aka The Iron Horse; 1903-1941), played to perfection by Cooper, one of the greatest (if not the nicest) baseball players in the game. Cooper is an unassuming and shy student at New York's Columbia University, working at odd jobs and even waiting on upper classmen while his mother, Janssen, and father, Stossel, work hard to help pay his tuition. He spends his every spare moment playing baseball, excelling in that sport since childhood and, after sportswriter Brennan sees him perform, he contacts the New York Yankees and urges the front office to sign Cooper to the roster. Offered a contract, Cooper, even though the offer is his dream come true, declines to please his mother, who is opposed to such a "waste of time," insisting that Cooper finish college and become an engineer. When Cooper learns that Janssen requires an expensive operation, however, he goes back to the Yankees and takes the lucrative deal in order to pay his mother's medical expenses. Joining the team in June 1925, Cooper meets his boyhood idol, Babe Ruth (who plays himself) and also meets the beautiful Wright, who is sitting in a box and makes fun of him after he fails to watch where he is walking and slips and falls on a row of bats when going toward home plate. Wright calls him "tanglefoot," a nickname that will stay with him. Janssen and Stossel attend Cooper's first game; Janssen still disapproves of her son's new profession, but they soon become avid baseball fans as Cooper quickly becomes a star player when displaying his outstanding batting and fielding skills. Brennan, who serves as Cooper's mentor, promotes him in the press whenever Cooper makes an outstanding play

Babe Ruth and Gary Cooper in *The Pride of the Yankees,* **1942.**

or hits a home run and that is more often than not. When Cooper helps the Yankees to the World Series, he travels to Chicago and there visits Wright, going to her home late at night and soon proposes. She accepts and the two are married, but the dominating Janssen tries to organize their lives. Cooper, however, who has always been a dutiful son, finally stands up to her and tells her that he and Wright are going to live their own lives as they see fit. The two then enjoy marital bliss as Cooper sets one baseball record after another, rivaling the feats of the great Babe Ruth. The future seems bright and promising, but, in 1939, Cooper's batting average tumbles and he goes into a slump. He consults physicians and learns that he has a rare and lethal neurological disease (amyotrophic lateral sclerosis), which will later be called Lou Gehrig's Disease. He is told that he does not have long to live and he quits his beloved Yankees. On July 4, 1939, Cooper addresses the crowd at Yankee Stadium (reenacting the emotion-packed appearance Gehrig made that day), stating: "Some people say I've had a bad break, but I consider myself to be the luckiest man on earth…" The crowd applauds and Ruth moves to the plate where Cooper is standing and embraces him (as Ruth did on that momentous and emotion-packed day in 1939 where the crowd shouted: "We love you, Lou!" and even the most cynical of sportswriters openly wept as did Gehrig and Ruth). Cooper then slowly walks from the field, steps into a dugout and the camera stops to film him walk away down a long hallway for the sad finale. This prosaic story is told with the lighthearted mirth and boyish excitement that truly embodies the game of baseball, and only toward the end does it embrace the tragic realities of its fascinating subject. Cooper's natural mannerisms and common man personality fully captures this simple man of sports, who possessed indefatigable spirit and the astounding skills of a Hercules, a man who was the living idol of every boy in America in his day. Director Wood does not rush this story, but allows it to unfold in one gentle scene after another, where the funny and touching romance between Cooper and Wright nurtures and fulfills the human heart. Maté's lensing is a masterpiece of seamless scenes, beautifully photographed and crisply lighted so that each visual moment becomes memorable. Harline's score is as energetic as the action on the field and where many great old songs are interspersed to give a deep sense of instant nostalgia, comfortable sounds of the past that warm each scene like small crackling fires. Editor Mandell won an Oscar and the film received ten Oscar nominations, including Best Picture, Best Actor (Cooper) and Best Actress (Wright). Songs: "Take Me Out to the Ball Game" (1908; Jack Norworth, Albert von Tilzer), "I'm Just Wild About Harry" (1921; Eubie Blake), "Ain't We Got Fun" (1921; music: Richard A. Whiting; lyrics: Gus Kahn, Ray Egan), "Chicago (That Toddlin' Town" (1922; Fred Fisher), "Always" (1925; Irving Berlin), "I'll See You in My Dreams" (1924; Isham Jones), "Auld Lang Syne" (tradi-

Emma Thompson and John Travolta in *Primary Colors*, 1998.

tional). ***Author's Note***: The film does not exhibit a lot of baseball playing (some shown in archive footage with the real Gehrig, Ruth and Yankees at play) because Cooper was not skilled at fielding or hitting, but the romance story brilliantly takes up the slack. Cooper nevertheless researched his subject, telling this author: "I worked for weeks with a fine baseball coach, Lefty O'Doul, and he had me fielding and batting left-handed so that I looked like Gehrig, at least from a distance. I still looked awkward, so they had me batting right-handed and then they [production director Menzies] reversed the print so that I looked as if I was batting left-handed, because Gehrig was a southpaw." Goldwyn had never produced a biographical drama until undertaking this film, telling this author that "I knew that most women had no interest in baseball then, so I had Sam [Wood] and the writers [Swerling and Mankiewicz] put most of the attention on the romantic part of the story and that brought the ladies into the theaters." Brennan, who had befriended Cooper in 1925 and appeared in many films with him (**The Westerner**, 1940; **Sergeant York**, 1941, **Meet John Doe**, 1941), believed, as he told this author, that Cooper's portrayal of Gehrig "was just about as close as one man can come to be another. They both had the same kind of down-to-earth personalities and both were great at baseball—Coop watching the game and Lou playing it." Gehrig played in 2,130 consecutive games, scored more runs (1,188) than any other first baseman, a seven-time AL All Star, and twice an AL MVP (1927, 1936), a six-time World Series champion (1927, 1928, 1932, 1936, 1937, 1938) and was inducted into the National Baseball Hall of Fame on November 7, 1939. His number "4" was retired by the Yankees. He was AL homerun champion in 1931 (shared with Babe Ruth, each with 46), in 1934 (49) and 1936 (49). On June 3, 1932, Gehrig hit four home runs in one game. In addition to this production, the New York Yankees and their spectacular managers and players have received more film profiles than any other baseball team in history, those films including **The Babe**, 1992; **Babe Ruth**, 1991 (made-for-TV); **The Babe Ruth Story**, 1948; **Damn Yankees**, 1958; **Damn Yankees!**, 1967 (made-for-TV); **Everyone's Hero**, 2006; **Fireman, Save My Child**, 1932; **For the Love of the Game**, 1999; **Joe Torre: Curveballs Along the Way**, 1997; **Safe at Home**, 1962; **The Scout**, 1994; **Slide, Kelly, Slide**, 1927; and **Speedy**, 1928. For a breakdown on all American baseball teams profiled in films, see Baseball Teams, Subject Index, Volume II of this work. **p**, Samuel Goldwyn; **d**, Sam Wood; **cast**, Gary Cooper, Teresa Wright, Babe Ruth, Walter Brennan, Dan Duryea, Elsa Janssen, Ludwig Stossel, Virginia Gilmore, Bill Dickey, Dane Clark, Bill Stern, Rex Lease, Tom Neal, Douglas Croft, David Holt, Ray Noble and His Orchestra, Velzs and Yolanda; **w**, Jo Swerling, Herman J. Mankiewicz (based on a story by Paul Gallico); **c**, Rudolph Matté; **m**, Leigh Harline; **ed**, Daniel Mandell; **prod d**, William Cameron Menzies; **art d**, Perry Ferguson; **set d**, Howard Bristol; **spec**

eff, Jack Cosgrove, R.O. Binger, Albert Simpson.

Primary Colors ★★★ 1998; France/U.K./Germany/ U.S./Japan; 143m; Award Entertainment/UNIV; Color; Comedy/Drama; Children: Unacceptable (MPAA: R); **BD**; **DVD**. Well-made political spoof sees Travolta playing a charismatic young Southern governor attempting to win the Democratic Party's nomination for President of the United States, and Thompson is his strong-willed wife. Lester, a young political idealist, joins the campaign, along with ruthless campaigner Thornton. Opponents try to discredit Travolta for his previous arrest for alleged past sexual indiscretions and make use of unstable Bates to support their scandalous contentions. Then Travolta is accused of making a sixteen-year-old girl pregnant. Much political dirty tricks follow and Lester considers dropping out of the campaign but remains; Travolta wins the nomination and the presidency. Loosely based on the 1992 presidential campaign of President Bill Clinton (1946-), this film capitalizes on Clinton's involvement with the Monica Lewinsky scandal wherein he was accused of having illicit sex with a naïve White House intern, which brought about impeachment proceedings against him and where he narrowly escaped being thrown out of office. Songs: "Primrose Lane" (Wayne Shanklin, George Callender); "On the Road Again" (Willie Nelson); "You Are My Sunshine" (Jimmie Davis, Charles Mitchell); "Shane" (Victor Young); "Happy Meeting in Glory," "Jericho Blues" (Ry Cooder); "Yum Yum Yum" (Joseph Accrington, Joe Tax); "Unforgettable" (Irving Gordon); "Please, Mr. Please" (Bruce Welch, John Rostill); "D-I-V-O-R-C-E" (Claude Putnam, Jr., Bobby Braddock); "Still the One" (John Hall, Johanna Hall); "Over There," "You're a Grand Old Flag," (George M. Cohan); "Battle Hymn of the Republic" (music, 1856: William Steffe; lyrics, 1861: Julia Ward Howe); "Happy Days Are Here Again" (Milton Ager, Jack Yellen); "Silbano Mambo" (Damaso Perez Prado as Perez Prado); "Toot Toot Tootsie/Goodbye" (Gus Kahn, Ernie Erdman, Ted Fio Rito); "Wide Sky" (Ry Cooder, Jon Hassell, Ronu Majumdar); "Good Ole Boys Like Me" (Bob McDill); "Tennessee Waltz" (Redd Stewart, Pee Wee King). Mature subject matter prohibits viewing by children. **p**, Mike Nichols, Michele Imperato; **d**, Nichols; **cast**, John Travolta, Emma Thompson, Billy Bob Thornton, Kathy Bates, Adrian Lester, Maura Tierney, Larry Hagman, Diane Ladd, Rob Reiner, Paul Guilfoyle; **w**, Elaine May (based on the novel by Joe Klein); **c**, Michael Ballhaus; **m**, Ry Cooder; **ed**, Arthur Schmidt; **prod d**, Bo Welch; **art d**, Tom Duffield; **set d**, Cheryl Carasik; **spec eff**, Alan Lorimer.

The Prime of Miss Jean Brodie ★★★★ 1969; U.K.; 116m; FOX; Color; Comedy/Drama; Children: Unacceptable (MPAA: M); **DVD**; **VHS**. Smith is outstanding as a slightly unbalanced teacher at a private girls' school in Edinburgh in the 1930s, and where she coddles three particular students, Grayson, Carr and Franklin, while inserting her right-wing politics into her lessons. She is an admirer of fascist dictators Francisco Franco of Spain and Benito Mussolini of Italy and is forever extolling their virtues while setting her romantic goal on Stephens, a bachelor teacher who has ambitions of becoming an artist. Smith's chances of landing Stephens are next to impossible in that he is Catholic, a father, and has an entrenched marriage, so Smith spends most of her off-duty hours with Jackson, another teacher, going with him to his country home, although she is only mildly interested in him. Meanwhile, Smith begins having trouble with her idolizing charges. Franklin resents Smith's constant praising of Grayson's beauty and spitefully seduces Stephens after he paints her portrait, one which she hates because her image looks more like Smith than herself. Smith then learns that Carr's brother is going to Spain to fight on the side of the fascist forces led by Franco, who is attempting to overthrow the legally elected Republic, and Smith urges Carr to join her brother in Franco's cause. She does, but she is killed when the train on which she is traveling is bombed. Smith begins to preach fascist dogma to her students and for which she is fired by Johnson, the school supervisor, who has been constantly at odds with

Smith about her teaching habits. Smith is further crushed when learning that Jackson, the suitor she has taken for granted, is planning to marry Anderson, a chemistry teacher at the school. Franklin delivers the coup de grace by then telling Smith that she has had a secret affair with Stephens, the only man Smith has loved, to spite her for having sent the naïve Carr to her death in war-torn Spain. Smith is a marvel to behold as she submerges her obsessive spinster character into one meddling crisis after another, all at her own manipulative doings, a bravura performance of far-reaching emotions for which she deservedly won an Oscar as Best Actress. McKuen's song was nominated for an Oscar, but lost out to "Raindrops Keep Falling on My Head" (Burt Bacharach and Hal David) that appeared in **Butch Cassidy and the Sundance Kid**, 1969. Songs: "Jean" (1969; Rod McKuen), "On the Beautiful Blue Danube" (1867; Johann Strauss), "Lock Lomand" (traditional Scottish folk song), "For He's a Jolly Good Fellow" (traditional). *Author's Note*: The novel by Sparks had only a limited success, but it was successfully adapted for the stage by Allen and became a hit in London where Vanessa Redgrave enacted the Smith role and where Zoe Caldwell scored an equal triumph in the Broadway production. Exteriors for this film were shot in Edinburgh and interiors at Pinewood Studios. **p**, Robert Fryer, James Cresson; **d**, Ronald Neame; **cast**, Maggie Smith, Robert Stephens, Pamela Franklin, Gordon Jackson, Celia Johnson, Diane Grayson, Jane Carr, Shirley Steedman, Rona Anderson, Lavinia Lang, Antoinette Biggerstaff; **w**, Jay Presson Allen (based on his play from the novel by Muriel Spark); **c**, Ted Moore (DeLuxe Color); **m**, Rod McKuen; ed, Norman Savage; **prod d**, John Howell; **art d**, Brian Herbert.

The Prince and the Pauper ★★★★ 1937; U.S.; 118m; First National Pictures/WB; B/W; Adventure; Children: Cautionary; **DVD**; **VHS**. The great Mark Twain adventure is brought to the screen in a sumptuous production with the Mauch twins exchanging roles, one a street urchin, the other a prince, and where the dashing Flynn saves them both from doom and destruction. Set in 16th, Century London, Billy Mauch, a poor boy living in the slums, is much abused by his drunken father, MacLane and he runs away, sneaking into the royal palace where he meets his lookalike, Bobby Mauch, who is the pampered and protected Prince Edward (later Edward VI; 1537-1553). The boys play games with the royal seal and other precious objects and then decide to exchange their roles in life, although Billy has his doubts that he can play the role of a prince. Bobby then lives the life of a beggar boy, learning the hard knocks of the street, but he is rescued by soldier-of-fortune Flynn, who takes him under his wing because he is amused at the boy's claims that he is a member of the royal household and insists upon being treated with great respect. When he tells Flynn that his father is the king (Henry VIII; 1491-1547, played with gusto by Love), Flynn is seized with rollicking laughter. He pretends to recognize the boy's claims, mockingly bowing and scraping before him, but he slowly comes to realize that Bobby is truly the heir to the English throne. Meanwhile, Billy is imperiled after treasonous nobleman Rains plots to seize the throne after he learns that Billy is an imposter. Rains plans to have Billy crowned after the death of Love and then rule England while controlling the boy with the threat of exposing his true identity. He must first get rid of the real prince and sends assassin Hale to accomplish that grisly deed. While Flynn is elsewhere, Hale finds Bobby and takes him to a remote spot, agonizing over the murder he is about to commit, but Flynn, who is hot on Hale's trail, overtakes the assassin and both duel with swords, with Flynn killing the assassin. Rains, assuming that Bobby is dead, proceeds to have Billy crowned king. Just before Billy is crowned, however, Flynn arrives at the lavish ceremony with the real prince and exposes Rains' plot. Bobby convinces everyone that he is the true prince by racing to a royal chamber where he hid the royal seal, retrieving it, and returning it to show it to his doubters. Billy thankfully exchanges places with Bobby so that the rightful heir can become the king of England and Bobby promises to have Billy at his side in the future. Keighley directs this action-packed tale with great skill, and the Mauch twins are superb in their roles as is

Billy and Bobby Mauch, the twins playing *The Prince and the Pauper*, 1937.

the energetic and charismatic Flynn while the rest of the cast render standout performances. The production values can be seen in the magnificent sets and rich costuming for this film, and Korngold's stirring score underscores and emphasizes each exciting scene. Song: "The Roost Song" (Erich Wolfgang Korngold, M. K. Jerome). *Author's Note*: Rains, who is outstanding as the insidious and manipulative nobleman, told this author that "in my reading of history, most noblemen in the courts of old England spent their time plotting against the throne or their superiors and that was my assignment in **The Prince and the Pauper**. It was a role that I would play again and again, also with the indomitable Mr. Flynn [in such films as **The Adventures of Robin Hood**, 1938, and **The Sea Hawk**, 1940]. Errol once asked me: 'Don't you ever get tired of playing these disgusting villains?' I replied by asking him: 'Don't you ever get tired of saving the world?' He gave me that wolf's grin of his and said: 'Never!'" Director Keighley told this author that the Mauch twins, who were twelve at the time they made this remarkable epic, "were really gifted boys who responded well to direction and came up with a lot of little funny gestures and tricks that I kept in their scenes. Their playful ideas worked so well that it makd them appear natural and that was exactly what they were supposed to be—boys playing at being princes." Flynn at this time was enjoying the great successes of **Captain Blood**, 1935, and **The Charge of the Light Brigade**, 1936, which had been huge box office hits, and therefore demanded a substantial raise in salary from studio boss Jack Warner. He had been recognized as the undisputed king of swashbuckling films and wanted to capitalize on his great fame, but Warner, always a money-minded mogul, bristled at the idea of paying Flynn more than the $500 a week he had started with when making **Captain Blood**. Flynn was adamant about getting more money, and Warner looked about for someone to replace him in **The Prince and the Pauper** before production began. "Hal [Wallis, the producer of the film] told me to test several other actors for the leading part in that picture," Keighley told this author, "because Jack Warner wanted to get rid of Flynn since he was demanding too much money. Well, I tested Ian Hunter, Patric Knowles and George Brent, but they were just too wooden in a role that called for a flamboyant and dashing actor and I knew that that was Flynn. I told Hal that only Flynn could play the part if he wanted a picture that could make money. Wallis went back to Jack Warner and the boss finally gave in. Flynn got the part and he was marvelous in the role, swaggering through every scene as if he owned the story, and he did. He was exuberant and charming and no one in the world could resist that Irish smile on that handsome face of his, a face that half the women in America had already fallen in love with." Warner increased Flynn's salary to $2,500 a week, and, in the future, Warner would go on giving Flynn raises, renewing lucrative contracts so that, by the early 1940s, the actor was making $200,000 per film. "He was

Moses, Jethro and Tzipporah in *The Prince of Egypt*, 1998.

worth every penny of it," Keighley told this author, "and Jack Warner knew it every time he checked the box receipts of the pictures Flynn made with him. In many ways, Flynn was like the Mauch twins in **The Prince and the Pauper**. All he wanted to do in life was to have adventure and fun, and he got both. In exchange, the world got some of the greatest adventure pictures ever made with him in them. He made a great fortune and spent it all on wine, women and song. He was just like the heroes he played in his pictures and he was more fun to be with than any other man I met in my life." Keighley would go on to direct Flynn in **The Adventures of Robin Hood**, 1938 (sharing the director's credit with Michael Curtiz), **Rocky Mountain**, 1950, and **The Master of Ballantrae**, 1953, which was the director's last film. The Mauch Twins were born in 1921, Billy (William John) ten minutes before Bobby (Robert John). They appeared in a few more movies, then Billy became a film sound editor and Bobby a film editor, serving together in the Air Force in the Philippines in World War II (1939-1945). Billy died at the age of 85 in 2006, a year before Bobby. Other than this exceptional production, there were many films and remakes of this exciting Mark Twain tale, including two silent in 1915 and 1920, and talkie versions that included made-for-TV films and episodes in TV series in 1933, 1943, 1957, 1960, 1971, 1972, 1976, 1977, 1996, 2000, 2005, and 2008, but none compare to this 1937 film. **p**, Hal B. Wallis; **d**, William Keighley; **cast**, Errol Flynn, Claude Rains, Henry Stephenson, Barton MacLane, Billy Mauch, Bobby Mauch, Alan Hale, Eric Portman, Lionel Pape, Montagu Love, Fritz Leiber, Phyllis Barry, St. Luke's Episcopal Church Choristers; **w**, Laird Doyle (based on the novel by Mark Twain); **c**, Sol Polito; **m**, Erich Wolfgang Korngold; **ed**, Ralph Dawson; **art d**, Robert Haas; **spec eff**, Willard Van Enger, James Gibbons.

The Prince and the Showgirl ★★★ 1957; U.K./U.S.; 115m; WB; Color; Comedy/Romance; Children: Unacceptable; **DVD**; **IV**; Enjoyable romantic comedy sees the gifted Olivier as Grand duke Charles, the prince-regent of Carpathia, a fictitious Balkan country which could start a European war by switching alliances from England to Germany. In June 1911, Olivier goes to London for the coronation of the new King George V (1865-1936) and spends an evening at the Coconut Girl Club. He is a stuffy fellow, but is charmed by Monroe, a sexy showgirl, who is merely an American understudy in a review, and orders his British attaché to invite her to the Carpathian embassy for a private supper. She senses that he wants to seduce her, although he is not very good at it. They eventually kiss and Monroe feels as if she may be falling in love with him, but she passes out from the drinks he keeps pouring into her. Olivier has her put in an adjoining bedroom to spend the night sleeping it off. She understands German and, the next morning, overhears a plot Olivier's young son, Spenser, hatches with members of the German em-

bassy to overthrow Olivier. Monroe then meets Thorndike, the Carpathian dowager queen, who is Olivier's mother-in-law. She invites Monroe to join them for the coronation in place of her lady-in-waiting. Monroe does not tell Olivier of his son's treasonous plan and gets Spenser to confess his plot if Olivier agrees to a general election. Olivier is impressed with Monroe's diplomacy and realizes he has fallen in love with her. The morning after the coronation ball, Monroe irons out differences between Olivier and his son. Her honesty and sincerity inspire Olivier to show affection to his son, now in private as well as he has half-heartedly displayed in public. Olivier tells Monroe his regency will be over in eighteen months and his son will become king, so he will be a free citizen and they can marry. Monroe says her contract as a showgirl also will end then. They go their separate ways, leaving it unclear as to whether they will meet again. Olivier does a fine job directing this film as well as giving a standout performance as a reserved but fascinating prince, and Monroe is also exceptional in her role as a dumb blonde who really has an active brain and more savvy than anyone realizes. A film based on the making of this production, **My Week with Marilyn**, was a romantic comedy hit in 2011. Songs: "The Duke of York," "The British Grenadiers," "Naval March," "Hornpipe," "The Minstrel Boy" (traditional); "The Liberty Bell" (John Philip Sousa); "Milanollo" (music: Johann Valentin Hamm); "Light of Foot" (music: Carl Latann); "I Was Glad (When They Said Unto Me) (music: Sir Charles Hubert Hastings Parry); "See the Conquering Hero Comes" (George Frederic Handel); "I Found a Dream" (music: Richard Addinsell; lyrics: Christopher Hassall). Mature themes prohibit viewing by children. *Author's Note*: Olivier was comfortable in his role as he had appeared on stage in the stage version of this story with his wife, Vivien Leigh, who was thought to have been miscast in the role of the showgirl and where Monroe, in the film version, was much more in character in that role. Monroe appears in her twenty-fifth film in a production that her own newly organized company financed under the unusual proviso that she was to receive seventy-five percent of all of the profits from this film. The film was made for about $1 million, shot at Pinewood Studios in England, but did not do as well as expected at the box office, producing only $1.5 million in its initial release. Ironically, **My Week with Marilyn**, 2011, the film based upon the filming of **The Prince and the Showgirl**, was produced for $10 million and yielded more than $35 million at the box office. **p&d**, Laurence Olivier; **cast**, Marilyn Monroe, Olivier, Jeremy Spenser, Dame Sybil Thorndike, David Horne, Jean Kent, Charles Victor, Daphne Anderson, Vera Day, Gillian Owen, Richard Wattis; **w**, Terence Rattigan (based on his play "The Sleeping Prince"); **c**, Jack Cardiff; **m**, Richard Addinsell; **ed**, Jack Harris; **prod d**, Roger Furse; **art d**, Carmen Dillon; **spec eff**, Charles Staffell, Bill Warrington.

The Prince of Egypt ★★★ 1998; U.S.; 99m; DreamWorks SKG; Color; Animated Drama; Children: Unacceptable (MPAA: PG); **DVD**; **VHS**. This animated version of the classic biblical tale is beautifully and reverently portrayed, providing a well-written and sensitive script. In vivid scenes, the story shows the life of Moses (Kilmer voiceover), from the time he is a baby found in a basket on the Nile River by the queen of Egypt (Mirren voiceover). He becomes the best friend of the son (Fiennes voiceover) of the Pharaoh (Stewart voiceover), but, after he learns of his Jewish heritage, and after he receives a Heavenly message, he spends his time exhorting Fiennes to release the Israelites from bondage. Fiennes refuses and Kilmer calls upon God to visit Egypt with plagues and pestilence, until Fiennes allows the Israelites to go free. He changes his mind and then pursues Kilmer and the Jews, only to see his chariot legions consumed by the Red Sea. Kilmer goes on to lead his people and, in their nomadic trek, he comes down from a mountain with the Ten Commandments as written in fire by the hand of God. He then leads his people toward the Promised Land. Songs: "Deliver Us," "All I Ever Wanted," "Queen's Reprise," Through Heaven's Eyes," "Playing with the Big Boys," The Plagues," "When You Believe" (Stephen Schwartz); "I Will Get There" (Diane Warren). Moses has been portrayed by many actors in several other films, including **Are We Civilized?**, 1934 (Alin Cavin); **The Cradle of God**, 1926 (Victor Vina); **History of the World: Part I**, 1981 (Mel Brooks); **Moon of Israel**, 1924 (Henry Mar); **Moses**, 1995 (made-for-TV; Ben Kingsley); **Moses and Aaron**, 1975 (Gunter Reich); **Moses the Lawgiver**, 1974 (TV miniseries; Burt Lancaster as adult Moses, William Lancaster as young Moses); **The Story of Mankind**, 1957 (Francis X. Bushman); **The Ten Commandments**, 1923 (Theodore Roberts); **The Ten Commandments**, 1956 (Charlton Heston); **The Ten Commandments**, 2006 (made-for-TV; Dougray Scott); **The Ten Commandments**, 2007 (Christian Slater voiceover); and **The Ten Commandments: The Musical**, 2006 (Val Kilmer). Intense depictions of thematic elements prohibit viewing by children. **p**, Penney Finkelman Cox, Sandra Rabins; **d**, Brenda Chapman, Steve Hickner, Simon Wells; **cast** (voiceovers), Ralph Fiennes, Val Kilmer, Michelle Pfeiffer, Sandra Bullock, Jeff Goldblum, Danny Glover, Patrick Stewart, Helen Mirren, Steve Martin, Martin Short, Mel Brooks; Sally Dworsky singing voice for Bullock; Amick Byram singing voice for Kilmer; **w**, Philip LaZebnik, Nicholas Meyer; **m**, Hans Zimmer; **ed**, Nick Fletcher; **prod d**, Darek Gogol; **art d**, Kathy Altieri, Richard Chavez; **spec eff**, Don Paul, Dan Philips.

Prince of Foxes ★★★★ 1949; U.S.; 107m; FOX; B/W; Adventure; Children: Unacceptable; **DVD**; **VHS**. Stirring historical adventure tale mixes intrigue and romance during the Renaissance with Power as a nobleman and soldier of fortune in the service of the calculating and sinister Cesare Borgia (1475-1507), wonderfully played by Welles. The film begins in August 1500 with Welles describing how he plans to conquer one city state after another in Italy as he indicates his covetous terrain on a map of the country to his trusted aides, including Power. Welles explains that he plans to secure his next territory not by force but by guile and orders Power to persuade his next adversary to wed Welles' widowed sister, Lucrezia Borgia (1480-1519), her recent spouse having been murdered, so that this femme fatale can be available for such an arranged marriage. To raise expense money, Power goes to Venice art dealer Ciannelli to sell some of his paintings and there meets noblewoman Hendrix, wife of an elderly duke controlling a mountainous city state and who admires Power's artwork, not knowing he is in the employ of the dangerous Welles. Smitten with the beautiful young woman, Power makes a gift of his painting, forfeiting a payment of 100 ducats, hoping to see her again. Resuming his mission, Power is attacked on a dark street by assassin Sloane, but Power overcomes the attacker and spares his life so that he can learn who has hired him. Sloane tells him that he is in the employ of the Duke d'Este (1431-1505), played by Van Hulzen, the father of Alfonso d'Este (1476-1534), who is played by Carney. Van Hulzen, knowing Welles' intention of using his son to gain territory, has hired Sloane to kill Power and prevent him from arranging that marriage to Lucrezia Borgia. Shrewdly, Power hires the devious Sloane, who becomes his companion. En route, Power stops off at a blacksmith's home to visit his widowed mother, Paxinou, and where the spying Sloane learns that Power is not a nobleman at all, but a commoner who has taken the name of a long extinct noble family to gain his position in life. Paxinou pleads with Power to quit his impersonation and pursue his talents in painting, but the ambitious Power assures her that he will succeed with his plans. He then visits Carney in Ferrara, and masterfully convinces him to marry Lucrezia in order to enhance his own influence and power. By accomplishing this diplomatic mission, Power earns the praise and appreciation of Welles, who thinks to marry his attractive cousin, Angela Borgia (1486-1522), played by Berti, to the enterprising Power. A rising star among Welles' entourage, Power has now earned the enmity of Bradley, one of Welles' captains, especially after Welles now assigns Power another important mission. Power is to visit Hendrix and her elderly husband, Aylmer, and he is to woo the attractive Hendrix while Aylmer is eliminated by assassin Sloane, who is sent by Welles to accompany Power. Upon meeting Aylmer, however, his prey impresses Power with his wisdom and love for his people, so

Marina Berti, Tyrone Power and Orson Welles in *Prince of Foxes,* 1949.

much so that he prevents Sloane from assassinating the old nobleman. He then undertakes to paint Hendrix and both begin to fall in love with each other, a romance that the enfeebled Aylmer encourages as he believes Power would be a good husband for his wife after he dies. Welles grows tired of waiting for Power to accomplish his bloodless coup and sends his foremost military captain, Bradley, to order Aylmer to give Welles' forces free passage through his territory as well as provide more troops for Welles' next military venture. Aylmer refuses, and Bradley tells him that he will now suffer siege. The people of Aylmer's duchy support him and, in a meeting with its leaders, Power, who has come to despise the murderous machinations of Welles, appears and he offers "one more sword against Cesare Borgia." The defenders heroically battle Welles' superior forces while Aylmer grows ill and asks Power to marry Hendrix after he passes and gives both of them his blessing. Aylmer dies and his defenders are eventually defeated. Power, branded a traitor, is imprisoned and is later dragged dirty and disheveled before a feast presided over by Welles and his captains, and Hendrix is forced to see him humiliated. She begs for Power's life, but Welles is inclined to have him executed. Power's true identify is shown when his mother, Paxinou, is brought into the hall where she also begs for the life of her son. The insidious Sloane then states that Power should be cruelly punished but allowed to live as an example of his treason. He then leaps over the feasting table and, to amuse Welles and his minions, displays his thumbs as the instruments of punishment. He leans close to Power, who is strapped to a chair, and whispers to him, telling him to scream as he pretends to gouge out his eyes. Power shouts in agony as Sloane appears to dig out his eyes and holds the gory trophies to the shocked spectators, but he has merely crushed two grapes instead. Appearing to be brutally blinded, Powers is ordered to roam the countryside and beg for a living with his mother as Welles departs, even he appalled by Sloane's savage conduct. Hendrix is kept a prisoner in her palace, but Power organizes a revolt with the help of Sloane. He invades the palace, and while trying to rescue Hendrix is discovered by Bradley, who is shocked to see that Power has his sight. Both men duel and Power kills Bradley and then wins over another Welles captain, who is tired of killing for Welles, and the duchy falls into the hands of the rebels. The revolt against Welles spreads as Power becomes the lord of the duchy, and when the evil prince falls, Power and Hendrix wed for a happy ending. Power is superb in his role of the dashing adventurer and is greatly supported with outstanding performances from Welles, Sloane, Hendrix, Paxinou and Aylmer. King's firm hand is evident in every forceful and action-packed scene, and Shamroy's lensing is superlative in capturing the magnificent landscapes and Renaissance palaces and fortifications. The script is both literate and provocative, and the costuming and sets equal the splendor of the age they represent. Newman's dynamic and memorable score robustly

Treat Williams, Matthew Laurance and Richard Foronjy in
Prince of the City, **1981.**

enhances this swashbuckling tale, which proved to be a great success at the box office, earning more than $2.5 million in its initial U.S. release. Cesare Borgia has been profiled by many other actors in many films, including **The Black Duke**, 1964 (Cameron Mitchell); **The Borgia**, 2006 (Sergio Peris-Mencheta); **Borgia**, 2011 (TV series; Mark Ryder); **The Borgias**, 1981 (TV miniseries; Oliver Cotton); **The Borgias**, 2011 (TV series; Francois Arnaud); **Bride of Vengeance**, 1949 (Macdonald Carey); **Caterina Sforza, la leonessa di Romagna**, 1959 (Erno Crisa); **Der Schatten**, 1961 (made-for-TV; Edwin Marian); **Don Juan**, 1926 (Warner Orland); **Giovanni de Medici: The Leader**, 1940 (Erwin Klietsch); **Leonardo**, 2003 (made-for-TV; James Frain); **The Life of Leonardo Da Vinci**, 1971 (TV series; Federico Pietrabruna); **Les Borgia ou le sang dore**, 1977 (made-for-TV; Jean-Claude Bouillon); **Lucrece Borgia**, 1956 (Pedro Armendariz); **Lucrezia Boria**, 1928 (Conrad Veidt); **Lucrezia Borgia**, 1937 (Gabriel Gabrio); **Lucrezia Borgia**, 1968 (Lou Castel); **Lucrezia Borgia; or Plaything of Power**, 1923 (Russell Thorndike); **Lucrezia giovane**, 1974 (Massimo Foschi); **L'uomo che ride**, 1966 (aka **The Man with the Golden Mask**; Edmund Purdom); **The Mask of Cesare Borgia**, 1941 (Osvaldo Valenti); **Meriota, die Tanzerin**, 1922 (Oscar Beregi Sr.); **The Nights of Lucretia Borgia**, 1960 (Franco Fabrizi); **O Falcao Negro**, 1954 (TV series; Fernando Baleroni); **The Power of the Borgias**, 1920 (Enrico Piacentini); and **Prisoner in the Tower of Fire**, 1953 (Rossano Brazzi). *Author's Note*: Welles told this author that the only reason why he took the role of Cesare Borgia was "to pay the rent. I needed cash and they needed someone to play one of the most evil characters in history. Seemed like a reasonable bargain." Director King had a difficult time with Welles throughout the production, telling this author that "he took his role a little too seriously, acting as if he were the real Cesare Borgia. In one scene where Orson arrives in a town, he suddenly stopped the scene and said loudly to me: 'The actors [townspeople] are not showing me enough respect when I ride into town—they are not bowing low enough to the powerful man I am playing!' I shook my head and pointed a finger at him and replied: 'You're getting a damned sight more than you deserve, Orson! You play the part. The actors will do what *I* tell them!' He is a great actor and one of the great directors, but I had to keep reminding him that I was directing the picture, not him. A lot of other directors always bowed and scraped to him when he was only an actor in their films. I would not do that. Actors should take direction from directors for a picture to work out well, but Orson could not accept that limited role. He thought that he was *the* Cesare Borgia of Hollywood and he was in the minds of many, but never to me." The film's exteriors were shot on location throughout Italy and in San Marino, with interiors shot at Cinecitta Studios. Though this lavishly appointed period film cried out for color, it was filmed in black-and-white, only because

the cumbersome three-strip Technicolor cameras used in those days would have been too costly to ship abroad and executives at Fox believed that, even if they had used those cameras, the processing of the color film in Italy would have been hazardous and much too costly. **p**, Sol C. Siegel; **d**, Henry King; **cast**, Tyrone Power, Orson Welles, Wanda Hendrix, Marina Berti, Everett Sloane, Katina Paxinou, Felix Aylmer, Leslie Bradley, Eduardo Ciannelli, James Carney, Joop van Hulzen, Eva Brauer, Rena Lenart, Guiseppe Faeti, Eugene Deckers; **w**, Milton Krims (based on the novel by Samuel Shellabarger); **c**, Leon Shamroy; **m**, Alfred Newman; **ed**, Barbara McLean; **art d**, Lyle Wheeler, Mark-Lee Kirk; **set d**, Elso Valentini; **spec eff**, Fred Sersen.

Prince of Players ★★★★ 1955; U.S.; 102m; FOX; Color; Drama; Children: Unacceptable; **VHS**. Burton is magnificent in portraying Edwin Booth (1833-1893), of the "Mad Booths of Maryland," a family that included his actor-brother, John Wilkes Booth (1838-1865), the sinister assassin of President Abraham Lincoln (1809-1865), and who is well played by Derek. Edwin Booth was considered to be the greatest actor (this side of the Atlantic Ocean) of the 19th Century, so Burton's interpretation of that thespian's acting style can only be imagined. It is known that Edwin Booth was a much more reserved and restrained actor than those of his era, who traditionally enacted their roles with elaborate theatrics and histrionics. The film opens with an actor presenting a performance with that very theatrical style, his father, Junius Brutus Booth (1796-1852), extravagantly (and correctly) played by Massey, and Burton acts as his stage manager and even caretaker in that Massey is an alcoholic and slightly demented. (The elder Booth exhibited his madness by often visiting the old dungeon-like jail in New York City, called The Tombs, and where he paid warders to allow him to occupy cells next to criminally insane murderers while he shared with them catered meals and expensive wines while he regaled them with his most outlandish performances of "King Lear" and "Macbeth.") Burton avidly watches his father's performances, realizing that Massey is milking the audience for applause by overacting, but he nevertheless takes notes of Massey's most effective techniques. When Massey cannot remember his lines and cannot perform before some miners in San Francisco, Burton takes his place and delivers a much more reserved performance that first annoys the audience, its more rowdy members heaping ridicule upon him, but he perseveres and wins their approval by the finale. He then learns that his father has died, and he begins to fulfill Massey's theatrical bookings. He begins to win fame as one of the most riveting actors on the stage and is soon heralded as a foremost thespian. Burton marries, but his wife dies and he becomes afflicted with his father's curse of drink, but he manages to overcome his alcoholic bent. He, meanwhile, must deal with another demented member of his family, his younger brother, John Wilkes Booth, broodingly played by Derek, who has taken up the cause of the South during the Civil War and who resents his older brother's fame, seeking to outdo him by performing a mad act that will forever stain the name of Booth by assassinating President Lincoln, who is portrayed by Hall. After Derek shoots and kills Hall at Ford's Theater in Washington, D. C., he escapes and is then himself fatally shot. Burton, who has been acting in London, must now face audiences showing universal hostility toward him because of his brother's heinous crime. He returns to the U.S. and goes before an audience to perform "Hamlet," but he is met with derision; members of the audience pelt him with garbage and other objects, and the other actors on the stage flee from the violence. Burton, however, stoically remains in a chair at center stage, accepting the insults, and, while covered with refuse, he stares bravely at his attackers. One of the rowdies in the audience then shouts: "He's got guts!" He then delivers another shout: "Booth, you're all right!" He begins clapping and he is soon joined in by the rest of the audience to end this stirring film. Burton gives one of his best performances as the problem-plagued Edwin Booth (who was called "Ned"), and proves mesmerizing when delivering his lines in excerpted scenes from "Romeo and Juliet," "Richard III" and "Hamlet." Derek is also captivating as his ruthlessly ambitious brother. Massey, too, provides a riveting character fighting off madness while attempting to bring high drama to the stage. McNamara, who essays Burton's first wife, is both fetching and haunting, and Le Gallienne (appearing in her film debut) is outstanding as she enacts the role of Queen Gertrude in "Hamlet." Dunne's direction is taut, and the script from playwright Hart is exceptionally intelligent and sensitively correct to its characters. Clarke's photography is inventive and fluid, and Hermann provides a dynamic and memorable score befitting that turbulent era. Many actors have profiled the Booths in films, especially John Wilkes Booth, who is portrayed in **Abraham Lincoln**, 1930 (Ian Keith); **The Birth of a Nation**, 1915 (Raoul Walsh); **The Conspirator**, 2011 (Toby Kebbell); **Gods and Generals**, 2003 (Chris Conner); and **The Prisoner of Shark Island**, 1936 (Francis McDonald). *Author's Note*: Burton told this author that "it was impossible to fully capture the persona of a man like Edwin Booth. My goal was to give an overall impression of the man, who was unlike any other actor of his day. I studied his poses and facial expressions in many old photos of him, but could only guess at his mannerisms and the sound of his voice. In the end, I had to be my own version of the man and how he might have delivered his characters on stage. I hope that I did him justice for I knew that he had performed the greatest version of 'Hamlet' in the last century [19th Century] and to pretend to duplicate that performance would have been ridiculous." Unlike the finale in this film, Booth did not immediately take to the stage after his brother shot Lincoln. Instead, he instantly retired and then sent a letter to the world apologizing for his brother's murderous actions, a letter that was widely published. He thereafter refused to have his brother's name ever mentioned in his home. Edwin Booth thought long and hard about returning to the stage, but, at the urgings of family members and promoters, he courageously appeared nine months after the Lincoln assassination at New York's Winter Garden Theater in January 1866, to appear in "Hamlet," which became his signature role. When the curtain opened to show Booth seated center stage, the audience stood as one and gave him a thunderous ovation, a reporter in the crowd later writing: "The sight of that slight, black [attired], seated figure did something to them all. As one man, the audience leaped to its feet and cheered…[Booth] slowly stood up and bowed very deep. His eyes were swimming with tears." For more information on John Wilkes Booth, see my two-volume work *The Great Pictorial History of World Crime*, Volume I, (History, Inc., 2004; pages 26-44). **p&d**, Philip Dunne; **cast**, Richard Burton, Maggie McNamara, John Derek, Raymond Massey, Charles Bickford, Elizabeth, Sellars Eva Le Gallienne, Ian Keith, Mae Marsh, Richard Travis; **w**, Moss Hart (based on the book by Eleanor Ruggles); **c**, Charles G. Clarke (CinemaScope; DeLuxe Color); **m**, Bernard Herrmann; **ed**, Dorothy Spencer; **art d**, Lyle Wheeler, Mark-Lee Kirk; **set d**, Walter M. Scott, Paul S. Fox; **spec eff**, Ray Kellogg.

Prince of the City ★★★ 1981; U.S.; 167m; Orion Pictures; Color; Crime Drama; Children: Unacceptable (MPAA: R); **DVD**; **VHS**. In this well-made and very realistic crime yarn, Williams is a New York City narcotics detective who becomes involved in some legally questionable police practices. He is offered a deal by the police department's Internal Affairs officers where he will be let off the hook if he tells what he knows about police corruption involving drug cover-ups, bribery, kickbacks and other deals that allow officers to "go on the pad." He agrees if he does not have to turn in his partners, but soon learns he can't trust anyone, since everyone is fair game for arrest. Williams no longer knows who the good guys are and fears he may not be one of them. He plays a dangerous game not only with his fellow police officers, but some murderous Mafia gang members that begin to suspect him of being an informer (he wears wire-tapping devices most of the time). In the end, he winds up singing a song that engulfs almost all of his associates and close friends, bringing them to ruin and even suicide. Williams is superb in his role of a troubled informer trying to save his own career while vainly attempting to shield his closest friends. Songs: "Love Will Keep

Nick Nolte and Barbra Streisand in *The Prince of Tides*, 1991.

Us Together" (Neil Sedaka, Howard Greenfield). Excessive violence and gutter language prohibit viewing by children. *Author's Note*: This film mirrors the story Lumet directed for **Serpico**, 1973, which also deals with widespread NYPD corruption. **p**, Burtt Harris; **d**, Sidney Lumet; **cast**, Treat Williams, Jerry Orbach, Richard Foronjy, Don Billett, Kenny Marino, Carmine Caridi, Tony Page, Paul Roebling, Norman Parker, Bob Balaban; **w**, Jay Presson Allen, Lumet (based on the book by Robert Daley); **c**, Andrzej Bartkowiak; **m**, Paul Chihara; **ed**, John J. Fitzstephens; **prod d**, Tony Walton; **art d**, Edward Pisoni.

The Prince of Tides ★★★ 1991; U.S.; 132m; COL; Color; Drama; Children: Unacceptable (MPAA: R); **DVD**; **VHS**. Nolte gives another captivating performance, this time as a teacher and football coach in South Carolina, who goes to New York to help Streisand, a psychiatrist working with his twin sister, Dillon, after her latest suicide attempt. This happens while his wife, Danner, is having an affair with a man who says he wants to marry her. Dillon's mental condition stems largely from the time when she was a girl and when three escaped convicts invaded the family home and raped her, her mother, and Nolte, and where an older brother shot and killed two of them and their mother killed the third. The bodies of the invaders were buried beneath the house and police never knew of the gruesome event. Working with Streisand, Nolte falls in love with her, but later decides to go back to his wife and children. Streisand has made great strides returning Dillon to mental health, and Nolte knows he will always miss his love affair with Streisand. Songs: "Fui Tu Caceria" (Margarita Pinillos), "Monkey" (George Michael), "Keep on Movin" (Beresford Romeo), "The Very Thought of You" (Ray Noble), "Happy Birthday to You" (Mildred J. Hill, Patty S. Hill), "Honey Don't" (Carl Perkins), "That's What I Like 'Bout the South" (Andy Razaf), "For All We Know" (Sam Lewis, J. Alfred Coots), "Dixie" (Daniel Decatur Emmett). Excessive violence and sexuality prohibits viewing by children. **p**, Barbra Streisand, Andrew Karsch, Sheldon Schrager; **d**, Streisand; **cast**, Streisand, Nick Nolte, Blythe Danner, Kate Nelligan, Jeroen Krabbé, Melinda Dillon, George Carlin, Jason Gould, Brad Sullivan, Maggie Collier, Lindsay Wray; **w**, Pat Conroy, Becky Johnston (based on the novel by Conroy); **c**, Stephen Goldblatt; **m**, James Newton Howard; **ed**, Don Zimmerman; **prod d**, Paul Sylbert; **art d**, W. Steven Graham; **set d**, Caryl Heller, Arthur Howe, Jr., Leslie Ann Pope; **spec eff**, Peter Knowlton.

Prince Valiant ★★★ 1954; U.S.; 100m; FOX; Color; Adventure; Children: Cautionary; **DVD**; **VHS**; **IV**. Exciting adventure story based on the King Features Syndicate comic book character, Prince Valiant, is set in the days of King Arthur. Wagner plays the stalwart son of Crisp, king of mythical Scandia, who is exiled when the evil and powerful lord of

Robert Wagner, left, in *Prince Valiant*, 1954.

Carnera usurps power. Wagner journeys to Camelot to ask help from King Arthur, sympathetically played by Aherne. En route, Wagner overhears a plot in which "The Black Knight" plans to capture Crisp and his family and imprison them in Carnera's dungeons while overthrowing Aherne. Wagner reaches Camelot and warns Aherne, who thanks him by making him a squire to Sir Gawain (Hayden), one of his Knights of the Round Table. Wagner learns sword fighting and other knightly skills from Hayden and becomes an asset to Camelot. The blonde and buxom Leigh, a princess of the Camelot court, falls in love with Wagner whom she calls "Val," short for Valiant. When Wagner receives a message that Crisp has been imprisoned in Carnera, he rides off to free him. Along the way, he is ambushed by Mason, another of Aherne's knights, but who is also known as "The Black Knight." Wagner and Leigh are taken to Carnera's dungeons and imprisoned in a cell, but Wagner escapes and gets help from some Viking warriors led by McLaglen. They storm Carnera, rescue Leigh and Crisp, and burn the castle to the ground. Wagner and Leigh return to Camelot where he exposes Mason to Aherne. Wagner and Mason engage in exciting swordplay which ends with Mason being run through. Aherne dubs Wagner a Knight of the Round Table and the young hero weds Leigh. This fine adventure is packed with great action from director Hathaway and offers high production values with sumptuous sets and stunning costuming. A 1998 film with the same title was also about Camelot but had a different plot. Many actors have essayed King Arthur in numerous films, most notably **Camelot**, 1967 (Richard Harris as adult Arthur, Nicolas Beauvy as Arthur as a boy); **A Connecitcut Yankee**, 1931 (William Farnum); **A Connecticut Yankee in King Arthur's Court**, 1949 (Sir Cedric Hardwicke); **Dragonheart**, 1996 (John Guilgud voiceover); **Excalibur**, 1981 (Nigel Terry); **First Knight**, 1995 (Sean Connery); **King Arthur**, 2004 (Clive Owen as adult Arthur; Shane Murray-Corcoran as young Arthur); **Knights of the Round Table**, 1953 (Mel Ferrer); **The Last Legion**, 2007 (Rory James as the young Arthur); **Monty Python and the Holy Grail**, 1975 (Graham Chapman); and **The Sword and the Stone**, 1963 (Rickie Sorensen voiceover). *Author's Note*: Tony Curtis, who was married to Leigh at the time, was first thought to be starred as the courageous Prince Valiant, but Wagner was selected instead at the last moment. Later in the same year that this film was released Curtis and Leigh appeared in a similar period film about jousting knights called **The Black Shield of Falworth**, 1954, but one where Curtis was utterly miscast as his New York City accent lampooned his own character and where such lines as "my fadda's castle" brought hoots and howling from the audience. Hayden told this author that he thought his role as a jousting knight in **Prince Valiant** was "a tight fit because I had to clank around in a heavy iron suit. I don't know how those guys in those days got to the washroom in time while being dressed like that." Mason told

this author that "those heavy broadswords we used in that picture were real and just lifting one gave one a backache for a week. I mentioned to the director that we were lumbering around in our fights with these swords and looked very clumsy. He replied: 'That's what they were in those days, very clumsy, so it will all be realistic, will it not?'" **p**, Robert L. Jacks; **d**, Henry Hathaway; **cast**, James Mason, Janet Leigh, Robert Wagner, Debra Paget, Sterling Hayden, Victor McLaglen, Donald Crisp, Brian Aherne, Barry Jones, Mary Philips, Tom Conway, Neville Brand, Primo Carnera, Michael Rennie (narrator); **w**, Dudley Nichols (based on the comic strip by Harold "Hal" Foster); **c**, Lucien Ballard (CinemaScope; Technicolor); **m**, Franz Waxman; **ed**, Robert L. Simpson; **art d**, Lyle Wheeler, Mark-Lee Kirk; **set d**, Stuart Reiss, Walter M. Scott; **spec eff**, Ray Kellogg, Louis J. Witte, Matthew Yuricich.

The Princess and the Frog ★★★ 2009; U.S.; 97m; Disney; Color; Animated Fantasy; Children: Cautionary (MPAA: PG); **BD**; **DVD**. A modern telling of the fairy tale *The Frog Prince* sees hardworking waitress Rose at the Mardi Gras in Jazz-era 1926 New Orleans where she meets Campos, a carefree and arrogant prince. He is penniless and wants to marry a rich woman and thinks Rose is a wealthy princess because of her elaborate costume. David, a voodoo magician, transforms Campos into a frog in a plot to rule New Orleans. There are some voodoo adventures and, with help from a trumpet-playing alligator, a firefly, and Lewis, a good voodoo priestess, Rose and Campos are reunited as humans and open a restaurant together. Songs: "Never Knew I Needed" (Ne-Yo); "Down in New Orleans," "Almost There," "Friends on the Other Side," "When We're Human," "Gonna Take You There," "Ma Belle Evangeline," "Dig a Little Deeper" (Randy Newman); "Dippermouth Blues" (Joseph Oliver); "Cajun Love Song" (Leon Russell). Elements involving voodoo may frighten younger children. **p**, Peter Del Vecho; **d**, John Musker, Ron Clements; **cast** (voiceovers), Anika Noni Rose, Keith David, Oprah Winfrey, Bruno Campos, Michael-Leon Wooley, Jennifer Cody, Jim Cummings, Peter Bartlett, Jennifer Lewis, Terrence Howard, John Goodman; **w**, Musker, Clements, Rob Edwards (based on the story "The Frog Princess" by E.D. Baker and a story by Musker, Clements, Greg Erb, Jason Oremland, Don Hall, Chris Ure, Jared Stern, Dean Wellins, Will Csaklos, Ralph Eggleston; **m**, Randy Newman; **ed**, Jeff Draheim; **prod d**, James Aaron Finch; **art d**, Ian Gooding; **spec eff**, Kyle Odermatt, Dan Turner.

The Princess and the Pirate ★★★ 1944; U.S.; 94m; Samuel Goldwyn/RKO; Color; Adventure/Comedy; Children: Acceptable; **DVD**. Entertaining comedy sees Mayo as a princess traveling by ship to Jamaica incognito in the mid-1700s to elope with her true love, instead of marrying the man to whom her father has promised her. On the high seas, pirates, led by McLaglen who knows her identity, attack the ship, and McLaglen plans to hold Mayo for ransom. She is rescued by Hope, who is a coward but masquerades as Sylvester the Great, a fearsome pirate. Hope and Mayo have fallen in love and are about to sail off together into the sunset when Bing Crosby suddenly appears at the wacky finale to take Mayo away with him. This laugh-filled romp is marked with superlative production values—impressive period sets and richly appointed costuming, all in color, which was exceptional for the day. The story was aired by the Screen Guild Theater in a thirty-minute radio adaptation on March 26, 1945, and where Hope and Mayo reprised their roles. Song: "Kiss Me in the Moonlight" (music: Jimmy McHugh; lyrics: Harold Adamson). This swashbuckling farce has some pirate violence, but should be acceptable for children. *Author's Note*: This was one of the few times where Hope briefly left his home studio of Paramount, being acquired by Goldwyn on a loan for which Goldwyn paid that studio $133,500 for the twelve weeks it took to produce this film. "I had the right to refuse doing **The Princess and the Pirate**," Hope told this author, "but Sam [Goldwyn] promised me the moon to do the film—a lavish production in color with all of his luscious Goldwyn Girls to ogle at, script approval where I could insert my own bits of funny business, and he counted on that, and, best of all, his new leading lady, a bouncy blonde named Virginia Mayo, and she was really the frosting on that delicious piece of cake." Mayo (1920-2005; born Virginia Clara Jones) had been discovered by Goldwyn after one of Goldwyn's talent scouts saw her in a vaudeville show as a straight woman to a horse act performed by the Mayo Brothers; she changed her named from Jones to Mayo, borrowing that new name from her old act when she was signed up as a Goldwyn Girl. She appeared in supporting roles in a few films in the early 1940s, until Goldwyn decided to make her a star by casting her as the leading lady in this film, and she was the only Goldwyn Girl who ever achieved such stardom. "You could have knocked me for a loop," Mayo told this author, "after Mr. Goldwyn told me that I would be starring in a picture with the great Bob Hope. I had died and gone to Heaven." Goldwyn told this author that "one of my assistants pointed out that Virginia [Mayo] was a little bit cross-eyed, but I already knew that, and I always had the cameramen and directors shoot her in such a way where her eyeballs weren't banging up against each other. Nobody ever noticed that, I think, in all of her pictures. A lovely girl and with a very nice temperament and she proved me right in making her a big star because she had the talent to deserve it and became a very fine actress." Mazurki, who invariably played journeyman goons, plays one of McLaglen's henchmen in this film, but he found his job difficult in this production because, according to his statements to this author: "Every time I had to rough house Bob [Hope] I almost cracked up laughing at his crazy antics, so I had to bite my tongue to keep from ruining a scene. I had a sore mouth for weeks after we did that picture." **p**, Samuel Goldwyn; **d**, David Butler; **cast**, Bob Hope, Virginia Mayo, Walter Brennan, Walter Slezak, Hugo Haas, Maude Eburne, Robert Warwick, Francis Ford, Rondo Hatton, Mike Mazurki, Louanne Hogan (singing voice for Mayo), Bing Crosby; **w**, Don Hartman, Melville Shavelson, Everett Freeman, Allen Boretz, Curtis Kenyon (based on a story by Sy Bartlett); **c**, Victor Milner, William E. Snyder (Technicolor); **m**, David Rose; **ed**, Daniel Mandell; **art d**, Ernst Fegte; **set d**, Howard Bristol; **spec eff**, R.O. Binger, Clarence Slifer, Harry Redmond Jr. and Sr.

The Princess Bride ★★★★★ 1987; U.S.; 98m; Act III Communications/Buttercup Films/FOX; Color; Adventure/Comedy; Children: Cautionary (MPAA: PG); **BD**; **DVD**; **VHS**. In this very funny movie, Savage is an ill boy who is visited by his grandfather, Falk, who decides to cheer him up by reading this fairy tale to him and one where the story line is occasionally interrupted by Savage, who objects to love scenes and, particularly, kissing. The story opens on a peaceful farm in the mythical land of Florin where Wright lives. She is a beautiful young woman named Buttercup who has a farmworker, Elwes (Westley), performing all of her heavy chores. He is eager to aid her and, whenever she gives him a task to perform, he replies: "As you wish." Wright soon realizes that Elwes is in love with her and she also falls in love with him. He then leaves to make his fortune, promising to return to her so that they can be married. His ship, however, is attacked by fierce pirates and, after waiting five years, Wright comes to believe that Elwes has been killed by a notorious pirate named Roberts, so she reluctantly agrees to marry the local prince, Sarandon (called Prince Humperdinck), who is a vicious, scheming and sinister character. Before Wright's wedding, however, she is kidnapped by a Sicilian adventurer, Shawn, and with the help of two hirelings, Andre the Giant (Fezzik) and Patinkin, a Spanish fencing master. Patinkin has a special mission in that he seeks vengeance on a man with six fingers who killed his father. They are pursued by a man wearing a black mask (Elwes) as well as Sarandon and his men. Wright does not know that her abduction has been arranged by Sarandon, who has hired Shawn and his two minions to take her to the land of Guilder and kill her there so that he can use her murder as a provocation to start a war with this rival country. Elwes sails his ship after the one carrying Wright. When the kidnappers reach the Cliffs of Insanity, Andre the Giant carries Wright, Shawn and Pantinkin upward

Cary Elwes and Robin Wright in *The Princess Bride*, 1987.

hand over hand on a rope to reach the top while Elwes rapidly climbs after them. Patinkin is left behind to kill the pursuer with his masterful swordplay, but, after Elwes reaches the top of the cliff, he displays amazing skill with the sword and bests Patinkin, knocking him unconscious. Elwes then catches up with Andre the Giant and defeats him, too, by choking him unconscious. Elwes then finds Shawn waiting for him with a blindfolded Wright and offers Elwes one of two cups of wine sitting between them. One of the wine goblets contains poison and the two have a battle of wits to see which one will take the poisoned cup, with a lot of razzle-dazzle exchanging of the cups when their backs are turned. After the two finally drink from the goblets, Shawn arrogantly laughs, boasting that he has outwitted Elwes, but it is just the opposite, as Shawn keels over dead from the poison. When Wright sees her rescuer she at first thinks him to be the pirate Roberts, who has killed Westley and, in a rage, pushes him into a gorge, stating that he should meet the same fate that has befallen her true love, Westley. When Elwes calls out "as you wish," she realizes that he is Westley and she jumps into the gorge after him. We next see the couple wandering through a dark forest called the Fire Swamp, where they battle oversized rodents and avoid spouting fire fountains and sand traps, only to emerge beyond the forest to be captured by Sarandon and his men. Wright agrees to return with Sarandon and marry him if he spares Elwes, life. Sarandon promises her that her true love will not be harmed, but, before leaving with her, he tells his henchman, Guest, who is the six-fingered man Patinkin has been seeking, to first torture Elwes before killing him. Once back at Sarandon's castle, Wright learns of Elwes' fate and denounces Sarandon as a coward. Sarandon, meanwhile, plots to kill her after he marries her and blame her death on his enemies in Guilder so that he can nevertheless start that war. While Sarandon plots with Guest, Patinkin learns that Guest is the man he has been seeking and decides to invade Sarandon's castle to settle his old score with Guest, but he is convinced that he needs Elwes to help him accomplish that mission and enlists the aid of Andre the Giant to rescue Elwes. They find him in Guest's torture chamber, but he appears to be dead and they remove his body to the home of a healer named Miracle Max, who is hilariously played by Crystal, a broken-down second-rate herbs and potions peddler, living with a hag of a wife, Kane. Crystal examines the limp Elwes and pronounces that there is hope since Elwes is "only mostly dead." He prepares a vile potion and administers this swill to Elwes who, after drinking it, miraculously returns to life, but is suffering from paralysis in all of his limbs. Andre the Giant carries the inert Elwes to the palace with Patinkin and all three find their way into that inner sanctum where Patinkin finally confronts Guest. In a wild swordfight where Patinkin is wounded many times, he nevertheless manages to dispatch villain Guest. Meanwhile, Wright, who has been locked in her room after Sarandon has ordered a whirl-

Kevin Kline and Phoebe Cates in *Princess Caraboo*, 1994.

wind marriage, thinks to commit suicide, but Elwes, who has regained partial movement of his limbs, arrives to tell her that she was never legally married to Sarandon because she never said "I do." After binding Sarandon to a chair to contemplate his many sins, Elwes, Wright, Patinkin and Andre the Giant escape the castle by riding away on four white horses and the story ends, but not before Elwes and Wright exchange one last passionate embrace and kiss. Savage, who is feeling much better after hearing this story read to him by grandfather Falk, asks his grandfather to return the next day and read the story to him once more. Falk, before exiting the boy's room, smiles and says: "As you wish." Director Reiner does a great job in presenting this romantic adventure tale, packing it with one humorous scene after another, where the entire cast plays tongue-in-cheek with their outlandish characters, all brilliantly essayed in the script from Goldman, which is based upon his equally sardonic novel. The production values are superb, from the well-appointed and spacious sets to the impressive costuming, and Biddle's inventive lensing and Knopfler's enchanting score both excel. This delightful romp sustains interest in every scene for both child and adult, albeit some violence might disturb younger children, even though there is the added comfort that the tale is being related to a sick child by his loving grandfather and that it is, after all, only a fairy tale (or is it?). This film saw a fair success at the box office, earning more than $30.8 million in its initial release against a budget of $16 million, but has since become a cult classic. Songs: "Take Me Out to the Ballgame" (Albert von Tilzer; Jack Norworth); "Morning Ride," "The Friend Song," "Guide My Sword," "I Will Never Love Again," "Florin Dance," "A Happy Ending" (Mark Knopfler). *Author's Note*: The film rights to Goldman's novel were purchased by Fox for $500,000 in 1973 after the book was published, but production delays and changes in studio executives put the film on hold. Goldman later bought back the rights with his own funds and, over the years, unsuccessfully tried to interest other studios in producing the film. Rob Reiner then read the book and went to Norman Lear, who provided funds to produce the film, with Reiner directing. "That was the best thing that could happen to that story," Falk told this author. "Rob [Reiner] was an old hand at doing good satire as he had been doing comedy, like his father [Carl Reiner], for years. He had been in the long-running 'All in the Family,' where he played Carroll O'Connor's liberal-minded son-in-law [called Michael 'Meathead' Stivic], so this man knew what was funny and what was not. Here I am telling this story to my sick grandson [Savage] but I am enjoying this wild tale just as much as he is, maybe more, even though he doesn't like the kissing parts—all boys hate that gooey stuff, until they get to know what it's all about. Yes, sir, that picture's got it all—pirates, evil princes, palaces and dungeons, eels that try to eat Princess Buttercup, giants, swordfights, races, pursuits, and a crazy wizard who can bring people

back to life. What else would anyone want, I ask you?" The film was shot on location in England and Ireland. **p**, Rob Reiner, Andrew Scheinman; **d**, Reiner; **cast**, Carey Elwes, Mandy Patinkin, Chris Sarandon, Robin Wright, Andre the Giant, Billy Crystal, Carol Kane, Anne Dyson, Peter Cook, Christopher Guest, Wallace Shawn, Fred Savage, Peter Falk (also the narrator); **w**, William Goldman (based on his novel); **c**, Adrian Biddle; **m**, Mark Knopfler; **ed**, Robert Leighton; **prod d**, Norman Garwood; **art d**, Keith Pain, Richard Holland; **set d**, Maggie Gray; **spec eff**, Nick Allder.

Princess Caraboo ★★★ 1994; U.K./U.S.; 97m; Ardican Films/TriStar Pictures; Color; Comedy/Drama; Children: Unacceptable (MPAA: PG); **DVD**; **VHS**. This entertaining comedy is based on the adventures of Mary Willcocks Baker (1791-1864), an imposter who said she was Princess Caraboo from a faraway island and fooled a British town for some months. The film is set in Bristol, England, in the early 1800s. Cates is a beautiful stranger, who speaks a strange foreign language and who is tried for the crime of begging. She is rescued by a wealthy family headed by Broadbent and Hughes, who take her in to capitalize on her alleged royalty. A reporter, Rea, tries his utmost to learn her true identity, but fails to learn anything, except that he is in love with her, and, even after her ruse is exposed, he goes on protecting her. Good acting and a clever script provides a thoroughly entertaining film. Sexuality and gutter language prohibit viewing by children. Songs: "Minuetto" (Luigi Boccherini), "Air" (from "The Ephesian Matron"; music: Isaac Bickerstaffe; lyrics: Charles Dibden). *Author's Note*: Baker appeared in Gloucester, England, in April 1817, and where she was wearing exotic apparel and speaking in an unknown language (gibberish of her own creation) and communicated with sign language to convince naïve officials and well-placed society members that she was a foreign princess from the island of Javasu (a mythical isle supposedly located in the Indian Ocean, also of her own creation). She claimed that she had been kidnapped by pirates but managed to escape by jumping from their ship in the English Channel and swimming to shore to find her way to Gloucester where she was accepted as a royal personage and sheltered by wealthy patrons. She showed proficiency in shooting arrows, using a sword and swam naked before praying to a god she called Alla-Tallah. She was exposed as an impersonator after a woman identified her as a former tenant in her Bristol, England, boarding house. The press identified her as Mary Willcocks, a poor servant girl, who was unemployed and who traveled about England looking for work. She apparently was taken in by gypsies, who gave her strange-looking clothing, and it was their language or a version of it that she employed when creating her hoax with the rustics of Gloucester. Instead of being arrested for perpetrating a hoax, her hosts provided her with money and a passage to Philadelphia. She sailed for that port on June 28, 1817. By that time, she had been widely publicized and she used her impersonation to go on to the American stage. She returned to England in 1824 and married a man named Baker, having a daughter. She made her living as peddler of leeches to hospitals for some time and died in Bristol in 1864. **p**, Andrew Karsch, Simon Bosanquet; **d**, Michael Austin; **cast**, Phoebe Cates, Jim Broadbent, Wendy Hughes, Kevin Kline, John Lithgow, Steven Mackintosh, Dougray Scott; Stephen Rea, Peter Eyre, Jacqueline Pearce, John Sessions, John Wells; **w**, Austin, Wells; **c**, Freddie Francis; **m**, Richard Hartley; **ed**, George Akers; **prod d**, Michael Howells; **art d**, Sam Riley; **set d**, Sasha Schwerid; **spec eff**, Ian Wingrove.

The Princess Comes Across ★★★ 1936; U.S.; 76m; PAR; B/W; Comedy/Mystery; Children: Acceptable; **DVD**; **VHS**. There are more laughs than fright in this hilarious whodunit that sees Lombard as a Brooklyn actress-dancer who thinks she may further her career and become a movie star if she pretends to be a member of royalty. She sails on a cruise ship to Europe and intends to come back a princess. She is accompanied by a friend, Skipworth, who pretends to be her lady-in-waiting. Aboard ship on a return from Europe to New York, Lombard meets bandleader MacMurray and his tough-talking manager, Frawley. Hall, an acquaintance of Lombard's from Flatbush, threatens to extort money from her or he will expose her impersonation as a Swedish princess. Before she can come across with extortion money, Hall is killed and she and MacMurray become the prime suspects. Ironically, the ship is awash with European detectives en route to a convention in New York, and one of them, Rumann, a pompous German sleuth, thinks he is on the trail of the killer. Before he can identify the culprit, however, he is dispatched. MacMurray, however, solves the mystery and names Dumbrille as the murderer, but it's unclear as to his motive. In New York, MacMurray tries to establish Lombard as a princess so she can become a movie star. By then Lombard decides her princess ploy won't work and, when interviewed by the press, she deliberately speaks in a strong Brooklyn accent (in one of the funniest scenes in this very funny film). MacMurray is glad she has ended her charade and they embrace at the finale of what is a delightful romantic comedy. Lombard and MacMurray shine in their roles, both being two gifted stars adept at playing drama or comedy. Songs: "My Concertina" (Jack Scholl, Phil Boutelje), "Flight of the Bumble Bee" (1900; music: Nikolai Rimsky-Korsakov). *Author's Note*: MacMurray was not the first actor picked to play Lombard's leading man in this film. Her original costar was the temperamental George Raft, who had clicked well with Lombard in **Bolero**, 1934, and **Rhumba**, 1935, but, in the latter film, Raft complained that cinematographer Tetzlaff was giving all the close-ups to Lombard. When he learned that Tetzlaff had been assigned to this film, Raft quit the production and MacMurray replaced him. "It was sheer joy to work with Carole [Lombard] in **The Princess Comes Across**," MacMurray told this author. "She was a very down-to-earth lady and had a great sense of humor. She could always make a scene better than it was written and would add little bits of funny business to make a scene even funnier and she could do that simply by flaring her nostrils or arching an eyebrow. She told me that she planned to do a take-off on the great Greta Garbo and so she is really doing another impersonation in that picture. She was a scream as she hunched her shoulders and lowered the timber of her voice like Garbo, striking dramatic poses and slinking around from cabin to cabin on board that ship while everyone is looking for some crazy killer. Ah, there was no one like Carole. She was a natural born comedienne." Many years later when this author sat with Garbo in her New York City penthouse, that great actress told me that when she saw Lombard's impersonation of her in **The Princess Comes Across**, "she made me laugh when she exaggerated my movements and mannerisms. I was not offended and I thought her impersonation of me was a compliment. She was a very talented person." MacMurray, an accomplished musician, actually played the concertina in this film and did it exceptionally well. **p**, Arthur Hornblow, Jr.; **d**, William K. Howard; **cast**, Carole Lombard, Fred MacMurray, Douglass Dumbrille, Alison Skipworth, George Barbier, Porter Hall, Sig Rumann, William Frawley, Mischa Auer, Christian Rub, Milburn Stone, John Sutton; **w**, Walter DeLeon, Francis Martin, Frank Butler, Don Hartman, Claude Binyon, J.B. Priestley (based on the story by Philip MacDonald from the novel by Louis Lucien Rogger); **c**, Ted Tetzlaff; **m**, John Leipold; **ed**, Paul Weatherwax; **art d**, Hans Dreier, Ernst Fegté; **spec eff**, Farciot Edouart, Dewey Wrigley.

Princess Mononoke ★★★ 1999; Japan; 134m; DENTSU Music and Entertainment/Miramax Films; Color; Animated Fantasy; Children: Unacceptable (MPAA: PG-13); **DVD**; **VHS**. Well-animated fantasy begins when, on a journey to find a cure for a curse, Crudup, a young man named Ashitaka, walks into a war between supernatural guardians of a forest and humans in a mining town that consumes the forest's resources. Crudup tries to reconcile the warring factions, but each regards him as an enemy. He encounters a brave young woman, Danes (Princess Mononoke), who was raised by a wolf-god. Crudup is shot and Danes nurses him back to health. They develop strong feelings for each other, but, after the war ends with some degree of everyone getting along, she leaves and he remains to help the mining town residents. Violence and

Robert Cummings, Jack Carson and Jane Wyman in *Princess O'Rourke*, 1943.

gore prohibit viewing by children. (In Japanese; English subtitles.) **p**, Toshio Suzuki; **d&w**, Hayao Miyazaki; **cast** (voiceovers, Japanese version), Yôji Matsuda, Yuriko Ishida, Yûko Tanaka, Kaoru Kobayashi, Masahiko Nishimura, Tsunehiko Kamijô, Sumi Shimamoto, Tetsu Watanabe, Mitsuru Satô, Akira Nagoya; (voiceovers, English version), Claire Danes, Billy Crudup, Gillian Anderson, Minnie Driver, Jennifer Cihi, Jada Pinkett Smith, Keith David, Billy Bob Thornton, John DeMita, Debi Derryberry, John DiMaggio, Alex Fernandez; **c**, Atsushi Okui; **m**, Joe Hisaishi; **ed**, Hayao Miyazaki, Takeshi Seyama; **art d**, Satoshi Kuroda, Kazuo Oga, Yôji Takeshige, Naoya Tanaka, Nizou Yamamoto; **spec eff**, Yoshikazu Fukutome, Yoshinori Sugano.

Princess O'Rourke ★★★ 1943; U.S.; 93m; WB; B/W; Comedy; Children: Acceptable; **DVD**; **VHS**. In this pleasing comedy, de Havilland is a European princess, who visits New York City, but becomes bored with the social restrictions imposed upon her because of her station in life. Coburn, her uncle, suggests she might like San Francisco better, so she boards a plane, but is nervous about flying and takes a sleeping pill. Sensing she is nervous, Cummings, the pilot, Carson, the navigator, and Wyman, the flight attendant, each give her more pills without knowing the others have been dosing her. The plane is forced back to New York because of bad weather, and de Havilland arrives groggy so Cummings takes her to his apartment. She pretends she's a poor girl from Europe and goes to work as a maid. After a series of comic adventures, de Havilland and Cummings fall in love and they plan to marry. Then Cummings learns that he must give up his American citizenship to wed the royal de Havilland and this he refuses to do. De Havilland, however, is not about to give up this charming man and she then insists that she will abandon her royal standing, despite all of Coburn's fulminations and protests. Their wedding takes place in Washington, D.C., at the White House, with Davenport, playing the role of a U.S. Supreme Court Justice, officiating, and where President Franklin D. Roosevelt is actually present (in the background) to sanction the marriage. Director Krasna, who specialized in comedies, does a fine job with this one, both helming the film and writing the lively script. De Havilland is convincing as the headstrong princess and Cummings impressive as the man she can't live without. Song: "Honorable Moon" (Arthur Schwartz, Ira Gershwin, E.Y. Harburg. *Author's Note*: Wyman told this author that "I don't know how the Warner Brothers' front office talked President Roosevelt into making an appearance in that wedding scene at the end of **Princess O'Rourke**, but I was told that he loved doing his bit part and that darling little dog of his, Fala, was also running around in the picture, the little ham." Roosevelt liked the script and thought the film was patriotic and much needed at a time when the U.S. was still struggling to tip the balance in WWII. **p**, Hal B. Wallis; **d&w**, Norman Krasna; **cast**, Olivia de Havil-

Alec Guinness in *The Prisoner*, 1955.

land, Robert Cummings, Charles Coburn, Jack Carson, Jane Wyman, Harry Davenport, Gladys Cooper, Minor Watson, Nan Wynn, Curt Bois, Julie Bishop, Bill Edwards, Ruth Ford, Bill Kennedy, President Franklin D. Roosevelt, Fala the dog; **m**, Friedrich Hollaender **c**, Ernest Haller; **ed**, Warren Low; **art d**, Max Parker; **set d**, George James Hopkins.

The Prisoner ★★★★ 1955; U.K.; 91m; Facet Productions/COL; B/W; Drama; Children: Unacceptable. **DVD**; **VHS**. Guinness gives a powerful performance as an imprisoned Catholic clergyman in an unnamed East European country that has come under communist tyranny, replacing the Nazi tyranny during World War II (1939-1945). Guinness is a Roman Catholic cardinal, who is arrested for treason in the police state. He is psychologically tortured under the direction of Hawkins, a one-time boyhood friend who has become a member of the ruling military. Hawkins convinces Guinness that the prelate did not join the church for religious reasons, but to escape poverty and an unhappy home life. Guinness cracks under this accusation, admits to treason, and is sentenced to be executed. He is later pardoned and goes free except that the interrogation has left him questioning his motivation in becoming a priest and his love and loyalty to God. Glenville directs this taut drama with a firm hand and, in addition to Guinness' riveting performance, Hawkins is also mesmerizing as a former friend turned antagonist, who viciously rakes up a tawdry personal past to emotionally break the will of an otherwise devout and dedicated man. This superlative film that delineates the methodology of Soviet brainwashing was condemned by many countries for many reasons. In Ireland, officials labeled the film "pro-communist." In France, it was branded "anti-communist" and it was officially barred from appearing at the Cannes Film Festival. In Italy, it was called "anti-Catholic" and it was officially banned from the Venice Film Festival. A film that can so powerfully alienate so many diversified critics with so many opposing views more than proved its impactful and meaningful message. *Author's Note*: The fictional story was widely considered to be based on the real-life arrest of Hungarian cardinal Jozef Mindszenty (1892-1975) in 1944 when he refused to hold a mass in Budapest that was dictated by the Nazis, one that was to commemorate "the successful liberation of Budapest from the Jews." Mindszenty courageously branded such a mass a cruel farce and a lie and for which he was imprisoned. When the Soviets took control of Hungary, Mindszenty was again imprisoned for defying the communist regime and for practicing Catholic rites. Elements of this story also incorporate events involving the similar arrest of Croatian cardinal Aloysius Stepinac (1898-1960). Mindszenty's fate helped to spawn the 1956 Hungarian Revolution. He later took refuge in the U.S. Embassy in Budapest, living there for the next fifteen years, almost as a virtual prisoner. Guinness told this author that "**The Prisoner** was grueling to do, almost every

scene demanding such emotional stamina that it proved exhausting for me as well as Jack [Hawkins]. The dialog is as relentless as the most dedicated fanatics that made up those Cold War interrogators, who always seemed to find a way to destroy the will and resolve of even the strongest of men. Psychological fear is employed as ruthlessly as one might fire a machine gun and that can be more devastating to one with a well-ordered mind than facing actual bullets. That is the plight and the fate of the person I enact. It is not an optimistic picture, but certainly an honest one." Violence prohibits viewing by children. **p**, Vivian Cox; **d**, Peter Glenville; **cast**, Alec Guinness, Jack Hawkins, Wilfrid Lawson, Kenneth Griffith, Jeanette Sterke, Ronald Lewis, Raymond Huntley, Mark Dignam, Gerard Heinz, Jonathan Bailey; **w**, Bridget Boland (based on her play); **c**, Reginald Ho Wyer; **m**, Benjamin Frankel; **ed**, Frederick Wilson; **art d**, John Hawkesworth.

The Prisoner of Second Avenue ★★★ 1975; U.S.; 98m; WB; Color; Comedy; Children: Unacceptable (MPAA: PG); **DVD**; **VHS**. Lemmon and Bancroft are bright spots in this gloom-and-doom farce from the ever inventive Simon. They are a middle-aged, middle-class married couple living in a Manhattan high rise apartment building. He loses his job at an advertising agency, their apartment is robbed, she gets a job and he has a nervous breakdown, then she loses her job. They also have nosy neighbors and relatives who try to be helpful but who prove to be just the opposite. When they seem to be on the verge of surrendering to bad fortune, they snub their noses at adversity and prepare to battle to change their lives. There are many humorous moments in this offbeat comedy, especially when Lemmon shouts through the walls and ceiling at his annoying neighbors. The upstairs neighbor, Peck, whose stentorian deep voice indicating a Higher Power, drenches Lemmon on his balcony and serves as a goad to Lemmon's increasing tirades, prompting him to explode and finally yell at the ceiling: "You think that I don't know what you look like, but I do!" This is a rare inconsistency from Simon in that Peck knows he has been seen by Lemmon after dousing him with water from his upstairs balcony. (That scene was originally shot on a New York City apartment complex balcony, but the color in the scene did not blend with the rest of the scenes and that scene had to be reshot at a Warner Brothers soundstage in Burbank, California.) An entertaining black comedy that is too mature for children. *Author's Note*: Simon borrows heavily from himself in this film (and his Broadway stage production, which starred Peter Falk and Lee Grant) in that the dark cloud following its characters is also the main theme in Simon's earlier comedy, **The Out-of-Towners**, 1970, which also starred Lemmon. To that, Lemmon told this author that "a good idea is worth repeating, is it not?" He added: "I suppose one could also say that Neil [Simon] had his eye on Billy Wilder's **The Apartment** [1960, also starring Lemmon] when he wrote this comedy, but a good writer will naturally use any ingredients that will work well for his story, and Neil is a very good writer. Someone told me that **The Prisoner of Second Avenue** is really a lift job of **Will Success Spoil Rock Hunter?** [1957, starring Tony Randall as a rising executive in an advertising agency], but without the success. That idea is absolutely ridiculous—don't you think?" Sylvester Stallone makes a brief appearance in a bit part as a youth in Central Park. **p&d**, Melvin Frank; **cast**, Jack Lemmon, Anne Bancroft, Gene Saks, Elizabeth Wilson, Florence Stanley, Maxine Stuart, Ed Peck, Gene Blakely, Ivor Francis, F. Murray Abraham, Sylvester Stallone; **w**, Neil Simon (based on his play); **c**, Philip Lathrop; **m**, Marvin Hamlisch; **ed**, Bob Wyman; **art d**, Preston Ames; **set d**, Marvin March.

The Prisoner of Shark Island ★★★★ 1936; U.S.; 96m; FOX; B/W; Biographical Drama; Children: Unacceptable; **DVD**. Baxter gives one of his most impressive performances as Dr. Samuel Alexander Mudd (1833-1883), who was swept up in the conspiracy to assassinate President Abraham Lincoln (1809-1865), briefly played by McGlynn. Following Lincoln's killing, Baxter is aroused from his sleep at his rural Maryland home in the middle of the night by McDonald, a traveler seeking aid for a broken ankle. The patient is furtive and evasive, McDonald speaking in terse and guarded statements. As grim events unfold, Baxter later learns (and the film presumes his innocence in his not knowing the true identity of his patient) that he has mended the leg of the notorious assassin, John Wilkes Booth (1838-1865), Lincoln's assassin. While treating his patient, McDonald makes some strange remark about the present political climate, and Baxter (where director Ford earlier establishes Baxter's character as a law-abiding citizen), states: "I guess Old Abe [Lincoln] is all right after all. He's the only salvation we southerners can look for—him and God's mercy." After the shadowy McDonald departs with his accomplice, Fix (who plays Booth's accomplice, David Herold, 1842-1865), Baxter tells his wife, Stuart, that his patient "smells of snakes." A short time later, Baxter is summarily arrested and separated from wife Stuart and their small child, charged as an accomplice in the Lincoln murder, McDonald and his accomplice, Fix, by then having been brought to justice. Baxter is brought to trial with many other conspirators, and Fix offers no help in exonerating him (Herold and three others were summarily hanged). Baxter's case is largely ignored by inept defense attorneys, although Wood, playing Union General Thomas Ewing Jr. (1829-1896), who was also an attorney, comes to believe that Baxter is innocent. Despite pleas from his wife, Stuart, Baxter is convicted on thin circumstantial evidence and is given a life sentence and then sent to Fort Jefferson in the Dry Tortugas, a remote prison squatting on a sandbar nicknamed Shark Island, not unlike France's counterpart, Devil's Island off the coast of French Guiana. Believing that his case is hopeless, Baxter attempts to escape by stowing away on board a Union supply ship, but he is caught and thrown into the guard house. He nevertheless quickly earns the respect of his fellow prisoners, as well as the black guards, by tending to the ill, both inmates and warders, and is referred to as a "southern gentleman." When a Yellow Fever epidemic strikes the place, Carey, the sympathetic commandant, asks for Baxter's aid, but with no promises that his sentence will ever be reduced or that he can hope for any kind of release. Baxter nevertheless accepts the daunting chore of combating the virulent plague, working night and day to save the inmates and guards who are stricken by the fever, including Carradine, the vicious sergeant of the guards, a radical abolitionist who hates Baxter. All that changes after Baxter saves Carradine's life and Carradine becomes an advocate for Baxter's freedom as does the grateful Carey. Baxter's case is reviewed in Washington, D.C., and, in light of his humanitarian services in saving the lives of both prisoners and guards at Fort Jefferson, he is pardoned and released, the final scene showing Baxter happily reuniting with his family. Under the firm guidance of pantheon director Ford, who is extremely meticulous in observing the historical facts in this absorbing case while providing many exciting scenes, Baxter renders a sympathetic and dynamic performance as an innocent man trapped by the overwhelming grim events of that turbulent era. He is well supported by Carey, Carradine, Stuart and the rest of a fine cast. Despite misgiving by Fox studio boss Zanuck, this film did very well at the box office. It was later adapted for the radio for the Encore Radio Theater in 1946 and its story line was the basis for the film **Hellgate**, 1952, starring Sterling Hayden. Songs: "Dixie's Land" (Daniel Decatur Emmett), "Maryland, My Maryland" (traditional), "The Battle Cry of Freedom" (George Frederick Root), "Battle Hymn of the Republic" (music [1856]: William Steffe; lyrics [1861]: Julia Ward Howe), "Taps" (Daniel Butterfield). Other actors and films profiling Dr. Mudd include **The Day Lincoln Was Shot**, 1998 (made-for-TV; Gary Wheeler); **Killing Lincoln**, 2013 (made-for-TV; Raynor Scheine); **Laramie**, 1959-1963 (TV series; "Time of the Traitor," 1962 episode: Lew Ayres); **The Lincoln Conspiracy**, 1977 (Wallace K. Wilkinson); **The Ordeal of Dr. Mudd**, 1980 (made-for-TV; Dennis Weaver); **Telephone Time**, 1956-1958 (TV series; "The Quality of Mercy," 1958 episode: Harry Townes); **Westinghouse Desilu Playhouse**, 1958-1960 (TV series; "The Case for Dr. Mudd," 1958 episode: Lew Ayres); and **You Are There**, 1953-1957 (TV series; "The Capture of John Wilkes Booth," 1953 episode: Ernest Sarracino). *Au-*

Warner Baxter in *The Prisoner of Shark Island*, 1936.

thor's Note: Booth, after fatally shooting Lincoln at Ford's Theater in Washington, D.C., on the night of April 14, 1865, while Lincoln was watching a comedy, leaped from the presidential box and broke his ankle when landing on the stage. He fled through the theater's rear entrance and mounted a horse being held there by an innocent boy and fled the city, joined later in his flight by David Herold, one of the conspirators. They arrived at Mudd's Maryland home on horseback at about 4 a.m. on April 15, 1865; Lincoln died three hours later at 7:22 a.m. that day. It was later claimed that Mudd had met Booth some weeks before he appeared at his home seeking medical aid, but it remains unclear to this day that Mudd knew anything about Booth's intention to murder Lincoln and that Booth only knew that Mudd was a practicing physician in the area through which he was fleeing and might be available in treating his leg injury. Mudd admitted in court that he treated Booth as he would any other injured person, setting his broken leg and then bandaging it and supporting it with splints. Booth and Herold spent about fifteen hours at Mudd's residence in an upstairs bedroom while Booth recuperated, but apparently they had little or no communication with Mudd before they departed. For more details on Mudd and the Lincoln assassination, see my two-volume work, *The Great Pictorial History of World Crime*, Volume I (History, Inc., 2004; pages 26-44). Ford told this author that he took great pains to get the facts straight when making **The Prisoner of Shark Island**, stating: "We had researchers getting copies of all the records in the shooting and everything that had to do with Dr. Mudd. I was not about to change history and told that to everyone connected to that picture." Writer Johnson, who was one of Ford's mainstay scriptwriters, told this author that "Pappy [Ford] had me pour over mounds of records in that case to get everything right about Dr. Mudd. We did not alter or hide any facts and even showed that he once owned slaves and had once been a strong supporter of the Southern cause, but everything about him pointed to his innocence in the Lincoln killing and that's how I wrote about him in the script." Zanuck earlier on expressed concerns about how Mudd would be portrayed, telling this author: "There is no greater American icon than Abraham Lincoln and anything having to do with him in pictures is watched by an army of historian hawks, so I warned Pappy to walk on eggs in doing **The Prisoner of Shark Island**. I think Johnson did a very good script with reliable facts. I know I could not improve upon it and I even tried." Johnson added that "Pappy, like almost all Americans, thought Lincoln walked on water, and he was very careful in the brief scene where he shows the President being killed. In my original script, I showed Booth shooting him in the head, but Pappy took that out, saying 'it's too brutal,' and told me to write the scene so that when Booth fires the fatal bullet, the audience sees only Lincoln's hand quiver a bit and then go limp to indicate he has been shot. Pappy then showed him slumped in his chair, but only very

Ronald Reagan and Steve Forrest in *Prisoner of War*, 1954.

briefly and then had Glennon [the cinematographer of the film] quickly dissolve that shot into a fine portrait of Lincoln as that is what Pappy wanted the world to remember about that great man. That's how sensitive Pappy was about showing Abraham Lincoln." **p**, Darryl F. Zanuck; **d**, John Ford; **cast**, Warner Baxter, Gloria Stuart, Claude Gillingwater, Arthur Byron, O.P. Heggie, Harry Carey, Francis Ford, John McGuire, Francis McDonald, Douglas Wood, John Carradine, Joyce Kay, Fred Kohler Jr., Paul Fix, John McGuire, Paul McVey, Frank McGlynn Sr., Jan Duggan, Paul Stanton, Arthur Loft, Ernest Whitman, Frank Shannon, Ronald "Jack" Pennick; **w**, Nunnally Johnson (based on the life of Dr. Samuel A. Mudd); **c**, Bert Glennon; **m**, Louis Silvers; **ed**, Jack Murray; **art d**, William Darling; **set d**, Thomas Little.

Prisoner of the Mountains ★★★ 1997; Russia/Kazakhstan; 99m; Karavan/Orion Classics; Color; War Drama; Children: Unacceptable (MPAA: R); **DVD**; **VHS**. Taut war tale has two Russian soldiers, Menshikov and Bodrov, Jr., being ambushed by Muslim rebels in the stark Caucasus Mountains during the Chechnyan rebellion and they are made prisoners. Menshikov is a tough war-experienced sergeant, while Bodrov is a raw recruit, thrown together when Islamic separatists wage guerrilla war in the mountains. They begin to understand each other better and become friends. The leader of the Muslim forces, Sikharulidze, in a hideaway camp where they are held, has a son in the war, held prisoner by the Russians. He asks for the release of his son in exchange for sparing the two Russians. Negotiations fail and Sikharulidze's son is killed by the Russians; Menshikov is shot by the Muslims, but Sikharulidze takes pity on Bodrov and allows him to go free. This well-crafted and firmly directed film presents a strong and sensitive portrait about war and the human sacrifices it extols. Songs: "Go Down Moses" (traditional), "Proshchante Slavianki" (V. Agapkin, A. Fedotov), "Sinii Platochek" (E. Petersbursky, M. Maksoimov), "Na Sopkakh Manchzhurii" (Igor Shatrov, A. Mashistov), "Pesnia O Pogibshem Brate" (Radzhab Radzhabov). **p**, Sergey Bodrov, Boris Giller, Carolyn Cavallero, Eduard Krapivsky; **d**, Bodrov; **cast**, Oleg Menshikov, Sergey Bodrov, Jr., Susanna Mekhraliyeva, Jemal Sikharulidze, Aleksandr Bureyev, Valentina Fedotova, Aleksei Zharkov, T. Kibyev, Valeri Kostrin, Pavel Lebeshev; **w**, Bodrov, Arif Aliyev, Giller (based on a story by Leo Tolstoy); **c**, Lebeshev; **m**, Leonid Desyatnikov; **ed**, Alan Baril, Olga Grinshpun, Vera Kruglova; **prod d**, Valeri Kostrin; **art d**, Igor Morozov.

Prisoner of War ★★★ 1954; U.S.; 81m; MGM; B/W; War Drama; Children: Unacceptable; **VHS**. In this chilling and realistic war tale about American POWs, Reagan is a U.S. Army intelligence officer, who volunteers to go into enemy territory during the Korean War

(1950-1953) to learn if American prisoners of war are being treated brutally by their communist captors. He parachutes behind enemy lines and infiltrates a group of GIs being marched to one of the POW camps. There he sees GIs, including Forrest and Martin, being brainwashed, beaten, subjected to mock executions, deprived of food and water, and tortured under the supervision of a Russian colonel, Homolka, who provides a particularly insidious portrait of a calculating interrogator. Despite the terrible situation, Reagan is heartened to see that most American soldiers are bearing it all with courage and determination to survive. In the process, Reagan joins Martin as turncoats where Martin becomes an informer and despicable traitor merely to get extra rations and special treatment but where Reagan does so to obtain information on how captors manipulate their prisoners for their own communist propaganda purposes. The direction is firm from Marton and the script plausible. Reagan, Martin, Forrest, Stewart and others are standouts as they show how their courageous characters are systematically reduced to cringing and craven persons, with some notable exceptions. Many other films have portrayed the Korean War on the battlefield and at the home front, most notably **The Bridges at Toko-Ri**, 1954; **Fixed Bayonets!**, 1951; **Flat Top**, 1952; **The Glory Brigade**, 1953; **The Great Imposter**, 1961; **Heartbreak Ridge**, 1986; **I Want You**, 1951; **The Last Picture Show**, 1971; **Love Is a Many Splendored Thing**, 1955; **The Manchurian Candidate**, 1962; **MacArthur**, 1977; **The McConnell Story**, 1955; **Men in War**, 1957; **Men of the Fighting Lady**, 1954; **One Minute to Zero**, 1952; **Pork Chop Hill**, 1959; **The Rack**, 1956; **Retreat, Hell!**, 1952; **Sayonara**, 1957; **The Steel Helmet**, 1951; **Take the High Ground!**, 1953; **Time Limit**, 1957; **War Hunt**, 1962; and **War Is Hell**, 1963. *Author's Note*: This film, like so many others of its era, took a very strong anti-communist position, particularly since Hollywood was then under fire from Washington, D.C., for having so many of its personnel being accused of left-wing activities. "Producers saw communists lurking in every casting call," Stewart, who plays an officer in the film, told this author, "so this picture was one of those that more or less told Washington that Hollywood was loyal—and, to prove it, they starred Ronnie Reagan in that picture because he was then the most outspoken critic of Hollywood left-wingers and fellow travelers, but, mind you, he was a very good actor and did a great job as an American spy in **Prisoner of War**. MGM hired a former American rmy officer [Captain Robert H. Wise], who had been held prisoner by the North Koreans in that war and he verified all the brutalities and tortures shown in that picture. It was not a pretty picture, but nothing about war is attractive, not a bit of it." Violence prohibits viewing by children. **p**, Henry Berman; **d**, Andrew Marton; **cast**, Ronald Reagan, Steve Forrest, Dewey Martin, Oscar Homolka, Robert Horton, Paul Stewart, Henry (Harry) Morgan, Stephen Bekassy, Leonard Strong, Darryl Hickman, John Lupton, Struther Martin, Dick Sargent, Stuart Whitman; **w**, Allen Rivkin; **c**, Robert Planck; **m**, Jeff Alexander; **ed**, James Newcom; **art d**, Cedric Gibbons, Malcolm Brown; **set d**, Edwin B. Willis, Jack D. Moore; **spec eff**, A. Arnold Gillespie, Warren Newcombe.

The Prisoner of Zenda ★★★ 1922; U.S.; 125m; Metro Pictures Corporation; B/W; Adventure; Children: Cautionary. Director Ingram presents this classic Anthony Hope adventure tale with zest and packs it with exciting action. The film opens with Stone, who plays the dual roles of Prince Rudolf and his heroic cousin and lookalike Rudolf Rassendyll, as the dissolute monarch-to-be gets drunk in his rural retreat in the mythical kingdom of Ruritania. After he is kidnapped by Novarro (as Rupert of Hentzau, and who uses the stage name of Samaniegos before he changed his name to Novarro), Stone, the cousin, takes the missing prince's place, impersonating the royal member of the family. Only Edeson, the king's loyal aide, knows of the impersonation. Stone's appearance is so much like that of his cousin that he is able to convince the beautiful Terry (Princess Flavia), Rudolf's intended, that he is the real prince of the realm, charming her with the kind of consideration and gentleness, which his lookalike cousin has never displayed. When Holmes (as "Black" Michael), Rudolf's evil, power-mad brother, learns of the abduction and impersonation, he joins with Novarro in holding the royal prince hostage in a dungeon at a castle at Zenda. Holmes then forces the impersonating cousin, Stone, to go ahead with a coronation that will make him king, knowing that he can later expose the impersonator and take the throne. With help of the sultry La Marr, who is Holmes' mistress, Stone secretly enters the guarded castle at Zenda while Edeson and his troops stand by outside, waiting for Stone to release the drawbridge so they can cross the moat and enter the castle. Meanwhile, Novarro, who covets La Marr, interrupts her and Holmes and kills Holmes. Stone, by then, has entered the castle and, with the help of a loyal servant, attempts to release the drawbridge, but Novarro kills the servant and then engages Stone in mortal combat with swords. Stone manages to release the drawbridge during the fight, and, seeing that his position is hopeless when Edeson and his men storm into the castle, Novarro escapes "to fight again another day." Stone then releases his imprisoned royal cousin who later tells him that he is grateful for saving his crown and for teaching him how "to become a king." Stone meets one last time with Terry, telling her that he loves her and asks that she return with him to England, but Terry, although she states she also loves the dashing impersonator, replies that her duty compels her to remain in Ruritania and to wed the prince. The impersonating cousin is then escorted to the border of the country by Edeson, who bids him a fond farewell, and Stone rides away and into legend. Director Ingram, who had scored with an enormous hit a year earlier when directing **The Four Horsemen of the Apocalypse**, 1921, which also starred Terry and introduced as a leading man the great "Latin Lover" Rudolph Valentino, was the first choice by Metro to direct this film and he handles the elaborate production with great skill, getting top performances from Stone, Terry, Novarro, and especially the alluring La Marr. *Author's Note*: Hope, who was a practicing British attorney later turned novelist and playwright, enjoyed great success with the publication of his novel, *The Prisoner of Zenda*, in 1894, and followed up with an 1898 sequel, *Rupert of Hentzau*. Hope collaborated with playwright Edward E. Rose in adapting *Prisoner of Zenda* for the New York stage, the play opening at the Lyceum Theater on September 4, 1895, and in London the following year on January 7, 1896. Hope had the story presented as a musical on Broadway with stirring music by Sigmund Romberg under the title of "Princess Flavia," which opened on November 2, 1925 and ran for 153 performances. This great adventure story saw three silent film versions, the first in 1913, remade in 1915, and remade again with this lavish production in 1922. It was remade as the first talkie version in 1937, and again as a good color production in 1952. Subsequent remakes occurred in 1961 (made-for-TV); a Bengali version also in 1961; a road show musical version in 1963 based on the original 1925, musical adaptation; and in 1979 (played for laughs in a comedy version with Peter Sellers); 1984 (BBC production, a TV miniseries); in 1988; and in 1996 (as a made-for-TV film). **p&d**, Rex Ingram; **cast**, Lewis Stone, Alice Terry, Robert Edeson, Stuart Holmes, Ramon Samaniegos (Ramon Novarro), Barbara La Marr, Malcolm McGregor, Edward Connelly, Lois Lee, Snitz Edwards, John George; **w**, Mary O'Hara (based on the play by Edward E. Rose and the novel by Anthony Hope); **c**, John F. Seitz; **ed**, Grant Whytock; **art d**, Amos Myers.

The Prisoner of Zenda ★★★★★ 1937; U.S.; 101m; Selznick International/UA; B/W; Adventure/Romance; Children: Cautionary; **DVD**; **VHS**. This masterpiece film from director Cromwell (with assists from directors Cukor and Van Dyke) offers a sumptuous and utterly captivating adventure-romance tale with the stellar talents of Colman, Carroll, Fairbanks, Massey and Astor, as well as a great cast. Colman plays the dual role of commoner Rassendyll and his lookalike prince, the soon-to-be King Rudolf V of the mythical kingdom of Ruritania, located somewhere in central Europe. Colman arrives by train in the also mythical city of Strelsau. Officials are shocked to see him in that they believe

Madeleine Carroll and Ronald Colman in *The Prisoner of Zenda*, 1937.

Colman is the prince traveling in disguise (he wears a goatee and the prince has a mustache), that disguise alarming these officials further in that the prince is about to be crowned king of the country. Colman the commoner is on a fishing expedition and he is found fishing by Smith and Niven, who are aides to the prince. The prince (also Colman, shown in clever masking to exhibit the doubles) also meets his lookalike, realizing that Colman is a distant cousin of the royal Elfberg family who has arrived from England. He is invited to dine that night at the royal hunting lodge, where Colman and his royal counterpart partake in too much wine drinking. The next morning Colman is rudely awakened when Smith douses him with a pitcher of water, demanding to know what he and the prince had to drink the night earlier. The prince cannot be revived because he is in a coma. Smith explains that Colman must make amends for partaking in the revelry by impersonating the prince so that he can be crowned the king, but only until the prince can recover. Colman reluctantly agrees, shaving off his goatee. Meanwhile, Smith and Niven learn that a housekeeper has drugged the wine the prince drank and, while they put the prince into a locked wine cellar to sleep off the drug, they force the traitorous woman to drink the drugged wine before binding and gagging her outside the cellar. They then entrust the prince's safekeeping to a loyal valet with Smith telling the unconscious prince that he will guarantee his coronation by using his cousin as his stand-in to prevent the prince's sinister brother, Massey ("Black Michael"), from ever sitting on the throne. He and Niven then depart with Colman for the coronation. Meanwhile, Massey is shown at his castle where he receives word that his brother had been poisoned to death and is congratulated on the fact that he will now become king of the land. Massey, however, is cautious and demands confirmation that the prince is dead. At that moment, Colman, regally attired as the prince, sits inside a closed compartment on a train heading for Strelsau as Smith and Niven coach him in the lines he is to speak at his coronation and where Colman struggles to memorize that important speech. When the train arrives at Strelsau and a nervous Colman emerges, someone in the crowd shouts: "God save the king!" Smith replies in a low voice: "God save them *both*!" When Colman arrives at the royal hall where he is to be crowned king, Massey stands in shock, now realizing that his brother is very much alive and he turns to his evil henchman, Fairbanks (Rupert of Hentzau) and orders him to return to the royal lodge and discover what went awry with their plans. Massey, holding a monocle, then closely scrutinizes Colman, and, after accepting him as the real prince, bows and offers him his arm and then escorts Colman to the throne area where he is crowned after haltingly stating his memorized lines in accepting that crown. As he sits upon the throne, Colman is startled to see the ravishingly beautiful Carroll (Princess Flavia, his distant cousin and his betrothed) step forward to swear her allegiance to him. As she kneels

Douglas Fairbanks Jr. and Ronald Colman in *The Prisoner of Zenda,* **1937.**

before him, Colman whispers to Smith: "Do I kiss her?" Smith nods and Colman leans forward and kisses Carroll on her cheek. He then leads her from the throne room to be greeted by cheering crowds. They ride together in the royal coach, and Colman, who is completely smitten by the beautiful Carroll, learns that the prince has woefully neglected her in the past, having sent her only two postcards in the last three years to remind her of their engagement. He tells her that she is the loveliest woman in his kingdom, and, to be closer to her, he tells her to bow in his direction to the cheering crowds they pass and he will do the same. Carroll's heart is brightened by the attention Colman gives her, forgiving his mistreatment of the past and now warming to his gentle and romantic conduct. In character, he is a wholly different man from the prince she has known. When later meeting Massey, Colman offhandedly apologizes for slighting him by devoting all his attention to Carroll and that he has acted impetuously because of "the excitement...[since it is] the first time I have ever been crowned." To taunt Massey, Colman tells him that he had an excellent wine the previous night, knowing full well that it was Massey's agents who drugged the prince's wine. After Colman yawns in his face, the offended Massey states: "I see that I bore your majesty," and he withdraws. Carroll knows the evil side of Massey and warns Colman against him, reminding him to be on guard because his life is important to "your country, your friends, and...your cousin and your most loving servant." That night, Colman and Smith secretly depart the palace, leaving Niven behind to guard the king's chamber and where Smith tells him that if anyone forces the door to draw his sword and prevent anyone from entering at the cost of his life. Colman and Smith then go to the royal hunting lodge to retrieve the prince and restore him to the throne Colman has only temporarily occupied. To their shock, they find that the valet has been murdered and the prince is gone. They discover a note left behind by the prince's kidnappers, one ostensibly written by Fairbanks, and reading: "One king is enough for any kingdom." Smith then asks Colman to continue his impersonation, but he has had enough of the charade. Smith reminds him that as long as he continues that impersonation the kidnappers cannot kill the king or even accuse Colman of being an imposter without revealing their own culpability. Smith warns that if Colman quits his role, the king, indeed, will be found dead, and that Massey will not only assume the throne, but will marry Carroll. "You cannot let that happen to her," says Colman. Knowing that Colman has fallen in love with Carroll, Smith responds: "Can you?" Colman agrees to go on playing the king and later escorts Carroll to the royal ball that celebrates his crowning. They step down a resplendent staircase (one of the largest ever offered in any film in one of the most elegant ballroom scenes ever shown) to waltz together. However, whenever Colman stops to talk to Carroll, all of the hundreds of dancers also come to a halt. Seeing that he controls the movement of

everyone in the grand hall, Colman tells Carroll that he will order the celebration to cease unless she agrees to step onto the terrace with him. She smilingly agrees, and they enter a beautiful terrace and enchanting garden, strolling along tranquil lagoons that are gracefully alive with swimming swans. Colman cannot control his passion for this beautiful woman, telling her in one of the most tender love scenes in any film: "I love you...I love you more than truth, or life or honor." They embrace and kiss and Carroll tells Colman that she loves him. He then asks her if she could love him if he were not the king. She gives him the response he longs to hear when she says: "In my heart, there is no king, no crown, only you." Colman is about to reveal his true identity to Carroll when the ever alert Smith arrives to interrupt him, telling him he is called away on important business. When Colman is alone with Smith, he tells Smith that he loves Carroll and that he has been thinking of forever continuing his impersonation so that he can remain with Carroll, so he urges Smith to find the king, "before it is too late." Meanwhile, Fairbanks meets with Massey, informing him that there are "two kings," the one they have abducted and Colman the impersonator. Massey proposes that they kill Colman, bury him as if he were the real king, and then murder the true king, so that he can then take the throne. To that end, Fairbanks sends a message to Colman that will arrange a meeting with Astor, Massey's mistress, and where Astor will tell Colman where the king is being held. Astor, who pretends to be part of Fairbanks' scheme but works against it since she believes that Fairbanks is only using Massey for his own evil purposes, meets with Colman at a remote cottage. She warns Colman that Fairbanks and some henchmen are close by and intend to murder him. To protect Massey against Fairbanks' murderous schemes, Astor then reveals to Colman that the king is being held a prisoner at Fairbanks' castle at Zenda and that she will later give him information on how to rescue the king. When Fairbanks arrives at the cottage, Colman bars the door and Fairbanks, calling Colman "play actor," promises to let him live if he leaves the country, but this is only a ruse as Fairbanks and his two men hold drawn guns and are waiting for Colman to step from the cottage so they can kill him. Distrusting Fairbanks, Colman escapes the cottage and climbs over a wall while Fairbanks and his men exchange shots with Colman and Niven, who has accompanied Colman to the meeting. Once back at the palace, Colman meets briefly with Carroll, telling her he must keep an important rendezvous, but will soon return to her side. Along with Smith and Niven, Colman returns to the king's hunting lodge where Smith assembles some loyal soldiers and they await word from Astor as to how they might invade the castle at Zenda. Fairbanks arrives and attempts to buy off Colman, offering him a fortune to leave the country, but Colman refuses and again escapes death when the treacherous Fairbanks hurls a knife at him that narrowly misses its mark. Fairbanks then successfully flees through a window and rides away on horseback with Smith's men firing after him. After arriving at his castle at Zenda, Fairbanks smirks as Astor tends to the ailing king, who languishes in a dungeon and where he is closely guarded by Fairbanks' henchmen. Fairbanks then taunts the king by opening a trapdoor and telling him that, should anyone try to rescue him, his guards will toss him through that opening, where he will meet a watery death by drowning. Massey then arrives and demands that the king sign a document of abdication, but the king refuses, weakly saying with courage he has not earlier exhibited: "I will not disgrace a crown I never wore." Then Astor sends her trusted servant, Foulger, to meet with Colman, Smith and Niven. Foulger gives them a map of the castle at Zenda, showing them where one man can swim the moat and enter a window of the room occupied by Astor so that he can then get into the dungeon and prevent the guards from drowning the king while he, Foulger, lowers the drawbridge that will allow Smith and Niven to enter the castle with their men. Colman insists that he be the one to swim the moat and enter the castle and rescue the king, telling Smith: "I have been an imposter for your sake. I won't be one for my own." They later go to the castle and Colman swims the moat, climbing into Astor's chamber and, from there, makes his way through the castle hallways to the dungeon while Foulger goes to the mechanism to lower the drawbridge. Fairbanks then invades Astor's room in an attempt to seduce her; he is confronted by Massey and Fairbanks kills Massey. After hearing some noise, Fairbanks rushes into a castle hallway to where Foulger is struggling to lower the drawbridge and kills him by crushing his skull with a pike. Meanwhile, Colman has entered the dungeon and struggles with two guards, killing both of them and telling the ailing king that he will be safe. He locks the door to the king's cell, but is confronted by Fairbanks in the anteroom. There Colman barters for time until he can seize a sword and begins fighting with Fairbanks, and Fairbanks is surprised at Colman's dexterous swordplay. Both men fight through the corridors of the castle, thrusting and parrying frantically, neither able to best the other. When Fairbanks sees that Colman is working his way toward the rope that holds the drawbridge and attempts to cut it, he blocks his path, saying smugly: "I just killed a man for trying that!" As they battle, Colman replies: "An unarmed man, of course." Fairbanks, a blackguard to the core, grins and says: "Of course!" While they battle, Fairbanks taunts Colman with the thought of death and losing Carroll, saying: "Your golden-haired goddess will look well in black, Rassendyll! I'll console her for you...kiss away her tears. What? No quotations?" Colman thrusts his sword forward, saying: "Yes—a barking dog never bites!" Back and forth the two men fight until Colman manages to sever the rope holding the drawbridge, which crashes down and where Smith and Niven lead their men on horseback to thunder across it and into the castle as they shoot down guards protecting the castle. Fairbanks, realizing that his plans have been shattered, jumps to a high window and says, "Farewell play-actor!" He dives through the window and into the moat, swimming away (to survive in the sequel). Colman, though wounded from his fight with Fairbanks, then rushes to the dungeon to remain with the king. Once the king is removed to his palace, he is visited one last time by his lookalike, and the king tells his savior that he is his "best and dearest friend," thanking him for all he has heroically done. Colman then meets with Carroll, begging her to go away with him to England so they can be happy together. Though she tells him that she loves him, she refuses to leave, saying that she is born to the purple and must meet her obligations to her people and her country. Sadly, Colman departs, seen to the border by Smith and Niven and where Niven tells Colman: "Fate does always make the right men kings." Colman turns to Smith and says: "Goodbye, Colonel. We've run a good course together." Smith replies: "Goodbye, Englishman. You are the finest Elfberg of them all!" With that, Colman spurs his horse forward and rides up a hill, waving from a distance before he disappears to end this great film. Cromwell directs with consummate skill in handling the complex plot and its many characters while brilliantly balancing the action and romance scenes and where Colman and Carroll are perfect together as the star-crossed lovers. Fairbanks provides a grinning villain who is also memorable, relishing his role as an evil-doer, and Massey is also chilling as the power-mad brother who will stop at nothing to gain a throne. Astor, although she appears briefly, is both enigmatic and sympathetic as a woman tormented by her lover's ambitions. Howe, a master cinematographer, captures the story with awe-inspiring panoramic scenes, and his shooting of the Colman-Carroll entrance into the grand ballroom is a feast for the eyes. Newman's score is regal and stirring, and the script from Balderston, Root and Stewart is lyrical and packed with wit, its love scenes hauntingly poetic and poignant, wholly capturing that elegant Victorian era of noble-minded adventurers and lovely princesses. Though staged and filmed many times (see the list of all productions for this story in the entry for the 1922 film version), no other production has matched the eloquence and majesty of this stirring classic. The production values for this film are unparalleled as would be expected from the meticulous Selznick, who doted on every aspect of the film. The sets are awe inspiring in their ornate and elaborate construction, and the rich costuming spectacularly adorns all of the players. This film beguiles and inspires with each new viewing, never wearing out its welcome. The cost for this film, $1,250,000, was exor-

Ronald Colman and Madeleine Carroll in *The Prisoner of Zenda*, 1937.

bitant for its day, but it earned back that budget in its initial box office release, returning about $200,000 in profit. Over the years, through rereleases, the film gleaned several more millions. The film received an Oscar nomination for Best Art Direction (Wheeler), and Best Musical Score (Newman, his first of forty-five nominations). Douglas Fairbanks Jr. reprised his role in this film version in a thirty-minute radio adaptation produced by Academy Award Theater on July 17, 1946. A thirty-minute radio adaptation of this version of the story was produced by Screen Director's Playhouse and aired on February 20, 1949, with Ronald Colman reprising his role. Songs: "Artist's Life, Op. 316" (1867; Johann Strauss), "On the Beautiful Blue Danube, Op. 314" (1866; Johann Strauss). *Author's Note*: Producer Selznick was warned by aides not to make this film in that it had worn thin with the public with so many previous productions, but Selznick believed that the story's rich background, intrigue and deep romance had never been fully developed and believed that, as the first talkie version, it would be the success it subsequently became. He shrewdly and correctly believed that the film would benefit from the added public attention riveted upon the upcoming coronation of England's Edward VIII (1894-1972), a reign that lasted only twelve months, until Edward abdicated to marry the woman he loved, Wallis Simpson, a divorced American citizen and a commoner. Cromwell, who was more comfortable with dramas, was beset with many problems during the production, not the least of which was the traditional meddling from Selznick, even though Selznick had hand-picked Cromwell to direct, rightly believing that he would illicit the best performances from the cast. Cromwell told this author that "Jimmy [James Wong Howe] came to me and told me that Colman had a 'bad side' or a profile that might not photograph too well and we had to be careful about that. Well, Madeleine heard about that and then she came to me and said she had a 'bad side,' too, and asked that she only be photographed on her 'good side.' I went to Jimmy and he said that her profiles were perfect and 'you couldn't fault her if you stood her on her head.' I then talked with Madeleine and told her that she photographed beautifully from either profile and, if we tried to photograph her only with Colman and used both of their same sides, we could not make the picture." She got so upset with me that she refused to talk to me for the rest of the production. I could not win." Selznick did mollify Carroll by bringing in director George Cukor, noted for being a "woman's director," to shoot the final love scene between her and Colman; Cukor urged her to become much more assertive and she does by aggressively telling Colman that, though she loves him and will love him as long as she lives, she cannot go away with him and desert her regal duties. So pleased with that scene was Carroll that she forever told anyone who wanted to know that **The Prisoner of Zenda** was her favorite film. Colman, who received $200,000 for his performance in this

Madeleine Carroll and Ronald Colman in *The Prisoner of Zenda*, 1937.

film, was always Selznick's first choice to play the dual roles of commoner and prince. The producer believed Colman was one of the greatest actors alive and took great pains to please him, "although Colman was no Errol Flynn," Cromwell told this author, "and Selznick was not happy with the dueling scene between him and Doug [Fairbanks], so he brought action director Woody [W.S. Van Dyke] to redo that scene and where Woody wore out poor Colman to the point of exhaustion in that swordfight. It was all fun and play for Doug, who was a much younger man, but Colman was forty-five then and no spring chicken. Yet, he somehow managed to keep pace with Doug. When it was finished, Colman said to me: 'I never want to see a sword again as long as I live, now that I have outlived this picture.'" For his part, Fairbanks had been reluctant to take the role of the sinister Hentzau. He had originally wanted to play the dual roles and even tested for the part and was then astonished to hear that Selznick had given the role to Colman. When Selznick offered him the role of the conniving count, Fairbanks stalled and thought to refuse the role. His father, Douglas Fairbanks Sr., however, told him that the character of Rupert of Hentzau was "the best part and the most interesting character in the story," according to Fairbanks' statement to this author. "I decided that if I was going to play this villain I would play him to the hilt, and I did, right up to hilt of my sword. That part did a lot of good as that character and all of his swordplay was remembered by almost every producer I talked to for years after." Astor, who has a small but solid supporting role in the film, told this author that "George Cukor was upset with Selznick for not letting him direct the entire picture and letting Cromwell do it, although George came on the set to direct the last love scene with Madeleine and Ronnie [Colman]. I always thought Cukor was arrogant and much too fussy for my likes. He was gay, you know, and gays have their own mean little agendas. George later claimed that he was behind all of what went on with **The Prisoner of Zenda** and that he insisted that Selznick make the picture to put the Duke of Windsor in his place for shirking his duties as the King of England to marry Mrs. Simpson. Well, all of that is nothing more than George's nonsense. He was not the power behind the picture at all. Cromwell was. And Selznick did not spend more than a million dollars just to teach the Duke of Windsor a lesson. Hollywood producers do a lot of nutty things, believe me, but Selznick was never nutty enough to spend his money so that he could scold the Duke of Windsor. I mentioned this fairy tale—forgive my pun—to Selznick and all he said was 'Oh, you know George thinks he's really the king of Ruritania.'" Massey, the man Astor's character loves, was somewhat nonplussed by the character he was playing, stating to this author that "I never quite understood the nature of 'Black Michael.' I told C. Aubrey Smith, who appeared in that picture with me, that I could not quite get a grasp on my character and he said that he had played every character 'except

Princess Flavia,' in **The Prisoner of Zenda** at one time or another and he never understood the character of 'Black Michael' either. Smith was by then stone deaf and had to use a hearing aid to communicate with anyone. He was the dean of the British community in Hollywood and had his own captain's chair with his name on it on the set. When not before the cameras he sat there with his hearing aid turned off reading the London *Times*, until someone tapped him on the shoulder to indicate that it was time to do another shot or tea time." Cosgrove's special effects are stunning in this film, particularly where Colman shakes hands with his double and drinks wine with him, all of the action achieved through a split screen process and where a stunt man's arm reaches out to actually grasp Colman's hand. The director of the orchestra during the grand ball is Al Shean, who was the legendary costar of the vaudeville team of Gallagher and Shean, as well as the uncle to the Marx Brothers. **p**, David O. Selznick; **d**, John Cromwell (not credited: W.S. Van Dyke, George Cukor); **cast**, Ronald Colman, Madeleine Carroll, Douglas Fairbanks, Jr., Mary Astor, Raymond Massey, C. Aubrey Smith, David Niven, Montagu Love, Philip Sleeman, Wilhel von Brincken, Ralph Faulkner, Torben Meyer, Eleanor Wesselhoeft, Byron Foulger, Francis Ford, Margaret Tallichet, Alexander D'Arcy, Al Shean; **w**, John L. Balderston, Wells Root, Donald Ogden Stewart (based on the novel by Anthony Hope, and the play by Edward Rose); **c**, James Wong Howe; **m**, Alfred Newman; **ed**, James E. Newcom; **art d**, Lyle Wheeler; **spec eff**, Jack Cosgrove.

The Prisoner of Zenda ★★★ 1952; U.S.; 96m; MGM; Color; Adventure/Romance; Children: Cautionary; **DVD**; **VHS**. In this fine remake of the classic adventure tale the swashbuckling Granger essays in grand style the dual roles of the commoner and the king of the mythical Balkan kingdom of Ruritania. He is an Englishman on a fishing vacation when he encounters his royal cousin and lookalike (also played by Granger), discovering they are distant cousins. After spending an evening with the profligate prince, who is about to be crowned king, he, along with the prince's two loyal aides, Calhern and Coote, find that the prince has been drugged and is in a coma. While the prince is placed in the safekeeping of a loyal servant, Calhern convinces Granger to impersonate the prince at his coronation, until the prince can recover. Granger reluctantly agrees and, after a crash course in memorizing his lines and speech for the coronation, attends that lavishly shown event, his likeness to the prince even convincing Douglas, his evil-minded brother, who covets the throne, that he is the real prince. Douglas, however, is amazed that Granger has so quickly recovered from his drugged state in that it was he, while in league with his henchman, Mason (in an outstanding performance as the sinister Rupert of Hentzau), who had arranged the drugging. Granger also wins over the heart of Kerr (Princess Flavia), who is his long-neglected fiancé, and he falls in love with this beautiful woman. Douglas and Mason, however, are not that easily foiled and kidnap the drugged king (by proxy through his cousin's coronation), but dare not kill him until they can get rid of the imposter without exposing their evil plot to seize the throne for Douglas. Granger continues his impersonation at Calhern's insistence until the missing king can be found, but the imposter tells Calhern that he is in love with Kerr and is thinking of remaining in his role so that he can marry the woman he has come to love and therefore urges Calhern and Coote to find the king quickly. Mason and Douglas then lure Granger to a secret meeting with Greer, who is Douglas' mistress, but she tells him that Mason is really out to get rid of the king as well as Douglas so that he can take the throne, and she warns Granger that he is about to be killed by Mason and some of his men. Greer also tells Granger, before he escapes the lethal rendezvous with her, that the real king is being held in a strongly guarded castle at Zenda, and that she will help Granger and his supporters free the king. Granger meets again with Kerr, telling her of his love for her and then departs for the royal hunting lodge with Calhern and Coote to await word from Greer as to how to penetrate the castle at Zenda. Mason, meanwhile, visits Granger and offers him a great deal of money if he will leave the country and the fate of the king to him and Douglas, but the noble-minded Granger refuses and Mason flees after vainly trying once more to kill Granger. Greer sends a trusted servant to Granger, Calhern and Coote, who tells them that one man must swim the moat of the castle at Zenda, climb into the chamber occupied by Greer, and then go to the dungeon and prevent guards from killing the king until he, that servant, can lower the castle's drawbridge that will allow Calhern and Coote to lead their men into the castle. Granger swims that moat, meets with Greer and then goes to the dungeon where he battles with two guards, overpowering them and then locking the king inside his cell. Mason, meanwhile, kills Douglas over Greer's affections, and then kills the servant who is attempting to lower the drawbridge. He then faces Granger and both men begin to battle with swords (one of the outstanding action scenes in this film), but Granger, though wounded, manages to cut the rope holding the drawbridge that allows Calhern and Coote to charge with their men across the drawbridge and into the castle. Knowing his murderous scheme is shattered, Mason bids Granger a mocking farewell, dives into the moat and swims away (one of the most sinister villains ever to make an escape in any romantic adventure, albeit his character, Rupert of Hentzau, meets his comeuppance in a sequel written by author Hope). The king expresses his gratitude to his commoner cousin for saving his life and preserving his kingdom. When Granger the commoner goes to Kerr and begs her to run away with him to England, she tells him that even though she loves him more than any other man and always will, her place is in Ruritania and that she must fulfill her royal obligations to her people and they part forever. Granger is escorted to the border by the grateful Calhern and Coote, and Calhern tells Granger that he is the greatest member of the royal family before Granger rides away at the finale. Director Thorpe, an expert hand at adventure films and period productions, having directed the superlative **Ivanhoe**, 1952, provides a top-flight action tale where Granger, Kerr, Mason, Greer and Calhern excel in their roles, capturing the romance and dash of that Victorian era. Quality and care shows in the film's lavish and well-conceived sets and the costuming is stunning, particularly in this first color version of the Hope tale. Newman's memorable and dynamic score from the 1937 production is offered again note for note. *Author's Note*: Thorpe told this author that directing this exceptional remake of the Hope story was "a walk-through as I worked from the original 1937 shooting script that Selznick and his writers produced and it was about as detailed as anyone could hope to have. I really did not have any problems with the cast as all of the players were very cooperative, except for maybe Mason, who complained about his costumes." In that regard, Mason told this author that "the wardrobe people at MGM simply duplicated the same costumes that had been worn in the 1937 picture, changing a few buttons and frills here and there. To tell you the truth, the costumes I wore in that picture made me look like a liveried chauffeur instead of a powerful count. When I complained about that to Thorpe, he told me to talk to wardrobe and they told me to talk to Thorpe so I quit talking about it." A workhorse at MGM, Thorpe was much appreciated by the front office in that he invariably brought his films within budget and under schedules simply through his methodical shooting procedures. Granger, who would be under Thorpe's direction the following year in **All the Brothers Were Valiant**, 1953, told this author that "Thorpe did not like doing retakes and avoided that at every turn. In **The Prisoner of Zenda**, he did what he always did, and that is start shooting with a long shot and then go to a medium shot of, say, two or three actors, and keep shooting until someone miscued or fluffed a line. He would then stop, eliminate the botched part of the scene, and continue the same scene with a close-up. He had his own assembly-line method of making films and as long as everyone stayed with their roles and followed their movement cues, and spoke their lines without mistakes, everything worked out fine. They called Thorpe a 'money director' because he saved the studio money." Kerr told this author that "it was impossible for me to duplicate the role Madeleine Carroll had so well created in the 1937 version of that picture—and what a beautiful

Stewart Granger and James Mason in *The Prisoner of Zenda*, 1952.

woman she truly was—so I played the role with even more reserve. Someone said I was turning my character into a little mouse, but I reminded that person that I was playing a princess in a day when women had little or nothing to say about anything, even princesses, and that my character was, indeed, a bird in a gilded cage." The equally beautiful Greer, who had made a career of playing femme fatales, particularly in **Out of the Past**, 1947, and **The Big Steal**, 1948 (both with Robert Mitchum), told this author: "Before I appeared as the mistress in **The Prisoner of Zenda**, I talked with Mary Astor, who had played that part in the 1937 version. Her only advice to me was: 'Your character is an unmarried woman sleeping with a murderous aristocrat, and why she loves this man I do not know. Do your best, dearie.'" Ironically, Stone, who starred in the 1922 film version of this exciting adventure tale, plays the part of the Cardinal who officiates in the coronation scene of this production. **p**, Pandro S. Berman; **d**, Richard Thorpe; **cast**, Stewart Granger, Deborah Kerr, James Mason, Jane Greer, Louis Calhern, Lewis Stone, Robert Douglas, Robert Coote, Peter Brocco, Francis Pierlot, Thomas Browne Henry, Eric Alden, Stephen Roberts, Bud Wolfe; **w**, John L. Balderston, Noel Langley, Wells Root, Donald Ogden Stewart (based on the novel by Anthony Hope, and the play by Edward Rose); **c**, Joseph Ruttenberg; **m**, Alfred Newman; **ed**, George Boemler; **art d**, Cedric Gibbons, Hans Peters; **set d**, Edwin B. Willis, Richard Pefferle; **spec eff**, Warren Newcombe.

Prisoners of the Sun ★★★ 1990; Australia; 108m; Blood Oath Productions/Skouras Pictures; Color; War Drama; Children: Unacceptable (MPAA: R); **DVD**; **VHS**. This gripping tale depicts an investigation into a WWII Japanese atrocity. During World War II (1939-1945), more than a thousand Australian soldiers were held as prisoners of war in a Japanese camp on the island of Ambon just north of Australia. After the war, Brown, an Australian army captain, investigates the deaths of 300 Australian airmen whose bodies are found in a mass grave. He suspects they were executed on orders of the camp's commander, Takei, who is returned to the island in the custody of O'Quinn, an American major, who does not seem to want Takei convicted. Politics become involved and the Japanese government lobbies for Takei's release from a war crimes trial while the U.S. does not want to expose the Japanese atrocity because of post-war efforts in peace-making. No one is blamed but everyone knows it was an example of war crimes. Excessive violence prohibits viewing by children. **p**, Denis Whitburn, Charles Waterstreet, Annie Bleakley; **d**, Stephen Wallace; **cast**, Bryan Brown, George Takei, Terry O'Quinn, John Bach, Toshi Shioya, John Clarke, Deborah Unger, John Polson, Russell Crowe, Nicholas Eadie, Jason Donovan, Tetsu Watanabe, Sokyu Fujita; **w**, Whitburn, Brian A. Williams; **c**, Russell Boyd; **m**, David McHugh; **ed**, Nicholas Beauman; **prod d**, Bernard

Goldie Hawn in *Private Benjamin*, 1980.

Hides; **art d**, Virginia Bieneman; **set d**, Susan Maybury; **spec eff**, Brian Pearce.

The Private Affairs of Bel Ami ★★★ 1947; U.S.; 112m; UA; B/W; Drama; Children: Unacceptable; **VHS**. Sanders gives a wonderful performance as a consummate rake as he uses women to climb up the social ladder in Paris in the 1850s. He has an affair with Wilson, a café frequenter, and goes on to charm Lansbury into a relationship. Carradine gets him a job as a writer on a French newspaper and, after his benefactor dies, Sanders marries his widow, Dvorak, for her money. He soon abandons her in his pursuit of a royal title. This leads him to learn that he may get away with dalliances with common women, but he cannot romance his way into France's most noble houses. In addition to standout acting from Sanders, Lansbury, Dvorak, Dee and Carradine, Lewin provides a seamless tale with superb lensing from Metty and an exceptional score from Milhaud. Song: "My Bel Ami" (Jack Lawrence, Irving Drutman). *Author's Note*: The Motion Picture Production Code of that day demanded that the more explicit sexual elements of the Maupassant tale be subdued and, to that end, the streetwalkers in the original story are portrayed as dancers with loose morals. Sanders told this author that "my character in that picture is a total libertine, my kind of man, but the old censorship board they had in Hollywood then insisted that he pay for his immorality and endless dalliances and trysts by being killed in the end. What a waste of a great scoundrel!" To characterize Sanders' amoral character, a painting by Max Ernst, "The Temptation of St. Anthony," is shown briefly in Technicolor, a ploy used two years earlier where the rotting soul of a similar and more lethal mountebank is also revealed in a portrait and also briefly shown in color (in an otherwise black-and-white film as is this one) in **The Picture of Dorian Gray**, 1945, which also featured Sanders. Sexual themes prohibit viewing by children. **p**, David L. Loew; **d&w**, Albert Lewin (based on the novel *Bel Ami* by Guy de Maupassant); **cast**, George Sanders, Angela Lansbury, Ann Dvorak, Frances Dee, John Carradine, Susan Douglas, Warren William, Hugo Haas, Albert Bassermann, Marie Wilson, Katherine Emery; **c**, Russell Metty; **m**, Darius Milhaud; **ed**, Albrecht Joseph; **prod d**, Gordon Wiles; **art d**, Frank Sylos; **set d**, Edward Boyle; **spec eff**, Tom Lawless, Robert Moreland.

Private Benjamin ★★★ 1980; U.S.; 109m; WB; Color; Comedy; Children: Unacceptable (MPAA: R); **DVD**; **VHS**. Hawn proves exceptional while enacting a "Jewish princess," a society girl whose husband dies on their wedding night while making love to her. She decides to get a new life by joining the Women's Army Corps, but gets more reality than she expects from Brennan, her tough-as-nails captain, and a colonel, Webber, a philanderer who is always making sexual advances. She is transferred

to NATO headquarters in Europe and has a brief affair with Assante, a French physician, who is also Jewish, a relationship that ends after it is learned that he belonged to a communist organization. This delightful comedy about a misfit in the peacetime army provides a lot of laughs through a clever script. Songs: "Hava Nagila" (Israeli folk song), "Down by the Riverside" (traditional), "Body and Soul" (Edward Heyman, Robert Sour, Frank Eyton, Johnny Green), "We Are Family" (Bernard Edwards, Nile Rodgers), "Bridal Chorus" (from "Lohengrin" by Richard Wagner). Sexuality prohibits viewing by children. **p&w**, Nancy Meyers, Charles Shyer, Harvey Miller; **d**, Howard Zieff; **cast**, Goldie Hawn, Eileen Brennan, Armand Assante, Robert Webber, Sam Wanamaker, Barbara Barrie, Mary Kay Place, Harry Dean Stanton, Albert Brooks, Alan Oppenheimer; **c**, David M. Walsh (Technicolor); **m**, Bill Conti; **ed**, Sheldon Kahn; **prod d**, Robert Boyle, Jeffrey Howard; **set d**, Arthur Jeph Parker; **spec eff**, Robert Peterson.

The Private Files of J. Edgar Hoover ★★★ 1977; U.S.; 112m; Larco Productions/American International; B/W; Biographical Drama; Children: Unacceptable (MPAA: PG); **VHS**. The tyrannical J. Edgar Hoover (1895-1972) is aptly portrayed in one of the first theatrically released feature films to depict his widespread abuse of power. The ambitious Hoover is shown in young adulthood by Wainwright when he joins the Department of Justice as a young attorney, focusing upon the then terrorist acts practiced by anarchists and how he comes to obsessively believe that these political malcontents present the most serious danger to the U.S., a lifelong obsession that would deflect Hoover's more needed attention to organized crime, which Hoover consistently claimed never existed. He is then assigned to the Bureau of Investigation, but, after he complains about the Bureau's ineptitude and outright corruption to U.S. Attorney General Harlan Fiske Stone (1872-1946), well played by Nolan, he is made head of the bureau with orders to clean up the agency. This he does, renaming the agency the Federal Bureau of Investigation or FBI, and roots out the deadwood and boondoggling agents, establishing many new crime techniques and forensic departments such as the Bureau's renowned fingerprint division. As time passes, however, and where an aging Hoover is played by a jowly and paunchy Crawford, his character takes on a more sinister personality, where he begins to abuse his office of authority. Although he curries favor with many U.S. Presidents to fatten the Bureau's budgets and broaden his powers, he is at loggerheads with the newly elected President John F. Kennedy (1917-1963), played by Jordan, disliking his liberal policies, and soon develops a contentious relationship with Kennedy's younger, feisty brother, Robert F. Kennedy (1925-1968), the newly appointed U.S. Attorney General, played by Parks. When both of these men are later assassinated, Crawford shows no sympathy for their terrible fates, seeming to gloat in surviving them and believing that their policies were irresponsible and reckless and actually brought about their demises. Crawford further becomes irrationally angered by the nation-wide attention created by civil rights activist Martin Luther King Jr. (1929-1968), played by St. Jacques, and attempts to discredit the black leader by monitoring his private life with his agents and even with illegal wiretaps. Crawford obtains this information (its credibility always in question) so that he can leak King's supposed extramarital affairs to the press, particularly through his crony, nationally syndicated newspaper columnist Walter Winchell (1897-1972), ironically played by Gough (Gough was blacklisted in Hollywood in the early 1950s as a communist sympathizer much through the efforts of Hoover). Crawford continues to assemble such illegal files on politicians and personalities, using them as dangerous tools by which he blackmails and coerces his political opponents into granting him more and more power while they bend to his tyrannical procedures and dictates, until he becomes the most powerful and dreaded man in the country after the President, the real power behind the throne. Countless such victims are relieved when Crawford suddenly dies of a heart attack and this dark nemesis is no longer alive to continue his misuse of power. Wainwright is believable as the young Hoover, and Crawford is the epitome of the aging Hoover, a fulminating, dour, and oppressive man without humor and as dangerous as a loaded gun in the hand of an irrational human being. The film presents a good case against this dictatorial bureaucrat and even provides a very humorous scene, albeit unintentional, when Crawford and Dailey, who plays Clyde Tolson (1900-1975), Associate Director of the FBI and Hoover's closest friend, explode with anger after learning that a Washington reporter has stated that they are lovers (this tale was always a closet rumor about Hoover and Tolson, but one never proved). Many actors have portrayed Hoover in films, notably **Bananas**, 1971 (Dorthi Fox, a black actress, cast by comedian Woody Allen to mock Hoover's dislike for blacks and to enforce rumors that Hoover was a cross-dresser or transvestite, none of which was ever supported in fact; Hoover died a year after this film was released); **The Brink's Job**, 1978 (Sheldon Leonard); **The FBI Story**, 1959 (Will J. White; and Hoover in archival footage); **G-Men**, 1935 (role model for Addison Richards, who plays the FBI leader under the name of Bruce J. Gregory); **The House on 92nd Street**, 1945 (himself); **J. Edgar**, 2011 (Leonardo DiCaprio); **Nixon**, 1995 (Bob Hoskins); **No God, No Master**, 2012 (Sean McNall); and **Public Enemies**, 2009 (Billy Crudup). For a complete list of such biopics and the actors who played Hoover, see Index, Historical Persons, Volume II of this work. For further details on Hoover, see my book *Citizen Hoover: A Critical Study of the Life and Times of J. Edgar Hoover and His FBI* (Nelson-Hall, 1972). *Author's Note*: Holm (who was a lifelong liberal Democrat) told this author that "the only reason I agreed to appear in that picture about Hoover is because I thought him to be an ogre and I knew it was going to rake him over the coals. He had that coming for a long time. I believed him to be a bigot and tin-pot dictator, who had made life miserable for thousands and thousands of innocent people. J. Edgar Hoover was a nightmare banging on your door in the middle of the night and threatening you with extinction." Nolan told this author that he was selected for his brief role as U.S. Attorney General Harlan Fiske Stone "simply because I had appeared in many films where I played the role of FBI agents [**G-Men**, 1935; **The House on 92nd Street**, 1945, and **The Street with No Name**, 1948]. Cohen [the director] tried to get approval to shoot at important locations in Washington, D.C., like the inner sanctum of the FBI, but he got nowhere. Then Betty Ford learned that Dan Dailey was in Washington to make a film—she didn't really know what it was about and probably thought it was a musical. She had been a dancer and always liked Dailey's musical films so she invited him and Crawford to the White House to have lunch. Well, when Cohen heard about that, he began making calls to the Bureau and everywhere else in Washington, saying that he wanted to film scenes at the Bureau, but could not do it until the day after his cast members had lunch at the White House. The Bureau people thought that the White House was behind the film, so they all opened their doors to him. Next thing you know he is shooting scenes in Hoover's old office with Crawford sitting at his desk, and in and out of the Bureau's corridors and departments and even at the FBI training area in Quantico [Virginia]. He even got the Mayflower Hotel to let him shoot there because Hoover ate lunch there every day and he had Hoover's favorite waiter in the film. He even used Hoover's barber at that hotel for one scene. Cohen was a very clever fellow, I can tell you. Everyone got a big surprise when Cohen premiered the film at the Kennedy Center in Washington, to see how he lambasted Hoover, but most of those in the audience were carping and complaining about how the picture was critical of both Democrats and Republicans, because it did not show the Kennedys or Richard Nixon in any kind of favorable light." Two decades earlier, Frank Capra got the same kind of disdainful response when he premiered **Mr. Smith Goes to Washington**, 1939, before Washington dignitaries and where they walked out almost to a man and woman. **p,d&w**, Larry Cohen; **cast**, Broderick Crawford, José Ferrer, Michael Parks, Ronee Blakley, Rip Torn, Celeste Holm, Dan Dailey, Howard Da Silva, William Jordan, Michael Parks, John Marley, Raymond St. Jacques, June Havoc, Lloyd Nolan, Andrew Duggan,

Charles Laughton and Elsa Lanchester in *The Private Life of Henry VIII*, 1933.

George Plimpton, Jack Cassidy, Brad Dexter, William Wellman, Jr.; **c**, Paul Glickman; **m**, Miklós Rózsa; **ed**, Christopher Lebenzon; **prod d**, Cathy Davis; **set d**, Carolyn Lowenstein.

The Private Life of Henry VIII ★★★★ 1933; U.K.; 97m; London Film Productions/UA; Biographical Drama; Children: Unacceptable; **DVD**; **VHS**. Laughton gives a bravura performance of England's dynamic and defiant Henry VIII (1491-1547), oozing tyranny and terror as he struts and stomps his way through his rule, discarding queens and acquiring mistresses at will. Laughton's Henry is seen in his palace where he treats state and international problems as pesky details, concentrating on marrying a wife that will produce a son and heir. To that obsessive end, we see him with Oberon, who plays Anne Boleyn (1501/1507-1536), the woman that started Henry's problems with the Catholic Church, after Laughton has divorced, in defiance of the Church, his first wife, Catherine of Aragon (1485-1536), who is not shown in the film, the prologue explaining that she was "far too respectable to be included." The fetching Oberon, however, has a short-lived reign as England's consort queen in that, failing to produce a son at birth, although she did produce a girl, who later became Elizabeth I (1533-1603), she becomes a doomed woman. Unable to provide Laughton with that much-desired male heir, she is sent to the block to lose her head. Oberon is charged and convicted of treason, adultery and incest in a trumped up case after Laughton decides to discard her after dallying with Jane Seymour (1508-1537), played by Barrie. That wife dies in childbirth, giving Laughton that male heir (Edward VI, 1537-1553), and Laughton's roving eye next focuses upon Lanchester, who plays German princess Anne of Cleves (1515-1557), and who was married to Laughton in real life (since 1929). Lanchester is wary of the king's terrible manners, profligacy and promiscuity and wants nothing to do with this slob of a man. In some of the most humorous moments in the film, Lanchester goes out of her way to make herself unattractive, adorning herself with dowdy attire, ungainly hairdos and a grimacing sour face, all done so that Laughton will not want her for a wife, their marriage having been established through state arrangements. When Laughton arrives at the regal bed chamber to consummate his marriage to Lanchester and sees this hideous looking woman, he utters a line that would become a classic in film history, sighing to himself: "The things I've done for England!" Lanchester employs a German accent so thick that it is often hard to understand her words, but that is a device she is using to free herself from this demanding monarch. She achieves that end on her wedding night when besting Laughton in a game of cards (another memorable scene in this immensely enjoyable film). Laughton is so disgusted with this woman that he divorces Lanchester and sends her packing. He next marries Barnes, the alluring Catherine Howard (1523-1542), but Laughton

Robert Stephens, Genevieve Page and Colin Blakely in *The Private Life of Sherlock Holmes,* 1970.

finds her cheating on him with his most trusted friend, Donat, who plays Thomas Culpepper (1514-1541), and sends them both to the chopping block. By the end of the film, Laughton has used up all his energy as a manic monarch and is no longer a table-thumping, ravenously eating glutton, but a subdued and docile king, easily ordered about by Gregg, who plays his last wife, Catherine Parr (1512-1548) as a bossy shrew, who, unlike most of Henry's wives, managed to survive him, but only by a year. The film belongs wholly to Laughton, who won an Oscar for his outstanding (if not incredibly obnoxious and repulsive) performance, the first actor in a British production to win that coveted award. The film was also nominated as Best Picture, another precedent for the British film industry. No one in the film comes anywhere near his extravagant and outlandish performance, but Lanchester comes close to stealing some of his scenes. Korda directs this film with a sure hand and was shrewd enough to employ the gifted French cinematographer Perinal, who captured all of Laughton's amazing tantrums, perfectly providing close-ups of his eating binges to show how he shovels food into a gaping mouth while manhandling without utensils a roasted chicken, which he tears apart with bare hands and gnaws upon, its grease and residue coating his otherwise luxuriant beard. Further, the elaborate costumes are appropriate for the era and the majestic and awe-inspiring sets from Vincent Korda (the producer-director's brother) are stunning, but only because of the way Perinal masterfully photographed them as they were really threadbare sets from long-ago films. Many actors have portrayed Henry VIII in numerous films, notably **Anne of the Thousand Days**, 1969 (Richard Burton); **A Man for All Seasons**, 1966 (Robert Shaw); **The Pearls of the Crown**, 1938 (Lyn Harding); **The Prince and the Pauper**, 1937 (Montagu Love); **When Knighthood Was in Flower**, 1922 (Lyn Harding); and Laughton again in **Young Bess**, 1953. *Author's Note*: The Hungarian-born Korda was at financial loose ends when thinking to produce and direct this film. He admired Laughton, who had appeared in several major films to this time, and was looking about for a vehicle that would fit that actor's unusual personality when he reportedly saw a statue of Henry VIII and thought its facial likeness to that of Laughton was almost identical. Another tale had it that Korda got the idea for the film when joking with a London cabdriver, who repeated the old line, "I'm Enery the Eighth I am, I am!" At the time, Korda found it difficult to find funding for the film, scraping up £60,000 to produce it, and where all the cast members, including Laughton, took deferred salaries. It saw an instant overnight success at the box office, however, producing more than £500,000 in its initial release (and would produce another £300,000 in rereleases). The film made Laughton and Oberon overnight international stars and so well established Korda that he became one of the top British filmmakers; United Artists, the U.S. distributor of this film (the U.S. being the largest and most lucrative

market), then one of the foremost film distributors, gave him a contract for sixteen more films. Director Alfred Hitchcock, who directed Laughton in **Jamaica Inn**, 1939, and **The Paradine Case**, 1947, told this author that "Charles did as he pleased in playing Henry VIII as Korda gave him all the latitude he wanted in portraying that incredible character. I asked Charles how he went about it and he said: 'Henry was an utter pig with women and had no manners at all. Having a porcine-looking face, I intended to play him just like that. The more I played the slobbering glutton [in the unforgettable feast scene], the more Korda loved it. No one ever forgot that scene where I am gnawing on a mutton chop or a chicken leg or whatever it was. I looked like some animal out of the woods, gulping and talking at the same time, with food flying from my mouth to land everywhere. I found that scene difficult as the food they gave me was cold and had no seasoning.'" Hitchcock added: "For some time after that picture, when Charles would go into a restaurant, the waiters would bring him a whole roast chicken on a large platter and give him no utensils with which to eat it. Of course, it was a joke, but Charles did not laugh. His performance had caught up with him." **p**, Alexander Korda, Ludovico Toeplitz; **d**, Korda; **cast**, Charles Laughton, Robert Donat, Binnie Barnes, Elsa Lanchester, Merle Oberon, Wendy Barrie, Everley Gregg, Lady Tree, Franklin Dyall, Miles Mander, Lawrence Hanray, Claude Allister, John Loder, William Austin, John Turnbull, Frederick Culley, Judy Kelly; **w**, Lajos Biro, Arthur Wimperis; **c**, Georges Perinal; **m**, Kurt Schroeder; **ed**, Stephen Harrison; **art d**, Vincent Korda; **spec eff**, W. Percy Day.

The Private Life of Sherlock Holmes ★★★ 1970; U.K.; 125m; Mirisch/UA; Color; Mystery; Children: Cautionary (MPAA: GP); **DVD**; **VHS**. Stephens is convincing as the great detective, who takes on a case involving the disappearance of a family of midgets. He and his friend, Blakely (Dr. Watson) enter an adventure with humor that includes some villainous monks, a Scottish castle, the Loch Ness monster, and some covert British naval experiments. Queen Victoria (1819-1901), who is played by Maureen, also appears, and Stephens deduces that the alluring Page is a German spy behind all the mysteries, chiefly where the Germans are trying to learn the British plans for a new type of warship, a submarine, which is being secretly constructed in Scotland (it's a mini-sub and therefore requires a crew of midgets). Wilder directs this mystery with a lot of comic flair, and the cast, particularly Lee, who plays Sherlock's older brother, a member of the British intelligence community, render top-flight performances. Rozsa's dynamic and memorable score strongly supports the mystery and the action. Music: "Concerto for Violin and Orchestra Opus 24" (Miklos Rozsa). **p&d**, Billy Wilder; **cast**, Robert Stephens, Colin Blakely, Genevieve Page, Christopher Lee, Tamara Toumanova, Clive Revill, Irene Handl, Mollie Maureen, Stanley Holloway, Catherine Lacey; **w**, Wilder, I.A.L. Diamond (based on characters created by Sir Arthur Conan Doyle); **c**, Christopher Challis; **m**, Miklos Rozsa; **ed**, Ernest Walter; **prod d**, Alexander Trauner; **art d**, Tony Inglis; **set d**, Harry Cordwell; **spec eff**, Cliff Richardson, Wally Veevers.

Private Lives ★★★ 1931; U.S.; 84m; MGM; B/W; Comedy; Children: Acceptable; **DVD**; **VHS**. Though this ultra-sophisticated tale from playwright Coward has aged somewhat, it remains a thoroughly entertaining and charming film, crackling with humor and wit. Shearer and Montgomery are divorced and have married two decidedly boring people. She has just wed stuffed shirt Denny and Montgomery has recently tied the knot with methodical Merkel. Ironically the newlyweds arrive at the very French hotel where Shearer and Montgomery spent their honeymoon some years ago, and when each momentarily leaves their spanking new spouses and stroll onto adjoining balconies, they are surprised and delighted to see each other. Separately, they have not been having a very good time with their newly acquired mates and are relieved to be in each other's company again as they are imaginative persons, sharing their love for caprice and adventure. In short order, the newlyweds begin arguing with each other, and Shearer and Montgomery come to suspect that they have made terrible mistakes in remarrying. Denny is a stick-in-the-mud conservative and Merkel is as dull as a rusty knife. The old spark between Shearer and Montgomery soon becomes a flame and both realize that they are still deeply in love with each other. Ignoring the strict social and legal rules of divorce, they slip away from their present spouses and go to a mountain retreat and are soon making torrid love, but their passion is also fueled by fiery temperaments that soon explode and they fall back to the old bickering and wild arguments that brought about their separation. In their rages, both become very physical, and Shearer finally lands a haymaker on Montgomery's chin (she was not expert in pulling her punches and actually knocked out Montgomery in this wild fracas, one that director Franklin believed was so hilarious that he decided to keep the shot in the movie). Then Denny and Merkel track down their missing mates at the retreat, and are so indignant at their spouses' promiscuous misbehavior that they get into a vicious argument, each accusing the other of making the mistake of marrying irresponsible people. Witnessing this explosive confrontation, Shearer and Montgomery are reminded that, despite their contentious natures, they are, as they have always been, made for each other, and that they can surmount and survive any contretemps as long as their intense love for one another exists. Shearer and Montgomery embrace and they leave Denny and Merkel to their own fates and go off to make another new life together, proving to the world that love is stronger than regimen and protocol. Director Franklin presents this charming tale with an adept and sure hand, but admitted that he had much to work with in that the original Coward play was almost translated word for word and scene for scene from the stage to the film production. The film was a great success, and furthered the careers of all the fine players, who are standouts in their distinctive roles. The play is a perennial that has been revived many times over the decades and with many noted actresses appearing on the stage in the role that Gertrude Lawrence (who appeared in the original stage production) and Shearer made famous, including Tallulah Bankhead, Maggie Smith and Elizabeth Taylor. *Author's Note*: MGM's head of production, Irving Thalberg, purchased the rights to the Coward play as a vehicle for his wife, Shearer. The play had first been staged in Edinburgh, Scotland, opening on August 18, 1930, with Gertrude Lawrence and Laurence Olivier in the leading roles and then went on to a five-week tour throughout England before opening in London on September 24, 1930, with Coward limiting its run for three months. The play sold out throughout that period, ending December 20, 1930. Coward then brought the play to New York, where it opened at Times Square Theater on January 27, 1931, and where it enjoyed 256 performances. By that time, Thalberg had seen the play and quickly bought the film rights from Coward. Thalberg then had the New York performance filmed so that director Franklin could translate the work as it originally appeared on the stage. (Such filming of a play today would not be tolerated by Actor's Equity, but in those days Hollywood did mostly as it pleased.) A lot of the lines of dialog in this elegant production are tied to smoking cigarettes, which is a decided taboo these days, and the word "God" in the original film was a word not to be employed lightly in Hollywood, so when one character asks for a cigarette in the original play, saying "For God's sake, give me one," that line was changed in the film to "Give me one for the love of Heaven." Shearer personally selected Montgomery as her leading man as she had worked harmoniously with the actor in three previous and successful films (**Their Own Desire**, 1929; **The Divorcee**, 1930; and **Strangers May Kiss**, 1931). "Norma [Shearer] took me into big time comedy with **Private Lives**," Montgomery told this author, "a picture that assured my acting career for some time to come. She was a darling person, kind and considerate to all and the most gentle lady I ever met, but she surprised me when, in one scene in that picture, she is compelled to strike me. Well, she was not experienced with hitting people on camera and was unsteady in pulling her punches, and she landed a terrific blow that put stars in my eyes. I was unconscious for some time and when I came to, Norma was

Robert Montgomery and Norma Shearer in *Private Lives*, **1931**.

crying and so upset with what she had done that I wound up consoling her instead of the other way around. Sidney [Franklin] was so delighted with that knockout that he told us that he would keep it in the picture. Norma kept apologizing to me for days after that, but I told her not to worry about it. From that point on, however, I was very careful in protecting my chin in doing any scene with any person, and that went for small children, animals, and swinging overhead microphones." Songs: "Someday I'll Find You" (1931; music and lyrics: Noel Coward), "Bridal Chorus (Here Comes the Bride)" (1850; from "Lohengrin" by Richard Wagner), "Chansonette (The Donkey Serenade)" (1923; Rudolf Friml), "A Shady Tree" (1927; music: Walter Donaldson). **p**, Irving Thalberg (not credited); **d**, Sidney Franklin; **cast**, Norma Shearer, Robert Montgomery, Reginald Denny, Una Merkel, Jean Hersholt, George Davis, Herman Bing, Ferike Boros, Alphonse Martell, Wilfrid North; **w**, Hans Kraly, Richard Schayer, Claudine West (based on the play by Noel Coward); **c**, Ray Binger; **m**, William Axt; **ed**, Conrad A. Nervig; **art d**, Cedric Gibbons.

The Private Lives of Elizabeth and Essex ★★★ 1939; U.S.; 106m; WB; Color; Adventure/Romance; Children: Unacceptable; **DVD**; **VHS**. The dynamic Davis gives a bravura performance of Queen Elizabeth I (1533-1603), while being romanced almost from her throne by military adventurer Robert Devereux (1565-1601), played by the dashing Flynn. This lavishly produced film begins when Flynn arrives triumphant in England after sacking Cadiz. Although he is much admired by the public, when Flynn arrives at the royal court, he is treated with disdain and anger by Davis. She humiliates him before the entire court by publicly chastising him for not bringing her the riches of Spain, and where, in order to deny England of this vast treasure, Flynn has allowed the Spanish to simply sink their treasure ships. She then turns to Price, who plays a slavish Sir Walter Raleigh (1554-1618), and who has long been a rival in seeking Davis' favors, and where she appoints him to a new high office, making him Flynn's superior. Before the emotionally damaged Flynn retires to his estates, de Havilland, who is Davis' most trusted lady-in-waiting, and who loves Flynn deeply, goes to him and warns him against any rash actions, knowing that he has a deep ambition to acquire power at almost any cost. She tells him to be on guard as Davis is a fiercely dominating monarch who will tolerate no rebellious nobles in her court, a court that is thick with intrigue, and where almost all of her courtiers are self-serving and few can be called Flynn's friends. He does have one powerful friend in that court, Crisp, who plays Francis Bacon (1561-1626), Davis's foremost statesman and adviser. Crisp, a gifted orator and author, who has a way with words, soothes the feisty monarch and convinces her to meet with Flynn, assuring her that, though headstrong, Flynn is utterly loyal to her. Davis meets with Flynn and

Bette Davis and Errol Flynn in *The Private Lives of Elizabeth and Essex,* **1939.**

they begin, as usual, to argue about state matters and what might be best for England's future. Davis is as wary as was the real Elizabeth in dealing with this clever young man, half romancer, half rogue, knowing full well that he intends to marry her and become king, sharing the throne with her, but the thought of her giving up any of her power is, in her mind, unthinkable. She calls a cabinet meeting where several conniving courtiers attend, including Price, Daniell (playing Robert Cecil, 1563-1612), and Stephenson (playing William Cecil or Lord Burghley, 1520-1598), and where these artful and manipulative men goad Flynn into accepting a next-to-impossible mission. He is to crush the widespread rebellion in Ireland led by the powerful Hugh O'Neill, Earl of Tyrone (1550-1616), played by Hale. Davis sees that such an expedition might lead to disaster, but Flynn's pride overcomes his reason when he insists on leading an English army to Ireland to stamp out the rebellion led by Hale. Davis, angered at Flynn's rash judgment, nevertheless gives him the authority to take troops to Ireland. Flynn is next seen leading those forces through the swamps and bogs of Ireland as he gropes for the elusive enemy, an enemy always beyond his reach. Meanwhile, Hale uses guerrilla tactics to make lighting attacks against Flynn's troops, gradually reducing those forces in a prolonged war of attrition. Flynn writes to Davis, urgently requesting supplies and reinforcements, but receives no response. Matters become worse when all of Flynn's communications to Davis are intercepted by Price and Stephenson, his avowed enemies, and who dupe the trusting de Havilland into turning over those important missives to them, which are then kept from Davis, who becomes increasingly angered over not hearing from Flynn. With his men near starvation, Flynn is finally surrounded by overwhelming forces led by Hale, who gives him honorable terms. He must surrender and quit Ireland, but will be allowed to leave the country with what remains of his army. Having no other recourse, Flynn accepts and returns in disgrace to England where he is received by an enraged Davis, who accuses him of irresponsibility, chiefly in that he has neglected to communicate with her. Flynn, however, is also enraged, believing that Davis has allowed him and his forces to die on the vine without supporting them with much-needed supplies and reinforcements. In fact, he has the advantage with her at this point since he has entered London with his army and where he still remains popular with the public. He has entered Davis' palace with his own men and has, for all purposes, seized her government. Knowing she is a prisoner, Davis uses her considerable diplomacy, telling Flynn that she never received his messages and that they were obviously intercepted and kept from her by scheming members of her court. None of that matters now to Flynn as he is consumed by only one ambition, that Davis marry him and share her power with him and where he will be king of England. Davis stalls for time, looking for a way out while the troubled de Havilland realizes that she has been hoodwinked by

Price, Daniell and Stephenson in turning over to them all of Flynn's messages to Davis. She plans to reveal this cabalistic scheme to Davis, but the insidious Daniell terrifies her into silence by telling her: "You have a lovely head and neck, milady. It would be a pity to separate them." Flynn then begins to outline his plans for England as its new ruler; Davis appears to accept his proposal, but demands his trust by telling him he must dismiss his men and that her regular palace guard be returned to duty. The wary Flynn is won over by Davis when she infers that she will marry him and announce him as joint ruler of England. He sends his men away, but, as soon as the old palace guards return, Davis coldly orders Flynn arrested and sent to the Tower of London, to be held there on charges of treason. He is condemned to death, but Davis, who loves him, meets with Flynn once more, offering to marry him and make him her consort, but telling him that he will not rule with her and that she alone will be the only monarch in England. Flynn refuses, telling her that even though he loves her, he insists that he alone shall rule England and, if denied the crown, he prefers death. Davis cannot give up her throne and, her heart torn apart, allows the man she loves most to go to his death, the film ending as this star-crossed romance and struggle for absolute power is sadly concluded. In addition to Davis' magnificent performance where she wholly captures the tenacious personality of Elizabeth I, Flynn is memorable as the dashing cavalier out for glory and power and where the rest of the cast are standouts. The direction from action helmsman Curtiz is superbly shown from one lavishly appointed scene to the next, and the sets and costuming awesomely and correctly represent that long ago Elizabethan golden age. Veteran cinematographer Polito does a marvelous job in fluidly capturing the sumptuous courtroom scenes as well as the murky, fog-filled expedition in Ireland where Flynn and his soldiers stagger toward ignominious defeat, all of it shown in the rich hues of the old Technicolor process. Korngold's heraldic score is rich and melodic with pomp and circumstance, thundering in the lower register and mounting to poetic crescendos. The film was successful in that it more than returned its $1 million budget in its initial release and it received five Oscar nominations as Best Art Direction (Grot), Best Cinematography (Polito), Best Music (Korngold), Best Special Effects (Haskin and Koenekamp), and Best Sound Recording (Nathan Levinson). Songs: "The Passionate Shepherd to His Love (Come Live with Me and Be My Love)" (music, 1939: Erich Wolfgang Korngold; lyrics,1599: Christopher Marlowe), "Love's Answer" (Walter Raleigh). *Author's Note*: Crisp, who plays the accomplished Sir Francis Bacon, told this author that "I saw the original play by Maxwell Anderson [produced in New York in 1930 and starring the married team of Alfred Lunt and Lynn Fontaine], which offered its lines in blank verse, and I must say that Bette [Davis] was just as good as Fontaine was in that play when delivering such marvelous lines in the picture version of the play." No greater example of her magnificent delivery of those lines can be found than at the very finale of the film when Davis sends Flynn to his doom and where she states: "I could be young with you, but now I'm old. I know how it will be without you. The sun will be empty and circle around an empty earth—and I will be queen of emptiness and death. Why could you not have loved me enough to give me your love and let me keep as I was?" Price, who plays the Elizabethan fop and adventurer, Sir Walter Raleigh, told this author that "my appearance in **The Private Lives of Elizabeth and Essex** was a godsend. It was my first feature part in a major picture and it helped my career enormously, although, as a devoted historian [Price graduated from Yale with a degree in history], I can tell you that the script for that picture took great liberties with the facts. Elizabeth was really an old woman when she met Essex, who was a much younger man, and there is still a lot of debate as to whether or not they were really lovers or if their relationship was simply platonic, and it was probably the latter. You know, my height almost got me cut from that picture after I did a rehearsal scene with Errol Flynn. Michael Curtiz, the director, stopped the scene and said: 'Oh this won't do—Vincent is too much taller than Errol. [Flynn stood six foot, two inches, Price stood six foot, four inches.] We need a shorter man.' I told Curtiz that I would hunch down a bit, but I was only about two inches taller than Errol, and Curtiz shook his head and I think was about to fire me, when Errol said: 'Forget it, Mike, Vincent is fine. If his height bothers you, have him stand a little away from me and we will look about the same size. Now let's get on with it. I want to go fishing later and land a marlin to put over my fireplace or maybe in my bathtub.' Curtiz agreed and Errol saved my job on the spot. I never forgot that about him. He was a naturally generous man and a great gentleman, and anyone who criticizes him will have to deal with me, except for Bette Davis, of course, because the only person who can deal with her is the Almighty." Davis went after her role as Elizabeth I with great dedication, studying all she could find about that legendary queen and even went to the length of cutting two inches of hairline from her head so that she could appear somewhat bald (as was Elizabeth I) beneath the colorful wigs she wears. She also helped the makeup people age her face with crow's feet about the eyes and some thickening at the neck, but kept her trim thirty-one-year-old figure while playing a monarch who was a woman in her early sixties at the setting of the film and where her lover Essex was thirty-two years her junior at that time. Davis also had her eyebrows plucked and later complained that they never really grew back so that she was compelled to use pencil liner for the rest of her life to fill them in. She was the first choice to play Elizabeth I, and she lobbied hard to have British actor Laurence Olivier as her leading man. Warner Brothers, however, was leery of hiring a foreign actor who was, at that time, little known in the U.S., and hired Flynn instead. Davis rebelled against hiring Flynn, telling Jack Warner that he was "irresponsible and too fun-loving" and that he would never take his role seriously. She had had some bad experiences with Flynn earlier when they appeared together in **Sisters**, 1938, and where Flynn had gotten top billing. In mollifying the feisty Davis, and at her insistence as a way of getting back at Flynn for all the pranks he had played on her in their previous experience together, she was given top billing for **The Private Lives of Elizabeth and Essex**. So much did Davis dislike Flynn at that time, as she told this author, that, to make her lines believable, "I made myself believe that I was acting opposite the great Olivier, mentally blanking out Errol's grinning wolf's head." She underestimated Flynn, however, for he was immensely popular and, ironically, they were the king and queen at Warner Brothers at that time. There is irony in their exchanges of dialog in this film that reflects their real-life studio stations. At one point, Davis says: "You believe you'd rule England better because you are a man." Flynn replies: "I would indeed! And that is why you fail. Because you can't act and think like a man!" The animus between these two tempestuous actors was consistent and often intense. Flynn, at one time, stated that Davis was "not physically my type…dominating everybody around and, especially, me," although he admitted that, as an actress, she was "the greatest thing in the movies." Davis remarked that Flynn "was, when we made **Elizabeth and Essex**, an overpaid glamour boy in tights." The actor was then receiving $6,000 a week, but Davis was being paid much less and she knew it. Their contentious relationship culminated in one explosive scene during the production when Davis is required to slap Flynn's face for being disrespectful. Davis, wearing heavy bracelets, in the first take of this scene, swung her arm in an arching loop and struck Flynn full force on his cheek, stunning him and reddening his face. Flynn later stated that the blow had created "comets, shooting stars, all in one flash. It didn't knock me to the ground. She had given me that dainty little hand, laden with a pound of costume jewelry, right across the ear. I felt as if I were deaf." Curtiz, who did not know if Davis had struck Flynn intentionally or not, called a brief recess and scheduled another take of that scene. During the interim, Flynn went to Davis' dressing room and confronted her, but, before he could say a word, she said: "Oh, I know what you are going to say…but, if you can't take a little slap, well, that's just too bad. What a pity. I knew you were going to complain. I can't do it any other way. If I have to pull my punches, I can't do this. That's the kind of actress I am. I am a *stress* actress!" Flynn left without saying a

Bette Davis and Olivia de Havilland in *The Private Lives of Elizabeth and Essex*, 1939.

word, but then returned to her dressing room where Davis exploded, saying while applying her makeup: "What's your problem now? I am telling you that I can't do it any other way!" Flynn lowered his voice and said with considerable menace: "I am going to give you one more chance to try [to pull your punches]. Do you get me?" Davis stood up and said: "What the hell are you talking about?" Flynn replied: "Just what I said." He walked away and resolved, as he later stated, that, if she struck him again, he would "whack her and drop her, and I believed that, after what I had been through, I would break her jaw. When Curtiz called for the retake of that violent scene, Flynn resolutely approached Davis and both stood glaring at each other. Flynn recalled: "I braced myself for this hit and the counterpunch to it. True, I would be disgraced. Me, a man, hitting the world's favorite on the chin was not going to look pretty, but I had to do it. I didn't care." Davis swung her arm, but she narrowly missed Flynn's face (he stated that "I could feel the wind go by"). Apparently, the talented Davis could pull her punches, if that was her desire. This second take was the scene that Curtiz used in the film. Flynn, however, was not one to let Davis' impactful insult go unanswered. In another scene where he and Davis are frisking about the palace, Flynn swung his arm with a flat hand "and it went right through her Elizabethan dress," he said, "slappo, smack on her Academy Award behind. She went about two feet off the ground." Davis turned about, furious, but Flynn only grinned at her, mimicking her earlier statement to him: "I'm awfully sorry, but I don't know how to do it any other way." She never again spoke to the actor off camera. Whenever the two met at the studio, Flynn would cordially say hello to her, but Davis never replied, only turned her head away from him, and Flynn invariably laughed and went his capricious way. Although Flynn received second billing in this film, he tried to position his character first and have the film's title changed to **The Knight and the Lady**, but when Davis heard about this, she went to Jack Warner and demanded that the original title from the Maxwell Anderson play, *The Private Lives of Elizabeth and Essex*, be used. Warner went through many stressful moments over this, since he disliked the original title and wanted to shorten it to simply **Elizabeth and Essex**, but he was informed that that particular title had been employed in a novel by Lytton Strachey and agents for that work were demanding $10,000 for its use by Warner. The studio chief had spent a fortune on the film already and refused to pay another dime, so the Anderson title was used, even though studio booking agents hated it, telling Warner that theater exhibitors believed it represented some earlier Alexander Korda films and would be confused with Korda's superlative **The Private Life of Henry VIII**, 1933 and his mediocre **The Private Life of Don Juan**, 1934. Davis, however, then the reigning queen at Warner Brothers, insisted that the Anderson title be used, and Warner reluctantly agreed. She had

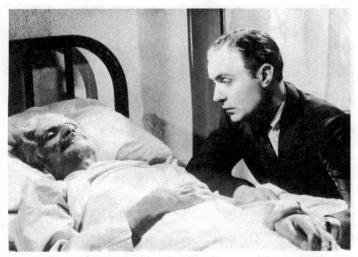

Charles Boyer in *Private Worlds*, 1935.

won another battle with her antagonist, Errol Flynn. After the film was released, Davis complained that Flynn was wooden throughout the film and that she was essentially playing opposite "a good looking prop." Davis told this author that she had seen the film many years later when her good friend Olivia de Havilland (this was the sixth of eight films de Havilland did with Flynn) showed Davis her own print of the film. "I was amazed at Errol's performance. He was really brilliant in that picture and I had been terribly wrong about his acting abilities and I told Olivia that. Errol Flynn was an incorrigible scamp, but he was truly a superb actor, far greater than anyone ever realized because his incredible daring-do blinded everyone to his great talent in playing serious characters and he was wonderful at drama as well as comedy. I must admit that I did hit him on purpose in that scene and I hit him as hard as I could and when I told him that I did not know how to pull my punches, well, that was absurd. I was an accomplished actress then and was easily able to do it." Davis then stared out of the window of the plane on which we were traveling, growing pensive and saying: "We often let our own lives get in the way of appreciating the truly wonderful people we meet along the way. God love him, Errol Flynn was one of those wonderful people." A number of actresses have portrayed Elizabeth in many films, most notably **Elizabeth**, 1998 (Cate Blanchett); **Elizabeth: The Golden Age**, 2007 (Cate Blanchett); **Fire Over England**, 1937 (Flora Robson); **Mary of Scotland**, 1936 (Florence Eldridge); **The Pearls of the Crown**, 1938 (Yvette Pienne); **The Sea Hawk**, 1940 (Flora Robson); **Tower of London**, 1939 (Barbara O'Neil); **The Virgin Queen**, 1955 (Bette Davis as a much older Elizabeth and a film she said she truly loved); and **Young Bess**, 1953 (Jean Simmons). **p**, Hal B. Wallis; **d**, Michael Curtiz; **cast**, Bette Davis, Errol Flynn, Olivia de Havilland, Donald Crisp, Alan Hale, Vincent Price, Henry Stephenson, Henry Daniell, James Stephenson, Nanette Fabares (Nanette Fabray), Ralph Forbes, Robert Warwick, Leo G. Carroll, Doris Lloyd, John Sutton; **w**, Norman Reilly Raine, Aeneas MacKenzie (based on the play "Elizabeth the Queen" by Maxwell Anderson); **c**, Sol Polito (Technicolor); **m**, Erich Wolfgang Korngold; **ed**, Owen Marks; **art d**, Anton Grot; **spec eff**, Byron Haskin, Hans F. Koenekamp.

Private Worlds ★★★ 1935; U.S.; 84m; PAR; B/W; Drama; Children: Unacceptable; **DVD**. Colbert is outstanding as a psychiatrist whose one great love is killed in World War I (1914-1918), so she pours herself into her work at a mental hospital. She and McCrea, the hospital's resident physician, are disappointed when he loses a promotion to head the institution to an outsider, Boyer, who is also a foreigner and has difficulty accepting women in medicine, which causes him to be cold toward Colbert. Boyer's wife, Vinson, is a mental case, thinking she may have killed her previous husband. Colbert becomes romantically interested in McCrea, who is married to Bennett, a situation causing jealous Bennett to have an emotional breakdown. Colbert's more modern and innovative treatment of mental patients then causes friction with Boyer, who is a traditionalist. They clash over treating emotionally disturbed patients, but this strained relationship is somewhat resolved when Boyer sees that some of Colbert's techniques do help patients. Director LaCava, usually a director of comedies, does a fine job of presenting a reasonable and convincing portrait of mental health while providing sustaining interest in this above-average drama. For a list of all films dealing with this subject, see Mental Illnesses, Index, Volume II. **p**, Walter Wanger; **d**, Gregory La Cava; **cast**, Claudette Colbert, Charles Boyer, Joan Bennett, Joel McCrea, Helen Vinson, Esther Dale, Guinn "Big Boy" Williams, Samuel S. Hinds, Theodore von Eltz, Stanley Andrews, Bess Flowers; **w**, Lynn Starling, La Cava, Gladys Unger (based on the novel by Phyllis Bottome); **c**, Leon Shamroy; **m**, Heinz Roemheld; **ed**, Aubrey Scotto; **art d**, Alexander Toluboff; **spec eff**, George J. Teague.

The Prize ★★★ 1952; France.; 122m; Eminente Films/Classic Pictures; B/W; Comedy; Children: Unacceptable; **VHS**. This delightful French farce sees Bouvril as a young village idiot, who is not afraid of bulls but frightened of women, especially those who play jokes on him. He becomes depressed and considers drowning himself but is rescued by Perrey, a countess who takes him to her Paris apartment. Under her influence, he becomes a ladies' man and, after he returns to his village, he is a changed man. Sexuality prohibits viewing by children. (In French; English subtitles.) **p**, Georges Agiman, Jean Darvey; **d**, Jean Boyer; **cast**, Bourvil, Jacqueline Pagnol, Mireille Perrey, Pauline Carton, Henri Vilbert, Jeanne Veniat, Albert Duvaleix, Germaine Reuver, Jean Dunot, Nina Myral; **w**, Marcel Pagnol (based on the novel *Le Rosier de Madame Husson* by Guy de Maupassant); **c**, Charles Suin; **m**, Etienne Lorin, Paul Misraki; **ed**, Fanchette Mazin; **prod d**, Robert Giordani.

The Prize ★★★ 1963; U.S.; 134m; Roxbury/MGM; Color; Spy Drama; Children: Unacceptable (MPAA: PG); **VHS**. Newman is exceptional as he plays an alcoholic American author who reluctantly accepts the Nobel Peace Prize for literature in Stockholm, Sweden, but nevertheless fearing that the prize will interfere with his private life. In preparing his acceptance speech he invents a story that one of the other recipients has been kidnapped. It turns out that the Russians have done exactly that, kidnapping Robinson, a German-American physicist who is traveling with his beautiful niece, Baker, and has replaced him with a lookalike actor. Though the story line takes a large leaf from Hitchcock's classic **Foreign Correspondent**, 1940 (where a lookalike impersonates a Dutch statesman before being killed and the real statesman kidnapped), this exciting tale sustains interest throughout as clever Newman solves the mystery, saves Robinson, and gets the girl. Mature themes prohibit viewing by children. Songs: "Winter Garden," "The Villa" (Harold Gelman). **p**, Pandro S. Berman; **d**, Mark Robson; **cast**, Paul Newman, Elke Sommer, Edward G. Robinson, Diane Baker, Micheline Presle, Sergio Fantoni, Kevin McCarthy, Leo G. Carroll, Virginia Christine, Karl Swenson, John Qualen, Anna Lee, Peter Coe, Brit Ekland, Queenie Leonard, Sam Harris, Jerry Dunphy, Gregg Palmer; **w**, Ernest Lehman (based on the novel by Irving Wallace); **c**, William H. Daniels (Panavision; Metrocolor); **m**, Jerry Goldsmith; **ed**, Adrienne Fazan; **art d**, Urie McCleary, George W. Davis; **set d**, Henry Grace, Richard Pefferle; **spec eff**, A. Arnold Gillespie, Robert R. Hoag, J. McMillan Johnson, Matthew Yuricich.

A Prize of Arms ★★★ 1962; U.K.; 105m; George Maynard Productions/Bryanston; B/W; Crime Drama; Children: Unacceptable; **VHS**. In a well-crafted and taut crime yarn, Baker, a British career captain, is cashiered out of the army for black-market dealings in Hamburg, Germany, in 1956. He plans revenge by robbing an army barracks payroll, and gets help from Bell and Schmid, all three posing as soldiers. They infiltrate the army camp and plan to get away with the payroll in a truck, but their careful plans begin to disintegrate in one foul-up after another. One of the accomplices gets assigned to mess hall duties, and the other becomes ill from a bad reaction to an inoculation. Baker eventually pulls off the heist alone and is escaping with the money in the truck when he is followed by military police and the truck and money are blown up. Violence prohibits viewing by children. **p,** George Maynard; **d,** Cliff Owen; **cast,** Stanley Baker, Helmut Schmid, Tom Bell, John Phillips, Patrick Magee, John Westbrook, Kenneth MacKintosh, Jack May, Frank Gatliff, Michael Ripper, Rio Fanning, John Rees; **w,** Paul Ryder (based on a story by Nicolas Roeg, Kevin Kavanagh); **c,** Gilbert Taylor, Gerald Gibbs; **m,** Robert Sharples; **ed,** John Jympson; **art d,** Jim Morahan, Bernard Sarron; **spec eff,** Brian Gamby, Martin Gutteridge, Jimmy Harris, Jim Hole, Garth Inns.

A Prize of Gold ★★★ 1955; U.K.; 98m; Warwick/COL; Color; Crime Drama; Children: Unacceptable. Widmark gives a riveting performance as a U.S. Army sergeant in Berlin after World War II (1939-1945). He falls in love with refugee Zetterling whose main goal is to take some war orphans to Brazil to start a new life. She needs money, so Widmark recruits some friends to help him steal a shipment of gold being flown from England to Germany. He, Cole, and Patrick hijack a plane carrying the gold and land the plane on an abandoned airstrip. Widmark and Cole then change their minds and want to give the gold back, but Patrick wants to keep it. They fight about it, and Widmark is eventually blamed for the caper. He nevertheless manages to supply the needed money to help Zetterling and the orphans. Action packed, this film also provides some good comic moments. Songs: "A Prize of Gold" (Lester Lee, Ned Washington), "In Love, In Love" (Gerhard Bronner, Tommie Connor). **p,** Irving Allen, Albert R. Broccoli, Phil C. Samuel; **d,** Mark Robson; **cast,** Richard Widmark, Mai Zetterling, Nigel Patrick, George Cole, Donald Wolfit, Joseph Tomelty, Andrew Ray, Karel Stepanek, Eric Pohlmann, Robert Ayres; **w,** Robert Buckner, John Paxton (based on the novel by Max Catto); **c,** Ted Moore (Technicolor); **m,** Malcolm Arnold; **ed,** William Lewthwaite; **art d,** John Box.

The Prize Winner of Defiance, Ohio ★★★★ 2005; U.S.; 99m; Revolution Eire Productions Ltd./DreamWorks; Color; Biographical Drama; Children: Unacceptable (MPAA: PG-13); **DVD.** Based on a true story, the Ryans (Moore, Harrelson) live with their ten children in the town of Defiance, Ohio. Harrelson works in a factory and barely makes enough money to support the family and retreats to drinking while becoming an angry man. Moore, who stays home to take care of their children, enters jingle contests and wins some prizes, including household appliances, a pony, a sports car, a lifetime supply of bird food and some free groceries, but her success makes Harrelson jealous and even more insecure. He even destroys some of the things she wins. He doesn't tell her he has taken out a second mortgage and can't make its payments, now further troubled in that the bank may take over the house in a foreclosure. Moore and the children pray for a miracle and it happens when she wins a Dr. Pepper contest and pays off the mortgage, which brings the family together again, thanks to what can only be called the luck of the Irish. Well made, Moore, Harrelson and the rest of the cast are standouts in this engrossing domestic tale. Songs: "Sitting on Top of the World" (Ray Henderson, Sam Lewis, Joe Young), "Bye Bye Blues" (Fred Hamm, Dave Bennett, Bert Lown, Chauncey Gray), "Rag Mop" (Johnny Lee Wills, Deacon Anderson), "The Sandwich Song" (Brian Kirk, Freddy Cannon), "Frisk the Frigidaire" (Brian Kirk, Evelyn Ryan), "Wrap Your Troubles in Dreams" (Harry Barris, Ted Koehler, Billy Moll), "The World Is Waiting for the Sunrise" (Ernest Seitz, Eugene Lockhart), "Wheel of Fortune" (Bennie Benjamin, George David Weiss), "Row Row Row Your Boat" (traditional). Gutter language, thematic elements, and disturbing images prohibit viewing by children. **p,** Robert Zemeckis, Jack Rapke, Steve Starkey; **d&w,** Jane Anderson (based on the book *The Prize Winner of Defiance, Ohio: How My Mother Raised 10 Kids on 25 Words or Less* by Terry Ryan); **cast,** Ju-

Jack Nicholson and Kathleen Turner in *Prizzi's Honor,* 1985.

lianne Moore, Woody Harrelson, Laura Dern, Trevor Morgan, Ellary Porterfield, Simon Reynolds, Monté Gagné, Robert Clark, Michael Seater, Erik Knudsen, Jake Scott, Jordan Todosey; **c,** Jonathan Freeman; **m,** John Frizzell; **ed,** Robert Dalva; **prod d,** Edward T. McAvoy; **art d,** Andrew Stern; **set d,** Clive Thomasson; **spec eff,** Martin Malivoire, Barry Watkins.

Prizzi's Honor ★★★ 1985; U.S.; 130m; ABC Motion Pictures/FOX; Color; Crime Comedy; Children: Unacceptable (MPAA: R); **DVD; VHS.** Nicholson, in another mesmerizing role that mixes menace with mirth, is a rather thick-headed enforcer for a Mafia family in New York. He slavishly follows the lethal orders of family don Hickey, a crotchety but shrewd old man who spends most of his time deciding which person will be eliminated, such unsavory jobs invariably addressed by his sons, Loggia and Richardson, with the help of Nicholson's father, Randolph. While attending a family wedding, Nicholson's roving eye focuses upon Turner, an attractive woman he has never before met and he asks Huston, his former lover, if she knows anything about Turner. Huston, who is Richardson's errant daughter and out of favor for having run off with another lover after ditching Nicholson, is reluctant to tell Nicholson anything about Turner as she still loves him. Nicholson nevertheless discovers that Turner is an independent "contractor," an assassin who takes assignments from the mob, but at a very heavy price per hit. Nicholson is so infatuated with Turner that he flies to California to be with her and they fall in love, and then Nicholson is assigned to kill Ruskin for robbing a mob-controlled casino, finding out that the man he has dispatched is really Turner's husband. After Turner repays the casino owners some of their lost money, she and Nicholson go to Mexico and tie the knot. After the possessive and jealous Huston learns that Nicholson has married Turner, she takes revenge and restores her honor with the Mafia hierarchy. She travels to the West Coast to inform the casino owners that Turner has held out considerable amounts of money her now deceased husband filched from them, and this information reinstates her position with her father, Richardson, who now wants Nicholson eliminated and orders him hit, but without knowing that the person assigned to that job is none other than Turner. Randolph, however, is incensed when hearing that Richardson has ordered a hit on his son, as is Loggia, Richardson's brother, who considers Nicholson a loyal member of the family, and he, in turn, orders a hit on Richardson. To satisfy all parties, Nicholson and Turner hatch a kidnapping ransom scheme that will repay everyone and enrich Mafia coffers, but things go awry and Turner shoots the wife of a police captain, which enrages the cops, who now threaten to cease all of their illegal ties to the Mafia and organized crime. This crisis causes Hickey to order a hit on the gun-happy Turner, giving the assignment to none other than Nicholson, who glumly complies. He returns home

Anjelica Huston and Jack Nicholson in *Prizzi's Honor*, 1985.

to be greeted by Turner and both pull guns. Turner is killed and Nicholson returns to New York where Huston, the spider woman who has woven this intricate web to eliminate romantic rival Turner, now consoles Nicholson while she plans to make him her own. Complex, tricky and sometimes downright perplexing, this film is nevertheless absorbing as it unravels an outlandish underworld tale; all the cast members are standouts in their grim, lethal and often lunatic roles, and the clever script is laced with dark humor and street wit. Songs: "Una furtiva lagrima" (from "L'elisir d'amore" by Gaetano Donizetti), "Overture to 'La Gazza ladra,'" "Overture to 'Semiramide'" (Gioachina Rossini), "Overture to 'Gianni Schicchi,' "Le Villi" (Giacomo Puccini), "O mio Babbino caro" (from "Gianni Schicchi" by Giacomo Puccini). **p**, John Foreman; **d**, John Huston; **cast**, Jack Nicholson, Kathleen Turner, Anjelica Huston, Robert Loggia, John Randolph, William Hickey, Lee Richardson, Lawrence Tierney, Michael Lombard, C.C.H. Pounder, Stanley Tucci, Joseph Ruskin; **w**, Richard Condon, Janet Roach (based on the novel by Condon); **c**, Andrzej Bartkowiak; **m**, Alex North; **ed**, Kaja Fehr, Rudi Fehr; **prod d**, Dennis Washington; **set d**, Bruce Weintraub; **spec eff**, R. Bruce Seinheimer, Connie Brink Tony, Parmelee.

The Prodigal Son ★★★ 1923 (silent); U.K./Iceland; 17 reels; Stoll Picture Productions; B/W; Drama; Children: Unacceptable. A completely faithful adaptation of the novel, this longest British film up to that time was made two years before Austrian genius Josef von Sternberg filmed the biblical story in two parts, the second titled **The Return of the Prodigal**. The story opens in the hostile winter environment of Iceland where Rome, a young man, steals Bishop, the woman loved by his brother, Victor. She dies in childbirth and Rome deserts her, going off to Nice, Italy, where he seduces her sister. He eventually returns home to seek forgiveness. An excellent film but unavailable in any home viewing format. Remade in 1931 with a somewhat similar plot as **The Prodigal** and again in 1955, and in 2012, but not related to the 1935 or 1981 kung fu film **The Prodigal Son**. **d&w**, A. E. Coleby (based on the novel by Hall Caine); **cast**, Stewart Rome, Henry Victor, Edith Bishop, Colette Brettel, Adeline Hayden Coffin, Frank Wilson, Henry Nicholls-Bates, Louise Conti, Peter Upcher, Sam Austin.

The Producers ★★★★★ 1968; U.S.; 88m; Embassy Pictures/AVCO; Color; Comedy; Children: Unacceptable (MPAA: PG); **DVD**; **VHS**. Mostel is utterly captivating in this masterpiece of mirth from the brilliant Brooks, a film that hilariously and acerbically spoofs the haughty powers that control New York theater, except that, as a theatrical producer, Mostel has no power at all. In fact, he is so down-and-out, that he is about to be evicted from his sleazy office until he meets accountant

whiz Wilder, who also renders one of his most side-splitting performances. The roly-poly Mostel longs to reestablish himself as a theatrical impresario (if he ever was that), but for all his thundering posturing, wearing of cravats and velvet lounging jackets, he is, as Wilder tells him, on the verge of financial and disgraceful collapse. The only salvation for Mostel, says the withdrawn Wilder, is that he either produce a smash hit or, and in this Wilder ruminates with whimsy, collects a lot of money from investors for a play that will be a surefire failure and retain whatever investment money that remains. This second alternative notion from Wilder sparks a wild idea in Mostel's desperation-controlled brain. He will find the worst play ever written and produce it and when it fails, sail off to Rio de Janeiro to live the high life (and where he impulsively clutches the startled Wilder and waltzes about his office with him while chanting "Rio—Rio by the sea-O!"). But, to achieve this ridiculous planned theatrical failure, Mostel needs Wilder's accounting wizardry. The shy and phobia-prone Wilder, however, becomes uncontrollably alarmed, having a fit after Mostel proposes that he doctor his books and become a partner in his wild scheme as a co-producer. Mostel uses everything in his palavering arsenal, from threats to promises, from cajoling and begging to bombastic demands to finally convince the cowering Wilder to agree to the scheme. Mostel and Wilder then celebrate their illicit union by cavorting about the Lincoln Square Fountain and where Wilder frenetically dances in joy as he envisions his share of the illegal riches that might flow from the scheme, shouting: "I want...I want...everything I've ever seen...in the movies!" Both then exhaustively read through piles of scripts, wearily plodding through one dull tale after another, searching frantically for a colossal dud, and they finally find a guaranteed flop when discovering a play titled "Springtime for Hitler." They track down its author, Mars, a former German soldier from WWII who lives in Yorkville and they find him tending to his pigeons atop a tenement rooftop and where he is wearing his German helmet from that war. He is a nutty Nazi zealot, who longs for the return of Adolf Hitler and becomes ecstatic when Mostel and Wilder tell him that they are going to produce his play. Then Mostel bids a brief farewell to Wilder, telling him that he is launching himself into "Little Old Lady Land," where he intends to gull endless spinsters into investing into this new and certifiably doomed play. We next see Mostel pitching and wooing these elderly women into giving him hundreds of thousands of dollars for this sight-unseen new theatrical production. When Mostel returns to his office with these bountiful funds, Wilder tallies the investments only to learn that Mostel has sold much more than 100% of the production, but since it is scheduled to fail, none of his investors will ever know about Mostel's illegal padding of the percentages and where Wilder cooks Mostel's books to simply reflect a total loss. The two begin to enjoy their newly acquired wealth by renting a new and lavish office, and Mostel hires the statuesque and voluptuous Meredith, a Swedish bombshell, who speaks no English and has no secretarial skills, but does a jiggling disco dance on orders and adeptly lights Mostel's cigarettes. To assure the failure of the play, Mostel hires Hewett, a flagrant transvestite, to direct "Springtime for Hitler," and then hires Shawn, a flaky hippie, to play the lead role of Der Fuhrer. On the opening night, Mostel goes so far as to assure a damning review from the New York *Times*, by openly trying to bribe its theater critic. The play then opens as a musical with chorines dressed as SS storm troopers doing high kicks, which enrages playwright Mars, and shocks and stuns the sophisticated audience, but, when theatergoers are about to leave in the first act, Shawn appears to perform as a "cool" and swinging Hitler, unintentionally turning the play into a wild comedy that lampoons Hitler, his minions, and the Third Reich in general, and theatergoers now begin to laugh. Meanwhile, Mostel and Wilder have retired to the bar across the street where they begin to prematurely celebrate the play's utter collapse, but are amazed and crestfallen when, after the first act, theatergoers rush into the place to ecstatically praise this new brilliant satire. Mostel, Wilder and Mars see that the play is going to be a big hit, and, to prevent that from happening, they decide to have Mars blow up the theater (he is willing to perform this sabotage because he is incensed at Shawn's depreciating profile of his idol, Adolf Hitler), but Mars botches the charges of dynamite and blows them all up so that when they later appear in court, charged with fraud by overselling the play, they are wearing casts and bandages. Wilder makes an impassioned plea on Mostel's behalf, calling him a genius. They are nevertheless convicted and sent to prison where they are next shown rehearsing a new and extravagant prison production, a musical, and where Wilder is again overselling percentages in the play to prisoners, guards and even the warden and where the capricious Mostel is on the stage, leading a line of prison inmates in a male chorus line to end this wacky and thoroughly entertaining masterpiece comedy. This was Brooks' first feature film as a director (and where his voiceover can also be heard in the chorus singing solo in "Springtime for Hitler"), and he made a side-splitting comedy out of cliché-ridden bad taste, so outlandish and impossible (as is the play that Mostel and Wilder produce) that it becomes an irresistible comedic tour de force. Almost every one of its characters, and they are all played to their hysterical hilt, are lunatics in a savage burlesque of the legitimate stage and the American Theater. Brooks simply trashes the shrewd perceptions and savoir faire of every first-nighter, profiling such discernible theater-goers as nincompoops while reducing ethos and ethics to the crud and crude along Broadway. All of this, however, is plausible and entertaining through the brilliantly intentional overacting from Mostel and Wilder, who consummately represent the flaky fringe characters inhabiting the wannabe world of New York's main stem. It is truly a laugh riot from beginning to end and gets better with each viewing. The film, shot on location in New York, earned more than $1,680,000 in its initial box office release against a budget of $940,000, even though New York City film critics lambasted it as "shoddy, cruel, gross, and grotesque," to name a few negative remarks. It nevertheless won an Oscar for Brooks (Best Original Screenplay) and an Oscar nomination for Wilder (Best Supporting Actor), the film that launched his career (and where the neurotic character he plays is never far from those he would go on to enact). Songs: "The Producers" (John Morris, M. Goode), "Love Power" (music: Norman Blagman; lyrics: Herb Hartig), "We're Prisoners of Love," "Springtime for Hitler" (Mel Brooks), "By the Light of the Silvery Moon" (Gus Edwards, Edward Madden), "Flying Down to Rio" (Vincent Youmans, Gus Kahn, Edward Ekiscu), "Beautiful Dreamer" (Stephen Foster), "Das Lied der Deutschen" (music, 1791: Joseph Haydn; lyrics, 1841: August Heinrich Hoffman von Fallersleben), "Die Wacht am Rhein" (music: Karl Wilhelm; lyrics: Max Schneckenburger). *Author's Note*: Mostel told this author that "Mel [Brooks] let me let loose with every expression, mannerism and movement I had in my bag of tricks when we did **The Producers**. At one point, I asked myself—'Is this too much?' Then I realized that nothing could be too much for this picture, because my character is as much as much can be. Now munch on that a little much." **p**, Sidney Glazier; **d&w**, Mel Brooks; **cast**, Zero Mostel, Gene Wilder, Dick Shawn, Kenneth Mars, Lee Meredith, Christopher Hewett, Andreas Voutsinas, Estelle Winwood, Renee Taylor, David Patch, Bill Hickey; **c**, Joseph Coffey (Pathe Color); **m**, John Morris; **ed**, Ralph Rosenblum; **prod d**, Charles Rosen; **set d**, James Dalton.

Professional Sweetheart ★★★ 1933; U.S.; 73m; RKO; B/W; Comedy; Children: Acceptable. Live-wire Rogers is a radio singer publicized as the squeaky-clean ideal of American womanhood to sell her sponsor's product, Ippsie-Wippsie Washcloths. She is not quite that girl and wants to sample booze, jazz, gambling, and men. When she rebels, Ratoff, who is her sponsor, hires Foster, a "sweetheart" from her fan mail, and lo and behold, that turns to love between the two young people. This above-average comedy pokes fun at advertising and a number of its products and does so with a bright and funny script backed up by good acting. Songs: "The Wedding March" (Felix Mendelssohn-Bartholdy), "My Imaginary Sweetheart" (Harry Akst, Edward Eliscu), "Daybreak" (Hoagy Carmichael). **p**, H.N. Swanson; **d**, William A. Seiter; **cast**, Gin-

Gene Wilder, Zero Mostel and Lee Meredith in *The Producers*, 1968.

ger Rogers, Norman Foster, Zasu Pitts, Frank McHugh, Allen Jenkins, Gregory Ratoff, Franklin Pangborn, Lucien Littlefield, Edgar Kennedy, Sterling Holloway, Betty Furness, Edward Everett Horton, Akim Tamiroff; **w**, Maurine Watkins (based on a story by Watkins); **c**, Edward Cronjager; **m**, Edward Eliscu, Harry Akst; **ed**, James B. Morley; **set d**, Van Nest Polglase, Carroll Clark.

The Professionals ★★★★ 1966; U.S.; 117m; Pax Enterprises/COL; Color; Western; Children: Unacceptable; **DVD**; **VHS**. This superb action-packed western begins when wealthy cattle baron Bellamy hires four professional soldiers-of-fortune to find and return to him his attractive, young wife, Cardinale, who has been abducted by ruthless bandit Palance, and who is holding her for a large ransom. To accomplish the arduous rescue and overcome Palance and his large gang of bandits, Bellamy first enlists the aid of Marvin, a former U.S. soldier and marksman, who, in turn, hires Lancaster, a dynamiter, then Ryan, an expert horse trainer, and finally Strode, a black man who is an expert archer. The four men are to be paid a handsome fee after they find and return Cardinale to Bellamy and, to that hazardous end, ride into Mexico, knowing that they are facing a wary enemy as Marvin and Lancaster once fought with Palance when they all rode with Pancho Villa during the Mexican Revolution. After riding deep into Mexico, they encounter some of Palance's men, who capture Lancaster and hang him upside down in his underwear as their leader questions him about his associates, but, before Lancaster is killed, Marvin, Strode and Ryan appear and rescue Lancaster at the last moment and where they shoot down the bandits. They then proceed to a goat herder's ranch and from whom they learn about Palance's guarded camp. They infiltrate that camp, and Strode creates diversions by shooting arrows with attached sticks of dynamite that explode throughout the place while Lancaster and Marvin invade Palance's home, taking Cardinale from her bed while holding an incensed Palance at gunpoint. They flee the camp with Palance and his men in hot pursuit, a chase that leads across deserts and through caverns. Meanwhile, the rescuers discover, to their surprise, that Cardinale does not want to be rescued, but wants only to remain with the man she loves, Palance. She explains that it was Bellamy who forced her into a loveless marriage with him and that she hates Bellamy. The foursome, however, intend to stick to their agreement with Bellamy, all needing the $10,000 each man is to receive for returning Cardinale to the cattle baron, even though they have also learned that Palance has only demanded the ransom for Cardinale to fund his ongoing revolution against tyrannical forces in Mexico and that Cardinale agreed to that ruse as she considers Palance not only her lover but a true patriot. At one point, Lancaster dynamites a narrow gorge, closing the gap with rocks to prevent Palance and his men from continuing their pursuit, but only for a time. He later

Burt Lancaster in *The Professionals*, 1966.

waylays what remains of Palance's forces, killing all of them and wounding Palance while Marvin, Ryan and Strode ride across the border into the U.S. with Cardinale. They are then joined by Lancaster, who has brought the wounded Palance along with him. When they arrive at the appointed rendezvous with Bellamy, the cattle baron expresses his gratitude for returning Cardinale to him, and then orders one of his guards to shoot and kill Palance. Marvin, however, regaining his scruples, refuses to let that happen, and shoots the guard. He then allows Palance and Cardinale to flee back to Mexico. The enraged Bellamy shouts at Marvin: "You bastard!" Marvin (in delivering one of the best lines of this gritty film, or any other for that matter), replies: "Yes, an unfortunate accident of birth, but you, sir, are a self-made man!" With that, he, Lancaster, Ryan and Strode, mount their horses and ride away without receiving their much-needed payments, but with the satisfaction that they have performed a noble deed. Director Brooks presents an almost nonstop action oater, thanks to the outstanding cinematography from Hall, and his well-written script provides good character development and witty dialog, far superior to the usual western. Marvin, Lancaster and Palance give exceptional performances, and the rest of the cast are standouts in their hard-barked roles. *Author's Note*: The film was shot on location at the Valley of Fires State Park near Lake Mead, Nevada, at Death Valley, and along the railway line at Indio, California. Brooks told this author that "we did a whirlwind job with **The Professionals**, shooting the entire film in nine weeks, but we had to overcome a lot of problems, including dust storms and a flash flood that trapped most of us in a box canyon for a few days. Thankfully, Claudia [Cardinale] did not have a lot of speaking lines because her Italian accent fractured the English so much it was often difficult to understand her and I did not have enough time to put her through speaking lessons." Cinematographer Hall shot the night scenes during the day because of the darkening landscapes of the locales, but that also eliminated the capturing of the many spectacular landscapes, causing Brooks to compensate by shooting many close-ups during the night scenes. Columbia spent lavishly on the film, the cost of Palance's fortified hacienda alone costing $200,000 to build. "That picture just about killed me," Ryan told this author, "because the heat was so intense when we were shooting at Death Valley, and, in fact, there is a scene where my character collapses from the heat. Well, I can tell you that I was not acting in that scene and felt that my brain was being fried. I was about fifty-six when I did that film and I think Burt [Lancaster] was only a few years younger than me [he was fifty-three] so I don't have any idea how he was able to do his own stunts in **The Professionals** without croaking himself, but he did them all right. He even scaled a cliff hand over hand on a rope. I later saw the rope burns on his hands, but he never said a word about that. He was once a circus acrobat, so he took all that in stride." For Lan-

caster's part, he told this author that "doing my own stunts in that picture was par for the course. My thinking was—'why should some stuntman double do all the crazy things I do in that film when I am enough of a damned fool to do them myself?" Marvin and Lancaster did not get along well during the production as Marvin spent most of his time drinking (and was accused later of being half drunk while appearing in most of his scenes). "Every day in making that picture was like stepping into an oven," Marvin told this author, "and there was no way to beat the heat except to take more than a few stiff ones and I took a lot of those. Burt [Lancaster] got very upset with me for doing that and, before we did one scene together, told me that he was going to throw me off a cliff if I did not stop the boozing. I told him that I would stop when the temperature dropped down about thirty degrees. I think that if his six-shooter had real bullets in it he might have shot me in the foot or something. Burt was a tough bird. He was just as intense off camera as he was in front of it, so I steered as clear of him as I could until we finished the picture and I got the hell out of there." **p,d&w**, Richard Brooks (based on the novel *A Mule for the Marquesa* by Frank O'Rourke); **cast**, Burt Lancaster, Lee Marvin, Robert Ryan, Jack Palance, Claudia Cardinale, Ralph Bellamy, Woody Strode, Joe De Santis, Rafael Bertrand, Jorge Martinez de Hoyos, Marie Gomez; **c**, Conrad Hall (Panavision; Technicolor); **m**, Maurice Jarre; **ed**, Peter Zinner; **art d**, Edward S. Haworth; **set d**, Frank Tuttle; **spec eff**, Willis Cook.

The Projectionist ★★★ 1971; U.S.; 88m; Maglan/Maron; Color; Comedy; Children: Unacceptable; **DVD**; **VHS**. Very funny film sees McCann as a movie projectionist in a Manhattan theater who loves his work and the movies he shows, often impersonating his favorite stars, but hates Dangerfield, his bossy employer. He fantasizes that he is a movie superhero named Captain Flash and Dangerfield is the villain called The Bat, who wants to take over the world as well as Balin, the girl McCann sees as the girl of his dreams. They all "live" in a movie in McCann's imagination. Hurwitz does a good job presenting this telescoping production which is really a movie within a movie showing movies, and McCann and Dangerfield as the contentious antagonists are exceptional in their roles, as is Kohout, an immigrant actor, who was known as "the Charlie Chaplin of Czechoslovakia." Through clever special effects and rear screen projection, McCann is shown as a character in many of his favorite films, standing at the bar in Bogart's saloon in **Casablanca**, 1942, as a witness inside the gloomy temple where murderous Thugs are gathered in **Gunga Din**, 1939, and, at the finale, standing with and taking bows with stars Ruby Keeler and Dick Powell in **Dames**, 1934. *Author's Note*: Dangerfield told this author that "the director [Hurwitz] used so many clips from other pictures in **The Projectionist** that I sometimes didn't know what picture I was in, but I always understood my character because I always play myself, whether I get respect or not." The use of interjecting characters from one film into another was begun by Orson Welles in his making of the masterpiece **Citizen Kane**, 1941, and where he shows in newsreels his character of Kane (Welles) socializing with real-life worldwide personalities, such as standing on a balcony with Adolf Hitler. Woody Allen would mimic that technique in **Zelig**, 1983, and the same technique would be employed in **Dead Men Don't Wear Plaid**, 1982, where comedian Steve Martin interacts with a bevy of movie tough guys such as Alan Ladd, Humphrey Bogart and James Cagney in clips from many film noir productions. Made on a shoestring budget, this film was completed within four weeks, but another eighteen months were spent in editing (and splicing scenes from other films). Some of Hurwitz's superimpositions do not work well, but the film nevertheless offers a lot of eye appeal for classic film fans who are challenged to identify some of their favorite movies. Hurwitz, a movie maven to the core, plays an usher in this film. Violent war and atrocity scenes prohibit viewing by children. **p,d,w&ed**, Harry Hurwitz; **cast**, Chuck McCann, Ina Balin, Rodney Dangerfield, Jára Kohout, Hurwitz, Mike Gentry, Lucky Kargo, David Holliday, Sam Stewart, Robert Lee; **c**, Victor Petrashevic (Technicolor); **m**, Igo Kantor, Erma E. Levin.

The Promoter ★★★ 1952; U.K.; 88m; British Film Makers/UNIV; B/W; Comedy/Drama; Children: Unacceptable; **VHS**. Guinness is compelling in this Horatio Alger tale where he is an impoverished student who alters the grade on his high school entrance exam so he can ensure his enrollment. A talented self-promoter, he "achieves" his way up the educational ladder and becomes a law clerk, then becomes successful in business. He starts his own loan company and becomes mayor of his town. Over the years, he comes under the sway of several charming women. One of these attractive ladies is Johns, who is unable to pay the rent that Guinness has to collect. Another woman, Clark, becomes his wife, although she is a predatory female who dominates him. A pleasant tale, this film sustains interest throughout while providing many humorous moments via the exceptional performances from Guinness, Johns and Clark. Songs: "The Man Who Broke the Bank at Monte Carlo" (Fred Gilbert), "Colonel Bogey March" (music: Kenneth Alford). *Author's Note*: Guinness told this author that "my character in **The Promoter** is like any average fellow trying to advance himself, but he bends some corners along the way. He is not an essentially venal person, but his ambition often gets in the way of his best interests and I would say that that applies to half the people living on this planet." At the finale of this film, a band marching in a parade strikes up a tune called the "Colonel Bogey March," the signature tune used five years later in **The Bridge on the River Kwai**, 1957, which starred Guinness in one of his most memorable roles. **p**, John Bryan; **d**, Ronald Neame; **cast**, Alec Guinness, Glynis Johns, Valerie Hobson, Petula Clark, Edward Chapman, Veronica Turleigh, Joan Hickson, Michael Hordern, Wilfrid Hyde-White; **w**, Eric Ambler (based on the novel by Arnold Bennett); **c**, Oswald Morris; **m**, William Alwyn; **ed**, Clive Donner; **art d**, T. Hopewell Ash; **spec eff**, Bill Warrington.

Proof ★★★ 2005; U.S.; 100m; UNIV; Color; Drama; Children: Unacceptable (MPAA: PG-13); **DVD**. In this well-crafted and absorbing drama, Paltrow gives an exceptional performance as Hopkins' daughter and where Hopkins is a mentally disturbed but famous mathematician who recently died. She believes she may have inherited his insanity. One of her father's former students, Gyllenhaal, wants to go through Hopkins' papers, and her estranged elder sister, Davis, shows up to help settle their father's affairs but troubles Paltrow because of her own domineering and intrusive actions. Paltrow allows Gyllenhaal to read her father's papers about a complex discovery in the field of prime numbers. She then claims she wrote the papers, but no one believes her and it is next to impossible for her to prove that she is the author. Songs: "El chocha loca" (Claudio Quattrocchi), "We Can Be Free" (Bruce Elliott-Smith, Frantic, Mark Lord, Lucy Wells, Steve Juneo), "String Quartet No. 4 in C" (Wolfgang Amadeus Mozart), "Uganda" (Bob Ward, Larry Goldings), "Inhaler" (Dave Warrin, John Warrin, Guy Gershoni), "I'm Ready" (Willie Dixon), "I'll Never Be Your Maggie May" (Suzanne Vega). Sexual content, drugs, and gutter language prohibit viewing by children. **p**, John N. Hart, Jr., Robert Kessel, Alison Owen, Jeffrey Sharp, Mark Cooper, Bob and Harvey Weinstein; **d**, John Madden; **cast**, Gwyneth Paltrow, Anthony Hopkins, Jake Gyllenhaal, Hope Davis, Tobiacz Daszkiewicz, Gary Houston, Danny McCarthy, Colin Stinton, Anne Whitman, Leigh Zimmerman, Leland Burnett; **w**, David Auburn, Rebecca Miller (based on the play by Auburn); **c**, Alwin Kuchler; **m**, Stephen Warbeck; **ed**, Mick Audsley; **prod d**, Alice Normington; **art d**, Keith Slote; **set d**, Barbara Herman-Skedling; **spec eff**, Stuart Brisdon, Nigel Wilkinson, Simon Frame.

The Proposal ★★★ 2009; U.S.; 108m; Touchstone/Disney; Color; Comedy/Romance; Children: Unacceptable (MPAA: PG-13); **DVD**. Cute comedy with above-average performances sees the fetching Bullock working as an editor at a New York publishing company, but she is faced with a dilemma. She is a Canadian facing deportation for an ex-

Gwyneth Paltrow and Jake Gyllenhaal in *Proof*, 2005.

pired visa and the only way she can remain in the U.S. is to marry an American citizen. She offers her male assistant, Reynolds, a promotion if he will marry her and he agrees. An Immigration Department officer is to test the couple's feelings for each other after a weekend. Bullock goes home with Reynolds to Sitka, Alaska, for the weekend to attend his grandmother's 90th birthday. It's a nightmare weekend with a dysfunctional family and, on Monday, immigration people may charge the couple with fraud. But all ends well because, despite their differences, Bullock and Reynolds find that they really love each other. Songs: "Relax" (Peter Gill, William Johnson, Mark O'Toole), "U Can't Touch This" (M.C. Hammer, Alonzo Miller, Rick James), "Cult of Personality" (Will Calhoun, Corey Glover, Vernon Reid, Muzzy Skillings), "It Takes Two" (James Brown, Robert Ginyard), "Find My Way" (Dan Wilson, Gabe Dixon), "So Danco Samba" (Antonio Carlos Jobim, Vinicius de Moraes), "I've Got You Under My Skin" (Cole Porter), "Canon in D" (Johann Pachelbel),"Coolin" (Alex Wilson, Paul Booth), "Freedom" (Matt Starr, Alex Grossi, Anthony Fox, Kenny Kweens, Joe Leste), "Woosh Xhant Wuda.aat" (Anne Fletcher, Buck Damon), "Get Low" (Deongelo Holmes, Eric Jackson, Jonathan Smith), "Love Me Tenderly" (Leonard Raymond Gehl, Sr.). Sexual content, nudity, and gutter language prohibit viewing by children. **p**, David Hoberman, Todd Lieberman; **d**, Anne Fletcher; **cast**, Sandra Bullock, Ryan Reynolds, Mary Steenburgen, Craig T. Nelson, Betty White, Denis O'Hare, Malin Akerman, Oscar Nuñez, Aasif Mandvi, Michael Nouri, Michael Mosley; **w**, Peter Chiarelli; **c**, Oliver Stapleton; **m**, Aaron Zigman; **ed**, Priscilla Nedd-Friendly; **prod d**, Nelson Coates; **art d**, Scott Meehan; **set d**, Denise Pizzini; **spec eff**, Sean Devereaux.

The Proud Ones ★★★ 1956; U.S.; 94m; FOX; Color; Western; Children: Unacceptable; **DVD**; **VHS**. Gritty and well-acted western sees U.S. Marshal Ryan as the tough lawman who keeps the peace in a town about to be impacted by the arrival of a railroad line and cattle drives. He expects trouble from Middleton, the owner of the local saloon, who plans to get rich. Hunter, the son of a hired gun Ryan earlier killed in the line of duty, comes to town seeking revenge. Hunter changes his attitude toward the principled Ryan and helps him clean up the town run by Middleton, but this is no easy chore in that Ryan begins to experience bouts of blindness, stemming from a wound in an earlier gun battle, and, during one of those hazardous spells, is almost killed in gunfights with Middleton's goons. Song: "Sweet Betsy from Pike" (John A. Stone). *Author's Note*: Ryan told this author that "I was not the first actor to get the leading part in **The Proud Ones**. In fact, I was low man on the totem pole. About four years before that picture was made, Fox bought the film rights from the novelist [Athanas], and they announced that Victor Mature would play the local lawman. Three years went by and

Robert Ryan and Virginia Mayo in *The Proud Ones*, 1956.

they resurrected the script and announced that Gregory Peck would play the leading role. Some months after that, Fox sent out a press release that Gary Cooper would play the part. After all of these fine actors dropped out or refused the role, Fox finally got around to me. I wanted that part because it had a lot of substance to it. The marshal is not just a stoic man with a gun, but has a conscience and must also deal with psychological problems when he hides from everyone who loves him the fact that he suffers from spells of blindness. **The Proud Ones** is a thinking man's western and that's a rarity in that genre." **p**, Robert L. Jacks; **d**, Robert D. Webb; **cast**, Robert Ryan, Virginia Mayo, Jeffrey Hunter, Robert Middleton, Walter Brennan, Arthur O'Connell, Ken Clark, Rodolfo Acosta, George Mathews, Fay Roope, Whit Bissell, Jackie Coogan; **w**, Edmund North, Joseph Petracca (based on the novel by Verne Athanas); **c**, Lucien Ballard (CinemaScope; DeLuxe Color); **m**, Lionel Newman; **ed**, Hugh S. Fowler; **art d**, Lyle R. Wheeler, Leland Fuller; **set d**, Walter M. Scott, Fred R. Simpson; **spec eff**, Ray Kellogg.

The Proud Rebel ★★★ 1958; U.S.; 103m; Formosa/Buena Vista; Color; Western; Children: Unacceptable; **DVD**; **VHS**. Ladd gives a compelling performance as a victimized Confederate veteran of the American Civil War (1861-1865). He is sentenced to thirty days in jail when he is falsely accused of starting a brawl in a small town. A local woman, de Havilland, pays his fine on the condition he work off the thirty days on her ranch. (This story line twist takes a leaf from **The Man from Laramie**, 1955, where rancher Aline MacMahon bails James Stewart out of jail to work on her ranch as a foreman after he is wrongly accused of killing a town drunk.) Ladd soon finds himself involved in trying to keep her ranch from the covetous clutches of a local landowner and whose men started the fight for which Ladd had been blamed. Ladd had been traveling with his young son (David Ladd, his real-life son) who became mute after seeing his mother (Ladd's wife) die in a fire when Yankees burned down their house in Atlanta during the war. De Havilland takes in Ladd, the boy, and their dog and, when the bad guys are about to shoot his father, young Ladd regains his voice and warns him, saving his life. It all ends well with father and son remaining on de Havilland's ranch and where all form a new family. Alan and David Ladd, along with de Havilland, are standouts in their roles, and Stanton, who has made a career of playing offbeat characters, is exceptional as a menacing villain whose mental stability is always one step away from utter collapse. **p**, Samuel Goldwyn, Jr.; **d**, Michael Curtiz; **cast**, Alan Ladd, Olivia de Havilland, Dean Jagger, David Ladd, Cecil Kellaway, James Westerfield, Henry Hull, Harry Dean Stanton, Thomas Pittman, Eli Mintz, John Carradine, Percy Helton, Mary Wickes; **w**, Joseph Petracca, Lillie Hayward (based on the story "Journal of Linnett Moore" by James Edward Grant); **c**, Ted D. McCord (Technicolor); **m**, Jerome

Moross; **ed**, Aaron Stell; **art d**, McClure Capps; **set d**, Victor Gangelin.

Providence ★★★★ 1977; France/Switzerland/U.K.; 104m; Action Films/Cinema 5 Distributing; Color; Children: Unacceptable (MPAA: R); **DVD**; **VHS**. This brilliant film merges literature and film through the agonized imagination of novelist Gielgud, who renders one of his most stunning performances. He is presumably dying from a rectal disorder and, while battling his pain with liquor, struggles to envision the last elements of a novel he is writing. All of this happens on the night before his 78th birthday, a commemorative occasion Gielgud does not anticipate with any relish or joy. In creating new scenes for what might be his last book, Gielgud bases his characters on his own family members, chiefly Bogarde, his son, and Burstyn, his daughter-in-law, who are constantly bickering and barbing each other with acerbic exchanges. He also profiles his illegitimate son, Warner, who is presently facing charges of murder in court for killing an old man and who claims innocence in that he was compelled to kill this elderly man because he had turned into a werewolf. As Gielgud continues drinking and his mind become muddled with booze, his characters become more and more bizarre and he begins to lose control over his plotline. Warner, who is prosecuted by Bogarde, is found innocent and, upon his release, he begins to make sexual advances toward Burstyn, which, instead of alarming Bogarde only produces disgust in him for both his half-brother and his wife. In his weakening mental state, Gielgud decides to give Bogarde a mistress, Stritch, who is based on his own deceased wife, a woman with a terminal illness, but Gielgud finds it difficult to distinguish Stritch from his real-life wife. As Gielgud slips into drunkenness, his characters also slip from their roles. Warner seems to forget his own identity and delivers Bogarde's lines while Bogarde and Burstyn play out one scene, but then reverse their roles by repeating each other's lines. The settings change abruptly. At one point, Bogarde is shown before a seaside and is then shown with a large city in the background, all of this being jumbled by Gielgud, who is losing control of sequence and continuity in his story. Rogue characters then begin to invade the tale, none of them having any reason to exist as they abruptly appear and disappear, such as soccer player Lawson, who races into a scene only to exit as quickly as he appeared, and physician Luckham, who performs a grisly autopsy that has nothing to do with the plot. By morning, Gielgud has slept off his pain and alcoholic stupor and, sober, he is visited by his children, all of whom are very normal people, Bogarde and Burstyn being a pleasant couple and Warner a considerate son, all of whom showing deep affection for their father by giving Gielgud thoughtful birthday presents that consist of a novel titled *The Scales of Time* showing its author to be Mercer (an in-joke as Mercer is the scriptwriter for this film), as well as a pen-knife that once belonged to Ernest Hemingway. The family then enjoys an elaborate and delightful outdoor dinner and then Gielgud asks them to leave so he can go back to work on his novel, a chore he does not welcome since he knows he will again take to booze in attempting to finish his novel. Gielgud presents a bravura performance that displays his incredible range of emotions and where he is utterly riveting in his role as a writer both physically and intellectually tortured over his own creation. The film perfectly melds the visual images Gielgud envisions while transmitting his abrupt mood and intellectual changes that alter and distort his story, all of this achieved through Resnais' brilliant direction and Mercer's incisive script, which is packed with wit and humor that ameliorates its more dire elements. Resnais always worked closely and well with authors, one of the few directors to understand their creative mindsets, as was demonstrated through his experiences with Marguerite Duras's **Hiroshima Mon Amour**, 1960; Alain Robbe-Grillet's **Last Year at Marienbad**, 1962; and Jorge Semprun's **The War Is Over**, 1967. **p**, Yves Gasser, Yves Peyrot, Klaus Hellwig; **d**, Alain Resnais; **cast**, John Gielgud, Dirk Bogarde, Ellen Burstyn, David Warner, Elaine Stritch, Cyril Luckham, Dennis Lawson, Kathryn Leigh Scott, Milo Sperber, Anna Wing; **w**, David Mercer; **c**, Ricardo Aronovich (Eastmancolor); **m**, Miklós Rózsa; **ed**, Albert Jurgenson;

prod d, Jacques Saulnier; **art d**, Michel Breton, Jean-Claude Cabouret, Daniel Pierre; **art d**, Claude Serre.

The Prowler ★★★★ 1951; U.S.; 92m; Horizon Pictures/UA; B/W; Crime Drama; Children: Unacceptable; **VHS**. The pensive Heflin gives a riveting performance as a venal cop with a covetous eye toward a married woman, Keyes. Heflin and his partner, Maxwell, respond to a call about a potential prowler in a Los Angeles neighborhood and go to Keyes' home, but they find no one in the area. Heflin is attracted to the alluring Keyes and returns to see her, asking if she is all right, but his real reason for being there is to subtly make advances on the married Keyes. He praises her good looks while he tells her how he envisions sometime buying a motel in Las Vegas where one can "make money while you sleep." Learning that her husband, Treacy, is an all-night disc jockey and leaves Keyes alone at night, and, after Heflin returns again and seduces the lonely woman, he learns that, if Treacy were to die, Keyes would inherit a sizeable amount of money, the very funds he needs to buy that motel. Heflin is visited by Keyes at his sleazy, cramped room, but he tells her that they have no future together, a ruse, since he plans to later make her his own, but through a murderous scheme he hatches when he goes to her home and pretends to be a prowler, on a night he knows Treacy will be at home. Treacy, as Heflin has anticipated, steps from his home with a gun in his hand, looking for the prowler and Heflin, then enacting his legitimate role as a policeman, responds to the call about the prowler, a call he himself has prompted. When he confronts Treacy outside in the shadows of his home, Heflin shoots and kills Treacy and then fires a bullet into his own leg so that it will appear that he has only acted in self-defense after Treacy has ostensibly shot him. Heflin answers a court of inquiry where he is suspected of killing Treacy by Keyes, and where she believes he arranged for the incident so that Heflin could be with her, but Heflin is exonerated. Keyes later accepts the story that Heflin acted in self-defense and marries him with blessings from her relatives, who think that Heflin is a decent man. They move to Las Vegas and, using Keyes' inheritance, buy the motel Heflin has always wanted. Business is booming and all seems well until Heflin learns that Keyes is pregnant following a short period since they have been married and he is how haunted with the impending birth of a child. That birth, he knows, will implicate him in Treacy's murder in that it is well known that Treacy was sterile and could never have children. Heflin explains his dilemma to Keyes, and she agrees to go to a remote location to have the baby. They drive to the desert and Heflin finds an abandoned house where Keyes goes into labor, but she begs that he summon a regular doctor. Heflin drives to a nearby town and brings back a physician, Chambers, who delivers the baby. Heflin impulsively admits murdering Treacy to Keyes and she realizes that he will now murder Chambers to cover up the birth of the child. Keyes helps the doctor escape and Heflin drives after him. Chambers, however, is able to contact the police, who are now in pursuit of Heflin. He is cornered by officers in the desert and, while fleeing and refusing to heed their orders to stop, is shot and killed by the officers, ironically in the same fashion as Heflin has claimed Treacy's life. In addition to Heflin's powerfully sinister performance, Keyes is also riveting in her role as the lovesick housewife who comes to realize too late that the man she has married is a ruthless killer. Director Losey helms this chilling film noir entry with a deft hand, carefully unfolding its story and the dark motivations of its developing characters with mounting suspense. Song: "Baby" (music: Lyn Murray; lyrics: Dick Mack). *Author's Note*: Heflin told this author that he felt that his role in this film was "extremely challenging because my character is not an out-and-out villain. He slowly becomes one through lust and greed, two of the most powerful influences that can send someone in the wrong direction. Everything about this man is repulsive and I don't think a lot of actors want to play such ugly characters, but I always thought that such characters offered the greatest challenge in testing your talents and your ability." The producer for this film is S. P. Eagle, which stands for

Van Heflin and Evelyn Keyes in *The Prowler,* 1951.

Sam Spiegel, who owned the company that produced this film, along with his partner and co-owner of that company, the gifted director John Huston. Keyes was married to Huston at the time, and Huston selected this film as a vehicle for her considerable acting talents. Screenwriter Dalton Trumbo, who was then blacklisted in Hollywood for his involvement in the probes in the U.S. House of Un-American Activities Committee (HUAC) as a labeled communist (or pro-communist activist), wrote the script for this thriller under the pseudonym of Hugo Butler. Losey also ran afoul of HUAC, but, rather than face that committee about his political past, the director went to England to bide his time. **p**, S.P. Eagle (Sam Spiegel); **d**, Joseph Losey; **cast**, Van Heflin, Evelyn Keyes, John Maxwell, Katherine Warren, Emerson Treacy, Madge Blake, Wheaton Chambers, Robert Osterloh, George Nader; **w**, Dalton Trumbo, Hugo Butler [Dalton Trumbo] (based on a story by Robert Thoeren, Hans Wilhelm); **c**, Arthur Miller; **m**, Lyn Murray; **ed**, Paul Weatherwax; **art d**, Boris Leven; **set d**, Jacques Mapes.

Prunella ★★★ 1918 (silent); U.S.; 50m/5 reels; Famous Players-Lasky; B/W; Romance; Children: Cautionary. Pantheon director Tourneur provides a lyrical and poetic romance between the attractive Clark and the handsome Raucourt. Clark dwells with her three protective aunts, Harris, Berwin and Cecil (who are named respectively "Prude," "Prim," and "Privacy"), living an idyllic life in their comfortable home and dreaming in their exquisite garden. When a troupe of traveling pantomime players pass that garden, one of them, Raucourt, sees the alluring Clark, and she is equally thunderstruck by him. It is love at first sight, and both are soon courting and are then married. Clark goes away with Ruycourt and they soon become stars on the Paris stage. Raucourt's roving eye, however, disrupts the marriage. After he dallies with another woman, Clark leaves him and becomes a lost woman, but Raucourt, still loving her, searches for her and finds her and they are reunited at the end. The film is superbly directed by Tourneur, and van den Broek's cinematography beautifully captures the gossamer scenes; the stunning sets and costuming constitute the kind of tasteful high production values for which Tourneur is known. **d**, Maurice Tourneur; **cast**, Marguerite Clark, Jules Racourt, Harry Leone, Marcia Harris, Isabel Berwin, Nora Cecil, William J. Gross, A.Voorhes Wood, Charles Hartley; **w**, Charles Maigne (based on a play by Harley Granville-Barker, Laurence Housman); **c**, John van den Broek, **art d**, Ben Carre.

The Psychic ★★★ 1979; Italy; 95m; Rizzoli Film/International Distributing Organization; Color; Horror/Mystery; Children: Unacceptable; **DVD**. O'Neill is absorbing as a clairvoyant woman who has recurring visions of a murder being committed. She slashes open part of a wall in her husband's home and finds a skeleton behind it. She enlists the aid

Janet Leigh in *Psycho*, 1960.

of her psychiatrist in trying to find out who the dead person might have been and who put the body behind that wall, believing it is a woman's skeleton. She begins to fear that she may share the same fate as the victim. For those who like strange and spooky films, this chilling entry will fit the bill. Mature themes prohibit viewing by children. (In Italian; dubbed in English.) Songs: "With You" (Franco Bixio, Fabio Frizzi, Vince Tempera), "Sette Note in Nero." **p**, Fulvio Frizzi, Franco Cuccu; **d**, Lucio Fulci; **cast**, Jennifer O'Neill, Gabriele Ferzetti, Marc Porel, Gianni Garko, Ida Galli (as Evelyn Stewart), Jenny Tamburi, Fabrizio Jovine, Loredana Savelli, Salvatore Puntillo; **w**, Fulci, Roberto Gianviti, Dardano Sacchetti; **c**, Sergio Salvati (DeLuxe Color); **m**, Franco Bixio, Fabio Frizzi, Vince Tempera; **ed**, Ornella Micheli; **art d**, Luciano Spadoni.

Psycho ★★★★ 1960; U.S.; 109m; Shamley Productions/PAR; B/W; Horror; Children: Unacceptable (MPAA: R); **BD**; **DVD**; **VHS**. Hitchcock was deservedly blamed for breaking almost all Hollywood taboos when making this bone-chilling horror film. The story blatantly plays to shock values, and created an avalanche of poorly made and tasteless imitations, but this brilliantly conceived and inventively presented tale nevertheless remains the watershed film of its genre. Perhaps no other director could have gotten away at that time with such a horrendously shocking film other than the redoubtable Hitchcock, and, as such, must take responsibility (as he did in his admissions to this author) for introducing and exposing a new kind of ruthless savagery and myriad perversities to the screen and to mainstream audiences. It is not a film for the squeamish, the faint of heart, or any child. As is the case with many another film, Hitchcock opens this creepy tale with his camera panning the skyline of a city, in this case Phoenix, Arizona, its focus narrowing to one building, then one window, until entering a hotel room to reveal the voluptuous Leigh wearing only a slip and a bursting bra after concluding a sexual tryst with lover Gavin. As Leigh slowly gets dressed, the two sadly discuss their inability to get married for lack of funds. When Leigh later goes to her job as a secretary for realtor Taylor she meets garrulous, wealthy Albertson, who has been drinking and celebrating the fact that he has just purchased a house for his daughter, giving Taylor $40,000 in cash to buy that home. Taylor, nervous about keeping such a large amount in his office, entrusts the cash to Leigh, asking her to take the cash to the bank and deposit it. Leigh, instead, takes the cash to her apartment and packs her bags, and then leaves, taking the money with her with the tenuous intent of starting life all over again. She buys a new car with some of the cash, but her nervous behavior alerts car salesman Anderson and traffic cop Mills. As Leigh drives away in the new car, Mills follows her on his motorcycle. Anxious and weary, Leigh pulls her car to the side of the road and goes to sleep.

She is awakened by Mills, who asks for her identification. (This scene shows Mills in extreme close-up as he grills Leigh, his eyes covered with dark glasses, a looming and foreboding figure, even though he is a representative of the law and where Hitchcock again emphasizes his traditional distrust of such authority as he has demonstrated in many previous films where the police symbolize as much menace as any villain.) When reaching for her driver's license to show Mills, Leigh almost reveals the stolen cash, which she has hidden in a folded newspaper. After Mills slowly examines her license and suspiciously examines Leigh's behavior, he allows her to go on her way, but warns her never again to sleep along a roadway. Leigh drives through the day and into the night, again becoming exhausted and much distracted by the glaring headlights of oncoming traffic. She then spots a sign off the main road that reads "Bates Motel" and drives into its parking area. She is greeted by Perkins, a nervous young man who operates the place and who is attracted to her. He gives her a room that adjoins his office and, before she retires for the night, invites her to have dinner with him, sandwiches that he makes after going to an old house sitting atop a hill behind the motel and where Leigh hears the carping voice of an elderly woman who is ostensibly Perkins' mother and is chastising her son for allowing a single woman to stay the night at their motel where Leigh is the only customer. When Perkins returns to his office, he and Leigh eat their meager dinner. In their conversation, the naïve but apparently well-meaning Perkins inquires about Leigh's ultimate destination. She thinks hard about this and realizes that she has no destination other than to escape a dreary and unpromising life. The outgoing Perkins talks like an adolescent boy even though he is in his twenties. He tells Leigh that his mother has mental problems, but bristles with hostility when Leigh suggests that he might want to institutionalize her. It is unclear whether Leigh now resolves to return the money and make amends for her wrongdoing when she goes to her room, but that is indicated when she counts up the money that is left and then flushes the tally sheet down the toilet (this being the first American film to show a flushing toilet). It is very clear that Perkins is not what he seems to be to Leigh when he goes to his office and opens a peephole that allows him to peer into Leigh's room where he watches her undress, stripping to her black bra and slip (she was wearing a white bra and slip when first shown, Hitchcock later stating that he had her dress that way when she was pure and innocent and then wear black to indicate her evil-doing). She packs her bags for her early morning departure, leaving the stolen money in the folded newspaper on a bed table and then strips naked and steps into the bathtub, drawing the plastic curtains before turning on the shower. Leigh lathers her body (Hitchcock is careful to show only her topside; the shooting had a closed set to protect the actress) and, as steam rises from the hot running water, the camera briefly focuses upon the shower head, this unusual close-up showing the water spraying downward or straight at the viewer (to achieve the shot, Hitchcock ordered a six-foot shower head constructed so that the water would spray from that nozzle in a circular fashion past the lens of his camera without blurring or obstructing the view). Then, through the obscuring shower curtain is seen an approaching figure; the shower curtain is suddenly swept aside to reveal the barely discernible figure of a woman wearing an old-fashioned granny dress, her face in shadows, with a long, upraised knife clutched in her hand, that knife slashing repeatedly downward into Leigh's flesh as she vainly struggles in agony to fend off each terrible thrust of the knife, which produces spouts of blood that run down her legs and flow into the drain. (Hitchcock later stated that at no time did he allow the blade wielded by the attacker to be shown penetrating the flesh, as if that somehow exonerated the overall intent of this horrific scene.) Exhausted in the struggle and drained of life, Leigh clutches the shower curtain and each of its clasps come loose from the overhead pole holding the curtain so that she collapses forward on it and to the bathroom floor, her dead eyes still open, one staring into the camera, which closes upon it to dissolve into the bathtub drain where her blood is washed downward in a rushing swirl. (The shower scene was the most elaborate to construct in the film, Hitchcock later stating that it took "seventy-eight separate pieces of film in forty-five seconds," indicating that the scene was laboriously spliced, albeit in only two split seconds does the slashing knife appear to touch or penetrate Leigh's flesh.) Only seconds after the mysterious assailant departs, Perkins then runs into the unlocked room that has been abandoned by the killer to find in horror the sprawled body of Leigh and where he agonizingly shouts about his mother's maniacally murderous act. After wrapping Leigh's body in the shower curtain and taking it to her car to place it in the trunk, he returns to the room and meticulously mops the bathroom floor. He cleans up the room, and then collects all of Leigh's belongings, including the folded newspaper containing the stolen money, and places these items in the car, which he then drives to a nearby swamp, sending the car into its murky bottom. Meanwhile, Miles, who is Leigh's sister and is worried about her disappearance, goes to Gavin and implores him to search for Leigh. They then meet Balsam, a private detective, who tells them that he, too, is looking for Leigh as he has been hired by Taylor, Leigh's employer, to find her and the missing $40,000. (Taylor has been seen earlier after Leigh left his office to ostensibly deposit that money in the bank and while she is driving in the wrong direction from the bank and Taylor is crossing a street, seeing her with a questioning look on his face.) Balsam is then shown as he dogs Leigh's trail, his investigation leading him to the Bates Motel where he interviews a jittery Perkins, who denies ever having seen a woman of Leigh's description. After Balsam finds an entry in the motel registry book to indicate that a woman had recently rented a room there, Perkins admits that that young woman could have been Leigh. He makes a flimsy excuse about business elsewhere and Balsam returns to his car, but then goes back to the motel office to find Perkins gone. Balsam sees lights go on in the second floor of the old, towering house at the rear of the motel and he climbs the stairs to the house, going inside. Finding no one about, Balsam then climbs the long stairs going to the second floor (the camera focused downward toward him as he plods upward and toward its lens). Just as Balsam reaches the top of the stairs, the camera, from a high angle, shows a lean woman race from a bedroom with a large knife clutched in her hand and which she drives repeatedly into Balsam, bloodying his face and where he falls backward down that long flight of stairs to the bottom, dead. Again, we hear Perkins yelling at his mother for committing another horrendous and inexplicable murder. When Balsam fails to contact Miles and Gavin as promised after calling them from the Bates Motel, they both go in search of him and the trail leads them to the area near the Bates Motel; where they meet with the local sheriff, McIntire. They tell McIniyre that Balsam had met with Perkins and also mentioned that Perkins' mother was living in the old house next to the motel. McIntire is astounded to hear this and tells Miles and Gavin that Perkins' mother has been dead and buried for the last eight years and he now wonders what woman is living in that house with Perkins. Gavin and Miles then drive to the Bates Motel where Gavin questions an anxiety-ridden Perkins, and Miles stealthily goes to the old mansion on the hill, entering it, and calling out for any occupant. She goes to the second floor and enters a bedroom that is decorated with old, ornate women's bric-a-brac and sees on the bed a deep depression or imprint of a human body, as if the person lying there had occupied only that single spot. Miles goes downstairs and, when hearing footsteps approaching the house, flees downstairs to the basement. The footsteps are those of Perkins, who has knocked Gavin unconscious when realizing the reason for his visit. Once in the basement, Miles enters a room with a single glaring light bulb and sees the figure of a woman sitting in a chair with her back to Miles. She calls out to the old lady, but, after getting no response, Miles steps forward, knocking the low-hanging light that begins to sway back and forth as Miles turns around the swivel chair in which the woman is sitting, so that she sees to her horror, as the overhead lamp jumps glaringly back and forth, a hideously decomposed corpse with a skull wearing a wig, dark sockets for eyes and clenched teeth and jawbone. She screams in horror as the molding cadaver sways grotesquely before her and as Perkins then arrives wearing one of his

Anthony Perkins in *Psycho*, 1960.

mother's old dresses and a wig and with a knife menacingly raised above his head. Before Perkins can stab Miles, however, Gavin, who has regained his consciousness and has raced after Perkins, overtakes him and wrestles the knife from his hand while subduing him. We next see Miles and Gavin in a police office where psychiatrist Oakland attempts to explain the strange and murderous doings at the Bates Motel. He says that Perkins has long been deranged, ever since his mother and her lover were murdered, and that his schizoid personality is divided between Perkins and his mother and where the mother's personality, which Perkins has adopted as part of his own, has slowly become the dominating personality, overcoming reason and sensibility and bringing about the murders, all created by the mother half of Perkins' split personality. Oakland goes on to explain that Perkins had disinterred his mother's body from her grave and kept the corpse so that he could have his mother nearby and so that he could transfer to her any guilt he might have felt in committing the murders. We now see Perkins sitting in a chair wearing a strait jacket in a padded cell and where he stares directly at the camera, his thoughts vocalized by his mother's voice, now that the mother's personality has totally taken over his character, as Oakland has stated. That altered personality states to the viewer that she/he will do nothing to alarm his warders and that she/he is completely harmless, and, to prove it, she/he will not even bother to harm a fly that is buzzing nearby, and that she/he is a tranquil person, utterly innocent and gentle as a lamb. The camera slowly closes on Perkins' face and even closer on his penetrating eyes that peer eerily at the viewer in a slightly alarming and cross-eyed fashion, this shot dissolving into a shot of Leigh's car being hauled from the swamp, where this classic shocker ends. Hitchcock holds back nothing in portraying this masterpiece of horror, incorporating just about every Hollywood taboo, including transvestitism, necrophilia, voyeurism, explicit and bloody murder and myriad personality disorders. Perkins is superlative in his role as the quiet young man who erupts into a raging lunatic in the disguise of his mother's personality. The rest of the cast do fine jobs in their roles, and Russell's cinematography is outstanding, his fluid and inventively angled shots enhancing the mounting suspense from scene to scene. The film proved to be a smash box office hit, earning more than $50 million against a budget of about $850,000. A sequel was made in 1983, with Perkins reprising his role, and it was remade several times thereafter, but none of these productions provide the enormous impact made by the original. Hitchcock makes his traditional cameo appearance in this film by strolling past Leigh's office at the beginning of the film. *Author's Note*: Hitchcock purchased the film rights to Bloch's novel for $9,000 and then pitched the story to Paramount, but the studio thought the tale "too repulsive" to put on the screen and wanted Hitchcock to finish up his contract with the studio with one last film that would star

Anthony Perkins next to "Mother's House" in *Psycho*, 1960.

Audrey Hepburn. That actress, however, was not available as she had become pregnant, and Paramount reluctantly agreed to have Hitchcock go ahead with **Psycho**. This was the last film Hitchcock would make in black-and-white, but that was in keeping with the many TV productions he had been doing for his own TV series and where Hitchcock told this author: "I wanted to use the same technical crew I had for the TV series as I was very comfortable with their abilities and talents, so I used most of them when we made **Psycho**." When this author asked Hitchcock his motivation for making such a blatant horror film, he unabashedly replied: "The money. I knew it had little or nothing to do with art and that it would make a lot of money. It did and so did I." (Actually, Hitchcock saw millions from this production because he later got stock options with MCA, becoming in the early 1960s its third-largest stockholder when he exchanged the rights for this film, as well as his TV Productions for that stock.) The film, however, has many fine elements of art, not the least of which is Herrmann's brilliant score, which provides eerie and memorably chilling passages (the composer called it "murder music") by having a number of violinists rapidly screeching the same discordant notes over and over again, producing strange sounds not dissimilar to shrieking birds, this furious bleating underscoring and then dominating each of the killing scenes. Hitchcock originally thought not to use any score at all for **Psycho**, but hired Herrmann on second thought, paying him $17,500 for the score. After he heard its arresting passages, however, Hitchcock was so impressed that he doubled Herrmann's payment. 'When a murder occurs," Hitchcock told this author, "everything goes out of order and that is exactly what Bernard Herrmann gave me when he did that amazing score—sounds you have never heard before and all of them in disorder and chaos. These were the sounds of a maniac, so his score was perfect for **Psycho**." Hitchcock pointed out that Paramount "hated the idea of **Psycho** and they gave me such a limited budget that I told them I would produce the picture with my own money, and that gave them the relief they wanted because all Paramount had to do then was to distribute the picture." In return for financing the film, Hitchcock deferred his usual $250,000 payment for directing a film in lieu of receiving sixty percent of all of its enormous profits. Hitchcock spent stingily on the production, having the mansion behind the motel built for only $15,000, but, though the old Victorian ramshackle of a house appears to be a looming structure, it is really a scaled down building that appears much larger when Hitchcock shot the building from a distance. Elements of that old house were used from cannibalized portions of the set for James Stewart's home in **Harvey**, 1950, which was produced at Universal. In creating the decrepit mansion, set designers used as a role model a memorable oil painting titled "House by the Railroad," produced in 1925 by renowned artist Edward Hopper and which hangs in New York City's Museum of Modern Art. The motel

was constructed on the Universal back lot as Hitchcock had already moved from Paramount to that studio (and where he would end his career), severing his relationship with Paramount when completing **Psycho**. "Yes, the motel appears to be seedy and looks like it was made of clapboard," Hitchcock told this author, "but that is an image I intended. Everything about **Psycho** is seedy, the characters, the settings, the murders, all tawdry and seedy because that is part of the story." Hitchcock was not looking for any Hollywood stars for this film, but intended to use what he called "pedestrian players," although he had a high regard for Vera Miles and said so to this author. Miles told this author at a dinner party in Chicago some years later that she "followed the script and stayed within character and that is the only way to stay on Hitch's safe side." Miles, like the corpse she confronts, wore a wig throughout the film because she had been compelled to shave her head in the recently and earlier produced film, **5 Branded Women**, 1960. Perkins told this author that "I knew that I would be dog-tagged with the character of Norman Bates forever if I took the role, but it was a rare opportunity to work with one of the world's greatest directors, so I did it. Hitch directed everything in his films, every little detail. After Janet [Leigh] is killed, and I have to wrap her body in the shower curtain, Hitch showed me exactly how to fold that curtain over her body and, after wrapping it, how to carry it from the room. He did that with everyone in the picture. Anyone who says that Hitch was lazy, and left all the details to others is completely wrong. He was obsessed with details and handled each detail like a gem-cutter shaping a diamond. I actually did not appear in the shower scene where Janet [Leigh] is killed. Hitch had a double [Ann Dore] do that bit, but you could not see her face, and for some of the slashing close-ups he used another double [Marli Renfro] to stand in for Janet. I never saw that murder scene in the shower until I saw it in a theater and it gave me what it gave everybody else—the willies. **Psycho** changed my career forever and for a long time, I did not want to talk about it, because I was so identified with that picture. Some people actually thought I was deranged or demented, and maybe Hitch did, too, because I think he hired me after seeing a picture I made some years earlier. I had appeared in **Fear Strikes Out** [1957] and where I played Jimmy Piersall (1929-), the Boston Red Sox baseball player, who had mental problems. Those problems, stemming from a dominating father, were a far cry from the lunatic I play in **Psycho**. Do I have regrets about doing **Psycho**? Sometimes I do and other times I do not—I guess that's what you might call a split personality response [and where the actor laughed]." To hide from audiences the plot and finale of the film, Hitchcock had publicists and theater owners tell filmgoers that they would not be admitted after the film began, only before it began. The director further went to the extent of employing a ruse through a publicity statement where he said he was considering hiring one of two illustrious actresses, either Helen Hayes or Judith Anderson, to play the role of the mother, implying that that character would be a very much alive person, instead of the rotting corpse that represents that deceased mother. "I must admit," Hitchcock told this author, "that I was as deceptive in how I talked about **Psycho** before it was released as Norman Bates is when talking to those who are so foolish as to pay a visit to his motel." There were many in Hollywood who never forgave Hitchcock for making this film, one of whom was the celebrated Walt Disney. When, some years later, Hitchcock asked Disney if he could shoot a few scenes at Disneyland for an upcoming production, Disney adamantly refused, saying: "[because] you made that disgusting movie, **Psycho**." One might convincingly say the same thing about **Hitchcock**, 2012, an extremely pretentious and wholly unreliable film that poorly mimics the style and concept of **Shadow of the Vampire**, 2000, an imaginary insider's view of the making of Murnau's 1922 horror classic, **Nosferatu**. Aimed at blatantly capitalizing upon Hitchcock's esteemed reputation, **Hitchcock** is based upon the director's making of **Psycho** and where Wisconsin's cannibal-serial killer, Ed Gein (upon whom the Bloch novel is based) ridiculously interplays as an illusionary character with the director while he is making that film. In one of my many meetings with Hitchcock, the director told me that he had "no interest whatsoever in knowing the mindset of Mr. Gein." For reliable information on Gein, see my two-volume work, *The Great Pictorial History of World Crime*, Volume I (History, Inc., 2004; pages 306-309). **p&d**, Alfred Hitchcock; **cast**, Anthony Perkins, Janet Leigh, Vera Miles, John Gavin, Martin Balsam, John McIntire, Simon Oakland, Frank Albertson, Pat Hitchcock, Lurene Tuttle, Vaughn Taylor, Alfred Hitchcock, Ann Dore (Perkins' double in the shower scene), Marli Renfro (Leigh's double in the shower scene); **w**, Joseph Stefano (based on the novel by Robert Bloch); **c**, John L. Russell; **m**, Bernard Herrmann; **ed**, George Tomasini; **art d**, Joseph Hurley, Robert Clatworthy; **set d**, George Milo; **spec eff**, Clarence Champagne.

PT 109 ★★★ 1963; U.S.; 140m; WB; Color; Biographical Drama/War Drama; Children: Cautionary; **VHS**. Robertson is exceptional in portraying a young and courageous John F. Kennedy (1917-1963), who would become the 35th President of the U.S. He is shown arriving (Kennedy actually arrived on April 14, 1943) at Tulagi Island in the Solomon Islands as a lieutenant junior grade to take command of a PT boat in Pacific operations during WWII (1939-1945). He is greeted by operations commander Gregory, a no-nonsense officer. Robertson asks that he be given command of a PT-boat and the badly damaged PT-109 comes under his command. He rounds up a crew, including executive officer Hardin and retread sailors Blake, Fell and others and they go to work repairing the boat so that it becomes serviceable. Following sea trials and where Robertson commits some errors when docking (destroying a dock and some clapboard buildings), much to the chagrin of Gregory, he receives his first battle assignment, and that is to rescue some U.S. Marines that are trapped on a nearby Japanese-occupied island. He and his crew are given such short notice in this assignment that they leave home port with the boat's fuel tanks only partially filled. After arriving at the island, the boat picks up the stranded Marines while conducting a firefight with Japanese machine gunners firing at it from the shore. Having run out of fuel, the boat perilously begins to drift back toward the shore and the waiting enemy, but another PT-boat, earlier summoned by Robertson via radio, arrives just in time to tow the PT-109 and its passengers back to home port and safety. Robertson is then ordered to take his boat once more into harm's way where it is to support other PT-boats in preventing Japanese troops from landing on a nearby island. In that nighttime sortie, however, the PT-109 is struck by an enemy destroyer, slicing the plywood craft in two and killing two of its crew members. Robertson swims through the burning wreckage to rescue some of his men, returning them to the half of the boat that has remained afloat, but, by dawn, fearing that that portion of the boat will soon sink, Robertson orders his men to swim to a nearby deserted island where they will await rescue. While on that island, Robertson keeps up the morale of his men by assuring them they are going to survive, even though some of them are badly burned and injured. When two natives appear on the island, Robertson carves a message in English on a coconut since the natives do not understand his language and gives it to them to take to, hopefully, some friendly English-speaking contacts on another island. The natives take the coconut to Pate, an Australian coast-watcher, who sends the natives back to the island to retrieve Robertson so that he can arrange for his men to be picked up later. Robertson returns a short time later with a PT-boat and swims to shore to guide his men to that boat and safety. This action-packed and stirring film is well acted, and the script is both believable and convincing. Lensing from accomplished cinematographer Surtees is outstanding, capturing the tropical terrain and sea battles with exciting, finely choreographed scenes. *Author's Note*: Pantheon director Milestone was originally slated to helm this film, and he supervised much of the initial shooting, but then left the production when studio chief Jack Warner, who personally supervised this film, felt that Milestone was running over budget (the film cost more than $4 million and returned only $3.5 million from its initial box office release). "That was the excuse they used at Warner Brothers to explain my departure from the picture after I got into a con-

Cliff Robertson (as John F. Kennedy) and Ty Hardin in *PT 109*, 1963.

frontation with Jack [Warner]," Milestone told this author. "The real reason I left was that I thought the script was not up to par and since Kennedy was then President, everyone at Warner Brothers was walking on eggs and they refused to make any of the changes I wanted. Kennedy's father, old Joe Kennedy, was a millionaire banker and had been a film producer back in the silent era when he was cheating on his wife [Rose Kennedy] by running around with Gloria Swanson. He thought he knew everything about making pictures, so he was really calling the shots on **PT-109**, and Jack Warner listened to Joe Kennedy and his people, not to me. I figured that I would not get into any brawl with the Kennedy family—that Irish clan was too tough to take on in addition to making a picture, so I bowed out." Jack Warner brought in Martinson, a TV director, to finish up the film, which nevertheless remains a superior biopic and war tale. Although several actors were considered for the role of Kennedy, including Warren Beatty, who was Jacqueline Kennedy's choice, Robertson was personally selected by President Kennedy after he saw Robertson in a screen test. The three PT-boats used in the film were actually 85-foot-long U.S. Coast Guard launches that were modified to look like the 80-foot Elco PT-boats that were used by Kennedy and U.S. Navy officers during WWII and were no longer in existence or could not be located. **p**, Bryan Foy; **d**, Leslie H. Martinson; **cast**, Cliff Robertson, Ty Hardin, James Gregory, Robert Culp, Grant Williams, Lew Gallo, Errol John, Michael Pate, Robert Blake, William Douglas, Biff Elliot, Norman Fell, George Takei, Andrew Duggan (narrator); **w**, Richard L. Breen, Howard Sheehan, Vincent X. Flaherty (based on the book *PT 109: John F. Kennedy in WWII* by Robert J. Donovan); **c**, Robert Surtees (Panavision; Technicolor); **m**, William Lava, David Buttolph; **ed**, Folmar Blangsted; **art d**, Leo K. Kuter; **set d**, John P. Austin; **spec eff**, Ralph Webb.

Public Enemies ★★★ 2009; U.S.; 140m; UNIV; Color; Crime Drama; Children: Unacceptable (MPAA: R); **BD**; **DVD**. Although the production values (costuming, sets, props and cinematography) are high for this film, it must be considered a work of fanciful fiction in that it has really little or nothing to do with the actual events and persons it depicts. The tale weaves the criminal careers of several bank robbers in the early 1930s, including, among others, John Dillinger (1903-1934?), woefully underplayed by the miscast Depp; Baby Face Nelson (Lester Gillis; 1908-1934), played by Graham; and Charles Arthur "Pretty Boy" Floyd (1904-1934), played by Tatum, as well as Evelyn "Billie" Frechette (1907-1969), who was Dillinger's foremost girlfriend and is played by Cotillard, as well as FBI agent Melvin Purvis (1903-1960), played by Bale, and FBI director J. Edgar Hoover (1895-1972), played by Crudup, the two lawmen who were most doggedly in pursuit of the elusive and wily Dillinger and others of his ilk during that period. Several bank rob-

Christian Bale (as Melvin Purvis) and Billy Crudup (as J. Edgar Hoover) in *Public Enemies*, 2009.

beries, Dillinger's meeting and relationship with Frechette, and the FBI's machinations in rounding up and eliminating the independent bank robbers of that day are shown in one episodic scene after another, but with somewhat confused continuity, until Dillinger and others are finally brought to justice. This is really a comic book version of that turbulent era with all characters in stereotypical poses, and, as such, it provides a lot of exciting if not bloody entertainment, but it is otherwise not to be viewed as a reliable visual record of those actual bandits and bullet-ridden times. The book by Burrough, upon which this film is based, is a little more than a hackneyed version of an FBI release that the publicity-conscious Hoover might have given to the press in those days. This film's consistent theme that shows Dillinger and other bank robbers directly dealing with members of organized crime, chiefly members of the Capone mob in Chicago, is pure humbug as such close associations never existed. This exorbitant production (at $100 million budget) earned back more than $200 million in its initial release. Many actors in other films have profiled Dillinger (and none of them reliable as to the facts), including **Baby Face Nelson**, 1957 (Leo Gordon); **Baby Face Nelson**, 1996 (Martin Kove); **Dillinger**, 1945 (Lawrence Tierney); **Dillinger**, 1973 (Warren Oates); **Dillinger and Capone**, 1995 (Martin Sheen); **The FBI Story**, 1959 (Scott Peters); **Guns Don't Argue**, 1957 (Myron Healey); **The Kansas City Massacre**, 1975 (made-for-TV; William Jordan); **The Lady in Red**, 1979 (Robert Conrad); **The Private Files of J. Edgar Hoover**, 1977 (Reno Carrel); and **Young Dillinger**, 1965 (Nick Adams). *Author's Note*: As the only non-law enforcement person to ever personally interview Evelyn "Billie" Frechette, who was Dillinger's girlfriend, this author can state with complete confidence that the profile of her, as well as all others in this filmic fantasy, has no basis in reliable fact. Only one of the many preposterously fabricated scenes in this fictional film has Depp seeing Cotillard (playing Frechette) being arrested by law enforcement officials and he later goes into the deserted detective headquarters where she has earlier been taken in a vain effort to retrieve her, and, finding no one, departs. This is utter nonsense as John Dillinger, daring as he was, would never have stepped into the lion's mouth for Frechette or any other woman with whom he had a relationship. For the true story of John Dillinger, see my books *The Dillinger Dossier* (December Press, 1983), and my two-volume reference work *The Great Pictorial History of World Crime*, Volume II (History, Inc., 2004; pages 1374-1442). **p**, Michael Mann, Kevin Misher, Bryan H. Carroll, Gusmano Cesaretti, Kevin De La Noy; **d**, Mann; **cast**, Christian Bale, Johnny Depp, Billy Crudup, Marion Cotillard, Stephen Dorff, James Russo, Casey Siemaszko, Leelee Sobieski, David Wenham, Channing Tatum, Christian Stolte, Jason Clarke, Stephen Graham; **w**, Mann, Ann Biderman, Ronan Bennett (based on the book *Public Enemies* by Bryan Burrough); **c**, Dantße Spinotti; **m**, Elliot Goldenthal;

ed, Jeffrey Ford, Paul Rubell; **prod d**, Nathan Crowley; **art d**, Patrick Lumb, William Ladd Skinner; **set d**, Rosemary Brandenburg; **spec eff**, Bruno Van Zeebroeck, Jamie Dixon, Syd Dutton, Robert Stadd, Dick Edwards, Fortunato Frattasio, Don Lee, Bill Taylor.

The Public Enemy ★★★★★ 1931; U.S.; 83m; WB; B/W; Crime Drama; Children: Unacceptable; **DVD**; **VHS**. This gritty and grimly realistic story startled viewing audiences with its candid portrait of a ruthless criminal and made a superstar out of its leading man, the inimitable James Cagney, who plays Tom Powers, that savage criminal. As one of the first talkie films to portray the actual modus operandi and behavior of organized crime figures in the U.S., this classic tale from pantheon director Wellman pulls no punches as it excitingly and often frighteningly shows the rise of a petty criminal to big time gangster, its violence and sex portrayed as the director saw fit since this production was made before the Hays Office, Hollywood's official censor, established strict codes for all U.S. films. Beginning in 1909 and set in the working-class neighborhood of Southside Chicago, two boys are playing on a wooden sidewalk, one of them, Coghlan (playing Cagney's character as a boy) underhandedly setting a trap for the sister of the other boy, Darro (playing Woods' character as a boy, and where Woods later becomes Cagney's erstwhile criminal sidekick). The girl tumbles when the boy raises a rope that tangles her skates, indicating that boy's devious and somewhat vicious nature. Coghlan is the son of Pratt, a heavy-handed Chicago cop who routinely beats him with a strap for any wrongdoing, and when caught after ensnaring the girl, he is ordered into the house where his father (who wears his police helmet inside that house), takes him into a bedroom with a razor strap. The defiant Coghlan sneers at his father, saying: "How do you want 'em? Up or down?" (He means is he to remove his trousers or not.) He is forced over his father's knees with the trousers still on and is soundly strapped. The boys are next seen when they attend a seedy club run by Kinnell, a Fagin-like character who hosts a group of street boys doing his criminal bidding. He sends the boys out to steal items, fencing these stolen goods and giving the boys pittance in return for their criminal efforts. Years later, we see Cagney, Woods and another youth break into a fur warehouse to steal its contents, but, after Cagney moves a rack of fur coats and sees a stuffed bear's head glaring at him, he impulsively fires several shots at it and, now that the neighborhood has been alerted by the gunfire, the boys flee, sliding down a drainpipe from the second floor to an alleyway, but where a police officer responding to an alarm bell, shoots and kills one of the boys as Cagney and Woods run into a dark alley. The cop pursues, but is killed by Cagney and Woods who then emerge from the alley, throwing the guns away before running off, the dead cop's hand still clutching a revolver to fade the scene. Cagney and Woods return to Kinnell's alleyway club, but the door is barred and a goon behind the door tells them through an open door panel that Kinnell has left town. Deserted by their sponsor, Cagney and Woods threaten reprisal, the goon stating: "You and who else?" Cagney smashes the door panel open in an attempt to retaliate and they then leave. At a wake for the dead boy, Mercer, who is Cagney's mother, consoles the bereaved wife of the slain accomplice and then Cagney and Woods apprehensively appear to peak into the open coffin of their slain associate. They later visit a saloon operated by O'Connor, who tells them that they were "saps" for listening to Kinnell and that he will have some good "jobs" for them to later perform, meaning criminal capers. Both are by then working as delivery men in 1917, when WWI is declared in the U.S., and Cook, Cagney's older brother, enlists with the Marines to fight in Europe. Before Cook leaves for duty, he lectures Cagney about his underworld activities, stealing while using his delivery job as a cover, and Cagney accuses Cook of being a penny-ante crook stealing coins on the streetcar where he had formerly worked as a conductor. The angry Cook hits Cagney, knocking him to the floor before leaving, such is the strained relationship between these two brothers, one that has existed since childhood where Cook has been an upright person and Cagney a venal character (and where director

Wellman told this author that he purposely positioned the brothers as Cain and Abel figures). It is then 1919, and Prohibition is about to go into law where all alcoholic beverages will be outlawed. Cagney and Woods meet with O'Connor, who tells them that he wants them to be part of a powerful gang that will obtain and supply liquor and beer not only to his saloon but scores of others, promising them a fortune in this new illegal racket called bootlegging. They eagerly volunteer for this work. Before the new law takes effect, panic ensues and Wellman depicts an utterly frenetic scene where liquor store operators are frantically selling out their inventory to desperate customers, the wealthy and the poor alike, who load their cars and trucks with bottles of liquor or carry as many bottles as they can. A well-dressed man hands a number of paper wrapped bottles of liquor to his wife through the window of their limousine, and, after one falls to the pavement and breaks, the elegantly dressed woman quickly steps from the car in an attempt to desperately preserve the contents of the broken bottle. Another man is shown going home as he pushes a baby carriage loaded with bottles of liquor while his wife carries their child in her arms along a street packed with drunken citizens also loaded with bottles of liquor. The crowd revels in its possession of the now illegal booze, which symbolizes the manic demand of the public to later obtain liquor in defiance of the new draconian law. Meanwhile, Cook returns home as an exhausted war hero, only to learn from a local cop who is a family friend that Cagney and Woods have become bootleggers and that "they will stop at nothing," including killing anyone who attempts to foil their operations. At a family dinner, Cagney and Woods place a huge keg of beer upon the dining room table of Cagney's home before Mercer sits down with her family to have dinner. Cook stares silently at the huge keg of beer that blocks his view of his mother. Woods pours glasses of beer from the keg, offering one to Cook, who does not drink from it. When Cagney asks him to drink up and toast the family, Cook not only refuses, but tells Cagney and Woods he knows what they have been doing and says: "You think I don't know what you two have been up to? That's not just beer in that keg—it's *blood* and beer!" He seizes the keg and smashes it against a wall before collapsing into a chair. Disgusted, Cagney states: "You ain't changed a bit…Your hands ain't so clean. You killed and liked it! You didn't get them medals for holding hands with them Germans!" Before leaving with Woods, Cagney tells Mercer to send his belongings to a hotel where he intends to live apart from the family. Cagney and Woods are next shown working for O'Connor and where they back up an oil truck to the wall of a closed warehouse containing bonded liquor and beer, running a hose from the truck and up and through a drainpipe to the warehouse's second floor. Inside the warehouse, others tap into a huge liquor vat, inserting the hose into it, causing the vat's contents to course through the hose and into the truck parked outside. Once the oil truck has been filled with the siphoned-off booze, Cagney and Woods drive the truck away, its contents to be distributed by O'Connor's mobsters to numerous speakeasies. This caper and others soon enrich Cagney and Woods, who buy expensive wardrobes (and where Cagney becomes angry with an effeminate tailor when he too closely measures him while Cagney stands for a fitting) and they purchase a high-powered and expensive roadster which they are shown driving up to a nightclub. As they stand in the street adorned with their vicuna coats and rakish fedoras, Cagney hears a porter grinding the gears of his new car and shouts: "Hey, mug! That ain't no Ford. It's got gears!" Cagney and Woods enter the speakeasy, and they order waiters to remove two passed-out drunks from a table at which two girls, Clarke and Blondell, are sitting. Cagney and Woods immediately take the place of the drunks, quickly establishing relationships with Clarke and Blondell. They later meet with O'-Connor, who introduces them to his new partner, the slick Fenton (who plays Nails Nathan), a big-time bootlegging boss with a huge gang behind him. Fenton describes how he plans to take over the city's bootlegging operations, even if it means killing any competitors and those reluctant to buy his booze. Cagney and Woods become even richer and more powerful as they climb the criminal ladder to success. They move

Mae Clarke and James Cagney in *The Public Enemy,* 1931.

into a luxurious apartment with Clarke and Blondell and Cagney later goes to see his mother, Mercer, giving her a wad of bills, but Cook arrives and tells him that he does not want Cagney's "blood" money going to their mother and throws it back at him. Cagney, enraged, tears up the money and departs as the brokenhearted Mercer weeps over the strife existing between her two sons. The following morning, Cagney awakes and goes to a table where Clarke has prepared his breakfast. She tells him that she wishes he would treat her better, but Cagney is now bored with Clarke, sneering: "I wish you was a wishing well so I could tie a bucket to you and sink you!" Clarke makes the mistake of saying: "Maybe you've found someone you like better?" With that, Cagney takes a half-sliced grapefruit and jams it into Clarke's face, leaving her to cry in humiliation. (This crude and vicious action by Cagney stunned worldwide audiences and permanently entrenched his tough guy image within the public mind.) In response to a request by Fenton to keep a speakeasy owner in line, Cagney and Woods then go to the speakeasy, and Cagney samples the owner's beer and then spits it into the owner's face, growling: "That ain't our beer." The owner tells him that he is buying cheaper beer from a competitive bootlegger, and Cagney goes behind the bar, opening all of the taps so that the beer flows freely; when the owner tries to stop him, Cagney slaps the owner into submission and compels him to order more beer from him. Cagney is next shown riding along a Chicago street (which was shot in Los Angeles where the entire production was made) with Woods at the wheel, and when Cagney sees Harlow, a curvaceous blonde walking on the street, he orders Woods to stop the car. Cagney alights and asks Harlow if he can give her a ride and she accepts. Deeply attracted to Harlow, he asks for her phone number before he drops her off at her destination, and she gives him that number. Cagney is later shown escorting Harlow to a swanky nightclub with Fenton and O'Connor and their girlfriends, along with Woods and Blondell and where they are celebrating the marriage between Woods and Blondell. While Cagney dances with Harlow, he sees his old mentor, Kinnell, sitting at a table with a henchman, and after returning to the table, Fenton tells him that Kinnell has played him as a sucker when he was a kid and that "he has the Indian sign on you." Goaded by Fenton and O'Connor into taking reprisal against Kinnell for his long ago desertion of them, Cagney and Woods leave the nightclub, following Kinnell to his home. Kinnell puts them off, saying that he can't invite them inside because he has a woman waiting for him. They nevertheless go inside with him and find no one there, Kinnell's lie enraging them. Cagney hits Kinnell, knocking him down, and it is then that Kinnell realizes that he is about to be killed and begs for his life, playing upon old sympathies by reminding Cagney and Woods, now dedicated killers, that they all had once been friends. Kinnell goes to a piano and begins to play an old song he played for Cagney and

Edward Woods, James Cagney and Lee Phelps in *The Public Enemy*, 1931.

Woods when they were boys, but Cagney, standing behind Kinnell, draws a gun and shoots him dead while he is in the middle of delivering the last word of that song, although the viewer does not see Kinnell die, as the camera is focused upon Woods as he watches apprehensively as Cagney commits the murder and we hear a shot and Kinnell cry out and the sound of piano keys all discordantly crashing together as Kinnell falls to his death. Cagney then walks into the scene, calmly telling the stunned Woods that he is going to call up Harlow and both leave. Cagney is then shown with Harlow in her luxurious apartment (it is obvious that she is a well-kept woman) and he sits complaining to her about their unfulfilled sexual relationship, saying: "How long can a guy wait—I'll go screwy!" Just as he is about to leave, she stops him, sits in his lap and caresses him while tossing his hat away and tells him: "You don't give—you take…Tommy. I could love you to death!" As she kisses him, the phone rings and Cagney learns from Woods that their boss, Fenton, has been killed, kicked to death by a temperamental horse while riding on the Chicago bridle path. Cagney and Woods immediately go to the stable, pay a trainer the cost for the horse and then go into its berth and, off camera, shoot and kill the animal. When Cagney emerges, he drops the horse's saddle blanket next to the startled trainer. Following Fenton's death, a widespread gang war erupts, and O'Connor takes over the gang. After his saloon is bombed and his breweries and distilleries destroyed, O'Connor gathers what is left of his gang, including Cagney and Woods, and tells them that they must all go into hiding until he can recruit more gang members and reorganize. He takes them to a bordello and hideout operated by Marvin. O'Connor collects all the money and guns his gang members have, saying they will not go onto the streets without either and to stay at Marvin's place until he contacts them. After he leaves, Cagney hears a loud noise from the street and, looking from the second-floor window of Marvin's place, sees that the racket has been created by a coal truck delivering coal through a chute and he then ignores the workers below. One of the workers, however, signals to an upstairs window across the street where two men raise a shade behind which sits two machine guns aimed at the building where Cagney and Woods have taken refuge. That night, Cagney gets drunk and, instead of playing cards with Woods and two other gang members, staggers into a bedroom where Marvin helps him undress and kisses him. She is about to leave the room, but, instead, turns out the light, walking off camera to return to Cagney and we hear him say: "You're Paddy's girl [O'Connor's girl]—get away from me!" When he wakes the next morning with a hangover, Cagney sits at a dining room table and Marvin pours him a cup of coffee, asking how he slept and then teases him so that he realizes she has slept with him. Enraged, he slaps her and then grabs his hat, telling Woods he is leaving with or without O'Connor's permission. Just as Cagney steps outside, Woods catches up with him, reminding him

that "we're together, aren't we?" Cagney grins at him and they begin to walk down the street, but they hear a racket and instinctively crouch on the street, but when they realize that the noise is again being made by the coal truck delivering coal. Just as they resume walking, the gangsters perched in the upstairs window across the street open fire with their machine guns, and Woods is shot down while Cagney manages to slip into an alleyway, bullets chipping away at the cornerstone of the building only inches from his head. He watches as the fallen Woods, mortally wounded, raises his arm in a grim farewell and dies. Cagney next goes to a shop where he asks to see some pistols, and, after the shopkeeper shows him two .38 caliber revolvers, he loads one of them with bullets and then aims it at the shopkeeper, who laughs, thinking Cagney is joking. He is not joking, when he barks: "Stick 'em up!" and then retreats from the store. He later waits in a rain storm outside the headquarters of Schemer Burns, the opposing gang leader who has brought about the gang war and Woods' death and where Cagney, armed with the two revolvers he has stolen, seeks revenge. He sees the mob boss arrive with a bevy of guards and enter his headquarters. Cagney then enters the place while the camera remains outside the building as rain continues to fall and suddenly wild gunfire is heard, along with the dying screams of the rival gangsters. Cagney emerges from the building, wounded and staggering into the street, hurling the two revolvers into the windows of the building, and then moving down the street wobbly-legged, blood gushing from a head wound, until he sinks to his knees with the camera at the street level to show the rushing rainwater swirling around him and where he says before collapsing: "I ain't so tough!" We next see Cook arriving at a hospital with Mercer and Flynn, Woods' sister and Cook's wife. They visit Cagney, who is heavily bandaged and recovering from his wounds. Cagney tells Cook and Mercer that he is "sorry" for everything and that he is through with the rackets. They are overjoyed to hear this and make preparations to welcome him home. Cook, Mercer and Flynn return home and make preparations for Cagney's return. O'Connor appears and tells Cook that Cagney has been kidnapped from the hospital by members of Burns' gang, adding that he has talked with the abductors and promised them that he would quit the rackets and leave them to his rivals if Cagney is returned home, and he departs. A short time later, Cook receives a phone call that Cagney will soon be delivered. While Mercer happily makes up the bed in Cagney's old room, Cook opens the front door of the house to see Cagney trussed up in ropes, dead eyes staring vacantly as his body collapses face forward to the floor with a thud. After kneeling beside the corpse and realizing that his brother is dead, Cook shakily gets to his feet and, while the song "I'm Forever Blowing Bubbles" is playing on a record player, slowly staggers in shock toward the camera to end this shuddering and terrifying film. Wellman's succinct, almost clinical direction provides a devastating portrait without frills or glamour, revealing in one mesmerizing scene after another the making of a predatory killer while documenting with great incisive skill the gangster era and all of its synthetic and deceptive attractions and allures. This classic masterpiece of crime set the precedent, along with **Little Caesar**, 1931, which was released in the same year and also produced by Warner Brothers, for all of the gangster films to come and where Wellman takes a dedicated documentary approach to his grim subject. Cagney, in a virtuoso performance of corruption and evil embodied in a single person, also established an unforgettable image that would be forever linked to his persona. The supporting cast, especially Cook and Mercer, are standouts, as is Woods as the faithful sidekick willing to go to hell with Cagney, and Fenton, who renders an equally impressive performance as one of the oiliest gang bosses in filmic record. Produced on a budget of $150,000, the film grossed almost $1 million at the box office in its initial release, a staggering success for that day and it earned twice that amount through several rereleases. Songs: "I'm Forever Blowing Bubbles" (1919; James Kendis, James Brockman, Nat Vincent), "Hesitation Blues" (1915; Billy Smythe, Scott Middleton, Art Gillham), "Toot, Toot, Tootsie (Goodbye!)" (Gus Khan, Ernie Erdman, Dan Russo), "Maple Leaf Rag" (1899;

Scott Joplin), "Brighten the Corner Where You Are" (1913; Charles H. Gabriel), "Smiles" (1917; Lee S. Roberts), "I Surrender Dear" (1931; Harry Barris). *Author's Note*: Much of what appears in this startling film is based on actual fact and real persons. Cagney's character is based on bootlegger and gangster Charles Dion "Deanie" O'Banion (1892-1924), who was the crime boss of Chicago's North Side, until murdered in his flower shop (unlike Cagney being delivered dead to his home) in 1924 by rival gangsters working for South Side crime boss Al Capone. "I did a lot of reading about O'Banion," Cagney told this author, "and learned that he had been a choir boy and an altar boy and attended Catholic Church every Sunday with his wife, even though he was bumping off his competitors on almost every other day of the week. I wanted to show that part of his character in the film, but when I mentioned that to Bill [Wellman], he said: 'I'm not giving that killer any breaks in this film. He was a murdering thug like all of the others we are showing, so forget the Church angle, Jimmy.' I was just starting out in pictures and was in no position to argue, especially in a picture where I first made my mark, so I kept my mouth shut about getting my character into any kind of church." Cagney went on to emphasize that his role in **The Public Enemy** was a very dangerous one, telling this author that "in the scene where Eddie [Woods] and I leave the apartment building and he is shot, Bill [Wellman] had an expert machine gunner fire real bullets at the wall where I was hiding and some of the cement chipped away and bits flew into my face. Those bullets were only inches away from my head and when Bill told me that he wanted another take of that scene, I told him that I was an actor, not a stunt man, and that I was not there to get shot, so he lived with the take he got on film and that is the one you see in the picture. They kept trying to do that with me in a lot of other pictures, like **Angels with Dirty Faces** [1938] and I was almost shot in that picture, too, until I finally put my foot down, and told them that I would never again play a clay pigeon for any director and I did not care how many expert marksmen they had or the promises they made that I would never be harmed. A stray bullet can't keep any promises." As to the celebrated grapefruit scene in the film, Cagney told this author: "It was a joke dreamed up by Bill and some of the crew members and poor Mae [Clarke] was not told that I was going to slam a wet grapefruit into her face, so when I did that, she was really surprised and startled and when she cried, I think she was crying because she had been humiliated. I felt very bad about that. It was cruel and not funny at all and I probably apologized to her dozens of times for years after that, but, by then, she had forgiven me. Bill Wellman was a great director, but I think he was an all-man director and insensitive to female emotions. Years after we did that to poor Mae, I asked Bill: 'Do you think if I smashed a grapefruit into your face, Bill, you would laugh?' He said: 'Hell, no, I would punch you in the nose.' 'There you have it, Bill,' I told him. I get embarrassed just thinking about that scene." Harlow, who appears in the only film she would ever do with Cagney, would so impress MGM executives with her brief but torrid performance, that she would be signed to a long-term contract by that studio and where she would become a superstar until prematurely dying six years later. Her blonde bombshell character in **The Public Enemy** is based upon Louise Rolfe (1906-1995), a showgirl and the mistress of Capone enforcer "Machine Gun Jack" McGurn, who orchestrated the 1929 St. Valentine's Day Massacre. McGurn married Rolfe so that she could not, as his wife, testify against him in refuting her statements that McGurn had been with her in her hotel room at the time of that 1929 massacre in Chicago (where seven members of O'Banion's old gang were summarily slaughtered) and Rolfe would be thereafter known as "The Blonde Alibi." Other characters in this pyrotechnic film were also based on members of O'Banion's North Side gang, including Hendricks, who plays a character called "Bugs Moran," as George "Bugs" Moran (1891-1957) was O'Banion's erstwhile friend and who eventually succeeded O'Banion as the boss of the gang. Fenton's character, called "Nails Nathan," is based on early-day Chicago bootlegger Samuel J. "Nails" Morton (1894-1923), who was a Chicago bootlegger

Jean Harlow, Edward Woods and James Cagney in *The Public Enemy*, 1931.

and an O'Bannion associate. Morton had been a WWI hero, serving in the U.S. Army as a lieutenant and, at the dawn of Prohibition, established his own gang of bootleggers working closely with O'Banion and his henchmen. Morton, as is shown in this film, was an avid horse rider and who was thrown from a horse he was riding on a bridle path in Chicago's Lincoln Park on May 13, 1923, kicked to death in the head by that horse. One of O'Banion's more flamboyant lieutenants, Louis "Two-Gun" Alterie (Leland Verain; 1886-1935), went to the stable to locate that horse and shot it to death in retaliation for Morton's demise, that scene reenacted in this film. The rival gang boss, "Schemer Burns," who is not clearly shown in the film, takes his name from another O'Banion lieutenant, Vincent "The Schemer" Drucci (1895-1927). Another member of the O'Banion gang, Earl "Hymie" Weiss (1898-1926), according to Cagney, was the source of the grapefruit scene in that the writers for the film told him that Weiss had awakened one morning and, angered by the incessant chatter from his mistress, smashed an omelet into her face, one that she had just prepared for him. "That grapefruit scene in **The Public Enemy** was really an out-take, a prank we all pulled on Mae Clarke," Wellman told this author, "and I did not intend to use that shot in the picture, but, after I watched it, and saw how painfully mortified Mae appeared, and how such a crude act by Cagney would symbolize his vicious nature, I decided to keep that shot in the picture. Mae was giving me a hard time and seemed to lack energy, although she said she had a cold at the time we were making the picture, but I never liked that dame, so I wanted to get back at her for the way she had been ignoring my directions and that is why I cooked up that gag, which, when looking back on it all, was pretty mean of me. The scene was important, though, because it typified the nature of those Chicago gangsters." Cagney told this author that "gangsters in Chicago were wild men back in the Twenties, much different than the bootleggers we saw in New York and on the Coast. They went around with guns bulging in their pockets just looking for any kind of excuse to shoot someone. A few years after we made **The Public Enemy**, I was in Chicago and a dapper looking man came up to me in a hotel lobby and told me how he admired my performance in that picture. When he patted me on the back, his suit coat opened a bit and I could see that he was wearing a gun in a holster beneath that coat. He was Louis Alterie, a member of the old O'Banion gang. I was glad to see him walk away from me because standing next to people like that was a very dangerous proposition. They could be shot and killed at any moment and nobody cared about bystanders, at least not in Chicago. Alterie was shot to death about a year after I met him." Darryl Zanuck, who was then head of production at Warner Brothers, did not initially want to do this film. "When Bill [Wellman] came to me and pitched the story for **The Public Enemy**," Zanuck told this author, "I turned him down. I pointed out

Joe Pesci and Barbara Hershey in *The Public Eye*, 1992.

that we had just recently made two tough gangster pictures, **Doorway to Hell** [1930] and **Little Caesar** [1931] and I said to Bill: 'What kind of picture could you give me that would top those two pictures?,' and he said: 'I'll give you the most violent and most realistic gangster picture ever made.' I let him go ahead with it, but I gave him such a restricted budget that I thought he would never be able to complete the picture. Well, he did, and he delivered exactly what he promised, the most violent gangster film ever made. No one has ever forgotten it, including me." Wellman effectively used the approximately $150,000 budget Zanuck gave him, shooting the film in his typical lightning-speed fashion and completing the film within a hectic schedule of twenty-six days. "I had to fight to get Jimmy [Cagney] in the lead role of that picture," Wellman told this author. "He had appeared in four other films up to that time and the front office thought of him only as a promising novice. We already had Eddie [Woods] in the leading part as Tom Powers, but, after I looked at some rushes, I said, 'we've got the wrong guy playing the leading man. It's Cagney who is the real tough guy, so I went back to Darryl [Zanuck] and told him I wanted Jimmy and Eddie to switch parts and he didn't like that, but I argued him into it and Cagney took over the role that would make him famous and a superstar. Darryl later took credit for all that, right down to the grapefruit scene, but I didn't care. I got what I wanted." Wellman wanted realism above all, and in the scene between Cagney and Cook where Cook hits him and knocks him down, Wellman told Cook not to pull his punches, telling Cook: "Go ahead, let him have it. He can take it." Cook, a larger man, landed a haymaker on Cagney's jaw that, according to what Cagney told this author, "had me seeing every star in the universe. I fell down like a brick and broke a chair when I went down. When I stood up, I could taste blood in my mouth and I later saw that Donald [Cook] had chipped one of my teeth. I did not complain about it. Bill [Wellman] had given me the greatest opportunity of my life by insisting that I play the leading role in **The Public Enemy**, so I showed my gratitude by taking all kinds of abuse without saying a word. That's how it was in those days—you couldn't be running to Actors' Equity with complaints. You took it and went on if you wanted to keep working in Hollywood then. Warner Brothers was probably the toughest studio to work at in those days because almost all of the studio's pictures were right out of the newspapers, rough and tumble stories. The actors over at Paramount and MGM were a lot safer, I think, because they were doing comedies and musicals and drawing room dramas. At Warner Brothers the actors were getting blown up and shot down in sound stages every hour of the day. We might as well have been living in Chicago." The tempestuous and volatile nature of some of that studio's executives reflected the violence-prone films for which Warner Brothers quickly became known. Wellman exampled that when telling this author: "I sat in a screen room with Jack Warner,

Michael Curtiz, who was Jack's workhorse director, and Zanuck, and we all watched **The Public Enemy** after I had completed the picture. After watching it, Jack Warner shook his head and said the film upset him and that it might be just too violent for the public. Well, Curtiz, who was forever agreeing with Jack, played the lap dog and began repeating every one of Jack's complaints about the picture. Zanuck, who loved what I had done with the picture, sat glaring at Curtiz until he could not take his slavish remarks anymore and jumped up and smashed his fist right into Curtiz's startled face. Curtiz was smoking a cigar then and I think it went right down his throat. Curtiz was also a hothead, but, before he could get at Zanuck, Jack and I got between them and calmed them down. I said to myself, 'I love this guy Zanuck and I do not care what he does from now on.' He went to bat for my picture and he put his fist where Curtiz's mouth was to prove it." After Zanuck left Warner Brothers to become head of Fox, he would always remember Wellman as a director he could depend upon in delivering outstanding films, and Wellman would go on to direct superior Fox westerns for Zanuck such as **The Ox-Bow Incident**, 1943, **Buffalo Bill**, 1944, and **Yellow Sky**, 1948. For more details on O'Banion, Morton, and other members mentioned in connection with the North Side Chicago gang of the 1920s, see my books *Bloodletters and Badmen*, 1973 (M. Evans, New York, 1973), *World Encyclopedia of Organized Crime* (Paragon House, New York, 1992), and *The Great Pictorial History of World Crime*, Volume I (History, Inc., Wilmette, Ill., 2004). **p**, Darryl F. Zanuck; **d**, William A. Wellman; **cast**, James Cagney, Jean Harlow, Edward Woods, Joan Blondell, Donald Cook, Leslie Fenton, Beryl Mercer, Robert Emmett O'Connor, Murray Kinnell, Rita Flynn, Mae Clarke, Mia Marvin, Frank Coghlan, Jr., Frankie Darro, Purnell Pratt, Helen Parrish, Ben Hendricks, Jr., Robert Homans, Snitz Edwards; **w**, Kubec Glasmon, John Bright, Harvey Thew (based on the story "Beer and Blood" by Bright); **c**, Dev Jennings; **m**, David Mendoza; **ed**, Edward M. McDermott; **art d**, Max Parker.

The Public Eye ★★★ 1992 U.S.; 108m; UNIV; Color; Crime Drama; Children: Unacceptable (MPAA: R); **DVD**; **VHS**. Pesci does an outstanding job as a scuzzy freelance news photographer for sensational tabloid newspapers in New York City in 1942, equally at home with cops or crooks. His photos with a big Speed Graphic camera are often of pain and death, but they are the ones readers want to see and other cameramen wish they had snapped. Glamorous Hershey seeks his help when mobsters begin muscling in on the nightclub she owns due to an arrangement with her late husband. Pesci isn't too good with women but agrees to help and does, freeing her from the gangsters. She falls in love with him, but the squat little man prefers freelancing, with women and photography, and goes his separate paparazzi way. The sets, cars, props, and costuming well capture the period and setting of the early 1940s. Songs: "You Can't Say No to a Soldier" (Harry Warren, Mack Gordon); "Embraceable You" (George Gershwin. Ira Gershwin). Excessive violence prohibits viewing by children. **p**, Sue Baden-Powell; **d&w**, Howard Franklin; **cast**, Joe Pesci, Barbara Hershey, Richard Riehle, Bryan Travis Smith, Richard Schiff, Timothy Hendrickson, Jack Denbo, Del Close, David Gianopoulos, Steve Forleo; **c**, Peter Suschitzky; **m**, Mark Isham; **ed**, Evan Lottman; **prod d**, Marcia Hinds-Johnson; **art d**, Bo Johnson, Dina Lipton; **set d**, Jan Bergstrom; **spec eff**, Martin Bresin.

Public Hero No. 1 ★★★ 1935; U.S.; 89m; MGM; B/W; Crime Drama; Children: Unacceptable. In this well-crafted crime tale, Morris poses as a convict to get into a prison to help inmate Calleia escape, so he can be followed and authorities can break up Detroit's notorious "Purple Gang" of bootleggers, which Calleia heads. Arthur is Calleia's innocent sister, who begins to fall for Morris and vice versa. Barrymore is an alcoholic doctor, who will perform any surgery for a bottle of whiskey. After Calleia is seriously wounded, Barrymore patches him up, but saves his life only after Morris donates some of his blood to keep Calleia alive long enough so that he can detail his gang operations to Morris. The murderous mobster gets his just deserts when Calleia is gunned down outside a movie theater, the incident borrowing from real life when bank robber John Dillinger (1903-1934?) was reportedly shot dead outside a Chicago movie theater on July 22, 1934. Morris is a standout in this tough crime yarn, which is packed with a lot of exciting action, and director Ruben does not stint on gang wars, muttering machineguns and well-orchestrated mayhem. Calleia (born on Malta as Joseph Spurin-Calleja) is excellent in the role of the sinister gang boss, providing a chilling essay of a cold-blooded killer who murders without remorse and at the drop of his Homburg hat. This film was remade as **Get-Away**, 1941, starring Dan Dailey, the remake using a lot of the action scenes from this production. The Purple Gang was additionally profiled under that title in 1960. The tactic of having an innocent person pose as a criminal to bring about imprisonment in order to effect the release of another prisoner has been employed in other films, most notably in **Strange Cargo**, 1940, but in that film the one impersonating a prisoner is God, and His motive is to redeem the soul of another prisoner by effecting that prisoner's escape. **p**, Lucien Hubbard; **d**, J. Walter Ruben; **cast**, Chester Morris, Jean Arthur, Lionel Barrymore, Joseph Calleia, Paul Kelly, Lewis Stone, Paul Hurst, George E. Stone, Sam Baker, Cora Sue Collins, Zeffie Tilbury; **w**, Wells Root (based on the story by Ruben, Root); **c**, Gregg Toland; **m**, Edward Ward; **ed**, Frank Sullivan; **art d**, Cedric Gibbons.

Puccini for Beginners ★★★ 2007; U.S.; 82m; Eden Wurmfeld Films/Strand Releasing; Color; Comedy/Romance; Children: Unacceptable; **DVD**. Reaser is entertaining in this partner exchanging sex farce, where she is an opera-loving writer in New York, who is reluctant to make a commitment to her girlfriend, Nicholson, and who leaves her. Reaser misses Nicholson, who begins dating a man. At a party, Reaser meets college professor Kirk, who has recently broken off with his girlfriend, Mol, and Reaser and Kirk go to bed together. Kirk gets serious about Reaser, but she says their relationship was only a fling on her part. Though Reaser becomes interested in Mol, Kirk and Mol wind up together and we get the hint that Reaser and Nicholson will, too. This low-budget, independently made, and offbeat film saw success at the 2006 Sundance Film Festival, although its lesbian themes proved unpopular with mainstream audiences. Music: Giacomo Puccini. Sexuality prohibits viewing by children. **p**, Jake Abraham, Gary Winick, Eden Wurmfeld; **d&w**, Maria Maggenti; **cast**, Elizabeth Reaser, Julianne Nicholson, Gretchen Mol, Justin Kirk, Ken Barnett, Brian Letscher, Tina Benko, Kate Simses, Natalie Havermeyer, Mimi Molligher; **c**, Mauricio Rubinstein; **m**, Terry Dame; **ed**, Susan Graef; **prod d**, Aleta Shaffer; **set d**, Valerie Nolan.

Pulp ★★★ 1972; U.K.; 95m; Three Michaels Film Productions/UA; Color; Crime Drama; Children: Unacceptable (MPAA: PG); **DVD**; **VHS**. Caine is a standout as a writer of sleazy pulp novels. He is hired to write the biography of a former movie star, Rooney, who is living reclusively in Malta. While working on the book with him, Rooney is murdered, and Caine becomes one of the suspects along with an odd assortment of others including Scott, a princess. Rooney had mob connections, and Caine finally discovers that a mob hit man is responsible for Rooney's death. This film pokes fun at *film noir* productions and is loaded with a lot of black humor. Songs: "Primitive People," "African Mood" (Hugo de Groot); "Victoria's Valse," "George Leybourne's Polka" (Leslie Bridgewater); "Grand Hotel" (John Hawksworth); "In a Quiet Corner" (William Millen, Jack Hylton, Reginald Connelly); "Little White Lies" (Walter Donaldson); "Funiculi Funicula" (Luigi Denza, Peppino Turco); "Santa Lucia" (Teodoro Cottrau); "O Sole Mio," "Maria Mari" (Eduardo Di Capua); "Remembrance" (Antonio Melfi); "Greensleeves" (traditional). Excessive violence prohibits viewing by children. **p**, Michael Klinger; **d&w**, Mike Hodges; **cast**, Michael Caine, Mickey Rooney, Lizabeth Scott, Lionel Stander, Nadia Cassini, Dennis Price, Al Lettieri, Leopoldo Trieste, Amerigo Tot, Roberto Sacchi,

Michael Caine and Nadia Cassini in *Pulp*, 1972.

Giulio Donnini, Joe Zammit Cordina; **c**, Ousama Rawi (DeLuxe Color); **m**, George Martin; **ed**, John Glen; **prod d**, Patrick Downing; **art d**, Darrell Lass; **spec eff**, Ron Ballanger.

The Pumpkin Eater ★★★ 1964; U.K.; 118m; Romulus Films/Royal Films; B/W; Drama; Children: Unacceptable; **VHS**. Taut domestic tale sees Finch as a film writer, and he and his wife, Bancroft, live in London with six of her eight children from three previous marriages while the two eldest boys are at boarding school. Only one of the children is Finch's with Bancroft. She becomes depressed, and psychiatrist Porter concludes that she uses childbirth as a rationale for sex, which she otherwise finds to be vulgar or repulsive. Finch and Bancroft say they love each other, but, when she asks him why he married her, he can give her no reasonable answer. Rather than dissolve their relationship, this odd couple decides to continue their marriage, but we are left at the finale not knowing what kind of relationship it will be. Sexual content and gutter language prohibit viewing by children. **p**, James Woolf; **d**, Jack Clayton; **cast**, Anne Bancroft, Peter Finch, James Mason, Sir Cedric Hardwicke, Janine Gray, Rosalind Atkinson, Alan Webb, Richard Johnson, Maggie Smith, Eric Porter; **w**, Harold Pinter (based on the novel by Penelope Mortimer); **c**, Oswald Morris; **m**, Georges Delerue; **ed**, James Clark; **art d**, Edward Marshall.

The Purple Gang ★★★ 1960; U.S.; 85m; AA; B/W; Crime Drama; Children: Unacceptable; **DVD**. Provocative crime tale records the bloody exploits of Detroit's infamous Purple Gang, which begins with a teenage rat pack headed by a psychopathic killer, Blake. The gang is made up of bootleggers, hijackers, and killers in Detroit during the Roaring Twenties. They team with adult hijackers during the Prohibition Era (1919-1933) when it is illegal to make, sell, or drink alcoholic beverages. In three years, the gang controls the city's underworld. Detective Sullivan is given a special assignment to break up the gang. To intimidate him, Blake has his number one henchman, Cavell, terrorize Sullivan's pregnant wife, Edwards, and then push her out a window to her death. The gang moves in on the cleaning and dyeing industry whose owners call in the Mafia for protection. Cavell tries to tip off Sullivan as to where the Mafia hoods are holed up, but Blake, mistaking his intentions, has Dubov seal him alive in a coffin and dump it into the Detroit River. Blake locates the Mafia headquarters hideout in an apartment building and goes there with two of his goons. They break in and machine-gun three Mafia leaders. Sullivan finally catches up with Blake and he is put behind bars, and his gang is destroyed. This effective crime drama is told in a semi-documentary style, but its excessive violence prohibits viewing by children. An earlier film, **Public Hero No. 1**, 1935, also profiles the criminal exploits of the Purple Gang. Song: "Runnin'

Richard Loo and Dana Andrews in *The Purple Heart*, 1944.

Wild" (Joe Gray, Leo Wood, A. Harrington Gibbs). Remade in 2008 but with much less impact. **p**, Lindsley Parsons; **d**, Frank McDonald; **cast**, Barry Sullivan, Robert Blake, Elaine Edwards, Marc Cavell, Jody Lawrance, Suzanne Ridgeway (as Suzy Marquette), Joseph Turkel, Victor Creatore, Paul Dubov, Ray Boyle, Kathleen Lockhart, Nestor Piava; **w**, Jack DeWitt; **c**, Ellis Carter; **m**, Paul Dunlap; **ed**, Maurice Wright; **art d**, David Milton; **set d**, Frank Lombardo.

The Purple Heart ★★★★ 1944; U.S.; 99m; FOX; B/W; War Drama; Children: Unacceptable; **DVD**; **VHS**. This stirring and memorable war tale from pantheon director Milestone records the fate of crew members from two of the sixteen B-25 Mitchell bombers in the Doolittle Raid that bombed Tokyo and other cities in April 1942. This grim tale (its title signifying those U.S. servicemen given the Purple Heart medal for being wounded or killed in combat) depicts those hapless fliers who were captured by the Japanese and put on trial as war criminals. Andrews represents the senior officer, a captain, who is imprisoned with seven other U.S. airmen, all falsely charged with purposely dropping bombs on Japanese schools, hospitals and other non-military targets. The airmen are all housed in a large cell and, after none will admit to committing any atrocities during the raid, they are taken from that cell one by one, each tortured in separate ways, this torture supervised by Loo, a clever and insidious Japanese officer (who was really a Hawaiian actor and who specialized in such despicable roles during WWII). Loo's purpose is not chiefly to obtain confessions from these fliers that they are guilty of the charges, but to learn the base from which the bombers flew. The Japanese high command is shown arguing about that source, Navy officers contending that the bombers came from an aircraft carrier, Army officers insisting that they flew from a land based location before attacking Japan. (At the time of the famous Doolittle Raid, U.S. President Franklin D. Roosevelt, while talking on the radio in one of his celebrated "Fireside Chats," jocularly and misleadingly stated that the bombers in the Doolittle Raid came from "Shangri La," a reference to the mythical and idyllic sanctuary somewhere in the Himalayas as depicted in James Hilton's 1933 popular fantasy novel, *Lost Horizon*.) While each flier anxiously awaits his turn to be brutally tortured, or after having returned from such painful brutalities (one is made senseless, another loses his memory, another has his arm broken, another has his hands mangled and yet another is rendered speechless) they think back on their fondest home-based memories. Andrews, who is one of the few who is not tortured, recalls his home life with his wife, Marshall, and his small son, these pleasing flashbacks all the more emphasizing the dire straits and dreadful future that awaits these heroic men. The fact that the tribunal hearing this case is no more than a kangaroo court is established when representatives of the international press witness the

high-handed tactics of the judges, presided over by Mitsuru Toyama (1855-1944), played by Chong. (Mitsuru Toyama led Japan's right-wing Black Dragon Society that had for decades encouraged and prodded Japan into its wars of aggression.) Despite all efforts made by the assiduous Loo and his henchmen, he is unable to learn from the tortured airmen the source of their base. The fliers are then returned to the court when some indicate that are now willing to speak. Levene, a tough sergeant, speaks for them, especially Granger, a young airman who has been tortured into silence, but he makes no admission on Granger's behalf, instead indicting the brutality of their captors. Andrews then appears in the witness box to denounce the court and all of its trumped up charges against him and his men, ending his impassioned speech with: "You started this war! You wanted it, and now you're going to get it, and it won't be finished until your dirty little empire is wiped off the face of the earth!" At that moment, Loo, who has lost all face in his inability to learn the source of the bomber base (the Doolittle bombers flew from the aircraft carrier USS *Hornet*), openly commits suicide in court by shooting himself. The eight U.S. airmen are found guilty and sentenced to death (three of the actual Doolittle airmen were executed, one died of illness while imprisoned and the others were released following the war). The convicted fliers then file from the dock and begin marching down a long corridor to meet their fates and in this last and most movingly memorable scene the viewer hears the "Army Air Corps Song" and "Battle Hymn of the Republic." Though inescapably propagandistic, the film is masterfully and sensitively handled by Milestone, where he carefully develops and reveals each character of the eight doomed fliers. Andrews, Levene, Granger, Conte, Barry and the rest are superlative as the American fliers, and those playing their Japanese oppressors are impressive in their sinister and repulsive roles. Newman's wonderful and patriotic score wholly captures the flavor of this unforgettable story while underscoring the characters of the gallant men being portrayed, and Miller's crisp and fluid lensing is superb. Songs: "Memories" (Egbert van Alstyne), "The Army Air Corps Song" (Robert Crawford), "The Battle Hymn of the Republic" (music: William Steffe; lyrics: Julia Ward Howe), "America (My Country Tis of Thee)" (from "God Save the King"; traditional), "Hail to the Chief" (James Sanderson), "Red River Valley" (traditional), "Turkey in the Straw" (traditional). The film was not only a box office success, but served as a powerful recruiting tool in that recruitment officers were present in the lobbies of the theaters showing this film and, following its showings, thousands of young males viewing this film immediately enlisted to serve in WWII. The 2005 film by the same name depicts a different subject. Several other notable films have profiled the 1942 Doolittle Raid, including **Destination Tokyo**, 1943; **Midway**, 1976; **Pearl Harbor**, 2001; and **Thirty Seconds over Tokyo**, 1944. *Author's Note*: Of the eighty airmen who participated in the famous Doolittle Raid, sixty-nine reached safety, escaping capture or death after completing the mission, three were killed and the remaining eight were taken prisoner by the Japanese when their planes went down in Japanese-occupied areas of China. Those eight included lieutenants Dean F. Hallmark, Chase Nielsen, Robert J. Meder, Robert L. Hite, William G. Farrow, and George Barr and corporals Harold A. Spatz and Jacob DeShazer. Hallmark, Farrow and Spatz were found guilty of committing atrocities and were executed by beheading on October 14, 1942, in Shanghai where the supposed war crimes trial was held in a Japanese Police headquarters court, while the other five were given life sentences. Meder died of maltreatment and illness on December 1, 1943. The remaining four survived the war and of all those imprisoned fliers, only Hite is alive at this 2013 writing. Three other Doolittle airmen who reached safety following the raid, are also alive at this writing: Richard E. Cole, who was the co-pilot of aircraft number one, which was piloted by the famed Colonel (later General) James Harold "Jimmy" Doolittle (1896-1993); engineer Edward Joseph Saylor;and gunner David J. Thatcher. Andrews told this author that "playing that role in **The Purple Heart** of a pilot in the Doolittle Raid was an honor and all of the other actors in that picture felt the same way. Those brave guys who flew on that near suicidal mission were all heroes and when we learned that some of them had been captured and sentenced to death for crimes they never committed we wanted to hit back at the Japanese for such underhanded tactics. That's what that picture did, creating so much hatred for the enemy that poor Richard Loo, who played the Japanese officer who mistreats all of the prisoners was afraid to be seen on the streets in Los Angeles. Women hissed at him and boys threw rocks and rotten apples at him. When going about in those days, he put bandages on his face to pretend he had been injured just so people could not recognize him. He wasn't even Japanese, but had been born in Hawaii. All of the others playing Japanese judges and officers in that picture were really Chinese actors, but they also got a lot of abuse." Zanuck had wanted to produce this film for some time, but held off until the U.S. government admitted that some of the Doolittle airmen had been tortured and executed, as he stated to this author: "I knew from insiders about a year before we made **The Purple Heart** that the Japanese had murdered three of our airman from the Doolittle Raid and I wrote the script for the picture under a pseudonym [Melville Crossman] and sat on it until I got a green light from Washington, D.C. The Government wanted that story to be told then to emphasize the war in the Pacific because too many stories and films had been centered on the war in Europe. We told that tragic story and we did not hold anything back, not anything." **p**, Darryl F. Zanuck; **d**, Lewis Milestone; **cast**, Dana Andrews, Richard Conte, Farley Granger, Kevin O'Shea, Don "Red" Barry, Trudy Marshall, Sam Levene, Charles Russell, Tala Birell, Richard Loo, Philip Ahn, Peter Chong; **w**, Jerome Cady (based on a story by Melville Crossman (Zanuck); **c**, Arthur Miller; **m**, Alfred Newman; **ed**, Douglass Biggs; **art d**, James Basevi, Lewis Creber; **set d** Thomas Little; **spec eff**, Fred Sersen.

The Purple Plain ★★★ 1954; U.K.; 100m; Two Cities Films/UA; Color; War Drama; Children: Unacceptable; **DVD**; **VHS**; **IV**. Peck gives a riveting performance as an Allied airman in WWII, haunted by a terrible past that creates a death wish in his military exploits. After Peck's bride is killed in a German air raid over London, a few years later, in 1945, he becomes a Canadian pilot determined to shoot down as many enemy planes as he can. Taking great risks, he becomes both admired and feared by others in his squadron in Burma in World War II (1939-1945). Peck and fellow officer Denham are flying over the jungle with Brook, their navigator, when their plane is shot down over Japanese-held territory. Brook is injured and can't walk, but they manage to escape into the jungle, Peck carrying Brook on his back. Denham becomes discouraged and takes his own life, but Peck struggles on with Brook. They reach an outpost of English-speaking refugees, which includes a beautiful young Burmese woman, Min Than. She and Peck become romantically interested in each other, and her loving care helps him to recover from his psychological problems. Songs: "Onward Christian Soldiers," "Jesus Christ Is Risen Today" (music: Robert Williams; lyrics: traditional, from Bohemia). This well-directed film from Parrish proved to be an effective war drama that was filmed in Ceylon (now Sri Lanka), but its violence prohibits viewing by children. *Author's Note*: Peck told this author: "There is a great deal of introspection in **The Purple Plain** only because it was written by a terrific writer, Ambler, who specialized in espionage stories, but always placed importance on the mindsets of his characters. He did that in the script for that picture, having my character mentally scarred by an earlier trauma, and when you have such characters to play, you also have many subtle facets in such characters that allow a much wider range in showing that character." Novelist Eric Ambler wrote the screenplay in between writing such books as *The Mask of Dimitrios, Journey into Fear*, and others. Bates was a prolific and popular British novelist whose books included *Love for Lydia* and *The Darling Buds of May*. **p**, John Bryan; **d**, Robert Parrish; **cast**, Gregory Peck, Maurice Denham, Win Min Than, Bernard Lee, Brenda de Banzie, Lyndon Brook, Anthony Bushell, Josephine Griffin, Dorothy Alison, Peter Arne; **w**, Eric Ambler (based on the novel

Mia Farrow and Jeff Daniels in *The Purple Rose of Cairo,* **1985.**

by H.E. Bates); **c**, Geoffrey Unsworth (Technicolor); **m**, John Veale; **ed**, Clive Donner; **art d**, Jack Maxsted, Donald M. Ashton; **spec eff**, Charles Staffell, Bill Warrington.

The Purple Rose of Cairo ★★★ 1985; U.S.; 82m; Orion Pictures; Color/B/W; Comedy/Fantasy/Romance; Children: Unacceptable (MPAA: PG); **DVD**; **VHS**. In this film within a film within a film, Allen presents a fascinating portrait of Farrow, a young woman yearning for love in a loveless marriage to brutish lout Aiello during the Great Depression. She is an inept waitress and finds what little happiness she can by going regularly to the local movie theater to see the latest romance film, her only way of escaping a dire life where she is both emotionally and financially impoverished. While watching these romance films, Farrow fantasizes about being in the arms of one of the romantic leads in the films she watches and so powerful is her longing that that very thing comes true. Farrow becomes enthralled with watching a melodramatic romance film titled *The Purple Rose of Cairo*, about Daniels, an adventurous and handsome young archeologist who meets some visiting Manhattan socialites when they arrive in Cairo, Egypt. They take him as a guest when they return to New York, and he falls madly in love with a performer at the Copacabana. Farrow, while sitting in the audience and watching the film many times, falls in love with Daniels. While she is watching a scene, Daniels suddenly breaks conformity with the script and ends his dialog with others in the film and looks at the camera, or the audience and sees Farrow, so attracted by her that he defies the fourth wall and steps literally from the screen and the black-and-white film in which he is appearing and into the colorful world of reality in that theater. He tells Farrow that he has the ability to come into her real world because she has seen the film so many times and he has felt her love for him. She takes Daniels on a tour of her New Jersey town, and he, in turn, takes her into the film where he upsets its story line and continuity. By breaking in and out of the film, Daniels has begun a series of other disruptions in theaters showing the same film and where other characters have inexplicably left the screen. None of this seems to matter to Daniels and Farrow as they have fallen deeply in love. The producer of the film, however, tries to correct the chaos Daniels or his screen persona has created by flying to New Jersey with the real actor, also Daniels, and where a strange ménage á trois takes place between Farrow, Daniels the real actor and Daniels the screen image. She ends her marriage to worthless Aiello and finally agrees to live her life with Daniels, the real-life-actor, and the screen image of Daniels returns to the screen where the film returns to its original state. Daniels the actor, however, has deceived Farrow and goes to Hollywood without her now that he has achieved his goal and that is having his screen persona return to the film. He suffers guilt about his deception in misleading a young

Robert Mitchum, Teresa Wright and Judith Anderson in *Pursued*, 1947.

woman who has placed her love in his hands, and resolves to make amends. Surrealistic in nature, this clever film captures Allen's own fascination with the Golden Era of films, which undoubtedly molded his own oddball form of humor from childhood and where he now pays homage to the pervasive influence that has helped to create his career. He enacts a fantasy that has been held universally by millions who so closely associate and identify with certain films, transitioning their characters from the mind's imagination to the actuality of real life, and Farrow, Daniels, Aiello and the rest of the cast are superb in their roles, real and imagined. The film was expensive to produce, more than $15 million, and did not do well at the box office, earning back only a little more than $10 million in its initial box office release. Songs: "Cheek to Cheek" (1935; Irving Berlin), "I Love My Baby, My Baby Loves Me" (1925; music: Harry Warren; lyrics: Bud Green), "Albany Bound" (1925; music: Ray Henderson; lyrics: Buddy G. De Sylva, Bud Green), "One Day at a Time" (Dick Hyman). *Author's Note*: Michael Keaton originally appeared in the leading role of the film, but, after some shooting, Allen felt that he was too "contemporary" for the character of the historic film actor and he was replaced by Daniels. **p**, Robert Greenhut; **d&w**, Woody Allen; **cast**, Mia Farrow, Jeff Daniels, Danny Aiello, Irving Metzman, Stephanie Farrow, Edward Herrmann, John Wood, Deborah Rush, Van Johnson, Zoe Caldwell, Milo O'Shea, Dianne Wiest; **c**, Gordon Willis; **m**, Dick Hyman; **ed**, Susan E. Morse; **prod d**, Stuart Wurtzel; **art d**, Edward Pisoni; **set d**, Carol Joffe; **spec eff**, Andrew and Don Hansard, Mitch Wilson.

Pursued ★★★★ 1947; U.S.; 101m; United States Pictures/WB; B/W; Western; Children: Unacceptable; **DVD**; **VHS**. Pantheon director Walsh presents an offbeat, sometimes bizarre western where the rugged and independent-minded Mitchum is routinely and inexplicably victimized again and again. This strangely compelling oater opens with Mitchum hiding in an abandoned, remote ranch in New Mexico at the turn of the 20th Century, awaiting the arrival of a lynch posse led by Jagger, his own stepfather. In flashback, we see Mitchum in childhood (at age seven, played by Severn) and where he goes to live with Jagger and Anderson and their children, Wright (Miller as a child) and Rodney (Bates as a child), after Mitchum's father is killed. He is treated as a stepson by both adoptive parents and where Jagger openly shows his favoritism to Rodney and Wright and demands that Mitchum perform impossible tasks. When the Spanish-American War begins, Jagger tells the two boys that one must uphold the family honor by fighting in that war. He tosses a coin and Mitchum, the loser, goes off to fight in the war. He surprisingly returns a hero, but Jagger is not impressed, and, in fact, seems to resent Mitchum's military achievements. Moreover, Rodney and Mitchum then get into a fight over the family rights to the ranch and

Mitchum loses out again after another toss of the coin. He is, however, lucky as a gambler, and wins a fortune, but Rodney, who detests Mitchum for some unexplained reason, attacks him and, in a wild struggle, Mitchum kills Rodney and then flees for his life with Jagger and a lynch posse in pursuit. Wright, who is really Mitchum's stepsister, then tells Jagger and Anderson that she will find and kill Mitchum after pretending to love him and marry him. She accomplishes that goal, but fails to kill Mitchum and then comes to believe that he is innocent and that she loves him. Jagger, however, is not so forgiving and resolves to kill Mitchum at all costs, but when he is about to take Mitchum's life, Anderson shoots and kills her husband, an act prompted by her own guilt. It is then revealed that Mitchum's father was murdered by Jagger and that Rodney had been insane all his life. Mitchum can finally see some happiness as he and Wright plan a peaceful life together. Walsh presents a grim but tense and realistic "modern" western, adeptly infusing into its scenes and characters emotional and intellectual disorders that tilt the story line away from traditional themes to take the tale and its troubled characters into a more surreal and subliminal world of anxiety and insanity. Mitchum, Wright, Jagger, Anderson and Rodney excel in their roles, and the script is as intelligent as the well-orchestrated action; where master cinematographer Howe brilliantly employs his cameras to present this western with the images of a film noir production, its scenes often as murky and moody as its mentally troubled characters. Songs: "Wedding March" (Felix Mendelssohn-Bartholdy), "Danny Boy" (Frederick Weatherly), "Streets of Laredo" (traditional), "The Girl I Left Behind Me" (Irish folk song), "When Johnny Comes Marching Home" (Irish folk song). *Author's Note*: Mitchum told this author that "**Pursued** is a first, I think, because it is a psychological western dealing with insanity and guilt complexes, and audiences had never seen characters with such mental disorders in westerns until that picture. Teresa's husband, Niven Busch, a fine writer, actually wrote the script for her and she did a great job with her character. Strangely enough, my character in that picture is more normal than almost everyone else, and that says a lot because I am usually the one playing the wacko." **p**, Milton Sperling; **d**, Raoul Walsh; **cast**, Teresa Wright, Robert Mitchum, Judith Anderson, Dean Jagger, Alan Hale, John Rodney, Harry Carey, Jr., Clifton Young, Ernest Severn, Peggy Miller, Charles Bates; **w**, Niven Busch; **c**, James Wong Howe; **m**, Max Steiner; **ed**, Christian Nyby; **art d**, Ted Smith; **set d**, Jack McConaghy; **spec eff**, William McGann, Willard Van Enger.

Pursuit to Algiers ★★★ 1945; U.S.; 65m; UNIV; B/W; Mystery; Children: Unacceptable; **DVD**; **VHS**. The great deductive sleuth Sherlock Holmes (Rathbone) and his friend Dr. Watson (Bruce) are in top form in this fine whodunit where they are searching for an assassin. The victim is the father of Vincent, a prince who is visiting London and must return to his fictitious home country in Europe. Rathbone takes Vincent aboard a private plane while Bruce takes a Mediterranean ship. Aboard ship, Bruce becomes friends with attractive singer Riordan, who is from Brooklyn. Also aboard ship is Ivan, a sinister-looking spinster, who carries a pistol in her handbag. Bruce learns that a plane has crashed in the Pyrenees and worries that Rathbone and Vincent may have been aboard. The ship's captain asks Bruce to look in on an ailing passenger in the cabin next to his and sees it is Rathbone, who is accompanied by Vincent. They never took a plane, Rathbone explains, but boarded the ship incognito. The prince is to travel pretending to be Bruce's nephew. After the ship stops at Lisbon, three strange men board the vessel. They are Evans, a gregarious man; Davis, a giant-sized mute; and Kosleck, is a small man, who is an accomplished knife-throwing performer. Someone then tries to kill Vincent. Poison is found, and Rathbone stops Kosleck from throwing a knife. Rathbone had recognized Kosleck from when the man was a knife-thrower in a circus. Before the ship reaches its destination, Algiers, Rathbone discovers that Riordan is an unwilling courier for an international jewel thief. Rathbone promises to help her and that night they attend a party given by Ivan. Bruce entertains at the party by describing an old Sherlock Holmes case called "The Giant Rat of Sumatra." Also at the party, Rathbone discovers a bomb hidden in a party favor and throws it into the sea where it harmlessly explodes. When the ship docks at Algiers, Rathbone is bound and gagged while Vincent is kidnapped from the ship by Evans and his henchmen. Rathbone, however, has hoodwinked the kidnappers into abducting Vincent, revealing that the real prince is alive and well and aboard ship working as a steward, Lowry, and that Vincent has been rescued by shore police and Evans and company arrested. Rathbone and Bruce have saved the prince's life and all ends well. Songs: "Loch Lomand" (traditional); "There Isn't Any Harm in That," "Cross My Heart" (Everett Carter, Milton Rosen); "Flow Gently, Sweet Afton" (music: Alexander Hume; lyrics: Robert Burns). This entry is entertaining and as clever as all of the Rathbone-Bruce films dealing with the inimitable Sherlock Holmes. Some violence prohibits viewing by children. *Author's Note*: This was the twelfth of fourteen films Rathbone and Bruce did in the Holmes series at Universal. Rathbone told this author that, by the time he did this film with Bruce, "I was growing very weary with the Holmes character. With the exception of the action scenes, I felt as if I were striking heroic poses of the immortal sleuth. By that time, people on the street were calling me "Mr. Holmes" and I suppose his image had somewhat taken over my own. I could not escape the man any more than [Arthur] Conan Doyle could get rid of the unforgettable character he had created. Nigel [Bruce] astounded all of us in **Pursuit to Algiers** by singing "Loch Lomand" with his own fine voice. When I complimented him about that, he said with that choppy laugh of his: 'You're not the only one with hidden talents, my dear Holmes." **p&d**, Roy William Neill; **cast**, Basil Rathbone, Nigel Bruce, Marjorie Riordan, Rosalind Ivan, Morton Lowry, Leslie Vincent, Martin Kosleck, John Abbott, Rex Evans, Gerald Hamer; **w**, Leonard Lee (based on a story in *The Return of Sherlock Holmes* by Sir Arthur Conan Doyle); **c**, Paul Ivano; **ed**, Saul A. Goodkind; **art d**, John B. Goodman, Martin Obzina; **set d**, Russell A. Gausman, Ralph Sylos.

Pushover ★★★ 1954; U.S.; 88m; COL; B/W; Crime Drama; Children: Unacceptable; **DVD VHS**. In this offbeat, tense crime tale MacMurray is an honest cop assigned to recover $200,000 after a bank robbery. He and other officers keep a round-the-clock surveillance on Novak, a girlfriend of one of the suspected robbers. MacMurray quickly falls in love with Novak. After she learns that he is a cop, she tries to persuade him to kill Richards, the ringleader of the robbers, so she and MacMurray can take off with the loot, but, he, at first, resists. Meanwhile, Carey, MacMurray's partner, meets Novak's neighbor, Malone, in their apartment building and falls for her. After a few days, MacMurray is so obsessed with Novak that he agrees to her plan. She arranges for Richards to come to her apartment where MacMurray kills him. But Nourse, another officer on the stakeout, sees the killing, so MacMurray kills him, too. Carey and detective lieutenant Marshall are looking for Richards, who was seen near Novak's apartment building. MacMurray knows he's in deep trouble and takes Malone hostage in an attempt to escape the building, but, after seeming to escape and get to a car, Carey shoots him dead and Novak, the catalyst of MacMurray's fall from grace, stands by mutely witnessing his demise and waiting to be arrested. Song: "There Goes That Song Again" (Jule Styne). This suspenseful crime drama is well directed by former actor Quine with MacMurray as a standout in playing a role similar to that in **Double Indemnity**, 1944. *Author's Note*: **Pushover** was Novak's first feature film. She had been groomed for stardom by Columbia chief Harry Cohn, who widely promoted this thriller, which proved to be a hit at the box office and established Novak as a top female star, while Malone, two years after this film, won a Best Supporting Actress Oscar for her portrayal of a society boozer in **Written on the Wind**, 1956. Multitalented MacMurray never won an Oscar, stating to this author that "although I play the central character in **Pushover**, the film was made to promote Kim [Novak] to the top of the heap. Harry Cohn, who ran Columbia, hovered over that picture when

Basil Rathbone (as Sherlock Holmes) and Nigel Bruce (as Dr. Watson) in *Pursuit to Algiers*, 1945.

it was being made like a mother hen. He thought he could make Kim into another Marilyn Monroe, but she has a much more reserved personality than Marilyn. She is an ultra-cool blonde. There is always something distant or far-away about her and I think that's one of her greatest attractions." **p**, Jules Schermer; **d**, Richard Quine; **cast**, Fred MacMurray, Phil Carey, Kim Novak, Dorothy Malone, E.G. Marshall, Allen Nourse, Paul Richards, Paul Picerni, James Anderson, Joe Bailey, Richard Bryan, Phil Chambers; **w**, Roy Huggins (based on the story "The Killer Wore a Badge" and the novels *The Night Watch* by Thomas Walsh and *Rafferty* by Bill S. Ballinger); **c**, Lester H. White; **m**, Arthur Morton; **ed**, Jerome Thoms; **art d**, Walter Holscher; **set d**, James Crowe.

Pygmalion ★★★★★ 1938; U.K.; 96m; Gabriel Pascal Productions; MGM; B/W; Comedy; Children: Acceptable; **DVD**; **VHS**. Howard and Hiller are perfect as unlikely lovers in this superlative comedy from Shaw (first produced in 1913 and remade several times). A rich phonetics teacher and language expert, Howard is slumming through Covent Garden with his equally well-to-do friend, Sunderland, when they meet Hiller quite by accident. She is a Cockney girl selling flowers on the street and her atrocious accent, in Sunderland's estimation, utterly defies correction or alteration. He places a large wager with Howard that Howard could never train this uncouth young woman to properly speak the King's English, let alone turn this smudge-faced girl into anything that would remotely resemble a grand lady. Howard takes up the challenge and entices Hiller to become his ward or pupil and, for his payment, she readily accepts his role as her mentor, moving into his luxurious residence, but where she initially balks at taking a bath at the firm insistence of Howard's no-nonsense housekeeper, Cadell. Before Hiller begins her transformational education, Lawson, her workingman father, appears at Howard's residence, wanting to know what Howard wants with his daughter. He is a clever old rogue, a besmirched dustman, who has never given Hiller much thought, but he sees an opportunity to enrich himself by implying that Howard has ulterior motives regarding Hiller and he artfully convinces Howard to pay him a modest sum of money for the "use" of his daughter before going on his merry way to the nearest pub. Though she bristles at Howard's regimen, Hiller undergoes endless and rigorous speaking lessons where Howard trains and refines her tonal delivery, enunciation, pronunciation and articulation. He also imposes a severe regimen of how to sit, stand and walk with elegant grace and fashionable style. Howard is merciless in his instructions, imposing tortuous elocution exercises upon Hiller, insisting that she speak precisely while placing next-to-impossible barriers in the way. He orders her to talk correctly while he places marbles in her mouth, adding one marble after another so that it is almost impossible for her to speak, let alone be understood. The always self-assured and confident

Wendy Hiller and Leslie Howard in *Pygmalion*, **1938.**

Howard enlarges upon his chore in turning this "guttersnipe" into an impressively poised, well-speaking lady. He now plans to pass the formerly ignorant and uncouth Hiller off as a stunning duchess at a grand ball which will be attended by London's social elite and royalty, the supreme test of his ability to transform ungainly clay into admirable marble. He uses a metronome to measure her verbal responses to his incessant questions, refining her diction and expanding her lexicon, reshaping and softening the words most mangled by her Cockney accent as would a hammering blacksmith even and smooth an otherwise lumpy slab of molten lead. Hiller slowly but surely achieves Howard's goals until she walks in a courtly manner and speaks elegantly, although Howard explodes with rage whenever a random "ain't" accidentally slips from her lovely mouth. Though incessantly challenged by Howard's exhausting verbal routines to quit his rigorous program, she matches his own stubbornness by keeping to her bargain with him, ritualistically repeating again and again such lines as "the rain in Spain stays mainly on the plain" (these lines would later be implanted in one of the many hit tunes stemming from the musical version of this stellar play, **My Fair Lady**, 1964). Before Hiller is put on display before London's elite, Howard introduces her to Tree and his high society family, and Tree, an impoverished playboy, falls in love with Hiller, which Howard finds unnerving, realizing that he is also deeply fond of her if not in love with her and that he is amazingly feeling pangs of jealousy. Finally, Hiller is ready for the supreme test, and Howard and Sunderland escort her to the Ambassador's Ball where she startles everyone with her stylish bearing, charming wit and eloquent speech. She is radiant and beautiful to the royal members she meets and she even dances with an enamored prince, who is utterly taken by the exquisite Hiller. Not for a moment does anyone believe that she might be the complete and dazzling fabrication the vain Howard has created out of whole cloth, and he revels in that very achievement. Howard is ecstatic in winning his bet from Sunderland and, now that he has no more use for Hiller, he tells her that she can go back to the streets and resume selling her flowers. Hiller is angry at the situation Howard has created for her, telling him that though he may be a brilliant man, he lacks compassion for others and now that he has changed her identity, she has no social place to take it. "What's to become of me?" she asks. "Now that you have made a lady of me, I am not fit for anything else!" She throws his slippers at him where, in previous evenings she lovingly brought those slippers to him. Howard now knows he loves Hiller as much as she loves him. He sits down and then, knowing she is still in the room behind his chair, asks her to retrieve his slippers, implying that these two mismatched lovers will be forever matched together. Everything about this masterpiece comedy is delightful and entertaining, its dialog contentiously sparking and endearingly sparkling. Asquith (as well as Howard who

co-directed) provides an unforgettable, heartwarming film that also renders great entertainment, revealing not merely Henry Higgins' great social experiment but his inescapable journey to happiness and love with the woman of his mind as well as his heart. Howard and Hiller are magnificent together, and Lawson gives one of the greatest performances of his life as Hiller's irascible father, and Sunderland, Tree and all the rest of the cast are outstanding in their roles. This film proved to be an enormous success worldwide and remains one of the great romance classics. *Author's Note*: This was Hiller's second film, and she became a superstar in British films. She had appeared in only one earlier film, a British programmer, **Lancashire Luck**, 1937, and was little known until Shaw saw that B-film, as well as her stage performances, and urged producer Pascal to costar Hiller with Howard. Shaw patterned this story after the Greek tale of the sculpturing king who chisels a statue of Aphrodite with such skill that he falls in love with his own magnificent creation. The only reason why Shaw allowed Pascal to produce this film version was that Pascal promised that not one word of Shaw's play would be changed or altered and that Shaw could approve of everything. Shaw initially wanted Charles Laughton to play Henry Higgins, but later agreed that Howard, who was widely popular in U.S. films, would be more widely received when the film was released in America. Howard proved to be the epitome of the intellectual tyrant created by Shaw and reportedly achieved that image by studying and copying in his great portrayal the very mannerisms and attitudes of the great Shaw. The shrewd Pascal did manage to alter some of the play's scenes, as well as adding the lavish ball sequence, but got Shaw to do the writing for those altered or new scenes, as well as having the playwright delete or shorten some of his own longer diatribes that appear in the original play. Though Hiller was widely in demand in Hollywood after the success of this film, she remained in England and pursued her stage career there. She seldom appeared in films thereafter, but when she did, those appearances were invariably great treats to viewing audiences. **p**, Gabriel Pascal; **d**, Anthony Asquith, Leslie Howard; **cast**, Howard, Wendy Hiller, Wilfrid Lawson, Marie Lohr, Scott Sunderland, Jean Cadell, David Tree, Everley Gregg, Leueen MacGrath, Esme Percy, Cathleen Nesbitt, Leo Genn, Patrick Macnee, Anthony Quayle; **w**, George Bernard Shaw, W.P. Lipscomb, Cecil Lewis, Ian Dalrymple, Anatole de Grunwald, Kay Walsh, Asquith (based on the play by Shaw); **c**, Harry Stradling; **m**, Arthur Honegger; **ed**, David Lean; **art d**, John Bryan.

Q ★★★ 1982; U.S.; 93m; Arkoff International/United Film Distribution Co. (UFDC); Color; Horror; Children: Unacceptable (MPAA: R); **DVD**; **VHS**. This offbeat but fascinating horror film begins when New York police get reports of a giant flying lizard sailing over the rooftops of the city. In one instance, forty-three witnesses describe in detail how a man is plucked by the beast from his swimming pool and devoured. Detectives David Carradine and Roundtree don't believe the reports until they verify that the creature is actually feasting on people. Moriarty, an unemployed piano player and former convict, thinks he can make money and a name for himself if he captures the creature. After committing a jewel robbery, he hides from police and learns the monster's nest is atop the Chrysler Building, discovering several partially eaten bodies there. David Carradine and Roundtree learn that the murders have been committed as sacrifices to the Aztec flying serpent god Quetzalcoatl, part bird and part serpent. Moriarty cuts a deal with New York City officials, who promise him $1 million if he tells them where the monster can be found, but they renege when the serpent escapes its nest and is later killed by cops firing submachine guns after it perches atop the Manhattan Bankers Trust Building. Its slayings have been committed at the bidding of a lunatic professor of Aztec history, although the menace promises to continue since the beast has left an egg that is about to be hatched. Solid direction, good acting and a literate script peppered with a lot of dark humor sustains interest from beginning to end, even though the film takes a large leaf from **King Kong**, 1933. Songs: "Dancing Too Close to the Flame" (Robert O. Ragland, Robert J. Walsh), "Evil Dream" (Michael Moriarty). Excessive violence prohibits viewing by children. **p, d & w**, Larry Cohen; **cast**, Michael Moriarty, Candy Clark, David Carradine, Richard Roundtree, James Dixon, Malachy McCourt, Fred J. Scollay, Peter Hock, Ron Cey, Mary Louise Weller, Bruce Carradine; **c**, Robert Levi, Fred Murphy; **m**, Robert O. Ragland; **ed**, Armond Lebowitz; **spec eff**, David Allen, Peter Kuran, Randall William Cook.

Quadrophenia ★★★ 1979; U.K.; 117m; The Who Films/World Northal; Color; Crime Drama; Children: Unacceptable (MPAA: R); **DVD**; **VHS**. Set in London, 1965, this well-crafted coming-of-age tale is laden with wrongdoing by Daniels, a drug-addicted teenager, who loathes his parents and job in a company mail room. He only feels free and accepted when with his Mod friends and cruising the city with them on motor scooters while listening to deafening rock music. He and his gang get into a rumble with another gang on Brighton Beach that ends badly with Daniels on a downward spiral into paranoia and isolation. Songs: "Hi-Heel Sneakers," "Dimples," "Wishin' & Hopin'," "Blazing Fire," "Night Train," "Be My Baby," "Da Doo Ron Ron," "Wah-Watusi," "Rhythm of the Rain," "Baby Love," "Baby Don't You Do It," "He's So Fine," "Louie, Louie," "5-4-3-2-1," "Anyway, Anyhow, Anywhere," "My Generation," "Green Onions," "Love Reign Over Me," "Zoot Suit." Excessive violence prohibits viewing by children. **p**, Roy Baird, Bill Curbishley; **d**, Franc Roddam; **cast**, Phil Daniels, Mark Wingett, Philip Davis, Leslie Ash, Ray Winstone, Sting (Gordon Matthew Sumner), Garry Cooper, Gary Shail, Toyah Willcox, Trevore Laird, Timothy Spall, Jesse Birdsall; **w**, Dave Humphries, Martin Stellman, Roddam, Pete Townshend; **c**, Brian Tufano (Eastmancolor); **m**, The Who (Pete Townshend, Roger Daltry, John Entwistle, Keith Moon); **ed**, Mike Taylor, Sean Barton; **prod d**, Simon Holland; **spec eff**, Steve Hamilton.

The Quare Fellow ★★★ 1963; U.K.; 85m; Liger Films/Astor Pictures; B/W; Crime Drama; Children: Unacceptable; **DVD**. Tough crime tale sees McGoohan become a new warden at an Irish prison. He is young, naïve, and believes in capital punishment. Macken, the senior warden, is older and more experienced in dealing with prisoners, and wants them treated as human beings. He is opposed to the death penalty, believing that capital punishment achieves no positive end. Two inmates are on Death Row, and one hangs himself. The other is to be executed for killing his brother in a jealous rage after he found him in bed with his wife, Syms. McGoohan becomes attracted to Syms during interviews, and, after her husband is hanged, that gruesome execution changes McGoohan's position on the death penalty. Violence prohibits viewing by children. **p**, Anthony Havelock-Allan; **d**, Arthur Dreifuss; **cast**, Patrick McGoohan, Sylvia Syms, Walter Macken, Dermot Kelly, Jack Cunningham, Hilton Edwards, Philip O'Flynn, Leo McCabe, Norman Rodway, Marie Kean; **w**, Dreifuss, Jacqueline Sundstrom (based on the play by Brendan Behan); **c**, Peter Hennessy; **m**, Alexander Farris; **ed**, Gitta Zadek; **art d**, Ted Marshall.

Quartet ★★★★ 1949; U.K.; 120m; Gainsborough Pictures/Eagle-Lion Films; B/W; Comedy/Drama; Children: Acceptable; **VHS**. Although segmented films seldom sustain interest throughout, this film proves the exception in that the four Somerset Maugham tales presented in this production are all handled with great skill, each complementing the other. The lofty Maugham introduces each story, the first titled "The Facts of Life," showing Radford as a father counseling son Watling not to waste money on gambling or women while he is on a tennis tour that takes him to Monte Carlo. Watling nevertheless plunges at the roulette table and surprisingly wins big, only to be seemingly gulled by femme fatale Zetterling. Watling, however, is not the naïve, young man he

David Carradine and "Q" in *Q*, **1982.**

seems to be, and cunningly turns the tables on the adventuress, not only recouping his own money, but making off with her own fortune. When learning of this, Radford tells his friend Wayne (both of these two fine actors appeared as a duo in the classic Hitchcock thriller **The Lady Vanishes**, 1938) how disappointed he is with his son after learning that Watling profited by totally ignoring his advice. In the second tale, "The Alien Corn," Bogarde (this being his sixth film and in one of his best roles to date) is in love with his cousin, the alluring Blackman. On his twenty-first birthday, Bogarde is offered a position with his father's firm, but he dumbfounds his wealthy family members when he tells them he wants to become a musician. He is obsessed with the thought of becoming an international success as a concert pianist. Blackman encourages his ambition by suggesting that he study hard to become that famous pianist and then accept the judgment of musical experts about his abilities. After devoting himself to two years of study in Paris, Bogarde returns to London for a recital arranged by Blackman, and Rosay, a noted composer, will judge his performance. Following Bogarde's recital, Rosay tells him that he has admirable skills, but that he lacks inspiration and the special talents that make up a great artist and that he will never be anything but a gifted amateur. So crushed by this news is Bogarde that he commits suicide, but his wealthy relatives, to preserve the family name, insist that Bogarde died through an accident when cleaning his gun. A coroner's jury agrees, rendering a verdict of accidental death, ironically stating that no high-born gentleman such as Bogarde would take his own life simply because he could not perform well at the piano. In the more light hearted third tale, "The Kite," we see Cole as a withdrawn man with Baddeley as his dominating mother. His only joy in life is flying kites, a hobby he has developed with his father since childhood. Against Baddeley's harsh advice, he meets and marries Shaw, who turns out to be the same kind of shrewish, hen-pecking woman as Baddeley, and who ridicules Cole whenever he flies his kite, saying that such recreation is reserved for children, not grown men, and he promises to quit flying kites. He nevertheless longs for the fun he misses and again flies a kite, and Shaw upbraids him for it, causing Cole to finally stand up to her by leaving their home, he goes to live once more with his mother, a move that delights Baddeley. So angered by his actions is Shaw that she destroys a mammoth kite that Cole had been building for a special outing and, after learning of this destruction, Cole refuses to financially support her. For this stubborn act, he is thrown into prison. Lee, an influential man who visits the prison, hears about Cole's strange story. He goes to Shaw and counsels her on how to preserve her marriage while Lee also arranges to have Cole released from jail. After Cole goes to the park where he invariably flew his kites, he is overjoyed to see Shaw there and where she is flying a kite. In the final and fourth story, "The Colonel's Lady," Parker's quiet

Greta Garbo and John Gilbert in *Queen Christina*, 1933.

and reserved wife, Swinburne, authors a book of poetry, which soon becomes a bestseller and a local scandal because she had written passionate sonnets about a man much younger than her husband, Parker. After Parker's mistress, Travers, reads the book, she concludes, as does everyone else, that Swinburne had a torrid affair with a young man other than her husband, Parker, but that that wonderful lover died many years ago. (Like Radford and Wayne, Travers and Parker had also appeared in **The Lady Vanishes**, and had played the same kind of roles, where Travers plays Parker's mistress, but poses as his wife.) When Travers tells this to Parker, he immediately dismisses the idea, saying that Swinburne is "too much of a lady" to ever enter an illicit love affair with another man, but the thought of Swinburne's betrayal nags and haunts him, although he is too frightened to confront her with his suspicions since such cheating mirrors his own conduct. Swinburne senses Parker's uneasiness about the passionate contents of her book and then admits that she did write those poems about another man she passionately loved, Parker himself as a young man and gave her his love when both were young together and where she blames herself for destroying that love. This admission and revelation suddenly dissolves the years of estrangement between Parker and Swinburne and they embrace to signal that their love for one another will be rekindled and nurtured in the future. Poignant and ironic, all four divergent stories make up consistent entertainment and their direction and acting from all helmsmen and players superbly conveys those stories with outstanding sensitivity and telling awareness. Maugham's similar **Trio**, 1950, which also portrays three separate tales, is just as effective and memorable as is this fine film. Songs: "Alouette" (French-Canadian traditional), "Impromptu" (Franz Schubert). **p**, Antony Darnborough; **d**, Ralph Smart ("The Facts of Life"); Harold French ("The Alien Corn"); Arthur Crabtree ("The Kite"); Ken Annakin ("The Colonel's Lady"); **cast**, Maugham (host); "The Facts of Life" segment: Basil Radford, Jack Watling, Naunton Wayne, Ian Fleming, Angela Baddeley, James Robertson Justice, Mai Zetterling; "The Alien Corn" segment: Dirk Bogarde, Honor Blackman, Raymond Lovell, Francoise Rosay, Irene Browne; "The Kite" segment: Bernard Lee, George Cole, Hermoine Baddeley, Susan Shaw, Mervyn Johns; "The Colonel's Lady" segment: Cecil Parker, Nora Swinburne, Linden Travers, Wilfrid Hyde-White, Felix Aylmer; **w**, R.C. Sheriff (from the stories by W. Somerset Maugham); **c**, Ray Elton, Reginald H. Wyer ("The Colonel's Lady" segment); **m**, John Greenwood; **ed**, A. Charles Knott, Jean Barker; **art d**, George Provis, Cedric Dawe, Norman G. Arnold; **spec eff**, Philippo Guidobaldi, Albert Whitlock.

Quebec ★★★ 1951; U.S.; 85m; PAR; Color; Adventure; Children: Unacceptable. Exciting adventure tale is set during a revolt that takes place between French and English forces in British-controlled Quebec, Canada, in 1837, and where the predominantly French Canadians revolt against the minority of English, who dictate the city's and Canada's destiny. Barrymore thinks his mother, Calvet, is dead, and he does not know that she is actually leading the Canadians in the revolution under the name of Lafleur. Calvert is also the mother of the British governor of the province, which creates many problems for the pro-British forces. Barrymore no sooner discovers Calvert's revolutionary identity than she sacrifices herself to save his life. This well-made adventure, based on actual facts, is packed with action, and Calvet, Knowles and Barrymore, along with the two young beauties who vie for Barrymore's attention, Rush and Duval, are standouts in their roles. *Author's Note*: This film was shot on location at Quebec and its neighboring countryside and the lensing from Green is beautifully breathtaking. Silent screen star Miller, who had starred with Lon Chaney Sr. in **The Hunchback of Notre Dame**, 1923, came out of retirement to appear in this film, her last feature film having been **Night Beat**, 1931. Violence prohibits viewing by children. **p & w**, Alan Le May; **d**, George Templeton; **cast**, John Barrymore, Jr., Corinne Calvet, Barbara Rush, Patric Knowles, Jon Hoyt, Arnold Moss, Nikki Duval, Don Haggerty, Patsy Ruth Miller, Howard Joslin, Paul Guévrement; **c**, W. Howard Green (Technicolor); **m**, Van Cleave, Edward H. Plumb; **ed**, Jack Ogilvie; **art d**, Ernst Fegté.

The Queen ★★★ 2006; U.K./France/Italy; 103m; Pathe Productions; Miramax; Color; Biographical Drama; Children: Unacceptable (MPAA: PG-13); **BD**; **DVD**. Absorbing biopic begins after the death of Princess Diana (Princess of Wales, 1961-1997) in a car accident in Paris, and where Queen Elizabeth II (1926-), played by Mirren, has a difficult time with her public grieving because of the conflicting personalities that had distanced Elizabeth and her deceased daughter-in-law. Mirren decides it best that she and the rest of the royal family remain secluded at Balmoral Castle for a time. The public does not understand and requests that their queen comfort them over the loss of the "People's Princess." They also pressure the newly elected Prime Minister Tony Blair (1953-), played by Sheen, to convince her to address the public, which the queen finally does and satisfies her adoring public. Mirren won an Oscar as Best Actress for her performance. The film was a great box office success, earning more than $100 million against its $15 million budget. Songs: "Oft in the Stilly Night," "Highland Laddie," "Creag Ghuanach" (traditional); "Heaven Must Be Missing an Angel" (Freddie Perren, Kenneth St. Lewis); "GMTV Reuters" (Tom Blades); "CNN World News Theme" (Herb Avery); "Libera me" (Giuseppe Verdi). Gutter language prohibits viewing by children. **p**, Andy Harries, Christine Langan, Tracey Seaward; **d**, Stephen Frears; **cast**, Helen Mirren, James Cromwell, Alex Jennings, Sylvia Syms, Roger Allam, Tim McMullan, Robin Soans, Lola Peploe, Douglas Reith, Joyce Henderson, Pat Laffan, Michael Sheen; **w**, Peter Morgan; **c**, Affonso Beato; **m**, Alexandre Desplat; **ed**, Lucia Zucchetti; **prod d**, Alan MacDonald; **art d**, Peter Wenham, Matthew Broderick, Franck Schwarz, Ben Smith; **set d**, Tina Jones; **spec eff**, Steve Breheney, Evan Green-Hughes.

Queen Christina ★★★★★ 1933; U.S.; 99m; MGM/B/W; Biographical Drama; Children: Acceptable; **DVD**; **VHS**. The great Greta Garbo was never more mystically alluring and enchanting than in this masterpiece film, which is brilliantly directed by Mamoulian and where Garbo is poignantly matched with her on-screen and off-screen lover, John Gilbert, providing memorable, smoldering love scenes yet to be equaled. We first see Garbo as Christina, Queen of Sweden (1626-1689, who reigned from 1632 to 1654), a firm and compassionate monarch, who is beset by court intrigues and critical matters of state. Further, she is endlessly plied by her ministers to marry a suitable husband, especially by Keith (playing Magnus Garbriel De la Gardie, 1622-1686), who is her former lover and one of her chief counselors and who urges her to wed Owen (playing Karl Gustav, 1622-1660, who later became Charles X, King of Sweden). Owen is a popular prince, but Garbo wants nothing to do with politically arranged marriages and is not attracted to Owen, who is her cousin. She has been queen since the age of six and, as queen regent and in her twenties, Garbo is now a clear-headed and decisive ruler, who is tired of the seemingly endless wars of attrition that engulf her country. When she meets with her cabinet members and they outline more battles to be waged in an ongoing war, she rebels. Garbo states: "Spoils, glory, flags and trumpets! What is behind these high-sounding words? Death and destruction…crippled men, Sweden victorious in a ravaged Europe…an island in a dead sea! I tell you, I want no more of it! I want for my people security and happiness. I want to cultivate the arts of peace, the arts of life. I want peace and peace I will have!" She is later shown stepping onto a balcony where its railings are coated with snow, scooping up some snow to rub upon her face. (The snow was oatmeal as director Mamoulian could not manufacture snow, and, to show Garbo exhaling steam, had her inhale some smoke from a cigarette before the camera rolled.) No longer able to endure the pressures of her throne, Garbo decides to go among her people, but incognito and disguises herself as a man by donning men's attire. Smith, one of her more avuncular advisers, enters her chambers and reluctantly helps her dress in such clothing, including leather pants, and Smith upbraids her for not wedding Owen, stating: "You cannot die an old maid." Garbo responds (in a prophetic statement that encompasses the actress' zealously guarded private life): "I have no intention to. I shall die a bachelor!" Traveling to a remote, snow-bound inn, Garbo, in the guise of a young man, meets Gilbert, who is a newly arrived Spanish envoy to the Swedish court. Pretending to be a wealthy youth seeking adventure, Garbo befriends Gilbert, who accepts her identity but advises her to be on guard when dealing with strangers and to always follow the noble and virtuous path. When some rowdy men appear at the inn's tavern where Garbo and Gilbert are sitting in the tavern, they begin arguing about the number of lovers their queen has had, until Garbo can no longer tolerate their bickering. Swaggering forward, she leaps upon a table where she fires a pistol shot, startling them. She declares in the throaty voice of a young man: "Well, gentlemen, I have the painful duty of telling you that you are both wrong—the sixes and the nines. The truth is that the Queen has had twelve lovers this past year, a round dozen. And now, if you will permit, I shall stand a round of drinks for all of you. Landlord, the punch!" The protective Gilbert invites Garbo to share his room and she accepts, but he is still unaware of the fact that she is a female, let alone the Queen of Sweden. She eventually discloses the fact that she is a woman and the two become lovers, spending a few idyllic days together, but Garbo keeps from Gilbert her identity as the Queen. The love scenes depicted during this two-day hiatus are marvels to behold as Garbo seems to float about the room, long arms outstretched, gently fondling the ornate furniture, a spinning wheel, the very walls, until gliding to the love bed to caress its sheets and pillows and embrace a bedpost (as a phallic symbol), all of this done while Mamoulian shoots Garbo from the waist up, purposely hiding her long and rather thin legs and large feet. These gossamer images constitute some of the most exquisite love scenes ever put on film and where Gilbert, along with the viewer, can only admire the stunningly beautiful woman so gracefully enlivening these tranquil sequences. The mesmerized Gilbert finally finds his voice, saying: "What are you doing?" While continuing to touch objects in the room, Garbo replies: "Memorizing this room.…In the future, in my memory, I shall live a great deal in this room…I have imagined happiness, but happiness you cannot imagine. You must feel it. This is how the Lord must have felt when He beheld the finished world with all His creatures, loving, breathing." (This magnificent scene and the unforgettable words uttered by Garbo stands as one of the greatest moments in film, epitomizing this great actress's unique charisma and persona. To achieve this scene, Mamoulian provided a metronome that measured Garbo's floating-like movements throughout the room and had faint and inspiring music playing in the background, a technique employed in the silent era to inspire players in romantic scenes.) When they must part, Garbo tells Gilbert that she will later see him at court when he presents himself to the Queen as the Span-

Greta Garbo in *Queen Christina*, 1933.

ish Ambassador. She then leaves for the capital and, when Gilbert arrives to pay homage to the Queen, he is startled to see that the Queen and his lover are one and the same person. Garbo is formal with Gilbert, pretending to recognize Gilbert only as a foreign ambassador and, he, in turn, upholds courtly decorum, by asking that she give her hand in marriage, not to him, but to the King of Spain. Garbo does not respond to this request, but nevertheless continues to secretly meet with Gilbert, whom she truly loves. In the next encounter, Gilbert is angry with Garbo, feeling that she has compromised his loyalty to his sovereign, the King of Spain, but his love for her is so overwhelming that he forgives her and they continue their hidden affair. The conniving Keith, however, learns of their secret relationship and exposes it, rousing the public and branding Gilbert a foreign seducer, who has sullied the Swedish throne. Garbo now fears for Gilbert's life, and, to protect him, orders him to leave, but telling him that she will quit her throne and meet him later and they will live out a happy life together. Against the pleas and urgings of her counselors, Smith chief among them, Garbo abdicates, and then hurries to her rendezvous with Gilbert. She then discovers that Gilbert has been mortally wounded by Keith in a sword fight and Gilbert dies in Garbo's arms. She takes his body to her ship and then sails for Spain, where she plans to live in Gilbert's home overlooking the sea. The final scene in this superb film shows Garbo standing at the prow of the ship, peering into the mists, envisioning, as she predicted earlier, a lonely future that will offer her only the wonderful memories of her blissful moments with the man she loved. Mamoulian is to be credited in exacting from Garbo one of her greatest performances if not her greatest, one where she grandly exhibits every passion, from sorrow to joy, from weakness to strength, her loving sensitivity present in every unforgettable scene. Gilbert, too, is wonderful in his role as the noble-hearted lover, and the cast members are outstanding in their roles. The lensing from Daniels stunningly captures the 17th-Century period and its rich costuming and sumptuous sets, and, most particular, the effervescent Garbo, while Stothart's score haunts and inspires. The film was expensive to make, costing more than $1,114,000, but it proved to be an enormous box office smash, producing more than $2,880,000 and it remains one of Garbo's most successful films. This film saw a miserable remake in 1974 under the title of **Abdication**. *Author's Note*: Garbo insisted that Gilbert play her leading man in this film, although their off-screen romance had long earlier waned. MGM boss Louis B. Mayer was opposed to having Gilbert in the film and had decided to get rid of Gilbert from the MGM roster, even going to the extent of spreading the false claim that his early talkies failed because Gilbert's voice was unmanly and too high-pitched, a claim made ridiculous in **Queen Christina** as Gilbert speaks with a well modulating baritone. However, Garbo was the top star at MGM at that time and Mayer bowed to her wishes. She

Lewis Stone and Greta Garbo in *Queen Christina*, **1933.**

had an almost unbreakable contract with MGM, where she not only received $250,000 for each film, but had complete approval of the director, cinematographer (she selected Daniels for this production as he was her favorite cinematographer), her leading men and each and every supporting player. "A lot of people in Hollywood said that John Gilbert was through as an actor," Garbo told this author, "but he disproved that claim when he appeared with me in **Queen Christina**. He was perfect in his part as my lover and I don't think any other actor could have given the performance he did. He was not drinking then and was sober and serious…and full of fond memories about our pictures together." (Garbo and Gilbert had made four films together, **Queen Christina** being the fourth and final film.) Gilbert, however, was not the first actor Garbo selected to play opposite her in this film. She had seen a young British actor named Laurence Olivier in a British melodrama, **Westward Passage**, 1932, and told MGM that Olivier should most probably be her leading man in **Queen Christina**. MGM did not like the idea, as Olivier was a virtually unknown actor in the U.S., but he was nevertheless signed to the role and his passage was paid for by the studio. When he arrived in Hollywood, Mamoulian told him that he wanted to have a rehearsal with him and Garbo, selecting what later became Garbo's signature scene in the bedroom of the inn. Olivier dressed in full costume for that scene and when he appeared in the set, Garbo entered wearing lounge pajamas and was smoking a cigarette. Olivier tried a friendly approach, chatting with Garbo, but she responded with only terse, one-word responses. Mamoulian then asked Olivier to 'grasp Garbo's body tenderly, look into her eyes, and, in the gesture, awaken the passion within her." Olivier later stated: "At the touch of my hand, Garbo became frigid. I could feel the sudden tautness in her." Mamoulian called a break and Olivier and Garbo sat down together and smoked cigarettes, but Olivier's small talk produced few responses from Garbo. Mamoulian asked both of them to try the scene again, and, according to Olivier, "Garbo froze up as before." Garbo walked from the set and Olivier also departed, both in separate directions. "I sat there alone in my director's chair with no one to direct and with the crew members standing about with nothing to do," Mamoulian told this author. "I was so disgusted that I threw down the script and shouted: 'For God's sake, is there *any* man this woman will warm to?' One of the technicians standing in the dark behind me gave me the answer when he said: 'John Gilbert!' Well, I knew he was right as Gilbert had been wonderful in playing with Garbo in several silent films together. I knew that Gilbert was always in love with Garbo and that she was sometimes in love with him. I called him at his home and I told him about the problem I had and asked him if he would help out and just warm up Garbo by doing that scene with her. He was a good-hearted fellow and instantly agreed. A short time later, Gilbert was wearing the costume Olivier had worn and, as soon as he

appeared in that scene with Garbo, she instantly relaxed and it was evident to me and everyone else that the old passion between these two was still there. Garbo was vibrant and gave of herself in that scene, although Gilbert was still just a stand-in for Olivier." Garbo, apparently, was so comfortable with being with Gilbert once more that she refused to have Olivier in the film and also rejected a bevy of other leading men MGM suggested for the part, including Leslie Howard, Nils Asther (who was Garbo's leading man in **Wild Orchids**, 1929), Franchot Tone and Bruce Cabot. Garbo had made up her mind. It was Gilbert or no one. She sent a formal message to MGM chief Louis B. Mayer that read: "This is to confirm the approval heretofore given by me that John Gilbert shall be substituted therein, in lieu and instead of Laurence Olivier." (MGM honored its agreement with Olivier, paying him $1,500 per month for four months, which ended its agreement with the actor, who returned to England and with little regard for whimsical Hollywood.) Garbo appeared to be magnanimous in resurrecting Gilbert's career, but, as she told this author, "I felt deeply obligated to John. He had insisted that I be his co-star in **Flesh and the Devil** [1926] and that picture, perhaps more than any other up to that time, helped to establish my career. I was returning his great generosity at a time he needed help, that's all." If there was more, her old and deep and passionate love for Gilbert, Garbo did not indicate it. That Garbo insisted on having Gilbert in this film came as good news to Irving Thalberg, who was head of production at MGM, and who was a close friend of Gilbert's, since he and his actress-wife, Norma Shearer, had both stood up at Gilbert's wedding with actress Virginia Bruce, in 1932, a year before this film was made. Gilbert, though outstanding in this film, did not see his career resuscitated (he was paid only $20,000 for his role, about one tenth of what he received in his silent days as a romantic leading man) and as hoped for by Garbo and Thalberg. He was later divorced from Bruce and, after long bouts of drinking, he died prematurely at age thirty-eight in 1936. The woman that was most profoundly saddened by his death was not Greta Garbo, but Marlene Dietrich, who had befriended him (or even, perhaps, had fallen in love with him, or the image of what Gilbert represented). Mamoulian employed many new technical applications when making **Queen Christina**, particularly when shooting the stirring finale where Garbo stands at the prow of the ship and peers into an uncertain future. For that scene, Mamoulian told this author: "I wanted to do a gradual closing toward her, ending with an extreme close-up of that unbelievably beautiful face, but I realized that such a close-up in those days would show every pore on her face, so, to eliminate those flaws, we made a ruler-shaped glass filter strip clear at one end and diffused at the other so that when we got that extreme close-up it was muted to soften her features." It was Garbo who actually prompted this production, one that would take only sixty-eight days to complete. Garbo had not made a film in eighteen months and was residing in Sweden when a friend of hers, Salka Viertel (who eventually wrote the story for this film, along with H. M. Harwood, with dialog written by S. N. Behrman), gave her two books to read about Queen Christina, a somewhat mysterious monarch in which Garbo had shown some interest. Those works were *Christina of Sweden* by Margaret Goldsmith and *Sybil of the North* by Faith Compton, both books being romanticized tales about Christina that nevertheless detailed her perversities and unorthodox lifestyle, including her penchant for wearing male attire, as Garbo demonstrates in this film. After reading these books, Garbo told Viertel that she was interested in doing a film about Christina and Viertel wrote a screenplay loosely based upon the monarch. Garbo liked the script and wired MGM to state that this would be her next film and left Sweden so quickly for the U.S. that the only available stateroom she could book was on a slow freighter and where, on board that ship, as she stated to this author, she went to its prow and preemptively practiced the final scene in that script where she is standing on the prow with the wind blowing in her hair. MGM, along with the new censoring organization, the Hays Office, had deep reservations about making this film as Queen Christina, in real life, was certainly a great lover, but a woman who loved other women, a decided lesbian. Further, she was short, fat and ugly with a large, beaked nose and bulbous, glaring eyes. She openly dallied with her favorite lady-in-waiting, and was so notorious for her penchant of refusing to bathe that her offensive body odor compelled her courtiers to stand well apart from her, some claiming that less than twenty feet distant from the monarch proved stiflingly dangerous. Christina did not abdicate of her own accord, as is shown in the film, but under blackmailing pressure from her counselors and high-ranking nobles, who, more or less, ordered her to either marry her lady-in-waiting and face public ridicule or quit the throne, and, to preserve Sweden's royal image, she opted for the latter, although Christina, at one point, actually thought to have herself crowned *king* of the country. Following her abdication, Christina sailed to Italy, not Spain, and lived out her life with other women in that country under an alias, "Count Dohna," and she was buried with that man's name, which is carved on her tombstone. Ironically, when Garbo appeared in one of her early films, **The Saga of Gosta Berling** (1924, released in the U.S. in 1928), the name of her character is "Martha Dohna." Garbo was twenty-eight when she made **Queen Christina**, the very age that the actual queen abdicated her throne. The fears and apprehensions expressed by MGM studio executives about doing this film, however, were soon abandoned when they read the script to learn that Christina's story was a highly romanticized version of her life and that her notorious lesbianism was only obliquely referenced in Garbo's wearing of male attire. Garbo's version of Christina is the one that remains in the mind of the public, particularly that unforgettable ending where she peers sphinx-faced from the prow of the ship, a scene that should be credited to not only Garbo, but to Mamoulian's great artistry. The director told this author that "I wanted Garbo to show an enigmatic face to the world in that scene. I told her: 'I want your face to be a blank piece of paper. I want the writing on that blank piece of paper to be done by everyone sitting in the audience of the theater. Try to avoid blinking your eyes so that your face is only a beautiful mask.' She understood perfectly, nodded, and we shot the scene and she did exactly as I asked her to do." **p**, Walter Wanger; **d**, Rouben Mamoulian; **cast**, Greta Garbo, John Gilbert, Ian Keith, Lewis Stone, Elizabeth Young, Sir C. Aubrey Smith, Reginald Owen, Georges Renavent, David Torrence, Gustav Von Seyffertitz;. Akin Tamiroff; **w**, H.M. Harwood, Salka Viertel, S.N. Behrman (based on a story by Viertel, Margaret P. Levino); **c**, William Daniels; **m**, Herbert Stothart; **ed**, Blanche Sewell; **prod d**, Edgar G. Ulmer; **art d**, Alexander Toluboff; **set d**, Edwin B. Willis.

Queen Kelly ★★★★ 1929 (silent); U.S.; 101m; Gloria Swanson Productions/UA; B/W; Drama; Children: Unacceptable; **DVD**. The tempestuous Swanson and the equally mercurial Stroheim combine to provide a stunning drama that remains a cult classic to this day. Von Swanson is an American girl attending a European convent and while she is walking along a country road with classmates her pantaloons fall off just at the time when some officers on military maneuvers appear. One of those officers is Byron, a profligate prince, who has been sent on those maneuvers as punishment by sadistic Owen, the queen of the mythical kingdom of Kronberg, for dallying with too many women. Owen, a certifiably insane monarch, is displeased by Byron since he has sullied his engagement to her by carrying on endless affairs. When Byron meets Swanson, however, he is smitten by the attractive young girl. After returning to the convent, Swanson is upbraided by the mother superior for her conduct on the country road and for flirting with Byron. She is ordered to go to bed without dinner and to pray for forgiveness. That night, Swanson prays, but her prayers ask that she see Byron again. Byron himself is in need of Divine aid in that he attends a dinner party at the palace that night and is shocked to hear Owen announce that he will marry her the next day. Haunted by Swanson's beauty and determined to have one last fling, Byron rides to the convent and sets a fire as a diversion that allows him to sneak into the convent and where he abducts Swanson. He takes her to his lavish suite in the palace where she is greeted by a candlelight dinner. As she sits with Byron, Owen is

Greta Garbo in *Queen Christina*, **1933.**

shown bathing in her luxurious sunken tub, emerging naked, except for a white cat she clutches to her bosom to shield her privates. Owen, after putting on a robe, then strolls to the adjoining suite occupied by Byron and becomes enraged at seeing Swanson. Owen then selects the most punishing whip from her collection of such instruments of torture and begins lashing Swanson, who cringes, cowers and cries out in pain, as Owen whips her about the cavernous palace suite. A title card shows Swanson crying out: "But, he's going to marry you!" Owen, displaying a wicked smile, replies on a title card: "No! I'm going to marry him!" Thoroughly disgraced and barred from reentering the convent, Swanson (in the original version) commits suicide by drowning, and Byron, so horrified by the death of the girl he has come to love, goes to the convent, finds her body, and, he, too, ends his life. Von Stroheim, however, tacked on an additional story where Swanson, having no place to go after being disgraced by Owen, learns that her wealthy aunt, Gibson, who operates a business in East Africa, is dying, and has sent for her. Swanson goes to East Africa, only to discover that Gibson owns and runs the most notorious whorehouse in the area, and she is forced to marry a repulsive, ugly, crippled millionaire, Marshall, who is more degenerate than Owen and Gibson or anyone else on the planet. Gibson then dies, but Swanson cannot tolerate the presence of the vile Marshall and refuses to cohabit with him. Meanwhile, Byron, who has not committed suicide, is imprisoned by Owen for refusing to marry her and the now loveless Swanson makes the best of her miserable lot in East Africa by living eccentrically as the owner of her aunt's brothel, becoming so infamous that she is dubbed "Queen Kelly." Though the story line for this bizarre drama is fractured and outlandish, Swanson is mesmerizing in her role and her wonderful close-ups with Byron at that candlelight dinner are enchantingly memorable (and are shown when Swanson views them two decades later as her own silent films when enacting silent screen star Norma Desmond in Billy Wilder's classic **Sunset Boulevard**, 1950). Stroheim's direction is masterful, and he captures one alarming and arresting image after another, at the expense of continuity and a comprehensive story line to achieve his end goal, and that is to present scenes so startling if not shocking that all else becomes incidental and even unnecessary, at least in his mind's eye. *Author's Note*: This strange but obsessively absorbing film was made by Stroheim when he was at the end of his directorial tether. His boundless excesses in ignoring budgets and schedules, his extravagant expenses in making films, and his dictatorial Teutonic manners and savage conduct had caused him to become a pariah at every major Hollywood studio. He had worn out his welcome at Universal, MGM and Paramount, even though his last film, **The Wedding March**, 1928, made at Paramount, had been a great success. "A lot of people in Hollywood thought Stroheim belonged in a lunatic asylum," film editor Gene Ruggiero told this author. "He con-

Seena Owen whipping Gloria Swanson in *Queen Kelly*, 1929.

sidered all women whores, including his own mother, and, after he told that to Louis B. Mayer [head of MGM], the chief exploded and Mayer beat him so badly that Stroheim had to go to a hospital for treatment. Gloria [Swanson] was having a hard time of it when she hooked up with Stroheim. Her own films were not doing well and she wanted to make a big commercial film, so she got her lover, Joseph Kennedy, the banker and who was the father of the Kennedy Boys who later took over the White House [John F. Kennedy and Robert F. Kennedy] to put up a fortune to back **Queen Kelly**. Well, poor Gloria got a lot more than what she bargained for…Stroheim made her almost as nuts as he was when they did that picture together." Swanson, at that time, had left Paramount and established her own production company, financed by Kennedy. Through that company, Swanson starred and produced **Sadie Thompson**, 1928, which was based on Somerset Maugham's play "Rain," and was released through United Artists (the same firm that would distribute **Queen Kelly**), that film proving to be a great box office success. Kennedy had been financing programmers and melodramas, but had ambitions to produce films that would be of great quality and he envisioned Swanson appearing in a film that would last throughout time. To that end, Swanson and Kennedy contacted the errant Stroheim. The three met in one of Kennedy's luxurious Hollywood hideouts where Kennedy, a married man, conducted his ongoing and torrid affair with Swanson. Stroheim was exuberant in explaining the storyline for the film they would make together and stated that he had written a script exclusively for Swanson which he had titled "The Swamp." After Swanson and Kennedy read the script, which was later retitled **Queen Kelly**, Kennedy told Stroheim that he was personally going to back the film and even went so far as to buy out Stroheim's contract from Paramount so that the director would be exclusively free to direct Swanson in this opus. Stroheim, by that time, was already ordering expensive wardrobes for his yet to be casted players for the film, and hiring experienced cavalry officers to play the roles of the troopers who accompany Byron in only a few scenes. He took over sound stages at UA and began ordering mammoth sets to be constructed, all of this costing Kennedy a fortune. "Kennedy was one of those Big Shot money guys who would get excited about something, then get interested in something else and walk away from his investment, leaving others to manage things," Ruggiero told this author, "and that's what he did with **Queen Kelly**, leaving Swanson in the lurch with that cuckoo, Stroheim, and, sure enough, Stroheim turns her into a whore in that picture like he did with almost of all his actresses in his pictures. As I said, he thought all women were whores and he went out of his way to show them as whores. That's how sick Stroheim really was, but nobody caught on to that, not even Kennedy and Swanson, until it was too late." Actually, Kennedy, at that time, had the opportunity to create a new

studio, RKO, and he gave that new project his undivided attention, turning over the production of **Queen Kelly** to producers Benjamin Glazer and William Le Baron. "I talked with Bill [Le Baron] about that," Ruggiero said, "and he told me that 'Hell, we were not about to tell Stroheim anything. That man walked about with a loaded gun and he once threatened to shoot a producer who even suggested that a few buttons be changed on an actor's costume. Do you think we were going to aggravate a loony like him?" Swanson became apprehensive almost from the beginning of the production, particularly after Stroheim told her that she had to bear some whiplashing from Owen in order to achieve "realism." According to Ruggiero, Stroheim "went out of his way to degrade and demean Gloria [Swanson] throughout the making of that picture, even telling one of the actors to spit on her." In the scene where Swanson is more or less ordered to marry the repulsive Marshall while a bevy of prostitutes serve as her bridal party in the brothel, Marshall's spit, mingled with juice from tobacco he is chewing, splattered Swanson's hand. The actress flared up and demanded to know why Marshall had done that. Marshall sheepishly replied that Stroheim had ordered him to do it. Swanson exploded, quit the scene, and immediately went to a phone where she got Kennedy on the line and demanded that "you fire this madman right now!" Kennedy, however, was too immersed in putting RKO into existence and Stroheim stayed with the production, until Kennedy finally got around to firing him. Swanson later scrapped the African element of the story (although some of this footage survived), and, with cinematographer Gregg Toland, reshot the film to have a different ending where Byron goes to the convent to visit Swanson's body after she has committed suicide following her being whipped from the palace by Owen and where Byron, so consumed by guilt over her death, also takes his own life, this version called "the Swanson ending." The film was not originally released in the U.S., but saw widespread distribution in Europe and South America. Both versions were later restored in 1985, but with stills replacing some of the missing scenes. **Queen Kelly** was Stroheim's swan song. He would never again direct a major film. Though well remembered for his classic film, **Greed**, Stroheim, like most unbalanced people, had blinding and brilliant flashes of insightful vision, almost wholly unrelated to logic, reason, and discipline, these filmic lightning strikes remaining his foremost legacy, bursting revelations of artistry possessing the strange and unpredictable compulsions of a mind unlike any other director in the history of films. **p**, Joseph P. Kennedy; **d&w**, Erich von Stroheim (titles by Marian Ainslee); **cast**, Gloria Swanson, Walter Byron, Seena Owen, Sylvia Ashton, Wilson Benge, Sidney Bracey, Rae Daggett, Florence Gibson, Madge Hunt, Tully Marshall, Madame SulTe-Wan; **c**, Paul Ivano, Gordon Pollock, Ben F. Reynolds, Gregg Toland; **m**, Adolf Tandler, Ugo Derouard (1985 restored version); **ed**, Viola Lawrence; **art d**, Robert Day, Stroheim, Harold Miles.

Queen of Hearts ★★★ 1989; U.S./U.K.; 112m; Channel Four Films/Cinecom Pictures; Color; Comedy; Children: Unacceptable; **DVD**; **VHS**. An Italian family moves to London and the father wins at cards and opens a café in an Italian neighborhood. Later, he loses the café and his wedding ring through gambling. The youngest son, Hawkes, who is eleven, tries to find a way to save their home and café, but Armandola, an old family enemy from Italy, arrives and tries to drive them into bankruptcy. This well-made comedy depicts a caring and feuding Italian family that may never make it rich, but there will be love along the way. Gutter language prohibits viewing by children. **p**, John Hardy; **d**, Jon Amiel; **cast**, Ian Hawkes, Vittorio Duse, Joseph Long, Anita Zagaria, Eileen Way, Vittorio Amandola, Roberto Scateni, Stefano Spagnoli, Alec Bregonzi, Ronan Vibert, Matilda Thorpe; **w**, Tony Grisoni; **c**, Mike Southon; **m**, Michael Convertino; **ed**, Peter Boyle; **prod d**, Jim Clay; **art d**, Philip Elton.

The Queen of Spades ★★★★ 1949; U.K.; 95m; De Grunwald Productions/Monogram Pictures; Drama; Children: Unacceptable; **DVD**.

Pushkin's supernatural tale about a man who seeks to make a pact with the Devil comes eerily to life in this fine atmospheric production that offers a standout performance from the gifted and intense Walbrook. He is a Russian captain in the Imperial Army, but so penniless that he cannot partake in the exciting gambling his fellow officers enjoy. Walbrook then hears about a mysterious, elderly countess, Evans, who is rumored to win all the time at faro, but her success at that gaming table is assured only because she sold her soul to the Evil One. To learn Evans' secret on how she always wins at faro, Walbrook seduces Mitchell, her companion, who tells him that he can learn the secret only by going up a staircase in Evans' home. Walbrook sneaks into the mansion at night, but, when ascending that staircase, he meets Evans, a horrid-looking old woman, who dies of fright at the sight of him. Fleeing the mansion, Walbrook dreams that night that he has learned the secret of winning at faro by being able to play three cards. He goes to the gambling casino and begins to win at faro, besting his rival at that game and knowing that if he wins, he will also win the affections of a young woman his rival also covets. The last card is the winning one he hopes for, an ace, but, before he plays it, it turns into the Queen of Spades and its face is exactly that of Evans, who winks at him in a sinister fashion. He not only loses all of his stakes, but his mind in the bargain and winds up in a lunatic asylum. Dickinson directs with great skill in providing this thriller, which is enhanced by a stellar cast, and the costuming and sets richly capture the period of the early 19th Century. Though several silent and talkie versions of this story have been filmed, this one is by far and away the best. *Author's Note*: Evans makes her appearance in this film after a thirty-three-year hiatus from the screen, having made only a few forgettable silent films before this production. Her appearance here was so impressive that it launched her into a new and successful film career that lasted almost another thirty years until her death in 1976 at age eighty-eight. **p**, Anatole de Grunwald; **d**, Thorold Dickinson; **cast**, Anton Walbrook, Edith Evans, Yvonne Mitchell, Ronald Howard, Mary Jerrold, Anthony Dawson, Miles Malleson, Michael Medwin, Athene Seyler, Ivor Barnard; **w**, Rodney Ackland, Arthur Boys (based on the story by Alexander Pushkin); **c**, Otto Heller; **m**, Georges Auric; **ed**, Hazel Wilkinson; **art d**, William Kellner.

Queen of the Mob ★★★ 1940; U.S.; 61m; PAR; B/W; Crime Drama; Children: Unacceptable. Yurka is chilling in playing the real mob boss Ma Barker (Arizona Donnie "Kate" Barker; 1873-1935). She and her three sons, Denning, Seay, and Kelly, take part with her in a series of bank robberies and a kidnapping, killing as they go along from state to state. They are unaware that, in one bank robbery, $400,000 of the money is marked, but the FBI knows and goes on their trail, led by super G-man agent Bellamy. Two of Yurka's sons are shot dead by FBI agents before Bellamy reaches her home where she is trimming a Christmas tree for local kids, and her surviving son dons a Santa Claus suit. He is shot and killed, and Yurka gives herself up. The real Ma Barker was much meaner and she and her surviving son were killed in a 45-minute shootout with G-men in Florida. Although the script plays fast and loose with the true facts surrounding Ma Barker and her brood, the film provides an action-packed tale that captures the flavor and times of that turbulent era. *Author's Note*: Yurka, an actress with decidedly unattractive features, was particularly selected for the role of Ma Barker based upon the savage nature she had displayed in her blood-thirsty character of Madame DeFarge in the classic **A Tale of Two Cities**, 1935, where she takes a special delight as a witness in seeing aristocrats going to the guillotine. The hatchet-faced Yurka (as she appeared in later years) was chiefly a stage actress and appeared in mostly crime and horror B films. She always felt that the Hollywood community did not really appreciate her acting talents, stating at one point: "Hollywood missed out on Blanche Yurka." She is also quoted as saying, "I never met a single person who lived the way the public believed we lived." This cryptic remark is made clear when one understands that Yurka was a member of the lesbian coterie of actresses that included Alla Nazimova, Natasha

J. Carrol Naish, Richard Denning, Blanche Yurka and Raymond Hatton in *Queen of the Mob*, 1940.

Rambova (who was once married to Rudolph Valentino), and others, and it was Nazimova who secured the role of Madame DeFarge in **A Tale of Two Cities** for Yurka. Three years before Yurka's appearance in that film, she was involved in a sensational murder case, the violent gunshot death of multimillionaire Zachary Smith Reynolds, heir to the great tobacco fortune, on July 5-6, 1932, at the sprawling Reynolds estate at Winston-Salem, North Carolina. Reynolds was then married to actress and torch singer Libby Holman, who was a close friend of Yurka's, and who invited Yurka to a party at that estate where she and others participated in an all-night drinking binge and, after Reynolds was found fatally shot, Yurka helped Holman and Ab Walker, a family friend (who might have been having an affair with Holman), to carry the dying Reynolds to a car before he was rushed to hospital where he was pronounced dead. Although Holman was suspected of having murdered Reynolds, perhaps even with the help of Walker and Yurka (who was thought to be Holman's lesbian lover at one point), the death was ruled an accident. "We all knew about Blanche's [Yurka's] strange past when we did **Queen of the Mob** together," Bellamy told this author some years after Yurka's death (she died in 1976 at age eighty-six): "We did not talk about it, but Blanche did. She was playing J. Edgar Hoover's version of Ma Barker in that picture and she was acting like her character off-camera. At one point, she invited me into her dressing room where she poured two stiff drinks and, after I declined to take one, she belted down both of them and then a few more. I asked her about what went on down there at the Reynolds estate, a case that always fascinated me, and she shrugged and said: 'Oh, we were all drunk that night and I guess Libby [Holman], who was so pie-eyed that she could hardly walk, shot Reynolds when he objected to her fooling around with his friend, Walker. She told me later that she couldn't really remember who pulled the trigger because she was so drunk that night.' Blanche later invited me to attend a party at the Garden of Allah, a fancy courthouse area where her good friend, Alla Nazimova, lived, but I did not want to be part of that crowd and found an excuse not to go. Everyone who went to those Nazimova parties were very light on their feet, men and women alike [lesbians and homosexuals]…not my kind of people." For more details on the Reynolds death, see my two-volume work *The Great Pictorial History of World Crime*, Volume II (History, Inc., 2004; pages 1238-1246). Robert Ryan makes his film debut in the film and James Cagney's sister, Jeanne Cagney, has a supporting role. This was the fourth and final crime picture based on *Persons in Hiding* by FBI Director J. Edgar Hoover (1895-1972), the other films being **Persons in Hiding**, 1939; **Undercover Doctor**, 1939; and **Parole Fixer**, 1940; all made before **Queen of the Mob**. The profiles in this film and others from Hoover's book are chiefly fictional accounts the FBI director concocted to promote his own image. There is debate to this day that Ma

Rae Dawn Chong, Everett McGill and Ron Perlman in *Quest for Fire,* **1982.**

Barker was anything other than a tagalong mother who accompanied her sons during their crime spree in the early 1930s and never planned anything, including dinner. For reliable details on the Barker gang, see my eight-volume reference work *Encyclopedia of World Crime,* Volume I (CrimeBooks, Inc., 1990; pages 235-243). **p**, William LeBaron; **d**, James Hogan; **cast**, Ralph Bellamy, Blanche Yurka, William Henry, Richard Denning, James Seay, J. Carrol Naish, Jeanne Cagney, Paul Kelly, Hedda Hopper, Jack Carson, Billy Gilbert, Paul Fix, Neil Hamilton, Mary Gordon, Raymond Hatton, Charles Lane, Robert Ryan, Sheila Ryan, Mary Treen; **w**, Horace McCoy, William R. Lipman (based on the book *Persons in Hiding* by J. Edgar Hoover); **c**, Theodor Sparkhul; **m**, Friedrich Hollaender, John Leipold; **ed**, Arthur Schmidt; **art d**, Hans Dreier, Ernst Fegté.

Queen of the Night Clubs ★★★ 1929; U.S.; 60m; WB; B/W; Biographical Drama; Children: Unacceptable. This lively film colorfully recreates the period of speakeasies during the Prohibition Era in America (1919-1933) when it was illegal to make, sell, or drink alcoholic beverages. Guinan plays a woman much like herself, Texas Guinan (Mary Louise Cecilia Guinan, 1884-1933), who was an American saloon keeper and actress, famous for jokingly greeting her patrons with: "Hello, sucker!" and telling them, "Give the little lady a great big hand," meaning to applaud her female entertainers. She plays Tex Malone, owner of a nightclub who hires Lee as a performer, causing Lee to break up with her partner, Foy. Davidson, a friend of Guinan's, is murdered by Housman, an old business associate of Guinan's. Evidence implicates Foy and he is arrested. Guinan discovers that Foy is her long-lost son. At his trial, she convinces jurors to come to her nightclub where they find evidence clearing Foy and which sends Housman to prison. Soon afterward, Norworth, her long-lost husband, returns to her. *Author's Note*: Jack Norworth (1879-1959) was a real-life songwriter who, with his fourth wife, singer Nora Bayes (1880-1928) wrote "Shine on Harvest Moon." A 1944 film with that title profiles these stellar entertainers and stars Dennis Morgan and Ann Sheridan. Norworth also wrote, with Albert Von Tilzer, "Take Me Out to the Ballgame" in 1908, which has become one of the most sung songs in America, the anthem for ball games, although neither of the composers had ever attended a baseball game. Song: "It's Tough to Be a Hostess on Broadway." George Raft makes his film debut in this film dancing the Charleston, which he did in one of Guinan's speakeasies when he began his career and after he quit working as a bootlegger for NYC gangster Owney Madden. For more details on the colorful Texas Guinan, see my book *Zanies: The World's Greatest Eccentrics* (New Century, Piscataway, N.J., 1982; pages 164-172). **p&d**, Bryan Foy; **cast**, Texas Guinan, John Davidson, Lila Lee, Arthur Housman, Eddie Foy, Jr., Jack Norworth, George Raft, Jimmy

Phillips, John Miljan, Lee Shumway; **w**, Addison Burkhard, Murray Roth (based on their story); **c**, Ed Du Par.

Quentin Durward ★★★ 1955; U.S.; 102m; MGM; Color; Adventure; Children: Unacceptable; **VHS**. In this exciting tale by Sir Walter Scott, stalwart Scottish nobleman Taylor travels to France in 1465 to marry Kendall, a countess. The wedding has been arranged for political reasons by Taylor's uncle, Thesiger. Taylor is a man of honor who rebels at the thought that he and Kendall are being used as pawns by Clunes, the Duke of Burgundy, and Morley, who plays Louis XI (1423-1483). Taylor and Kendall, however, fall in love, and, after overcoming attempts on his life and many hazardous exploits, Taylor finally goes to the altar with the lovely Kendall. Director Thorpe presents an action-loaded adventure tale, and the sets, costuming, lensing and score enhance this fine period production. *Author's Note*: Taylor told this author that "by the time I appeared in **Quentin Durward**, I was getting typecast into historical epics, and that all started with **Quo Vadis** [1951], until I was clanking around in armor from one picture to the next [**Ivanhoe**, 1952; **Knights of the Round Table**, 1953]. I don't mean to complain because all of those pictures were top-flight productions, but, after a while, I got a little tired of lugging around all those heavy swords and shields. I was almost matched with Grace Kelly in **Quentin Durward**, but she bowed out and I got Kay Kendall as my co-star, which was fine with me because Kay was one of the most beautiful actresses in the business." **p**, Pandro S. Berman; **d**, Richard Thorpe; **cast**, Robert Taylor, Kay Kendall, Robert Morley, George Cole, Alec Clunes, Marius Goring, Wilfrid Hyde-White, Eric Pohlmann, Harcourt Williams, Ernest Thesiger; **w**, Robert Ardrey (based on an adaptation by George Froeschel of the novel by Sir Walter Scott); **c**, Christopher Challis, Desmond Dickinson; **m**, Bronislau Kaper; **ed**, Ernest Walter; **art d**, Alfred Junge; **spec eff**, Tom Howard.

Quest for Fire ★★★ 1982; Canada/France/U.S.; 100m; International Cinema Corporation/FOX; Color; Historical Drama; Children: Unacceptable (MPAA: R); **DVD**; **VHS**. Primitive man is excitingly and realistically portrayed in this absorbing tale. When a tribe loses the source of its fire and knows no way to recreate the needed flames, three of its members are sent in search of that elusive blaze. McGill, Perlman and El-Kadi explore unknown and dangerous territory until they locate another tribe, a fierce clan of cavemen that kills without hesitation or mercy. The searchers, however, discover that this tribe has learned how to create fire by using flints and sticks and, after learning this technique, they escape back to their own tribe, rescuing the attractive Chong in the process. Although several cave men films, including **One Million, B.C.**, 1940, and **One Million Years, B.C.**, 1966, along with many other films, have profiled what Hollywood thinks early human life on this planet may have been, this film presents a much more credible portrait in that the cavemen use body language adopted from simian gestures and mannerisms created by Desmond Morris, author of *The Naked Ape*, and the primitive language employed was created by celebrated novelist Anthony Burgess. Made for $12 million, this film reaped more than $55 million at the box office in its initial release. **p**, John Kemeny, Denis Heroux, Jacques Dorfmann, Vera Belmont; **d**, Jean-Jacques Annaud; **cast**, Everett McGill, Ron Perlman, Nameer El-Kadi, Rae Dawn Chong, Gary Schwartz, Naseer El-Kadi, Frank Olivier Bonnet, Jean-Michel Kindt, Kurt Schiegl, Brian Gill; **w**, Gerard Brach (based on the novel *La guerre de feu* by J.H. Rosny, Sr.); **c**, Claude Agostini (Panavision; Bellevue-Pathe Color); **m**, Philippe Sarde; **ed**, Yves Langlois; **prod d**, Brian Morris, Guy Comptois; **art d**, Clinton Cavers; **spec eff**, Martin Malivoire.

Quick Change ★★★ 1990; U.S.; 92m; Devoted Productions/WB; Color; Comedy; Children: Unacceptable (MPAA: R); **DVD**; **VHS**. Funny film sees Murray dressing as a clown to rob a New York City bank and where he succeeds with the help of accomplices Davis and Quaid. Robbing the bank appears to be easy, but the hard part is getting to the airport with cops led by Robards on their trail. A hilarious series of misadventures follow until the trio is finally caught to prove that crime does not pay, at least for these inept jokers. Songs: "L-O-V-E" (Bert Kaempfert, Milt Farler), "Baila Mi Ritmo" (C. Valdez, B. Coteaux), "Tive um coracao, perdi-o" (Jose Fontes Rocha), "Dertfick Confiance/Nakaar" (Chab Mami). Gutter language and violence prohibit viewing by children. **p**, Robert Greenhut, Bill Murray; **d**, Howard Franklin, Murray; **w**, Franklin (based on the novel by Jay Cronley); **cast**, Murray, Geena Davis, Randy Quaid, Dale Grand, Bob Elliott, Kimberleigh Aarn, Ron Ryan, Brian McConnachie, Jack Gilpin, Jordan Cael; **c**, Michael Chapman; **m**, Randy Edelman; **ed**, Alan Heim; **prod d**, David Gropman; **art d**, Speed Hopkins; **set d**, Susan Bode.

Quick Millions ★★★★ 1931; U.S.; 72m; FOX; B/W; Crime Drama; Children: Unacceptable. The inimitable Tracy is a truck driver with a lot of bright ideas, some of them leading him down the dark path of crime. Too lazy to work, he dreams up a racket where he organizes a group of thugs to purposely wreck cars so that he will get a share of the money from the garage owners repairing those vandalized autos. He soon graduates to more serious crimes, including extortion, protection, and finally muscles in on all of the trucking firms so that he controls their operations. As Tracy grows wealthy, he seeks to add social stature to his riches by dumping his girlfriend, the common Eilers, for uncommon society lady Churchill, but Churchill wants no part of the conniving gangster, especially after Tracy compels her brother, Wray, to become an unwilling partner in his illegal enterprises. Meanwhile, Raft, who is Tracy's top enforcer and loyal friend, kills a reformer through a ruse concocted by Richmond, who is Tracy's underworld rival. To shield himself from blame in the killing, Tracy ruthlessly orders Raft murdered by his own men, a killing they reluctantly commit. When Churchill is about to marry another man, Tracy loses all sense of reason and plans to kidnap her from the altar and somehow compel this unwilling woman to marry him. When he tells his gang members to prepare for that kidnapping, his minions now feel that Tracy's wild scheme is driven only by his obsession to obtain recognition in the world of high society and, instead of executing that kidnapping for him, his men execute Tracy by taking him for a "one-way ride." Director Brown helms a fast-paced, underrated gangster film with stunning and realistic scenes, where Tracy excels as a good man gone wrong through warped ambitions. Raft, in his second film, is a standout as the victimized sidekick. Another film with the same title made by Fox in 1939 is a comedy and is unrelated to this story. *Author's Note*: Brown, who also co-authored the script, based many incidents in this film (as he would again in **Blood Money**, 1933) on the exploits of real-life NYC bootleggers of his personal acquaintance, especially Owen "Owney" Madden (1891-1965), who would be well essayed in **The Cotton Club**, 1984, by Bob Hoskins. Madden asked Brown if he could introduce one of his former employees, a rumrunner turned speakeasy dancer, George Raft, to some people in Hollywood with the thought of casting Raft in some films, the dancer then having ambitions of becoming a screen actor. Brown secured small parts for Raft in several films until he thought to give him a featured role in this film. Tracy, who was then a rising star at Fox, was, as he told this author, "amazed to see this guy [George] Raft show up at the studio in a limousine. He gets out of that wagon with his thick black hair parted in the middle and slicked down with pomade and he is dressed to the nines. He says to me as I am standing outside a sound stage: 'Hey, buddy, where do I go for a picture called **Quick Millions**?' I took him inside the sound stage and Rowland [Brown] spots him and runs over to shake his hand like it is old home week. Rowland told us that Raft was going to be in the picture and then all hell breaks loose when the casting director tells Rowland that Raft has no acting experience and Rowland, a very tough bird, grabs the casting director and threatens to bop him in the nose. And poor George was in the middle, trying to pry the two of them apart. What an entrance!" Raft told this author that "Rowland [Brown] had gotten me a few small roles in some pictures

Sally Eilers and Spencer Tracy in *Quick Millions*, 1931.

before he called me up and said he was giving me a beefy part in **Quick Millions** and he sent a limousine to pick me up at the hotel where I was staying that took me to the studio, and I met the star of the film, Spence [Spencer Tracy]. Rowland was a tough nut and when the casting director objected to my being in the film because of my lack of acting experience, I thought Rowland was going to knock him out, so I jumped in and stopped the fight and then I said: 'Why don't I do an audition for the part and, if you like what I do, hire me?' The casting director nodded and that settled the matter. I did the audition and got the part. Howard Hughes saw me in **Quick Millions** and decided to put me into another gangster picture called **Scarface** [1932], which was written by Ben Hecht, and it was that picture that really established my movie career, but it would never have happened without Rowland's great help." Brown was well known to screenwriter Ben Hecht, who contributed some passages of dialog to **Quick Millions**, but was not credited. Hecht, who was this author's mentor, told this author that "Rowland Brown was a gifted writer and film director, but he had the temperament of a volcano. He was a born adventurer. Before he arrived in Hollywood in the 1920s, he had been a prizefighter and even sparred with Jack Dempsey. He worked briefly in New York for gangster Owney Madden as a bodyguard, and then began writing stories and plays. He had met George Raft when Raft was also working for Madden, driving trucks loaded with illegal booze from Canada to New York during Prohibition and when Raft told Madden that he wanted to go into the movies, Madden called Rowland, who welcomed his pal George with open arms and got him parts in some early talkies and then put him into **Quick Millions** with Spencer Tracy and that part really started George's career. **Quick Millions** was the first picture Rowland directed, but he had scored big when writing the story for **The Doorway to Hell** [1930], which was based on his play. Raft went up fast after **Quick Millions** and Rowland went slowly down, but it was his own fault. Rowland only did a few films as a director and they were mostly gangster films in the early Thirties, but they were very good ones [**Quick Millions**, 1931; **Hell's Highway**, 1932; **Blood Money**, 1933; and **The Devil Is a Sissy**, 1936, not credited]. Rowland could not compromise with producers and whenever any of them asked him to make any changes, Rowland either threatened to knock them for a loop or walk out of the picture, a very stubborn guy. Alexander Korda, the British producer and director, saw some of Rowland's early films and asked him to go to England and direct a Leslie Howard picture [**The Scarlet Pimpernel**, 1934], but he got into trouble after he told Korda that he was directing that film like he would a gangster film and, if Korda did not like that, he would walk. Korda told him to walk and he did. Rowland was a brilliant man and could have had a great career as a film director, but there was a hotheaded man who prevented that from happening, himself." For details about the man who

Mickey Rooney, Jeanne Cagney and Peter Lorre in *Quicksand*, 1950.

once employed Brown and Raft, the enigmatic gangster Owen "Owney" Madden, see my book *World Encyclopedia of Organized Crime* (Paragon House, New York, 1992; pages 262-263). **p**, William Fox; **d**, Rowland Brown; **cast**, Spencer Tracy, Marguerite Churchill, Sally Eilers, Bob Burns, Warner Richmond, George Raft, John Swor, Leon Ames, Oscar Apfel, Ward Bond, Edgar Kennedy, Dixie Lee; **w**, Brown, Courtney Perrett (based on their story); **c**, Joseph H. August; **ed & art d**, Duncan Cramer.

Quicksand ★★★ 1950; U.S.; 79m; Samuel H. Stiefel Productions/UA; B/W; Crime Drama; Children: Unacceptable; **DVD**; **VHS**. Rooney proved his dramatic talents as an intense and riveting actor in this absorbing crime tale. He is an on-the-level, hardworking mechanic, who is suddenly taken by alluring Cagney (sister of actor James Cagney). To impress her by taking her on the town one night, the impoverished Rooney borrows $20 from his boss's till, thinking he has enough time to return the money before an accountant shows up to check the books. That night, Rooney meets Lorre, who owns an arcade and who has been one of Cagney's former sugar daddies, and Rooney now realizes that the woman he loves is a gold digger, but that does not matter because he is daffy about her. When Rooney appears at his job the next morning, he is alarmed to see that the accountant has arrived days earlier to balance the books. He panics and goes to a jewelry store where he buys an expensive watch on credit and then pawns the watch for $30, racing back to his garage to place the missing $20 in the till just before the accountant checks the money on hand. But, in replacing the missing money, Rooney has compounded his problems in that creditors now hound him for payments on the watch he has pawned and which he cannot afford to reclaim. Further, he needs money to also wine and dine Cagney, and, in desperation, he rolls a drunk for his cash, but the insidious Lorre (when was he not?) witnesses Rooney's crime and begins blackmailing him, telling Rooney he will keep his mouth shut if Rooney steals a car for him from the garage where he works. Rooney takes a car from the garage and delivers it to Lorre, but Rooney's boss, Smith, discovers that Rooney has taken the auto and demands that Rooney pay for it. To obtain enough money to pay off Smith, Rooney and Cagney then rob Lorre's arcade, obtaining a substantial amount of cash, but the greedy Cagney spends most of it on a fur coat, leaving Rooney with only $1,800 to pay Smith for the stolen car. Smith takes the money, but then holds a gun on Rooney as he reaches for a phone to call police, proving he is just as crooked as everyone else in Rooney's twisted world, as Smith intends to keep the money and still claim the car has been stolen. Rooney can no longer bear the quicksand of events that have sucked him into debt impossible to repay and a life of crime that assures him of imprisonment. He jumps forward, wrestling the gun from Smith

and then strangles him, leaving him for dead as he flees. He carjacks an auto driven by Holmes, telling him his story, and Holmes, who is an attorney, seems sympathetic to his plight. Police then stop the car and corner Rooney. Thinking he is now facing a murder charge, Rooney shoots it out with the cops and is wounded and captured. A glimmer of hope appears when he learns that Smith is alive and Holmes tells him that he will represent him in court and that Rooney should be facing a light term in prison since he is a first- time offender. Grim and fatalistic, this film is yet compelling due to Pichel's taut direction and Rooney's outstanding performance and where Cagney, Lorre, Smith and the rest of the cast are convincing in their roles. The 2003 film with the same title presents a much different story line. *Author's Note*: Rooney and Lorre formed a partnership company that produced this film, one of three films envisioned by the two actors, but the film did not do well at the box office, and the two additionally envisioned films were never made by Rooney and Lorre. **Quicksand** most likely failed with the public because Rooney fans were expecting another one of his lighthearted comedies and were, instead, presented with a mature and unnerving film noir story that went against the grain of Rooney's former juvenile persona, despite the fact that **Quicksand** proved to be a superior crime yarn. Lorre not only lost his investment, but, according to what he told this author, "my manager squandered most of my reserve cash and that forced me into bankruptcy. I went back to Europe and was at loose ends, until I got the opportunity to make a significant picture, **The Lost One** [1951, released in the U.S. in 1984], the only film I ever directed [and starred in]. Like **Quicksand**, that picture never got the recognition it deserved." **p**, Mort Briskin; **d**, Irving Pichel; **cast**, Mickey Rooney, Jeanne Cagney, Barbara Bates, Peter Lorre, Taylor Holmes, Art Smith, Wally Cassell, Richard Lane, Patsy O'Connor, John Gallaudet, Jack Elam, Red Nichols and His Five Pennies (performing in the nightclub scenes); **w**, Robert Smith; **c**, Lionel Lindon; **m**, Louis Gruenberg; **ed**, Walter Thompson; **prod d & art d**, Boris Leven; **set d**, Robert Priestley.

The Quiet American ★★★ 1958; U.S.; 120m; Figaro/UA; B/W; Drama; Children: Unacceptable; **DVD**. This incisive film about the U.S. foreign policy failure in pre-war Indochina is seen through the eyes of Murphy, an innocent young American, who arrives in Vietnam representing a privately funded aid effort to help the South Vietnamese in their fight against the communists and the French. He meets Redgrave, a cynical British reporter, and they not only have opposing views in trying to win the hearts and minds of the Vietnamese people, but they compete over the affections of a young Vietnamese woman, Moll. Murphy wants to reform her and make her a typical middle-class American housewife. Redgrave accepts her inability to take any political stance and does not promise her any real future, but objects to Murphy's attempts to change her. Redgrave eventually is duped by the communists into taking part in the murder of Murphy. The story is told in flashback, opening with Dauphin investigating Murphy's murder. It's never clear whether Murphy is the naïve American do-gooder he appears to be, or if he is an agent of U.S. covert operations, but he nevertheless ends up being an expendable pawn and killed. Song: "La Cathedrale engloutie" (Claude Debussy). Filmed in Vietnam, the movie was not very successful at the box office, but its top-flight direction and standout performances from Murphy, Redgrave and Moll nevertheless recommend viewing. Mature themes and violence prohibit viewing by children. The story was remade in 2002. **p&d**, Joseph L. Mankiewicz; **cast**, Audie Murphy, Michael Redgrave, Claude Dauphin, Giorgia Moll, Bruce Cabot, Fred Sadoff, Richard Loo, Peter Trent, Georges Brehat, Clinton Anderson, Yôko Tani; **w**, Mankiewicz (based on the novel by Grahame Greene); **c**, Robert Krasker; **m**, Mario Nascimbene; **ed**, William Hornbeck; **set d**, Rino Mondellini; **spec eff**, Roscoe "Rocky" Cline.

The Quiet Man ★★★★★ 1952; U.S.; 129m; Argosy Pictures/REP; Color; Drama/Romance; Children: Cautionary; **DVD**; **VHS**. Of the many superlative films produced by pantheon director Ford, this film ranks as one of his foremost and memorable masterpieces. It is the poignant story of a two-fisted Irish-American, Wayne, returning to his homeland of Ireland, just as Ford returns with his cameras to the land of his ancestors to film this wonderful, peerless tale. Set in the 1920s, Wayne, an ex-prizefighter, arrives from America on a train that slices through green hills and meadows, viewing the verdant landscape from his compartment with admiration and anticipation. When arriving at the village of Innisfree, Wayne is met by the colorful Fitzgerald, a local solicitor, who also narrates this charming tale, and who, without being asked, places Wayne's luggage on his pony cart and then drives Wayne to a remote and beautiful little cottage in a quiet glen next to a running brook, Wayne's birthplace, which is called "White O'Morning." As Wayne fondly gazes at his ancestral home, he sees in the distance a beautiful, red-haired woman, O'Hara, tending some sheep, her long hair flowing in the wind. Stunned by this gorgeous creature, Wayne says: "Is that real?" Fitzgerald replies: "Only a mirage brought on by your terrible thirst!" Wayne then goes to see Natwick, a rich widow, who owns the cottage, and purchases the place from her, but only after she is satisfied that he should be the rightful owner since the cottage was once owned by Wayne's now deceased relatives. This causes strife from McLaglen, a man as towering and massive as Wayne, and who owns the large and lucrative farm adjacent to the cottage and who has long wanted to acquire the property. McLaglen is further incensed in that, as a widower and the richest farmer in the area, Natwick has sold the cottage to a foreigner, "a dirty Yank" from America, as he puts it, especially since he thinks Natwick will sometime accept his proposal of marriage. Natwick flares up at McLaglen's presumptions that the two have a more than a neighborly relationship and angrily tells him that she will sell her property to anyone she pleases. Meanwhile, when Wayne goes to the cottage to make it his home, he finds the door open and a broom on the floor where someone has been sweeping. Behind the door, he finds O'Hara, who is McLaglen's sister and Wayne's neighbor and who has made an effort to clean the cottage as a welcoming gesture. She attempts to flee, but Wayne catches her by the hand and brings her to him, kissing her. She slaps him and then, before leaving, leans forward and kisses him back, and she then races off as if she were some fleeting gossamer vision imagined by Wayne. Wayne next devotes his time to fixing up the cottage while attempting to farm the land, which, like most of Ireland, is studded with rocks, and which he laboriously unearths as he ploughs its challenging loam. He is visited by the affable Shields (who is Fitzgerald's real-life brother), the local Protestant vicar, and his doting wife, Crowe, who compliments Wayne about how he has immaculately and charmingly repaired the cottage, saying: "It looks the way all Irish cottages should, and only an American would think of painting it emerald green." When Wayne plants roses nearby in memory of his mother, O'Hara, a practical woman, later tells him that planting vegetables would be more productive. Wayne is taken with the unwed O'Hara, but when he then meets her brother, McLaglen, he is confronted in a pub by a man who seethes with hate for him, McLaglen accusing Wayne of disrupting his relationship with Natwick and "back-dealing" him out of the farm Wayne has purchased from Natwick. Wayne nevertheless extends his hand in friendship, and the powerful McLaglen grips his hand with all of his might, as does Wayne, both men pulling their hands away with painful expressions on their faces. McLaglen, as the richest farmer in the area, is also a boisterous and bragging bully of a man, and who is much disliked by the locals, including Catholic priests Bond and Lilburn and members of the IRA (Irish Republican Army), and who side with Wayne in his ongoing feud with McLaglen. Wayne, however, goes out of his way to avoid a fight with McLaglen as he is shielding a past he wants to forget as a prizefighter. Only kindhearted clergyman Shields knows about Wayne's secret, the fact that Wayne, when fighting in the ring in the U.S., accidentally killed an opponent and for which he bears not only deep remorse but haunting guilt. He has therefore resolved never to fight another man (the same resolve is maintained by Montgomery Clift, a former boxer who has blinded one of his best friends in

Maureen O'Hara and John Wayne in *The Quiet Man,* 1952.

a fight and refuses to become part of a boxing team in **From Here to Eternity**, 1953, made a year after this film). Shields is not only a boxing enthusiast, but had been an amateur boxer in his early days and has kept clippings of reports on all notable prizefights, including the one where Wayne's blows brought about the death of his adversary in the ring. Shields promises to keep Wayne's past a secret as Wayne then pursues the fetching O'Hara after he meets her when attending Mass on Sunday. When O'Hara leaves the church, Wayne scoops up some holy water from a container outside the church and offers it to her and O'Hara dips her fingers into the water and uses it to make the sign of the cross before hurrying away. Wayne then later carries flowers to O'Hara's doorstep while accompanied by Fitzgerald, his official matchmaker, and both meet with the heavy-handed McLaglen, who is eating breakfast, and where Fitzgerald asks on Wayne's behalf that McLaglen allow Wayne to court his beautiful spinster sister. As Wayne stands silent with hat in hand before McLaglen, listening to Fitzgerald's request, McLaglen, who has been waiting to do any mean thing he can to Wayne, delights in telling Fitzgerald: "If he was the last man on earth and my sister the last woman, I'd still say no!" O'Hara, who has been anxiously waiting in an upstairs room of her home watches sadly as Wayne and Fitzgerald leave the house and where Wayne tosses away the roses he intended to give to O'Hara. Fitzgerald tells Wayne that, without McLaglen's approval, there can be no courtship or subsequent marriage as that is the way things are done in Ireland. When McLaglen next meets Wayne in the local pub, he tries to start a fight, mocking Wayne for his inability to marry his sister, but Wayne, instead of giving the bully a good thrashing, refuses to fight, all because he fears he might again kill another man as he did when he was a prizefighter. Meanwhile, O'Hara is desolate at not being able to marry the man she loves and is further frustrated when, during a horse race, the winner, Wayne, does not claim the prize, her bonnet, but, instead, snatches the hat owned by Natwick. All seems hopeless for any future between Wayne and O'Hara, until Priest Bond joins in what he believes to be a harmless conspiracy. Bond convinces McLaglen to allow Wayne to court O'Hara, implying that, should he so good-naturedly grant his approval, McLaglen will ingratiate himself to the widow Natwick and his own marital ambitions with her will most likely become a reality. Wayne and the overjoyed O'Hara then embark upon their courtship with Fitzgerald acting as their chaperone and where he cautions them as he drives them about with his pony cart to observe proprieties, adding: "And no paddy-fingers, if you please." Following their marriage, O'Hara demands from her brother that he pay Wayne her dowry. She also wants her prized furniture delivered to her new home, Wayne's cottage. McLaglen, however, learns from Natwick that she has no intentions of wedding him and now McLaglen accuses Bond, Fitzgerald and others of hoodwinking him

John Wayne and Maureen O'Hara in *The Quiet Man,* 1952.

into permitting O'Hara to marry Wayne. When McLaglen refuses to pay O'Hara's dowry and will not send her furniture to Wayne's cottage, Wayne tells McLaglen that he can keep the money and the furniture. O'Hara is angry at being denied what is rightfully hers, and she and Wayne get into such a fierce argument on their wedding night that he carries her into the bedroom and tosses her onto the bed which promptly collapses while he retreats to the living room where he spends the night sleeping alone on the floor. O'Hara's feelings are soothed the next morning when Fitzgerald and others arrive with her furniture, these well-wishing friends having convinced McLaglen to release O'Hara's prized possessions under threat of physical reprisals. O'Hara is delighted when her furnishings are carried into the cottage, directing movers as to where each piece of furniture, particularly her piano, should be placed. When Fitzgerald sees the bed flattened to the floor he is astounded at what he thinks has happened on Wayne's wedding night, exclaiming: "Impetuous! Homeric!" (Fitzgerald had added to that: "The strength of the man!" but that phrase was cut from the film as it was thought to be too risqué at that time.) The marriage between Wayne and O'Hara, however, remains deeply troubled in that O'Hara feels that she is married "in name only," because Wayne has refused to demand the dowry that is hers and will not fight for it (or her) in maintaining a long-lasting Irish tradition. Wayne, too, is angry with O'Hara over her stubborn claim about her dowry, so much so that he sleeps apart from her in a sleeping bag. O'Hara goes to priest Bond, interrupting him just as he is about to catch a large trout in a nearby stream, a fish he has been seeking to bag for many a long year. O'Hara's arrival causes Bond to lose concentration and, just as he is about to land that prize trout, the fish escapes his hook and net and Bond explodes, especially after O'Hara whispers in his ear (not in English but in Gaelic because her confidence is so sensitive) that her husband will not sleep with her and instead reposes at night in a sleeping bag. "Ireland may be a poor country," exclaims Bond, "but here a man sleeps in a bed not in a bag!" So strained is the relationship between Wayne and O'Hara that she finally decides to leave Wayne and goes to a nearby train station, getting into one of its compartments to await its departure and where she plans to live with distant relatives. When Wayne discovers what O'Hara has done, he races to the train station where the conductors and engineers are involved in a hot-headed argument about train schedules and as to when the train should actually depart. (This is another wonderful scene in many such scenes that emphasizes the fact that temperament and not timetables dictates small and large events in Ireland.) This fortuitous delay allows Wayne to walk down the length of the train to inspect each compartment in his search for O'Hara, angrily slamming the door of each compartment he finds empty. He then discovers O'Hara cowering in a compartment and drags her from it, pulling her from the train station as he stalks in the direction

of McLaglen's farm, which is five miles distant. Seeing this, and knowing the strife between the pair, the conductors, engineers and others gathered at the station now know that Wayne intends to confront the fierce McLaglen in what must be the fight of the decade if not the century, and they eagerly abandon everything in their lives to follow the couple as Wayne drags O'Hara forward. A woman in the crowd races ahead to hand Wayne a piece of wood, saying: "And here's a stick with which to beat the lovely lady!" News quickly spreads that Wayne is manhandling O'Hara "the whole long way" back to her brother's farm, and everyone expects a physical confrontation between the two powerful men, that inevitable donnybrook anticipated in relish by one and all. People leave their homes and businesses and join the crowd following Wayne and the struggling O'Hara as they cross streams and meadows. The commotion resuscitates even Francis Ford (the director's older brother who has appeared in almost every one of Ford's films, almost as a good luck charm, this being his 29th appearance in one of his brother's films). Ford is an ancient man with a flowing white beard who is on his deathbed and receiving the Last Rites from priest Lilburn. When hearing about the impending battle between Wayne and McLaglen, the ailing Ford throws back the blankets of his bed, gets to his feet and begins slipping his trousers over his nightshirt, and he is seen struggling up the street after the crowd running in Wayne's direction while Lilburn races off to find and inform his superior, Bond, about the climactic event that is about to happen. McLaglen is then shown supervising some of his workmen at his farm, amazed to see Wayne approaching with the struggling, slipping and sliding O'Hara in his firm grasp as he tows her toward his destination and where one of McLaglen's employees sardonically tells him that his relatives are "paying you a visit." Wayne then swings O'Hara by her arm so that she sails and falls at McLaglen's feet and where Wayne shouts: "No dowry, no marriage—it's your custom, not mine!" The assembled crowd waits with bundled anticipation for McLaglen's response. Embarrassed and ashamed before the whole community, McLaglen withdraws the amount of the dowry and throws it at Wayne, shouting: "Here's your filthy money, you spawn!" Wayne scoops it up and, O'Hara, now that her honor and dowry has been upheld, opens the door to a nearby heating unit and Wayne tosses the money into the fire. O'Hara, now knowing her marriage is intact, and, despite the battle between her husband and brother that is about to commence, smiles at Wayne, telling him that his dinner will be waiting for him and begins walking home. As he walks past McLaglen, the incensed McLaglen hits Wayne full force in the face, sending Wayne flying. Wayne now abandons his reservations about fighting and readily goes to battle, smashing the hulking McLaglen and sending him to the ground while Fitzgerald, the ever enterprising businessman, begins to take bets on the two contestants. The battle is Olympian, as each man knocks, pummels and strikes the other, their fight extending across meadows, over stone walls, through running brooks and where Wayne finally slams McLaglen into a river. Rising from its shallows, McLaglen wipes water from his face and says to Wayne: "Have you had enough?" Wayne says no, and helpfully pulls McLaglen from the river; McLaglen then lands another powerful blow in Wayne's face, sending him sailing once more. The men battle right into the streets of the village where Bond and Lilburn watch from hiding and where Lilburn tells Bond that they should stop the fight. Bond agrees, but is much too excited in seeing the fight as he watches the battlers from afar while shadow-boxing, for he, like all others in Ireland (it is more than implied) love nothing better on earth than a good fight. Even the mild-mannered Shields watches the fighters bash each other along the streets while he and his visiting bishop view the fight through binoculars and make private wagers on who will emerge the winner. Natwick, too, watches the fight from a window, and, when seeing that McLaglen is losing that battle, bursts forth with a statement that reveals her true and deep affections for McLaglen, and where she repeats McLaglen's own often-stated boast, saying: "The best man in Innisfree! As if I didn't know it!" The entire community is now following and attending this heroic battle of two titans, the crowds enlarging as word about the titanic struggle has spread to other towns and villages and where those residents, all with their blood up, flock into the village to witness a fight they know will become a significant moment in the annals of Ireland's history. When both fighters stagger each other outside the local pub, Fitzgerald calls a halt, suggesting that the contestants take a brief respite inside that pub to take refreshing drinks of stout. Inside the pub, Wayne orders two large glasses of stout, and the proprietor happily complies. After being served, Wayne and McLaglen, now having deep respect for each other's prowess, if not personalities, toast each other's abilities. These compliments quickly dissolve after Wayne throws money on the bar to pay for the drinks. McLaglen indignantly sweeps Wayne's money from the bar and throws down his own money, insisting he pay for the drinks. Wayne then does the same, but McLaglen throws the contents of his glass into Wayne's face. The incensed Wayne asks for a bar towel from the proprietor and, after wiping his face, lands a tremendous blow against McLaglen that sends him crashing through the door of the pub to land outside and where the fight begins anew and continues into dusk. O'Hara, by then, waits at her cottage and looks out at the lush and rolling hills while a nearby brook bubbles and through which splash two battered men, staggering with the support of each other and singing "The Wild Colonial Boy." They are Wayne and McLaglen, their legendary fight ended and their friendship begun, now that they have bloodied each other in an exhaustive test of each other's indefatigable physical stamina and indomitable wills, only to find themselves equals in manliness and spirit. They enter the cottage and both sit down to a table, Wayne saying: "I've brought the brother to dinner." O'Hara, who has already prepared that dinner, as if expecting the good outcome from the day's tumultuous events, serves the food and all sit in silence, heads bowed, as they pray in thankfulness and where the bruised and now subdued McLaglen concludes with: "And bless all in this house." Ford ends his heartfelt salute to Old Ire by showing his fine players in an epilogue. Natwick and McLaglen begin their courtship while sitting in Fitzgerald's pony cart as they proudly wave to their neighbors and where all of the other players appear in fresco to take bows and curtsies for their appearances in this masterpiece film. Ford presents a tender but also tempestuous love story, mixed with brawls and spirited songs and drinking that captures the mercurial Irish temperament, his scenes fondling the lush landscapes and caressing the faces of young and old in sensitive close-ups. The acting from all is superlative, each perfect in their lively and colorful characterizations, and where each is charmingly unforgettable, right down to the last bit player. Wayne was never more the resolute hero and O'Hara was never lovelier and alluring, each rendering the performance of their lives. McLaglen is as magnificent a heavy as he was when winning an Oscar as Best Actor in Ford's earlier classic film about Ireland, **The Informer**, 1935, albeit he is truculently endearing in this film in lieu of being the bumbling turncoat and traitor as depicted in the earlier production. The supporting players, Fitzgerald, Shields, Bond, Natwick and all others represent the strong emotional cement that firmly holds this Ford cottage together and where the director welcomes the world to warm its hands at its fireplace and sing its songs within the comforting framework of that enchanted cottage. Cinematographers Hoch and Stout provide stunning sequences that reflect the Wayne-O'Hara love story, such as where they run through fields in a rainstorm to reach some abandoned ruins and where they passionately kiss as a purple sky spliced by bolts of white lightning accentuate their torrid lovemaking. Young's lilting and often poetic score is both stirring and fanciful, studded with traditional Irish ballads, tunes now endemic to this memorable film. **The Quiet Man** earned Ford his fifth Oscar as Best Director (his previous Oscars in that category being **The Informer**, 1935; **Stagecoach**, 1939; **The Grapes of Wrath**, 1940; and **How Green Was My Valley**, 1941). The film also won an Oscar for Best Cinematography, Color (Hoch and Stout). McLaglen, who had won an Oscar as Best Actor for Ford's classic film, **The Informer**, also received an Oscar nomination for this film as Best Supporting Actor. The film was ex-

John Wayne, Ward Bond and Victor McLaglen in *The Quiet Man*, 1952.

tremely popular with the public, gleaning $3.8 million from the box office in its initial release against a budget of $1,750,000. Songs: "The Wild Colonial Boy" (traditional; adapted by Sean O'Casey and Dennis O'Casey), "The Young May Moon" (Thomas Moore), "The Humor Is on Me Now" (traditional; adapted by Richard Hayward), "Mush-Mush-Mush, Tural-l-addy" (traditional; adapted by Sean O'Casey and Dennis O'Casey), "The Isle of Innisfree" (1950; music and lyrics: Dick Farrelly), "Galway Bay" (1947; music and lyrics: Arthur Colahan), "Rakes of Mallow" (traditional), "Rising of the Moon" (traditional), "Garryowen" (traditional), "I'll Take You Home Again Kathleen" (1875; music and lyrics: Thomas Payne Westendorf), "The Kerry Dance" (traditional), "Barbary Bell" (traditional), "Believe Me If All Those Endearing Young Charms" (traditional), "Mitty Matty Had a Hen" (traditional). *Author's Note*: The director had long wanted to make this film, buying the film rights of the story for a pittance in 1933, but he could not interest any studio in financially backing the production until many years after he had established his reputation and convinced Republic to back the film with more money than it had heretofore done with almost any other film, but the studio imposed two conditions on Ford and one was that the film not exceed two hours. It ran nine minutes over that time when Ford completed the film. The second condition imposed by studio chief Herbert J. Yates was that Ford would agree to do a western film starring Wayne and O'Hara, which became the third film in Ford's U.S. Cavalry trilogy, **Rio Grande**, 1950, a film Republic rightly believed would make enough money to offset the loss they expected from **The Quiet Man**. Yates did not believe **The Quiet Man** would see any success, at one time describing the film when it was in production as "a silly Irish story that won't make a penny." Studio executives were elated when the film was nominated for an Oscar as Best Film, that nomination being the only one that studio ever received in that category. Exteriors were shot in Ireland in the counties of Galway and Mayo. Ford told this author that "**The Quiet Man** is a picture of salvation. The hero finds himself again by going back to the land of his people and his birth. What does the little girl say in **The Wizard of Oz** [1939]? 'There's no place like home.' The hero finds the woman of his heart when he finds that home, and a lot of loveable lunatics, too." Ford presents an Ireland with common values and with little or no social or religious distinctions and only obliquely refers to the IRA (Irish Republican Army, an underground organization that had for years been battling the British for Irish independence). At one point, when Wayne demands O'Hara's dowry, McLaglen looks at two men in the crowd who represent the IRA and asks them if the IRA "has a hand in this." One of them replies: "If it were, not a scorched stone of your fine house would be left standing." These IRA men are shown to be well dressed and more financially substantial than others in the film and they are the ones who convince McLaglen to release

Tom Selleck and Laura San Giacomo in *Quigley Down Under*, 1990.

O'Hara's furniture and deliver those furnishings to her. "I had relatives who had fought with the IRA," Ford told this author, "and, in the old days, they were looked upon as patriots and honorable men, especially in the 1920s, which is the setting for that picture, and when the country was not a republic, but a free state still trying to get out from under the British yoke. I showed my story of the IRA in **The Informer** [1935; and would touch upon that subject in a later film, **The Rising of the Moon**, 1957], so there was no need to go into details about that organization when we did **The Quiet Man**. I had enough battles going on in that picture anyway, especially the one between Duke [Wayne] and Vic [Victor McLaglen]. You know, Vic was really getting on when we did that picture. I think he was in his sixties [he was sixty-four], but he still had the strength and stamina of a bull and he showed that in the many fine scenes he did with Duke when they get into it with their fists, both of them big, bruising fellows." Wayne stood six-feet-four-inches in real life and McLaglen six-feet-three inches, but McLaglen, even though older than Wayne by twenty-one years, had been a professional prizefighter and, in fact, the British-born McLaglen moved to Canada, where he became a professional prizefighter, becoming so adept and powerful in the ring as a heavyweight boxer that he was once thought to be a potential contender to the heavyweight crown. He fought a grueling six-round fight in 1909 with U.S. Heavyweight Champion Jack Johnson, right after Johnson became champion, a fight with no decision as it was an exhibition match, but where Johnson later stated that McLaglen "wore me down considerably, a man I could not knock out with any punch." During the prolonged fight with McLaglen in the film, Wayne took considerable punishment from the massive McLaglen, telling this author that "Vic [Victor McLaglen] had the biggest fists I have ever seen and when he failed to pull some of his punches in that never-ending fight we had before the cameras, he knocked me for a loop, and I felt pain all over my head and body for weeks after that. It was like getting hit with large, iron frying pans. Vic was not really a boxer, but a clubber. He clubbed you with those massive fists of his like hammering a metal mallet on raw beef to tenderize it. And he tenderized me plenty in that picture. I got compensated for that because my leading lady was the wonderful Maureen O'Hara, a great actress and one of the most beautiful women in the world." O'Hara and Wayne became life-long friends after they appeared together in **Rio Grande**, 1950, **The Quiet Man** being their second film together, followed by three more, **The Wings of Eagles**, 1957; **McLintock!**, 1963, and **Big Jake**, 1971. Wayne, when going to Ireland for on-location shooting (all interiors were shot at the Republic Studios in California), brought along his four children and, after one of them said to director Ford: "Can we be in the picture, too?" Ford laughed and said: "Why not?" All four children appear in some of the crowd scenes. **p**, Merian C. Cooper, John Ford; **d**,

Ford; **cast**, John Wayne, Maureen O'Hara, Barry Fitzgerald, Ward Bond, Victor McLaglen, Mildred Natwick, Francis Ford, Eileen Crowe, May Craig, Arthur Shields, James O'Hara, Sean McClory, Ken Curtis, Mae Marsh, James Lilburn, Charles FitzSimons, Jack McGowran, Joseph O'Dea, Eric Gorman, Kevin Lawless, Paddy O'Donnell, Web Overlander, Harry Tenbrook, and Melinda, Michael, Patrick, Toni Wayne; **w**, Frank S. Nugent, (not credited) Richard Llewellyn (based on the story by Maurice Walsh); **c**, Winton C. Hoch (Technicolor); **m**, Victor Young; **ed**, Jack Murray; **art d**, Frank Hotaling; **set d**, John McCarthy, Jr., Charles Thompson; **spec eff**, Howard and Theodore Lydecker (not credited).

Quigley Down Under ★★★ 1990; Australia; 119m; Pathe Entertainment/MGM; Color; Adventure; Children: Unacceptable (MPAA: PG-13); **DVD**; **VHS**. Selleck gives a powerful performance as an American cowboy with an unerring eye for long-distance shooting. He uses an 1874 Sharps buffalo rifle (even though the film is set in the 1860s) and is accurate up to 900 yards. He answers an ad for long-distance sharpshooters and is hired by Rickman, a wealthy Australian rancher. But when Selleck arrives in Australia and learns what his job entails, the killing of aborigines who are invading the ranch to steal livestock and get food to survive, he refuses. He has earlier run afoul of Rickman's bully boy henchmen when he beats up a few of these roughnecks after they try to molest Giacomo, a young woman with an erratic personality that has branded her "Crazy Cora." Rickman is a misanthropic character, who thinks that he has been born on the wrong side of the earth and that he really belongs in the American Old West, as he fancies himself a quick-draw artist and imitates the notorious gunmen he has read about in dime novels. Selleck believes he has been tricked into going to Australia, believing that he would be shooting wild animals, such as dingoes, but he will not become a hired killer of human beings. Meanwhile, Selleck becomes Giacomo's protector after learning that she is from Texas and had suffered great trauma after Comanche Indians attacked her ranch when she was alone with her infant child and when she accidentally suffocated her baby when trying to keep the child quiet while they hid in a storm cellar from the Indians. She was later found by her husband, who then shipped her off on the next freighter, which landed her in Australia and where she has no way of supporting herself. Selleck, meanwhile, takes up the cause of the aborigines and begins shooting Rickman's men when they attack these outback dwellers. He continues to wage this one-man war, even against the local military forces, its commander in Rickman's employ, who looks the other way whenever Rickman kills any aborigines. Eventually, using his long-range buffalo gun, Selleck picks off Rickman's men one by one, until only Rickman remains to confront him and here Rickman believes he has the edge since he and Selleck face each other wearing six-guns and Selleck is no longer using his buffalo rifle. Fast draw artist Rickman, however, discovers to his shock that Selleck is not only proficient with a rifle, but is also quick on the draw when using a six-gun and, after both men draw and fire, it is Selleck who hits his mark, fatally shooting Rickman. The military police arrive and are about to shoot down Selleck, but they then see hundreds of aborigines surrounding them, and, thinking better of their actions, allow Selleck to go on his way. Selleck then goes to a ticket agent to buy passage for America, but the agent sees an old wanted poster that appears to be that of Selleck. When he asks for Selleck's name, Giacomo suddenly runs to Selleck's side, pretending to be his wife, and Selleck gives the ticket agent the nickname Giacomo has given him. The agent, instead of reaching for a gun, sells Selleck two tickets he requests as Selleck decides to take Giacomo along with him so that they can make a life together. Director Wincer does a fine job in presenting this exciting, action-packed and offbeat western taking place "down under." Selleck, Rickman and Giacomo give standout performances, and the film is inventively lensed by Eggby, who stunningly captures the outback landscapes. This film did not do as well at the box office as expected, taking in more than $21 million in its initial release against a budget of $18 million. *Author's Note*: The script for this film was written as early as 1978, but few studios expressed a strong interest in producing the story, even though Clint Eastwood and Steve McQueen were originally considered for the leading role. Sometime in the 1980s, Selleck learned about the story and it went into production after Alan Ladd Jr. got behind the project. **p**, Stanley O'Toole, Alexandra Rose, Megan Rose; **d**, Simon Wincer; **cast**, Tom Selleck, Laura San Giacomo, Alan Rickman, Chris Haywood, Ron Haddrick, Tony Bonner, Jerome Ehlers, Conor McDermottroe, Roger Ward, Ben Mendelsohn; **w**, John Hill; **c**, David Eggby; **m**, Basil Poledouris; **ed**, Peter Burgess; **prod d**, Ross Major; **art d**, Ian Gracie; **set d**, Brian Dusting, Brian Edmonds; **spec eff**, Steve Courtley, Conrad Rothman.

The Quiller Memorandum ★★★ 1966; U.K./U.S.; 104m; Ivan Foxwell/Carthay Films/Rank/FOX; Color; Spy Drama; Children: Unacceptable; **DVD**; **VHS**. Two British agents are murdered by a neo-Nazi organization in West Berlin. British Secret Service chief Guinness gets the help of U.S. agent Segal, who follows a lead that a teacher has hanged himself after being accused of being a war criminal in World War II (1939-1945). Segal meets voluptuous teacher Berger, who knew the deceased teacher and, from her, learns that Sydow is behind the murders and the neo-Nazi group. Segal, in searching for the hiding place of Sydow and his neo-Nazi goons, finds it, but is imprisoned and held as a hostage there, until Sydow decides to have him killed. Segal nevertheless escapes, goes to Guinness with his information, and Sydow and his associates are brought to justice. Berger, who is not ensnared in the espionage roundup, and to whom Segal is romantically drawn, is seen by Segal at the finale, but they separate forever as she returns to her teaching job and he to his covert activities. Segal's name in the film is Quiller. Anderson uses a firm hand in presenting this thriller, maintaining taut suspense throughout, and Segal, Sydow and Berger give outstanding performances. Songs: "Wednesday's Child" (John Barry, Mack David), "Downtown" (Tony Hatch), "Alte Kameraden/Old Comrades" (Carl Teike). Mature themes prohibit viewing by children. **p**, Ivan Foxwell; **d**, Michael Anderson; **cast**, George Segal, Alec Guinness, Max von Sydow, Senta Berger, George Sanders, Robert Helpmann, Robert Flemyng, Peter Carsten, Ernst Walder, John Moulder-Brown; **w**, Harold Pinter (based on the novel by Trevor Dudley Smith), **c**, Erwin Hillier (Panavision; DeLuxe Color); **m**, John Barry; **ed**, Frederick Wilson; **art d**, Maurice Carter; **set d**, Arthur Taksen; **spec eff**, Arthur Beavis, Les Bowie.

Quiz Show ★★★★ 1994; U.S. 133m; Baltimore Pictures/Buena Vista; Color; Drama; Children: Unacceptable (MPAA: PG-13); **DVD**; **VHS**. Incisive and compelling, this superlative drama savagely exposes the widespread fraud exercised by TV producers presenting rigged quiz shows in the late 1950s. Contestants, as exposes later revealed, appeared in those TV quiz shows as if they were full of wisdom and knowledge in answering difficult questions involving all types of subjects and winning small fortunes, but their answers were secretly provided to them beforehand in order to rivet audience attention upon those well-rehearsed contestants. The film opens with Turturro (as Herbert Stempel; 1926-), appearing on "Twenty One" (1956-1958) a TV show hosted by NBC, one of the most popular quiz shows on national television at that time. He answers one challenging question after another, but with some apparent difficulty, sometimes wiping away perspiration from his face with a handkerchief. While watching the show in a control booth, producers Paymer (as Dan Enright; 1917-1992), and Azaria (Albert Freedman) receive a phone call from Scorsese, who heads the firm producing Geritol, which sponsors the show, and who tells Paymer that Turturro's approval ratings as an on-air contestant are beginning to fall and he suggests that Turturro be replaced by another more appealing contestant. While quickly screening contestant applicants for the show, the producers discover that Fiennes (as Charles Van Doren; 1926-), a handsome, young instructor at New York City's Columbia University, has

Senta Berger and Max von Sydow in *The Quiller Memorandum,* 1966.

applied to become a contestant and they quickly recruit him, believing he will be more popular as a winning contestant than the ungainly looking Turturro. Paymer takes Turturro to an expensive restaurant and buys him dinner and then tells him that, because the show's ratings are falling and his own ratings have leveled out, Turturro must purposely lose in his next on-air appearance by giving the wrong answer and allowing Fiennes to win. Since Turturro has been winning all along with answers to questions that have been provided to him, he has no choice but to go along with the continuing fraud, although he gets Paymer to promise him that he will hire him for another TV show and will get more money for such appearances, which also soothes Turturro's ego since playing to the vanity of such publicity-seeking contestants is one of the manipulative enticements used by Paymer and his ilk. Though he is reluctant to do so, Turturro nevertheless appears on "Twenty One" with Fiennes, and, after each contestant seems to battle each other by answering one correct difficult question after another, Turturro stumbles and fails to answer a rather simple question, and that is what film won the Oscar for Best Film in 1955. Even though he knows the answer is **Marty**, 1954, he purposely gives the wrong answer, saying that the winner was **On the Waterfront**, 1954, and where Fiennes answers with **Marty**, the correct answer, becoming the show's new champion contestant. Fiennes has won with some of his own acumen in that he has initially refused to be given the answers and is allowed to feel that he has, at least, a modicum of honesty by receiving the questions in advance of the shows on which he appears and provides the answers on his own by doing his own research. Week after week, Fiennes wins and wins and becomes enormously popular with TV audiences as a wizard of intelligence, seeming to know almost everything there is to know. He grows rich and revels in the attention he gets from fans, especially young women who swarm him when he arrives at the NBC headquarters to make his appearances. He even amazes his brilliant parents, his father, Scofield (as Pulitzer Prize-winning poet and intellectual Mark Van Doren; 1894-1972), who also teaches as a professor at Columbia University, and his mother, Wilson (as novelist Dorothy Van Doren; 1896-1993). The fly in Fiennes' ointment becomes Turturro, who, bitter about being forced from "Twenty One," is shown going to the offices of the local district attorney. We next see Morrow (as Richard N. "Dick" Goodwin; 1931-), a U.S. Congressional attorney, who becomes intrigued with Tuturro's report to the district attorney after learning that a grand jury's findings resulting from the district attorney's investigation have been sealed. Morrow launches his own probe and visits many former contestants of "Twenty One." Most refuse to talk to him, but Turturro tells Morrow how the TV show is nothing but a fraud and that all the questions and answers are rigged. Morrow goes to Fiennes, who more or less tells Morrow, a graduate of the esteemed Harvard Law School, that Tur-

The chariot race in *Quo Vadis,* **1913.**

turro's accusations and complaints come from a man consumed with envy for his, Fiennes', success. Fiennes labels Turturro's claims as nothing more than sour grapes, inferring, as does Paymer when Morrow interviews him, that Turturro has become unbalanced after losing all of his contestant winnings to bookies as he is an inveterate gambler. In fact, Paymer says, he even tried to help Turturro, by paying for some psychiatric treatment Turturro received. Morrow is almost swayed to believe that Tuturro's claims are bogus, especially when Morrow is invited to visit Fiennes at his parents' residence and where Morrow is impressed at meeting Fiennes' famous parents and illustrious intellectual friends, such as Edmund Wilson (1895-1972), America's foremost man of letters, played by O'Brien, and Thomas Merton (1915-1968), poet and monk, who is played by Kilgour. Morrow now comes to believe that a man of Fiennes' stature and intellectual heritage would never stoop to being part of a TV swindle. Morrow nevertheless provides the evidence gotten from Turturro to the House Committee for Legislative Oversight that holds hearings about the quiz shows and where Turturro not only tells the U.S. Congressmen that "Twenty-One" is rigged but that he *and* Fiennes were part of that ongoing fraud. During his testimony, which is accompanied by scenes from the show that are witnessed by the Congressional panel and a packed hearing room, Turturro delights in describing how he, as a contestant, and other contestants were coached by Paymer and others to appear nervous by wiping sweat from their brows with handkerchiefs, that sweat produced when the sealed contestant booths were purposely overheated with extremely bright lights. His comments prompt Rich (as Robert Kintner, 1909-1980, who was president of NBC) to pressure Fiennes into issuing a statement that "Twenty One" is legitimate and above-board. Fiennes, now sensing that his own reputation has been compromised by Turturro's statements to Congress, purposely misses an easy question and leaves the show, only to be rehired by the same network to appear as a brains trust for talk show host Dave Garroway (1913-1982), played by Levinson. But Fiennes is not off the hook. He is eventually summoned to testify before Congress and appears (with Turturro on hand to witness Fiennes' comeuppance), with his parents, Scofield and Wilson, accompanying him. (Fiennes, in a moving scene, has already told Scofield that he has been part of a fraud, shocking and dismaying his famous father.) Fiennes, in a forthright statement to the Congressmen, admits his participation in the rigged TV quiz show, and several Congressmen congratulate him for his candor which brings scattered applause of appreciation, but another Congressman states that he does not share the same appreciation his colleagues have expressed for Fiennes simply and finally "telling the truth," a remark that brings thunderous applause that universally condemns instead of exonerates the now thoroughly disgraced Fiennes, who walks with his parents, shocked and dazed from the hearings. Paymer, however, then testifies without impli-

cating either his sponsor or the network and Morrow now realizes that, instead of his "getting" the goods on television, television "has gotten us." Redford directs this film with a careful, firm hand, delivering a story more suspenseful than waiting for any anxious response on any quiz show, and he brilliantly develops his fascinating characters while exposing the sleazy corruption by repulsively arrogant media moguls and their slavish surrogates. Fiennes, one of the finest actors of the modern era, is superb in his painfully measured role as the self-misguided Van Doren, as is the manic Turturro, a man whose insatiable craving for recognition and attention sends him over the brink. Morrow, too, is riveting as a do-gooder attorney met with barricades at every turn, and Scofield, although his part is small, is wonderful as a brilliant father brought to sorrow by a brilliant son who has betrayed, for TV's thirty pieces of silver, the integrity of a great family. This was an expensive film for its day, with a budget of $31 million, and it did not recoup its investment at the box office in its initial release, taking in about $25 million. Songs: "Mack the Knife" (Kurt Weill, Bertolt Brecht, Marc Blitzstein), "Dancing in the Dark" (Arthur Swartz, Howard Dietz), "Moritat" (Kurt Weill, Bertolt Brecht). **p**, Robert Redford, Michael Jacobs, Julian Krainin, Michael Nozik, Richard N. Goodwin, Jeff McCracken, Gail Mutrux; **d**, Redford; **cast**, John Turturro, Rob Morrow, Ralph Fiennes, Paul Scofield, David Paymer, Elizabeth Wilson, Mira Sorvino, Martin Scorsese, Allan Rich, Hank Azaria, Barry Levinson, Jeffrey Nordling, Vince O'Brien, Adam Kilgour; **w**, Paul Attanasio (based on the book *Remembering America: A Voice from the Sixties* by Goodwin; **c**, Michael Ballhaus; **m**, Mark Isham; **ed**, Stu Linder; **prod d**, Jon Hutman; **art d**, Tim Galvin; **set d**, Samara Schaffer.

Quo Vadis ★★★ 1913 (silent); Italy; 120m; Societa Italiana Cines/George Kleine Attractions; B/W; Historical Drama; Children: Unacceptable. This sweeping epic was one of the first feature films produced and its enormous popularity initiated the making of feature films thereafter. It is the classic Roman tale of the despotic emperor Nero (37-68 A.D.), played by Carlo Cattaneo, who lusts after the fair Giunchi, a beautiful woman who has become a Christian in an age when adopting that religion was a dangerous move as Nero has branded all Christians as outlaws. Novelli, a Roman Tribune, falls in love with Giunchi, but rejects her religion until he learns its great human and spiritual values from Gizzi, who plays St. Peter (d. 67 A.D.), who was one of Jesus' apostles and who has become the leader of the Christina Church, and, who, like Jesus, is crucified for preaching Christianity. After Giunchi rebuffs Nero's advances, he orders her to be sacrificed in the arena and while he orders Rome burned so that he can rebuild the city to his liking and blames the arson his soldiers create on the Christians, using this lie to send countless Christians to their deaths in the arena. Giunchi is taken to the Circus Maximus where she is tied to the back of a raging bull, but she is saved by her lifelong protector, Castellani, a giant, who struggles with the bull and, in a titanic battle, finally breaks the beast's neck, saving Giunchi. Novelli races into the arena to stand by Giunchi and denounce Nero, who flees to his palace and where he first murders his sinister wife, Brandini (Poppaea) before he commits suicide as his regime is being overthrown by Roman citizens who have now learned the truth about his burning of their city. Well crafted and with thousands of extras featured in the many crowd scenes, this early epic presents many breathtaking scenes, particularly the sequences in the arena. When released in the U.S., the film drew hundreds of thousands of viewers to special screenings where admission was ten times the amount usually paid to watch the one-and two-reel silent films of that era, which was fifteen cents, producing enormous profits for its U.S. distributor, George Kleine. Master filmmaker D.W. Griffith viewed this film with actress Blanche Sweet and was inspired to produce in the following year his own first feature film, **Judith of Bethulia**, 1914, another historical epic that set the standard for its day. Several versions of **Quo Vadis** were made in the silent and talkie eras, the most significant being the masterpiece version in 1951 from pantheon director Mervyn LeRoy. **d&w**, Enrico Guazzoni (based on the novel by Henryk Sienkiewicz); **cast**, Amleto Novelli, Gustavo Serena, Amelia Cattaneo, Carlo Cattaneo, Lea Giunchi, Bruto Castellani, Augusto Mastripietri, Cesare Moltini, Olga Brandini, Ignazio Lupi, Giovanni Gizzi; **c**, Eugenio Bava, Alessandro Bona; **ed**, Guazzoni, **prod d**, Guazzoni, Camillo Innocenti; **art d**, Guazzoni.

Quo Vadis ★★★★★ 1951; U.S.; 171m; MGM; Color; Historical Drama; Children: Unacceptable; **DVD**; **VHS**. One of the greatest historical epic films ever made, this version (of many silent and talkie productions) offers superb acting from Taylor, Kerr, Genn and, particularly, Ustinov, who plays a certifiably insane Emperor Nero (37-68 A.D.) in what is undoubtedly his greatest performance. The film opens with Taylor, a Roman commander, entering Rome with his troops to receive accolades for his recent military victories. Laffan, who plays Poppaea Sabina (30-65 A.D.), the conspiratorial and manipulative second wife of the degenerate Ustinov, greets Taylor, plying her sultry charms in order to seduce the virile and robust soldier, but Taylor avoids her sexual entrapments and thus evades Ustinov's wrath. He then meets lovely Kerr, who lives in comfortable and protective custody with Aylmer and his family at a luxurious villa. Aylmer is a retired and distinguished Roman general who earlier defeated and killed Kerr's father, a foreign king, and Kerr is ostensibly a hostage, but is treated like an adopted daughter by the compassionate Aylmer. Taylor lusts for Kerr, but when she learns that he embraces pagan beliefs, although he thinks little of such Roman gods, Kerr rebuffs his advances as she is a devout Christian, her religious beliefs kept secret as Ustinov has outlawed all Christians. When Taylor tries to force himself on Kerr, he is confronted by Baer, a massive and towering giant, who serves as Kerr's personal bodyguard, and Taylor quickly thinks twice about simply abducting the beautiful woman who has captured his passions. Taylor then uses his influence with Ustinov to have Kerr placed within the royal harem and where she is dressed in alluring attire and compelled to attend a feast with Taylor, presided over by the gluttonous Ustinov, who, while peering at Kerr through a colored eyeglass, announces that she is "too narrow in the hips" for his liking. Though passively obedient to Taylor's commands, Kerr is released after Taylor realizes that he cannot force this beautiful woman to love him. He follows her when Kerr goes to a secret meeting where Currie, who plays St. Peter the Apostle (d. 67 A.D.), preaches good will and love for others to the large throng of Christians gathered there. Learning about the Christians and their nonviolent religion, Taylor softens toward Kerr and her fellow Christians and, when seeing this, Kerr, who has fallen in love with the stalwart and noble-minded Taylor, and against the advice of friends, agrees to marry him. Taylor, however, has a difficult time in embracing Christianity and he cannot persuade Kerr to give up her religious beliefs, which Taylor believes to be the teachings of fanatics. Even after meeting the kindly Sofaer, who plays St. Paul (5-67 A.D.), and who describes how Christianity is based on peace and love, Taylor decides that Christians are nothing more than foolish dreamers deluded by their faith into thinking they can overcome the might of Rome and any other oppressive regime with their peaceful credo and he leaves Kerr, now believing that she and her fellow Christians are hopeless visionaries who will not face the realities of life. Ustinov, by this time, is consumed by his vanity and power, which goes unchecked as all fear this maniac, who orders the death of anyone daring to displease him. Genn, his closest adviser, detests the despot, but cleverly manipulates him through his well-chosen words of advice (laced with acerbic wit and subliminal criticism). Genn attempts to persuade Ustinov from not fulfilling his most ruthless ambition, that of burning down the entire city of Rome so that he can rebuild it to his liking (Ustinov is offended by the stench coming from the poor districts of the city that suffer from faulty sanitary systems). The lunatic emperor, however, orders his minions to torch the city. Ustinov stands on a terrace of his palace high above the city and becomes ecstatic as would a pyromaniac after he witnesses sections of the city burst into flames, deliriously de-

Finlay Currie in *Quo Vadis*, 1951.

lighting in the destruction. In accordance with legend, he clutches a lyre and begins to chant his own forced poetry as he strokes that lyre, warbling in a terrible singing voice a paean of praise to himself. Genn and other Roman leaders are not only disgusted at Ustinov's total disregard for his people and empire, but now know they are dealing with an utter lunatic who has abandoned reason and rationality. As the fires begin to consume whole sections of Rome, Taylor, fearing for Kerr's life, battles through the panicking, fleeing crowds up and down streets engulfed by flames to finally find Kerr, but she and he are then arrested and imprisoned as Christians, falsely blamed by Ustinov for creating the devastating blazes. Meanwhile, Genn, who can no longer tolerate the excesses and insane persecutions meted out by Ustinov, holds a feast with his friends, telling them that it is better to die at one's own hands than to serve a mindless idiot like Ustinov. He has taken poison and slowly dies, but not before sending a final message to Ustinov. When Ustinov receives that last message, which he thinks is from a dying friend whose last fond thoughts were of him, he pretentiously tells his lickspittle subordinates that he is so moved by Genn's dying gesture that he will now weep and calls for a weeping vial in which to preserve his sacred tears, for he has proclaimed himself a god. He then reads Genn's message, which acidly damns him as a talentless cretin not worthy of the company of intelligent persons and that Genn is finally happy to meet death only to escape hearing any more of Ustinov's inane, boring and meritless poetry. This sends Ustinov into another wild rage where he orders Genn's estate confiscated, his home burned to the ground, and all of his servants killed. He then proceeds to seek more vengeance by going to the arena where he orders thousands of Christians to be fed to lions and tigers. He is dismayed to hear these hapless victims go to their deaths singing Christian hymns. Aylmer is, along with many others, tied to a cross, which is set afire. Aylmer cries out to the crowd that it was Ustinov, not the Christians, who set Rome ablaze and that he is a despot not worthy of being emperor. The crowd becomes unnerved and angry at this, and Ustinov now fears that the crowd may turn upon him. Aylmer is whipped into silence and perishes. Currie, meanwhile, appears in the arena to comfort the Christians and denounce Ustinov. He is imprisoned in one of the dungeons where he marries Taylor and Kerr and is later crucified, but stating that he is not worthy of dying by execution in the manner of Jesus and his captors accommodate him by crucifying him upside down. The following day, more Christians are sacrificed in the arena, but again, the cries of agony of some are drowned out by the hymn singing of most others. Taylor is brought to Ustinov's royal box, where he is tied to a post to watch the Christians die. Incensed at Ustinov's brutality, Taylor shouts at Ustinov: "These people know how to die, Nero! In death, you will squeal like a hog!" Ustinov orders Taylor killed on the spot, but his scheming wife, Laffan, persuades Ustinov to spare Taylor's life, at least

Leo Genn, Marina Berti and Robert Taylor in *Quo Vadis*, 1951.

for the moment, because she had arranged a special entertainment for her husband and for Taylor, one that presents a horrible fate for Kerr. In making arrangements for the grim event to come, Laffan is viciously taking vengeance on Taylor for his earlier rejection of her. Kerr is then brought into the arena where she is tied to a stake and then a wild bull is released and where Ustinov and Laffan expect the beast to gore Kerr to death while Taylor watches in agony. However, the tyrant allows Kerr a chance to live by having her bodyguard, the giant Baer, stand next to her. If Baer can somehow kill the bull, Ustinov promises to release Kerr, an empty promise in that he and no one else believe that Baer can save Kerr from the bull. The bull charges and Baer grapples the beast by its horns and is bucked high and thrown by the bull. Baer nevertheless gets to his feet and again wraps his arms around the bull's lethal horns, both struggling for balance and advantage, and Taylor cries out "God, help him!" In a fierce struggle, Baer finally turns the bull's head, forcing the beast to its knees and then snaps its neck, killing the bull. Ustinov, as expected, then goes back on his word, and orders both Kerr and Baer killed, but Taylor manages to work his way free from his bonds, leaping into the arena and going to Kerr's side. When one of Ustinov's guards is about to throw a spear into Taylor, the guard is killed by one of the many soldiers loyal to Taylor, who have joined him in the arena. Taylor now denounces Ustinov, telling the crowd how their emperor destroyed Rome for his own pleasure and falsely accused the Christians of burning the city and that the lunatic Ustinov is a tyrant and, at that moment, General Galba (3 B.C.-69 A.D.) is marching on Rome with his legions to become their new emperor. "Hail, Galba!" Taylor shouts, and the crowd echoes his shout with approval, instantly turning on Ustinov, who, now terrified, flees to his palace. From the balcony of that palace, Ustinov trembles in fear as he sees thousands of Roman citizens pour into the palace below where no guards oppose them. He locks himself within his private chambers, sitting on his throne and, when seeing Laffan, blames her for all of his troubles, calling her his "evil self' and the true architect who urged him to use the Christians as scapegoats for his maniacal arson. He grabs her by the throat and strangles her to death. Thousands of Romans are now racing through the palace searching for the tyrant, and Ustinov, eyes rolling in terror, sweat pouring from his porcine face, his flabby body quivering and his arms flailing in a vain effort to find safety and preserve his life, realizes that he must now commit suicide, but he does not have the will power to end his life, which he thinks, even in these final moments of that hideous life, that he is more precious and sacrosanct than any other human being. Crutchley, a slave who has always loved Ustinov (and we cannot fathom why she could have an ounce of affection for this repulsive creature), comes to him. While he holds a dagger to his heart and pleads for her help, she plunges the blade into him and he painfully dies. We see an expression of shock and sur-

prise upon Ustinov's face that declares him mortal and where he recognizes in abject terror the kind of violent death he has so liberally and ruthlessly administered to countless others. Crutchley weeps over Ustinov's bloated corpse, most likely the only person within the empire who inexplicably mourns his passing. Taylor is then seen watching Galba, played by Tordi, enter Rome with his legions. He and Kerr are then shown leaving Rome, and, along the way, they are shown the place where Currie was crucified and, as they ride away, the camera closes in on Currie's staff. It stands at the side of the roadway, encircled by a flowering vine while shafts of radiant light beaming through the overhead trees fall upon it, and where we hear the words: "I am the Way, the Truth, and the Life." Few historical epics reach the magnitude and scope of this wonderful, impeccably produced film from pantheon director LeRoy. The director carefully unfolds this stirring and exciting tale (the entire film shot in historical sequence) with meticulous care, where he elicits superb performances from the entire cast. The cast is truly in the thousands, and the film's costuming and sets (especially those in the palace, the burning of Rome, and the scenes in the arena) are some of the most lavish and richly appointed ever created; cinematographers Surtees and Skall marvelously capture the action through their deep focus photography. Rozsa's score is dynamic and lyrical, filled with marital music and strange and fugitive melodies that are somewhat discordant at times to indicate the perversions and bloodletting by the despotic Ustinov. The film received an Oscar nomination as Best Picture, and Ustinov received an Oscar nomination as Best Supporting Actor while Rozsa received an Oscar nomination for Best Score, and an Oscar nomination was received for Best Art Direction, as well as Best Cinematography, Color (Surtees and Skall). It also won Oscar nominations for Best Costuming, Color, and Best Editing. The film was an enormous box office success, earning more than $30 million against its initial $7 million budget (not including pre-production costs). The story was also filmed as a TV miniseries in 1985 and remade in 2002 (a Polish production). ***Author's Note***: This story had been filmed many times in the silent era, the most notable production being in 1913 (made in Italy in 1912 and released the following year in the U.S.). It was remade again in Italy in 1924 as a silent and that version was enhanced with sound effects and rereleased in 1929. In the mid-1930s, MGM producer Hunt Stromberg revived the story and sent director Robert Z. Leonard to Italy to scout locations, but Leonard ran into problems with the fascist regime under Mussolini, who controlled all film production at that time, the fascists proved uncooperative, stating that any new version of **Quo Vadis** might depict Italians in a bad light. The talkie version as a project was further delayed when WWII (1939-1945) broke out. The story was again revived by production chief Dore Schary, who was then battling Louis B. Mayer for control of MGM. Schary launched the production in 1949, naming John Huston as its director. This version of the tale under Schary's guidance was long in development, although Ustinov tested at MGM for his role of Nero as early as 1949, and he was the first of the leading players selected for this epic. The production was put on hold, but MGM executives still thought to keep Ustinov in his pivotal part, although one executive wired his concerns to Ustinov, stating that he might be too young for the role of Nero. Ustinov jocularly wired back: "If you wait much longer, I shall be too old." Meanwhile, Gregory Peck and Elizabeth Taylor were signed for the leading roles and they traveled with Huston to Italy to begin some initial shooting. Huston ran into mounting problems right from the start, finding that, in 1949, the Italian film studios were a shambles and almost in ruins because of the war; his pre-production costs soared to more than $2 million with only a few scenes to show for the expense. The production bogged down and then came to a halt, especially when Huston and MGM producers began arguing about how Huston intended to make this version a modern interpretation of the historical epic. Schary abandoned the project for reasons of seemingly insurmountable expenses, but then Mayer took up the banner, crowing that he was right all along, that the public would never accept the modern interpretation of the story, and that the historical version was the only one that would see good box office results. Mayer hired Zimbalist, a workhorse producer, to put a new production in motion, hiring Robert Taylor and Deborah Kerr in the lead roles. "I was surprised to hear that MGM had spent so much money on a modern version of the story and then scrapped that whole project," Kerr told this author. "I was glad that I was to appear in the historical version, which I thought more suitable to the story line and where I would be able to wear some of the most beautiful costumes I would ever wear in any picture. They were absolutely stunning, some of them with expensive diamonds, rubies, sapphires and emeralds actually sewn into the design of those costumes. I shimmered and glittered so much, they had to use filters on the cameras so as not to have flashes of light ruin some of my scenes." There were more than 32,000 costumes designed for this film, which was probably a record in the history of film wardrobes. LeRoy was then named director of the film and inherited a production nightmare, not the least of which included dozens of wild lions he had to let loose in the arena to somehow devour the Christians but without having the lions injure any of the extras playing those sacrificial victims. "LeRoy went nuts over those damned lions," Taylor told this author. "He was terrified that they would start biting the extras and, God forbid, actually kill some of them. At first he had a bunch of lion tamers stand by in the arena when he had the lions set free from the tunnels where they were being held. He told the lion tamers to shoot any lion that might go after one of the extras. But when the cats came out into the arena and saw the hot, glaring sunlight, they turned around and went right back into the tunnels. The lion tamers told LeRoy to starve the lions for about a week or so, and he did, but when those starving cats came out into the arena again, they did the same thing, going right back into the tunnels. LeRoy tore his hair out trying to figure a way to have those lions look fierce inside the arena while keeping his extras safe, and, by that time, he had to pay those extras hazardous money because they all knew they were in danger. He came running up to me one day with a wide grin on his face and said: 'I figured it out, Bob! I am going to put raw, bloody meat inside a lot of dummy figures in the arena and then let those lions go at them and tear them to pieces. No one gets hurt, the lions are fed, the dummies are dirt cheap, and I get what I need on film!' When LeRoy again let loose the lions, they raced into the arena and, smelling the blood-soaked dummies containing the raw meat, savagely tore into those dummies, tearing them to shreds while devouring the implanted meat. The director, however, used only a small amount of that footage as most of that action, even when shot from a distance, still appeared that the lions were mangling dummies, not real humans. LeRoy told this author that "**Quo Vadis** was the toughest job I ever tackled. I had to supervise more than 8,000 extras in the stands of the arena and twice that in the scenes where we burn Rome. It was like directing an army, so I broke down sections of extras like you would military organizations, you know, companies, platoons, squads, and so on, and had a lot of assistant directors, my sergeants, keeping these groups in order and doing what they were supposed to do on camera. I did not get any help from the local filmmakers. Italy's studios were a mess and most of the industry's technicians were either killed off in the war or were crippled or had just quit, so I had a lot of inexperienced young Italian film technicians who really didn't know what they were doing, although they always smiled and nodded and told me that everything was 'okay, boss.' I was using Italian cameras and they were all screwed up. When I started shooting, the film went backward instead of forward because the technicians had installed the wrong switches. The lighting crews, who were also Italian, did not know that it required four times the light to capture good images on color film and they set up the wrong lighting for a lot of my early scenes that were ruined after I shot them." The most challenging chore in the production, according to LeRoy, was building the colossal sets that profiled Rome during the burning scenes. Scores of workmen spent several months building a four-block area of buildings that reflected the architecture of ancient Rome and to hundreds of the doors and windows of all of these buildings

Robert Taylor, Deborah Kerr and Buddy Baer in *Quo Vadis,* 1951.

they connected two miles of iron pipe. Through these pipes flowed untold gallons of inflammable mixed liquids, including gasoline, naphthalene, butane, fuel oil, which were set aflame through opening and closing valves to create jets of leaping, soaring flames, the process taking twenty-four nights until LeRoy was satisfied with the all-consuming fire he managed to capture on film (and where it took Nero only six days to burn down most of Rome). To his directorial brilliance and life-saving credit, LeRoy achieved these awesome scenes without a single person being injured or burned. Much of the new scenes added to this version that had not appeared in previous productions was "borrowed" from Cecil B. DeMille's **The Sign of the Cross**, 1933, which starred Fredric March and Elissa Landi as the hero and heroine and where Claudette Colbert plays the evil and sensuous Poppaea Sabina and the inimitable Charles Laughton plays Nero (and where Ustinov's portrayal of that tyrant is undoubtedly patterned after Laughton's extravagant and profligate performance). The outstanding and unusual score from Rozsa is as historically accurate as is everything else about this masterpiece production (with the exception of some historical time frames as to actual events). Before writing his great score for this film, Rozsa had MGM librarian George Schneider research and locate just about every type of instrument used and played in that long-ago Roman era, including lyres, harps and ancient horns, Rozsa employing and incorporating the sounds of these instruments within his score and where he had to ferret out and use expert musicians proficient in playing such instruments. Thus, this gifted composer was able to bring the musical sound of the ancient world into the modern era and onto the screen. **p**, Sam Zimbalist; **d**, Mervyn LeRoy; **cast**, Robert Taylor, Deborah Kerr, Leo Genn, Peter Ustinov, Patricia Laffan, Finlay Currie, Abraham Sofaer, Marina Berti, Buddy Baer, Felix Aylmer, Nora Swinburne, Peter Miles, Ralph Truman, Norman Wooland, Geoffrey Dunn, Nicholas Hannen, D.A. Clarke-Smith, Rosalie Crutchley, John Ruddock, Arthur Walge, Elspeth March, Strelsa Brown, Pietro Tordi, Walter Pidgeon (narrator), and (not credited) Sophia Loren, Elizabeth Taylor; **w**, John Lee Mahin, S.N. Behrman, Sonya Levien (based on the novel by Henryk Sienkiewicz); **c**, Robert Surtees, William V. Skall (Technicolor); **m**, Miklos Rozsa; **ed**, Ralph E. Winters; **art d**, William A. Horning, Cedric Gibbons, Edward Carfagno; **set d**, Hugh Hunt; **spec eff**, Thomas Howard, A. Arnold Gillespie, Donald Jahraus, Peter Ellenshaw.

Rabbit-Proof Fence ★★★ 2002; Australia; 94m; Rumbalara Films/Miramax; Color; Drama; Children: Unacceptable (MPAA: PG); **DVD**; **VHS**. This moving and well-acted drama is set in 1931 Australia where three aboriginal girls escape after being taken from their homes to be

William Holden and Loretta Young in *Rachel and the Stranger,* **1948.**

trained as domestic workers. It is a government policy to take half-caste children from their aboriginal mothers and send them into what amounts to indentured servitude "to save them from themselves." The girls are two sisters, Daisy, age eight (Sansbury), and Molly, thirteen (Sampi), and a cousin, Gracie (Monaghan), age ten. They escape a camp where they are being held and follow a fence that keeps rabbits out, making an incredible trek across the outback wilderness. They walk 1,500 miles in nine weeks to finally get back to their home village, but Gracie dies along the way. It would be many years before the cruel practice would be abolished. Songs: "Blue Sky" (Peter Gabriel), "Swanee River" (Stephen Foster), "The Man Who Broke the Bank at Monte Carlo" (Fred Gilbert), "All Things Bright and Beautiful" (William H. Monk, Cecil F. Alexander). Disturbing privation scenes prohibit viewing by children. (In Aboriginal; English subtitles.) **p**, Phillip Noyce, Christine Olsen, John Winter, Oliver Huzly; **d**, Noyce; **cast**, Everlyn Sampi, Tianna Sansbury, Laura Monaghan, Kenneth Branagh, David Gulpilil, Ningali Lawford, Myarn Lawford, Deborah Mailman, Jason Clarke, Natasha Wanganeen; **w**, Olsen (based on the book *Follow the Rabbit-Proof Fence* by Doris Pilkington Garimara); **c**, Christopher Doyle; **m**, Peter Gabriel; **ed**, Veronika Jenet, John Scott; **prod d**, Roger Ford; **art d**, Laurie Faen; **set d**, Rebecca Cohen; **spec eff**, Jonathan Blaikie, Paul Butterworth, Murray Pope.

The Racers ★★★ 1955; U.S.; 88m; FOX; Color; Sports Drama; Children: Unacceptable; **VHS**. This exciting film chronicles European-style road racing in France, Italy, and Germany and provides a lot of daredevil action in the bargain. Douglas is an Italian bus driver, who aspires to become a winning race car driver and will risk his life and the lives of other drivers to do it. He lives with Darvi, a beautiful ballerina, but he keeps her on the back burner, telling her that driving comes first with him. He gets a race car and wins his first race, then is hired by a successful racing team managed by Cobb, who becomes anxious about Douglas' reckless driving. Douglas becomes one of the top racers that include Roland and Romero, but, unlike his competitors, he displays a cold heart, exhibiting a callous attitude when a mechanic is accidentally killed at a race. Douglas is then injured in a crash at a race in Brussels and is close to losing a leg, but Darvi persuades doctors not to perform the operation. He loses Darvi after he relentlessly wins the final race of Romero's career, even after Cobb instructs him to let Romero have one last victory. In time, Douglas loses races and he is alone. He begs Darvi to return to him, but she has become involved with another driver, Hudson. In his next race, Douglas lets Hudson speed past him, indicating that Douglas has become human after all. Song: "I Belong to You" (music: Alex North; lyrics: Jack Brooks). Douglas gives another fine performance, this time as a self-centered and rather ruthless character,

learning too late about compassion and generosity to keep the love of a good woman. Mature themes prohibit viewing by children. **p**, Julian Blaustein; **d**, Henry Hathaway; **cast**, Kirk Douglas, Gilbert Roland, Bella Darvi, Cesar Romero, Lee J. Cobb, Katy Jurado, John Hudson, Charles Goldner, George Dolenz, Agnes Laury; **w**, Charles Kaufman (based on the novel by Hans Ruesch); **c**, Joseph MacDonald (CinemaScope; DeLuxe Color); **m**, Alex North; **ed**, James B. Clark; **art d**, Lyle R. Wheeler, George Patrick; **set d**, Stuart A. Reiss, Walter M. Scott; **spec eff**, Ray Kellogg, Louis J. Witte.

Rachel and the Stranger ★★★ 1948; U.S.; 80m; RKO; B/W; Adventure/Romance; Children: Cautionary; **DVD**; **VHS**. Holden, Young and Mitchum are standouts in this well-crafted adventure tale set during the early 1800s on the frontier of the Great Northwest. Farmer and widower Holden is struggling to raise his young son, Gray, but he thinks that he needs a woman around the house, mostly to help with the chores and provide some motherly care for his boy. To that end, he travels to a nearby town and buys an indentured servant, Young. To quell gossip and subdue scandal, Holden marries Young, but the union is in name only and is both loveless and sexless. Young finds herself becoming a combination house servant and nanny for Gray, but the boy resents Young as a replacement for a mother Gray still remembers and for whom he longs, and that is Holden's perspective, too, as he can only look to yesterday when he was happy with his first wife. Young works hard in trying to endear herself to both Holden and Gray, but the only person who seems to appreciate her is Mitchum. A scout and woodsman, Mitchum arrives to stay with the family and, after he sees that Holden or Gray pay little or no attention to Young, he begins to make subtle passes at the beautiful woman. Holden grows jealous and asks Mitchum to leave, but he says that he loves Young and wants to buy her and marry her, just as Holden has. Young, feeling as though she is nothing more than chattel to be bought and sold, becomes so angry that she moves back to the town. Holden, Gray and Mitchum go after her, but she wants nothing to do with any of them. Then news arrives that Indians are ravaging the area and attacking and burning farms. Holden, Gray and Mitchum are joined by Young when they race back to Holden's farm just in time as Indians arrive. They manage to hold off the Indians until townsmen come to their rescue and drive the heathens back to their hinterlands. Mitchum, during the attack (a fierce, prolonged and very harrowing sequence) sees that Young truly loves Holden and Gray, and, after peace is restored, he decides to move on, wishing the family well. Foster does an exceptional job in helming this warm-hearted film, injecting considerable comedy into its many action-packed scenes. Songs: "Rachel," "Tall, Dark Stranger," "Foolish Pride," "Summer Song," "O-he-o-hi-o-ho," "Just Like Me" (music: Roy Webb; lyrics: Waldo Salt). *Author's Note*: Mitchum, in addition to his lively and charismatic acting in **Rachel and the Stranger**, strums a guitar and sings a few songs that surprised his fans with a pleasant singing voice heretofore unheard. Mitchum told this author that "I don't know who got the idea that I should sing in that picture, but I went along with it as a lark. I may have a better singing voice than some other actors, but that doesn't say much. I never had any ambitions to sing in any other pictures, although I hum an old hymn when I am hunting two kids in **Night of the Hunter** [1955], but that doesn't pass for singing. If I had to make a living doing that, I would be sleeping in a shack by the side of a railroad in Mississippi." **p**, Richard H. Berger; **d**, Norman Foster; **cast**, Loretta Young, William Holden, Robert Mitchum, Gary Gray, Tom Tully, Sara Haden, Frank Ferguson, Walter Baldwin, Regina Wallace, Frank Conlan; **w**, Waldo Salt (based on the stories "Rachel" and "Neighbor Sam" by Howard Fast); **c**, Maury Gertsman; **m**, Roy Webb; **ed**, Les Millbrook; **art d**, Albert S. D'Agostino, Jack Okey; **set d**, Darrell Silvera, John Sturtevant; **spec eff**, Russell A. Cully.

Rachel Getting Married ★★★ 2008; U.S.; 113m; Armian Pictures/Sony; Color; Drama/Romance; Children: Unacceptable

(MPAA: R); **BD**; **DVD**. This tense and emotionally draining drama sees Hathaway as a young woman with drug addiction problems and who is released from rehab for a few days to go home to her father's (Irwin) house and attend the wedding of her sister Rachel, played by DeWitt. Their parents are either estranged or divorced and their mother, Winger, lives nearby in her own house. Relationships at home are strained between Hathaway and family members as they all try to reconcile themselves with her past and present. Irwin is concerned about her well-being, which Hathaway misinterprets as mistrust. She also resents DeWitt's choice of her best friend, George, rather than her, to be her maid of honor. DeWitt also resents the attention that Hathaway's drug addiction is distracting from her wedding. These apprehensions are publicly exposed at a rehearsal dinner where Hathaway takes the microphone to apologize for her past actions, as part of her twelve-step drug rehab program. Behind the family tensions is a tragedy that happened years before, when, as a teenager, Hathaway was responsible for the death of her younger brother. He was left in her care one day when, driving home from a nearby park while intoxicated, Hathaway lost control of the car and drove over a bridge into a lake where the boy drowned. The day before the wedding, Hathaway is approached by a man she knew from an early stay in rehab. He thanks her for helping him deal with his own problems, stemming from the time when he was molested by an uncle. DeWitt becomes furious when she learns his story was all a lie, an attempt by Hathaway to evade responsibility for her drug addiction. Tension between the sisters climaxes that night at their father's house when Hathaway comes home and DeWitt reveals that she has never forgiven Hathaway for their brother's death. She further maintains that Hathaway's rehab has been a hoax since she has been lying about the cause of her problems. Hathaway finally admits being responsible for her brother's death and says she has been relapsing into drugs in order to cope with her guilt. She then gets into her father's car and leaves the house, going to the home of her mother, hoping to find comfort from her. But an argument breaks out between them when Hathaway asks Winger why she left the boy in her care on the night of his death, knowing that she was often on drugs. Hathaway says it would have been better if Winger had left him in DeWitt's care. Winger says it was because Hathaway was "good with him" and that DeWitt is a hypocrite for blaming Hathaway for her son's death. Hathaway now blames her mother for being partly responsible in the death, causing Winger to slap her face. Hathaway strikes her mother back and drives off in her father's car. While sobbing uncontrollably because her mother has not accepted any responsibility in the tragedy, Hathaway accidentally drives the car off the road and it crashes into a boulder. Instead of seeking help, she spends the night in the car while those at home worry about her whereabouts. The next morning, the day of the wedding, Hathaway's car is spotted by joggers who call police. Officers awaken Hathaway and give her a sobriety test, which she passes. She gets a ride home with the driver of a tow truck who is towing the wrecked car. Hathaway goes to DeWitt's room as the bride is dressing. When DeWitt sees Hathaway's bruised face and having heard about the fight Hathaway had the previous night with their mother, her anger from the previous night is gone and she tenderly bathes and dresses her sister. DeWitt and the groom are married in a festive Indian-themed ceremony and Hathaway is the maid of honor, overcome with emotion as the newlyweds exchange their vows. Hathaway tries to enjoy the wedding reception, but still feels out of place and troubled by the unresolved dispute with her mother. Winger leaves the party early, despite DeWitt's efforts to reconcile her sister and mother. The mother-daughter estrangement is left unresolved, leaving viewers to suspect that the main cause of the family's problems is Winger's inability to accept any responsibility for her son's death. The next morning, Hathaway must return to rehab. As she is leaving, DeWitt runs out of the house and hugs her. At least the sisters have reconciled with each other, if not with their mother. Songs: "Here Comes the Bride"(Richard Wagner); "Could It Be Magic" (Barry Manilow, Adrienne Anderson); "Rice Field Chant," "Dancing with Shiva" (Roberto

Anne Hathaway and Rosemarie DeWitt in *Rachel Getting Married,* **2008.**

Colella, Riccardo Mazzamauro); "Biddar" (Gaida Hinnawi); "Peace Like a River" (traditional); "It's Been Done" (Per Sunding, Nathan Larson, Angela McCluskey); "Unknown Legend" (Neil Young); "America," "Up to Our Nex" (Robyn Hitchcock); "Dread Natty Congo" (Carol T. East); "Samba for Shiva" (Cyro Baptista); "Lower Ninth Ward Blues" (Al "Carnival Time" Johnson); "Golden Hen" (Clive Bright, Stephen Thomas, Keith Wignall); "In My Soul" (Tavish Graham); "Trilla" (Brooklyn Demme). Gutter language and sexuality prohibit viewing by children. **p**, Jonathan Demme, Marc Platt, Neda Armian, H.H. Cooper; **d**, Demme; **cast**, Anne Hathaway, Rosemarie DeWitt, Bill Irwin, Debra Winger, Tunde Adebimpe, Mather Zickel, Anna Deavere Smith, Anisa George, Victoria Haynes, Jerome LePage, Carol-Jean Lewis; **w**, Jenny Lumet; **c**, Declan Quinn; **m**, Donald Harrison, Jr., Zafer Tawil; **ed**, Tim Squyres; **prod d**, Ford Wheeler; **art d**, Kim Jennings; **set d**, Chryss Hionis; **spec eff**, Glenn Allen, Peter Amante, Richard Friedlander, Eric J. Robertson.

Rachel, Rachel ★★★ 1968; U.S.; 101m; Kayos Productions/WB-Seven Arts; Color; Drama; Children: Unacceptable (MPAA: R); **DVD**; **VHS**. Woodward (Rachel) gives an outstanding performance as a thirty-five-year-old spinster and virgin, a sad and lonely woman living with her highly demanding widowed mother and where Woodward has no man in her life. She teaches second grade at a school in a small Connecticut town where she grew up. Olson, a friend from her childhood, returns from the big city to visit his family for the summer. He makes overtures while he is in town, but Woodward fears getting involved with any man. Gradually, Woodward warms to him and, after they have sex, she thinks she is pregnant. Happy about the possibility, she soon learns she is not going to have a child. Olson ends his relationship with Woodward by lying, saying that he is married, and leaves. She and Harrington, a girlfriend, go to Oregon for a vacation and Woodward hopes she will yet meet a decent man and be married. Sexuality prohibits viewing by children. **p&d**, Paul Newman; **cast**, Joanne Woodward, James Olson, Kate Harrington, Estelle Parsons, Donald Moffat, Terry Kiser, Frank Corsaro, Bernard Barrow, Geraldine Fitzgerald, Nel Potts, Shawn Campbell, Violet Dunn; **w**, Stewart Stern (based on the novel *A Jest of God* by Margaret Laurence); **c**, Gayne Rescher (Technicolor); **m**, Jerome Moross; **ed**, Dede Allen; **art d**, Arthur Gundlach; **set d**, Richard Merrell.

The Rack ★★★ 1956; U.S.; 100m; MGM; B/W; Drama; Children: Unacceptable; **DVD**; **VHS**. Taut drama from the gifted Serling sees Newman returning home from the Korean War where he faces a court martial, charged with collaboration with the enemy. Pigdeon, his father, a career officer, stands by his son as Corey is a reluctant prosecutor and O'Brien serves as Newman's defense counsel, both attorneys being dis-

Paul Newman and Edmond O'Brien in *The Rack*, 1956.

tinguished U.S. Army officers. A tribunal of officers hears the case and it is obvious that Newman is guilty of treason, but O'Brien presents a compelling defense in outlining how Newman was put on an emotional and psychological rack by his captors, who eventually wore down his resistance and broke his spirit and will, turning him into a manipulated traitor. Further, Newman has lived a lonely life since his mother died and where his father, Pidgeon, has never shown any real affection toward him. He found little friendship in the service from fellow officers, all of this causing him to become dependent upon his captors after they insidiously pretended to be the kind of friends he has always wanted and never had. His case is dissected by the testimony of other officers who were imprisoned with Newman, but who resisted all efforts by enemy interrogators to turn them into the kind of traitor Newman became. Marvin is one of those officers testifying against Newman, having been imprisoned with him and having suffered the same kind of psychological tortures endured by Newman, as well as undergoing terrible physical torture that Newman evaded. His testimony is as damning to Newman's case as is many others. While listening to that testimony, Newman is filled with remorse and guilt (especially over the fact that his brother was killed in that war and he survived) and, when he takes the witness stand, he more or less admits his culpability, which brings about his inevitable conviction. At the end of this unnerving and tense story, Newman finds some comfort in that Pidgeon now shows him the kind of love that he has withheld throughout his life. Director Laven presents a fast-paced tale and the dialog is crisp, intelligent and revealing; Newman gives a fine performance, which is equaled by strong supporting players. The film was made for about $800,000, but it failed to recoup its investment, earning $750,000 at the box office when initially released. Song: "The Last Time I Saw Paris" (music: Jerome Kern; lyrics: Oscar Hammerstein). *Author's Note*: Newman told this author that "I made my first feature with the **The Silver Chalice** [1954], but I got my biggest boosts from **Somebody Up There Likes Me** [1956] and **The Rack**. Those pictures were released in the same year. **The Rack** was really a script written for television by Rod Serling, a talented writer with a knack for good dialog. It was adapted by another good writer, Stewart Stern, and he later wrote the script for the first film I directed, **Rachel, Rachel** [1968]. **The Rack** had great dialog and very strong characters, but it did not go over too well with the public. I think that was because very few wanted to remember the Korean War, and I play a victim of brainwashing in that war. Like Vietnam, it was a war we did not win. It was a draw and the American public likes winners." Marvin told this author that "I served in the Pacific during the big war [WWII and where Marvin was painfully wounded] and the enemy in that war did not take you captive and try to bend your mind to their thinking. They just killed you, so when I played an officer tes-

tifying against Paul [Newman] in **The Rack** over his being brainwashed, I did not have any personal sympathy for him, just like the character I was playing. I suppose that's why I felt that I was convincing in that part. I never bought that brainwashing crap anyway." This was Pidgeon's last film for MGM, having been with the studio for nineteen years. Other films dealing with the brainwashing of American POWs during the Korean War include **The Manchurian Candidate**, 1962, and **Prisoner of War**, 1954. For an extensive listing on films dealing with the Korean War, see Index, Volume II, of this work. **p**, Arthur M. Loew Jr.; **d**, Arnold Laven; **cast**, Paul Newman, Wendell Corey, Walter Pidgeon, Edmond O'Brien, Anne Francis, Lee Marvin, Cloris Leachman, Robert Burton, Robert Simon, Trevor Bardette, Adam Williams, James Best, Fay Roope, Barry Atwater, Charles Evans; **w**, Stewart Stern (based on the teleplay by Rod Serling); **c**, Paul C. Vogel; **m**, Adolph Deutsch; **ed**, Harold F. Kress, Marshall Neilan Jr.; **art d**, Cedric Gibbons, Merrill Pye; **set d**, Edwin B. Willis, Fred MacLean.

The Racket ★★★★ 1928 (silent); U.S.; 84m/8 reels; The Caddo Company/PAR; B/W; Crime Drama; Children: Unacceptable. Pantheon director Milestone offers a no-holds-barred gangster film, based on Chicago crime boss Al Capone (1899-1947), who is savagely played by Wolheim. Set during Prohibition in the mid-1920s in Chicago, Wolheim is shown as a ruthless boss heading a bootlegging gang that stops at nothing in peddling its illegal booze while controlling most of the town's speakeasies. His lucrative business allows Wolheim to bribe almost all in the hierarchy of the city's police department to work with him in ignoring his illegal operations, including countless murders where rivals are shot down in droves by his machine gun-wielding thugs. Meighan is one of the few police captains refusing to cooperate with Wolheim, waging a one-man war against the gangster and his minions. Meighan personally supervises police raids on Wolheim's speakeasies, still-operations and warehouses, and a small army of Wolheim's men are jailed. These widespread arrests, however, come to nothing. Wolheim has bribed almost all the other police commanders and also owns the judges in the city, who routinely release Wolheim's men after Meighan puts them behind bars. Wolheim then openly threatens Meighan with death, but that threat only inspires the intrepid cop to increase his crusade against Wolheim. The crime boss then uses his influence to have Meighan transferred to a remote district where he is unable to raid any of Wolheim's operations. Meighan, however, continues to goad and aggravate Wolheim by using wisecracking newspaper reporters as his surrogates to pass along to Wolheim insults and dire predictions about Wolheim's future. Then Stone, who is Wolheim's irresponsible brother, is arrested after a hit-and-run accident, and Meighan uses this arrest, along with Prevost, a gold-digging singer in one of Wolheim's nightclubs, and the up-coming elections, as well as turncoats in Wolheim's organization, to destroy the crime boss. Milestone robustly directs this crime yarn, packing its scenes with exciting action and depicts the grim lifestyle of the Chicago underworld in memorable sequences of sleazy speakeasies; posturing, well-dressed gangsters; and speeding cars, where gunfire erupts at the drop of a fedora. Other than the upstanding Meighan, the city's politicians and police commanders are shown to be utterly corrupt, the bought stooges of Wolheim, who gives a great performance of a grotesque, power-made crime boss, a thug who kills without mercy. Meighan is riveting as the incorruptible police commander. Gaudio's crisp and inventive lensing is superb, vividly capturing the gloomy and grim atmosphere of the Chicago underworld. This film was extremely popular and did well at the box office, except in the city of Chicago, where it was banned. *Author's Note*: Wolheim possessed the perfect image as a repulsive-looking gangster, with his broken nose (gotten in his youth when playing football at Cornell); massive jaw; heavy, turkey-like neck; and bulbous eyes. This superlative character actor would, two years later, render one of his greatest performances under Milestone's direction when appearing in **All Quiet on the Western Front**, 1930, as the veteran German soldier in that masterpiece film about WWI, and for which Milestone would win an Oscar as Best Director. Wolheim's role in **The Racket** is a thinly disguised character that is unmistakably based upon crime czar Al Capone. Wolheim's name in the film is "Scarsi," a synonym for "Scarface," which was Capone's underworld nickname due to the scars he bore on his left cheek from an attack by a barber, who used a razor to slash his face when Capone, as a youth in Brooklyn, started a fight with that barber. Meighan's character as the honest police captain, who doggedly battles with Wolheim, is based upon Chicago Police Captain John Stege, one of the few Chicago police commanders who could not be bought off by Capone and was forever detaining him for the myriad murders Capone and his henchmen committed during Chicago's gang wars. Stege was unable to make a case against the crime boss, invariably ordered by paid-off judges to release him. **The Racket** was later reworked and modified by MGM as **The Beast of the City**, 1932, where Walter Huston plays the Meighan role and Jean Hersholt plays the omnipotent gangster essayed by Wolheim. **The Racket** was, for some years, lost to the public after most of its original prints either vanished or were destroyed. I viewed this film when director Milestone ran his own print of the film for this author in one of our several meetings. Milestone told this author that he had deep reservations about directing this film, which was a pet project of movie mogul Howard Hughes, and who had, only a few years earlier entered the film business as a producer, using his father's vast wealth (from a patented tool and die business that monopolized the use of oil drilling bits) to make his own films. Milestone stated to this author: "Howard [Hughes] hated Capone, and he made **The Racket** as a matter of ego or personal pride. When Capone heard through the grapevine that Howard was thinking about making a picture about him and was going to portray him like a murderous ape, he sent a Chicago attorney to see Hughes, who warned Howard not to make the picture—just like the lawyer in **The Godfather** [1972]. Howard said to me: 'That god-damned Capone isn't going to tell me what to do with my business. He might run Chicago, but he doesn't run Los Angeles. I want Wolheim to play that guy as the rottenest bastard on earth because that's what that stinking Capone is!' Howard was a young man and I don't think he knew how dangerous Capone really was, that Capone might send his killers out to the Coast and bump Howard off any time he wanted. It was all about ego with Howard. Capone wasn't going to tell him what to do. Nobody could ever tell Howard Hughes what to do. Well, I got a call from someone who gave me the same warning when we went into production for **The Racket**. The caller would not give me his name over the phone. He said that, if I directed the film, I might be found floating face down off Catalina [Catalina Island, twenty-six miles from the Los Angeles coast]. I told Howard about that call and he laughed and said, 'Oh, that's probably some guy playing a prank on you. Forget it.' I didn't forget it and thought about it all the time while we were making that picture. Howard had a fixation about Capone and he went after him again when he did **Scarface** [1932], a talkie, where Paul Muni plays Capone and there's no mistaking his character, and Howard got another message from Capone about that picture, too, and so did Ben Hecht, who wrote the script for **Scarface**. Both of them were told to dump the production. That was like waving a red flag at a bull. Howard opened up his checkbook and I think he would have spent every dime he had to make **Scarface**, just to spit in Capone's eye. Howard and Capone were just like the two guys in **The Racket**, the cop and the gangster, each one of them determined to destroy the other. Howard's hatred for Capone was permanent. When Capone died in 1947, Howard called me and said: 'That rotten son-of-a-bitch just died. I hope he suffered!'" Cormack, who had been a Chicago newspaperman, wrote this story as a play that was produced on Broadway, opening on November 22, 1927, and closing in March 1928, after 119 performances. Its original cast had Edward G. Robinson in the leading role as the gangster, a role that more or less typecast Robinson as an underworld boss, and he

Louis Wolheim, Thomas Meighan and Marie Prevost in *The Racket,* **1928.**

would play that kind of character again and again. Robinson essays a loose characterization of Capone in **Little Caesar**, 1931. The Cormack play stirred a lot of passions in Chicago where the play and its film version were banned by local politicians headed by Mayor William Hale "Big Bill" Thompson (1869-1944), who, like most politicians and cops in Chicago at that time, was on Capone's payroll. Playwright, screenwriter and novelist Ben Hecht told this author that "I knew Bart [Bartlett Cormack, 1898-1942] from the old days in Chicago when we were newspaper reporters. He worked for the *American* when I was writing for the *Daily News*, and we covered a lot of crime together, always trying to scoop the other, but there were so many gang gunfights and killings that there was plenty of news like that to go around. Bart really wanted to write plays and he told me that he was going to write a gangster play and have Capone as one of his leading characters. I told him that he was looking for a one-way ride or a cement jacket. [The "one-way ride" was where gangsters took victims for a ride in their cars and shot them to death, leaving the victims in remote areas; "cement jackets" refers to how gangsters encased their victims in cement while they were alive before dumping them into rivers or lakes to drown.] He only laughed at me and said: 'Aw, come on, Ben. Those people [gangsters] don't kill writers.' I reminded him of his statement to me a few years later after Capone had Jake Lingle [1891-1931, a reporter for the Chicago *Tribune*] killed. Lingle was crooked and on the take from Capone. He double-crossed Scarface, but he was still a reporter. Bart wasn't laughing about that. After I wrote the screenplay for **Scarface**, some of Capone's goons tracked me down and wanted to know if I had written about their boss, and I nervously told them, no, that I just made up the character. I told Bart about this jittery visitation and he laughed, and this time the laugh was on me, because I had not taken my own advice. Well, we were all in the writing business and gangsters were good grist for our mill. We used their stories so we had to take the threats that went with them." For more details on Hecht's encounter with gangsters over his writing **Scarface**, see my *Author's Note* for that entry in this work. For detailed information about Al Capone and the bootleggers of Chicago in the Prohibition era, see my books *Bloodletters and Badmen* (M. Evans, New York, 1973, 1983, 1991, 1995); my eight-volume *Encyclopedia of World Crime*, Volume I (Vols. I-VI; CrimeBooks, 1990; Vols. VII-VIII; History, Inc., 1999), and my two-volume work *The Great Pictorial History of World Crime*, Volume I (History, Inc., Wilmette, Ill., 2004). **p**, Howard Hughes; **d**, Lewis Milestone; **cast**, Thomas Meighan, Marie Prevost, Louis Wolheim, Pat Collins, Henry Sedley, George E. Stone, Sam DeGrasse, Skeets Gallagher, Lee Moran, Walter Brennan, Milestone; **w**, Harry Behn, Bartlett Cormack, Tom Miranda (titles), Del Andrews, (based on the play by Cormack); **c**, Tony Gaudio; **m**, Robert Israel; **ed**, Eddie Adams; **art d**, Julian Fleming.

Gangsters destroying produce in *Racket Busters*, 1938.

The Racket ★★★ 1951; U.S.; 88m; RKO; B/W; Crime Drama; Children: Unacceptable; **VHS**. Solid and absorbing remake of the 1928 silent film, updated with contemporary themes based on the televised Kefauver Crime hearings, has Mitchum as a crusading police captain battling crime boss Ryan, both actors rendering compelling and intense performances. Ryan, who heads the rackets in an unnamed midwestern city, is working hard to promote his hand-picked candidates for an upcoming election, looking to see these political stooges take office and thereafter do his bidding. Mitchum works hard to sully those venal candidates as well as find enough evidence to arrest and subsequently send Ryan to prison. Whenever Mitchum orders a raid or any police action against Ryan's operations, he is met with obstacles placed in his way by prosecuting attorney Collins and special inspector Conrad, both being Ryan's bought surrogates. Mitchum focuses upon a nightclub owned by Ryan, which is the headquarters of all his criminal enterprises, and tries to use torch singer Scott, who works there, to turn the tables on Ryan. Mitchum arrests King, who is Ryan's younger brother, for carrying a concealed weapon and then compels Scott to become a material witness against King, even though she has been King's sweetheart. She is meanwhile offered support and affection from newspaperman Hutton, who is smitten by her. When Ryan learns that Scott is about to testify against his brother, he orders her murdered, but Talman, another honest and dedicated officer working closely with Mitchum, prevents that hit and, in turn, is killed. Ryan is then captured by Mitchum as he attempts to flee over some rooftops and he admits to an earlier killing. While he is jailed, Collins and Conrad tell Ryan that his old-fashioned violence has jeopardized their crooked rackets and they want him to remain behind bars, at least until the impending elections are over and their candidates have taken office. Ryan threatens to expose them unless he is released on bail. When they balk, Ryan tells Conrad that he should allow him to escape while being held at police headquarters and Conrad pretends to go along with that scheme, but kills Ryan when he attempts to escape. Mitchum, however, has arranged for all of these underhanded machinations to take place in order to not only finish off the murderous Ryan but ensnare Collins and Conrad, which he does, bringing about the destruction of their criminal operations. Director Cromwell does a good job in maintaining a swift pace for this film noir story, and the stalwart Mitchum is convincing as the no-nonsense cop and Ryan captivating as his sinister nemesis, while Collins, Conrad and Scott are effective in their roles. Song: "A Lovely Way to Spend an Evening" (music: Jimmy McHugh; lyrics: Harold Adamson). Despite criticism from reviewers that this film had too many loose ends (and that is truly befitting of how law enforcement invariably deals with crime in that not all the pieces of the puzzle fit comfortably in every slot), this thoroughly suspenseful film did well at the box office in its initial release,

taking in more than $1,750,0000. *Author's Note*: Cromwell told this author that "Bob [Mitchum] was cast in the role of the police captain because he fit the part, an actor who kept a lot of emotion in reserve. I had personal experience with the role that Bob played because I played it myself when the story was produced in New York in 1927 when I was part of the original cast." Mitchum, on the other hand, told this author that "I had no choice but to play my character cool and detached to give contrast to Ryan's character, who is a wacko crime boss. His character called for him to chew on everybody like a hungry lion, and he chewed up the sets, too, but that's the way the director [Cromwell] wanted it. He is one hell of an actor. We were together in **Crossfire** [1947] and, in that picture he is a racist wacko." Ryan echoed Mitchum's statements when telling this author that "I had to be another nutcase in **The Racket**, a gangster who is out of fashion because he uses the kind of muscle they flexed in the Twenties. You know, bump everyone off who talks back. I got a little tired of playing those lunatics, but that's about all that kept coming my way in those days. I got good at it because every time a scene called for me to blow my stack, I would think about every casting director that shoved me into such roles." Collins and Talman would appear together in the long-running TV series "Perry Mason"albeit Collins had long established his onscreen persona as a corrupt politician when appearing as Orson Welles' political nemesis in **Citizen Kane**, 1941, as "James W. 'Big Jim' Gettys," and would go on playing that kind of role in such films as **Touch of Evil**, 1958, which also starred Welles and where Collins is a waffling, conniving politician. **p**, Edmund Grainger; **d**, John Cromwell, Nicholas Ray; **cast**, Robert Mitchum, Lizabeth Scott, Robert Ryan, William Talman, Ray Collins, Joyce MacKenzie, Robert Hutton, Virginia Huston, William Conrad, Walter Sande, Les Tremayne, Don Porter, Walter Reed, Milburn Stone; **w**, William Wister Haines, W.R. Burnett (based on the play by Bartlett Cormack); **c**, George E. Diskant; **m**, Paul Sawtell; **ed**, Sherman Todd; **art d**, Albert S. D'Agostino, Jack Okey.

Racket Busters ★★★ 1938; U.S.; 71m; Cosmopolitan/WB; Crime; Children: Unacceptable; Unavailable. Bogart is again exceptional in this tough crime tale, this time playing John "Czar" Martin, a top Manhattan gangster, who sets his sights on controlling the produce trucking business in the city by forcing drivers to pay him protection money (some of the story line takes a leaf from an earlier crime film, **Quick Millions**, 1931). At first, the truckers resist, but, after Bogart's goons beat some of them to a pulp, they agree to pay him a large share of their salaries. Brent is a trucker who resists, needing all his pay because his wife, Dickson, is pregnant. His partner, Jenkins, agrees to help him stand up to Bogart, but Bogart has his goons burn their truck. A special prosecutor, Abel, is appointed to end Bogart's racket, but Jenkins has had enough and quits, resorting to selling tomatoes. Brent is broke so he breaks into Bogart's trucking office and steals enough money to have Dickson moved to a safe place to have their baby. Bogart and his thugs go to Brent's apartment and promise Brent that his wife won't be harmed if he agrees to join the other truckers into agreeing to pay for protection. Brent sees no other choice so he agrees. Bogart then sends his men on a rampage beating up any drivers who won't cooperate, including Jenkins, who, by then, is operating a produce shop. An old trucker, O'Shea, offers to give Abel evidence against Bogart, but he is killed by Bogart's men. The drivers blame Brent for the killing, and Abel arrests him in order to get information from him. Bogart then has all the truckers go on strike, which stops delivery of fruit and vegetables to shops and restaurants in New York City. Abel lets Brent go so he can work undercover in Bogart's racket. Brent organizes the truckers to oppose Bogart, winning them over after Jenkins is shot and killed by Bogart's goons. The truckers have had enough of Bogart and break the strike, getting the trucks rolling again to deliver produce to the city. Brent goes to Bogart's apartment and beats him up just before police arrive to arrest Bogart. Brent provides evidence at Bogart's trial to get him convicted and is then reunited with his wife and their baby while the truckers go back to work without any further trouble from Bogart and his men. Director Bacon, a workhorse helmsman at Warner Brothers who specialized in crime films, provides a lot of action, from the wrecking of vehicles to bombings and fist-flying donnybrooks, and the cast members, especially Bogart and Brent, are standouts in their roles. *Author's Note*: Rossén, who wrote the screenplay for this solid crime story, and who would go on to write and direct other film noir entries (**Johnny O'Clock**, 1947; **Body and Soul**, 1947; and his masterpiece, **The Hustler**, 1961), told this author that "Bogey [Bogart] was appearing in so many gangster films for Warner Brothers that he could not keep count of them, but he said that **Racket Busters** was better than most because the script 'made sense' of the characters, but maybe he was just being kind because I wrote that script. He was right when he said that 'this picture has a much better cast than a lot of others I have done.' Bogey liked Lloyd [Bacon] because they had gotten along well when doing some previous pictures together [**Marked Woman**, 1937; **San Quentin**, 1937]. When Lloyd was directing pictures like **Racket Busters** he always let Bogey develop his characters in his own style. I wrote the script for **Marked Woman**, and Lloyd directed that picture, which starred Bette Davis, but Bogey was her costar and he got, for a change, to play a good guy, a crusading district attorney. He told me years later that that role, more than a lot of others he played in those days, 'put me on the track to getting better parts.' We all had to work very hard back then to get where we wanted to be. Don't forget, everyone was starving back then during the Depression, but we were eating in Hollywood." Penny Singleton, a supporting actress in this film, appeared in several other productions in 1938 and ended the year by playing the lead in **Blondie**, 1938, which led to her becoming a star after she made that role her own and continued in that role in the ongoing delightful comedy series during the 1940s. **p**, Samuel Bischof; **d**, Lloyd Bacon; **cast**, Humphrey Bogart, George Brent, Gloria Dickson, Allen Jenkins, Walter Abel, Henry O'Neill, Penny Singleton, Oscar O'Shea, Anthony Averill, Fay Helm, Elliott Sullivan, Vera Lewis, John Ridgely; **w**, Robert Rosson, Leonardo Bercovici, (not credited) Warren Duff, Mark Hellinger; **c**, Arthur Edeson; **m**, Adolph Deutsch; **ed**, James Gibbon; **art d**, Esdras Hartley.

Radio Days ★★★★ 1987; U.S.; 88m; Orion Pictures; Color; Comedy/Drama; Children: Unacceptable (MPAA: PG); **DVD**; **VHS**. Allen provides a poignant and memorable recalling of another era, the days of his youth, when the airways were filled with the mostly pleasant sounds of radio and not the traumatic images of television. Allen narrates this amusing and thoroughly entertaining stroll into the past of the 1930s and 1940s, his most cherished recollected years of youth, and where he seamlessly intersperses the great music of those periods with a wonderful kaleidoscope of characters, based upon family members. In various episodes, we see Green (Allen) as a boy longing for a decoder ring while daydreaming about movie stars and an attractive substitute teacher who flits in and out of his life. He lives with his good-hearted Jewish-American family at Rockaway Beach, and he recalls through his innocent youth the aspirations of young hopefuls. We see his Aunt Bea, movingly played by Wiest, who seems doomed to never find the man of her heart in her desperate quest for elusive love, and Farrow, an aspiring actress, who struggles to get a break on radio and become a star of the airways. Weaving in and out of the many well-constructed and related vignettes are radio news stories, such as that of a little girl who falls into a well in Pennsylvania and where the country holds its breath in waiting for her rescue (a leaf from the sensational Floyd Collins story, a man trapped in a Kentucky cave in 1925 and the desperate effort to rescue him as was reported on radio), the gossip of Hollywood buzzing from radios, and the news of the Pearl Harbor attack. Throughout we hear, as do Allen's absorbing and colorful characters, the wonderful and unforgettable music of that era (almost as if Allen had constructed this brilliant piece of nostalgia in order to showcase his fondest tunes). Like the music it offers, this film is sweet and charming as it takes the viewer down a memory lane where Mom's good cooking can almost be smelled coming

The cast of *Radio Days*, 1987.

from the kitchen and Dad's cigar smoke drifting from the den. The color photography is outstanding, capturing the flavor of the period, including the hazy bars, busy radio sound stages, all-night eateries, and rooftops where denizens-dream. This slice of Americana is a generous one from Allen, and he serves it on a large and attractive platter. Enjoy. Songs: "The Flight of the Bumblebees" (1899; Nicolai Rimsky-Korsakov), "Dancing in the Dark" (music: Arthur Schwartz; lyrics: Howard Dietz), "Chinatown, My Chinatown" (1906; music: Jean Schwartz; lyrics: William Jerome), "Let's All Sing Like the Birdies Sing" (1932; music: Tolchard Evans; lyrics: Stanley J. Damerell and Robert Hargreaves), "September Song" (1944; music: Kurt Weill; lyrics: Maxwell Anderson), "Body and Soul" (1930; music: John W. Green; lyrics: Edward Heyman, Robert Sour and Frank Eyton), "In the Mood" (1939; Joe Garland), "Radio Show Themes" (1987; Dick Hyman), "You're Getting to Be a Habit with Me" (1932; music: Harry Warren; lyrics: Al Dubin), "La Cumparsita" (1916; Matos Rodriguez), "Carioca" (1933; music: Vincent Youmans; lyrics: Gus Kahn and Edward Eliscu), "Tico Tico" (1942; music: Zequinha Abreu; lyrics: Aloysio Oliveira), "Begin the Beguine" (1935; Cole Porter); "Opus One" (1943; Sy Oliver), "Frenesi" (1939; music: A Dominguez; English lyrics: Ray Charles and S. K. Russell), "All or Nothing at All" (1940; music: Arthur Altman; lyrics: Jack Lawrence), "The Donkey Serenade" (1923; music: Rudolf Friml and Herbert Stothart; lyrics: Chet Forrest and Bob Wright), "You and I" (1941; Meredith Wilson), "Paper Doll" (1915; Johnny S. Black), "Pistol Packin' Mama" (1943; Al Dexter), "South American Way" (1939; music: Jimmy McHugh; lyrics: Al Dubin), "Mairzy Doats" (1943; Milton Drake, Al Hoffman and Jerry Livingston), "If You Are But a Dream" (1941; Moe Jaffe, Nat Bonx and Jack Fulton), "If I Didn't Care" (1939; Jack Lawrence), "I Don't Want to Walk Without You" (1941; music: Jule Styne; lyrics: Frank Loesser), "Schloff mein kind" (traditional), "Remember Pearl Harbor" (1941; music: Don Reid and Sammy Kaye; lyrics: Don Reid), "Babalu" (1941; music: Margarita Lecuona; English lyrics: S. K. Russell), "They're Either Too Young or Too Old" (1943; music: Arthur Schwartz; lyrics: Frank Loesser), "That Old Feeling" (1937; music: Sammy Fain; lyrics: Lew Brown), "Re-Lax Jingle" (1987; Dick Hyman), "(There'll Be Blue Birds Over) The White Cliffs of Dover" (1941; music: Walter Kent; lyrics: Nat Burton), "Goodbye" (1934; Gordon Jenkins), "I'm Getting' Sentimental Over You" (1932; music: George Bassman; lyrics: Ned Washington), "Lullaby of Broadway" (1934; music: Harry Warren; lyrics: Al Dubin), "American Patrol" (1891; F. W. Meacham), "Take the 'A' Train" (1941; Billy Strayhorn), "You'll Never Know" (1943; music: Harry Warren; lyrics: Mack Gordon), "One, Two, Three, Kick" (1933; music: Xavier Cugat; lyrics: Albert Stillman), "Just One of Those Things" (1935; Cole Porter), "You'd Be So Nice to Come Home To" (1943; Cole Porter), "Night and Day"

John Rogers and Ronald Colman in *Raffles*, 1930.

(1932; Cole Porter), "The Sailor's Hornpipe" (traditional), "Auld Lang Syne" (traditional). Brief nudity and mature themes prohibit viewing by children. **p**, Robert Greenhut; **d&w**, Woody Allen; **cast**, Dianne Wiest, Jeff Daniels, Kenneth Mars, Mia Farrow, Larry David, Danny Aiello, Todd Field, Kitty Carlisle, Mercedes Ruehl, Tony Roberts, Diane Keaton, William H. Macy, Allen (narrator); **c**, Carlo Di Palma; **m**, various popular song writers of the 1930s and 1940s; **ed**, Susan E. Morse; **prod d**, Santo Loquasto; **art d**, Speed Hopkins; **set d**, Leslie Bloom, Carol Joffe.

Raffles ★★★★ 1930; U.S.; 72m; Samuel Goldwyn Company/UA; B/W; Crime Drama; Children: Unacceptable; **VHS**. Colman fascinates in his performance of the slick A. J. Raffles, gentleman cricket player at day and cat burglar at night. Playing a cat-and-mouse game with Scotland Yard, Colman consistently burglers the homes of the wealthy, making off with cash and rare jewels, reveling in the name he is given, the "Amateur Cracksman." He meets and falls in love with socialite Francis, who invites him to an upscale social affair in the country where he hobnobs with the social elite, his hosts being aristocrats Kerr and Skipworth. Scotland Yard inspector Torrence also attends this soiree, believing that his prey is the charming Colman, but he must wait for the suave and sophisticated crook to make the first move. Colman is not unaware of Torrence's suspicions, but he is determined to steal a priceless necklace owned by Skipworth so that he can financially aid Fletcher, a close friend who is bordering on the suicidal for lack of funds. While romancing Francis at Skipworth's country estate, the clever Colman finds enough time to slip into Skipworth's boudoir, but, as he is about to filch the coveted necklace, another thief, Rogers, beats him to it and takes the necklace. Colman, however, recoups the necklace while Rogers is left holding an empty bag and is also arrested by Torrence and taken away. Colman goes to Fletcher and gives him the necklace, allowing him to return the priceless heirloom in order to receive a sizeable reward that ameliorates Fletcher's debts. Meanwhile, Torrence, realizing that he has been hoodwinked in arresting the wrong man, Rogers, goes after Colman. The master jewel thief, however, escapes the clutches of Scotland Yard by slipping into a large grandfather clock in his residence, one that leads to a secret passageway and his freedom. Once outside the residence, Colman blithely walks through a bevy of Scotland Yard detectives, free to take Francis to Paris where he plans to continue that promising romance. Well directed and enacted by the entire cast, this polished production sees sumptuous sets, stunning costumes and a taut script offering plenty of suspense and excitement, as well as a lot of witty dialog and humorous scenes. Colman, who had scored big with the public as an indefatigable detective in **Bulldog Drummond**, 1929, won another great audience with his charismatic performance of the noble-minded thief. He would not again play that rascally thief, but he would reprise his character of Hugh Drummond in **Bulldog Drummond Strikes Back**, 1934. *Author's Note*: This was the first sound version of the enormously popular novel by Hornung, which had been published in 1899 and adapted for the theater in 1903, the first film version being produced as a silent in 1914 and starring John Barrymore. It was produced as another silent in 1925, starring House Peters. This version, released in 1930 in the U.S., was made as both silent and sound productions. Its producer, Goldwyn, believed that sound films would soon replace the silent movies and he heavily invested in sound equipment and hired sound technicians for his next films, closing his door on the silent era. "**Raffles** was the perfect picture to start with for sound," Goldwyn told this author. "It starred an actor with one of the most wonderful-sounding male voices ever recorded and that was Ronald Colman. Every male actor was jealous of that voice and every woman in the world swooned when listening to it. When **Raffles** had its premiere, we had people sign cards with their comments on them. One woman wrote: 'When I listened to Mr. Colman speak in **Raffles**, I closed my eyes and felt that he was standing next to me and softly talking into my ear. Listening to his voice was thrilling. I will remember that voice as long as I live, even though my husband is very angry about that.' We got a lot of cards with the same kind of remarks from female viewers, so Ronald Colman was well on his way into the talkies." **p**, Samuel Goldwyn; **d**, George Fitzmaurice; **cast**, Ronald Colman, Kay Francis, Bramwell Fletcher, Frances Dade, David Torrence, Alison Skipworth, Frederick Kerr, John Rogers, Wilson Benge, Virginia Bruce; **w**, Sidney Howard (based on the novel *Raffles, The Amateur Cracksman* by E.W. Hornung, and the play of the same name by Eugene Wiley Presbrey); **c**, George Barnes, Gregg Toland; **ed**, Stuart Heisler; **art d**, William Cameron Menzies, Park French.

Raffles ★★★ 1939; U.S.; 72m; Howard Productions/UA; B/W; Crime Drama; Children: Unacceptable; **VHS**. Niven admirably reprises the role Ronald Colman made famous in the 1930 production about the charming rogue, who is a famous cricket player by day and a jewel thief by night. Director Wood faithfully follows the 1930 script to show how Niven consistently outwits Scotland Yard detective Digges, who is in dogged pursuit of him, although he is never able to secure enough evidence to put the wily Niven behind bars. Niven almost gives himself away when he loses his heart to socialite de Havilland (playing the role essayed by Kay Francis in 1930). He accepts her invitation to a social bash at a country estate where the hosts are the wealthy Whitty and Pape, and Niven resolves to steal Whitty's priceless necklace, planning to return it. His cat burglary routines make up an exciting if not dangerous game for Niven, who risks all in order to fool Digges, his ardent pursuer, in a game of wits. Niven does not steal for profit, only to acquire items and then return them, to prove that he is smarter than Scotland Yard. Digges is on hand at that social gathering, waiting for Niven to make the mistake that will allow him cuff him, but Niven again outwits him, putting the blame on a real thief while still pocketing the necklace. He gives it to Walton, who is de Havilland's financially strapped brother and who returns that necklace, receiving a sizeable reward that enables him to retire his debts. Digges is once more left standing out in the cold, and Niven then proceeds to romance de Havilland while promising to reform his errant ways (perhaps). *Author's Note*: Niven had made more than twenty films before appearing in this film, telling this author that "**Raffles** was the first picture where I got top billing, but I had to fight for that billing with Sam Goldwyn because we were, just before that production, in negotiating the renewing of my contract with him. At one point, he threatened to put Dana Andrews in the leading role of **Raffles** instead of me, but I kept to my guns and he gave me what I wanted. You could always negotiate with Sam, and even come out on top a little bit. He was a softie at heart, God love him." Niven, although he had achieved stardom, enlisted in the British armed services after making this film, serving his country, England, which was then at war, and, during a six-year hiatus from the screen, except for two propaganda films, **Spitfire**, 1942, and **The Way Ahead**, 1944, did not return to the screen until appearing in **Stairway to Heaven**, 1946, where he played the leading role. He was still a star and remained so until his death in 1983. **p**, Samuel Goldwyn; **d**, Sam Wood; **cast**, David Niven, Olivia de Havilland, Dame May Whitty, Dudley Digges, Douglas Walton, E.E. Clive, Lionel Pape, Peter Godfrey, Margaret Seddon, James Finlayson; **w**, John Van Druten, Sidney Howard, (not credited) F. Scott Fitzgerald (based on the novel *Raffles, The Amateur Cracksman* by E.W. Hornung, and the play of the same name by Eugene Wiley Presbrey); **c**, Gregg Toland; **m**, Victor Young; **ed**, Sherman Todd; **art d**, James Basevi; **set d**, Julia Heron.

Rage at Dawn ★★★ 1955; U.S.; 87m; RKO; Color; Western; Children: Unacceptable; **DVD**; **VHS**; **IV**. Scott is a special agent assigned by the Peterson Detective Agency in Chicago to track down an infamous gang of train robbers led by the Reno Brothers (Tucker, Naish, and Healey) who are terrorizing Indiana in 1866 by looting, burning, and killing in the process of robbing trains. Scott poses as a bank robber to gain their confidence, but complicates matters by falling in love with their sister, Powers, who is not part of the gang but, out of family loyalty, merely keeps house for the outlaws in their home base at Seymour, Indiana. Also, the brothers have paid off crooked local politicians so they can get away with their robberies and escape the law. Scott manages to entrap the brothers in a train robbery he has planned. The brothers are put in jail, but an angry mob lynches them before they can be brought to trial. This well-made western sees good performances from Scott, Tucker, Naish, Powers and the rest of the cast and presents a strong anti-mob violence message, a subject treated in detail in the classic **The Ox-Bow Incident**, 1943. Violence prohibits viewing by children. *Author's Note*: The Reno Brothers and their accomplices were the first to rob trains during peacetime in the U.S. Scott told this author that "the production people and the scriptwriter for that picture spent a great deal of time researching the background of the members of the actual Reno Gang, who were shown in that picture. I play an agent who goes undercover to expose the gang and its operations, working for a detective agency called Peterson. It was really the Pinkerton Detective Agency that went after the gang, but, because the gang members wound up being lynched instead of imprisoned, that agency was blamed for their unlawful deaths, so the Pinkerton Agency did not want its name used in the picture. That's why the name was changed." For details on the Reno Gang, see my book, *Encyclopedia of Western Lawmen and Outlaws* (Paragon House, New York, 1992). **p**, Nat Holt; **d**, Tim Whelan; **cast**, Randolph Scott, Forrest Tucker, Mala Powers, J. Carrol Naish, Edgar Buchanan, Myron Healey, Howard Petrie, Ray Teal, Denver Pyle, Dennis Moore; **w**, Horace McCoy (based on a story by Frank Gruber); **c**, Ray Rennahan; **m**, Paul Sawtell; **ed**, Harry Marker; **art d**, Walter Keller.

Raggedy Ann & Andy; A Musical Adverture ★★★ 1977; U.S.; 84m; International Telephone & Telegraph/FOX; Color; Animated Comedy; Children: Acceptable (MPAA: G); **DVD**; **VHS**. Williams is a little girl who spends a lot of time telling her dolls stories, and those cute and colorful tales come to vivid life in this entertaining film. Raggedy Ann (Conn voiceover) and Andy (Baker voiceover) look inside a package that has arrived in their playroom and find a beautiful French doll, Babette (Flacks voiceover). A pirate captain (Irving voiceover) falls in love with and kidnaps Babette, flying out a window. Conn and Baker get into many fascinating adventures before they finally rescue Babette. Songs: "I Look, and What Do I See?," "No Girl's Toy," "I'm Just a Rag Doll/Poor Babette/A Miracle," "The Pirate Song," "Candy Hearts and Paper Flowers," "Blue," "Camel's Mirage," "I Never Get Enough," "Because I Love You," "It's Not Easy Being King When You're Short," "Hooray for Me," "You're My Friend," "I'm Home" (Joe Raposo). **p**, Richard Horner, Stanley Sills; **d**, Richard Williams; **cast**, Claire Williams and (voiceovers) Didi Conn, Mark Baker, Fred Stuthman, Niki

Sissy Spacek and Eric Roberts in *Raggedy Man*, 1981.

Flacks, George S. Irving, Arnold Stang, Joe Silver, Alan Sues, Marty Brill, Paul Dooley; **w**, Patricia Thackray, Max Wilk (based on stories and characters created by Johnny Gruelle); **c**, Dick Mingalone, Al Rezek (Panavision; DeLuxe Color); **m**, Joe Raposo; **ed**, Harry Chang, Lee Kent, Ken McIlwaine, Maxwell Seligman; **prod d**, Cornelius "Corny" Cole; **art d**, William Mickley; **spec eff**, Lisa Atkinson.

Raggedy Man ★★★ 1981; U.S.; 94m; UNIV; Color; Drama; Children: Unacceptable (MPAA: PG); **DVD**; **VHS**. Spacek gives an exceptional performance as a divorced young woman, who is the mother of two small boys, Thomas and Hollis Jr. She goes to work as a telephone company switchboard operator in a small Texas town during World II in 1944. The little family lives in the office building where Spacek works day and night. Sanderson and Walter, two local drunks, want to have their way with her, but she and her boys are befriended by Shepard, a facially disfigured homeless rag man, and he scares off the drunks. One evening, Roberts, a handsome sailor, arrives while on a four-day furlough, hitchhiking to his home in Oklahoma. Spacek and Roberts fall in love, but, when Roberts' furlough is up, he leaves, so Sanderson and Walter try once more to seduce Spacek. This time Shepard nearly kills them. He is really her husband and father of the boys, but does not reveal that and continues to remain close to Spacek and the boys to look after their safety, symbolically representing the raggedy men or scarecrows farmers erect in their fields to scare off predatory or hungry birds. Fisk directs this compelling film with a firm hand, and Shepard renders a strong and compelling performance as the disfigured and socially disenfranchised raggedy man. Songs: "Rum and Coca Cola" (Lord Invader, Lionel Belasco), "The Lady's in Love With You" (Frank Loesser, Burton Lane). Sexuality prohibits viewing by children. **p**, Burt Weissbourd, William D. Wittliff; **d**, Jack Fisk; **cast**, Sissy Spacek, Eric Roberts, Sam Shepard, William Sanderson, Tracey Walter, R.G. Armstrong, Henry Thomas, Carey Hollis, Jr., Ed Geldart, Bill Thurman; **w**, Wittliff; **c**, Ralf Bode (Technicolor); **m**, Jerry Goldsmith; **ed**, Edward Warschilka; **art d**, John Lloyd; **set d**, Hal Gausman; **spec eff**, Russ Hessey.

Raging Bull ★★★★★ 1980; U.S.; 129m; Chartoff-Winkler Productions/UA; B/W; Biographical Drama/Sports Drama; Children: Unacceptable (MPAA: R); **BD**; **DVD**; **VHS**. In what is inarguably De Niro's finest performance (for which he won an Oscar as Best Actor), this sterling actor not only plays World Middleweight Champion Jake La Motta (1921-), but chillingly exposes in that bravura performance the ruthless and topsy-turvy mind-set of this driven man, an Italian-American born and raised in the Bronx, New York. This is not a film for children, the weak of heart or those with squeamish stomachs as director Scorsese provides a scathing indictment of professional boxing, which, by any

Robert De Niro as prizefighter Jake La Motta in *Raging Bull*, 1980.

other name, is a decided blood sport, and does not spare or stint on savage beatings where flesh welts and blood gushes before the viewer's eyes. De Niro is shown early in his career as a promising middleweight in 1941, where he routinely wins every bout, quickly dispatching his opponents with powerful blows from both left and right hands (La Motta was dazzlingly effective with the jab, uppercut and right and left crosses). He is not merely a prizefighter, but a destroyer of men, a boxer who pounds his adversaries into submission with a strange and inexplicable vengeance that seethes with hate if not malevolence (and was nicknamed "The Raging Bull," ergo the title of this film). His manager is Pesci, his own brother, Joey La Motta (1925-), who is also his sparring partner and closest confidantt. Though he is married to Saldana, De Niro is forever leaving her at home alone and carousing through sleazy nightclubs and dance halls with Pesci, always on the alert for any stray attractive females, a lifestyle that causes Saldana to shriek curses and vile epithets at him. They do not have a happy marriage. When De Niro spots the tall, blonde Moriarty at a public pool (where she is conversing with several Mafia goons), he has Pesci arrange to have Moriarty accompany him for a drive in his new convertible. Moriarty, who plays Bronx-born Vikki La Motta (Beverly Thailer; 1930-2005), soon becomes enamored of the aggressive and dominating De Niro, who takes her to his apartment and, while his wife is absent, has sex with her. They later marry, Moriarty becoming De Niro's second wife, but she lives in apprehension of his brutish nature and worries about his intense jealousy whenever she speaks to another man. Pesci also goes out of his way to shield the sexy Moriarty from the Mafia thugs who infest the nightclubs she attends and, in one instance, when he finds Moriarty at a table with Mafia sub-boss Vincent and others, he attacks Vincent, savagely breaking Vincent's arm, before battling him and other Mafioso down the stairs of the second-floor club to the outside and where he continues to batter these goons. Pesci, who made a film career of playing tough characters and psychopathic killers, such as the wannabe Mafia member in **Goodfellas**, 1990, is just as violent a man as De Niro in this shuddering film. Meanwhile De Niro begins a series of fights with the only other middleweight contender for the crown, Barnes, who plays Sugar Ray Robinson (1921-1989; who was former Welterweight Champion when he first met La Motta in their match at New York's Madison Square Garden, which La Motta lost). The two fighters would see five fights together. By this time, De Niro is yearning to fight for the championship, but he believes that the only way that fight will be set is through the crooked operations of the Mafa. Although the Mafia has attempted many times to woo De Niro into its camp, he has resisted the temptation of taking money from Mafia don Colasanto and keeps his record clean. He finally succumbs, however, on the promise that, if he throws a fight so that Mafia dons can win on that fixed match, he will be promised a shot at the champi-

onship title with Champion Middleweight and French boxer Marcel Cerdan (1916-1949), who is played by Raftis. In that thrown fight, De Niro, although his opponent hardly puts up any kind of battle, pretends to be hit hard and knocked down and out (the only time he has been floored up to this time), losing the bout. He is so upset at having discarded his closely guarded ethics, however, that he weeps openly in his dressing room, and Pesci and his trainer tell him that it is not worth it and he should hang up his gloves. (The thrown fight occurred on November 14, 1947, when Billy Fox ostensibly knocked La Motta out in the fourth round; La Motta later admitted that he had thrown the fight.) Since authorities cannot determine that De Niro has actually thrown the match, he continues fighting, winning his bouts straightforwardly and this time, he is allowed a shot at the championship title by being matched with Cerdan (Raftis), ostensibly the match arranged through Colasanto's influence. Before that fight, De Niro is shown with Pesci, Moriarty and his trainer in a Detroit hotel suite where De Niro becomes abrasive with his wife. When Colasanto arrives to wish De Niro well in his forthcoming championship fight, he sees Moriarty give Colasanto a kiss (on the cheek, more social than passionate). De Niro, who is insanely jealous of Moriarty, upbraids her for such conduct, humiliating her before others when he slaps her face and then goes into a bedroom, slamming the door behind him. De Niro has earlier beaten a ring opponent to a pulp after Moriarty made a passing remark that that opponent was a handsome young man, such is his jealousy about his attractive wife. De Niro and Cerdan (Raftis) meet and battle for the title on June 16, 1949, and De Niro brutally manhandles the champion, knocking Raftis down in the first round (Cerdan actually dislocated an arm during the knockdown, which incapacitated him for the remainder of the fight). By the tenth round, Raftis is unable to continue the fight and the title goes to De Niro. As champion, De Niro becomes idle, grows fat and refuses to train. He obsesses about his voluptuous wife, accusing Moriarty of sleeping not only with others, but with his own brother, Pesci. In a wild fight, Moriarty angrily and mockingly (without sincerity) tells De Niro that she has not only slept with everyone he names, but spitefully cites her sexual acts with these persons. These remarks send De Niro over the brink and he not only beats Moriarty, but storms out of his house and goes to Pesci's nearby residence, barging into the dining room where Pesci is eating with his family and viciously attacks his brother, beating him senseless before departing. After ruining his family relationships, De Niro goes on to fight more bouts, but now faces his old nemesis, Barnes (Robinson), who, in their fifth match together, soundly beats De Niro so that his face is left with a bloody mask, although Barnes is unable (as was Robinson) to knock down the obstinate De Niro, who loses the title to Barnes. De Niro has also lost Moriarty, who has divorced him (Vikki La Motta divorced Jake La Motta in 1957 after eleven years of marriage that produced three children). De Niro, grown fat, is next seen managing a modest bar in Florida, where he acts as a stand-up comedian, telling terrible jokes that few laugh at and posturing as a celebrity to his back-slapping patrons. (La Motta was arrested in 1958 for allowing men to buy drinks for an underage girl; he was convicted and sent to prison, serving time on a Florida chain gang, albeit La Motta always claimed to be innocent.) At the finale, De Niro is, as he is shown at the beginning of the film, struggling to recall the lines that actor Marlon Brando, playing an ex-prizefighter, states in **On the Waterfront**, 1954, which he intends to use in his present act at a New York lounge and we hear him rattling on, mumble-mouthed, if not addle-brained, a surviving hulk from yesteryear's boxing ring, who is all but forgotten and who only listens to the cheers of the past. This memorable masterpiece from Scorsese is presented almost as a documentary, filmed in black and white, his cameras mimicking the stark news reel footage of yesteryear's fights, and where the director adeptly intersperses the fighter's personal life with his bouts in the ring. Scorsese depicts in detail and in many close-ups the savage beatings De Niro administers, as well as the ones he receives, where the faces of the fighters explode in bloody eruptions as powerful bone-crushing blows are landed in slow-motion. The violence is excessive, but necessarily so in that this is the only way in which Scorsese can truly example the violent life of his subject and the vicious, almost bestial world he inhabits. (This is not the case with some of Scorsese's other productions, such as **Gangs of New York**, 2002, or **Taxi Driver**, 1976, the latter starring De Niro, and which are so overwhelming and purposely dominated by gratuitous violence that they do not qualify for inclusion in this work.) De Niro's performance is unforgettable as a rather dim-witted prizefighter with the cretin-like personality and mentality of a street thug. Relentless violence is integral to his nature and endemic to his economic survival, and his success in the ring only exacerbates the trauma he imposes on those he ostensibly loves. He is an American Neanderthal, glorified and manipulated by gangsters and whose corruptive violence finally consumes and destroys his own life. All of the cast members, especially Pesci, Moriarty, Colasanto, and Vincent, superbly enact their unsophisticated characters to tellingly illustrate the sleazy and compromising lifestyles of their times. Chapman's crisp and sharply defined cinematography is outstanding as he captures that thumb-in-the-eye era when Americans lived more in the streets than behind locked doors and in front of TV sets, and Scorsese nostalgically underscores that period by lacing it with the plaintive sounds of that era through many memorable tunes (as can be noted from the extensive list of songs cited below), contrastingly more gentle and tender than the brutal scenes he exhibits. The sets, costumes and cars are perfect to the era, presenting an evocative image of the Forties and Fifties. The film did not see the success expected, taking in about $23 million from the box office in its initial release against a budget of $18 million. Songs: "Cavalleria rusticana: Intermezzo" (1890; Pietro Mascagni), "Guglielmo Ratcliff: Intermezzo" (1895; Pietro Mascagni), "Silvano: Barcarolle" (1895; Pietro Mascagni), "A New King of Love" (1930; Sammy Fain, Irving Kahal, Pierre Norman), "At Last" (1941; music: Harry Warren; lyrics: Mack Gordon), "Vivere" (1937; Cesare A. Bixio), "Webster Hall' (Garth Hudson), "Stornelli florentini" (1949; Cesare A. Bixio), "Turi Giuliano" (S. Bella, O. Strano), "Scapricciatiello (Infatuation)" (1956; Fernando Albano), "Cow Cow Boogie" (1941; Benny Carter, Don Raye, Gene de Paul), "Stone Cold Dead in the Market" (1946; Frederick W. Hendricks), "Whispering Grass" (1940; music: Doris Fisher; lyrics: Fred Fisher), "Till Then" (1944; Sol Marcus, Eddie Seiler, Guy Wood), "Heartaches" (1931; music: Al Hoffman; lyrics: John Klenner), "Big Noise from Winnetka" (1938; music: Ray Bauduc, Bob Haggart; lyrics: Ben Pollock, Bob Crosby), "Do I Worry" (1940; Bobby Worth, Stanley Cowan), "Drum Boogie" (1941; Gene Krupa, Roy Eldridge), "Two O'Clock Jump" (1939; Count Basie, Harry James); "All or Nothing at All" (1940; music: Arthur Altman; lyrics: Jack Lawrence), "Flash" (1939; Harry James), "Blue Velvet" (1951; music: Lee Morris; lyrics: Bernie Wayne), "Jersey Bounce" (1936; music: Bobby Plater, Tiny Bradshaw, Edward Johnson; lyrics: Bob Wright, Buddy Feyne), "Mona Lisa" (1949; Jay Livingston, Ray Evans), "Come Fly With Me" (1957; music: Jimmy Van Heusen; lyrics: Sammy Cahn), "Nao tenho lagrimas" (1937; Max Bulhoes, Milton de Oliveira), "I Ain't Got Nobody" (1915; music: Spencer Williams; lyrics: Roger Graham), "Prisoner of Love" (1931; music: Russ Columbo, Clarence Gaskill; lyrics: Leo Robin), "My Reverie" (1938; Larry Clinton; based on "Reverie," 1880, by Claude Debussy), "Frenesi" (1939; music: A Dominguez; English lyrics: Ray Charles and S. K. Russell), "Just One More Chance" (1931; music: Arthur Johnston; lyrics: Sam Coslow), "Bye, Bye, Baby" (1953; music: Jule Styne; lyrics: Leo Robin), "That's My Desire" (1947; music: Helmy Kresa; lyrics: Carroll Loveday), "Tell the Truth" (1956; Lowman Pauling), "Lonely Nights" (1955; Zell Sanders). *Author's Note*: Jake La Motta was reportedly dissatisfied with this film, despite the fact that Scorsese had faithfully shown the true events of that prizefighter's career and personal life, based on La Motta's own admissions. On the strength of the success (or notoriety) of this film, La Motta's ex-wife, Vikki La Motta, still attractive while in her early fifties, was signed by *Playboy Magazine* and where she posed nude in its pages. Many other films have

Robert De Niro in *Raging Bull,* 1980.

profiled prizefighters in and out of the ring, notably **The Abysmal Brute**, 1923; **Adventures of a Young Man**, 1962; **Against the Ropes**, 2004; **Ali**, 2001 (Muhammad Ali); **Ali: An American Hero**, 2000 (made-for-TV; Muhammad Ali); **Any Which Way You Can**, 1980 (Bare Knuckle); **April Showers**, 1923; **Behind the Rising Sun**, 1943; **The Big Man**, 1991; **Body and Soul**, 1947; **The Boxer**, 1997; **Broken Blossoms**, 1919; **Buck Privates**, 1941; **Cain and Mabel**, 1936; **Carnera: The Walking Mountain**, 2008 (Primo Carnera); **The Champ**, 1931; **The Champ**, 1979; **Champion**, 1949; **Cinderella Man**, 2005 (James J. Braddock, Max Baer); **City for Conquest**, 1940; **City Lights**, 1931; **The Crooked Circle**, 1957; **Dempsey**, 1983 (made-for-TV; Jack Dempsey); **Detective**, 1985; **Diggstown**, 1992; **Duke of Chicago**, 1949; **Every Which Way But Loose**, 1978 (Bare Knuckle); **Fat City**, 1972; **The Fighter**, 1952; **The Fighter**, 2010; **Flying Fists**, 1937; **Footlight Serenade**, 1942; **From Here to Eternity**, 1953; **From Mexico with Love**, 2009; **Gentleman Jim**, 1942 (James J. Corbett, John L. Sullivan); **Glory Alley**, 1952; **The Great John L**, 1945 (John L. Sullivan); **The Great White Hope**, 1970 (Jack Johnson); **The Greatest**, 1977 (Muhammad Ali); **Halls of Montezuma**, 1950; **The Hammer**, 2007; **Hard Times**, 1975 (Bare Knuckle); **The Harder They Fall**, 1956 (Primo Carnera); **Heart of a Champion: The Ray Mancini Story**, 1985 (made-for-TV; Ray "Boom Boom" Mancini); **Here Comes Mr. Jordan**, 1941; **Homeboy**, 1988; **How Green Was My Valley**, 1941; **The Hurricane**, 1999; **Iron Man**, 1951; **It's Always Fair Weather**, 1955; **Joe and Max**, 2002 (made-for-TV; Joe Louis, Max Schmeling); **The Joe Louis Story**, 1953; **The Kid: Chamaco**, 2010; **The Kid from Brooklyn**, 1946; **Kid Galahad**, 1937; **Kid Galahad**, 1962; **Killer McCoy**, 1947; **The Killers**, 1946; **L.A. Confidential**, 1997; **Lady and the Gent**, 1932; **Laughing Irish Eyes**, 1936; **Lionheart**, 1990 (Bare Knuckle); **The Main Event**, 1979; **Max Schmeling**, 2010; **Million Dollar Baby**, 2004; **Night and the City**, 1992; **On the Waterfront**, 1954; **Pat and Mike**, 1952; **Phantom Punch**, 2008 (Sonny Liston); **Pittsburgh**, 1942; **Play It to the Bone**, 1999; **Prison Shadows**, 1936; **The Prizefighter**, 1979; **The Prizefighter and the Lady**, 1933 (Max Baer, Primo Carnera); **The Quiet Man**, 1952; **Random Harvest**, 1942; **Requiem for a Heavyweight**, 1962; **Right Cross**, 1950; **The Ring**, 1927; **Rocky**, 1976 (and its many sequels); **The Set-Up**, 1949; **Somebody Up There Likes Me**, 1956 (Rocky Graziano); **Split Decisions**, 1988; **Strength and Honor**, 2007; **The Street With No Name**, 1948; **They Never Come Back**, 1932; **Tough Enough**, 1983; **World in My Corner**, 1956; for a more extensive listing, see Index, Volume II, under Prizefighters and Prizefighting. **p**, Irwin Winkler, Robert Chartoff; **d**, Martin Scorsese; **cast**, Robert De Niro, Cathy Moriarty, Joe Pesci, Frank Vincent, Nicholas Colasanto, Theresa Saldana, Mario Gallo, Frank Adonis, Joseph Bono, Johnny Barnes, Louis Raftis, Charles Scorsese, Martin

Mary Pickford in *Rags*, 1915.

Scorsese, John Turturro; **w**, Paul Schrader, Mardik Martin (based on the book by Jake La Motta with Joseph Carter, Peter Savage); **c**, Michael Chapman; **ed**, Thelma Schoonmaker; **prod d**, Gene Rudolf; **art d**, Alan Manser, Kirk Axtell, Sheldon Haber; **set d**, Fred Weiler, Phil Abramson; **spec eff**, Raymond Klein, Max E. Wood.

Rags ★★★ 1915 (silent); U.S.; 50m/5 reels; Famous Players Film Company/PAR; B/W; Comedy/Drama; Children: Acceptable. Pickford is endearing in this touching tale where she plays mother and daughter. As her mother, Pickford is wooed by ambitious MacDonald, who works for banker Manning, and who is also Pickford's guardian. After Manning discovers that MacDonald has been cooking the books and embezzling from his bank, he fires him, but allows him to leave the city for the sake of Pickford. MacDonald and Pickford marry and move west to a mining town, but she dies in childbirth, leaving MacDonald to fend for the child, who grows up to be Pickford, a warmhearted tomboy. MacDonald, by this time, has become a roustabout and drunk and Pickford must deal with insults and ridicule for being his daughter, but she manages to keep a smile on her face and makes the best of her miserable life. As she grows up and matures, Pickford meets and falls in love with Neilan (who would later write many scripts for Pickford's films and become one of Pickford's favorite directors). Neilan is a rich engineer, who more pities Pickford than loves her, and, unbeknownst to Pickford, is also Manning's nephew. In one of the many poignant scenes offered in this film, Pickford invites Neilan to dinner at her shack, having used up all of her resources so that she can offer him a good meal. Before Neilan arrives, however, MacDonald and some of his drunken friends stagger into the shack and devour most of the food Pickford had prepared for Neilan and herself. After discovering this awful pillaging, Pickford finds enough scraps of food to place on Neilan's plate, placing a note next to that plate that reads: "I was so hungry I just couldn't wait for you." (This memorable scene did not go unnoticed by Charles Chaplin, who would more or less duplicate it in the New Year's Eve dinner he prepares and is shown in his classic comedy **The Gold Rush**, 1925.) Meanwhile, Pickford learns that her thoroughly corrupted father plans to rob the payroll of the local mining company where Neilan works and is a partner. Pickford, who has put up with years of abuse from her father and has nevertheless defended him against town slander, can no longer tolerate MacDonald's evil doings and she goes to the sheriff, telling him about the impending robbery. The sheriff and his men confront MacDonald and his friends when they attempt to steal the payroll, and a gunfight ensues where MacDonald is fatally shot. Before he dies, the repentant MacDonald writes a letter to his former employer, Manning, in which he begs Manning to take care of "Rags," the nickname by which Pickford is known. The kindhearted Manning takes Pickford in,

making her his ward, as he had her mother, and Pickford becomes an attractive and refined young lady and, at that point, Manning summons his nephew, Neilan, who arrives to see a beautiful woman. He promptly falls in love with her and they shortly plan a life together after they go to the altar. **Rags** was an enormous success, filling the coffers of Paramount, further cementing Pickford's image as "America's Sweetheart." ***Author's Note***: When Pickford was leaving Paramount Studios in New York (most films were then being produced in that city at that time as Hollywood had not yet become the center of U.S. filmmaking) and was driving along Broadway, she saw dense lines of moviegoers waiting to purchase tickets at a theater showing **Rags**, a Paramount release, but some time later, when passing another theater showing a Paramount film that did not have Pickford in it, there were no lines waiting to buy tickets. Pickford confronted Adolph Zukor, head of Paramount, with this information and he reluctantly admitted that her films invariably saw sold-out audiences, even though Paramount doubled the price to see a Pickford film. He also admitted that Paramount saddled less popular films to Pickford's movies on a double billing (or block booking), in order to capitalize on its investment for both films. Armed with these admissions, the actress, along with her mother, Charlotte Smith Pickford, who served as her manager, later met with Zukor, demanding a new contract where Pickford would receive a substantial weekly increase in her payments from Paramount. Zukor grudgingly signed that new contract, rather than see Pickford go to another studio, such as Universal, which had recently offered to pay her $10,000 a week. Zukor stated at that time: "Mary, sweetheart, I don't have to diet. Every time I talk over a new contract with you and your mother I lose ten pounds." **p&d**, James Kirkwood; **cast**, Mary Pickford, Marshall Neilan, Joseph Manning, J. Farrell MacDonald; **w**, Frances Marion, Pickford (based on the novel by Edith Barnard Delano); **c**, Emmett A. Williams; **art d**, Jack Holden.

Ragtime ★★★★ 1981; U.S.; 155m; Sunley Productions/PAR; Color; Drama; Children: Unacceptable (MPAA: PG); **DVD**; **VHS**. Though somewhat splintered in its kaleidoscopic and episodic presentation of several stories, this well-acted and intelligently scripted film nevertheless captures with great panache many colorful and controversial events in 1906, while blending fact with fiction. The absorbing tale begins with Dourif, who lives with his sister, Steenburgen, and her husband, Olson, in a comfortable Edwardian mansion in New Rochelle, New York. Dourif is obsessed with beautiful showgirl Evelyn Nesbit (1884-1967), essayed by McGovern, giving her gifts to be in her beauteous company. She tolerates his puppy-like love, but she is married to mad millionaire Harry K. Thaw (1871-1947), played by Joy, and keeps Dourif at a distance. Thaw then disrupts Dourif's idylls with Nesbit when he shoots and kills the celebrated architect Stanford White (1853-1906), played by Mailer, over the earlier affections White had shown to Thaw's wife and former showgirl Nesbit, even though White had not seen Nesbit since she married Thaw. The murder is all the more sensational in that Joy arrogantly kills Mailer at the rooftop theater of Madison Square Garden in front of hundreds of horrified spectators. While Joy goes on trial for his killing of Mailer, his wealthy family, particularly Joy's dominating mother (Mrs. Thaw stated that she would spend $1 million or more to see her son go free), who is played by Eloise O'Brien, treats McGovern with disdain and even outright resentment, blaming her and her beauty for causing Joy's insane jealousy to burst into murder. Meanwhile, Olson, who runs a tight household where he keeps Steenburgen in tight harness, senses that all is not right with his family when Steenburgen takes in a black baby that is abandoned at her doorstep and she later hires the baby's mother, Allen, to work as a maid in her home. These actions distress Olson, as does Rollins, a black piano player who has gotten rich by playing Ragtime tunes, when he arrives with his newly purchased Model T Ford. Rollins tells Olson that he is the father of Allen's baby and wants to marry her, but Olson, an always in-control man, puts him off. Rollins returns to his car, which he has parked next to a firehouse, only to find that bigoted white firemen had vandalized the brand new-car and where he finds human feces smeared on its seats. Enraged, Rollins calls police, but, instead of arresting the vandalizing firemen, especially their racist leader, McMillan, they arrest Rollins and put him in jail. Rollins demands an attorney and Olson agrees to have him represented. While on bail, Rollins plants a bomb at the firehouse and he then invades the ornate and elegant J. P. Morgan Library with a few other blacks, all armed and wearing hoods, and where Rollins demands that his car be returned to him in mint condition and that McMillan be turned over to him so that he can administer justice to the vandal. By this time, Steenburgen has flown the coop, leaving the oppressive Olson, going to Atlantic City, where she meets and falls in love with entrepreneurial film director Patinkin, beginning an affair with him. (Steenburgen's character is one of a woman who has thrown off her marital chains and represents the early-day suffragettes that predate the women's liberation movement.) Feeling responsible for events, do-gooder Olson goes to the J. P. Morgan Library and tries to persuade Rollins to give up his radical cause, but Rollins holds him a near-willing hostage and continues his demands, threatening that he will blow up the library unless those demands are met. Olson does not know that his brother-in-law, Dourif, has joined Rollins and is disguised from him while wearing a hood. Meanwhile, Pat O'Brien, playing the flamboyant defense attorney Delphin Michael Delmas (1844-1928), asks McGovern to go the witness stand and where she is to say that Mailer, the man murdered by her husband, Joy, made unwanted advances to her and that her husband was never really mentally stable, O'Brien already preparing his defense based on insanity. McGovern is promised a substantial amount of money by Joy's mother if she cooperates. At the library, Rollins remains defiant, holding at bay a small army of police that surround the place. The esteemed black leader and educator Booker T. Washington (1856-1915), played by Gunn, goes to the library and attempts to persuade Rollins and his associates to give up their mad scheme, which Gunn describes as irrational and unreasonable, pointing out that Rollins is now breaking the law and inviting his own destruction. Rollins refuses to surrender, and Gunn sadly leaves the young man to his fate. Meanwhile, Pat O'Brien manages to persuade a jury to declare his client Joy not guilty of murdering Mailer by reason of insanity and Joy is then sent to an asylum for the criminally insane. Now that Joy's wealthy mother, Eloise O'Brien, has saved her son's life, she has no more use for his wife, McGovern, who is left a pittance of money and, having no means of support, agrees to return to the stage to tell audiences the torrid and lurid tales of her personal life. By this time, Cagney, who plays the decisive Rhinelander Waldo (1877-1927), who was, at that time, the First Deputy Commissioner of the NYPD, orders fireman McMillan to appear before him; he lambasts the bigot for creating the police confrontation with Rollins, calling McMillan "a piece of slime," and menacingly threatens to turn over McMillan to Rollins, which terrifies the fireman into admitting that he and his fellow fireman did, indeed, vandalize Rollins' car. Cagney, however, realizes that he must do his duty and he demands that Rollins surrender under the promise that his fellow blacks inside the library will be allowed to go free. Rollins, to save his supporters from harm and imprisonment, finally decides to relent and, after his associates flee the library, he steps forth to surrender, only to be shot dead by policemen, this action against Cagney's wishes, and that is where this fascinating, extravagant and somewhat unrealistic film ends. Forman, a gifted and skilled director, does a herculean job in balancing the many divergent stories and merges and meshes them with clever visual segues. Cagney, though he appears briefly, is his old dynamic and captivating self as an official confronted with an impossible dilemma, and Rollins is dynamically convincing as the idealistic but misguided black activist defying a rigid Edwardian age with tactics that can only assure his doom. Olson, Dourif and Steenburgen are perfectly anemic as is called for by their bloodless, fickle characters, the former two clinging to the clichés of their day and the latter pursuing happiness at any hazard, an altruistic and decidedly far-afield

James Cagney in *Ragtime,* 1981.

female ambition in a day when most women still opted for the comforts and security of home, irrespective of the dictatorial conditions accompanying such security. McGovern is empathetic as a pawn in a sensational murder case, as was the actual position of the real Evelyn Nesbit, and Joy is effective as the lunatic Thaw. The cinematography, sets, costumes and props all marvelously reflect that gentler age of parasols and winged collars. Forman makes a great effort to authenticate the story by presenting many real-life persons, along with the tale's stranger fictional characters, and where the viewer sees, in addition to Thaw, Nesbit, White, Washington and Waldo, such distinguished actual persons as President Theodore Roosevelt (1858-1919), played by Boyd; Vice President Charles Warren Fairbanks (1852-1918), played by Carlin; J. P. Morgan (1837-1913), played by Bisset; and even famed magician Harry Houdini (1874-1926), played by DeMunn. The film received eight Oscar nominations, including those for McGovern (Best Supporting Actress), Rollins (Best Supporting Actor), and Newman (Best Original Score), this being Newman's first score for a feature film. The film grossed a little more than $1 million at the box office in its initial release. Song: "One More Hour" (1981; Randy Newman). *Author's Note*: This was the last film in which Cagney and O'Brien appeared, both having made many films together. Cagney, who was eighty-one when he came out of retirement to make this film, was actually fifty years older than the real Waldo was at this film's 1906 setting, Waldo being only thirty years old at that time. The script, as did the Doctorow novel, takes great liberties with real-life characters and their functions in this tale are as mythical as the fictional characters cleverly woven into their historical fabrics. For extensive details on the actual Thaw case, see my work, *The Great Pictorial History of World Crime*, Volume II (History, Inc., 2004; pages 819-826). **p**, Dino De Laurentiis; **d**, Milos Forman; **cast**, James Cagney, Brad Dourif, Moses Gunn, Elizabeth McGovern, Kenneth McMillan, Pat O'Brien, Robert Joy, Donald O'Connor, James Olson, Mandy Patinkin, Howard E. Rollins Jr., Mary Steenburgen, Debbie Allen, Norman Mailer, Jeff Daniels, Eloise O'Brien, Robert Boyd, Donald Bisset, Thomas A. Carlin, Jeffrey DeMunn, Samuel L. Jackson, Bessie Love, Jack Nicholson; **w**, Michael Weller (based on the novel by E.L. Doctorow); **c**, Miroslav Ondrícek (Todd-AO; Technicolor); **m**, Randy Newman; **ed**, Anne V. Coates, Antony Gibbs, Stanley Warnow; **prod d**, John Graysmark; **art d**, Patrizia Von Brandenstein, Anthony Reading; **spec eff**, Ed Drohan, George Gibbs, Charles D. Staffell.

The Raid ★★★★ 1954; U.S.; 82m; Panoramic Productions/FOX; Color; War Drama; Children: Unacceptable; **VHS**. This tense and well-enacted Civil War tale is based on an actual event that took place on October 19, 1864, when a group of Confederate soldiers raided and robbed several banks in St. Albans, Vermont, in order to secure funds for the

Van Heflin, right, in *The Raid*, 1954.

starving Confederacy. The film opens with Heflin, a Confederate officer, escaping with some of his men from a Union prison camp. They flee to Canada where Heflin meets with Confederate agents, who supply him and his men with cash and provisions, and they plan a daring raid at St. Albans, Vermont, which is only fifteen miles from the Canadian border. Heflin arrives in St. Albans in the disguise of a Canadian businessman, where he stays as a paying boarder in the home of Bancroft, an attractive widow. Her son, Rettig, befriends Heflin and he treats the boy with kindness and compassion, almost becoming a surrogate father while he secretly scouts the town and cases its three banks, all of which are fat with gold and cash. While Bancroft warms toward Heflin because of his considerate attitude toward her son, she draws the ire of another boarder, Boone, a Union officer, who has lost an arm in the war. Boone is also one of her boarders, a deeply embittered veteran, who is in love with Bancroft and is jealous of the friendly attentions Bancroft shows to Heflin. Meanwhile, Heflin makes arrangements to purchase a nearby vacant ranch, which is used as a hiding place by his Confederates, all experienced cavalry troopers, where those men gather as Heflin organizes the raid to be made against the St. Albans' banks. The money taken from those banks is earmarked for the Confederacy, which is losing the war and desperately needs funds to continue its almost Lost Cause. The Rebels, all wearing civilian clothes, have also brought along many four-ounce bottles of Greek fire, a highly flammable liquid (made from saltpeter) with which to burn down the town after robbing its banks. Meanwhile, Heflin ingratiates himself with the residents of the town, and he attends social functions with Bancroft, much to the dislike of Boone. While attending church with her and Rettig, the pastor of the church, Spencer, delivers a fiery sermon in which he lambasts the Confederacy, damning it for rebelling against the Union. Unknown to Heflin, Marvin, one of his men, an alcoholic who has become half-crazed by drinking some of the Greek fire and who has slipped into the church, becomes incensed at Spencer's remarks and stands up, drawing a gun as he walks toward the reverend, shouting at him with intent to kill Spencer. Stunned at seeing Marvin, Heflin, to protect the secret of his mission and his other men, pulls his own weapon and shoots and kills Marvin, becoming the town hero and Rettig's idol. A short time later, however, a column of Union cavalry arrives in St. Albans, which compels Heflin to postpone the raid. When the Federals depart, Heflin goes to his room and dons his Confederate uniform, but is discovered by Rettig, who is crushed to see that his hero is a Rebel. Heflin then joins with his men, who have come into town in small groups and then throw off long coats to reveal that they, too, are Confederate soldiers. Following Heflin's orders, some Rebels quickly rob the local banks while others hold the citizens of the town at gunpoint in the local square. Boone shows his mettle when he wages a one-man war against the Rebels by

firing at them and, after being disarmed, is placed among the group of residents in the town square, and now he has earned the respect from Bancroft and Rettig that he has so long wanted. Notified of the raid, the commander of the Union cavalry returns to St. Albans, but his column is held up by the town citizens, who have been forced by the Rebels to block the road while Heflin and his men toss bottles of Greek fire into the town buildings to set them afire and then ride away. As the town residents scatter, the Union cavalry pursues, but Heflin and his men burn the bridge across a roaring river that prevents pursuit, and then safely ride back into Canada. Firm direction from Fregonese and inventive lensing from Ballard provides a taut tale packed with suspense and well-choreographed action, and Heflin, Bancroft, Boone, Rettig and Marvin, as well as the rest of the cast, are standouts in their roles. The film was made on a budget of $650,000. *Author's Note*: Heflin never had any illusions about becoming a leading man. When once encountered by Louis B. Mayer, boss of MGM, Mayer brutally told him that he did not possess the good looks to be a romantic lead, adding: "You will never get the girl at the end [of a film]." Heflin told this author that "I never forgot what Mayer said, and he was right, so I figured I had better concentrate on acting instead of wooing any leading lady. I did not get the beautiful Anne Bancroft at the end of **The Raid**, but my character's purpose is noble enough to gain her respect and that's about as close to being loved by a leading lady I ever got." Marvin, then a supporting player before becoming a leading man, told this author that "I play another nutcase in **The Raid**, a guy who craves booze so much that he drinks an inflammable liquid designed to burn down buildings, which sets my brain on fire and gets me killed after I go berserk in a church. I like drinking, always have, but I would never gulp down any kind of swill like that and I did not think my character would either. I told the director about that and he only patted me on the back and said: 'He's not all there, Lee. Your character will drink anything.'" The actual raid that took place in St. Albans in 1864 was conducted as a reprisal for the burning of Atlanta, Georgia, by troops commanded by Union General William T. Sherman (1820-1891), and where the twenty-one Confederate raiders, led by Lieutenant Bennett H. Young (1843-1919), netted more than $200,000 from the three banks they robbed. The raiders attempted to burn down the town before fleeing, and used Greek fire to set ablaze its buildings, but only a shed was destroyed. A townsman was killed and another wounded during the raid. Canadian authorities detained the raiders after they arrived in that country, but later released them, returning $88,000 of the stolen money to U.S. authorities that had been found on the raiders, the balance never recovered, thought to have been passed on to secret Rebel agents in Canada before the raiders were rounded up. Young, the leader of the raid, did not qualify for amnesty and, following the war, went to Ireland. He was permitted to return to his native Kentucky in 1868 where he practiced law, becoming a leading citizen and established the first orphanage for black children in Louisville, Kentucky, as well as supporting a school for the blind. He remains one of the state's leading citizens. Youngstown, Kentucky, was named after him. **p**, Robert L. Jacks, Leonard Goldstein; **d**, Hugo Fregonese; **cast**, Van Heflin, Anne Bancroft, Richard Boone, Lee Marvin, Tommy Rettig, Peter Graves, Will Wright, James Best, Douglas Spencer, Lee Aaker, Claude Akins, John Dierkes, Paul Cavanagh, Helen Ford, William Schallert, Kermit Maynard; **w**, Sydney Boehm (based on the story by Francis Cockrell, from the article "Affair at St. Albans" by Herbert Ravenal Sass); **c**, Lucien Ballard (Technicolor); **m**, Roy Webb; **ed**, Robert Golden; **art d**, George Patrick; **set d**, Glen Daniels.

The Raiders ★★★ 1963; U.S.; 75m; Revue Studios/UNIV; Color; Western; Children: Unacceptable; **DVD**. Keith, a former colonel in the Confederate army, is the head of a group of seven West Texas cattle ranchers who are poverty stricken after the U.S. Civil War (1861-1865) and attempt to drive their herds to the rail-head at Hays City, Kansas. Along the way, at the borders of the Six Nations Indian country in the Territory of Oklahoma, they encounter Indian trouble. Surviving that, and now convinced that they must have an extension to the rail line into Texas, they continue to Hays City to demand that the railroad build that spur. The manager of the Kansas & Pacific Railroad is behind schedule in building tracks to Pueblo, Colorado, and refuses to do anything for the Texas cattlemen. They retaliate by starting a war of attrition against the railroad that brings them into conflict with James Butler "Wild Bill" Hickok (1837-1876), played by Culp, and William F. "Buffalo Bill" Cody (1846-1917), played by McMullan, who are both hired by the railroad and the U.S. Army, along with Martha "Calamity Jane" Canary (1852-1876), played by Meredith, who has an equipment-freighting contract for the railroad's construction work. Culp and McMullan try to defend the railroad's interests against those of the Texas cattlemen. Soldiers are about to intervene in a shoot-out with the ranchers, but Culp, McMullan, and Meredith save them. Keith then convinces railroad executives to build a spur line to the ranches in Texas. This well-made action western sees top-flight performances from the entire cast, although the producers play fast and loose with the actual facts concerning Hickok, Cody and Calamity Jane. For more information about Hickok and Calamity Jane, see my book *Encyclopedia of Western Lawmen and Outlaws* (Paragon House, New York, 1992). For extensive listings about films profiling Hickok, Cody and Calamity Jane, see Index, under Historical Characters, Volume II of this work. **p**, Howard Christie; **d**, Herschel Daugherty; **cast**, Robert Culp, Brian Keith, Jim McMullan, Judi Meredith, Alfred Ryder, Ben Cooper, Harry Carey Jr., Trevor Bardette, Dick Cutting, Addison Richards, Cliff Osmond, Rodolfo Acosta, Walter Woolf King; **w**, Gene L. Coon; **c**, Bud Thackery; **m**, Morton Stevens, David Buttolph; **ed**, Gene Palmer; **art d**, Alexander A. Mayer; **set d**, Robert C. Bradfield, John McCarthy, Jr.

Raiders of the Lost Ark ★★★★★ 1981; U.S.; 115m; Lucasfilm/PAR; Color; Adventure; Children: Unacceptable (MPAA: PG); **DVD**; **VHS**. Spectacular, stupendous and terrific is the best description for this masterpiece adventure film, one that offers more astounding action and mesmerizing scenes than any viewer has the right to expect or demand. This quintessential cliffhanger that wonderfully glorifies and commemorates the 1930s and 1940s action serials also provides superlative production values, a witty and humorous script, and excellent performances from the entire cast. Ford is the superhero of this unforgettable saga, undaunted by any challenge and unconquered by any foe while nobly disdaining the foibles and follies of the fairer sex, certainly a shining knight by anyone's standards, but less than a saint by virtue (or the lack of it) of his impetuous willingness to go into harm's way for the sake of a just cause. He is a dedicated college professor and archeologist named Indiana Jones, first seen as he fearlessly enters a cave-like tomb in South America (ostensibly Peru), accompanied by an undependable guide, and where they evade all of the many booby traps implanted there eons ago, including lurching tarantulas, poisoned darts activated by any light or movement and pop-up impaling spikes, so that they can arrive before an altar on which sits a golden idol. Ford scoops up this treasure with one hand while replacing it with a sack of weights he thinks is equal to the weight of the idol and then he and his guide retrace their steps, only to instantly discover that Ford has misjudged the counterbalancing weight, which has released a huge round boulder that now pursues them through the cavernous chamber as they run for their lives. As they race forward a chasm opens before them and Ford uses his whip, curling it about a rock on the other side of the chasm, allowing his guide to swing across that chasm to safety. The guide asks Ford to throw the golden treasure to him and he does, but the treacherous guide refuses to return the end of the whip to Ford so that he can save himself, racing off with the treasure. Ford, however, leaps forward, reaching the other side of the chasm, holding on with his fingertips, pulling himself to momentary safety as the enormous boulder continues to thunder after him. He races forward to see that the guide is dead, studded with poisoned darts, and he snatches the idol as he continues running, diving from the cave just ahead of the boulder that shoots harmlessly past him. Ford is then

Harrison Ford in *Raiders of the Lost Ark*, 1981.

greeted by Freeman, his arch rival in their competitive search for the world's treasures, and who demands that he turn over the idol while a small army of armed natives stand threateningly nearby, ready to spear Ford if he makes any wrong move. Turning over the idol, Ford then makes a break for the river, dodging the many spears thrown after him. He reaches the river and dives into it, desperately swimming toward a seaplane that has been waiting for him and where the pilot has already started its engines. As natives swarm to the river's shoreline and hurl spears after Ford, he reaches forward to grab and hold on to one of the plane's pontoons as the pilot sends the plane quickly up the river. Ford clambers onto the pontoon and then climbs into the plane just as it takes flight, but he is horrified to see a large snake curling about the cabin, cowering before it and shouting, "I hate snakes!" He learns that the snake is the pilot's pet, but that does not disquiet him while the pilot states ironically (in light of what Ford has just endured): "Show a little backbone, will you?" (This scene, although it has no connection to the basic plot of this film, is designed by director Spielberg to set the adventurous nature of Ford's indomitable character as was the case in the old serials Spielberg obliquely honors.) After Ford returns to his college in the U.S., he is visited by members of American intelligence, who tell him about reports they have received concerning the Ark of the Covenant, the sacred container that holds the two tablets on which are written the Ten Commandments as given by God to Moses. The agents tell Ford that Nazi agents are now searching for the Ark so that Hitler, who is obsessed with the occult, can possess and somehow use the Ten Commandments in his aim of world conquest. Ford is asked to find and obtain the Ark before the Nazis can find it and return the Ark to the U.S. where it can be protected. Ford does not believe that his mission is utterly impossible if he can acquire a hieroglyphic artifact, which, when its message is deciphered, can tell him where the Ark is hidden. To obtain that necessary medallion, Ford travels to the high mountains of Nepal, going to a saloon run by a former flame, Allen, who is still angry with Ford for having earlier deserted her, but he soothes her injured feelings since he knows she possesses the hieroglyphic medallion he is seeking. Just before Allen turns over the medallion to Ford, Lacey, leading a contingent of heavily armed Nazis, enters the saloon and begins firing at everyone and everything as these Nazis are also searching for the same clue-revealing medallion. Ford and Allen, however, dodging bullets and the fire that consumes the saloon, escape into the mountain snows and then travel to Cairo to see Rhys-Davies, an Egyptian curio dealer and one of Ford's old friends. Ford learns from Rhys-Williams that Nazis are very busy nearby at a ruins as they desperately search for a hidden treasure. Ford and Allen are later waylaid by several paid assassins, who kidnap Allen while Ford battles these death-dealing killers. In one instance, he is confronted by a towering man who brandishes a

Harrison Ford and cobra in *Raiders of the Lost Ark*, 1981.

menacing sword, but, instead of using his whip or a knife in battling this assassin, as might be expected, Ford expeditiously and perfunctorily whips out a pistol and simply shoots his foe to death. (This is the kind of visual if not grim humor that is surprisingly expressed by Spielberg throughout this utterly unpredictable film.) While scouting the ruins, Ford sees that his old foe, Freeman, is openly working with the Nazis in their desperate search for the Ark while excavating some ruins. (Here Spielberg defies chronological history in that he shows scores of German troops dressed in the uniform of the Africa Corps when WWII has not yet begun at the time set of this film, 1936, and that the Africa Corps did not arrive in North Africa until 1940 under the command of General, later Field Marshal, Erwin Rommel). Lacey, meanwhile, is shown as Allen's captor, bearing scars he received in the battle in Nepal, but Allen's fate is secondary to Ford's purpose in locating the Ark and he deciphers the message on the medallion he has gotten from Allen to locate a tomb that has already been excavated but overlooked by the Nazis. He lowers himself into this dark cavern, only to discover to his horror that the floor is moving in that it is almost completely covered by slithering, squirming snakes, the creatures he most fears in life. Lighting one torch after another to keep the snakes at bay, Ford locates and ties up the Ark, having Rhys-Davies and his men slowly lift the sacred Ark from the tomb. Just then, Freeman, along with Lacey, who has brought Allen in tow, arrives with a bevy of Nazi troops and they seize the Ark and toss Allen into the tomb where she and Ford must now fend off the snakes. Ford and Allen use up one torch after another as they desperately search for a way out while the poisonous pythons and cobras squirm closer and closer. Ford finally finds a wall through which he makes a hole to a passageway and, as the last torch burns out, they scramble from the tomb and to safety. Ford then races after the Nazis, who have loaded the Ark onto a truck. Ford leaps into the cab of the truck, knocking Nazis onto the road and causing other vehicles driven by Nazis to crash or go off the road. He is then knocked from the truck, falling in front of it, but, as it passes over him, he grabs the rear bumper and hauls himself onto its bumper and then works his way back to the cabin, throwing the last Nazi to the road. (This spectacular stunt was first enacted by Yakima Canutt in John Ford's classic western **Stagecoach**, 1939, where Canutt falls from the front of a racing stagecoach, falls beneath it and between its churning wheels, only to grab a handle at its rear when the coach passes over him and to lift himself back onto the stagecoach.) He sees Allen by the road, and picks her up and then both drive the truck through a hail of bullets. Once back in Cairo, Ford and Allen take ship on a freighter headed for the U.S., that vessel containing the Ark in its hold and where the Ark radiates a mystical light. The ship is halted in its voyage, however, by a German submarine and where the Nazis recoup the Ark, again abducting Allen in the process.

Ford stows away on the U-boat that sails to a remote island in the Aegean Sea. The Ark is taken to a protected area where Freeman thinks to test the powers of the Ark before he presents it to Adolf Hitler. Ford arrives to prevent him from doing that by threatening to blow up the Ark with a bazooka, but Freeman is confident that Ford will never really destroy such a precious and sacred treasure. He is right, as Ford surrenders and is then tied with Allen to a post to await execution. Meanwhile, Freeman gathers all of the Nazis around the Ark and, defying the ancient warning that to open the Ark is to invite death, opens the Ark and sees what appears to be a mound of sand. Ford and Allen close their eyes under Ford's direction (he knows well that ancient warning) and from the Ark emerges terrible apparitions that make up the Angels of Death, who engulf Freeman and the Nazis with a lethal cloud that reduces them to agonizing death as their flesh shreds and their bones crumble to dust. Ford and Allen are spared and Ford is later shown in Washington, D.C., where he is informed by U.S. intelligence agents that the Ark is now safe and secure in a well-protected government warehouse and we see in the last scene the Ark residing in a huge warehouse, simply as a large crate among thousands of other crates that store the world's antiquity. (This last scene by Spielberg is a respectful and nostalgic nod to the finale of the classic film, **Citizen Kane**, 1941, where the lifelong and seemingly endless collections of art and antiquity are shown in a vast warehouse in a sweeping boom shot to represent the legacy of its now deceased media mogul and chief character, Charles Foster Kane, enacted by Orson Welles, who also directed that masterpiece film.) Impossible as this outlandish and extravagant film truly is, **Raiders of the Lost Ark** is nevertheless mesmerizing, so well conceived and so convincingly portrayed in its detailed action scenes that the viewer is compelled to suspend any disbelief in its herculean tale and mythical characters. Spielberg, one of the last great film directors, uses every visual technique from the past to this production's present to achieve that eventual and everlasting impactful image. The characters are perfectly played by all cast members as the prosaic and predictable persons they enact, each decidedly a good or bad guy or girl, as was the case in all serials. Williams' score is haunting and evocative, containing the memorable "Raiders March." The film received an Oscar for Best Art Direction (Reynolds, Dilley and Ford) and for Best Film Editing (Kahn), as well as Best Visual Effects (Edlund, West, Nicholson and Johnston), and received Oscar nominations for Best Picture, Best Director (Spielberg), Best Original Score (Williams), and Best Cinematography (Slocombe). This film was a great box office success, grossing almost $390 million against a $22 million budget. Songs: "I Am the Monarch of the Sea," "A British Tar" (1878; from "H.M.S. Pinafore"; music: Arthur Sullivan; lyrics: William S. Gilbert). ***Author's Note***: Although the film was expensive to make for its day, Spielberg minimalized the importance of the production by later stating: "I made it as a B-Movie. I didn't see the film as anything more than a better made version of the Republic [Studio] serials." The film was shot on location in La Rochelle, France; Tunisia, Hawaii and in California. Stuntman Terry Leonard performed the daring stunt where Ford slips beneath the front of the moving truck that passes over him only to grab its rear bumper and haul himself upward to get back onto the truck. The road on which this truck rumbled was hollowed out at the center to allow Leonard more clearance in performing that great stunt. For some close-ups, Ford was actually dragged behind the truck and suffered some bruised ribs in the process. Ford later stated with sardonic humor that he was not worried about doing that part of the stunt because, if his contribution to that stunt as the star was truly dangerous, "they would have filmed more of the movie first," indicating that if there had been any possibility of the film's star being injured, Spielberg would have callously caught Ford on film far ahead of being injured in that stunt that might have prevented Ford from finishing the film. Ford did get ill, along with others in the cast after eating some bad food that gave them all food poisoning, but Spielberg avoided that illness by bringing along and eating his own food, an abundant supply of Spaghetti-O's. Ford was still ill from that food poisoning when

Spielberg was about to make the shot in the bazaar where the assassin confronts Ford. Too ill to perform the action written for that shot, where Ford is to use his whip to disarm the assassin, Ford suggested to Spielberg that he simply "shoot the sucker," and Spielberg seized upon that inventive thought and shot the scene that way. The stoic Ford was not the first choice to play the lead in this film. He was signed only three weeks before it went into production and only after Jeff Bridges, Nick Nolte, Tom Selleck, Jack Nicholson and several others proved unavailable to play the heroic Indiana Jones. The wardrobe department was busy on the many period costumes for this film, not the least of which was the worn-out leather jacket Ford wears. They made ten of these jackets and then spent hours scuffing, scratching and sand-boarding the jackets to make them appear as if they had been worn through innumerable revolutions, wars and harrowing adventures. The special visual effects by Edlund and others are marvels to behold and were created through inventive and masterfully executed techniques. For instance, the "angels of death" emerging from the Ark of the Covenant at the end of the film were created by filming remotely controlled mannequins underwater in slow motion through a clouded lens to present that chilling other-world image. The unique and eerie sounds permeating this film were also inventively created. The creepy sounds of the thousands of snakes filling the horrific tomb in which Ford and Allen are trapped were produced by sound designer Ben Burtt, who recorded the sound of his own fingers squiggling inside a cheese casserole, augmenting that sound by adding the noise of sponges being scraped on a rubber skateboard. In his salute to the Absurd, Spielberg went to great lengths to incorporate little bits of business that mocked his story, such as having a monkey raise its arm in a Nazi salute and, in slightly discernible monkey gibberish state "Heil Hitler." This ridiculous little scene, suggested by producer Lucas, maker of the staggering **Star Wars** series (a scene that Spielberg later said was one of his favorites) was achieved by having the monkey reach for a grape that was dangled from a fishing pole just out of camera range, a shot that took more than fifty takes before Spielberg pronounced it perfect. The monkey gibberish was provided by Frank Welker, a voice expert, who went on to provide the voiceover of Abu, the spider monkey in Disney's **Aladdin**, 1992. Had this film been made twenty years earlier it would most likely have been a miserable flop since Spielberg portrays the Nazis as little more than vicious clowns, moronic thugs more gangster-like than the well-organized and lethal military organization that brought about the deaths of millions. Living memories of the genocidal Nazis had, for Spielberg's purposes, conveniently and comfortably diminished, so that his version of the Nazis as serial menaces were tolerated and accepted by the public as oafish buffoons. Watching this film is like turning the pages of a comic book, both Spielberg and Lucas being avid readers of such published lore, which explains how the tremendous opening scene came into existence. That scene mimics a Disney comic book story where Donald Duck and his errant nephews enter a cave in search of a treasure and are confronted by the same perils that Ford faces—flying darts, a descending blade and a mammoth boulder that threatens to make them all into a duck soufflé. What was good for Disney's goose was also good for Spielberg's gander. **p**, Frank Marshall (George Lucas, Howard Kazanjian); **d**, Steven Spielberg; **cast**, Harrison Ford, Karen Allen, Paul Freeman, Ronald Lacey, John Rhys-Davies, Denholm Elliott, Alfred Molina, Wolf Kahler, Anthony Higgins, Vic Tablain, Don Fellows, William Hootkins; **w**, Lawrence Kasdan (based on a story by George Lucas, Philip Kaufman); **c**, Douglas Slocombe (Panavision; Metrocolor); **m**, John Williams; **ed**, Michael Kahn; **prod d**, Norman Reynolds; **art d**, Leslie Dilley; **set d**, Michael Ford; **spec eff**, Richard Edlund, Kit West, Bruce Nicholson, Joe Johnston.

Railroaded ★★★★ 1947; U.S.; 72m; Producers Releasing Corporation (PRC)/Eagle-Lion; B/W; Crime Drama; Children: Unacceptable; **VHS**. Ireland is chillingly outstanding in his role as a psychopathic killer in this well-made film noir entry. Detective Beaumont and others respond

Hugh Beaumont and Sheila Ryan in *Railroaded,* 1947.

to a bloody robbery of a beauty shop that has been used as a front for a gambling den and where a policeman has been killed, and Brasselle, badly disfigured in the robbery, is captured and taken to a hospital. From his hospital bed, the conniving Brasselle implicates Kelly in the robbery, but Kelly's sister, Ryan, tells Beaumont that her brother is innocent and begs the detective to probe further. When both take the investigation into the seamy areas of the city to find witnesses to the crime, they unearth one witness after another, but all have been killed, frustrating their efforts to vindicate Kelly. They finally learn that the killer is Ireland, who has been silencing witnesses to the robbery he has committed, one where he robbed the gambling parlor on behalf of the mob, but, instead of turning over the loot to the mobsters, has kept the cash for himself. Ireland is no average thug, but a cunning murderer and thief, who is in love with violence and relishes killing people. He is forever fondling and petting his gun and, to leave his murderous imprimatur at crime scenes, coats his bullets with a distinctive perfume (a clue that helps his pursuers identify him). The dogged and dedicated Beaumont, however, tracks down Ireland, trapping him in a deserted eatery, where they shoot it out and where Ireland is killed. Director Mann does a great job in maintaining suspense throughout this thriller, its simple tale dynamically cemented with a bravura performance from Ireland. *Author's Note*: Ireland told this author that "I was amazed that we got away with showing the character I played in that picture. He is just about the most perverse killer one could imagine. He is actually making love to his gun most of the time—not only a phallic symbol but an instrument of death. I mentioned to Tony [Anthony Mann] that he would not get that character past the censors, but he said 'they will stamp him okay because he gets his just deserts by being killed.' Well, that's what happened and all of my purring and petting in that offbeat crime picture stayed in." **p**, Charles F. Riesner; **d**, Anthony Mann; **cast**, John Ireland, Sheila Ryan, Hugh Beaumont, Jane Randolph, Ed Kelly, Charles D. Brown, Clancy Cooper, Peggy Converse, Hermine Sterler, Keefe Brasselle, Ellen Corby; **w**, John C. Higgins (based on a story by Gertrude Walker); **c**, Guy Roe; **m**, Alvin Levin; **ed**, Louis H. Sackin; **art d**, Perry Smith; **set d**, Robert P. Fox, Armor Marlowe; **spec eff**, George J. Teague.

Rain ★★★ 1932; U.S. 94m; Feature Productions/UA; B/W; Drama; Children: Unacceptable; **DVD**; **VHS**. Crawford is mesmerizing as that shady lady, Sadie Thompson, in Maugham's tale of sex and salvation and where Huston, as a religious zealot, also provides a shuddering and memorable performance. After a deadly disease breaks out on a tramp steamer, the ship makes an unscheduled stop at Pago Pago in the Samoan Islands. Crawford, one of its passengers, disembarks, her tight skirt and curvaceous body attracting the ogling eyes of many of the U.S. soldiers stationed on that island, particularly Gargan, a rather naïve ser-

Joan Crawford as Sadie Thompson in *Rain*, 1932.

geant, who thinks Crawford is upright and clean, oblivious to her street-walking character and tawdry background. Crawford jokes with the soldiers, but her teasing behavior is interpreted as sexually suggestive by missionaries Huston and his wife Bondi, both Old Testament fanatics and who lecture anyone who will listen (most will not) about the shoddy morals of mankind. Crawford enrages Huston with her taunts and defiance until he threatens to have her deported to San Francisco where she might face imprisonment for an unspecified criminal act, one that Crawford denies having committed. Huston tells Crawford that if she gives up her sinful way of living and reforms, confessing all of her sins to him, she will not only receive his blessing, but support in making a better life. Crawford continues to resist repentance and remorse for her notorious past behavior and further angers Huston when answering him with wisecracks. Gargan then discovers that the woman of his dreams has had a shadowy and unsavory history, but he forgives that, telling her that she can have a much better way of life if she marries him. Meanwhile, the incessant rain beats down on rooftops and walkways, its noise mixing with drums and chants coming from the natives, their incantations sent to their pagan gods. All of this unnerves Crawford, who finally relents and confesses all to Huston, who tells her to go her way and sin no more, but, hypocrite that he is, Huston himself is jarred by the endless rain and the jungle drums, all of which brings to the surface his own deep and suppressed lust for Crawford. He goes to her room to find her face scrubbed clean of the heavy makeup and mascara that has ordinarily adorned that face and she wears a plain dress, an image that goes with her newly found salvation through Huston's spiritual efforts. Huston, however, is no longer concerned with saving Crawford's soul, but is all consumed by Crawford's former sexual allure as he attacks and rapes her. Crawford's newly acquired religious beliefs are destroyed by Huston's bestial conduct and she emerges from her room the next morning wearing her old come hither attire and wearing heavy makeup, resorting to her old way of life and where her previous cynicism and jaded perspective of life is back in full force. When she is informed that Huston has committed suicide, she exhibits no sorrow or pity. Gargan, not knowing of Crawford's horrible experience, meets with her just before she is about to depart the island and proposes marriage, promising her that she and he will make a home together in Australia. Crawford, instead of discarding all hope for a better future, grasps for that last straw of happiness and agrees as she leaves with Gargan for Sydney, Australia. Though Milestone does a fine job in faithfully following the stage version of the story, which was a smash hit, the public did not respond well to this film, shocked to see a glamorous film star depicted as a sleazy streetwalker. Most critics demeaned **Rain** as a production that cheapened Crawford's reputation and one that also depreciated if not condemned religious leaders as bigoted hypocrites, as manifested in

Huston's powerful performance. Fundamentalism in the U.S. in those days of the Depression was at high tide, and the religious community also condemned the film. The story had been made as a silent, **Sadie Thompson**, 1928, with Gloria Swanson as the leading lady, Lionel Barrymore as the religious zealot and Raoul Walsh as the sergeant. It was remade as **Miss Sadie Thompson**, 1953, with Rita Hayworth as Sadie, Jose Ferrer as the preacher and Aldo Ray as the fun-loving sergeant. Songs: "St. Louis Blues" (1914; W. C. Handy), "Wabash Blues" (1921; music: Fred Meinken; lyrics: Dave Ringle). *Author's Note*: **Rain** was shot on location at Catalina Island (twenty-six miles off the Southern California coast), which provided the tropical setting for the story, but the production was hampered by many problems, chiefly dealing with the cast. Milestone told this author that "Joan [Crawford] made life not only difficult for me but for herself when we did that picture together. She had deep reservations about playing Sadie Thompson, believing that the role of the tart would injure her reputation. Joe Schenck [producer of this film] convinced Joan to leave MGM briefly to make the picture and Joe was the boss of most of Hollywood, including MGM and a lot of studios because he and his brother Nick [Nicholas Schenck] controlled most of the distribution of pictures in all the major theaters in the country. Well, she gave me trouble right from the beginning when she complained about doing rehearsals." For her part, Crawford told this author: "Lewis [Milestone] was one of those directors that want to rehearse and rehearse until you wore out the words you were to speak and that slowed down the action in any scene." She felt that the film was doomed from the beginning and that she could never match the previous performances of Sadie Thompson by Jeanne Eagels, who first played the part in the smash stage hit, and Gloria Swanson's enactment of the same role in the successful 1928 silent film version. Moreover, she and her costar, Walter Huston, did not get along well. Huston was a polished stage actor where Crawford's acting career had been established in films. Most of the supporting players were also chiefly denizens of the Broadway stage and these rather haughty thespians "gave me the cold shoulder," according to Crawford's statements to this author. "Mr. Gargan and Mr. Catlett thought that they were better than I was as actors, and, maybe, as human beings. They looked down their long noses at me as if I truly was Sadie Thompson." Crawford made a strong effort to befriend both of these actors, initiating a conversation with them while they were all sitting off-camera and waiting to enact a scene. She began talking to Gargan about her film career and he stared at her vacantly, letting her run on until he interrupted her and rather cruelly stated: "Miss Crawford—I've never seen you on the screen in my life!" Gargan at that time was enjoying considerable success, having scored big in the stage version of "The Animal Kingdom." Catlett, too, was outright insulting toward Crawford. He was by nature an acerbic, heavy-drinking and rather obnoxious person (and he played that kind of character on the stage and on the screen to the hilt). After Crawford tried to chat with Catlett, the actor, who, as usual, had belted down several stiff drinks, leaned close to her, breathing his boozy breath into her startled face and said: "Listen, fish-cake, when Jeanne Eagels died, **Rain** died with her!" Milestone later commented: "Gargan and Catlett were just awful to Joan, driving her to her cabin and where she locked herself in and played Bing Crosby records all hours of the night, which caused a lot of the crew and cast members to come to me with complaints about all that crooning in the middle of the night, but I told them that that was not my problem and to live with it." Crawford became so hostile to everyone that one day she told Milestone that she would not perform any more scenes while visitors were allowed on the set, a custom that had been tolerated up to that time. Milestone then delayed the production while he shielded the set with large black drapes that prevented anyone from watching Crawford's scenes. After the film was released and got bad reviews, Crawford blamed herself, later stating: "I did it badly, I know it. I would have given anything to recall it....The two ghosts of Sadie Thompson [Eagels and Swanson] rose up to haunt me." Her director of that film did not ultimately agree with her. "You know," Milestone recalled for this author, "looking back on it, Joan did a very good job in her role in that picture, better than she knew herself. And where are the actors like Gargan and Catlett, who treated her like dirt when we did that picture? They didn't go anywhere, but the world sure knows who Joan Crawford is." The world also remembers the dynamic Gloria Swanson, but it has only fading memories of Jeanne Eagels, the actress who made this story famous on the Broadway stage. The remark made to Crawford by acid-tongued Catlett, as cited above, was true. Eagels truly owned the role of Sadie Thompson. She had actually played a similar part, that of a prostitute who becomes a faith healer in a play called "The Outcast," patterning her performance after actress Elsie Ferguson, the star of that stage production, and she appeared in its silent film version, **The World and the Woman**, 1916. Unlike the fictional portrait of Eagels in the dismal biopic, **Jeanne Eagels**, 1957, where Kim Novak essays the actress, Eagels was a well-established stage actress when she starred in the stage version of "Rain." The Somerset Maugham story was adapted for the stage by John Colton and Clemence Randolph, opening on Broadway at Maxine Elliott's Theater on November 7, 1922, starring Eagels. "Rain" was a smash hit, thanks to Eagel's electrifying portrait of Sadie, the show running for 256 performances. So successful was the play that it became a road show, starring Eagels, and then returned to Broadway, reopening at the Gaiety Theater on September 1, 1924 (transferring to the New Park Theater on December 15, 1924), and ran for another astounding 648 performances. The play was revived twice, the last in 1935 and starring Tallulah Bankhead. The play also saw a musical version, opening at the Alvin Theater on November 16, 1944, but enjoyed only sixty performances. More than any other actress, Jeanne Eagels truly owned the role of Sadie Thompson, a role that made her one of the great actresses of the American theater, but, sadly, the troubled nature of the character she had made famous overwhelmed and somewhat replaced her own persona, Eagels becoming dissolute with booze and drugs and dying from a heroin overdose at the age of thirty-nine on October 3, 1929. **p**, Joseph M. Schenck; **d**, Lewis Milestone; **cast**, Joan Crawford, Walter Huston, William Gargan, Guy Kibbee, Walter Catlett, Beulah Bondi, Matt Moore, Kendall Lee, Ben Hendricks, Frederic Howard, Mary Shaw; **w**, Maxwell Anderson (based on the play "Rain" by John Colton, Clemence Randolph, and the story "Miss Thompson" by W. Somerset Maugham); **c**, Oliver Marsh; **m**, Alfred Newman; **ed**, W. Duncan Mansfield; **art d**, Richard Day.

Rain Man ★★★★ 1988; U.S.; 133m; Guber-Peters Company/UA; Color; Drama; Children: Unacceptable (MPAA: R); **BD**; **DVD**; **VHS**. Hoffman and Cruise give memorable performances as brothers crossing America on a journey to resolve the inheritance of a great fortune, a trip that also takes them into the past to resolve their mysterious relationship. Cruise is a self-centered salesman peddling expensive foreign cars in Los Angeles, who takes his girlfriend, Golino, to Palm Springs for a weekend vacation. That idyll is interrupted when Cruise learns that his estranged father has died and left a great fortune. Cruise goes with Golino to Cincinnati, Ohio, to learn about that inheritance, but, when he arrives, he discovers to his shock that his father has left him only a 1949 Buick Roadmaster and some rose bushes. The bulk of the estate, about $3 million, has been left for the care of Hoffman, a brother who resides in a local mental institution, a brother Cruise knows nothing about. He learns that Hoffman is an autistic savant, who has brilliant recall of everything he has remembered and also has amazing abilities to calculate numbers. Determined to get his share of the inheritance, Cruise takes custody of Hoffman, and both set out for Los Angeles where Cruise plans to have his attorneys change his father's will so that he receives half of the fortune, the rest going to the mental institution for its continued support and maintenance of his mentally deficient brother. When Golino hears of this, she becomes disgusted with Cruise's selfish motives and permanently leaves him. Since Hoffman has a fear of flying, the brothers travel westward by car, but the trip proves frustrating for Cruise in that Hoffman is often frightened of any sudden change and

Dustin Hoffman and Tom Cruise in *Rain Man*, 1988.

finds security only in reliable routines (and to allay his fears Hoffman repetitively recites the old Abbott and Costello routine of "Who's On First?"). Hoffman, when not distressed, displays little or no emotion, his face a blank, and he avoids eye contact with Cruise and other humans. During the trip, Cruise thinks that Hoffman's autism is not authentic, but he slowly realizes that his brother's condition is real when dimly recalling how Hoffman was injured in an accident while protecting him, Cruise, his younger brother. After Hoffman sings "I Saw Her Standing There," an old Beatles song, Cruise then remembers Hoffman as that protective brother whom he called "Rain Man," instead of his real name, "Raymond." Although Cruise is annoyed by Hoffman's strange behavior, he begins to warm toward his brilliant brother, but nevertheless exploits his ability to calculate cards when both arrive in Las Vegas, where Cruise uses Hoffman to win at blackjack. By the time they arrive in Los Angeles, Cruise's attitude has drastically changed. He now truly loves his older but mentally impaired brother, and is no longer interested in the money from his father's estate. His only concern now is that he retains permanent custody of Hoffman so that he can be the protector of a brother who had been his protector in childhood. Hoffman cannot decide whether or not to stay with Cruise, so he opts for the security of the institution he has always known in Cincinnati, and Cruise obliges by putting Hoffman on an Amtrak train bound for that city, promising him that he will visit him within a few weeks. Levinson brilliantly directs this sensitive story with great care, fully developing the characters through one memorable and moving scene after another so that at the finale, these two strangers are now closely bonded brothers in blood and in spirit. There is a hint in **Rain Man** of the relationship between Lenny and George from Steinbeck's **Of Mice and Men**, 1940, but Hoffman's character is much more complex but no less empathetic than the groping and adolescent-minded Lenny of that tale. This film proved to be an enormous success at the box office, taking in almost $355 million against a budget of $25 million. It won Oscars for Best Picture, Best Director (Levinson), Best Actor (Hoffman), Best Original Screenplay (Bass, Morrow), and received Oscar nominations for Best Film Editing (Linder), Best Original Score (Zimmer), Best Art Direction (Random, DeScenna), and Best Cinematography (Seale). Songs: "Iko Iko" (1965; Rosa Lee Hawkins, Joe Jones, Barbara Hawkins, Sharon Jones, John Johnson, Marilyn Jones, Jesse Thompson), "Scatterlings of Africa" (1986; Johnny Clegg), "Lonely Avenue" (1956; Doc Pomus), "Please Love Me Forever" (1961; Johnny Malone, Ollie Blanchard), "Dry Bones" (1927; music: James Weldon Johnson; lyrics: traditional), "Beyond the Blue Horizon" (1930; music: Richard A. Whiting, W. Franke Harling; lyrics: Leo Robin), "Star Dust" (1927; music: Hoagy Carmichael; lyrics, 1929; Mitchell Parish), "At Last" (1941; music: Harry Warren; lyrics: Mack Gordon), "Lonely Women Make Good

Bruce Jones and Ricky Tomlinson in *Raining Stones*, 1994.

Lovers" (1973; Freddy Weller, Spooner Oldham), "Wishful Thinking" (Jocko Marcellino, Randy Handley), "Nathan Jones" (1971; Leonard Caston, Kathy Wakefield), "Lovin' Ain't So Hard" (Jocko Marcellino), "After Midnight" (1966; J. J. Cale), "I Saw Her Standing There" (1963; John Lennon, Paul McCartney), "Bouncin' the Blues" (1948; Harry Warren), "They Can't Take That Away from Me" (1937; music: George Gershwin; lyrics: Ira Gershwin), "Shoes with Wings On" (1948; Harry Warren). **p**, Mark Johnson, Gerald R. Molen; **d**, Barry Levinson; **cast**, Dustin Hoffman, Tom Cruise, Valeria Golino, Jack Murdock, Michael D. Roberts, Ralph Seymour, Lucinda Jenney, Bonnie Hunt, Molen, Levinson; **w**, Ronald Bass, Barry Morrow (based on a story by Morrow); **c**, John Seale; **m**, Hans Zimmer; **ed**, Stu Linder; **prod d**, Ida Random; **art d**, William A. Elliott; **set d**, Linda DeScenna; **spec eff**, Don Myers.

The Rain People ★★★ 1969; U.S.; 101m; WB; Color; Drama; Children: Unacceptable (MPAA: R); **DVD**; **VHS**. Absorbing drama sees Knight as an unhappily married New York housewife. She panics when she discovers she is pregnant and leaves her husband, Modica. While driving to California, she picks up Caan, a handsome hitch hiking ex-college football player, who is mentally disabled from a sports injury. She plans to have one night with him, but her plans become complicated when Duvall, a Nebraska highway patrolman, takes an interest in her. This romantic triangle becomes stormy and Duvall fights with Caan over Knight's affections. Zimmet, who is Duvall's daughter, shoots Caan, and he dies. Little is resolved at the finale since no one has managed to solve the problems of their earlier lives or where they are going, people who not only have been out in the rain too long, but are drowning in it. Sexuality and violence prohibit viewing by children. **p**, Bart Patton, Ronald Colby; **d&w**, Francis Ford Coppola; **cast**, James Caan, Shirley Knight, Robert Duvall, Marya Zimmet, Tom Aldredge, Laurie Crews, Andrew Duncan, Margaret Fairchild, Sally Gracie, Alan Manson; **c**, Wilmer Butler (Technicolor); **m**, Ronald Stein; **ed**, Blackie Malkin; **art d**, Leon Ericksen.

Raining Stones ★★★ 1994; U.K.; 90m; Channel Four Films/Northern Arts; Color; Comedy; Children: Acceptable; **DVD**; **VHS**. Pleasant comedy has Jones as a devoted husband and father, proud though poor, in the north of England. His six-year-old daughter, Phoenix, needs an expensive white dress for her upcoming First Communion, but Jones does not have the money to buy that gown. He and a friend, Tomlinson, steal a sheep to sell the meat for money, but they find it is all mutton and won't bring a good price. They sell the meat, and then Jones' van is stolen. To obtain more cash for that all-important Communion dress, Jones works at opening clogged sewers and being a nightclub bouncer,

anything for some money. He could rent a dress, but is determined that Phoenix will wear a new one. With the help of his wife, Brown, and parish priest Hickey, he finally achieves that goal in an often very funny film that has plenty of heart. **p**, Sally Hibbin; **d**, Ken Loach; **cast**, Bruce Jones, Julie Brown, Gemma Phoenix, Ricky Tomlinson, Tom Hickey, Mike Fallon, Ronnie Ravey, Lee Brennan, Karen Henthorn, Christine Abbott; **w**, Jim Allen; **c**, Barry Ackroyd; **m**, Stewart Copeland; **ed**, Jonathan Morris; **prod d**, Martin Johnson; **art d**, Fergus Clegg.

The Rainmaker ★★★ 1956; U.S.; 121m; Hal Wallis Productions; PAR; Color; Comedy/Romance; Children: Acceptable; **DVD**; **VHS**. Hepburn and Lancaster are exceptional in this romantic comedy set in the arid Southwest. Hepburn is a flighty and somewhat protected spinster living on a large farm when back country confidence man Lancaster rolls into the area. He claims that he can create rain for the parched crops, but insists that he be paid $100 for conjuring up the heavens to produce that much-needed deluge. The desperate Prud'Homme, owner of the farm and father to Hepburn and two strapping sons, tells Lancaster that he will pay the required sum if he produces that rain. Lancaster takes residence in one of the outbuildings on the sprawling farm, impressing Holliman, the oafish, younger son, with his palaver and rainmaking talents, even though Lancaster has not produced a single drop of water from the reluctant skies. Holliman is more interested in wooing Lime, a local beauty, than worrying about irrigating his father's crops. Bridges, the older and wiser son, does not buy into Lancaster's glib spiel, pronouncing him a fraud, but Hepburn, who is lovestarved, wants to believe in Lancaster only because he is an exciting available bachelor. Knowing this, the enterprising Lancaster makes amorous advances that Hepburn cautiously accepts, but only to goad Corey, the local lawman, who has been tepidly courting Hepburn for years. Hepburn has little or no self-confidence. She is constantly reminded by the tactless Bridges that she is plain-looking, if not unattractive, and that is why she has not been taken to the altar by hesitant suitor Corey. The slick Lancaster, however, convinces Hepburn that she is beautiful and desired by any sane man, and Hepburn begins to think of herself that way. Corey, seeing that Lancaster is making romantic inroads with Hepburn, becomes much more aggressive in courting Hepburn, now realizing that she is a wonderful female and he will be lucky to win her hand, if Lancaster does not beat him to it. Meanwhile, Lancaster is hounded by Prud'Homme and Bridges to produce that downpour he has promised and he works hard with his charms, strange incantations, rattling tambourine and other rainmaking gadgets of his own creation, desperately summoning the gods to send down those droplets while figuring out a way to leave the area without losing too much face. To his amazement and the universal joy of all, the skies respond to Lancaster's shenanigans and, by fortuitous happenstance, the skies cloud up and a rainstorm ensues, drenching the area and replenishing the drying crops, reassuring Prud'Homme and the farmers of a promising season. (No one is more surprised than Lancaster at this providential downpour, exclaiming to himself: "I did it! I actually did it!") Lancaster says farewell to Hepburn, who loves him for helping to establish her confidence, but she also loves the patient and gentle Corey. Hepburn and Corey then plan their wedding as the charming Lancaster goes on his conniving way to another town to ply his colorful confidence games, now believing that he truly is a rainmaker. Anthony skillfully presents this romantic comedy by faithfully following the stage version (the sets are accordingly stagey but do not distract from the story or its compelling characters), and all the players are standouts in their roles. This film saw great success at the box office, gleaning more than $2 million in its initial release. It received two Oscar nominations, for Best Actress (Hepburn, her seventh such nomination), and Best Musical Score (Bernstein). It was remade in 1982 as a made-for-TV production with Tuesday Weld, Tommy Lee Jones, James Cromwell and William Katt in the leading roles. Song: "She'll Be Coming 'Round the Mountain" (traditional). *Author's Note*: This story undoubtedly influenced composer Meredith

Wilson to create his top-flight musical, which appeared on Broadway in the same year that this film was released, and was later adapted for film, **The Music Man**, 1962, a story identical in modus operandi in that a confidence man comes to a small town to woo a spinster, but, instead of peddling rain he is out to sell the small town expensive band instruments. Playwright and screenwriter N. Richard Nash (Nathan Richard Nusbaum; 1913-2000), originally wrote **The Rainmaker** as a teleplay before adapting it to the stage, the play produced on Broadway at the Court Theater, opening on October 28, 1954, and running for 125 performances and starring Geraldine Page in the Hepburn role, Darrin McGavin in the Lancaster part, and Prud'Homme in the role of the father; it was directed by Anthony, who also directed the 1956 film. The play was produced as a Broadway musical, "110 in the Shade" in 1963 and that version saw many revivals up to 2007. Producer Wallis had long wanted to make this film, buying the film rights from Nash for $300,000, outbidding RKO studio for those rights. His first choice for the love-starved spinster was Hepburn, who told this author: "By that time in my career, I had typecast myself as an old maid after I appeared in **The African Queen** [1951], where I played a spinster, so Hollywood thought of me as a spinster on screen ever afterward. My Lord, did producers not think I could play anyone else other than some old bag that nobody wanted to take home?" Hepburn was fifty-one years old when making **The Rainmaker** while Lancaster was forty-three and Corey was forty-two, so, indeed, these two suitors are wooing a woman decidedly older than themselves (as the unkindly close-ups of Hepburn in the film affirm when showing the crow's feet at her eyes). Lancaster told this author that "I was not the first choice for the con man in **The Rainmaker**. Paramount wanted Bill [William] Holden in that role, but he was then a big star at that studio, having won an Oscar for his terrific role in **Stalag 17** [1953]. I was reading Hedda Hopper's Hollywood gossip column one day where she reported that Holden had turned down the role and I got Hal Wallis on the line and told him that I wanted to play the role of the confidence man. I had known such wily birds when I was performing in carnivals and circuses as an acrobat and I felt I could capture the personality of that character." Wallis thought Lancaster would be good in the role, but the always opportunistic producer would only give Lancaster the role if the actor agreed to star in a western, the following year, **Gunfight at the O.K. Corral**, 1957 (which proved to be an enormous success) and Lancaster agreed. For his part, Holden told this author that "I did not like the character Wallis wanted me to play in **The Rainmaker**, an out and out confidence man who plays up to an older woman to gain her trust. I had already done that kind of role, or a version of it, when I appeared with Gloria Swanson in **Sunset Boulevard** [1950] and where I con an older woman into supporting me by pretending to help her write a screenplay, which is awful. That was the reason why I backed out of **The Rainmaker**." The playwright, N. Richard Nash (no relation to this author), admitted to this author that, although he wrote the original play for his older sister, he had in mind as the confidence man a spectacular character named Charles Mallory Hatfield (1875-1958), a sewing machine salesman, who turned professional "rainmaker" after creating a secret formula of twenty-three chemicals that would produce rain. The Kansas-born Hatfield called himself a "moisture accelerator," and, at the turn of the 20th Century began promoting himself as a rainmaker. A group of California ranchers hired him in 1904 to make rain for their thirsty cattle and Hatfield and his brother, Paul, went to the top of Mount Lowe in the San Gabriel Mountains and reportedly released Hatfield's mixture into the air and, lo and behold, rain fell throughout the area, although many later claimed that the rainstorm was on its way before Hatfield invoked the heavens to yield its contents. So grateful were the ranchers that they paid Hatfield $100 (the very amount Lancaster demands in this film), instead of the $50 he had asked for his unusual services. Hatfield's exploits thereafter were hit and miss propositions, but, in late 1915, a drought struck San Diego and its city fathers, after exhausting all other avenues, went to Hatfield, imploring him to sell them his miraculous

Katharine Hepburn, Lloyd Bridges, Burt Lancaster, Cameron Prud'Homme and Earl Holliman in *The Rainmaker*, 1956.

services. Hatfield promised that he would fill up the city's reservoirs if they would pay him $1,000 for every inch of water he produced. The City Council voted to give him a flat $10,000. Hatfield went to work with his brother Paul and some workmen, who constructed a twenty-foot tower next to Lake Morena. Hatfield, in the first few days of early January 1916 began releasing his mixture into the air and the results were much more than he or anyone else could have anticipated. On January 15, torrential rains poured down on San Diego, and the rain increased with each succeeding day until the reservoirs were not only filled, but all the bone-dry riverbeds were filled and then overflowing as widespread flooding ensued and everyone became alarmed, thinking that Hatfield had gone overboard with his magical mixture (not unlike the unending floods created by the capricious and irresponsible Mickey Mouse in the Sorcerer's Apprentice segment of **Fantasia**, 1940). The rainstorms kept coming, and soon the entire San Diego area was deluged with water and everything was at flood stage. Trains were marooned, bridges destroyed, and miles of telephone and telegraph poles and wires were snapped and demolished as the waters swelled and rolled. Farms and homes went underwater as dams broke and more than twenty people lost their lives. Nevertheless, Hatfield demanded his fee. The San Diego City Council told him that they would pay him his $10,000, but only if he assumed the responsibility for the widespread damage he had created when calling forth the deluge, those damages now amounting to more than $3.5 million. He disavowed all responsibility, saying that the city officials should have heeded his warnings and taken precautions. He said he promised to deliver the water, but he added that he had given no assurances that he could stop the seven-day downpour that had inundated the area. When the city refused to pay him, Hatfield entered a prolonged suit that went on for many years, concluding when the courts decided that the great flood had been created by an "Act of God," not the conjuring Hatfield. By that time, Hatfield's wife had divorced him and his friends abandoned him to his own follies. He did contract for more rainmaking jobs, but they were mostly unsuccessful. Hatfield stubbornly insisted until his death in 1958 that his secret formula could, indeed, produce rain, perhaps in more quantities than desired. He took that formula to his grave with him. His many detractors stated that Hatfield was nothing more than a clever confidence man who possessed extremely good meteorological knowledge that allowed him to ascertain when rain would indeed fall from the skies and that he used that knowledge in pretending that his own formula was the source of all that water. **p**, Hal B. Wallis; **d**, Joseph Anthony; **cast**, Burt Lancaster, Katharine Hepburn, Wendell Corey, Lloyd Bridges, Earl Holliman, Cameron Prud'Homme, Wallace Ford, Yvonne Lime, Michael Bachus, Dottie Bee Baker; **W**, N. Richard Nash (based on his play); **c**, Charles Lang Jr. (VistaVision; Technicolor); **m**, Alex North; **ed**, Warren Low; **art d**,

Myrna Loy and George Brent in *The Rains Came*, 1939.

Hal Pereira, Walter Tyler; **set d**, Sam Comer, Arthur Krams; **spec eff**, John P. Fulton.

The Rainmaker ★★★ 1997; U.S.; 135m; American Zoetrope/PAR; Color; Drama; Children: Unacceptable (MPAA: PG); **DVD**; **VHS**. Not a remake but the same title as the 1956 film, this intriguing drama sees Damon as a struggling young lawyer working with his cynical partner, DeVito, who takes on a powerful Tennessee law firm representing a corrupt insurance company. That company has refused to pay for an operation that could have saved the life of Whitworth, the son of an elderly couple, Place and West. During a wrongful death trial, Damon falls for Danes, a hospital patient whose husband beat her severely, but she will not leave him for fear that he will kill her. With evidence provided by an employee of the insurance firm, Damon wins the trial, but not the girl. Songs: "Woman You Must Be Crazy" (T-Bone Walker), "You Are My Sunshine" (Jimmie Davis, Charles Mitchell), "How Blue Can You Get" (Jane Feather), "Five Long Years" (Eddie Boyd), "Baby, Scratch My Back" (James Moor). Excessive violence and domestic abuse prohibit viewing by children. **p**, Fred Fuchs, Steven Reuther, Michael Douglas, Georgia Kacandes; **d**, Francis Ford Coppola; **cast**, Matt Damon, Danny DeVito, Claire Danes, Jon Voight, Mary Kay Place, Dean Stockwell, Teresa Wright, Virginia Madsen, Mickey Rourke, Andrew Shue, Roy Scheider, Randy Travis, Danny Glover; **w**, Coppola, Michael Herr (based on the novel by John Grisham); **c**, John Toll; **m**, Elmer Bernstein; **ed**, Melissa Kent, Barry Malkin; **prod d**, Howard Cummings; **art d**, Robert Shaw; **set d**, Barbara Munch; **spec eff**, Guy Clayton, Mike Ahasay.

The Rains Came ★★★★ 1939; U.S.; 104m; FOX: B/W; Drama; Children: Acceptable; **DVD**; **VHS**. Loy and Power are standouts in this exotic romantic tale about a mythical province in India that is beset with calamities and where both vainly struggle against a relationship involving miscegenation and a rigid caste system. Loy is the pampered but bored wife of wealthy businessman Bruce, longing for a flesh-and-blood lover. She and Bruce travel to the Indian province of Ranchipur, where Loy renews her friendship with former lover Brent, a well-educated Englishman, who has elected to live in this remote area because his heavy drinking has made of him a social pariah with his own class. While Brent fends off advances from Joyce, a beautiful but naïve young girl whose missionary parents seek to have her marry a British aristocrat, he also attempts to rekindle his old love affair with Loy. She is having none of that, however, after Loy meets the swarthy, handsome Power, a gifted and dedicated Indian physician and a court favorite of Warner and Ouspenskaya, the aging rulers of Ranchipur. Loy plies her considerable charms on Power, but, although he is attracted to the sultry

Loy, he resists by immersing himself in his busy medical practice, where taking care of the sick is more important than dallying with a straying wife. His chores become overwhelming when an earthquake, followed by torrential rains, causes the dam to break, flooding most of the town. Thousands are killed in the calamity, including Bruce and Warner, and Brent proves himself a hero by saving many from drowning and carrying important messages from Ouspenskaya to her subordinates. Power's clinic swells with the injured from the disaster and increases when malaria breaks out. Loy, by this time, has come to appreciate human life as never before and volunteers to work at Power's clinic without him knowing it. She is regarded as a useless worker with no medical skills and is given the most menial and dirty jobs, such as disposing of disease-ridden bandages and scrubbing the bloodstained floors of surgeries. Exhausted, Loy thoughtlessly drinks from a glass of water contaminated by malaria and grows so ill that she collapses. Power finds her and puts her to bed, patiently treating her. Loy has now found happiness in realizing that Power loves her. However, Ouspenskaya has earlier warned Loy that, if she were to inveigle Power into marrying her, Power's own position in the caste-sensitive makeup of Ranchipur would be jeopardized to where he would not be able to become the province's prime minister, a position Ouspenskaya has long envisioned for Power, who is her political protégé. Ouspenskaya also obliquely warns that such a union would make both Loy and Power pariahs in their own races that would not sanction or tolerate such a marriage of two persons from different races. None of that comes about as Loy, after becoming a compassionate and giving person, tragically dies in Power's arms. Power then becomes the prime minister of the country while Brent has reformed and has found happiness with Joyce. Brown directs this film with a sturdy hand; the disaster scenes are wonderfully choreographed, an astounding sequence that earned for Sersen and Hansen an Oscar for Best Visual Effects, the first such award given in that category. The film also received Oscar nominations for Best Original Score (Newman), Best Sound Recording (Hansen), Best Art Direction (Darling and Dudley), and Best Cinematography, Black and White (Miller). Songs: "The Rains Came" (1939; Mack Gordon), "Hindoo Love Song" (1939; Lal Chand Mehra), "God Save the King" (1744; Henry Carey), "Piano Concerto No. 14 in C Sharp Minor, Op.27 No.2 (Moonlight)" (1802; Ludwig van Beethoven). ***Author's Note***: Director Brown told this author that "Darryl Zanuck [head of Fox Studio] was one hundred percent behind **The Rains Came** and gave me an almost unlimited budget, because it was a very expensive picture to make. [The budget exceeded $2.5 million, one of the largest ever given to any film to that time by the studio.] More than half of the budget went into the making of the huge sets—the palace and part of the town and into the disaster scenes where the dam breaks and the town is flooded following the earthquake and the rains. I got the picture into the can in about one hundred days, but half of that time was spent in working with Sersen and others to get the disaster scenes right and believable. Most of that was done in miniature, but it was still a very costly affair." The town of Ranchipur was built on eighteen acres of the Fox back lot, and the construction of the elaborately appointed palace cost $75,000 to build, which it was systematically wrecked in the disaster scenes. Those particular scenes taking took days to shoot with fourteen cameras, and more than 350 carpenters, grips and workmen labored to do the overall dam-breaking and flooding scenes for more than a month. A tank containing more than 50,000 gallons of water was specially constructed on a Fox sound stage that eventually released its contents to represent the flood scenes in the film. Loy told this author that "what the audiences saw was a very carefully constructed earthquake and flood in **The Rains Came**, and it was very frightening to see, but more frightening for me in that picture was when I had to ride a horse in one scene and it suddenly bolted and I was thrown. I came close to hitting my head and could have been killed. One of the first persons who came running to make sure I was all right was Ty [Tyrone Power], my co-star and one of the finest gentlemen of Hollywood. He was a matinee idol in those days, but that never went to his head. He thought and cared about others before he thought about himself and I want to emphasize that he was a great actor. He had a vivid imagination about the characters he played and he discussed those ideas with me. Ty was always open with his thoughts and that is a form of his generosity, too." **p**, Darryl F. Zanuck; **d**, Clarence Brown; **cast**, Myrna Loy, Tyrone Power, George Brent, Brenda Joyce, Nigel Bruce, Maria Ouspenskaya, Joseph Schildkraut, Mary Nash, Jane Darwell, Marjorie Rambeau, Henry Travers, H.B. Warner, Laura Hope Crews, **w**, Philip Dunne, Julien Josephson (based on the novel by Louis Bromfield); **c**, Arthur Miller; **m**, Alfred Newman; **d**, Barbara McLean; **art d**, William Darling, George Dudley; **set d**, Thomas Little; **spec eff**, Fred Sersen, (not credited, special effects, sound) Edmund H. Hansen.

The Rains of Ranchipur ★★★ 1955; U.S.; 104m; FOX; Color; Drama; Children: Unacceptable; **DVD**. This good remake of the 1939 version of the Bromfield tale sees Turner as the wayward wife of Rennie randomly cheating on a very tolerant husband, her promiscuous ways unchanged when they visit the mythical Indian province of Ranchipur at the invitation of Leontovich, the ruling maharani. Once Turner sees handsome Burton, a dedicated Indian physician, she sets her trap for him, but Burton fends off her amorous advances after Leontovich warns him about the lady's notorious reputation. Meanwhile, MacMurray, an alcoholic but noble-minded recluse living as an expatriate in India, becomes involved with young Caulfield, the daughter of ambitious missionaries. The cynical MacMurray thinks Caulfield is naïve, but he tolerates her bursts of emotion while he attempts to aid Leontovich with political problems. Burton, by this time, can no longer resist Turner and they enter into a passionate affair, but that tryst troubles Burton's conscience to the point where he confesses his love for Turner to husband Rennie, who is grateful for his candor and also for Burton saving his life from a tiger while both were earlier on a safari. The Turner-Burton affair comes to a standstill when the province is struck by its seasonal heavy rains followed by a tremendous earthquake that devastates the area. After a massive dam bursts, the area is flooded and thousands are killed and injured, and Burton's clinic is overwhelmed with suffering patients. MacMurray proves to be a hero by saving many lives during the calamity while Burton gives all his time and energy to treating his patients. Turner, who has come to love Burton, forsakes selfish motives and, following Burton's idealistic lifestyle, returns to the arms of her always forgiving husband, Rennie. Through the crisis, MacMurray has regained his self-respect and belief in mankind by the finale and decides to make a life with Caulfield. Director Negulesco faithfully follows the script of the 1939 production, but Turner's fate is altered in that she does not die of malaria, as did Myrna Loy in the 1939 version when playing the promiscuous wife turned self-sacrificing hospital worker. Taut direction, good acting and sumptuous sets, as well as breathtaking and well-choreographed disaster scenes and crisp cinematography from Krasner makes for a thoroughly absorbing production. *Author's Note*: Though throughout this intriguing melodrama there runs a streak of old colonialism, as depicted in the attitudes of all of the characters in both film versions (as was the case in Bromfield's novel), its main attraction is the development and change of the chief characters, and, in both film versions, the interrupting earthquake and flood cathartically levels the emotional problems of its characters to basic good instincts and action. Director Negulesco told this author that "most of the problems with that picture involved the disaster scenes and they took a long time to get that all on film and that was the most costly part of **The Rains of Ranchipur**." Fox spent from between $3 to $4 million on the overall production and did not recoup its investment from its initial box office release, which yielded about $3 million. There were also problems on the sets with some of the actors. MacMurray did not like his character, telling this author that "I was little more than the town drunk in that picture and Jean [Negulesco] had me belting down so many drinks that I could hardly get my lines out through the gulping. Of course the booze

Lana Turner and Richard Burton in *The Rains of Ranchipur*, 1955.

I was supposed to be drinking was tea but even that stuff dries out your mouth." Turner and Burton did not get along well during the production. Turner told this author: "He [Burton] was acting as an Indian doctor, and his role called for him to be passive and unresponsive to me at first, but he stayed with that attitude while we were making that picture, so, by the end, I was still throwing my lines at a statue." Turner's feelings toward Burton never changed, which eventually ruptured Turner's friendship with Burton's wife, Elizabeth Taylor. Burton's performance, however, was highly praised and rightly so, for he revealingly struggles with the additional deep problems of caste and miscegenation in presenting his character. **p**, Frank Ross; **d**, Jean Negulesco; **cast**, Lana Turner, Richard Burton, Fred MacMurray, Joan Caulfield, Michael Rennie, Eugenie Leontovich, Gladys Hurlbut, Madge Kennedy, Carlo Rizzo, Beatrice Kraft; **w**, Merle Miller (based on the novel *The Rains Came* by Louis Bromfield); **c**, Milton Krasner (CinemaScope; DeLuxe Color); **m**, Hugo Friedhofer; **ed**, Dorothy Spencer; **art d**, Lyle R. Wheeler, Addison Hehr; **set d**, Walter M. Scott, Paul S. Fox; **spec eff**, Ray Kellogg.

Raintree County ★★★ 1957; U.S.; 187m; MGM; Color; Drama; Children: Unacceptable; **DVD**; **VHS**. Somewhat overlong but intriguing Civil War drama sees fine performances from a sterling cast and solid direction from Dmytryk. The beautiful Taylor arrives in Raintree County, Indiana, catching the eyes of every young swain, including Clift, a student wanting to become a teacher. A spoiled Southern belle, Taylor can pick any available suitor, but she wants only the withdrawn and shy Clift and, working her sultry wiles, captures his lust and love, even though he is engaged to Saint, a practical woman. Other than physical attraction, Taylor and Clift have little in common as he is deeply opposed to slavery and Taylor looks upon that "peculiar institution" as an agrarian necessity for her beloved South. Clift has second thoughts during his torrid romance with Taylor, but when he seems to stray, Taylor, desperate to keep Clift for her own, lies to him when telling him that she is pregnant. His conscience will not permit him to do anything other than take Taylor to the altar while the deserted Saint can only watch as her only love is lost to her. Clift then gets his degree and becomes a teacher, but he is inveigled with arguments with Taylor and others in his community over the new federal administration headed by President Abraham Lincoln and his anti-slavery policies. (The Taylor-Clift strife over the politics of the North and South mirror Lincoln's own marriage in that his wife Mary was also a Southern belle with strong sentiments for the South.) While Clift teaches at a school Taylor gives birth to a son, and the family relocates in the South, but the marriage is further troubled when the Civil War erupts and Clift thinks to join the Union Army against strong opposition from wife Taylor. Clift nevertheless returns to Indiana with Taylor and their son, joining the Federal

Montgomery Clift and Elizabeth Taylor in *Raintree County,* 1957.

troops and going off to battle with friends he has known since childhood, including Marvin, his most devoted and closest friend. Clift is shown involved in many terrible battles (shown in montage as was the case with **Gone with the Wind**, 1939, which this film attempted to emulate but could never surpass). Meanwhile, Taylor flees Indiana, returning to her home in Georgia, and is caught up in the fighting; the bloodshed and violence jars her mind and she slowly begins to lose her sanity, her mother having died insane in a suspicious fire, as Clift has earlier learned. As the war wanes on, Clift and Marvin become foragers (scavengers or "bummers' as these irregular troops were called) for Sherman's army as it ravages Georgia, and Clift finds the home where Taylor has taken his son. Taylor is gone, having been placed in an insane asylum. Clift takes his son in tow just as a skirmish breaks out with Southern militia led by Confederate officer Kelley. Marvin is fatally shot in the stomach, poignantly crying out before dying: "I am from Raintree County!" (This evocative declaration reveals the secular perspectives of those living in a chiefly agricultural America in that era and who thought of their native state or even their homeland county as their country and viewed all territory beyond the borders of their homesteads as foreign lands.) Clift and his son escape pursuing Rebels and regain the Union lines. The war ends and, after Clift is mustered out, he returns to Georgia and finds a thoroughly disoriented Taylor in a shabby asylum, taking her back to Indiana, where he hopes to help her regain her sanity. Thinking about the future, Clift decides to run for office at the urging of Saint, who still loves him. Taylor, by this time, has lost all reason and, believing that she will die in the same manner as her deranged mother, grabs her boy and flees the house during a fierce rainstorm. A frantic Clift conducts a desperate search for them and finally finds his son alive, sitting next to the body of Taylor, both found beneath a legendary raintree that Clift has been searching for since boyhood. Clift is now free to make a future with Saint, who has all along waited for him through years of seemingly endless mental illusions and delusions. The film was a success at the box office, earning more than $9 million against a whopping $6 million budget. Taylor received an Oscar nomination as Best Actress for her role as the mad Southern belle, and the film also received Oscar nominations for Best Score, Best Art Direction and Best Costuming. Songs: "Battle Cry of Freedom" (George Frederick Root); "The Battle Hymn of the Republic" (lyrics: Julia Ward Howe); "Raintree County," "Never Till Now" (music: Johnny Green; lyrics: Paul Francis Webster). *Author's Note*: The film was shot in a new 65 millimeter widescreen process titled MGM Camera 65; this process was also employed when MGM produced **Ben-Hur**, 1959. Locations used for the production included Lorman, Mississippi (to include the antebellum plantation mansions Windsor Ruins and Dunleith), Reelfoot Lake in Tennessee and at Danville and Frankfort, Kentucky. The pro-

duction was hampered by many problems, not the least of which was an accident involving Clift, where the actor was almost killed. "We closed down all production when Monty [Clift] got seriously injured," Dmytryk told this author, "and, at one point, we did not know if he would live or not." Taylor, who had appeared with Clift in the classic **A Place in the Sun**, 1951, actually raced to the scene of the accident on the night of May 12, 1956, after Clift had left Taylor's home (and that of her then husband, Michael Wilding) following a dinner party, where Clift had crashed his car into a telephone pole. Learning of the wreck, Taylor got to the accident site to find Clift choking on one of his own teeth that had broken off and had been embedded in his tongue and Taylor manually pulled that tooth from his mouth. "He was in great pain when he returned to the production [of **Raintree County**] and a part of the left side of his face had become paralyzed," Taylor told this author. "I agonized over him for weeks and weeks, but he never complained about the pain he was enduring and performed his part brilliantly in the picture." According to Dmytryk's statements to this author, "one of the biggest problems I had when working on that picture was Dore Schary, who was running things at MGM then. He kept coming to the set and asking the principal players—Elizabeth [Taylor] Monty [Clift] and others to cold read the script with him while he read all the lines of the supporting players—the guy was a ham at heart, and a bad one. [Schary secretly desired to be an actor and took delight in appearing before the camera when introducing shorts that showcased upcoming MGM releases. Schary also appeared in a bit part when playing a politician in his own production of **Sunrise at Campobello**, 1960.] I had to put up with this guy butting in any time he wanted while he played director and he did not know the first thing about directing pictures. Not only that, but Schary saddled me with a lot of old camera technicians who should have retired by then because they were using equipment that dated back to the silent era. When I told them that a lot of new techniques and equipment had been developed since then, they got mad at me and complained to Schary and that is only one of the reasons why I never worked at MGM after making that picture." MGM spent lavishly, if not recklessly, on this film, having Taylor's wardrobe made of the finest cloth, even her petticoats that were hidden beneath her expensive dresses. It also spent a good deal of money on having all the actors in full costume for old-fashioned color tests when, according to Dmytryk, color had been refined by that time to show exactly what colors were being worn in those costumes. Dmytryk, unlike most everyone in Hollywood, had little respect for Clift, blaming him for a lot of the delays in the production. "He got into that accident," Dmytryk told this author, "because he was groggy with a hangover and had no sleep when he was driving away from Elizabeth's home. The guy was always looped with booze or drugs and sometimes we could not find him to do his scenes. I found him dead drunk in his hotel room one day, passed out on his bed. A cigarette had burned between two of his fingers but he was too drunk to know it. I searched his room and found more than one hundred different kinds of drugs and also a leather-bound case with syringes and needles. When I checked Monty's arms, I found dozens of old puncture marks and then I knew he was a hopeless druggie. What a shame, because he was a hell of an actor and could have done much more with his life. The trouble was that he had a lot of rich women who felt sorry for him and mothered him—and he was a mother's boy all the way—and he used them to keep up that rotten way of life of his. I'm not talking about his homosexuality, but his self-destructive lifestyle." Oddly, Clift's widespread use of drugs actually saved his co-star's life. In one scene being shot in Mississippi during intense heat, Taylor, wearing a seventy-five-pound dress, collapsed from hyperventilation. She found it difficult to breathe, and when a physician was called, he said he could not, under the local law, prescribe the necessary medication. Clift, however, suddenly appeared with a clean syringe and a full bottle of Demerol, which the physician promptly used to restore Taylor's breathing to normal, even though she was later bedridden for about a week after suffering an attack of tachycardia (quickened heartbeat). Clift, however, proved incorrigible when the cast and crew were on location. When in Danville, Kentucky, Clift left his hotel room in the middle of the night without a stich of clothing and ran through the upscale area of the town hooting and hollering, causing the leading citizens of that town to demand that the actor be taken in tow. Policemen were assigned to guard Clift's hotel room each night and prevent him from re-enacting his naked marathon through their town. 'Everything about **Raintree County** reminds me of tragedy," Dmytryk told this author. "Monty was as suicidal as the heroine Elizabeth plays and even Ross Lockridge, the author of the novel on which the picture is based, committed suicide, just like his heroine." **p**, David Lewis; **d**, Edward Dmytryk; **cast**, Montgomery Clift, Elizabeth Taylor, Eva Marie Saint, Nigel Patrick, Lee Marvin, Rod Taylor, Agnes Moorehead, Walter Abel, Jarma Lewis, Tom Drake, Rhys Williams, Russell Collins, DeForest Kelley, John Eldredge, Myrna Hansen, Oliver Blake, Isabelle Cooley; **w**, Millard Kaufman (based on the novel by Ross Lockridge Jr.); **c**, Robert Surtees (Panavision; Technicolor); **m**, Johnny Green; **ed**, John Dunning; **art d**, William A. Horning, Urie Mc-Cleary; **set d**, Edwin B. Willis, Hugh Hunt; **spec eff**, Warren Newcombe.

Raise the Red Lantern ★★★ 1991; China; 125m; Salon Films/Orion Classics; Color; Drama; Children: Unacceptable (MPAA: PG); **DVD**; **VHS**. Exciting drama set in 1920s northern China sees the beautiful nineteen-year-old Li, following the death of her father, being forced to marry the fifty-year-old Jingwu, a lord of a powerful family. He already has three wives who live in separate small houses in his walled estate, and Li is also awarded her own house. Each evening, Jingwu has a servant hang a red lantern outside the house of the wife with which he will spend the night. Competition is fierce among the wives for Jingwu's attentions, and they plot against each other, but, especially, against Li, who is Jingwu's new favorite. During her first night with Jingwu, he is called away to tend to his spoiled third wife, Saifei, a former opera singer. The second wife offers Li friendship and advice, but she is secretly conniving with Li's maid to undermine both Saifei and Li. A little shed stands atop the roof of the main house, and we learn, at the end of the film, that an earlier wife, who did not adjust well, is confined there. Li has to watch herself or she might also become a similar captive, another victim of the jealous wives. Beautifully filmed and well acted, this absorbing drama does what some movies do best, taking the viewer over a rainbow, even though, in this case, the destination is not fairyland. Sexuality prohibits viewing by children. (In Mandarin; English subtitles.) **p**, Fu-Sheng Chiu; **d**, Yimou Zhang; **cast**, Li Gong, Jingwu Ma, Saifei He, Cuifen Cao, Qi Zhao, Lin Kong, Shuyuan Jin, Weimin Ding, Zhengyin Cao, Zhihgang Cui, Chu Xiao, Baotain Li; **w**, Ni Zhen (based on the novel by Su Tong); **c**, Lun Yang, Fei Zhao; **m**, Naoki Tachikawa, Jiping Zhao; **ed**, Yuan Du; **art d**, Juiping Cao.

A Raisin in the Sun ★★★★ 1961; U.S.; 128m; COL; B/W; Drama; Children: Unacceptable; **DVD**; **VHS**. Poignant and compelling story deals with a black family struggling to improve its lot while living in a Chicago slum area. McNeil, the sensible matriarch, is the recipient of a $10,000 insurance payment following her husband's death. She plans to put that much-needed money to good use by putting $3,500 down on a nice house in a better neighborhood, which is predominantly inhabited by whites and use the balance to put her daughter Sands through medical school. Her son, Poitier, however, who works hard as a limousine driver, thinks that the family should, instead, allow him to buy a liquor store, which he believes is a moneymaking proposition. McNeil and Dee, who is Poitier's wife, are dead set against the liquor store idea, and McNeil objects on the basis of her religious beliefs. Poitier becomes angry, believing that his family is sabotaging his ambitious dreams of becoming a successful businessman and he leaves the house. After Poitier has been gone for three days, McNeil and Dee begin searching for him and McNeil finds him in a bar. She tells him that he can have the balance of the money after her payment on the house for his investment in the liquor store, but must hold on to $3,000 for Sands' education. The family is

Nicolas Cage and T. J. Kuhn in *Raising Arizona,* 1987.

then shocked to learn that Poitier has been victimized and has lost all of that money in a fraudulent scheme operated by hustler Glenn. All is not lost, however, when Fiedler (the only white actor in this all-black cast) arrives, telling the family that he will buy the house McNeil has purchased as part of the neighborhood's "improvement association." This means that the family will see a profit from their investment, but family members unite and turn him down. They unite in their resolve to have a better way of life, planning to move to that new home, even though paying off its mortgage will mean great sacrifice for all and that they will all have to work together to meet that goal. Poitier, too, has altered his mindset for the betterment of the family where all the family members now look forward to a hopeful future. The film was produced on a budget of about $1.5 million. It was remade as an American Playhouse TV production in 1989, and as a made-for-TV production in 2008. *Author's Note*: Producers found it difficult to fund the Hansberry play, but managed to acquire enough financing to bring the story to the boards on Broadway, the play opening on March 11, 1959, at the Ethel Barrymore Theater. It proved to be a smash hit, with 530 performances. The play was set in Chicago's Woodland neighborhood, which is inhabited by poor blacks and most of its action is confined to the cramped apartment inhabited by the family, but director Petrie, with the inventive aid of cinematographer Lawton, gave the film a fluid and expansive look to keep it from appearing stagey. Most of the actors in the film reprise their roles from the stage version and Lou Gossett Jr. debuts in his first feature film (he added the "Jr." later). McNeil was only about ten years older than Poitier when playing his mother in this film. Glenn, the no-good who runs off with Poitier's money, played Poitier's father in **Guess Who's Coming to Dinner**, 1967. Fiedler reprised his role in the 1989 TV remake of the story. **p**, David Susskind, Philip Rose, Ronald H. Gilbert; **d**, Daniel Petrie; **cast**, Sidney Poitier, Claudia McNeil, Ruby Dee, Diana Sands, Ivan Dixon, John Fiedler, Louis Gossett, Stephen Perry, Joel Fluellen, Louis Terrel; **w**, Lorraine Hansberry (based on her play); **c**, Charles Lawton Jr.; **m**, Laurence Rosenthal; **ed**, William A. Lyon, Paul Weatherwax; **art d**, Carl Anderson; **set d**, Louis Diage.

Raising Arizona ★★★★ 1987; U.S.; 94m; Circle Films/FOX; Color; Comedy; Children: Unacceptable (MPAA: PG-13); **BD**; **DVD**; **VHS**. Nutty, flamboyant and absurd, this film nevertheless provides a bevy of belly laughs from a superlative cast and an intentionally crackbrained script from the invariably unpredictable Coen brothers. Cage is a professional thief and robber, meeting Hunter, a policewoman, after she takes his mug shots to update his long criminal record. Attracted to each other, Hunter visits Cage while he is imprisoned, and Cage learns that Hunter's fiancé has deserted her. When he is released, Cage asks Hunter to marry him, and she accepts. Following their marriage, they take res-

Don DeFore and Joel McCrea on horseback in *Ramrod*, 1947.

idence at a mobile home in the desert, and Cage gets a job at a nearby machine shop. Both want to have children, but Hunter is unable to give birth, so they opt to kidnap one of the celebrated "Arizona Quintuplets," one of the children belonging to wealthy Nathan Arizona (Wilson), a furniture tycoon. They believe they have abducted Nathan Junior and while they go about raising this kidnapped child, they receive a visit from Goodman and Forsythe, two of Cage's former prison pals, these dim-witted brothers having just escaped and are close to persuading Cage into resuming his old criminal pursuits. Meanwhile, McMurray, who is Cage's boss at the machine shop, suggests that he and Cage swap wives, which enrages Cage, who promptly thrashes him. The fact that Cage is hard to give up his errant ways is demonstrated while he goes shopping with Hunter. Cage decides to steal some diapers for their child, but the angry Hunter departs, driving away. Cage steals the diapers, but is then pursued by gun-toting store workers and a small army of police and a pack of police dogs. Narrowly escaping, he is picked up by Hunter and taken home with a lecture. McMurray has by then deduced that Cage and Hunter have stolen the Arizona child. He fires Cage and then blackmails him, saying that if he doesn't turn over the stolen child to him and his wife, McDormand, he will turn Cage over to the police. Overhearing this, Goodman and Forsythe tie up Cage and take the child with them while they plan to rob a small-town bank. When Hunter returns home, she finds Cage and unties him and they then both arm themselves and go in pursuit of Goodman and Forsythe, Cage telling Hunter that, after they retrieve the child, they should call their marriage quits as he is too much of a liability. Meanwhile, Cobb, a bounty hunter, goes to Wilson and offers to recoup his child, but Wilson is wary of him, believing that Cobb is the actual abductor of his child. Cobb then decides that he will track down the kidnappers, snatch the child and sell the boy on the black market. Cobb is always armed to the teeth for any emergency, carrying not only automatic weapons but hand grenades affixed to his vest. After Goodman and Forsythe rob the bank, they depart in such a hurry that the child is left behind, and they are undone when an anti-theft device explodes inside a sack carrying the stolen money, destroying their getaway car and wounding them. Cobb then arrives at the bank and grabs the child, but Cage and Hunter show up and, while Cage struggles with Cobb, Hunter snatches the baby and runs off. Cage is losing his fight with wild man Cobb, who knocks Cage down and is about to kill him when Cage pulls one of the pins from a grenade attached to Cobb's vest, blowing Cobb to pieces. Cage and Hunter then decide that the child is a greater liability than Cage and sneak him back into Wilson's home, but they are discovered by Wilson, who takes a kindly avuncular attitude toward them after they explain why they abducted the boy. When they tell him that they are planning to divorce, Wilson tells them to go home and sleep on it before they come to a final decision. They

go home, and Cage has a strange dream where he envisions Goodman and Forsythe returning to prison and where Goodman gets his comeuppance for telling one too many "Pollock" jokes and Forsythe later becomes a football star after receiving a football at Christmas from an elderly couple, who wish to remain unknown. The dream, like this oddball film, ends with Cage dreaming of the elderly couple enjoying a family get-together with many children and grandchildren. The film is replete with a lot of clever wit and humor mixed with many forced funny scenes that are so skillfully handled by the cast members that they succeed, turning the ridiculous into reality or vice-versa. The characters and their crackpot schemes and perspectives are in keeping with the low-level mentality of their lowlife personalities. Like most of the Coen films, this comedy allows the most cretin-like viewer to feel mentally superior to the idiots paraded on the screen. No viewer is compelled to unscramble any perplexing concept for this impossible film. All is understandable and in plain sight, like a custard pie crashing into a dilettante's face. As such, **Raising Arizona** presents a perfect presentation of perfidious piffle. Songs: "Down in the Willow Garden" (Arthur Gorson), "Goofing-Off Suite" (Pete Seeger), "Home on the Range" (traditional), "She'll Be Coming 'Round the Mountain" (traditional), "Ode to Joy" (from Symphony No. 9 by Ludwig van Beethoven). **p**, Ethan and Joel Coen, Mark Silverman; **d&w**, Ethan and Joel Coen; **cast**, Nicolas Cage, Holly Hunter, Trey Wilson, John Goodman, William Forsythe, Sam McMurray, Frances McDormand, Randall "Tex" Cobb, T.J. Kuhn Jr., Lynne Dumin Kitei, Ron Cobert; **c**, Barry Sonnenfeld; **m**, Carter Burwell; **ed**, Michael R. Miller; **prod d**, Jane Musky; **art d**, Harold Thrasher; **set d**, Robert Kracik; **spec eff**, Peter and Tom Chesney.

Rambling Rose ★★★ 1991; U.S.; 112m; Carolco Studios/New Line Cinema; Color; Drama; Children: Unacceptable (MPAA: R); **DVD**; **VHS**. This compelling drama sees Dern, a destitute young woman, being taken in by a family headed by Duvall and Ladd in Alabama during the 1930s, so she can avoid becoming a prostitute. Dern works for them by watching over Haas, their fourteen-year-old son, and his younger siblings. She is so attractive that men easily fall for her, and she knows it, but she finds that she is strongly attracted to Duvall. Haas watches from behind a door as she throws herself at Duvall. He resists her, saying he can only kiss his wife. Duvall keeps the incident from Ladd, and then strange men show up at the house. Dern is arrested and bites a policeman's thumb. Duvall wants her to leave them, but Ladd says Dern only wants love, and sex is the only way she knows how to get it. The problem about what to do with her is tragically solved when Dern dies of cancer. Coolidge does a good job helming this intricate tale while Dern, Duvall and Ladd render top-flight performances. The casting for this film adds more luster in that Ladd and Dern are real-life mother and daughter. Songs: "Dixie" (Daniel Decatur Emmett); "If I Could Be with You One Hour Tonight" (James P. Johnson, Henry Creamer); "Collegiate Rhythm," "Blue Moan" (Keith Nichols);"Lover's Serenade" (Alan Moorhouse); "Sidewalk Stomp Rag" (Richard Myhill). Sexuality prohibits viewing by children. **p**, Renny Harlin; **d**, Martha Coolidge; **cast**, Laura Dern, Robert Duvall, Diane Ladd, Lukas Haas, John Heard, Kevin Conway, Robert Burke, Lisa Jakub, Evan Lockwood, Matt Sutherland; **w**, Calder Willingham (based on the novel by Willingham); **c**, Johnny E. Jensen; **m**, Elmer Bernstein; **ed**, Steven Cohen; **prod d**, John Vallone; **art d**, Christiaan Wagener; **set d**, Bob Gould; **spec eff**, Lorenzo T. Hall.

Ramrod ★★★ 1947; U.S.; 95m; Enterprise Productions/UA; B/W; Western; Children: Unacceptable; **BD**; **DVD**; **VHS**. Gritty and revealing oater works well the old theme of the cattlemen-vs.-sheep-men feud. Lake loses her fiancé, but gets his sheepherding ranch, which she is determined to run alone. This will be in opposition to Foster, who is the cattleman "boss" of the valley and whom her father, Ruggles, wanted her to marry. Lake hires McCrea, a recovering alcoholic, to be her ranch foreman (ramrod) and a crew of Foster's enemies. Foster fights back with violence and destruction, so McCrea decides to get the best of him legally. Before he can get anywhere with attorneys, Lake and Foster and their men go to war with each other, and McCrea puts an end to it by fatally shooting Foster. McCrea, who has vainly tried to avoid the senseless bloodshed, then rides off into the sunset without Lake. Great action and beautiful black-and-white photography highlights this exceptional western, but the film was not the success producers expected. *Author's Note*: McCrea and Lake made the film six years after they co-starred in the classic comedy-drama **Sullivan's Travels**, 1941, in which they showed more romantic chemistry than in this western. Lake was married to director de Toth at the time of the filming of **Ramrod**. Many other films have profiled the range wars between sheep ranchers and cattle ranchers, including: **The Ballad of Josie**, 1967; **The Ballad of Little Jo**, 1993; **Code of the Range**, 1936; **The Fighting Peacemaker**, 1926; **Frontier**, 1955-1956 (TV series; "A Stillness in Wyoming," 1955 episode); **How the West Was Won**, 1962 (briefly in cameo scene); **In Old Montana**, 1939; **Law of the Range**, 1941; **Man from Music Mountain**, 1943; **Montana**, 1950; **Roll on Texas Moon**, 1946; **The Sheepman**, 1958; **Springtime in the Rockies**, 1937; and **Table Top Ranch**, 1922. **p**, Harry Sherman; **d**, Andre de Toth; **cast**, Joel McCrea, Veronica Lake, Preston Foster, Don DeFore, Donald Crisp, Arleen Whalen, Charlie Ruggles, Lloyd Bridges, Nestor Paiva, Ray Teal, Housely Stevenson, Jeff Corey, **w**, Jack Moffitt, Graham Baker, Cecile Kramer (based on a story by Luke Short); **c**, Russell Harlan; **m**, Adolph Deutsch; **ed**, Sherman A. Rose; **prod d**, Lionel Banks; **set d**, Allan O'Dea; **spec eff**, Harry Redmond, Jr.

Ran ★★★ 1985; Japan; 162m; Greenwich Film Productions/Rialto Pictures; Color; War; Children: Unacceptable (MPAA: R); **BD**; **DVD**; **VHS**. This epic presents a monumental Japanese version of "King Lear" by William Shakespeare. Nakadai, an elderly warlord in feudal Japan, abdicates to the authority of his three sons, Terao, Nezu and Ryû. He hopes to retire as an honored guest in the castle of each of his sons, but the two eldest sons turn against him. The youngest son warns Nakadai that his brothers are plotting against him, but is considered a troublemaker and banished. He is nevertheless right and his brothers conspire to take everything away from Nakadai, even his title. What follows is a saga of greed, lust for power, and ultimate revenge, presented by visually stunning photography, including a magnificently staged huge battle as Nakadai defeats his bad sons and gives everything to the good one. Kurosawa, a master filmmaker, presents much less character development in this production than in many of his other films (thirty in all over a fifty-seven-year period), depending more on spectacle than introspection, and his protagonists are somewhat cliché-ridden. His brilliantly choreographed battle scenes, however, are breathtaking and make the film worthwhile. Kurosawa, like all Japanese filmmakers of his era and earlier, was restricted in mindset to the traditional warlike nature of his country's feudalistic history, and tribal mentality rigidly bound by a draconian social caste system that allowed little intellectual exegesis, where individuality was outlawed if not unthinkable. Excessive violence prohibits viewing by children. (In Japanese; English subtitles.) **p**, Masato Hara, Serge Silberman; **d**, Akira Kurosawa; **cast**, Tatsuya Nakadai, Akira Terao, Jinpachi Nezu, Daisuke Ryû, Mieko Harada, Yoshiko Miyazaki, Hisashi Igawa, Pita, Masayuki Yui, Kazuo Katô; **w**, Kurosawa, Hideo Oguni, Masato Ide (based on the play "King Lear" by William Shakespeare); **c**, Asakazu Nakai, Takao Saitô, Shôji Ueda; **m**, Tôru Takemitsu; **ed**, Kurosawa; **prod d**, Shinobu and Yoshiro Muraki; **set d**, Jiro Hirai, Mitsuyuki Kimura, Yasuyoshi Ototake, Tsuneo Shimura, Osumi Tousho.

Rancho Notorious ★★★★ 1952; U.S.; 89m; Fidelity Pictures/RKO; Color; Western; Children: Unacceptable; **DVD**; **VHS**. Pantheon director Lang offers an offbeat if not bizarre tale in this, the third of his western trilogy (the others being **The Return of Frank James**, 1940, and **Western Union**, 1941). This fascinating saga retells the age-old story of love

Peter and Tatsuya Nakadai in *Ran*, 1985.

and revenge that begins with cowboy Kennedy meeting his betrothed, Henry, where they make plans for their upcoming wedding, daydreaming bright thoughts of children and happiness to come. He gives her a brooch and then leaves for work on a ranch while Henry minds a store in town. Shortly after Kennedy's departure, two scurrilous types, Gough and Doucette, arrive and go into the store to rob it. The sleazy and lustful Gough manhandles Henry, and the viewer then sees the exterior of the store and hears a gunshot with Gough and Doucette fleeing to their horses and riding away. Kennedy is summoned and enters the store, pushing his way through a silent crowd, where he sees the fallen Henry's hand clenched in death, the brooch he had given her, taken by the outlaws, and a physician telling him: "She wasn't spared anything." (This remark signifies that the defenseless young woman was raped.) Kennedy and a posse then set out to track down the robbers and the killer of his beloved, but the pursuers weary of the chase and drop out, leaving Kennedy to continue alone. He later finds Doucette fatally shot in the back by his companion, Gough, the dying outlaw giving Kennedy his only clue with one word from his dying breath: "Chuck-A-Luck." He then discovers that the name is that of a town where outlaws and brigands are welcomed by corrupt politicians and businessmen and he travels to that place, further learning that the criminal masterminds controlling the area are Dietrich, a hard-headed and beautiful ranch owner, and her erstwhile lover and gunslinger, Ferrer. In flashback, we see Dietrich, a former saloon lady, winning a fortune at the gambling tables with the help of Ferrer and then buying her large ranch, which is manned by outlaws controlled by Ferrer. To find out more information, Kennedy starts a ruckus and is thrown into jail so that he can befriend Ferrer, who is presently behind bars. (This ploy is shown in many westerns, including **The Man from the Alamo**, 1953, where Glenn Ford purposely has himself arrested and jailed in order to befriend inmate and outlaw Neville Brand in order to learn who burned his ranch and killed his wife and children.) The two break jail, and Ferrer takes Kennedy to the huge ranch that Dietrich rules with an iron hand. Dietrich welcomes Kennedy as she does any other outlaw (there are invariably eight or ten such wanted felons at the ranch at any given time), but she has strict conditions that tolerate their presence, not the least of which is that no one asks questions and that the outlaws pay her five percent of all their loot in return for her sheltering them. Dietrich seems to be drawn to Kennedy, even though she is Ferrer's woman. When meeting other outlaws, Kennedy focuses upon Reeves, thinking that this ladies' man, who bears a recent scar on his face from one of his rough romantic escapades, is most likely the man who attacked and killed Henry, and that Henry left that mark on Reeves' face for Kennedy's future identification of her attacker. When Kennedy sees Dietrich dress for dinner and wearing the very brooch he had given Henry, he makes a play for her,

Arthur Kennedy and Marlene Dietrich in *Rancho Notorious*, 1952.

believing that she will tell him the name of the man who gave her that brooch. Dietrich, however, fends off Kennedy's advances, telling him as she does all others, except the faithful Ferrer, that she is too old for him, emphasizing that contention by singing a song titled "Get Away, Young Man." Kennedy is uncertain as to whether or not Ferrer gave Dietrich that brooch, his search interrupted when Dietrich learns that a sheriff's posse from the neighboring town is about to arrive. She orders all of the outlaws to ride away to a nearby hideout, but Kennedy pretends to get lost and returns to the ranch to see the sheriff and his men arrive. One of the sheriff's deputies points out that he has found numerous fresh horse tracks at the ranch, but Kennedy explains that he is a cowhand working for Dietrich and has just rounded up some stray horses and that explains those tracks. The sheriff and his men are satisfied and depart and then Kennedy grabs Dietrich and passionately kisses her. She slaps him, saying: "That was for trying." She then slaps him again, adding: "That was for trying too hard!" When the outlaws return to the ranch they plan a dangerous bank robbery, but Dietrich demands 10 percent of their loot, which puts them off, but Dietrich is doing this to dampen the plan so that Ferrer and Kennedy (she now loves both men) will not go in harm's way. By this time, Kennedy learns that it was Gough who had given Dietrich the telltale brooch as part of his payment to her for providing a safe haven. Kennedy then begins a fight with Gough, prompting him to draw his six-gun, but the wily Gough, who knows that fast-draw Ferrer has taught Kennedy his tricks, evades the gunfight. The sheriff reappears, and Kennedy exposes Gough as Henry's killer and Gough is arrested and jailed. The rest of the outlaws feel betrayed by Dietrich, and they break Gough from jail and then return to the ranch where they shoot it out with Ferrer and Kennedy, who have become fast friends. Gough and others are killed and Kennedy and Ferrer are victorious, but at a terrible price as Dietrich, after leaping before a bullet to save Kennedy's life, has been mortally shot and dies in Kennedy's arms. He and Ferrer then ride away from the ranch together, ostensibly to continue a life of crime. Although Kennedy has gotten his revenge, the cost for that revenge is his own virtue, as he has become, like his friend Ferrer, an outlaw. Lang directs this offbeat western with a firm hand, many of his Germanic techniques in evidence (with the camera POV, tracking and dolly shots); he takes the story line from its comfortable and predictable western genre and into elements of modern film noir (taking a leaf from his classic **M**, 1931, which deals with modern city-based murder and revenge). Dietrich, Kennedy and Ferrer are standouts in their striking roles, and no one other than Dietrich could have been more convincing as the manipulative ranch lady whose final grasp at fading love compels her tragic demise. Gough is also riveting as the evasive and evil-minded killer while Mohr's photography is superb, capturing the action and subterfuge in rich color. Songs: "Get Away, Young Man,"

"Gypsy Davey," "Legend of Chuck-A-Luck" (Ken Darby). *Author's Note*: "I suppose I was a little too demanding with poor Fritz [Lang] when we made **Rancho Notorious**," Dietrich told this author. "He objected to my going directly to Hal [Mohr, the cinematographer] to ask him to soften some of my close-ups, just as he had when we did **Destry Rides Again** [1939], and that was my first big western picture." Mohr had shown Dietrich in that earlier film in muted close-ups that projected an image of youth, the very thing that Dietrich wanted him to achieve once more in **Rancho Notorious**. In **Destry Rides Again**, where Dietrich starred with James Stewart, she plays a singer in a western saloon and where she dies at the end, saving the man she loves by stepping in front of a bullet, which is what she does in **Rancho Notorious**. In one respect, **Rancho Notorious** is almost a sequel to her character in **Destry Rides Again**, except that she has escaped the dance hall to a luxurious ranch where she nevertheless once more dies of unrequited love. Dietrich also told this author that "Fritz became annoyed and upset when I suggested that he use some of the camera techniques that worked so well in my pictures with Josef von Sternberg. Well, I learned that was a big mistake, because you simply cannot tell a director to copy the work of another director, even though that might help the picture. An actor will use anyone's ideas to make a performance better, but a director is someone who is ruled by vanity and the single thought that only he or she knows what is the best thing to do. When giving these good suggestions to Fritz, he only stared at me and said nothing. I was talking to a stone statue." Dietrich did not mention to this author the fact that she had, in separate periods of her life, been romantically involved with both Sternberg and Lang, although Sternberg had and always remained her most cherished director, as well as her mentor in molding and advancing her acting career. By the time that **Rancho Notorious** was completed, Lang and Dietrich were not talking to each other, on or off camera. Two years after this film was released, Nicholas Ray presented an almost identical tale titled **Johnny Guitar**, 1954, where Joan Crawford modeled her character after the character Dietrich essays in **Rancho Notorious**. Ray told this author: "Joan wanted to outdo Marlene's flamboyant character in **Rancho Notorious** so when we did **Johnny Guitar**, she pulled out all of the stops. When I tried to have her use some reserve, she ran over me like a steamroller. At one point, I told her that she did not need to compete with Marlene and that she was her own inimitable person. She replied in typical Joan Crawford style: 'I am going to show that German bitch that she knows nothing about how to act in a western!' Joan ate up everything in sight in that picture, not only the sets, but the furniture and costumes, proving that Marlene was an actress and that Joan Crawford was Joan Crawford everywhere she went, including her sleep. She was acting every second of her life and I don't think she ever knew who the hell she really was." Howard Hughes, who was then head of RKO, learned that Gough, the villain in this film, had been an uncooperative witness at the House of Un-American Activities Committee in Washington, D.C., then probing subversive communist activities. Hughes personally ordered that Gough's name be removed from the credits of this film and Gough was then placed on the unwritten Blacklist that prohibited work in films for the foreseeable future. **p**, Howard Welsch; **d**, Fritz Lang; **cast**, Marlene Dietrich, Arthur Kennedy, Mel Ferrer, Gloria Henry, Lloyd Gough (not credited); William Frawley, Lisa Ferraday, John Raven, Jack Elam, George Reeves, John Doucette, Frank Ferguson, Dan Seymour, John Kellogg, Charlita, Fuzzy Knight, Kermit Maynard; **w**, Daniel Taradash (based on the story "Gunsight Whitman" by Silvia Richards); **c**, Hal Mohr (Technicolor); **m**, Emil Newman, Ken Darby; **ed**, Otto Ludwig; **prod d**, Wiard Ihnen; **set d**, Robert Priestley.

Random Harvest ★★★★★ 1942; U.S.; 126m; MGM; B/W; Romance; Children: Acceptable; **DVD**; **VHS**. This superlative and movingly tender romance film sees two magnificent performances from Colman and Garson, where the theme of amnesia was never more effectively served. Based on the 1940 best-selling novel by James Hilton, the story begins just after WWI ends. Colman, a former British officer who was wounded in France on the Western Front, suffers from amnesia. He resides in an asylum where he anxiously awaits a visit from a kind and considerate elderly couple, who think he might be their son. When they meet, however, they sadly inform psychiatrist Dorn that Colman is not their son and they depart. In a brief bittersweet scene, the noble Colman wistfully tells Dorn: "I would have liked to have belonged to them." The compassionate and understanding Dorn then tells Colman that there is always hope that his real relatives might be located and that he can be restored to his family, although Colman has no recollection of his own past. The Armistice is declared and the town celebrates, and Colman, seeing the guards at the asylum relax their guard, puts on the coat and hat of a British officer and simply walks out of the institution, which is shrouded in fog, calling it a "Pea Souper." He wanders into the town of Medbury, going to a local pub where he meets Garson, who lives above the pub and performs as a singer and dancer at a nearby theater. When Colman has a dizzy spell, Garson takes him to the theater with her, allowing her to view her dancing and singing routine from the wings, but he becomes dizzy. She later takes him to her room above the pub, which is owned by former prizefighter Owen. Garson then realizes that Colman has escaped from the asylum and is suffering from amnesia. She resolves to take care of him and, with the help of kindly Owen, who thinks Colman is a fine gentleman, escorts him to a remote village inn where Colman regains his speech and faculties, albeit he still has no recollections of his past. He and Garson fall deeply in love as Colman discovers that he has a writing talent and begins writing stories, but without being able to use his own forgotten past for those tales. He and Garson then marry and move into a small cottage. They have a child, and Colman begins selling his stories until he is offered a job at a newspaper in Liverpool. He bids Garson and the baby farewell and travels to that city, but, while crossing a street, he is struck by a car and knocked unconscious. He is taken to a nearby apothecary where his memory is restored, but does not understand why he is wearing civilian clothes and is not wearing his uniform. He startles a policeman who asks him his current residence and Colman replies: "The trenches…Arras," meaning that his current address is the Western Front as the war is still raging to Colman's mind, and where he no longer has any recollections of the period from the time he lost his memory to the time he has been struck by that car in Liverpool. (The Battle of Arras occurred in April-May 1917, which is the time when Colman has been wounded and shell-shocked into amnesia that led him to be institutionalized in the asylum at Medbury.) Garson, his child, and the cottage in rural England he has called his home for three years no longer exist in Colman's mind. Colman returns to his family estate as he is a member of the landed gentry, only to discover on the night of his arrival that his father, the lord of the estate, has died. He is now the head of the estate and meets once more with his relatives, busying himself by heading the family's vast industrial operations. Meanwhile, Garson is grief stricken over the disappearance of her husband and struggles to survive, but her child dies, and, with the help of Dorn, the very psychiatrist who once counseled Colman at the asylum, locates Colman, who is now a nationally famous businessman (labeled by the press as "the industrial prince of England"). Using a different name, she goes to work for him as his private secretary, but not telling him about their former relationship, of which Colman has no memory. Garson proves to be the perfect secretary, efficient in all of her duties, and Colman is extremely pleased with her, somehow looking upon her with hazy fondness and emotional dependency he cannot explain. There is something about her manner and bearing that stirs the shadows of the three years of his life that remain a blank, and he always carries a key on a chain that somehow might explain those missing years. When Garson tells Dorn about this, the psychiatrist cautions her not to attempt to force Colman's memory, which, he says, might cause dangerous psychological trauma for Colman. Desperate for Colman's love, however, Garson accompanies Colman to a hotel in Liverpool he has managed to recollect, the very place where he stayed before being struck by that

Greer Garson and Ronald Colman in *Random Harvest,* **1942.**

auto and when he regained his old memory. They find his old valise containing the clothes he wore at that time, and a few mementoes that Garson remembers giving him, but Colman's mind remains a blank about those vanished years with only that key to a lock on a door he cannot find to open. Peters, who is Colman's attractive young niece, who has always been in love with him, then begins a relationship with the tycoon and they eventually make plans to marry, but before the nuptials are announced, Colman seems withdrawn and reserved when discussing that impending marriage; Peters realizes that somewhere in Colman's past is an unknown woman. They break off their engagement, and Colman immerses himself in his business and then decides to run for office in the House of Lords. He makes a brilliant speech in that august house, with Garson complimenting him afterward at lunch. Colman then states that he cannot be a successful politician and industrialist at the same time without a good wife at his side and proposes to her. Garson, who was officially divorced from Colman following his disappearance years earlier, reluctantly accepts, knowing the psychological dangers that might be involved and while Colman is still oblivious to the fact that Garson is the woman of his past. Garson knows that her marriage to Colman is in name only, but, despite warnings from Dorn, attempts to rekindle Colman's memory of her. He gives her a stunning diamond necklace on one occasion and, when she places it within her jewelry box, Colman sees an old, cheap necklace that seems reminiscent, but cannot remember that he had given that very necklace to Garson when they were married many years earlier. Garson agonizes over her strange emotional predicament and finally decides that she needs to separate from Colman and returns alone to the town of Medbury. Colman, ironically, is called to that very town after a labor dispute arises there that involves one of his companies. After arriving in Medbury, Colman settles the dispute, giving the workers better terms and then strolls through the town with an aide, somehow recalling town landmarks, and even remembering a tobacco shop where he first met Garson years earlier. He then recalls a pub run by Owen, the place jarring his memory, and he later goes to the inn where Garson first took him to begin their romance. Colman describes a small cottage and is told by the proprietor where such a cottage is located. He leaves the inn just as Garson comes downstairs to check out, and she learns that Colman has left in search of that cottage. She follows his trail to stand outside the fence of the cottage, watching Colman fingering that key he has kept all these years and, when he tries it in the lock of the cottage door, it opens and so does his memory of his first and only wife, Garson. He turns to see her standing there, smiling and crying with joy; he smiles at her, calling out her original name, "Paula!" They race into each other's arms as Garson calls him by the name she first knew him, "Smithy, Smithy, Smithy!" They kiss and embrace as their old love

Greer Garson and Ronald Colman in *Random Harvest*, 1942.

flames anew, a love that is now all-knowing. This finale is one of the most thrilling and satisfying romantic moments ever put on a screen, and few romantic leads could have equaled its telling impact other than Colman and Garson. Master helmsman LeRoy carefully directs this sensitive tale, fully developing its mature and intelligent characters with endearing personalities and seamlessly unfolding one memorable scene after another, visually transcending many lost years into precious days and hours, until allowing love to find its way back into the human heart where all true and best memories reside. LeRoy takes enough time to cement the love between Colman and Garson through their deepening friendship, unflagging loyalty and profound respect for each other. Unlike the star-crossed lovers of other masterpiece romance films, such as **Casablanca**, 1942, and **Now, Voyager**, 1942 (ironically three of these films made in the same year), and **Waterloo Bridge**, 1940, **Random Harvest** generously allows its lovers a magnificent triumph in the end, a great victory of the heart shared by every viewer. In other directorial hands, this fragile and vulnerable story might have drowned in sloppy sentimentality, but the always deliberate LeRoy maintains a wonderful balance between eerie happenstance and stark reality, sustaining suspense and angst throughout, and the pensive Colman, through his inimitable physical gestures and facial nuances, is utterly convincing and empathetic as a man afflicted by amnesia. Garson, never more charming and beautiful than in this stirring film, radiates confidence and hope that she will regain the love of her life, despite all odds and obstacles. The film received Oscar nominations for Best Picture and Best Director (LeRoy). Colman was rightly nominated for a Best Actor Oscar, as was Peters for Best Supporting Actress. Garson won an Oscar as Best Actress that year, but for **Mrs. Miniver**, 1942, although her performance in **Random Harvest** was no less outstanding. The film was an enormous box office success, taking in more than $8 million (domestic and foreign) against a $2 million budget. Songs: "Viva La Company!" (traditional), "God Save the King!" (Henry Carey), "Pack Up Your Troubles in Your Old Kit Bag and Smile, Smile, Smile" (1915; music: Felix Powell; lyrics: George Asaf), "Sombre las olas (Over the Waves)" (Juventino Rosas), "She's My Daisy" (1905; music: Harry Lauder; lyrics: Harry Lauder and J.D. Harper), "It's a Long Way to Tipperary" (Jack Judge, Harry Williams), "The Voice That Breathed O'er Eden" (1857; music [1852]: Henry J. Gauntlett; lyrics: John Keble), "Symphony No. 5 in E Minor, Op. 64" (1888; Peter Ilyich Tchaikovsky), "Oh Perfect Love" (1889; music: Joseph Barnby; lyrics: Dorothy B. Gurney), "For He's a Jolly Good Fellow" (traditional). *Author's Note*: "The story for **Random Harvest** was tricky," LeRoy told this author, "because it had so many twists and turns and because I did not shoot the picture chronologically, it was a complicated production, making sure all the plot twists worked. That's where continuity be-

comes very important, especially when you deal with costuming. We had to have Ronnie [Colman] in rather shabby clothes when he is a struggling writer, but wearing a lot of finery when he is a rich lord, right down to his shoes. Louis B. Mayer, who ran MGM then, loved this story and thought Greer [Garson] walked on water, and, in those days, she did, what a marvelous actress. Like Ronnie, she was faultless in every one of her scenes and so stunningly beautiful that I think almost every male above the age of fifteen was in love with her." Garson had some apprehension about doing a dance routine on a theater stage at the beginning of the film where she wears a short kilt and exposes her legs. "I was concerned about that scene," she told this author, "and told Mr. Mayer that I would only do it if it was done with taste. He replied: 'Oh, legs are legs, my dear, and they are only tastefully shown by tasteful ladies like you.' Since the scene was a musical comedy routine there was no suggestiveness in showing my legs. I later got fan mail from men asking for cheesecake photos, which I did not do." Amnesia is a mental condition stemming from physical or psychological injuries, or is induced through drugs, where the victim suffers a momentary or prolonged loss of memory. That loss of memory can afflict those who have no recollections of information before the time of an accident or operation that can date back for decades, but otherwise allow such victims to have full use of all other mental faculties. Amnesia is one of the most popular themes in films as it inherently presents dynamic drama packed with mystery and quest and where significant revelations are often sought under harrowing conditions, or where amnesia is feigned to achieve comedic or dramatic results. Other notable films dealing with amnesia include **The Addams Family**, 1991; **The Adventures of Baron Munchausen**, 1989; **Anastasia**, 1956; **As You Desire Me**, 1932; **Away from Her**, 2007; **Black Angel**, 1946; **Blind Alley**, 1939; **The Blue Dahlia**, 1946; **The Bourne Identity**, 2002; **Charlie Chan at the Opera**, 1936; **The Chase**, 1946; **Conspiracy Theory**, 1997; **The Constant Husband**, 1955; **Courage of Lassie**, 1946; **The Dark Past**, 1948; **A Double Life**, 1947; **The English Patient**, 1996; **The Great Dictator**, 1940; **Hallelujah, I'm a Bum!**, 1933; **High Wall**, 1947; **The Howling**, 1981; **I Love You Again**, 1940; **Impact**, 1949; **A Little Princess**, 1995; **The Long Wait**, 1954; **Love Letters**, 1945; **Madonna of the Seven Moons**, 1946; **Marnie**, 1964; **Me after the Show**, 1951; **Men in Black**, 1997; **Men in Black II**, 2002; **Mirage**, 1965; **Mr. Arkadin**, 1962; **Muholland Dr.**, 2001; **The Muppets Take Manhattan**, 1984; **Murder!**, 1930; **Murder on Monday**, 1953; **Nightmare**, 1956; **Nosferatu: The Vampire**, 1979; **Paris, Texas**, 1984; **Possessed**, 1947; **RoboCop**, 1987; **Shadow on the Wall**, 1950; **The Snake Pit**, 1948; **Somewhere in the Night**, 1946; **Spellbound**, 1945; **Star Trek: The Search for Spock**, 1984; **Suddenly, Last Summer**, 1959; **Sullivan's Travels**, 1941; **Sundays and Cybele**, 1962; **Tenebre**, 1987; **The Thief of Bagdad**, 1940; **36 Hours**, 1965; **Total Recall**, 1990; **Ulysses**, 1955; **Unknown**, 2011; **The Unsuspected**, 1947; **The Walking Dead**, 1926; **Without Love**, 1945; **The Woman in Green**, 1945; **X-Men**, 2000; **X2**, 2003; and **X-Men Origins: Wolverine**, 2009. For a more extensive list of films profiling amnesia, see Index, Volume II, of this work. **p**, Sidney Franklin; **d**, Mervyn LeRoy; **cast**, Ronald Colman, Greer Garson, Philip Dorn, Susan Peters, Henry Travers, Reginald Owen, Bramwell Fletcher, Rhys Williams, Una O'Connor, Margaret Wycherly, Melville Cooper, Alan Napier, Ann Richards, Peter Lawford, Terry Kilburn, St. Luke's Episcopal Church Choristers; **w**, Claudine West, George Froeschel, Arthur Wimperis (based on the novel by James Hilton); **c**, Joseph Ruttenberg; **m**, Herbert Stothart; **ed**, Harold F. Kress; **art d**, Cedric Gibbons; **set d**, Edwin B. Willis.

Rango ★★★ 2011; U.S.; 107m; Nickelodeon Movies/PAR; Color; Animated Adventure; Children: Unacceptable (MPAA: PG); **BD**; **DVD**. Amusing and entertaining, this well-crafted animated film sees Rango (Depp voiceover) as an ordinary everyday chameleon, who accidentally finds himself in the 21st-century Wild West town of Dirt, a woebegone town that desperately needs a new sheriff. He takes the job, which involves finding the town's missing water. Through some uncommon and exciting exploits, he accomplishes his tasks by outwitting the villain, Rattlesnake Jack (Nighy voiceover). Songs: "Rango," "Walk Don't Rango," "Rango Theme Song" (John Thum, David Thum), "Latin Lounge"(Mike Radovsky, Paul Martin); "Ave Maria" (Franz Schubert); "Forkboy" (Jello Biafra, Paul Barker, Al Jourgensen, Jeff Ward, Bill Rieflin); "Welcome Amigo," "The Banks Been Robbed," "La Muerte a Llegado" (Rick Garcia, Kenneth Karman, Gore Verbinski, James Ward Byrkit); "Cool Water" (Bob Nolan); "Selenger's Round" (Nicholas Parker, Francis Silkstone); "Ride of the Valkyries" (Richard Wagner); "On the Beautiful Blue Danube" (Johann Strauss, Jr.); "Finale" (from **The Kingdom** by Danny Elfman); "Right on Target" (Hans Zimmer); "El Canelo" (traditional). Crude humor, gutter language, violence and smoking prohibit viewing by children. **p**, Gore Verbinski, John B. Carls, Graham King, Adam Cramer, Shari Hanson, David Shannon; **d**, Verbinski; **cast** (voiceovers), Johnny Depp, Isla Fisher, Abigail Breslin, Ned Beatty, Alfred Molina, Bill Nighy, Stephen Root, Harry Dean Stanton, Timothy Olyphant, Ray Winstone, Ian Abercrombie; **w**, John Logan (based on a story by Logan, Verbinski, James Ward Byrkit); **m**, Hans Zimmer; **ed**, Craig Wood; **prod d**, Mark "Crash" McCreery; **art d**, John Bell; **spec eff**, Tim Alexander, John Knoll.

Ransom! ★★★★ 1956; U.S.; 109m; MGM; B/W; Crime Drama; Children: Unacceptable; **VHS**. Taut and well-acted crime tale sees Clark, the son of wealthy businessman Ford, kidnapped and held for ransom. The entire town shows its empathy toward Ford and his distraught wife, Reed, while Police Chief Keith attempts to locate the hideout of the kidnappers. Meanwhile, Nielsen (in his feature film debut), a cold-blooded newsman, is more concerned with getting a provocative story for his avid crime readers than having any consideration for the emotionally torn Ford and Reed. Ford manages to collect the $500,000 ransom demanded by the kidnappers, but, at the last minute, stubbornly refuses to deliver that ransom money to his son's abductors, fatalistically believing that they will nevertheless kill the boy. He appears on television and offers the money as a reward for the capture of the kidnappers, instead of offering it as ransom, which devastates Reed, as she now believes Ford has consigned her son to death. Ford's troubled reasoning concludes that the kidnappers no longer have any reason to murder Clark, since they would also face charges for that killing in addition to charges of kidnapping, and therefore gain nothing by holding on to the boy or injuring him in any way. Though Ford's actions have ruptured his relationship with Reed, he is supported in his actions by compassionate house servants Hernandez and Moore, and Nielsen then gains great respect for Ford's courageous but dangerous decision. When Ford hears nothing from the kidnappers, he is overwhelmed with a sense of guilt, believing that he may have brought about his son's death, but, at the end, Clark appears in the backyard of his home while Ford is agonizing over the dilemma and he embraces the boy, who has been released by his kidnappers, who have, fortunately, acted as Ford had hopefully anticipated. Director Segal maintains suspense and a deep sense of anxiety throughout this taut thriller, particularly by never showing the kidnappers of Clark's ongoing plight, and Ford, Reed and the rest of the cast are standouts in their roles. *Author's Note*: Ford told this author that "my role in that picture was very demanding. I have to visually translate what my character is thinking while risking the life of his son with dangerous kidnappers. Are his actions based on the best interests of his son or himself? That is what I must keep the viewer guessing about. It's a psychological drama and they are the hardest to perform because you somehow have to allow the viewer to get into your character's mind, not an easy chore." The film was based upon a teleplay, "Fearful Decision," which was aired on the United States Steel Hour on June 22, 1954. The telecast had such an enormous and popular impact that MGM decided to produce the story as a feature film, as did Ron Howard in producing its superior remake in **Ransom**, 1996, starring Mel Gibson and Gary Sinise. **p**, Nicholas Nayfack; **d**, Alex Segal; **cast**, Glenn Ford, Donna Reed,

Mel Gibson offering millions on television for the return of his son (photo of Brawley Nolte behind him) in *Ransom*, 1996.

Leslie Nielsen, Juano Hernandez, Robert Keith, Richard Gaines, Mabel Albertson, Alexander Scourby, Bobby Clark, Juanita Moore; **w**, Cyril Hume, Richard Maibaum; **c**, Arthur E. Arling; **m**, Jeff Alexander; **ed**, Ferris Webster; **art d**, Cedric Gibbons, Arthur Lonergan; **set d**, Edwin B. Willis, Richard Pefferle.

Ransom ★★★★ 1996; U.S.; 121m; Touchstone Pictures/Buena Vista; Color; Crime Drama; Children: Unacceptable (MPAA: R); **DVD**; **VHS**. A rugged Gibson and a devious Sinise play a dangerous game of wits in this taut kidnapping yarn, remade from the 1956 film. This production proved to be a superior version, one presenting nonstop suspenseful and bone-chilling scenes that make up its grim and fascinating story. Gibson, a multimillionaire, attends a science fair with his wife, Russo, and son, Nolte, where Nolte is kidnapped. The boy is taken to a basement apartment occupied by Taylor, who works as a caterer for Gibson and Russo and has arranged for the abduction through her inside information regarding the family's day-to-day routines and whereabouts. She is accompanied by professional criminals Schreiber, Wahlberg and Handler, who tie up the boy and blindfold him so that he cannot recognize his abductors. Gibson then receives an email, demanding that he pay a ransom of $2 million to recover Nolte alive. Gibson contacts the FBI, its agents establishing a headquarters operation inside of Gibson's lavish NYC penthouse. As agents attempt to identify the kidnappers, Sinise, a clever NYPD detective, sees Wahlberg purchase an item in a convenience store, following him to Taylor's apartment where Sinise finds Nolte tied to a bed. Sinise then holds a gun on Wahlberg while he berates Wahlberg for being too obvious in his actions, as Sinise has masterminded the kidnapping right from the beginning and is the boss of the abduction ring. Disguising his voice with an electronic device, Sinise then contacts Gibson by phone and gives him instructions as to where to take the ransom money, saying that someone will be waiting to receive the $2 million payoff at a New Jersey quarry and where that person will tell Gibson to retrieve his son after making the payoff. Gibson meets with Wahlberg, but the kidnapper has either forgotten or not received Sinise's instructions on where Gibson can find Nolte and simply demands that Gibson turn over the money to him. Without knowing where he can recoup his son, Gibson refuses to make the payoff and, when an FBI helicopter appears, Wahlberg makes a break and then begins firing at the helicopter and is shot to death by return fire, never revealing Nolte's whereabouts of that orhis criminal associates. Sinise calls Gibson again and sets up another rendezvous where Gibson is to deliver the ransom money. This time, Gibson balks, enraged over the fact that the FBI interfered in his meeting with Wahlberg, trailing him instead of the money he might have given Wahlberg. Believing that any repeat of that original plan will most likely result in Nolte's death, he has developed

Maureen O'Hara and James Stewart in *The Rare Breed*, 1966.

a new and very dangerous plan to which Russo hysterically objects in that she believes that plan will assure her son's death. Gibson is adamant in taking a new approach, and despite strong objections from FBI Special Agent Lindo, he appears on television, showing the amount of cash the kidnappers demand, but as a bounty to anyone who will save his son and bring in the kidnappers. He tells the kidnappers over the airways that they have only one chance in saving themselves: turn over his son safely to him, and, once that is done, he will withdraw the bounty and press no charges against them. Sinise will not be out-maneuvered by Gibson, retaliating by enticing Russo to a meeting where he tells her that unless her husband pays the ransom and quickly, Nolte will be killed. Russo goes to Gibson and pleads with him to make the $2 million payoff, but he obstinately refuses, going back on TV and now offering $4 million as a bounty to bring in the kidnappers. Sinise then calls Gibson and tells him to either pay the money or his son will be killed. Gibson tells him to turn over his son or he will use the payoff money to have him tracked down. Sinise then allows Nolte to cry out to Gibson for help and then fires a shot and the line goes dead and now Gibson and Russo shockingly think that their son has been murdered. Sinise then formulates another, more sinister plan. He goes to Taylor's apartment and calls for backup from the NYPD, stating that he has discovered a possible kidnapping. As Schreiber and Handler leave the apartment and are about to get into a van, Sinise blocks their way, drawing his gun. Both Schreiber and Handler now realize that their boss is betraying them and attempt to escape, but Sinise shoots them both dead. As he approaches the apartment, Taylor emerges, realizing what her lover has done, and draws a gun, firing at Sinise and wounding him in the shoulder. He returns fire and kills her. He then enters the apartment, and, pretending to be Nolte's rescuer (as well as later claiming the bounty of $4 million Gibson has offered), goes to the boy and poses as his protector as NYPD officers rush into the place to hail him a courageous hero. Alerted to events, Gibson and Russo rush to the crime scene and are joyously reunited with Nolte, and Gibson gives his deep thanks to Sinise for ostensibly saving his son as the wounded Sinise is placed into an ambulance. FBI agent Lindo then shows Gibson the body of Taylor so that Gibson now realizes that one of his own employees had arranged to kidnap his son. The nerveless Sinise later arrives to claim his $4 million reward from Gibson by going to Gibson's penthouse, his arm in a sling as he is recovering from the gunshot wound. Gibson happily begins to write out a check for the reward, but then sees Nolte standing some distance away in shock and terror, the boy recognizing Sinise's voice as one of his kidnappers. Gibson also identifies Sinise as the man who has called him on the phone as he has repeated some of the same phrases stated by the kidnapper. Alerted to the fact that he is dealing with a cleaver criminal, Gibson writes a false signature on the check and hands

it to Sinise, but Sinise realizes that he has been identified as the criminal mastermind and now threatens to kill Gibson and everyone in his family. Gibson frantically negotiates, telling Sinise he will personally escort him to his bank and where he will have Sinise's $4 million wired to any other bank around the world and then arrange for Sinise to fly out of the country with him as a hostage on Gibson's private jet. Sinise agrees, and, while pretending to call his private jet, Gibson actually calls Lindo, alerting him that he is taking Sinise to his bank and to get his plane ready to fly out to a foreign country. Lindo then orders FBI agents to converge on the bank. When inside the bank, the $4 million is wired to a bank account Sinise has designated in a foreign country and when he and Gibson leave the bank, a NYC policeman tells Sinise that he is being detained for questioning. Realizing that his game is up, the desperate Sinise shoots and kills his fellow officer, and then races into the street with Gibson pursuing him. They struggle and Gibson knocks the wounded Sinise and himself into a plate glass window, breaking it, and they collapse into the store. Gibson retrieves Sinise's fallen gun and aims it at Sinise, who now struggles to breathe as a jagged piece of plate glass has penetrated his throat. Lindo has arrived with his agents and orders Gibson to drop the gun, which he does. Sinise, however, reaches for a backup revolver strapped to his ankle, but before he can fire at Gibson, Gibson retrieves the fallen gun, and he and Lindo both fire shots into Sinise, killing him. Lindo then orders police to release Gibson and that is where this action-packed and very tense thriller ends. Director Howard does an outstanding job in unfolding this absorbing crime yarn, carefully detailing its tricky plot turns and drawing forth excellent portrayals from Gibson, Sinise, Russo, Nolte, Lindo and others in the sterling cast. The film was a box office smash, earning more than $300 million in its initial box office release against an $80 million budget. Songs: "Lizards," "Rats," "Rats with Tails," "Spiders," "Squirrels," "Worms" (Billy Corgan of Smashing Pumpkins). **p**, Brian Grazer, Scott Rudin, B. Kipling Hagopian, Susan Merzbach, Adam Schroeder; **d**, Ron Howard; **cast**, Mel Gibson, Rene Russo, Gary Sinise, Brawley Nolte, Liev Schreiber, Donnie Wahberg, Evan Handler, Lili Taylor, Delroy Lindo, Paul Guilfoyle; **w**, Richard Price, Alexander Ignon (based on a story by Cyril Hume, Richard Maibaum); **c**, Piotr Sobocinski; **m**, James Horner; **ed**, Dan Hanley, Mike Hill; **prod d**, Michael Corenblith; **art d**, John Kasarda; **set d**, Susan Bode; **spec eff**, Wilfred Caban.

The Rare Breed ★★★ 1966; U.S.; 97m; UNIV; Color; Western; Children: Acceptable; **DVD**. Exceptional western sees O'Hara and her husband and daughter, Mills, travel by ship from England to America, but he dies en route and she tries to carry out his dream of introducing British Hereford cattle into the American West and crossbreed them with traditional longhorns. O'Hara takes her prize Hereford bull named "Vindicator" to the St. Louis Exposition and looks for a rancher willing to help her. Keith, a fiery Scotsman, agrees to become a partner and he hires a drifter, Stewart, to lead them on a journey to transport the bull to Keith's ranch in Texas. Before leaving for Texas, Stewart accepts a bribe from Elam to swindle O'Hara, but, on the trail while protecting her and her daughter from stampedes, cattle rustlers, and other hazards, he decides against the swindle when he becomes romantically interested in O'Hara, as does Keith. They arrive safely in Texas, but Keith has doubts that Herefords can withstand a cold Texas winter. O'Hara and Mills stay in Keith's house over the winter and O'Hara begins to share Keith's doubts about the rare breed of cattle surviving the cold, but Stewart has faith in the Herefords. "Vindicator" dies and spring arrives. O'Hara thinks she may marry Keith, while Stewart rides back over their trail from the previous autumn in hopes that "Vindicator" mated with a longhorn and he may find a half-Hereford calf. After a long search, he finds one and takes it to Keith's ranch. O'Hara changes her mind and now decides to marry Stewart and they will start their own crossbreeding cattle business. This exciting and absorbing western is a fictionalized account of how British-bred cattle came to become part of the American beef industry. Another film, **Rare Breed**, 1954, had a different plot. **p**,

William Alland; **d**, Andrew V. McLaglen; **cast**, James Stewart, Maureen O'Hara, Brian Keith, Juliet Mills, Don Galloway, David Brian, Jack Elam, Ben Johnson, Harry Carey Jr., Gregg Palmer, Perry Lopez; **w**, Ric Hardman; **c**, William H. Clothier (Panavision; Technicolor); **m**, John "Johnny" Williams; **ed**, Russell F. Schoengarth; **art d**, Alexander Golitzen, Alfred Ybarra; **set d**, Oliver Emert, John McCarthy; **spec eff**, Albert Whitlock.

Rascal ★★★ 1969; U.S.; 85m; Disney/Buena Vista; Color; Adventure; Children: Recommended (MPAA: G); **DVD**; **IV**. A wonderful family film about a boy, Mumy, and his mischievous pet raccoon named "Rascal," who saves his life from an attacking lynx. The story is set in the summer of 1918 in northern Wisconsin, where Mumy lives with his widowed father, Forrest, who is often away from home on business sales trips. Mumy is left mostly alone to play with Rascal and his dog, Wowser. He lets Rascal run free at times, and it gets into a neighbor's corn patch. When summer ends and Mumy must go back to school, he is comforted by knowing that Rascal and its female partner will be there to play with after school is out for the day and on weekends. Song: "Summer Sweet" (Bobby Russell). *Author's Note*: The film is based on the novel by North, which was based on his boyhood experiences with a pet raccoon. **p**, James Algar; **d**, Norman Tokar; **cast**, Steve Forrest, Bill Mumy, Pamela Toll, Elsa Lanchester, Henry James, Steve Carlson, Bettye Ackerman, Jonathan Daly, John Fiedler, Richard Erdman, Herbert Anderson, Robert Emhardt, Maudie Prickett, (narrator) Walter Pidgeon; **w**, Harold Swanton (based on the novel by Sterling North); **c**, William Snyder; **m**, Buddy Baker; **ed**, Norman R. Palmer; **art d**, John B. Mansbridge; **set d**, Emile Kuri, Frank R. McKelvy; **spec eff**, Eustace Lycett, Alan Maley.

Rashomon ★★★★★ 1951; Japan; 88m; Daiei Motion Picture Company/RKO; Drama; Children: Unacceptable; **DVD**; **VHS**. This is one of Kurosawa's greatest films, if not his finest. Set in 8th-Century medieval Japan, there is widespread unrest and chaos since most are starving. Three persons from a village—Shimura, a woodcutter; Ueda, a peasant; and Chiaki, a priest—find themselves together when they seek shelter beneath the ruined gate of the city of Kyoto during a torrential rainstorm. As the three wait out the storm, Shimura tells the other two men a tale drawn from his own experience. He relates how he found a dead body in a forest, the corpse being that of a wealthy man, and we now see four different versions of how that victim came to his fate. Mifune, a bandit, is accused of killing the rich man, Mori, and then raping his beautiful wife, Kyo. Mifune admits his guilt, stating (to the camera as if testifying before a magistrate presiding over the case) that he, because he could not resist Kyo's beauty, tied up Mori and then had his way with Kyo, and where Kyo states that she cannot live with the humiliation of having been defiled before two men. Kato, a policeman, listens to the testimony without comment as he attempts to organize the contradictory statements of the witnesses. Mifune claims that after he has assaulted Kyo he released Mori and both men dueled and where Mifune honorably killed Mori in combat. Kyo's story refutes Mifune's account as she claims that Mifune tied up and raped her husband and then assaulted her, but she later freed Mori, and, when he showed nothing but contempt for her, now that she is despoiled, she flew into a rage and killed her husband. Honma, a medium, then recounts a third version of the event as she speaks through the voice and eyes of the murdered Mori, describing how, after Mifune assaulted Kyo, she pleaded with Mifune to kill her husband, but he refused, believing such an act to be dishonorable and then left with Kyo, after she begged Mifune to take her along with him. Mori, mortified at being cuckolded, admits through medium Honma that he withdrew his bejeweled dagger and committed hara-kiri (suicide). Shimura, the only witness not involved in the incident, then testifies, and his perspective presents yet a fourth version of the story. He states that even though Mori was a cringing coward, Kyo goaded him into attacking Mifune and, to defend his life, Mifune killed

Toshiro Mifune and Daisuke Kato in *Rashomon*, 1951.

Mori. Shimura's tale is looked upon with suspicion since he stole the jeweled dagger from Mori's corpse. Chiaki, the priest, after listening to these disturbing versions of the same tale, becomes disillusioned with mankind. As the rain lets up, the trio discovers an infant beneath a pile of rags, and Ueda attempts to rob the baby of its clothes, but Shimura, who has many children of his own, decides to take the child with him; this act of kindness restores Chiaki's belief in humanity, and this is where this fascinating film ends. In this riveting film, Kurosawa challenges the validity of truth, presenting the many-sided aspects of truth as seen by several persons with different motivations. There is no declarative answer, only varying perspectives where what is reality becomes fragmented through the prism-like views of witnesses seeing the same thing but through their own self-serving interpretations of that reality. Simply stated, Kurosawa takes the position that "truth is in the eye of the beholder." The director displays his mastery in economically depicting this complex story through more than 400 separate cuts within the framework of its 88 minutes, cohesively joining all of the varied perspectives as uniform but with slight variations that otherwise alter the placing of guilt and responsibility. The film was remade as **The Outrage**, 1964, starring Paul Newman, but which proved to be much less impactful than this masterpiece. *Author's Note*: Kurosawa and scriptwriter Hashimoto, like the author of the original story upon which this strange but compelling tale is based, Ryunosuke Akutagawa, asks the viewer to determine the truth of the story they present. Akutagawa, a brilliant author, who is called "the father of the Japanese short story," centered his literature upon the ambiguities of life, which eventually overwhelmed his own. Fearing that he had inherited his mother's insanity, he took his own life on July 24, 1927, with an overdose of barbital, his last written words reportedly stating that he was fearful and had a "vague insecurity about the future." (In Japanese; English subtitles.) **p**, Minoru Jingo; **d**, Akira Kurosawa; **cast**, Toshiro Mifune, Machiko Kyo, Masayuki Mori, Takashi Shimura, Minoru Chiaki, Kichijiro Ueda, Noriko Honma, Daisuke Kato; **w**, Shinobu Hashimoto, Kurosawa (based on the short story "Nabu no Naka" and the novel *Rasho-Mon* by Ryunosuke Akutagawa); **c**, Kazuo Miyagawa; **m**, Fumio Hayasaka; **ed**, Kurosawa; **prod d**, Takashi Matsuyama; **set d**, H. Motsumoto.

Rasputin ★★★★ 1985; USSR; 151m; Mosfilm/International Film Exchange; Color; Biographical Drama; Children: Unacceptable; **DVD**; **VHS**. Petrenko is mesmerizing in the role of the "Mad Monk," Grigori Rasputin (1869-1916), in this elaborately produced baroque film that also dynamically profiles the last years of the Russian royal family. Rasputin's almost mystical powers of hypnotism are emphasized as he acts as a healer for the czar's hemophiliac son, able to stop the boy's internal bleeding as the result of any minor injury. As such, the profligate

Anatoliy Romashin and Alisa Freyndlikh in *Rasputin*, 1985.

Petrenko wields such great power with the royal couple, Emperor Nicholas II (1868-1918), played by Romashin, and, especially the always worried Empress Alexandra (1872-1918), played by Line, that he alarms many Russian aristocrats. Petrenko's meddling in state affairs and his persuasive efforts to dangerously guide the czar in the course of the war (WWI, 1914-1918) convinces Romantsov, playing Prince Felix Yusupov (1887-1967), a Russian member of the royal family, to plot Petrenko's assassination. Petrenko uses his influence with the weak-willed Romashin to appoint a new prime minister and create new policies that alienate the Duma (the Russian parliament). Any criticism of the monk's manipulative practices causes the protective empress to defend the holy man as she believes him to be a saint by repeatedly saving her son's life. Thus shielded, Petrenko acts with impunity, hosting wild bacchanalian parties where he promiscuously dallies with the wives of noblemen. After he assaults a baroness, her husband attacks Petrenko and is imprisoned for the attack. His wife, in order to have her husband released, is forced to grant Petrenko sexual favors. Pressured by aristocrats to remove the irresponsible and dangerous Petrenko from power, Romashin finally banishes Petrenko from the royal palace in St. Petersburg, ordering him to leave the city. Drunk and disheveled, Petrenko nevertheless secretly reenters the royal palace one night and uses his hypnotic powers with the gullible Romashin to reinstate him. He further convinces the czar to take command of all the Russian armies in the field, which will certainly bring Russia to defeat in the eyes of militarists as Romashin has no military expertise. Romantsov and others then decide to end the monk's disastrous power behind the throne. Petrenko is invited to a party (at Yusupov's Moika Palace in St. Petersburg on the night of December 29, 1916) where he anticipates enjoying the sexual favors of Romantsov's beautiful wife, but, instead, is poisoned, shot four times, beaten with an iron bar, and stabbed, his body, bound with heavy ropes, then thrown into the frozen Neva River. (When the body was later found, it was theorized that, despite all of his wounds, the powerful Rasputin, whose body was jammed through a hole in the ice of the river, nevertheless briefly survived underwater and broke through the ice down river, struggling to the bank where he was later found dead.) This Soviet-sponsored film takes no moral position about the hedonistic Rasputin. It therefore focuses more on Rasputin's political machinations to show disfavor upon the royal couple, in keeping with the peculiar and bizarre events of that time, all viewed by the communist regime as corrupt. The film is nevertheless superbly directed by Klimov and its sets, costuming and score are all outstanding and in keeping with the period profiled. (In Russian; English subtitles.) **p&d**, Elem Klimov; **cast**, Aleksey, Petrenko, Anatoliy Romashin, Velta Line, Alisa Freyndlikh, Alexkandr Romantsov, Yuri Katin-Yartsev, Leonid Bronevoy, Pavel Pankov, Mikhail Danilov, Mikhail Svetin, Nelli Pshyonnaya; **w**, Semyon

Lungin, Ilya Nusinov; **c**, Leonid Kalashnikov (Sovcolor); **m**, Alfred Schnittke; **ed**, Valeriya Belova; **prod d**, Sergey Voronkov, Shavkat Abdusalamov; **art d**, Abdusalamov.

Rasputin and the Empress ★★★★ 1932; U.S.; 135m; MGM; B/W; Biographical Drama/Horror; Children: Unacceptable; **DVD**; **VHS**. Two royal families are superbly presented in this excellent historical drama, the first family being the last ill-fated royal Romanov family of Russia. The second is the royal family of Broadway—John, Lionel and Ethel Barrymore—who play the principal characters and play them to the hilt while fiercely competing with each other for every scene in this exciting film. The setting is the last stages of the Romanov dynasty during WWI, where the throne must contend with widespread unrest and brewing revolution. John Barrymore, a prince of the royal family and a reformer at heart, arrives at the royal palace in St. Petersburg to urge Emperor Nicholas II (1868-1918), played by Morgan, to institute reforms to ease the suffering of his people, but Morgan and his wife, Empress Alexandra (1872-1918), played by Ethel Barrymore, are too obsessed and worried about their son and heir to the throne, Alexei (1904-1918), played by Alexander. The boy is afflicted by a dangerous hemophilia that, whenever he experiences a slight bruise, begins internal bleeding that might end his life. After the royal physician, Arnold, informs the royal couple that he cannot stop the bleeding from a recent accident and that Alexander might die, Ethel becomes desperate for any kind of cure. Wynyard, her lady-in-waiting, and who is also John's fiancé, tells Ethel about a mystical monk named Rasputin (1869-1916), played by Lionel Barrymore, who has great healing powers and that this strange clergyman might be able to save Alexander's life. Lionel is summoned to the St. Petersburg palace, this brooding and cunning character telling Ethel that God has sent him to save her son, but he must be left alone with the boy while he works a miraculous cure. The royal couple agrees, and Lionel enters Alexander's bedroom chamber, hypnotizing him, and is able to stop his internal bleeding by commanding the boy to become well. Insidious to his core, the devious and manipulating Lionel is out for power and intends to obtain that power by making Alexander a total slave to his will. With the boy and his royal parents now wholly dependent upon Lionel for his survival, the monk begins to expand his influence at the royal court. At Ethel's insistence, Lionel has free access to the royal palace, where he begins to meddle in Morgan's shaky government, persuading the weak monarch to name Lionel's cronies to high office positions after Lionel has been heavily bribed by these office-seekers and who now do Lionel's bidding. The lascivious Lionel then eyes the beautiful elder daughters of the czar, using his hypnotic powers to put them under his sway (and it is suggested in one scene that he has raped one of the daughters). John Barrymore, who has demeaned Lionel from the start, branding him nothing more than a conniving, crude peasant, realizes that Lionel is destroying the government and, through his irresponsible dictates, is causing revolt among the masses. He decides to get rid of Lionel by assassinating him. (John's role is decidedly based upon Prince Felix Yusupov, 1887-1967, who headed the small cabal that brought about Rasputin's assassination on the night of December 29, 1916, in St. Petersburg, Russia.) Lionel is invited to a party in St. Petersburg, not knowing that it is the home of his arch enemy, John, and where he is given wine and cakes that have been dosed with "enough poison to kill five men," according to court physician Von Seyffertitz, who has provided John with that poison (cyanide was the poison used in the assassination). Lionel grows wary when he sees Auer, whom he knows is John's butler, and now believes that he has been trapped. He finds John lurking nearby and both men battle, the powerful Lionel struggling with John in a cellar room, where Lionel tries to shoot John. The monk's enormous stamina, however, begins to wane when the poisoned cakes and wine he has consumed begin to take effect, and John knocks him unconscious. Lionel nevertheless regains his senses and staggers to his feet, his face a hideous mask of blood, snarling that, if he dies, Russia will die, as he believes that his hypnotic powers control the royal family and the fate of its only male heir as well as the destiny of Russia. Furious, John wrestles the weakened Lionel from the house (Yusupov actually invited Rasputin to his own palace in St. Petersburg, enticing the sexually ravenous monk to a party by using his own beautiful wife, Princess Irina, 1895-1970, who was the czar's niece, as bait). John drags the semi-conscious Lionel through the snows of a street to a nearby river, throwing him into the rushing waters to his death. (After being poisoned, stabbed, beaten with an iron bar and shot, Rasputin was taken to the Neva River, where the conspirators chopped a hole in the frozen river, stuffing the monk's corpse into it, but, amazingly, the body was later found downstream, where Rasputin apparently had survived underwater, breaking through the ice and crawling to shore, only to die at that spot.) John is brought before Morgan and Ethel Barrymore where he is publicly chastised for bringing about Lionel's death, and he and his wife, Wynyard, are banished from Russia. Morgan, however, takes John aside to express his gratitude for ridding Russia of a lunatic. John begs Morgan to abdicate and take his family to a foreign country, telling the monarch that revolution will soon erupt and destroy the Romanov dynasty. Morgan tells John that his people will never overturn the monarchy, and John, full of misgivings, departs to live in another country. (The monarchy was overthrown a year later, and a year after that, in 1918, Nicholas II and his entire family were assassinated by Bolsheviks.) Director Boleslawsky helms this epic film with great care, developing the characters with skill while faithfully following the brilliant script from MacArthur (who wrote most of his screenplays in cooperation with Ben Hecht); MacArthur religiously presents the then known facts about Rasputin with accuracy, emphasizing the monk's profligate lifestyle, as well as his mystical hypnotic powers. All of the cast members are outstanding in their riveting roles, Morgan as the indecisive czar, Ethel as the empress living in constant fear that her son may die at any moment from his malady, John Barrymore as the prince dedicated to ending Rasputin's evil machinations and Lionel Barrymore, in a bravura performance where he wholly captures the creepy, diabolical character of the conniving monk. The film was lavishly produced with sumptuous sets and meticulous and impressive costumes, all appropriate for the era; MGM spent more than $800,000 to produce the film. Songs: "Russian National Anthem" (composer unknown), "Waltz of the Flowers" (1892; from "Nutcracker Suite, Op. 71a by Peter Ilyich Tchaikovsky). *Author's Note*: The USSR banned this film upon its release at the personal direction of Joseph Stalin, who was then the Communist dictator of the country and viewed the profiling of the revolutionaries in the film as savage and murderous, but MacArthur had done his research well in profiling the Bolshevik-Communist leaders of that era as the bloodthirsty creatures they truly were. This production had long been in the mind of MGM production chief, Irving Thalberg, who wanted to have all three of the Barrymore family in one film (and this is the only film in which the three ever appeared together). He signed John Barrymore for the role of the prince at $150,000, and had no difficulty in casting Lionel as Rasputin as Lionel was then a contract actor at the studio, being paid $1,500 a week. His greatest difficulty was enlisting Ethel Barrymore. She was then one of the foremost actresses of the theater in New York, and she resisted Thalberg's entreaties for some time, until she agreed to play the empress for a payment of $100,000, but only on the strict proviso that the production take place during the summer months and was limited to an eight-week shooting schedule so that she would be able to return to the stage in the fall. She also had reservations about appearing with her two temperamental brothers. She and her brothers had not appeared together for sixteen years when they all performed in a theatrical production of "Camille" in Baltimore, Maryland, in 1916 (ironically the year in which Rasputin was assassinated). As a grand dame of American theater, Ethel had unreserved contempt for Hollywood, thinking it nothing more than a bastardized version of legitimate theater, a garish sideshow pandering piffle to unsophisticated audiences. She once described Hollywood as nothing more than "a set, a glaring, gaudy, nightmarish set built up in the desert.

Lionel Barrymore and John Barrymore in *Rasputin and the Empress*, 1932.

[Hollywood] has not been thought in. There is no sediment of thought there. It looks, it feels, as if it had been invented by a Sixth Avenue peep show man." Ethel had not appeared in a film since 1919, when playing in the silent film **The Divorcee**, and that experience had created considerable embarrassment for her. When she was asked at that time by the director of that film to appear on location in front of a New York mansion, Ethel balked after learning that she would be filmed while standing in front of the huge home owned by her friend and millionaire socialite, Mrs. Whitelaw Reid. She insisted that another location be selected, and the director bowed to her wishes. Her two brothers were interviewed before Ethel arrived in Hollywood, neither of them looking forward to appearing in the film with her or each other. Lionel stated: "The three Barrymores are going to be in one picture—can you imagine what will happen to the poor director?" John sardonically remarked: "You need not worry about Mrs. Colt [Ethel's married name]. Our sister will be standing right before the camera—in front of us!" John and Lionel, however, were fiercely competitive with each other. In a story conference with Thalberg where John discussed how he was to assassinate Lionel at the end of the film, John stated: "The way Lionel is going to steal this picture, I ought to shoot him in the *first* reel!" Only John was on hand to greet his sister when she got off the train in Los Angeles. He rushed to her and embraced her and whispered something in her ear that the crowd assembled around them thought was nothing more than an endearing remark. Ethel later stated that her brother had whispered: "For God's sake, get Bill Daniels [William Daniels, the noted cinematographer who lensed **Rasputin and the Empress**]...he's a cameraman, best in the world. He takes all those sweetbreads away from under my eyes. [Greta] Garbo won't make a picture without him." When she met Thalberg, the first thing Ethel requested was that Daniels be the cinematographer for the film, and Thalberg, impressed with her knowledge about such an accomplished artist, immediately granted her request. MGM chief Louis B. Mayer then met with Ethel, and she asked that director Charles Brabin, an old friend, direct the film; Mayer granted that request, too, telling Ethel that she should call on him at any time (an open invitation that he lived to regret). Thalberg was then embarrassed to tell Ethel that no script had yet been written for the film. Thalberg stated that he wanted Charles MacArthur to write the screenplay for **Rasputin and the Empress**, but that "he won't do it." MacArthur had written the smash film adaptation for the play, **The Front Page**, 1931, which had received three Oscar nominations for Best Film, Best Director (Lewis Milestone) and Best Actor (Adolphe Menjou), a play and film he had co-authored with Ben Hecht. Unfortunately, Thalberg explained to Ethel, the writer had stated to him that he was exhausted from his Hollywood writing chores and he had taken up residence with his wife (actress Helen Hayes0 at the posh Garden of Allah bungalow apartments and intended

Ethel Barrymore and John Barrymore in *Rasputin and the Empress,* **1932.**

to rest there without interruptions. Ethel Barrymore was not a person to whom someone said no, and she told Thalberg: "I will make him do it!" According to the statements that Ben Hecht gave to this author: "Helen [Hayes] got a call from Ethel [Barrymore], and Ethel told her that she was coming right over to visit her and Charlie [MacArthur]. Helen was a powerful name on Broadway at that time, but Ethel was the reigning queen of New York Theater, so Helen bowed to Ethel's wishes. Well, when Ethel showed up, she immediately ordered Charlie to write the script for **Rasputin and the Empress**, and he refused. She exploded and grabbed him by the lapels of his suit coat, shouting at him. He had to pull her grasp away and then ran behind Helen, who is a very small woman, while Ethel shouted at him [screaming: 'You lazy, incompetent, good-for-nothing ass!']. She grabbed some of Charlie's books and began hurling them at him while he and Helen dodged those flying tomes. She then took hold of a floor lamp, ripping its cord from its socket, and threatened to drive him ['through a wall'] with it unless he agreed to write the script. Charlie threw up his hands and told her would do it. Ethel put down the lamp, sweetly kissed Helen on the forehead as if nothing had happened, and departed for her luxury suite at a nearby hotel, saying that there was no time to waste because she had to complete the picture soon so she could appear in a play in New York. 'That woman was the fiercest lady I think I ever met,' Charlie told me. 'She kept calling me every day to ask me how many lines I had written for the picture and on some days, she called four or five times. When I had the phone removed, Ethel sent her chauffeur to my door, this towering geek smashing his leather-gloved hand into the palm of his other leather-gloved hand, demanding to know how many lines I had written that day. It was a nightmare where the Great Hounds of Hell were on my tail!' Charlie begged me to take over the writing for that picture, or, at least, work with him on it. 'No thanks, Charlie,' I told him. 'I would like to keep my sanity this year.' I knew he was in the lion's den, poor fellow, but I did not want Ethel and her brothers chewing on me, too." The much-harassed MacArthur actually wrote six different scripts for the film, much of the time rewriting scenes only a few minutes before those scenes were enacted by the Barrymore trio before the cameras and while the three temperamental actors waited impatiently on the set, Lionel thumping on furniture, John flicking burning cigarettes in MacArthur's direction and Ethel shouting: "Will you hurry it up, Mr. MacArthur!" Desperately, MacArthur would write new lines of dialog and set up new scenes by jotting down this new text on envelopes and then handing them separately to the actors. "I would learn a scene, "Ethel stated," and then find that I would have to learn an entirely new one after I was on the set." Director Brabin, who was initially assigned to direct the film at Ethel's request, quickly fell afoul of the actress when he made some mild suggestions as to her comportment as the Empress of Russia. Ethel

gave him a cold glare and stated imperiously: "*I knew her majesty personally!*" When Brabin appeared to be slowing down the production, Ethel then went to MGM boss Mayer and said: "See here, Mayer, let's get rid of Mr. Theda Bara [Ethel's demeaning name for Brabin as he was then married to silent screen star Theda Bara]." Mayer, desirous of appeasing Ethel in any way in order to get the film completed, agreed and, at her suggestion, replaced Brabin with Boleslavsky, a Polish actor-turned-director, who had been part of the Moscow Theater during the days of the czar and was considered a white Russian émigré, who was intimate with the Romanov story. Ethel seemed to work well with Boleslavsky, but Lionel and John did not care who was directing this film as they were mostly directing themselves where, in one scene after another, they tenaciously tried to steal each scene from one another. In one scene where Lionel, playing the crude and unsophisticated monk, belches while dining with the royal family, John reacts (with a close-up done by his favorite cinematographer, Daniels) by rolling his eyes in disgust. In another scene, Lionel is bragging about the power he has gained by controlling the impressionable mind of the emperor's son and stating: "In less than one year, *I* will be Russia!" John responds while Lionel is delivering his diatribe before the camera by turning his back on him and withdrawing a sword, wildly slicing the air with the blade in a mighty effort to take the scene from his brother. Following this distracting but effective swordplay by John, Lionel exploded and raced from the set after the scene was completed. He went to a phone and got Thalberg on the line yelling at him, saying that if he, Thalberg, did not curb his brother's outlandish scene-stealing antics, "I will be tempted to lay one on him!" Hecht told this author that "John and Lionel Barrymore loved each other very much as brothers, but they had nothing but contempt for each other's acting abilities, each thinking that the other was the worst kind of ham, so histrionic and theatrical that they deserved thrashings and they got into it with their fists with each other on more than one occasion." John Barrymore was really the provocateur, who loved pulling pranks and had a fatalistic view of everything. As a young actor, John had been appearing in a play in San Francisco when the earthquake struck and devastated that city in 1906. He later wandered through the ruins wearing his stage apparel, a tuxedo, and sipping from a bottle of warm champagne. He encountered at that time a terrified Enrico Caruso, the great tenor, who was sitting atop a wagon where its driver and the horses had deserted him. Barrymore looked up at Caruso and toasted him with the champagne bottle and said: "Feeling down in the dumps about this whole thing, are you? Well, perk up, old fellow. You're alive and able to go on drinking some more good Italian wine." He then strolled away. John was also imbibing throughout the production of **Rasputin and the Empress**, and, when it came to the final scene where he assassinates Lionel, he appears to be a wild man, struggling and fighting with Lionel until subduing him. (Lionel later complained about having received numerous bruises and cuts from the struggle.) When dragging the limp body of his brother from the house to dump it into the river, John, however, having had one too many, toppled into that river, which had been man-made by art director Cedric Gibbons and his crew, a rushing flow of water, and, while the cameras were still running, several crew members dove into that ersatz but dangerous river to save John's life. Sobered by the icy experience, the actor redid the scene within an hour, but this time correctly pushing Lionel into that river. Ethel Barrymore more than once rebuked her brothers for their on-screen excesses. At one point, she ordered Boleslavsky to stop a scene while she upbraided both of them: "I want you two boys to stop your nonsense and act like adults," she lectured both John and Lionel. "I am sick and tired of these ridiculous competitive games you are playing with each other! You are staining our family's reputation! Now, stop it, and I mean now!" John bowed and kissed her hand. Lionel pointed a finger at John, as if to put all the blame on his rascally brother. True to her word, Ethel promptly left the production after the eight weeks of her agreement ended, leaving Boleslavsky to complete the film by shooting around her scenes. The production also had a serious external problem, one predicted by Mercedes de Acosta, a White Russian émigré, who worked as a researcher with MacArthur when he was writing the script. When Thalberg told Acosta to insert in her notes that Wynyard, who is playing John Barrymore's wife, Natasha, was to be shown as being raped by Rasputin (Lionel Barrymore), or that she appears to be raped, Acosta objected. She told Thalberg that he was inviting a libel suit, informing him that the woman upon which Wynyard's role was based was Princess Irina, the wife of Prince Felix Yusupov, the man who engineered Rasputin's assassination in St. Petersburg in 1916 and that the prince and princess were then alive and living in exile in Paris. "I don't need you to tell me a lot of nonsense about what is libelous," Thalberg responded. "I want this sequence in and that's all there is to it!" The scene went in, and Acosta's prediction became a reality in that Yusupov and his wife sued MGM when the film was released, even though MacArthur had changed John Barrymore's name from Yusupov to Prince Chegodieff. The Yusupovs won the case and were awarded $127,000. Another Russian prince, named Chegodieff, who had nothing to do with Rasputin's murder, also sued MGM and he reportedly received about $125,000 in an out-of-court settlement. When the Barrymore members departed, each for their inner sanctums, the press published many rumors about their joint efforts in this memorable production. To quiet gossip, John held a press conference and announced: "They [the press] seem to think that the three Barrymores are just three damned fools! They say we are jealous of one another, that we won't do what the director tells us, that we want to change the story, each for his selfish glorification...Ethel has been marvelous [in her portrayal in the film]; Lionel, who loves his sarcasm, has never been in better humor. I have, ladies and gentlemen, conducted myself magnificently!" Ethel was not so forgiving, saying about her brothers before she departed for the East: "They are nothing more than overpublicized and overpaid factory hands!" Many actors have profiled Rasputin in numerous films, including **Anastasia**, 1997 (Christopher Lloyd voiceover; Jim Cummings singing voiceover); **BBC Play of the Month**, 1965-1983 (TV series; "Rasputin," 1971 episode: Robert Stephens); **A Beautiful Stranger**, 1993 (Ivan Krasko); **Die Brandstifter Europas**, 1926 (Max Neufeld); **Dornenweg einer Furstin**, 1928 (Gregori Chmara); **Fall of Eagles**, 1974 (TV miniseries; "Tell the King the Sky Is Falling," 1974 episode: Michael Aldridge); **The Fall of the Romanovs**, 1917 (Edward Connelly); **Forever Knight**, 1989-1996 (TV series; "Strings," 1995 episode: Sam Malkin); **Going Hollywood**, 1933 (Sam McDaniel); **Nicholas and Alexander**, 1971 (Tom Baker); **The Night They Killed Rasputin**, 1962 (Edmund Purdom); **Raspoutine**, 2011 (made-for-TV; Gerard Depardieu); **Rasputin**, 1939 (Harry Baur); **Rasputin**, 1954 (Pierre Brasseur); **Rasputin**, 1958 (made-for-TV; Narciso Ibanez Menta); **Rasputin**, 1966 (made-for-TV; Herbert Stass); **Rasputin**, 1967 (Gert Frobe); **Rasputin**, 1985 (Aleksey Petrenko); **Rasputin**, 1996 (made-for-TV; Alan Rickman); **Rasputin**, 2010 (Francesco Cabras); **Rasputin and the Holy Devil**, 1928 (Nikolai Malikoff); **Rasputin, Demon with Women**, 1932 (Conrad Veidt); **Rasputin, the Black Monk**, 1917 (Montagu Love); **Rasputin: The Mad Monk**, 1966 (Christopher Lee); **Rasputins Liebesabenteuer**, 1928 (Nikolai Malikoff); **The Red Dance**, 1928 (Demetrius Alexis); **Suspense**, 1949-1954 (TV series; "The Black Prophet," 1953 episode: Boris Karloff); **The Successor**, 1996 (Igor Solovyov); and **Why Russians Are Revolting**, 1970 (Wes Carter). For more details showing those who enacted the parts of Nicholas II, Empress Alexandra, members of the Russian royal family and their ministers and military aides, see Index, Historical Characters, Volume II, of this work. Details about Rasputin and his gruesome assassination, as well as that of the Russian royal family, can be found in my two-volume work, *The Great Pictorial History of World Crime*, Volume I (History, Inc., 2004; Rasputin: pages 73-78; Nicholas II and his family: pages 79-84. **p**, Bernard H. Hyman; **d**, Richard Boleslavsky, (not credited) Charles Brabin; **cast**, John Barrymore, Ethel Barrymore, Lionel Barrymore, Ralph Morgan, Diana Wynyard, Tad Alexander, C. Henry Gordon, Edward Arnold, Luis Alberni, Henry Armetta, Mischa Auer, Gustav von

Harry Baur and Jany Holt in the French version of *Rasputin*, 1939.

Seyffertitz, Louise Closser Hale, Charlotte Henry, Dave O'Brien, Jean Parker, Anne Shirley (Dawn O'Day), Sarah Padden, Henry Kolker, Frank Reicher; **w**, Charles MacArthur; **c**, William Daniels; **m**, Herbert Stothart; **ed**, Tom Held; **art d**, Cedric Gibbons, Alexander Toluboff.

Rasputin the Mad Monk ★★★ 1966; U.K.; 92m; Seven Arts/Hammer/FOX; Color; Biographical Drama/Horror; Children: Unacceptable (MPAA: R); **BD**; **DVD**; **VHS**; **IV**. Though not entirely historically accurate, this exciting film about the Russian monk, Grigori Rasputin (1869-1916), played by Lee, focuses upon his corrupt and degenerate lifestyle rather than his extraordinary power and influence on Emperor Nicholas II (1868-1918), played by Duncan, and Empress Alexandra (1872-1918), played by Asherson. Lee is thrown out of his monastery for drunken behavior and sexual dalliances. He uses hypnotism to win over two court aides, Shelley and Pasco, thereby gaining access to the royal court. Shelley commits suicide and Pasco sees the evil in Rasputin, using every method to kill him including poisoned food and lethal injections. Lee simply won't die, but eventually does. In a vampire-like setting and mood, Rasputin is depicted as being one of the most diabolical men of all time. An effective horror film, but too violent for children. See Index, Historical Characters, Volume II of this work for all films depicting Rasputin and Nicholas II and members of the royal Romanov family. **p**, Anthony Nelson Keys; **d**, Don Sharp; **cast**, Christopher Lee, Barbara Shelley, Renee Asherson, Richard Pasco, Nicholas Pennell, Francis Matthews, Suzan Farmer, Dinsdale Landen, Derek Francis, Joss Ackland, Robert Duncan, Alan Tilvern, John Welsh, John Bailey; **w**, Anthony Hinds (as John Elder); **c**, Michael Reed (CinemaScope; DeLuxe Color); **m**, Don Banks; **ed**, Roy Hyde; **prod d**, Bernard Robinson; **art d**, Don Mingaye.

Rat Fink ★★★ 1965; U.S.; 80m; Genesis/Cinema Distributors of America; B/W; Drama; Children: Unacceptable; **VHS**. Gritty and grim tale depicts the story of a heartless rock singer, Haydn, his ruthless ambition to get to the top of the heap causing him to commit endless offenses. He sleeps with an older woman just to steal from her purse in order to get to Hollywood, where he hires a top agent, Bokar. He becomes involved with the agent's wife, Ott, and also with a teenager, Hughes, whom he later takes to a veterinarian for an abortion, then dumps her on his climb up the ladder of success. It's a realistic and hard-hitting portrayal of a man who, while smiling, makes you cringe in every frame. Song: "My Soul Runs Naked," "One on Every Corner" (Ronald Stein). **p**, Lewis Andrews; **d&w**, James Landis (based on a story by Matthew Cheney, Jack Miller); **cast**, Schuyler Haydn, Hal Bokar, Warrene Ott, Judy Hughes, Eve Brenner, Alice Reinheart, Jack Lester, Ernie Crites, Chuck Harrod, Richard Jeffries; **c**, Vilmos Zsigmond; **m**, Ronald

Boris Karloff sees for the first time the monstrous face given to him by surgeon Bela Lugosi in *The Raven*, 1935.

Stein; **ed**, Tom Boutross; **art d**, Daniel Toledo.

Ratatouille ★★★ 2007; U.S.; 111m; Disney/Pixar/Buena Vista; Color; Drama; Children: Acceptable (MPAA: G); **BD**; **DVD**. A thoroughly delightful film about a loveable rat named Remy (Oswalt voiceover), who dreams of becoming a great French chef although his family doesn't think it's a good idea because working with gourmet dishes isn't exactly acceptable work for his species. Looking for food in the sewers of Paris, he finds himself beneath a restaurant made famous by his culinary hero (Garrett voiceover). With help from some friends, he concocts the best workingman's soup/stew called ratatouille. One taste of it and the toughest culinary critic in Paris (O'Toole voiceover) calls it perfection, and Oswalt achieves his dream of fame as a chef. The film was a huge hit, gleaning more than $623 million in its initial box office release against a budget of $150 million. Song: "Le Festin" (Michael Giacchino). **p**, Brad Lewis; **d**, Brad Bird, Jan Pinkava; **cast** (voiceovers), Patton Oswalt, Ian Holm, Lou Romano, Brian Dennehy, Peter Sohn, Peter O'-Toole, Brad Garrett, Janeane Garofalo, Will Arnett, Julius Callahan, Bird, Stephane Roux (narrator); **w**, Bird (based on a story by Bird, Pinkava, Jim Capobianco, Emily Cook, Kathy Greenberg, Bob Peterson); **m**, Michael Giacchino; **ed**, Darren Holmes; **prod d**, Harley Jessup; **spec eff**, Spiro Carras.

The Raven ★★★ 1935; U.S.; 61m; UNIV; B/W; Horror; Children: Unacceptable; **DVD**; **VHS**. Poe's classic horror tale serves as an inspiration other than being realistically adapted in this chilling film. Lugosi is a demented physician, who has constructed a dungeon in his home, filling it with all the cruel, medieval instruments of torture and death as described in Poe's grotesque stories. He encounters Karloff, who is a much-wanted criminal, and performs plastic surgery to alter his face, but he badly botches the operation so that Karloff looks even more monstrous than before. Lugosi promises the murderous Karloff that he will correct his medical mistakes in a future operation that will make him appear more attractive, but, in the meanwhile, he demands and gets Karloff's henchman services. Lugosi has had in mind to purposely bungle Karloff's operation in order to have him do his bidding. Hinds, who is a respected judge, has earlier asked Lugosi to come out of retirement to save the life of his daughter, Ware. After she has been crippled and brain damaged in a car accident, Lugosi restores her to perfect health. Falling in love with Ware, Lugosi asks Hinds for Ware's hand in marriage, but Hinds only scoffs at him, pointing out that his daughter is engaged to Matthews and they look forward to a happy life together. Seething with revenge, Lugosi plans to lure Hinds, Matthews and Ware to his home, and where he plans to torture Hinds and Matthews to death and then keep Ware for himself, thinking her to be the reincarnation of

Poe's "Lenore." When the trio appear at Lugosi's home, he realizes that Ware will never be his own and he straps Hinds to a table where a slowly descending scythe (as in Poe's "The Pit and the Pendulum") comes closer and closer to his chest while he imprisons Matthews and Ware in a shrinking room where the walls slowly close, promising to crush the occupants to death. Karloff is enlisted in these grisly chores, but, deadly criminal that he is, his conscience will not permit such wanton slaughter. He rescues Ware and Matthews and places Lugosi into the shrinking room where the lethal doctor meets the gruesome end he had so insidiously designed for his victims. Well directed, scripted and acted, this chiller is above the usual horror film fare of that day, and both Lugosi and Karloff are standouts in essaying their evil characters. Made for only $115,000, this film proved to be a modest hit at the box office, recouping its budget for Universal, but audiences were generally repelled by its tortures and disfigurements, and anti-horror film sentiment was so strong in England at that time that such films were generally banned. Songs: "The Black Cat" (Heinz Roemheld), "Sonata in B Minor" (Franz Liszt), "Destination Unknown" (W. Franke Harling), "Romeo and Juliet Overture" (Peter Ilyich Tchaikovsky), "Toccata and Fugue in D Minor DWV.565" (Johann Sebastian Bach). *Author's Note*: Karloff told this author that "Although I got top billing in **The Raven**, Bela [Lugosi] was my co-star. I was told that he resented my success after my appearance in **Frankenstein** [1931], made about the same time he starred in **Dracula** [1931] and that he felt that Universal was promoting me rather than him. Bela never said a word about that to me and we remained friends throughout our careers. To tell you the truth, I look more hideous than anyone in **The Raven**, but Bela is a lot more frightening as the lunatic doctor he portrays." **p**, David Diamond; **d**, Louis Friedlander [Lew Landers]; **cast**, Boris Karloff, Bela Lugosi, Irene Ware, Lester Matthews, Samuel S. Hinds, Spencer Charters, Inez Courtney, Ian Wolfe, Maidel Turner, Raine Bennett; **w**, David Boehm (based on the poem by Edgar Allan Poe); **c**, Charles Stumar; **m**, Clifford Vaughan; **ed**, Albert Akst; **art d**, Albert S. D'Agostino; **spec eff**, John P. Fulton.

The Raven ★★★ 1963; U.S.; 86m; Alta Vista/American International Pictures (AIP); Color; Horror; Children: Unacceptable; **DVD**; **VHS**. Producer Corman offers this grim horror tale with a tongue-in-cheek attitude, a broad-based farce on the genre where the entire cast, chiefly masters of horror Price, Karloff and Lorre, excel in their menacing roles while providing a lot of dark humor. Price is the son of a deceased wizard who suffers the loss of his alluring wife, Court, and, following her untimely death, goes into seclusion, meditating upon the grim tales of Edgar Allan Poe. He is then visited by a talking raven with a barbed tongue spewing insult, but the darkly capricious Price nevertheless entertains this obnoxious aviary by holding lengthy conversations with it. The bird insists that it, too, is a wizard, but that he was transformed into a raven by Karloff, after provoking this most powerful magician on earth. Price, goaded by his own self-aggrandizement as a wizard, decides to use his own powerful potions to restore the wizard to human form. To that end, Price brews a concoction of God-awful glutinous glop, mixed with spiders and even the hairs of a dead man, which Price clips from his own father's corpse after opening that crypt, and feeds this swill to the raven. The bird is transformed back into the original state of Lorre, but the potion only works halfway, leaving the squat little man with flopping wings. Price tries again, this time using more of his strange ingredients, and the next time he administers the potion, Lorre is fully restored to human form. Lorre then tells his story about how he challenged Karloff's great powers, but, in their battle together, Lorre lost that battle, attributing his defeat to the sorry fact that he had been drinking too much. In describing his experience with the omnipotent Karloff, Lorre describes a woman living with Karloff who bears a striking resemblance to Price's deceased wife, Court. This so haunts Price that he decides to investigate, and he and Lorre travel to Karloff's castle with Price's daughter, Sturgess, and Lorre's son, Nicholson. To his shock and amazement, Price, upon arriving at Karloff's bastion, sees that his wife, Court, is very much alive and bitterly learns that she faked her death so that she could become Karloff's mistress, preferring to live with a more powerful wizard. Price then realizes that the calculating Karloff has planned all of the events that have lured him to Karloff's castle only so that Karloff can acquire the skills of wizardry that Price possesses. Price, however, shocks Karloff in that he proves a match for Karloff's powers, both fighting each other in a colossal battle filled with flashing light bolts and fireballs (that must have inspired the laser battles shown decades later in the Star Wars films); Karloff loses the awesome confrontation after all his energies and powers are debilitated and drained, so that the now all-powerful Price emerges the victor. Price then leaves Karloff's castle, glad to also rid himself of Court, who remains behind as a hectoring banshee screaming invective at a now much hen-pecked and ignominiously disgraced Karloff, his castle in ruins and his powers gone forever. Before this titanic battle of wizards ensues, Lorre is turned back into a raven by Karloff at his own request in order to escape torture for betraying the magician. He later begs Price to restore him to human form again, but this time Price is fed up with the laborious transformations and tells Lorre to shut his beak! Corman does a top flight-job in offering this horror spoof and his fright-makers, Price, Karloff and Lorre (who appeared together for the first time and were billed in its promotion as "The Great Triumvirate of Terror"), give priceless (no pun intended) performances in this outlandish and hugely entertaining lampoon as horrific lunatics gone weirdly amuck. Lorre, whether as the raven, human or a bit of both, steals many scenes since Corman allowed him to insert his witty and sardonic remarks as he shot the film, his infectious dark humor challenging the straight-faced and often startled responses of Price and Karloff in fending off these unwritten cue lines. The film was a success at the box office, taking in more than $1.4 million against a budget of $350,000 (high for the standard horror films produced by AIP). *Author's Note*: Price told this author that "Peter [Lorre], a dear, old friend, was in fine form when we made **The Raven**, his acerbic wit peppering the dialog and where he inventively inserted those bon mots as we went along. He thought to rattle Boris [Karloff] and me, but he did not get away with it. We were ready for his quick artist lines and gave him back some of our own unexpected ad libs." Lorre stated to this author that "I was more or less trussed up with a lot of feathers when I was handed the bird in **The Raven**. The apparatus the crew members constructed allowed me to flutter my wings, but it was very uncomfortable and gave me back pains for some time. I knew I looked ridiculous made up like that bird, so I decided to make the most of it and have the bird be a wise guy, like a sassy parrot. What else could one do with such an absurd part?" Karloff, who had appeared in another version of **The Raven** three decades earlier, took all the shenanigans in stride, telling this author that "Vincent [Price] and Peter [Lorre] were having a lot of fun with the picture we made together. They played capricious magicians, but I am the evil member of the Brotherhood of Magicians, so I had to keep a straight face when they were throwing all those funny lines at me. *Someone* had to be sinister in that picture, so I was elected to be the real heavy." This was one of Nicholson's earliest films before he became a superstar six years later in **Easy Rider**, 1969. He reportedly enjoyed partaking in this farce, but complained that the actual bird playing the raven, a trained aviary, had little regard for its fellow actors and freely defecated throughout the set, making occasional deposits on the cast and crew, including Nicholson, who was quoted as saying: "I hated that bird." Corman, who always directed his films with lightning speed, finished **The Raven** three days ahead of schedule, and decided to use that time in making another horror film, that quickie titled **The Terror**, 1963, which stars Karloff and Nicholson, still under contract for those three days, and where Corman used the same sets with some revision as were used for **The Raven** when rushing **The Terror** into completion. **The Raven** was the fifth of eight AIP films based on Edgar Allan Poe's works. This film is not a remake from the 1935 production, which has a wholly different plotline, and is not to be confused with the 2012 film by the same title, which

Dennis O'Keefe and Marsha Hunt in *Raw Deal*, 1948.

centers on author Edgar Allan Poe (Nicolas Cage) tracking down a serial killer. **p&d**, Roger Corman; **cast**, Vincent Price, Peter Lorre, Boris Karloff, Hazel Court, Olive Sturgess, Jack Nicholson, Connie Wallace, William Baskin, Aaron Saxon; **w**, Richard Matheson (based on the poem by Edgar Allan Poe); **c**, Floyd Crosby (Panavision; Pathe Color); **m**, Les Baxter; **ed**, Ronald Sinclair; **prod d** & **art d**, Daniel Haller; **set d**, Harry Reif; **spec eff**, Pat Dinga.

Raw Deal ★★★★ 1948; U.S.; 79m; Edward Small Productions/Eagle-Lion Films; B/W; Crime Drama; Children: Unacceptable; **DVD**; **VHS**. Iconic film noir tale that packs a terrific wallop with a fine script and top-flight acting from O'Keefe, Trevor, Hunt, and a great supporting cast. O'Keefe is doing time in prison for a crime he did not commit, framed by gang boss Burr, and all he thinks about is settling that old score. He is visited by pretty Hunt, a straight-laced social worker who has his best interests at heart, and O'Keefe plays her along, thinking to later use her in his scheme of revenge. Trevor, who is O'Keefe's lover (superb again as a gun moll, the type of role she made her own in many crime films), helps him break out of prison. While both are en route to wreak havoc on Burr, O'Keefe abducts Hunt, intending to use her as a hostage if police corner him. The jealous Trevor wants no part of Hunt, but she tolerates her presence for the sake of O'Keefe, even after he appears to be falling in love with Hunt. For her part, Hunt, an otherwise upstanding citizen, becomes erotically fascinated with O'Keefe's criminal lifestyle, excited by its dangerous prospects. She becomes a willing participant in that lifestyle after O'Keefe is attacked by Ireland, one of Burr's gunmen. When it appears that Ireland is about to kill O'Keefe, he cries out for Hunt's aid, and she shoots Ireland in the back, killing him. O'Keefe has now made Hunt part of his criminal pursuits, but she is in love with him by now and nothing else matters. In a moment of righteous conscience, O'Keefe decides to shield Hunt from his underworld activities by sending her away while he goes after the insidious Burr, who has become an arsonist in addition to his other rackets. O'-Keefe finds Burr in his hideout testing flammable liquids and where the gang boss shoots O'Keefe after a struggle that sets the place on fire. As the blaze begins to consume the hideout, a desperate Burr tries to escape the flames by leaping from a window but is killed in the fall. O'Keefe has gotten his revenge, but at a terrible price. He is dying when Hunt and Trevor find him. Hunt holds O'Keefe in her arms as he passes from this world while Trevor grimly witnesses her lover's death. Both women are now without the man they both love at the grim finale of this tale. No one wins in **Raw Deal**, a film that dispassionately portrays its top-to-bottom characters as people who lose everything for the sake of their obsessive and sinister goals, a hard-hitting morality film well crafted by director Mann; the script is taut and its scenes riveting and

Tyrone Power and Susan Hayward in *Rawhide,* **1951.**

tense throughout, exceptionally lensed by Alton. Two films by the same title but having nothing to do with the plotline of this film were produced in 1977 and 1986. *Author's Note*: O'Keefe, who had specialized in comedies during the early 1940s, gravitated into film noir a few years later; he appeared in many outstanding film noir productions like this excellent entry, as well as the classic **T-Men**, 1947; **Cover-Up**, 1949, and **Abandoned**, 1949; Trevor told this author that "I do my usual stand-by-your gangster role in **Raw Deal**. Marsha [Hunt] wins the heart of my man and I am left standing out in the cold again. The man I am nutty about is Dennis [O'Keefe] who was always a much underrated actor. He had great talent and a very strong presence before the cameras. He was a heavy smoker and died of lung cancer much too early in life. I think he was sixty when he died, a great loss. Dennis could do good comedy and drama as easy as using one hand or the other. Actors like him don't come along like that anymore." **p**, Edward Small; **d**, Anthony Mann; **cast**, Dennis O'Keefe, Claire Trevor, Marsha Hunt, John Ireland, Raymond Burr, Curt Conway, Chili Williams, Regis Toomey, Whit Bissell, Cliff Clark; **w**, Leopold Atlas, John C. Higgins (from a story by Arnold B. Armstrong, Audrey Ashley); **c**, John Alton; **m**, Paul Sawtell; **ed**, Alfred DeGaetano; **art d**, Edward L. Ilou; **set d**, Armor Marlowe, Clarence Steenson; **spec eff**, Jack R. Rabin, George J. Teague.

Rawhide ★★★★ 1951; U.S.; 89m; FOX; B/W; Western; Children: Unacceptable; **DVD**; **VHS**. This suspense-packed western offers many unusual twists and a more modern plotline, dialog and deeper character development than found in most oaters, where Power, Hayward and Marlowe are standouts in their contentious roles. Power is a young assistant to grouchy, old Buchanan, both operating a remote horse relay station for passing stagecoaches. Squatting in the middle of the desert, this barren place, called Rawhide, offers little creature comforts for those briefly visiting. Hayward, a feisty lady who formerly entertained riverboat audiences with her songs, arrives with her toddler niece, Dunn, but she is told that she must wait for the next stage as a band of ruthless robbers is terrorizing the area. Those robbers show up a short time later in the form of Marlowe, an intelligent but ruthless thief, and his three henchmen, oafish Tobias, loafer Jagger and gun-happy Elam. They have arrived to set an ambush for the next stage, which is reportedly carrying more than $100,000 in gold bullion. Buchanan telegraphs the fact that he has recognized Marlowe and is summarily shot to death, leaving Power to provide food for the invaders. Marlowe believes that Hayward and Power are man and wife, locking them and Dunn into a small room at the back of the small inn. Without a gun, Power does not stand a chance against the four gunmen, but he has secreted a knife, which he uses to start digging a hole in the adobe wall to the outside. It is too

small for Power or Hayward to slip through, but toddler Dunn, unbeknownst to Hayward, squirms through the hole and begins running about outside. When Hayward discovers her niece gone, she panics and begins pounding on the door. The lecherous Elam opens it and tries to molest her and when Marlowe and Tobias try to intervene, Elam shoots and kills them both while Jagger flees. Power, meanwhile, escapes to the corral and finds a gun he has hidden. Just before Power is about to shoot Elam, the gunman grabs Dunn and uses her as a shield, saying that if Power does not throw down his gun, he will kill the toddler. Power tosses the gun aside and is about to be shot down by the savage Elam, but Hayward finds a rifle and shoots Elam, killing him. Jagger is easily captured, and after the stagecoach arrives, Hayward and Dunn depart while Power remains at the station as its new manager. The story is a simple one, but it is fraught with tension as the lives of Power, Hayward and Dunn hang in the balance at the whims of the gunmen, where Power uses many ploys to stave off execution until the outlaws are overcome, much of this due to the taut direction of action director Hathaway. Song: "A Rollin' Stone" (music: Lionel Newman; lyrics: Bob Russell). *Author's Note*: Hathaway admitted to this author that "**Rawhide** is not an average western even though it has a western setting. There are no wild horse rides or open space pursuits and chases and we shot most of the picture inside the single adobe inn where the desperadoes hold Susan [Hayward] and Ty [Power] and the little child [Dunn] captive. After they are used to decoy the stagecoach, they will be killed so all of the suspense is not knowing if they will survive or not. The suspense is sustained in the fine script that Dudley [Nichols] wrote, which shows how clever and unpredictable the outlaws are and how inventive the victims can be in managing to survive." Hayward liked this film, telling this author that "it was, for a change, an intelligent picture with solid characters and a lot of good lines. I got a lot of those good lines, so I had nothing to complain about." **p**, Samuel G. Engel; **d**, Henry Hathaway; **cast**, Tyrone Power, Susan Hayward, Hugh Marlowe, Dean Jagger, Edgar Buchanan, Jack Elam, George Tobias, Jeff Corey, James Millican, Louis Jean Heydt, Max Terhune, Gary Merrill (narrator); **w**, Dudley Nichols; **c**, Milton Krasner; **m**, Sol Kaplan; **ed**, Robert Simpson; **art d**, Lyle Wheeler, George W. Davis; **set d**, Thomas Little, Stuart Reiss; **spec eff**, Fred Sersen.

Ray ★★★ 2004; U.S.; 152m; UNIV; Color; Biographical Drama; Children: Unacceptable (MPAA: PG-13); **BD**; **DVD**. The life and career of legendary singer, pianist, and composer Ray Charles (1930-2004), played by Foxx, comes to impressive life in this jarring biopic. Blind since the age of seven, Foxx comes from dirt-poor Georgia roots and battles racism besides blindness as well as a troubled personal life created by his womanizing, which defies and upsets his marriage to Washington. He rises by the early 1960s to stardom at Carnegie Hall and tours Europe, blending gospel and blues to become the master of soul music. Throughout his hectic life, Foxx also deals with his plaguing heroin addiction while otherwise conducting his business dealings in an utterly ruthless manner. Foxx is superlative in essaying this legendary artist, a musical giant, offering a tragic portrait that pulls no punches while serving as a grand showcase of Charles' most memorable hits. Songs: "What'd I Say," "Hard Times (No One Knows Better Than I)," "I Believe to My Soul," "Rockhouse," "Baby Let Me Hold Your Hand," "Leave My Woman Alone," "Mary Ann," "What Kind of Man Are You?," "I Got a Woman," "Hallelujah I Love Her So," "The Key of G," "Pete Johnson's Stride" (Ray Charles); "Anytime" (Herbert Lawson); "Emanon" (John "Dizzy" Gillespie, Milton Shaw); "Route 66" (Bobby Troup); "Straighten Up and Fly Right" (Nat King Cole, Irving Mills); "Yesterdays" (Jerome Kern, Otto A. Harbach); "Red Wing Boogie" "My Little Pal Ray" (Willie Metcalf Jr.); "Rock This House" (Lowell Fulson); "Everyday I Have the Blues" (Memphis Slim as Peter Chatman); "Drinkin' Wine Spo-Dee-O-Dee" (Stick McGhee, J. Mayo Williams); "We Will Walk Through the Streets of the City" (traditional); "Walk Around" (R. H. Harris); "Roll with My Baby," The Midnight Hour"

(Sam Sweet); "Mess Around" (Ahmet Ertegun); "Drown in My Own Tears" (Henry Glover); "Moonlight Sonata" (Ludwig Von Beethoven), "The Night Is the Right Time" (Lew Herman, Samuel Mathews); "As It Falls" (Wilson Turbinton); "Georgia on My Mind" (Hoagy Carmichael, Stuart Gorrell); "Montuno Uno" (Curt Sobel, Gary Schreiner); "Hit the Road Jack"(Percy Mayfield); "Unchain My Heart" (Bobby Sharp, Teddy Powell); "You Don't Know Me" (Eddy Arnold, Cindy Walker); "I Can't Stop Loving You" (Don Gibson); "Bye Bye Love" (Boudleaux Bryant, Felice Bryant); "Born to Lose" (Ted Daffan). Drug addiction, sexuality, and thematic material prohibit viewing by children. **p,** Taylor Hackford, Howard Baldwin, Karen Elise Baldwin, Stuart Benjamin, Alise Benjamin; **d,** Hackford; **cast,** Jamie Foxx, Regina King, Kerry Washington, Clifton Powell, Harry Lennix, Bokeem Woodbine, Aunjanue Ellis; Sharon Warren, C.J. Sanders, Curtis Armstrong, Richard Schiff; Nick Morton, Ray Charles Robinson, Jr.; **w,** James L. White (based on a story by White, Hackford); **c,** Pawel Edelman; **m,** Craig Armstrong; **ed,** Paul Hirsch; **prod d,** Stephen Altman; **art d,** John E. Bucklin, Scott Plauche; **set d,** Maria Nay; **spec eff,** Chris Bailey, Robert H . Cooper.

Anne Baxter and John Payne in *The Razor's Edge,* 1946.

The Razor's Edge ★★★★ 1946; U.S.; 145m; FOX; B/W; Drama; Children: Unacceptable; **DVD**; **VHS**. In one of his finest performances, Power is riveting and empathetic as a war-disillusioned young man named Larry Darrell, who is searching for significant meaning in life. In what was the most costly version of any Maugham story to date, this fascinating tale begins in Chicago, with Power returning home after serving in WWI as a fighter pilot. He meets with his fiancé, Tierney, at her lavish North Shore home where she tells him that she has arranged to have him work at a high-salaried job so that they can soon begin to plan their marriage. He shocks the high society woman when telling her that he wants time to think things out while he tries to learn the secrets of spiritual and intellectual freedom. Power, like so many expatriates of his lost generation (as coined by Jazz Age author F. Scott Fitzgerald), goes to Paris to live, and the wealthy Tierney, accompanied by her mother, Watson, follows him there, taking residence in a sumptuous villa. She meets Power at a party, and he proposes that they get married, although he insists that he must continue his quest for spiritual truth and happiness. Tierney grows tired of Power's inexplicable and almost mystical ambitions, considering his statements adolescent daydreams. When visiting his meager one-room apartment, Tierney realizes that, though she loves Power, he will never be able to afford her lifestyle and she rejects his proposal, especially after her wealthy uncle Webb, a shallow snob and lifelong dilettante, tells her that Power will never amount to anything and to forget him and marry someone of substance. Yet Tierney makes one last effort to bring Power to her frame of mind, but he refuses and departs for India where the secrets of life may be found. He travels to the high Himalayas, finding a Hindu sanctuary high in the mountains, where Humphreys, a mystical religious leader' slowly brings peace of mind to Power. Many years later, Power returns to Paris where he encounters writer W. Somerset Maugham (1874-1965), who is played by Marshall (and who narrates this strange tale, the author making himself one of his own characters). Marshall tells Power that Tierney is now married to Power's boyhood friend, Payne, who was once rich, but lost everything during the 1929 stock market crash, and he, Tierney and their two little girls, have moved to Paris to live with the still wealthy Webb. Power also learns from Maugham that another old friend, Baxter, has vanished. Shown earlier marrying Latimore, Baxter lost her husband and their child in an accident and gave up on life. When Power meets Tierney once more, she suggests they all go nightclubbing, and they make the rounds of several night spots, including a sleazy dump where they find Baxter, who has become an alcoholic and is under the sway of a pimp, who orders her to go to a back room. Power forcefully tells Baxter to remain with him and his friends and then yanks the earring from the earlobe of the pimp, producing a gush of blood. He then shocks Tierney by stating that he is going to take Baxter under his wing and bring

about her social and spiritual rehabilitation. Power also aids the ailing Payne, who seems to have lost his will to make anything of his shambled business. He patiently sits with Payne and, using autosuggestion and a form of hypnosis learned from his guru in India, Power instills within Payne new and healthy perspectives that bring about his mental recovery and hopes for a better future. The married Tierney is nevertheless still in love with Power and, after seeing that he has also rehabilitated Baxter and that Power and Baxter plan to wed, she puts in motion an insidious plan. Tierney invites Baxter to her uncle's lavish abode and reminds Baxter of her sordid past, as well as blaming her for the deaths of her child and husband. She leaves Baxter alone with ample liquor. Baxter again takes to drink and vanishes. Meanwhile, Webb, who has wasted his meaningless life with social fetes and affairs, spending his wealth on his own selfish whims, grows ill, and the compassionate Power has the influential Marshall arrange for a Catholic bishop to give the old man his Last Rites while he is dying in his lavish estate on the Riviera. When Webb learns that he has not been included in the guest list of one of the most important social affairs of the season, Power persuades Lanchester, a social secretary sending out invitations for that affair, to look the other way while he takes an invitation from her desk and delivers it to Webb, who, on his deathbed, states that he will be unable to attend due "to a previous appointment" with the Almighty. Power has brought gratification to the supercilious Webb in his last moments on earth. He then finds that Baxter has been murdered, her body thrown into the Seine. He sadly inspects her family mementos in a cheap room, the last remnants of her miserable existence. Power then has a final meeting with Tierney, who admits that she was instrumental in sending Baxter away from him, believing her to be a "derelict" and that she did the right thing in protecting Power from Baxter's corruptive way of life. Power sees through her self-aggrandizing machinations and blames her for Baxter's death. Tierney throws herself at him, telling him that she still loves him and that she will abandon her family for him, but Power rejects her and her useless upper-class way of life. After he leaves, Marshall later tells Tierney that Power has not thrown away his own life, but enriched it greatly and wherever Power goes, goodness and human compassion goes with him. The viewer sees Power in the final dynamic scene while working as a seaman on a freighter as the seas lash the sailing ship with crashing waves, his future uncertain, but his confidence in himself and mankind firmly set in his mind and heart. Director Goulding carefully helms this sensitive tale, and outstanding performances are rendered by Power, Tierney, Baxter, Webb, Marshall and the rest of the fine cast. Miller's photography is stunning as it portrays the sumptuously decorated residences of the rich, the ethereal setting of the Himalayas and the sordid byways and hovel-like dwellings of the other half of life. The sets, costuming and locales are meticulously appropriate

Gene Tierney and Tyrone Power in *The Razor's Edge*, 1946.

to the eras presented, and Newman's dynamic score is compelling and haunting. The script diligently follows Maugham's best-selling novel that amalgamates and balances spirituality and intellectualism with just enough hedonism, greed, envy and jealousy (as well as alcoholism, prostitution and murder) to produce a fascinating melodrama of the first order. This is really a 19th-Century morality tale relocated in the more turbulent and unpredictable 20th Century, where rigid but aging Victorian principles clash with modern perspectives and are infused with Hindu mysticism that transcends those epochs. It is a heady drink to swallow but made more palatable by being served on the platter of the common man. Power's character is decidedly bereft of permanent female companionship, losing Tierney as well as Baxter to their own self-destructive pursuits, as is the case in the novel. (Maugham's female characters in most of his works are invariably menacing, afflicted with subtle but damning character flaws; they are either too frail or too dominating to make healthy mates for worthy males.) The true nature of the character essayed by Power is subliminally suggested by Maugham to be homosexual when shown in sharp contrast to the two women in his life, the spiritually draining character enacted by Baxter and the conniving, destructive vixen essayed by Tierney. The latter's character is not unlike the vicious and scheming Mildred portrayed in Maugham's masterpiece, **Of Human Bondage**, 1934, so magnificently portrayed by Bette Davis. Maugham himself was a closet homosexual throughout life and his two socially oppressed heroes in both of these films really represent the author's persona (and where film reviewer Roger Ebert once off-handedly remarked about this film to this author by cruelly describing the character of Larry Darrell as Maugham's own thinly disguised human shell in **The Razor's Edge** as "Larry the Fairy"). In **The Razor's Edge**, the hero is spiritually crippled by the traumatic events of World War I, and in **Of Human Bondage** the hero is socially crippled by having an ungainly looking clubfoot, both of these afflictions representing Maugham's own homosexuality, which, in his day, was widely seen as a repulsive disease as hideous as leprosy. All of this was mostly lost on a rather unsophisticated viewing audience that largely embraced and liked this superlative production, which viewed Power as simply a young man trying to make sense of his life in a confusing and conflicting society. The film gleaned a then whopping $5 million in box office receipts against a then also staggering budget of $1.2 million (not including payments to the author Maugham, on-location shooting, second unit expenses, and promotion expenses that soared that budget to perhaps as much as $4 million). Baxter, who gives an amazing performance as the fallen woman, won an Oscar as Best Supporting Actress, and Webb, playing the rich, old roué, one of his prissy specialties, was nominated for an Oscar as Best Supporting Actor. The film also received an Oscar nomination for Best Art Direction (and Set Decoration; Day, Juran, Lit-

tle and Fox). A lifeless remake was produced in 1984 at $12 million and earned back only half of its investment, and where the otherwise effective comedian Bill Murray stumbles stoically through the role that Power made his own in the original production. The presumptuous 1984 remake, like so many costly attempts by Hollywood to cash in on a good thing, disgraced a fine story with an anemic production and dead-stick performances, where the vanity of wealth and star power deservedly fell flat on its arrogant face with audiences. Songs: "April Showers" (1921; Louis Silvers); "I'll See You in My Dreams" (1924; Isham Jones); "I'm Forever Blowing Bubbles" (1919; James Kendis, James Brockman, Nat Vincent); "Mam'selle" (music: Ray Dorey; [1946] Edmund Goulding; lyrics [English]: Mack Gordon); "The Miner's Song," "M'aime ta pomme" (1946; music: Edmund Goulding; lyrics: Jacques Surmagne); "Frere Jacques" (traditional); "Loch Lomond" (Scottish traditional); "Night Was So Dark" (1946: music: Edmund Goulding; lyrics: Nina Koshetz); "Aupres de ma blonde" (traditional). *Author's Note*: This was a pet project of Fox studio boss Darryl Zanuck, who told this author that "I was determined to show how the leading character rejects materialism for the sake of spiritual peace, and, to do that, we had to show the opulence of the rich in many scenes and that was a very costly proposition." To that end, Zanuck used the most expensive props available, including more than $800,000 worth of handmade ornate fountains, chandeliers; candelabra; imported, hand-woven tapestries and carpets; paintings and antique furniture used in the film's eighty-nine sets. In one dinner scene, so much expensive silverware was used that Pinkerton detectives were on hand to make sure none of the extras walked away with silver and gold-plated utensils. Zanuck paid Maugham $250,000 for the film rights to the story. "Maugham and his agents were very tough to deal with,' Zanuck told this author. "They insisted that, if shooting for the picture did not start in early February 1946, I had to pay Maugham an additional $50,000. We were not ready to shoot by that time since I was waiting for Ty [Tyrone Power] to get mustered out of the Marine Corps [Power had been serving as a Marine Corps pilot during WWII, not unlike the character he would play in the film where he is recently mustered out of the service as a fighter pilot in WWI]. I got around that problem by having a second unit go in the late summer of 1945 [August] to shoot exteriors of the mountains near Denver [Colorado], which served as the location of the high Himalayas, scenes we would use later in the picture." Although Zanuck always had Power in mind to play the idealistic character in **The Razor's Edge**, he toyed with the idea of using rising Fox star Gregory Peck in that role. He offered Power the leading role in another Fox film, **Gentleman's Agreement**, 1947, a hard-hitting story that dealt with anti-Semitism. Power, however, turned down that role and elected to make **The Razor's Edge**, and Peck went on to star in **Gentleman's Agreement**, a film that made him a superstar. The part of the tragic Sophie was originally planned for Alice Faye, Zanuck thinking to lure her back to his studio with this meaty role, but the actress, who had chiefly been a singing star in Fox musicals, refused to ever work at Fox again and turned down the role. Baxter got the part by default and went on to win an Oscar for her memorably empathetic performance and would go on to deservedly receive an Oscar nomination as Best Actress for her stunning performance in **All about Eve**, 1950. "Someone suggested that I get Betty Grable to play the part of Sophie in **The Razor's Edge**," Zanuck told this author, "but that was ridiculous. Betty was great as a singing and dancing star at Fox, but she did not have the emotional equipment for a role like that and I knew it. We had Anne [Baxter] under a long-term contract and we tried her out in that role and she proved to be perfect." George Cukor was originally hired to direct the film, but, after some preliminary shooting, he and Zanuck argued and Zanuck replaced him with the more agreeable and less temperamental Goulding. Zanuck reportedly approached Maureen O'Hara with the part of the leading lady in **The Razor's Edge**. (O'Hara later claimed that Zanuck offered the role, but that she was to keep mum about it, and when he learned that she had mentioned this to Linda Darnell, a Fox contract actress, who parroted her remarks back to Zanuck, the studio boss canceled O'Hara from the film.) Tierney, however, was always Zanuck's first choice, as she was also Maugham's first selection. "We had the most beautiful actress in the world at Fox and that was Gene Tierney," Zanuck told this author. "She was always my first and only choice to play that spoiled rotten society girl." Tierney told this author that "I think they wanted me to play that terrible bitch in **The Razor's Edge** because of my role in **Leave Her to Heaven** [1945], a picture we made only a year before we did **The Razor's Edge**. In **Leave Her to Heaven**, I played an awful, scheming rich woman, a murderess really, who will kill just to keep her husband's love all to herself. I played about the same kind of person in **The Razor's Edge**, jealous of any other woman interested in Ty [Tyrone Power]. If that is not typecasting, I don't know what isn't." Payne, who has a small but significant role in **The Razor's Edge**, told this author that "I play a rich guy who loses everything and his will to live, too, until Ty [Tyrone Power] hypnotizes me back into my right mind. I always thought that that was pretty far-fetched, since I don't believe anyone can be so easily hypnotized unless they are a half-wit at the start. I was under contract at Fox then, so I was not about to argue with the scriptwriter or the director. After my scene with Ty [Tyrone Power] when he does his swami routine with me, I asked him if he believed that such powers really existed and he laughed and said: 'Only at carnivals and sideshows and only if some poor sap wants to believe that he has had his mind cooked by some con artist.' So he wasn't about to argue either about all that goofy palaver. The strange thing is that in Ty's next picture, **Nightmare Alley** [1947] he plays that kind of sideshow con artist, and he did a damned good job of it, too. Everything about the movies is sleight-of-hand. In **The Razor's Edge**, Ty had millions believing in mind over matter, but, the next year, he is convincing them in **Nightmare Alley** that spiritualism is nothing more than a big swindle." **p**, Darryl F. Zanuck; **d**, Edmund Goulding; **cast**, Tyrone Power, Gene Tierney, John Payne, Anne Baxter, Clifton Webb, Herbert Marshall, Lucile Watson, Frank Latimore, Elsa Lanchester, Fritz Kortner, Cobina Wright Sr., John Wengraf, Cecil Humphreys, Jack Wagner; **w**, Lamar Trotti (based on the novel by W. Somerset Maugham); **c**, Arthur Miller; **m**, Alfred Newman; **ed**, J. Watson Webb Jr.; **art d**, Richard Day, Nathan Juran; **set d**, Thomas Little, Paul S. Fox; **spec eff**, Fred Sersen.

Reach for the Sky ★★★ 1957; U.K.; 135m; Rank; B/W; War Drama; Children: Unacceptable; **DVD**; **VHS**. This stirring and true story profiles the heroic exploits of British aviator Douglas Bader (1910-1982), played by More. Despite losing both legs in a 1931 plane accident, he uses artificial legs to fly again, joining the Royal Air Force and becoming a hero early in World War II (1939-1945). He is shot down again during the Battle of Britain (1940) when the German Luftwaffe bombs England, and he is captured by the Germans. After three failed attempts to escape from a prisoner-of-war camp, More is imprisoned in an escape-proof old castle, but is released when war ends. More gives a standout performance as the legless Bader and is supported by a strong cast in this exciting production. Songs: "Love Is the Sweetest Thing" (Ray Noble), "All By Yourself in the Moonlight" (Jay Wallis as Ralph T. Butler), "Goodnight Sweetheart" (Ray Noble, Reginald Connelly, Jimmy Campbell). Violence prohibits viewing by children. **p**, Daniel M. Angel; **d**, Lewis Gilbert; **cast**, Kenneth More, Muriel Pavlow, Lyndon Brook, Lee Patterson, Alexander Knox, Anton Diffring, Dorothy Alison, Michael Warre, Eric Pohlmann, Michael Gough; **w**, Gilbert, Vernon Harris (based on the book *The Story of Douglas Bader* by Paul Brickhill); **c**, Jack Asher; **m**, John Addison; **ed**, John Shirley; **art d**, Bernard Robinson; **spec eff**, Bryan Langley, Bert Marshall, Bill Warrington.

The Reader ★★★ 2009; U.S./Germany; 124m.; Weinstein Company; Color; Drama/Romance; Children: Unacceptable (MPAA: R); DVD; VHS. Set in post-World War II Germany, this riveting tale sees Kross as a teenage boy, who falls ill and is helped home by Winslet, a stranger

Kate Winslet in *The Reader,* 2009.

twice his age. He recovers from scarlet fever, and the two have a passionate but secret affair. He discovers that she likes to be read to, so he reads to her sections of *The Odyssey, Huckleberry Finn,* and *The Lady with the Little Dog.* After she mysteriously disappears, Kross is left confused and heartbroken. As Fiennes, an adult eight years later, he is a law student observing the Nazi war crime trials, and is stunned to see that Winslet is one of the defendants in the courtroom. As her past is revealed, Fiennes uncovers a deep secret that will impact both of their lives. Well written and acted, this impactful drama closely examines how one generation comes to terms with the crimes of another. Songs: "Musik Liegt in her Luft" (Heinz Gietz, Kurt Feltz), "Pueri Hebraeorum" (Giovanni Pierluigi da Palestrina), "Making Time" (Edwin Phillips, Kenneth Pickett), "Don't Look Back" (Jackson C. Frank). Sexual scenes and mature subject matter prohibit viewing by children. **p**, Sydney Pollack, Donna Gigliotti, Anthony Minghella, Redmond Morris, Christopher Fisser, Henning Molfenter, Bob Weinstein, Harvey Weinstein; **d**, Stephen Daldry; **cast**, Ralph Fiennes, Kate Winslet, David Kross, Jeanette Hain, Susanne Lothar, Alissa Wilms, Florian Bartholomai, Friederike Becht, Matthias Habich, Frieder Venus; **w**, David Hare (based on the novel *Der Vorleser* by Bernhard Schlink; **c**, Roger Deakins, Chris Menges; **m**, Nico Muhly; **ed**, Claire Simpson; **prod d**, Brigitte Broch; **art d**, Stefan Hauck, Erwin Prib, Yeshim Zolan; **set d**, Karin Betzler, Eva Stiebler; **spec eff**, Adolf Wojtinek, Bernd Wildau.

The Real Glory ★★★★ 1939; U.S.; 96m; Samuel Goldwyn Company/UA; B/W; Adventure/War Drama; Children: Unacceptable; **DVD**; **VHS**. Action-packed and with fine performances from Cooper, Leeds, Niven and others, this exciting war tale takes place in the exotic southern Philippines during the Moro Rebellion (1899-1913), following the Spanish-American War of 1898. The film opens in 1906 with a small cadre of American officers commanding Filipino troops at a small base in Mindanao, and who are defending a local village at Mysang from the oppressive fanatical Muslims of the Moro Rebellion. The Moro rebels are raiding nearby villages, murdering men and abducting women and children to use as slaves. Gordon, the colonel in charge of the base, is killed by the rebels and he is replaced by Hicks. Shown emerging onto a veranda after a social affair, Hicks is assaulted by a Moro stupefied with drugs as he mindlessly plods toward him, murdering Hicks in front of his wife, Johnson, and his daughter, Leeds, with a slashing machete. The drug-controlled assassin is only killed after many bullets from shocked officers are fired into him. Owen, who has received a blow to the head that causes him to gradually grow blind, takes command. Meanwhile, Cooper, a medical officer, arrives to supervise the local clinic while lieutenants Niven and Crawford are assigned to train the local Filipino recruits as part of the constabulary designed to combat

Gary Cooper and Andrea Leeds in *The Real Glory,* 1939.

the Moro rebels, but the local priest, Waldron, has little belief that the Moro rebels can be overcome. Owen, who stubbornly runs everything by the book, ignores advice from Cooper, especially prohibiting Cooper from conducting surveillance in the countryside beyond the village fortifications. Cooper nevertheless disobeys orders and, with Inocencio, a native boy who knows the area, goes into the interior to reconnoiter the enemy's position and operations, learning much about the Moro modus operandi and rituals and its fanatical leader, Komai. They see Komai ordering another drugged assassin to go to Mysang and kill Owen, but Cooper intercepts this would-be killer and returns him to his base as a captive. When he returns to base, however, Owen is enraged at his unmilitary conduct, and Cooper is arrested and confined to his quarters. Meanwhile, Leeds falls in love with Cooper and refuses to leave the base when her mother, Johnson, departs, staying on to help Cooper administer to the sick in the village, especially when the base is struck by cholera after the rebels build a dam that prevents the river from flowing into the village and the local water supply from an old well becomes contaminated. Owen is then compelled to send Crawford and a small unit of soldiers to destroy the dam in reopening the flowing river to replenish the village's water supply, but Crawford does not return. Sokoloff, a supposedly friendly Moro, offers to guide Owen and his men to the dam, and Owen and most of his men set off to demolish that dam. Sokoloff, however, plans to lead them into an ambush, just as he has insidiously done with Crawford. Meanwhile, Cooper learns from Inocencio that Crawford and all the others in his unit have been killed and that Sokoloff is leading Owen into a trap. Cooper leaves Niven and only a handful of men to defend the village, which, after Cooper departs, comes under heavy Moro attack, that assault ensuing now that Owen and his men have been decoyed by Sokoloff. Cooper finds Crawford's body and is able to catch up with Owen and his men before Sokoloff can signal his Moro allies to attack. Cooper kills Sokoloff and manages to blow up the dam, and then takes command of Owen's forces as Owen is now completely blind. Cooper orders rafts to be quickly built and he and his men board these rafts, which are hurried down the river with now rushing waters toward the besieged fortifications of Mysang. Within the village, Niven, grown ill from cholera, just barely manages to man the defenses with his scant force as Leeds helps him supply ammunition to his men, but the ammunition begins to run out as the Moro rebels creep closer and closer to the barricaded village. Cooper arrives with an advance party of men to help stave off the attackers, throwing lighted sticks of dynamite at the Moro invaders, blowing them up. When running out of dynamite, he lights candles from Waldron's church, tossing these in front of the attackers to ward them off until they realize the ruse and rush the barricades. Just at that moment, Owen and his main force arrive on rafts through the rushing river and beat back the Moro attack

and secure the village. As the evil leader, Komai, is about to escape, a dedicated Filipino officer, Robles, kills him. At the finale, with peace restored, Cooper departs with Leeds, leaving the command of the new reinforced Filipino garrison in charge of Robles. Hathaway, a foremost action director, outdoes himself in this exceptional and adventurous war tale, one where the exotic jungles of the Philippines are wholly captured through Maté's crisp lensing and the many battle scenes are amazingly well choreographed—some of the most exciting action scenes put on film to that time—where Cooper, Niven, Owen, Leeds, Crawford and the rest of the cast shine in their captivating roles. *Author's Note*: "We wanted to tell this story for some time," producer Goldwyn told this author, "because it was based on true events that happened in the Philippines and because we wanted to build up the image of the great Filipino people. We knew the Philippines would soon be in harm's danger from the Japanese, who were then invading China and had plans to go everywhere in the Pacific back then and because the Philippines were then part of the United States territories. We had promised the Philippines independence and they got it in 1946, but that great people had to go through hell during World War II before that happened." Cooper echoed those sentiments when telling this author that "**The Real Glory** was really a tribute to the Filipino constabulary that later became the famous Filipino Scouts that fought on Bataan and Corregidor in the early part of the war [WWII]. Thousands of those brave men died in the Bataan Death March and in Japanese prison camps, but the Filipinos never surrendered, really, and fought for more than three years in the hills against the Japanese until the U.S. returned with MacArthur to the Philippines in 1944." Hathaway pointed out to this author: "We did a good deal of research on the Moro behavior before we did that picture. One of the most telling scenes is where Coop [Gary Cooper] captures a Moro and makes him give information after he threatens to stick him into a slaughtered pig. Muslims want nothing to do with pigs and consider them unholy and are frightened to death of those little oinkers." U.S. General John J. Pershing (1860-1948), while serving as commander in Manila in 1911, harshly dealt with Moro insurgents. After learning their Muslim credo and avid aversion to pigs, he ordered several captured Moro terrorists to be shot to death following their murderous rampages, having them tied to posts after they dug their own graves. Pershing had many pigs slaughtered, their guts and blood smeared onto the bullets fired into the convicted terrorists and their graves coated with this gore and into which the bodies of the Moro rebels were dumped and buried. He allowed one Moro to escape to tell the tale of this horrible sacrilege and that reportedly stopped all Moro activity in the islands for many years to come. It was this tale that inspired Hathaway to use that scene of pig intimidation in **The Real Glory**. (One might wonder if a similar result could be achieved by dropping a million pigs by parachute into any hostile Muslim country.) Niven, who has a supporting role in this film, stated that "I was playing second fiddle to a lot of big-name stars in those days. If it wasn't Errol Flynn, it was Gary Cooper in **The Real Glory**, but, I must admit that Coop was a real gentleman and treated me like an equal, or, at least, a bass fiddle." **p**, Samuel Goldwyn; **d**, Henry Hathaway; **cast**, Gary Cooper, David Niven, Andrea Leeds, Reginald Owen, Broderick Crawford, Kay Johnson, Russell Hicks, Vladimir Sokoloff, Roy Gordon, Charles Waldron, Benny Inocencio, Tetsu Komai, Rudy Robles, Elmo Lincoln, Lotus Long; **w**, Jo Swerling, Robert R. Presnell (based on the novel by Charles L. Clifford); **c**, Rudolph Maté; **m**, Alfred Newman; **ed**, Daniel Mandell; **art d**, James Basevi; **set d**, Julia Heron; **spec eff**, Paul Widlicska, R.O. Binger, Paul Eagler.

Real Life ★★★ 1979; U.S.; 99m; PAR; Color; Comedy; Children: Unacceptable (MPAA: PG); **DVD**; **VHS**. Brooks gives another uproarious performance as an obnoxious documentary filmmaker who persuades a Phoenix, Arizona, family (Grodin and McCain) to let him and his crew film their everyday lives. However, not enough happens to satisfy Brooks, so, instead of merely allowing the family to do its thing, he tries to control every aspect of their lives, saying: "It's for the good of the show." Grodin and McCain's home life becomes so upset that they decide the only way to save their marriage is to call off the filming and tell everyone to leave the house. When things go from bad to worse, Brooks sets the house on fire. This very funny film was based on the concept of a television documentary, "American Family." Songs: "Something's Gotta Give" (Johnny Mercer), "Tara Theme" (Max Steiner), "Jump Into the Fire" (Harry Nillson). Gutter language and violence prohibit viewing by children. **p**, Penelope Spheeris; **d**, Albert Brooks; **cast**, Dick Haynes, Brooks, Matthew Tobin, J.A. Preston, Joseph Schaffler, Phyllis Quinn, James Ritz, Clifford Einstein, Harry Einstein, Mandy Einstein, Karen Einstein, Charles Grodin; **w**, Brooks, Monica Mcgowan Johnson, Harry Shearer; **c**, Eric Saarinen (Panavision; Technicolor); **m**, Mort Lindsey; **ed**, David Finfer; **art d**, Linda Marder, Linda Spheeris; **spec eff**, Dick Albain, Mark Jaffe.

Reap the Wild Wind ★★★★ 1942; U.S.; 124m; PAR; Color; Adventure; Children: Cautionary; **DVD**; **VHS**. That grand maker of epics DeMille does not disappoint with this roaring sea saga that showcases the considerable talents of Wayne, Milland, Goddard, Hayward, Preston and Massey. Set in the 1840s when the tall sailing ships were giving way on the seas to steam engine vessels, and located in the Florida Keys, the film opens with a fierce hurricane sweeping through the area. As the storm subsides, a bevy of salvage hunters, not unlike the lower beasts of prey searching for carcasses on the savannas of Africa, swarm out to sea to claim the cargoes of any stricken ship. One of these is Goddard, who runs a salvage operation inherited from her deceased father. She sails her schooner to the sinking wreck of a cargo ship that has been shattered on some shoals by the storm. She finds its captain, Wayne, lashed to its mast and rescues him, but she cannot claim salvage since another sea scavenger, Massey, and his brother, Preston, have arrived first and claim the ship's cargo. It soon becomes suspicious that Massey and Preston have arrived to make their claim with more than fortuitous alacrity and that they may have had a hand in "arranging" that wreck and its cargo-seizing salvage through the underhanded collusion of the otherwise upright Wayne. Those suspicions have surfaced since Massey and Preston have invariably arrived at wrecks before any other salvage operators. Goddard nurses Wayne through his injuries, but he worries that by losing his ship he may also have lost his captaincy of a new steam vessel. Goddard tells him that she will journey to the company's headquarters in Charleston, South Carolina, and convince investigators that he was not responsible for the loss of the ship, attributing it to the work of pirates. When arriving in Charleston with her cousin, Hayward, Goddard meets with company attorney Milland, who holds Wayne's new commission papers, but is reluctant to release them until he thoroughly investigates the wreck and is satisfied that Wayne is innocent of any wrongdoing. Meanwhile, Hayward falls for Milland, and Goddard leads Milland on in order to soften his attitude toward Wayne. While Hayward sails to her home in Havana, Milland and Goddard travel to Florida. When Massey sees Milland present, he becomes alarmed, believing that his piratical operations will be discovered. He orders Milland shanghaied, but, after Goddard learns of Massey's plot, she persuades Wayne to intervene and he and Milland have a savage fight with Massey's goons, beating them off. Milland loses Wayne's commission papers during the battle, and Wayne is now convinced that Milland is not only trying to sabotage his career, but is attempting to steal Goddard's affections. Wayne meets with the devious Massey and agrees to sabotage his new ship so that Massey can claim salvage. To that end, Wayne travels to Havana to take command of his new ship, and Milland later becomes suspicious that Wayne's new ship, the *Southern Cross*, is imperiled because of the wildly fluctuating prices for that ship's cargo, which is yet to be delivered. Thinking that Wayne plans to wreck the ship, Milland commandeers a ship with Goddard on board and sails for Havana, but Goddard, believing that Wayne is innocent of any wrongdoing, disables the ship so that it drifts aimlessly through a fog bank

John Wayne in *Reap the Wild Wind*, 1942.

while the *Southern Cross* crashes onto a reef and sinks. Preston, Massey's brother who has served on the *Southern Cross* to make sure that it is wrecked, survives the wreck, along with Wayne and others, but Hayward, who has stowed away on the ship to be with Preston, the man she loves, is drowned when the ship goes down, this grim fact unknown to its captain and crew. Wayne is then charged with malfeasance and stands trial where evidence indicates that a woman was on board the lost ship. To determine that fact, Milland and Wayne agree to go to the site of the sunken wreck and dive to its depths. Both men sail to the area and, donning diving suits, descend into the deeps where they enter the hull of the wrecked ship and find evidence that proves Hayward's death by drowning. While they are searching, a giant squid attacks Milland, threatening to crush him, but Wayne heroically goes to his rescue, chopping away some of the squid's tentacles. In the titanic struggle Wayne is himself ensnared in other tentacles from the squid, and, while attempting to escape, the wrecked ship slides from its precarious perch on the edge of an underwater shelf and falls into a deep chasm, taking the squid and Wayne with it. Milland surfaces carrying a scarf that proves Hayward's death and Preston, who is seized with grief and remorse over Hayward's death, turns on his brother Massey and brands him with piracy. The merciless Massey shoots and kills Preston and, in turn, is shot to death by Milland. Goddard, meanwhile, attempts to comfort the dying Preston while Milland recognizes that Wayne has given his life to save him. DeMille directs this fine adventure tale with his usual flamboyant flair, presenting a lavish and exciting film replete with great action and stirring seascape scenes awash with howling winds and roiling seas and most likely the largest and menacing squid ever known to mankind. The color lensing from Milner and Skall is exceptionally eye-popping, and Young's dynamic score befits the wild exploits of the daring seagoing fortune seekers. Paramount, DeMille's home studio, gave the director a huge budget of more than $2 million, which was recouped with a handsome profit from the box office, returning more than $4 million in the film's initial release. The film received an Oscar for Best Visual Effects (Special Effects; Jennings, Pereira, Edouart, Wrigley and Lerpae) and received Oscar nominations for Best Cinematography (Color; Milner and Skall), and for Best Art Direction (Color; Drier, Anderson and Sawley). The story was aired in a sixty-minute radio broadcast by Lux Radio Theater on March 8, 1943, with Ray Milland and Paulette Goddard reprising their roles. Songs: "Columbia, the Gem of the Ocean" (1843; David T. Shaw); "Sea Chantey (The Nellie B)" (1942; music: Victor Young; lyrics: Frank Loesser); "Bye and Bye," "When I'm Gone Away" (both 1942; music and lyrics: Troy Sanders); "Tis But A Little Faded Flower" (1860; music: John Rogers Thomas; lyrics: Frederick Enoch; adaptation, 1942: Troy Sanders); "Reap the Wild Wind" (1942; music: Lew Pollack; lyrics: Ned Washington; published in order

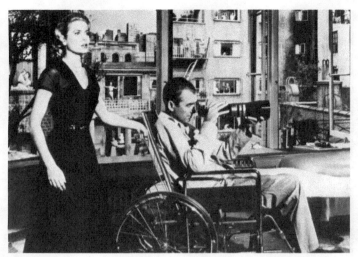

Grace Kelly and James Stewart in *Rear Window*, 1954.

to promote this film). ***Author's Note***: DeMille, with his usual penchant for everything big, insisted that studio craftsmen build a gigantic squid (which was pinkish red in color), this formidable deep sea creature constructed at a cost of $12,000 and which was operated through a series of complex hydraulic pistons and steel cables that allowed technicians to move its tentacles in any direction. The creature served as the action highlight of the film and was much talked about for years by viewers, these exciting underwater scenes taking about five weeks to accomplish. Because the U.S. lacked rubber during WWII after the Japanese cornered that raw material by occupying Indochina and Malaya, Paramount donated the rubber squid to the war effort following the completion of the film. DeMille was not impressed with John Wayne and originally wanted Errol Flynn to play his part, but Jack Warner at Warner Brothers adamantly refused to loan Flynn to Paramount, so DeMille signed on "that cowboy star," as he called Wayne. "I knew that DeMille did not like me," Wayne told this author, "and he showed it when we made **Reap the Wild Wind** by giving almost all of his attention to Milland, and Paulette his little pet [Paulette Goddard, who appeared in other De-Mille films, including **North West Mounted Police**, 1940, and **Unconquered**, 1947]. DeMille was building Milland up to be a rugged guy, but at my expense." Milland and Goddard got top billing when the film was released, but when it was rereleased in 1954, new promotion had Wayne and Hayward with top billing since both had become superstars and Milland and Goddard had faded from that stellar status. Hayward told this author that "Mr. DeMille was very gracious toward me and I took his direction as gospel and that was the only way to stay on that man's good side. He acted like a field marshal on a battlefield and called the shots on everything. He had an eagle eye for detail and could tell if a bow was out of place on a dress or someone's coat was unbuttoned. You never wanted to get on that man's bad side, unless you wanted to be humiliated by him in front of the entire cast and crew. He was like that enormous squid he had in **Reap the Wild Wind**. His tentacles were everywhere." Massey told this author: "You could only get along with Mr. DeMille if you followed the script and his instructions to the letter. To ad lib a line or make the wrong movement was a cardinal sin with him. We all knew it, so we towed his mark, except for Duke [Wayne], who seemed to taunt him at times by delivering his lines slowly. I don't think Duke and Mr. DeMille had any love for each other." Character actor Victor Kilian was seriously injured when enacting one of the goons trying to shanghai Milland and Wayne, where Wayne accidentally and permanently injured one of Kilian's eyes. Kilian later stated: "It was not his [Wayne's] fault, but I don't like him. Not for what he did but for the person he is." Kilian was referring to Wayne's political views, which were decidedly conservative and Republican while Kilian was a dedicated liberal, if not a fellow traveler, who later came under the scrutiny

of the U.S. House of Un-American Activities Committee (HUAC) during the McCarthy era, and was for some time on the Hollywood blacklist. **p&d**, Cecil B. DeMille; **cast**, Ray Milland, John Wayne, Paulette Goddard, Raymond Massey, Robert Preston, Lynne Overman, Susan Hayward, Charles Bickford, Walter Hampden, Louise Beavers, Martha O'Driscoll, Elisabeth Risdon, Hedda Hopper, Barbara Britton, Dorothy Sebastian, Akim Tamiroff, Victor Kilian, DeMille (prologue speaker); **w**, Alan LeMay, Charles Bennett, Jesse Lasky, Jr., (uncredited) Jeanie Macpherson, Theodore St. John, Thelma Strabel (based on a story by Strabel); **c**, Victor Milner, William V. Skall (Technicolor); **m**, Victor Young; **ed**, Anne Bauchens; **art d**, Hans Dreier, Roland Anderson; **set d**, George Sawley; **spec eff**, Gordon Jennings, W. L. Pereira, Farciot Edouart, Dewey Wrigley, Paul K. Lerpae.

Rear Window ★★★★ 1954; U.S.; 112m; PAR; Color; Crime Drama; Children: Unacceptable; **BD**; **DVD**; **VHS**. Another masterpiece thriller from Hitchcock is as riveting a film as is the obsessive view of its wheelchair-bound protagonist, Stewart, who thinks he has seen a murder committed by his across-the-way neighbor, the burly Burr. Stewart is a professional action photographer who has broken a leg and is incapacitated and confined to his wheelchair and apartment, a condition that causes him endless and sleepless hours of anxiety and frustration. To while away his time and feed his fertile imagination, he uses his telescopic camera lens to spy on his neighbors from the rear window of his apartment, one that gives him a complete view of many backyard apartments surrounding a court and a small garden area. His sharp-tongued and always advising housekeeper, Ritter, condemns Stewart's conduct as nothing more than the activities of an offensive Peeping Tom. (Voyeurism is replete in this film, but appears to be excusable in that Stewart has no perverse reasons for his ogling other than as an inquiring photojournalist preoccupying himself with the nuances and behaviors of his neighbors, unlike the decidedly degenerate Peeping Tom that is Tony Perkins in Hitchcock's later thriller, the grim **Psycho**, 1960.) Stewart shrugs off such criticism, saying that he is innocently studying his neighbors to learn more about them. These include a lonely woman Stewart calls Miss Lonely Hearts (Evelyn), who never seems to have any gentleman callers, an apprentice ballerina, a composer who has the most expensive apartment with a huge skylight window, and a married couple with a little dog they send from their third floor window in lowering and raising basket so that he can perform his daily ablutions. He also watches a buxom blonde whom Stewart calls Miss Torso (Darcy), who gets a lot of male visitors and loving newlyweds, but only when their shade is not drawn, which is seldom. He begins to focus on Burr, a heavyset traveling salesman, who has a shrewish wife, Winston, and is routinely henpecked while he walks from one room to another, brooding. Stewart's ritualistic neighbor-watching is then interrupted by Kelly, a beautiful and well-to-do blonde model, who is engaged to him and dotes upon Stewart, attention he finds too fussy and even annoying, though he knows he is very lucky to have this wonderful woman in his life. After Kelly arrives, she withdraws a skimpy nightgown from a small carrying bag to show that she has brought along her wardrobe for the evening and then surprises Stewart by having a catered meal of haute cuisine brought into his apartment by a waiter from a posh restaurant. She has also selected the finest wine to go along with that sumptuous meal, but the down-to-earth Stewart seems somehow vexed with all this grand attention, telling Kelly that the meal is perfect and that she is perfect and everything she does is perfect and that perfection is what creates his distemper. Meanwhile, Stewart begins to pay more and more attention to Burr, particularly after Burr and Winston get into a shouting match and, the following day, after the shades on the window of Burr's bedroom are drawn for some time. Stewart then sees Burr wrapping a saw and a large butcher knife in a newspaper and where there is no more sign of the hectoring Winston. When he tells all this to Kelly and Ritter both women take a deeper interest in this neighbor, becoming convinced that Winston is now the victim of foul play. Stewart calls an old friend,

Corey, who is a NYPD detective. Corey visits him and Kelly, patiently listening to their story and suspicions about Burr. He dismisses their notions that Burr has killed and vivisected his wife, saying that there is no evidence that would compel him to investigate the salesman. Corey tolerates their arguments and then promises that he will look into the matter, but he indicates a decided reluctance to do so. He later calls Stewart to tell him that Winston may have left her husband, but there is nothing to indicate that she was injured in any way by her now estranged spouse, Burr, further telling Stewart that he and Kelly should leave crime investigations to professional criminologists. Stewart, Kelly and Ritter then take matters into their own hands. After they see that the little dog, who has been digging at some bushes in the courtyard has been found dead, killed by someone unknown and causing the owners to cry out in anguish at their neighbors with accusations, Ritter digs up the area, but finds nothing, all concluding that Burr had buried something there but found the dog, killed it, and then retrieved the item he had buried. Burr then ships a rope-bound trunk to an unknown destination and Stewart learns of the shipment, informing Corey, who believes he is being sent on a wild goose chase and later reports that the trunk was delivered and claimed by a woman he believes to be Burr's estranged wife. Stewart counters by saying that the woman may be Burr's mistress and in league with Burr in disposing of Winston. Corey tells him that he is inventing a murder mystery and to forget about Burr. To find concrete evidence that will convince Corey, Kelly then boldly invades Burr's apartment while he is gone and finds Winston's wedding ring, but just as she is about to leave, Burr returns and finds her in his apartment. Seeing all this, Stewart panics and calls police, who rush to the apartment just as Burr is manhandling Kelly. Police arrest Kelly for breaking and entering, but, before she is taken away, she signals to Stewart that she is wearing Winston's wedding ring and now has the needed evidence to implicate Burr. Stewart sends Ritter to the local precinct station to bail out Kelly, but, by then, Burr, peering across the courtyard, sees and identifies his antagonist, Stewart. He calls Stewart, who is now left alone and helpless in his wheelchair and Stewart hangs up on him, knowing that Burr will soon be at his door. Burr does arrive at Stewart's apartment, which Stewart has kept dark, turning off all the lights. Burr barges into the place, demanding to know what Stewart seeks from him. Stewart demands to know what Burr has done with his wife. Enraged, the myopic Burr (who wears thick glasses) stumbles forward, realizing that Stewart is on to him, but Stewart repeatedly blinds Burr by setting off flashbulbs from his camera. Burr nevertheless reaches Stewart and drags the helpless man to the open rear window, attempting to throw him out. They struggle frantically with Stewart clinging to the window's ledge and shouting for help. Corey, along with Kelly, who has been released from custody, accompanied by several policemen, rush through the courtyard just as Stewart plunges downward, but his fall is broken by cops with outstretched arms. Other officers charge into Stewart's apartment and corral Burr, who admits that he has killed his wife and he is taken away. We next see victorious Stewart back in his wheelchair, and this time he has *two* broken legs in casts, the second broken leg as a result of his encounter with the killer he has brought to justice. Kelly is seen nearby, curled up with a fashion magazine. Their harrowing experience has cemented their future life together. Hitchcock takes his time in building suspense in this superlative thriller, but so carefully mounts anxiety that the climax is both frightening and breathtaking, a fingernail biter to the very end. Stewart perfectly fits the mold as an adventurous photographer upset at being confined to his abode and restricted from action by his impaired leg. The effervescent Kelly shines in all of her scenes where she displays considerable wisdom and wit, at one point stating that she and Stewart are "two of the most frightening ghouls I have ever known." Hayes' script is taut and well crafted, and Waxman's score keeps pace with the unfolding drama, interspersed with some lively tunes that add irony, as well as the day and night noises of the neighbors, all presenting a feeling of misleading comfort while a sinister murder is in progress. The cameo scenes of the neighbors are straight out of Norman Rockwell,

Raymond Burr and James Stewart in *Rear Window,* 1954.

but they are presented by Hitchcock so seamlessly with the main story line involving Stewart and Kelly that they all work well. The film was an enormous success, taking in more than $5 million against a $1 million budget (its total receipts to date are estimated to between $27 and $36 million), and Hitchcock, as usual, brought the film in on schedule. The film received Oscar nominations for Best Director (Hitchcock), Best Color Cinematography (Burks), and Best Sound Recording. Songs: "Fancy Free" (1944; excerpt from Ballet Music by Leonard Bernstein), "That's Amore" (1952; music: Harry Warren), "To See You (Is to Love You)" (1952; music: Jimmy Van Heusen; lyrics: Johnny Burke), "Lisa" (1954; music: Franz Waxman; lyrics: Harold Rome), "Mona Lisa" (1950; Ray Evans and Jay Livingston), "Red Garters' (1954; excerpt by Ray Evans and Jay Livingston), "Martha" (1847; music: Friedrich von Flotow; lyrics: Friedrich Wilhelm Riese), "Many Dreams Ago" (1954; music: Franz Waxman; lyrics: Mack David). *Author's Note*: Hitchcock works with only one set in this film, the interior of Stewart's apartment and the exterior of the courtyard and the back windows and interiors of the surrounding apartments, a marvelous lifelike set that perfectly fits the story line. (He appears in his traditional cameo role as a man winding a clock in the composer's apartment.) Hitchcock made continuous fluid takes, which proved amazingly effective despite the set's confining restrictions, unlike the same kind of single apartment set he employed in the much less effective **Rope**, 1948. Hitchcock told this author that "in **Rear Window**, I had a lot more interaction going on because I involved the neighbors and little slices of their lives to work with what was going on in Jimmy's [Stewart's] little apartment and while he is preoccupied with the murderous goings-on in Mr. Burr's apartment. I did not have that extra and much-needed element when we did **Rope**. My window dressing for **Rear Window** was, of course, the beautiful Grace Kelly, if you forgive the terrible pun. The presence of such a beautiful woman is really incongruous to the story. You would never believe that such a stunning person would sink to being a lowly detective, but it's all an adventure for her, more to satisfy Jimmy than to solve a real murder. She wants to please this street photographer and show him she has the same kind of nerve he has. That way she can convince him that she is just as common as he is and not the above-it-all lady he thinks she is. When she risks her life with Mr. Burr to prove his point, well, then Jimmy knows that she loves him, but it scares the hell out of him, too." Stewart enjoyed doing **Rear Window**, but had some reservations about his character, telling this author: "I had a queasy feeling about the role I was playing. I am supposed to be a news photographer and everyone's story is grist for my mill, but spying on my neighbors as I do in that picture made me feel uncomfortable and I told that to Hitch. He only patted that prop of a cast I had on my leg and said, 'don't give it a guilty thought, my boy. The audience will

Joan Fontaine and Judith Anderson in *Rebecca,* 1940.

be peeping along with you and will love doing it.' I didn't know if he was joking or not. You never knew that about him and he made sure you never knew because of the way he threw out those lines at you. I learned one thing about him, though, early on, and that was if you said something he did not really like, he would stop talking and abruptly get up and walk away and he was not smiling when he did that." The construction of the thirty-one full-scale apartments for the set, the largest ever built at Paramount, was personally supervised by Hitchcock, who also dictated the furnishing of twelve of those apartments, all of it done to his specifications in order to achieve the right kind of lighting. "We could never have had those apartments properly lit if we used real locations," he told this author. "When you control the lighting, you control every mood for every character and scene and that is absolutely essential in filmmaking." Hitchcock also selected all of the dresses and shoes Kelly wore in the film, specifically telling costume designer Edith Head how to adorn the actress, which caused Head to later state: "He was really putting a dream together in the studio." Along with **Shadow of a Doubt**, 1943, this production was one of the director's two favorite films. Similar films where murders are briefly seen through windows that also lead to chilling, near-lethal encounters include **Lady on a Train**, 1945; **The Window**, 1949; and **Witness to Murder**, 1954. **p&d**, Alfred Hitchcock; **cast**, James Stewart, Grace Kelly, Wendell Corey, Thelma Ritter, Raymond Burr, Judith Evelyn, Irene Winston, Ross Bagdasarian, Georgine Darcy, Sara Berner, Frank Cady, Kathryn Grant, Gig Young, Hitchcock; **w**, John Michael Hayes (based on the story "It Had to Be Murder" by Cornell Woolrich); **c**, Robert Burks (Technicolor); **m**, Franz Waxman; **ed**, George Tomasini; **art d**, Hal Pereira, Joseph MacMillan Johnson; **set d**, Sam Comer, Ray Moyer; **spec eff**, John P. Fulton.

Rebecca ★★★★★ 1940; U.S.; 130m; Selznick/UA; B/W; Crime Drama/Mystery; Children: Unacceptable; **BD**; **DVD**; **VHS**. Another classic thriller from Hitchcock takes a different turn as an eerie psychological crime tale when a beautiful young woman enters her new husband's world of wealth and is engulfed by his mysterious past. Fontaine, who narrates her own journey into that strange past, is working as a paid companion for a rich dowager, Bates, who is vacationing on the Riviera. She encounters Olivier, a handsome man, as he stands at the edge of a cliff, pensively peering out to sea. Thinking that he is contemplating suicide, Fontaine calls out to him, and he is so startled that he barks a rebuke, but then thinks better of his abrupt remark and apologizes. They become friends, and Fontaine continues to see Olivier, a wealthy widower, whenever she can break away from the demanding and obnoxious Bates, never telling her employer that she is seeing this well-to-do vacationer. The shy and unassuming Fontaine captures Olivier's heart while she falls in love with him and his gentle and considerate ways. When Bates decides to leave Monte Carlo, Fontaine makes an excuse at the last minute and slips away to say goodbye to Olivier, but he tells her that she is not leaving with Bates but that he intends to marry her. Overwhelmed and overjoyed, Fontaine bids farewell to the snobbish Bates, who is shocked to see Fontaine becoming the new wife of the much-sought-after Olivier, snidely calling Fontaine a "fast worker," and telling her that she will never fit in as a grand lady in high British society. After an idyllic honeymoon with Olivier, Fontaine is taken to his sprawling estate and palatial home, Manderley, in Cornwall, England. They are greeted by the staff of the estate, headed by Anderson, the housekeeper, a severe and dominating woman who shows Fontaine a lavishly adorned bedroom in an unused wing of the palace that had been occupied by Olivier's deceased wife, Rebecca. These rooms have been kept in pristine condition, representing sacred ground for Anderson, who maintains this area as a shrine in memory of Rebecca, whom Anderson considers a saint. Rebecca's embroidered imprimatur appears on the pillows of the silk-encompassed bed and everywhere else in this anointed sanctuary. Rebecca's presence is everywhere Fontaine goes, including a huge oil portrait of her (the only image we ever see of this enigmatic woman) that hangs in the grand hall of the palace, one that haunts Fontaine as much as Anderson's constant reminders of Rebecca's perfect conduct and how Fontaine, as the new mistress of the estate, fails in every respect in taking her place. Anderson appears everywhere Fontaine goes in this cavernous palace, frightening her as the grim-looking, wide-eyed housekeeper suddenly steps from shadowy hallways and darkened rooms, appearing to be as much a specter as the mysterious Rebecca. She then meets Sanders, who is Rebecca's cousin and who implies that he had a close relationship with her (suggesting an incestuous alliance), but is not really welcomed at the estate by Olivier, who becomes closed-mouthed and even sullen whenever Rebecca's name is mentioned. Anderson, meanwhile, works her psychological wiles on Fontaine, constantly reminding her of how Rebecca was so wonderful and perfect. Fontaine, when attending a small party of Olivier's friends, wears a gown selected by the insidious and manipulative Anderson that disturbs Olivier when he sees Fontaine wearing it. Fontaine does not realize that Anderson has selected one of Rebecca's gowns for her, knowing this would disturb Olivier. Fontaine becomes so insecure that she actually contemplates suicide while peering down at a courtyard from a high window and where Anderson, standing next to her, tells her that by leaping to her death, Fontaine's anxieties and haunting memories of Rebecca will cease and she will find peace. Fontaine manages to resist this terrible impulse and, instead, begins to assert herself with Anderson, telling her that she will now take charge of the household and begins giving Anderson instructions which she reluctantly obeys. Meanwhile, another threat arises when a storm at sea disgorges the boat which Rebecca had been sailing and sank and where she was presumed lost. It is learned that the sailboat was intentionally scuttled, and the vindictive Sanders points an accusing finger at Olivier, implying that he purposely killed Rebecca, placed her body in that boat and then sank it to hide the murder. During an inquest, little is learned and proven against Olivier, although Sanders tries to blackmail Olivier to keep him silent, and family friend and government official Smith, who is presiding over the case, warns Sanders about his conduct. When the haunted Olivier is alone with Fontaine, he admits his involvement in Rebecca's death, telling her that she was anything but the perfect woman everyone believed her to be. She was, Olivier states, cruel, vicious and unfaithful to him. When she bragged to him that she was pregnant with another man's child, he struck her and she fell, accidentally hitting her head and dying. Olivier recounts how he then placed her body in their sailboat, took it out to sea and then sank it to shroud his actions. While suspicion still hangs over Olivier's head, Fontaine remains loving and loyal to him. He then learns that Rebecca had been seeing a physician in London and Sanders believes that she went there because she was pregnant, ostensibly with his child. Should that doctor confirm that belief, Sanders is convinced,

Olivier will be trapped into a murder charge. Accompanied by Sanders, his close friend, Denny, and Smith, Olivier pays a visit on that doctor, Carroll. Instead of confirming a pregnancy, Carroll shocks his visitors by telling them that Rebecca had terminal cancer. It is then assumed that she had taken her own life, based upon her fatalistic statements to Carroll. Following this meeting, Sanders calls Anderson and glumly tells her that "Rebecca fooled us all...yes...suicide." Before he departs, Smith warns Sanders that the law "takes a dim view toward blackmailers." Olivier then drives home with Denny to his estate that night, but, as they approach Olivier's palatial home, they see the dark skies brightened with flames and then see that the sprawling and elegant mansion is on fire. Rushing to find Fontaine, Olivier finds her and they embrace as they watch Anderson furtively move from one burning room to another, Fontaine telling Olivier how Anderson, now completely insane, had set fire to the place. The fires begin to consume the rich interior of the palace, chandeliers and ceilings crashing downward to kill Anderson while the camera closes upon the bed and its satin pillow case bearing an embroidered "R" (standing for Rebecca), which slowly burns away as if to eradicate the memory of this repulsive and repugnant woman. (This stunning finale was not lost on Orson Welles, who uses a similar symbolic "K" to represent his enigmatic character in **Citizen Kane**, 1941, made a year after this film, and where Welles also uses fire to obliterate the last boyhood vestiges of that character at the finale of that equally classic film.) Hitchcock masterfully directs this film with infinite care, developing Fontaine's character to the point where the viewer shares her apprehensions and eerie thoughts that Rebecca is lurking behind every door and trailing her footsteps and where Olivier is almost as enigmatic as the unseen Rebecca. Both Fontaine and Olivier render superlative performances as does the creepy Anderson, the supportive Denny, the oily Sanders and the rest of the fine cast. The script from Sherwood and Harrison bristles with brilliant scenes and crisp dialog, and Barnes' lensing is outstanding, as is Waxman's angst-filled score. The film won Oscars for Best Picture and Best Cinematography, Black-and-White (Barnes), as well as Oscar nominations for Best Director (Hitchcock); Best Actor (Olivier); Best Actress (Fontaine); Best Supporting Actress (Anderson); Best Art Direction, Black-and-White (Wheeler); Best Film Editing (Hayes); Best Original Score (Waxman); and Best Special Effects (Cosgrove). The film saw great success at the box office, taking in more than $6 million in its initial release, against a budget of more than $1,200,000. Song: "Love's Old Sweet Song (Just a Song at Twilight)" (1884: J.L. Molloy). *Author's Note*: Hitchcock, who makes his traditional cameo appearance as a man outside a phone booth, was particularly meticulous in making this film, the first he made in the U.S., after migrating to Hollywood under an exclusive contract with producer Selznick. In heralding this film, Selznick told the press that it would, in many respects, equal his beloved and eternally successful **Gone with the Wind**, 1939, and went out of his way to make sure that the fire that consumes Manderley had the trappings of the burning of Atlanta shown in GWTW, even though the inferno shown in **Rebecca** was mostly achieved in miniature. Selznick, who purchased the film rights for the novel at $50,000, originally talked with Carole Lombard, thinking to cast her in the leading part on the proviso that she could persuade Ronald Colman to play the role of the husband. Colman declined the part, thinking that Selznick would, as did the novel, focus upon the leading lady (as Selznick did when faithfully following the plotline for GWTW). Colman further resisted doing the part because he did not like the fact that a killing, accidental or not, was attached to the character he would have to play. As was the case with GWTW, Selznick created considerable hoopla for **Rebecca** by conducting a nationwide search for his leading lady, but this was more of a promotion gimmick than his real intent as he had several Hollywood stars in mind for the role of Olivier's second wife, chiefly Loretta Young, but he could not work out a deal with that actress. Olivier was signed after Ronald Colman turned down the part of the haunted husband, although Selznick had approached William Powell and Leslie Howard to play that part, but both proved to

Joan Fontaine and Laurence Olivier in *Rebecca,* 1940.

be more expensive than the British actor. Olivier then urged Selznick to cast his wife, Vivien Leigh, in the leading female part. Although she was Selznick's greatest asset at that time, having become an international superstar as Scarlett O'Hara in GWTW, Selznick reportedly had second thoughts, believing that Leigh simply would not be convincing enough as the starry-eyed, naïve young lady who marries the sophisticated and somewhat older Olivier. He thought about Olivia de Havilland, Margaret Sullavan and Anne Baxter (the latter actress was Hitchcock's nomination as he thought Baxter a promising actress and would later cast her in his **I Confess**, 1953) for that part, but then decided to cast Fontaine, then only twenty-two years old, in the role. Fontaine had appeared in only a few B-films up to that time, and neither Hitchcock nor Olivier wanted her in the film after seeing tests of her. Hitchcock told this author that Fontaine "was called 'The Wooden Woman' at that time because she did very little emoting and she talked in such a quiet voice that I had to constantly ask her to speak louder." Olivier told this author that "I did not think she [Fontaine] was right for the part as the second wife, but she proved me wrong by delivering a startling performance. She turned from mousey and cringing to assertive and reliable as the production progressed, but I think Mr. Hitchcock's patient direction had much to do with that." Hitchcock's patience grew thin after a few weeks when working with the nagging Selznick, who was noted for sending endless memos to his directors dealing with the smallest detail of his productions. "He drove me crazy," Hitchcock told this author, "but I would not let him know that. I simply got his memos and acknowledged receiving them and then proceeded to do what I thought best." Selznick had a lifelong desire to control every aspect of any film production he financed, much more so than Samuel Goldwyn, another producer who "meddled" with his directors, but his intrusions were much more in the line of "fiddling" with directors than Selznick's incessant and exhausting detailed changes and alterations, even though, and in fairness, Selznick's obsession in this regard was to present the highest quality values with his productions. "He watched me like a hawk," Hitchcock told this author, "when we did **Rebecca** and I had the devil of a time with some of its scenes with him." One of those scenes, later edited out of the final print, showed Olivier smoking a cigar on board a ship as he travels to the Riviera and where other passengers so affected by the smoke from that stogie, coupled with their motion sickness, vomit on camera. When Selznick saw this scene, he exploded, sending Hitchcock another scolding memo: "I think the scenes of the seasickness are cheap beyond words, and old-fashioned in the bargain. We bought *Rebecca*, and we intend to make *Rebecca*, not a distorted and vulgarized version of a provenly successful work." Hitchcock, in creating that scene out of thin air, was expressing his own concerns about his own motion sickness, which he told this author was acute when he traveled by ship.

Mary Pickford in *Rebecca of Sunnybrook Farm*, 1917.

"Selznick communicated with me mostly by memo since he wanted all of his endless details in print and on record. We had very few personal meetings when doing **Rebecca**. I recall one meeting he called at his summer house where the scriptwriter [Sherwood] spent most of his time drinking and sailing little boats in Selznick's pool rather than talking about the picture and Selznick walked around delivering instructions until I almost dozed off in my chair. He kept us there until four o'clock in the morning and we accomplished nothing." Selznick later complained that Hitchcock exercised a sly attitude with everyone involved with **Rebecca**, "needling those around him. He needled stars, staff, press agents, any and all." Hitchcock, according to Selznick, made demeaning remarks to many involved in the production as to their drinking habits and their lethargic movements as a result of those habits. He admitted to this author that he many times took Fontaine aside and whispered in her ear that Olivier did not want her in the film, that others had severely criticized her, but that he was in her corner and was supporting her. He said he did this to "give the lady the right attitude of insecurity her character embodies and, only toward the end when her character becomes more confident, did I stop all that. Any good director must use psychology to get things done." Selznick was happy with Fontaine's performance, but grew to dislike Olivier's manner of delivering his character and his lines, at one point sending a memo to Hitchcock that read: "His [Olivier's] pauses and spacing in the scene with the girl in which she tells him about the ball are the most ungodly, slow and deliberate reactions I have ever seen. It is played as though he were deciding whether or not to run for President instead of whether or not to give a ball." Selznick held on to his criticism about Olivier and had serious misgivings about the success of **Rebecca**, but all of that came to nothing after the film was released and it became an enormous success, establishing Olivier in America as a superstar as well as that of Fontaine and cemented Hitchcock's ongoing love affair with American audiences that would continue until his demise forty years later. "Oh, I always knew from the beginning that **Rebecca** would be a hit," Sanders told this author. "It was a great suspense story that would do well with the public. Anyone could see that when we were doing that picture with the illustrious Mr. Hitchcock. He went out of his way to compliment me on my performance, even though I appear in only a few scenes. 'Marvelous,' Hitchcock told me, 'you have brilliantly transcended your rotten character from a lowly cad to a despicable mountebank.'" **p**, David O. Selznick; **d**, Alfred Hitchcock; **cast**, Laurence Olivier, Joan Fontaine, George Sanders, Judith Anderson, Nigel Bruce, Reginald Denny, C. Aubrey Smith, Gladys Cooper, Florence Bates, Melville Cooper, Leo G. Carroll, Hitchcock; **w**, Robert E. Sherwood, Joan Harrison (based on an adaptation by Philip MacDonald and Michael Hogan of the novel by Daphne Du Maurier); **c**, George Barnes; **m**, Franz Waxman; **ed**, W. Donn Hayes; **art d**, Lyle Wheeler; **spec eff**, Jack Cosgrove, Albert Simpson.

Rebecca of Sunnybrook Farm ★★★★ 1917 (silent); U.S.; 78m; Mary Pickford Company/Artcraft Pictures; B/W; Comedy/Drama; Children: Recommended; **DVD**. Pickford shines bright in this delightful tale, set in the pre-auto era of 1903, where she again plays a little girl. When her mother can no longer take care of her family brood, she sends Pickford off to live in a small New England community with her aunts, Crowell and Kelso, two crotchety, elderly women. Crowell is especially cantankerous and as strict as a whipping stick. Crowell cannot tolerate children and persistently shows her grumpy side whenever the impish Pickford pulls one of her many pranks. Pickford is insulted by an obnoxious local girl, Wilkey (who is called Minnie Smellie), and Pickford holds her little parasol to Wilkey's midsection, threatening to run her through with it. (Little comedic touches such as these pepper the scenes, along with numerous sight gags). To befriend local children, Pickford hosts an amateur circus in her aunt's barn and appears as the star performer, hoisted into the air with a harness before riding a horse around the ring, but she becomes stuck in mid-air, twirling about as Crowell enters, shocked to see her place turned into amusement center, where children are hooting and hollering. Rebuking her for her outlandish behavior, Crowell confines Pickford to her room, but she decides to run away. Pickford crawls from her second-story bedroom window and onto a trellis at the height of a fierce thunderstorm. She flees into the storm only to be knocked unconscious by a piece of flying timber shattered from a nearby church tower that is struck by lightning. She is rescued and returned home by O'Brien, the town's most eligible bachelor and Pickford's youthful heartthrob. This final exploit enrages the dowdy Crowell to the point where she decides to get rid of the little "troublemaker" by sending the lonely girl to a boarding school (and in these scenes Pickford wrenches the heart, mixing pathos with mirth). Pickford goes off to that school, but returns to the town as an adult, lovely woman, having successfully graduated with top grades. She is saddened to find Crowell dying and, before the old lady passes on, Pickford tells Crowell that, no matter their differences, she still loves her, the old lady then dying peacefully. Pickford is not alone in the world, however. O'Brien, who she has always loved, is smitten with her and they soon make plans to go to the altar. Nielan, who became one of Pickford's favorite directors, helms this film with great care, inserting many distinctive touches, from facial expressions to physical mannerisms by Pickford and other children, to create a superlatively lively and endearing film, one of Pickford's best. Her scenes where she attempts to sell soap door to door and where she recites her own poetry on Visitor's Day at school are priceless. The 1903 novel by Wiggin was first adapted for the stage by the author and Charlotte Thompson, the play opening on Broadway at the Theater Republic on October 3, 1910, running for 216 performances. ***Author's Note***: Although this film proved to be a great box office success, Wiggin did not like this first film adaptation of her classic story, believing that too much comedy and clowning antics had been inserted into the film script. Pickford's career had slumped until she made this film, along with **The Poor Little Rich Girl**, 1917, also with Neilan, and with Frances Marion working on the script. Both films reaffirmed her status as "America's Sweetheart" with the public. Some of the stunts Pickford herself performed were not only demanding, but were also hazardous. The scene where she is held aloft in a harness caused her considerable discomfort. According to her statements later: "The harness made me so sore on the first night that I couldn't move, sleep or breathe." **d**, Marshall Neilan; **cast**: Mary Pickford, Eugene O'Brien, Helen Jerome Eddy, Josephine Crowell, Mayme Kelso, Charles Ogle, Marjorie Daw, Violet Wilkey, Jane Wolff, Jack McDonald, Frank Turner, Zau Pitts; **w**, Frances Marion (based on the novel by Kate Douglas Wiggin and the play by Wiggin and Charlotte Thompson); **c**, Walter Stradling.

Rebecca of Sunnybrook Farm ★★★ 1938; U.S.; FOX; 80m; B/W; Musical; Children: Recommended; **DVD**; **VHS**. In this delightful version of the Wiggin tale, lovable Temple plays Rebecca, who is a ten-year-old orphan living on a farm with her aunt, Westley, after an uncle, Demarest, fails to get the child a job singing on a radio show, although she has an excellent singing voice. Westley disapproves of show business for Rebecca, but a next-door neighbor, Scott, is a talent scout who discovers her and she becomes a great success on the radio. Temple's movies like this one cheered up audiences during the Great Depression (1929-1939), and two of her signature songs in the film are "On the Good Ship Lollipop" and "Animal Crackers in My Soup," and her tap dancing with Bill "Bojangles" Robinson in "Parade of the Wooden Soldiers" is a memorable highlight. Songs: "Happy Endings" (1938; music: Lew Pollack; lyrics: Sidney D. Mitchell), "You've Gotta Eat Your Spinach, Baby" (1936; music: Harry Revel; lyrics: Mack Gordon), "An Old Straw Hat" (1938; Revel, Gordon), "Crakly Grain Flakes" (1938; music: Lew Pollack; lyrics: Sidney D. Mitchell), "Alone with You" (1938; Pollack, Mitchell), "Come and Get Your Happiness" (1938; music: Samuel Pokrass; lyrics: Jack Yellen), "On the Good Ship Lollipop" (1934; music: Richard A. Whiting; lyrics: Sidney Clare), "Animal Crackers in My Soup" (1935; music: Ray Henderson; lyrics: Ted Koehler, Irving Caesar), "When I'm with You" (1936; music: Harry Revel; lyrics: Mack Gordon); "Oh My Goodness" (1936; Revel, Gordon), "Goodnight, My Love" (1936; Revel, Gordon), "Parade of the Wooden Soldiers" (1897; music: Leon Jessel; lyrics: Ballard MacDonald), "The Toy Trumpet" (1938: music: Raymond Scott; lyrics: Sydney D. Mitchell, Lew Pollack). **p**, Raymond Griffith, (not credited) Darryl F. Zanuck; **d**, Allan Dwan; **cast**, Shirley Temple, Randolph Scott, Jack Haley, Gloria Stuart, Phyllis Brooks, Helen Westley, William Demarest, Slim Summerville, Bill Robinson, Raymond Scott, Lynn Bari, Dixie Dunbar; **w**, Karl Tunberg, Don Ettlinger (based on the novel by Kate Douglas Wiggin and the play by Wiggin and Charlotte Thompson); **c**, Arthur C. Miller; **ed**, Allen McNeil; **art d**, Bernard Herzbrun, Hans Peters; **set d**, Thomas Little.

Rebel in Town ★★★ 1956; U.S.; 78m; Schenck-Koch/Bel-Air/UA; B/W; Western; Children: Unacceptable; **VHS**. Exciting oater sees Naish and his four sons (Cooper, Smith, Mason (Franck), Johnson) taking to a life of crime. Former Confederate soldiers shortly after the American Civil War (1861-1865), they ride toward a small Western town, intending to rob the bank. While they are drinking from a well outside of town, a boy aims a toy gun at them, and, mistaking it for a real one, Cooper shoots the boy dead. The clan flees the area, but Cooper goes into the town and winds up at the home of Payne and Roman, not knowing they are the parents of the boy he has killed. When Payne learns of Cooper's identity as his son's killer, he seeks revenge for his son's death. He enlists the aid of townspeople to help him attack the former Rebels until peace is finally restored. An offbeat and well-crafted western, this film is nevertheless too violent for children. **p**, Howard W. Koch; **d**, Alfred L. Werker; **cast**, John Payne, Ruth Roman, J. Carrol Naish, Ben Cooper, John Smith, James Griffith, Mary Adams, Bobby Clark, Ben Johnson, Cain Mason (Sterling Franck), Kermit Maynard; **w**, Danny Arnold; **c**, Gordon Avil; **m**, Les Baxter; **ed**, John F. Schreyer.

Rebel Without a Cause ★★★★ 1955; U.S.; 111m; WB; Color; Children: Unacceptable; **DVD**; **VHS**. Dean gives a bravura performance as a 1950s teenager struggling for love from parents and recognition from peers in this taut and sometimes traumatic drama. Dean is a malcontent youth who has caused his parents, Backus and Doran, endless frustration and dilemmas, so much so that they have repeatedly relocated from one town after another to escape his notorious troublemaking, finally settling in Los Angeles. He is shown being arrested for being drunk and disorderly, but the booking detective, Platt, is an understanding type, who learns from Dean how he hates Doran for smothering him with superficial motherly affection while dominating his good-natured father,

James Dean in *Rebel Without a Cause*, 1955.

Backus, whom he thinks has no backbone. While being examined by Platt, Dean sees two other teenagers brought into the precinct headquarters, Wood, a girl picked up for wandering the streets, and Mineo, who has been arrested for killing a litter of puppies and who is the unsupervised son of wealthy parents never at home. Doran and Backus then arrive to bail out Dean, both upset by the fact that they have been called away from a posh dinner party at an upscale club to retrieve their unruly son. When Dean sees Wood the next day at the high school they attend and where he is a new boy at that school, he asks her for a date, but she ignores him, going with Allen, who always wears a cool leather jacket and drives a fast car. Allen is the leader of a clan who all ape his mannerisms and dress, all wearing the popular zippered leather jackets of the day. After their class attends the Griffith Observatory, Allen confronts Dean outside the planetarium, picking a fight with him, ostensibly over Wood's attentions and where she perversely enjoys both fighting over her. After Dean and Allen draw switchblades, the only person supporting Dean is the troubled Mineo, who is quickly silenced by Allen's slavish and goon-like followers. Dean defeats Allen, but their dislike for each other accelerates to another disastrous confrontation where both Dean and Allen, to prove their mettle, risk their lives in what is described as a "chickie run." Allen challenges Dean to perform in this near suicidal match where each boy will drive a beat-up car to the edge of a cliff and jump from that speeding car at the last moment before each car goes over the cliff. The one who jumps last wins the match and will prove himself the most daring and courageous. That night, the teenagers collect at near a remote cliff and Dean and Allen get into their heaps and roar toward the edge of the cliff. Dean jumps safely before his car goes over the cliff, but a strap on Allen's leather jacket gets tangled in the door handle of the car and he is taken to his death with that plunging auto. Now the fetching Wood is Dean's girl. He takes her home to discover that she has the same difficulties with her parents as he endures. When Dean tell his parents about Allen's death, Doran becomes hysterical, insisting that they again move, her invariable answer to any crisis her son creates, and when Backus refuses to defy her orders, Dean, so disgusted with his lack of will, attacks and knocks his father down. He then runs from the house and collects Mineo and Wood. The trio goes to a deserted mansion to take refuge from Allen's goons, who are now seeking revenge for their leader's demise. Mazzola, Hopper and others search the mansion and they find Mineo, who shoots Mazzola, one of the gang members who has long been persecuting him. When an officer investigates the break-in at the mansion, Mineo shoots him, too. He goes to the planetarium to hide out, and Dean, Wood, their parents and a small army of cops flock to the area; Dean enters the planetarium to talk Mineo into surrendering, promising him that everything will be settled and that he has nothing to fear. He removes the remaining

Sal Mineo, James Dean and Corey Allen in *Rebel without a Cause*, 1955.

bullets from Mineo's gun, and they step outside. When Mineo sees an officer approaching, however, he panics and begins to run. The officer, thinking Mineo means to shoot him, fires and kills Mineo. Dean weeps as he holds the dead Mineo in his arms. Backus then finds enough courage to overrule Doran's dictates, telling his son that no matter what comes, they will stay where they are and work for a better life. At the end, Dean and Wood embrace, having learned some hard but significant meanings about growing up. Ray directs this supercharged film with great intensity like a whirring dynamo that eventually goes out of control, scattering its characters into chaos and tragedy. The director portrays adults as a separate species from the teenage principals of the story as shown from the hostile and contemptuous perspective of those teenagers, as if the adults have no more relationships with their offspring than that of keeping them as untrained and bothersome pets. Ray's teenagers and adults live in two alien worlds, one challenging with defiance, the other dominating with crushing and compassionless authority. The acting from all is superb, and Haller's sharp lensing is outstanding. This film inspired a spate of other similar films, as did **Black Board Jungle**, 1955, but few of them have the impact and significance of these films. Songs: "Ride of the Valkyries" (1856; Richard Wagner), "I'll String Along with You" (1934; Harry Warren), "Five O'-Clock Whistle" (1936; Gene Irwin, Josef Myrow), "Wiegenlied, Op. 49, No. 4 (Lullaby)" (Johannes Brahms). *Author's Note*: Ray told this author that he shot this film in black-and-white with the CinemaScope process for "a few weeks to get a feel for the dark mood that invades every scene of the picture. When we went to color, I made sure that all the scenes had muted color to keep that mood. The kids in the picture are really walking volcanoes, ready to explode at any moment." There is no doubt that Dean, who dominates the film and became the idol of teenagers in the 1950s because of his electrifying performance in this film, modeled his character after Marlon Brando's rebel in **The Wild One**, 1953, emulating Brando's hesitant delivery and blurting monologues. "Yeah, man," Dennis Hopper told this author, "Jimmy [Dean] was doing Brando all through that picture, and we were doing him. I had a bit part as a thug in that picture and had only a few lines to deliver, and I could not find a better model than Jimmy to use. We all aped the guy because he was so terrific in that part. He was terrific in all the parts he played in all the movies he was in, but the sad thing was that there were so few of them, man." Where teenagers embraced this film and perpetuated it through the decades as a cult movie, adults of its day universally condemned it, stating that it showed only the violent and virulent side of youth, emphasizing a morose and fatalistic fixation on death, those adult critics pointing out that youth invariably embodies vitality and hope. The idea for this offbeat film was pitched to executives at Warner Brothers by Ray, who told this author that "they went for it right

away, but, can you believe it, they wanted me to put Tab Hunter in the lead role and Jayne Mansfield as his teenage girlfriend! I wanted Dean and Wood right from the start and I had to battle to get them." Years later when Ray was making a film in Chicago I went to a restaurant in Chinatown to have dinner with him and film reviewer Roger Ebert, and Ebert said to Ray: "You lucked out when Warner Brothers told you that you had to use James Dean and Natalie Wood in **Rebel without a Cause**." Ray, who was then wearing an eye patch after having lost the use of an eye, stared at Roger with his one good eye for some time and then said: "You don't know what you're talking about. I had to fight like hell to get them into that picture. Where do you get your information—from press agents?" In this Ray's assumption was right since Roger was a press agent's dream, a welcoming depository into which they dumped their most outlandish claims and assertions, and Roger happily recycled those tales into his own brand of hearsay. Ironically, the three principals of this film met the kind of tragedy exhibited in the somewhat grim plot. Wood (1938-1981), who had been a precocious child star with such films as **Miracle on 34th Street**, 1947, went on to become an adult star, but mysteriously drowned after falling from a boat off Catalina Island. Mineo (1939-1976) was so convinced that he would win the Oscar as Supporting Actor in **Rebel without a Cause** that he gave a huge party at his West Hollywood apartment with a sign saying: "Congratulations, Sal!" He did not win and he burned the banner. Mineo spent lavishly on clothes and cars after making that film and was the star of the homosexual community in West Hollywood, appearing in many more films, but was stabbed to death in West Hollywood on the night of February 12, 1976, by black drifter and mugger Lionel Ray Williams, who was sent to prison for life. (For more details on the Mineo slaying, see my two-volume work, *The Great Pictorial History of World Crime*, Volume II (History, Inc., 2004; pages: 894-896.) Dean (1931-1955), like his adversary in **Rebel without a Cause**, met the same kind of violent end. Dean was driving a Porsche sports car at high speeds on September 30, 1955, and was stopped by a cop and given a ticket for driving 75mph in a 45mph speed zone. He said to the cop "so what?" before he drove off. A short time later, driving near Cholame, California, at more than 100 mph, he struck another car, killing himself (a broken neck) and seriously injuring two others. He was twenty-four years old. **p**, David Weisbart; **d**, Nicholas Ray; **cast**, James Dean, Natalie Wood, Sal Mineo, Jim Backus, Ann Doran, Corey Allen, William Hopper, Rochelle Hudson, Dennis Hopper, Edward Platt, Virginia Brissac, Nick Adams; **w**, Stewart Stern (based on an adaptation by Irving Shulman of a story line by Ray inspired from the story "The Blind Run" by Robert M. Lindner); **c**, Ernest Haller (CinemaScope; Warner Color); **m**, Leonard Rosenman; **ed**, William H. Ziegler; **prod d** & **art d**, Malcolm C. Bert; **set d**, William Wallace.

Reckless ★★★ 1935; U.S.; 97m; MGM; B/W; Drama/Musical; Children: Unacceptable; **VHS**. An excellent cast and Fleming's lively and inventive direction makes this tale a standout. Harlow is a Broadway singing and dancing star who meets Tone, a wealthy industrialist. He buys out every ticket for one performance so he can have Harlow to himself as the only spectator (a ploy also used by director William Wyler when making **The Westerner**, 1940, where renegade Walter Brennan buys all the tickets for a performance by his idol, Lily Langtry to become the only spectator). Tone throws over his girlfriend Russell and concentrates on Harlow, much to the dismay of Powell, her agent, who has always loved Harlow, but has not had the nerve to tell her so. Tone sweeps Harlow off her feet with his aggressive passion and incredible wealth and they soon marry. Not all is well between them, however. After Russell marries, Tone attends the reception, getting drunk and telling Russell that Harlow forced him to marry her, which has created great friction with his father, Stephenson. Moreover, Tone states, his marriage is hollow and without love. After Harlow learns of Tone's feelings, she seeks solace from Powell. Tone thinks this is a rejection of him and takes his life. Hearsay and gossip mount to the point where many believe that Harlow murdered Tone so that she could be with Powell. Harlow, who is pregnant with Tone's baby, is then forced to give up her inheritance by Stephenson under the threat of taking custody of the child when born. Powell stands by Harlow, putting together a new musical for her, but the public has turned against the showgirl due to the rumors involving Tone's death. When Harlow appears on stage she is met with hooting and jeering. She stops to confront her accusers, sincerely stating to the audience her side of the story with Tone and is so convincing that she turns the attitude of the crowd around to the point where they begin cheering her and her star is now again in the ascendancy. Somewhat trite and where Harlow is lacking in singing and dancing skills (her singing voice was dubbed by Virginia Verrill and a double did most of her more difficult dancing), the production values are high as well as the acting from the cast. Songs: "Reckless" (1935; music: Jerome Kern; lyrics: Oscar Hammerstein II), "Trocadero" (1934; music: Burton Lane; lyrics: Harold Adamson), "Everything's Been Done Before" (1935; music: Jack King; lyrics: Edwin Knopf, Harold Adamson), "Bridal Chorus (Here Comes the Bride)" (from "Lohengrin" by Richard Wagner), "Hear What My Heart Is Saying" (1935; music: Burton Lane; lyrics: Harold Adamson), "I'm Going Down to Dance at Clancy's," "Hi-Deedle-De-Dum" (1935; Con Conrad and Herb Magidson). *Author's Note*: Powell admitted to this author that "**Reckless** was popular with the public because the story was similar to the death of tobacco tycoon Zachary Smith Reynolds, who was married to torch singer Libby Holman. He was mysteriously shot to death a few years [on July 5-6, 1932] before we made **Reckless**, and Libby—I knew her well—was brought to trial, but the death was never solved and she was not charged. David O. Selznick wrote the story upon which **Reckless** is based, and he wrote that story under a pen name [Oliver Jeffries]. I asked him if he had used the Holman-Reynolds case for the story and he said: 'Of course, but don't ever tell anyone I said so.' I am telling you that now since Selznick is long gone and most people don't remember that case." For more details about the unsolved killing of Reynolds, see my two-volume work, *The Great Pictorial History of World Crime*, Volume II (History, Inc., 2004; pages: 1238-1246). Ironically, Harlow's own life mirrors elements of this film. Her second husband, MGM producer Paul Bern, committed suicide much the same way Tone takes his life in **Reckless** (Bern allegedly shot himself over his impotence in 1932). She was then briefly married to cinematographer Harold Rosson, and was romantically involved with Powell right up to the time of her premature death on June 7, 1937, from cerebral edema (dropsy), at the age of twenty-six, a death that devastated Powell. **p**, David O. Selznick; **d**, Victor Fleming; **cast**, Jean Harlow, William Powell, Franchot Tone, May Robson, Ted Healy, Nat Pendleton, Rosalind Russell, Mickey Rooney, Henry Stephenson, Man Mountain Dean, Farina (Allen Hoskins), Allan Jones, James Ellison, Margaret Dumont, Paul Fix, Harold Huber, Charles Middleton, Akim Tamiroff, Virginia Verrill (dubbing singing voice for Harlow); **w**, P.J. Wolfson (based on the story "A Woman Called Cheap" by Oliver Jeffries (Selznick); **c**, George Folsey; **m**, Jack Virgil; **d**, Margaret Booth; **art d**, Cedric Gibbons.

The Reckless Moment ★★★★ 1949; U.S.; 82m; COL; B/W; Crime Drama; Children: Unacceptable; **VHS**. This tension-filled film noir tale from the gifted Opuls, one of the few films he made in the U.S., sees stellar performances from Mason and Bennett. The film opens on a peaceful setting in Balboa Island in southern California, where Bennett lives in a luxurious home with her husband; her teenage children, son Bair, daughter Brooks; her father-in-law, O'Neill; and a devoted maid, Williams. While her husband is away on business (he is never seen), Bennett discovers that Brooks is carrying on an affair with a much older man, Strudwick. Brooks tearfully explains to Bennett that she has written a number of torrid love letters to Strudwick and he is now demanding a lot of money or will expose those letters and ruin the family name. Bennett tells Brooks to put a stop to all that, and Brooks meets with Strudwick at the family boathouse. When Strudwick refuses to return

William Powell and Jean Harlow in *Reckless*, 1935.

the letters, Brooks angrily and impulsively strikes him with a flashlight and leaves. Strudwick, dazed, attempts to follow Brooks, but slips over a railing and falls to his death. The next morning, Bennett finds the body, and, now terrified, thinks that Brooks has murdered Strudwick. She hides the body in a boat, worrying how she might dispose of it. At the same time, Strudwick's shady past is revealed in that he has given Brooks' incriminating letters to a loan shark, Roberts, to whom he owes money. When Roberts learns of Strudwick's death, he intends to collect the blackmail money that Strudwick failed to secure in his attempt to pay him his juice money. He sends Mason to collect the money. Mason is an odd sort of an underworld character, intelligent and compassionate. He patiently explains to Bennett the fix she is in and demands a $5,000 payoff in return for her daughter's letters, which would implicate Brooks in the death of Strudwick. Bennett agrees to raise the money and begins pawning her most expensive jewels. She tries to get a loan and to raise more money, but is unable to do so, collecting only a small amount of money to give to Mason. He, on the other hand, becomes deeply sympathetic to Bennett's plight, commiserating over her frantic efforts to save her daughter and realizing the sacrifices a mother will make to protect her child while having second thoughts about his own sleazy way of life, which he would like to abandon. (Mason's attitude is reflected in many other films that show strong-armed collectors reluctant to hurt a debtor, most notably as seen in Sylvester Stallone's portrayal of a juice collector in **Rocky**, 1976.) Bennett becomes desperate and frantic after she realizes that she cannot meet the blackmail demands, but Mason then tells her that another person has been arrested for Strudwick's murder and that her daughter will not be charged. Bennett, however, is now haunted by the nagging guilt that an innocent man might be executed for a crime he did not commit. Angry at Mason over his inability or unwillingness to collect the blackmail money from Bennett, the oily Roberts travels to Balboa Island to confront Bennett. Instead, he meets Mason and the two men battle. Though severely wounded in the fight, Mason manages to kill Roberts. When Bennett arrives, Mason tells her to help him get Roberts' body into his car and he then drives away, intending to dispose of the body elsewhere. Bennett and Williams follow in Bennett's car, where Bennett tells the surprised Williams the whole sordid story. Mason grows weak from his wound and crashes his car. When police arrive, Mason, who is dying and seeing Bennett at a distance, tells the police that he killed Strudwick and Roberts. Mason dies, retrieving his honor in his final, noble act, and Bennett returns home with Williams, never to say a word about what has transpired; Williams promises never to reveal her secret, admiring Bennett for having saved her daughter and family from ruination. Opuls does a masterful job with this complex but intriguing story, using his many European techniques to heighten suspense, including distorted angle shots, fluid tracking

Rachel Roberts and Nicol Williamson in *The Reckoning*, 1971.

shots and crane shots, all amazingly effective through cinematographer Guffey's innovative lensing. *Author's Note*: Bennett told this author that "poor Max [Opuls] had one bad break after another with **The Reckless Moment**. Equipment was always failing and when it came time to preview the film, he took it to small theater where the film broke. It took minutes to splice it together and then the soundtrack went out of sync. By the time they fixed that, most of the audience had walked out." Mason had a high regard for the director, having appeared in another top-flight film noir production helmed by Opuls, **Caught**, 1949, telling this author that "he was not treated well by Hollywood producers, who stinted on his budgets and even prevented him from using elaborate lighting that would make his sets more expensive, as they did in **The Reckless Moment**. He was as much a master filmmaker as was Alfred Hitchcock and I worked for both of those directors, but Max [Opuls] never got the credit he was due." Wanger, the producer of this film, was then married to Bennett, their union lasting from 1940 until 1965. The producer, always possessive and deeply jealous of his wife, created a scandal similar to this tale when, in 1951, he shot Jennings Lang, who was Bennett's agent, believing that Lang was attempting to steal his wife from him, a scandal that lingered long in Hollywood. **p**, Walter Wanger; **d**, Max Ophuls; **cast**, James Mason, Joan Bennett, Geraldine Brooks, Henry O'Neill, Shepperd Strudwick, David Bair, Roy Roberts, Jessie Arnold, Pat Barton, Ann Shoemaker; **w**, Henry Garson, Robert W. Soderberg (based on an adaptation by Mel Dinelli, Robert E. Kent of the story "The Blank Wall" by Elisabeth Sanxay Holding); **c**, Burnett Guffey; **m**, Hans Salter; **ed**, Gene Havlick; **art d**, Cary Odell; **set d**, Frank Tuttle.

The Reckoning ★★★ 1971; U.K.; 111m; COL; Color; Drama; Children: Unacceptable; **VHS**. Williamson gives a superb performance as a lower-class Irishman from Liverpool who claws his way to the top as a successful London businessman. He's unhappily married to Bell, who is wealthy, but they have little in common beyond their accumulating wealth. The death of his father takes Williamson back to Liverpool after an absence of thirty-seven, years and he finds himself confronted by his lost Irish roots. He learns that his father died because of a fight with some vicious Anglo-Saxon youths. It becomes a matter of honor for him to take his revenge without involving the British police. He returns to London and has a torrid affair with Roberts, a medical receptionist. He gets drunk and disorderly at a company party and his boss, Rogers, considers firing him, then Bell walks out on him. He returns to Liverpool for the revenge he wants and finds the boy who killed his father, beating him with an iron pipe. It's not known if the boy lives, but Williamson is satisfied that he has meted out "Irish justice." He returns to London and has an affair with Rogers' secretary, getting information from her about

Roberts that causes his boss' downfall. Williamson is on track again to the top and he and Bell reconcile. Williamson gives a riveting performance as a ruthless man intending to succeed at any cost in this fine drama. Violence and mature scenes prohibit viewing by children. **p**, Ronald Shedlo; **d**, Jack Gold; **cast**, Nicol Williamson, Ann Bell, Lilita De Barros, Tom Kempinski, Kenneth Hendel, Douglas Wilmer, Barbara Ewing, Zena Walker, Paul Rogers, Rachel Roberts; **w**, John McGrath (based on the novel *The Harp That Once* by Patrick Hall); **c**, Geoffrey Unsworth (Technicolor); **m**, Malcolm Arnold; **ed**, Peter Weatherley; **art d**, Ray Simm; **set d**, Peter James.

Red ★★★ 1994; France/Switzerland/Poland; 94m; Zespol Filmowy Tor/Miramax; Color; Drama; Children: Unacceptable (MPAA: R); **DVD**; **VHS**. This intriguing drama is the final installment of a three-film series, **Blue**, 1993, and **White**, 1994, and with red representing the three colors of the flag of France. The story begins when Jacob accidentally injures a dog while driving and takes it to its owner, Trintignant, a retired judge, who is obsessed with spying on the phone calls of a law student and neighbor, Lorit, and who is having an affair with Feder. Trintignant does this not to bribe anyone, but to feed his cynicism. The four people become impacted in this tale of compassion, redemption, and forgiveness. At the end of this film, the major characters from all three films meet through a coincidence. Sexual scenes prohibit viewing by children. (In French; English subtitles.) **p**, Marin Karmitz; **d**, Krzysztof Kieslowski; **cast**, Juliette Binoche, Jean-Louis Trintignant, Julie Delpy, Irene Jacob, Benoit Regent, Frederique Feder, Jean-Pierre Lorit, Samuel Lebihan, Marion Stalens, Teco Celio, Bernard Escalon; **w**, Kieslowski, Krzysztof Piesiewicz; **c**, Piotr Sobocinski; **m**, Zbigniew Preisner; **ed**, Jacques Witta; **prod d**, Claude Lenoir; **set d**, Pierre Agoston, Paola Andreani, Marc Babel, Jean-Pierre Balsiger, Jean-François Despres, Patrick Flumet, Patrick Lehmann, Daniel Mercier, David Stadelmann, Patrick Stoll.

The Red Badge of Courage ★★★★★ 1951; U.S.; 69m; MGM; B/W; War Drama; Children: Unacceptable; **DVD**; **VHS**. Pantheon director John Huston always thought that this stirring film he so faithfully adapted from Stephen Crane's masterpiece novella was one of his greatest works and could have been his greatest if MGM had not tampered with it. Meddling from the front office or not, this superlative production, indeed, remains a classic film that acutely examines the harrowingly thin differences between cowardice and courage while depicting the soldiers on both sides fighting that terrible American Civil War (1861-1865). The film opens in the spring of 1862, where Murphy plays a youth named Henry Fleming, who has, like many others, joined a Union regiment that is untested in battle. (It is not ironic that Murphy was selected to play the lead role in this war film as he had been the most decorated American soldier during WWII for his incredible feats of bravery on the battlefields of North Africa, Italy and France.) Murphy is a withdrawn and apprehensive youth who recently joined the Union army and is shown training with other raw recruits who constantly speculate about the battles to come in which they may be involved, listening to endless gossip and brags about their heroic deeds to come. He asks Dierkes, an older soldier, if he thinks that any of the boys in his regiment will run at the first sound of battle, and Dierkes tells him that he thinks that "there's some that will" but that most will stay at their posts. Murphy's question is rooted to his own uneasy conduct, obsessed with his dread of battle and how he might cowardly shirk his duty. His closest friend, Mauldin (who later became a Pulitzer Prize-winning illustrator) boasts that he and the rest of "the boys" will give the Rebels "a good thumping" when they meet the Confederate enemy in battle. Mauldin's bragging so much irritates Murphy that he turns on Mauldin, chastising him for making such outlandish claim,s and Mauldin, his feelings hurt, tells Murphy that he only meant that he would do his part as a soldier. Anxious and nervous, Murphy and Mauldin, while filling canteens at a river, overhear officers talking about taking their troops into battle that day and they race back to their friends to impart this information, but where most accuse them of simply spreading more fanciful rumors. Then word comes that what Murphy and Mauldin have said is true. The regiment is going into battle. Murphy and his companions are marched toward the front and, at one point ordered to construct defensive positions behind which they can crouch and fire at an advancing enemy. Hunnicutt, an older, bewhiskered soldier, refuses to crouch down, saying that he intends to "do my fighting standing up." The troops are then ordered to abandon their position and march again, this time coming to an open valley where troops on both sides are in positions, the area cloudy with cannon smoke as barrages erupt and through which cavalry units ride madly about. As Murphy and others are put into the front line of the Union defenses by their company commander, Dick, one in the number gazes at the erupting battle, stating in naïve awe: "Humpy-dady! Everybody fighting! Blood and destruction!" Murphy and others take shelter inside a gulley, including Hunnicutt. Another soldier sees Hunnicutt in a crouching position and snorts: "I thought you were going to do your fighting standing up?" Hunnicutt snaps back: "Shut your dad-burned mouth!" Then Murphy sees what he has so long feared, Confederate troops advancing, a Rebel officer riding at the head of the infantry, waving a sabre and riding far in front to be shot from his horse. His troops, however, press forward and are greeted with a searing volley from the Union ranks. The Rebels, staggered, retreat; Murphy momentarily relaxes but is then gripped with terror when he sees the enemy lines rally and press forward again, coming closer and closer, firing as they come. Several men near Murphy fall dead or wounded from the enemy fire, and Murphy sees several men suddenly break ranks and race toward the rear, fleeing the battle. The Rebels doggedly come forward, sustaining the Union fire and returning their own blistering volleys, and, just as they appear to break through, panic seizes Murphy and he runs from the defense line, which is now enshrouded with billowing smoke, he races past Dick who tries to stop him and others with his waving sword. Murphy, feeling that he has utterly disgraced and dishonored himself through his cowardly actions, runs madly through the mists of battle until he gets into a clearing and sees Union troops coming from some woods. He stops one soldier and asks him where the troops are going, but the man refuses to answer and, when Murphy clings to him, demanding an answer, the soldier raises his rifle and slams its butt into Murphy's head, knocking him unconscious. After he regains consciousness, Murphy staggers to a road where long lines of wounded Union soldiers slowly move along, all bearing wounds with bandaged heads, arms and legs. Dano, a soldier with a bloody bandage wrapped around his head and his uniform shot to rags, approaches Murphy and asks him where he has been hit, but Murphy only holds his head as an explanation. Murphy then sees Dierkes staggering within the agonizing ranks; when he learns that Dierkes has been shot when Dierkes, hesitantly and while catching his breath, describes the battle he has endured. He then begs Murphy and Dano to keep him out of the road so that ordnance carrions rumbling along the road will not run him over. When some of these horse-drawn cannons approach, Dierkes bolts from the road, going up a hill with Murphy and Dano following him. Out of breath and weaving back and forth, Dierkes stands atop the hill, telling Murphy not to touch him. He then tilts crazily back and forth until toppling dead to the earth. Dano admires the stamina and strength displayed by Dierkes in managing to climb that hill while fatally shot, saying with praise: "He were a Jim-dandy, weren't he?" Murphy wanders away from the road and, by nightfall, finds jovial Devine, a roly-poly sergeant oozing with endless and hopeful optimism about life. Devine treats Murphy as a slightly wounded soldier, guiding him back to his regiment and telling him how countless soldiers like him have been accidentally separated from their units in the confusion of the day's battle. Before sending him into the campground where his fellow soldiers are camped around burning fires, Devine wishes Murphy good luck and saunters away singing "Oh happy am I…" When Mauldin sees Murphy he welcomes him with open arms, delighted to see him alive, and Murphy tells Mauldin that

Audie Murphy in *The Red Badge of Courage*, 1951.

he got separated from his regiment during the battle and struck on the head. Mauldin examines his wound and assumes that Murphy had been struck by a Minnie ball that has "raised a large lump on your head." Company commander Dick sees Murphy and routinely accepts him back into the fold without recognizing him as being one of the deserters that fled the battle that day. Murphy goes to sleep, thanking the confusion of battle for invisibly disguising his cowardice, that dark and haunting secret known only to him. The following day, Murphy and his regiment are once more marched to the front, and, again, the enemy attacks. The Union troops again fire a volley into the midst of the Confederates. This time, angered over the enemy's threat to compel his shirking behavior of the day earlier and that the persistent Rebel attacks again threaten to test his valor, Murphy creeps forward from the Union line, firing at the Rebels and shouting vengeance and retribution. Some Union soldiers join him, cautiously moving forward as Murphy slowly advances against the enemy. Loading and firing his rifle musket rapidly, Murphy advances and his unit follows him, Dick, the company commander, urging his men to follow Murphy's lead. The Rebels retreat from this unexpected counterattack, and Murphy, grabbing the U.S. banner, leads his fellows forward, first at a walk, then on the run, advancing toward the Rebel defense line in what becomes a wild charge that carries the Union soldiers over a low wall, where the Rebels surrender. Murphy follows a dying Confederate soldier, who is crawling away while holding the Confederate battle flag. When the man dies at his feet, Murphy clutches that Rebel banner, holding both flags symbolically in his hands as they flutter above him and that fallen foe. Those two flags represent the powerful symbols of a divided nation, both now held in the hands of an impetuous youth, who has regained his resolve and proven his bravery. Meanwhile, other Union soldiers talk with their Confederate prisoners to find that their captives are the same kind of men as themselves, plain-speaking soldiers fighting for a cause and far from home. Murphy and the men of his regiment are then ordered to march from the battlefield, feeling confident in their ability to survive battle and grateful for that survival, sensing the basic joys of life as they move from that battlefield. Director Huston closes this masterpiece with an overhead shot to show those soldiers marching away while the narrator (Whitmore) quotes the final immortal lines of Stephen Crane's great work that summarize Murphy's character and his baptism of fire: "So it came to pass as he trudged from the place of blood and wrath his soul changed. He had been to touch the Great Death and found that, after all, it was but the Great Death. Scars faded as flowers and the youth saw that the world was a world for him. He had rid himself of the red sickness of battle and the sultry nightmare was in the past. He turned now with a lover's thirst to images of tranquil skies, fresh meadows, cool brooks, an existence of soft and eternal peace." Director Huston masterfully helms this film with infinite care,

Audie Murphy in *The Red Badge of Courage*, 1951.

his powerful and telling scenes all fluid as he employs crane, dolly, tracking and panning shots to capture the breathtaking, well-choreographed action while seamlessly unfolding its prosaic tale. Murphy and Mauldin are astoundingly effective in that they were both newcomers to film, and veteran actors Dierkes, Devine, Hunnicutt, Dano and others are outstanding in their roles. They all present themselves as simple men turned soldiers caught up in the maelstrom of battle. They are all members of clashing ignorant armies, who know nothing about the grandiose schemes and machinations of those directing their fates. There are countless memorable scenes in this riveting film. At one point, Durant, the general commanding the Union troops, just before the battle, rides along the lines of his men, telling each unit that he will have dinner with them that night after the battle is over, a promise he knows he cannot keep as do his troops, but they all take that promise as an endearing gesture of his fondness for them. Durant then rides to the crest of a hill to hear in the distance the defiant martial music of "Dixie" coming from the Confederate lines, and he smiles and says to an aide: "Hark to the gamecock!" He then removes his hat and bows his white-haired head and prays before sending his men into battle. There is poignancy and passion and no little humor throughout this wonderful film, all convincingly expressed through the down-home dialog of uneducated but well-intentioned men, that brilliant script also provided by the gifted Huston. Typical of the raw humor Huston faithfully infuses into Crane's characters are lines delivered by Hunnicutt, who, after surviving the battle, expresses his gratitude thusly: "I got holes in my pants, holes in my shoes, but there ain't no holes in me other than the ones God intended." Rosson's lensing is superb and the costuming exceptionally accurate to the period. The film was expensively produced at a budget of more than $1.6 million, and it did not initially recoup its investment. Songs: "Taps" (Daniel Butterfield), "The Battle Hymn of the Republic" (music, 1856: William Steffe; lyrics, 1862: Julia Ward Howe), "Yankee Doodle" (traditional), "Dixie" (Daniel Decatur Emmett), "Camptown Races" (Stephen Foster). *Author's Note*: This outstanding film did not do well at the box office at its initial release only because of the way in which it was mishandled by the MGM front office where a battle was ongoing for control of the studio by old chief Louis B. Mayer and his production chief, Dore Schary. "Mayer initially rejected the idea of making **The Red Badge of Courage**," Huston told this author, "insisting that no one would want to see a picture with a bunch of boys wearing funny caps and shooting pop-guns at each other. Of course, Mr. Mayer knew nothing about the American Civil War or anything else about the real world. He lived in Hollywood's fantasyland where the problems of families consisted of having to decide what to eat for dinner each night. He had successfully been making tidy romance films that always ended in a happy embrace. But the public wanted to see the real world on the screen

after the end of the war [WWII] because that war compelled Americans to touch the grim realities of life. Mayer was as old-fashioned as high-button shoes and winged collars. Schary, on the other hand, was in touch with public tastes and he went to war with Mayer over **The Red Badge of Courage** and that war was not settled until Nick Schenck, who really held the purse strings at MGM, backed Schary. When Schary was out of town for some time, I went to Mayer and he tried to persuade me to forget about doing the picture. He was so upset about it that he stormed around his office, reenacting what he thought the battles would look like on the screen. I told him: 'If you feel that strongly about it, L.B., I won't do the picture.' His face went red and he shouted: 'What's the matter with you, John? Don't you have the guts to back up your own faith in a picture you want to make? I don't like the idea for the picture. I don't think it will make any money and I will continue to fight against doing it, but you should fight to make that picture if you believe in it!' I was amazed. Mayer had always been the most decisive man in Hollywood, but here he was contradicting and subverting his own efforts to quash the production. I think he was becoming paranoid and felt that he was on his way out, and he was, because Schary took over the studio a short time after we did that picture. But Mayer got his licks in, meddling and tampering with that picture, which I thought could have been my greatest picture. I broke my back on that picture. You know, the author, Crane, never fought in that war. He wrote that book thirty years after that war started and was inspired to write that book by going to the New York Public Library where he studied the amazing Civil War photographs of Mathew Brady and others, and I studied those photos, too, before I did the first scene in **The Red Badge of Courage**. I left the production to make **The African Queen**, [1951] and a pack of editors went to work on it, following Mayer's instructions to clip out some of the death scenes. They chopped it up considerably so that it was as wounded as some of the men I showed in that picture." One of the scenes deleted was that of Dano, who is last seen when Murphy leaves the road trodden by wounded men, but Dano is originally seen, like Diekes, realizing that he himself has a mortal wound and falls down dead in the road. The film was originally completed at 78 minutes, but its truncated version (the only edition available) presents only 69 minutes. Huston also told this author that "in many respects, the three pictures I made around that time, **The Red Badge of Courage**, **The African Queen** [1951] and **The Asphalt Jungle** [1950] all dealt with courage, but shown by much different characters. In **The African Queen**, that courage is shown by an alcoholic river rat and a barren spinster when they take on the might of the German navy and, in **The Asphalt Jungle**—another picture Mayer hated—an unsophisticated strong-arm man shows courage after he is betrayed by a powerful attorney. There are all kinds of courage from all kinds of people in this world—just getting up in the morning shows a lot of courage, young man." Huston also told this author that character actor James Whitmore was selected to narrate this film after he had left the production, but that he was impressed with Whitmore's narration "because he had the kind of voice that held authority, the kind of voice you would hear from an uncle who had been to battle and back." Whitmore told this author that "I was flabbergasted when they asked me to narrate that great picture. I was nervous about that because what Stephen Crane wrote was Holy Scripture in the world of literature, a soldier's poetry, plain and simple and with greatness in every line. I felt when I spoke Crane's chilling words that I was walking on hallowed ground." Mauldin, who only appeared in two films, this one and **Teresa**, 1951, had been an illustrator for *Stars and Stripes* during WWII, where he became famous for drawing the inimitable, dog-weary GI characters, Willie and Joe. He went on to become a Pulitzer Prize-winning newspaper cartoonist. This author befriended him when Mauldin was working as an illustrator for the Chicago *Sun-Times* and who told this author that "appearing in **The Red Badge of Courage** was one of my most enjoyable experiences. The director [Huston] knew I was not a professional actor, but he assured me that I would be fine in my role as Audie's [Murphy's] best friend in that picture and that I should not try to act, just be myself, and that is what I did. He did that with all the actors, including Audie, and that is why that picture looks natural and is believable. I thought it was ironic that Audie, of all people, was playing a young soldier who has to deal with a streak of cowardice in him because Audie, as you know, was one of the bravest soldiers we had in World War II. He killed more than two dozen enemy soldiers in that war, wiped out machine-gun nests, turned back an armored column—he was a one-man army. I asked him when we were doing that picture if he had any remorse about what he did and he said: 'Are you kidding, Bill? Those bastards were shooting at us and killing my friends. Regrets? Hell, no! They had it coming. Those Germans were trying to push the world around and they murdered millions. They had it coming and I give them what they had been giving to everybody else.' Audie was still angry at the Germans, even then, about five years after the war, and he told me that he was recalling his experiences in battle when he did the battle scenes in **The Red Badge of Courage** and he said, 'This war is just as bad as the one we were in, Bill, but maybe our food and medicine was a little bit better.'" At one point in my relationship with Mauldin, this author asked him to draw a color illustration for the cover of *ChicagoLand Magazine*, for which I was then editor-in-chief. I was running a story about the crime syndicate's operations in Chicago and in bordering northern Indiana. Mauldin, within twenty-four hours of my assignment to him, gave me an astounding cover. He had drawn a squatting, wide-hatted, cigar-chomping gangster in a loud suit and with many arms outreaching toward the viewer as a grotesque Buddha, with the caption "How does this grab you?" It was the perfect image I wanted to convey for the lead story. The day that issue of *ChicagoLand* was published and distributed, I got a call from someone with a gravelly voice that snarled: "You publish another article like the one you just did and you will be floating face down in the Little Calumet River where we dumped the copies of your magazine!" I then learned that all the copies of *ChicagoLand* that had been scheduled for distribution in northern Indiana had somehow been mysteriously seized and had been thrown into that river. I called Mauldin and told him about that and he laughed and said: "Yeah, I got the same call. It looks like we won't die alone, pal. We will both be floating down that river together!" **p**, Gottfried Reinhardt; **d&w**, John Huston (based on an adaptation by Albert Band of the novel by Stephen Crane); **cast**, Audie Murphy, Bill Mauldin, Douglas Dick, Royal Dano, John Dierkes, Arthur Hunnicutt, Tim Durant, Andy Devine, Robert Easton Burke, Smith Ballew, Whit Bissell, James Whitmore (narrator); **c**, Harold Rosson; **m**, Bronislau Kaper; **ed**, Ben Lewis; **art d**, Cedric Gibbons, Hans Peters; **set d**, Edwin B. Willis, Fred MacLean; **spec eff**, Warren Newcombe.

The Red Baron ★★★ 2010; Germany/U.S./106m; Miama Film; Monterey Media; Color; Biographical Drama/War Drama; Children: Unacceptable (MPAA: PG-13); **DVD**. Well made and action filled, this intriguing biopic and war drama accurately profiles German Baron Manfred von Richthofen (1892-1918), played as an adult by Schweighofer. He was called "The Red Baron" because he was a nobleman and for the red color of his plane. He was the most famous and decorated pilot of the Imperial German Army Air Force in World War I (1914-1918) and feared by American and Allied nation combat fliers. To Schweighofer and his fellow aces, air combats are sporting events providing technical challenge and honorable skills. They blithely ignore the fact that they might be killed and are callous about the Allied pilots they shoot down. Injured in a crash, Schweighofer is hospitalized and falls in love with his nurse, Headey. He comes to realize he is only being used for German propaganda and grows disgusted with war, but feeling responsible for the safety of his unit's fighting wing, he flies again, but to his death, shot down near Amiens, in northern France. It is still unknown as to who shot down his plane, albeit a Canadian fighter pilot named Roy Brown is credited with that kill. He was the top German ace of the war, shooting down eighty Allied combat planes. Song: "Open Skies" (Reamonn rock band: Rea Garvey, Uwe Bossert, Mike Gommeringer, Phillip

Clark Gable and Jean Harlow in *Red Dust*, 1932.

Rfauenbusch, Sebastian Padotzke). War violence and sexuality prohibit viewing by children. *Author's Note*: Manfred von Richthofen has been profiled by many actors in several films, notably **The Blue Max**, 1966 (Carl Schell); **Darling Lili**, 1970 (Ingo Morgendorf); **The Great Waldo Pepper**, 1975 (Art Scholl); **The Red Baron**, 2010 (Matthias Schweighofer as the adult Manfred von Richthofen; Tomas Koutnik as the young Manfred von Richthofen); **Richthofen**, 1929 (George Burghardt); and **Von Richthofen and Brown**, 1971 (John Phillip Law). **p**, Nikolai Mullerschoen, Dan Maag, Thomas Reisser, Philip Schulz-Deyle, Marisa Kagan, Rene Kock; **d&w**, Mullerschoen; **cast**, Matthias Schweighofer, Lena Headey, Joseph Fiennes, Maxim Mehmet, Hanno Koffler, Til Schweiger, Richard Krajco, Steffan Schroeder, Lukas Prikazky, Iveta Jirickova, Tomas Koutnik; **c**, Klaus Merkel; **m**, Stefan Hansen, Dirk Reichardt; **ed**, Emmelie Mansee, Olivia Retzer, Adam P. Scott; **prod d**, Yvonne von Wallenberg; **art d**, Jindrich Koci, Milena Koubkova, Thomas Molt; **set d**, Petra Klimek; **spec eff**, Jens Doldissen.

Red Desert ★★★ 1965; France/Italy; U.K. 116m; Film Duemila/Criterion; Drama; Children: Unacceptable; **DVD**; **VHS**. Beautiful Vitti is married to Chionetti, manager of a factory in Ravenna, Italy, where waste material from that factory pollutes area lakes. She is mentally ill but keeps it from her husband as best she can. She meets Harris, an engineer en route to Patagonia to start a factory there. They become attracted to each other at a dinner party that leads to a sexual dalliance. Chionetti leaves town on business, and Vitti fears that her son, Bartoleschi, has polio. She later discovers that he is faking that illness and goes to Harris because she feels no one needs or loves her. Harris takes advantage of her sexually before leaving her, and she is left alone and still mentally ill at the conclusion of this somewhat depressing but interesting and beautifully filmed tale. (In Italian; English subtitles.) **p**, Antonio Cervi, Angelo Rizzoli; **d**, Michelangelo Antonioni; **cast**, Monica Vitti, Richard Harris, Carlo Chionetti, Valerio Bartoleschi, Xenia Valderi, Rita Renoir, Lili Rheims, Aldo Grotti, Emanuela Paola Carboni, Bruno Borghi; **w**, Antonioni, Tonino Guerra; **c**, Carlo Di Palma (Eastmancolor); **m**, Giovanni Fusco, Vittorio Gelmetti; **ed**, Eraldo Da Roma; **art d**, Piero Poletto; **spec eff**, Franco Freda.

Red Dust ★★★★ 1932; U.S.; 83m; MGM; B/W; Drama; Children: Unacceptable; **DVD**; **VHS**. Gable and Harlow sizzle in this steamy tale set in exotic Indochina, where Gable runs a rubber plantation and plays host to two women who vie for his attentions. When one of his assistants, Crisp, arrives on a boat from Saigon he brings along Harlow, a shady lady trying to evade the long arm of the law. Harlow manages to also evade the advances of a drunken Crisp until Gable arrives and nobly allows her to stay on the plantation, but only until the next departing

Jean Harlow and Clark Gable in *Red Dust*, 1932.

boat arrives in a week's time. Harlow makes a play for the tough, no-nonsense Gable, but she gets nowhere, her wisecracks and street savvy palaver only reminding him of the kind of disreputable lifestyle she has had, something he deeply dislikes. Harlow's endearing and charismatic ways, however, finally soften Gable attitude and they have an affair. When the boat arrives, Harlow says goodbye and now Gable is greeted by Raymond, a young engineer Gable has hired to help him run the plantation, along with Raymond's attractive wife, Astor. The eager Raymond, however, quickly comes down with fever, and Gable helps Astor tend to him. Meanwhile, Harlow returns, explaining that the boat that was taking her back to civilization broke down and she needs a place to stay. She tries to resume her relationship with Gable, but he is now preoccupied with the alluring and manipulative Astor. When Raymond recovers, Gable sends him, along with Crisp and Marshall, another one of Gable's assistants, to work on a bridge. While Raymond is gone, Gable succumbs to Astor's enticing arms and they have an affair, much to the anger and resentment of the now abandoned Harlow. Raymond completes his assignment and returns to show nothing but loyalty and respect to Gable, which causes him to feel guilty for dallying with Raymond's wife, so, to get rid of Raymond and Astor, Gable turns his attentions back to Harlow, who is delighted in his renewed passions toward her. Astor, the betraying wife, is now enraged at being betrayed and, unable to take a dose of her own bad medicine, shoots Gable, wounding him in his side. Raymond appears, and Harlow covers for Astor by telling him that his wife was merely defending herself against the unwanted advances of Gable. Crestfallen at seeing that his idol Gable is nothing more than common clay, Raymond resigns and he and Astor leave the plantation, much to the joy of the quick-thinking Harlow. Gable is stunned by Harlow's actions, where she has not only preserved Raymond's marriage (until, it is assumed, Astor can find another lover with whom to cuckold her naïve husband), but has managed to rid him of Astor, an unwanted and deceitful woman. Harlow remains at Gable's side, and he has now fallen in love with this big-hearted woman, planning to make a life with her. Fleming, one of Gable's favorite directors, helms this film with gusto, emphasizing Gable's rugged character and eliciting fine performances from the cast. The challenging and enjoyable chemistry between Gable and Harlow is evident in every scene as each tries to cheapen the other but, in the process, building a very earthy romance. The lensing from master cinematographer Rosson is exceptional; the sets are outstanding, capturing the exotic and sultry landscapes, where the oppressive monsoons and sweltering heat seems to radiate from the screen, mixing with the equally tempestuous love scenes between Gable, Harlow and Astor. Made on a budget of about $400,000, this film was an enormous success with the public, quickly recouping its investment at the box office in its initial release. The story was re-

made as **Congo Maisie**, 1940, a programmer for Ann Sothern, and as **Mogambo**, 1953, where Gable reprises his role with Ava Gardner and Grace Kelly, a film directed by John Ford and is as impactful and fascinating at the original. ***Author's Note***: This film flirts with a number of Hollywood taboos, including infidelity, adultery and prostitution, all of which threatens to bubble to the surface at any moment in almost every scene, not to mention Harlow's (implied) nude bathing scene in a makeshift outdoor shower where she flirts with Gable. The Hollywood censorship organizations were not then fully organized, but this film, among many others, provoked so much scandal that that organization (the Hays Office, later the Breen Office) was soon exercising more authority. "I would say that **Red Dust** was a lot more than peppered with sex," Astor told this author. "It was salacious and it offended a lot of church leaders and reformers, and I was leading the way on that as an idiotic rabbit hopping from one bin to another to mate with anything that moved. My character in that picture is about as trustworthy as any snake in the grass, a woman who has no morality whatsoever. But that makes for the most interesting characters, don't you think?" The straightlaced Gable disliked playing a man who would randomly sleep with any available woman. He told director Fleming that "I don't know which one of us is the whore in this picture, Jean [Harlow] or me." He nevertheless became an international star after this film was released, particularly with women who swooned at his rugged, dark good looks, his unshaven, jutting jaw, brawny physique, and where he often appears bare-chested. Harlow and Gable had not gotten along too well in their first film, **The Secret Six**, 1931, but they had had only a few scenes together in that early talkie. In **Red Dust**, they became good friends and enjoyed the double entendre exchanges with each other. Fleming had the lighting crews use all available lighting to show an almost blinding sun beating down upon the players in their scenes together. When Harlow and Astor complained about the intense heat from the lights, Fleming shouted: "So what? Everybody sweats in the tropics! Let it show! That's the way it is!" Astor recalled when talking to this author that "we perspired so much under those blistering lights that we left little puddles every time we took a step." Tragedy stalked Harlow at this time in that her sexually impotent new husband, Paul Bern, unable to perform on their wedding night, later doused himself with Harlow's perfume and then sent a bullet into his head, the suicide rocking Hollywood. The scandal so unnerved MGM boss Louis B. Mayer that he thought to replace Harlow with Tallulah Bankhead, but Bankhead refused to replace Harlow, telling Mayer that "to damn the radiant Jean [Harlow] for the misfortune of another would be the shabbiest act of all time." When Mayer was informed that the public was widely sympathetic to Harlow, Mayer then wanted to cash in on that sentiment by telling Fleming to hurriedly complete **Red Dust**, which he did. Harlow, while attempting to recuperate from Bern's death, was consoled and comforted by Rosson, the cinematographer of this film, and they married a short time later, a union that lasted for only six months. **p**, Victor Fleming, (not credited) Hunt Stromberg, Irving Thalberg; **d**, Fleming; **cast**, Clark Gable, Jean Harlow, Gene Raymond, Mary Astor, Donald Crisp, Tully Marshall, Forrester Harvey, Willie Fung; **w**, John Mahin (based on the play by Wilson Collison); **c**, Harold Rosson; **ed**, Blanche Sewell; **art d**, Cedric Gibbons.

Red-Headed Woman ★★★ 1932; U.S.; 79m; MGM; B/W; Drama; Children: Unacceptable; **DVD**; **VHS**. Harlow gives an exceptional performance in this raucous and risqué tale of a vixen out to vamp her way into riches and high society. After becoming the personal secretary to business tycoon Morris, Harlow makes advances toward the boss, her sensual allures so overwhelming the staid Morris that he abandons his caring wife, Hyams, divorcing her. When Hyams realizes that she has lost her husband to the conniving Harlow, she tries to reconcile with Morris but is shocked to see that he has married Harlow, who now puts in motion her campaign to entrench herself with the social elite. Harlow is angered when Morris' father, Stone, rejects her, branding her a home-wrecking lowlife with no social background. After meeting Stephenson, a coal magnate and one of Stone's business associates, Harlow seduces Stephenson and then uses blackmail to compel him to have a lavish party at her posh mansion where Harlow expects to meet the leading figures of high society. The guests arrive, but soon depart to attend a surprise party at a mansion across the street, and Harlow learns from her hairdresser (Merkel) that her guests have left to be with Hyams, who occupies that mansion opposite her own. This social rebuff so insults and enrages Harlow that she deserts Morris, going to live alone in New York. Stone later visits his friend Stephenson, and he finds Harlow's handkerchief at Stephenson's abode and realizes that Harlow is two-timing his son. When Stone offers this evidence to Morris, the angered husband employs private detectives to trail Harlow and they soon discover that she is not only having an affair with the gullible Stephenson, but is carrying on a torrid romance with Stephenson's suave chauffeur, Boyer. After Harlow discovers that Morris now knows about her not-so-secret affairs with Stephenson and Boyer, she tries to reinstate herself with Morris, but when she returns to him, she finds him with Hyams; playing the role of the betrayed wife, even though she has done most of the betraying, Harlow withdraws a gun and shoots Morris and then flees. Morris survives as a much wiser man, showing his noble nature by refusing to have Harlow charged with attempted murder. He remarries Hyams and looks forward to a happier and more tranquil life. Sometime later, he and Hyams, while on a vacation to France, see Harlow at the Grand Prix, accepting the winning trophy on behalf of a nobleman, who sponsors the winning racing team and for whom Harlow is now that wealthy man's mistress. At her side, Morris and Hyams see the ubiquitous French chauffeur, Boyer, knowing that Harlow is up to her own tricks in juggling love affairs with two men. Conway directs this film with vitality and the cast members render fine performances in this titillating sex farce. Harlow, wearing a red wig throughout, is riveting as a sexy siren using all of her considerable charms to get to the top. Although this film agitated reformers and church groups with its blatant exhibition of promiscuity, the production was an enormous hit at the box office, securing stardom for Harlow, along with another MGM film released that year, **Red Dust**, 1932, where she plays a more empathetic character, a warm-hearted lady who is nevertheless another trollop. Songs: "Red-Headed Woman" (music: Richard A. Whiting; lyrics: Raymond B. Egan), "I'm Nobody's Baby" (Benny Davis, Milton Ager, Lester Santley), "Frankie and Johnnie" (traditional), "St. Louis Blues" (W. C. Handy), "The Stars and Stripes Forever" (John Philip Sousa), "We'll Dance Till Dawn" (music: Jimmy McHugh; lyrics: Dorothy Fields). *Author's Note*: The gifted F. Scott Fitzgerald wrote the original story and first draft of the screenplay for this film. After Irving Thalberg, who was head of production at MGM, read the script, he concluded that it was too serious and he had Loos rewrite the screenplay, injecting light-hearted moments in its more somber scenes and where Harlow's character became more brassy than sinister. Thalberg initially offered the role of the vamp to Clara Bow, who accepted the part but then backed away when Thalberg insisted that she commit to several other future films in the same agreement. Harlow, an MGM ingénue and contract player, was then given the part. Thalberg had great difficulties with the Hays Office, Hollywood's censoring organization. It objected to many of the scenes where Harlow was skimpily dressed and, especially, her sultry seductions of her victims. More than a dozen cuts were made to tone down those scenes, but the film still saw widespread complaints from social and religious leaders objecting to its sexually provocative scenes. Despite all the controversy, the film made considerable profit, even though it was banned in the U.K. and not shown in England until 1965. Boyer, who was yet to become a romantic matinee idol and who had appeared in small parts in only two other U.S. films for Paramount, **The Magnificent Lie**, 1931, and **The Man from Yesterday**, 1932, told this author that he eagerly sought out his role as the slippery and unsavory chauffeur in **Red-Headed Woman** "because it was an MGM production and MGM was the foremost studio making pictures. In France,

Chester Morris and Jean Harlow in *Red-Headed Woman*, 1932.

MGM pictures were considered to be the finest products in the movie-making industry, so I thought it would be a large feather in my hat if I appeared in that picture. It was a pleasure to work with Jean [Harlow], one of the most considerate actresses of that day, a totally charming lady. She would go on to marry the producer of that picture, Paul Bern, but he committed suicide over very strange circumstances [his impotence on his wedding night with Harlow] and I don't think Jean ever recovered from that. She died prematurely about five years after we made **Red-Headed Woman** together and I can tell you with certainty that there has never been another actress to replace her." Ironically, Boyer would commit suicide on August 26, 1978, two days after the death of his wife, Pat Patterson, their happy marriage having lasted forty-four years. **p**, Paul Bern, (not credited) Albert Lewin, Irving Thalberg; **d**, Jack Comway; **cast**, Jean Harlow, Chester Morris, Lewis Stone, Leila Hyams, Una Merkel, Henry Stephenson, May Robson, Charles Boyer, Harvey Clark, Henry Armetta; **w**, Anita Loos, (not credited) F. Scott Fitzgerald (based on a novel by Katharine Brush); **c**, Harold Rosson; **ed**, Blanche Sewell; **art d**, Cedric Gibbons.

Red, Hot and Blue ★★★ 1949; U.S; 84m.; PAR; B/W; Musical Comedy; Crime; Children: Unacceptable; **DVD**; **VHS**. Lively musical sees Broadway singer Hutton dating Mature, a stage manager, when a gangster backing the show is murdered and she becomes a suspect because his body is found in her apartment. The gangster's minions kidnap her in trying to learn about his death. She manages to wriggle out of her predicament while delivering some perky tunes. Hutton's firecracker personality is much in evidence, and Mature gives her fine (if not the only sane) support while press agent Demarest and Havoc, Hutton's roommate, provide a lot of wisecracks and funny moments. Composer Loesser makes a rare appearance as the gangster abducting Hutton. It's mainly a film to show off Hutton's vitality and singing and achieves that goal while sustaining interest throughout. Songs: "That's Loyalty," "I Wake Up in the Morning Feeling Fine," "Hamlet," "Now That I Need You" (Frank Loesser). *Author's Note*: "That picture was done with a bolt of lightning by the director [Farrow]," Hutton told this author. "He was one of those directors that wasted no time in his setups or shooting schedules and he drove us all like race horses going down a fast track." **p&d**, John Farrow; **cast**, Betty Hutton, Victor Mature, William Demarest, Robert Kellard, June Havoc, Jane Nigh, Frank Loesser, William Talman, Art Smith, Raymond Walburn, Jack Kruschen, Julie Adams; **w**, Farrow, Hagar Wilde (based on a story by Charles Lederer); **c**, Daniel L. Fapp; **ed**, Eda Warren; **art d**, Hans Dreier, Franz Bachelin; **set d**, Sam Comer, Ross Dowd.

The Red House ★★★★ 1947; U.S.; 100m; Sol Loesser Productions;

Allene Roberts and Edward G. Robinson in *The Red House*, 1947.

UA; B/W; Crime Drama; Children: Unacceptable; **DVD**; **VHS**. Robinson excels as a deranged man in this thriller. He is a farmer, crippled years earlier; he owns a large piece of property on which is a red house, and which, under his orders, no one can visit. Living with his equally strange sister, Anderson (who played the weird and eerie housekeeper in Hitchcock's **Rebecca**, 1940), Robinson is so fearful that someone might discover the secrets of that red house that he hires woodsman Calhoun to protect the property against trespassers, giving him orders to shoot to kill anyone who gets near that red house. Roberts, who is the ward of Robinson and Anderson and whose parents disappeared years ago, is in love with MCallister and persuades him to take a job on the farm. Robinson repeatedly warns Roberts and MCallister to stay away from the red house, which is secluded in a wood, because that eerie house emits strange shrieks of terror. Curiosity gets the better of the youthful lovers, but when they attempt to investigate the red house they are frightened off after Calhoun shoots at them. Realizing that her brother will never have any peace of mind until the red house is destroyed, Anderson attempts to burn it to the ground, but Calhoun mortally shoots her. As Anderson is dying, she reveals the secret of the red house to Roberts and MCallister. She explains that Robinson murdered Roberts' mother and father in the red house fifteen years ago after Roberts' mother rejected his advances, and, out of guilt and remorse, he and Anderson adopted and raised Roberts. After Anderson dies, Robinson loses his faculties and tries to entice Roberts to the red house so that she can meet the same kind of lethal fate he administered to her parents. MCallister, however, comes to the rescue with police and Roberts is saved at the last moment. Rather than be captured by the police, Robinson elects to take his own life by wildly driving his truck into the swamp where he buried the bodies of his victims so many years ago. Daves directs this chilling story with a sure hand, carefully unfolding its grim tale while mounting and sustaining suspense; Robinson, Anderson, MCallister and Roberts are standouts. Rozsa's lower register and edgy score underline and enhance the mystery and tension of this thriller. *Author's Note*: The finale, where Robinson ends up in the swamp, was not lost on Alfred Hitchcock, who employs a similar ending to **Psycho**, 1960, but where a victim's car is being dragged from a swamp, and, to a larger extent, in **The Enforcer**, 1951, directed by Bretaigne Windust and Raoul Walsh, and starring Humphrey Bogart, where a huge swamp is dredged to uncover countless bodies of murder victims dying at the hands of Murder, Inc. Robinson enjoyed playing his part as the demented killer, telling this author that "such roles are always the most challenging. One must walk the fine line between sanity and insanity. My character hides his insanity by appearing to be protective and avuncular, but a maniac lurks just beneath the surface of that fragile sanity and, deep down, he knows it. The script for **The Red House** is very

much like Edgar Allan Poe's story 'The Tell-Tale Heart' [1843] where a man murders another man and dismembers the body and then hides the remains under some floorboards, but he can still hear his victim's heart pounding, and that drives him insane. **The Red House** is similar because it represents murders committed many years ago, but it stands as a reminder of that crime, the victims calling out to the killer until his mind is unhinged. The picture, like that story, reminds the viewer that "murder will - out." **p**, Sol Lesser; **d&w**, Delmer Daves (based on the novel by George Agnew Chamberlain); **cast**, Edward G. Robinson, Lon McCallister, Judith Anderson, Rory Calhoun, Allene Roberts, Julie London, Ona Munson, Harry Shannon, Arthur Space, Pat Flaherty, Walter Sande; **c**, Bert Glennon; **m**, Miklos Rozsa; **ed**, Merrill White; **art d**, McClure Capps; **spec eff**, Warren Lynch.

The Red Inn ★★★★ 1954; France; 98m; Memmon Films/Cocinor; B/W; Comedy; Children: Unacceptable; **VHS**. French comedian Fernandel captivates in this very dark comedy. He is a monk traveling with a group of tourists when they take refuge at a remote inn from a blinding snowstorm, where Fernandel quickly discovers to his dismay the sinister goings-on by the innkeepers. Rosay, the wife of the innkeeper, confesses her sins to Fernandel, and from these admissions he learns that she and her husband have been routinely murdering guests by poisoning the soup served to them and then stealing their belongings. Knowing the couple intends to do the same thing to their present group of guests, but prevented from talking about it through his vow of silence dealing with confessions, Fernandel sets out to prevent these murders. He employs a number of outlandish tricks to save the lives of his fellow travelers, producing many comedic scenes by using many burlesque routines in a black satire that will amuse many but where others may find the story line a bit too grim. Song: "Le Complainte de l'auberge rouge" (Rene Cloerec). *Author's Note*: This film takes a large leaf from Alfred Hitchcock's **I Confess**, 1953, where a priest, played by Montgomery Clift, hears the confession of a killer and is then faced with either keeping his religious vow of silence or revealing the identity of the murderer. Many films deal with someone with secret knowledge attempting to prevent the deaths of several persons connected to each other through circumstance or relationship, such as **And Then There Were None**, 1945, and **The List of Adrian Messenger**, 1963, but the Fernandel outing transforms this concept into macabre and ridiculous hilarity. In reality, the most notorious serial killers who played hosts to guests at an inn before killing them to obtain their riches were the Benders, a family of four, father, mother, son and daughter. This family killed at least twenty travelers who made the mistake of stopping at their two-room inn on the Kansas prairie in 1872-1873, none of these sinister culprits ever apprehended. For more information on the notorious Bender family, see my two-volume work, *The Great Pictorial History of World Crime*, Volume II (History, Inc., 2004; pages 1036-1046). (In French; English subtitles.) **p**, Simon Schiffrin; **d**, Claude Autant Lara; **cast**, Fernandel, Francoise Rosay, Marie-Claire Olivia, Jean-Roger Caussimon, Nane Germon, Didier d'Yd, Lud Germain, Jacques Charon, Robert Berri, Andre Cheff, Yves Montand; **w**, Pierre Bost, Jean Aurenche, Autant-Lara (based on the story "L'Auberge Sanglante de Peyrebelle" by Honore de Balzac); **c**, Andre Bac, Jacques Natteau; **m**, Rene Cloerec; **ed**, Madeleine Gug; **prod d** & **set d**, Max Douy; **spec eff**, Nicolas Wilke.

Red Mountain ★★★ 1951; U.S.; 84m; PAR; Color; Western; Children: Unacceptable; **VHS**. Ladd is a standout in this action-packed, mature western set at the closing of the American Civil War (1861-1865). He is a Confederate captain fleeing to Colorado to join a band of Southern guerrillas led by William Quantrill (1837-1865), played by Ireland. On his way there, he stops in a pro-Northern town to get revenge against White, who stole his land before the war. Ladd shoots White dead, but Kennedy is blamed for the killing because the shell used in the shooting is a Confederate casing and Kennedy is known to have been on the South's side before coming to the town. Feeling guilty about an innocent man being hanged for his crime, Ladd rescues Kennedy and they ride away. They hide out in a mountain cabin where Ladd meets Scott, who is about to marry Kennedy. Kennedy realizes that Ladd killed White and wants to turn him in, but, when they fight, Kennedy breaks a leg. Ladd and Scott fall in love, and Ireland and his men arrive. Ladd realizes Ireland is nothing more than an outlaw gang leader so he arranges for Union troops to go after him. In a gun fight with Ireland and his men, Kennedy is killed, but Ladd arrives with the Union soldiers and they wipe out Ireland and his gang. News arrives that the war has ended and Ladd and Scott can ride off into the sunset as he has made his own peace with the North. Dieterle provides a lot of well-choreographed action in this film that nevertheless plays fast and loose with historical facts dealing with Quantrill. Similar films that show Confederates going to the far West to continue their Lost Cause in the Civil War include **The Last Outpost**, 1951; **The Outriders**, 1950; **Rocky Mountain**, 1950; **Two Flags West**, 1950; and **Virginia City**, 1940. Quantrill has been essayed by many actors in several other films, including **Dark Command**, 1940 (role model for Walter Pidgeon); **Fighting Man of the Plains**, 1949 (James Griffith); **Kansas Pacific**, 1953 (Reed Hadley); **Kansas Raiders**, 1950 (Brian Donlevy); **The Legend of the Golden Gun**, 1979 (made-for-TV; Robert Davi); **Quantrill's Raiders**, 1958 (Leo Gordon); **Renegade Girl**, 1946 (Ray Corrigan); **Ride with the Devil**, 1999 (John Ales); **The Stranger Wore a Gun**, 1953 (James Millican); **Woman They Almost Lynched**, 1953 (Brian Donlevy); and **Young Jesse James**, 1960 (Emile Meyer). *Author's Note*: Director Dieterle told this author that "we shot most of the exteriors, especially the battle scenes, outside of Gallup, New Mexico, and we used a lot of the local Indians as extras. I had a difficult time with some of those extras, who wanted me to provide them with bottles of booze along with their daily wages. This I refused to do and one of them said to me: 'That's why we hate the white man!'" Violence prohibits viewing by children. **p**, Hal B. Wallis; **d**, William Dieterle; **cast**, Alan Ladd, Lizabeth Scott, Arthur Kennedy, John Ireland, Jeff Corey, James Bell, Bert Freed, Walter Sande, Neville Brand, Carleton Young, Whit Bissell, Jay Silverheels, Iron Eyes Cody; **w**, John Meredyth Lucas, George F. Slavin, George W. George (based on a story by Slavin, George); **c**, Charles B. Lang Jr. (Technicolor); **m**, Franz Waxman; **ed**, Warren Low; **art d**, Hal Pereira, Franz Bachelin; **set d**, Sam Comer, Ray Moyer; **spec eff**, Farciot Edouart, W. Wallace Kelley.

The Red Pony ★★★ 1949; U.S.; 89m; REP; Color; Drama; Children: Acceptable; **DVD**; **VHS**. Based on a fine story by Steinbeck, this warm-hearted family film is set on a ranch in the coast range of mountains near Salinas Valley, California. Miles is a ten-year-old boy who loves his red pony; he lives on the ranch with his mother, Loy, father, Strudwick, as well as Strudwick's father, Calhern, and a seasoned ranch hand, Mitchum. Strudwick becomes jealous of the friendship Miles feels for Mitchum, who helps him train the pony. The pony is frightened during a storm, falls ill, and dies. Miles blames Mitchum, who soon gives him a colt and Miles warms to him again. Strudwick accepts Miles' and Mitchum's friendship and also grows closer to his son. Milestone directs this film with great care, where the characters are well developed, with Mitchum and Miles giving strong performances. The story was remade in 1973 as a made-for-TV production. Songs: "Shall We Gather at the River?" (Robert Lowry), "Marche Militaire" (Franz Schubert). *Author's Note*: Director Milestone told this author that "I took a great deal of time in shooting **The Red Pony** because I wanted to present the Steinbeck characters exactly the way he portrayed them in his stories about them, and that irked the front office at Republic Studios because it cost them more than what they scheduled for the picture. Republic was the top studio of the Poverty Row studios, but its boss, Herbert J. Yates, watched where every penny went. I caught his usual hell for going over budget and stretching out the shooting schedule." The shooting schedule went to eighty-one days, the costliest such schedule Republic had to that time. Mitchum liked his role in this

Alan Ladd and Lizabeth Scott in *Red Mountain*, 1951.

film, stating to this author that "my part as the ranch hand who befriends the son of the ranch owner in that picture got me a lot of sympathy. I'm an old cowhand with a lot of bruises to prove it, and that part impressed a lot of producers and probably got me the role I played in a film a few years later called **The Lusty Men** [1952], where I am playing another seasoned westerner, but as a rodeo rider." Steinbeck told this author that "Milestone did a great job with my story about the boy and his pony and got it onto the screen just about the way I envisioned it. I actually wrote that story as a series of four stories [that appeared in magazines from 1933 to 1937] and then patched them all into the novella called *The Red Pony*." **p&d**, Lewis Milestone; **cast**, Myrna Loy, Robert Mitchum, Louis Calhern, Shepperd Strudwick, Peter Miles, Margaret Hamilton, Patty King, Jackie Jackson, Beau Bridges, Don Reynolds; **w**, John Steinbeck (based on his novel); **c**, Tony Gaudio (Technicolor); **m**, Aaron Copland; **ed**, Harry Keller; **prod d**, Nicolai Remisoff; **art d**, Victor Greene; **set d**, Charles Thompson, John McCarthy, Jr.; **spec eff**, Howard and Theodore Lydecker.

Red River ★★★★★ 1948; U.S.; 133m; Monterey Productions/UA; B/W; Western; Children: Unacceptable; **DVD**; **VHS**. This magnificent western from pantheon director Hawks ranks as one of the top ten films in that vast and popular genre and it is closer to the top than the bottom in that elite group of masterpiece productions. Wayne is the stalwart lynchpin of this sweeping saga of the Old West, seen at the beginning driving a prairie schooner in a long wagon train heading west with a lone bull tied to it and accompanied by his loyal friend, Brennan. At one point, Wayne pulls his wagon out of line and begins to head south toward Texas and the Red River, but the wagon master objects, telling Wayne that he signed on to stay with the wagon train and now that they are entering Indian country, his gun will be needed to fend off any attacks. Wayne is adamant, saying: "I signed nothing. If I had, I'd stay." As Wayne rides off, Brennan sums up Wayne's resolute and deliberate character for the wagon master, telling him: "He's a mighty set man. When his mind is made up even you can't change it." Before departing, Wayne meets with Gray, a young, beautiful woman who is traveling with the wagon train with her family and who is in love with him. He tells her that after he has found and established his ranch in Texas, he will send for her, giving her a bracelet his mother wore. She begs him to stay with her, but Wayne is determined to carve out an empire on a huge cattle ranch by claiming vast unclaimed lands to the south. He kisses Gray goodbye, and he and Brennan ride southward. Hours later, they see black smoke curling skyward in the distance and realize that the wagon train has been attacked by Indians. That night, Wayne and Brennan await their own attack by those Indians. When Wayne hears Indians using night bird signals, he crawls away from the wagon and

John Ireland and Montgomery Clift in *Red River*, 1948.

kills several Indians while Brennan shoots down other Indians attacking the wagon. In a final battle with the last Indian, Wayne kills his opponent only to find to his shock that the Indian is wearing the bracelet he had given to Gray, and he now knows that the only woman he has loved is dead. The following morning, Kuhn, a dazed boy from the wagon train and its only survivor of the Indian attack, stumbles on to Wayne's campsite, dragging a cow by a rope, the only other living creature from that ill-fated wagon train. Wayne stands before him to listen to Kuhn's jumbled account of the attack, and, to stop him from babbling, slaps him to his senses. Kuhn immediately draws a gun and aims it at Wayne while Brennan stands helplessly nearby. Wayne employs a ruse to quickly take the six-gun from the youth and tells him that he can accompany him and Brennan in their search for new lands and they travel southward. Crossing the Red River, they continue southward, going deep into southwestern Texas until they are close to the Rio Grande. The far vistas Wayne sees at this point show rich grazing lands thick with grass and running water, and Wayne declares that they have reached their goal and that these are now the lands of his own vast ranch. He sets the bull and cow free and Kuhn says: "They'll get away." Wayne replies: "Wherever they go they will be on my land." At that moment, two riders approach. The apprehensive Brennan states that he never likes to see strangers, stating: "No stranger ever good-newsed me." The two riders are Mexican wranglers working for a wealthy Mexican landlord who lives hundreds of miles distant in Mexico across the Rio Grande. The lead wrangler tells Wayne that he and his friends are welcome to stay on the lands for some time, but must then move on. Wayne tells him that his boss owns too much land and that the land upon which he stands and all the land to the Rio Grande is now his own. The wrangle states: "I am sorry for you, senor," and goes for his gun, but Wayne draws his gun faster and shoots and kills the wrangler, telling his companion to take the body back to his employer and that he now owns the land. Kuhn is impressed with Wayne's fast draw and asks him how he knew when the wrangler was going to go for his gun. "By watching his eyes," Wayne tells him. As the rider departs with his dead companion, Wayne kneels down to draw in the dirt two squiggling lines to indicate the Red River and the letter "D" standing for his name, Dunson, stating that this is the brand upon which they will mark all their cattle and, the sign of the Red River D signifying his great ranch. Kuhn reminds Wayne that he has contributed his cow to Wayne's ambitious empire and says: "I don't see my name on that brand [Matthew Garth]." Wayne promises that he will add his name to that brand, but only "when you've earned it." In the next scene, fourteen years later, we see that Wayne now owns that great ranch and has the largest cattle herd in Texas. He has aged with white streaks in his hair. The youth he took along with him has now grown to manhood in the form of Clift, who has fought in the Civil War on the side of the

Confederacy and has returned just after the end of that war. Clift learns from Brennan that though Wayne has more cattle than any rancher could ever envision, his enormous herds of cattle are all but worthless as there is no market in Texas for them. Wayne, who is broke, has an ambitious plan and that is to drive his entire herd northward to Missouri and the railroad where he can sell the much-wanted cattle at a substantial profit. He orders his men to begin rounding up all the cattle grazing on his lands and has them all branded with the Red River D brand, despite the fact that some of the cattle represent strays from herds owned by other cattlemen. Clark, one of those cattlemen, arrives with some of his cowhands, one of whom is a professional gunman, Ireland, and asks Wayne if he is branding cattle owned by him. Wayne admits that he is doing that but has no time to weed out stray cattle. He promises Clark to pay him for the sale of any of his cattle he can make when and if he gets to Missouri. Ireland asks Wayne for a job, saying that he wants to go along on his historic cattle drive (the first to be made from Texas) and Wayne hires him. That night, Wayne addresses all of his men, asking them to sign a document that they will not only go on the drive but that they will not quit until they reach their destination. A few refuse and leave the bunkhouse, but most sign on, including Brennan, who serves as the cook on the drive, and who drives the chuck wagon. Before the drive takes place, Clift and Ireland, both fast guns, test each other's firing accuracy by shooting at a can, keeping it in the air shot after shot. With the cattle rounded up, Wayne turns to Clift and says: "Take them to Missouri!" With that, one cowboy after another lets out a long hoot to rouse the cattle (Hawks provides many quick cuts to show these leathered, bearded and mustachioed faces shouting, hooting and bellowing, an electrifying sequence that remains memorable to this day.) Brennan starts the drive with considerable discomfort in that he has lost his false teeth in an earlier poker game to fellow cowhand Chief Yowlatchie (Daniel Simmons, a Yakima Indian and a veteran character actor since the 1920s who started his career as an opera singer and played mostly Apache Indians in films), and is given those teeth only at meal times so that he can eat his vittles, but must return them to Chief Yowlatchie until he pays the dollar owed to his poker-playing opponent. Brennan is constantly arguing with the stubborn Indian, who stoically replies: "Come grub, you get 'em tooth." Brennan has another nagging problem and that is Parry, a cowboy with a sweet tooth, who is forever raiding the sugar container in one of the two chuck wagons; Brennan, when catching Parry filching sugar, drives him off with a whip, and Parry good naturedly says: "I could take that personal." At the end of a long day, the cowboys make camp, but Wayne tells his night herders to calm down the cattle, which have become restless after hearing the yowling of coyotes. One of those cowboys, Harry Carey Jr., rides slowly through the herd, softly singing to the cattle. Worden, another cowboy, beds down next to Clift, Ireland and Beery, telling them that he is worried about the cattle and thinks that they are "spooked" and can be easily aroused into a stampede and then describes the horrors of such outbursts where campsites have been destroyed and many men killed by panicking cattle trampling everyone and everything in sight. The disaster that all these cowboys dread comes to grim reality when Parry, again searching for sugar at Brennan's chuck wagon, unhinges pots and pans at the wagon, causing them to fall down in a loud clamor and this so startles the restless cattle that the herd stampedes. The cowboys mount their horses and wildly ride after the cattle, shooting guns in the air and driving the herd into a box canyon, but much of the campsite is destroyed, including one of the chuck wagons, and many of the riders are injured. Wayne and others then find Carey trampled to death, all saddened as he was one of the most liked cowboys in the drive; Wayne orders him buried and sats that he will "read over him," meaning that he will quote some phrases from his Bible at his burial. He also promises that, when the drive is over and the cattle sold, Carey's recently married wife, now a widow, will receive Carey's full salary and he tells Clift to also buy a pair of red shoes for that woman, which is what Carey hoped to do at the end of that drive. Later, Wayne confronts a remorseful Parry, telling him that he has caused widespread damage, injuries and the death of Carey and that he intends to punish him for that transgression by whipping him. Parry tells Wayne that he is sorry for what he has done, but that no one is going to whip him. He defiantly stands with his hand next to his gun, but before Wayne can draw his six-gun, fast-draw Clift pulls his own gun and wounds Parry, who thanks him, knowing that Wayne would have shot to kill. This is the first act of defiance Clift shows to his adopted father, Wayne, that defiance growing as the drive continues, where Wayne acts like a ruthless dictator as he and his men push the herd northward. The men are on short rations since one of the chuck wagons was destroyed during the stampede and the cowboys are reduced to eating only beef, slaughtering the cattle they are herding as this now becomes their main food supply. Wayne pushes his men to the point of exhaustion, insisting that the drive continue through dusk and halting to make camp only at night. Morale sinks and even the most loyal men begin to grumble and complain. Ireland tells Clift that there is a shorter route in taking the cattle to market, and that is to drive them up the old Chisholm Trail to Kansas, believing that there is a railhead in Kansas where they might sell the cattle. The cowboys come across Self, a wounded man, one night, the only survivor of a cattle drive heading for Missouri. He croaks from a wounded neck that he and others were ambushed by Missouri renegades and the herd stolen, but when asked if the railroad had reached Kansas, the man is uncertain. Wayne puts a stop to the suggestion that Wayne alter the course of the drive and head for Kansas, stubbornly saying that they are going to Missouri. Wayne's rigid supervision turns into relentless dictatorship, although Brennan explains to Clift, Ireland and others than Wayne is going without sleep and is haunted by the fact that he has no idea of the perils awaiting them in the days to come. Three of the cowboys, Fiero, Strange and Tyler, finally tell Wayne that they have had enough and that they are quitting and returning to Texas. Wayne tells them that they signed on to stay with the herd until it was delivered to market and that he is going to hold them to their promise. The men go for their guns, but Wayne, with gunplay from Brennan and Clift, shoot down the would-be deserters, killing all three of them. Wayne, who is wounded in the foot, states: "Bury them and I will read over them." Worden, one of the cowboys, says: "Planting and reading, planting and reading. Fill a man full of lead, stick him in the ground and then read words at him. Why, when you kill a man, why try to read the Lord in as a partner on the job?" All of the men now know that if anyone attempts to desert, Wayne will mete out the same kind of punishment. Still, three others, Fix, White and another rider (named Bill Kelsey, never seen), desert the drive, stealing cartridges and food. Wayne sends Ireland and Beery after them, ordering them to return the deserters to him. Meanwhile, Wayne ruthlessly drives his men onward, nursing his wound and going without sleep, telling Brennan that he intends to stay awake so that no more of his men will desert. The herd is then driven across the Red River, which symbolizes Wayne's ranch; the cowboys herd more than 9,000 cattle across that river. Sometime later, Ireland and Beery return with Fix and White in tow, reporting that they have killed the other deserter when he refused to return with them. Fix knows that Wayne intends to shoot him and White, saying to Wayne, "You're crazy. You've been drinking and not sleeping. If you ain't crazy, you're close....There's a good way to Abilene [Kansas], but you won't listen to that. You want to drive them [the cattle] to Missouri when you've got the high-and-low Jack against you....This herd doesn't belong to you. It belongs to every poor hoping and praying cattleman in the state. I shouldn't have run away. I should have stayed and put a bullet in you. I signed a pledge, sure, but you ain't the man I signed it with.... Now you can get your Bible and read over us after you shoot us." Wayne, who has patiently listened to Fix, replies: "I'm going to hang you." Clift, who has tolerated Wayne's oppressive ways for the sake of their father-son relationship, takes his stand, saying to Wayne: "No, you're not....You're not going to hang them." Wayne stares at Clift, asking: "Who will stop me?" Clift answers: "I will." Wayne goes for his gun, but Ireland shoots it out of his hand; when he reaches for it again,

John Wayne and Montgomery Clift in *Red River*, 1948.

Beery fires a shot that sends slivers of wood from a tree limb into Wayne's fingers. He stands helpless as Clift tells everyone that he is taking the herd to Abilene, Kansas, and that Wayne is staying behind. The cowboys all enthusiastically back Clift, including Brennan, who has always been loyal to Wayne, but, in this instance, tells Wayne: "You was wrong, Mr. Dunson." The next day they drive the herd toward Kansas. The wounded Wayne stands by his horse. He has been given supplies and Clift tells him that "if there's any chance at all we'll get your herd to Kansas," but Wayne vows vengeance. "You should have let them kill me, 'cause I'm going to kill you. I'll catch up with you. I don't know when, but I'll catch up. Every time you turn around expect to see me, 'cause one time you turn around, I'll be there. I'm going to kill you." Clift and his cowboys drive the herd toward Abilene with the same desperation shown earlier by Wayne, but what drives them now is the fear that Wayne will recuperate and follow them, full of awful vengeance. The herd is stopped when Clift and others find one of their wayward steers killed, an arrow sticking in its hide. Clift hands the arrow to Chief Yowlatchie, who tells him that it is a Comanche arrow. He sends Ireland and Beery to scout ahead for about ten miles so that they can give warning if they see Indians. Some days later, Beery comes riding back with news that he and Ireland have encountered a wagon train of gamblers and showgirls who are en route to Utah to open a saloon and tells how he was given biscuits, beans, coffee and pie by these hosting travelers and how Ireland has stayed behind with them because he has met one of the attractive dance hall girls. Clift decides to drive the entire herd in the direction of that camp, but when they approach that area, he and some others riding ahead of the herd see Indians attacking that wagon train. Clift sends one of his riders back to get all of his cowboys to attack the Indians while he and three others ride toward the wagon train, which is encircled by the attacking Indians. Clift and three others fire their six-guns as they ride pell-mell forward, shooting down the attackers and riding into the center of the circle of wagons, where Clift sees and joins Ireland. While battling the attackers, Clift meets Dru, the dark-haired young showgirl who has caught Ireland's eye (Dru and Ireland would marry in 1949, a year after this film was released, a union that ended in divorce in 1957) and who knows from Ireland all about Clift and how he has taken the herd away from Wayne to save the lives of his cowboys and in jeopardy of his life. Clift orders her to load weapons as he fires at the enemy. During the attack, Dru is wounded, an arrow penetrating her shoulder. After Clift's men arrive and drive off the Indians, Clift pulls the arrow from Dru's shoulder (and sucking any contaminated blood from the wound) and Dru then slaps his face hard in response to his harsh treatment of her before she collapses unconscious. He has Ireland carry her to a safe place where she can be further treated while Cording, the boss of the wagon train, invites

John Wayne and Joanne Dru in *Red River,* 1948.

Clift and his cowboys to enjoy their hospitality, including their good food and drinks. While Clift and his men briefly stay with the wagon train, Dru and Clift have a brief affair and Clift then takes the herd toward Abilene. Dru has only one memento of her meeting with Clift, a metal snake bracelet he has worn for fourteen years, one that Wayne has given him, the very bracelet that Wayne had given to the slain Gray and had recouped from the Indian who killed the woman he loved. While Clift is gone, Wayne arrives with a group of gunmen he has hired to help him track down and confront Clift and his men, staying briefly with the wagon train. Wayne meets Dru, who tries to persuade Wayne from going after Clift, the man she loves, but he tells her that "nothing you can say or do" will prevent him from exacting the revenge he seeks against Clift and his fellow usurpers. Wayne tells her that he had thought of Clift as his son, the one who would inherit his ranch when he died. He says that Clift is the son he worked so hard for to establish that great ranch, but Clift's betrayal ended that dream and he now wants to have another son to inherit that ranch. Dru offers to have his child, if he will give up his plan to kill Clift, but Wayne refuses. He then tells her that she can remove the small derringer she has hidden in her arm-sling (as a result of her wound) with which she intends to shoot him, saying "it wouldn't have done you any good," producing his own six-gun, which he has hidden beneath a table, resting that weapon menacingly on that table. Wayne will not alter his course of vengeance. Meanwhile, Clift and his men, while driving the herd northward, hear the faint sounds of a strange wailing in the distance and ride forward to see to their joy what they thought to be only a myth, the railroad, and where an engineer has halted his engine and cars to marvel at the sight of the great herd of cattle crossing its tracks. The jubilant engineer encourages the cowboys to keep bringing the cattle across those tracks, so delighted is he at the welcoming sight of the arriving fresh beef on the hoof. At the request of Beery, the engineer hoots the whistle of the train repeatedly to hurry the cattle along, the herd now only a few miles away from its goal, Abilene, Kansas. When arriving at Abilene, Clift meets with Harry Carey Sr. (the real life father of the young cowboy who had been killed in the stampede, this being the only film in which the father and son appeared). Carey is a cattle buyer and who purchases the entire herd, making a check out to Wayne, as per Clift's instruction. Carey learns about Clift's problem with Wayne, offering to talk to Wayne on his behalf, but Clift tells him that "I will only have to talk to him after that." That night, Clift enters his hotel room to find Dru waiting for him. She tells him that she tried to argue Wayne into not taking any revenge against Clift, but failed and that Wayne is camped outside of Abilene and will arrive the next morning. Clift accepts his fate as he embraces Dru. The next morning, Clift steps from the hotel where his cowboys are gathered, all loyally protective of him as they await the arrival of Wayne and his gunmen.

Beery, who has been watching for Wayne atop his horse inside the milling herd of cattle outside of town, sees Wayne and his men approaching on horseback and rides hooting through the herd to meet with Ireland, who is waiting for Wayne and inserting cartridges into his six-gun. Beery tells Ireland that Wayne is approaching and that "he has plenty with him, ten or twelve." Beery then rides on to meet with Clift and the other cowboys, telling them the same thing. Clift and his men then walk stoically forward to meet Wayne and his gunmen. Wayne rides forward with his gunslingers, moving slowly through the dense herd of cattle. Wayne stops and, while his gunmen remain behind, dismounts and begins walking through the herd, grim-faced, his hand close to his holstered six-gun. He passes Ireland, who calls out his name, but Wayne ignores him. Ireland shouts: "Mr. Dunson—I'll say it just one more time!" Wayne wheels about and fires off a shot that wounds and downs Ireland, whose return fire wounds Wayne in the side, but does not stop his resolute march forward until he confronts Clift. Wayne stands before his prey, ordering Clift to draw his gun, but Clift does nothing. Wayne shouts: "Then, I'll make you!" He fires a shot at Clift's feet. He then fires another that shoots off his hat, then another that nicks Clift's cheek, but Clift gives him back only a grim smile. Wayne marches up to Clift, saying: "You're soft! Won't anything make a man out of you? You once told me to never take your gun away from you." Wayne takes Clift's gun from its holster and throws it away while Clift stands motionless. "You yellow-bellied, chicken-livered…" Wayne snarls as he smashes his fist into Clift's jaw, knocking him down. He picks Clift up before knocking him down again and again. Then Clift rises from the dust and hits Wayne with a powerful blow, knocking Wayne down and surprising him. Brennan is delighted to see Clift fight back, saying: "For fourteen years I've been scared, but it's going to be all right!" Now it is Wayne's turn to take punishment as Clift hammers him with a barrage of powerful blows, knocking him down again and again, and then driving him into the side of a wagon with a running head thrust until they both collapse as baggage tumbles on top of them. Before they can resume their Homeric fight, Dru leaps forward, grabbing a gun from Worden, one of the cowboys, and fires a shot between the two disheveled and bruised men, shouting: "Stop it! I'm mad, good and mad, and who wouldn't be? You Dunson—pretending that you were going to kill him….It's the last thing in the world….Stay still!" She fires another shot. "And you, Matthew Garth, getting your face all beat up and all bloody! You should see how silly you look, like something the cat dragged in….Anybody with half a mind would know that you two love each other." Dru looks at Wayne, saying: "It took somebody else to shoot you [Ireland]. He wouldn't do it….Are you hurt?" Wayne points to his side, saying that Ireland's shot "only nicked the fat." Dru, beside herself, adds: "I changed my mind. Go ahead, beat each other crazy. Maybe it will put some sense in both of you!" She throws the gun back to Worden. Wayne looks in amazement at Dru and then at Clift, saying: "You better marry that girl, Matt." Clift smiles and nods and says: "Yeah, I think I'd…" He turns to his adopted father and replies: "When are you going to stop telling people what to do?" Wayne smiles and says: "Right now…as soon as I tell you one more thing…When we get back to the ranch I want you to change the brand. It'll be like this…" He draws a squiggly line in the dust to represent the Red River, along with the letter "D" representing his name, and then adds the letter "M" standing for Clift's name. "You don't mind that, do you?" Wayne asks. "No," replies Clift. The camera focuses upon that new, proud brand and Wayne says in voiceover: "You've earned it." Hawks directs this great western saga with enormous vitality and gusto, profiling the cattle drive as a frontier achievement of magnitude, and Harlan's gritty black-and-white photography captures in absorbing detail the sweeping motion of the cowboys and the prized possessions of their future, the cattle. Hawks uses every visual technique, panning, tracking and overhead shots, to heighten the drama of this tale. He films the giant herd as if it were an army on the move, its ranks spreading across plains, pouring over embankments and swimming across rivers in its relentless march toward its objective—

the railroad—while its supervising cowboys, from point to drag, herd them along. The performances from Wayne, Clift, Brennan, Ireland and the rest of the cast are superlative in essaying the hardscrabble and un-compromising men they characterize. Wayne's riveting performance as the ruthless ramrod so startled director John Ford, who directed Wayne in many films, that Ford told Hawks: "I didn't know the big s.o.b. could act!" Gifted composer Tiomkin enhances every scene with one of the finest scores ever composed for a western. The film received only two Oscar nominations for Best Story (Chase) and Best Film Editing (Nyby), but this was in a day when westerns seldom commanded Academy Award attention. The film was nevertheless an enormous box office suc-cess, grossing $4,150,000, the third largest box office return in the U.S. for the year 1948, exceeded only by **Easter Parade**, 1948 ($4.2 million), and **The Road to Rio**, 1948 ($4.5 million), against a $2.7 million budget; the film would add in rereleases another $5 million. The story was aired on Lux Radio Theater in a sixty-minute adaptation on March 7, 1949, where Wayne, Brennan and Dru reprised their roles. Songs: "Settle Down" (1947; Dimitri Tiomkin), "Bury Me Not on the Lone Prairie" (traditional). ***Author's Note***: In the original story written by Chase, and which ran in the *Saturday Evening Post*, the character played by Wayne is mortally shot at the end, his body taken back to Texas so that it can be interred at his ranch. Hawks told this author that "we changed that ending because I did not want to see either of the two main characters die at the end of the picture—they were just too damned good to be killed off." Wayne told this author that "I had to die in a lot of my pictures, but Howard [Hawks] told me that 'I am not going to bump you off in this picture, Duke, so that you live to tell the tale.' It was a wise decision because it showed how my character makes up for all of his abuse by bonding with Clift's character at the end, and it also makes Clift look better, too, by not gunning me down as in the original story." This production marked Clift's film debut, although he appeared in **The Search**, 1948, which was made later and released in the same year **Red River** was released, this film having been put on hold for some time be-cause of a legal battle. Although the chemistry between Wayne, Brennan and Clift worked well on screen, the three actors did not get along with each other, or, specifically, Wayne and Brennan, who were politically conservative, and Clift, who was a progressive liberal, held strong di-vergent political views. Hawks told this author: "They agreed not to talk about politics when we were making that picture. I made sure of that by telling them to keep those opinions to themselves. Duke [Wayne] and Walter [Brennan] did not like Monty [Clift] for other reasons, mostly because Monty was a method actor from the East and they thought he was also a little too light on his feet [Clift's known homosexuality]. They also did not like Monty's use of drugs and neither did I, but as long as he did his job before the cameras, I was satisfied with him and his work. The job of a director is to make a good film, not play nursemaid to a bunch of actors. I did have a few problems with Walter and John Ire-land." Hawks' problem with Brennan came when he told the fifty-two-year-old actor (at the beginning of shooting in 1946) that he had to remove his teeth and mostly gum his words throughout the film to con-tinue the running gag with Chief Yowlatchie, who has won his false teeth in a poker game. "I did not want to do that and told Howard [Hawks] that if I removed my false teeth, I would not be understood when I spoke, but he told me that that would only add more personality to my character and get me some laughs and he said he needed all the laughs he could get in a western where the real star was the herd of cows we are trying to get to market. Well, I owed Howard a lot. He was the director of **Come and Get It** [1936], along with William Wyler, and I got an Oscar as Best Supporting Actor for that picture, and I got another Oscar nomination in the same category for **Sergeant York** [1941], which Howard also directed. So I agreed to go along with him and took out my false teeth and mumbled my way through **Red River**, spitting and slobbering all over the place and I even sent some spit into Joanne Dru's eye in one scene and apologized, but I told her that it was Howard's fault. In one scene where Chief Yowlatchie is supposed to

John Wayne and Montgomery Clift in *Red River,* 1948.

give me back my teeth to eat, I could not find my own choppers and, before we shot that scene, that old Indian actor took out his own false teeth and handed them to me, spit and all and said: 'Here, use mine.' He was a funny old guy and we got a lot of laughs from his stone-faced de-liveries. I handed him back his own teeth and found my own for that scene." The problem Hawks had with Ireland was over personal matters and it had to do with the sultry Dru. Ireland was enamored of the actress and made advances to her whenever the cameras stopped rolling, all of this irritating Hawks, who had designs on the actress himself, even though he was then married. When Ireland appeared to be making ro-mantic headway with Dru, Hawks took revenge by cutting Ireland's role down to the bare minimum, deleting some of his scenes and treating Ire-land as an unwanted talisman. "Hawks acted like a jerk on that picture," Ireland told this author. "He complained that I was drinking all the time and even smoked pot with Monty, which I did not do, although Monty was always sucking on a joint when we made that picture. Hawks said I was unprepared when I did my scenes in that picture and he cut my part down, but that was just an excuse, because the problem between us was personal and had nothing to do with the picture." Hawks, who had never before directed a western, originally asked Gary Cooper to star in **Red River**. Cooper had starred in Hawks' great WWI film, **Sergeant York**, and for which Cooper won an Oscar as Best Actor. Cooper, how-ever, after reading the script, said that the character of the savage Dun-son was not the kind of person he wanted to enact. Wayne had no such reservations. Clift, on the other hand, was Hawks, first choice in playing the part of the rebellious adopted son. The director had seen Clift on Broadway when he appeared in *The Searching Wind* by Lillian Hellman, and he signed him for the part (Clift would receive $60,000 for his por-trayal). Clift had some deep apprehensions about his role in **Red River**, a film he never liked, even though he told Hawks that he knew how to ride horses. Clift had learned how to ride horses while attending a mil-itary school in Germany where he and his parents were once vacation-ing, but riding western style was another matter. Early during the production, Clift got help from seasoned horse riders Noah Beery Jr. and Hank Worden. "Noah and I taught Monty how to sit in the saddle like a cowpoke," Worden told this author, "and how to use his spurs to guide his horse and how to mount a horse. I don't think, until then, he knew one stirrup from another. He was a nice young fellow, but I had to tell him that I did not smoke his brand when he offered me a marijuana cigarette. I told him that I would take a shot of booze if he had one handy but that was it. He didn't spend much time with the other actors and I don't think he liked Duke [Wayne] much because Duke towered over him like a big oak tree and I think that made Monty feel insecure." Wayne stood six-foot-four-inches; Clift stood five-feet-ten-inches. Hawks took advantage of Clift's insecurity with Wayne by telling him

Montgomery Clift and John Wayne in *Red River*, 1948.

to think about his role as that of "David against Goliath." When Clift told Hawks that he should be as firm as Wayne in the scene where Wayne threatens to hang Fix and White, Hawks countermanded him, saying: "No, that won't work. Don't try to get hard because that will mean nothing compared to Wayne." He told Clift to underplay Wayne by simply taking a cup of coffee and looking him over and this worked so well in that scene that Wayne later went to Hawks and told the director that "any doubts I had about that fellow are gone. He's going to be okay." Hawks did the same thing in reverse when Clift leaves Wayne wounded and alone on the prairie after taking his herd. Wayne, following Hawks' direction, turns away from Clift when he tells him he is going to kill him, a move that so startled Clift that he stood stunned and uncertain, staring at Wayne, the kind of reaction Hawks wanted. "I left him [Clift] standing there dumbfounded just as long as I wanted," Hawks said. "Then I said: 'Get the hell out of there, Monty!' He turned and walked away. I knew my voice could be edited out later." Clift later went to Hawks and said: "My big scene [with Wayne] didn't amount to much, did it? I didn't have a chance...He [Wayne] was just marvelous." Wayne, who received $150,000 and 10 percent of the profits from this film, thought his appearance in **Red River** would be his swansong, figuring that his career was almost at an end and that he might be washed up in films. "I really felt that my role in that picture was that of a character actor, not the lead, which went to Monty, and no one was more surprised than me when the public opened its arms and gave me a great big hug for doing that picture. Looking back on **Red River**, I think it is a greater picture than what I thought it was when we made it. So many fine scenes, but that's all due to Howard [Hawks], one of the finest directors in the world. He is the kind of director who sits on a scene like a mother hen until he hatches it as a good one and then goes on to hatch another one. He once told me that if you can make a great scene in one picture, you have a good picture, and if you have more than one great scene in a picture you have a great picture. Well, **Red River** has so many great scenes in it that it is one of the greatest pictures ever made, and that is all due to Howard." Much of it was also due to Wayne, who gave Hawks a lot of advice when making the film, especially urging the director to employ as many seasoned cowboy actors as he could and Hawks agreed, doubling the number of cowboys originally slated for the film, more than seventy, which, along with Hawks' decision to make an epic western, almost doubled his original budget of $1.5 million. "Noah [Beery], Hal [Taliaferro] and I were only a few of the fellows Mr. Hawks put into **Red River** at Duke's suggestion," Worden told this author. "Duke was always wonderful to all of us, getting us jobs in all of his westerns whenever he could, especially whenever he was in a picture directed by the great John Ford." (Worden is especially endeared to this author as he was the first person to buy my 29-volume work, *The*

Motion Picture Guide, when it was first advertised in a prepublication offer.) Hawks spent a great deal of time and expenses scouting the locales for **Red River**, including Texas, Oklahoma, Arizona, New Mexico and northern Mexico. The locale of Wayne's huge ranch was based upon the sprawling King ranch in Texas by Chase in his original story (the largest ranch in the U.S.). Hawks shot on location near Elgin, Texas, in the southern portion of the state, which offered a 5,000-foot plateau, and in and around the Whetstone Mountains in southeastern Arizona, which offered the broad landscapes and magnificent mountain ranges shown in the film. The crossing of the Red River really involved almost 10,000 head of cattle that were driven across the San Pedro River and where, in many scenes, more than 25,000 gallons of water were used to settle the enormous clouds of dust kicked up by the cattle to allow shooting, all of this adding more than $1 million to Hawks' original budget. More than 500 actors and crew members were involved in the prolonged on-location shootings, providing an ongoing nightmare for wardrobe personnel since tears and rips and daily abuse of costumes were routine and repairs always in widespread demand. The costuming cost a small fortune, each cowboy actor having two pairs of boots at a cost of $150 per pair. More than $150,000 went into the expense for the costuming of all of the actors, Dru's own wardrobe soaring more than $20,000 (and where she later complained that "those long dresses with boned bodices were miserable" to wear). "Howard [Hawks] was a general in that picture," Wayne told this author. "He had a half dozen assistant directors who were positioned at all points of the moving herd and he talked with them over walkie-talkies he got from army surplus, so he could coordinate with them all the movements of the herd and the direction he wanted the cattle to take. Howard drove himself and all of us as much as I drove my cowboys in that picture. We were all worn out in the first few weeks and we had a long way to go. The weather turned rotten and a lot of us got sick, including me." Wayne was bedridden for days with a virulent cold and Dru came down with influenza. The indefatigable Hawks was slowed down after he was bitten by a centipede. "They took him to a hospital where they had to slowly drain off the poison," Brennan told this author, "but even then Howard was giving the doctors instructions on how to hurry up to save his life so he could get back to making that picture. We all went a little crazy when making **Red River**. I must have swallowed about five pounds of dust and was coughing it up for months after we finished." When Hawks finally did finish, his masterpiece western was almost stillborn in that he was prevented from releasing it by movie mogul Howard Hughes. A lawsuit held up release while Hughes argued that the end of **Red River** had been directly plagiarized from his own western film, **The Outlaw**, 1943. Hawks was in despair, realizing that Hughes had all the money in the world to keep **Red River** in the can forever and that he could make no personal appeal to Hughes as they were then on shaky social ground. Wayne came to the rescue. "I told Howard [Hawks] that I would talk to Hughes and when I went to Hughes I told him that, sure, there were some scenes in **Red River** that were like some of those in the Hughes picture. I pointed out that those similarities could be found in dozens of other western pictures. Hughes shrugged and said he would drop the lawsuit and that was the end of it and **Red River** was released a short time later. I knew that Hughes liked me because I always talked to him in plain-speaking terms, and that was not the way they talked in Hollywood where everybody is trying to confuse and mislead everybody else to get them to do what they want. Hughes hated that Hollywood crap and that is why he did me and Howard [Hawks] the favor of dropping that suit. The rest, as they say, is history." The history of **Red River**, or the memory of it, recalls a particular personal experience of this author. Many years ago while traveling on a luxury train heading for San Francisco, that train was briefly halted in cattle country by a small avalanche of snow and, while waiting for the tracks to be cleared, I stood between cars and where the conductor opened the doors. From that perch, I saw a cowboy, his chaps so weathered that they looked like burnt parchment. His jacket was several times patched, his hat ragged like everything he wore. Upon his hands were old leather gloves so thin that some of his fingers protruded. This seasoned cowboy was then struggling to free a calf that had gotten ensnared by a barbed wired fence that bordered the railroad tracks. He pried the barbs from the bloody flesh of the struggling calf one by one and where, without a sign or sound of complaint from him, his fingers bled, his own gore fusing with that of his ward, that calf, in his exhausting chore. He freed the calf, which ambled up a small hill, leaving a deep furrow in the snow. The cowboy rested a while at the fence line, looking at the train and directly at me. I stood wearing a three-piece suit and highly polished shoes. We were total opposites from different worlds. "Don't you ever get tired of your kind of work, cowboy?" I called out to him. He shook his head emphatically and replied: "Mister, wherever you are going on that nice warm train, I don't think it will ever finally take you to a place like this, to God's country where everything is beautiful night and day. How could you ever get tired of working in a place like this?" Then he said with telling words, but with a sympathetic tone: "*I'm the free man, mister, not you.* I'm sorry for you, mister, really sorry." His poignant words harkened to the dreams of my boyhood, the truth of those words making everything modern and sophisticated as hollow as a dead birch tree. I knew in that moment that this man possessed the kind of full and meaningful life that so sadly evades most of us. Feeling a bittersweet nostalgia for a life I had never lived, I watched with a strange and nagging envy while that cowboy led his horse on foot as they waded together through snow before disappearing over a small rise. Whenever I think of that truly heroic man and that is often when wanting to recall any real value in life, I think also of the film **Red River** and its rough-hewn, intrepid characters that cowboy so dramatically symbolized. Men like that never die. They are always there, alive, somewhere in the West, or within the frames of such great films as **Red River**. **p&d**, Howard Hawks; **cast**, John Wayne, Montgomery Clift, Joanne Dru, Walter Brennan, Colleen Gray, Harry Carey, Sr., John Ireland, Noah Beery, Jr., Harry Carey, Jr., Chief Yowlatchie, Paul Fix, Hank Worden, Mickey Kuhn, Hal Taliaferro, Tom Tyler, Paul Fiero, Glenn Strange, Davison Clark, William Self, Dan White, Harry Cording, Chief Sky Eagle, Shelley Winters, Richard Farnsworth; **w**, Borden Chase, Charles Schnee (based on the novel *The Chisholm Trail* by Chase); **c**, Russell Harlan; **m**, Dimitri Tiomkin; **ed**, Christian Nyby; **art d**, John Datu Arensma; **spec eff**, Donald Steward, Allan Thompson.

The Red Shoes ★★★★ 1948; U.K.; 133m; The Archers/Eagle-Lion Films; Color; Drama/Fantasy; Children: Cautionary; **BD**; **DVD**; **VHS**. Undoubtedly the preeminent ballet film, this marvelous production presents an intriguing backstage romance tied to the slippers of a ravishing ballerina and the brilliant Svengali, who mercilessly shapes her spectacular dancing career. Walbrook is an uncompromising ballet impresario, who sees great promise in novice ballerina Shearer. (He is not unlike the draconian Serge Diaghilev, 1872-1929, who ruled the Ballet Russe with an iron hand and who molded the dancing career of the peerless Russian ballerina, Anna Pavlova, 1881-1931, the role model for Shearer.) Walbrook's company has recently seen a great success after the performance of "Heart of Fire," a ballet authored by Trevor, and the impresario celebrates by attending a party where he meets fledgling dancer Shearer. She so impresses him with her fever to become a ballerina that he arranges an audition for her. Then Walbrook receives a letter from Goring, a young composer, the missive explaining that Trevor, who is Goring's teacher, stole his composition, "Heart of Fire." To prove this claim, Goring plays for Walbrook, who realizes that the novice composer is correct, and gives him a relatively unimportant position with his company. He then attends Shearer's audition and sees that the beautiful, young dancer has much to learn, but that she possesses a natural talent and gives her a job with his company. He soon decides to reward Goring by allowing him to arrange all the music for an ongoing production. The company is thrown into turmoil, however, when Walbrook's lead ballerina, Tcherina, quits the company, telling Walbrook that she is getting married and would rather be a wife than a prima ballerina, a de-

Robert Helpmann, Moira Shearer and Leonide Massine in *The Red Shoes*, 1948.

cision Walbrook cannot understand. He decides to mount a new production based on Hans Christian Andersen's story, "The Red Shoes," and assigns the gifted Goring to write the ballet. Shearer, meanwhile, has proven to be an astonishingly accomplished dancer, and Walbrook decides to take a chance and casts her as the leading ballerina in Goring's new ballet. (The original Andersen story is a grim tale, one where a dancer dons a pair of red shoes that control her feet and dances the girl to the point of total exhaustion and where her life is only saved when an executioner chops off her feet. Those feet and shoes go on crazily dancing while the girl's feet are replaced with wooden replicas and where she must hobble miserably throughout the rest of her life.) Shearer, who secretly loves Walbrook, throws herself completely into the new production, working closely with Goring. They are both stubborn geniuses, who are often at odds about the nuances of the ballet and, while they argue, they also draw closer together, falling in love. A magnificent ballet is then produced (shown as an awe-inspiring twenty-minute segment, replete with resplendent sets and where Shearer's flaming red hair is offset by a white and blue costume, the ensemble accompanying her marvelous dancing equal to anything ever choreographed by Busby Berkeley). The production meets with universal approval from critics and audiences alike, and Walbook is so elated that he offers Shearer the next leading part in his new production. When he learns, however, that Shearer and Goring are in love, Walbrook's mood darkens to seething anger as they have violated one of his cardinal rules. That rule is that any romances between his performers and artists are strictly prohibited as such emotional relationships only serve to disrupt his strict control of his company and might interfere with the total commitment to art that he demands. The reclusive and self-sustaining Walbrook looks upon such emotional commitments as human weaknesses that detract if not destroy the needed dedication to the ballet. He turns on the two persons he has selected to head his company, severely and unjustly criticizing Goring's new composition, which is in sharp contrast to all others who think that score is brilliant. Goring tenders his resignation, and Shearer, loyal to him, also resigns. They leave the company and marry. Walbrook shows indifference to their departure, saying that Shearer will never be able to reach the top of her dancing profession without his guidance. Goring then writes another composition that is to be performed at Covent Garden. Shearer, meanwhile, returns to Paris and meets Walbrook, who asks if she will perform one more performance of "The Red Shoes," which is booked at Monaco. Since Shearer has not been able to find work because of the strict contract she earlier signed with Walbrook, she accepts the assignment. On the night she is to perform "The Red Shoes" in Monaco, Goring suddenly appears in her dressing room, telling her that he has left another person to conduct his new composition in London to be at her side and to tell her that she

Richard Widmark in *Red Skies of Montana*, 1952.

is making a mistake by performing that night. Walbrook then enters the dressing room, and he and Goring get into a shouting match. Shearer, it seems, is determined to go ahead with the performance as she finishes dressing and puts on the red shoes, but the shoes have compelled her to this action and they now, like those in the Andersen story, take on a life of their own. The shoes hurry Shearer from the dressing room, but not to the stage. She, instead, despite her struggle to do otherwise, goes outside the theater and scurries to a high balcony overlooking some railroad tracks. She belongs to the phenomenon of the shoes now, and, unable to resist their controlling action, leaps from the balcony and onto the tracks, just as the speeding Nice Express is racing toward her and which strikes her. Goring finds her and removes the shoes, but it is too late. Shearer dies in his arms. Walbrook refuses to cancel the production and the curtain opens with only a spotlight where Shearer was to have danced and that spotlight moves to the music of Goring's ballet as if Shearer were performing on that empty stage to end this stunning film of dazzling pirouettes and entrechats. This great tale so well directed by Powell and Pressburger presents ballet as a surrealistic portrait of that high creative art instead of the more realistic viewpoint shown in **The Turning Point**, 1977; Walbrook, Shearer, Goring and the rest of the cast give superlative performances. The obsessive personas of the principal players are decidedly self-destructive in that their fanatical love for art battles their indomitable love for one another, these passions in mortal combat with each other. Their collective journey to triumph and tragedy is preordained by a third and equally uncontrollable passion, ambition, represented by those red shoes that determine their disastrous destiny. Melodramatic and even affected in spots, this powerful film nevertheless offers a uniquely mythical image of ballet that has seen no equal. It won an Oscar for Best Dramatic or Comedy Score (Easdale), and Best Art Direction, Color (Heckroth); and Set Decoration (Lawson), and received Oscar nominations as Best Picture, Best Story (Pressburger) and Best Film Editing (Mills). The film was a great success at the box office, first in the U.S., taking in more than $5 million against a budget of £500,000. The story was adapted as a Broadway musical in 1993, but saw only five performances. Songs: "The Ballet of the Red Shoes," "Bougainvillia" (Brian Easdale), "Aria" (unknown composer), "Swan Lake" (Peter Ilyich Tchaikovsky), "La Boutique Fantasque" (Ottorino Respighi; based on the music of Gioachino Rossini), "Les Sylphides" (Franz Liszt), "Giselle" (Adolphe Adam), "Danse de la poupee" (from "Coppelia" by Leo Delibes). *Author's Note*: The history of this film began many years earlier with film producer Alexander Korda, who hired Pressburger to write the story for his actress-wife Merle Oberon, who was to act the role of the ballerina, but where a double would do all of her dancing. The project remained on the shelf for some time, and, after Pressburger joined with Powell, he purchased the rights to the story from

Korda and he and Powell went to work developing the production. Pressburger rewrote many scenes expressly for Shearer, a Sadler's Wells ballerina, who proved that her acting ability equaled her dancing mastery, as did that of Tcherina, Massine and Helpmann, who brilliantly choreographed the "Red Shoes" sequence. Many on-location shots were taken in London, Paris and Monaco, adding an international flavor to the production. When this film opened in England, it met with lukewarm reception by audiences and the producer-directors were urged to change the tragic ending to a happy one, but they adamantly refused to alter that finale. They glumly looked forward to an artistic failure, but, when the film was released in the U.S., American audiences flocked to see it and the same public response was seen in many other countries until, to the surprise and edification of Powell and Pressburger, the film made millions. American actor-dancer Gene Kelly considered **The Red Shoes** a classic, and it inspired him to include his own marvelous ballet sequence when he made **An American in Paris**, 1951. Kelly told this author that "Vincent Minnelli [the director of **An American in Paris**] and I had a hard time convincing anyone at MGM to allow us to include that ballet sequence until we persuaded some front office executives to watch **The Red Shoes**. They were so impressed with that great picture that they gave us the green light to include the ballet, which is the centerpiece of our picture." The rich hues shown in **The Red Shoes** are the result of the producers using the old, expensive Technicolor process, which employed the use of vegetable dyes. **p&d**, Michael Powell, Emeric Pressburger; **cast**, Anton Walbrook, Moira Shearer, Marius Goring, Leonide Massine, Ludmilla Tcherina, Robert Helpmann, Albert Basserman; Austin Trevor, Esmond Knight, Irene Browne, Jean Short, Gordon Littmann, Julia Lang, **w**, Powell, Pressburger, Keith Winter (based on the fairy tale by Hans Christian Andersen); **c**, Jack Cardiff (Technicolor); **m**, Brian Easdale; **ed**, Reginald Mills; **prod d**, Hein Heckroth; **art d**, Arthur Lawson; **spec eff**, W. Percy Day, Peter Ellenshaw, F. George Gunn, E. Hague, Les Bowie.

Red Skies of Montana ★★★ 1952; 89m.; FOX; Color; Drama/Adventure; Children: Cautionary; **DVD**; **VHS**. Action-packed adventure tale sees a squad of firefighters from the U.S. Forest Services being flown into the mountains of Montana to fight a large forest fire. They put out the blaze under the leadership of Widmark, but several firefighters are killed. Hunter, son of one of those who died in the fire, thinks his father died because Widmark acted cowardly while fighting the blaze and sets out to prove it. Hunter joins Widmark and his crew in fighting another fire and Widmark saves his life, Hunter concluding that Widmark is not a coward but in fact a hero. *Author's Note*: Widmark told this author that "we had to learn from the Forestry people how to combat fires when we did that picture and some of us got properly singed in some of those scenes when we forgot what we had learned. I don't know how those firefighters can go day and night in battling those fires and still keep their sanity. They are the bravest of the brave." The story for this film was based upon the devastating fire that roared through Mann Gulch along the Upper Missouri River in the Gates of the Mountains Wilderness in Montana's Helena National Forest in August 1949. Of the fifteen firefighters who parachuted into the area to fight the fire, thirteen were killed. Crew Chief Robert Wagner Dodge (the role model for Widmark's character in this film), who had been separated from his men, survived the fire, along with two others. Dodge was later accused of deserting his men, but a thorough investigation proved him innocent. **p**, Samuel G. Engel; **d**, Joseph M. Newman; **cast**, Richard Widmark, Jeffrey Hunter, Constance Smith, Richard Boone, Warren Stevens, Joe Sawyer, James Griffith, Robert Adler, Richard Crenna, John Close; **w**, Harry Kleiner (based on a story by Art Cohn from the novel by George R. Stewart); **c**, Charles G. Clarke (Technicolor); **m**, Sol Kaplan; **ed**. William Reynolds; **art d**, Lyle Wheeler; **set d**, Thomas Little, Bruce MacDonald; **spec eff**, Fred Sersen.

The Red Tent ★★★ 1971; USSR/Italy; 121m; Mosfilm/PAR; Color;

Adventure/Fantasy; Children: Unacceptable; **DVD**; **VHS**. Absorbing adventure deals with early exploration by air of Antarctica. Finch is the commander of a failed 1928 airship expedition in Antarctica, who remembers events of the ill-fated *Italia* dirigible flight, its crash, and subsequent rescue efforts. The "ghosts" of those involved come to his memories to help him determine any guilt on his part in the affair. Connery plays Norwegian polar region explorer Roald Amundsen (1872-1928), who dies in attempts to rescue the survivors. The story is based on true events and is well directed and acted. (In Russian; English subtitles.) **p**, Franco Cristaldi; **d**, Mickail K. Kalatozov; **cast**, Sean Connery, Claudia Cardinale, Hardy Kruger, Peter Finch, Massimo Girotti, Luigi Vannucchi, Mario Adorf, Eduard Martsevich, Grigori Gaj, Nikolai Ivanov; **w**, Ennio De Concini, Richard DeLong Adams; **c**, Leonid Kalashnikov (Technicolor); **m**, Ennio Morricone; **ed**, Peter Zinner, John Shirley; **prod d**, Mikhail Fishgojt; **art d**, Giancarlo Bartolini Salimbeni, David Vinitsky; **set d**, Franco D'Andria, Yuri Ekonomtsev.

The Red Violin ★★★ 1999; Canada/Italy/U.S./ U.K./Austria; 130m; Color; Drama; Children: Unacceptable (MPAA: R); **DVD**. Fascinating episodic film centers on a famous Nicolo Bussotti violin that is being auctioned off in present-day Montreal. During the auction the film has flashbacks and flashforwards to chronicle the history of the violin, first at its creation in 17th-century Italy, then in an 18th-century Austrian monastery, then when owned by a violinist in 19th-century Oxford, and then in China during that country's cultural revolution. The violin finally reaches Montreal where a collector attempts to establish its identity and its secrets. Exciting and well acted, the film is enhanced by beautiful violin music performed by Joshua Bell. Sexuality prohibits viewing by children. **p**, Niv Fichman, Daniel Iron, Giannandrea Pecorelli; **d**, Francois Girard; **cast**, Carlo Cecchi, Jason Flemhng, Greta Scacchi, Irene Grazioli, Anita Laurenzi, Jean-Luc Bideau, Christoph Koncz, Clotilde Mollet, Dimitri Andreas, Sylvia Chang, Zifeng Liu; **w**, Girard, Don McKellar; **c**, Alain Dostie; **m**, John Corigliano; **ed**, Gaetan Huot; **prod d**, Francois Seguin; **art d**, Martyn John; **set d**, Judy Farr.

Reds ★★★★ 1981; U.S.; 195m; Barclays/PAR; Color; Biographical Drama; Children: Unacceptable (MPAA: R); **DVD**; **VHS**. Though disjointed and somewhat confusing, this riveting, episodic biopic nevertheless tells a great story. Through a series of documentary-type interviews with those who knew them, the film captures and dynamically relates the tempestuous love affair and political machinations of two fascinating Americans, writer and socialist John Reed (John Silas "Jack" Reed; 1887-1920), essayed by Beatty, and Marxist-anarchist journalist Louise Bryant (1885-1936), played by Keaon. Their colorful lives and careers were enmeshed with the lives of many leading personalities of their tumultuous era, including playwright Eugene O'Neill (1888-1953), played by Nicholson; anarchist Emma Goldman (1869-1940), portrayed by Stapleton; writer and socialist Max Eastman (1883-1969), essayed by Herrmann; novelist Floyd Dell (1887-1969), played by Wright; writer Jane Heap (1883-1964), portrayed by Duiguid; and union leader Big Bill Haywood (William Dudley Haywood; 1869-1928), essayed by Sweet. Intertwined in this romantic saga are the socialist upheavals occurring in the U.S. and in Russia before, during and after WWI (1914-1918). The film opens when Beatty makes a brief visit to Portland, Oregon, in 1915 and meets Keaton, quickly exciting her with his socialist-based political visions, which she passionately shares, and she falls in love with him. After Keaton interviews Beatty for a small magazine, he leaves to return to his journalistic life in New York's Greenwich Village. Keaton severs all ties with family, divorces her dentist husband and travels east to be with Beatty. There she meets the new literary lights of the day, Nicholson (O'Neill), Herrmann (Eastman), Wright (Dell), Stapleton (Goldman), and Duiguid (Heap), all either dedicated socialists or Marxists or even anarchists, who feed the flames of Keaton's burning radical political beliefs. When she tries to contribute her ideas, she is, however, largely ignored and she feels left out, an out-

Warren Beatty directing *Reds,* 1981, in which he also appears as American communist writer John Reed.

cast from the inner intellectual circle she so desperately wants to join. Thinking that she is being treated as a hanger-on or an attractive wannabe, Keaton decides to depart, but Beatty saves their relationship by taking her to Provincetown, where she better fits into a group of left-wing writers, who establish a small theater where their radical plays are produced. The real star of that operation is Nicholson (and where O'Neill's brilliant, natural plays soon draw attention and praise from critics and theatrical bigwigs who produced those plays on Broadway's legitimate stage). Beatty, meanwhile, is caught up in the war fever that grips America, which has yet to enter the conflict raging in Europe. He abruptly leaves for Chicago to participate in a new union movement, leaving Keaton behind, where she develops an affair with Nicholson. That affair is short-lived when Beatty returns and Keaton realizes that he is the only man for her. Realizing that he has almost lost the woman he loves, Beatty goes against his grain by marrying Keaton and they move into a small cottage. The couple argues after Beatty discovers a love note left for Keaton by Nicholson, and the relationship becomes so strained that Keaton takes a job as a foreign correspondent and departs for Europe to cover the war. Beatty, meanwhile, is hospitalized by a kidney ailment, and he is warned to slow down his hectic lifestyle, which he ignores. He travels to Europe and meets with Keaton, asking her to travel with him to Russia, which is erupting in revolution. They travel by train to St. Petersburg, now called Petrograd, but their relationship is now platonic in that Keaton insists that she establish her own literary reputation by not sharing any bylines with her now famous husband and further curtails his sexual relationship with her. They interview a number of the revolutionary leaders, including interim prime minister Alexander Kerensky (1881-1970), who is played by Oleg Kerensky, the real-life grandson of that beleaguered and well-intentioned leader, whose noble policies were undermined by the plotting Bolsheviks. Beatty and Keaton also talk with Bolsheviks Leon Trotsky (1879-1940), played by Richman, and Vladimir Lenin (1870-1924), who is essayed by Sloman. Beatty abandons his neutral position as a journalist, however, when attending a workers' rally, where he hears through an interpreter that American workers have failed to support the Bolshevik movement. He mounts the podium and, with an interpreter relating his comments to the assembled crowd, tells those assembled that American workers stand behind the revolution and all but promises that they will do the same thing in America, which brings tumultuous cheers from the Bolsheviks (even though Beatty knows that such a widespread political movement does not exist in the U.S.). Now that he has put his political beliefs where his mouth is, Beatty is committed fully to the Bolshevik cause and becomes a cause célèbre among the elitist Bolshevik circles, as well as inspiring Keaton to resume her sexual relationship with Beatty and which is where the first half of this saga concludes. The second half

Warren Beatty as John Reed in *Reds*, 1981.

begins with Beatty and Keaton returning to New York where, despite his notes on his experience in Russia being appropriated, he nevertheless writes his monumental work, *Ten Days That Shook the World*, which becomes an overnight bestseller and vaults Beatty to the foremost literary ranks. (Lenin read the book and pronounced it the definitive work of the Russian Revolution, demanding that it be translated into all languages.) Beatty, by this time, forsakes his writing and becomes totally involved in communist activities in the U.S., so committed to his political activities that he again ignores Keaton. She has come to believe that Beatty's ambitions for a communist state in America is nothing more than a pipe dream and that workers will never wholly embrace his ideologies. Beatty has turned from writing to politics and now becomes a political leader for radical communists. He forces a split of the Socialist Party and establishes his own faction, which designates him as a representative going to the new Soviet regime in Russia, seeking acknowledgment and recognition of his political organization from Lenin and other Bolshevik leaders. Returning to Russia at this time is a risky business as that country is now ravaged by a civil war between Bolsheviks and retaliating white Russian forces representing the old czarist regime. Further, the U.S. has restricted travel to the newly established USSR, an administration that is not recognized by the U.S. and most western powers. Keaton no longer shares Beatty's dream for a communist America and she is so disillusioned with what she now feels is his naïve political perspectives and ambitions that she tells him that she may not be waiting for him when and if he returns from Russia. Beatty is oblivious to all this as he is consumed by his political mission to Moscow, but promises Keaton he will return by Christmas. Keaton retreats into old friendships, particularly with Nicholson, who savagely vivisects her relationship with Beatty, whom he lambasts as a political stooge for the communists. Keaton has more problems when she discovers that federal agents are dogging her steps as they are searching for Beatty, who is considered a traitor in that he is now leading a crusade to violently overthrow the U.S. in the manner the czarist regime was destroyed through revolution. Beatty, too, is in trouble. When he arrives in Moscow, he finds the euphoric attitude of the Bolsheviks has faded with their revolution and a new grim political climate shrouds the country. Communist bureaucrats such as Grigory Zinoviev (1883-1936), who is played by Kosinski, prevent him from accomplishing his goals. Kosinski looks suspiciously upon Beatty as a novice communist and refuses to recognize his worker's party in the U.S. He further refuses to allow Beatty to leave Russia, believing that Beatty may impart unfavorable reports on the new and harsh Bolshevik regime to the western world. Beatty frantically seeks to escape and manages to reach the Finnish border, but he is arrested by the Finns and imprisoned where he is denied outside communication and given food and water so sparingly that he develops ty-

phus. Lenin, hearing of Beatty's plight, reportedly trades three Finnish teachers held in Bolshevik captivity for Beatty's release. Meanwhile, Keaton hears of her lover's dire situation and, with Nicholson's help, she travels to Finland only to discover that Beatty has gone back to Russia. The ill Beatty is barely surviving in Moscow when he meets Stapleton, who has been deported from the U.S. as an undesirable alien. (Emma Goldman, who is played by Stapleton, was deported along with Alexander Berkman, and 247 other communists and anarchists, their deportations in 1920 brought about by legal briefs provided by a youthful a staunch anti-communist attorney, J. Edgar Hoover of the Department of Justice, who would later head the FBI.) Stapleton derides the present communist regime to Beatty. She is disillusioned with its leaders and she likens the oppressive Bolsheviks with the earlier oppressions of the czar. (Goldman would later leave Russia and take up residence in Canada where she penned a scathing indictment of the Soviet regime titled *My Disillusionment with Red Russia*.) Beatty refuses to give up on Soviet philosophy and, ignoring Stapleton's warnings, goes to Kosinski and offers to help him spread communist propaganda. He and Kosinski travel by train to eastern Russia to spread the communist gospel to Arab nationalities, but Beatty becomes enraged when he learns that his written words have been changed to indict the U.S. While he and Kosinski are returning to Moscow, their train is attacked by White Russian forces, and the heavily armed communists (Reds) on the train then counterattack the Whites. Beatty, eager to take part in the action, is left behind. Weak with illness, he is placed on board the train, which continues its journey toward Moscow. Meanwhile, Keaton arrives in Moscow and learns from Stapleton just how sick Beatty is and she waits at the train station, not knowing if Beatty will arrive from the east dead or alive. When the train arrives, Keaton finds Beatty still alive, but he is dying. "Don't leave me," he whispers to her before he is rushed to a hospital where he breathes his last. (In reality, Reed and Bryant did not have that last meeting, albeit Bryant had received a communication from Reed that he would soon see her while he was returning from the eastern provinces.) Throughout this journey into violence and political upheaval, director Beatty offers many interjected cameo appearances from famous and obscure persons who knew Reed and Bryant, although he does not identify these persons in any of their segments (due to Beatty's fear that by having their names superimposed in their scenes would make his film appear to be too much of a documentary). The use of such interrupting scenes presents sometimes cogent and sometimes idiotic comments from these persons (especially from song-and-dance man George Jessel, who seems not to know where he is or who he is talking about while wearing a ridiculous self-styled uniform). This technique both enhances and detracts from the overall dramatization of this intriguing tale, which combines an intimate romance and a historical epic. As such this film is a brilliant experiment that, for the most part, is faithful to the facts if not the best rumors surrounding these legendary personalities. The acting is superlative, and the period sets and costuming are stunning to behold. Storaro's lensing is outstanding, and the musical score from Sondheim, which mixes the poignant tunes of the era, is both evocative and impressively applicable to that truly frightening era when half the world was in chaos. Beatty, who proves his mastery of films in this marvelous production, won an Oscar as Best Director. Stapleton won an Oscar as Best Supporting Actress (and who is much less dowdy and more animated than was the real Emma Goldman), and Storaro got an Oscar for Best Cinematography. The film received Oscar nominations for Best Picture, Best Actor (Beatty), Best Actress (Keaton), Best Supporting Actor (Nicholson), Best Original Screenplay (Beatty and Griffiths), Best Sound (Dick Vorisek, Tom Fleischman and Simon Kaye), and Best Art Direction (Sylbert and Holland). The film saw an initial box office return of more than $50 million against its enormous budget of $32 million or more. Songs: "You're a Grand Old Flag," "Over There," "Yankee Doodle Boy" (George M. Cohan); "Onward Christian Soldiers" (S. Baring-Gould, Arthur Sullivan); "Liebesfreud" (Fritz Kreisler); "Waiting for the Robert E. Lee" (Wolfe Gilbert, Louis

F. Muir); "America the Beautiful" (Katherine L. Bates, Samuel A. Wood); "I Don't Want to Play in Your Yard" (music: H. W. Petrie; lyrics: Philip Wingate); "Oh, You Beautiful Doll" (A.S. Brown, Nat D. Ayer); "St. Louis Tickle" (Barney & Seymour & Glen Snelgrove); "Rattlesnake Rag" (Louis F. Bush, Eddy Hanson); "Dill Pickles" (Al Bryan, Charles L. Johnson); "The Crazy Otto Rag" (Edward R. White, Maxwell A. Wolfson, Luigi Creatore); "Stop Your Ticklin' Me" (Jack Little, Walter Hirsch); "Cartoon Rag" (Michael Karp); "Just a Little Love Song" (Joseph Young, Samuel M. Lewis, Joe Cooper); "Country Club, Rag Time Two Step" (Scott Joplin); "The Internationale" (Pierre Degeyter, Eugene Pottier); Valse Bluette" (Leopold Auer); "The Red Army Is the Most Powerful of All" (traditional); "The Engine" (traditional). *Author's Note*: This was a pet project for Beatty, who envisioned making this film sometime in the 1960s. He began working on the story in 1976, spending more than four years researching Reed and developing the project and while writing the script with British playwright Griffiths. He thought the finished script too somber, so he hired comedy writer Elaine May to insert some funny moments and jokes into the screenplay, but some of these offhanded tidbits seem a bit too cutely modern for the tale, these offhanded asides apparently modeled for Keaton and seem more fitting for her role in the comedy **Annie Hall**, 1977, than for the more deadly serious Louise Bryant character of the Woodrow Wilson era. Throughout Beatty's memorable film there is the unmistakable visual influence of the great British director David Lean, as can be seen in Beatty's gloomy, cavernous interiors, the surging crowd scenes, and, particularly, his panoramic scenes of the train traveling to and from the eastern provinces, all closely reminiscent of Lean's classic romantic epic about Russia of the same period, **Dr. Zhivago**, 1965. Paramount provided enormous funding for this epic and became worried when more and more funding was needed to complete the film (a reported total of $45 million went into the production). The reason why this excellent film was poorly received by the public was due to the conservative tide that had swept the country, the film being released in the first year of the Ronald Reagan presidency. Many theaters showing **Reds** were picketed by conservative activists and, even though Beatty emphatically degrades and indicts the communist philosophy and its draconian regime in **Reds**, the film was thought to be Marxist propaganda, which it is not. It is essentially the story of a principled journalist, who lived and died according to his ideals and the woman who loved him and those ideals. Without question, this film is Beatty's finest work on film, one he never duplicated. Other actors and films profiling John Reed include **And Starring Pancho Villa as Himself**, 2003 (made-for-TV: Matt Day); **Red Bells Part I: Mexico on Fire**, 1982 (Franco Nero); **Reed, Mexico Insurgente**, 1974 (Claudio Obregon); and **V dni oktyabrya**, 1958 (A. Fyodorinov). p&d, Warren Beatty; cast, Beatty, Diane Keaton, Edward Herrmann, Jack Nicholson, Gene Hackman, Paul Sorvino, Maureen Stapleton, Jerzy Kosinski, Nicolas Coster, M. Emmet Walsh, Bessie Love, Max Wright, George Plimpton, Dolph Sweet, Nancy Duiguid, Stuart Richman, Oleg Kerensky, Roger Sloman; commentators: Henry Millier, George Jessel, Adela Rogers St. Johns, Dora Russell, Scott Nearing, Tess Davis, Hamilton Fish, Heaton Vorse, Will Durant, Rebecca West, George Seldes, Kenneth Chamberlain, Blanch Hays Fagen; w, Beatty, Trevor Griffiths; c, Vittorio Storaro (Technicolor); m, Stephen Sondheim; ed, Dede Allen, Craig McKay; prod d, Richard Sylbert; art d, Simon Holland; spec eff, Bob Dawson, Ian Wingrove, Doug Hubbard, Antonio Parra.

Reign of Terror ★★★ 1949; U.S.; 89m.; Walter Wanger/Eagle-Lion Films; B/W; Adventure/Horror; Children: Unacceptable. Basehart gives a riveting performance of lawyer-patriot Maximilian Robespierre (1758-1794), architect of the Reign of Terror during the French Revolution (1789-1799). He is desperately looking for his missing black book, a death list of those he has marked for the guillotine. If not found, it could mean his political downfall and likely death. Basehart meets with Cummings, thinking he is the ruthless prosecutor of Strasbourg, entrusting

Diane Keaton and Warren Beatty in *Reds*, 1981.

Cummings with the assignment of finding that black book within twenty-four hours and giving complete authority over everyone, except himself, of course. No one knows that book is missing except Basehart, Cummings and Moss, the latter being the dreaded head of the French secret police, Joseph Fouche (1759-1820). What these diabolical men do not know is that Cummings has killed that prosecutor and has taken his place, knowing that neither Basehart nor Moss have ever met that slain man. In his assignment to obtain the black book, Cummings meets with Dahl, who puts him on to Hart, who plays Paul Francois de Barras (1755-1829), Basehart's rival and one of the leaders of the revolutionary Directory. Hart, however, is arrested by Barker, who plays another revolutionary leader, Louis Antoine de Saint-Just (1767-1794), a staunch ally of Basehart's. Cummings then realizes that three of the homes once occupied by those suspected of stealing the black book have never been thoroughly searched and he concludes that the book has not been stolen and that Basehart is merely using that claim as a ruse to root out those opposed to his reign of terror. He goes to Basehart's dwelling and finds the book, but is interrupted by Moss. Both men struggle and Cummings escapes. He later learns that Dahl has been arrested, and knowing that he is in love with her, Moss tries to trade her for Basehart's incriminating book. Cummings refuses and, instead, releases the book at the Convention where all suspected traitors of France are tried and where the delegates inspect Basehart's death list as they pass the black book from hand to hand. Basehart then tries to indict Hart, but the delegates, many of their names appearing in Basehart's book, turn against him, branding him a traitor. Basehart attempts to save his life by giving an eloquent speech, but Moss silences his golden tongue by shooting him in the jaw. Basehart is then condemned and sent to the same guillotine where so many of his own victims have been decapitated. Hart is then set free. Cummings, by this time, has invaded the secret room where Dahl has been held captive, and he and she escape to seek happiness beyond the borders of unhappy France. At the finale of this exciting thriller, Moss meets a man at the Convention, and after he asks him his name, he replies that he is Napoleon Bonaparte (1769-1821), who is played by Strudwick. Moss promises Strudwick that he will remember his name (Fouche later became the head of the secret police under Napoleon I). *Author's Note*: Basehart told this author that "**Reign of Terror** was shot on a shoestring budget [about $770,000, and it did not return that investment at the box office, producing less than $700,000 in its initial release] and was made to look like a very costly production because Menzies [William Cameron Menzies] cannibalized a lot of sets from old movie musicals. They patched up hand-me-down costumes from other pictures about the French revolutionary period and all of us were walking around in costumes that promised to fall apart if we made the wrong moves. In one scene I stretched out an arm and the seam of my

Don Knotts (left) in *The Reluctant Astronaut*, 1967.

sleeve gave way and we had to have it sewn up and the scene reshot. A lot of thread held that picture together, but it looked and sounded pretty good when Anthony [Mann] finally got it into the can." **p**, William Cameron Menzies; **d**, Anthony Mann; **cast**, Robert Cummings, Richard Basehart, Arlene Dahl, Richard Hart, Arnold Moss, Jess Barker, Shepperd Strudwick, Norman Lloyd, Wade Crosby, Charles McGraw, Ellen Lowe; **w**, Philip Yordan, Aeneas MacKenzie (based on their story); **c**, John Alton; **m**, Sol Kaplan; **ed**, Fred Allen; **art d**, Edward Ilou, (not credited) William Cameron Menzies; **set d**, Armor Marlowe.

Relentless ★★★ 1948; U.S.; 91m.; Cavalier/COL; Color; Western; Children: Cautionary; **VHS**. Young gives an exceptional performance in this offbeat but absorbing oater. He as a man falsely accused of murder and is hounded by Parker, a sheriff, while searching for the real killer. Along the way, Young is befriended by Chapman, who owns a traveling covered wagon store, and they fall in love. Young finally tracks down the murderer, MacLane, finding him in the desert where the killer confesses, but only under the threat of being left to die in the hot sun. Good direction and acting contribute to an above-average western, where some stunning photography captures the western landscapes in rich color. *Author's Note*: Young told this author that "**Relentless** is an unusual western, a picture that offers really two good character studies. One is of a man pursued for a crime he did not commit and the other is the man pursuing him. Both of these men are searching for the truth until one of them catches up with the guilty man. George [Sherman] is known as an action director, but he is very good at showing scenes with very effective subtle touches that allow for that kind of character development." **p**, Eugene B. Rodney; **d**, George Sherman; **cast**, Robert Young, Marguerite Chapman, Willard Parker, Akim Tamiroff, Barton MacLane, Mike Mazurki, Robert Barrat, Clem Bevans, Will Wright; **w**, Winston Miller (based on the story "Three Were Thoroughbreds" by Kenneth Perkins); **c**, Edward Cronjaeger (Technicolor); **m**, Marlin Skiles; **ed**, Gene Havlick; **art d**, Stephen Goosson, Walter Holscher; **set d**, Wilbur Menefee, James Roach.

The Reluctant Astronaut ★★★ 1967; U.S.; 101m; UNIV; Color; Comedy; Children: Acceptable; **DVD**. The unforgettable Knotts provides a lot of hilarious moments in this clever comedy. He is a small-town operator of a carnival kiddie ride and is deathly afraid of heights. His domineering father, O'Connell, signs him up for a space program, and Knotts is terrified, until he arrives at NASA headquarters in Houston, Texas, and learns that his job is simply to be a janitor, not an astronaut. But O'Connell keeps telling everyone Knotts is, indeed, going to be an astronaut fearlessly exploring space. NASA officials decide to prove the worthiness of a new automated spacecraft, and Knotts is given

a chance to confront his fears. He does so well on the space mission that he becomes a hero and wins the heart of the fetching Freeman. There are some good sight gags and enough funny scenes to sustain interest throughout while providing many laughs. Comedic character actor White adds much to the mirth. Song: "Space Song" (music: Joseph Gershenson; lyrics: James Fritzell and Everett Greenbaum). *Author's Note*: Knotts told this author when recalling this film: "I am smart enough to get into the space program and graduate from idiot to nincompoop. But the question really is, how smart is NASA to hire a birdbrain like me?" **p&d**, Edward J. Montagne; **cast**, Don Knotts, Leslie Nielsen, Joan Freeman, Jesse White, Jeanette Nolan, Frank McGrath, Arthur O'Connell, Nydia Westman, Guy Raymond, Joan Shawlee; **w**, Jim Fritzell, Everett Greenbaum (based on an idea by Knotts); **c**, Rexford Wimpy (Technicolor); **m**, Vic Mizzy; **ed**, Sam E. Waxman; **art d**, Alexander Golitzen, William D. DeCinces; **set d**, John McCarthy, John Austin; **spec eff**, Albert Whitlock.

The Reluctant Dragon ★★★ 1941; U.S.; 72m; Disney/RKO; Color; Animation Fantasy/Live Action; Children: Acceptable; **DVD**; **VHS**. Humorist Benchley tours the Walt Disney Studios and learns about the animation process while hoping to influence Disney in the idea of making a cartoon about a shy dragon. He succeeds and the film is made about a gentle dragon that is reluctant to live up to its reputation as a ferocious beast. The animated fantasy portion of this film was later released as a short and was very successful. The live action scenes involving Benchley are fascinating to watch as he and viewers learn just how Disney artists work their technical magic, from storyboarding to superimposition of frame after frame of their wonderful black-and-white drawings that are then converted to brilliant colors to piece together their many celluloid masterpieces. In the process, we hear the inimitable voiceovers of many Disney characters, including Mickey Mouse and Donald Duck. Songs: "The Reluctant Dragon" (Charles Wolcott, T. Hee, Ed Penner); "Casey, Jr." (Frank Churchill). **p**, Walt Disney; **d**, Alfred L. Werker (cartoon sequences, Hamilton Luske, Jack Cutting, Ub Iwerks, Jack Kinney); **cast**, Robert Benchley, Frances Gifford, Buddy Pepper, Nana Bryant, Alan Ladd, Disney, Truman Woodworth, and voiceovers, Claud Allister, Barnett Parker, Billy Lee, Florence Gill, Clarence Nash; **w**, Ted Sears, Al Perkins, Larry Clemmons, Bill Cottrell, Harry Clork (based on a story by Kenneth Grahame, Erdman Penner, T. Hee, Joe Grant, Dick Heumer, John P. Miller); **c**, Winton Hoch, Bert Glennon; **m**, Frank Churchill, Larry Morey; **ed**, Paul Weatherwax; **art d**, Ken Anderson, Yale Gracey, Hugh Hennesy, Lance Nolley, Gordon Wiles; **set d**, Earl Woodin; **spec eff**, Iwerks, Joshua L. Meador.

The Remains of the Day ★★★★ 1993; U.K./U.S.; 134m; Merchant Ivory Productions/COL; Color; Drama; Children: Cautionary (MPAA: PG); **DVD**; **VHS**. Sedate and isolated to the perfunctory lifestyle of a proper head butler, this film nevertheless provides an utterly riveting performance from Hopkins. An equally compelling performance is seen from Thompson as the head housekeeper of a sprawling mansion called Darlington Hall and whose love for the kind and considerate Hopkins goes sadly unrequited. The story opens in the 1950s when Hopkins is now serving Reeve, an American politician who has purchased the estate where Hopkins has worked for so many years and where his former employer, Fox, has recently died. To improve the household service and because he still remembers Thompson with fondness, Hopkins goes to visit her to ask her to return to her position, one she left twenty years earlier. In flashback, we see Hopkins in those pre-WWII years efficiently catering to the needs of Fox and his family and where he demands from all the household workers their utmost in servicing his employer. He is a perfectionist, who will not tolerate any slacking or an undusted speck of dirt, although he is always civil when firmly giving orders to those beneath his station. Thompson, who is just as efficient, is nevertheless more outgoing and exhibits the kind of warmth and care that Hopkins purposely represses. Both clash on procedures and the manner in which employees are treated, but Hopkins refuses to become emotionally involved. He is a man of iron will who upholds the protocol of his lofty station as head butler. He does not display any great deal of emotion when his own father, Vaughan, who is also a butler, begins to lose his memory, which causes Hopkins to relegate Vaughan to menial duties after he shows signs of senility (grimly noticed when Vaughan's nose is running and dripping while he is serving his employer's guests and where the old man is oblivious to his offensive conduct). Even when Vaughan dies, Hopkins demonstrates very little emotional response. Fox, the aristocratic lord of the household, is shown to be a political dilettante, who, during the crisis with Germany just before the war, takes a strong position for appeasement with Adolf Hitler. Siding with him are other wealthy aristocrats, who meet with Fox at the estate, holding conferences on just how to avoid war with Germany. Reeve, who is shown as a much younger American politician attending one of those conferences, denounces their plans of appeasement, telling them they are all dangerous political amateurs that do not understand the ruthlessness of Hitler, and are simply fuelling his plans for world conquest. Fox, influenced by the writings of a right-wing British author, decides to get rid of two German-Jewish maids, having Hopkins fire them, but Thompson strongly objects, telling Hopkins that these two girls, if they lose their employment, will be sent back to Germany' where they will face the racial persecution of the Nazis. After Hopkins dismisses the two maids, Fox regrets his decision, asking that the girls be reinstated, but they cannot be located and the viewer is left to conclude that these two unfortunate young women have been sent to a terrible fate because of the political whims of their irresponsible employer. Retribution for Fox's irresponsible politics is seen when he is branded a traitor in the British press. He files a libel suit, but that legal action exhausts his wealth and he dies a financially and spiritually broken man. Hopkins, at one point, is asked for his advice by Fox, but he tells Fox that he has no political opinions and if he has, he will never express them to anyone lest he betray his credo of being next to invisible to those he serves, a policy he demands of all other household workers. Hopkins takes the same attitude in his relationship with Thompson, displaying the same cold and impassive manner he shows to all others, even when she teases him about his unwavering policies and always proper conduct. He seems to warm to her a bit, but can never bring himself to establish a relationship deeper than the professional cordiality Hopkins shows to all other employees. Thompson nevertheless falls in love with him. When he refuses to return her expressions of affection, Thompson meets another man and marries him and then resigns. She insults Hopkins before she leaves because he has rejected her love and chiefly because he has sacrificed his own love for her in order to maintain his dedicated position as guardian of the estate's household. In flash-forward, Hopkins meets once more with Thompson, but she refuses to return to Darlington Hall as its housekeeper, saying that she is happily married and has a daughter who is also married and is about to have a child. Hopkins accepts her decision and leaves, but Thompson is not as happy as she has indicated to Hopkins. She cries when seeing Hopkins depart, her tears shed for his terrible inability to have accepted hers or any other person's love those long, sad years ago. Hopkins, in a final salute to Thompson, tips his hat. He then meets with Reeve, who is waiting for his family to arrive from America and take residence at the great mansion and the two enter the grand hall. Reeve then recalls his meeting many years earlier with Fox and his well-meaning but politically misguided associates. Reeve admits that he was then a brash, young man who expressed cruel but truthful remarks that typified the weak-willed British aristocrats of that day, describing their lives much like that of the automaton-like Hopkins, ambiguous and unresolved, lives lived without real purpose. While they stand in the grand hall, a pigeon flies into the cavernous room, fluttering about and looking to escape. Reeve and Hopkins chase the bird and capture it and then release it so that it flies away, that pigeon symbolically having more freedom than Hopkins has ever enjoyed throughout his long life of silent servitude. This powerful film so carefully directed by Ivory conveys an

Anthony Hopkins and Emma Thompson in *The Remains of the Day,* **1993.**

overall feeling of elegant emptiness where lives are lived without any significant fulfillment, except for that of Thompson, who escapes that all-confining estate, like that pigeon, to find a modicum of happiness. The framework of the film is the harboring estate that sanctions the crusty foibles of peerage and wealth and keeps in tidy and unemotional place its worker ant employees. Its maintenance is rigidly managed by a man, Hopkins, who has eliminated his identity as a human being for the sake of a lofty but loveless role in life. The story is a simple one, but the complex nuances and the struggle to utterly suppress human emotion on the part of Hopkins is nothing short of acting genius, presenting one of this great actor's finest performances. Few actors, other than, perhaps, Charles Laughton or Alec Guinness, could have so well captured that unforgettable character. It is a role that the gifted Hopkins will be remembered for long decades after we have all passed. There is something obsessively funereal about it all where the living willingly bury themselves within creaking, musty traditions and where Darlington Hall is the ornate mortuary housing the remains of its ancient antecedents and present-day inhabitants. The film received Oscar nominations for Best Picture, Best Director (Ivory), Best Actor (Hopkins), Best Actress (Thompson), Best Adapted Screenplay (Prawer Jhabvala), Best Original Score (Robbins), Best Art Direction (Arrighi, Ralph, Whittaker) and Best Costume Design (Jenny Beavan, John Bright). This film that so subtly indicts the ruling class of England and acerbically depicts those who serve that class was surprisingly successful at the box office, gleaning almost $64 million in its initial release against a $15 million budget. Songs: "Blue Moon" (music: Richard Rodgers; lyrics: Lorenz Hart); "Roll Along Prairie Moon" (Ted Fio Rito, Albert von Tilzer, Harry MacPherson), "Sei mir gegrusst" (Franz Schubert). *Author's Note*: The script for this story was originally written by Harold Pinter, but, after it was considerably altered, Pinter asked that he not be given credit, even though he was paid according to original agreements. Mike Nichols was to direct this film, but Ivory took over the reins, although Nichols remained with the production thereafter. Producers were persuasive in getting permission to shoot several elegant British manor houses for this film, estates otherwise not open to the public, including the Dyrham Park estate, which represents the exteriors of Darlington Hall, and the resplendent interiors being shot at Powderham Castle, Badminton House, and Corsham Court. **p,** Ismail Merchant, John Calley, Mike Nichols; **d,** James Ivory; **cast,** Anthony Hopkins, Emma Thompson, Christopher Reeve, James Fox, Hugh Grant, Tim Pigott-Smith, Peter Halliday, Peter Cellier, Jeffry Wickham; Peter Vaughan, John Haycraft, Paula Jacobs, Patrick Godfrey; **w,** Ruth Prawer Jhabvala (based on the novel by Kazuo Ishiguro); **c,** Tony Pierce-Roberts (Technicolor); **m,** Richard Robbins; **ed,** Andrew Marcus; **prod d,** Luciana Arrighi; **art d,** John Ralph; **set d,** Ian Whittaker; **spec eff,** Garth Inns, Karin Hanson.

William Holden, center, meets the ghost of President Andrew Jackson (Brian Donlevy) in *The Remarkable Andrew,* 1942.

The Remarkable Andrew ★★★ 1942; U.S.; 80m; PAR; B/W; Comedy/Fantasy; Children: Acceptable. Absorbing fantasy tale sees Holden playing an honest young accountant in a small town, while also serving as a secretary for a local society that honors Andrew Jackson (1767-1845). He idolizes the memory of the former President of the United States, after whom he was named. He discovers a $1,240 discrepancy in the city budget and is wary when town fathers try to explain it away. This leads to him being blamed for the loss, but "Old Hickory," played by Donlevy, materializes, along with other famous deceased American leaders, to help Holden discover who stole the town's money. Aiding in that sleuthing effort are the spirits of George Washington (1732-1799), played by Love; Benjamin Franklin (1706-1790), played by Watts; Thomas Jefferson (1743-1826), played by Emery; John James Marshall (1755-1835), played by Hurst; and, of all people, outlaw Jesse James (1847-1882), who is played by Cameron. There are many humorous moments as Holden and his helpful spirits track down the culprit, and the special effects showing the spirits materializing and dematerializing is exceptional. *Author's Note*: Trumbo pitched this story to Arthur Hornblow Jr., who was an executive producer at Paramount, but Hornblow, according to Trumbo's statements to this author, "turned it down as an original screenplay. He then suggested that I could make a lot more money if the story was published as a novel and he would then buy the book rights, as well as paying me to write the adaptation for the screen. I followed his advice and cashed in on his idea." Donlevy told this author that "I enjoyed playing Andrew Jackson, an ornery cuss even though he was a great President. I played Jackson like the backwoodsman he was, not the shrewd politician, who wound up in the White House." Holden told this author that "the writer for that picture [Trumbo] was very impressed with another fantasy picture called **The Devil and Daniel Webster** [1941] where a lot of historical characters are brought back to life to judge a guy who has sold his soul to Satan, and he told me when we did that picture that he was using the same device for **The Remarkable Andrew**. It was a good idea that had been used once too often, because our picture did not do as well as **The Devil and Daniel Webster**, but it was still a very inventive and lively production." Other actors have essayed Andrew Jackson in many films, including **Bad Blood: The Border War That Triggered the Civil War**, 2007 (made-for-TV; Robert Eckhoff); **Bridger**, 1976 (made-for-TV; John Anderson); **The Buccaneer**, 1938 (Hugh Sothern); **The Buccaneer**, 1958 (Charlton Heston); **Davy Crockett: King of the Wild Frontier**, 1955 (Basil Ruysdael); **The Eagle and the Sea**, 1926 (George Irving); **The Fighting Kentuckian**, 1949 (Steve Darrell); **First Ladies Diaries: Rachel Jackson**, 1975 (made-for-TV; Gerald Gordon); **The First Texan**, 1956 (Carl Benton Reid); **The Frontiersman**, 1927 (Russell Simpson); **Gone to Texas**, 1986 (made-for-TV; G. D. Spradlin);

The Gorgeous Hussy, 1936 (Lionel Barrymore); **Lone Star**, 1952 (Lionel Barrymore); **Man of Conquest**, 1939 (Edward Ellis); **My Own United States**, 1918 (F. C. Earle); **Pirates of Treasure Island**, 2006 (Thomas Downey); **The President's Lady**, 1953 (Charlton Heston); **Privateer**, 2009 (Corin Nemec); **The Wedding of Lilli Marlene**, 1953 (Robert Ayres); and **War of 1812**, 1999 (TV miniseries; Richard Clarkin). **p**, Richard Blumenthal; **d**, Stuart Heisler; **cast**, William Holden, Brian Donlevy, Ellen Drew, Montagu Love, Gilbert Emery, Brandon Hurst, George Watts, Rod Cameron, Frances Gifford, Martha O'Driscoll; **w**, Dalton Trumbo (based on his novel); **c**, Theodor Sparkuhl; **m**, Victor Young; **ed**, Archie Marshek; **art d**, Hans Dreier, Earl Hedrick.

Rembrandt ★★★★ 1936; U.K.; 85m; London Film Productions/UA; B/W; Biographical Drama; Children: Acceptable. This superb biopic is undoubtedly one of the finest portraits of an artist, his techniques and his lifestyle; Laughton gives a magnificent restrained performance of the great Rembrandt (1606-1669). The film spans the last twenty-seven years of the artist's life, shown in episodic sequences and each sequence is a marvel to behold. The viewer sees Rembrandt reduced over those span of years from one of the most esteemed artists in Europe to a miserable and groveling person, who must scrape to sustain his work and life. Laughton is at the peak of his career when the film begins and where his cherished first wife dies just as he completes his majestic painting, "The Night Watch." The distinguished men portrayed in that painting, however, all of whom having paid a princely sum to sit before and be painted by the master, are deeply disappointed in that their faces seem to retreat into the background of the artwork. Laughton ignores their criticism as he tolerates no debates about his art. This treatment alienates some of his wealthy supporters who later take financial revenge upon him. With his first wife gone, Laughton feels that he should marry again for he is a family man and needs the emotional support of a good woman. He marries Lawrence, but she is far from the good woman Laughton has envisioned. Vulgar and shrewish, Lawrence makes Laughton's life miserable as she constantly carps and complains. His well-ordered life begins to come apart and, unable to pay off his creditors, including those he has earlier offended, he must sell his resplendent home and move into a crude dwelling. Further, he finds solace only with an uneducated but empathetic maid, Lanchester (she and Laughton were married in real life, a union that lasted until his death). When Lawrence discovers Laughton giving attention to Lanchester, she leaves him and then Lanchester becomes pregnant. Laughton does the right thing and, after the child is born, marries her. After Lanchester dies, however, Laughton becomes nearly senile and almost helpless, slavishly groveling before anyone who will advance small sums to keep him alive and where he struggles to go on painting. He looks upon himself as a miserable failure and a doddering fool as old age and eventually death engulfs him. Korda directs this tale with a loving hand, one where Rembrandt's paintings are displayed in impressive arrays (and where the use of color would have greatly enhanced the production). Laughton presents a masterpiece profile of the great painter, and Lawrence, Lanchester and the rest of the distinguished cast members are outstanding. The cinematography from Perinal and Agst astoundingly captures the Dutch landscape and lifestyle during the period of the artist, as well showcasing many Rembrandt masterpieces. *Author's Note*: Producer Korda, after having directed Laughton in **The Private Life of Henry VIII**, 1933 (Laughton won an Oscar for his dynamic performance in that film), had long wanted to have Laughton appear in another biographical drama. They chose the life of the Dutch painter, mostly based upon his universal popularity and because Korda, who was a collector of fine art, felt that Rembrandt's story was one well suited to dramatization. Laughton threw himself into this role with great vitality, traveling to Holland to study the history of the country at the time of Rembrandt, as well as the man's life, and immersed himself in many biographical accounts about the painter before the production began.

The film was not the success Korda envisioned, but this was mostly due to the fact that Laughton plays a mostly introverted person and he was less animated than in his role as Henry VIII, the kind of performance his fans expected and did not get. It nevertheless remains a classic tale that accurately and memorably records and relates the life of one of the world's greatest artists and is truly the forerunner to such future classics as **Moulin Rouge**, 1953 (where José Ferrer portrays painter Henri de Toulouse-Lautrec) and **Lust for Life**, 1956 (where Kirk Douglas portrays painter Vincent van Gogh). **p&d**, Alexander Korda; **cast**, Charles Laughton, Gertrude Lawrence, Elsa Lanchester, Edward Chapman, Walter Hudd, Roger Livesey, John Clements, Abraham Sofaer, Evelyn Ankers, Marius Goring, Wilfrid Hyde-White, Alexander Knox; **w**, Carl Zuckmayer, Lajos Biró, June Head, Arthur Wimperis; **c**, Georges Perinal; **m**, Geoffey Toye; **ed**, William Hornbeck, Francis Lyon; **prod d**, Vincent Korda; **spec eff**, Ned Mann.

Remember Last Night? ★★★ 1935; U.S.; 81m; UNIV; B/W; Mystery; Children: Unacceptable. Intriguing whodunit begins when a group of wealthy socialites go out on a night of drinking during which a murder is discovered. Arnold, a good-natured detective, investigates, only to discover a total of four murders and two suicides that night. To his puzzlement, none of the revelers can recall anything that happened the previous night, most likely due to their head-banging hangovers. Arnold calls in a hypnotist, von Seyffertitz, to jar the memories of the heavy drinkers, and he seems to make headway, but he, too, is murdered before he can disclose his discoveries. Arnold nevertheless identifies and catches the culprit. Song: "Lookie Lookie Lookie, Here Comes Cookie" (1935; Mack Gordon). *Author's Note*: Young told this author, "The director, James Whale, was in trouble at Universal at the time we made **Remember Last Night?** He had had a blowout with the front office after he did **The Bride of Frankenstein** [1935], a classic horror film, like his earlier **Frankenstein** [1931] and he told the bosses that he was fed up with making more horror pictures. So they gave him a programmer called **Remember Last Night?**, but he did a hell of a job with that mystery story even though they did not promote the film like they did his earlier pictures. The next year, Whale directed a tremendous musical, **Show Boat** [1936], and proved that he could make great pictures without having a monster throttling innocent people." **p**, Carl Laemmle Jr.; **d**, James Whale; **cast**, Edward Arnold, Robert Young, Constance Cummings, George Meeker, Sally Eilers, Reginald Denny, Gregory Ratoff, Robert Armstrong, Jack LaRue, Edward Brophy, Gustav von Seyffertitz, Arthur Treacher, Dewey Robinson; **w**, Harry Clork, Doris Malloy, Dan Totheroh (based on the novel *Hangover Murders* by Adam Hobhouse); **c**, Joseph Valentine; **m**, Franz Waxman; **ed**, Ted Kent; **art d**, Charles D. Hall; **spec eff**, John P. Fulton.

Remember the Day ★★★ 1941; U.S.; 85m; FOX; B/W; Drama; Children: Acceptable. Colbert gives a memorable performance as an aging schoolteacher about to meet a presidential candidate, Sheppard, who was one of her pupils twenty-five years earlier. She reflects on that time (1916) when, as a boy, Sheppard had a crush on her and became jealous when he learned she was married to another teacher, Payne, so she gives the boy special attention, encouraging him to do great things with his life. World War I (1914-1918) breaks out and Payne joins the Canadian Air Force and is killed in battle. It's a heartwarming "Mrs. Chips" story well played by the leads, especially Colbert. *Author's Note*: Shepperd Strudwick later changed his acting name to John Sheppard, but never became a star, although he remained a fine supporting actor. Director King told this author that "there weren't too many actresses who could so beautifully age on film as Claudette [Colbert] as she does in **Remember the Day**. In fact, I thought she was more beautiful in old age than when she was younger, but that's the warm character coming from that great lady." Colbert told this author that "no actress wants to look old on the screen, but the makeup people in that picture were very kind to me, especially to my eyes and neck and let me keep a youthful

Barbara Stanwyck and Fred MacMurray in *Remember the Night*, 1940.

look in my old age." Payne thought his role in this film "was another short-lived love interest since I get killed in the war. It was a pretty easy part to play—kiss the girl, say goodbye, and then get bumped off." Songs: "Chatanooga Choo Choo" (Harry Warren), "Indiana" (music: James F. Hanley; lyrics: Ballard MacDonald), "The Sailor's Hornpipe" (traditional), "In the Good Old Summertime" (George Evans), "O Come, All Ye Faithful" (traditional), "It Came Upon a Midnight Clear" (Richard Stoors Willis), "Pretty Baby" (music: Egbert Van Alstyne, Tony Jackson; lyrics: Gus Kahn), "It's a Long, Long Way to Tipperary" (Jack Judge, Harry Williams), "Till We Meet Again" (Richard A. Whiting). **p**, William Perlberg; **d**, Henry King; **cast**, Claudette Colbert, John Payne, Shepperd Strudwick (John Shapperd), Ann Todd, Douglas Croft, Jayne Seymour, Anne Revere, Frieda Inescourt, Marie Blake, David Holt, Robert Lowery, Mae Marsh; **w**, Tess Slesinger, Frank Davis, Allan Scott (based on the play by Philo Higley, Phillip Dunning); **c**, George Barnes; **m**, Alfred Newman; **ed**, Barbara McLean; **art d**, Richard Day.

Remember the Night ★★★★ 1940; U.S.; 94m; PAR; B/W; Comedy/Drama/Romance; Children: Acceptable; **DVD**; **VHS**. Stanwyck and MacMurray click with great romantic chemistry in this heart warmer from aesthetic director Leisen and comedic writer Sturges. Stanwyck is a professional shoplifter, who decides to give herself the gift of a diamond necklace at Christmastime, but, adept as she is in filching, she is caught and jailed. The presiding judge, Waldron, puts off his sentencing until after Christmas, but Stanwyck's sentence may be severe as she is a repeating offender, having been convicted twice earlier for the same offense. MacMurray, who is an assistant prosecutor, is returning to Indiana for the holidays and, after he learns that Stanwyck comes from the same state, bails her out of jail. He tells her that he will drop her off at her mother's home, but makes her promise that she will return after Christmas to face the music. When they arrive at Stanwyck's home, she is met by Caine, a mother who has long ago given up on Stanwyck. When Caine insults and hurts Stanwyck, the sympathetic MacMurray decides to take her to his mother's home to celebrate Christmas and where he knows she will be treated with kindness and consideration. She is warmly welcomed by MacMurray's mother, Bondi, his dithering but adorable aunt, Patterson, and their fun-loving handyman, Holloway. Stanwyck's hard shell softens when exposed to these affectionate and caring people and she quickly falls in love with MacMurray, and he with her. Stanwyck toys with the idea of fleeing and almost flies the coop, but she is drawn back to this loving family, one she has never known and has always yearned to have. Thinking she may never really have a future with MacMurray, she leaves for parts unknown, but then reconsiders and returns to New York where MacMurray is relieved to see that

William Powell and Rosalind Russell in *Rendezvous*, 1935.

she has honored her promise to return. When Stanwyck stands trial before Waldron, her defense attorney, Robertson, attempts to overwhelm MacMurray's prosecution, which is lame to say the least as he does not want Stanwyck to go behind bars. Robertson offers a blathering, bathos-splashed summation in an effort to get Stanwyck released, but she cuts him off and admits her guilt. Waldron, impressed with her repentant attitude and honest admission, gives her a minimal sentence, which Stanwyck accepts with the hope that MacMurray will be waiting for her when she is released. Director Leisen carefully develops his down-to-earth characters so that they are natural with each other and prevents the tale from becoming maudlin or syrupy, and MacMurray, Stanwyck and the rest of the cast give understated performances that resonate with reality and empathy. Scriptwriter Sturges, who went on to direct many classic comedies, injects a great deal of wisecracking humor to soften the hard edges of an otherwise worldly, hardened shoplifter and a cynical prosecutor. This film did well at the box office and was aired three times in 1940, 1941 and 1949, in radio shows, and remains a film invariably shown at Christmas. Songs: "Jingle Bells" (James Pierpont), "Easy Living" (Leo Robin, Ralph Rainger), "(Back Home Again In) Indiana" (1917; music: James F. Hanley; lyrics: Ballard MacDonald), "Old Folks at Home (Swanee River)" (Stephen Foster), "A Perfect Day" (1910; Carrie Jacobs Bond), "Auld Lang Syne" (1788; traditional Scottish ballad; lyrics: Robert Burns). ***Author's Note***: "I suppose that when you look back on that picture, you might think it is something Frank Capra might make," MacMurray told this author. "It is a very realistic story with a lot of good scenes, and that's the kind of pictures Capra made." Stanwyck told this author that "Sturges wrote in a lot of little scenes that made the picture a heart warmer—making popcorn and singing at Christmastime. He has a canary chirping in a cage and everyone is having fun at a barn dance. Nothing spectacular, but these were scenes that showed the very human side of the characters and audiences always relate to that, always." Many memorable films have as their centerpiece the Christmas season, most notably: **Arthur Christmas**, 2011; **Babes in Toyland**, 1934; **The Bishop's Wife**, 1947; **The Cheaters**, 1945; **A Christmas Carol**, 1938; **A Christmas Carol**, 1951; **Christmas Eve**, 1947; **Christmas in Connecticut**, 1945; **A Christmas Story**, 1983; **Come to the Stable**, 1949; **Holiday Inn**, 1942; **The Holly and the Ivy**, 1954; **Home Alone**, 1990; **It's a Wonderful Life**, 1946; **Joyeux Noel**, 2005; **The Lemon Drop Kid**, 1951; **Miracle on 34th Street**, 1947; **O. Henry's Full House**, 1952 ("The Gift of the Magi" sequence); **One Magic Christmas**, 1985; **The Santa Clause**, 1994; **The Santa Clause 2**, 2002; **Scrooge**, 1970; and **White Christmas**, 1954. **p&d**, Mitchell Leisen; **cast**, Barbara Stanwyck, Fred MacMurray, Beulah Bondi, Elizabeth Patterson, Sterling Holloway, Willard Robertson, Charles Waldron, Paul Guilfoyle, Charlie Arnt, Fred

"Snowflake" Toones, Fuzzy Knight, Georgia Caine, Virginia Brissac, James Flavin, Thomas W. Ross, Spencer Charters; **w**, Preston Sturges; **c**, Ted Tetzlaff; **m**, Frederick Hollander; **ed**, Doane Harrison; **art d**, Hans Dreier, Roland Anderson.

Remember the Titans ★★★ 2000; U.S; 113m.; Jerry Bruckheimer Films/Buena Vista; Color; Sports Drama; Children: Unacceptable (MPAA: PG); **BD**; **DVD**. This well-made sports drama is based on actual events in 1971, where schools have been segregated for generations in suburban Virginia, within sight of the Washington Monument over the river at the nation's capital. One black and one white school are closed and the students sent to T.S. Williams High School under federal mandate to integrate. The year is seen through the eyes of the football team, where Washington, the man hired to coach the black school, is made head coach over the highly successful white coach. The integrated team becomes the unifying symbol for the community as the boys and adults learn to depend on and trust each other. Songs: "Ain't No Mountain High Enough" (Nick Ashford, Valerie Simpson), "Spirit in the Sky" (Norman Greenbaum), "Spill the Wine" (Harold R. Brown, Morris D. Dickerson, Lonnie Jordan, Lee Oskar, Charles Miller, Howard E. Scott, Thomas Allen), "Na Na Hey Hey Kiss Him Goodbye" (Gary DeCarlo, Dale Frashuer, Paul Leka), "House of the Rising Sun" (traditional), "Venus" (Robbie van Leeuwen), "Fire and Rain" (James Taylor), "I Heard It Through the Grapevine" (Norman Whitfield, Barrett Strong), "Up Around the Bend" (John Fogerty), "Long Cool Woman/in a Black Dress" (Allan Clarke, Roger Greenaway, Roger Cook), "Peace Train" (Cat Stevens), "Express Yourself" (Charles Wright, The Watts 103rd Street Rhythm Band: James Gadson, Melvin Dunlap, Ray Jackson, Al McKay, Benorce Blackmon), "Act Naturally" (Vonnie Morrison, Johnny Russell), "A Hard Rain's A-Gonna Fall" (Bob Dylan), "I Want to Take You Higher" (Sly Stone), "Superstar/Remember How You Got Where You Are," "You've Got to Earn It" (The Temptations: David Ruffin, Melvin Franklin, Paul Williams, Otis Williams, Eddie Kendricks), "Them Changes" (George Buddy Miles), "Time Has Come Today" (Joseph Chambers, Willie Chambers), "Amazing Grace" (John Newton), "The Way You Do the Things You Do" (Smokey Robinson, Bobby Rogers), "Call On Me" (Deadric Malone), "Ain't Too Proud to Bed" (Norman J. Whitfield, Edward Holland Jr.), "No Surrender" (Chris Goulstone), "Let's Go Blue" (Joseph Carl, Albert Ahronheim), "Quiet Home" (Jesse Greer). Thematic elements and gutter language prohibit viewing by children. **p**, Jerry Bruckheimer, Chad Oman; **d**, Boaz Yakin; **cast**, Denzel Washington, Will Patton, Ryan Gosling, Wood Harris, Ryan Hurst, Donald Faison, Craig Kirkwood, Ethan Suplee, Kip Pardue, Kate Bosworth; **w**, Gregory Allen Howard; **c**, Philippe Rousselot; **m**, Trevor Rabin; **ed**, Michael Tronick; **prod d**, Deborah Evans; **art d**, Jonathan Short; **set d**, Anne Kuljian; **spec eff**, Bob Shelley.

Rendezvous ★★★ 1935; U.S.; 91m; MGM; B/W; Comedy; Children: Acceptable; **DVD**; **IV**. Clever comedy combines romance and espionage beginning when Powell, a puzzle editor for a Washington newspaper, joins the army at the outbreak of World War I (1914-1918). He falls in love with Russell, whose uncle has an important position with the War Department. She saves him from being sent into combat by getting him assigned to a code-breaking unit in the capital where German messages are being sent out of the Soviet embassy. Powell then discovers that sensuous Barnes is a German spy and mole at the Soviet embassy. He dallies with her to get information, but that almost upsets his romantic applecart with Russell. After some very funny exploits, Powell exposes the spy ring after breaking a code. He is about to be sent into combat when Russell again gets him assigned a desk job at the code-breaking unit, and where they can safely plan a life together. Songs: "You're in the Army Now" (traditional), "My Buddy" (Walter Donaldson), "The Stars and Stripes Forever" (John Philip Sousa), "Smiles" (Lee S. Roberts), "Till We Meet Again" (Richard A. Whiting). ***Author's Note***: Powell told this author that his role in **Rendezvous** "was based on real persons who were recruited by U.S. code breakers. They sought out and hired editors at newspapers and magazines who were in charge of putting together puzzles because they were good at figuring out ciphers." Russell told this author that "I did not know a thing about spies, codes or cloak and dagger people when we did **Rendezvous**. My character doesn't give a hoot about such things. She is daffy over William Powell and she pulls a lot of strings to keep him from becoming cannon fodder on the Western Front. Not a very patriotic thing to do, but she's in love and that excuses everything." Oddly, this story was originally purchased by MGM with thoughts of producing a serious spy drama, but it was turned into a lighthearted and well-written, urbane and witty comedy, albeit a bit of somber menace was injected into some of its scenes. The film was designed as a vehicle for Powell and Russell, who were then being promoted as a romantic film duo. The Powell-Russell teaming never surpassed the Powell-Myrna Loy love team that was enormously popular as a result of the Thin Man series. The author of the book, Herbert O. Yardley, was a brilliant code breaker, who was the first to establish a U.S. cipher service during WWI. He and his embryonic intelligence service are profiled in my work *Spies: A Narrative Encyclopedia of Dirty Deeds and Double Dealing from Biblical Times to Today* (M. Evans, New York, 1997; pages 519-521). **p**, Lawrence Weingarten, William K. Howard; **d**, Howard; **cast**, William Powell, Rosalind Russell, Binnie Barnes, Lionel Atwill, Cesar Romero, Samuel S. Hinds, Henry Stephenson, Charley Grapewin, Melville Cooper, Milburn Stone, Margaret Dumont, Mary Forbes, Sterling Holloway, Mickey Rooney; **w**, P.J. Wolfson, George Oppenheimer (adapted by Bella Spewack, Samuel Spewack from the book *American Black Chamber* by Herbert O. Yardley); **c**, William H. Daniels, (not credited) James Wong Howe; **m**, William Axt; **ed**, Hugh Wynn; **art d**, Cedric Gibbons.

Rendez-vous ★★★ 1987; France; 82m; Films A2/International Spectrafilm; Color; Drama; Children: Unacceptable; **DVD**; **VHS**. Absorbing tale focuses on Binoche, a young woman going to Paris to become an actress. She sleeps around before meeting Stanczack, who falls in love with her. She is stalked by Wilson, his former roommate, and plays both men against each other. Finally, Binoche and Stanczak share an apartment, but she still won't take him as a lover, concentrating on appearing in a stage production of *Romeo and Juliet*, which is directed by Trintignant, who becomes her father figure. She winds up with none of the men in her life, settling for an acting career instead of any permanent romantic relationships. Song: "Au clair de la lune" (Jean-Baptiste Lully). Sexuality prohibits viewing by children. (In French; English subtitles.) **p**, Alain Terzian; **d**, Andre Techine; **cast**, Juliette Binoche, Lambert Wilson, Jean-Louis Trintignant, Wadeck Stanczak, Dominique Lavanant, Anne Wiazemsky, Jean-Louis Vitrac, Philippe Landoulsi, Olimpia Carlisi, Caroline Faro; **w**, Techine, Olivier Assayas; **c**, Renato Berta (Eastmancolor); **m**, Philippe Sarde; **ed**, Martine Giordano; **prod d**, Jean-Pierre Kohut-Svelko; **spec eff**, Georges Demetrau.

Rendezvous in Paris ★★★ 1996; France; 94m; Compagnie Eric Rohmer/Artificial Eye; Color; Comedy/Drama; Children: Unacceptable; DVD; VHS. Well-made episodic tales present four stories of young men and women coming together in Paris before their relationships fall apart. Stories are titled: "The 7 p.m. Rendezvous," "The Next Morning," and two set in 1907: "The Seats of Paris Parks" and "Mother and Child." (In French; English subtitles.) **p**, Francoise Etchegaray; **d&w**, Eric Rohmer; **cast**, Clara Bellar, Antoine Basler, Mathias Megard, Judith Chancel, Malcolm Conrath, Aurore Rauscher, Serge Renko, Benedicte Loyen, Veronika Johansson, Florence Levu; **c**, Diane Baratier; **m**, Sebastien Erms; **ed**, Mary Stephen; **art d**, Pierre De Chevilly.

Repulsion ★★★ 1965; U.K.; 104m; Compton Films/Royal International; B/W; Horror; Children: Unacceptable; **BD**; **DVD**; **IV**. Offbeat and often frightening character study sees beautiful Deneuve as a very troubled person. She is a young Belgian woman working as a mani-

Juliette Binoche and Lambert Wilson in *Rendez-vous,* 1987.

curist in a London beauty salon. She has lunch at a restaurant where she meets a good-looking young man, John Fraser, who makes a date with her. She shares an apartment with her sister, Furneaux, whose lover, Hendry, is a married man. That uneasy relationship causes Deneuve to fear for her sister while developing a strong dislike of men in general. This causes her to have a strained relationship with Fraser, but, when he probes her discontent, she can't or won't explain her feelings to him. After Hendry takes Furneaux on a holiday abroad, the insecure Deneuve is left alone in the apartment where she drifts into moments of catalepsy and hallucination that end in madness. Again, the odd-minded Polanski presents a strange tale, peppering it with his weird, if not degenerate perspectives of life and love, where Deneuve offers a riveting performance of a woman slowly losing her sanity. **p**, Gene Gutowski; **d**, Roman Polanski; **cast**, Catherine Deneuve, Ian Hendry, John Fraser, Yvonne Furneaux, Patrick Wymark, Renee Houston, Valerie Taylor, James Villiers, Helen Fraser, Hugh Futcher, Monica Merlin, Imogen Graham, Polanski; **w**, Polanski, Gerard Brach, David Stone; **c**, Gilbert Taylor; **m**, Chico Hamilton; **ed**, Alastair McIntyre; **art d**, Seamus Flannery.

Requiem for a Heavyweight ★★★★ 1962; U.S.; 85m; COL; B/W; Sports Drama; Children: Unacceptable; **DVD**; **VHS**. This brilliantly savage indictment of prizefighting from the gifted Serling sees a stunning performance from Quinn. He plays Mountain Rivera, a fighter who has fought for seventeen years in the ring, has beaten 111 opponents, and has nothing to show for all his pain and suffering but an addled brain and empty pockets. The film opens with Quinn, now a stumbling and pawing fighter with no agility or stamina left, being pounded to pieces by a young contender, Clay (who would become in real life Muhammad Ali, heavyweight champion of the world). The camera shows Quinn's POV as Clay sends powerhouse blows directly at the audience (or Quinn). The brutal punishment ends when Quinn is knocked out in the seventh round. When he is examined by a doctor after the fight, Quinn is told that his boxing days are over and, if he attempts to fight again, he would most likely be blinded for life. Quinn hangs up his gloves, but his slippery manager, Gleason, is now in serious trouble. He had placed a bet with Spivy, a rough customer, that Quinn would never last beyond the fourth round with Clay, and since he went three rounds beyond that grueling time span, Gleason is now obligated to pay that debt, one he cannot meet. Quinn, meanwhile, goes to an employment agency where sympathetic Harris works hard to find him a job. It appears that he may have the opportunity of becoming the athletic director for a summer camp, but, when Gleason hears of this, he sabotages that chance by getting Quinn drunk so that he fails to get the job. Gleason wants Quinn to go on working for him so that he can pay off that debt to Spivy and con-

Anthony Quinn in *Requiem for a Heavyweight*, 1962.

vinces the simple-minded Quinn that he can have a new and sterling career as a performer in the fake wrestling racket. At first, Quinn refuses
to lose the last vestiges of his shattered dignity by sinking to such impersonating charades. Harris, who has fallen in love with the gentle and
caring Quinn, tries to get him employment, but he is all but unemploy-
able. Quinn then changes his mind about Gleason's offer when he learns
that Gleason faces injury or even death from Spivy unless he repays the
$3,000 owed to the thug. Rooney, who is Quinn's loyal handler, lam-
basts Gleason for attempting to use a fighter who has given his all to
Gleason over the years. Gleason, though remorseful for his conduct,
tells Rooney that he, too, is at the end of his career and rope and is too
desperate to care about anything except his own survival. For the sake
of his old friend, Quinn, sacrifices his self-respect by accepting Gleason's proposal. Using his Indian heritage, he gets into the ring as a
wrestling Indian chief, wearing an Indian loin cloth and headdress, he
dances around, waving a tomahawk, whooping and yelping like the Indians of the Old West, or his idea of such ancestors as he is ridiculed by
jeering spectators. It is the last, degrading act of a man who has no future
except that of a freakish performer in a crude sideshow. All values in
his life have been stripped from him, including his integrity, honor and
manhood. Mountain Rivera exists only as a mocking impersonator of
his former self. Sad, even depressing, this powerful film presents the
decline and fall of an honorable man whose grim fate is exacerbated by
a manipulative manager he has trusted with his future all of his life.
Gleason also gives a memorable performance as that manager as does
the intense Rooney as Quinn's long-lasting and loyal friend. Harris renders an outstanding performance of a woman consumed by apathy in
her inability to help the man she has come to love. Tension is maintained
throughout by Nelson's taut direction, and the brilliant script from Serling is both literate and compassionate. Song: "Home on the Range"
(Daniel E. Kelley). *Author's Note*: This story was originally written by
Serling as a teleplay, which earned for him an Emmy and where Jack
Palance gave a fine performance as the fighter who falls from grace, but
that performance was given greater stature when Quinn reprised the role
six years later when this theatrical film was produced. Serling told this
author that many classic films about prizefighters influenced him when
he wrote this story, including **City for Conquest**, 1940, **Body and Soul**,
1947, and **Champion**, 1949, telling this author: "Any writer who does
not use the best elements of stories and characters that have been written
by good writers in the past is not much of a writer, but just as long as he
works his own original ideas into his story. I knew a man who had been
a prizefighter and had been punched so badly that he could hardly recall
his own name. He was really the person I used for that story, but I won't
deny that a lot of those great old boxing pictures helped me tailor and
trim that tale." Quinn told this author that **"Requiem for a Heavyweight**

was one of my best pictures, but it is ironic that, at the end of that picture,
I wind up playing an Indian. That is where I started my career in Hollywood, playing Indians, so even in that very good story I revert to my
typecasting. [He laughed loudly and long.] Many years ago, I used to
go to see an old woman who read palms and every time she read my
palm, she always ended her spiel with: 'You can't escape your destiny.'
Was she right? I always wound up playing an Indian. So she was right."
Gleason thought his role in this film was "pretty close to the kind of
person I played in **The Hustler** [1962], a super pool shark, a guy who
is under the thumb of a petty gangster. In **Requiem for a Heavyweight**
I am a fight manager who is under the thumb of a loan shark, so I sell
out my best friend, my own prizefighter, to get out from under. Nobody
ever gets out from under the thumb, my young friend." **p**, David
Susskind; **d**, Ralph Nelson; **cast**, Anthony Quinn, Jackie Gleason,
Mickey Rooney, Julie Harris, Stanley Adams, Madame Spivy, Val Avery,
Herbie Faye, Jack Dempsey, Barney Ross, Rory Calhoun, Cassius Clay
(Muhammad Ali), Willie Pep; **w**, Rod Serling (based on his TV play);
c, Arthur J. Ornitz; **m**, Laurence Rosenthal; **ed**, Carl Lerner; **prod d**,
Burr Smidt; **set d**, Francis J. Brady.

Rescue Dawn ★★★ 2007; U.S./Luxembourg; 126m; MGM; Color;
War Drama; Children: Unacceptable (MPAA: PG-13); **BD**; **DVD**. Exciting war tale is set in 1965, where Bale is shown as a U.S. fighter pilot.
He is shot down over the jungle while bombing Laos during the Vietnam
War. Bale is arrested by peasants, tortured by the Vietcong, and sent to
a prison camp. He becomes friends with another prisoner, Zahn, and
they plan an escape. Davies, an unstable prisoner, opposes the plan and
upsets it, leaving Bale and Zahn on their own in the jungle, which be-
comes their prison. Despite hazards and perils, they eventually survive.
Songs: "Mantra of the Touching Heart" (Florian Fricke); "Dangerous
Games," "River in the Rain," "Monsoon," "Voice from Another World,"
"Phantom of the Night" (Ernst Reijseger); "Double 2 Bows," "Alleluja"
(Frances-Marie Uitti); "Happy Birthday to You" (Mildred J. Hill, Patty
S. Hill). Excessive violence and torture prohibit viewing by children. **p**,
Elton Brand, Harry Knapp, Steve Marlton; **d&w**, Werner Herzog; **cast**,
Christian Bale, Steve Zahn, Jeremy Davies, Zach Grenier, Marshall Bell,
Toby Huss, Pat Healy, Gregory J. Qaiyum, James Oliver, Brad Carr; **c**,
Peter Zeitlinger; **m**, Klaus Badelt; **ed**, Joe Bini; **art d**, Arin "Aoi" Pini-
jvararak; **spec eff**, Adam Howarth, Chalempol Panichsuk, Watcharachai
"Sam" Panicsuk.

The Rescuers ★★★ 1977; U.S.; 78m; Disney/Buena Vista; Color; Animated Adventure; Children: Acceptable (MPAA: G); **DVD**; **VHS**. Delightful animated tale from Disney begins with a brave mouse named
Bianca (Gabor voiceover), who is a leader of the Rescue Aid Society, a
mouse organization in the basement of the United Nations building in
New York City. When a bottle containing a plea for help from a little
girl, Stacy, makes its way to her, Gabor enlists the help of a shy janitor,
Newhart, to rescue the girl. They learn she has been kidnapped by Page,
an evil treasure-hunter, and her companion, Flynn. After many exciting
adventures the rescuers find Stacy in a pirate's cave and get her safely
back home. Songs: "The Journey," "Rescue Aid Society," "Tomorrow
Is Another Day" (Carol Connors, Ayn Robbins); "Someone's Waiting
for You"(Sammy Fain, Connors, Robbins); "The U.S. Air Force"
(Robert Crawford); "For He's a Jolly Good Fellow" (traditional). **p**,
Wolfgang Reitherman; **d**, Reitherman, John Lounsbery, Art Stevens;
cast, Eva Gabor, Bob Newhart, Geraldine Page, Joe Flynn, Jeanette
Nolan, Pat Buttram, Jim Jordan, Michelle Stacy, John McIntire, Bernard
Fox; **w**, Larry Clemmons, Ken Anderson, Frank Thomas, Vance Gerry,
David Michener, Ted Berman, Fred Lucky, Burny Mattinson, Dick Se-
bast (based on stories by Margery Sharp); **m**, Artie Butler; **ed**, James
Koford, James Melton; **art d**, Don Griffith.

The Rescuers Down Under ★★★ 1990; U.S.; 77m; Disney/Buena
Vista; Color; Animated Adventure; Children: Acceptable (MPAA: G);

DVD; **VHS**. Entertaining sequel to the 1977 Disney film sees an Australian boy (Ryen voiceover) from Mugwomp Flats getting a distress call about a trapped giant golden eagle. He frees the bird and they become friends. Soon, Ryen is abducted by a poacher (Scott voiceover), who wants the eagle because it is an endangered species and very valuable. Ryen contacts the Rescue Aid Society, a mouse organization in the basement of the United Nations building in New York City. Their top agents (Gabor and Newhart voiceovers) go to the rescue, riding their albatross friend. In Australia, they join forces with Jake, the Kangaroo Rat (Rogers voiceover) and save the eagle. This good family film was also seen in 3-D. Songs: "Black Slacks" (Joe Bennett, Jimmy Denton), "Waltzing Matilda" (A.B. Paterson, Marie Cowan). **p**, Thomas Schumacher; **d**, Mike Gabriel, Hendel Butoy; **cast** (voiceovers), Bob Newhart, Eva Gabor, Adam Ryen, John Candy, George C. Scott, Tristan Rogers, Wayne Robson, Douglas Seale, Frank Welker, Bernard Fox, Peter Firth; **w**, Joe Ranft, Jim Cox, Karey Kirkpatrick, Byron Simpson (based on characters created by Margery Sharp); **m**, Bruce Broughton; **ed**, Michael Kelly; **art d**, Maurice and Pixote Hunt.

Reservoir Dogs ★★★ 1992; U.S.; 99m; Live America/Miramax; Color; Crime Drama; Children: Unacceptable (MPAA: R); **BD**; **DVD**. Taut crime tale profiles six criminals who are strangers to each other and are hired by crime boss Tierney to pull off a diamond robbery. He gives them assumed names and does not want them to become friendly so they will concentrate on the job. They are surprised when police arrive at the scene of the robbery and panic. One of the crooks is killed in a gunfight with police where several cops and civilians also are killed. The surviving crooks go to a prearranged rendezvous in a warehouse, all suspecting that one of them is an undercover police informer. Tarantino directs this thriller with a firm hand, but its plotline takes several large leafs from many film noir classics, including **The Killers**, 1946, and **The Thomas Crown Affair**, 1968. Songs: "Green Bag" (Jan Gerbrand Visser, Benjamino Boiuwens), "Stuck in the Middle with You" (Gerry Rafferty, Joe Egan), "I Gotcha" (Joe Tex), "Fool for Love" (Sandy Rogers), "Hooked on a Feeling" (Mark James), "Coconut" (Harry Nilsson), "Harvest Moon" (Jay Joyce), "Magic Carpet Ride" (Rushton Moireve, John Kay), "Wes Turned Country" (Nikki Bernard), "Country's Cool" (Peter Morris), "It's Country" (Henrick Nielson). Excessive violence and gutter language prohibit viewing by children. **p**, Lawrence Bender, Harvey Keitel; **d&w**, Quentin Tarantino; **cast**, Tarantino, Keitel, Tim Roth, Michael Madsen, Chris Penn, Steve Buscemi, Edward Bunker, Lawrence Tierney, Randy Brooks, Kirk Baltz, Steven Wright, Rich Turner; **c**, Andrzej Sekula; **ed**, Sally Menke; **prod d**, David Wasco; **set d**, Sandy Reynolds-Wasco; **spec eff**, Larry Fioritto.

Restoration ★★★ 1995; U.S./U.K. 117m; Miramax; Color; Drama; Children: Unacceptable (MPAA: R); **DVD**; **VHS**. This fascinating historical drama is set in 1660 when the English, Scottish, and Irish monarchies were all restored under Charles II (1630-1685) after the Wars of the Three Kingdoms. Downey, Jr. is young physician in the service of Charles, who is played by Neill. He becomes one of Neill's favorites after he saves the life of a spaniel dear to the king. Downey joins the royal court and is ordered to marry Walker, one of the king's mistresses, in order to divert attention from Charles' affair with her. Downey marries Walker and then finds that he loves her. The king becomes angered at this and relieves Downey of his position and wealth. Banished, Downey begins a journey of self-discovery where he learns that his true love is practicing medicine. This richly mounted film relates a fine tale of royal court intrigues while also re-creating the twin 1666 tragedies of the Black Plague and the Great Fire of London. Sexuality prohibits viewing by children. **p**, Sarah Black, Cary Brokaw, Andy Paterson, Donna Gigliotti, Bob and Harvey Weinstein; **d**, Michael Hoffman; **cast**, Robert Downey, Jr., Sam Neill, David Thewlis, Polly Walker, Meg Ryan, Ian McKellen, Hugh Grant, Ian McDiarmid, Mary MacLeod, Mark Letheren; **w**, Rupert Walters (based on the novel by Rose

The gang of thieves, Harvey Keitel in foreground, in *Reservoir Dogs,* 1992.

Tremain); **c**, Oliver Stapleton; **m**, James Newton Howard; **ed**, Garth Craven; **prod d**, Eugenio Zanetti; **art d**, Jonathan Lee, Lucy Richardson, Alan Cassie; **set d**, Mark Jury, Zanetti; **spec eff**, Peter Hutchinson.

Resurrection ★★★ 1963; USSR; 152m; Mosfilm/Artkino Pictures; B/W/Color; Drama; Children: Unacceptable; **DVD**; **VHS**. Strange but compelling Tolstoy tale is centered upon Syomina, a Russian country girl, who is seduced and abandoned by Matveev, a prince. Years later, Matveev serves on a jury trying Syomina for a crime he now realizes his actions drove her to commit when his child died and she became a prostitute. He proposes to her, but she declines and goes to prison. He follows her to imprisonment in Siberia in hopes of redeeming himself for his crimes against her. This is a better remake of a 1931 U.S. film by the same title. Sexuality prohibits viewing by children. (In Russian; English subtitles.) **d**, Mikhail Shvejtser; **cast**, Tamara Syomina, Yevgeni Matveyev, Pavel Massalsky, Viktor Kulakov, Vasili Bokarev, Lev Zolotukhin, Vladimir Sez, Nikolai Svobodin, Vyacheslav Sushkevich, Aleksandr Khvylya; **w**, Shevejtser, Yevgeni Gabrilovich (based on the novel by Leo Tolstoy); **c**, Sergei Poluyanov, Era Savelyeva; **m**, Georgi Sviridov; **ed**, Klavdiya Aleyeva; **prod d** & **art d**, Abram Freydin, David Vinitsky; **spec eff**, Grigory Ayzenberg, A. Vinokurov.

Retreat, Hell! ★★★★ 1952; U.S. 95m; United States Pictures/WB; B/W; War Drama; Children: Unacceptable; **DVD**; **VHS**. Superior war story profiles the heroic exploits of elements of the 1st Marine Division in its fighting retreat from the Chosin Reservoir during the Korean War (1950-1953). The film begins when the war breaks out and with the recalling of several retreads to service, including Lovejoy, who leaves his post at an American embassy to take command of a newly forming Marine battalion. Carlson, a captain and communications expert, is also recalled from his Marine reserve. Joining that battalion is raw recruit Tamblyn, who has lied about his underage status so that he can enlist and be with his older brother, who is serving somewhere with the Marines. He and many other recruits are shown being trained under the demanding discipline of Young, a tough and savvy sergeant, until they are ready for combat and then shipped to Korea. The unit takes part in the amphibious Inchon landings (September 10-19, 1950) and then proceeds to drive back the North Korean invaders through North Korea until hundreds of thousands of communist Chinese troops join the North Koreans and attack and drive back the Allied forces. Lovejoy and his men struggle through freezing mountain passes as they make their way toward the Chosin Reservoir (this was a seventeen-day brutal battle where the 1st Marine Division fought its way to the staging area at Hungnam Harbor in 1950). En route, Tamblyn learns that his brother is among those slain during the fighting. Since he is the sole surviving son

Richard Carlson, Frank Lovejoy and Russ Tamblyn in *Retreat, Hell!*, 1952.

of his family, Lovejoy orders that he be sent stateside, but Tamblyn is almost killed when the Chinese mount a savage counterattack, where enemy troops penetrate Lovejoy's campsite, even shooting their way into his command tent, only to be killed by the scores and driven back. Tamblyn survives and is sent home while the Marines make an honorable and historic retreat. At one point, when asked if his men are withdrawing in the face of the enemy, Lovejoy shouts: "Retreat, hell! We're not retreating! We're just advancing in another direction!" (This memorable statement was made by General Oliver Prince Smith, 1893-1977, who commanded the 1st Marine Division at that time.) Director Lewis maintains a brisk pace in this well-made war story, keeping close to the real facts and drawing good performances from all the cast members. The battle scenes are particularly good, the action effectively choreographed and appearing grimly realistic. This film was very popular at the box office, returning $2 million to its producers in its initial release. *Author's Note*: Carlson told this author that "the producer for that war picture got a lot of cooperation from the Marine Corps, which allowed us to shoot the training scenes at Camp Pendleton [California] and where we used a lot of those Marine recruits in those scenes. The War Department almost cancelled us out when top brass learned that the word "hell" was going to be in the title, but the Marine Corps intervened, pointing out that the title was actually a quote from one of their own generals [Smith], and they gave us the go-ahead." Many films have profiled the Korean War, those most notably including the battlefield actions being **The Bridges at Toko-Ri**, 1954; **Fixed Bayonets!**, 1951; **Flat Top**, 1952; **The Glory Brigade**, 1953; **MacArthur**, 1977; **The McConnell Story**, 1955; **Men in War**, 1957; **Men of the Fighting Lady**, 1954; **Pork Chop Hill**, 1959; **The Steel Helmet**, 1951; **War Hunt**, 1962; and **War is Hell**, 1963. p, Milton Sperling; d, Joseph H. Lewis; cast, Frank Lovejoy, Richard Carlson, Anita Louise, Russ Tamblyn, Ned Young, Lamont Johnson, Robert Ellis, Paul Smith, Peter Ortiz, Dorothy Patrick, Morton C. Thompson, Joseph Keane; w, Ted Sherdeman, Sperling (based on a story by Sperling); c, Warren Lynch; m, William Lava; ed, Folmar Blangsted; art d, Edward Carrere; set d, William Wallace.

The Return of Dr. X ★★★ 1939; U.S.; 62m.; WB; B/W; Horror; Children: Unacceptable; **DVD**. Eerie and genuinely frightening, this horror tale begins with Morris, a New York newspaper reporter. He loses his job after he claims to have found Lys, an actress, dead in her apartment, and is proved a liar when she turns up alive the next day and threatens to sue the paper. Investigating, Morris discovers that Lys is involved with Litel and Bogart, two strange doctors experimenting with human blood. Morris then discovers a connection with some gruesome murders where the victims were all found drained of blood. With Morgan, a young intern, Morris learns that Litel has been developing synthetic

blood fused with human blood and has used this concoction to bring small, dead animals back to life. Litel has used his serum on Bogart, which is why he looks like a walking corpse, his face pallid white and a thick streak of white covering the top of his closely cropped and otherwise black hair. Litel is finally pressured by Morris into admitting that his experiments have drastically backfired and that Bogart, Lys and others he has injected with his serum are not dissimilar to stalking vampires, who crave fresh blood from the living, which explains a number of unsolved murders in the area. Then Morris and Morgan learn that Bogart is hunting Lane, who is Morgan's girlfriend, because she possesses the very rare blood type he needs to sustain his life. A chase ensues that ends up in the New Jersey marshes where Morris and Morgan, accompanied by police, rescue the terrified Lane just before Bogart can drain her every drop of blood. Bogart is shot to pieces once more by a bevy of cops, this time not as a gangster, which was his usual end in films in those days, but as a bloodthirsty ghoul. This was a remake, and a good one, of **Dr. X**, 1932, which starred Lionel Atwill as the mad doctor. *Author's Note*: Bogart hated playing this part, but he was then a contract player at Warner Brothers and did as he was told, but not without protest. After he made this film, he barged into Jack Warner's office and demanded a pay raise, telling Warner that he had given him a part that "Bela Lugosi or Boris Karloff should have played." Bogart later stated: "I was this doctor brought back to life and the only thing that nourished this poor bastard was blood. I wouldn't have minded if it had been Jack Warner's blood." p, Bryan Foy; d, Vincent Sherman; cast, Humphrey Bogart, Rosemary Lane, Wayne Morris, Dennis Morgan, John Litel, Lya Lys, Huntz Hall, Vera Lewis, John Ridely, Glenn Langan, William Hopper; w, Lee Katz (from a story by William J. Makin); c, Sidney Hickox; m, Bernhard Kaun; ed, Thomas Pratt; art d, Esdras Hartley.

The Return of Frank James ★★★★ 1940; U.S.; 92m; FOX; Color; Biographical Drama/Western; Children: Unacceptable; **DVD**; **VHS**. Few sequels to hit films are as successful as the original, but this one is, where Fonda presents a riveting portrayal of western outlaw Frank James (Alexander Franklin "Frank" James; 1843-1915), the taciturn, deliberate brother of the most notorious bandit of the Old West, Jesse James (1847-1882). This rousing and action-packed biopic opens where the original left off, with Jesse (portrayed by Tyrone Power) being shot (in the back) and killed by gang members Robert Ford (1861-1892), played by Carradine, and Charles Ford (1857-1884), played by Tannen. Fonda is then shown working at a farm with the help of a black field hand, Whitman, and Cooper, who is Fonda's teenage ward, the son of one of the gang's deceased members. Fonda has put away his gun and given up a life of crime, living under an alias and wanting nothing more than to live a peaceful life on his farm. When he hears that his brother has been shot and killed, he takes no action, despite the urgings of hothead Cooper, who wants Fonda to take immediate revenge on his brother's killers. Fonda tells Cooper that the law will mete out justice for the killers. Cooper later shows Fonda a newspaper with a report that Carradine and Tannen have not only been pardoned for killing Jesse James, but have been given thousands of dollars in reward money for committing the heinous deed. Fonda then resolves to bring justice to these killers himself by going after the two men. He retrieves his six-gun while Whitman provides him with supplies and saddles his horse, telling Cooper and Whitman to tend to the farm. Cooper begs to go with him, but Fonda tells him that what he must do he must do alone. Meanwhile, Carradine and Tannen enter a saloon in Liberty, Missouri, offering to buy drinks all around since they are flush with the reward money, but no one wants anything to do with them. Hull, who is the fiery editor of the local newspaper and a friend of the James family, confronts Carradine and Tannen, telling them that they have killed Jesse James, but that his brother, Fonda, is still alive and that they can expect a visit from him at any time. Bromberg, a detective who has schemed to destroy the James gang and has arranged for Carradine and Tannen to work out a deal with authorities and get the reward for killing Jesse, asks the two killers about their plans. Carradine, heeding Hull's words and believing that Fonda will soon be on his trail, tells Bromberg that he and his brother are leaving immediately for parts unknown in the west. That night, Fonda arrives in Liberty and meets secretly with Hull, who tells him that the culprits have left town and Fonda resolves to pursue them, Hull wishing him well when he departs and saying: "Good hunting." Fonda, needing money to pursue the villains, decides to rob a railroad express station since he believes that Meek, the president of the railroad (that the James gang had so routinely robbed in the past), had financed and backed the killers of his brother and, by stealing from the railroad, Fonda is simply seeking retribution. He robs the local express station at night, but Cooper, who has been trailing him, sees him enter the station and goes to help him, but accidentally discharges his six-gun, which alerts Bromberg and other men in the town. Bromberg leads a posse that surrounds the express station and they begin firing into the small building, and the station clerk (Mason) is killed by one of their stray bullets. Fonda and Cooper climb through a hatch to the roof and jump into an alleyway where they overcome two posse members and mount their horses, riding away. As Fonda follows the trail of the killers, he orders Cooper to go back to the farm. Cooper insists that he help Fonda bring the murderers to justice, and Fonda reluctantly allows the youth to accompany him. Meanwhile, Bromberg wrongly affixes the death of the station clerk onto Fonda, who is now wanted for a murder he did not commit. Fonda and Cooper ride after Carradine and Tannen (the Ford Brothers) and find them in a mining town where they are appearing on stage in a dime novel version of how they killed Jesse James. Fonda buys a ticket and tells Cooper to stay outside the theater and watch their horses while he attends the performance. He sits in a box seat and grimly watches Carradine and Tannen reenact their killing of Jesse James, but where Carradine and Tannen alter the facts by not showing how Bob Ford actually shot James in the back. They depict the outlaw's death as a result of a fair gunfight with the Ford Brothers. As Carradine is taking a bow for his hokey and extremely theatrical performance, he glances upward to see Fonda staring down at him. Terrified, Carradine grabs a burning oil lamp and hurls it at Fonda, who ducks, and the lamp sets fire to the box. Carradine and Tannen flee the stage with Fonda in close pursuit, but Fonda is thwarted by an excited Cooper, who has not, as instructed, tended to their horses, but entered the theater to see the show. This delay allows Carradine and Tannen to ride from the town. Fonda and Cooper ride after them, and when they close in on Tannen, who lags behind Carradine, Tannen begins firing at Fonda, who is close behind. They race through a mountainous area, crossing rushing rivers over log bridges and in and around huge rock formations, Fonda and Tannen exchanging shots as they ride pell-mell and where their gunfire ominously echoes through the canyons. (Technicians at Fox Studios had created a method by which gunfire was distinctively heard in only Fox films, one where they fired live rounds into a metal container wadded with cotton and other substances that produced prolonged, hollow and echoing sounds of gunfire, these sounds then applied to the sound track for the appropriate shootout scenes in a film.) Tannen's horse stumbles and he is thrown from his mount, scrambling to a high rocky area as Fonda pursues him on foot, both firing from behind huge boulders as bullets zing and whine about them. Just as Tannen is about to shoot Fonda, he loses his footing and slips from his precarious perch, falling to his death below. Fonda then looks down upon the crumpled body of Tannen, saying: "That's one of them, Jesse." Meanwhile, Carradine, who has callously deserted his brother, has escaped. While looking for Carradine, Fonda and Cooper go to Denver, Colorado, taking a room in an upscale hotel, and Cooper pretends to be an old friend of Fonda's just arriving from Mexico, saying before many persons sitting on the hotel's veranda that he has witnessed the death of Frank James. Cooper states that the notorious brother of Jesse James was shot by outlaws south of the border. This fabricated story has been concocted by Cooper and Fonda to cover Fonda's true identity and to persuade lawmen to cease their pursuit of him. Hearing about this tale, Tierney (in her film debut), who is the

Henry Fonda and Henry Hull in *The Return of Frank James,* 1940.

daughter of Corrigan, owner of the local newspaper, and who has ambitions to become a newspaper reporter, visits Fonda and Cooper at their hotel. She gets an interview with Cooper, who tells about the death of Frank James in Mexico, grandly embellishing his tale to elaborately portray Fonda as a hero who died while attempting to save the virtue of a young girl. His story thrills Tierney, who now looks upon Frank James as a heroic figure, although Fonda, who is using the alias of "Woodson" (his outlaw brother was named Jesse "Woodson" James) seems embarrassed by Cooper's grandiose account. After Tierney's story about the alleged death of Frank James appears in her father's newspaper, Tierney is contacted by Bromberg, who has been on Fonda's trail, and who tells her that the man she met with Cooper, Fonda, is not the person he represents himself to be, but is none other than the much-wanted outlaw, Frank James. He tells Tierney that Fonda is wanted for killing the guard in an express station. Tierney is startled and confused, refusing to believe that Fonda is the cruel and cunning killer Bromberg has described. A short time later, Bromberg captures Fonda and Cooper when they enter their hotel room where he has been awaiting them, but Cooper, in a ruse, pulls the rug from beneath the chair where Bromberg sits holding a gun on them and Fonda wrestles Bromberg to the floor. Bromberg is then tied up and hanged on a hook in a closet like an old coat while Fonda and Cooper prepare to leave town. Before they continue their search for Carradine, however, Fonda meets with Tierney, who tells him that she believes him to be a good and innocent man. She also tells him that Whitman, the black farm hand who has worked so many years with Fonda, has been arrested in Missouri and has been charged with killing the station clerk. Fonda tells her that Whitman is innocent and that the clerk had been killed by someone outside the building during the robbery. When she begs him to do the honorable thing and return to Missouri to save Whitman, he tells her that he must continue to search for Carradine and bring him to justice for murdering his brother. Tierney's fine illusions about Fonda are shattered when he rides off with Cooper in search of Carradine. While Fonda is pursuing Carradine, he suddenly stops and tells Cooper that he is returning to Missouri, where he will turn himself in to authorities since he cannot allow Whitman to be found guilty and hanged for a crime that he did not commit. Cooper argues with him, telling him that he has become weak due to the pleadings of Tierney, and Fonda slaps him for this insult and then begins riding back toward Missouri. Cooper joins him and Fonda reluctantly accepts his companionship. They come upon some stray horses and swap these fresh mounts for their exhausted mounts, leaving money for the owner. They then ride to a train depot and compel at gunpoint its station agent, Collins, to flag down the express train going eastward. Fonda arrives in time to save Whitman and is then put on trial for the murder of the station clerk, Mason. Hull, his good friend,

Jackie Cooper, Eddie Collins and Henry Fonda in *The Return of Frank James,* **1940.**

defends him in court where railroad boss Meek sits with the prosecutor, Hicks. The jury is decidedly partial toward the defendant, who was once a member of guerrilla forces fighting for the Confederacy during the Civil War. One of the jury members wears an old Confederate uniform, and Barbier, the presiding judge, was once a Confederate officer during that war. Hull, in his histrionic defense, contends that Mason was killed by a shot fired by someone outside the express office while Hicks, the prosecutor, insists that Fonda deliberately killed Mason. When it appears that Fonda might be convicted, Carradine enters the court, smugly standing in the rear of the room, obviously there to see Fonda convicted and with a gloating look upon his face in anticipation of that conviction. His presence is noted by the judge and jury, all of whom know that Carradine was the man who cowardly shot and killed Fonda's brother. The jury quickly deliberates and then renders its decision, its foreman saying that "Frank James is not guilty of anything." Fonda, now that he is free to pursue Carradine, who has fled the courthouse, is stopped by Tierney, who has traveled to attend Fonda's trial, and where she begs him not to take revenge against Carradine. Meanwhile, several shots are heard outside the courtroom, and Fonda and the crowd rush to the town square where Fonda finds Cooper mortally wounded. Cooper tells him that he tried to stop Carradine, and may have seriously wounded him before Carradine shot him. Cooper dies in Fonda's arms, and Fonda then goes to a livery stable where Carradine has taken refuge. Fonda stalks Carradine, who fires at him from grain sacks and then retreats into a room in the loft and where Fonda fires a shot through the door. He enters the room to see Carradine dead, sprawled on the floor and where Fonda says: "That's the other one, Jesse." Fonda then says farewell to Tierney, telling her that he might pay her a visit in the future. She turns the corner of a building, smiling and waving goodbye to him, and disappears. The camera closes upon an old and weathered poster announcing a reward for the capture of Frank and Jesse James and a gust of wind then blows away those names from the poster to symbolically and evocatively state that those outlaw years are dead and gone and that violent era of the Old West is no more. Lang directs this superb biopic and western with great care, and Fonda and the rest of the cast provide absorbing character portraits. The western landscapes are beautifully photographed by Barnes in lush Technicolor (the older process that provides deeper and more inspiring hues, more natural than the newer process where color is less rich and seemingly flat). Although many exciting action scenes are presented, Lang offers a more introspective portrait of the outlaws, and his sets and lighting present a special haunting atmosphere seldom seen in other westerns (except, perhaps, his own later production, **Rancho Notorious**, 1952, the only other western Lang directed). The result is a distinctive classic western, despite the fact that the script, which is well written and intelligent, took great liberties with the facts involving the

James gang. Songs: "Old Ironsides March" (Hugo Riesenfeld), "Ring, Ring the Banjo," "Jeannie with the Light Brown Hair" (Stephen Foster). *Author's Note*: When Zanuck decided to assign this film to director Lang a lot of eyebrows were raised at his studio. Zanuck told this author: "Some people told me that Lang was all wrong to direct **The Return of Frank James**, and that his background in Germany was centered on dark dramas and offbeat crime stories like **M** [1931], a pretty grim story about a child-killer. I told these self-styled critics that Lang had a keen perception and would see things about the western story that we would not and that his viewpoint would make for a better picture. What I meant by that was that I knew Lang had been working for some years on a project about the Navajo Indians and had traveled throughout the Southwest and learned a lot about the Old West. Though that project never got on film, Lang had a treasure trove of western culture and behavior and all that shows in the fine picture he made." Fonda, the star of this film, did not share Zanuck's confidence in Lang and, after he learned that Lang would be again directing him, he went to Zanuck and complained. "I told the boss [Zanuck] that I would not work with Lang," Fonda told this author. "He was a monster when we did **You Only Live Once** [1937]. He abused every actor and crew member to the point where we all wanted to find new professions. He used an iron-fist policy that was part of his German training, I guess, but that translated into him insulting everyone every time he gave instructions." When Zanuck repeated Fonda's statements to Lang, the director promised that he would talk to Fonda and assure him that their relationship while making **The Return of Frank James** would be cordial and pleasant. Lang did go to Fonda and, according to Fonda's statements to this author: "He actually cried tears when he said he had heard my unkind remarks about him. He promised me that he would be kind and considerate to everyone while we made the picture, so I agreed to do it. Well, that was a big mistake, because, as soon as Lang sat down in that director's chair on the set, or stood behind the cameras, he was his old self, a dictator acting like the Kaiser, abruptly bossing people about and snapping orders like a field marshal. So all those crocodile tears he was shedding earlier was just a trick to get me to do the picture. It was the last one I ever did with him." Tierney, who appeared in her first feature film with this production, thought that "the picture was beautifully made and all the mountain areas are breathtaking. My role was created to have some love interest for Hank [Fonda] and I was not happy with how I delivered some of my lines, especially when I get frantic at the end and try to stop Hank from killing the man who killed his brother. When I heard my voice in that scene, I was horrified. I sounded like a shrieking mouse that had been bitten by a cat. Awful, just awful, I thought. I vowed that whenever I had to raise my voice in another picture I would purposely lower the tone of my voice and I practiced that for months and months after **The Return of Frank James** was released. In those days in Hollywood you could learn from your mistakes on the screen and still survive." The film basically ignores the background of Jesse and Frank James and centers on telling a story of revenge. That story nevertheless softens Fonda's character to an acceptable level while he is shown more of a hero than a lawbreaker. It is true that Frank James turned himself in after his brother was killed and that he was tried and acquitted in a sensation trial, set free to live out a long life as a gentleman farmer and celebrated former outlaw. He did not, however, seek any revenge against Bob and Charlie Ford, who killed his brother. Charlie, apparently haunted by his act, committed suicide and Bob was killed in Creede, Colorado, in his own saloon by an irate drunk, Edward C. Kelley, on June 8, 1892, about ten years after Bob Ford had murdered Jesse James. Many other actors have portrayed Frank James in several films, most notably **The Adventures of Frank and Jesse James**, 1948 (Steve Darrell); **Alias Jesse James**, 1959 (Jim Davis); **American Outlaws**, 2001 (Gabriel Macht); **The Assassination of Jesse James by the Coward Robert Ford**, 2007 (Sam Shepard); **Bad Man's Territory**, 1946 (Tom Tyler); **Belle Starr**, 1980 (made-for-TV; Gary Combs); **Best of the Badmen**, 1951 (Tom Tyler); **Bitter Heritage**, 1958 (made-for-TV; Franchot Tone); **Days of**

Jesse James, 1939 (Harry Worth); **Frank and Jesse**, 1995 (Bill Paxton); **The Great Missouri Raid**, 1951 (Wendell Corey); **The Great Northfield, Minnesota Raid**, 1972 (John Pearce); **Gunfire**, 1950 (Don "Red" Barry); **Hell's Crossroads**, 1957 (Douglas Kennedy); **I Shot Jesse James**, 1949 (Tom Tyler); **The James Brothers of Missouri**, 1949 (Robert Bice); **Jesse James**, 1927 (James Pierce); **Jesse James**, 1939 (Henry Fonda): **Jesse James at Bay**, 1941 (Al Taylor); **Jesse James' Hidden Treasure**, 2009 (made-for-TV; Bill Armstrong); **Jesse James' Women**, 1954 (Jack Buetel); **Kansas Raiders**, 1950 (Richard Long); **The Last Days of Frank and Jesse James**, 1986 (made-for-TV; Johnny Cash); **The Legend of Jesse James**, 1965-1966 (TV series; Allen Case); **The Long Riders**, 1980 (Stacy Keach); **Outlaw Treasure**, 1955 (Robert Hinkle); **The Return of Frank James**, 1940 (Henry Fonda); **The Return of Jesse James**, 1950 (Reed Hadley); **A Time for Dying**, 1982 (Willard Willingham); **The True Story of Jesse James**, 1957 (Jeffrey Hunter); **Two Gangsters in the Wild West**, 1964 (Tony Casale); **Woman They Almost Lynched**, 1953 (James Brown); **Young Jesse James**, 1960 (Robert Dix); and **The Young Riders**, 1989-1992 (TV series; Jamie Walters). For more details about Frank and Jesse James and their criminal exploits and associates, see my works *Bloodletters and Badmen: A Narrative Encyclopedia of American Criminals from the Pilgrims to the Present* (M. Evans, 1995); *Encyclopedia of Western Lawmen and Outlaws* (Paragon House, 1992); and *The Great Pictorial History of World Crime* (History, Inc., 2004; pages 1342-1360). **p**, Darryl F. Zanuck; **d**, Fritz Lang; **cast**, Henry Fonda, Gene Tierney, Jackie Cooper, Henry Hull, John Carradine, J. Edward Bromberg, Donald Meek, Ernest Whitman, Eddie Collins, George Barbier, Russell Hicks, Charles Tannen, Lloyd Corrigan, Louis Mason, Barbara Pepper; **w**, Sam Hellman; **c**, George Barnes (Technicolor); **m**, David Buttolph; **ed**, Walter Thompson; **art d**, Richard Day, Wiard Ihnen; **set d**, Thomas Little; **spec eff**, Larry Chapman.

The Return of Martin Guerre ★★★ 1983; France; 111m; Dussault; European International; Color; Drama/Mystery; Children: Unacceptable; **DVD**; **VHS**. Depardieu gives a disturbing and compelling performance in this classic mystery tale. Set in 16th-Century France, a young husband named Martin Guerre goes off to war, and when he does not return, his wife, Baye, believes he is dead. Depardieu reappears nine years later, claiming to be her long-lost husband. He is welcomed by most of the townspeople in his village, including Baye, but some state that he is not the same man who went off to war those many years earlier. He cannot recall some of the people who have known him, and his lapses of memory fuel the flames of suspicion. Some of his detractors insist that the real Martin Guerre lost a leg in battle during the war and that he never returned home. These naysayers brand Depardieu an imposter. Throughout the film short sequences depict an ongoing judicial inquiry into whether or not Depardieu is who he claims to be. At times, Baye is very supportive of him, insisting that he is her husband, but, on other occasions where Depardieu seems to have no contact with his surroundings, she seems to lose confidence in him as signaled by her stony silence. The end is grim and final: The magistrate concludes that Depardieu is an imposter and sentences him to death by hanging. Based on a true story, the viewer is left to decide if Depardieu is the real Martin Guerre or not. Sexuality prohibits viewing by children. (In French; English subtitles.) **p&d**, Daniel Vigne; **cast**, Gérard Depardieu, Bernard-Pierre Donnadieu, Nathalie Baye, Roger Planchon, Maurice Jacquemont, Isabelle Sadoyan, Rose Thiéry, Chantal Deruaz, Maurice Barrier, Francis Arnaud; **w**, Vigne, Jean-Claude Carriére, Natalie Zemon Davis (based on the novel *The Wife of Martin Guerre* by Janet Lewis); **c**, André Neau (Fujicolor); **m**, Michel Portal; **ed**, Denise de Casabianca; **art d**, Alain Négre.

Return of the Bad Men ★★★ 1948; U.S.; 90m.; RKO; B/W; Western; Children: Unacceptable; **DVD**; **VHS**. In this exciting sequel to **Badmen's Territory**, 1946, Scott is a U.S. marshal, who wants to retire, but

George "Gabby" Hayes and Randolph Scott in *Return of the Bad Men*, 1948.

finds no peace when part of the Oklahoma Territory becomes officially part of the United States. His problems increase when outlaw Ryan (playing the Sundance Kid), forms a gang including Billy the Kid, the Younger Brothers, and the Dalton Brothers to rob stage coaches and trains in the area. Scott manages to survive a shootout with the outlaws, scattering them hither and yon. There's a lot of well-choreographed action in this above-average oater, but the story line plays fast and loose with Western history. *Author's Note*: Scott told this author that "to make characters more credible, the Hollywood writers in the late 1940s inserted real-life western bad men into scripts and they threw almost every outlaw they could think of into that picture. They did not concern themselves with the real facts, figuring that no one would check up on what these folks really did or what happened to them. They traded on those notorious names that everyone would recognize and that was enough for them." Of his unsavory character in this film, Ryan stated to this author: "I don't think that the real Sundance Kid was ever as mean and vicious as I was in **Return of the Bad Men**. I admit that I was damned mad about being typecast again as a heavy, so I took it out on my character and I guess I made him look like a lunatic, who just could not wait to get up in the morning and shoot someone." **p**, Nat Holt; **d**, Ray Enright; **cast**, Randolph Scott, Robert Ryan, Anne Jeffreys, George "Gabby" Hayes, Jacqueline White, Steve Brodie, Tom Keene, Robert Bray, Lex Barker, Walter Reed, Dean White, Michael Harvey, Tom Tyler; **w**, Charles O'Neal, Jack Natteford, Luci Ward (based on a story by Natteford, Ward); **c**, J. Roy Hunt; **m**, Paul Sawtell; **ed**, Samuel E. Beetley; **art d**, Albert S. D'Agostino, Ralph Berger; **set d**, Darrell Silvera, James Altwies.

The Return of the Pink Panther ★★★ 1975; U.K.; 115m; UA; Color; Comedy/Crime/Mystery; Children: Acceptable (MPAA: G); **DVD**; **VHS**. A lot of fun and no little mirthful mayhem takes place when a master thief called "The Phantom" returns and is suspected of having stolen the famous jewel, The Pink Panther. French Police Inspector Clouseau (Sellers) and his Asian manservant Cato (Kwouk) set out to catch and identify him, and, while going along their hilarious and bungling ways, drive Chief Inspector Dreyfus (Lom) to near insanity. Plummer, a retired jewel thief, is a prime suspect, but Sellers' dragnet includes just about everyone else as he stumbles toward the eventual culprit. Edwards directs this film with whirlwind speed, and Sellers, as always, is marvelous to behold as he fractures the English language with his wrongly accented deliveries; the cast all render top-flight performances. A sequel to **The Pink Panther**, 1963, this very funny film was a big hit at the box office, producing more than $40 million in its initial release against a $5 million budget. It was followed by **The Pink Panther Strikes Again**, 1976, **Revenge of the Pink Panther**, 1978, **The**

David Alan Grier and David Duchovny in *Return to Me*, 2000.

Pink Panther, 2006, and **The Pink Panther 2**, 2009. Songs: "The Pink Panther Theme" (Henry Mancini), "The Greatest Gift" (music: Mancini; lyrics: Hal David), "The Ride of the Valkyries" (Richard Wagner). *Author's Note*: The film was shot on location at Casablanca, Marrakesh, at Gstaad, Switzerland (the resort there being Ernest Hemingway's favorite recreation spot for winter sports), and the French Riviera, which accelerated its budget. United Artists rejected the story after producer Walter Mirisch and Edwards pitched it to its executives because Edwards and his star, Sellers, had seen declining popularity at the box office. That all changed after British producer Lew Grade (his critics called him "Low Grade") backed the production. Plummer (while we sat talking one evening in the old Blue Room Bar of New York's Algonquin Hotel) told this author that "working with Peter [Sellers] always presented a number of surprises. It was hard to keep a straight face as he went through his unexpected antics. His facial expressions were priceless and his pratfalls were as natural as taking one step after another. He had a genius for comedy." **p&d**, Blake Edwards; **cast**, Peter Sellers, Christopher Plummer, Catherine Schell, Herbert Lom, Burt Kwouk, Peter Arne, Peter Jeffrey, Gregoire Aslan, David Lodge, Eric Pohlmann, Peter Jones; **w**, Edwards, Frank Waldman; **c**, Geoffrey Unsworth (Panavision; DeLuxe Color); **m**, Henry Mancini; **ed**, Tom Priestley; **prod d**, Peter Mullins; **spec eff**, John Gant.

The Return of the Vampire ★★★ 1943; U.S.; 69m; COL; B/W; Horror; Children: Unacceptable; **DVD**; **IV**. Creepy, well-made horror tale is set in 1918 England, where a family is terrorized by vampires. These creatures are defeated and thought to be extinct, but German bombs in World War II (1939-1945) unearth the patriarchal vampire (Lugosi). He reclaims the soul of his werewolf servant, Willis, and assumes the identity of a scientist, who has just escaped from a Nazi concentration camp. Lugosi then starts out on a plan to get revenge on the family that wiped out his bloodsucking clan twenty years earlier. He meets his match in Inescort, a staunch female vampire slayer who operates an asylum where the unstable Willis works. When Lugosi goes after Foch, who is the apple of Willis' eye, the tormented Willis, weary of periodically changing into a werewolf at Lugosi's bidding, turns on his master and fends him off with a crucifix. Lugosi is then driven into the sunlight where daylight destroys him. Well-directed and acted by Lugosi, Willis, Inescort and Mander, the latter an outstanding British supporting actor with an always refined persona, give top-notch performances. The film was shot on a shoestring budget of less than $100,000 and returned five times that amount at the box office. *Author's Note*: Lugosi, though he was known for playing vampires, only enacted a few such roles, but his impact on international audiences with **Dracula**, 1931, was so long-lasting that he personified these sinister mythical creatures. (At his request

before he died, he was buried in the cloak he wore in **Dracula**; friends Vincent Price and Peter Lorre attended his funeral and Lorre acidly quipped: "Do you think we should drive a stake through his heart just to be on the safe side?") In this film, Lugosi (who received $3,500 for his four weeks of work on this film) uses the name of "Armand Tesla," enacting the demonstrative mannerisms of Nikola Tesla (1856-1943), the brilliant inventor and engineer, although the use of the same last name was undoubtedly lost on audiences at that time, even though that genius died the same year this film was released. Makeup artist Clay Campbell does some fine work in this film, particularly when recreating Willis into a werewolf. The final scene in the film belongs to Campbell in that he created a horrifying death scene for Lugosi's vampire. He recreated Lugosi's head in wax over a human skull. As Lugosi is trapped by the rays of the sun and collapses in an open lot, the camera closes on that wax replica, which melts into ghastly looking shreds (through a heating device Campbell inserted in the skull), this repulsive-looking sludge falling from the bone to expose the gruesome skull. This last scene was thought to be too ghoulishly grim for British audiences and it was edited out before the film was released in England. **p**, Sam White; **d**, Lew Landers; **cast**, Bela Lugosi, Frieda Inescort, Nina Foch, Miles Mander, Roland Varno, Matt Willis, William Austin, Jeanne Bates, Billy Bevan, Sydney Chatton; **w**, Griffin Jay, Randall Faye (from a story idea by Kurt Neumann); **c**, L. William O'Connell, John Stumar; **m**, Mario Castelnuovo-Tedesco; **ed**, Paul Borofsky; **art d**, Lionel Banks, Victor Greene; **set d**, Louis Diage.

Return to Me ★★★ 2000; U.S.; 115m; JLT Productions/MGM; Color; Comedy/Romance; Children: Unacceptable (MPAA: PG); **DVD**; **VHS**. Lively romantic comedy sees Duchovny and Richardson as a happily married couple living in the Windy City. Duchovny is a Chicago architect, and Richardson is a zoologist at the city's Lincoln Park Zoo, the film opening as they are preparing for a fund-raising dinner. However, the evening ends tragically with Richardson dying in an automobile accident. Her heart is transplanted into another woman, Driver. Duchovny's heart is broken by his loss, but Grier, a friend, fixes him up with a blind date at a restaurant. Duchovny is more interested in the waitress, Driver, and they eventually fall in love, but only later does he learn that the heart Driver possesses once belonged to his late wife. He is now faced with wondering if he has fallen in love with a new woman or is she the reincarnation of his former wife. Songs: "Return to Me" (Danny DiMinno, Carmen Lombardo); "The Lion Sleeps Tonight" (Solomon Linda, Hugo Poeretti, George David Weiss, Luigi Creatore); "Soon," "But Not for Me" "Someone to Watch Over Me" (George and Ira Gershwin); "Return to Sorrento" (Giambattista De Curtis, Ernesto De Curtis); "Angel Standing By" (Jewel Kilcher); "The Best Is Yet to Come" (Cy Coleman, Carolyn Leigh); 'It's Such a Happy Day' (Jackie Gleason); "Buona Sera" (Peter De Rose, Carl Sigman); "Maria Mari" (Eduardo Di Capua, V. Russo); "Danny Boy" (Rory Dall O'Cahan, Frederick Edward Weatherly); "When Irish Eyes Are Smiling" (Ernest Ball, George Graff, Chauncey Olcott); "O Sole Mio" (Eduardo Di Capua, Giovanni Capurro, Alfredo Mazzucchi); "Tenderly" (Walter Gross, Jack Lawrence); "Where or When" (Richard Rodgers, Lorenz Hart); "Good Mornin' Life" (Joseph Meyer, Robert Allen); "I Second That Emotion" (Al Cleveland, William "Smokey" Robinson, Jr.); "At Long Last Love" (Cole Porter); "What If I Loved You" (Joseph Gian); "Here I Am" (Charley Midnight, Joseph Gian). Gutter language and thematic elements prohibit viewing by children. **p**, Jennie Lew Tugend; **d**, Bonnie Hunt; **cast**, David Duchovny, Minnie Driver, Carroll O'Connor, Robert Loggia, Hunt, David Alan Grier, Joely Richardson, Eddie Jones, James Belushi, Marianne Muellerleile; **w**, Hunt, Don Lake (based on a story by Hunt, Lake, Andrew Stern, Samantha Goodman); **c**, Laszlo Kovacs; **m**, Nicholas Pike; **ed**, Garth Craven; **prod d**, Brent Thomas; **art d**, David W. Krummel; **set d**, Daniel Clancy; **spec eff**, Rodman Kiser, Mark Hogan.

Reunion ★★★ 1989; France/West Germany/U.K.; 110m; TAG/Las

Films Ariane/Castle Hill; Color; Drama; Children: Unacceptable (MPAA: PG-13); **VHS**. Fascinating period drama begins when two teenage boys from very different backgrounds become best friends in 1933 Stuttgart, Germany. Anholt is Jewish, the son of a doctor, and West comes from a German autocratic family. With Hitler gaining power, anti-Semitism and politics drive a wedge between them. Anholt escapes the Nazi persecution of Jews by going to America and, as a grown man, Robards has a reunion with the past, learning that his boyhood friend became a Nazi, but fell into disfavor for opposing Hitler and was executed by a firing squad. This compelling and well-made film subtly depicts the virulent anti-Semitism that the Hitler regime sowed in Germany, and how, as this film shows in microcosm, it destroyed the social fabric of the country. Excessive violence prohibits viewing by children. **p**, Anne Francois; **d**, Jerry Schatzberg; **cast**, Jason Robards, Christien Anholt, Samuel West, Francoise Fabian, Maureen Kerwin, Dorothea Alexander, Frank Baker, Tim Barker, Imke Barnstedt, Rupert Degas; **w**, Harold Pinter (based on a novel by Fred Uhlman); **c**, Bruno de Keyzer; **m**, Philippe Sarde; **ed**, Martine Barraque; **prod d**, Alexandre Trauner, Didier Naert; **art d**, Thomas Schappert; **spec eff**, Adolf Wojtinek.

Reunion in France ★★★ 1942; U.S.; 104m; MGM; B/W; Drama/Romance; Children: Unacceptable; **DVD**. Superior drama sees Frenchwoman Crawford living in luxury in Paris with her successful husband Dorn. All that changes when Germany invades France in WWII (1939-1945) and Nazi troops occupy the city. Her mansion is turned into a German bureau that dispenses coal, and she is compelled to live in less comfortable quarters. After she learns that Dorn has turned collaborator in order to hold on to his possessions, Crawford denounces him, becoming, to her surprise, a patriot. She encounters Wayne, a downed American flying with the RAF who is being hunted by the Gestapo, and she hides him, falling in love with him. She attempts to smuggle Wayne out of the country, but all her considerable efforts fail. Desperate, Crawford goes to Dorn, begging him for help. To her amazement, she finds that her husband is not the lowly collaborator he led her to believe, but has been working with the French Resistance, and has been sabotaging Nazi operations ever since the Germans marched into Paris. He has also been energetically smuggling to freedom many Allied servicemen trapped in France. Dorn, at great risk, arranges for Wayne to escape by sending him to the South of France, and he eventually makes his way back to England to fly again. Crawford, who had originally thought to leave with Wayne, has found new respect and affection for the heroic Dorn, and elects to stay at his side, where both will continue to fight against the oppressors. The gifted Dassin directs this good melodrama with a deft hand, carefully developing the principal characters while peppering the film with many harrowing scenes embodied by such evil Nazi personifications as Carradine and Owen, who play Gestapo agents. Songs: "La Marseillaise" (1792; Claude Joseph Rouget de Lisle), "Frere Jacques" (traditional), "March" (from the opera "Die Meistersinger von Nurnberg"; 1868, by Richard Wagner), "Concerto for Violin in D Minor, second movement" (1844; Felix Mendelssohn-Bartholdy), "Symphony No, 5 in C Minor" (1809; Ludwig van Beethoven), "I'll Be Glad When You're Dead, You Rascal You" (1931; Spo-De-Odee), "Taps" (1862, Daniel Butterfield). *Author's Note*: Wayne told this author that "**Reunion in France** was a vehicle for Joan Crawford. I played a romantic prop in that picture as Joan was then the reigning queen at MGM, although I must admit that she treated me with great respect. She was no grand dame, but a very elegant woman, who was always nice to everyone." Crawford told this author that she "objected to some of the scenes in the film, especially where I go on wearing designer dresses and my wardrobe seems to expand even after the Germans march into Paris. I told the director [Dassin] that seemed out of place. He said: 'You're playing the wife of a collaborator and that brings special privileges so you must go on wearing those wonderful gowns.'" **p**, Joseph L. Mankiewicz; **d**, Jules Dassin; **cast**, Joan Crawford, John Wayne, Philip Dorn, Reginald Owen, Albert Bassermann, John Carradine, Ann Ayars,

Glenn Close and Jeremy Irons in *Reversal of Fortune*, 1990.

J. Edward Bromberg, Moroni Olsen, Henry Daniell, Howard Da Silva, and Ava Gardner seen briefly as a salesgirl; **w**, Marc Connelly, Jan Lustig, Marvin Borowsky, Charles Hoffman (from a story by Ladislas Bus-Fekete); **c**, Robert Planck; **m**, Franz Waxman; **ed**, Elmo Veron; **art d**, Cedric Gibbons; **set d**, Edwin B. Willis; **spec eff**, Warren Newcombe.

Revenge of the Pink Panther ★★★ 1978; U.K./U.S.; 98m; Jewel Productions/UA; Color; Comedy; Children: Acceptable (MPAA: G); **DVD**; **VHS**. Many comedic moments are presented in this delightful comedy, the fifth picture of the "Pink Panther" series. Sellers is again the bumbling French Inspector Clouseau, this time assigned by his boss, Chief Inspector Dreyfus (Lom) to break a narcotics ring run by Webber. Lom thinks he will help matters by announcing that Sellers is dead, although he isn't, and the ruse only creates more comedic situations. The bumbling and stumbling Sellers receives much-needed help in Webber's capture by the drug lord's dumped girlfriend, the savvy Cannon, who proves to be a more effective shamus than the hilariously posturing French sleuth. Edwards directs with his usual lightning speed, and Sellers is the whole show, well supported by Cannon and the exceptional Stewart, who plays the heavy, and the always perplexed and vexed Lom. Songs: "Move 'Em Out" (music: Henry Mancini; lyrics: Leslie Bricusse), "M' appari tutt' amor" (from the opera "Martha" by Friedrich von Flotow), "Thank Heaven for Little Girls," "A Touch of Red" (Mancini). Other films in the enormously successful series are **The Pink Panther**, 1963, **Return of the Pink Panther**, 1975, **The Pink Panther Strikes Again**, 1976, **Revenge of the Pink Panther**, 1978, **The Pink Panther**, 2006, and **The Pink Panther 2**, 2009. **p&d**, Blake Edwards; **cast**, Peter Sellers, Herbert Lom, Burt Kwouk, Dyan Cannon, Robert Webber, Robert Loggia, Tony Beckley, Paul Stewart, Andre Maranne, Graham Stark; **w**, Edwards, Frank Waldman, Ron Clark (from a story by Edwards); **c**, Ernest Day (Panavision; Technicolor); **m**, Henry Mancini; **ed**, Alan Jones; **prod d**, Peter Mullins; **art d**, John Siddall, Benjamin Fernandez; **spec eff**, Brian Johnson.

Reversal of Fortune ★★★ 1990; U.S./111m; WB; Color; Crime Drama; Children: Unacceptable (MPAA: R); **DVD**; **VHS**. Riveting and often frightening tale sees wealthy socialite Bunny von Bulow (1931-2008), played by Close, lying brain-dead in a coma as her husband Claus von Bulow (1926-), played by Irons, is charged with attempted murder by giving her an overdose of insulin, ostensibly to acquire her vast fortune. He hires a top criminal defense lawyer, Alan Dershowitz (1938-), played by Silver, to defend him. Silver thinks Irons is guilty, but takes the case when Irons agrees to fund Silver's defense of two poor black teenagers accused of murder. Silver brings about an acquittal for Irons in this mainly good courtroom drama that is based on a celebrated true

Jennifer Salt and Jon Voight in *The Revolutionary*, 1970.

crime story. Songs: "3 Strange Days" (Josh Clayton-Felt, Michael Ward), "Sing a Happy Funky Song" (Paul Politi), "Gimme a Little Sign" (Jerry Winn, Alfred Smith, Joseph Hooven), "Hot Shot" (Andy Kahn, Burt Boruslewicz), "Late Night Goings On" (Les Hooper), "The Mercenaries" (Dennis Farnon). ***Author's Note***: Bulow had been convicted of attempted murder on March 16, 1982, but remained free on bail while awaiting sentencing. In 1984, Dershowitz, a very savvy Harvard Law School professor, took on his case and got Bulow's conviction overturned on a technicality. He later brought about an acquittal on appeal based upon the same legal argument. Most crime authorities, however, including this author, remained convinced that Bulow was guilty. I profiled the Bulow case in my book, *Murder among the Mighty* (Delacorte Press, New York, 1983), a year before Dershowitz undertook that case. I first met Dershowitz many years earlier when we both appeared on a TV talk show in Cincinnati. I had appeared on that show to discuss one of the dozens of books I had written on true crime. After that show, when we were being driven back to our hotels in a limousine (provided by the producers of that show), Dershowitz bombarded me with endless questions about the success of my published true crime works. He wanted to know how I approached the subject and asked me to detail my methods of research. I gave him some perfunctory responses as I thought him naïve when he asked me to detail the involved methodology of research for those detailed works that had taken years to develop. "Do you make any money with these books?" he asked. "Oh, yes," I replied (with no little sarcastic implication), adding: "The royalties roll in so fast that I don't have the time to spend all the money." I played him along, painting a picture of the fabulous bounties—mansions, yachts and bulging bank accounts that awaited him if he entered that field of endeavor. He then told me that he was thinking of going into the true crime publishing field "to cash in on such a lucrative market." I wished him well. Dershowitz later "cashed in" when he began writing true crime books based on his cases, as well as selling those books for film adaptations to Hollywood, including the Bulow affair, and went on years later to "cash in" on his legal participation in the O. J. Simpson case (where Dershowitz provided some key points that helped acquit Simpson, who nevertheless remains guilty of murdering his wife in this author's perspective). Dershowitz nevertheless remains one of the country's most brilliant legal experts in criminal justice (his specialty is overturning cases on appeal), as well as an enterprising entrepreneur, who did "cash in" after he entered the true crime publishing field. In addition to the above-mentioned book, more details on the Bulow case, as well as the Simpson case, can been found in my two-volume work, *The Great Pictorial History of World Crime* (History, Inc., 2004; Bulow: pages 898-902; Simpson: pages 920-933). Dershowitz, in addition to his legal and writing chores, loves the camera, and he appears in this film as a judge; he often appears

these days as a talking head on legal matters on TV, and he regularly appears on Fox News as such. All good attorneys are also good actors, and Dershowitz is no exception. Violence shown in this film prohibits viewing by children. **p**, Oliver Stone, Edward R. Pressman, Nicholas Kazan, Elon Dershowitz; **d**, Barbet Schroeder; **cast**, Glenn Close, Jeremy Irons, Ron Silver, Annabella Sciorra, Uta Hagen, Fisher Stevens, Jack Gilpin, Christine Baranski, Stephen Mailer, Felicity Huffman, Close (narrator); **w**, Kazan (based on the book by Alan Dershowitz); **c**, Luciano Tovoli; **m**, Mark Isham; **ed**, Lee Percy; **prod d**, Mel Bourne; **art d**, Dan Davis; **set d**, Beth Kushnick.

The Revolutionary ★★★ 1970; U.K.; 101m; Pressman-Williams; UA/Color; Drama; Children: Unacceptable (MPAA: R); **DVD**. Solid drama has Voight as a radical university student in a fictitious country in the 1960s. He opposes the campus association to which he belongs because it is cooperating with a political regime he believes should be overthrown by violent means. He and his girlfriend, Wilcox-Horn, quit the university and join with Duvall, a factory owner, who leads the opposition, an organization that is thinly disguised as being communist. Voight joins a general strike and is arrested, but is not jailed because he is drafted into military service. He is assigned to break the strike he once led, but goes A.W.O.L. rather than fight against his political beliefs. This leads him into joining with another revolutionary, Cassel, an alliance that ends with him holding a bomb as he confronts a judge sympathetic to the establishment. Offbeat but compelling, this tale follows the then popular sentiment that opposed the Vietnam War (1961-1975). Violence prohibits viewing by children. **p**, Edward Rambach Pressman; **d**, Paul Williams; **cast**, Jon Voight, Robert Duvall, Seymour Cassel, Collin Wilcox-Horn, Jennifer Salt, Elliott Sullivan, Alexandra Berlin, Warren Stanhope, Peter Carlisle, Bill Nagy; **w**, Hans Koningsberger (based on his novel); **c**, Brian Probyn; **m**, Michael Small; **ed**, Henry Richardson; **prod d**, Disley Jones.

Rhapsody ★★★ 1954; U.S.; 115m; MGM; Color; Musical/Romance; Children: Acceptable; **DVD**; **IV**. Taylor was never lovelier than when playing a beautiful, rich, and spoiled young woman, who wants to be needed and even recognized as an accomplished pianist. She studies in Europe, but her teachers sadly inform her that she has little aptitude for classical music. She then devotes her time to a concert violinist, Gassman, at a conservatory in Zurich, Switzerland. He is a gifted musician dedicated to his studies, and Taylor, who has fallen in love with him, hopes Gassman will marry her. Ericson, an ex-GI and a promising pianist, who is attending the same conservatory, falls in love with Taylor, but she has eyes only for Gassman, who, in turn, only loves his music and is ruthlessly ambitious to make himself one of Europe's foremost violinists. This Calhern, Taylor's wealthy dilettante father, knows well, and even after he tells his daughter that Gassman is only out for himself, Taylor insists that Gassman loves her and that they will be married and live happily together. Calhern knows his pampered daughter very well, telling her that she will get bored with Gassman and resent being his camp-follower as she trots after him from one concert after another. Ericson, on the other hand, places Taylor first and his music second. Taylor decides to marry Ericson, but is still drawn to the egocentric Gassman. She finally decides to stay with Ericson after he proves himself as a gifted pianist in a virtuoso performance and, in her eyes, is now an equal to that of Gassman as an artist. Vidor directs this romantic melodrama with a sure hand, and Taylor, Gassman, Ericson and Calhern are standouts in their roles, as is Chekhov as the demanding music professor decreeing which person will have a future in classical music and which person will not. The excerpts from the Tchaikovsky and Rachmaninoff masterpieces (their best known pieces) are stunningly and inspirationally offered through Kaper's arrangements, a rich treat for classical music lovers. Music: "Concerto in D Major for Violin and Orchestra" (Pyotr Ilyich Tchaikovsky), "Concerto No, 2 in C Minor for Piano and Orchestra" (Sergei Rachmaninoff), "Gypsy Airs" (Pablo de Sarasate). ***Author's***

Note: Taylor told this author that **Rhapsody** "was one of the most enjoyable pictures I ever made and where I had two wonderful leading men [Gassman and Ericson], but I was very busy that year. **Rhapsody** was one of four pictures I made that year [in 1954, the others being **Beau Brummell, Elephant Walk**, and **The Last Time I Saw Paris**]. I had a lot more energy in those days, so I was able to keep up with all the production schedules [she was only twenty-two years old, and considered one of the most beautiful women in the world, married at that time to British actor Michael Wilding]. Hollywood was a wonderful place to work at in those days. Everyone was handsome, rich and famous." **p**, Lawrence Weingarten; **d**, Charles Vidor; **cast**, Elizabeth Taylor, Vittorio Gassman, John Ericson, Louis Calhern, Michael Chekhov, Barbara Bates, Richard Hageman, Richard Lupino, Celia Lovsky, Stuart Whitman, Madge Blake; **w**, Fay Kanin, Michael Kanin (adapted by Ruth Goetz, Augustus Goetz from the novel *Maurice Guest* by Henry Handel Richardson); **c**, Robert Planck (CinemaScope; Technicolor); **m**, Bronislau Kaper; **ed**, John Dunning; **art d**, Cedric Gibbons, Paul Groesse; **set d**, Edwin B. Willis, Hugh Hunt; **spec eff**, A. Arnold Gillespie, Warren Newcombe.

Rhapsody in Blue ★★★ 1945; U.S.; 135m; WB; B/W; Biographical Drama/Musical; Children: Acceptable; **DVD**; **VHS**. This delightful biopic rightly concentrates on the timeless music of the great composer George Gershwin (1898-1937), who is aptly played by Alda, and his equally gifted brother Ira Gershwin (1896-1983), played by Rudley. They are two Jewish youths from an immigrant family living in the Lower East Side of NYC's Manhattan. While struggling to make their names in the music world, Alda and Rudley work the byways of New York's Tin Pan Alley, plugging their own tunes to music publishers. They see little success until Coburn, one of those music publishers, sees the light and begins publishing Alda's music. Alda's songs begin to take hold, and he and Rudley, along with other lyricists, soon become involved in musical revues before graduating to the big time with George White's Scandals. Finally Alda's songs are being played and sung everywhere. Alda then struggles to compose more difficult compositions, wanting to be identified with classical music. Carnovsky, his father, attends all of the Broadway productions where his son's music is performed, timing the length of each composition, believing that the longer the composition, the more important it will become in the annals of music. Alda is briefly involved with Leslie, a young singer, and later develops a romance with attractive socialite Smith (wholly fictitious characters), but these romances go nowhere as Alda, consumed by ambition, works night and day on his compositions. He is forever racing off to Europe and elsewhere to supervise his own masterpieces while meeting with musical giants Maurice Ravel (1875-1937), played by Loraine, and Sergei Rachmaninoff (1873-1943), played by Wright. He seeks out these great composers in order to learn from them but is amazed when they tell him that *they* want to learn from *him* about his ability to create his unique type of modern American music. His more classical pieces are performed as Alda exhausts himself, growing ill and prematurely dying from an operation to remove a brain tumor at Cedars of Lebanon Hospital in Los Angeles on July 11, 1937, at the age of thirty-eight. Thin on story line, the plentiful music makes up for the lack of an exacting biography. The film is peppered with cameo appearances of real-life entertainers and music masters, including Paul Whiteman, who plays himself and was the first conductor of Gershwin's unforgettable "Rhapsody in Blue." Oscar Levant, the acerbic and gifted pianist, who was a close friend of Gershwin's and a great, sharp-tongued wit, appears throughout, getting most of the best lines. In one classic scene, Levant is traveling on board a luxury train with Alda, and they are sharing the same compartment that has two berths, but where Alda tops Levant's lines by saying: "That's the difference between genius and talent, Oscar, lower berth and upper berth," as he directs Levant to occupy the upper berth. (According to Levant, that scene and those words actually occurred between Gershwin and him.) Rapper does a fine job balancing

Elizabeth Taylor and Vittorio Gassman in *Rhapsody*, 1954.

the story line while infusing a great deal of musical works, mostly by Gershwin, into this irresistible songfest. Although most of the tunes are truncated, viewers are treated to the complete rendition of "Rhapsody in Blue," as it is played by Levant, although this immortal composition was first heard in its entirety in film in **King of Jazz**, 1930, a color film that offers a number of songs as conducted by Paul Whiteman, the conductor best known for conducting "Rhapsody in Blue" at Carnegie Hall. Songs: "Embraceable You," "The Man I Love," "I Got Rhythm," "Love Walked In," "'S Wonderful," "Drifting Along with the Tide," "Oh, Lady Be Good," "Clap Yo' Hands," "Fascinating Rhythm," "Bidin' My Time," "Mine," "Delishious," "It Ain't Necessarily So," "Someone to Watch Over Me" (music: George Gershwin; lyrics: Ira Gershwin), "(I'll Build a Stairway to Paradise" (music: George Gershwin; lyrics: Buddy G. DeSylva and Ira Gershwin as Arthur Jackson); "Liza (All the Clouds'll Roll Away" (music: George Gershwin; lyrics: Ira Gershwin and Gus Kahn); "Somebody Loves Me" (music: George Gershwin; lyrics: Ballard MacDonald and Buddy G. DeSylva); "Swanee" (music: George Gershwin; lyrics: Irving Caesar); "Summertime" (music: George Gershwin; lyrics: DeBose Heyward); "Blue Monday Blues," "I'm Gonna See My Mother," "Do It Again," "Has One of You Seen Joe?" (music: George Gershwin; lyrics: Buddy G. DeSylva); "The Yankee Doodle Blues" (music: George Gershwin; lyrics: Irving Caesar and Buddy G. DeSylva); "Cuban Overture," "Rhapsody in Blue," "Concerto in F for Piano and Orchestra," "An American in Paris," (music: George Gershwin); "Melody in F" (music: Anton Rubinstein); "The Sidewalks of New York" (music: Charles Lawlor); "Nocturne, Op. 9, No. 2 in E flat major," "Prelude, Op. 28, No. 7 in A major" (music: Frederic Chopin); "Smiles" (music: Lee S. Roberts; lyrics: J. Will Callahan); "Some Sunday Morning" (music: Richard A. Whiting; lyrics: Ray Egan and Gus Kahn); "Where the Black-Eyed Susans Grow" (music: Richard A. Whiting; lyrics: Dave Radford); "Cleopatra" (music: Harry Tierney; lyrics: Al Bryan); "Pretty Baby" (music: Egbert Van Alstyne and Tony Jackson; lyrics: Gus Kahn), "Wiegenlied Op 49, No. 4 (aka: "Brahms' Lullaby" by Johannes Brahms). *Author's Note*: Koch, who was one of the many writers working on the script for this film, told this author that "Oscar Levant mostly wrote his own lines for that picture and who was to challenge him as he knew more about George Gershwin than almost anybody else. Actually, his lines are funnier than the ones we came up with. Oscar was a guy who always put his money where his mouth was and that money was his ability to play the piano. No one played Gershwin music better than Oscar, except Gershwin himself." The love interest shown in the film on the part of Leslie and Smith is merely window-dressing and white-washing by Warner Brothers as it did not want to expose the fact that Gershwin was a homosexual or bisexual, then a Hollywood taboo in films. The same white-washing was applied

Ray Milland and cat in *Rhubarb*, 1951.

when a musical biopic was made involving composer Cole Porter (1891-1964), who was portrayed in **Night and Day**, 1946, with Cary Grant playing Porter and Smith (almost reprising her role from **Rhapsody in Blue**) as his mythical love interest. Such convenient white-washing was made when **Words and Music**, 1948, was produced; it treated one of its two principals, Lorenz Hart (1895-1943), appropriately played by pint-sized Mickey Rooney as Hart stood less than five feet, as a man who can't get a girl because of his dwarf-like stature. The real-life Hart was tormented throughout his life because of his hidden homosexual lifestyle, as well as becoming an alcoholic, which foreshortened his life. The other principal in that film was the masterful composer Richard Rodgers (1902-1979), played by Tom Drake, and who was a heterosexual. Relative to the above, I was once walking down Broadway with my good friend Stanley Ralph Ross (1935-2000), a film and TV producer, scriptwriter and a composer in his own right and who possessed an amazing amount of knowledge regarding the personal lifestyles of noted musicians. As we walked along, I asked him about the sexual habits of a number of American composers. I would mention a name and Stanley would (apparently too loudly) respond with a one-word description of their sexual profiles. "Jerome Kern," I said. "Straight [meaning heterosexual]," Stanley replied. "George Gershwin?" I asked, "Homosexual," Stanley replied. "Irving Berlin," I asked. "Straight," Stanley replied. "Cole Porter," I asked. "Homosexual," Stanley replied. We continued this rather childish game until we came to a stoplight and became silent, only to have our coattails yanked by a little man who had been closely following us and avidly listening to our every word. As we turned around to see this fellow, he said: "Go on, will you? Go on!" **p**, Jesse L. Lasky; **d**, Irving Rapper; **cast**, Robert Alda, Joan Leslie, Alexis Smith, Charles Coburn, Julie Bishop, Albert Bassermann, Herbert Rudley, Morris Carnovsky, Rosemary DeCamp, Darryl Hickman, Johnny Downs, Lynn Baggett, Mark Stevens, Robert Shayne, Oscar Levant, Paul Whiteman, Al Jolson, Oscar Loraine, Will Wright, Elsa Maxwell; **w**, Howard Koch, Elliot Paul (based on a story by Sonya Levien); **c**, Sol Polito; **m**, George and Ira Gershwin; musical adaptations: Max Steiner; musical arrangements: Ray Heindorf, Ferde Grofe; **ed**, Folmar Blangsted; **art d**, Anton Grot, John Hughes; **set d**, Fred M. MacLean; **spec eff**, Willard Van Enger, Roy Davidson.

Rhino! ★★★ 1964; U.S.; 92m; MGM; Color; Adventure/Drama; Children: Cautionary; **DVD**; **VHS**. Exciting animal protection tale has Culp as a zoologist trying to save two white rhinos in Africa. His compassionate efforts, however, are hampered when he has to deal with poachers and local tribesmen, who do not understand his methods. He enlists a big game hunter, Guardino, to capture the animals, not knowing Guardino plans to sell the endangered animals on the black market.

Guardino steals Culp's equipment, including a tranquilizer gun, but Guardino's girlfriend, Eaton, a district nurse, helps Culp track him down. They find him and both men have a fight during which Guardino is bitten by a snake. After Culp saves his life, Guardino has a change of heart, and the two become friends and devote themselves to animal protection and research. Good family adventure but it may be too violent for children. **p**, Ben Chapman; **d**, Ivan Tors; **cast**, Harry Guardino, Shirley Eaton, Robert Culp, Harry Mekela, George Lane; **w**, Art Arthur, Arthur Weiss (based on a story by Arthur); **c**, Sven Persson, Lamar Boren (Metrocolor); **m**, Lalo Schifrin; **ed**, Warren Adams.

Rhodes of Africa ★★★ 1936; U.K.; 94m; Gaumont British; B/W; Biographical Drama; Children: Unacceptable; **IV**. Well-made biopic profiles British empire-builder Cecil Rhodes (1853-1902), played by Huston. After traveling to Africa, Huston finds a rich diamond mine, and establishes the Kimberley Mines Company. He tries to unite warring tribes so as to improve their living conditions and helps found the South African colonies. An ardent believer in British colonialism, he founds the South African territory of Rhodesia which is named after him in 1895. The Rhodes Scholarship Foundation is funded by his estate, which originally included the DeBeers Company, and which has a virtual monopoly on all mined diamonds in Africa. Huston, always a forceful and commanding actor, gives a powerful performance of this dynamic man, who became the prime minister of Cape Colony in 1890, and the following year, pioneered the copper mining industry. He died at age forty-eight. **p**, Geoffrey Barkas; **d**, Berthold Viertel; **cast**, Walter Huston, Oskar Homolka, Basil Sydney, Frank Cellier, Peggy Ashcroft, Renee De Vaux, Percy Parsons, Ndaniso Kumala, Felix Aylmer, Leo Genn (narrator). **w**, Michael Barringer, Leslie Arliss, Miles Malleson (based on the book *Rhodes* by Sarah Gertrude Millin); **c**, S.R. Bonnett, Bernard Knowles; **m**, Hubert Bath; **ed**, Derek N. Twist; **art d**, Oscar Friedrich Werndorff.

Rhubarb ★★★ 1951; U.S.; 94m; PAR; B/W; Comedy; Children: Acceptable; **DVD**. Delightful and entertaining comedy begins when Lockhart, an eccentric millionaire, adopts Rhubarb, a feral cat that becomes his beloved pet. When Lockhart dies, he leaves most of his fortune and a professional baseball team, the Brooklyn Loons, to the cat. The team protests, but the club's publicist, Milland, convinces them that Rhubarb is a symbol of good luck. Crooked gamblers kidnap Rhubarb because they believe the cat is helping the club win games. Milland's fiancée, Sterling, who is allergic to cats, uses her allergy to lead Milland to Rhubarb, who is rescued and the crooks are caught. Songs: "Friendly Finance Company," "It's a Priv'ledge to Live in Brooklyn" (Jay Livingston, Ray Evans). *Author's Note*: Milland told this author that "**Rhubarb** was the only picture I ever made where I was constantly upstaged by a cat. That clever little creature knew how to steal every scene by simply blinking innocently at the camera. Any actor knows that he or she will lose out when acting against any animal because viewers worldwide love their pets more than they do people." **p**, William Perlberg, George Seaton; **d**, Arthur Lubin; **cast**, Ray Milland, Jan Sterling, Gene Lockhart, William Frawley, Elsie Holmes, Donald MacBride, Madge Blake, Paul Douglas, Strother Martin, Leonard Nimoy; **w**, Dorothy Davenport, Francis M. Cockrell, David Stern (based on the novel by H. Allen Smith); **c**, Lionel Lindon; **m**, Van Cleave; **ed**, Alma Macrorie; **prod d**, Hal Pereira, Henry Bumstead; **set d**, Sam Comer, Ross Dowd; **spec eff**, Gordon Jennings.

Rhythm on the Range ★★★ 1936; U.S.; 87m; PAR; B/W; Musical Comedy/Western; Children: Acceptable; **DVD**; **VHS**. Crosby is a standout as a singing cowboy who manages a dude ranch in California with his partner Burns. They go to New York, and their bull wins a prize at Madison Square Garden. Crosby takes the bull back home via freight train while Burns goes by passenger train. Crosby meets Farmer, who is a stowaway escaping a boyfriend in New York. Her parents want her to marry this young man, but she finds him to be a bore. Crosby invites her to his ranch and she accepts. Burns arrives there first with his new lady love, Raye, a garrulous society woman. Crosby and Farmer fall in love and there will be a double wedding with them and Burns and Raye. This is Raye's film debut, and her comical antics steal the show, although Crosby holds his own when delivering his inimitable crooning. Songs: "I'm an Old Cowhand from the Rio Grande" (Johnny Mercer); "I Can't Escape from You" (Richard A. Whiting, Leo Robin); "Empty Saddles" (Billy Hill, J. Keirn Brennan); "Roundup Lullaby" (Clifton W. Barnes, Badger Clark); "If You Can't Sing It/You'll Have to Swing It" (Sam Coslow); "Love in Bloom," "Drink It Down" (Ralph Rainger, Leo Rubin); "Arkansas Traveler" (Sanford Faulkner); "One More Ride" (Bob Nolan). This film was one of the top moneymakers for Paramount in 1936. It was remade as a tepid comedy, **Pardners**, 1956, with Dean Martin and Jerry Lewis. *Author's Note*: One of the singers appearing in this film is an obscure young actor-singer called Leonard Slye, who later changed his name to Dick Weston and then changed it to a name that would live forever in Hollywood lore, Roy Rogers. **p**, Benjamin Glazer; **d**, Norman Taurog; **cast**, Bing Crosby, Frances Farmer, Bob Burns, Martha Raye, Samuel S. Hinds, Warren Hymer, Lucile Gleason, George E. Stone, Martha Sleeper, Clem Bevans, Leonid Kinskey, Ellen Drew, Dennis O'Keefe, Louis Prima, Leonard Slye (Roy Rogers); **w**, John C. Moffitt, Sidney Salkow, Francis Martin, Walter DeLeon (based on a story by Mervin J. Houser); **c**, Karl Struss, **m**, John Leipold; **ed**, Ellsworth Hoagland; **art d**, Hans Dreier, Robert Usher; **set d**, A.E. Freudeman; **spec eff**, Gordon Jennings, Devereaux Jennings.

Rhythm on the River ★★★ 1940; U.S.; 92m; PAR; B/W; Musical Comedy; Children: Acceptable; **DVD**; **VHS**. This entertaining songfest begins with songwriter Rathbone, who has been fooling the public for years by using one ghost writer for his music and another for the lyrics. Both ghost writers, Crosby and Martin, meet at an inn, fall in love, and try selling their songs under their own names. That's not easy because all the big song publishers think they're copying Rathbone's style. Rathbone needs a hit song for his new show and uses a love song Crosby and Martin wrote to each other. Crosby hears it and is ready to take legal action, so Rathbone tells the world the song was written by his collaborators Crosby and Martin and they finally get the credit and money they deserve, as well as each other. This film presents a lot of laughs and is brilliantly written by Taylor and Wilder, who later became a stellar film director. Crosby wonderfully warbles some great tunes, and Rathbone is superb as an egomaniacal person whose insecurity rivals that of Rodney Dangerfield and Woody Allen in films decades to come. Songs: "I Don't Want to Cry Anymore" (Victor Schertzinger); "Ain't It a Shame About Mame," "Only Forever," "Rhythm on the River," "When the Moon Comes Over Madison Square Garden," "What Would Shakespeare Have Said?," "That's for Me" (James V. Monaco, Johnny Burke); "Tiger Rag" (Edwin B. Edwards, Nick LaRocca, Tony Sbarbaro, Henry Ragas, Larry Shields). *Author's Note*: Rathbone told this author that "again I play a villain in that Crosby vehicle, and I thought that I might be typecast with such villainous roles until I returned to the Sherlock Holmes character [Rathbone had played Holmes in **The Hound of the Baskervilles** and **The Adventures of Sherlock Holmes**, both in 1939 from Fox, going into the Universal Studios series on that character with **Sherlock Holmes and the Voice of Terror**, 1942]. But once I donned Sherlock's cap and cloak, I found that I could not escape that character either." **p**, William LeBaron; **d**, Victor Schertzinger; **cast**, Bing Crosby, Mary Martin, Basil Rathbone, Oscar Levant, Oscar Shaw, Charley Grapewin, William Frawley, John Scott Trotter, Jeanne Cagney, Charles Lane, Douglas Kennedy, Janet Waldo; **w**, Dwight Taylor (based on a story by Billy Wilder, Jacques Thery); **c**, Ted Tetzlaff; **m**, Victor Young; **ed**, Hugh Bennett; **art d**, Hans Dreier, Ernst Fegte.

Rich and Strange ★★★ 1932; U.K.; 83m; British International Pictures (BIP)/Powers Pictures, Inc.; B/W; Drama; Children: Cautionary; **DVD**; **VHS**. Offbeat and sometimes weird, this drama was one of Hitch-

Henry Kendall, Joan Barry and Edward Underwood in *Rich and Strange*, 1932.

cock's earliest talkies. Kendall and Barry, a married couple living in a small English town, are shown bickering until a telegram arrives to inform them that an uncle is going to advance them considerable money against their eventual inheritance so that they can enjoy life earlier than later. They decide to make their dreams come true by taking a world cruise. That dream turns into a nightmare after they board a luxury liner where the naïve couple attempt to mix in with upper-class passengers. The gullible couple is gulled by two smooth operators, Barry inveigled into a romance by a middle-aged lothario and Kendall enticed by a vamp, who impersonates a princess and who swindles him out of all of his funds. Almost broke and stranded, Kendall and Barry secure passage on a tramp steamer, but that vessel is abandoned after it collides with another ship in a dense fog. The couple is rescued by Chinese fishermen, who take them aboard their junk and where they are subjected to a crude and offensive lifestyle that would turn even the most iron-cast stomach. At one point, the Chinese cook on that junk makes chop suey by chopping up a cat and using its grisly remains as the main ingredient, serving this to Kendall and Barry as if it were haute cuisine. When the junk finally reaches port, Kendall and Barry regain a more civilized way of life by securing passage on a more conventional ship that sails them back to England, sadder but not much wiser for their unfortunate experiences as they are shown as vigorously arguing as they were when the film opens. Hitchcock employs in this intriguing tale many of the techniques he later used in his more celebrated films, including overhead and tracking shots. The film was originally released in the U.S. with the title **East of Shanghai**, and ran at 83 minutes, cut down from the original British release from 92 minutes. Through subsequent U.S. rereleases, the film's original title was employed. *Author's Note*: Hitchcock used for this film a large water tank and with a recreation of a full-sized ship, much as he did with his later sea saga, **Lifeboat**, 1944. The director had written the story for this film shortly after he married his lifelong wife, Alma Reville, in 1926. Hitchcock based its story line on a cruise he and his wife took as newlyweds, although the more harrowing and adulterous scenes in this film were strictly generated by Hitchcock's fertile imagination. The film is only a part talkie, about one fifth of the film offering dialog while the remainder is presented visually with sound effects. Its primitive construction, however, makes it all the more interesting in how Hitchcock achieves those visually presented dramatic moments. "I had great difficulties with that picture," Hitchcock admitted to this author. "My problems centered on its two leading players, both of whom were foisted upon me by producers that also gave me a very limited budget. I had to do with what I had been given, period. Well, Miss Barry, the leading lady, was an actress I had used in my picture **Blackmail** [1929], where she dubbed the voice of the leading lady in that picture [Anny Ondra, a Czech actress], but, as it turned out, she was

Kathryn Walker and Trini Alvarado in *Rich Kids*, 1979.

utterly terrified of microphones when acting before the cameras. Whenever she had to deliver a line, she froze up like a wooden Indian. I had to beg and plead with her to speak her lines clearly without spitting them out like morsels of food that had gotten stuck in her teeth. I can't remember how many retakes I had to make with that lady to finally get acceptable scenes from her. Mr. Kendall was an entirely different problem. He was a comic character actor, who had made his reputation in the music halls of London's West End, and was decidedly on the light-footed side. His swishy mannerisms were so blatantly obvious that I had to repeatedly tell him to 'put more masculinity' into his scenes. At one point, I could no longer bear to see him sashaying about on the set like some woebegone drag queen. I took him aside and quietly and patiently said to him: 'If you do not start walking like a man, or what you think a man walks like, I will have to have an iron bar attached to your spine for all of your next scenes, Mr. Kendall.' He glared at me, but he made a special effort after that to successfully disguise himself as a man." **p**, John Maxwell; **d**, Alfred Hitchcock; **cast**, Henry Kendall, Joan Barry, Percy Marmont, Betty Amann, Elsie Randolph, Aubrey Dexter, Hannah Jones; **w**, Val Valentine, Alma Reville (based on an adaptation of a novel by Dale Collins); **c**, Charles Martin, John Cox; **m**, Adolph Hallis; **ed**, Rene Marrison, Winifred Cooper; **art d**, C. Wilfred Arnold.

Rich Kids ★★★ 1979; U.S.; 101m; Lion's Gate/UA; Color; Comedy; Children: Unacceptable (MPAA: PG); **DVD**; **VHS**. Entertaining comedy sees two very precocious twelve-year-old children, Franny (Alvarado) and Jamie (Levy) as best friends. They live in Upper West Side New York City where Levy's parents are divorced and Alvarado senses that her parents are not happy in their marriage. Levy tries to help her through her own parents' possible divorce, telling her that there are advantages to being a "child of divorce," and he is so convincing that she almost believes him. One night, Alvarado convinces her still-married parents to allow her to go to a sleepover with Levy, one where the children innocently explore their curiosity about the opposite sex. Over time, Alvarado gains confidence, believing that, even if her parents do split up, she will not have to assume responsibility for that failed marriage and that her parents will nevertheless continue to love her. Songs: "Happy Ida and Broken-Hearted John," "Fast Asleep" (Craig Doerge, Judy Henske); "Reasons," "Hot Love in a Minute," "I Don't Want to Dance," "You Knock Me Out" (Craig Doerge, Allan Nicholls); "Goodbye Yesterday" (John Alper, Alan Bellink, Ted Drachman). Sexuality prohibits viewing by children. **p**, George W. George, Michael Hausman; **d**, Robert M. Young; **cast**, Trini Alvarado, Jeremy Levy, Kathryn Walker, John Lithgow, Terry Kiser, David Selby, Irene Worth, Olympia Dukakis, Jill Eikenberry, Kathryn Grody; **w**, Judith Ross; **c**, Ralf D. Bode (Panavision; Technicolor); **m**, Craig Doerge; **ed**, Edward Beyer;

art d, David Mitchell; **set d**, Richard Merrell, Harold Sasso.

Rich, Young and Pretty ★★★ 1951; U.S.; 95m.; MGM; Color; Musical Comedy/Romance; Children: Acceptable; **DVD**; **VHS**. Delightful songfest features Powell (having one of the most wonderful singing voices in films), who is a Texas girl visiting Paris with Corey, her single-parent rancher father. There she meets the man of her dreams, Damone, and also a beautiful woman, Darrieux, not knowing she is her birth mother, who deserted Corey shortly after giving birth and remained in Europe. Complications arise when Powell tries to reunite her parents while a Latin lover, Lamas, pursues Darrieux. Lovely Powell does a lot of singing in between love-matching. This film was a box office hit, gleaning more than $1.7 million in its initial release. Songs: "Tonight for Sure," "Paris," "Dark Is the Night," "Wonder Why" (music: Nicholas Brodsky; lyrics: Sammy Cahn); "I Can See You," "There's Danger in Your Eyes," "We Never Talk Much," Cherie," "How D'Ya Like Your Eggs in the Morning" (Peter Wendling, Harry Richman, Jack Meskill); "Old Piano Roll Blues" (Cy Cohen); "Deep in the Heart of Texas" (music: Don Swander; lyrics: June Hershey). *Author's Note*: My good friend, Gene Ruggiero, who edited this film, told this author that "**Rich, Young and Pretty** was one of those light-as-a-feather pictures Joe Pasternak was always producing. It was good entertainment, but did not have much of a story. Who needed one, when you had Janie Powell singing her heart out?" This was the film debut for both Vic Damone and Lamas. "There were two prima donnas that the director [Taurog] had to put up with when we did that production," Ruggiero told this author. "One was the famous French actress, Danielle Darrieux, and the other was Fernando Lamas. Both of them thought they were God's gifts to Hollywood and strutted about like peacocks throughout that production. Lamas was even more vain that Darrieux, jutting his jaw into every scene he could steal, or try to steal, and Taurog had to tell him more than once not to stand in front of the leading lady. He was an Argentine and he acted like he was some Gaucho riding in from the pampas to do us all a favor. What a cornball!" **p**, Joe Pasternak; **d**, Norman Taurog; **cast**, Jane Powell, Danielle Darrieux, Wendell Corey, Vic Damone, Fernando Lamas, Una Merkel, Marcel Dalio, Richard Anderson, Hans Conried, The Four Freshman (Bob Flanagan, Don Barbour, Hal Kratzsch, Ken Errair); **w**, Sidney Sheldon, Dorothy Cooper (based on a story by Cooper); **c**, Robert Planck (Technicolor); **ed**, Gene Ruggiero; **art d**, Cedric Gibbons, Arthur Lonergan; **set d**, Edwin B. Willis; **spec eff**, Warren Newcombe.

Richard ★★★ 1972; U.S.; 83m; Aurora City Group/Billings; B/W/Color; Comedy; Children: Unacceptable (MPAA: PG); **DVD**. This offbeat and largely fictional biography of Richard M. Nixon (1913-1994; 37th President of the United States), played by Resin, presents an absorbing and biting political satire (and was produced before Nixon destroyed his career in the Watergate scandal). As a young political hopeful, Resin answers an advertisement for a Congressional candidate and becomes subject to Gifford, Garrett, and Forrest, three unholy advisers. They advise him to get some plastic surgery from a facial reconstruction whiz, Carradine, and he becomes a new man with a new face, played by Dixon. He goes on to see a spectacular if not a bizarre political career. This film was sparsely distributed upon its initial release, but it remains a fascinating curiosity with a clever, witty script and some good acting. Mature subject matter prohibits viewing by children. **p**, Lorees Yerby, Bertrand Castelli; **d**, Yerby, Harry Hurwitz; **cast**, Richard M. Dixon, Dan Resin, Lynn Lipton, Hazen Gifford, Hank Garrett, Paul Forrest, Mickey Rooney, John Carradine, Paul Ford, Kevin McCarthy, Vivian Blaine; **w**, Castelli, Yerby, Hurwitz; **c**, Victor Petrashevic; **ed**, Emil Haviv; **set d**, Raymond Maynard.

Richard III ★★★★★ 1956; U.K.; 161m; London Film Productions; Lopert Pictures; Color; Drama; Children: Unacceptable; **DVD**; **VHS**. Olivier, who had magnificently scored with two previous Shakespeare tales (**Henry V**, 1946, and **Hamlet**, 1948), outdoes all other portraits of Richard III (1452-1485), the power mad king of England, who is crippled in mind, body and spirit. Opening with the coronation of Edward IV (1442-1483), who is played by Hardwicke, Olivier stands by to witness that crowning, seething with jealousy and envy over his brother's ascendancy to the throne. When all depart, Olivier addresses the viewer with a begging soliloquy where he bemoans the fact that he carries the burden of having a withered arm and a hunchback and that he has been relegated to a lowly position. His sinister plans to change all that and become king are evident when he puts in motion a plot to destroy his other brother, George (1449-1478), played by Gielgud. Olivier tells Hardwicke that Gielgud secretly plans to murder him and arranges for Gielgud to be imprisoned in the Tower of London. When Hardwicke hears of this, he sends an order to release Gielgud, but Olivier intercepts and stops that order. He then sends two thugs, Gough and Ripper, to the Tower to murder Gielgud, who is drowned in a vat of wine. Olivier, to strengthen his position at court, then crudely woos Lady Anne Neville (1456-1485), played by Bloom. Though she despises Olivier for his murderous ways as well as his hideous deformities, she marries him. The ever busy Olivier then creates dissension in the court by spreading slanderous gossip about the Queen Consort, Elizabeth (1437-1492), played by Kerridge, all of this so exhausting for an already ill Hardwicke that he turns to Olivier for support, appointing him Lord Protector of England. When Hardwicke dies after learning about the gruesome death of his brother George, his young son, Huson, who plays Edward V (1470-1483?) becomes king. Olivier, however, arranges for Huson and his younger brother Richard (1473-1483?), played by Shine, to be sent to the Tower of London. Olivier then asks Richardson, who plays the Duke of Buckingham (1455-1483) to create a good image for him with the public, which Richardson does on Olivier's promise of giving him a wealthy land grant. When Olivier then asks Richardson to dispatch the annoying princes in the Tower of London, he balks. Olivier finds an ambitious knight, Troughton, who plays Sir James Tyrrell (1455-1502), to perform the heinous deed. (The fate of the two young princes was never determined, but it is safely assumed by many historians that Richard III had then both killed.) After he has finally achieved his goal and is crowned king, Olivier again meets with Richardson, who reminds him of his promise to give him that large estate. Olivier, however, angered over Richardson's refusal to murder the princes in the Tower, angrily denies him that estate, shouting: "I am not in the giving vein today!" Richardson now knows that he, like so many others, is marked for death. He joins the growing opposition to Olivier, which mounts to armed insurrection on the part of many knights, led by Baker (as Henry, Earl of Richmond, 1457-1509, who later became Henry VII), and including Richardson. These forces are met by Olivier and his army at the Battle of Bosworth Field (the last significant battle of the War of the Roses, occurring on August 22, 1485). Before the battle, Richardson is captured and Olivier takes his revenge by having him executed. On the night before the battle, Olivier sleeps fitfully, his nightmares recalling all his foul deeds so that he awakes screaming from these hauntings. By dawn, Olivier has regained his confidence and meets with his generals to plan tactics and then appears before his troops where he delivers a rousing speech to inspire them to battle on his behalf. As the battle ensues, Olivier finds himself in the thick of the conflict, fighting alongside Naismith, who plays Lord Thomas Stanley (1435-1504), whom Olivier has suspected for some time as being disloyal. His suspicions become a frightening reality when Naismith suddenly betrays Olivier and allies himself with the enemy, fighting with Baker. Olivier is now in a desperate position, and while attempting to escape enemy soldiers, he is knocked from his horse, losing his crown, his cherished symbol of power. Now on foot and having no means of escape, Olivier cries out those memorable Shakespearean lines: "A horse! A horse! My kingdom for a horse!" Naismith then finds Olivier and both engage in mortal combat as they frantically wield their swords in savage blows against each other. Before Naismith can dispatch Olivier, however, some of Nai-

Laurence Olivier in *Richard III*, 1956.

smith's troops mortally wound Olivier and he dies in agony while offering his sword to the sky rather than surrendering it to the enemy, defiant to the end of what has been a hideous life. Naismith then wanders through the battlefield to find Olivier's crown. He takes it to Baker and offers it to him in recognition of Baker becoming the new king (Henry VII). Olivier and Bushell direct this film with meticulous care, where Olivier appears in almost every scene, as is befitting to his character and where he makes that character his own in one of his most memorable performances. Olivier's Richard is a limping, hunchbacked person who speaks in a raspy voice, higher pitched than the actor's normal tone, to imply an effeminate streak (that works well with his incongruous-looking dark-haired pageboy wig). That only adds a more sinister aspect to his most villainous persona. Olivier truly represents the most deceitful and evil monarch that ever ruled England. His incisive and devastatingly revealing characterization of Richard is wholly in keeping with the Immortal Bard's perspective of that conniving character, and who was never intended to be anything other than that when first represented on the stage to an audience. Only a few cuts and a few characters were added in an otherwise superlative production that remains a faithful adaptation to Shakespeare's original work. This mesmerizing film further benefits from lush color lensing by the gifted Heller and presents a score as haunting as Richard's nightmares from composer Walton. The film was expensive to produce with an estimated budget of £6 million, and though it produced good box office receipts in its initial release, it did not recoup its original investment, returning about $2.6 million in the U.S., where it was widely popular and about £400,000 in England where it was not initially well received. Olivier was nominated for an Oscar as Best Actor, but lost out to Yul Brynner for his performance in **The King and I**, 1956. *Author's Note*: Olivier had long wanted to make this film ever since enacting "Richard III" at the Old Vic in 1944. He found the money to produce this film from British movie mogul Alexander Korda, who had produced several films in the past that starred Olivier. When the film showed little profit in England, Korda inventively recouped some of his investment by setting a precedent in having the film premiered on NBC-TV in the U.S., and receiving a then whopping payment of $500,000 for its one-time TV showing. Three scenes thought to be too violent were excised from the TV showing, including scenes involving the Battle of Bosworth Field, which was shot in Spain. Olivier was injured in the battle scenes, an arrow entering his right shin, causing him excruciating pain, but he continued his enactment until the scene was over before seeking medical treatment. Since he was required throughout the film to limp on that very right leg, his hobbling about was not affected but very real. All of the interiors were shot at Shepperton Studios in England. Olivier told this author that "**Richard III** looks like a production that took a long time to produce, but we were able to

Laurence Olivier in *Richard III*, 1956.

complete that picture in about seventeen weeks. I took some liberties, by inserting two characters [monks played by Fisher and Bosco] into the scenario and who act as a Greek chorus to witness Richard's dark intrigues, but, other than that, all remains as it was in the original work." In his previous two ventures into Shakespearean works, **Henry V** and **Hamlet**, Olivier had not spoken soliloquies, but stared vacantly into nothingness while the words were heard in his voiceover. He changed that with **Richard III**, telling this author that "I purposely broke the fourth wall [staring directly into the camera and the viewer] to isolate the character from his environment and all other characters, as if he is stepping from himself to confess to anyone or no one his guilt, although this is a man who really feels no guilt except in his subconscious. The character's loneliness is enforced when he breaks that fourth wall. It does not stop the action, but accelerates it, for Richard is the catalyst, who makes all things happen." It was a brilliant ploy and was a first in any dramatic film, although comedians Groucho Marx, Oliver Hardy and Bob Hope routinely broke the fourth wall in their films, but as permissible comedic asides. This technique as used by Olivier, however, startled viewers and critics alike then as it does today, personalizing the character while Olivier's genius achieved the impossible by creating empathy for the utterly despicable Richard. **p**, Laurence Olivier, (not credited) Alexander Korda; **d**, Olivier, Anthony Bushell; **cast**, Olivier, Ralph Richardson, Claire Bloom, John Gielgud, Cedric Hardwicke, Pamela Brown, Laurence Naismith, Alec Clunes, Mary Kerridge, Paul Huson, Andy Shine, Patrick Troughton, Michael Gough, John Laurie, Stanley Baker, Michael Ripper, Norman Fisher, Wally Bosco; **w**, Alan Olivier, Colley Cibber, David Garrick (based on the play by William Shakespeare); **c**, Otto Heller (VistaVision; Technicolor); **m**, Sir William Walton; **ed**, Helga Cranston; **prod d**, Roger Furse; **art d**, Carmen Dillon; **spec eff**, Wally Veevers.

The Richest Girl in the World ★★★ 1934; U.S.; 76m; MGM; B/W; Comedy/Romance; Children: Acceptable; **VHS**. Delightful comedy sees Hopkins as an heiress, who is afraid no man will love her for herself and will only be interested in her vast wealth. To find the right mate, she trades places with her secretary, Wray. Hopkins becomes attracted to handsome young McCrea, but matches him with Wray to test whether or not he is only after her money. Things get out of control until Hopkins finally gets McCrea, the man she loves, after she is convinced he loves her for herself. The script is clever and witty, and Hopkins, Wray and McCrea are standouts; Seiter directs with a lively eye and firm hand. The film was remade as **Bride by Mistake**, 1944. *Author's Note*: McCrea told this author that "Krasna, the scriptwriter for that picture, started as a playwright. He had a natural bent for comedy and he gave us some great lines in that very good comedy. The leading lady [Hop-

kins] was named Dorothy Hunter, but that was a smokescreen for the real-life character she is playing and that was Barbara Hutton [1912-1979, heiress of the Woolworth fortune] and she was one of the richest girls in the world." Wray told this author that "I liked playing in that picture with Joel [McCrea] again. We did **The Most Dangerous Game** [1932] together and we got along famously, but I had some problems with the leading lady, Miss Hopkins, who more or less warned me not to upstage her. I steered clear of her as I knew she could create a lot of problems for any actress and I wanted no part of that. Bette Davis was the only actress in Hollywood who dared to face that lady down and she did it so much that it drove Miss Hopkins a little batty." **p**, Pandro S. Berman; **d**, William A. Seiter; **cast**, Miriam Hopkins, Joel McCrea, Fay Wray, Henry Stephenson, Reginald Denny, Beryl Mercer, George Meeker, Wade Boteler, Herbert Bunston, Edgar Norton; **w**, Norman Krasna (based on his story); **c**, Nick Musuraca; **ed**, George Crone; **art d**, Van Nest Polglase, Charles Kirk; **spec eff**, Harry Redmond Sr.

The Rickshaw Man ★★★ 1960; Japan; 103m; Toho Company/Cory Film Corp.; Color; Comedy/Drama; Children: Unacceptable (MPAA: PG); **VHS**. Solid and provocative drama has Mifune as a poor Japanese rickshaw driver. He is a favorite of those in his town because of his vitality and optimism. Mifune helps an injured boy, Kasahara, and is hired by the boy's parents to take Kasahara to and from his doctor's appointments. Mifune comes to love the boy and his parents, so, when the father dies, he becomes a surrogate father. While helping raise the boy, Mifune falls in love with his mother, Takamine, but the gulf between their social classes is so wide that he knows that he can only be a rickshaw man to her. As Kasahara grows into manhood he has less time for Mifune, who becomes so lonely and unhappy that he drinks himself to death. Mifune is wonderful in this sensitive story, which is beautifully lensed by Yamada. Stark reality scenes and suicide prohibit viewing by children. (In Japanese; English subtitles.) **p**, Tomoyuki Tanaka; **d**, Hiroshi Inagaki; **cast**, Toshiro Mifune, Hideko Takamine, Hiroshi Akutagawa, Chishu Ryu, Choko Iida, Haruo Tanaka, Jun Tatara, Kenji Kasahara, Kaoru Matsumoto, Nobuo Nakamura; **w**, Inagaki, Mansaku Itami (based on a story by Shunsaku Iwashita); **c**, Kazuo Yamada (CinemaScope; Agfacolor); **m**, Ikuma Dan; **ed**, Yoshitami Kuroiwa; **prod d**, Hiroshi Ueda.

Ride a Crooked Mile ★★★ 1938; U.S.; 70m; PAR; B/W; Western; Children: Unacceptable. The tempestuous Tamiroff plays the wealthy leader of a gang of cattle rustlers. He is joined by his estranged son, Erickson, who tries to outdo his father in outlawry and feats of daring. They form a bond, but Tamiroff is captured and is sent to Leavenworth prison. Erickson joins a cavalry unit in hopes of helping his father escape, but Tamiroff breaks prison without his help and Erickson becomes part of a posse assigned to track him down. When Erickson does find Tamiroff, he tells him that his loyalty to the cavalry is stronger than his love for him, so Tamiroff jumps off a cliff to his death. Offbeat, but exciting, this well-crafted tale has a strong subplot where Erickson and his then real-life wife, Frances Farmer, who plays a Russian émigré saloon singer, develop a strong romance. Farmer, a gifted but troubled actress, mainly critical of the Hollywood studio system, had a breakdown in real life and left the movies, some years later recovering and hosting a radio show. Her harrowing life story is told in the film **Frances**, 1983. **p**, Jeff Lazarus; **d**, Alfred E. Green; **cast**, Akim Tamiroff, Leif Erickson, Frances Farmer, Lynne Overman, John Miljan, J.M. Kerrigan, Vladimir Sokoloff, Wade Crosby, Gloria Williams, Fred "Snowflake" Toones; **w**, Jack Moffitt, Ferdinand Reyher; **c**, William C. Mellor; **m**, Gregory Stone; **ed**, James Smith; **art d**, Hans Dreier, Robert Usher; **spec eff**, Farciot Edouart.

The Ride Back ★★★ 1957; U.S.; 79m; Associates and Aldrich Company/UA; B/W; Western; Children: Unacceptable; **VHS**. In this fascinating and gritty western Conrad is a resolute lawman pursuing Quinn, a wanted man. He finds and arrests him in Mexico and then begins to ride back to the U.S. with Quinn in tow. Quinn tells Conrad that he is innocent, but Conrad has little or no sympathy for him. Though manacled, Quinn repeatedly tries to escape, but Conrad is too smart for him. After they pass a small group of Apaches, who are drinking and wearing obviously stolen clothes, the two make camp for the night, but hear the Indians nearby. Quinn asks for a gun by which he can defend himself, but Conrad ignores him. Conrad then hears the Indians signaling to each other and leaves the camp, gun in hand. He fires a shot at a figure darting in the dark and then returns to the camp to find that Quinn has found his rifle and is pointing it at him. Conrad gives him a knowing grin, saying: "You didn't think I would leave it loaded, did you?" Quinn, realizing that the rifle has no cartridges, gives up his attempt to escape. The next day, they see a deserted farm house and, after entering it, find the residents, a man, woman and girl, all killed by the Indians. They bury the bodies and, when returning to the house, are shot at by the Apaches, who have surrounded the building and driven off their horses. Quinn then ventures outside to find Monroe, another girl, the twin sister of the girl earlier found slain. Quinn rushes her back to the house where she stares coldly at him in shock. He gives her a doll he has found and tells her that he is her friend and she warms to him. Quinn then retrieves one of the horses and the animal is hitched to a wagon. Conrad, Quinn and Hope then escape the farmhouse by driving the horse-drawn wagon onto the prairie, but the Indians doggedly follow their trail. When they make camp, Quinn breaks through Monroe's wall of silence by telling her that she is going to be all right and she is going to have a happy future. Monroe, who looks upon Quinn as her protector, places her trust in him. When Quinn sees that the exhausted Conrad has fallen asleep, he gets the girl to retrieve Conrad's six-gun, as he is bound to a tree, but, when she returns to Quinn with the six-gun, Conrad awakes and stops her. Conrad takes back the weapon, telling Quinn that he has never accomplished anything in life. He tells Quinn that he knows Quinn has a wife and family and friends who love hom, but that Conrad's wife hates him for the failure he has been in life. That is why Conrad vows to take Quinn to justice, so that he can achieve the only significant accomplishment in his otherwise empty and useless life. The trio continues its journey with only the one horse to carry Monroe until the Apaches catch up with them just before they reach a nearby town. The Indians fire at them from a high ridge, wounding Conrad and disabling him. Quinn takes Conrad and Monroe to the shelter of some rocks and, taking Conrad's gun, climbs upward, battling the Indians and shooting three of them dead before a lone Apache flees. Quinn returns to Conrad and Monroe, finding that Conrad is seriously wounded. He tells Conrad that he is going back to his family and leaves him and Monroe to their fate, riding away on the only horse left to them. Monroe, lonely and afraid, reaches out and clutches Conrad's hand and the lawman responds by warmly clasping her hand, realizing that someone in the world cares for him. Conrad lapses into semi-consciousness, but then sees the shadow of a man on a horse towering over him and Monroe, realizing that it is Quinn. He has returned out of conscience to save Conrad and Monroe and, helping the wounded Conrad to the saddle of the horse, leads it toward the town. Quinn says that he will take his chances with the law, willing to stand trial for murder as he holds Monroe's hand and they all move off in the distance. Miner, who debuts as a director with his film, helms this stark oater with a sure hand, with Quinn, Conrad and Monroe giving outstanding performances in what is a simple but revealing story and where the few characters are wonderfully developed. It is a story of redemption and honor, but told in such natural and down-to-earth terms that every scene is compelling. The black-and-white lensing by Biroc (the film originally released in Sepiatone) is superbly uncompromising, showing the unwelcoming western vistas where nothing moves and silence is everywhere, all appearing as lonely lunar landscapes. Much of the look of the film was influenced by Robert Aldrich, who was the executive producer of the film, and who was noted for making realistic films. The film received little attention when it was released and remains somewhat obscure, but it deserves strong recommendation for its many

Anthony Quinn in *The Ride Back*, 1957.

good production values. Song: "The Ride Back" (Frank De Vol). *Author's Note*: Quinn told this author that "**The Ride Back** was produced on a shoestring budget that was actually financed by Bill Conrad, a great actor. The distributor [United Artists] did not get behind the picture, so it never got the attention it deserved. A few years later, I did a picture [**Last Train from Gun Hill**, 1959] that had the same kind of story line about a dedicated lawman, played by Kirk Douglas, who is bound hell for leather to bring a lawbreaker to justice, and in that picture, I played the father of the boy Douglas wants to send to prison." Douglas earlier played the same kind of dogged sheriff who risks everything to bring Walter Brennan to justice for a crime committed by another in **Along the Great Divide**, 1951. Douglas' co-star in many films, Burt Lancaster, also plays the same kind of unrelenting sheriff in **Lawman**, 1971. Such incorruptible lawmen were exampled by Walter Huston in **Law and Order**, 1932; George Bancroft in **Stagecoach**, 1939; Randolph Scott in **Frontier Marshal**, 1939; Henry Fonda in **My Darling Clementine**, 1946; Alan Ladd in **Whispering Smith**, 1948; Lancaster again in **Gunfight at the O.K. Corral**, 1957; Clint Eastwood in **Hang 'Em High**, 1968; Gene Hackman in **Unforgiven**, 1992; Kurt Russell in **Tombstone**, 1993; and Kevin Costner in **Wyatt Earp**, 1994. **p**, William Conrad, Robert Aldrich (not credited); **d**, Allen H. Miner; **cast**, Anthony Quinn, William Conrad, Ellen Hope Monroe, Lita Milan, George Trevino, Victor Millan, Joe Dominguez, Louis Towers; **w**, Antony Ellis; **c**, Joseph Biroc (Sepiatone); **m**, Frank De Vol; **ed**, Michael Luciano; **art d**, William Glasgow; **set d**, Glen Daniels; **spec eff**, Lee Zavitz.

Ride Clear of Diablo ★★★ 1954; U.S.; 80m, UNIV; Color; Western; Children: Unacceptable; **DVD**; **VHS**. This action-packed western opens with Murphy working as a railroad surveyor. After his father and brother are murdered by town sheriff Birch and lawyer Pullen, he sets out to bring them to justice. With the help of a gunfighter, Duryea, Murphy identifies the killers. The bad guys are killed in a shootout, and Murphy rides off with lovely Cabot, who had been engaged to Pullen. Good acting and a well-written script sustains interest throughout. Songs: "Noche de Ronda" (Maria Teresa Lara), "Wanted" (Frederick Herbert, Arnold Hughes). **p**, John W. Rogers; **d**, Jesse Hibbs; **cast**, Audie Murphy, Susan Cabot, Dan Duryea, Abbe Lane, Russell Johnson, Paul Birch, William Pullen, Jack Elam, Denver Pyle, Hamilton Camp; **w**, George Zuckerman, D.D. Beauchamp (based on a story by Ellis Marcus); **c**, Irving Glassberg (Technicolor); **m**, Milton Rosen, Herman Stein; **ed**, Edward Curtiss; **art d**, Bernard Herzbrun, Robert Boyle; **set d**, Russell A. Gausman.

Ride 'Em Cowboy ★★★ 1942; U.S.; 86m; UNIV; B/W; Musical Comedy; Children: Acceptable; **DVD**; **VHS**. A lot of laughable action is pres-

Randolph Scott and Karen Steele in *Ride Lonesome*, 1959.

ent in this well-made Abbott and Costello vehicle. They are peanut vendors at a rodeo show who get in trouble with their boss and hide out on a railroad train going west. Even though they know nothing about horses, they are hired as cowboys on a dude ranch. Gwynne, whose father, Hinds, owns the ranch, and Foran, a western novelist, are in love, but their romance is short-circuited by the disrupting, wacky antics of Bud and Lou. The lively and delightful musical numbers make this film exceptional, particularly with the sterling performance of the great Ella Fitzgerald, who does an unforgettable rendition of "A Tisket, A Tasket" while singing as she rides along in a packed bus. The Merry Macs replace the inimitable Andrews Sisters and do a fine job with their numbers. Songs: "I'll Remember April," "Give Me My Saddle," "Wake Up, Jacob," "Beside the Rio Tonto Shore," "Ride 'em Cowboy," "Rockin' and Reelin'" (Gene de Paul, Don Raye); "A Tisket, a Tasket" (Ella Fitzgerald, Van Alexander). **p**, Alex Gottlieb; **d**, Arthur Lubin; **cast**, Bud Abbott, Lou Costello, Dick Foran, Johnny Mack Brown, Anne Gwynne, Samuel S. Hinds, Douglass Dumbrille, Chief Yowlachie, Iron Eyes Cody, Ella Fitzgerald, Dorothy Dandridge, The Merry Macs (Joe, Judd, Ted McMichael, Mary Lou Cook); **w**, True Boardman, John Grant, Harold Shumate (based on a story by Edmund L. Hartmann); **c**, John W. Boyle; **m**, Frank Skinner; **ed**, Philip Cahn; **art d**, Jack Otterson; **set d**, Russell A. Gausman.

Ride Lonesome ★★★★ 1959; U.S.; 73m; COL; Color; Western; Children: Unacceptable; **DVD**. This was one of Boetticher's "modern" westerns where an intelligent script and outstanding acting presents a tense and fascinating tale. Scott, as the always resolute man of the Old West, is a bounty hunter searching for killer Best, but his real aim is to find his murderous brother, Van Cleef, who has slain Scott's wife. After Scott captures Best, he encounters Steele, an attractive widow, along with outlaws Roberts and Coburn (in his film debut), who have also been searching for Best, so that they can turn Best in and receive pardons. Scott keeps his plans to himself, using Best as bait to draw Van Cleef out into the open and where Scott finally takes his revenge on his murderous brother. Instead of taking Best in, however, Scott turns out to be a magnanimous bounty hunter in that he turns Best over to Roberts so he can deliver the felon to officials and receive his pardon. By that time, Steele and Scott have developed a close relationship and they depart to make a new life together. Boetticher's no-nonsense, taut and economical direction provides a lot of well-orchestrated action, and the script from Kennedy is both intelligent and filled with offbeat humor, mostly provided by Best, who plays a laughing, joke-telling killer. Scott and the rest of the cast are superlative in their roles, all of their characters well defined and sustaining interest throughout. The main theme that involves Scott searching for a lethal brother takes a leaf from Anthony Mann's

classic western, **Winchester '73**, 1950, which stars James Stewart, who is throughout that film doggedly searching for his murderous brother, Stephen McNally, who had killed their father. **Ride Lonesome** did well at the box office, as did most of Scott's westerns, particularly when teamed with Boetticher, their other films together including **Decision at Sundown**, 1957; **Buchanan Rides Alone**, 1958; **Westbound**, 1959; and **Comanche Station**, 1960. *Author's Note*: Scott told this author that "**Ride Lonesome** was another one of those very realistic westerns I did with the very talented Budd Boetticher. He had a gift for portraying western characters that were believable and who spoke as intelligent persons. The characters in his films only go for their guns when they have to, not every other few minutes as you would often see in the old shoot-'em-ups." **p&d**, Budd Boetticher; **cast**, Randolph Scott, Karen Steele, Pernell Roberts, James Best, Lee Van Cleef, James Coburn, Bennie E. Dobbins, Roy Jensen, Dyke Johnson, Boyd "Red" Morgan, Boyd Stockman; **w**, Burt Kennedy; **c**, Charles Lawton, Jr. (CinemaScope; Eastmancolor); **m**, Heinz Roemheld; **ed**, Jerome Thoms; **art d**, Robert Peterson; **set d**, Frank A. Tuttle.

Ride the High Country ★★★★ 1962; 94m; MGM; Color; Western; Children: Unacceptable; **DVD**; **VHS**. Few westerns so evocatively depict the passing of the Old West as does this marvelous western, as epitomized by two aging westerners, McCrea and Scott, old friendly enemies who take a last and fateful ride together. In this, Peckinpah's second feature film (following **The Deadly Companions**, 1961), viewers are treated to one of the finest westerns ever produced. The film opens when the Old West was fading fast and as McCrea, an aging, unemployed former lawman, rides into a small town and down its main street, pleasantly surprised to see its citizens seemingly cheering him. He sheepishly tips his hat to the spectators he passes until a policeman rudely tells him to get out of the way and McCrea then realizes that the hooting and hollering from citizens is to inform McCrea that he is blocking a race being run down that very street. Embarrassed, he moves his horse to the side of the street as the racers go past him, horse riders competing against a fast-moving camel. When McCrea crosses the street, he is almost struck by an automobile, which represents the modern era to which McCrea does not belong. McCrea enters the local bank to inform bankers Helton and Foulger that he is the man they sent for to serve as a guard taking gold from a mountainous mining town to the bank. Seeing that McCrea has gotten on in years, the elderly bankers are skeptical about McCrea's abilities to do the job. McCrea, while hiding the frayed cuffs on his shirt, affirms that the can handle the job and then takes the contract the bankers have given him to a washroom where he can review it, but without his employers seeing that he needs to use his spectacles to read the fine print in that contract. He emerges to say that all is in accordance with his understanding of the job and he is then reluctantly but officially hired. McCrea decides to stay in town, looking for a second man to serve as a fellow guard, and he runs into Scott, hardly recognizing his own friend, a former lawman like himself. Scott is running a sideshow where he performs as a sharpshooter called "The Oregon Kid," wearing a false beard, a wig with long hair and an outlandish out-sized Stetson hat. He tells McCrea that his ridiculous impersonation serves to provide him enough money to eat in a quick-changing West where he and others like him, including McCrea, must now struggle to survive. McCrea invites Scott to have dinner with him that night after McCrea describes the job at hand and Scott becomes interested, but not as a guard. He and his young companion, Starr, plan to serve as guards with McCrea, but, somewhere along the way, they intend to rob the gold. They meet with McCrea that night and are having dinner in a Chinese restaurant where McCrea thinks that Starr is not enough of a man to handle the job of a guard. He changes his mind, however, after Starr gets into a fight with several other young men and bests them in a wild battle that causes considerable wreckage in the restaurant. The following day, the three men begin riding toward the high country and the mining town. McCrea and Scott exchange stories about the better days of their lives, the jobs they have held, and how they have fallen on hard times. Though Scott is a man who has tried to adapt to the changing times, he no longer feels an obligation to obey the law. McCrea, on the other hand, is as resolute in purpose as he was when young, telling Scott that he has held on to his honor and dignity in spite of the reversals he has suffered. "All I want is to enter my house justified," McCrea tells Scott, meaning that he wants to die without betraying his code of decency and with the knowledge that has upheld the law to the last. McCrea, Scott and Starr arrive at a farm owned by Armstrong and pay him to stay there for the night. They have dinner with Armstrong and his attractive daughter, Hartley, soon realizing that Armstrong is a Bible-quoting religious zealot, who has repressed his daughter and who considers women untrustworthy. Armstrong has buried his wife on the farm, and her tombstone brands her a "harlot." Starr is attracted to Hartley and she is equally drawn to him, but later Hartley asks McCrea if she can ride with him and his friends to the mining camp where she plans to marry Drury, a handsome but roughhouse miner, having made this secret plan without her father's knowledge. Seeing that Hartley is desperate to escape the domination of the draconian Armstrong, McCrea takes pity on her and allows her to ride with him, Scott and Starr, and all set out together for the mining camp. When they arrive at that camp, with its seedy shacks and stained tents, Hartley is reunited with Drury. They are married in a bordello by Buchanan, a drunken justice of the peace. Hartley soon realizes her mistake as Drury is nothing more than a crude and unthinking miner, as savage and cruel as his father, Anderson, and his filth-ridden brothers, Jones, Oates and Chandler, all of whom passionately kiss her after her wedding. She is shocked and frightened by their lascivious attitude, which indicates to her that she will be their common sexual slave. The brothers begin to battle with each other as to which one will sleep with Hartley after Drury has consummated his marriage. Hartley's romantic dream has turned into a hideous nightmare. To escape her cruel fate, she again seeks Starr's help, knowing that he loves her and he, in turn, asks McCrea to intervene. McCrea, a by-the-book westerner, sees no legal way by which Hartley can abandon a legal marriage to which she gave her willing approval, but he says that a miner's court can judge her case. The compassionate Scott knows Hartley has no case, but he intends to make one for her by going to the besotted Buchanan. He orders Buchanan to testify at the hearing that he has no legal right to marry anyone and that the marriage between Hartley and Drury is therefore illegal. Scott emphasizes that if Buchanan does not so testify, he will shoot him. To make sure Buchanan keeps his word, Scott takes Buchanan's license for safe-keeping. Buchanan then appears before the miner's court and hesitantly states that he has no license to perform marriages, a statement that is technically true in that that license is in the hands of Scott. The miner's court then decrees that Hartley is not married to Drury and is free to go her own way, and she does, riding off with McCrea, Scott and Starr. McCrea by that time has collected the gold he is to deliver to the bank, but does not know that Scott and Starr are planning to take the gold from him. Meanwhile, Hartley is happy and relieved that she has escaped a terrible fate and warms to Starr, falling in love with the sensitive young man. Starr, by this time, has reservations about joining with Scott to rob McCrea of the gold they have been entrusted to guard. Scott, too, is hesitant to go against his old friend and tries to subtly persuade McCrea to join with him in taking the gold, saying that it is rightly theirs anyway since they have spent their lives upholding the law and have received nothing but poverty and misery in return. McCrea tells him that such thinking goes against his beliefs and that one must live by the contracts one signs in life, as he has with the bank. When they make camp that night, Scott and Starr make an attempt to take the gold from McCrea, even though Starr has earlier told Scott that he does not want any part of it, but will live up to his agreement in going along with the robbery. McCrea is too fast for Scott, however, and holds him at gunpoint, telling him that Scott has betrayed their friendship and slaps him in the face. After Scott drops his gun belt and Starr surrenders his gun, both of them are tied up. Hart-

Ron Starr and Joel McCrea in *Ride the High Country,* 1962.

ley is crestfallen in that Starr has turned bad, but she quickly realizes that he acted reluctantly and is not a thief at heart. The next day, Drury and his family members appear in the high mountains through which McCrea and the others are traveling, intent on taking back Hartley. They fire at McCrea and his party, and he allows Scott and Starr to use their guns in the ensuing gun battle. Jones and Chandler are killed, and Drury, Oates and Anderson flee. That night, Scott complains that "I don't sleep so good anymore," and asks McCrea to untie him. The compassionate McCrea complies and Scott later escapes, returning to the site of the gunfight and retrieves a horse and a gun. The next day, McCrea, Starr and Hartley arrive at Hartley's farm. They see Hartley's father, Armstrong, kneeling at the grave of his wife, apparently praying, but McCrea's weak eyesight does not allow him to see that Armstrong is dead with a bullet in his head. His killers, Anderson, Drury and Oates, are hiding in the farmhouse, rightly believing that Hartley and her protectors would return there. When McCrea, Hartley and Starr approach the house, the three killers fire at them, wounding Starr and McCrea. Pinned down, McCrea decides to stand his ground and make a fight of it, but realizes that he and the disabled Starr do not stand much of a chance. Just then, Scott appears, riding forward and firing at the killers, returning to aid McCrea in an effort to regain his lost respect. McCrea and Scott then decide to call the killers out and have a face-to-face gunfight as in days of old. They shout insults at Drury, Oates and Anderson, and when McCrea and Scott stand up and begin walking toward the farmhouse, Anderson thinks to shoot them from cover. Drury, however, says to him: "Don't you have any family pride?" Anderson then joins Drury and Oates as they all step from cover and stand in the open to face McCrea and Scott. They resolutely move toward each other and then open fire at each other. In the blazing gunfire, Anderson, Oates and Drury are killed and McCrea and Scott wounded. Scott's wound is superficial, but McCrea is mortally wounded and collapses. McCrea tells Scott that he does not want Hartley and Starr to see him die, and Scott waves the young couple away. "I'll go it alone," McCrea says. Scott then tells the dying McCrea: "Don't worry about anything. I'll take care of it, just like you would have." McCrea replies: "Hell, I know that. I always did. You just forgot it for a while...so long, partner." Scott replies: "I'll see you later." He walks back to Hartley and Starr and they begin to leave as the camera closes on the prone McCrea. He takes a last look at the blue sky, the sunlit farm, and the mountains rising behind it, and then slips downward, almost in slow motion, to the earth, to end this great film. Peckinpah takes great care to develop the wonderful characters of this film, giving each special attention to define their personality traits and quirks. McCrea, Scott, Hartley, Starr and Drury, as well as his deadly family members, along with the boozy Buchanan, are superlative in playing their sharply etched characters. It is a bittersweet film that says farewell

Joel McCrea, Ron Starr and Randolph Scott in *Ride the High Country,* 1962.

to the Old West, but not without a figh; its dynamic characters refuse to go gentle into that good night. The director adds many touches to emphasize the changing world which engulfs old-timers McCrea and Scott. That is shown not only in the appearance of the auto (as Peckinpah also exhibits in his other westerns, **The Wild Bunch**, 1969, and **The Ballad of Cable Hogue**, 1970) to show the intrusion of modernity, but in singular signs of aging (McCrea's failing eyesight, Scott's inability to sleep), as well as the loss of ethical behavior (Scott breaking his word, the Drury clan making a mockery of marriage) that hallmarked the cherished traditions and honorable codes, mythical or not, of the Old West. This film was not a success at the box office in the U.S., and did not return its original budget of a little over $800,000, but this was due to the indifferent distribution by MGM. Songs: "When the Roll Is Called Up Yonder" (James Milton Black), "For She's a Jolly Good Fellow" (traditional). *Author's Note*: Peckinpah was notorious for feuding with producers, mostly due to his inability or unwillingness to complete films on schedule, which invariably skyrocketed budgets. He nevertheless got along famously with Lyons, the producer of this film. The story was Lyons' pet project from the start, having acquired the story about two aging lawmen; he envisioned McCrea and Scott in those roles right from the beginning, but not as they appeared in the film. He persuaded McCrea, who had not made a feature film in some years, to play the part of the old lawman-turned-thief and convinced Scott to play the part of the dedicated protector of the gold shipment. McCrea, however, had second thoughts. He told this author: "The more I thought about that character, the more uncomfortable I became with his character. He was a man, who redeems himself in the end, but he is nevertheless a villain, and I never played villains in my life. I called Richard [Lyons] and asked him if he would talk with Scott about changing roles. Well, I almost fell on the floor when I got a call back from him telling me that Scott felt the same way, that he did not like the other part. So we each gladly switched roles and that worked out swell for the both of us and I think helped that picture a lot." Scott echoed McCrea's words when telling this author: "I thought that the backsliding partner was a better role for me. Joel [McCrea] and I had always played heroes, but I don't think he ever played the bad guy, but I did. I played the outlaw, Bill Doolin [William "Bill" Doolin; 1858-1896] in **The Doolins of Oklahoma** [1949], so I was not unfamiliar with that kind of role. I really thought that my part in **Ride the High Country** was a little more sympathetic than Joel's, except at the end when he dies the way he has lived, as a hero." Lyons personally selected Peckinpah to direct this film after seeing some TV shows he had directed and he eventually convinced MGM studio chief Sol Siegel to give him the green light to hire Peckinpah, but only after Siegel watched some of those TV shows and thought Peckinpah had a special talent. Peckinpah took on the directorial chore, but only under

the proviso that he could rewrite the script. He stayed mostly with the original script, but he inserted some lines that were straight out of his family album, including the line McCrea utters: "All I want is to enter my house justified," a line that Peckinpah's own father often stated. He also altered the ending, having McCrea die at the end, instead of having Scott perish in redeeming himself, so that McCrea could, indeed, enter that house justified. "Peckinpah's changes in the script," Scott told this author, "were inspired." Both McCrea and Scott were top stars, and their billing was decided when they tossed a coin while they were having lunch at the Brown Derby and Scott won. Scott's name came first in the billing but McCrea's name appears right after it and on the same line. Peckinpah shot some scenes in the high mountains at Mammoth Lake in the High Sierras, but, after four days of shooting, the weather closed in with snowstorms that threatened to delay the production and increase costs. Peckinpah reluctantly shot most of the remaining exteriors at Bronson Canyon at Griffith Park, where so-called snow machines produced endless soap suds to simulate snow. Other scenes were shot at the Fox Studio ranch at Malibu Creek State Park, Inyo National Forest at Bishop, and near Merrimac, California. By the time the film was completed, Siegel had been replaced at MGM by Joseph R. Vogel, and who, for some reason, prohibited Peckinpah from being involved with the editing of the film. Vogel also barred Peckinpah from the first studio screening of the film. Vogel reportedly fell asleep when the film was screened and when he awoke he offhandedly stated that it was the worst film he had ever seen (or not seen). He dumped the film into the B-programming distributional schedule where it was not treated like the major film it truly was and that limited distribution hampered its box office receipts, although it was critically acclaimed. It nevertheless was a big hit in Europe (the biggest grossing MGM film to that time) and elsewhere and it saw growing enthusiasm from the public in its rereleases. It remains today as a western classic of the first order, and rightly so. Like the memorable westerner he plays in **Ride the High Country**, this was the movie swansong for Randolph Scott. "It was time to put those six-shooters away," Scott said to this author with a wide grin. He never made another film. **p**, Richard E. Lyons; **d**, Sam Peckinpah; **cast**, Randolph Scott, Joel McCrea, Mariette Hartley, Ron Starr, Edgar Buchanan, R.G. Armstrong, Jenie Jackson, James Drury, L.Q. Jones, John Anderson, John Davis Chandler, Warren Oates, Percy Helton, Byron Foulger; **w**, N.B. Stone, Jr.; **c**, Lucien Ballard (Metrocolor); **m**, George Bassman; **ed**, Frank Santillo; **art d**, Leroy Coleman, George W. Davis; **set d**, Henry Grace, Otto Siegel.

Ride the Pink Horse ★★★★ 1947: U.S.; 101m; UNIV; B/W; Crime Drama; Children: Unacceptable; **DVD**. Montgomery gives a mesmerizing performance as a shifty, laconic character with some strange ethics, who tries blackmail to get rich before seeking revenge against a mob boss. He shows up in a small New Mexico town looking for Clark, a cunning gang boss, who has been operating several rackets. Montgomery meets and befriends Gomez, the operator of a small carousel that features a pink horse among its lifeless animal effigies (ergo the title of this offbeat tale), along with fetching Hendrix, a Mexican girl who falls in love with the smooth operator. Before Montgomery can find Clark, he is visited by Smith, a shrewd FBI agent who has been trailing him, believing that Montgomery can lead him to Clark. Smith asks for Montgomery's cooperation in getting evidence that will send Clark to prison where he belongs, but Montgomery pretends that he does not know a thing about Clark. He certainly does. He knows that Clark is operating rackets and he has the evidence that will send Clark to prison, a canceled check that proves Clark's profits from his illegal operations. When Montgomery does track down Clark and confronts him, his blackmail scheme falls apart and, instead of a payoff, he gets the beating of his life from Clark's thugs. Montgomery vows revenge, especially after he learns that a close friend has been murdered on Clark's orders. Montgomery recuperates from that savage beating by staying with Gomez and Hendrix, who nurse him back to health. Hendrix pleads with Montgomery to give up his vengeful plan against Clark. Though he is fond of the girl, Montgomery thinks her naïve. He is a street savvy guy, who doesn't need her advice or help. Montgomery goes back to Clark, but this time traps the gang boss with a ruse, although he is almost murdered by Clark's killers. Thanks to Hendrix, who goes to Smith and tells him the whereabouts of Montgomery, the FBI agent arrives just in time to save Montgomery's life, and Montgomery turns over his evidence to Smith that will smash Clark's operations. Montgomery then leaves town as inauspiciously as he arrived. Montgomery directs this exceptional film noir entry with great skill, fully developing all the main characters and where he stars in the film but as a low-profile fast-buck hustler. His character is not unlike his restrained role as the cunning private eye, Philip Marlowe, in **Lady in the Lake**, 1947, a film Montgomery also directed and one that was made just before he did **Ride the Pink Horse**. Montgomery allows his lowlife character in this film to regain a conscience, but only through the sincerity and emotional generosity of Gomez and Hendrix, who are both outstanding in their roles. So, too, is Clark as the sleazy, conniving and lethal operator that no one would ever want to meet. This story was aired in a sixty-minute broadcast by Lux Radio Theater on December 8, 1947, with Montgomery, Hendrix and Gomez reprising their roles. The film saw a poor remake etitled **The Hanged Man**, 1964. *Author's Note*: Montgomery had scored well when directing a riveting Raymond Chandler story, **Lady in the Lake**, 1947, a film made just before **Ride the Pink Horse**, where he played the role of private eye Philip Marlowe. "I tried to repeat that success," Montgomery told this author, "but it was not to be. I think **Ride the Pink Horse** was just a little too off-the-beaten track for audiences, although it deserved more success than what it saw." Gomez told this author that Montgomery "is one of the most talented men I ever met. Not only a fine actor, but a brilliant director, and that shows in the films he directed. He was selfish in everything he did in **Ride the Pink Horse**, letting all of us other actors take the scenes, but only as long as we hit our marks. Would that there were more of him in Hollywood." **p**, Joan Harrison; **d**, Robert Montgomery; **cast**, Montgomery, Thomas Gomez, Wanda Hendrix, Andrea King, Fred Clark, Art Smith, Richard Gaines, Tito Renaldo, Martin Garralaga, Grandon Rhodes, **w**, Ben Hecht, Charles Lederer (based on the novel by Dorothy B. Hughes); **c**, Russell Metty; **m**, Frank Skinner; **ed**, Ralph Dawson; **art d**, Bernard Herzbrun, Robert Boyle; **set d**, Russell A. Gausman, Oliver Emert.

Ride with the Devil ★★★★ 1999; U.S.; 138m; Good Machine/MCA UNIV; Color; War Drama; Children: Unacceptable (MPAA: R); **DVD**; **VHS**. Set during the American Civil War (1861-1865), this action-packed tale provides a well-written script that accurately describes the lifestyles and perspectives of guerrilla warfare. Beginning in 1861, Maguire (star of the Spider-Man trilogy, 2002-2007), a German-American youth living in rural Missouri, aligns himself with pro-Confederate factions just before the eruption of the Civil War. His hard-working father, Judd, is a staunch pro-Unionist and who more or less disowns his son for siding with the Rebels. When the war breaks out, Maguire rides with other Southern guerrillas such as his close friend, Ulrich, but he later learns that Judd has been murdered by Union Jayhawkers simply because he was Maguire's father. He and Ulrich then meet Baker, who comes from a wealthy family that owned slaves and who has granted freedom to Wright, a former slave who has been his childhood companion, both of whom having joined the Southern guerrillas known as Bushwhackers. They join with other Rebel guerrillas and use hit-and-run tactics in battling the enemy, and when they are on the run, they find refuge with a family with Southern sympathies; Ulrich falls in love with Jewel, the daughter of that protective farm family. Ulrich is wounded in a skirmish and later dies from that wound when gangrene sets in. Jewel, who has become pregnant, is then protected by the sympathetic and compassionate Maguire, who is also attracted to her. Meanwhile, the Bushwhackers swell in numbers and they are soon joined by the pro-Confederate forces led by William Clarke Quantrill (1837-1865), played

Jeffrey Wright, Tobey Maguire and Jewel in *Ride with the Devil*, 1999.

by Ales, who gathers hundreds of Bushwhackers and calls upon them to accompany him to Lawrence, Kansas, a Unionist town where they will destroy that Union bastion in retaliation for the Unionist murders of Rebels, including Quantrill's female relatives. Disguised as Union troopers, the Bushwhackers then ride to Lawrence. When arriving at that tranquil town, the Bushwhackers discard their Union uniforms and ride wildly into the town, shooting down all the members of the small Federal garrison and then go about randomly shooting and killing all the town's males, including teenage boys and even women who try to prevent the wholesale slaughter. (The attack conducted by Quantrill and 300 to 400 raiders was labeled the Lawrence Massacre, that attack occurring on August 21, 1863, and where 164 Union casualties were inflicted by the raiders.) Among the most rampant and ruthless killers is Rhys Meyers, a psychopathic killer who delights in slaying anyone he thinks is pro-Unionist. Disgusted with the senseless murders, Maguire and Wright go to a small restaurant with some others and demand that the frightened proprietors, an elderly man and woman, serve them breakfast. This they readily do while other Bushwhackers roam the streets, shooting down citizens and setting fire to buildings. The bloodthirsty Rhys Meyers enters the restaurant and orders the terrified owners to step into the street, but Maguire countermands that order, telling Rhys Meyers that these people are serving him and others breakfast, and to leave them alone. When Rhys Meyers tells Maguire that he is a traitor and that he would just as soon shoot him, Maguire and others draw their weapons, pointing them at the unbalanced Rhys Meyers. "When are you going to do this mean thing to me?" says Maguire. Rhys Meyers, in the face of these cocked guns, then retreats into the street to continue wreaking more mayhem on the suffering citizens, but not before threatening Maguire with deadly reprisals to come. When the elderly owner of the restaurant thanks Maguire for saving his life, Maguire angrily tells him to go to hell as he thinks of this harmless and doddering old man as the enemy. After sacking Lawrence, Ales leads his men from the town, all riding away with stolen loot. While riding away, Maguire is approached by Caviezel, one of the most fanatical Rebels, menacingly asking him if he is a traitor, his question obviously prompted by the trouble-making Rhys Meyers; Maguire replies: "You know that I am not." Maguire's friend, Baker, who is now a member of the hierarchy with the Bushwhackers, rides to Maguire to tell him that he "will do what I can" to allay the suspicions about Maguire's loyalty that have been instigated by the maniacal Rhys Meyers. Knowing that his life is now in danger, Maguire becomes apprehensive as he rides along with the guerrillas. The next day, Union forces arrive in pursuit of the guerrillas, the federal cavalry first chasing a group of the Rebels, only to be counterattacked in a savage charge by the guerrillas, who ride among the Union troopers, shooting many of them down before retreating. The Union cavalry re-

Jewel and Skeet Ulrich in *Ride with the Devil*, 1999.

groups and then attacks, following the retreating Rebels, only to find them waiting in the cover of a tree line and where many more federal troopers are shot from their racing horses. During this wild battle (expertly choreographed and one of the most realistically recreated guerrilla actions about that war ever filmed), Maguire is almost killed by a bullet fired from behind him. He turns to see that Rhys Meyers has shot at him, such is the zealot's seething hatred for Maguire in earlier backing him down at Lawrence. At the same time, Wright is wounded and Baker, seeing his friend disabled, dismounts his horse and goes to him, shielding him with his body, but is then struck by a fatal bullet and dies on the spot. Wright refuses to leave Baker, but Maguire pulls him away as the Rebels retreat, scattering in small groups as they are now hunted by Union forces, all branded as murderous criminals for their actions at Lawrence. Maguire and Wright recuperate at the farm where Jewel has taken refuge and where she later gives birth. Pressured to marry Jewel by those who think the child is his, he nevertheless weds Jewel since he loves her, and they then prepare to migrate to California following the war's end and with Wright accompanying them. En route, they encounter the deadly Rhys Meyers, who is now a wanted criminal and who invites Maguire and Wright to accompany him to a nearby town occupied by Union troops. Maguire tells Rhys Meyers that he will be killed, but the savage killer does not care. Thinking that Rhys Meyers is seeking to settle old scores, Maguire and Wright pull guns and aim them at Rhys Meyers and a companion. "You got me now," Rhys Meyers says as he turns his horse in the direction toward the town and slowly rides away. Maguire and Wright allow him to go as good riddance. Wright then tells Maguire that he will not be going to California with him, but, instead, is traveling to Texas to try to find his mother. The two friends part and go their separate ways and that is where this dynamic film ends. Lee does a marvelous job in recreating that turbulent era, all of the props and costumes appropriate to that period. All of the cast members underplay their roles, restraining their emotions and allowing the action to engulf them, except for the horrific and realistic enactment of the sacking of Lawrence. For the most part, the actors speak with monotone voices, flat and unemotional as was the actual case with these plain-speaking middle-westerners, who were mostly farm boys fighting for a mythical cause in that they did not own slaves and where their loyalty to the Confederacy was emotional rather than practical. The film did not see the success it deserved, taking in only about $600,000 at the box office when initially released against a whopping $38 million budget. *Author's Note*: The film advanced the careers of several actors, who later became superstars, including Maguire as Spider-Man, and Caviezel, a superb actor, appearing as Jesus in Mel Gibson's **The Passion of the Christ**, 2004, and as master golfer Bobby Jones in **Bobby Jones: Stroke of Genius**, 2004, as well as Baker, who

began with a small part as a homosexual actor in **L.A. Confidential**, 1997, and eventually graduated to the leading player in the enormously popular TV series, **The Mentalist**, 2008- . The commercial failure of **Ride with the Devil** was due to undeservedly bad reviews from such film gurus as Roger Ebert, who condemned this film as being "not a very entertaining movie" best employed as "a discussion in a history class." However, Ebert's self-admitted ignorance about that national conflict ("I don't know anything about the Civil War," he once admitted to this author), dismissed his ability to understand the dramatic and historical significance of this powerful film and its subject, particularly the uneducated and life-taking guerrillas who fought that war and are so accurately profiled in this stellar production. I knew Ebert throughout the life of his writing career and also knew him to be brilliantly perceptive on social issues, but he was woefully lacking in any knowledge when it came to history or real-life historical persons, and as dismally ignorant of the era of the youths so well depicted in this film. That is sadly the case with most film reviewers, who presumptively arbitrate the worth of films without a scintilla of expertise about their basic subjects, substituting their highly promoted personas for actual research and validation of the factual truth. Unfortunately this was Ebert's eventual and permanent "pop star" posture where his celebrated image created an ersatz authority that conveniently shielded his inability to incisively determine intrinsic values in such history-based films. This is one of those films, which is certainly "entertaining" as well as informative and, most importantly, socially revealing for the period it so well captures and portrays. Since most films are taken from real life, the credibility of any film reviewer is endemic to being a reliable historian, and Roger Ebert was never among those exclusive ranks. Quantrill has been played by many actors in numerous other films, including **Arizona Raiders**, 1965 (Fred Graham); **Dark Command**, 1940 (role model for Walter Pidgeon); **Fighting Man of the Plains**, 1949 (James Griffith); **Hondo**, 1967 (TV series; "Hondo and the Judas," 1967 episode: Forrest Tucker); **Jesse James under the Black Flag**, 1921 (Harry Hall); **Kansas Pacific**, 1953 (Reed Hadley); **Kansas Raiders**, 1950 (Brian Donlevy); **The Legend of Jesse James**, 1965-1966 (TV series; Peter Whitney); **The Legend of the Golden Gun**, 1979 (made-for-TV; Robert Davi); **Quantrill's Raiders**, 1958 (Leo Gordon); **Red Mountain**, 1951 (John Ireland); **Renegade Girl**, 1946 (Ray Corrigan); **The Stranger Wore a Gun**, 1953 (James Millican); **Woman They Almost Lynched**, 1953 (Brian Donlevy); and **Young Jesse James**, 1960 (Emile Meyer). **p**, Anne Carey, James Schamus, Robert F. Colesberry, Ted Hope; **d**, Ang Lee; **cast**; Tobey Maguire, Skeet Ulrich, Jewel [Kilcher], Jeffrey Wright, Simon Baker, Jonathan Rhys Meyers, Jim Caviezel, Tom Guiry, Jonathan Brandis, Mark Ruffalo, Tom Wilkinson, Margo Martindale, John Ales, John Judd; **w**, Daniel Woudrell, Schamus; **c**, Frederick Elmes; **m**, Mychael Dana; **ed**, Tim Squyres; **prod d**, Mark Friedberg; **art d**, Steve Arnold; **set d**, Stephanie Carroll, Bryan E. Jordan; **spec eff**, Allen Hall.

The Rider of Death Valley ★★★ 1932; U.S.; 76m; UNIV; B/W; Western; Children: Unacceptable. Exciting oater sees Wilson's gold-prospecting brother striking it rich in Death Valley, California. After he is murdered, Wilson goes to the valley to look for the gold mine and is closely watched by greedy Kohler and Stanley. Mix is a stalwart cowboy, who meets Wilson and helps her keep the mine away from Kohler and Stanley. This fine early sound western provides a lot of rock-'em-sock-'em action from Tom Mix, who was the most popular cowboy star of his day. Violence prohibits viewing by children. Songs: "In the Hills of Montana" (Billy Barry), "Little Sweetheart of the Mountains" (Herb Pinkert, Billy Barry, Lou Handman). **p**, Carl Laemmle, Jr.; **d**, Albert Rogell; **cast**, Tom Mix, Lois Wilson, Fred Kohler, Forrest Stanley, Edith Fellows, Mae Busch, Francis Ford, Willard Robertson, Otis Harlan, Iron Eyes Cody, Tony the Horse; **w**, Jack Cunningham, Al Martin (based on a story by Cunningham, Stanley Bergerman); **c**, Daniel B. Clark; **ed**, Robert Carlisle; **art d**, Thomas F. O'Neill.

Rider on the Rain ★★★ 1970; Italy/France; 120m; Greenwich Film Productions/AVCO Embassy; Color; Drama; Children: Unacceptable (MPAA: PG-13); **VHS**. Jobert is a beautiful young woman living at a small seaside resort in the south of France, who is married to Tinti, a jealous airline pilot. While he is away at work, a masked man invades their home and rapes her. She shoots him dead and dumps the body in the sea. The body washes ashore a few days later, and she meets Bronson, a U.S. Army colonel. He accuses her of murdering a sex fiend, who escaped from prison after he stole $60,000 from the U.S. Army. Bronson is convinced that Jobert has the loot. Wilder events unfold as Jobert's early life is revealed, including the adulterous lifestyle of her mother and her father's desertion. Jobert then finds the bag containing the stolen money and tries to return it to Bronson. He then informs her that another woman has been arrested and charged with the invader's murder, and this prompts Jobert to conduct her own investigation, which leads her to Paris. While interviewing the sister of the arrested woman, who resides in a brothel, Jobert is endangered by several crooks also looking for that stolen loot. Bronson arrives to save Jobert from harm, returning with her to the South of France. Eventually, Bronson gets Jobert to confess about the shooting and gets the money back for the army, but decides not to involve Jobert, compassionately concluding that Jobert has had enough problems in her troubled life. Clement directs this rather complex crime tale with a taut hand, sustaining tension and anxiety throughout to produce a superior thriller. Song: "Le passager de la pluie" (Francis Lai, Sebastien Japrisot, Peggy Lee). Violence and rape prohibit prohibits viewing by children. (In French; English subtitles.) **p**, Serge Silberman; **d**, Rene Clement; **cast**, Marlene Jobert, Charles Bronson, Annie Cordy, Jill Ireland, Gabriele Tinti, Jean Gaven, Jean Piat, Corinne Marchand, Ellen Bahl, Steve Eckhardt, Jean-Daniel Ehrmann; **w**, Sebastien Japrisot, Lorenzo Ventavoli; **c**, Andreas Winding (Eastmancolor); **m**, Francis Lai; **ed**, Francoise Javet; **art d**, Pierre Guffroy.

Riders of the Timberline ★★★ 1941; U.S.; 59m; PAR; B/W; Western; Children: Acceptable; **DVD**. In what is an offbeat but superior entry in the series, Boyd is again the indefatigable Hopalong Cassidy, western hero fighting against outlaws. Keane, an Easterner who wants everything in sight, has hired Taliaferro and his gang to stop logger MacDonald from fulfilling a contract so he can get his land and the contract. When Tyler, one of Taliaferro's men, gets the loggers to walk off the job, MacDonald's daughter, Stewart, arrives with a new crew. Boyd builds an overhead line to transport the logs, so Taliaferro sets out to blow up a dam, but Boyd gets there first to stop him. Hoppy then rounds up the rest of the villains, saving MacDonald's business and winning Stewart's gratitude. Director Selander provides nonstop action in this very exciting oater. Song: "The Fighting Forty" (Grace Hamilton, Jack Stern). **p**, Harry Sherman; **d**, Lesley Selander; **cast**, William Boyd, Andy Clyde, Brad King, Victor Jory, Eleanor Stewart, J. Farrell MacDonald, Anna Q. Nilsson, Tom Tyler, Edward Keane, Hal Taliaferro; **w**, J. Benton Cheney (based on a story by Cheney and characters created by Clarence E. Mulford); **c**, Russell Harlan; **m**, John Leipold; **ed**, Fred Feitshans Jr.; **art d**, Ralph Berger; **set d**, Emile Kuri.

The Riders of the Whistling Skull ★★★ 1937; U.S.; 58m; REP; B/W; Western; Children: Acceptable. Exceptional entry in the Three Mesquiteer's series involves an expedition to find an ancient lost Indian city and a pair of scientists who have disappeared while looking for it. The city is surrounded by rocks that give off a whistling sound when the wind blows through the formations. The Mesquiteers (Livingston, Corrigan, Terhune) discover that greedy Williams and an Indian (Canutt) are the villains who have been raiding the city of its treasures. They are also holding the two scientists hostage, Van Pelt, an archeology professor, and his daughter, Russell. Without food or water, the Mesquiteers move fast, as does this action-loaded film, to rescue the captives and bring the villains to justice. Song: "Bury Me Not on the Lone Prairie" (traditional). **p**, Nat Levine; **d**, Mack V. Wright; **cast**, Robert Livingston,

Ray Corrigan and Indians in *The Riders of the Whistling Skull*, 1937.

Ray "Crash" Corrigan, Max Terhune, Mary Russell, John Van Pelt, Roger Williams, Fern Emmett, Yakima Canutt, John Ward, Chief Thunder Cloud, Iron Eyes Cody; **w**, Oliver Drake, John Rathmell (based on a story by Bernard McConville, Drake from the novels *Riders of the Whistling Skull* and *The Singing Scorpion* by William Colt MacDonald); **c**, Jack Marta; **m**, Hugo Riesenfeld, Karl Hajos, Arthur Kay, Leon Rosebrook, J. S. Zamecnik, Jacques Aubran, Sidney Cutner; **ed**, Murray Seldeen, Tony Martinelli.

Riding Alone for Thousands of Miles ★★★ 2006; Hong Kong; China/Japan; 107m; Toho Co./Sony; Color; Drama; Children: Unacceptable (MPAA: PG); **DVD**. Takakura is a fisherman and devoted father living in a small Japanese coastal village, who misses his son, Nakai, from whom he has been estranged for years. Terajima, his daughter-in-law, who resides in Tokyo, informs him that her husband Nakai is sick and has been hospitalized in that city. She suggests that Takakura visit his son and restore their relationship. Takakura undertakes the long journey, but, when he gets to the hospital, Nakai refuses to see him. Terajima gives Takakura a videotape that shows how much Nakai loves Chinese opera. When he returns home, Terajima tells Takakura that Nakai has a terminal liver cancer. Takakura travels to a far province to videotape Nakai's favorite singer. Jiamin Li, in an opera, to give to his dying son, and when he returns with it, the father and son are finally reunited. This sad but beautifully made film tellingly depicts the love of a father for his offspring and is well enacted by the entire cast. Thematic elements prohibit viewing by children. (In Mandarin/Japanese; English subtitles.) **p**, William Kong, Jian Xiu, Weiping Zhang; Yimou Zhang; **d**, Yimou Zhang; **cast**, Ken Takakura, Shinobu Terajima, Kiichi Nakai (voice), Ken Nakamoto, Jiamin Li, Jiang Wen, Lin Qiu, Bin Li, Ziliang Chen, Zezhou He, Zhenbo Yang; **w**, Jingzhi Zou (based on a story by Zhang, Zou, Bin Wang); **c**, Xiaoding Zhao; **m**, Wenjing Guo; **ed**, Long Cheng; **prod d**, Li Sun; **spec eff**, Graeme Pitt, Tony Poriazis.

Riding High ★★★ 1950; U.S.; 112m; PAR; B/W; Musical Comedy; Children: Acceptable; **IV**. Crosby is delightful as a down-on-his-luck horse trainer who puts all his bets on a horse, Broadway Bill, to win the big race. He and wealthy Gray love each other, but she's jealous of the horse, so she makes Crosby choose between them. He chooses the horse (naturally), and it does gallop off to win the big race, making Crosby rich, but then Bill dies after the end of the race. Gray goes off with boxing champion Max Baer while Crosby, heartbroken at his horse's death, attends Bill's funeral. A terrific supporting cast includes legendary film comic Oliver Hardy in a cameo role. Crosby has a lot to croon about as he wonderfully delivers a bevy of memorable tunes. Capra, who directed the original talkie version of this story in 1934, adds a lot of very funny

Raymond Walburn, Coleen Gray, Clarence Muse, Bing Crosby and William Demarest in *Riding High*, 1950.

sequences to this updated and more entertaining entry. One of those set pieces involves Crosby trying to wheedle money out of Demarest and Walburn, thinking they are wealthy plungers, but they do not have a dime, and are trying to do the same thing to him. Songs: "We've Got a Sure Thing," "Someplace on Anywhere Road," "Sunshine Cake," "The Horse Told Me" (1950; music; Jimmy Van Heusen; lyrics: Johnny Burke), "The Camptown Races" (1850: Stephen Foster), "Home, Sweet Home" (1823; H.R. Bishop); "The Whiffenpoof Song" (1909: music; Tod B. Galloway; lyrics: Meade Minnigerode, George S. Pomeroy). This is a much better remake of two previous films made in 1918 and 1934 and both titled **Broadway Bill**. *Author's Note*: Capra told this author that "I really enjoyed remaking that story, which is a turf legend and it was all made a lot easier for me because I was working with Bing [Crosby], who is the nicest guy in the world to get along with." Crosby told this author that "I have been known to visit the track on occasions and place a modest bet now and then, so the story for that picture was familiar to me. I didn't have to tell Frank [Capra] to include all the necessary boosters, hustlers and race track touts. They were all there in **Riding High**." p&d, Frank Capra; **cast**, Bing Crosby, Coleen Gray, Charles Bickford, Frances Gifford, William Demarest, Raymond Walburn, James Gleason, Ward Bond, Percy Kilbride, Harry Davenport, Margaret Hamilton, Gene Lockhart, Douglass Dumbrille, Marjorie Hoshelle, Rand Brooks, Marjorie Lord, Joe Frisco, Frankie Darro, Charles Lane, Max Baer, Clara Blandick, Ann Doran, Fritz Feld; **w**, Robert Riskin, Melville Shavelson, Jack Rose (based on the story "Broadway Bill" by Mark Hellinger); **c**, George Barnes, Ernest Laszlo; **m**, Victor Young; **ed**, William Hornbeck; **art d**, Hans Dreier, Walter Tyler; **set d**, Emile Kuri, Sam Comer; **spec eff**, Farciot Edouart.

Riffraff ★★★ 1936; U.S.; 94m; MGM; B/W; Drama; Children: Cautionary; **DVD**; **VHS**. In another memorable role, Tracy is a good-natured, rough-house fisherman who falls for Harlow (wearing a brown wig this time instead of her platinum blonde hair), a girl who works in a cannery. They marry and all seems well with them until Hurst, a strikebreaker, convinces Tracy to lead all the workers in a strike to better their earnings. Tracy does not know that he is being set up in that Hurst is acting on behalf of Calleia, owner of the cannery, since the strike will get him better terms when it is settled in negotiations. When this happens, Tracy is blamed for worsening the workers' conditions instead of improving them and he becomes a pariah. Depressed and disillusioned, Tracy, after being ejected from the union, abandons his home and Harlow. After the ever faithful Harlow learns that Tracy is ill and is also penniless, so goes to wealthy Calleia and begs him for money to help Tracy. When Calleia coldheartedly refuses, Harlow steals some money, but the proud Tracy refuses her financial aid. Harlow then asks Hurst to

give the money to Tracy. Hurst breaks his promise by keeping the money and Harlow is caught and sent to prison for the theft. Tracy, back on his feet, returns to the waterfront where he learns about Hurst's sneaky mistreatment of his wife and gives him a good beating. He then gets on Calleia's good side by preventing Hurst from sabotaging the tuna boats. Harlow, who has given birth behind bars, the child unknown to Tracy, hears that Tracy has been injured during the sabotage attempt on the boats and, desperate, escapes from prison to be at his side. She finds him safe and sound and they reconcile. Harlow agrees to return to prison to serve out her time, and Tracy promises to be waiting for her when she is released. The film is well written with a lot of tough-talking lines from Tracy, Harlow and the rest of the fine cast, written by two leading female writers, Loos and Marion. The acting is outstanding as are the waterfront location scenes where a lot of exciting roustabout action takes place. *Author's Note*: Tracy told this author that "**Riffraff** is not one of my favorite pictures, although I liked working with Jean [Harlow], a grand gal with a great sense of humor. I did not like the character I was playing much. He is a bit of a lout and is just dumb enough to get suckered into being the pawn of others. When he loses out, he runs away like a coward and that I did not like. Well, it was really Jean's picture, so maybe I should shut up about that. I made up for that role a year later when I played a fisherman in **Captains Courageous** [1937] and I did not like my character in that one either, or the look of that character. They made me wear a mop of curly hair and speak with what was supposed to be a Portuguese accent—good luck! I must have done something good, since they gave me an Oscar [as Best Actor] for my performance in that picture. I played another fisherman when we did Hemingway's **The Old Man and the Sea** [1958]. That one I liked, but Hemingway didn't." **p**, Irving Thalberg; **d**, J. Walter Ruben; **cast**, Jean Harlow, Spencer Tracy, Una Merkel, Joseph Calleia, Victor Kilian, Mickey Rooney, J. Farrell MacDonald, Roger Imhof, Juanita Quigley, Vince Barnett; **w**, Frances Marion, H.W. Hanemann, Anita Loos (based on a story by Marion); **c**, Ray June; **m**, Edward Ward; **ed**, Frank Sullivan; **art d**, Cedric Gibbons, Stanwood Rogers.

Riffraff ★★★ 1947; U.S.; 80m; RKO; B/W; Drama; Children: Unacceptable. Well-directed drama sees private eye O'Brien searching for a map that could lead him to some rich oil deposits in Panama. Slezak, the leader of some unscrupulous businessmen, is also after that prized map. Jeffreys, a nightclub singer, provides romantic interest for O'Brien, and Kilbride offers some very funny moments as O'Brien overcomes Slezak and all odds to win through. Not related to several other films of the same title. Song: "Money Is the Root of All Evil" (Alex Kramer, Joan Whitney). *Author's Note*: This film sees fine direction from Tetzlaff, his debut at helming a feature film. He was earlier a top-notch cameraman, lensing some superlative films such as the **Talk of the Town**, 1942; **The More the Merrier**, 1943; **The Enchanted Cottage**, 1945; and Hitchcock's **Notorious**, 1946. Hitchcock's influence can be seen in this film, where Tetzlaff employs the same kind of menacing shadows and lighting to heighten tension. *Author's Note*: O'Brien told this author that "I always liked that picture because I liked playing a private detective, the kind of freelance operator who can bend the corners of the law a little to get things done and that's where you can pack in a lot more drama. I'm no Bogart in that picture, but I get my licks in against the bad guys all the same. Yeah, that picture was a lot of fun." **p**, Nat Holt; **d**, Ted Tetzlaff; **cast**, Pat O'Brien, Anne Jeffreys, Walter Slezak, Percy Kilbride, Jerome Cowan, George Givot, Tommy Noonan, Jason Robards Sr., Marc Krah, Ernest Anderson; **w**, Martin Rackin; **c**, George E. Diskant; **m**, Roy Webb; **ed**, Philip Martin; **art d**, Albert S. D'Agostino, Walter E. Keller; **set d**, Darrell Silvera, Michael Ohrenbach; **spec eff**, Russell A. Cully.

RiffRaff ★★★ 1993; U.K.; 95m; Parallax Pictures; Fine Line Features; Color; Comedy/Drama/Romance; Children: Unacceptable; **DVD**. Carlyle, a construction worker, and his girlfriend, McCourt, an unemployed pop singer, barely survive from week to week among the poor class in 1990s London. The film centers on proletarian-type workers resentful over reconstructing 19th-Century buildings into luxury homes for the upscale wealthy class. Director Loach provides enough humor to sustain interest and sympathy for Carlyle, McCourt and the rest of the truculent cast members while he moves this offbeat tale along at a brisk pace. Songs: "Always On My Mind" (Johnny Christopher, Francis Zambon as Mr. Jones, Wayne Carson Thompson), "With a Little Help from My Friends" (John Lennon, Paul McCartney), "Won't You Charleston with Me" (Sandy Wilson), "Spread a Little Happiness" Gordon Sumner, Vivian Ellis), "I'm So Excited" (Trevor Lawrence, Anita Pointer, June Pointer, Ruth Pointer), "Good Morning" (Nacio Herb Brown, Arthur Freed), "Everytime I Say Goodbye" (Cole Porter), "The Sun Has Got His Hat On" (Ralph Butler, Noel Gay). **p**, Sally Hibbin; **d**, Ken Loach; **cast**, Robert Carlyle, Emer McCourt, Jimmy Coleman, George Moss, Ricky Tomlinson, David Finch, Richard Belgrave, Ade Sapara, Derek Young, Bill Moores; **w**, Bill Jesse; **c**, Barry Ackroyd; **ed**, Jonathan Morris; **prod d**, Martin Johnson; **art d**, Jonathan Lee; **spec eff**, Graham Riddell, Nick Smith.

RiffRaff ★★★ 2009; U.S.; 106m; Naughty Otter Productions/Midnight Films; Color; Comedy/Romance; Children: Unacceptable (MPAA: R); **DVD**. Two lifeguards try to keep their minds on life-saving at Chicago's trendy North Avenue Beach, which is always packed with beauties in bikinis. The boys are Wells, a hopeless romantic, and Belushi, a lady-killer, who gets involved in one love triangle after another as young sex kitten O'Hagan and tomboy Whitehead become their main focus of attention. Meanwhile, the beach guard boss patrol is watching to foil their trysting and dampen their often amusing shenanigans. Songs: "For One Day," "Merry-Go-Round," "Offshore Bank Accounts" (Paul Chesne); "Cowboy Boots," You're Stupid" (Graham Elvis); "Lust" (Jeff Pahiti), "Sex and Violins" (Brad Elvis); "Dennehy" (David Cohn); "Darkness" (Rebecca Shaheen, Christina Isabel Jones); "Crack Whore" (Ross May), "Jimmy's New Board," "I Think It Means Death" (Steven Panchism); "Southside/Remix," "Chi City" (Chi-Town Kids: Mark Wlodarski, Ryan O'Malley, Chris Walsh); "Blue Eyes" (Mick Radichel); "Golden Lies," "Left Behind" (Derek E. Phillips). **p**, David J. Miller, John Otterbacher; **d&w**, Justen Naughton; **cast**, Ben Wells, Robert Belushi, Katie O'Hagan, Chryssie Whitehead, Joe Farina, Justen Naughton, Sonny Jaramilla, Alissa Bailey, Tavares Davis, Kyle Lane; **c**, Kuba Zelazek; **ed**, **set d**, Justen Naughton, John Otterbacher.

Rififi ★★★★★ 1956; France; 122m; Pathe Consortium Cinema; United Motion Pictures; B/W; Crime Drama; Children: Unacceptable; **DVD**; **VHS**. Masterful crime tale from the gifted Dassin presents a quintessential caper film, although it owes much to John Huston's film noir classic, **The Asphalt Jungle**, 1950. The Dassin production involves four conniving thieves, who conspire to rob an upscale jewelry store on the Rue de Rivoli in Paris. Servais is the criminal mastermind planning the dangerous robbery and keeping his fellow thieves (Vita, Manuel and Mohner) in line as he drills them in procedures and their specific assignments. The robbery, taking about thirty minutes in the film, depicts the elaborate theft without dialog or musical score, and where only the sounds of the thieves and their criminal labors are heard. After going to an apartment above the jewelry store, the thieves drill a small hole in the floor, slipping an umbrella through it and then opening the umbrella to catch any falling debris so that it does not fall on the floor of the jewelry store to trip the sensitive alarm system. They further disable the alarm bell by inserting the contents of a fire extinguisher into the bell so that when it does go off, it resonates with only a soft purr. Slipping through the drilled hole, the thieves work the safe containing the precious gems and easily open it, scooping up its expensive contents before departing. Fate then steps in to destroy this criminal triumph. When rival gang members Lupovici and Hossein learn of the spectacular robbery, they demand a cut of the spoils, and, to insure payment, they kidnap a

Jean Harlow and Spencer Tracy in *Riffraff*, 1936.

child of one of the thieves. Meanwhile, the thieves all meet separate and disastrous ends. One thief dies after he gives one of the stolen gems to a girl, others in shootouts, and the remaining survivor eventually succumbs from wounds while driving his car. Dassin's inventive and provocative camera angles, his stark sets and sparse dialog all work in harmony to provide a gritty and realistic portrait of a criminal enterprise gone wrong. The grim conclusion is achieved through misadventure and misfortune where fate, not law enforcement, takes a grim hand in meting out justice. "Rififi" is French slang meaning "trouble" or "brawl" and the characters in this film get plenty of both. *Author's Note*: Dassin, who appears in the film as one of the thieves, using the acting alias of Perlo Vita, had a penchant for making exceptional films that rank high in the history of film noir, including **Brute Force**, 1947; **Naked City**, 1948; and **Thieves' Highway**, 1949; all were Hollywood productions. He ran afoul of the U.S. House of Un-American Activities Committee and, rather than face contempt charges and imprisonment for his involvement with left-wing activities, departed the U.S., restarting his career as a film director, writer and actor in Europe; this was his second film made during that new career. Just as Dassin appropriated for **Rififi** the criminal modus operandi so startlingly depicted and detailed in Huston's **The Asphalt Jungle**, **Rififi** was subsequently emulated, if not blatantly lifted for subsequent crime films such as **The Killing**, 1956 (and where the director of that film, Stanley Kubrick, admitted to this author that "**Rififi** was not far from my mind when we did that picture, but Dassin leaned very heavily on John Huston's **The Asphalt Jungle**, so I was leaning on both of them"); **Big Deal on Madonna Street**, 1960; **Topkapi**, 1964; **Gambit**, 1966; **The Hot Rock**, 1972; **Bank Shot**, 1974; **Thief**, 1981; and **Crackers**, 1984, to name a few. **p**, Rene Bezard, Henri Berard, Pierre Cabaud; **d**, Jules Dassin; **cast**, Jean Servais, Carl Mohner, Robert Manuel, Perlo Vita (Jules Dassin), Janine Darcey, Pierre Grasset, Robert Hossein, Marcel Lupovici, Dominique Maurin, Magali Noel, Marie Sabouret; **w**, Dassin, Rene Wheeler, Auguste Le Breton (based on the novel by Le Breton); **c**, Philippe Agostini; **m**, Georges Auric; **ed**, Roger Dwyre; **prod d**, Alexandre Trauner; **set d**, Auguste Capelier.

Right Cross ★★★ 1950; U.S.; 90m; MGM; B/W; Boxing Drama; Children: Unacceptable; **DVD**. Montalban, a promising prizefighter, is in love with Allyson, the daughter of his promoter, Barrymore. But Powell, a reporter and his best friend, is also is in love with her even though he knows that she loves Montalban. Powell also knows he's going to lose Allyson so he takes to drink and strikes up a quickie romance with sexy Monroe after meeting her in a nightclub. Meanwhile, Montalban knows his right hand is going bad and needs to win a fight for big money before it's too late. To obtain enough money to marry Allyson and take care of the ailing, wheelchair-bound Barrymore, Montalban leaves Barrymore

Sam Shepard as the greatest of American test pilots Chuck Yeager in *The Right Stuff*, 1983.

to fight for a big purse, signing with another manager, Kelley. Barrymore is so depressed and upset with Montalban's departure that he dies of a heart attack. Allyson is incensed at Montalban's actions, believing him to be cruel and ungrateful, but not knowing the reasons for his actions. Montalban then enters the ring and fights his heart out, but loses the match, even though he gains a heavy purse for his painful labors. Powell meets with him in his dressing room after the fight, and they get into an argument where Montalban begins throwing punches and permanently injures his already disabled right hand, which ends his prizefighting career. When Powell and Allyson learn Montalban's true motivations, they reunite with him. Allyson decides to make a life with Montalban, and Powell is content to remain the boxer's friend. *Author's Note*: Sturges told this author that "Dick [Powell] and June [Allyson] were terrific to work with on **Right Cross**, always cooperative and helpful, but Montalban was a prima donna, always wanting to change his lines, mostly for the worse, and insisting he get more camera shots, even though he was not the star of the film. Marilyn Monroe, who was not too well known then [her eighth film appearance for which she received no billing], played a bar girl and she was very good in that little role. Who knew that a few years later she would be Hollywood's greatest sex symbol." **p**, Armand Deutsch; **d**, John Sturges; **cast**, June Allyson, Dick Powell, Ricardo Montalban, Lionel Barrymore, Tom Powers, Teresa Celli, Barry Kelley, Kenneth Tobey, Larry Keating, Chester Conklin, Marilyn Monroe; **w**, Charles Schnee; **c**, Norbert Brodine; **m**, David Raksin; **ed**, James E. Newcom; **art d**, Cedric Gibbons, Gabriel Scognamillo; **set d**, Edwin B. Willis.

The Right Stuff ★★★★★ 1983; U.S.; 193m; Ladd Company/WB; Color; Adventure/Biographical Drama; Children: Unacceptable (MPAA: R); **BD**; **DVD**; **VHS**. Stirring and historically memorable, this adventurous biopic depicts the heroic exploits of Air Force, Marine and Navy test pilots, who pioneered America's probes into high-speed air flights and eventual space exploration. This fascinating film opens in 1947 at California's Muroc Army Airfield, where test pilots have been testing high-speed planes and dying in the process. Slick Goodlin (Chalmers "Slick" Goodlin, 1923-2005), played by Russ, agrees to test the dangerous rocket-propelled Bell X-1 in an attempt to break the sound barrier, but he demands a prohibitive payment of $150,000. Captain Chuck Yeager (Charles Elwood "Chuck" Yeager; 1923-), played by Shepard, who agrees to fly the test plane for only his monthly payment of $283, is then given the assignment. Before attempting that hazardous flight, Shepard injures his ribs while horseback riding with his wife, Glennis Yeager, who is played by Hershey. In considerable pain, Shepard worries about his inability to close the hatch of the X-1 due to his debilitating injury, but a fellow pilot, Jack Ridley (1915-1957), played

by Helm, breaks the handle of a broomstick and shows Shepard how to use it in closing that hatch. Shepard climbs into the Bell X-1 on October 13, 1947, using the portion of the broomstick to close its hatch, and then powers the plane to 47,000 feet, where he breaks the sound barrier at Mach 1.07. It is next 1953 and the scene is the same base, now renamed Edwards Air Force Base, and Shepard is a colonel and encourages young test pilots to their missions, all of these brave airmen having "the right stuff" to achieve the goals needed. Shepard and his friendly rival, Wilson, who plays pilot Scott Crossfield (1921-2006) awe the younger pilots by consistently breaking more speed and altitude records. Those younger pilots include Gordon Cooper (Leroy Gordon Cooper Jr.; 1927-2004), played by Quaid; Virgil I. "Gus" Grissom (1926-1967), played by Ward; and Donald D. "Deke" Slayton (1924-1993), played by Paulin. Reed, who plays Cooper's wife, along with some of the other wives, expresses deep concern, if not outright fear, that their husbands might be killed at any moment while testing U.S. planes. With the launching of the Soviet Sputnik into space in 1957, U.S. President Lyndon B. Johnson (1908-1973), played by Moffat, demands that NASA (National Aeronautics and Space Administration) step up its programs in order to compete with the Soviets in the Space Race. The search for the first American astronauts begins, but Shepard is excluded because of his lack of a college education. Selected for the program are Quaid, Ward and Paulin; added to that sterling group are John Glenn (1921-), played by Harris; Scott Carpenter (1925-2013), played by Frank, Alan Shepard (1923-1998), played by Glenn, and Walter Schirra (1923-2007), played by Henriksen. Many tests are made in the new Mercury program, but test rockets explode on launching and technicians and inventors labor long to prevent such accidents from happening when live astronauts occupy spacecraft to be sent into space. The Soviets beat the U.S. by launching Vostok 1, a spacecraft that carries Yuri Gagarin into space on April 12, 1961. America responds by launching Mercury-Redstone 3, on May 5, 1961, carrying Glenn (Shepard) in a fifteen-minute sub-orbital space flight. His feat is repeated by Ward (Grissom) on July 21, 1961, but, when reentering the earth's atmosphere and crashing into the ocean, the hatch of the capsule blows open, rapidly filling the capsule with water; Ward narrowly escapes with his life. Harris (Glenn) is the next astronaut to enter space, becoming the first American to orbit the earth on February 20, 1962, in Mercury-Atlas 6. Hailed a hero, he is given a tickertape parade and the American public now gets behind the U.S. space program. Because of Harris' feat, the Manned Space Center is established in Houston, Texas, and the country now goes full tilt into that program. Some of the traditional test pilots at Edwards Air Force Base demean the space program by calling it nothing more than sending "spam in a can" into space, but Shepard (Yeager) defends the space program and considers its astronauts brave men. He himself attempts another altitude test and is almost killed in the process, his Lockheed NF-104A crashing. Those at the base believe he has been killed, but they see in the distance that the aging test pilot has ejected and has again survived, proving that he, along with the heroic astronauts he respects, still retains "the right stuff." Quaid (Cooper) ends the Mercury program with the successful launch of Mercury Atlas-9, on May 15, 1963, where the astronaut is hailed as having flown higher, farther and faster than any other American and has, for a moment, become the greatest pilot anyone has ever known. This monumental film, meticulously directed by Kaufman and superbly acted by Shepard, Harris, Quaid and the rest of the cast, remains a great tribute to a rare breed of heroic men who risked their lives to prove the human ability to enter space with the promise of exploring the vast universe beyond. The film was three years in the making at a cost of more than $25 million, but unfortunately saw only about $21 million at the box office upon its initial release. It nevertheless remains a classic tale showing the embryonic growth of the American space program that later developed into the Apollo program that took more lives in America's quest to conquer space and provided greater achievements in the process. **p**, Irwin Winkler, Robert Chartoff; **d&w**, Philip Kaufman (based on the book by Tom

Wolfe); **cast**, Sam Shepard, Scott Glenn, Ed Harris, Dennis Quaid, Fred Ward, Barbara Hershey, Kim Stanley, Veronica Cartwright, Charles Frank, Lance Henriksen, Scott Wilson, Scott Paulin, Kathy Baker, Pamela Reed, Jeff Goldblum, Chuck Yeager, Donald Moffat, Levon Helm, William Russ; **c**, Caleb Deschanel (Technicolor); **m**, Bill Conti; **ed**, Glenn Farr, Lisa Fruchtman, Tom Rolf, Stephen A. Rotter, Douglas Stewart; **prod d**, Geoffrey Kirkland; **art d**, Richard J. Lawrence, W. Stewart Campbell, Peter Romero; **set d**, Craig Edgar, Joel David Lawrence, Nicanor Navarro, George R. Nelson, Pat Pending; **spec eff**, Ken Pepiot, Stan Parks, David Pier, Gary Gutierrez, Jordan Belson.

Righteous Kill ★★★ 2008; U.S.; 101m; Millennium Films/Overture Films; Color; Crime Drama; Children: Unacceptable (MPAA: R); **BD**; **DVD**. This frightening and often eerie film sees Turk (De Niro) and Rooster (Pacino) as two aging New York Police Department detectives and longtime partners, investigating a serial killer whose victims are sociopathic criminals. The killer, called "Poetry Boy," leaves poems behind explaining that his deeds are righteous kills because he is slaying dangerous murderers. De Niro and Pacino have seen many guilty killers go free in the courts so they are somewhat sympathetic to the serial killer. They are teamed with two younger detectives, Leguizamo and Wahlberg, and tensions surface among the four, especially since De Niro is sleeping with Leguizamo's ex-girlfriend, Gugino, who is also a homicide detective. During all of this, Pacino kills Jackson, a drug dealer, and De Niro finds Pacino's diary, and from that he learns that his partner is the serial killer, a man who had lost his faith in justice. The film ends with a shootout between De Niro and Pacino in which Pacino dies. Grim and sometimes perplexing, this riveting story is nevertheless well directed and enacted, ending on a much-needed light note when De Niro is shown coaching a Police Athletic League baseball game while Gugino watches. Songs: "We Fly High" (James Jones, Zukham Bey); "Cast a Spell," "Nocturne" (Homer Greencastle); "War" (Darryl Pittman, Tyrone Smith); "Chicago Style" (Larry Cohn); "Jaybird" (Timothy S. Jones, Johnny Lee Schell); "Blue Dreams" (D. DiFonzo, Scott Schreer); "Stylin" (Willie Mackie, Robert Smith, Michael Clervoix). Violence, gutter language, sexuality and drug use prohibit viewing by children. **p**, Jon Avnet, Rob Cowan, Randall Emmett, Lati Grobman, Avi Lerner, Alexandra Milchan, Daniel M. Rosenberg, Marsha Oglesby; **d**, Avnet; **cast**, Robert De Niro, Al Pacino, Curtis Jackson (50 Cent), Carla Gugino, John Leguizamo, Donnie Wahlberg, Brian Dennehy, Trilby Glover, Saidah Arrika Ekulona, Alan Rosenberg, Melissa Leo; **w**, Russell Gewirtz; **c**, Denis Lenoir; **m**, Edward Shearmur; **ed**, Paul Hirsch; **prod d**, Tracey Gallacher; **art d**, Christina Ann Wilson; **set d**, Kathy Lucas; **spec eff**, Vesselina Hary Georgieva, Velichko Ivanov, Ajoy Mani, Leo Vezzali.

The Ring ★★★ 1927 (silent); U.K.; 116m; British International Pictures (BIP)/Wolfe and Freedman; B/W; Sports Drama; Children: Unacceptable. Hitchcock presents a combative tale of two prizefighters, Brisson and Hunter, who not only battle in the ring, but fight for the affections of Hall-Davis. Brisson works for a circus where he takes on all comers and is known as "Round One," and where Hall-Davis sells tickets for customers to see him in the ring. Falling in love with him, Hall-Davis marries Brisson, but she is soon swayed by the amorous attentions of professional prizefighter Hunter. A love triangle ensues and ends with a fierce battle between Brisson and Hunter, who are finally matched in the ring. Hall-Davis attends the fight and initially gives her support to the swaggering Hunter, jeering and hooting at her husband. Brisson starts to take a terrible beating, and Hall-Davis becomes frightened for him, realizing that she truly loves Brisson. She goes to his corner and gives him encouragement to fight on, her comforting and loving words giving Brisson renewed strength. He then begins to fight back and lands some powerful blows on Hunter that finally defeat him. Brisson returns to his corner where Hall-Davis is waiting for him and he knows that she will be in his corner in all of his days to come. The script is rather pedes-

Carla Gugino and Robert De Niro in *Righteous Kill*, 2008.

trian (written by Hitchcock and his wife Alma Reville). However, Hitchcock's clever use of cameras and unusual angle shots, along with a hurried pace to all of his action to increase tension and excitement, sustains absorbing interest. The director uses as a plot element a bracelet that Hunter gives to Hall-Davis, one that becomes repeatedly symbolic as the story unfolds. *Author's Note*: Hitchcock admitted to this author that this silent film was "rather primitive compared to my later work, but I was able to experiment quite a bit with camera shots in **The Ring**, and that was part of learning my craft. Fortunately, I was allowed to learn as I went along, and at the expense of producers, something that is not allowed today by studios. You must come fully equipped or don't come at all is today's message." **p**. John Maxwell; **d**, Alfred Hitchcock; **cast**, Carl Brisson, Lillian Hall-Davis, Ian Hunter, Forrester Harvey, Harry Terry, Gordon Harker, Billy Wells, Charles Farrell, Clare Greet, Tom Helmore, Brandy Walker, Minnie Rayner; **w**, Hitchcock, Alma Reville (based on a story by Hitchcock); **c**, John J. Cox; **art d**, C. Wilfred Arnold.

Ring ★★★ 1998; Japan; 96m; Omega Project/DreamWorks; B/W/Color; Horror/Mystery; Children: Unacceptable; **DVD**. Frightening tale begins when Matushima, a woman, interviews teenagers in Japan about a mysterious "cursed video tape," after her niece, Nakatani, dies of "sudden heart failure" with an unnaturally horrified look on her face. Matushima begins an investigation, revealing that Nakatani and some friends had been on a holiday the week before her death. Nakatani's friends had died on exactly the same night, at the exact time and place, and in the same way. Matushima goes to a cottage where the friends had stayed and finds an unlabeled videotape that she decides is the cursed videotape. This leads to a volcanic island where she learns that the video has a connection to a psychic, who died thirty years earlier and that discovery opens another series of terrifying experiences. This story was remade in English in 2002. (In Japanese; English subtitles.) **p**, Takashige Ichise, Shin'ya Kawai, Takenori Sento; **d**, Hideo Nakata; **cast**, Nanako Matsushima, Miki Nakatani, Yuko Takeuchi, Hitomi Sato, Yoichu Numata, Yutaka Matsushige, Katsui Muramatsu, Rikiya Otaka, Daisuke Ban, Kanehiro Ri; **w**, Hiroshi Takahashi (based on the novel by Koji Suzuki); **c**, Jun'ichiro Hayashi; **m**, Kenji Kawai; **ed**, Nobuyuki Takahashi; **prod d**, Iwao Saito; **spec eff**, Hajime Matsumoto.

The Ring ★★★ 2002; U.S./Japan; 115m; DreamWorks;Color; Horror; Mystery; Thriller; Children: Unacceptable (MPAA: PG-13); **BD**; **DVD**. Watts is a journalist, who investigates a videotape that may have killed four teenagers, including her niece. An urban legend about the tape is that anyone viewing it will die seven days after watching it. She must race against time to solve the mystery or she and her son may be the

Martin Henderson and Naomi Watts in *The Ring*, 2002.

tape's next victims. Song: "Hey John" (Scott Leger, Nate Navarro, Eddie Willis, Steve Rude, Curtis Ryker). Thematic elements, disturbing images, gutter language, and drug references prohibit viewing by children. This is a U.S. remake of the 1998 Japanese film. **p**, Laurie MacDonald, Walter F. Parkes, Christine Iso; **d**, Gore Verbinski; **cast**, Naomi Watts, Martin Henderson, Jane Alexander, David Dorfman, Brian Cox, Lindsay Frost, Amber Tamblyn, Rachael Bella, Daveigh Chase, Michael Spound; **w**, Ehren Kruger (based on the 1998 screenplay **Ringu** by Hiroshi Takahashi and the novel by Koji Suzuki); **c**, Bojan Bazelli; **m**, Hans Zimmer; **ed**, Craig Wood; **prod d**, Tom Duffield; **art d**, Patrick M. Sullivan Jr.; **set d**, Rosemary Brandenburg; **spec eff**, Rodney M. Byrd, Burt Dalton.

Ring of Bright Water ★★★ 1969; U.K.; 94m; Brightwater Film Productions/Rank Organization/Cinerama; Color; Drama; Children: Acceptable (MPAA: PG); **DVD**; **VHS**. Good family film sees Travers as a London clerk who aspires to become a writer. He buys a playful otter at a pet shop and strikes up a man-dog friendship with the playful creature. He calls the otter Mij and soon realizes that his big city apartment is no place to raise it, so he takes Mij to a cottage on the coast of Scotland. Together they explore the area's wildlife, including geese and sharks. Travers falls in love with the town doctor, McKenna, and the three become inseparable friends. Called to London on business, he leaves the otter in the care of a veterinarian, but, when he returns, he is told that Mij was killed in a road accident. Soon he sees a female otter and her three cubs and realizes they are Mij's family. He takes the otters home as his new pets, knowing that they will always remind him of Mij, and writes a book about it all. The popular book became this wonderful family film. Song: "Ring of Bright Water" (Frank Cordell, Betty Botley). **p**, Joseph Strick; **d**, Jack Couffer; **cast**, Bill Travers, Virginia McKenna, Peter Jeffrey, Jameson Clark, Helena Gloag, Willie Joss, Roddy McMillan, Jean Taylor-Smith, Christopher Benjamin, Kevin Collins; **w**, Couffer, Travers (based on the book by Gavin Maxwell); **c**, Wolfgang Suschitzky (Technicolor); **m**, Frank Cordell; **ed**, Reginald Mills; **prod d**, Terry Lewis; **art d**, Ken Ryan.

Ring of Fire ★★★ 1961; U.S.; 91m; MGM; Color; Adventure/Crime Drama; Children: Unacceptable. Taut tale sees three young thieves, Taylor, Gorshin, and Johnson, arrested by a sheriff, Janssen, for robbing a gas station in Oregon. Taylor, the female of the captives, pulls a gun on Janssen, and they take him prisoner as they try to escape through a forest. Gorshin carelessly discards a lighted cigarette butt and starts a forest fire. A town is threatened by the fire, and Janssen, who has freed himself, manages to get the townspeople onto a train. Gorshin dies when a trestle collapses under the train, and Janssen takes the remaining robbers into custody. Footage of two real forest fires in Oregon and California were

used in this exciting film. Song: "Ring of Fire" (Duane Eddy). **p**, Virginia and Andrew L. Stone; **d&w**, Andrew L. Stone; **cast**, David Janssen, Joyce Taylor, Frank Gorshin, Joel Marston, James Johnson, Ron Myron, Marshall Kent, Doodles Weaver; **c**, William H. Clothier; **ed**, Virginia L. Stone; **spec eff**, Herman E. Townsley.

Rio ★★★★ 2011; U.S.; 96m; FOX; Color; Animated Adventure; Comedy; Children: Recommended (MPAA: G); **BD**; **DVD**; **IV**. This delightful and lively romp is a superlative example of animation at its very best and where the colorization is so excitingly rich that it threatens to leap from the screen and nest in your best vase. A baby macaw, Blu (voice of Eisenberg) is captured in Rio de Janeiro by dealers in exotic birds and smuggled to the U.S. While driving through Moose Lake, Minnesota, the truck transporting Blu accidentally drops his box on the road where a girl finds Blu and raises him as her pet. Fifteen years pass and Blu is domesticated and intelligent, but cannot fly. An ornithologist tells the girl (now an adult woman) that Blu is the last male of his species and he has a female in Rio with whom Blu can be mated. The ornithologist and the woman take Blu to Rio where smugglers steal both birds to sell them, but the girl and the ornithologist rescue them for a happy ending. The adventures of the macaws and other South American birds in Rio are delightfully shown with a lot of inventive and exciting soaring and sky-sailing until Blu eventually learns how to fly. Songs: "Real in Rio" (music: Sergio Mendes, Carlinhos Brown, Mikael Mutti, John Powell; lyrics: Siedah Garrett), "Whoomp! There it Is" (Stephen Gibson, Cecil Glenn), "Let Me Take You to Rio" (Ester Dean, Carlinhos Brown, Mikael Mutti), "Say You, Say Me" (Lionel Richie), "Sapo Cai" (Sergio Mendes, Carlinhos Brown), "Copacabana Dreams" (Sergio Mendes, John Powell), "Pretty Bird" (music: Jemaine Clement, John Powell; lyrics: Jemaine Clement, Yoni Brenner, Mike Reiss), "Girl from Ipanema" (Antonio Carlos Jobin, Vinicius De Moraes, Norman Gimbel), "Funky Monkey" (music: Brown, Mutti; lyrics: Garrett, Brown, Mutti), "Mas Que Nada" (Jorge Ben), "Forro Da Fruta (Brown, Mutti), "Balanco Carioca" (Mutti), "Hot Wings/I Wanna Party," "Drop it Low" (William Adams), "Fly Love" (Brown, Garrett), "The Chicken Dance" (Werner Thomas, Terry Rendall), "Take You to Rio" (Ester Dean, Mikkel S. Eriksen, Tyor Eriok Hermansen). **p**, Bruce Anderson, John C. Donkin; **d**, Carlos Saldanha; **cast** (voiceovers), Jesse Eisenberg, Anne Hathaway, Wanda Sykes, Jamie Foxx, Rodrigo Santoro, Bernardo de Paula, Saldanha, Renato D'Angelo, Carlos Ponce, George Lopez; **w**, Don Rhymer, Joshua Sternin, Jeffrey Ventimilia, Sam Harper (based on a story by Saldanha, Earl Richey Jones, Todd Jones); **c**, Renato Falcao; **m**, John Powell; **ed**, Harry Hitner; **set d**, Melanie Martini.

Rio Bravo ★★★★★ 1959; U.S.; 141m; Armada Productons/WB; Color; Western; Children: Unacceptable; **BD**; **DVD**; **VHS**. The versatile and gifted Hawks, who had earlier directed one of the truly great westerns (**Red River**, 1948), presents another classic in this always popular genre. This exciting and evergreen tale begins when Martin, a former deputy sheriff, who has become an alcoholic over a failed love affair, enters a saloon in a small Texas border town. Penniless, dirty and woebegone, he sacrifices what little is left of his pride by begging for a drink. Akins, the brutal brother of cattle baron Russell, who is playing cards at a nearby table, tosses a coin in Martin's direction, but it lands, as Akins intends, in an odorous spittoon loaded with tobacco juice and human saliva. Desperate to quench his raging thirst for liquor, Martin degrades himself by kneeling down to reach into that container of glutinous glop when the spittoon is abruptly kicked away from him by his former employer, Wayne, who is the town sheriff. Enraged, Martin knocks Wayne senseless and then attacks Akins, who, along with his cronies, beat Martin and Wayne. When a well-intentioned bystander attempts to stop Akins, Akins mindlessly draws a gun and shoots and kills the bystander. Wayne frees himself and then arrests Akins, charging him with murder, and takes him to the small jail, placing him behind bars. Akins brags that he will not be in a cell for long as his brother, Russell, will soon appear with his armed cowboys and release him. Wayne tells him that if that occurs, Akins will be the first one to die. Meanwhile, the only aid Wayne can count on is from toothless, hobbling old jail guard Brennan (called "Stumpy" because of his limping gait) and who thumps about the jail while holding a loaded shotgun, eager to shoot any invader. Bond, who operates a freighting business, arrives in town with some of his wagons. An old friend of Wayne's, he offers to help him ward off the attack expected from cattle boss Russell, but Wayne tells him that he and his men are not gunslingers and would only add to his problems by getting hurt or even killed. Wayne does notice one of Bond's men, Nelson, a young man who is very fast on the draw. "He's so good, he doesn't feel like he's got to prove it," says Bond, but Nelson refuses to join Wayne, saying that he does not want to become involved with the problems of others. Meanwhile, Wayne thinks that Dickinson, a beautiful woman playing poker with some men in a saloon, is cheating and he takes her upstairs to her room, telling her that he doesn't like cardsharps. She denies being a card cheat and dares him to search her for any hidden cards. Wayne becomes embarrassed at the thought, and after Nelson exposes the real card cheat at the poker table, Wayne rescinds his order to Dickinson to leave town. (This scene takes a leaf from the western, **Gunfight at the O.K. Corral**, 1957, where lawman Wyatt Earp, played by Burt Lancaster, arrests lady card player Rhonda Fleming, only to later release her as he falls in love with her, and as is the case with Wayne in this film.) Bond is later shot and killed by one of Russell's gunmen, and Martin, seeking redemption for his miserable lifestyle, goes after that gunman, wounding him. He tells Wayne that the killer has run into a saloon, and both he and Wayne enter the saloon, which is packed with Russell's gunslingers. Martin tells Wayne that Bond's murderer ran through a mud puddle and should have mud on his boots. Wayne orders the gunmen to drop their gun belts, and he and Martin inspect their boots. They are clean. The gunmen then insult Martin about his drunkenness, although he has been sober for some time, goading him to take a drink. Wayne grills the gunmen, all of them saying they saw no one run into the bar with muddy boots. Martin appears to be weakening and goes to the bar where the bartender, an ally of Russell and his men, offers him a free drink to mock his malady. Martin stands at the end of the bar, considering the drink before him when he notices blood dripping from above and into a glass of beer on the bar. Instead of taking the drink, Martin spins quickly about and fires a single shot into the man lurking in the rafter above who is about to shoot him. The man, who is Bond's killer, crashes to the floor dead. He is wearing muddy boots. Wayne, staring at one of Russell's men who had denied seeing the killer smashes his rifle into the gunman's face, knocking him senseless. He and Martin then leave the saloon, and Wayne tells Martin: "You were good in there," and reinstates Martin as his deputy, even though he does not know how long Martin can manage to stay on the wagon. Martin, his confidence renewed, takes a bath and acquires a new set of clothes, now proud to wear his deputy badge. He is assigned to stand at the edge of the town where he orders Russell and his men to unbuckle their gun belts as Russell arrives and before Russell goes to the jail to visit with his brother, Akins. Russell tells Akins that he will not remain behind bars too long, implying to Wayne that he intends to free Akins at any cost before a judge arrives to hear his case and most likely find Akins guilty of murder and mete out punishment. Wayne tells him that he is prepared to keep Akins in jail at all costs. When Russell leaves, Wayne goes to a nearby hotel, not knowing that Martin has been waylaid by some of Russell's men and one of them has donned Martin's hat and vest so that Wayne, looking down the road, thinks Martin is still at his post. Meanwhile several of Russell's gunmen surround Wayne, drawing guns while he is off guard. Dickinson and Nelson, who are standing inside the hotel lobby, sees this and Nelson, who has remained in town to seek vengeance for the murder of his boss, tells Dickinson to throw a flower pot through a hotel window to distract Russell's gunmen. Nelson steps outside, and as Dickenson crashes the pot through the window and when the gunmen turn toward that smashed window, Nelson

Ricky Nelson and John Wayne in *Rio Bravo*, 1959.

goes for his guns, blazing away as Wayne goes for his rifle. Both of them shoot down and kill the gunslingers. (This action is not dissimilar to a scene in Hawks' western of a decade earlier, **Red River**, where Wayne is confronted by three rebellious cowboys, who are shot down by fast-drawing Montgomery Clift and where Wayne and Brennan, who appear in that film, also use rifles to help dispatch their opponents.) Meanwhile, Martin has freed himself and joins Wayne. A grateful Wayne makes Nelson a deputy, and he joins with Martin and Wayne in patrolling the town, ever watchful for Russell's men. While Wayne deepens his relationship with the fetching Dickinson, Martin, Nelson and Brennan develop a close bond with each other as dedicated lawmen intent on maintaining law and order and, especially, holding on to Akins until he can be tried for his crime. At one point, Martin and Nelson sing a song together, their separate styles of singing blending well in harmony. Later, Wayne and Martin are trapped by more of Russell's gunmen (Russell has what appears to be an inexhaustible army of gunslingers willing to fight and die for him). While Martin is held hostage, two of the gunmen escort Wayne at gunpoint to the jail, where they order Wayne to tell his guard, Brennan, to release Akins. Wayne then calls out to Brennan, but steps aside quickly, knowing what is coming. That is a shotgun blast that Brennan releases, which immediately kills the two gunmen. Meanwhile, Martin is taken hostage and Wayne is informed that, unless he swaps Akins for Martin the next morning, Martin will be killed. Wayne, realizing that he has no choice, agrees to the swap. While he and Nelson prepare for the meeting, Brennan grabs a shotgun, expecting to be present, but Wayne tells him that, because of his crippled leg, he will be of no use to them. Wayne and Nelson then go to the edge of town with Akins in tow, standing in some deserted adobe buildings to look at a large wooden storehouse in which Russell and his men are positioned and holding Martin. Wayne calls out to Russell, telling him that he is sending Akins toward the distant storehouse and that he is to send Martin toward him at the same time. Wayne then tells Akins to start walking slowly toward the storehouse. Both Akins and Martin begin walking toward one another. Martin looks for a chance to waylay Akins, and, just as the two men come abreast, Martin dives at Akins, driving him behind some adobe ruins where both men struggle. Russell and his men then open fire at Wayne and Nelson, who return fire as Martin and Akins struggle. Martin succeeds in knocking out Akins, and Wayne tosses him a gun so that he can also fire at Russell and his men in the storehouse. Several of Russell's men then make a break from the storehouse to skirt Wayne's position, but Wayne is surprised to see them suddenly blown dead from a shotgun blast on his flank. He sees that Brennan is there and has fired that shotgun. While Nelson and Martin keep Russell's men pinned down in the storehouse, Wayne joins Brennan, telling him that he must get out of the area. "No," Brennan insists, "this is a good spot."

Angie Dickinson and John Wayne in *Rio Bravo*, 1959.

Wayne then points out that he is standing next to a wagon loaded with dynamite. This gives them an idea. They collect several sticks of dynamite and move to a safer position. Brennan begins to throw sticks of dynamite at the storehouse while Wayne fires shots to explode them. A few come close to the storehouse, but the explosions do little damage. "Can't you throw any farther?" Wayne shouts. Brennan tells him he can and throws a stick landing squarely on the loading deck of the storehouse, and when Wayne fires a shot that explodes that stick of dynamite, part of the building disintegrates in a tremendous blast. Russell and his men are defeated and stagger from the building with their hands in the air. "That took the fight out of them!" Brennan victoriously exclaims. Wayne and his rag-tag group of deputies have overcome a fierce and oppressive gang of killers and have brought peace and law and order to the town. Wayne is seen meeting Dickinson in her room where she is dressed in tights and corset, telling Wayne that she plans to wear this alluring outfit while she performs as a singer, but Wayne tells her that she is not going to go before an audience dressed like that and that if she does, he will arrest her. Dickinson smiles, knowing that the tough lawman's threat means that he is in love with her and that he does not want to share her with anyone else. This she more or less tells him as she changes clothes behind a screen, draping the tights over it. Fully dressed, she emerges and she and Wayne embrace, with Wayne throwing the tights out of the window. They fall in front of Brennan, who is patrolling the street with Martin, and he picks them up, draping them around his neck and he and Martin laugh as they continue down the street to end this rousing and utterly wonderful western. Hawks directs this simple story without frills, but keeps the action moving at all times, as was his traditional habit, and where all the twists and turns of the basic plot are tied neatly together. Wayne is his old reliable self, but he has a few exceptional scenes where he steps out of character, such as brutally slamming his rifle into a gunman's face out of sheer anger and where he is as sheepish as a young boy when dealing with sultry Dickinson. Exceptional performances are seen from Martin and Brennan, as two misfit deputies who prove their mettle, despite their mental and physical ailments. None of the bad men are sympathetic, all of them sinister and evil-minded as their leaders, Akins and Russell, which is what Hawks intended them to be. The excellent script provides a great deal of witty one-liners sprinkled through all the character roles and the good guy characters act, as was also Hawks' intention, as close family members, unafraid to speak their minds while displaying concern and affection for one another. Though packed with violent scenes, this is a gentler western than Hawks' scruffy and uncompromising **Red River**, but one no less important in the genre, greatly enhanced by Harlan's inventive lensing and Tiomkin's dynamic score. It was a box office smash, earning more than $5.5 million in its initial release, returning more than five times its budget. Songs: "Rio Bravo," "My Rifle, My Pony and Me" (music: Dimitri Tiomkin; lyrics: Paul Francis Webster from the original song "Settle Down" by Tiomkin, first appearing in **Red River**, 1948, which was also scored by Tiomkin); "Cindy" (composer unknown); "Deguello (The Cutthroat Song)" (Mexican traditional). *Author's Note*: The reason why this film saw hundreds of thousands of teenage girls flocking to see it was the presence of Ricky Nelson, who was then the singing rage among those young females. Hawks shrewdly knew this would be the case when he cast Nelson in a supporting role, stating to this author: "He was worth a million dollars at the box office then." Wayne thought that Nelson was miscast and looked too modern for a western, telling this author; "He was a nice kid, but he could not really act. Well, he didn't have to, because all those teeny-boppers came to see him in **Rio Bravo**, because of those sappy love songs he had been singing. He sings a song with Dean in that picture ["My Rifle, My Pony and Me"] and they both sounded pretty good, but, as you know, Dean is a professional singer. Dean amazed all of us by giving the performance of his life in that picture, playing a filthy drunken bum and he did that so well that you could almost smell his stench coming right off the screen. He was just great." Hawks echoed those words when he told this author that "Martin showed up on the set for the first scene all duded up in brand new western regalia, squeaky clean. I told him: 'Look, Dean, you are playing a broken down drunken guy who wears a dirty shirt and pants. He is as grubby as the winos you see in alleyways in downtown L.A.' Well, he turned around, changed his clothes, dirtied himself up, and came back very quickly and, lo and behold, he looked worse than Charles Laughton when he played a sweating, dirty drunken bum in **The Bribe** [1949]. He was perfect." So perfect was Martin that when studio boss Jack Warner saw some of the early rushes of the film, he asked Hawks: "Where is Dean Martin? I thought we hired him for this picture?" Hawks replied: "He's the funny-looking guy in the old hat." Warner slapped his forehead, saying: "Holy Cow! Is that Dean Martin?" Hawks, along with Wayne, reportedly wanted to do this film in response to the classic western **High Noon**, 1952, where Gary Cooper, realizing he is facing a gang of ruthless killers, seeks help (and gets none) from the townspeople he is supposed to protect. Hawks hated the story line in that film, one that insisted that a lawman in the Old West could not stand alone against any odds. In response, he made **Rio Bravo** to show just such a lawman (Wayne), who nevertheless gets some help, but from a drunk, a grouchy old man, and a teenager (Nelson was nineteen when making this film). p&d, Howard Hawks; cast, John Wayne, Dean Martin, Ricky Nelson, Angie Dickinson, Walter Brennan, Ward Bond, John Russell, Pedro Gonzalez-Gonzalez, Estelita Rodriguez, Claude Akins, Sheb Wooley, Yakima Canutt, Bob Steele, Malcolm Atterbury, Myron Healey; w, Jules Furthman, Leigh Brackett (based on a story by Barbara Hawks McCampbell); c, Russell Harlan (Technicolor); m, Dimitri Tiomkin; ed, Folmar Blangsted; art d, Leo K. Kuter; set d, Ralph S. Hurst.

Rio Grande ★★★★★ 1950; U.S.; 105m; Argosy Pictures/REP; B/W; Western; Children: Unacceptable; **DVD**; **VHS**. Another superb western from Ford, this is the third film in the director's classic trilogy about the U.S. Cavalry in the Old West (the previous two being **Fort Apache**, 1948, and **She Wore a Yellow Ribbon**, 1949). The film opens with Wayne, who commands a U.S. Cavalry post in the southwest near the Rio Grande, returning from a long and tiring patrol, only to discover that his son, Jarman, whom he has not seen in years, is a new recruit among his troopers. Jarman, who has dropped out of military school and joined the U.S. Army against the wishes of his mother, O'Hara, is brought before Wayne by top sergeant McLaglen. Jarman stands at attention before father Wayne and there is little civility existing between them. Wayne tells Jarman that, because he is his son, he cannot seek any special privileges and Jarman replies by saying that he wants no special favors and that he did make any request to be sent to the post his father commands. (In establishing this early-on conflict, Ford employs a plotline from other films showing hostility between father and son on military posts such as **Lives of a Bengal Lancer**, 1935, and **Geronimo**, 1939.) When Jarman leaves Wayne's quarters he measures the height of his son where he stood with his head against the tent and then his own height to see that there is little difference. While Jarman befriends other new recruits Johnson and Carey, Wayne suddenly gets a visit from O'Hara, his estranged wife, whom he has not seen for fifteen years. Their separation occurred during the Civil War when Wayne was ordered to burn down her family mansion by Union General Philip Sheridan (1831-1888), played by Naish, as O'Hara's family was then supporting the Confederacy. O'Hara has never forgiven Wayne for this act, and where she points to his old sergeant, McLaglen, as the chief "arsonist" who carried out Wayne's orders. Meanwhile, Jarman shows his mettle while in training when he and others are being trained in riding horses. McLaglen encourages his new recruits to daringly ride two horses at once, or "Roman style," where one rider stands with separate feet on separate horses, riding them while standing and leading them close together in a gallop to hurdle a high fence. Johnson and Carey accomplish these spectacular deeds; Jarman then follows but takes a dangerous spill when his horses strike the top-most rail of the fence and Jarman is thrown. Wayne watches this mishap from a distance with deep fatherly concern but does nothing as Jarman is helped to his feet unharmed. Jarman later gets into a fight with another trooper, Kennedy, and when Wayne arrives to ask the reason for the fight, Jarman and Kennedy refuse to tell him the reason for their quarrel. Wayne walks off, telling them to continue, but both men shake hands, now friends in that both withheld that reason, which involved Kennedy making a critical remark about Wayne and Jarman coming to his father's defense. At this time, O'Hara, who has taken over Wayne's quarters, tells Wayne that she wants him to sign a release that will allow Jarman to leave the U.S. Army and where she will take custody of him. Wayne refuses, saying that Jarman must meet his obligations as a soldier. Meanwhile, some renegade Apaches who are being held in a stockade are freed when other Apaches raid the post, wildly riding through the area, shooting down guards and tearing down the stockade fence to free the imprisoned renegades. As the Apaches escape, Wayne races to Jarman's tent, finding O'Hara safe, protected by Jarman, Carey and Johnson. A short time later, Withers, a sheriff, shows up at the post, demanding that the army turn over Johnson, who is wanted on a murder charge in Texas. He says that he will return to pick up Johnson the next day. Johnson is held in custody that night and tells McLaglen and surgeon Wills that he shot and killed a man in Texas who attacked his sister and then joined the army so that he would not interfere with his sister's impending wedding. He asks for time to "disappear" until his sister is happily married and, at that time, will turn himself into authorities and will ask for the legal help O'Hara has offered him. McLaglen and Wills then pretend that they do not see Johnson leave their cabin as Johnson saddles none other than Wayne's horse, and rides away from the post. Wayne is told about this "arranged" desertion, but he has other, more serious problems at hand. He is visited by Naish (as General Sheridan), who gives him "unofficial" orders to lead an expedition against the renegade Apaches, who have fled the post, as well as those who have freed those renegades, even if that expedition means going across the Rio Grande River and into Mexico to apprehend the renegades and return them to the reservation. If Wayne is later charged for violating foreign territory, Naish promises that he and other friendly officers will be those presiding over his court martial. Wayne accepts this thankless assignment and leads his troops in search of the Apaches, while sending all the women and children in a separate wagon train to a safer destination. That wagon train, however, is attacked by the renegade Apaches, all but one of the heavily guarded wagons reaching the momentary safety of a high ridge. Jarman is sent on horseback to find and bring Wayne's troops to the rescue. He rides away as O'Hara worriedly looks after him and while troopers, using the wagons as shields, continue to fight off the attacking Apaches. As Jarman rides away several Apaches ride after him. Before the Indians can catch up

John Wayne and Maureen O'Hara in *Rio Grande,* 1950.

with Jarman, Johnson appears, cutting off a closely pursuing Apache and killing him, then shouting to Jarman to continue while he stays behind to hold off more oncoming Indians. Wayne, along with Jarman and his troops, later reach the wagon train to find the Apaches gone and the wagon train intact, except for one wagon loaded with children and a woman, which has been captured by the Apaches. Wayne and his troops pursue the Apaches, finding the captured wagon. It has been burned and the children missing. The lone woman, the wife of a corporal riding with Wayne, has been raped and killed, and Wayne restrains the emotionally disturbed husband from going to see her violated body, telling him: "Stay with me, son." Johnson then joins Wayne to tell him that he has located the Apaches, who have occupied a small village across the Rio Grande in Mexico and where they are drinking and dancing before a church where the children are being held. Johnson believes that, at dawn, the renegades will kill all the children, unless he and a few others can sneak into that village and into the church and hold off the Apaches until Wayne arrives with his troops to rescue them. Johnson then asks Wayne for two men that he trusts to accompany him in this dangerous assignment, one being Carey and the other Jarman. Wayne approves and the three troopers ride off. They infiltrate the village and then enter the church where they find the children alive. The three troopers then take up defensive positions in the church and wait for Wayne and his men. Before dawn, Wayne aligns his troops before the village and then orders a charge. With his bugler sounding that charge, Wayne and his men dash forward in a wild race into the village, firing at the Apaches, who take refuge in the deserted adobe buildings while others rush the church, only to be shot down by Johnson, Carey and Jarman as one of the little girls, Grimes, pulls a rope that rings the church bell to signal to Wayne that the children are safe. At the same time, troopers arrive with wagons in front of the church and the children flee the church and are loaded into the wagons as troopers give them protective fire. McLaglen and Grimes are the last to leave the church, but not before McLaglen quickly genuflects before they depart. Wayne and his charging troops receive intense gunfire and arrows from the Apaches as they repeatedly charge up and down the main street of the village. In one such sortie, Wayne is struck in the chest by an arrow, causing him to slip from his horse. Jarman and other troopers go to his aid, and Wayne tells his son: "Pull it out, Jeff!" Jarman grits his teeth and yanks the arrow from Wayne's chest. The troopers regroup and begin their return to their post. By that time, O'Hara and the other women have already returned to that post and they watch in apprehension when the main force returns, women searching for their husbands, including O'Hara, who finds Wayne wounded and being dragged on a litter. She holds his hand as she accompanies that litter forward. At a later ceremony, Johnson, Carey, Jarman and others are awarded medals for their heroism and Wayne's victory over the

John Wayne in *Rio Grande*, 1950.

Apaches is celebrated when his troops pass in review before Naish, O'Hara and Wayne. The band strikes up the song "Dixie," which Naish has ordered in honor of the southern-born O'Hara, who twirls her parasol in delight at hearing that evocative song. Withers, the sheriff who is still searching for Johnson, arrives again to serve his warrant. Seeing Withers arrive, Wayne steps forth and shouts to Johnson, telling him that he has a ten-day furlough and orders him from the post. Johnson readily complies by racing to a nearby horse, Naish's own mount, taking it and riding off. The camera then closes in on the parading troopers to end this stirring and thoroughly entertaining western saga. Ford presents a lively portrait of cavalry life, providing many humorous and action-packed scenes, and where he candidly shows the grim and gruesome side of Indian savagery that was always present in the Old West. His fully developed characters have distinctive personalities, most of whom are empathetic and where decency and honor are present in the personas of these everyday heroes wearing dirty uniforms, frayed hats and muddy boots. **Rio Grande** offers an unforgettable, realistic western, the third and last of Ford's monumental trilogy (with **Fort Apache** and **She Wore a Yellow Ribbon**) that significantly honors the old U.S. Cavalry. The acting by Wayne, O'Hara, Jarman, McLaglen, Johnson and others is superlative, all in keeping with their fascinating characters. Glennon's gritty black-and-white cinematography and Young's wonderful score that mixes martial and lyrical passages add greatly to all the fine production values embodied in this outstanding film. The film, like all of Ford's westerns, did well at the box office, taking in more than $2,250,000 in box office receipts in its initial release against a $1,200,000 budget. Songs: "My Gal Is Purple," "Footsore Cavalry," "Yellow Stripes" (Stan Jones); "Aha, San Antone" (Dale Evans); "Low Bridge (Fifteen Miles on the Erie Canal)" (Thomas S. Allen); "Down by the Glenside" (Peadar Kearney); "Cattle Call" (Tex Owens), "I'll Take You Home Again Kathleen" (Thomas Payne Westendorf); "The Girl I Left Behind Me" (traditional); "Dixie" (Daniel Decatur Emmett), "Reveille" (traditional). *Author's Note*: Oddly, this last of Ford's U.S. Cavalry trilogy was not a film he originally thought to make, at least at the time he made this film. Ford had lobbied Republic Studios for backing so he could make **The Quiet Man**, 1952, a very costly project for that smaller studio. To hedge his bets, Republic boss Herbert J. Yates asked Ford to make **Rio Grande**, knowing the great successes he had achieved with his two previous U.S. Cavalry films, **Fort Apache**, 1948, and **She Wore a Yellow Ribbon**, 1949. "I agreed to do **Rio Grande** so that Republic would back **The Quiet Man**," Ford told this author. "It was that simple, although I had the story for **Rio Grande** in my pocket for some time. Republic did not think that **The Quiet Man** would make any money, so they figured they would cover their loss by releasing **Rio Grande** first. Well, both of those pictures made a lot of money for that

studio. You had to play the game to get anything done in Hollywood." Wayne liked **Rio Grande**, telling this author that "it was another Ford picture that portrayed the old U.S. Cavalry very accurately. Pappy [Ford] always took great care to present historical figures and events, right down to the correct belt buckle and button on every man's tunic. What you see on the screen in the picture is about as close to what you would ever see if you were living back then in the days of those troopers. You had to give Pappy credit for that. That picture told a great story, but I did not like wearing the little goatee under my lower lip and told Pappy about that, but he insisted I wear it. I knew why. Hank Fonda wore just such a goatee in **Fort Apache**, an earlier picture that showed the U.S. Cavalry, and Pappy thought that that little tuff of ugly hair represented authority. He showed me pictures of U.S. Cavalry commanders in the Old West wearing goatees, so I had no argument. I grew that damned hank of hair and I don't think Maureen [O'Hara] liked it much when I had to kiss her. That picture was the first one we made together and we played man and wife a few years later when we did **The Quiet Man**. She is a terrific actress with the kind of strong personality that worked well with the kind of rugged films we did together." Wayne and O'Hara appeared in five films together: **Rio Grande**, 1950; **The Quiet Man**, 1953; **The Wings of Eagles**, 1957; **McLintock!**, 1963; and **Big Jake**, 1971. Also appearing in this film is a real-life adventurer and soldier-of-fortune Peter Ortiz, who plays a French-American officer under Wayne's command named Captain St. Jacques. "Peter had a spectacular background," Wayne told this author, "a larger-than-life guy, who had as many adventures as any cavalryman ever had in the Old West." Pierre "Peter" Julien Ortiz (1913-1988) was one of the most decorated U.S. Marine officers in WWII. In 1932, at the age of nineteen, Ortiz joined the French Foreign Legion, serving in North Africa for five years, rising to the rank of sergeant and twice receiving the Croix de Guerre for actions against the Rif. When his enlistment expired, he went to Hollywood and worked as an adviser on war films, but, when WWII began in 1939, Ortiz reenlisted in the Legion (since the U.S. was then neutral and did not get into that war until 1941). He fought in the Battle of France in 1940 and was captured and imprisoned by the Germans. He escaped prison in 1941 and returned to the U.S. In 1942, he enlisted in the U.S. Marines and, because of his considerable military training, was promoted to the rank of lieutenant within forty days and then to the rank of captain a short time later. Because of his experiences in North Africa, he was assigned to the OSS (Office of Strategic Services), which was then U.S. Intelligence and the precursor of the CIA). He went behind German lines to conduct secret reconnaissance. When on that mission, he encountered a German patrol but fought his way out. Wounded, he managed to return to U.S. lines where his wound was so serious that he was sent back to the U.S. to recuperate. He refused to remain in the States and rejoined the OSS as an intelligence officer, parachuting into France in 1944 to help organize French resistance to German forces then occupying the country. Before leaving France, Ortiz smuggled four downed RAF pilots out of France and into Spain. In August 1944, Ortiz again parachuted behind German lines, but was captured and spent the rest of the war in a German concentration camp from which he repeatedly attempted to escape. For his incredible heroic services, Ortiz was awarded two Navy Crosses, two Purple Hearts, the Legion of Merit, the Order of the British Empire, and five Croix de Guerre medals, along with other French citations, becoming the most decorated OSS agent in WWII. His daring espionage exploits were later used as the basis for the plots and characters in two spy films, **13 Rue Madeleine**, 1947, and **Operation Secret**, 1952. "It was men like Peter, who were the first to fight fascism and it was men like Peter who truly saved the world," Wayne said to this author. Ortiz is buried at Arlington National Cemetery. "Peter was an excellent horseman," Ford told this author, and Duke [Wayne] had a hell of a time keeping up with him when I ordered those charges into the village to rescue the kids from the Apaches. I shot several scenes where the troopers are charging up and down the street of the village and, at one point, Duke said to me:

'I think Peter is too reckless with himself. He's out in front of all of us, riding his horse like a madman. He might break his neck.' I told Duke: 'Not that guy. He loves danger and, as far as I am concerned, I am going to let him charge like hell—that's what this is all about.' I knew all about Peter's experiences in World War II and earlier. He was my kind of man." Ford provided masterfully orchestrated cavalry charges in his U.S. Cavalry trilogy (films cited herein), while many other films have depicted well-choreographed cavalry charges in the Old West by the U.S. Cavalry during the Indian wars, including **Arrowhead**, 1953; **Buffalo Bill**, 1944; **Comanche**, 1956; **Custer of the West**, 1967; **Geronimo**, 1939 (footage from **The Plainsman**, 1936); **Geronimo: An American Legend**, 1993; **The Great Sioux Massacre**, 1965; **The Last Outpost**, 1951; **Little Big Man**, 1970; **Major Dundee**, 1965; **The Plainsman**, 1936; **The Searchers**, 1956 (Ford); **Sitting Bull**, 1954; **Stagecoach**, 1939 (Ford); **They Died with Their Boots On**, 1941; **Two Flags West**, 1950; and **Ulzana's Raid**, 1972. Other cavalry charges of note throughout history depicted in films include: **Abraham Lincoln** (Union cavalry during the Civil War); **Alexander**, 2004 (Greek cavalry charge against Persian forces in Asia Minor, 333 BC); **The Charge of the Light Brigade**, 1936 (British cavalry in 19th Century India and the charge at the Battle of Balaclava, 1854, in the Crimean War); **The Charge of the Light Brigade**, 1968 (remake of the 1936 film); **Gunga Din**, 1939 (British Cavalry charge against Thug forces in 19th-Century India); **The Horse Soldiers**, 1959 (John Ford; Union cavalry during the American Civil War); **Juarez**, 1939 (French cavalry charge against the forces of Juarez during the ill-fated brief reign of Maximilian I of Mexico, 1864-1867); **The Lighthorsemen**, 1987 (Australian cavalry charge at the Battle of Beersheeba in 1917 in WWI); **The Lives of a Bengal Lancer**, 1935 (British cavalry in 19th Century India); **The Red Badge of Courage**, 1951; (U.S. and Confederate cavalry during the Civil War); **Rocky Mountain**, 1950 (Confederate cavalry against Indians during the Civil War); **Santa Fe Trail**, 1940 (U.S. troops at Harpers Ferry during the John Brown insurrection in 1859); **They Came to Cordura**, 1959 (U.S. cavalry in its campaign in Mexico in 1916 against Pancho Villa); **War Horse**, 2011 (British cavalry charge in 1914 during WWI); **Waterloo**, 1970 (French cavalry at the Battle of Waterloo, 1815). For a comprehensive list of films dealing with the U.S. Cavalry, see Subject Index, U.S. Cavalry, Volume II of this work. **p**, John Ford, Merian C. Cooper; **d**, Ford; **cast**, John Wayne, Maureen O'Hara, Ben Johnson, Claude Jarman Jr., Harry Carey Jr., Chill Wills, J. Carrol Naish, Victor McLaglen, Grant Withers, Peter Ortiz, Fred Kennedy, Karolyn Grimes, Steve Pendleton, Alberto Morin, Stan Jones, Ken Curtis, Jack Pennick, Barlow Simpson, Patrick Wayne, Sons of the Pioneers; **w**, James Kevin McGuinness (based on the story "Mission with No Record" by James Warner Bellah); **c**, Bert Glennon; **m**, Victor Young; **ed**, Jack Murray; **art d**, Frank Hotaling; **set d**, John McCarthy, Jr., Charles Thompson; **spec eff**, Howard and Theodore Lydecker.

Rio Rita ★★★★ 1929; U.S.; 140m; RKO; B/W/Color; Musical Comedy; Children: Acceptable; **DVD**. This terrific early-day talkie presents some spectacular dance productions and a bevy of great tunes while also providing a lot of laughs from the clever comedy team of Wheeler and Woolsey. The plot involves Boles, a Texas Ranger in pursuit of a mysterious bandit named El Kinkajou. He arrives at a border town where he meets and falls in love with Daniels, although he suspects that her brother, Alvarado, is the much-wanted outlaw, which causes their romance to be strained. After Boles indicates that Alvarado is the man he is looking for, Daniels breaks off her relationship and begins seeing Renavent, an oily and repulsive character, who is the quintessential villain (and who invariably caused audiences to hiss). Throughout this fragile romance triangle is a subplot involving Wheeler, who is trying to get out of his marriage while taking all the wrong advice from a bloviating divorce lawyer, Woolsey, their bantering routines together providing considerable mirth. In the end, Renavent is discovered to be the insidi-

Bebe Daniels and John Boles in *Rio Rita,* 1929.

ous El Kinkajou. While the ranger gets his man, Boles also gets Daniels back in his arms for a kissing finale. Director Reed does a marvelously good job at mixing the story with many superb ensemble dance sequences, as excitingly exhibited as any Busby Berkeley spectacular, where the choreography is often breathtaking. The singing, too, is exceptional, particularly Boles, who had a fine voice, and who would go on to become a popular matinee idol, although he is best remembered for his role as the lover of one of Bela Lugosi's blood-drained victims in **Dracula**, 1931. The film proved to be a great box office success, taking in more than $2.4 million against a $675,000 budget, replenishing the coffers of RKO, which had been suffering financial problems. This film was remade in 1942, with John Carroll as the ranger and Kathryn Grayson as Rita; Bud Abbot and Lou Costello replaced comedians Wheeler and Woolsey. Songs: "Jumping Bean," "The Kinkajou," "Sweethearts," "Rio Rita," "River Song," "Espanola," "Siesta Time," "Are You There," "The Ranger's Song," "You're Always in My Arms," "If You're in Love You'll Waltz," "The Spanish Shawl," "Out on the Loose," "Poor Fool," "Sweetheart, We Need Each Other," "Over the Boundary Line," "Following the Sun Around," "Long Before You Came" (1927; music: Harry Tierney; lyrics: Joseph McCarthy). *Author's Note*: This was the film debut for comedians Wheeler and Woolsey, and they would remain a very popular screen duo throughout the 1930s. This was also Daniels' first talkie, which director Reed shot at high speed and got into the can within twenty-four days. The reason why Reed worked with such alacrity was due to the fact that he made only a few minor changes in this adaptation of the successful Florenz Ziegfeld production by the same name. That original stage musical opened at the Ziegfeld Theater in NYC on February 2, 1927 and proved to be a smash hit, running for 494 performances. Wheeler and Woolsey were the only two original cast members appearing in the film version. Ziegfeld was on hand as a co-producer, but did not receive credit. Ziegfeld suggested that the film be shot entirely in color, but it was shot in black-and-white and in color and his advice should have been taken. The name of the villain, El Kinkajou, was apparently selected by original writers Bolton and Thompson through a random dictionary search; the name represents the adorable little creatures (related to the raccoon family) found in Australia and used in advertising for Qantas Airlines. **p**, William LeBaron, (not credited) Florenz Ziegfeld, Jr.; **d&w**, Luther Reed (based on the musical by Guy Bolton, Fred Thompson); **cast**, Bebe Daniels, John Boles, Bert Wheeler, Robert Woolsey, Dorothy Lee, Don Alvarado, Georges Renavent, Helen Kaiser, Richard Alexander, Hank Bell; **c**, Robert Kurrle; **m**, Harry Tierney; **ed**, William Hamilton; **art d**, Max Ree; **spec eff**, Lloyd Knechtel.

Rio Rita ★★★ 1942; U.S.; 91m; MGM; B/W; Comedy; Children: Ac-

Ray Danton in *The Rise and Fall of Legs Diamond*, 1960.

ceptable; **DVD**; **VHS**. Fun-filled comedy sees Abbott and Costello trying to stop Nazi spy Conway from attempting to smuggle bombs into the U.S. from a Texas-Mexico border town hotel. Lovely Grayson, who owns the hotel, sings and is sung to and romanced by stalwart John Carroll. The boys manage to foil Conway while Carroll wraps his arms around Grayson for the happy finale. This is a remake of the 1929 version, offering less music but some good routines by the comics. Songs: "Rio Rita," "The Ranger's Song" (1927; music: Harry Tierney; lyrics: Joseph McCarthy); "Before You Came Along," A Couple of Caballeros" "Poor Whipporwill," "Such Unusual Weather" (1942; music: Harold Arlen; lyrics: E.Y. Harburg); "Shadow Song" (1859; from the opera "Dinorah, ou le pardon de Ploemel; music: Giacomo Meyerbeer; lyrics: Jules Barbier, Michel Carre); "Brazilian Dance" (Nilo Barnet); "Ora O Conga" (Lacerdo). **p**, Pandro S. Berman; **d**, S. Sylvan Simon; **cast**, Bud Abbott, Lou Costello, Kathryn Grayson, John Carroll, Patricia Dane, Tom Conway, Peter Whitney, Barry Nelson, Arthur Space, Dick Rich, Eva Puig; **w**, Richard Connell, Gladys Lehman, John Grant. The film bears no resemblance to the 1929 film of the same name. **c**, George Folsey; **m**, Herbert Stothart; **ed**, Ben Lewis; **art d**, Cedric Gibbons; **set d**, Edwin B. Willis; **spec eff**, Warren Newcombe.

Riot in Cell Block 11 ★★★ 1954; U.S.; 80m; AA; B/W; Crime Drama; Children: Unacceptable; **DVD**; **VHS**. Grim but riveting prison tale has inmates staging a violent uprising to protest against substandard food, brutal guards, overcrowding, and barely livable conditions. Most inmates join, taking several guards hostage. Negotiations between the inmates and prison officials are stymied by politicians interfering with the prison administration and by dissension and infighting in the inmates' own ranks. Brand leads the inmates, honestly attempting to establish reforms, but his efforts are hampered by homicidal Gordon (who in real life was an unruly actor acting much like the thug he plays in this film). The riot is finally quelled, but Brand, mostly because of Gordon's violent actions, has another thirty years added to his sentence for leading the riot, although some reforms are achieved. *Author's Note*: Producer Wanger wanted to make a film about prison life after serving four months for shooting and wounding Jennings Lang on December 15, 1951. Lang had been for fifteen years the agent for actress Joan Bennett, who was then married to Wanger. When seeing that his wife had left her car at a lot and had driven off with Lang and returned with him sometime later, Wanger thought Lang was having an affair with Bennett. He served his sentence at an honor farm, unlike the prison in the film. Bennett denied having had any kind of romantic relationship with Lang and blamed Wanger's actions on a nervous breakdown as a result of financial problems. She remained married to the producer until 1965 when she divorced him. **p**, Walter Wanger; **d**, Don Siegel; **cast**, Neville Brand,

Emile Meyer, Frank Faylen, Leo Gordon, Robert Osterloh, Paul Frees, Don Keefer, Alvy Moore, Whit Bissell, Carleton Young; **w**, Richard Collins (based on his story); **c**, Russell Harlan; **m**, Herschel Burke Gilbert; **ed**, Bruce B. Pierce; **art d**, David Milton; **set d**, Robert Priestley; **spec eff**, Ray Mercer.

Riptide ★★★ 1934; U.S.; 92m; MGM; B/W; Drama; Children: Unacceptable; **VHS**. Infidelity among the wealthy class was a popular theme in 1930s films, but this similar tale rises above the melodramatic soap suds because of superlative performances from its cast. Shearer is a fun-loving American who meets British lord Marshall and they have an affair. She becomes pregnant and gives birth, but the noble Marshall does the right thing and marries her. Their love is genuine and they enjoy a happy marriage until Marshall is called away on business. Left with nothing to do, Shearer attends an upscale party and meets Montgomery, who is an old flame. The earlier romance was abandoned by Shearer when she realized that the charming Montgomery was nothing more than a self-centered playboy. However, their passions are renewed when they meet at this party, but Shearer remains loyal to Marshall by rebuffing Montgomery's advances. She goes home, but the aroused Montgomery persistently follows her. Though he is drunk, Montgomery attempts to climb to Shearer's terrace, but falls and is injured. After Montgomery arrives at a hospital for treatment, the scandal breaks. Marshall returns and believes that Shearer has been unfaithful. He dismisses her explanation that nothing happened between her and Montgomery and separates from her. Shearer then plays the field and winds up again with Montgomery, but her heart is not with Montgomery. Marshall, meanwhile, comes to believe that his wife was telling the truth all along, but when he finds her again with Montgomery, he files for divorce. Before their divorce is finalized, however, Shearer and Marshall realize that the love they had for each other remains strong and enduring and they reunite for a blissful finale. Songs: "We're Together Again" (1932; music: Nacio Herb Brown; lyrics: Arthur Freed), "Riptide" (1934; music: Walter Donaldson; lyrics: Gus Kahn), "La Marseillaise" (Claude Joseph Rouget de Lisle). *Author's Note*: Shearer, the reigning queen at MGM, was married to the studio's production chief, Irving Thalberg, and this was another film in which she plays a sexually liberated woman in a sophisticated drama (although comedies were her specialty), which was handcrafted by her husband. She had won an Oscar for Best Actress for her appearance in **The Divorcee**, 1930, a film in which Montgomery also appeared; she considered the actor her "good luck guy." Montgomery had appeared with Shearer in **Their Own Desire**, 1929, and went on to play opposite that fine actress in the sterling comedy **Private Lives**, 1931. Montgomery told this author that "I don't get Norma at the end of **Riptide** and I don't deserve her because I play a wealthy wastrel out for fun and no responsibilities. To tell you the truth, I got more than a little tired of playing all those rich playboys and, if I really had the money my characters were supposed to have, I would have retired from making pictures." **p**, Irving Thalberg; **d&w**, Edmund Goulding; **cast**, Norma Shearer, Robert Montgomery, Herbert Marshall, Mrs. Patrick Campbell, Richard "Skeets" Gallagher, Ralph Forbes, Lilyan Tashman, Helen Jerome Eddy, Walter Brennan, Arthur Treacher; **c**, Ray June; **m**, Herbert Stothart; **ed**, Margaret Booth; **art d**, Alexander Toluboff, Fredric Hope; **set d**, Edwin B. Willis.

The Rise and Fall of Legs Diamond ★★★ 1960; U.S.; 101m; WB; B/W; Biographical Drama; Children: Unacceptable; **VHS**. Top-drawer biopic depicts the brief, spectacular criminal career of NYC bootlegger Jack "Legs" Diamond (1897-1931), well essayed by Danton. The film begins with Danton working as a dancer at the Hotsy Totsy Club (which Diamond owned in real life). To get some gems for his girlfriend, he robs a jewelry store with his slow-witted brother, Oates. He continues as a petty thief until he works his way into the good graces of rackets boss Arnold Rothstein (1882-1928), played by Lowery, by romancing Stewart, who is Lowery's mistress. Danton becomes a bodyguard for the boss and rises in the mob after he is wounded in saving his employer's life. Learning how Lowery operates his rackets, Danton begins to take them over, growing rich and marrying childhood sweetheart Steele, although he is invariably unfaithful to her. When Lowery is murdered by killers unknown (Danton is suspected of having a hand in the mysterious slaying), gang members split up the boss's rackets, with Danton taking over most of Lowery's bootlegging operations. Now rich and powerful, he ruthlessly dumps Stewart, who has helped him to climb the ladder of criminal success, and buys the nightclub where he once worked as a dancer. He sends his brother, Oates, to Denver to recover from his tuberculosis, but then refuses to pay for his medical treatment. After Oates dies miserable and alone, Danton shows no remorse. He then gets into a gang war with rival bootleg boss White (who plays a role model based on Diamond's true underworld nemesis, Dutch Schultz, 1901-1935), but, though wounded several times by White's gunmen, Danton survives and egotistically comes to believe that "the bullet hasn't been made that can kill me." He is undone, however, when Stewart, seeking revenge for being abandoned, sets Danton up by getting him drunk and sending him to a NYC boarding house where hired killers finally succeed in killing him, firing many bullets into him and ending his meteoric criminal career. The darkly handsome Danton is convincing as the arrogant gangster and he is supported by a fine cast. Boetticher's fast-paced and well-controlled direction, along with fine lensing from Ballard, makes this an exciting biopic where a fascinating portrait of a gangster is uncompromisingly etched. Richard Gardner has a small but significant role while playing NYC gangster Vincent "Mad Dog" Coll (1908-1932), kidnapper and freelance mob killer, who was later the role model for Nicolas Cage's character in **The Cotton Club**, 1984. Songs: "It Had To Be You" (Isham Jones, Gus Kahn), "Avalon" (Buddy DeSylva, Al Jolson, Vincent Rose), "I'm Just Wild About Harry" (Eubie Blake, Noble Sissle), "Sweet Georgia Brown" (Ben Bernie, Kenneth Casey, Maceo Pinkard), "If I Could Be With You One Hour Tonight" (Henry Creamer, James P. Johnson), "Your Eyes Have Told Me So" (Walter Blaufuss, Gus Kahn, Egbert Van Alstyne), "Blue Room" (Richard Rodgers, Lorenz Hart), "The Japanese Sandman" (Richard A. Whiting, Ray Egan), "Black and White Rag" (George Botsford), "Charleston" (James P. Johnson, Cecil Mack), "Documentary March" (William Lava), "Marche Grave" (Howard Jackson), "I Wonder What's Become of Sally" (Milton Ager, Jack Yellen). *Author's Note*: Diamond, from 1916 to 1931, was wounded so many times by rival gangsters that he was given the underworld sobriquet of "The Clay Pigeon of the Underworld." Most of those wounds were received at the hands of gunmen working for crime boss Dutch Schultz, who, vexed and angered over the inability of his henchmen to dispatch Diamond, once moaned: "Ain't there nobody who can shoot this guy so that he don't bounce back?" For more details on Coll, Diamond, Rothstein and Schultz see my book *World Encyclopedia of Organized Crime* (Paragon House, New York, 1992; Coll: pages 107-110; Diamond: pages 134-139; Rothstein: pages 337-341; Schultz: pages 353-360). **p**, Milton Sperling; **d**, Budd Boetticher; **cast**, Ray Danton, Karen Steele, Elaine Stewart, Jesse White, Simon Oakland, Robert Lowery, Judson Pratt, Warren Oates, Frank DeKova, Gordon Jones, Dyan Cannon, Joseph Ruskin, Richard Gardner, Sid Melton, Robert "Buzz" Henry; **w**, Joseph Landon; **c**, Lucien Ballard; **m**, Leonard Rosenman; **ed**, Folmar Blangsted; **art d**, Jack Poplin; **spec eff**, Clarence I. Steensen.

Rise of the Planet of the Apes ★★★ 2011; U.S.; 105m; FOX; Science Fiction; Children: Unacceptable (MPAA: PG); **BD**, **DVD**. This chilling entry of the popular series sees a chimpanzee called Caesar (Serkis) gain human-like intelligence and emotions from an experimental drug. Raised like a child by Franco, the drug's creator, and a primatologist, Pinto, he is ultimately taken away from the humans he loves and imprisoned in an ape sanctuary in San Bruno, California. Man and ape are put on a collision course that leads to a terrible battle between apes and humans on the Golden Gate Bridge, after which Serkis leads the apes

Cyril Cusack and Noel Purcell in *The Rising of the Moon*, 1957.

to escape into the Redwood Forest. Serkis is home at last with his own kind. Earlier films were **Beneath the Planet of the Apes**, 1970; **Escape from the Planet of the Apes**, 1971; **Conquest of the Planet of the Apes**, 1972; **Battle for the Planet of the Apes**, 1973; and television films and series. Frightening action and violence prohibit viewing by children. **p**, Peter Chernin, Dylan Clark, Rick Jaffa, Amanda Silver, Kurt Williams; **d**, Rupert Wyatt; **cast**, James Franco, Freida Pinto, John Lithgow, Brian Cox, Tom Felton, David Oyelowo, Tyler Labine, Jamie Harris, David Hewlett, Ty Olsson, Madison Bell; **w**, Jaffa, Silver (suggested by the novel *Planet of the Apes* by Pierre Boulle); **c**, Andrew Lesnie; **m**, Patrick Doyle; **ed**, Conrad Buff IV, Mark Goldblatt; **prod d**, Claude Pare; **art d**, Dan Hermansen, Grant Van Der Slagt, Helen Jarvis; **set d**, Elizabeth Wilcox; **spec eff**, Justin Cornish, Dan Lemmon, Brooke Lyndon-Stanford, Kevin Romond, R. Chistopher White, Erik Winquist.

The Rising of the Moon ★★★★ 1957; Ireland/U.S.; Four Provinces Films/WB; B/W; Drama; Children: Cautionary. Entertaining and masterfully directed by pantheon director Ford, this episodic film presents three fascinating and colorful tales centered in Ireland, the land of Ford's heritage. Actor Tyrone Power, who starred in Ford's **The Long Gray Line**, 1955, introduces and narrates these memorable sequences, the first of which is titled "The Majesty of the Law." In this story, Cyril Cusack is an Irish policeman who must serve a warrant on Purcell, a proud, old fellow who has been accused of striking a neighbor for selling him undrinkable moonshine whiskey. Cusack goes to Purcell's home, and the old man invites him inside. They sit together as Cusack hesitantly brings up the issue of the assault, telling Purcell that he can pay a fine and avoid a short jail term. Purcell refuses on principle, telling Cusack that the old Irish values and the country's wonderful heritage are eroding because of modern films, radio and other modern inventions. Cusack more or less agrees and then asks Purcell to accompany him to jail, which the old man does. As they walk along, the man whom Purcell has attacked runs up to them, offering to pay the fine to keep Purcell from jail, but the old man is too proud to accept such generosity. He and Purcell continue their walk toward jail as most of the townspeople step from their homes to pay homage to the elderly Purcell, who is the symbol of an unyielding and fighting Ireland. "A Minute's Wait," the second episode, depicts the stopping of an Irish train at a small village. The train has been held up so that fresh lobsters can be loaded on board in order to be delivered in time to be served at the Bishop's Jubilee Dinner. The delay, of course, leads to a lot of comic situations that take much more than "a minute." The engineer, for instance, refuses to start the engine and move the train until he has finished a lengthy ghost story he has been telling to his avid listener, a barmaid. Meanwhile, several passengers are moved from their seats, including a stuffy British couple, who

Rebecca De Mornay and Tom Cruise in *Risky Business*, 1983.

are displaced from their first-class compartment by a goat being delivered to its new owner. (This sequence borrows heavily from a lengthy scene in Ford's own classic film, **The Quiet Man**, 1952, where engineers and conductors hold up a train to argue and threaten to fight over trivial issues while John Wayne searches the train to find his runaway wife, Maureen O'Hara, and drag her back to her wifely duties.) "1921," the third and final episode, is more somber, dealing with the escape of an IRA prisoner, Donnelly, who eludes captors with the help of Abbey Theatre players. Donnelly, who is considered a great Irish patriot and who is awaiting execution, is visited in his cell by two actresses from the theater group, who are disguised as nuns. While one of the women distracts a guard, Donnelly exchanges his prison clothes with the nun's habit the other woman wears and then steps from the cell, head down and face shrouded as he and the other nun leave the prison. He makes it to a waterfront area, waiting for a chance to set to sea in a small boat, but the area is heavily patrolled by British Black and Tan men, avowed enemies of the IRA. Also patrolling the waterfront is O'Dea, an Irish police sergeant. He is not a member of the IRA but he also is no friend of the Black and Tans, an organization he dislikes because of its oppressive and brutal tactics. O'Dea encounters a ragged street singer, delighted at the songs the man warbles for him, and, when he turns his back, the singer is gone. O'Dea becomes suspicious, but his wife appears and appeals to his Irish patriotism to quit any search for the singer, and this he does. O'Dea then sees a man rowing a small boat out to sea and realizes that he has allowed the much-wanted Donnelly, who disguised himself as that singer, to escape. O'Dea is not upset about it, and, in fact, takes a secret Irish pride in helping that patriot and that is where this charming and heartwarming film ends. This much view-worthy film nevertheless did not do well at the box office, taking in a little more than $100,000 in its initial release against a $500,000 budget. Songs: "Slattery's Mounted Fut" (Percy French), "She Is Far from the Land" (Frank Lambert). *Author's Note*: Ford told this author that he had long wanted to do this film, "but when I made that picture, I had next to nothing to cover expenses and was unable to bring big name stars into the production. That is the reason, I believe, why the picture didn't do very well when it was released, although all the actors in the picture are marvelous." He wanted Maureen O'Hara, Barry Fitzgerald and Tyrone Power to play roles in one of the episodes, but none were available when Ford when into production with this film. Power, however, later offered to introduce the episodes for a next-to-nothing fee. **p**, Michael Killanin; **d**, John Ford; **cast**, Tyrone Power (host), Noel Purcell, Cyril Cusack, Jack MacGowran, Jimmy O'Dea, Paul Farrell, Maureen Potter, May Craig, Denis O'Dea, Eileen Crowe, Frank Lawton, Donal Donnelly, Maureen Cusack; **w**, Frank S. Nugent (based on the stories "The Majesty of the Law" by Frank O'Connor, "A Minute's Wait" by Michael

J. McHugh, and "The Rising of the Moon" by Lady Augusta Gregory); **c**, Robert Krasker; **m**, Eamonn O'Gallagher; **ed**, Michael Gordon; **art d**, Raymond Simm.

Risky Business ★★★ 1939; U.S.; 65m; UNIV; B/W; Crime Drama; Children: Unacceptable. Good crime tale has Murphy as a Los Angeles radio gossip columnist who attempts to expose mob criminal activities in Hollywood. This leads to him rescuing a producer's kidnapped daughter. Murphy kills the kidnapper, Ciannelli, only to be killed by mob members just before he goes on the air with his expose. Offbeat but fascinating film sustains interest throughout, thanks to Murphy's fine performance. This film has no relation to the Tom Cruise 1983 comedy of the same name, but it is a remake of **Okay, America!**, 1932. **p**, Burt Kelly; **d**, Arthur Lubin; **cast**, George Murphy, Dorothea Kent, Eduardo Ciannelli, Leon Ames, El Brendel, John Wray, Arthur Loft, Mary Forbes, Lane Chandler, Mark Daniels; **w**, Charles Grayson (based on the story "Okay America" by William Anthony McGuire); **c**, Stanley Cortez.

Risky Business ★★★ 1983; U.S.; 98m.; Geffen/WB; Color; Comedy; Children: Unacceptable (MPAA: R); **BD**; **DVD**; **VHS**. Very funny film has parents Pryor and Carroll leaving their upscale suburban Chicago home to go on a weekend trip, leaving their residence in the care of their model teenage son, Cruise. He invites his school pals over for a big poker game, drinking liquor, smoking cigars, and playing a blaring stereo. De Mornay, a prostitute, arrives, and Cruise, to prove his entrepreneurial skills, goes into business, turning the house into an upscale suburban whorehouse. Everything goes from bad to worse, and Cruise's goofy plans to grow rich as an entrepreneur crash everywhere about him. Typical of these endless disasters is when Cruise watches horrified as, accidentally, his father's prize Porsche nose-dives into Lake Michigan. All ends well as Cruise gets the house back in order and the car repaired, just moments before his parents return home none the wiser for the menacing mayhem he has created. This film became a surprise megahit, giving teenagers just the kind of movie they wanted, one that showed them in control, even though Cruise's authority is exercised over endless chaos, which also appealed to the more anarchistic emotions of teenagers. It made a fortune for the producers and catapulted Cruise to superstardom. An early scene showing Cruise sliding across the floor in his jockey shorts while wearing sunglasses became a classic and unforgettable "cool" scene, an image cherished forever by his generation. The film was a smash at the box office, taking in $63,500,000 in its initial release against a budget of $6.2 million. Songs: "Every Breath You Take" (Sting: Gordon Matthew Sumner), "My Heart Tells Me" (Harry Warren), "Old Time Rock and Roll" (George Jackson, Tom Jones III), "The Pump" (Tony Hymans, Simon Phillips), "Hungry Heart" (Bruce Springsteen), "Mannish Boy" (Bo Diddley, Melvin London, Muddy Waters), "Swamp" (Music: Talking Heads: David Byrne, Chris Frantz, Tina Weymouth, Jerry Harrison), "After the Fall" (Jonathan Cain, Steve Perry), "D.M.S.R." (Prince: Rogers Nelson), "In the Air Tonight" (Phil Collins), "Love on a Real Train/Risky Business" (Tangerine Dream: Peter Baumann, Johannes Schmoelling, Paul Haslinger, Jerome Froese). Sexuality, smoking, drinking and prostitution prohibit viewing by children. **p**, Jon Avnet, Steve Tisch; **d&w**, Paul Brickman; **cast**, Tom Cruise, Rebecca De Mornay, Joe Pantoliano, Richard Masur, Bronson Pinchot, Curtis Armstrong, Nicholas Pryor, Janet Carroll, Shera Danese, Bruce A. Young, Sean Penn; **c**, Bruce Surtees, Reynaldo Villalobos (Technicolor); **m**, Tangerine Dream; **ed**, Richard Chew; **prod d**, William J. Cassidy; **set d**, Ralph Hall; **spec eff**, Steve Purcell.

The River ★★★★★ 1951; France/India/U.S.; 99m; Oriental International Films/UA; Color; Drama; Children: Unacceptable; **DVD**; **VHS**. This magnificently photographed film is set in India, following WWII, and where an upscale British family lives in idyllic comfort close to the flowing Ganges River. The father, Knight, who has lost an eye during the war, operates a jute mill while his pregnant wife, Swinburne, supervises their large family of five daughters and a young son, and with the aid of a governess or nanny, Suprova Mukerjee. The story is narrated by one of the daughters, Walters, reading from her diary as an adult and looking back upon this tale when she was a young teenager. Though steeped in colonial traditions, the family embraces the varied philosophies of Hinduism, Buddhism and other religions, observing and respecting the customs of India's many cultures. Their tranquil and uneventful lifestyle is disrupted when Breen, a handsome, young American, who has lost a leg in the war, comes to live on a nearby plantation at the invitation of his cousin, Shields. The daughters are all attracted to this charming and sophisticated American, even though he only wants to be alone. He accepts their invitation to a Diwali (a five-day Hindu celebration), and Walters competes for Breen's attentions by sharing her diary with him. Breen, who is tolerantly avuncular toward her and the rest of the girls, including Walters' keenest competitors, Corri, a friend, and Radha, who is Shields' daughter, both of these vying girls older than Walters. After her young brother, Foster, dies through mishap and she witnesses Breen passionately kiss Corri, Walters loses her will to live. She believes that she has somehow brought about her brother's death and, having lost any chance at romance with Breen, decides to end her life in the Ganges. She runs away from home, going to the river, getting into a small skiff where the treacherous night currents threaten to take her life. To be sure of that, Walters slips into the water. However, she has been seen by fishermen along the shore, who rescue her, taking her back to the shore and resuscitating her. She later discovers that Breen does not really love Corri, but has fallen deeply in love with Radha , but he and she are troubled by their relationship because she is of Radha mixed blood. Her father, Shields, expresses his regret at having married her mother because of the social and emotional trouble his own mixed marriage has produced, and he fears that his daughter will suffer the same troubling fate brought on by miscegenation. Moreover, the love affair between Radha and Breen is tenuous at best since she finds him, for all his kindness, stiffly overbearing, but this is based upon her own misgivings and self-worthiness relative to her mixed blood that places her in two separate caste systems. Through these travails, director Renoir consistently reverts to scenes of the always busy Ganges River, where its energy compels endless workers to their labors. The viewer sees along its winding waters constantly moving vessels, fishermen and peddlers along its shores, the comings and goings of passengers, a series of ever-changing events, and persons in motion, all umbilical to the eternal flow of that river. The Ganges itself is the lynchpin to the story that links its characters, and, like Walter's evocative and era-recalling diary, visually testifies to their eventful days along its banks. This film deservedly saw a great success at the box office, taking in more than $1 million in its initial release. *Author's Note*: Renoir left France, where he had established his name as a pantheon director with such classic films as **Grand Illusion**, 1938; **The Human Beast**, 1940; and **The Rules of the Game** (1939), 1950. He migrated to Hollywood, but found only a few stories he felt suited to his talents, the best of these being **The Southerner**, 1945. Before he left Hollywood, he had befriended Kenneth McEldowney, who owned considerable real estate and a string of florist shops in Los Angeles. He mentioned to McEldowney that he always wanted to make a film in India, and outlined his ideas for **The River**. McEldowney's wife at that time was a publicist for MGM Studio, and, after McEldowney complained repeatedly about the pedestrian fare being produced by her studio and others in Hollywood, she challenged him to make a better film. McEldowney took her up on that dare and sold off much of his holdings to provide Renoir with most of the initial money to make **The River**, working with the director for several years (from 1947 until the film's release). He saw that film open at reserved seat prices in New York, where it ran before packed houses for thirty-four weeks. McEldowney then returned to his real estate business and never again made another film. Renoir, to present a natural family setting, purposely selected, for the most part, non-professional actors

Patricia Walters and Radha in *The River*, 1951.

to essay his characters. His love of nature is evident everywhere in the film as is his affection for the teeming river life he so brilliantly captures in this awe-inspiring masterpiece. Renoir provided what is most likely one of the most sumptuous-looking color films ever made, carefully supervising the Technicolor process then used (which incorporated the use of vegetable dyes), and he used intensive lighting to accentuate the coloring, measuring that coloring with a spectrometer and photometer. When he thought certain objects or even landscapes did not provide enough lush coloring, such as a lawn being shown in one scene, Renoir had some of the frames in the film hand-painted, such elaborate and laborious work adding six months to the production schedule. This technique was also used for the first time in the U.S., by Oscar-winning film editor Gene Ruggiero when he had some action scenes hand-painted for **Men of the Fighting Lady**, 1954 (see details in *Author's Note* for that entry). Knight, who plays the father in **The River**, actually lost an eye while serving in WWII during the sea battle with the German pocket battleship *Bismarck* in May 1941 when Knight was on board the British battleship *Prince of Wales*. In the exciting recreation of that battle in **Sink the Bismarck!**, 1960, Knight played the captain of the *Prince of Wales*. Breen, who is missing a leg in this film, lost that leg in real life. Indian filmmaker Satyajit Ray began his career with this film as one of Renoir's assistants, and this film also launched the career of Subrata Mitra, who later became Ray's chief cinematographer. **p**, Jean Renoir, Kenneth McEldowney; **d**, Renoir; **cast**, Nora Swinburne, Esmond Knight, Arthur Shields, Thomas E. Breen, Suprova Mukerjee, Patricia Walters, Radha (Radha Burnier), Adrienne Corri, Nimai Barik, Richard R. Foster, June Hillman (narrator); **w**, Renoir, Rumer Godden (based on the novel by Godden); **c**, Claude Renoir (Technicolor); **m**, M.A. Partha Sarathy; **ed**, George Gale; **prod d**, Eugene Lourie; **art d**, Bansi Chandragupta.

River of No Return ★★★★ 1954; U.S.; 91m; FOX; Color; Adventure/Western; Children: Unacceptable; **DVD**; **VHS**. Set in the Northwest in 1875, this action-loaded and well-acted western depicts the saga of three persons, Mitchum; his young son, Rettig; and Monroe, a dance hall girl, all surviving on a raft while going down a dangerous river as Indians pursue them. The film opens with Mitchum arriving at a mining town to find his young son, Rettig. Mitchum has been released from prison after serving a term for murder, although he claims he killed a man in order to stop him from shooting a friend. His conviction has not been made known to Rettig, who had been taken care of by friends. Mitchum finds Rettig in the care of Monroe, who has established a protective if not motherly bond with Rettig. Mitchum thinks of her only as a singer in a tent saloon, another loose woman in the untamed frontier and he is also disdainful of her shifty boyfriend, Calhoun, a darkly hand-

Marilyn Monroe as a dance hall singer in *River of No Return*, 1954.

some but decidedly devious cardsharp. Mitchum tells his trusting and impressionable son that they will have a good time together at their homestead next to a large river, where they will be hunting and fishing. After Mitchum and Rettig depart for Mitchum's small farm and log cabin, Calhoun tells Monroe that he has won a deed to a gold mine in a poker game and they must leave immediately for Council City to file a claim on that deed. They depart on a raft, going down the river, but, after having difficulty, they stop at Mitchum's homestead. Calhoun decides that it will be faster to get to his destination if he uses Mitchum's horse, but Mitchum refuses to sell the animal to the gambler. Calhoun hits him over the head, taking the horse and Mitchum's rifle. Rettig thinks his father is dead and is so upset that Monroe's compassion for him compels her to tell Calhoun to go on alone while she helps Mitchum recuperate. The self-serving Calhoun tells her that he will see her in Council City and rides off. Mitchum regains consciousness, looking up to see Indians riding down a ridge and approaching the homestead. He tells Monroe and Rettig to gather up their things, realizing that the hostiles will soon be upon them. Mitchum, Monroe and Rettig climb aboard the raft, shoving off and sailing down the river just as the Indians arrive at the cabin and set it afire. The hostiles shoot arrows and throw spears at the raft, but the river has carried Mitchum, Monroe and Rettig to relative safety. The fugitives guide the raft to shore and camp that night, eating berries Monroe has gathered and small game that Mitchum has been able to capture. Monroe becomes alarmed when Mitchum admits that he is going after Calhoun to make him pay for attacking him and stealing his horse and rifle, asking Monroe why she would want to marry a man who would endanger a child by leaving him to the mercy of savage Indians. She angrily responds that he is worse than Calhoun in that he shot a man in the back and was sent to prison for that crime. Rettig overhears this story about his father and is shocked, his idealistic notions about Mitchum now shattered. The following day while the furtive trio raft down the river, the Indians again attack, doggedly seeking to kill Mitchum, Monroe and Rettig as if they were hunting wild animals. Their prey nevertheless manages to escape these attacks. When making camp again, a mountain lion looking for food enters the camp, and Mitchum, with only a hunting knife to use for defense, confronts the ferocious beast. He struggles wildly with the cougar, killing it. Later, while Mitchum, Monroe and Rettig are eating, they are visited by two seedy-looking prospectors, Vye and Spencer. Mitchum offers them some roasted meat, but Vye's roving eye focuses upon Monroe, and when he attempts to assault her, Mitchum intervenes and both men fight. Mitchum gets the upper hand and, while holding his knife to Vye's throat, orders Spencer to leave the camp with his horse and that of Vye's, waiting for Vye up river. Mitchum then releases the miner, but keeps his rifle, as he orders Vye to join his friend. The fugitives then resume their

trip down the river, but they are almost killed when they encounter vicious rapids that threaten to overturn the raft. They are then attacked again by Indians, who ride along the shores of the river, firing arrows and hurling spears. A few of the hostiles dive into the river and attempt to board the raft, but Mitchum, Monroe and Rettig beat them off and continue their hazardous journey until they finally reach Council City. While Monroe goes to a local saloon to resume her singing career, Mitchum and Rettig go to a store to buy provisions to set up a new homestead. Just then Calhoun appears. Believing that Mitchum is seeking revenge, Calhoun strikes first, firing a shot at Mitchum that barely misses him. Before Calhoun can fire another shot at the helpless Mitchum, Rettig uses a gun from the store to fire at Calhoun, killing him. Rettig now realizes how his father came to be imprisoned by doing about the same thing many years earlier. That night, before Mitchum and Rettig set out to make a new home, Mitchum enters the saloon where Monroe is performing and, just as she finishes her song, Mitchum picks her up and carries her outside to the wagon in which Rettig sits. She realizes now that Mitchum loves her and that he and Rettig want her to spend the rest of her days with them as a happy family. She is overjoyed with the prospect as she, too, has come to love Mitchum as she has Rettig. The wagon rolls away, and Monroe removes her dance-hall slippers, dropping them onto the street; the camera closes upon these discarded symbols of a life abandoned for a better, happier future. Director Preminger does a fine job in unfolding this exciting saga, sharply defining all of his characters as he surrounds them with the majestic landscape of the Rockies and the rushing, rapids-infested river where its swirling pools and waves crashing over dangerous rocky outcroppings are breathtakingly shown. Mitchum, sleepy-eyed as ever, is superlative as the taciturn but principled father and reluctant lover; Monroe, even though she later said this was her "worst picture," is outstanding as the down-and-out showgirl, and her tender scenes with Rettig are touching and compelling. Rettig, a fine young actor (eleven years old at the time), is perfect as a young boy learning life the hard way and becoming wiser for his harrowing experiences, and Calhoun is just right as the deceitful gambler. La Shelle's lensing is outstanding as is Mockridge's stirring score, which is peppered with some fine songs from Newman and Darby. The film was a success at the box office at a time when Monroe's popularity was reaching its peak, taking in $3,800,000 against a budget of $2,200,000. Songs: "River of No Return," "I'm Gonna File My Claim," "One Silver Dollar," "Down in the Meadow" (music: Lionel Newman; lyrics: Ken Darby); "Red River Valley" (traditional). *Author's Note*: The always dictatorial Preminger was an odd choice as the director of this film, as his career had been centered on making somber film noir productions (**Laura**, 1944; **Fallen Angel**, 1945; **Whirlpool**, 1949; **Angel Face**, 1952). Rubin, the producer of the film, objected to Preminger, telling Fox studio boss Darryl Zanuck that he thought William Wellman or Raoul Walsh would be more suited to helm **River of No Return**. Zanuck told this author that "I had already assigned Otto [Preminger] to direct that picture and told Rubin that Otto was doing it, period. Otto was fulfilling a contract with our studio and I thought he would do a good job with the picture, even though he had never directed a western. I took the same chance years earlier with Fritz Lang, another German director, when I gave him **The Return of Frank James** [1940] to direct and he did a bang-up job with that picture. I told Stanley [Rubin] to cover himself by having some of our assistant directors make a lot of good on-location shots where we had doubles for the stars in long shots and that would make up for anything lacking from Otto." The on-location shots were taken in Alberta, in the heart of the Canadian Rockies, including Baniff National Park, Jasper National Park, and Lake Louise. Preminger liked the script for this film and eagerly looked forward to doing the picture (which he brought in on schedule and within budget), and he also looked forward to using some experimental shots for the widescreen CinemaScope process being used for the film. However, according to his statements to this author, Preminger "had some difficulties with Miss Monroe. She was getting to be a big star, a very voluptuous young woman, but a bundle of nerves. She had this ridiculous dramatic coach [Natasha Lytess], who followed her everywhere and gave her all the wrong advice about everything." Lytess instructed Monroe to clearly articulate each and every word of her lines. When doing so, the actress, according to Preminger's comments to this author, "looked like the worst amateur before the cameras, very affected and pretentious, and that was the doing of her lady friend. I took Marilyn aside and told her: 'You must speak naturally. We are not making a film about how to teach little children to speak clearly. We are not doing a course in diction.' She got sullen about that and told her coach. Then this coach came to me and accused me of undermining her instructions to Marilyn. That was about enough. I told her: 'I am directing this picture, not you. And you are now leaving the set and are never to return.' Well, Marilyn, who was a bigger star at Fox than most others at that time, called Zanuck to complain about my little run-in with Natasha whatever-her-name-was, and Zanuck called me and asked that I put up with that crazy woman. I did, but I gave her as much hell as she gave me. Marilyn depended on that coach like she depended on too many people. She never owned her own mind. She let others do her thinking for her, except for me when we did that picture. But I wore out her affected way of talking by having so many retakes that she got weary and then talked normally and those were the scenes I used in the picture. When the picture was finished, I took this Natasha aside and whispered in her ear: 'If I ever see you walking on the street when I am in my car [limousine], I will instruct my driver to run you over.' Some months later, she was walking on Sunset Boulevard and saw me sitting in my car and she ran like a rabbit up a side street. Of course, my statement to her was not a literal threat, but she thought it was. That's the only satisfaction I ever got when dealing with that creature." Mitchum, who had been the leading man in Preminger's thriller, **Angel Face**, 1952, told this author that "that wacky drama coach of Marilyn's caused a lot of headaches for Otto [Preminger], and me, too, when we did **River of No Return**. She told Marilyn to keep in constant motion, no matter what kind of scene she was doing. At one point, I had to kiss Marilyn, but she was bobbing her head around and I stopped the scene and told Otto: "I can't plant a kiss on her if she keeps dodging me like some halfback trying to get into the end zone.' Marilyn did not really need that goofy coach. She was a fine actress and could do any kind of picture, comedy or drama. The trouble was that she never believed that she had any talent. All of those expensive hangers-on convinced her that she needed them to hold on to her career. In the end, they wrecked her until she gulped down enough pills to end her life. Marilyn Monroe was a true tragedy." Mitchum, always a heavy drinker, appeared sluggish in a few scenes, and Preminger went to him and said, according to the director's statements to this author: "Bob, I think you should alter your diet, which I believe now consists of beer for breakfast and hard liquor for lunch. He said to me: 'You live your life and I will live mine.' But I think my remarks took hold because he was sober in all of his scenes after that." **p**, Stanley Rubin; **d**, Otto Preminger; **cast**, Robert Mitchum, Marilyn Monroe, Rory Calhoun, Tommy Rettig, Murvyn Vye, Douglas Spencer, Fred Aldrich, Claire Andre, Hal Baylor, Don Beddoe, John Doucette, Barbara Nichols; **w**, Frank Fenton (based on a story by Louis Lantz); **c**, Joseph La Shelle (CinemaScope; Technicolor); **m**, Cyril J. Mockridge; **ed**, Louis Loeffler; **art d**, Lyle Wheeler, Addison Hehr; **set d**, Walter M. Scott, Chester Bayhi; **spec eff**, Ray Kellogg.

A River Runs Through It ★★★ 1992; U.S.; 123m; Allied Filmmakers/COL; Color; Drama; Children: Cautionary (MPAA: PG); **BD**; **DVD**. This moving film, based on an autobiographical novel about fly fishing, presents a touching portrait of fatherly and brotherly love. Two brothers with vastly divergent natures grow up in 1920s Missoula, Montana. Norman (Sheffer) is obedient, intellectual, and studious while younger Paul (Pitt) is more of a free spirit and sometime hell raiser. Their father, Skerritt, is a stoic Presbyterian minister, who is adept at fly fishing for trout in the nearby Blackfoot River. He teaches both sons how to fly fish, in-

Director Robert Redford, right, with Brad Pitt and Craig Sheffer on the set of *A River Runs Through It,* 1992.

stilling them with a passion for the sport. Sheffer goes east to college, and Pitt remains at home working as a reporter for the local newspaper and develops a need to drink and gamble. The brothers only seem to connect when fly fishing together, a sport that Pitt masters, to his father's great pleasure. Pitt, however, gets killed in a gambling dispute, leaving Sheffer and Skerritt to grieve for a member of the family they loved but hardly knew. The film's title poetically refers to the river that ran through and spiritually connected their lives. Songs: "The Sheik of Araby" (Harry B. Smith, Ted Snyder, Francis Wheeler), "Bye Bye Blackbird" (Mort Dixon, Ray Henderson), "Muskrat Ramble" (Ray Gilber, Edward "Kid" Ory), "Yes, We Have No Bananas" (Frank Silver, Irving Cohn). *Author's Note*: Although the book and film is set in Missoula, Montana, along the Blackfoot River, the film's on-location shots were taken at Livingston and Bozeman, Montana, and the rivers portrayed are the Upper Yellowstone, Boulder and Gallatin rivers. Gutter language and brief nudity prohibit viewing by children. **p**, Robert Redford, Patrick Markey, Amalia Mato, William Kittredge, Barbara Maltby, Annick Smith; **d**, Redford; **cast**, Craig Sheffer, Brad Pitt, Tom Skerritt, Brenda Blethyn, Emily Lloyd, Edie McClurg, Stephen Shellen, Vann Gravage, Nicole Burdette, Susan Traylor, Redford (narrator); **w**, Richard Friedenberg (based on the novel by Norman Maclean); **c**, Philippe Rousselot; **m**, Mark Isham; **ed**, Robert Estrin, Lynzee Klingman; **prod d**, Jon Hutman; **art d**, Walter P. Martishius; **set d**, Gretchen Rau; **spec eff**, Richard Stutsman, Mark Yuricich.

The Road ★★★ 2009; U.S.; 111m; 2929 Productions/Dimension Films; Color; Drama; Children: Unacceptable (MPAA: R); **BD**; **DVD**. Exciting but sometimes depressing post-apocalyptic adventure focuses upon Mortensen and his young son, Smit-McPhee, who are trying to survive in a hostile world. They walk alone through a burned-out America where nothing moves but ash on the wind and water, and snow falling in the bitter cold. They head south, hoping to find a warmer climate, and Mortensen is armed only with a pistol to defend them against lawless, cannibalistic bands that stalk the road along which they travel. They scavenge food, carrying these meager vittles in a rusting shopping cart. After several months, they reach a southern clime, which is along the California coast, but conditions are no better, so they move back inland. Mortensen falls ill and dies, leaving Smit-McPhee alone. Several days later, Smit-McPhee encounters an old man, Duvall, who has been following them with a wife and young son and daughter. Duvall takes him in as part of the family and they resolve to survive together. Although this film takes a large leaf from the Mad Max films, it nevertheless provides a riveting tale. Songs: "Westerly," "Green Eyes" (Viggo Mortensen); "Sonata for Violin and Harpsichord No. 3" (Johann Sebastian Bach). Violence and gutter language prohibit viewing by children.

Charlize Theron in *The Road*, 2009.

p, Steve Schwartz, Paula Mae Schwartz, Nick Wechsler, Erik Hodge; **d,** John Hillcoat; **cast,** Viggo Mortensen, Charlize Theron, Kodi Smit-McPhee, Robert Duvall, Guy Pearce, Molly Parker, Michael Kenneth Williams, Garret Dillahunt, Bob Jennings, Agnes Herrmann, Buddy Sosthand; **w,** Joe Penhall (based on the novel by Cormac McCarthy); **c,** Javier Aguirresarobe; **m,** Nick Cave, Warren Ellis; **ed,** Jon Gregory; **prod d,** Chris Kennedy; **art d,** Gershon Ginsburg; **set d,** Robert Greenfield; **spec eff,** Glenn Allen, Mark O. Forker, Paul Graff, Noel Hooper.

The Road Back ★★★ 1937; U.S.; 97m (103m original release); UNIV; Drama; Children: Unacceptable. Many powerful and poignant scenes can be found in this mostly forgotten film, a good sequel to **All Quiet on the Western Front**, 1930. The film opens with one last and titanic battle that ends WWI (1914-1918), after which the Armistice (November 11, 1918) is signed. Emery, the commander of a German company, orders a final roll call of his remaining troops, but only a few return to the ranks as most of his men have been killed (and where the viewer sees those fallen soldiers as specters filling in the gaps of the company's lines). Each surviving soldier then trudges homeward through a defeated Germany, all haunted by the grim and terrible memories of their years of trench warfare along the Western Front. When reaching home, they find it difficult to adjust to civilian life. One ex-soldier, Devine, returns to the school where he was inspired to go to war four years earlier and where a former teacher happily hands him a toy gun that teacher took from him, that model gun now representing destruction and death. Inflation has gripped the country and this is demonstrated when a mob, desperate for goods and food, begins storming stores. When an angry crowd assembles before a shop owned by the town's mayor, Summerville, another ex-soldier, steps before the mob and persuades its members not to loot the place and to go home peacefully. So grateful is the mayor for Summerville's intervention that he allows the ex-soldier to marry his daughter. A much less happy outcome results after another mob assembles before a store and Blake, another ex-solider from that same company, steps forth to make revolutionary demands as he has become a Marxist dreaming of a communist state. His utopian vision is shattered with the arrival of Emery, his old company commander. Emery has remained in the army and now commands regular troops; he orders those troops to shoot Blake for leading an insurrection. Yet another veteran from the same company, Murphy, meets a similar tragic end. He returns home to find that his sweetheart is now involved with a sleazy racketeer trading in the black market. Murphy kills the racketeer and is placed on trial, charged with murder. His defense is that since he was trained to kill men in battle he did not know or dislike, by killing a sinister man, he was simply carrying on the skills he had been taught in war while ridding society of an evil person, who had robbed him of his

happiness in life. The film ends with school children gathered in a playground where, instead of enjoying games, they are being trained to march in goosestep by Nazi instructors, who are training the next generation for the next war. Director Whale presents a grim but fascinating portrait of post-war Germany where returning war veterans are wholly displaced and disassociated from their society as if they are aliens arriving from another world. Song: "Mademoiselle from Armentieres" (Joseph Turnbridge). *Author's Note*: Universal purchased the rights to novelist Remarque's novel, *The Road Back*, when it was published in 1931, thinking to make the picture on the heels of its enormous success with **All Quiet on the Western Front**, 1930, which was based on Remarque's popular 1929 novel. The studio, at the time it purchased the rights to *The Road Back*, was chiefly owned and controlled by Carl Laemmle and his son, Carl Laemmle Jr., both having a dislike for **All Quiet on the Western Front** because of its grim story line, even though that film greatly enriched Universal. The Laemmle family simply sat on the rights for *The Road Back* until they were ousted and new management took over the studio and then reactivated the project. The film, however, ran into serious trouble even in production after Nazi propaganda minister Joseph Goebbels learned it was going into production. Universal was officially informed by Goebbels that not only would the film be banned in Germany but in all other countries where Germany had widespread influence and that also applied to *all* of Universal films thereafter. The Nazis did not stop there. Many of the actors received letters from Nazi officials saying that if they acted in **The Road Back**, all of the films in which they might later appear would also be banned in Germany. Germany went so far as to file an official protest with the U.S. State Department, which caused widespread furor as well as a great deal of unwanted publicity, but Universal, caving in to Nazi demands, softened some of the scenes indicting the oppressive Nazis (cutting out about six minutes of the film) before it was released. That did not help. The film was nevertheless banned in Germany as had been the Remarque novel when it was first published. This author met Remarque in 1958 when he was living in a villa in Switzerland, and where he told me that "the Nazis had a very long arm in those days. They knew I hated them and their tactics and they took all the reprisals they could against my published works, including films based on those works. They did not ban the film version of my book *All Quiet on the Western Front* because they were not in power when that book and its film were released, but they made sure to burn copies of that book when they came into power years later. They were relentless." The failure of this film at the box office depressed director Whale, who felt that the film had been sabotaged by Universal to appease the Nazis. It nevertheless remains an incisive indictment against war and warmongers such as the Nazis Whale's and many eye-arresting techniques are much in evidence, such as a huge, mobile crane he had constructed for his well-choreographed battle scenes and which he used in many subsequent scenes when depicting street mobs and riots. **p,** Edmund Grainger, Charles R. Rogers; **d,** James Whale; **cast,** John "Dusty" King, Richard Cromwell, Slim Summerville, Andy Devine, Barbara Read, Spring Byington, Frank Reicher, John Emery, Noah Beery, Jr., Laura Hope Crews, Louise Fazenda, Lionel Atwill, Al Shean, Clara Blandick, Francis Ford, Dwight Frye; **w,** R.C. Sherriff, Charles Kenyon (based on the novel by Erich Maria Remarque); **c,** George Robinson, John J. Mescall; **m,** Dimitri Tiomkin; **ed,** Ted J. Kent, Charles Maynard; **art d,** Charles D. Hall, **spec eff,** John P. Fulton.

Road House ★★★★ 1948; U.S.; 95m; FOX; B/W; Crime Drama; Children: Unacceptable; **DVD; VHS**. This intense drama is infused with considerable fright through the chilling performance of Widmark, an insidious road house owner bent on killing his best friend. The film opens with Widmark, who operates an upscale club in a small community close to the Canadian border. Wilde is his best friend, who manages Widmark's club. They have enjoyed hunting and fishing together since their youthful days, but their camaraderie disintegrates as soon as Lupino arrives to be Widmark's star attraction as a torch singer. Her throaty blues singing soon packs in audiences captivated by her sultry style and smoky delivery. Widmark is immediately attracted to her, but she only has eyes for the darkly handsome Wilde, who keeps his distance from her, knowing that his boss and buddy Widmark has made an unofficial claim on the sexy Lupino. Holm, who works at the club as its bookkeeper and cashier, loves Wilde from afar, but never lets him know about her deep affection for him. After Widmark leaves to go hunting, however, Wilde eventually succumbs to Lupino's advances and they fall in love, and get married. Wilde breaks that jolting news to Widmark when he returns, and Widmark abruptly breaks off his friendship with Wilde, who quits. Wilde later leaves a note for Widmark, telling him that he has taken $600 for back wages due him. Widmark, seething with hatred for Wilde for winning Lupino's heart, destroys Wilde's note, and then accuses Wilde of stealing all of the week's receipts from the club, about $2,600. Wilde is arrested and charged with robbery while the savvy Lupino immediately deduces that Widmark has set up Wilde and accuses Widmark of framing her husband. Convicted of grand larceny, Wilde is sentenced to two years, but Widmark, playing the part of an old and forgiving friend, prevents Wilde from going to prison. He convinces the judge to parole Wilde into his custody for that two-year period and where Wilde will continue to work for Widmark, the amount stolen deducted from his paychecks. Wilde and Lupino now realize that Widmark has trapped both of them by compelling Wilde to his servitude where he can control both of their lives. Widmark then begins a sadistic routine of demeaning Wilde and Lupino as they continue to work at his club and where their lives are strained and tormented by Widmark's constant insinuation that Wilde is a thief not to be trusted and must be always watched. He then pretends to soften his attitude, arranging for a friendly hunting trip at his remote lodge, which is located only a few miles from the Canadian border. Widmark believes that that proximity to the border will tempt Wilde to make a break for freedom by slipping into Canada to escape Widmark's stranglehold on his life. At that time, Widmark plans to kill Wilde as an escaped felon breaking his parole. He, Wilde, Lupino and Holm go to the lodge where Widmark pretends to be careless with his rifle, hoping that Wilde will attempt to take it and where he can then shoot Wilde. He insults both Wilde and Lupino until Lupino explodes and outwardly accuses Widmark of stealing his own money and wrongly blaming Wilde for the theft. Widmark hits her so hard that he knocks her down, and Wilde leaps forward, struggling with Widmark, knocking him unconscious. He and Lupino then flee, running through the dense woods and heading for the Canadian border. Meanwhile, Holm rummages through the pockets of the unconscious Widmark, and finds a deposit slip for the stolen money. This evidence will prove that Widmark banked the money and then falsely claimed it was stolen to frame Wilde. She runs through the woods with this evidence to give to Wilde, but Widmark, who has regained consciousness, tracks her and shoots Holm, who nevertheless manages to find Wilde and Lupino and where she delivers that evidence before collapsing. Widmark is now hunting the fugitives in the dense wood, which is also shrouded by a thick fog. As he approaches their position, Wilde and Lupino find a motorboat, but, instead of escaping in it, they start the boat and send it into the lake without any occupants. Widmark arrives at the shore and begins firing at the boat sputtering through the fog, but Wilde attacks him, knocking the rifle from his hands. When Widmark breaks free, he sees Lupino holding the rifle and he grabs a rock, intending to crush her head with it. Lupino acts first, firing the rifle before Widmark can reach her and Widmark falls dead. Wilde then picks up the wounded Holm and he begins to carry her back to safety with Lupino at his side. Negulesco directs this film noir tale with great style, using deep focus and many long shots to accent Lupino's singing performances and where his fog-bound wilderness scenes are fraught with tension. Widmark's performance oozes evil, and Lupino is superb as the world weary honky-tonk singer. Wilde is impressive as the deliberate and resolute lover, and Holm gives an empathetic performance as a selfless woman loving a man who belongs to

Richard Widmark and Celeste Holm in *Road House*, 1948.

someone else. The script presents a twisty tale that is peppered with sharp-tongued dialog, all of its characters sharply defined as they are eventually engulfed by the machinations of a sinister man with only homicide on his mind. (Widmark's plan to set up Wilde as his human prey at the end of this film where he plans to hunt him like a wild animal in the wilderness is not unlike the maniacal lifestyle exampled by the lunatic hunter in **The Most Dangerous Game**, 1932.) Songs: "One for My Baby (And One More for the Road)" (music: Harold Arlen; lyrics: Johnny Mercer), "Again" (1948; music: Lionel Newman; lyrics: Dorcas Cochran), "The Right Kind" (music: Lionel Newman, Charles Henderson; lyrics: Don George), "There'll Be Changes Made" (Billy Higgins, W. Benton Overstreet), "Elsa's Dream" (from "Lohengrin" by Richard Wagner). *Author's Note*: Zanuck told this author that "a lot of directors turned down the script for **Road House**, all telling me that they could never get the right actor to play the murderous nightclub owner. I knew that we had just such an actor under contract and that was Dick [Widmark], who had already played ruthless killers in his first two pictures for us [**The Kiss of Death**, 1947, and **The Street with No Name**, 1948]. I finally hired Jean Negulesco, who had been fired at Warner Brothers after he had a run-in with Jack Warner. Jean was a master at directing top crime pictures, such as **The Mask of Dimitrios** [1944] and **Three Strangers** [1946], pictures he had done for Warner Brothers, and I knew he was perfect for **Road House**." Negulesco agreed with Zanuck, telling this author that "Dick Widmark was the only actor I ever met who could give you a smile with a snarl behind it. He has an expressive face that can telegraph insincerity while he appears to be sincere. There is an uncanny sneakiness about him that no other actor possesses, so he was just right for the role of Jefty [Widmark's character] in **Road House**. The only thing I told him before we went into production for that picture was 'just be your old evil self, Dick.'" Lupino enjoyed making this film, telling this author that "they let me sing my own songs in that picture instead of dubbing my voice, which always happened when I was at Warner Brothers. **Road House** was a breakaway picture for me where I escaped from the contract clutches of Jack Warner, who was always giving me hand-me-down scripts Bette Davis had rejected. At Warner Brothers I was a second-hand substitute for Bette. At Fox I was my own person." Holm, who liked appearing in **Road House**, had nothing but admiration for Lupino, who went on to become the only female director of note during the late 1940s. Holm told this author: "Ida was a tough cookie, who learned all about directing when she was an actress at Warner Brothers. In those days, she always paled around with directors, picking up their tricks and techniques, and she would later use all that when directing her own films. She is not only a gifted actress, but one of the best directors around, male or female. She was terrific in **Road House** as a torch singer. When we did that picture together, she re-

Warner Baxter and Fredric March in *The Road to Glory*, 1936.

minded me much of Bette Davis. Ida has a strong personality and is very forceful before the cameras. Both of these actresses are small women [Lupino standing five feet, four-inches; Davis at five feet, three inches], and I always thought that the smaller the package, the bigger is the firecracker inside of it. [Holm stood five feet, six-inches.] Both have explosive temperaments, but Ida has a slow fuse and Bette short one. When they ignite, it's the Fourth of July." Widmark was grateful to Zanuck and Negulesco for casting him in the role of the homicidal club owner, but, as he told this author: "Zanuck promised me that he would be giving me different parts in the future where I would be playing the hero and not the crumb-bum. He pointed out to me that my character in **Road House** had a lot more depth to him than the nutcases I had played in a couple of previous pictures for Fox, and he was right. **Road House** is a different kind of crime picture because of its psychological approach to my character, a guy who slowly turns into a slippery killer. It took a very careful director like Jean Negulesco to effectively develop that kind of character with me. That was all Zanuck's doing. The reason why Fox films were mostly always successful was because Zanuck had started as a writer and was always a writer at heart when he ran the studio. He knew what stories would click with the public and **Road House** was one of those stories." **p**, Edward Chodorov; **d**, Jean Negulesco; **cast**, Ida Lupino, Cornel Wilde, Celeste Holm, Richard Widmark, O.Z. Whitehead, Robert Karnes, George Beranger, Ian MacDonald, Grandon Rhodes, Louis Bacigalupi; **w**, Chodorov (based on a story by Margaret Gruen, Oscar Saul); **c**, Joseph LaShelle; **m**, Cyril Mockridge; **ed**, James B. Clark; **art d**, Lyle Wheeler, Maurice Ransford; **set d**, Thomas Little; **spec eff**, Fred Sersen.

Road to Bali ★★★ 1952; U.S.; 91m; PAR; Color; Comedy/Musical; Children: Acceptable; **DVD**; **VHS**; **IV**. Good entertainment can be found in Hope and Crosby's sixth "Road" film in more than twelve years where the boys are vaudevillians in Australia. They are run out of Melbourne by fathers of young women to whom they have made marriage promises they didn't intend to keep. They take jobs as divers for Vye, who sails them to a Pacific island where they meet wealthy Lamour, wearing her traditional sarong. There they prevent Vye from stealing her fortune and Crosby winds up with both Lamour and Jane Russell in a cameo role. Along the way, the boys fight cannibals, a giant squid, crazed animals, and predatory women. Dean Martin and Jerry Lewis appear in cameo roles as does Bing's brother, Bob Crosby, and there is a scene from **The African Queen**, 1951, with Humphrey Bogart and Katharine Hepburn hauling the boat of that name through a swamp. A lot of laughs are provided in this delightful romp, including some very good songs: "Chicago Style," "Moon Flowers," "Hoot Moon," "The Merry Go Runaround," "To See You" (music: Jimmy Van Heusen;

lyrics: Johnny Burke); "The Whiffenpoof Song" (music: Tod B. Galloway; lyrics: George S. Pomeroy, Meade Minnigerode). This film was the only one in the series that was shot in color. The other six films in the seven-film series are **The Road to Hong Kong**, 1962; **Road to Morocco**, 1942; **Road to Rio**, 1947; **Road to Singapore**, 1940; **Road to Utopia**, 1946; and **Road to Zanzibar**, 1941. **p**, Harry Tugend, Daniel Dare; **d**, Hal Walker; **cast**, Bing Crosby, Bob Hope, Dorothy Lamour, Murvyn Vye, Peter Coe, Ralph Moody, Leon Askin, Michael Ansara, Carolyn Jones, Patricia Dane; **w**, Frank Butler, Hal Kanter, William Morrow (based on a story by Butler, Tugend); **c**, George Barnes (Technicolor); **m**, Joseph J. Lilley; **ed**, Archie Marshek; **art d**, Hal Pereira, J. McMillan Johnson; **set d**, Sam Cromer, Ross Dowd; **spec eff**, Farciot Edouart, Gordon Jennings, Paul K. Lerpae.

The Road to Glory ★★★ 1936; U.S.; 103m; FOX; B/W; War Drama; Children: Unacceptable; **DVD**. Gritty, grim war tale sees a powerful performance from Baxter, who is a regimental commander of French troops during WWI (1914-1918). Living on aspirin and cognac, he is shown addressing new replacements, giving them an encouraging speech about duty, honor and country, but knowing that many of these young men will soon die in taking only a small amount of territory that will be lost the next day to the German enemy. He and his men are fighting an attritional war where great numbers of lives are spent in capturing a line of trenches in see-saw battles that never end in victory for either side. March, a young officer full of ideals and hope for the future, joins the unit and is soon in conflict with Baxter over the affections of Lang, a beautiful nurse. Baxter's life becomes more complicated when his own aged father, Barrymore, arrives as a replacement, a man who has fought at Sedan during the Franco-Prussian War (1870-1871). Barrymore's presence and Baxter's deep concerns about his safety causes Baxter to more heavily depend on liquor. When ordered to mount another senseless attack, Baxter leads the assault himself and is blinded by an explosion. When he returns for aid to a field hospital, Barrymore offers to be his eyes and patriotically leads Baxter to the front where they both spot enemy positions for French artillery and are killed in the intensive barrage. March is then promoted to the command of the regiment, supported by Lang, but he winds up giving the same routine speech to newly arriving replacements earlier uttered by the slain Baxter. Like Baxter, he knows he has spoken empty words to inspire his men to battle and, like Baxter, no longer believes in those words, as he, too, is completely disillusioned with the seemingly endless war. Hawks does a fine job with this good character study of soldiers at war, dwelling on the demands of command and the cruel orders given to men without much hope of survival (not unlike the commanding officers in **The Dawn Patrol**, 1930, and its fine 1938 remake, as well as **Journey's End**, 1930, and **What Price Glory**, 1926, and its good 1952 remake). Baxter gives an extraordinary performance as the commander haunted by guilt for sending men to their death, as do Barrymore as the old soldier and March as the young officer who assumes Baxter's terrible mantle at the end. Song: "La Marseillaise" (Claude Joseph Roget de Lisle), "Ave Maria" (Franz Schubert). *Author's Note*: Unlike the jarring and memorable battle scenes Hawks would direct in another stirring film about WWI, **Sergeant York**, 1941(although he would also borrow some scenes for that film from **The Fighting 69th**, 1940), he relied almost entirely on battle scenes from a French film, **Wooden Crosses**, 1932, when making **The Road to Glory**. "I had no choice," he told this author, "as Fox had purchased the rights to that French production, but never had any intention of distributing it in the U.S. Producers only wanted the superb battle scenes from that picture and intended to wrap a different story line around those scenes. That's where I came in. They hired me to put that story together and I did, with the help of a great writer, William Faulkner. He wrote in long hand and I picked up what he wrote every day, about thirty finely written pages each day. I think Bill finished the script in about a week and then went on a two-week bender. I called him some time after that and asked him about a scene he had written for **The Road to Glory** and he said: 'I can't remember a word I wrote about that picture.'" March was full of praise for Hawks and his co-stars in this film, telling this author that "Warner [Baxter] was always a much underrated actor. He was never more intense and effective than as the tormented commander of troops at the front in **Road to Glory**. He gave a performance that I could never have equaled. Lionel was also excellent in his role as the old soldier and I still recall one of his most memorable scenes in that picture just before he and Warner are about to be killed in action and where Lionel produces his old bugle from an earlier war and patriotically blows upon it, as if summoning the ghosts of those long-ago soldiers to come to their aid. That was one of the last pictures where Lionel was able to walk and move around freely. He suffered from severe arthritis in his legs and even took morphine to dull the pain. He later broke his hip, not once, but twice, and, by the late 1930s, he was acting from a wheelchair. He was just as powerful in that wheelchair as he was when he was moving up and down trenches in **The Road to Glory**. Hawks did a wonderful job with that picture and presented many tension-filled scenes. One of them is where the French troops are listening to German sappers digging beneath our position, knowing they are planting explosives and intending to blow us all up. All the French soldiers can do is wait for their own deaths and those scenes of waiting that Hawks filmed are some of the most anxious moments ever put on the screen." **p**, Darryl F. Zanuck; **d**, Howard Hawks; **cast**, Fredric March, Warner Baxter, Lionel Barrymore, June Lang, Gregory Ratoff, Victor Kilian, John Qualen, Theodore von Eltz, Paul Fix, Leonid Kinskey; **w**, Joel Sayre, William Faulkner (based on the film "Les croix des bois" directed by Raymond Bernard and the novel by Roland Dorgeles); **c**, Gregg Toland; **m**, R.H. Bassett; **ed**, Edward Curtiss; **art d**, Hans Peters; **set d**, Thomas Little.

The Road to Hong Kong ★★★ 1962; U.S./U.K.; 91m; Melnor/UA; B/W; Comedy/Musical; Children: Acceptable; **DVD**; **VHS**; **IV**. In their seventh and final "Road" film, Crosby and Hope give up being vaude-villains to become con men trying to sell a "Fly-it-Yourself" space kit for interplanetary travel. When police pursue them, Hope takes a fall and is then taken to a hospital where he is treated by Sellers, an Indian doctor, who says Hope has amnesia and has forgotten that women exist. Crosby learns of a drug that can restore Hope's memory, but it can only be found in a Tibetan lamasery. They go there and meet Niven, a monk, and the head lama, Aylmer, who administers the drug, which restores Hope's memory. They go to an airport intending to return to the U.S. and meet beautiful Collins, who is a spy for an organization planning to conquer the world by taking over space. She thinks Hope is a fellow spy and reveals to him a stolen Russian formula for a secret rocket fuel. The villains, led by Morley, capture the boys and put them aboard a rocket ship that sends them around the moon before returning them safely to Hong Kong. They escape up some alleys and encounter Lamour, in a cameo role, singing in a nightclub. She helps them capture Morley and his gang. The boys then stumble into a rocket ship that takes them to a remote planet where they meet Frank Sinatra and Dean Martin, also in cameo roles as space travelers. This entry provides a lot of fun and some memorable songs, including "Personality," "Teamwork," "Warmer Than a Whisper," "The Road to Hong Kong," "Let's Not Be Sensible" (music: Jimmy Van Heusen; lyrics: Sammy Cahn). The other six films in the seven-film series are **Road to Bali**, 1952; **Road to Morocco**, 1942; **Road to Rio**, 1947; **Road to Singapore**, 1940; **Road to Utopia**, 1946; and **Road to Zanzibar**, 1941. **p**, Melvin Frank; **d**, Norman Panama; **cast**, Bing Crosby, Bob Hope, Joan Collins, Peter Sellers, Robert Morley, Felix Aylmer, Katya Douglas, Roger Delgado, Robert Ayres, Mei Ling; **w**, Panama, Frank; **c**, Jack Hildyard; **m**, Robert Farnon; **ed**, Alan Osbiston, John C. Smith, John Victor-Smith; **prod d**, Roger K. Furse; **art d**, Syd Cain, William Hutchinson; **set d**, Maurice Fowler; **spec eff**, Wally Veevers, Ted Samuels.

Road to Morocco ★★★★ 1942; U.S.; 81m; PAR; B/W; Comedy; Chil-

Bing Crosby, Dorothy Lamour and Bob Hope in *Road to Morocco,* **1942.**

dren: Acceptable; **DVD**; **VHS**. In this third of the series, which is arguably the best of the seven films, the inimitable crooner, Crosby, and irrepressible comic, Hope, provide non stop entertainment with a bevy of good songs and a gaggle of laughable gags. Having established their winning formula by spoofing film genres in **The Road to Singapore**, 1940 (adventure films), and **The Road to Zanzibar**, 1941 (jungle films), the boys present a grand lampoon of the Arabian Nights. Again, the object of their collective eyes is the sultry Lamour, and this time their sword-slashing nemesis is the villainous hoarse-voiced and swarthy Quinn. The boys are shown as the lone survivors of a shipwreck, making it ashore to wander around in the desert until saved by a meandering camel that takes them to a Moroccan town. They soon discover that not is all well in this land of a 1001 nights, the people suffering from poverty and oppression from the local sheik, Quinn. Worse, Crosby and Hope are starving and do not have a penny to buy a stale crust of bread. When the boys enter a restaurant, the proprietor is leery about their ability to pay for their meals, especially when they start ordering everything on the menu. Smoothie Crosby settles that problem by selling Hope to slave-buyer Seymour, without Hope's knowledge, of course. Hope has a conniption fit over such flesh peddling, but soon warms to the idea when he learns that he is to be the personal pet of alluring princess Lamour. Meanwhile, Crosby receives a visit in his dreams from the ghost of Hope's aunt, played by Hope in wig and nanny dress, who berates him for selling her naïve nephew. Now full of suitable guilt, Crosby ventures to the palace in an attempt to rescue his suckered partner, only to find Hope living in the lap of Lamour and luxury. He learns that Hope is to be Lamour's next husband, a fate Hope looks forward to with salivating lips. Little does he know (and Hope knows little or nothing about the plot turns of this or any other film in the wacky series) that his marriage to Lamour will be short-lived. Sokoloff, who is Lamour's personal astrologer, has read in the stars that Hope is the man she is to marry, but as the first of two husbands, in that he will die a short time after the nuptials and she will then marry the man of her dreams. Crosby arrives at the palace and is barely tolerated by Hope, who wants his former friend to disappear, but Lamour is enchanted by Crosby's singing and the two begin a relationship. Meanwhile, Drake, Lamour's foremost lady-in-waiting, falls for Hope, telling him of his dire fate as predicted by Sokoloff. Quinn then storms into the palace as he has staked a claim on Lamour and, when hearing that Hope is her intended, thinks to behead the interloper on the spot. He searches the palace for Hope, as well as chum Crosby, and both disguise themselves as two nodding decapitated heads along a line of other such gruesome artifacts in a strange trophy room where Quinn ignores them. Lamour then tells Quinn that poor Hope has but a short time on earth, according to soothsayer Sokoloff. She promises Quinn, more to save Hope's life at the moment than any

Jude Law, cameraman and killer, in *Road to Perdition*, 2002.

real desire to marry ruffian Quinn, that, after Hope goes to the beyond, she will wed him. The mollified Quinn storms off, and Crosby and Hope now try to figure a way to get out of their dangerous dilemma. Sokoloff then reveals a new discovery in his telescope, saying that his original prediction was all wrong because a swarm of insects clouded his vision. When Quinn learns that Hope will have a long life after marrying Lamour, he takes action, capturing Crosby and Hope and taking them into the desert where he expects they will soon perish for lack of water. Instead, they find a tribe of Arabs opposed to Quinn and they lead these insurgents in an attack against Quinn's bastion just before he is about to marry Lamour. Quinn is defeated, and Lamour is rescued. The next scene has Crosby paired with Lamour and Hope with Drake as they sail on board a ship bound for more civilized climes, but Hope ends that idyllic cruise when he wanders into the ship's hold with a lighted cigarette that eventually ignites a cargo of explosives that blows up the vessel. Crosby, Lamour, Hope and Drake are next seen on a raft drifting to nowhere and where thirst and hunger take over Hope's fragile mind, causing him to go into hysterics, crying out: "No food, no water—I can't take it!" He raves on until Crosby quietly points out to him that they are sailing into New York harbor, which is shown in the background, and will soon be safe. Hope then shouts at Crosby: "You spoiled the only good scene I had in the movie! If you had kept your mouth shut I might have won an Academy Award!" (Hope was forever bemoaning over the decades how he had been overlooked by the Academy in not bestowing upon him the coveted Oscar.) The wacky film comes to an end when the camel that had rescued Crosby and Hope in the early scenes reappears to address the viewer by saying: "This is the screwiest picture I have ever been in!" Screwy or not, this one was a delight, packed with inside jokes of the day. The paddy-cake routine between Crosby and Hope where they slap each other's hands before throwing punches at adversaries in opposite directions backfires on them in this film when Quinn steps aside and knocks their heads together. At that moment, Crosby, shaking away double vision, says: "That gag sure got around." In the scene where Hope's aunt lambasts Crosby in his dreams, the old lady, speaking from a heavenly domain, says: "I can't talk now—here comes Mr. Jordan," which is a reference to the popular fantasy film of that era, **Here Comes Mr. Jordan**, 1941. Crosby's singing voice was never in better pitch, and Hope's funny antics highlight the hilarity in this Middle East sendup. Songs: "Moonlight Becomes You," "Constantly," "Ain't Got a Dime to My Name (Ho Hum)," "(We're Off on the) Road to Morocco" (1942; music: Jimmy Van Heusen; lyrics: Johnny Burke). *Author's Note*: Hope told this author that "Bing is victimizing me again in that picture, but his schemes only land me into Dorothy Lamour's harem. What a way to be victimized!" Crosby told this author that "**The Road to Morocco** was very funny because Tony

[Quinn] played his role of the slaughtering sheik as a straight man, just like he did in **Road to Singapore** [1940]. If you don't have a good straight man to bounce the jokes off of, nothing really works well. Tony was a great bouncing board." The other six films in the seven-film series are **Road to Bali**, 1952; **The Road to Hong Kong**, 1962; **Road to Rio**, 1947; **Road to Singapore**, 1940; **Road to Utopia**, 1946; and **Road to Zanzibar**, 1941. **p**, Paul Jones; **d**, David Butler; **cast**, Bing Crosby, Bob Hope, Dorothy Lamour, Anthony Quinn, Dona Drake, Vladimir Sokoloff, Mikhail Rasumny, George Givot, Abner Biberman, Monte Blue, Yvonne De Carlo; **w**, Frank Butler, Don Hartman; **c**, William C. Mellor; **m**, Victor Young; **ed**, Irene Morra; **art d**, Hans Dreier, Robert Usher; **spec eff**, Farciot Edouart, Gordon Jennings.

Road to Perdition ★★★ 2002; U.S.; 117m; DreamWorks; Color; Crime Drama; Children: Unacceptable (MPAA: R); **BD**; **DVD**; **VHS**. Gritty and absorbing crime tale set in the early 1930s presents a lot of fanciful mob characters based on real persons, but have no credibility in fact as is the case in the pulp novel upon which this film is based. Hanks' is a family man who also works as an enforcer for an Irish mob in a northern Indiana town that borders on Chicago. Newman is the old man who heads that mob and who has raised the orphaned Hanks since boyhood and considers him a second son to his real offspring, Craig, an irresponsible killer insanely jealous of Hanks' close association with his father. Newman gives Craig and Hanks orders to quell the violent activities of a satellite gang by sending them to see that mob boss, Hinds. The impulsive Craig, however, shoots and kills Hinds, compelling enforcer Hanks to mow down Hinds' henchmen, all of this witnessed by Hanks young son, Hoechlin, who has stowed away in Hanks' car on that stormy and fateful night. Newman does not sanction his son's actions, but he wants Craig to go on living as his closest blood relative. Craig, to cover his tracks, thinks to kill everyone knowing of the hit, and murders Hanks' wife and younger son. Hanks pursues the evasive Craig, but Craig disappears, going into hiding. Realizing he is out of a job, Hanks travels with Hoechlin to Chicago where he tries to get a job as an enforcer with the Al Capone mob. He gets an appointment with mob underboss Frank Nitti (1886-1943), played by Tucci, but not before Tucci meets with Newman. Tucci politely turns down Hanks and then tells Newman that Hanks has departed, and Newman, knowing that Hanks' is seeking vengeance for the murders of his family members and fearing for Craig's life, gives Law a murder contract for Hanks. Law is a crime scene photographer, who also works as a killer for hire and, he begins tracking Hanks. Now on the run, Hanks drives away and stops at a remote diner to have dinner with Hoechlin, but he realizes that Law is trailing him and he escapes with his son, puncturing the tires of Law's car before driving away. Hanks then takes on the Capone mob by robbing banks where Capone money is stashed and where Hoechlin acts as his getaway driver after Hanks teaches the boy how to drive a car. The mob then begins withdrawing its hidden caches of money from these small-town banks, and Hanks then meets with Newman's accountant, Baker, in order to obtain the mob's ledgers that will prove to Newman that his son, Craig, has been embezzling great sums of money from him over the years. The meeting is a setup where Law is waiting for Hanks. In the ensuing gun battle, Baker is killed and both Hanks and Law are wounded. Hanks, who has taken the revealing ledgers, has been wounded in the shoulder and cannot drive. Hoechlin drives him to a remote farm where an elderly couple tends to Hanks' wound, and he and his son grow closer together. Before they depart, Hanks gives the couple some of his stolen money and then meets with Newman while the mob boss is attending church. He gives Newman the ledgers, but Newman already knows that his son has been embezzling from him and says that he believes that Craig will be killed either by mobsters or by Hanks, but he cannot give up on his own son. He tells Hanks to escape with his own son while he can and says a sad goodbye. Instead, Hanks waits for Newman to show up with his entire mob and, during a rainstorm, withdraws a Thompson submachine gun and begins firing away, mowing down all of Newman's gunmen. He then walks up to Newman, who tells him he is glad he is about to be killed by him, and Hanks shoots Newman to death. Now that Newman is gone, Tucci tells Hanks where Craig is hiding, but on the promise that, after he dispatches the berserk Craig, the blood feud will end. Hanks goes to the hotel where Craig is hiding and kills him and then takes Hoechlin to a remote cottage on the shores of Lake Michigan. Law finds him there and mortally wounds Hanks. Hoechlin aims a gun at Law, but does not have the will to kill him. Hanks, however, withdraws his own gun and kills Law and then dies in Hoechlin's arms, hoping he will not grow up to lead his kind of life. Hoechlin goes to live with the childless elderly couple and, growing up and recalling all these terrible events from his childhood, is asked if his father was a good or bad man and he only replies: "He was my father." Somber, even depressing at times, this film presents superlative production values with great cinematography that captures all the gruesome action and where the period sets, costume and cars are appropriate to the era they represent. The acting is sometimes superior, except that the adults often appear too stoic, some to the point of being automatons and as if mimicking each other's pensiveness to give deeper meaning to characters that inherently have no deeper meaning. The sound throughout is too often unprofessional and where many of the actors swallow their words or simply cannot be understood through mumbling and here director Mendes is to blame. This is an ongoing problem with even the best films in the last twenty or so years where directors fail to have leading players simply pronounce and articulate words that can be understood by the viewer, this most likely resulting from star status intimidation where directors are secondary to present-day leading players. Such titular directors would never dare to demand that a Tom Hanks or a Russell Crowe speak from the diaphragm so that their words could be understood as clearly as was that of Cary Grant, Clark Gable, Errol Flynn, Humphrey Bogart, or even Peter Lorre in every one of his clearly enunciated lines in the Mr. Moto series. The viewer must suspend any belief in the preposterous story line of **Road to Perdition**, which is as childishly far-fetched as is Hoechlin's perspectives of his errant father, naively relying upon boogeymen stereotypes, but this is more of a grim comic version of that mobster era than a film purporting to present any accurate recreations based upon known reality. The use of the ledgers to implicate a thieving member of the mob is lifted from scenes in **The Untouchables**, 1987, where ledgers were acquired to bring about the tax evasion conviction and imprisonment of mob boss Al Capone (1899-1947), who is played in this film by Anthony LaPaglia. His only scene in the film was deleted before the film's theatrical release, although it appears in the DVD release as an outtake. For reliable details on Capone and Nitti, see my books *World Encyclopedia of Organized Crime* (Paragon House, 1992; Capone: pages 78-98; Nitti: page 302) and *The Great Pictorial History of World Crime*, Volume I (History, Inc., 2004; Capone and Nitti: pages 503-541). **p**, Sam Mendes, Richard D. Zanuck, Dean Zanuck; **d**, Mendes; **cast**, Tom Hanks, Tyler Hoechlin, Paul Newman, Jude Law, Daniel Craig, Jennifer Jason Leigh, Stanley Tucci, Liam Aiken, Ciarán Hinds, Craig Spidle, Dylan Baker, Ian Barford; **w**, David Self (based on the graphic novel by Max Allan Collins, Richard Piers Rayner); **c**, Conrad L. Hall (Technicolor); **m**, Thomas Newman; **ed**, Jill Bilcock; **prod d**, Dennis Gassner; **art d**, Richard L. Johnson; **set d**, Nancy Haigh; **spec eff**, Allen L. Hall, William Dambra.

Road to Rio ★★★★ 1947; U.S.; 100m; PAR; B/W; Comedy/Musical; Children: Acceptable; **DVD**; **VHS**. Delightful film where Paramount writers discarded the zaniness and talking animals of the earlier entries in the series, opting for a straightforward comedy that proved to be the top box office grosser of the year. In this fifth entry of the series, Crosby and Hope are bumbling circus musicians who accidentally set fire to the big tent and flee from the police, stowing away on board a luxury liner heading for Rio de Janeiro. They meet ravishing Lamour, preventing her from jumping overboard in what seems to be a suicidal act. She thanks them, but is alternately friendly and outgoing toward them and,

Bing Crosby, Dorothy Lamour and Bob Hope in *Road to Rio*, 1947.

without reason or rhyme, suddenly gives them the cold shoulder as if they were suffering from leprosy. She turns them over to the ship's captain as stowaways. Her inexplicably weird attitude dumbfounds them, but provides for many hilarious scenes. They then meet Lamour's eerie-looking aunt, Sondergaard, who is a hypnotist. The boys finally realize that Lamour is under the manipulative mental sway of the evil Sondergaard. Meanwhile, when landing at Rio, the boys look about for employment and hear that Paiva, who operates an upscale nightclub, is looking for an act featuring Americans. Crosby and Hope then find the three Wiere Brothers, who are performers that do a manic acrobatic act. Unfortunately, they do not speak a word of English. To pass them off to Paiva as Americans and as part of their act, Crosby and Hope train these three weirdo brothers to utter a few American phrases, assigning a phrase to each brother: "You're in the groove, Jackson"; "This is murder"; and "You're telling me." They then all go to work at Paiva's nightclub, but he soon discovers the ruse (in what is another hilarious scene where the Weire Brothers misapply their phrases to all the wrong meanings and drive Paiva to the brink of a nervous breakdown). Again out of work, Crosby and Hope discover that the sinister Sondergaard has been hypnotizing Lamour into believing that she wants to marry Sondergaard's brother so that Sondergaard can control some secret papers connected to Lamour. At the last minute, Crosby and Hope crash the wedding ceremony with Crosby impersonating a pirate and Hope as a Latin American bombshell in drag á la Carmen Miranda. The guests believe them to be entertainers hired for the occasion, but their ruse is exposed by Sondergaard and her henchmen. A chase ensues, but the boys find the "secret papers" Sondergaard so jealously covets. Crosby and Hope bring the baddies to justice, but not without the help of zany comedian Jerry Colonna, who was a regular on Bob Hope's popular radio show, and who rides to the rescue with a horde of U.S. cavalry troopers, at the end of that scene the pop-eyed Colonna saying: "Exciting, wasn't it?" After Hope asks Crosby what the secret papers were all about (a question undoubtedly asked by every viewer of this film), he turns to the camera to say: "The world must never know." Unlike the endings of other films in the series, it is Hope, not Crosby, who ends up with the luscious Lamour. Crosby cannot figure that out and, after Hope and Lamour marry and go to Niagara Falls on their honeymoon, Crosby tags along, to make a startling discovery. He peeps through the keyhole of their honeymoon suite (the camera POV) to see that Hope is again hypnotizing Lamour as he has been doing all along in getting her to marry him. Director McLeod, who specialized in comedies, provides a great one here with so many sight gags and comedic routines that it is hard to keep up with them as they whizz from scene to scene and where Crosby and Hope are at their delightful best. Lamour provides just the right amount of allure and romance and the eyebrow-arched Sondergaard is

Dorothy Lamour, Bing Crosby and Bob Hope in *Road to Singapore*, 1940.

energetically evil. This film was an enormous success at the box office, taking in more than $4.5 million in its initial release. Songs: "You Don't Have to Know the Language," "Experience," "Apalachicola, FLA," "But Beautiful," "For What?" (music: Jimmy Van Heusen; lyrics: Johnny Burke); "Tiz Que Tem" (Hannibal Cruz, Vicente Paiva); "Batuque Nio Morro [Jam Session in the Hills]" (Russo de Pandeiro, Sa Roris); "Maria" (Luiz Peixoto); "Olha Ella" (Russo de Pandeiro); "Cavaquinho" (Ernesto Nazareth). *Author's Note*: Director McLeod told this author that "Paramount wanted a more structured comedy for **Road to Rio** than what Bing [Crosby] and Bob [Hope] had been doing in that series in the past. In those earlier pictures, their scenes were more or less ad-libbed. Not to say that they both didn't do that very same thing when we made **Road to Rio** together. I got a tight script and tried to have them stick to it, but that was impossible with those two. They did not stray too far from the script and what they added was pretty funny, so I kept those zinging one liners in the picture." Hope told this author that "**Road to Rio** had three of the goofiest-looking comedians I ever met, the Wiere Brothers. They cracked me up. They were a rage in Europe, but never caught on in pictures, which was too bad, because they really had great talent." Crosby praised another act appearing in this film, saying: "The Andrews Sisters were in that one with us and those gals were terrific. Their beat, tempo and harmony were the very best. No one could swing it better than those lovely ladies, absolutely no one." The other six films in the seven-film series are **Road to Bali**, 1952; **The Road to Hong Kong**, 1962; **Road to Morocco**, 1942; **Road to Singapore**, 1940; **Road to Utopia**, 1946; and **Road to Zanzibar**, 1941. **p**, Daniel Dare; **d**, Norman Z. McLeod; **cast**, Bing Crosby, Bob Hope, Dorothy Lamour, Gale Sondergaard, Jerry Colonna, Frank Faylen, Joseph Vitale, The Andrews Sisters (Patty, Maxene, Laverne Andrews), The Wiere Brothers; **w**, Edmund Beloin, Jack Rose; **c**, Ernest Laszlo; **m**, Robert Emmett Dolan; **ed**, Ellsworth Hoagland; **art d**, Hans Dreier, Earl Hedrick; **set d**, Sam Comer, Ray Moyer; **spec eff**, Farciot Edouart, Gordon Jennings, Paul Lerpae.

Road to Singapore ★★★ 1940; 84m; PAR; B/W; Comedy; Children: Acceptable; **DVD**; **IV**. The first of the Crosby-Hope "Road" pictures, this entertaining romp opens with Coburn, a millionaire shipping tycoon, wanting his playboy son, Crosby, to shape up and take over the family business, but the son opts instead to go off with his pal, Hope, to the most remote place they can think of, which is Singapore, mostly to have Crosby escape his family responsibilities. The boys encounter adventure and romance with a beautiful native girl, Lamour. She is in a nightclub act with Quinn, who snaps a cigarette out of her mouth with a bullwhip. When Quinn becomes too demanding, the boys take her in as their housekeeper and vie over her affections. In the end, Crosby asks Lamour

to choose and she selects Hope, which shocks Crosby. He later learns that Lamour only picked Hope because she did not want to come between Crosby and a former flame, Barrett, even though she loves Crosby. After learning that Lamour longs only for him, Crosby books passage back to Singapore and finds Lamour, and the two get together, with Hope looking for romance elsewhere, which was the case in most of the "Road" films. This film does not have too many Hope one-liners, which were later to come in the series, but the film is nevertheless an entertaining comedy. The other six films in the series are: **Road to Zanzibar**, 1941, **Road to Morocco**, 1942, **Road to Utopia**, 1946, **Road to Rio**, 1947, **Road to Bali**, 1951, and **The Road to Hong Kong**, 1962. Songs: "Too Romantic," "Kaigoon," "Sweet Potato Piper," (1940: music: James V. Monaco; lyrics: Johnny Burke); "The Moon and the Willow Tree," "Captain Custard" (1940: music: Victor Schertzinger; lyrics: Johnny Burke). **p**, Harlan Thompson; **d**, Victor Schertzinger; **cast**, Bing Crosby, Dorothy Lamour, Bob Hope, Charles Coburn, Judith Barrett, Anthony Quinn; Jerry Colonna, Elvia Allman, Monte Blue, Bobby Barber; **w**, Don Hartman, Frank Butler, Barney Dean, Ray Golden, Sid Kuller (based on a story by Harry Hervey); **c**, William C. Mellor; **m**, Victor Young; **ed**, Paul Weatherwax; **art d**, Hans Dreier, Robert Odell; **spec eff**, Farciot Edouart.

Road to Utopia ★★★★ 1946; U.S.; 90m; PAR; B/W; Comedy/Musical; Children: Acceptable; **DVD**; **VHS**. In one of their most hilarious outings (fourth in the series), Crosby and Hope are inept miners during the Gold Rush. Their story is told in flashback as Hope and the fetching Lamour, shown in old age, recall their adventurous days in the Klondike. They are living in a mansion and enjoying the riches from a gold mine that brought them together, but at the expense of their close friend, Crosby. As they are musing through their memories, they hear the crooning voice of Crosby (singing "Sunday, Monday or Always," a tune he originally sang in the film **Dixie**, 1943, which also co-starred Lamour), and he appears to join in with their reminiscences. The viewer then sees in flashback how Crosby and Hope are San Francisco sideshow entertainers pretending to be magicians, gulling customers by doubling the money of the first sucker only to trick other suckers into losing their cash. When their scam is exposed, they run for their lives, stowing away on board a ship heading for the Klondike during the Gold Rush. In the process, they tie up two lethal miners, Barrat and Paiva, impersonating them by wearing fake beards and taking the deed to their gold mine. They are mistaken for these two roughnecks when they appear in Skagway where they meet Dumbrille, who believes they are the two killers he has sent for, hiring them to act as his bodyguards. They then meet seductive Lamour, who is singing in a dance hall, and she quickly makes a move on them in an attempt to get the deed to the gold mine, one that has been earlier stolen from her deceased father. Lamour first plies her wiles on Hope, but she quickly dumps him after learning that Crosby is holding the deed. When she goes after Crosby, she falls in love with him, losing her focus on the deed, even after he tells her that he and Hope are nothing but a couple of huckstering impersonators. The boys then include Lamour on the deal, agreeing to share the spoils from the gold mine, but they are then endangered when Barrat and Paiva show up, looking to even the score. By that time, the shifty Dumbrille has learned about the deed and he, too, is after the trio, who flee in a dogsled, racing across the frozen wastes with the bad guys in hot pursuit. The quarry is cornered on a frozen lake where the ice begins to break. Hope and Lamour are separated from Crosby as their section of ice begins to float away to safety, and it appears that Crosby will be left to the doom of drowning or being captured by the pursuing villains. Lamour goes on to marry Hope (in one of the rare instances of the series as Crosby usually gets Lamour), and, in flash,forward, we again see the trio talking in the mansion. Just as Crosby is about to depart, wishing his old friends well, they ask him to stay a moment so that he can meet their son, Junior. The son appears and he is the exact image of Crosby, and where the older Crosby gapes and gulps, until Hope turns to the camera, saying:

"We adopted him!" A lot of zany action and many sight gags (mostly culled from Hope's ongoing radio program, written by Panama and Frank, who also scripted this film and received an Oscar nomination) pepper the lively scenes, and several tunes from Jimmy van Heusen and Johnny Burke enliven and enchant along the way. This very funny film saw another great box office success, producing more than $4 million in its initial release. Songs: "Put It There, Pal," "It's Anybody's Spring," "Good Time Charlie," "Sunday, Monday or Always," "Welcome to My Dream," "Personality," "Would You?" (music: Jimmy Van Heusen; lyrics: Johnny Burke); "Jingle Bells" (1857; James Pierpont); "Bridal Chorus (Here Comes the Bride)" (1850; from "Lohengrin" by Richard Wagner). *Author's Note*: Crosby told this author that "Bob [Hope] had his jokesters working night and day producing gags for that picture and they produced so many one-liners that even a Henny Youngman couldn't count them." Hope told this author that "Bing [Crosby] gets to sing a lot in **The Road to Utopia**, but I get the girl at the end and if that isn't justice nothing is. He'd been hogging Dottie [Lamour] in the earlier films, but the writers turned the table on him in that picture." The other six films in the seven-film series are **Road to Bali**, 1952; **The Road to Hong Kong**, 1962; **Road to Morocco**, 1942; **Road to Rio**, 1947; **Road to Singapore**, 1940; and **Road to Zanzibar**, 1941. **p**, Paul Jones; **d**, Hal Walker; **cast**, Bing Crosby, Bob Hope, Dorothy Lamour, Hillary Brooke, Douglass Dumbrille, Jack La Rue, Robert Barrat, Nestor Paiva, George Anderson, Robert Benchley (narrator); **w**, Norman Panama, Melvin Frank; **c**, Lionel Lindon; **m**, Leigh Harline; **ed**, Stuart Gilmore; **art d**, Hans Dreier, Roland Anderson; **set d**, George Sawley; **spec eff**, Farciot Edouart.

Road to Zanzibar ★★★ 1941; U.S.; 90m; PAR; B/W; Comedy; Children: Acceptable; **DVD**; **IV**. In this second entry of the entertaining series, Crosby and Hope sell a phony gold mine to shady dealer Royce, escaping from him by going to Zanzibar. There they meet showgirls Lamour and Merkel, who are looking for Lamour's lost brother. The ladies talk the boys into taking them on a safari into the jungle to find that lost brother. From there, the film becomes a satire on jungle films in which the boys almost become dinner for hostile and hungry natives. Songs: "Road to Zanzibar," "You Lucky People," "African Etude," "You're Dangerous," "It's Always You" (music: Jimmy Van Heusen; lyrics: Johnny Burke); "Birds of a Feather" (Jimmy Van Heusen); "A'Frangesa" (Don Costa); "There's No Place Like Home/Home, Sweet Home" (1823: music: H.R. Bishop; lyrics: John Howard Payne); "Rockabye Baby" (traditional). *Author's Note*: The other six films in the seven-film series are **Road to Bali**, 1952; **The Road to Hong Kong**, 1962; **Road to Morocco**, 1942; **Road to Rio**, 1947; **Road to Singapore**, 1940; and **Road to Utopia**, 1946. **p**, Paul Jones; **d**, Victor Schertzinger; **cast**, Bing Crosby, Bob Hope, Dorothy Lamour, Una Merkel, Eric Blore, Douglass Dumbrille, Iris Adrian, Lionel Royce, Buck Woods, Leigh Whipper, Noble Johnson, Joan Marsh; **w**, Don Hartman, Frank Butler, Barney Dean (based on the story "Find Colonel Fawcett" by Hartman, Sy Bartlett); **c**, Ted Tetzlaff; **m**, Victor Young; **ed**, Alma Macrorie; **art d**, Hans Dreier, Robert Usher.

The Road Warrior ★★★ 1982; Australia; 94m; Kennedy Miller Productions/WB; Color; Adventure; Children: Unacceptable (MPAA: R); **BD**; **DVD**; **VHS**. Action-packed thriller sees Gibson (as Max), a cynical drifter, attempting to survive in a post-apocalyptic Australian wasteland. He is a former police officer whose wife and child were killed by marauding bikers. He wanders alone, except for his dog, in a supercharged car, armed with a sawed-off shotgun. He helps a small, gasoline-rich community of settlers to escape a horde of motorcycle-riding bandits who killed his family and want the gas, which has become a scarce and priceless commodity. Gibson leads a battle against the bikers that allows the settlers to reach the coast to establish a new civilization, but Gibson leaves the settlers, continuing his lonely life as a drifter. This film made a superstar of Gibson and became a huge financial success, taking in

Bruce Spence as gyro captain in *The Road Warrior*, 1982.

more than $23 million at the box office in its initial release against a $4.5 million budget. This is the sequel to **Mad Max**, 1979, which was followed by **Mad Max, Beyond the Thunderdome**, 1985. Excessive violence prohibits viewing by children. **p**, Byron Kennedy; **d**, George Miller; **cast**, Mel Gibson, Bruce Spence, Mike Preston, Max Phipps, Vernon Wells, Kjell Nilsson, Emil Minty, Virginia Hey, William Zappa, Arkie Whiteley; **w**, Terry Hayes, Miller, Brian Hannant; **c**, Dean Semler; **m**, Brian May; **ed**, David Stiven, Tim Wellburn, Michael Balson; **art d**, Graham "Grace" Walker; **spec eff**, Jeff Clifford, Kim Priest.

Roadblock ★★★ 1951; U.S; 73m; RKO; B/W; Crime Drama; Children: Unacceptable; **VHS**. McGraw gives an exceptional performance as an honest insurance investigator, who is corrupted by his greedy girlfriend, Dixon. She says she loves him, but wants a richer lifestyle than what he can provide from his job. They marry, and soon he becomes involved in a scheme to steal more than a million dollars in paper money before the cash can be destroyed. Events turn bad when a postal employee is killed and McGraw is framed for the man's death. He and Dixon try leaving a mountain hideout but are detoured by roadblocks. McGraw panics and drives through a concreted Los Angeles riverbed, and police, following his car, shoot and kill him. Song: "So Swell of You" (Leona Davidson). *Author's Note*: The vast concrete river drainage system in Los Angeles has been used for many action scenes in several films, most notably in **Them!**, 1954, where mutant ants take refuge and must be blasted and burned to extinction before they threaten all life on earth. **p**, Lewis J. Rachmil; **d**, Harold Daniels; **cast**, Charles McGraw, Joan Dixon, Lowell Gilmore, Louis Jean Heydt, Milburn Stone, Peter Brocco, Barry Brooks, John Butler, Ben Cameron, Dave Willock; **w**, Steve Fisher, George Bricker (based on a story by Richard Landau, Geoffrey Homes); **c**, Nicholas Musuraca; **m**, Paul Sawtell; **d**, Robert Golden; **art d**, Albert S. D'Agostino, Walter E. Keller; **set d**, Darrell Silvera, Jack Mills.

The Roaring Twenties ★★★★ 1939; U.S.; 104m; WB; B/W; Crime Drama; Children: Unacceptable; **DVD**; **VHS**. Cagney rivets as a tough gangster in this well-crafted crime saga that documents the rise and fall of the bootlegging era (Prohibition; 1919-1933). This compelling tale begins on the Western Front where doughboys Cagney, Bogart and Lynn are fighting in WWI (1914-1918). Bogart is clinging to the earth inside a crater in the middle of No-Man's-Land during a fierce barrage when another soldier, Cagney, dives into the crater to save his life. He lands squarely on top of Bogart, who roars: "You always come into a rat-hole like that?" Cagney spits back: "What do you want me to do? Knock?" Then Lynn spills into the crater to further annoy Bogart, who has a miserable temper and the character of a killer. The three of them are seen a

James Cagney and Humphrey Bogart in _The Roaring Twenties_, 1939.

short time later in a trench and, realizing that the war is coming to an end, talk about what they might do in civilian life. Bogart does not have time for such chatter as he peers intently through a gun port, adjusting the sight on his rifle and then slowly squeezes off a round, killing a young German soldier in the opposite trench. Bogart reveals his blood-thirsty nature by exclaiming about the young German soldier he has just killed: "He jumped up three feet and came down like a board!" Lynn says that, after the war, he plans to complete his studies and become an attorney, and Cagney says he will look up his old boss, who has been holding on to his job for him as a mechanic at a garage. Nothing so docile is envisioned by the ruthless Bogart. He fondles his rifle, more or less saying that the government spent a lot of money training him how to use his weapon and he intends to put it to good use when he is mustered out. Returning to New York, the three doughboys go their separate ways, Cagney returning to the garage where he once worked. His old boss welcomes him warmly and then asks him what he plans to do. Cagney tells him he wants his old job back, but the oily boss responds by saying that he had to hire replacements while he and others were overseas and he cannot fire those new employees. As Cagney leaves, two of the mechanics insult him, and he punches one of them, knocking him backward to take the other mechanic to the floor with him; Cagney gloats: "Two for one!" Cagney then looks up McHugh, an old friend who works as a cabdriver. He renews that friendship, giving McHugh a war souvenir, a German helmet, which McHugh fondly stores beneath his bed. Cagney then shows McHugh a picture of a beautiful girl (Lane), a young lady he has never met and who was his pen pal while he served overseas. He decides to see this girl for the first time, and McHugh drives him to Mineola, N.Y. (which is fifteen miles from Manhattan), but Cagney is in for the surprise of his life when he discovers that the girl in the picture is Lane, an impressionable teenager, who has a crush on him. Cagney makes excuses to leave immediately. When Lane asks him when she will see him again, he smiles and says: "When you grow up." Unable to find work, Cagney goes to work as a cabdriver, using McHugh's taxi when McHugh is off duty. One of his fares, a man, gives Cagney a few dollars to deliver a package to a nearby club, but when Cagney takes the package to George, who manages the club, she pretends she knows nothing about the package as two plainclothes policemen are present. One grabs the package and finds that it contains illegal liquor and he arrests Cagney and George for violating the newly established Prohibition Act that prohibits any making, distribution or consumption of alcohol. Cagney covers for George, and she is released, but he is thrown into a jail. He shares a cell with another former doughboy, who complains about not being able to find any work and how, if he had his old service rifle with him, he would use it to kill himself. Cagney tells him to forget about such thinking as he is bailed out of jail. He sees

McHugh and thanks him, but McHugh points out that George, the woman Cagney has shielded, has bailed him out. Cagney, who blames George for his arrest, grudgingly thanks her and she tells him that she thinks he is a "right guy" for not giving her away and shouldering the responsibility for delivering the liquor to her. She tells him that she may have a job for him, one that pays more money than he can ever spend, and he accompanies her to a speakeasy (the kind of hidden saloons that sprang up overnight during Prohibition, this one secreted in the back of a hardware store). George tells Cagney that she can set him up with some big time bootleggers and where he can make good money by delivering illegal booze. He hesitates, remembering his recent arrest and reminding George that bootlegging is illegal. She tells him that Prohibition is a bad law and everybody is breaking it because everyone wants to drink beer, wine, and hard liquor and no one will ever stop the public from doing that. At that moment, and almost as to emphasize George's statements, a beat cop appears in the speakeasy and demands to know who has illegally parked a car near a fire hydrant. A nervous patron admits to the offense, and the cop orders him to move his car. The cop then steps up to the bar to receive a free drink of booze, so even the long arm of the law is reaching for liquor. Cagney takes the job and enlists McHugh's aid as they begin to distribute booze, growing rich as they make their deliveries. When one of the gangsters providing the bottled booze increases his price, Cagney and McHugh quit, Cagney defiantly saying: "I can make this tiger sweat myself!" He and McHugh are then shown making gin in a bathtub, tempering raw alcohol with other ingredients to make this swill somewhat palatable. They are later shown operating their own manufacturing center where they produce their own beer, wine, liquor and even champagne, selling these illegal wares for a fortune and growing rich. Lynn, Cagney's old war buddy, who has become an attorney, works for him, chiefly buying him fleets of cabs, which are used to deliver Cagney's illegal booze. Lynn urges Cagney to use his cabs for legal fares, telling him that he can become even richer by pursuing legitimate ways of life, but Cagney tells him that he is out for the fast dollar. When one of Cagney's collectors tells him that a Broadway producer has not paid his substantial liquor bill, Cagney goes to the producer's theater to collect himself. He is surprised, however, to see an all-grown-up Lane performing in the chorus and he asks her for a date, but she puts him off. He persists, riding her home on the train to Mineola, and to her home where she tells him that her mother has died and that she is trying to get a singing job to keep the family house. Cagney later arranges for Lane to sing at the Panama Club where George is the hostess (her name is Panama Smith and she emulates the celebrated speakeasy hostess of that era, Texas Guinan, who greeted her customers with: "Hello, suckers!"). Meanwhile, Cagney and his henchmen ride motor launches beyond the twelve mile limit where a rum-running ship is awaiting a pickup of its cargo of illegal liquor. Cagney and his men board the ship, holding its crew at bay with guns while others unload the liquor onto the launches. The captain of the ship turns out to be Bogart, who, instead of resisting the wholesale theft of the booze, makes a partnership deal with Cagney while betraying his former boss, Kelly, a ruthless bootlegger. Cagney reluctantly agrees, thinking he has made a bad bargain since he does not trust Bogart, who becomes his top aide. They are next seen raiding a warehouse that contains impounded liquor, loading their trucks with cases of that liquor until they hear a night watchman approaching. The watchman is Sawyer, who had once been their sergeant during the war, a man Bogart detests. Out of his seething hatred for Sawyer, Bogart shoots Sawyer to death before the bootleggers roar away with the stolen liquor. Meanwhile, Lane goes to work as a singer at the Panama Club, which Cagney packs with customers paid to applaud her performance. When the owner of the club, Keane, ridicules Cagney for being a sucker by paying for customers, Cagney smashes the cigar clenched in Keane's mouth and later tells him that he is buying the club. Lynn arranges for the purchase of the club and comes to meet Lane. They are attracted to each other and soon fall in love, but do not tell Cagney, who has eyes only for Lane, even though

George loves him and always has. Rival gangster Kelly later visits the club and confronts Cagney and Bogart, telling them that if they continue to invade his bootlegging territory there will be a gang war. Bogart angers Kelly to the point where the gang boss pulls a gun, but Cagney knocks Kelly senseless and Kelly's minions are also subdued and then carried from the place. Kelly retaliates by killing McHugh, his body dumped in front of Cagney's club with a note pinned to McHugh's coat reading: "Let me alone and maybe I will let you alone." Cagney tells Bogart that he is going to raid Kelly's spaghetti restaurant, but Bogart refuses to take part in the attack. After Cagney and some of his men leave, Bogart betrays Cagney, calling Kelly and telling him that Cagney and his boys are going to pay him a visit. The alerted Kelly chases customers from his restaurant, except for an elderly couple, ordering them to stay in their places. He then positions his gunmen within the restaurant. Cagney appears with a number of his own gunmen, and both gangs open fire, filling the place with gun smoke. Several of Kelly's men are shot down and Kelly makes a break for the rear entrance, but Cagney cuts him off, shooting through a door and killing Kelly. When Cagney returns to his club, George tells him that Lane has quit and has left with Lynn, further informing him that Lane loves Lynn, not him. When Cagney later steps from his club to see Lynn and Lane walking toward him, he goes to Lynn and knocks him down. He then apologizes, and returns to his club where he begins to drink hard liquor, something he has never done before. Cagney's empire begins to disintegrate as rival gangs make inroads into his bootlegging operations and he then loses a fortune when the Stock Market begins to crash. To cover his stock losses, he sells his fleet of cabs to Bogart for $250,000, who allows him to keep one cab, telling him: "You are going to need it, pal." The Stock Market collapses and with it goes Cagney's wealth. Further, Prohibition is repealed and his nightclub and bootlegging operations evaporate. Cagney is now reduced to his old job, driving a cab, the very one that Bogart let him keep. He scrapes along in life, spending his nights drinking in a low dive where George works as a singer. One day, Lane gets into his cab and she tells him that she is glad to see him and that her husband, Lynn, is now a district attorney. Cagney drives her home and he meets her little son and then meets Lynn once more when he returns home. Cagney wishes Lane and Lynn well and departs, but not before he warns Lynn about Lynn's probes into Bogart's rackets as Bogart has survived the bootlegging era and has become an underworld kingpin. Lynn, by this time, has earned the animosity of Bogart as Lynn has caused some of Bogart's operations to close down. Incensed, Bogart sends Biberman, one of his goons, to visit Lane while her husband is gone. Biberman tells Lane that if Lynn does not stop his probes into Bogart's rackets, Lynn will be killed. Terrified, the panicked Lane searches for Cagney and finds him at the club where George is singing. Knowing that Cagney knows Bogart well, she asks Cagney to stop Bogart from harming her husband. Cagney tells her that he can do nothing about Lynn's problems with Bogart and she departs weeping. Cagney, still in love with Lane, decides that he will talk with Bogart and he pays a visit to the gangster's mansion. When meeting with Bogart, Cagney asks Bogart to forget about killing Lynn and that their days of violence are over and they have finished out of the money. Bogart tells him that he is doing fine and that he intends to take care of Lynn in his own way and that Cagney is only pleading for Lynn because he is still carrying a torch for Lane. Bogart then says that Cagney knows too much about his operations and he orders his goons to "take care of him." Realizing that Bogart has just ordered him killed, Cagney spins about and takes a gun away from Biberman, knocking him out. He then trains the gun on Bogart and kills him. Cagney then shoots his way out of the mansion with Bogart's gunmen firing after him. As he runs along a street, one of the gunmen fires and mortally wounds Cagney, who staggers forward and then up some stairs of a church where he finally collapses. George, who has followed Cagney to Bogart's mansion, finds Cagney and cradles him in her arms. A policeman arrives, looking down and begins to write up a report, asking the name of the dead man. "His name is Eddie

Humphrey Bogart and James Cagney in *The Roaring Twenties,* **1939.**

Bartlett," George tells the cop. "What did he do?" asks the cop. The camera slowly pulls backward as snow begins falling and we hear George's reply: "He used to be a big shot!" Thus ends the story of a good man corrupted by a bad law, Prohibition. This message is repeatedly emphasized throughout the film by a narrator and through introductory comments from producer-writer Mark Hellinger, who brainstormed this film into production, based upon characters and events he recorded as a NYC journalist in the Roaring Twenties. Director Walsh presents lightning-fast action, his forte, in this absorbing melodrama, and where the acting from Cagney, Bogart, Lynn, Lane and the rest of the fine cast superbly represents their memorable characters. Songs: "Mademoiselle from Armentieres" (traditional), "Smiles" (1917; music: Lee S. Roberts), "I'm Forever Blowing Bubbles" (1918; John W. Kellette), 'Swanee" (1919; George Gershwin), "Carolina in the Morning" (1922; Walter Donaldson), "Ain't We Got Fun" (1921; Richard A. Whiting), "The Japanese Sandman" (1920; Richard A. Whiting), "Bye Bye Blackbird" (1926; Ray Henderson), "Tip Toe Through the Tulips With Me" (1929; Joseph Burke), "If I Could Be with You" (1926; music: James P. Johnson), "Sweet Georgia Brown" (1925; music: Maceo Pinkard), "Dancing with Tears in My Eyes" (1930; Joseph Burke), "Cryin' for the Carolinas" (1929; music: Harry Warren), "I'm Just Wild About Harry" (1921; music: Eubie Blake; lyrics: Noble Sissle), "My Melancholy Baby" (1912; music: Ernie Burnett; lyrics: George A. Norton), "It Had to Be You" (1924; music: Isham Jones; lyrics: Gus Kahn), "In a Shanty in Old Shanty Town" (1932; music: Jack Little, John Siras; lyrics: Joe Young). *Author's Note*: Hellinger based Cagney's character on wealthy NYC bootlegger Larry Fay, who was killed by a disgruntled employee at one of his nightclubs in 1932, and who was the role model for the bootlegger protagonist in F. Scott Fitzgerald's classic 1925 novel, *The Great Gatsby*. Director Walsh told this author that "I knew Larry Fay when he was running speakeasies in New York and where Texas Guinan was his hostess, a very raucous lady, who insulted customers in such a way that they liked it. Guinan died in 1933, about six years before we made **The Roaring Twenties**, but she had appeared in a picture called **Queen of the Nightclubs** [1929] where she played herself. I had Gladys [George] watch that picture and told her to act like Guinan as the hostess in **The Roaring Twenties**, and she was better than I expected. In fact, she was terrific and Guinan would have said of her "give the little lady a great big hand," which is what Guinan said about the singers in her clubs when ordering audiences to applaud for them. Jimmy [Cagney] was just magnificent in **The Roaring Twenties**, even in the scene where he appears to be drunk. Well, Jimmy did not really drink, but he was the most convincing drunk on the screen that anyone ever saw. He learned all about drunks and how they acted when he was a kid. His father ran a saloon in New York and the place was always reeling with

James Cagney, Priscilla Lane and Gladys George in *The Roaring Twenties*, 1939.

drunks and Jimmy never forgot those poor, slobbering, staggering stiffs. About ten years after we made **The Roaring Twenties** Jimmy made another picture about a recovering alcoholic [**Come Fill the Cup**, 1951] and he did a scene in that picture where he is a raging drunk that is stunning and unforgettable. Burt Lancaster later told me that he studied that picture before he played an alcoholic in **Come Back, Little Sheba** [1952] and admitted that he copied a lot of Jimmy's mannerisms. Everybody copied Cagney." **The Roaring Twenties** was the last gangster film Cagney would play until enacting a psychopathic gangster in **White Heat**, 1949. Cagney told this author that "I agreed to do **The Roaring Twenties** because it had a good script and because Uncle [Walsh] was directing that film and he was one of the best in the business. Mark Hellinger, who wrote that script, was a good friend, so I was in good company when we did that picture. Those gangster parts were getting very thin with me by then and I was looking for different kinds of roles. So was poor Bogey [Bogart], who carped his way all through **The Roaring Twenties**, although we always got along well together. I knew he was tired of playing second fiddle to me as he had in **Angels with Dirty Faces** [1938]. He did not get along too well with Jack Warner, who ran things at Warner Brothers where we all worked, but none of us really got along with Jack, who was a smiling slave driver. I remember Bogey telling me before the scene when I shoot him, and I was always shooting him: 'As far as Jack Warner is concerned you might as well be firing real bullets into me. He hates my guts because I tell him off every time I get the chance. Well, here I am cringing and cowering again while you pump lead into me, Jimmy.' We walked on to the set and he said: 'Go ahead, let me have it.' We had to stop because we started laughing. That's how ridiculous it all was." Lane told this author that "I played a small-town girl who meets a big-time gangster. He makes a singing star out of me and I then run off with his lawyer, so how nice of a person am I? Well, Doris Day did the same thing to Jimmy [Cagney] in **Love Me or Leave Me** [1955]. Some women are fickle, aren't they?" **d**, Raoul Walsh, Anatole Litvak; **cast**, James Cagney, Priscilla Lane, Humphrey Bogart, Jeffrey Lynn, Gladys George, Frank McHugh, Paul Kelly, Edward Keane, Elisabeth Risdon, Joe Sawyer, Abner Biberman, George Meeker, Jack Norton, Robert Armstrong, John Ridgely; **w**, Jerry Wald, Richard Macaulay, Robert Rossen (based on a story by Mark Hellinger); **c**, Ernest Haller; **m**, Heinz Roemheld, Ray Heindorf; **ed**, Jack Killifer; **art d**, Max Parker; **spec eff**, Byron Haskin, Edwin B. DuPar.

Rob Roy ★★★ 1995; U.S./U.K.; 139m; UA; Color; Biographical Drama; Children: Unacceptable (MPAA: R); **BD**; **DVD**. This good remake of the 1954 film is set in the highlands of Scotland in the 1700s. A rebel leader, Rob Roy MacGregor (1671-1734), essayed by Neeson, tries to lead his small town to a better future by borrowing money from

the local nobility to buy cattle to herd to market. When the money is stolen, he takes on a Robin Hood lifestyle to defend his family and honor. Songs: "Ailein Duinn," "Blunt Reels," Gaelic Reels," "Morag's Lament" (traditional, Capercailli); "Green Garters," "Hard Earth" (Carter Burwell); "MacPherson's Farewell" (traditional); "Mrs. MacDonald of Sunach," "Nutmigs and Ginger;" "O'Sullivan's March" (Michael Tubridy); "The High Road to Linton," I'll Go Home" (traditional), "Walter Douglas MBE" (Mark Duff). Violence and sexuality prohibit viewing by children. **p**, Peter Broughan, Richard Jackson, Larry DeWaay; **d**, Michael Caton-Jones; **cast**, Liam Neeson, Jessica Lange, John Hurt, Eric Stoltz, Tim Roth, Andrew Keir, Brian Cox, Brian McCardie, Gilbert Martin, Vicki Masson, Jason Flemyng; **w**, Alan Sharp; **c**, Karl Walter Lindenlaub; **m**, Carter Burwell; **ed**, Peter Honess; **prod d**, Assheton Gorton; **art d**, John Ralph, Alan Tomkins; **set d**, Ann Mollo; **spec eff**, Yves De Bono, David Harris.

Rob Roy: The Highland Rogue ★★★ 1954; U.K./U.S.; 81m; Disney/RKO; Color; Adventure; Children: Unacceptable; **VHS**. This exciting action-packed tale is set in 1715, after the British defeat the Scottish clans. One of the highland leaders, Rob Roy MacGregor (1671-1734), played by Todd, escapes. He becomes a rogue and enough of a nuisance to George I (1660-1727) that he is outlawed and hunted. Todd becomes known as the Scottish Robin Hood, and, after many adventures, he is forced to surrender. Imprisoned, he is later pardoned. The film deals mainly with Todd's adventures, which were toned down for children, yet there is some violence. The film was remade as **Rob Roy**, 1995. *Author's Note*: Because of infighting and poor distribution of this film, Disney severed its relationship with RKO after having made almost two dozen films with this studio. **p**, Perce Pearce; **d**, Harold French; **cast**, Richard Todd, Glynis Johns, James Robertson Justice, Michael Gough, Finlay Currie, Jean Taylor Smith, Geoffrey Keen, Eric Pohlman, Archie Duncan, Russell Waters; **w**, Lawrence Edward Watkin (based on the novel by Sir Walter Scott); **c**, Guy Green; **m**, Cedric Thorpe Davie; **ed**, Geoffrey Foot; **prod d**, Carmen Dillon; **art d**, Geoffrey Drake; **spec eff**, George Blackwell.

Robbery ★★★ 1967; U.K.; 94m; Oakhurst Productions/Embassy; Color; Crime Drama; Children: Unacceptable; **DVD**. Well-executed crime caper sees Baker planning a jewelry heist to fund his larger goal of robbing £3 million from a mail train heading south from Glasgow, Scotland, to London. He succeeds with the jewelry robbery, and then arranges for Finlay to be released from prison to help him and others with the train robbery. Baker and his criminal associates are successful in robbing the train and capturing the loot and then go to a deserted airfield to escape. Scotland Yard detectives, however, get there first, and arrest everyone but Baker, who escapes with the money to the U.S. The film is based on what is called England's "Great Train Robbery," which occurred on August 8, 1963. The actual thieves were captured, but their leader, Ronald Arthur "Ronnie" Biggs (1929-2013) escaped with the money to Brazil. Song: "Born to Lose"(Johnny Keating, Tommy Scott). Excessive violence prohibits viewing by children. *Author's Note*: For extensive details on the "Great Train Robbery," see my two-volume work *The Great Pictorial History of World Crime*, Volume II (History, Inc., 2004; pages 1430-1433). **p**, Michael Deeley, Stanley Baker; **d**, Peter Yates; **cast**, Baker, Joanna Pettet, James Booth, Frank Finlay, Barry Foster, William Marlowe, Clinton Greyn, George Sewell, Glynn Edwards, Michael McStay, Martin Wyldeck; **w**, Edward Boyd, Yates, George Markstein; **c**, Douglas Slocombe; **m**, Johnny Keating; **ed**, Reginald Beck; **art d**, Michael Seymour.

The Robe ★★★★ 1953; U.S.; 135m; FOX; Color; Historical Drama; Children: Unacceptable; **DVD**; **VHS**. Superlative production offers a stirring tale centered on the crucifixion of Christ and the man who crucified him, a Roman tribune played by Burton. He is a profligate officer and womanizer serving in the Roman army of Emperor Tiberius (42

BC-37 AD), played by Thesiger. Burton creates the animosity of Robinson, playing Caligula (12 AD-41 AD), who is the emperor's erratic and high-strung nephew, when Burton thinks to develop a romance with alluring Simmons. She is the emperor's ward and has been promised in marriage to Robinson. Burton angers Robinson when outbidding him at a slave auction where, to spite Robinson, Burton buys a powerful Greek slave, Mature. In retaliation, Robinson has Burton transferred to the hinterlands of Palestine. Before his ship sails for that destination, Simmons, who has fallen in love with Burton, visits him and tells him that she will try to persuade the emperor to recall him to Rome and that she will be waiting for him. Burton tells her that he loves her and also asks that she persuade the emperor not to sanction her marriage to Robinson. When arriving in Palestine, Burton, accompanied by a junior officer, Morrow, watch as Jesus, played by Klune, a celebrated rabbi, triumphantly enters Jerusalem with a large crowd of supporters. Mature, who has accompanied Burton, sees Jesus and becomes one of His most ardent followers. When Jesus is later arrested Mature begs Burton to intervene in His case. Burton tells Mature that he will look into the matter as he is recovering from a severe hangover. Burton then meets with Boone, who plays Pontius Pilate (d. 36 AD). Boone, who appears agitated and mentally disturbed, orders Burton to crucify a man he has just judged while Boone repeatedly washes his hands, as if to rid himself of an unclean act (as was the recorded case of Pilate). Burton methodically goes about that duty, telling the pleading Mature, who has embraced Jesus' benign teachings, that he can do nothing but execute his orders. Burton then presides over the crucifixion of Jesus, showing an indifferent attitude toward his gruesome chore and even throwing dice with some of his men for the prize of Jesus' red homespun robe. A storm erupts as Jesus dies on the cross, and Burton is startled when he leans against that cross and blood from the victim trickles onto his hand. As he leaves the site of execution, Burton is confronted by an enraged Mature, accusing him of murdering the Son of God. Burton holds on to the robe of the crucified Jesus, but is suddenly gripped by remorse in having crucified him, interpreting his guilty feelings as a curse the robe carries and has attached to him. Mature takes the robe from Burton, damning him and the oppressive Roman Empire and runs off. Haunted by the memory of the crucifixion and his part in the death of Jesus, Burton has become deranged, constantly besieged with nightmares of that execution. He sails to the island of Capri where Simmons is waiting for him. She takes him to see Thesiger, who plays an avuncular and considerate Tiberius and who patiently listens to Burton's ravings that describe how the robe is cursed and that Jesus' followers possess through that robe great and terrible powers. Thesiger gives Burton a royal commission to return to Palestine and find that robe and destroy it, as well as to identify all of Jesus' followers and provide him with a list of such rebels. Burton tells Simmons that once he rids himself of the robe's curse, he will return to her and they will marry. After Burton has departed, Thesiger tells Simmons that she should forget Burton because he has gone mad. After Burton returns to Palestine, he befriends Jagger, a leader of a Christian community, who eventually leads him to Mature, who guards the robe of Jesus. Burton demands that he turn over the robe to him, and when he does, Burton is first terrified by the magical powers he believes the robe possesses. He buries his head in the robe, but, instead of being struck dead, as he envisioned, he becomes tranquil and at peace with himself. Burton's nightmares have fled and he now embraces Christianity. He becomes a member of the community, where he meets Peter (d. c.67 AD), an Apostle of Jesus, who is portrayed by Rennie and whose inspiring teachings further deepen Burton's allegiance to Christianity. Jagger then gathers all the Christians together so they can hear Rennie speak, but he is killed by an arrow shot by a Roman soldier. Morrow, the centurion, who has earlier been a subordinate to Burton, now commands a Roman troop that has surrounded the Christians and are about to put them all to death. Burton confronts Morrow and asks him if he has orders to commit such an atrocity. "I need no orders to clear out a nest of traitors," Morrow replies. He then tells Burton that his commis-

Richard Burton in *The Robe,* 1953.

sion from the emperor is invalid as Thesiger is now dead and a new emperor, Robinson, has taken his place. Burton reminds Morrow that his commission is valid until Robinson personally revokes it and tells Morrow to obey his order. Morrow tells Burton: "Make me obey, Tribune." Both men draw their swords and fight savagely. Though wounded, Burton bests Morrow by knocking him down. Instead of killing Morrow, Burton follows the Christian ethic by not slaying him, and, instead, drives his sword into a tree. Morrow, humbled and beaten, salutes Burton, and orders his men to withdraw. Rennie then asks Burton to accompany him and Mature to travel to other countries to spread the teachings of Jesus, but Burton tells Rennie that he is not worthy, admitting that he crucified Jesus. Rennie tells him he knows that and that he also injured Jesus by denying he knew Him not once but three times when Romans were searching for Jesus. Burton agrees to go on the mission that eventually takes them to Rome where Christians are compelled to meet in secret hiding areas. Meanwhile, Robinson, who has become power-mad after assuming the throne, summons Simmons to his palace and there tells her that Burton has become an outlaw, and that he has branded Burton a traitor for becoming a Christian. He takes her to his royal dungeon to see Mature, who has been captured and is being tortured in order to find out where Burton and other Christians are hiding. When Simmons leaves the palace, she sees Leonard, a household servant of Burton's family with whom she has been staying. Believing that Leonard is a secret Christian, she convinces Leonard to take her to Burton and he does, leading her into the labyrinthine catacombs. She meets with Burton, who tells her of his conversion to Christianity and that the robe is holy and sacred, not a talisman of evil. Simmons tells him that Mature is held captive, and Burton gathers some followers and then invades the dungeon and, after struggling with guards, manages to free Mature. In their escape, Burton sends the weakened Mature away to safety while he stays behind to hold off pursuing Roman cavalry at a bridge. He delays these pursuers until Mature is safely beyond reach and is then captured. Returned to the palace, Burton is confronted by a berserk Robinson, who denounces him and all Christians. He demands that Burton announce his allegiance to only one god, himself, which Burton refuses to do. Robinson sentences him to death, but Simmons, who is nearby, joins Burton, telling Robinson she no longer wishes to live in a world ruled by a lunatic such as Robinson. Robinson then sentences both Simmons and Burton to death at the royal archery field and both solemnly leave the palace, but not before Simmons hands the cherished robe to house servant Leonard, telling him to take it to Rennie. She and Burton are then shown walking to their deaths, which transcends into a scene where they ascend into the heavens, the fate envisioned by all good practicing Christians. Director Koster does a great job in telling his inspiring story, filling his scenes with sumptuous

Fred Astaire and Ginger Rogers in *Roberta*, 1935.

pageantry; the majestic sets of the palace and Rome are breathtaking to behold, especially when seen through the CinemaScope process, which was then being pioneered by Fox and its studio chief, Zanuck. The script is well adapted from Douglas' best-selling biblical novel. The acting is excellent, particularly from Burton, Simmons, Mature, Rennie and Robinson, that actor's hysterically shuddering performance of a deranged Caligula (which he reprised in the sequel, **Demetrius and the Gladiators**, 1954) establishing a theatrical hallmark. This film, due to the then new novelty of CinemaScope, was an enormous success at the box office, reaping more than $36 million against a budget of $4 million. Oscars were received for Best Art Direction, Color (Wheeler, Davis, Scott and Fox), and Best Costume Design, Color (Charles LeMaire and Emile Santiago). The film was nominated for an Oscar as Best Picture, Best Actor (Burton), and Best Color Cinematography (Shamroy). ***Author's Note***: Fox purchased the rights to the 1942 Douglas novel for $100,000 from RKO, which had originally purchased the rights in the 1940s, and where studio boss Zanuck planned to use the biblical epic as the first film to be released with Fox's CinemaScope process. The first film shot at Fox in that process was **How to Marry a Millionaire**, 1953, but that film was released on November 4, 1953, where **The Robe** preceded it, being released on September 16, 1953, becoming the first Fox CinemaScope film to be seen by the public. CinemaScope was Fox's answer to its foremost competitor; this new process offered films on a gigantic screen (sixty-eight feet by twenty-four feet) against which no television screen could hope to compete and was the brainchild of Fox boss, Darryl Zanuck. He personally convinced money-man Spros Skouras to get behind it. Zanuck had seen a demonstration of the new screen process as developed by Professor Henri Cretien, who created an anamorphic lens to show that wide-screen process, and while at that demonstration, Zanuck purchased that first anamorphic lens on the spot. Since Koster complained about having only one camera with such a lens in shooting **The Robe** and that its limited use was delaying production, Zanuck closed down the production while a second anamorphic lens was constructed and then had both lenses during that production guarded night and day by armed detectives. "I worried that they might be stolen by a competitor," Zanuck told this author, "so I had them watched night and day as if they were as precious as the most guarded secret in World War II, the Norden Bombsight." Skouras held a press conference on the eve of the release of this film, announcing to the press: "We are hoping to establish a hallmark in the highest of entertainment. We want the public to say that there never was a bad CinemaScope film, just like there never was a bad Cadillac." To make sure that all theaters in the U.S. converted to the wide-screen process, Zanuck called the heads of all the Hollywood studios together, including Warner Brothers, MGM, RKO, Universal,

Paramount, United Artists and Columbia, where they all agreed, except for Paramount, to adopt the new process. Paramount later created its own wide-screen version called Panavision. Sometime later, Zanuck admitted that "CinemaScope was all wrong mechanically. We cut too low and too circular. Visual experts told us, not then but later, that the correct proportion is Panavision. Panavision is the perfect proportion to fit the eyes." Zanuck's first choice for the Roman soldier who accepts Christianity was his most favorite actor, Tyrone Power, but Power refused to play the part, opting instead to appear in a Broadway play, "John Brown's Body," which, unfortunately, had a limited run of only sixty-five performances. Then Zanuck decided to gamble on Burton, who had appeared in only a handful of theatrically released feature films. Burton was at first enthusiastic about his role, stating: "After what I am and what I have come from, where can I go but to the top?" That is exactly where he went after this film was released, one that made him an international star. He threw himself into this production heart and soul, delivering 313 speeches in the more than 700 speeches in the film. Burton was so consumed by his part that he often wore his costumes, togas and Tribune uniform, home with him and went to sleep thusly attired. "That role about wrecked me," Burton told this author. "It was one of the most exhausting and demanding parts I ever played. After watching the rushes, I started to dislike what I saw. Some critics later described my character as 'wooden,' but that did not disturb me since I was playing a Roman robot of a soldier. I never seemed to be able to make the transition from the time he goes mad to the time he becomes enlightened with the teachings of Christianity and that has always upset me. No one was more surprised than I was when I heard that I had been nominated for an Academy Award as Best Actor in that film. Most actors look back on their performances and think that they could have done better and **The Robe** was one such performance for me." Burton would be nominated for an Oscar seven times and never win one. Burton's co-star, Simmons, did not share his opinion of his performance, telling this author that "Richard gave one of his best performances in **The Robe**. He radiated power. It was like touching a live wire." **p**, Frank Ross; **d**, Henry Koster; **cast**, Richard Burton, Jean Simmons, Victor Mature, Michael Rennie, Jay Robinson, Dean Jagger, Torin Thatcher, Richard Boone, Betta St. John, Jeff Morrow, Ernest Thesiger, Dawn Addams, Michael Ansara, Donald C. Klune, David Leonard, Cameron Mitchell (voice of Jesus Christ); **w**, Philip Dunne (based on an adaptation by Gina Kaus of the novel by Lloyd C. Douglas); **c**, Leon Shamroy (CinemaScope; Technicolor); **m**, Alfred Newman; **ed**, Barbara McLean; **art d**, Lyle Wheeler, George W. Davis; **set d**, Paul S. Fox, Walter M. Scott; **spec eff**, Ray Kellogg, James B. Gordon.

Roberta ★★★★ 1935; U.S.; 105m; RKO; B/W; Musical Comedy; Children: Acceptable; **DVD**; **VHS**. Entertaining songfest offers a bevy of great songs, mostly from Jerome Kern, and some wonderful dancing from Astaire and Rogers. The film begins when football player Scott tags along as his friend, Astaire, and a music group called the Wabash Indianians, who travel by steamship to play a gig in Paris. After arriving, the group loses the gig and Scott takes Astaire to visit his aunt, Roberta (Westley), who owns a posh fashion house run by her assistant, Dunne. There they meet Rogers, a woman claiming to be a Polish countess (and she is hilarious when doing that impersonation), but Astaire recognizes her as an old friend named Lizzie, who gets the band a job. Meanwhile, Westley dies and leaves the business to Scott, and he and Dunne become partners in the fashion house. They fall in and out of love and, finally, in love again. Astaire and Rogers become dance partners, and Dunne sings some wonderful songs. Lucille Ball, early in her film career, has a bit role as one of the fashion models. This film, based on the popular Broadway show, was a huge hit at the box office, taking in more than $2.3 million in its initial release against a $600,000 budget. Songs: "(Back Home Again In) Indiana" (1917; James F. Hanley); "Let's Begin," "Russian Lullaby," "It'll Be Hard to Handle," "Yesterdays," "I Won't Dance," "Smoke Gets in Your Eyes," "Lovely to Look At,"

(1933; music: Jerome Kern; lyrics: Otto A. Harbach). *Author's Note*: Dunne, who possessed a fine singing voice, told this author that "I have fond memories of **Roberta** and its wonderful cast, such great talents as Fred [Astaire], Ginger [Rogers] and Randy [Scott]. I also got to sing one of my favorite songs in that picture, 'Yesterdays.'" Rogers told this author that "I had done a few pictures with Fred [Astaire] before we did **Roberta**, and I knew how demanding he could be because he was a perfectionist. As long as you stayed with his routines, you were okay. He had a lot of intricate steps and movements and they were always different than what other dancers did. They always talk about how he improvised in his dancing numbers, but there was never any ad-libbing in our routines. I never had to worry about my weight in those days. When you worked with Fred, you burned off every ounce of fat you had and then some." Astaire told this author that "**Roberta** had one of the best dance numbers I ever performed with Ginger [Rogers]. It combined ballroom and tap dancing and it required some very close coordination. We challenged each other with some pretty fancy steps. We were speed demons in that number and Ginger never missed a step. She was very fast and light as a feather. She later got the nickname "feathers" because of the feathery gowns they gave her for some of our numbers together, not because she looked like she was dancing on air. We rehearsed that number until we could do it in our sleep and I was dreaming about it for months after we finished that picture. Nobody was faster than Ginger, nobody. Dancing comes naturally to some people and I think Ginger was one of those persons. Even back then, Ginger was aiming at serious dramatic roles, but she didn't get a shot at that until some years later. Meanwhile, she was dancing her way toward heavy drama and that's why I think dancing came so easily for her. Her primary ambition was not dancing. It was drama, and when she got into that she showed the world that she was a great actress. She has an Oscar [**Kitty Foyle**, 1940] to prove it." **p**, Pandro S. Berman; **d**, William A. Seiter; **cast**, Irene Dunne, Fred Astaire, Ginger Rogers, Randolph Scott, Helen Westley, Claire Dodd, Mary Forbes, William Frawley, Lynne Carver, Candy Candido; **w**, Jane Murfin, Sam Mintz, Allan Scott, Glenn Tryon (based on the novel *Gowns by Roberta* by Alice Duer Miller and the play by Jerome Kern and Otto A. Harbach); **c**, Edward Cronjager; **ed**, William Hamilton; **art d**, Van Nest Polglase; **spec eff**, Harry Redmond Sr.

Robin and Marian ★★★★ 1976; U.S.; 106m; Rastar/COL; Color; Adventure/Romance; Children: Unacceptable (MPAA: PG); **DVD**; **VHS**. Unlike the many versions of Robin Hood, this offbeat but superb adventure tale shows the knight errant, Connery, in his aging years rekindling his love for the woman of his heart. That woman is Hepburn, who has taken refuge from his rebellious antics in a convent, only to discover that her own deep love for this always enchanting rogue is undying. The film opens with Connery as Robin loyally serving his king, Harris, who plays Richard I (Richard the Lion-Heart; 1157-1199). They have gone on crusades together and are now attacking rebellious fiefdoms. Harris orders Connery and his close friend, Williamson, playing Little John, to attack a castle and retrieve a priceless gold statue. Connery discovers that the castle is sparsely defended and is the haven for many orphaned children and that there is no gold statue to be found. He refuses to launch the attack, and Harris, who has lost his faculties, orders Connery and Williamson to be executed. Before that happens, Harris is mortally wounded by an arrow in his neck and, as he is dying, Harris rescinds his order of execution, setting Connery and Williamson free. Returning to England, they are warmly greeted by old friends Elliott (Will Scarlet) and Barker (Friar Tuck), who still reside in Sherwood Forest. Connery learns that Hepburn is the abbess of a nunnery and is now in trouble with Connery's old nemesis, Shaw, the resolute Sheriff of Nottingham. Hepburn has been ordered to leave England as are all the leading Roman Catholic leaders of the land, but she refuses, telling Connery that his presence only adds to her problems and she wants no more to do with him. When she is about to be arrested, however, Connery rescues her, disabling Haigh, one of Shaw's knights. They spend

Sean Connery and Audrey Hepburn in *Robin and Marian*, 1976.

some idyllic moments in Sherwood Forest, recalling their former love affair and Connery's daring deeds. They rekindle their deep love for one another, but their time together is cut short when Shaw arrives just outside of the forest with two hundred men, intent on capturing Connery and his ragtag band of rebels. Hepburn begs Connery not to confront Shaw, realizing that he and his aging men will soon be overcome. Connery, however, cannot go against his adventurous grain and proposes to Shaw that they settle all matters by having hand-to-hand combat to the death and, whichever one wins, that winner will not allow further bloodshed to take place. Shaw agrees and both men go at each other in a grueling, savage fight that reduces both men to exhausted staggering figures. Shaw severely wounds Connery, who has enough strength to deliver a mortal blow to Shaw, killing him. Haigh then attacks Connery and his men, and Williamson kills Haigh before Connery is removed to Hepburn's nunnery where she tells Williamson that she will tend to Connery. She realizes, however, that Connery has suffered a wound that will forever cripple him and that they are now wanted outlaws and have no future. She doses a goblet of wine with poison, drinking from it before she hands it to Connery. He drinks from the goblet and then realizes that he has been poisoned by the only woman he has ever loved. When he asks her why she has done such a thing, Hepburn replies: "I love you more than all you know. I love you more than children, more than fields I've planted with my hands. I love you more than morning prayers or peace or food to eat. I love you more than sunlight, more than flesh or joy, or one more day. I love you…more than God." Before the two star-crossed lovers die, Connery shoots an arrow through the window and tells the loyal Williamson to bury Hepburn and himself wherever that arrow falls. Poignant and powerful, this film remains a classic tale with outstanding acting from Connery, Hepburn, Harris, Shaw and Williamson, offering superb production values with costumes and sets appropriate to that ancient era. *Author's Note*: Although Hepburn was forty-seven when she made this film (she had not appeared in a film within nine years as she had been devoting her time to her family), her acting skills are at their peak and she is mesmerizing in her role of an aging woman whose passion for a man has never aged. Connery was reunited with Harris in another film after appearing together in **The Molly Maguires**, 1970, and Harris agreed to play Richard I because he and Connery had become friends in that earlier film. Ironically, Connery went on to play Richard I in **Robin Hood: Prince of Thieves**, 1991. **p**, Denis O'Dell; **d**, Richard Lester; **cast**, Sean Connery, Audrey Hepburn, Robert Shaw, Richard Harris, Nicol Williamson, Denholm Elliott, Kenneth Haigh, Ronnie Barker, Ian Holm, Esmond Knight; **w**, James Goldman; **c**, David Watkin (Technicolor); **m**, John Barry; **ed**, John Victor-Smith; **prod d**, Michael Stringer; **art d**, Gil Parrondo; **spec eff**, Eddie Fowlie.

Frank Sinatra, Bing Crosby and Dean Martin in *Robin and the 7 Hoods,* **1964.**

Robin and the 7 Hoods ★★★ 1964; U.S.; 123m; P-C Productions; WB; Color; Comedy; Children: Unacceptable; **DVD**; **VHS**. Broad parody of Prohibition and Chicago gangsters of the late 1920s begins when Robinson, boss of bosses, is shot to death and the spoils of his empire are mostly gathered by runty Falk. (This scene takes a large leaf from Billy Wilder's classic comedy, **Some Like It Hot**, 1959, which opens when two musicians inadvertently witness the 1929 St. Valentine's Day Massacre, and must then run for their lives from searching gangsters.) Sinatra agrees to Falk's new underworld position, but warns Falk that the North Side is his exclusive rackets domain and, to protect that territory, Sinatra gathers a small coterie of bootleggers, including Martin, Davis, and others to his ranks, adding do-gooder Crosby to give him a good front. After Robinson is bumped off, Rush, his sultry daughter, gives Sinatra $50,000 to kill whoever was responsible for her father's untimely demise. Sinatra wants nothing to do with such a bloody assignment and gives the money to Davis, telling him to do what he wants with that large loose cash. Davis "donates" the cash to Crosby's orphanage, and when Crosby learns that the source of such munificent funds is Sinatra, he releases that information to the press. Newspapers then promote the story that Sinatra is a modern-day Robin Hood, using his ill-gotten wealth to help the needy. Sinatra accepts the role, hiring Crosby to set up his private charities, but only to give the public the good side of his social profile while continuing to operate his illegal rackets. (Again, this film takes another leaf from **Pocketful of Miracles**, 1961, where a racketeer and gambler sets up a charitable organization, this plot element also employed in **The Lemon Drop Kid**, 1951.) Sinatra begins to establish a relationship with Rush, doubting, however, that he can ever match the elegant style of this well-educated and refined woman. Sinatra loses all his illusions about this grand lady after he learns that she is using Crosby's charities as a cover for a counterfeiting ring, along with Martin. Sinatra banishes Martin from his mob and tells Rush to get out of town. She retaliates by offering a lot of money to Falk to kill Sinatra and Martin, too, since he exposed and ruined her counterfeiting operation. Falk happily agrees, but he is so unsuccessful in dispatching his erstwhile enemies that he goes to the bottom of a river encased in cement. Martin gets back into Sinatra's good graces, but Rush is not finished with him, Sinatra and their pals. She teams with Crosby and begins a reformer group that brings about the destruction of Sinatra's rackets, and he and his pals are reduced to penniless bums begging for handouts on the street. The finale sees them approach a limousine where its occupants, Rush and Crosby, toss them a few coins before entering their reform headquarters. A lot of outlandish gangster action is shown in this underworld send-up, and Sinatra and his clan do a good job providing many funny scenes while lampooning their pinstripe-suited characters while doffing fedoras and toting gats and submachine guns. In the entertaining process some good tunes are warbled by Sinatra, Martin, Crosby and Davis. Songs: "My Kind of Town," "Mr. Booze," "All for One and One for All," "Don't Be a Do-Badder," "Any Man Who Loves His Mother," "Style," "Bang! Bang!" (music: Jimmy Van Heusen; lyrics: Sammy Cahn); "Jingle Bells" (1857; James Pierpont). *Author's Note*: Sinatra told this author that "We were accused of stealing a lot of characters from the stories of Damon Runyon when I produced **Robin and the 7 Hoods**, but that was all nonsense. I had already appeared in Runyon's story, **Guys and Dolls** [1955], so that's where that all started, but my picture about Chicago gangsters was an entirely different story. I wore a loud suit in **Robin and the 7 Hoods** as I did in **Guys in Dolls**, so I guess you could say I lifted some wardrobe ideas, big deal." Sinatra's son was kidnapped while his father was making this picture. The nineteen-year-old Frank Sinatra Jr., was kidnapped on December 8, 1963, at Harrah's Lake Tahoe and was released unharmed two days later after his father reportedly paid a ransom of $240,000. The culprits were later apprehended and imprisoned. President John F. Kennedy was assassinated shortly after this film went into production, that killing hitting home in that Sinatra had campaigned hard for Kennedy's election and was a close friend until Kennedy refused to stay at Sinatra's home as originally planned after his brother, Robert Kennedy, then U.S. Attorney General advised his brother to stay at Bing Crosby's home instead. Sinatra had made expensive arrangements for that Kennedy visit, including the construction of a heliport, but was told that Sinatra's home was not secure enough for Secret Service agents to protect the President. The real reason why the President did not stay at Sinatra's home was because Robert Kennedy told his brother that Sinatra had too many underworld contacts and that such unsavory liaisons might harm the President's public image. Sinatra asked actor Peter Lawford, who had married into the Kennedy family, to intercede in that planned visit, but when Kennedy changed his plans at the last minute and stayed with Crosby, Sinatra blamed Lawford for the social fiasco and both men never spoke to each other again. For that reason, Lawford does not appear in this film. Oddly, Crosby, a lifelong Republican, does appear in this film. Crosby told this author that "I appeared with Frank in **High Society** [1956], so it was old home week when we made that gangster spoof some years later. I understood that some people in Chicago did not like the picture. They thought we were making fun of some of their relatives in that Toddling Town. You can't please them all." **p**, Frank Sinatra; **d**, Gordon Douglas; **cast**, Sinatra, Dean Martin, Sammy Davis, Jr., Bing Crosby, Peter Falk, Barbara Rush, Victor Buono, Allen Jenkins, Jack La Rue, Phillip Crosby, Richard Simmons, Tony Randall, Edward G. Robinson, Sig Ruman; **w**, David R. Schwartz; **c**, William H. Daniels (Panavision; Technicolor); **m**, Nelson Riddle; **ed**, Sam O'Steen; **art d**, LeRoy Deane; **set d**, Raphael Bretton.

Robin Hood ★★★★★ 1922 (silent); U.S.; 127m/11 reels; UA; B/W; Adventure; Children: Cautionary; **DVD**. One of the great majestic epics of the silent era, this lavishly produced adventure tale is one of Fairbanks' most significant films and it remains a classic to this day. The film opens with royal jousts over which Richard I (Richard the Lion-Heart; 1157-1199) presides, and who is played by Beery. The king's champion is Fairbanks, who plays the Earl of Huntingdon. He meets Dickey, playing Sir Guy of Gisbourne, who is Fairbanks' avowed enemy and who has unfairly strapped himself onto his horse so that he cannot be so easily unseated. Fairbanks nevertheless manages to drive his lance into Dickey enough times to finally win the match, and he is pronounced the triumphant hero of that day. Fairbanks then joins Beery when the king leads his mighty army in the Third Crusade in the Holy Land, leaving his treacherous brother, Prince John (John, King of England; John Lackland; 1166-1216), played by De Grasse, to rule as regent in his place. The conniving Dickey easily persuades De Grasse to abuse his authority by oppressing British subjects with unjust taxes to enrich their personal coffers, and Dickey also goads De Grasse into illegally seizing Beery's throne. Bennett, who plays Lady Marian and who is betrothed to Fairbanks, writes her lover a letter explaining these terrible transgressions. When Fairbanks asks Beery for permission to leave his ranks and return to England, Beery interprets this request as a sign of cowardice, believing that Fairbanks has lost his nerve to fight the Saracens. Beery refuses that permission. When Fairbanks disobeys and starts for England, Dickey and his men ambush him and he is imprisoned. Fairbanks escapes and returns to England, Beery now believing him to be a traitor. After he arrives in England, Fairbanks is told that Bennett is dead and most of his friends have been outlawed. He gathers those friends in Sherwood Forest and, assuming the name of Robin Hood, begins a guerrilla campaign against the cruel De Grasse, and his evil henchman, Lowery, who plays the Sheriff of Nottingham. With Hale (Little John), Geary (Will Scarlet), Louis (Friar Tuck), and Talman (Allan-a-Dale), he gathers many followers, leading them into wild skirmishes and outright battles with the forces of De Grasse and Lowery. Throughout, Fairbanks' legend of taking from the oppressing rich and giving the spoils to the poor spreads throughout England. He then learns that Bennett is alive, but is held a prisoner in De Grasse's castle. Fairbanks invades the castle and rescues her and then defeats Dickey in a final battle. He is nevertheless captured and is sentenced to death. Fairbanks' life is spared and he is reunited with Bennett when, at the last moment, Beery returns from the Crusades and removes the ruthless De Grasse from power. Fairbanks is then reinstated as Beery's foremost champion. Dwan presents a sweeping and breathtaking adventure tale in this superbly mounted film, which is the director's masterpiece. Fairbanks shines as the daring Robin Hood, performing his own amazing acrobatic stunts in some of the best action scenes ever put on film. He was the foremost swashbuckler of the silent screen, and this magnificent production perfectly examples his great talents in wielding swords, shooting arrows and riding horses. In his time, he had no equal in that genre. His supporting cast, particularly Beery, render equally memorable performances. This film was a huge success at the box office, replenishing its investment of $1.4 million many times over. This was the first picture to be premiered at Grauman's newlybuilt Egyptian Theater in Hollywood, that gala event occurring on October 18, 1922. *Author's Note*: Dwan had been making two-reel films with Fairbanks from the earliest silent days and would go on to make eleven feature films with him, including Fairbanks' last film, **The Man in the Iron Mask**, 1929. By the time Fairbanks bankrolled this film, he was already enjoying great profits from his previous films, especially after he, his wife Mary Pickford, Charles Chaplin and master director D. W. Griffith established their own studio, United Artists, in 1919. While envisioning the production for **Robin Hood**, Fairbanks and Pickford bought the old Jesse Hampton Studio in Santa Monica where Fairbanks ordered enormous sets built for **Robin Hood**, larger than anything before or since, including Griffith's monumental sets for **Intolerance**, 1916. In a preproduction meeting, Fairbanks announced that the film would be titled **The Spirit of Chivalry**, a title later discarded for the more recognizable title of **Robin Hood**. He stated at that meeting that he wanted to build "really big sets—Nottingham in the 12th Century, Richard the Lion Heart's castle, the town in Palestine, Sherwood Forest and the outlaw's lair. There's a big field to the south [of the former Hampton Studio] where we can set up the crusaders' camp in France. We'll have several thousand costumes designed from contemporary documents. We'll order shields, lances and swords by the thousand and we'll stage a tournament." The ebullient Fairbanks was interrupted by his brother, John Fairbanks, who controlled finances for the production company, stating that such a production would be extremely expensive. Fairbanks waved him away, saying: "That's not the point. These things have to be done properly or not at all." After Fairbanks and Pickford left for New York on a business trip, more than 500 craftsmen went to work on the enormous sets. Some of their interiors were so huge that they could not be properly lighted with electricity so they were painted to effectively show atmospheric images that presented nighttime shadows and dazzling sunlight pouring through towering windows. The sets were so enormous that they were

Charles Stevens and Douglas Fairbanks Sr. in *Robin Hood*, 1922.

seen from a distance of many miles. (One of the many architects working on those sets was Lloyd Wright, 1890-1978, the son of famed architect Frank Lloyd Wright, 1867-1959, and who later remodeled one of those sets as a band shell for the Hollywood Bowl.) When Fairbanks returned by train from New York, a huge throng awaited him at the Pasadena train station, his associates and fans anxious to see his reaction to the towering sets, which had been completed. When Fairbanks arrived at the location, he was overwhelmed at what he saw. Even though the vast sets had been precisely constructed as he had envisioned them, their enormity staggered him, and he felt dwarfed by their intimidating presence. All of his enthusiasm evaporated and he became instantly depressed, telling Dwan: "I can't compete with that. My work is intimate. People know me as an intimate actor. I can't work in a vast thing like that. What could I do in there?" Dwan told him to go home and think about it and then return in a few days. When Fairbanks did return, Dwan described a great action scene he had envisioned, only one of many he would create for Fairbanks. He pointed to a forty-foot balcony where Dwan had had a huge drape that hung from that balcony to the ground. He described to Fairbanks how he would be chased by several knights to that balcony and would escape from them by using the drape. "I showed him," Dwan later stated. "I climbed on to the balcony and jumped into this drape. I had a kid's slide hidden inside of it and I slid right down that curtain to the ground with a gesture like he [Fairbanks] used to make, and I ran through the arch to freedom." Fairbanks was suddenly full of enthusiasm. "I'll do it!" he exclaimed. Fairbanks duplicated Dwan's actions, improving on them with his always considerable flourishing and was so pleased with the action that, according to Dwan, "he did a thousand times—like a kid!" This spectacular feat would later be duplicated with slight variations by Fairbanks when making **The Black Pirate**, 1926, and where he uses his sword to slice through a huge sail on a ship, sliding down that sail to the deck, while being held by guidelines unseen behind that sail. No film would eclipse **Robin Hood** until the coming of **The Adventures of Robin Hood**, 1938, starring the inimitable Errol Flynn as the daring outlaw. Dwan presents many innovative techniques in this wonderful epic, not the least of which is an eye-opening beginning shot where the huge drawbridge of the castle lowers straight into the camera. Over that drawbridge rides Beery as Richard I, accompanied by knights, squires and footmen, all carrying banners that flap in the breeze as they journey toward the jousting fields. So impressed with the sets for **Robin Hood** was Fairbanks that he invited the great comedian, Charles Chaplin, his partner at United Artists, to visit the sprawling fields and those sets. Said Chaplin later: "He built a sixteen-acre set for **Robin Hood**, a castle with enormous drawbridges and ramparts, far bigger than any castle that ever existed. With great pride, Douglas showed me the huge drawbridge. 'Magnificent,' I said. 'What a wonderful opening for one

Danny Huston as Richard the Lion-Heart in *Robin Hood*, 2010.

of my comedies. The drawbridge comes down, and I put out the cat and take in the milk.'" **p**, Douglas Fairbanks; **d**, Allan Dwan; **cast**, Fairbanks, Wallace Beery, Sam De Grasse, Enid Bennett, Paul Dickey, William Lowery, Roy Coulson, Billie Bennett, Merrill McCormick, Alan Hale, Maine Geary, Willard Louis, Lloyd Talman, Ann Doran; **w**, Lotta Woods (based on a story by Elton Thomas [Fairbanks]); **c**, Arthur Edeson; **m**, John Scott; **ed**, William Nolan; **art d**, Wilfred Buckland, Irvin J. Martin, Edward M. Langley; **spec eff**, Paul Eagler.

Robin Hood ★★★★ 1973; U.S.; 83m; Disney; Buena Vista; Color; Animation, Adventure, Comedy; Children: Acceptable (MPAA: G); **BD**; **DVD**; **IV**. The Robin Hood legend sees an inventive version in this delightful animation comedy that is laugh-packed and song-filled. The story follows the traditional legend with animals standing in for the live characters. Robin Hood (Bedford voiceover) is an outlaw who forms a gang in Sherwood Forest to fight the injustices of the evil Sheriff of Nottingham (Buttram voiceover), who levies unreasonably high taxes on the people. Bedford goes on to defeat the bully, rescue Lady Marian, and make things right for the world. Songs: "Oo-de-lally," "Not in Nottingham," "Whistle Stop" (1972: Roger Miller); "Love" (1972: Floyd Huddleston, George Bruns); "The Phony King of England" (1972: Johnny Mercer);"Fight On" (University of Southern California fight song; 1922; Milo Sweet); "On Wisconsin" (University of Wisconsin fight song; 1909; William T. Purdy); "Happy Birthday" (1893: Mildred J. Hill, Patty S. Hill); "Rock-a-Bye Baby" (1886: Effie I. Canning). **p&d**, Wolfgang Reitherman; **cast** (voiceovers), Brian Bedford, Roger Miller, Phil Harris, Peter Ustinov, Terry-Thomas, Andy Devine, Monica Evans, Carole Shelley, George Lindsey, Ken Curtis; **w**, Ken Anderson, Vance Gerry, Frank Thomas, Eric Cleworth, Julius Svendsen, Dave Michener (based on a story by Larry Clemmons, Anderson); **m**, George Bruns; **ed**, Tom Acosta, Jim Melton; **art d**, Don Griffith; **spec eff**, Jack Buckley, Dan MacManus.

Robin Hood ★★★★ 2010; U.S./U.K.; 140m; UNIV; Color; Adventure; Children: Unacceptable (MPAA: PG-13); **BD**; **DVD**. Though this gritty and very realistic version of the legendary outlaw somewhat alters the original story and ignores some historical hard facts, it is nevertheless a superlative and mesmerizing film, and director Scott and actor Crowe masterfully recreate the indefatigable Robin. Crowe is first seen in 1199 as an archer fighting with Richard I (Richard the Lion-Heart, 1157-1199), played by Huston, as he and other archers and friends (Doyle as Allan A'Dayle; Grimes as Will Scarlet; and Durand as Little John) besiege a castle in France. Crowe and his friends are war weary, having fought with Huston in the Third Crusade in Palestine and are now engulfed in Huston's seemingly endless attritional war with Philip II of

France (1165-1223), played by Zaccaï. One night, Huston moves among his soldiers, asking their opinions about his conduct of the war, inviting open remarks and promising no reprisals for any criticisms they may make. Crowe takes Huston at his word and speaks freely, delivering some unflattering remarks. Huston ignores his promise and angrily responds by having Crowe and his friends arrested and placed in stocks, saying that he will judge them after he has successfully concluded the siege of the castle. Huston is then mortally struck by an arrow by one of the defending archers, and when Crowe learns that Huston is dying, he and his friends free themselves and flee. The deserters later see a English horse troop being attacked by French forces in a forest, those enemy troops led to that spot by Strong, a traitorous English knight, who has been collaborating with the French, secretly working with Zaccaï to assassinate Huston. Crowe and his friends take sides by assaulting the ambushing French, killing several of the attackers with will-aimed arrows. Crowe shoots an arrow at Strong that scars his face, but Strong nevertheless escapes. Crowe and his friends then find all of the English knights either dead or dying. One of those mortally stricken knights is Hodge, who plays Sir Robert Loxley. Crowe kneels beside Hodge to hear him ask that he take his sword to his father at Nottingham in England, and Crowe promises that he will do so. Hodge dies and Crowe then learns that he and other knights were carrying Huston's crown to the coast where a waiting ship is to take that crown to Huston's brother, Isaac, who plays John (King John; John Lackland; 1866-1216). Crowe decides to impersonate Hodge, and take the crown to Isaac, although his friends believe that such an act borders on lunacy. They ride to the coast, and the captain of a waiting ship, who has never met Hodge, accepts Crowe in that role and they sail for England. When arriving at London, Crowe brings the crown to the royal family to indicate that Huston is dead and he witnesses the crowning of Isaac, who first thinks to reward him for bringing the crown, but, when he hears his name, Isaac rescinds that offer, saying that his father, Sydow (who plays the father of the slain Hodge) has not paid his taxes. Isaac, an unthinking and mean-streaked tyrant, then orders heavy taxes to be levied on his citizens and orders the conniving Strong to collect those taxes in the Northern shires, though Isaac does not know that Strong is still secretly in league with the French under Zaccaï and who is plotting to create a civil aware that will more easily allow Zaccaï to invade England and where Strong expects to share in the spoils resulting from a French victory. Crowe travels on to Nottingham where he presents Hodge's sword to his father, Sydow, an elderly lord who has gone blind. He nevertheless warms to Crowe after Crowe admits that he has impersonated his son in order to return to England. Believing Crowe to be brave and artless, Sydow asks Crowe to go on pretending to be his son in order to protect the family's estate from being seized by tax collectors. Crowe agrees and his friends remain with him to help him keep order and run the estate, but Blanchett, who is Hodge's widow, initially distrusts Crowe. She begins to gain respect for him as he improves working methods at the estate and then is full of admiration for him when he recoups the estate's grain from a ruthless tax collector. In another adventure, Crowe and his friends come upon Friar Tuck, played by Addy, befriending him and making him part of their coterie. Meanwhile, Strong has stirred up such strife in the North that local barons are in revolt against Isaac, who now realizes that Strong is a traitor working with the French. Isaac bends to the pressure of the English barons and promises to later sign the Magna Carta, which will grant widespread rights to his subjects and where unfair taxation cannot be levied, a historic agreement that is suggested by none other than Crowe, who has gone to the North to aid the local barons. Strong by this time arrives in Nottingham where he searches for Crowe, believing him to be Sydow's son. When not finding him, Strong attacks Sydow. The old blind knight attempts to put up a fight, but Strong mercilessly kills him. The French soldiers under Strong's command then pillage the village, looting and killing at will. They lock up most of the villagers in a large storage building and set fire to it, but Blanchett, who has escaped with the help of some others, returns to the village and unlocks the door to the building, allowing the villagers to flee to safety. At that moment, Crowe returns with English forces that attack the French, killing most of them, but Strong escapes. From French survivors, Crowe learns that Zaccaï will soon invade England and he warns Isaac of that impending invasion. Crowe leads a contingent of Isaac's army to the Cliffs of Dover where the French invasion fleet lands on the beaches. The British and French forces battle in the surf, and Crowe then sees Blanchett arrive in armor; she attempts to kill Strong, who is fighting with the French. She is almost killed by the villain, but Crowe intervenes and drives off Strong. The tide of victory turns in favor of the English, who defeat the French, and Zaccaï returns to France with his shattered fleet. Meanwhile, Strong, while attempting to escape, is killed after Crowe sends an arrow at a long distance that pierces his neck. When Strong topples from his horse, the English army cheers not its king, Isaac, but the valiant Crowe. Realizing that Crowe is more popular as a heroic figure than he is, the jealous Isaac reneges on his promise to sign the Magna Carta and brands Crowe an outlaw for impersonating a knight. Crowe is then joined by Blanchett and his friends as they take refuge in the dense Sherwood Forest, preparing to fend off the oppressive forces of Isaac and his equally cruel minions and where many followers flock to Crowe's banner, the film ending where most other films about the legendary outlaw start with the words: "So the legend begins." Scott's direction is sure-handed as he orchestrates eye-popping action and his breathtaking battles (for which he is best known) are as well choreographed as is his fine development of characters. Crowe, Isaac, Strong, Blanchett and the rest of the cast render top-flight performances in this sweeping epic that sustains and builds tension throughout. The film has a natural feel for the primitive era it depicts, its clumpy home-spun costuming, rough-hewn jewelry, and cold and uninviting makeshift buildings appropriate to that era's hardscrabble way of life. Everything about this intriguing film is earthy, dirty and crude. Everywhere there is evidence of a lack of creature comforts, and its characters show little regard for hygiene. Most of the players are routinely shown besmirched with dirt and mud, seldom washing or bathing, and rats are routinely shown scurrying along stone floors and eating the leftovers on messy wooden dining room tables. These miserable lifestyles and unhealthy conditions would contribute over the centuries to the eventual Black Plague that stamped out a third of the world's population. The film nevertheless portrays in many telling scenes the courage, honor and dedication of its heroes, which staunchly maintains the legend of Robin Hood in spirit if not in the polished glamour to be found in most other productions about this eternally celebrated character. This film was very costly to produce, its budget exceeding $155 million, returning more than $320 million at the box office. **p**, Ridley Scott, Brian Grazer, Russell Crowe, Nikolas Korda; **d**, Scott; **cast**, Russell Crowe, Cate Blanchett, Matthew Macfadyen, Max von Sydow, William Hurt, Eileen Atkins, Mark Strong, Oscar Isaac, Danny Huston, Mark Addy, Kevin Durand, Scott Grimes, Alan Doyle, Douglas Hodge, Jonathan Zaccaï; **w**, Brian Helgeland (based on a story by Helgeland, Ethan Reiff, Cyrus Voris); **c**, John Mathieson; **m**, Marc Streitenfeld; **ed**, Pietro Scalia; **prod d**, Arthur Max; **art d**, John King, David Allday, Karen Wakefield, Ray Chan; **set d**, Sonja Klaus; **spec eff**, Trevor Wood.

Robin Hood: Men in Tights ★★★ 1993; U.S.; 104m; Brooksfilms; FOX; Color; Comedy; Children: Unacceptable (MPAA: PG-13); **3-D**; **DVD**; **VHS**. Funny spoof of the Robin Hood legend in which the Rogue of Sherwood Forest is incredibly stalwart and handsome (Elwes) and his band of merry men dress in tights. Otherwise it's the familiar story with laughs and songs as Elwes jousts with greedy Prince John (Lewis) and the Sheriff of Nottingham (Rees) and woos Maid Marian (Yasbeck). Songs: "Men in Tights," "Marian" (Mel Brooks); "Sherwood Forest Rap" (Brooks, Hummie Mann); "The Night Is Young and You're So Beautiful" (Billy Rose, Irving Kahall, Dana Suesse). Crude and off-color humor prohibit viewing by children. **p&d**, Mel Brooks; **cast**, Cary Elwes, Richard Lewis, Roger Rees, Amy Yasbeck, Mark Blankfield,

Kevin Costner as Robin Hood, about to unleash a flaming arrow in *Robin Hood: Prince of Thieves*, 1991.

Davie Chappelle, Tracy Ullman, Patrick Stewart, Dom DeLuise, Dick Van Patten, Avery Schreiber, Clive Revill, Brooks; **w**, Brooks, Evan Chandler, J. David Shapiro (based on a story by Chandler, Shapiro); **c**, Michael D. O'Shea; **m**, Hummie Mann; **ed**, Stephen E. Rivkin; **prod d**, Roy Forge Smith; **art d**, Stephen Myles Berger; **set d**, Ronald R. Reiss; **spec eff**, Richard Ratliff, Mat Beck.

Robin Hood of El Dorado ★★★ 1936; U.S.; 85m; MGM; B/W; Biographical Drama/Western; Children: Unacceptable. Baxter is exceptional as a celebrated real-life Mexican outlaw in this well-made western biopic. Mexico cedes California to the United States in the 1840s, making life almost impossible for Mexicans due to the influx of Americans seeking land and gold prospecting. A poor Mexican farmer, Joaquin Murrieta (c.1829-1853), played by Baxter, takes revenge against four Americans who killed his wife (Margo), and is then branded an outlaw. The bounty on him increases after he kills a man who brutally murders his brother. Baxter then joins with another outlaw, "Three-Fingered Jack" (Naish), and they raise an army of disgruntled Mexicans, going on a killing rampage against Americans. The Americans respond through Cabot, a friend, who leads a posse against them, until they are brought to justice. Songs: "Oh Susanna" (1846; Stephen Foster), "Bridal Chorus/Here Comes the Bride" (1850; from the opera "Lohengrin" by Richard Wagner). *Author's Note*: The almost mythical Murrieta has been profiled by many actors in several films, including **The Avenger**, 1931 (Buck Jones); **The Bandit Queen**, 1950 (Phillip Reed); **Behind the Mask of Zorro**, 2005 (made-for-TV; Jesse Borrego); **The Firebrand**, 1962 (Valentin de Vargas); **The Gay Defender**, 1927 (Richard Dix); **The Last Rebel**, 1958 (Carlos Thompson); **The Man behind the Gun**, 1953 (Robert Cabal); **The Mask of Zorro**, 1998 (Victor Rivers); **Murrieta**, 1965 (Jeffrey Hunter); **Robin Hood of El Dorado**, 1936 and **Vengeance of the West**, 1942 (Bill Elliott). For more details on Murrieta, see my book *Encyclopedia of Western Lawmen and Outlaws* (Paragon House, 1992). **p**, John W. Considine Jr.; **d**, William A. Wellman; **cast**, Warner Baxter, Ann Loring, Bruce Cabot, Margo, J. Carrol Naish, Soledad Jimenez, Eric Linden, Edgar Kennedy, Carlos de Valdez, Harvey Stephens, Marc Lawrence; Carlotta Monti; **w**, Wellman, Joseph Calleia, Melvin Levy, Peter B. Kyne, James Kevin McGuinness, Howard Emmett Rogers, Lynn Starling, C. Gardner Sullivan, Dan Totheroh (based on a novel by Walter Noble Burns); **c**, Chester Lyons; **m**, Herbert Stothart; **ed**, Robert J. Kern; **art d**, Gabriel Scognamillo, David Townsend.

Robin Hood: Prince of Thieves ★★★ 1991; U.S.; 143m; Morgan Creek/WB; Color; Adventure; Children: Unacceptable (MPAA: PG-13); **DVD**; **IV**. Costner does a good job playing British nobleman Robin of

Peter Weller in *RoboCop*, 1987.

Locksley. He is first shown saving the life of a Moor, Freeman, after they are captured by Turks during the Crusades in the Holy Land. Freeman vows to remain with Costner until he repays him for saving his life, so he goes to England with him. Costner discovers that, during his absence, his father, Blessed, a nobleman loyal to Richard I (Richard the Lion-Heart; 1157-1199), played by Connery, has been murdered by the brutal Sheriff of Nottingham, Rickman. Costner also learns that Rickman has helped install Richard's evil brother, Prince John, as king, while Richard is fighting in the Crusades. Costner returns home vowing to avenge his father's death and restore Richard to the throne, so he becomes leader of a band of exiled villagers in Sherwood Forest, who rob from the rich and give to the poor. This leads to many adventures until Costner's vow is fulfilled. Along the way, Freeman saves Costner's life and goes on his merry way while Costner is reunited with his love, Lady Marian (Mastrantonio). A top-drawer script and good action sustains interest throughout. This film was a huge box office success, taking in more than $165 million in its initial release against a budget of $48 million. Songs: "Everything I Do/ I Do It for You" (Robert John Lange, Michael Kamen, Bryan Adams), "Wild Times" (Kamen, Jeff Lynne). **p**, Pen Densham, Richard Barton Lewis, John Watson, Kevin Costner, Michael J. Kagan; **d**, Kevin Reynolds; **cast**, Kevin Costner, Morgan Freeman, Mary Elizabeth Mastrantonio, Alan Rickman, Christian Slater, Geraldine McEwan, Brian Blessed, Michael McShane, Michael Wincott, Nick Brimble; **w**, Pen Densham, John Watson (based on the Robin Hood legend and a story by Densham); **c**, Douglas Milsome; **m**, Michael Kamen; **ed**, Peter Boyle; **prod d**, John Graysmark; **art d**, Fred Carter; **spec eff**, Barry Whitrod, Craig Barron.

RoboCop ★★★★ 1987; U.S.; 102m; Orion Pictures; Color; Crime Drama/Science Fiction; Children: Unacceptable (MPAA: R); **BD**; **DVD**; **VHS**. Stunning special effects and almost nonstop action permeate this excellent sci-fi crime thriller that is set in Detroit, Michigan, in the near future. The city is beset with widespread crime and underworld thugs endless abound to create constant mayhem and murder. To combat the incessant crime waves, the city signs a deal with a mega corporation that now administers law and order. At the same time, "Old Detroit" is slowly demolished and a utopian metropolis is constructed in its place, which is to be called "Delta City." O'Herlihy, who heads the corporation, approves of a new program that will create cyborg policemen, all reconstructed from deceased officers, these law enforcement robots to be called "RoboCops." Weller, who has been teamed with female officer Allen, becomes the first cyborg after he is killed when chasing a group of maniacal thieves, led by Smith. His body is encased with bullet-proof armor and implanted with cybernetic elements that allow him to reason and even have sporadic memories of his former life. He is programmed

to stop and destroy all lethal lawbreakers and he embarks on his mission as a dedicated RoboCop. He is a one-man army that deals with any crisis and soon brings law and order to Detroit. His flashes of memory, however, compel him to locate his former home where he searches for his wife and son, but he finds them gone and that they believe him to be dead. He eventually locates his own killer, Smith, but his programming will not allow him to kill Smith, only arrest him. When Weller also discovers that Smith has been working with Cox, another corporation executive, who has been conducting underworld operations with Smith, he is also prevented by secret programming Cox has ordered, from taking the corporate boss into custody. Further, Cox tries to take over the government with a monstrous droid, ED-209, which has malfunctioned in the past and killed a government director. Weller confronts ED-209, but he cannot overcome the droid's firepower, which annihilates everything and everyone in its path. Cox then attempts to kill O'Herlihy at a board meeting, believing that Weller's programming will prevent him from intervening, but when O'Herlihy simply fires Cox, Weller's programming then allows him to dispatch the culprit while he later outwits and defeats the droid, dispatches Smith, and finally brings peace to the city. Verhoeven does a great job helming this thriller, and the robots and their actions fill the screen with eye-popping action. Though **RoboCop** bears a marked similarity to the powerful and deadly robot appearing in **The Day the Earth Stood Still**, 1951, the director and scriptwriters infused enough humanity into this marvelous automated character to make him distinctive and empathetic. This film did well at the box office, taking in more than $53 million against a $13 million budget. **p**, Arne Schmidt; **d**, Paul Verhoeven; **cast**, Peter Weller, Nancy Allen, Dan O'Herlihy, Ronny Cox, Kurtwood Smith, Miguel Ferrer, Robert DoQui, Ray Wise, Felton Perry, Paul McCrane; **w**, Edward Neumeier, Michael Miner; **c**, Jost Vacano, Sol Negrin; **m**, Basil Poledouris; **ed**, Frank J. Urioste; **prod d**, William Sandell; **art d**, Gayle Simon; **set d**, Robert Gould; **spec eff**, Peter Kuran, William Purcell.

The Rocketeer ★★★ 1991; U.S.; 108m; Disney/Buena Vista; Color; Adventure; Children: Unacceptable (MPAA: PG); **BD**; **DVD**, **VHS**. Good action and special effects crown this cartoon-strip type adventure tale. Campbell is a stalwart young pilot, who, along with his friend, Arkin, stumbles upon a prototype backpack that allows Campbell to become a high-flying masked rocket hero. The adventure is set in the 1930s pioneering age of aviation with gangsters and a Nazi spy, Dalton, who all want the invention for a war weapon while Dalton also wants Campbell's beautiful girlfriend, Connelly, for himself. While soaring about California and even through and about a vast nightclub, Campbell manages to defeat the villains, protecting the important rockets for America. Enjoyable and entertaining throughout, this film is evocatively reminiscent of the many popular futuristic serials of the late 1930s and early 1940s. It took in more than $62 million against a $42 million budget. Songs: "Der Hoelle Rache" (Wolfgang Amadeus Mozart); "You're a Sweet Little Headache" (Ralph Rainger, Leo Robin); "Drum Majorette" (Arnold Steck); "Amboss Polka" (A. Parlow); "Vilia" (Franz Lehar, Paul Francis Webster); "Begin the Beguine," "Night and Day," "Easy to Love" (Cole Porter); "Any Old Time" (Artie Shaw); "In a Sentimental Mood" (Duke Ellington); "When Your Lover Has Gone" (E.A. Swan); "Barrage" (Charles Williams); "All Dressed Up and No Place to Go" (Oscar Levant, Edward Heyman). Mature themes prohibit viewing by children. **p**, Charles Gordon, Lawrence Gordon, Lloyd Levin, Dave Stevens; **d**, Joe Johnston; **cast**, Billy Campbell, Jennifer Connelly, Alan Arkin, Timothy Dalton, Paul Sovino, Terry O'Quinn, Ed Lauter, James Handy, Robert Guy Miranda, John Lavachielli, Jon Polito, Eddie Jones; **w**, Danny Bilson, Paul De Meo (based on the graphic novel by Stevens); **c**, Hiro Narita; **m**, James Horner; **ed**, Arthur Schmidt; **prod d**, James D. Bissell; **art d**, Christopher Burian-Mohr; **set d**, Linda DeScenna; **spec eff**, Jon G. Belyeu.

Rock 'n' Roll High School ★★★ 1979; U.S.; 93m; New World Pictures; Color; Comedy; Children: Unacceptable (MPAA: PG); **DVD**; **VHS**. A ridiculous script and inane acting is overcome by a bevy of outstanding tunes that caption the rock 'n' roll craze that has gone with the Charleston, swing, disco and innumerable other musical vogues. A high school has a hard time keeping principals, all succumbing to nervous breakdowns because of the students' fanatical love of rock 'n' roll and their lack of interest in studies. Their leader, Soles, loves the music of the rock band the Ramones. A new rock-hating principal, Woronov, vows to end the music craze and gets help from parents, who attempt to burn a pile of rock 'n' roll records. The students retaliate by taking over the school. The Ramones join them and are made honorary students. Police demand that the students evacuate the building, but, instead, they blow up the school (and what other reasonable conclusion could be expected). Songs: "Alley Cat" (Bent Fabric), "School Day (Ring! Ring Goes the Bell)" (Chuck Berry); "Smokin' in the Boy's Room" (Brownsville Station); "School's Out" (Alice Cooper); "Come Back Jonee" (Devo); "Teenage Depression," "Albatross," "Jigsaw Puzzle Blues" (Fleetwood Mac); "So It Goes" (Nick Lowe); "Did We Meet Somewhere Before?" (Paul McCartney, Denny Laine); "High School," "C'mon Let's Go," "You're the Best" (The Paley Brothers); "A Dream Goes on Forever" (Todd Rundgren); "Rock 'n' Roll," "Spirits Drifting," "Alternative 3," "M386," Energy Fools the Magician" (Brian Eno); "Blitzkrieg Bop," "I Just Wanna Have Something to Do," "I Wanna Be Sedated," "I Wanna Be Your Boyfriend," "I Want You Around," "Pinhead," "She's the One," "Questioningly," "Rock 'n' Roll High School," "Sheena Is a Punk Rocker," "Teenage Lobotomy," "California Sun," "Do You Wanna Dance?" (The Ramones). Gutter language and excessive violence prohibit viewing by children. **p**, Michael Finnell; **d**, Allan Arkush; **cast**, P.J. Soles, Vincent Van Patten, Clint Howard, Dey Young, Mary Woronov, Paul Bartel, Dick Miller, Don Steele, Alix Elias, Loren Lester; **w**, Richard Whitely, Russ Dvonch, Joseph McBride (based on a story by Arkush, Joe Dante); **c**, Dean Cundey (Metrocolor); **m**, The Ramones (Joey, Johnny, Dee Dee, Marky Ramone); **ed**, Larry Bock, Gail Werbin; **art d**, Marie Kordus; **set d**, Linda Pearl.

Rock around the Clock ★★★ 1956; U.S.; 77m; Clover Productions; COL; B/W; Biographical Drama/Musical; Children: Unacceptable (MPAA: G); **DVD**; **VHS**. In the first true rock 'n' roll feature film, a band promoter, Freed, meets Bill Haley and the Comets at a small-town dance and becomes their manager and takes them to New York where they become a sensation. The fictionalized film of the beginning of rock 'n' roll caused riots in some cities and was banned in some countries as teenagers were so excited about the new sound of pop music that they rioted. Songs: "Rock around the Clock" (Max C. Freedman, Jimmy de Knight); "Happy Baby" (Frank Pingatore); "Razzle-Dazzle" (Charles E. Calhoun); "A.B.C. Boogie" (Max Spickol, A. Russell); "Mambo Rock," "Mambo Capri," "Sad and Lonely," "Skins," "Codfish and Potatoes" (Tony Martinez); "The Great Pretender," "Only You" (Buck Ram); "See You Later, Alligator" (Robert C. Gurdy); "R-O-C-K" (Bill Haley, Arrett Keefer, Ruth Keefer); "Rudy's Rock" (Haley, Rudy Pompilii); "We're Gonna Teach You to Rock" (Fred Bell); "Giddy Up Ding Dong" (Pep Lantanzi, Bell); "Rock-a-Beatin' Boogie" (Haley). Violence prohibits viewing by children. **p**, Sam Katzman; **d**, Fred F. Sears; **cast**, Bill Haley and the Comets (Rudy Pompilli, Al Rex, Franny Beecher, Johnny Grande, Ralph Jones, Billy Williamson), The Platters (Tony Williams, Zola Taylor, Herb Reed, David Lynch, Paul Robi), Tony Martinez, Freddie Bell, Alan Freed, Johnny Johnston, Alix Talton; **w**, Robert E. Kent, James B. Gordon (based on their story); **c**, Benjamin. H. Kline; **m**, Fred Karger; **ed**, Saul A. Goodkind, Jack Ogilvie; **art d**, Paul Palmentola.

Rocketship X-M ★★★ 1950; U.S.; 71m; Lippert Pictures; B/W; Science Fiction; Children: Unacceptable; **DVD**; **IV**. Well-made sci-fi thriller sees a spaceship heading for the Moon when it is sent far off-course by meteors, causing the craft to land on Mars where its astronauts

John Mills and John Howard Davies in *The Rocking Horse Winner*, 1950.

discover ruins of a great civilization that was destroyed in a nuclear war. Blind, mutilated survivors of this civilization attack the crew and kill some of them, leaving only three survivors. Their three survivors manage to leave Mars, but their spacecraft, while reentering Earth's atmosphere, begins to disintegrate, killing them before they can land safely. **p,d&w**, Kurt Neumann; **cast**, Lloyd Bridges, Osa Massen, John Emery, Noah Beery Jr., Hugh O'Brian, Morris Ankrum, Patrick Ahern, Sherry Moreland, John Dutra, Katherine Marlowe; **c**, Karl Struss; **m**, Ferde Grofe; **ed**, Harry Gerstad; **prod d & art d**, Theobold Holsopple; **set d**, Clarence Steensen; **spec eff**, Jack Rabin, Irving A. Block, Don Stewart, Tom Scherman.

The Rocking Horse Winner ★★★★ 1950; U.K.; 91m; Two Cities Films/UNIV; B/W; Drama/Fantasy; Children: Unacceptable; **DVD**; **VHS**. Riveting tale sees a memorable performance from Davies as a boy possessed of a strange and destructive gift after he receives a rocking horse as a present. Davies lives with his dominating mother, Hobson, and his weak-willed father, Sinclair, in an upscale London residence. Hobson, though she possesses most creature comforts, is constantly complaining about family expenses, although she compulsively buys hats, dresses and jewelry she really does not need, exhausting the family coffers. Sinclair is a hopeless gambler, who invariably loses at the racetrack, never being able to pick a winning race horse. The family is forever being bailed out of their financial problems by Squire, a rich uncle. After the impressionable Davies receives as a Christmas gift a new but odd-looking hobby horse, Mills, the family man, shows him how to ride that horse as if he were a jockey furiously riding at the races. Davies begins to ride the horse, and, the faster he rocks, the more he is inspired to recall from thin air the name of a winning horse in a race that has yet to be run. Hobson learns of this, and she and Sinclair place a bet on the name of that horse predicted by Davies and it wins. As Hobson encourages Davies to ride again, he predicts another winning horse and his parents begin to grow rich from enormous winnings. Hobson's greed is insatiable and she demands that Davies ride again and again to provide the names of winning horses, but, each time Davies rides the rocking hobby horse, he becomes exhausted and emotionally drained. Hobson ignores the trauma caused by Davies' experiences and continues to urge her son to ride his hobby horse again. He does, but the effort leaves him in a state of complete collapse. Davies is now obsessed with appeasing his profligate mother, and, to find the name of just one more winner, he fearfully rides the hobby horse one more time, hearing his house crying out to him: "We need more money!" He frenetically rides the hobby horse and the winning horse's name comes to him, but the emotional task is too much for him as he dies in the process. Mills, who has been Davies' only real friend, goes to Hobson after her son's burial and offers

Sylvester Stallone in *Rocky*, 1976.

her a fortune in winnings from the Derby, winnings achieved by her son's last desperate and deathly ride. Hobson now realizes what she has done to her child and recoils in horror at the sight of the money, telling Mills that it is "blood money" and he is to burn it. She has sadly learned her lesson too late as this somber allegorical tale emphasizes. Pelissier, who directed and wrote this absorbing and chilling film presents a faithful adaptation of the original short story from the gifted Lawrence, and Davies' mesmerizing performance is a sight to behold. Davies had earlier appeared as the leading character in David Lean's classic **Oliver Twist**, 1948, a film in which he also gave another great performance. **p**, John Mills; **d&w,** Anthony Pelissier (based on the story by D.H. Lawrence); **cast**, Valerie Hobson, John Howard Davies, Ronald Squire, John Mills, Hugh Sinclair, Charles Goldner, Susan Richards, Cyril Smith, Anthony Holles, Melanie McKenzie; **c**, Desmond Dickinson; **m**, William Alwyn; **ed**, John Seabourne; **art d**, Carmen Dillon; **spec eff**, Francis Carver.

Rocky ★★★★★ 1976; U.S.; 119m; Chartoff-Winkler Productions; UA; Color; Sports Drama; Children: Unacceptable (MPAA: PG); **BD**; **DVD**; **VHS**. Touching, powerful and forever fondly memorable, this classic rags-to-riches-in-the-ring tale was the brainchild of its star, Stallone, and his sudden and startling appearance in this wonderful film deservedly made of him a superstar. Stallone is first shown as a club fighter (named Rocky Balboa, "The Italian Stallion"), picking up short money for going a few rounds with punch-drunk boxers while he also works as an enforcer for loan shark Spinell. He does not like his job much as he chases down debtors, threatening to break their fingers, arms and legs if they do not pay the exorbitant interest due on their loans. Spinell, who likes Stallone and thinks he has promise as a boxer, nevertheless takes him aside and lectures him, telling him he must punish delinquent borrowers or that he, Spinell, will lose face as a no-nonsense loan shark. Stallone promises to do better, but his heart is not in such oppressive work. He stops by a pet store to see Shire, a shy, pretty young woman, who works there, making small talk with her. She barely responds, although she knows Stallone has an interest in her and she also likes him because he has bought pets from her in the past and loves animals. Stallone lives alone in a small, cheap apartment in a Philadelphia tenement area where the walls are adorned with pictures of his childhood. He works out at a small gym operated by aging boxing trainer Meredith, who has long earlier given up on Stallone as a contending prizefighter, telling Stallone he has no discipline, has not trained properly, and that his once-in-a-while fighting matches offer him opponents who are basically "bums." To show his utter disregard for the slovenly Stallone, Meredith has his locker cleaned out and gives it to another boxer Meredith deems worthy, having the cleaning man place Stallone's belongings

in a bag that hangs on a rack and where Stallone complains that he has been moved to "skid row." Meanwhile, Stallone visits with his friend, Young, who works at a meat packing firm and is Shire's brother. He asks Young why his sister is not friendlier toward him. Young, who wants to marry Shire off to anyone, takes Stallone to his home, surprising the withdrawn Shire, who hides out in her room. Encouraged by Young, the bashful Stallone asks Shire to go on a date while shouting to her as he stands on the other side of a door. Her unresponsive silence so angers Young that he tosses a chicken Shire has been cooking out the back door and begins yelling at her. Shire then opens the door, dressed in coat and hat, ready to go anywhere to escape her brother's wrath. Stallone takes Shire to dinner and then to an ice-skating rink where an attendant tells him that it is closed. Stallone persuades the attendant to allow them to use the rink for a few minutes for $10 and Stallone walks with Shire, telling her about his life as she awkwardly skates on the ice. The two then go to Stallone's cramped apartment, although Shire is reluctant to enter. When she does, he shows her the turtles he keeps, reminding her that he bought these pets from her. Shire slowly warms to Stallone and they finally kiss and then become lovers. Stallone's life vastly improves with Shire in his life while, unknown to him, others are remolding that life. Weathers, a black fighter and the heavyweight champion, is having a hard time in getting anyone to fight him. Weathers then gets a big promotional idea. He will fight an unknown in Philadelphia to celebrate the 1976 bicentennial, giving that opponent an equal opportunity at the title, thinking that he will have to carry the novice fighter for a few rounds until he knocks him out. He scans the available prizefighters in the area in the current boxing registry and spots Stallone's picture and his boxing nickname, "The Italian Stallion," mocking that name and saying that this is the man he will make famous before sending him to the canvas with stars in his eyes. David, the local fight promoter, goes big for the idea and he summons Stallone to his office where he offers Stallone the opportunity to fight Weathers. Stallone is shocked and refuses, saying that he is no match for the heavyweight champion of the world. David asks Stallone if he believes that America is the land of opportunity, and Stallone agrees that it is. Then David points out that that opportunity, which comes only once in a lifetime, is at his door and that he should take advantage of the offer. Stallone thinks about it and agrees to fight Weathers. Both fighters appear on a prerecorded television press conference that Stallone watches with Shire in Young's home; Young tells Stallone that he needs him to be one of his trainers. In that press conference the flamboyant Weathers brags that he will give Stallone a good fight before he puts him away, comments that do not disturb Stallone, who is only grateful for the opportunity to make substantial money so that he and Shire can be married. At first, and having no place to train, Stallone goes to the meat-packing plant where Young works and uses the frozen carcasses of meat hanging from meat hooks as punching bags, hammering away at the frozen slabs of meat. Young tells the press about this, and Stallone is then interviewed while slamming his fists into that stiff beef in the frozen meat locker. Hearing the news that Stallone is going to fight Weathers, fight manager Meredith goes to Stallone's apartment one night and, hat in hand, tells him that he needs a good manager for his upcoming fight. Stallone more or less ignores him, and Meredith practically begs Stallone for the opportunity to manage him. Stallone is still bristling over the way Meredith earlier treated him and cuts off the conversation by going into the bathroom and closing the door. Meredith now realizes that Stallone wants nothing more to do with him and the old man leaves, walking slowly down the stairs from Stallone's miserable dwelling. Stallone cannot resist venting his spleen on Meredith, shouting after him that Meredith earlier called him a bum and ranting about having to live in a "stinking" little apartment. Meredith, an utterly defeated man, turns a deaf ear to Stallone's invective, slowly leaving the apartment building and walking down the street. In a long shot, however, we see Stallone revert to his compassionate nature as he runs from the apartment building and after Meredith, catching up with the old man. We cannot hear the words they exchange, but it is evident that Stallone wants Meredith to manage him for the fight when they shake hands. When loan shark Spinell sees Stallone on the street and knowing he is about to fight Weathers, he gives him some cash to pay for his training, wishing him well, and then yanks a cigarette from Stallone's mouth, saying: "You're in training!" Meredith then puts Stallone through grueling training, compelling him to do endless sit-ups, pushups, bag-punching, sparring with opponents, until his muscles are toned, his breathing improves and he becomes a fine specimen of a prizefighter. Stallone captions this training by running through the streets of Philadelphia and where its citizens recognize him as a contender to the title, their pride swelling in knowing that he is one of their own, a nobody from nowhere, who has suddenly captured the public's attention and imagination. Shire makes a gift of a large dog that Stallone has always admired in her shop (this was Stallone's dog in real life) and the devoted animal accompanies him on some of his running jaunts. The scenes of Stallone running through the neighborhoods and marketplaces of Philadelphia, along its waterfront and thoroughfares, is thrilling to watch as Conti's dynamic score and the lyrics "getting strong now" accompanies the pounding steps of Stallone. Children begin to follow him in his dawn runs, more and more of them collecting, all of these youngsters now looking upon Stallone as their hero. They emulate him by racing behind him as he swiftly enters a park and then dashes up a tremendous flight of stairs to reach the top (of Philadelphia's Museum of Art) and jubilantly jumps with the joy of victory, and those ecstatic children leap and jump with him, one of the most electrifying and triumphant scenes in any picture. Stallone is now ready to go into that ring with the heavyweight champion of the world. Stallone has second thoughts about the fight and tells Shire that he really has no chance of beating Weathers. She nevertheless supports him, although she cannot bear to go to the area to see him fight, so fearful is she of his being injured. When visiting the empty arena before the fight begins, Stallone sees huge pictures of Weathers and himself. Promoter David appears and calms him down, but he is apprehensive as he is dressed and prepared in his locker room by Meredith and Young, and he is still on edge when he later goes into that packed arena, receiving applause from supporters. As he stands in the ring, he sees Weathers saunter down an aisle dressed in an Uncle Sam outfit, waving to his admirers; Meredith tells Stallone to ignore the fanfare and concentrate on the fight. When the fight begins, the overly confident Weathers playfully jabs at Stallone, staggering him. Awkward by comparison to Weathers' stylish fight manners, Stallone wades in toward his opponent and surprising staggers and knocks him down with a powerful blow. Weathers now knows he is in for a real fight, but he finds it difficult to combat Stallone since he is fighting a southpaw who leads with his right, an unorthodox way of fighting that keeps Weathers off balance. The two ferociously battle round after round, landing haymakers that stagger each other. Meanwhile, Shire, who had refused to attend the fight, appears, and the sight of her encourages Stallone to go the distance. At the end of the brutal, relentless fight, each man lands powerful blows against the other, but neither goes to the canvas. In the end, Weathers barely wins the fight in a close decision. He tells Stallone that he will never give him a rematch and Stallone tells him that he does not want one. He feels, as does everyone watching this epic ring struggle that he has nevertheless triumphed and the film concludes with the badly beaten Stallone clutching the woman he loves for a freeze-frame ending. Alvidsen directs this inspiring film with a firm hand, taking great care to develop Stallone's character as well as that of Shire, Meredith, Young, Weathers, Spinell and the rest of the cast, while providing many tender and touching moments that humanize these memorable characters. The titanic fight at the end is brilliantly choreographed and so realistic that these traumatic scenes excitingly reenact the vivid ring battles that can be seen in newsreels of classic title bouts. Stallone's script is superb, masterfully working one seamless scene into another, and the dialog is down to earth and believable. He provides no outlandish heroics, only the dedicated resolve of a man to seek and find a better way of life that will include the two things

Sylvester Stallone and Burgess Meredith in *Rocky*, 1976.

that he has always been denied—love and respect. Its appealing simplicity encompasses complex and conflicting emotions, all resolved when its courageous protagonist overcomes an oppressive lifestyle while gaining the affection of a loving and caring woman. Production values are superlative, the lensing crisp and innovative from Crabe, and Conti's brilliant score is a heart-lifting gem. This magnificent film ranks with the very best prizefighting productions (**Body and Soul**, 1947; **Champion**, 1949; **Cinderella Man**, 2005; **City for Conquest**, 1940; **Golden Boy**, 1939; **Requiem for a Heavyweight**, 1962; and **Somebody Up There Likes Me**, 1956, to name a few). The film deservedly won Oscars for Best Picture, Best Director (Alvidsen) and Best Film Editing (Halsey and Conrad). It received Oscar nominations for Best Actor (Stallone), Best Actress (Shire), Best Supporting Actor (Meredith), Best Original Screenplay (Stallone), Best Original Song ("Gonna Fly Now" by Conti, Connors and Robbins), and Best Sound Mixing (Bud Alper, Lyle J. Burbridge, William McCaughey, and Harry W. Tetrick). The film was box office dynamite, producing more than $225 million against a $1 million budget. Songs: "Take Me Back" (Frank Stallone Jr.); "Rocky's Theme," "Gonna Fly Now" (music: Bill Conti; lyrics: Carol Connors, Ayn Robbins); "You Take My Heart Away" (Deetta Little); "Summer Madness" (composer unknown); "The First Noel" (traditional); "Jingle Bells" (1857; James Pierpont); "Silent Night, Holy Night" (1818; Franz Gruber), "Deck the Halls" (traditional Welsh song), "U.S. Marine Corps Hymn" (1868, from "Genevieve de Brabant" by Jacques Offenbach). ***Author's Note***: Like the story of this film, its genesis produced a rags-to-riches success for the gifted Stallone. Before making this film, Stallone was a supporting actor with only a few credits to his name. He decided to write scripts and wrote one after another without success while struggling to support his wife and child, all living in a West Hollywood apartment that was about as cramped as the one in which Rocky Balboa resides. Stallone struggled for two years at writing scripts that no one bought. One night, while he was close to being broke, Stallone watched a televised fight between heavyweight champion Muhammad Ali and New Jersey club fighter Chuck Wepner. No one expected Wepner to last more than a round or two, but he doggedly stayed in the fight almost to the very end before losing the match. Wepner became an overnight hero by demonstrating his courage in refusing to quit against a man who greatly overmatched him, and this gave Stallone the idea to write **Rocky**. He reportedly wrote the screenplay in three days and gave it to Gene Kirkwood, who, in turn, submitted the script to Winkler and Chartoff. They offered Stallone $75,000 for the script, thinking to make an inexpensive film about the subject. Though he was close to starving at that time, Stallone stubbornly held out and the price for the script soared upward to $250,000, but Stallone held firm, saying that he wanted to star in the film. The producers were so

Errol Flynn in *Rocky Mountain*, 1950.

impressed with his passionate insistence that only he could make **Rocky** come to life (having lived about the same existence as his character) that they convinced United Artists to allow him to star in the film, which was then produced for about $1 million and the rest is history, or, the stuff that dreams are made of. **p**, Irwin Winkler, Robert Chartoff; **d**, John G. Avildsen; **cast**, Sylvester Stallone, Talia Shire, Burt Young, Carl Weathers, Burgess Meredith, Thayer David, Joe Spinell, Frank Stallone, Christopher Avildsen, George O'Hanlon, Joe Frazier; **w**, Stallone; **c**, James Crabe (Technicolor); **m**, Bill Conti; **ed**, Richard Halsey, Scott Conrad; **prod d**, Bill Cassidy; **art d**, James H. Spencer; **set d**, Ray Molyneaux.

Rocky Mountain ★★★ 1950; U.S.; 83m; WB; B/W; Western; Children: Unacceptable; **DVD**. Exciting and action-loaded, this well-written and superbly acted western takes place during the waning days of the Civil War. The indefatigable Flynn leads a small band of Confederate soldiers to the mountains of Nevada on a secret and desperate mission in an effort to turn the tide of war in favor of the failing South. Flynn and his men go to a rocky outcropping in the desert to await contact from a Rebel agent who has been organizing a small army in California and Nevada to fight for the South in order to draw large Union forces from the East to relieve dwindling Confederate armies. While waiting, Flynn and his men see in the distance a stagecoach that is being attacked by Indians. They ride to the rescue, beating off the Indians and saving the lives of stage driver Johnson and his lone passenger, Wymore, a beautiful, young woman who has been traveling to see her fiancé, Forbes, a Union commander in the area. Flynn and his men take these survivors to their mountain lair for protection, but do not tell them about their mission. Meanwhile, Petrie, a mysterious character, arrives, saying that he represents the leader of the southern guerrilla forces they are to meet, but he gives them little information while they all await the expected arrival of Forbes, Flynn believing that that Union officer will now be searching for Wymore. He is right. Forbes arrives on the scene with a few soldiers and three Indian guides, and Flynn and his men quickly capture them. The Indians make an escape, and one of them is killed. He is identified by Johnson as the son of the elderly Indian who has escaped and who is a chief. Petrie then departs, promising that he will return with the Confederate guerrillas. After gunshots are heard in the night, it is assumed that Petrie has been killed by Indians led by the escaped chief, and the Rebels now believe that they are surrounded by hostiles. Forbes then escapes, Wymore telling Flynn (they are attracted to each other even though her heart belongs to Forbes) that Forbes will return with his Union forces to save them from the Indians that surround them. Flynn has no intention of being captured by Federal troops as he plans an escape for his small contingent. Realizing that Wymore will

not have a chance when the Indians close in, Flynn and his men all decide to leave their rocky perch and lead the Indians away from her as Flynn orders Johnson to take Wymore in the opposite direction and to safety. Seeing hordes of Indians collecting on the plains in the distance, Flynn rides out from the mountainous hideout with his men, drawing the Indians after them. Johnson and Wymore ride off to find Forbes, who has arrived with his entire troop. Wymore begs Forbes to ride after Flynn and save the noble Rebels from annihilation. This Forbes does while Flynn and his men are pursued by the hostiles. The Rebels ride furiously through the desert plains until they race into a boxed canyon where no escape is possible. Flynn turns his men about, saying: "They've seen our backs. Now let's show them our faces!" As the Indians charge forward, Flynn orders his men to fire a volley from their rifles, and many Indians topple from their horses. Flynn then leads his men in a charge right into the hordes of Indians, and each man is overwhelmed while battling with the hostiles, the last to die being Flynn as two arrows are sent into him before he topples dead to the earth (in much the same manner Flynn died as George Armstrong Custer when leading his men at the 1876 battle of Little Bighorn in **They Died with Their Boots On**, 1941). Forbes and his Union troopers, along with Wymore and Johnson, then arrive at the scene to see the Indians gone and Flynn and his heroic men all dead. Forbes finds among the dead a Confederate flag, and, in honor of the sacrifice made by the Rebels, orders that that flag be raised atop a nearby mountain. After the flag is raised, Forbes and his men draw sabers and salute their fallen foe to end this stirring film. Keighley's direction is firm in unfolding the intriguing story, building suspense throughout as the impending Indian attack is slowly mounted; the acting is outstanding from the entire cast, Flynn giving one of his more reserved performances. The script is intelligent and witty, and Steiner's dynamic score gives great emphasis to the harrowing plotline. *Author's Note*: This was the film debut of character actors Wooley and Pickens (his first speaking role), the latter's real name being Louis Burton Lindley Jr., and would go on to be a very popular supporting player in many films, especially as the gung ho bomber pilot who starts WWIII in **Dr. Strangelove**, 1964. Keighley told this author that "**Rocky Mountain** was really promised to Ronald Reagan first, not Errol [Flynn]. Ronnie went to Jack Warner and complained about the second-rate films he was being given and said he wanted to do a western. Jack told him that if he brought him a good western story, he would put Ronnie in it. Ronnie came up with a story called "Ghost Mountain" that had been written by Alan Le May, and Jack like that story. So what does he do? He casts Errol in that picture, not Ronnie. Errol was Jack's favorite actor at Warner Brothers at the time and he did a great job in **Rocky Mountain**, his last western. Well, Ronnie was used to playing second fiddle, but he got to be the conductor when he became President, so Lady Fortune remembered him after all. Le May was a really good writer. He later wrote **The Searchers** [1956] and westerns don't come any better than that one." Flynn's career was in decline when he made this film, but his amorous nature was in full force. He was immediately attracted to the attractive Wymore, and she fell in love with him. They married shortly after this film was completed, a union that ended with Flynn's untimely death in 1959. **p**, William Jacobs; **d**, William Keighley; **cast**, Errol Flynn, Patrice Wymore, Scott Forbes, Guinn "Big Boy" Williams, Dick Jones, Howard Petrie, Slim Pickens, Chubby Johnson, Buzz Henry, Sheb Wooley, Peter Coe, Yakima Canutt; **w**, Alan Le May, Winston Miller (based on the story "Ghost Mountain" by Le May); **c**, Ted McCord; **m**, Max Steiner; **ed**, Rudi Fehr; **art d**, Stanley Fleischer; **set d**, L.S. Edwards.

Rocky II ★★★ 1979; U.S.; 119m; UA; Color; Sports Drama; Children: Unacceptable (MPAA: PG); **BD**; **DVD**; **VHS**. In this good sequel to **Rocky**, 1976, Rocky Balboa (Stallone), a little-known boxer, did so well in a boxing match against champion Apollo Creed (Weathers) in the first film in the series that the champ is embarrassed by not doing better against a fighter he considers to be an amateur. Weathers wants to have a rematch, something he said in the first film he would never allow. Shire, who is Stallone's pregnant wife, tries to dissuade Stallone from boxing again, fearing for his safety, but he needs the money, so he agrees to the rematch. She relents and gives him her approval and, with Meredith as his demanding but avuncular trainer, and Young as his assistant, Stallone readies himself for another titanic ring battle. When he does get into the ring with Weathers, Stallone endures an even bloodier fight than the previous one, this time winning and becoming the heavyweight champion of the world. At the end of that grueling fight, a badly beaten but victorious Stallone holds the championship belt high above his head as the watching crowd goes wild and he shouts Shire's name in recognition to the woman of his heart: "Yo, Adrian!" Stallone cast a gaggle of his relatives in the film and even cast his dog (that canine had also appeared in the original film). Songs: "Scat Street," "Two Kinds of Love" (Frank Stallone). Excessive violence prohibits viewing by children. Sequel to **Rocky**, 1976, followed by **Rocky III**, 1982, **Rocky IV**, 1985, **Rocky V**, 1990, and **Rocky Balboa**, 2006. **p**, Irwin Winkler, Robert Chartoff; **d&w**, Sylvester Stallone; **cast**, Stallone, Talia Shire, Burt Young, Carl Weathers, Burgess Meredith, Tony Burton, Joe Spinell, Leonard Gaines, Sylvia Meals, Frank McRae, Al Silvani; **c**, Bill Butler (Panavision; Technicolor); **m**, Bill Conti; **ed**, Stanford C. Allen, Janice Hampton; **art d**, Richard Berger; **set d**, Ed Baer.

Rogue Cop ★★★ 1954; U.S./U.K.; 92m; MGM; B/W; Crime Drama; Children: Unacceptable; **DVD**; **VHS**. Taut crime yarn sees veteran cop Taylor on the take from crime boss Raft. Taylor's younger brother, Forrest, also a cop, witnesses a murderer running away from the scene of a crime. Mobster Raft offers Taylor $15,000 if he gets Forrest not to testify at the suspect's trial. Forrest, an honest cop, refuses, so Raft puts out a hit on him. Taylor, consumed by vengeance, then tries to track down his brother's killer and, in the harrowing process, dismantles Raft and his illegal operations. Taylor, Forrest and Raft are standouts in this above-average film noir entry, stemming from a story by McGivern, who also wrote the novel upon which another fine film noir film is based, **The Big Heat**, 1953, that story, too, dealing with corrupt police officials. **p**, Nicholas Nayfack; **d**, Roy Rowland; **cast**, Robert Taylor, Janet Leigh, George Raft, Steve Forrest, Anne Francis, Alan Hale Jr., Vince Edwards, Olive Carey, Roy Barcroft, Connie Marshall. **w**, Sydney Boehm (based on the novel by William P. McGivern); **c**, John Seitz; **m**, Jeff Alexander; **ed**, James E. Newcom; **art d**, Cedric Gibbons, Hans Peters; **set d**, Edwin B. Willis, Keogh Gleason; **spec eff**, A. Arnold Gillespie.

Rogue's Regiment ★★★ 1948; U.S.; 85m.; UNIV; B/W; Adventure; Children: Unacceptable. A tough and uncompromising Powell is a U.S. Intelligence agent, who enlists in the French Foreign Legion in order to track down a Nazi war criminal, McNally. McNally's character is likened to Martin Bormann (1900-1945), the third highest ranking Nazi during World War II (1939-1945). While serving in the Legion and probing for McNally, Powell encounters Price, who is a gun dealer and whose front is being an antique seller. Powell finally nabs his man, but not without overcoming many perils and at the close risk of his life. Powell rivets in his role as the dogged agent, and McNally and Price prove exceptional villains. Songs: "Just for a While," "Who Can Tell" (music: Serge Walter; lyrics: Jack Brooks). *Author's Note*: Price told this author that "I got to play another devious person in **Rogue's Regiment**, a man you can trust no farther than a gnat's eyelash. It was a delightful role." **p**, Robert Buckner; **d**, Robert Florey; **cast**, Dick Powell, Marta Toren, Vincent Price, Stephen McNally, Edgar Barrier, Henry Rowland, Carol Thurston, Richard Loo, Philip Ahn, Richard Fraser; **w**, Buckner (based on a story by Buckner, Florey); **c**, Maury Gertsman; **m**, Daniele Amfitheatrof; **ed**, Ralph Dawson; **art d**, Bernard Herzbrun, Gabriel Scognamillo; **set d**, Russell A. Gausman, Oliver Emert.

Rollerball ★★★ 1975; U.S.; 125m; Algonquin/UA; Color; Science Fic-

James Caan, left, fighting for his life in *Rollerball*, 1975.

tion; Children: Unacceptable (MPAA: R); **DVD**; **VHS**. Chilling sci-fi entry depicts a futuristic society in 2018 where corporations have replaced countries and control energy, transportation, housing, and communication on a global basis. The game of Rollerball, similar to Roller Derby but much more violent with some players riding motorcycles, is used to control people by demonstrating the futility of individuality. The object of the game, a substitute for warfare, is for players to kill their opponents. However, one player, Caan, who becomes a superstar at the sport, fights for his personal freedom and comes to threaten corporate control. (The same theme, but one set against a Roman tyrant and former general turned arena fighter is seen in **Gladiator**, 2000.) Houseman, a corporate leader, slackens the game's rules to intentionally cause more deaths. Caan goes ballistic in a climactic game on roller-skates, where he refuses to kill his main opponent, and the crowd roars its approval. (In this sequence the storyline freely borrows a significant scene from **Spartacus**, 1960, where gladiator Kirk Douglas refuses to kill his opponent in the arena after that opponent, Woody Strode, has spared his life.) Caan has defeated the purpose of the game, Houseman runs for an exit, and it is the start of a return to personal freedom that can crush the oppressive corporate control of everyone's lives. Songs/Music: "Adagio for Strings and Organ in G minor" (Tomaso Albinoni); "Toccata and Fugue in D minor" (Johann Sebastian Bach); "Glass Sculpture," "Executive Party" (Andre Previn); "Sleeping Beauty Waltz" (Pyotr Ilyich Tchaikovsky; "Symphony No. 5, Fourth Movement" (Dmitri Shostakovich). Excessive violence prohibits viewing by children. A remake of this story was produced in 2002. **p&d**, Norman Jewison; **cast**, James Caan, John Houseman, Maud Adams, John Beck, Moses Gunn, Pamela Hensley, Barbara Trentham, John Normington, Ralph Richardson, Robert Ito; **w**, William Harrison (based on his story "Roller Ball Murder"); **c**, Douglas Slocombe (Technicolor); **m**, Andre Previn; **ed**, Antony Gibbs; **prod d**, John Box; **art d**, Robert Laing; **spec eff**, Sass Bedig, John Richardson.

Rollercoaster ★★★ 1977; U.S.; 119m; UNIV; Color; Crime Drama; Children: Unacceptable (MPAA: PG); **DVD**; **VHS**. Well-made thriller sees Bottoms as a young terrorist, who plants a radio-controlled time bomb under the tracks of rollercoasters at big amusement parks. People are injured or killed as rollercoasters blow up or fly off their tracks. Police consider the bomber to be a psychopath, and learn he is also an extortionist, demanding a million dollars to stop his deadly game. He is paid the ransom, but he nevertheless plans to go ahead and blow up another rollercoaster, this one at a major park in California. FBI agents Segal and Widmark are kept very busy in trying to stop him. Songs: "Big Boy," "Fill 'Er Up" (Ron Mael). Excessive violence prohibits viewing by children. *Author's Note*: Widmark told this author that "we

Audrey Hepburn and Gregory Peck in *Roman Holiday*, 1953.

were very concerned when making **Rollercoaster** that we might be giving some wacko the idea to start planting bombs at amusement parks and we held our breaths for some time about that, but no such thing happened, although I think a lot of those parks put on extra security just in case." **p**, Jennings Lang; **d**, James Goldstone; **cast**, George Segal, Richard Widmark, Timothy Bottoms, Henry Fonda, Harry Guardino, Susan Strasberg, Helen Hunt, William Prince, Steve Guttenberg, Dorothy Tristan; **w**, Richard Levinson (based on a screen story by Levinson, Sanford Sheldon, William Link from a story by Tommy Cook); **c**, David M. Walsh (Panavision; Technicolor); **m**, Lalo Schifrin; **ed**, Edward A. Biery, Richard Sprague; **prod d**, Henry Bumstead; **art d**, James W. Payne; **spec eff**, Albert Whitlock.

Roman Holiday ★★★★★ 1953; U.S.; 118m; PAR; B/W; Comedy; Romance; Children: Acceptable; **DVD**; **VHS**. Delightful, charming, insouciant are only a few praiseworthy words that can be said of this classic comedy-romance where a captivating screen novice, Hepburn, won an Oscar, and where stalwart Peck renders an equally wonderful performance. In the hands of another director, this film might have been just another amusing love story, but master helmsman Wyler deftly turned it into a masterpiece. Hepburn is a princess from a small unspecified country arriving for the first time in Rome with Rawlings as her chaperone and Carminati as her aide, both watchdogs regulating and monitoring her every royal move. She is in her late teens and as innocent as a spring daisy unfolding petals eager for sunlight. Once ensconced with her coterie, Hepburn burns with a desire to see the Eternal City on her own, but her strict itinerary confines her to humdrum protocol at her embassy. When Hepburn appears to be too excited about the sights to be seen, her physician gives her a sedative, but she has no intention of sleeping through her visit. Rebelling as would a wild bird to escape a cage, Hepburn runs off alone, eluding her benign supervisors and determined to explore life in the city. Meanwhile, a small army of reporters, learning about her presence in Rome, begin searching for her, as do police of her own country as well as that of Italy. Peck, a hard-boiled reporter who gets a story at any cost, meets Hepburn by happy happenstance, finding her sleeping on a park bench as the result of the sedative. At first, he does not recognize her as the much-sought-after princess and, to keep her out of harm's way, benignly takes her to his small apartment, fascinated by her regal bearing. She quickly falls asleep on his bed, but he moves her to his couch. She is still sleeping when Peck awakes, and he goes off to his office where he fibs to his editor, Power, telling him that he attended the press conference where the princess was interviewed. Power then informs him that the princess failed to show up at the press conference because she had fallen ill. Peck then sees a photo of Hepburn and realizes that he is sitting on a great

scoop. He tells Power that he can get an exclusive interview with the princess and asks for a $5,000 payment. Power agrees, but bets him $500 that he will never get that interview. Peck calls his friend and photographer, Albert, asking him to later meet him to take photos of Hepburn. When he returns to his apartment, Peck hides the fact that he is a reporter and offers to serve as Hepburn's guide to the city. She declines and promptly departs. Excited and exhilarated at the thought of her newfound freedom, Hepburn stops at a barbershop and has her hair cropped short. Peck, who has been dogging her, then pretends to accidently come across her as she strolls about the Spanish Steps and this time he persuades Hepburn to allow him to show her the wonders of Rome. One of those sights they visit is the legendary Mouth of Truth, a face carved in marble on the side of a wall with a gaping mouth. Legend has it that anyone making a false statement and then placing their hand in that mouth will have it bitten off. Peck, after explaining all this, tells a whopper and then slips his hand into the mouth, extending his arm far into it. He then quickly withdraws his arm, pretending to wince in pain, and showing an empty sleeve to indicate that his hand has been devoured by the Mouth of Truth. Hepburn screams in horror, but Peck then produces his hand as he has merely slipped it upward in his sleeve, reenacting an old theater gag. This delights the innocent Hepburn and further endears him to her as her entertaining escort. The two then go on a scooter ride, with Hepburn driving through the streets of Rome as Peck rides behind her, quipping about Rome's sights and scenes, but Hepburn's speeding brings the attention of a cop and they are taken to a police station and given a ticket and a warning. As the day fades to evening, Hepburn and Peck slowly fall in love. They go dancing that night on a river boat, but detectives on Hepburn's trail arrive to disrupt that romantic interlude. A melee ensues and Hepburn and Peck escape, only to realize that Hepburn's 24-hour idyllic jaunt of freedom is coming to an end. Though they are now deeply in love, they also know and accept some hard facts. Hepburn and Peck live in two decidedly separate worlds—she is royalty and he a commoner and never the twain shall meet (at least in the more rigid social era of this film, years before commoner Diana became Princess Di). Hepburn accepts her role as a royal princess, and Peck resigns himself to his life as a journalist, and they say farewell to each other in a poignantly remembered parting. Peck nobly decides that he will not write this story, but will protect Hepburn's cherished spree of freedom from the prying eyes of the world, a private and enduring memory they will share with only themselves. Only a brilliant and gifted director such as the sensitive Wyler could have made such an endearing film, one so evocative and heart-enriching that it stands as a towering lighthouse, its far-reaching and comforting beacon-like rays warmly inspiring lovers everywhere. Hepburn's performance is perfection. She captures and projects the innocence of a fun-loving young woman seeking and finding, if only for a moment, the kind of romantic interlude her station in life has otherwise denied her. Peck is her knight in shining armor, wonderfully enacting a difficult role where he convincingly transitions from opportunistic newshound to that of a gentle and selfless lover. Peck's magnificent performance is reminiscent of Ronald Colman's role in **The Prisoner of Zenda**, 1937, where Colman plays a commoner who pretends to be a king, falling in love with a beautiful princess, Madeleine Carroll, and nobly forsakes their love to protect her station in life. Hepburn received an Oscar as Best Actress for her stunning performance, as did Trumbo for Best Story, and Edith Head for Best Costume Design (Black and White). The film received Oscar nominations for Best Picture, Best Director (Wyler), Best Supporting Actor (Albert), Best Story and Screenplay (Hunter [Trumbo]; and Dighton), Best Cinematography (Black and White; Alekan and Planer), and Best Film Editing (Swink). The film was a box office success, taking in more than $12 million against a $1.5 million budget. ***Author's Note***: Director Frank Capra originally purchased the film adaptation of this story in 1949 from writer Dalton Trumbo, and he thought to cast Elizabeth Taylor in the role of the princess and Cary Grant as the reporter. "I thought it was a cute variation on my film **It Happened One Night**

[1934]," Capra told this author, "but I ran into financial problems involving my own production company [Liberty Films], so I sold the rights to the story to Paramount. They still wanted me to direct the film, but I was unhappy about the limited budget they offered, especially when they knew the picture had to be shot on location in Italy. Paramount wanted to use only the frozen assets they had in Italy for the picture, I did not think enough would be available to do a first-class job, especially since I wanted to shoot the picture in color and they wanted it in black-and-white to save money [which is the way the film was eventually shot]. I was also disturbed that Dalton Trumbo, who was then in big trouble with the House Committee on Un-American Activities [HUAC], was to write the screenplay and I did not need to inherit his problems, too, so I bowed out." Paramount then contacted pantheon director George Stevens, but he declined the job and it is not known if his decision was based on working with Trumbo. The studio then approached another great director, Wyler, and asked if he would work with Trumbo, although studio executives were already gun shy about using Trumbo's name, as was Trumbo, who was then on Hollywood's unwritten blacklist. Wyler told this author that "I did not give a damn about such politics. I was only concerned about directing a good story. On the safe side, however, Paramount and Trumbo agreed not to credit Trumbo for the screenplay, even though he did most of the writing for the script as the story came from him. Two other writers who worked on that script, Ian Hunter and John Dighton, were the only ones who got credit for the screenplay." Trumbo went unrecognized for the wonderful script, although he told this author: "I did not really care if I got credit or not. I was working and getting paid for it and that is all that mattered to me then." When the Oscar was awarded for that screenplay in 1954, only writers Hunter and Dighton stepped up at the Academy Awards to receive that coveted award while Trumbo stayed at home. Trumbo did receive proper recognition for his work, but posthumously, the Oscar given to his wife, Cleo, in 1993 (that gifted writer having died in 1976). Trumbo received much belated credit for that script in 2002 in the restored edition of that film. Hepburn was not Wyler's first choice for the capricious princess. "When we started doping out the script," Wyler told this author, "I thought I would use Jean Simmons for the role of the princess. I was told that she was not available for the production and I had second thoughts about even doing it. I had barely heard about Audrey Hepburn until a short time later when we did a screen test with her, which proved her perfect for the role." That screen test is now legend. Hepburn, up to the time she made this film, had appeared in some European films before she met French novelist Colette in the south of France while Hepburn was working on the in-production of **Monte Carlo Baby**, 1953. Colette was so taken with Hepburn's frothy effervescence and fresh-faced innocence that she contacted New York producers and told them to give Hepburn the lead in her play "Gigi," which proved to be a smash hit. That play brought her to the attention of Paramount and Wyler at that time and was asked to make a screen test for **Roman Holiday**. "I wanted to see how natural and down-to-earth this girl was," Wyler told this author, "so I told the cameraman to keep the camera going after she did a short scene from the script. Audrey kept talking and thought she was off-camera. Her friendly behavior and sweet smile and those innocent saucer eyes—the kind of trusting eyes a baby shows to you when smiling back at you when standing in a crib—were so engaging that I knew she was right for the part of the naïve princess." Peck dragged his feet before signing on. He was reluctant to play Hepburn's leading man in that he thought his role to be more a supporting one instead of being the leading man, but he then changed his mind. Peck told this author: "I realized that I had been playing some tough roles in recent pictures [**David and Bathesheba**, 1951; **The World in His Arms**, 1952; **The Snows of Kilimanjaro**, 1952] and that my part in **Roman Holiday** would soften my image. I quickly realized when making that picture that I was appearing opposite a superb actress and that she was giving such a startling performance that she would win an Academy Award. I went to Willy [Wyler] and told him that he should

Goldwyn Girls appearing in _Roman Scandals_, 1933.

put Audrey's name above the title because she deserved it and also told Willy that Audrey would get an Oscar." Wyler agreed, and Hepburn's name went above the title. As Peck predicted, she did win the Oscar. "That girl deserved it," Wyler told this author. "Everything about that sweet lady was so spontaneous, and that shows in every frame in **Roman Holiday**. When it came to doing the scene where Greg [Peck] inserts his hand in the Mouth of Truth and lies and then yanks it out without showing his hand, Audrey's eyes popped and she let out a genuine scream of horror. We did not tell her before Greg did that that we had set her up, not telling her what Greg was going to do, which was an old burlesque gag Greg remembered Red Skelton doing. Her reaction was so spontaneous and sincere that I did only one take for that scene as I could never improve on it and everybody knows that I probably do more takes in a film than any other director and that is the curse of all perfectionists. After that scene Greg patted me on the back and said, 'you had better be careful—people might start calling you 'One-Take Willy.'" **p&d**, William Wyler; **cast**, Gregory Peck, Audrey Hepburn, Eddie Albert, Hartley Power, Harcourt Williams, Margaret Rawlings, Tullio Carminati, Paolo Carlini, Paola Borboni, Alfredo Rizzo; **w**, Ian McLellan Hunter (Dalton Trumbo), John Dighton (based on a story by Hunter [Trumbo]); **c**, Henri Alekan, Franz Planer; **m**, Georges Auric; **ed**, Robert Swink; **art d**, Hal Pereria, Walter Tyler.

Roman Scandals ★★★ 1933; U.S.; 85m; Howard Productions/UA; B/W; Comedy; Children: Acceptable; **VHS**. Cantor is very funny in this zany comedy. He is a delivery man in West Rome, Oklahoma, who dreams he is a slave in ancient Rome as a food-taster to evil emperor Arnold, whom he proves is a fraud. Along the way there is a romance between Stuart and Manners before Cantor gets back to Oklahoma. One of the more spectacular scenes in this lavishly produced film (at $1 million) is a wild chariot race that lampoons **Ben Hur**, 1925. Songs: "Build a Little Home," "No More Love," "Keep Young and Beautiful" (1933; music: Harry Warren; lyrics: Al Dubin); "Put a Tax on Love" (1933: music: Harry Warren; lyrics: Al Dubin, L. Wolfe Gilbert); "All of Me" (1931: music: Gerald Marks; lyrics: Seymour Simons); "Dinah" (music: Harry Akst; lyrics: Sam Lewis, Joe Young); "Kickin' the Gong Around" (1931: music: Harold Arlen; lyrics: Ted Koehler); "Turkey in the Straw" (traditional). *Author's Note*: Goldwyn told this author that "I thought about putting Eddie [Cantor] into a comical version of "Androcles and the Lion" by George Bernard Shaw, but, when we could not get the rights for that play, I had a lot of writers to do a story about a working man who dreams he is back in ancient Rome. I got two top writers, George S. Kaufman and Robert E. Sherwood to do the first draft of the script, but I did not like it because I thought that all they did was to rewrite a picture that starred Will Rogers called **A Connecticut Yankee**

Jack Carson and Doris Day in *Romance on the High Seas*, 1948.

[1931], so I had to hire more writers to give me a story that stood on its own head [own two feet?]. When I refused to pay Kaufman and Sherwood, what do those two guys do? They sue me!" Goldwyn settled out of court with both writers. This film also marked the last production Busby Berkeley worked on at United Artists, one where he choreographed only one scene, but a spectacular and rather risqué one that showed all the Goldwyn Girls naked, except for their long blonde hair, which was discreetly positioned to ward off the censors of that era. Goldwyn, who always meddled in his productions, much to the vexing ire of directors, was opposed to one aspect of Berkeley's extravagant ensemble in that sequence, not its choreography, but the presence of one of the statuesque ladies. Goldwyn walked up to a tall girl wearing only that long, blonde hair and said to Berkeley: "This is not one of my Goldwyn Girls!" Berkeley replied: "She is now, Sam." Goldwyn was furious, saying: "What's the idea of hiring a Goldwyn Girl without getting my approval?" Berkeley stated: "I needed an extra girl to make this scene work. Now, please, Sam, let me get on with this shot. You are costing yourself a lot of extra money by delaying me." Berkeley quickly won the argument. Sam Goldwyn fretted about costs the way some people worry about the weather, and he quickly left the set. The girl remained and Berkeley completed the scene. The girl's name was Lucille Ball. **p**, Samuel Goldwyn; **d**, Frank Tuttle; **cast**, Eddie Cantor, Ruth Etting, Gloria Stuart, David Manners, Edward Arnold, Verree Teasdale, Alan Mowbray, John Rutherford, Willard Robertson, Paulette Goddard and Lucille Ball as two of the Goldwyn Girls; **w**, William Anthony McGuire, George Oppenheimer, Arthur Sheekman, Nat Perrin (based on a story by George S. Kaufman, Robert E. Sherwood); **c**, Ray June, Gregg Toland; **m**, Alfred Newman; **ed**, Stuart Heisler, Sherman Todd.

The Roman Spring of Mrs. Stone ★★★ 1961; U.S./U.K.; 103m; Seven Arts/WB; Color; Drama/Romance; Children: Unacceptable; **DVD**; **VHS**. Offbeat but compelling romantic drama sees Leigh as a beautiful and famous Broadway star. She is approaching fifty and in delicate emotional health. She and Phillips, her ailing producer-husband, start for a holiday to Rome, but he suffers a fatal heart attack on the plane. Now a widow, Leigh leases a luxury apartment in Rome and Lenya, a countess, comes to visit, bringing along a handsome young man, Beatty. Lenya makes a good living by foisting gigolos like Beatty on wealthy widows, and they split money the hustling young men bilk from these love-starved females. Leigh is lonely and falls for Beatty's attentions and, despite criticism from her friends, pursues an affair with him. Even though gigolo Beatty receives no payment from Leigh for his affectionate attentions, he falls in love with her. When Beatty fails to provide any cash for his liaison with Leigh, Lenya threatens to expose him and break up the love affair. Beatty, though he has received

some expensive trinkets from Leigh, tires of the affair and, at Lenya's instructions, switches his affections to the newly arrived St. John, a younger film actress. Leigh, learning of this, goes to Beatty and openly begs him to return to her, losing all dignity and for which Beatty scorns her. She returns to her hotel room and looks down to the street to see Spenser, a mysterious person who is seen periodically trailing Leigh. She tosses the key to her apartment to him and sits down. Spenser then enters her room, slowly going toward Leigh, his long black coat eventually blanketing the screen as to suggest that he is the Angel of Death. Song: "Love Is a Bore" (music: Richard Addinsell; lyrics: Paddy Roberts). **p**, Louis de Rochemont; **d**, Jose Quintero; **cast**, Vivien Leigh, Warren Beatty, Lotte Lenya, Jill St. John, Coral Browne, Jeremy Spenser, Bessie Love, Ernest Thesiger, Jean Marsh; **w**, Gavin Lambert, Jan Read (based on the novel by Tennessee Williams); **c**, Harry Waxman; **m**, Richard Addinsell; **ed**, Ralph Kemplen; **prod d**, Roger Furse; **art d**, Herbert Smith.

The Romance of Rosy Ridge ★★★ 1947; U.S; 105m.; MGM; B/W; Drama; Children: Unacceptable; **DVD**. Above-average romantic drama sees Johnson as a veteran of the American Civil War (1861-1865). He finds work on a farm in Missouri owned by Mitchell. The locals in the area have divided loyalties to the Union and the Confederacy and are still fighting the war even after a peace treaty has been signed. Johnson falls in love with Mitchell's daughter, Leigh (in her film debut), while fighting barn-burning night raiders. It's a struggle, but the compassionate Johnson manages to bring a reasonable and lasting peace to the area while winning the hand of the fetching Leigh. **p**, Jack Cummings; **d**, Roy Rowland; **cast**, Van Johnson, Thomas Mitchell, Janet Leigh, Marshall Thompson, Selena Royle, Charles Dingle, Dean Stockwell, Guy Kibbee, Elisabeth Risdon, Jim Davis, William Bishop, Paul Langton, Barbara Billingsley, May McAvoy, Marie Windsor; **w**, Lester Cole (based on a story by MacKinlay Kantor); **c**, Sidney Wagner; **m**, George Bassman; **ed**, Ralph E. Winters; **art d**, Cedric Gibbons, Richard Duce, Eddie Imazu; **set d**, Edwin B. Willis, Elliot Morgan; **spec eff**, Warren Newcombe.

Romance on the High Seas ★★★ 1948; U.S.; 99m; WB; Color; Musical Comedy; Children: Acceptable; **DVD**; **VHS**. Zany comedy peppered with many good songs has wealthy socialite Paige suspecting her husband, DeFore, of having an affair with another woman, especially after he says he can't join her on an ocean voyage. She hires Day, a nightclub singer, to pose as her on the cruise while she stays home to spy on her husband. But Paige is unaware that DeFore has hired a detective, Carson, to keep an eye on her while she is aboard the luxury liner. Carson doesn't realize that Day is not Paige and romantic bedlam follows. Everyone pairs off appropriately in the end, and Day makes a terrific movie debut. Songs: "It's Magic," "Put 'Em in a Box, Tie 'Em with a Ribbon, and Throw 'Em in the Deep Blue Sea," "It's You or No One," "I'm in Love," "The Tourist Trade," "Run, Run, Run," "Romance on the High Seas" (Jule Styne, Sammy Cahn); 'She's a Latin from Manhattan" (Harry Warren, Al Dubin); "Brazilian Rhapsody" (Styne, Ray Heindorf, Oscar Levant). **p**, Alex Gottlieb, Michael Curtiz; **d**, Curtiz; **cast**, Jack Carson, Janis Paige, Don DeFore, Doris Day, Oscar Levant, S.Z. Sakall, Fortunio Bonanova, Eric Blore, Franklin Pangborn, Leslie Brooks, William Bakewell, John Alvin, Barbara Bates, Ray Montgomery, Grady Sutton, Vampira; **w**, Julius J. and Philip G. Epstein, I.A.L. Diamond (based on the story "Romance in High C" by S. Pondal Rios, Carlos A. Olivari); **c**, Elwood Bredell (Technicolor); **m**, Ray Heindorf, Levant; **ed**, Rudi Fehr; **art d**, Anton Grot; **set d**, Howard Winterbottom; **spec eff**, David Curtiz, Wilfred M. Cline, Robert Burks.

Romancing the Stone ★★★ 1984; Mexico/U.S.; 106m; FOX; Adventure/Comedy; Children: Unacceptable (MPAA: PG); **BD**; **DVD**; **VHS**. Action-packed tale with a lot of comedic moments sees some fine acting from Turner, Douglas, DeVito and the rest of the cast. This wild tale begins when Turner, a romance novelist, gets a treasure map in the mail from her recently murdered brother-in-law. Meanwhile, her sister is kidnapped in Colombia and the two kidnappers contact Turner demanding that she travel there to exchange the map for her sister. Turner goes there, but gets lost in the jungle after being waylaid by a corrupt Colombian cop, who also wants the map. Turner gets help from soldier-of-fortune Douglas, who reluctantly agrees to bring her back to civilization. They become involved in adventures that surpass any Turner could ever envision for her books while Douglas and Turner fall in love. A sequel, **Jewel of the Nile**, 1985, was as exciting and delightful as this film, a female version of the "Indiana Jones" movies. Songs: "Romancing the Stone" (Eddy Grant), "How the West Was Won" (Alfred Newman). **p**, Michael Douglas, Jack Brodsky, Joel Douglas; **d**, Robert Zemeckis; **cast**, Douglas, Kathleen Turner, Danny DeVito, Manuel Ojeda, Zack Norman, Alfonso Arau, Holland Taylor, Mary Ellen Trainor, Eve Smith, Joe Nesnow; **w**, Diane Thomas, Lem Dobbs, Howard Franklin, Treva Silverman; **c**, Dean Cundey; **m**, Alan Silvestri; **ed**, Donn Cambern, Frank Morriss; **prod d**, Lawrence G. Paull; **art d**, Agustin Ituarte; **set d**, Enrique Estevez; **spec eff**, Laurencio Cordero, Billy Myatt.

Romanoff and Juliet ★★★ 1961; U.S.; 103m; Pavla/UNIV; Color; Comedy; Children: Acceptable; **DVD**; **VHS**. Entertaining throughout, Shakespeare's play "Romeo and Juliet" is updated to the Cold War and moved to a middle European country ruled by a general, who arranges for the sons and daughters of U.S. and Soviet ambassadors to fall in love. The situation develops into a delightful farce until the main lovers, Dee and Gavin, are finally united. This was a filmic tour de force from Ustinov, who produced, directed and starred in this modern-day version of the Immortal Bard's love tale. **p,d&w**, Peter Ustinov (from the play by Ustinov and William Shakespeare); **cast**, Ustinov, Sandra Dee, John Gavin, Akim Tamiroff, Alix Talton, Rik Von Nutter, John Phillips, Peter Jones, Tamara Shayne, Suzanne Cloutier; **c**, Robert Krasker (Technicolor); **m**, Mario Nascimbene; **ed**, Renzo Lucidi; **art d**, Alexander Trauner; **set d**, Maurice Barnathan.

Romeo and Juliet ★★★★ 1936; U.S.; 125m; MGM; B/W; Drama/Romance; Children: Unacceptable; **DVD**; **VHS**. Though they are much older than the teenage star-crossed lovers originally portrayed in Shakespeare's classic tale, Howard and Shearer nevertheless present riveting performances in this superlative production brilliantly directed by Cukor. Howard and Shearer, despite the fact that their families (the Capulets and Montagues) have been lethally feuding in Verona for decades, meet and fall deeply in love. The distempered Rathbone, who is Shearer's cousin, disrupts their poetic romance after he insults and inveigles the outgoing and life-loving Barrymore into a duel, ruthlessly killing his opponent, running Barrymore through (and where that actor renders one of his finest death scenes on film). Howard becomes enraged at the killing of his closest friend Barrymore and retaliates by dueling with the insidious Rathbone, killing him. As a result, Howard is banished from the city. Meanwhile, the pining Shearer is, against her will, pledged to marry Forbes by her family, albeit none in her clan know of her deep love for Howard and that she and Howard have secretly married. Shearer confides her love for Howard to adviser Kolker, but he offers her a way by which she can be with Howard. He gives her a powerful sleeping potion that will make her appear dead, but she will only be in a deep sleep. After her body is placed in a vault, Howard can come to her and both can then flee Verona to live happily in Mantua. Shearer dutifully follows Kolker's plan and, after she takes the sleeping potion, she is placed in the family crypt. Kolker then sends a message to Howard that informs him that Shearer is only in a deep sleep and waiting for him to revive her so that they can be together. All goes awry after that message is waylaid. When Howard arrives at the vault to see Shearer, he believes that she is truly dead and, in grief, takes his own life. Shearer revives and, after finding the one and true love of her life dead, drives a knife into her own heart, ending her young life. Remorse

Kathleen Turner and Michael Douglas in *Romancing the Stone*, 1984.

and regret then drives the two warring families to settle their ancient feud, their peaceful reconciliations coming at a terrible price. Howard and Shearer exquisitely recreate this immortal tragedy with sensitive performances that only the passionate Cukor could have elicited. The director lovingly dotes on each memorable character, developing their distinctive personalities through his own gifted persona and interpretation of those characters, providing what is most likely the best version of this tale on film. It received Oscar nominations for Best Picture, Best Actress (Shearer), Best Supporting Actor (Rathbone) and Best Art Direction (Gibbons, Hope and Willis). This film was an expensive production, costing more than $2 million and it barely recouped its investment from worldwide receipts. It nevertheless remains the classic version of the Shakespeare tale. Songs/Music: "Romeo and Juliet" (1869; Peter Ilyich Tchaikovsky), "Pavane" (1926; from "Capriol Suite" by Peter Warlock). *Author's Note*: MGM's production chief Irving Thalberg had for years envisioned this film as vehicle for his actress-wife, Shearer. He fought tooth and nail with MGM boss Louis B. Mayer over the project, Mayer telling Thalberg that "Shakespeare is too arty for the public. All of his plays go right over the viewer's head." When Mayer heard that his arch rival, Jack Warner, had given the green light for the production of Shakespeare's **A Midsummer Night's Dream**, 1935, Mayer, not to be outdone by a major Shakespeare film, changed his mind and told Thalberg to go ahead with **Romeo and Juliet**. Thalberg spared no expense in preparing the film, sending a second unit to Verona to photograph the city's ancient buildings and make copies of Italian Renaissance artworks. Oddly, when discussing the production with other MGM brass, Thalberg also announced his wife's swansong on the screen (although she would go on to appear in many more films after this production), stating: "I believe that Norma can play anything and do it better than anyone else. **Marie Antoinette** [still in project and not produced until 1938] and [**Romeo and**] **Juliet** mark the end of Norma Shearer's acting career. Too many stars stay on camera too long. I want her to bow out at her highest point." Shearer was thirty-one when she did this film, and her leading man, Howard, was forty-three. Howard knew he was too old for the part and did not really want to enact the boyish Romeo, but the ever persuasive Thalberg convinced him to take the part, especially because Shearer wanted him in that role. Howard was not Thalberg's first choice for Romeo. He approached Fredric March and offered him the role, but March promptly declined. Thalberg even toyed with having rugged Clark Gable, then MGM's top male star, play the part of Romeo. When Thalberg mentioned this to Gable, the actor thought Thalberg had "lost some of his screws." He told Thalberg: "I don't look Shakespeare. I don't talk Shakespeare. I don't like Shakespeare and I won't do Shakespeare." The producer even went to Robert Donat and Errol Flynn with the proposal, but both actors said no. Shearer, however,

Claire Danes and Leonardo DiCaprio in *Romeo + Juliet*, 1996.

always wanted Howard, who had appeared with her in **A Free Soul**, 1931; Shearer had gotten an Oscar nomination for her performance in that film, believing Howard was her "good luck charm." Barrymore was easily persuaded to play the ill-fated Mercutio in that he desperately needed money at that time as he was then romancing Elaine Barrie. He took a flat $20,000 payment for the part, a bargain basement deal for MGM in that it had paid Barrymore as much as $150,000 per film only a few years earlier. Barrymore gives one of the most flamboyant performances of his life (and more demonstrative than any other Shakespearean character ever played) in this film, employing what is a slight Irish accent and demonstrating airy gestures that were interpreted by some to be the mannerisms of a homosexual. "Oh, he was incorrigible in **Romeo and Juliet**," Cukor told this author. "Jack [Barrymore] was drunk most of the time, or pretty close to it, when we did that picture with him. He got so bad that Irving [Thalberg] had him stay at a rehabilitation home and had detectives watching him night and day to keep booze from him. Jack was too clever for them. He still managed to find plenty to drink and when he appeared on the set, he was always slightly tipsy, or he seemed that way. Still, he delivered his speeches magnificently and, after one scene, we all applauded him. Jack turned to me and some others and said: 'To hell with the applause. Get me a drink.'" Rathbone did not agree with Cukor, telling this author that "I thought Barrymore was stone cold sober in our scenes together. He knew that everyone thought about him as a heavy drinker so he played that part as a little game. No one could have delivered his lines so eloquently while being drunk or so actively sword-fighting me in our scenes together as he did if they had been intoxicated. I think Barrymore pretended to be slightly inebriated so that he would get even more respect from us when doing a good scene in spite of the alcohol he wanted everyone to believe he had absorbed. John Barrymore was an actor within an actor within an actor and anyone who did not know that about him, did not know him at all. He had little ways about him that mocked those he worked with. He inserted some prissy mannerisms into his part in **Romeo and Juliet** just to provoke George [Cukor], who was gay. Barrymore was the consummate ladie's man and disdained homosexuals, although he never openly criticized them. He was smart enough to know that there were too many homosexuals in our business that would find ways to retaliate. As I have said, Barrymore was a telescopic actor, who could show many personalities, almost at the same time. He was dangerous to play against because he knew that he could distract you and draw you away from the character you were playing to create more self-attention, so you always had to be on guard with him. As such, he challenged your discipline with his own iron will, and that is the sign of greatness." Although much criticism of this film is based upon the fact that the principals are much older than the teenagers Shakespeare

profiled, one must fault the author for that, not the actors, in that Shakespeare's sophisticated and erudite speeches are not those generated by teenage minds, but from incisive adult perspectives that decidedly display the wisdom of age and not the naiveté of inexperienced youth. **p**, Irving Thalberg; **d**, George Cukor; **cast**, Norma Shearer, Leslie Howard, John Barrymore, Edna May Oliver, Basil Rathbone, C. Aubrey Smith, Andy Devine, Conway Tearle, Ralph Forbes, Henry Kolker, Robert Warwick, Reginald Denny, Violet Kemble Cooper, Katherine DeMille, Lon McCallister; **w**, Talbot Jennings (based on the play by William Shakespeare); **c**, William Daniels; **m**, Herbert Stothart; **ed**, Margaret Booth; **art d**, Cedric Gibbons; **set d**, Gibbons, Oliver Messel; **spec eff**, Slavko Vorkapich.

Romeo and Juliet ★★★ 1954; Italy/U.K.; 138m; Rank/UA; Color; Drama/Romance; Children: Unacceptable; **DVD**. In this well-crafted version of Shakespeare's play, the story gets a fine but altered treatment in this production with handsome Harvey as Romeo in an impossible romance with lovely Shentall as Juliet. They are from rival feuding families in Verona, Italy, which, as expected, comes to no good for them. The director-screenplay writer Castellani took liberties with the play, deleting parts of it, but it is nonetheless moving in its own right and is gorgeous looking. Two better-looking young leads would be hard to find. **p**, Sandro Ghenzi, Joseph Janni; **d&w**, Renato Castellani (adapted from the play by William Shakespeare); **cast**, Lawrence Harvey, Susan Shentall, Flora Robson, Norman Wooland, Mervyn Johns, John Gielgud, Bill Travers, Sebastian Cabot, Ubaldo Zollo, Enzo Fiermonte; **c**, Robert Krasker; **m**, Roman Vlad; **ed**, Sidney Hayers.

Romeo and Juliet ★★★ 1968; U.K.; Italy; 139m; BHE Films/PAR; Color; Drama/Romance; Children: Unacceptable; **DVD**; **IV**. A visually sumptuous telling of the Shakespeare tragedy with two very attractive teenage actors (Hussey was fifteen and Whiting was seventeen) performing well as the young lovers from feuding families that leads both to their tragic deaths. Filmed in Tuscany, it is mainly a drama but has more humor and sexuality than most other filmed adaptations of the play. This attracted young audiences that were mainly then watching beach party films. Zeffirelli gave them that and a dose of the bard besides, which they enjoyed. Song: "What Is Youth?" (music: Nino Rota; lyrics: Eugene Walter). **p**, Anthony Havelock-Allan, John Brabourne; **d**, Franco Zeffirelli; **cast**, Leonard Whiting, Olivia Hussey, Michael York, John McEnery, Milo O'Shea, Pat Heywood, Robert Stephens, Bruce Robinson, Paul Hardwick, Laurence Olivier (narrator); **w**, Franco Zeffirelli, Franco Brusati, Masolino D'Amico (based on the play by William Shakespeare); **c**, Pasqualino De Santis (Technicolor); **m**, Nino Rota; **ed**, Reginald Mills; **prod d**, Lorenzo Mongiardino; **art d**, Emilio Carcano, Luciano Puccini.

Romeo + Juliet ★★★ 1996; U.S.; 120m; FOX; Color; Drama/Romance; Children: Unacceptable (MPAA: PG-13); **BD**; **DVD**. Australian director Luhrmann updates Shakespeare's play to a hip modern-day suburb of Verona, Italy, while retaining its original dialogue. Gun-toting members of rival families wage a vicious war against each other on the streets as the star-crossed lovers (DiCaprio, Danes) become the feud's victims. Songs: "Number One Crush" (Garbage: Shirley Manson, Duke Erikson, Steve Marker, Butch Vig), "Local God" (Art Alexakis, Everclear: Art Alexakis, Dave French, Freddy Herrera, Josh Crawley, Sean Winchester), "Angel" (Gavin Friday, Maurice Seezer), "Pretty Piece of Flesh" (Nellee Hooper, Marius De Vris, Justin Warfield), "I'm Kissing You/Love Theme from Romeo + Juliet" (Des'ree: Desiree Annette Weeks, Tim Atack), "Whatever/I Had a Dream" (Butthole Surfers: Gibby Haynes, Paul Leary, King Coffey, Jeff Pinkus), "Lovefool" (Peter Svensson, Nina Persson), "Young Hearts Run Free" (David Crawford), "Everybody's Free/To Feel Good" (Tim Cox, Nigel Swanston), "To You I Bestow" (Mundy: Edmund Enright), "Talk Show Host, "Exit Music/For a Film" (Thom Yorke, Jonny Greenwood, Ed O'Brien, Colin

Greenwood, Phil Selway), "Little Star" (Stina Nordenstam), "You and Me Song" (Par Wiksten, Fredrik Schoenfeldt, Stefan Schoenfeldt, Gunnar Karlsson, Christina Bergmark), "When Doves Cry" (Prince: Rogers Nelson), "Slow Movement" (Craig Armstrong), "KTTV News Theme" (Gary S. Scott), "Symphony No. 25" (Wolfgang Amadeus Mozart), "Liebestod" (from the opera "Tristan and Isolde" by Richard Wagner). Violence and sexuality prohibit viewing by children. **p**, Baz Luhrmann, Gabriella Martinelli, Martin Brown; **d**, Luhrmann; **cast**, Leonardo Di-Caprio, Claire Danes, John Leguizamo, Harold Perrineau, Pete Postleth-waite, Paul Sorvino, Brian Dennehy, Paul Rudd, Jesse Bradford, Miriam Margolyes; **w**, Luhrmann, Craig Pearce (based on the play by William Shakespeare); **c**, Donald M. McAlpine; **m**, Nellee Hooper; **ed**, Jill Bil-cock; **prod d**, Catherine Martin; **art d**, Doug Hardwick; **set d**, Brigitte Broch; **spec eff**, Laurencio "Chovy" Cordero.

Ronin ★★★ 1998; U.S./U.K.; 122m; FGM Entertainment/UA; Color; Crime Drama; Children: Unacceptable (MPAA: R); **DVD**; **VHS**. De Niro renders another riveting performance, this time as a CIA agent in-filtrating a leaderless rogue unit of the outlawed IRA (called "ronin" after a Samurai legend), which is involved in obtaining arms for the IRA's ongoing struggle with the British government. The film begins when an IRA group attempts to hijack a shipment of arms in Paris and the operation goes wrong when a sniper begins firing on the participants. The arms dealer is killed, and the attackers escape with a mysterious case that becomes the focal point of the film. Several wild gun battles and killings occur as members of "ronin," and Russian gangsters who are formerly members of the KGB and foreign intelligence agents com-pete to obtain that case, all ending with the shooting of a championship ice skater. Complex and sometimes confusing due to a disjointed script, the cops-and-robbers action is almost nonstop, having many shootouts and wild car chases in this exciting thriller, where Reno, McElhone, Bean, Pryce and Skarsgard turn in good performances. The film was costly, shot on location in Paris and in Southern France, and it did not do well at the box office, taking in only a little more than $70 million against a heavy budget of $55 million. Songs: "Time to Say Goodbye" (music: Francesco Sartori; English lyrics: Frank Peterson), "Our Favorite Son" (music: Cy Coleman; lyrics: Betty Comden, Adolph Green), "The Sleeping Beauty: Ballet Suite" (Peter Tchaikovsky), "Rhapsody on a Theme of Paganini, Variation 18" (Sergei Rachmaninoff), "Les Anges dans nos campagnes" (traditional), "Adeste Fideles" (traditional). *Au-thor's Note*: Director Frankenheimer told this author that "I thought that the action scenes in **Ronin** would be more effective if we shot those scenes as if news cameramen were filming the action on the run. I think that proved successful, but I may have overworked it. You can some-times have too much of a good thing." Gutter language and excessive violence prohibit viewing by children. **p**, Frank Mancuso Jr.; **d**, John Frankenheimer; **cast**, Robert De Niro, Jean Reno, Natascha McElhone, Stellan Skarsgard, Sean Bean, Jonathan Pryce, Skipp Sudduth, Michael Lonsdale, Jan Triska, Ron Perkins; **w**, J.D. Zeik, Richard Weisz [David Mamet] (from a story by Zeik); **c**, Robert Fraisse; **m**, Elia Cmiral; **ed**, Tony Gibbs; **prod d**, Michael Z. Hanan; **art d**, Gerard Viard; **set d**, Robert Le Corre; **spec eff**, Georges Demetrau.

Rookie of the Year ★★★ 1993; U.S.; 99m; FOX; Color; Comedy; Chil-dren: Unacceptable (MPAA: PG); **BD**; **DVD**; **VHS**. Entertaining com-edy sees twelve-year-old Nicholas dreaming of being a professional baseball player. His late father was a minor league baseball player, but Nicholas thinks that his dreams of becoming a player like his father have been shattered after he suffers a broken arm while trying to catch a base-ball at school. That injury is, however, a blessing in disguise. The tendon in his arm heals too tightly, allowing him to throw pitches as fast as 103 mph. He is spotted by the Chicago Cubs' general manager, Hedaya, who decides Nicholas may be the hot pitcher that team owner Bracken has been praying for. Nicholas is hired, but the club's manager, Hall, is not keen on it. Hall soon warms to the boy after Nichols' rookie season per-

Patrick LaBrecque, Robert Gorman and Thomas Ian Nicholas in *Rookie of the Year*, **1993.**

formance scores many wins for the team and fans love it and him. Songs: "The Second Time Around" (Sammy Cahn, Jimmy Van Heusen), "Get Up" (Mike Rutherford, Paul Carrack), "You Don't Know What You Got" (Walter Kahn, Tom Uzzo, Deborah Stevens), "You Got the Right One Baby, Uh Huh" (Ray Charles), "All of My Days" (Angie Rubin, Shelley Speck), "In the Mood" (Joe Garland). Gutter language prohibits viewing by children. **p**, Robert Harper; **d**, Daniel Stern; **cast**, Thomas Ian Nicholas, Gary Busey, Albert Hall, Amy Morton, Dan Hedaya, Bruce Altman, Eddie Bracken, Robert Gorman, Patrick LaBrecque, Stern; **w**, Sam Harper; **c**, Jack N. Green; **m**, Bill Conti; **ed**, Donn Cambern, Raja Gosnell; **prod d**, Steven Jordan; **art d**, William Arnold; **set d**, Leslie Bloom; **spec eff**, Dieter and Yvonne Sturm, Erik Henry, Daniel Chuba.

Room at the Top ★★★★ 1959; U.K.; 115m; Romulus Films/Conti-nental Distributing; B/W; Drama; Children: Unacceptable; **DVD**; **VHS**. In one of his finest and intense roles, Harvey is a former P.O.W. seeking the better things of life he thinks that can be found only at the top. He secures a job as a government accountant in the soot-filled town of Warnley, a small community where the social classes rigidly conform to their stations. Dominating the town is millionaire indus-trialist Wolfit, who acts like a feudal lord keeping everyone in their slavish places. Harvey, knowing he is at a social dead end, focuses upon young and impressionable Sears, who is Wolfit's protected daughter. Harvey romances Sears, although he does not love her, be-lieving that by marrying the girl, he will also marry into wealth and the kind of social position he so desperately craves. Wolfit, however, is on to the young man, seeing Harvey with grudging admiration as a younger version of his own rise to power and wealth. He has no in-tention, however, of allowing this social interloper to gain a foothold in his family. Wolfit ships Sears off to the Continent, and Harvey is left in the cold. He warms himself with the company of love-craving Signoret, who is an aging actress heading a local theater group. Though married to stick-in-the-mud Cuthbertson, Signoret soon de-velops an affair with Harvey and Harvey strangely finds himself feel-ing genuine love for this caring woman. When Sears returns from her European jaunt, Harvey leaves Signoret and resumes his ambitious pursuit of Sears. He ruthlessly cements that relationship by seducing and impregnating Sears. Wolfit tries everything he can think to do in ridding himself of this unwanted son-in-law, from threats to outright bribery, but nothing works and Harvey's wedding to Sears is then scheduled. Meanwhile, the deserted Signoret, who has failed to get a divorce from Cuthbertson so that she can marry Harvey, the only man she loves, then learns that that man is about to marry the wealthy Sears. When Harvey refuses to see her again, the forlorn Signoret takes to drink and then gets into a car and drives wildly to her crashing

Julian Sands and Helena Bonham Carter in *A Room with a View,* **1986.**

death. Harvey begins to feel for the first time deep remorse for deserting Signoret. His troubling emotions are compounded when he is then, as if beset by retribution from On High, attacked by a group of vicious Teddy Boys, England's version of Hell's Angels, except they are dressed in fashionable attire and pose as socially acceptable human beings. Harvey takes a terrible beating from these thugs, who randomly seek victims to satisfy their sadistic lust, accepting this punishment as if doing penance for committing his victimizing sins against Sears and Signoret. He nevertheless survives in time to go to the altar, but he feels no satisfaction in gaining the world at the loss of the woman he loved. Harvey is a British version of the scheming and conniving character so expertly played by Montgomery Clift in **The Heiress**, 1949. The difference is that where Clift fails in his insidious ambitions to capture the heart of wealthy and perceptive heiress Olivia de Havilland, Harvey achieves his goal to find a room at the top of wealth and prestige, only to find that room empty of love and integrity. Harvey, Signoret, Sears and Baddeley render outstanding performances in this compelling tale. Signoret's great performance of the scorned, aging woman won her an Oscar and the film received Oscar nominations for Best Picture, Best Director (Clayton), Best Actor (Harvey), and Best Supporting Actress (Baddeley). Songs: "Roses from the South" (Johann Strauss), "The Wedding March" (Felix Mendelssohn-Bartholdy). **p**, John and James Woolf; **d**, Jack Clayton; **cast**, Simone Signoret, Laurence Harvey, Heather Sears, Donald Wolfit, Donald Houston, Hermione Baddeley, Allan Cuthbertson, Raymond Huntley, Wilfrid Lawson, John Moulder-Brown; **w**, Neil Paterson (based on the novel by John Braine); **c**, Freddie Francis; **m**, Mario Nascimbene; **ed**, Ralph Kemplen; **art d**, Ralph Brinton.

Room for One More ★★★ 1952; 95m; WB; B/W; Comedy; Children: Acceptable; **DVD**; **IV**. Good performances are seen in this heartwarming story of a married middle-class couple with three children, who take in a withdrawn thirteen-year-old girl for two weeks. She becomes like one of the family, which encourages the couple to then take in a crippled orphan boy. The heart of this family most strongly beats within Drake, who has to not only win the confidence of her adopted children, but who slowly instills the same charitable feelings in husband Grant, who has resisted the adoptions all along. Songs: "Can't We Be Friends" (Kay Swift), "Auld Lang Syne" (traditional; lyrics: Robert Burns), "Good King Wenceslas" (traditional). *Author's Note*: Grant and Drake were married in real life when making this film, a union that ended in divorce in 1962. Grant told this author that "**Room for One More** was a very enjoyable picture and it was based on a real couple [Poppy and Anna Perrot Rose of Lynwood, New Jersey], who kept adopting orphaned children. We had George Winslow in that pic-

ture. He was called "Foghorn" because of his unusual low-timbered voice, a very cute little fellow." It was Grant who specifically had Winslow cast in this film after seeing him on the televised "Art Linkletter Show" when five-year-old Winslow first bellowed in that low-registered voice that brought about the sobriquet of "Foghorn." **p**, Henry Blanke; **d**, Norman Taurog; **cast**, Cary Grant, Betsy Drake, Lurene Tuttle, Randy Stuart, John Ridgely, Irving Bacon, Mary Treen, George Winslow, William Bakewell, Douglas Fowley, Hayden Rorke; **w**, Melville Shavelson, Jack Rose (based on the book by Anna Perrot Rose); **c**, Robert Burks; **m**, Max Steiner; **ed**, Alan Crosland Jr.; **art d**, Douglas Bacon; **set d**, William L. Kuehl.

Room Service ★★★ 1938; U.S.; 78m; RKO; B/W; Comedy; Children: Acceptable; **DVD**. Amusing outing from the Marx Brothers is based on the Broadway comedy about financing the staging of a new Broadway musical comedy. Their secretary, Ball, charms a playwright, Albertson, into letting the brothers produce his drama, not knowing they intend to turn it into a musical with lots of dancing girls. Most of the humor involves the inventive ways the brothers have in keeping their hotel room without paying rent, which, at the beginning of this film, is already at $1,000 in arrears. The boys are up to the old zany antics in this funny outing, but Chico does not play the piano and Harpo does not strum his harp. *Author's Note*: Groucho told this author that "we decided to give the public a break by keeping Chico away from the keyboard and Harpo from his strings. We somehow misplaced Margaret Dumont, who did not appear with us in that picture, but I think she was counting her blessings and not bruises by missing that one." Songs: "Merrily We Roll Along" (traditional, based on "Good Night Ladies" [1894] by Edwin P. Christy), "Song of the Volga Boatmen" (traditional), "The Last Round-Up" (1933; Billy Hill), "Swing Low, Sweet Chariot" (1872; Wallis Willis). This film was remade as **Step Lively**, 1944, as a vehicle for Frank Sinatra. **p**, Pandro S. Berman; **d**, William A. Seiter; **cast**, The Marx Brothers (Groucho, Harpo, Chico Marx), Lucille Ball, Ann Miller; Frank Albertson, Donald MacBride, Cliff Dunstan, Philip Loeb, Charles Halton, Philip Wood, Alexander Asro; **w**, Morrie Ryskind, Loeb, Glenn Tryon (from the play by John Murray, Allen Boretz); **c**, J. Roy Hunt; **ed**, George Crone; **art d**, Van Nest Polglase.

A Room with a View ★★★★ 1986; U.K.; 117m; Goldcrest Films/Cinecom Pictures; Color; Drama/Romance; Children: Cautionary; **BD**; **DVD**. Set at the time of the turn of the 20th Century, two upper-class women, Bonham Carter and her older cousin and chaperone, Smith, take residence in a small hotel in Florence, Italy. Both are refined ladies restricted by Victorian manners and protocols. Bonham Carter, however, is more free-spirited while the older Smith insists on formalities when dealing with other tourists as she invariably manipulates Bonham Carter into following her stand-offish attitude. Among the other tourists, they meet Elliott, a decided nonconformist, and his handsome son, Sands, who is a free thinker. Elliott suggests that the two ladies switch rooms with him and his son so that they can have a better room with a view, but Smith considers this a breach of her strict code of etiquette, a familiarity she also considers tactless in that she and her ward will then be indebted to persons who are otherwise total strangers. When the two women take a short touring jaunt, an Italian carriage driver purposely misdirects Bonham Carter to a field where Sands is standing, and when she appears Sands impulsively embraces and kisses her. Smith then arrives and stops this momentary romantic interlude, chastising Sands for taking liberties. Bonham Carter, however, is thrilled by the experience and she begins to nurture hopes for her first romance. Smith, however, brands Sands a rake, if not an outright masher, recalling a similar experience she had years earlier with a young man, one that turned her heart into the stone that presently resides within her as she fears and dislikes men. Smith swears Bonham Carter to secrecy, and when they return to England, neither of them mentions the incident to family members. A short time later, Bonham Carter accepts a marriage proposal from wealthy Day-Lewis, a rather stuffy young man. At the same time, Elliott and Sands move into the area and Sands repeatedly attempts to see Bonham Carter, but she puts him off. Finally, Bonham Carter, disturbed at her persistent deep feelings for Sands, breaks off her marriage plans with Day-Lewis and announces that she is going to Greece for a vacation. Before she departs, Bonham Carter meets Elliott and then realizes that the only reason why she has broken off her engagement to Day-Lewis and is leaving on an extended visit to Greece is because she truly loves Sands. She does not go to Greece after all, but is seen back at the small hotel in Florence where she is honeymooning with her husband, Sands, and where they have that room with a view. Ivory directs this film with great care, developing all the subtle nuances endemic to its absorbing characters, and Bonham Carter, Smith, Sands, Elliott and the rest of the cast shine in their roles. This film was a great success at the box office, gleaning more than $20 million in its initial release against a $3 million budget. The film won Oscars for Best Adapted Screenplay (Jhabvala), Best Art Direction (Ackland-Snow, Quaranta, Savegar, Altramura), and Best Costume Design (Jenny Beavan, John Bright). It received Oscar nominations for Best Picture, Best Director (Ivory), Best Supporting Actress (Smith), and Best Cinematography (Pierce-Roberts). Songs: "O mio babbino caro," "Chi il bel sogno di doretta" (Giacomo Puccini); "Mademoiselle Moidiste" (Victor Herbert). **p**, Ismail Merchant; **d**, James Ivory; **cast**, Maggie Smith, Helena Bonham Carter, Denholm Elliott, Julian Sands, Simon Callow, Judi Dench, Daniel Day-Lewis, Rosemary Leach, Rupert Graves, James Wilby; **w**, Ruth Prawer Jhabvala (based on the novel by E.M. Forster); **c**, Tony Pierce-Roberts; **m**, Richard Robbins; **ed**, Humphrey Dixon; **prod d**, Brian Ackland-Snow, Gianni Quaranta; **art d**, Brian Savegar, Elio Altamura.

Rooster Cogburn ★★★ 1975; U.S.; 108m; Hal Wallis Productions; UNIV; Color; Western; Children: Cautionary (MPAA: PG); **DVD**; **VHS**. This lively production is a much better western than most in that genre and it particularly entertains throughout via the sterling performances of two great stars, Wayne and Hepburn, appearing in their first and only film together. Wayne loses his badge again (as he briefly had in **True Grit**, 1969, and this film serves as its loose sequel) after he proves a bit too trigger-happy for McIntire, the presiding judge in his territory. McIntire, however, needs the fiery old U.S. marshal once more after a gang of murderous raiders, led by Jordan, waylays and captures a U.S. Army wagon loaded with dynamite. McIntire goes to Wayne at his residence, which he shares with Lee, a Chinese merchant, and a cat, and asks him to put that badge back on and go after Jordan. Wayne dutifully agrees, but not before shooting a scurrying rat in the back room of Lee's store and then blaming his cat (named "General Sterling Price" after a Confederate general under which Wayne once served) for not doing his job in attending to such pesky rodents. Meanwhile, Jordan and his cutthroats stop at a small mission operated by Lormer and his daughter, Hepburn, where Jordan shoots and kills Lormer when he attempts to stop Jordan from molesting some of the Indians in Lormer's care. Hepburn chases away all the Indian girls to keep them from harm, and after Jordan and his ruffians depart, she is left alone with Romancito, a young Indian boy, who is devoted to her. Wayne then comes upon Hepburn and Romancito, promising them that he will bring Jordan and his gang to justice, but they do not know how he can accomplish that alone without help, even though Wayne has dismissed the deputies McIntire offered him as useless lawmen who "will only get in the way." Despite his protests, Hepburn and Romancito insist on accompanying him, and he takes them along, thinking to later drop them off at a safe location. Hepburn, however, is set on seeing justice meted out to the ruthless Jordan for the murder of her father and intends to stay at Wayne's side until he triumphs over the bad men. Wayne, who is prone to imbibing while hunting men, gets tipsy and falls from his horse more than once, while Hepburn lectures him on the evils of drink. Romancito, however, thrills to the har-

Strother Martin, Katharine Hepburn and John Wayne in *Rooster Cogburn*, 1975.

rowing stories Wayne spins about his career as a lawman and the various outlaws he has bested, telling Wayne that he wants to become a lawman just like him. Wayne then takes a route where he will be able to cut off the fleeing Jordan and sets up an ambush, using Hepburn and Romancito to fire weapons from hiding to make the outlaws think they are facing a large posse. Several of the outlaws driving the wagon with dynamite become separated from Jordan and the main gang, and Wayne shoots down these men with the help of Hepburn and Romancito, capturing the wagon and its dynamite. He, Hepburn and Romancito then ride to a river crossing where Martin operates a ferry that consists of a large raft. Wayne tells Martin that he is appropriating the raft to carry the dynamite down the river to avoid its being recaptured by Jordan, telling Martin he will later be compensated by the government, a prospect that does not make Martin too happy. Wayne and his two "deputies" then load the dynamite, along with a deadly Gatling gun, onto the raft and begin rafting down the river. Enraged at losing the load of dynamite, which Jordan intended to use in future raids, the outlaw chief orders his men to line the river downstream and wait for Wayne, Hepburn and Romancito to arrive. At that time, he and his men will shoot down the lawman and his friends and recoup the explosives. Jordan sends Zerbe, one of his top gunmen, along with another outlaw, far down the river to wait for Wayne and to notify him when Wayne will be abreast of the outlaw ambush. Zerbe, however, who is an old friend of Wayne's, betrays Jordan. When the other outlaw sets a trap for the raft by affixing a rope across the narrows of the river, the raft is stopped, but Zerbe, who feels he has a debt to Wayne, shoots his fellow outlaw while Wayne cuts the rope. "I owed you one," Zerbe tells Wayne, but warns him that he cannot help him farther down river where Jordan and his main gang are waiting. Zerbe then rides back to tell Jordan that he and the other outlaw "gun fought" Wayne, but "he was too much for us." The suspicious Jordan grabs Zerbe's six-gun and finds only one bullet fired and knows Zerbe has betrayed him. He promptly kills Zerbe and then warns the rest of his men that the same fate awaits them if they duplicate Zerbe's traitorous actions. Jordan then waits for Wayne, Hepburn and Romancito at a point where the river widens, and he and his men ride in its shallows toward the raft when it comes into sight. Jordan orders Wayne to throw down his guns, but Wayne, instead, tells Hepburn and Romancito to take cover as he ignites fuses affixed to sticks of dynamite, throwing them at Jordan and his men and blowing them all to pieces. Finally delivering Hepburn and Romancito to safety, Wayne bids his newfound friends goodbye while Hepburn embarrasses Wayne by praising his great courage and indefatigable nature. The film borrows heavily from the plotlines of many other productions (to name a few: **The African Queen**, 1951, where Hepburn was also a missionary and where she is displaced in her village when her brother is killed;

Trevor Howard, Errol Flynn and Juliette Greco in *The Roots of Heaven*, 1958.

River of No Return, 1954, where a man, woman and boy escape down a river from pursuing Indians on a raft; and **Rio Bravo**, 1959, where Wayne, as a sheriff, uses dynamite to subdue a large outlaw gang), but it is nevertheless thoroughly entertaining, thanks to the sterling performances of Wayne and Hepburn, who show great chemistry in their scenes together. The well-written script is witty, and the exciting action is well choreographed. This film did well at the box office, taking in more than $8 million (half of its international receipts). *Author's Note*: Wayne told this author that "working with Kate [Hepburn] in **Rooster Cogburn** was like working with Hollywood royalty. That gal is a great actress and a great woman. She was so very down to earth that you never had to talk up to her. We shot most of that picture on location in Oregon [along the Deschutes and Rogue rivers] and Kate never complained about the hardships we had to put up with. If she had lived in the Old West, she would have been a great pioneer." Hepburn told this author that "Duke [Wayne] was one of the most natural actors I ever met in my life. He never seemed to have any trouble with his lines or action and he was flawless in his delivery. For many years, I had wanted to work with him in a picture, but never got the chance until **Rooster Cogburn**. That was one of the treats of my life. He was exactly what I expected, a man bigger than life, and as big as the great outdoors the world always envisioned him riding through. There will never be anyone to walk in those big cowboy boots." **p**, Hal B. Wallis; **d**, Stuart Millar; **cast**, John Wayne, Katharine Hepburn, Anthony Zerbe, Richard Jordan, John McIntyre, Strother Martin, Richard Romancito, Warren Vanders, Tommy Lee, Jon Lormer, Paul Koslo; **w**, Martin Julien (based on the characters created by Charles Portis in his novel, *True Grit*); **c**, Harry Stradling Jr. (Panavision; Technicolor); **m**, Laurence Rosenthal; **ed**, Robert Swink; **art d**, Preston Ames; **set d**, George Robert Nelson; **spec eff**, Jack McMasters.

The Roots of Heaven ★★★ 1958; U.S.; 121m; FOX; Color; Adventure/Drama; Children: Unacceptable; **DVD**; **VHS**. Absorbing offbeat adventure begins with Howard, a former POW, who survived the brutalities of the Nazis in WWII (1939-1945) and who is consumed by the overpowering ambition to save the ever decreasing herds of elephants in French Equatorial Africa. All he could think about in that German concentration camp was elephants and the freedom these great beasts have enjoyed throughout history. When he is free and goes to Africa, he sees that ivory poachers, big game hunters and starving natives are ruthlessly preying upon the elephants, drastically reducing their numbers almost to extinction. Howard begins a one-man crusade to save the elephants from slaughter, but he meets with widespread indifference, most of those he solicits for help thinking him to be a hopeless idealist or a crackpot zealot. Greco, a prostitute with deep compassion, sees

Howard's crusade as something out of King Arthur and the quest for the Holy Grail and she becomes his avid supporter. Slowly, the social flotsam and jetsam of Africa are attracted to this inspiring man. Flynn, a former and disgraced British officer, who has long been a hopeless alcoholic after he was accused of betraying his own men during WWII, also joins Howard. Officials, however, turn a deaf ear to Howard's plea that the hunting of elephants be restricted. When Welles, a famous American radio commentator, arrives in Africa, he publicly announces that he is there to see the great sport of shooting elephants, and goes along on a hunting safari. Howard teaches him a lesson in false pride by firing a load of rock salt into his backside from a shotgun, which uncomfortably debilitates Welles, causing him to rest on his belly while his mutilated behind is medically treated. Instead of becoming enraged at Howard, Welles recognizes Howard's cause as worthwhile. After recuperating and returning to the U.S., he becomes an advocate for Howard's unorthodox crusade, praising Howard and urging all to save the elephants. Added to Howard' coterie of dedicated supporters is Ledebur, a Danish scientist, and Hussenot, a European baron, who refuses to speak to anyone, such is his resentment of his fellow human beings for their savage inhumanity toward all living things. Albert, an opportunistic photojournalist, arrives to record Howard's actions, thinking to enrich himself by documenting Howard's crusade. (Albert's role is modeled after that of Lowell Thomas, who became the unofficial biographer of the nonconforming T. E. Lawrence during the Arab uprisings in WWI, promoting Lawrence into the heroic image of "Lawrence of Arabia.") Howard then attracts the attention of Connor, who heads a Pan-African liberation organization. Connor thinks to use Howard to further his group's political ends, but, after Howard sees through Connor's machinations and subterfuge, Connor sides with Howard's most avowed enemy, Lom, who is the leader of bloodthirsty poachers after the ivory tusks of elephants. Howard learns that Lom and his small army of poachers plan to attack one of the last great elephant herds in the territory. Howard leads his small group to where the herd is grazing, and before the poachers can open fire, Howard, Flynn, Ledebur, Hussenot, and Greco, all situated in different locations around that herd, begin firing into the air to begin an elephant stampede. The great beasts move as a crushing tide through the jungles, overrunning some of the poachers, these natives fleeing in terror. The group's heroic efforts are not without sacrifice. Lom takes revenge by having his top killers track down and kill Flynn and Hussenot. Howard, Greco, Ledebur then defy authorities and head back into the wilds to continue their cause, and Albert, who has become inspired by their courageous and noble efforts, discards the tools of his trade, his cameras, and follows after them, becoming as dedicated as Howard in preserving the elephants of Africa. Huston does a terrific job with this strange tale, carefully unfolding the story to build growing suspense and tension that finally leads up to the elephant stampede, and he draws fine performances from Howard, Flynn and Albert. This was a costly film to make, Fox spending more than $3.3 million on the production, which was shot on location in Chad for many months. The offbeat theme did not resonate with the public; box office receipts from the film's initial release came to only $3 million. Song: "Minna's Theme" (Henri Patterson). *Author's Note*: Zanuck told this author that "the shooting of that film in Africa was a nightmare. The temperature averaged 130 degrees during the day and it never went below ninety degrees at night. Almost everyone caught one disease or another, from dysentery to malaria, and many had to be hospitalized. I vowed that I would never again return to Africa." Greco, a French singer and actress, who was Zanuck's hand-picked protégé, and who was personally promoted by Zanuck in many films produced during his reign at Fox, complained that Huston's direction of **The Roots of Heaven** was haphazard at best. She stated after the film was released that the director's only instructions to her and other players in the production invariably consisted of "'show me what you are feeling…Do what you want to do.'" In his defense, Huston told this author that "I gave Juliette [Greco] very little direction because she was under Darryl's [Zanuck's] direct sponsorship. She was not an actress with a wide range of emotions." Huston and Flynn were the only members of the cast who did not come down with one tropical ailment or another. "I think that was due to the fact that Errol [Flynn] and I did not drink any of the local water," Huston told this author. "We confined our drinking to vodka, which we sipped throughout each day and that insulated us, I think, against the virulent malaria most others contracted. I was an old hand at that. When I did **The African Queen** [1951] with Bogey [Humphrey Bogart] and Kate Hepburn, Bogey and I did the same thing, sipping vodka throughout that on-location shooting in Africa." Huston would, three years after his death, be profiled as a ruthless game hunter with a savage personality in **White Hunter, Black Heart**, 1990. He had long earlier forsaken such blood sports, according to his statements to this author: "I wanted to make **The Roots of Heaven** because I had come to realize how pointless and inhuman it was in killing those magnificent elephants or any other endangered species. By then I shared the viewpoints expressed by the characters in that picture, who only wanted those elephants to go on living." Howard was one of the few principals who did not suffer the severe effects of malaria. As good as Howard is in this film, he was not the first choice for the leading role, which was originally offered to actor William Holden. That actor told this author that "I had to drop out of that picture as I had too many other projects in the works and I am glad that I did not go to Africa with the rest of the gang because most of them wound up in hospitals from every disease known to man." Holden was himself a dedicated advocate of animal preservation in Africa and elsewhere and actively sponsored a wildlife reservation for such animals in that country. Greco was stricken with malaria after she finished her scenes and became so ill that she was flown out of the country to recuperate in a European hospital. Albert, too, was stricken with a strange fever that reduced him to constant shivering. According to Zanuck, Albert was so ill for three weeks that all he could do was to remain prone on the concrete floor of his hut and shiver. He had to be helped to the latrine to relieve himself, and after he recovered, he reportedly had no recollection of his ailment. Welles appears only briefly in this film. He was, according to his statements to this author, "very grateful that I was not subjected to the prolonged shooting schedule in Africa for **The Roots of Heaven**. Otherwise, I believe I would have been another malaria victim like most of the cast and crew." Welles received only $15,000 for his cameo role in this film, but he was also grateful to get the work as, according to his further statements to the author: "I needed to pay creditors as I was seriously in debt at that time, still paying off expenses for other productions that did not do as well as expected. In this business, you pay as you go. If you do not have the cash, you pay with your talent, your brains, or, in my case in that picture, you allow yourself to be shot in the butt without complaint." **p**, Darryl F. Zanuck; **d**, John Huston; **cast**, Errol Flynn, Juliette Greco, Trevor Howard, Eddie Albert, Orson Welles, Paul Lukas, Herbert Lom, Gregoire Aslan, Andre Luguet, Friedrich Ledebur; **w**, Romain Gary, Patrick Leigh-Fermor (based on the novel by Gary); **c**, Oswald Morris (CinemaScope; DeLuxe Color); **m**, Malcolm Arnold; **ed**, Russell Lloyd; **art d**, Stephen Grimes; **set d**, Bruno Avesani; **spec eff**, L.B. Abbott, Fred Etcheverry.

Rope ★★★ 1948; U.S.; 80m; Transatlantic Pictures/WB; Color; Crime Drama; Children: Unacceptable; **DVD**; **VHS**. A chilling and technically experimental film from pantheon director Hitchcock, this offbeat murder tale was shot on one elaborate set and took only ten takes to put into the can. The action takes place in a NYC penthouse apartment of two wealthy young homosexual men, Dall and Granger (who are prototypes for thrill Chicago killers Richard Loeb, 1905-1936, and Nathan Leopold, 1904-1971). The film opens with both of them plotting to murder Hogan, one of their college friends, a mild-mannered and too-trusting young fellow. Their only motivation is to demonstrate their intellectual ability and superiority in getting away with such a ruthless crime. They invite Hogan to their residence and mercilessly strangle him with a short piece of rope (ergo the title of the film). They hide the body in an antique

Farley Granger, James Stewart and John Dall in *Rope,* **1948.**

wooden chest in their living room and place the rope in a drawer. Toasting their grim deed with champagne, Dall and Granger then go about arranging the place with food and drinks they intend to serve to their upscale guests at a cocktail party that evening. Their guest list reflects the insidious minds of the hosts as they have invited Hardwicke, Hogan's father, and Chandler, the victim's fiancée, to attend. They have also invited, among other guests, their old college professor, Stewart, who has previously discussed and advanced the so-called "superman" theories of Friedrich Nietzsche, and which have inspired these two merciless killers to perform their heinous deed. To further mock their murder, the killers think it amusing to serve their guests food from the top of the large wooden chest that holds the corpse of their victim. As guests arrive and begin to chit-chat, Dall purposely flaunts the murder by dropping hints in his conversation ("I could kill you" and "Knock 'em dead."), all of which unnerves Granger, who is urged by Dall to play the piano, telling him ruefully that "these hands will bring you great fame," the very hands used to strangle Hogan. Some of the guests become uneasy when Hogan fails to make his appearance and they begin to wonder if he has fallen victim to foul play or misadventure. To heighten the suspense, Dall takes Stewart aside and morosely begins to talk about killing "undesirables" as a moral responsibility to rid the world of weak-minded persons. He then offers Hardwicke some books, tying them together with the very rope he and Granger used to murder Hardwicke's son. The guests then make their farewells and all leave. Stewart, however, returns. He has grown suspicious of the two young men, alerted by their innuendoes and, especially, Granger's edgy behavior and the fact that he takes too much liquor and becomes drunk, acting even more erratically. Stewart puts all the pieces Dall has placed before him together and then realizes that Granger and Dall have murdered Hogan and he finds the body in the wooden chest. Granger feebly produces a gun and points it at him, but Stewart disarms Granger, slightly wounding him. He then opens a window and fires a few shots from the gun to summon police. Dall pleads with Stewart to abandon any thought of turning him and Granger over to the law, arguing that they committed their deed because of Stewart's intellectual support of Nietzsche's teachings, but Stewart dismisses such influence as degenerate perversions of his earlier statements to these two young killers. He intends to see them brought to justice and they all grimly wait for the police to arrive as the film ends. The film, though a fascinating experiment and one that offers many tense moments and good acting from Stewart, Dall and Granger, was not a success, and did not initially earn back its $1.5 million budget. Songs: "Movement Perpetual No. 1" (1919; Francis Poulenc), "I'm Looking Over a Four-Leaf Clover" (Harry M. Woods). *Author's Note*: Hitchcock shot this film in ten eight-minute continuous takes, having the entire set, including its walls and furnishings, on coasters, so that

Peter Lorre and Burt Lancaster in *Rope of Sand,* **1949.**

when the cameras dollied to new positions, portions of the set broke away for those new angles. Hitchcock told this author that: "I had experimented with continuous long takes in some early films like **Blackmail** [1929] and **Murder!** [1930], and I always wanted to do an entire picture with nothing but continuous takes. **Rope** gave me that opportunity as it all takes place in one apartment [other than the opening street scene credit shots]. The actors had to move lively during the production and I think it annoyed some of them. It was more theatrical than filmic and it gave them a chance to act as if they were on the stage, but there was no live audience except the crew. In the end, the technique gave the story fluid visuals, but I thought later that it had a claustrophobic feel to it as it was confined to that one set. They all do not work out as you might hope." Stewart, who appeared in several later films by Hitchcock (**Rear Window**, 1954; **The Man Who Knew Too Much**, 1956; **Vertigo**, 1958), had a strong dislike for the film. He first appears twenty-eight minutes into the film and felt that "I was just one more prop in that moveable set. I did not like my role. I am supposed to be a professor who gives these two creeps the idea of killing someone because of his superiority theories. Well, that alone made me feel very uncomfortable because I have never held such ideas and the role reminded me of the one that Orson Welles did a few years earlier in a film called **The Stranger** [1946] where he is an escaped Nazi hiding out in a New England town and is a professor with those same fascist ideas about superiority. No, I never liked that picture at all. About ten years later, I appeared in another picture with a grim theme like **Rope**, called **Anatomy of a Murder**, but that picture was handled much differently and where I played a criminal defense attorney defending the accused killer [Ben Gazzara]. That picture was really a good courtroom drama that did not dwell on the rape and murder involved in the case where **Rope** sits right on top of the murder committed by two arrogant punks like Lady Godiva riding naked right down the middle of the street, and I think that Hitch missed a bit on that one. He did not miss many." Hume Cronyn (who had debuted as an actor in Hitchcock's **Shadow of a Doubt**, 1943; and had appeared in Hitchcock's **Lifeboat**, 1944) worked on the script, and also told this author that "the story is really about two homosexuals who select a heterosexual victim to murder. Their sexual relationship is evident in the picture and that's why a lot of theaters refused to show the picture when it was released. Homosexuality was taboo in those days. In Hitch's **Shadow of a Doubt**, I played a meek neighbor who is always talking about clever murder methods with Henry Travers, the head of the household where the killer [Cotten] is living and that grim little game so intrigued me that I did some research on the two Chicago killers [upon which **Rope** is based] and provided some of that information for the script." The film was initially banned in Chicago, Memphis, Spokane, Seattle and several other towns. Nov-

elist and screenwriter Ben Hecht, who worked on many scripts for Hitchcock (**Foreign Correspondent**, 1940; **Lifeboat**, 1944; **Spellbound**, 1945; **Notorious**, 1946), also worked on the screenplay for this film, telling this author: "The story was reworked from a 1929 play and that play was based on the 1924 thrill killing in Chicago by Richard Loeb and Nathan Leopold, two rich kids from millionaire families, who were homosexuals and murdered a boy [Bobby Franks, age fourteen] just to see if they could get away with it. They didn't. It was a sordid tale and Hitch did his best with it, but the story never gets out of its box because everything happens inside of that apartment. I wrote some exterior shots to give the story some air, but Hitch never used those scenes. He was a budget and schedule man to the bone." For more details on Loeb and Leopold, see my entries on these two horrific killers in my works *Bloodletters and Badmen* (M. Evans, 1973, 1995), *Encyclopedia of 20th-Century Murder* (Paragon House, 1992), and *The Great Pictorial History of World Crime*, Volume II (History, Inc., 2004; pages 840-858). **p**, Sidney Bernstein, Alfred Hitchcock; **d**, Hitchcock; **cast**, James Stewart, John Dall, Farley Granger, Sir Cedric Hardwicke, Constance Collier, Douglas Dick, Dick Hogan, Edith Evanson, Joan Chandler, Hitchcock; **w**, Arthur Laurents, Hume Cronyn, (not credited) Ben Hecht (based on the play "Rope's End" by Patrick Hamilton); **c**, Joseph Valentine, William V. Skall (Technicolor); **m**, David Buttolph; **ed**, William H. Ziegler; **art d**, Perry Ferguson; **set d**, Emile Kuri, Howard Bristol.

Rope of Sand ★★★ 1949; U.S.; 104m; PAR; B/W; Adventure; Children: Unacceptable; **DVD**. Taut tale has the brawny and canny Lancaster serving as a guide in a mining town in South Africa. He takes a hunter who has stolen a cache of priceless diamonds out of the area, but, while crossing the desert, the hunter dies. Henreid, who is chief of security for the diamond company, learns of Lancaster's role and arrests him, demanding to know where the stolen diamonds are hidden. A sadistic brute that enjoys inflicting pain, Henreid savagely beats Lancaster to compel him to disclose the whereabouts of the missing diamonds, but his victim is too tough and taciturn to give him any information. Henreid then reluctantly releases Lancaster, but Rains, the cunning and calculating owner of the diamond mine, who will not tolerate a single gem escaping his grasp, then uses psychology to have Lancaster return to the location where the diamonds are hidden. When Henreid asks Rains for permission to again arrest and torture Lancaster, the mine owner refuses, saying he is going to try another tactic. He hires Calvet, an alluring prostitute, to wangle information about the hidden diamonds from Lancaster, but Lancaster resists her wiles. She meanwhile falls in love with her prey while Henreid falls in love with Calvet. Lancaster, in a turnabout move, forces Henreid to take him and Calvet into the forbidden zone where the diamonds are hidden. After Lancaster retrieves the gems and escapes, Henreid takes revenge by murdering Jaffe, the company physician who is one of Lancaster's few friends and has aided him in his quest to escape the territory. Because Calvet has rebuffed his advances, Henreid frames her for Jaffe's killing by leaving evidence that will implicate her in the doctor's death. Lancaster then learns that Calvet is being held and is about to be executed for Jaffe's murder, information supplied by local barfly and sleazy informant Lorre, who is aptly named "Toady." Lancaster, who has fallen in love with Calvet, then goes to Rains and offers him a deal, the missing diamonds for Calvet. The ever possessive Rains accepts and compels Henreid to sign a document that absolves Lancaster and Calvet of any wrongdoing in Jaffe's murder, but, before Lancaster and Calvet flee, the always conniving Rains hands Henreid a gun to dispatch the two. At the last minute, either out of guilt or whim, Rains shouts a warning to Lancaster, who turns about and shoots Henreid dead before he can kill him and the fetching Calvet, who then both flee to freedom and a happier life. Well directed and acted, this gritty tale did well at the box office. Three of the actors—Henreid, Rains and Lorre—were reunited after appearing in **Casablanca**, 1942; this film attempts to recapture the flavor and mystique of that classic film. The story was aired in a thirty-minute radio broadcast by Screen Director's Playhouse on April 28, 1950, where Lancaster reprised his role. Song: "Zulu Warrior" (Josef Marais). *Author's Note*: Dieterle told this author that "**Rope of Sand** was a vehicle hatched by producer Hal Wallis, who wanted to recreate **Casablanca**, as the setting was in the desert. He tried to get Ingrid Bergman and Humphrey Bogart into the picture, but they were not available, so he got Burt [Lancaster] and put Corinne [Calvet] into the production and that was Corinne's first film." Lancaster was never enthusiastic about the film, telling this author that "I never liked it, even though it had a good story and cast. I was going through a lot of personal troubles then, which I associated with the picture. I guess that is an unfair way to look at things, but making films is an emotional experience and the emotions you have when making a picture stay with you forever." Rains told this author that "my role in **Rope of Sand** is pretty much like the character I played in **Casablanca**, always self-serving and manipulating everybody else. Poor Paul [Henreid], who played a hero in **Casablanca**, is a vicious villain in **Rope of Sand**, but he did an amazingly convincing job as a sadistic enforcer heading a private police force, a consummate actor to be sure." Jaffe had no misgivings about his supporting role, stating to this author that "I only had a few scenes in that picture, but I appear to be the only person in the cast who has any scruples—the rest are the flotsam and jetsam of the earth." Lorre thought he had, as usual, been typecast, saying to this author: "I played another slimy squealer, just like the part I had in **Strange Cargo** [1940], but one had to work and pay the bills, so it was squeal like a pig to get the paycheck." **p**, Hal B. Wallis; **d**, William Dieterle; **cast**, Burt Lancaster, Paul Henreid, Claude Rains, Peter Lorre, Corinne Calvet, Sam Jaffe, John Bromfield, Mike Mazurki, Ida Moore, Hayden Rorke; **w**, Walter Doniger, John Paxton (based on a story by Doniger); **c**, Charles B. Lang, Jr.; **m**, Franz Waxman; **ed**, Warren Low; **art d**, Hans Dreier, Franz Bachelin; **set d**, Sam Comer, Grace Gregory; **spec eff**, Farciot Edouart, Gordon Jennings.

Rosa Luxemburg ★★★ 1987; Czechoslovakia/Germany; 122m; Bioskop Film/New Yorker Films; Color; Biographical Drama; Children: Unacceptable; **VHS**. This riveting biopic sees Marxist and social democrat Rosa Luxemburg (1871-1919), brilliantly played by Sukowa, risking her life as she denounces war and militarism in Germany at the start of World War I (1914-1918), and where she helps form a revolutionary German party, the Spartacist League. The film begins in 1916 in a prison where she faces a mock execution, then flashes back twenty years as she struggles for a socialist government in Germany and revolution in Poland. As international tensions mount, Sukowa makes speeches against militarism and war, seeming to be too radical even for her fellow socialists as World War I begins. She and her fellow socialist leader, Karl Liebknecht (1871-1919), superbly played by Sander, are then kidnapped by right-wing militarists, the precursors to the Nazis, and are summarily executed. This fine production, which presents many astounding period sets and locations, as well as the appropriate period costuming, is dedicated to its talented costume designer Monika Hasse, who died while the film was in production. *Author's Note*: For details on Luxemburg and Liebknecht, see my work *The Great Pictorial History of World Crime*, Volume I (History, Inc., 2004; pages 118-120). (In German; English subtitles.) **p**, Eberhard Junkersdorf, Regina Ziegler; **d&w**, Margarethe von Trotta; **cast**, Barbara Sukowa, Daniel Olbrychski, Otto Sander, Adelheid Arndt, Jurgen Holtz, Doris Schade, Hannes Jaenicke, Jan Biczycki, Karin Baal, Winfried Glatzeder; **c**, Franz Rath; **m**, Nicolas Economou; **ed**, Dagmar Hirtz, Galip Iyitanir; **set d**, Stepan Exner, Bernd Lepel; **spec eff**, Ben De Jong, Harry Wiessenhaan.

Rosalie ★★★ 1937; U.S.: 123m; MGM; B/W/ Musical Comedy; Children: Acceptable; **DVD**. This broad-based musical extravaganza offers a complex plot that involves Eddy as a conceited football player at West Point, who becomes the hero of the big game against Navy, which nonetheless ends in a tie. He falls in love with Powell, a Vassar girl, who

Nelson Eddy and Eleanor Powell in *Rosalie*, 1937.

is really a European princess, and who tells no one about her royal ties. She thinks Eddy is too arrogant for her, but she agrees to see him later in the European principality where she lives. Powell returns to her country where a marriage between her and Rutherford, the son of Owen, the country's chancellor, has been arranged. She does not like the idea of marrying a man she does not love, but Eddy solves that when he flies his own plane to her country and where comics Gilbert (and his famous sneezing) and Colonna and (his zany double talk) almost cause him to crash as they guide him to a landing from the airport radio they control. After Eddy lands like an arriving Lindbergh, Morgan befriends him and helps him search for Powell, Eddy thinking she is only a common citizen, and, in their search, a subplot between Grey and Bolger blossoms. The country then erupts in revolution, and Powell and her royal family flee to the U.S.; the indefatigable Eddy nevertheless finds Powell, and they return to West Point where they sing out their love for one another in a spectacular finale. Though Eddy is a bit long in the tooth (he was thirty-seven when making this film), his wonderful tenor voice is in full and lyrical force; Powell's dancing and singing (her singing voice dubbed by Marjorie Lane) is worth the film itself. The sets and costuming are staggering in size and enriched finery in one of the most expensive and sumptuous musicals ever produced by MGM. Songs: "Rosalie," "Who Knows?," I've a Strange New Rhythm in My Heart," "Why Should I Care?," "Spring Love Is in the Air," "Close," "In the Still of the Night," "It's All Over But the Shouting," "To Love or Not to Love" (1937; Cole Porter), "The Caisson Song" (1907; Edmund L. Gruber), "On, Brave Old Army Team" (1910; Philip Egner), "Anchors Aweigh" (1906; music: Charles A. Zimmerman; lyrics: Alfred Hart Miles, R. Lovell), "M'appari tutt'amor" (1847; from the opera "Martha" by Friedrich von Flotow), "Dance russe" (1911; from "Petrouchka" by Igor Stravinsky), "Polovetsian Dances" (1887; from "Prince Igor" by Aleksandr Borodin), "Caucasian Sketches, Op. 10" (1894; Mikhail Ippolitov-Ivanov), "Symphony No. 6 in B Flat," "Pathétique' Op.74" (1893; Pyotr Ilyich Tchaikovsky), "Goodbye Forever" (Francesco Paolo Tosti), "The Washington Post" (1889; John Philip Sousa), "The Stars and Stripes Forever" (1896; Sousa), "El Capitan" (1896; Sousa), "Semper Fidelis" (1888; Sousa), "Parade" (Herbert Stothart), "Gaudeamus Igitur" (traditional), "The Wedding March" (1893; from "A Midsummer Night's Dream" by Felix Mendelssohn-Bartholdy), "Oh Promise Me" (1889; from the opera "Robin Hood"; music: Reginald De Koven; lyrics: Clement W. Scott). *Author's Note*: The film is based upon a successful Broadway musical produced by impresario Florenz Ziegfeld, opening in New York at the New Amsterdam Theater on January 10, 1928, and running for 335 performances with Marilyn Miller as the princess and Frank McLennan as the football hero and Frank Morgan as the king of the principality. Morgan reprised that role in this film version. At a cost of more than $2 mil-

Bette Midler in *The Rose*, 1979.

take their toll on her and she breaks down under alcohol and drugs. Though Bates is obliquely blamed for Midler's collapse, the real Janis Joplin went busily about destroying herself with dangerous drugs and without any help from anyone. Songs: "The Rose" (Amanda McBroom), "Whose Side Are You On" (Kenny Hopkins), "Midnight in Memphis" (Tony Johnson), "When a Man Loves a Woman" (Calvin Lewis, Andrew Wright), "Sold My Soul to Rock 'N' Roll" (Gene Pistilli), "Keep on Rockin' (Sammy Hagar, John Carter), "Love Me with a Feeling" (Hudson Whittaker), "Camellia" (Stephen Hunter), "Stay with Me" (Jerry Ragovoy, George Weiss), "Let Me Call You Sweetheart" (Beth Slater Whitson, Leo Friedman), "Fire Down Below" (Bob Seger). Excessive drinking, drug use and sexuality prohibit viewing by children. **p**, Marvin Worth, Aaron Russo; **d**, Mark Rydell; **cast**, Bette Midler, Alan Bates, Frederic Forrest, Harry Dean Stanton, Barry Primus, David Keith, Sandra McCabe, Will Hare, Rudy Bond, Doris Roberts; **w**, Bo Goldman, Bill Kerby, Michael Cimino (based on a story by Kerby); **c**, Vilmos Zsigmond (DeLuxe Color); **m**, Paul A. Rothchild; **ed**, Robert L. Wolfe, C. Timothy O'Meara; **prod d**, Richard Macdonald; **art d**, Jim Schoppe; **set d**, Bruce Weintraub; **spec eff**, Jay King.

Rose Marie ★★★★ 1936; U.S.; 113m; MGM; B/W; Musical/Romance; Children: Acceptable; **DVD**; **VHS**. This smash musical hit is the one for which the celebrated musical team of MacDonald and Eddy are best remembered. Its light operetta music is superb, their performances excellent and the story is both absorbing and exciting. MacDonald is a successful opera star touring Canada who, while performing in Montreal, goes to Mowbray, the Premier of the country, to beg for her errant brother, Stewart (in his second film), who has been jailed for robbing a bank. MacDonald asks that Stewart be released, pending trial, but before such a request can be granted, Stewart breaks loose and kills a Mountie in the process. Now the Mounties are after him and so is MacDonald, who searches for her escaped brother. She quits her opera troupe, hires Regas, an untrustworthy half-breed guide out for money, and, without the proper clothing and equipment, sets out for the wilderness. At the last outpost, a crude mining town, Regas makes off with MacDonald's purse, and Littlefield, a kindly shopkeeper, urges her to tell the Mounties about the theft. Knowing that these upright defenders of the law are also searching for Stewart, she is disinclined to talk to anyone wearing one of those red coats. She goes to a roughhouse saloon where Gray (Gilda Gray of the "Shimmy" fame), an old hand at entertaining the tough prospectors, shows her how to sing songs that these lowbrow miners like. She sings a few songs, awkwardly imitating the brassy delivery of Gray, but Eddy, a Mountie who visits the saloon, realizes that MacDonald is the newly arrived visitor he is looking for. When she leaves the saloon, Eddy follows her and tells her that her stolen suitcase is being held at his office. He then takes her to an Indian ceremony, and while they are watching tribal dances, MacDonald spots Regas, who embarrassingly returns her purse and money and promises to take her into the wilds to find her brother. Eddy, by this time, realizes that MacDonald is the sister of the man he is sworn to capture, but he is torn between his love for her and his duty-bound oath to get his man. When she and Regas sneak out of town, Eddy follows them. As MacDonald and Regas struggle through the wilderness, the guide sees Eddy trailing them and deserts MacDonald. Eddy finds her and uses her to finally capture Stewart and bring him to justice. MacDonald returns to her singing, but, while appearing in "Tosca," she finds that she cannot sing a word and breaks down. She is in a total state of collapse, but, Owen, her avuncular manager, knows the reason for MacDonald's emotional stress, and he summons the true man of MacDonald's heart. When Eddy arrives, MacDonald becomes her old self, and they are united for a happy ending. This great songfest was an enormous hit at the box office, gleaning more than $3.5 million in domestic and foreign receipts against a budget of $875,000, and it cemented the singing love duo of MacDonald and Eddy with the public. The film was shot on location at Lake Tahoe during the summer since even the Canadian Rockies at that time

lion, the production numbers showed every penny spent on the film. More than 1,200 extras appeared in the Drum Dance sequence, which cost more than $30,000 to light. The original music, which was a mixture of an operetta and a campus musical, originated with Sigmund Romberg and George Gershwin, but all of those fine tunes were abandoned, including Gershwin's memorable "How Long Has This Been Going On?" A new score and tunes were then substituted by Porter and other composers. Marion Davies had appeared in an earlier silent film version of the story, only partially produced by Cosmopolitan and MGM in 1928; it was halted after the studio converted its operations to sound. Some of the exterior scenes from that silent version, however, appear in this film. Director Van Dyke, who was otherwise known for his quick takes, redid many scenes, which increased the burgeoning budget, and, in some of the musical numbers, he used up to twenty cameras to capture the action and the epic ensembles. Massey makes her debut in the film after she was discovered by MGM boss Louis B. Mayer on one of his rare European trips. Mayer also put under contract Hedy Lamarr, Greer Garson and others while on that European jaunt, including a budding actress named Rose Stradner. After making a few films, Stradner gave up her acting career when meeting producer-director Joseph Mankiewicz, marrying him and forsaking the allure of the silver screen. She resented her life as a housewife and later became alcoholic and mentally unstable, throwing violent tirades and threatening suicide. She finally took her life with an overdose of sleeping pills in 1958, which ended her almost twenty years of marriage to Mankiewicz. Two minor players, Barcroft, who appears as a conspirator, and Aldridge, playing a lady-in-waiting, went on to become staples at Republic, the topmost studio along Poverty Row. **p**, William Anthony McGuire; **d**, W.S. Van Dyke; **cast**, Nelson Eddy, Eleanor Powell, Frank Morgan, Edna May Oliver, Ray Bolger, Ilona Massey, Reginald Owen, Tom Rutherford, Billy Gilbert, George Zucco, Virginia Grey, Jerry Colonna, William Demarest, Phillip Terry, Clay Clement, Oscar O'Shea, Janet Beecher, Rush Hughes, Al Shean, Purnell Pratt, Richard Tucker, Roy Barcroft, Kay Aldridge; **w**, McGuire (based on the play by McGuire, Guy Bolton); **c**, Oliver T. Marsh; **m**, Cole Porter; **ed**, Blanche Sewell; **art d**, Cedric Gibbons; **spec eff**, Slavko Vorkapich.

The Rose ★★★ 1979; U.S.; 125m; FOX; Color; Drama; Children: Unacceptable (MPAA: R); **DVD**; **VHS**. Midler does an exceptional job in this tragic tale of a self-destructive rock star, which is modeled after the drug-addicted Janis Joplin (1943-1970). Midler plays Rose, and the film follows her career during her last tour. She wants to take a year off, but her self-serving manager, Bates, pushes her into the grueling tour even though she is exhausted from road appearances. She goes on the tour and has a very satisfying affair with a chauffeur, Forrest, but the gigs were too cold and forbidding for the extended production. The story was remade in 1954 by the same studio with Ann Blyth and Howard Keel in the leading roles. Songs: "Romeo and Juliette" (1867; music: Charles Gounod; lyrics: Jules Barbier, Michel Carre); "God Save the King" (1744; Henry Carey); "Pardon Me Madame" (1936; music: Herbert Stothart; lyrics: Gus Kahn); "Dinah" (1925; music: Harry Akst; lyrics: Sam Lewis, Joe Young); "Some of These Days" (1910; Shelton Brooks); "The Mounties," "Rose Marie," "Totem Tom-Tom" (1924; music: Rudolf Friml; lyrics: Oscar Hammerstein II, Otto A. Harbach); "Just for You" (1936; Rudolf Friml and Herbert Stothart; lyrics: Gus Kahn); "Indian Love Call" (1924; music: Rudolf Friml; lyrics: Oscar Hammerstein II); "Three Blind Mice" (traditional); "Tosca" (1900; music: Giacomo Puccini; lyrics: Luigi Illica and Giuseppe Giacosa). *Author's Note*: Director Van Dyke, as was his custom, shot this film in a whirlwind schedule, although he realized that MacDonald, who had by then become a big MGM star, was attempting to manipulate him and successfully manipulated Eddy so that she appeared most prominent in their two-shots together and where she insisted, without Eddy's knowledge, that Van Dyke give her most of the close-ups in such scenes, a trick that Eddy did not discover until he saw the finished film. Van Dyke was a facile and easy-going director who could animate just about any actor or animal, but he had difficulty with Eddy, who had no self-esteem as an actor and only projected with confidence when he was singing. Eddy was conscious of another fine tenor appearing in this film, the personable and handsome Allan Jones, who sings with MacDonald in the opera scenes; MacDonald actually upbraids Jones in one of their performances together by saying on camera: "What's the idea of holding every high A longer than I did?" As Eddy watched these scenes with MacDonald and Jones, he thought that Jones was being allowed too much time on screen and complained about it to the front office. Jones' scenes were cut down, but he went on to establish his own career as a singing star, including a role opposite MacDonald in **The Firefly**, 1937. Stewart told this author that "**Rose Marie** was a big break for me. It was my second feature film and it was a strong supporting role, even though I play an irresponsible young man who turns into a rather savage killer, the kind of character that goes against my own nature. I had appeared only in one other feature before that, one with the great Spencer Tracy, in **Murder Man** [1935] and I played a reporter. Tracy helped me a lot in that picture and told me to take any kind of part I could get and that the better parts would come later. Jeanette [MacDonald] and Nelson [Eddy] were very nice to me, but you didn't dare get in front of Jeanette when the cameras rolled because she was one of the great scene-stealers and Nelson let her steal all she wanted. She did not get away with that when she did a picture with John Barrymore, one called **Maytime** [1937]. She tried to steal scenes from the Great Profile by hauling out a handkerchief and playing with it in her scenes with him, but he caught her doing that just once and stopped the scene. He leaned close to her and said with a smile and a whisper: 'If you ever try to steal a scene from me again with that delicate little handkerchief, dear, I will stuff it down your pretty throat.' **p**, Hunt Stromberg; **d**, W.S. Van Dyke; **cast**, Jeanette MacDonald, Nelson Eddy, Reginald Owen, Allan Jones, James Stewart, Alan Mowbray, Gilda Gray, Robert Greig, George Regas, Una O'Connor, David Nivens (Niven), Herman Bing, Bill Cody, Jr., Iron Eyes Cody; **w**, Frances Goodrich, Albert Hackett, Alice Duer Miller (based on the operetta by Otto A. Harbach, Oscar Hammerstein II, Rudolf Friml from the play by Herbert Stothart); **c**, William Daniels; **m**, Friml, Stothart; **ed**, Blanche Sewell; **art d**, Cedric Gibbons.

Rose Marie ★★★ 1954; U.S.; 115m; MGM; Color; Musical/Romance; Children: Acceptable; **DVD**; **VHS**. Blyth is outstanding while playing pretty tomboy, Rose Marie, the orphaned ward of Canadian Mountie Keel. They fall in love, and she insists upon becoming a lady. In this effort, she meets outlaw trapper Lamas, who also falls in love with her. Lamas is in a dispute with an Indian chief (Yowlachie), who is found murdered, and Keel hunts down Lamas who is the killer. He is captured

Nelson Eddy and Jeanette MacDonald in *Rose Marie*, 1936.

after Keel hears Lamas and Blyth singing the "Indian Love Call" song to each other in the mountainous wilds, which allows Keel to locate the evasive outlaw. Blyth, however, loves the rugged Mountie more and she and Keel embrace at the finale. This is a tongue-in-cheek remake of the classic 1936 musical, but offers a much different plot, although it sustains interest throughout with one fine song after another. Songs: "The Right Place for a Girl," "Free to Be Me," "I Have the Love" (music: Rudolf Friml; lyrics: Paul Francis Webster); "Rose Marie," "Indian Love Call," "Mounties" (music: Friml; lyrics: Otto A. Harbach, Oscar Hammerstein II); "Free to Be Free," "I'm a Mountie Who Never Got His Man" (music: George Stoll; lyrics: Stoll, Herbert Baker), "Totem Tom-Tom" (music: Friml, Herbert Stothart; lyrics: Harbach, Hammerstein II); "Alouette" (traditional). **p&d**, Mervyn LeRoy; **cast**, Ann Blyth, Howard Keel, Fernando Lamas, Burt Lahr, Marjorie Main, Joan Taylor, Ray Collins, Chief Yowlachie, Fred Aldrich, Robert Anderson; **w**, Ronald Millar, George Froeschel (based on the operetta by Otto A. Harbach, Oscar Hammerstein II, Rudolf Friml, Herbert Stothart); **c**, Paul Vogel (CinemaScope; Eastmancolor); **m**, George Stoll, Robert Van Eps, Albert Sendrey; **ed**, Harold F. Kress; **art d**, Cedric Gibbons, Merrill Pye; **set d**, Edwin B. Willis, Ralph Hurst; **spec eff**, A. Arnold Gillespie, Warren Newcombe.

Rose of Washington Square ★★★★ 1939; U.S.; 86m; FOX; B/W; Drama/Musical; Children: Cautionary; **DVD**; **VHS**. Lively and entertaining, this songfest features the great Al Jolson singing many of his most celebrated songs, and Faye shines by equally delivering her tunes with panache and gusto. Faye is a newly arrived singer, who tries to get ahead by appearing in endless amateur night singing contests in NYC. When she tires of this dead-end routine, she and her friend, Compton, go on vacation to Long Island. There she meets Power, a handsome and charming young man, who soon proves to be a smooth operator obsessed with get-rich schemes he flirts dangerously with the law. When police arrive, Power suddenly disappears, and Faye returns to Manhattan to discover that her former partner, Jolson, has gotten the break he has been looking for when he appears on stage with several important showmen in the audience. His singing act is, however, interrupted by Cavanaugh, an insulting drunk, who sits in a box hurling wisecracks at Jolson. The heckler gets more laughs than Jolson, who manages to sing a few songs before exiting. He thinks his opportunity has been crushed by Cavanaugh, but the showmen think the drunk is part of Jolson's new hilarious act and he is signed to a contract. To make sure of his continued success, Jolson finds Cavanaugh and puts him under contract, but, now sober, the meek little Cavanaugh is apprehensive about having to make a living as a pickled heckler. Faye, too, sees success, but where she gets a job singing in a speakeasy. Power sud-

Tyrone Power, Alice Faye and Al Jolson in *Rose of Washington Square*, 1939.

denly reappears with some of his shady friends, and he comes to Faye's rescue when the place is raided by police, hurrying her out of the dive to safety. They renew their friendship, which blossoms into love and, while they attend a party honoring Jolson, Faye sings a song that interests talent agent Frawley, who wants to sign her to a contract, but the manipulative Power attempts to act as her manager. This upsets Jolson, who becomes deeply distrustful of Power. Faye, however, is under Power's charming sway, and after he sells off some expensive furniture in an upscale apartment where he has been living, he and Faye are married and go off to Cuba on a honeymoon. When they return, Power is in big trouble because he sold off someone else's furniture as the apartment where he was living was on loan to him by a friend, who now threatens legal and criminal action. Faye by then learns that she has been selected to star in a new Ziegfeld Follies show, and after she makes her appearance, she becomes the toast of Broadway. Power then becomes involved with a gang of thieves, who botch a robbery, and he is arrested. The magnanimous Jolson, who has always loved Faye, posts Power's bond, but Power betrays Jolson and Faye by going into hiding while Faye pines for him. Power slips back into the city to see Faye perform, watching her sing the plaintive "My Man," which describes their troubled life together. Guilt and what is left of his decency and honor now compels Power to do the right thing. He faces his own music and turns himself in and is convicted and sentenced to prison for five years. Faye accompanies him to Grand Central Station where a train will take Power to Sing Sing Prison, and where the ever loyal Faye tells Power that she will be waiting for him. Power and Faye are very good together, giving convincing performances as star-crossed lovers, but Jolson steals this film hands down by belting out a bevy of his most memorable tunes. Songs: "Rose of Washington Square" (music: James F. Hanley; lyrics: Ballard MacDonald), "Yaaka Hula Hickey Dula (Hawaiian Love Song)" (music: Pete Wendling; lyrics: E. Ray Goetz, Joe Young), "Pretty Baby" (music: Egbert Van Alstyne and Tony Jackson; lyrics: Gus Kahn), "The Vamp" (Byron Gay), "Smiles" (Lee S. Roberts), "I'm Sorry I Made You Cry" (N. J. Clesi), "Mother Machree" (music: Ernest Ball and Chauncey Olcott; lyrics: Rida Johnson Young), "I'm Always Chasing Rainbows" (Harry Carroll), "Ja-Da" (Bob Carleton), "Rock-a-Bye Your Baby With a Dixie Melody" (music: Jean Schwartz; lyrics: Sam Lewis, Joe Young), "Toot, Toot, Tootsie (Goo' Bye!)" (Dan Russo, Ernie Erdman, Gus Kahn), "I'm Just Wild About Harry" (music: Eubie Blake; lyrics: Noble Sissle), "Shine On, Harvest Moon" (Nora Bayes), "California, Here I Come" (Joseph Meyer, Buddy G. DeSylva, Al Jolson), "The Curse of an Aching Heart" (music: Al Piantadosi; lyrics: Henry Fink), "I Never Knew Heaven Could Speak" (music: Harry Revel; lyrics: Mack Gordon), "I'll See You in My Dreams" (music: Isham Jones; lyrics: Gus Kahn), "The Japanese Sandman" (Richard A. Whiting), "My Mammy"

(music: Walter Donaldson; lyrics: Sam Lewis, Joe Young), "My Man" (music: Maurice Yvain; lyrics: Albert Willemetz, Jacques Charles; English lyrics: Channing Pollock). *Author's Note*: This was the third and final film in which Faye and Power would appear (the first two being **In Old Chicago**, 1937, and **Alexander's Ragtime Band**, 1938), and Faye told this author that "I never had a more handsome and attractive leading man than Ty [Power]. He was a delight to work with and there was not an ounce of conceit in him. He was friendly and outgoing at all times, but he took his work seriously and worked without ever complaining. I once asked him if he ever got tired of doing pictures and he said, 'heck no, it's all fun, isn't it?'" This film was attached with considerable notoriety since everyone knew it was based upon the spectacular career of Ziegfeld Follies star Fanny Brice (1891-1951) and her errant gambler-husband, Nicky Arnstein (1879-1965), who was associated with big time NYC crooks like Arnold Rothestein (1882-1928). Brice and Arnstein developed a torrid romance while Arnstein was still married, and when he was convicted of swindling and sent to Sing Sing Prison, Brice visited him every week and married him when he was released. He nevertheless refused to reform and was later convicted of peddling stolen securities stolen in Washington, D.C. When Brice was told that her husband had engineered this spectacular robbery, she replied: "My Nicky? He couldn't engineer a light bulb into a socket." He was nevertheless sent to Leavenworth federal prison, and Brice, tired of her husband's crooked ways, divorced him upon his release in 1927. Brice saw this film and realized that it was based wholly on her life with Arnstein, and she filed a suit for using the events of her life without permission, invasion of privacy and defamation of character. Her signature song, "My Man," which had been sung by Faye in the film, was cited in the suit to prove the film's association with Brice. Zanuck told this author that "I didn't think she would do it because the events of her life with Arnstein had been made public in the press through his notorious conduct. I thought we were protected by that public record, but Fanny sued us all the same." Brice filed for damages amounting to $750,000, but later settled out of court for $25,000. Her life with Arnstein was later profiled in two enormously successful films, **Funny Girl**, 1968, and its sequel, **Funny Lady**, 1975. For more details on the Brice-Arnstein union and Arnstein's criminal pursuits, see my work *Encyclopedia of World Crime*, Volume I (CrimeBooks, 1990; pages 163-166). **p**, Darryl F. Zanuck; **d**, Gregory Ratoff; **cast**, Tyrone Power, Alice Faye, Al Jolson, William Frawley, Joyce Compton, Hobart Cavanaugh, Moroni Olsen, E.E. Clive, Louis Prima, Horace McMahon; **w**, Nunnally Johnson (based on a story by John Larkin, Jerry Horwin); **c**, Karl Freund; **m**, Louis Silvers, various composers of 1920s popular songs; **ed**, Louis R. Loeffler; **art d**, Richard Day, Rudolph Sternad; **set d**, Thomas Little.

The Rose Tattoo ★★★★ 1955; U.S.; 117m; PAR; B/W; Drama; Children: Unacceptable; **DVD**; **VHS**. Earthy and riveting, this dynamic tale from gifted playwright Williams sees Magnani, in her first U.S. film, living as a widow and taking care of her fifteen-year-old daughter, Pavan, following the death of her beloved husband. After she has her hubby's remains cremated, even though this is in defiance of her Catholic religion, she is beset with new emotional problems. The Sicilian-born Magnani is so devoted to her husband's memory because he was loyal to her, that she wants to keep what is left of him close to her by housing his ashes in her home. She is overly protective of her daughter, and after Cooper, a sailor, is attracted to Pavan, Magnani extracts a promise from Cooper that he will not touch the girl until after they are married sometime in the unspecified future. Meanwhile, brawny Lancaster, who works as a banana hauler, as was her husband's job, enters Magnani's life. He wears a rose tattoo as had her husband, symbolically representing virility among the Sicilian inhabitants of the small Louisiana town where they all live. Magnani is attracted to the robust and lusty Lancaster, but she resists his advances out of respect for her deceased spouse. After she learns that her husband was not the true blue mate she always believed, and that he was having an affair with Grey,

Magnani now feels that it is all right to carry on an affair with Lancaster, and they begin their tempestuous love affair with grunting gusto. The Williams-Kanter script tiptoes around the censorship rules of the day to present a steamy story of lustful sex, although it is all presented with an almost comical lowbrow approach where the participants are simply too ignorant to appear intentionally salacious or lascivious. It is a well-produced story of peasant emotions and superstitions, where romance is reduced to sweat-dripping anxieties that awkwardly grope toward love through raw sensuality and sex. Typical of Williams' intellectual contempt for such inferior creatures (he was a lifelong gay and haughtily above all such heterosexual folly), he portrays his characters as almost comical caricatures, who tastelessly and relentlessly seek the satisfaction of their loins, as he arrogantly does in his smug portraits of the equally cretin-like, sex-enslaved characters in **A Streetcar Named Desire**, 1951. The much less sophisticated and sexually naïve public of that day, however, accepted this drama for what it was worth on its face, and the film became a huge box office success, gleaning more than $4.2 million. Magnani's powerful and compelling performance rightly earned for her an Oscar as Best Actress, and Oscars were also given for Best Art Direction Black and White (Pereira, Larsen, including set decoration: Comer and Krams) and for Best Cinematography Black and White (Howe). Songs: "The Sheik of Araby" (Ted Snyder, Francis Wheeler and Harry B. Smith), "Come le rose" (music: Adolfo Genise; lyrics: Gaetano Lama), "Out of Nowhere" (Johnny Green). *Author's Note*: Lancaster told this author that "some critics said I was miscast in **The Rose Tattoo**, but I think my personality fit the character I played. They say that only a Sicilian can play a Sicilian in pictures, but that's just nonsense. Any good actor can play any kind of character. Look at Edward G. Robinson—he played a Chinese assassin in **The Hatchet Man** [1932] and was more convincing than any Chinese actor could have been in that role. But nobody, I think, could have played the role Anna [Magnani] played in **The Rose Tattoo**. She is not an attractive woman [with a long, hooked nose, close-set eyes and a thick body], but she makes herself desirable through her great performance." Williams actually wrote the play with Magnani in mind, but she refused the role for some years until she could manage to speak enough English to make her lines understandable in this U.S. production. **p**, Hal B. Wallis; **d**, Daniel Mann; **cast**, Anna Magnani, Burt Lancaster, Marisa Pavan, Ben Cooper, Virginia Grey, Jo Van Fleet, Sandro Giglio, Mimi Aguglia, Florence Sundstrom, Wallis, Tennessee Williams; **w**, Williams, Hal Kanter (based on the play by Williams); **c**, James Wong Howe; **m**, Alex North; **ed**, Warren Low; **art d**, Hal Pereira, Tambi Larsen; **set d**, Sam Comer, Arthur Krams; **spec eff**, Farciot Edouart, John P. Fulton.

Roseanna McCoy ★★★ 1949; U.S.; 100m; Samuel Goldwyn; RKO; B/W; Drama/Romance; Children: Unacceptable; **VHS**. Powerful and riveting tale sees an American Romeo and Juliet story in which a young man and woman fall in love who, like the star-crossed lovers of the Shakespeare classic, are members of two feuding families in the Blue Ridge Mountains. It is the story of the hillbilly blood feud between the Hatfield and McCoy clans, two large families that fought to the death against each other along the West Virginia and Kentucky border (1863-1891). Young Granger is a Hatfield, who meets the fetching Evans, a member of the McCoy family, and both fall in love. Granger abducts Evans after she tells him that nothing can come of their love for one another. He takes her back to the Hatfield stronghold, but Bickford, the Hatfield patriarch, sends Evans back to her family, hoping to restore peace and finally settle the long-standing feud. Basehart, however, a Hatfield zealot and hothead, renews the feud when he mindlessly guns down Miles, a McCoy member. Granger finds Evans and they decide to leave the area and live apart from their lethal families, but, when they try to escape, they find themselves in a gun-shooting war zone. Their presence, however, brings all parties to their senses, and the feud stops so that these lovers can find some happiness. Strong performances from all of the fine cast members, along with great lensing from Garmes and

Anna Magnani and Burt Lancaster in *The Rose Tattoo*, 1955.

Crosby that captures the moody and murky mountainous atmosphere contribute to an impressive production. Song: "Roseanna" (Frank Loesser). *Author's Note*: Goldwyn told this author that "I know the story is sort of a modern-day Romeo and Juliet romance, but I wanted to show those hill people as they really were when they were all shooting at each other. I wanted Teresa Wright to play the girl, but she was very uncooperative at that time. I suppose she had gotten to be just another big movie star and did not want to listen to people like me." Director Ray told this author that "Sam [Goldwyn] was meddling with that production as he did with all of his pictures, and decided that Irving [Reis] was not putting enough blood and thunder into the picture, so he brought me in to do some of the action shots, but the picture was really Irving's production from beginning to end." Goldwyn also brought in veteran screenwriter Hecht to enliven the story, but Hecht, as he told this author, "did very little work on that script, only punched up a few scenes with some additional dialog and inserted some pot-shooting scenes." Massey told this author that "my role as the patriarch of the McCoy family shows me in a half-way decent light as a loving father and someone who really wants peace, not bloodshed. I understand that the real person I was playing was not so benevolent and routinely went hunting for Hatfield members like one might track down and shoot a possum." **p**, Samuel Goldwyn; **d**, Irving Reis, (not credited) Nicholas Ray; **cast**, Farley Granger, Joan Evans, Charles Bickford, Raymond Massey, Richard Basehart, Gigi Perreau, Aline MacMahon, Marshall Thompson, Peter Miles, Mabel Paige, William Mauch [Billy Mauch]; **w**, John Collier, (not credited) Ben Hecht (based on the novel by Alberta Hannum); **c**, Lee Garmes, Floyd Crosby; **m**, David Buttolph; **ed**, Daniel Mandell; **art d**, George Jenkins; **set d**, Julia Heron.

Rosemary ★★★ 1960; West Germany; 105m; Roxy Films/Films Around the World; B/W; Drama; Children: Unacceptable. This well-produced story is set after World War II (1939-1945), where West Germany is becoming an economic superpower in the 1950s. Tiller is Rosemary (or Rosemarie), a young woman, who uses her charms to get ahead by sleeping with members of the West German industrial elite. This leads her to learning business secrets she sells to French competitors. Her world comes crashing down when scandal reveals her shady dealings. The sensuous Tiller is impressive as the conniving courtesan, and she receives strong support from a gifted cast in a tale that sustains riveting interest throughout. **p**, Luggi Waldleitner; **d**, Rolf Thiele; **cast**, Nadja Tiller, Peter van Eyck, Carl Raddatz, Gert Frobe, Hanne Wieder, Mario Adorf, Jo Herbst, Werner Peters, Karin Baal, Horst Frank; **w**, Thiele, Jo Herbst, Erich Kuby, Rolf Ulrich; **c**, Rolf von Rautenfeld; **m**, Norbert Schultze; **ed**, Elisabeth Kleinert-Neumann; **prod d**, Wolf Englert, Ernst Richter.

Patsy Kelly, Ruth Gordon and Mia Farrow in *Rosemary's Baby*, 1968.

Rosemary's Baby ★★★★ 1968; U.S.; 136m; William Castle Productions/PAR; Color; Horror; Children: Unacceptable (MPAA: R); **BD**; **DVD**; **VHS**. Polanski patiently directs this eerie tale to a mounting, flesh-tingling thriller awash with Devil-worshippers and unholy visitations by the Evil One. The film begins modestly enough when struggling actor Cassavetes rents an old and spacious apartment at an ancient building in central Manhattan, moving in with his new bride, Farrow. Evans, who is a friend of Farrow's, tells her that the building has a strange and somewhat macabre history and, for her welfare, suggests that she and her husband leave the premises immediately and do not return. They ignore this obtuse warning and move in, befriending some of the building's odd occupants. Farrow, when visiting the building's laundry, meets Dorian, who is the ward of Blackmer and Gordon, the elderly couple living next door to Cassavetes and Farrow. Farrow is shocked to learn a few days later that Dorian, for no explained reason, has committed suicide by leaping from one of the windows high up in the building. In fact, Farrow seems more upset about Dorian's death than do the young woman's guardians, Blackmer and Gordon, who take an uncommon interest in Farrow's welfare. Further, Cassavetes seems somehow attached to the elderly couple, acting solicitous and overly respectful to the couple, particularly toward Blackmer, who flatters the unemployed actor by telling him that he has seen some of his performances in a few TV productions and he predicts good things for Cassavetes. At that time, Cassavetes has auditioned for an important role in an upcoming Broadway production, but he has lost out to another actor, Baumgart. He suddenly gets the part, however, when the other actor inexplicably goes blind. Now that he has a good paying job, Cassavetes tells Farrow that they can afford to have the child they have long envisioned. To commemorate that so-called blessed event, Blackmer and Gordon visit them, and Gordon brings along a dessert of her own concoction that Cassavetes, out of politeness to their guests, encourages Farrow to eat. The strange dessert causes Farrow to become ill, and as Blackmer and Gordon leave, Cassavetes tends to his ailing wife, putting her to bed. She has a bizarre dream where a group of strange people sit as spectators in her bedroom as she is visited and sexually assaulted by a demonic creature. She describes this nightmare to Cassavetes, who tells her that the bad dream was most likely a by-product of the food she ate the night earlier. Farrow insists that the nightmare was all too real because she shows her husband many bruises and scratch marks she received from that hideous night visitor. Cassavetes then admits that he was probably the source of such strange marks as he got drunk that night and apologizes for his unusual roughhouse lovemaking. When she learns that she is pregnant, Farrow is put into the care of Bellamy, an aging but seemingly kindhearted obstetrician, who tells her to take a special food Gordon prepares that has aided many another pregnant young woman.

Farrow dutifully follows this regimen, although the food Gordon gives her is vile to the taste and causes her to lose weight and suffer stomach cramps. She complains about taking this God-awful food to Evans (Farrow actually ate bloody, raw liver in one scene), who becomes alarmingly suspicious and has some of Gordon's concoctions analyzed, and discovers that it does not have the contents Gordon claims to have used in her special food-making. Before Evans can warn Farrow not to consume any more of Gordon's food, he dies of mysterious causes. In his will, however, Evans has left for Farrow an obscure book titled *All of Them Witches*. It describes a Devil-worshipping warlock, and after Farrow anagrams the name of that character, she sees that it spells out the name of her neighbor, Blackmer. Becoming alarmed and thinking that she is now seized by paranoid impulses and unreasoning thoughts, Farrow nevertheless concludes that a cabal consisting of Cassavetes, Blackmer, Gordon, Bellamy and others have somehow manipulated her pregnancy. She turns to Grodin, her former gynecologist, telling him about her suspicions as she seeks refuge at his office. Grodin assures her that he will contact the authorities and set matters right, but he, instead, contacts Cassavetes, believing Farrow is having a nervous breakdown. Cassavetes retrieves her, and she is put to bed where she gives birth at home with Bellamy in attendance to deliver the child. She awakes to hear Cassavetess sorrowfully tell her that the baby has died. She remains bed-ridden but later hears a baby crying in the next-door apartment that is occupied by Blackmer and Gordon. Weak and filled with dread, Farrow goes to the kitchen and retrieves a butcher knife to take matters into her own hands, now convinced that her hellish nightmare was a reality. She goes to Blackmer's apartment to find Blackmer, Gordon, Bellamy, Cassavetes and many others in attendance as they pay slavish honor to the child squirming within a bassinet, all celebrating the birth of what is the Anti-Christ, the child of Satan, who has been spawned through Farrow and permitted by the insidious and conniving Cassavetes so that he could achieve success in life with the help of the Devil-worshipping cult to which he now belongs. As she peers down into the bassinet to look at the child, she hears someone in the room say: "He has his father's eyes." Instead of driving the knife into this child of Satan, Farrow sheds her horror and hatred for this progeny of the Devil and is consumed by motherly love. She drops the knife and begins to sing a lullaby to the child as this grim and terrifying film ends. Polanski does an outstanding job in presenting this truly frightening tale, taking his time in developing the story line and its lurking, evil-minded characters, the most riveting of the lot being the weird Gordon, who plays one of the most sinister witches if there ever was one, an unforgettable performance that earned her an Oscar as Best Supporting Actress. The script from Polanski, from the popular novel from Levin, who consistently churned out bestsellers that made their way to the screen (**The Boys from Brazil**, 1978; **Deathtrap**, 1982; and **No Time for Sergeants**, 1958), is carefully written and is packed with devilish innuendoes and subtle signs that herald the devastating event to come, effectively unfolding the oozing of evil, which would be taken to even greater and more horrific conclusions in **The Omen**, 1976. The film was a huge box office success, earning more than $33 million against a $2.3 million budget. A sub-standard sequel was made for TV in 1976. Songs: "Lullaby" (Krzysztof Komeda), "Fur Elise" (Ludwig van Beethoven). Violence, Devil-worship and gutter language prohibits viewing by children. *Author's Note*: A number of bad and sorrowful events attended the production of this film. Farrow received divorce papers from husband Frank Sinatra while she was working on one of the film's sets. It is grimly ironic that a year after this film was released, Polanski's own wife, the beautiful actress Sharon Tate (1943-1969), was, along with others, brutally murdered by the slavish and ruthless members of the Charles Manson (1934-) Family and while she was then pregnant with Polanski's child (he was away at the time). Moreover, also gruesomely ironic is the fact that the building in which this film was shot in NYC, the Dakota apartment building (renamed The Bramford in this film), was also the location where singer-composer

John Lennon (1940-1980), of the Beatles fame, was shot and killed by berserk groupie Mark David Chapman (1955-). For extensive details on the Manson mass murders, and the Chapman killing, see my work, *The Great Pictorial History of World Crime*, Volume II (History, Inc., 2004; Manson Family: pages 898-997; Mark David Chapman: pages 908-911). Polanski kept Farrow on edge throughout this production, capturing her genuinely expressed concerns and confusions by pulling little tricks on her. For instance, he has Farrow hear the voice of the actor Cassavetes replaces, Baumgart, but the director had accomplished actor Tony Curtis speak those lines without telling Farrow who was speaking so that she thought she recognized the voice, but could not identify it. The producer for this film, William Castle, had acquired the film rights for the Levin novel, but he was told by Paramount chief Robert Evans that he would approve of the production only if Castle did not direct as Evans believed Castle's talents as a helmsman was limited to low-budget exploitation horror films. Polanski got the nod and embarked on adapting the Levin story, changing whatever he liked to suit his filmic perceptions (Levin later stated that Polanski's adaptation was the best ever applied to any of his works). The director wanted Robert Redford to play the role of the husband, but that actor was then embroiled in a legal dispute with Paramount. Jack Nicholson, Warren Beatty, Laurence Harvey, Richard Chamberlain and James Fox were also considered, but all either declined or were not available. Cassavetes was a last choice for the role and proved to be exceptional as the ruthlessly ambitious husband, making a pact with the Devil in exchange for theatrical success (which some evangelical film reviewers claimed was the actual case with the film itself in its relationships with other horrendous events that attached themselves to some of its principals). Bellamy, who plays the avuncular physician attending the birth of the Devil child, had apprehensions about appearing in this film, telling this author: "I read the script and realized that the story was about as sinister as any screenplay ever written. I knew that the director [Polanski], who wrote that script, had doted on every detail, almost as if he personally relished this terrible tale. I had to make up my mind whether I would sit in judgment of this story or take a part that was demanding and important. In such cases, the actor, not the person, always comes first. So I performed the role, but, as a person, I still have regrets about doing it. The picture is powerful and terrifying, but I think it sends out the wrong message that evil easily triumphs. Try as it might, evil does not eventually triumph in this world. The stamp of history identifies evil for what it truly is, like turning over a rock and finding a poisonous viper slithering from its hiding place. That's how we came to know the truth about Adolf Hitler and Joseph Stalin, two of Satan's most cherished children." Bellamy's comments about these two very sinister historical characters may have been brought to mind as he recalled his own portrayal of Franklin D. Roosevelt in **Sunrise at Campobello**, 1960, the American President who had to contend with both of these decidedly evil persons during his lifetime. Producer Castle, not incidentally, begged to play the role that Bellamy essayed, but was refused the part, and had to settle for his appearance as an extra in a crowd scene. Other films depicting Devil-worshipping include **Cry of the Werewolf**, 1944; **Danger Island**, 1931; **The Dunwich Horror**, 1970; **The Masque of the Red Death**, 1964; **The Mephisto Waltz**, 1971; **The Ninth Gate**, 1999; **The Omen**, 1976; **The Omen**, 2006; **Perils of the Jungle**, 1927; **Robin Hood: Prince of Thieves**, 1991; **The Seventh Victim**, 1943; and **Sinbad and the Eye of the Tiger**, 1977. p, William Castle; d&w, Roman Polanski (based on the novel by Ira Levin); cast, Mia Farrow, John Cassavetes, Ruth Gordon, Sidney Blackmer, Maurice Evans, Ralph Bellamy, Patsy Kelly, Elisha Cook, Jr., Emmaline Henry, Charles Grodin, Hope Summers, Patricia O'Neal, Tony Curtis (voice); c, William Fraker (Technicolor); m, Christopher Komeda; ed, Sam O'Steen, Bob Wyman; prod d, Richard Sylbert; art d, Joel Schiller; set d, Robert Nelson; spec eff, Farciot Edouart.

Rosewood ★★★★ 1997; U.S.; 140m; Peters Entertainment/WB;

Mia Farrow (back to camera) and Ralph Bellamy in *Rosemary's Baby*, 1968.

Color; Crime Drama/Horror; Children: Unacceptable (MPAA: R); **DVD**; **VHS**. Racist lynch law comes to chilling life in this mesmerizing historical crime drama that also, through its excellent portrayal of mass hysteria and mob violence, produces a first-rate horror film. This film is accurately based (with the exception of a few fictional characters) on historical events that occurred in Rosewood, Florida, in the first week of January 1923 (called the Rosewood Massacre), where six blacks and two whites were killed in a savage race riot and the town of Rosewood was destroyed by fire. The story opens with Kellner, an emotionally unstable housewife, who has been cheating on hubby Dean with white lover Patrick. When she quarrels with Patrick, some blacks hear of the disturbance coming from Kellner's ramshackle home and later spread the gossip that a white man has attacked the white housewife. Hearing this tale, Dean questions his wife, and Kellner, to cover up her relationship, tells him that she had been attacked by an unknown black man (these events are fictional and unsupported by the actual events leading up to the real Rosewood riot). Dean and other white racists, all living in Sumner, Florida, a town adjacent to the all-black Rosewood, quickly accept Kellner's claim, and they set in motion violent retribution, forming mobs that also include members of the Ku Klux Klan. Rhames, a black veteran of WWI, is visiting his girlfriend, Neal, who lives in Rosewood, and cares for a number of children, but, after he hears the story of the attack against white woman Kellner, he leaves the area, believing that he, as a black stranger, will be accused of the crime. Meanwhile, wholesale attacks are made on blacks. Their shacks and their local church are burned to the ground. Several are killed by white mobs led by racist McGill and others. Voight owns a local store where whites and blacks trade. He finds Benjamin, a wounded black man, hiding in his store. Instead of turning Benjamin over to the mob, he risks his own life and that of his family members by shielding him from the mob. The local sheriff, Rooker, who makes a halfhearted effort to maintain peace in the area, learns that Benjamin is being protected by Voight, and tells the storekeeper that he only wants to question the wanted black man. Voight makes the mistake of turning Benjamin over to Rooker. After Benjamin can give no answers to Rooker's questions, McGill shoots and kills him. Meanwhile, a mob attacks the home of Rolle, a black woman who has been much loved by whites as she has taken care of many white children and served as a cleaning lady in many white homes. Rolle and several of her family members are shot to death by an attacking mob, many of its white members later expressing regret that she has been killed, including Dean as Rolle has worked in his own home. However, Cheadle, one of Rolle's black family members, escapes by lying beneath Rolle's corpse, which is carried out of the area in a wooden coffin. By this time, Rhames has returned to the area carrying his two automatic pistols and rifle, riding his horse into the area to rescue girlfriend

Dexter Gordon and Lonette McKee in *Round Midnight*, 1986.

Neal. He battles some of the whites in a cornfield, chasing them off but is later captured that night after sending Neal and many of her children into a hiding place. Rhames refuses to give mob members any information on his fellow blacks and is lynched, but, while Voight distracts lynch members, Rhames frees himself from the rope by which he has been hanging and escapes. He rejoins Neal and the children and begins to lead them from white posse members who pursue them through woods and swamps with barking bloodhounds leading the way (not unlike the chilling scenes depicted in Harriet Beecher Stowe's *Uncle Tom's Cabin*). Rhames attempts to lead his wards toward the distant railroad tracks where he hopes that Voight will have a train waiting for them to escape the area. Voight, meanwhile, persuades two reluctant engineers to use their train to escort all the blacks they can carry from the area and the train races to a rendezvous point where Rhames, Neal, the children and many other blacks arrive, including Cheadle. They board the train with Voight's help, and as it starts to leave, white mobs break into the area, chasing the train with wagons and horses, Rhames and Voight shooting these attackers down. The blacks on the train survive, but the town of Rosewood is shown as destroyed, only charred ashes remaining where homes once stood. McGill and others, who have so senselessly killed the hapless blacks, are shown having no remorse, but McGill's own son, Hook, who has been lectured by McGill on the right of whites to wantonly kill blacks at will, rejects his father, telling him that he never wants to see him again and leaves home forever. Although the story takes some liberties with the real facts in the case, the film is brilliantly directed by Singleton, who captures the period violence and incisively portrays the riotous mindset of the lynch mobs. Voight, Rhames, Cheadle, Benjamin, Rolle and others in the fine cast give stellar performances in an unforgettable visual document of one of America's most devastating crimes. This film was expensive to produce, its budget exceeding $30 million, and it unfortunately did not recoup its investment, returning only a little more than $13 million from the box office in its initial release. Songs: "Sylvester's Blues, " "Tom Cat Blues," "New Year's Eve Fiddle Music" (Wynton Marsalis); "The Town Burns" (John Williams); "Happy Birthday to You" (Patty S. Hill and Mildred J. Hill). *Author's Note*: The Ku Klux Klan (KKK), which is shown to have its ugly presence throughout this film, is extensively profiled in my work *The Great Pictorial History of World Crime*, Volume II (History, Inc., 2004; pages: 1481-1494). Racism inspiring the violence of lynch mobs (and chiefly involving the KKK) in the South has been profiled in many films, notably in **The Birth of a Nation**, 1915; **Intruder in the Dust**, 1949; **Journey to Shiloh**, 1968; **Mississippi Burning**, 1988; **O Brother, Where Art Thou**, 2000; **Storm Warning**, 1951; and **To Kill a Mockingbird**, 1962. **p**, Jon Peters, Penelope L. Foster; **d**, John Singleton; **cast**, Jon Voight, Ving Rhames, Don Cheadle, Bruce McGill, Loren Dean, Esther Rolle,

Paul Benjamin, Elise Neal, Robert Patrick, Michael Rooker, Catherine Kellner, Akosua Busia, Tristan Hook; **w**, Gregory Poirier; **c**, Johnny E. Jensen (Technicolor); **m**, John Williams; **ed**, Bruce Cannon; **prod d**, Paul Sylbert; **art d**, Chris Gorak; **set d**, Dan May; **spec eff**, Michael N. Arbogast, Joey Digaetano, Jesse Silver.

Rosita ★★★ 1923 (silent); U.S.; 90m; Mary Pickford Productions; UA; B/W; Drama; Children: Unacceptable. Well-made film directed by the talented Lubitsch has Pickford in the unusual role of a Spanish street singer. The beautiful girl is loved by Blinn, the King of Spain, but she loves the dashing Walsh, a penniless nobleman. Blinn intends to possess Pickford at any costs but is finicky about her social position in life. Blinn can only tryst with Pickford after she has transitioned from commoner to the aristocracy so that she will be worthy of a kingly bed. To that end, Blinn has both Pickford and Walsh blindfolded and then married in a palace wedding so that Pickford is worthy of him since she now has the title of a countess. Walsh is ordered executed by Blinn for the crime of love, but he is saved by the queen, Rich. She wants Walsh to live so he can marry Pickford and Rich can thus preserve her marriage to the impulsive Blinn. Rich orders that blank cartridges be put in the rifles of the firing squad. Walsh feigns death, but, when he goes in search of Pickford, he finds that she is about to assassinate Blinn with a knife for ordering Walsh's death. Walsh prevents Pickford from dispatching the reckless ruler and, by doing so, wins Blinn's gratitude. He pardons Walsh and Pickford and allows them to be reunited for a happy ending. Lubitsch keeps a fast pace with this romantic tale, and Pickford shines as the alluring street singer, strongly supported by Walsh, Rich, Blinn and the rest of the cast. *Author's Note*: The gifted Lubitsch was brought from Germany by Pickford to direct another film titled **Dorothy Vernon of Haddon Hall**, 1924 (in which Pickford appeared with Marshall Neilan directing), but Lubitsch did not like the story for that film and opted to make this film with Pickford. The two did not get along well together throughout the production, and she later complained that Lubitsch's directorial talents were best achieved with male actors and that his high-handed and arrogant Teutonic behavior proved to be insulting. Lubitsch took the film much over the budget Pickford originally allowed (the film was made through her company), and the actress bristled over the additional expenses. Although the film is well made and highly watchable, Pickford, influenced by her personal dislike for Lubitsch, called this her worst film, which it was not. She so disliked Lubitsch that she refused to watch this film after it was released and also refused to watch any film Ernst Lubitsch made in the future. Walsh told this author: "Mary [Pickford] was so upset by Ernst's [Lubitsch's] indifference to her star status that she asked me to direct some of our scenes together, and I did. Ernst did not like a bit of that, although he used a few of those scenes in the final release, especially the wedding scene where Mary and I are blindfolded and do not know that we are marrying each other. The public suspended a lot of disbelief in those days so that scenes like that actually sailed down the river." **p**, Mary Pickford; **d**, Ernst Lubitsch, (not credited) Raoul Walsh; **cast**, Mary Pickford, Holbrook Blinn, George Walsh, Irene Rich, Charles Belcher, Frank Leigh, Mathilde Comont, Marian Nixon, Charles Farrell; **w**, Edward Knoblock (based on an adaptation by Knoblock of a story by Norbert Falk and the play "Don Cesar de Bazan" by Philippe Francois Pinel Dumanoir and Adolphe d'Ennery); **c**, Charles Rosher; **m**, Louis F. Gottschalk; **art d**, William Cameron Menzies; **set d**, Svend Gade.

Round Midnight ★★★★ 1986; U.S.; France; 133m; Little Bear; WB; Color; Drama; Children: Unacceptable (MPAA: R.); **DVD**; **IV**. Well-crafted drama presents real-life jazz legend Dexter Gordon portraying the fictional black tenor sax player Dale Turner, a hopeless alcoholic in the 1950s New York jazz scene. He takes a gig in Paris where he is accepted despite his color. A sympathetic Parisian man who loves Turner's music befriends him and it results in a poignant relationship with the man and his young daughter, but they cannot save him from his own self-destructive ways. The film is reminiscent of **Paris Blues**, 1961, where black jazz musician Sidney Poitier prefers to work in Paris because there is little or no prejudice against his race, albeit he is not plagued by the use of alcohol or drugs in that film. Black performers like the celebrated dancer Josephine Baker (1906-1975) had migrated to Paris during the 1920s in order to escape race prejudice in the U.S., and where they found widespread success and social acceptance. Born and raised in a St. Louis slum, Baker went to New York where, like the character portrayed by Gordon in this film, sees some success before going on to Paris in 1925 and becoming a cause célèbre. The same was the case of Ada "Brick Top" Smith (1894-1984), a black dancer from West Virginia, who, after working in NYC, migrated to Paris in 1924 and later opened her own nightclub, Chez Bricktop (1924-1961, located at 66 Rue Pigale). She became the rage by teaching her many distinguished guests to perform popular dances like the Charleston and the Black Bottom. Her protégés included Josephine Baker, Duke Ellington and Mabel Merceer. Songs: "'Round Midnight" (Thelonious Monk, Cootie Williams, Bernie Hanighen); "As Time Goes By" (Herman Hupfeld); "Society Red," "Tivoli" (Dexter Gordon); "Fairweather" (Kenny Dorham); "Now's the Time," "Ina Noche Con Francis" (Charlie Parker); "Autumn in New York" (Vernon Duke); "Body and Soul" (Edward Heyman, Robert Sour, Frank Eyton, Johnny Green);, "I Cover the Waterfront" (Heyman, Green); "Watermelon Man" (Herbie Hancock); "It's Only a Paper Moon" (Billy Rose, E. Y. Harburg, Harold Arlen); "How Long Has This Been Going On?" (music: George Gershwin; lyrics" Ira Gershwin); "Put It Right Here" (Bessie Smith); "Rhythm-A-Ning" (Thelonious Monk); "I Love Paris," "What Is This Thing Called Love?" (Cole Porter); "Chan's Song/Never Said" (Herbie Hancock, Stevie Wonder). **p**, Irwin Winkler; **d**, Bertrand Tavernier; **cast**, Dexter Gordon, Francois Cluzet, Gabrielle Haker, Sandra Reaves-Phillips, Lonette McKee, Christine Pascal, Herbie Hancock, Bobby Hutcherson, Pierre Trabaud, Frederique Meininger; **w**, Tavernier, David Rayfiel, Colo Tavernier; **c**, Bruno de Keyzer (Eastmancolor); **m**, Herbie Hancock; **ed**, Armand Psenny; **prod d**, Alexandre Trauner; **art d**, Pierre Duquesne.

The Rounders ★★★ 1965; U.S; 85m.; MGM; B/W; Western/Comedy; Children: Acceptable; **DVD; VHS**. Amusing oater has Ford and Fonda as aging cowboys who break broncos for Wills, a rancher in Sedona, Arizona. Aging sisters Joan Freeman and Kathleen Freeman would like the boys to marry them, but they aren't yet ready to be branded and settle down. Their dream is to go to Tahiti and open a bar. When winter comes, the boys usually spend it in the high country corralling more than 100 stray cattle at $7 a head for Wills. They then spend their winter's pay in one spring night at a Sedona bar. They try something new this spring, betting their winter's pay that they can ride an ornery roan at the Sedona rodeo. If one of them rides the horse and wins, they will be able to afford a trip to Tahiti. But the horse proves too much for them and they lose their savings, forcing them to go back to work for Wills and spend another winter in the mountains. *Author's Note*: Ford told this author that he believed "**The Rounders** was a down-to-earth western without all the phony heroics. Anyone can relate to these two cowboys. They have ordinary dreams and work hard at capturing a few of them. Like most people, they don't win any prizes, but they enjoy their lives as they live them." Similar films that most realistically profile the gritty cowboy lifestyle include **Cowboy**, 1958; **The Culpepper Cattle Co.**, 1972; **Monte Walsh**, 1970 (and its 2003 remake); and **Will Penny**, 1968. **p**, Richard E. Lyons; **d**, Burt Kennedy; **cast**, Glenn Ford, Henry Fonda, Sue Ann Langdon, Hope Holiday, Chill Wills, Edgar Buchanan, Kathleen Freeman, Joan Freeman, Denver Pyle, Barton MacLane, Doodles Weaver, Peter Fonda, Peter Ford, Warren Oates; **w**, Kennedy (based on the novel by Max Evans); **c**, Paul C. Vogel (Panavision; Metrocolor); **m**, Jeff Alexander; **ed**, John McSweeney; **art d**, Urie McCleary, George W. Davis; **set d**, Henry Grace, Jack Mills.

Roxie Hart ★★★★ 1942; U.S.; 75m; FOX; B/W; Comedy; Children:

Ginger Rogers, Adolphe Menjou and William Frawley in *Roxie Hart*, **1942.**

Cautionary; **DVD; VHS**. Rogers is sensational in this broad satire on crime, criminal defense attorneys and the outlandish press in Chicago's Roaring Twenties. The film opens with aging reporter Montgomery buying drinks at a Chicago bar where he recalls one of the most spectacular stories he covered during the Jazz Age. As he buys drinks for the locals, Montgomery recalls how Rogers, a sexy, ambitious dance hall girl advances her career through the press after her jealous but mousy husband, Chandler, shoots and kills an overly amorous talent agent trying to make moves on his leggy wife. His story then unfolds in flashback to portray the wisecracking, gum-chewing Rogers, who is the very essence of the brassy, "liberated" flapper of the day. After the agent is found shot dead in her bedroom, Rogers, although she is innocent, is persuaded to take the blame for the killing by veteran newspaper reporter Overman, who is Montgomery's avuncular guide through the zany news world of Chicago during the Twenties. Overman tells Rogers that the publicity that she will receive will make her an overnight star and she will be able to name her own ticket in show business after she is acquitted. Her acquittal is assured by the brash Overman, who tells Rogers that no Chicago jury has ever convicted and sent a woman to the gallows for shooting a rakish man attempting to take advantage of a defenseless woman. Coming to Rogers' rescue is flamboyant criminal defense attorney Menjou, who tells Rogers that he can get her acquitted, but only if she religiously follows his instructions, and those draconian directions include putting on a good show for the all-male jury and the judge. Meanwhile, Rogers is swarmed by reporters, including Byington, who plays Miss Sunshine, a female sob sister columnist, during her stay at the female prison block at Cook County Jail. Rogers tells the reporters a lot of tall tales and gives confusing versions of the shooting of her alleged victim before, at Menjou's urgings, she performs her trademark dance, "The Black Hula." One of the reporters is novice scribe Montgomery, who falls in love with her. At one point, before returning to her cell, Rogers provides a show-stopping tap dance for him, dazzlingly clicking her heels up and down some metal stairs and sexily snapping her fingers and chewing gum to capture Montgomery's palpitating, puppy dog heart. Rogers also begins to lose her heart to the adoring Montgomery. Rogers is now the star boarder at the Cook County Jail, her notorious case preempting another femme fatale, Reynolds, who had been earlier charged with murdering her lover, but who now resents Rogers replacing her as the new female sensation in Chicago's headlines. During Rogers' trial, Menjou pleads self-defense, and, at the same time, Montgomery learns from Darien, the janitor of Roger's apartment building, that Chandler is the real culprit. In court, Rogers puts on a gaudy show, flashing her legs to the thighs, causing jurors and judge to ogle and gape while Menjou delivers elaborate and plaintive pleas on her behalf. Menjou then creates more sympathy for his client by con-

Ina Claire, Fredric March and Henrietta Crosman in *The Royal Family of Broadway*, 1930.

vincing the thick-witted Chandler to divorce Rogers. She, however, is becoming concerned that she might very well be convicted and urges Menjou to have Darien testify on her behalf and where he will name Chandler as the killer. This effort fails when Darien is reported dead and his signed statements are found to be inadmissible in court. Moreover, the sensational allure Rogers has held for the press quickly fades as a new and bombastic blonde, Adrian (who is called "Two-Gun Gertie"), arrives at the jail, charged with crimes more sensational than that allegedly committed by Rogers. It now looks black for Rogers, but Menjou has her dressed in a funereal mourning dress, carrying flowers into court and where she makes her own heart-wrenching plea before fainting before the stunned jury. She and Menjou have rung every drop of empathy and sympathy from the jurors' and this pays off when they find her not guilty and Rogers is released while Menjou takes his bows as the great Svengali of the courtroom. Rogers is now free to marry any number of available swains, including rich stockbroker Frawley, who had been a member of the jury that acquitted her. The viewer is left in a quandary as to her final decision. In flash-forward, Montgomery concludes his laudatory tale about Rogers and then leaves his cronies, including Frawley, who is now the bartender, having lost his fortune in the 1929 Stock Market Crash. Montgomery steps into a driving rain and goes to a parked car where his wife is waiting for him, and that woman is none other than Rogers. The car is packed with their six children, and Rogers announces that she is again pregnant and they will be adding another member to their burgeoning family. The car drives away through the rainstorm to conclude a happy domestic setting, far from the clamoring days of Rogers' and Montgomery's turbulent, wacky youth. Wellman, as usual, directs this film with lightning speed, the bon mots and action coming so fast that the viewer hardly has time to catch a breath between sensations. Rogers is outstanding as the sassy heroine, and Menjou is hilarious as the cynical, conniving shyster who will do any outlandish thing to win a case. The film was a great success at the box office and furthered Rogers' career as a gifted actress for comedy (she had already earned a Best Actress Oscar for her dramatic essay in **Kitty Foyle**, 1940). The story was originally filmed as a silent in 1927 with Mack Sennett bathing beauty Phyllis Haver as Roxie Hart. The film was remade as a musical version on Broadway by Bob Fosse, which was later made into a 2002 film under the title of **Chicago**, the original title of the story that was initially produced on Broadway. Songs: "Chicago (That Toddlin' Town)" (Fred Fisher), "Pretty Baby" (Egbert Van Alstyne, Tony Jackson), "Black Bottom," "Here I Am (Broken Hearted)" (music: Ray Henderson; lyrics: Lew Brown and Buddy G. DeSylva). *Author's Note*: The play, written by Maurine Dallas Watkins (1896-1969), upon which the 1927 silent film and this production is based, was originally directed by George Abbott and opened on Broadway at the Music Box Theater on December 30, 1926, running for 172 performances. "Maurine's play appeared about a year before Charlie [MacArthur] and I wrote and produced *The Front Page* in New York," screenwriter Ben Hecht told this author. "She worked at the Chicago *Tribune* with Charlie about the same time Charlie and I became friends and she covered a lot of the murder cases we all wrote about. In her play she concentrated on two goofy dames, Beulah Annan and Belva Gaertner, who each bumped off a guy and both copped pleas to escape the gallows. Her character Roxie is Beulah and another character she has is based on Belva. Both of these women were loud-mouthed drunks, who were lucky enough to get two smart lawyers [W. W. O'Brien, who represented Annan and who is essayed by Menjou in **Roxie Hart**; and William Scott Stewart, who represented Gaertner]. Those sharp attorneys showed those lethal ladies to juries as innocent victims and got them acquitted. Since I knew all about these two harridans, I was asked to work on the script for **Roxie Hart**, and I contributed some of the dialog that Ginger [Rogers] rattles off to the jury. Chicago was and is a blue-collar town, not very sophisticated, and any half-sober defense attorney could easily pull the wool over the eyes of a jury. In those days, the juries were made up of men who looked upon female defendants in such cases as their own mothers, so getting an acquittal was a cinch. They didn't hang women in Chicago and both of those female killers knew it when they pulled the triggers on their sugar daddies. After Beulah shot her man, she sat staring at the body for several hours, boozing gin and listening to her favorite Jazz tune, "Hula Lou," and that's where they got the idea for Ginger to dance to her favorite song, "The Black Hula" when they did **Roxie Hart**. I must admit that we made heroines and heroes out of the worst lowlifes to be found in the Chicago gutters. We called it entertainment." Wellman told this author that he was so impressed with the performance of George Chandler, who plays Rogers' dim-witted husband, that "I more or less adopted him and put him into a lot of my pictures after we made **Roxie Hart**. George has the kind of sad-looking puppy dog face that makes people feel sorry for him and his dead-pan deliveries are perfect for the pipsqueak roles he plays." Chandler appeared in twenty films made by Wellman, notably in **Battleground**, 1950, where Chandler plays a mess sergeant pressed into fighting in the front lines and, while going to the front, is given a rifle he has never before fired. Another GI begins to give Chandler detailed information about the rifle until Chandler interrupts him, delivering a classic line: "Look, you're not selling it to me—you're only showing me how it works!" Though she is ideal in her role, Rogers was not the first selection to play the leading lady in **Roxie Hart**. "They wanted Alice Faye to play that part," Rogers told this author, "but she was pregnant at the time, so I got the role. Alice later told me that she thought she could never have done the job I did in that picture, but she was being kind. Alice could do anything better than most actresses." p&w, Nunnally Johnson (based on the play "Chicago" by Maurine Watkins); d, William Wellman; cast, Ginger Rogers, Adolphe Menjou, George Montgomery, Lynne Overman, Nigel Bruce, Phil Silvers, Sara Allgood, William Frawley, Spring Byington, Ted North, Helene Reynolds, George Chandler, Iris Adrian, Frank Darien; c, Leon Shamroy; m, Alfred Newman; ed, James B. Clark; art d, Richard Day, Wiard B. Ihnen; set d, Thomas Little.

The Royal Family of Broadway ★★★ 1930; U.S; 38m.; PAR; Comedy; Children: Acceptable. In this thinly disguised but excellent portrait of the Barrymore family, Claire plays a stage actress from a famous family of Broadway actors. Her mother, Crosman, is still acting, but her womanizing actor brother, March, is on the run from a breach of promise suit in Hollywood after reneging on a promise to marry a Polish actress. Her daughter, Brian, is trying to decide whether to go on stage like the others in the family or settle down and get married to handsome and rich but dull Starrett. Claire thinks it would be nice to retire and get married, when a former boyfriend, Conroy, shows up, now a viable spouse since he has become a wealthy platinum mining magnate in South

America. After many ups and downs and much thinking, everyone stays the same, not marrying and continuing the royal family of the Broadway stage. Cukor direct this film with great skill (with some fine directorial assistance from Gardner), carefully developing the many characters in this entertaining film. March, although he appears only briefly in this film, is exceptional in essaying John Barrymore. The story was aired in a sixty-minute radio show by Theater Guild on December 16, 1945, with March reprising his role. *Author's Note*: March told this author that he spent months preparing for his role in this film, stating: "I got the part in **The Royal Family of Broadway** after I appeared in a road show version of the play in Los Angeles, and some Paramount executives saw my performance, a lucky break. I was really doing John Barrymore in that role. I watched every silent and talkie film Barrymore appeared in and studied his mannerisms, from his trademark sneer to his raised eyebrows. I particularly copied the little gestures he made with his hands, especially in scenes with others so he could steal scenes. I must have done something right since I received an Oscar nomination for that part. Ironically, John's brother, Lionel, received the Oscar that year for his great performance in **A Free Soul** [1931]." Cukor told this author that "that picture had many great funny lines about the temperamental Barrymore family members, although we really did not profile Lionel in that picture. The humor came from Kaufman, who wrote the original play with Edna Ferber. He was a born humorist, who saw something funny in everyone." The original play was produced on Broadway, opening at the Selwyn Theater on December 28, 1927, and ran for 345 performances with Otto Kruger playing the role based on John Barrymore. "We changed the original title of the play when we did the screen adaptation," Cukor told this author. "It was originally called 'The Royal Family' and we changed the title to 'The Royal Family of Broadway' so that the public would not think that the story had anything to do with European royalty, but the esteemed family that literally owned American theater at that time and everyone knew that that was the Barrymore family." The editor for this film, Dmytryk, went on to become a distinguished film director, helming such stellar productions as **Murder, My Sweet**, 1944; **Crossfire**, 1947; and **The Young Lions**, 1958. d, George Cukor, Cyril Gardner; cast, Ina Claire, Fredric March, Mary Brian, Henrietta Crosman, Charles Starrett, Arnold Korff, Frank Conroy, Royal C. Stout, Elsie Esmond, Lucile Watson; w, Herman J. Mankiewicz, Gertrude Purcell (adapted from the play "The Royal Family" by Edna Ferber and George S. Kaufman); c, George J. Folsey; ed, Edward Dmytryk.

Royal Flash ★★★ 1975; U.K./U.S.; 102m; FOX; Color; Adventure/Comedy; Children: Unacceptable (MPAA: PG); **DVD**; **VHS**. Good send-up presents the humorous adventures of an 1800s British officer, Harry Flashman, well essayed by McDowell. He is an admitted rogue and coward but who is invariably successful in his pursuit of happiness and riches. He has a chance meeting with Reed and Bates, who have a plan to use him to get rich and win political favor. They send him on a wild journey to a small European province where he is to imitate a Prussian prince and marry Ekland, a duchess. The masquerade works, he gets a title, and the royal girl of his heart, coming out a winner again. Sexuality prohibits viewing by children. p, David V. Picker, Denis O'Dell; d, Richard Lester; cast, Malcolm McDowell, Alan Bates, Florinda Bolkan, Oliver Reed, Tom Bell, Joss Ackland, Christopher Cazenove, Henry Cooper, Lionel Jeffries, Alastair Sim, Michael Hordern, Britt Ekland, Bob Hoskins; w, George MacDonald Frsaser (based on his novel); c, Geoffrey Unsworth (DeLuxe Color); m, Ken Thorne; ed, John Victor-Smith; prod d, Terence Marsh; art d, Alan Tomkins; set d, Peter Howitt; spec eff, John Richardson.

A Royal Scandal ★★★ 1945; U.S.; 94m; FOX; B/W; Comedy/Romance; Children: Acceptable; **DVD**. A lot of humor is seen in this romp through the court of Russian royalty. The setting is 18th-Century St. Petersburg, Russia, where Eythe is a handsome but minor cavalry officer.

Anne Baxter and Tallulah Bankhead in *A Royal Scandal*, 1945.

He wins favor with Empress Catherine the Great (1729-1796), who is broadly played by Bankhead. She appoints him chief of the Imperial Guard, so he can be close to her bed chambers. Eythe tells Bankhead about a plot to overthrow her, one hatched by some of her generals led by Coburn, the grand chancellor. While Bankhead ferrets out the villains, she pays more attention to Eythe and promotes him a general. Eythe worships Bankhead as an empress but is not in love with her. His heart, instead, belongs to Baxter, one of Bankhead's ladies in waiting. Jealous, Bankhead banishes Baxter from the palace, but, after she sees how heartbroken Eythe becomes, she allows Baxter to return and reunite with Eythe. Bankhead then turns her romantic attentions toward Price, the French ambassador. A delightful, sophisticated comedy and remake of the silent film **Forbidden Paradise**, 1924, also directed by Lubitsch and starring Pola Negri, his discovered star, who plays Catherine the Great. *Author's Note*: "Ernst [Lubitsch] got ill after preparing everything for **A Royal Scandal**," Preminger told this author, "so he called me in to direct most of the picture. This was the film debut of John Russell, a tall, dark-haired young actor. I always thought he showed considerable promise, but his career in pictures never really got him to the top." Price told this author that "my role in **A Royal Scandal** was that of a conniving ambassador from France and I used all the tricks I could to bring attention to that character, but no one in the world could ever upstage Tallulah Bankhead. That woman not only chewed up the scenery, but she swallowed the sets, too!" Many actresses have played Catherine the Great in other films, including **Admiral Ushakov**, 1954 (Olga Zhiznyeva); **The Adventures of Baron Munchausen**, 1943 (Brigitte Horney); **The Captain's Daughter**, 2001 (Olga Antonova); **Catherine of Russia**, 1963 (Hildegard [Hildegarde] Knef [Neff]); **Catherine the Great**, 1996 (made-for-TV; Catherine Zeta-Jones); **Catherine the Great**, 2005 (made-for-TV; Emily Bruni); **The Chess Player**, 1930 (Marcelle Charles Dullin); **Chess Player**, 1939 (Francoise Rosay); **Cossacks in Exile**, 1939 (L. Biberowich); **The Eagle**, 1925 (Louise Dresser); **Forbidden Paradise**, 1924 (Pola Negri); **Grafinya Sheremeteva**, 1994 (made-for-TV; Lidya Fedoseeva-Shukshina); **Great Catherine**, 1948 (made-for-TV; Gertrude Lawrence); **Great Catherine**, 1958 (made-for-TV; Sydney Sturgess); **Great Catherine**, 1969 (Jeanne Moreau); **John Paul Jones**, 1959 (Bette Davis); **The Loves of Casanova**, 1929 (Suzanne Bianchetti); **Meeting of the Minds**, 1977-1981 (TV series; "Catherine the Great," 1981 episode: Jayne Meadows); **Pugachev**, 1980 (Vija Artmane); **The Queen of Spades**, 1999 (made-for-TV; Inga Rappaport); **The Ring of the Empress**, 1930 (Lil Dagover); **The Rise of Catherine the Great**, 1934 (Elizabeth Bergner); **Russia**, 1986 (TV miniseries; Valentina Azovskaya); **Russian Ark**, 2002 (Maria Kuznetsova/Natalia Nikulenko); **The Scarlet Empress**, 1934 (Marlene Dietrich); **Seven Faces**, 1929 (Salka [Walka] Stener-

Fred Astaire, Jane Powell and Keenan Wynn in *Royal Wedding,* **1951.**

mann [Viertel]); **Shadow of the Eagle**, 1950 (Binnie Barnes); **Tempest**, 1959 (Viveca Lindfors); **Tsigni pitsisa**, 1984 (Nina Yurasova); **Wednesday Theater**, 1951-1953 (TV series; "Great Catherine," 1953 episode: Mary Ellis); and **Young Catherine**, 1991 (made-for-TV; Julia Ormond). **p**, Ernst Lubitsch; **d**, Lubitsch, Otto Preminger; **cast**, Tallulah Bankhead, Charles Coburn, Anne Baxter, William Eythe, Vincent Price, Mischa Auer, Sig Ruman, Vladimir Sokoloff, Mikhail Rasumny, Feodor Chaliapin Jr. John Russell, Eva Gabor, Grady Sutton; **w**, Edwin Justus Mayer (adapted by Bruno Frank from the play "The Czarina" by Lajos Biro, Melchior Lengyel); **c**, Arthur Miller); **m**, Alfred Newman; **ed**, Dorothy Spencer; **art d**, Lyle Wheeler, Mark-Lee Kirk; **set d**, Thomas Little; **spec eff**, Fred Sersen, Rolla Flora.

Royal Wedding ★★★ 1951; U.S; 93m; MGM; Color; Musical; Children: Acceptable; **DVD**; **IV**. This lively and very entertaining musical features some of Astaire's best solo dancing. He and Powell are a brother and sister Broadway song and dance team whose show is closing. Their agent books them a gig in London during the 1947 wedding of Queen Elizabeth (1926-) and Prince Philip (1921-). Aboard ship and en route to England, Powell falls for Lawford, a young British nobleman while Astaire keeps himself in dancing shape by dancing with a coat rack in his stateroom. Arriving in London, Powell and Lawford begin a romance while Astaire occupies his time dancing on the walls and ceiling in his hotel room (this great scene became historic for its cleverness). Astaire falls for a British woman, Churchill, while Powell and Lawford pair off. Songs: "Too Late Now," "E'very Night at Seven," "Open Your Eyes," "The Happiest Day of My Life," "You're All the World to Me," "I Left My Hat in Haiti," "What a Lovely Day for a Wedding," "How Could You Believe Me When I Said I Loved You When You Know I've Been a Liar All My Life" (music: Burton Lane; lyrics: Alan Jay Lerner); "Sunday Jumps" (Lane). *Author's Note*: This was Donen's first helming as a solo director and he does a marvelous job with a lot of inventive dance routines (he had worked closely in the past with that other great dancer of film musicals, Gene Kelly). The astounding sequence where Astaire seems to dance on the walls and ceiling of his room was achieved after the room was built like a rotating box that moved at the same speed as the camera. The cameraman was strapped to his chair for this sequence as Astaire, at one point, appears to be dancing on the floor of the room, but the cameraman and the camera were actually hanging upside down from the ceiling. "I really followed the point of gravity," Astaire told this author. "I was actually dancing at the floor level all the time, stepping onto the sections of the wall or ceiling as the room rotated under my feet. I did a lot of similar routines in other films, like **The Band Wagon** [1953], where we had breakaway sets quickly change into other settings to keep the dancing going in one take. But I think we never re-

ally equaled that dancing on the walls and ceiling routine in **Royal Wedding**. I thought that routine was one of the cleverest visuals ever produced on film." So did everyone else. **p**, Arthur Freed; **d**, Stanley Donen; **cast**, Fred Astaire, Jane Powell, Peter Lawford, Sarah Churchill, Keenan Wynn, Albert Sharpe, Les Baxter, Bea Allen, Wilson Benge, Mae Clarke. **w**, Alan Jay Lerner (from his story); **c**, Robert Planck (Technicolor); **m**, Albert Sendrey; **ed**, Albert Akst; **art d**, Cedric Gibbons, Jack Martin Smith; **set d**, Edwin B. Willis; **spec eff**, Warren Newcombe.

Rudy ★★★★ 1993; U.S.; 114m; TriStar Pictures; Color; Sports Drama; Children: Cautionary (MPAA: PG); **DVD**; **VHS**. A moving and compelling story sees Astin playing Daniel "Rudy" Ruettiger (1948-), shown as a youth living in Joliet, Illinois, where he attends high school and has dreams of attending the University of Notre Dame and playing for its football team. Everything is against his reaching his goal in that he has no money, inadequate grades and lacks the physical stature and ability to play intercollegiate football. Upon graduation, he goes to work at the steel mill where his father, Beatty, works, both sharing their enthusiasm for Notre Dame's football future. After his best friend, Reed, is killed in a mill accident, Astin decides that his own future will take a different course and he resolves to go to Notre Dame. Traveling to South Bend, Indiana, he fails to gain admission to Notre Dame, but, with the help of a local priest, he is admitted to Holy Cross, a nearby junior college. He struggles to achieve good grades, learns that he has dyslexia, but he overcomes this handicap and eventually gets good grades. He does not achieve the same results on the home front where he loses his fiancée to one of his brothers, his siblings mocking his pronounced ambitions to eventually get into Notre Dame and play on its football team. Astin perseveres and does achieve, for him, the impossible, by being admitted to Notre Dame, and he further convinces its football coach, Ara Parseghian (1923-), played by Miller, to play on the practice squad. Miller, seeing how dedicated Astin proves to be on that squad, despite his undersized build against taller and heavier players, agrees to let him suit up in the last game of his senior year so that his family members and friends can see him on the squad in that last game. Miller, however, steps down from his post before that game, and he is replaced by no-nonsense coach Dan Devine (1924-2002), played by Ross, who refuses to let Astin suit up for that last game. The senior football players, however, place their jerseys on Ross' desk, asking that Astin suit up instead of themselves. Ross is so shocked by this sacrifice that he allows Astin to suit up. Astin's fellow seniors have him lead the team onto the field, and Beatty and his family are overjoyed to see their son running onto that field, hopefully to play against Georgia Tech. Ross, however, refuses to allow Astin to get into the game, despite the pleadings of the senior Notre Dame players. As the game is coming to a close, however, a chant of "Rudy, Rudy, Rudy" comes from the crowd, and Ross relents, sending Astin in to play defense. He then proves himself a hero by sacking the quarterback of Georgia Tech on the final play of the game and is carried from the field on the shoulders of his teammates in joyful triumph. Anspaugh directs this touching film with exceptional skill as he carefully develops his characters in unfolding Ruettiger's simple but heroic story, symbolizing the indomitability of the human spirit. Astin is superb as the youth who will not surrender his boyhood dreams, which, through hard work and dedication, he achieves in all of its innocent glory. The film did well at the box office, realizing almost $23 million in its initial release against a $12 million budget. Songs: "Notre Dame Victory March" (John F. Shea, Michael J. Shea), "Rakes of Mallow" (traditional), "Nitanny Lion" (James A. Leyden), "Walking Dream" (Ginger Willis, Hal Willis), "Run Through the Jungle" (John Fogerty), "Ring of Fire" (Merle Kilgore, June Carter Cash), "Hike Notre Dame!" (Vincent Fagan, Joseph J. Casasanta), "The Victory Clog" (Robert F. O'Brien), "When the Irish Backs Go Marching By" (Eugene Burke, Joseph J. Casasanta), "Merrily Kiss the Quaker's Wife" (traditional). *Author's Note*: Devine agreed to allow writers to portray him as the heavy in the film for dramatic purposes, but he was upset when seeing the film upon its release, saying that the scene where the senior players lay their jerseys on his desk in protest of his refusal to allow Rudy to suit up never happened. It is a matter of record, however, that those senior players did urge Devine to allow Rudy to play in that final game. The many scenes shot on location at Notre Dame were allowed by university officials, who had prohibited such on-location shooting since the making of **Knute Rockne, All American**, 1940, which lionized Rockne, the great Notre Dame coach. **p**, Robert N. Fried, Cary Woods, Angelo Pizzo; **d**, David Anspaugh; **cast**, Sean Astin, Jon Favreau, Ned Beatty, Greta Lind, Scott Benjaminson, Mary Ann Thebus, Charles S. Dutton, Lili Taylor, Christopher Reed, Deborah Wittenberg, Jason Miller, Chelcie Ross; **w**, Pizzoe; **c**, Oliver Wood (Technicolor); **m**, Jerry Goldsmith; **ed**, David Rosenbloom; **prod d**, Robb Wilson King; **set d**, Martin Price; **spec eff**, Joey Digaetano.

Ruggles of Red Gap ★★★★ 1935; U.S.; 90m; PAR; B/W; Comedy; Children: Acceptable; **DVD**; **VHS**. Delightful comedy where Laughton first exhibited the humorous side of his nature after having proven to the world that he could be the most pompous and ruthless tyrant in **The Private Life of Henry VIII**, 1933. Here he is the obsequious English butler for Young, a poor gentleman, who is entertaining Ruggles and his wife, Boland, when they visit England. Though Boland has aspirations of becoming a British lady, Ruggles has no ambitions to buy a title for her and is dedicated to his life in the American West where he owns vast holdings. He wears cowboy boots and a wide-brimmed Stetson hat that symbolizes his American heritage. Young and Ruggles get into a tenacious poker game where Young loses all he has. He makes one more bet, wagering his devoted butler, Laughton, and loses him, too, to the canny Ruggles. Taking Laughton in tow, Ruggles, along with a fellow Westerner, Burke, go on a spree in Paris and where very funny moments occur, especially due to Laughton's stiff reservations about observing social protocol and his station in life. (Laughton's name in the film is Ruggles, ergo the title of this film, and he is not to be confused with Charles Ruggles, the name of the actor playing the rich rancher who has won Laughton while playing poker.) Ruggles and Boland then decided to return to their home in America and Laughton dutifully accompanies them to their ranch, which is located outside of Red Gap. Laughton attempts to maintain his dignity as a proper butler, but he soon realizes that he is living in the land of the free and is entitled to abandon the slavish duty of a butler and go his own way in the world. After he meets and falls for the ungainly but endearing Pitts, he decides to open a restaurant with her, one that becomes immensely popular since most locals believe Laughton is a member of the British aristocracy who has sacrificed his lofty station in life to be among the common people. Young then shows up and he meets and falls in love with Eburne, deciding he, too, will settle in Red Gap to live next to his former butler. The film ends with a poignant and memorable scene where Laughton, who has taken a bit too much to drink, emotionally recites Lincoln's "Gettysburg Address," which wholly captures the sympathy and affection of the local residents, as it did movie audiences the world over. McCarey, who is noted for his lighthearted films that have remained in fond human memory (**The Awful Truth**, 1937; **Love Affair**, 1939; **Going My Way**, 1944; **The Bells of St. Mary's**, 1945; and **An Affair to Remember**, 1957), tells an uncomplicated story of a prosaic man (Laughton), who is rooted to servitude, only to discover to his spiritual joy that opportunity in a free America welcomes his adventurous individuality. McCarey uses no stars here, only great character actors, to bring this tale to entertaining life, and Laughton and the fine cast effectively act as normal, down-to-earth human beings. Along the way, as was always McCarey's wont, he includes within his doting scenes all the delightful mannerisms and quirks his characters inhabit to make them even more memorable. The film was nominated for an Oscar as Best Film and did very well at the box office in its initial release. It was aired as a sixty-minute program by Lux Radio Theater on July 10, 1939, with Ruggles, Laughton and Pitts reprising their roles. It was again aired

Charles Ruggles, Charles Laughton and Mary Boland in *Ruggles of Red Gap*, 1935.

as a thirty-minute radio adaptation by the Screen Guild Theater on December 17, 1945, with Laughton and Ruggles reprising their roles. A thirty-minute radio adaptation was aired through Academy Award Theater on June 8, 1946, with Laughton and Ruggles reprising their roles. A remake, **Fancy Pants**, 1950, starring Bob Hope as the wagered-away butler, proved to be a much inferior adaptation. Songs: "By the Light of the Silvery Moon" (music: Gus Edwards; lyrics: Edward Madden), "You're the Flower of My Heart, Sweet Adeline" (Harry Armstrong), "Maple Leaf Rag" (Scott Joplin), "Mariette" (Sterny-Courquin), "Nights of Gladness" (Charles Ancliffe), "Cheyenne" (music: Egbert Van Alstyne; lyrics: Harry Williams), "Pretty Baby" (music: Egbert Van Alstyne and Tony Jackson; lyrics: Gus Kahn), "Alexander's Ragtime Band" (Irving Berlin), "Quintet in E Major Op 12(11) No. 5 Minuet" (Luigi Boccherina). *Author's Note*: The 1915 Wilson novel, upon which this film is based, was adapted for Broadway by Harrison Rhoades, and that play opened at the Fulton Theater on December 25, 1915, running for thirty-three performances. It was adapted for the screen and first produced as a film in 1918 with Taylor Holmes as the butler. Paramount bought the rights to the film and remade it as another silent in 1923 with Edward Everett Horton as the servile Ruggles. When Paramount decided to make a talkie of the tale, its producers had a stroke of genius by casting Laughton in the lead role. The actor, in turn, asked that McCarey direct the film. Laughton had seen the Marx Brothers in the hilarious **Duck Soup**, 1933, a film directed by McCarey, and thought that only a master of comedy films such as McCarey could bring **Ruggles of Red Gap** to life. McCarey told this author that "Charles [Laughton] gave many great performances on the screen, but he always remembered **Ruggles of Red Gap** as one of his favorite pictures and thought his performance in that picture was one of his best. He was so emotional when he recited Lincoln's 'Gettysburg Address' at the end of that picture, that he broke up several times and we had to do several retakes over two days to get it right. So proud of that scene was Laughton that he redid the scene for the actors with him when he did **Mutiny on the Bounty** [1936]. When Clark Gable came back from Catalina Island where they were shooting that picture, he told me: 'That guy Laughton is one of the world's greatest actors. He was so damned vicious when playing Captain Bligh that we all carried over our dislike for him when we stopped shooting. He knew it, so he turned us all around at the end of the picture by reciting Lincoln's "Gettysburg Address". That touched our hearts. We went away loving the guy, instead of hating him. Only a great actor can get away with doing something like that.'" **p**, Arthur Hornblow, Jr.; **d**, Leo McCarey; **cast**, Charles Laughton, Mary Boland, Charles Ruggles, Zasu Pitts, Roland Young, Leila Hyams, Maude Eburne, Lucien Littlefield, Leota Lorraine, James Burke; **w**, Walter DeLeon, Harlan Thompson (based on an adaptation by Humphrey Pearson of the novel

The many characters of *Rugrats of Paris*, 2000.

by Harry Leon Wilson); **c**, Alfred Gilks; **m**, Ralph Rainger, Sam Coslow; **ed**, Edward Dmytryk; **art d**, Hans Dreier, Robert Odell.

Rugrats in Paris ★★★ 2000; U.S./Germany; 78m; Nickelodeon Pictures/PAR; Color; Animated Adventure; Children: Acceptable (MPAA: G); **DVD**; **VHS**. In this superior and entertaining sequel to **The Rugrats Movie**, 1998, based on the television cartoon series, the adorable and mischievous babies travel to Paris where Chuckie (Cavanaugh voiceover) hopes to find a new mother while keeping his father (Bell voiceover) from marrying an evil business woman. They also help Stu Pickles (Riley voiceover) work on his invention at the Reptard amusement park. As the babies see the sights of Paris they learn new lessons about courage, loyalty, trust and, above all, true love. Songs: "Who Let the Dogs Out" (Baha Men), "I Want a Mom That Will Last Forever" (Cyndi Lauper), "My Getaway" (Brycn Evans), "Life Is a Party" (Andy Goldmark), "Final Heartbreak" (Eric Fos White), "When You Love" (Adam Anders), "I'm Telling You This" (Steve Miligore), "These Boots Are Made for Walkin'" (Nancy Walker), "L'Chuckie Chan" (Mark Mothersburg), "Excuse My French" (Desmond Child), "Bad Girls" (Angela Pickles), "Packin' to Go" (Elizabeth Daily). **p**, Arlene Klasky, Tracy Kramer, Terry Thoren, Norton Virgien; **d**, Paul Demeyer, Stig Bergqvist; **cast** (voiceovers), Debbie Reynolds, Susan Sarandon, John Lithgow, Jack Riley, Christine Cavanaugh, Elizabeth Daily, Cheryl Chase, Mako, Tara Strong, Cree Summer, Kath Soucie, Michael Bell; **w**, Klasky, David N. Weiss, J. David Stern, Jill Gorey, Barbara Herndon, Kate Boutilier, Paul Germain, Peter Chung, Gabor Csupo; **m**, Mark Mothersbaugh; **ed**, John Bryant; **prod d**, Dima Malanitchev; **art d**, Gena Kornyshev; **spec eff**, Ko Hashiguchi, Mary Mullen, Allen Stovall.

The Rules of the Game ★★★★★ [1939] 1950; France; 110m; Nouvelles Editions de Films (NEF)/Janus Films; B/W; Drama; Children: Cautionary; **DVD**; **VHS**. One of the most significant films ever produced in France by the gifted Renoir, this film revealingly documents the social caste system that existed just before WWII, incisively examining the ruling bourgeoisie in all of its varied complexities. The film opens with Renoir and other members of the press and dignitaries welcoming Toutain, a heroic French aviator who has just achieved a flight over the Atlantic, a feat that now places him within the illustrious pantheon of Charles Lindbergh. Toutain's bubble bursts, however, when he sees that the woman he made the flight for, Gregor, has failed to appear at the airport and he rashly and emotionally blurts this admission over the airways to reporters holding microphones in his face. This is not what the newspersons want to hear, nor does the aloof upper class, so the reporters quickly ignore the aviator and begin to interview the en-

gineer of the plane that carried Toutain, focusing upon the more mundane subject of its gas tanks. Oblivious to her ignored lover, the pampered Gregor, meanwhile, is being dressed by her high-spirited maid, Dubost. Gregor apparently has given no thought to her lover, Toutain, as she prepares to go out on the town with her wealthy husband, Dalio, a detached person whose only joy in life is doting upon his mechanical toy collection. Dalio is aware of his wife's relationship with Toutain, and he thinks to change things by breaking off with his mistress, the beautiful Parely, but, not wanting to injure her feelings, continues to maintain that affair. Everyone, it seems, in Dalio's household, which is representative of the overall bourgeoisie class in France, is having extramarital affairs, including the maid, Dubost. She routinely cheats on her husband, Modot, the estate's groundskeeper, dallying with a rather thick-witted poacher, so that the morals and manners of the upper class are broadly emulated by those who serve the socially elite. Renoir, who is the catalyst or centerpiece of the film, is driving home with Toutain when the aviator, distracted by depression over not seeing Gregor, drives the car into a ditch. He and Renoir then proceed on foot with Renoir sarcastically resentful of Toutain's actions. When Toutain asks him if he is hurt, Renoir retorts: "I don't know if I am alive. Your dashboard sneaked up and slugged me!" (The accident Renoir shows in this scene is one he himself experienced some years earlier and almost at the same location depicted in the film.) Renoir admits to his friend that he, too, is attracted to Gregor, but goes on to say that his attraction to her is one of friendship rather than deep emotional attachment (and here he may be hiding his true feelings for this woman, who seems to arouse the carnal inclinations of the entire male population of the country). Renoir concedes that he will never possess Gregor because he refuses to adhere to the "rules" that dictate the social mores of French society. Renoir then buoys Toutain's spirits after he arranges for the aviator to be invited to a shooting party that is taking place over a weekend at Dalio's estate. When they arrive, they are cordially greeted by their hosts, Dalio and Gregor (and where many of the impressionist works by Auguste Renoir, the director's father, are exhibited). Dalio has invited everyone to this shooting party, including his mistress, Parely, and everyone pretends that their lovers are merely friends while they jockey for emotional positions that will allow them to continue their extramarital charades without dangerous confrontations. Renoir acts as a subtle and tactful referee as he loves everyone, but has no lover. The hunt ensues where the guests track and shoot rabbits and pheasant, but the game turns brutal when the jealous lovers begin taking potshots at their rivals. Meanwhile, Dalio puts on a farcical show where he employs his mechanical toys, and Renoir takes part while dressed in a bear costume from which he finds it almost impossible to escape. He later takes a walk with Gregor to the greenhouse and dallies with her, but cannot bring himself to betray his friend Toutain. He finds Toutain and sends him to the greenhouse to be with Gregor, but Modot, who is hunting his wife's lover, mistakes Toutain for his prey and shoots and kills the aviator. Dalio, who knows that murder has really been committed, sloughs off the killing as an unfortunate hunting accident. In so doing, Dalio has maintained the regimen or "the rules of the game," to end this complex and always intriguing film. Renoir labored long in preparing and making this film, one which is both a broad and scathing indictment of the French bourgeoisie, and, in so doing, indicts the ruling class of France that, through indifference and fumbling subterfuge, allowed the Nazi regime to subsequently conquer and occupy its country. The selfish follies and foibles of Dalio, Gregor and the class they represent ignores the responsibilities they owe to their nation and its welfare, a theme that is also reflected in a latter-day film, **The Remains of the Day**, 1993, where the British ruling class ineffectively dabbles in well-meaning but ineffective politics that allows the Nazis to succeed as the German "rules of the game" are decisive and ruthless. *Author's Note*: Renoir originally wanted Simone Simon to play Dalio's pampered wife, but she demanded too much money and the director settled for Gregor, an Austrian princess with limited acting ability, a woman with whom

Renoir was then personally involved. Gregor, an ungainly and even awkward-appearing actress, was labeled "ugly" by film critic Andre Bazin, who addressed this remark directly to his close friend, Renoir, not knowing that the director was then having an affair with this novice actress. Renoir made no reply to Bazin's brutal but accurate remark. Renoir, however, was keenly aware of Gregor's shortcomings and minimized her role in the film while enlarging those playing character parts. The film was not well received and was widely booed at its premiere; and one person hated the film's implications so much that Renoir had to personally prevent this would-be arsonist from burning down the theater. The French government banned its showing before France fell to the German's and then the French puppet government controlled by the Nazis went on to also ban this film. In an attempt to appease audiences, Renoir cut the film down several times, until the running time was at 85 minutes, but that did not alter the widespread negative reaction to this masterpiece. The film was shelved by the Nazis. Prints were recovered after the war, and in 1959, an almost intact restored version was completed and rereleased, the film finally receiving the accolades it justly deserved. Songs: "Dreizehn deutsche Tänze, K. 605, No. 1" (1791; Wolfgang Amadeus Mozart), "C'est la guinguette" (Gaston Claret and Camille Francois), "Cors de chasse (Hunting Horns)" (composer unknown), "En revenant d'la revue" (Louis Desormes, Lucien Delormel, Leon Garnier), "Valse No. 7 op. 64, 2 'Petit chien'" (Fredric Chopin), "Danse macabre, Op. 40" (1874; Camille Saint-Saens), "Tout le long de la Tamise" (Eugene Rosi), "Nous avons l'vé l'pied" (Francis Salabert), "A Barbizon" (Vincent Scotto), "Die Fledermaus Overture" (1874; Johann Strauss), "Le déserteur" (1762; Pierre-Alexandre Monsigny; adaptation by Roger Desormiere). **p&d**, Jean Renoir; **cast**, Marcel Dalio, Nora Gregor, Roland Toutain, Renoir, Mila Parely, Paulette Dubost, Odette Talazac, Claire Gerard, Anne Mayen, Lise Elina, Gaston Modot; **w**, Renoir, in collaboration with Carl Koch, Camille Francois, and the cast); **c**, Jean Bachelet, Jean-Paul Alphen, Jacques Lemare, Alain Renoir; **m**, Roger Desormieres, Joseph Kosma; **ed**, Marguerite Renoir, Marthe Huget; **prod d**, Max Douy, Eugene Louri.

The Ruling Class ★★★ 1972; U.K.; 154m; Keep Films/AVCO Embassy; Color; Comedy; Children: Unacceptable (MPAA: PG); **DVD**; **VHS**. This witty satire scathingly indicts England's social and political institutions and still manages to provide an entertaining story in the process, especially through O'Toole's exceptional performance. After a member of the House of Lords dies, he leaves his estate to a son, O'Toole, who is, unfortunately, a paranoid schizophrenic and who thinks he is Jesus Christ. Other members of the family plot to steal the estate from him, creating elaborate schemes that result in murder and mayhem. The first half of the film is very funny where O'Toole displays his antics, the last half turning dark and sinister when he is cured of his Christ image and then thinks that he is serial killer Jack the Ripper, looking for his victims among members of the House of Lords. The film incisively depicts government supporting patronage and privilege by England's ruling class. Songs/Music: "Onward, Christian Soldiers" (Arthur Sullivan, Sabine Baring-Gould), "Pomp and Circumstance" (Edward Elgar), "Mairzy Doats and Dozy Doats" (Milton Drake, Al Hoffman, Jerry Livingston), "Requiem Mass in D Minor" (Wolfgang Amadeus Mozart), "The Internationale" (Pierre Degeyter), "I'm Gilbert the Filbert" (Basil Hallam), "All Things Bright and Beautiful" (William H. Monk, Cecil F. Alexander), "La Traviata" (Giuseppe Verdi), "The Varsity Drag" (Buddy G. DeSylva, Lew Brown, Ray Henderson), "My Blue Heaven" (Walter Donaldson, George Whiting), "Largo from Xerxes" (George Frideric Handel)" "Wedding March" and "Oh for the Wings of a Dove" (Felix Mendelssohn), "Poor Wand'ring One" (Arthur Sullivan, William S. Gilbert), "Dry Bones" (William Osborne, Dick Rogers), "Kes" (John Cameron), "The Eton Boating Song" (William Johnson XV, Algernon Drummond), "Ten Little Nigger Boys" (traditional), "Goodnight" (Eduard Kunneke, Adrian Ross). Gutter language and adult themes prohibit viewing by children. **p**, Jules Buck, Jack Hawkins; **d**,

Matt Dillon and Mickey Rourke in *Rumble Fish*, 1983.

Peter Medak; **cast**, Peter O'Toole, Alastair Sim, Arthur Lowe, Harry Andrews, Coral Browne, Michael Bryant, Nigel Green, Kay Walsh, William Mervyn, Carolyn Seymour; **w**, Peter Barnes (based on his play); **c**, Ken Hodges; **m**, John Cameron; **ed**, Ray Lovejoy; **prod d**, Peter Murton; **spec eff**, Roy Whybrow.

Rumble Fish ★★★ 1983; U.S.; 74m; Zoetrope Films/UNIV; B/W/Color; Drama; Children: Unacceptable (MPAA: R); **DVD**; **VHS**. Disturbing but compelling tale sees Rusty James (Dillon) as the teenage leader of a small gang in an industrial town where gangs are dying out. He lives in the shadow of the memory of his older brother, Rourke, known as "The Motorcycle Boy," who was shot dead by police when he stole fish from a pet shop and tried to set them free in a river. Dillon was along and fled to California. He has a relationship with Lane, but deceitful Cage takes her away from him. His father, Hopper, is an alcoholic, his mother has left, and he takes no interest in school, believing that his relationships are shallow. He longs for the days when gang warfare was rampant, but that won't happen for him and he knows he will never be the action hero his brother embodied. The film's title comes from rumble fish, Siamese fighting fish that, when put together, try to kill each other, used here as a metaphor for gangs heading into self-destruction through pointless street warfare. Song: "Don't Box Me In" (Stewart Copeland, Stan Ridgway). Excessive violence and gutter language prohibit viewing by children. *Author's Note*: "I played an alcoholic father in that picture," Hopper told this author, "a part that was just about what I did in **Hoosiers** [1986] and, I think I got the part in **Hoosiers** because producers thought I was convincing as a drunken father in **Rumble Fish**. Okay, man, call it typecasting. So what? Just as long as you get the gig, man." **p**, Fred Roos, Doug Claybourne; **d**, Francis Ford Coppola; **cast**, Matt Dillon, Mickey Rourke, Diane Lane, Dennis Hopper, Vincent Spano, Diana Scarwid, Nicolas Cage, Chris Penn, Laurence Fishburne, William Smith, Tom Waits, Sofia Coppola, Gian-Carlo Coppola; **w**, S.E. Hinton, Francis Ford Coppola (based on the novel by Hinton); **c**, Stephen H. Burum (Technicolor); **m**, Stewart Copeland; **ed**, Barry Malkin; **prod d**, Dean Tavoularis; **set d**, Mary Swanson; **spec eff**, David Marconi, Dennis Dion.

Run for Cover ★★★ 1955; U.S.; 93m; PAR; Color; Western; Children: Unacceptable; **BD**. Cagney gives a riveting performance as a man who has served six years in prison for a crime he did not commit, having been mistaken for a train robber. He teams up with Derek, a young man who reminds him of his son who died in his late youth. A posse goes after train robbers and suspects them, and Derek is wounded in gunplay by the posse. They escape and Cagney takes wounded Derek to a farm owned by Hersholt whose daughter, Lindfors, nurses Derek. Cagney

Jane Greer and Richard Widmark in *Run for the Sun,* 1956.

and Lindfors fall in love, and townspeople elect Cagney as their sheriff and Derek as his deputy. Derek, however, is not the honest fellow Cagney thinks he is, and Derek tries to get money from a bank robber, Withers, by letting him escape jail. Derek sets out to have Withers kill Cagney but comes to his senses and, in a gunfight, Derek is killed by Withers while saving Cagney's life. A lot of action and a good script make this oater worthwhile. Song: "Run for Cover" (music: Howard Johnson; lyrics: Jack Brooks). *Author's Note*: Cagney told this author that "**Run for Cover** is not one of those run-of-the-mill westerns. Its characters have a lot of complexities and it tests friendship and loyalty on a psychological level you don't find in most of those shoot-'em-ups." The film's gifted director, Ray, had nothing but profound respect for his star in this film, telling this author: "No actor I know could take a plain-speaking character and turn him into a believable hero better than Jimmy [Cagney]. He has a common dirt personality that always attracts audiences and that's why I was able to do such a good job with **Run for Cover**." **p**, William H. Pine, William C. Thomas; **d**, Nicholas Ray; **cast**, James Cagney, Viveca Lindfors, John Derek, Jean Hersholt, Grant Withers, Jack Lambert, Ernest Borgnine, Ray Teal, Irving Bacon, Denver Pyle; **w**, Winston Miller (based on a story by Harriet Frank Jr., Irving Ravetch); **c**, Daniel Fapp (VistaVision; Technicolor); **m**, Howard Johnson; **ed**, Howard Smith; **art d**, Hal Pereira, Henry Bumstead; **set d**, Sam Comer, Frank McKelvy; **spec eff**, Farciot Edouart, John P. Fulton.

Run for the Sun ★★★ 1956; U.S.; 99m; Russ-Field, UA; Color; Adventure; Children: Unacceptable; **DVD**. Exciting and well-scripted, this tale has Widmark as an adventurer and novelist. He puts his writing on hold as he takes time off in Mexico. He is followed by Greer, a reporter who hopes to write an article about why he has stopped writing. They fall in love, but, on a flight to Mexico City, their small plane, which is flown by Widmark, is forced down. They survive in a remote jungle and meet up with van Eyck, who, Widmark learns, is trying to escape as a Nazi war criminal. Van Eyck is assisted by Howard, a suave British traitor, both of them residing in a luxurious, remote estate where they play host to the stranded Widmark and Greer. After van Eyck and Howard realize that Widmark and Greer are on to them and know their true identities, the culprits make them prisoners. Before they can decide how they will dispose of these two interlopers, Widmark and Greer escape into the jungle. Van Eyck and Howard then hunt them as one might hunt wild animals. Widmark, however, outwits the two men in the jungle in a cat-and-mouse game that ends when he brings them to justice and giving Greer an even bigger story than what she had envisioned. Songs: "Taco," "Triste Ranchero" (music: Frederick Steiner; lyrics: Nestor Amaral). *Author's Note*: Widmark told this author that "we remade that frightening picture, **The Most Dangerous Game** [1932] when we made **Run**

for the Sun, and I never thought that we could recreate the tension Joel McCrea and Fay Wray created in the original picture, but we put together a lot of good action scenes and kept the suspense going to put it across. I thought the scenes where Jane [Greer] and I get trapped in some ruins and still find a way to eliminate our pursuers had a lot of tense moments. The picture did better at the box office than what was expected." The film saw more than $1,250,000 in box office receipts in its initial release, becoming one of the top grossing feature films for the year. Greer told this author that "**Run for the Sun** was a little too exciting for me. I contracted some sort of jungle virus when we were on location in Mexico shooting that film and that eventually led to a heart operation. So you might say that that film is close to my heart and the pun is definitely intended." This was one of four films produced by a company owned by film actress Jane Russell and her husband and former football star Bob Waterfield. Although the film made money, it was a costly production, almost all of its scenes shot on location in the jungles southeast of Cuernavaca, the ruins of a huge 16th-Century hacienda established by explorer Henan Cortes was used for van Eyck's hideout. The interior and house, as well as the hotel where Widmark and Greer originally meet were enormous sets built for the film, the largest sets built for any film in Mexico up to that time. Leo Genn was originally signed to play the British traitor, but he did not like the script. Since his agreement allowed Genn script approval, a second draft was written and he did not like that version either, so he quit, but his contract nevertheless compelled Russell and Waterfield to pay him his full salary. He was then replaced with Howard, who does a great job as the insidious British traitor. **p**, Harry Tatelman, Jane Russell; **d**, Roy Boulting; **cast**, Richard Widmark, Trevor Howard, Jane Greer, Peter van Eyck, Juan Garcia, Jose Antonio Carbajal, Jose Chavez Trowe, Guillermo Calles, Margarito Luna, Ededina Diaz de Leon; **w**, Boulting, Dudley Nichols (based on the story "The Most Dangerous Game" by Richard Connell); **c**, Joseph LaShelle (SuperScope; Eastmancolor); **m**, Frederick Steiner; **ed**, Frederic Knudtson; **art d**, Alfred C. Ybarra.

Run of the Arrow ★★★★ 1957; U.S.; 86m; RKO/UNIV; Color; Western; Children: Unacceptable; **VHS**. Steiger renders a memorable performance in this offbeat but fascinating western. He is a former Rebel, who refuses to admit that the Confederacy has lost the Civil War, although he knows that Robert E. Lee has surrendered all Confederate forces at Appomattox. Just before that surrender, on April 9, 1865, Steiger fires the last bullet of the war, one that strikes Union lieutenant Meeker, who recovers from that wound. The bullet Steiger has fired is returned to him with the note: "To Private O'Meara, Virginia 6th Volunteers, who shot this last bullet of the war and missed." Steiger keeps the bullet as a souvenir and, because he cannot tolerate the North winning the war, migrates to the West. There he encounters a tribe of Sioux Indians, who have been warring with whites. He is given the opportunity to save his life through a ritual known as "the run of the arrow." Steiger is stripped to the waist and allowed to run for his life, an arrow shot high into the air as he begins to run and, when it lands on the earth, braves pursue him. Steiger outdistances most of his pursuers and bests those who catch up with him. He is further aided by a beautiful Indian girl, Montiel, who risks her life in preventing Steiger from being skinned alive. Instead of being killed, Steiger is adopted by the tribe and learns the lifestyle of the Sioux, coming to respect their credos and ethics while he and Montiel fall in love. Tension mounts as a U.S. Cavalry unit erects Fort Abraham Lincoln just outside Sioux boundaries. Steiger tries to keep the peace between the U.S. troops and the Indians, but Wynant, a Sioux brave who distrusts the white troopers, kills their commander, Keith, who has tried to treat the Indians with honor and respect. Keith is replaced by Meeker, the very man Steiger shot during the last day of the Civil War, and Meeker, a vicious and ruthless officer, wages war with the Sioux. Steiger goes to the fort in an attempt to reason with Meeker and is knocked senseless by Meeker for his peace-seeking efforts. Meeker's outrages against the Sioux, however, are answered when the tribe attacks and destroys the fort in a bloody battle where most of the troopers are slaughtered. Meeker and others are taken captive and Meeker is tied to a post and is about to be skinned alive. Rather than see such torture inflicted, even against a man he hates, Steiger inserts the bullet he used to shoot Meeker during the war and fires it into his head, ending his suffering. He then makes peace with the Sioux and leads the surviving troopers from the area, with Montiel, his Indian wife, accompanying him, along with their adopted Indian son, Miller. Steiger, who carries the Union flag with him from the devastated area at the end of the film, symbolizes his acceptance of the end of the Civil War as he plans to make a life for himself and his adopted Indian family. Fuller directs this unorthodox western with great skill, carefully developing his characters and his choreographing of the action and the battles between the troopers and the Indians, is outstanding. *Author's Note*: Fuller told this author that Steiger "had sprained an ankle early in the production of **Run of the Arrow** and, by the time we came to shoot the scene where he must run for his life, he could hardly walk. I covered his injury by showing some medium shots of him from the waist up as he appeared to be running and then cut to running feet, his own, which a double substituted for him, and that of the pursuing Indians. Film reviewers thought that that visual approach was very effective, but they did not know that I had no other way to show those scenes." Steiger told this author that "I have always felt that Native Americans in this country were mistreated and abused from the very first time white settlers went west, so my sympathetic attitude toward the Sioux in **Run of the Arrow** is really genuine. I was on their side long before I made that picture." Keith enjoyed making this film, telling this author that "Sam [Fuller] is a director who does his job without acting like a prima donna. I can't tell you how refreshing that is, working with a man who only asks you to do your best with your role without expecting anyone to bow down to him as if he was some Hollywood rajah. And believe you me there are plenty of directors in this town who expect that kind of slavish behavior from actors." Meeker, however, thought he was again typecast for his role as the unethical cavalry officer, telling this author that "I pretty much played the same kind of sneaking and vicious character I played some years earlier in another western, **The Naked Spur** [1953]. In that picture I was a Union officer who had been kicked out of the service for raping a woman, and all I do in that picture is try to kill someone to get a big reward. In **Run of the Arrow**, I played a sadist persecuting Indians. I just couldn't get a part where I played a decent guy, but that changed in a big way when, in the same year that I did **Run of the Arrow** with Rod [Steiger] I was cast in Kirk Douglas' great war picture, **Paths of Glory** [1957]. In that one, I played an honorable soldier, who is victimized by his drunken superior, Wayne Morris. Wayne complained about his role in that picture, telling me: 'I hate myself for playing such a boozy coward. I feel like a creep.' I told him: 'Well, Wayne, now you know how I have been feeling for about five years because those are the only kind of people I have been playing on the screen.'" Montiel, who spoke with a thick accent, had her voice dubbed by studio contract player Angie Dickinson. This was one of the last films produced by RKO, but the studio went broke before it was released and Universal bought the rights to this film (and others), and released it through its own distribution arm. **p,d&w**, Samuel Fuller; **cast**, Rod Steiger, Sarita Montiel, Brian Keith, Ralph Meeker, Jay C. Flippen, Charles Bronson, Olive Carey, H. M. Wynant, Neyle Morrow, Frank DeKova, Col. Tim McCoy, Billy Miller, Roscoe Ates, Angie Dickinson; **c**, Joseph Biroc (RKO-Scope; Technicolor); **m**, Victor Young; **ed**, Gene Fowler, Jr.; **art d**, Albert S. D'Agostino, Jack Okey; **set d**, Bert Granger; **spec eff**, Norman Breedlove.

Run Silent, Run Deep ★★★★ 1958; U.S.; 98m; Hill-Hecht-Lancaster Productions/UA; B/W; War Drama; Children: Unacceptable; **DVD**; **VHS**. Gable, in one of his last films, along with the equally dynamic Lancaster, give powerful performances in this tense war tale of American submariners battling the Japanese in the Pacific in WWII (1939-

Rod Steiger in *Run of the Arrow*, 1957.

1945). Gable commands a submarine that is sunk by a superfast Japanese destroyer in the Bongo Straits. He survives and, with a few others, manages to return to base at Pearl Harbor, but he is left without a command and given a desk job with loyal seaman Warden at his side. Gable manages to persuade the brass to give him another submarine. Before departing with that new sub, Gable receives a visit at his home by Lancaster, who tells him that he does not want to serve under him as his executive officer and that he expected to receive his own command of a submarine. He further tells Gable that he believes that the only way Gable was given a command of a new sub was because he asked for an experienced executive officer, Lancaster, and got him. Gable tells Lancaster that he will not transfer him from his command and Lancaster leaves, setting the scene for a continued confrontation between these two strong-headed men. When the sub embarks on its mission, Gable opens his sealed orders to learn that he is to operate in all enemy waters except the Bongo Straits. He begins drilling his crew relentlessly to cut down the time it normally takes to submerge and does not tell his men or even his officers the reasons for such demanding drills. After some enemy ships are sighted, Gable ignores the opportunity to attack them, and most of his crew, except for the loyal Warden, thinks that Gable has either lost his nerve or is losing his mind. When Dexter, an abrasive officer, calls Gable a coward, Warden knocks him down and is put on report. Lancaster challenges Gable's decision but reluctantly abides by it, reminding crew members that Gable is still the skipper of the boat. Defying orders, Gable then takes his submarine into the dangerous Bongo Straits, hunting for "Bongo Pete," the superfast destroyer that sank his first submarine. He soon meets the adversary, and as expected, the Japanese destroyer bears down upon the submarine with incredible speed. Gable orders a crash dive, firing two torpedoes straight at "Bongo Pete" as the destroyer advances, and Gable's intense drilling pays off in that the submarine manages to submerge just when the Japanese warship opens fire, missing its mark. The torpedoes fired by Gable, however, do not miss, both striking the Japanese destroyer squarely at its bow and blowing it to pieces. The sub's radio operator, however, hears a strange radio signal he cannot interpret. At that time, Gable, who has suffered a blow to his head during the crash dive, is put to bed in his cabin and remains unconscious while Lancaster takes command of the boat. Lancaster then realizes that the strange signal being picked up by the radio operator is that of a Japanese submarine that has been working with the sunken Japanese destroyer and is now attempting to contact it. Both the American and Japanese submarines then stalk each other, both running silent and groping for their positions as they stealthily sail underwater. Lancaster causes the Japanese submarine to go to the surface and follows it. By this time, Gable, though still seriously injured, goes to the conning tower to join Lancaster. They see the Japanese submarine sail-

Rebecca De Mornay, Eric Roberts and Jon Voight in *Runaway Train*, 1985.

ing on the surface, but it slips behind a Japanese freighter. Gable realizes that the freighter has a shallow draft and orders two torpedoes fired at it. As suspected, the torpedoes sail unobstructed by the freighter, running beneath it and strike the Japanese submarine, destroying it. Japanese planes then close in on the American submarine, and Gable collapses from the strain of battle and is dragged down a hatch. The sub submerges in time to avoid the aerial attack. The final scene shows Lancaster and the crew members holding a burial ceremony at sea. Gable is dead, and they slip his body into the sea with Lancaster stating: "Let no one on board this boat say that we did not have a commander." The submarine then sails toward home base through tranquil waters to end this exciting and superbly acted film. Director Wise displays great expertise in building tension and providing many harrowing moments in the claustrophobic atmosphere of the sub. The film received widespread acclaim and did well at the box office. *Author's Note*: Gable would make three more films before his death two years later. He was feeling his age when he did this film, refusing to work beyond five p.m. each day, as Wise later noted, stating that "he was just physically wrung out by then." Lancaster told this author that "I had great respect for Gable, who was still on his toes when we did **Run Silent, Run Deep**. He never flubbed a line or missed a cue, but he was pretty much set in his ways and would not tolerate any changes in the script, no matter how small they might be." In truth, Gable and Lancaster did not get along well together since Lancaster was invariably given to improvising story lines as he went along, seeking to improve and tighten plots and trim characters for the sake of speeding up the action. At one point, Lancaster wanted the script changed so that he becomes mutinous and takes over command of the ship. Gable strongly objected, saying that that would destroy his image of the commander. Lancaster got around that objection by having Gable grow ill from suffering a head injury so that he becomes the skipper by default. The U.S. Navy proved very cooperative with Lancaster's company, loaning it the use of the USS *Redfish* (SS-395), exterior shots of this submarine shot on and near the U.S. submarine base at San Diego, California. The outstanding underwater sequences showing the dueling submarines were done in miniature and are considered some of the best such scenes ever created. This was the film debut of comedian Don Rickles, who was then attempting serious acting. He clowned around on the set, at one time pretending to be gay and was found in bed with another sailor by Gable when he entered his wardroom. Gable went to director Wise and said: "These boys are a little light on their feet. Have them play in some other area of the sub instead of my room." It took some time before Rickles convinced Gable that he was only pretending to be gay. Gable then told him that he was pretty convincing at it and should seek another avenue of entertainment, suggesting that he become a comedian, a suggestion that the actor embraced wholeheartedly. Other

films depicting submarines in the Pacific during WWII include **Battle of the Coral Sea**, 1959; **Destination Tokyo**, 1943; **Gung Ho!**, 1943; **Hellcats of the Navy**, 1957; **I Was an American Spy**, 1951; **The Incredible Mr. Limpet**, 1964; **1941**, 1979; **Okinawa**, 1952; **Operation Pacific**, 1951; **Operation Petticoat**, 1959; **Pearl Harbor**, 2001; **Prisoner of Japan**, 1942; **Sea Wife**, 1957; **Submarine Command**, 1951; **Submarine Seahawk**, 1958; **Task Force**, 1949; **They Were Expendable**, 1945; **Tora! Tora! Tora!**, 1970; **Torpedo Run**, 1958; and **Up Periscope**, 1959. For a more extensive listing of submarines portrayed in films, see Index, Volume II of this work, under Submarines. **p**, Harold Hecht; **d**, John Gay (based on the novel by Comdr. Edward L. Beach); **cast**, Clark Gable, Burt Lancaster, Jack Warden, Brad Dexter, Don Rickles, Nick Cravat, Joe Maross, Mary LaRoche, Eddie Foy III, Skip Ward; **c**, Russell Harlan; **m**, Franz Waxman; **ed**, George Boemler; **art d**, Edward Carrere; **set d**, Ross Dowd; **spec eff**, Gerald Endler, A. Arnold Gillespie, Howard Lydecker.

Runaway Jury ★★★ 2003; U.S.; 127m; Regency Enterprises/FOX; Color; Drama; Children: Unacceptable (MPAA: PG-13); **BD**; **DVD**; **VHS**. This absorbing courtroom drama begins in New Orleans where a failed day trader at a stock brokerage fires on his former colleagues, then turns the gun on himself. His victims include McDermott. Two years later, with pro bono attorney Hoffman, Going, who is McDermott's widow, takes Vicksburg Firearms to court on the grounds that the company's gross negligence led to her husband's death. During jury selection, jury consultant Hackman gives background information on each of the jurors to lead defense attorney Davison in the courtroom through electronic surveillance. In the jury pool, Cusack, a conniving clerk at an electronics store, and his girlfriend, Weisz, conspire to sell his verdict to the highest bidder. This leads to deep waters including blackmail and Griffis, one of the jurors, attempting suicide. Eventually, the gun manufacturer is found liable and the jury awards $110 million to Going. The story, however, does not end on that note. We learn that, after the trial, Cusack and Weisz confront Hackman with a receipt for a $15 million bribe he accepted to influence the verdict, and the money will benefit shooting victims in an earlier case against the gun lobby. Songs: "Happy Birthday to You" (Mildred J. Hill, Patty S. Hill), "Big Rock Candy Mountain" (Harry McClintock), "The Habanera from Carmen" (Georges Bizet), "A Bitter Tree" (David Baerwald), "It's Your Thing" (O'Kelly Isley, Ronald Isley, Rudolph Isley), "Heart of Mine" (Bob Dylan), "When the Saints Go Marching In" (James Milton Black, Katharine E. Purvis). Excessive violence and gutter language prohibit viewing by children. **p**, Gary Fleder, Arnon Milchan, Christopher Mankiewicz; **d**, Fleder; **cast**, John Cusack, Gene Hackman, Dustin Hoffman, Rachel Weisz, Bruce Davison, Jennifer Beals, Joanna Going, Rusty Schwimmer, Rhoda Griffis, Margo Moorer, Ed Nelson, Dylan McDermott; **w**, Brian Koppelman, David Levien, Rick Cleveland, Matthew Chapman (based on the novel *The Runaway Jury* by John Grisham); **c**, Robert Elswit; **m**, Christopher Young; **ed**, William Steinkamp; **prod d**, Nelson Coates; **art d**, Scott Plauche; **set d**, Tessa Posnasky; **spec eff**, John H. Hartigan, Robert C. Cooper.

Runaway Train ★★★ 1985; U.S.; 111m; Northbrook Films/Cannon Group; Color; Adventure; Children: Unacceptable (MPAA: R); **DVD**; **VHS**. Many exciting moments can be found in this harrowing adventure tale. Two escaped convicts, a hardened criminal and bank robber, Voight, and a younger prisoner, Roberts, escape from a brutal prison in Alaska in the middle of winter and find themselves on an-out-of-control train with no brakes and the driver having died from a heart attack. With them is De Mornay, a female railway worker, and pursuing them by helicopter is the prison's vengeful warden, Ryan. The efforts of Voight, Roberts and De Mornay to control the train as it races through frozen tundra provides a lot of fright and tension, the wild ride ending when Ryan is lowered onto the train and arrests the fugitives. Music: "Gloria in D Major" (Antonio Vivaldi). Violence prohibits viewing by children. **p**, Menahem

Golan, Yoram Globus; **d**, Andrei Konchalovsky; **cast**, Jon Voight, Eric Roberts, Rebecca De Mornay, Kyle T. Heffner, John P. Ryan, T. K. Carter, Kenneth McMillan, Stacey Pickren, Hank Wardon, Dennis Franz; **w**, Djordje Milicevic, Paul Zindel, Edward Bunker (based on a story by Ryuzo Kikushima, Hideo Oguni and a screenplay by Akira Kurosawa); **c**, Alan Hume; **m**, Trevor Jones; **ed**, Henry Richardson; **prod d**, Stephen Marsh; **art d**, Joseph T. Garrity; **set d**, Anne Kuljian; **spec eff**, Rick Josephsen, Keith Richins.

The Running Man ★★★ 1963; U.K.; 103m; Peet/COL; Color; Drama; Children: Unacceptable. Well-directed and exceptionally acted tale sees Harvey taking vengeance on an insurance company at what appears to be the cost of his own life. Unable to collect from that huge insurance firm because he missed a premium payment by one day, Harvey fakes his death in a staged plane crash, and, after things quiet down, meets up with his wife, Remick, collecting her and the money in Malaga, Spain. The good life starts coming unglued when Bates, an insurance investigator, suspects something is wrong in Remick's claim and goes to Spain looking for her and, eventually, Harvey. Harvey, by this time, has turned into a stealthy and conniving crook. After finding the passport of a millionaire, he plans to murder the wealthy man and collect on his policy. Bates, meanwhile, seems to accept Harvey's false identity as he falls for Remick and pursues her since she is reportedly now a widow, which she is not. When Harvey thinks Bates is on to him, he plots to kill the insurance investigator, but then thinks to leave the country altogether. He flees in a small plane, but neglects to see that the gas tanks are empty, and, as he flies over the sea, runs out of gas and plummets to his death almost in the same manner he earlier faked his own demise, irony becoming reality in this last twist of fate. A similar story was released the same year, **Five Miles to Midnight**, starring Sophia Loren, who is married to the same kind of fraudulent person, Tony Perkins, who fakes his own death for insurance money and he does not get away with it any more than Harvey does. **p&d**, Carol Reed; **cast**, Laurence Harvey, Lee Remick, Alan Bates, Felix Aylmer, Eleanor Summerfield, Allan Cuthbertson, Harold Goldblatt; Noel Purcell, Ramsay Ames, Fernando Rey; **w**, John Mortimer (based on the novel *The Ballad of the Running Man* by Shelley Smith); **c**, Robert Krasker (Panavision; Eastmancolor); **m**, William Alwyn; **ed**, Bert Bates; **art d**, John Stoll.

Running on Empty ★★★ 1988; U.S.; 116m; Lorimar/WB; Color; Drama; Children: Unacceptable (MPAA: PG-13); **DVD**; **VHS**. This intriguing but disturbing tale begins in 1971 when Arthur and his wife Annie Pope (Hirsch and Lahti) blow up a napalm laboratory to protest the Vietnam War. Since then, they have been on the run from the FBI and living under false identities. Now residing in New York City, their seventeen-year-old son, Phoenix, wants a life of his own, even though he is aware that his parents could get caught and/or he might never see them again. Phoenix has ability as a pianist and studies at the Julliard School of Music. He decides to put his parents' problem behind him and start a new life, trying for a piano scholarship at Julliard and seeing a possible future with his girlfriend Plimpton. Songs: "Fire and Rain" (James Taylor); "Lucky Star" (Madonna); "Oh Pretty Woman" (Roy Orbison, Bill Dees); "Happy Birthday to You" (Mildred J. Hill, Patty S. Hill). Excessive violence prohibits viewing by children. Lumet does a good job with this socially conscious story, offering fully developed characters, who, through some fine acting from Hirsch, Phoenix, Lahti and Plimpton, gain considerable empathy. **p**, Griffin Dunne, Amy Robinson; **d**, Sidney Lumet; **cast**, River Phoenix, Christine Lahti, Judd Hirsch, Jonas Abry, Martha Plimpton, Ed Crowley, L.M. Kit Carson, Steven Hill, Augusta Dabney, David Margulies, Lynne Thigpen; **w**, Naomi Foner; **c**, Gerry Fisher; **m**, Tony Mottola; **ed**, Andrew Mondshein; **prod d**, Philip Rosenberg; **art d**, Robert Guerra; **set d**, Philip Smith.

Running Wild ★★★★ 1927 (silent); U.S.; 68m; PAR; B/W; Comedy;

Jonas Abry, Christine Lahti and River Phoenix in *Running on Empty,* **1988.**

Children: Acceptable; **VHS**. The inimitable Fields is a scream in this comedy that establishes many of his plots to come in the talkie era. He is a meek and much maligned man, incessantly henpecked by his shrew of a wife, Shotwell, and constantly harassed and humiliated by his overweight stepson, Raskin. His boss, Burton, treats him like a slave and is forever berating Fields for the slightest error. Only Brian, who is Fields' adoring and loving daughter, brings him any happiness. Fields suffers from a serious inferiority complex, but all that changes when Roseman hypnotizes Fields and he becomes a changed man. He stands up to his wife, disciplines his surprised stepson and talks back to his boss Burton while plunging into a venture that has a $15,000 reward. Fields' antics as a newborn man of independence and free will causes him endless problems and no little hazards, but he survives his own self-destructive mistakes to find bliss at the end of this very funny comedy. Fields would take this same story to a masterpiece conclusion when making **It's a Gift**, 1934, the talkie version of the little man who finally asserts himself, despite the obstacles fate and fortune set in his ambling path. **p**, Gregory La Cava, William LeBaron; **d**, La Cava; **cast**: W. C. Fields, Mary Brian, Marie Shotwell, Frederick Burton, Barnett Raskin, Claude Buchanan, Frank Evans, Edward Roseman, J. Moy Bennett, Tom Madden, John Merton; **w**, Roy Briant (based on a story by La Cava); **c**, Paul Vogel; **ed**, Ralph Black.

The Russians Are Coming! The Russians Are Coming! ★★★★ 1966; U.S.; 126m; Mirisch Corporation/UA; Color; Comedy; Children: Acceptable; **DVD**; **VHS**. This hilarious mix of mayhem and manic clowning lampoons the anxieties the U.S. harbored during the Cold War. That war threatens to turn hot when a Soviet submarine malfunctions and stalls near an island off the New England coast. The Russian commander, Bikel, orders his submarine too close to the American shores to get a good look at the "other half" and promptly gets the boat stuck on a sandbar. He orders Arkin, his down-to-earth first officer, to go ashore with some sailors to see if they can find a boat large enough that might pull the submarine to open water, but without alarming the inhabitants, a chore next to impossible to accomplish. Arkin and his men skulk along the beaches and in the sand dunes until they come upon a beach house occupied by TV writer Reiner and his wife Saint, and their children, Putnam and Golomb. Reiner hates the island and its damp climate and longs to return to the confines of Manhattan. Arkin and his men invade the beach house, and he points a gun at Reiner. Arkin's actions alarm the American family, but Arkin apologetically explains that he and his men are peaceful and are only seeking help as he tries to convey his message in broken English. Arkin takes Reiner captive and orders him to drive him and his men to an area where they can get a motorboat to pull the submarine from the sandbar. He leaves Law, a

Alan Arkin and Carl Reiner in *The Russians Are Coming! The Russians Are Coming!* 1966.

young sailor, behind to guard Saint and her children, along with Dromm, a visiting eighteen-year-old girl, who is quickly attracted to the handsome, tall sailor. Arkin and his men then pay a visit to the local postmistress and, after tying her up with Reiner, escape in her small car. They then tie up the local telephone operator, tying her to a chair and placing her and the chair on a wall with a gag in her mouth. They are then off searching for a motorboat. Meanwhile, word has spread through the little island that the Russians have landed, and Sheriff Keith and his oafish deputy, Winters, must now contend with Ford, en elderly army reservist, who dons his old uniform and grabs a sword to summon the locals to arms. Meanwhile, Blue rides on a horse through the community like a latter-day Paul Revere, shouting out the title of this film: "The Russians are coming! The Russians are coming!" Blue suffers from inebriation, however, and, in his drunken antics, manages to get himself repeatedly thrown by the uncooperative animal. Keith, meanwhile, tries to calm the residents, who have armed themselves and are ready to wage World War Three with the Russians, encouraged by the saber-rattling Ford, the most blathering zealot bleating patriotic slogans if there ever was one. While the armed-to-the-teeth locals search for the elusive Russians, Reiner later befriends Arkin after they are brought together by the warm relationship between Law and Dromm, and Reiner aids Arkin in getting a boat that helps pull the Russian sub off the sandbar. Arkin, however, loses track of Law and goes back for him. Bikel, the obstreperous commander of the Soviet sub, then sails his boat into the town's harbor and all the locals think he is about to open fire on them. They level their weapons at the sub and its crew, but a boy, Whitaker, falls from a bell tower and is hanging by a thread. Residents and Russian sailors then band together to form a human pyramid to reach the boy, with Law at the top and reaching out to save the boy before he plummets to his doom. (A similar scene is shown in **The Eagle Has Landed**, 1976, made ten years after this film, where a German parachutist saves a child from drowning, but with much more gruesome results in that espionage thriller.) The saving of the boy immediately cements a deep bond between the Americans and the Russians, and, after Ford announces that he has contacted the U.S. Air Force and that fighter jets are on their way to blow up the Russian submarine, the entire town takes to all of its large and small boats and escorts the Soviet sub out to sea. The jets arrive overhead, but, when seeing the Americans protectively sailing with the Russian boat, they abandon their mission and fly off. The Soviets wave farewell, and the sub safely submerges while the locals cheer its departure. The very talented Jewison directs this manic and mirthful film with alacrity, effectively cross-cutting the activities of the Russians and the alarmed residents while inserting many humorous isolated scenes to increase the hilarity. Arkin, in his film debut, is superb as the compassionate Russian officer as is the discombobulated Reiner and all the rest of

the fine cast, from Keith to Winters, the helpless lawmen, to Law and Dromm as the young lovers, give standout performances. The film received Oscar nominations for Best Picture, Best Actor (Arkin), Best Film Editing (Ashby and Williams), and Best Adapted Screenplay (Rose). It did big box office in its initial release, producing $21.7 million against a budget of $3.9 million. Song: "The Shining Sea" (Johnny Mandel and Peggy Lee). *Author's Note*: Winters told this author that he felt that his role in this comedy "was one of my best as the goofball deputy, who routinely fouls up every assignment he gets. If deputies everywhere acted like that they'd be in the pokey and the crooks would be wearing the badges. **The Russians Are Coming!** was a lot like an earlier picture I made, **It's a Mad, Mad, Mad, Mad World** [1963]—did I get enough "Mads" in there? Both pictures had a collection of comedians packed into them and both pictures allowed enough room for those madcaps to do their own little routines, although I think the earlier picture had more of us clowns in it. I know that the director, Stanley Kramer, rounded up every guy and gal that ever took a funny pratfall and put them into that one." Keith told this author that "I was really impressed with the performance of Johnny Whitaker, the kid who falls from the bell tower and is saved by everyone, so when they began casting for my TV show, "A Family Affair" [1966], I asked that he be part of the cast. He was a great little performer." The locale of the film is a mythical New England island town called "Glouchester," which was really shot at Mendocino, California, a town in the northern part of the state that bears a resemblance to New England locales. The U.S. Navy refused to loan a submarine to represent the Soviet sub, so the boat was constructed for the film. The fighter jets that overfly the town and its fleet of residents and the Russian boat as it goes out to sea, however, were real U.S. fighter planes, a group of McDonnell-Douglas F-101B Voodoo fighter jets from the 437th Fighter Interceptor Squadron located at Oxnard Air Force Base (presently called Camarillo Airport). **p&d**, Norman Jewison; **cast**, Carl Reiner, Eva Marie Saint, Alan Arkin, Brian Keith, Jonathan Winters, Paul Ford, Theodore Bikel, John Phillip Law, Andrea Dromm, Sheldon Golomb, Cindy Putnam, Ben Blue, Michael J. Pollard, Johnny Whitaker; **w**, William Rose (based on the novel *The Off-Islanders* by Nathaniel Benchley); **c**, Joseph Biroc (Panavision; DeLuxe Color); **m**, Johnny Mandel; **ed**, Hal Ashby, J. Terry Williams; **art d**, Robert F. Boyle; **set d**, Darrell Silvera; **spec eff**, Daniel W. Hays.

Ryan's Daughter ★★★ 1970; U.K.; 195m; Faraway Productions MGM; Color; Drama/Romance; Children: Unacceptable (MPAA: R); **DVD**; **VHS**. Lush Irish landscapes are beautifully photographed by skilled cinematographer Young in this torrid love triangle tale set in 1916 while WWI (1914-1918) is raging. Taciturn teacher Mitchum, who has been trying to keep the peace between the local IRA (Irish Republican Army) and the occupying British in a small Irish coastal town, marries Miles, the sex-craving daughter of McKern, who owns a prosperous pub. The union is an unhappy one from the start as Mitchum, for arcane reasons, disdains sex (the viewer never knows if he is homosexual or too saintly to consummate his marital vows and bedroom obligations). Miles becomes so frustrated that she seeks advice from parish priest Howard. Instead of helpful hints on how to improve her sexual life with Mitchum, Howard lectures her on celibacy and tells her that she should be grateful that she has married such a devout man. (This scene is reminiscent of another film with an Irish setting that depicts the clandestine meeting between Maureen O'Hara and priest Ward Bond in **The Quiet Man**, 1952, where O'Hara whispers about her strained sexual relations with her husband, John Wayne, telling Bond that Wayne is not in her bed at night, but sleeping on the floor in a sleeping bag.) Jones, a shell-shocked British officer, arrives in the area to quell the subversive doings of the IRA and trouble-making German spies. Miles quickly attaches herself to Jones, and the two begin a reckless affair where they abandon all caution in having sex in open fields and deserted buildings, the imprudent trysts tracked by town idiot Mills. After Mills finds a button torn from Jones' uniform by Miles during one of their tempestuous clinches, he parades about town with that button, displaying it as a love trophy that indicts Miles and Jones and further increases the raging gossip about the adulterous pair. Mitchum hears these tales but does nothing, thinking that the best course is to allow the affair to exhaust itself. IRA leader Foster then appears with a large cache of guns he has received from German agents, which is to be used in an uprising against the British. Mitchum wants no part of such a rebellion, reasoning that the British will ruthlessly take reprisals that will damage all of the townspeople, so he informs on Foster and his fellow gun-runners and the British trap them and make them prisoners. So enraged at this betrayal are the local residents that they invade Mitchum's home, all believing that it was Miles who told her British lover Jones about the guns. She is stripped and her head shaved, the symbolic punishment meted out to those who collaborate with the enemy. Jones, who realizes that his indiscreet affair is now a matter of public record, is so mortified that he kills himself by exploding a grenade that blows him to pieces. Mitchum, the ever forgiving husband, then reconciles with Miles and both of them leave the town, heading for Dublin and a new and, hopefully, better life together. Pantheon director Lean provides an absorbing story that is well enacted by Mitchum, Miles, Jones and the rest of the cast, albeit its conclusion is grim and less than satisfying. The story line for this film is reminiscent of **The Eye of the Needle**, 1981, which deals with German agents in Ireland and a love triangle between Donald Sutherland, Kate Nelligan and disabled British officer Stephen MacKenna, and even, to some degree, the plotline of **The Eagle Has Landed**, 1976, where Sutherland is an IRA operative working with the Nazis in WWII and dallying with a local Irish lady. The film was a box office success, gleaning more than $30 million in U.S. receipts and an additional $15 million in foreign receipts against a $13 million budget. The film, however, received negative reviews, particularly those aimed at Mitchum, who was accused of "sleepwalking" his way through his role. Mills received an Oscar as Best Supporting Actor, and Miles received an Oscar nomination as Best Actress as did Gordon K. McCallum and John Bramall for Best Sound Mixing. Songs: "Mary of the Curling Hair," "Saddle the Pony," "Guinea Willie," "Drowsy Maggie," "Rose Tree" (traditional), "It's a Long Way to Tipperary" (Jack Judge and Harry Williams). *Author's Note*: Mitchum was not Lean's first choice for the role of the cuckolded husband, the director wanting Paul Scofield to play that role, but Scofield's theatrical commitments prevented him from taking the part. When he was not available Lean thought about casting Anthony Hopkins, George C. Scott and Patrick McGoohan in that role. "I must admit that I went after that part," actor Gregory Peck told this author, "but I backed off after I learned that Lean had approached Mitchum." Mitchum read the script and liked it, but he had reservations about working with Lean, a director who liked to make epics out of stories with limited scope of action. "He is a director that makes an army out of a small crowd," Mitchum told this author. "Even when small is fascinating, David Lean wants to make it all bigger and grander." Mitchum was having personal problems at the time Lean approached him, and after he dragged his feet and did not give the director a quick response, Lean asked him why he was not responding. "I was thinking of committing suicide, instead of doing your picture," Mitchum jocularly told Lean. This caused the scriptwriter, Bolt, to tell Mitchum that "if you finish working on this wretched little film and then do yourself in, I would be happy to stand the expenses of your burial." Mitchum went ahead with the role, but his relationship with Lean remained strained and contentious. Mitchum, nevertheless, told this author that "Lean did a brilliant job in directing that film, despite all the headaches I gave him as did a lot of others. I thought my part was one of the best I ever did, and that I got a bum rap from film reviewers." Lean also had problems with Miles and Jones, who did not get along with each other, and the director had to struggle with both of them in creating passionate scenes. "Oh, they hated each other," Mitchum told this author. "Jones was not happy because he knew that Lean did not want him for the part of the British officer. He had offered that role to Marlon Brando, but

Sarah Miles and Christopher Jones in *Ryan's Daughter*, 1970.

Brando backed out because he was doing another picture [**Burn!**, 1969], so Lean went after a lot of other leading guys [Richard Burton, Richard Harris, Peter O'Toole], and wound up with Jones." Jones was reportedly upset through most of the production as Sharon Tate (the wife of film director Roman Polanski), with whom he had an alleged affair, had been murdered by the Manson Family while the film was in production. The role of the priest essayed by Howard went to that fine actor by default because Alec Guinness refused to play that part. Guinness, who was a practicing Catholic, thought the role, which was reportedly written for him, inaccurately portrayed Catholic priests. Guinness told this author that "I had had enough of Mr. Lean's perception of history. After our experience together in **Dr. Zhivago**, 1965, I wanted to stay clear of his all-encompassing productions where all characters are swallowed by the whale Mr. Lean rides." Other films depicting the IRA and its struggles for independence against the British include **Beloved Enemy**, 1936; **The Boxer**, 1997; **The Eagle Has Landed**, 1976; **The Enigma of Frank Ryan**, 2012; **Five Minutes of Heaven**, 2009; **Hunger**, 2008; **I See a Dark Stranger**, 1947; **The Informer**, 1935; **The Man Who Never Was**, 1956; **Michael Collins**, 1996; **The Night Fighters**, 1960; **Odd Man Out**, 1947; **Patriot Games**, 1998; **The Plough and the Stars**, 1936; **The Quiet Man**, 1952; **The Rising of the Moon**, 1957; **Ronin**, 1998; **Shake Hands with the Devil**, 1959; **Sword in the Desert**, 1949; **Veronica Guerin**, 2003; and **The Wind That Shakes the Barley**, 2007. **p**, Anthony Havelock-Allan; **d**, David Lean; **cast**, Robert Mitchum, Sarah Miles, Christopher Jones, Trevor Howard, John Mills, Leo McKern, Barry Foster, Marie Kean, Arthur O'Sullivan, Evin Crowley; **w**, Robert Bolt; **c**, Freddie Young (Super Panavision; Metrocolor); **m**, Maurice Jarre; **ed**, Norman Savage; **prod d**, Stephen Grimes; **art d**, Roy Walker; **set d**, Josie MacAvin.